PrincetonReview.com

COMPLETE
BOOK OF COLLEGES

Random House, Inc., New York
2011 Edition

The Princeton Review, Inc.
111 Speen St., Suite 550
Framingham, MA 01701
Email: bookeditor@review.com

ISBN 978-0-375-42805-0

SVP, Publisher: Robert Franek
Editor: Laura Braswell
Production: Best Content Solutions, LLC
Production Editor: Kristen O'Toole

Printed in the United States of America.

9 8 7 6 5 4 3 2 1

2011 Edition

ACKNOWLEDGMENTS

Each year we assemble an awe-inspiringly talented group of colleagues who work together to produce our guidebooks; this year is no exception. Everyone involved in this effort—authors, editors, data collectors, production specialists, and designers—gives so much more than is required to make *The Complete Book of Colleges* an exceptional student resource guide.

My sincere thanks go to the many who contributed to this tremendous project. Very special thanks go to Seamus Mullarkey and Laura Braswell for their editorial commitment and vision. A warm and special thank you goes to our Student Survey Team, Andrea Kornstein, Adrinda Kelly, Abe Koogler and Steven Aglione, who continue to work in partnership with school administrators and students alike. My continued thanks go to our data collection pros, Ben Zelevansky and David Soto, for their successful efforts in collecting and accurately representing the statistical data that appear with each college profile. The enormousness of this project and its deadline constraints could not have been realized without the calm presence of our production partner, Scott Harris. Scott and his team's many years of dedication, focus, and most important, careful eyes, continue to delight and remind me of what a pleasure it is to work together on this project each year. Special thanks also go to Jeanne Krier, our Random House publicist, for the dedicated work she continues to do on this book and the overall series since its inception. Jeanne continues to be my trusted colleague, media advisor, and friend. I would also like to make special mention of Tom Russell and Nicole Benhabib, our Random House publishing team, for their continuous investment and faith in our ideas. Last, I thank my TPR Partner Team, Scott Kirkpatrick, Michael Bleyhl, Paul Kanarek, Robin Staley, Brian Healy and Tom Modero for their confidence in me and my content team and for their commitment to providing students the resources they need to find the right fit school for them. Again, to all who contributed so much to this publication, thank you for your efforts; they do not go unnoticed.

Robert Franek
SVP—Publisher

CONTENTS

FOREWORD

Welcome. You have found the best place to begin, fine-tune, and execute the search for your perfect college. With the understanding that choosing a school wisely is a top priority for each prospective student, we have provided a significant breadth of information in this text to help you navigate the exciting, amazing, and sometimes confusing process of choosing the right college.

The design of this guidebook will allow you to narrow your search of colleges from 1,762 to a few dozen. Here you'll find all the individual college statistics you'll need to make informed choices about the competitiveness, size, location, and academic offerings of the schools available to you. In addition, you can find even more information about individual schools at The Princeton Review's website, PrincetonReview.com. The site includes college search features, college profiles, college discussion boards, a college majors search engine, and much more.

By using this book, you can search for, choose, and apply to colleges with the confidence of a pro—or at the very least a well-informed undergraduate hopeful! We supply the information and guidance, and you ultimately make your own decision.

The college selection, application, and interview processes can be overwhelming at times. They can also be rewarding experiences. For most, choosing a college is the first major life decision. I know it was mine. Remember that your college decision is yours alone, so arm yourself with the best available information. Badger teachers, friends, high school and college admissions counselors, brothers, sisters, and parents; ask them how they chose their colleges and why. The more you know when beginning the process, the more in control of the situation you'll feel.

Whatever it is that you choose as your path in life, your college selection will forever be your first step in that direction. The friends you make, the professors you meet, and the classes you take are all springboards to the next phase of your life.

I wish you much luck and success at whichever college you decide to attend. My sincere hope is that this publication and other Princeton Review tools will be helpful in the process.

Robert Franek
SVP, Publisher

INTRODUCTION

Before you dive into the *Complete Book of Colleges*, we want to give you some tips for your college search—especially on how to get the most out of this book and what to do once you've made your choices and are ready to apply. Since the most important thing for you to do now is to start your search, we want to start right off by revealing the secret to getting admitted to the college of your choice.

It's almost never the focus of talk about college admissions in the media, and parents and students discuss the subject all the time without even realizing that it's the crucial element to getting admitted. We're talking about matchmaking: That is, finding colleges that have the educational and social environments you're looking for, where you are well-suited academically and have something the college is looking for in return. You have a lot more control over where you end up going to college than you might think.

Matchmaking is a two-step process. You should begin with a thorough self-examination or personal inventory. Your personal inventory is best structured in the form of a spreadsheet or chart, so that when you begin to consider your options, you can check off those colleges that satisfy the various needs or wants you've identified. In this way, your best college choices will gradually begin to identify themselves.

Divide your inventory into two sections. One section should be biographical, including your high school course selection, GPA, SAT or ACT scores, class rank, and personal information like extracurricular activities—especially those you plan to continue in college. This will help you to assess how you stack up against each college's admissions standards and student body. The second section is a listing of the characteristics you need or want in the college you'll choose to attend. This list should include anything and everything you consider important, such as location, size of the student body, availability of scholarships, dormitory options, clubs and activities, even school colors if you want. This part of your inventory should grow continuously as you become more and more aware of what is important to you in your choice of colleges.

Armed with your personal inventory, you can begin to take advantage of the numerous resources available to help you narrow your choices of where to apply. There are five sources for information and advice that have become standard for most college-bound students:

1. College admissions viewbooks, videos, brochures, and catalogs

If you are a junior or senior in high school, you probably know more about the kinds of information these materials should include than the people who are responsible for designing and writing them. No college that spends half a million dollars on glossy literature is going to be objective about its content. In the best of this material, you can probably get a decent idea of the academic offerings and the basic admissions requirements. In all of it, you will never see anything but the most appealing architecture and the best-looking students on campus, nor will you hear about the recent tuition increases that were greater than the rate of inflation. Look these materials over, but don't make any decisions based solely on what you read or see.

2. Your friends

No one knows colleges and universities better than the students who currently attend them. Seek out any and all of your friends, sons and daughters of family friends, and recent graduates of your high school who attend colleges that you are considering. Talk to them when they come home. Arrange to stay with them when you visit their colleges. Pick their brains for everything they know. It doesn't get any more direct and honest than this.

3. Books and college guides

There are two types of books that can be helpful to you in your search: those that discuss specific aspects of going to college and college guides. A great narrative guide that stresses students' own opinions of colleges is our own *The Best 373 Colleges*. In addition, look at *The Fiske Guide to Colleges* or the *Yale Daily News' Insiders Guide to Colleges* for good second opinions. As for comprehensive guides—those that emphasize data over narrative content—you're holding the most up-to-date and useful one in your hands.

4. Computers

There's a lot of help out there. Using our site, PrincetonReview.com, is the best way to find the right school for you and prepare for college. For more information about our *free* online tools and features see page 9.

5. Your counselor

Since it's *critically* important, we'll say it again: Once you've developed some ideas about your personal inventory and college options, schedule a meeting with your guidance counselor. The more research you've done before you get together, the more help you're likely to get. Good advice comes out of thoughtful discussion, not from the expectation that your counselor will do your work. When it comes time to file applications, look over the materials and requirements together, and allow plenty of time to put forth your best.

USING COLLEGE INFORMATION IN THE *COMPLETE BOOK OF COLLEGES* AND ELSEWHERE

Throughout the course of your college search, you'll confront an amazing array of statistics and other data related to every college you consider. In order for all of this information to be helpful, you need to have some sense of how to interpret it. We've included a detailed key to the college entries in this book a few pages deeper into this introduction. Almost all the statistics we've compiled are self-explanatory, but there are a few that will be more useful with some elaboration.

Let's start with student/teacher ratio. Don't use it to assess average class size; they are not interchangeable terms. At almost every college, the average class size is larger than its student/teacher ratio. At many big universities, it is considerably larger. What is useful about the ratio is that it can give you an idea of how accessible your professors will be outside of the classroom. Once you are in college, you'll grow to realize just how important this is.

In the same way, the percentage of faculty who hold PhDs is useful information. When you're paying thousands of dollars in tuition each year, there's something comforting about knowing that your professors have a considerably broader and deeper grasp of what you're studying than you do. In contrast, teaching assistants (TAs) may often be just one or two steps ahead of you.

Another interesting group of statistics deals with the percentage of students who go on to graduate or professional school. Never allow yourself to be swayed by such statistics, unless you've taken the time to ponder their meaning and visited the college in question. High percentages almost always mean one of two things: that the college is an intellectual enclave that inspires students onward to further their education, or that it is a pre-professional bastion of aggressive careerists. There isn't anything inherently wrong with either scenario, but neither has universal appeal to prospective students. Colleges that are exceptions to this rule are rare and precious. The most misleading figures provided to prospective students are those for medical school acceptance rates. Virtually every college in the country can boast of high acceptance rates to medical school for its graduates; pre-med programs are designed to weed out those who will not be strong candidates before they even get to apply! If you're thinking about medical school, ask colleges how many of their students apply to medical school each year. Also, try to get a sense of the attrition rate within the premed program.

One final piece of advice about statistics relates to the college's acceptance rate. Simply knowing the percentage of applicants who are admitted each year is helpful, but it is even more helpful if you know how many applied, as well. When you compare these figures to the freshman profile, you have the most accurate picture of just how tough it is to get in. An 80 percent acceptance rate doesn't mean there's an open door if you don't match up well to the academic achievements of the college's typical freshman. Beyond this, keep an eye out for colleges that have relatively self-selecting applicant pools. In these cases, high acceptance rates may be misleading. When evaluating highly selective public colleges as an out-of-state applicant, remember that you will likely face a more selective evaluation than state residents.

A Few Final Thoughts

Once you've narrowed down your options and decided where to apply, find the applications on PrincetonReview.com and get to work filling them out. The admissions process is stressful enough without putting extra pressure on yourself by waiting until the last minute. The first thing you should do when you receive the necessary forms is go over them with your guidance counselor. Immediately remove the recommendation forms (if they are required) and give them to the teachers and counselor(s) who will be completing them for you. They'll have a better opportunity to write a thorough and supportive recommendation if you give them enough time to complete them. This is also the time to make your request for official transcripts. Again, it takes time to do these things. Plan ahead.

As for completing the applications, organize yourself and all the materials. Keep everything in folders and accessible in case you need to speak with an admissions officer over the telephone. When essays and information on your extracurricular activities are required, do some outlining and rough draft-writing before you commit yourself to the actual forms or online tools.

Paying for college requires some of your attention too. Though we don't have nearly enough space to go into such a complicated and stressful subject now, it's very important that you get to work on your financial circumstances right away. Keep in mind that while college is costly, few people pay the "sticker price." Regardless, you have to have your finances in order before you can get the most financial aid possible. We've developed a financial center on PrincetonReview.com to help demystify the sometimes bewildering task of financing your education. You can also find the most exhaustive strategies for financing your education in our book *Paying for College Without Going Broke.*

Last but not least, **don't take it easy during your senior year!** Colleges routinely request mid-year grades, and they expect you to continue taking challenging academic courses and keep your grades up throughout your high school career. Doing so takes you one step closer to getting good news. On behalf of The Princeton Review, have a good time, and good luck. See you on campus!

Nota Bene

The data reported in this book, unless otherwise noted, was collected from the profiled colleges from the fall of 2009 through the spring of 2010. In some cases, we were unable to publish the most recent data because schools did not report the necessary statistics to us in time, despite our repeated outreach efforts. Because enrollment and financial statistics as well as application and financial aid deadlines fluctuate from one year to another, we recommend that you check to make sure you have the most current information before applying. Best of luck!

HOW THE *COMPLETE BOOK* OF *COLLEGES* IS ORGANIZED

There are two types of profiles in this book. Not every school listed will have both. All of the 1,762 colleges and universities included in this book have their own informational profiles, and each entry follows the same basic format. Many of the institutions also have special two-page portraits located at the back of the book. These are written by the colleges and universities that wanted to present detailed descriptions of their campuses and programs.

Unless noted in the descriptions below, the Admissions Services Division of The Princeton Review collected all of the data presented in the informational profiles. As is customary with college guides, all data reflect figures for the academic year prior to publication, unless otherwise indicated. Since college offerings and demographics vary significantly from one institution to another and some colleges report data more thoroughly than others, few entries will include all of the individual data points described below.

The Heading

This section includes school name, address, telephone number, fax number, e-mail address, Internet site, financial aid telephone number, and college code numbers for both the College Board (CEEB) and the American College Testing Program (ACT) when applicable. All Internet site addresses were accurate and functioning at the time of publication. Check PrincetonReview.com for the most up-to-date links to colleges.

The Icons

The icons are a feature we hope will make using the *Complete Book of Colleges* easier. Icons appear under the school name for schools that are profiled in *The Best 373 Colleges*.

The Blurb

Describes the college or university. Includes all available data that relate to the date of founding of the school, religious affiliation, whether the school is public or private, and campus size.

Ratings

This section includes the school's Fire Safety Rating, its Admissions Selectivity Rating, and its Green Rating.

Selectivity Rating

The number listed for each college is The Princeton Review's exclusive rating of admissions competitiveness. It is a very general assessment determined by several factors, among which are the school's acceptance rate, and the class rank and average test scores of entering first-year students. By incorporating all these factors, the rating adjusts for "self-selecting" applicant pools. *Note:* The Selectivity Rating for visual and performing arts schools are approximations only. Estimated Selectivity Ratings are included to give you a general idea of where they fit in the selectivity scale, but auditions and portfolios carry the greatest weight in admissions decisions.

Schools that received an Admissions Selectivity rating of 60* did not supply sufficient data for proper calculation of this rating. By default, these schools are given this rating, although their rating may have been significantly higher had they supplied sufficient data.

Fire Safety

We asked all the schools from which we collect data annually to answer several questions about their efforts to ensure fire safety for campus residents. Each school's responses to nine of those questions were considered when calculating its Fire Safety Rating. The questions were developed in consultation with the Center for Campus Fire Safety (www.campusfire.org), and they cover: 1) The percentage of student housing sleeping rooms protected by an automatic fire sprinkler system with a fire sprinkler head located in the individual sleeping rooms; 2) The percentage of student housing sleeping rooms equipped with a smoke detector connected to a supervised fire alarm system; 3) The number of malicious fire alarms that occur in student housing per year; 4) The number of unwanted fire alarms that occur in student housing per year; 5) The banning of certain hazardous items and activities in residence halls, like candles, smoking, halogen lamps, etc.; 6) The percentage of student housing building fire alarm systems that, if activated, result in a local alarm only; 7) The percentage of student housing building fire alarm systems that, if activated, result in a signal being transmitted to a monitored location, where security investigates before notifying the fire department; 8) The percentage of student housing building fire alarm systems that, if activated, result in a signal being transmitted immediately to a continuously monitored location which can then immediately notify the fire department to initiate a response; 9) How often fire safety rules-compliance inspections are conducted each year.

Schools that did not report answers to any of the above questions receive a Fire Safety Rating of 60*. The schools have an opportunity to update their fire safety data every year and will have their fire safety ratings re-calculated and published annually.

Each individual rating places a college on a continuum for purposes of comparing all colleges within this academic year only. Though similar, these ratings are not intended to be compared directly to those that appeared on PrincetonReview.com in any prior academic year or within any Princeton Review print publication, except for *The Best 373 Colleges, 2011 Edition* and *The Best Northeastern Colleges, 2011 Edition*. Our ratings computations are refined and change annually.

Green Rating

We asked all the schools we collect data from annually to answer a number of questions that evaluate the comprehensive measure of their performance as an environmentally aware and responsible institution. The questions were developed in consultation with ecoAmerica, a research and partnership-based environmental nonprofit that convened an expert committee to design this comprehensive rating system, and cover: 1) whether students have a campus quality of life that is both healthy and sustainable; 2) how well a school is preparing students not only for employment in the clean energy economy of the 21st century, but also for citizenship in a world now defined by environmental challenges; and 3) how environmentally responsible a school's policies are.

Colleges that did not supply answers to a sufficient number of the green campus questions for us to fairly compare them to other colleges receive a Green Rating of 60*. The schools have an opportunity to update their green data every year and will have their green ratings re-calculated and published annually.

Each individual rating places a college on a continuum for purposes of comparing all colleges within this academic year only. Though similar, these ratings are not intended to be compared directly to those that appeared on PrincetonReview.com in any prior academic year or within any Princeton Review print publication, except for the those editions published in the same year, as our ratings computations are refined and change annually.

Students & Faculty

Enrollment
The total number of full-time undergraduates.

Student Body
The percentage of male, female, out-of-state, and international students, and the number of foreign countries represented.

Ethnic Representation
By percentage according to ethnic group. Figures may not add up to 100 percent, as student reporting of ethnicity is voluntary by law.

Retention and Graduation
The percentage of freshmen who return for sophomore year. The percentage of last year's seniors who entered as freshmen and graduated in four years. The percentage of graduates who pursue further study within one year. The percentage of graduates who pursue further study at law school. The percentage of graduates who pursue further study at business school. The percentage of graduates who pursue further study at medical school.

Faculty
The ratio of undergraduates to full-time faculty. The number of full-time instructional faculty. The percentage of faculty who hold PhDs. The percentage of faculty members who teach undergraduates.

Academics

Degrees
The types of degrees awarded to students.

Academic Requirements
Areas in which all or most students are required to complete some course work prior to graduation. Can include general education (nonspecific), arts/fine arts, computer literacy, philosophy, foreign languages, history, humanities, mathematics, English (including composition), sciences (biological or physical), social sciences, and other requirements as specified by each school.

Classes
Number of students in an average regular class and an average lab/discussion section.

Majors with Highest Enrollment
The most popular majors.

Special Study Options
May include accelerated programs, cross registration, cooperative (work-study) program, distance learning, double majors, dual enrollment, English as a Second Language, student exchange programs (domestic), external degree programs, honors programs, independent study, internships, liberal arts/career combinations, student-designed majors, study abroad, teacher certification programs, weekend college, and other options as specified by each school.

Facilities

Housing
Types of school-owned or affiliated housing available. May include coed dorms, women's dorms, men's dorms, apartments for married students, apartments for single students, special housing for disabled students, special housing for international students, fraternity/sorority housing, cooperative housing, and other options as specified by the school. The availability of assistance in finding off-campus housing. Any housing requirements that may exist, such as required on-campus residence for freshmen.

Special Academic Facilities/Equipment
Other facilities and equipment of note (e.g., nuclear reactor, on-campus elementary school for student teachers, scanning electron microscopes, and so forth).

Campus Life

Activities
Standard activities available. May include campus ministries, choral groups, concert band, dance, drama/theater, international student organization, jazz band, literary magazine, Model UN, musical ensembles, musical theater, opera, pep band, radio station, student film society, student government, student newspaper, symphony orchestra, television station, and yearbook.

Organizations
Total number of registered organizations, honor societies, religious organizations, fraternities, sororities.

Athletics
Intercollegiate athletics available, listed by sex.

Admissions

Freshman Academic Profile
Average high school GPA. Class rank distribution. The percentage from public high schools. Average SAT (Math, Critical Reading, and Writing sections) and/or ACT composite scores. Median range of SAT (Math, Critical Reading, and Writing sections) and/or ACT composite scores. Test of English as a Foreign Language (TOEFL) requirements for international studies.

Basis for Candidate Selection
The criteria considered by the admissions committee in evaluating candidates. May include secondary school record, class rank, recommendations, standardized test scores, essay, interview, extracurricular activities, talent/ability, character/personal qualities, alumni/-ae relations, geographic residence, state residency, religious affiliation/commitment, minority status, volunteer work, work experience.

Freshman Admission Requirements
High school diploma/GED requirements. The number of academic units required or recommended in total and by academic subject. (Individual subject totals may not equal the complete sum of academic units required; in most cases, the difference is made up with electives. Check with the admissions office for any additional requirements.)

Freshman Admissions Statistics
The number of students who applied, the percentage of applicants who were accepted, and the percentage of those accepted who ultimately enrolled.

Transfer Admissions Requirements
Application requirements (may include high school transcript, college transcript, essay, interview, standardized tests, statement of good standing from prior school). Minimum high school GPA required. Minimum college GPA required. Lowest course grade transferable.

General Admissions Information

Application fee. Application deadlines. Admission notification date. "Rolling" indicates that decisions are sent to candidates as they are made, rather than held for a common notification date. Registration policy for terms other than the fall term. Common Application participation. Credit policies for College Entrance Examination Board Advanced Placement tests. Deferred admission policy.

Costs and Financial Aid

Tuition, room & board, fees, and books.

Required Forms and Deadlines

Forms that applicants for financial aid must file and their respective deadlines. May include FAFSA, institution's own financial aid form, CSS/Financial Aid PROFILE, business/farm supplement, state aid form, noncustodial (divorced/separated) parent statement, and other forms specified by the school. Deadlines for filing financial aid forms.

Notification of Awards

The date that notification of financial aid awards occurs. "Rolling" indicates that notification is ongoing—the sooner you complete all of your required financial aid paperwork, the sooner you'll hear about your package.

Types of Aid

Need-based scholarships and grants may include Federal Pell, SEOG, state scholarships/grants, private scholarships, college/university gift aid from institutional funds, United Negro College Fund, Federal Nursing Scholarship, and other resources as specified by the school. Loans may include Direct Subsidized Stafford Loans, Direct Unsubsidized Stafford Loans, Direct PLUS Loans, Direct Consolidation Loan, FFEL Subsidized Stafford Loans*, FFEL Unsubsidized Stafford Loans*, FFEL PLUS Loans*, FFEL Consolidation Loans*, Federal Perkins Loans, Federal Nursing Loans, state loans, college/university loans from institutional funds, and other resources as specified by the school.

*As of printing, the Federal Family Education Loan (FFEL) no longer exists. Due to the passage of the Health Care and Reconciliation Act of 2010, the program was eliminated, and new loans will not be issued under the program. You may be eligible to receive loans through the Federal Direct Student Loan Program. For more detailed information about your financial aid options, please contact the admissions offices of the schools you are interested in.

Student Employment

Availability of Federal Work-Study, a federal program that is need-based and part of most financial aid packages. Availability of part-time jobs direct from the college that are not based on need. The college's own assessment of part-time employment opportunities off campus.

Financial Aid Statistics

The percentage of freshmen who received some form of need-based financial aid. The percentage of undergraduates who received some form of need-based financial aid. The number of freshmen and undergrads who received an athletic scholarship or grant. The average amount of freshman scholarships and grants. The average amount of freshman loans. The average income from an on-campus job.

The Best 373 Colleges Icon

 Indicates whether the school can be found in our book, *The Best 373 Colleges*. In that book, each school has a detailed profile that includes the results of our surveys regarding students' opinion, about many aspects of their schools and their educations.

COLLEGE DIRECTORY

ABILENE CHRISTIAN UNIVERSITY

ACU Box 29000, Abilene, TX 79699
Phone: 325-674-2650 **Financial Aid Phone:** 325-674-2300
E-mail: info@admissions.acu.edu **CEEB Code:** 6001
Fax: 325-674-2130 **Website:** www.acu.edu **ACT Code:** 4050

This private school, affiliated with the Church of Christ Church, was founded in 1906. It has a 208-acre campus.

RATINGS
Admissions Selectivity Rating: 84   **Fire Safety Rating:** 66   **Green Rating:** 75

STUDENTS AND FACULTY
Enrollment: 3,787. **Student Body:** 54% female, 46% male, 16% out-of-state, 3% international (40 countries represented). Asian 1%, African American 8%, Caucasian 77%, Hispanic 8%, Native American 1%.
Retention and Graduation: 75% freshmen return for sophomore year. 41% freshmen graduate within 4 years. 35% grads go on to further study within 1 year. 16% grads pursue arts and sciences degrees. 3% grads pursue law degrees. 8% grads pursue business degrees. 4% grads pursue medical degrees. **Faculty:** Student/faculty ratio 15:1. 236 full-time faculty, 82% hold PhDs, 9% are members of minority groups, 34% are women. 1% of classes are taught by teaching assistants.

ACADEMICS
Degrees: Associate, bachelor's, master's, post-bachelor's certificate, post-master's certificate. **Classes:** Most classes have 20–29 students. Most lab/discussion sessions have 10–19 students. **Majors with Highest Enrollment:** Accounting and finance; business administration and management; psychology. **Special Study Options:** Cross-registration, distance learning, double major, dual enrollment, English as a Second Language (ESL), honors program, independent study, internships, student-designed major, study abroad, teacher certification program. **Honors programs:** The Honors College offers highly motivated students extra stimulation and recognition in their course work, opportunities to work with selected faculty members, and the chance to do independent projects in their major field. Ten percent of the ACU students participate. To graduate with University Honors will require 30 hours of Honors Courses. Special programs offered to physically disabled students include note-taking services, reader services, tape recorders. **Career services:** Alumni network, alumni services, career/job search classes, career assessment, internships. **Career services highlights include:** Body and Soul Pre-med program. College of Business Administration Leadership Deveopment.

FACILITIES
Housing: Special housing for disabled students, men's dorms, special housing for international students, women's dorms. 95% of campus accessible to physically disabled. **Special Academic Facilities/Equipment:** Museum of university's history, biblical restoration studies center, voice institute, demonstration farm and ranch, observatory. **Computers:** 100% of classrooms, 100% of dorms, 100% of libraries, 100% of dining areas, 100% of student union, 87% of common outdoor areas have wireless network access. Students can register for classes online. Administrative functions (other than registration) can be performed online.

CAMPUS LIFE
Environment: City. **Activities:** Choral groups, concert band, drama/theater, jazz band, literary magazine, marching band, music ensembles, musical theater, opera, radio station, student government, student newspaper, symphony orchestra, television station, yearbook, campus ministries, international student organization. **Organizations:** 108 registered organizations, 14 honor societies, 16 religious organizations. 4 fraternities, 7 sororities. **Athletics (Intercollegiate):** *Men:* Baseball, basketball, cross-country, football, tennis, track/field (outdoor), track/field (indoor). *Women:* Basketball, cross-country, soccer, softball, tennis, track/field (outdoor), track/field (indoor), volleyball. **On-Campus Highlights:** Learning Commons in Brown Library, Jacob's Dream Sculpture, World Famous Bean in McGlothlin Campus Center, Hunter Welcome Center, Williams Performing Arts Building. Abilene Christian University remains proud to be one of the first to catch the vision of the learning commons nationwide. The Learning Commons combines group work space with computers and Starbucks coffee inside the Library.

ADMISSIONS
Freshman Academic Profile: Average high school GPA 3.49. 23% in top 10% of high school class, 49% in top 25% of high school class, 78% in top 50% of high school class. 63% from public high schools. SAT Math middle 50% range 490–620. SAT Critical Reading middle 50% range 480–600. ACT middle 50% range 21–27. Minimum paper TOEFL 525. Minimum computer TOEFL 197. Minimum web-based TOEFL 70. **Basis for Candidate Selection:** *Very important factors considered include:* Class rank, application essay, rigor of secondary school record, standardized test scores. *Important factors considered include:* Academic GPA, character/personal qualities, talent/ability. *Other factors considered include:* Recommendation(s), alumni/ae relation, extracurricular activities, first generation, level of applicant's interest, volunteer work, work experience. **Freshman Admission Requirements:** High school diploma is required and GED is accepted. *Academic units recommended:* 4 English, 3 mathematics, 3 science, (2 science labs), 2 foreign language. **Freshman Admission Statistics:** 3,712 applied, 49% admitted, 54% enrolled. **Transfer Admission Requirements:** High school transcript, college transcript(s), interview, minimum college GPA of 2.0 required. Lowest grade transferable C. **General Admission Information:** Application fee $50. Regular application deadline 2/15. Regular notification 2/15. Nonfall registration accepted. Credit offered for CEEB Advanced Placement tests.

COSTS AND FINANCIAL AID
Annual tuition $19,200. Room and board $7,510. Required fees $1,090. Average book expense $1,200. **Required Forms and Deadlines:** FAFSA, institution's own financial aid form. Priority financial aid filing date 3/1. **Notification of Awards:** Applicants will be notified of awards on a rolling basis beginning 4/1. **Types of Aid:** *Need-based scholarships/grants:* Federal Pell, SEOG, state scholarships/grants, private scholarships, the school's own gift aid, United Negro College Fund. *Loans:* Federal Perkins, state loans, college/university loans from institutional funds. **Student Employment:** Federal Work-Study Program available. Institutional employment available. Highest amount earned per year from on-campus jobs $1,500. Off-campus job opportunities are good. **Financial Aid Statistics:** 67% freshmen, 63% undergrads receive need-based scholarship or grant aid. 55% freshmen, 56% undergrads receive non-need-based scholarship or grant aid. 47% freshmen, 49% undergrads receive need-based self-help aid. 6% freshmen, 7% undergrads receive athletic scholarships. 93% freshmen, 87% undergrads receive any aid. 71% undergrads borrow to pay for school. Average cumulative indebtedness $35,453. **Criteria for awarding institutional aid:** *Non-need-based:* Academics, art, athletics, leadership, minority status, music/drama, religious affiliation, state/district residency.

ACADEMY OF ART UNIVERSITY

79 New Montgomery St, San Francisco, CA 94105
Phone: 415-274-2222 **Financial Aid Phone:** 800-544-2787
E-mail: info@academyart.edu
Fax: 415-618-6287 **Website:** www.academyart.edu **ACT Code:** 155

This proprietary school was founded in 1929. It has a 20-acre campus.

RATINGS
Admissions Selectivity Rating: 60*   **Fire Safety Rating:** 60*   **Green Rating:** 60*

STUDENTS AND FACULTY
Enrollment: 10,724. **Student Body:** 56% female, 44% male, 42% out-of-state, 14% international (116 countries represented). Asian 10%, African American 6%, Caucasian 34%, Hispanic 8%, Native American 1%.
Retention and Graduation: 57% freshmen return for sophomore year. **Faculty:** Student/faculty ratio 20:1. 196 full-time faculty, 22% hold PhDs, 15% are members of minority groups, 44% are women.

ACADEMICS
Degrees: Associate, bachelor's, certificate, master's. **Classes:** Most classes have 10–19 students. **Majors with Highest Enrollment:** Animation, interactive technology, video graphics and special effects; cinematography and film/video production; fashion/apparel design. **Special Study Options:** Accelerated program, cooperative education program, distance learning, English as a Second Language (ESL), independent study, internships, weekend college, portfolio development, Personal Enrichment program. Special programs offered to physically disabled students include note-taking services, reader services, tape recorders, tutors. **Career services:** Alumni network.

FACILITIES
Housing: Coed dorms, men's dorms, women's dorms, apartments for married students, apartments for single students. 80% of campus accessible to physically disabled. **Special Academic Facilities/Equipment:** 3 art galleries (public) for display of student work. **Computers:** Students can register for classes online. Administrative functions (other than registration) can be performed online.

CAMPUS LIFE
Environment: Metropolis. **Activities:** Dance, drama/theater, musical theater, student newspaper, student-run film society, international student organization. **Organizations:** 27 registered organizations. **Athletics (Intercollegiate):** *Men:* Baseball, basketball, cross-country, golf, soccer, tennis, track/field (outdoor). *Women:* Basketball, cross-country, golf, soccer, softball, tennis, track/field (outdoor), volleyball.

ADMISSIONS

Freshman Admission Requirements: High school diploma is required and GED is accepted. **Freshman Admission Statistics:** 4,716 applied, 100% admitted, 63% enrolled. **Transfer Admission Requirements:** High school transcript, college transcript(s), minimum college GPA of 2.0 required. Lowest grade transferable C. **General Admission Information:** Application fee $100. Nonfall registration accepted. Admission may be deferred for a maximum of 24 months.

COSTS AND FINANCIAL AID

Annual tuition $22,200. Room and board $13,400. Required fees $290. Average book expense $1,638. **Required Forms and Deadlines:** FAFSA, institution's own financial aid form. Priority financial aid filing date 7/10. **Notification of Awards: Types of Aid:** *Need-based scholarships/grants:* Federal Pell, SEOG, state scholarships/grants. *Loans:* Direct Subsidized Stafford, Direct Unsubsidized Stafford, Direct PLUS. **Student Employment:** Federal Work-Study Program available. Off-campus job opportunities are good. **Financial Aid Statistics:** 31% freshmen, 30% undergrads receive need-based scholarship or grant aid. 3% freshmen, 2% undergrads receive non-need-based scholarship or grant aid. 59% freshmen, 51% undergrads receive need-based self-help aid. 6% freshmen, 2% undergrads receive athletic scholarships. 63% freshmen, 60% undergrads receive any aid. **Criteria for awarding institutional aid:** *Non-need-based:* Academics, art, athletics.

ACADIA UNIVERSITY

Admissions Office, Wolfville, NS B4P 2R6 Canada
Phone: 1-902-585-1446 **Financial Aid Phone:** 902-585-1016
E-mail: pam.dimock@acadiau.ca
Fax: 902-585-1092 **Website:** www.acadiau.ca

This public school was founded in 1838. It has a 200-acre campus.

RATINGS

Admissions Selectivity Rating: 60* **Fire Safety Rating:** 60* **Green Rating:** 60*

STUDENTS AND FACULTY

Enrollment: 2,928. **Student Body:** 55% female, 45% male, 42% out-of-state. **Retention and Graduation:** 83% freshmen return for sophomore year. **Faculty:** Student/faculty ratio 10:1. 243 full-time faculty, 36% are women.

ACADEMICS

Degrees: Bachelor's, certificate, diploma, master's. **Special Study Options:** Cooperative education program, distance learning, double major, English as a Second Language (ESL), exchange student program (domestic), honors program, independent study, internships, study abroad. **Career services:** Career/job search classes, career assessment, internships.

FACILITIES

Housing: Coed dorms, special housing for disabled students, men's dorms, women's dorms, apartments for single students. **Computers:** Students can register for classes online. Administrative functions (other than registration) can be performed online.

CAMPUS LIFE

Environment: Rural. **Activities:** Choral groups, concert band, dance, drama/theater, jazz band, literary magazine, music ensembles, musical theater, opera, pep band, radio station, student government, student newspaper, symphony orchestra, yearbook, campus ministries, international student organization. **Organizations:** 60 registered organizations, 3 religious organizations. **Athletics (Intercollegiate):** *Men:* Basketball, cheerleading, cross-country, football, ice hockey, rugby, soccer, track/field (outdoor), volleyball. *Women:* Basketball, cheerleading, cross-country, ice hockey, rugby, soccer, track/field (outdoor), volleyball. **On-Campus Highlights:** KC Irving Environmental Science Centre, The Sheldon L. Fountain Learning Commons.

ADMISSIONS

Freshman Academic Profile: 80% from public high schools. Minimum paper TOEFL 550. **Basis for Candidate Selection:** *Very important factors considered include:* Academic GPA, rigor of secondary school record. *Important factors considered include:* Recommendation(s), talent/ability. *Other factors considered include:* Class rank, standardized test scores, character/personal qualities, extracurricular activities, geographical residence, volunteer work, work experience. **Freshman Admission Requirements:** High school diploma is required and GED is not accepted. *Academic units required:* 1 English, 1 mathematics. *Academic units recommended:* 1 English, 2 mathematics, 1 science, 1 foreign language, 1 social studies, 1 history, 2 academic electives. **Freshman Admission Statistics:** 1,600 applied, 49% admitted, 68% enrolled. **Transfer Admission Requirements:** College transcript(s). **General**

Admission Information: Application fee $25. Notification on a rolling basis, beginning on or about 11/1. Nonfall registration accepted. Admission may be deferred for a maximum of 1 year. Credit and/or placement offered for CEEB Advanced Placement tests.

COSTS AND FINANCIAL AID

Annual in-state tuition $8,062. Annual out-of-state tuition $8,062. Room and board $8,284. Required fees $180. Average book expense $1,200. **Required Forms and Deadlines: Notification of Awards:** Applicants will be notified of awards on or about 4/15. **Types of Aid:** *Loans:* Direct Subsidized Stafford, Direct Unsubsidized Stafford, Direct PLUS. **Student Employment:** Off-campus job opportunities are excellent. **Criteria for awarding institutional aid:** *Non-need-based:* Academics, leadership, music/drama, state/district residency.

ADAMS STATE COLLEGE

208 Edgemont Blvd, Alamosa, CO 81102
Phone: 719-587-7712 **Financial Aid Phone:** 719-587-7306
E-mail: ascadmit@adams.edu **CEEB Code:** 4001
Fax: 719-587-7522 **ACT Code:** 496

This public school was founded in 1921. It has a 90-acre campus.

RATINGS

Admissions Selectivity Rating: 72 **Fire Safety Rating:** 60* **Green Rating:** 78

STUDENTS AND FACULTY

Enrollment: 2,347. **Student Body:** 56% female, 44% male, 11% out-of-state, international (13 countries represented). Asian 2%, African American 5%, Caucasian 47%, Hispanic 29%, Native American 2%. **Retention and Graduation:** 58% freshmen return for sophomore year. 14% freshmen graduate within 4 years. **Faculty:** Student/faculty ratio 20:1. 111 full-time faculty, 68% hold PhDs, 18% are members of minority groups, 48% are women.

ACADEMICS

Degrees: Associate, bachelor's, master's. **Classes:** Most classes have fewer than 10 students. Most lab/discussion sessions have 10–19 students. **Majors with Highest Enrollment:** Business administration and management; kinesiology and exercise science; teacher education, multiple levels. **Special Study Options:** Accelerated program, distance learning, double major, independent study, internships, study abroad, teacher certification program, weekend college, High School dual enrollment. Special programs offered to physically disabled students include note-taking services, reader services, tutors. **Career services:** Alumni network, career/job search classes, career assessment, internships. **Career services highlights include:** on-campus interviews, career fair career counseling services.

FACILITIES

Housing: Coed dorms, men's dorms, women's dorms, apartments for married students, apartments for single students, learning community. 95% of campus accessible to physically disabled. **Special Academic Facilities/Equipment:** Luther Bean Museum, Hatfield Gallery, Gallery 114, Leon Memorial Music Hall, Zacheis Planetarium, Ryan Geology Museum. **Computers:** 10% of classrooms, 100% of dorms, 100% of libraries, 100% of dining areas, 99% of student union, have wireless network access. Students can register for classes online. Administrative functions (other than registration) can be performed online.

CAMPUS LIFE

Environment: Village. **Activities:** Choral groups, concert band, dance, drama/theater, jazz band, literary magazine, marching band, music ensembles, musical theater, pep band, radio station, student government, student newspaper, campus ministries, Model UN. **Organizations:** 23 registered organizations, 2 religious organizations. **Athletics (Intercollegiate):** *Men:* Basketball, cross-country, football, golf, soccer, track/field (outdoor), track/field (indoor), wrestling. *Women:* Basketball, cross-country, golf, soccer, softball, swimming, track/field (outdoor), track/field (indoor), volleyball. **On-Campus Highlights:** Leon Memorial Concert Hall, Zacheis Planetarium, Nielson Library, Plachy Hall, Rex Activity Center, Student Union Building (SUB). **Environmental Initiatives:** Establishment of EARTH (Environmental Action for Resources, Transportation, & Health) group on campus; partnering with the city of Alamosa and Habitat for Humanity to increase recycling opportunities on campus. Water Project: Phase 1, convert supply to non-potable water; Phase 2, update inefficient system with one with a weather station. Note that Phase 2 has not been implemented yet, and may not be for a few years.

ADMISSIONS

Freshman Academic Profile: Average high school GPA 2.97. 7% in top 10% of high school class, 20% in top 25% of high school class, 53% in top 50% of

high school class. SAT Math middle 50% range 420–545. SAT Critical Reading middle 50% range 400–550. SAT Writing middle 50% range 398–513. ACT middle 50% range 17–22. Minimum paper TOEFL 550. Minimum computer TOEFL 213. Minimum web-based TOEFL 79. **Basis for Candidate Selection:** *Very important factors considered include:* Rigor of secondary school record, standardized test scores. *Important factors considered include:* Academic GPA. *Other factors considered include:* Class rank, recommendation(s), character/personal qualities, extracurricular activities, geographical residence, interview, state residency. **Freshman Admission Requirements:** High school diploma is required and GED is accepted. *Academic units recommended:* 4 English, 2 mathematics, 2 science, 2 foreign language, 3 social studies, 1 history, 0 computer applications. For the required units, 10 must come from the fields of English, foreign language. **Freshman Admission Statistics:** 2,332 applied, 57% admitted, 42% enrolled. **Transfer Admission Requirements:** College transcript(s), minimum college GPA of 2.0 required. Lowest grade transferable D. **General Admission Information:** Application fee $30. Nonfall registration accepted. Admission may be deferred for a maximum of 2 years. Credit offered for CEEB Advanced Placement tests.

COSTS AND FINANCIAL AID
Required Forms and Deadlines: FAFSA. **Notification of Awards:** Applicants will be notified of awards on a rolling basis beginning 3/1. **Types of Aid:** *Need-based scholarships/grants:* Federal Pell, SEOG, state scholarships/grants, private scholarships, the school's own gift aid. *Loans:* Direct Subsidized Stafford, Direct Unsubsidized Stafford, Direct PLUS, Federal Perkins, Alternative Loans. **Student Employment:** Federal Work-Study Program available. Institutional employment available. Highest amount earned per year from on-campus jobs $1,854. Off-campus job opportunities are good. **Financial Aid Statistics:** 68% freshmen, 731% undergrads receive need-based scholarship or grant aid. 41% freshmen, 293% undergrads receive non-need-based scholarship or grant aid. 52% freshmen, 620% undergrads receive need-based self-help aid. 7% freshmen, 49% undergrads receive athletic scholarships. 89% freshmen, 92% undergrads receive any aid. 65% undergrads borrow to pay for school. Average cumulative indebtedness $21,211. **Criteria for awarding institutional aid:** *Non-need-based:* Academics, alumni affiliation, art, athletics, leadership, minority status, music/drama, state/district residency.

ADELPHI UNIVERSITY

Levermore Hall 114, 1 South Avenue, Garden City, NY 11530
Phone: 516-877-3050 **Financial Aid Phone:** 516-877-2240
E-mail: admissions@adelphi.edu **CEEB Code:** 2003
Fax: 516-877-3039 **Website:** www.adelphi.edu **ACT Code:** 2664

This private school was founded in 1896. It has a 75-acre campus.

RATINGS
Admissions Selectivity Rating: 81   **Fire Safety Rating:** 99   **Green Rating:** 87

STUDENTS AND FACULTY
Enrollment: 4,923. **Student Body:** 71% female, 29% male, 8% out-of-state, 3% international (63 countries represented). Asian 6%, African American 11%, Caucasian 55%, Hispanic 7%.
Retention and Graduation: 52% freshmen graduate within 4 years. 44% grads go on to further study within 1 year. 2% grads pursue law degrees. 11% grads pursue business degrees. 7% grads pursue medical degrees. **Faculty:** Student/faculty ratio 9:1. 308 full-time faculty, 86% hold PhDs, 21% are members of minority groups, 55% are women.

ACADEMICS
Degrees: Associate, bachelor's, master's, post-bachelor's certificate, post-master's certificate. **Classes:** Most classes have 10–19 students. Most lab/discussion sessions have 10–19 students. **Majors with Highest Enrollment:** Business/commerce; education; nursing, other. **Special Study Options:** Accelerated program, cross-registration, distance learning, double major, dual enrollment, English as a Second Language (ESL), honors program, independent study, internships, liberal arts/career combination, student-designed major, study abroad, teacher certification program, weekend college, joint degrees; learning disabilities program; distance learning program is being restructured. **Honors programs:** The Honors College seeks to prepare highly talented and motivated students to face the 21st century by providing them with the intellectual perspectives and critical skills necessary to exercise responsible leadership. It involves an intense curricular and extracurricular program that asks students to view themselves and their work with integrity, passion, and seriousness. **Combined degree programs:** BA/JD, BA/MA, BA/DDS, BA/MEng, optometry, dentistry, physical therapy, law, environment studies, osteopathic. Special

programs offered to physically disabled students include note-taking services, reader services, tape recorders, tutors. **Career services:** Alumni network, alumni services, career/job search classes, career assessment, internships, regional alumni.

FACILITIES
Housing: Coed dorms, special housing for disabled students, theme housing; honors students live in the same residence hall; EXCEL mentoring program. 95% of campus accessible to physically disabled. **Special Academic Facilities/Equipment:** Art gallery, sculpture and ceramics studios, bronze-casting foundry, theatre, language labs. **Computers:** 90% of dorms, 99% of libraries, 99% of dining areas, 90% of student union, 75% of common outdoor areas have wireless network access. Students can register for classes online. Administrative functions (other than registration) can be performed online.

CAMPUS LIFE
Environment: Metropolis. **Activities:** Choral groups, concert band, dance, drama/theater, jazz band, literary magazine, music ensembles, musical theater, opera, radio station, student government, student newspaper, student-run film society, symphony orchestra, yearbook, campus ministries, international student organization, Model UN. **Organizations:** 80 registered organizations, 21 honor societies, 5 religious organizations. 3 fraternities, 7 sororities. **Athletics (Intercollegiate):** *Men:* Baseball, basketball, cross-country, golf, lacrosse, soccer, swimming, tennis, track/field (outdoor), track/field (indoor). *Women:* Basketball, bowling, cross-country, field hockey, lacrosse, soccer, softball, swimming, tennis, track/field (outdoor), track/field (indoor), volleyball. **On-Campus Highlights:** Ruth S. Harley University Center, UnderGround Cafe, Swirbul Library, New Fine Arts Building, New Recreational Center. **Environmental Initiatives:** LEED Silver rating for the CSPA project; 100% green electricity; use of geothermal heating and cooling systems in the newly constructed and proposed residence halls.

ADMISSIONS
Freshman Academic Profile: Average high school GPA 3.37. 24% in top 10% of high school class, 60% in top 25% of high school class, 87% in top 50% of high school class. 73% from public high schools. SAT Math middle 50% range 500–600. SAT Critical Reading middle 50% range 480–580. SAT Writing middle 50% range 498–590. ACT middle 50% range 20–26. Minimum paper TOEFL 550. Minimum computer TOEFL 80. **Basis for Candidate Selection:** *Very important factors considered include:* Rigor of secondary school record. *Important factors considered include:* Class rank, application essay, academic GPA, standardized test scores, character/personal qualities, extracurricular activities, talent/ability, volunteer work. *Other factors considered include:* Alumni/ae relation, first generation, interview, level of applicant's interest, work experience. **Freshman Admission Requirements:** High school diploma is required and GED is accepted. *Academic units recommended:* 4 English, 3 mathematics, 3 science, 2 foreign language, 4 social studies, history, English, math, science, or foreign language. **Freshman Admission Statistics:** 7,359 applied, 70% admitted, 20% enrolled. **Transfer Admission Requirements:** College transcript(s), essay or personal statement, minimum college GPA of 2.3 required. **General Admission Information:** Application fee $35. Notification on a rolling basis, beginning on or about 10/1. Nonfall registration accepted. Credit and/or placement offered for CEEB Advanced Placement tests.

COSTS AND FINANCIAL AID
Annual tuition $24,100. Room and board $10,500. Required fees $1,200. Average book expense $1,000. **Required Forms and Deadlines:** FAFSA, state aid form. Priority financial aid filing date 3/1. **Notification of Awards:** Applicants will be notified of awards on a rolling basis beginning 2/15. **Types of Aid:** *Need-based scholarships/grants:* Federal Pell, SEOG, state scholarships/grants, private scholarships, the school's own gift aid, United Negro College Fund. *Loans:* Direct Subsidized Stafford, Direct Unsubsidized Stafford, Direct PLUS, Federal Perkins, Federal Nursing, New York HELP Program (private alternative). **Student Employment:** Federal Work-Study Program available. Institutional employment available. Highest amount earned per year from on-campus jobs $20,594. Off-campus job opportunities are good. **Financial Aid Statistics:** 54% freshmen, 45% undergrads receive need-based scholarship or grant aid. 47% freshmen, 43% undergrads receive non-need-based scholarship or grant aid. 62% freshmen, 54% undergrads receive need-based self-help aid. 2% freshmen, 2% undergrads receive athletic scholarships. 90% freshmen, 88% undergrads receive any aid. 69% undergrads borrow to pay for school. Average cumulative indebtedness $28,307. **Criteria for awarding institutional aid:** *Non-need-based:* Academics, alumni affiliation, art, athletics, leadership, minority status, music/drama, religious affiliation.

ADRIAN COLLEGE

110 South Madison Street, Adrian, MI 49221
Phone: 517-265-5161 **Financial Aid Phone:** 517-265-5161
E-mail: admissions@adrian.edu **CEEB Code:** 1001
Fax: 517-264-3331 **Website:** www.adrian.edu **ACT Code:** 1954

This private school, affiliated with the Methodist Church, was founded in 1859. It has a 100-acre campus.

RATINGS

Admissions Selectivity Rating: 78   **Fire Safety Rating:** 60*   **Green Rating:** 60*

STUDENTS AND FACULTY

Enrollment: 1,308. **Student Body:** 47% female, 53% male, 24% out-of-state, 4% international (6 countries represented). Asian 1%, African American 4%, Caucasian 77%, Hispanic 2%.
Retention and Graduation: 73% freshmen return for sophomore year. 40% freshmen graduate within 4 years. 25% grads go on to further study within 1 year. 51% grads pursue arts and sciences degrees. 9% grads pursue law degrees. 9% grads pursue business degrees. 22% grads pursue medical degrees. **Faculty:** Student/faculty ratio 12:1. 78 full-time faculty, 82% hold PhDs, 9% are members of minority groups, 41% are women.

ACADEMICS

Degrees: Associate, bachelor's, transfer associate. **Classes:** Most classes have 10–19 students. Most lab/discussion sessions have 10–19 students. **Majors with Highest Enrollment:** Business/commerce; English language and literature; kinesiology and exercise science. **Special Study Options:** Double major, dual enrollment, honors program, independent study, internships, student-designed major, study abroad, teacher certification program. **Combined degree programs:** BA/MEng. Special programs offered to physically disabled students include note-taking services, reader services, tape recorders, tutors. **Career services:** Alumni network, alumni services, career assessment, internships, regional alumni. **Career services highlights include:** internships.

FACILITIES

Housing: Coed dorms, men's dorms, women's dorms, fraternity/sorority housing, apartments for single students, special-interest houses. 50% of campus accessible to physically disabled. **Special Academic Facilities/Equipment:** Art gallery, studio theatre, arboretum, education resource center, language lab, observatory, planetarium, solar greenhouse, nuclear magnetic resonance spectrometer, differential scanning calorimeter. **Computers:** 100% of classrooms, 100% of dorms, 100% of libraries, 100% of dining areas, 100% of student union, 100% of common outdoor areas have wireless network access. Students can register for classes online. Administrative functions (other than registration) can be performed online.

CAMPUS LIFE

Environment: Town. **Activities:** Choral groups, concert band, dance, drama/theater, jazz band, literary magazine, marching band, music ensembles, musical theater, pep band, radio station, student government, student newspaper, symphony orchestra, yearbook, campus ministries, international student organization. **Organizations:** 68 registered organizations, 13 honor societies, 8 religious organizations. 4 fraternities, 3 sororities. **Athletics (Intercollegiate):** *Men:* Baseball, basketball, cross-country, football, golf, ice hockey, lacrosse, soccer, tennis, track/field (outdoor). *Women:* Basketball, bowling, cross-country, golf, ice hockey, lacrosse, soccer, softball, tennis, track/field (outdoor), volleyball. **On-Campus Highlights:** Caine Student Center, Shipman Library, Merillat Sport and Fitness Center.

ADMISSIONS

Freshman Academic Profile: Average high school GPA 3.3. 17% in top 10% of high school class, 46% in top 25% of high school class, 81% in top 50% of high school class. SAT Math middle 50% range 410–535. SAT Critical Reading middle 50% range 430–515. ACT middle 50% range 20–25. Minimum paper TOEFL 500. Minimum computer TOEFL 173. **Basis for Candidate Selection:** *Very important factors considered include:* Class rank, rigor of secondary school record. *Important factors considered include:* Academic GPA, standardized test scores, talent/ability. *Other factors considered include:* Alumni/ae relation, character/personal qualities, extracurricular activities, interview, level of applicant's interest, volunteer work, work experience. **Freshman Admission Requirements:** High school diploma is required and GED is accepted. *Academic units recommended:* 4 English, 3 mathematics, 2 science, (1 science labs), 2 foreign language, 1 social studies, 1 history, 2 academic electives. **Freshman Admission Statistics:** 3,709 applied, 64% admitted, 21% enrolled. **Transfer Admission Requirements:** High school transcript, college transcript(s), minimum college GPA of 2.7 required. Lowest grade transferable C. **General Admission Information:** Notification on a rolling basis, beginning on or about 9/1. Nonfall registration not accepted. Admission may be deferred for a maximum of 1 year. Credit and/or placement offered for CEEB Advanced Placement tests.

COSTS AND FINANCIAL AID

Annual tuition $23,090. Room and board $7,600. Required fees $300. Average book expense $400. **Required Forms and Deadlines:** FAFSA Financial aid filing deadline 3/1. Priority financial aid filing date 3/1. **Notification of Awards:** Applicants will be notified of awards on a rolling basis beginning 3/15. **Types of Aid:** *Need-based scholarships/grants:* Federal Pell, SEOG, state scholarships/grants, private scholarships, the school's own gift aid. *Loans:* Direct Subsidized Stafford, Direct Unsubsidized Stafford, Direct PLUS, Federal Perkins. **Student Employment:** Federal Work-Study Program available. Institutional employment available. Highest amount earned per year from on-campus jobs $1,700. Off-campus job opportunities are good. **Financial Aid Statistics:** 67% freshmen, 67% undergrads receive need-based scholarship or grant aid. 67% freshmen, 68% undergrads receive non-need-based scholarship or grant aid. 68% freshmen, 70% undergrads receive need-based self-help aid. 98% freshmen, 92% undergrads receive any aid. 81% undergrads borrow to pay for school. Average cumulative indebtedness $20,000. **Criteria for awarding institutional aid:** *Non-need-based:* Academics, alumni affiliation, art, leadership, music/drama, religious affiliation.

AGNES SCOTT COLLEGE

141 East College Avenue, Atlanta/Decatur, GA 30030-3797
Phone: 404-471-6285 **Financial Aid Phone:** 404-471-6395
E-mail: admission@agnesscott.edu **CEEB Code:** 5002
Fax: 404-471-6414 **Website:** www.agnesscott.edu **ACT Code:** 780

This private school, affiliated with the Presbyterian Church, was founded in 1889. It has a 100-acre campus.

RATINGS

Admissions Selectivity Rating: 92   **Fire Safety Rating:** 91   **Green Rating:** 95

STUDENTS AND FACULTY

Enrollment: 784. **Student Body:** 100% female, 42% out-of-state, 7% international (27 countries represented). Asian 4%, African American 25%, Caucasian 49%, Hispanic 5%.
Retention and Graduation: 86% freshmen return for sophomore year. 60% freshmen graduate within 4 years. 25% grads go on to further study within 1 year. 15% grads pursue arts and sciences degrees. 4% grads pursue law degrees. 2% grads pursue business degrees. 2% grads pursue medical degrees. **Faculty:** Student/faculty ratio 9:1. 82 full-time faculty, 98% hold PhDs, 20% are members of minority groups, 61% are women.

ACADEMICS

Degrees: Bachelor's, master's, post-bachelor's certificate. **Classes:** Most classes have 10–19 students. Most lab/discussion sessions have 10–19 students. **Majors with Highest Enrollment:** English language and literature; history; psychology. **Special Study Options:** Accelerated program, cross-registration, double major, dual enrollment, exchange student program (domestic), external degree program, independent study, internships, student-designed major, study abroad, teacher certification program, Woodruff Scholars program for women beyond traditional college age; exchange program with Mills College; Atlanta Semester. **Combined degree programs:** BA/MA, BA/MA Arch. w/Wash. U, BA/BS Eng, BA/BSN w/Emory. Special programs offered to physically disabled students include note-taking services, reader services, tape recorders, tutors. **Career services:** Alumni network, alumni services, career/job search classes, career assessment, internships, regional alumni. **Career services highlights include:** internships.

FACILITIES

Housing: Women's dorms, apartments for single students, theme housing 90% of campus accessible to physically disabled. **Special Academic Facilities/Equipment:** Art galleries, state-of-the-art science building opened in January 2003, collaborative learning centers, language lab, electron microscope, observatory, 30-inch Beck telescope, planetarium, interactive learning center, multimedia presentation classrooms, instructional technology center, multi-media production facility. **Computers:** 50% of classrooms, 100% of libraries, 100% of student union, 10% of common outdoor areas have wireless network access. Students can register for classes online. Administrative functions (other than registration) can be performed online.

CAMPUS LIFE

Environment: Metropolis. **Activities:** Choral groups, dance, drama/theater, literary magazine, marching band, music ensembles, musical theater, pep band, student government, student newspaper, symphony orchestra, television station, yearbook, campus ministries, international student organization, Model UN. **Organizations:** 80 registered organizations, 12 honor societies, 12 religious organizations. **Athletics (Intercollegiate):** *Women:* Basketball, lacrosse, soccer, softball, tennis, volleyball. **On-Campus Highlights:** New $36.5 million Science Center, Alston Campus Center, newly renovated Bradley Observatory, McCain Library, Several residence halls are on the National Regist. **Environmental Initiatives:** Converted to campus-wide single stream recycling and composting. Agnes Scott is committed to Zero Waste, and has already achived a 62% waste diversion rate. Implementing a climate action plan with major efficiency and renewable energy commitments. Continued guidance and leadership from an inclusive sustainability steering committee with active Board and alumnae representatives as well as students, faculty, staff, and all management.

ADMISSIONS

Freshman Academic Profile: Average high school GPA 3.57. 33% in top 10% of high school class, 66% in top 25% of high school class, 93% in top 50% of high school class. 80% from public high schools. SAT Math middle 50% range 490–620. SAT Critical Reading middle 50% range 520–650. SAT Writing middle 50% range 520–640. ACT middle 50% range 22–28. Minimum paper TOEFL 577. Minimum computer TOEFL 233. **Basis for Candidate Selection:** *Very important factors considered include:* Class rank, application essay, academic GPA, recommendation(s), rigor of secondary school record, standardized test scores, character/personal qualities, talent/ability. *Important factors considered include:* Extracurricular activities, volunteer work, work experience. *Other factors considered include:* Alumni/ae relation, first generation, geographical residence, interview, level of applicant's interest, racial/ethnic status, state residency. **Freshman Admission Requirements:** High school diploma is required and GED is accepted. *Academic units recommended:* 4 English, 3 mathematics, 2 science, (2 science labs), 2 foreign language, 2 social studies, 2 history. **Freshman Admission Statistics:** 1,984 applied, 46% admitted, 26% enrolled. **Transfer Admission Requirements:** High school transcript, college transcript(s), essay or personal statement, statement of good standing from prior institution(s). Minimum college GPA of 3.0 required. Lowest grade transferable C. **General Admission Information:** Application fee $35. Nonfall registration accepted. Admission may be deferred for a maximum of 1 year. Credit and/or placement offered for CEEB Advanced Placement tests.

COSTS AND FINANCIAL AID

Annual tuition $31,068. Room and board $9,850. Required fees $215. Average book expense $1,000. **Required Forms and Deadlines:** FAFSA Financial aid filing deadline 5/1. Priority financial aid filing date 2/15. **Notification of Awards:** Applicants will be notified of awards on a rolling basis beginning 3/1. **Types of Aid:** *Need-based scholarships/grants:* Federal Pell, SEOG, state scholarships/grants, private scholarships, the school's own gift aid. *Loans:* Direct Subsidized Stafford, Direct Unsubsidized Stafford, Direct PLUS. **Student Employment:** Federal Work-Study Program available. Institutional employment available. Off-campus job opportunities are excellent. **Financial Aid Statistics:** 77% freshmen, 73% undergrads receive need-based scholarship or grant aid. 23% freshmen, 19% undergrads receive non-need-based scholarship or grant aid. 61% freshmen, 65% undergrads receive need-based self-help aid. 100% freshmen, 98% undergrads receive any aid. 69% undergrads borrow to pay for school. Average cumulative indebtedness $23,176. **Criteria for awarding institutional aid:** *Non-need-based:* Academics, leadership, minority status, music/drama, religious affiliation, state/district residency.

ALABAMA A&M UNIVERSITY

P.O. Box 908, Normal, AL 35762
Phone: 256-851-5245 **Financial Aid Phone:**
E-mail: juan.alexander@aamu.edu **CEEB Code:** 1003
Fax: 256-851-5249 **ACT Code:** 2

This public school was founded in 1875. It has a 880-acre campus.

RATINGS

Admissions Selectivity Rating: 60*   **Fire Safety Rating:** 60*   **Green Rating:** 60*

STUDENTS AND FACULTY

Enrollment: 4,489. **Student Body:** 52% female, 48% male, 31% out-of-state, 1% international (42 countries represented). African American 70%, Caucasian 2%.
Retention and Graduation: 77% grads go on to further study within 1 year. 40% grads pursue arts and sciences degrees. 2% grads pursue law degrees. 45% grads pursue business degrees. 11% grads pursue medical degrees. **Faculty:** Student/faculty ratio 14:1. 314 full-time faculty, 45% hold PhDs, 55% are members of minority groups, 39% are women. 1% of classes are taught by teaching assistants.

ACADEMICS

Degrees: Bachelor's, master's, post-master's certificate. **Classes:** Most classes have fewer than 10 students. Most lab/discussion sessions have 20–29 students. **Majors with Highest Enrollment:** Biology/biological sciences; elementary education and teaching; mechanical engineering related technologies/technicians, other. **Special Study Options:** Accelerated program, cooperative education program, distance learning, double major, dual enrollment, exchange student program (domestic), honors program, independent study, internships, study abroad, teacher certification program, weekend college. Special programs offered to physically disabled students include note-taking services, reader services, tape recorders, tutors. **Career services:** Career/job search classes, career assessment, internships, regional alumni.

FACILITIES

Housing: Men's dorms, women's dorms, apartments for single students. 65% of campus accessible to physically disabled. **Special Academic Facilities/Equipment:** State Black Archives **Computers:** Students can register for classes online.

CAMPUS LIFE

Environment: City. **Activities:** Choral groups, concert band, dance, drama/theater, jazz band, literary magazine, marching band, music ensembles, pep band, radio station, student government, student newspaper, symphony orchestra, television station, yearbook, campus ministries, international student organization. **Organizations:** 76 registered organizations, 14 honor societies, 3 religious organizations. 4 fraternities, 4 sororities. **Athletics (Intercollegiate):** *Men:* Baseball, basketball, cross-country, football, golf, soccer, track/field (outdoor). *Women:* Basketball, cross-country, soccer, softball, track/field (outdoor), volleyball. **On-Campus Highlights:** Engineering building, cafeteria, gym, business school, Dawson Building.

ADMISSIONS

Freshman Academic Profile: 90% from public high schools. SAT Math middle 50% range 380–470. SAT Critical Reading middle 50% range 400–470. SAT Writing middle 50% range 380–460. ACT middle 50% range 16–19. Minimum paper TOEFL 550. Minimum computer TOEFL 213. **Basis for Candidate Selection:** *Very important factors considered include:* Standardized test scores, alumni/ae relation, geographical residence, state residency. *Important factors considered include:* Racial/ethnic status. *Other factors considered include:* Class rank, recommendation(s). **Freshman Admission Requirements:** High school diploma is required and GED is accepted. *Academic units required:* 4 English, 4 mathematics, 4 science, (2 science labs), 4 social studies, 4 history. **Freshman Admission Statistics:** 5,697 applied, 47% admitted, 39% enrolled. **Transfer Admission Requirements:** High school transcript, college transcript(s), standardized test scores, statement of good standing from prior institution(s). Minimum college GPA of 2.5 required. Lowest grade transferable C. **General Admission Information:** Application fee $10. Regular application deadline 7/1. Notification on a rolling basis, beginning on or about 4/15. Nonfall registration accepted. Admission may be deferred for a maximum of 1 year. Neither credit nor placement offered for CEEB Advanced Placement tests.

COSTS AND FINANCIAL AID

Annual in-state tuition $3,948. Annual out-of-state tuition $7,896. Room and board $5,350. Required fees $744. **Required Forms and Deadlines:** FAFSA, institution's own financial aid form. Priority financial aid filing date 4/15. **Types of Aid:** *Need-based scholarships/grants:* Federal Pell, SEOG, state scholarships/grants, private scholarships, the school's own gift aid, United Negro College Fund. *Loans:* Direct Subsidized Stafford, Direct Unsubsidized Stafford, Direct PLUS, Federal Perkins, state loans, college/university loans from institutional funds. **Student Employment:** Highest amount earned per year from on-campus jobs $5,400.

ALABAMA STATE UNIVERSITY

915 South Jackson Street, Montgomery, AL 36104
Phone: 334-229-4291 **Financial Aid Phone:**
E-mail: dlamar@asunet.alasu.edu
Fax: 334-229-4984 **Website:** www.alasu.edu **ACT Code:** 8

This public school was founded in 1867.

RATINGS
Admissions Selectivity Rating: 60*   **Fire Safety Rating:** 60*   **Green Rating:** 60*

STUDENTS AND FACULTY
Enrollment: 5,125. **Student Body:** 59% female, 41% male, 35% out-of-state. African American 95%, Caucasian 4%.
Retention and Graduation: 68% freshmen return for sophomore year. 50% grads go on to further study within 1 year. **Faculty:** Student/faculty ratio 19:1. 229 full-time faculty, 59% hold PhDs, 67% are members of minority groups, 54% are women.

ACADEMICS
Degrees: Bachelor's, master's. **Majors with Highest Enrollment:** Computer and information science; criminal justice/safety studies; elementary education and teaching. **Special Study Options:** Cooperative education program, cross-registration, double major, honors program, internships, teacher certification program. Special programs offered to physically disabled students include note-taking services, tape recorders. **Career services:** Career/job search classes, internships.

FACILITIES
Housing: Men's dorms, women's dorms, apartments for single students, Honor dorms. 90% of campus accessible to physically disabled. **Special Academic Facilities/Equipment:** Levi Watkins Learning Center Special Collections. **Computers:** Students can register for classes online. Administrative functions (other than registration) can be performed online.

CAMPUS LIFE
Activities: Choral groups, concert band, dance, drama/theater, jazz band, marching band, music ensembles, musical theater, pep band, radio station, student government, student newspaper, symphony orchestra, yearbook. **Organizations:** 64 registered organizations, 17 honor societies. 5 fraternities, 4 sororities. **Athletics (Intercollegiate):** *Men:* Baseball, basketball, cheerleading, cross-country, football, golf, tennis, track/field (outdoor), track/field (indoor). *Women:* Basketball, cheerleading, cross-country, golf, softball, tennis, track/field (outdoor), track/field (indoor), volleyball.

ADMISSIONS
Freshman Academic Profile: Average high school GPA 2.67. SAT Math middle 50% range 340–444. SAT Critical Reading middle 50% range 350–457. ACT middle 50% range 14–18. Minimum paper TOEFL 500. **Basis for Candidate Selection:** *Very important factors considered include:* Rigor of secondary school record. *Important factors considered include:* Class rank, standardized test scores. *Other factors considered include:* recommendation(s). **Freshman Admission Requirements:** High school diploma is required and GED is accepted. *Academic units recommended:* 3 English, 2 mathematics, 2 science, 2 foreign language, 2 social studies. **Freshman Admission Statistics: Transfer Admission Requirements:** College transcript(s), minimum college GPA of 2.0 required. Lowest grade transferable C. **General Admission Information:** Regular application deadline 7/30. Notification on a rolling basis, beginning on or about 8/30. Nonfall registration accepted. Admission may be deferred for a maximum of 1 semester. Credit and/or placement offered for CEEB Advanced Placement tests.

COSTS AND FINANCIAL AID
Annual in-state tuition $2,904. Annual out-of-state tuition $5,808. Room and board $3,700. Average book expense $800. **Required Forms and Deadlines:** FAFSA, state aid form. Priority financial aid filing date 5/1. **Notification of Awards:** Applicants will be notified of awards on a rolling basis beginning 5/15. **Types of Aid:** *Need-based scholarships/grants:* Federal Pell, SEOG, state scholarships/grants, private scholarships, the school's own gift aid. *Loans:* Direct Subsidized Stafford, Direct Unsubsidized Stafford, Direct PLUS, Federal Perkins. **Student Employment:** Federal Work-Study Program available. Institutional employment available. Highest amount earned per year from on-campus jobs $2,400. Off-campus job opportunities are good. **Financial Aid Statistics:** 70% freshmen, 68% undergrads receive need-based scholarship or grant aid. 17% freshmen, 20% undergrads receive non-need-based scholarship or grant aid. 73% freshmen, 72% undergrads receive need-based self-help aid. 3% freshmen, 5% undergrads receive athletic scholarships. 72% undergrads borrow to pay for school. Average cumulative indebtedness $34,430. **Criteria for awarding institutional aid:** *Non-need-based:* Academics, athletics.

ALASKA BIBLE COLLEGE

P.O. Box 289, Glennallen, AK 99588
Phone: 907-822-3201 **Financial Aid Phone:**
E-mail: info@akbible.edu **Fax:** 907-822-5027 **Website:** www.akbible.edu

This private school, affiliated with the Christian (Nondenominational) Church, was founded in 1966. It has a 90-acre campus.

RATINGS
Admissions Selectivity Rating: 60*   **Fire Safety Rating:** 60*   **Green Rating:** 60*

STUDENTS AND FACULTY
Student Body: 60% out-of-state.
Retention and Graduation: 67% freshmen return for sophomore year. **Faculty:** Student/faculty ratio 7:1. 4 full-time faculty, 25% hold PhDs.

ACADEMICS
Degrees: Associate, bachelor's, certificate, terminal associate, transfer associate. **Special Study Options:** Cooperative education program, double major, independent study, internships.

FACILITIES
Housing: Men's dorms, women's dorms, apartments for married students, apartments for single students.

CAMPUS LIFE
Environment: Rural. **On-Campus Highlights:** Annette Ball Memorial Library, Food Cache, Murdock Campus Center, Vince Joy Hall, Firebreak.

ADMISSIONS
Freshman Academic Profile: Minimum paper TOEFL 500. Minimum computer TOEFL 173. **Basis for Candidate Selection:** *Very important factors considered include:* Application essay, recommendation(s), rigor of secondary school record, standardized test scores, character/personal qualities, interview, religious affiliation/commitment. *Important factors considered include:* Volunteer work, work experience. *Other factors considered include:* Extracurricular activities, racial/ethnic status, talent/ability. **Freshman Admission Requirements:** High school diploma is required and GED is accepted. **Freshman Admission Statistics:** 11 applied, 100% admitted, 100% enrolled. **Transfer Admission Requirements:** High school transcript, college transcript(s), essay or personal statement, interview, standardized test scores, statement of good standing from prior institution(s). Minimum college GPA of 2.0 required. Lowest grade transferable C. **General Admission Information:** Application fee $35. Regular application deadline 7/1. Nonfall registration accepted. Admission may be deferred for a maximum of 1 year.

COSTS AND FINANCIAL AID
Annual tuition $5,720. Room and board $4,570. Average book expense $400.

ALASKA PACIFIC UNIVERSITY

4101 University Drive, Anchorage, AK 99508
Phone: 907-564-8248 **Financial Aid Phone:** 907-564-8341
E-mail: admissions@alaskapacific.edu **CEEB Code:** 4201
Fax: 907-562-4276 **Website:** www.alaskapacific.edu **ACT Code:** 62

This private school was founded in 1957. It has a 170-acre campus.

RATINGS
Admissions Selectivity Rating: 85   **Fire Safety Rating:** 83   **Green Rating:** 85

STUDENTS AND FACULTY
Enrollment: 493. **Student Body:** 67% female, 33% male, 13% out-of-state (2 countries represented). Asian 3%, African American 3%, Caucasian 56%, Hispanic 5%, Native American 18%.
Retention and Graduation: 75% freshmen return for sophomore year. 17% freshmen graduate within 4 years. **Faculty:** Student/faculty ratio 8.5:1. 53 full-time faculty, 58% hold PhDs, 4% are members of minority groups, 57% are women.

ACADEMICS
Degrees: Associate, bachelor's, certificate, master's, post-bachelor's certificate, terminal associate. **Classes:** Most classes have fewer than 10 students. Most lab/discussion sessions have fewer than 10 students. **Majors with Highest Enrollment:** Business administration and management; elementary education and teaching; parks, recreation and leisure facilities management. **Special**

Study Options: Distance learning, double major, exchange student program (domestic), independent study, internships, student-designed major, study abroad, teacher certification program. Degree Completion program for adult students and a distance education program for rural Alaskan Native adults. Special programs offered to physically disabled students include note-taking services, tape recorders, tutors. **Career services:** Career/job search classes, career assessment, internships.

FACILITIES

Housing: Coed dorms, cooperative housing, several theme houses, such as the Nordic Skiers House for ski team members. 75% of campus accessible to physically disabled. **Special Academic Facilities/Equipment:** Alaskana collection; GIS lab gym with pool; Student Center with weight room and indoor climbing wall; outdoor recreation center with classes and rental equipment; lake for canoeing and kayaking; trails for running, skiing, hiking, biking, etc. connected to city's trail system. **Computers:** 100% of classrooms, 100% of dorms, 100% of libraries, 100% of dining areas, 100% of student union, 100% of common outdoor areas have wireless network access. Students can register for classes on-line. Administrative functions (other than registration) can be performed online.

CAMPUS LIFE

Environment: City. **Activities:** Drama/theater, literary magazine, music ensembles, student government, student newspaper, yearbook. **Organizations:** 15 registered organizations, 1 religious organization. **On-Campus Highlights:** Student Center, climbing wall and weight room, pool, lounges in Grant Hall and in Carr Gottst. **Environmental Initiatives:** Kellogg Farm dedicated to organic and sustainable enterprises. APU does not use paper plates, plastic silverware, etc. Also paperless initiative. Committed to building a LEED level student center.

ADMISSIONS

Freshman Academic Profile: Average high school GPA 3.22. 24% in top 10% of high school class, 50% in top 25% of high school class, 76% in top 50% of high school class. 95% from public high schools. SAT Math middle 50% range 490–600. SAT Critical Reading middle 50% range 510–630. ACT middle 50% range 22–26. Minimum paper TOEFL 550. Minimum computer TOEFL 79. **Basis for Candidate Selection:** *Very important factors considered include:* Application essay, academic GPA, rigor of secondary school record. *Important factors considered include:* Recommendation(s), standardized test scores, alumni/ae relation, level of applicant's interest. *Other factors considered include:* Extracurricular activities, talent/ability, volunteer work, work experience. **Freshman Admission Requirements:** High school diploma is required and GED is accepted. *Academic units recommended:* 4 English, 3 mathematics, 2 science, (1 science labs), 2 foreign language, 1 social studies, 1 history. **Freshman Admission Statistics:** 1,353 applied, 35% admitted, 14% enrolled. **Transfer Admission Requirements:** College transcript(s), essay or personal statement, statement of good standing from prior institution(s). Minimum college GPA of 2.0 required. Lowest grade transferable C. **General Admission Information:** Application fee $25. Regular application deadline 8/15. Notification on a rolling basis, beginning on or about 1/15. Nonfall registration accepted. Admission may be deferred for a maximum of 1 year. Credit offered for CEEB Advanced Placement tests.

COSTS AND FINANCIAL AID

Annual tuition $22,500. Room and board $8,884. Required fees $110. Average book expense $1,000. **Required Forms and Deadlines:** FAFSA. Priority financial aid filing date 4/1. **Notification of Awards:** Applicants will be notified of awards on a rolling basis beginning 2/1. **Types of Aid:** *Need-based scholarships/grants:* Federal Pell, SEOG, state scholarships/grants, private scholarships, the school's own gift aid. *Loans:* Direct Subsidized Stafford, Direct Unsubsidized Stafford, Direct PLUS, state loans, college/university loans from institutional funds. **Student Employment:** Federal Work-Study Program available. Institutional employment available. Off-campus job opportunities are good. **Financial Aid Statistics:** 72% freshmen, 24% undergrads receive need-based scholarship or grant aid. 72% freshmen, 62% undergrads receive non-need-based scholarship or grant aid. 64% freshmen, 65% undergrads receive need-based self-help aid. 6% freshmen, 2% undergrads receive athletic scholarships. 88% freshmen, 92% undergrads receive any aid. 93% undergrads borrow to pay for school. Average cumulative indebtedness $16,750. **Criteria for awarding institutional aid:** *Non-need-based:* Academics, alumni affiliation, leadership, religious affiliation, state/district residency.

ALBANY COLLEGE OF PHARMACY

106 New Scotland Avenue, Albany, NY 12208
Phone: 518-694-7221 **Financial Aid Phone:** 518-694-7256
E-mail: admissions@acp.edu **CEEB Code:** 2013
Fax: 518-694-7322 **Website:** www.acp.edu **ACT Code:** 2672

This private school was founded in 1881. It has a 21-acre campus.

RATINGS
Admissions Selectivity Rating: 91 **Fire Safety Rating:** 60* **Green Rating:** 60*

STUDENTS AND FACULTY

Enrollment: 1,015. **Student Body:** 58% female, 42% male, 10% out-of-state, 8% international (6 countries represented). Asian 13%, African American 2%, Caucasian 73%, Hispanic 1%.
Retention and Graduation: 79% freshmen return for sophomore year. **Faculty:** Student/faculty ratio 16:1. 82 full-time faculty, 74% hold PhDs, 12% are members of minority groups, 49% are women.

ACADEMICS

Degrees: Bachelor's, certificate, first professional. **Classes:** Most classes have 20–29 students. Most lab/discussion sessions have 20–29 students. **Majors with Highest Enrollment:** Pharmacy (PharmD [US], PharmD or BS/BPharm [Canada]). **Special Study Options:** Accelerated program, cross-registration. **Combined degree programs:** BA/JD, PharmD/MS, PharmD/MBA, BS/Phy Asst. Special programs offered to physically disabled students include tutors. **Career services:** Career/job search classes, career assessment.

FACILITIES

Housing: Coed dorms, apartments for single students. 100% of campus accessible to physically disabled. **Special Academic Facilities/Equipment:** Throop Pharmaceutical Museum. **Computers:** Students can register for classes online. Administrative functions (other than registration) can be performed online. Undergraduates are required to own a computer.

CAMPUS LIFE

Environment: City. **Activities:** Choral groups, concert band, dance, literary magazine, student government, student newspaper, yearbook, international student organization. **Organizations:** 2 honor societies, 1 religious organizations. **Athletics (Intercollegiate):** *Men:* Basketball, soccer. *Women:* Basketball, soccer. **On-Campus Highlights:** NEW—ACP Student Center.

ADMISSIONS

Freshman Academic Profile: Average high school GPA 92. 47% in top 10% of high school class, 86% in top 25% of high school class, 99% in top 50% of high school class. SAT Math middle 50% range 570–650. SAT Critical Reading middle 50% range 530–620. SAT Writing middle 50% range 510–600. ACT middle 50% range 23–28. Minimum paper TOEFL 600. Minimum computer TOEFL 250. **Basis for Candidate Selection:** *Very important factors considered include:* Academic GPA, standardized test scores. *Important factors considered include:* Class rank, rigor of secondary school record. *Other factors considered include:* Application essay, recommendation(s), alumni/ae relation, character/personal qualities, extracurricular activities, geographical residence, level of applicant's interest, talent/ability, volunteer work, work experience. **Freshman Admission Requirements:** High school diploma is required and GED is accepted. *Academic units required:* 4 English, 4 mathematics, 3 science, (3 science labs), 4 social studies. *Academic units recommended:* 4 science, (4 science labs), 4 foreign language. **Freshman Admission Statistics:** 1,050 applied, 54% admitted, 43% enrolled. **Transfer Admission Requirements:** College transcript(s), essay or personal statement, statement of good standing from prior institution(s). Minimum college GPA of 3.2 required. Lowest grade transferable B. **General Admission Information:** Application fee $75. Early decision application deadline 11/1. Regular application deadline 3/1. Regular notification 3/15. Nonfall registration not accepted. Admission may be deferred for a maximum of 1 year. Credit offered for CEEB Advanced Placement tests.

COSTS AND FINANCIAL AID

Required Forms and Deadlines: FAFSA. Financial aid filing deadline 3/1. Priority financial aid filing date 2/1. **Notification of Awards:** Applicants will be notified of awards on a rolling basis beginning 3/25. **Types of Aid:** *Need-based scholarships/grants:* Federal Pell, SEOG, state scholarships/grants, private scholarships, the school's own gift aid. *Loans:* FFEL Subsidized Stafford, FFEL Unsubsidized Stafford, FFEL PLUS, Federal Perkins. **Financial Aid Statistics:** 68% freshmen, 49% undergrads receive need-based scholarship or grant aid. 9% freshmen, 4% undergrads receive non-need-based scholarship or grant aid. 62% freshmen, 56% undergrads receive need-based self-help aid. 92% undergrads borrow to pay for school. Average cumulative indebtedness $20,010. **Criteria for awarding institutional aid:** *Non-need-based:* Academics, alumni affiliation, leadership.

ALBANY STATE UNIVERSITY

504 College Drive, Albany, GA 31705
Phone: 229-430-4646 **Financial Aid Phone:** 229-430-4650
E-mail: admissions@asurams.edu **CEEB Code:** 5004
Fax: 229-430-3936 **Website:** www.asurams.edu **ACT Code:** 0782

This public school was founded in 1903. It has a 232-acre campus.

RATINGS
Admissions Selectivity Rating: 74   **Fire Safety Rating:** 60*   **Green Rating:** 77

STUDENTS AND FACULTY
Enrollment: 3,753. **Student Body:** 67% female, 33% male, 3.9% out-of-state, 1% international (27 countries represented). African American 92%, Caucasian 6%.
Retention and Graduation: Faculty: Student/faculty ratio 21.03:1. 152 full-time faculty, 40% are women.

ACADEMICS
Degrees: Associate, bachelor's, master's, post-master's certificate. **Classes:** Most classes have 20–29 students. **Majors with Highest Enrollment:** Business administration and management; early childhood education and teaching; nursing/registered nurse (RN, ASN, BSN, MSN). **Special Study Options:** Cooperative education program, cross-registration, distance learning, double major, dual enrollment, honors program, independent study, internships, liberal arts/career combination, study abroad, teacher certification program, weekend college, 3+2 and 2+2 engineering program with GA Tech. Pre-med, pre-med technology, pre-pharmacy study options. Online degree programs. **Honors programs:** The Velma Fudge Grant Honors Program represents a commitment made by Albany State University (ASU) to broaden and enrich educational experiences of bright, highly motivated and creative students. Honors Program students are provided opportunities for scholarships, access to special extracurricular programs, a chance to pursue independent projects and research interests, professional experience through internship programs and special service options. Through its specially designed curriculum, the university provides the opportunity for faculty to teach academically talented students in inventive, interdisciplinary, small class settings designed to fulfill core curriculum requirements, as well as in advanced or intensive classes in particular disciplines. The Honors Program is specifically designed for academic scholarship recipients, academically talented students and entering freshman and transfer students with a proven dedication to academic excellence and scholarship. The Honors Program student must reach beyond good grades for success and have the courage to demonstrate superior ethical leadership in his/her chosen field of study. Special programs offered to physically disabled students include note-taking services, reader services, tape recorders, tutors. **Career services:** Alumni network, alumni services, career assessment, internships, regional alumni. All opportunities are welcomed to provide experiential learning experiences for ASU students, especially those that result in employment opportunities.

FACILITIES
Housing: Coed dorms, men's dorms, women's dorms, apartments for single students, Upper classmen and graduate halls. 50% of campus accessible to physically disabled. **Computers:** 67% of dorms, have wireless network access.

CAMPUS LIFE
Environment: City. **Activities:** Choral groups, concert band, dance, drama/theater, jazz band, marching band, opera, radio station, student government, student newspaper, television station, campus ministries, international student organization, Model UN. **Organizations:** 70 registered organizations, 10 honor societies. 6 fraternities, 4 sororities. **Athletics (Intercollegiate):** *Men:* Baseball, basketball, cross-country, football, track/field (outdoor). *Women:* Basketball, cross-country, softball, tennis, track/field (outdoor), volleyball. **On-Campus Highlights:** Student Affairs Building, gymnasium, housing, stadium. **Environmental Initiatives:** Hazardous Waste Lab; recycling toner cartridges, paper and paper products, used motor oil, used cooking oil; containment for elevator reserviors.

ADMISSIONS
Freshman Academic Profile: Average high school GPA 2.81. SAT Math middle 50% range 410–480. SAT Critical Reading middle 50% range 420–480. ACT middle 50% range 17–19. Minimum paper TOEFL 523. Minimum computer TOEFL 193. **Basis for Candidate Selection:** *Very important factors considered include:* Academic GPA, standardized test scores. *Other factors considered include:* Interview. **Freshman Admission Requirements:** *Academic units required:* 4 English, 4 mathematics, 3 science, (2 science labs), 2 foreign language, 3 social studies. **Freshman Admission Statistics:** 4,773 applied, 42% admitted, 37% enrolled. **Transfer Admission Requirements:** College transcript(s), minimum college GPA of 2.0 required. Lowest grade transferable D. **General Admission Information:** Application fee $20. Regular application deadline 7/1. Nonfall registration accepted. Admission may be deferred for a maximum of 1 year.

COSTS AND FINANCIAL AID
Student Employment: Federal Work-Study Program available. Institutional employment available. Off-campus job opportunities are poor. **Financial Aid Statistics:** 98% freshmen, 93% undergrads receive any aid.

ALBERTA COLLEGE OF ART & DESIGN

1407 14 Avenue NW, Calgary, AB T2N 4R3 Canada
Phone: 403-284-7617 **Financial Aid Phone:** 403-284-7600
E-mail: admissions@acad.ca
Fax: 403-284-7644 **Website:** www.acad.ca

This public school was founded in 1926.

RATINGS
Admissions Selectivity Rating: 60*   **Fire Safety Rating:** 60*   **Green Rating:** 60*

STUDENTS AND FACULTY
Enrollment: 1,135. **Student Body:** 70% female, 30% male, 13% out-of-state, 5% international (49 countries represented).
Retention and Graduation: 73% freshmen return for sophomore year. 33% freshmen graduate within 4 years. **Faculty:** Student/faculty ratio 16.5:1. 44 full-time faculty, 36% are women.

ACADEMICS
Degrees: Bachelor's. **Majors with Highest Enrollment:** Drawing; painting; sculpture. **Special Study Options:** Cross-registration, exchange student program (domestic), internships, study abroad, mobility and exchange. Special programs offered to physically disabled students include reader services, tutors.

FACILITIES
Housing: Coed dorms, assisted off-campus housing search. 100% of campus accessible to physically disabled. **Special Academic Facilities/Equipment:** 2 art galleries. **Computers:** 100% of classrooms, have wireless network access. Students can register for classes online. Administrative functions (other than registration) can be performed online.

CAMPUS LIFE
Environment: Metropolis. **Activities:** Student government. **Athletics (Intercollegiate):** *Men:* Basketball, ice hockey, volleyball. *Women:* Basketball, volleyball. **On-Campus Highlights:** Facilities, glass department, graffiti stairwell, residence.

ADMISSIONS
Freshman Academic Profile: Minimum paper TOEFL 560. Minimum computer TOEFL 220. Minimum web-based TOEFL 83. **Basis for Candidate Selection:** *Very important factors considered include:* Application essay, academic GPA, level of applicant's interest, talent/ability. *Other factors considered include:* Recommendation(s), standardized test scores, character/personal qualities, extracurricular activities, work experience. **Freshman Admission Requirements:** High school diploma is required and GED is not accepted. *Academic units required:* 4 English. **Freshman Admission Statistics:** 740 applied, 46% admitted, 96% enrolled. **Transfer Admission Requirements:** College transcript(s), essay or personal statement. **General Admission Information:** Application fee $85. Early decision application deadline 2/1. Regular application deadline 4/1. Regular notification 5/15. Nonfall registration accepted. Credit and/or placement offered for CEEB Advanced Placement tests.

COSTS AND FINANCIAL AID
Annual in-state tuition $4,123. Annual out-of-state tuition $4,123. Room and board $10,000. Required fees $805. Average book expense $3,000. **Required Forms and Deadlines:** FAFSA. **Student Employment:** Off-campus job opportunities are good. **Criteria for awarding institutional aid:** *Non-need-based:* Academics, art.

ALBERTUS MAGNUS COLLEGE

700 Prospect Street, New Haven, CT 06511
Phone: 203-773-8501 **Financial Aid Phone:** 203-773-8508
E-mail: admissions@albertus.edu **CEEB Code:** 3001
Fax: 203-773-5248 **Website:** www.albertus.edu **ACT Code:** 549

This private school, affiliated with the Roman Catholic Church, was founded in 1925. It has a 50-acre campus.

RATINGS
Admissions Selectivity Rating: 71   **Fire Safety Rating:** 60*   **Green Rating:** 60*

STUDENTS AND FACULTY
Enrollment: 1,682. **Student Body:** 68% female, 32% male, 15% out-of-state. Asian 1%, African American 27%, Caucasian 55%, Hispanic 10%.
Retention and Graduation: 78% freshmen return for sophomore year. 49% freshmen graduate within 4 years. **Faculty:** Student/faculty ratio 13:1. 42 full-time faculty, 79% hold PhDs, 43% are women.

ACADEMICS
Degrees: Associate, bachelor's, certificate, master's. **Classes:** Most classes have 10–19 students. **Majors with Highest Enrollment:** Business/commerce; education; psychology. **Special Study Options:** Accelerated program, double major, honors program, independent study, internships, student-designed major, teacher certification program. **Honors programs:** Students may apply to follow the Honors Program, which involves work in special courses designated each semester as honors courses and the development of individual projects designed in consultation with faculty mentors. Entering qualified students are assigned to special honors courses and returning students interested in such a program should consult, by the spring of their sophomore year or earlier, with their advisor and the Director of the Honors Program. Special programs offered to physically disabled students include note-taking services, reader services, tape recorders, tutors. **Career services:** Alumni network, career/job search classes, career assessment, internships.

FACILITIES
Housing: Coed dorms, women's dorms, mansion-style residence halls. Substance free and quiet halls. 70% of campus accessible to physically disabled. **Special Academic Facilities/Equipment:** Margart McDonough Art Gallery.

CAMPUS LIFE
Environment: City. **Activities:** Choral groups, dance, drama/theater, literary magazine, musical theater, student government, yearbook, campus ministries. **Organizations:** 1 honor societies, 1 religious organizations. **Athletics (Intercollegiate):** *Men:* Baseball, basketball, cross-country, lacrosse, soccer, tennis, volleyball. *Women:* Basketball, cross-country, lacrosse, soccer, softball, tennis, volleyball. **On-Campus Highlights:** Center for Science, Art and Technology; athletic center, library, Campus Center, art gallery.

ADMISSIONS
Freshman Academic Profile: Average high school GPA 3.0. 10% in top 10% of high school class, 29% in top 25% of high school class, 68% in top 50% of high school class. 70% from public high schools. SAT Math middle 50% range 470–500. SAT Critical Reading middle 50% range 490–560. SAT Writing middle 50% range 430–560. Minimum paper TOEFL 550. Minimum computer TOEFL 213. **Basis for Candidate Selection:** *Very important factors considered include:* Academic GPA, rigor of secondary school record. *Important factors considered include:* Recommendation(s), standardized test scores. *Other factors considered include:* Class rank, application essay, alumni/ae relation, character/personal qualities, extracurricular activities, first generation, interview, level of applicant's interest, talent/ability, volunteer work, work experience. **Freshman Admission Requirements:** High school diploma is required and GED is accepted. *Academic units required:* 4 English, 2 mathematics, 2 science, 2 foreign language, 2 social studies, 2 history, 2 academic electives. *Academic units recommended:* 3 mathematics, 3 science, (1 science labs), 3 foreign language, 1 social studies, 2 history. **Freshman Admission Statistics:** 587 applied, 82% admitted, 21% enrolled. **Transfer Admission Requirements:** College transcript(s), minimum college GPA of 2.0 required. Lowest grade transferable C. **General Admission Information:** Application fee $35. Notification on a rolling basis, beginning on or about 12/1. Nonfall registration accepted. Admission may be deferred for a maximum of 1 year. Credit offered for CEEB Advanced Placement tests.

COSTS AND FINANCIAL AID
Annual tuition $20,166. Room and board $8,907. Required fees $908. Average book expense $920. **Required Forms and Deadlines:** FAFSA, institution's own financial aid form. Priority financial aid filing date 2/28. **Notification of Awards:** Applicants will be notified of awards on a rolling basis beginning 3/1. **Types of Aid:** *Need-based scholarships/grants:* Federal Pell, SEOG, state

scholarships/grants, the school's own gift aid. *Loans:* Direct Subsidized Stafford, Direct Unsubsidized Stafford, Direct PLUS, FFEL Subsidized Stafford, FFEL Unsubsidized Stafford, FFEL PLUS, Federal Perkins. **Student Employment:** Federal Work-Study Program available. **Financial Aid Statistics:** 87% freshmen, 75% undergrads receive any aid. Average cumulative indebtedness $15,625. **Criteria for awarding institutional aid:** *Non-need-based:* Academics, leadership, religious affiliation.

See page 1006.

ALBION COLLEGE

611 East Porter, Albion, MI 49224
Phone: 517-629-0321 **Financial Aid Phone:** 517-629-0440
E-mail: admissions@albion.edu **CEEB Code:** 1007
Fax: 517-629-0569 **Website:** www.albion.edu **ACT Code:** 1956

This private school, affiliated with the Methodist Church, was founded in 1835. It has a 585-acre campus.

RATINGS
Admissions Selectivity Rating: 84   **Fire Safety Rating:** 68   **Green Rating:** 85

STUDENTS AND FACULTY
Enrollment: 1,722. **Student Body:** 52% female, 48% male, 8% out-of-state, 2% international (21 countries represented). Asian 3%, African American 3%, Caucasian 86%, Hispanic 1%.
Retention and Graduation: 85% freshmen return for sophomore year. 63% freshmen graduate within 4 years. 41% grads go on to further study within 1 year. 18.5% grads pursue arts and sciences degrees. 3% grads pursue law degrees. 2% grads pursue business degrees. 5% grads pursue medical degrees. **Faculty:** Student/faculty ratio 13.29:1. 124 full-time faculty, 94% hold PhDs, 14% are members of minority groups, 39% are women.

ACADEMICS
Degrees: Bachelor's. **Classes:** Most classes have 10–19 students. Most lab/discussion sessions have 10–19 students. **Majors with Highest Enrollment:** Biology/biological sciences; economics; psychology. **Special Study Options:** Double major, dual enrollment, honors program, independent study, internships, liberal arts/career combination, student-designed major, study abroad, teacher certification program, Environmental Institute, Ford Institute for Public Service, Gerstacker Liberal Arts Program in Professional Management. **Honors programs:** The Honors Program at Albion was founded in 1976, and in August of 2004 it was renamed The Prentiss M. Brown Honors Institute. We provide an exciting and unique variety of academic experiences for highly motivated and talented students. The Institute's mix of small discussion classes, independent research, academic rigor, and personal attention provides Honors students with special challenges and opportunities for growth. Many of the college's finest teachers and scholars regularly contribute to the Institute's curriculum. **Combined degree programs:** BA/MEng. Special programs offered to physically disabled students include note-taking services, reader services, tape recorders, tutors. **Career services:** Alumni network, alumni services, career assessment, internships, regional alumni. **Career services highlights include:** our six academic institutes: Professional Management, Environmental, Education, Public Policy & Service, Honors and Pre-Health. All incorporate internships or experiential learning into the curriculum.

FACILITIES
Housing: Coed dorms, special housing for disabled students, women's dorms, fraternity/sorority housing, apartments for married students, cooperative housing, apartments for single students, special interest annexes available. 90% of campus accessible to physically disabled. **Special Academic Facilities/Equipment:** Visual arts museum, nature center, science complex museum, shark aquarium, greenhouse, geographic information systems/computer-aided mapping lab, observatory. **Computers:** 95% of classrooms, 100% of dorms, 100% of libraries, 100% of dining areas, 100% of student union, 25% of common outdoor areas have wireless network access. Students can register for classes online. Administrative functions (other than registration) can be performed online.

CAMPUS LIFE
Environment: Village. **Activities:** Choral groups, concert band, dance, drama/theater, jazz band, literary magazine, marching band, music ensembles, musical theater, pep band, radio station, student government, symphony orchestra,

yearbook, campus ministries, international student organization, Model UN. **Organizations:** 122 registered organizations, 17 honor societies, 11 religious organizations. 6 fraternities, 7 sororities. **Athletics (Intercollegiate):** *Men:* Baseball, basketball, cross-country, diving, equestrian sports, football, golf, soccer, swimming, tennis, track/field (outdoor), track/field (indoor). *Women:* Basketball, cross-country, diving, equestrian sports, golf, soccer, softball, swimming, tennis, track/field (outdoor), track/field (indoor), volleyball. **On-Campus Highlights:** Kellogg Student Center, Dow Recreation Center (athletic facility), quad, Baldwin Dining Hall, Science Center Atrium, Albion is often lauded for the amount of student space available. Whether it's lounge areas, computer classrooms, meeting spaces, or the myriad rooms in the Kellogg Center, Albion students find many areas to congregate socially and academically. **Environmental Initiatives:** Development of Institute for the Study of the Environment, to foster involvement and projects by students. Examples include development of residential E-house (2006–present), EPA P3 grant (2006–2007), two National Wildlife Federation Sustainability Fellows (2008), CREATE (a student-run environmental program), and active "Focus the Nation" and "Step it Up" participation (2007–2008). Development of an environmental category requirement as a graduation requirement for all students. This has fostered development of over 20 environmental courses spread over the arts, humanities, natural sciences and social sciences divisions of the college. Sustainability identified as one of four themes in current strategic planning process. Active research team and establishment of Sustainability Council advisory to the President.

ADMISSIONS

Freshman Academic Profile: Average high school GPA 3.51. 27% in top 10% of high school class, 56% in top 25% of high school class, 86% in top 50% of high school class. 75% from public high schools. SAT Math middle 50% range 560–670. SAT Critical Reading middle 50% range 530–660. ACT middle 50% range 22–28. Minimum paper TOEFL 550. Minimum computer TOEFL 270. **Basis for Candidate Selection:** *Very important factors considered include:* Application essay, academic GPA, recommendation(s), rigor of secondary school record, standardized test scores, alumni/ae relation, character/personal qualities, extracurricular activities, first generation, geographical residence, level of applicant's interest, state residency, talent/ability, volunteer work, work experience. **Freshman Admission Requirements:** High school diploma is required and GED is accepted. *Academic units required:* 4 English, 3 mathematics, 3 science, (2 science labs), 2 foreign language, 3 social studies, 1 history. *Academic units recommended:* 4 mathematics, 4 science, 3 foreign language, 4 social studies. **Freshman Admission Statistics:** 1,780 applied, 79% admitted, 31% enrolled. **Transfer Admission Requirements:** High school transcript, college transcript(s), essay or personal statement, interview, standardized test scores, statement of good standing from prior institution(s). Minimum college GPA of 2.5 required. Lowest grade transferable C. **General Admission Information:** Application fee $40. Notification on a rolling basis, beginning on or about 11/1. Nonfall registration accepted. Admission may be deferred for a maximum of 1 year. Credit and/or placement offered for CEEB Advanced Placement tests.

COSTS AND FINANCIAL AID

Average book expense $900. **Required Forms and Deadlines:** FAFSA. Priority financial aid filing date 3/1. **Notification of Awards:** Applicants will be notified of awards on a rolling basis beginning 3/15. **Types of Aid:** *Need-based scholarships/grants:* Federal Pell, SEOG, state scholarships/grants, private scholarships, the school's own gift aid. *Loans:* Direct Subsidized Stafford, Direct Unsubsidized Stafford, Direct PLUS, Federal Perkins.. **Student Employment:** Federal Work-Study Program available. Institutional employment available. Highest amount earned per year from on-campus jobs $5,330. Off-campus job opportunities are fair. **Financial Aid Statistics:** 71% freshmen, 65% undergrads receive need-based scholarship or grant aid. 70% freshmen, 62% undergrads receive non-need-based scholarship or grant aid. 57% freshmen, 52% undergrads receive need-based self-help aid. 100% freshmen, 99% undergrads receive any aid. 55% undergrads borrow to pay for school. Average cumulative indebtedness $30,149. **Criteria for awarding institutional aid:** *Non-need-based:* Academics, alumni affiliation, art, leadership, music/drama.

ALBRIGHT COLLEGE

PO Box 15234, 13th and Bern Streets, Reading, PA 19612-5234
Phone: 610-921-7799 **Financial Aid Phone:** 610-921-7515
E-mail: admission@albright.edu **CEEB Code:** 2004
Fax: 610-921-7294 **Website:** www.albright.edu **ACT Code:** 2004

This private school, affiliated with the Methodist Church, was founded in 1856. It has a 118-acre campus.

STUDENTS AND FACULTY

Enrollment: 2,074. **Student Body:** 58% female, 42% male, 33% out-of-state, 3% international (26 countries represented). Asian 2%, African American 9%, Caucasian 78%, Hispanic 4%.
Retention and Graduation: 76% freshmen return for sophomore year. 52% freshmen graduate within 4 years. **Faculty:** Student/faculty ratio 14:1. 103 full-time faculty, 83% hold PhDs, 7% are members of minority groups, 46% are women.

ACADEMICS

Degrees: Bachelor's, certificate, master's. **Classes:** Most classes have 10–19 students. Most lab/discussion sessions have 10–19 students. **Majors with Highest Enrollment:** Business/commerce; sociology. **Special Study Options:** Accelerated program, cross-registration, dual enrollment, English as a Second Language (ESL), exchange student program (domestic), honors program, independent study, internships, liberal arts/career combination, student-designed major, study abroad, teacher certification program, interdisciplinary.

FACILITIES

Housing: Coed dorms, men's dorms, women's dorms, apartments for single students, honors, special interest, freshmen floors vs dorms. **Special Academic Facilities/Equipment:** Freedman Art Gallery.

CAMPUS LIFE

Environment: City. **Activities:** Choral groups, concert band, dance, drama/theater, jazz band, literary magazine, music ensembles, musical theater, pep band, radio station, student government, student newspaper, television station, yearbook. **Organizations:** 84 registered organizations, 10 honor societies, 3 religious organizations. 4 fraternities, 3 sororities. **Athletics (Intercollegiate):** *Men:* Baseball, basketball, cheerleading, cross-country, football, golf, soccer, swimming, tennis, track/field (outdoor), track/field (indoor), wrestling. *Women:* Badminton, basketball, cheerleading, cross-country, field hockey, soccer, softball, swimming, tennis, track/field (outdoor), track/field (indoor), volleyball. **On-Campus Highlights:** Student Center, Jake's Place, Wachovia Theatre, Sports Center, Natatorium.

ADMISSIONS

Freshman Academic Profile: Average high school GPA 3.3. 23% in top 10% of high school class, 48% in top 25% of high school class, 79% in top 50% of high school class. 77% from public high schools. SAT Math middle 50% range 460–570. SAT Critical Reading middle 50% range 470–580. **Basis for Candidate Selection:** *Very important factors considered include:* Rigor of secondary school record. *Important factors considered include:* Class rank, application essay, academic GPA, recommendation(s), standardized test scores, character/personal qualities. *Other factors considered include:* Alumni/ae relation, extracurricular activities, talent/ability, volunteer work, work experience. **Freshman Admission Requirements:** High school diploma is required and GED is accepted. *Academic units required:* 4 English, 2 mathematics, 3 science, (1 science labs), 2 foreign language, 2 social studies, 1 history, 2 academic electives. *Academic units recommended:* 4 English, 3 mathematics, 4 science, (2 science labs), 3 foreign language, 2 social studies, 2 history, 2 academic electives. **Freshman Admission Statistics:** 3,013 applied, 71% admitted, 21% enrolled. **Transfer Admission Requirements:** College transcript(s), essay or personal statement, statement of good standing from prior institution(s). Minimum college GPA of 2.0 required. Lowest grade transferable C–. **General Admission Information:** Application fee $25. Notification on a rolling basis, beginning on or about 10/1. Nonfall registration accepted. Admission may be deferred for a maximum of 1 year. Credit and/or placement offered for CEEB Advanced Placement tests.

COSTS AND FINANCIAL AID

Annual tuition $25,232. Room and board $7,888. Required fees $800. Average book expense $800. **Required Forms and Deadlines:** FAFSA. Priority financial aid filing date 3/1. **Notification of Awards:** Applicants will be notified of awards on a rolling basis beginning 2/14. **Types of Aid:** *Need-based scholarships/grants:* Federal Pell, SEOG, state scholarships/grants, private scholarships, the school's own gift aid. *Loans:* Direct Subsidized Stafford, Direct Unsubsidized Stafford, Direct PLUS, Federal Perkins, private educational loans. **Student Employment:** Federal Work-Study Program available. Institutional employment available. Highest amount earned per year from on-campus jobs $1,100. Off-campus job opportunities are good. **Financial Aid Statistics:** 81% freshmen, 68% undergrads receive need-based scholarship or grant aid. 11% freshmen, 9% undergrads receive non-need-based scholarship or grant aid. 67% freshmen, 59% undergrads receive need-based self-help aid. 95% freshmen, 94% undergrads receive any aid. 88% undergrads borrow to pay for school. Average cumulative indebtedness $24,671. **Criteria for awarding institutional aid:** *Non-need-based:* Academics, alumni affiliation, art, leadership, minority status, music/drama, religious affiliation, state/district residency.

RATINGS

Admissions Selectivity Rating: 79   **Fire Safety Rating:** 60*   **Green Rating:** 60*

ALCORN STATE UNIVERSITY

1000 ASU Drive #300, Alcorn State, MS 39096
Phone: 601-877-6147 **Financial Aid Phone:**
E-mail: ksampson@alcorn.edu **CEEB Code:** 1008
Fax: 601-877-6347 **ACT Code:** 2176

This public school was founded in 1871. It has a 1756-acre campus.

RATINGS
Admissions Selectivity Rating: 75   **Fire Safety Rating:** 60*   **Green Rating:** 60*

STUDENTS AND FACULTY
Enrollment: 2,700. **Student Body:** 67% female, 33% male, 13% out-of-state, 1% international (14 countries represented). African American 93%, Caucasian 5%, Hispanic 1%.
Retention and Graduation: 70% freshmen return for sophomore year. 22% freshmen graduate within 4 years. 38% grads go on to further study within 1 year. **Faculty:** Student/faculty ratio 15:1. 183 full-time faculty, 63% hold PhDs, 77% are members of minority groups, 50% are women.

ACADEMICS
Degrees: Associate, bachelor's, master's, post-master's certificate. **Classes:** Most classes have 20–29 students. Most lab/discussion sessions have fewer than 10 students. **Majors with Highest Enrollment:** Biology; elementary education and teaching; liberal arts and sciences/liberal studies. **Special Study Options:** Accelerated program, cooperative education program, distance learning, double major, dual enrollment, honors program, independent study, internships, liberal arts/career combination, study abroad, teacher certification program, undergrads may take grad level classes (restrictions apply). **Combined degree programs:** Cooperative physics program with Howard U. **Career services:** Internships.

FACILITIES
Housing: Men's dorms, women's dorms, Honors Dorm. **Special Academic Facilities/Equipment:** Honors Resident Hall. **Computers:** Students can register for classes online. Administrative functions (other than registration) can be performed online.

CAMPUS LIFE
Environment: Rural. **Activities:** Choral groups, concert band, dance, drama/theater, jazz band, marching band, music ensembles, radio station, student government, student newspaper, television station, yearbook. **Organizations:** 120 registered organizations, 10 honor societies, 8 religious organizations. 8 fraternities, 7 sororities. **Athletics (Intercollegiate):** *Men:* Baseball, basketball, cross-country, football, golf, tennis, track/field (outdoor). *Women:* Basketball, cross-country, golf, soccer, softball, tennis, track/field (outdoor), volleyball.

ADMISSIONS
Freshman Academic Profile: Average high school GPA 2.76. 71% in top 50% of high school class. 99% from public high schools. SAT Math middle 50% range 400–460. SAT Critical Reading middle 50% range 390–470. ACT middle 50% range 16–19. Minimum paper TOEFL 525. **Basis for Candidate Selection:** *Very important factors considered include:* Class rank, academic GPA, rigor of secondary school record. *Important factors considered include:* Standardized test scores. *Other factors considered include:* Recommendation(s), interview. **Freshman Admission Requirements:** High school diploma is required and GED is accepted. *Academic units required:* 4 English, 3 mathematics, 3 science, (2 science labs), 3 social studies, 2 academic electives. *Academic units recommended:* 1 foreign language. **Freshman Admission Statistics:** 3,195 applied, 40% admitted, 50% enrolled. **Transfer Admission Requirements:** College transcript(s), statement of good standing from prior institution(s). Minimum college GPA of 2.0 required. Lowest grade transferable C. **General Admission Information:** Nonfall registration accepted. Credit and/or placement offered for CEEB Advanced Placement tests.

COSTS AND FINANCIAL AID
Required Forms and Deadlines: FAFSA, institution's own financial aid form. Priority financial aid filing date 4/1. **Notification of Awards:** Applicants will be notified of awards on a rolling basis beginning 4/1. **Types of Aid:** *Need-based scholarships/grants:* Federal Pell, SEOG, state scholarships/grants, private scholarships, the school's own gift aid. *Loans:* Direct Subsidized Stafford, Direct Unsubsidized Stafford, Direct PLUS. **Student Employment:** Federal Work-Study Program available. Institutional employment available. Highest amount earned per year from on-campus jobs $500. Off-campus job opportunities are poor. **Financial Aid Statistics:** 93% freshmen, 84% undergrads receive need-based scholarship or grant aid. 33% freshmen, 23% undergrads receive non-need-based scholarship or grant aid. 78% freshmen, 74% undergrads receive need-based self-help aid. 7% freshmen, 8% undergrads receive athletic scholarships. 73% undergrads borrow to pay for school. **Criteria for awarding institutional aid:** *Non-need-based:* Academics, athletics.

ALDERSON-BROADDUS COLLEGE

101 College Hill Drive, Campus Box 2003, Philippi, WV 26416
Phone: 800-263-1549 **Financial Aid Phone:** 304-457-6354
E-mail: admissions@ab.edu **CEEB Code:** 5005
Fax: 304-457-6239 **Website:** www.ab.edu **ACT Code:** 4508

This private school, affiliated with the American Baptist Church, was founded in 1871. It has a 170-acre campus.

RATINGS
Admissions Selectivity Rating: 75   **Fire Safety Rating:** 67   **Green Rating:** 70

STUDENTS AND FACULTY
Enrollment: 582. **Student Body:** 66% female, 34% male, 21% out-of-state, 2% international (9 countries represented). Asian 1%, African American 4%, Caucasian 89%, Hispanic 2%.
Retention and Graduation: 71% freshmen return for sophomore year. 28% freshmen graduate within 4 years. 15% grads go on to further study within 1 year. 18.5% grads pursue arts and sciences degrees. 4% grads pursue law degrees. 7% grads pursue business degrees. 11% grads pursue medical degrees. **Faculty:** Student/faculty ratio 10:1. 59 full-time faculty, 46% hold PhDs, 10% are members of minority groups, 59% are women.

ACADEMICS
Degrees: Associate, bachelor's, certificate, master's, post-bachelor's certificate. **Classes:** Most classes have fewer than 10 students. Most lab/discussion sessions have 10–19 students. **Majors with Highest Enrollment:** Biology/biological sciences; health services/allied health/health sciences; nursing/registered nurse (RN, ASN, BSN, MSN). **Special Study Options:** Double major, honors program, independent study, internships, liberal arts/career combination, study abroad, teacher certification program, business department offers online certificate program. Special programs offered to physically disabled students include note-taking services, reader services, tape recorders, tutors. **Career services:** Alumni network, career/job search classes, career assessment, internships.

FACILITIES
Housing: Coed dorms, special housing for disabled students, women's dorms, apartments for married students, apartments for single students, Wellness Housing. 70% of campus accessible to physically disabled. **Special Academic Facilities/Equipment:** Art Gallery in Burbick Hall. Campbell School House. **Computers:** 75% of classrooms, 100% of dorms, 90% of libraries, 100% of dining areas, 100% of student union, have wireless network access. Administrative functions (other than registration) can be performed online.

CAMPUS LIFE
Environment: Rural. **Activities:** Choral groups, concert band, drama/theater, jazz band, literary magazine, music ensembles, musical theater, radio station, student government, student newspaper, television station, yearbook, campus ministries. **Organizations:** 49 registered organizations, 2 honor societies, 2 religious organizations. 2 fraternities, 3 sororities. **Athletics (Intercollegiate):** *Men:* Baseball, basketball, cross-country, soccer, track/field (outdoor), track/field (indoor). *Women:* Basketball, cross-country, soccer, softball, track/field (outdoor), track/field (indoor), volleyball. **On-Campus Highlights:** Cave, Burbick Hall, Rex Pyles Arena, Wilcox Chapel. **Environmental Initiatives:** Recycling efforts, electric maintenance vehicles, sustainability survey.

ADMISSIONS
Freshman Academic Profile: Average high school GPA 3.3. 21% in top 10% of high school class, 41% in top 25% of high school class, 81% in top 50% of high school class. 97% from public high schools. SAT Math middle 50% range 420–510. SAT Critical Reading middle 50% range 440–530. SAT Writing middle 50% range 430–500. ACT middle 50% range 19–23. Minimum paper TOEFL 500. Minimum computer TOEFL 173. **Basis for Candidate Selection:** *Very important factors considered include:* Academic GPA, rigor of secondary school record, standardized test scores. *Important factors considered include:* Application essay. *Other factors considered include:* Recommendation(s), alumni/ae relation, first generation, interview, level of applicant's interest, talent/ability. **Freshman Admission Requirements:** High school diploma is required and GED is accepted. *Academic units required:* 4 English, 3 mathematics, 3 science, (1 science lab), 1 social studies. *Academic units recommended:* 4 English, 3 mathematics, 3 science, (3 science labs), 1 foreign language, 3 social studies. **Freshman Admission Statistics:** 597 applied, 74% admitted, 37% enrolled. **Transfer Admission Requirements:** High school transcript, college transcript(s), statement of good standing from prior institution(s). Minimum college GPA of 2.0 required. Lowest grade transferable C. **General Admission Information:** Application fee $25. Nonfall registration accepted. Admission may be deferred for a maximum of 1 year. Placement offered for CEEB Advanced Placement tests.

COSTS AND FINANCIAL AID

Annual tuition $21,444. Room and board $7,002. Required fees $210. Average book expense $800. **Required Forms and Deadlines:** FAFSA, state aid form. Priority financial aid filing date 3/1. **Notification of Awards:** Applicants will be notified of awards on a rolling basis beginning 2/15. **Types of Aid:** *Need-based scholarships/grants:* Federal Pell, SEOG, state scholarships/grants, private scholarships, the school's own gift aid, Federal Nursing Scholarships. , National Health Service Corp, Scholarship for disadvantaged students. *Loans:* Direct Subsidized Stafford, Direct Unsubsidized Stafford, Direct PLUS, Federal Perkins, Federal Nursing, college/university loans from institutional funds. **Student Employment:** Federal Work-Study Program available. Highest amount earned per year from on-campus jobs $1,400. Off-campus job opportunities are fair. **Financial Aid Statistics:** 94% freshmen, 91% undergrads receive need-based scholarship or grant aid. 20% freshmen, 13% undergrads receive non-need-based scholarship or grant aid. 74% freshmen, 74% undergrads receive need-based self-help aid. 3% freshmen, 5% undergrads receive athletic scholarships. 100% freshmen, 99% undergrads receive any aid. 98% undergrads borrow to pay for school. Average cumulative indebtedness $29,613. **Criteria for awarding institutional aid:** *Non-need-based:* Academics, athletics, music/drama.

ALFRED UNIVERSITY

Alumni Hall, One Saxon Drive, Alfred, NY 14802-1205
Phone: 607-871-2115 **Financial Aid Phone:** 607-871-2159
E-mail: admissions@alfred.edu **CEEB Code:** 2005
Fax: 607-871-2198 **Website:** www.alfred.edu **ACT Code:** 2666

This private school was founded in 1836. It has a 600-acre campus.

RATINGS

Admissions Selectivity Rating: 80   **Fire Safety Rating:** 60*   **Green Rating:** 72

STUDENTS AND FACULTY

Enrollment: 1,971. **Student Body:** 49% female, 51% male, 35% out-of-state, 3% international. Asian 2%, African American 4%, Caucasian 64%, Hispanic 2%.
Retention and Graduation: 82% freshmen return for sophomore year. 49% freshmen graduate within 4 years. 30% grads go on to further study within 1 year. **Faculty:** Student/faculty ratio 12:1. 172 full-time faculty, 44% are women.

ACADEMICS

Degrees: Bachelor's, master's, post-master's certificate. **Classes:** Most classes have 10–19 students. Most lab/discussion sessions have fewer than 10 students. **Majors with Highest Enrollment:** Business/commerce; ceramic sciences and engineering; fine/studio arts. **Special Study Options:** Cooperative education program, cross-registration, double major, English as a Second Language (ESL), exchange student program (domestic), honors program, independent study, internships, liberal arts/career combination, student-designed major, study abroad, teacher certification program. **Honors programs:** The Alfred University Honors Program is designed to enrich the lives of exceptional students. It has two components: An honors seminar that meets one evening a week and the senior thesis. **Combined degree programs:** 4+1 MBA program for business, liberal arts and sciences. Special programs offered to physically disabled students include note-taking services, tape recorders, tutors. **Career services:** Alumni network, career assessment, internships. Career services highlights include: We are extremely proud of all of the services offered by the staff at the Robert R. McComsey Career Development Center.

FACILITIES

Housing: Coed dorms, apartments for single students, theme housing (i.e., Environmental Studies House, Language House, etc.). 50% of campus accessible to physically disabled. **Special Academic Facilities/Equipment:** Art museums, carillon, language labs, electron microscope, observatory, extensive engineering equipment, performing arts center. **Computers:** 90% of classrooms, 100% of dorms, 100% of libraries, 100% of student union, have wireless network access. Students can register for classes online. Administrative functions (other than registration) can be performed online.

CAMPUS LIFE

Environment: Rural. **Activities:** Choral groups, concert band, dance, drama/theater, literary magazine, music ensembles, musical theater, pep band, radio station, student government, student newspaper, student-run film society,

television station, yearbook, campus ministries, international student organization. **Organizations:** 90 registered organizations, 13 honor societies, 3 religious organizations. **Athletics (Intercollegiate):** *Men:* Basketball, cross-country, diving, equestrian sports, football, lacrosse, skiing (downhill/alpine), soccer, swimming, tennis, track/field (outdoor), track/field (indoor). *Women:* Basketball, cross-country, diving, equestrian sports, lacrosse, skiing (downhill/alpine), soccer, softball, swimming, tennis, track/field (outdoor), track/field (indoor), volleyball. **On-Campus Highlights:** Powell Campus Center, Binns Merrill Hall, Schein-Joseph International Museum of Ceramic Art, John L. Stull Observatory, Robert Turner Student Art Gallery.

ADMISSIONS

Freshman Academic Profile: 18% in top 10% of high school class, 46% in top 25% of high school class, 85% in top 50% of high school class. SAT Math middle 50% range 500–620. SAT Critical Reading middle 50% range 440–610. ACT middle 50% range 22–27. Minimum paper TOEFL 550. Minimum computer TOEFL 213. **Basis for Candidate Selection:** *Very important factors considered include:* Class rank, recommendation(s), rigor of secondary school record, character/personal qualities, extracurricular activities. *Important factors considered include:* Application essay, standardized test scores, volunteer work, work experience. *Other factors considered include:* Interview, racial/ethnic status, talent/ability. **Freshman Admission Requirements:** High school diploma is required and GED is accepted. *Academic units required:* 4 English, 2 mathematics, 2 science, (2 science labs), 2 social studies. *Academic units recommended:* 4 mathematics, 3 science, (3 science labs), 3 social studies. **Freshman Admission Statistics:** 2,355 applied, 74% admitted, 28% enrolled. **Transfer Admission Requirements:** College transcript(s), statement of good standing from prior institution(s). Minimum college GPA of 2.5 required. Lowest grade transferable C. **General Admission Information:** Application fee $40. Early decision application deadline 12/1. Notification on a rolling basis, beginning on or about 2/15. Nonfall registration accepted. Admission may be deferred for a maximum of 2 years. Credit offered for CEEB Advanced Placement tests.

COSTS AND FINANCIAL AID

Annual tuition $23,428. Room and board $10,796. Required fees $850. Average book expense $900. **Required Forms and Deadlines:** FAFSA, institution's own financial aid form, state aid form, noncustodial PROFILE, business/farm supplement. Financial aid filing deadline 3/15. **Notification of Awards:** Applicants will be notified of awards on a rolling basis beginning 2/15. **Types of Aid:** *Need-based scholarships/grants:* Federal Pell, SEOG, state scholarships/grants, private scholarships, the school's own gift aid. *Loans:* Direct Subsidized Stafford, Direct Unsubsidized Stafford, Direct PLUS, Federal Perkins, college/university loans from institutional funds, Private alternative loans. **Student Employment:** Federal Work-Study Program available. Institutional employment available. Off-campus job opportunities are poor. **Financial Aid Statistics:** 74% freshmen, 73% undergrads receive need-based scholarship or grant aid. 44% freshmen, 39% undergrads receive non-need-based scholarship or grant aid. 66% freshmen, 66% undergrads receive need-based self-help aid. 92% freshmen, 90% undergrads receive any aid. 82.5% undergrads borrow to pay for school. Average cumulative indebtedness $23,292. **Criteria for awarding institutional aid:** *Non-need-based:* Academics, art, leadership, music/drama.

ALICE LLOYD COLLEGE

100 Purpose Road, Pippa Passes, KY 41844
Phone: 606-368-6036 **Financial Aid Phone:**
E-mail: admissions@alc.edu **CEEB Code:** 1098
Fax: 606-368-6215 **Website:** www.alc.edu **ACT Code:** 1502

This private school was founded in 1923. It has a 225-acre campus.

RATINGS

Admissions Selectivity Rating: 84   **Fire Safety Rating:** 87   **Green Rating:** 60*

STUDENTS AND FACULTY

Enrollment: 607. **Student Body:** 51% female, 49% male, 13% out-of-state, (1 countries represented). African American 1%, Caucasian 99%.
Retention and Graduation: 63% freshmen return for sophomore year. 25% freshmen graduate within 4 years. 55% grads go on to further study within 1 year. 35% grads pursue arts and sciences degrees. 5% grads pursue law degrees. 10% grads pursue business degrees. 5% grads pursue medical degrees. **Faculty:** Student/faculty ratio 18:1. 29 full-time faculty, 59% hold PhDs, 10% are members of minority groups, 41% are women.

ACADEMICS

Degrees: Bachelor's. **Classes:** Most classes have 20–29 students. **Majors with Highest Enrollment:** Biology/biological sciences; business/commerce; education. **Special Study Options:** Cooperative education program, double major, honors program, independent study, internships, liberal arts/career combination, study abroad, teacher certification program. Special programs offered to physically disabled students include reader services, tutors. **Career services:** Alumni network, alumni services, career assessment, internships, regional alumni.

FACILITIES

Housing: Men's dorms, women's dorms. 90% of campus accessible to physically disabled. **Special Academic Facilities/Equipment:** Photographic archives, oral history museum, Appalachian collection, on-campus day care center, kindergarten, elementary, and secondary school. **Computers:** 100% of classrooms, 50% of dorms, 100% of libraries, 100% of dining areas, 75% of common outdoor areas have wireless network access.

CAMPUS LIFE

Environment: Rural. **Activities:** Choral groups, drama/theater, music ensembles, musical theater, pep band, radio station, student government, student newspaper, yearbook. **Organizations:** 19 registered organizations, 2 honor societies, 1 religious organizations. **Athletics (Intercollegiate):** *Men:* Baseball, basketball, cheerleading, cross-country, golf, tennis. *Women:* Basketball, cheerleading, cross-country, golf, softball, tennis. **On-Campus Highlights:** Jerry Davis Student Center, Historical Tour, Grady Nutt Athletic Center, Campbell Arts Center, Cushing Hall.

ADMISSIONS

Freshman Academic Profile: Average high school GPA 3.39. 30% in top 10% of high school class, 58% in top 25% of high school class, 86% in top 50% of high school class. 90% from public high schools. SAT Math middle 50% range 480–570. SAT Critical Reading middle 50% range 440–590. SAT Writing middle 50% range 430–520. ACT middle 50% range 17–23. Minimum paper TOEFL 550. Minimum computer TOEFL 213. **Basis for Candidate Selection:** *Very important factors considered include:* Rigor of secondary school record, standardized test scores, character/personal qualities, geographical residence. *Important factors considered include:* Class rank, recommendation(s), alumni/ae relation, state residency. *Other factors considered include:* Application essay, extracurricular activities, interview, talent/ability, volunteer work, work experience. **Freshman Admission Requirements:** High school diploma is required and GED is accepted. *Academic units required:* 4 English, 3 mathematics, 2 science, 2 social studies, 1 history. *Academic units recommended:* 4 English, 3 mathematics, 2 science, 2 foreign language, 2 social studies. **Freshman Admission Statistics:** 994 applied, 56% admitted, 32% enrolled. **Transfer Admission Requirements:** High school transcript, college transcript(s), standardized test scores, statement of good standing from prior institution(s). Minimum college GPA of 2.0 required. Lowest grade transferable C. **General Admission Information:** Regular application deadline 5/1. Nonfall registration accepted. Credit and/or placement offered for CEEB Advanced Placement tests.

COSTS AND FINANCIAL AID

Room and board $4,250. Required fees $1,300. Average book expense $850. **Required Forms and Deadlines:** FAFSA. Priority financial aid filing date 3/15. **Notification of Awards:** Applicants will be notified of awards on a rolling basis beginning 4/1. **Types of Aid:** *Need-based scholarships/grants:* Federal Pell, SEOG, state scholarships/grants, private scholarships, the school's own gift aid. *Loans:* Direct Subsidized Stafford, Direct Unsubsidized Stafford, Direct PLUS, college/university loans from institutional funds. **Student Employment:** Federal Work-Study Program available. Institutional employment available. Off-campus job opportunities are fair. **Financial Aid Statistics:** 83% freshmen, 81% undergrads receive need-based scholarship or grant aid. 9% freshmen, 13% undergrads receive non-need-based scholarship or grant aid. 74% freshmen, 68% undergrads receive need-based self-help aid. 7% freshmen, 5% undergrads receive athletic scholarships. 100% freshmen, 100% undergrads receive any aid. 33% undergrads borrow to pay for school. Average cumulative indebtedness $4,653. **Criteria for awarding institutional aid:** *Non-need-based:* Athletics, minority status, state/district residency.

ALLEGHENY COLLEGE

Allegheny College, Admissions Office, Box 5, 520 North Main Street, Meadville, PA 16335
Phone: 814-332-4351 **Financial Aid Phone:** 800-835-7780
E-mail: admissions@allegheny.edu **CEEB Code:** 2006
Fax: 814-337-0431 **Website:** www.allegheny.edu **ACT Code:** 3520

This private school was founded in 1815. It has a 565-acre campus.

RATINGS

Admissions Selectivity Rating: 90 **Fire Safety Rating:** 79 **Green Rating:** 93

STUDENTS AND FACULTY

Enrollment: 2,099. **Student Body:** 55% female, 45% male, 43% out-of-state, 1% international (38 countries represented). Asian 3%, African American 4%, Caucasian 89%, Hispanic 3%.
Retention and Graduation: 88% freshmen return for sophomore year. 66% freshmen graduate within 4 years. 43% grads go on to further study within 1 year. 8% grads pursue arts and sciences degrees. 5% grads pursue law degrees. 4% grads pursue business degrees. 11% grads pursue medical degrees. **Faculty:** Student/faculty ratio 13:1. 152 full-time faculty, 93% hold PhDs, 14% are members of minority groups, 44% are women.

ACADEMICS

Degrees: Bachelor's. **Classes:** Most classes have 10–19 students. Most lab/discussion sessions have 10–19 students. **Majors with Highest Enrollment:** Biology/biological sciences; economics; psychology. **Special Study Options:** double major, dual enrollment, English as a Second Language (ESL), exchange student program (domestic), independent study, internships, student-designed major, study abroad, pre-professional programs, teacher preparation partnerships, combined degree programs, experiential learning terms (summer study program), marine biology study program, Washington Semester, medical school partnerships, graduate school partnerships, double minor, domestic off campus semester away study programs, accelerated masters and doctorate degree programs. **Combined degree programs:** BA/MA, BA/MEng, management, public policy, teachng, nursing, occupational and physical therapy, osteopathic medicine, physician's assistant. Special programs offered to physically disabled students include note-taking services, tape recorders, tutors. **Career services:** Alumni network, alumni services, career/job search classes, career assessment, internships, regional alumni. **Career services highlights include:** experiential learning which connects classroom learning to the wider world, including social issues, international relations, key concepts in leadership development, and ultimately career and life goals. Through internships, community service programs and service learning, off-campus study, and other leadership opportunities students become active participants in the learning process by adapting academic skills and knowledge to meet new challenges. ACCEL, Allegheny College Center for Experiential Learning, unites resources, personnel, and funding sources to create experiential learning initiatives for Allegheny students.

FACILITIES

Housing: Coed dorms, special housing for disabled students, men's dorms, women's dorms, fraternity/sorority housing, apartments for single students, wellness program, theme housing, quiet study floors, environmentally-sensitive LEED-certified townhouses with low-fume material. 35% of campus accessible to physically disabled. **Special Academic Facilities/Equipment:** New Center For Communication Arts with a trap stage and green and blue screen room; radio and television stations; state-of-the-art, nationally acclaimed science complex; videoconference facilities; planetarium; observatory; GIS lab; state-of-the-art language-learning center; smart classrooms; renovated dance and art studios and performance spaces; art galleries; world's largest solid-volume glass sculpture grouping; 283-acre environmental research reserve; 80–acre protected forest; new alumni center; comprehensive sports and fitness center, seismographic network station, Center for Political Participation, Center for Economic and Environmental Development, environmental roof garden. **Computers:** 50% of classrooms, 100% of dorms, 100% of libraries, 100% of dining areas, 100% of student union, 100% of common outdoor areas have wireless network access. Students can register for classes online. Administrative functions (other than registration) can be performed online.

CAMPUS LIFE

Environment: Town. **Activities:** Choral groups, concert band, dance, drama/theater, jazz band, literary magazine, music ensembles, musical theater, radio station, student government, student newspaper, symphony orchestra, television station, yearbook, campus ministries, international student organization,

Model UN. **Organizations:** 113 registered organizations, 15 honor societies, 8 religious organizations. 5 fraternities, 5 sororities. **Athletics (Intercollegiate):** *Men:* Baseball, basketball, cross-country, diving, football, golf, soccer, swimming, tennis, track/field (outdoor), track/field (indoor). *Women:* Basketball, cross-country, diving, golf, lacrosse, soccer, softball, swimming, tennis, track/field (outdoor), track/field (indoor), volleyball. **On-Campus Highlights:** Rustic Bridge; Wise Sport and Fitness Center; Henderson Campus Center, Pelletier Library, world's largest solid-volume glass sculpture group; state-of-the-art, nationally acclaimed science complex dedicated to biology, chemistry and environmental science; Patricia Bush Tippie Alumni Center; seismographic network station; Center for Political Participation; Center for Economic & Environmental Development; radio and TV stations, Grounds For Change Coffeehouse; Vukovich Communication Arts Building; Environmental Roof Garden; Robertson athletic fields and recreation area. **Environmental Initiatives:** Climate action plan; energy efficiency through energy audit, retrofits, geothermal wells, education, green building, submetering, dorm competitions, wind energy; composting.

ADMISSIONS

Freshman Academic Profile: Average high school GPA 3.75. 45% in top 10% of high school class, 76% in top 25% of high school class, 97% in top 50% of high school class. 82% from public high schools. SAT Math middle 50% range 560–650. SAT Critical Reading middle 50% range 550–660. SAT Writing middle 50% range 550–640. ACT middle 50% range 23–29. Minimum paper TOEFL 550. Minimum computer TOEFL 213. Minimum web-based TOEFL 80. **Basis for Candidate Selection:** *Very important factors considered include:* Class rank, academic GPA, rigor of secondary school record. *Important factors considered include:* Recommendation(s), standardized test scores, character/personal qualities, extracurricular activities, interview, level of applicant's interest. *Other factors considered include:* Application essay, alumni/ae relation, first generation, geographical residence, racial/ethnic status, talent/ability, volunteer work, work experience. **Freshman Admission Requirements:** High school diploma is required and GED is accepted. *Academic units required:* 4 English, 3 mathematics, 3 science, 2 foreign language, 3 social studies, 1 academic electives. **Freshman Admission Statistics:** 3,916 applied, 66% admitted, 22% enrolled. **Transfer Admission Requirements:** High school transcript, college transcript(s), essay or personal statement, standardized test scores, minimum college GPA of 2.5 required. Lowest grade transferable C. **General Admission Information:** Application fee $35. Early decision application deadline 11/15. Regular application deadline 2/15. Regular notification 4/1. Nonfall registration accepted. Admission may be deferred for a maximum of 1 year. Credit and/or placement offered for CEEB Advanced Placement tests.

COSTS AND FINANCIAL AID

Annual tuition $33,240. Room and board $8,440. Required fees $320. Average book expense $1,000. **Required Forms and Deadlines:** FAFSA. Priority financial aid filing date 2/15. **Notification of Awards:** Applicants will be notified of awards on a rolling basis beginning 3/1. **Types of Aid:** *Need-based scholarships/grants:* Federal Pell, SEOG, state scholarships/grants, private scholarships, the school's own gift aid, Federal Academic Competitiveness Grant, National SMART Grant, Veterans Educational Benefits, Yellow Ribbon Program. *Loans:* Direct Subsidized Stafford, Direct Unsubsidized Stafford, Direct PLUS, Federal Perkins, private loans from commercial lenders. **Student Employment:** Federal Work-Study Program available. Institutional employment available. Highest amount earned per year from on-campus jobs $8,350. Off-campus job opportunities are excellent. **Financial Aid Statistics:** 69% freshmen, 69% undergrads receive need-based scholarship or grant aid. 12% freshmen, 9% undergrads receive non-need-based scholarship or grant aid. 58% freshmen, 61% undergrads receive need-based self-help aid. 99% freshmen, 98% undergrads receive any aid. **Criteria for awarding institutional aid:** *Non-need-based:* Academics, leadership, minority status, state/district residency.

ALLEN COLLEGE

1825 Logan Avenue, Waterloo, IA 50703
Phone: 319-226-2000 **Financial Aid Phone:** 319-226-2003
E-mail: allenCollegeAdmissions@ihs.org
Fax: 319-226-2051 **Website:** www.allencollege.edu **ACT Code:** 30691

This private school was founded in 1989.

RATINGS
Admissions Selectivity Rating: 91   **Fire Safety Rating:** 88   **Green Rating:** 60*

STUDENTS AND FACULTY
Enrollment: 314. **Student Body:** 93% female, 7% male, 4% out-of-state, African American 2%, Caucasian 96%, Native American 1%.
Retention and Graduation: 89% freshmen return for sophomore year. 41%

freshmen graduate within 4 years. 10% grads go on to further study within 1 year. **Faculty:** Student/faculty ratio 12:1. 29 full-time faculty, 24% hold PhDs, 3% are members of minority groups, 97% are women.

ACADEMICS
Degrees: Associate, bachelor's, certificate, master's, post-master's certificate. **Classes:** Most classes have fewer than 10 students. Most lab/discussion sessions have fewer than 10 students. **Majors with Highest Enrollment:** Family practice nurse/nurse practitioner; health services/allied health/health sciences; nursing/registered nurse (RN, ASN, BSN, MSN). **Special Study Options:** Accelerated program, cooperative education program, distance learning, honors program, independent study, internships. Special programs offered to physically disabled students include tutors.

FACILITIES
Housing: Coed dorms, housing also available at a cooperating institution. 100% of campus accessible to physically disabled. **Computers:** 100% of classrooms, 100% of dorms, 100% of libraries, 100% of student union, 100% of common outdoor areas have wireless network access. Administrative functions (other than registration) can be performed online.

CAMPUS LIFE
Environment: City. **Activities:** Choral groups, student government, student newspaper, yearbook. **Organizations:** 4 registered organizations, 1 honor societies, 1 religious organizations.

ADMISSIONS
Freshman Academic Profile: Average high school GPA 3.54. 33% in top 10% of high school class, 67% in top 25% of high school class, 100% in top 50% of high school class. ACT middle 50% range 21–24. Minimum paper TOEFL 550. Minimum computer TOEFL 213. **Basis for Candidate Selection:** *Very important factors considered include:* Class rank, academic GPA, rigor of secondary school record, standardized test scores. *Important factors considered include:* Application essay, recommendation(s). *Other factors considered include:* Character/personal qualities, extracurricular activities, first generation, interview, talent/ability. **Freshman Admission Requirements:** High school diploma is required and GED is accepted. *Academic units required:* 8 English, 6 mathematics, 6 science, 6 social studies. **Freshman Admission Statistics:** 40 applied, 10% admitted, 75% enrolled. **Transfer Admission Requirements:** High school transcript, college transcript(s), essay or personal statement, standardized test scores, minimum college GPA of 2.7 required. Lowest grade transferable C. **General Admission Information:** Application fee $50. Regular application deadline 3/1. Notification on a rolling basis, beginning on or about 3/15. Nonfall registration accepted. Credit offered for CEEB Advanced Placement tests.

COSTS AND FINANCIAL AID
Annual tuition $13,458. Room and board $6,816. Required fees $1,537. Average book expense $1,012. **Required Forms and Deadlines:** FAFSA, institution's own financial aid form. Priority financial aid filing date 6/30. **Notification of Awards:** Applicants will be notified of awards on a rolling basis beginning 4/1. **Types of Aid:** *Need-based scholarships/grants:* Federal Pell, SEOG, state scholarships/grants, private scholarships, the school's own gift aid, Federal Nursing Scholarships. Various funds from HRSA (SDS—Scholarship for Disadvantaged Students, NSP—Nursing Scholarship Program, AENT—Advanced Education Nurse Traineeship. *Loans:* Direct Subsidized Stafford, Direct Unsubsidized Stafford, Direct PLUS, Federal Perkins, Federal Nursing, college/university loans from institutional funds, alternative Loans. **Student Employment:** Federal Work-Study Program available. Off-campus job opportunities are excellent. **Financial Aid Statistics:** 50% freshmen, 70% undergrads receive need-based scholarship or grant aid. 50% freshmen, 75% undergrads receive need-based self-help aid. 100% freshmen, 97% undergrads receive any aid. 100% undergrads borrow to pay for school. Average cumulative indebtedness $29,010. **Criteria for awarding institutional aid:** *Non-need-based:* Academics, alumni affiliation, leadership, minority status, state/district residency.

ALLEN UNIVERSITY

1530 Harden Street, Columbia, SC, 29204

This is a private school.

RATINGS
Admissions Selectivity Rating: 60*   **Fire Safety Rating:** 60*   **Green Rating:** 60*

ACADEMICS
Degrees: Bachelor's.

ADMISSIONS

Freshman Academic Profile: Minimum paper TOEFL 550. Minimum computer TOEFL 213. Minimum web-based TOEFL 75. **General Admission Information:** Credit offered for CEEB Advanced Placement tests.

ALMA COLLEGE

614 West Superior Street, Alma, MI 48801-1599
Phone: 989-463-7139 **Financial Aid Phone:** 989-463-7347
E-mail: admissions@alma.edu **CEEB Code:** 1010
Fax: 989-463-7057 **Website:** www.alma.edu **ACT Code:** 1958

This private school, affiliated with the Presbyterian Church, was founded in 1886. It has a 125-acre campus.

RATINGS

Admissions Selectivity Rating: 83 **Fire Safety Rating:** 60* **Green Rating:** 70

STUDENTS AND FACULTY

Enrollment: 1,394. **Student Body:** 55% female, 45% male, 4.8% out-of-state, international (16 countries represented). Asian 2%, African American 2%, Caucasian 91%, Hispanic 3%, Native American 1%.
Retention and Graduation: 51% freshmen graduate within 4 years. **Faculty:** Student/faculty ratio 13.9:1. 85 full-time faculty, 89% hold PhDs, 8% are members of minority groups, 38% are women.

ACADEMICS

Degrees: Bachelor's. **Classes:** Most classes have 10–19 students. Most lab/discussion sessions have 10–19 students. **Majors with Highest Enrollment:** Biological and physical sciences; business/commerce; education. **Special Study Options:** Double major, dual enrollment, exchange student program (domestic), honors program, independent study, internships, student-designed major, study abroad, teacher certification program. **Honors programs:** Students in the Honors Program participate in special seminar opportunities and enroll in courses designed for honors scholars. **Combined degree programs:** 3-2 occupational therapy. Special programs offered to physically disabled students include note-taking services, reader services, tape recorders, tutors. **Career services:** Alumni services, career assessment, internships.

FACILITIES

Housing: Coed dorms, fraternity/sorority housing, theme housing. 75% of campus accessible to physically disabled. **Special Academic Facilities/Equipment:** Music and arts centers, science lab, planetarium, a DNA synthesizer and sequencer, and a multinuclear magnetic resonance spectrometer. **Computers:** 60% of classrooms, 100% of libraries, 100% of dining areas, 100% of student union, have wireless network access. Students can register for classes online.

CAMPUS LIFE

Environment: Village. **Activities:** Choral groups, concert band, dance, drama/theater, jazz band, marching band, music ensembles, radio station, student government, student newspaper, symphony orchestra, yearbook, campus ministries, international student organization, Model UN. **Organizations:** 75 registered organizations, 20 honor societies, 4 religious organizations. 6 fraternities, 5 sororities. **Athletics (Intercollegiate):** *Men:* Baseball, basketball, cross-country, diving, football, golf, soccer, swimming, tennis, track/field (outdoor). *Women:* Basketball, cross-country, diving, golf, soccer, softball, swimming, tennis, track/field (outdoor), volleyball. **On-Campus Highlights:** Joe's Place, Stone Center for Recreation, Library, Remick Heritage Center, Wright Hall (residence hall). **Environmental Initiatives:** Alma's green residence hall, Wright Hall, was completed in January 2005. The modern, 60–bed, apartment-style hall features a number of environmentally friendly features, including geothermal heating and cooling, recycled-content ceiling tiles and carpeting, energy-efficient windows, rooftop solar heating panels, energy-efficient showers and washing machines, and a computerized energy monitoring system. Alma College's partnership with the Pine River Superfund Citizen Task Force was selected as the winner of Michigan's 2008 Carter Partnership Award. Organized by Michigan Campus Compact, the Jimmy and Rosalynn Carter Partnership Award for Campus-Community Collaboration recognizes colleges and community groups that work together in exceptional ways to improve peoples' lives and help college students learn the value of community service. The Task Force works to clean the Pine River. Alma College and the Pine River Superfund Task Force organized an international conference that examined the impact of DDT on human health and the environment. The Eugene Kenaga International DDT Conference on Environment and Health took place March 14, 2008, at Alma College. It brought together international experts to frame and lead discussions of current knowledge of DDT and other persistent organic pollutants (POPs).

ADMISSIONS

Freshman Academic Profile: Average high school GPA 3.48. 30% in top 10% of high school class, 57% in top 25% of high school class, 87% in top 50% of high school class. 91% from public high schools. SAT Math middle 50% range 483–668. SAT Critical Reading middle 50% range 470–708. SAT Writing middle 50% range 503–710. ACT middle 50% range 21–27. Minimum paper TOEFL 525. Minimum computer TOEFL 195. Minimum web-based TOEFL 69. **Basis for Candidate Selection:** *Very important factors considered include:* Academic GPA, standardized test scores. *Important factors considered include:* Application essay. *Other factors considered include:* Class rank, recommendation(s), rigor of secondary school record, alumni/ae relation, character/personal qualities, extracurricular activities, geographical residence, interview, level of applicant's interest, state residency, talent/ability, volunteer work, work experience. **Freshman Admission Requirements:** High school diploma is required and GED is accepted. *Academic units required:* 4 English, 3 mathematics, 3 science, 3 social studies. *Academic units recommended:* 2 foreign language. **Freshman Admission Statistics:** 1,778 applied, 75% admitted, 30% enrolled. **Transfer Admission Requirements:** High school transcript, college transcript(s), statement of good standing from prior institution(s). Minimum college GPA of 3.0 required. Lowest grade transferable C. **General Admission Information:** Application fee $25. Notification on a rolling basis, beginning on or about 9/1. Nonfall registration accepted. Admission may be deferred for a maximum of 1 year. Credit and/or placement offered for CEEB Advanced Placement tests.

COSTS AND FINANCIAL AID

Average book expense $800. **Required Forms and Deadlines:** FAFSA. Priority financial aid filing date 3/1. **Notification of Awards:** Applicants will be notified of awards on a rolling basis beginning 3/1. **Types of Aid:** *Need-based scholarships/grants:* Federal Pell, SEOG, state scholarships/grants, the school's own gift aid. *Loans:* Direct Subsidized Stafford, Direct Unsubsidized Stafford, Direct PLUS, Federal Perkins, college/university loans from institutional funds, alternative loans. **Student Employment:** Federal Work-Study Program available. Institutional employment available. Off-campus job opportunities are good. **Financial Aid Statistics:** 84% freshmen, 81% undergrads receive need-based scholarship or grant aid. 17% freshmen, 13% undergrads receive non-need-based scholarship or grant aid. 64% freshmen, 60% undergrads receive need-based self-help aid. 99% freshmen, 99% undergrads receive any aid. 74% undergrads borrow to pay for school. Average cumulative indebtedness $31,476. **Criteria for awarding institutional aid:** *Non-need-based:* Academics, alumni affiliation, art, minority status, music/drama.

ALVERNIA COLLEGE

400 St. Bernardine Street, Reading, PA 19607
Phone: 610-796-8220 **Financial Aid Phone:** 610-796-8356
E-mail: admissions@alvernia.edu
Fax: 610-796-8336

This private school, affiliated with the Roman Catholic Church, was founded in 1958. It has a 80-acre campus.

RATINGS

Admissions Selectivity Rating: 70 **Fire Safety Rating:** 60* **Green Rating:** 60*

STUDENTS AND FACULTY

Enrollment: 2,019. **Student Body:** 71% female, 29% male, 14% out-of-state, international (9 countries represented). Asian 1%, African American 11%, Caucasian 74%, Hispanic 6%.
Retention and Graduation: 77% freshmen return for sophomore year. 40% freshmen graduate within 4 years. **Faculty:** Student/faculty ratio 13:1. 74 full-time faculty, 68% hold PhDs, 7% are members of minority groups, 57% are women.

ACADEMICS

Degrees: Associate, bachelor's, certificate, master's, post-bachelor's certificate, post-master's certificate. **Classes:** Most classes have 10–19 students. Most lab/discussion sessions have 10–19 students. **Majors with Highest Enrollment:** Criminal justice/law enforcement administration; elementary education and teaching; substance abuse/addiction counseling. **Special Study Options:** Accelerated program, cross-registration, double major, dual enrollment, English as a Second Language (ESL), honors program, independent study, internships, student-designed major, study abroad, teacher certification program. **Honors programs:** Alvernia College Honors Program. **Combined degree programs:** BA/MA, BS/MS occupational therapy. Special programs offered to physically disabled students include note-taking services, tape recorders, tutors. **Career services:** Career/job search classes, career assessment, internships. **Career**

services highlights include: The Washington Center and many local internship opportunities.

FACILITIES

Housing: Coed dorms, special housing for disabled students, women's dorms, single-sex suites in townhouses. Single-sex floors in dorms. 90% of campus accessible to physically disabled. **Computers:** Students can register for classes online. Administrative functions (other than registration) can be performed online.

CAMPUS LIFE

Environment: Village. **Activities:** Choral groups, dance, drama/theater, literary magazine, music ensembles, student government, student newspaper, yearbook. **Organizations:** 35 registered organizations, 5 honor societies, 5 religious organizations. **Athletics (Intercollegiate):** *Men:* Baseball, basketball, cross-country, golf, lacrosse, soccer, tennis. *Women:* Basketball, cheerleading, cross-country, field hockey, lacrosse, soccer, softball, tennis, volleyball. **On-Campus Highlights:** Student center, Crusader Cafe, library, gym, Residence Hall Lounge.

ADMISSIONS

Freshman Academic Profile: Average high school GPA 2.88. 8% in top 10% of high school class, 27% in top 25% of high school class, 53% in top 50% of high school class. 74% from public high schools. SAT Math middle 50% range 420–530. SAT Critical Reading middle 50% range 420–520. Minimum paper TOEFL 550. Minimum computer TOEFL 213. **Basis for Candidate Selection:** *Very important factors considered include:* Academic GPA, standardized test scores. *Important factors considered include:* Class rank, application essay, recommendation(s), rigor of secondary school record, character/personal qualities, extracurricular activities, interview, level of applicant's interest, talent/ability, volunteer work, work experience. *Other factors considered include:* Religious affiliation/commitment. **Freshman Admission Requirements:** High school diploma is required and GED is accepted. **Freshman Admission Statistics:** 922 applied, 76% admitted, 41% enrolled. **Transfer Admission Requirements:** High school transcript, college transcript(s), essay or personal statement, minimum college GPA of 2.0 required. Lowest grade transferable C. **General Admission Information:** Application fee $25. Nonfall registration accepted. Admission may be deferred for a maximum of 1 year. Credit and/or placement offered for CEEB Advanced Placement tests.

COSTS AND FINANCIAL AID

Annual tuition $20,220. Room and board $8,220. Required fees $202. Average book expense $1,200. **Required Forms and Deadlines:** FAFSA Financial aid filing deadline 5/1. **Notification of Awards:** Applicants will be notified of awards on a rolling basis beginning 2/10. **Types of Aid:** *Need-based scholarships/grants:* Federal Pell, SEOG, state scholarships/grants, private scholarships. *Loans:* Direct Subsidized Stafford, Direct Unsubsidized Stafford, Direct PLUS. **Student Employment:** Highest amount earned per year from on-campus jobs $3,886. **Financial Aid Statistics:** 84% freshmen, 94% undergrads receive need-based scholarship or grant aid. 1% freshmen, 11% undergrads receive non-need-based scholarship or grant aid. 80% freshmen, 90% undergrads receive need-based self-help aid. 94% freshmen, 98% undergrads receive any aid. 91% undergrads borrow to pay for school. Average cumulative indebtedness $6,985. **Criteria for awarding institutional aid:** *Non-need-based:* Academics, alumni affiliation.

See page 1008.

ALVERNO COLLEGE

3400 South 43rd Street, PO Box 343922, Milwaukee, WI 53234-3922
Phone: 414-382-6101 **Financial Aid Phone:** 414-382-6046
E-mail: admissions@alverno.edu **CEEB Code:** 1012
Fax: 414-382-6055 **Website:** www.alverno.edu **ACT Code:** 4558

This private school, affiliated with the Roman Catholic Church, was founded in 1887. It has a 47-acre campus.

RATINGS

Admissions Selectivity Rating: 67   **Fire Safety Rating:** 73   **Green Rating:** 73

STUDENTS AND FACULTY

Enrollment: 2,307. **Student Body:** 100% female, 3% out-of-state, 1% international (19 countries represented). Asian 5%, African American 18%, Caucasian 62%, Hispanic 13%, Native American 1%.
Retention and Graduation: 73% freshmen return for sophomore year. 17% freshmen graduate within 4 years. **Faculty:** Student/faculty ratio 13:1. 118 full-time faculty, 92% hold PhDs, 9% are members of minority groups, 75% are women.

ACADEMICS

Degrees: Associate, bachelor's, master's, post-bachelor's certificate, post-master's certificate. **Classes:** Most classes have 20–29 students. Most lab/discussion sessions have 20–29 students. **Majors with Highest Enrollment:** Business administration and management; education; nursing/registered nurse (RN, ASN, BSN, MSN). **Special Study Options:** Double major, independent study, internships, student-designed major, study abroad, teacher certification program, weekend college. Special programs offered to physically disabled students include note-taking services, reader services, tape recorders, tutors. **Career services:** Alumni services, career/job search classes, career assessment, Career services highlights include: We are proudest of our integration into the Alverno curriculum. Counselors design and teach 3 courses that are required by various disciplines (one at the first-year level and two at the senior level), as well as teach segments in several additional courses. The result is that virtually every student has done in-class work with a career counselor prior to graduation.

FACILITIES

Housing: Women's dorms. 95% of campus accessible to physically disabled. **Special Academic Facilities/Equipment:** Art & Culture Gallery, career center, fitness center, Reiman Gymnasium, Nursing Skills Lab, student-centered multi-media production facility, Diagnostic Digital Portfolio, computer center, science labs, theatre venue. **Computers:** 35% of classrooms, 100% of dorms, 100% of libraries, 100% of dining areas, 100% of student union, have wireless network access. Students can register for classes online. Administrative functions (other than registration) can be performed online.

CAMPUS LIFE

Environment: Metropolis. **Activities:** Choral groups, dance, drama/theater, literary magazine, music ensembles, student government, student newspaper, campus ministries, international student organization. **Organizations:** 37 registered organizations, 1 honor societies, 1 religious organization. 2 sororities. **Athletics (Intercollegiate):** *Women:* Basketball, cross-country, soccer, softball, tennis, volleyball. **On-Campus Highlights:** Teaching, Learning and Technology Center, The Mug Coffee House, fitness center, The Pipeline Activity Center, Reiman Gymnasium. **Environmental Initiatives:** Recycle paper, plastic, cans. When remodeling, we use energy efficient lighting in areas we changed over from steam to hot water heat.

ADMISSIONS

Freshman Academic Profile: Average high school GPA 2.9. 78% from public high schools. ACT middle 50% range 17–22. Minimum paper TOEFL 520. Minimum computer TOEFL 190. Minimum web-based TOEFL 68. **Basis for Candidate Selection:** *Very important factors considered include:* Academic GPA, standardized test scores. *Important factors considered include:* Application essay, rigor of secondary school record. *Other factors considered include:* Recommendation(s), character/personal qualities, extracurricular activities, interview, level of applicant's interest, talent/ability, volunteer work, work experience. **Freshman Admission Requirements:** High school diploma is required and GED is accepted. *Academic units required:* 4 English, 3 mathematics, 3 science, 3 social studies, 4 academic electives. *Academic units recommended:* 2 foreign language. **Freshman Admission Statistics:** 525 applied, 85% admitted, 55% enrolled. **Transfer Admission Requirements:** High school transcript, college transcript(s), essay or personal statement, minimum college GPA of 2.0 required. Lowest grade transferable C. **General Admission Information:** Application fee $20. Notification on a rolling basis, beginning on or about 9/1. Nonfall registration accepted. Admission may be deferred for a maximum of 1 year. Credit and/or placement offered for CEEB Advanced Placement tests.

COSTS AND FINANCIAL AID

Average book expense $1,050. **Required Forms and Deadlines:** FAFSA, institution's own financial aid form. Priority financial aid filing date 3/15. **Notification of Awards:** Applicants will be notified of awards on a rolling basis beginning 3/15. **Types of Aid:** *Need-based scholarships/grants:* Federal Pell, SEOG, state scholarships/grants, private scholarships, the school's own gift aid, Federal Nursing Scholarships. *Loans:* Direct Subsidized Stafford, Direct Unsubsidized Stafford, Direct PLUS, Federal Perkins, state loans. **Student Employment:** Federal Work-Study Program available. Institutional employment available. Highest amount earned per year from on-campus jobs $8,830. Off-campus job opportunities are good. **Financial Aid Statistics:** 78% freshmen, 71% undergrads receive need-based scholarship or grant aid. 81% freshmen, 66% undergrads receive non-need-based scholarship or grant aid. 83% freshmen, 78% undergrads receive need-based self-help aid. 100% freshmen, 98% undergrads receive any aid. 83% undergrads borrow to pay for school. Average cumulative indebtedness $32,142. **Criteria for awarding institutional aid:** *Non-need-based:* Academics, alumni affiliation.

AMERICAN CONSERVATORY OF MUSIC

252 Wildwood Road, Hammond, IN 46324
Phone: 219-931-6000 **Financial Aid Phone:**
E-mail: registrar@americanconservatory.edu
Fax: 219-931-6089

This private school, affiliated with the Greek Orthodox Church, was founded in 1886.

RATINGS
Admissions Selectivity Rating: 60*   **Fire Safety Rating:** 60*   **Green Rating:** 60*

STUDENTS AND FACULTY
Faculty: Student/faculty ratio 1:1.

ACADEMICS
Degrees: Associate, bachelor's, certificate, diploma, master's. **Special Study Options:** Accelerated program, distance learning, double major, English as a Second Language (ESL).

FACILITIES
Housing: Apartments for married students, apartments for single students. **Computers:** Undergraduates are required to own a computer.

CAMPUS LIFE
Environment: Metropolis. **Activities:** Choral groups, jazz band, music ensembles, opera, symphony orchestra.

ADMISSIONS
Transfer Admission Requirements: High school transcript, college transcript(s), essay or personal statement, interview, statement of good standing from prior institution(s). Minimum college GPA of 2.0 required. Lowest grade transferable C.

COSTS AND FINANCIAL AID
Average book expense $2,400. **Types of Aid:** *Need-based scholarships/grants:* the school's own gift aid. **Criteria for awarding institutional aid:** *Non-need-based:* Music/drama.

AMERICAN INDIAN COLLEGE OF THE ASSEMBLIES OF GOD, INC.

10020 N. 15th Ave, Phoenix, AZ 85021
Phone: 602-944-3335 **Financial Aid Phone:**
E-mail: aicadm@aicag.edu
Fax: 602-943-8299 **Website:** www.aicag.edu **ACT Code:** 6005

This private school, affiliated with the Assemblies of God Church, was founded in 1957. It has a 10-acre campus.

RATINGS
Admissions Selectivity Rating: 60*   **Fire Safety Rating:** 60*   **Green Rating:** 60*

STUDENTS AND FACULTY
Enrollment: 70. **Student Body:** 44% female, 56% male, 69% out-of-state, 1% international (2 countries represented). Asian 6%, African American 4%, Caucasian 14%, Hispanic 6%, Native American 69%.
Retention and Graduation: Faculty: Student/faculty ratio 5:1. 8 full-time faculty, 88% hold PhDs, 38% are women.

ACADEMICS
Degrees: Associate, bachelor's. **Classes:** Most classes have fewer than 10 students. Most lab/discussion sessions have fewer than 10 students. **Special Study Options:** Double major.

FACILITIES
Housing: Special housing for disabled students, men's dorms, women's dorms, apartments for married students.

CAMPUS LIFE
Environment: Metropolis. **Activities:** Choral groups, drama/theater, literary magazine, music ensembles, musical theater, student government, student newspaper, yearbook, campus ministries. **On-Campus Highlights:** Gymnasium, Cree Student Union, Ramsey Cafeteria, Chapel, Prayer Mountain Trail.

ADMISSIONS
Freshman Academic Profile: Average high school GPA 2.5. 60% in top 50% of high school class. Minimum paper TOEFL 500. Minimum computer TOEFL 150. **Basis for Candidate Selection:** *Very important factors considered include:* Class rank, recommendation(s), rigor of secondary school record, standardized test scores, character/personal qualities, religious affiliation/commitment. *Important factors considered include:* Application essay. *Other factors considered include:* Extracurricular activities, interview, talent/ability, volunteer work, work experience. **Freshman Admission Requirements:** High school diploma is required and GED is accepted. **Freshman Admission Statistics:** 18 applied, 44% admitted, 113% enrolled. **Transfer Admission Requirements:** High school transcript, college transcript(s), standardized test scores, minimum college GPA of 2.0 required. Lowest grade transferable C. **General Admission Information:** Nonfall registration accepted.

COSTS AND FINANCIAL AID
Annual tuition $4,950. Room and board $3,850. Required fees $605. Average book expense $500. **Required Forms and Deadlines:** FAFSA, institution's own financial aid form, CSS/Financial Aid PROFILE, state aid form, noncustodial PROFILE, business/farm supplement. **Types of Aid:** *Need-based scholarships/grants:* Federal Pell, SEOG, state scholarships/grants, private scholarships, the school's own gift aid. *Loans:* Direct Subsidized Stafford, Direct Unsubsidized Stafford, Direct PLUS. **Student Employment:** Off-campus job opportunities are fair. **Financial Aid Statistics:** 46% undergrads receive any aid.

AMERICAN INTERNATIONAL COLLEGE

1000 State Street, Springfield, MA 01109-3184
Phone: 413-205-3201 **Financial Aid Phone:** 413-205-3259
E-mail: inquiry@aic.edu **CEEB Code:** 3002
Fax: 413-205-3051 **Website:** www.aic.edu **ACT Code:** 1772

This private school was founded in 1885. It has a 58-acre campus.

RATINGS
Admissions Selectivity Rating: 71   **Fire Safety Rating:** 86   **Green Rating:** 60*

STUDENTS AND FACULTY
Enrollment: 1,729. **Student Body:** 58% female, 42% male, 35% out-of-state, 2% international (44 countries represented). Asian 3%, African American 27%, Caucasian 44%, Hispanic 9%, Native American 1%.
Retention and Graduation: 60% freshmen return for sophomore year. 20% grads go on to further study within 1 year. 9% grads pursue arts and sciences degrees. 5% grads pursue law degrees. 15% grads pursue business degrees. 2% grads pursue medical degrees. **Faculty:** Student/faculty ratio 15:1. 89 full-time faculty, 47% hold PhDs, 7% are members of minority groups, 60% are women.

ACADEMICS
Degrees: Associate, bachelor's, master's, post-master's certificate, terminal associate. **Classes:** Most classes have 10–19 students. Most lab/discussion sessions have 10–19 students. **Majors with Highest Enrollment:** Criminal justice/safety studies; nursing/registered nurse (RN, ASN, BSN, MSN); psychology. **Special Study Options:** Accelerated program, cross-registration, distance learning, double major, dual enrollment, English as a Second Language (ESL), honors program, independent study, internships, liberal arts/career combination, study abroad, teacher certification program, weekend college, off-campus study in Washington, DC; upper division undergrads may take grad level courses. **Honors programs:** Four Year Honors program open to students in any major with appropriate credentials. **Combined degree programs:** BA/MA, 4-1 bachelor's/MBA program. Special programs offered to physically disabled students include note-taking services, reader services, tape recorders, tutors. **Career services:** Alumni services, career/job search classes, career assessment, internships.

FACILITIES
Housing: Coed dorms, women's dorms, wellness housing 75% of campus accessible to physically disabled. **Special Academic Facilities/Equipment:** Centers for child development, cultural arts, and human technology. **Computers:** 100% of classrooms, 90% of dorms, 100% of libraries, 100% of dining areas, 100% of student union, 100% of common outdoor areas have wireless network access. Students can register for classes online. Administrative functions (other than registration) can be performed online.

CAMPUS LIFE
Environment: City. **Activities:** Choral groups, dance, drama/theater, literary magazine, musical theater, pep band, radio station, student government, student newspaper, yearbook, campus ministries, international student organization.

Organizations: 45 registered organizations, 5 honor societies, 3 religious organizations. 4 fraternities, 5 sororities. **Athletics (Intercollegiate):** *Men:* Baseball, basketball, cheerleading, cross-country, football, golf, ice hockey, lacrosse, soccer, tennis, track/field (outdoor), track/field (indoor), wrestling. *Women:* Basketball, cheerleading, cross-country, field hockey, lacrosse, soccer, softball, tennis, track/field (outdoor), track/field (indoor), volleyball. **On-Campus Highlights:** Courniotes Hall for Health Sciences, Karen Sprague Cultural Arts Center, Butova & Metcalf Gymnasiums, WAIC–FM (radio station).

ADMISSIONS

Freshman Academic Profile: Average high school GPA 2.5. 22% in top 10% of high school class, 28% in top 25% of high school class, 23% in top 50% of high school class. 79% from public high schools. SAT Math middle 50% range 420–520. SAT Critical Reading middle 50% range 420–510. SAT Writing middle 50% range 420–500. ACT middle 50% range 17–23. Minimum paper TOEFL 550. Minimum computer TOEFL 213. Minimum web-based TOEFL 80. **Basis for Candidate Selection:** *Important factors considered include:* Class rank, academic GPA, rigor of secondary school record, standardized test scores. *Other factors considered include:* Application essay, recommendation(s), alumni/ae relation, character/personal qualities, extracurricular activities, first generation, interview, level of applicant's interest, racial/ethnic status, volunteer work, work experience. **Freshman Admission Requirements:** High school diploma is required and GED is accepted. *Academic units required:* 4 English, 3 mathematics, 2 science, (2 science labs), 1 foreign language, 1 social studies, 2 history, 4 academic electives. *Academic units recommended:* 4 English, 4 mathematics, 3 science, (2 science labs), 2 foreign language, 2 social studies. **Freshman Admission Statistics:** 1,469 applied, 79% admitted, 30% enrolled. **Transfer Admission Requirements:** High school transcript, college transcript(s), minimum college GPA of 2.0 required. Lowest grade transferable C. **General Admission Information:** Application fee $25. Notification on a rolling basis, beginning on or about 12/15. Nonfall registration accepted. Admission may be deferred for a maximum of 2 years. Credit and/or placement offered for CEEB Advanced Placement tests.

COSTS AND FINANCIAL AID

Required Forms and Deadlines: FAFSA, state aid form. Priority financial aid filing date 5/1. **Notification of Awards:** Applicants will be notified of awards on a rolling basis beginning 3/15. **Types of Aid:** *Need-based scholarships/grants:* Federal Pell, SEOG, state scholarships/grants, private scholarships, the school's own gift aid, Federal Nursing Scholarships. *Loans:* Direct Subsidized Stafford, Direct Unsubsidized Stafford, Direct PLUS, Federal Perkins, college/university loans from institutional funds. **Student Employment:** Federal Work-Study Program available. Institutional employment available. Highest amount earned per year from on-campus jobs $2,200. Off-campus job opportunities are good. **Financial Aid Statistics:** 110% freshmen, 88% undergrads receive need-based scholarship or grant aid. 11% freshmen, 8% undergrads receive non-need-based scholarship or grant aid. 102% freshmen, 81% undergrads receive need-based self-help aid. 16% freshmen, 8% undergrads receive athletic scholarships. 100% freshmen, 85% undergrads receive any aid. 100% undergrads borrow to pay for school. Average cumulative indebtedness $25,378. **Criteria for awarding institutional aid:** *Non-need-based:* Academics, alumni affiliation, athletics, leadership.

See page 1010.

AMERICAN JEWISH UNIVERSITY

15600 Mulholland Drive, Familian Campus, Bel Air, CA 90077
Phone: 310-440-1247 **Financial Aid Phone:** 310-440-1252
E-mail: admissions@ajula.edu **CEEB Code:** 2741
Fax: 310-471-3657 **Website:** www.ajula.edu **ACT Code:** 0462

This private school, affiliated with the Jewish Church, was founded in 1947. It has a 28-acre campus.

RATINGS
Admissions Selectivity Rating: 87   **Fire Safety Rating:** 73   **Green Rating:** 66

STUDENTS AND FACULTY
Enrollment: 108. **Student Body:** 52% female, 48% male, 21% out-of-state, 2% international (1 countries represented). Asian 1%, African American 4%, Caucasian 48%, Hispanic 6%, Native American 2%.
Retention and Graduation: 78% freshmen return for sophomore year. 37% freshmen graduate within 4 years. **Faculty:** Student/faculty ratio 4:1. 13 full-time faculty, 92% hold PhDs, 38% are women.

ACADEMICS

Degrees: Bachelor's, master's. **Classes:** Most classes have fewer than 10 students. Most lab/discussion sessions have fewer than 10 students. **Majors with Highest Enrollment:** Business administration and management; political science and government; psychology. **Special Study Options:** Cross-registration, double major, independent study, internships, student-designed major, study abroad. **Combined degree programs:** BA/MA, BA/MBA, BA/MAEd. **Career services:** Career assessment, internships, **Career services highlights include:** internships: Our students have had internships with American Jewish Joint Distribution Committee, Anti-Defamation League, Cedars-Sinai Medical Center, Jewish Federation of Greater Los Angeles, Jewish Telegraphic Agency, Jewish Television Network, Los Angeles Holocaust Museum, Museum of Tolerance, New Line Cinema, and the Simon Wiesenthal Center.

FACILITIES

Housing: Coed dorms, special housing for disabled students, apartments for married students, apartments for single students. 90% of campus accessible to physically disabled. **Special Academic Facilities/Equipment:** Art Gallery, Ostrow Library **Computers:** 100% of dorms, 100% of libraries, 100% of student union, 50% of common outdoor areas have wireless network access. Administrative functions (other than registration) can be performed online.

CAMPUS LIFE

Environment: Metropolis. **Activities:** Choral groups, drama/theater, literary magazine, student government, student newspaper, Model UN. **Organizations:** 17 registered organizations, 1 religious organizations. **On-Campus Highlights:** Residence Halls, Auerbach Student Union, The Berg, our kosher dining hall, Sculpture Garden, Ostrow Library. **Environmental Initiatives:** Energy management, conserving water, recycling.

ADMISSIONS

Freshman Academic Profile: Average high school GPA 3.11. 11% in top 25% of high school class, 45% in top 50% of high school class. 74% from public high schools. SAT Math middle 50% range 425–500. SAT Critical Reading middle 50% range 450–530. SAT Writing middle 50% range 420–540. ACT middle 50% range 18–20. Minimum paper TOEFL 530. Minimum computer TOEFL 215. Minimum web-based TOEFL 75. **Basis for Candidate Selection:** *Very important factors considered include:* Application essay, recommendation(s), character/personal qualities, extracurricular activities, interview, talent/ability, volunteer work. *Important factors considered include:* Academic GPA, standardized test scores, level of applicant's interest. *Other factors considered include:* Class rank, rigor of secondary school record, alumni/ae relation, geographical residence, religious affiliation/commitment, state residency, work experience. **Freshman Admission Requirements:** High school diploma is required and GED is accepted. **Freshman Admission Statistics:** 49 applied, 96% admitted, 49% enrolled. **Transfer Admission Requirements:** College transcript(s), essay or personal statement. Lowest grade transferable C. **General Admission Information:** Application fee $35. Regular application deadline 5/31. Notification on a rolling basis, beginning on or about 9/15. Nonfall registration accepted. Admission may be deferred for a maximum of 1 year. Credit offered for CEEB Advanced Placement tests.

COSTS AND FINANCIAL AID

Required Forms and Deadlines: FAFSA, institution's own financial aid form, tax form, verification form. **Notification of Awards:** Applicants will be notified of awards on a rolling basis beginning 1/1. **Types of Aid:** *Need-based scholarships/grants:* Federal Pell, SEOG, state scholarships/grants, private scholarships, the school's own gift aid. *Loans:* Direct Subsidized Stafford, Direct Unsubsidized Stafford, Direct PLUS. **Student Employment:** Federal Work-Study Program available. Institutional employment available. Highest amount earned per year from on-campus jobs $1,000. Off-campus job opportunities are good. **Financial Aid Statistics:** 96% freshmen, 25% undergrads receive need-based scholarship or grant aid. 100% freshmen, 56% undergrads receive non-need-based scholarship or grant aid. 100% freshmen, 36% undergrads receive need-based self-help aid. 100% freshmen, 75% undergrads receive any aid. 75% undergrads borrow to pay for school. Average cumulative indebtedness $66,000. **Criteria for awarding institutional aid:** *Non-need-based:* Leadership, minority status, music/drama, state/district residency.

AMERICAN UNIVERSITY

4400 Massachusetts Ave, NW, Washington, DC, 20016-8001
Phone: 202-885-6000 **Financial Aid Phone:** 202-885-6100
E-mail: admissions@american.edu **CEEB Code:** 5007
Fax: 202-885-1025 **Website:** www.american.edu **ACT Code:** 648

This private school, affiliated with the Methodist Church, was founded in 1893. It has a 84-acre campus.

RATINGS
Admissions Selectivity Rating: 91   **Fire Safety Rating:** 91   **Green Rating:** 86

STUDENTS AND FACULTY
Enrollment: 6,028. **Student Body:** 62% female, 38% male, 84% out-of-state, 6% international (137 countries represented). Asian 5%, African American 4%, Caucasian 62%, Hispanic 4%.
Retention and Graduation: 70% freshmen graduate within 4 years. **Faculty:** Student/faculty ratio 13.5:1. 578 full-time faculty, 94% hold PhDs, 17% are members of minority groups, 46% are women.

ACADEMICS
Degrees: Associate, bachelor's, certificate, first professional, master's, post-bachelor's certificate. **Majors with Highest Enrollment:** Business/commerce; international relations and affairs; mass communication/media studies. **Special Study Options:** Accelerated program, cooperative education program, cross-registration, double major, exchange student program (domestic), honors program, independent study, internships, student-designed major, study abroad, teacher certification program, weekend college. AU Abroad offers more than 100 study abroad programs in 33 geographic locations around the world. Earn college credit, learn a foreign language, pursue and internship and gain international experience and contacts. One-semester, full year, alternative spring break, and language immersion options are available. With AU Abroad partner universities in Canada, Mexico, England, Scotland, Ireland, Argentina, Australia, Egypt,the United Arab Emirates, and numerous other countries around the world, you have the ability to go almost anywhere. **Honors programs:** The University Honors Program is designed to promote a continuous learning environment, making optimum use of AU's outstanding faculty, campus facilities and the numerous resources available in the Washington, DC, area and abroad. Students enjoy small classes, proven instructors, cultural events, a wide range of social activities, and the option of living in Honors housing. Members of the University Honors Program can major in any discipline at the university and can also participate in multidisciplinary Honors Colloquia. **Combined degree programs:** BA/MA, BS/MS, BA/MPA, BA/MS. Special programs offered to physically disabled students include note-taking services, reader services, tape recorders, tutors. **Career services:** Alumni network, alumni services, career/job search classes, career assessment, internships, regional alumni.

FACILITIES
Housing: Coed dorms, special housing for disabled students, special housing for international students, apartments for married students, apartments for single students. 94% of campus accessible to physically disabled. **Special Academic Facilities/Equipment:** Student-run radio and TV facilities, Watkins Art Gallery, Katzen Arts Center, Experimental Theatre, Greenberg Theatre, Friedheim Journalism Center, William I Jacobs Fitness Center, language resource center, multimedia center, audiotechnology lab, UNIX and Oracle labs, Kay Spiritual Life Center (interdenominational). **Computers:** 100% of classrooms, 100% of dorms, 100% of libraries, 100% of dining areas, 100% of student union, 100% of common outdoor areas have wireless network access. Students can register for classes online. Administrative functions (other than registration) can be performed online.

CAMPUS LIFE
Environment: Metropolis. **Activities:** Choral groups, dance, drama/theater, jazz band, literary magazine, music ensembles, musical theater, opera, pep band, radio station, student government, student newspaper, student-run film society, symphony orchestra, television station, yearbook, international student organization. **Organizations:** 180 registered organizations, 15 honor societies, 15 religious organizations. 11 fraternities, 12 sororities. **Athletics (Intercollegiate):** *Men:* Basketball, cross-country, diving, soccer, swimming, track/field (outdoor), track/field (indoor), wrestling. *Women:* Basketball, cross-country, diving, field hockey, lacrosse, soccer, swimming, track/field (outdoor), track/field (indoor), volleyball. **On-Campus Highlights:** Mary Graydon Center, Sports Center Complex and Jacobs Fitness, Katzen Arts Center, The Quad, Ter-

race Dining Room. **Environmental Initiatives:** Signatory of the American College's and President's Climate Commitment (ACUPCC) and currently completing our GHG Inventory. Signatory of the Talloires Declaration and have established a "Green Teaching Certification Program" to reward professors using sustainable practices and incorporting sustainabilty content into curriculum. Staffing of a full-time Manager of Sustainability Programs.

ADMISSIONS
Freshman Academic Profile: 46% in top 10% of high school class, 79% in top 25% of high school class, 97% in top 50% of high school class. SAT Math middle 50% range 570–670. SAT Critical Reading middle 50% range 580–700. SAT Writing middle 50% range 580–680. ACT middle 50% range 25–30. Minimum paper TOEFL 610. Minimum computer TOEFL 263. Minimum web-based TOEFL 101. **Basis for Candidate Selection:** *Very important factors considered include:* Academic GPA, rigor of secondary school record, standardized test scores, level of applicant's interest. *Important factors considered include:* Application essay, recommendation(s), extracurricular activities, volunteer work. *Other factors considered include:* Alumni/ae relation, character/personal qualities, first generation, geographical residence, racial/ethnic status, talent/ability, work experience. **Freshman Admission Requirements:** High school diploma is required and GED is accepted. *Academic units required:* 4 English, 3 mathematics, 3 science, (2 science labs), 2 foreign language, 2 social studies, 3 academic electives. *Academic units recommended:* 4 English, 4 mathematics, 4 science, 3 foreign language, 4 social studies, 4 academic electives. **Freshman Admission Statistics:** 15,413 applied, 53% admitted, 19% enrolled. **Transfer Admission Requirements:** College transcript(s), essay or personal statement, minimum college GPA of 2.5 required. Lowest grade transferable C. **General Admission Information:** Application fee $60. Early decision application deadline 11/15. Regular application deadline 1/15. Regular notification 4/1. Nonfall registration accepted. Admission may be deferred for a maximum of 1 year. Credit and/or placement offered for CEEB Advanced Placement tests.

COSTS AND FINANCIAL AID
Annual tuition $34,456. Room and board $12,930. Required fees $517. Average book expense $1,000. **Required Forms and Deadlines:** FAFSA, institution's own financial aid form. Financial aid filing deadline 2/15. **Notification of Awards:** Applicants will be notified of awards on or about 4/1. **Types of Aid:** *Need-based scholarships/grants:* Federal Pell, SEOG, state scholarships/grants, private scholarships, the school's own gift aid, academic merit scholarships: Presidential Scholarships, Dean's Scholarships, Leadership Scholarships, Phi Theta Kappa Scholarships (transfers only), Tuition Exchange Scholarships, United Methodist Scholarships, and other private/restricted scholarships are awarded by the Undergraduate Admissions Office. Most scholarships do not require a separate application and are renewable for up to three years if certain criteria are met. *Loans:* Direct Subsidized Stafford, Direct Unsubsidized Stafford, Direct PLUS, Federal Perkins, college/university loans from institutional funds. **Student Employment:** Federal Work-Study Program available. Institutional employment available. Off-campus job opportunities are excellent. **Financial Aid Statistics:** 2% freshmen, 25% undergrads receive need-based scholarship or grant aid. 27% freshmen, 20% undergrads receive non-need-based scholarship or grant aid. 38% freshmen, 42% undergrads receive need-based self-help aid. 3% freshmen, 3% undergrads receive athletic scholarships. 82% freshmen, 69% undergrads receive any aid. **Criteria for awarding institutional aid:** *Non-need-based:* Academics, alumni affiliation, athletics, leadership, minority status, music/drama, religious affiliation, state/district residency.

See page 1012.

AMERICAN UNIVERSITY IN CAIRO

AUC Avenue, P.O. Box 74 New Cairo 11835, New Cairo, Egypt
Phone: 20.2.26151459 **Financial Aid Phone:** 2.02.26151480
E-mail: enrolauc@aucegypt.edu
Fax: Website: www.aucegypt.edu

This private school was founded in 1919. It has a 260-acre campus.

RATINGS
Admissions Selectivity Rating: 60*   **Fire Safety Rating:** 60*   **Green Rating:** 60*

STUDENTS AND FACULTY
Enrollment: 5,055. **Student Body:** 51% female, 49% male, % out-of-state, international (77 countries represented).
Retention and Graduation: 94% freshmen return for sophomore year. 35% freshmen graduate within 4 years. **Faculty:** Student/faculty ratio 12.3:1. 394 full-time faculty, 69% hold PhDs, 48% are women.

ACADEMICS

Degrees: Bachelor's, diploma, master's. **Classes:** Most classes have 10–19 students. Most lab/discussion sessions have 10–19 students. **Majors with Highest Enrollment:** Business administration, management and operations, other, mechanical engineering; political science and government. **Special Study Options:** Double major, English as a Second Language (ESL), independent study, internships, liberal arts/career combination, study abroad. **Career services:** Alumni network, alumni services, career/job search classes, career assessment, internships. **Career services highlights include:** job shadowing and internships to help students explore career options. Online recruitment and employment fairs generate employment opportunities.

FACILITIES

Housing: Men's dorms, women's dorms, apartments for married students, apartments for single students. 100% of campus accessible to physically disabled. **Computers:** 100% of classrooms, 100% of dorms, 100% of libraries, 100% of dining areas, 100% of student union, 100% of common outdoor areas have wireless network access. Students can register for classes online. Administrative functions (other than registration) can be performed online.

CAMPUS LIFE

Environment: Metropolis. **Activities:** Choral groups, dance, drama/theater, literary magazine, music ensembles, radio station, student government, student newspaper, student-run film society, yearbook, international student organization, Model UN. **Organizations:** 62 registered organizations, **Athletics (Intercollegiate):** *Men:* Basketball, boxing, fencing, football, gymnastics, handball, rugby, soccer, squash, swimming, table tennis, tennis, track/field (outdoor), volleyball, water polo, wrestling. *Women:* Basketball, fencing, football, gymnastics, handball, soccer, squash, swimming, table tennis, tennis, track/field (outdoor), volleyball. **On-Campus Highlights:** Athletic facility, food court, library, student center.

ADMISSIONS

Freshman Academic Profile: SAT Math middle 50% range 530–640. SAT Critical Reading middle 50% range 410–520. SAT Writing middle 50% range 500–580. Minimum paper TOEFL 557. Minimum computer TOEFL 220. Minimum web-based TOEFL 83. **Basis for Candidate Selection:** *Very important factors considered include:* Academic GPA, standardized test scores. *Important factors considered include:* Recommendation(s), extracurricular activities, state residency, talent/ability. *Other factors considered include:* Application essay, alumni/ae relation, character/personal qualities, geographical residence, interview, work experience. **Freshman Admission Requirements:** High school diploma is required and GED is accepted. *Academic units recommended:* 3 English, 3 mathematics, 2 science, 2 foreign language, 3 social studies. **Freshman Admission Statistics:** 2,686 applied, 56% admitted, 81% enrolled. **Transfer Admission Requirements:** College transcript(s), essay or personal statement, standardized test scores, statement of good standing from prior institution(s). Minimum college GPA of 2 required. Lowest grade transferable 2. **General Admission Information:** Application fee $45. Regular application deadline 5/15. Notification on a rolling basis, beginning on or about 7/20. Nonfall registration accepted.

COSTS AND FINANCIAL AID

Average book expense $700. **Required Forms and Deadlines:** Institution's own financial aid form. Financial aid filing deadline 5/15. **Notification of Awards:** Applicants will be notified of awards on or about 8/15. **Types of Aid:** *Need-based scholarships/grants:* Private scholarships, the school's own gift aid. **Financial Aid Statistics:** 2% undergrads receive athletic scholarships. 46% undergrads receive any aid. **Criteria for awarding institutional aid:** *Non-need-based:* Academics, art, athletics, leadership, music/drama, state/district residency.

THE AMERICAN UNIVERSITY OF PARIS (CO)

US Admissions Office, 950 South Cherry Street Suite 210, Denver, CO 80246
Phone: 303-757-6333 **Financial Aid Phone:** +1 40620720
E-mail: usoffice@aup.edu **CEEB Code:** 866
Fax: 303-757-6444 **ACT Code:** 5295

This private school was founded in 1962.

RATINGS

STUDENTS AND FACULTY

Enrollment: 925. **Student Body:** 67% female, 33% male, % out-of-state, (100 countries represented).

Retention and Graduation: 64% freshmen return for sophomore year. 32% freshmen graduate within 4 years. **Faculty:** Student/faculty ratio 12:1. 56 full-time faculty, 80% hold PhDs, 46% are women.

ACADEMICS

Degrees: Bachelor's, master's. **Classes:** Most classes have 10–19 students. Most lab/discussion sessions have 10–19 students. **Special Study Options:** Double major, exchange student program (domestic), independent study, internships, study abroad. **Combined degree programs:** BA/MA, BA/MA. **Career services:** Alumni network, alumni services, career assessment, internships.

FACILITIES

Housing: Students are housed in independent rooms or with French families. 60% of campus accessible to physically disabled. **Computers:** Administrative functions (other than registration) can be performed online.

CAMPUS LIFE

Environment: Metropolis. **Activities:** drama/theater, literary magazine, musical theater, student government, student newspaper, yearbook. **Organizations:** 20 registered organizations. **Athletics (Intercollegiate):** *Men:* Basketball, football, rugby, soccer, swimming, volleyball. *Women:* Basketball, football, soccer, swimming, volleyball.

ADMISSIONS

Freshman Academic Profile: SAT Math middle 50% range 520–640. SAT Critical Reading middle 50% range 550–660. Minimum paper TOEFL 600. Minimum computer TOEFL 250. **Basis for Candidate Selection:** *Very important factors considered include:* Class rank, application essay, recommendation(s), rigor of secondary school record. *Important factors considered include:* Academic GPA, standardized test scores, character/personal qualities, extracurricular activities, level of applicant's interest. *Other factors considered include:* Alumni/ae relation, interview, talent/ability, volunteer work, work experience. **Freshman Admission Requirements:** High school diploma is required and GED is accepted. *Academic units recommended:* 4 English, 3 mathematics, 2 science, (1 science labs), 3 foreign language, 3 social studies, 2 history. **Freshman Admission Statistics:** 541 applied, 71% admitted, 41% enrolled. **Transfer Admission Requirements:** College transcript(s), essay or personal statement, statement of good standing from prior institution(s). Minimum college GPA of 3.0 required. Lowest grade transferable C. **General Admission Information:** Application fee $50. Nonfall registration accepted. Admission may be deferred for a maximum of 1 year. Credit and/or placement offered for CEEB Advanced Placement tests.

COSTS AND FINANCIAL AID

Average book expense $1,200. **Required Forms and Deadlines:** FAFSA, institution's own financial aid form. **Types of Aid:** *Need-based scholarships/grants:* the school's own gift aid. *Loans:* Direct Subsidized Stafford, Direct Unsubsidized Stafford, Direct PLUS **Student Employment:** Highest amount earned per year from on-campus jobs $2,500. **Financial Aid Statistics:** 37% freshmen, 33% undergrads receive need-based scholarship or grant aid. 12% freshmen, 10% undergrads receive need-based self-help aid. **Criteria for awarding institutional aid:** *Non-need-based:* Academics, alumni affiliation.

AMERICAN UNIVERSITY OF PUERTO RICO

PO Box 2037, Bayamon, PR 00960-2037
Phone: 787-740-6410
E-mail: mcruz@aupr.edu
Fax: 787-785-7377 **Website:** www.aupr.edu

This private school was founded in 1963.

RATINGS

STUDENTS AND FACULTY

Enrollment: 4,060. **Student Body:** 59% female, 41% male. Hispanic 100%.

ACADEMICS

Degrees: Associate, bachelor's, master's. **Special Study Options:** Cooperative education program, distance learning, English as a Second Language (ESL), honors program, independent study, liberal arts/career combination, student-designed major. **Career services:** Career/job search classes.

CAMPUS LIFE

Activities: Dance, drama/theater, literary magazine. **Athletics (Intercollegiate):** *Men:* Baseball, basketball, soccer, tennis, volleyball. *Women:* Baseball, basketball, soccer, tennis, volleyball.

ADMISSIONS

Freshman Academic Profile: Average high school GPA 2.49. 66% from public high schools. **Basis for Candidate Selection:** *Very important factors considered include:* Rigor of secondary school record, standardized test scores. *Other factors considered include:* Character/personal qualities, interview, talent/ability. **Freshman Admission Requirements:** High school diploma is required and GED is accepted. **Freshman Admission Statistics:** 1,131 applied, 100% admitted, 71% enrolled. **General Admission Information:** Application fee $15. Nonfall registration accepted.

COSTS AND FINANCIAL AID

Annual tuition $1,740. Required fees $160. Average book expense $160. **Required Forms and Deadlines: Notification of Awards: Types of Aid:** *Need-based scholarships/grants:* Federal Pell, SEOG, state scholarships/grants *Loans:* Direct Subsidized Stafford, state loans. **Student Employment:** Federal Work-Study Program available. Off-campus job opportunities are good. **Financial Aid Statistics:** 87% freshmen, 85% undergrads receive need-based scholarship or grant aid. 80% freshmen, 46% undergrads receive need-based self-help aid. 4% freshmen, 3% undergrads receive athletic scholarships. **Criteria for awarding institutional aid:** *Non-need-based:* Academics, alumni affiliation, art, athletics, job skills, leadership, minority status, music/drama, religious affiliation, state/district residency.

AMHERST COLLEGE

Campus Box 2231, PO Box 5000, Amherst, MA 01002
Phone: 413-542-2328 **Financial Aid Phone:** 413-542-2296
E-mail: admission@amherst.edu **CEEB Code:** 3003
Fax: 413-542-2040 **Website:** www.amherst.edu **ACT Code:** 1774

This private school was founded in 1821. It has a 999-acre campus.

RATINGS

Admissions Selectivity Rating: 99 **Fire Safety Rating:** 60* **Green Rating:** 60*

STUDENTS AND FACULTY

Enrollment: 1,744. **Student Body:** 50% female, 50% male, 89% out-of-state, 8% international (24 countries represented). Asian 10%, African American 11%, Caucasian 39%, Hispanic 11%.
Retention and Graduation: 94% freshmen return for sophomore year. 85% freshmen graduate within 4 years. **Faculty:** Student/faculty ratio 8:1. 206 full-time faculty, 98% hold PhDs, 21% are members of minority groups, 42% are women.

ACADEMICS

Degrees: Bachelor's. **Classes:** Most classes have 10–19 students. Most lab/discussion sessions have fewer than 10 students. **Majors with Highest Enrollment:** Economics; political science and government; psychology. **Special Study Options:** Cross-registration, double major, exchange student program (domestic), honors program, independent study, student-designed major, study abroad, teacher certification program. **Honors programs:** Senior Honors Thesis—an opportunity to engage in extensive research with a professor as the student's advisor. Special programs offered to physically disabled students include note-taking services, reader services, tape recorders, tutors. **Career services:** Alumni network, alumni services, career/job search classes, career assessment, internships, regional alumni.

FACILITIES

Housing: Coed dorms, cooperative housing, French/Spanish language house, German/Russian language house, Latino culture house, African American culture house, Health and Wellness house, Arts house, Food Cooperative house, and single sex floors for men and women within specific dorms. **Special Academic Facilities/Equipment:** Art, natural history, geology museums, language labs, observatory, planetarium, The Amherst Center for Russian Culture, The Dickinson Homestead. **Computers:** Administrative functions (other than registration) can be performed online.

CAMPUS LIFE

Environment: Town. **Activities:** Choral groups, concert band, dance, drama/theater, jazz band, literary magazine, music ensembles, musical theater, opera, radio station, student government, student newspaper, student-run film society, symphony orchestra, yearbook, international student organization, Model UN. **Organizations:** 100 registered organizations, 2 honor societies, 7 religious or-

ganizations. **Athletics (Intercollegiate): Men:** Baseball, basketball, cross-country, diving, football, golf, ice hockey, lacrosse, soccer, squash, swimming, tennis, track/field (outdoor), track/field (indoor). *Women:* Basketball, cross-country, diving, field hockey, golf, ice hockey, lacrosse, soccer, softball, squash, swimming, tennis, track/field (outdoor), track/field (indoor), volleyball. **On-Campus Highlights:** Mead Art Museum, Pratt Museum of Natural History, Russian Cultural Center, Japanese Peace Garden, Observatory.

ADMISSIONS

Freshman Academic Profile: 85% in top 10% of high school class, 94% in top 25% of high school class, 100% in top 50% of high school class. 58% from public high schools. SAT Math middle 50% range 650–780. SAT Critical Reading middle 50% range 660–760. SAT Writing middle 50% range 660–770. ACT middle 50% range 30–34. Minimum paper TOEFL 600. Minimum computer TOEFL 250. Minimum web-based TOEFL 100. **Basis for Candidate Selection:** *Very important factors considered include:* Application essay, academic GPA, recommendation(s), rigor of secondary school record, standardized test scores, character/personal qualities, extracurricular activities, first generation, talent/ability. *Important factors considered include:* Class rank, alumni/ae relation, volunteer work. *Other factors considered include:* Geographical residence, state residency, work experience. **Freshman Admission Requirements:** High school diploma or equivalent is not required. *Academic units recommended:* 4 English, 4 mathematics, 3 science, (1 science labs), 4 foreign language, 2 social studies, 2 history. **Freshman Admission Statistics:** 7,679 applied, 16% admitted, 38% enrolled. **Transfer Admission Requirements:** High school transcript, college transcript(s), essay or personal statement, statement of good standing from prior institution(s). Minimum college GPA of 3.5 required. Lowest grade transferable C. **General Admission Information:** Application fee $60. Early decision application deadline 11/15. Regular application deadline 1/1. Regular notification 4/5. Nonfall registration not accepted. Admission may be deferred for a maximum of 2 years. Neither credit nor placement offered for CEEB Advanced Placement tests.

COSTS AND FINANCIAL AID

Annual tuition $38,250. Room and board $10,150. Required fees $678. Average book expense $1,000. **Required Forms and Deadlines:** FAFSA, CSS/Financial Aid PROFILE, noncustodial PROFILE, business/farm supplement. Income documentation submitted through college. Priority financial aid filing date 2/15. **Notification of Awards:** Applicants will be notified of awards on or about 4/1. **Types of Aid:** *Need-based scholarships/grants:* Federal Pell, SEOG, state scholarships/grants, private scholarships, the school's own gift aid. *Loans:* Direct Subsidized Stafford, Direct Unsubsidized Stafford, Direct PLUS, Federal Perkins, college/university loans from institutional funds. **Student Employment:** Federal Work-Study Program available. Institutional employment available. Off-campus job opportunities are excellent. **Financial Aid Statistics:** 53% freshmen, 56% undergrads receive need-based scholarship or grant aid. 56% undergrads receive non-need-based scholarship or grant aid. 45% freshmen, 50% undergrads receive need-based self-help aid. 44% freshmen, 54% undergrads receive any aid. 41% undergrads borrow to pay for school. Average cumulative indebtedness $11,347.

ANDERSON UNIVERSITY (IN)

1100 East Fifth Street, Anderson, IN 46012
Phone: 765-641-4080 **Financial Aid Phone:** 765-641-4180
E-mail: info@anderson.edu **CEEB Code:** 1016
Fax: 765-641-4091 **Website:** www.anderson.edu **ACT Code:** 1174

This private school, affiliated with the Church of God Church, was founded in 1917. It has a 100-acre campus.

RATINGS

Admissions Selectivity Rating: 75 **Fire Safety Rating:** 62 **Green Rating:** 60*

STUDENTS AND FACULTY

Enrollment: 2,194. **Student Body:** 58% female, 42% male, 34% out-of-state, 2% international (31 countries represented). Asian 1%, African American 5%, Caucasian 89%, Hispanic 1%.
Retention and Graduation: 77% freshmen return for sophomore year. 39% freshmen graduate within 4 years. 20% grads go on to further study within 1 year. **Faculty:** Student/faculty ratio 15:1. 141 full-time faculty, 65% hold PhDs, 3% are members of minority groups, 43% are women.

ACADEMICS

Degrees: Associate, bachelor's, first professional, master's. **Classes:** Most classes have 10–19 students. Most lab/discussion sessions have 10–19 students. **Majors with Highest Enrollment:** Business administration and management;

elementary education and teaching; nursing/registered nurse (RN, ASN, BSN, MSN). **Special Study Options:** Accelerated program, cross-registration, double major, honors program, independent study, internships, student-designed major, study abroad, teacher certification program, Summer over seas service program. **Honors programs:** The Honors Program at Anderson University is devoted to fostering within its honors scholars a passionate dedication to intellectual inquiry and spiritual development so that they may serve as vibrant leaders in their professions and in their communities. Special programs offered to physically disabled students include note-taking services, reader services, tape recorders, tutors.

FACILITIES

Housing: Coed dorms, men's dorms, women's dorms, apartments for married students, apartments for single students, one house. 95% of campus accessible to physically disabled. **Special Academic Facilities/Equipment:** Gustav Jeeninga Museum of Bible and Near Eastern Studies, Wilson Galleries, Archives of the Church of God. **Computers:** Students can register for classes online. Administrative functions (other than registration) can be performed online.

CAMPUS LIFE

Environment: Town. **Activities:** Choral groups, concert band, dance, drama/theater, jazz band, literary magazine, music ensembles, musical theater, opera, pep band, radio station, student government, student newspaper, symphony orchestra, yearbook. **Organizations:** 33 registered organizations, 12 honor societies, 15 religious organizations. **Athletics (Intercollegiate):** *Men:* Baseball, basketball, cheerleading, cross-country, football, golf, soccer, tennis, track/field (outdoor). *Women:* Basketball, cheerleading, cross-country, golf, soccer, softball, tennis, track/field (outdoor), volleyball. **On-Campus Highlights:** Kardatzke Wellness Center, Mocha Joe's in the Olt Student Center, Decker Commons and Cafe Ole, Reardon Auditorium.

ADMISSIONS

Freshman Academic Profile: Average high school GPA 3.33. 22% in top 10% of high school class, 46% in top 25% of high school class, 78% in top 50% of high school class. 95% from public high schools. SAT Math middle 50% range 460–580. SAT Critical Reading middle 50% range 460–580. ACT middle 50% range 20–26. Minimum paper TOEFL 515. Minimum computer TOEFL 187. **Basis for Candidate Selection:** *Very important factors considered include:* Recommendation(s), rigor of secondary school record, religious affiliation/commitment. *Important factors considered include:* Class rank, standardized test scores, character/personal qualities, extracurricular activities, interview, volunteer work. *Other factors considered include:* Application essay, alumni/ae relation, first generation, level of applicant's interest, racial/ethnic status, talent/ability. **Freshman Admission Requirements:** High school diploma is required and GED is not accepted. *Academic units required:* 4 English, 3 mathematics, 3 science, (3 science labs), 2 foreign language, 1 social studies, 1 history. *Academic units recommended:* 4 English, 4 mathematics, 4 science, (4 science labs), 3 foreign language, 2 social studies, 2 history, 5 academic electives. **Freshman Admission Statistics:** 1,986 applied, 91% admitted, 25% enrolled. **Transfer Admission Requirements:** High school transcript, college transcript(s), standardized test scores, statement of good standing from prior institution(s). Minimum college GPA of 2.0 required. Lowest grade transferable C–. **General Admission Information:** Application fee $25. Regular application deadline 7/1. Notification on a rolling basis, beginning on or about 9/1. Nonfall registration accepted. Admission may be deferred for a maximum of 1 year. Credit and/or placement offered for CEEB Advanced Placement tests.

COSTS AND FINANCIAL AID

Annual tuition $19,990. Room and board $6,460. Average book expense $850. **Required Forms and Deadlines:** FAFSA. Priority financial aid filing date 3/1. **Notification of Awards:** Applicants will be notified of awards on a rolling basis beginning 2/15. **Types of Aid:** *Need-based scholarships/grants:* Federal Pell, SEOG, state scholarships/grants, private scholarships, the school's own gift aid. *Loans:* Direct Subsidized Stafford, Direct Unsubsidized Stafford, Direct PLUS, Federal Perkins, college/university loans from institutional funds. **Student Employment:** Federal Work-Study Program available. **Financial Aid Statistics:** 79% freshmen, 76% undergrads receive need-based scholarship or grant aid. 58% freshmen, 48% undergrads receive non-need-based scholarship or grant aid. 78% freshmen, 75% undergrads receive need-based self-help aid. 76% undergrads borrow to pay for school. Average cumulative indebtedness $17,439. **Criteria for awarding institutional aid:** *Non-need-based:* Academics.

ANDERSON UNIVERSITY (SC)

316 Boulevard, Anderson, SC 29621
Phone: 864-231-5607 **Financial Aid Phone:** 864-231-2073
E-mail: admissions@andersonuniversity.edu **CEEB Code:** 5008
Fax: 864-231-2033 **Website:** www.andersonuniversity.edu **ACT Code:** 3832

This private school, affiliated with the Southern Baptist Church,, affiliated with the South Carolina Baptist Convention Church, was founded in 1911. It has a 56-acre campus.

RATINGS

Admissions Selectivity Rating: 80 **Fire Safety Rating:** 79 **Green Rating:** 60*

STUDENTS AND FACULTY

Enrollment: 2,127. **Student Body:** 67% female, 33% male, 15.84% out-of-state, 2% international (12 countries represented). Asian 1%, African American 9%, Caucasian 65%, Hispanic 2%.
Retention and Graduation: 74% freshmen return for sophomore year. 46% freshmen graduate within 4 years. 15% grads go on to further study within 1 year. **Faculty:** Student/faculty ratio 19:1. 72 full-time faculty, 56% hold PhDs, 7% are members of minority groups, 45% are women.

ACADEMICS

Degrees: Bachelor's, master's. **Classes:** Most classes have 20–29 students. Most lab/discussion sessions have 20–29 students. **Majors with Highest Enrollment:** Business administration and management; elementary education and teaching; kinesiology and exercise science. **Special Study Options:** Accelerated program, cooperative education program, distance learning, double major, dual enrollment, honors program, independent study, internships, liberal arts/career combination, study abroad, teacher certification program, Washington Semester. Special programs offered to physically disabled students include note-taking services, reader services, tape recorders, tutors. **Career services:** Career/job search classes, career assessment, internships.

FACILITIES

Housing: Men's dorms, women's dorms. **Special Academic Facilities/Equipment:** Electronic classroom, art galleries, recording studio. **Computers:** Students can register for classes online. Administrative functions (other than registration) can be performed online.

CAMPUS LIFE

Environment: Town. **Activities:** Choral groups, concert band, dance, drama/theater, jazz band, literary magazine, music ensembles, musical theater, student government, student newspaper, symphony orchestra, yearbook, campus ministries. **Organizations:** 27 registered organizations, 1 honor societies, 6 religious organizations. **Athletics (Intercollegiate):** *Men:* Baseball, basketball, cross-country, equestrian sports, golf, soccer, tennis, track/field (outdoor), wrestling. *Women:* Basketball, cheerleading, cross-country, equestrian sports, golf, soccer, softball, tennis, track/field (outdoor), volleyball. **On-Campus Highlights:** Java City, Student Center, Bunton Computer Lab, Thrift Libary, Fitness Center.

ADMISSIONS

Freshman Academic Profile: Average high school GPA 3.28. 32.63% in top 10% of high school class, 51.88% in top 25% of high school class, 79.81% in top 50% of high school class. 94% from public high schools. SAT Math middle 50% range 450–580. SAT Critical Reading middle 50% range 440–580. SAT Writing middle 50% range 430–570. ACT middle 50% range 18–24. Minimum paper TOEFL 550. Minimum computer TOEFL 220. **Basis for Candidate Selection:** *Very important factors considered include:* Academic GPA, standardized test scores. *Important factors considered include:* Class rank, rigor of secondary school record. *Other factors considered include:* Application essay, recommendation(s), alumni/ae relation, character/personal qualities, first generation, interview, racial/ethnic status, religious affiliation/commitment, talent/ability, volunteer work. **Freshman Admission Requirements:** High school diploma is required and GED is accepted. *Academic units required:* 4 English, 3 mathematics, 3 science, (2 science labs), 2 foreign language, 2 social studies, 2 history, 4 academic electives. *Academic units recommended:* 4 mathematics, 4 science. **Freshman Admission Statistics:** 1,926 applied, 68% admitted, 38% enrolled. **Transfer Admission Requirements:** College transcript(s), minimum college GPA of 2.0 required. Lowest grade transferable C. **General Admission Information:** Application fee $25. Notification on a rolling basis, beginning on or about 9/2. Nonfall registration accepted. Admission may be deferred for a maximum of 1 year. Credit and/or placement offered for CEEB Advanced Placement tests.

COSTS AND FINANCIAL AID

Annual tuition $17,876. Room and board $6,750. Required fees $1,336. Average book expense $1,650. **Required Forms and Deadlines:** FAFSA. Financial aid filing deadline 6/30. Priority financial aid filing date 3/1. **Notification of**

Awards: Applicants will be notified of awards on a rolling basis beginning 3/15. **Types of Aid:** *Need-based scholarships/grants:* Federal Pell, SEOG, state scholarships/grants, the school's own gift aid. *Loans:* Direct Subsidized Stafford, Direct Unsubsidized Stafford, Direct PLUS, Federal Perkins.. **Student Employment: Financial Aid Statistics:** 64% freshmen, 70% undergrads receive need-based scholarship or grant aid. 64% freshmen, 50% undergrads receive non-need-based scholarship or grant aid. 59% freshmen, 64% undergrads receive need-based self-help aid. 16% freshmen, 14% undergrads receive athletic scholarships. 76% undergrads borrow to pay for school. Average cumulative indebtedness $15,150. **Criteria for awarding institutional aid:** *Non-need-based:* Academics, alumni affiliation, art, athletics, leadership, minority status, music/drama, religious affiliation, state/district residency.

ANDREWS UNIVERSITY

Office of Admissions, Andrews University, Berrien Springs, MI 49104
Phone: 269-471-6343 **Financial Aid Phone:**
E-mail: enroll@andrews.edu **CEEB Code:** 1030
Fax: 269-471-2670 **Website:** www.andrews.edu **ACT Code:** 1992

This private school, affiliated with the Seventh Day Adventist Church, was founded in 1874. It has a 1600-acre campus.

RATINGS
Admissions Selectivity Rating: 80   **Fire Safety Rating:** 60*   **Green Rating:** 60*

STUDENTS AND FACULTY
Enrollment: 1,746. **Student Body:** 56% female, 44% male, 42% out-of-state, 15% international. Asian 10%, African American 21%, Caucasian 52%, Hispanic 8%.
Retention and Graduation: 69% freshmen return for sophomore year. 24% grads go on to further study within 1 year. 24% grads pursue arts and sciences degrees. **Faculty:** 10% of classes are taught by teaching assistants.

ACADEMICS
Degrees: Associate, bachelor's, diploma, first professional, master's. **Special Study Options:** Study abroad, undergrads may take grad level classes. **Combined degree programs:** BA/MD, BA/DDS, BA/MEng, Co-op in dental assisting, hygiene; med record admin. **Career services:** Internships.

FACILITIES
Housing: Men's dorms, women's dorms, apartments for married students, apartments for single students. **Special Academic Facilities/Equipment:** Audio-visual center, lab school, natural history and archaeological museums, observatory, physical therapy facilities.

CAMPUS LIFE
Environment: Rural. **Activities:** Choral groups, concert band, radio station, student government, student newspaper, yearbook. **Organizations:** 2 religious organizations.

ADMISSIONS
Freshman Academic Profile: 23% from public high schools. SAT Math middle 50% range 420–600. SAT Critical Reading middle 50% range 440–610. ACT middle 50% range 19–27. **Basis for Candidate Selection: Freshman Admission Requirements:** High school diploma is required and GED is accepted. *Academic units recommended:* 4 English, 2 mathematics, 2 science, 2 history. **Freshman Admission Statistics:** Minimum college GPA of 2.0 required. Lowest grade transferable C. **General Admission Information:** Application fee $30. Early decision application deadline 1/1. Nonfall registration accepted. Credit offered for CEEB Advanced Placement tests.

COSTS AND FINANCIAL AID
Annual tuition $11,685. Room and board $3,630. Required fees $285. Average book expense $1,128. **Required Forms and Deadlines:** FAFSA, institution's own financial aid form, state aid form. **Notification of Awards: Types of Aid:** *Need-based scholarships/grants:* State scholarships/grants. *Loans:* Direct Subsidized Stafford, Direct PLUS. **Student Employment:** Federal Work-Study Program available. Institutional employment available. Highest amount earned per year from on-campus jobs $1,200. Off-campus job opportunities are good.

ANGELO STATE UNIVERSITY

Best 373

2601 West Avenue N, San Angelo, TX 76909
Phone: 325-942-2041 **Financial Aid Phone:** 325-942-2246
E-mail: admissions@angelo.edu **CEEB Code:** 6644
Fax: 325-942-2078 **Website:** www.angelo.edu **ACT Code:** 4164

This public school was founded in 1928. It has a 268-acre campus.

RATINGS
Admissions Selectivity Rating: 63   **Fire Safety Rating:** 90   **Green Rating:** 73

STUDENTS AND FACULTY
Enrollment: 5,725. **Student Body:** 55% female, 45% male, 3% out-of-state, 1% international (22 countries represented). Asian 1%, African American 5%, Caucasian 49%, Hispanic 18%.
Retention and Graduation: 59% freshmen return for sophomore year. 21% freshmen graduate within 4 years. **Faculty:** Student/faculty ratio 19:1. 246 full-time faculty, 76% hold PhDs, 17% are members of minority groups, 44% are women. 2% of classes are taught by teaching assistants.

ACADEMICS
Degrees: Associate, bachelor's, master's. **Classes:** Most classes have 20–29 students. Most lab/discussion sessions have 20–29 students. **Majors with Highest Enrollment:** Business/commerce; nursing/registered nurse (RN, ASN, BSN, MSN); psychology. **Special Study Options:** Distance learning, double major, dual enrollment, honors program, independent study, internships, study abroad, teacher certification program, 4+1 programs in various disciplines allowing students to complete a bachelor's degree in four years and a master's degree in a related field in one year at Texas Tech University. Also, 3+2 physics/pre-engineering program allowing three years of study in applied physics and two years at an affiliated university for an engineering degree. **Honors programs:** www.angelo.edu/dept/honors/ **Combined degree programs:** BBA/MBA. Special programs offered to physically disabled students include note-taking services, tutors. **Career services:** Alumni network, alumni services, career/job search classes, career assessment, internships. **Career services highlights include:** ASU's multiple internship programs have provided exceptional worklife experiences for undergraduates with students interning in positions ranging from the Los Alamos National Labs to Washington, DC, news services. Additionally, the Career Development Office Career Exploration and Planning classes, which help broaden student understanding of career possibilities and the value of internships.

FACILITIES
Housing: Coed dorms, women's dorms, apartments for single students, theme housingRooms for disabled and Honors students. 99% of campus accessible to physically disabled. **Special Academic Facilities/Equipment:** Planetarium; West Texas Collection; Management, Instruction, and Research (Agricultural)Center; Food Safety and Product Development Lab. **Computers:** 100% of classrooms, 100% of dorms, 100% of libraries, 100% of dining areas, 100% of student union, 100% of common outdoor areas have wireless network access. Students can register for classes online. Administrative functions (other than registration) can be performed online.

CAMPUS LIFE
Environment: City. **Activities:** Choral groups, concert band, dance, drama/theater, jazz band, literary magazine, marching band, music ensembles, musical theater, pep band, radio station, student government, student newspaper, student-run film society, television station, campus ministries, international student organization. **Organizations:** 76 registered organizations, 11 honor societies, 9 religious organizations. 4 fraternities, 2 sororities. **Athletics (Intercollegiate):** *Men:* Baseball, basketball, cross-country, football, track/field (outdoor). *Women:* Basketball, cross-country, golf, soccer, softball, track/field (outdoor), volleyball. **On-Campus Highlights:** Houston Harte University Center, Junell Center/Stephens Arena, ASU Planetarium, ASU Lake House, West Texas Collection, ASU Mall, and Student Gathering Areas Porter Henderson Library. **Environmental Initiatives:** LEED Certification initiatives in all new buildings. Recycling programs. Moving to green cleaning products.

ADMISSIONS
Freshman Academic Profile: 15% in top 10% of high school class, 31% in top 25% of high school class, 74% in top 50% of high school class. 96% from public high schools. SAT Math middle 50% range 430–540. SAT Critical Reading middle 50% range 410–520. SAT Writing middle 50% range 400–510. ACT middle

50% range 18–23. Minimum paper TOEFL 550. Minimum computer TOEFL 213. **Basis for Candidate Selection:** *Very important factors considered include:* Class rank, rigor of secondary school record, standardized test scores. **Freshman Admission Requirements:** High school diploma is required and GED is accepted. *Academic units recommended:* 4 English, 3 mathematics, 3 science, 2 foreign language, 3 social studies, 1 computer science, 1 academic electives. **Freshman Admission Statistics:** 2,920 applied, 92% admitted, 55% enrolled. **Transfer Admission Requirements:** College transcript(s), statement of good standing from prior institution(s). Minimum college GPA of 2.0 required. Lowest grade transferable D. **General Admission Information:** Application fee $25. Nonfall registration accepted. Credit offered for CEEB Advanced Placement tests.

COSTS AND FINANCIAL AID
Annual in-state tuition $4,245. Annual out-of-state tuition $12,675. Room and board $6,612. Required fees $1,893. Average book expense $1,000. **Required Forms and Deadlines:** FAFSA. Priority financial aid filing date 4/1. **Notification of Awards:** Applicants will be notified of awards on a rolling basis beginning 4/1. **Types of Aid:** *Need-based scholarships/grants:* Federal Pell, SEOG, state scholarships/grants, private scholarships, the school's own gift aid, Federal Nursing Scholarships. *Loans:* Direct Subsidized Stafford, Direct Unsubsidized Stafford, Direct PLUS, Federal Perkins, Federal Nursing, state loans, college/university loans from institutional funds. **Student Employment:** Federal Work-Study Program available. Institutional employment available. Off-campus job opportunities are good. **Financial Aid Statistics:** 53% freshmen, 50% undergrads receive need-based scholarship or grant aid. 32% freshmen, 25% undergrads receive non-need-based scholarship or grant aid. 42% freshmen, 43% undergrads receive need-based self-help aid. 1% freshmen, 2% undergrads receive athletic scholarships. 79% freshmen, 74% undergrads receive any aid. 37% undergrads borrow to pay for school. Average cumulative indebtedness $16,372. **Criteria for awarding institutional aid:** *Non-need-based:* Academics, art, athletics, leadership, music/drama, state/district residency.

ANNA MARIA COLLEGE

50 Sunset Lane, Box O, Paxton, MA 01612-1198
Phone: 508-849-3360 **Financial Aid Phone:** 508-849-3366
E-mail: admission@annamaria.edu **CEEB Code:** 3005
Fax: 508-849-3362 **Website:** www.annamaria.edu **ACT Code:** 3232

This private school, affiliated with the Roman Catholic Church, was founded in 1946. It has a 190-acre campus.

RATINGS
Admissions Selectivity Rating: 63   **Fire Safety Rating:** 69   **Green Rating:** 77

STUDENTS AND FACULTY
Enrollment: 978. **Student Body:** 56% female, 44% male, 12% out-of-state, 1% international. Asian 1%, African American 6%, Caucasian 73%, Hispanic 5%.
Retention and Graduation: 70% freshmen return for sophomore year. 50% freshmen graduate within 4 years. 47% grads go on to further study within 1 year. 19% grads pursue arts and sciences degrees. 2% grads pursue law degrees. 1% grads pursue business degrees. **Faculty:** Student/faculty ratio 10:1. 50 full-time faculty, 72% hold PhDs, 66% are women.

ACADEMICS
Degrees: Associate, bachelor's, certificate, master's, post-bachelor's certificate, post-master's certificate. **Classes:** Most classes have 10–19 students. Most lab/discussion sessions have fewer than 10 students. **Majors with Highest Enrollment:** Business administration and management; criminal justice/safety studies; fire science/fire-fighting. **Special Study Options:** Accelerated program, cooperative education program, cross-registration, double major, independent study, internships, liberal arts/career combination, student-designed major, study abroad, teacher certification program. **Honors programs:** The Honors Program at Anna Maria College is designed to intellectually challenge highly motivated scholastic achievers. The Program is now a member of "National Collegiate Honors Programs," the national association of Honors Programs. Each Honors Program participant will have the opportunity to engage directly in foreign culture through interesting study abroad programs, such as a semester abroad experience,or a focused Urban Seminar that meets in a city like Paris, Vienna, Rome, or Berlin that is sponsored by the college and supervised by a professor who oversees the program. **Combined degree programs:** BA/MA. Special programs offered to physically disabled students include note-taking services, reader services, tape recorders, tutors. **Career services:** Alumni services, career assessment, internships.

FACILITIES
Housing: Coed dorms, special housing for disabled students, wellness housing. **Special Academic Facilities/Equipment:** The Mondor-Eagan Library houses Anna Maria College's volumes, stacks, periodicals, study rooms, computer center, resource centers, and language laboratory. Classrooms are located in Trinity Hall, Cardinal Cushing Hall, and Foundress Hall. Foundress Hall houses the Zecco Performing Arts Center. Trinity Hall also houses the learning center. Among the other buildings are Madore Chapel, St. Joseph's Hall for sciences and Miriam Hall for music, performance, and art. **Computers:** 100% of classrooms, 100% of dorms, 100% of libraries, 100% of dining areas, 100% of student union, 100% of common outdoor areas have wireless network access. Administrative functions (other than registration) can be performed online.

CAMPUS LIFE
Environment: Rural. **Activities:** Choral groups, dance, drama/theater, jazz band, pep band, student government, student newspaper, yearbook, campus ministries. **Organizations:** 17 registered organizations, 5 honor societies, 1 religious organizations. **Athletics (Intercollegiate):** *Men:* Baseball, basketball, cross-country, football, golf, lacrosse, soccer, tennis *Women:* Basketball, field hockey, lacrosse, soccer, softball, tennis, volleyball. **On-Campus Highlights:** NEW: residence hall, NEW: exercise/weight room, NEW: Art building w/ gallery, snack bar/lounge, student center. **Environmental Initiatives:** There is a Green Committee that meets regularly to discuss environmental issues and ways that the college can be be more sustainable. Efforts are ongoing in moving to a paperless environment. We have made significant progress in this area.

ADMISSIONS
Freshman Academic Profile: Average high school GPA 2.62. 2% in top 10% of high school class, 13% in top 25% of high school class, 41% in top 50% of high school class. SAT Math middle 50% range 378–480. SAT Critical Reading middle 50% range 378–490. ACT middle 50% range 18–21. Minimum paper TOEFL 500. Minimum computer TOEFL 150. **Basis for Candidate Selection:** *Very important factors considered include:* Academic GPA, standardized test scores. *Other factors considered include:* Application essay, recommendation(s), rigor of secondary school record, extracurricular activities, level of applicant's interest, volunteer work, work experience. **Freshman Admission Requirements:** High school diploma is required and GED is accepted. *Academic units required:* 4 English, 3 mathematics, 3 science, (1 science labs), 2 foreign language, 2 social studies, 2 history, 4 academic electives. **Freshman Admission Statistics:** 935 applied, 89% admitted, 30% enrolled. **Transfer Admission Requirements:** High school transcript, college transcript(s), essay or personal statement, statement of good standing from prior institution(s). Minimum college GPA of 2.0 required. Lowest grade transferable C. **General Admission Information:** Application fee $40. Notification on a rolling basis, beginning on or about 12/1. Nonfall registration accepted. Admission may be deferred for a maximum of 1 year. Credit and/or placement offered for CEEB Advanced Placement tests.

COSTS AND FINANCIAL AID
Annual tuition $23,500. Room and board $9,350. Required fees $2,350. Average book expense $800. **Required Forms and Deadlines:** FAFSA, state aid form. Priority financial aid filing date 3/1. **Notification of Awards:** Applicants will be notified of awards on a rolling basis beginning 4/1. **Types of Aid:** *Need-based scholarships/grants:* Federal Pell, SEOG, state scholarships/grants, private scholarships, the school's own gift aid, United Negro College Fund. *Loans:* Direct Subsidized Stafford, Direct Unsubsidized Stafford, Direct PLUS, Federal Perkins, college/university loans from institutional funds. **Student Employment:** Federal Work-Study Program available. Off-campus job opportunities are good. **Financial Aid Statistics:** 81% freshmen, 78% undergrads receive need-based scholarship or grant aid. 81% freshmen, 78% undergrads receive non-need-based scholarship or grant aid. 75% freshmen, 73% undergrads receive need-based self-help aid. 98% freshmen, 95% undergrads receive any aid. 92% undergrads borrow to pay for school. Average cumulative indebtedness $35,575. **Criteria for awarding institutional aid:** *Non-need-based:* Academics, alumni affiliation, music/drama, religious affiliation, state/district residency.

ANTIOCH COLLEGE

795 Livermore Street, Yellow Springs, OH 45387
Phone: 937-769-1100 **Financial Aid Phone:**
E-mail: admissions@antioch-college.edu **CEEB Code:** 1017
Fax: 937-769-1111 **Website:** www.antioch-college.edu **ACT Code:** 3232

This private school was founded in 1852. It has a 100-acre campus.

RATINGS
Admissions Selectivity Rating: 82   **Fire Safety Rating:** 60*   **Green Rating:** 60*

STUDENTS AND FACULTY

Enrollment: 120. **Student Body:** 68% female, 33% male, 66% out-of-state, international.
Retention and Graduation: 60% freshmen return for sophomore year. 28% freshmen graduate within 4 years. **Faculty:** Student/faculty ratio 8:1. 45 full-time faculty, 78% hold PhDs, 13% are members of minority groups, 56% are women.

ACADEMICS

Degrees: Bachelor's. **Classes:** Most classes have fewer than 10 students. **Special Study Options:** Cooperative education program, cross-registration, dual enrollment, independent study, internships, liberal arts/career combination, student-designed major, study abroad. Special programs offered to physically disabled students include note-taking services, reader services, tape recorders, tutors. **Career services:** Alumni services, career/job search classes, career assessment, internships.

FACILITIES

Housing: Coed dorms, special housing for disabled students, special housing for international students, gender specific floors. 25% of campus accessible to physically disabled. **Special Academic Facilities/Equipment:** 1,000–acre nature preserve.

CAMPUS LIFE

Environment: Rural. **Activities:** Choral groups, dance, drama/theater, literary magazine, music ensembles, musical theater, radio station, student government, student newspaper. **Organizations:** 16 registered organizations. **On-Campus Highlights:** Herndon Gallery, Glen Hellen Nature Preserve, Japanese Tea Garden, Community Bike Shop, Alternative Library.

ADMISSIONS

Freshman Academic Profile: Average high school GPA 3.3. 14% in top 10% of high school class, 42% in top 25% of high school class, 70% in top 50% of high school class. SAT Math middle 50% range 500–620. SAT Critical Reading middle 50% range 550–690. ACT middle 50% range 22–27. Minimum paper TOEFL 525. **Basis for Candidate Selection:** *Very important factors considered include:* Application essay, academic GPA, recommendation(s), rigor of secondary school record, character/personal qualities, interview, level of applicant's interest. *Important factors considered include:* Class rank, volunteer work, work experience. *Other factors considered include:* Standardized test scores, alumni/ae relation, extracurricular activities, first generation, talent/ability. **Freshman Admission Requirements:** High school diploma is required and GED is accepted. *Academic units required:* 4 English. *Academic units recommended:* 4 mathematics, 4 science, (3 science labs), 4 foreign language, 4 social studies, 4 history, 2 academic electives. **Freshman Admission Statistics:** 1,204 applied, 60% admitted, 15% enrolled. **Transfer Admission Requirements:** High school transcript, college transcript(s), essay or personal statement, statement of good standing from prior institution(s). **General Admission Information:** Notification on a rolling basis, beginning on or about 1/1. Nonfall registration not accepted. Admission may be deferred for a maximum of 1 year. Credit and/or placement offered for CEEB Advanced Placement tests.

COSTS AND FINANCIAL AID

Annual tuition $27,800. Room and board $7,354. Required fees $750. Average book expense $2,000. **Required Forms and Deadlines:** FAFSA, institution's own financial aid form. Priority financial aid filing date 3/1. **Notification of Awards:** Applicants will be notified of awards on a rolling basis beginning 3/15. **Types of Aid:** *Need-based scholarships/grants:* Federal Pell, SEOG, state scholarships/grants, private scholarships, the school's own gift aid. *Loans:* Direct Subsidized Stafford, Direct Unsubsidized Stafford, Direct PLUS, Federal Perkins.. **Student Employment:** Federal Work-Study Program available. Institutional employment available. Off-campus job opportunities are fair. **Financial Aid Statistics:** 61% freshmen, 72% undergrads receive need-based scholarship or grant aid. 77% freshmen, 81% undergrads receive non-need-based scholarship or grant aid. 63% freshmen, 69% undergrads receive need-based self-help aid. 85% undergrads borrow to pay for school. Average cumulative indebtedness $17,112. **Criteria for awarding institutional aid:** *Non-need-based:* Academics.

ANTIOCH SOUTHERN CALIFORNIA— LOS ANGELES

Office of Admissions, Culver City, CA 90230
Phone: 310-578-1090 **Financial Aid Phone:**
E-mail: admissions@atiochla.edu **CEEB Code:** 1862
Fax: 310-822-4824 **Website:** www.antiochla.edu

This private school was founded in 1852. It has a 800-acre campus.

RATINGS

Admissions Selectivity Rating: 60*   **Fire Safety Rating:** 60*   **Green Rating:** 60*

STUDENTS AND FACULTY

Enrollment: 188. **Student Body:** 100% female, 9% out-of-state, (20 countries represented). Asian 5%, African American 24%, Caucasian 80%, Hispanic 11%, Native American 2%.
Retention and Graduation: 73% grads go on to further study within 1 year. 82% grads pursue arts and sciences degrees. 4% grads pursue law degrees. 12% grads pursue business degrees. **Faculty:** Student/faculty ratio 14:1. 21 full-time faculty, 81% hold PhDs, 24% are members of minority groups, 71% are women.

ACADEMICS

Degrees: Bachelor's, certificate, diploma, master's, post-bachelor's certificate, post-master's certificate. **Classes:** Most classes have 10–19 students. **Special Study Options:** cross-registration, double major, independent study, internships, teacher certification program, weekend college. **Combined degree programs:** BA/MA. Special programs offered to physically disabled students include note-taking services, tape recorders. **Career services:** Internships.

FACILITIES

Housing: Coed dorms 100% of campus accessible to physically disabled.

CAMPUS LIFE

Environment: City. **Activities:** Radio station, student government, campus ministries. **Organizations:** 1 registered organizations. **On-Campus Highlights:** Student lounge, campus services, classrooms, computer lab, faculty and Student Services Offices.

ADMISSIONS

Freshman Academic Profile: Minimum paper TOEFL 600. Minimum computer TOEFL 250. **Transfer Admission Requirements:** College transcript(s), essay or personal statement, Lowest grade transferable C. **General Admission Information:** Application fee $60. Regular application deadline 8/1. Notification on a rolling basis, beginning on or about 9/1. Nonfall registration not accepted. Admission may be deferred for a maximum of 1 year. Credit and/or placement offered for CEEB Advanced Placement tests.

COSTS AND FINANCIAL AID

Annual tuition $15,380. Required fees $260. **Required Forms and Deadlines:** FAFSA, institution's own financial aid form. Priority financial aid filing date 3/24. **Notification of Awards:** Applicants will be notified of awards on a rolling basis beginning 4/15. **Types of Aid:** *Need-based scholarships/grants:* Federal Pell, SEOG, state scholarships/grants, private scholarships, the school's own gift aid. *Loans:* FFEL Subsidized Stafford, FFEL Unsubsidized Stafford, FFEL PLUS, Federal Perkins. **Student Employment:** Federal Work-Study Program available. Institutional employment available. Off-campus job opportunities are excellent. **Financial Aid Statistics:** 67% undergrads receive need-based scholarship or grant aid. 74% undergrads receive need-based self-help aid. **Criteria for awarding institutional aid:** *Non-need-based:* Academics, leadership.

ANTIOCH UNIVERSITY SANTA BARBARA

801 Garden Street, Suite 101, Santa Barbara, CA 93101
Phone: 805-962-8179 **Financial Aid Phone:** 805-962-8179
E-mail: admissions@antiochsb.edu
Fax: 805-962-4786 **Website:** www.antiochsb.edu

This private school was founded in 1852.

RATINGS

Admissions Selectivity Rating: 60*   **Fire Safety Rating:** 60*   **Green Rating:** 60*

STUDENTS AND FACULTY

Enrollment: 105. **Student Body:** 75% female, 25% male, (11 countries represented).
Retention and Graduation: Faculty: 16 full-time faculty, 69% are women.

ACADEMICS

Degrees: Bachelor's, master's. **Special Study Options:** Cross-registration, double major, independent study, internships, liberal arts/career combination, study abroad, teacher certification program, weekend college.

FACILITIES

Computers: Students can register for classes online. Administrative functions (other than registration) can be performed online.

CAMPUS LIFE

Environment: City.

ADMISSIONS

Freshman Admission Requirements: High school diploma is required and GED is accepted. **Freshman Admission Statistics: Transfer Admission Requirements:** High school transcript, college transcript(s), essay or personal statement, interview, statement of good standing from prior institution(s). Minimum college GPA of 2.0 required. Lowest grade transferable C. **General Admission Information:** Application fee $60. Nonfall registration not accepted.

COSTS AND FINANCIAL AID

Annual tuition $15,375. Required fees $26. **Required Forms and Deadlines:** FAFSA, institution's own financial aid form. Priority financial aid filing date 4/15. **Notification of Awards: Types of Aid:** *Need-based scholarships/grants:* Federal Pell, SEOG, state scholarships/grants, private scholarships, the school's own gift aid. *Loans:* Direct Subsidized Stafford, Direct Unsubsidized Stafford, Direct PLUS, Federal Perkins. **Student Employment: Financial Aid Statistics:** 75% undergrads borrow to pay for school. Average cumulative indebtedness $25,000.

APPALACHIAN STATE UNIVERSITY

Office of Admissions, ASU Box 32004, Boone, NC 28608-2004
Phone: 828-262-2120 **Financial Aid Phone:** 828-262-2190
E-mail: admissions@appstate.edu **CEEB Code:** 5010
Fax: 828-262-3296 **Website:** www.appstate.edu **ACT Code:** 3062

This public school was founded in 1899. It has a 1300-acre campus.

RATINGS

Admissions Selectivity Rating: 86   **Fire Safety Rating:** 71   **Green Rating:** 98

STUDENTS AND FACULTY

Enrollment: 14,698. **Student Body:** 52% female, 48% male, 9% out-of-state, international (54 countries represented). Asian 1%, African American 3%, Caucasian 88%, Hispanic 2%.
Retention and Graduation: 39% freshmen graduate within 4 years. **Faculty:** Student/faculty ratio 17:1. 824 full-time faculty, 99% hold PhDs, 10% are members of minority groups, 44% are women.

ACADEMICS

Degrees: Bachelor's, certificate, master's, post-bachelor's certificate, post-master's certificate. **Classes:** Most classes have 20–29 students. Most lab/discussion sessions have 20–29 students. **Majors with Highest Enrollment:** Business administration and management; elementary education and teaching; psychology. **Special Study Options:** Distance learning, double major, dual enrollment, English as a Second Language (ESL), exchange student program (domestic), honors program, independent study, internships, liberal arts/career combination, student-designed major, study abroad, teacher certification program.
Honors programs: Heltzer Honors Program offers promising and highly motivated students opportunities by providing honors classes in many fields. Special programs offered to physically disabled students include note-taking services, reader services, tape recorders, tutors. **Career services:** Alumni network, alumni services, career/job search classes, career assessment, internships, regional alumni.

FACILITIES

Housing: Coed dorms, special housing for disabled students, men's dorms, special housing for international students, women's dorms, apartments for married students, apartments for single students, wellness housing, theme housingSorority housing. 100% of campus accessible to physically disabled. **Special Academic Facilities/Equipment:** Language lab, Dark Sky Observatory www.dancaton.physics.appstate.edu/Observatories/DSO/index.htm, meteorological reporting station, art gallery, Living Learning Center, geology museum and

rock garden www.geology.appstate.edu/museum/museum.htm, wind research site www.wind.appstate.edu/swiwind/smallwindrdsite.php, library Special Collections www.library.appstate.edu/collections/sc/index.html. **Computers:** 95% of classrooms, 70% of dorms, 90% of libraries, 90% of dining areas, 85% of student union, 5% of common outdoor areas have wireless network access. Students can register for classes online. Administrative functions (other than registration) can be performed online.

CAMPUS LIFE

Environment: Village. **Activities:** Choral groups, concert band, dance, drama/theater, jazz band, literary magazine, marching band, music ensembles, musical theater, opera, pep band, radio station, student government, student newspaper, student-run film society, symphony orchestra, campus ministries, international student organization, Model UN. **Organizations:** 270 registered organizations, 20 honor societies, 25 religious organizations. 18 fraternities, 11 sorority. **Athletics (Intercollegiate):** *Men:* Baseball, basketball, cross-country, football, golf, soccer, tennis, track/field (outdoor), track/field (indoor), wrestling. *Women:* Basketball, cross-country, field hockey, golf, soccer, softball, tennis, track/field (outdoor), track/field (indoor), volleyball. **On-Campus Highlights:** Student Union, Central Dining Hall, Belk Library, Student Recreation Center, Holmes Convocation Center. **Environmental Initiatives:** Significant recent institutional commitments Establishment of the Office of Sustainability reporting to the Vice Chancellor, creation of 35 member interdisciplinary, cross-campus Sustainability Council Signatory of the American College and University Presidents Climate Commitment. On track with the target requirements. Climate Action Plan creation in process currently. Numerous operation commitments including policy that mandates all new buildings will be LEED Silver certified or higher.

ADMISSIONS

Freshman Academic Profile: Average high school GPA 3.92. 22% in top 10% of high school class, 62% in top 25% of high school class, 93% in top 50% of high school class. 87.7% from public high schools. SAT Math middle 50% range 540–630. SAT Critical Reading middle 50% range 530–620. SAT Writing middle 50% range 510–600. ACT middle 50% range 22–26. Minimum paper TOEFL 500. Minimum computer TOEFL 173. Minimum web-based TOEFL 61. **Basis for Candidate Selection:** *Very important factors considered include:* Class rank, academic GPA, rigor of secondary school record, standardized test scores. *Other factors considered include:* Application essay, recommendation(s), character/personal qualities, extracurricular activities, first generation, racial/ethnic status, talent/ability, volunteer work, work experience. **Freshman Admission Requirements:** High school diploma is required and GED is not accepted. *Academic units required:* 4 English, 4 mathematics, 3 science, (1 science labs), 2 foreign language, 1 social studies, 1 history. **Freshman Admission Statistics:** 13,039 applied, 63% admitted, 33% enrolled. **Transfer Admission Requirements:** High school transcript, college transcript(s), minimum college GPA of 2.0 required. Lowest grade transferable C. **General Admission Information:** Application fee $50. Nonfall registration accepted. Admission may be deferred for a maximum of 1 yr. Credit and/or placement offered for CEEB Advanced Placement tests.

COSTS AND FINANCIAL AID

Annual in-state tuition $2,341. Annual out-of-state tuition $12,692. Room and board $6,400. Required fees $2,150. Average book expense $700. **Required Forms and Deadlines:** FAFSA. Priority financial aid filing date 3/15. **Notification of Awards:** Applicants will be notified of awards on a rolling basis beginning 4/1: **Types of Aid:** *Need-based scholarships/grants:* Federal Pell, SEOG, state scholarships/grants, private scholarships, the school's own gift aid. *Loans:* Direct Subsidized Stafford, Direct Unsubsidized Stafford, Direct PLUS, Federal Perkins. **Student Employment: Financial Aid Statistics:** 29% freshmen, 32% undergrads receive need-based scholarship or grant aid. 12% freshmen, 8% undergrads receive non-need-based scholarship or grant aid. 22% freshmen, 29% undergrads receive need-based self-help aid. 2% freshmen, 2% undergrads receive athletic scholarships. 50% undergrads borrow to pay for school. Average cumulative indebtedness $15,080. **Criteria for awarding institutional aid:** *Non-need-based:* Academics, alumni affiliation, art, athletics, job skills, leadership, minority status, music/drama, religious affiliation, state/district residency.

AQUINAS COLLEGE

1607 Robinson Road SE, Grand Rapids, MI 49506-1799
Phone: 616-632-2900 **Financial Aid Phone:** 616-632-2893
E-mail: admissions@aquinas.edu **CEEB Code:** 1018
Fax: 616-732-4469 **Website:** www.aquinas.edu **ACT Code:** 1962

This private school was founded in 1886. It has a 107-acre campus.

RATINGS

Admissions Selectivity Rating: 79   **Fire Safety Rating:** 70   **Green Rating:** 83

STUDENTS AND FACULTY

Enrollment: 1,879. **Student Body:** 64% female, 36% male, 4% out-of-state, international (8 countries represented). Asian 2%, African American 4%, Caucasian 88%, Hispanic 4%.

Retention and Graduation: 72% freshmen return for sophomore year. 33% freshmen graduate within 4 years. 21% grads go on to further study within 1 year. 5% grads pursue arts and sciences degrees. 2% grads pursue law degrees. 2% grads pursue business degrees. 4% grads pursue medical degrees. **Faculty:** Student/faculty ratio 12.68:1. 94 full-time faculty, 87% hold PhDs, 9% are members of minority groups, 49% are women.

ACADEMICS

Degrees: Associate, bachelor's, master's. **Classes:** Most classes have 20–29 students. **Special Study Options:** Accelerated program, cooperative education program, cross-registration, distance learning, double major, dual enrollment, exchange student program (domestic), honors program, independent study, internships, liberal arts/career combination, student-designed major, study abroad, teacher certification program, Service learning experiences in Peru, Haiti, Mexico. Semester abroad in Costa Rica, France, Germany, Spain,Italy, Japan and Ireland. Domestic exchange in California, Florida and Chicago. **Honors programs:** Insignis Honors Program Special programs offered to physically disabled students include note-taking services, reader services, tape recorders, tutors. **Career services:** Alumni services, career/job search classes, career assessment, internships.

FACILITIES

Housing: Coed dorms, women's dorms, apartments for single students, theme housing 95% of campus accessible to physically disabled. **Special Academic Facilities/Equipment:** Observatory and Jarecki Center for Advanced Learning featuring high-speed, two-way interactive video conferencing for courses and a virtual connection for external experts to interact with classes (sound, video, graphics) using a laptop computer equipped with a camera that is housed in a self-contained briefcase. The package includes all the technology needed to accomplish the connection through a standard phone jack. This "virtual faculty briefcase" can be shipped to a guest lecturer at another location anywhere in the world and they are able to conduct an interactive lecture or discussion with an Aquinas classroom. **Computers:** 100% of classrooms, 100% of dorms, 100% of libraries, 100% of dining areas, 100% of student union, 80% of common outdoor areas have wireless network access. Administrative functions (other than registration) can be performed online.

CAMPUS LIFE

Environment: Metropolis. **Activities:** Choral groups, concert band, dance, drama/theater, jazz band, literary magazine, music ensembles, radio station, student government, student newspaper, campus ministries, Model UN. **Organizations:** 71 registered organizations, 4 honor societies, 2 religious organizations. **Athletics (Intercollegiate):** *Men:* Baseball, basketball, cheerleading, cross-country, golf, lacrosse, soccer, tennis, track/field (outdoor), track/field (indoor). *Women:* Basketball, cheerleading, cross-country, golf, lacrosse, soccer, softball, tennis, track/field (outdoor), track/field (indoor), volleyball. **On-Campus Highlights:** Physical Education Building, Jarecki Center, Moose Cafe, Wege Student Center, Performing Arts Center. The new, state-of-the-art, Grace Hauenstein Library located in the Jarecki Center opened in August 2006. With ample parking, many meeting rooms, and the latest technology, it is now the most popular meeting place on the campus. **Environmental Initiatives:** Sustainable Business practices restore environmental quality, promote stable and healthy communities, and increase long-term profitability. The Aquinas Sustainable Business Degree program fosters ecological and social intelligence in all business decisions and is the only undergraduate program of its kind in Michigan and possibly the United States. The West Michigan Sustainable Business Forum is an association of over 90 businesses, including Aquinas College, that have come together to research and promote "best sustainable business practices" in West Michigan. Aquinas is offering employees of any member business a 20% tuition discount for SB program classes. The Aquinas Campus Sustainability Initiative process has begun. There are currently 14 proposals in progress, 6 more that are of preliminary status (in need of further development) and 3 which have been accepted and implemented. Proposals focus on a variety of campus processes including native plant landscaping, healthy cleaning products, an intelligent campus-wide recycling system, food waste composting with a campus vegetable garden, a smokeless campus, and a number of energy related proposals. Ideas are submitted to the student senate sustainability committee who help to further develop the proposals. For more information see: www. aquinas.edu/sustainability.

ADMISSIONS

Freshman Academic Profile: Average high school GPA 3.4. 19% in top 10% of high school class, 48% in top 25% of high school class, 77% in top 50% of high school class. 80% from public high schools. ACT middle 50% range 20–26. Minimum paper TOEFL 550. Minimum computer TOEFL 213. **Basis for Candidate Selection:** *Very important factors considered include:* Academic GPA, rigor of secondary school record, standardized test scores. *Other factors*

considered include: Character/personal qualities, extracurricular activities, first generation, talent/ability, volunteer work, work experience. **Freshman Admission Requirements:** High school diploma is required and GED is not accepted. *Academic units required:* 4 English, 4 mathematics, 3 science, 4 social studies. **Freshman Admission Statistics:** 2,192 applied, 80% admitted, 23% enrolled. **Transfer Admission Requirements:** High school transcript, college transcript(s), minimum college GPA of 2.0 required. Lowest grade transferable D. **General Admission Information:** Notification on a rolling basis, beginning on or about 9/15. Nonfall registration accepted. Admission may be deferred for a maximum of 1 year. Credit offered for CEEB Advanced Placement tests.

COSTS AND FINANCIAL AID

Annual tuition $22,314. Room and board $7,014. Average book expense $798. **Required Forms and Deadlines:** FAFSA. Priority financial aid filing date 3/1. **Notification of Awards:** Applicants will be notified of awards on a rolling basis beginning 3/1. **Types of Aid:** *Need-based scholarships/grants:* Federal Pell, SEOG, state scholarships/grants, private scholarships, the school's own gift aid. *Loans:* Direct Subsidized Stafford, Direct Unsubsidized Stafford, Direct PLUS, Federal Perkins. **Student Employment:** Federal Work-Study Program available. Institutional employment available. Highest amount earned per year from on-campus jobs $13,040. Off-campus job opportunities are good. **Financial Aid Statistics:** 86% freshmen, 82% undergrads receive need-based scholarship or grant aid. 86% freshmen, 56% undergrads receive non-need-based scholarship or grant aid. 86% freshmen, 82% undergrads receive need-based self-help aid. 17% freshmen, 15% undergrads receive athletic scholarships. 86% freshmen, 82% undergrads receive any aid. 66% undergrads borrow to pay for school. Average cumulative indebtedness $14,983. **Criteria for awarding institutional aid:** *Non-need-based:* Academics, alumni affiliation, art, athletics, leadership, music/drama.

AQUINAS COLLEGE (TN)

4210 Harding Road, Nashville, TN 37205
Phone: 615-297-7545 **Financial Aid Phone:**
E-mail: admissions@aquinas-tn.edu
Fax: 615-297-7970 **Website:** www.aquinas-tn.edu **ACT Code:** 3942

This private school, affiliated with the Roman Catholic Church, was founded in 1961. It has a 80-acre campus.

RATINGS

Admissions Selectivity Rating: 60*   **Fire Safety Rating:** 60*   **Green Rating:** 60*

STUDENTS AND FACULTY

Enrollment: 329. **Student Body:** 77% female, 23% male, 12% out-of-state, international.

Retention and Graduation: Faculty: Student/faculty ratio 12:1. 21 full-time faculty, 43% hold PhDs, 5% are members of minority groups, 67% are women.

ACADEMICS

Degrees: Associate, bachelor's, post-bachelor's certificate, terminal associate, transfer associate. **Special Study Options:** Liberal arts/career combination, teacher certification program, weekend college. **Career services:** Career/job search classes, career assessment.

FACILITIES

Housing: 70% of campus accessible to physically disabled.

CAMPUS LIFE

Activities: student government, student newspaper **Organizations:** 5 registered organizations, **Athletics (Intercollegiate):** *Men:* Baseball, basketball. *Women:* Cheerleading.

ADMISSIONS

Freshman Academic Profile: 80% from public high schools. Minimum paper TOEFL 525. **Basis for Candidate Selection:** *Very important factors considered include:* Rigor of secondary school record, standardized test scores. *Other factors considered include:* Recommendation(s), alumni/ae relation, character/personal qualities, extracurricular activities, interview, work experience. **Freshman Admission Requirements:** High school diploma is required and GED is accepted. *Academic units recommended:* 4 English, 3 mathematics, 3 science, 1 foreign language, 1 social studies, 1 history. **Freshman Admission Statistics:** 329 applied, 73% admitted, 28% enrolled. **Transfer Admission Requirements:** college transcript(s), minimum college GPA of 2.0 required. Lowest grade transferable C. **General Admission Information:** Application fee $10. Notification on a rolling basis, beginning on or about 10/1. Nonfall registration accepted. Admission may be deferred for a maximum of 1 year. Credit offered for CEEB Advanced Placement tests.

COSTS AND FINANCIAL AID

Required Forms and Deadlines: FAFSA, institution's own financial aid form. Priority financial aid filing date 2/15. **Notification of Awards:** Applicants will be notified of awards on a rolling basis beginning 3/1. **Types of Aid:** *Need-based scholarships/grants:* Federal Pell, SEOG, state scholarships/grants, private scholarships, the school's own gift aid. *Loans:* Direct Subsidized Stafford, Direct Unsubsidized Stafford, Direct PLUS. **Student Employment:** Federal Work-Study Program available. Off-campus job opportunities are excellent. **Financial Aid Statistics:** 33% undergrads receive need-based scholarship or grant aid. 51% undergrads receive need-based self-help aid. 2% undergrads receive athletic scholarships. **Criteria for awarding institutional aid:** *Non-need-based:* Academics, athletics, leadership, religious affiliation.

ARCADIA UNIVERSITY

450 South Easton Road, Glenside, PA 19038
Phone: 215-572-2910 **Financial Aid Phone:** 215-572-2980
E-mail: admiss@arcadia.edu **CEEB Code:** 2039
Fax: 215-572-4049 **Website:** www.arcadia.edu

This private school, affiliated with the Presbyterian Church, was founded in 1853. It has a 60-acre campus.

RATINGS
Admissions Selectivity Rating: 80   **Fire Safety Rating:** 60*   **Green Rating:** 60*

STUDENTS AND FACULTY
Enrollment: 2,063. **Student Body:** 73% female, 27% male, 36% out-of-state, 1% international (13 countries represented). Asian 2%, African American 8%, Caucasian 81%, Hispanic 3%.
Retention and Graduation: 80% freshmen return for sophomore year. 54% freshmen graduate within 4 years. 25% grads go on to further study within 1 year. 18% grads pursue arts and sciences degrees. 2% grads pursue law degrees. 3% grads pursue business degrees. 2% grads pursue medical degrees. **Faculty:** Student/faculty ratio 13:1. 102 full-time faculty, 16% are members of minority groups, 47% are women.

ACADEMICS
Degrees: Bachelor's, master's, post-bachelor's certificate, post-master's certificate. **Classes:** Most classes have 10–19 students. Most lab/discussion sessions have 10–19 students. **Majors with Highest Enrollment:** Business/commerce; education; psychology. **Special Study Options:** Cooperative education program, cross-registration, double major, exchange student program (domestic), honors program, independent study, internships, liberal arts/career combination, student-designed major, study abroad, teacher certification program, Arcadia also offers programs in Washington, DC, and a Philadelphia Urban Semester. Undergraduate students may also take gradutate courses. The university also offers evening and some weekend classes. **Honors programs:** Honors program for invited students **Combined degree programs:** BA/MA, 4-2 1/2 PT; 4+2 PA, 4+2, FS, 7-yr optometry. Special programs offered to physically disabled students include reader services, tape recorders, tutors. **Career services:** Alumni network, alumni services, career assessment, internships.

FACILITIES
Housing: Coed dorms, special housing for disabled students, women's dorms, apartments for single students, Living Learning Communities. 99% of campus accessible to physically disabled. **Special Academic Facilities/Equipment:** Art gallery, language lab, observatory. **Computers:** Students can register for classes online. Administrative functions (other than registration) can be performed online.

CAMPUS LIFE
Environment: Town. **Activities:** Choral groups, dance, drama/theater, literary magazine, music ensembles, musical theater, radio station, student government, student newspaper, television station, yearbook. **Organizations:** 40 registered organizations, 8 honor societies, 3 religious organizations. **Athletics (Intercollegiate):** *Men:* Baseball, basketball, cheerleading, golf, soccer, swimming, tennis. *Women:* Basketball, cheerleading, field hockey, lacrosse, soccer, softball, swimming, tennis, volleyball. **On-Campus Highlights:** Grey Towers Castle, Kuch Center, The Chat, Walk of Pride, Landman Library.

ADMISSIONS
Freshman Academic Profile: 31% in top 10% of high school class, 62% in top 25% of high school class, 93% in top 50% of high school class. 72% from public high schools. SAT Math middle 50% range 500–590. SAT Critical Reading middle 50% range 510–610. SAT Writing middle 50% range 510–610. ACT middle 50% range 21–27. Minimum paper TOEFL 550. Minimum computer TOEFL 213. **Basis for Candidate Selection:** *Very important factors con-*

sidered include: Academic GPA, rigor of secondary school record. *Important factors considered include:* Class rank, application essay, recommendation(s), standardized test scores, extracurricular activities. *Other factors considered include:* Alumni/ae relation, character/personal qualities, interview, talent/ability, volunteer work, work experience. **Freshman Admission Requirements:** High school diploma is required and GED is accepted. *Academic units recommended:* 4 English, 3 mathematics, 3 science, (3 science labs), 2 foreign language, 2 social studies, 2 history. **Freshman Admission Statistics:** 4,750 applied, 67% admitted, 20% enrolled. **Transfer Admission Requirements:** College transcript(s), essay or personal statement, minimum college GPA of 2.5 required. Lowest grade transferable C–. **General Admission Information:** Application fee $30. Early decision application deadline 10/15. Regular application deadline 8/1. Notification on a rolling basis, beginning on or about 11/1. Nonfall registration accepted. Admission may be deferred for a maximum of 1 year. Credit and/or placement offered for CEEB Advanced Placement tests.

COSTS AND FINANCIAL AID
Annual tuition $29,340. Room and board $10,280. Required fees $360. Average book expense $1,000. **Student Employment:** Off-campus job opportunities are good. **Financial Aid Statistics:** 97% freshmen receive any aid.

See page 1014.

ARIZONA STATE UNIVERSITY

PO Box 870112, Tempe, AZ 85287-0112
Phone: 480-965-7788 **Financial Aid Phone:** 480-965-3355
E-mail: ugradinq@asu.edu **CEEB Code:** 4007
Fax: 480-965-3610 **Website:** www.asu.edu **ACT Code:** 88

This public school was founded in 1885. It has a 1963.73-acre campus.

RATINGS
Admissions Selectivity Rating: 77   **Fire Safety Rating:** 87   **Green Rating:** 99

STUDENTS AND FACULTY
Enrollment: 53,902. **Student Body:** 51% female, 49% male, 20.4% out-of-state, 2% international (130 countries represented). Asian 6%, African American 5%, Caucasian 64%, Hispanic 16%, Native American 2%.
Retention and Graduation: 30% freshmen graduate within 4 years.

ACADEMICS
Degrees: Bachelor's, master's, post-bachelor's certificate, post-master's certificate. **Classes:** Most classes have 10–19 students. Most lab/discussion sessions have 20–29 students. **Majors with Highest Enrollment:** Business, management, marketing, and related support services, other; multi-/interdisciplinary studies, other; psychology. **Special Study Options:** Accelerated program, cooperative education program, distance learning, double major, exchange student program (domestic), honors program, independent study, internships, study abroad, teacher certification program, ASU offers internships in many disciplines, study abroad in 60 countries, work-study programs, accelerated degree programs and a variety of interdisciplinary undergraduate programs. Students may participate in educational programs supported by several institutes and centers. Also available are continuing education programs and a summer programs for high school students. **Honors programs:** The Honors College at ASU, Barrett, is a selective, residential college that educates academically outstanding undergraduates from across the nation. Students enrolled in Barrett are part of both the honors college community and an ASU disciplinary college of their choice. They may major in any field offered at any one of ASU's four campuses. Honors courses are taught by honors faculty within the college and within a variety of departments and programs. **Combined degree programs:** BA/MA, MBA/MSE EE; MBA/MHSM; MArch/MBS; MAIS/MBA; JD/MBA; JD/MHSM; MPA/MSW. Special programs offered to physically disabled students include note-taking services, reader services, tape recorders, tutors. **Career services:** Alumni network, alumni services, career/job search classes, career assessment, internships. Career services highlights include: ASU Career Services worked with APPLE during the Spring 2009 semester to educate the campus community on a new Summer Customer Support program that is full-time during the Summer and then continues on a part-time basis for the following academic year. ASU was one of only 5 schools selected for this program, and attracted the most students of any of the 5 schools (about 80 students were hired). APPLE will continue recruiting for the 2010 year at ASU because of the coordination support from ASU and the positive results of this program.

FACILITIES

Housing: Coed dorms, fraternity/sorority housing, apartments for married students, apartments for single students, Freshmen Housing Please visit: www.asu.edu/housing. 99% of campus accessible to physically disabled. **Special Academic Facilities/Equipment:** Art, anthropology, geology, history, and sports museums, early childhood development lab, herbarium, robotics lab, semiconductor clean room, high-resolution electron microscope facility, gamma cell irradiation chamber, solar research facilities, nuclear reactor, biodesign institute, thermal emission imaging system, melikian center, KAET (public television station), KASR 1260 AM, Phoenix urban research laboratory, Arizona biomedical collaborative, altitude chamber, simulator building, planetarium. **Computers:** 100% of classrooms, 100% of dorms, 100% of libraries, 100% of dining areas, 100% of student union, 70% of common outdoor areas have wireless network access. Students can register for classes online. Administrative functions (other than registration) can be performed online.

CAMPUS LIFE

Environment: Metropolis. **Activities:** Choral groups, concert band, dance, drama/theater, jazz band, literary magazine, marching band, music ensembles, musical theater, opera, pep band, radio station, student government, student newspaper, student-run film society, symphony orchestra, television station, campus ministries, international student organization, Model UN. **Organizations:** 675 registered organizations, 16 honor societies, 15 religious organizations. 32 fraternities, 22 sororities. **Athletics (Intercollegiate): Men:** Baseball, basketball, cross-country, diving, football, golf, swimming, track/field (outdoor), wrestling. *Women:* Basketball, cross-country, diving, golf, gymnastics, soccer, softball, swimming, tennis, track/field (outdoor), volleyball, water polo. **On-Campus Highlights:** ASU Memorial Union—Tempe campus, Grady Gammage Auditorium—Tempe campus, Barrett Honors Complex—Tempe campus, Fletcher Library—West campus, Union—Polytechnic campus, Hayden Library—Tempe campus, Walter Cronkite School of Journalism and Mass Communication—Downtown Phoenix campus, Academic Complex—Polytechnic campus, Las Casas Residence Hall—West campus, Taylor Place—Downtown Phoenix campus. **Environmental Initiatives:** Carbon Neutrality Energy Efficiency/Conservation/Renewable Generation ° Transportation ° Solid Waste ° Misc. Zero Solid Waste and Water Waste Averting and Diverting Solid Waste ° Conserving Water and Reducing Water Consumption and Waste Water Active Community Engagement, Principled Practice 81k Potential Change Agents in our ASU Community ° The Campus as a Living Laboratory ° Demonstrating Sustainability Values Through a Productive-Healthy-Quality Work/Learning Environment.

ADMISSIONS

Freshman Academic Profile: Average high school GPA 3.38. 31% in top 10% of high school class, 57% in top 25% of high school class, 84% in top 50% of high school class. SAT Math middle 50% range 480–620. SAT Critical Reading middle 50% range 470–590. ACT middle 50% range 20–26. Minimum paper TOEFL 500. Minimum computer TOEFL 173. Minimum web-based TOEFL 61. **Basis for Candidate Selection:** *Very important factors considered include:* Class rank, academic GPA, standardized test scores. *Important factors considered include:* State residency. **Freshman Admission Requirements:** High school diploma is required and GED is accepted. *Academic units required:* 4 English, 4 mathematics, 3 science, (3 science labs), 2 foreign language, 1 social studies, 1 history, 1 fine arts. **Freshman Admission Statistics:** 28,304 applied, 91% admitted, 36% enrolled. **Transfer Admission Requirements:** College transcript(s), standardized test scores, minimum college GPA of 2.0 required. Lowest grade transferable C. **General Admission Information:** Application fee $50. Regular application deadline 2/1. Nonfall registration accepted. Credit and/or placement offered for CEEB Advanced Placement tests.

COSTS AND FINANCIAL AID

Annual in-state tuition $5,679. Annual out-of-state tuition $18,582. Room and board $9,210. Required fees $337. Average book expense $1,270. **Required Forms and Deadlines:** FAFSA. Priority financial aid filing date 3/1. **Notification of Awards: Types of Aid:** *Need-based scholarships/grants:* Federal Pell, SEOG, state scholarships/grants, private scholarships, the school's own gift aid, Federal Nursing Scholarships. *Loans:* Direct Subsidized Stafford, Direct Unsubsidized Stafford, Direct PLUS, Federal Perkins. **Student Employment:** Federal Work-Study Program available. Institutional employment available. Off-campus job opportunities are good. **Financial Aid Statistics:** 44% freshmen, 39% undergrads receive need-based scholarship or grant aid. 9% freshmen, 4% undergrads receive non-need-based scholarship or grant aid. 24% freshmen, 34% undergrads receive need-based self-help aid. 1% freshmen, 1% undergrads receive athletic scholarships. 78.4% freshmen, 70.2% undergrads receive any aid. 45% undergrads borrow to pay for school. Average cumulative indebtedness $17,008.

ARIZONA STATE UNIVERSITY AT THE WEST CAMPUS

PO Box 37100, Phoenix, AZ 85069-7100
Phone: 602-543-8203 **Financial Aid Phone:** 602-543-8178
E-mail: west-admissions@asu.edu **CEEB Code:** 4007
Fax: 602-543-8312 **Website:** www.west.asu.edu **ACT Code:** 880

This public school was founded in 1984. It has a 300-acre campus.

RATINGS
Admissions Selectivity Rating: 84   **Fire Safety Rating:** 60*   **Green Rating:** 60*

STUDENTS AND FACULTY
Enrollment: 5,860. **Student Body:** 64% female, 36% male, 7% out-of-state, 1% international (81 countries represented). Asian 5%, African American 5%, Caucasian 60%, Hispanic 20%, Native American 3%.
Retention and Graduation: 77% freshmen return for sophomore year. 36% freshmen graduate within 4 years.

ACADEMICS
Degrees: Bachelor's, master's, post-bachelor's certificate. **Classes:** Most classes have 20–29 students. Most lab/discussion sessions have 10–19 students. **Majors with Highest Enrollment:** Criminal justice/law enforcement administration; elementary education and teaching; international business/trade/commerce. **Special Study Options:** Distance learning, double major, honors program, independent study, internships, student-designed major, study abroad, teacher certification program. Special programs offered to physically disabled students include note-taking services, reader services, tape recorders, tutors. **Career services:** Alumni network, career/job search classes, career assessment, internships.

FACILITIES
Housing: Special housing for disabled students, apartments for single students. 100% of campus accessible to physically disabled. **Computers:** 100% of classrooms, 100% of dorms, 100% of libraries, 100% of dining areas, 100% of student union, have wireless network access. Students can register for classes online. Administrative functions (other than registration) can be performed online.

CAMPUS LIFE
Environment: City. **Activities:** Drama/theater, literary magazine, student government, student newspaper, student-run film society. **Organizations:** 36 registered organizations, 3 honor societies, 3 religious organizations. **On-Campus Highlights:** Library, Cafe West, ASU West Gallery, Backstage West, ISM Technology Lab.

ADMISSIONS
Freshman Academic Profile: Average high school GPA 3.39. 28% in top 10% of high school class, 61% in top 25% of high school class, 89% in top 50% of high school class. 92% from public high schools. SAT Math middle 50% range 440–570. SAT Critical Reading middle 50% range 450–560. ACT middle 50% range 19–25. Minimum paper TOEFL 500. Minimum computer TOEFL 173. Minimum web-based TOEFL 61. **Basis for Candidate Selection:** *Very important factors considered include:* Class rank, academic GPA, rigor of secondary school record, standardized test scores. *Important factors considered include:* State residency. *Other factors considered include:* Application essay, recommendation(s), extracurricular activities, interview, talent/ability. **Freshman Admission Requirements:** High school diploma is required and GED is accepted. *Academic units required:* 4 English, 4 mathematics, 3 science, (3 science labs), 2 foreign language, 1 social studies, 1 history, 1 fine arts. **Freshman Admission Statistics:** 1,549 applied, 93% admitted, 42% enrolled. **Transfer Admission Requirements:** College transcript(s), minimum college GPA of 2.0 required. Lowest grade transferable C. **General Admission Information:** Application fee $25. Nonfall registration accepted. Credit and/or placement offered for CEEB Advanced Placement tests.

COSTS AND FINANCIAL AID
Annual in-state tuition $4,620. Annual out-of-state tuition $16,853. Required fees $146. Average book expense $950. **Required Forms and Deadlines:** FAFSA Financial aid filing deadline 3/1. Priority financial aid filing date 2/1. **Notification of Awards:** Applicants will be notified of awards on a rolling basis beginning 3/15. **Types of Aid:** *Need-based scholarships/grants:* Federal Pell, SEOG, state scholarships/grants, private scholarships, the school's own gift aid. *Loans:* Direct Subsidized Stafford, Direct Unsubsidized Stafford, Federal Perkins, college/university loans from institutional funds. **Student Employment:** Federal Work-Study Program available. Institutional employment available. Highest amount earned per year from on-campus jobs $13,306. Off-campus job opportunities are excellent. **Financial Aid Statistics:** 47% freshmen, 47%

undergrads receive need-based scholarship or grant aid. 5% freshmen, 2% undergrads receive non-need-based scholarship or grant aid. 19% freshmen, 37% undergrads receive need-based self-help aid. 72% freshmen, 56% undergrads receive any aid. 54% undergrads borrow to pay for school. Average cumulative indebtedness $15,586. **Criteria for awarding institutional aid:** *Non-need-based:* Academics.

ARIZONA STATE UNIVERSITY POLYTECHNIC CAMPUS

AZ State University, PO Box 870112, Tempe, AZ 85287-0112
Phone: 480-965-7788 **Financial Aid Phone:** 480-727-1041
E-mail: poly@asu.edu **CEEB Code:** 4007
Fax: 480-727-1008 **Website:** www.asu.edu **ACT Code:** 88

This public school was founded in 1994. It has a 605-acre campus.

RATINGS
Admissions Selectivity Rating: 74   **Fire Safety Rating:** 60*   **Green Rating:** 60*

STUDENTS AND FACULTY
Enrollment: 2,590. **Student Body:** 44% female, 56% male, 12% out-of-state, 2% international (44 countries represented). Asian 4%, African American 3%, Caucasian 72%, Hispanic 12%, Native American 3%.
Retention and Graduation: 70% freshmen return for sophomore year. **Faculty:** Student/faculty ratio 16:1. 158 full-time faculty, 77% hold PhDs, 16% are members of minority groups, 36% are women.

ACADEMICS
Degrees: Bachelor's, master's, post-bachelor's certificate. **Classes:** Most classes have 10–19 students. Most lab/discussion sessions have 10–19 students. **Special Study Options:** distance learning, double major, English as a Second Language (ESL), honors program, independent study, internships, liberal arts/career combination, student-designed major, study abroad, teacher certification program **Honors programs:** The Barrett Honors College at Arizona State University is a living and learning community of bright scholars, caring advisers and enthusiastic professors. We represent a powerful and unique combination of the special care and attention an honors student should expect in academics and advising from an excellent residential liberal arts college with the vast program choice and research mentoring resources of a vibrant Research I university. From the President of the University to the caretakers of our honors campus, there is unwavering support of our purpose: to promote and enable the very best education possible for intellectually-engaged students from Arizona, from America and from the world. Special programs offered to physically disabled students include note-taking services, reader services, tape recorders, tutors. **Career services:** Alumni services, career/job search classes, career assessment, internships.

FACILITIES
Housing: Coed dorms, special housing for disabled students, apartments for married students, apartments for single students, theme housing based on academic interest; "Single Family Style" housing for students with families and single students. There is also a special dorm for freshmen. 90% of campus accessible to physically disabled. **Computers:** Students can register for classes online. Administrative functions (other than registration) can be performed online.

CAMPUS LIFE
Environment: Metropolis. **Activities:** Choral groups, student government **Organizations:** 31 registered organizations, 3 honor societies, **On-Campus Highlights:** Williams Campus Student Union, Physical Activity Center (PAC)/ Fitness Center, Learning Center/Computer Commons, Agribusiness, Technology Building.

ADMISSIONS
Freshman Academic Profile: Average high school GPA 3.2. 23% in top 10% of high school class, 51% in top 25% of high school class, 79% in top 50% of high school class. SAT Math middle 50% range 480–610. SAT Critical Reading middle 50% range 460–570. ACT middle 50% range 19–25. Minimum paper TOEFL 500. Minimum computer TOEFL 173. **Basis for Candidate Selection:** *Very important factors considered include:* Academic GPA, rigor of secondary school record, standardized test scores, state residency. **Freshman Admission Requirements:** High school diploma is required and GED is accepted. *Academic units required:* 4 English, 4 mathematics, 3 science, (3 science labs), 2 foreign language, 1 social studies, 1 history, 1 fine arts. **Freshman Admission Statistics:** 1,151 applied, 87% admitted, 25% enrolled. **Transfer Admission Requirements:** College transcript(s), statement of good standing

from prior institution(s). Lowest grade transferable C. **General Admission Information:** Application fee $50. Notification on a rolling basis, beginning on or about 8/1. Nonfall registration accepted. Credit offered for CEEB Advanced Placement tests.

COSTS AND FINANCIAL AID
Annual in-state tuition $4,400. Annual out-of-state tuition $15,750. Room and board $6,150. Average book expense $950. **Required Forms and Deadlines:** FAFSA. Priority financial aid filing date 3/1. **Notification of Awards:** Applicants will be notified of awards on a rolling basis beginning 4/15. **Types of Aid:** *Need-based scholarships/grants:* Federal Pell, SEOG, state scholarships/grants, private scholarships, the school's own gift aid. *Loans:* Direct Subsidized Stafford, Direct Unsubsidized Stafford, Direct PLUS, Federal Perkins. **Student Employment: Financial Aid Statistics:** 45% freshmen, 41% undergrads receive need-based scholarship or grant aid. 3% freshmen, 1% undergrads receive non-need-based scholarship or grant aid. 26% freshmen, 40% undergrads receive need-based self-help aid. **Criteria for awarding institutional aid:** *Non-need-based:* Academics, art, athletics, music/drama.

ARKANSAS STATE UNIVERSITY

PO Box 1630, State University, AR 72467
Phone: 870-972-3024 **Financial Aid Phone:**
E-mail: admissions@astate.edu **CEEB Code:** 6011
Fax: 870-910-8094 **Website:** www.astate.edu **ACT Code:** 116

This public school was founded in 1909. It has a 941-acre campus.

RATINGS
Admissions Selectivity Rating: 74   **Fire Safety Rating:** 60*   **Green Rating:** 60*

STUDENTS AND FACULTY
Enrollment: 9,000. **Student Body:** 59% female, 41% male, 10% out-of-state, 1% international (56 countries represented). Asian 1%, African American 15%, Caucasian 82%, Hispanic 1%.
Retention and Graduation: 70% freshmen return for sophomore year. 15% freshmen graduate within 4 years. 3% grads go on to further study within 1 year. 1% grads pursue arts and sciences degrees. 1% grads pursue law degrees. 2% grads pursue business degrees. 1% grads pursue medical degrees. **Faculty:** Student/faculty ratio 19:1. 446 full-time faculty, 62% hold PhDs, 11% are members of minority groups, 43% are women. 3% of classes are taught by teaching assistants.

ACADEMICS
Degrees: Associate, bachelor's, certificate, master's, post-bachelor's certificate, post-master's certificate. **Classes:** Most classes have 20–29 students. Most lab/discussion sessions have fewer than 10 students. **Majors with Highest Enrollment:** Business/commerce; data processing and data processing technology/ technician; early childhood education. **Special Study Options:** Accelerated program, cooperative education program, distance learning, double major, dual enrollment, English as a Second Language (ESL), exchange student program (domestic), honors program, independent study, internships, study abroad, teacher certification program. Special programs offered to physically disabled students include note-taking services, reader services, tape recorders, tutors. **Career services:** Alumni services, career/job search classes, career assessment, internships.

FACILITIES
Housing: Men's dorms, women's dorms, fraternity/sorority housing, apartments for married students, apartments for single students, Married and graduate student housing. 95% of campus accessible to physically disabled. **Special Academic Facilities/Equipment:** Art gallery, museum of Native American cultures and Arkansas artifacts. Ecotoxicology research facility, electron microscope facility, geographic information system facility. Equine center. **Computers:** Students can register for classes online. Administrative functions (other than registration) can be performed online.

CAMPUS LIFE
Environment: Town. **Activities:** Choral groups, concert band, dance, drama/ theater, jazz band, marching band, music ensembles, musical theater, opera, pep band, radio station, student government, student newspaper, symphony orchestra, television station, yearbook. **Organizations:** 192 registered organizations, 42 honor societies, 16 religious organizations. 12 fraternities, 9 sororities. **Athletics (Intercollegiate):** *Men:* Baseball, basketball, cross-country, football, golf, track/field (outdoor), track/field (indoor). *Women:* Basketball, cross-country, golf, soccer, tennis, track/field (outdoor), track/field (indoor), volleyball. **On-Campus Highlights:** New Student Union, Fowler Center for Performing Arts, ASU Convocation Center, Outdoor theatre, ASU Museum.

ADMISSIONS

Freshman Academic Profile: Average high school GPA 3.2. 93% from public high schools. ACT middle 50% range 18–25. Minimum paper TOEFL 500. Minimum computer TOEFL 173. **Basis for Candidate Selection:** *Very important factors considered include:* Rigor of secondary school record, standardized test scores. *Other factors considered include:* Class rank, recommendation(s), talent/ability. **Freshman Admission Requirements:** High school diploma is required and GED is accepted. *Academic units recommended:* 4 English, 3 mathematics, 3 science, (3 science labs), 2 foreign language, 1 social studies, 2 history. **Freshman Admission Statistics:** 3,088 applied, 66% admitted, 75% enrolled. **Transfer Admission Requirements:** College transcript(s), minimum college GPA of 2.0 required. Lowest grade transferable C. **General Admission Information:** Application fee $15. Regular application deadline 8/23. Nonfall registration accepted. Admission may be deferred for a maximum of no maximum. Credit offered for CEEB Advanced Placement tests.

COSTS AND FINANCIAL AID

Annual in-state tuition $3,750. Annual out-of-state tuition $9,660. Room and board $3,640. Required fees $1,060. Average book expense $1,000. **Required Forms and Deadlines:** FAFSA, institution's own financial aid form Financial aid filing deadline 7/1. Priority financial aid filing date 2/15. **Notification of Awards:** Applicants will be notified of awards on a rolling basis beginning 6/1. **Types of Aid:** *Need-based scholarships/grants:* Federal Pell, SEOG, state scholarships/grants, private scholarships, the school's own gift aid. *Loans:* Direct Subsidized Stafford, Direct Unsubsidized Stafford, Direct PLUS, Federal Perkins. **Student Employment:** Federal Work-Study Program available. Institutional employment available. Highest amount earned per year from on-campus jobs $3,600. Off-campus job opportunities are good. **Financial Aid Statistics:** 78% freshmen, 53% undergrads receive need-based scholarship or grant aid. 20% freshmen, 25% undergrads receive non-need-based scholarship or grant aid. 33% freshmen, 37% undergrads receive need-based self-help aid. 3% freshmen, 3% undergrads receive athletic scholarships. 76% freshmen, 67% undergrads receive any aid. 63% undergrads borrow to pay for school. Average cumulative indebtedness $14,900. **Criteria for awarding institutional aid:** *Non-need-based:* Academics, alumni affiliation, art, athletics, leadership, minority status, music/drama, state/district residency.

ARKANSAS TECH UNIVERSITY

1605 Coliseum Dr Suite 141, Doc Bryan #141, Russellville, AR 72801
Phone: 479-968-0343 **Financial Aid Phone:** 479-968-0399
E-mail: tech.enroll@atu.edu **CEEB Code:** 6010
Fax: 479-964-0522 **Website:** www.atu.edu/ **ACT Code:** 0114

This public school was founded in 1909. It has a 541-acre campus.

RATINGS

Admissions Selectivity Rating: 81   **Fire Safety Rating:** 60*   **Green Rating:** 60*

STUDENTS AND FACULTY

Enrollment: 7,331. **Student Body:** 53% female, 47% male, 4% out-of-state, 3% international (31 countries represented). Asian 2%, African American 5%, Caucasian 85%, Hispanic 4%, Native American 2%.
Retention and Graduation: 71% freshmen return for sophomore year. 23% freshmen graduate within 4 years. **Faculty:** Student/faculty ratio 18:1. 293 full-time faculty, 63% hold PhDs, 8% are members of minority groups, 47% are women. 1.69% of classes are taught by teaching assistants.

ACADEMICS

Degrees: Associate, bachelor's, certificate, master's, post-master's certificate, terminal associate. **Classes:** Most classes have 20–29 students. Most lab/discussion sessions have 10–19 students. **Majors with Highest Enrollment:** Business administration and management; mechanical engineering; nursing/registered nurse (RN, ASN, BSN, MSN). **Special Study Options:** Distance learning, double major, dual enrollment, English as a Second Language (ESL), honors program, independent study, internships, study abroad, teacher certification program. Special programs offered to physically disabled students include note-taking services, reader services, tape recorders, tutors. **Career services:** Career assessment, internships.

FACILITIES

Housing: Coed dorms, special housing for disabled students, men's dorms, women's dorms, fraternity/sorority housing, apartments for single students. 100% of campus accessible to physically disabled. **Special Academic Facilities/Equipment:** Arkansas Center for Energy, Natural Resources, and Environmental Studies; Crabaugh Communications Center; Museum of Prehistory

and History; Technology Center. **Computers:** Students can register for classes online. Administrative functions (other than registration) can be performed online.

CAMPUS LIFE

Environment: Town. **Activities:** Choral groups, concert band, dance, drama/theater, jazz band, literary magazine, marching band, music ensembles, musical theater, pep band, radio station, student government, student newspaper, television station, campus ministries, international student organization. **Organizations:** 130 registered organizations, 14 honor societies, 13 religious organizations. 6 fraternities, 4 sororities. **Athletics (Intercollegiate):** *Men:* Baseball, basketball, cheerleading, football, golf. *Women:* Basketball, cheerleading, cross-country, golf, softball, tennis, volleyball. **On-Campus Highlights:** Ross Pendergraft Library and Technology Center, Tech Fit, Doc's Place, Summit Hall, Tucker Coliseum.

ADMISSIONS

Freshman Academic Profile: Average high school GPA 3.23. 19% in top 10% of high school class, 45% in top 25% of high school class, 71% in top 50% of high school class. SAT Math middle 50% range 460–620. SAT Critical Reading middle 50% range 370–530. ACT middle 50% range 20–26. Minimum paper TOEFL 500. Minimum computer TOEFL 173. Minimum web-based TOEFL 61. **Basis for Candidate Selection:** *Very important factors considered include:* Academic GPA, standardized test scores. *Important factors considered include:* Rigor of secondary school record. **Freshman Admission Requirements:** High school diploma is required and GED is accepted. *Academic units required:* 4 mathematics. *Academic units recommended:* 4 English, 3 science, (3 science labs), 2 foreign language, 3 social studies, 4 academic electives, 1 various: Consult the ATU Online Catalog. **Freshman Admission Statistics:** 3,304 applied, 94% admitted, 59% enrolled. **Transfer Admission Requirements:** College transcript(s), minimum college GPA of 2.0 required. Lowest grade transferable D. **General Admission Information:** Nonfall registration accepted. Admission may be deferred for a maximum of 1 semester. Credit and/or placement offered for CEEB Advanced Placement tests.

COSTS AND FINANCIAL AID

Annual in-state tuition $5,010. Annual out-of-state tuition $10,020. Room and board $5,156. Required fees $600. Average book expense $1,380. **Required Forms and Deadlines:** FAFSA, institution's own financial aid form. Priority financial aid filing date 4/15. **Notification of Awards:** Applicants will be notified of awards on a rolling basis beginning 5/1. **Types of Aid:** *Need-based scholarships/grants:* Federal Pell, SEOG, state scholarships/grants, private scholarships. *Loans:* Direct Subsidized Stafford, Direct Unsubsidized Stafford, Direct PLUS, Federal Perkins. **Student Employment:** Federal Work-Study Program available. Institutional employment available. Off-campus job opportunities are excellent. **Financial Aid Statistics:** 52% freshmen, 48% undergrads receive need-based scholarship or grant aid. 31% freshmen, 19% undergrads receive non-need-based scholarship or grant aid. 33% freshmen, 42% undergrads receive need-based self-help aid. 4% freshmen, 4% undergrads receive athletic scholarships. 51% undergrads borrow to pay for school. Average cumulative indebtedness $12,562. **Criteria for awarding institutional aid:** *Non-need-based:* Academics, athletics, leadership, music/drama, state/district residency.

ARLINGTON BAPTIST COLLEGE

Admissions Office, 3001 W. Division, Arlington, TX 76012
Phone: 817-461-8741 **Financial Aid Phone:** 817-461-8741, ext 110
E-mail: jtaylor@abconline.edu
Fax: 817-274-1138 **Website:** www.abconline.edu **ACT Code:** 4163

This private school, affiliated with the Baptist Church, was founded in 1939. It has a 35-acre campus.

RATINGS

Admissions Selectivity Rating: 61   **Fire Safety Rating:** 83   **Green Rating:** 60*

STUDENTS AND FACULTY

Enrollment: 138. **Student Body:** 53% female, 47% male, 19% out-of-state, 4% international (1 countries represented). Asian 1%, African American 7%, Caucasian 84%, Hispanic 4%.
Retention and Graduation: 68% freshmen return for sophomore year. 20% freshmen graduate within 4 years. 15% grads go on to further study within 1 year. **Faculty:** Student/faculty ratio 7:1. 8 full-time faculty, 13% are members of minority groups, 50% are women.

ACADEMICS

Degrees: Bachelor's, certificate, diploma, master's. **Classes:** Most classes have fewer than 10 students. Most lab/discussion sessions have 10–19 students.

Majors with Highest Enrollment: Pastoral studies/counseling; religious education; theological and ministerial studies, other. **Special Study Options:** Distance learning, double major, dual enrollment, external degree program, teacher certification program.

FACILITIES

Housing: Men's dorms, women's dorms, wellness housing. **Special Academic Facilities/Equipment:** Heritage Collection. **Computers:** 100% of classrooms, 100% of dorms, 100% of libraries, have wireless network access.

CAMPUS LIFE

Environment: Metropolis. **Activities:** Choral groups, student government, yearbook, campus ministries **Organizations:** 5 religious organizations. **Athletics (Intercollegiate):** *Men:* Baseball, basketball. *Women:* Basketball, cheerleading, volleyball. **On-Campus Highlights:** Student Union Building, Library, Heritage Collection.

ADMISSIONS

Freshman Academic Profile: Average high school GPA 3.3. 8% in top 10% of high school class, 17% in top 25% of high school class, 58% in top 50% of high school class. 80% from public high schools. Minimum paper TOEFL 550. Minimum computer TOEFL 213. **Basis for Candidate Selection:** *Very important factors considered include:* Application essay, recommendation(s), religious affiliation/commitment. *Important factors considered include:* Interview, level of applicant's interest. *Other factors considered include:* Character/personal qualities, extracurricular activities. **Freshman Admission Requirements:** High school diploma is required and GED is accepted. *Academic units required:* 3 English, 2 mathematics, 1 science, 2 social studies. **Freshman Admission Statistics:** 20 applied, 100% admitted, 55% enrolled. **Transfer Admission Requirements:** High school transcript, college transcript(s), essay or personal statement, Lowest grade transferable C. **General Admission Information:** Application fee $15. Nonfall registration accepted. Admission may be deferred for a maximum of three semesters. Neither credit nor placement offered for CEEB Advanced Placement tests.

COSTS AND FINANCIAL AID

Annual tuition $6,000. Room and board $4,200. Required fees $540. Average book expense $750. **Required Forms and Deadlines:** FAFSA. Financial aid filing deadline 8/15. **Notification of Awards:** Applicants will be notified of awards on a rolling basis beginning 6/1. **Types of Aid:** *Need-based scholarships/grants:* Federal Pell, SEOG, private scholarships, the school's own gift aid. *Loans:* Direct Subsidized Stafford, Direct Unsubsidized Stafford, Direct PLUS. **Student Employment:** Institutional employment available. Highest amount earned per year from on-campus jobs $5,600. Off-campus job opportunities are excellent. **Financial Aid Statistics:** 82% freshmen, 50% undergrads receive need-based scholarship or grant aid. 91% freshmen, 82% undergrads receive need-based self-help aid. 69% freshmen, 64% undergrads receive any aid. 70% undergrads borrow to pay for school. Average cumulative indebtedness $9,500.

ARMSTRONG ATLANTIC STATE UNIVERSITY

11935 Abercorn Street, Savannah, GA 31419-1997
Phone: 912-927-5277 **Financial Aid Phone:**
E-mail: adm-info@mail.armstrong.edu **CEEB Code:** 5012
Fax: 912-927-5462 **Website:** www.armstrong.edu **ACT Code:** 786

This public school was founded in 1935. It has a 250-acre campus.

RATINGS
Admissions Selectivity Rating: 73   **Fire Safety Rating:** 60*   **Green Rating:** 60*

STUDENTS AND FACULTY
Enrollment: 5,281. **Student Body:** 68% female, 32% male, 8% out-of-state, 2% international (71 countries represented). Asian 3%, African American 22%, Caucasian 65%, Hispanic 3%.
Retention and Graduation: Faculty: Student/faculty ratio 19:1. 229 full-time faculty, 70% hold PhDs, 16% are members of minority groups, 51% are women.

ACADEMICS
Degrees: Associate, bachelor's, master's, post-bachelor's certificate, post-master's certificate. **Classes:** Most classes have 20–29 students. Most lab/discussion sessions have fewer than 10 students. **Majors with Highest Enrollment:** Early childhood education; liberal arts and sciences/liberal studies; nursing/registered nurse (RN, ASN, BSN, MSN). **Special Study Options:** Cooperative education program, cross-registration, distance learning, double major, dual enrollment, honors program, independent study, internships, study abroad, teacher certification program, weekend college. **Combined degree programs:** BSPT/MSPT, BSN/MSN. Special programs offered to physically

disabled students include note-taking services, reader services, tape recorders, tutors. **Career services:** Alumni services, career/job search classes, career assessment, internships.

FACILITIES

Housing: Apartments for single students 80% of campus accessible to physically disabled. **Special Academic Facilities/Equipment:** Language lab. Criminal justice training center. Sports medicine clinic. Speech/lang. pathology lab. **Computers:** Students can register for classes online. Administrative functions (other than registration) can be performed online.

CAMPUS LIFE

Environment: City. **Activities:** Choral groups, concert band, drama/theater, jazz band, literary magazine, music ensembles, musical theater, pep band, student government, student newspaper, symphony orchestra. **Organizations:** 55 registered organizations, 7 honor societies, 3 religious organizations. 1 fraternities, 1 sorority. **Athletics (Intercollegiate):** *Men:* Baseball, basketball, golf, tennis. *Women:* Basketball, softball, tennis, volleyball. **On-Campus Highlights:** Library, Main computer lab, Compass Point (on-campus apartments), Gym, Cafeteria.

ADMISSIONS

Freshman Academic Profile: Average high school GPA 3.05. SAT Math middle 50% range 450–550. SAT Critical Reading middle 50% range 470–570. ACT middle 50% range 18–23. Minimum paper TOEFL 523. Minimum computer TOEFL 193. **Basis for Candidate Selection:** *Important factors considered include:* Rigor of secondary school record, standardized test scores. *Other factors considered include:* Extracurricular activities, volunteer work. **Freshman Admission Requirements:** High school diploma is required and GED is accepted. *Academic units required:* 4 English, 4 mathematics, 3 science, (2 science labs), 2 foreign language, 3 social studies. **Freshman Admission Statistics:** 1,685 applied, 65% admitted, 75% enrolled. **Transfer Admission Requirements:** College transcript(s), minimum college GPA of 2.0 required. Lowest grade transferable D. **General Admission Information:** Application fee $20. Regular application deadline 7/1. Notification on a rolling basis, beginning on or about 1/1. Nonfall registration accepted. Admission may be deferred for a maximum of 1 year. Credit and/or placement offered for CEEB Advanced Placement tests.

COSTS AND FINANCIAL AID

Annual in-state tuition $2,212. Annual out-of-state tuition $8,842. Room and board $4,500. Required fees $390. Average book expense $800. **Required Forms and Deadlines:** FAFSA. Priority financial aid filing date 3/15. **Notification of Awards:** Applicants will be notified of awards on or about 2/1. **Types of Aid:** *Need-based scholarships/grants:* Federal Pell, SEOG, state scholarships/grants, private scholarships, the school's own gift aid, Federal Nursing Scholarships. *Loans:* Direct Subsidized Stafford, Direct Unsubsidized Stafford, Direct PLUS, state loans. **Student Employment:** Federal Work-Study Program available. Institutional employment available. Off-campus job opportunities are excellent. **Financial Aid Statistics:** 13% freshmen, 36% undergrads receive need-based scholarship or grant aid. 15% freshmen, 22% undergrads receive non-need-based scholarship or grant aid. 11% freshmen, 53% undergrads receive need-based self-help aid. 6% freshmen, 3% undergrads receive athletic scholarships. 90% freshmen, 90% undergrads receive any aid. 55% undergrads borrow to pay for school. Average cumulative indebtedness $11,000. **Criteria for awarding institutional aid:** *Non-need-based:* Academics, athletics, leadership, minority status, religious affiliation, state/district residency.

ARNOLD AND MARIE SCHWARTZ COLLEGE OF PHARMACY AND HEALTH SCIENCE

Long Island University, 75 DeKalb Avenue, Brooklyn, NY 11201
Phone: 718-403-1011 **Financial Aid Phone:**
E-mail: admissions@brooklyn.liu.edu
Fax: 718-797-2399 **Website:** www.liu.edu

This is a private school.

RATINGS
Admissions Selectivity Rating: 60*   **Fire Safety Rating:** 60*   **Green Rating:** 60*

ACADEMICS
Degrees: First professional, master's. **Special Study Options:** Honors program.

FACILITIES
Housing: Coed dorms, women's dorms, apartments for single students.

CAMPUS LIFE

Organizations: 3 honor societies, 2 religious organizations. **Athletics (Intercollegiate):** *Men:* Basketball, cross-country, softball, tennis, track/field (outdoor), track/field (indoor).

ADMISSIONS

Freshman Academic Profile: Minimum paper TOEFL 500. **Basis for Candidate Selection:** *Very important factors considered include:* Rigor of secondary school record, standardized test scores. *Important factors considered include:* Character/personal qualities, extracurricular activities, talent/ability. *Other factors considered include:* Class rank, recommendation(s), interview, volunteer work, work experience. **Freshman Admission Requirements:** High school diploma is required and GED is accepted. *Academic units required:* 2 mathematics, 1 science, (1 science labs). *Academic units recommended:* 2 science, (2 science labs). **Transfer Admission Requirements:** College transcript(s), minimum college GPA of 3.0 required. Lowest grade transferable C. **General Admission Information:** Application fee $30. Nonfall registration not accepted.

COSTS AND FINANCIAL AID

Comprehensive fee $7,900. **Required Forms and Deadlines:** FAFSA. Priority financial aid filing date 3/15. **Notification of Awards: Types of Aid:** *Need-based scholarships/grants:* Federal Pell, SEOG, state scholarships/grants, private scholarships, the school's own gift aid. *Loans:* Direct Subsidized Stafford, Direct Unsubsidized Stafford, Direct PLUS, Federal Perkins, Health Professions Student Loan (HPSL). **Student Employment:** Federal Work-Study Program available. **Criteria for awarding institutional aid:** *Non-need-based:* Academics.

ART ACADEMY OF CINCINNATI

1212 Jackson Street, Cincinnati, OH 45202
Phone: 513-562-8740 **Financial Aid Phone:** 513-562-8751
E-mail: admissions@artacademy.edu
Fax: 513-562-8778 **Website:** www.artacademy.edu **ACT Code:** 003011

This private school was founded in 1887.

RATINGS

Admissions Selectivity Rating: 60*   **Fire Safety Rating:** 60*   **Green Rating:** 60*

STUDENTS AND FACULTY

Enrollment: 159. **Student Body:** 64% female, 36% male, % out-of-state, 1% international (2 countries represented). Asian 1%, African American 4%, Caucasian 90%, Hispanic 1%.
Retention and Graduation: Faculty: Student/faculty ratio 6:1. 14 full-time faculty, 100% hold PhDs, 7% are members of minority groups, 57% are women.

ACADEMICS

Degrees: Associate, bachelor's, master's. **Majors with Highest Enrollment:** Graphic design; illustration; painting. **Special Study Options:** Cooperative education program, cross-registration, double major, internships. Special programs offered to physically disabled students include note-taking services, tape recorders, tutors.

FACILITIES

Housing: Coed dorms.

CAMPUS LIFE

Environment: Metropolis. **Activities:** Literary magazine, student government, student-run film society, yearbook. **On-Campus Highlights:** New building, dorms, student studios, student commons, 3 art galleries. **Environmental Initiatives:** Received Leadership in Energy and Environmental Design (LEED) Green Building certification by the United States Green Building Council. On-going recycling program.

ADMISSIONS

Freshman Academic Profile: SAT Math middle 50% range 420–570. SAT Critical Reading middle 50% range 480–600. ACT middle 50% range 18–24. Minimum paper TOEFL 550. Minimum computer TOEFL 213. Minimum web-based TOEFL 80. **Basis for Candidate Selection:** *Very important factors considered include:* Rigor of secondary school record, interview, talent/ability. *Important factors considered include:* Application essay, academic GPA. *Other factors considered include:* Recommendation(s), standardized test scores, character/personal qualities, extracurricular activities. **Freshman Admission Requirements:** High school diploma is required and GED is accepted. *Academic units recommended:* 4 English, 3 mathematics, 2 science, 1 social studies. **Freshman Admission Statistics:** 541 applied, 21% admitted, 42% enrolled. **Transfer Admission Requirements:** High school transcript, college

transcript(s), essay or personal statement, interview, minimum college GPA of 2.0 required. Lowest grade transferable C. **General Admission Information:** Regular application deadline 6/30. Notification on a rolling basis, beginning on or about 9/1. Nonfall registration accepted. Admission may be deferred for a maximum of 1 year.

COSTS AND FINANCIAL AID

Annual tuition $21,500. Room and board $6,000. Required fees $380. Average book expense $1,200. **Required Forms and Deadlines:** FAFSA, state aid form **Notification of Awards:** Applicants will be notified of awards on a rolling basis beginning 3/1. **Types of Aid:** *Need-based scholarships/grants:* Federal Pell, SEOG, state scholarships/grants, private scholarships, the school's own gift aid. *Loans:* Direct Subsidized Stafford, Direct Unsubsidized Stafford, Direct PLUS, Federal Perkins. **Student Employment:** Federal Work-Study Program available. Institutional employment available. Off-campus job opportunities are good. **Financial Aid Statistics:** 95% undergrads receive any aid. **Criteria for awarding institutional aid:** *Non-need-based:* Academics, art.

ART CENTER COLLEGE OF DESIGN

1700 Lida Street, Pasadena, CA 91103-1999
Phone: 626-396-2373 **Financial Aid Phone:** 626-396-2215
E-mail: admissions@artcenter.edu **CEEB Code:** 4009
Fax: 626-795-0578 **Website:** www.artcenter.edu

This private school was founded in 1930. It has a 175-acre campus.

RATINGS

Admissions Selectivity Rating: 60*   **Fire Safety Rating:** 60*   **Green Rating:** 60*

STUDENTS AND FACULTY

Enrollment: 1,485. **Student Body:** 40% female, 60% male, 23% out-of-state, 16% international (32 countries represented). Asian 35%, African American 2%, Caucasian 35%, Hispanic 11%.
Retention and Graduation: 86% freshmen return for sophomore year. 62% freshmen graduate within 4 years. **Faculty:** Student/faculty ratio 9:1. 66 full-time faculty, 9% are members of minority groups, 27% are women.

ACADEMICS

Degrees: Bachelor's, master's. **Classes:** Most classes have 10–19 students. **Majors with Highest Enrollment:** Graphic design; illustration; industrial design. **Special Study Options:** Cooperative education program, independent study, internships. Special programs offered to physically disabled students include note-taking services, tape recorders, tutors. **Career services:** Alumni network, alumni services, internships.

FACILITIES

Housing: 100% of campus accessible to physically disabled. **Special Academic Facilities/Equipment:** 2 art galleries. **Computers:** Administrative functions (other than registration) can be performed online.

CAMPUS LIFE

Environment: City. **Activities:** Student government. **Organizations:** 12 registered organizations. **On-Campus Highlights:** Student gallery.

ADMISSIONS

Freshman Academic Profile: Average high school GPA 3.3. Minimum paper TOEFL 550. Minimum computer TOEFL 213. **Basis for Candidate Selection:** *Very important factors considered include:* Application essay, academic GPA, rigor of secondary school record, talent/ability. *Important factors considered include:* Class rank, standardized test scores. *Other factors considered include:* Recommendation(s), character/personal qualities, extracurricular activities, interview, racial/ethnic status, volunteer work, work experience. **Freshman Admission Requirements:** High school diploma is required and GED is accepted. **Freshman Admission Statistics:** 543 applied, 71% admitted, 65% enrolled. **Transfer Admission Requirements:** College transcript(s), essay or personal statement, Lowest grade transferable c. **General Admission Information:** Application fee $50. Notification on a rolling basis, beginning on or about 1/1. Nonfall registration accepted. Admission may be deferred for a maximum of 1 consecutive semest. Credit offered for CEEB Advanced Placement tests.

COSTS AND FINANCIAL AID

Annual tuition $27,710. Required fees $200. **Required Forms and Deadlines:** FAFSA. Priority financial aid filing date 1/1. **Notification of Awards: Types of Aid:** *Need-based scholarships/grants:* Federal Pell, SEOG, state scholarships/grants, private scholarships, the school's own gift aid. *Loans:* Direct Subsidized Stafford, Direct Unsubsidized Stafford, Direct PLUS. **Student Employment:** Federal Work-Study Program available. Institutional employment available. **Financial Aid Statistics:** 43% freshmen, 55% undergrads receive need-based scholarship or grant aid. 69% freshmen, 68% undergrads receive need-based self-help aid. 78% freshmen, 79% undergrads receive any aid. 61% undergrads borrow to pay for school. Average cumulative indebtedness $51,864.

THE ART INSTITUTE OF ATLANTA

6600 Peachtree Dunwoody Road, 100 Embassy Row, Atlanta, GA 30328
Phone: 770-394-8300 **Financial Aid Phone:** 770-689-4824
E-mail: aia-admis@aii.edu
Fax: 770-394-0008 **Website:** www.artinstitutes.edu/atlanta/ **ACT Code:** 859

This proprietary school was founded in 1949. It has a 7-acre campus.

RATINGS
Admissions Selectivity Rating: 60*   **Fire Safety Rating:** 60*   **Green Rating:** 60*

STUDENTS AND FACULTY
Enrollment: 3,839. **Student Body:** 44% female, 56% male, % out-of-state, international (33 countries represented). African American 22%, Caucasian 19%, Hispanic 2%.
Retention and Graduation: Faculty: Student/faculty ratio 20.5:1. 131 full-time faculty, 48% hold PhDs, 21% are members of minority groups, 45% are women.

ACADEMICS
Degrees: Associate, bachelor's, certificate, diploma. **Classes:** Most classes have 10–19 students. **Majors with Highest Enrollment:** Commercial and advertising art; culinary arts/chef training; interior design. **Special Study Options:** Accelerated program, distance learning, dual enrollment, honors program, independent study, internships, study abroad, weekend college. **Honors programs:** Design Honors Studio for graphic design students: students work with clients in the community. Special programs offered to physically disabled students include note-taking services, reader services, tape recorders, tutors. **Career services:** Alumni network, alumni services, career/job search classes, internships.

FACILITIES
Housing: Coed dorms. 100% of campus accessible to physically disabled. **Special Academic Facilities/Equipment:** Art gallery, multi-camera video studio with digital and non-linear video editing suites, and an audio studio and control room featuring Protools stations. Professional photography studios with traditional and digital darkroom facilities containing high-end professional equipment such as the Imacon scanner, Cone Piezograph black and white printers, Epson 5500 printer, and Epson 10000 printer. Photographic video editing stations consist of Dual Processor G4s with cinema displays that are color managed with Greytag MacBeth equipment. Culinary facilities with five teaching kitchens and a dining lab. **Computers:** Students can register for classes online.

CAMPUS LIFE
Environment: Metropolis. **Activities:** Student government, international student organization. **Organizations:** 16 registered organizations. **On-Campus Highlights:** Gallery, supply store, coffee bar, snack bar, Creations Dining Lab. Entertainers perform in the coffee bar and reduced-price tickets are often available for events in Atlanta. The student affairs department also coordinates college community service programs and quarterly blood drives. Besides being enjoyable, student activities provide opportunities for making new friends and trying new experiences, as well as offering a great way to gain leadership experience.

ADMISSIONS
Freshman Academic Profile: Minimum paper TOEFL 500. Minimum computer TOEFL 173. **Basis for Candidate Selection:** *Very important factors considered include:* Application essay, academic GPA, recommendation(s), standardized test scores. *Important factors considered include:* Interview. **Freshman Admission Requirements:** High school diploma is required and GED is accepted. **Freshman Admission Statistics: Transfer Admission Requirements:** High school transcript, college transcript(s), essay or personal statement, interview, standardized test scores, statement of good standing from prior institution(s). Lowest grade transferable C. **General Admission Information:** Application fee $50. Nonfall registration accepted. Admission may be deferred for a maximum of 4 quarters. Credit and/or placement offered for CEEB Advanced Placement tests.

COSTS AND FINANCIAL AID
Annual tuition $23,535. Room and board $9,984. Average book expense $1,700. **Required Forms and Deadlines:** FAFSA, state aid form **Notification of Awards:** Applicants will be notified of awards on a rolling basis beginning 3/15. **Types of Aid:** *Need-based scholarships/grants:* Federal Pell, SEOG, state

scholarships/grants, private scholarships, the school's own gift aid. *Loans:* Direct Subsidized Stafford, Direct Unsubsidized Stafford, Direct PLUS, Federal Perkins. **Student Employment:** Federal Work-Study Program available. Institutional employment available. Off-campus job opportunities are good. **Financial Aid Statistics:** 50% freshmen, 63% undergrads receive need-based scholarship or grant aid, 38% freshmen, 7% undergrads receive non-need-based scholarship or grant aid. 97% freshmen, 87% undergrads receive need-based self-help aid. 19% freshmen, 81% undergrads receive any aid. 90% undergrads borrow to pay for school. Average cumulative indebtedness $6,375. **Criteria for awarding institutional aid:** *Non-need-based:* Academics, art, state/district residency.

ART INSTITUTE OF COLORADO

1200 Lincoln St, Denver, CO 80203
Phone: 303-837-0825 **Financial Aid Phone:**
E-mail: aicinfo@artinstitutes.edu
Fax: 303-860-8520 **Website:** www.aic.artinstitutes.edu **ACT Code:** 495

This proprietary school was founded in 1952.

RATINGS
Admissions Selectivity Rating: 60*   **Fire Safety Rating:** 60*   **Green Rating:** 60*

STUDENTS AND FACULTY
Enrollment: 2,320. **Student Body:** 48% female, 52% male. Asian 2%, African American 1%, Caucasian 43%, Hispanic 6%, Native American 1%.
Retention and Graduation: Faculty: Student/faculty ratio 20:1. 64 full-time faculty, 17% hold PhDs, 11% are members of minority groups, 38% are women.

ACADEMICS
Degrees: Associate, bachelor's, certificate, diploma. **Majors with Highest Enrollment:** Missions/missionary studies and missiology; pastoral studies/counseling; pre-theology/pre-ministerial studies. **Special Study Options:** Independent study, internships, study abroad. **Career services:** Alumni services, career/job search classes, internships.

FACILITIES
Housing: Apartments for single students. **Computers:** Administrative functions (other than registration) can be performed online.

CAMPUS LIFE
Organizations: 3 honor societies.

ADMISSIONS
Freshman Academic Profile: Minimum paper TOEFL 480. **Basis for Candidate Selection:** *Important factors considered include:* Application essay, standardized test scores, interview. *Other factors considered include:* Rigor of secondary school record. **Freshman Admission Requirements:** High school diploma is required and GED is accepted. **Freshman Admission Statistics:** 748 applied, 52% admitted, 96% enrolled. **Transfer Admission Requirements:** High school transcript, essay or personal statement, interview, lowest grade transferable C. **General Admission Information:** Application fee $50. Nonfall registration accepted. Admission may be deferred for a maximum of 1 yr. Credit offered for CEEB Advanced Placement tests.

COSTS AND FINANCIAL AID
Annual tuition $14,880. Room and board $6,048. Required fees $50. Average book expense $2,250. **Required Forms and Deadlines:** FAFSA, institution's own financial aid form. Priority financial aid filing date 3/15. **Notification of Awards: Types of Aid:** *Need-based scholarships/grants:* Federal Pell, SEOG, state scholarships/grants, private scholarships, the school's own gift aid. *Loans:* Direct Subsidized Stafford, Direct Unsubsidized Stafford, Direct PLUS, Federal Perkins, state loans. **Student Employment:** Federal Work-Study Program available. Institutional employment available. Off-campus job opportunities are excellent. **Financial Aid Statistics:** 97% undergrads borrow to pay for school. Average cumulative indebtedness $30,000.

THE ART INSTITUTE OF BOSTON AT LESLEY UNIVERSITY

700 Beacon Street, Boston, MA 02215-2598
Phone: 617.585.6710 **Financial Aid Phone:** 617-349-8710
E-mail: admissions@aiboston.edu **CEEB Code:** 3777
Fax: 617.585.6720 **Website:** aiboston.edu **ACT Code:** 1850

This private school was founded in 1912. It has a 1-acre campus.

RATINGS
Admissions Selectivity Rating: 81   **Fire Safety Rating:** 88   **Green Rating:** 72

STUDENTS AND FACULTY
Enrollment: 1,261. **Student Body:** 75% female, 25% male, 44% out-of-state,
3% international (15 countries represented). Asian 3%, African American 4%,
Caucasian 63%, Hispanic 5%.
Retention and Graduation: 66% freshmen return for sophomore year. 37%
freshmen graduate within 4 years. **Faculty:** Student/faculty ratio 10:1. 73 full-
time faculty, 68% hold PhDs, 12% are members of minority groups, 55% are
women.

ACADEMICS
Degrees: Associate, bachelor's, master's, post-master's certificate. **Classes:**
Most classes have 10–19 students. **Majors with Highest Enrollment:**
Graphic design; illustration; photography. **Special Study Options:** Accelerated
program, cross-registration, distance learning, double major, dual enrollment,
exchange student program (domestic), honors program, independent study,
internships, liberal arts/career combination, student-designed major, study
abroad, teacher certification program, Studio Courses. **Honors programs:**
First year foundation students are eligible for advanced placement, foundation
studio exemptions, and enrolling in Honors Studio and Honors English. **Combined degree programs:** BFA/MEd. Special programs offered to physically
disabled students include note-taking services, reader services, tape recorders, tutors. **Career services:** Alumni network, alumni services, career/job
search classes, career assessment, internships, regional alumni. Career services
highlights include: We are proud of the wide range of services available to our
students and alumni through our new online system, Lesley Career Connection,
which includes job listings, internships, career fairs, career center workshops,
employer directory and more.

FACILITIES
Housing: Coed dorms, women's dorms, Special Interest and themed housing.
90% of campus accessible to physically disabled. **Special Academic Facilities/
Equipment:** Art Gallery with regular shows of prominant artists; art library;
applied art facilities, including state of the art photo and computer labs, annima-
tion studio, ceramics studio, wood shop, metals studio, and printmaking studio.
Computers: 100% of classrooms, 10% of dorms, 100% of libraries, 100%
of dining areas, 100% of student union, 25% of common outdoor areas have
wireless network access. Students can register for classes online. Administrative
functions (other than registration) can be performed online.

CAMPUS LIFE
Environment: Metropolis. **Activities:** Choral groups, dance, drama/theater,
literary magazine, musical theater, student government, student newspaper,
campus ministries, International student organization. **Organizations:** 25
registered organizations, 2 honor societies, 2 religious organizations. **Athletics
(Intercollegiate):** *Men:* Basketball, cross-country, soccer, tennis, volleyball.
Women: Basketball, crew/rowing, cross-country, soccer, softball, tennis, volleyball. **On-Campus Highlights:** Gallery, computer labs, animation studio, photo
labs, student lounge. **Environmental Initiatives:** Continual enhancement of
recycling, waste management and composting programs on campus. The formation of sustainability recommendations for faculty, staff and students. Student
groups on campus are involved with and sponsor sustainability events.

ADMISSIONS
Freshman Academic Profile: Average high school GPA 3. 12% in top 10%
of high school class, 38% in top 25% of high school class, 70% in top 50% of
high school class. 84% from public high schools. SAT Math middle 50% range
460–560. SAT Critical Reading middle 50% range 490–600. SAT Writing middle
50% range 490–590. ACT middle 50% range 19–26. Minimum paper TOEFL
500. Minimum computer TOEFL 173. Minimum web-based TOEFL 61.
Basis for Candidate Selection: *Very important factors considered include:*
Academic GPA, rigor of secondary school record. *Important factors considered include:* Class rank, application essay, recommendation(s), standardized
test scores, character/personal qualities, extracurricular activities, interview,
talent/ability. *Other factors considered include:* Alumni/ae relation, first generation, geographical residence, level of applicant's interest, racial/ethnic status,
volunteer work, work experience. **Freshman Admission Requirements:** High

school diploma is required and GED is accepted. *Academic units required:* 4
English. *Academic units recommended:* 4 English, 1 mathematics, 1 science,
1 foreign language, 2 social studies, 2 history, 2 academic electives, 2 studio
art. **Freshman Admission Statistics:** 2,523 applied, 65% admitted, 20%
enrolled. **Transfer Admission Requirements:** High school transcript, college
transcript(s), essay or personal statement, interview, statement of good standing from prior institution(s). Minimum college GPA of 2.0 required. Lowest
grade transferable C. **General Admission Information:** Application fee $50.
Notification on a rolling basis, beginning on or about 1/15. Nonfall registration
accepted. Admission may be deferred for a maximum of 1 year. Credit and/or
placement offered for CEEB Advanced Placement tests.

COSTS AND FINANCIAL AID
Annual tuition $25,780. Required fees $750. Average book expense $1,575.
Required Forms and Deadlines: FAFSA. Priority financial aid filing date
2/15. **Notification of Awards:** Applicants will be notified of awards on a rolling
basis beginning 2/15. **Types of Aid:** *Need-based scholarships/grants:* Federal
Pell, SEOG, state scholarships/grants, private scholarships, the school's own gift
aid. *Loans:* Direct Subsidized Stafford, Direct Unsubsidized Stafford, Direct
PLUS, Federal Perkins, state loans **Student Employment:** Federal Work-
Study Program available. Institutional employment available. Highest amount
earned per year from on-campus jobs $1,200. Off-campus job opportunities are
excellent. **Financial Aid Statistics:** 73% freshmen, 51% undergrads receive
need-based scholarship or grant aid. 18% freshmen, 34% undergrads receive
non-need-based scholarship or grant aid. 69% freshmen, 63% undergrads receive need-based self-help aid. 70% freshmen, 70% undergrads receive any aid.
93% undergrads borrow to pay for school. Average cumulative indebtedness
$17,000. **Criteria for awarding institutional aid:** *Non-need-based:* Academ-
ics, art, leadership, minority status, state/district residency.

THE ART INSTITUTE OF LAS VEGAS

2350 Corporate Circle, Henderson, NV, 89074,
Phone: 702.369.9944 **Financial Aid Phone:**
E-mail: ailvadm@aii.edu
Fax: 702.992.8458 **Website:** www.artinstitutes.edu/lasvegas/

This is a proprietary school. It has a 1.5-acre campus.

RATINGS
Admissions Selectivity Rating: 60*   **Fire Safety Rating:** 60*   **Green Rating:** 60*

STUDENTS AND FACULTY
Enrollment: 1,301. **Student Body:** 48% female, 52% male. Asian 12%, Afri-
can American 9%, Caucasian 35%, Hispanic 14%, Native American 1%.
Retention and Graduation: 54% freshmen return for sophomore year.
Faculty: Student/faculty ratio 17:1. 27 full-time faculty, 7% hold PhDs, 22% are
women.

ACADEMICS
Degrees: Associate, bachelor's. **Classes:** Most classes have 10–19 students.
Majors with Highest Enrollment: Culinary arts/chef training; digital communication and media/multimedia. **Special Study Options:** Distance learning,
independent study, internships, study abroad. Special programs offered to
physically disabled students include note-taking services, reader services, tape
recorders, tutors. **Career services:** Alumni network, alumni services, career/
job search classes, career assessment, internships, regional alumni.

FACILITIES
Housing: Apartments for single students, wellness housing.

CAMPUS LIFE
Environment: City. **Activities:** Student-run film society. **On-Campus Highlights:** Student lounge.

ADMISSIONS
Freshman Academic Profile: Average high school GPA 2.61. Minimum paper
TOEFL 500. Minimum computer TOEFL 173. **Basis for Candidate Selec-
tion:** *Very important factors considered include:* Application essay, interview.
Important factors considered include: Level of applicant's interest, talent/abil-
ity. *Other factors considered include:* Academic GPA, standardized test scores,
character/personal qualities. **Freshman Admission Requirements:** High
school diploma is required and GED is accepted. **Freshman Admission
Statistics:** 436 applied, 68% admitted, 78% enrolled. **Transfer Admission
Requirements:** High school transcript, college transcript(s), essay or personal
statement, interview, statement of good standing from prior institution(s).
Minimum college GPA of 2.0 required. Lowest grade transferable C. **General
Admission Information:** Application fee $150. Nonfall registration accepted.

COSTS AND FINANCIAL AID

Annual tuition $21,552. Required fees $450. **Student Employment:** Federal Work-Study Program available.

THE ART INSTITUTE OF PITTSBURGH

420 Blvd. of The Allies, Pittsburgh, PA 15219
Phone: 412-263-6600 **Financial Aid Phone:** 412-291-6376
E-mail: aip_admissions@aii.edu
Fax: 412-263-6667 **Website:** www.aip.aii.edu

This proprietary school was founded in 1921.

RATINGS

Admissions Selectivity Rating: 60*   **Fire Safety Rating:** 60*   **Green Rating:** 60*

STUDENTS AND FACULTY

Enrollment: 4,864. **Student Body:** 55% female, 45% male, 0.5% out-of-state, international (20 countries represented). African American 2%, Caucasian 30%. **Retention and Graduation: Faculty:** Student/faculty ratio 20:1. 44 full-time faculty, 50% hold PhDs, 102% are members of minority groups, 70% are women.

ACADEMICS

Degrees: Associate, bachelor's, diploma, transfer associate. **Special Study Options:** Distance learning, English as a Second Language (ESL), internships Special programs offered to physically disabled students include note-taking services, tape recorders, tutors. **Career services:** Alumni services, career/job search classes, internships, regional alumni.

FACILITIES

Housing: 100% of campus accessible to physically disabled.

CAMPUS LIFE

Activities: Student government, student newspaper, student-run film society **Organizations:** 21 registered organizations, 2 honor societies, 1 religious organizations.

ADMISSIONS

Basis for Candidate Selection: *Very important factors considered include:* Application essay, rigor of secondary school record. *Important factors considered include:* Talent/ability. *Other factors considered include:* Recommendation(s), extracurricular activities. **Freshman Admission Requirements:** High school diploma is required and GED is accepted. *Academic units recommended:* 3 English, 3 mathematics, 3 science. **Freshman Admission Statistics:** 2,177 applied, 46% admitted, 100% enrolled. **Transfer Admission Requirements:** High school transcript, essay or personal statement, interview, Lowest grade transferable C. **General Admission Information:** Application fee $150. Nonfall registration accepted. Admission may be deferred for a maximum of 1 year. Neither credit nor placement offered for CEEB Advanced Placement tests.

COSTS AND FINANCIAL AID

Annual tuition $16,740. Room and board $6,525. Average book expense $900. **Required Forms and Deadlines:** FAFSA, institution's own financial aid form, state aid form. **Types of Aid:** *Need-based scholarships/grants:* Federal Pell, SEOG, state scholarships/grants, private scholarships, the school's own gift aid. *Loans:* Direct Subsidized Stafford, Direct Unsubsidized Stafford, Direct PLUS, Federal Perkins, state loans, college/university loans from institutional funds. **Student Employment:** Federal Work-Study Program available. Institutional employment available. Off-campus job opportunities are excellent. **Financial Aid Statistics:** 88% undergrads receive any aid.

THE ART INSTITUTES INTERNATIONAL MINNESOTA

15 South 9th Street, Minneapolis, mn 55402
Phone: 612-332-3361 **Financial Aid Phone:** 612-332-3361
E-mail: aimadm@aii.edu
Fax: 612-332-3934 **Website:** www.artinstitutes.edu/minneapolis

This proprietary school was founded in 1997.

RATINGS

Admissions Selectivity Rating: 60*   **Fire Safety Rating:** 60*   **Green Rating:** 60*

STUDENTS AND FACULTY

Enrollment: 1,974. **Student Body:** 61% female, 39% male, 20% out-of-state, international.
Retention and Graduation: 60% freshmen return for sophomore year. **Faculty:** Student/faculty ratio 20:1. 56 full-time faculty, 36% are women.

ACADEMICS

Degrees: Associate, bachelor's, certificate. **Special Study Options:** distance learning, independent study, internships, study abroad, Evening & Weekend. Special programs offered to physically disabled students include note-taking services, tape recorders, tutors. **Career services:** Alumni network, alumni services, career/job search classes, internships, regional alumni.

FACILITIES

Housing: Apartments for single students. 100% of campus accessible to physically disabled. **Computers:** 100% of classrooms, 100% of dorms, 100% of libraries, 100% of dining areas, 100% of student union, have wireless network access. Students can register for classes online. Administrative functions (other than registration) can be performed online.

CAMPUS LIFE

Environment: Metropolis. **Activities:** literary magazine, student newspaper, campus ministries, International student organization. **Organizations:** 16 registered organizations, 1 honor societies, **On-Campus Highlights:** School dining lab, art galleries, connection to the city's skyway system, new second campus.

ADMISSIONS

Freshman Academic Profile: Basis for Candidate Selection: *Very important factors considered include:* Application essay, interview. *Important factors considered include:* Talent/ability. *Other factors considered include:* Academic GPA, standardized test scores, character/personal qualities, extracurricular activities, level of applicant's interest. **Freshman Admission Requirements:** High school diploma is required and GED is accepted. **Freshman Admission Statistics: Transfer Admission Requirements:** High school transcript, college transcript(s), essay or personal statement, interview, minimum college GPA of 2.0 required. Lowest grade transferable C. **General Admission Information:** Application fee $50. Nonfall registration accepted.

COSTS AND FINANCIAL AID

Annual tuition $22,416. **Required Forms and Deadlines:** FAFSA. **Types of Aid:** *Need-based scholarships/grants:* Federal Pell, SEOG, state scholarships/grants, private scholarships, the school's own gift aid, United Negro College Fund. *Loans:* Direct Subsidized Stafford, Direct Unsubsidized Stafford, Direct PLUS, FFEL Subsidized Stafford, FFEL Unsubsidized Stafford, FFEL PLUS, state loans, college/university loans from institutional funds. **Student Employment:** Federal Work-Study Program available. Institutional employment available. Off-campus job opportunities are good.

ASBURY COLLEGE

1 Macklem Drive, Wilmore, KY 40390
Phone: 859-858-3511 **Financial Aid Phone:**
E-mail: admissions@asbury.edu **CEEB Code:** 1019
Fax: 859-858-3921 **Website:** www.asbury.edu **ACT Code:** 1486

This private school was founded in 1890. It has a 400-acre campus.

RATINGS

Admissions Selectivity Rating: 85   **Fire Safety Rating:** 60*   **Green Rating:** 60*

STUDENTS AND FACULTY

Enrollment: 1,167. **Student Body:** 58% female, 42% male, 70% out-of-state, 1% international (10 countries represented). Asian 1%, African American 1%, Caucasian 96%, Hispanic 1%.
Retention and Graduation: 82% freshmen return for sophomore year. 49% freshmen graduate within 4 years. **Faculty:** Student/faculty ratio 11:1. 90 full-time faculty, 78% hold PhDs, 27% are women.

ACADEMICS

Degrees: Bachelor's, master's. **Classes:** Most classes have 10–19 students. **Majors with Highest Enrollment:** Communications technologies/technicians and support services, other; elementary education and teaching; psychology. **Special Study Options:** Double major, internships, teacher certification program, 3-2 programs in engineering and computer science with the University of Kentucky. Special programs offered to physically disabled students include tape recorders, tutors. **Career services:** Alumni services, career/job search classes, career assessment, internships.

FACILITIES

Housing: Special housing for disabled students, men's dorms, women's dorms, apartments for married students, apartments for single students, Spanish House. 70% of campus accessible to physically disabled. **Special Academic Facilities/Equipment:** Art gallery, Art Annex, practice rooms, theatre building, Luce Physical Activities Center, TV/radio studios and Mac lab. **Computers:** Administrative functions (other than registration) can be performed online.

CAMPUS LIFE

Environment: Rural. **Activities:** Choral groups, concert band, drama/theater, jazz band, literary magazine, music ensembles, opera, radio station, student government, student newspaper, symphony orchestra, television station, yearbook. **Organizations:** 41 registered organizations, 6 honor societies, 8 religious organizations. **Athletics (Intercollegiate):** *Men:* Baseball, basketball, cross-country, diving, soccer, swimming, tennis, track/field (outdoor). *Women:* Basketball, cross-country, diving, soccer, softball, swimming, tennis, track/field (outdoor), volleyball.

ADMISSIONS

Freshman Academic Profile: Average high school GPA 3.55. 30% in top 10% of high school class, 60% in top 25% of high school class, 86% in top 50% of high school class. 65% from public high schools. SAT Math middle 50% range 490–620. SAT Critical Reading middle 50% range 530–650. ACT middle 50% range 21–28. Minimum paper TOEFL 550. Minimum computer TOEFL 213. **Basis for Candidate Selection:** *Very important factors considered include:* Recommendation(s), rigor of secondary school record, standardized test scores, character/personal qualities, racial/ethnic status, religious affiliation/commitment. *Important factors considered include:* Class rank, application essay, volunteer work, work experience. *Other factors considered include:* Alumni/ae relation, extracurricular activities, geographical residence, state residency, talent/ability. **Freshman Admission Requirements:** High school diploma is required and GED is accepted. *Academic units recommended:* 4 English, 4 mathematics, 3 science, 2 foreign language, 2 social studies. **Freshman Admission Statistics:** 820 applied, 73% admitted, 49% enrolled. **Transfer Admission Requirements:** High school transcript, college transcript(s), essay or personal statement, standardized test scores, minimum college GPA of 2.5 required. Lowest grade transferable C–. **General Admission Information:** Application fee $30. Nonfall registration accepted. Admission may be deferred for a maximum of 1 year. Neither credit nor placement offered for CEEB Advanced Placement tests.

COSTS AND FINANCIAL AID

Annual tuition $17,660. Room and board $4,494. Required fees $148. Average book expense $600. **Required Forms and Deadlines:** FAFSA, institution's own financial aid form. Financial aid filing deadline 6/30. Priority financial aid filing date 3/1. **Notification of Awards:** Applicants will be notified of awards on a rolling basis beginning 3/1. **Types of Aid:** *Need-based scholarships/grants:* Federal Pell, SEOG, state scholarships/grants, the school's own gift aid. *Loans:* Direct Subsidized Stafford, Direct Unsubsidized Stafford, Direct PLUS, Federal Perkins, college/university loans from institutional funds, Private alternative loans. **Student Employment:** Federal Work-Study Program available. Institutional employment available. Highest amount earned per year from on-campus jobs $1,200. Off-campus job opportunities are good. **Financial Aid Statistics:** 72% freshmen, 69% undergrads receive need-based scholarship or grant aid. 25% freshmen, 2% undergrads receive non-need-based scholarship or grant aid. 67% freshmen, 61% undergrads receive need-based self-help aid. 1% freshmen, 68% undergrads borrow to pay for school. Average cumulative indebtedness $18,885. **Criteria for awarding institutional aid:** *Non-need-based:* Academics, alumni affiliation, athletics, leadership, music/drama

ASHLAND UNIVERSITY

401 College Ave, Ashland, OH 44805
Phone: 419-289-5052 **Financial Aid Phone:** 419-289-5002
E-mail: enrollme@ashland.edu **CEEB Code:** 1021
Fax: 419-289-5999 **Website:** www.ashland.edu **ACT Code:** 3234

This private school, affiliated with the Church of Brethren Church, was founded in 1878. It has a 12-acre campus.

RATINGS

Admissions Selectivity Rating: 78   **Fire Safety Rating:** 60*   **Green Rating:** 60*

STUDENTS AND FACULTY

Enrollment: 2,612. **Student Body:** 52% female, 48% male, 7% out-of-state, 2% international (14 countries represented). African American 5%, Caucasian 71%, Hispanic 2%.
Retention and Graduation: 71% freshmen return for sophomore year. 46% freshmen graduate within 4 years. 13% grads go on to further study within 1

year. 2% grads pursue arts and sciences degrees. 1% grads pursue law degrees. 1% grads pursue business degrees. 1% grads pursue medical degrees. **Faculty:** Student/faculty ratio 16:1. 234 full-time faculty, 84% hold PhDs, 6% are members of minority groups, 41% are women.

ACADEMICS

Degrees: Associate, bachelor's, certificate, diploma, doctoral, master's, terminal associate, transfer associate. **Classes:** Most classes have 10–19 students. Most lab/discussion sessions have 10–19 students. **Majors with Highest Enrollment:** Business/commerce; education; psychology. **Special Study Options:** Double major, English as a Second Language (ESL), honors program, independent study, internships, student-designed major, study abroad, teacher certification program, weekend college, Ashbrook Center for Public Affairs. **Honors programs:** Ashland University Honors Program. Special programs offered to physically disabled students include note-taking services, reader services, tape recorders, tutors. **Career services:** Alumni network, alumni services, career/job search classes, career assessment, internships.

FACILITIES

Housing: Coed dorms, special housing for disabled students, men's dorms, women's dorms, fraternity/sorority housing, apartments for single students, theme housing. 70% of campus accessible to physically disabled. **Special Academic Facilities/Equipment:** Neumismatic Center, Patterson Technology Center, Coburn Art Gallery, Hugo Young Theatre, Studio Theatre, 33 room Radio/Television Condex, Media Center, Pre-Columbian Art Exhibit, Ashbrook Center. **Computers:** 90% of classrooms, 50% of dorms, 100% of libraries, 50% of dining areas, 100% of student union, 50% of common outdoor areas have wireless network access. Students can register for classes online. Administrative functions (other than registration) can be performed online.

CAMPUS LIFE

Environment: Town. **Activities:** Choral groups, concert band, dance, drama/theater, jazz band, literary magazine, marching band, music ensembles, musical theater, pep band, radio station, student government, student newspaper, symphony orchestra, television station, yearbook, campus ministries, international student organization. **Organizations:** 102 registered organizations, 18 honor societies, 9 religious organizations. 4 fraternities, 5 sororities. **Athletics (Intercollegiate):** *Men:* Baseball, basketball, cross-country, diving, football, golf, soccer, swimming, track/field (outdoor), track/field (indoor), wrestling *Women:* Basketball, cheerleading, cross-country, diving, golf, soccer, softball, swimming, tennis, track/field (outdoor), track/field (indoor), volleyball. **On-Campus Highlights:** Kettering Science Center, Recreation and Sport Sciences Center, Schar College of Education, Dauch College of Business and Economics, National ranked food service, NCAA Division II Athletics 2009–2010 New football stadium, new soccer complex, new track and field complex.

ADMISSIONS

Freshman Academic Profile: Average high school GPA 3.36. 17.6% in top 10% of high school class, 47.1% in top 25% of high school class, 78.9% in top 50% of high school class. 89% from public high schools. SAT Math middle 50% range 470–590. SAT Critical Reading middle 50% range 460–560. SAT Writing middle 50% range 440–550. ACT middle 50% range 20–25. Minimum paper TOEFL 500. Minimum computer TOEFL 173. Minimum web-based TOEFL 65. **Basis for Candidate Selection:** *Very important factors considered include:* rigor of secondary school record, standardized test scores. *Important factors considered include:* Class rank, academic GPA, alumni/ae relation, character/personal qualities, extracurricular activities, interview, level of applicant's interest. *Other factors considered include:* Application essay, recommendation(s), geographical residence, religious affiliation/commitment, state residency, talent/ability, volunteer work, work experience. **Freshman Admission Requirements:** High school diploma is required and GED is accepted. *Academic units required:* 3 English, 2 mathematics, 2 science, 2 social studies, 1 history. *Academic units recommended:* 4 English, 3 mathematics, 3 science, 2 foreign language, 3 social studies, 1 history. **Freshman Admission Statistics:** 2,903 applied, 94% admitted, 23% enrolled. **Transfer Admission Requirements:** college transcript(s), essay or personal statement, minimum college GPA of 2.5 required. Lowest grade transferable C–. **General Admission Information:** Regular application deadline 8/15. Notification on a rolling basis, beginning on or about 10/15. Nonfall registration accepted. Admission may be deferred for a maximum of 1 semester. Credit and/or placement offered for CEEB Advanced Placement tests.

COSTS AND FINANCIAL AID

Annual tuition $24,414. Room and board $9,352. Required fees $818. Average book expense $900. **Required Forms and Deadlines:** FAFSA. Priority financial aid filing date 3/15. **Notification of Awards:** Applicants will be notified of awards on a rolling basis beginning 3/1. **Types of Aid:** *Need-based scholarships/grants:* Federal Pell, SEOG, state scholarships/grants, private scholarships, the school's own gift aid. *Loans:* Direct Subsidized Stafford, Direct Unsubsidized Stafford, Direct PLUS, Federal Perkins, Federal Nursing, state loans, college/university loans from institutional funds. **Student Employment:** Federal Work-Study Program available. Institutional employment available. Highest amount earned per year from on-campus jobs $2,800. Off-campus job opportunities are good. **Financial Aid Statistics:** 86% freshmen, 82% undergrads receive need-based scholarship or grant aid. 86% freshmen, 82% undergrads receive non-need-based scholarship or grant aid. 76% freshmen, 73% undergrads receive need-based self-help aid. 3% freshmen, 3% undergrads receive athletic scholarships. 99% freshmen, 98% undergrads receive any aid. 82% undergrads borrow to pay for school. Average cumulative indebtedness $36,545. **Criteria for awarding institutional aid:** *Non-need-based:* Academics, alumni affiliation, art, athletics, job skills, leadership, minority status, music/drama, religious affiliation.

ASSUMPTION COLLEGE

500 Salisbury Street, Worcester, MA 01609-1296
Phone: 508-767-7285 **Financial Aid Phone:** 508-767-7158
E-mail: admiss@assumption.edu **CEEB Code:** 3009
Fax: 508-799-4412 **Website:** www.assumption.edu **ACT Code:** 1782

This private school, affiliated with the Roman Catholic Church, was founded in 1904. It has a 180-acre campus.

RATINGS
Admissions Selectivity Rating: 77   **Fire Safety Rating:** 84   **Green Rating:** 65

STUDENTS AND FACULTY
Enrollment: 2,163. **Student Body:** 59% female, 41% male, 32% out-of-state, 1% international (8 countries represented). Asian 2%, African American 2%, Caucasian 76%, Hispanic 3%.
Retention and Graduation: 73% freshmen graduate within 4 years. 22% grads go on to further study within 1 year. **Faculty:** Student/faculty ratio 12:1. 155 full-time faculty, 92% hold PhDs, 6% are members of minority groups, 41% are women.

ACADEMICS
Degrees: Bachelor's, master's, post-master's certificate. **Classes:** Most classes have 20–29 students. Most lab/discussion sessions have 10–19 students. **Majors with Highest Enrollment:** Accounting; psychology; rehabilitation and therapeutic professions, other. **Special Study Options:** Cross-registration, double major, honors program, independent study, internships, student-designed major, study abroad, teacher certification program. **Honors programs:** The Assumption College Honors Program is a selective program designed to foster academic engagement inside and outside the classroom. The program promotes intellectual friendship and discourse while providing a common, intensive learning experience in small seminar classes. **Combined degree programs:** BA/MA, BA/MAs SP ED, Rehab Couns, School Couns; BA/MBA. Special programs offered to physically disabled students include note-taking services, reader services, tape recorders, tutors. **Career services:** Alumni network, career/job search classes, career assessment, internships, regional alumni.

FACILITIES
Housing: Coed dorms, special housing for disabled students, women's dorms, wellness housing, theme housing, freshmen dorms. 71% of campus accessible to physically disabled. **Special Academic Facilities/Equipment:** French Institute museum, Institute for Social and Rehabilitation Services, language lab, media center Living/Learning Center Testa Science Center Information Technology Center. **Computers:** 100% of classrooms, 100% of libraries, 50% of dining areas, 100% of student union, 25% of common outdoor areas have wireless network access. Students can register for classes online. Administrative functions (other than registration) can be performed online.

CAMPUS LIFE
Environment: City. **Activities:** Choral groups, concert band, drama/theater, literary magazine, musical theater, pep band, student government, student newspaper, student-run film society, television station, yearbook, campus ministries. **Organizations:** 50 registered organizations, 12 honor societies, 1 religious organizations. **Athletics (Intercollegiate):** *Men:* Baseball, basketball, cross-country, football, golf, ice hockey, lacrosse, soccer, tennis, track/field (outdoor), track/field (indoor). *Women:* Basketball, crew/rowing, cross-country, field hockey, lacrosse, soccer, softball, swimming, tennis, track/field (outdoor), track/field (indoor), volleyball. **On-Campus Highlights:** Testa Science Center, Living Learning Center, Plourde Recreation Center, Charlie's Cafe, D'Alzon Library.

ADMISSIONS
Freshman Academic Profile: Average high school GPA 3.44. 14% in top 10% of high school class, 43% in top 25% of high school class, 82% in top 50% of high school class. 68% from public high schools. SAT Math middle 50% range 480–580. SAT Critical Reading middle 50% range 470–580. ACT middle 50%

range 20–25. Minimum paper TOEFL 550. Minimum computer TOEFL 213. Minimum web-based TOEFL 80. **Basis for Candidate Selection:** *Very important factors considered include:* Application essay, academic GPA. *Important factors considered include:* recommendation(s), rigor of secondary school record, interview, level of applicant's interest, volunteer work. *Other factors considered include:* Class rank, standardized test scores, alumni/ae relation, character/personal qualities, extracurricular activities, first generation, racial/ethnic status, talent/ability. **Freshman Admission Requirements:** High school diploma is required and GED is accepted. *Academic units required:* 4 English, 3 mathematics, 2 science, 2 foreign language, 2 history, 5 academic electives. **Freshman Admission Statistics:** 3,889 applied, 71% admitted, 22% enrolled. **Transfer Admission Requirements:** High school transcript, college transcript(s), essay or personal statement, statement of good standing from prior institution(s). Minimum college GPA of 2.5 required. Lowest grade transferable C. **General Admission Information:** Application fee $50. Regular application deadline 2/15. Nonfall registration accepted. Admission may be deferred for a maximum of 1 year. Credit and/or placement offered for CEEB Advanced Placement tests.

COSTS AND FINANCIAL AID
Annual tuition $29,806. Room and board $10,070. Required fees $365. Average book expense $1,000. **Required Forms and Deadlines:** FAFSA. Financial aid filing deadline 2/1. **Notification of Awards:** Applicants will be notified of awards on a rolling basis beginning 2/16. **Types of Aid:** *Need-based scholarships/grants:* Federal Pell, SEOG, state scholarships/grants, private scholarships, the school's own gift aid. *Loans:* Direct Subsidized Stafford, Direct Unsubsidized Stafford, Direct PLUS. **Student Employment:** Federal Work-Study Program available. Institutional employment available. Highest amount earned per year from on-campus jobs $2,948. Off-campus job opportunities are good. **Financial Aid Statistics:** 74% freshmen, 71% undergrads receive need-based scholarship or grant aid. 12% freshmen, 8% undergrads receive non-need-based scholarship or grant aid. 59% freshmen, 59% undergrads receive need-based self-help aid. 1% freshmen, 1% undergrads receive athletic scholarships. 94% freshmen, 95% undergrads receive any aid. 93% undergrads borrow to pay for school. Average cumulative indebtedness $26,691. **Criteria for awarding institutional aid:** *Non-need-based:* Academics, athletics.

See page 1018.

ATHABASCA UNIVERSITY

1 University Drive, Athabasca, AB T9S 3A3 Canada
Phone: 780-675-6100 **Financial Aid Phone:** 800-788-9041
E-mail: admissions@athabascau.ca
Fax: 780-675-6174 **Website:** www.athabascau.ca

This public school was founded in 1970.

RATINGS
Admissions Selectivity Rating: 60*   **Fire Safety Rating:** 60*   **Green Rating:** 74

STUDENTS AND FACULTY
Student Body: 87 countries represented.
Faculty: 123 full-time faculty.

ACADEMICS
Degrees: Bachelor's, certificate, diploma, master's, post-bachelor's certificate, post-master's certificate. **Majors with Highest Enrollment:** Criminal justice/safety studies; elementary education and teaching; nursing/registered nurse (RN, ASN, BSN, MSN). **Special Study Options:** Accelerated program, cross-registration, distance learning, English as a Second Language (ESL), external degree program. Special programs offered to physically disabled students include tape recorders, tutors.

FACILITIES
Housing: Coed dorms. **Computers:** Students can register for classes online. Administrative functions (other than registration) can be performed online.

CAMPUS LIFE
Environment: Rural. **Activities:** Student government, yearbook.

ADMISSIONS
Transfer Admission Requirements: High school transcript, college transcript(s). **General Admission Information:** Application fee $56. Nonfall registration accepted. Admission may be deferred for a maximum of 1 year.

COSTS AND FINANCIAL AID
Annual in-state tuition $591. Annual out-of-state tuition $689.

ATLANTA CHRISTIAN COLLEGE

Office of Admissions, 2605 Ben Hill Rd, East Point, GA 30344
Phone: 404-669-3202 **Financial Aid Phone:**
E-mail: admissions@acc.edu
Fax: 404-460-2451 **Website:** www.acc.edu **ACT Code:** 785

This private school, affiliated with the Christian (Nondenominational) Church, was founded in 1937. It has a 52-acre campus.

RATINGS
Admissions Selectivity Rating: 60*   **Fire Safety Rating:** 60*   **Green Rating:** 60*

STUDENTS AND FACULTY
Student Body: 10% out-of-state.
Faculty: Student/faculty ratio 16:1.

ACADEMICS
Degrees: Associate, bachelor's. **Majors with Highest Enrollment:** Bible/biblical studies; elementary education and teaching; social work. **Special Study Options:** Double major, dual enrollment, independent study, internships. **Career services:** Alumni services, career/job search classes, internships.

FACILITIES
Housing: Men's dorms, women's dorms, apartments for married students, apartments for single students. 95% of campus accessible to physically disabled. **Computers:** Students can register for classes online.

CAMPUS LIFE
Environment: Village. **Activities:** Choral groups, music ensembles, student government, yearbook. **Organizations:** 2 fraternities, 2 sororities. **Athletics (Intercollegiate):** *Men:* Baseball, basketball, golf, soccer. *Women:* Basketball, soccer, volleyball.

ADMISSIONS
Freshman Academic Profile: 10% in top 10% of high school class, 15% in top 25% of high school class, 90% in top 50% of high school class. 85% from public high schools. Minimum paper TOEFL 500. Minimum computer TOEFL 173. **Basis for Candidate Selection:** *Very important factors considered include:* Recommendation(s), rigor of secondary school record, standardized test scores. *Important factors considered include:* Character/personal qualities. **Freshman Admission Requirements:** High school diploma is required and GED is accepted. **Transfer Admission Requirements:** College transcript(s), statement of good standing from prior institution(s). Minimum college GPA of 2.0 required. Lowest grade transferable C. **General Admission Information:** Application fee $25. Early decision application deadline 11/15. Regular application deadline 8/1. Notification on a rolling basis, beginning on or about 8/20. Nonfall registration accepted. Admission may be deferred for a maximum of 1 semester. Credit and/or placement offered for CEEB Advanced Placement tests.

COSTS AND FINANCIAL AID
Annual tuition $10,800. Room and board $4,400. Required fees $560. Average book expense $800. **Student Employment:** Federal Work-Study Program available. Institutional employment available. Off-campus job opportunities are excellent.

AUBURN UNIVERSITY

Quad Center, Auburn, AL 36849-5149
Phone: 334-844-4080 **Financial Aid Phone:** 334-844-4634
E-mail: admissions@auburn.edu **CEEB Code:** 1005
Fax: 334-844-6436 **Website:** www.auburn.edu **ACT Code:** 11

This public school was founded in 1856. It has a 1875-acre campus.

RATINGS
Admissions Selectivity Rating: 86   **Fire Safety Rating:** 60*   **Green Rating:** 85

STUDENTS AND FACULTY
Enrollment: 19,916. **Student Body:** 48% female, 52% male, 35% out-of-state, 1% international (78 countries represented). Asian 2%, African American 8%, Caucasian 86%, Hispanic 2%, Native American 1%.
Retention and Graduation: 86% freshmen return for sophomore year. 37% freshmen graduate within 4 years. 34% grads go on to further study within 1 year. 5% grads pursue arts and sciences degrees. 6% grads pursue law degrees. 18% grads pursue business degrees. 7% grads pursue medical degrees. **Faculty:** Student/faculty ratio 18:1. 1184 full-time faculty, 16% are members of minority groups, 33% are women.

ACADEMICS
Degrees: Bachelor's, doctoral, master's, post-master's certificate. **Classes:** Most classes have 20–29 students. Most lab/discussion sessions have 20–29 students. **Majors with Highest Enrollment:** Business administration and management; mechanical engineering; secondary education and teaching. **Special Study Options:** Accelerated program, cooperative education program, distance learning, double major, dual enrollment, English as a Second Language (ESL), honors program, independent study, internships, liberal arts/career combination, study abroad, teacher certification program. **Honors programs:** The Auburn University's Honors College offers qualified students a unique academic experience, designed to provide many of the advantages of a small college in the midst of the many diverse opportunities available at a large university. It is designed for students capable of academic excellence. The program selects 200 entering freshmen each year, who may be enrolled in any College or School of the University which has undergraduate programs or offerings. Students already enrolled at Auburn can also qualify for the Honors College. **Combined degree programs:** Liberal Arts or Agriculture. Special programs offered to physically disabled students include note-taking services, reader services, tape recorders, tutors. **Career services:** Alumni network, alumni services, career/job search classes, career assessment, internships.

FACILITIES
Housing: Coed dorms, special housing for disabled students, men's dorms, women's dorms, fraternity/sorority housing, apartments for married students, apartments for single students, Housing for students enrolled in Honors College and academiC–themed learning communities (i.e., Agriculture Pre-Vet, AT&T Minority Engineering Program, Conservation Biology). 95% of campus accessible to physically disabled. **Special Academic Facilities/Equipment:** Nuclear Science Center; Hybridoma Facility; Freeman Herbarium; Jule Collins Smith Art Museum; Hypervelocity Impact Facility; Advanced Microscopy & Imaging Laboratory; Alabama Microelectronics Science & Technology Center; Alabama Water Resources Research Institute; AU Airport with single/multi-engine aircraft and flight simulators; Center for Forest Sustainability; Center for Governmental Services; Center for Pharmacy Operations & Designs; Drug Information & Learning Resources Center; Economic & Community Development Institute; Fish Molecular Genetics & Biotechnology Laboratory; Forest Policy Center; Forest Products Development Center; Fusion Lab; Harris Early Learning Center; Dept of Psychology Health Behavior Assessment Center; Highway Research Center; Marriage & Family Therapy Center; Microfibrous Materials Manufacturing Center; Dept of Kinesiology Biomechanics Lab, and Motor Behavior Center; Plasma Sciences Lab; Veterinary Medicine Radiology Clinic, Scott-Ritchey Research Center, Southeastern Raptor Rehabilitation Center, Small & Large Animal Health Clinics. **Computers:** 35% of classrooms, 100% of dorms, 95% of libraries, 50% of dining areas, 100% of student union, 30% of common outdoor areas have wireless network access. Students can register for classes online. Administrative functions (other than registration) can be performed online.

CAMPUS LIFE
Environment: Town. **Activities:** Choral groups, concert band, dance, drama/theater, jazz band, literary magazine, marching band, music ensembles, musical theater, opera, pep band, radio station, student government, student newspaper, student-run film society, symphony orchestra, television station, yearbook, international student organization. **Organizations:** 300 registered organizations, 56 honor societies, 15 religious organizations. 30 fraternities, 19 sororities. **Athletics (Intercollegiate):** *Men:* Baseball, basketball, cheerleading, cross-country, diving, football, golf, swimming, tennis, track/field (outdoor), track/field (indoor). *Women:* Basketball, cheerleading, cross-country, diving, equestrian sports, golf, gymnastics, soccer, softball, swimming, tennis, track/field (outdoor), track/field (indoor), volleyball. **On-Campus Highlights:** Telfair B. Peet Theatre, Student Activity Center, Haley Center Concourse, Library Coffee Shop, War Eagle Dining, Student Center; Arboretum; Agricultural Heritage Park; Forest Ecology Preserve. **Environmental Initiatives:** Incorporation of sustainability initiatives into university curricula, including one of the first truly interdisciplinary sustainability minors in the country. 2007 Campus Master Plan weaves sustainability throughout, including: pedestrianization of core campus, establishment of campus development boundary, evaluation of flat roof space for solar energy, and expansion of non-paved green spaces on campus. 2008 Campus Strategic Plan incorporating commitment to sustainability as guiding concept in campus development: "As an institution devoted to learning, Auburn must constantly strive to improve itself. Making better use of scarce resources is an evergreen management challenge that is made even more important by

our deepening commitment to sustainability. This priority will steadily increase in importance as the proportion of Auburn's funding provided by the State of Alabama continues to decline."

ADMISSIONS

Freshman Academic Profile: Average high school GPA 3.69. 40% in top 10% of high school class, 65% in top 25% of high school class, 91% in top 50% of high school class. 86% from public high schools. SAT Math middle 50% range 540–660. SAT Critical Reading middle 50% range 520–640. SAT Writing middle 50% range 510–620. ACT middle 50% range 23–29. Minimum paper TOEFL 550. Minimum computer TOEFL 213. Minimum web-based TOEFL 79. **Basis for Candidate Selection:** *Very important factors considered include:* Application essay, academic GPA, standardized test scores. *Important factors considered include:* Rigor of secondary school record, alumni/ae relation, character/personal qualities, extracurricular activities, first generation, geographical residence, level of applicant's interest, state residency, talent/ability, volunteer work, work experience. *Other factors considered include:* Recommendation(s). **Freshman Admission Requirements:** High school diploma is required and GED is accepted. *Academic units required:* 4 English, 3 mathematics, 2 science, (1 science labs), 3 social studies. *Academic units recommended:* 4 English, 3 mathematics, 3 science, (2 science labs), 1 foreign language, 4 social studies. **Freshman Admission Statistics:** 14,862 applied, 80% admitted, 33% enrolled. **Transfer Admission Requirements:** college transcript(s), minimum college GPA of 2.5 required. Lowest grade transferable C. **General Admission Information:** Application fee $40. Regular application deadline 6/1. Regular notification 2/15. Notification on a rolling basis, beginning on or about 10/15. Nonfall registration accepted. Admission may be deferred for a maximum of 1 year. Credit and/or placement offered for CEEB Advanced Placement tests.

COSTS AND FINANCIAL AID

Annual in-state tuition $6,240. Annual out-of-state tuition $18,720. Room and board $8,972. Required fees $732. Average book expense $1,100. **Required Forms and Deadlines:** FAFSA. Priority financial aid filing date 3/1. **Notification of Awards:** Applicants will be notified of awards on a rolling basis beginning 10/2. **Types of Aid:** *Need-based scholarships/grants:* Federal Pell, SEOG, state scholarships/grants, private scholarships, the school's own gift aid. *Loans:* Direct Subsidized Stafford, Direct Unsubsidized Stafford, Direct PLUS, Federal Perkins, Federal Nursing, college/university loans from institutional funds. **Student Employment:** Federal Work-Study Program available. Institutional employment available. Highest amount earned per year from on-campus jobs $10,920. Off-campus job opportunities are good. **Financial Aid Statistics:** 22% freshmen, 20% undergrads receive need-based scholarship or grant aid. 4% freshmen, 3% undergrads receive non-need-based scholarship or grant aid. 19% freshmen, 25% undergrads receive need-based self-help aid. 2% freshmen, 2% undergrads receive athletic scholarships. 63% freshmen, 54% undergrads receive any aid. 40% undergrads borrow to pay for school. Average cumulative indebtedness $22,232.

AUBURN UNIVERSITY MONTGOMERY

P.O. Box 244023, Montgomery, AL 36124-4023
Phone: 334-244-3615 **Financial Aid Phone:** 334-244-3571
E-mail: admitme@aum.edu
Fax: 334-244-3795 **Website:** www.aum.edu **ACT Code:** 57

This public school was founded in 1967. It has a 500-acre campus.

RATINGS

Admissions Selectivity Rating: 69   **Fire Safety Rating:** 60*   **Green Rating:** 75

STUDENTS AND FACULTY

Enrollment: 4,525. **Student Body:** 62% female, 38% male, 4% out-of-state, 3% international (37 countries represented). Asian 2%, African American 32%, Caucasian 60%, Hispanic 1%, Native American 1%.
Retention and Graduation: 58% freshmen return for sophomore year. 11% freshmen graduate within 4 years. **Faculty:** Student/faculty ratio 18:1. 187 full-time faculty, 19% are members of minority groups, 45% are women. 3% of classes are taught by teaching assistants.

ACADEMICS

Degrees: Bachelor's, master's, post-master's certificate. **Classes:** Most classes have 20–29 students. Most lab/discussion sessions have 20–29 students. **Majors with Highest Enrollment:** Business/commerce; elementary education and teaching; nursing/registered nurse (RN, ASN, BSN, MSN). **Special Study Options:** Accelerated program, cooperative education program, cross-registration, distance learning, double major, dual enrollment, English as a Second Language (ESL), honors program, independent study, internships, liberal arts/career

combination, study abroad, teacher certification program, weekend college, Joint PhD in public administration with Auburn University; EdD in cooperation with Auburn University. Special programs offered to physically disabled students include note-taking services, reader services, tape recorders, tutors. **Career services:** Alumni network, alumni services, career/job search classes, career assessment, internships.

FACILITIES

Housing: Coed dorms, special housing for disabled students, apartments for married students, apartments for single students. 100% of campus accessible to physically disabled. **Computers:** Students can register for classes online. Administrative functions (other than registration) can be performed online.

CAMPUS LIFE

Environment: City. **Activities:** Choral groups, dance, drama/theater, musical theater, student government, student newspaper, student-run film society, campus ministries, international student organization. **Organizations:** 50 registered organizations, 10 honor societies, 7 religious organizations. 3 fraternities, 6 sororities. **Athletics (Intercollegiate): Men:** Baseball, basketball, cheerleading, soccer, tennis. *Women:* Basketball, cheerleading, soccer, softball, tennis. **On-Campus Highlights:** Senator's Cafe, Computer Labs, Taylor Center/Student Union, Residence Hall, Athletic Facility. **Environmental Initiatives:** Recycling, campus beautification—plant trees educating the campus on Sustainability Initiative.

ADMISSIONS

Freshman Academic Profile: Average high school GPA 3.02. 14% in top 10% of high school class, 36% in top 25% of high school class, 67% in top 50% of high school class. ACT middle 50% range 18–23. Minimum paper TOEFL 500. Minimum web-based TOEFL 61. **Basis for Candidate Selection:** *Very important factors considered include:* Class rank, academic GPA, rigor of secondary school record, standardized test scores. *Other factors considered include:* Recommendation(s), alumni/ae relation, extracurricular activities, geographical residence, state residency. **Freshman Admission Requirements:** High school diploma is required and GED is accepted. *Academic units recommended:* 3 English, 3 mathematics, 2 science, (2 science labs), 2 foreign language, 2 social studies, 2 history, 2 academic electives. **Freshman Admission Statistics:** 1,409 applied, 95% admitted, 65% enrolled. **Transfer Admission Requirements:** college transcript(s), minimum college GPA of 2.0 required. Lowest grade transferable D. **General Admission Information:** Application fee $25. Nonfall registration accepted. Admission may be deferred for a maximum of 1 year. Credit offered for CEEB Advanced Placement tests.

COSTS AND FINANCIAL AID

Annual in-state tuition $5,640. Annual out-of-state tuition $16,920. Room and board $3,640. Required fees $300. Average book expense $900. **Required Forms and Deadlines:** FAFSA. Priority financial aid filing date 3/1. **Notification of Awards:** Applicants will be notified of awards on a rolling basis beginning 6/1. **Types of Aid:** *Need-based scholarships/grants:* Federal Pell *Loans:* Direct Subsidized Stafford, Direct Unsubsidized Stafford, Direct PLUS, Federal Perkins. **Student Employment:** Federal Work-Study Program available. Institutional employment available. **Financial Aid Statistics: Criteria for awarding institutional aid:** *Non-need-based:* Academics, alumni affiliation, art, athletics, job skills, leadership, minority status, music/drama.

AUGSBURG COLLEGE

2211 Riverside Avenue South, Minneapolis, MN 55454
Phone: 612-330-1001 **Financial Aid Phone:** 612-330-1046
E-mail: admissions@augsburg.edu **CEEB Code:** 6014
Fax: 612-330-1590 **Website:** www.augsburg.edu **ACT Code:** 2080

This private school, affiliated with the Lutheran Church, was founded in 1869. It has a 23-acre campus.

RATINGS

Admissions Selectivity Rating: 80   **Fire Safety Rating:** 60*   **Green Rating:** 60*

STUDENTS AND FACULTY

Enrollment: 2,979. **Student Body:** 54% female, 46% male, 13% out-of-state, 1% international (24 countries represented). Asian 6%, African American 8%, Caucasian 71%, Hispanic 3%, Native American 2%.
Retention and Graduation: 81% freshmen return for sophomore year. 37% freshmen graduate within 4 years. 27% grads go on to further study within 1 year. 15% grads pursue arts and sciences degrees. 2% grads pursue law degrees. 4% grads pursue business degrees. 5% grads pursue medical degrees. **Faculty:** Student/faculty ratio 13:1. 200 full-time faculty, 73% hold PhDs, 10% are members of minority groups, 49% are women.

ACADEMICS

Degrees: Bachelor's, certificate, master's. **Classes:** Most classes have 10–19 students. Most lab/discussion sessions have 10–19 students. **Majors with Highest Enrollment:** Business/commerce; education; psychology. **Special Study Options:** Cooperative education program, cross-registration, double major, dual enrollment, honors program, independent study, internships, liberal arts/career combination, student-designed major, study abroad, teacher certification program, weekend college. **Honors programs:** First, the Honors Signature Courses, based on the medieval divisions of knowledge, automatically satisfy all of the College's general education requirements (except health/physical education and modern language) in a simple sequence of challenging courses, created just for Honors students. Second, Student-Created Courses allow students to design their own courses—as either a replacement or supplement to the established Honors courses. Students can learn through one-on-one tutoring, small reading groups, or out-of-classroom experiences. Third, Honors Leadership Activities give Honors students access to the The Augsburg Review, Honors Debate League, Faculty/Student Research Collaboration, and the Honors Houses. Through these activities, students can engage in travel abroad, service-learning, social justice activities, political activism, leadership, research, and social gatherings with their friends. **Combined degree programs:** BA/MEng. Special programs offered to physically disabled students include note-taking services, reader services, tape recorders, tutors. **Career services:** Career/job search classes, internships.

FACILITIES

Housing: Coed dorms, special housing for disabled students, special housing for Step-Up program students (i.e., sober student program). 99% of campus accessible to physically disabled. **Special Academic Facilities/Equipment:** Electron microscope, center for atmospheric science research, theatre, pipe organ. **Computers:** Students can register for classes online. Administrative functions (other than registration) can be performed online.

CAMPUS LIFE

Environment: Metropolis. **Activities:** Choral groups, concert band, dance, drama/theater, jazz band, literary magazine, music ensembles, opera, radio station, student government, student newspaper, yearbook, campus ministries, international student organization. **Organizations:** 35 registered organizations, 1 honor societies, 1 religious organizations. **Athletics (Intercollegiate):** *Men:* Baseball, basketball, cross-country, football, golf, ice hockey, soccer, tennis, track/field (outdoor), track/field (indoor), wrestling. *Women:* Basketball, cheerleading, cross-country, golf, ice hockey, soccer, softball, swimming, tennis, track/field (outdoor), track/field (indoor), volleyball. **On-Campus Highlights:** Christensen Center/Starbucks Coffee Shop, Si Melby Athletic Fieldhouse, Lindell Library, Foss Center/Atrium, Gateway Center.

ADMISSIONS

Freshman Academic Profile: Average high school GPA 3.27. 11% in top 10% of high school class, 37% in top 25% of high school class, 69% in top 50% of high school class. SAT Math middle 50% range 500–640. SAT Critical Reading middle 50% range 510–640. SAT Writing middle 50% range 480–600. ACT middle 50% range 19–25. Minimum paper TOEFL 550. Minimum computer TOEFL 213. **Basis for Candidate Selection:** *Very important factors considered include:* Class rank, application essay, academic GPA, recommendation(s), rigor of secondary school record. *Important factors considered include:* standardized test scores, alumni/ae relation, extracurricular activities, level of applicant's interest. *Other factors considered include:* first generation, interview, talent/ability, volunteer work, work experience. **Freshman Admission Requirements:** High school diploma is required and GED is accepted. *Academic units required:* 4 English, 3 mathematics, 3 science, 2 foreign language, 2 social studies. *Academic units recommended:* 4 social studies, 2 history. **Freshman Admission Statistics:** 2,330 applied, 52% admitted, 37% enrolled. **Transfer Admission Requirements:** College transcript(s), statement of good standing from prior institution(s). Minimum college GPA of 2.5 required. Lowest grade transferable B. **General Admission Information:** Application fee $25. Regular application deadline 8/15. Notification on a rolling basis, beginning on or about 11/1. Nonfall registration accepted. Admission may be deferred for a maximum of 24 mos. Neither credit nor placement offered for CEEB Advanced Placement tests.

COSTS AND FINANCIAL AID

Annual tuition $27,628. Room and board $7,514. Required fees $608. Average book expense $1,000. **Required Forms and Deadlines:** FAFSA. Financial aid filing deadline 8/1. Priority financial aid filing date 5/1. **Notification of Awards:** Applicants will be notified of awards on a rolling basis beginning 3/1. **Types of Aid:** *Need-based scholarships/grants:* Federal Pell, SEOG, state scholarships/grants, private scholarships, the school's own gift aid. *Loans:* Direct Subsidized Stafford, Direct Unsubsidized Stafford, Direct PLUS, Federal Perkins, Federal Nursing, state loans, Supplemental Loans from Private Lenders. **Student Employment:** Institutional employment available. Highest amount earned per year from on-campus jobs $3,000. Off-campus job opportunities are good. **Financial Aid Statistics:** 80% freshmen, 68% undergrads receive need-based scholarship

or grant aid. 8% freshmen, 9% undergrads receive non-need-based scholarship or grant aid. 64% freshmen, 63% undergrads receive need-based self-help aid. 90% freshmen, 86% undergrads receive any aid. 90% undergrads borrow to pay for school. Average cumulative indebtedness $25,155. **Criteria for awarding institutional aid:** *Non-need-based:* Academics, alumni affiliation, art, leadership, minority status, music/drama, religious affiliation.

AUGUSTA STATE UNIVERSITY

2500 Walton Way, Augusta, GA 30904-2200
Phone: 706-737-1632 **Financial Aid Phone:** 706-737-1431
E-mail: admissio@aug.edu **CEEB Code:** 5336
Fax: 706-667-4355 **ACT Code:** 796

This public school was founded in 1925. It has a 76-acre campus.

RATINGS

Admissions Selectivity Rating: 73   **Fire Safety Rating:** 60*   **Green Rating:** 60*

STUDENTS AND FACULTY

Enrollment: 5,394. **Student Body:** 64% female, 36% male, 9% out-of-state, 1% international (60 countries represented). Asian 3%, African American 28%, Caucasian 59%, Hispanic 3%.
Retention and Graduation: 69% freshmen return for sophomore year. 4% freshmen graduate within 4 years. **Faculty:** Student/faculty ratio 18:1. 236 full-time faculty, 64% hold PhDs, 16% are members of minority groups, 51% are women.

ACADEMICS

Degrees: Associate, bachelor's, master's, post-master's certificate, terminal associate, transfer associate. **Classes:** Most classes have 20–29 students. Most lab/discussion sessions have 20–29 students. **Majors with Highest Enrollment:** Biology/biological sciences; elementary education and teaching; psychology. **Special Study Options:** Cooperative education program, cross-registration, distance learning, double major, dual enrollment, English as a Second Language (ESL), honors program, independent study, internships, study abroad, teacher certification program, Paralegal Certification. **Honors programs:** Augusta State University's Honors Program provides about 100 of our best students with special sections of classes in the core curriculum. Those classes are usually smaller, involve much closer interaction with the professor, and encourage more independent and collaborative work than non-honors sections of these courses. In their Junior and Senior years, Honors students take two interdisciplinary courses, prepare, write, and defend a thesis, and conclude their undergraduate program with a Capstone course. Special programs offered to physically disabled students include note-taking services, reader services, tape recorders, tutors. **Career services:** Alumni services. **Career services highlights include:** Our outreach to students via the classrooms and appointments for individualized help.

FACILITIES

Housing: Apartments for single students. 90% of campus accessible to physically disabled. **Special Academic Facilities/Equipment:** Performing Arts Theatre, Christenberry Field House, Forest Hill Golf Course. **Computers:** 95% of classrooms, 5% of dorms, 100% of libraries, 100% of dining areas, 100% of student union, have wireless network access. Students can register for classes online. Administrative functions (other than registration) can be performed online.

CAMPUS LIFE

Environment: City. **Activities:** Choral groups, concert band, drama/theater, jazz band, literary magazine, pep band, radio station, student government, student newspaper. **Organizations:** 60 registered organizations, 5 honor societies, 5 religious organizations. 3 fraternities, 3 sororities. **Athletics (Intercollegiate):** *Men:* Baseball, basketball, golf, tennis. *Women:* Basketball, golf, softball, tennis, volleyball. **On-Campus Highlights:** Allgood Hall, Christenberry Field House, University Hall, Jaguar Student Activities Center, Maxwell Performing Arts Theater.

ADMISSIONS

Freshman Academic Profile: Average high school GPA 2.93. 95% from public high schools. SAT Math middle 50% range 430–540. SAT Critical Reading middle 50% range 440–540. ACT middle 50% range 17–21. Minimum paper TOEFL 500. Minimum computer TOEFL 250. **Basis for Candidate Selection:** *Important factors considered include:* Academic GPA, rigor of secondary school record, standardized test scores. **Freshman Admission Requirements:** High school diploma is required and GED is accepted. *Academic units required:* 4 English, 4 mathematics, 3 science, 2 foreign language, 3 social studies. **Freshman Admission Statistics:** 2,418 applied, 57% admitted, 68%

enrolled. **Transfer Admission Requirements:** College transcript(s), minimum college GPA of 2.0 required. Lowest grade transferable D. **General Admission Information:** Application fee $20. Nonfall registration accepted. Admission may be deferred for a maximum of unlimited. Credit and/or placement offered for CEEB Advanced Placement tests.

COSTS AND FINANCIAL AID
Average book expense $1,000. **Required Forms and Deadlines:** FAFSA, state aid form. Financial aid filing deadline 4/1. **Notification of Awards:** Applicants will be notified of awards on or about 6/1. **Types of Aid:** *Need-based scholarships/grants:* Federal Pell, SEOG, state scholarships/grants, private scholarships, the school's own gift aid. *Loans:* Direct Subsidized Stafford, Direct Unsubsidized Stafford, Direct PLUS, Federal Perkins, state loans, college/university loans from institutional funds, Alternative loans. **Student Employment:** Highest amount earned per year from on-campus jobs $10,637. **Financial Aid Statistics:** 36% freshmen, 37% undergrads receive need-based scholarship or grant aid. 12% freshmen, 16% undergrads receive non-need-based scholarship or grant aid. 33% freshmen, 36% undergrads receive need-based self-help aid. 2% undergrads receive athletic scholarships. 36% undergrads borrow to pay for school. Average cumulative indebtedness $5,961. **Criteria for awarding institutional aid:** *Non-need-based:* Academics, alumni affiliation, art, athletics, job skills, leadership, minority status, music/drama, state/district residency.

AUGUSTANA COLLEGE (IL)

639 38th Street, Rock Island, IL 61201-2296
Phone: 309-794-7341 **Financial Aid Phone:** 309-794-7449
E-mail: admissions@augustana.edu **CEEB Code:** 1025
Fax: 309-794-7422 **Website:** www.augustana.edu **ACT Code:** 946

This private school, affiliated with the Lutheran Church, was founded in 1860. It has a 115-acre campus.

RATINGS
Admissions Selectivity Rating: 85   **Fire Safety Rating:** 64   **Green Rating:** 79

STUDENTS AND FACULTY
Enrollment: 2,457. **Student Body:** 57% female, 43% male, 11% out-of-state, 1% international (18 countries represented). Asian 2%, African American 2%, Caucasian 81%, Hispanic 3%.

Retention and Graduation: 82% freshmen return for sophomore year. 72% freshmen graduate within 4 years. 45% grads go on to further study within 1 year. 25% grads pursue arts and sciences degrees. 3% grads pursue law degrees. 10% grads pursue business degrees. 7% grads pursue medical degrees. **Faculty:** Student/faculty ratio 11:1. 174 full-time faculty, 89% hold PhDs, 18% are members of minority groups, 43% are women.

ACADEMICS
Degrees: Bachelor's. **Classes:** Most classes have 10–19 students. **Majors with Highest Enrollment:** Business/commerce; pre-medicine/pre-medical studies; psychology. **Special Study Options:** Accelerated program, double major, honors program, independent study, internships, liberal arts/career combination, student-designed major, study abroad, teacher certification program. **Honors programs:** Augustana has two tracks in first-year honors studies, Foundations and Logos. The Foundations program is a challenging interdisciplinary honors curriculum offering an intensive examination of the basic questions that have perplexed humans for centuries, and focuses on integrated learning and the development of critical thinking and writing skills. Logos is a challenging interdisciplinary honors curriculum with a special focus on how science has evolved across the centuries, how science has been used and viewed at particular historical moments, and how we live with the fruits of science today. **Combined degree programs:** Env. Mgt, Forestry, Occ. Therapy, Landscape Arch. Special programs offered to physically disabled students include reader services, tape recorders, tutors. **Career services:** Alumni network, alumni services, career/job search classes, career assessment, internships.

FACILITIES
Housing: Coed dorms, men's dorms, women's dorms, apartments for single students. 80% of campus accessible to physically disabled. **Special Academic Facilities/Equipment:** Educational technology building, art gallery, black culture house, Hispanic culture house, geology museum, on-campus preschool, immigration research center, scanning and transmission electron microscopes, nuclear magnetic resonance, atomic absorption, and diode array mass spectrophotometers, planetarium, observatory with celestron telescope, environmental field stations. **Computers:** 50% of classrooms, 30% of dorms, 100% of libraries, 100% of dining areas, 90% of student union, 25% of common outdoor areas have wireless network access. Students can register for classes online. Administrative functions (other than registration) can be performed online.

CAMPUS LIFE
Environment: City. **Activities:** Choral groups, concert band, dance, drama/theater, jazz band, literary magazine, music ensembles, musical theater, opera, pep band, radio station, student government, student newspaper, symphony orchestra, yearbook, campus ministries, international student organization, Model UN. **Organizations:** 128 registered organizations, 15 honor societies, 5 religious organizations. 7 fraternities, 6 sororities. **Athletics (Intercollegiate):** *Men:* Baseball, basketball, cross-country, diving, football, golf, soccer, swimming, tennis, track/field (outdoor), track/field (indoor), wrestling. *Women:* Basketball, cross-country, diving, golf, lacrosse, soccer, softball, swimming, tennis, track/field (outdoor), track/field (indoor), volleyball. **On-Campus Highlights:** Thomas Tredway Libarary, Pepsico Recreation Center, Java 101-Coffee shop, F.W. Olin Center for Educational Technology, College Center. **Environmental Initiatives:** Recycling Program; LEED certification for new construction, including geothermal heating for newest housing; Farm to Fork Program—food services practices with partnerships involving local agriculture producers, keeping small-scale and family businesses profitable.

ADMISSIONS
Freshman Academic Profile: 35% in top 10% of high school class, 64% in top 25% of high school class, 90% in top 50% of high school class. 85% from public high schools. ACT middle 50% range 23.4–28.7. Minimum paper TOEFL 550. Minimum computer TOEFL 213. **Basis for Candidate Selection:** *Very important factors considered include:* Class rank, academic GPA, rigor of secondary school record. *Important factors considered include:* Application essay, recommendation(s), standardized test scores, character/personal qualities, extracurricular activities, interview, level of applicant's interest, talent/ability. *Other factors considered include:* Alumni/ae relation, geographical residence, racial/ethnic status, religious affiliation/commitment, volunteer work, work experience. **Freshman Admission Requirements:** High school diploma is required and GED is accepted. *Academic units required:* 3 English, 3 mathematics, 3 science, (2 science labs), 1 foreign language, 1 social studies, 1 history. *Academic units recommended:* 4 English, 4 mathematics, 4 science, (2 science labs), 2 foreign language, 2 social studies, 1 history, 4 academic electives. **Freshman Admission Statistics:** 3,633 applied, 73% admitted, 23% enrolled. **Transfer Admission Requirements:** High school transcript, college transcript(s), statement of good standing from prior institution(s). Minimum college GPA of 2.0 required. Lowest grade transferable D. **General Admission Information:** Application fee $35. Nonfall registration accepted. Credit and/or placement offered for CEEB Advanced Placement tests.

COSTS AND FINANCIAL AID
Required Forms and Deadlines: FAFSA, institution's own financial aid form. Priority financial aid filing date 4/1. **Notification of Awards: Types of Aid:** *Need-based scholarships/grants:* Federal Pell, SEOG, state scholarships/grants, private scholarships, the school's own gift aid. *Loans:* Direct Subsidized Stafford, Direct Unsubsidized Stafford, Direct PLUS, Federal Perkins. **Student Employment:** Federal Work-Study Program available. Institutional employment available. Highest amount earned per year from on-campus jobs $900. Off-campus job opportunities are excellent. **Financial Aid Statistics:** 67% freshmen, 66% undergrads receive need-based scholarship or grant aid. 15% freshmen, 10% undergrads receive non-need-based scholarship or grant aid. 50% freshmen, 52% undergrads receive need-based self-help aid. 98% freshmen, 98% undergrads receive any aid. **Criteria for awarding institutional aid:** *Non-need-based:* Academics, alumni affiliation, art, leadership, music/drama, religious affiliation

AUGUSTANA COLLEGE (SD)

2001 South Summit Avenue, Sioux Falls, SD 57197
Phone: 605-274-5516 **Financial Aid Phone:** 605-274-5216
E-mail: admissions@augie.edu **CEEB Code:** 6015
Fax: 605-274-5518 **Website:** www.augie.edu **ACT Code:** 3902

This private school, affiliated with the Lutheran Church, was founded in 1860. It has a 100-acre campus.

RATINGS
Admissions Selectivity Rating: 84   **Fire Safety Rating:** 71   **Green Rating:** 80

STUDENTS AND FACULTY
Enrollment: 1,771. **Student Body:** 63% female, 37% male, 49% out-of-state, 2% international (14 countries represented). Asian 1%, African American 1%, Caucasian 94%.

Retention and Graduation: 82% freshmen return for sophomore year. 51% freshmen graduate within 4 years. 22% grads go on to further study within 1 year. 9% grads pursue arts and sciences degrees. 2% grads pursue law degrees. 1% grads pursue business degrees. 9% grads pursue medical degrees. **Faculty:**

Student/faculty ratio 11.9:1. 125 full-time faculty, 79% hold PhDs, 2% are members of minority groups, 45% are women.

ACADEMICS

Degrees: Bachelor's, master's. **Classes:** Most classes have 10–19 students. Most lab/discussion sessions have fewer than 10 students. **Majors with Highest Enrollment:** Biology/biological sciences; business/commerce; nursing/registered nurse (RN, ASN, BSN, MSN). **Special Study Options:** Cooperative education program, cross-registration, double major, dual enrollment, exchange student program (domestic), external degree program, honors program, independent study, internships, liberal arts/career combination, study abroad, teacher certification program, Metro-Urban Studies through HECUA. January Abroad program through UMAIE. Washington, DC, Semesters. Study Austrailia through EAN. Dual Degree Program in Engineering. Service-Learning Spring Breaks trips; Faculty-led Spring Breaks Abroad; Honors Courses in Western Civilization, Chemistry, and Religion. Civitas honors program for students with 27 ACT and 3.5 GPA. **Honors programs:** Our campus-wide, interdisciplinary Honors program is called Civitas (citizenship). Specific majors also offer departmental honors programs for students willing to accept academic challenges that go well beyond those required for graduation. Special programs offered to physically disabled students include note-taking services, reader services, tape recorders, tutors. **Career services:** Alumni network, alumni services, career/job search classes, career assessment, internships, regional alumni. Career services highlights include: The city of Sioux Falls (151,000), along with Augustana alumni and connections, provides excellent opportunities for internships and research opportunities. It is the best laboratory for our students to apply their knowledge.

FACILITIES

Housing: Coed dorms, special housing for disabled students, apartments for married students, apartments for single students, theme housing, housing is available for students with children. 80% of campus accessible to physically disabled. **Special Academic Facilities/Equipment:** Center for Western Studies, Archeology Lab, Eide/Dalrymple Gallery, Center for Liturgical Art. **Computers:** 25% of classrooms, 25% of dorms, 100% of libraries, 100% of dining areas, 75% of student union, have wireless network access. Students can register for classes online. Administrative functions (other than registration) can be performed online.

CAMPUS LIFE

Environment: City. **Activities:** Choral groups, concert band, dance, drama/theater, jazz band, literary magazine, music ensembles, musical theater, opera, pep band, student government, student newspaper, student-run film society, symphony orchestra, yearbook, campus ministries, international student organization. **Organizations:** 92 registered organizations, 13 honor societies, 9 religious organizations. **Athletics (Intercollegiate):** *Men:* Baseball, basketball, cross-country, football, golf, tennis, track/field (outdoor), track/field (indoor), wrestling. *Women:* Basketball, cheerleading, cross-country, golf, soccer, softball, tennis, track/field (outdoor), track/field (indoor), volleyball. **On-Campus Highlights:** Morrison Commons, The Huddle, Mikkelson Library, Elmen Center, Center for Visual Arts, The Madsen Center, home to our social science programs, is also a popular place for students to gather and study, or use the computer lab. With newly renovated and refurbished lounges, our resident halls also serve as gathering areas for students to converse, watch TV, play ping pong or pool. **Environmental Initiatives:** Examples include: Additional recycle bins placed in all campus buildings; Sodexho Dining Services has decreased food and beverage waste by 50% through redesigning of trays and cups. They have also cut back on paper waste by installing high-definition televisions to post announcements and by substituting post-recycled cups and napkins for students on-the-go. Green bike program offers students the chance to use bikes for free transportation on and around campus. Student group, Augie Green, has started an Augustana garden and a program called "trash talkers."

ADMISSIONS

Freshman Academic Profile: Average high school GPA 3.6. 29% in top 10% of high school class, 61% in top 25% of high school class, 89% in top 50% of high school class. 91% from public high schools. ACT middle 50% range 22–28. Minimum paper TOEFL 550. Minimum computer TOEFL 213. Minimum web-based TOEFL 79. **Basis for Candidate Selection:** *Very important factors considered include:* Academic GPA, standardized test scores. *Important factors considered include:* Class rank, application essay, recommendation(s), rigor of secondary school record, extracurricular activities. *Other factors considered include:* interview, volunteer work, work experience. **Freshman Admission Requirements:** High school diploma is required and GED is accepted. *Academic units recommended:* 4 English, 3 mathematics, 2 science, (2 science labs), 2 foreign language, 3 social studies, 2 history, 1 visual/performing arts, 1 computer science. **Freshman Admission Statistics:** 1,284 applied, 81% admitted, 42% enrolled. **Transfer Admission Requirements:** High school transcript, college transcript(s), essay or personal statement, minimum college GPA of 2.2 required. Lowest grade transferable C–. **General Admission Information:** Notification on a rolling basis, beginning on or about 10/1. Nonfall

registration not accepted. Admission may be deferred for a maximum of 1 year. Credit offered for CEEB Advanced Placement tests.

COSTS AND FINANCIAL AID

Annual tuition $23,276. Room and board $6,188. Required fees $274. Average book expense $1,000. **Required Forms and Deadlines:** FAFSA. Priority financial aid filing date 3/1. **Notification of Awards:** Applicants will be notified of awards on a rolling basis beginning 4/1. **Types of Aid:** *Need-based scholarships/grants:* Federal Pell, SEOG, state scholarships/grants, private scholarships, the school's own gift aid. *Loans:* Direct Subsidized Stafford, Direct Unsubsidized Stafford, Direct PLUS, Federal Perkins, Federal Nursing, college/university loans from institutional funds. **Student Employment:** Federal Work-Study Program available. Institutional employment available. Highest amount earned per year from on-campus jobs $1,794. Off-campus job opportunities are excellent. **Financial Aid Statistics:** 74% freshmen, 69% undergrads receive need-based scholarship or grant aid. 73% freshmen, 68% undergrads receive non-need-based scholarship or grant aid. 57% freshmen, 56% undergrads receive need-based self-help aid. 10% freshmen, 9% undergrads receive athletic scholarships. 100% freshmen, 100% undergrads receive any aid. 76% undergrads borrow to pay for school. Average cumulative indebtedness $29,531. **Criteria for awarding institutional aid:** *Non-need-based:* Academics, alumni affiliation, art, athletics, leadership, minority status, music/drama, religious affiliation, state/district residency.

AURORA UNIVERSITY

347 South Gladstone Ave, Aurora, IL 60506
Phone: 630-844-5533 **Financial Aid Phone:** 630-844-6190
E-mail: admission@aurora.edu **CEEB Code:** 1027
Fax: 630-844-5535 **Website:** www.aurora.edu **ACT Code:** 950

This private school was founded in 1893. It has a 30-acre campus.

RATINGS

Admissions Selectivity Rating: 74   **Fire Safety Rating:** 89   **Green Rating:** 64

STUDENTS AND FACULTY

Enrollment: 2,181. **Student Body:** 68% female, 32% male, 7% out-of-state, international (2 countries represented). Asian 3%, African American 10%, Caucasian 73%, Hispanic 12%.
Retention and Graduation: 73% freshmen return for sophomore year. 33% freshmen graduate within 4 years. **Faculty:** Student/faculty ratio 14:1. 112 full-time faculty, 81% hold PhDs, 7% are members of minority groups, 52% are women.

ACADEMICS

Degrees: Bachelor's, master's, post-bachelor's certificate, post-master's certificate. **Classes:** Most classes have 10–19 students. Most lab/discussion sessions have 10–19 students. **Majors with Highest Enrollment:** Elementary education and teaching; nursing/registered nurse (RN, ASN, BSN, MSN); social work. **Special Study Options:** Accelerated program, cross-registration, double major, honors program, independent study, internships, liberal arts/career combination, student-designed major, study abroad, teacher certification program. **Honors programs:** Honors Program including honors seminars, honors section of some general education courses and a senior honors project. Special programs offered to physically disabled students include note-taking services, reader services, tape recorders, tutors. **Career services:** Alumni network, alumni services, career/job search classes, career assessment, internships.

FACILITIES

Housing: Coed dorms. 95% of campus accessible to physically disabled. **Special Academic Facilities/Equipment:** Schingoethe Center for Native American Culture, Downstairs Dunham Gallery Center For Faith And Action, Perry Theatre in the Aurora Foundation Center for Community Education. **Computers:** 100% of classrooms, 80% of dorms, 100% of libraries, 100% of dining areas, 100% of student union, 90% of common outdoor areas have wireless network access. Administrative functions (other than registration) can be performed online.

CAMPUS LIFE

Environment: City. **Activities:** Choral groups, drama/theater, literary magazine, pep band, radio station, student government, student newspaper, campus ministries, Model UN. **Organizations:** 49 registered organizations, 2 honor societies, 1 religious organizations. 1 fraternities, 4 sororities. **Athletics (Intercollegiate):** *Men:* Baseball, basketball, cross-country, football, golf, soccer, tennis, track/field (outdoor), track/field (indoor). *Women:* Basketball, cross-country, golf, soccer, softball, tennis, track/field (outdoor), track/field (indoor), volleyball. **On-Campus Highlights:** The Spartan Spot, Fitness Center, The Learning

Center, Computer Labs, Vago Stadium. **Environmental Initiatives:** Campus-wide recycling. Use of green chemicals for cleaning. Energy conservation audit for campus-wide lighting.

ADMISSIONS
Freshman Academic Profile: Average high school GPA 3.37. 14% in top 10% of high school class, 41% in top 25% of high school class, 80% in top 50% of high school class. 92% from public high schools. SAT Math middle 50% range 440–540. SAT Critical Reading middle 50% range 440–570. ACT middle 50% range 20–24. Minimum paper TOEFL 550. Minimum computer TOEFL 213. Minimum web-based TOEFL 79. **Basis for Candidate Selection:** *Very important factors considered include:* Class rank, academic GPA, rigor of secondary school record, standardized test scores, interview. *Important factors considered include:* Alumni/ae relation, character/personal qualities, extracurricular activities. *Other factors considered include:* Application essay, recommendation(s), first generation, level of applicant's interest, talent/ability, volunteer work, work experience. **Freshman Admission Requirements:** High school diploma is required and GED is accepted. *Academic units required:* 4 English, 3 mathematics, 3 science, 3 social studies, 3 academic electives. **Freshman Admission Statistics:** 1,443 applied, 79% admitted, 33% enrolled. **Transfer Admission Requirements:** college transcript(s), statement of good standing from prior institution(s). Minimum college GPA of 2.0 required. Lowest grade transferable C. **General Admission Information:** Application fee $25. Regular application deadline 5/1. Notification on a rolling basis, beginning on or about 9/1. Nonfall registration accepted. Admission may be deferred for a maximum of two years. Credit and/or placement offered for CEEB Advanced Placement tests.

COSTS AND FINANCIAL AID
Annual tuition $18,000. Room and board $8,270. Required fees $100. Average book expense $1,000. **Required Forms and Deadlines:** FAFSA. Priority financial aid filing date 4/15. **Notification of Awards:** Applicants will be notified of awards on a rolling basis beginning 3/1. **Types of Aid:** *Need-based scholarships/grants:* Federal Pell, SEOG, state scholarships/grants, private scholarships, the school's own gift aid. *Loans:* Direct Subsidized Stafford, Direct Unsubsidized Stafford, Direct PLUS, Federal Perkins, college/university loans from institutional funds. **Student Employment:** Federal Work-Study Program available. Institutional employment available. Highest amount earned per year from on-campus jobs $4,960. Off-campus job opportunities are excellent. **Financial Aid Statistics:** 55% freshmen, 53% undergrads receive need-based scholarship or grant aid. 79% freshmen, 71% undergrads receive non-need-based scholarship or grant aid. 63% freshmen, 61% undergrads receive need-based self-help aid. 99% freshmen, 98% undergrads receive any aid. 79% undergrads borrow to pay for school. Average cumulative indebtedness $20,092. **Criteria for awarding institutional aid:** *Non-need-based:* Academics, alumni affiliation, art, music/drama, religious affiliation, state/district residency.

See page 1020.

AUSTIN COLLEGE

900 North Grand Ave, Suite 6N, Sherman, TX 75090-4400
Phone: 903-813-3000 **Financial Aid Phone:** 903-813-2900
E-mail: admission@austincollege.edu **CEEB Code:** 6016
Fax: 903-813-3198 **Website:** www.austincollege.edu **ACT Code:** 4058

This private school, affiliated with the Presbyterian Church, was founded in 1849. It has a 70-acre campus.

RATINGS
Admissions Selectivity Rating: 86   **Fire Safety Rating:** 68   **Green Rating:** 60*

STUDENTS AND FACULTY
Enrollment: 1,328. **Student Body:** 54% female, 46% male, 7% out-of-state, 2% international (13 countries represented). Asian 15%, African American 3%, Caucasian 66%, Hispanic 10%, Native American 1%.
Retention and Graduation: 86% freshmen return for sophomore year. 67% freshmen graduate within 4 years. 44% grads go on to further study within 1 year. 22% grads pursue arts and sciences degrees. 2.99% grads pursue law degrees. 0.6% grads pursue business degrees. 8.66% grads pursue medical degrees. **Faculty:** Student/faculty ratio 13.57:1. 91 full-time faculty, 93% hold PhDs, 8% are members of minority groups, 31% are women.

ACADEMICS
Degrees: Bachelor's, master's. **Classes:** Most classes have 10–19 students. Most lab/discussion sessions have fewer than 10 students. **Majors with Highest Enrollment:** Biology/biological sciences; business/commerce; psychology. **Special Study Options:** Double major, exchange student program (domestic), honors program, independent study, internships, student-designed major, study abroad, teacher certification program, Phi Beta Kappa. **Combined degree programs:** 3-2 Program in Engineeri with UT, Dal and Wash Univ. Special programs offered to physically disabled students include tutors. **Career services:** Alumni network, alumni services, career/job search classes, career assessment, internships.

FACILITIES
Housing: Coed dorms, special housing for disabled students, men's dorms, women's dorms, apartments for single students, Jordan Family Language House. 99% of campus accessible to physically disabled. **Special Academic Facilities/Equipment:** Tissue culture facility, high-performance numerics and graphics computing facility. **Computers:** 30% of classrooms, 100% of dorms, 100% of libraries, 100% of dining areas, 100% of student union, 30% of common outdoor areas have wireless network access. Students can register for classes online. Administrative functions (other than registration) can be performed online.

CAMPUS LIFE
Environment: Town. **Activities:** Choral groups, dance, drama/theater, jazz band, literary magazine, music ensembles, musical theater, pep band, student government, student newspaper, symphony orchestra, yearbook, campus ministries, international student organization, Model UN. **Organizations:** 52 registered organizations, 15 honor societies, 6 religious organizations. 6 fraternities, 6 sororities. **Athletics (Intercollegiate):** *Men:* Baseball, basketball, football, soccer, swimming, tennis. *Women:* Basketball, soccer, softball, swimming, tennis, volleyball. **On-Campus Highlights:** Wright Campus Center, Jordan Family Language House, Verde Dickey Fitness Pavilion, Abell Library, Residence hall facilities, Roo Suites, a suite-style residence facility for upperclass students is the favored residential experience.

ADMISSIONS
Freshman Academic Profile: Average high school GPA 3.56. 41% in top 10% of high school class, 70% in top 25% of high school class, 92% in top 50% of high school class. 85.7% from public high schools. SAT Math middle 50% range 570–670. SAT Critical Reading middle 50% range 560–680. SAT Writing middle 50% range 540–650. ACT middle 50% range 24–28. Minimum paper TOEFL 550. Minimum computer TOEFL 213. **Basis for Candidate Selection:** *Very important factors considered include:* Academic GPA, rigor of secondary school record. *Important factors considered include:* Class rank, application essay, recommendation(s), standardized test scores, character/personal qualities, extracurricular activities, talent/ability. *Other factors considered include:* Alumni/ae relation, first generation, geographical residence, interview, racial/ethnic status, religious affiliation/commitment, state residency, volunteer work, work experience. **Freshman Admission Requirements:** High school diploma is required and GED is accepted. *Academic units required:* 4 English, 3 mathematics, 3 science, (2 science labs), 2 foreign language, 2 social studies, 1 visual/performing arts, 1 academic electives. *Academic units recommended:* 4 English, 4 mathematics, 4 science, (3 science labs), 3 foreign language, 3 social studies, 2 visual/performing arts. **Freshman Admission Statistics:** 1,750 applied, 80% admitted, 30% enrolled. **Transfer Admission Requirements:** College transcript(s), essay or personal statement, statement of good standing from prior institution(s). Minimum college GPA of 3.0 required. Lowest grade transferable C. **General Admission Information:** Application fee $35. Regular application deadline 5/1. Notification on a rolling basis, beginning on or about 12/15. Nonfall registration accepted. Admission may be deferred for a maximum of 1 year. Credit and/or placement offered for CEEB Advanced Placement tests.

COSTS AND FINANCIAL AID
Annual tuition $29,075. Room and board $9,549. Required fees $160. Average book expense $1,000. **Required Forms and Deadlines:** FAFSA. Priority financial aid filing date 4/1. **Notification of Awards:** Applicants will be notified of awards on a rolling basis beginning 3/1. **Types of Aid:** *Need-based scholarships/grants:* Federal Pell, SEOG, state scholarships/grants, private scholarships, the school's own gift aid. *Loans:* Direct Subsidized Stafford, Direct Unsubsidized Stafford, Direct PLUS, Federal Perkins, state loans, college/university loans from institutional funds, alternative loans through various sources. **Student Employment:** Federal Work-Study Program available. Institutional employment available. Highest amount earned per year from on-campus jobs $1,164. Off-campus job opportunities are good. **Financial Aid Statistics:** 68% freshmen, 61% undergrads receive need-based scholarship or grant aid. 41% freshmen, 30% undergrads receive non-need-based scholarship or grant aid. 49% freshmen, 48% undergrads receive need-based self-help aid. 99% freshmen, 99% undergrads receive any aid. **Criteria for awarding institutional aid:** *Non-need-based:* Academics, alumni affiliation, art, leadership, music/drama, religious affiliation, state/district residency.

AUSTIN PEAY STATE UNIVERSITY

P.O. Box 4548, Clarksville, TN 37044
Phone: 931-221-7661 **Financial Aid Phone:**
E-mail: admissions@apsu.edu **CEEB Code:** 1028
Fax: 931-221-6168 **Website:** www.apsu.edu **ACT Code:** 3944

This public school was founded in 1927. It has a 210-acre campus.

RATINGS
Admissions Selectivity Rating: 76   **Fire Safety Rating:** 60*   **Green Rating:** 60*

STUDENTS AND FACULTY
Enrollment: 9,084. **Student Body:** 61% female, 39% male, 10% out-of-state, (13 countries represented).
Retention and Graduation: 68% freshmen return for sophomore year. 13% freshmen graduate within 4 years. **Faculty:** Student/faculty ratio 20:1. 310 full-time faculty, 10% are members of minority groups, 45% are women.

ACADEMICS
Degrees: Associate, bachelor's, certificate, master's, post-bachelor's certificate, post-master's certificate, terminal associate, transfer associate. **Classes:** Most classes have 20–29 students. Most lab/discussion sessions have 20–29 students. **Special Study Options:** Accelerated program, cooperative education program, distance learning, double major, dual enrollment, English as a Second Language (ESL), honors program, independent study, internships, study abroad, teacher certification program, Servicemembers Opportunity College (SOC) for associate and bachelor's degrees. Special programs offered to physically disabled students include note-taking services, reader services, tutors. **Career services:** Career/job search classes, career assessment, internships.

FACILITIES
Housing: Coed dorms, special housing for disabled students, men's dorms, women's dorms, fraternity/sorority housing, apartments for married students, apartments for single students, for faculty/staff. 100% of campus accessible to physically disabled. **Special Academic Facilities/Equipment:** Art museum, biology museum, language lab, demonstration farm, 21st century classroom.

CAMPUS LIFE
Environment: Village. **Activities:** Choral groups, concert band, dance, drama/theater, jazz band, literary magazine, marching band, music ensembles, musical theater, opera, pep band, radio station, student government, student newspaper, student-run film society, symphony orchestra, television station, yearbook, campus ministries, international student organization. **Organizations:** 50 registered organizations, 13 honor societies, 10 religious organizations. 8 fraternities, 6 sororities. **Athletics (Intercollegiate):** *Men:* Baseball, basketball, cheerleading, cross-country, football, golf, tennis *Women:* Basketball, cheerleading, cross-country, golf, riflery, soccer, softball, tennis, track/field (outdoor), volleyball. **On-Campus Highlights:** University Center, Sundquist Science Complex, Hand Village, Dunn Center.

ADMISSIONS
Freshman Academic Profile: Average high school GPA 3.11. 14% in top 10% of high school class, 39% in top 25% of high school class, 75% in top 50% of high school class. 95% from public high schools. SAT Math middle 50% range 450–538. SAT Critical Reading middle 50% range 443–550. ACT middle 50% range 19–23. Minimum paper TOEFL 500. Minimum computer TOEFL 173. **Basis for Candidate Selection:** *Very important factors considered include:* Academic GPA, standardized test scores. *Other factors considered include:* rigor of secondary school record. **Freshman Admission Requirements:** High school diploma is required and GED is accepted. *Academic units required:* 4 English, 3 mathematics, 2 science, (1 science labs), 2 foreign language, 1 social studies, 1 history, 1 Visual/Performing Arts **Freshman Admission Statistics:** 3,111 applied, 90% admitted, 59% enrolled. **Transfer Admission Requirements:** College transcript(s), Lowest grade transferable D. **General Admission Information:** Application fee $15. Regular application deadline 7/29. Nonfall registration accepted. Admission may be deferred for a maximum of 1 year. Credit offered for CEEB Advanced Placement tests.

COSTS AND FINANCIAL AID
Annual in-state tuition $4,584. Annual out-of-state tuition $16,512. Room and board $6,120. Required fees $1,224. Average book expense $1,550. **Required Forms and Deadlines:** FAFSA. Priority financial aid filing date 4/1. **Notification of Awards:** Applicants will be notified of awards on a rolling basis beginning 5/1. **Types of Aid:** *Need-based scholarships/grants:* Federal Pell, SEOG, state scholarships/grants, private scholarships, the school's own gift aid, Corporate. *Loans:* Direct Subsidized Stafford, Direct Unsubsidized Stafford, Direct PLUS, Federal Perkins. **Student Employment:** Federal Work-Study Program available. Institutional employment available. Off-campus job opportunities are good. **Financial Aid Statistics:** 37% freshmen, 41% undergrads

receive need-based scholarship or grant aid. 53% freshmen, 31% undergrads receive non-need-based scholarship or grant aid. 45% freshmen, 52% undergrads receive need-based self-help aid. 3% freshmen, 2% undergrads receive athletic scholarships. 55.6% undergrads borrow to pay for school. Average cumulative indebtedness $20,158. **Criteria for awarding institutional aid:** *Non-need-based:* Academics, alumni affiliation, art, athletics, leadership, music/drama, state/district residency.

AVERETT UNIVERSITY

420 West Main Street, Danville, VA 24541
Phone: 434-791-4996 **Financial Aid Phone:** 434-791-5890
E-mail: admit@averett.edu **CEEB Code:** 5017
Fax: 434-797-2784 **Website:** www.averett.edu **ACT Code:** 4338

This private school was founded in 1859. It has a 19-acre campus.

RATINGS
Admissions Selectivity Rating: 72   **Fire Safety Rating:** 71   **Green Rating:** 76

STUDENTS AND FACULTY
Enrollment: 763. **Student Body:** 47% female, 53% male, 35% out-of-state, 4% international (15 countries represented). Asian 1%, African American 33%, Caucasian 61%, Hispanic 3%, Native American 1%.
Retention and Graduation: 50% freshmen return for sophomore year. 34% freshmen graduate within 4 years. **Faculty:** Student/faculty ratio 12:1. 52 full-time faculty, 71% hold PhDs, 6% are members of minority groups, 44% are women.

ACADEMICS
Degrees: Associate, bachelor's, master's, transfer associate. **Classes:** Most classes have 10–19 students. Most lab/discussion sessions have 10–19 students. **Majors with Highest Enrollment:** Management science; sport and fitness administration/management; teacher education, multiple levels. **Special Study Options:** Accelerated program, cooperative education program, cross-registration, distance learning, double major, dual enrollment, exchange student program (domestic), honors program, independent study, internships, student-designed major, study abroad, teacher certification program, Also offered: Inter-disciplinary studies and Leadership studies. Undergraduates may take grad level classes. Some online courses available. **Honors programs:** Averett's Honors Program gives students the opportunity to go a step beyond regular classroom study. Honors students explore, in-depth, selected areas of academics. Participation in the Honors Program demonstrates a commitment to scholarship and will give students an edge in graduate study or in the job market. To earn the honors distinction, approximately 20% of all coursework completed must carry honors credit. The program culminates with a senior honors project. Honors Program students may also participate in the Honors Association and attend conferences, social activities and cultural performances. Special programs offered to physically disabled students include note-taking services, reader services, tape recorders, tutors. **Career services:** Alumni network, alumni services, career/job search classes, career assessment, internships, regional alumni.

FACILITIES
Housing: Coed dorms, men's dorms, women's dorms, apartments for single students. 73% of campus accessible to physically disabled. **Special Academic Facilities/Equipment:** Averett's Flight Center located 4 miles from the main campus at Danville Regional Airport has two runways (one with ILS approach), automated weather system, and UNICOM service. Averett's facility houses aircraft, areas for ground instruction, simulator rooms, technology center. Averett's 100–acre Equestrian Center is a 15-minute drive from the main campus. It houses an indoor ring, 40 stalls with removable partitions, 3 tack rooms, wash room for horses and equipment, breeding area, offices, and a laboratory. The outdoor facilities include a round pen, riding ring, jumping area, pastures, and cross-country trails. **Computers:** 100% of libraries, 100% of dining areas, 100% of student union, have wireless network access. Students can register for classes online. Administrative functions (other than registration) can be performed online.

CAMPUS LIFE
Environment: Town. **Activities:** Choral groups, drama/theater, literary magazine, musical theater, student government, student newspaper, international student organization. **Organizations:** 30 registered organizations, 4 honor societies, 4 religious organizations. 1 fraternities, 1 sorority. **Athletics (Intercollegiate):** *Men:* Baseball, basketball, cheerleading, cross-country, equestrian sports, football, golf, soccer, tennis. *Women:* Basketball, cheerleading, cross-country, equestrian sports, soccer, softball, tennis, volleyball. **On-Campus Highlights:** Student Center, Grant Athletic Center (North Campus), Equestrian Center, Airport Facilities, Jut's Cafe.

ADMISSIONS

Freshman Academic Profile: Average high school GPA 3.03. 5% in top 10% of high school class, 29% in top 25% of high school class, 62% in top 50% of high school class. 95% from public high schools. SAT Math middle 50% range 420–525. SAT Critical Reading middle 50% range 410–510. ACT middle 50% range 17–21. Minimum paper TOEFL 500. Minimum computer TOEFL 173. Minimum web-based TOEFL 61. **Basis for Candidate Selection:** *Very important factors considered include:* Academic GPA, rigor of secondary school record. *Important factors considered include:* Class rank, standardized test scores. *Other factors considered include:* Application essay, recommendation(s), alumni/ae relation, character/personal qualities, extracurricular activities, interview, level of applicant's interest, talent/ability, volunteer work, work experience. **Freshman Admission Requirements:** High school diploma is required and GED is accepted. *Academic units required:* 4 English, 3 mathematics, 3 science, (3 science labs), 3 social studies, 3 academic electives, 0 *Academic units recommended:* 4 English, 4 mathematics, 4 science, (3 science labs), 3 foreign language, 4 social studies, 3 history, 1 visual/performing arts, 2 computer science. **Freshman Admission Statistics:** 1,159 applied, 91% admitted, 21% enrolled. **Transfer Admission Requirements:** College transcript(s), statement of good standing from prior institution(s). Minimum college GPA of 2.0 required. Lowest grade transferable C. **General Admission Information:** Regular application deadline 7/15. Nonfall registration accepted. Admission may be deferred for a maximum of 1 year. Credit and/or placement offered for CEEB Advanced Placement tests.

COSTS AND FINANCIAL AID

Annual tuition $21,112. Required fees $1,000. **Required Forms and Deadlines:** FAFSA, state aid form. Priority financial aid filing date 4/1. **Notification of Awards:** Applicants will be notified of awards on a rolling basis beginning 2/15. **Types of Aid:** *Need-based scholarships/grants:* Federal Pell, SEOG, state scholarships/grants, private scholarships, the school's own gift aid. *Loans:* Direct Subsidized Stafford, Direct Unsubsidized Stafford, Direct PLUS, Federal Perkins, state loans, college/university loans from institutional funds, Private. **Student Employment:** Federal Work-Study Program available. Institutional employment available. Highest amount earned per year from on-campus jobs $2,000. Off-campus job opportunities are fair. **Financial Aid Statistics:** 79% freshmen, 79% undergrads receive need-based scholarship or grant aid. 8% freshmen, 11% undergrads receive non-need-based scholarship or grant aid. 68% freshmen, 67% undergrads receive need-based self-help aid. 67% undergrads borrow to pay for school. Average cumulative indebtedness $30,943. **Criteria for awarding institutional aid:** *Non-need-based:* Academics, alumni affiliation, art, leadership, minority status, music/drama, state/district residency.

AVILA UNIVERSITY

11901 Wornall Road, Kansas City, MO 64145-1698
Phone: 816-942-8400 **Financial Aid Phone:**
E-mail: admissions@mail.avila.edu **CEEB Code:** 6109
Fax: 816-942-3362 **Website:** www.avila.edu **ACT Code:** 2278

This private school, affiliated with the Roman Catholic Church, was founded in 1916. It has a 48-acre campus.

RATINGS

Admissions Selectivity Rating: 81   Fire Safety Rating: 60*   Green Rating: 60*

STUDENTS AND FACULTY

Enrollment: 1,096. **Student Body:** 64% female, 36% male, 34% out-of-state, 3% international. Asian 1%, African American 18%, Caucasian 70%, Hispanic 4%, Native American 1%.
Retention and Graduation: 69% freshmen return for sophomore year. 30% freshmen graduate within 4 years. 40% grads go on to further study within 1 year. 20% grads pursue arts and sciences degrees. 2% grads pursue law degrees. 15% grads pursue business degrees. 3% grads pursue medical degrees. **Faculty:** Student/faculty ratio 12:1. 63 full-time faculty, 71% hold PhDs, 3% are members of minority groups, 63% are women.

ACADEMICS

Degrees: Bachelor's, certificate, master's. **Classes:** Most classes have fewer than 10 students. **Majors with Highest Enrollment:** Business/commerce; nursing, other; psychology. **Special Study Options:** Accelerated program, double major, dual enrollment, English as a Second Language (ESL), independent study, internships, study abroad, teacher certification program.

FACILITIES

Housing: Coed dorms.

CAMPUS LIFE

Environment: Metropolis. **Activities:** Choral groups, drama/theater, literary magazine, student government, student newspaper, television station. **Organizations:** 12 religious organizations. **Athletics (Intercollegiate):** *Men:* Baseball, basketball, football, soccer, volleyball. *Women:* Basketball, cheerleading, golf, soccer, softball, volleyball.

ADMISSIONS

Freshman Academic Profile: Average high school GPA 3.2. 17% in top 10% of high school class, 39% in top 25% of high school class, 74% in top 50% of high school class. 92% from public high schools. ACT middle 50% range 18–25. Minimum paper TOEFL 550. Minimum computer TOEFL 213. **Basis for Candidate Selection:** *Very important factors considered include:* rigor of secondary school record, standardized test scores. *Other factors considered include:* Class rank, application essay, recommendation(s), character/personal qualities, extracurricular activities, interview, talent/ability. **Freshman Admission Requirements:** High school diploma is required and GED is accepted. *Academic units recommended:* 4 English, 3 mathematics, 2 science, (1 science labs), 2 foreign language, 3 social studies, 2 history. **Freshman Admission Statistics:** 936 applied, 42% admitted, 38% enrolled. **Transfer Admission Requirements:** college transcript(s), minimum college GPA of 2.0 required. Lowest grade transferable C. **General Admission Information:** Notification on a rolling basis, beginning on or about 9/4. Nonfall registration accepted. Admission may be deferred for a maximum of 1 year. Credit and/or placement offered for CEEB Advanced Placement tests.

COSTS AND FINANCIAL AID

Annual tuition $14,700. Room and board $5,300. Required fees $187. Average book expense $800. **Required Forms and Deadlines:** FAFSA, institution's own financial aid form. Priority financial aid filing date 4/1. **Notification of Awards:** Applicants will be notified of awards on a rolling basis beginning 2/15. **Types of Aid:** *Need-based scholarships/grants:* Federal Pell, SEOG, state scholarships/grants *Loans:* Direct Subsidized Stafford, Direct Unsubsidized Stafford, Direct PLUS, Federal Perkins. **Student Employment:** Federal Work-Study Program available. Institutional employment available. Highest amount earned per year from on-campus jobs $1,500. **Financial Aid Statistics:** 30% freshmen, 44% undergrads receive need-based scholarship or grant aid. 46% freshmen, 50% undergrads receive non-need-based scholarship or grant aid. 46% freshmen, 57% undergrads receive need-based self-help aid. 100% freshmen, 70% undergrads receive athletic scholarships. 75% undergrads borrow to pay for school. Average cumulative indebtedness $20,000. **Criteria for awarding institutional aid:** *Non-need-based:* Academics, alumni affiliation, art, athletics, music/drama, religious affiliation, state/district residency.

AZUSA PACIFIC UNIVERSITY

901 East Alosta Avenue, Azusa, CA 91702-7000
Phone: 626-812-3016 **Financial Aid Phone:** 626-812-3009
E-mail: admissions@apu.edu **CEEB Code:** 4596
Fax: 626-812-3096 **Website:** www.apu.edu

This private school, affiliated with the Christian (Nondenominational) Church, was founded in 1899. It has a 103-acre campus.

RATINGS

Admissions Selectivity Rating: 90   Fire Safety Rating: 60*   Green Rating: 62

STUDENTS AND FACULTY

Enrollment: 4,874. **Student Body:** 64% female, 36% male, 19% out-of-state, 2% international (41 countries represented). Asian 8%, African American 5%, Caucasian 60%, Hispanic 15%, Native American 1%.
Retention and Graduation: 82% freshmen return for sophomore year. 55% freshmen graduate within 4 years. **Faculty:** Student/faculty ratio 12:1. 339 full-time faculty, 74% hold PhDs, 22% are members of minority groups, 47% are women.

ACADEMICS

Degrees: Bachelor's, master's. **Classes:** Most classes have 10–19 students. Most lab/discussion sessions have 10–19 students. **Majors with Highest Enrollment:** Business, management, marketing, and related support services, other; nursing, other; psychology. **Special Study Options:** Accelerated program, cooperative education program, distance learning, double major, English as a Second Language (ESL), exchange student program (domestic), honors program, independent study, internships, study abroad, teacher certification program. **Combined degree programs:** BA/MA. **Career services:** Career/job search classes, career assessment, internships.

FACILITIES

Housing: Coed dorms, men's dorms, women's dorms, apartments for single students 100% of campus accessible to physically disabled. **Special Academic Facilities/Equipment:** Electron microscope. **Computers:** 100% of classrooms, 100% of dorms, 100% of libraries, 100% of dining areas, 100% of student union, 100% of common outdoor areas have wireless network access. Students can register for classes online. Administrative functions (other than registration) can be performed online.

CAMPUS LIFE

Environment: Town. **Activities:** Choral groups, concert band, drama/theater, jazz band, marching band, music ensembles, musical theater, opera, pep band, radio station, student government, student newspaper, symphony orchestra, television station, yearbook. **Organizations:** 30 registered organizations, 7 honor societies. **Athletics (Intercollegiate):** *Men:* Baseball, basketball, cross-country, football, soccer, tennis, track/field (outdoor), volleyball. *Women:* Basketball, cheerleading, cross-country, diving, soccer, softball, swimming, tennis, track/field (outdoor), volleyball, water polo. **On-Campus Highlights:** Coffee Shops, Cougars' Den (Dining Facility), An Athletic Facility, Darling Library, Cougar Dome.

ADMISSIONS

Freshman Academic Profile: Average high school GPA 3.62. 32% in top 10% of high school class, 63% in top 25% of high school class, 86% in top 50% of high school class. SAT Math middle 50% range 480–600. SAT Critical Reading middle 50% range 490–590. SAT Writing middle 50% range 970–1180. ACT middle 50% range 21–27. Minimum paper TOEFL 500. Minimum computer TOEFL 173. **Basis for Candidate Selection:** *Very important factors considered include:* Class rank, application essay, academic GPA, recommendation(s), standardized test scores. *Important factors considered include:* Character/personal qualities, state residency. *Other factors considered include:* Rigor of secondary school record, alumni/ae relation, extracurricular activities, first generation, interview, level of applicant's interest, racial/ethnic status, talent/ability, volunteer work, work experience. **Freshman Admission Requirements:** High school diploma is required and GED is accepted. *Academic units recommended:* 4 English, 3 mathematics, 2 science, 3 foreign language, 1 social studies, 2 history. **Freshman Admission Statistics:** 5,262 applied, 59% admitted, 33% enrolled. **Transfer Admission Requirements:** college transcript(s), essay or personal statement, statement of good standing from prior institution(s). Minimum college GPA of 2.2 required. Lowest grade transferable C. **General Admission Information:** Application fee $45. Regular application deadline 6/1. Regular notification 4/1. Nonfall registration accepted. Credit offered for CEEB Advanced Placement tests.

COSTS AND FINANCIAL AID

Annual tuition $26,950. Room and board $8,314. Required fees $800. Average book expense $1,638. **Required Forms and Deadlines:** FAFSA, institution's own financial aid form. Financial aid filing deadline 7/1. Priority financial aid filing date 3/2. **Notification of Awards:** Applicants will be notified of awards on a rolling basis beginning 3/1. **Types of Aid:** *Need-based scholarships/grants:* Federal Pell, SEOG, state scholarships/grants, private scholarships, the school's own gift aid, Federal Nursing Scholarships. *Loans:* Direct Subsidized Stafford, Direct Unsubsidized Stafford, Direct PLUS, Federal Perkins, Federal Nursing **Student Employment:** Federal Work-Study Program available. Institutional employment available. Highest amount earned per year from on-campus jobs $8,000. Off-campus job opportunities are good. **Financial Aid Statistics:** 66% freshmen, 61% undergrads receive need-based scholarship or grant aid. 57% freshmen, 57% undergrads receive non-need-based scholarship or grant aid. 51% freshmen, 52% undergrads receive need-based self-help aid. 2% freshmen, 2% undergrads receive athletic scholarships. 90% undergrads receive any aid. **Criteria for awarding institutional aid:** *Non-need-based:* Academics, athletics, leadership, minority status, music/drama, religious affiliation.

BABSON COLLEGE

Lunder Hall, Babson Park, MA 02457
Phone: 781-239-5522 **Financial Aid Phone:** 781-239-4219
E-mail: ugradadmission@babson.edu **CEEB Code:** 3075
Fax: 781-239-4135 **Website:** www3.babson.edu **ACT Code:** 1780

This private school was founded in 1919. It has a 370-acre campus.

RATINGS

Admissions Selectivity Rating: 93   **Fire Safety Rating:** 83   **Green Rating:** 60*

STUDENTS AND FACULTY

Enrollment: 1,799. **Student Body:** 41% female, 59% male, 46% out-of-state, 18% international (60 countries represented). Asian 11%, African American 4%, Caucasian 44%, Hispanic 8%.
Retention and Graduation: 93% freshmen return for sophomore year. 85% freshmen graduate within 4 years. **Faculty:** Student/faculty ratio 16:1. 150 full-time faculty, 90% hold PhDs, 14% are members of minority groups, 33% are women.

ACADEMICS

Degrees: Bachelor's, master's, post-master's certificate. **Classes:** Most classes have 30–39 students. **Majors with Highest Enrollment:** Accounting; entrepreneurial and small business operations, other; finance. **Special Study Options:** Cross-registration, exchange student program (domestic), honors program, independent study, internships, liberal arts/career combination, study abroad. We offer 26 concentrations which provide groupings of courses that help students choose a coherent set of courses for academic and external recognition. **Honors programs:** The Honors Program consists of three components in which participants add to their academic and cocurricular development. These include honors courses, an honors project and an international experience. **Combined degree programs:** BS/MS in accounting. Special programs offered to physically disabled students include note-taking services, reader services, tape recorders. **Career services:** Alumni network, alumni services, career/job search classes, career assessment, internships, regional alumni. Career services highlights include: Coaching for Leadership and Teamwork.

FACILITIES

Housing: Coed dorms, special housing for disabled students, fraternity/sorority housing, substance free, special interest housing. 50% of campus accessible to physically disabled. **Special Academic Facilities/Equipment:** The Babson World Globe, Roger Babson Museum, Isaac Newton Museum, Arthur M. Blank Center for Entrepreneurship. **Computers:** 100% of classrooms, 100% of dorms, 100% of libraries, 100% of dining areas, 100% of student union, 100% of common outdoor areas have wireless network access. Students can register for classes online. Administrative functions (other than registration) can be performed online. Undergraduates are required to own a computer.

CAMPUS LIFE

Environment: Village. **Activities:** dance, drama/theater, jazz band, literary magazine, musical theater, radio station, student government, student newspaper, yearbook. **Organizations:** 78 registered organizations, 3 religious organizations. 4 fraternities, 3 sororities. **Athletics (Intercollegiate):** *Men:* Baseball, basketball, cross-country, diving, golf, ice hockey, lacrosse, skiing (downhill/alpine), soccer, swimming, tennis, track/field (outdoor), track/field (indoor). *Women:* Basketball, cross-country, diving, field hockey, lacrosse, skiing (downhill/alpine), soccer, softball, swimming, tennis, track/field (outdoor), track/field (indoor), volleyball. **On-Campus Highlights:** Sorenson Arts Center, Blank Center for Entrepeneurship, Glavin Family Chapel, Reynolds Student Center, Webster Athletic Center.

ADMISSIONS

Freshman Academic Profile: 22% in top 10% of high school class, 17% in top 25% of high school class, 99% in top 50% of high school class. 50% from public high schools. SAT Math middle 50% range 610–690. SAT Critical Reading middle 50% range 555–650. SAT Writing middle 50% range 580–660. ACT middle 50% range 25–29. Minimum paper TOEFL 600. Minimum computer TOEFL 250. Minimum web-based TOEFL 100. **Basis for Candidate Selection:** *Very important factors considered include:* Application essay, academic GPA, recommendation(s), rigor of secondary school record, standardized test scores, character/personal qualities. *Important factors considered include:* Class rank, extracurricular activities. *Other factors considered include:* Alumni/ae relation, first generation, geographical residence, interview, level of applicant's interest, racial/ethnic status, state residency, talent/ability, volunteer work, work experience. **Freshman Admission Requirements:** High school diploma is required and GED is accepted. *Academic units recommended:* 4 English, 4 mathematics, 4 science, (3 science labs), 4 foreign language, 2 social studies, 2 history, 1 precalculus. **Freshman Admission Statistics:** 3,530 applied, 38% admitted, 34% enrolled. **Transfer Admission Requirements:** High school transcript, college transcript(s), essay or personal statement, statement of good standing from prior institution(s). Lowest grade transferable C. **General Admission Information:** Application fee $65. Early decision application deadline 11/1. Regular application deadline 1/15. Regular notification 4/1. Nonfall registration not accepted. Admission may be deferred for a maximum of 1 year. Credit and/or placement offered for CEEB Advanced Placement tests.

COSTS AND FINANCIAL AID

Annual tuition $37,824. **Required Forms and Deadlines:** FAFSA, CSS/Financial Aid PROFILE, noncustodial PROFILE, business/farm supplement. Federal tax returns, W-2s, and Verification Worksheet. Financial aid filing deadline 2/15. Priority financial aid filing date 2/15. **Notification of Awards:** Applicants will be notified of awards on or about 4/1. **Types of Aid:** *Need-based* *scholarships/grants:* Federal Pell, SEOG, state scholarships/grants, the school's own gift aid. *Loans:* Direct Subsidized Stafford, Direct Unsubsidized Stafford, Direct PLUS, Federal Perkins, state loans. **Student Employment:** Federal Work-Study Program available. Institutional employment available. Highest amount earned per year from on-campus jobs $5,400. Off-campus job opportunities are good. **Financial Aid Statistics:** 40% freshmen, 38% undergrads receive need-based scholarship or grant aid. 6% freshmen, 6% undergrads receive non-need-based scholarship or grant aid. 44% freshmen, 41% undergrads receive need-based self-help aid. 44% freshmen, 42% undergrads receive any aid. 51% undergrads borrow to pay for school. Average cumulative indebtedness $28,902. **Criteria for awarding institutional aid:** *Non-need-based:* Academics, leadership.

See page 1022.

BAKER UNIVERSITY

P.O. Box 65, Baldwin City, KS 66006
Phone: 785-594-8307 **Financial Aid Phone:** 785-594-4595
E-mail: admissions@bakeru.edu **CEEB Code:** 6031
Fax: 785-594-8372 **Website:** www.bakerU.edu **ACT Code:** 1386

This private school, affiliated with the Methodist Church, was founded in 1858. It has a 36-acre campus.

RATINGS
Admissions Selectivity Rating: 84   **Fire Safety Rating:** 79   **Green Rating:** 60*

STUDENTS AND FACULTY
Enrollment: 903. **Student Body:** 52% female, 48% male, 27% out-of-state, 1% international (7 countries represented). Asian 1%, African American 8%, Caucasian 81%, Hispanic 1%, Native American 1%.
Retention and Graduation: 36% freshmen graduate within 4 years. 30% grads go on to further study within 1 year. 17% grads pursue arts and sciences degrees. 2% grads pursue law degrees. 4% grads pursue business degrees. 5% grads pursue medical degrees. **Faculty:** Student/faculty ratio 12:1. 65 full-time faculty, 86% hold PhDs, 5% are members of minority groups, 42% are women.

ACADEMICS
Degrees: Bachelor's. **Classes:** Most classes have 10–19 students. Most lab/discussion sessions have fewer than 10 students. **Majors with Highest Enrollment:** Biology/biological sciences; business/commerce; elementary education and teaching. **Special Study Options:** Accelerated program, double major, honors program, independent study, internships, liberal arts/career combination, student-designed major, study abroad, teacher certification program, Students can transfer to the School of Nursing (located in a clinical setting in Topeka, KS) after completing their first two years of general education and pre-nursing course work. Baker also offers an Interterm program (3 weeks in January), during which students can take classes on campus, pursue travel courses, or work in internships. **Honors programs:** Honors Program, Bronston Fellows Program. **Combined degree programs:** 3-2 forestry program with Duke U. Special programs offered to physically disabled students include note-taking services, reader services, tape recorders, tutors. **Career services:** Alumni services, career/job search classes, career assessment, internships. Career services highlights include: Professional project-based practicum experiences sponsored by local businesses and organizations (facilitated by faculty within the Business and Economics Department).

FACILITIES
Housing: Coed dorms, special housing for disabled students, men's dorms, women's dorms, fraternity/sorority housing, apartments for single students. 85% of campus accessible to physically disabled. **Special Academic Facilities/Equipment:** Old Castle Museum, Quayle Bible Collection. **Computers:** 95% of classrooms, 100% of dorms, 100% of libraries, 100% of dining areas, 100% of student union, have wireless network access. Students can register for classes online. Administrative functions (other than registration) can be performed online.

CAMPUS LIFE
Environment: Rural. **Activities:** Choral groups, concert band, dance, drama/theater, jazz band, literary magazine, music ensembles, pep band, radio station, student government, student newspaper, television station, yearbook, international student organization. **Organizations:** 60 registered organizations, 18 honor societies, 2 religious organizations. 5 fraternities, 5 sororities. **Athletics (Intercollegiate):** *Men:* Baseball, basketball, cheerleading, cross-country, football, golf, soccer, tennis, track/field (outdoor), track/field (indoor), wrestling. *Women:* Basketball, bowling, cheerleading, cross-country, golf, soccer, softball, tennis, track/field (outdoor), track/field (indoor), volleyball. **On-Campus Highlights:** Library, Wildcat Cafe, Osborne Chapel, Fitness Center, Living Learning Center.

ADMISSIONS
Freshman Academic Profile: Average high school GPA 3.48. 24% in top 10% of high school class, 54% in top 25% of high school class, 84% in top 50% of high school class. 95% from public high schools. SAT Math middle 50% range 433–563. SAT Critical Reading middle 50% range 453–575. ACT middle 50% range 21–26. Minimum paper TOEFL 525. Minimum computer TOEFL 195. **Basis for Candidate Selection:** *Very important factors considered include:* Academic GPA, recommendation(s), rigor of secondary school record, standardized test scores, level of applicant's interest. *Important factors considered include:* Class rank. *Other factors considered include:* Application essay, alumni/ae relation, character/personal qualities, extracurricular activities, geographical residence, interview, talent/ability, volunteer work, work experience. **Freshman Admission Requirements:** High school diploma is required and GED is accepted. *Academic units recommended:* 4 English, 3 mathematics, 3 science, (1 science labs), 2 foreign language, 3 social studies, 2 fine arts/computing. **Freshman Admission Statistics:** 1,266 applied, 56% admitted, 36% enrolled. **Transfer Admission Requirements:** High school transcript, college transcript(s), standardized test scores, minimum college GPA of 2.3 required. Lowest grade transferable C. **General Admission Information:** Nonfall registration accepted. Admission may be deferred for a maximum of 1 year. Credit and/or placement offered for CEEB Advanced Placement tests.

COSTS AND FINANCIAL AID
Required Forms and Deadlines: FAFSA, institution's own financial aid form. Priority financial aid filing date 3/1. **Notification of Awards:** Applicants will be notified of awards on a rolling basis beginning 3/1. **Types of Aid:** *Need-based scholarships/grants:* Federal Pell, SEOG, state scholarships/grants, private scholarships, the school's own gift aid. *Loans:* Direct Subsidized Stafford, Direct Unsubsidized Stafford, Direct PLUS, Federal Perkins. **Student Employment:** Federal Work-Study Program available. Institutional employment available. Off-campus job opportunities are good. **Financial Aid Statistics:** 38% freshmen, 38% undergrads receive need-based scholarship or grant aid. 67% freshmen, 67% undergrads receive non-need-based scholarship or grant aid. 67% freshmen, 67% undergrads receive need-based self-help aid. 8% freshmen, 7% undergrads receive athletic scholarships. **Criteria for awarding institutional aid:** *Non-need-based:* Academics, alumni affiliation, art, athletics, leadership, music/drama, religious affiliation.

BALDWIN-WALLACE COLLEGE

275 Eastland Rd, Berea, OH 44017
Phone: 440-826-2222 **Financial Aid Phone:** 440-826-2108
E-mail: admission@bw.edu **CEEB Code:** 1050
Fax: 440-826-3830 **Website:** www.bw.edu **ACT Code:** 3236

This private school was founded in 1845. It has a 100-acre campus.

RATINGS
Admissions Selectivity Rating: 83   **Fire Safety Rating:** 64   **Green Rating:** 76

STUDENTS AND FACULTY
Enrollment: 3,561. **Student Body:** 57% female, 43% male, 13% out-of-state, 2% international (22 countries represented). Asian 1%, African American 7%, Caucasian 84%, Hispanic 3%.
Retention and Graduation: 85% freshmen return for sophomore year. 50% freshmen graduate within 4 years. **Faculty:** Student/faculty ratio 15:1. 167 full-time faculty, 79% hold PhDs, 8% are members of minority groups, 41% are women.

ACADEMICS
Degrees: Bachelor's, certificate, master's. **Classes:** Most classes have 10–19 students. Most lab/discussion sessions have 20–29 students. **Majors with Highest Enrollment:** Accounting; business administration and management; psychology. **Special Study Options:** Accelerated program, cross-registration, distance learning, double major, dual enrollment, English as a Second Language (ESL), exchange student program (domestic), honors program, independent study, internships, liberal arts/career combination, student-designed major, study abroad, teacher certification program, weekend college, 3-2 in Engineering with Case Western Reserve University and Columbia University; 3-2 in Social Work with Case Western Reserve University; 3/2 Accounting MBA, 3/2 Human Resources MBA and 3/2 Computer Science/Info. Systems MBA Programs. **Honors programs:** Liberal Arts Program. **Combined degree programs:** BA/MBA Acct, BA/MBA HR, BS-CompSci/MBA, BS-Comp Info Syst/MBA, BA/MSSA Social Work. Special programs offered to physically disabled students include note-taking services, reader services, tutors. **Career services:** Alumni network, alumni services, career assessment, internships. Career services highlights include: It is hard to pick just one of the programs, because part of

their strength is the combination of them all: On Campus Recruiting Services, Employer Meet and Greets, Career and Internship Expo (annual job fair) and Career Connections (alumni network and mentor program), Fall Career Week and Spring Career Week that coincide with job fairs.

FACILITIES

Housing: Coed dorms, special housing for disabled students, special housing for international students, women's dorms, fraternity/sorority housing, apartments for single students, Carmel Living Learning Center (Education-based), Student-Directed Learning Communities (Sustainability, Art, Women's Christian, Men's Christian), themed housing (STEM, Language, Conservatory, SPROUT-for single mothers and children). 80% of campus accessible to physically disabled. **Special Academic Facilities/Equipment:** Art gallery, electron microscope, observatory. **Computers:** 100% of classrooms, 100% of dorms, 100% of libraries, 100% of dining areas, 100% of student union, 100% of common outdoor areas have wireless network access. Students can register for classes online. Administrative functions (other than registration) can be performed online.

CAMPUS LIFE

Environment: Village. **Activities:** Choral groups, concert band, dance, drama/theater, jazz band, literary magazine, marching band, music ensembles, musical theater, opera, pep band, radio station, student government, student newspaper, student-run film society, symphony orchestra, television station, yearbook, campus ministries, international student organization, Model UN. **Organizations:** 136 registered organizations, 25 honor societies, 7 religious organizations. 5 fraternities, 5 sororities. **Athletics (Intercollegiate):** *Men:* Baseball, basketball, cross-country, diving, football, golf, soccer, swimming, tennis, track/field (outdoor), track/field (indoor), wrestling. *Women:* Basketball, cross-country, diving, golf, soccer, softball, swimming, tennis, track/field (outdoor), track/field (indoor), volleyball. **On-Campus Highlights:** CyberCafe, The Hive, The S.A.C. (Student Activities Center), Conservatory/Theatre performances, Recreation Center, The new Lou Higgins Recreation Center features a Fitness Center, Weight Room, Dance Studio, multipurpose basketball, volleyball, badminton courts and racquetball courts, swimming pool, indoor batting cage and second-floor computer lab. The Student Activities Center provides a club-like atmosphere for entertainment programming on campus. It features a pulsating sound and dance light system, a 10' x 12' video screen, neon lights and snack bar. Comedians, live bands, disc jockeys, multi-media capabilities and special snack foods attracting students to all-campus events. **Environmental Initiatives:** Commitment to geo-thermal energy with all new buildings and major renovations. Creation of Ohio's first undergraduate major in Sustainability. Considerable investments in electricity energy conservation and renewable energy sources.

ADMISSIONS

Freshman Academic Profile: Average high school GPA 3.5. 28% in top 10% of high school class, 54% in top 25% of high school class, 81% in top 50% of high school class. 83% from public high schools. SAT Math middle 50% range 490–590. SAT Critical Reading middle 50% range 480–610. SAT Writing middle 50% range 470–600. ACT middle 50% range 21–26. Minimum paper TOEFL 500. Minimum computer TOEFL 173. Minimum web-based TOEFL 61. **Basis for Candidate Selection:** *Very important factors considered include:* Academic GPA, rigor of secondary school record. *Important factors considered include:* Class rank, application essay, character/personal qualities, extracurricular activities, talent/ability. *Other factors considered include:* recommendation(s), standardized test scores, alumni/ae relation, first generation, geographical residence, interview, level of applicant's interest, racial/ethnic status, state residency, volunteer work, work experience. **Freshman Admission Requirements:** High school diploma is required and GED is accepted. *Academic units required:* 4 English, 3 mathematics, 3 science, (2 science labs), 1 foreign language, 2 social studies, 1 history. *Academic units recommended:* 4 English, 4 mathematics, 4 science, (2 science labs), 2 foreign language, 3 social studies, 1 history, 3 academic electives. **Freshman Admission Statistics:** 3,498 applied, 67% admitted, 32% enrolled. **Transfer Admission Requirements:** High school transcript, college transcript(s), statement of good standing from prior institution(s). Minimum college GPA of 2.5 required. Lowest grade transferable C. **General Admission Information:** Application fee $25. Notification on a rolling basis, beginning on or about 11/1. Nonfall registration accepted. Admission may be deferred for a maximum of 1 year. Credit and/or placement offered for CEEB Advanced Placement tests.

COSTS AND FINANCIAL AID

Annual tuition $24,230. Room and board $7,960. Average book expense $1,220. **Required Forms and Deadlines:** FAFSA. Financial aid filing deadline 9/1. Priority financial aid filing date 5/1. **Notification of Awards:** Applicants will be notified of awards on a rolling basis beginning 2/14. **Types of Aid:** *Need-based scholarships/grants:* Federal Pell, SEOG, state scholarships/grants, private scholarships, the school's own gift aid. *Loans:* Direct Subsidized Stafford, Direct Unsubsidized Stafford, Direct PLUS, Federal Perkins, college/university loans from institutional funds. **Student Employment:** Federal Work-Study Program available. Institutional employment available. Highest amount earned per

year from on-campus jobs $2,400. Off-campus job opportunities are excellent. **Financial Aid Statistics:** 80% freshmen, 80% undergrads receive need-based scholarship or grant aid. 10% freshmen, 13% undergrads receive non-need-based scholarship or grant aid. 80% freshmen, 80% undergrads receive need-based self-help aid. 98% freshmen, 98% undergrads receive any aid. 67% undergrads borrow to pay for school. Average cumulative indebtedness $17,716. **Criteria for awarding institutional aid:** *Non-need-based:* Academics, alumni affiliation, minority status, music/drama, religious affiliation, state/district residency.

BALL STATE UNIVERSITY

Office of Admissions, Lucina Hall, Muncie, IN 47306
Phone: 765-285-8300 **Financial Aid Phone:** 765-285-5600
E-mail: askus@bsu.edu **CEEB Code:** 1051
Fax: 765-285-1632 **Website:** www.bsu.edu **ACT Code:** 1176

This public school was founded in 1918. It has a 1035-acre campus.

RATINGS

Admissions Selectivity Rating: 76   **Fire Safety Rating:** 72   **Green Rating:** 93

STUDENTS AND FACULTY

Enrollment: 17,403. **Student Body:** 52% female, 48% male, 11% out-of-state, 2% international (76 countries represented). Asian 1%, African American 7%, Caucasian 84%, Hispanic 2%.
Retention and Graduation: 32.4% grads go on to further study within 1 year. **Faculty:** Student/faculty ratio 18.3:1. 940 full-time faculty, 74% hold PhDs, 14% are members of minority groups, 43% are women. 6.7% of classes are taught by teaching assistants.

ACADEMICS

Degrees: Associate, bachelor's, doctoral, master's, post-bachelor's certificate, post-master's certificate. **Classes:** Most classes have 20–29 students. **Majors with Highest Enrollment:** Elementary education and teaching; family and consumer sciences/human sciences; radio and television. **Special Study Options:** Accelerated program, distance learning, double major, dual enrollment, English as a Second Language (ESL), exchange student program (domestic), external degree program, honors program, independent study, internships, student-designed major, study abroad, teacher certification program. **Honors programs:** BSU offers an Honors College which has its own curriculum, undergraduate research fellowships and study abroad programs. Special programs offered to physically disabled students include note-taking services, reader services, tape recorders, tutors. **Career services:** Alumni services, career assessment, internships, regional alumni. **Career services highlights include:** The professional skills development programs and services provided by the career center offer the highest level of staff expertise and training methods. Student use of these services has grown an average of 86% over the past three years. Students and alumni use the online resume review program, professional etiquette dinners, and individual appointments for job coaching including video-taped practice interviews to prepare for internships and job searches.

FACILITIES

Housing: Coed dorms, special housing for disabled students, men's dorms, special housing for international students, women's dorms, fraternity/sorority housing, apartments for married students, apartments for single students, wellness housing, theme housing, Living/Learning Communities. 95% of campus accessible to physically disabled. **Special Academic Facilities/Equipment:** Art gallery, museum, on-campus school (K–12), learning center, weather station, physical therapy lab, human performance lab, planetarium/observatory, wildlife and nature preserve. **Computers:** 100% of classrooms, 100% of dorms, 100% of libraries, 100% of dining areas, 100% of student union, 100% of common outdoor areas have wireless network access. Students can register for classes online. Administrative functions (other than registration) can be performed online. Undergraduates are required to own a computer.

CAMPUS LIFE

Environment: City. **Activities:** Choral groups, concert band, dance, drama/theater, jazz band, literary magazine, marching band, music ensembles, musical theater, opera, pep band, radio station, student government, student newspaper, student-run film society, symphony orchestra, television station, campus ministries. **Organizations:** 355 registered organizations, 31 honor societies, 32 religious organizations. 15 fraternities, 12 sororities. **Athletics (Intercollegiate):** *Men:* Baseball, basketball, cheerleading, cross-country, diving, football, golf, swimming, tennis, volleyball. *Women:* Basketball, cheerleading, cross-country, diving, field hockey, golf, gymnastics, soccer, softball, swimming, tennis, track/field (outdoor), volleyball. **On-Campus Highlights:** Museum of

Art, Worthen Arena, Emens Auditorium, Atrium, Letterman Communication & Media Bldg, Emens Auditorium, Music Building/Sursa Hall, Bracken Library. **Environmental Initiatives:** Council on the environment which represents every constituency group on campus and in the surrounding community. Creating unit-level sustainability plans for 102 administrative units on campus. Requiring that all new construction be LEED Silver Certified at minimum and that all renovation and remodeling seek the same performance levels.

ADMISSIONS

Freshman Academic Profile: Average high school GPA 3.28. 16% in top 10% of high school class, 45% in top 25% of high school class, 87% in top 50% of high school class. 91% from public high schools. SAT Math middle 50% range 470–580. SAT Critical Reading middle 50% range 470–570. SAT Writing middle 50% range 460–560. ACT middle 50% range 19–24. Minimum paper TOEFL 550. Minimum computer TOEFL 213. Minimum web-based TOEFL 79. **Basis for Candidate Selection:** *Very important factors considered include:* Academic GPA, rigor of secondary school record, standardized test scores. *Other factors considered include:* Class rank, application essay, recommendation(s), character/personal qualities, extracurricular activities, talent/ability, volunteer work, work experience. **Freshman Admission Requirements:** High school diploma is required and GED is accepted. *Academic units required:* 4 English, 3 mathematics, 3 science, (2 science labs), 3 social studies. *Academic units recommended:* 3 foreign language. **Freshman Admission Statistics:** 13,022 applied, 74% admitted, 44% enrolled. **Transfer Admission Requirements:** College transcript(s), minimum college GPA of 2.0 required. Lowest grade transferable C. **General Admission Information:** Application fee $25. Regular application deadline 8/15. Nonfall registration accepted. Admission may be deferred for a maximum of 1 year. Credit and/or placement offered for CEEB Advanced Placement tests.

COSTS AND FINANCIAL AID

Annual in-state tuition $7,228. Annual out-of-state tuition $19,796. Room and board $8,052. Required fees $602. Average book expense $970. **Required Forms and Deadlines:** FAFSA. Priority financial aid filing date 3/10. **Notification of Awards:** Applicants will be notified of awards on a rolling basis beginning 4/1. **Types of Aid:** *Need-based scholarships/grants:* Federal Pell, SEOG, state scholarships/grants, private scholarships, the school's own gift aid. *Loans:* Direct Subsidized Stafford, Direct Unsubsidized Stafford, Direct PLUS, Federal Perkins. **Student Employment:** Federal Work-Study Program available. Institutional employment available. Off-campus job opportunities are good. **Financial Aid Statistics:** 37% freshmen, 38% undergrads receive need-based scholarship or grant aid. 30% freshmen, 22% undergrads receive non-need-based scholarship or grant aid. 54% freshmen, 52% undergrads receive need-based self-help aid. 2% freshmen, 2% undergrads receive athletic scholarships. 94% freshmen, 90% undergrads receive any aid. 67% undergrads borrow to pay for school. Average cumulative indebtedness $22,598. **Criteria for awarding institutional aid:** *Non-need-based:* Academics, athletics, leadership, minority status, music/drama, state/district residency.

BALTIMORE HEBREW UNIVERSITY

5800 Park Heights, Baltimore, MD 21215
Phone: 410-578-6967 **Financial Aid Phone:**
E-mail: bhu@bhu.edu **CEEB Code:** 5035
Fax: 410-578-6940 **Website:** www.bhu.edu **ACT Code:** 20093

This private school was founded in 1919.

RATINGS
Admissions Selectivity Rating: 60*   **Fire Safety Rating:** 60*   **Green Rating:** 60*

STUDENTS AND FACULTY
Enrollment: 75. **Student Body:** 63% female, 37% male, (4 countries represented). African American 3%, Caucasian 139%.
Retention and Graduation: 67% freshmen return for sophomore year. 33% freshmen graduate within 4 years. **Faculty:** Student/faculty ratio 8:1.

ACADEMICS
Degrees: Associate, bachelor's, certificate, master's. **Special Study Options:** cross-registration, double major, dual enrollment, independent study, internships, study abroad, teacher certification program, English language skills program for non-native speakers. Special programs offered to physically disabled students include tape recorders.

FACILITIES
Housing: 65% of campus accessible to physically disabled. **Special Academic Facilities/Equipment:** Joseph Meyerhoff Library Cohen Auditorium.

CAMPUS LIFE
Organizations: 2 registered organizations.

ADMISSIONS
Freshman Academic Profile: Minimum paper TOEFL 250. Minimum computer TOEFL 250. **Basis for Candidate Selection:** *Very important factors considered include:* recommendation(s), interview. *Other factors considered include:* Class rank, rigor of secondary school record, standardized test scores, character/personal qualities. **Freshman Admission Requirements:** High school diploma is required and GED is accepted. **Freshman Admission Statistics:** 6 applied, 100% admitted, 67% enrolled. **Transfer Admission Requirements:** College transcript(s), minimum college GPA of 2.0 required. Lowest grade transferable C. **General Admission Information:** Application fee $20. Nonfall registration accepted. Admission may be deferred for a maximum of 1 year.

COSTS AND FINANCIAL AID
Annual tuition $6,400. Required fees $30. Average book expense $600. **Required Forms and Deadlines:** FAFSA. **Types of Aid:** *Need-based scholarships/grants:* Federal Pell, state scholarships/grants, private scholarships, the school's own gift aid. *Loans:* FFEL Subsidized Stafford, FFEL Unsubsidized Stafford, FFEL PLUS. **Student Employment:** Off-campus job opportunities are excellent. **Financial Aid Statistics:** 2% undergrads receive need-based scholarship or grant aid. 2% undergrads receive need-based self-help aid. **Criteria for awarding institutional aid:** *Non-need-based:* Academics.

BAPTIST BIBLE COLLEGE AND SEMINARY

538 Veanrd Rd, Clarks summit, PA, 18411,
Phone: 570-586-2400 **Financial Aid Phone:** 570-585-9206
E-mail: admissions@bbc.edu **CEEB Code:** 2036
Fax: 570-585-9299 **Website:** www/bbc/edu **ACT Code:** 3523

This private school, affiliated with the Baptist Church, was founded in 1932. It has a 121-acre campus.

RATINGS
Admissions Selectivity Rating: 73   **Fire Safety Rating:** 61   **Green Rating:** 60*

STUDENTS AND FACULTY
Enrollment: 668. **Student Body:** 59% female, 41% male, 68% out-of-state, 2% international (13 countries represented). Asian 1%, African American 1%, Caucasian 94%, Hispanic 2%.
Retention and Graduation: 69% freshmen return for sophomore year. **Faculty:** 35 full-time faculty, 57% hold PhDs, 3% are members of minority groups, 29% are women.

ACADEMICS
Degrees: Associate, bachelor's, certificate, master's. **Classes:** Most classes have fewer than 10 students. **Majors with Highest Enrollment:** Counseling psychology; elementary education and teaching; theology and religious vocations, other. **Special Study Options:** Distance learning, double major, dual enrollment, independent study, internships, study abroad, teacher certification program. **Career services:** Alumni services, internships.

FACILITIES
Housing: Men's dorms, women's dorms. **Computers:** 100% of classrooms, 100% of libraries, 100% of dining areas, 100% of student union, 100% of common outdoor areas have wireless network access. Students can register for classes online. Administrative functions (other than registration) can be performed online.

CAMPUS LIFE
Environment: Town. **Activities:** Choral groups, concert band, drama/theater, music ensembles, student government, yearbook, campus ministries. **Athletics (Intercollegiate):** Men: Baseball, basketball, cross-country, golf, soccer. Women: Basketball, cross-country, soccer, softball, tennis, volleyball. **On-Campus Highlights:** Underground Cafe, dorm, student center, classroom building.

ADMISSIONS
Freshman Academic Profile: 40% from public high schools. SAT Math middle 50% range 430–560. SAT Critical Reading middle 50% range 460–570. ACT middle 50% range 20–24. Minimum paper TOEFL 500. Minimum computer TOEFL 173. **Basis for Candidate Selection:** *Very important factors considered include:* Application essay, recommendation(s), rigor of secondary school record, standardized test scores, character/personal qualities, religious affiliation/commitment. *Important factors considered include:* Academic GPA. *Other factors considered include:* Extracurricular activities, interview, level of applicant's interest, talent/ability, volunteer work, work experience. **Freshman**

Admission Requirements: High school diploma is required and GED is accepted. **Freshman Admission Statistics:** 452 applied, 76% admitted, 48% enrolled. **Transfer Admission Requirements:** High school transcript, college transcript(s), essay or personal statement, minimum college GPA of 2 required. Lowest grade transferable 2. **General Admission Information:** Application fee $30. Regular application deadline 8/15. Nonfall registration accepted. Credit offered for CEEB Advanced Placement tests.

COSTS AND FINANCIAL AID

Annual tuition $6,840. Room and board $5,900. Required fees $468. **Required Forms and Deadlines:** FAFSA, institution's own financial aid form. Financial aid filing deadline 5/1. Priority financial aid filing date 5/1. **Notification of Awards:** Applicants will be notified of awards on a rolling basis beginning 10/1. **Types of Aid:** *Need-based scholarships/grants:* Federal Pell, state scholarships/grants, the school's own gift aid. *Loans:* Direct Unsubsidized Stafford, FFEL Subsidized Stafford, FFEL Unsubsidized Stafford, FFEL PLUS, state loans. **Student Employment:** Federal Work-Study Program available. Institutional employment available. Off-campus job opportunities are excellent. **Financial Aid Statistics:** 100% freshmen, 96% undergrads receive any aid. **Criteria for awarding institutional aid:** *Non-need-based:* Academics, leadership.

BAPTIST COLLEGE OF FLORIDA

5400 College Drive, Graceville, FL 32440-1898
Phone: 850-263-3261 **Financial Aid Phone:** 18003282660 ext. 461
E-mail: admissions@baptistcollege.edu
Fax: 850-263-9026 **ACT Code:** 6870

This private school, affiliated with the Southern Baptist Church, was founded in 1943. It has a 217-acre campus.

RATINGS
Admissions Selectivity Rating: 64   **Fire Safety Rating:** 60*   **Green Rating:** 60*

STUDENTS AND FACULTY
Enrollment: 546. **Student Body:** 38% female, 62% male, 26% out-of-state, (4 countries represented). Asian 1%, African American 3%, Caucasian 88%, Hispanic 2%.
Retention and Graduation: 60% grads go on to further study within 1 year. 60% grads pursue arts and sciences degrees. **Faculty:** Student/faculty ratio 13:1. 23 full-time faculty, 65% hold PhDs, 22% are women.

ACADEMICS
Degrees: Associate, bachelor's, certificate, terminal associate. **Classes:** Most classes have fewer than 10 students. Most lab/discussion sessions have 10–19 students. **Majors with Highest Enrollment:** Pastoral studies/counseling; religious education; theology/theological studies. **Special Study Options:** Distance learning, double major, independent study, internships, teacher certification program, academic remediation, Advanced Placement credit, Learning Disabilities Services. Special programs offered to physically disabled students include note-taking services, reader services, tape recorders, tutors. **Career services:** Alumni services, internships.

FACILITIES
Housing: Special housing for disabled students, men's dorms, women's dorms, apartments for married students. 100% of campus accessible to physically disabled. **Special Academic Facilities/Equipment:** Florida Baptist Historical Society; Heritage Village; Weight Rooms in Assembly Center. **Computers:** 100% of classrooms, 100% of dorms, 100% of libraries, 100% of dining areas, 100% of student union, 100% of common outdoor areas have wireless network access. Students can register for classes online. Administrative functions (other than registration) can be performed online.

CAMPUS LIFE
Environment: Rural. **Activities:** Choral groups, concert band, drama/theater, jazz band, music ensembles, radio station, campus ministries. **Organizations:** 3 registered organizations, 2 religious organizations. **Athletics (Intercollegiate):** *Men:* Golf. *Women:* Volleyball. **On-Campus Highlights:** Athletic Center, Coffee Shop, Courtyard, Student Center, Chapel.

ADMISSIONS
Freshman Academic Profile: 90% from public high schools. Minimum paper TOEFL 500. **Basis for Candidate Selection:** *Very important factors considered include:* Recommendation(s), character/personal qualities, level of applicant's interest, religious affiliation/commitment. *Important factors considered include:* Academic GPA, alumni/ae relation, talent/ability. *Other factors considered include:* Class rank, rigor of secondary school record, standardized test scores, extracurricular activities, interview, volunteer work.

Freshman Admission Requirements: High school diploma is required and GED is accepted. *Academic units recommended:* 4 English, 4 mathematics, 3 science, 1 social studies, 2 history. **Freshman Admission Statistics: Transfer Admission Requirements:** High school transcript, college transcript(s), essay or personal statement, minimum college GPA of 2.0 required. Lowest grade transferable C. **General Admission Information:** Application fee $25. Regular application deadline 8/15. Notification on a rolling basis, beginning on or about 9/1. Nonfall registration accepted. Admission may be deferred for a maximum of 2 semesters. Neither credit nor placement offered for CEEB Advanced Placement tests.

COSTS AND FINANCIAL AID

Annual tuition $7,800. Room and board $3,886. Required fees $350. Average book expense $900. **Required Forms and Deadlines:** FAFSA, institution's own financial aid form, state aid form. Financial aid filing deadline 5/15. Priority financial aid filing date 4/1. **Notification of Awards:** Applicants will be notified of awards on a rolling basis beginning 6/15. **Types of Aid:** *Need-based scholarships/grants:* Federal Pell, SEOG, state scholarships/grants, private scholarships, the school's own gift aid. *Loans:* FFEL Subsidized Stafford, FFEL Unsubsidized Stafford, FFEL PLUS, college/university loans from institutional funds, Alternative Loans. **Student Employment:** Federal Work-Study Program available. Institutional employment available. Highest amount earned per year from on-campus jobs $7,600. Off-campus job opportunities are good. **Financial Aid Statistics:** 52% freshmen, 60% undergrads receive need-based scholarship or grant aid. 6% freshmen, 5% undergrads receive non-need-based scholarship or grant aid. 34% freshmen, 47% undergrads receive need-based self-help aid. **Criteria for awarding institutional aid:** *Non-need-based:* Academics, minority status, music/drama, religious affiliation.

BARBER SCOTIA COLLEGE

145 Cabarrus Avenue, Concord, NC 28025
Phone: 704-789-2901 **Financial Aid Phone:**
E-mail: wwhite@b-sc.edu
Fax: 704-789-2624 **Website:** www.barber-scotia.edu **ACT Code:** 3060

This private school, affiliated with the Presbyterian Church, was founded in 1867. It has a 40-acre campus.

RATINGS
Admissions Selectivity Rating: 60*   **Fire Safety Rating:** 60*   **Green Rating:** 60*

STUDENTS AND FACULTY
Enrollment: 475. **Student Body:** 45% female, 55% male, 45% out-of-state, international (2 countries represented). African American 101%, Caucasian 1%.
Retention and Graduation: 61% freshmen return for sophomore year. 9% grads go on to further study within 1 year. 7% grads pursue arts and sciences degrees. 2% grads pursue business degrees.

ACADEMICS
Degrees: Bachelor's. **Special Study Options:** cooperative education program, double major, dual enrollment, honors program, internships, student-designed major, teacher certification program **Combined degree programs:** BA/JD, BA/BSN. Special programs offered to physically disabled students include note-taking services, reader services, tape recorders, tutors. **Career services:** Alumni services, career/job search classes, career assessment, internships

FACILITIES
Housing: Special housing for disabled students, men's dorms, women's dorms, apartments for married students 50% of campus accessible to physically disabled. **Special Academic Facilities/Equipment:** Barber-Scotia's African-American Women's History Collection: This Collection houses one of the largest bodies of documents related to African-American women in the united States. Major areas of interest are the Reconstruction-Jim Crow Era.

CAMPUS LIFE
Environment: Village. **Activities:** Choral groups, dance, pep band, student government, student newspaper, yearbook. **Organizations:** 18 registered organizations, 2 honor societies, 2 religious organizations. 4 fraternities, 4 sororities. **Athletics (Intercollegiate):** *Men:* Basketball, cross-country, track/field (outdoor). *Women:* Basketball, cheerleading, cross-country, softball, track/field (outdoor), volleyball.

ADMISSIONS
Freshman Academic Profile: 98% from public high schools. **Basis for Candidate Selection:** *Very important factors considered include:* Class rank, application essay, recommendation(s), interview. *Important factors considered include:* Rigor of secondary school record, extracurricular activities, talent/abil-

ity, volunteer work. *Other factors considered include:* Alumni/ae relation, character/personal qualities, state residency. **Freshman Admission Requirements:** High school diploma is required and GED is accepted. *Academic units required:* 4 English, 3 mathematics, 3 science, 2 social studies, 1 history. **Freshman Admission Statistics:** 840 applied, 64% admitted, 32% enrolled. **Transfer Admission Requirements:** College transcript(s), minimum college GPA of 2.0 required. Lowest grade transferable C. **General Admission Information:** Application fee $15. Regular application deadline 7/1. Nonfall registration accepted. Credit and/or placement offered for CEEB Advanced Placement tests.

COSTS AND FINANCIAL AID
Annual tuition $7,400. Room and board $3,500. Required fees $466. Average book expense $250. **Required Forms and Deadlines:** FAFSA. Financial aid filing deadline 8/1. Priority financial aid filing date 5/30. **Notification of Awards:** Applicants will be notified of awards on or about 6/15. **Types of Aid:** *Need-based scholarships/grants:* Federal Pell, SEOG, state scholarships/grants, private scholarships, the school's own gift aid, United Negro College Fund. *Loans:* Direct Subsidized Stafford, Direct Unsubsidized Stafford, Direct PLUS, FFEL Subsidized Stafford, FFEL Unsubsidized Stafford, FFEL PLUS. **Student Employment:** Federal Work-Study Program available. Institutional employment available. Off-campus job opportunities are excellent. **Financial Aid Statistics:** 87% freshmen, 93% undergrads receive need-based scholarship or grant aid. 7% freshmen, 27% undergrads receive non-need-based scholarship or grant aid. 80% freshmen, 66% undergrads receive need-based self-help aid. 8% freshmen, 10% undergrads receive athletic scholarships. 84% undergrads borrow to pay for school. Average cumulative indebtedness $14,629. **Criteria for awarding institutional aid:** *Non-need-based:* Academics, alumni affiliation, athletics, leadership, minority status, music/drama, religious affiliation, state/district residency.

BARD COLLEGE

Best 373

Office of Admissions, Annandale-on-Hudson, NY 12504
Phone: 845-758-7472 **Financial Aid Phone:** 845-758-7526
E-mail: admission@bard.edu **CEEB Code:** 2037
Fax: 845-758-5208 **Website:** www.bard.edu **ACT Code:** 2674

This private school was founded in 1860. It has a 600-acre campus.

RATINGS
Admissions Selectivity Rating: 96   **Fire Safety Rating:** 80   **Green Rating:** 89

STUDENTS AND FACULTY
Enrollment: 1,900. **Student Body:** 57% female, 43% male, 67% out-of-state, 12% international (57 countries represented). Asian 3%, African American 2%, Caucasian 55%, Hispanic 3%, Native American 1%.
Retention and Graduation: 87% freshmen return for sophomore year. 71% freshmen graduate within 4 years. **Faculty:** Student/faculty ratio 10.2:1. 145 full-time faculty, 96% hold PhDs, 15% are members of minority groups, 44% are women.

ACADEMICS
Degrees: Associate, bachelor's, doctoral, master's. **Majors with Highest Enrollment:** English language and literature; social sciences; visual and performing arts. **Special Study Options:** Cross-registration, double major, dual enrollment, English as a Second Language (ESL), independent study, internships, student-designed major, study abroad, Intensive language studies in Italy, Germany, France, Mexico, Russia, China, program in International Education (Central and Eastern Europe and Southern Africa). **Combined degree programs:** BA/MA, BA/MEng, See catalog, pp. 244. Special programs offered to physically disabled students include note-taking services, reader services, tape recorders, tutors. **Career services:** Alumni network, alumni services, career/job search classes, career assessment, internships, regional alumni. Career services highlights include: The Career Office offers over 30 career information workshops a year.

FACILITIES
Housing: Coed dorms, women's dorms, cooperative housing, wellness housing, theme housing. 70% of campus accessible to physically disabled. **Special Academic Facilities/Equipment:** Performing arts center, gallery, art museum, collection of contemporary art, center for curatorial studies, language lab, nursery school, ecology field station, archaeology field school, economics institute.

Computers: 5% of classrooms, 50% of dorms, 100% of libraries, 100% of dining areas, 100% of student union, have wireless network access. Students can register for classes online. Administrative functions (other than registration) can be performed online.

CAMPUS LIFE
Environment: Rural. **Activities:** Choral groups, concert band, dance, drama/theater, jazz band, literary magazine, music ensembles, musical theater, opera, radio station, student government, student newspaper, student-run film society, symphony orchestra, campus ministries, international student organization, Model UN. **Organizations:** 120 registered organizations, 5 religious organizations. **Athletics (Intercollegiate):** *Men:* Basketball, cross-country, soccer, squash, tennis, track/field (outdoor), volleyball. *Women:* Basketball, cross-country, soccer, tennis, track/field (outdoor), volleyball. **On-Campus Highlights:** Richard B Fisher Center for the Performing Arts, Stevenson Library, Bertelsmann Campus Center, Museum @ Center for Curatorial Studies, Levy Economics Institute—Blithewood Mansion, A new Center for Science and Computation designed by the renowned firm Rafael Vinoly Architects opened in the fall of 2007. **Environmental Initiatives:** Renewable energy (geothermal) installed in new buildings and currently in place in 20 existing buildings. 100% food composting onsite. (#1 in "Food Scrap" category in 2009 RecycleMania). Performance contract for 7% energy reduction and contracts in progress for solar-thermal and photovoltaic installations.

ADMISSIONS
Freshman Academic Profile: Average high school GPA 3.5. 64% in top 10% of high school class, 95% in top 25% of high school class, 100% in top 50% of high school class. 64% from public high schools. SAT Math middle 50% range 650–680. SAT Critical Reading middle 50% range 680–740. Minimum paper TOEFL 600. Minimum computer TOEFL 250. **Basis for Candidate Selection:** *Very important factors considered include:* Application essay, academic GPA, recommendation(s), rigor of secondary school record, character/personal qualities, extracurricular activities, talent/ability. *Important factors considered include:* Volunteer work, work experience. *Other factors considered include:* Class rank, standardized test scores, alumni/ae relation, first generation, geographical residence, interview, level of applicant's interest, racial/ethnic status, religious affiliation/commitment, state residency. **Freshman Admission Requirements:** High school diploma is required and GED is accepted. *Academic units recommended:* 4 English, 4 mathematics, 4 science, (3 science labs), 4 foreign language, 4 social studies, 4 history. **Freshman Admission Statistics:** 5,510 applied, 33% admitted, 28% enrolled. **Transfer Admission Requirements:** College transcript(s), essay or personal statement, statement of good standing from prior institution(s). Minimum college GPA of 3.0 required. Lowest grade transferable C. **General Admission Information:** Application fee $50. Regular application deadline 1/15. Regular notification 4/1. Nonfall registration not accepted. Admission may be deferred for a maximum of 1 year. Credit offered for CEEB Advanced Placement tests.

COSTS AND FINANCIAL AID
Average book expense $850. **Required Forms and Deadlines:** FAFSA, CSS/Financial Aid PROFILE, state aid form, noncustodial PROFILE, business/farm supplement. Financial aid filing deadline 2/15. Priority financial aid filing date 2/1. **Notification of Awards:** Applicants will be notified of awards on or about 4/1. **Types of Aid:** *Need-based scholarships/grants:* Federal Pell, SEOG, state scholarships/grants, private scholarships, the school's own gift aid. *Loans:* FFEL Subsidized Stafford, FFEL Unsubsidized Stafford, FFEL PLUS, Federal Perkins, Loans from institutional funds (for international students only). **Student Employment:** Federal Work-Study Program available. Institutional employment available. Highest amount earned per year from on-campus jobs $1,800. Off-campus job opportunities are good. **Financial Aid Statistics:** 62% freshmen, 56% undergrads receive need-based scholarship or grant aid. 51% freshmen, 48% undergrads receive need-based self-help aid. 72% freshmen, 66% undergrads receive any aid. 52% undergrads borrow to pay for school. Average cumulative indebtedness $26,131. **Criteria for awarding institutional aid:** *Non-need-based:* Academics.

BARD COLLEGE AT SIMON'S ROCK

Best 373

84 Alford Road, Great Barrington, MA 01230
Phone: 413-528-7312 **Financial Aid Phone:** 413-528-7249
E-mail: admit@simons-rock.edu **CEEB Code:** 3795
Fax: 413-528-7334 **Website:** www.simons-rock.edu **ACT Code:** 1893

This private school was founded in 1964. It has a 275-acre campus.

RATINGS
Admissions Selectivity Rating: 90   **Fire Safety Rating:** 60*   **Green Rating:** 60*

STUDENTS AND FACULTY
Enrollment: 368. **Student Body:** 57% female, 43% male, 80% out-of-state, 4% international. Asian 4%, African American 7%, Caucasian 58%, Hispanic 6%, Native American 1%.
Retention and Graduation: 82% freshmen return for sophomore year. 73% freshmen graduate within 4 years. **Faculty:** Student/faculty ratio 8:1. 37 full-time faculty, 95% hold PhDs, 14% are members of minority groups, 30% are women.

ACADEMICS
Degrees: Associate, bachelor's. **Classes:** Most classes have 10–19 students. Most lab/discussion sessions have 10–19 students. **Majors with Highest Enrollment:** Cell/cellular biology and histology; creative writing; psychology. **Special Study Options:** Accelerated program, cooperative education program, cross-registration, dual enrollment, exchange student program (domestic), independent study, internships, student-designed major, study abroad, Study Abroad Program(s) within in the last two years: In Hondorus, Spain, England, Germany, Thailand, South Africa, Japan, China. **Combined degree programs:** BA/BS Eng) from Dartmouth/Washington U/or Columbia. Special programs offered to physically disabled students include tape recorders, tutors. **Career services:** Alumni network, career/job search classes, internships, regional alumni.

FACILITIES
Housing: Coed dorms, men's dorms, women's dorms, apartments for single students; if students propose a plan for cooperative housing it will be considered by Dean of Student Life. 75% of campus accessible to physically disabled. **Special Academic Facilities/Equipment:** Daniel Arts Center, Fisher Science and Academic Center. **Computers:** Administrative functions (other than registration) can be performed online.

CAMPUS LIFE
Environment: Village. **Activities:** Choral groups, dance, drama/theater, jazz band, literary magazine, music ensembles, radio station, student government, student newspaper, student-run film society, yearbook. **Organizations:** 21 registered organizations, 3 religious organizations. **Athletics (Intercollegiate):** *Men:* Basketball, soccer, swimming, tennis. *Women:* Basketball, soccer, swimming, tennis. **On-Campus Highlights:** Fisher Science and Academic Center, Daniel Arts Center, Alumni Library, Kellogg Music Center, Kilpatrick Athletic Center, Livingston Hall Student Union.

ADMISSIONS
Freshman Academic Profile: Average high school GPA 3.36. 60% in top 10% of high school class, 82% in top 25% of high school class, 94% in top 50% of high school class. SAT Math middle 50% range 530–680. SAT Critical Reading middle 50% range 560–690. ACT middle 50% range 25–30. Minimum paper TOEFL 550. Minimum computer TOEFL 200. **Basis for Candidate Selection:** *Very important factors considered include:* Application essay, recommendation(s), rigor of secondary school record, character/personal qualities, interview, talent/ability. *Important factors considered include:* Class rank, academic GPA, level of applicant's interest. *Other factors considered include:* standardized test scores, alumni/ae relation, extracurricular activities, first generation, racial/ethnic status, volunteer work, work experience. **Freshman Admission Requirements:** High school diploma or equivalent is not required. *Academic units recommended:* 2 English, 2 mathematics, 2 science, (1 science labs), 2 foreign language, 2 social studies, 2 history. **Freshman Admission Statistics:** 204 applied, 84% admitted, 74% enrolled. **Transfer Admission Requirements:** college transcript(s), essay or personal statement, interview, minimum college GPA of 2.0 required. Lowest grade transferable C. **General Admission Information:** Application fee $50. Regular application deadline 5/31. Notification on a rolling basis, beginning on or about 9/1. Nonfall registration accepted. Admission may be deferred for a maximum of 1 year. Credit and/or placement offered for CEEB Advanced Placement tests.

COSTS AND FINANCIAL AID
Annual tuition $34,804. Room and board $9,260. Required fees $530. Average book expense $1,000. **Required Forms and Deadlines:** FAFSA, CSS/Financial Aid PROFILE, business/farm supplement. Parent and Student Federal Taxes/ Federal Verification Worksheet. Priority financial aid filing date 4/15. **Notification of Awards:** Applicants will be notified of awards on a rolling basis beginning 4/15. **Types of Aid:** *Need-based scholarships/grants:* Federal Pell, SEOG, state scholarships/grants, private scholarships, the school's own gift aid. *Loans:* FFEL Subsidized Stafford, FFEL Unsubsidized Stafford, FFEL PLUS, Federal Perkins, state loans, Alternative Educational Loans. **Student Employment:** Federal Work-Study Program available. Institutional employment available. Highest amount earned per year from on-campus jobs $1,300. Off-campus job opportunities are good. **Financial Aid Statistics:** 51% freshmen, 39% undergrads receive need-based scholarship or grant aid. 50% freshmen, 33% undergrads receive non-need-based scholarship or grant aid. 47% freshmen, 43% undergrads receive need-based self-help aid. 78% freshmen, 71% undergrads receive any aid. 70% undergrads borrow to pay for school. Average cumulative indebtedness $15,000. **Criteria for awarding institutional aid:** *Non-need-based:* Academics, alumni affiliation, leadership, state/district residency.

BARNARD COLLEGE

Best 373

3009 Broadway, New York, NY 10027
Phone: 212-854-2014 **Financial Aid Phone:** 212-854-2154
E-mail: admissions@barnard.edu **CEEB Code:** 2038
Fax: 212-854-6220 **Website:** www.barnard.edu **ACT Code:** 2718

This private school was founded in 1889. It has a 4-acre campus.

RATINGS
Admissions Selectivity Rating: 97   **Fire Safety Rating:** 66   **Green Rating:** 83

STUDENTS AND FACULTY
Enrollment: 2,417. **Student Body:** 100% female, 67% out-of-state, 5% international (32 countries represented). Asian 16%, African American 4%, Caucasian 66%, Hispanic 9%.
Retention and Graduation: 93% freshmen return for sophomore year. 22% grads go on to further study within 1 year. 6% grads pursue arts and sciences degrees. 7% grads pursue law degrees. 1% grads pursue business degrees. 5% grads pursue medical degrees. **Faculty:** Student/faculty ratio 10:1. 208 full-time faculty, 94% hold PhDs, 15% are members of minority groups, 58% are women.

ACADEMICS
Degrees: Bachelor's. **Classes:** Most classes have 10–19 students. Most lab/discussion sessions have 10–19 students. **Majors with Highest Enrollment:** Economics, other; English language and literature; psychology. **Special Study Options:** Accelerated program, cross-registration, double major, dual enrollment, exchange student program (domestic), honors program, independent study, internships, liberal arts/career combination, student-designed major, study abroad, teacher certification program, independant scholars program, BA/BS in engineering and applied science. **Honors programs:** The Barnard Centennial Scholars Program, established in 1984, offers selected students the opportunity to pursue courses of independent study early in their college careers. Working closely with mentors of their choice over a period of several semesters, these young women undertake investigations in areas of personal interest that culminate in projects presented to faculty and peers. The Athena Center for Leadership Studies was launched in September of 2009 and offers a range of academic courses that examines all aspects of women's leadership, sponsored lectures, mentoring and leadership opportunities and a lab which offers a wide range of workshops designed to teach practical elements of leadership to students, alums and other leaders in New York. **Combined degree programs:** BA/JD, BA/DDS, BA/MIA or BA/MBA Col. Schl. of Intern. and Public Af. Special programs offered to physically disabled students include note-taking services, reader services, tape recorders, tutors. **Career services:** Alumni network, alumni services, career/job search classes, career assessment, internships, regional alumni. Career services highlights include: Because of our urban setting, our students are exposed to extremely wide range of internship opportunities. Barnard also offers funding for some unpaid internships.

FACILITIES
Housing: Coed dorms, special housing for disabled students, women's dorms, apartments for single students. 100% of campus accessible to physically

disabled. **Special Academic Facilities/Equipment:** Black Box theater, infant-toddler center, greenhouse, academic computer center, advanced architecture labs. **Computers:** 60% of classrooms, 80% of dorms, 80% of libraries, 100% of dining areas, 100% of student union, 100% of common outdoor areas have wireless network access. Students can register for classes online. Administrative functions (other than registration) can be performed online.

CAMPUS LIFE

Environment: Metropolis. **Activities:** Choral groups, concert band, dance, drama/theater, jazz band, literary magazine, marching band, music ensembles, musical theater, opera, pep band, radio station, student government, student newspaper, student-run film society, symphony orchestra, television station, yearbook, campus ministries. **Organizations:** 100 registered organizations, 1 honor societies. **Athletics (Intercollegiate):** *Women:* Archery, basketball, crew/rowing, cross-country, diving, fencing, field hockey, golf, lacrosse, soccer, softball, swimming, tennis, track/field (outdoor), volleyball. **On-Campus Highlights:** Diana Center, Arthur Ross Greenhouse, Held Auditorium, Smart Media Classrooms, Liz's Place Cafe. **Environmental Initiatives:** Engaged an energy consulting firm to provide energy modeling for all new building systems design and create an inventory of existing equipment to be upgraded or modified to reduce consumption, model the savings and provide a prioritized list of initiative and payback periods. We are working with the USGBC, Con Edison and NYSERDA on other incentive-based or life cycle initiatives. We have set up a tripartite committee to study sustainable business practices and a website to report and track our performance.

ADMISSIONS

Freshman Academic Profile: 75% in top 10% of high school class, 93% in top 25% of high school class, 98% in top 50% of high school class. 53% from public high schools. SAT Math middle 50% range 620–710. SAT Critical Reading middle 50% range 630–730. SAT Writing middle 50% range 660–740. ACT middle 50% range 28–32. Minimum paper TOEFL 600. Minimum computer TOEFL 250. **Basis for Candidate Selection:** *Very important factors considered include:* Academic GPA, recommendation(s), rigor of secondary school record, standardized test scores, character/personal qualities, extracurricular activities. *Important factors considered include:* Application essay, talent/ability, volunteer work. *Other factors considered include:* Class rank, alumni/ae relation, first generation, geographical residence, interview, level of applicant's interest, racial/ethnic status, work experience. **Freshman Admission Requirements:** High school diploma or equivalent is not required. *Academic units recommended:* 4 English, 3 mathematics, 3 science, (2 science labs), 3 foreign language. **Freshman Admission Statistics:** 4,174 applied, 31% admitted, 45% enrolled. **Transfer Admission Requirements:** High school transcript, college transcript(s), essay or personal statement, standardized test scores, statement of good standing from prior institution(s). Lowest grade transferable C–. **General Admission Information:** Application fee $55. Early decision application deadline 11/15. Regular application deadline 1/1. Regular notification 4/1. Nonfall registration not accepted. Admission may be deferred for a maximum of 1 year. Credit and/or placement offered for CEEB Advanced Placement tests.

COSTS AND FINANCIAL AID

Annual tuition $37,051. Room and board $12,319. Required fees $1,599. Average book expense $1,146. **Required Forms and Deadlines:** FAFSA, institution's own financial aid form, CSS/Financial Aid PROFILE, state aid form, noncustodial PROFILE, business/farm supplement, federal income tax returns. Financial aid filing deadline 2/1. **Notification of Awards:** Applicants will be notified of awards on or about 3/31. **Types of Aid:** *Need-based scholarships/grants:* Federal Pell, SEOG, state scholarships/grants, private scholarships, the school's own gift aid. *Loans:* FFEL Subsidized Stafford, FFEL Unsubsidized Stafford, FFEL PLUS, Federal Perkins, state loans, college/university loans from institutional funds. **Student Employment:** Federal Work-Study Program available. Institutional employment available. Highest amount earned per year from on-campus jobs $8,325. Off-campus job opportunities are excellent. **Financial Aid Statistics:** 38% freshmen, 42% undergrads receive need-based scholarship or grant aid. 40% freshmen, 44% undergrads receive need-based self-help aid. 53% freshmen, 51% undergrads receive any aid. 44% undergrads borrow to pay for school. Average cumulative indebtedness $14,706.

See page 1024.

BARRY UNIVERSITY

11300 North East Second Avenue, Miami Shores, FL 33161-6695
Phone: 305-899-3100 **Financial Aid Phone:** 305-899-3673
E-mail: Des-forms@mail.barry.edu **CEEB Code:** 5053
Fax: 305-899-2971 **Website:** www.barry.edu **ACT Code:** 718

This private school, affiliated with the Roman Catholic Church, was founded in 1940. It has a 122-acre campus.

RATINGS

Admissions Selectivity Rating: 76   **Fire Safety Rating:** 60*   **Green Rating:** 60*

STUDENTS AND FACULTY

Enrollment: 5,053. **Student Body:** 68% female, 32% male, 26% out-of-state, 4% international (101 countries represented). Asian 1%, African American 22%, Caucasian 23%, Hispanic 29%.
Retention and Graduation: 64% freshmen return for sophomore year. **Faculty:** Student/faculty ratio 13:1. 340 full-time faculty, 84% hold PhDs, 26% are members of minority groups, 53% are women.

ACADEMICS

Degrees: Bachelor's, first professional, master's, post-bachelor's certificate, post-master's certificate. **Classes:** Most classes have 10–19 students. **Majors with Highest Enrollment:** Business/commerce; elementary education and teaching; information science/studies. **Special Study Options:** Accelerated program, double major, English as a Second Language (ESL), honors program, internships, study abroad, teacher certification program. **Combined degree programs:** DPM/MBA; JD/MBA; MSN/MBA. Special programs offered to physically disabled students include note-taking services, reader services, tape recorders, tutors. **Career services:** Alumni services.

FACILITIES

Housing: Coed dorms, special housing for disabled students, men's dorms, women's dorms. 82% of campus accessible to physically disabled. **Special Academic Facilities/Equipment:** Human performance lab, broadcasting studio, radio station, athletic training room, cell biology/biotechnology labs, Classroom of Tomorrow, Biomechanics lab, Photogrpahy lab, darkroom, and studio, language lab, athletic training room. **Computers:** Students can register for classes online. Administrative functions (other than registration) can be performed online.

CAMPUS LIFE

Environment: Village. **Activities:** Choral groups, dance, drama/theater, literary magazine, music ensembles, musical theater, radio station, student government, student newspaper, television station, campus ministries, international student organization. **Organizations:** 67 registered organizations, 20 honor societies, 5 religious organizations. 2 fraternities, 2 sororities. **Athletics (Intercollegiate):** *Men:* Baseball, basketball, golf, soccer, tennis. *Women:* Basketball, crew/rowing, golf, soccer, softball, tennis, volleyball. **On-Campus Highlights:** Thompson Hall-Student Center, Human Performance Leisure Sciences-Athletic Complex, Penaport Pool, Residence Halls, Library.

ADMISSIONS

Freshman Academic Profile: Average high school GPA 3.14. 100% in top 50% of high school class. SAT Math middle 50% range 420–520. SAT Critical Reading middle 50% range 440–520. ACT middle 50% range 18–22. Minimum paper TOEFL 550. Minimum computer TOEFL 213. **Basis for Candidate Selection:** *Very important factors considered include:* Academic GPA, standardized test scores. *Important factors considered include:* character/personal qualities, interview, talent/ability. *Other factors considered include:* Class rank, application essay, recommendation(s), rigor of secondary school record, extracurricular activities, volunteer work, work experience. **Freshman Admission Requirements:** High school diploma is required and GED is accepted. *Academic units recommended:* 4 English, 3 mathematics, 3 science, 3 social studies. **Freshman Admission Statistics:** 3,315 applied, 57% admitted, 25% enrolled. **Transfer Admission Requirements:** College transcript(s), minimum college GPA of 2.0 required. Lowest grade transferable C. **General Admission Information:** Application fee $30. Notification on a rolling basis, beginning on or about 9/8. Nonfall registration accepted. Admission may be deferred for a maximum of 1 year. Credit offered for CEEB Advanced Placement tests.

COSTS AND FINANCIAL AID

Required Forms and Deadlines: FAFSA. **Notification of Awards:** Applicants will be notified of awards on a rolling basis beginning 1/25. **Types of Aid:** *Need-based scholarships/grants:* Federal Pell, SEOG, state scholarships/grants, private scholarships, the school's own gift aid, Federal Nursing Scholarships. *Loans:* FFEL Subsidized Stafford, FFEL Unsubsidized Stafford, FFEL PLUS, Federal Perkins, Federal Nursing, college/university loans from institutional funds, Alternative Loans. **Student Employment:** Federal Work-Study Program available. Institutional employment available. Highest amount earned per year from on-campus jobs $7,400. Off-campus job opportunities are good. **Financial Aid Statistics:** 48% freshmen, 45% undergrads receive need-based scholarship or grant aid. 74% freshmen, 71% undergrads receive non-need-based scholarship or grant aid. 66% freshmen, 67% undergrads receive need-based self-help aid. 5% freshmen, 3% undergrads receive athletic scholarships. 98% freshmen, 85% undergrads receive any aid. 76% undergrads borrow to pay for school. Average cumulative indebtedness $20,619. **Criteria for awarding institutional aid:** *Non-need-based:* Academics, art, athletics, music/drama.

BARTON COLLEGE

Box 5000, Wilson, NC 27893-7000
Phone: 252-399-6317 **Financial Aid Phone:** 252-399-6316
E-mail: enroll@barton.edu **CEEB Code:** 5016
Fax: 252-399-6572 **Website:** www.barton.edu **ACT Code:** 3066

This private school, affiliated with the Disciples of Christ Church, was founded in 1902. It has a 76-acre campus.

RATINGS
Admissions Selectivity Rating: 73   **Fire Safety Rating:** 78   **Green Rating:** 60*

STUDENTS AND FACULTY
Enrollment: 1,126. **Student Body:** 71% female, 29% male, 14% out-of-state, 1% international (8 countries represented). Asian 2%, African American 26%, Caucasian 58%, Hispanic 2%, Native American 1%.
Retention and Graduation: 67% freshmen return for sophomore year. 33% freshmen graduate within 4 years. **Faculty:** Student/faculty ratio 12:1. 68 full-time faculty, 69% hold PhDs, 9% are members of minority groups, 47% are women.

ACADEMICS
Degrees: Bachelor's. **Classes:** Most classes have 10–19 students. Most lab/discussion sessions have fewer than 10 students. **Majors with Highest Enrollment:** Business administration and management; elementary education and teaching; nursing/registered nurse (RN, ASN, BSN, MSN). **Special Study Options:** Cooperative education program, double major, honors program, independent study, internships, liberal arts/career combination, study abroad, teacher certification program, weekend college. **Honors programs:** Three competitive international travel scholarships awarded to entering honors students Special programs offered to physically disabled students include note-taking services, reader services, tape recorders, tutors. **Career services:** Alumni services, career/job search classes, career assessment, internships.

FACILITIES
Housing: Coed dorms, special housing for disabled students, women's dorms, fraternity/sorority housing. 90% of campus accessible to physically disabled. **Special Academic Facilities/Equipment:** TV station, art museum, music recording studio, greenhouse. **Computers:** 90% of libraries, 90% of dining areas, have wireless network access. Administrative functions (other than registration) can be performed online.

CAMPUS LIFE
Environment: Town. **Activities:** Choral groups, dance, drama/theater, musical theater, pep band, student government, student newspaper, symphony orchestra, campus ministries. **Organizations:** 51 registered organizations, 7 honor societies, 4 religious organizations. 3 fraternities, 3 sororities. **Athletics (Intercollegiate):** *Men:* Baseball, basketball, cross-country, golf, soccer, tennis. *Women:* Basketball, cross-country, soccer, softball, tennis, volleyball. **On-Campus Highlights:** Hamlin Student Center, Sam and Marjorie Ragan Writing Center, Kennedy Recreation and Intramural Center, Hackney Library, Barton Art Museum.

ADMISSIONS
Freshman Academic Profile: Average high school GPA 3. 7% in top 10% of high school class, 36% in top 25% of high school class, 68% in top 50% of high school class. 87% from public high schools. SAT Math middle 50% range 420–560. SAT Critical Reading middle 50% range 400–550. ACT middle 50% range 17–20. Minimum paper TOEFL 525. Minimum computer TOEFL 195. **Basis for Candidate Selection:** *Very important factors considered include:* Academic GPA, standardized test scores. *Other factors considered include:* Class rank, recommendation(s), rigor of secondary school record, extracurricular activities, interview, volunteer work, work experience. **Freshman Admission Requirements:** High school diploma is required and GED is accepted. *Academic units required:* 4 English, 3 mathematics, 2 science, (1 science labs), 1 academic electives. *Academic units recommended:* 2 foreign language, 2 social sciences. **Freshman Admission Statistics:** 2,681 applied, 51% admitted, 17% enrolled. **Transfer Admission Requirements:** College transcript(s), statement of good standing from prior institution(s). Minimum college GPA of

2.0 required. Lowest grade transferable C. **General Admission Information:** Application fee $25. Notification on a rolling basis, beginning on or about 8/15. Nonfall registration accepted. Admission may be deferred for a maximum of 1 year. Credit and/or placement offered for CEEB Advanced Placement tests.

COSTS AND FINANCIAL AID
Required Forms and Deadlines: FAFSA. Priority financial aid filing date 4/1. **Notification of Awards: Types of Aid:** *Need-based scholarships/grants:* Federal Pell, SEOG, state scholarships/grants, private scholarships, the school's own gift aid. *Loans:* FFEL Subsidized Stafford, FFEL Unsubsidized Stafford, FFEL PLUS, Federal Perkins. **Student Employment:** Federal Work-Study Program available. Institutional employment available. Highest amount earned per year from on-campus jobs $1,500. Off-campus job opportunities are good. **Financial Aid Statistics:** 67% freshmen, 64% undergrads receive need-based scholarship or grant aid. 87% freshmen, 82% undergrads receive non-need-based scholarship or grant aid. 33% freshmen, 28% undergrads receive need-based self-help aid. 5% freshmen, 5% undergrads receive athletic scholarships. 98% freshmen, 93% undergrads receive any aid. **Criteria for awarding institutional aid:** *Non-need-based:* Academics, alumni affiliation, art, athletics, leadership, minority status, music/drama, religious affiliation, state/district residency.

BASTYR UNIVERSITY

14500 Juanita Drive NE, Kenmore, WA 98028
Phone: 4256023330 **Financial Aid Phone:** 425-602-3329
E-mail: admissions@bastyr.edu
Fax: 4256023090 **Website:** www.bastyr.edu

This private school was founded in 1978. It has a 51-acre campus.

RATINGS
Admissions Selectivity Rating: 60*   **Fire Safety Rating:** 60*   **Green Rating:** 60*

STUDENTS AND FACULTY
Enrollment: 173. **Student Body:** 84% female, 16% male, 35% out-of-state, 4% international (35 countries represented). Asian 5%, African American 2%, Caucasian 61%, Hispanic 3%.
Retention and Graduation: **Faculty:** Student/faculty ratio 9:1. 38 full-time faculty, 87% hold PhDs, 21% are members of minority groups, 71% are women.

ACADEMICS
Degrees: Bachelor's, certificate, master's, post-master's certificate. **Majors with Highest Enrollment:** Acupuncture; naturopathic medicine/naturopathy (nd); nutrition sciences. **Special Study Options:** Double major, internships, selected tracks within major. **Combined degree programs:** Naturopathic medicine and acupuncture. **Career services:** Career/job search classes, career assessment, internships.

FACILITIES
Housing: Coed dorms, wellness housing.

CAMPUS LIFE
Environment: Town. **Activities:** Choral groups, student government. **On-Campus Highlights:** Vegetarian cafeteria, medicinal herb garden, spacious campus grounds and playfields, adjacent state park, bookstore.

ADMISSIONS
Freshman Academic Profile: Minimum paper TOEFL 550. Minimum computer TOEFL 213. Minimum web-based TOEFL 79. **Transfer Admission Requirements:** College transcript(s), essay or personal statement, minimum college GPA of 2.25 required. Lowest grade transferable C. **General Admission Information:** Application fee $60. Notification on a rolling basis, beginning on or about 4/15.

COSTS AND FINANCIAL AID
Annual tuition $19,050. **Required Forms and Deadlines:** FAFSA, institution's own financial aid form. Priority financial aid filing date 5/15. **Notification of Awards:** Applicants will be notified of awards on a rolling basis beginning 5/15. **Types of Aid:** *Need-based scholarships/grants:* Federal Pell, SEOG, state scholarships/grants, private scholarships, the school's own gift aid. *Loans:* Direct Subsidized Stafford, Direct Unsubsidized Stafford, Direct PLUS, FFEL Subsidized Stafford, FFEL Unsubsidized Stafford, FFEL PLUS, Federal Perkins. **Student Employment:** Federal Work-Study Program available. **Financial Aid Statistics:** 75% undergrads receive need-based scholarship or grant aid. 2% undergrads receive non-need-based scholarship or grant aid. 85% undergrads receive need-based self-help aid. 85% undergrads borrow to pay for school. Average cumulative indebtedness $32,500. **Criteria for awarding institutional aid:** *Non-need-based:* Academics, alumni affiliation.

BATES COLLEGE

Best 373

23 Campus Avenue, Lindholm House, Lewiston, ME 04240
Phone: 207-786-6000 **Financial Aid Phone:** 207-786-6096
E-mail: CEEB Code: 3076
Fax: 207-786-6025 **Website:** www.bates.edu **ACT Code:** 1634

This private school was founded in 1855. It has a 109-acre campus.

RATINGS
Admissions Selectivity Rating: 95 **Fire Safety Rating:** 90 **Green Rating:** 97

STUDENTS AND FACULTY
Enrollment: 1,660. **Student Body:** 52% female, 48% male, 89% out-of-state, 5% international (65 countries represented). Asian 6%, African American 3%, Caucasian 81%, Hispanic 2%.
Retention and Graduation: 83% freshmen graduate within 4 years. **Faculty:** Student/faculty ratio 10:1. 162 full-time faculty, 93% hold PhDs, 14% are members of minority groups, 46% are women.

ACADEMICS
Degrees: Bachelor's. **Classes:** Most classes have 10–19 students. Most lab/discussion sessions have 10–19 students. **Majors with Highest Enrollment:** Economics; political science and government; psychology. **Special Study Options:** Accelerated program, cooperative education program, double major, honors program, independent study, internships, liberal arts/career combination, student-designed major, study abroad, teacher certification program. **Honors programs:** The Honors Program Special programs offered to physically disabled students include note-taking services, reader services, tape recorders, tutors. **Career services:** Alumni network, alumni services, career/job search classes, career assessment, internships, regional alumni. **Career services highlights include:** Finance Boot Camp. A day long introductory workshop presented by alumni working in all facets of the industy. The day provides a soup to nuts look at the industry with class specific small group options and networking opportunities.

FACILITIES
Housing: Coed dorms, men's dorms, women's dorms, theme houses, quiet/study houses and halls, chem-free and low chem houses and halls. 65% of campus accessible to physically disabled. **Special Academic Facilities/Equipment:** Art gallery, Edmund S. Muskie Archives, language labs, planetarium, 600-acre conservation area on seacoast for environmental studies, scanning electron microscope, Imaging Center. **Computers:** 40% of classrooms, 100% of dorms, 100% of libraries, 100% of dining areas, 100% of student union, 10% of common outdoor areas have wireless network access. Students can register for classes online. Administrative functions (other than registration) can be performed online.

CAMPUS LIFE
Environment: Town. **Activities:** Choral groups, dance, drama/theater, jazz band, literary magazine, music ensembles, pep band, radio station, student government, student newspaper, student-run film society, symphony orchestra, yearbook, campus ministries, international student organization. **Organizations:** 99 registered organizations, 3 honor societies, 9 religious organizations. **Athletics (Intercollegiate):** *Men:* Baseball, basketball, crew/rowing, cross-country, diving, football, golf, lacrosse, skiing (downhill/alpine), skiing (nordic/cross-country), soccer, squash, swimming, tennis, track/field (outdoor), track/field (indoor). *Women:* Basketball, crew/rowing, cross-country, diving, field hockey, golf, lacrosse, skiing (downhill/alpine), skiing (nordic/cross-country), soccer, softball, squash, swimming, tennis, track/field (outdoor), track/field (indoor), volleyball. **On-Campus Highlights:** Pettengill Hall, Bates College Museum of Art, Dining Commons, The George and Helen Ladd Library, Merrill Gymnasium/Underhill Arena. **Environmental Initiatives:** In the process of developing a climate neutral action plan. Working with Committee on Environmental Responsibility to update a sustainability plan for the college. Recently formed an Energy Task Force to reduce energy consumption, costs, and emissions across campus.

ADMISSIONS
Freshman Academic Profile: 55% in top 10% of high school class, 86% in top 25% of high school class, 99% in top 50% of high school class. 57% from public high schools. SAT Math middle 50% range 630–700. SAT Critical Reading middle 50% range 635–710. **Basis for Candidate Selection:** *Very important factors considered include:* Class rank, application essay, academic GPA, recommendation(s), rigor of secondary school record, character/personal qualities, extracurricular activities, interview, level of applicant's interest, talent/ability. *Other factors considered include:* standardized test scores, alumni/ae relation, first generation, geographical residence, racial/ethnic status, state residency, volunteer work, work experience. **Freshman Admission Requirements:** High school diploma is required and GED is not accepted. *Academic units required:* 4 English, 3 mathematics, 3 science, (2 science labs), 2 foreign language, 3 social studies. *Academic units recommended:* 4 English, 4 mathematics, 4 science, (3 science labs), 4 foreign language, 4 social studies. **Freshman Admission Statistics:** 4,434 applied, 30% admitted, 34% enrolled. **Transfer Admission Requirements:** High school transcript, college transcript(s), essay or personal statement, statement of good standing from prior institution(s). Lowest grade transferable C. **General Admission Information:** Application fee $60. Early decision application deadline 11/15. Regular application deadline 1/1. Regular notification 3/31. Nonfall registration accepted. Admission may be deferred for a maximum of 1 year. Credit and/or placement offered for CEEB Advanced Placement tests.

COSTS AND FINANCIAL AID
Comprehensive fee $51,300. Average book expense $1,150. **Required Forms and Deadlines:** FAFSA, CSS/Financial Aid PROFILE, noncustodial PROFILE, business/farm supplement. Financial aid filing deadline 2/1. **Notification of Awards:** Applicants will be notified of awards on or about 4/1. **Types of Aid:** *Need-based scholarships/grants:* Federal Pell, SEOG, state scholarships/grants, private scholarships, the school's own gift aid. *Loans:* FFEL Subsidized Stafford, FFEL Unsubsidized Stafford, FFEL PLUS, Federal Perkins, state loans. **Student Employment:** Federal Work-Study Program available. Institutional employment available. Off-campus job opportunities are good. **Financial Aid Statistics:** 41% freshmen, 39% undergrads receive need-based scholarship or grant aid. 40% freshmen, 39% undergrads receive need-based self-help aid. 44% freshmen, 41% undergrads receive any aid. 40% undergrads borrow to pay for school. Average cumulative indebtedness $18,785.

BAY PATH COLLEGE

588 Longmeadow Street, Longmeadow, MA 01106-2292
Phone: 413-565-1331 **Financial Aid Phone:** 413-565-1345
E-mail: admiss@baypath.edu
Fax: 413-565-1105 **Website:** www.baypath.edu

This private school was founded in 1897. It has a 48-acre campus.

RATINGS
Admissions Selectivity Rating: 74 **Fire Safety Rating:** 99 **Green Rating:** 70

STUDENTS AND FACULTY
Enrollment: 1,409. **Student Body:** 100% female, % out-of-state, 1% international (8 countries represented). Asian 2%, African American 11%, Caucasian 71%, Hispanic 12%.
Retention and Graduation: 73% freshmen return for sophomore year. 49% freshmen graduate within 4 years. **Faculty:** Student/faculty ratio 14:1. 44 full-time faculty, 52% hold PhDs, 7% are members of minority groups, 70% are women.

ACADEMICS
Degrees: Associate, bachelor's, certificate, master's, post-bachelor's certificate. **Classes:** Most classes have 10–19 students. Most lab/discussion sessions have 10–19 students. **Majors with Highest Enrollment:** Business administration and management; forensic science and technology; psychology. **Special Study Options:** Accelerated program, cooperative education program, cross-registration, distance learning, double major, English as a Second Language (ESL), exchange student program (domestic), honors program, independent study, internships, student-designed major, study abroad, teacher certification program, weekend college, directed study program. **Honors programs:** The Bay Path Honors Program offers unique learning experiences to the most qualified undergraduate students through honors courses, service projects, on and off campus events and participation in and development of the Bay Path College Honors Program community. The Honors Program at Bay Path provides academically talented and motivated students with uniquely challenging and intellectually stimulating educational opportunities. In the first two years, Honors students take team-taught, interdisciplinary seminars on specific topics, such as Darwin Across the Disciplines. This innovative approach broadens exposure to areas outside the major and provides connections with other Honors students. In the last two years, under the guidance of a faculty mentor, students are immersed in their field of study, and are urged to explore new areas of knowledge with an Honors thesis or creative project. Special programs offered to physically

disabled students include tutors. **Career services:** Alumni network, alumni services, career/job search classes, career assessment, internships, regional alumni. **Career services highlights include:** We have a very strong internship program, with all students required in each respective major to perform fieldwork, an internship, student teaching, or experiential learning. Internships are listed in the top 3 important experiences employers wish to see on a college student's resume, aside from major and degree achieved.

FACILITIES

Housing: Women's dorms. 50% of campus accessible to physically disabled. **Special Academic Facilities/Equipment:** Blake Student Commons, Bashevkin Academic Development Center, Breck Fitness Center, occupational therapy laboratory, and D'Amour Hall for Business, Communications and Technology. **Computers:** 100% of libraries, 100% of dining areas, 100% of student union, 25% of common outdoor areas have wireless network access. Students can register for classes online. Administrative functions (other than registration) can be performed online.

CAMPUS LIFE

Environment: Village. **Activities:** Choral groups, dance, drama/theater, literary magazine, musical theater, student government, student newspaper, international student organization, Model UN. **Organizations:** 42 registered organizations, 3 honor societies, 1 religious organizations. **Athletics (Intercollegiate):** *Women:* Basketball, cross-country, field hockey, soccer, softball, tennis, volleyball. **On-Campus Highlights:** Carpe Diem Cafe, Toner/Helliwell Hearth and Lounge, Game Room, Breck Fitness Center, D'Amour Hall for Business, Communications and Tech. **Environmental Initiatives:** Recycling program; Energy Conservation Efforts—conversion of electric heat in student residence hall to gas heat.

ADMISSIONS

Freshman Academic Profile: Average high school GPA 3.15. 16% in top 10% of high school class, 47% in top 25% of high school class, 77% in top 50% of high school class. 93% from public high schools. SAT Math middle 50% range 420–530. SAT Critical Reading middle 50% range 430–540. SAT Writing middle 50% range 420–540. ACT middle 50% range 17–21. Minimum paper TOEFL 500. Minimum computer TOEFL 177. Minimum web-based TOEFL 62. **Basis for Candidate Selection:** *Very important factors considered include:* Academic GPA, rigor of secondary school record. *Important factors considered include:* Standardized test scores. *Other factors considered include:* Class rank, application essay, recommendation(s), alumni/ae relation, character/personal qualities, extracurricular activities, first generation, geographical residence, interview, level of applicant's interest, state residency, talent/ability, volunteer work, work experience. **Freshman Admission Requirements:** High school diploma is required and GED is accepted. *Academic units required:* 4 English, 3 mathematics, 2 science, (2 science labs), 2 social studies, 1 history. *Academic units recommended:* 4 English, 4 mathematics, 3 science, (2 science labs), 2 foreign language, 2 social studies, 2 history. **Freshman Admission Statistics:** 635 applied, 83% admitted, 29% enrolled. **Transfer Admission Requirements:** College transcript(s), minimum college GPA of 2.0 required. Lowest grade transferable C–. **General Admission Information:** Application fee $25. Notification on a rolling basis, beginning on or about 9/15. Nonfall registration accepted. Placement offered for CEEB Advanced Placement tests.

COSTS AND FINANCIAL AID

Annual tuition $23,840. Room and board $9,750. Average book expense $1,200. **Required Forms and Deadlines:** FAFSA, institution's own financial aid form. Priority financial aid filing date 3/15. **Notification of Awards:** Applicants will be notified of awards on a rolling basis beginning 3/1. **Types of Aid:** *Need-based scholarships/grants:* Federal Pell, SEOG, state scholarships/grants, private scholarships, the school's own gift aid. *Loans:* FFEL Subsidized Stafford, FFEL Unsubsidized Stafford, FFEL PLUS, Federal Perkins, state loans. **Student Employment:** Federal Work-Study Program available. Institutional employment available. Highest amount earned per year from on-campus jobs $2,000. **Financial Aid Statistics:** 85% freshmen, 815% undergrads receive need-based scholarship or grant aid. 5% freshmen, 47% undergrads receive non-need-based scholarship or grant aid. 76% freshmen, 731% undergrads receive need-based self-help aid. 96% freshmen, 94% undergrads receive any aid. 90% undergrads borrow to pay for school. Average cumulative indebtedness $20,662. **Criteria for awarding institutional aid:** *Non-need-based:* Academics, state/district residency.

BAYLOR UNIVERSITY

One Bear Place #97056, Waco, TX 76798-7056
Phone: 254-710-3435 **Financial Aid Phone:** 254-710-2611
E-mail: admissions@baylor.edu **CEEB Code:** 6032
Fax: 254-710-3436 **Website:** www.baylor.edu **ACT Code:** 4062

This private school was founded in 1845. It has a 508-acre campus.

RATINGS

Admissions Selectivity Rating: 87   **Fire Safety Rating:** 91   **Green Rating:** 80

STUDENTS AND FACULTY

Enrollment: 12,101. **Student Body:** 59% female, 41% male, 18% out-of-state, 2% international (85 countries represented). Asian 7%, African American 8%, Caucasian 69%, Hispanic 11%, Native American 1%.
Retention and Graduation: 84% freshmen return for sophomore year. 47% freshmen graduate within 4 years. **Faculty:** Student/faculty ratio 15:1. 859 full-time faculty, 81% hold PhDs, 11% are members of minority groups, 37% are women.

ACADEMICS

Degrees: Bachelor's, master's, post-master's certificate. **Classes:** Most classes have 10–19 students. Most lab/discussion sessions have 10–19 students. **Majors with Highest Enrollment:** Biology/biological sciences; marketing/marketing management; psychology. **Special Study Options:** Accelerated program, double major, honors program, internships, student-designed major, study abroad, teacher certification program. **Honors programs:** Honors Program, University Scholars Program, Great Texts Program. **Combined degree programs:** , BBA/MAccounting, BBA/MTax, BSN/MSNursing, BBA/MBA, BSE/MSBE, BSE/ME, etc. Special programs offered to physically disabled students include note-taking services, reader services. **Career services:** Alumni network, alumni services, career/job search classes, career assessment, internships.

FACILITIES

Housing: Special housing for disabled students, men's dorms, special housing for international students, women's dorms, apartments for married students, apartments for single students, theme housing, living-learning centers. **Special Academic Facilities/Equipment:** Language and environmental studies labs, natural science museum, high definition television, Armstrong Browning library, Texas Collection Library, Strecker Museum/Bill and Vara Daniel Historical Village, TV station, radio station. **Computers:** 98% of classrooms, 10% of dorms, 95% of libraries, 95% of dining areas, 95% of student union, 50% of common outdoor areas have wireless network access. Students can register for classes online. Administrative functions (other than registration) can be performed online.

CAMPUS LIFE

Environment: City. **Activities:** Choral groups, concert band, dance, drama/theater, jazz band, literary magazine, marching band, music ensembles, musical theater, opera, pep band, radio station, student government, student newspaper, student-run film society, symphony orchestra, television station, yearbook, campus ministries, international student organization, Model UN. **Organizations:** 222 registered organizations, 32 honor societies, 11 religious organizations. 22 fraternities, 20 sororities. **Athletics (Intercollegiate):** *Men:* Baseball, basketball, cheerleading, cross-country, football, golf, tennis, track/field (outdoor), track/field (indoor). *Women:* Basketball, cheerleading, cross-country, equestrian sports, golf, soccer, softball, tennis, track/field (outdoor), track/field (indoor), volleyball. **On-Campus Highlights:** Mayborn Museum Complex, Armstrong Browning Library, Baylor Sciences Building, Student Life Center, Chili's Too—1st on a University Campus. **Environmental Initiatives:** Campus wide recycling, with over 700 locations on campus to recycle in which to recycle, and collaboration with Athletics Department to recycle at all university sporting events. Financing wind power generation facilities through our contract for the next 10 years to finance the construction of wind turbines. Campus-wide commitment to energy conservation through campaigns such as Last Out, Lights Out.

ADMISSIONS

Freshman Academic Profile: 40% in top 10% of high school class, 73% in top 25% of high school class, 95% in top 50% of high school class. SAT Math middle 50% range 550–650. SAT Critical Reading middle 50% range 530–640. SAT Writing middle 50% range 510–620. ACT middle 50% range 23–29. Minimum paper TOEFL 540. Minimum computer TOEFL 207. Minimum web-based TOEFL 76. **Basis for Candidate Selection:** *Very important factors consid-*

ered include: Class rank, rigor of secondary school record, standardized test scores. *Important factors considered include:* Academic GPA. *Other factors considered include:* Application essay, recommendation(s), alumni/ae relation, character/personal qualities, extracurricular activities, first generation, interview, level of applicant's interest, religious affiliation/commitment, talent/ability, volunteer work. **Freshman Admission Requirements:** High school diploma is required and GED is accepted. *Academic units required:* 4 English, 3 mathematics, 3 science, (2 science labs), 2 foreign language, 1 social studies, 1 history. **Freshman Admission Statistics:** 31,440 applied, 50% admitted, 20% enrolled. **Transfer Admission Requirements:** College transcript(s), minimum college GPA of 2.5 required. Lowest grade transferable C. **General Admission Information:** Application fee $50. Nonfall registration accepted. Credit and/or placement offered for CEEB Advanced Placement tests.

COSTS AND FINANCIAL AID

Annual tuition $26,996. Room and board $8,331. Required fees $2,758. Average book expense $1,398. **Required Forms and Deadlines:** FAFSA, State Residency Affirmation. Financial aid filing deadline 8/15. Priority financial aid filing date 1/15. **Notification of Awards:** Applicants will be notified of awards on a rolling basis beginning 3/1. **Types of Aid:** *Need-based scholarships/grants:* Federal Pell, SEOG, state scholarships/grants, the school's own gift aid. *Loans:* FFEL Subsidized Stafford, FFEL Unsubsidized Stafford, FFEL PLUS, Federal Perkins, Federal Nursing, state loans. **Student Employment:** Federal Work-Study Program available. Institutional employment available. Highest amount earned per year from on-campus jobs $9,325. Off-campus job opportunities are good. **Financial Aid Statistics:** 64% freshmen, 52% undergrads receive need-based scholarship or grant aid. 63% freshmen, 47% undergrads receive non-need-based scholarship or grant aid. 55% freshmen, 45% undergrads receive need-based self-help aid. 3% freshmen, 3% undergrads receive athletic scholarships. 94% freshmen, 86% undergrads receive any aid. **Criteria for awarding institutional aid:** *Non-need-based:* Academics, art, athletics, job skills, leadership, music/drama.

BEACON COLLEGE

105 E. Main Street, Leesburg, FL 34748
Phone: 352-638-9731 **Financial Aid Phone:** 352-787-6306
E-mail: admissions@beaconcollege.edu
Fax: 352-787-0721 **Website:** www.beaconcollege.edu **ACT Code:** 704

This private school was founded in 1989.

RATINGS
Admissions Selectivity Rating: 60*   **Fire Safety Rating:** 88   **Green Rating:** 60*

STUDENTS AND FACULTY
Enrollment: 128. **Student Body:** 38% female, 63% male, 80% out-of-state, (2 countries represented). Asian 2%, African American 10%, Caucasian 85%, Hispanic 3%.
Retention and Graduation: 73% freshmen return for sophomore year. 50% freshmen graduate within 4 years. **Faculty:** Student/faculty ratio 714:1. 17 full-time faculty, 65% hold PhDs, 6% are members of minority groups, 59% are women.

ACADEMICS
Degrees: Associate, bachelor's. **Classes:** Most classes have 10–19 students. **Special Study Options:** Cooperative education program, independent study, internships, study abroad. **Honors programs:** Psi Tau Omega is the academic honor society at Beacon College. Special programs offered to physically disabled students include note-taking services, reader services, tape recorders, tutors.

FACILITIES
Housing: Special housing for disabled students, apartments for single students, Students enjoy 1, 2, and 3 bedroom apartment style living accommodations. **Computers:** 100% of classrooms have wireless network access.

CAMPUS LIFE
Environment: Village. **Activities:** Choral groups, drama/theater, literary magazine, student government, student newspaper, yearbook. **Organizations:** 13 registered organizations, 1 honor societies, 1 fraternities, 1 sorority. **On-Campus Highlights:** New Resident Apartment Complex, Student Center, Stoer Building—Office of Student Services, Beacon College Library, Administration Building.

ADMISSIONS
Freshman Academic Profile: Average high school GPA 2.8. Minimum paper TOEFL 525. **Basis for Candidate Selection:** *Very important factors*

considered include: Recommendation(s). *Important factors considered include:* Application essay, rigor of secondary school record, standardized test scores, character/personal qualities, talent/ability. *Other factors considered include:* Class rank, academic GPA, extracurricular activities, interview, volunteer work, work experience. **Freshman Admission Requirements:** High school diploma is required and GED is accepted. *Academic units required:* 4 English, 1 mathematics, 1 science, 1 social studies, 2 history, 3 academic electives. **Freshman Admission Statistics:** 53 applied, 92% admitted, 59% enrolled. **Transfer Admission Requirements:** High school transcript, college transcript(s), essay or personal statement, interview, Lowest grade transferable C. **General Admission Information:** Application fee $50. Regular application deadline 8/1. Notification on a rolling basis, beginning on or about 9/1. Nonfall registration accepted. Credit offered for CEEB Advanced Placement tests.

COSTS AND FINANCIAL AID

Annual tuition $27,000. Room and board $8,150. Required fees $700. Average book expense $900. **Required Forms and Deadlines:** FAFSA, institution's own financial aid form, state aid form. Financial aid filing deadline 4/1. Priority financial aid filing date 3/1. **Notification of Awards:** Applicants will be notified of awards on or about 2/1. **Types of Aid:** *Need-based scholarships/grants:* Federal Pell, SEOG, state scholarships/grants, private scholarships, the school's own gift aid. **Student Employment:** Federal Work-Study Program available. Highest amount earned per year from on-campus jobs $6,000. Off-campus job opportunities are good. **Financial Aid Statistics:** 21% freshmen, 17% undergrads receive need-based scholarship or grant aid. 21% freshmen, 17% undergrads receive need-based self-help aid. 67% undergrads borrow to pay for school. Average cumulative indebtedness $28,000.

BELHAVEN UNIVERSITY

1500 Peachtree Street, Box 153, Jackson, MS 39202
Phone: 601-968-5940 **Financial Aid Phone:** 601-968-5933
E-mail: admission@belhaven.edu **CEEB Code:** 1055
Fax: 601-968-8946 **Website:** www.belhaven.edu **ACT Code:** 2180

This private school, affiliated with the Presbyterian Church, was founded in 1883. It has a 42-acre campus.

RATINGS
Admissions Selectivity Rating: 85   **Fire Safety Rating:** 60*   **Green Rating:** 60*

STUDENTS AND FACULTY
Enrollment: 2,298. **Student Body:** 65% female, 35% male, 45% out-of-state, international (18 countries represented). Asian 1%, African American 9%, Caucasian 27%, Hispanic 1%.
Retention and Graduation: 67% freshmen return for sophomore year. 35% freshmen graduate within 4 years. **Faculty:** Student/faculty ratio 10:1. 63 full-time faculty, 73% hold PhDs, 35% are women.

ACADEMICS
Degrees: Associate, bachelor's, certificate, master's. **Classes:** Most classes have fewer than 10 students. Most lab/discussion sessions have fewer than 10 students. **Majors with Highest Enrollment:** Business/commerce; dance; elementary education and teaching; history; social sciences. **Special Study Options:** Accelerated program, distance learning, double major, dual enrollment, English as a Second Language (ESL), honors program, independent study, internships, student-designed major, study abroad, teacher certification program. **Honors programs:** The Honors College at Belhaven College gives academically advanced, highly motivated students a forum in which to deepen and expand their college education, both intellectually and spiritually. Enrollment in the Honors College is limited to students who demonstrate a past record of academic achievement, seriousness about their calling, and enthusiasm for challenging dialogue with students and scholars from a variety of fields. **Combined degree programs:** BA/MEng **Career services:** Internships.

FACILITIES
Housing: Men's dorms, women's dorms. **Special Academic Facilities/Equipment:** Bitsy Irby art gallery. **Computers:** 100% of dorms, 100% of libraries, 100% of student union, have wireless network access. Students can register for classes online. Administrative functions (other than registration) can be performed online.

CAMPUS LIFE
Environment: City. **Activities:** Choral groups, dance, drama/theater, jazz band, literary magazine, marching band, music ensembles, pep band, student government, student newspaper, yearbook, international student organization. **Organizations:** 29 registered organizations, 5 religious organizations. **Athletics (Intercollegiate):** *Men:* Baseball, basketball, cheerleading, cross-country,

football, golf, soccer, tennis. *Women:* Basketball, cheerleading, cross-country, golf, soccer, softball, tennis, volleyball.

ADMISSIONS

Freshman Academic Profile: Average high school GPA 3.33. 33% in top 10% of high school class, 55% in top 25% of high school class, 80% in top 50% of high school class. SAT Math middle 50% range 460–570. SAT Critical Reading middle 50% range 490–610. ACT middle 50% range 19–24. Minimum paper TOEFL 500. Minimum computer TOEFL 173. Minimum web-based TOEFL 61. **Basis for Candidate Selection:** *Very important factors considered include:* Academic GPA, standardized test scores. *Other factors considered include:* Application essay, recommendation(s), interview. **Freshman Admission Requirements:** High school diploma is required and GED is accepted. *Academic units required:* 4 English, 2 mathematics, 1 science, 1 history, 8 academic electives. **Freshman Admission Statistics:** 1,380 applied, 52% admitted, 27% enrolled. **Transfer Admission Requirements:** college transcript(s), minimum college GPA of 2.0 required. Lowest grade transferable D. **General Admission Information:** Application fee $25. Nonfall registration accepted. Admission may be deferred for a maximum of 12. Credit and/or placement offered for CEEB Advanced Placement tests.

COSTS AND FINANCIAL AID

Annual tuition $17,700. Room and board $6,500. Average book expense $1,400. **Required Forms and Deadlines:** FAFSA, state aid form. Priority financial aid filing date 3/1. **Notification of Awards:** Applicants will be notified of awards on a rolling basis beginning 2/1. **Types of Aid:** *Need-based scholarships/grants:* Federal Pell, SEOG, state scholarships/grants, private scholarships, the school's own gift aid. *Loans:* FFEL Subsidized Stafford, FFEL Unsubsidized Stafford, FFEL PLUS, Federal Perkins. **Student Employment:** Federal Work-Study Program available. **Financial Aid Statistics:** 72% freshmen, 72% undergrads receive need-based scholarship or grant aid. 6% freshmen, 5% undergrads receive non-need-based scholarship or grant aid. 59% freshmen, 60% undergrads receive need-based self-help aid. 15% freshmen, 9% undergrads receive athletic scholarships. 100% undergrads borrow to pay for school. Average cumulative indebtedness $32,728. **Criteria for awarding institutional aid:** *Non-need-based:* Academics, alumni affiliation, art, athletics, music/drama.

BELLARMINE UNIVERSITY

2001 Newburg Road, Louisville, KY 40205
Phone: 502-452-8131 **Financial Aid Phone:** 502-452-8124
E-mail: admissions@bellarmine.edu **CEEB Code:** 1056
Fax: 502-452-8002 **Website:** www.bellarmine.edu **ACT Code:** 1490

This private school, affiliated with the Roman Catholic Church, was founded in 1950. It has a 135-acre campus.

RATINGS
Admissions Selectivity Rating: 85   **Fire Safety Rating:** 91   **Green Rating:** 78

STUDENTS AND FACULTY
Enrollment: 2,139. **Student Body:** 64% female, 36% male, 30% out-of-state, 1% international (20 countries represented). Asian 3%, African American 3%, Caucasian 82%, Hispanic 2%. **Retention and Graduation:** 52% freshmen graduate within 4 years. 23% grads go on to further study within 1 year. 4% grads pursue arts and sciences degrees. 1% grads pursue law degrees. 2% grads pursue business degrees. 2% grads pursue medical degrees. **Faculty:** Student/faculty ratio 12:1. 150 full-time faculty, 78% hold PhDs, 6% are members of minority groups, 48% are women.

ACADEMICS
Degrees: Bachelor's, master's, post-bachelor's certificate. **Classes:** Most classes have 10–19 students. Most lab/discussion sessions have 10–19 students. **Majors with Highest Enrollment:** Business/commerce; nursing/registered nurse (RN, ASN, BSN, MSN); psychology. **Special Study Options:** Accelerated program, cross-registration, double major, dual enrollment, honors program, independent study, internships, liberal arts/career combination, student-designed major, study abroad, teacher certification program. **Honors programs:** Bellarmine Honors Program, Bellarmine Brown Scholars Program. **Combined degree programs:** Accounting BA and MBA. Special programs offered to physically disabled students include note-taking services, reader services, tutors. **Career services:** Alumni network, alumni services, career/job search classes, career assessment, internships. Career services highlights include: 80% of Bellarmine

undergraduates will complete an internship or another form of experiential learning before graduating (Source NSSE 2007 BU Seniors).

FACILITIES
Housing: Coed dorms, special housing for disabled students, men's dorms, women's dorms, 4 bedroom or 2 bedroom suites. 85% of campus accessible to physically disabled. **Special Academic Facilities/Equipment:** McGrath Art Gallery; Thomas Merton Center. **Computers:** 50% of classrooms, 100% of dorms, 100% of libraries, 25% of dining areas, 100% of student union, 25% of common outdoor areas have wireless network access. Students can register for classes online. Administrative functions (other than registration) can be performed online.

CAMPUS LIFE
Environment: Metropolis. **Activities:** Choral groups, concert band, dance, drama/theater, jazz band, literary magazine, music ensembles, musical theater, pep band, radio station, student government, student newspaper, yearbook, campus ministries, international student organization. **Organizations:** 70 registered organizations, 3 honor societies, 6 religious organizations. 1 fraternities, 1 sorority. **Athletics (Intercollegiate):** *Men:* Baseball, basketball, bowling, cross-country, golf, lacrosse, soccer, tennis, track/field (outdoor). *Women:* Basketball, bowling, cheerleading, cross-country, field hockey, golf, soccer, softball, tennis, track/field (outdoor), volleyball. **On-Campus Highlights:** Norton Health Science Center, Our Lady of the Woods Chapel, Siena Halls, Owsley B. Frazier Stadium, The Thomas Merton Center, The $5.1 million Owsley B. Frazier Stadium has taken approximately 18 months to build and will be the new home for Bellarmine's soccer, field hockey, lacrosse, and track teams. The new facility has several outstanding features which are outlined below: • Artificial Turf – The artificial turf product, called "24/7," was produced and installed by the Motz Group. It has permanent markings for soccer, field hockey, and lacrosse and has an exceptional drainage system to allow for extensive play in all weather conditions. • Lighting – Lighting has been installed at the field to allow for night play. The Musco Lighting system features redirected lighting which bends spill lighting back on to the field, drastically reducing the amount of light which will fall outside the stadium's perimeter. • Track Surface – The track is an eight-lane, 400–meter track, featuring three long jump pits, two pole vault areas, a high jump pit, and a steeplechase water jump pit. The surface is a dual-durometer, polyurethane poured surface provided by Beynon Sport Surfaces, the same company which has installed tracks at other top college facilities over the past three years including Illinois, Maryland, and Purdue. • Capacity – Chairback bench seating is available for 2,000 spectators. • Scoreboard – A Daktronics scoreboard featuring a 17 x 3' scrolling message board is installed on the three-story clock tower at the south end of the stadium. • Press Box – The fully enclosed press box features seating for 14 people and wireless Internet access. The stadium also has a concession stand, public address system, officials' locker rooms, storage areas, and public restrooms. **Environmental Initiatives:** Development of an on-campus fruit/vegetable garden. Our major geothermal heating/cooling project and improved energy efficiency in new dormitory construction. Establishment of the Center for Regional Environmental Studies in July 2009.

ADMISSIONS
Freshman Academic Profile: Average high school GPA 3.49. 23% in top 10% of high school class, 51% in top 25% of high school class, 84% in top 50% of high school class. 63% from public high schools. SAT Math middle 50% range 510–600. SAT Critical Reading middle 50% range 480–600. ACT middle 50% range 22–27. Minimum paper TOEFL 550. Minimum computer TOEFL 213. Minimum web-based TOEFL 80. **Basis for Candidate Selection:** *Very important factors considered include:* Academic GPA, recommendation(s), rigor of secondary school record, standardized test scores, character/personal qualities, level of applicant's interest. *Important factors considered include:* Class rank, extracurricular activities. *Other factors considered include:* Application essay, alumni/ae relation, first generation, geographical residence, interview, racial/ethnic status, state residency, talent/ability, volunteer work, work experience. **Freshman Admission Requirements:** High school diploma is required and GED is accepted. *Academic units required:* 4 English, 3 mathematics, 3 science, (2 science labs), 2 foreign language, 2 social studies, 1 history, 5 academic electives. *Academic units recommended:* 4 English, 4 mathematics, 4 science, (2 science labs), 2 foreign language, 3 social studies, 3 history, 7 academic electives. **Freshman Admission Statistics:** 6,021 applied, 53% admitted, 19% enrolled. **Transfer Admission Requirements:** College transcript(s), minimum college GPA of 2.0 required. Lowest grade transferable D. **General Admission Information:** Application fee $25. Regular application deadline 8/15. Notification on a rolling basis, beginning on or about 10/1. Nonfall registration accepted. Admission may be deferred for a maximum of 1 year. Credit offered for CEEB Advanced Placement tests.

COSTS AND FINANCIAL AID
Annual tuition $29,160. Room and board $8,550. Required fees $1,150. Average book expense $764. **Required Forms and Deadlines:** FAFSA. Priority financial aid filing date 3/1. **Notification of Awards:** Applicants will be

notified of awards on a rolling basis beginning 4/1. **Types of Aid:** *Need-based scholarships/grants:* Federal Pell, SEOG, state scholarships/grants, private scholarships, the school's own gift aid. *Loans:* FFEL Subsidized Stafford, FFEL Unsubsidized Stafford, FFEL PLUS, Federal Perkins, state loans, college/university loans from institutional funds. **Student Employment:** Federal Work-Study Program available. Institutional employment available. Highest amount earned per year from on-campus jobs $2,500. Off-campus job opportunities are excellent. **Financial Aid Statistics:** 79% freshmen, 74% undergrads receive need-based scholarship or grant aid. 27% freshmen, 26% undergrads receive non-need-based scholarship or grant aid. 53% freshmen, 49% undergrads receive need-based self-help aid. 6% freshmen, 8% undergrads receive athletic scholarships. 100% freshmen, 98% undergrads receive any aid. 69% undergrads borrow to pay for school. Average cumulative indebtedness $21,639. **Criteria for awarding institutional aid:** *Non-need-based:* Academics, alumni affiliation, art, athletics, leadership, minority status, music/drama, religious affiliation, state/district residency.

BELMONT ABBEY COLLEGE

100 Belmont-Mount Holly Road, Belmont, NC 28012
Phone: 704-825-6665 **Financial Aid Phone:** 704-461-718
E-mail: admissions@bac.edu **CEEB Code:** 5055
Fax: 704-825-6220 **Website:** www.belmontabbeycollege.edu **ACT Code:** 3070

This private school, affiliated with the Roman Catholic Church, was founded in 1876. It has a 650-acre campus.

RATINGS
Admissions Selectivity Rating: 71   **Fire Safety Rating:** 60*   **Green Rating:** 60*

STUDENTS AND FACULTY
Enrollment: 1,625. **Student Body:** 63% female, 37% male, 28% out-of-state, 3% international (16 countries represented). Asian 2%, African American 27%, Caucasian 55%, Hispanic 5%.
Retention and Graduation: 59% freshmen return for sophomore year. 39% freshmen graduate within 4 years. 35% grads go on to further study within 1 year. 20% grads pursue arts and sciences degrees. 2% grads pursue law degrees. 8% grads pursue business degrees. 5% grads pursue medical degrees. **Faculty:** Student/faculty ratio 17:1. 69 full-time faculty, 64% hold PhDs, 3% are members of minority groups.

ACADEMICS
Degrees: Bachelor's. **Classes:** Most classes have 10–19 students. **Special Study Options:** Accelerated program, cooperative education program, double major, dual enrollment, external degree program, honors program, independent study, internships, liberal arts/career combination, study abroad, teacher certification program, weekend college. **Honors programs:** Anne Horne Little Honors Program, Hintemeyer Scholars Program. Special programs offered to physically disabled students include tutors. **Career services:** Alumni network, alumni services, career/job search classes, career assessment, internships, regional alumni. **Career services highlights include:** Internships.

FACILITIES
Housing: Coed dorms, men's dorms, women's dorms, apartments for single students **Special Academic Facilities/Equipment:** Museum with rare book collection. **Computers:** 10% of classrooms, 100% of libraries, 100% of dining areas, 100% of student union, have wireless network access.

CAMPUS LIFE
Environment: Village. **Activities:** Choral groups, drama/theater, literary magazine, musical theater, student government, student newspaper, campus ministries, international student organization. **Organizations:** 21 registered organizations, 5 honor societies, 3 religious organizations, 5 fraternities, 4 sororities. **Athletics (Intercollegiate):** *Men:* Baseball, basketball, cross-country, golf, soccer, tennis, wrestling. *Women:* Basketball, cross-country, soccer, softball, tennis, volleyball. **On-Campus Highlights:** Church/Basillica, Weeler Center Athletic Center, dining hall, Holy Grounds Coffee Shop.

ADMISSIONS
Freshman Academic Profile: Average high school GPA 3.11. 10% in top 10% of high school class, 29% in top 25% of high school class, 63% in top 50% of high school class. 65% from public high schools. SAT Math middle 50% range 460–550. SAT Critical Reading middle 50% range 450–570. ACT middle 50% range 17–23. Minimum paper TOEFL 550. Minimum computer TOEFL 213. **Basis for Candidate Selection:** *Very important factors considered include:* Rigor of secondary school record, standardized test scores, character/personal qualities. *Important factors considered include:* Class rank, alumni/ae relation, extracurricular activities, interview, volunteer work. *Other factors considered*

include: Application essay, recommendation(s), talent/ability, work experience. **Freshman Admission Requirements:** High school diploma is required and GED is accepted. *Academic units required:* 4 English, 3 mathematics, 2 science, 1 social studies, 1 history, 3 academic electives. *Academic units recommended:* 4 mathematics, 3 foreign language. **Freshman Admission Statistics:** 1,762 applied, 75% admitted, 31% enrolled. **Transfer Admission Requirements:** college transcript(s), minimum college GPA of 2.0 required. Lowest grade transferable C. **General Admission Information:** Application fee $35. Regular application deadline 8/2. Notification on a rolling basis, beginning on or about 9/15. Nonfall registration accepted. Admission may be deferred for a maximum of 1 yr. Credit offered for CEEB Advanced Placement tests.

COSTS AND FINANCIAL AID
Annual tuition $19,114. Room and board $9,620. Required fees $1,925. Average book expense $900. **Required Forms and Deadlines:** FAFSA. Priority financial aid filing date 4/1. **Notification of Awards:** Applicants will be notified of awards on a rolling basis beginning 3/10. **Types of Aid:** *Need-based scholarships/grants:* Federal Pell, SEOG, state scholarships/grants, private scholarships, the school's own gift aid. *Loans:* Direct Subsidized Stafford, Direct Unsubsidized Stafford, Direct PLUS, Federal Perkins. **Student Employment:** Federal Work-Study Program available. Institutional employment available. Highest amount earned per year from on-campus jobs $1,800. Off-campus job opportunities are fair. **Financial Aid Statistics:** 71% freshmen, 79% undergrads receive need-based scholarship or grant aid. 11% freshmen, 6% undergrads receive non-need-based scholarship or grant aid. 60% freshmen, 72% undergrads receive need-based self-help aid. 13% freshmen, 7% undergrads receive athletic scholarships. 90% freshmen, 81% undergrads receive any aid. 79% undergrads borrow to pay for school. Average cumulative indebtedness $19,000. **Criteria for awarding institutional aid:** *Non-need-based:* Academics, athletics, leadership, religious affiliation, state/district residency.

BELMONT UNIVERSITY

1900 Belmont Boulevard, Nashville, TN 37212-3757
Phone: 615-460-6785 **Financial Aid Phone:** 615-460-6403
E-mail: buadmission@belmont.edu **CEEB Code:** 1058
Fax: 615-460-5434 **Website:** www.belmont.edu **ACT Code:** 3946

This private school, affiliated with the Christian (Nondenominational) Church, was founded in 1860. It has a 66-acre campus.

RATINGS
Admissions Selectivity Rating: 87   **Fire Safety Rating:** 88   **Green Rating:** 74

STUDENTS AND FACULTY
Enrollment: 4,339. **Student Body:** 57% female, 43% male, 56% out-of-state, 1% international (30 countries represented). Asian 3%, African American 4%, Caucasian 86%, Hispanic 2%.
Retention and Graduation: 82% freshmen return for sophomore year. 53% freshmen graduate within 4 years. 18% grads go on to further study within 1 year. 15% grads pursue arts and sciences degrees. 1% grads pursue law degrees. 6% grads pursue business degrees. 2% grads pursue medical degrees. **Faculty:** Student/faculty ratio 12:1. 269 full-time faculty, 80% hold PhDs, 11% are members of minority groups, 50% are women.

ACADEMICS
Degrees: Bachelor's, master's, post-bachelor's certificate, post-master's certificate. **Classes:** Most classes have 10–19 students. Most lab/discussion sessions have 10–19 students. **Majors with Highest Enrollment:** Business/commerce; music management and merchandising; music performance. **Special Study Options:** Accelerated program, cooperative education program, distance learning, double major, honors program, independent study, internships, liberal arts/career combination, student-designed major, study abroad, teacher certification program. **Career services:** Alumni network, alumni services, career/job search classes, career assessment, internships. Career services highlights include: Campus-based business program—Our undergraduate students run five campus-based businesses that are collaborations with other programs on campus. This offers experiential learning for students who do not have a business of their own. Three of these businesses are retail oriented—located in 3,400 square feet of prime retail space in our student life building facing the edge of campus, and the other two are service business. These programs involve as many as 60 students at any given time.

FACILITIES
Housing: Men's dorms, women's dorms, apartments for single students. 98% of campus accessible to physically disabled. **Special Academic Facilities/Equipment:** Language lab, recording studio, the Belmont Mansion, Little Theatre.

Computers: 100% of classrooms, 100% of dorms, 100% of libraries, 100% of dining areas, 100% of student union, 100% of common outdoor areas have wireless network access. Students can register for classes online. Administrative functions (other than registration) can be performed online.

CAMPUS LIFE

Environment: Metropolis. **Activities:** Choral groups, concert band, dance, drama/theater, jazz band, literary magazine, marching band, music ensembles, musical theater, opera, pep band, radio station, student government, student newspaper, symphony orchestra, television station, campus ministries, international student organization. **Organizations:** 80 registered organizations, 17 honor societies, 12 religious organizations. 3 fraternities, 4 sororities. **Athletics (Intercollegiate):** *Men:* Baseball, basketball, cross-country, golf, soccer, tennis, track/field (outdoor). *Women:* Basketball, cross-country, golf, soccer, softball, tennis, track/field (outdoor), volleyball. **On-Campus Highlights:** Beaman Student Life Center, Curb Event Center, Belmont Mansion, Center for Music Business Recording Studios, Massey Courtyard. **Environmental Initiatives:** Recycle, composting of all leaves, conservation.

ADMISSIONS

Freshman Academic Profile: Average high school GPA 3.53. 35% in top 10% of high school class, 68% in top 25% of high school class, 95% in top 50% of high school class. 57% from public high schools. SAT Math middle 50% range 530–640. SAT Critical Reading middle 50% range 540–640. ACT middle 50% range 23–29. Minimum paper TOEFL 550. Minimum computer TOEFL 213. **Basis for Candidate Selection:** *Very important factors considered include:* Class rank, academic GPA, rigor of secondary school record, standardized test scores. *Important factors considered include:* Application essay, recommendation(s). *Other factors considered include:* Alumni/ae relation, character/personal qualities, extracurricular activities, first generation, racial/ethnic status, talent/ability, volunteer work, work experience. **Freshman Admission Requirements:** High school diploma is required and GED is accepted. *Academic units required:* 4 English, 3 mathematics, 3 science, 2 foreign language, 3 social studies, 3 academic electives. *Academic units recommended:* 4 mathematics, 4 science, 2 foreign language, 3 social studies, 3 academic electives. **Freshman Admission Statistics:** 3,220 applied, 77% admitted, 40% enrolled. **Transfer Admission Requirements:** High school transcript, college transcript(s), essay or personal statement, standardized test scores, minimum college GPA of 2.0 required. Lowest grade transferable C. **General Admission Information:** Application fee $50. Regular application deadline 8/1. Notification on a rolling basis, beginning on or about 9/1. Nonfall registration accepted. Admission may be deferred for a maximum of 1 year. Credit and/or placement offered for CEEB Advanced Placement tests.

COSTS AND FINANCIAL AID

Annual tuition $21,270. Room and board $8,590. Required fees $1,090. Average book expense $1,300. **Required Forms and Deadlines:** FAFSA. Priority financial aid filing date 3/1. **Notification of Awards:** Applicants will be notified of awards on a rolling basis beginning 3/15. **Types of Aid:** *Need-based scholarships/grants:* Federal Pell, SEOG, state scholarships/grants, private scholarships, the school's own gift aid. *Loans:* Direct PLUS, FFEL Subsidized Stafford, FFEL Unsubsidized Stafford, FFEL PLUS, Federal Perkins, college/university loans from institutional funds. **Student Employment:** Federal Work-Study Program available. Highest amount earned per year from on-campus jobs $4,000. Off-campus job opportunities are excellent. **Financial Aid Statistics:** 29% freshmen, 31% undergrads receive need-based scholarship or grant aid. 37% freshmen, 27% undergrads receive non-need-based scholarship or grant aid. 31% freshmen, 38% undergrads receive need-based self-help aid. 5% freshmen, 5% undergrads receive athletic scholarships. 85% freshmen, 80% undergrads receive any aid. 56.6% undergrads borrow to pay for school. Average cumulative indebtedness $29,268. **Criteria for awarding institutional aid:** *Non-need-based:* Academics, art, athletics, leadership, music/drama, religious affiliation, state/district residency.

See page 1026.

BELOIT COLLEGE

700 College Street, Beloit, WI 53511
Phone: 608-363-2500 **Financial Aid Phone:** 608-363-2663
E-mail: admiss@beloit.edu **CEEB Code:** 1059
Fax: 608-363-2075 **Website:** www.beloit.edu **ACT Code:** 4564

This private school was founded in 1846. It has a 75-acre campus.

RATINGS

Admissions Selectivity Rating: 88 **Fire Safety Rating:** 66 **Green Rating:** 70

STUDENTS AND FACULTY

Enrollment: 1,323. **Student Body:** 57% female, 43% male, 78% out-of-state, 6% international (32 countries represented). Asian 3%, African American 4%, Caucasian 74%, Hispanic 4%, Native American 1%.
Retention and Graduation: 90% freshmen return for sophomore year. 73% freshmen graduate within 4 years. 34% grads go on to further study within 1 year. **Faculty:** Student/faculty ratio 11:1. 123 full-time faculty, 93% hold PhDs, 11% are members of minority groups, 49% are women.

ACADEMICS

Degrees: Bachelor's. **Classes:** Most classes have 10–19 students. **Majors with Highest Enrollment:** Anthropology; international relations and affairs; political science and government. **Special Study Options:** Double major, English as a Second Language (ESL), exchange student program (domestic), independent study, internships, liberal arts/career combination, student-designed major, study abroad, teacher certification program, 3-2 Programs in Engineering and Forestry. Over half of our graduates earn credit off-campus for at least a semester through our comprehensive study abroad and "field term" programs. **Combined degree programs:** BA/MEng, Rush University—Nursing and Med. Tech. Special programs offered to physically disabled students include note-taking services, tape recorders, tutors. **Career services:** Alumni network, alumni services, career assessment, internships, regional alumni. Career services highlights include: Beloit offers career exploration programs and services that connect students with alumni and other professionals for job shadowing, informational interviews and internships. Programs can be reviewed at www.beloit.edu/facs/.

FACILITIES

Housing: Coed dorms, women's dorms, fraternity/sorority housing, cooperative housing, apartments for single students, theme housingWide variety of special-interest housing, particularly for languages. See Beloit College's web site for a current list of special-interest housing. 35% of campus accessible to physically disabled. **Special Academic Facilities/Equipment:** Wright Museum of Art, Logan Museum of Anthropology, Center for Language Study, student-run market research company (BELMARK), Alfred S. Thompson Observatory Center for Entrepreneurial Leadership (CELEB). **Computers:** 80% of classrooms, 10% of dorms, 100% of libraries, 100% of dining areas, 80% of student union, 4% of common outdoor areas have wireless network access. Administrative functions (other than registration) can be performed online.

CAMPUS LIFE

Environment: Town. **Activities:** Choral groups, dance, drama/theater, jazz band, literary magazine, music ensembles, musical theater, radio station, student government, student newspaper, student-run film society, symphony orchestra, television station, yearbook, international student organization. **Organizations:** 95 registered organizations, 6 honor societies, 3 religious organizations. 3 fraternities, 3 sororities. **Athletics (Intercollegiate):** *Men:* Baseball, basketball, cross-country, football, golf, soccer, swimming, tennis, track/field (outdoor), track/field (indoor). *Women:* Basketball, cross-country, soccer, softball, swimming, tennis, track/field (outdoor), track/field (indoor), volleyball. **On-Campus Highlights:** Logan Museum of Anthropology, Wright Museum of Art, Center for the Sciences, Alfred S. Thompson Observatory, Laura H. Idrich Neese Theatre Complex. Other popular spaces include the Poetry Garden, the Java Joint, Morse Library, Sports Center, and Pearsons Hall. **Environmental Initiatives:** New Science Center has been platinum-level LEED-certified, one of only three such buildings in the state. Campus-wide recycling program; in 2009 Beloit recycled 72 tons of material, 15% of the total waste stream. Green meal plan for food service is under continuous discussion and development. The introduction of trayless dining in 2008 has reduced waste by 35%, locally sourced food and produce from the campus vegetable garden are used whenever possible, and two campus dining options have switched to bio-degradable utensils and plates.

ADMISSIONS

Freshman Academic Profile: Average high school GPA 3.41. 32% in top 10% of high school class, 69% in top 25% of high school class, 93% in top 50% of high school class. 79% from public high schools. SAT Math middle 50% range 560–670. SAT Critical Reading middle 50% range 575–710. ACT middle 50% range 25–30. Minimum paper TOEFL 550. Minimum computer TOEFL 213. Minimum web-based TOEFL 80. **Basis for Candidate Selection:** *Very important factors considered include:* Application essay, academic GPA, recommendation(s), rigor of secondary school record. *Important factors considered include:* Class rank, standardized test scores, interview. *Other factors considered include:* Alumni/ae relation, character/personal qualities, extracurricular activities, first generation, level of applicant's interest, talent/ability, volunteer work, work experience. **Freshman Admission Requirements:** High school diploma is required and GED is accepted. *Academic units recommended:* 4 English, 4 mathematics, 3 science, 2 foreign language, 4 social studies. **Freshman Admission Statistics:** 1,962 applied, 73% admitted, 23% enrolled. **Transfer Admission Requirements:** College transcript(s), essay or personal statement, statement of good standing from prior institution(s). Minimum college GPA of 3.00 required. Lowest grade transferable C. **General Admission Information:** Application fee $35. Notification on a rolling basis, beginning on or about 2/15. Nonfall registration accepted. Admission may be deferred for a maximum of 1 year. Credit and/or placement offered for CEEB Advanced Placement tests.

COSTS AND FINANCIAL AID

Required Forms and Deadlines: FAFSA, institution's own financial aid form, state aid form Financial aid filing deadline 3/1. Priority financial aid filing date 3/1. **Notification of Awards:** Applicants will be notified of awards on a rolling basis beginning 4/1. **Types of Aid:** *Need-based scholarships/grants:* Federal Pell, SEOG, state scholarships/grants, private scholarships, the school's own gift aid. *Loans:* FFEL Subsidized Stafford, FFEL Unsubsidized Stafford, FFEL PLUS, Federal Perkins, college/university loans from institutional funds. **Student Employment:** Federal Work-Study Program available. Institutional employment available. Highest amount earned per year from on-campus jobs $3,000. Off-campus job opportunities are good. **Financial Aid Statistics:** 64% freshmen, 63% undergrads receive need-based scholarship or grant aid. 65% freshmen, 61% undergrads receive need-based self-help aid. 94% freshmen, 90% undergrads receive any aid. 69% undergrads borrow to pay for school. Average cumulative indebtedness $17,909. **Criteria for awarding institutional aid:** *Non-need-based:* Academics, leadership, minority status, music/drama.

BEMIDJI STATE UNIVERSITY

1500 Birchmont Dr. NE, Deputy Hall, Bemidji, MN 56601
Phone: 218-755-2040 **Financial Aid Phone:** 218-755-4143
E-mail: admissions@bemidjistate.edu **CEEB Code:** 6676
Fax: 218-755-2074 **Website:** www.bemidjistate.edu **ACT Code:** 2084

This public school was founded in 1919. It has a 90-acre campus.

RATINGS

Admissions Selectivity Rating: 76   **Fire Safety Rating:** 61   **Green Rating:** 86

STUDENTS AND FACULTY

Enrollment: 4,362. **Student Body:** 52% female, 48% male, 9% out-of-state, international (35 countries represented). **Retention and Graduation:** 33% freshmen graduate within 4 years. 34% grads go on to further study within 1 year. 27% grads pursue arts and sciences degrees. 1% grads pursue law degrees. 5% grads pursue business degrees. 1% grads pursue medical degrees. **Faculty:** Student/faculty ratio 19:1. 192 full-time faculty, 60% hold PhDs, 6% are members of minority groups, 40% are women. 5% of classes are taught by teaching assistants.

ACADEMICS

Degrees: Associate, bachelor's, master's. **Classes:** Most classes have 10–19 students. Most lab/discussion sessions have 20–29 students. **Majors with Highest Enrollment:** Business/commerce; education; industrial production technologies/technicians, other. **Special Study Options:** Accelerated program, cooperative education program, distance learning, double major, dual enrollment, English as a Second Language (ESL), exchange student program (domestic), external degree program, honors program, independent study, internships, liberal arts/career combination, study abroad, teacher certification program, Eurospring Semester, Sino-Summer, exchange program with other Minnesota state universities, other study-travel. Special programs offered to physically disabled students include note-taking services, reader services, tutors. **Career services:** Alumni network, career/job search classes, career assessment, regional alumni.

FACILITIES

Housing: Coed dorms, men's dorms, special housing for international students, women's dorms, apartments for married students, cooperative housing, apartments for single students, two floors for SOTA (Students Older Than Average age.), cooperative housing for international students. 95% of campus accessible to physically disabled. **Special Academic Facilities/Equipment:** Aquatics lab. Waterfront. C.V. Hobson Forest. Center for Research and Innovation (CRI). **Computers:** 90% of classrooms, 90% of dorms, 100% of libraries, 100% of student union, have wireless network access. Students can register for classes online. Administrative functions (other than registration) can be performed online.

CAMPUS LIFE

Environment: Village. **Activities:** Choral groups, concert band, dance, drama/theater, jazz band, literary magazine, music ensembles, musical theater, opera, pep band, radio station, student government, student newspaper, student-run film society, symphony orchestra, television station, campus ministries, international student organization, Model UN. **Organizations:** 83 registered organizations, 1 honor societies, 8 religious organizations. 2 fraternities, 1 sorority. **Athletics (Intercollegiate):** *Men:* Baseball, basketball, cross-country, football, golf, ice hockey, soccer, softball, tennis, track/field (outdoor), track/field (indoor), volleyball. *Women:* Basketball, cross-country, golf, ice hockey, soccer, softball, tennis, track/field (outdoor), track/field (indoor), volleyball. **On-Campus Highlights:** Recreation Center, Student Union, library, dormitories, computer labs. **Environmental Initiatives:** Signature theme of Environmental Stewardship, ACUPCC signatory, Talloires Declaration signatory.

ADMISSIONS

Freshman Academic Profile: Average high school GPA 3.33. 4% in top 10% of high school class, 27% in top 25% of high school class, 62% in top 50% of high school class. 95% from public high schools. ACT middle 50% range 19–24. Minimum paper TOEFL 550. Minimum computer TOEFL 200. **Basis for Candidate Selection:** *Very important factors considered include:* Class rank, standardized test scores. *Important factors considered include:* rigor of secondary school record. *Other factors considered include:* Application essay, recommendation(s). **Freshman Admission Requirements:** High school diploma is required and GED is accepted. *Academic units required:* 4 English, 3 mathematics, 3 science, (1 science labs), 2 foreign language, 3 social studies, 1 history, 1 art/music/world culture. *Academic units recommended:* 4 English, 3 mathematics, 3 science, (1 science labs), 2 foreign language, 3 social studies, 1 history, 1 academic electives, 1 art/music/world culture. **Freshman Admission Statistics:** 2,062 applied, 83% admitted, 45% enrolled. Minimum college GPA of 2.0 required. Lowest grade transferable C. **General Admission Information:** Application fee $20. Regular application deadline 8/15. Nonfall registration accepted. Admission may be deferred for a maximum of 1 year. Placement offered for CEEB Advanced Placement tests.

COSTS AND FINANCIAL AID

Annual in-state tuition $6,410. Annual out-of-state tuition $6,410. Room and board $6,325. Required fees $950. Average book expense $800. **Required Forms and Deadlines:** institution's own financial aid form. Priority financial aid filing date 5/15. **Notification of Awards:** Applicants will be notified of awards on a rolling basis beginning 5/15. **Types of Aid:** *Need-based scholarships/grants:* Federal Pell, SEOG, state scholarships/grants, private scholarships, the school's own gift aid. *Loans:* Direct Subsidized Stafford, Direct Unsubsidized Stafford, Direct PLUS, Federal Perkins, state loans. **Student Employment:** Federal Work-Study Program available. Institutional employment available. Highest amount earned per year from on-campus jobs $2,700. Off-campus job opportunities are good. **Financial Aid Statistics:** 41% freshmen, 44% undergrads receive need-based scholarship or grant aid. 44% freshmen, 42% undergrads receive non-need-based scholarship or grant aid. 52% freshmen, 52% undergrads receive need-based self-help aid. 13% freshmen, 4% undergrads receive athletic scholarships. 77% freshmen, 77% undergrads receive any aid. 67% undergrads borrow to pay for school. Average cumulative indebtedness $21,931. **Criteria for awarding institutional aid:** *Non-need-based:* Academics, alumni affiliation, art, athletics, music/drama.

BENEDICT COLLEGE

1600 Harden St, Columbia, SC 29204
Phone: 803-705-4491 **Financial Aid Phone:**
E-mail: thompso@benedict.edu
Fax: 803-253-5167 **Website:** www.benedict.edu

This private school, affiliated with the Baptist Church, was founded in 1870. It has a 110-acre campus.

RATINGS

Admissions Selectivity Rating: 62   **Fire Safety Rating:** 60*   **Green Rating:** 60*

STUDENTS AND FACULTY

Enrollment: 2,641. **Student Body:** 51% female, 49% male, 40% out-of-state. African American 99%, Hispanic 1%.
Retention and Graduation: 53% freshmen return for sophomore year. 11% freshmen graduate within 4 years. **Faculty:** Student/faculty ratio 19:1. 117 full-time faculty, 65% hold PhDs, 95% are members of minority groups, 58% are women.

ACADEMICS

Degrees: Bachelor's. **Classes:** Most classes have fewer than 10 students. Most lab/discussion sessions have fewer than 10 students. **Special Study Options:** Accelerated program, double major, dual enrollment, external degree program, honors program, internships, teacher certification program, weekend college

FACILITIES

Housing: Men's dorms, women's dorms.

CAMPUS LIFE

Environment: City. **Activities:** Choral groups, concert band, marching band, student government, student newspaper, campus ministries, international student organization.

ADMISSIONS

Freshman Academic Profile: Average high school GPA 2.54. 5% in top 10% of high school class, 15% in top 25% of high school class, 39% in top 50% of high school class. 63% from public high schools. SAT Math middle 50% range 320–430. SAT Critical Reading middle 50% range 320–430. ACT middle 50% range 13–17. Minimum paper TOEFL 550. Minimum computer TOEFL 213. Minimum web-based TOEFL 80. **Basis for Candidate Selection: Freshman Admission Requirements:** High school diploma is required and GED is accepted. *Academic units recommended:* 4 English, 3 mathematics, 2 science, 3 social studies. **Freshman Admission Statistics:** 4,624 applied, 83% admitted, 17% enrolled. **Transfer Admission Requirements:** High school transcript, college transcript(s), statement of good standing from prior institution(s). Minimum college GPA of 2.0 required. Lowest grade transferable C. **General Admission Information:** Application fee $25. Nonfall registration accepted. Credit offered for CEEB Advanced Placement tests.

COSTS AND FINANCIAL AID

Annual tuition $12,516. Room and board $6,444. Required fees $1,494. Average book expense $1,000. **Required Forms and Deadlines:** FAFSA Financial aid filing deadline 4/15. **Notification of Awards: Types of Aid:** *Need-based scholarships/grants:* Federal Pell, SEOG, state scholarships/grants, private scholarships, the school's own gift aid, United Negro College Fund. *Loans:* Direct Subsidized Stafford, Direct Unsubsidized Stafford, Direct PLUS.

BENEDICTINE COLLEGE

1020 North Second Street, Atchison, KS 66002
Phone: 913-360-7476 **Financial Aid Phone:** 913-360-7480
E-mail: bcadmiss@benedictine.edu **CEEB Code:** 6056
Fax: 913-367-5462 **Website:** www.benedictine.edu **ACT Code:** 1444

This private school, affiliated with the Roman Catholic Church, was founded in 1859. It has a 225-acre campus.

RATINGS

Admissions Selectivity Rating: 83 **Fire Safety Rating:** 62 **Green Rating:** 60*

STUDENTS AND FACULTY

Enrollment: 1,382. **Student Body:** 53% female, 47% male, 44% out-of-state, 2% international (18 countries represented). Asian 1%, African American 4%, Caucasian 81%, Hispanic 5%, Native American 1%.
Retention and Graduation: 76% freshmen return for sophomore year. 43% freshmen graduate within 4 years. 28% grads go on to further study within 1 year. 20% grads pursue arts and sciences degrees. 1% grads pursue law degrees. 7% grads pursue business degrees. 3% grads pursue medical degrees. **Faculty:** Student/faculty ratio 14:1. 76 full-time faculty, 68% hold PhDs, 7% are members of minority groups, 26% are women.

ACADEMICS

Degrees: Associate, bachelor's, master's. **Classes:** Most classes have 20–29 students. Most lab/discussion sessions have 10–19 students. **Majors with Highest Enrollment:** Business/commerce; elementary education and teaching; religion/religious studies. **Special Study Options:** Cooperative education program, double major, dual enrollment, English as a Second Language (ESL), independent study, internships, liberal arts/career combination, student-designed major, study abroad, teacher certification program. **Combined degree programs:**

BA/MA, BA/MEng, 3-2 occupational therapy with Washington U. Special programs offered to physically disabled students include tutors. **Career services:** Alumni services, career/job search classes, career assessment, internships.

FACILITIES

Housing: Coed dorms, men's dorms, women's dorms. Off-campus college-owned housing. 80% of campus accessible to physically disabled. **Special Academic Facilities/Equipment:** Language and special education labs, high tech classroom, stadium, student union. **Computers:** 60% of classrooms, 100% of dorms, 100% of libraries, 100% of dining areas, 100% of student union, 75% of common outdoor areas have wireless network access. Administrative functions (other than registration) can be performed online.

CAMPUS LIFE

Environment: Town. **Activities:** Choral groups, concert band, dance, drama/theater, jazz band, literary magazine, music ensembles, musical theater, pep band, student government, student newspaper, symphony orchestra, yearbook. **Organizations:** 38 registered organizations, 14 honor societies, 4 religious organizations. **Athletics (Intercollegiate):** *Men:* Baseball, basketball, cheerleading, cross-country, football, golf, soccer, tennis, track/field (outdoor), track/field (indoor). *Women:* Basketball, cheerleading, cross-country, golf, soccer, softball, tennis, track/field (outdoor), track/field (indoor), volleyball. **On-Campus Highlights:** Raven Roost, Ferrell Hall, Student Union, Abbey Church, River Lookout.

ADMISSIONS

Freshman Academic Profile: Average high school GPA 3.32. 5% in top 10% of high school class, 15% in top 25% of high school class, 36% in top 50% of high school class. 44% from public high schools. ACT middle 50% range 21–27. Minimum paper TOEFL 535. Minimum computer TOEFL 200. **Basis for Candidate Selection:** *Very important factors considered include:* Class rank, rigor of secondary school record, standardized test scores. *Other factors considered include:* Application essay, recommendation(s), alumni/ae relation, character/personal qualities, extracurricular activities, interview, racial/ethnic status, talent/ability, volunteer work, work experience. **Freshman Admission Requirements:** High school diploma is required and GED is accepted. *Academic units required:* 4 English, 3 mathematics, 2 science, 2 foreign language, 2 social studies, 2 history, 1 academic electives. *Academic units recommended:* 4 mathematics, 4 science, 4 foreign language. **Freshman Admission Statistics:** 2,192 applied, 20% admitted, 91% enrolled. **Transfer Admission Requirements:** college transcript(s), minimum college GPA of 2.0 required. Lowest grade transferable C. **General Admission Information:** Application fee $25. Notification on a rolling basis, beginning on or about 3/1. Nonfall registration accepted. Admission may be deferred for a maximum of 1 year. Credit and/or placement offered for CEEB Advanced Placement tests.

COSTS AND FINANCIAL AID

Annual tuition $18,800. Room and board $6,400. Average book expense $1,000. **Required Forms and Deadlines:** FAFSA. Priority financial aid filing date 3/15. **Notification of Awards:** Applicants will be notified of awards on a rolling basis beginning 2/1. **Types of Aid:** *Need-based scholarships/grants:* Federal Pell, SEOG, state scholarships/grants, private scholarships, the school's own gift aid. *Loans:* FFEL Subsidized Stafford, FFEL Unsubsidized Stafford, FFEL PLUS, Federal Perkins, Alternative Loans. **Student Employment:** Federal Work-Study Program available. Institutional employment available. Off-campus job opportunities are good. **Financial Aid Statistics:** 48% freshmen, 46% undergrads receive need-based scholarship or grant aid. 74% freshmen, 71% undergrads receive non-need-based scholarship or grant aid. 60% freshmen, 61% undergrads receive need-based self-help aid. 35% freshmen, 35% undergrads receive athletic scholarships. 98% freshmen, 77% undergrads receive any aid. 98% undergrads borrow to pay for school. Average cumulative indebtedness $26,000. **Criteria for awarding institutional aid:** *Non-need-based:* Academics, alumni affiliation, art, athletics, job skills, leadership, minority status, music/drama, religious affiliation.

BENEDICTINE UNIVERSITY

5700 College Road, Lisle, IL 60532-0900
Phone: 630-829-6300 **Financial Aid Phone:** 630-829-6100
E-mail: admissions@ben.edu **CEEB Code:** 1707
Fax: 630-829-6301 **Website:** www.ben.edu **ACT Code:** 1132

This private school, affiliated with the Roman Catholic Church, was founded in 1887. It has a 108-acre campus.

RATINGS

Admissions Selectivity Rating: 74 **Fire Safety Rating:** 86 **Green Rating:** 73

STUDENTS AND FACULTY

Enrollment: 3,244. **Student Body:** 57% female, 43% male, 4% out-of-state, (16 countries represented).
Retention and Graduation: 74% freshmen return for sophomore year. **Faculty:** Student/faculty ratio 13:1. 103 full-time faculty, 88% hold PhDs, 18% are members of minority groups, 46% are women.

ACADEMICS

Degrees: Associate, bachelor's, certificate, master's, post-bachelor's certificate, transfer associate. **Classes:** Most classes have 10–19 students. **Majors with Highest Enrollment:** Biology/biological sciences; business administration, management and operations, other; computer science. **Special Study Options:** Accelerated program, cross-registration, distance learning, double major, dual enrollment, English as a Second Language (ESL), honors program, independent study, internships, study abroad, teacher certification program, weekend college, Engineering degree program with Illinois Institute of Technology. **Honors programs:** University Scholars Program Special programs offered to physically disabled students include note-taking services, reader services, tape recorders, tutors. **Career services:** Alumni network, alumni services, career/job search classes, career assessment, internships. **Career services highlights include:** Internship program.

FACILITIES

Housing: Coed dorms, men's dorms, women's dorms, apartments for married students, apartments for single students, wellness housing 100% of campus accessible to physically disabled. **Special Academic Facilities/Equipment:** Natural science and history museums, www.ben.edu/museum/; Exercise physiology lab. **Computers:** 100% of dorms, 100% of libraries, 100% of student union, have wireless network access. Students can register for classes online. Administrative functions (other than registration) can be performed online.

CAMPUS LIFE

Environment: Town. **Activities:** Choral groups, concert band, dance, drama/theater, jazz band, literary magazine, music ensembles, pep band, student government, student newspaper, student-run film society, symphony orchestra, television station, campus ministries, international student organization, Model UN. **Organizations:** 40 registered organizations, 3 religious organizations. **Athletics (Intercollegiate):** *Men:* Baseball, basketball, cross-country, football, golf, soccer, track/field (outdoor), track/field (indoor). *Women:* Basketball, cross-country, golf, soccer, softball, tennis, track/field (outdoor), track/field (indoor), volleyball. **On-Campus Highlights:** Jurica Nature Museum, Kindlon Hall and Benedictine Library, Birck Hall of Science, Krasa Center: Chapel, cafeteria, snack bar, The Sports Complex, Coal Ben. **Environmental Initiatives:** Energy reduction, education, recycling.

ADMISSIONS

Freshman Academic Profile: Average high school GPA 3.29. 15% in top 10% of high school class, 39% in top 25% of high school class, 70% in top 50% of high school class. 71% from public high schools. ACT middle 50% range 20–26. Minimum paper TOEFL 550. Minimum computer TOEFL 213. Minimum web-based TOEFL 76. **Basis for Candidate Selection:** *Very important factors considered include:* Class rank, academic GPA, rigor of secondary school record, standardized test scores. *Other factors considered include:* Application essay, recommendation(s), extracurricular activities, interview. **Freshman Admission Requirements:** High school diploma is required and GED is accepted. *Academic units required:* 4 English, 3 mathematics, 2 science, (1 science labs), 2 foreign language, 3 social studies, 1 history. *Academic units recommended:* 4 mathematics, 3 science, (2 science labs). **Freshman Admission Statistics:** 1,667 applied, 79% admitted, 34% enrolled. **Transfer Admission Requirements:** college transcript(s), statement of good standing from prior institution(s). Minimum college GPA of 2.0 required. Lowest grade transferable D. **General Admission Information:** Application fee $40. Regular application deadline 8/30. Nonfall registration accepted. Admission may be deferred for a maximum of 4. Credit offered for CEEB Advanced Placement tests.

COSTS AND FINANCIAL AID

Annual tuition $21,600. Room and board $7,300. Required fees $720. Average book expense $1,260. **Required Forms and Deadlines:** FAFSA. Priority financial aid filing date 4/15. **Notification of Awards:** Applicants will be notified of awards on a rolling basis beginning 2/15. **Types of Aid:** *Need-based scholarships/grants:* Federal Pell, SEOG, state scholarships/grants, private scholarships, the school's own gift aid. *Loans:* FFEL Subsidized Stafford, FFEL Unsubsidized Stafford, FFEL PLUS, Federal Perkins. **Student Employment:** Federal Work-Study Program available. Institutional employment available. Highest amount earned per year from on-campus jobs $11,506. Off-campus job opportunities are excellent. **Financial Aid Statistics:** 47% freshmen, 44% undergrads receive need-based scholarship or grant aid. 69% freshmen, 53% undergrads receive non-need-based scholarship or grant aid. 49% freshmen, 58% undergrads receive need-based self-help aid. 96% freshmen, 88% undergrads receive any aid. 67% undergrads borrow to pay for school. Average cumulative indebtedness $34,640. **Criteria for awarding institutional aid:** *Non-need-based:* Academics, alumni affiliation, leadership, music/drama, religious affiliation, state/district residency.

BENNETT COLLEGE

900 East Washinton Street, Greensboro, NC 27401
Phone: 336-370-8624 **Financial Aid Phone:** 336-517-2220
E-mail: admiss@bennett.edu **CEEB Code:** 5058
Fax: 336-370-8653 **Website:** www.bennett.edu **ACT Code:** 3072

This private school, affiliated with the Methodist Church, was founded in 1873. It has a 55-acre campus.

RATINGS

Admissions Selectivity Rating: 70   **Fire Safety Rating:** 67   **Green Rating:** 60*

STUDENTS AND FACULTY

Enrollment: 711. **Student Body:** 100% female, 65% out-of-state, 1% international (5 countries represented). African American 96%, Hispanic 1%.
Retention and Graduation: 75% freshmen return for sophomore year. 17% freshmen graduate within 4 years. 30% grads go on to further study within 1 year. 20% grads pursue arts and sciences degrees. 5% grads pursue law degrees. 5% grads pursue business degrees. 15% grads pursue medical degrees. **Faculty:** Student/faculty ratio 11:1. 56 full-time faculty, 61% hold PhDs, 64% are members of minority groups, 71% are women.

ACADEMICS

Degrees: Bachelor's. **Classes:** Most classes have fewer than 10 students. Most lab/discussion sessions have 30–39 students. **Majors with Highest Enrollment:** Communication and media studies, other; psychology; social work. **Special Study Options:** Accelerated program, cooperative education program, cross-registration, double major, dual enrollment, honors program, independent study, internships, student-designed major, study abroad, teacher certification program, collaborative degree program with Howard University in Nursing (2x2). Special programs offered to physically disabled students include tape recorders, tutors. **Career services:** Alumni services, career/job search classes.

FACILITIES

Housing: Women's dorms, wellness housing. 21% of campus accessible to physically disabled. **Special Academic Facilities/Equipment:** Children's House, Constance Maiteena collection, college archives, telecommunications satellite dish. **Computers:** Students can register for classes online.

CAMPUS LIFE

Environment: City. **Activities:** Choral groups, dance, drama/theater, literary magazine, music ensembles, student government, student newspaper, campus ministries, international student organization. **Organizations:** 34 registered organizations, 5 honor societies, 1 religious organization. 4 sororities. **Athletics (Intercollegiate):** *Women:* Basketball, cheerleading, cross-country, softball, swimming, tennis, track/field (outdoor), volleyball. **On-Campus Highlights:** Student Union, Chapel, Little Theathre, Holgate Library, Lda Goode Gym.

ADMISSIONS

Freshman Academic Profile: Average high school GPA 2.61. 3% in top 10% of high school class, 10% in top 25% of high school class, 39% in top 50% of high school class. 92% from public high schools. SAT Math middle 50% range 320–420. SAT Critical Reading middle 50% range 350–450. ACT middle 50% range 15–18. Minimum paper TOEFL 500. **Basis for Candidate Selection:** *Very important factors considered include:* Academic GPA, rigor of secondary school record, standardized test scores. *Important factors considered include:* Class rank, application essay, recommendation(s), alumni/ae relation, talent/ability. *Other factors considered include:* Character/personal qualities, extracurricular activities, first generation, geographical residence, interview, level of applicant's interest, racial/ethnic status, religious affiliation/commitment, state residency, volunteer work, work experience. **Freshman Admission Requirements:** High school diploma is required and GED is accepted. *Academic units required:* 4 English, 3 mathematics, 2 science, 2 foreign language, 2 social studies, 5 academic electives. **Freshman Admission Statistics:** 1,676 applied, 54% admitted, 26% enrolled. **Transfer Admission Requirements:** college transcript(s), essay or personal statement, minimum college GPA of 2.0 required. Lowest grade transferable C. **General Admission Information:** Application fee $30. Nonfall registration accepted. Credit offered for CEEB Advanced Placement tests.

COSTS AND FINANCIAL AID

Annual tuition $13,258. Room and board $6,736. Required fees $1,976. Average book expense $1,200. **Required Forms and Deadlines:** FAFSA, institution's own financial aid form. Financial aid filing deadline 4/15. **Notification of Awards:** Applicants will be notified of awards on or about 7/15. **Types of Aid:** *Need-based scholarships/grants:* Federal Pell, SEOG, state scholarships/grants, private scholarships, the school's own gift aid, United Negro College Fund, Federal Nursing Scholarships. *Loans:* FFEL Subsidized Stafford, FFEL Unsubsidized Stafford, FFEL PLUS, Federal Perkins, The College has emergency funds available. **Student Employment:** Federal Work-Study Program available. Institutional employment available. Highest amount earned per year from on-campus jobs $1,500. Off-campus job opportunities are good. **Financial Aid Statistics:** 88% freshmen, 83% undergrads receive need-based scholarship or grant aid. 1% freshmen, 2% undergrads receive non-need-based scholarship or grant aid. 89% freshmen, 88% undergrads receive need-based self-help aid. 98% undergrads borrow to pay for school. Average cumulative indebtedness $37,667. **Criteria for awarding institutional aid:** *Non-need-based:* Academics, alumni affiliation, leadership, minority status, religious affiliation, state/district residency.

BENNINGTON COLLEGE

Office of Admissions, Bennington, VT 05201-6003
Phone: 802-440-4312 **Financial Aid Phone:**
E-mail: admissions@bennington.edu **CEEB Code:** 3080
Fax: 802-440-4320 **Website:** www.bennington.edu **ACT Code:** 4296

This private school was founded in 1932. It has a 470-acre campus.

RATINGS
Admissions Selectivity Rating: 89 | **Fire Safety Rating:** 79 | **Green Rating:** 83

STUDENTS AND FACULTY
Enrollment: 664. **Student Body:** 67% female, 33% male, 95% out-of-state, 6% international (29 countries represented). Asian 2%, African American 2%, Caucasian 86%, Hispanic 2%.
Retention and Graduation: 90% freshmen return for sophomore year. 49% freshmen graduate within 4 years. 14% grads go on to further study within 1 year. **Faculty:** Student/faculty ratio 9:1. 62 full-time faculty, 73% hold PhDs, 10% are members of minority groups, 48% are women.

ACADEMICS
Degrees: Bachelor's, master's, post-bachelor's certificate. **Classes:** Most classes have 10–19 students. Most lab/discussion sessions have 10–19 students. **Majors with Highest Enrollment:** English language and literature; visual and performing arts. **Special Study Options:** Accelerated program, cross-registration, double major, English as a Second Language (ESL), independent study, internships, student-designed major, study abroad, teacher certification program, Postbaccalaureate program in preparation for Medical or Allied Health School Grad Programs. **Combined degree programs:** BA/MAT. Special programs offered to physically disabled students include note-taking services, reader services, tape recorders. **Career services:** Alumni network, alumni services, career/job search classes, career assessment, internships. Career services highlights include: Each academic year at Bennington College includes a seven-week winter term of field work off campus. During Field Work Term, students take their interests to the world beyond the college, where they work at jobs or internships in fields that complement their studies, clarify their interests, and open possibilities for their future.

FACILITIES
Housing: Coed dorms, cooperative housing, theme housing, off-campus. 78% of campus accessible to physically disabled. **Special Academic Facilities/Equipment:** Observatory; greenhouse; digital arts lab; architecture, drawing, painting, printmaking, and sculpture studios; ceramics studio and kilns; color and black-and-white photography darkrooms; film and video editing studio; fully equipped professional theaters; scripts library; dance studios and archives; electronic music and sound recording studios; music practice rooms and music library. **Computers:** 100% of classrooms, 100% of dorms, 100% of libraries, 100% of dining areas, 100% of student union, 75% of common outdoor areas have wireless network access. Administrative functions (other than registration) can be performed online.

CAMPUS LIFE
Environment: Town. **Activities:** Choral groups, dance, drama/theater, literary magazine, music ensembles, musical theater, radio station, student government, student newspaper, international student organization. **Organizations:** 21 registered organizations, **On-Campus Highlights:** Edward Clark Crossett Library, Visual and Performing Arts Center, Student Center, Commons Dining Hall and Lounge, Meyer Recreation Barn, Opening in 2011, the Center for the Advancement of Public Action (CAPA), is a $20–million, state-of-the-art, green, academic facility for Bennington's new citizenship curriculum. It morphs the studio of the artist, the laboratory of a scientist, the workshop of a craftsman,

and the think tank of policy work. **Environmental Initiatives:** Converting to a campus-wide biomass heating system, new green construction, energy conservation program.

ADMISSIONS
Freshman Academic Profile: Average high school GPA 3.45. 31% in top 10% of high school class, 63% in top 25% of high school class, 85% in top 50% of high school class. 59% from public high schools. SAT Math middle 50% range 560–640. SAT Critical Reading middle 50% range 620–720. SAT Writing middle 50% range 610–710. ACT middle 50% range 26–31. Minimum paper TOEFL 577. Minimum computer TOEFL 233. **Basis for Candidate Selection:** *Very important factors considered include:* Class rank, application essay, academic GPA, recommendation(s), rigor of secondary school record, character/personal qualities, extracurricular activities, interview, talent/ability. *Other factors considered include:* standardized test scores, alumni/ae relation, first generation, geographical residence, level of applicant's interest, racial/ethnic status, volunteer work, work experience. **Freshman Admission Requirements:** High school diploma is required and GED is accepted. *Academic units recommended:* 4 English, 4 mathematics, 3 science, 2 foreign language, 4 social studies, 4 history. **Freshman Admission Statistics:** 1,054 applied, 66% admitted, 28% enrolled. **Transfer Admission Requirements:** High school transcript, college transcript(s), essay or personal statement, statement of good standing from prior institution(s). Lowest grade transferable C. **General Admission Information:** Application fee $60. Regular application deadline 1/3. Regular notification 4/1. Nonfall registration accepted. Admission may be deferred for a maximum of 1 year. Neither credit nor placement offered for CEEB Advanced Placement tests.

COSTS AND FINANCIAL AID
Required Forms and Deadlines: FAFSA, institution's own financial aid form, CSS/Financial Aid PROFILE, noncustodial PROFILEStudent and Parent Federal Tax Returns and W-2s. Financial aid filing deadline 2/15. Priority financial aid filing date 2/1. **Notification of Awards:** Applicants will be notified of awards on or about 4/1. **Types of Aid:** *Need-based scholarships/grants:* Federal Pell, SEOG, state scholarships/grants, private scholarships, the school's own gift aid. *Loans:* Direct Subsidized Stafford, Direct Unsubsidized Stafford, Direct PLUS, college/university loans from institutional funds. NOTE: College/university loans from institutional funds for International students only. **Student Employment:** Federal Work-Study Program available. Institutional employment available. Highest amount earned per year from on-campus jobs $1,900. Off-campus job opportunities are good. **Financial Aid Statistics:** 69% freshmen, 67% undergrads receive need-based scholarship or grant aid. 10% freshmen, 5% undergrads receive non-need-based scholarship or grant aid. 59% freshmen, 63% undergrads receive need-based self-help aid. 81% freshmen, 80% undergrads receive any aid. Average cumulative indebtedness $22,402. **Criteria for awarding institutional aid:** *Non-need-based:* Academics.

BENTLEY UNIVERSITY

175 Forest Street, Waltham, MA 02452
Phone: 781-891-2244 **Financial Aid Phone:** 781-891-3441
E-mail: ugadmission@bentley.edu **CEEB Code:** 3096
Fax: 781-891-3414 **Website:** www.bentley.edu **ACT Code:** 1783

This private school was founded in 1917. It has a 163-acre campus.

RATINGS
Admissions Selectivity Rating: 90 | **Fire Safety Rating:** 99 | **Green Rating:** 93

STUDENTS AND FACULTY
Enrollment: 4,179. **Student Body:** 40% female, 60% male, 52% out-of-state, 9% international (89 countries represented). Asian 7%, African American 3%, Caucasian 58%, Hispanic 5%.
Retention and Graduation: 93% freshmen return for sophomore year. 80% freshmen graduate within 4 years. 18% grads go on to further study within 1 year. 1% grads pursue law degrees. 13% grads pursue business degrees. **Faculty:** Student/faculty ratio 14:1. 279 full-time faculty, 82% hold PhDs, 13% are members of minority groups, 39% are women.

ACADEMICS
Degrees: Associate, bachelor's, doctoral, master's, post-bachelor's certificate, post-master's certificate, terminal associate, transfer associate. **Classes:** Most

classes have 30–39 students. **Majors with Highest Enrollment:** Accounting and related services, other; business administration and management; marketing/marketing management. **Special Study Options:** Accelerated program, cross-registration, double major, honors program, independent study, internships, liberal arts/career combination, student-designed major, study abroad, 5 year Bachelors/Masters program in Business Administration, Accountancy, Finance, Marketing, Analytics, Info Technology, Financial Planning, Taxation. **Honors programs:** The Honors Program is a four-year journey that provides special challenge and fulfillment to select Bentley students. Students in approximately the top ten percent of the entering class are invited to participate in this four-year program. **Combined degree programs:** BA-MS, BS-MS, BA-MBA, BS-MBA. Special programs offered to physically disabled students include note-taking services, reader services, tape recorders, tutors. **Career services:** Alumni network, alumni services, career/job search classes, career assessment, internships, regional alumni. **Career services highlights include:** For the past several years, Bentley students have journeyed to Ghana, West Africa, to work on a long-term economic development partnership focused on helping an orphanage become self-sustaining. This effort has expanded to include students who now implement and train Ghanian NGOs in the use of accounting software to allow them to apply for an receive USAID funding.

FACILITIES

Housing: Coed dorms, special housing for disabled students, apartments for single students, wellness housing, theme housing, three Wellness Houses with an overall health and wellness theme are available. Global living floors with a focus on connecting international and US students are available to residents. 70% of campus accessible to physically disabled. **Special Academic Facilities/Equipment:** Academic Technology Center, Alliance for Ethics and Social Responsibility, Center for Business Ethics, Center for International Students and Scholars, Center for Quantitative Analysis, Art Gallery, Center for Marketing Technology, Center for Languages and International Collaboration, ESOL Center, Math Learning Center, Writing Center, Financial Trading Room, Design and Usability Center, Service Learning Center, Cronin International Center, Cyberlaw Center, Enterprise Risk Management Program, Hughey Center for Financial Services, Library, Media & Culture labs and studio, Valente Center for Arts and Sciences, Winer Accounting Center, Women's Leadership Institute, Academic Technology Center, Spiritual Life Center. **Computers:** 100% of classrooms, 100% of dorms, 100% of libraries, 100% of dining areas, 100% of student union, 100% of common outdoor areas have wireless network access. Students can register for classes online. Administrative functions (other than registration) can be performed online. Undergraduates are required to own a computer.

CAMPUS LIFE

Environment: Town. **Activities:** Choral groups, dance, drama/theater, jazz band, literary magazine, music ensembles, pep band, radio station, student government, student newspaper, television station, campus ministries, international student organization, Model UN. **Organizations:** 101 registered organizations, 3 honor societies, 4 religious organizations. 5 fraternities, 4 sororities. **Athletics (Intercollegiate):** *Men:* Baseball, basketball, cross-country, diving, football, golf, ice hockey, lacrosse, soccer, swimming, tennis, track/field (outdoor), track/field (indoor). *Women:* Basketball, cross-country, diving, field hockey, lacrosse, soccer, softball, swimming, tennis, track/field (outdoor), track/field (indoor), volleyball. **On-Campus Highlights:** Student Center, Dana Athletic Center, Currito Burrito, Einstein's Coffee Shop, library. **Environmental Initiatives:** Climate Action Plan has been completed. Goals: 50% reduction (over 2008 baseline) by 2015, 70% reduction by 2020, 100% reduction by 2030. Re-vamped single stream recycling program (increased education, awareness, training on recylcing). Upgrading HVAC equipment and building controls with the goal of tying all HVAC equipment into our central energy management system. Running HVAC equipment through this system allows for more efficient operation and helps to use less energy in our buildings.

ADMISSIONS

Freshman Academic Profile: 38% in top 10% of high school class, 79% in top 25% of high school class, 97% in top 50% of high school class. 73% from public high schools. SAT Math middle 50% range 600–680. SAT Critical Reading middle 50% range 540–630. SAT Writing middle 50% range 550–640. ACT middle 50% range 25–28. Minimum paper TOEFL 550. Minimum computer TOEFL 213. Minimum web-based TOEFL 80. **Basis for Candidate Selection:** *Very important factors considered include:* Academic GPA, rigor of secondary school record, standardized test scores. *Important factors considered include:* Application essay, recommendation(s), character/personal qualities, extracurricular activities, level of applicant's interest, volunteer work. *Other factors considered include:* Class rank, alumni/ae relation, first generation, geographical residence, interview, racial/ethnic status, state residency, talent/ability, work experience. **Freshman Admission Requirements:** High school diploma is required and GED is accepted. *Academic units recommended:* 4 English, 4 mathematics, 3 science, (3 science labs), 3 foreign language, 3 social studies, 2 additional English, mathematics, social or lab science, foreign language. **Freshman Admission Statistics:** 6,675 applied, 43% admitted, 33% enrolled. **Transfer**

Admission Requirements: High school transcript, college transcript(s), essay or personal statement, statement of good standing from prior institution(s). Lowest grade transferable C. **General Admission Information:** Application fee $50. Early decision application deadline 11/1. Regular application deadline 1/15. Regular notification 4/1. Nonfall registration accepted. Admission may be deferred for a maximum of 1 year. Credit and/or placement offered for CEEB Advanced Placement tests.

COSTS AND FINANCIAL AID

Annual tuition $34,360. Room and board $11,740. Required fees $1,468. Average book expense $1,050. **Required Forms and Deadlines:** FAFSA, CSS/Financial Aid PROFILE, noncustodial PROFILE, business/farm supplement. Federal Tax Returns, including all schedules for parents and student. Financial aid filing deadline 2/1. **Notification of Awards:** Applicants will be notified of awards on a rolling basis beginning 3/25. **Types of Aid:** *Need-based scholarships/grants:* Federal Pell, SEOG, state scholarships/grants, private scholarships, the school's own gift aid. *Loans:* FFEL Subsidized Stafford, FFEL Unsubsidized Stafford, FFEL PLUS, Federal Perkins, state loans **Student Employment:** Federal Work-Study Program available. Institutional employment available. Off-campus job opportunities are good. **Financial Aid Statistics:** 40% freshmen, 40% undergrads receive need-based scholarship or grant aid. 18% freshmen, 15% undergrads receive non-need-based scholarship or grant aid. 42% freshmen, 43% undergrads receive need-based self-help aid. 1% freshmen, 1% undergrads receive athletic scholarships. 64% undergrads borrow to pay for school. Average cumulative indebtedness $33,073. **Criteria for awarding institutional aid:** *Non-need-based:* Academics, athletics, leadership, minority status.

See page 1028.

BEREA COLLEGE

CPO 2220, Berea, KY 40404
Phone: 859-985-3500 **Financial Aid Phone:** 859-985-3310
E-mail: admissions@berea.edu **CEEB Code:** 1060
Fax: 859-985-3512 **Website:** www.berea.edu **ACT Code:** 1492

This private school was founded in 1855. It has a 140-acre campus.

RATINGS

Admissions Selectivity Rating: 92   **Fire Safety Rating:** 82   **Green Rating:** 80

STUDENTS AND FACULTY

Enrollment: 1,496. **Student Body:** 59% female, 41% male, 57% out-of-state, 7% international (58 countries represented). Asian 1%, African American 18%, Caucasian 68%, Hispanic 3%, Native American 1%.
Retention and Graduation: 51% freshmen graduate within 4 years. **Faculty:** Student/faculty ratio 10:1. 130 full-time faculty, 91% hold PhDs, 12% are members of minority groups, 38% are women.

ACADEMICS

Degrees: Bachelor's. **Classes:** Most classes have 10–19 students. **Majors with Highest Enrollment:** Biology/biological sciences; business/commerce; family and consumer sciences/human sciences. **Special Study Options:** Double major, English as a Second Language (ESL), exchange student program (domestic), honors program, independent study, internships, student-designed major, study abroad, teacher certification program, 3-2 engineering program with Washington University, St. Louis, and University of Kentucky. **Combined degree programs:** UK or Washington Univ (MO) resulting in BS. Special programs offered to physically disabled students include note-taking services, reader services, tape recorders. **Career services:** Alumni network, alumni services, career/job search classes, career assessment, internships.

FACILITIES

Housing: Men's dorms, women's dorms, apartments for married students, apartments for single parents and married students at our Ecovillage (see the following site for more information: www.berea.edu/sens/ecovillage/). 75% of campus accessible to physically disabled. **Special Academic Facilities/Equipment:** Appalachian Gallery, Special Collections and Sound Archives in the Hutchins Library, Planetarium and Observatory, Geology Museum, The Ecovillage, the Child Development Laboratory, extensive acreage of farmland and forestland, and the Monty Saulmon Early Technology Lab. **Computers:** 33% of classrooms, 100% of libraries, 100% of dining areas, 100% of student union,

33% of common outdoor areas have wireless network access. Students can register for classes online. Administrative functions (other than registration) can be performed online. Undergraduates are required to own a computer.

CAMPUS LIFE

Environment: Village. **Activities:** Choral groups, dance, drama/theater, jazz band, literary magazine, music ensembles, pep band, student government, student newspaper, yearbook, campus ministries, international student organization. **Organizations:** 75 registered organizations, 14 honor societies, 5 religious organizations. **Athletics (Intercollegiate):** *Men:* Baseball, basketball, cross-country, golf, soccer, swimming, tennis, track/field (outdoor). *Women:* Basketball, cross-country, soccer, softball, swimming, tennis, track/field (outdoor), volleyball. **On-Campus Highlights:** Carillon (in Draper building tower), Eco-Village (married and single parent housing), Alumni Building (cafeteria, lounge, gameroom), Woods-Penn Complex (post office, cafe, etc), Seabury Center (gym). **Environmental Initiatives:** 1. Sustainability and Environmental Studies academic program; 2. Ecological Renovations (including 1st LEED-certified building in KY and the Ecovillage residential complex for student families); 3. Local Food Initiative.

ADMISSIONS

Freshman Academic Profile: Average high school GPA 3.37. 25.9% in top 10% of high school class, 68.5% in top 25% of high school class, 91.4% in top 50% of high school class. SAT Math middle 50% range 465–585. SAT Critical Reading middle 50% range 500–620. SAT Writing middle 50% range 510–590. ACT middle 50% range 21–26. Minimum paper TOEFL 500. Minimum computer TOEFL 173. Minimum web-based TOEFL 61. **Basis for Candidate Selection:** *Very important factors considered include:* Class rank, academic GPA, rigor of secondary school record, standardized test scores, interview. *Important factors considered include:* Application essay, character/personal qualities. *Other factors considered include:* Recommendation(s), extracurricular activities, first generation, geographical residence, level of applicant's interest, racial/ethnic status, state residency, talent/ability, volunteer work, work experience. **Freshman Admission Requirements:** High school diploma is required and GED is accepted. *Academic units recommended:* 4 English, 3 mathematics, 2 science, (2 science labs), 2 foreign language, 1 social studies, 1 history. **Freshman Admission Statistics:** 2,745 applied, 19% admitted, 76% enrolled. **Transfer Admission Requirements:** High school transcript, college transcript(s), interview, minimum college GPA of 2.0 required. Lowest grade transferable C. **General Admission Information:** Regular application deadline 4/30. Notification on a rolling basis, beginning on or about 11/1. Nonfall registration accepted. Credit offered for CEEB Advanced Placement tests.

COSTS AND FINANCIAL AID

Required Forms and Deadlines: FAFSA. Priority financial aid filing date 3/15. **Notification of Awards:** Applicants will be notified of awards on a rolling basis beginning 4/1. **Types of Aid:** *Need-based scholarships/grants:* Federal Pell, SEOG, state scholarships/grants, private scholarships, the school's own gift aid. *Loans:* FFEL Subsidized Stafford, FFEL Unsubsidized Stafford, FFEL PLUS, Federal Perkins, college/university loans from institutional funds. **Student Employment:** Federal Work-Study Program available. **Financial Aid Statistics:** 100% freshmen, 100% undergrads receive need-based scholarship or grant aid. 100% freshmen, 100% undergrads receive need-based self-help aid. 100% freshmen, 100% undergrads receive any aid. 79% undergrads borrow to pay for school. Average cumulative indebtedness $8,133.

BERKELEY COLLEGE

44 Rifle Camp Road, West Paterson, NJ 07424
Phone: 973-278-5400 **Financial Aid Phone:**
E-mail: info@berkeleycollege.edu **CEEB Code:** 2061
Fax: 973-278-9141 **ACT Code:** 2576

This proprietary school was founded in 1931. It has a 25-acre campus.

RATINGS

Admissions Selectivity Rating: 60*   **Fire Safety Rating:** 60*   **Green Rating:** 60*

STUDENTS AND FACULTY

Enrollment: 2,709. **Student Body:** 72% female, 28% male, 4% out-of-state, 1% international. Asian 5%, African American 20%, Caucasian 35%, Hispanic 35%.
Retention and Graduation: 53% freshmen return for sophomore year.
Faculty: Student/faculty ratio 24:1. 54 full-time faculty, 15% are members of minority groups, 54% are women.

ACADEMICS

Degrees: Associate, bachelor's, certificate, terminal associate, transfer associate. **Majors with Highest Enrollment:** Accounting; business administration and management; fashion merchandising. **Special Study Options:** Accelerated program, distance learning, internships, study abroad, academic remediation, off-campus study at Berkeley College, New York City; Berkeley College, White Plains. Special programs offered to physically disabled students include tutors.

FACILITIES

Housing: Coed dorms. **Computers:** Administrative functions (other than registration) can be performed online.

CAMPUS LIFE

Environment: City. **Activities:** Choral groups, literary magazine, student government, student newspaper **Organizations:** 8 registered organizations, 1 honor societies.

ADMISSIONS

Freshman Academic Profile: Minimum paper TOEFL 500. Minimum computer TOEFL 173. **Basis for Candidate Selection:** *Very important factors considered include:* Rigor of secondary school record, interview. *Important factors considered include:* Standardized test scores. *Other factors considered include:* Class rank, academic GPA, recommendation(s), character/personal qualities, extracurricular activities, talent/ability, volunteer work, work experience. **Freshman Admission Requirements:** High school diploma is required and GED is accepted. **Transfer Admission Requirements:** High school transcript, college transcript(s), Lowest grade transferable C. **General Admission Information:** Application fee $50. Nonfall registration accepted. Credit and/or placement offered for CEEB Advanced Placement tests.

COSTS AND FINANCIAL AID

Annual tuition $17,400. Room and board $12,500. Required fees $750. Average book expense $1,200. **Required Forms and Deadlines:** FAFSA. **Notification of Awards:** Applicants will be notified of awards on a rolling basis beginning 3/1. **Types of Aid:** *Need-based scholarships/grants:* Federal Pell, SEOG, state scholarships/grants, private scholarships, the school's own gift aid. *Loans:* FFEL Subsidized Stafford, FFEL Unsubsidized Stafford, FFEL PLUS, state loans. **Financial Aid Statistics:** 85% freshmen receive any aid. 88% undergrads borrow to pay for school. Average cumulative indebtedness $5,000. **Criteria for awarding institutional aid:** *Non-need-based:* Academics, alumni affiliation

BERKELEY COLLEGE—NEW YORK CITY CAMPUS

3 East 43 Street, New York, NY 10017
Phone: 212-986-4343 **Financial Aid Phone:** 212-986-4343
E-mail: info@berkeleycollege.edu
Fax: 212-818-1079 **ACT Code:** 2688

This proprietary school was founded in 1936.

RATINGS

Admissions Selectivity Rating: 60*   **Fire Safety Rating:** 60*   **Green Rating:** 60*

STUDENTS AND FACULTY

Enrollment: 2,390. **Student Body:** 70% female, 30% male, 9% out-of-state, 15% international. Asian 5%, African American 22%, Caucasian 16%, Hispanic 23%.
Retention and Graduation: 51% freshmen return for sophomore year. **Faculty:** Student/faculty ratio 24:1. 40 full-time faculty.

ACADEMICS

Degrees: Associate, bachelor's, certificate. **Majors with Highest Enrollment:** Business administration and management; fashion merchandising; marketing/marketing management. **Special Study Options:** Accelerated program, distance learning, English as a Second Language (ESL), internships, study abroad, academic remediation, off campus study at Berkeley College, White Plains, and Berkley College, New Jersey. Special programs offered to physically disabled students include tutors. **Career services:** Alumni services, career/job search classes, career assessment, internships.

FACILITIES

Computers: Administrative functions (other than registration) can be performed online.

CAMPUS LIFE

Environment: Metropolis. **Activities:** Choral groups, student government. **Organizations:** 6 registered organizations, 4 honor societies.

ADMISSIONS

Freshman Academic Profile: Minimum paper TOEFL 500. Minimum computer TOEFL 173. **Basis for Candidate Selection:** *Very important factors considered include:* rigor of secondary school record. *Important factors considered include:* standardized test scores. *Other factors considered include:* Class rank, academic GPA, recommendation(s), character/personal qualities, extracurricular activities, talent/ability, volunteer work, work experience. **Freshman Admission Requirements:** High school diploma is required and GED is accepted. **Transfer Admission Requirements:** college transcript(s), Lowest grade transferable C. **General Admission Information:** Application fee $50. Nonfall registration accepted. Admission may be deferred for a maximum of no time limit. Credit and/or placement offered for CEEB Advanced Placement tests.

COSTS AND FINANCIAL AID

Annual tuition $17,400. Required fees $750. Average book expense $1,200. **Required Forms and Deadlines:** FAFSA, state aid form. **Notification of Awards:** Applicants will be notified of awards on or about 3/1. **Types of Aid:** *Need-based scholarships/grants:* Federal Pell, SEOG, state scholarships/grants, private scholarships, the school's own gift aid. *Loans:* FFEL Subsidized Stafford, FFEL Unsubsidized Stafford, FFEL PLUS. **Student Employment:** Federal Work-Study Program available. Institutional employment available. Off-campus job opportunities are excellent. **Financial Aid Statistics:** 85% freshmen receive any aid. 88% undergrads borrow to pay for school. Average cumulative indebtedness $5,000. **Criteria for awarding institutional aid:** *Non-need-based:* Academics, alumni affiliation.

BERKELEY COLLEGE—NEW YORK CITY CAMPUS

3 East 43 Street, New York, NY 10017
Phone: 212-986-4343 **Financial Aid Phone:** 212-986-4343
E-mail: info@berkeleycollege.edu
Fax: 212-818-1079 **ACT Code:** 2688

This proprietary school was founded in 1936.

RATINGS

Admissions Selectivity Rating: 60*   **Fire Safety Rating:** 60*   **Green Rating:** 60*

STUDENTS AND FACULTY

Enrollment: 2,595. **Student Body:** 69% female, 31% male, 13% out-of-state, 18% international. Asian 4%, African American 23%, Caucasian 15%, Hispanic 24%, Native American 1%.
Retention and Graduation: 52% freshmen return for sophomore year. **Faculty:** 73 full-time faculty.

ACADEMICS

Degrees: Associate, bachelor's, certificate. **Special Study Options:** Accelerated program, distance learning, English as a Second Language (ESL), internships, study abroad, academic remediation, off campus study at Berkeley College, White Plains, and Berkley College, New Jersey. Special programs offered to physically disabled students include tutors.

FACILITIES

Housing: Computers:

CAMPUS LIFE

Environment: Metropolis. **Activities:** Choral groups, student government. **Organizations:** 6 registered organizations, 4 honor societies.

ADMISSIONS

Freshman Academic Profile: Minimum paper TOEFL 500. Minimum computer TOEFL 173. **Basis for Candidate Selection:** *Very important factors considered include:* rigor of secondary school record, interview. *Important factors considered include:* standardized test scores. *Other factors considered include:* Class rank, academic GPA, recommendation(s), character/personal qualities, extracurricular activities, talent/ability, volunteer work, work experience. **Freshman Admission Requirements:** High school diploma is required and GED is accepted. **Transfer Admission Requirements:** college transcript(s), Lowest grade transferable C. **General Admission Information:** Application fee $50. Nonfall registration accepted. Admission may be deferred for a maximum of no time limit. Credit and/or placement offered for CEEB Advanced Placement tests.

COSTS AND FINANCIAL AID

Annual tuition $18,300. Required fees $750. Average book expense $1,300. **Required Forms and Deadlines:** FAFSA, state aid form. **Notification of Awards:** Applicants will be notified of awards on or about 3/1. **Types of Aid:**

Need-based scholarships/grants: Federal Pell, SEOG, state scholarships/grants, private scholarships, the school's own gift aid. *Loans:* FFEL Subsidized Stafford, FFEL Unsubsidized Stafford, FFEL PLUS. **Student Employment:** Federal Work-Study Program available. Institutional employment available. Off-campus job opportunities are excellent. **Financial Aid Statistics:** 85% freshmen receive any aid. **Criteria for awarding institutional aid:** *Non-need-based:* Academics, alumni affiliation.

BERKELEY COLLEGE—WESTCHESTER CAMPUS

99 Church Street, White Plains, NY 10601
Phone: 914-694-1122 **Financial Aid Phone:** 914-694-1122
E-mail: info@berkeleycollege.edu
Fax: 914-328-9470 **Website:** www.berkeleycollege.edu **ACT Code:** 2695

This proprietary school was founded in 1945.

RATINGS

Admissions Selectivity Rating: 60*   **Fire Safety Rating:** 60*   **Green Rating:** 60*

STUDENTS AND FACULTY

Enrollment: 608. **Student Body:** 72% female, 28% male, 15% out-of-state, 6% international. Asian 3%, African American 26%, Caucasian 35%, Hispanic 21%.
Retention and Graduation: 50% freshmen return for sophomore year. **Faculty:** Student/faculty ratio 24:1. 17 full-time faculty.

ACADEMICS

Degrees: Associate, bachelor's, certificate. **Majors with Highest Enrollment:** Business administration and management; business administration, management and operations, other; marketing/marketing management. **Special Study Options:** Accelerated program, distance learning, English as a Second Language (ESL), internships, study abroad, academic remediation, off-campus study at Berkley College, New York City and Berkeley College, New Jersey. Special programs offered to physically disabled students include tutors.

FACILITIES

Housing: Coed dorms. **Computers:** Administrative functions (other than registration) can be performed online.

CAMPUS LIFE

Environment: Town. **Activities:** Student government. **Organizations:** 6 registered organizations, 4 honor societies, 1 fraternities, 1 sorority.

ADMISSIONS

Freshman Academic Profile: Minimum paper TOEFL 500. Minimum computer TOEFL 173. **Basis for Candidate Selection:** *Very important factors considered include:* Rigor of secondary school record, interview. *Important factors considered include:* Standardized test scores. *Other factors considered include:* Class rank, academic GPA, recommendation(s), character/personal qualities, extracurricular activities, talent/ability, volunteer work, work experience. **Freshman Admission Requirements:** High school diploma is required and GED is accepted. **Freshman Admission Statistics: Transfer Admission Requirements:** College transcript(s), Lowest grade transferable C. **General Admission Information:** Application fee $50. Nonfall registration accepted. Admission may be deferred for a maximum of no time limi. Credit and/or placement offered for CEEB Advanced Placement tests.

COSTS AND FINANCIAL AID

Annual tuition $16,950. Room and board $9,000. Required fees $750. Average book expense $1,200. **Required Forms and Deadlines:** FAFSA, state aid form. **Notification of Awards:** Applicants will be notified of awards on a rolling basis beginning 3/1. **Types of Aid:** *Need-based scholarships/grants:* Federal Pell, SEOG, state scholarships/grants, private scholarships, the school's own gift aid. *Loans:* FFEL Subsidized Stafford, FFEL Unsubsidized Stafford, FFEL PLUS. **Financial Aid Statistics:** 88% undergrads borrow to pay for school. Average cumulative indebtedness $5,000. **Criteria for awarding institutional aid:** *Non-need-based:* Academics, alumni affiliation

BERKLEE COLLEGE OF MUSIC

1140 Boylston Street, Boston, MA 02215-3693
Phone: 617-747-2222 **Financial Aid Phone:** 617-747-2274
E-mail: admissions@berklee.edu **CEEB Code:** 3107
Fax: 617-747-2047 **Website:** www.berklee.edu **ACT Code:** 1789

This private school was founded in 1945.

RATINGS
Admissions Selectivity Rating: 60*   **Fire Safety Rating:** 60*   **Green Rating:** 60*

STUDENTS AND FACULTY
Enrollment: 3,531. **Student Body:** 29% female, 71% male, 76.9% out-of-state, 20% international (70 countries represented). Asian 4%, African American 8%, Caucasian 52%, Hispanic 8%.
Retention and Graduation: Faculty: Student/faculty ratio 12:1. 234 full-time faculty, 17% are members of minority groups, 21% are women.

ACADEMICS
Degrees: Bachelor's, diploma. **Classes:** Most classes have fewer than 10 students. **Majors with Highest Enrollment:** Music performance; music, other. **Special Study Options:** Cooperative education program, cross-registration, distance learning, double major, dual enrollment, English as a Second Language (ESL), independent study, internships, student-designed major, study abroad, teacher certification program, Berkleemusic.com is the online continuing education division of Berklee College of Music. Study is online with Berklee's renowned faculty in areas that include Music Business, Music Production, Guitar, Theory, Harmony & Ear Training, and Songwriting. Special programs offered to physically disabled students include reader services, tape recorders, tutors. **Career services:** Alumni services, career/job search classes, internships.

FACILITIES
Housing: Coed dorms 80% of campus accessible to physically disabled. **Special Academic Facilities/Equipment:** Ensemble library, 10 professional recording studios, film scoring and editing studio, analog and digital music synthesis labs, 1,200–seat performance center, learning center.

CAMPUS LIFE
Environment: Metropolis. **Activities:** Choral groups, concert band, dance, jazz band, literary magazine, music ensembles, musical theater, radio station, student government, student newspaper, student-run film society, international student organization. **Organizations:** 47 registered organizations, 2 honor societies, 4 religious organizations. **On-Campus Highlights:** Student Activities Center, Berklee Performance Center, practice rooms; Stan Getz Media Center.

ADMISSIONS
Freshman Academic Profile: Minimum paper TOEFL 500. **Basis for Candidate Selection:** *Very important factors considered include:* Character/personal qualities, interview, talent/ability. *Important factors considered include:* Application essay, academic GPA, rigor of secondary school record. *Other factors considered include:* Class rank, recommendation(s), standardized test scores, alumni/ae relation, extracurricular activities, first generation, level of applicant's interest, volunteer work, work experience. **Freshman Admission Requirements:** High school diploma is required and GED is accepted. **Freshman Admission Statistics:** 3,636 applied, 42% admitted, 56% enrolled. **Transfer Admission Requirements:** High school transcript, college transcript(s), essay or personal statement, interview, Lowest grade transferable C. **General Admission Information:** Application fee $150. Regular application deadline 1/15. Regular notification 3/31. Nonfall registration accepted. Admission may be deferred for a maximum of 1 year. Credit offered for CEEB Advanced Placement tests.

COSTS AND FINANCIAL AID
Student Employment: Federal Work-Study Program available. Highest amount earned per year from on-campus jobs $2,000. Off-campus job opportunities are good. **Financial Aid Statistics:** 27% freshmen, 24% undergrads receive need-based scholarship or grant aid. 26% freshmen, 23% undergrads receive non-need-based scholarship or grant aid. 53% freshmen, 45% undergrads receive need-based self-help aid. 57% freshmen, 38% undergrads receive any aid.

BERRY COLLEGE

P.O. Box 490159, Mount Berry, GA 30149-0159
Phone: 706-236-2215 **Financial Aid Phone:** 706-236-1714
E-mail: admissions@berry.edu **CEEB Code:** 5059
Fax: 706-290-2178 **Website:** www.berry.edu **ACT Code:** 798

This private school was founded in 1902. It has a 26000-acre campus.

RATINGS
Admissions Selectivity Rating: 86   **Fire Safety Rating:** 85   **Green Rating:** 88

STUDENTS AND FACULTY
Enrollment: 1,756. **Student Body:** 69% female, 31% male, 20% out-of-state, 2% international (19 countries represented). Asian 2%, African American 5%, Caucasian 83%, Hispanic 3%.
Retention and Graduation: 74% freshmen return for sophomore year. 48% freshmen graduate within 4 years. 27% grads go on to further study within 1 year. 19% grads pursue arts and sciences degrees. 3% grads pursue law degrees. 1% grads pursue business degrees. 2% grads pursue medical degrees. **Faculty:** Student/faculty ratio 12:1. 145 full-time faculty, 90% hold PhDs, 4% are members of minority groups, 39% are women.

ACADEMICS
Degrees: Bachelor's, master's, post-master's certificate. **Classes:** Most classes have 10–19 students. Most lab/discussion sessions have 20–29 students. **Majors with Highest Enrollment:** Animal sciences; communication, journalism, and related programs, other; psychology. **Special Study Options:** Cooperative education program, cross-registration, double major, dual enrollment, honors program, independent study, internships, student-designed major, study abroad, teacher certification program, 3-2 nursing with Emory University, 3-2 engineering with Georgia Institute of Technology. **Honors programs:** The Berry College Honors Program provides students with an opportunity to learn within an intellectually challenging community of peers and instructors. Honors courses familiarize students with works that have been central to our past and contemporary intellectual traditions, while encouraging them to examine issues or themes from multiple and conflicting perspectives. All Honors courses are taught as seminars that provide an ideal environment for the development of effective communication and critical-thinking skills. As part of the Honors program the Oxbridge Lecture Series uses the English model of instruction with public lectures and private tutorials. Students enrolled benefit from small group, intensive student-faculty interaction, and exploratory assignments that stimulate inquiry and intellectual growth. Additionally, the Berry College Honors Program now offers a unique education abroad opportunity in conjunction with the University of Glasgow in Scotland and Berry College International Programs. **Combined degree programs:** 3-2 Nursing with Emory University. Special programs offered to physically disabled students include note-taking services, reader services, tape recorders, tutors. **Career services:** Alumni network, alumni services, career/job search classes, career assessment, internships, regional alumni.

FACILITIES
Housing: Coed dorms, men's dorms, women's dorms, apartments for single students, wellness housing. Traditional residence halls are single sex; apartments and townhouses are co-ed by site or apartment. Special-interest houses for Women in Math and Science (primarily first-year students). 80% of campus accessible to physically disabled. **Special Academic Facilities/Equipment:** The 131,000–square-foot Steven J. Cage Athletic and Recreation Center, National Historic Site containing Oak Hill and The Martha Berry Museum, 34-foot overshot waterwheel, Georgia wildlife management area and refuge, equine center, dairy and beef cattle research center, on-campus elementary and middle schools, child development center, science center featuring 60–foot Foucault pendulum. **Computers:** 100% of classrooms, 100% of dorms, 100% of libraries, 100% of dining areas, 100% of student union, 10% of common outdoor areas have wireless network access. Students can register for classes online. Administrative functions (other than registration) can be performed online.

CAMPUS LIFE
Environment: Town. **Activities:** Choral groups, concert band, dance, drama/theater, jazz band, literary magazine, music ensembles, musical theater, student government, student newspaper, symphony orchestra, television station, yearbook, campus ministries, international student organization, Model UN. **Organizations:** 75 registered organizations, 15 honor societies, 11 religious organizations. **Athletics (Intercollegiate):** *Men:* Baseball, basketball, cross-country, diving, golf, lacrosse, soccer, swimming, tennis. *Women:* Basketball, cross-country, diving, equestrian sports, golf, lacrosse, soccer, softball, swimming, tennis, volleyball. **On-Campus Highlights:** Steven J. Cage Athletic & Recreation Ctr, Ford Complex, Science Center, Gunby Equestrian Center (Mountain Campus), The Old Mill (Mountain Campus), the 131,000–square-foot Steven

J. Cage Athletic and Recreation Center houses an indoor swimming pool, three basketball courts, two racquetball courts, one multi-purpose court and a jogging track. Berry Beanery (Starbucks) in Krannert Student Center. **Environmental Initiatives:** President's Climate Commitment: Energy Star Policy, RecycleMania; Environmental Land Management: Carbon Reserve, wetland banking, and EPA Compliance-Peer Audit; establishing an environmental science major.

ADMISSIONS

Freshman Academic Profile: Average high school GPA 3.64. 32% in top 10% of high school class, 66% in top 25% of high school class, 92% in top 50% of high school class. 75% from public high schools. SAT Math middle 50% range 510–610. SAT Critical Reading middle 50% range 520–640. SAT Writing middle 50% range 510–620. ACT middle 50% range 22–28. Minimum paper TOEFL 550. Minimum computer TOEFL 213. Minimum web-based TOEFL 80. **Basis for Candidate Selection:** *Very important factors considered include:* Academic GPA, rigor of secondary school record, standardized test scores. *Important factors considered include:* Extracurricular activities. *Other factors considered include:* Class rank, application essay, recommendation(s), interview, volunteer work, work experience. **Freshman Admission Requirements:** High school diploma is required and GED is accepted. *Academic units required:* 4 English, 4 mathematics, 3 science, 2 foreign language, 3 social studies. **Freshman Admission Statistics:** 2,412 applied, 67% admitted, 35% enrolled. **Transfer Admission Requirements:** College transcript(s), statement of good standing from prior institution(s). Minimum college GPA of 2.5 required. Lowest grade transferable C. **General Admission Information:** Application fee $50. Regular application deadline 7/23. Notification on a rolling basis, beginning on or about 11/1. Nonfall registration accepted. Admission may be deferred for a maximum of Up to one year. Credit and/or placement offered for CEEB Advanced Placement tests.

COSTS AND FINANCIAL AID

Annual tuition $23,160. Room and board $8,340. Required fees $200. Average book expense $1,200. **Required Forms and Deadlines:** FAFSA. Priority financial aid filing date 4/1. **Notification of Awards:** Applicants will be notified of awards on a rolling basis beginning 2/1. **Types of Aid:** *Need-based scholarships/grants:* Federal Pell, SEOG, state scholarships/grants, private scholarships, the school's own gift aid. *Loans:* FFEL Subsidized Stafford, FFEL Unsubsidized Stafford, FFEL PLUS, Federal Perkins, college/university loans from institutional funds. **Student Employment:** Federal Work-Study Program available. Institutional employment available. Highest amount earned per year from on-campus jobs $5,873. Off-campus job opportunities are good. **Financial Aid Statistics:** 73% freshmen, 68% undergrads receive need-based scholarship or grant aid. 15% freshmen, 12% undergrads receive non-need-based scholarship or grant aid. 58% freshmen, 56% undergrads receive need-based self-help aid. 5% undergrads receive athletic scholarships. 99% freshmen, 99% undergrads receive any aid. 82% undergrads borrow to pay for school. Average cumulative indebtedness $17,502. **Criteria for awarding institutional aid:** *Non-need-based:* Academics, art, job skills, leadership, minority status, music/drama, state/district residency.

BETHANY COLLEGE (KS)

335 E Swensson, Lindsborg, KS 67456-1897
Phone: 785-227-3311 **Financial Aid Phone:** 785-227-3311
E-mail: admissions@bethanylb.edu **CEEB Code:** 6034
Fax: 785-227-8993 **Website:** www.bethanylb.edu **ACT Code:** 1388

This private school, affiliated with the Lutheran Church, was founded in 1881. It has a 62-acre campus.

RATINGS

Admissions Selectivity Rating: 77   **Fire Safety Rating:** 94   **Green Rating:** 60*

STUDENTS AND FACULTY

Enrollment: 569. **Student Body:** 48% female, 52% male, 49% out-of-state, 6% international (29 countries represented). Asian 1%, African American 11%, Caucasian 71%, Hispanic 7%, Native American 1%.
Retention and Graduation: 61% freshmen return for sophomore year. 32% freshmen graduate within 4 years. 20% grads go on to further study within 1 year. 1% grads pursue law degrees. 3% grads pursue medical degrees. **Faculty:** Student/faculty ratio 9:1. 44 full-time faculty, 57% hold PhDs, 5% are members of minority groups, 36% are women.

ACADEMICS

Degrees: Bachelor's. **Classes:** Most classes have fewer than 10 students. Most lab/discussion sessions have fewer than 10 students. **Majors with Highest Enrollment:** Biology/biological sciences; business administration and manage-

ment; elementary education and teaching. **Special Study Options:** Accelerated program, cross-registration, double major, dual enrollment, exchange student program (domestic), honors program, independent study, internships, liberal arts/career combination, student-designed major, study abroad, teacher certification program. **Honors programs:** Honors program offered. **Combined degree programs:** BA/MEng. Special programs offered to physically disabled students include note-taking services, reader services, tape recorders, tutors. **Career services:** Alumni network, alumni services, career/job search classes, career assessment, internships, regional alumni. Career services highlights include: experience-based education.

FACILITIES

Housing: Coed dorms, women's dorms, apartments for single students, special interest housing-bid on by student groups, community service and house improvements. 80% of campus accessible to physically disabled. **Special Academic Facilities/Equipment:** Mingenback Gallery, Bethany College Archives, Plym Gallery, Sandzen Gallery.

CAMPUS LIFE

Environment: Rural. **Activities:** Choral groups, concert band, dance, drama/theater, jazz band, music ensembles, musical theater, pep band, student government, student newspaper, symphony orchestra, yearbook, campus ministries, international student organization. **Organizations:** 49 registered organizations, 8 honor societies, 9 religious organizations. 3 fraternities, 3 sororities. **Athletics (Intercollegiate):** *Men:* Baseball, basketball, cheerleading, cross-country, football, golf, soccer, tennis, track/field (outdoor), track/field (indoor). *Women:* Basketball, cheerleading, cross-country, golf, soccer, softball, tennis, track/field (outdoor), track/field (indoor), volleyball. **On-Campus Highlights:** Student Union, Walderstadt Library, Mingenback Art Gallery, Residence Halls, Athletic Fields.

ADMISSIONS

Freshman Academic Profile: Average high school GPA 3.33. 15% in top 10% of high school class, 42% in top 25% of high school class, 76% in top 50% of high school class. 97% from public high schools. SAT Math middle 50% range 420–560. SAT Critical Reading middle 50% range 370–500. SAT Writing middle 50% range 380–490. ACT middle 50% range 19–24. Minimum paper TOEFL 525. Minimum computer TOEFL 195. Minimum web-based TOEFL 71. **Basis for Candidate Selection:** *Very important factors considered include:* Academic GPA, rigor of secondary school record, standardized test scores. *Other factors considered include:* Application essay, recommendation(s), character/personal qualities, extracurricular activities, racial/ethnic status, talent/ability, volunteer work. **Freshman Admission Requirements:** High school diploma is required and GED is accepted. *Academic units recommended:* 4 English, 3 mathematics, 3 science, (2 science labs), 2 foreign language, 3 social studies. **Freshman Admission Statistics:** 811 applied, 65% admitted, 34% enrolled. **Transfer Admission Requirements:** College transcript(s), statement of good standing from prior institution(s). Minimum college GPA of 2.3 required. Lowest grade transferable D. **General Admission Information:** Application fee $20. Regular application deadline 7/1. Notification on a rolling basis, beginning on or about 10/1. Nonfall registration accepted. Neither credit nor placement offered for CEEB Advanced Placement tests.

COSTS AND FINANCIAL AID

Annual tuition $17,824. Room and board $5,650. Required fees $300. Average book expense $1,000. **Required Forms and Deadlines:** FAFSA. Priority financial aid filing date 3/15. **Notification of Awards:** Applicants will be notified of awards on a rolling basis beginning 3/1. **Types of Aid:** *Need-based scholarships/grants:* Federal Pell, SEOG, state scholarships/grants, private scholarships, the school's own gift aid, Federal ACG and Federal SMART and TEACH Grant. *Loans:* FFEL Subsidized Stafford, FFEL Unsubsidized Stafford, FFEL PLUS, Federal Perkins. **Student Employment:** Federal Work-Study Program available. Institutional employment available. Highest amount earned per year from on-campus jobs $1,500. Off-campus job opportunities are good. **Financial Aid Statistics:** 70% freshmen, 68% undergrads receive need-based scholarship or grant aid. 33% freshmen, 26% undergrads receive non-need-based scholarship or grant aid. 63% freshmen, 64% undergrads receive need-based self-help aid. 7% undergrads receive athletic scholarships. 100% freshmen, 98% undergrads receive any aid. 82% undergrads borrow to pay for school. Average cumulative indebtedness $17,161. **Criteria for awarding institutional aid:** *Non-need-based:* Academics, alumni affiliation, art, athletics, leadership, music/drama, religious affiliation.

BETHANY COLLEGE (WV)

Office of Admission, Bethany, WV 26032
Phone: 304-829-7611 **Financial Aid Phone:** 304-829-7141
E-mail: admission@bethanywv.edu **CEEB Code:** 5060
Fax: 304-829-7142 **Website:** www.bethanywv.edu **ACT Code:** 4512

This private school, affiliated with the Disciples of Christ Church, was founded in 1840. It has a 400-acre campus.

RATINGS
Admissions Selectivity Rating: 80   **Fire Safety Rating:** 60*   **Green Rating:** 60*

STUDENTS AND FACULTY
Enrollment: 887. **Student Body:** 49% female, 51% male, 74% out-of-state, 4% international (13 countries represented). Asian 1%, African American 2%, Caucasian 92%, Hispanic 1%.
Retention and Graduation: 79% freshmen return for sophomore year. 51% freshmen graduate within 4 years. 10% grads go on to further study within 1 year. 30% grads pursue arts and sciences degrees. 4% grads pursue law degrees. 2% grads pursue business degrees. 3% grads pursue medical degrees. **Faculty:** Student/faculty ratio 12:1. 66 full-time faculty, 65% hold PhDs, 2% are members of minority groups.

ACADEMICS
Degrees: Bachelor's. **Classes:** Most classes have 10–19 students. Most lab/discussion sessions have 10–19 students. **Majors with Highest Enrollment:** Education; mass communication/media studies; psychology. **Special Study Options:** double major, exchange student program (domestic), independent study, internships, liberal arts/career combination, student-designed major, study abroad, teacher certification program, Off Campus Study: Washington, DC. **Combined degree programs:** BA/JD, BA/MEng, BA/JD with Duquesne University. Special programs offered to physically disabled students include note-taking services, reader services, tape recorders, tutors.

FACILITIES
Housing: Coed dorms, special housing for disabled students, men's dorms, women's dorms, fraternity/sorority housing, apartments for married students, apartments for single students. **Computers:** Administrative functions (other than registration) can be performed online.

CAMPUS LIFE
Environment: Rural. **Activities:** Choral groups, concert band, drama/theater, jazz band, literary magazine, music ensembles, musical theater, pep band, radio station, student government, student newspaper, student-run film society, television station, yearbook. **Organizations:** 38 registered organizations, 16 honor societies, 3 religious organizations. 6 fraternities, 3 sororities. **Athletics (Intercollegiate):** *Men:* Baseball, basketball, cross-country, diving, football, golf, soccer, swimming, tennis, track/field (outdoor), track/field (indoor). *Women:* Basketball, cross-country, diving, golf, soccer, softball, swimming, tennis, track/field (outdoor), track/field (indoor), volleyball. **On-Campus Highlights:** Old Main, Bethany House, Athletic Facilities, Campbell Village, Campbell Mansion.

ADMISSIONS
Freshman Academic Profile: Average high school GPA 3.16. 10% in top 10% of high school class, 35% in top 25% of high school class, 79% in top 50% of high school class. 75% from public high schools. SAT Math middle 50% range 460–560. SAT Critical Reading middle 50% range 450–540. ACT middle 50% range 19–25. Minimum paper TOEFL 500. Minimum computer TOEFL 173. **Basis for Candidate Selection:** *Very important factors considered include:* Class rank, application essay, recommendation(s), rigor of secondary school record, standardized test scores. *Important factors considered include:* Interview. *Other factors considered include:* Alumni/ae relation, character/personal qualities, extracurricular activities, talent/ability, volunteer work, work experience. **Freshman Admission Requirements:** High school diploma is required and GED is accepted. *Academic units required:* 4 English, 3 mathematics, 3 science, 2 foreign language, 3 social studies. **Freshman Admission Statistics:** 860 applied, 75% admitted, 35% enrolled. **Transfer Admission Requirements:** College transcript(s), essay or personal statement, statement of good standing from prior institution(s). Minimum college GPA of 2.0 required. Lowest grade transferable D. **General Admission Information:** Application fee $25. Notification on a rolling basis, beginning on or about 10/1. Nonfall registration accepted. Admission may be deferred for a maximum of 1 year. Credit and/or placement offered for CEEB Advanced Placement tests.

COSTS AND FINANCIAL AID
Annual tuition $15,750. Room and board $7,770. Required fees $800. Average book expense $1,000. **Required Forms and Deadlines:** FAFSA, institution's own financial aid form. Priority financial aid filing date 4/1. **Notification of Awards:** Applicants will be notified of awards on a rolling basis beginning 3/1.

Types of Aid: *Need-based scholarships/grants:* Federal Pell, SEOG, state scholarships/grants, private scholarships, the school's own gift aid. *Loans:* Direct Subsidized Stafford, Direct Unsubsidized Stafford, Direct PLUS, Federal Perkins. **Student Employment:** Federal Work-Study Program available. Institutional employment available. Highest amount earned per year from on-campus jobs $1,000. Off-campus job opportunities are fair. **Financial Aid Statistics:** 78% freshmen, 77% undergrads receive need-based scholarship or grant aid. 76% freshmen, 79% undergrads receive non-need-based scholarship or grant aid. 88% freshmen, 88% undergrads receive need-based self-help aid. 95% freshmen, 92% undergrads receive any aid. 76% undergrads borrow to pay for school. Average cumulative indebtedness $18,000. **Criteria for awarding institutional aid:** *Non-need-based:* Academics, alumni affiliation, leadership, music/drama, religious affiliation.

See page 1030.

BETHANY UNIVERSITY

800 Bethany Drive, Scotts Valley, CA 95066
Phone: 831-438-3800 **Financial Aid Phone:**
E-mail: info@bethany.edu **CEEB Code:** 4021
Fax: 831-438-6104 **Website:**

This is a private school.

RATINGS
Admissions Selectivity Rating: 62   **Fire Safety Rating:** 60*   **Green Rating:** 60*

STUDENTS AND FACULTY
Enrollment: 504. **Student Body:** 60% female, 40% male, 15% out-of-state, 2% international. Asian 5%, African American 10%, Caucasian 62%, Hispanic 18%, Native American 1%.
Retention and Graduation: 59% freshmen return for sophomore year. 6% grads go on to further study within 1 year. 6% grads pursue arts and sciences degrees. **Faculty:** Student/faculty ratio 12:1. 25 full-time faculty, 84% hold PhDs, 40% are women.

ACADEMICS
Degrees: Associate, bachelor's, certificate, master's, post-bachelor's certificate. **Classes:** Most classes have 10–19 students. Most lab/discussion sessions have fewer than 10 students. **Special Study Options:** Accelerated program, distance learning, double major, external degree program, independent study, internships, teacher certification program, weekend college.

FACILITIES
Housing: Coed dorms, special housing for disabled students, men's dorms, women's dorms, fraternity/sorority housing, apartments for married students, apartments for single students, theme housing.

CAMPUS LIFE
Activities: Choral groups, concert band, dance, drama/theater, jazz band, literary magazine, marching band, music ensembles, musical theater, opera, pep band, radio station, student government, student newspaper, student-run film society, symphony orchestra, television station, yearbook, campus ministries, international student organization. **Organizations:** 1 honor societies, 1 religious organizations. **Athletics (Intercollegiate):** *Men:* Basketball, cheerleading, golf *Women:* Basketball, cheerleading, softball, volleyball.

ADMISSIONS
Freshman Academic Profile: 16% in top 10% of high school class, 59% in top 25% of high school class, 75% in top 50% of high school class. Minimum paper TOEFL 500. **Basis for Candidate Selection:** *Very important factors considered include:* Application essay, academic GPA, recommendation(s), standardized test scores, religious affiliation/commitment. *Other factors considered include:* Class rank, rigor of secondary school record, character/personal qualities, extracurricular activities, level of applicant's interest. **Freshman Admission Statistics:** 228 applied, 55% admitted, 67% enrolled. **Transfer Admission Requirements:** College transcript(s), essay or personal statement, minimum college GPA of 2.0 required. **General Admission Information:** Application fee $35. Regular application deadline 7/1. Nonfall registration accepted. Admission may be deferred for a maximum of 2 years.

COSTS AND FINANCIAL AID
Annual tuition $14,300. Room and board $6,320. Required fees $715. Average book expense $500. **Required Forms and Deadlines:** FAFSA, institution's own financial aid form. Priority financial aid filing date 3/2. **Notification of Awards: Types of Aid:** *Need-based scholarships/grants:* Federal Pell, SEOG, state scholarships/grants, private scholarships, the school's own gift aid. *Loans:* FFEL Subsidized Stafford, FFEL Unsubsidized Stafford, FFEL PLUS,

Federal Perkins, college/university loans from institutional funds. **Student Employment:** Federal Work-Study Program available.

BETHEL COLLEGE (IN)

1001 W McKinley Avenue, Mishawaka, IN 46545
Phone: 574-257-3339 **Financial Aid Phone:** 574-257-3316
E-mail: admissions@bethelcollege.edu **CEEB Code:** 1079
Fax: 574-257-3335 **Website:** www.bethelcollege.edu **ACT Code:** 1178

This private school was founded in 1947. It has a 75-acre campus.

RATINGS
Admissions Selectivity Rating: 72   **Fire Safety Rating:** 60*   **Green Rating:** 69

STUDENTS AND FACULTY
Enrollment: 1,974. **Student Body:** 34% female, 66% male, 27% out-of-state, 2% international (18 countries represented). Asian 2%, African American 10%, Caucasian 80%, Hispanic 3%.
Retention and Graduation: 79% freshmen return for sophomore year. 37% freshmen graduate within 4 years. **Faculty:** Student/faculty ratio 13:1. 97 full-time faculty, 10% are members of minority groups, 43% are women.

ACADEMICS
Degrees: Associate, bachelor's, master's. **Classes:** Most classes have 10–19 students. Most lab/discussion sessions have fewer than 10 students. **Majors with Highest Enrollment:** Business/commerce; elementary education and teaching; nursing/registered nurse (RN, ASN, BSN, MSN). **Special Study Options:** Accelerated program, cross-registration, double major, English as a Second Language (ESL), exchange student program (domestic), independent study, internships, student-designed major, study abroad, teacher certification program. Special programs offered to physically disabled students include note-taking services, reader services, tape recorders, tutors. **Career services:** Alumni services, career/job search classes, career assessment, internships. Career services highlights include: Reputation of Career Service Office usership is up.

FACILITIES
Housing: Special housing for disabled students, men's dorms, women's dorms 90% of campus accessible to physically disabled. **Special Academic Facilities/Equipment:** Bowen Museum, Weaver Gallery. **Computers:** 25% of classrooms, 100% of dorms, 100% of libraries, 100% of dining areas, 100% of student union, 25% of common outdoor areas have wireless network access. Administrative functions (other than registration) can be performed online.

CAMPUS LIFE
Environment: City. **Activities:** Choral groups, concert band, dance, drama/theater, jazz band, literary magazine, music ensembles, musical theater, pep band, radio station, student government, student newspaper, yearbook. **Organizations:** 18 registered organizations, 1 honor societies, 5 religious organizations. **Athletics (Intercollegiate):** *Men:* Baseball, basketball, cheerleading, cross-country, golf, soccer, tennis, track/field (outdoor), track/field (indoor). *Women:* Basketball, cheerleading, cross-country, golf, soccer, softball, tennis, track/field (outdoor), track/field (indoor), volleyball. **On-Campus Highlights:** Acorn Student Center, Everst Rohrer Chapel, Sufficient Grounds Coffee House, Wiekamp Athletic Center, Dining Commons, workout and weight rooms. **Environmental Initiatives:** Recycle trash, working with local community on MS4 program, recycle leaves.

ADMISSIONS
Freshman Academic Profile: Average high school GPA 3. 15% in top 10% of high school class, 39% in top 25% of high school class, 74% in top 50% of high school class. 70% from public high schools. SAT Math middle 50% range 460–590. SAT Critical Reading middle 50% range 450–570. SAT Writing middle 50% range 435–560. ACT middle 50% range 19–25. Minimum paper TOEFL 540. Minimum computer TOEFL 207. Minimum web-based TOEFL 76. **Basis for Candidate Selection:** *Important factors considered include:* Class rank, application essay, academic GPA, recommendation(s), rigor of secondary school record, standardized test scores, character/personal qualities, extracurricular activities. *Other factors considered include:* Interview, racial/ethnic status, volunteer work. **Freshman Admission Requirements:** High school diploma is required and GED is accepted. *Academic units recommended:* 4 English, 3 mathematics, 1 science, (1 science labs), 2 foreign language, 1 social studies, 2 history, 3 academic electives. **Freshman Admission Statistics:** 645 applied, 91% admitted, 53% enrolled. **Transfer Admission Requirements:** High school transcript, college transcript(s), essay or personal statement, standardized test scores, statement of good standing from prior institution(s). Minimum college GPA of 2.0 required. Lowest grade transferable C–. **General Admission Information:** Application fee $25. Regular application deadline 8/15. Notification on a rolling basis, beginning on or about 10/1. Nonfall registration

---

accepted. Admission may be deferred for a maximum of 1 year. Credit and/or placement offered for CEEB Advanced Placement tests.

COSTS AND FINANCIAL AID
Annual tuition $17,450. Room and board $5,380. Average book expense $1,600. **Required Forms and Deadlines:** FAFSA. Priority financial aid filing date 3/10. **Notification of Awards:** Applicants will be notified of awards on a rolling basis beginning 4/15. **Types of Aid:** *Need-based scholarships/grants:* Federal Pell, SEOG, state scholarships/grants, private scholarships, the school's own gift aid, Federal Nursing Scholarships. *Loans:* FFEL Subsidized Stafford, FFEL Unsubsidized Stafford, FFEL PLUS, Federal Perkins, college/university loans from institutional funds. **Student Employment:** Federal Work-Study Program available. Institutional employment available. Highest amount earned per year from on-campus jobs $2,500. Off-campus job opportunities are excellent. **Financial Aid Statistics:** 60% freshmen, 53% undergrads receive need-based scholarship or grant aid. 73% freshmen, 64% undergrads receive non-need-based scholarship or grant aid. 73% freshmen, 67% undergrads receive need-based self-help aid. 25% freshmen, 17% undergrads receive athletic scholarships. 76% freshmen, 73% undergrads receive any aid. 83% undergrads borrow to pay for school. Average cumulative indebtedness $15,990. **Criteria for awarding institutional aid:** *Non-need-based:* Academics, art, athletics, job skills, leadership, minority status, music/drama, religious affiliation, state/district residency.

BETHEL COLLEGE (KS)

300 E 27th St, North Newton, KS 67117-8061
Phone: 316-284-5230 **Financial Aid Phone:** 316-284-5232
E-mail: admissions@bethelks.edu **CEEB Code:** 6037
Fax: 316-284-5870 **Website:** www.bethelks.edu **ACT Code:** 1390

This private school was founded in 1887. It has a 60-acre campus.

RATINGS
Admissions Selectivity Rating: 85   **Fire Safety Rating:** 67   **Green Rating:** 60*

STUDENTS AND FACULTY
Enrollment: 437. **Student Body:** 49% female, 51% male, 25% out-of-state, 3% international (13 countries represented). Asian 2%, African American 5%, Caucasian 81%, Hispanic 7%, Native American 1%.
Retention and Graduation: 76% freshmen return for sophomore year. 51% freshmen graduate within 4 years. **Faculty:** Student/faculty ratio 9:1. 40 full-time faculty, 63% hold PhDs, 5% are members of minority groups, 43% are women.

ACADEMICS
Degrees: Bachelor's, certificate. **Classes:** Most classes have 10–19 students. Most lab/discussion sessions have 10–19 students. **Majors with Highest Enrollment:** Biology/biological sciences; business/commerce; nursing/registered nurse (RN, ASN, BSN, MSN). **Special Study Options:** Cross-registration, double major, dual enrollment, independent study, internships, liberal arts/career combination, study abroad, teacher certification program. **Combined degree programs:** BA/MEng. Special programs offered to physically disabled students include note-taking services, reader services, tape recorders, tutors. **Career services:** Alumni network, career/job search classes, career assessment. **Career services highlights include:** The liberal arts program provides students with a foundational, broad understanding of the social and natural world. Focused study in a major field equips students with the intellectual achievement vital to vocational success. Internships are thus an additional, integrated component of a larger academic program that fosters in students a powerful sense of purpose. The skills developed in a liberal education—the ability to speak, read and write correctly, clearly and cogently—are the skills needed in employment. Internship experiences help students understand the relationship of their educational experience to potential careers.

FACILITIES
Housing: Coed dorms, special housing for disabled students, apartments for married students, apartments for single students. 75% of campus accessible to physically disabled. **Special Academic Facilities/Equipment:** Art gallery, natural history and midwestern/Kansas history museums, 80 acre natural history field laboratory for biological studies, Mennonite Historical Library and Archives, Institute for Peace and Conflict Resolution, observatory. **Computers:** 25% of classrooms, 75% of libraries, 100% of dining areas, 100% of student union, 50% of common outdoor areas have wireless network access. Administrative functions (other than registration) can be performed online.

CAMPUS LIFE
Environment: Village. **Activities:** Choral groups, concert band, dance, drama/theater, jazz band, literary magazine, music ensembles, musical theater, opera,

radio station, student government, student newspaper, symphony orchestra, television station, yearbook, campus ministries, international student organization. **Organizations:** 50 registered organizations, 2 religious organizations. **Athletics (Intercollegiate):** *Men:* Basketball, cross-country, football, golf, soccer, tennis, track/field (outdoor), track/field (indoor). *Women:* Basketball, cross-country, golf, soccer, tennis, track/field (outdoor), track/field (indoor), volleyball. **On-Campus Highlights:** Student Center, Krehbiel Science Center, Athletic Complex, The Green, Warkentine Court.

ADMISSIONS

Freshman Academic Profile: Average high school GPA 3.6. 36% in top 10% of high school class, 58% in top 25% of high school class, 86% in top 50% of high school class. 97% from public high schools. SAT Math middle 50% range 460–730. SAT Critical Reading middle 50% range 420–700. SAT Writing middle 50% range 430–690. ACT middle 50% range 21–29. Minimum paper TOEFL 540. Minimum computer TOEFL 207. Minimum web-based TOEFL 76. **Basis for Candidate Selection:** *Very important factors considered include:* Academic GPA, standardized test scores, level of applicant's interest. *Important factors considered include:* Class rank, alumni/ae relation, character/personal qualities, extracurricular activities. *Other factors considered include:* recommendation(s), rigor of secondary school record. **Freshman Admission Requirements:** High school diploma is required and GED is accepted. *Academic units recommended:* 4 English, 4 mathematics, 3 science, 2 foreign language, 3 social studies, 1 history, 1 computer science. **Freshman Admission Statistics:** 386 applied, 75% admitted, 32% enrolled. **Transfer Admission Requirements:** High school transcript, college transcript(s), statement of good standing from prior institution(s). Lowest grade transferable D–. **General Admission Information:** Application fee $20. Notification on a rolling basis, beginning on or about 9/1. Nonfall registration accepted. Admission may be deferred for a maximum of 1 yr. Credit and/or placement offered for CEEB Advanced Placement tests.

COSTS AND FINANCIAL AID

Required Forms and Deadlines: FAFSA. Priority financial aid filing date 4/1. **Notification of Awards:** Applicants will be notified of awards on a rolling basis beginning 2/1. **Types of Aid:** *Need-based scholarships/grants:* Federal Pell, SEOG, state scholarships/grants, private scholarships, the school's own gift aid. *Loans:* Direct Subsidized Stafford, Direct Unsubsidized Stafford, Direct PLUS, FFEL Subsidized Stafford, FFEL Unsubsidized Stafford, FFEL PLUS, Federal Perkins. **Student Employment:** Federal Work-Study Program available. Institutional employment available. Highest amount earned per year from on-campus jobs $9,278. Off-campus job opportunities are good. **Financial Aid Statistics:** 64% freshmen, 55% undergrads receive need-based scholarship or grant aid. 79% freshmen, 72% undergrads receive non-need-based scholarship or grant aid. 51% freshmen, 58% undergrads receive need-based self-help aid. 53% freshmen, 41% undergrads receive athletic scholarships. 100% freshmen, 94% undergrads receive any aid. 81% undergrads borrow to pay for school. Average cumulative indebtedness $24,241. **Criteria for awarding institutional aid:** *Non-need-based:* Academics, alumni affiliation, art, athletics, minority status, music/drama, religious affiliation, state/district residency.

BETHEL UNIVERSITY

Office of Admissions–CAS, 3900 Bethel Drive, Saint Paul, MN 55112
Phone: 651-638-6242 **Financial Aid Phone:** 651-638-6241
E-mail: BUadmissions-cas@bethel.edu **CEEB Code:** 6038
Fax: 651-635-1490 **Website:** www.bethel.edu **ACT Code:** 2088

This private school was founded in 1871. It has a 247-acre campus.

RATINGS
Admissions Selectivity Rating: 81   **Fire Safety Rating:** 76   **Green Rating:** 77

STUDENTS AND FACULTY
Enrollment: 3,335. **Student Body:** 61% female, 39% male, 22% out-of-state, international (45 countries represented). Asian 2%, African American 4%, Caucasian 82%, Hispanic 1%.
Retention and Graduation: 85% freshmen return for sophomore year. 63% freshmen graduate within 4 years. 23% grads go on to further study within 1 year. 8% grads pursue arts and sciences degrees. 1% grads pursue law degrees. 3% grads pursue business degrees. 3% grads pursue medical degrees. **Faculty:** Student/faculty ratio 12:1. 188 full-time faculty, 78% hold PhDs. 11% are members of minority groups, 42% are women.

ACADEMICS
Degrees: Associate, bachelor's, master's, post-bachelor's certificate, post-master's certificate. **Classes:** Most classes have 10–19 students. Most lab/discussion sessions have 10–19 students. **Majors with Highest Enrollment:** Business administration and management; education; nursing/registered nurse (RN, ASN,

BSN, MSN). **Special Study Options:** Double major, exchange student program (domestic), honors program, independent study, internships, student-designed major, study abroad, teacher certification program. **Honors programs:** The program consists of two honors courses in the freshman year, one in the sophomore year and one in the junior year. In their senior year the student will complete an Honors Senior Project. The two courses in the sophomore year and junior year, as well as the Honors Senior Project are geared toward a discipline of the students choosing. This program also consists of other Honors classes and Honors Forums throughout all four years. **Combined degree programs:** Dual degree BA/BS Program in Engineering. Special programs offered to physically disabled students include note-taking services, reader services, tape recorders, tutors. **Career services:** Alumni services, career/job search classes, career assessment, internships. Career services highlights include. We have a very collaborative network of colleagues around the state and provide high quality job fairs through our joint effort.

FACILITIES
Housing: Coed dorms, special housing for disabled students, apartments for single students. 99% of campus accessible to physically disabled. **Special Academic Facilities/Equipment:** Two art galleries, media center, closed circuit TV, television studio, and radio station, cadaver lab. **Computers:** 100% of classrooms, 50% of dorms, 100% of libraries, 100% of dining areas, 100% of student union, 50% of common outdoor areas have wireless network access. Students can register for classes online. Administrative functions (other than registration) can be performed online.

CAMPUS LIFE
Environment: Metropolis. **Activities:** Choral groups, concert band, dance, drama/theater, jazz band, literary magazine, music ensembles, musical theater, radio station, student government, student newspaper, student-run film society, symphony orchestra, campus ministries, international student organization. **Organizations:** 55 registered organizations, 5 honor societies, 20 religious organizations. **Athletics (Intercollegiate):** *Men:* Baseball, basketball, cross-country, football, golf, ice hockey, soccer, tennis, track/field (outdoor), track/field (indoor). *Women:* Basketball, cross-country, golf, ice hockey, soccer, softball, tennis, track/field (outdoor), track/field (indoor), volleyball. **On-Campus Highlights:** Brushaber Commons (new student facility), SRC–Student Recreation Center, Market Square/Dining Center, Lissner Hall-New Dorm/ Lounges, Ona Orth Athletic Complex, Brushaber Commons: All new student facility. Great Hall: seats 1600 people; location of Chapel services, Vespers, concerts, musicals and large on-campus events. **Environmental Initiatives:** Green Roof and Permeable Pavers for Brushaber Commons, Day Lighting Control for Monson Dining Center, North Village Composting

ADMISSIONS
Freshman Academic Profile: Average high school GPA 3.5. 31% in top 10% of high school class, 55% in top 25% of high school class, 84% in top 50% of high school class. 80% from public high schools. SAT Math middle 50% range 510–667.5. SAT Critical Reading middle 50% range 512.5–677.5. ACT middle 50% range 21–28. Minimum paper TOEFL 525. Minimum computer TOEFL 195. Minimum web-based TOEFL 70. **Basis for Candidate Selection:** *Very important factors considered include:* Academic GPA, rigor of secondary school record, standardized test scores, character/personal qualities, religious affiliation/commitment. *Important factors considered include:* Class rank, application essay, extracurricular activities. *Other factors considered include:* Recommendation(s), alumni/ae relation, first generation, geographical residence, interview, level of applicant's interest, racial/ethnic status, state residency, talent/ability, volunteer work. **Freshman Admission Requirements:** High school diploma is required and GED is accepted. *Academic units required:* 4 English, 3 mathematics, 3 science, (3 science labs), 4 social studies. *Academic units recommended:* 2 foreign language, 1 history, 1 visual/performing arts, 1 computer science. **Freshman Admission Statistics:** 2,179 applied, 80% admitted, 42% enrolled. **Transfer Admission Requirements:** College transcript(s), essay or personal statement, minimum college GPA of 2.5 required. Lowest grade transferable C. **General Admission Information:** Notification on a rolling basis, beginning on or about 10/1. Nonfall registration accepted. Admission may be deferred for a maximum of 1 term. Credit and/or placement offered for CEEB Advanced Placement tests.

COSTS AND FINANCIAL AID
Required Forms and Deadlines: FAFSA, institution's own financial aid form. Priority financial aid filing date 4/15. **Notification of Awards:** Applicants will be notified of awards on a rolling basis beginning 3/1. **Types of Aid:** *Need-based scholarships/grants:* Federal Pell, SEOG, state scholarships/grants, private scholarships, the school's own gift aid. *Loans:* Direct Subsidized Stafford, Direct Unsubsidized Stafford, Direct PLUS, Federal Perkins, state loans. **Student Employment:** Federal Work-Study Program available. Institutional employment available. Highest amount earned per year from on-campus jobs $6,500. Off-campus job opportunities are excellent. **Financial Aid Statistics:** 74% freshmen, 71% undergrads receive need-based scholarship or grant aid. 6% freshmen, 7% undergrads receive non-need-based scholarship or grant

aid. 65% freshmen, 63% undergrads receive need-based self-help aid. 99% freshmen, 97% undergrads receive any aid. 80% undergrads borrow to pay for school. Average cumulative indebtedness $30,496. **Criteria for awarding institutional aid:** *Non-need-based:* Academics, alumni affiliation, art, leadership, music/drama, state/district residency.

BETHUNE-COOKMAN COLLEGE

640 Dr. Mary McLeod Bethune Boulevard, Daytona Beach, FL 32114-3099
Phone: 386-481-2600 **Financial Aid Phone:** 386-481-2626
E-mail: admissions@cookman.edu **CEEB Code:** 5061
Fax: 386-481-2601 **Website:** www.bethune.cookman.edu **ACT Code:** 720

This private school, affiliated with the Methodist Church, was founded in 1904. It has a 78-acre campus.

RATINGS
Admissions Selectivity Rating: 64   **Fire Safety Rating:** 60*   **Green Rating:** 60*

STUDENTS AND FACULTY
Enrollment: 3,093. **Student Body:** 58% female, 42% male, 30% out-of-state, 3% international (25 countries represented). African American 91%, Caucasian 1%, Hispanic 2%.
Retention and Graduation: 69% freshmen return for sophomore year. 13% freshmen graduate within 4 years. 28% grads go on to further study within 1 year. 12% grads pursue arts and sciences degrees. 1% grads pursue law degrees. 14% grads pursue business degrees. 1% grads pursue medical degrees. **Faculty:** Student/faculty ratio 17:1. 161 full-time faculty, 57% hold PhDs, 58% are members of minority groups, 50% are women.

ACADEMICS
Degrees: Bachelor's, master's. **Classes:** Most classes have 20–29 students. Most lab/discussion sessions have fewer than 10 students. **Majors with Highest Enrollment:** Business/commerce; corrections and criminal justice, other; elementary education and teaching. **Special Study Options:** Accelerated program, distance learning, double major, honors program, independent study, internships, study abroad, teacher certification program, weekend college. **Honors programs:** The Honors program is designed to provide expanded study opportunities for highly motivated and exceptionally qualified students, broaden their intellectual horizons, integrate various areas of knowledge, and explore intensively major fields of study through innovative techniques of individualized learning and independent research, preparing students more adequately for graduate school. Special programs offered to physically disabled students include tutors. **Career services:** Internships. Career services highlights include: Opportunities in the Teacher Education Internships.

FACILITIES
Housing: Men's dorms, women's dorms, Scholarship Housing. 70% of campus accessible to physically disabled. **Special Academic Facilities/Equipment:** Historic archives, founder's home and gravesite (historic landmark), outreach center, telecommunications satellite network, art gallery/studio, audiologic recording studio, observatory. **Computers:** Students can register for classes online. Administrative functions (other than registration) can be performed online.

CAMPUS LIFE
Environment: Town. **Activities:** Choral groups, concert band, drama/theater, jazz band, marching band, music ensembles, radio station, student government, student newspaper, yearbook. **Organizations:** 40 registered organizations, 9 honor societies, 2 religious organizations. 5 fraternities, 4 sororities. **Athletics (Intercollegiate):** *Men:* Baseball, basketball, cross-country, football, golf, tennis, track/field (outdoor), track/field (indoor). *Women:* Basketball, cross-country, golf, softball, tennis, track/field (outdoor), track/field (indoor), volleyball. **On-Campus Highlights:** Bethune Foundation (the Founder's Home), Bethune Performing Arts Center, Bethune Fine Arts studio and Gallery, Swisher Library Archives and Exhibit Rooms, Heyn Memorial Chapel (White Hall).

ADMISSIONS
Freshman Academic Profile: Average high school GPA 2.75. 5% in top 10% of high school class, 15% in top 25% of high school class, 48% in top 50% of high school class. 90% from public high schools. SAT Math middle 50% range 360–460. SAT Critical Reading middle 50% range 360–460. ACT middle 50% range 14–18. Minimum paper TOEFL 550. Minimum computer TOEFL 213. **Basis for Candidate Selection:** *Very important factors considered include:* Academic GPA, rigor of secondary school record, standardized test scores. *Important factors considered include:* Recommendation(s), character/personal qualities. *Other factors considered include:* Class rank, application essay, alumni/ae relation, extracurricular activities, first generation, interview, level of applicant's interest, talent/ability, volunteer work, work experience. **Fresh-**

man **Admission Requirements:** High school diploma is required and GED is accepted. *Academic units required:* 4 English, 3 mathematics, 3 science, (1 science labs), 1 social studies, 2 history, 6 academic electives. *Academic units recommended:* 2 foreign language, 1 computer literacy **Freshman Admission Statistics:** 4,129 applied, 78% admitted, 28% enrolled. **Transfer Admission Requirements:** College transcript(s), essay or personal statement, statement of good standing from prior institution(s). Minimum college GPA of 2.2 required. Lowest grade transferable C. **General Admission Information:** Application fee $25. Nonfall registration accepted. Admission may be deferred for a maximum of 1 year. Credit offered for CEEB Advanced Placement tests.

COSTS AND FINANCIAL AID
Annual tuition $11,792. Room and board $7,206. Average book expense $850. **Required Forms and Deadlines:** FAFSA. Priority financial aid filing date 4/1. **Notification of Awards:** Applicants will be notified of awards on a rolling basis beginning 4/1. **Types of Aid:** *Need-based scholarships/grants:* Federal Pell, SEOG, state scholarships/grants, private scholarships, the school's own gift aid, United Negro College Fund, Federal Nursing Scholarships. *Loans:* Direct Subsidized Stafford, Direct Unsubsidized Stafford, Direct PLUS, FFEL Subsidized Stafford, FFEL Unsubsidized Stafford, FFEL PLUS **Student Employment:** Federal Work-Study Program available. Institutional employment available. Highest amount earned per year from on-campus jobs $2,500. Off-campus job opportunities are good. **Financial Aid Statistics:** 76% freshmen, 71% undergrads receive need-based scholarship or grant aid. 11% freshmen, 12% undergrads receive non-need-based scholarship or grant aid. 84% freshmen, 79% undergrads receive need-based self-help aid. 8% freshmen, 9% undergrads receive athletic scholarships. 94% freshmen, 93% undergrads receive any aid. 85% undergrads borrow to pay for school. Average cumulative indebtedness $32,500. **Criteria for awarding institutional aid:** *Non-need-based:* Academics, athletics, leadership, music/drama, religious affiliation, state/district residency.

BIOLA UNIVERSITY

13800 Biola Avenue, La Mirada, CA 90639
Phone: 562-903-4752 **Financial Aid Phone:** 562-903-4752
E-mail: admissions@biola.edu **CEEB Code:** 4017
Fax: 562-903-4709 **Website:** www.biola.edu **ACT Code:** 172

This private school, affiliated with the Christian (Nondenominational) Church, was founded in 1908. It has a 95-acre campus.

RATINGS
Admissions Selectivity Rating: 76   **Fire Safety Rating:** 83   **Green Rating:** 60*

STUDENTS AND FACULTY
Enrollment: 3,452. **Student Body:** 62% female, 38% male, 27% out-of-state, international (40 countries represented).
Retention and Graduation: 86% freshmen return for sophomore year. 51% freshmen graduate within 4 years. **Faculty:** Student/faculty ratio 17:1. 213 full-time faculty, 75% hold PhDs, 15% are members of minority groups, 27% are women.

ACADEMICS
Degrees: Bachelor's, first professional, master's, post-master's certificate. **Classes:** Most classes have 10–19 students. Most lab/discussion sessions have 10–19 students. **Majors with Highest Enrollment:** Business/commerce; elementary education and teaching; psychology. **Special Study Options:** Double major, English as a Second Language (ESL), exchange student program (domestic), honors program, internships, study abroad, teacher certification program. Special programs offered to physically disabled students include note-taking services, reader services, tape recorders, tutors. **Career services:** Alumni network, alumni services, career/job search classes, career assessment, internships, regional alumni. **Career services highlights include:** Biola University provides internships applicable to a student's major allowing them to gain academic credit and career development.

FACILITIES
Housing: Coed dorms, special housing for disabled students, men's dorms, women's dorms, apartments for married students, apartments for single students, flex style dorms—separate floors and wings for specific genders off campus apartments, on campus apartments. 70% of campus accessible to physically disabled. **Special Academic Facilities/Equipment:** Art gallery, electron microscope, TV production facility, film editing facility, media center, writing center, Student Ministry Union and tutoring services. **Computers:** 100% of dorms, 100% of libraries, 100% of student union, 75% of common outdoor areas have wireless network access. Students can register for classes online. Administrative functions (other than registration) can be performed online.

CAMPUS LIFE

Environment: Town. **Activities:** Choral groups, concert band, drama/theater, jazz band, music ensembles, musical theater, opera, radio station, student government, student newspaper, student-run film society, symphony orchestra, television station, yearbook. **Organizations:** 33 registered organizations, 2 honor societies. **Athletics (Intercollegiate):** *Men:* Baseball, basketball, cross-country, golf, soccer, swimming, tennis, track/field (outdoor). *Women:* Basketball, cross-country, golf, soccer, softball, swimming, tennis, track/field (outdoor), volleyball. **On-Campus Highlights:** Common Grounds, The Eagle's Nest, Art Gallery, McNally Field, The Sub (Student Union Building).

ADMISSIONS

Freshman Academic Profile: Average high school GPA 3.52. SAT Math middle 50% range 490–620. SAT Critical Reading middle 50% range 500–620. SAT Writing middle 50% range 500–610. ACT middle 50% range 21-26. Minimum paper TOEFL 500. Minimum computer TOEFL 173. **Basis for Candidate Selection:** *Very important factors considered include:* Application essay, academic GPA, recommendation(s), standardized test scores, character/personal qualities, religious affiliation/commitment. *Important factors considered include:* rigor of secondary school record, extracurricular activities, interview. *Other factors considered include:* Class rank, alumni/ae relation, first generation, geographical residence, level of applicant's interest, state residency, volunteer work, work experience. **Freshman Admission Requirements:** High school diploma is required and GED is accepted. *Academic units recommended:* 4 English, 3 mathematics, 2 science, 4 foreign language, 2 social studies, 1 history. **Freshman Admission Statistics:** 2,252 applied, 84% admitted, 50% enrolled. **Transfer Admission Requirements:** High school transcript, college transcript(s), essay or personal statement, statement of good standing from prior institution(s). Minimum college GPA of 2.0 required. Lowest grade transferable C. **General Admission Information:** Application fee $45. Regular application deadline 3/1. Regular notification 4/1. Nonfall registration not accepted. Admission may be deferred for a maximum of 2 years. Credit offered for CEEB Advanced Placement tests.

COSTS AND FINANCIAL AID

Annual tuition $24,998. Room and board $7,770. Average book expense $1,386. **Required Forms and Deadlines:** FAFSA, state aid form. **Notification of Awards:** Applicants will be notified of awards on a rolling basis beginning 3/1. **Types of Aid:** *Need-based scholarships/grants:* Federal Pell, SEOG, state scholarships/grants, private scholarships, the school's own gift aid. *Loans:* FFEL Subsidized Stafford, FFEL Unsubsidized Stafford, FFEL PLUS, Federal Perkins, Federal Nursing, college/university loans from institutional funds. **Student Employment:** Highest amount earned per year from on-campus jobs $2,000. Off-campus job opportunities are good. **Financial Aid Statistics:** 56% freshmen, 52% undergrads receive need-based scholarship or grant aid. 59% freshmen, 50% undergrads receive non-need-based scholarship or grant aid. 69% freshmen, 64% undergrads receive need-based self-help aid. 2% freshmen, 3% undergrads receive athletic scholarships. 89% freshmen, 96% undergrads receive any aid. 75% undergrads borrow to pay for school. Average cumulative indebtedness $27,628. **Criteria for awarding institutional aid:** *Non-need-based:* Academics, alumni affiliation, art, athletics, leadership, minority status, music/drama.

BIRMINGHAM-SOUTHERN COLLEGE

Best 373

Box 549008, Birmingham, AL 35254
Phone: 205-226-4696 **Financial Aid Phone:** 205-226-4688
E-mail: admission@bsc.edu **CEEB Code:** 1064
Fax: 205-226-3074 **Website:** www.bsc.edu **ACT Code:** 1012

This private school, affiliated with the Methodist Church, was founded in 1856. It has a 196-acre campus.

RATINGS

Admissions Selectivity Rating: 88   **Fire Safety Rating:** 98   **Green Rating:** 75

STUDENTS AND FACULTY

Enrollment: 1,412. **Student Body:** 51% female, 49% male, 34% out-of-state, international (12 countries represented). Asian 3%, African American 8%, Caucasian 84%, Hispanic 1%.
Retention and Graduation: 75% freshmen return for sophomore year. 53% freshmen graduate within 4 years. 42% grads go on to further study within 1

year. 27% grads pursue arts and sciences degrees. 17% grads pursue law degrees. 13% grads pursue business degrees. 24% grads pursue medical degrees. **Faculty:** Student/faculty ratio 12:1. 104 full-time faculty, 94% hold PhDs, 2% are members of minority groups, 43% are women.

ACADEMICS

Degrees: Bachelor's, master's. **Classes:** Most classes have 10–19 students. Most lab/discussion sessions have 10–19 students. **Majors with Highest Enrollment:** Business/commerce; English language and literature; psychology. **Special Study Options:** Cooperative education program, cross-registration, double major, dual enrollment, exchange student program (domestic), honors program, independent study, internships, liberal arts/career combination, student-designed major, study abroad, teacher certification program. **Honors programs:** The Honors Program at Birmingham-Southern is designed to engage students' intellectual curiosity, enhance their oral and written communications skills, and further develop their ability to think and study independently. The importance of viewing issues from interdisciplinary perspectives and of integrating—as well as analyzing—knowledge is a special focus of the program's courses and requirements. The program addresses its mission through small, interdisciplinary seminars developed specifically for Honors students and through upper-level courses with an interdisciplinary focus. The Honors Program serves as a complementary approach to fulfilling the requirements of the College's Foundations Plan for General Education. "…Honors students are open to new ideas, aware of expanding horizons, and willing to change their own ideas to make room for the knowledge that they gain. They incorporate, embrace, and encourage differences. 'Honors' is not synonymous with straight A's and valedictorians. Ideal Honors students would participate in the program even if it did not appear on their transcripts." Excerpted from "The Ideal Student in the Honors Program" as adopted by the Honors Committee 2002. The Honors Program component of Honors student's general education consists of five units of Honors seminars and one unit of independent study, known as the Honors Project. The specific general education requirements met by Honors courses and those met by regular courses will vary from student to student, depending on which Honors courses the student elects to take. Students may take one January Interim Term Honors project which will count toward the five units of Honors seminars. Students who participate in study abroad programs that include interdisciplinary courses also may petition to count one such course toward their Honors requirements. Honors students' remaining general education coursework is completed in the regular curriculum of the College. The student's sixth unit in independent study is typically taken over two terms. One-half unit is taken while the project is being designed by the student, the program director, and a faculty sponsor. The project must be interdisciplinary in nature and outside the student's major. Once approved by the Honors Program Committee, the independent study is completed the next term, giving the second half-unit of credit. All Honors Senior, or independent study, projects are presented publicly as part of the program's requirements. **Combined degree programs:** BA/MEng, BS/MSN (with Vanderbilt University; BS/MF or BS/MEM (with Duke Univ.). **Career services:** Alumni network, alumni services, career/job search classes, career assessment, internships, regional alumni. **Career services highlights include:** The Mentor Program is a unique job shadowing program that matches students with local successful professionals in the student's field of interest.

FACILITIES

Housing: Special housing for disabled students, men's dorms, special housing for international students, women's dorms, fraternity/sorority housing, apartments for married students, apartments for single students, wellness housing, theme housing, "Honors" floors in residence halls. 90% of campus accessible to physically disabled. **Special Academic Facilities/Equipment:** Theater, planetarium, Environmental Center, Urban Environmental Park, Kennedy Art Center, Ropes Course for Leadership Training. **Computers:** 100% of classrooms, 100% of dorms, 100% of libraries, 100% of dining areas, 100% of student union, 90% of common outdoor areas have wireless network access. Students can register for classes online. Administrative functions (other than registration) can be performed online.

CAMPUS LIFE

Environment: Metropolis. **Activities:** Choral groups, dance, drama/theater, jazz band, literary magazine, musical theater, opera, pep band, student government, student newspaper, yearbook, campus ministries, international student organization. **Organizations:** 70 registered organizations, 18 honor societies, 5 religious organizations. 6 fraternities, 6 sororities. **Athletics (Intercollegiate):** *Men:* Baseball, basketball, cheerleading, cross-country, football, golf, lacrosse, soccer, tennis, track/field (outdoor), track/field (indoor). *Women:* Basketball, cheerleading, cross-country, golf, lacrosse, riflery, soccer, softball, tennis, track/field (outdoor), track/field (indoor), volleyball. **On-Campus Highlights:** Urban Environmental Park, Striplin Physical Fitness Center, The Cellar—Coffee House, The Court. **Environmental Initiatives:** 10 compressed natural gas operations vehicles will come on line this spring. Campus police vehicles are hybrids. The Southern Environmental Center (SEC) is the largest educational facility of its kind in Alabama. In addition to its award winning interactive museum and Ecoscape Gardens, the SEC is also active in the community. Annually, 15,000 school children visit the center. See www.myecoscapes.org. An Urban Environmental Park, which opened in the fall of 2009, serves as both a place of recreation for students, as well as an academic laboratory for the study of environmental issues.

ADMISSIONS

Freshman Academic Profile: Average high school GPA 3.4. 32% in top 10% of high school class, 53% in top 25% of high school class, 82% in top 50% of high school class. 65% from public high schools. SAT Math middle 50% range 510–630. SAT Critical Reading middle 50% range 520–540. ACT middle 50% range 23–28. Minimum paper TOEFL 500. Minimum computer TOEFL 173. Minimum web-based TOEFL 61. **Basis for Candidate Selection:** *Very important factors considered include:* Application essay, academic GPA, recommendation(s), rigor of secondary school record, standardized test scores. *Important factors considered include:* character/personal qualities. *Other factors considered include:* extracurricular activities, interview, level of applicant's interest, talent/ability, work experience. **Freshman Admission Requirements:** High school diploma is required and GED is accepted. *Academic units required:* 4 English. *Academic units recommended:* 4 mathematics, 4 science, (2 science labs), 2 foreign language, 2 social studies, 2 history, 10 academic electives. **Freshman Admission Statistics:** 2,101 applied, 69% admitted, 31% enrolled. **Transfer Admission Requirements:** High school transcript, college transcript(s), essay or personal statement, standardized test scores, statement of good standing from prior institution(s). Minimum college GPA of 2.0 required. Lowest grade transferable D. **General Admission Information:** Application fee $40. Notification on a rolling basis, beginning on or about 7/1. Nonfall registration accepted. Admission may be deferred for a maximum of 1 year. Credit and/or placement offered for CEEB Advanced Placement tests.

COSTS AND FINANCIAL AID

Annual tuition $25,800. Room and board $9,236. Required fees $946. Average book expense $1,100. **Required Forms and Deadlines:** FAFSA. Priority financial aid filing date 3/1. **Notification of Awards:** Applicants will be notified of awards on a rolling basis beginning 3/1. **Types of Aid:** *Need-based scholarships/grants:* Federal Pell, SEOG, state scholarships/grants, private scholarships, the school's own gift aid, United Negro College Fund. *Loans:* FFEL Subsidized Stafford, FFEL Unsubsidized Stafford, FFEL PLUS, Federal Perkins. **Student Employment:** Federal Work-Study Program available. Institutional employment available. Highest amount earned per year from on-campus jobs $1,800. Off-campus job opportunities are excellent. **Financial Aid Statistics:** 44% freshmen, 38% undergrads receive need-based scholarship or grant aid. 53% freshmen, 48% undergrads receive non-need-based scholarship or grant aid. 41% freshmen, 38% undergrads receive need-based self-help aid. 4% undergrads receive athletic scholarships. 99% freshmen, 98% undergrads receive any aid. 79% undergrads borrow to pay for school. Average cumulative indebtedness $27,798. **Criteria for awarding institutional aid:** *Non-need-based:* Academics, alumni affiliation, art, leadership, minority status, music/drama, religious affiliation.

BISHOP'S UNIVERSITY

2600 College Street, Sherbrooke, QC J1M0C8 Canada
Phone: 819-822-9600 **E-mail:** admissio@ubishops.ca
Fax: 819-822-9616 **Website:** www.ubishops.ca

This public school was founded in 1843. It has a 550-acre campus.

RATINGS

Admissions Selectivity Rating: 60*   **Fire Safety Rating:** 60*   **Green Rating:** 60*

STUDENTS AND FACULTY

Retention and Graduation: 78% freshmen return for sophomore year. 57% freshmen graduate within 4 years. 50% grads go on to further study within 1 year. **Faculty:** Student/faculty ratio 12:1. 120 full-time faculty, 68% hold PhDs, 30% are women.

ACADEMICS

Degrees: Bachelor's, certificate, master's. **Classes:** Most classes have 10–19 students. Most lab/discussion sessions have 10–19 students. **Majors with Highest Enrollment:** Biology; business/commerce; education. **Special Study Options:** Double major, English as a Second Language (ESL), exchange student program (domestic), honors program, independent study, liberal arts/career combination, student-designed major, study abroad, teacher certification program. Special programs offered to physically disabled students include note-taking services, reader services, tape recorders, tutors. **Career services:** Alumni services, career/job search classes, career assessment.

FACILITIES

Housing: Coed dorms, special housing for disabled students, women's dorms. 75% of campus accessible to physically disabled. **Special Academic Facilities/Equipment:** Eastern Townships, Research Centre, Cormier Economics Centre, Dobson-Lagasse Entrepренneurship Centre, Molson Fine Arts Building, Art Gallery.

CAMPUS LIFE

Environment: Rural. **Activities:** Choral groups, concert band, dance, drama/theater, jazz band, literary magazine, music ensembles, musical theater, radio station, student government, student newspaper, yearbook. **Organizations:** 60 registered organizations, 2 religious organizations. **Athletics (Intercollegiate):** *Men:* Basketball, football, golf, rugby, skiing (downhill/alpine). *Women:* Basketball, rugby, skiing (downhill/alpine), soccer.

ADMISSIONS

Freshman Academic Profile: Minimum paper TOEFL 550. Minimum computer TOEFL 213. **Basis for Candidate Selection:** *Very important factors considered include:* Rigor of secondary school record. *Important factors considered include:* Standardized test scores. *Other factors considered include:* Class rank, application essay, recommendation(s), character/personal qualities, extracurricular activities, talent/ability, volunteer work. **Freshman Admission Requirements:** High school diploma is required and GED is accepted. **Freshman Admission Statistics: Transfer Admission Requirements:** college transcript(s), **General Admission Information:** Application fee $55. Notification on a rolling basis, beginning on or about 2/1. Nonfall registration accepted. Admission may be deferred for a maximum of 1 year. Credit offered for CEEB Advanced Placement tests.

COSTS AND FINANCIAL AID

Annual in-state tuition $1,668. Annual out-of-state tuition $3,438. Room and board $4,000. Required fees $525. Average book expense $625. **Required Forms and Deadlines:** state aid form **Types of Aid:** *Loans:* Direct Subsidized Stafford, Direct Unsubsidized Stafford, FFEL Subsidized Stafford, FFEL Unsubsidized Stafford, state loans. **Student Employment:** Off-campus job opportunities are good. **Financial Aid Statistics:** 33% undergrads borrow to pay for school.

BLACK HILLS STATE UNIVERSITY

1200 University Street Unit 9502, Spearfish, SD 57799-9502
Phone: 605-642-6343
E-mail: admissions@bhsu.edu **CEEB Code:** 6042
Fax: 605-642-6254 **ACT Code:** 3904

This public school was founded in 1883. It has a 123-acre campus.

RATINGS

Admissions Selectivity Rating: 66   **Fire Safety Rating:** 60*   **Green Rating:** 60*

STUDENTS AND FACULTY

Enrollment: 3,138. **Student Body:** 63% female, 37% male, 21% out-of-state, 1% international (6 countries represented). Asian 1%, African American 1%, Caucasian 87%, Hispanic 2%, Native American 4%.
Retention and Graduation: 55% freshmen return for sophomore year. 10% freshmen graduate within 4 years. 20% grads go on to further study within 1 year. 1% grads pursue arts and sciences degrees. 2% grads pursue law degrees. 2% grads pursue business degrees. 2% grads pursue medical degrees. **Faculty:** Student/faculty ratio 21:1. 117 full-time faculty, 71% hold PhDs, 8% are members of minority groups, 39% are women.

ACADEMICS

Degrees: Associate, bachelor's, master's, post-bachelor's certificate. **Classes:** Most classes have 20–29 students. Most lab/discussion sessions have 20–29 students. **Special Study Options:** cooperative education program, distance learning, double major, dual enrollment, honors program, independent study, internships, study abroad, teacher certification program. Special programs offered to physically disabled students include note-taking services, reader services, tape recorders, tutors.

FACILITIES

Housing: Coed dorms, men's dorms, women's dorms, apartments for married students, apartments for single students. **Special Academic Facilities/Equipment:** Art galleries, museum collections, western historical studies library, center for Indian studies, center for advancement and study of tourism, small business institute, center of excellence for math and science education. **Computers:** Students can register for classes online.

CAMPUS LIFE

Environment: Village. **Activities:** Choral groups, concert band, drama/theater, jazz band, music ensembles, pep band, radio station, student government, student newspaper, television station. **Organizations:** 60 registered organizations, 5 honor societies, 3 religious organizations. 1 fraternities, 1 sorority. **Athletics (Intercollegiate):** *Men:* Basketball, cross-country, football, track/field (outdoor), track/field (indoor). *Women:* Basketball, cross-country, track/field (outdoor), track/field (indoor), volleyball. **On-Campus Highlights:** Clare and Josef Meier Hall, Donald E. Young Sports and Fitness Center, David B. Miller Yellow Jacket Student Union, Woodburn Hall, Jonas Hall.

ADMISSIONS

Freshman Academic Profile: Average high school GPA 3.09. 6% in top 10% of high school class, 24% in top 25% of high school class, 60% in top 50% of high school class. ACT middle 50% range 18–23. Minimum paper TOEFL 520. **Basis for Candidate Selection:** *Very important factors considered include:* Class rank, rigor of secondary school record, standardized test scores. *Other factors considered include:* Character/personal qualities, extracurricular activities, talent/ability. **Freshman Admission Requirements:** High school diploma is required and GED is accepted. *Academic units required:* 4 English, 3 mathematics, 3 science, (3 science labs), 3 social studies, 1 fine arts. **Freshman Admission Statistics:** 1,341 applied, 93% admitted, 52% enrolled. **Transfer Admission Requirements:** High school transcript, college transcript(s), minimum college GPA of 2.0 required. Lowest grade transferable D. **General Admission Information:** Application fee $20. Nonfall registration accepted. Credit and/or placement offered for CEEB Advanced Placement tests.

COSTS AND FINANCIAL AID

Annual in-state tuition $2,382. Annual out-of-state tuition $8,074. Room and board $4,667. Required fees $2,619. Average book expense $800. **Required Forms and Deadlines:** FAFSA. Priority financial aid filing date 3/1. **Notification of Awards:** Applicants will be notified of awards on or about 5/15. **Types of Aid:** *Need-based scholarships/grants:* Federal Pell, SEOG, state scholarships/grants, private scholarships, the school's own gift aid. *Loans:* FFEL Subsidized Stafford, FFEL Unsubsidized Stafford, FFEL PLUS, Federal Perkins. **Student Employment:** Highest amount earned per year from on-campus jobs $1,700. **Financial Aid Statistics:** 75% undergrads borrow to pay for school. Average cumulative indebtedness $12,701. **Criteria for awarding institutional aid:** *Non-need-based:* Academics, art, athletics.

BLACKBURN COLLEGE

700 College Ave, Carlinville, il 62626
Phone: 217-854-3231
E-mail: admit@blackburn.edu
Fax: 217-854-3713 **Website:** www.blackburn.edu **ACT Code:** 0958

This private school, affiliated with the Presbyterian Church, was founded in 1837. It has a 80-acre campus.

RATINGS

Admissions Selectivity Rating: 68   **Fire Safety Rating:** 60*   **Green Rating:** 60*

STUDENTS AND FACULTY

Enrollment: 603. **Student Body:** 59% female, 41% male.
Retention and Graduation: Faculty: Student/faculty ratio 17:1. 31 full-time faculty, 6% are members of minority groups, 35% are women.

ACADEMICS

Degrees: Bachelor's. **Special Study Options:** Double major, exchange student program (domestic), honors program, independent study, internships, liberal arts/career combination, student-designed major, study abroad, teacher certification program.

FACILITIES

Housing: Coed dorms, men's dorms, women's dorms, theme housing.

CAMPUS LIFE

Environment: Village. **Activities:** Choral groups, dance, drama/theater, jazz band, literary magazine, music ensembles, musical theater, radio station, student government, student newspaper, student-run film society, yearbook, campus ministries, international student organization.

ADMISSIONS

Freshman Academic Profile: Average high school GPA 3.45. 16% in top 10% of high school class, 22% in top 25% of high school class, 37% in top 50% of high school class. 80% from public high schools. Minimum paper TOEFL 525. Minimum computer TOEFL 195. Minimum web-based TOEFL 70. **Basis for**

Candidate Selection: *Very important factors considered include:* Academic GPA, rigor of secondary school record, standardized test scores. *Important factors considered include:* Class rank, level of applicant's interest. *Other factors considered include:* Application essay, recommendation(s), alumni/ae relation, character/personal qualities, extracurricular activities, talent/ability, volunteer work, work experience. **Freshman Admission Requirements:** High school diploma is required and GED is accepted. *Academic units recommended:* 4 English, 3 mathematics, 3 science, 2 foreign language, 3 social studies. **Freshman Admission Statistics:** 893 applied, 64% admitted, 26% enrolled. **Transfer Admission Requirements:** High school transcript, college transcript(s), standardized test scores, minimum college GPA of 2.0 required. Lowest grade transferable C. **General Admission Information:** Nonfall registration accepted. Credit and/or placement offered for CEEB Advanced Placement tests.

COSTS AND FINANCIAL AID

Average book expense $1,000.

BLESSING-RIEMAN COLLEGE OF NURSING

Broadway at 11th Street, PO Box 7005, Quincy, IL 62305-7005
Phone: 217-228-5520 **Financial Aid Phone:**
E-mail: hmutter@blessinghospital.com
Fax: 217-223-4661 **Website:** www.brcn.edu **ACT Code:** 956

This private school was founded in 1891. It has a 1-acre campus.

RATINGS

Admissions Selectivity Rating: 89   **Fire Safety Rating:** 60*   **Green Rating:** 60*

STUDENTS AND FACULTY

Enrollment: 177. **Student Body:** 97% female, 3% male, 28% out-of-state,. African American 2%, Caucasian 84%, Hispanic 1%, Native American 1%. **Retention and Graduation:** 76% freshmen return for sophomore year. 47% freshmen graduate within 4 years. **Faculty:** Student/faculty ratio 9:1. 13 full-time faculty, 31% hold PhDs, 100% are women.

ACADEMICS

Degrees: Bachelor's. **Classes:** Most classes have 10–19 students. Most lab/discussion sessions have fewer than 10 students. **Special Study Options:** Double major.

FACILITIES

Housing: Apartments for single students, men's and women's dormitories available at Culver-Stockton College and Quincy University. 100% of campus accessible to physically disabled. **Computers:** Students can register for classes online. Administrative functions (other than registration) can be performed online.

CAMPUS LIFE

Activities: Student government. **Organizations:** 1 registered organizations, 1 honor societies.

ADMISSIONS

Freshman Academic Profile: Average high school GPA 3.63. 20% in top 10% of high school class, 97% in top 25% of high school class, 100% in top 50% of high school class. 89% from public high schools. ACT middle 50% range 22–27. Minimum paper TOEFL 550. **Basis for Candidate Selection:** *Very important factors considered include:* Class rank, rigor of secondary school record, standardized test scores. **Freshman Admission Requirements:** High school diploma is required and GED is accepted. *Academic units required:* 4 English, 2 mathematics, 3 science, (2 science labs), 3 social studies. **Freshman Admission Statistics:** 153 applied, 50% admitted, 34% enrolled. **Transfer Admission Requirements:** High school transcript, college transcript(s), minimum college GPA of 2.0 required. Lowest grade transferable C. **General Admission Information:** Notification on a rolling basis, beginning on or about 9/1. Nonfall registration accepted.

COSTS AND FINANCIAL AID

Annual tuition $11,200. Room and board $4,975. Required fees $300. Average book expense $800. **Required Forms and Deadlines:** FAFSA. **Notification of Awards:** Applicants will be notified of awards on a rolling basis beginning 9/1. **Types of Aid:** *Need-based scholarships/grants:* Federal Pell, state scholarships/grants, Federal Nursing Scholarships. *Loans:* FFEL Subsidized Stafford, FFEL Unsubsidized Stafford, FFEL PLUS, Federal Nursing, college/university loans from institutional funds. **Student Employment:** Institutional employment available. Off-campus job opportunities are excellent. **Financial Aid Statistics:** 94% undergrads receive need-based scholarship or grant aid. 40% undergrads receive need-based self-help aid. 75% undergrads borrow to pay for school. Average cumulative indebtedness $20,000.

BLOOMFIELD COLLEGE

1 Park Place, Bloomfield, NJ 07003
Phone: 973-748-9000 **Financial Aid Phone:** 973-748-9000 x212
E-mail: admission@bloomfield.edu **CEEB Code:** 2044
Fax: 973-748-0916 **Website:** www.bloomfield.edu **ACT Code:** 2540

This private school, affiliated with the Presbyterian Church, was founded in 1868. It has a 12.5-acre campus.

RATINGS
Admissions Selectivity Rating: 70   **Fire Safety Rating:** 88   **Green Rating:** 64

STUDENTS AND FACULTY
Enrollment: 2,131. **Student Body:** 65% female, 35% male, 5% out-of-state, 1% international (38 countries represented). Asian 3%, African American 50%, Caucasian 15%, Hispanic 20%.
Retention and Graduation: 71% freshmen return for sophomore year. 11% freshmen graduate within 4 years. 7% grads go on to further study within 1 year.
Faculty: Student/faculty ratio 15:1. 68 full-time faculty, 74% hold PhDs, 21% are members of minority groups, 57% are women.

ACADEMICS
Degrees: Bachelor's, certificate, post-bachelor's certificate. **Classes:** Most classes have 10–19 students. Most lab/discussion sessions have 10–19 students. **Majors with Highest Enrollment:** Nursing/registered nurse (RN, ASN, BSN, MSN); psychology; sociology. **Special Study Options:** Accelerated program, distance learning, double major, dual enrollment, English as a Second Language (ESL), honors program, independent study, internships, liberal arts/career combination, student-designed major, study abroad, teacher certification program, Four-year clinical laboratory science program and allied health technologies major offered in conjunction with University of Medicine and Dentistry of New Jersey. Joint BS/MS in computer information systems program offered with NJIT. Special programs offered by the Institute of Technology and Professional Studies. **Honors programs:** Honors program open to new and enrolled students consisting of interdisciplinary courses, honors seminars in the arts and sciences, special courses, and honors projects. **Combined degree programs:** BA/MA, Joint BS/MS Comp Inform Sys Dgr with NJ Inst Tech. Special programs offered to physically disabled students include note-taking services, reader services, tape recorders, tutors. **Career services:** Alumni network, alumni services, career/job search classes, career assessment, internships, regional alumni. **Career services highlights include:** Personalized career counseling to indentify individual skills and abilities as the relate to career options and internship opportunities.

FACILITIES
Housing: Coed dorms, theme housing 55% of campus accessible to physically disabled. **Special Academic Facilities/Equipment:** Westminster Theatre, art gallery, state-of-the-art library. **Computers:** 20% of classrooms, 100% of dorms, 100% of libraries, 100% of dining areas, 100% of student union, have wireless network access. Administrative functions (other than registration) can be performed online.

CAMPUS LIFE
Environment: Town. **Activities:** dance, drama/theater, radio station, student government, campus ministries, international student organization. **Organizations:** 40 registered organizations, 4 honor societies, 1 religious organizations. 6 fraternities, 6 sororities. **Athletics (Intercollegiate):** *Men:* Baseball, basketball, cross-country, soccer, tennis *Women:* Basketball, cross-country, soccer, softball, volleyball. **On-Campus Highlights:** Library, Art Gallery, College Center, Deacons Den, Gymnasium, Quad. **Environmental Initiatives:** Campus-wide recycling program; E-waste recycling. Continued upgrading of newer, more efficient heating systems.

ADMISSIONS
Freshman Academic Profile: Average high school GPA 2.56. 8% in top 10% of high school class, 24% in top 25% of high school class, 60% in top 50% of high school class. 74% from public high schools. SAT Math middle 50% range 360–460. SAT Critical Reading middle 50% range 370–450. Minimum paper TOEFL 550. Minimum computer TOEFL 213. Minimum web-based TOEFL 79. **Basis for Candidate Selection:** *Very important factors considered include:* Application essay, academic GPA, recommendation(s), rigor of secondary school record, standardized test scores. *Important factors considered include:* Class rank, extracurricular activities, interview, talent/ability, volunteer work. *Other factors considered include:* Alumni/ae relation, work experience. **Freshman Admission Statistics:** 3,242 applied, 52% admitted, 29% enrolled. **Transfer Admission Requirements:** college transcript(s), minimum college GPA of 2.0 required. Lowest grade transferable 2. **General Admission Information:** Application fee $40. Regular application deadline 8/1. Notification on a rolling

basis, beginning on or about 10/1. Nonfall registration accepted. Admission may be deferred for a maximum of 1 Year. Credit and/or placement offered for CEEB Advanced Placement tests.

COSTS AND FINANCIAL AID
Average book expense $1,000. **Required Forms and Deadlines:** FAFSA Financial aid filing deadline 6/1. Priority financial aid filing date 3/15. **Notification of Awards:** Applicants will be notified of awards on a rolling basis beginning 3/15. **Types of Aid:** *Need-based scholarships/grants:* Federal Pell, SEOG, state scholarships/grants, private scholarships, the school's own gift aid. *Loans:* FFEL Subsidized Stafford, FFEL Unsubsidized Stafford, FFEL PLUS **Student Employment:** Federal Work-Study Program available. Institutional employment available. Highest amount earned per year from on-campus jobs $2,400. Off-campus job opportunities are good. **Financial Aid Statistics:** 92% freshmen, 86% undergrads receive need-based scholarship or grant aid. 53% freshmen, 40% undergrads receive non-need-based scholarship or grant aid. 82% freshmen, 81% undergrads receive need-based self-help aid. 2% undergrads receive athletic scholarships. 96% freshmen, 89% undergrads receive any aid. 87% undergrads borrow to pay for school. Average cumulative indebtedness $28,310. **Criteria for awarding institutional aid:** *Non-need-based:* Academics, alumni affiliation, athletics, music/drama, religious affiliation.

See page 1032.

BLOOMSBURG UNIVERSITY OF PENNSYLVANIA

104 Student Services Center, 400 East Second Street, Bloomsburg, PA 17815
Phone: 570-389-4316 **Financial Aid Phone:** 570-389-4279
E-mail: www.bloomu.edu/admissions/ **CEEB Code:** 2646
Fax: 570-389-4741 **Website:** www.bloomu.edu **ACT Code:** 3692

This public school was founded in 1839. It has a 282-acre campus.

RATINGS
Admissions Selectivity Rating: 77   **Fire Safety Rating:** 93   **Green Rating:** 60*

STUDENTS AND FACULTY
Enrollment: 8,377. **Student Body:** 58% female, 42% male, 11% out-of-state, 1% international (31 countries represented). Asian 1%, African American 7%, Caucasian 79%, Hispanic 3%.
Retention and Graduation: 81% freshmen return for sophomore year. 41% freshmen graduate within 4 years. 21.5% grads go on to further study within 1 year. **Faculty:** Student/faculty ratio 21:1. 400 full-time faculty, 84% hold PhDs, 13% are members of minority groups, 41% are women.

ACADEMICS
Degrees: Bachelor's, certificate, master's, post-bachelor's certificate, post-master's certificate. **Classes:** Most classes have 20–29 students. Most lab/discussion sessions have 10–19 students. **Majors with Highest Enrollment:** Business administration and management; elementary education and teaching; special education and teaching. **Special Study Options:** Cooperative education program, cross-registration, distance learning, double major, dual enrollment, English as a Second Language (ESL), exchange student program (domestic), honors program, independent study, internships, liberal arts/career combination, study abroad, teacher certification program. **Honors programs:** The Honors Program's goals are: to challenge students to perform at the highest level of excellence to encourage independent thinking and learning; to create a supportive environment that encourages the aspirations and achievements of students and fosters their dignity, self esteem and sense of initiative; to encourage creativity, intellectual independence, analytical thinking and problem solving and the growth of communication skills through a strong emphasis on reading, writing and research; to provide opportunities for students to develop a broader perspective on national and global issues; to provide forums for symposia, experiential learning and independent study; to create a meaningful learning community; to develop students' leadership potential; to enable students to engage in a rigorous, coherent, integrated academic experience with a high degree of student-faculty interaction Special programs offered to physically disabled students include note-taking services, reader services, tape recorders, tutors. **Career services:** Career/job search classes, career assessment. **Career services highlights include:** http://internships.bloomu.edu/.

FACILITIES
Housing: Coed dorms, apartments for single students, affiliated off-campus apartments operated by the Community Government Association. 100% of campus accessible to physically disabled. **Special Academic Facilities/Equipment:** Art gallery, language lab, TV studio, radio station. **Computers:** 100% of classrooms, 100% of libraries, 100% of student union, 50% of common outdoor areas have wireless network access. Students can register for classes online. Administrative functions (other than registration) can be performed online.

CAMPUS LIFE

Environment: Village. **Activities:** Choral groups, concert band, dance, drama/theater, literary magazine, marching band, music ensembles, pep band, radio station, student government, student newspaper, television station, yearbook, campus ministries, international student organization, Model UN. **Organizations:** 195 registered organizations, 19 honor societies, 8 religious organizations. 15 fraternities, 13 sororities. **Athletics (Intercollegiate):** *Men:* Baseball, basketball, cheerleading, cross-country, football, soccer, swimming, tennis, track/field (outdoor), track/field (indoor), wrestling. *Women:* Basketball, cheerleading, cross-country, field hockey, lacrosse, soccer, softball, swimming, tennis, track/field (outdoor), track/field (indoor). **On-Campus Highlights:** Kehr Student Union, Dining Hall/Food Court, Climbing Wall, Recreation Center, Redman Stadium, Starbucks.

ADMISSIONS

Freshman Academic Profile: 12% in top 10% of high school class, 36% in top 25% of high school class, 76% in top 50% of high school class. 87% from public high schools. SAT Math middle 50% range 460–560. SAT Critical Reading middle 50% range 450–540. SAT Writing middle 50% range 440–540. Minimum paper TOEFL 550. Minimum computer TOEFL 213. **Basis for Candidate Selection:** *Very important factors considered include:* Class rank, academic GPA, rigor of secondary school record, standardized test scores. *Other factors considered include:* Application essay, recommendation(s), character/personal qualities, extracurricular activities, geographical residence, interview, state residency, talent/ability, volunteer work, work experience. **Freshman Admission Requirements:** High school diploma is required and GED is accepted. *Academic units required:* 4 English, 3 mathematics, 3 science, 2 social studies, 2 history, 2 academic electives. *Academic units recommended:* 4 English, 4 mathematics, 4 science, 2 foreign language, 2 social studies, 2 history, 1 computer science. **Freshman Admission Statistics:** 11,749 applied, 64% admitted, 27% enrolled. **Transfer Admission Requirements:** High school transcript, college transcript(s), minimum college GPA of 2.0 required. Lowest grade transferable C. **General Admission Information:** Application fee $30. Notification on a rolling basis, beginning on or about 9/18. Nonfall registration accepted. Admission may be deferred for a maximum of 1 year. Credit and/or placement offered for CEEB Advanced Placement tests.

COSTS AND FINANCIAL AID

Required Forms and Deadlines: FAFSA. Priority financial aid filing date 3/15. **Notification of Awards:** Applicants will be notified of awards on a rolling basis beginning 4/1. **Types of Aid:** *Need-based scholarships/grants:* Federal Pell, SEOG, state scholarships/grants, private scholarships, the school's own gift aid, Federal ACG and Federal Smart Grants. *Loans:* FFEL Subsidized Stafford, FFEL Unsubsidized Stafford, FFEL PLUS, Federal Perkins, state loans, Alternative Loans. **Student Employment:** Federal Work-Study Program available. Institutional employment available. Highest amount earned per year from on-campus jobs $4,640. **Financial Aid Statistics:** 44% freshmen, 40% undergrads receive need-based scholarship or grant aid. 21% freshmen, 15% undergrads receive non-need-based scholarship or grant aid. 53% freshmen, 51% undergrads receive need-based self-help aid. 3% freshmen, 3% undergrads receive athletic scholarships. 74% freshmen receive any aid. 71% undergrads borrow to pay for school. Average cumulative indebtedness $21,322. **Criteria for awarding institutional aid:** *Non-need-based:* Academics, art, athletics, job skills, leadership, minority status, music/drama, state/district residency.

BLUE MOUNTAIN COLLEGE

PO Box 160, Blue Mountain, MS 38610
Phone: 662-685-4771 **Financial Aid Phone:** 662-685-4771
E-mail: admissions@bmc.edu
Fax: 662-685-4776 **Website:** bmc.edu

This private school, affiliated with the Baptist Church, was founded in 1873. It has a 44-acre campus.

RATINGS
Admissions Selectivity Rating: 79 **Fire Safety Rating:** 61 **Green Rating:** 60*

STUDENTS AND FACULTY
Enrollment: 406. **Student Body:** 64% female, 36% male, 12% out-of-state, international (1 countries represented). African American 12%, Caucasian 87%. **Retention and Graduation:** 72% freshmen return for sophomore year. 31% freshmen graduate within 4 years. 14% grads go on to further study within 1 year. 14% grads pursue arts and sciences degrees. 1% grads pursue business degrees. 2% grads pursue medical degrees. **Faculty:** Student/faculty ratio 13:1. 24 full-time faculty, 67% hold PhDs, 54% are women.

ACADEMICS

Degrees: Bachelor's, master's. **Classes:** Most classes have 10–19 students. Most lab/discussion sessions have 10–19 students. **Majors with Highest Enrollment:** Bible/biblical studies; elementary education and teaching; psychology. **Special Study Options:** double major, honors program, internships, teacher certification program. **Honors programs:** Academic Honors Program Special programs offered to physically disabled students include note-taking services, tutors.

FACILITIES

Housing: Men's dorms, women's dorms. 50% of campus accessible to physically disabled.

CAMPUS LIFE

Environment: Rural. **Activities:** Choral groups, drama/theater, literary magazine, musical theater, student government, yearbook. **Organizations:** 28 registered organizations, 4 honor societies, 2 religious organizations. **Athletics (Intercollegiate):** *Women:* Basketball, tennis. **On-Campus Highlights:** Johnnie Armstrong Gal-ry, Student Union Building, Tyler Gymnasium, Broach Hall, Fisher-Washburn Hall.

ADMISSIONS

Freshman Academic Profile: Average high school GPA 3.3. 19% in top 10% of high school class, 50% in top 25% of high school class, 86% in top 50% of high school class. 73% from public high schools. ACT middle 50% range 18–23. Minimum paper TOEFL 500. Minimum computer TOEFL 173. **Basis for Candidate Selection:** *Important factors considered include:* Class rank, academic GPA, rigor of secondary school record, standardized test scores. *Other factors considered include:* Recommendation(s), alumni/ae relation, character/personal qualities. **Freshman Admission Requirements:** High school diploma is required and GED is accepted. *Academic units required:* 4 English, 3 mathematics, 3 science, (2 science labs), 2 foreign language, 1 social studies, 2 history. *Academic units recommended:* 4 English, 3 mathematics, 3 science, (2 science labs), 2 foreign language, 1 social studies, 2 history. **Freshman Admission Statistics:** 197 applied, 50% admitted, 60% enrolled. **Transfer Admission Requirements:** College transcript(s), Lowest grade transferable C. **General Admission Information:** Application fee $10. Notification on a rolling basis, beginning on or about 10/1. Nonfall registration accepted. Admission may be deferred for a maximum of semester. Credit offered for CEEB Advanced Placement tests.

COSTS AND FINANCIAL AID

Annual tuition $6,900. Room and board $3,766. Required fees $540. Average book expense $650. **Required Forms and Deadlines:** FAFSA, institution's own financial aid form. Priority financial aid filing date 3/31. **Notification of Awards:** Applicants will be notified of awards on a rolling basis beginning 4/1. **Types of Aid:** *Need-based scholarships/grants:* Federal Pell, SEOG, state scholarships/grants, private scholarships. *Loans:* FFEL Subsidized Stafford, FFEL Unsubsidized Stafford, FFEL PLUS, Federal Perkins. **Student Employment:** Federal Work-Study Program available. Institutional employment available. Highest amount earned per year from on-campus jobs $1,400. Off-campus job opportunities are good. **Financial Aid Statistics:** 79% freshmen, 41% undergrads receive need-based scholarship or grant aid. 79% freshmen, 64% undergrads receive non-need-based scholarship or grant aid. 61% freshmen, 11% undergrads receive need-based self-help aid. 8% freshmen, 6% undergrads receive athletic scholarships. 95% freshmen, 96% undergrads receive any aid. 83% undergrads borrow to pay for school. Average cumulative indebtedness $11,484. **Criteria for awarding institutional aid:** *Non-need-based:* Academics, alumni affiliation, athletics, religious affiliation, state/district residency.

BLUEFIELD COLLEGE

3000 College Drive, Bluefield, VA 24605
Phone: 540-326-4214 **Financial Aid Phone:** 800-872-0175
E-mail: thavens@mail.bluefield.edu **CEEB Code:** 5063
Fax: 540-326-4288 **Website:** www.bluefield.edu **ACT Code:** 4340

This private school, affiliated with the Baptist Church, was founded in 1922.

RATINGS
Admissions Selectivity Rating: 80 **Fire Safety Rating:** 60* **Green Rating:** 60*

STUDENTS AND FACULTY
Enrollment: 776. **Student Body:** 60% female, 40% male, 22% out-of-state. Asian 1%, African American 18%, Caucasian 78%, Hispanic 1%.

Retention and Graduation: 66% freshmen return for sophomore year. 36% freshmen graduate within 4 years. 23% grads go on to further study within 1 year. 10% grads pursue arts and sciences degrees. 3% grads pursue law degrees. 8% grads pursue business degrees. 2% grads pursue medical degrees. **Faculty:** Student/faculty ratio 12:1. 33 full-time faculty, 64% hold PhDs, 30% are women.

ACADEMICS

Degrees: Bachelor's. **Classes:** Most classes have fewer than 10 students. Most lab/discussion sessions have 10–19 students. **Majors with Highest Enrollment:** Business/commerce; christian studies; criminal justice/law enforcement administration. **Special Study Options:** Accelerated program, double major, dual enrollment, honors program, internships, student-designed major, study abroad, teacher certification program, weekend college. Special programs offered to physically disabled students include tape recorders, tutors. **Career services:** Alumni network, alumni services, career/job search classes, internships.

FACILITIES

Housing: Coed dorms, men's dorms, women's dorms 50% of campus accessible to physically disabled. **Special Academic Facilities/Equipment:** Art center.

CAMPUS LIFE

Environment: Rural. **Activities:** Choral groups, drama/theater, literary magazine, music ensembles, student government, student newspaper, yearbook. **Organizations:** 18 registered organizations, 7 honor societies, 6 religious organizations. 2 fraternities, 2 sororities. **Athletics (Intercollegiate):** *Men:* Baseball, basketball, golf, soccer, tennis. *Women:* Basketball, soccer, softball, tennis, volleyball.

ADMISSIONS

Freshman Academic Profile: Average high school GPA 3.2. 23% in top 10% of high school class, 44% in top 25% of high school class, 83% in top 50% of high school class. 95% from public high schools. SAT Math middle 50% range 420–520. SAT Critical Reading middle 50% range 440–530. ACT middle 50% range 19–24. **Basis for Candidate Selection:** *Very important factors considered include:* rigor of secondary school record, standardized test scores, character/personal qualities. *Important factors considered include:* Class rank, interview. *Other factors considered include:* Application essay, recommendation(s), alumni/ae relation, extracurricular activities, talent/ability, volunteer work, work experience. **Freshman Admission Requirements:** High school diploma is required and GED is accepted. *Academic units required:* 4 English, 3 mathematics, 3 science, (1 science labs), 3 social studies, 6 academic electives. **Freshman Admission Statistics:** 537 applied, 50% admitted, 40% enrolled. **Transfer Admission Requirements:** college transcript(s), minimum college GPA of 2.0 required. Lowest grade transferable D. **General Admission Information:** Application fee $30. Notification on a rolling basis, beginning on or about 9/1. Nonfall registration accepted. Admission may be deferred for a maximum of semester.

COSTS AND FINANCIAL AID

Annual tuition $6,900. Room and board $4,890. Average book expense $900. **Required Forms and Deadlines:** FAFSA, institution's own financial aid form, state aid form. Priority financial aid filing date 3/10. **Notification of Awards:** Applicants will be notified of awards on a rolling basis beginning 3/10. **Types of Aid:** *Need-based scholarships/grants:* Federal Pell, SEOG, state scholarships/grants, private scholarships, the school's own gift aid. *Loans:* FFEL Subsidized Stafford, FFEL Unsubsidized Stafford, FFEL PLUS, Keesee Foundation. **Student Employment:** Highest amount earned per year from on-campus jobs $700. Off-campus job opportunities are good. **Financial Aid Statistics:** 53% freshmen, 70% undergrads receive need-based scholarship or grant aid. 9% freshmen, 9% undergrads receive non-need-based scholarship or grant aid. 39% freshmen, 60% undergrads receive need-based self-help aid. 80% undergrads borrow to pay for school. Average cumulative indebtedness $12,177. **Criteria for awarding institutional aid:** *Non-need-based:* Academics, art, athletics, leadership, minority status, music/drama, religious affiliation, state/district residency.

BLUEFIELD STATE COLLEGE

219 Rock Street, Bluefield, WV 24701
Phone: 304-327-4065 **Financial Aid Phone:**
E-mail: bscadmit@bluefieldstate.edu **CEEB Code:** 5064
Fax: 304-325-7747 **Website:** www.bluefieldstate.edu **ACT Code:** 4514

This public school was founded in 1895. It has a 40-acre campus.

RATINGS
Admissions Selectivity Rating: 64   **Fire Safety Rating:** 60*   **Green Rating:** 60*

STUDENTS AND FACULTY

Enrollment: 3,092. **Student Body:** 65% female, 35% male, 5% out-of-state, (15 countries represented). African American 11%, Caucasian 100%, Hispanic 1%.
Retention and Graduation: 76% freshmen return for sophomore year. 24% freshmen graduate within 4 years. 9% grads go on to further study within 1 year. 4% grads pursue arts and sciences degrees. 1% grads pursue law degrees. 3% grads pursue business degrees. 1% grads pursue medical degrees. **Faculty:** Student/faculty ratio 17:1. 92 full-time faculty, 40% hold PhDs, 9% are members of minority groups, 55% are women.

ACADEMICS

Degrees: Associate, bachelor's, certificate, terminal associate, transfer associate. **Classes:** Most classes have 10–19 students. Most lab/discussion sessions have 10–19 students. **Majors with Highest Enrollment:** Business/commerce; elementary education and teaching; nursing/registered nurse (RN, ASN, BSN, MSN). **Special Study Options:** Distance learning, dual enrollment, honors program, internships, student-designed major, teacher certification program. **Honors programs:** Bluefield State College Honors Program. Special programs offered to physically disabled students include note-taking services, reader services, tape recorders, tutors. **Career services:** Career/job search classes.

FACILITIES

Housing: Off-campus housing services provided, including referrals and resources. 100% of campus accessible to physically disabled. **Computers:** Students can register for classes online. Administrative functions (other than registration) can be performed online.

CAMPUS LIFE

Environment: Village. **Activities:** Choral groups, student government, student newspaper, yearbook. **Organizations:** 28 registered organizations, 6 honor societies, 1 religious organizations. 3 fraternities, 4 sororities. **Athletics (Intercollegiate):** *Men:* Baseball, basketball, cross-country, golf, tennis. *Women:* Basketball, cheerleading, cross-country, softball, tennis, volleyball.

ADMISSIONS

Freshman Academic Profile: Average high school GPA 3.15. 10% in top 10% of high school class, 27% in top 25% of high school class, 73% in top 50% of high school class. 98% from public high schools. ACT middle 50% range 21–16. Minimum paper TOEFL 550. Minimum computer TOEFL 250. **Basis for Candidate Selection:** *Important factors considered include:* rigor of secondary school record, standardized test scores. **Freshman Admission Requirements:** High school diploma is required and GED is accepted. *Academic units required:* 4 English, 3 mathematics, 3 science, (2 science labs), 0 foreign language, 3 social studies, 1 history, 1 academic electives. *Academic units recommended:* 2 foreign language. **Freshman Admission Statistics:** 1,135 applied, 98% admitted, 53% enrolled. **Transfer Admission Requirements:** College transcript(s), Lowest grade transferable D. **General Admission Information:** Nonfall registration accepted. Admission may be deferred for a maximum of 1 semester. Credit and/or placement offered for CEEB Advanced Placement tests.

COSTS AND FINANCIAL AID

Annual in-state tuition $3,114. Annual out-of-state tuition $6,894. Average book expense $1,200. **Required Forms and Deadlines:** FAFSA, institution's own financial aid form, state aid form. Financial aid filing deadline 3/1. Priority financial aid filing date 3/1. **Notification of Awards:** Applicants will be notified of awards on a rolling basis beginning 6/1. **Types of Aid:** *Need-based scholarships/grants:* Federal Pell, SEOG, state scholarships/grants, private scholarships, the school's own gift aid. *Loans:* Direct Subsidized Stafford, Direct Unsubsidized Stafford, Direct PLUS, Federal Perkins. **Student Employment:** Highest amount earned per year from on-campus jobs $1,500. **Financial Aid Statistics:** 66% freshmen, 38% undergrads receive need-based scholarship or grant aid. 11% freshmen, 7% undergrads receive non-need-based scholarship or grant aid. 53% freshmen, 29% undergrads receive need-based self-help aid. 5% freshmen, 5% undergrads receive athletic scholarships. 50% undergrads borrow to pay for school. Average cumulative indebtedness $10,500. **Criteria for awarding institutional aid:** *Non-need-based:* Academics, alumni affiliation, athletics, leadership, minority status, state/district residency.

BLUFFTON UNIVERSITY

Office of Admissions, 1 University Drive, Bluffton, OH 45817
Phone: 419-358-3257
E-mail: admissions@bluffton.edu **CEEB Code:** 1067
Fax: 419-358-3081 **Website:** www.bluffton.edu **ACT Code:** 3238

This private school, affiliated with the Mennonite Church, was founded in 1899. It has a 65-acre campus.

RATINGS
Admissions Selectivity Rating: 74   **Fire Safety Rating:** 60*   **Green Rating:** 60*

STUDENTS AND FACULTY
Enrollment: 943. **Student Body:** 51% female, 49% male, 12% out-of-state, 2% international. Asian 1%, African American 7%, Caucasian 85%, Hispanic 2%.
Retention and Graduation: 75% freshmen return for sophomore year. 56% freshmen graduate within 4 years. 9% grads go on to further study within 1 year. 9% grads pursue arts and sciences degrees. 1% grads pursue law degrees. 1% grads pursue medical degrees. **Faculty:** Student/faculty ratio 13:1. 62 full-time faculty, 73% hold PhDs, 2% are members of minority groups, 34% are women.

ACADEMICS
Degrees: Bachelor's, master's. **Classes:** Most classes have 10–19 students. Most lab/discussion sessions have 10–19 students. **Special Study Options:** distance learning, double major, dual enrollment, English as a Second Language (ESL), honors program, independent study, internships, student-designed major, study abroad, teacher certification program. Special programs offered to physically disabled students include reader services, tape recorders, tutors. **Career services:** Alumni services, career/job search classes.

FACILITIES
Housing: Coed dorms, men's dorms, women's dorms, theme housing 99% of campus accessible to physically disabled. **Special Academic Facilities/Equipment:** Mennonite historical library, peace arts center, nature preserve.

CAMPUS LIFE
Environment: Rural. **Activities:** Choral groups, concert band, dance, drama/theater, jazz band, literary magazine, music ensembles, musical theater, pep band, radio station, student government, campus ministries, international student organization. **Organizations:** 50 registered organizations, 19 honor societies, 10 religious organizations. **Athletics (Intercollegiate):** *Men:* Baseball, basketball, cheerleading, cross-country, football, golf, soccer, tennis, track/field (outdoor), track/field (indoor). *Women:* Basketball, cheerleading, cross-country, golf, soccer, softball, tennis, track/field (outdoor), track/field (indoor), volleyball. **On-Campus Highlights:** Centennial Hall-academic center, Marbeck Center-student union, College Hall-administrative/classroom building, Salzman Stadium-Football Stadium, Founders Hall-gymnasium.

ADMISSIONS
Freshman Academic Profile: Average high school GPA 3.18. 14% in top 10% of high school class, 33% in top 25% of high school class, 67% in top 50% of high school class. 98% from public high schools. SAT Math middle 50% range 450–600. SAT Critical Reading middle 50% range 420–570. ACT middle 50% range 19–24. Minimum paper TOEFL 500. **Basis for Candidate Selection:** *Very important factors considered include:* Class rank, academic GPA, standardized test scores. *Important factors considered include:* Recommendation(s). *Other factors considered include:* Application essay, rigor of secondary school record, character/personal qualities, religious affiliation/commitment, talent/ability, volunteer work. **Freshman Admission Requirements:** High school diploma is required and GED is accepted. *Academic units recommended:* 4 English, 4 mathematics, 4 science, 3 foreign language, 3 social studies. **Freshman Admission Statistics:** 1,674 applied, 66% admitted, 23% enrolled. **Transfer Admission Requirements:** High school transcript, college transcript(s), statement of good standing from prior institution(s). Minimum college GPA of 2.0 required. Lowest grade transferable C–. **General Admission Information:** Application fee $20. Regular application deadline 8/15. Nonfall registration accepted. Admission may be deferred for a maximum of two years. Credit and/or placement offered for CEEB Advanced Placement tests.

COSTS AND FINANCIAL AID
Annual tuition $23,594. Room and board $8,170. Required fees $450. Average book expense $1,400. **Required Forms and Deadlines:** FAFSA Financial aid filing deadline 10/1. Priority financial aid filing date 5/1. **Notification of Awards:** Applicants will be notified of awards on a rolling basis beginning 3/1. **Types of Aid:** *Need-based scholarships/grants:* Federal Pell, SEOG, state scholarships/grants, private scholarships, the school's own gift aid. *Loans:* FFEL Subsidized Stafford, FFEL Unsubsidized Stafford, FFEL PLUS, Federal Perkins. **Student Employment:** Federal Work-Study Program available.

Institutional employment available. Highest amount earned per year from on-campus jobs $1,350. Off-campus job opportunities are good. **Financial Aid Statistics:** 91% freshmen, 86% undergrads receive need-based scholarship or grant aid. 1% freshmen, 4% undergrads receive non-need-based scholarship or grant aid. 86% freshmen, 82% undergrads receive need-based self-help aid. 88% undergrads borrow to pay for school. Average cumulative indebtedness $26,896. **Criteria for awarding institutional aid:** *Non-need-based:* Academics, art, job skills, leadership, minority status, music/drama, religious affiliation, state/district residency.

BOB JONES UNIVERSITY

1700 Wade Hampton Boulevard, Greenville, SC 29614
Phone: 864-242-5100 Ext 205 **Financial Aid Phone:** 864-242-5100 Ext 3040
E-mail: admissions@bju.edu **CEEB Code:** 5065
Fax: 800-232-9258 **Website:** www.bju.edu **ACT Code:** 3836

This proprietary school was founded in 1927. It has a 225-acre campus.

RATINGS
Admissions Selectivity Rating: 77   **Fire Safety Rating:** 65   **Green Rating:** 60*

STUDENTS AND FACULTY
Enrollment: 3,437. **Student Body:** 55% female, 45% male, 73% out-of-state, (47 countries represented). Asian 5%, African American 1%, Caucasian 85%, Hispanic 3%.
Retention and Graduation: 18.4% grads go on to further study within 1 year. 1.2% grads pursue arts and sciences degrees. 1% grads pursue law degrees. 1.5% grads pursue business degrees. 3.1% grads pursue medical degrees. **Faculty:** Student/faculty ratio 13:1. 228 full-time faculty, 40% hold PhDs, 3% are members of minority groups, 41% are women.

ACADEMICS
Degrees: Associate, bachelor's, certificate, doctoral, master's, transfer associate. **Classes:** Most classes have fewer than 10 students. Most lab/discussion sessions have fewer than 10 students. **Majors with Highest Enrollment:** Accounting; elementary education and teaching; nursing/registered nurse (RN, ASN, BSN, MSN). **Special Study Options:** Accelerated program, distance learning, English as a Second Language (ESL), internships, teacher certification program. Special programs offered to physically disabled students include note-taking services, reader services, tape recorders, tutors. **Career services:** Alumni services, career/job search classes, career assessment.

FACILITIES
Housing: Special housing for disabled students, men's dorms, women's dorms, apartments for married students, apartments for single students. 90% of campus accessible to physically disabled. **Special Academic Facilities/Equipment:** Museum & gallery, Davis Field House, Rodeheaver Auditorium, Bob Jones Jr. Memorial Seminary & Evangelism Center. **Computers:** 85% of classrooms, 100% of dorms, 100% of libraries, 20% of dining areas, 100% of student union, 70% of common outdoor areas have wireless network access. Students can register for classes online. Administrative functions (other than registration) can be performed online.

CAMPUS LIFE
Environment: City. **Activities:** Choral groups, concert band, drama/theater, music ensembles, opera, radio station, student government, student newspaper, symphony orchestra, television station, yearbook, campus ministries. **Organizations:** 31 registered organizations, 18 religious organizations. **On-Campus Highlights:** University Student Center, Davis Field House, Cuppa Jones coffee shop, Fast Break lunch area, BJU Museum & Gallery.

ADMISSIONS
Freshman Academic Profile: Average high school GPA 3.42. 8% in top 10% of high school class, 38% in top 25% of high school class, 65% in top 50% of high school class. 11% from public high schools. ACT middle 50% range 20–26. Minimum paper TOEFL 500. Minimum computer TOEFL 173. Minimum web-based TOEFL 61. **Basis for Candidate Selection:** *Very important factors considered include:* Academic GPA, recommendation(s), character/personal qualities, level of applicant's interest, religious affiliation/commitment. *Important factors considered include:* Application essay, rigor of secondary school record. *Other factors considered include:* Class rank, standardized test scores, alumni/ae relation, extracurricular activities, first generation, talent/ability, volunteer work, work experience. **Freshman Admission Requirements:** High school diploma is required and GED is accepted. *Academic units recommended:* 3 English, 2 mathematics, 1 science, 2 foreign language, 2 social studies, 6 academic electives. **Freshman Admission Statistics:** 1,610 applied, 75% admitted, 71% enrolled. **Transfer Admission Requirements:** High

school transcript, college transcript(s), essay or personal statement, standardized test scores, statement of good standing from prior institution(s). Minimum college GPA of 2.0 required. Lowest grade transferable C. **General Admission Information:** Application fee $45. Regular application deadline 8/1. Nonfall registration accepted. Admission may be deferred for a maximum of 1 year. Credit offered for CEEB Advanced Placement tests.

COSTS AND FINANCIAL AID

Annual tuition $11,920. Room and board $5,100. Required fees $610. Average book expense $1,336. **Required Forms and Deadlines: Notification of Awards: Types of Aid:** *Need-based scholarships/grants:* Federal Pell, SEOG, state scholarships/grants, private scholarships, the school's own gift aid, United Negro College Fund. *Loans:* FFEL Subsidized Stafford, FFEL Unsubsidized Stafford, FFEL PLUS, college/university loans from institutional funds. **Student Employment:** Federal Work-Study Program available. Institutional employment available. Highest amount earned per year from on-campus jobs $5,000. Off-campus job opportunities are good. **Financial Aid Statistics:** 60% freshmen, 61% undergrads receive any aid. **Criteria for awarding institutional aid:** *Non-need-based:* Alumni affiliation.

BOISE BIBLE COLLEGE

8695 W Marigold Street, Boise, ID 83714-1220
Phone: 208-376-7731
E-mail: boisebible@boisebible.edu **CEEB Code:** 891
Fax: 208-376-7743 **ACT Code:** 917

This private school, affiliated with the Christian (Nondenominational) Church, was founded in 1945. It has a 16-acre campus.

RATINGS

Admissions Selectivity Rating: 69   **Fire Safety Rating:** 60*   **Green Rating:** 60*

STUDENTS AND FACULTY

Enrollment: 175. **Student Body:** 50% female, 50% male, 55% out-of-state, 2% international (3 countries represented). Asian 2%, African American 1%, Caucasian 89%, Hispanic 3%, Native American 1%.
Retention and Graduation: 60% freshmen return for sophomore year. **Faculty:** Student/faculty ratio 16:1. 8 full-time faculty, 13% hold PhDs, 13% are women.

ACADEMICS

Degrees: Associate, bachelor's, certificate. **Majors with Highest Enrollment:** Pastoral studies/counseling; religious education; theological and ministerial studies, other. **Special Study Options:** Double major, internships, teacher certification program.

FACILITIES

Housing: Men's dorms, women's dorms.

CAMPUS LIFE

Environment: Village. **Activities:** Choral groups, music ensembles, student government.

ADMISSIONS

Freshman Academic Profile: Average high school GPA 3.22. 8% in top 10% of high school class, 40% in top 25% of high school class, 70% in top 50% of high school class. SAT Math middle 50% range 410–540. SAT Critical Reading middle 50% range 460–550. ACT middle 50% range 16–21. Minimum paper TOEFL 500. Minimum computer TOEFL 173. **Basis for Candidate Selection:** *Important factors considered include:* Class rank, application essay, academic GPA, recommendation(s), standardized test scores, character/personal qualities, religious affiliation/commitment. *Other factors considered include:* interview, level of applicant's interest. **Freshman Admission Requirements:** High school diploma is required and GED is accepted. **Freshman Admission Statistics:** 80 applied, 99% admitted, 75% enrolled. **Transfer Admission Requirements:** College transcript(s), essay or personal statement, statement of good standing from prior institution(s). Minimum college GPA of 2.0 required. Lowest grade transferable C. **General Admission Information:** Application fee $25. Regular application deadline 8/15. Notification on a rolling basis, beginning on or about 2/15. Nonfall registration accepted. Admission may be deferred for a maximum of 1 year. Credit offered for CEEB Advanced Placement tests.

COSTS AND FINANCIAL AID

Annual tuition $6,840. Room and board $4,800. Required fees $49. Average book expense $450. **Required Forms and Deadlines:** FAFSA, institution's own financial aid form. **Types of Aid:** *Need-based scholarships/grants:* Federal Pell, SEOG, private scholarships. *Loans:* Direct Subsidized Stafford, Direct Unsubsidized Stafford, Direct PLUS. **Student Employment:** Federal Work-

Study Program available. **Criteria for awarding institutional aid:** *Non-need-based:* Academics, leadership, music/drama.

BOISE STATE UNIVERSITY

1910 University Drive, Boise, ID 83725
Phone: 208-426-1156 **Financial Aid Phone:** 208-426-1664
E-mail: bsuinfo@boisestate.edu **CEEB Code:** 4018
Fax: 208-426-3765 **ACT Code:** 914

This public school was founded in 1932. It has a 150-acre campus.

RATINGS

Admissions Selectivity Rating: 72   **Fire Safety Rating:** 60*   **Green Rating:** 60*

STUDENTS AND FACULTY

Enrollment: 15,997. **Student Body:** 54% female, 46% male, 11% out-of-state, 2% international (42 countries represented). Asian 3%, African American 2%, Caucasian 80%, Hispanic 7%, Native American 1%.
Retention and Graduation: 69% freshmen return for sophomore year. 6% freshmen graduate within 4 years. 15% grads go on to further study within 1 year. 4% grads pursue arts and sciences degrees. 1% grads pursue law degrees. 2% grads pursue business degrees. 1% grads pursue medical degrees. **Faculty:** Student/faculty ratio 20.8:1. 562 full-time faculty, 75% hold PhDs, 9% are members of minority groups, 44% are women. 1% of classes are taught by teaching assistants.

ACADEMICS

Degrees: Associate, bachelor's, doctoral, master's, post-bachelor's certificate. **Classes:** Most classes have 20–29 students. Most lab/discussion sessions have 20–29 students. **Majors with Highest Enrollment:** Communication studies/speech communication and rhetoric; computer science; information science/studies. **Special Study Options:** Cooperative education program, distance learning, double major, dual enrollment, English as a Second Language (ESL), exchange student program (domestic), honors program, independent study, internships, liberal arts/career combination, study abroad, teacher certification program, weekend college Special programs offered to physically disabled students include note-taking services, reader services, tape recorders, tutors. **Career services:** Alumni network, alumni services, career assessment, internships. **Career services highlights include:** one of the larger internship programs in the Northwest.

FACILITIES

Housing: Coed dorms, special housing for disabled students, men's dorms, women's dorms, fraternity/sorority housing, apartments for married students, apartments for single students. 95% of campus accessible to physically disabled. **Computers:** Students can register for classes online. Administrative functions (other than registration) can be performed online.

CAMPUS LIFE

Environment: City. **Activities:** Choral groups, drama/theater, literary magazine, marching band, music ensembles, musical theater, pep band, radio station, student government, student newspaper, student-run film society, international student organization. **Organizations:** 180 registered organizations, 4 fraternities, 3 sororities. **Athletics (Intercollegiate):** *Men:* Basketball, cheerleading, cross-country, football, golf, tennis, track/field (outdoor), track/field (indoor), wrestling. *Women:* Basketball, cheerleading, cross-country, golf, gymnastics, skiing (downhill/alpine), soccer, tennis, track/field (outdoor), track/field (indoor), volleyball.

ADMISSIONS

Freshman Academic Profile: Average high school GPA 3.3. 13% in top 10% of high school class, 36% in top 25% of high school class, 71% in top 50% of high school class. 94% from public high schools. SAT Math middle 50% range 470–590. SAT Critical Reading middle 50% range 460–570. SAT Writing middle 50% range 440–560. ACT middle 50% range 19–25. Minimum paper TOEFL 500. Minimum computer TOEFL 173. **Basis for Candidate Selection:** *Very important factors considered include:* Academic GPA, rigor of secondary school record, standardized test scores. *Other factors considered include:* Class rank, extracurricular activities, first generation, racial/ethnic status, talent/ability. **Freshman Admission Requirements:** High school diploma is required and GED is accepted. *Academic units required:* 4 English, 3 mathematics, 3 science, 1 foreign language, 2 social studies, 1 academic electives. **Freshman Admission Statistics:** 4,127 applied, 87% admitted, 61% enrolled. **Transfer Admission Requirements:** college transcript(s), minimum college GPA of 2.0 required. Lowest grade transferable c. **General Admission Information:** Application fee $50. Regular application deadline 6/30. Notification on a rolling basis, beginning on or about 4/1. Nonfall registration accepted. Credit offered for CEEB Advanced Placement tests.

COSTS AND FINANCIAL AID

Annual in-state tuition $3,106. Annual out-of-state tuition $12,110. Room and board $5,114. Required fees $1,758. Average book expense $1,168. **Required Forms and Deadlines:** FAFSA. Financial aid filing deadline 4/1. Priority financial aid filing date 2/1. **Notification of Awards:** Applicants will be notified of awards on a rolling basis beginning 4/1. **Types of Aid:** *Need-based scholarships/grants:* Federal Pell, SEOG, state scholarships/grants, private scholarships, the school's own gift aid. *Loans:* Direct Subsidized Stafford, Direct Unsubsidized Stafford, Direct PLUS, Federal Perkins, college/university loans from institutional funds. **Student Employment:** Federal Work-Study Program available. Institutional employment available. Highest amount earned per year from on-campus jobs $10,000. Off-campus job opportunities are excellent. **Financial Aid Statistics:** 56% freshmen, 50% undergrads receive need-based scholarship or grant aid. 8% freshmen, 3% undergrads receive non-need-based scholarship or grant aid. 44% freshmen, 50% undergrads receive need-based self-help aid. 70% freshmen, 80% undergrads receive any aid. 64% undergrads borrow to pay for school. Average cumulative indebtedness $23,256. **Criteria for awarding institutional aid:** *Non-need-based:* Academics, art, athletics, music/drama.

BOSTON ARCHITECTURAL COLLEGE

320 Newbury Street, Boston, MA 02115-2703
Phone: 617-585-0123
E-mail: admissions@the-bac.edu **CEEB Code:** 1168
Fax: 617-585-0121 **Website:** www.the-bac.edu

This private school was founded in 1889.

RATINGS
Admissions Selectivity Rating: 60*   **Fire Safety Rating:** 60*   **Green Rating:** 60*

STUDENTS AND FACULTY
Faculty: Student/faculty ratio 15:1.

ACADEMICS
Degrees: Bachelor's, certificate, first professional, master's. **Majors with Highest Enrollment:** Computer and information sciences; elementary education and teaching; psychology. **Special Study Options:** Cross-registration, distance learning, study abroad, concurrent academic and practice-based learning. **Career services:** Career/job search classes, internships.

FACILITIES
Housing: 100% of campus accessible to physically disabled. **Special Academic Facilities/Equipment:** McCormick Gallery.

CAMPUS LIFE
Activities: Student newspaper. **Organizations:** 2 registered organizations.

ADMISSIONS
Freshman Academic Profile: Minimum paper TOEFL 550. **Freshman Admission Requirements:** High school diploma is required and GED is accepted. **Freshman Admission Statistics:** 368 applied, 94% admitted, 32% enrolled. **Transfer Admission Requirements:** High school transcript, college transcript(s), Lowest grade transferable C. **General Admission Information:** Application fee $50. Nonfall registration accepted. Admission may be deferred for a maximum of 1 Semester. Credit and/or placement offered for CEEB Advanced Placement tests.

COSTS AND FINANCIAL AID
Annual tuition $7,438. Required fees $150. Average book expense $1,105. **Required Forms and Deadlines:** FAFSA, institution's own financial aid form. Financial aid filing deadline 3/31. Priority financial aid filing date 3/31. **Notification of Awards:** Applicants will be notified of awards on a rolling basis beginning 4/30. **Types of Aid:** *Need-based scholarships/grants:* Federal Pell, state scholarships/grants, private scholarships. *Loans:* FFEL Subsidized Stafford, FFEL Unsubsidized Stafford, FFEL PLUS, state loans **Student Employment:** Off-campus job opportunities are excellent. **Financial Aid Statistics:** 50% undergrads borrow to pay for school. Average cumulative indebtedness $40,000. **Criteria for awarding institutional aid:** *Non-need-based:* Academics, job skills.

BOSTON COLLEGE

Best 373

140 Commonwealth Avenue, Devlin Hall 208, Chestnut Hill, MA 02467-3809
Phone: 617-552-3100 **Financial Aid Phone:** 617-552-3300
E-mail: CEEB Code: 3083
Fax: 617-552-0798 **Website:** www.bc.edu **ACT Code:** 1788

This private school, affiliated with the Roman Catholic Church, was founded in 1863. It has a 386.1-acre campus.

RATINGS
Admissions Selectivity Rating: 97   **Fire Safety Rating:** 89   **Green Rating:** 86

STUDENTS AND FACULTY
Enrollment: 9,171. **Student Body:** 52% female, 48% male, 73% out-of-state, 3% international (96 countries represented). Asian 10%, African American 5%, Caucasian 68%, Hispanic 8%.
Retention and Graduation: 96% freshmen return for sophomore year. 21.6% grads go on to further study within 1 year. 6.6% grads pursue arts and sciences degrees. 4.9% grads pursue law degrees. 2% grads pursue business degrees. 3.3% grads pursue medical degrees. **Faculty:** Student/faculty ratio 13:1. 708 full-time faculty, 98% hold PhDs, 13% are members of minority groups, 38% are women.

ACADEMICS
Degrees: Bachelor's, doctoral, master's, post-master's certificate. **Classes:** Most classes have 10–19 students. **Majors with Highest Enrollment:** Communication and media studies, other; English language and literature; finance. **Special Study Options:** Accelerated program, cross-registration, distance learning, double major, English as a Second Language (ESL), exchange student program (domestic), honors program, independent study, internships, liberal arts/career combination, student-designed major, study abroad, teacher certification program. **Honors programs:** Multiple Honors Programs in various Schools and Departments, along with a Presidential Scholars Program. **Combined degree programs:** BA/MD, BA/MA, MD with Tufts Medical School. Special programs offered to physically disabled students include note-taking services, reader services, tape recorders, tutors. **Career services:** Alumni network, alumni services, career/job search classes, career assessment, internships, regional alumni. **Career services highlights include:** internships.

FACILITIES
Housing: Coed dorms, special housing for disabled students, women's dorms, Greycliff Honors House, multicultural and intercultural floors, a quiet floor, social justice floor, a community living floor, and a leadership house. Also apartment style housing and Townhouse apartments. 95% of campus accessible to physically disabled. **Special Academic Facilities/Equipment:** Art museum, theatre arts center, on-campus school for multihandicapped students, athletic facility, state-of-the-art science facilities. **Computers:** 100% of classrooms, 100% of dorms, 100% of libraries, 100% of dining areas, 100% of student union, 100% of common outdoor areas have wireless network access. Students can register for classes online. Administrative functions (other than registration) can be performed online.

CAMPUS LIFE
Environment: City. **Activities:** Choral groups, concert band, dance, drama/theater, jazz band, literary magazine, marching band, music ensembles, musical theater, pep band, radio station, student government, student newspaper, student-run film society, symphony orchestra, television station, yearbook, campus ministries, international student organization. **Organizations:** 225 registered organizations, 12 honor societies, 14 religious organizations. **Athletics (Intercollegiate):** *Men:* Baseball, basketball, cross-country, diving, fencing, football, golf, ice hockey, lacrosse, sailing, skiing (downhill/alpine), soccer, swimming, tennis, track/field (outdoor), track/field (indoor). *Women:* Basketball, crew/rowing, cross-country, diving, fencing, field hockey, golf, ice hockey, lacrosse, sailing, skiing (downhill/alpine), soccer, softball, swimming, tennis, track/field (outdoor), track/field (indoor), volleyball. **On-Campus Highlights:** McMullen Museum of Art, Alumni Stadium/Conte Forum, Robsham Theater, Bapst Library, McElroy Commons/Bookstore. **Environmental Initiatives:** Master Plan—5 buildings are registered w/USGBC. Silver is the targeted certification. Energery Conservation program and procurement. (40.5% of electricity is from hydropower). Carbon footprint calculation is nearly complete and plan to reduce footprint will be issued within 1 year.

ADMISSIONS

Freshman Academic Profile: 79% in top 10% of high school class, 95% in top 25% of high school class, 99% in top 50% of high school class. 51% from public high schools. SAT Math middle 50% range 640–730. SAT Critical Reading middle 50% range 610–700. SAT Writing middle 50% range 630–720. ACT middle 50% range 29–32. Minimum paper TOEFL 600. Minimum computer TOEFL 250. Minimum web-based TOEFL 100. **Basis for Candidate Selection:** *Very important factors considered include:* Academic GPA, rigor of secondary school record, standardized test scores. *Important factors considered include:* Class rank, application essay, recommendation(s), alumni/ae relation, character/personal qualities, extracurricular activities, religious affiliation/commitment, talent/ability, volunteer work. *Other factors considered include:* first generation, racial/ethnic status, work experience. **Freshman Admission Requirements:** High school diploma is required and GED is accepted. *Academic units recommended:* 4 English, 4 mathematics, 4 science, (4 science labs), 4 foreign language, 4 social studies. **Freshman Admission Statistics:** 29,289 applied, 30% admitted, 25% enrolled. **Transfer Admission Requirements:** High school transcript, college transcript(s), essay or personal statement, standardized test scores, statement of good standing from prior institution(s). Minimum college GPA of 3.0 required. Lowest grade transferable C. **General Admission Information:** Application fee $70. Regular application deadline 1/1. Regular notification 4/15. Nonfall registration accepted. Admission may be deferred for a maximum of 2 years. Placement offered for CEEB Advanced Placement tests.

COSTS AND FINANCIAL AID

Annual tuition $38,530. Room and board $12,909. Required fees $600. Average book expense $900. **Required Forms and Deadlines:** FAFSA, CSS/Financial Aid PROFILE, noncustodial PROFILE, business/farm supplement. Priority financial aid filing date 2/1. **Notification of Awards:** Applicants will be notified of awards on or about 4/1. **Types of Aid:** *Need-based scholarships/grants:* Federal Pell, SEOG, state scholarships/grants, private scholarships, the school's own gift aid. *Loans:* FFEL Subsidized Stafford, FFEL Unsubsidized Stafford, FFEL PLUS, Federal Perkins, Federal Nursing, state loans. **Student Employment:** Federal Work-Study Program available. Institutional employment available. Highest amount earned per year from on-campus jobs $2,400. Off-campus job opportunities are good. **Financial Aid Statistics:** 39% freshmen, 35% undergrads receive need-based scholarship or grant aid. 1% freshmen, 1% undergrads receive non-need-based scholarship or grant aid. 42% freshmen, 40% undergrads receive need-based self-help aid. 4% freshmen, 4% undergrads receive athletic scholarships. 63% freshmen, 69% undergrads receive any aid. 52% undergrads borrow to pay for school. Average cumulative indebtedness $19,358. **Criteria for awarding institutional aid:** *Non-need-based:* Academics, athletics, leadership.

BOSTON CONSERVATORY

8 The Fenway, Boston, MA 02215
Phone: 617-912-9153
E-mail: admissions@bostonconservatory.edu **CEEB Code:** 3084
Fax: 617-247-3159 **Website:** www.bostonconservatory.edu **ACT Code:** 1790

This private school was founded in 1867.

RATINGS

Admissions Selectivity Rating: 60*   **Fire Safety Rating:** 60*   **Green Rating:** 60*

STUDENTS AND FACULTY

Enrollment: 450. **Student Body:** 63% female, 37% male, 60% out-of-state, international (26 countries represented).
Retention and Graduation: 68% freshmen return for sophomore year. 35% freshmen graduate within 4 years. **Faculty:** Student/faculty ratio 4:1. 44 full-time faculty, 59% are women.

ACADEMICS

Degrees: Bachelor's, diploma, master's, post-bachelor's certificate, post-master's certificate. **Classes:** Most classes have fewer than 10 students. **Special Study Options:** cross-registration, double major, English as a Second Language (ESL), independent study, teacher certification program. **Career services:** Alumni services, career/job search classes, career assessment, internships,

FACILITIES

Housing: Coed dorms, women's dorms, Graduate house.

CAMPUS LIFE

Activities: Literary magazine, student government, student newspaper. **Organizations:** 11 registered organizations, 1 honor societies, 1 religious organizations.

ADMISSIONS

Freshman Academic Profile: 90% from public high schools. **Basis for Candidate Selection:** *Very important factors considered include:* Recommendation(s), character/personal qualities, talent/ability. *Important factors considered include:* Class rank, application essay, rigor of secondary school record, interview. *Other factors considered include:* Extracurricular activities. **Freshman Admission Requirements:** High school diploma is required and GED is accepted. *Academic units required:* 4 English, 3 mathematics, 2 science, 2 foreign language, 2 social studies, 2 history. **Freshman Admission Statistics:** 989 applied, 43% admitted, 28% enrolled. **Transfer Admission Requirements:** High school transcript, college transcript(s), essay or personal statement, minimum college GPA of 2.5 required. Lowest grade transferable C. **General Admission Information:** Application fee $100. Regular notification 4/1. Nonfall registration accepted. Admission may be deferred for a maximum of 12. Credit offered for CEEB Advanced Placement tests.

COSTS AND FINANCIAL AID

Annual tuition $2,194. Room and board $15,640. Required fees $2,690. **Required Forms and Deadlines:** FAFSA, institution's own financial aid form. Financial aid filing deadline 2/1. Priority financial aid filing date 2/1. **Notification of Awards:** Applicants will be notified of awards on or about 4/1. **Types of Aid:** *Need-based scholarships/grants:* Federal Pell, SEOG, state scholarships/grants, private scholarships, the school's own gift aid. *Loans:* FFEL Subsidized Stafford, FFEL Unsubsidized Stafford, FFEL PLUS, college/university loans from institutional funds, Private Educational Loans. **Student Employment:** Federal Work-Study Program available. Institutional employment available. Highest amount earned per year from on-campus jobs $830. Off-campus job opportunities are excellent. **Financial Aid Statistics:** 16% freshmen, 16% undergrads receive need-based scholarship or grant aid. 39% freshmen, 46% undergrads receive non-need-based scholarship or grant aid. 49% freshmen, 52% undergrads receive need-based self-help aid. 76% undergrads borrow to pay for school. Average cumulative indebtedness $15,000. **Criteria for awarding institutional aid:** *Non-need-based:* Music/drama.

BOSTON UNIVERSITY

Best 373

121 Bay State Road, Boston, MA 02215
Phone: 617-353-2300 **Financial Aid Phone:** 617-353-4176
E-mail: admissions@bu.edu **CEEB Code:** 3087
Fax: 617-353-9695 **Website:** www.bu.edu **ACT Code:** 1794

This private school was founded in 1839. It has a 132-acre campus.

RATINGS

Admissions Selectivity Rating: 94   **Fire Safety Rating:** 60*   **Green Rating:** 86

STUDENTS AND FACULTY

Enrollment: 16,673. **Student Body:** 60% female, 40% male, 77% out-of-state, 6% international (100 countries represented). Asian 13%, African American 3%, Caucasian 56%, Hispanic 7%.
Retention and Graduation: 91% freshmen return for sophomore year. 76% freshmen graduate within 4 years. 29% grads go on to further study within 1 year. 26% grads pursue arts and sciences degrees. 1% grads pursue law degrees. 1% grads pursue medical degrees. **Faculty:** Student/faculty ratio 14:1. 1512 full-time faculty, 77% hold PhDs, 11% are members of minority groups, 34% are women. 6% of classes are taught by teaching assistants.

ACADEMICS

Degrees: Bachelor's, first professional, first professional certificate, master's, post-bachelor's certificate, post-master's certificate. **Classes:** Most classes have 10–19 students. Most lab/discussion sessions have 20–29 students. **Majors with Highest Enrollment:** Business/commerce; international relations and affairs; psychology. **Special Study Options:** Accelerated program, cooperative education program, cross-registration, distance learning, double major, dual enrollment, English as a Second Language (ESL), honors program, independent study, internships, liberal arts/career combination, student-designed major, study abroad, teacher certification program, weekend college, Field study in Marine Science at the Woods Hole Institute and in Environmental/Ecological Science in Ecuador at the Biodiversity Station in the tropical rain forest. The Photonics Center. **Honors programs:** Honors Programs are offered in the College of Arts and Sciences and the School of Management. **Combined degree programs:** BA/MD, BA/MA, BA/DMD, BS/MS, BA/MD, BS/MSOT, BS/DPT.

Special programs offered to physically disabled students include note-taking services, reader services, tape recorders, tutors. **Career services:** Alumni network, alumni services, career/job search classes, career assessment, internships, regional alumni. **Career services highlights include:** Our internship program provides opportunities for student to work with early stage companies at the BU incubators, as well as in the community. One particularly unusual aspect of the program is that we provide opportunities for non-business students to intern with startups our business students are creating. One such program this year had Graphic Design students working with MBA student entrepreneurs to develop corporate identity programs for them.

FACILITIES

Housing: Coed dorms, special housing for disabled students, women's dorms, apartments for married students, cooperative housing, apartments for single students, Specialty dorms/floors for groups of students with a common interest or academic major. 90% of campus accessible to physically disabled. **Special Academic Facilities/Equipment:** Center for Computational Science, Center for Advanced Biotechnology, Center for Photonics Research, art galleries, planetarium, commercial TV station, National Public Radio station, 20th century archives, professional theatre and theatre company, Center for Remote Sensing, Geddes Language Labratory, speech, language and hearing clinic, Culinary Center, Metcalf Center for Science and Engineering, Tsai Performance Center, and College of Communication Multimedia Lab. **Computers:** Students can register for classes online. Administrative functions (other than registration) can be performed online.

CAMPUS LIFE

Environment: Metropolis. **Activities:** Choral groups, concert band, dance, drama/theater, jazz band, literary magazine, marching band, music ensembles, musical theater, opera, radio station, student government, student newspaper, student-run film society, symphony orchestra, yearbook, international student organization. **Organizations:** 400 registered organizations, 11 honor societies, 26 religious organizations. 9 fraternities, 9 sororities. **Athletics (Intercollegiate):** *Men:* Basketball, crew/rowing, cross-country, diving, golf, ice hockey, soccer, swimming, tennis, track/field (outdoor), track/field (indoor), wrestling. *Women:* Basketball, crew/rowing, cross-country, diving, field hockey, golf, ice hockey, lacrosse, soccer, softball, swimming, tennis, track/field (outdoor), track/field (indoor). **On-Campus Highlights:** Marsh Chapel Plaza, Mugar Memorial Library, special collections, DeWolfe Boathouse, George Sherman Student Union, The Photonics Center. **Environmental Initiatives:** Energy Efficiency Retrofits, Recycling Program, Water Efficiency Upgrades.

ADMISSIONS

Freshman Academic Profile: Average high school GPA 3.45. 55% in top 10% of high school class, 87% in top 25% of high school class, 99% in top 50% of high school class. 74% from public high schools. SAT Math middle 50% range 600–690. SAT Critical Reading middle 50% range 580–670. SAT Writing middle 50% range 590–680. ACT middle 50% range 25–30. Minimum paper TOEFL 550. Minimum computer TOEFL 215. **Basis for Candidate Selection:** *Very important factors considered include:* Rigor of secondary school record. *Important factors considered include:* Class rank, application essay, academic GPA, recommendation(s), standardized test scores. *Other factors considered include:* Alumni/ae relation, character/personal qualities, extracurricular activities, first generation, geographical residence, level of applicant's interest, racial/ethnic status, state residency, volunteer work, work experience. **Freshman Admission Requirements:** High school diploma is required and GED is accepted. *Academic units required:* 4 English, 3 mathematics, 3 science, (3 science labs), 2 foreign language, 3 social studies. *Academic units recommended:* 4 English, 4 mathematics, 4 science, (4 science labs), 4 foreign language, 4 social studies. **Freshman Admission Statistics:** 33,390 applied, 56% admitted, 22% enrolled. **Transfer Admission Requirements:** High school transcript, college transcript(s), essay or personal statement, standardized test scores, statement of good standing from prior institution(s). Minimum college GPA of 3.5 required. Lowest grade transferable C. **General Admission Information:** Application fee $75. Early decision application deadline 11/1. Regular application deadline 1/1. Nonfall registration accepted. Admission may be deferred for a maximum of 1 year. Credit and/or placement offered for CEEB Advanced Placement tests.

COSTS AND FINANCIAL AID

Annual tuition $37,910. Room and board $11,848. Required fees $530. Average book expense $940. **Required Forms and Deadlines:** FAFSA, CSS/Financial Aid PROFILE, state aid form, noncustodial PROFILE, business/farm supplement. Financial aid filing deadline 2/15. **Notification of Awards:** Applicants will be notified of awards on a rolling basis beginning 3/15. **Types of Aid:** *Need-based scholarships/grants:* Federal Pell, SEOG, state scholarships/grants, private scholarships, the school's own gift aid. *Loans:* Direct Subsidized Stafford, Direct Unsubsidized Stafford, Direct PLUS, Federal Perkins, state loans. **Student Employment:** Federal Work-Study Program available. Institutional employment available. Off-campus job opportunities are excellent. **Financial Aid Statistics:** 41% freshmen, 39% undergrads receive need-based scholarship

or grant aid. 17% freshmen, 11% undergrads receive non-need-based scholarship or grant aid. 40% freshmen, 38% undergrads receive need-based self-help aid. 2% freshmen, 2% undergrads receive athletic scholarships. 46% freshmen, 44% undergrads receive any aid. 60% undergrads borrow to pay for school. Average cumulative indebtedness $24,939. **Criteria for awarding institutional aid:** *Non-need-based:* Academics, alumni affiliation, art, athletics, leadership, music/drama, religious affiliation, state/district residency.

See page 1034.

BOWDOIN COLLEGE

5000 College Station, Bowdoin College, Brunswick, ME 04011-8441
Phone: 207-725-3100 **Financial Aid Phone:** 207-725-3273
E-mail: admissions@bowdoin.edu **CEEB Code:** 3089
Fax: 207-725-3101 **Website:** www.bowdoin.edu **ACT Code:** 1636

This private school was founded in 1794. It has a 205-acre campus.

RATINGS

Admissions Selectivity Rating: 98   **Fire Safety Rating:** 95   **Green Rating:** 97

STUDENTS AND FACULTY

Enrollment: 1,772. **Student Body:** 51% female, 49% male, 88% out-of-state, 3% international (38 countries represented). Asian 12%, African American 6%, Caucasian 66%, Hispanic 10%, Native American 1%.
Retention and Graduation: 96% freshmen return for sophomore year. 89% freshmen graduate within 4 years. 15% grads go on to further study within 1 year. 8% grads pursue arts and sciences degrees. 4% grads pursue law degrees. 1% grads pursue business degrees. 2% grads pursue medical degrees. **Faculty:** Student/faculty ratio 9:1. 177 full-time faculty, 98% hold PhDs, 18% are members of minority groups, 48% are women.

ACADEMICS

Degrees: Bachelor's. **Classes:** Most classes have 10–19 students. Most lab/discussion sessions have 10–19 students. **Majors with Highest Enrollment:** Biology/biological sciences; economics; political science and government. **Special Study Options:** Accelerated program, double major, exchange student program (domestic), independent study, liberal arts/career combination, student-designed major, study abroad, teacher certification program, 3-2 or 4-2 Engineering Degree Programs with Dartmouth College, California Institute of Technology, Columbia University and the University of Maine; and 3-3 Legal Studies Degree Program with Columbia University Law School. Pass/Fail grading options are available. **Combined degree programs:** BA/JD, BA/MEng, 3-3 Law—Columbia University Law. Special programs offered to physically disabled students include note-taking services, reader services, tape recorders, tutors. **Career services:** Alumni network, alumni services, career/job search classes, career assessment, internships, regional alumni. **Career services highlights include:** paid internship opportunities through the generosity of donors. Many of these internships serve the needs of underserved and disadvantaged populations.

FACILITIES

Housing: Coed dorms, special housing for disabled students, apartments for single students, wellness housing, 3 small college houses, and 8 college house system houses. 70% of campus accessible to physically disabled. **Special Academic Facilities/Equipment:** Art museum; Arctic Museum; Arctic Studies Center; coastal marine biology and ornithology research facility on Orr's Island; scientific station on Kent Island; black box theater; Pickard Theater; Baldwin Center for Learning and Teaching; Outdoor Leadership Center; Visual Arts Center; Crafts Center; 8 specialized libraries, including the Language Media Center; Coleman Farm; Quantitative Skills Program; The Writing Project; Gibson Hall of Music; Recital Hall; Educational Technology Center; Environmental Studies Center; Russwurm African-American Center; Women's Resource Center; Off-Campus Study Office; Office of Health Professions Advising; Pre-Law Advising Office; Career Planning Center; Community Service Resource Center; Electronic Classroom; Recording Studio; and a state-of-the-art science facility. **Computers:** 100% of classrooms, 100% of dorms, 100% of libraries, 100% of dining areas, 100% of student union, 100% of common outdoor areas have wireless network access. Administrative functions (other than registration) can be performed online.

CAMPUS LIFE

Environment: Village. **Activities:** Choral groups, concert band, dance, drama/theater, jazz band, literary magazine, music ensembles, musical theater, radio station, student government, student newspaper, student-run film society, symphony orchestra, television station, yearbook, international student organization. **Organizations:** 109 registered organizations, 1 honor societies, 4 religious organizations. **Athletics (Intercollegiate):** *Men:* Baseball, basketball, cross-country, diving, football, golf, ice hockey, lacrosse, sailing, skiing (nordic/cross-country), soccer, squash, swimming, tennis, track/field (outdoor), track/field (indoor). *Women:* Basketball, cross-country, diving, field hockey, golf, ice hockey, lacrosse, rugby, sailing, skiing (nordic/cross-country), soccer, softball, squash, swimming, tennis, track/field (outdoor), track/field (indoor), volleyball. **On-Campus Highlights:** Bowdoin College Museum of Art, Druckenmiller Science Building, Studzinski Recital Hall, Schwartz Outdoor Leadership Center, Wish / Pickard Theater, Peary MacMillan Arctic Museum; Visual Arts Center and McLellan art studios; Hawthorne-Longfellow Library; Smith Student Union; Thorne Dining Hall; top of Coles Tower (for birds-eye view); athletic facilities and playing fields/trails; walk the Bowdoin Quad and the Bowdoin Pines. **Environmental Initiatives:** Bowdoin has committed to becoming a carbon neutral campus by 2020 and detailed a Climate Action Plan, moving forward to begin implementation of which with the installation of a co-generation system at its campus steam plant over the next 2 summers. The Co-Gen system will reduce the College's net 2008 emissions by 18%. Bowdoin is also currently implementing a Building Dashboard system on 35 campus buildings that will allow the campus community to track the electricity use of its buildings in real-time. Bowdoin has established a campus-managed, certified organic garden that provides produce to the dining halls, a year-round composting program, a small hoop house, academic and co-curricular opportunities for students and bicycle delivery carts to provide carbon neutral produce. Bowdoin has implemented a comprehensive approach to alternative transportation on campus that includes a bike sharing program, Zipcars, a free campus shuttle for students, promotions for faculty and staff who carpool, bike and walk to work as well as reserved parking for carpoolers and low-emitting, fuel-efficient vehicles and increased emphasis on biking infrastructure on campus.

ADMISSIONS

Freshman Academic Profile: Average high school GPA 3.8. 81% in top 10% of high school class, 96% in top 25% of high school class, 100% in top 50% of high school class. 56% from public high schools. SAT Math middle 50% range 660–750. SAT Critical Reading middle 50% range 660–750. SAT Writing middle 50% range 660–750. ACT middle 50% range 30–33. Minimum paper TOEFL 600. Minimum computer TOEFL 250. Minimum web-based TOEFL 100. **Basis for Candidate Selection:** *Very important factors considered include:* Class rank, application essay, academic GPA, recommendation(s), rigor of secondary school record, character/personal qualities, extracurricular activities, talent/ability. *Important factors considered include:* Standardized test scores, alumni/ae relation, first generation. *Other factors considered include:* Geographical residence, interview, racial/ethnic status, state residency. **Freshman Admission Requirements:** High school diploma is required and GED is not accepted. *Academic units recommended:* 4 English, 4 mathematics, 4 science, (3 science labs), 4 foreign language, 4 social studies. **Freshman Admission Statistics:** 5,940 applied, 19% admitted, 43% enrolled. **Transfer Admission Requirements:** High school transcript, college transcript(s), essay or personal statement, statement of good standing from prior institution(s). Minimum college GPA of 3.0 required. Lowest grade transferable C–. **General Admission Information:** Application fee $60. Early decision application deadline 11/15. Regular application deadline 1/1. Regular notification 4/5. Nonfall registration not accepted. Admission may be deferred for a maximum of 1 year. Credit and/or placement offered for CEEB Advanced Placement tests.

COSTS AND FINANCIAL AID

Annual tuition $39,605. Room and board $10,880. Required fees $415. Average book expense $800. **Required Forms and Deadlines:** FAFSA, CSS/Financial Aid PROFILE, noncustodial PROFILE, business/farm supplement. Financial aid filing deadline 2/15. **Notification of Awards:** Applicants will be notified of awards on or about 4/5. **Types of Aid:** *Need-based scholarships/grants:* Federal Pell, SEOG, state scholarships/grants, private scholarships, the school's own gift aid. *Loans:* FFEL Subsidized Stafford, FFEL Unsubsidized Stafford, FFEL PLUS, Federal Perkins, state loans. **Student Employment:** Federal Work-Study Program available. Institutional employment available. Highest amount earned per year from on-campus jobs $2,000. Off-campus job opportunities are good. **Financial Aid Statistics:** 41% freshmen, 43% undergrads receive need-based scholarship or grant aid. 32% freshmen, 35% undergrads receive need-based self-help aid. 45% freshmen, 47% undergrads receive any aid. 45% undergrads borrow to pay for school. Average cumulative indebtedness $18,135. **Criteria for awarding institutional aid:** *Non-need-based:* Academics, leadership.

BOWIE STATE UNIVERSITY

14000 Jericho Park Road, Henry Administration Bldg, Bowie, MD 20715
Phone: 301-860-3415 **Financial Aid Phone:** 301-860-3543
E-mail: dkiah@bowiestate.edu **CEEB Code:** 5401
Fax: 301-860-3438 **Website:** www.bowiestate.edu

This public school was founded in 1865. It has a 312-acre campus.

RATINGS

Admissions Selectivity Rating: 75   **Fire Safety Rating:** 60*   **Green Rating:** 60*

STUDENTS AND FACULTY

Enrollment: 3,953. **Student Body:** 64% female, 36% male, 8% out-of-state, 1% international (48 countries represented). Asian 1%, African American 74%, Caucasian 5%, Hispanic 1%.
Retention and Graduation: 72% freshmen return for sophomore year. 11% freshmen graduate within 4 years. 30% grads go on to further study within 1 year. **Faculty:** Student/faculty ratio 19:1. 191 full-time faculty, 68% hold PhDs, 73% are members of minority groups, 45% are women.

ACADEMICS

Degrees: Bachelor's, certificate, master's, post-bachelor's certificate, post-master's certificate. **Classes:** Most classes have 20–29 students. **Special Study Options:** Cooperative education program, cross-registration, distance learning, double major, dual enrollment, exchange student program (domestic), honors program, independent study, internships, liberal arts/career combination, study abroad, teacher certification program, Dual degree Mathematics/Engineering Program. **Combined degree programs:** BA/MEng. Special programs offered to physically disabled students include note-taking services, reader services, tape recorders, tutors. **Career services:** Career/job search classes, internships

FACILITIES

Housing: Coed dorms, men's dorms, women's dorms, apartments for single students, Honors' Residence available; Special interest floors. 100% of campus accessible to physically disabled. **Special Academic Facilities/Equipment:** Science and math labs, computer academy, art galleries. **Computers:** Students can register for classes online. Administrative functions (other than registration) can be performed online.

CAMPUS LIFE

Environment: Town. **Activities:** Choral groups, concert band, dance, drama/theater, jazz band, literary magazine, marching band, music ensembles, musical theater, pep band, radio station, student government, student newspaper, television station, yearbook. **Organizations:** 71 registered organizations, 17 honor societies, 2 religious organizations. 4 fraternities, 4 sororities. **Athletics (Intercollegiate):** *Men:* Basketball, cross-country, football, track/field (outdoor) *Women:* Basketball, cross-country, softball, tennis, track/field (outdoor), volleyball. **On-Campus Highlights:** New Science Bldg, The Jazz man Coffee Shop

ADMISSIONS

Freshman Academic Profile: Average high school GPA 3.11. 88% from public high schools. SAT Math middle 50% range 400–480. SAT Critical Reading middle 50% range 400–490. Minimum paper TOEFL 500. Minimum computer TOEFL 173. **Basis for Candidate Selection:** *Very important factors considered include:* Rigor of secondary school record, standardized test scores. *Other factors considered include:* Application essay, recommendation(s), extracurricular activities, interview. **Freshman Admission Requirements:** High school diploma is required and GED is accepted. *Academic units required:* 4 English, 3 mathematics, 3 science, 2 foreign language, 1 social studies, 2 history. **Freshman Admission Statistics:** 2,826 applied, 52% admitted, 44% enrolled. **Transfer Admission Requirements:** college transcript(s), minimum college GPA of 2.0 required. Lowest grade transferable C. **General Admission Information:** Application fee $40. Notification on a rolling basis, beginning on or about 4/3. Nonfall registration accepted. Admission may be deferred for a maximum of 1 year. Credit and/or placement offered for CEEB Advanced Placement tests.

COSTS AND FINANCIAL AID

Annual in-state tuition $4,286. Annual out-of-state tuition $13,591. Room and board $6,823. Required fees $1,195. Average book expense $1,388. **Required Forms and Deadlines:** FAFSA. **Notification of Awards: Types of Aid:** *Need-based scholarships/grants:* Federal Pell, SEOG, state scholarships/grants, private scholarships, the school's own gift aid. *Loans:* Direct Subsidized Stafford, Direct Unsubsidized Stafford, Direct PLUS, Federal Perkins. **Student Employment:** Federal Work-Study Program available. **Financial Aid Statistics:** 46% freshmen, 44% undergrads receive need-based scholarship or grant aid. 32% freshmen, 33% undergrads receive non-need-based scholarship or grant aid. 38% freshmen, 44% undergrads receive need-based self-help aid. 7% freshmen, 8% undergrads receive athletic scholarships. 34% undergrads borrow to pay for school. Average cumulative indebtedness $10,842. **Criteria for awarding institutional aid:** *Non-need-based:* Academics, art, athletics, music/drama, state/district residency.

BOWLING GREEN STATE UNIVERSITY

110 McFall Center, Admissions, Bowling Green, OH 43403-0085
Phone: 419-372-BGSU **Financial Aid Phone:** 419-372-2651
E-mail: choosebgsu@bgsu.edu **CEEB Code:** 1069
Fax: 419-372-6955 **Website:** www.bgsu.edu **ACT Code:** 3240

This public school was founded in 1910. It has a 1250-acre campus.

RATINGS
Admissions Selectivity Rating: 71   **Fire Safety Rating:** 76   **Green Rating:** 79

STUDENTS AND FACULTY
Enrollment: 14,023. **Student Body:** 53% female, 47% male, 10% out-of-state, 2% international (91 countries represented). Asian 1%, African American 11%, Caucasian 80%, Hispanic 3%, Native American 1%.
Retention and Graduation: 75% freshmen return for sophomore year. 34% freshmen graduate within 4 years. **Faculty:** Student/faculty ratio 18.4:1. 795 full-time faculty, 75% hold PhDs, 17% are members of minority groups, 45% are women. 11% of classes are taught by teaching assistants.

ACADEMICS
Degrees: Bachelor's, doctoral, master's, post-master's certificate. **Classes:** Most classes have 20–29 students. **Majors with Highest Enrollment:** Biology/biological sciences; sport and fitness administration/management; teacher education, multiple levels. **Special Study Options:** Accelerated program, cooperative education program, cross-registration, distance learning, double major, dual enrollment, English as a Second Language (ESL), exchange student program (domestic), honors program, independent study, internships, liberal arts/career combination, student-designed major, study abroad, teacher certification program. **Honors programs:** www.bgsu.edu/offices/honors/. Special programs offered to physically disabled students include note-taking services, reader services, tape recorders, tutors. **Career services:** Alumni network, alumni services, career/job search classes, career assessment, internships, regional alumni. Career services highlights include: see www.bgsu.edu/offices/sa/career/.

FACILITIES
Housing: Coed dorms, fraternity/sorority housing, wellness housing, theme housingresidental learning communities (including Wellness Community), no-alcohol wings. **Special Academic Facilities/Equipment:** http://go2.bgsu.edu/choose/campus/tour/, www.bgsu.edu/map/buildings/. **Computers:** 99% of classrooms, 64% of dorms, 100% of libraries, 100% of dining areas, 100% of student union, 40% of common outdoor areas have wireless network access. Students can register for classes online. Administrative functions (other than registration) can be performed online.

CAMPUS LIFE
Environment: Town. **Activities:** Choral groups, concert band, dance, drama/theater, jazz band, literary magazine, marching band, music ensembles, musical theater, radio station, student government, student newspaper, student-run film society, symphony orchestra, television station, yearbook, international student organization. **Organizations:** 20 honor societies, 24 fraternities, 19 sororities. **Athletics (Intercollegiate):** *Men:* Baseball, basketball, cross-country, football, golf, ice hockey, soccer. *Women:* Basketball, cross-country, golf, gymnastics, soccer, softball, swimming, tennis, track/field (outdoor), track/field (indoor), volleyball. **On-Campus Highlights:** Bowen Thompson Student Union, Jerome Library, McFall Center, College of Business Administration, Residence Halls, http://go2.bgsu.edu/choose/campus/tour/. **Environmental Initiatives:** Developing a acedemic program for Sustainability LEED cerfification for new building construction. Student funded green fee.

ADMISSIONS
Freshman Academic Profile: Average high school GPA 3.2. 12% in top 10% of high school class, 35% in top 25% of high school class, 69% in top 50% of high school class. SAT Math middle 50% range 450–570. SAT Critical Reading middle 50% range 450–580. SAT Writing middle 50% range 450–550. ACT middle 50% range 19–24. Minimum paper TOEFL 500. Minimum computer TOEFL 173. Minimum web-based TOEFL 61. **Basis for Candidate Selection:** *Very important factors considered include:* Academic GPA, rigor of secondary school record, standardized test scores. *Important factors considered include:* Class rank, talent/ability. *Other factors considered include:* Application essay, recommendation(s), alumni/ae relation, character/personal qualities, extracurricular activities, first generation, interview, level of applicant's interest, racial/ethnic status, volunteer work, work experience. **Freshman Admission Requirements:** High school diploma is required and GED is accepted. *Academic units required:* 4 English, 3 mathematics, 3 science, (2 science labs), 2 foreign language, 3 social studies, 1 visual/performing arts. *Academic units recommended:* 4 English, 3 mathematics, 3 science, (2 science labs), 2 foreign language, 3 social studies, 1 visual/performing arts. **Freshman Admission Statistics:** 10,418 applied, 89% admitted, 34% enrolled. Minimum college GPA of 2.5 required. Lowest grade transferable C. **General Admission Information:** Application fee $40. Regular application deadline 7/15. Notification on a rolling basis, beginning on or about 10/1. Nonfall registration accepted. Admission may be deferred for a maximum of 1 year. Credit and/or placement offered for CEEB Advanced Placement tests.

COSTS AND FINANCIAL AID
Required Forms and Deadlines: FAFSA. **Notification of Awards:** Applicants will be notified of awards on a rolling basis beginning 4/15. **Types of Aid:** *Need-based scholarships/grants:* Federal Pell, SEOG, state scholarships/grants, private scholarships, the school's own gift aid. *Loans:* Direct Subsidized Stafford, Direct Unsubsidized Stafford, Direct PLUS, Federal Perkins, Federal Nursing, state loans, college/university loans from institutional funds. **Student Employment:** Federal Work-Study Program available. Institutional employment available. Highest amount earned per year from on-campus jobs $13,544. Off-campus job opportunities are good. **Financial Aid Statistics:** 58% freshmen, 45% undergrads receive need-based scholarship or grant aid. 6% freshmen, 4% undergrads receive non-need-based scholarship or grant aid. 60% freshmen, 57% undergrads receive need-based self-help aid. 2% freshmen, 2% undergrads receive athletic scholarships. 93% freshmen, 86% undergrads receive any aid. 72% undergrads borrow to pay for school. Average cumulative indebtedness $28,542. **Criteria for awarding institutional aid:** *Non-need-based:* Academics, alumni affiliation, art, athletics, leadership, minority status, music/drama, state/district residency.

BRADLEY UNIVERSITY

1501 West Bradley Avenue, Peoria, IL 61625
Phone: 309-677-1000 **Financial Aid Phone:** 309-677-3089
E-mail: admissions@bradley.edu **CEEB Code:** 1070
Fax: 309-677-2797 **Website:** www.bradley.edu **ACT Code:** 960

This private school was founded in 1897. It has a 85-acre campus.

RATINGS
Admissions Selectivity Rating: 75   **Fire Safety Rating:** 69   **Green Rating:** 60*

STUDENTS AND FACULTY
Enrollment: 5,047. **Student Body:** 54% female, 46% male, 11% out-of-state, 1% international (28 countries represented). Asian 4%, African American 8%, Caucasian 81%, Hispanic 4%.
Retention and Graduation: 17% grads go on to further study within 1 year. 3% grads pursue arts and sciences degrees. 1% grads pursue law degrees. 2% grads pursue business degrees. 2% grads pursue medical degrees. **Faculty:** Student/faculty ratio 13:1. 345 full-time faculty, 83% hold PhDs, 14% are members of minority groups, 38% are women.

ACADEMICS
Degrees: Bachelor's, master's. **Classes:** Most classes have 20–29 students. **Majors with Highest Enrollment:** Mechanical engineering; nursing/registered nurse (RN, ASN, BSN, MSN); organizational communication. **Special Study Options:** Accelerated program, cooperative education program, distance learning, double major, honors program, independent study, internships, liberal arts/career combination, student-designed major, study abroad, teacher certification program, Limited distance learning courses available. Collaborative classes with other institutions taught through Internet. **Honors programs:** The Honors Program is structured so that students majoring in any department are eligible to participate. The programs builds progressively through a student's four years, beginning with special honors sections of General Education courses and leading to interdisciplinary seminars and possibilities for independent research. **Combined degree programs:** BA/MSA. Special programs offered to physically disabled students include tutors. **Career services:** Alumni network, alumni services, career/job search classes, career assessment, internships, regional alumni. Career services highlights include: Bradley recently established the Marjorie and Bill Springer Center for Excellence in Internships. The Center will focus on five areas: expanding opportunities for students to gain career-related experience; generating more student participation in the cooperative education and internship program; increasing awareness of international internship opportunities; enhancing activities that assist students in conducting their job searches and preparing them for on-the-job success; and providing continuous evaluation and improvement of the cooperative education and internship program policies, procedures, and data collected.

FACILITIES

Housing: Coed dorms, fraternity/sorority housing, apartments for single students, wellness housing, service and leadership floor. 75% of campus accessible to physically disabled. **Special Academic Facilities/Equipment:** Caterpillar Global Communication Center, two art galleries on campus. **Computers:** 95% of classrooms, 5% of dorms, 100% of libraries, 80% of dining areas, 100% of student union, 30% of common outdoor areas have wireless network access. Students can register for classes online. Administrative functions (other than registration) can be performed online.

CAMPUS LIFE

Environment: City. **Activities:** Choral groups, concert band, dance, drama/theater, jazz band, literary magazine, music ensembles, musical theater, pep band, radio station, student government, student newspaper, student-run film society, symphony orchestra, television station, yearbook, campus ministries, international student organization, Model UN. **Organizations:** 220 registered organizations, 31 honor societies, 17 religious organizations. 16 fraternities, 11 sorority. **Athletics (Intercollegiate):** *Men:* Baseball, basketball, cross-country, golf, soccer, tennis. *Women:* Basketball, cross-country, golf, softball, tennis, track/field (outdoor), track/field (indoor), volleyball. **On-Campus Highlights:** Markin Family Student Recreation Center, Caterpillar Global Communications Center, Olin Hall of Science, Michel Student Center, Cullom-Davis Library, Bradley's 85 acre campus, is the heart of a residential neighborhood just 1 mile from downtown. Peoria is the largest metropolitan area in Illinois south of Chicago.

ADMISSIONS

Freshman Academic Profile: 26% in top 10% of high school class, 60% in top 25% of high school class, 91% in top 50% of high school class. 85% from public high schools. SAT Math middle 50% range 510–640. SAT Critical Reading middle 50% range 480–600. ACT middle 50% range 22–27. Minimum paper TOEFL 550. Minimum computer TOEFL 197. **Basis for Candidate Selection:** *Very important factors considered include:* Academic GPA, rigor of secondary school record. *Important factors considered include:* Class rank, standardized test scores. *Other factors considered include:* Application essay, recommendation(s), alumni/ae relation, character/personal qualities, extracurricular activities, geographical residence, interview, level of applicant's interest, racial/ethnic status, talent/ability, volunteer work, work experience. **Freshman Admission Requirements:** High school diploma is required and GED is accepted. *Academic units required:* 4 English, 3 mathematics, 2 science, (2 science labs), 2 social studies. *Academic units recommended:* 5 English, 4 mathematics, 3 science, (3 science labs), 2 foreign language, 3 social studies, 2 history. **Freshman Admission Statistics:** 6,221 applied, 74% admitted, 24% enrolled. **Transfer Admission Requirements:** College transcript(s), statement of good standing from prior institution(s). Minimum college GPA of 2.0 required. Lowest grade transferable C. **General Admission Information:** Application fee $35. Notification on a rolling basis, beginning on or about 9/15. Nonfall registration accepted. Admission may be deferred for a maximum of 1 year. Credit and/or placement offered for CEEB Advanced Placement tests.

COSTS AND FINANCIAL AID

Average book expense $1,200. **Required Forms and Deadlines:** FAFSA. Priority financial aid filing date 3/1. **Notification of Awards: Types of Aid:** *Need-based scholarships/grants:* Federal Pell, SEOG, state scholarships/grants, private scholarships, the school's own gift aid. *Loans:* Direct Subsidized Stafford, Direct Unsubsidized Stafford, Direct PLUS, FFEL PLUS, Federal Perkins, Federal Nursing. **Student Employment:** Federal Work-Study Program available. Institutional employment available. **Financial Aid Statistics:** 68% freshmen, 70% undergrads receive need-based scholarship or grant aid. 9% freshmen, 8% undergrads receive non-need-based scholarship or grant aid. 61% freshmen, 56% undergrads receive need-based self-help aid. 1% freshmen, 1% undergrads receive athletic scholarships. 97% freshmen, 93% undergrads receive any aid. **Criteria for awarding institutional aid:** *Non-need-based:* Academics, alumni affiliation, art, athletics, leadership, music/drama, state/district residency.

BRANDEIS UNIVERSITY

415 South St, MS003, Waltham, MA 02454-9110
Phone: 781-736-3500 **Financial Aid Phone:** 781-736-3700
E-mail: admissions@brandeis.edu **CEEB Code:** 3092
Fax: 781-736-3536 **Website:** www.brandeis.edu/ **ACT Code:** 1802

This private school was founded in 1948. It has a 235-acre campus.

RATINGS

Admissions Selectivity Rating: 97   **Fire Safety Rating:** 87   **Green Rating:** 90

STUDENTS AND FACULTY

Enrollment: 3,299. **Student Body:** 56% female, 44% male, 74% out-of-state, 10% international (97 countries represented). Asian 11%, African American 5%, Caucasian 47%, Hispanic 5%.
Retention and Graduation: 94% freshmen return for sophomore year. 83% freshmen graduate within 4 years. 31% grads go on to further study within 1 year. **Faculty:** Student/faculty ratio 9:1. 358 full-time faculty, 96% hold PhDs, 11% are members of minority groups, 39% are women.

ACADEMICS

Degrees: Bachelor's, doctoral, master's, post-bachelor's certificate. **Classes:** Most classes have 10–19 students. **Majors with Highest Enrollment:** Biology/biological sciences; economics; psychology. **Special Study Options:** cross-registration, double major, independent study, internships, student-designed major, study abroad. **Combined degree programs:** BA/MA, Early admission to Mt. Sinai;Tufts medical schools. Special programs offered to physically disabled students include note-taking services, tape recorders. **Career services:** Alumni network, alumni services, career/job search classes, career assessment, internships, regional alumni.

FACILITIES

Housing: Coed dorms, men's dorms, women's dorms, apartments for single students, Thematic Learning Communities. 78% of campus accessible to physically disabled. **Special Academic Facilities/Equipment:** Art museum, multicultural library, intercultural center, theater arts complex, language lab, spatial orientation lab, research centers on aging, basic medical sciences, complex systems, family/children's policy, health policy, mental retardation, public policy, study of European Jewry, student leadership Development Room. **Computers:** 100% of classrooms, 100% of dorms, 100% of libraries, 100% of dining areas, 100% of student union, 100% of common outdoor areas have wireless network access. Students can register for classes online. Administrative functions (other than registration) can be performed online.

CAMPUS LIFE

Environment: City. **Activities:** Choral groups, concert band, dance, drama/theater, jazz band, literary magazine, music ensembles, musical theater, radio station, student government, student newspaper, student-run film society, symphony orchestra, television station, yearbook, campus ministries, international student organization. **Organizations:** 253 registered organizations, 4 honor societies, 19 religious organizations. **Athletics (Intercollegiate):** *Men:* Baseball, basketball, cross-country, diving, fencing, soccer, tennis, track/field (outdoor), track/field (indoor), wrestling. *Women:* Basketball, cheerleading, cross-country, diving, fencing, soccer, softball, tennis, track/field (outdoor), track/field (indoor), volleyball, wrestling. **On-Campus Highlights:** Shapiro Science Center, Spingold Theater, Usen Castle, Shapiro Campus Center, Rapaporte Treasure Hall. **Environmental Initiatives:** The Brandeis University Climate Action Plan was completed in Fall of 2009. This plan sets aggressive goals for future energy and climate impact reductions. Brandeis has invested significantly since 2005 in energy reduction efforts—realizing an over 10% drop in campus energy use. The Climate Action Plan builds on these past successes to further reduce cost and environmental impact. A 277 kW sized Solar Photovolatic Array, was installed on the Gosman Sports Center. The solar array is one of the larges in Massachusetts. This system is owned by a for profit business, while Brandeis essentially "rents" the power affordably. This innovative financing structure has allowed Brandeis to support the renewable energy industry, educate students about a growing technology, and reduce world wide carbon impact. To be clear, as the array is not currently owned by the University we can not claim the % of solar energy generated in other questions on this survey because of federal marketing regulations. However, the solar generated at Brandeis is improving air quality for the region. Brandeis is proud of the active student engagement in activism and education on environmental issues. Students are involved in Eco-Reps, where each residential building as a environmental peer educator. Many other accomplishments for sustainability have been brought about through student innovation and education.

ADMISSIONS

Freshman Academic Profile: Average high school GPA 3.77. 79% in top 10% of high school class, 97% in top 25% of high school class, 100% in top 50% of high school class. 70% from public high schools. SAT Math middle 50% range 640–730. SAT Critical Reading middle 50% range 620–730. SAT Writing middle 50% range 620–720. ACT middle 50% range 27–31. Minimum paper TOEFL 600. Minimum computer TOEFL 250. Minimum web-based TOEFL 100. **Basis for Candidate Selection:** *Very important factors considered include:* Class rank, academic GPA, rigor of secondary school record, standardized test scores, character/personal qualities. *Important factors considered include:* Application essay, recommendation(s), extracurricular activities, level of applicant's interest, talent/ability, volunteer work, work experience. *Other factors considered include:* Alumni/ae relation, first generation, geographical residence, interview, racial/ethnic status. **Freshman Admission Requirements:** High school diploma is required and GED is accepted. *Academic units recommended:* 4 English, 4 mathematics, 4 science, (2 science labs), 4 foreign language, 4 social studies. **Freshman Admission Statistics:** 6,815 applied, 40% admitted, 28% enrolled. **Transfer Admission Requirements:** High school transcript, college transcript(s), essay or personal statement, standardized test scores, statement of good standing from prior institution(s). Minimum college GPA of 3.20 required. Lowest grade transferable C–. **General Admission Information:** Application fee $55. Early decision application deadline 11/15. Regular application deadline 1/15. Regular notification 4/1. Nonfall registration accepted. Admission may be deferred for a maximum of 1 year. Credit and/or placement offered for CEEB Advanced Placement tests.

COSTS AND FINANCIAL AID

Annual tuition $37,530. Room and board $10,792. Required fees $1,232. Average book expense $1,000. **Required Forms and Deadlines:** FAFSA, CSS/Financial Aid PROFILE, noncustodial PROFILE, business/farm supplement. Priority financial aid filing date 2/1. **Notification of Awards: Types of Aid:** *Need-based scholarships/grants:* Federal Pell, SEOG, state scholarships/grants, private scholarships, the school's own gift aid. *Loans:* Direct Subsidized Stafford, Direct Unsubsidized Stafford, Direct PLUS, Federal Perkins, state loans, college/university loans from institutional funds. **Student Employment:** Federal Work-Study Program available. Institutional employment available. Off-campus job opportunities are fair. **Financial Aid Statistics:** 53% freshmen, 48% undergrads receive need-based scholarship or grant aid. 4% freshmen, 4% undergrads receive non-need-based scholarship or grant aid. 52% freshmen, 45% undergrads receive need-based self-help aid. 57% freshmen, 51% undergrads receive any aid. 58% undergrads borrow to pay for school. Average cumulative indebtedness $26,078. **Criteria for awarding institutional aid:** *Non-need-based:* Academics.

BRANDON UNIVERSITY

270-18TH Street, Brandon, MB R7A 6A9 Canada
Phone: 204-727-9784
E-mail: admission@brandonu.ca
Fax: 204-728-3221 **Website:** www.brandonu.ca

This public school was founded in 1899. It has a 3-acre campus.

RATINGS
Admissions Selectivity Rating: 60*   **Fire Safety Rating:** 60*   **Green Rating:** 60*

STUDENTS AND FACULTY

Enrollment: 3,097. **Student Body:** 68% female, 32% male, 55% out-of-state, (30 countries represented).
Retention and Graduation: 65% freshmen return for sophomore year. **Faculty:** Student/faculty ratio 11:1. 215 full-time faculty.

ACADEMICS

Degrees: Bachelor's, certificate, master's. **Classes:** Most classes have fewer than 10 students. **Majors with Highest Enrollment:** Pharmacy (PharmD [US], PharmD or BS/BPharm [Canada]). **Special Study Options:** distance learning, double major, English as a Second Language (ESL), teacher certification program **Combined degree programs:** BMus/BEd (AD). Special programs offered to physically disabled students include note-taking services, reader services, tape recorders, tutors.

FACILITIES

Housing: Men's dorms, women's dorms. 80% of campus accessible to physically disabled. **Special Academic Facilities/Equipment:** B.J. Hales Museum. **Computers:** Administrative functions (other than registration) can be performed online.

CAMPUS LIFE
Environment: Town. **Activities:** Choral groups, music ensembles, student government **Athletics (Intercollegiate):** *Men:* Basketball, volleyball. *Women:* Basketball, volleyball.

ADMISSIONS

Freshman Academic Profile: Minimum paper TOEFL 550. Minimum computer TOEFL 213. **Basis for Candidate Selection:** *Very important factors considered include:* Academic GPA, rigor of secondary school record. **Freshman Admission Requirements:** High school diploma is required and GED is accepted. **Transfer Admission Requirements:** college transcript(s), statement of good standing from prior institution(s). **General Admission Information:** Application fee $125. Notification on a rolling basis, beginning on or about 11/1. Nonfall registration accepted. Admission may be deferred for a maximum of nil.

COSTS AND FINANCIAL AID

Annual in-state tuition $3,354. Annual out-of-state tuition $3,354. Room and board $6,270. Required fees $345. Average book expense $1,000. **Required Forms and Deadlines:** Institution's own financial aid form.

BRENAU UNIVERSITY THE WOMEN'S COLLEGE

500 Washington St SE, Gainesville, GA 30501
Phone: 770-534-6100 **Financial Aid Phone:** 770-534-6152
E-mail: wcadmissions@lib.brenau.edu **CEEB Code:** 5066
Fax: 770-538-4306 **Website:** www.brenau.edu **ACT Code:** 800

This private school was founded in 1878. It has a 56-acre campus.

RATINGS
Admissions Selectivity Rating: 60*   **Fire Safety Rating:** 60*   **Green Rating:** 60*

STUDENTS AND FACULTY

Enrollment: 805. **Student Body:** 100% female, 13% out-of-state, 6% international (11 countries represented). Asian 2%, African American 18%, Caucasian 54%, Hispanic 4%.
Retention and Graduation: 74% freshmen return for sophomore year. 37% freshmen graduate within 4 years. **Faculty:** Student/faculty ratio 9:1. 71 full-time faculty, 83% hold PhDs, 10% are members of minority groups, 66% are women.

ACADEMICS

Degrees: Bachelor's, master's. **Classes:** Most classes have 10–19 students. Most lab/discussion sessions have 10–19 students. **Majors with Highest Enrollment:** Nursing/registered nurse (RN, ASN, BSN, MSN); psychology. **Special Study Options:** Cross-registration, distance learning, double major, dual enrollment, English as a Second Language (ESL), honors program, independent study, internships, student-designed major, study abroad, teacher certification program, weekend college. **Honors programs:** The Honors Program at the Women's College of Brenau University begins in the freshman year and is followed throughout the student's entire college career at Brenau. Special classes reserved for honors students are taught in an enriched manner, affording these students an approach to their general education courses which enables them to study these subjects at an advanced level. **Combined degree programs:** BS/MS in Occupational Therapy. Special programs offered to physically disabled students include note-taking services, tape recorders, tutors.

FACILITIES

Housing: Special housing for disabled students, special housing for international students, women's dorms, fraternity/sorority housing, cooperative housing, apartments for single students. 90% of campus accessible to physically disabled. **Special Academic Facilities/Equipment:** Simmons Art Gallery, Wages House, Whitepath House, Natatorium Physical Fitness Center, Leo Castelli Art Gallery. **Computers:** Students can register for classes online. Administrative functions (other than registration) can be performed online.

CAMPUS LIFE

Environment: Town. **Activities:** Choral groups, dance, drama/theater, literary magazine, music ensembles, musical theater, radio station, student government, student newspaper, television station, yearbook, campus ministries, international student organization. **Organizations:** 54 registered organizations, 12 honor societies, 2 religious organizations. 8 sororities. **Athletics (Intercollegiate):** *Women:* Basketball, cross-country, soccer, softball, swimming, tennis, volleyball. **On-Campus Highlights:** Pearce Auditorium, Burd Center for Performing Arts, Fitness Center, Dining Hall and Tea Room, Northeast Georgia History Center.

ADMISSIONS

Freshman Academic Profile: SAT Math middle 50% range 450–520. SAT Critical Reading middle 50% range 460–560. ACT middle 50% range 19–23. Minimum paper TOEFL 550. Minimum computer TOEFL 173. **Basis for Candidate Selection:** *Important factors considered include:* Academic GPA, rigor of secondary school record, standardized test scores. *Other factors considered include:* Class rank, character/personal qualities, extracurricular activities, first generation, interview, level of applicant's interest, talent/ability, volunteer work, work experience. **Freshman Admission Requirements:** High school diploma is required and GED is accepted. **Freshman Admission Statistics:** 2,556 applied, 42% admitted, 16% enrolled. **Transfer Admission Requirements:** College transcript(s), minimum college GPA of 2.0 required. Lowest grade transferable C. **General Admission Information:** Application fee $35. Notification on a rolling basis, beginning on or about 10/1. Nonfall registration accepted. Credit and/or placement offered for CEEB Advanced Placement tests.

COSTS AND FINANCIAL AID

Annual tuition $19,106. Room and board $9,772. Required fees $250. Average book expense $1,050. **Required Forms and Deadlines:** FAFSA, state aid form. Priority financial aid filing date 4/1. **Notification of Awards:** Applicants will be notified of awards on a rolling basis beginning 3/1. **Types of Aid:** *Need-based scholarships/grants:* Federal Pell, SEOG; state scholarships/grants, private scholarships, the school's own gift aid, National Smart Grant. *Loans:* FFEL Subsidized Stafford, FFEL Unsubsidized Stafford, FFEL PLUS, Federal Perkins, state loans, Private Alternative Loans. **Student Employment:** Off-campus job opportunities are excellent. **Financial Aid Statistics:** 76% freshmen, 71% undergrads receive need-based scholarship or grant aid. 14% freshmen, 10% undergrads receive non-need-based scholarship or grant aid. 51% freshmen, 52% undergrads receive need-based self-help aid. 8% freshmen, 6% undergrads receive athletic scholarships. 97% freshmen, 97% undergrads receive any aid. 68% undergrads borrow to pay for school. Average cumulative indebtedness $16,975. **Criteria for awarding institutional aid:** *Non-need-based:* Academics, art, athletics, leadership, minority status, music/drama.

BRESCIA UNIVERSITY

717 Frederica Street, Owensboro, KY 42301-3023
Phone: 270-686-4241
E-mail: admissions@brescia.edu **CEEB Code:** 1071
Fax: 270-686-4314 **Website:** www.brescia.edu **ACT Code:** 14980

This private school, affiliated with the Roman Catholic Church, was founded in 1950. It has a 9-acre campus.

RATINGS

Admissions Selectivity Rating: 75   **Fire Safety Rating:** 87   **Green Rating:** 62

STUDENTS AND FACULTY

Enrollment: 571. **Student Body:** 64% female, 36% male, 23% out-of-state, 3% international (17 countries represented). Asian 1%, African American 5%, Caucasian 66%, Hispanic 2%.
Retention and Graduation: 57% freshmen return for sophomore year. 26% freshmen graduate within 4 years. **Faculty:** Student/faculty ratio 10.7:1. 41 full-time faculty, 66% hold PhDs, 12% are members of minority groups, 54% are women.

ACADEMICS

Degrees: Associate, bachelor's, master's, post-bachelor's certificate. **Classes:** Most classes have fewer than 10 students. Most lab/discussion sessions have fewer than 10 students. **Majors with Highest Enrollment:** Elementary education and teaching; general studies; social work, other. **Special Study Options:** Accelerated program, cross-registration, distance learning, double major, English as a Second Language (ESL), exchange student program (domestic), honors program, independent study, internships, liberal arts/career combination, student-designed major, teacher certification program, weekend college Special programs offered to physically disabled students include note-taking services, tape recorders, tutors. **Career services:** Alumni services, career/job search classes, career assessment, internships.

FACILITIES

Housing: Coed dorms, special housing for disabled students, men's dorms, women's dorms, apartments for single students, theme housing. **Special Academic Facilities/Equipment:** Art Gallery, computer labs, campus center, greenhouse, observatory, science building. **Computers:** 100% of classrooms, 100% of dorms, 100% of libraries, 100% of dining areas, 100% of common outdoor areas have wireless network access. Administrative functions (other than registration) can be performed online.

CAMPUS LIFE

Environment: City. **Activities:** Choral groups, dance, drama/theater, literary magazine, pep band, student government, student newspaper, campus ministries, international student organization. **Organizations:** 22 registered organizations, 3 honor societies, 2 religious organizations. **Athletics (Intercollegiate):** *Men:* Baseball, basketball, cross-country, golf, soccer, tennis, track/field (outdoor). *Women:* Basketball, cross-country, golf, soccer, softball, tennis, track/field (outdoor), volleyball. **Environmental Initiatives:** Recycling; purchasing more energy efficient windows; purchasing more energy efficient equipment when needed.

ADMISSIONS

Freshman Academic Profile: Average high school GPA 3.27. 61% from public high schools. SAT Math middle 50% range 440–510. ACT middle 50% range 18–24. Minimum paper TOEFL 550. Minimum computer TOEFL 213. **Basis for Candidate Selection:** *Very important factors considered include:* Academic GPA, standardized test scores. **Freshman Admission Requirements:** High school diploma is required and GED is accepted. *Academic units recommended:* 4 English, 3 mathematics, 2 science, 2 foreign language, 2 social studies, 2 history, 2 academic electives. **Freshman Admission Statistics:** 677 applied, 67% admitted, 27% enrolled. **Transfer Admission Requirements:** High school transcript, college transcript(s), minimum college GPA of 2.0 required. Lowest grade transferable C. **General Admission Information:** Application fee $25. Notification on a rolling basis, beginning on or about 9/1. Nonfall registration accepted. Admission may be deferred for a maximum of 1 year. Credit and/or placement offered for CEEB Advanced Placement tests.

COSTS AND FINANCIAL AID

Annual tuition $15,600. Room and board $7,600. Required fees $440. **Required Forms and Deadlines:** FAFSA. Priority financial aid filing date 8/1. **Notification of Awards:** Applicants will be notified of awards on a rolling basis beginning 3/1. **Types of Aid:** *Need-based scholarships/grants:* Federal Pell, SEOG, state scholarships/grants, private scholarships, the school's own gift aid. *Loans:* Direct Subsidized Stafford, Direct Unsubsidized Stafford, Direct PLUS, FFEL Subsidized Stafford, FFEL Unsubsidized Stafford, FFEL PLUS, Federal Perkins, college/university loans from institutional funds. **Student Employment:** Federal Work-Study Program available. Institutional employment available. Highest amount earned per year from on-campus jobs $1,236. Off-campus job opportunities are excellent. **Financial Aid Statistics: Criteria for awarding institutional aid:** *Non-need-based:* Academics, alumni affiliation, art, athletics, minority status, music/drama, religious affiliation, state/district residency.

BREVARD COLLEGE

One Brevard College Drive, Brevard, NC 28712
Phone: 828-884-8300 **Financial Aid Phone:** 828-884-8287
E-mail: admissions@brevard.edu **CEEB Code:** 5067
Fax: 828-884-3790 **ACT Code:** 3074

This private school, affiliated with the Methodist Church, was founded in 1853. It has a 120-acre campus.

RATINGS

Admissions Selectivity Rating: 72   **Fire Safety Rating:** 68   **Green Rating:** 81

STUDENTS AND FACULTY

Enrollment: 651. **Student Body:** 43% female, 57% male, 49% out-of-state, 3% international (13 countries represented). African American 12%, Caucasian 77%, Hispanic 2%, Native American 1%.
Retention and Graduation: 58% freshmen return for sophomore year. 20% freshmen graduate within 4 years. **Faculty:** Student/faculty ratio 10:1. 55 full-time faculty, 73% hold PhDs, 40% are women.

ACADEMICS

Degrees: Bachelor's. **Classes:** Most classes have 10–19 students. Most lab/discussion sessions have 10–19 students. **Majors with Highest Enrollment:** Business administration and management; music; parks, recreation and leisure studies. **Special Study Options:** Double major, dual enrollment, honors program, independent study, internships, student-designed major, study abroad, teacher certification program. **Honors programs:** To complete the Honors Program, students must take a minimum of 19 s.h. in honors courses during the typical 4-year period of their enrollment at Brevard College. These hours include honors enrichment seminar courses, honors-designated sections of courses, and a senior project. The only coursework of these 19 hours that is not directly attributable to core or major requirements is 4 s.h. of ENR (Enrichment) seminars. Special programs offered to physically disabled students include note-taking services, reader services, tape recorders, tutors. **Career services:** Career/job search classes, career assessment, internships.

FACILITIES
Housing: Coed dorms, special housing for disabled students, men's dorms, women's dorms, coed upper classperson dorm. 100% of campus accessible to physically disabled. **Special Academic Facilities/Equipment:** Porter Center for Performing Arts; Sims Art Center; Morrison Playhouse; Fitness Appraisal Laboratory; Academic Enrichment Center; Center for Career, Service, and Learning; Medical Services Building; Stamey Counseling Center; 24-hour computer lab; Library with wireless connection; Moore Science Annex Building. **Computers:** 25% of dorms, 100% of libraries, 100% of dining areas, 100% of student union, have wireless network access. Administrative functions (other than registration) can be performed online.

CAMPUS LIFE
Environment: Village. **Activities:** Choral groups, concert band, dance, drama/theater, jazz band, literary magazine, music ensembles, musical theater, opera, pep band, student government, student newspaper, yearbook, campus ministries. **Organizations:** 32 registered organizations, 3 honor societies, 1 religious organizations. **Athletics (Intercollegiate):** *Men:* Baseball, basketball, cheerleading, cross-country, cycling, football, golf, soccer, tennis, track/field (outdoor). *Women:* Basketball, cheerleading, cross-country, cycling, golf, soccer, softball, tennis, track/field (outdoor), volleyball. **On-Campus Highlights:** Food Court & Dining Hall, Porter Center for Performing Arts, The Village, MG Super Lab, Moore Science Annex Building, Academic Enrichment Center. **Environmental Initiatives:** Campus wide recycling program, HVAC renovations to increase energy efficiency, master landscaping plan that focuses on native vegetation.

ADMISSIONS
Freshman Academic Profile: Average high school GPA 2.86. 7% in top 10% of high school class, 22% in top 25% of high school class, 49% in top 50% of high school class. 86% from public high schools. SAT Math middle 50% range 430–550. SAT Critical Reading middle 50% range 420–540. ACT middle 50% range 16–21. Minimum paper TOEFL 537. Minimum computer TOEFL 203. **Basis for Candidate Selection:** *Very important factors considered include:* Academic GPA, rigor of secondary school record, standardized test scores, level of applicant's interest. *Important factors considered include:* Class rank, application essay, character/personal qualities, extracurricular activities, interview, talent/ability, volunteer work. *Other factors considered include:* Recommendation(s), alumni/ae relation, work experience. **Freshman Admission Requirements:** High school diploma is required and GED is accepted. *Academic units recommended:* 4 English, 3 mathematics, 3 science, (1 science labs), 2 foreign language, 4 social studies, 1 history, 4 academic electives. **Freshman Admission Statistics:** 1,191 applied, 54% admitted, 30% enrolled. **Transfer Admission Requirements:** High school transcript, college transcript(s), essay or personal statement, standardized test scores, statement of good standing from prior institution(s). Minimum college GPA of 2.0 required. Lowest grade transferable C–. **General Admission Information:** Application fee $30. Notification on a rolling basis, beginning on or about 7/1. Nonfall registration accepted. Admission may be deferred for a maximum of one semester. Credit and/or placement offered for CEEB Advanced Placement tests.

COSTS AND FINANCIAL AID
Average book expense $1,000. **Required Forms and Deadlines:** FAFSA, state aid form. Priority financial aid filing date 4/15. **Notification of Awards:** Applicants will be notified of awards on a rolling basis beginning 2/1. **Types of Aid:** *Need-based scholarships/grants:* Federal Pell, SEOG, state scholarships/grants, private scholarships, the school's own gift aid. *Loans:* Direct Subsidized Stafford, Direct Unsubsidized Stafford, Direct PLUS, FFEL Subsidized Stafford, FFEL Unsubsidized Stafford, FFEL PLUS, Federal Perkins, state loans. **Student Employment:** Federal Work-Study Program available. Institutional employment available. Highest amount earned per year from on-campus jobs $1,860. Off-campus job opportunities are fair. **Financial Aid Statistics:** 69% freshmen, 72% undergrads receive need-based scholarship or grant aid. 8% freshmen, 9% undergrads receive non-need-based scholarship or grant aid. 68% freshmen, 58% undergrads receive need-based self-help aid. 7% freshmen, 10% undergrads receive athletic scholarships. 87% freshmen, 91% undergrads receive any aid. 59% undergrads borrow to pay for school. Average cumulative indebtedness $20,770. **Criteria for awarding institutional aid:** *Non-need-based:* Academics, art, athletics, job skills, leadership, minority status, music/drama, religious affiliation, state/district residency.

BREWTON-PARKER COLLEGE

P.O. Box 2011, Mt. Vernon, GA 30445
Phone: 912-583-3265
E-mail: admissions@bpc.edu
Fax: 912-583-3598 **Website:** www.bpc.edu

This private school, affiliated with the Baptist Church, was founded in 1904. It has a 270-acre campus.

RATINGS
Admissions Selectivity Rating: 70   **Fire Safety Rating:** 60*   **Green Rating:** 60*

STUDENTS AND FACULTY
Enrollment: 1,124. **Student Body:** 64% female, 36% male, 5% out-of-state, 2% international (19 countries represented). African American 20%, Caucasian 65%, Hispanic 2%.
Retention and Graduation: 59% freshmen return for sophomore year. 8% freshmen graduate within 4 years. 10% grads go on to further study within 1 year. **Faculty:** Student/faculty ratio 9:1. 52 full-time faculty, 73% hold PhDs, 38% are women.

ACADEMICS
Degrees: Associate, bachelor's. **Classes:** Most classes have fewer than 10 students. **Majors with Highest Enrollment:** Business/commerce; education; psychology; **Special Study Options:** Double major, dual enrollment, exchange student program (domestic), honors program, independent study, internships, teacher certification program, weekend college. Special programs offered to physically disabled students include note-taking services, reader services, tape recorders, tutors. **Career services:** Alumni services, career assessment, internships.

FACILITIES
Housing: Men's dorms, women's dorms 80% of campus accessible to physically disabled. **Special Academic Facilities/Equipment:** Library. **Computers:** Students can register for classes online.

CAMPUS LIFE
Environment: Rural. **Activities:** Choral groups, concert band, drama/theater, jazz band, literary magazine, music ensembles, musical theater, student government, student newspaper, yearbook. **Organizations:** 24 registered organizations, 1 honor societies, 5 religious organizations. 3 fraternities, 3 sororities. **Athletics (Intercollegiate):** *Men:* Baseball, basketball, cheerleading, soccer. *Women:* Basketball, cheerleading, soccer, softball, volleyball. **On-Campus Highlights:** New Student Activities Center, Upstairs Cafe, Phillips Student Center Lobby, McAllister Lobby, Baseball/Softball Field.

ADMISSIONS
Freshman Academic Profile: 12% in top 10% of high school class, 26% in top 25% of high school class, 62% in top 50% of high school class. 80% from public high schools. SAT Math middle 50% range 400–500. SAT Critical Reading middle 50% range 390–510. ACT middle 50% range 17–21. **Basis for Candidate Selection:** *Very important factors considered include:* Standardized test scores. *Important factors considered include:* Class rank, rigor of secondary school record. **Freshman Admission Requirements:** High school diploma is required and GED is accepted. *Academic units required:* 4 English, 3 mathematics, 3 science, 3 social studies. **Freshman Admission Statistics:** 498 applied, 48% admitted, 49% enrolled. **Transfer Admission Requirements:** college transcript(s), statement of good standing from prior institution(s). Minimum college GPA of 2.0 required. Lowest grade transferable D. **General Admission Information:** Application fee $25. Regular notification 1/1. Nonfall registration accepted. Admission may be deferred for a maximum of 1 year.

COSTS AND FINANCIAL AID
Annual tuition $11,500. Room and board $5,200. Required fees $1,100. Average book expense $1,000. **Required Forms and Deadlines:** FAFSA, state aid form, Certification Statement. Priority financial aid filing date 4/1. **Notification of Awards:** Applicants will be notified of awards on a rolling basis beginning 2/1. **Types of Aid:** *Need-based scholarships/grants:* Federal Pell, SEOG, state scholarships/grants, private scholarships, the school's own gift aid, Georgia Baptist Funds. *Loans:* FFEL Subsidized Stafford, FFEL Unsubsidized Stafford, FFEL PLUS, Federal Perkins, state loans, college/university loans from institutional funds. **Student Employment:** Federal Work-Study Program available. Institutional employment available. Highest amount earned per year from on-campus jobs $1,235. Off-campus job opportunities are fair. **Financial Aid Statistics:** 88% freshmen, 90% undergrads receive need-based scholarship or grant aid. 8% freshmen, 7% undergrads receive non-need-based scholarship or grant aid. 62% freshmen, 67% undergrads receive need-based self-help aid. 6% freshmen, 6% undergrads receive athletic scholarships. 82% undergrads borrow to pay for school. Average cumulative indebtedness $21,169. **Criteria**

for awarding institutional aid: *Non-need-based:* Academics, art, athletics, leadership, music/drama, religious affiliation, state/district residency.

BRIAR CLIFF UNIVERSITY

Admissions Office, PO Box 2100, Sioux City, IA 51104-0100
Phone: 712-279-5200 **Financial Aid Phone:** 712-279-5239
E-mail: admissions@briarcliff.edu **CEEB Code:** 1846
Fax: 712-279-1632 **Website:** www.briarcliff.edu **ACT Code:** 1276

This private school, affiliated with the Roman Catholic Church, was founded in 1930. It has a 70-acre campus.

RATINGS
Admissions Selectivity Rating: 76   **Fire Safety Rating:** 88   **Green Rating:** 67

STUDENTS AND FACULTY
Enrollment: 1,018. **Student Body:** 56% female, 44% male, 39% out-of-state, international (4 countries represented). Asian 3%, African American 7%, Caucasian 82%, Hispanic 6%, Native American 2%.
Retention and Graduation: 66% freshmen return for sophomore year. 40% freshmen graduate within 4 years. 20% grads go on to further study within 1 year. 2% grads pursue arts and sciences degrees. 9% grads pursue law degrees. 3% grads pursue business degrees. 44% grads pursue medical degrees. **Faculty:** Student/faculty ratio 13:1. 60 full-time faculty, 72% hold PhDs, 3% are members of minority groups, 53% are women.

ACADEMICS
Degrees: Associate, bachelor's, master's, post-bachelor's certificate, post-master's certificate. **Classes:** Most classes have 10–19 students. Most lab/discussion sessions have fewer than 10 students. **Majors with Highest Enrollment:** Business/commerce; elementary education and teaching; nursing/registered nurse (RN, ASN, BSN, MSN). **Special Study Options:** Accelerated program, cross-registration, distance learning, double major, dual enrollment, honors program, independent study, internships, liberal arts/career combination, student-designed major, study abroad, teacher certification program, weekend college. **Honors programs:** Briar Cliffs Honor Program involves elements of leadership, service and character as well as academics, and is led by the Student Honors Executive Board. In addition to talking Honors courses with small enrollments, Honors students perform individual research work with faculty at the upper levels. Special programs offered to physically disabled students include note-taking services, reader services, tape recorders, tutors. **Career services:** Alumni services, career/job search classes, career assessment, internships. Career services highlights include: The Chicago Semester allows students from any major field of study to work, study, and live in Chicago for a semester.

FACILITIES
Housing: Coed dorms, men's dorms, women's dorms, apartments for single students. 90% of campus accessible to physically disabled. **Special Academic Facilities/Equipment:** Nursing Simulation Lab, Integrated Multimedia Center, Human Anatomy Lab, Clausen Art Gallery. **Computers:** 100% of classrooms, 100% of libraries, 100% of dining areas, 100% of student union, have wireless network access. Administrative functions (other than registration) can be performed online.

CAMPUS LIFE
Environment: City. **Activities:** Choral groups, drama/theater, jazz band, literary magazine, music ensembles, musical theater, opera, radio station, student government, student newspaper, campus ministries. **Organizations:** 36 registered organizations, 2 honor societies, 3 religious organizations. **Athletics (Intercollegiate):** *Men:* Baseball, basketball, cross-country, football, golf, soccer, tennis, track/field (outdoor), track/field (indoor), wrestling. *Women:* Basketball, cross-country, golf, soccer, softball, tennis, track/field (outdoor), track/field (indoor), volleyball. **On-Campus Highlights:** Java City, Stark Student Center, Newman Flanagan Athletic Center, Game Room, tunnels, The McCoy Arnold Athletic Facility was completed in 2004. This multi-use athletic facility provides additional facilities for students to work on personal training and fitness. **Environmental Initiatives:** Recycling, Prairie Restoration, trayless dining.

ADMISSIONS
Freshman Academic Profile: Average high school GPA 3.19. 11% in top 10% of high school class, 34% in top 25% of high school class, 64% in top 50% of high school class. 82% from public high schools. ACT middle 50% range 19–25. Minimum paper TOEFL 525. Minimum computer TOEFL 193. Minimum web-based TOEFL 70. **Basis for Candidate Selection:** *Very important factors considered include:* Academic GPA, rigor of secondary school record, standardized test scores. *Other factors considered include:* Class rank, application essay, recommendation(s), alumni/ae relation, character/personal qualities,

extracurricular activities, first generation, interview, talent/ability. **Freshman Admission Requirements:** High school diploma is required and GED is accepted. *Academic units recommended:* 4 English, 3 mathematics, 3 science, 2 foreign language, 3 social studies, 1 academic electives. **Freshman Admission Statistics:** 1,579 applied, 62% admitted, 23% enrolled. **Transfer Admission Requirements:** High school transcript, college transcript(s), statement of good standing from prior institution(s). Minimum college GPA of 2.0 required. Lowest grade transferable D. **General Admission Information:** Application fee $20. Nonfall registration accepted. Admission may be deferred for a maximum of 1 year. Credit offered for CEEB Advanced Placement tests.

COSTS AND FINANCIAL AID
Annual tuition $21,867. Room and board $6,978. Required fees $669. Average book expense $900. **Required Forms and Deadlines:** FAFSA. Priority financial aid filing date 3/15. **Notification of Awards: Types of Aid:** *Need-based scholarships/grants:* Federal Pell, SEOG, state scholarships/grants, private scholarships, the school's own gift aid. *Loans:* FFEL Subsidized Stafford, FFEL Unsubsidized Stafford, FFEL PLUS, Federal Perkins, state loans. **Student Employment:** Federal Work-Study Program available. Institutional employment available. Highest amount earned per year from on-campus jobs $2,500. Off-campus job opportunities are excellent. **Financial Aid Statistics:** 80% freshmen, 70% undergrads receive need-based scholarship or grant aid. 80% freshmen, 70% undergrads receive non-need-based scholarship or grant aid. 80% freshmen, 70% undergrads receive need-based self-help aid. 61% freshmen, 47% undergrads receive athletic scholarships. 100% freshmen, 98% undergrads receive any aid. 89% undergrads borrow to pay for school. Average cumulative indebtedness $30,865. **Criteria for awarding institutional aid:** *Non-need-based:* Academics, alumni affiliation, art, athletics, leadership, music/drama, religious affiliation, state/district residency.

BRIDGEWATER COLLEGE

402 East College Street, Bridgewater, VA 22812-1599
Phone: 540-828-5375 **Financial Aid Phone:** 540-828-5376
E-mail: admissions@bridgewater.edu **CEEB Code:** 5069
Fax: 540-828-5481 **Website:** www.bridgewater.edu **ACT Code:** 4342

This private school, affiliated with the Church of Brethren Church, was founded in 1880. It has a 190-acre campus.

RATINGS
Admissions Selectivity Rating: 75   **Fire Safety Rating:** 61   **Green Rating:** 60*

STUDENTS AND FACULTY
Enrollment: 1,575. **Student Body:** 59% female, 41% male, 19% out-of-state, 1% international (10 countries represented). Asian 1%, African American 7%, Caucasian 80%, Hispanic 2%.
Retention and Graduation: 74% freshmen return for sophomore year. 54% freshmen graduate within 4 years. 29% grads go on to further study within 1 year. **Faculty:** Student/faculty ratio 14:1. 101 full-time faculty, 79% hold PhDs, 4% are members of minority groups, 40% are women.

ACADEMICS
Degrees: Bachelor's. **Classes:** Most classes have 10–19 students. Most lab/discussion sessions have 10–19 students. **Majors with Highest Enrollment:** Biology/biological sciences; business administration and management; liberal arts and sciences/liberal studies. **Special Study Options:** Double major, honors program, independent study, internships, liberal arts/career combination, study abroad, teacher certification program. Dual Degree Programs: 3-2 Engineering Program with George Washington University (BA/BA), 3-2 Engineering Program with Virginia Tech (BA/BA), 3-2 Nursing Program with Vanderbilt University (BA/MN), 3-4 Veterinary Science Program with Virginia Tech (BA/DVM), 3-4 Physical Therapy Program with Shenandoah University (BA/DPT), Pre-professional Programs in dentistry, engineering, law, medicine, ministry, nursing, occupational therapy, pharmacy, physical therapy, and veterinary science. **Honors programs:** The Honors Program is designed to provide additional challenges and opportunities for outstanding students. Honors courses are taught as smaller classes and provide opportunities for different types of student learning and faculty teaching--greater independence, research, and discussion formats. An Honors Project is one in which a student researches a subject, by examination of relevant literature or by experimentation or both; the student reports the results in an accurately documented and well-written paper or appropriate representation of the work. **Combined degree programs:** BA/MA, vet. science, physical therapy, nursing. Special programs offered to physically disabled students include note-taking services, reader services, tape recorders, tutors. **Career services:** Alumni services, career/job search classes, career assessment, internships. Career services highlights include: The internship program promotes student participation and establishes new opportunities/sites for internships within the local, regional, and distant communities.

FACILITIES

Housing: Coed dorms, special housing for disabled students, men's dorms, women's dorms, apartments for single students, wellness housing, theme housing, honor housing. 95% of campus accessible to physically disabled. **Special Academic Facilities/Equipment:** Museum of Shenandoah region and Brethren history. **Computers:** 5% of classrooms, 10% of dorms, 75% of libraries, 100% of dining areas, 100% of student union, have wireless network access. Students can register for classes online. Administrative functions (other than registration) can be performed online.

CAMPUS LIFE

Environment: Village. **Activities:** Choral groups, concert band, dance, drama/theater, jazz band, literary magazine, music ensembles, musical theater, pep band, radio station, student government, student newspaper, yearbook, campus ministries, international student organization. **Organizations:** 74 registered organizations, 8 honor societies, 9 religious organizations. **Athletics (Intercollegiate):** *Men:* Baseball, basketball, cross-country, equestrian sports, football, golf, soccer, tennis, track/field (outdoor), track/field (indoor). *Women:* Basketball, cross-country, equestrian sports, field hockey, lacrosse, soccer, softball, swimming, tennis, track/field (outdoor), track/field (indoor), volleyball. **On-Campus Highlights:** McKinney Center for Science and Mathematics, Kline Campus Center, Funkhouser Center for Health and Wellness, Carter Center for Worship and Music, Eagle's Nest (snack shop).

ADMISSIONS

Freshman Academic Profile: Average high school GPA 3.4. 20.4% in top 10% of high school class, 46.5% in top 25% of high school class, 83.9% in top 50% of high school class. 88% from public high schools. SAT Math middle 50% range 460–560. SAT Critical Reading middle 50% range 450–550. SAT Writing middle 50% range 430–550. ACT middle 50% range 18–23. Minimum paper TOEFL 500. Minimum computer TOEFL 173. Minimum web-based TOEFL 65. **Basis for Candidate Selection:** *Very important factors considered include:* Academic GPA, rigor of secondary school record, standardized test scores. *Important factors considered include:* Class rank, recommendation(s), character/personal qualities, extracurricular activities, interview, talent/ability. *Other factors considered include:* Geographical residence, level of applicant's interest, state residency, volunteer work, work experience. **Freshman Admission Requirements:** High school diploma is required and GED is accepted. *Academic units required:* 4 English, 3 mathematics, 2 science, (2 science labs), 4 academic electives, 2 social studies and history. *Academic units recommended:* 4 English, 4 mathematics, 4 science, (2 science labs), 3 foreign language, 4 academic electives, 3 social studies and history. **Freshman Admission Statistics:** 3,186 applied, 86% admitted, 18% enrolled. **Transfer Admission Requirements:** High school transcript, college transcript(s), standardized test scores, statement of good standing from prior institution(s). Minimum college GPA of 2.2 required. Lowest grade transferable C. **General Admission Information:** Application fee $30. Notification on a rolling basis, beginning on or about 9/1. Nonfall registration accepted. Admission may be deferred for a maximum of 1 year. Credit and/or placement offered for CEEB Advanced Placement tests.

COSTS AND FINANCIAL AID

Annual tuition $25,500. Room and board $10,350. Average book expense $1,100. **Required Forms and Deadlines:** FAFSA, state aid form. Priority financial aid filing date 3/1. **Notification of Awards:** Applicants will be notified of awards on a rolling basis beginning 3/16. **Types of Aid:** *Need-based scholarships/grants:* Federal Pell, SEOG, state scholarships/grants, private scholarships, the school's own gift aid. *Loans:* FFEL Subsidized Stafford, FFEL Unsubsidized Stafford, FFEL PLUS, Federal Perkins. **Student Employment:** Federal Work-Study Program available. Institutional employment available. Highest amount earned per year from on-campus jobs $1,947. Off-campus job opportunities are good. **Financial Aid Statistics:** 82% freshmen, 76% undergrads receive need-based scholarship or grant aid. 80% freshmen, 73% undergrads receive non-need-based scholarship or grant aid. 61% freshmen, 58% undergrads receive need-based self-help aid. 99% freshmen, 99% undergrads receive any aid. 74% undergrads borrow to pay for school. Average cumulative indebtedness $29,331. **Criteria for awarding institutional aid:** *Non-need-based:* Academics, music/drama, religious affiliation.

BRIDGEWATER STATE COLLEGE

Gates House, Bridgewater State College, Bridgewater, MA 02325
Phone: 508-531-1237 **Financial Aid Phone:** 508-531-1341
E-mail: admission@bridgew.edu **CEEB Code:** 3517
Fax: 508-531-1746 **Website:** www.bridgew.edu **ACT Code:** 1900

This public school was founded in 1840. It has a 235-acre campus.

RATINGS

Admissions Selectivity Rating: 71 **Fire Safety Rating:** 60* **Green Rating:** 60*

STUDENTS AND FACULTY

Enrollment: 8,310. **Student Body:** 60% female, 40% male, 5% out-of-state, 1% international (52 countries represented). Asian 2%, African American 6%, Caucasian 81%, Hispanic 2%.
Retention and Graduation: 80% freshmen return for sophomore year. 22% freshmen graduate within 4 years. 16% grads go on to further study within 1 year. 2% grads pursue law degrees. 1% grads pursue business degrees. **Faculty:** Student/faculty ratio 18.6:1. 306 full-time faculty, 90% hold PhDs, 11% are members of minority groups, 48% are women.

ACADEMICS

Degrees: Bachelor's, master's, post-bachelor's certificate, post-master's certificate. **Classes:** Most classes have 20–29 students. Most lab/discussion sessions have 10–19 students. **Majors with Highest Enrollment:** Business/commerce; elementary education and teaching; psychology. **Special Study Options:** Accelerated program, cross-registration, distance learning, double major, dual enrollment, English as a Second Language (ESL), exchange student program (domestic), honors program, independent study, internships, study abroad, teacher certification program. **Combined degree programs:** BS/MSM in Management, BSE/M.Ed in Elem/Spec. Ed. Special programs offered to physically disabled students include note-taking services, reader services, tape recorders, tutors. **Career services:** Alumni services, career/job search classes, career assessment, internships.

FACILITIES

Housing: Coed dorms, special housing for disabled students, apartments for single students, break housing for athletes, student teachers, international students, visiting lecturers. 95% of campus accessible to physically disabled. **Special Academic Facilities/Equipment:** On-campus school, children's physical development clinic, human performance lab, TV studio, observatory, flight simulators, electron microscope, Moakley Technology Center. **Computers:** Students can register for classes online. Administrative functions (other than registration) can be performed online. Undergraduates are required to own a computer.

CAMPUS LIFE

Environment: Village. **Activities:** Choral groups, concert band, dance, drama/theater, jazz band, literary magazine, marching band, music ensembles, musical theater, radio station, student government, student newspaper, yearbook, campus ministries, international student organization. **Organizations:** 67 registered organizations, 11 honor societies, 1 religious organizations. **Athletics (Intercollegiate):** *Men:* Baseball, basketball, cross-country, football, soccer, swimming, tennis, track/field (outdoor), wrestling. *Women:* Basketball, cross-country, field hockey, lacrosse, soccer, softball, swimming, tennis, track/field (outdoor), volleyball.

ADMISSIONS

Freshman Academic Profile: Average high school GPA 3.01. 8% in top 10% of high school class, 32% in top 25% of high school class, 77% in top 50% of high school class. SAT Math middle 50% range 470–560. SAT Critical Reading middle 50% range 460–560. ACT middle 50% range 19–23. Minimum paper TOEFL 500. **Basis for Candidate Selection:** *Very important factors considered include:* Academic GPA, rigor of secondary school record. *Important factors considered include:* Class rank, standardized test scores. *Other factors considered include:* Application essay, recommendation(s), alumni/ae relation, character/personal qualities, extracurricular activities, racial/ethnic status, talent/ability, volunteer work, work experience. **Freshman Admission Requirements:** High school diploma is required and GED is accepted. *Academic units required:* 4 English, 3 mathematics, 3 science, (2 science labs), 2 foreign language, 1 social studies, 1 history, 2 academic electives. *Academic units recommended:* 4 English, 3 mathematics, 3 science, (2 science labs), 2 foreign language, 1 social studies, 1 history, 2 academic electives. **Freshman Admission Statistics:** 6,226 applied, 72% admitted, 33% enrolled. **Transfer Admission Requirements:** College transcript(s), essay or personal statement, minimum college GPA of 2.0 required. Lowest grade transferable C–. **General Admission Information:** Notification on a rolling basis, beginning on or about 12/15. Nonfall registration accepted. Credit and/or placement offered for CEEB Advanced Placement tests.

COSTS AND FINANCIAL AID

Annual in-state tuition $910. Annual out-of-state tuition $7,050. Room and board $6,852. Required fees $532,700. Average book expense $1,000. **Required Forms and Deadlines:** FAFSA. Priority financial aid filing date 3/1. **Notification of Awards: Types of Aid:** *Need-based scholarships/grants:* Federal Pell, SEOG, state scholarships/grants, private scholarships, the school's own gift aid. *Loans:* Direct Subsidized Stafford, Direct Unsubsidized Stafford, Direct PLUS, Federal Perkins, state loans. **Student Employment:** Federal Work-Study Program available. Institutional employment available. Highest amount earned per year from on-campus jobs $4,000. Off-campus job opportunities are good. **Financial Aid Statistics:** Average cumulative indebtedness $21,399. **Criteria for awarding institutional aid:** *Non-need-based:* Academics, leadership, minority status, state/district residency.

BRIERCREST COLLEGE

510 College Drive, Caronport, SK S0H 0S0 Canada
Phone: 800-667-5199 **Financial Aid Phone:**
E-mail: admissions@briercrest.ca
Fax: 800-667-5500 **Website:** www.briercrest.ca

This private school was founded in 1935. It has a 160-acre campus.

RATINGS

Admissions Selectivity Rating: 60*   **Fire Safety Rating:** 60*   **Green Rating:** 60*

STUDENTS AND FACULTY

Student Body: 11% out-of-state.
Faculty: Student/faculty ratio 16:1. 30 full-time faculty.

ACADEMICS

Degrees: Associate, bachelor's, certificate, master's, post-bachelor's certificate. **Special Study Options:** Distance learning, double major, English as a Second Language (ESL), independent study, internships, study abroad. **Career services:** Alumni services, career assessment.

FACILITIES

Housing: Coed dorms, special housing for disabled students, suite, corridor, singles, smoke-free, over 21 yrs, over 24 yrs, wellness living, quiet study, same curriculum housing, baccalaureate, single room options, and computer life style, new upperclassmen apartment suite complex. **Computers:** Students can register for classes online.

CAMPUS LIFE

Environment: Rural. **Activities:** Choral groups, concert band, drama/theater, jazz band, literary magazine, music ensembles, musical theater, radio station, student government, student newspaper, symphony orchestra, yearbook. **Athletics (Intercollegiate):** *Men:* Basketball, ice hockey, volleyball. *Women:* Basketball, volleyball.

ADMISSIONS

Transfer Admission Requirements: High school transcript, college transcript(s), essay or personal statement. **General Admission Information:** Nonfall registration accepted.

COSTS AND FINANCIAL AID

Room and board $2,000. Required fees $150. Average book expense $500.

BRIGHAM YOUNG UNIVERSITY (UT)

A-153 ASB, Provo, UT 84602-1110
Phone: 801-422-2507 **Financial Aid Phone:** 801-378-4104
E-mail: admissions@byu.edu **CEEB Code:** 4019
Fax: 801-422-0005 **Website:** www.byu.edu **ACT Code:** 4266

This private school, affiliated with the Church of Jesus Christ of Latt Church, was founded in 1875. It has a 557-acre campus.

RATINGS

Admissions Selectivity Rating: 92   **Fire Safety Rating:** 62   **Green Rating:** 60*

STUDENTS AND FACULTY

Enrollment: 30,745. **Student Body:** 49% female, 51% male, 70% out-of-state, 3% international (121 countries represented). Asian 4%, Caucasian 87%, Hispanic 4%.
Retention and Graduation: 84% freshmen return for sophomore year. 30% freshmen graduate within 4 years. **Faculty:** Student/faculty ratio 21:1. 1286 full-time faculty, 86% hold PhDs, 5% are members of minority groups, 21% are women.

ACADEMICS

Degrees: Bachelor's, master's. **Classes:** Most classes have 10–19 students. **Majors with Highest Enrollment:** Business/commerce; elementary education and teaching; exercise physiology. **Special Study Options:** Accelerated program, cooperative education program, cross-registration, distance learning, double major, English as a Second Language (ESL), external degree program, honors program, independent study, internships, liberal arts/career combination, study abroad, teacher certification program. **Honors programs:** The Honors Program, participation in which is open to all BYU students, complements the university's expansive educational agenda by providing the benefits of a small liberal arts learning community. These benefits include offering small classes with high-quality teaching and learning that challenge students to reach their highest potential; fostering a spirit of ongoing inquiry that includes undergraduate research in a mentored environment; and underscoring the importance of combining personal excellence, faithful discipleship, and meaningful service. **Combined degree programs:** BA/JD, BA/MA, BA/Macc, BS/MS. Special programs offered to physically disabled students include note-taking services, reader services, tape recorders, tutors.

FACILITIES

Housing: Special housing for disabled students, men's dorms, women's dorms, apartments for married students, apartments for single students, Language houses are available. 97% of campus accessible to physically disabled. **Special Academic Facilities/Equipment:** Art, peoples/cultures, life science, and earth science museums, film studio, on-campus nursery school, language research center, seismography equipment, electron microscope. **Computers:** 10% of classrooms, 100% of libraries, 100% of dining areas, 100% of student union, have wireless network access. Students can register for classes online. Administrative functions (other than registration) can be performed online.

CAMPUS LIFE

Environment: City. **Activities:** Choral groups, concert band, dance, drama/theater, jazz band, literary magazine, marching band, music ensembles, musical theater, opera, pep band, radio station, student government, student newspaper, student-run film society, symphony orchestra, television station. **Organizations:** 390 registered organizations, 22 honor societies, 25 religious organizations. **Athletics (Intercollegiate):** *Men:* Baseball, basketball, cheerleading, cross-country, diving, football, golf, swimming, tennis, track/field (outdoor), track/field (indoor), volleyball. *Women:* Basketball, cheerleading, cross-country, diving, golf, gymnastics, soccer, softball, swimming, tennis, track/field (outdoor), track/field (indoor), volleyball. **On-Campus Highlights:** Monte L. Bean Life Science Museum, The Museum of Art, Gordon B. Hinckley Alumni & Visitors Cen, Harold B. Lee Library, Wilkinson Student Center, Some of the popular places on campus are the HFAC theatres and music halls, the Creamery on 9th, and the Marriott Center (where weekly devotionals and forums as well as sports events are held). Campus highlights also include BYU's new Student Athlete Building houses the impressive Legacy Hall (BYU sports Hall of Fame) and the popular Legends Grille, the very large (athletic teams') Indoor Practice Facility is completed, the newly remodeled Brimhall Building is housing the Communications Department, and the new Joseph F. Smith Building (which replaced the Smith Family Living Center) has been completed and now houses the College of Family, Home and Social Sciences.

ADMISSIONS

Freshman Academic Profile: Average high school GPA 3.8. 51% in top 10% of high school class, 83% in top 25% of high school class, 98% in top 50% of high school class. SAT Math middle 50% range 570–680. SAT Critical Reading middle 50% range 550–670. ACT middle 50% range 25–30. Minimum paper TOEFL 500. Minimum computer TOEFL 173. **Basis for Candidate Selection:** *Very important factors considered include:* Academic GPA, rigor of secondary school record, standardized test scores, character/personal qualities, interview, religious affiliation/commitment. *Important factors considered include:* Application essay, recommendation(s), extracurricular activities, racial/ethnic status, volunteer work. *Other factors considered include:* First generation, talent/ability, work experience. **Freshman Admission Requirements:** High school diploma is required and GED is accepted. *Academic units required:* 4 English, 3 mathematics, 2 science, (2 science labs), 2 foreign language, 2 history, 2 literature or writing. *Academic units recommended:* 4 English, 4 mathematics, 3 science, (3 science labs), 4 foreign language. **Freshman Admission Statistics:** 10,081 applied, 69% admitted, 78% enrolled. **Transfer Admission Requirements:** College transcript(s), essay or personal statement, minimum college GPA of 3.0 required. Lowest grade transferable C–. **General Admission Information:** Application fee $30. Regular application deadline

2/1. Nonfall registration accepted. Admission may be deferred for a maximum of 2 years. Credit and/or placement offered for CEEB Advanced Placement tests.

COSTS AND FINANCIAL AID
Annual tuition $4,420. **Required Forms and Deadlines:** FAFSA, Institutional Application for Financial Aid. Priority financial aid filing date 4/15. **Notification of Awards:** Applicants will be notified of awards on a rolling basis beginning 5/1. **Types of Aid:** *Need-based scholarships/grants:* Federal Pell, state scholarships/grants, private scholarships, the school's own gift aid. *Loans:* FFEL Subsidized Stafford, FFEL Unsubsidized Stafford, FFEL PLUS. **Student Employment: Financial Aid Statistics:** 12% freshmen, 29% undergrads receive need-based scholarship or grant aid. 13% freshmen, 16% undergrads receive non-need-based scholarship or grant aid. 6% freshmen, 15% undergrads receive need-based self-help aid. 3% freshmen, 2% undergrads receive athletic scholarships. 53% freshmen, 64% undergrads receive any aid. 24% undergrads borrow to pay for school. Average cumulative indebtedness $10,730. **Criteria for awarding institutional aid:** *Non-need-based:* Academics, art, athletics, leadership, minority status, music/drama, religious affiliation, state/district residency.

BRIGHAM YOUNG UNIVERSITY—HAWAII

BYU- Hawaii # 1973, 55—220 Kulanui, Laie, HI 96762
Phone: 808-675- 3738 **Financial Aid Phone:** 808-293-3530
E-mail: admissions@byuh.edu **CEEB Code:** 4106
Fax: 808-675-3741 **ACT Code:** 899

This private school, affiliated with the Church of Jesus Christ of Latter-day Saints, was founded in 1955. It has a 60-acre campus.

RATINGS
Admissions Selectivity Rating: 85　　**Fire Safety Rating:** 60*　　**Green Rating:** 60*

STUDENTS AND FACULTY
Enrollment: 2,312. **Student Body:** 56% female, 44% male, 68% out-of-state, 44% international (67 countries represented). Asian 22%, African American 1%, Caucasian 29%, Hispanic 2%, Native American 1%.
Retention and Graduation: 57% freshmen return for sophomore year. 25% freshmen graduate within 4 years. **Faculty:** Student/faculty ratio 14:1. 122 full-time faculty, 80% hold PhDs, 23% are members of minority groups, 21% are women.

ACADEMICS
Degrees: Bachelor's. **Classes:** Most classes have 10–19 students. Most lab/discussion sessions have 10–19 students. **Majors with Highest Enrollment:** Information science/studies; intercultural/multicultural and diversity studies; international business/trade/commerce. **Special Study Options:** Accelerated program, cooperative education program, distance learning, English as a Second Language (ESL), exchange student program (domestic), honors program, independent study, internships, student-designed major, teacher certification program. **Honors programs:** The University Honors Program is open to all interested students who feel they are capable of accepting the challenge of an Honors Education. You will have the opportunity to participate in a stimulating class environment with other top students and the best professors. Special programs offered to physically disabled students include note-taking services, reader services, tape recorders, tutors.

FACILITIES
Housing: Men's dorms, women's dorms, apartments for married students 90% of campus accessible to physically disabled. **Special Academic Facilities/Equipment:** Museum of Natural History Media Lab. **Computers:** 100% of classrooms, 100% of libraries, 100% of dining areas, 100% of student union, 100% of common outdoor areas have wireless network access. Students can register for classes online. Administrative functions (other than registration) can be performed online.

CAMPUS LIFE
Environment: Village. **Activities:** Choral groups, concert band, dance, jazz band, literary magazine, music ensembles, pep band, student government, student newspaper, student-run film society. **Organizations:** 52 registered organizations, 3 honor societies. **Athletics (Intercollegiate):** *Men:* Basketball, cross-country, golf, soccer, tennis. *Women:* Basketball, cross-country, soccer, softball, tennis, volleyball. **On-Campus Highlights:** Joseph F. Smith Library, Cannon Activities Center, The Club Cafe, The Seasider Snackbar, Aloha Center.

ADMISSIONS
Freshman Academic Profile: Average high school GPA 3.42. SAT Math middle 50% range 480–600. SAT Critical Reading middle 50% range 460–580. ACT middle 50% range 20–27. Minimum paper TOEFL 475. Minimum com-

puter TOEFL 153. **Basis for Candidate Selection:** *Very important factors considered include:* Application essay, recommendation(s), rigor of secondary school record, standardized test scores, character/personal qualities, extracurricular activities, geographical residence, interview, religious affiliation/commitment. *Important factors considered include:* Class rank, alumni/ae relation, talent/ability, volunteer work, work experience. *Other factors considered include:* State residency. **Freshman Admission Requirements:** High school diploma is required and GED is not accepted. *Academic units recommended:* 4 English, 2 mathematics, 2 science, (2 science labs), 2 foreign language, 2 history. **Freshman Admission Statistics:** 1,268 applied, 48% admitted, 49% enrolled. **Transfer Admission Requirements:** College transcript(s), essay or personal statement, statement of good standing from prior institution(s). Minimum college GPA of 3.0 required. Lowest grade transferable C–. **General Admission Information:** Application fee $30. Regular application deadline 2/15. Regular notification 4/1. Nonfall registration accepted. Admission may be deferred for a maximum of 1 semester. Credit offered for CEEB Advanced Placement tests.

COSTS AND FINANCIAL AID
Annual tuition $3,600. Room and board $5,568. Average book expense $900. **Required Forms and Deadlines:** FAFSA, institution's own financial aid form. Financial aid filing deadline 3/31. Priority financial aid filing date 3/1. **Notification of Awards:** Applicants will be notified of awards on or about 6/30. **Types of Aid:** *Need-based scholarships/grants:* Federal Pell, private scholarships, the school's own gift aid. *Loans:* FFEL Subsidized Stafford, FFEL Unsubsidized Stafford, FFEL PLUS, college/university loans from institutional funds. **Student Employment:** Institutional employment available. Highest amount earned per year from on-campus jobs $4,500. Off-campus job opportunities are fair. **Financial Aid Statistics:** 71% freshmen, 62% undergrads receive need-based scholarship or grant aid. 19% freshmen, 40% undergrads receive non-need-based scholarship or grant aid. 57% freshmen, 40% undergrads receive need-based self-help aid. 13% freshmen, 7% undergrads receive athletic scholarships. 70% freshmen, 72% undergrads receive any aid. 36% undergrads borrow to pay for school. Average cumulative indebtedness $12,418. **Criteria for awarding institutional aid:** *Non-need-based:* Academics, art, athletics, leadership, music/drama, state/district residency.

BROCK UNIVERSITY

500 Glenridge Avenue, St. Catharines, ON L2S 3A1 Canada
Phone: 905-688-5550 **Financial Aid Phone:**
E-mail: admissns@brocku.ca
Fax: 905-988-5488 **Website:** www.brocku.ca

This public school was founded in 1964. It has a 457-acre campus.

RATINGS
Admissions Selectivity Rating: 60*　　**Fire Safety Rating:** 60*　　**Green Rating:** 60*

STUDENTS AND FACULTY
Student Body: 8% out-of-state, international (80 countries represented). **Retention and Graduation:** 52% freshmen graduate within 4 years. **Faculty:** Student/faculty ratio 27:1. 577 full-time faculty, 43% are women.

ACADEMICS
Degrees: Bachelor's, certificate, master's. **Majors with Highest Enrollment:** Business/commerce; education; health professions and related clinical sciences, other. **Special Study Options:** Cooperative education program, double major, English as a Second Language (ESL), exchange student program (domestic), honors program, internships, liberal arts/career combination, student-designed major, study abroad, teacher certification program. Liberal arts/career combination: Students may choose from 7 Concurrent Education programs, combining their undergraduate degree and Bachelor of Education degree. **Combined degree programs:** BA/BEd; BSc/BEd; BPHEd/BEd. Special programs offered to physically disabled students include note-taking services, reader services, tape recorders, tutors. **Career services:** Career/job search classes, internships. Career services highlights include: Brock offers the third largest selection of co-op programs in Ontario. A variety of additional experiential learning opportunities are built into virtually all of our programs.

FACILITIES
Housing: Coed dorms, special housing for disabled students, women's dorms, Village Residence and Quarry View Residence (townhouses). 100% of campus accessible to physically disabled. **Special Academic Facilities/Equipment:** Cool Climate Oenology and Viticulture Institute Map Library, Intructional Resource Centre, Rodman Hall Arts Centre, Cypriote Museum. **Computers:** 100% of classrooms, 100% of libraries, 100% of student union, have wireless network access. Students can register for classes online. Administrative functions (other than registration) can be performed online.

CAMPUS LIFE

Environment: City. **Activities:** Choral groups, concert band, dance, drama/theater, literary magazine, music ensembles, musical theater, radio station, student government, student newspaper, student-run film society, symphony orchestra, television station, yearbook, campus ministries. **Organizations:** 40 registered organizations, 6 religious organizations. **Athletics (Intercollegiate):** *Men:* Baseball, basketball, cheerleading, crew/rowing, cross-country, curling, fencing, ice hockey, lacrosse, rugby, soccer, squash, swimming, wrestling. *Women:* Basketball, cheerleading, crew/rowing, cross-country, curling, fencing, ice hockey, rugby, soccer, swimming, volleyball, wrestling. **On-Campus Highlights:** Residences, Walker Complex—athletic facility, Computer Commons, Isaacs, Plaza Building. **Environmental Initiatives:** Our newest building earned LEED Silver certification. The energy cost performance is almost 43 per cent better than the Model National Energy Code. Brock's campus has been designated as a UNESCO Biosphere Reserve.

ADMISSIONS

Freshman Academic Profile: Minimum computer TOEFL 237. Minimum web-based TOEFL 88. **Basis for Candidate Selection:** *Very important factors considered include:* Academic GPA, rigor of secondary school record. *Important factors considered include:* Standardized test scores. *Other factors considered include:* Class rank, recommendation(s), talent/ability. **Freshman Admission Requirements:** High school diploma is required and GED is accepted. **Freshman Admission Statistics: Transfer Admission Requirements:** High school transcript, college transcript(s). **General Admission Information:** Application fee $155. Regular application deadline 4/1. Notification on a rolling basis, beginning on or about 1/1. Nonfall registration not accepted. Neither credit nor placement offered for CEEB Advanced Placement tests.

COSTS AND FINANCIAL AID

Annual in-state tuition $4,852. Room and board $8,215. Average book expense $900. **Required Forms and Deadlines:** Institution's own financial aid form, Ontario Student Assistance Program. **Types of Aid:** *Need-based scholarships/grants:* The school's own gift aid. *Loans:* Ontario Student Assistance Program. **Student Employment:** Federal Work-Study Program available. Institutional employment available. Off-campus job opportunities are good. **Financial Aid Statistics:** 12% undergrads receive need-based scholarship or grant aid. 39% undergrads receive any aid. **Criteria for awarding institutional aid:** *Non-need-based:* Academics, athletics, leadership.

BROWN UNIVERSITY

Box 1876, 45 Prospect St, Providence, RI 02912
Phone: 401-863-2378 **Financial Aid Phone:** 401-863-2721
E-mail: admission_undergraduate@brown.edu **CEEB Code:** 3094
Fax: 401-863-9300 **Website:** www.brown.edu **ACT Code:** 3800

This private school was founded in 1764. It has a 146-acre campus.

RATINGS

Admissions Selectivity Rating: 99   **Fire Safety Rating:** 86   **Green Rating:** 91

STUDENTS AND FACULTY

Enrollment: 6,013. **Student Body:** 52% female, 48% male, 95% out-of-state, 9% international (106 countries represented). Asian 16%, African American 7%, Caucasian 44%, Hispanic 9%, Native American 1%.
Retention and Graduation: 97% freshmen return for sophomore year. 86% freshmen graduate within 4 years. 35% grads go on to further study within 1 year. 10% grads pursue arts and sciences degrees. 10% grads pursue law degrees. 1% grads pursue business degrees. 9% grads pursue medical degrees.
Faculty: Student/faculty ratio 8:1. 787 full-time faculty, 95% hold PhDs, 16% are members of minority groups, 36% are women.

ACADEMICS

Degrees: Bachelor's, master's. **Classes:** Most classes have 10–19 students.
Majors with Highest Enrollment: Biology/biological sciences; economics; international relations and affairs. **Special Study Options:** Cross-registration, double major, exchange student program (domestic), honors program, independent study, internships, student-designed major, study abroad, teacher certification program, 8-year medical program (AB or SCB plus MD) 5-year degree program (AB and SCB). **Combined degree programs:** BA/MD, BA/MA, BS/MD, BS/MS, BA/BS. Special programs offered to physically

disabled students include note-taking services, reader services, tape recorders, tutors. **Career services:** Alumni network, career/job search classes, career assessment, internships, regional alumni. **Career services highlights include:** Each year, hundreds of brown students receive funding to pursue independent research, internships, projects, or faculty collaborations to deepen and connect their learning and experience. The Brown Internship Award Program provides funding on a competitive basis for students pursuing unpaid or low-paying summer internships. The program has two components, a living stipend and, for students on financial aid, the opportunity to have their summer earnings requirement waived. The Royce Fellowship is one of several Brown fellowships which invite proposals for summer projects of students' own design. They Royce provides not only a financial award for research projects but ongoing seminars and programs for fellows in the academic year following their award. Each of the fellowships has a particular focus: research, international service, social entrepreneurship, public interest law, sports and human rights, etc. The Undergraduate Teaching and Research Award supports nearly 300 students each year to collaborate with a Brown faculty member on course development or research. More information on these programs can be found at www.brown.edu/Administration/Dean_of_the_College/fellowships/.

FACILITIES

Housing: Coed dorms, special housing for disabled students, fraternity/sorority housing, cooperative housing, apartments for single students, wellness housing, theme housing. **Special Academic Facilities/Equipment:** Art gallery, anthropology museum, language lab, information technology center, NASA research center, center for modern culture/media. **Computers:** 50% of classrooms, 100% of dorms, 100% of libraries, 100% of dining areas, 100% of student union, 50% of common outdoor areas have wireless network access. Students can register for classes online. Administrative functions (other than registration) can be performed online.

CAMPUS LIFE

Environment: City. **Activities:** Choral groups, concert band, dance, drama/theater, jazz band, literary magazine, marching band, music ensembles, musical theater, opera, pep band, radio station, student government, student newspaper, student-run film society, symphony orchestra, television station, yearbook, campus ministries, international student organization, Model UN. **Organizations:** 400 registered organizations, 3 honor societies, 20 religious organizations. 8 fraternities, 2 sororities. **Athletics (Intercollegiate):** *Men:* Baseball, basketball, crew/rowing, cross-country, diving, fencing, football, golf, ice hockey, lacrosse, soccer, squash, swimming, tennis, track/field (outdoor), track/field (indoor), water polo, wrestling. *Women:* Basketball, crew/rowing, cross-country, diving, equestrian sports, fencing, field hockey, golf, gymnastics, ice hockey, lacrosse, skiing (downhill/alpine), soccer, softball, squash, swimming, tennis, track/field (outdoor), track/field (indoor), volleyball. **On-Campus Highlights:** The College Green, Bell Gallery, Libraries—Jon Hay, John Carter Brown, Watson Institute, Lyman Hall & Dill Center. **Environmental Initiatives:** Reduce GHG emissions to 42% (15% below 1990) below 2007 for existing buildings by 2020. Reduce GHG emissions for all newly constructed facilities between 25% and 50% below code requirements. Reduce GHG emissions for all newly acquired facilities by a minimum of 15% and as much as 30%.

ADMISSIONS

Freshman Academic Profile: 92% in top 10% of high school class, 99% in top 25% of high school class, 100% in top 50% of high school class. 56% from public high schools. SAT Math middle 50% range 670–770. SAT Critical Reading middle 50% range 650–760. SAT Writing middle 50% range 670–770. ACT middle 50% range 29–34. Minimum paper TOEFL 600. Minimum computer TOEFL 250. Minimum web-based TOEFL 100. **Basis for Candidate Selection:** *Very important factors considered include:* Rigor of secondary school record, character/personal qualities, level of applicant's interest, talent/ability. *Important factors considered include:* Class rank, application essay, academic GPA, recommendation(s), standardized test scores, extracurricular activities. *Other factors considered include:* Alumni/ae relation, first generation, geographical residence, interview, racial/ethnic status, state residency, volunteer work, work experience. **Freshman Admission Requirements:** High school diploma is required and GED is not accepted. *Academic units required:* 4 English, 3 mathematics, 3 science, (2 science labs), 3 foreign language, 2 history, 1 academic electives. *Academic units recommended:* 4 English, 4 mathematics, 4 science, (3 science labs), 4 foreign language, 2 history, 1 visual/performing arts, 1 academic electives. **Freshman Admission Statistics:** 24,988 applied, 11% admitted, 54% enrolled. **Transfer Admission Requirements:** High school transcript, college transcript(s), essay or personal statement, standardized test scores, statement of good standing from prior institution(s). Lowest grade transferable C. **General Admission Information:** Application fee $75. Early decision application deadline 11/1. Regular application deadline 1/1. Regular notification 4/1. Nonfall registration not accepted. Admission may be deferred for a maximum of 1 year. Placement offered for CEEB Advanced Placement tests.

COSTS AND FINANCIAL AID

Required Forms and Deadlines: FAFSA, CSS/Financial Aid PROFILE, noncustodial PROFILE. Financial aid filing deadline 2/1. **Notification of**

Awards: Applicants will be notified of awards on or about 4/1. **Types of Aid:** *Need-based scholarships/grants:* Federal Pell, SEOG, state scholarships/grants, private scholarships, the school's own gift aid. *Loans:* Direct Subsidized Stafford, Direct Unsubsidized Stafford, Direct PLUS, Federal Perkins, college/university loans from institutional funds. **Student Employment:** Federal Work-Study Program available. Institutional employment available. Off-campus job opportunities are excellent. **Financial Aid Statistics:** 41% freshmen, 40% undergrads receive need-based scholarship or grant aid. 35% freshmen, 39% undergrads receive need-based self-help aid. 39% freshmen, 42% undergrads receive any aid. 41% undergrads borrow to pay for school. Average cumulative indebtedness $21,858.

BRYAN COLLEGE

The Office of Admissions, Bryan College, Dayton, TN 37321
Phone: 800 277-9522 **Financial Aid Phone:** 423-775-7339
E-mail: admissions@bryan.edu **CEEB Code:** 001908
Fax: 423-775-7199 **Website:** www.bryan.edu **ACT Code:** 4038

This private school was founded in 1930. It has a 125-acre campus.

RATINGS
Admissions Selectivity Rating: 79   **Fire Safety Rating:** 60*   **Green Rating:** 60*

STUDENTS AND FACULTY
Enrollment: 1,011. **Student Body:** 54% female, 46% male, 46% out-of-state, 2% international. Asian 1%, African American 5%, Caucasian 90%, Hispanic 2%.
Retention and Graduation: 74% freshmen return for sophomore year. 45% freshmen graduate within 4 years. **Faculty:** Student/faculty ratio 17:1. 43 full-time faculty, 79% hold PhDs, 19% are women.

ACADEMICS
Degrees: Associate, bachelor's, master's. **Classes:** Most classes have 10–19 students. **Majors with Highest Enrollment:** Business administration and management; communication studies/speech communication and rhetoric; English language and literature. **Special Study Options:** Distance learning, dual enrollment, honors program, independent study, internships, study abroad. Special programs offered to physically disabled students include note-taking services, reader services, tape recorders, tutors. **Career services:** Alumni network, alumni services, career/job search classes, career assessment, internships.

FACILITIES
Housing: Men's dorms, women's dorms, apartments for married students, apartments for single students. **Special Academic Facilities/Equipment:** Willard Henning Natural History Museum. **Computers:** 100% of classrooms, 100% of dorms, 100% of libraries, 100% of dining areas, 100% of student union, 80% of common outdoor areas have wireless network access. Administrative functions (other than registration) can be performed online.

CAMPUS LIFE
Environment: Town. **Activities:** Choral groups, drama/theater, musical theater, radio station, student government, student newspaper, yearbook, campus ministries. **Athletics (Intercollegiate):** *Men:* Baseball, basketball, cross-country, golf, soccer, track/field (outdoor), track/field (indoor). *Women:* Basketball, cross-country, golf, soccer, softball, track/field (outdoor), track/field (indoor). **On-Campus Highlights:** Student Center, Library, The "Grassy Bowl," The Commons.

ADMISSIONS
Freshman Academic Profile: Average high school GPA 3.62. 31% from public high schools. SAT Math middle 50% range 480–610. SAT Critical Reading middle 50% range 520–660. SAT Writing middle 50% range 480–620. ACT middle 50% range 20–28. **Basis for Candidate Selection:** *Very important factors considered include:* Application essay, academic GPA, rigor of secondary school record, standardized test scores. *Important factors considered include:* Character/personal qualities, level of applicant's interest, religious affiliation/commitment. *Other factors considered include:* Class rank, recommendation(s), alumni/ae relation, extracurricular activities, interview, talent/ability, volunteer work. **Freshman Admission Requirements:** High school diploma is required and GED is accepted. *Academic units required:* 4 English, 3 mathematics, 3 science, 2 foreign language, 3 social studies. *Academic units recommended:* 4 English, 3 mathematics, 3 science, 2 foreign language, 3 social studies. **Freshman Admission Statistics:** 462 applied, 75% admitted, 55% enrolled. **Transfer Admission Requirements:** College transcript(s), essay or personal statement, standardized test scores, minimum college GPA of 2.75 required. Lowest grade transferable C. **General Admission Information:** Application fee $35. Non-fall registration accepted. Credit offered for CEEB Advanced Placement tests.

COSTS AND FINANCIAL AID
Average book expense $1,200. **Required Forms and Deadlines:** FAFSA. Priority financial aid filing date 2/15. **Notification of Awards:** Applicants will be notified of awards on a rolling basis beginning 2/15. **Types of Aid:** *Need-based scholarships/grants:* Federal Pell, SEOG, state scholarships/grants, private scholarships, the school's own gift aid. *Loans:* Direct Subsidized Stafford, Direct Unsubsidized Stafford, Direct PLUS, FFEL Subsidized Stafford, FFEL Unsubsidized Stafford, FFEL PLUS, Federal Perkins, college/university loans from institutional funds. **Student Employment:** Federal Work-Study Program available. Institutional employment available. Off-campus job opportunities are fair. **Financial Aid Statistics:** 74% freshmen, 66% undergrads receive need-based scholarship or grant aid. 43% freshmen, 26% undergrads receive non-need-based scholarship or grant aid. 55% freshmen, 56% undergrads receive need-based self-help aid. 7% freshmen, 5% undergrads receive athletic scholarships. 79% freshmen, 75% undergrads receive any aid. 74% undergrads borrow to pay for school. Average cumulative indebtedness $14,976. **Criteria for awarding institutional aid:** *Non-need-based:* Academics, alumni affiliation, athletics, leadership, minority status, music/drama, state/district residency.

BRYANT UNIVERSITY

1150 Douglas Pike Ste 3, Smithfield, RI 02917-1285
Phone: 401-232-6100 **Financial Aid Phone:** 401-232-6020
E-mail: admission@bryant.edu **CEEB Code:** 3095
Fax: 401-232-6741 **Website:** www.bryant.edu **ACT Code:** 3802

This private school was founded in 1863. It has a 420-acre campus.

RATINGS
Admissions Selectivity Rating: 88   **Fire Safety Rating:** 89   **Green Rating:** 77

STUDENTS AND FACULTY
Enrollment: 3,367. **Student Body:** 43% female, 57% male, 84% out-of-state, 5% international (51 countries represented). Asian 3%, African American 4%, Caucasian 82%, Hispanic 4%.
Retention and Graduation: 87% freshmen return for sophomore year. 72% freshmen graduate within 4 years. 6% grads go on to further study within 1 year. 4% grads pursue business degrees. **Faculty:** Student/faculty ratio 18:1. 158 full-time faculty, 85% hold PhDs, 10% are members of minority groups, 38% are women.

ACADEMICS
Degrees: Bachelor's, master's. **Classes:** Most classes have 30–39 students. Most lab/discussion sessions have fewer than 10 students. **Majors with Highest Enrollment:** Accounting; finance; marketing/marketing management. **Special Study Options:** double major, English as a Second Language (ESL), honors program, independent study, internships, study abroad. **Honors programs:** The Bryant University Honors Program offers its members a personalized, distinctive experience that enriches their academic, social, cultural and professional talents in a mentor-oriented environment. The Program offers its members a different experience to develop the unique talents of exceptionally prepared and focused individuals. Designated courses in the Honors Program are organized to encourage in-depth classroom discussions and application of business and liberal arts disciplines with reduced class sizes. Special programs offered to physically disabled students include note-taking services, tape recorders, tutors. **Career services:** Alumni network, alumni services, career/job search classes, career assessment, internships, regional alumni. Career services highlights include: In 2008, 343 companies participated in the Corporate Recruiting Program.

FACILITIES
Housing: Coed dorms, special housing for disabled students, women's dorms, apartments for single students, Honors, International Business. 90% of campus accessible to physically disabled. **Special Academic Facilities/Equipment:** George E. Bello Center for Information and Technology, Koffler Technology Center and Communications Complex, John H. Chafee Center for International Business, Koffler Television Studio, C.V. Starr Financial Markets Center, Learning and Language Lab. **Computers:** 100% of classrooms, 100% of dorms, 100% of libraries, 100% of dining areas, 100% of student union, 100% of common outdoor areas have wireless network access. Students can register for classes online. Administrative functions (other than registration) can be performed online. Undergraduates are required to own a computer.

CAMPUS LIFE

Environment: Village. **Activities:** Choral groups, dance, drama/theater, jazz band, literary magazine, music ensembles, musical theater, pep band, radio station, student government, student newspaper, television station, yearbook, campus ministries, international student organization. **Organizations:** 87 registered organizations, 6 honor societies, 5 religious organizations. 6 fraternities, 2 sororities. **Athletics (Intercollegiate):** *Men:* Baseball, basketball, cross-country, football, golf, lacrosse, soccer, swimming, tennis, track/field (outdoor), track/field (indoor). *Women:* Basketball, cross-country, field hockey, lacrosse, soccer, softball, swimming, tennis, track/field (outdoor), track/field (indoor), volleyball. **On-Campus Highlights:** Bello Center for Information and Technology, Chase Athletics and Wellness Center, Unistructure Rotunda, Koffler Technology and Communications Co, Bryant Center, The Bello Center for Information & Technology houses the Douglas & Judith Krupp Library, the Stepan Grand Hall, and the C.V. Starr Financial Markets Center (FMC) featuring real-time stock market data and Reuters 3000. The Wellness Center features a fitness center modeled after private health clubs and a six-lane, 25-yard swimming pool. The Bryant Center houses offices for student organizations around campus including The Archway, the student newspaper, as well as dining options including Subway, South Side Deli, the Scoop, South Cafe, and the Sky Ranch Grill. The Rotunda is a hub of student activity located in the main classroom building, the Unistructure. The Communication Complex houses the all-digital television studio and radio station, WJMF, as well as advanced multimedia editing rooms for use with AVID software. WJMF streams live over the Internet and offers podcasts on its website, www.wjmf887.com. **Environmental Initiatives:** Recycling program, purchasing renewable energy credits, environmental studies major.

ADMISSIONS

Freshman Academic Profile: Average high school GPA 3.35. 25% in top 10% of high school class, 58% in top 25% of high school class, 93% in top 50% of high school class. SAT Math middle 50% range 550–630. SAT Critical Reading middle 50% range 510–590. SAT Writing middle 50% range 510–600. ACT middle 50% range 23–26.5. Minimum paper TOEFL 550. Minimum computer TOEFL 213. Minimum web-based TOEFL 80. **Basis for Candidate Selection:** *Very important factors considered include:* Academic GPA, rigor of secondary school record. *Important factors considered include:* Class rank, application essay, recommendation(s), standardized test scores. *Other factors considered include:* Alumni/ae relation, character/personal qualities, extracurricular activities, first generation, geographical residence, interview, level of applicant's interest, racial/ethnic status, state residency, talent/ability, volunteer work, work experience. **Freshman Admission Requirements:** High school diploma is required and GED is accepted. *Academic units required:* 4 English, 4 mathematics, 2 science, (2 science labs), 2 foreign language, 2 history. *Academic units recommended:* 4 English, 4 mathematics, 3 science, (2 science labs), 3 foreign language, 3 history. **Freshman Admission Statistics:** 5,393 applied, 53% admitted, 26% enrolled. **Transfer Admission Requirements:** High school transcript, college transcript(s), essay or personal statement, minimum college GPA of 2.5 required. Lowest grade transferable C. **General Admission Information:** Application fee $50. Early decision application deadline 11/16. Regular application deadline 2/1. Regular notification 3/21. Nonfall registration accepted. Admission may be deferred for a maximum of 1 year. Credit and/or placement offered for CEEB Advanced Placement tests.

COSTS AND FINANCIAL AID

Annual tuition $31,974. Room and board $11,757. Required fees $300. Average book expense $1,200. **Required Forms and Deadlines:** FAFSA. Financial aid filing deadline 2/15. Priority financial aid filing date 2/15. **Notification of Awards:** Applicants will be notified of awards on or about 3/24. **Types of Aid:** *Need-based scholarships/grants:* Federal Pell, SEOG, state scholarships/grants, private scholarships, the school's own gift aid. *Loans:* Direct Subsidized Stafford, Direct Unsubsidized Stafford, FFEL PLUS, Federal Perkins, privately funded education loans. **Student Employment:** Federal Work-Study Program available. Institutional employment available. Highest amount earned per year from on-campus jobs $7,378. Off-campus job opportunities are fair. **Financial Aid Statistics:** 49% freshmen, 57% undergrads receive need-based scholarship or grant aid. 66% freshmen, 38% undergrads receive non-need-based scholarship or grant aid. 56% freshmen, 60% undergrads receive need-based self-help aid. 2% freshmen, 2% undergrads receive athletic scholarships. 81% freshmen, 79% undergrads receive any aid. 80% undergrads borrow to pay for school. Average cumulative indebtedness $34,268. **Criteria for awarding institutional aid:** *Non-need-based:* Academics, athletics, minority status.

See page 1036.

BRYN ATHYN COLLEGE OF THE NEW CHURCH

P.O. Box 462, Bryn Athyn, PA 19009
Phone: 267-502-6000 **Financial Aid Phone:** 267-502-2493
E-mail: admissions@brynathyn.edu **CEEB Code:** 2002
Fax: 267-502-2593 **Website:** www.brynathyn.edu **ACT Code:** 3228

This private school was founded in 1877. It has a 130-acre campus.

RATINGS

Admissions Selectivity Rating: 73   **Fire Safety Rating:** 68   **Green Rating:** 60*

STUDENTS AND FACULTY

Enrollment: 184. **Student Body:** 50% female, 50% male, 24% out-of-state, 22% international (15 countries represented). Asian 2%, African American 7%, Caucasian 72%.
Retention and Graduation: 74% freshmen return for sophomore year. 22% freshmen graduate within 4 years. **Faculty:** Student/faculty ratio 6:1. 24 full-time faculty, 58% hold PhDs, 46% are women.

ACADEMICS

Degrees: Associate, bachelor's, master's. **Classes:** Most classes have 10–19 students. **Majors with Highest Enrollment:** Elementary education and teaching; English language and literature; multi-/interdisciplinary studies, other. **Special Study Options:** Accelerated program, cooperative education program, cross-registration, distance learning, English as a Second Language (ESL), independent study, internships, student-designed major, study abroad, teacher certification program. Special programs offered to physically disabled students include tape recorders, tutors. **Career services:** Alumni network, internships. **Career services highlights include:** Internships at Bryn Athyn College are developed on an individual basis, and occur in places around the world. Opportunities can be arranged as early as the first year, founded on the belief that this applied learning can help new first-year students chart their academic programs of study.

FACILITIES

Housing: Men's dorms, women's dorms, on-campus cottages for upperclassmen. 65% of campus accessible to physically disabled. **Special Academic Facilities/Equipment:** Glencairn Museum Swedenborg Library Swedenborgiana Academy of the New Church Archives John Pitcairn Archives Raymond and Mildred Pitcairn Archives **Computers:** 100% of classrooms, 100% of dorms, 100% of libraries, 75% of common outdoor areas have wireless network access.

CAMPUS LIFE

Environment: Village. **Activities:** Choral groups, concert band, dance, drama/theater, music ensembles, student government, student newspaper, international student organization. **Organizations:** 15 registered organizations, **On-Campus Highlights:** College Grounds Cafe, Swedenborg Library, Brickman Center for Student Life, Asplundh Field House, Glencairn Museum. **Environmental Initiatives:** Chemical purchase, storage and disposal plan. LEED-certified construction. Recycling program for glass and paper in all buildings.

ADMISSIONS

Freshman Academic Profile: Average high school GPA 3.36. 61.4% from public high schools. SAT Math middle 50% range 470–600. SAT Critical Reading middle 50% range 490–630. SAT Writing middle 50% range 470–610. ACT middle 50% range 20–23. Minimum paper TOEFL 520. Minimum computer TOEFL 190. Minimum web-based TOEFL 70. **Basis for Candidate Selection:** *Very important factors considered include:* Application essay, academic GPA, recommendation(s), rigor of secondary school record, standardized test scores, level of applicant's interest. *Important factors considered include:* Character/personal qualities, religious affiliation/commitment, talent/ability. *Other factors considered include:* Class rank, alumni/ae relation, extracurricular activities, interview, volunteer work, work experience. **Freshman Admission Requirements:** High school diploma is required and GED is accepted. *Academic units required:* 4 English, 3 mathematics, 3 science, 2 foreign language, 3 social studies or history. **Freshman Admission Statistics:** 227 applied, 92% admitted, 34% enrolled. **Transfer Admission Requirements:** High school transcript, college transcript(s), essay or personal statement, minimum college GPA of 2.0 required. Lowest grade transferable C. **General Admission Information:** Regular application deadline 7/1. Notification on a rolling basis, beginning on or about 12/1. Nonfall registration accepted. Credit and/or placement offered for CEEB Advanced Placement tests.

COSTS AND FINANCIAL AID

Annual tuition $4,396. Room and board $5,281. Required fees $1,812. Average book expense $950. **Required Forms and Deadlines:** FAFSA, institution's own financial aid form, federal income tax forms (1040 or equivalent). Financial aid filing deadline 6/1. **Notification of Awards:** Applicants will be notified of awards on a rolling basis beginning 4/1. **Types of Aid:** *Need-based scholarships/*

grants: Federal Pell, SEOG, state scholarships/grants, private scholarships, the school's own gift aid. *Loans:* Direct Subsidized Stafford, Direct Unsubsidized Stafford, Direct PLUS, FFEL Subsidized Stafford, FFEL Unsubsidized Stafford, FFEL PLUS, college/university loans from institutional funds. **Student Employment:** Institutional employment available. Highest amount earned per year from on-campus jobs $13,780. Off-campus job opportunities are good. **Financial Aid Statistics:** 63% freshmen, 57% undergrads receive need-based scholarship or grant aid. 39% freshmen, 23% undergrads receive non-need-based scholarship or grant aid. 24% freshmen, 23% undergrads receive need-based self-help aid. 66% freshmen, 62% undergrads receive any aid. 57.1% undergrads borrow to pay for school. Average cumulative indebtedness $12,729. **Criteria for awarding institutional aid:** *Non-need-based:* Academics, leadership, religious affiliation.

See page 1038.

BRYN MAWR COLLEGE

101 North Merion Avenue, Bryn Mawr, PA 19010-2859
Phone: 610-526-5152 **Financial Aid Phone:** 610-526-5245
E-mail: admissions@brynmawr.edu **CEEB Code:** 2049
Fax: 610-526-7471 **Website:** www.brynmawr.edu **ACT Code:** 3526

This private school was founded in 1885. It has a 135-acre campus.

RATINGS
Admissions Selectivity Rating: 95   **Fire Safety Rating:** 71   **Green Rating:** 80

STUDENTS AND FACULTY
Enrollment: 1,274. **Student Body:** 100% female, 84% out-of-state, 7% international (46 countries represented). Asian 12%, African American 6%, Caucasian 46%, Hispanic 4%.
Retention and Graduation: 90% freshmen return for sophomore year. 81% freshmen graduate within 4 years. 29.5% grads go on to further study within 1 year. 18.7% grads pursue arts and sciences degrees. 5.1% grads pursue law degrees. 0.5% grads pursue business degrees. 2.6% grads pursue medical degrees. **Faculty:** Student/faculty ratio 8:1. 158 full-time faculty, 94% hold PhDs, 15% are members of minority groups, 49% are women.

ACADEMICS
Degrees: Bachelor's, master's, post-bachelor's certificate. **Classes:** Most classes have 10–19 students. **Majors with Highest Enrollment:** English language and literature; mathematics; psychology. **Special Study Options:** Accelerated program, cross-registration, double major, dual enrollment, exchange student program (domestic), independent study, internships, liberal arts/career combination, student-designed major, study abroad, teacher certification program, AB/MA City Planning 3-2 Program in City and Regional Planning offered with the University of Pennsylvania. AB/BS 3-2 engineering programs with Cal Tech. **Combined degree programs:** BA/MA, 3-2 progam in city planning w/U Penn. Special programs offered to physically disabled students include note-taking services, reader services, tape recorders, tutors. **Career services:** Alumni network, alumni services, career/job search classes, career assessment, internships, regional alumni. **Career services highlights include:** Praxis I for 3 hours per week, Praxis II for 6–8 hours per week and Praxis III as a supervised independent study involving 10–12 hours per week in the field. These are courses for full credit.

FACILITIES
Housing: Coed dorms, women's dorms, cooperative housing, apartments for single students, students may live at Haverford. Foreign language houses available to students studying Chinese, French, German, Hebrew, Italian, Russsian or Spanish. Coed housing is available. Special housing available for non-traditional-aged students. Co-ops, such as Vegan House, are available as well. **Special Academic Facilities/Equipment:** Museum of classical and Near Eastern archaeology, mineral collection, Child Study Institute, on-campus nursery school, Newfeld Collection of African Art, Language Learning Center. **Computers:** 60% of classrooms, 10% of dorms, 25% of libraries, 10% of dining areas, 100% of student union, 10% of common outdoor areas have wireless network access. Students can register for classes online. Administrative functions (other than registration) can be performed online.

CAMPUS LIFE
Environment: Metropolis. **Activities:** Choral groups, dance, drama/theater, jazz band, literary magazine, marching band, music ensembles, musical theater,

radio station, student government, student newspaper, student-run film society, yearbook. **Organizations:** 94 registered organizations, 10 religious organizations. **Athletics (Intercollegiate):** *Women:* Badminton, basketball, crew/rowing, cross-country, field hockey, lacrosse, soccer, swimming, tennis, track/field (outdoor), track/field (indoor), volleyball. **On-Campus Highlights:** Thomas Hall (on National Historic Landma, Erdman Hall (designed by famed architect, The Cloister and Great Hall, Taft Garden, Rhys Carpenter Library, Goodhart Theater. **Environmental Initiatives:** We have received two Pennsylvania Growing Greener Grants for watershed improvements under the Environmental improvement and Watershed Protection Act. We are committed to being good steward's of the waterway that pass through our campus. We currently removing all incandescent light bulbs from Campus. We are committed to reducing our consumption of electricity through the use of technology. All capital projects are required to be designed using the appropriate LEED checklist archiving a minimum of 26 points. We are committed to designing sustainability into the renovations of our buildings.

ADMISSIONS
Freshman Academic Profile: 65% in top 10% of high school class, 96% in top 25% of high school class, 99% in top 50% of high school class. 62% from public high schools. SAT Math middle 50% range 580–680. SAT Critical Reading middle 50% range 620–730. SAT Writing middle 50% range 620–710. ACT middle 50% range 27–31. Minimum paper TOEFL 600. Minimum computer TOEFL 250. Minimum web-based TOEFL 90. **Basis for Candidate Selection:** *Very important factors considered include:* Recommendation(s), rigor of secondary school record. *Important factors considered include:* Application essay, academic GPA, character/personal qualities, extracurricular activities. *Other factors considered include:* Class rank, standardized test scores, alumni/ae relation, first generation, geographical residence, interview, racial/ethnic status, talent/ability, volunteer work, work experience. **Freshman Admission Requirements:** High school diploma is required and GED is accepted. *Academic units required:* 2 academic electives. *Academic units recommended:* 4 English, 3 mathematics, 2 science, (1 science labs), 3 foreign language, 2 social studies, 2 history. **Freshman Admission Statistics:** 2,150 applied, 49% admitted, 35% enrolled. **Transfer Admission Requirements:** High school transcript, college transcript(s), essay or personal statement, standardized test scores, statement of good standing from prior institution(s). Lowest grade transferable C. **General Admission Information:** Application fee $50. Early decision application deadline 11/15. Regular application deadline 1/15. Regular notification 4/1. Nonfall registration not accepted. Admission may be deferred for a maximum of 1 year. Credit and/or placement offered for CEEB Advanced Placement tests.

COSTS AND FINANCIAL AID
Annual tuition $37,120. Room and board $12,000. Required fees $914. Average book expense $1,000. **Required Forms and Deadlines:** FAFSA, CSS/Financial Aid PROFILE, business/farm supplement. Statement of earnings from parents' employer. Financial aid filing deadline 3/1. Priority financial aid filing date 2/4. **Notification of Awards:** Applicants will be notified of awards on or about 3/23. **Types of Aid:** *Need-based scholarships/grants:* Federal Pell, SEOG, state scholarships/grants, the school's own gift aid, Federal Academic Competitiveness Grant (ACG), Federal National Science and Mathematics to Retain Talent Grant (SMART). *Loans:* FFEL Subsidized Stafford, FFEL Unsubsidized Stafford, FFEL PLUS, Federal Perkins. **Student Employment:** Highest amount earned per year from on-campus jobs $2,000. **Financial Aid Statistics:** 48% freshmen, 50% undergrads receive need-based scholarship or grant aid. 4% freshmen, 2% undergrads receive non-need-based scholarship or grant aid. 44% freshmen, 48% undergrads receive need-based self-help aid. 62% freshmen, 62% undergrads receive any aid. 54% undergrads borrow to pay for school. Average cumulative indebtedness $20,019. **Criteria for awarding institutional aid:** *Non-need-based:* Academics, leadership.

BUCKNELL UNIVERSITY

Freas Hall, Bucknell University, Lewisburg, PA 17837
Phone: 570-577-1101 **Financial Aid Phone:** 570-577-1331
E-mail: admissions@bucknell.edu **CEEB Code:** 2050
Fax: 570-577-3538 **Website:** www.bucknell.edu **ACT Code:** 3528

This private school was founded in 1846. It has a 446-acre campus.

RATINGS
Admissions Selectivity Rating: 96   **Fire Safety Rating:** 87   **Green Rating:** 83

STUDENTS AND FACULTY

Enrollment: 3,523. **Student Body:** 51% female, 49% male, 76% out-of-state, 3% international (52 countries represented). Asian 4%, African American 3%, Caucasian 82%, Hispanic 3%.

Retention and Graduation: 94% freshmen return for sophomore year. 88% freshmen graduate within 4 years. 24% grads go on to further study within 1 year. 9% grads pursue arts and sciences degrees. 3% grads pursue law degrees. 1% grads pursue business degrees. 3% grads pursue medical degrees. **Faculty:** Student/faculty ratio 10:1. 345 full-time faculty, 97% hold PhDs, 13% are members of minority groups, 39% are women.

ACADEMICS

Degrees: Bachelor's, master's. **Classes:** Most classes have 10–19 students. Most lab/discussion sessions have 10–19 students. **Majors with Highest Enrollment:** Business administration and management; economics; English language and literature. **Special Study Options:** Double major, dual enrollment, honors program, independent study, internships, liberal arts/career combination, student-designed major, study abroad, teacher certification program. **Combined degree programs:** BS/MS 5-year program in biology, chemistry, math, English. Special programs offered to physically disabled students include tape recorders, tutors. **Career services:** Alumni network, alumni services, career/job search classes, career assessment, internships, regional alumni. **Career services highlights include:** Bucknell's Institute for Leadership in Technology and Management (ILTM) was founded in 1993 to offer Bucknell students a unique learning experience that bridges the disciplines of engineering and management. Consisting of a two-summer sequence of programs, the ILTM brings together in the first summer 18 of the best and most highly motivated rising juniors in engineering and management to engage in an extremely intensive, six-week, on-campus program that focuses on globalization, ethics, communication skills, critical thinking, teamwork, and leadership.

FACILITIES

Housing: Coed dorms, special housing for disabled students, men's dorms, special housing for international students, women's dorms, fraternity/sorority housing, cooperative housing, apartments for single students, wellness housing, theme housing. 70% of campus accessible to physically disabled. **Special Academic Facilities/Equipment:** Art gallery, center for performing arts, poetry center, photography lab, observatory, 63-acre nature site, greenhouse, primate facility, gas chromatograph/mass spectrometer, electron microscope, herbarium, crafts center, engineering structural test lab, nuclear magnetic resonance spectrometer, 18-hole golf course, conference center, high ropes course. **Computers:** 100% of classrooms, 100% of dorms, 100% of libraries, 100% of dining areas, 100% of student union, 95% of common outdoor areas have wireless network access. Students can register for classes online. Administrative functions (other than registration) can be performed online.

CAMPUS LIFE

Environment: Village. **Activities:** Choral groups, concert band, dance, drama/theater, jazz band, literary magazine, music ensembles, musical theater, opera, pep band, radio station, student government, student newspaper, student-run film society, symphony orchestra, yearbook, campus ministries, international student organization, Model UN. **Organizations:** 150 registered organizations, 23 honor societies, 13 religious organizations. 12 fraternities, 8 sororities. **Athletics (Intercollegiate):** *Men:* Baseball, basketball, cross-country, diving, football, golf, lacrosse, soccer, swimming, tennis, track/field (outdoor), track/field (indoor), water polo, wrestling. *Women:* Basketball, crew/rowing, cross-country, diving, field hockey, golf, lacrosse, soccer, softball, swimming, tennis, track/field (outdoor), track/field (indoor), volleyball, water polo. **On-Campus Highlights:** Weis Center for the Performing Arts, Outdoor Primate Facilities, Uptown Night Club, Stadler Poetry Center, Library with Technology and Media Commons, Bertrand Library, Seventh Street Cafe, Elaine Langone Center (student center), Bucknell Observatory, Environmental Center, Samek Art Gallery. **Environmental Initiatives:** In September of 2007, the Bucknell University Environmental Center (BUEC) initiated a campus-wide environmental assessment of the university's operations, involving over 70 faculty, students, staff, and community members in a highly educational and collaborative project. Teams conducted research on ten indicators of sustainability, including administration/policy, education, energy, water, solid waste, hazardous materials, purchasing, dining, built environment, and landscape. Preliminary results of the assessment were presented at the 2nd Annual Environmental Assessment Summit on October 1st 2008. A full written report is scheduled to be completed at the end of January 2009. A campus master plan that embraces sustainable principles; Bucknell's campus master plan, completed in August 2008, calls for reducing the amount of asphalt on campus by removing cars and parking from some of the main campus arteries, making the campus more pedestrian friendly; restoring Miller Run, improving storm water runoff and collection, creating more natural buffer areas, recapturing access to the river, and creating new bike trails linking the campus to neighboring communities. Energy efficiency and renewable energy initiatives: In 1998 Bucknell University transitioned from a conventional coal-burning power plant to a highly efficient co-generation power plant fueled by cleaner-burning natural gas. The new power plant has allowed Bucknell to reduce its greenhouse gas emissions by 40% compared to pre-1998 levels, a fact that was established through the completion of the university's first greenhouse gas inventory in 2006. Bucknell also purchases 4 million kilowatt hours of wind power per year, accounting for 100% of Bucknell's purchased energy. Additionally, Bucknell maintains three photovoltaic arrays which are used in educational programming.

ADMISSIONS

Freshman Academic Profile: Average high school GPA 3.49. 59% in top 10% of high school class, 88% in top 25% of high school class, 99% in top 50% of high school class. 63% from public high schools. SAT Math middle 50% range 630–720. SAT Critical Reading middle 50% range 600–680. SAT Writing middle 50% range 600–690. ACT middle 50% range 27–31. Minimum paper TOEFL 550. Minimum computer TOEFL 213. Minimum web-based TOEFL 106. **Basis for Candidate Selection:** *Very important factors considered include:* Class rank, application essay, academic GPA, rigor of secondary school record, standardized test scores, character/personal qualities, talent/ability. *Important factors considered include:* Recommendation(s), extracurricular activities, level of applicant's interest, volunteer work, work experience. *Other factors considered include:* Alumni/ae relation, first generation, geographical residence, racial/ethnic status, religious affiliation/commitment. **Freshman Admission Requirements:** High school diploma is required and GED is accepted. *Academic units required:* 4 English, 3 mathematics, 2 science, 2 foreign language, 2 social studies, 2 history, 1 academic electives. *Academic units recommended:* 4 English, 4 mathematics, 3 science, 4 foreign language, 2 social studies, 2 history, 1 academic electives. **Freshman Admission Statistics:** 7,572 applied, 30% admitted, 41% enrolled. **Transfer Admission Requirements:** High school transcript, college transcript(s), essay or personal statement, standardized test scores, statement of good standing from prior institution(s). Minimum college GPA of 2.5 required. Lowest grade transferable C. **General Admission Information:** Application fee $60. Early decision application deadline 11/15. Regular application deadline 1/15. Regular notification 4/1. Nonfall registration not accepted. Admission may be deferred for a maximum of 2 years. Credit and/or placement offered for CEEB Advanced Placement tests.

COSTS AND FINANCIAL AID

Annual tuition $40,594. Room and board $9,504. Required fees $222. Average book expense $880. **Required Forms and Deadlines:** FAFSA, CSS/Financial Aid PROFILE, noncustodial PROFILE. Financial aid filing deadline 1/1. **Notification of Awards:** Applicants will be notified of awards on or about 4/1. **Types of Aid:** *Need-based scholarships/grants:* Federal Pell, SEOG, state scholarships/grants, private scholarships, the school's own gift aid, Federal ACG Grant, Federal SMART. *Loans:* FFEL Subsidized Stafford, FFEL Unsubsidized Stafford, FFEL PLUS, Federal Perkins. **Student Employment:** Federal Work-Study Program available. Institutional employment available. Highest amount earned per year from on-campus jobs $1,500. Off-campus job opportunities are poor. **Financial Aid Statistics:** 47% freshmen, 46% undergrads receive need-based scholarship or grant aid. 6% freshmen, 5% undergrads receive non-need-based scholarship or grant aid. 47% freshmen, 46% undergrads receive need-based self-help aid. 3% freshmen, 1% undergrads receive athletic scholarships. 62% undergrads receive any aid. 61% undergrads borrow to pay for school. Average cumulative indebtedness $18,800. **Criteria for awarding institutional aid:** *Non-need-based:* Academics, art, athletics, leadership, music/drama.

See page 1040.

BUENA VISTA UNIVERSITY

610 West Fourth Street, Storm Lake, IA 50588-1798
Phone: 712-749-2235 **Financial Aid Phone:** 712-749-2164
E-mail: admissions@bvu.edu **CEEB Code:** 6047
Fax: 712-749-1459 **Website:** www.bvu.edu **ACT Code:** 1278

This private school, affiliated with the Presbyterian Church, was founded in 1891. It has a 60-acre campus.

RATINGS

Admissions Selectivity Rating: 74	**Fire Safety Rating:** 69	**Green Rating:** 60*

STUDENTS AND FACULTY

Enrollment: 939. **Student Body:** 51% female, 49% male, 24% out-of-state, 4% international (10 countries represented). Asian 2%, African American 6%, Caucasian 82%, Hispanic 5%.

Retention and Graduation: 61% freshmen return for sophomore year. 46% freshmen graduate within 4 years. 17% grads go on to further study within 1

year. 8% grads pursue arts and sciences degrees. 1% grads pursue business degrees. 8% grads pursue medical degrees. **Faculty:** Student/faculty ratio 10:1. 83 full-time faculty, 69% hold PhDs, 5% are members of minority groups, 45% are women.

ACADEMICS
Degrees: Bachelor's, master's. **Classes:** Most classes have 10–19 students. Most lab/discussion sessions have 10–19 students. **Majors with Highest Enrollment:** Biology/biological sciences; elementary education and teaching; management science. **Special Study Options:** Distance learning, double major, dual enrollment, English as a Second Language (ESL), external degree program, honors program, independent study, internships, student-designed major, study abroad, teacher certification program, off-campus study, other semester-away programs available. Academic and cultural events series brings national and world leaders and performers to campus; students earn credits for attendance. **Combined degree programs:** BA/MEng. Special programs offered to physically disabled students include note-taking services, reader services, tape recorders, tutors. **Career services:** Alumni network, alumni services, career/job search classes, career assessment, internships.

FACILITIES
Housing: Coed dorms, men's dorms, women's dorms. **Special Academic Facilities/Equipment:** Art gallery, language lab, television station, radio station, satellite telecommunications system, computer labs/centers, electron microscope. **Computers:** 100% of classrooms, 100% of dorms, 100% of libraries, 100% of dining areas, 100% of common outdoor areas have wireless network access. Students can register for classes online. Administrative functions (other than registration) can be performed online.

CAMPUS LIFE
Environment: Village. **Activities:** Choral groups, concert band, dance, drama/theater, jazz band, music ensembles, musical theater, pep band, radio station, student government, student newspaper, television station, campus ministries, international student organization. **Organizations:** 65 registered organizations, 5 honor societies, 3 religious organizations. **Athletics (Intercollegiate):** *Men:* Baseball, basketball, cross-country, football, golf, soccer, tennis, track/field (outdoor), track/field (indoor), wrestling. *Women:* Basketball, cross-country, golf, soccer, softball, tennis, track/field (outdoor), track/field (indoor), volleyball. **On-Campus Highlights:** Recreation Center, Harold Walter Siebens Forum, Centennial Room, a huge cafeteria, suites are the biggest rooms on campus.

ADMISSIONS
Freshman Academic Profile: Average high school GPA 3.26. 15% in top 10% of high school class, 38% in top 25% of high school class, 71% in top 50% of high school class. 85% from public high schools. ACT middle 50% range 18–25. Minimum paper TOEFL 475. Minimum computer TOEFL 153. Minimum web-based TOEFL 60. **Basis for Candidate Selection:** *Very important factors considered include:* Class rank, academic GPA, recommendation(s), rigor of secondary school record, standardized test scores. *Other factors considered include:* Application essay, alumni/ae relation, character/personal qualities, extracurricular activities, first generation, interview, talent/ability, volunteer work, work experience. **Freshman Admission Requirements:** High school diploma is required and GED is accepted. *Academic units required:* 4 English, 2 science, 2 social studies. *Academic units recommended:* 4 mathematics, 4 science, 2 foreign language, 2 history, 1 computer science. **Freshman Admission Statistics:** 1,433 applied, 72% admitted, 27% enrolled. **Transfer Admission Requirements:** College transcript(s), statement of good standing from prior institution(s). Minimum college GPA of 2.0 required. Lowest grade transferable D. **General Admission Information:** Nonfall registration accepted. Admission may be deferred for a maximum of 1 year. Credit and/or placement offered for CEEB Advanced Placement tests.

COSTS AND FINANCIAL AID
Average book expense $1,500. **Required Forms and Deadlines:** FAFSA. Priority financial aid filing date 6/1. **Notification of Awards:** Applicants will be notified of awards on a rolling basis beginning 2/15. **Types of Aid:** *Need-based scholarships/grants:* Federal Pell, SEOG, state scholarships/grants, private scholarships, the school's own gift aid. *Loans:* FFEL Subsidized Stafford, FFEL Unsubsidized Stafford, FFEL PLUS, Federal Perkins, college/university loans from institutional funds. **Student Employment:** Federal Work-Study Program available. Institutional employment available. Off-campus job opportunities are excellent. **Financial Aid Statistics:** 81% freshmen, 74% undergrads receive need-based scholarship or grant aid. 88% freshmen, 86% undergrads receive non-need-based scholarship or grant aid. 78% freshmen, 76% undergrads receive need-based self-help aid. 99% freshmen, 98% undergrads receive any aid. 91% undergrads borrow to pay for school. Average cumulative indebtedness $40,569. **Criteria for awarding institutional aid:** *Non-need-based:* Academics, art, minority status, music/drama, religious affiliation.

95 North Ave, Admissions Offic, Burlington, VT 05401
Phone: 802-862-9616 x104 **Financial Aid Phone:** 802-862-9616 ext 110
E-mail: admissions@burlington.edu **CEEB Code:** 1119
Fax: 802/660-4331 **Website:** www.burlington.edu **ACT Code:** 4329

This private school was founded in 1972. It has a 1-acre campus.

RATINGS
Admissions Selectivity Rating: 60* **Fire Safety Rating:** 61 **Green Rating:** 74

STUDENTS AND FACULTY
Enrollment: 169. **Student Body:** 45% female, 55% male, 47% out-of-state, 1% international (5 countries represented). Asian 2%, African American 2%, Caucasian 80%, Hispanic 2%.
Retention and Graduation: 60% freshmen return for sophomore year. 20% freshmen graduate within 4 years. 42% grads go on to further study within 1 year. 90% grads pursue arts and sciences degrees. 5% grads pursue law degrees. **Faculty:** Student/faculty ratio 6:1. 6 full-time faculty, 33% hold PhDs, 67% are women.

ACADEMICS
Degrees: Associate, bachelor's, certificate. **Classes:** Most classes have fewer than 10 students. **Majors with Highest Enrollment:** Film/cinema studies; multi-/interdisciplinary studies, other; psychology, other. **Special Study Options:** Cross-registration, distance learning, double major, dual enrollment, external degree program, independent study, internships, liberal arts/career combination, student-designed major, study abroad, flexible, self-designed degree program, independent study option. **Honors programs:** A capstone Degree Project, equivalent to a graduate thesis, is required of all BA candidates. Special programs offered to physically disabled students include note-taking services, reader services, tape recorders, tutors. **Career services:** Career/job search classes, internships. **Career services highlights include:** Action Learning/Internship. There is an internship requirement for each major carrying a minimum of 3 academic credits (96 on-site hours). For each credit, the student must complete 32 hrs of field-supervised, hands-on experience and attend a concurrent seminar which provides guidance and support.

FACILITIES
Housing: Cooperative housing, apartments for single students 100% of campus accessible to physically disabled. **Special Academic Facilities/Equipment:** The main campus houses classrooms, film and video editing labs, a photography darkroom, a college-operated gallery and a community garden. We are within walking distance from the ECHO lake aquarium and science center, the Waterfront Blackbox Theatre and Cinema, the Community Sailing Center, the YMCA, and the Flynn Theatre. As Burlington's College, our downtown location also allows us to utilize multiple local art galleries and music venues for showcasing students arts and talents. **Computers:** 100% of classrooms, 100% of dorms, 100% of libraries, 100% of student union, have wireless network access.

CAMPUS LIFE
Environment: Town. **Activities:** Literary magazine, student government, student-run film society. **Organizations:** 1 registered organizations. **On-Campus Highlights:** Burlington College Community Gallery, Miller Studio, Photography Darkroom. **Environmental Initiatives:** Conducted energy audits on all buildings, completed 75% of recommendations and plan to complete the rest. Plan to build LEED-certified building; Organic Community Garden.

ADMISSIONS
Freshman Academic Profile: Average high school GPA 2.72. 71% from public high schools. Minimum paper TOEFL 550. Minimum computer TOEFL 213. Minimum web-based TOEFL 79. **Basis for Candidate Selection:** *Very important factors considered include:* Application essay, character/personal qualities, interview, level of applicant's interest. *Important factors considered include:* Recommendation(s), talent/ability, volunteer work. *Other factors considered include:* Academic GPA, rigor of secondary school record, standardized test scores, alumni/ae relation, extracurricular activities, first generation, work experience. **Freshman Admission Requirements:** High school diploma is required and GED is accepted. *Academic units recommended:* 4 English, 3 mathematics, 3 science, (2 science labs), 2 foreign language, 4 social studies, 3 history, 4 academic electives. **Freshman Admission Statistics:** 126 applied, 83% admitted, 23% enrolled. **Transfer Admission Requirements:** High school transcript, college transcript(s), essay or personal statement, Lowest grade transferable C. **General Admission Information:** Application fee $50. Regular application deadline 8/15. Nonfall registration accepted. Admission may be deferred for a maximum of 2 semesters. Credit and/or placement offered for CEEB Advanced Placement tests.

COSTS AND FINANCIAL AID

Annual tuition $20,424. Room and board $6,750. Average book expense $990. **Required Forms and Deadlines:** FAFSA, state aid form. **Notification of Awards:** Applicants will be notified of awards on a rolling basis beginning 3/15. **Types of Aid:** *Need-based scholarships/grants:* Federal Pell, SEOG, state scholarships/grants, private scholarships, the school's own gift aid. *Loans:* FFEL Subsidized Stafford, FFEL Unsubsidized Stafford, FFEL PLUS, Federal Perkins. **Student Employment:** Federal Work-Study Program available. Off-campus job opportunities are good. **Financial Aid Statistics:** 60% freshmen, 61% undergrads receive need-based scholarship or grant aid. 65% freshmen, 68% undergrads receive need-based self-help aid. 65% freshmen, 68% undergrads receive any aid. 80% undergrads borrow to pay for school. Average cumulative indebtedness $38,198. **Criteria for awarding institutional aid:** *Non-need-based:* Academics, leadership.

BUTLER UNIVERSITY

4600 Sunset Avenue, Indianapolis, IN 46208
Phone: 317-940-8100 **Financial Aid Phone:** 317-940-8200
E-mail: admission@butler.edu **CEEB Code:** 1073
Fax: 317-940-8150 **Website:** www.butler.edu **ACT Code:** 1180

This private school was founded in 1855. It has a 290-acre campus.

RATINGS

Admissions Selectivity Rating: 89   **Fire Safety Rating:** 71   **Green Rating:** 71

STUDENTS AND FACULTY

Enrollment: 3,715. **Student Body:** 60% female, 40% male, 42% out-of-state, 2% international (52 countries represented). Asian 2%, African American 4%, Caucasian 85%, Hispanic 2%.
Retention and Graduation: 90% freshmen return for sophomore year. 57% freshmen graduate within 4 years. 33% grads go on to further study within 1 year. 15% grads pursue arts and sciences degrees. 2% grads pursue law degrees. 3% grads pursue business degrees. 2% grads pursue medical degrees. **Faculty:** Student/faculty ratio 11:1. 327 full-time faculty, 83% hold PhDs, 13% are members of minority groups, 46% are women.

ACADEMICS

Degrees: Associate, bachelor's, master's. **Classes:** Most classes have 10–19 students. Most lab/discussion sessions have 20–29 students. **Majors with Highest Enrollment:** Biology/biological sciences; marketing/marketing management; pharmacy (PharmD [US], PharmD or BS/BPharm [Canada]). **Special Study Options:** Cross-registration, double major, dual enrollment, exchange student program (domestic), honors program, independent study, internships, student-designed major, study abroad, teacher certification program, cooperative program in business only. **Honors programs:** The Butler University Honors Program exists to meet the expectations of academically outstanding students in all colleges and majors who wish to develop their talents and potential to the fullest. Through a combination of honors courses, cultural events, independent study, creative activity and research, it is designed to foster a diverse and challenging intellectual environment for honors students and to enhance our academic community by adding a distinctive note of innovative thinking and interdisciplinary dialogue. **Combined degree programs:** BA/MEng. Special programs offered to physically disabled students include note-taking services, reader services. **Career services:** Alumni network, alumni services, career/job search classes, career assessment, internships, regional alumni. Career services highlights include: The College of Business assigns each student a career mentor and requires two internships for each of their majors; 75% of Butler undergraduates participate in some form of experiential learning.

FACILITIES

Housing: Coed dorms, women's dorms, fraternity/sorority housing, apartments for single students. 90% of campus accessible to physically disabled. **Special Academic Facilities/Equipment:** Holcomb Observatory, Clowes Memorial Hall (performing arts theatre). **Computers:** 100% of classrooms, 100% of dorms, 100% of libraries, 100% of dining areas, 100% of student union, have wireless network access. Students can register for classes online. Administrative functions (other than registration) can be performed online.

CAMPUS LIFE

Environment: Metropolis. **Activities:** Choral groups, concert band, dance, drama/theater, jazz band, literary magazine, marching band, music ensembles, musical theater, opera, pep band, student government, student newspaper, symphony orchestra, television station, yearbook, campus ministries, international student organization, Model UN. **Organizations:** 135 registered organizations, 8 honor societies, 6 religious organizations. 7 fraternities, 9 so-

rorities. **Athletics (Intercollegiate):** *Men:* Baseball, basketball, cross-country, football, golf, soccer, tennis, track/field (outdoor), track/field (indoor). *Women:* Basketball, cross-country, golf, soccer, softball, swimming, tennis, track/field (outdoor), track/field (indoor), volleyball. **On-Campus Highlights:** Starbucks in the Union, Carillon on Lake Road, Holcomb Gardens, Fairbanks Center, Lilly Music Hall (newly renovated). **Environmental Initiatives:** College of Pharmacy and Health Sciences building will be LEED certified Silver. IDEM grant for campus recycling, $25,000. Completely Green cleaning operations for our custodial operation.

ADMISSIONS

Freshman Academic Profile: Average high school GPA 3.75. 50.4% in top 10% of high school class, 78.8% in top 25% of high school class, 97.6% in top 50% of high school class. 85% from public high schools. SAT Math middle 50% range 540–650. SAT Critical Reading middle 50% range 520–630. SAT Writing middle 50% range 520–620. ACT middle 50% range 25–30. Minimum paper TOEFL 550. Minimum computer TOEFL 213. **Basis for Candidate Selection:** *Very important factors considered include:* Application essay, academic GPA, rigor of secondary school record, standardized test scores. *Important factors considered include:* Class rank, extracurricular activities, talent/ability. *Other factors considered include:* Recommendation(s), alumni/ae relation, character/personal qualities, volunteer work, work experience. **Freshman Admission Requirements:** High school diploma is required and GED is accepted. *Academic units required:* 4 English, 3 mathematics, 3 science, (2 science labs), 2 foreign language, 2 social studies, 2 history. **Freshman Admission Statistics:** 6,246 applied, 79% admitted, 19% enrolled. **Transfer Admission Requirements:** College transcript(s), essay or personal statement, statement of good standing from prior institution(s). Minimum college GPA of 2.0 required. Lowest grade transferable C. **General Admission Information:** Application fee $35. Regular application deadline 8/1. Notification on a rolling basis, beginning on or about 3/6. Nonfall registration accepted. Admission may be deferred for a maximum of 1 year. Credit offered for CEEB Advanced Placement tests.

COSTS AND FINANCIAL AID

Annual tuition $28,460. Room and board $9,740. Required fees $786. Average book expense $800. **Required Forms and Deadlines:** FAFSA. Priority financial aid filing date 3/1. **Notification of Awards:** Applicants will be notified of awards on a rolling basis beginning 3/15. **Types of Aid:** *Need-based scholarships/grants:* Federal Pell, SEOG, state scholarships/grants, the school's own gift aid. *Loans:* FFEL Subsidized Stafford, FFEL Unsubsidized Stafford, FFEL PLUS, Federal Perkins. **Student Employment:** Federal Work-Study Program available. Institutional employment available. Highest amount earned per year from on-campus jobs $3,000. Off-campus job opportunities are excellent. **Financial Aid Statistics:** 60% undergrads receive need-based scholarship or grant aid. 60% undergrads borrow to pay for school. Average cumulative indebtedness $23,500. **Criteria for awarding institutional aid:** *Non-need-based:* Academics, athletics, music/drama.

CABRINI COLLEGE

610 King of Prussia Road, Radnor, PA 19087-3698
Phone: 610-902-8552 **Financial Aid Phone:** 610-902-8420
E-mail: admit@cabrini.edu **CEEB Code:** 2071
Fax: 610-902-8508 **Website:** www.cabrini.edu **ACT Code:** 3532

This private school, affiliated with the Roman Catholic Church, was founded in 1957. It has a 112-acre campus.

RATINGS

Admissions Selectivity Rating: 70   **Fire Safety Rating:** 88   **Green Rating:** 60*

STUDENTS AND FACULTY

Enrollment: 1,820. **Student Body:** 66% female, 34% male, 34% out-of-state, 1% international (34 countries represented). Asian 2%, African American 6%, Caucasian 83%, Hispanic 3%.
Retention and Graduation: 66% freshmen return for sophomore year. 46% freshmen graduate within 4 years. 21% grads go on to further study within 1 year. 16% grads pursue arts and sciences degrees. 1% grads pursue law degrees. 3% grads pursue business degrees. 1% grads pursue medical degrees. **Faculty:** Student/faculty ratio 16:1. 64 full-time faculty, 80% hold PhDs, 5% are members of minority groups, 55% are women.

ACADEMICS

Degrees: Bachelor's, certificate, master's, post-bachelor's certificate. **Classes:** Most classes have 20–29 students. Most lab/discussion sessions have 10–19 students. **Majors with Highest Enrollment:** Business, management, marketing, and related support services, other; elementary education and teaching. **Special**

Study Options: Accelerated program, cooperative education program, cross-registration, double major, honors program, independent study, internships, liberal arts/career combination, student-designed major, study abroad, teacher certification program. **Honors programs:** Cabrini College Honors Program; Honors in the major. Special programs offered to physically disabled students include note-taking services, reader services, tape recorders, tutors. **Career services:** Alumni network, alumni services, career/job search classes, career assessment, internships. Career services highlights include: Parallel cooperative education program semester to semester.

FACILITIES

Housing: Coed dorms, special housing for disabled students, women's dorms, Special Interest Housing is available. 97% of campus accessible to physically disabled. **Special Academic Facilities/Equipment:** Exercise Science Lab, Communications center (includes a graphic design lab, radio station, newsroom, and television studio). Science Education and Technology building with state-of-the-art biology, chemistry, and physics labs, Instructional Technology labs, and research space. **Computers:** 100% of classrooms, 95% of dorms, 100% of libraries, 100% of dining areas, 100% of student union, 95% of common outdoor areas have wireless network access. Students can register for classes on-line. Administrative functions (other than registration) can be performed online.

CAMPUS LIFE

Environment: Town. **Activities:** Choral groups, dance, drama/theater, literary magazine, radio station, student government, student newspaper, student-run film society, television station, yearbook, campus ministries, international student organization. **Organizations:** 32 registered organizations, 18 honor societies, 1 religious organizations. **Athletics (Intercollegiate):** *Men:* Basketball, cross-country, golf, lacrosse, soccer, swimming, tennis, track/field (outdoor). *Women:* Basketball, cross-country, field hockey, lacrosse, soccer, softball, swimming, tennis, track/field (outdoor), volleyball. **On-Campus Highlights:** Dixon Center—athletic/recreation facility, Jazzman's Cafe, Holy Spirit Library, Mansion, Science Technology Education Building, The College also has a Communications Center with a radio station, newsroom, graphic design lab, and a television studio.

ADMISSIONS

Freshman Academic Profile: Average high school GPA 3.06. 6% in top 10% of high school class, 20% in top 25% of high school class, 49% in top 50% of high school class. 56% from public high schools. SAT Math middle 50% range 430–520. SAT Critical Reading middle 50% range 440–530. Minimum paper TOEFL 500. Minimum computer TOEFL 80. **Basis for Candidate Selection:** *Very important factors considered include:* Academic GPA, standardized test scores. *Important factors considered include:* Level of applicant's interest. *Other factors considered include:* Class rank, application essay, recommendation(s), rigor of secondary school record, alumni/ae relation, character/personal qualities, extracurricular activities, interview, talent/ability, volunteer work, work experience. **Freshman Admission Requirements:** High school diploma is required and GED is accepted. *Academic units required:* 4 English, 3 mathematics, 3 science, 2 foreign language, 3 social studies, 3 history. *Academic units recommended:* 4 English, 4 mathematics, 3 science, 2 foreign language, 3 social studies, 3 history, 2 academic electives. **Freshman Admission Statistics:** 4,015 applied, 75% admitted, 17% enrolled. **Transfer Admission Requirements:** College transcript(s), minimum college GPA of 2.2 required. Lowest grade transferable C–. **General Admission Information:** Application fee $35. Notification on a rolling basis, beginning on or about 8/1. Nonfall registration accepted. Admission may be deferred for a maximum of 1 year. Credit and/or placement offered for CEEB Advanced Placement tests.

COSTS AND FINANCIAL AID

Average book expense $960. **Required Forms and Deadlines:** FAFSA. Financial aid filing deadline 5/1. **Notification of Awards:** Applicants will be notified of awards on a rolling basis beginning 2/20. **Types of Aid:** *Need-based scholarships/grants:* Federal Pell, SEOG, state scholarships/grants, private scholarships, the school's own gift aid. *Loans:* FFEL Subsidized Stafford, FFEL Unsubsidized Stafford, FFEL PLUS, Federal Perkins. **Student Employment:** Highest amount earned per year from on-campus jobs $4,160. Off-campus job opportunities are good. **Financial Aid Statistics:** 63% freshmen, 55% undergrads receive need-based scholarship or grant aid. 71% freshmen, 66% undergrads receive non-need-based scholarship or grant aid. 62% freshmen, 59% undergrads receive need-based self-help aid. 98% freshmen, 97% undergrads receive any aid. 77% undergrads borrow to pay for school. Average cumulative indebtedness $22,700. **Criteria for awarding institutional aid:** *Non-need-based:* Academics, alumni affiliation.

See page 1042.

CALDWELL COLLEGE

9 Ryerson Avenue, Caldwell, NJ 07006-6195
Phone: 973-618-3500 **Financial Aid Phone:**
E-mail: admissions@caldwell.edu **CEEB Code:** 2072
Fax: 973-618-3600 **Website:** www.caldwell.edu **ACT Code:** 2542

This private school, affiliated with the Roman Catholic Church, was founded in 1939. It has a 80-acre campus.

RATINGS

Admissions Selectivity Rating: 70   **Fire Safety Rating:** 60*   **Green Rating:** 60*

STUDENTS AND FACULTY

Enrollment: 1,563. **Student Body:** 67% female, 33% male, 14% out-of-state, 5% international (26 countries represented). Asian 2%, African American 16%, Caucasian 61%, Hispanic 12%.
Retention and Graduation: 73% freshmen return for sophomore year. 45% freshmen graduate within 4 years. **Faculty:** Student/faculty ratio 12:1. 80 full-time faculty, 83% hold PhDs, 63% are women.

ACADEMICS

Degrees: Bachelor's, certificate, master's, post-bachelor's certificate, post-master's certificate. **Majors with Highest Enrollment:** Business/commerce; elementary education and teaching; psychology. **Special Study Options:** Accelerated program, cooperative education program, distance learning, double major, English as a Second Language (ESL), external-degree program, honors program, independent study, internships, liberal arts/career combination, student-designed major, study abroad, teacher certification program, weekend college. Special programs offered to physically disabled students include note-taking services, reader services, tape recorders, tutors. **Career services:** Alumni services, career/job search classes, career assessment, internships.

FACILITIES

Housing: Coed dorms 85% of campus accessible to physically disabled. **Special Academic Facilities/Equipment:** Art gallery, theatre, library with media center, TV studio, state-of-the-art technology building with Interactive Television Classroom, new student center. **Computers:** Students can register for classes online. Administrative functions (other than registration) can be performed online.

CAMPUS LIFE

Environment: Village. **Activities:** Choral groups, drama/theater, jazz band, literary magazine, music ensembles, musical theater, pep band, student government, student newspaper, yearbook. **Organizations:** 20 registered organizations, 15 honor societies, 1 religious organizations. **Athletics (Intercollegiate):** *Men:* Baseball, basketball, golf, soccer, tennis. *Women:* Basketball, golf, soccer, softball, tennis. **On-Campus Highlights:** Newly opened 60,000 square-foot recreation center, completed renovated science labs, brand new fitness center, radio and TV studios, art department galleries.

ADMISSIONS

Freshman Academic Profile: Average high school GPA 3.03. 7% in top 10% of high school class, 14% in top 25% of high school class, 47% in top 50% of high school class. 67% from public high schools. SAT Math middle 50% range 430–530. SAT Critical Reading middle 50% range 420–520. Minimum paper TOEFL 500. **Basis for Candidate Selection:** *Very important factors considered include:* Rigor of secondary school record, extracurricular activities. *Important factors considered include:* Class rank, academic GPA, standardized test scores, talent/ability. *Other factors considered include:* Application essay, recommendation(s), alumni/ae relation, character/personal qualities, interview, volunteer work, work experience. **Freshman Admission Requirements:** High school diploma is required and GED is accepted. *Academic units required:* 4 English, 2 mathematics, 2 science, (1 science labs), 2 foreign language, 1 history, 5 academic electives. **Freshman Admission Statistics:** 1,442 applied, 66% admitted, 30% enrolled. **Transfer Admission Requirements:** High school transcript, college transcript(s), minimum college GPA of 2.0 required. Lowest grade transferable C. **General Admission Information:** Application fee $40. Regular application deadline 4/1. Nonfall registration accepted. Admission may be deferred for a maximum of 1 semester. Credit and/or placement offered for CEEB Advanced Placement tests.

COSTS AND FINANCIAL AID

Annual tuition $12,400. Room and board $7,000. Required fees $100. Average book expense $800. **Required Forms and Deadlines:** FAFSA, institution's own financial aid form. Priority financial aid filing date 4/15. **Notification of Awards:** Applicants will be notified of awards on a rolling basis beginning 3/1. **Types of Aid:** *Need-based scholarships/grants:* Federal Pell, SEOG, state scholarships/grants, private scholarships, the school's own gift aid. *Loans:* FFEL Subsidized Stafford, FFEL Unsubsidized Stafford, FFEL PLUS, state loans,

Alternative Loans, such as Key, TERI, Signature. **Student Employment:** Federal Work-Study Program available. Institutional employment available. Highest amount earned per year from on-campus jobs $1,000. Off-campus job opportunities are excellent. **Financial Aid Statistics:** 66% freshmen, 79% undergrads receive need-based scholarship or grant aid. 58% freshmen, 60% undergrads receive need-based self-help aid. 79% undergrads borrow to pay for school. Average cumulative indebtedness $15,125. **Criteria for awarding institutional aid:** *Non-need-based:* Academics, alumni affiliation, art, athletics, leadership, music/drama, religious affiliation.

CALIFORNIA BAPTIST UNIVERSITY

8432 Magnolia Ave, Riverside, CA 92504
Phone: 951-343-4212 **Financial Aid Phone:** 951-343-4236
E-mail: admissions@calbaptist.edu **CEEB Code:** 4094
Fax: 951-343-4525 **ACT Code:** 4094

This private school, affiliated with the Southern Baptist Church, was founded in 1950. It has a 103-acre campus.

RATINGS
Admissions Selectivity Rating: 75   Fire Safety Rating: 63   Green Rating: 60*

STUDENTS AND FACULTY
Enrollment: 3,212. **Student Body:** 61% female, 39% male, 7.1% out-of-state, 4% international (26 countries represented). Asian 4%, African American 7%, Caucasian 57%, Hispanic 19%, Native American 1%.
Retention and Graduation: 73% freshmen return for sophomore year. 45% freshmen graduate within 4 years. **Faculty:** Student/faculty ratio 18:1. 164 full-time faculty, 52% hold PhDs, 15% are members of minority groups, 46% are women.

ACADEMICS
Degrees: Bachelor's, master's. **Classes:** Most classes have 10–19 students. Most lab/discussion sessions have 10–19 students. **Majors with Highest Enrollment:** Business/commerce; liberal arts and sciences/liberal studies; psychology. **Special Study Options:** Accelerated program, distance learning, double major, English as a Second Language (ESL), exchange student program (domestic), honors program, internships, liberal arts/career combination, study abroad, teacher certification program, weekend college. **Honors programs:** The Honors program offers students from all major areas of study the opportunity to participate in rigorous study, requiring diligence in reading primary sources and writing original essays thorough 8 intensive seminars. Honors students progressively investigate a single generative idea using primary texts, drawing upon the expertise of leading faculty. These seminars may be used to fulfill elective unit requirements and specially selected general education requirements. Successful completion of the Honors Program will be posted on the academic transcript and students will be designated as Honors Program graduates at commencement. Special programs offered to physically disabled students include note-taking services, tutors. **Career services:** Alumni services, career/job search classes, internships. Career services highlights include: Internship elective credit is available for students in all academic disciplines. In addition, a RE-FOCUS program is available which seeks to prepare students in their transition from the academic culture of the university to a professional culture. The program is designed for Juniors and Seniors and offers interactive workshops such as mock interviews hosted by a national employer, business etiquette dinners, resume and interview skills workshops and graduate school information sessions.

FACILITIES
Housing: Men's dorms, women's dorms, cooperative housing, apartments for single students. 95% of campus accessible to physically disabled. **Special Academic Facilities/Equipment:** Metcalf Art Gallery, Annie Gabriel Library, Wallace Theater, P. Boyd Smith Hymnology Collection, School of Music Performance and Recording Studios, Nie Wieder! Collection, Lancer Sports Complex and Aquatic Center. **Computers:** 40% of classrooms, 10% of dorms, 100% of libraries, 100% of dining areas, 100% of student union, 25% of common outdoor areas have wireless network access. Students can register for classes online. Administrative functions (other than registration) can be performed online.

CAMPUS LIFE
Environment: City. **Activities:** Choral groups, concert band, drama/theater, jazz band, music ensembles, musical theater, pep band, student government, student newspaper, symphony orchestra, yearbook, campus ministries, international student organization. **Organizations:** 30 registered organizations, 2 honor societies, 6 religious organizations. **Athletics (Intercollegiate):** *Men:* Baseball, basketball, cheerleading, cross-country, diving, golf, soccer, swimming, volleyball, water polo, wrestling. *Women:* Basketball, cheerleading, cross-country, diving, golf, soccer, softball, swimming, volleyball, water polo. **On-Campus Highlights:** Alumni Dining Commons, Student Activity Center, Wanda's (Coffee Shop), Van Dyne Gymnasium, Aquatic Center. **Environmental Initiatives:** Energy efficient lighting, HVAC regulators, strategic landscaping considerations.

ADMISSIONS
Freshman Academic Profile: Average high school GPA 3.4. 16% in top 10% of high school class, 43% in top 25% of high school class, 78% in top 50% of high school class. 82% from public high schools. SAT Math middle 50% range 440–560. SAT Critical Reading middle 50% range 450–570. SAT Writing middle 50% range 440–560. ACT middle 50% range 19–24. Minimum paper TOEFL 500. Minimum computer TOEFL 153. **Basis for Candidate Selection:** *Very important factors considered include:* Application essay, academic GPA, recommendation(s), rigor of secondary school record, standardized test scores, character/personal qualities. *Important factors considered include:* Level of applicant's interest. *Other factors considered include:* Class rank, extracurricular activities, talent/ability, volunteer work. **Freshman Admission Requirements:** High school diploma is required and GED is accepted. *Academic units required:* 4 English, 3 mathematics, 1 science, (1 science labs), 2 foreign language, 2 social studies, 2 history. *Academic units recommended:* 4 English, 4 mathematics, 2 science, (2 science labs), 3 foreign language, 2 social studies, 2 history, 3 academic electives. **Freshman Admission Statistics:** 1,734 applied, 74% admitted, 45% enrolled. **Transfer Admission Requirements:** College transcript(s), essay or personal statement, statement of good standing from prior institution(s). Minimum college GPA of 2.0 required. Lowest grade transferable C. **General Admission Information:** Application fee $45. Notification on a rolling basis, beginning on or about 11/9. Nonfall registration accepted. Admission may be deferred for a maximum of 1 year. Credit and/or placement offered for CEEB Advanced Placement tests.

COSTS AND FINANCIAL AID
Average book expense $1,638. **Required Forms and Deadlines:** FAFSA, state aid form. Priority financial aid filing date 3/2. **Notification of Awards:** Applicants will be notified of awards on a rolling basis beginning 3/2. **Types of Aid:** *Need-based scholarships/grants:* Federal Pell, SEOG, state scholarships/grants, private scholarships, the school's own gift aid, Federal Nursing Scholarships. *Loans:* FFEL Subsidized Stafford, FFEL Unsubsidized Stafford, FFEL PLUS, Federal Perkins, Federal Nursing, Alternative Loans. **Student Employment:** Federal Work-Study Program available. Institutional employment available. Highest amount earned per year from on-campus jobs $1,900. Off-campus job opportunities are good. **Financial Aid Statistics:** 64% freshmen, 58% undergrads receive need-based scholarship or grant aid. 50% freshmen, 40% undergrads receive non-need-based scholarship or grant aid. 59% freshmen, 58% undergrads receive need-based self-help aid. 18% freshmen, 10% undergrads receive athletic scholarships. 100% freshmen, 100% undergrads receive any aid. 82% undergrads borrow to pay for school. Average cumulative indebtedness $35,550. **Criteria for awarding institutional aid:** *Non-need-based:* Academics, art, athletics, music/drama, religious affiliation.

CALIFORNIA COLLEGE FOR HEALTH SCIENCES

2423 Hoover Avenue, National City, CA 91950
Phone: 619-477-4800
E-mail: admissns@cchs.edu
Fax: 619-477-4360 **Website:** www.cchs.edu

This proprietary school was founded in 1978. It has a 1-acre campus.

RATINGS
Admissions Selectivity Rating: 60*   Fire Safety Rating: 60*   Green Rating: 60*

STUDENTS AND FACULTY
Faculty: Student/faculty ratio 17:1. 5 full-time faculty.

ACADEMICS
Degrees: Associate, bachelor's, master's. **Special Study Options:** Distance learning.

CAMPUS LIFE
Environment: Metropolis. **Activities: Organizations:** 2 honor societies.

ADMISSIONS
Freshman Admission Requirements: High school diploma is required and GED is accepted. **Transfer Admission Requirements:** college transcript(s), Lowest grade transferable C. **General Admission Information:** Application fee $35. Notification on a rolling basis, beginning on or about 11/11. Nonfall

registration accepted. Admission may be deferred for a maximum of 11 months. Neither credit nor placement offered for CEEB Advanced Placement tests.

COSTS AND FINANCIAL AID
Annual tuition $3,000. Required fees $35.

CALIFORNIA COLLEGE OF THE ARTS

1111 Eighth Street, San Francisco, CA 94107
Phone: 415-703-9523 **Financial Aid Phone:** 415-703-9528
E-mail: enroll@cca.edu **CEEB Code:** 4031
Fax: 415-703-9539 **Website:** www.cca.edu **ACT Code:** 176

This private school was founded in 1907. It has a 4-acre campus.

RATINGS
Admissions Selectivity Rating: 77   **Fire Safety Rating:** 77   **Green Rating:** 85

STUDENTS AND FACULTY
Enrollment: 1,362. **Student Body:** 61% female, 39% male, 40% out-of-state, 9% international (32 countries represented). Asian 17%, African American 4%, Caucasian 46%, Hispanic 11%, Native American 1%.
Retention and Graduation: 73% freshmen return for sophomore year. 27% freshmen graduate within 4 years. **Faculty:** Student/faculty ratio 16:1. 81 full-time faculty, 80% hold PhDs, 19% are members of minority groups, 48% are women.

ACADEMICS
Degrees: Bachelor's, master's. **Classes:** Most classes have 10–19 students. **Majors with Highest Enrollment:** Architecture (BArch, BA/BS, MArch, MA/MS, PhD); graphic design; illustration. **Special Study Options:** Cross-registration, double major, English as a Second Language (ESL), exchange student program (domestic), independent study, internships, student-designed major, study abroad, Sponsored studios and project-based learning with community engagement courses integrated in the curriculum. Learning disability services also offered. **Combined degree programs:** MFA/MA, MFA/MBA. Special programs offered to physically disabled students include note-taking services, reader services, tape recorders, tutors. **Career services:** Alumni network, alumni services, career/job search classes, career assessment, internships. **Career services highlights include:** Engage at CCA combines project-based learning with community engagement throughout the curriculum of CCA's diverse programs. An example of an Engage course includes a furniture design class working with Lighthouse Community Charter School to create tables for the school's courtyard atrium.

FACILITIES
Housing: Coed dorms, special housing for disabled students, apartments for single students, theme housing, themed communities, and living-learning communities. 80% of campus accessible to physically disabled. **Special Academic Facilities/Equipment:** Logan Gallery on the San Francisco Campus, Wattis Institute for Contemporary Art. **Computers:** 100% of classrooms, 60% of dorms, 100% of libraries, 100% of dining areas, 90% of common outdoor areas have wireless network access. Students can register for classes online. Administrative functions (other than registration) can be performed online.

CAMPUS LIFE
Environment: Metropolis. **Activities:** Literary magazine, student government, student-run film society, international student organization. **Organizations:** 10 registered organizations, 1 fraternities. **On-Campus Highlights:** The Nave—San Francisco campus, The Foundry—Oakland campus, Individualized Painting Studios—SF, North/South Student Galleries—Oakland, Wattis Institute for Contemporary Art, Students learn from individuals, the inter-cultural community, and the myriad events and activities sponsored by the Center for Art and Public Life, the CCA Wattis Institute, and the Student Affairs Office. Activities range from social events, yoga classes, exhibition receptions, workshops, and topical forums to programs designed to engage the public and the academic community in a dialogue about the nature of arts and culture. Readings, lectures, performances, issue-based symposia, and panel discussions on the arts, architecture, design, and humanities are offered throughout the year. **Environmental Initiatives:** Largest solar heated facility in San Francisco, named Top Ten Green Building on Earth Day 2001. Curricular content commitment to sustainability with national experts teaching. Ongoing partnerships with Pacific Energy Center, Sustainable Cotton Project, IDSA's Okala curriculum standards, etc.

ADMISSIONS
Freshman Academic Profile: Average high school GPA 3.18. 73% from public high schools. SAT Math middle 50% range 480–610. SAT Critical Read-

ing middle 50% range 460–630. SAT Writing middle 50% range 460–596. ACT middle 50% range 20–26. Minimum paper TOEFL 550. Minimum computer TOEFL 213. Minimum web-based TOEFL 79. **Basis for Candidate Selection:** *Very important factors considered include:* Application essay, academic GPA, talent/ability. *Important factors considered include:* Recommendation(s). *Other factors considered include:* Rigor of secondary school record, standardized test scores, alumni/ae relation, character/personal qualities, extracurricular activities, first generation, interview, level of applicant's interest, racial/ethnic status, volunteer work, work experience. **Freshman Admission Requirements:** High school diploma is required and GED is accepted. **Freshman Admission Statistics:** 1,181 applied, 75% admitted, 24% enrolled. **Transfer Admission Requirements:** college transcript(s), essay or personal statement, minimum college GPA of 2.0 required. Lowest grade transferable C. **General Admission Information:** Application fee $60. Notification on a rolling basis, beginning on or about 1/15. Nonfall registration accepted. Admission may be deferred for a maximum of one semester. Credit and/or placement offered for CEEB Advanced Placement tests.

COSTS AND FINANCIAL AID
Annual tuition $32,904. Room and board $6,870. Required fees $350. Average book expense $1,500. **Required Forms and Deadlines:** FAFSA. Priority financial aid filing date 3/1. **Notification of Awards:** Applicants will be notified of awards on a rolling basis beginning 3/15. **Types of Aid:** *Need-based scholarships/grants:* Federal Pell, SEOG, state scholarships/grants, private scholarships, the school's own gift aid, Various. *Loans:* FFEL Subsidized Stafford, FFEL Unsubsidized Stafford, FFEL PLUS, Federal Perkins, state loans. **Student Employment:** Federal Work-Study Program available. Institutional employment available. Highest amount earned per year from on-campus jobs $1,800. Off-campus job opportunities are good. **Financial Aid Statistics:** 64% freshmen, 64% undergrads receive need-based scholarship or grant aid. 49% freshmen, 31% undergrads receive non-need-based scholarship or grant aid. 52% freshmen, 56% undergrads receive need-based self-help aid. 89% freshmen, 81% undergrads receive any aid. 63.9% undergrads borrow to pay for school. Average cumulative indebtedness $34,518. **Criteria for awarding institutional aid:** *Non-need-based:* Academics, art.

See page 1044.

CALIFORNIA INSTITUTE OF INTEGRAL STUDIES

1453 Mission St, 4th Floor, San Francisco, CA 94103
Phone: 415-575-6154 **Financial Aid Phone:** 415.575.6122
E-mail: admissions@ciis.edu
Fax: 415-575-1268 **Website:** www.ciis.edu

This private school was founded in 1968. It has a 1-acre campus.

RATINGS
Admissions Selectivity Rating: 60*   **Fire Safety Rating:** 60*   **Green Rating:** 60*

STUDENTS AND FACULTY
Student Body: 10% out-of-state, international (42 countries represented). **Faculty:** Student/faculty ratio 11:1. 62 full-time faculty, 19% are members of minority groups, 48% are women.

ACADEMICS
Degrees: Bachelor's, certificate, master's. **Majors with Highest Enrollment:** Dance therapy/therapist; marriage and family therapy/counseling; psychiatry. **Special Study Options:** Distance learning, dual enrollment, student-designed major, weekend college. **Combined degree programs:** BA/MA. Special programs offered to physically disabled students include note-taking services, reader services, tape recorders.

FACILITIES
Housing: 100% of campus accessible to physically disabled. **Computers:** 100% of classrooms, 100% of libraries, 100% of dining areas, 100% of student union, 100% of common outdoor areas have wireless network access. Students can register for classes online. Administrative functions (other than registration) can be performed online.

CAMPUS LIFE
Environment: Metropolis. **Activities:** Student government, international student organization. **On-Campus Highlights:** CIIS Cafe, Meditation Room, Roof Top Garden, library, bookstore.

ADMISSIONS
Freshman Academic Profile: Minimum paper TOEFL 550. Minimum computer TOEFL 213. Minimum web-based TOEFL 80. **Transfer Admission Requirements:** College transcript(s), essay or personal statement, minimum college GPA of 3.0 required. Lowest grade transferable C.

COSTS AND FINANCIAL AID

Annual tuition $21,285. Required fees $21,285.

CALIFORNIA INSTITUTE OF TECHNOLOGY

Best 373

1200 East California Boulevard, Mail Code 1-94, Pasadena, CA 91125
Phone: 626-395-6341 **Financial Aid Phone:** 626-395-6280
E-mail: ugadmissions@caltech.edu **CEEB Code:** 4034
Fax: 626-683-3026 **Website:** admissions.caltech.edu **ACT Code:** 182

This private school was founded in 1891. It has a 124-acre campus.

RATINGS

Admissions Selectivity Rating: 99   **Fire Safety Rating:** 60*   **Green Rating:** 60*

STUDENTS AND FACULTY

Enrollment: 921. **Student Body:** 34% female, 66% male, 65% out-of-state, 11% international (32 countries represented). Asian 40%, African American 1%, Caucasian 40%, Hispanic 6%.
Retention and Graduation: 98% freshmen return for sophomore year. 81% freshmen graduate within 4 years. 53% grads go on to further study within 1 year. 40% grads pursue arts and sciences degrees. 1% grads pursue law degrees. 3% grads pursue medical degrees. **Faculty:** Student/faculty ratio 2.7:1. 332 full-time faculty, 98% hold PhDs, 14% are members of minority groups, 14% are women.

ACADEMICS

Degrees: Bachelor's, master's, post-master's certificate. **Classes:** Most classes have fewer than 10 students. Most lab/discussion sessions have 20–29 students. **Majors with Highest Enrollment:** Mathematics; mechanical engineering; physics; physics. **Special Study Options:** Cooperative education program, cross-registration, double major, English as a Second Language (ESL), exchange student program (domestic), independent study, liberal arts/career combination, student-designed major, study abroad, "remedial services" are not formally offered. However, remediation is available for students who are deficient in basic scientific knowledge or technical skills. **Combined degree programs:** Caltech-UCSD Medical Scholars Program. Special programs offered to physically disabled students include note-taking services, reader services, tape recorders, tutors.

FACILITIES

Housing: Coed dorms, special housing for disabled students, apartments for married students, single-unit houses. 95% of campus accessible to physically disabled. **Special Academic Facilities/Equipment:** Jet Propulsion Laboratory, Palomar Observatory, Seismological Laboratory, Beckman Institute for Fundamental Research in Biology and Chemistry, Mead Chemistry Laboratory, Moore Laboratory. **Computers:** 50% of classrooms, 50% of dorms, 100% of libraries, 50% of dining areas, 100% of student union, 50% of common outdoor areas have wireless network access. Students can register for classes online. Administrative functions (other than registration) can be performed online.

CAMPUS LIFE

Environment: Metropolis. **Activities:** Choral groups, concert band, dance, drama/theater, jazz band, literary magazine, music ensembles, musical theater, opera, pep band, student government, student newspaper, student-run film society, symphony orchestra, yearbook. **Organizations:** 148 registered organizations, 2 honor societies, 6 religious organizations. **Athletics (Intercollegiate):** *Men:* Baseball, basketball, cross-country, diving, fencing, soccer, swimming, tennis, track/field (outdoor), water polo. *Women:* Basketball, cross-country, diving, fencing, swimming, tennis, track/field (outdoor), volleyball, water polo. **On-Campus Highlights:** Caltech Bookstore, Moore Laboratory, Mead Chemistry Laboratory, Broad Center for the Biological Sciences, Red Door Cafe.

ADMISSIONS

Freshman Academic Profile: 97% in top 10% of high school class, 100% in top 25% of high school class, 70% from public high schools. SAT Math middle 50% range 770–800. SAT Critical Reading middle 50% range 700–760. SAT Writing middle 50% range 690–770. ACT middle 50% range 33–35. **Basis for Candidate Selection:** *Very important factors considered include:* Rigor of secondary school record. *Important factors considered include:* Class rank, application essay, academic GPA, recommendation(s), standardized test scores, character/personal qualities, extracurricular activities. *Other factors considered include:* Alumni/ae relation, first generation, racial/ethnic status, talent/abil-

ity, volunteer work, work experience. **Freshman Admission Requirements:** High school diploma or equivalent is not required. *Academic units required:* 3 English, 4 mathematics, 2 science, (1 science labs), 1 social studies, 1 history. *Academic units recommended:* 4 English, 4 science, 3 foreign language, 3 social studies, 1 history. **Freshman Admission Statistics:** 3,957 applied, 17% admitted, 34% enrolled. **Transfer Admission Requirements:** High school transcript, college transcript(s), essay or personal statement, statement of good standing from prior institution(s). **General Admission Information:** Application fee $60. Regular application deadline 1/1. Regular notification 4/1. Nonfall registration not accepted. Admission may be deferred for a maximum of 1 year. Neither credit nor placement offered for CEEB Advanced Placement tests.

COSTS AND FINANCIAL AID

Room and board $10,755. Required fees $3,660. Average book expense $1,290. **Required Forms and Deadlines:** FAFSA, institution's own financial aid form, CSS/Financial Aid PROFILE, state aid form, noncustodial PROFILE, business/farm supplement. Priority financial aid filing date 1/15. **Notification of Awards:** Applicants will be notified of awards on or about 4/15. **Types of Aid:** *Need-based scholarships/grants:* Federal Pell, SEOG, state scholarships/grants, private scholarships. *Loans:* Direct Subsidized Stafford, Direct Unsubsidized Stafford, Direct PLUS, Federal Perkins, college/university loans from institutional funds. **Student Employment:** Federal Work-Study Program available. Institutional employment available. **Financial Aid Statistics:** 49% freshmen, 47% undergrads receive need-based scholarship or grant aid. 2% freshmen, 4% undergrads receive non-need-based scholarship or grant aid, 33% freshmen, 37% undergrads receive need-based self-help aid. 60% freshmen, 60% undergrads receive any aid. 39% undergrads borrow to pay for school. Average cumulative indebtedness $9,871. **Criteria for awarding institutional aid:** *Non-need-based:* Academics.

CALIFORNIA INSTITUTE OF THE ARTS

24700 McBean Parkway, 24700 McBean Pkw, Valencia, CA 91355
Phone: 661-255-1050 **Financial Aid Phone:** 661-253-7869
E-mail: admissions@calarts.edu **CEEB Code:** 4049
Fax: 661-253-7710 **Website:** www.calarts.edu **ACT Code:** 121

This private school was founded in 1961. It has a 60-acre campus.

RATINGS

Admissions Selectivity Rating: 60*   **Fire Safety Rating:** 61   **Green Rating:** 65

STUDENTS AND FACULTY

Enrollment: 888. **Student Body:** 49% female, 51% male, 49% out-of-state, 8% international (34 countries represented). Asian 12%, African American 8%, Caucasian 58%, Hispanic 12%, Native American 1%.
Retention and Graduation: 75% freshmen return for sophomore year. **Faculty:** Student/faculty ratio 7:1. 160 full-time faculty, 100% hold PhDs, 18% are members of minority groups, 44% are women.

ACADEMICS

Degrees: Bachelor's, certificate, doctoral, master's, post-bachelor's certificate. **Classes:** Most classes have fewer than 10 students. **Majors with Highest Enrollment:** Music performance. **Special Study Options:** Independent study, internships, student-designed major, study abroad. Special programs offered to physically disabled students include note-taking services, reader services, tape recorders, tutors. **Career services:** Career/job search classes, career assessment, internships. **Career services highlights include:** the new career mentorship program "Arts In the World Coaching."

FACILITIES

Housing: Coed dorms, special housing for disabled students, apartments for single students 98% of campus accessible to physically disabled. **Special Academic Facilities/Equipment:** 7 Art galleries, TV studio, Walt Disney Theater, Roy Disney Music Hall, Sharon Disney Lund Dance Theater, Bijou Film Theater. **Computers:** 20% of classrooms, 100% of libraries, 100% of dining areas, 20% of common outdoor areas have wireless network access. Students can register for classes online. Administrative functions (other than registration) can be performed online.

CAMPUS LIFE

Environment: City. **Activities:** Choral groups, dance, drama/theater, jazz band, literary magazine, music ensembles, opera, radio station, student government, student newspaper, student-run film society, symphony orchestra, television station. **Organizations:** 5 registered organizations, **On-Campus Highlights:** Modular Theater, Permanent Set, Gamelan Room, Main Gallery, Lund Dance Theater, Roy O. Disney Music Hall, Bijou Theater. **Environmental Initiatives:** Recycling program, boiler modernization, white energy efficient roofing in Ahmanson Building

ADMISSIONS

Freshman Academic Profile: Minimum paper TOEFL 550. Minimum computer TOEFL 213. Minimum web-based TOEFL 80. **Basis for Candidate Selection:** *Very important factors considered include:* Application essay, talent/ability. *Important factors considered include:* Recommendation(s), extracurricular activities. *Other factors considered include:* Academic GPA, rigor of secondary school record, character/personal qualities, interview, level of applicant's interest. **Freshman Admission Requirements:** High school diploma is required and GED is accepted. *Academic units recommended:* 4 English, 3 mathematics, 3 science, 2 foreign language, 3 social studies, 1 computer science, 2 academic electives. **Freshman Admission Statistics:** 1,186 applied, 33% admitted, 40% enrolled. **Transfer Admission Requirements:** High school transcript, college transcript(s), essay or personal statement, Lowest grade transferable C. **General Admission Information:** Application fee $70. Regular application deadline 1/5. Notification on a rolling basis, beginning on or about 4/1. Nonfall registration accepted. Credit offered for CEEB Advanced Placement tests.

COSTS AND FINANCIAL AID

Annual tuition $36,166. Room and board $9,293. Required fees $576. Average book expense $1,500. **Required Forms and Deadlines:** FAFSA. Priority financial aid filing date 3/2. **Notification of Awards:** Applicants will be notified of awards on a rolling basis beginning 4/1. **Types of Aid:** *Need-based scholarships/grants:* Federal Pell, SEOG, state scholarships/grants, private scholarships, the school's own gift aid. *Loans:* FFEL Subsidized Stafford, FFEL Unsubsidized Stafford, FFEL PLUS, Federal Perkins, college/university loans from institutional funds, Private/Alternative Loans. **Student Employment:** Federal Work-Study Program available. Institutional employment available. Highest amount earned per year from on-campus jobs $3,222. Off-campus job opportunities are good. **Financial Aid Statistics:** 62% freshmen, 64% undergrads receive need-based scholarship or grant aid. 58% freshmen, 61% undergrads receive need-based self-help aid. 71% freshmen, 77% undergrads receive any aid. 67% undergrads borrow to pay for school. Average cumulative indebtedness $39,286. **Criteria for awarding institutional aid:** *Non-need-based:* Art, minority status, music/drama.

CALIFORNIA LUTHERAN UNIVERSITY

60 West Olsen Road, 1350, Thousand Oaks, CA 91360
Phone: 805-493-3135
E-mail: cluadm@clunet.edu **CEEB Code:** 4088
Fax: 805-493-3114 **Website:** www.callutheran.edu **ACT Code:** 183

This private school, affiliated with the Lutheran Church, was founded in 1959. It has a 290-acre campus.

RATINGS

Admissions Selectivity Rating: 82   **Fire Safety Rating:** 60*   **Green Rating:** 60*

STUDENTS AND FACULTY

Enrollment: 1,959. **Student Body:** 56% female, 44% male, 21% out-of-state, 1% international. Asian 3%, African American 2%, Caucasian 52%, Hispanic 12%, Native American 1%.
Retention and Graduation: 78% freshmen return for sophomore year. 57% freshmen graduate within 4 years. 65% grads go on to further study within 1 year. **Faculty:** Student/faculty ratio 14:1. 118 full-time faculty, 86% hold PhDs, 15% are members of minority groups, 48% are women.

ACADEMICS

Degrees: Bachelor's, master's, post-bachelor's certificate, post-master's certificate. **Classes:** Most classes have 20–29 students. Most lab/discussion sessions have 10–19 students. **Majors with Highest Enrollment:** Biology; business/commerce; liberal arts and sciences/liberal studies. **Special Study Options:** Accelerated program, cooperative education program, double major, dual enrollment, exchange student program (domestic), honors program, independent study, internships, student-designed major, study abroad, teacher certification program. **Honors programs:** Honors Program. **Combined degree programs:** 3-2 with Washington University. Special programs offered to physically disabled students include note-taking services, reader services, tape recorders, tutors. **Career services:** Career/job search classes, career assessment, internships.

FACILITIES

Housing: Coed dorms, special housing for disabled students, apartments for single students. 90% of campus accessible to physically disabled. **Special Academic Facilities/Equipment:** On-campus pre-school, hypermedia lab, multimedia center and program, film studio, Kwan Fong Art Gallary, Scandinavian Center, Educational Technology Center. **Computers:** Students can register for classes online. Administrative functions (other than registration) can be performed online.

CAMPUS LIFE

Environment: Town. **Activities:** Choral groups, concert band, dance, drama/theater, jazz band, literary magazine, music ensembles, musical theater, pep band, radio station, student government, student newspaper, symphony orchestra, television station, yearbook. **Organizations:** 75 registered organizations, 11 honor societies, 3 religious organizations. **Athletics (Intercollegiate):** *Men:* Baseball, basketball, cheerleading, cross-country, diving, football, golf, soccer, swimming, tennis, track/field (outdoor), water polo. *Women:* Basketball, cheerleading, cross-country, diving, soccer, softball, swimming, tennis, track/field (outdoor), volleyball, water polo. **On-Campus Highlights:** Education and Technology Building, Soland Humanities Center, The Apartments, Kingsmen Park, Samuelson Chapel, Will begin construction on a new athletics complex and lab facilities for sports medicine in January 2004.

ADMISSIONS

Freshman Academic Profile: Average high school GPA 3.4. 29% in top 10% of high school class, 60% in top 25% of high school class, 95% in top 50% of high school class. SAT Math middle 50% range 500–600. SAT Critical Reading middle 50% range 480–590. ACT middle 50% range 21–26. Minimum paper TOEFL 550. Minimum computer TOEFL 213. **Basis for Candidate Selection:** *Very important factors considered include:* Recommendation(s), rigor of secondary school record, standardized test scores. *Important factors considered include:* Application essay, extracurricular activities, talent/ability, volunteer work, work experience. *Other factors considered include:* Class rank, alumni/ae relation, character/personal qualities, geographical residence, interview, racial/ethnic status, religious affiliation/commitment, state residency. **Freshman Admission Requirements:** High school diploma is required and GED is accepted. *Academic units required:* 4 English, 3 mathematics, 3 science, 2 foreign language, 2 social studies, 1 history, 2 humanities. **Freshman Admission Statistics:** 1,660 applied, 73% admitted, 33% enrolled. **Transfer Admission Requirements:** College transcript(s), essay or personal statement, statement of good standing from prior institution(s). Minimum college GPA of 2.8 required. Lowest grade transferable D. **General Admission Information:** Application fee $45. Notification on a rolling basis, beginning on or about 12/1. Nonfall registration accepted. Admission may be deferred for a maximum of 1 year. Credit and/or placement offered for CEEB Advanced Placement tests.

COSTS AND FINANCIAL AID

Annual tuition $21,820. Room and board $7,570. Required fees $465. Average book expense $1,260. **Required Forms and Deadlines:** FAFSA, Student Request Form. Priority financial aid filing date 3/2. **Notification of Awards:** Applicants will be notified of awards on a rolling basis beginning 4/1. **Types of Aid:** *Need-based scholarships/grants:* Federal Pell, SEOG, state scholarships/grants, private scholarships, the school's own gift aid. *Loans:* FFEL Subsidized Stafford, FFEL Unsubsidized Stafford, FFEL PLUS, Federal Perkins, Opportunity Loans From Loan Servicer. **Student Employment:** Federal Work-Study Program available. Institutional employment available. Highest amount earned per year from on-campus jobs $1,200. Off-campus job opportunities are good. **Financial Aid Statistics:** 72% freshmen, 65% undergrads receive need-based scholarship or grant aid. 29% freshmen, 24% undergrads receive non-need-based scholarship or grant aid. 56% freshmen, 54% undergrads receive need-based self-help aid. 83% undergrads receive any aid. 71% undergrads borrow to pay for school. Average cumulative indebtedness $17,598. **Criteria for awarding institutional aid:** *Non-need-based:* Academics, art, leadership, music/drama, religious affiliation.

CALIFORNIA MARITIME ACADEMY OF CALIFORNIA STATE UNIVERSITY

200 Maritime Academy, Vallejo, CA 94590-0644
Phone: 707-654-1330
E-mail: admission@csum.edu
Fax: 707-654-1336 **Website:** www.csum.edu **ACT Code:** 184

This public school was founded in 1929. It has a 67-acre campus.

RATINGS

Admissions Selectivity Rating: 60*   **Fire Safety Rating:** 60*   **Green Rating:** 60*

STUDENTS AND FACULTY

Enrollment: 606. **Student Body:** 17% female, 83% male, 13% out-of-state, 6% international. Asian 11%, African American 4%, Caucasian 59%, Hispanic 7%, Native American 1%.

Retention and Graduation: 93% freshmen return for sophomore year. **Faculty:** Student/faculty ratio 15:1. 49 full-time faculty, 53% hold PhDs, 12% are women.

ACADEMICS

Degrees: bachelor's. **Majors with Highest Enrollment:** heating, air conditioning and refrigeration technology/technician (ach/acr/achr/hrac/hvac/ac technology); international business/trade/commerce; logistics and materials management; mechanical engineering; **Special Study Options:** Cooperative education program, distance learning, double major, internships, all students participate in at least one 2-month training cruise around the Pacific rim over the summer on The GOLDEN BEAR. Special programs offered to physically disabled students include tutors. **Career services:** Alumni services, career/job search classes, internships.

FACILITIES

Housing: Coed dorms 70% of campus accessible to physically disabled. **Special Academic Facilities/Equipment:** Bookstore, library, gym, swimming pool.

CAMPUS LIFE

Activities: Student government. **Organizations:** 16 registered organizations. **Athletics (Intercollegiate):** *Men:* Basketball, crew/rowing, golf, sailing, soccer, water polo *Women:* Crew/rowing, sailing, volleyball.

ADMISSIONS

Freshman Academic Profile: Average high school GPA 3.05. 80% from public high schools. Minimum paper TOEFL 550. Minimum computer TOEFL 213. **Basis for Candidate Selection:** *Very important factors considered include:* Rigor of secondary school record, standardized test scores. *Other factors considered include:* Application essay, recommendation(s), alumni/ae relation, character/personal qualities, extracurricular activities, geographical residence, interview, state residency, talent/ability, volunteer work, work experience. **Freshman Admission Requirements:** High school diploma is required and GED is accepted. *Academic units required:* 4 English, 3 mathematics, 2 science, (2 science labs), 2 foreign language, 1 social studies, 1 history, 1 visual/performing arts, 1 academic electives. **Freshman Admission Statistics:** 432 applied, 83% admitted, 44% enrolled. **Transfer Admission Requirements:** College transcript(s), statement of good standing from prior institution(s). Minimum college GPA of 2.0 required. Lowest grade transferable C. **General Admission Information:** Application fee $55. Regular application deadline 5/1. Regular notification 5/1. Notification on a rolling basis, beginning on or about 11/30. Nonfall registration not accepted.

COSTS AND FINANCIAL AID

Annual in-state tuition $1,572. Annual out-of-state tuition $8,460. Room and board $6,750. Required fees $1,050. Average book expense $846. **Required Forms and Deadlines:** FAFSA. Priority financial aid filing date 3/2. **Notification of Awards:** Applicants will be notified of awards on a rolling basis beginning 4/15. **Types of Aid:** *Need-based scholarships/grants:* Federal Pell, SEOG, state scholarships/grants, private scholarships, the school's own gift aid. *Loans:* FFEL Subsidized Stafford, FFEL Unsubsidized Stafford, FFEL PLUS, Federal Perkins. **Student Employment:** Federal Work-Study Program available. Highest amount earned per year from on-campus jobs $750. Off-campus job opportunities are fair. **Financial Aid Statistics:** 42% freshmen, 59% undergrads receive need-based scholarship or grant aid. 8% freshmen, 7% undergrads receive non-need-based scholarship or grant aid. 63% freshmen, 71% undergrads receive need-based self-help aid. 96% undergrads borrow to pay for school. Average cumulative indebtedness $7,058.

CALIFORNIA POLYTECHNIC STATE UNIVERSITY

Admissions Office, Cal Poly, San Luis Obispo, CA 93407-0031
Phone: 805-756-2311 **Financial Aid Phone:** 805-756-2927
E-mail: admissions@calpoly.edu **CEEB Code:** 4038
Fax: 805-756-5400 **Website:** www.calpoly.edu **ACT Code:** 188

This public school was founded in 1901. It has a 9678-acre campus.

RATINGS

Admissions Selectivity Rating: 93 **Fire Safety Rating:** 84 **Green Rating:** 60*

STUDENTS AND FACULTY

Enrollment: 18,239. **Student Body:** 44% female, 56% male, 4% out-of-state, 1% international (73 countries represented). Asian 11%, African American 1%, Caucasian 65%, Hispanic 12%, Native American 1%.
Retention and Graduation: 24% freshmen graduate within 4 years. **Faculty:** Student/faculty ratio 19:1. 824 full-time faculty, 82% hold PhDs, 32% are women.

ACADEMICS

Degrees: bachelor's, master's. **Classes:** Most classes have 20–29 students. Most lab/discussion sessions have 20–29 students. **Special Study Options:** Cooperative education program, distance learning, double major, English as a Second Language (ESL), exchange student program (domestic), honors program, internships, liberal arts/career combination, study abroad, teacher certification program. **Combined degree programs:** , BS/MS. Special programs offered to physically disabled students include note-taking services, reader services, tape recorders, tutors. **Career services:** Alumni network, alumni services, career/job search classes, career assessment, internships, regional alumni. **Career services highlights include:** Cooperative Education Program.

FACILITIES

Housing: Coed dorms, special housing for disabled students, special housing for international students, apartments for single students, theme housing. **Special Academic Facilities/Equipment:** Dairy, veterinary clinic, printing museum, art gallery. **Computers:** 100% of classrooms, 5% of dorms, 100% of libraries, 100% of dining areas, 100% of student union, 5% of common outdoor areas have wireless network access. Students can register for classes online. Administrative functions (other than registration) can be performed online.

CAMPUS LIFE

Environment: Town. **Activities:** Choral groups, concert band, dance, drama/theater, jazz band, literary magazine, marching band, music ensembles, musical theater, opera, pep band, radio station, student government, student newspaper, symphony orchestra, television station, campus ministries, international student organization, Model UN. **Organizations:** 400 registered organizations, 14 religious organizations. 25 fraternities, 14 sororities. **Athletics (Intercollegiate):** *Men:* Baseball, basketball, cross-country, football, golf, soccer, swimming, tennis, track/field (outdoor), wrestling. *Women:* Basketball, cross-country, golf, soccer, softball, swimming, tennis, track/field (outdoor), track/field (indoor), volleyball. **On-Campus Highlights:** Performing Arts Center, Recreation Center, Julian's Coffee Shop, Spanos Stadium, University Union, El Corral Bookstore.

ADMISSIONS

Freshman Academic Profile: Average high school GPA 3.81. 48% in top 10% of high school class, 84% in top 25% of high school class, 98% in top 50% of high school class. 83.6% from public high schools. SAT Math middle 50% range 570–670. SAT Critical Reading middle 50% range 530–630. ACT middle 50% range 24–29. Minimum paper TOEFL 550. Minimum computer TOEFL 213. Minimum web-based TOEFL 80. **Basis for Candidate Selection:** *Very important factors considered include:* Academic GPA, rigor of secondary school record, standardized test scores. *Other factors considered include:* Extracurricular activities, first generation, geographical residence, talent/ability, volunteer work, work experience. **Freshman Admission Requirements:** High school diploma is required and GED is accepted. *Academic units required:* 4 English, 3 mathematics, 3 science, (1 science labs), 2 foreign language, 2 social studies, 1 history, 1 visual/performing arts, 1 academic electives. *Academic units recommended:* 5 English, 4 mathematics, 4 science, (2 science labs), 3 foreign language, 2 social studies, 1 history, 1 visual/performing arts. **Freshman Admission Statistics:** 31,489 applied, 37% admitted, 33% enrolled. **Transfer Admission Requirements:** College transcript(s), minimum college GPA of 2.0 required. Lowest grade transferable D. **General Admission Information:** Application fee $55. Early decision application deadline 10/31. Regular application deadline 11/30. Regular notification 4/1. Nonfall registration not accepted. Credit offered for CEEB Advanced Placement tests.

COSTS AND FINANCIAL AID

Room and board $9,623. Required fees $6,198. Average book expense $1,638. **Required Forms and Deadlines:** FAFSA. Priority financial aid filing date 3/2. **Notification of Awards:** Applicants will be notified of awards on a rolling basis beginning 4/1. **Types of Aid:** *Need-based scholarships/grants:* Federal Pell, SEOG, state scholarships/grants, private scholarships, the school's own gift aid, Federal TEACH Grant. *Loans:* Direct Subsidized Stafford, Direct Unsubsidized Stafford, Direct PLUS, Federal Perkins, college/university loans from institutional funds, alternative loans. **Student Employment:** Federal Work-Study Program available. Institutional employment available. Off-campus job opportunities are fair. **Financial Aid Statistics:** 25% freshmen, 24% undergrads receive need-based scholarship or grant aid. 2% freshmen, 1% undergrads receive non-need-based scholarship or grant aid. 20% freshmen, 23% undergrads receive need-based self-help aid. 2% freshmen, 2% undergrads receive athletic scholarships. **Criteria for awarding institutional aid:** *Non-need-based:* Academics, alumni affiliation, art, athletics, job skills, leadership, music/drama, state/district residency.

CALIFORNIA STATE POLYTECHNIC
UNIVERSITY—POMONA

3801 West Temple Avenue, Pomona, CA 91768
Phone: 909-869-3210 **Financial Aid Phone:** 909-869-3700
E-mail: admissions@csupomona.edu **CEEB Code:** 4082
Fax: 909-869-4529 **Website:** www.csupomona.edu/ **ACT Code:** 4048

This public school was founded in 1938. It has a 1437-acre campus.

RATINGS
Admissions Selectivity Rating: 76   **Fire Safety Rating:** 68   **Green Rating:** 94

STUDENTS AND FACULTY
Enrollment: 20,136. **Student Body:** 43% female, 57% male, 2% out-of-state, 5% international (118 countries represented). Asian 27%, African American 3%, Caucasian 25%, Hispanic 32%.
Retention and Graduation: 87% freshmen return for sophomore year. 15% freshmen graduate within 4 years. **Faculty:** Student/faculty ratio 25:1. 565 full-time faculty, 35% are members of minority groups, 41% are women. 3% of classes are taught by teaching assistants.

ACADEMICS
Degrees: bachelor's, master's. **Classes:** Most classes have 30–39 students. Most lab/discussion sessions have 20–29 students. **Majors with Highest Enrollment:** business administration and management; civil engineering; mechanical engineering; **Special Study Options:** Cooperative education program, cross-registration, distance learning, double major, dual enrollment, English as a Second Language (ESL), exchange student program (domestic), external degree program, honors program, internships, study abroad, teacher certification program, Ocean Studies Institute Desert Studies Consortium. **Honors programs:** See web site for complete information about The Kellogg Honors College: www.csupomona.edu/~honorscollege. Special programs offered to physically disabled students include note-taking services, reader services, tutors. **Career services:** Alumni network, alumni services, career/job search classes, career assessment, internships, regional alumni. **Career services highlights include:** Career Development/Counseling: The Career Center assists all students in selecting or changing their major, as well as, what students can do with their major. Students are offered a number of career assessment inventories to assist with career development. The Career Center at Cal Poly Pomona has one of the largest number of organizations recruiting Cal Poly Pomona students in the State of California.

FACILITIES
Housing: Coed dorms, apartments for single students 95% of campus accessible to physically disabled. **Special Academic Facilities/Equipment:** Center for hospitality management, art gallery, center for regenerative studies, citrus-packing house, meat-processing building, poultry plant, feed mill, beef, sheep, swine, Arabian horse units, horse show arena, and aerospace wind tunnel. **Computers:** 10% of classrooms, 10% of dorms, 100% of libraries, 100% of dining areas, 100% of student union, 60% of common outdoor areas have wireless network access. Students can register for classes online. Administrative functions (other than registration) can be performed online.

CAMPUS LIFE
Environment: City. **Activities:** Choral groups, concert band, dance, drama/theater, jazz band, literary magazine, music ensembles, musical theater, opera, pep band, student government, student newspaper, symphony orchestra, yearbook, campus ministries, international student organization. **Organizations:** 280 registered organizations, 26 honor societies, 10 religious organizations. 12 fraternities, 8 sororities. **Athletics (Intercollegiate):** *Men:* Baseball, basketball, cheerleading, cross-country, soccer, tennis, track/field (outdoor). *Women:* Basketball, cheerleading, cross-country, soccer, tennis, track/field (outdoor), volleyball. **On-Campus Highlights:** The Farmstore at Kellogg Ranch, Rain Bird Aquatic, Ethnobotany&Rainforest, W. K. Kellogg Arabian Horse Center, Kellogg House Pomona, John T. Lyle Center for Regenerative Studies, Full name for #2 above:The Rain Bird Aquatic, Ethnobotony & Rainforest Learning Centers .Cal Poly Pomona is located on the eastern edge of Southern California's San Gabriel Valley. The University's 1,400–acre campus features lush rolling hills; flowers, plants and trees from all seven continents; a rose garden personally built by W.K. Kellogg; and a beautifully landscaped Japanese garden. The university's aesthetic qualities are one of its best kept secrets. Some of the world's finest architects and landscape architects designed and built the ranch—a hybrid of architecture, which combined the formal courtyards, gardens and elements of Spanish, Italian and Islamic architecture with the informality of a growing nouveau-riche society. Pasadena architect Myron Hunt (Rose Bowl, Huntington Library) designed W.K. Kellogg's main house. Charles Gibbs Adams whose work included the Hearst Castle Gardens in San Simeon,

California was selected to landscape the grounds. Later, the landscape was completed by Florence Yoch and Lucile Council, widely recognized as two of the finest garden designers and landscape architects in California. More recently, Antoine Predock designed the University's administration building with a desert theme. **Environmental Initiatives:** Completed baseline inventory. Established LEED Silver Standard or Equivalent on all new buildings. Established Energy Star Policy on Purchase of Office Equipment and Appliances.

ADMISSIONS
Freshman Academic Profile: Average high school GPA 3.36. 84% from public high schools. SAT Math middle 50% range 470–610. SAT Critical Reading middle 50% range 450–560. ACT middle 50% range 19–25. Minimum paper TOEFL 525. Minimum computer TOEFL 195. **Basis for Candidate Selection:** *Very important factors considered include:* Academic GPA, rigor of secondary school record, standardized test scores. **Freshman Admission Requirements:** High school diploma is required and GED is accepted. *Academic units required:* 4 English, 3 mathematics, 2 science, (2 science labs), 2 foreign language, 1 social studies, 1 history, 1 visual/performing arts, 1 academic electives. *Academic units recommended:* 4 mathematics. **Freshman Admission Statistics:** 20,759 applied, 61% admitted, 23% enrolled. **Transfer Admission Requirements:** College transcript(s), statement of good standing from prior institution(s). Minimum college GPA of 2.0 required. **General Admission Information:** Application fee $55. Regular application deadline 11/30. Notification on a rolling basis, beginning on or about 10/2. Nonfall registration not accepted. Credit and/or placement offered for CEEB Advanced Placement tests.

COSTS AND FINANCIAL AID
Annual out-of-state tuition $11,160. Room and board $9,570. Required fees $4,551. Average book expense $1,500. **Required Forms and Deadlines:** FAFSA **Notification of Awards:** Applicants will be notified of awards on a rolling basis beginning 4/1. **Types of Aid:** *Need-based scholarships/grants:* Federal Pell, SEOG, state scholarships/grants, private scholarships, the school's own gift aid. *Loans:* FFEL Subsidized Stafford, FFEL Unsubsidized Stafford, FFEL PLUS, Federal Perkins, college/university loans from institutional funds. **Student Employment:** Federal Work-Study Program available. Institutional employment available. Off-campus job opportunities are good. **Financial Aid Statistics:** 37% freshmen, 42% undergrads receive need-based scholarship or grant aid. 4% freshmen, 3% undergrads receive non-need-based scholarship or grant aid. 42% freshmen, 46% undergrads receive need-based self-help aid. 1% freshmen, 1% undergrads receive athletic scholarships. 59% freshmen, 60% undergrads receive any aid. 36% undergrads borrow to pay for school. Average cumulative indebtedness $14,035. **Criteria for awarding institutional aid:** *Non-need-based:* Academics, alumni affiliation, athletics, leadership, state/district residency.

CALIFORNIA STATE UNIVERSITY—
BAKERSFIELD

9001 Stockdale Highway, Bakersfield, CA 93311
Phone: 661-664-3036
E-mail: swatkin@csub.edu **CEEB Code:** 4110
Fax: 661-664-3389 **Website:** www.csub.edu

This public school was founded in 1970. It has a 375-acre campus.

RATINGS
Admissions Selectivity Rating: 60*   **Fire Safety Rating:** 60*   **Green Rating:** 60*

STUDENTS AND FACULTY
Student Body: 10% out-of-state, international.
Retention and Graduation: 20% grads go on to further study within 1 year. 10% grads pursue arts and sciences degrees. 10% grads pursue business degrees. **Faculty:** Student/faculty ratio 19:1.

ACADEMICS
Degrees: Bachelor's, master's. **Majors with Highest Enrollment:** Business, management, marketing, and related support services, other; liberal arts and sciences/liberal studies; psychology. **Special Study Options:** Accelerated program, cooperative education program, cross-registration, distance learning, double major, dual enrollment, English as a Second Language (ESL), exchange student program (domestic), external degree program, honors program, independent study, internships, liberal arts/career combination, student-designed major, study abroad, teacher certification program. Special programs offered to physically disabled students include note-taking services, reader services, tape recorders, tutors. **Career services:** Alumni services, career/job search classes, career assessment, internships.

FACILITIES

Housing: Coed dorms, women's dorms 100% of campus accessible to physically disabled. **Special Academic Facilities/Equipment:** Todd Madigan Art Gallery, Frances Dor Theater, Calif. Well Sample Repository, Geotechnology Training Center, Family Business Institute. **Computers:** Students can register for classes online.

CAMPUS LIFE

Environment: Village. **Activities:** Choral groups, concert band, drama/theater, jazz band, literary magazine, music ensembles, musical theater, opera, pep band, student government, student newspaper. **Organizations:** 71 registered organizations, 1 honor societies, 2 religious organizations. 2 fraternities, 2 sororities. **Athletics (Intercollegiate):** *Men:* Basketball, diving, golf, soccer, swimming, track/field (outdoor), wrestling. *Women:* Basketball, cross-country, diving, soccer, softball, swimming, tennis, track/field (outdoor), volleyball, water polo.

ADMISSIONS

Freshman Academic Profile: 99% from public high schools. Minimum paper TOEFL 550. **Basis for Candidate Selection: Freshman Admission Requirements:** High school diploma is required and GED is accepted. *Academic units required:* 4 English, 3 mathematics, 1 science, (2 science labs), 2 foreign language, 2 history, 1 academic electives, 1 visual/performing arts. **Transfer Admission Requirements:** College transcript(s), minimum college GPA of 2.0 required. Lowest grade transferable D. **General Admission Information:** Application fee $55. Nonfall registration accepted. Admission may be deferred for a maximum of N/A. Credit and/or placement offered for CEEB Advanced Placement tests.

COSTS AND FINANCIAL AID

Required Forms and Deadlines: FAFSA, state aid form. Financial aid filing deadline 4/1. Priority financial aid filing date 4/1. **Notification of Awards:** **Types of Aid:** *Need-based scholarships/grants:* Federal Pell, SEOG, state scholarships/grants, private scholarships, the school's own gift aid, United Negro College Fund, Federal Nursing Scholarships. *Loans:* Direct Subsidized Stafford, FFEL Subsidized Stafford, Federal Perkins, Federal Nursing, state loans, college/university loans from institutional funds. **Student Employment:** Federal Work-Study Program available. Institutional employment available. Highest amount earned per year from on-campus jobs $3,916. Off-campus job opportunities are good. **Financial Aid Statistics:** 55% freshmen, 53% undergrads receive need-based scholarship or grant aid. 15% freshmen, 5% undergrads receive non-need-based scholarship or grant aid. 31% freshmen, 44% undergrads receive need-based self-help aid. 72% undergrads borrow to pay for school.

CALIFORNIA STATE UNIVERSITY, CHICO

400 West First Street, Chico, CA 95929-0722
Phone: 530-898-4428 **Financial Aid Phone:** 530-898-6451
E-mail: info@csuchico.edu **CEEB Code:** 4048
Fax: 530-898-6456 **Website:** www.csuchico.edu **ACT Code:** 212

This public school was founded in 1887. It has a 130-acre campus.

RATINGS

Admissions Selectivity Rating: 78   **Fire Safety Rating:** 60*   **Green Rating:** 94

STUDENTS AND FACULTY

Enrollment: 15,617. **Student Body:** 51% female, 49% male, 2% out-of-state, 3% international (42 countries represented). Asian 2%, African American 1%, Caucasian 83%, Hispanic 6%.
Retention and Graduation: 82% freshmen return for sophomore year. **Faculty:** 501 full-time faculty, 83% hold PhDs, 18% are members of minority groups, 42% are women. 1% of classes are taught by teaching assistants.

ACADEMICS

Degrees: bachelor's, certificate, master's, post-bachelor's certificate, post-master's certificate. **Classes:** Most classes have 20–29 students. Most lab/discussion sessions have 20–29 students. **Majors with Highest Enrollment:** Business administration, management and operations, other; liberal arts and sciences/liberal studies; psychology; **Special Study Options:** Cooperative education program, cross-registration, distance learning, double major, dual enrollment, English as a Second Language (ESL), exchange student program (domestic), external degree program, honors program, independent study, internships, student-designed major, study abroad, teacher certification program. **Honors programs:** Honors in General Education (HGE) Honors in the Major (HIM) **Combined degree programs:** We currently offer BA or BS combined with a post-bac credential. Special programs offered to physically disabled students

include note-taking services, reader services, tape recorders, tutors. **Career services:** Alumni network, career assessment, internships. **Career services highlights include:** We are most proud of the experiential learning that we afford our students. Typical of the types of projects our entrepreneurship students engage in is the collaboration between teams of students associated with our Center for Entrepreneurship (CFE) and teams of students enrolled in the College of Engineering's Manufacturing Technology Program. This collaboration takes these student teams out of the classroom and into the middle of one of the most important industries (rice) in the University's service region. In March 2007, Chico State Manufacturing Technology Program (MFP) students won the Grand Prize in the prestigious WESTEC (Western Tool Exposition and Conference) Manufacturing Challenge for building a bio-diesel reactor unit that they redesigned from an existing manually operated home bio-diesel kit. The bio diesel reactor unit was originally designed to reduce, reuse and recycle the used vegetable oil and animal fat from Chico State's residence hall kitchen. The project team also considered use of animal renderings from the university farm as a potential feedstock for bio-diesel fuel. While the Chico State bio-diesel reactor unit was built more for research than for commercial production, conversations between our CFE Director and the MFP Director led to a CFE-initiated assessment of the feasibility of alternative feed stock products from which bio-diesel could be produced. A study conducted by the interdisciplinary team of students led to the discovery that rice processing provides an effective feedstock for the production of bio-diesel. The study demonstrated that rice producing areas in Butte and Glenn counties may be capable of producing sufficient bio diesel from rice bran to substantially impact the amount of petroleum-based diesel fuel needed for the industry's production processes. The study concluded that feedstock within the university's 12-county service region would be plentiful, thereby creating new revenue sources for the local agricultural business community and facilitating new opportunities in the area of sustainable farming. This and other types of experiential learning projects that we make available for our students aligns perfectly with the college's vision for a world-class Center for Entrepreneurship at California State University, Chico. It also supports the University's strong commitment and unique competencies in the area of sustainability, it furthers our commitment to provide students with experiential learning opportunities, and it helps us mobilize campus resources that can contribute to the vibrancy of the local economy.

FACILITIES

Housing: Coed dorms, special housing for disabled students, special housing for international students, fraternity/sorority housing, apartments for single students, thematic housing for honors, engineering, minorities in engineering and science, business, and math. Theme floors include community service, recreational sports, leadership, and Adventure Outings. 95% of campus accessible to physically disabled. **Special Academic Facilities/Equipment:** Anthropology museum, center for intercultural studies, satellite communication dishes, biological field station, university farm, electron microscope. **Computers:** 100% of classrooms, 100% of dorms, 100% of libraries, 100% of dining areas, 100% of student union, 25% of common outdoor areas have wireless network access. Students can register for classes online. Administrative functions (other than registration) can be performed online.

CAMPUS LIFE

Environment: City. **Activities:** Choral groups, concert band, dance, drama/theater, jazz band, literary magazine, music ensembles, musical theater, opera, pep band, radio station, student government, student newspaper, student-run film society, symphony orchestra, yearbook. **Organizations:** 192 registered organizations, 18 honor societies, 12 religious organizations. 15 fraternities, 14 sororities. **Athletics (Intercollegiate):** *Men:* Baseball, basketball, cross-country, golf, soccer, track/field (outdoor). *Women:* Basketball, cross-country, golf, soccer, softball, track/field (outdoor), volleyball. **On-Campus Highlights:** Bell Memorial Union, Meriam Library, Turner Print Museum, Humanities Gallery/University Gallery, Wildcat Recreation Center, Nettleton Stadium; on-campus housing facilities; athletic facilities; recording arts studio. **Environmental Initiatives:** This Way to Sustainability Conference AASHE STARS Pilot Project At Chico State, we often purcahse environmentally friendly goods and services to show our support of environmental products and practices. Procurement and Contract Services supports and promotes the purchasing of environmentally friendly products on campus.

ADMISSIONS

Freshman Academic Profile: Average high school GPA 3.12. 35% in top 10% of high school class, 76% in top 25% of high school class, 100% in top 50% of high school class. 84% from public high schools. SAT Math middle 50% range 460–570. SAT Critical Reading middle 50% range 450–550. ACT middle 50% range 19–24. Minimum paper TOEFL 500. Minimum computer TOEFL 173. Minimum web-based TOEFL 173. **Basis for Candidate Selection:** *Very important factors considered include:* Academic GPA, standardized test scores. *Important factors considered include:* Geographical residence, state residency. **Freshman Admission Requirements:** High school diploma is required and GED is accepted. *Academic units required:* 4 English, 3 mathematics, 2 science, (2 science labs), 2 foreign language, 2 social studies, 1 visual/performing arts, 1 academic electives. **Freshman Admission Statistics:** 12,881 applied, 88% admitted, 22% enrolled. **Transfer Admission Requirements:** college transcript(s), statement of good standing from prior institution(s). Minimum college GPA of 2.0 required. Lowest grade transferable D. **General Admission Information:** Application fee $55. Regular application deadline 11/30. Regular notification 3/1. Nonfall registration accepted. Admission may be deferred for a maximum of 1 year. Credit offered for CEEB Advanced Placement tests.

COSTS AND FINANCIAL AID

Annual in-state tuition $5,336. Annual out-of-state tuition $16,496. Room and board $9,404. Required fees $960. Average book expense $1,656. **Required Forms and Deadlines:** FAFSA, Scholarship Application Form. Priority financial aid filing date 3/2. **Notification of Awards:** Applicants will be notified of awards on a rolling basis beginning 3/2. **Types of Aid:** *Need-based scholarships/grants:* Federal Pell, SEOG, state scholarships/grants, private scholarships, the school's own gift aid. *Loans:* Direct Subsidized Stafford, Direct Unsubsidized Stafford, Direct PLUS, Federal Perkins, college/university loans from institutional funds. **Student Employment:** Federal Work-Study Program available. Institutional employment available. Off-campus job opportunities are fair. **Financial Aid Statistics:** 31% freshmen, 36% undergrads receive need-based scholarship or grant aid. 12% freshmen, 8% undergrads receive non-need-based scholarship or grant aid. 17% freshmen, 37% undergrads receive need-based self-help aid. 1% freshmen, 1% undergrads receive athletic scholarships. 89% freshmen, 90% undergrads receive any aid. **Criteria for awarding institutional aid:** *Non-need-based:* Academics, art, athletics, leadership, minority status, music/drama, religious affiliation.

CALIFORNIA STATE UNIVERSITY— DOMINGUEZ HILLS

100 East Victoria Street, Carson, CA 90747
Phone: 310-243-3600 **Financial Aid Phone:**
E-mail: lwise@csudh.edu **CEEB Code:** 4098
Fax: 310-516-3609 **Website:** www.csudh.edu

This public school was founded in 1960. It has a 346-acre campus.

RATINGS
Admissions Selectivity Rating: 79   **Fire Safety Rating:** 60*   **Green Rating:** 60*

STUDENTS AND FACULTY
Enrollment: 8,698. **Student Body:** 69% female, 31% male, 1% out-of-state, 2% international. Asian 9%, African American 27%, Caucasian 13%, Hispanic 36%, Native American 1%. **Retention and Graduation:** 67% freshmen return for sophomore year. 5% freshmen graduate within 4 years. **Faculty:** Student/faculty ratio 22:1. 252 full-time faculty, 76% hold PhDs, 33% are members of minority groups, 48% are women.

ACADEMICS
Degrees: Bachelor's, certificate, master's, post-bachelor's certificate. **Classes:** Most classes have 20–29 students. Most lab/discussion sessions have 20–29 students. **Special Study Options:** Cooperative education program, cross-registration, distance learning, double major, dual enrollment, external degree program, honors program, independent study, internships, study abroad, teacher certification program, weekend college. Special programs offered to physically disabled students include note-taking services, reader services, tape recorders, tutors.

FACILITIES
Housing: Apartments for married students, apartments for single students 100% of campus accessible to physically disabled. **Special Academic Facilities/Equipment:** University Art Gallery. Olympic Velodrome University Theater.

CAMPUS LIFE
Environment: City. **Activities:** Choral groups, concert band, dance, drama/theater, jazz band, music ensembles, student government, student newspaper, symphony orchestra. **Organizations:** 65 registered organizations, 6 honor societies, 3 religious organizations. 4 fraternities, 4 sororities. **Athletics (Intercollegiate):** *Men:* Baseball, basketball, golf, soccer. *Women:* Basketball, cross-country, soccer, softball, tennis, track/field (outdoor), volleyball. **On-Campus Highlights:** Welch Hall, Student Union, Library, Athletic Fields/Home Depot Center, Sculpture Garden.

ADMISSIONS
Freshman Academic Profile: Average high school GPA 3.04. 50% in top 50% of high school class. 84% from public high schools. SAT Math middle

50% range 370–480. SAT Critical Reading middle 50% range 360–470. ACT middle 50% range 13–19. Minimum paper TOEFL 550. Minimum computer TOEFL 150. **Basis for Candidate Selection:** *Other factors considered include:* Recommendation(s), geographical residence, state residency. **Freshman Admission Requirements:** High school diploma is required and GED is accepted. *Academic units required:* 4 English, 3 mathematics, 2 science, (2 science labs), 2 foreign language, 2 social studies, 1 history, 1 academic electives, 1 visual/performing arts. **Freshman Admission Statistics:** 6,486 applied, 15% admitted, 75% enrolled. **Transfer Admission Requirements:** High school transcript, college transcript(s), minimum college GPA of 2.0 required. Lowest grade transferable C. **General Admission Information:** Application fee $55. Regular application deadline 6/1. Nonfall registration accepted. Credit offered for CEEB Advanced Placement tests.

COSTS AND FINANCIAL AID

Annual in-state tuition $1,815. Annual out-of-state tuition $7,380. Room and board $5,801. Required fees $300. Average book expense $630. **Required Forms and Deadlines:** FAFSA, institution's own financial aid form, state aid form. Financial aid filing deadline 4/15. Priority financial aid filing date 3/2. **Notification of Awards:** Applicants will be notified of awards on a rolling basis beginning 2/28. **Types of Aid:** *Need-based scholarships/grants:* Federal Pell, state scholarships/grants. *Loans:* Direct Subsidized Stafford, Direct Unsubsidized Stafford, FFEL PLUS, Federal Perkins. **Student Employment:** Highest amount earned per year from on-campus jobs $3,000. **Financial Aid Statistics:** 66% freshmen, 64% undergrads receive need-based scholarship or grant aid. 16% freshmen, 6% undergrads receive non-need-based scholarship or grant aid. 21% freshmen, 35% undergrads receive need-based self-help aid. 55% undergrads borrow to pay for school. Average cumulative indebtedness $15,112.

CALIFORNIA STATE UNIVERSITY—EAST BAY

25800 Carlos Bee Blvd, Hayward, CA 94542-3035
Phone: 510-885-2784 **Financial Aid Phone:** 510.885.2784
E-mail: admissions@csueastbay.edu **CEEB Code:** 4011
Fax: 510-885-3505 **Website:** www.csueastbay.edu **ACT Code:** 154

This public school was founded in 1957. It has a 342-acre campus.

RATINGS
Admissions Selectivity Rating: 78   **Fire Safety Rating:** 60*   **Green Rating:** 60*

STUDENTS AND FACULTY
Enrollment: 10,336. **Student Body:** 61% female, 39% male, 1.1% out-of-state, 6% international (86 countries represented). Asian 27%, African American 14%, Caucasian 23%, Hispanic 15%, Native American 1%. **Retention and Graduation:** 79% freshmen return for sophomore year. 17% freshmen graduate within 4 years. **Faculty:** Student/faculty ratio 20:1. 365 full-time faculty, 48% are women. 5% of classes are taught by teaching assistants.

ACADEMICS
Degrees: Bachelor's, certificate, master's, post-bachelor's certificate, post-master's certificate. **Special Study Options:** Cooperative education program, cross-registration, distance learning, double major, dual enrollment, English as a Second Language (ESL), exchange student program (domestic), external degree program, honors program, independent study, internships, liberal arts/career combination, student-designed major, study abroad, teacher certification program, weekend college, Year round operation with state supported summer quarter. Joint Master's Degree in Marine Science offered at Moss Landing Marine Lab. Joint MFA in Creative Writing in summer. Overseas MBA programs in Hong Kong, Moscow, Singapore, and Vienna. Special programs offered to physically disabled students include note-taking services, reader services, tape recorders, tutors. **Career services:** Alumni services, career/job search classes, career assessment, internships

FACILITIES
Housing: Apartments for single students, 95% of campus accessible to physically disabled. **Special Academic Facilities/Equipment:** Anthropology museum, art gallery, scanning electron microsope facility, marine lab, ecological field station, geology summer camp. **Computers:** Students can register for classes online. Administrative functions (other than registration) can be performed online.

CAMPUS LIFE
Environment: City. **Activities:** Choral groups, concert band, dance, drama/theater, jazz band, literary magazine, music ensembles, musical theater, opera, pep band, radio station, student government, student newspaper, symphony orchestra, television station **Organizations:** 100 registered organizations, 2 honor societies, 2 religious organizations. 7 fraternities, 7 sororities. **Athletics (In-**

tercollegiate): *Men:* Baseball, basketball, cross-country, golf, soccer *Women:* Basketball, cross-country, golf, soccer, softball, swimming, volleyball, water polo **On-Campus Highlights:** University Union, Gymnasium/Pools, Warren Hall /Administration, University Theatre, University Art Gallery.

ADMISSIONS

Freshman Academic Profile: Average high school GPA 3. SAT Math middle 50% range 390–510. ACT middle 50% range 15-21. Minimum paper TOEFL 525. Minimum computer TOEFL 197. **Basis for Candidate Selection:** *Very important factors considered include:* Academic GPA, rigor of secondary school record, standardized test scores. *Other factors considered include:* recommendation(s), state residency. **Freshman Admission Requirements:** High school diploma is required and GED is accepted. *Academic units required:* 4 English, 3 mathematics, 2 science, (2 science labs), 2 foreign language, 1 social studies, 1 history, 1 academic electives, 1 Visual/Performing Arts **Freshman Admission Statistics:** 7,189 applied, 75% admitted, 25% enrolled. **Transfer Admission Requirements:** college transcript(s), statement of good standing from prior institution(s). Minimum college GPA of 2.0 required. Lowest grade transferable D. **General Admission Information:** Application fee $55. Early decision application deadline 3/15. Regular application deadline 6/30. Notification on a rolling basis, beginning on or about 3/15. Nonfall registration accepted. Admission may be deferred for a maximum of 2 quarters. Credit and/or placement offered for CEEB Advanced Placement tests.

COSTS AND FINANCIAL AID

Annual in-state tuition $4,872. Annual out-of-state tuition $13,800. Room and board $10,430. Average book expense $1,734. **Required Forms and Deadlines:** FAFSA. Priority financial aid filing date 3/2. **Notification of Awards:** Applicants will be notified of awards on a rolling basis beginning 3/15. **Types of Aid:** *Need-based scholarships/grants:* Federal Pell, SEOG, state scholarships/grants, private scholarships, the school's own gift aid. *Loans:* FFEL Subsidized Stafford, FFEL Unsubsidized Stafford, FFEL PLUS, Federal Perkins. **Student Employment:** Federal Work-Study Program available. Institutional employment available. Off-campus job opportunities are excellent. **Financial Aid Statistics:** 79% freshmen, 42% undergrads receive need-based scholarship or grant aid. 57% freshmen, 34% undergrads receive need-based self-help aid. 43% freshmen, 42% undergrads receive any aid. 33.7% undergrads borrow to pay for school. Average cumulative indebtedness $12,385. **Criteria for awarding institutional aid:** *Non-need-based:* Academics

CALIFORNIA STATE UNIVERSITY, FRESNO

5150 North Maple Ave. M/S JA 57, Fresno, CA 93740-8026
Phone: 559-278-2261 **Financial Aid Phone:** 559-278-6558
E-mail: vivian_franco@csufresno.edu **CEEB Code:** 4312
Fax: 559-278-4812 **Website:** www.csufresno.edu **ACT Code:** 266

This public school was founded in 1911. It has a 388-acre campus.

RATINGS

Admissions Selectivity Rating: 71   **Fire Safety Rating:** 65   **Green Rating:** 89

STUDENTS AND FACULTY

Enrollment: 18,216. **Student Body:** 57% female, 43% male, 1% out-of-state, 1% international (103 countries represented). Asian 16%, African American 6%, Caucasian 34%, Hispanic 35%, Native American 1%.
Retention and Graduation: 14% freshmen graduate within 4 years. 5% grads go on to further study within 1 year. 1% grads pursue law degrees. 4% grads pursue business degrees. 1% grads pursue medical degrees. **Faculty:** Student/faculty ratio 20:1. 645 full-time faculty, 83% hold PhDs, 34% are members of minority groups, 46% are women. 1% of classes are taught by teaching assistants.

ACADEMICS

Degrees: Bachelor's, master's. **Classes:** Most classes have 20–29 students. Most lab/discussion sessions have 20–29 students. **Majors with Highest Enrollment:** Health services/allied health/health sciences; liberal arts and sciences/liberal studies. **Special Study Options:** Accelerated program, cooperative education program, cross-registration, distance learning, double major, dual enrollment, English as a Second Language (ESL), exchange student program (domestic), honors program, independent study, internships, student-designed major, study abroad, teacher certification program. Special programs offered to physically disabled students include note-taking services, reader services, tape recorders, tutors.

FACILITIES

Housing: Coed dorms, men's dorms, women's dorms, fraternity/sorority housing 100% of campus accessible to physically disabled. **Special Academic Facilities/Equipment:** Marine lab, Downing Planetarium. **Computers:** 100%

of classrooms, 100% of dorms, 100% of libraries, 100% of dining areas, 100% of student union, 20% of common outdoor areas have wireless network access. Students can register for classes online. Administrative functions (other than registration) can be performed online. Undergraduates are required to own a computer.

CAMPUS LIFE

Environment: Metropolis. **Activities:** Choral groups, concert band, dance, drama/theater, jazz band, marching band, music ensembles, musical theater, radio station, student government, student newspaper, symphony orchestra, television station, international student organization. **Organizations:** 250 registered organizations, 21 honor societies, 11 religious organizations. 19 fraternities, 13 sororities. **Athletics (Intercollegiate):** *Men:* Baseball, basketball, cheerleading, cross-country, football, golf, tennis, track/field (outdoor). *Women:* Basketball, cheerleading, cross-country, diving, equestrian sports, golf, lacrosse, light weight football, soccer, softball, swimming, tennis, track/field (outdoor), volleyball. **On-Campus Highlights:** Savemart Events Center, Downing Planetarium, Kennel Bookstore, New Ciminology Center, Henry Madden Library, Please check out our website for more inforamtion: www.gotofresnostate.com.

ADMISSIONS

Freshman Academic Profile: Average high school GPA 3.28. 99% from public high schools. SAT Math middle 50% range 420–540. SAT Critical Reading middle 50% range 400–520. ACT middle 50% range 17–22. Minimum paper TOEFL 500. Minimum computer TOEFL 173. Minimum web-based TOEFL 61. **Basis for Candidate Selection:** *Very important factors considered include:* Academic GPA, rigor of secondary school record, standardized test scores. **Freshman Admission Requirements:** High school diploma is required and GED is accepted. *Academic units required:* 4 English, 3 mathematics, 1 science, (1 science labs), 2 foreign language, 1 social studies, 1 history, 1 visual/performing arts, 1 academic electives. **Freshman Admission Statistics:** 14,025 applied, 72% admitted, 27% enrolled. **Transfer Admission Requirements:** College transcript(s), minimum college GPA of 2.4 required. Lowest grade transferable D. **General Admission Information:** Application fee $55. Regular application deadline 11/30. Notification on a rolling basis, beginning on or about 8/1. Nonfall registration accepted. Credit offered for CEEB Advanced Placement tests.

COSTS AND FINANCIAL AID

Annual out-of-state tuition $10,170. Room and board $8,590. Required fees $3,687. Average book expense $1,288. **Required Forms and Deadlines:** FAFSA. Priority financial aid filing date 3/3. **Notification of Awards:** Applicants will be notified of awards on a rolling basis beginning 4/1. **Types of Aid:** *Need-based scholarships/grants:* Federal Pell, SEOG, state scholarships/grants, private scholarships, the school's own gift aid. *Loans:* FFEL Subsidized Stafford, FFEL Unsubsidized Stafford, FFEL PLUS, Federal Perkins, Federal Nursing, college/university loans from institutional funds. **Student Employment:** Federal Work-Study Program available. Institutional employment available. Off-campus job opportunities are good. **Financial Aid Statistics:** 52% freshmen, 51% undergrads receive need-based scholarship or grant aid. 12% freshmen, 7% undergrads receive non-need-based scholarship or grant aid. 48% freshmen, 52% undergrads receive need-based self-help aid. 3% freshmen, 2% undergrads receive athletic scholarships. 65% freshmen, 62% undergrads receive any aid. 65% undergrads borrow to pay for school. Average cumulative indebtedness $10,406. **Criteria for awarding institutional aid:** *Non-need-based:* Academics, art, athletics, leadership, music/drama, state/district residency.

CALIFORNIA STATE UNIVERSITY, FULLERTON

800 North State College Boulevard, Fullerton, CA 92834-6900
Phone: 714-773-2370
E-mail: admissions@fullerton.edu **CEEB Code:** 4589
Fax: 714-278-2356 **Website:** www.fullerton.edu

This public school was founded in 1957. It has a 225-acre campus.

RATINGS

Admissions Selectivity Rating: 78   **Fire Safety Rating:** 78   **Green Rating:** 60*

STUDENTS AND FACULTY

Enrollment: 25,261. **Student Body:** 60% female, 40% male, 1% out-of-state, 4% international (78 countries represented). Asian 24%, African American 3%, Caucasian 34%, Hispanic 24%, Native American 1%.
Retention and Graduation: 80% freshmen return for sophomore year. 8% freshmen graduate within 4 years. **Faculty:** Student/faculty ratio 21:1. 754 full-time faculty, 84% hold PhDs, 24% are members of minority groups, 39% are women.

ACADEMICS

Degrees: Bachelor's, master's. **Classes:** Most classes have 20–29 students. Most lab/discussion sessions have 20–29 students. **Special Study Options:** Cooperative education program, double major, honors program, independent study, internships, student-designed major, study abroad. Special programs offered to physically disabled students include note-taking services, reader services, tape recorders. **Career services:** Alumni services, career/job search classes, career assessment, internships.

FACILITIES

Housing: Fraternity/sorority housing, apartments for single students. 90% of campus accessible to physically disabled. **Computers:** Students can register for classes online. Administrative functions (other than registration) can be performed online.

CAMPUS LIFE

Activities: Choral groups, concert band, dance, drama/theater, jazz band, music ensembles, musical theater, radio station, student government, student newspaper. **Athletics (Intercollegiate):** *Men:* Baseball, basketball, cross-country, fencing, soccer, track/field (outdoor), wrestling. *Women:* Basketball, cross-country, fencing, gymnastics, soccer, softball, tennis, track/field (outdoor), volleyball. **On-Campus Highlights:** Fullerton Arboretum, 5 Starbucks coffee shops, Titan Student Union Underground.

ADMISSIONS

Freshman Academic Profile: 82% from public high schools. SAT Math middle 50% range 440–560. SAT Critical Reading middle 50% range 420–530. ACT middle 50% range 17–23. Minimum paper TOEFL 500. Minimum computer TOEFL 173. **Basis for Candidate Selection:** *Very important factors considered include:* Rigor of secondary school record, standardized test scores. *Other factors considered include:* State residency. **Freshman Admission Requirements:** High school diploma is required and GED is accepted. *Academic units required:* 2 science, (2 science labs), 2 history, 1 academic electives, 1 visual/performing arts. **Freshman Admission Statistics:** 13,721 applied, 69% admitted, 30% enrolled. **Transfer Admission Requirements:** College transcript(s), statement of good standing from prior institution(s). Minimum college GPA of 2.0 required. Lowest grade transferable C. **General Admission Information:** Application fee $55. Regular application deadline 4/15. Notification on a rolling basis, beginning on or about 1/1. Nonfall registration accepted. Credit and/or placement offered for CEEB Advanced Placement tests.

COSTS AND FINANCIAL AID

Annual out-of-state tuition $5,904. Room and board $3,953. Required fees $1,881. Average book expense $1,080. **Required Forms and Deadlines:** FAFSA, state aid form. Priority financial aid filing date 3/2. **Notification of Awards:** Applicants will be notified of awards on a rolling basis beginning 3/1. **Types of Aid:** *Need-based scholarships/grants:* Federal Pell, SEOG, state scholarships/grants, private scholarships, the school's own gift aid. *Loans:* FFEL Subsidized Stafford, FFEL Unsubsidized Stafford, FFEL PLUS, Federal Perkins, college/university loans from institutional funds. **Student Employment:** Federal Work-Study Program available. Institutional employment available. Off-campus job opportunities are good. **Financial Aid Statistics:** 30% freshmen, 29% undergrads receive need-based scholarship or grant aid. 15% freshmen, 21% undergrads receive need-based self-help aid. 1% freshmen, 1% undergrads receive athletic scholarships. 41% undergrads borrow to pay for school. Average cumulative indebtedness $12,001. **Criteria for awarding institutional aid:** *Non-need-based:* Academics.

CALIFORNIA STATE UNIVERSITY, MONTEREY BAY

100 Campus Center, Bldg 47, Seaside, CA 93955
Phone: 831-582-3738 **Financial Aid Phone:** 831-582-5100
E-mail: admissions@csumb.edu **CEEB Code:** 1945
Fax: 831-582-3783 **Website:** http://csumb.edu **ACT Code:** 0321

This public school was founded in 1994. It has a 1387-acre campus.

RATINGS

Admissions Selectivity Rating: 71   **Fire Safety Rating:** 90   **Green Rating:** 90

STUDENTS AND FACULTY

Enrollment: 4,278. **Student Body:** 59% female, 41% male, 2% out-of-state, 1% international (15 countries represented). Asian 6%, African American 4%, Caucasian 48%, Hispanic 26%, Native American 1%. **Retention and Graduation:** 71% freshmen return for sophomore year. 14% freshmen graduate within 4 years. **Faculty:** Student/faculty ratio 27:1. 114

full-time faculty, 89% hold PhDs, 46% are members of minority groups, 48% are women.

ACADEMICS

Degrees: bachelor's, master's. **Classes:** Most classes have 20–29 students. Most lab/discussion sessions have 20–29 students. **Majors with Highest Enrollment:** Biology/biological sciences; business administration and management, humanities/humanistic studies; liberal arts and sciences/liberal studies; **Special Study Options:** cross-registration, distance learning, double major, exchange student program (domestic), independent study, internships, student-designed major, study abroad, teacher certification program, service learning. Special programs offered to physically disabled students include note-taking services, reader services, tape recorders. **Career services:** Alumni services, career/job search classes, career assessment, internships. **Career services highlights include:** Annual career conference that brings together students, alumni and other working professionals together for a day of networking and learning was featured in the "Good Ideas" section of Campus Career Counselor magazine.

FACILITIES

Housing: Coed dorms, special housing for disabled students, special housing for international students, apartments for married students, apartments for single students, wellness housing, theme housing, six-person suite-style living with living areas and kitchenette; substance-free residence hall. 75% of campus accessible to physically disabled. **Special Academic Facilities/Equipment:** Panetta Institute, Tanimura & Antle Family Memorial Library. **Computers:** 100% of classrooms, 100% of dorms, 100% of libraries, 100% of dining areas, 100% of student union, 25% of common outdoor areas have wireless network access. Students can register for classes online. Administrative functions (other than registration) can be performed online.

CAMPUS LIFE

Environment: Village. **Activities:** Choral groups, concert band, dance, drama/theater, jazz band, music ensembles, radio station, student government, student newspaper, campus ministries, international student organization, Model UN. **Organizations:** 71 registered organizations, 4 religious organizations. 5 fraternities, 8 sororities. **Athletics (Intercollegiate):** *Men:* Baseball, basketball, cross-country, golf, sailing, soccer. *Women:* Basketball, cross-country, golf, sailing, soccer, softball, volleyball, water polo. **On-Campus Highlights:** Black Box Cabaret, University Center, Student Center, Tanimura & Antle Library, Chapman Science Academic Center. **Environmental Initiatives:** We are an early signatory to the Presidents Climate Commitment. We have formed a revolving fund called the Energy Innovations Fund that will support energy saving projects and repay itself through energy savings. Our Food Service operations has a high commitment to organic foods, compostable packaging and serving products, and recycling of cooking oil.

ADMISSIONS

Freshman Academic Profile: Average high school GPA 3.11. 9% in top 10% of high school class, 34% in top 25% of high school class, 78% in top 50% of high school class. 84% from public high schools. SAT Math middle 50% range 440–560. SAT Critical Reading middle 50% range 440–550. SAT Writing middle 50% range 440–540. ACT middle 50% range 18–24. Minimum paper TOEFL 500. Minimum computer TOEFL 173. Minimum web-based TOEFL 61. **Basis for Candidate Selection:** *Important factors considered include:* Academic GPA, rigor of secondary school record, standardized test scores. *Other factors considered include:* Recommendation(s), state residency. **Freshman Admission Requirements:** High school diploma is required and GED is accepted. *Academic units required:* 4 English, 3 mathematics, 2 science, (2 science labs), 2 foreign language, 1 social studies, 1 history, 1 visual/performing arts, 1 academic electives. **Freshman Admission Statistics:** 9,938 applied, 81% admitted, 12% enrolled. **Transfer Admission Requirements:** college transcript(s), minimum college GPA of 2.0 required. Lowest grade transferable D–. **General Admission Information:** Application fee $55. Regular application deadline 11/30. Notification on a rolling basis, beginning on or about 10/2. Nonfall registration accepted. Admission may be deferred for a maximum of 1 semester. Credit and/or placement offered for CEEB Advanced Placement tests.

COSTS AND FINANCIAL AID

Average book expense $1,386. **Required Forms and Deadlines:** FAFSA, state aid form. Priority financial aid filing date 3/2. **Notification of Awards:** Applicants will be notified of awards on or about 3/1. **Types of Aid:** *Need-based scholarships/grants:* Federal Pell, SEOG, state scholarships/grants, private scholarships, the school's own gift aid. *Loans:* Direct Subsidized Stafford, Direct Unsubsidized Stafford, Direct PLUS, FFEL Subsidized Stafford, FFEL Unsubsidized Stafford, FFEL PLUS, Federal Perkins. **Student Employment:** Federal Work-Study Program available. Institutional employment available. Highest amount earned per year from on-campus jobs $12,914. Off-campus job opportunities are good. **Financial Aid Statistics:** 26% freshmen, 40% undergrads receive need-based scholarship or grant aid. 6% freshmen, 4% undergrads receive non-need-based scholarship or grant aid. 34% freshmen, 35% undergrads receive need-based self-help aid. 3% freshmen, 3% undergrads receive athletic scholarships. 69% freshmen, 63% undergrads receive any aid. 63% undergrads borrow to pay for school. Average cumulative indebtedness $15,254. **Criteria for awarding institutional aid:** *Non-need-based:* Academics, alumni affiliation, athletics, leadership, state/district residency.

CALIFORNIA STATE UNIVERSITY—LONG BEACH

1250 Bellflower Boulevard, Long Beach, CA 90840
Phone: 562-985-5471 **Financial Aid Phone:**
E-mail: eslb@csulb.edu **CEEB Code:** 4389
Fax: 562-985-4973 **Website:** www.csulb.edu

This public school was founded in 1949. It has a 322-acre campus.

RATINGS
Admissions Selectivity Rating: 93   **Fire Safety Rating:** 60*   **Green Rating:** 60*

STUDENTS AND FACULTY
Enrollment: 29,226. **Student Body:** 59% female, 41% male, 2% out-of-state, 4% international. Asian 24%, African American 5%, Caucasian 29%, Hispanic 29%, Native American 1%.
Retention and Graduation: 13% freshmen graduate within 4 years. **Faculty:** Student/faculty ratio 21:1. 1021 full-time faculty, 85% hold PhDs, 29% are members of minority groups, 46% are women. 8% of classes are taught by teaching assistants.

ACADEMICS
Degrees: Bachelor's, master's, post-bachelor's certificate. **Classes:** Most classes have 20–29 students. Most lab/discussion sessions have 20–29 students. **Majors with Highest Enrollment:** corrections and criminal justice, other; management information systems; psychology; **Special Study Options:** Accelerated program, cross-registration, distance learning, double major, dual enrollment, English as a Second Language (ESL), honors program, independent study, internships, student-designed major, study abroad, teacher certification program. Special programs offered to physically disabled students include note-taking services, reader services. **Career services:** Alumni services, career assessment, internships.

FACILITIES
Housing: Coed dorms, special housing for international students. 98% of campus accessible to physically disabled. **Special Academic Facilities/Equipment:** Art and science museums, Japanese garden, special events arena with meeting facilities.

CAMPUS LIFE
Activities: Choral groups, concert band, dance, drama/theater, jazz band, literary magazine, music ensembles, musical theater, opera, radio station, student government, student newspaper, student-run film society, symphony orchestra, television station, yearbook. **Organizations:** 300 registered organizations, 25 honor societies, 20 religious organizations. 16 fraternities, 15 sororities. **Athletics (Intercollegiate):** *Men:* Baseball, basketball, cross-country, golf, track/field (outdoor), volleyball, water polo *Women:* Basketball, cross-country, golf, soccer, softball, tennis, track/field (outdoor), volleyball, water polo.

ADMISSIONS
Freshman Academic Profile: Average high school GPA 3.42. 84% in top 25% of high school class, 100% in top 50% of high school class. 82% from public high schools. SAT Math middle 50% range 460–590. SAT Critical Reading middle 50% range 440–560. ACT middle 50% range 18–24. Minimum paper TOEFL 525. **Basis for Candidate Selection:** *Very important factors considered include:* Academic GPA, standardized test scores, geographical residence, state residency. *Important factors considered include:* Talent/ability. *Other factors considered include:* Application essay, recommendation(s), rigor of secondary school record, character/personal qualities, extracurricular activities, volunteer work, work experience. **Freshman Admission Requirements:** High school diploma is required and GED is accepted. *Academic units required:* 4 English, 3 mathematics, 2 science, (2 science labs), 2 foreign language, 1 social studies, 1 history, 1 academic electives, 1 fine arts. **Freshman Admission Statistics:** 45,771 applied, 32% admitted, 24% enrolled. **Transfer Admission Requirements:** College transcript(s), minimum college GPA of 2.0 required. Lowest grade transferable C. **General Admission Information:** Application fee $55. Regular application deadline 11/30. Notification on a rolling basis, beginning on or about 12/1. Nonfall registration accepted. Credit offered for CEEB Advanced Placement tests.

COSTS AND FINANCIAL AID
Annual out-of-state tuition $11,160. Room and board $11,038. Required fees $4,606. Average book expense $1,620. **Required Forms and Deadlines:**

FAFSA. Priority financial aid filing date 3/2. **Notification of Awards:** Applicants will be notified of awards on a rolling basis beginning 3/30. **Types of Aid:** *Need-based scholarships/grants:* Federal Pell, SEOG, state scholarships/grants, private scholarships, the school's own gift aid. *Loans:* Direct Subsidized Stafford, Direct Unsubsidized Stafford, Direct PLUS, Federal Perkins. **Student Employment:** Federal Work-Study Program available. Institutional employment available. Highest amount earned per year from on-campus jobs $3,000. Off-campus job opportunities are good. **Financial Aid Statistics:** 49% freshmen, 49% undergrads receive need-based scholarship or grant aid. 7% freshmen, 9% undergrads receive non-need-based scholarship or grant aid. 41% freshmen, 58% undergrads receive need-based self-help aid. 1% undergrads receive athletic scholarships. 43% undergrads borrow to pay for school. Average cumulative indebtedness $10,927. **Criteria for awarding institutional aid:** *Non-need-based:* Academics, art, athletics, music/drama.

CALIFORNIA STATE UNIVERSITY— LOS ANGELES

5151 State University Drive, Los Angeles, CA 90032
Phone: 323-343-3901 **Financial Aid Phone:** 323-343-6260
E-mail: admission@calstatela.edu **CEEB Code:** 4399
Fax: 323-343-6306 **ACT Code:** 320

This public school was founded in 1947. It has a 175-acre campus.

RATINGS
Admissions Selectivity Rating: 68   **Fire Safety Rating:** 60*   **Green Rating:** 60*

STUDENTS AND FACULTY
Enrollment: 15,588. **Student Body:** 61% female, 39% male, 4% out-of-state, 6% international. Asian 19%, African American 8%, Caucasian 10%, Hispanic 48%.
Retention and Graduation: 8% freshmen graduate within 4 years. **Faculty:** Student/faculty ratio 16:1. 585 full-time faculty, 43% are members of minority groups, 48% are women.

ACADEMICS
Degrees: Bachelor's, certificate, master's, post-bachelor's certificate. **Classes:** Most classes have 20–29 students. **Majors with Highest Enrollment:** Business administration and management; criminal justice/law enforcement administration; psychology. **Special Study Options:** Accelerated program, cooperative education program, cross-registration, distance learning, double major, dual enrollment, English as a Second Language (ESL), exchange student program (domestic), honors program, independent study, internships, student-designed major, study abroad, teacher certification program. Special programs offered to physically disabled students include note-taking services, reader. services **Career services:** Career/job search classes, internships.

FACILITIES
Housing: Coed dorms, special housing for international students, fraternity/sorority housing, apartments for single students, wellness housing, theme housing, (Special Interest Housing), First Year House, Quiet House, ACLP/International House, The Neighborhood Wellness/Substance Free House, The Village Quiet House. **Special Academic Facilities/Equipment:** Baroque pipe organ, bilingual center, entrepreneurship and small business institutes, center for study of armament and disarmament, Van de Graaff accelerator. **Computers:** Administrative functions (other than registration) can be performed online.

CAMPUS LIFE
Environment: Metropolis. **Activities:** Choral groups, dance, drama/theater, jazz band, literary magazine, music ensembles, musical theater, opera, radio station, student government, student newspaper, symphony orchestra, yearbook. **Organizations:** 130 registered organizations, 3 religious organizations. 7 fraternities, 4 sororities. **Athletics (Intercollegiate):** *Men:* Baseball, basketball, cross-country, soccer, track/field (outdoor). *Women:* Basketball, cross-country, soccer, tennis, track/field (outdoor), volleyball.

ADMISSIONS
Freshman Academic Profile: Average high school GPA 3.07. SAT Math middle 50% range 370–490. SAT Critical Reading middle 50% range 370–480. ACT middle 50% range 15–19. Minimum paper TOEFL 550. Minimum computer TOEFL 213. **Basis for Candidate Selection:** *Very important factors considered include:* Academic GPA, rigor of secondary school record, standardized test scores. *Other factors considered include:* State residency. **Freshman Admission Requirements:** High school diploma is required and GED is accepted. *Academic units required:* 4 English, 3 mathematics, 2 science, (2 science labs), 2 foreign language, 1 social studies, 1 history, 1 academic electives,

1 visual and performing arts. **Freshman Admission Statistics:** 18,785 applied, 77% admitted, 14% enrolled. **Transfer Admission Requirements:** College transcript(s), minimum college GPA of 2.0 required. Lowest grade transferable C. **General Admission Information:** Application fee $55. Regular application deadline 6/15. Nonfall registration accepted. Credit and/or placement offered for CEEB Advanced Placement tests.

COSTS AND FINANCIAL AID

Annual in-state tuition $3,377. Annual out-of-state tuition $11,513. Room and board $8,406. Required fees $605. Average book expense $1,566. **Required Forms and Deadlines:** FAFSA, Verification/Household Size. Financial aid filing deadline 3/2. Priority financial aid filing date 3/2. **Notification of Awards: Types of Aid:** *Need-based scholarships/grants:* Federal Pell, SEOG, state scholarships/grants, private scholarships, the school's own gift aid, Federal and State Work Study. *Loans:* Direct Subsidized Stafford, Direct Unsubsidized Stafford, FFEL PLUS, Federal Perkins, Federal Nursing. **Student Employment:** Federal Work-Study Program available. Institutional employment available. Off-campus job opportunities are good. **Financial Aid Statistics:** 78% freshmen, 52% undergrads receive need-based scholarship or grant aid. 16% freshmen, 12% undergrads receive need-based self-help aid. 55% freshmen, 61% undergrads receive any aid.

CALIFORNIA STATE UNIVERSITY—NORTHRIDGE

The Tseng College of Extended Learning, California State University, Northridge, Northridge, CA 91330-8365
Phone: 818-677-2270
E-mail: lorraine.newlon@csun.edu **CEEB Code:** 4707
Fax: 818-677-5088 **Website:** www.csun.edu **ACT Code:** 400

This public school was founded in 1956. It has a 350-acre campus.

RATINGS
Admissions Selectivity Rating: 60*   **Fire Safety Rating:** 60*   **Green Rating:** 60*

STUDENTS AND FACULTY
Student Body: 1% out-of-state.
Retention and Graduation: 78% freshmen return for sophomore year. 4% freshmen graduate within 4 years.

ACADEMICS
Degrees: Bachelor's, master's. **Special Study Options:** Accelerated program, English as a Second Language (ESL), honors program, student-designed major, study abroad Special programs offered to physically disabled students include note-taking services, reader services, tape recorders, tutors. **Career services:** Alumni services, career/job search classes.

FACILITIES
Housing: Coed dorms, special housing for international students, fraternity/sorority housing, apartments for married students, apartments for single students. **Special Academic Facilities/Equipment:** Anthropology museum, art galleries, deafness center, urban archives, map library, cancer research/developmental biology center, planetarium, observatory.

CAMPUS LIFE
Activities: Choral groups, concert band, drama/theater, jazz band, literary magazine, marching band, music ensembles, musical theater, radio station, student government, student newspaper, yearbook. **Organizations:** 267 registered organizations, 18 honor societies, 13 religious organizations. 24 fraternities, 12 sororities. **Athletics (Intercollegiate):** *Men:* Baseball, basketball, cross-country, diving, football, golf, soccer, swimming, track/field (outdoor), track/field (indoor), volleyball. *Women:* Basketball, cross-country, diving, football, golf, soccer, softball, swimming, tennis, track/field (outdoor), track/field (indoor), volleyball.

ADMISSIONS
Freshman Academic Profile: 81% from public high schools. Minimum paper TOEFL 500. **Basis for Candidate Selection:** *Very important factors considered include:* Standardized test scores. **Freshman Admission Requirements:** High school diploma is required and GED is accepted. High school diploma is required and GED is not accepted. *Academic units required:* 4 English, 3 mathematics, 1 science, (2 science labs), 2 foreign language, 2 history, 1 academic electives, 1 visual/performing arts. **Freshman Admission Statistics:** 7,931 applied, 78% admitted, 38% enrolled. Lowest grade transferable D. **General Admission Information:** Application fee $55. Notification on a rolling basis, beginning on or about 11/30. Nonfall registration accepted. Credit and/or placement offered for CEEB Advanced Placement tests.

COSTS AND FINANCIAL AID
Required Forms and Deadlines: Institution's own financial aid form. **Types of Aid:** *Need-based scholarships/grants:* Federal Pell, SEOG, state scholar-

ships/grants, private scholarships, the school's own gift aid, Federal Nursing Scholarships. *Loans:* FFEL Subsidized Stafford, FFEL Unsubsidized Stafford, FFEL PLUS, Federal Perkins, Federal Nursing, college/university loans from institutional funds. **Student Employment:** Federal Work-Study Program available. Institutional employment available. Highest amount earned per year from on-campus jobs $3,000. Off-campus job opportunities are good.

CALIFORNIA STATE UNIVERSITY— SACRAMENTO

6000 J Street, Lassen Hall, Sacramento, CA 95819-6048
Phone: 916-278-3901 **Financial Aid Phone:** 916-278-6554
E-mail: admissions@csus.edu **CEEB Code:** 4671
Fax: 916-278-5603 **Website:** www.csus.edu **ACT Code:** 382

This public school was founded in 1947. It has a 300-acre campus.

RATINGS
Admissions Selectivity Rating: 76   **Fire Safety Rating:** 61   **Green Rating:** 60*

STUDENTS AND FACULTY
Enrollment: 23,028. **Student Body:** 57% female, 43% male, 1% out-of-state, 1% international (122 countries represented). Asian 19%, African American 7%, Caucasian 43%, Hispanic 15%, Native American 1%. **Retention and Graduation:** 81% freshmen return for sophomore year. 10% freshmen graduate within 4 years. **Faculty:** Student/faculty ratio 22:1. 812 full-time faculty, 78% hold PhDs, 25% are members of minority groups, 43% are women.

ACADEMICS
Degrees: Bachelor's, master's. **Classes:** Most classes have 20–29 students. Most lab/discussion sessions have 10–19 students. **Majors with Highest Enrollment:** Business/commerce; criminal justice/law enforcement administration; nursing/registered nurse (RN, ASN, BSN, MSN); **Special Study Options:** Accelerated program, cooperative education program, cross-registration, distance learning, double major, dual enrollment, English as a Second Language (ESL), honors program, independent study, internships, student-designed major, study abroad, teacher certification program. **Combined degree programs:** BA/MA Special programs offered to physically disabled students include note-taking services, reader services, tape recorders, tutors. **Career services:** Alumni network, alumni services, career assessment, internships, regional alumni.

FACILITIES
Housing: Coed dorms 95% of campus accessible to physically disabled. **Special Academic Facilities/Equipment:** CSUS Museum of Anthropology, University Library Gallery (Art), Else Gallery (Art), Witt Gallery (Art). **Computers:** Students can register for classes online. Administrative functions (other than registration) can be performed online.

CAMPUS LIFE
Environment: Metropolis. **Activities:** Choral groups, concert band, dance, drama/theater, jazz band, marching band, music ensembles, musical theater, opera, pep band, radio station, student government, student newspaper, symphony orchestra. **Organizations:** 222 registered organizations, 7 honor societies, 13 religious organizations. 19 fraternities, 20 sororities. **Athletics (Intercollegiate):** *Men:* Baseball, basketball, cheerleading, cross-country, football, golf, soccer, tennis, track/field (outdoor). *Women:* Basketball, cheerleading, crew/rowing, cross-country, golf, gymnastics, soccer, softball, tennis, track/field (outdoor), volleyball. **On-Campus Highlights:** University Union, River Front Center, Guy West Bridge, Mariposa Hall, Hornet Stadium.

ADMISSIONS
Freshman Academic Profile: Average high school GPA 3.2. 100% in top 50% of high school class. 89% from public high schools. SAT Math middle 50% range 440–550. SAT Critical Reading middle 50% range 420–540. ACT middle 50% range 17–22. Minimum paper TOEFL 510. Minimum computer TOEFL 180. **Basis for Candidate Selection:** *Very important factors considered include:* Rigor of secondary school record, standardized test scores. *Important factors considered include:* State residency. *Other factors considered include:* Recommendation(s), extracurricular activities, geographical residence, interview, talent/ability. **Freshman Admission Requirements:** High school diploma is required and GED is accepted. *Academic units required:* 4 English, 3 mathematics, 2 science, (2 science labs), 2 foreign language, 1 social studies, 1 history, 1 academic electives, 1 visual/performing arts. **Freshman Admission Statistics:** 15,980 applied, 47% admitted, 34% enrolled. **Transfer Admission Requirements:** College transcript(s), statement of good standing from prior

institution(s). Minimum college GPA of 2.0 required. Lowest grade transferable D. **General Admission Information:** Application fee $55. Regular application deadline 11/30. Notification on a rolling basis, beginning on or about 11/1. Nonfall registration accepted. Admission may be deferred for a maximum of one semester. Credit and/or placement offered for CEEB Advanced Placement tests.

COSTS AND FINANCIAL AID
Annual in-state tuition $3,072. Annual out-of-state tuition $13,242. Room and board $7,052. Required fees $276. Average book expense $1,260. **Required Forms and Deadlines:** FAFSA. Priority financial aid filing date 3/2. **Notification of Awards:** Applicants will be notified of awards on a rolling basis beginning 4/1. **Types of Aid:** *Need-based scholarships/grants:* Federal Pell, SEOG, state scholarships/grants, private scholarships, Federal Nursing Scholarships. *Loans:* Direct Subsidized Stafford, Direct Unsubsidized Stafford, Direct PLUS, Federal Perkins, Federal Nursing. **Student Employment:** Federal Work-Study Program available. Institutional employment available. Off-campus job opportunities are fair. **Financial Aid Statistics:** 43% freshmen, 39% undergrads receive need-based scholarship or grant aid. 24% freshmen, 32% undergrads receive need-based self-help aid. 50% undergrads receive any aid. 41% undergrads borrow to pay for school. Average cumulative indebtedness $11,514.

CALIFORNIA STATE UNIVERSITY— SAN BERNARDINO

5500 University Parkway, CSUSB-IR, 5500 U, San Bernardino, CA 92407-2397
Phone: 909-537-5188 **Financial Aid Phone:** 909-537-7800
E-mail: moreinfo@mail.csusb.edu **CEEB Code:** 4099
Fax: 909-537-7034 **Website:** www.csusb.edu **ACT Code:** 205

This public school was founded in 1965. It has a 430-acre campus.

RATINGS
Admissions Selectivity Rating: 75   **Fire Safety Rating:** 60*   **Green Rating:** 60*

STUDENTS AND FACULTY
Enrollment: 14,416. **Student Body:** 64% female, 36% male, 0.9% out-of-state, 3% international (62 countries represented). Asian 8%, African American 11%, Caucasian 26%, Hispanic 43%, Native American 1%.
Retention and Graduation: 82% freshmen return for sophomore year. 13% freshmen graduate within 4 years. **Faculty:** Student/faculty ratio 21:1. 471 full-time faculty, 29% are members of minority groups, 46% are women.

ACADEMICS
Degrees: Bachelor's, doctoral, master's. **Classes:** Most classes have 20–29 students. Most lab/discussion sessions have 20–29 students. **Majors with Highest Enrollment:** Business/commerce; liberal arts and sciences/liberal studies; psychology. **Special Study Options:** Accelerated program, cooperative education program, cross-registration, distance learning, double major, dual enrollment, exchange student program (domestic), honors program, independent study, internships, study abroad, teacher certification program, School of Social and Behavioral Sciences offers Master's in National Security Studies. Special programs offered to physically disabled students include note-taking services, reader services, tape recorders.

FACILITIES
Housing: Coed dorms, women's dorms, apartments for single students, wellness housing. **Special Academic Facilities/Equipment:** Simulation labs, electronic music studios, language lab, desert studies center. Robert V. Fullerton Art Museum. Anthropology Museum. **Computers:** Students can register for classes online. Administrative functions (other than registration) can be performed online.

CAMPUS LIFE
Environment: City. **Activities:** Choral groups, dance, drama/theater, jazz band, music ensembles, musical theater, radio station, student government, student newspaper, television station, campus ministries, international student organization, Model UN. **Organizations:** 97 registered organizations, 3 religious organizations. 9 fraternities, 6 sororities. **Athletics (Intercollegiate):** *Men:* Baseball, basketball, golf, soccer, swimming, water polo. *Women:* Basketball, cross-country, soccer, softball, swimming, tennis, volleyball, water polo. **On-Campus Highlights:** Coussoulis Arena, Robert V. Fullerton Art Museum, Social and Behavioral Sciences Building, Santos Manuel Student Union, Pfau Library.

ADMISSIONS
Freshman Academic Profile: Average high school GPA 3.14. 81% from public high schools. SAT Math middle 50% range 400–500. SAT Critical Reading middle 50% range 400–500. SAT Writing middle 50% range 370–490. ACT middle 50% range 16–21. Minimum paper TOEFL 500. Minimum computer TOEFL 173. **Basis for Candidate Selection:** *Very important factors considered include:* Academic GPA, recommendation(s), standardized test scores. *Other factors considered include:* Geographical residence. **Freshman Admission Requirements:** High school diploma is required and GED is accepted. *Academic units required:* 4 English, 3 mathematics, 2 science, (2 science labs), 2 foreign language, 1 social studies, 1 history, 1 visual/performing arts. **Freshman Admission Statistics:** 9,963 applied, 70% admitted, 29% enrolled. **Transfer Admission Requirements:** College transcript(s), minimum college GPA of 2.0 required. Lowest grade transferable C. **General Admission Information:** Application fee $55. Nonfall registration accepted. Credit and/or placement offered for CEEB Advanced Placement tests.

COSTS AND FINANCIAL AID
Annual in-state tuition $5,373. Annual out-of-state tuition $11,445. Room and board $6,483. Average book expense $1,638. **Required Forms and Deadlines:** FAFSA. Priority financial aid filing date 3/2. **Notification of Awards:** Applicants will be notified of awards on a rolling basis beginning 4/1. **Types of Aid:** *Need-based scholarships/grants:* Federal Pell, SEOG, state scholarships/grants, private scholarships, the school's own gift aid. *Loans:* Direct Subsidized Stafford, Direct Unsubsidized Stafford, Direct PLUS, Federal Perkins. **Student Employment:** Federal Work-Study Program available. Institutional employment available. Off-campus job opportunities are fair. **Financial Aid Statistics:** 61% freshmen, 59% undergrads receive need-based scholarship or grant aid. 7% freshmen, 5% undergrads receive non-need-based scholarship or grant aid. 71% freshmen, 70% undergrads receive need-based self-help aid. 1% freshmen, 1% undergrads receive athletic scholarships. 71.2% freshmen, 75.86% undergrads receive any aid. **Criteria for awarding institutional aid:** *Non-need-based:* Academics, alumni affiliation, art, athletics, leadership, music/drama, state/district residency.

CALIFORNIA STATE UNIVERSITY— SAN MARCOS

CSU San Marcos, San Marcos, CA 92096-0001
Phone: 760-750-4848 **Financial Aid Phone:** 760-750-4850
E-mail: apply@csusm.edu **CEEB Code:** 5677
Fax: 760-750-3248 **Website:** www.csusm.edu

This public school was founded in 1989. It has a 304-acre campus.

RATINGS
Admissions Selectivity Rating: 60*   **Fire Safety Rating:** 60*   **Green Rating:** 60*

STUDENTS AND FACULTY
Enrollment: 8,686. **Student Body:** 61% female, 39% male, 1% out-of-state.
Retention and Graduation: 74% freshmen return for sophomore year. 14% freshmen graduate within 4 years. **Faculty:** Student/faculty ratio 25:1. 202 full-time faculty.

ACADEMICS
Degrees: Bachelor's, master's. **Classes:** Most classes have 30–39 students. **Special Study Options:** Accelerated program, cross-registration, distance learning, double major, dual enrollment, English as a Second Language (ESL), independent study, internships, student-designed major, study abroad, teacher certification program, weekend college, Evening degree program, Program for Adult College Education (PACE), Saturday classes, Air Force ROTC, extended studies, open university, special sessions, including winter. Special programs offered to physically disabled students include note-taking services, reader services, tape recorders, tutors. **Career services:** Alumni services, career assessment, internships.

FACILITIES
Housing: Special housing for disabled students, special housing for international students, apartments for single students. Our housing is privatized and operated by Allen and O'Hara. **Computers:** Students can register for classes online.

CAMPUS LIFE
Environment: Town. **Activities:** Choral groups, drama/theater, music ensembles, student newspaper. **Organizations:** 70 registered organizations, 5 honor societies, 2 religious organizations. 2 fraternities, 2 sororities. **Athletics (Intercollegiate):** *Men:* Baseball, cross-country, golf, soccer, track/field (out-

door). *Women:* Cross-country, golf, soccer, softball, track/field (outdoor)

ADMISSIONS

Freshman Academic Profile: Average high school GPA 3.15. SAT Math middle 50% range 430–540. SAT Critical Reading middle 50% range 430–530. Minimum paper TOEFL 550. Minimum computer TOEFL 200. **Basis for Candidate Selection:** *Very important factors considered include:* rigor of secondary school record, standardized test scores. *Other factors considered include:* geographical residence, state residency. **Freshman Admission Requirements:** High school diploma is required and GED is accepted. *Academic units required:* 4 English, 3 mathematics, 2 science, (2 science labs), 2 foreign language, 2 social studies, 1 academic electives, 1 visual performing arts. *Academic units recommended:* 4 English, 4 mathematics, 2 science, (2 science labs), 2 foreign language, 2 social studies, 1 academic electives, 1 visual performing arts. **Transfer Admission Requirements:** College transcript(s), minimum college GPA of 2.0 required. Lowest grade transferable C. **General Admission Information:** Application fee $55. Notification on a rolling basis, beginning on or about 12/1. Nonfall registration not accepted. Credit and/or placement offered for CEEB Advanced Placement tests.

COSTS AND FINANCIAL AID

Annual out-of-state tuition $8,136. Room and board $6,250. Required fees $3,650. Average book expense $1,386. **Required Forms and Deadlines:** FAFSA. Priority financial aid filing date 3/2. **Notification of Awards:** Applicants will be notified of awards on or about 4/15. **Types of Aid:** *Need-based scholarships/grants:* Federal Pell, SEOG, state scholarships/grants, private scholarships, the school's own gift aid. *Loans:* Direct Subsidized Stafford, Direct Unsubsidized Stafford, Direct PLUS, FFEL PLUS, Federal Perkins, college/university loans from institutional funds. **Student Employment: Financial Aid Statistics: Criteria for awarding institutional aid:** *Non-need-based:* Academics, athletics, leadership, state/district residency.

CALIFORNIA STATE UNIVERSITY—STANISLAUS

Best 373

One University Circle, Turlock, CA 95382
Phone: 209-667-3070 **Financial Aid Phone:** 209-667-3336
E-mail: Outreach_Help_Desk@csustan.edu **CEEB Code:** 4713
Fax: 209-667-3788 **Website:** www.csustan.edu **ACT Code:** 435

This public school was founded in 1957. It has a 228-acre campus.

RATINGS

Admissions Selectivity Rating: 80 **Fire Safety Rating:** 99 **Green Rating:** 92

STUDENTS AND FACULTY

Enrollment: 6,559. **Student Body:** 65% female, 35% male, 2% out-of-state, international (32 countries represented).
Retention and Graduation: 22% freshmen graduate within 4 years. **Faculty:** Student/faculty ratio 19:1. 302 full-time faculty, 84% hold PhDs, 23% are members of minority groups, 48% are women.

ACADEMICS

Degrees: Bachelor's, master's, post-bachelor's certificate, post-master's certificate. **Classes:** Most classes have 20–29 students. Most lab/discussion sessions have 20–29 students. **Majors with Highest Enrollment:** Business/commerce; liberal arts and sciences/liberal studies; psychology. **Special Study Options:** Cooperative education program, distance learning, double major, dual enrollment, English as a Second Language (ESL), exchange student program (domestic), honors program, independent study, internships, liberal arts/career combination, student-designed major, study abroad, teacher certification program. **Honors programs:** University Honors Program Special programs offered to physically disabled students include note-taking services, reader services, tape recorders, tutors. **Career services:** Alumni network, alumni services, career/job search classes, career assessment, internships, regional alumni. **Career services highlights include:** Our Internship Program is exceptional. We work with employers to develop internship and coop opportunities, post information online for students to help them connect with their college department internship coordinator for course credit, and post internship information in the Career Services Center to help students identify appropriate opportunities related to their major course of study.

FACILITIES

Housing: Coed dorms, apartments for single students, Housing available in the summer months. ADA compliant units available. 99% of campus accessible

to physically disabled. **Special Academic Facilities/Equipment:** Marine sciences station, laser lab, greenhouse, art gallery, mainstage theatre, recital hall, observatory, science building, art complex, distance learning studios, BioAg Eco building. **Computers:** 100% of classrooms, 100% of dorms, 100% of libraries, 100% of dining areas, 100% of student union, 10% of common outdoor areas have wireless network access. Students can register for classes online. Administrative functions (other than registration) can be performed online.

CAMPUS LIFE

Environment: Town. **Activities:** Choral groups, concert band, dance, drama/theater, jazz band, music ensembles, musical theater, opera, radio station, student government, student newspaper, symphony orchestra, television station, international student organization. **Organizations:** 76 registered organizations, 11 honor societies, 4 religious organizations. 7 fraternities, 9 sororities. **Athletics (Intercollegiate):** *Men:* Baseball, basketball, cross-country, golf, soccer, track/field (outdoor), track/field (indoor) *Women:* Basketball, cross-country, soccer, softball, tennis, track/field (outdoor), track/field (indoor), volleyball. **On-Campus Highlights:** Naraghi Hall of Science, MSR Educational Services Gateway Buildin, JFR Faculty Development Center, CSU Stanislaus University Art Gallery, Cafeteria and adjoining room, Student Union recently renovated; game room. **Environmental Initiatives:** Received LEED Silver certification on our new Naraghi Hall of Science. Scheduled to have solar-generating (Photovoltaic) equipment installed during Summer of 2009 that will deliver zero-emission renewable energy directly to the campus at economical costs. Campus paper/cardboard/waste recycling program, in addition to studnet club plastic/aluminum recycling program.

ADMISSIONS

Freshman Academic Profile: Average high school GPA 3.2. 93% from public high schools. SAT Math middle 50% range 420–540. SAT Critical Reading middle 50% range 420–530. ACT middle 50% range 17–22. Minimum paper TOEFL 500. Minimum computer TOEFL 173. Minimum web-based TOEFL 61. **Basis for Candidate Selection:** *Very important factors considered include:* Academic GPA, rigor of secondary school record, standardized test scores. *Important factors considered include:* Class rank. **Freshman Admission Requirements:** High school diploma is required and GED is accepted. *Academic units required:* 4 English, 3 mathematics, 2 science, (2 science labs), 2 foreign language, 1 social studies, 1 history, 1 visual/performing arts, 1 academic electives. **Freshman Admission Statistics:** 4,751 applied, 66% admitted, 31% enrolled. **Transfer Admission Requirements:** College transcript(s), statement of good standing from prior institution(s). Minimum college GPA of 2.0 required. Lowest grade transferable D. **General Admission Information:** Application fee $55. Regular application deadline 3/1. Notification on a rolling basis, beginning on or about 10/1. Nonfall registration accepted. Credit offered for CEEB Advanced Placement tests.

COSTS AND FINANCIAL AID

Annual out-of-state tuition $11,160. Room and board $7,936. Required fees $4,840. Average book expense $1,566. **Required Forms and Deadlines:** FAFSA. Priority financial aid filing date 3/2. **Notification of Awards:** Applicants will be notified of awards on a rolling basis beginning 3/15. **Types of Aid:** *Need-based scholarships/grants:* Federal Pell, SEOG, state scholarships/grants, private scholarships, the school's own gift aid, Federal Nursing Scholarships. *Loans:* FFEL Subsidized Stafford, FFEL Unsubsidized Stafford, FFEL PLUS, Federal Perkins, college/university loans from institutional funds. **Student Employment:** Federal Work-Study Program available. Institutional employment available. Highest amount earned per year from on-campus jobs $17,680. Off-campus job opportunities are good. **Financial Aid Statistics:** 36% freshmen, 57% undergrads receive need-based scholarship or grant aid. 3% freshmen, 4% undergrads receive non-need-based scholarship or grant aid. 32% freshmen, 49% undergrads receive need-based self-help aid. 2% freshmen, 1% undergrads receive athletic scholarships. 51% freshmen, 67% undergrads receive any aid. 23% undergrads borrow to pay for school. Average cumulative indebtedness $17,000. **Criteria for awarding institutional aid:** *Non-need-based:* Academics, alumni affiliation, art, athletics, leadership, minority status, music/drama, state/district residency.

CALIFORNIA UNIVERSITY OF PENNSYLVANIA

250 University Avenue, California, PA 15419
Phone: 724-938-4404 **Financial Aid Phone:** 724-938-4415
E-mail: inquiry@cup.edu **CEEB Code:** 2647
Fax: 724-938-4564 **Website:** www.cup.edu **ACT Code:** 3694

This public school was founded in 1852. It has a 188-acre campus.

RATINGS

Admissions Selectivity Rating: 73 **Fire Safety Rating:** 93 **Green Rating:** 98

STUDENTS AND FACULTY

Enrollment: 6,199. **Student Body:** 52% female, 48% male, 6% out-of-state, 1% international (18 countries represented). African American 6%, Caucasian 67%, Hispanic 1%. **Retention and Graduation:** 74% freshmen return for sophomore year. 25% freshmen graduate within 4 years. 16% grads go on to further study within 1 year. **Faculty:** Student/faculty ratio 19:1. 298 full-time faculty, 65% hold PhDs, 12% are members of minority groups, 43% are women.

ACADEMICS

Degrees: Associate, bachelor's, certificate, master's, post-bachelor's certificate, post-master's certificate, terminal associate. **Classes:** Most classes have 20–29 students. Most lab/discussion sessions have 20–29 students. **Majors with Highest Enrollment:** Business administration and management; criminal justice/safety studies; elementary education and teaching. **Special Study Options:** Accelerated program, cooperative education program, distance learning, double major, dual enrollment, exchange student program (domestic), honors program, independent study, internships, liberal arts/career combination, student-designed major, study abroad, teacher certification program, weekend college, undergrads may take grad classes. Special programs offered to physically disabled students include note-taking services, reader services, tape recorders, tutors. **Career services:** Alumni network, alumni services, career/job search classes, career assessment, internships, regional alumni. **Career services highlights include:** Extensive programs in Internships and training.

FACILITIES

Housing: Coed dorms, special housing for disabled students, men's dorms, special housing for international students, women's dorms, fraternity/sorority housing, cooperative housing, wellness housing, theme housing, Jefferson Apartments, garden style with outdoor pool/sandlot volleyball. court and extensive gym. 90% of campus accessible to physically disabled. **Special Academic Facilities/Equipment:** Manderino Gallery of Fine Arts, hosts top 40 corporate art collections in the world. **Computers:** Students can register for classes online. Administrative functions (other than registration) can be performed online.

CAMPUS LIFE

Environment: Village. **Activities:** Choral groups, concert band, dance, drama/theater, jazz band, literary magazine, marching band, music ensembles, musical theater, opera, pep band, radio station, student government, student newspaper, symphony orchestra, television station, yearbook, campus ministries, international student organization. **Organizations:** 25 honor societies, 1 religious organizations. 6 fraternities, 7 sororities. **Athletics (Intercollegiate):** *Men:* Baseball, basketball, cheerleading, cross-country, football, golf, rugby, soccer, softball, track/field (outdoor), track/field (indoor), volleyball. *Women:* Basketball, cheerleading, cross-country, diving, golf, rugby, soccer, softball, swimming, tennis, track/field (outdoor), track/field (indoor), volleyball. **On-Campus Highlights:** Residence Halls, Student Union, classrooms, Herron Rec Center, library. **Environmental Initiatives:** Multimillion Dollar Geothermal project plus replacing ALL residence halls in less than 5 years with green buildings. Massive implementation of Johnson Controls systems to reduce our carbon footprint and energy usage. Campus-wide sustainability awareness programs

ADMISSIONS

Freshman Academic Profile: Average high school GPA 3.3. 7% in top 10% of high school class, 28% in top 25% of high school class, 65% in top 50% of high school class. 80% from public high schools. SAT Math middle 50% range 460–540. SAT Critical Reading middle 50% range 460–536. Minimum paper TOEFL 450. Minimum computer TOEFL 133. **Basis for Candidate Selection:** *Very important factors considered include:* Class rank, rigor of secondary school record, standardized test scores. *Other factors considered include:* Application essay, recommendation(s), extracurricular activities, interview, talent/ability, work experience. **Freshman Admission Requirements:** High school diploma is required and GED is accepted. *Academic units required:* 4 English, 3 mathematics, 1 science, (1 science labs), 2 social studies, 2 history, 6 academic electives, 1 Arts and Humanities *Academic units recommended:* 4 English, 3 mathematics, 1 science, (1 science labs), 2 foreign language, 2 social studies, 2 history, 6 academic electives, 1 arts and humanities. **Freshman Admission Statistics:** 3,849 applied, 68% admitted, 51% enrolled. **Transfer Admission Requirements:** High school transcript, college transcript(s), statement of good standing from prior institution(s). Minimum college GPA of 2.3 required. Lowest grade transferable C. **General Admission Information:** Application fee $25. Nonfall registration accepted. Admission may be deferred for a maximum of one semester. Credit offered for CEEB Advanced Placement tests.

COSTS AND FINANCIAL AID

Annual in-state tuition $5,178. Annual out-of-state tuition $8,284. Room and board $8,466. Required fees $1,673. Average book expense $875. **Required Forms and Deadlines:** FAFSA. Priority financial aid filing date 5/1. **Notification of Awards:** Applicants will be notified of awards on a rolling basis beginning 4/1. **Types of Aid:** *Need-based scholarships/grants:* Federal Pell, SEOG, state scholarships/grants, private scholarships, the school's own gift aid. *Loans:*

FFEL Subsidized Stafford, FFEL Unsubsidized Stafford, FFEL PLUS, Federal Perkins. **Student Employment:** Federal Work-Study Program available. Institutional employment available. Off-campus job opportunities are good. **Financial Aid Statistics:** 45% freshmen, 49% undergrads receive need-based scholarship or grant aid. 21% freshmen, 13% undergrads receive non-need-based scholarship or grant aid. 55% freshmen, 60% undergrads receive need-based self-help aid. 2% freshmen, 3% undergrads receive athletic scholarships. 76% freshmen, 72% undergrads receive any aid. 83% undergrads borrow to pay for school. Average cumulative indebtedness $21,860. **Criteria for awarding institutional aid:** *Non-need-based:* Academics, athletics, leadership, minority status, music/drama, state/district residency.

See page 1046.

CALVARY BIBLE COLLEGE AND THEOLOGICAL SEMINARY

15800 Calvary Rd, Kansas City, MO 64147
Phone: 816-322-3960 **Financial Aid Phone:** 816-322-5152
E-mail: admissions@calvary.edu
Fax: 816-331-4474 **ACT Code:** 2312

This private school was founded in 1961. It has a 55-acre campus.

RATINGS

Admissions Selectivity Rating: 72   **Fire Safety Rating:** 60*   **Green Rating:** 60*

STUDENTS AND FACULTY

Enrollment: 230. **Student Body:** 51% female, 49% male, African American 7%, Caucasian 89%, Hispanic 1%, Native American 2%. **Retention and Graduation:** 57% freshmen return for sophomore year. **Faculty:** Student/faculty ratio 12:1. 13 full-time faculty, 38% hold PhDs, 31% are women.

ACADEMICS

Degrees: Associate, bachelor's, certificate, first professional, master's, terminal associate, transfer associate. **Majors with Highest Enrollment:** Bible/biblical studies; elementary education and teaching; pastoral studies/counseling; **Special Study Options:** Cooperative education program, double major, independent study, internships, student-designed major, teacher certification program.

FACILITIES

Housing: Men's dorms, women's dorms, apartments for married students, apartments for single students. Single students required to live in college housing unless living with parents or at least 23 years of age. Duplexes available for married students. **Computers:** 100% of dorms, 100% of libraries, 100% of student union, have wireless network access. Students can register for classes online.

CAMPUS LIFE

Environment: Village. **Activities:** Choral groups, drama/theater, music ensembles, musical theater, pep band, radio station, student government, yearbook. **Athletics (Intercollegiate):** *Men:* Basketball, soccer. *Women:* Basketball, volleyball. **On-Campus Highlights:** Student Lounge, The Point, gymnasium.

ADMISSIONS

Freshman Academic Profile: Average high school GPA 3.42. 14% in top 10% of high school class, 18% in top 25% of high school class, 68% in top 50% of high school class. ACT middle 50% range 19–24. **Basis for Candidate Selection:** *Very important factors considered include:* Academic GPA, recommendation(s), standardized test scores, religious affiliation/commitment. *Important factors considered include:* Character/personal qualities. *Other factors considered include:* Application essay. **Freshman Admission Requirements:** High school diploma is required and GED is accepted. **Freshman Admission Statistics:** 55 applied, 80% admitted, 95% enrolled. **Transfer Admission Requirements:** college transcript(s), essay or personal statement, minimum college GPA of 2.0 required. Lowest grade transferable C–. **General Admission Information:** Application fee $25. Regular application deadline 7/15. Nonfall registration accepted. Admission may be deferred for a maximum of 2 Semesters.

COSTS AND FINANCIAL AID

Annual tuition $8,100. Room and board $4,400. Required fees $772. Average book expense $500. **Required Forms and Deadlines:** FAFSA, institution's own financial aid form. Financial aid filing deadline 4/1. Priority financial aid filing date 3/1. **Notification of Awards:** Applicants will be notified of awards on a rolling basis beginning 5/1. **Types of Aid:** *Need-based scholarships/grants:* Federal Pell, SEOG, private scholarships, the school's own gift aid. *Loans:*

FFEL Subsidized Stafford, FFEL Unsubsidized Stafford, FFEL PLUS **Student Employment:** Federal Work-Study Program available. Institutional employment available. Off-campus job opportunities are good. **Financial Aid Statistics:** 63% undergrads receive any aid. **Criteria for awarding institutional aid:** *Non-need-based:* Academics, alumni affiliation, job skills, music/drama, religious affiliation.

CALVIN COLLEGE

3201 Burton Street S.E, Grand Rapids, MI 49546
Phone: 616-526-6106 **Financial Aid Phone:** 800-688-0122
E-mail: admissions@calvin.edu **CEEB Code:** 1095
Fax: 616-526-6777 **Website:** www.calvin.edu **ACT Code:** 1968

This private school, affiliated with the Christian Reformed Church, was founded in 1876. It has a 400-acre campus.

RATINGS
Admissions Selectivity Rating: 81 **Fire Safety Rating:** 65 **Green Rating:** 77

STUDENTS AND FACULTY
Enrollment: 3,939. **Student Body:** 54% female, 46% male, 44% out-of-state, 8% international (54 countries represented). Asian 3%, African American 2%, Caucasian 81%, Hispanic 2%.
Retention and Graduation: 55% freshmen graduate within 4 years. 41% grads go on to further study within 1 year. 16% grads pursue arts and sciences degrees. 2% grads pursue law degrees. 3% grads pursue business degrees. 3% grads pursue medical degrees. **Faculty:** Student/faculty ratio 11:1. 326 full-time faculty, 82% hold PhDs, 10% are members of minority groups, 34% are women.

ACADEMICS
Degrees: Bachelor's, master's, post-bachelor's certificate. **Classes:** Most classes have 20–29 students. Most lab/discussion sessions have 10–19 students. **Majors with Highest Enrollment:** Business/commerce; engineering; nursing/registered nurse (RN, ASN, BSN, MSN). **Special Study Options:** Accelerated program, double major, dual enrollment, honors program, independent study, internships, student-designed major, study abroad, teacher certification program, Academically-based Service-learning. **Honors programs:** For almost forty years Calvin College has challenged its best students with a campus-wide Honors Program—part of our overall mission to encourage academic excellence in a Christ-centered environment. The McGregor Sophomore Scholars Program develops targeted programming for sophomores in the Honors Program, such as one-on-one mentoring with faculty and program leaders and special events. Special programs offered to physically disabled students include note-taking services, reader services, tape recorders, tutors. **Career services:** Alumni network, alumni services, career/job search classes, career assessment, internships, regional alumni.

FACILITIES
Housing: men's dorms, women's dorms, apartments for single students, theme housing, Project Neighborhood Houses. 95% of campus accessible to physically disabled. **Special Academic Facilities/Equipment:** Art gallery, observatory, ecosystem preserve, electron microscope, seismograph lab. **Computers:** 40% of classrooms, 100% of dorms, 100% of libraries, 75% of dining areas, 20% of student union, 10% of common outdoor areas have wireless network access. Students can register for classes online. Administrative functions (other than registration) can be performed online.

CAMPUS LIFE
Environment: City. **Activities:** Choral groups, concert band, dance, drama/theater, jazz band, literary magazine, music ensembles, musical theater, pep band, student government, student newspaper, student-run film society, symphony orchestra, yearbook, campus ministries, international student organization, Model UN. **Organizations:** 60 registered organizations, 6 honor societies, 5 religious organizations. **Athletics (Intercollegiate):** *Men:* Baseball, basketball, cross-country, diving, golf, soccer, swimming, tennis, track/field (outdoor). *Women:* Basketball, cross-country, diving, golf, soccer, softball, swimming, tennis, track/field (outdoor), volleyball. **On-Campus Highlights:** Field House, Johnny's Cafe, Heckman Library, DeVos Communications Building, Engineering Projects and Design Building. **Environmental Initiatives:** Calvin Environmental Assessment Program (www.calvin.edu/admin/provost/ceap/); Bunker Interpretive Center and the Ecosystem Preserve (www.calvin.edu/aca-

demic/eco-preserve/bunker/); Sustainabilty Summit (www.calvin.edu/admin/provost/ceap/SustainabilitySummitSummaryReport2008.pdf).

ADMISSIONS
Freshman Academic Profile: Average high school GPA 3.6. 29.1% in top 10% of high school class, 57.4% in top 25% of high school class, 80.8% in top 50% of high school class. 43% from public high schools. SAT Math middle 50% range 550–660. SAT Critical Reading middle 50% range 520–670. ACT middle 50% range 23–29. Minimum paper TOEFL 550. Minimum computer TOEFL 213. Minimum web-based TOEFL 80. **Basis for Candidate Selection:** *Very important factors considered include:* Academic GPA, rigor of secondary school record, standardized test scores, religious affiliation/commitment. *Important factors considered include:* Application essay, recommendation(s), character/personal qualities, extracurricular activities. *Other factors considered include:* Class rank, level of applicant's interest, volunteer work, work experience. **Freshman Admission Requirements:** High school diploma is required and GED is accepted. *Academic units required:* 3 English, 3 mathematics, 2 science, 2 social studies, 3 academic electives. *Academic units recommended:* 4 English, 3 mathematics, 2 science, (1 science labs), 2 foreign language, 3 social studies, 3 academic electives. **Freshman Admission Statistics:** 2,529 applied, 94% admitted, 40% enrolled. **Transfer Admission Requirements:** High school transcript, college transcript(s), essay or personal statement, statement of good standing from prior institution(s). Minimum college GPA of 2.5 required. Lowest grade transferable C. **General Admission Information:** Application fee $35. Regular application deadline 8/15. Notification on a rolling basis, beginning on or about 11/1. Nonfall registration accepted. Admission may be deferred for a maximum of 1 year. Credit and/or placement offered for CEEB Advanced Placement tests.

COSTS AND FINANCIAL AID
Annual tuition $23,810. Room and board $8,275. Required fees $225. Average book expense $980. **Required Forms and Deadlines:** FAFSA. Priority financial aid filing date 2/15. **Notification of Awards:** Applicants will be notified of awards on a rolling basis beginning 3/15. **Types of Aid:** *Need-based scholarships/grants:* Federal Pell, SEOG, state scholarships/grants, private scholarships, the school's own gift aid. *Loans:* Direct Subsidized Stafford, Direct Unsubsidized Stafford, Direct PLUS, Federal Perkins, state loans, college/university loans from institutional funds, Alternative Educational Loans. **Student Employment:** Federal Work-Study Program available. Institutional employment available. Highest amount earned per year from on-campus jobs $5,000. Off-campus job opportunities are excellent. **Financial Aid Statistics:** 64% freshmen, 62% undergrads receive need-based scholarship or grant aid. 20% freshmen, 16% undergrads receive non-need-based scholarship or grant aid. 56% freshmen, 56% undergrads receive need-based self-help aid. 95% freshmen, 92% undergrads receive any aid. 68% undergrads borrow to pay for school. Average cumulative indebtedness $28,500. **Criteria for awarding institutional aid:** *Non-need-based:* Academics, alumni affiliation, art, leadership, minority status, music/drama, religious affiliation, state/district residency.

CAMERON UNIVERSITY

2800 West Gore Boulevard, Lawton, OK 73505
Phone: 580-581-2230 **Financial Aid Phone:** 580-581-2293
E-mail: admiss@cua.cameron.edu **CEEB Code:** 6080
Fax: 580-581-5514 **ACT Code:** 3386

This public school was founded in 1908. It has a 369-acre campus.

RATINGS
Admissions Selectivity Rating: 61 **Fire Safety Rating:** 82 **Green Rating:** 60*

STUDENTS AND FACULTY
Enrollment: 5,076. **Student Body:** 60% female, 40% male, 1% out-of-state, 3% international (50 countries represented). Asian 3%, African American 19%, Caucasian 58%, Hispanic 9%, Native American 8%.
Retention and Graduation: 56% freshmen return for sophomore year. 24% freshmen graduate within 4 years. **Faculty:** Student/faculty ratio 17:1. 180 full-time faculty, 69% hold PhDs, 14% are members of minority groups, 36% are women.

ACADEMICS
Degrees: Associate, bachelor's, master's. **Classes:** Most classes have 20–29 students. Most lab/discussion sessions have 10–19 students. **Special Study Options:** Accelerated program, distance learning, double major, dual enrollment, honors program, independent study, internships, liberal arts/career combination, teacher certification program, undergrads may take grad classes. Evening and saturday classes offered; extension study possible. **Honors programs:**

Honors programs have been created for exceptional scholars. This includes studies in Europe and travel to scholarly programs in the U.S.A. Courses and programs provide challenging multidisciplinary activities. **Combined degree programs:** BA/MD. Special programs offered to physically disabled students include note-taking services, reader services, tape recorders, tutors.

FACILITIES

Housing: Men's dorms, women's dorms, quiet and wellness (non-smoking) areas available. 88% of campus accessible to physically disabled. **Special Academic Facilities/Equipment:** Satellite labs. **Computers:** Administrative functions (other than registration) can be performed online.

CAMPUS LIFE

Environment: City. **Activities:** Choral groups, concert band, dance, drama/theater, jazz band, literary magazine, music ensembles, musical theater, pep band, radio station, student government, student newspaper, symphony orchestra, television station, yearbook. **Organizations:** 66 registered organizations, 19 honor societies, 4 religious organizations. 2 fraternities, 3 sororities. **Athletics (Intercollegiate):** Men: Baseball, basketball, cross-country, golf, tennis. Women: Basketball, golf, softball, tennis, volleyball. **On-Campus Highlights:** Student Union, Cameron Village, Moody Blue, Student Activities Building, Fitness Center.

ADMISSIONS

Freshman Academic Profile: 8% in top 10% of high school class, 28% in top 25% of high school class, 62% in top 50% of high school class. 99% from public high schools. ACT middle 50% range 16–22. Minimum paper TOEFL 500. Minimum computer TOEFL 173. **Basis for Candidate Selection:** Important factors considered include: Class rank, academic GPA, standardized test scores, geographical residence, state residency. **Freshman Admission Requirements:** High school diploma is required and GED is accepted. Academic units required: 4 English, 3 mathematics, 2 science, (2 science labs), 2 history, 3 academic electives. **Freshman Admission Statistics:** 1,357 applied, 100% admitted, 70% enrolled. **Transfer Admission Requirements:** College transcript(s), minimum college GPA of 2.0 required. Lowest grade transferable D. **General Admission Information:** Application fee $15. Nonfall registration accepted. Admission may be deferred for a maximum of 12. Credit and/or placement offered for CEEB Advanced Placement tests.

COSTS AND FINANCIAL AID

Average book expense $1,050. **Required Forms and Deadlines:** FAFSA. Priority financial aid filing date 6/15. **Notification of Awards:** Applicants will be notified of awards on a rolling basis beginning 4/1. **Types of Aid:** Need-based scholarships/grants: Federal Pell, SEOG, state scholarships/grants, private scholarships, the school's own gift aid. Loans: FFEL Subsidized Stafford, FFEL Unsubsidized Stafford, FFEL PLUS. **Student Employment: Financial Aid Statistics:** 36% freshmen, 26% undergrads receive need-based scholarship or grant aid. 23% freshmen, 14% undergrads receive non-need-based scholarship or grant aid. 29% freshmen, 18% undergrads receive need-based self-help aid. 1% undergrads receive athletic scholarships. 36% freshmen, 26% undergrads receive any aid. 30% undergrads borrow to pay for school. Average cumulative indebtedness $7,500. **Criteria for awarding institutional aid:** Non-need-based: Academics, alumni affiliation, art, athletics, leadership, music/drama.

CAMPBELL UNIVERSITY

Post Office Box 546, Buies Creek, NC 27506
Phone: 910-893-1290
E-mail: adm@mailcenter.campbell.edu **CEEB Code:** 5100
Fax: 910-893-1288 **Website:** www.campbell.edu **ACT Code:** 3076

This private school, affiliated with the Southern Baptist Church, was founded in 1887. It has a 850-acre campus.

RATINGS

Admissions Selectivity Rating: 86   **Fire Safety Rating:** 60*   **Green Rating:** 60*

STUDENTS AND FACULTY

Enrollment: 2,806. **Student Body:** 52% female, 48% male, 22% out-of-state, 3% international. African American 8%, Caucasian 56%, Hispanic 2%, Native American 1%.
Retention and Graduation: 71% freshmen return for sophomore year. 23% grads go on to further study within 1 year. 5% grads pursue arts and sciences degrees. 4% grads pursue law degrees. 7% grads pursue business degrees.
Faculty: Student/faculty ratio 14:1. 196 full-time faculty, 91% hold PhDs, 33% are women.

ACADEMICS

Degrees: Associate, bachelor's, first professional, master's. **Classes:** Most classes have fewer than 10 students. **Special Study Options:** Accelerated program, cooperative education program, distance learning, double major, dual enrollment, exchange student program (domestic), honors program, independent study, internships, liberal arts/career combination, study abroad, teacher certification program. **Combined degree programs:** BA/JD, BA/MA, BA/MBA PHD/MBA. Special programs offered to physically disabled students include note-taking services, tape recorders. **Career services:** Career/job search classes, career assessment, internships.

FACILITIES

Housing: Special housing for disabled students, men's dorms, women's dorms, apartments for married students, apartments for single students. Student apartments and suites for sophomores, juniors and seniors; also graduate apartments. All off-campus housing must be approved by the Office of Residence Life. 75% of campus accessible to physically disabled. **Special Academic Facilities/Equipment:** Taylor Bott-Rogers Fine Arts Bldg. Lundy-Fetterman School of Business museum and exhibit hall, School of Pharmacy Clinical Research Facility.

CAMPUS LIFE

Environment: Rural. **Activities:** Choral groups, concert band, drama/theater, jazz band, literary magazine, music ensembles, musical theater, pep band, radio station, student government, student newspaper, yearbook, campus ministries, international student organization. **Organizations:** 44 registered organizations, 14 honor societies, 20 religious organizations. **Athletics (Intercollegiate):** Men: Baseball, basketball, cross-country, golf, soccer, tennis, track/field (outdoor), wrestling. Women: Basketball, cheerleading, cross-country, golf, soccer, softball, swimming, tennis, track/field (outdoor), volleyball. **On-Campus Highlights:** Lundy-Fetterman School of Business, Wallace Student Center/Oasis Grill/Starbucks, Keith Hills Country Club and Golf Course, Eakes Sports Complex, D. Rich Memorial Hall, Saylor Park.

ADMISSIONS

Freshman Academic Profile: Average high school GPA 3.4. 38% in top 10% of high school class, 80% in top 25% of high school class, 92% in top 50% of high school class. 85% from public high schools. Minimum paper TOEFL 500. Minimum computer TOEFL 173. **Basis for Candidate Selection:** Very important factors considered include: Academic GPA, rigor of secondary school record, standardized test scores. Important factors considered include: Class rank, interview, talent/ability. Other factors considered include: Application essay, recommendation(s), alumni/ae relation, character/personal qualities, extracurricular activities, level of applicant's interest, volunteer work, work experience. **Freshman Admission Requirements:** High school diploma is required and GED is accepted. Academic units required: 4 English, 3 mathematics, 2 science, (1 science labs), 2 foreign language, 2 social science. **Freshman Admission Statistics:** 3,348 applied, 60% admitted, 45% enrolled. **Transfer Admission Requirements:** High school transcript, college transcript(s), standardized test scores, statement of good standing from prior institution(s). Minimum college GPA of 2.5 required. Lowest grade transferable C. **General Admission Information:** Application fee $35. Regular application deadline 8/19. Notification on a rolling basis, beginning on or about 9/1. Nonfall registration accepted. Admission may be deferred for a maximum of 12. Credit and/or placement offered for CEEB Advanced Placement tests.

COSTS AND FINANCIAL AID

Annual tuition $19,650. Room and board $6,830. Required fees $700. Average book expense $1,100. **Required Forms and Deadlines:** FAFSA. Priority financial aid filing date 3/15. **Notification of Awards:** Applicants will be notified of awards on a rolling basis beginning 3/1. **Types of Aid:** Need-based scholarships/grants: Federal Pell, SEOG, state scholarships/grants, private scholarships, the school's own gift aid. Loans: FFEL Subsidized Stafford, FFEL Unsubsidized Stafford, FFEL PLUS, Federal Perkins, state loans, college/university loans from institutional funds. **Student Employment:** Federal Work-Study Program available. Institutional employment available. Highest amount earned per year from on-campus jobs $600. Off-campus job opportunities are good. **Financial Aid Statistics:** 53% freshmen, 47% undergrads receive need-based scholarship or grant aid. 70% freshmen, 86% undergrads receive non-need-based scholarship or grant aid. 63% freshmen, 57% undergrads receive need-based self-help aid. 7% freshmen, 6% undergrads receive athletic scholarships. 97% freshmen, 92% undergrads receive any aid. 75% undergrads borrow to pay for school. Average cumulative indebtedness $21,703. **Criteria for awarding institutional aid:** Non-need-based: Academics, athletics, music/drama, religious affiliation, state/district residency.

CAMPBELLSVILLE UNIVERSITY

1 University Drive, Campbellsville, KY 42718-2799
Phone: 270-789-5220 **Financial Aid Phone:** 270-789-5013
E-mail: admissions@campbellsville.edu **CEEB Code:** 1097
Fax: 270-789-5071 **ACT Code:** 1500

This private school, affiliated with the Baptist Church, was founded in 1906. It has a 90-acre campus.

RATINGS
Admissions Selectivity Rating: 74   **Fire Safety Rating:** 60*   **Green Rating:** 60*

STUDENTS AND FACULTY
Enrollment: 1,888. **Student Body:** 54% female, 46% male, 12% out-of-state, international.
Retention and Graduation: 65% freshmen return for sophomore year. 26% freshmen graduate within 4 years. 20% grads go on to further study within 1 year. 25% grads pursue arts and sciences degrees. 1% grads pursue law degrees. 15% grads pursue business degrees. 1% grads pursue medical degrees. **Faculty:** Student/faculty ratio 13:1. 115 full-time faculty, 58% hold PhDs, 6% are members of minority groups, 51% are women.

ACADEMICS
Degrees: Associate, bachelor's, master's. **Classes:** Most classes have fewer than 10 students. **Majors with Highest Enrollment:** Accounting; business, management, marketing, and related support services, other; junior high/intermediate/middle school education and teaching. **Special Study Options:** Cooperative education program, distance learning, double major, dual enrollment, English as a Second Language (ESL), honors program, independent study, internships, liberal arts/career combination, study abroad, teacher certification program, weekend college. Special programs offered to physically disabled students include tutors. **Career services:** Alumni services, career assessment, internships.

FACILITIES
Housing: Men's dorms, women's dorms, apartments for married students, apartments for single students. 70% of campus accessible to physically disabled. **Special Academic Facilities/Equipment:** Computer labs: Technology lab. **Computers:** Students can register for classes online. Administrative functions (other than registration) can be performed online.

CAMPUS LIFE
Environment: Rural. **Activities:** Choral groups, concert band, dance, drama/theater, jazz band, literary magazine, marching band, music ensembles, musical theater, pep band, radio station, student government, student newspaper, television station, yearbook, campus ministries, international student organization. **Organizations:** 49 registered organizations, 1 honor societies, 7 religious organizations. **Athletics (Intercollegiate):** *Men:* Baseball, basketball, bowling, cheerleading, cross-country, football, golf, soccer, tennis, track/field (outdoor), wrestling. *Women:* Basketball, bowling, cheerleading, cross-country, golf, soccer, softball, swimming, tennis, track/field (outdoor), volleyball. **On-Campus Highlights:** Technology Center, Athletic Center, New Resident Village, Library, Fine Arts Center.

ADMISSIONS
Freshman Academic Profile: Average high school GPA 3.18. 17% in top 10% of high school class, 38% in top 25% of high school class, 69% in top 50% of high school class. 90% from public high schools. SAT Math middle 50% range 430–600. SAT Critical Reading middle 50% range 420–560. ACT middle 50% range 18–23. Minimum paper TOEFL 500. Minimum computer TOEFL 173. **Basis for Candidate Selection:** *Very important factors considered include:* Rigor of secondary school record. *Important factors considered include:* Class rank, recommendation(s), standardized test scores, character/personal qualities, interview. *Other factors considered include:* Application essay, alumni/ae relation, extracurricular activities, religious affiliation/commitment, talent/ability, volunteer work, work experience. **Freshman Admission Requirements:** High school diploma is required and GED is accepted. *Academic units recommended:* 4 English, 3 mathematics, 3 science, (1 science labs), 2 social studies, 1 history, 6 academic electives, 1 fine arts. **Freshman Admission Statistics:** 2,109 applied, 67% admitted, 36% enrolled. **Transfer Admission Requirements:** College transcript(s), lowest grade transferable C. **General Admission Information:** Application fee $20. Regular application deadline 8/15. Notification on a rolling basis, beginning on or about 9/1. Nonfall registration accepted. Admission may be deferred for a maximum of 12. Credit and/or placement offered for CEEB Advanced Placement tests.

COSTS AND FINANCIAL AID
Annual tuition $18,410. Room and board $6,540. Required fees $400. Average book expense $1,000. **Required Forms and Deadlines:** FAFSA. **Notification**

of Awards: Applicants will be notified of awards on a rolling basis beginning 2/15. **Types of Aid:** *Need-based scholarships/grants:* Federal Pell, SEOG, state scholarships/grants, private scholarships, the school's own gift aid. *Loans:* FFEL Subsidized Stafford, FFEL Unsubsidized Stafford, FFEL PLUS, Federal Perkins, college/university loans from institutional funds. **Student Employment:** Federal Work-Study Program available. Institutional employment available. Highest amount earned per year from on-campus jobs $2,000. Off-campus job opportunities are good. **Financial Aid Statistics:** 94% freshmen, 91% undergrads receive need-based scholarship or grant aid. 13% freshmen, 10% undergrads receive non-need-based scholarship or grant aid. 69% freshmen, 73% undergrads receive need-based self-help aid. 5% freshmen, 6% undergrads receive athletic scholarships. 95% freshmen, 92% undergrads receive any aid. 90% undergrads borrow to pay for school. Average cumulative indebtedness $21,500. **Criteria for awarding institutional aid:** *Non-need-based:* Academics, art, athletics, leadership, minority status, music/drama, religious affiliation, state/district residency.

CANISIUS COLLEGE

2001 Main Street, Buffalo, NY 14208
Phone: 716-888-2200 **Financial Aid Phone:** 716-888-2300
E-mail: admissions@canisius.edu **CEEB Code:** 2073
Fax: 716-888-3230 **Website:** www.canisius.edu **ACT Code:** 2690

This private school, affiliated with the Roman CatholiC–Jesuit Church, was founded in 1870. It has a 32-acre campus.

RATINGS
Admissions Selectivity Rating: 80   **Fire Safety Rating:** 60*   **Green Rating:** 66

STUDENTS AND FACULTY
Enrollment: 3,105. **Student Body:** 53% female, 47% male, 6.9% out-of-state, 4% international (32 countries represented). Asian 1%, African American 6%, Caucasian 78%, Hispanic 2%.
Retention and Graduation: 57% freshmen graduate within 4 years. **Faculty:** Student/faculty ratio 11.2:1. 230 full-time faculty, 94% hold PhDs, 7% are members of minority groups, 37% are women.

ACADEMICS
Degrees: Associate, bachelor's, master's, post-bachelor's certificate, post-master's certificate. **Classes:** Most classes have 20–29 students. Most lab/discussion sessions have 20–29 students. **Majors with Highest Enrollment:** Business administration and management; political science and government; psychology; **Special Study Options:** Cooperative education program, cross-registration, distance learning, double major, dual enrollment, English as a Second Language (ESL), exchange student program (domestic), honors program, independent study, internships, study abroad, teacher certification program, 4 + 1 BS/MBA 3 + 4 BS/DD (Bio and Dentistry)-Early Assurance guaranteed Medical School Admission). **Honors programs:** The All College Honors Program offers outstanding students the opportunity for a highly demanding and rewarding experience of the core curriculum. Students study under the college's most distinguished faculty, participate in educational travel, write a senior thesis and compete for special awards and honors. **Combined degree programs:** BA/DDS, BA/BS-MBA, BA/BS-MBAPA. Special programs offered to physically disabled students include note-taking services, reader services, tape recorders, tutors. **Career services:** Alumni network, alumni services, career/job search classes, career assessment, internships, regional alumni.

FACILITIES
Housing: Coed dorms, special housing for disabled students, special housing for international students, apartments for single students, Honors Student Housing. All college-owned housing is handicapped accessible. 95% of campus accessible to physically disabled. **Special Academic Facilities/Equipment:** TV studio, electron microscope, seismograph, language lab, digital lab, human performance lab, molecular biology and physics labs, mini-planetarium. **Computers:** 100% of classrooms, 100% of dorms, 100% of libraries, 100% of dining areas, 100% of student union, 100% of common outdoor areas have wireless network access. Students can register for classes online. Administrative functions (other than registration) can be performed online.

CAMPUS LIFE
Environment: Metropolis. **Activities:** Choral groups, concert band, dance, drama/theater, jazz band, literary magazine, music ensembles, musical theater, pep band, radio station, student government, student newspaper, student-run film society, television station, yearbook, campus ministries, international student organization, Model UN. **Organizations:** 102 registered organizations, 16 honor societies, 2 religious organizations. 1 fraternities, 1 sorority.

Athletics (Intercollegiate): *Men:* Baseball, basketball, cross-country, diving, golf, ice hockey, lacrosse, soccer, swimming. *Women:* Basketball, cross-country, diving, lacrosse, soccer, softball, swimming, synchronized swimming, volleyball. **On-Campus Highlights:** Montante Cultural Center, Delavan Townhouses, Palisano Pavillion, Koessler Athletic Center, Richard E. Winter Student Center. Canisius College sponsors a variety of on-campus entertainment to keep students busy throughout the year. Our highly popular Java Jams is a weekly coffee-style event offering entertainment in the Palisano Pavilion.

ADMISSIONS

Freshman Academic Profile: Average high school GPA 90.3. 28% in top 10% of high school class, 57% in top 25% of high school class, 87% in top 50% of high school class. 71% from public high schools. SAT Math middle 50% range 510–620. SAT Critical Reading middle 50% range 500–600. ACT middle 50% range 23–29. Minimum paper TOEFL 500. Minimum computer TOEFL 173. **Basis for Candidate Selection:** *Very important factors considered include:* Academic GPA, rigor of secondary school record. *Important factors considered include:* Application essay, recommendation(s), standardized test scores. *Other factors considered include:* Class rank, alumni/ae relation, character/personal qualities, extracurricular activities, first generation, interview, talent/ability, volunteer work, work experience. **Freshman Admission Requirements:** High school diploma is required and GED is accepted. *Academic units required:* 4 English, 3 mathematics, 2 science, (2 science labs), 2 foreign language, 4 social studies. *Academic units recommended:* 4 English, 4 mathematics, 4 science, (2 science labs), 4 foreign language, 4 social studies, 4 academic electives. **Freshman Admission Statistics:** 3,996 applied, 77% admitted, 23% enrolled. **Transfer Admission Requirements:** College transcript(s), statement of good standing from prior institution(s). Minimum college GPA of 2.0 required. Lowest grade transferable C. **General Admission Information:** Application fee $40. Regular application deadline 5/1. Notification on a rolling basis, beginning on or about 12/15. Nonfall registration accepted. Admission may be deferred for a maximum of 1 year. Credit and/or placement offered for CEEB Advanced Placement tests.

COSTS AND FINANCIAL AID

Average book expense $700. **Required Forms and Deadlines:** FAFSA, state aid form. Priority financial aid filing date 2/15. **Notification of Awards:** Applicants will be notified of awards on a rolling basis beginning 3/1. **Types of Aid:** *Need-based scholarships/grants:* Federal Pell, SEOG, state scholarships/grants, private scholarships, the school's own gift aid. *Loans:* FFEL Subsidized Stafford, FFEL Unsubsidized Stafford, FFEL PLUS, Federal Perkins. **Student Employment:** Federal Work-Study Program available. Institutional employment available. Highest amount earned per year from on-campus jobs $2,175. Off-campus job opportunities are excellent. **Financial Aid Statistics:** 82% freshmen, 75% undergrads receive need-based scholarship or grant aid. 19% freshmen, 14% undergrads receive non-need-based scholarship or grant aid. 68% freshmen, 63% undergrads receive need-based self-help aid. 2% freshmen, 3% undergrads receive athletic scholarships. 98% freshmen, 98% undergrads receive any aid. 77.2% undergrads borrow to pay for school. Average cumulative indebtedness $33,645. **Criteria for awarding institutional aid:** *Non-need-based:* Academics, alumni affiliation, art, athletics, job skills, music/drama, religious affiliation.

CAPE BRETON UNIVERSITY

PO Box 5300, Sydney, NS B1P 6L2 Canada
Phone: 902-563-1117 **Financial Aid Phone:** 902-563-1420
E-mail: registrar@uccb.ns.ca
Fax: 902-563-1371 **Website:** www.cbu.ca

This public school was founded in 1974. It has a 140-acre campus.

RATINGS
Admissions Selectivity Rating: 60*   **Fire Safety Rating:** 60*   **Green Rating:** 60*

STUDENTS AND FACULTY
Enrollment: 2,702. **Student Body:** 58% female, 42% male, % out-of-state, international (40 countries represented).
Retention and Graduation: 55% freshmen return for sophomore year. 54% freshmen graduate within 4 years. **Faculty:** Student/faculty ratio 15:1. 189 full-time faculty, 41% hold PhDs, 25% are women.

ACADEMICS
Degrees: Bachelor's, certificate, diploma, master's, post-bachelor's certificate. **Classes:** Most classes have fewer than 10 students. **Majors with Highest Enrollment:** Early childhood education and teaching; education; mathematics and computer science. **Special Study Options:** Cooperative education program, distance learning, double major, honors program, independent study, internships, liberal arts/career combination, study abroad. **Combined degree**

programs: BBA/BACS. Special programs offered to physically disabled students include note-taking services, reader services, tape recorders, tutors.

FACILITIES
Housing: Coed dorms 100% of campus accessible to physically disabled. **Special Academic Facilities/Equipment:** Art Gallery, Boardmore Playhouse CAPR Radio. **Computers:** Students can register for classes online. Administrative functions (other than registration) can be performed online.

CAMPUS LIFE
Environment: Town. **Activities:** Drama/theater, literary magazine, radio station, student government, student newspaper, yearbook. **Organizations:** 72 registered organizations, 1 honor societies, **Athletics (Intercollegiate):** *Men:* Basketball, soccer. *Women:* Basketball, soccer, volleyball. **On-Campus Highlights:** Pit Lounge, Sullivan Field House Athletic Centre, Great Hall, Boardmore Playhouse, Centre for Cape Breton Studies.

ADMISSIONS
Freshman Academic Profile: 80% from public high schools. Minimum paper TOEFL 550. Minimum computer TOEFL 213. **Basis for Candidate Selection:** *Important factors considered include:* Rigor of secondary school record. **Freshman Admission Requirements:** High school diploma is required and GED is not accepted. *Academic units required:* 3 English, 2 mathematics. *Academic units recommended:* 3 mathematics, 6 science, 3 history. **Freshman Admission Statistics:** 1,679 applied, 89% admitted, 85% enrolled. **Transfer Admission Requirements:** College transcript(s). **General Admission Information:** Application fee $20. Regular application deadline 8/1. Notification on a rolling basis, beginning on or about 3/1. Nonfall registration accepted. Admission may be deferred for a maximum of 1 year.

COSTS AND FINANCIAL AID
Annual in-state tuition $3,887. **Student Employment:** Institutional employment available. Off-campus job opportunities are good.

CAPITAL UNIVERSITY

Admission Office, 1 College and Main, Columbus, OH 43209
Phone: 614-236-6101 **Financial Aid Phone:** 614-236-6511
E-mail: admissions@capital.edu **CEEB Code:** 1099
Fax: 614-236-6926 **Website:** www.capital.edu **ACT Code:** 3242

This private school, affiliated with the Lutheran Church, was founded in 1830. It has a 48-acre campus.

RATINGS
Admissions Selectivity Rating: 77   **Fire Safety Rating:** 60*   **Green Rating:** 75

STUDENTS AND FACULTY
Enrollment: 2,634. **Student Body:** 62% female, 38% male, 5% out-of-state, 1% international. Asian 1%, African American 9%, Caucasian 82%, Hispanic 2%.
Retention and Graduation: 76% freshmen return for sophomore year. 46% freshmen graduate within 4 years. **Faculty:** Student/faculty ratio 9:1. 217 full-time faculty, 71% hold PhDs, 12% are members of minority groups, 45% are women.

ACADEMICS
Degrees: Bachelor's, first professional, master's. **Classes:** Most classes have 10–19 students. Most lab/discussion sessions have 20–29 students. **Majors with Highest Enrollment:** Education; multi-/interdisciplinary studies, other; nursing/registered nurse (RN, ASN, BSN, MSN). **Special Study Options:** Accelerated program, cooperative education program, cross-registration, double major, English as a Second Language (ESL), exchange student program (domestic), honors program, independent study, internships, liberal arts/career combination, student-designed major, study abroad, teacher certification program. **Honors programs:** Capital University Honors Program. **Combined degree programs:** , MSN/JD, MSN/MBA, MSN/Master's of Lay Ministry. Special programs offered to physically disabled students include tape recorders, tutors. **Career services:** Alumni network, alumni services, career/job search classes, career assessment, internships

FACILITIES
Housing: Coed dorms, special housing for disabled students, special housing for international students, fraternity/sorority housing, apartments for single students, student organization and special interest housing. 100% of campus accessible to physically disabled. **Special Academic Facilities/Equipment:** Art gallery, Conservatory of Music. **Computers:** Students can register for classes online. Administrative functions (other than registration) can be performed online.

CAMPUS LIFE

Environment: Metropolis. **Activities:** Choral groups, concert band, dance, drama/theater, jazz band, literary magazine, music ensembles, musical theater, radio station, student government, student newspaper, symphony orchestra, television station, yearbook, campus ministries, international student organization. **Organizations:** 63 registered organizations, 16 honor societies, 5 religious organizations. 5 fraternities, 5 sororities. **Athletics (Intercollegiate):** *Men:* Baseball, basketball, cross-country, football, golf, soccer, tennis, track/field (outdoor), track/field (indoor). *Women:* Basketball, cross-country, golf, soccer, softball, tennis, track/field (outdoor), track/field (indoor), volleyball. **On-Campus Highlights:** Capital Center, College Avenue Residence Hall, Schumacher Gallery. **Environmental Initiatives:** Energy management; solid waste recycling; behavior modification.

ADMISSIONS

Freshman Academic Profile: Average high school GPA 3.4. 18% in top 10% of high school class, 46% in top 25% of high school class, 82% in top 50% of high school class. 92% from public high schools. SAT Math middle 50% range 470–590. SAT Critical Reading middle 50% range 470–590. SAT Writing middle 50% range 460–570. ACT middle 50% range 21–26. Minimum paper TOEFL 500. Minimum computer TOEFL 173. **Basis for Candidate Selection:** *Very important factors considered include:* Academic GPA, rigor of secondary school record, standardized test scores. *Important factors considered include:* Class rank, extracurricular activities, interview. *Other factors considered include:* Recommendation(s), alumni/ae relation, character/personal qualities, level of applicant's interest, racial/ethnic status, religious affiliation/commitment, talent/ability. **Freshman Admission Requirements:** High school diploma is required and GED is accepted. *Academic units required:* 4 English, 3 mathematics, 3 science, (2 science labs), 2 foreign language, 3 social studies, 1 academic electives. *Academic units recommended:* 4 English, 3 mathematics, 3 science, (2 science labs), 2 foreign language, 3 social studies, 1 academic electives. **Freshman Admission Statistics:** 3,394 applied, 75% admitted, 25% enrolled. **Transfer Admission Requirements:** College transcript(s), minimum college GPA of 2.5 required. Lowest grade transferable C–. **General Admission Information:** Application fee $25. Notification on a rolling basis, beginning on or about 9/15. Nonfall registration accepted. Admission may be deferred for a maximum of 1 year. Credit and/or placement offered for CEEB Advanced Placement tests.

COSTS AND FINANCIAL AID

Annual tuition $27,680. Room and board $7,150. Average book expense $1,000. **Required Forms and Deadlines:** FAFSA. Priority financial aid filing date 2/28. **Notification of Awards:** Applicants will be notified of awards on a rolling basis beginning 3/1. **Types of Aid:** *Need-based scholarships/grants:* Federal Pell, SEOG, state scholarships/grants, private scholarships, the school's own gift aid. *Loans:* FFEL Subsidized Stafford, FFEL Unsubsidized Stafford, FFEL PLUS, Federal Perkins, Federal Nursing, state loans, college/university loans from institutional funds. **Student Employment:** Federal Work-Study Program available. Institutional employment available. Off-campus job opportunities are good. **Financial Aid Statistics:** 52% freshmen, 49% undergrads receive need-based scholarship or grant aid. 50% freshmen, 68% undergrads receive non-need-based scholarship or grant aid. 81% freshmen, 73% undergrads receive need-based self-help aid. 99% freshmen receive any aid.

---

sion sessions have fewer than 10 students. **Majors with Highest Enrollment:** Aerospace, aeronautical and astronautical engineering; computer engineering; electrical, electronics and communications engineering. **Special Study Options:** Cooperative education program, distance learning, double major, independent study, internships, weekend college. Special programs offered to physically disabled students include note-taking services, tape recorders, tutors. **Career services:** Alumni services, career/job search classes, career assessment, internships.

FACILITIES

Housing: Men's dorms, women's dorms, apartments for single students. 99% of campus accessible to physically disabled.

CAMPUS LIFE

Activities: Dance, drama/theater, literary magazine, radio station, student government, student newspaper. **Organizations:** 10 registered organizations, 3 honor societies.

ADMISSIONS

Freshman Academic Profile: 85% from public high schools. SAT Math middle 50% range 350–520. SAT Critical Reading middle 50% range 400–520. Minimum paper TOEFL 500. **Basis for Candidate Selection:** *Very important factors considered include:* Rigor of secondary school record. *Important factors considered include:* Application essay, standardized test scores. *Other factors considered include:* Recommendation(s), alumni/ae relation, character/personal qualities, extracurricular activities, interview, talent/ability, volunteer work, work experience. **Freshman Admission Requirements:** High school diploma is required and GED is accepted. *Academic units required:* 4 English, 3 mathematics, 3 science, (2 science labs). *Academic units recommended:* 4 English, 4 mathematics, 4 science, (2 science labs), 2 social studies, 2 history. **Freshman Admission Statistics:** 190 applied, 86% admitted, 21% enrolled. **Transfer Admission Requirements:** College transcript(s), essay or personal statement, minimum college GPA of 2.0 required. Lowest grade transferable C. **General Admission Information:** Application fee $25. Notification on a rolling basis, beginning on or about 11/15. Nonfall registration accepted. Admission may be deferred for a maximum of 1. Credit and/or placement offered for CEEB Advanced Placement tests.

COSTS AND FINANCIAL AID

Annual tuition $16,500. Room and board $3,710. Required fees $600. Average book expense $800. **Required Forms and Deadlines:** FAFSA, institution's own financial aid form. Priority financial aid filing date 3/1. **Notification of Awards:** Applicants will be notified of awards on a rolling basis beginning 6/30. **Types of Aid:** *Need-based scholarships/grants:* Federal Pell, SEOG, state scholarships/grants, private scholarships, the school's own gift aid. *Loans:* FFEL Subsidized Stafford, FFEL Unsubsidized Stafford, FFEL PLUS, Federal Perkins. **Student Employment:** Federal Work-Study Program available. Institutional employment available. Highest amount earned per year from on-campus jobs $2,000. Off-campus job opportunities are excellent. **Financial Aid Statistics:** 25% freshmen, 36% undergrads receive need-based scholarship or grant aid. 1% undergrads receive non-need-based scholarship or grant aid. 10% freshmen, 30% undergrads receive need-based self-help aid. 89% undergrads borrow to pay for school. Average cumulative indebtedness $18,000. **Criteria for awarding institutional aid:** *Non-need-based:* Academics, alumni affiliation, leadership, minority status.

CAPITOL COLLEGE

11301 Springfield Road, Laurel, MD 20708
Phone: 800-950-1992
E-mail: admissions@capitol-college.edu
Fax: 301-953-1442 **Website:** www.capitol-college.edu

This is a private school.

RATINGS

Admissions Selectivity Rating: 60*   **Fire Safety Rating:** 60*   **Green Rating:** 60*

STUDENTS AND FACULTY

Enrollment: 452. **Student Body:** 22% female, 78% male, 14% out-of-state, 4% international. Asian 7%, African American 36%, Caucasian 48%, Hispanic 2%.
Retention and Graduation: 60% freshmen return for sophomore year. 5% freshmen graduate within 4 years. 10% grads go on to further study within 1 year. 10% grads pursue arts and sciences degrees. **Faculty:** Student/faculty ratio 12:1. 21 full-time faculty, 33% hold PhDs, 14% are members of minority groups, 29% are women.

ACADEMICS

Degrees: Associate, bachelor's, certificate, master's, post-bachelor's certificate, transfer associate. **Classes:** Most classes have 10–19 students. Most lab/discus-

---

CARLETON COLLEGE

100 South College Street, Northfield, MN 55057
Phone: 507-222-4190 **Financial Aid Phone:** 507-222-4138
E-mail: admissions@carleton.edu **CEEB Code:** 6081
Fax: 507-222-4526 **Website:** www.carleton.edu **ACT Code:** 2092

This private school was founded in 1866. It has a 955-acre campus.

RATINGS

Admissions Selectivity Rating: 97   **Fire Safety Rating:** 60*   **Green Rating:** 60*

STUDENTS AND FACULTY

Enrollment: 1,975. **Student Body:** 52% female, 48% male, 76% out-of-state, 6% international (30 countries represented). Asian 10%, African American 5%, Caucasian 73%, Hispanic 5%, Native American 1%.

Retention and Graduation: 95% freshmen return for sophomore year. 90% freshmen graduate within 4 years. 23% grads go on to further study within 1 year. 12% grads pursue arts and sciences degrees. 3% grads pursue law degrees. 2% grads pursue medical degrees. **Faculty:** Student/faculty ratio 9:1. 215 full-time faculty, 96% hold PhDs, 21% are members of minority groups, 45% are women.

ACADEMICS

Degrees: Bachelor's. **Classes:** Most classes have 10–19 students. Most lab/discussion sessions have 10–19 students. **Majors with Highest Enrollment:** Biology/biological sciences; economics; political science and government. **Special Study Options:** Accelerated program, cross-registration, double major, dual enrollment, independent study, internships, student-designed major, study abroad, teacher certification program. **Combined degree programs:** BA/JD, 3-2 Nursing, Elementary Education. Special programs offered to physically disabled students include note-taking services, reader services, tape recorders, tutors. **Career services:** Alumni network, regional alumni.

FACILITIES

Housing: Coed dorms, special housing for disabled students, apartments for single students, 25 college-owned houses within 2 blocks of campus with varying meal plan options. Some are designated as special interest houses (ex: Green House, Culinary House). 28% of campus accessible to physically disabled. **Special Academic Facilities/Equipment:** Arboretum, greenhouse, observatory, scanning and transmission electron microscopes, refractor and reflector telescopes, nuclear magnetic resonance spectrometer, art gallery. **Computers:** 45% of classrooms, 15% of dorms, 85% of libraries, 50% of dining areas, 100% of student union, 15% of common outdoor areas have wireless network access. Students can register for classes online.

CAMPUS LIFE

Environment: Village. **Activities:** Choral groups, concert band, dance, drama/theater, jazz band, literary magazine, music ensembles, musical theater, radio station, student government, student newspaper, student-run film society, symphony orchestra, yearbook, campus ministries, international student organization, Model UN. **Organizations:** 132 registered organizations, 3 honor societies, 17 religious organizations. **Athletics (Intercollegiate):** *Men:* Baseball, basketball, cross-country, diving, football, golf, soccer, swimming, tennis, track/field (outdoor), track/field (indoor). *Women:* Basketball, cross-country, diving, golf, soccer, softball, swimming, synchronized swimming, tennis, track/field (outdoor), track/field (indoor), volleyball. **On-Campus Highlights:** Cowling Arboretum, Art Gallery, Historic Goodsell Observatory, Japanese Garden, Recreation Center, Sayles Campus Center, Library.

ADMISSIONS

Freshman Academic Profile: 74% in top 10% of high school class, 96% in top 25% of high school class, 100% in top 50% of high school class. 73% from public high schools. SAT Math middle 50% range 650–740. SAT Critical Reading middle 50% range 660–750. SAT Writing middle 50% range 650–750. ACT middle 50% range 29–33. Minimum paper TOEFL 600. Minimum computer TOEFL 250. **Basis for Candidate Selection:** *Very important factors considered include:* Class rank, academic GPA, rigor of secondary school record. *Important factors considered include:* Application essay, recommendation(s), standardized test scores, alumni/ae relation, character/personal qualities, extracurricular activities, racial/ethnic status, talent/ability, volunteer work, work experience. *Other factors considered include:* First generation, geographical residence, interview, state residency. **Freshman Admission Requirements:** High school diploma is required and GED is accepted. *Academic units recommended:* 4 English, 3 mathematics, 3 science, (1 science labs), 3 foreign language, 3 social studies and history. **Freshman Admission Statistics:** 4,956 applied, 27% admitted, 37% enrolled. **Transfer Admission Requirements:** High school transcript, college transcript(s), essay or personal statement, standardized test scores, statement of good standing from prior institution(s). Minimum college GPA of 2.0 required. Lowest grade transferable C–. **General Admission Information:** Application fee $30. Early decision application deadline 11/15. Regular application deadline 1/15. Regular notification 4/15. Nonfall registration not accepted. Admission may be deferred for a maximum of 1 year. Credit and/or placement offered for CEEB Advanced Placement tests.

COSTS AND FINANCIAL AID

Annual tuition $39,546. Room and board $10,428. Required fees $231. Average book expense $728. **Required Forms and Deadlines:** FAFSA, CSS/Financial Aid PROFILE, noncustodial PROFILE, business/farm supplement. Prior year tax forms. Financial aid filing deadline 2/15. Priority financial aid filing date 2/15. **Notification of Awards:** Applicants will be notified of awards on or about 4/1. **Types of Aid:** *Need-based scholarships/grants:* Federal Pell, SEOG, state scholarships/grants, private scholarships, the school's own gift aid. *Loans:* FFEL Subsidized Stafford, FFEL Unsubsidized Stafford, FFEL PLUS, Federal Perkins, state loans, college/university loans from institutional funds, Minnesota SELF Loan program. **Student Employment:** Federal Work-Study Program available. **Financial Aid Statistics:** 54% freshmen, 55% undergrads receive

need-based scholarship or grant aid. 10% freshmen, 10% undergrads receive non-need-based scholarship or grant aid. 50% freshmen, 53% undergrads receive need-based self-help aid. 50% freshmen, 54% undergrads receive any aid. 52% undergrads borrow to pay for school. Average cumulative indebtedness $20,083. **Criteria for awarding institutional aid:** *Non-need-based:* Academics.

CARLOS ALBIZU UNIVERSITY—CAU

2173 NW 99 Ave, Miami, FL 33172
Phone: 800-672-3246 **Financial Aid Phone:**
E-mail: admissions@albizu.edu
Fax: 305-593-1854 **Website:** www.mia.albizu.edu

This private school was founded in 1966. It has a 18-acre campus.

RATINGS

Admissions Selectivity Rating: 60*   **Fire Safety Rating:** 60*   **Green Rating:** 60*

STUDENTS AND FACULTY

Enrollment: 563. **Student Body:** 74% female, 26% male, % out-of-state, 2% international. African American 17%, Caucasian 6%, Hispanic 77%. **Retention and Graduation:** -33% freshmen graduate within 4 years. 60% grads go on to further study within 1 year. 85% grads pursue arts and sciences degrees. **Faculty:** Student/faculty ratio 13:1. 4 full-time faculty, 100% hold PhDs, 25% are members of minority groups, 50% are women.

ACADEMICS

Degrees: Bachelor's, diploma, master's. **Special Study Options:** Accelerated program, cooperative education program, cross-registration, double major, dual enrollment, English as a Second Language (ESL), independent study, internships, teacher certification program, weekend college.

CAMPUS LIFE

Activities: Student government, student newspaper. **Organizations:** 3 registered organizations, 1 honor societies.

ADMISSIONS

Freshman Academic Profile: Basis for Candidate Selection: *Very important factors considered include:* Rigor of secondary school record. **Freshman Admission Requirements:** High school diploma is required and GED is accepted. **Freshman Admission Statistics:** 185 applied, 64% admitted, 54% enrolled. Minimum college GPA of 2.0 required. Lowest grade transferable C. **General Admission Information:** Application fee $25. Nonfall registration accepted. Admission may be deferred for a maximum of 1 year.

COSTS AND FINANCIAL AID

Annual tuition $8,250. Average book expense $690. **Required Forms and Deadlines:** FAFSA, institution's own financial aid form. Priority financial aid filing date 6/1. **Notification of Awards:** Applicants will be notified of awards on a rolling basis beginning 2/1. **Student Employment:** Off-campus job opportunities are good. **Financial Aid Statistics:** 82% freshmen, 84% undergrads receive need-based scholarship or grant aid. 3% undergrads receive non-need-based scholarship or grant aid. 95% freshmen, 91% undergrads receive need-based self-help aid. 85% undergrads borrow to pay for school. Average cumulative indebtedness $23,500. **Criteria for awarding institutional aid:** *Non-need-based:* Academics.

CARLOW UNIVERSITY

3333 Fifth Avenue, Pittsburgh, PA 15213-3165
Phone: 412-578-6059
E-mail: admissions@carlow.edu
Fax: 412-578-6668 **Website:** www.carlow.edu

This private school, affiliated with the Roman Catholic Church, was founded in 1929. It has a 15-acre campus.

RATINGS

Admissions Selectivity Rating: 76   **Fire Safety Rating:** 60*   **Green Rating:** 60*

STUDENTS AND FACULTY

Enrollment: 1,502. **Student Body:** 94% female, 6% male, 3% out-of-state, international (5 countries represented). Asian 1%, African American 17%, Caucasian 67%, Hispanic 1%, Native American 1%.

Retention and Graduation: 73% freshmen return for sophomore year. 33% freshmen graduate within 4 years. **Faculty:** Student/faculty ratio 11:1. 93 full-time faculty, 71% hold PhDs, 8% are members of minority groups, 74% are women.

ACADEMICS

Degrees: Bachelor's, master's, post-bachelor's certificate, post-master's certificate. **Classes:** Most classes have 10–19 students. **Majors with Highest Enrollment:** Business/commerce; elementary education and teaching; nursing, other. **Special Study Options:** Accelerated program, cross-registration, distance learning, double major, dual enrollment, honors program, independent study, internships, liberal arts/career combination, student-designed major, study abroad, teacher certification program, weekend college, 3/2 programs with Carnegie Mellon for Chem. Engineering, Environmental Engineering, Mechanical Engineering. Other programs with Duquesne U. in Environmental Science and Mgt.(3/2), several programs with Art Institute of Pittsburgh. **Career services:** Alumni network, career/job search classes.

FACILITIES

Housing: Women's dorms. **Special Academic Facilities/Equipment:** The A.J. Palumbo Hall of Science and Technology features research labs, as well as a greenhouse, darkroom, biochamber, an on-site reference library and specially designed study and work zones on every floor to encourage team research. The building incorporates more than 1,000 outlets for Internet access. Also, on-campus preschool and elementary school. **Computers:** 100% of classrooms, 100% of dorms, 100% of libraries, 100% of dining areas, 100% of student union, have wireless network access. Students can register for classes online.

CAMPUS LIFE

Environment: City. **Activities:** Choral groups, drama/theater, literary magazine, student government, student newspaper, yearbook, campus ministries, international student organization. **Organizations:** 28 registered organizations, 5 honor societies, 1 religious organizations. **Athletics (Intercollegiate):** *Women:* Basketball, soccer, softball, tennis, volleyball.

ADMISSIONS

Freshman Academic Profile: Average high school GPA 3.27. 12% in top 10% of high school class, 39% in top 25% of high school class, 79% in top 50% of high school class. SAT Math middle 50% range 440–540. SAT Critical Reading middle 50% range 440–530. SAT Writing middle 50% range 420–540. ACT middle 50% range 18–23. **Basis for Candidate Selection:** *Very important factors considered include:* Academic GPA, rigor of secondary school record, standardized test scores. *Important factors considered include:* Class rank. *Other factors considered include:* Application essay, recommendation(s), alumni/ae relation, character/personal qualities, extracurricular activities, first generation, interview, level of applicant's interest, talent/ability, volunteer work, work experience. **Freshman Admission Requirements:** High school diploma is required and GED is accepted. *Academic units required:* 4 English, 3 mathematics, 3 science, 2 social studies, 2 history, 4 academic electives. *Academic units recommended:* 4 mathematics, 4 science, (2 science labs). **Freshman Admission Statistics:** 1,063 applied, 60% admitted, 38% enrolled. **Transfer Admission Requirements:** College transcript(s), minimum college GPA of 2.0 required. Lowest grade transferable C. **General Admission Information:** Application fee $20. Nonfall registration accepted. Credit and/or placement offered for CEEB Advanced Placement tests.

COSTS AND FINANCIAL AID

Average book expense $1,000. **Required Forms and Deadlines:** FAFSA. Priority financial aid filing date 4/1. **Notification of Awards:** Applicants will be notified of awards on a rolling basis beginning 2/15. **Types of Aid:** *Need-based scholarships/grants:* Federal Pell, SEOG, state scholarships/grants, private scholarships, the school's own gift aid. *Loans:* FFEL Subsidized Stafford, FFEL Unsubsidized Stafford, FFEL PLUS, Federal Perkins, Federal Nursing. **Financial Aid Statistics:** 85% undergrads borrow to pay for school. **Criteria for awarding institutional aid:** *Non-need-based:* Academics, athletics, leadership.

CARNEGIE MELLON UNIVERSITY

5000 Forbes Avenue, Pittsburgh, PA 15213
Phone: 412-268-2082 **Financial Aid Phone:** 412-268-8186
E-mail: undergraduate-admissions@andrew.cmu.edu **CEEB Code:** 2074
Fax: 412-268-7838 **Website:** www.cmu.edu **ACT Code:** 3534

This private school was founded in 1900. It has a 136-acre campus.

RATINGS

Admissions Selectivity Rating: 97   **Fire Safety Rating:** 75   **Green Rating:** 95

STUDENTS AND FACULTY

Enrollment: 5,951. **Student Body:** 41% female, 59% male, 79% out-of-state, 15% international (112 countries represented). Asian 24%, African American 5%, Caucasian 40%, Hispanic 5%, Native American 1%.

Retention and Graduation: 67% freshmen graduate within 4 years. 33% grads go on to further study within 1 year. 51% grads pursue arts and sciences degrees. 4% grads pursue law degrees. 7% grads pursue business degrees. 10% grads pursue medical degrees. **Faculty:** Student/faculty ratio 12:1. 883 full-time faculty, 98% hold PhDs, 16% are members of minority groups, 26% are women.

ACADEMICS

Degrees: Bachelor's, master's, post-master's certificate. **Classes:** Most classes have fewer than 10 students. Most lab/discussion sessions have 20–29 students. **Majors with Highest Enrollment:** Computer science. **Special Study Options:** Cooperative education program, cross-registration, distance learning, double major, dual enrollment, exchange student program (domestic), independent study, internships, liberal arts/career combination, student-designed major, study abroad, teacher certification program. **Combined degree programs:** BA/MA, BA/MEng, BS/MBA Industrial Admin; BS/MPM Public Management. Special programs offered to physically disabled students include note-taking services, reader services, tape recorders, tutors. **Career services:** Alumni network, alumni services, career/job search classes, career assessment, internships, regional alumni. Career services highlights include: Our internships mission: Students who value experiential learning and who have participated in internships; campus, summer, part-time employment; and/or community service opportunities. An energized and expanding employer base (artistic, corporate, public, service, campus) committed to long term relationships with Carnegie Mellon (and the Career Center) founded on the continual enhancement and development of employer relationships. Internship Development and Placement Programs: Student Employment; Experiential and Professional Development; Pittsburgh Funded Internships (provide funds for students to stay in Pittsburgh for a summer position); Employment Opportunities Conference (Job Fair); On-Campus Recruiting; Networking Events—New York, DC, Boston, Chicago, Silicon Valley, Pittsburgh, Baltimore; Internship Search Workshop Series.

FACILITIES

Housing: Coed dorms, special housing for disabled students, men's dorms, women's dorms, fraternity/sorority housing, apartments for single students, special interest housing. 95% of campus accessible to physically disabled. **Special Academic Facilities/Equipment:** Rare books collection, Entertainment Technology Center, art galleries, theatres, Botanical Institute, extensive lab facilities and equipment, recording studio, Robotics Institute, design studios, photo shoot studio and darkrooms, radio station, Collaborative Innovation Center, LEED-certified green residence hall, Campo Garden, observatory, wood shops. **Computers:** 100% of classrooms, 100% of dorms, 100% of libraries, 100% of dining areas, 100% of student union, 100% of common outdoor areas have wireless network access. Students can register for classes online. Administrative functions (other than registration) can be performed online.

CAMPUS LIFE

Environment: Metropolis. **Activities:** Choral groups, concert band, dance, drama/theater, literary magazine, marching band, music ensembles, musical theater, pep band, radio station, student government, student newspaper, student-run film society, symphony orchestra, television station, yearbook, campus ministries, international student organization. **Organizations:** 225 registered organizations, 18 religious organizations. 16 fraternities, 7 sororities. **Athletics (Intercollegiate):** *Men:* Basketball, cheerleading, cross-country, diving, football, golf, soccer, swimming, tennis, track/field (outdoor). *Women:* Basketball, cheerleading, cross-country, diving, soccer, swimming, tennis, track/field (outdoor), volleyball. **On-Campus Highlights:** Hunt Library, Skibo Coffee House, The Cut, The Underground, University Center Building—Student Center. **En-**

vironmental Initiatives: 1. Operations: USGBC LEED Silver required for all building projects and purchase of 29% renewable electricity. 2. Environmental Education: EDUCATION—We strive to make every student a steward of the environment through both formal and informal education. Informal education is delivered through our campus operations and promoted by our Green Practices Committee (discussed elsewhere) as well as our many student groups (discussed below). Formal education happens at both the undergraduate and graduate levels. Undergraduate offerings range from environmental art (and their award winning posters) www.cmu.edu/homepage/practical/2007/spring/influence-by-design.shtml to a public policy class that has evaluated the campus carbon footprint and has provided thoughtful discussion as to when Carnegie Mellon can feasibly make the commitments implied by the signing of the PCC www.cmu.edu/greenpractices/campus-energy/Reports%20and%20Presentations.html. 3. Research: Carnegie Mellon promotes interdisciplinary environmental research through more than 18 centers that span our 7 colleges. The centers most focused on climate change include: Climate Decision Making Center http://cdmc.epp.cmu.edu/ Carnegie Mellon Electricity Industry Center www.cmu.edu/ceic and the Green Design Institute www.ce.cmu.edu/GreenDesign/ Center creation and collaboration is facilitated with the help of the Steinbrenner Institute for Environmental Education and Research (www.cmu.edu/steinbrenner) which was formed in 2004 to promote Carnegie Mellon's strategic goal of 'transitioning to an environmentally sustainable society.'

ADMISSIONS

Freshman Academic Profile: Average high school GPA 3.62. 75% in top 10% of high school class, 93% in top 25% of high school class, 99% in top 50% of high school class. SAT Math middle 50% range 670–780. SAT Critical Reading middle 50% range 620–720. SAT Writing middle 50% range 620–720. ACT middle 50% range 28–34. Minimum paper TOEFL 600. Minimum computer TOEFL 250. **Basis for Candidate Selection:** *Very important factors considered include:* Class rank, academic GPA, rigor of secondary school record, standardized test scores. *Important factors considered include:* Application essay, recommendation(s), alumni/ae relation, character/personal qualities, extracurricular activities, first generation, interview, level of applicant's interest, racial/ethnic status, talent/ability, volunteer work, work experience. **Freshman Admission Requirements:** High school diploma is required and GED is accepted. *Academic units required:* 4 English, 4 mathematics, 3 science, (3 science labs), 2 foreign language, 3 academic electives. *Academic units recommended:* 4 English, 4 mathematics, 3 science, (3 science labs), 2 foreign language, 4 academic electives. **Freshman Admission Statistics:** 14,153 applied, 36% admitted, 28% enrolled. **Transfer Admission Requirements:** High school transcript, college transcript(s), essay or personal statement, standardized test scores, statement of good standing from prior institution(s). **General Admission Information:** Application fee $70. Early decision application deadline 11/1. Regular application deadline 1/1. Regular notification 4/15. Nonfall registration not accepted. Admission may be deferred for a maximum of 1 year. Credit offered for CEEB Advanced Placement tests.

COSTS AND FINANCIAL AID

Annual tuition $39,470. Room and board $10,340. Required fees $428. Average book expense $1,000. **Required Forms and Deadlines:** FAFSA, institution's own financial aid form, Parent and student Federal Tax Returns. Parent W2 Forms. Financial aid filing deadline 5/1. Priority financial aid filing date 2/15. **Notification of Awards:** Applicants will be notified of awards on or about 3/15. **Types of Aid:** *Need-based scholarships/grants:* Federal Pell, SEOG, state scholarships/grants, private scholarships, the school's own gift aid. *Loans:* FFEL Subsidized Stafford, FFEL Unsubsidized Stafford, FFEL PLUS, Federal Perkins. **Student Employment:** Federal Work-Study Program available. Institutional employment available. Off-campus job opportunities are good. **Financial Aid Statistics:** 53% freshmen, 47% undergrads receive need-based scholarship or grant aid. 21% freshmen, 18% undergrads receive non-need-based scholarship or grant aid. 49% freshmen, 46% undergrads receive need-based self-help aid. 50% undergrads borrow to pay for school. Average cumulative indebtedness $29,546. **Criteria for awarding institutional aid:** *Non-need-based:* Academics, art, leadership, minority status, music/drama, state/district residency.

CARROLL COLLEGE (MT)

1601 North Benton Avenue, Helena, MT 59625
Phone: 406-447-4384 **Financial Aid Phone:** 406-447-5423
E-mail: admission@carroll.edu **CEEB Code:** 4041
Fax: 406-447-4533 **Website:** www.carroll.edu **ACT Code:** 2408

This private school, affiliated with the Roman Catholic Church, was founded in 1909. It has a 63-acre campus.

STUDENTS AND FACULTY

Enrollment: 1,311. **Student Body:** 56% female, 44% male, 40% out-of-state, 1% international (15 countries represented). Asian 1%, African American 1%, Caucasian 83%, Hispanic 2%, Native American 1%.
Retention and Graduation: 80% freshmen return for sophomore year. 46% freshmen graduate within 4 years. 22% grads go on to further study within 1 year. **Faculty:** Student/faculty ratio 13:1. 80 full-time faculty, 70% hold PhDs, 3% are members of minority groups, 36% are women.

ACADEMICS

Degrees: Associate, bachelor's, certificate, transfer associate. **Classes:** Most classes have 10–19 students. Most lab/discussion sessions have 20–29 students. **Majors with Highest Enrollment:** Business/commerce; nursing/registered nurse (RN, ASN, BSN, MSN); psychology. **Special Study Options:** Accelerated program, cooperative education program, double major, dual enrollment, English as a Second Language (ESL), exchange student program (domestic), honors program, independent study, internships, liberal arts/career combination, student-designed major, study abroad, teacher certification program. Special programs offered to physically disabled students include tutors. **Career services:** Career/job search classes, career assessment, internships.

FACILITIES

Housing: Coed dorms, apartments for single students, theme housing. 75% of campus accessible to physically disabled. **Special Academic Facilities/Equipment:** Arts lab, observatory, seismograph station, engineering lab.

CAMPUS LIFE

Environment: Village. **Activities:** Choral groups, dance, drama/theater, literary magazine, music ensembles, musical theater, pep band, radio station, student government, student newspaper, student-run film society, yearbook, campus ministries, international student organization. **Organizations:** 34 registered organizations, 10 honor societies, 4 religious organizations. **Athletics (Intercollegiate):** *Men:* Basketball, cheerleading, football, golf. *Women:* Basketball, cheerleading, golf, soccer, volleyball. **On-Campus Highlights:** Science and Technology Center, Nelson Stadium, Campus Center, St. Charles Chapel, Fitness Center.

ADMISSIONS

Freshman Academic Profile: Average high school GPA 3.47. 26% in top 10% of high school class, 59% in top 25% of high school class, 87% in top 50% of high school class. 82% from public high schools. SAT Math middle 50% range 500–610. SAT Critical Reading middle 50% range 490–590. SAT Writing middle 50% range 480–580. ACT middle 50% range 21–26. **Basis for Candidate Selection:** *Very important factors considered include:* Rigor of secondary school record, standardized test scores. *Important factors considered include:* Class rank, application essay, academic GPA, recommendation(s), character/personal qualities. *Other factors considered include:* Alumni/ae relation, extracurricular activities, interview, level of applicant's interest, religious affiliation/commitment, talent/ability, volunteer work, work experience. **Freshman Admission Requirements:** High school diploma is required and GED is accepted. *Academic units recommended:* 4 English, 3 mathematics, 2 science, (1 science labs), 2 foreign language, 1 social studies, 2 history, 2 visual/performing arts, 1 technology. **Freshman Admission Statistics:** 1,174 applied, 76% admitted, 39% enrolled. **Transfer Admission Requirements:** College transcript(s), essay or personal statement, statement of good standing from prior institution(s). Minimum college GPA of 2.5 required. Lowest grade transferable C. **General Admission Information:** Application fee $35. Regular application deadline 6/1. Notification on a rolling basis, beginning on or about 9/10. Nonfall registration accepted. Admission may be deferred for a maximum of 1 year. Credit and/or placement offered for CEEB Advanced Placement tests.

COSTS AND FINANCIAL AID

Annual tuition $22,252. Room and board $7,118. Required fees $340. Average book expense $800. **Required Forms and Deadlines:** FAFSA. Priority financial aid filing date 3/1. **Notification of Awards:** Applicants will be notified of awards on a rolling basis beginning 3/1. **Types of Aid:** *Need-based scholarships/grants:* Federal Pell, SEOG, state scholarships/grants, private scholarships, the school's own gift aid. *Loans:* FFEL Subsidized Stafford, FFEL Unsubsidized Stafford, FFEL PLUS, Federal Perkins, private loans. **Student Employment:** Federal Work-Study Program available. Institutional employment available. Off-campus job opportunities are good. **Financial Aid Statistics:** 50% freshmen, 55% undergrads receive need-based scholarship or grant aid. 11% freshmen, 8% undergrads receive non-need-based scholarship or grant aid. 34% freshmen, 34% undergrads receive need-based self-help aid. 4% freshmen, 3% undergrads receive athletic scholarships. 67% freshmen, 67% undergrads receive any aid. 71% undergrads borrow to pay for school. Average cumulative indebtedness $25,246. **Criteria for awarding institutional aid:** *Non-need-based:* Academics, art, athletics, leadership, minority status, music/drama, religious affiliation.

RATINGS

Admissions Selectivity Rating: 83   **Fire Safety Rating:** 60*   **Green Rating:** 60*

CARROLL COLLEGE (WI)

100 North East Avenue, Waukesha, WI 53186
Phone: 262-524-7220 **Financial Aid Phone:** 262-524-7297
E-mail: ccinfo@ccadmin.cc.edu **CEEB Code:** 1101
Fax: 262-951-3037 **Website:** www.cc.edu **ACT Code:** 4570

This private school, affiliated with the Presbyterian Church, was founded in 1846. It has a 52-acre campus.

RATINGS
Admissions Selectivity Rating: 73 **Fire Safety Rating:** 60* **Green Rating:** 60*

STUDENTS AND FACULTY
Enrollment: 2,925. **Student Body:** 68% female, 32% male, 20% out-of-state, 2% international (39 countries represented). Asian 1%, African American 2%, Caucasian 87%, Hispanic 3%.
Retention and Graduation: 74% freshmen return for sophomore year. 41% freshmen graduate within 4 years. 13% grads go on to further study within 1 year. **Faculty:** Student/faculty ratio 16:1. 121 full-time faculty, 63% hold PhDs, 2% are members of minority groups, 46% are women.

ACADEMICS
Degrees: Bachelor's, master's, post-bachelor's certificate. **Classes:** Most classes have 10–19 students. Most lab/discussion sessions have 10–19 students. **Majors with Highest Enrollment:** Business/commerce; education; nursing/registered nurse (RN, ASN, BSN, MSN) **Special Study Options:** Distance learning, double major, exchange student program (domestic), honors program, independent study, internships, liberal arts/career combination, student-designed major, study abroad, teacher certification program. Special programs offered to physically disabled students include note-taking services, tape recorders, tutors. **Career services:** Alumni network, career/job search classes, career assessment, internships.

FACILITIES
Housing: Coed dorms, women's dorms, apartments for single students 50% of campus accessible to physically disabled. **Special Academic Facilities/Equipment:** A 60 acre scientific study and conservancy area with a class 1 trout stream and associated wetland and upland habitats. **Computers:** 80% of classrooms, 100% of dorms, 100% of libraries, 100% of dining areas, 100% of student union, 90% of common outdoor areas have wireless network access. Students can register for classes online. Administrative functions (other than registration) can be performed online.

CAMPUS LIFE
Environment: Town. **Activities:** Choral groups, concert band, dance, drama/theater, jazz band, literary magazine, music ensembles, pep band, radio station, student government, student newspaper, international student organization. **Organizations:** 40 registered organizations, 2 religious organizations. 2 fraternities, 4 sororities. **Athletics (Intercollegiate):** *Men:* Baseball, basketball, cross-country, football, golf, soccer, swimming, tennis, track/field (outdoor), track/field (indoor). *Women:* Basketball, cross-country, golf, soccer, softball, swimming, tennis, track/field (outdoor), track/field (indoor), volleyball. **On-Campus Highlights:** Main Hall, Van Male Fieldhouse, Campus Center, Shattuck, Physical Therapy Building.

ADMISSIONS
Freshman Academic Profile: 21% in top 10% of high school class, 55% in top 25% of high school class, 83% in top 50% of high school class. 87% from public high schools. ACT middle 50% range 20–25. Minimum paper TOEFL 550. Minimum computer TOEFL 213. **Basis for Candidate Selection:** *Very important factors considered include:* Class rank, academic GPA, rigor of secondary school record. *Important factors considered include:* Standardized test scores. *Other factors considered include:* Application essay, recommendation(s), alumni/ae relation, character/personal qualities, extracurricular activities, geographical residence, interview, racial/ethnic status, state residency, talent/ability, work experience. **Freshman Admission Requirements:** High school diploma is required and GED is accepted. *Academic units recommended:* 4 English, 4 mathematics, 3 science, (2 science labs), 3 social studies, 3 history. **Freshman Admission Statistics:** 2,728 applied, 72% admitted, 34% enrolled. **Transfer Admission Requirements:** High school transcript, college transcript(s), minimum college GPA of 2.0 required. Lowest grade transferable C. **General Admission Information:** Nonfall registration accepted. Credit and/or placement offered for CEEB Advanced Placement tests.

COSTS AND FINANCIAL AID
Annual tuition $20,400. Room and board $6,350. Required fees $430. Average book expense $1,060. **Required Forms and Deadlines:** FAFSA. **Notification of Awards:** Applicants will be notified of awards on a rolling basis beginning 2/15. **Types of Aid:** *Need-based scholarships/grants:* Federal Pell, SEOG, state scholarships/grants, private scholarships, the school's own gift aid, Federal Nursing Scholarships. *Loans:* FFEL Unsubsidized Stafford, FFEL PLUS, Federal Perkins, state loans. **Student Employment:** Federal Work-Study Program available. Institutional employment available. Highest amount earned per year from on-campus jobs $4,270. **Financial Aid Statistics:** 71% freshmen, 67% undergrads receive need-based scholarship or grant aid. 65% freshmen, 61% undergrads receive non-need-based scholarship or grant aid. 52% freshmen, 53% undergrads receive need-based self-help aid. 98% freshmen, 98% undergrads receive any aid. 73% undergrads borrow to pay for school. Average cumulative indebtedness $21,794. **Criteria for awarding institutional aid:** *Non-need-based:* Academics, alumni affiliation, art, leadership, minority status, religious affiliation

CARSON-NEWMAN COLLEGE

1646 Russell Avenue, Jefferson City, TN 37760
Phone: 865-471-3223 **Financial Aid Phone:**
E-mail: admitme@.cn.edu **CEEB Code:** 1102
Fax: 865-471-3502 **Website:** www.cn.edu **ACT Code:** 3950

This private school, affiliated with the Baptist Church, was founded in 1851. It has a 90-acre campus.

RATINGS
Admissions Selectivity Rating: 78 **Fire Safety Rating:** 60* **Green Rating:** 60*

STUDENTS AND FACULTY
Enrollment: 1,849. **Student Body:** 53% female, 47% male, 32% out-of-state, 3% international. African American 9%, Caucasian 85%, Hispanic 1%.
Retention and Graduation: 72% freshmen return for sophomore year. 45% freshmen graduate within 4 years. 25% grads go on to further study within 1 year. 20% grads pursue arts and sciences degrees. 3% grads pursue law degrees. 1% grads pursue business degrees. 2% grads pursue medical degrees. **Faculty:** Student/faculty ratio 13:1. 123 full-time faculty, 69% hold PhDs, 2% are members of minority groups, 49% are women.

ACADEMICS
Degrees: Associate, bachelor's, master's. **Classes:** Most classes have 10–19 students. Most lab/discussion sessions have 10–19 students. **Special Study Options:** Cooperative education program, double major, dual enrollment, English as a Second Language (ESL), honors program, independent study, internships, student-designed major, study abroad, teacher certification program. Special programs offered to physically disabled students include note-taking services, reader services, tape recorders, tutors. **Career services:** Alumni services, career/job search classes, career assessment.

FACILITIES
Housing: Men's dorms, women's dorms, apartments for married students, apartments for single students 80% of campus accessible to physically disabled. **Special Academic Facilities/Equipment:** Art galleries, Appalachian history museum, home management house, language lab.

CAMPUS LIFE
Environment: Rural. **Activities:** Choral groups, concert band, dance, drama/theater, jazz band, literary magazine, marching band, music ensembles, musical theater, opera, pep band, student government, student newspaper, television station, yearbook. **Organizations:** 45 registered organizations, 10 honor societies, 5 religious organizations. 2 fraternities, 2 sororities. **Athletics (Intercollegiate):** *Men:* Baseball, basketball, cheerleading, cross-country, football, golf, soccer, tennis, track/field (outdoor), wrestling. *Women:* Basketball, cheerleading, cross-country, soccer, softball, tennis, track/field (outdoor), volleyball. **On-Campus Highlights:** Maddox Student Activities Center, Coffee House (in MSAC) and TV lounge, Workout/Weight Rooms (in MSAC), Cafeteria, Swann Field (Intramurals).

ADMISSIONS
Freshman Academic Profile: Average high school GPA 3.3. 28% in top 10% of high school class, 49% in top 25% of high school class, 77% in top 50% of high school class. 87% from public high schools. Minimum paper TOEFL 550. Minimum computer TOEFL 213. **Basis for Candidate Selection:** *Very important factors considered include:* Rigor of secondary school record, standardized test scores. *Important factors considered include:* Class rank. *Other factors considered include:* Application essay, recommendation(s), alumni/ae relation, character/personal qualities, extracurricular activities, interview, religious affiliation/commitment, talent/ability, volunteer work, work experience. **Freshman Admission Requirements:** High school diploma is required and GED is accepted. *Academic units required:* 4 English, 2 mathematics, 2 science, (1 science labs), 1 social studies, 1 history, 4 academic electives. *Academic units recommended:* 2 foreign language. **Freshman Admission Statistics:**

1,694 applied, 82% admitted, 32% enrolled. **Transfer Admission Requirements:** college transcript(s), minimum college GPA of 2.0 required. Lowest grade transferable D. **General Admission Information:** Application fee $25. Notification on a rolling basis, beginning on or about 6/1. Nonfall registration accepted. Admission may be deferred for a maximum of 2 years. Credit and/or placement offered for CEEB Advanced Placement tests.

COSTS AND FINANCIAL AID

Annual tuition $17,000. Room and board $5,450. Required fees $800. Average book expense $990. **Required Forms and Deadlines:** FAFSA, institution's own financial aid form. Priority financial aid filing date 3/1. **Notification of Awards: Types of Aid:** *Need-based scholarships/grants:* Federal Pell, SEOG, state scholarships/grants, private scholarships, the school's own gift aid. *Loans:* Direct Subsidized Stafford, Direct Unsubsidized Stafford, Direct PLUS, Federal Perkins, Federal Nursing. **Student Employment:** Federal Work-Study Program available. Institutional employment available. Highest amount earned per year from on-campus jobs $900. Off-campus job opportunities are good. **Financial Aid Statistics:** 79% freshmen, 74% undergrads receive need-based scholarship or grant aid. 77% freshmen, 72% undergrads receive non-need-based scholarship or grant aid. 60% freshmen, 58% undergrads receive need-based self-help aid. 5% freshmen, 6% undergrads receive athletic scholarships. 74% undergrads borrow to pay for school. Average cumulative indebtedness $18,552. **Criteria for awarding institutional aid:** *Non-need-based:* Academics, art, athletics, leadership, minority status, music/drama, religious affiliation

CARTHAGE COLLEGE

2001 Alford Park Drive, Kenosha, WI 53140-1994
Phone: 262-551-6000 **Financial Aid Phone:** 262-551-6001
E-mail: admissions@carthage.edu **CEEB Code:** 1103
Fax: 262-551-5762 **Website:** www.carthage.edu **ACT Code:** 4571

This private school, affiliated with the Lutheran Church, was founded in 1847. It has a 95-acre campus.

RATINGS
Admissions Selectivity Rating: 78   **Fire Safety Rating:** 60*   **Green Rating:** 60*

STUDENTS AND FACULTY
Enrollment: 2,456. **Student Body:** 58% female, 42% male, 70% out-of-state, (16 countries represented).
Retention and Graduation: 75% freshmen return for sophomore year. 46% freshmen graduate within 4 years. 16% grads go on to further study within 1 year. 4% grads pursue arts and sciences degrees. 2% grads pursue law degrees. 1% grads pursue business degrees. 1% grads pursue medical degrees. **Faculty:** Student/faculty ratio 16:1. 126 full-time faculty, 87% hold PhDs, 6% are members of minority groups, 32% are women.

ACADEMICS
Degrees: Bachelor's, certificate, master's. **Classes:** Most classes have 20–29 students. **Majors with Highest Enrollment:** Biology/biological sciences; business administration and management; elementary education and teaching. **Special Study Options:** Accelerated program, cross-registration, double major, honors program, independent study, internships, student-designed major, study abroad, teacher certification program. **Honors programs:** We offer All College Honors as well as Honors in the Major. **Combined degree programs:** BA/MA, Occupational Therapy at Wash Univ—St. Louis. Special programs offered to physically disabled students include note-taking services, reader services, tape recorders, tutors. **Career services:** Career/job search classes, career assessment, internships.

FACILITIES
Housing: Coed dorms, men's dorms, women's dorms, fraternity/sorority housing, Best Western Harborside through Carthage. 99% of campus accessible to physically disabled. **Special Academic Facilities/Equipment:** H.F. Johnson Art Gallery, Center for Children's Literature, planetarium, undergraduate science research lab, graphic design lab, greenhouse, computer/math research lab, physics research lab, ScienceWorks lab, A.W. Clausen Center Boardroom. **Computers:** Students can register for classes online. Administrative functions (other than registration) can be performed online.

CAMPUS LIFE
Environment: City. **Activities:** Choral groups, concert band, dance, drama/theater, jazz band, literary magazine, music ensembles, musical theater, opera, pep band, radio station, student government, student newspaper, student-run film society, symphony orchestra, yearbook. **Organizations:** 90 registered organizations, 20 honor societies, 7 religious organizations. 8 fraternities, 7 sororities. **Athletics (Intercollegiate):** *Men:* Baseball, basketball, cross-coun-

try, football, golf, soccer, swimming, tennis, track/field (outdoor), track/field (indoor), volleyball. *Women:* Basketball, cross-country, golf, soccer, softball, swimming, tennis, track/field (outdoor), track/field (indoor), volleyball, water polo. **On-Campus Highlights:** Tarble Athletic and Recreation Center, Hedberg Library, A.W. Clausen Center for World Business, Oaks Residence Halls, Lake Michigan. Located midway between Chicago and Milwaukee, Carthage is easily accessible by car, airplane and train. Our 95 acre, park-like campus is on the shore of Lake Michigan.

ADMISSIONS
Freshman Academic Profile: Average high school GPA 3.23. 19% in top 10% of high school class, 43% in top 25% of high school class, 75% in top 50% of high school class. 91% from public high schools. SAT Math middle 50% range 490–620. SAT Critical Reading middle 50% range 470–630. ACT middle 50% range 21–26. Minimum paper TOEFL 500. Minimum computer TOEFL 173. **Basis for Candidate Selection:** *Very important factors considered include:* Academic GPA, rigor of secondary school record, standardized test scores. *Other factors considered include:* Class rank, application essay, recommendation(s), character/personal qualities, extracurricular activities, interview, talent/ability, volunteer work, work experience. **Freshman Admission Requirements:** High school diploma is required and GED is accepted. *Academic units recommended:* 4 English, 3 mathematics, 3 science, (2 science labs), 2 foreign language, 3 social studies, 3 academic electives. **Freshman Admission Statistics:** 4,495 applied, 77% admitted, 19% enrolled. **Transfer Admission Requirements:** college transcript(s), statement of good standing from prior institution(s). Minimum college GPA of 2.0 required. Lowest grade transferable C–. **General Admission Information:** Application fee $25. Notification on a rolling basis, beginning on or about 9/15. Nonfall registration accepted. Admission may be deferred for a maximum of 1 year. Credit and/or placement offered for CEEB Advanced Placement tests.

COSTS AND FINANCIAL AID
Annual tuition $25,000. Room and board $7,000. Average book expense $1,200. **Required Forms and Deadlines:** FAFSA. Priority financial aid filing date 2/15. **Notification of Awards:** Applicants will be notified of awards on a rolling basis beginning 3/1. **Types of Aid:** *Need-based scholarships/grants:* Federal Pell, SEOG, state scholarships/grants, private scholarships, the school's own gift aid. *Loans:* FFEL Subsidized Stafford, FFEL Unsubsidized Stafford, FFEL PLUS, Federal Perkins, state loans, college/university loans from institutional funds. **Student Employment:** Highest amount earned per year from on-campus jobs $1,000. **Financial Aid Statistics:** 73% freshmen, 69% undergrads receive need-based scholarship or grant aid. 11% freshmen, 10% undergrads receive non-need-based scholarship or grant aid. 59% freshmen, 56% undergrads receive need-based self-help aid. 97% freshmen, 97% undergrads receive any aid. **Criteria for awarding institutional aid:** *Non-need-based:* Academics, alumni affiliation, art, leadership, minority status, music/drama, religious affiliation.

CASCADE COLLEGE

9101 East Burnside Street, Portland, OR 97216-1515
Phone: 503-257-1202 **Financial Aid Phone:** 503-257-1241
E-mail: admissions@cascade.edu
Fax: 503-257-1222 **Website:** www.cascade.edu **ACT Code:** 3459

This private school, affiliated with the Church of Christ Church, was founded in 1993. It has a 12-acre campus.

RATINGS
Admissions Selectivity Rating: 60*   **Fire Safety Rating:** 61   **Green Rating:** 61

STUDENTS AND FACULTY
Enrollment: 262. **Student Body:** 59% female, 41% male, 64% out-of-state, 1% international (8 countries represented). Asian 3%, African American 5%, Caucasian 26%, Hispanic 5%.
Retention and Graduation: 46% freshmen return for sophomore year. 23% freshmen graduate within 4 years. 15% grads go on to further study within 1 year. 10% grads pursue arts and sciences degrees. 2% grads pursue law degrees. 1% grads pursue business degrees. **Faculty:** Student/faculty ratio 12:1. 15 full-time faculty, 60% hold PhDs, 13% are members of minority groups, 27% are women.

ACADEMICS
Degrees: Bachelor's. **Classes:** Most classes have 10–19 students. Most lab/discussion sessions have fewer than 10 students. **Majors with Highest Enrollment:** Business/commerce; psychology; teacher education, multiple levels. **Special Study Options:** Double major, dual enrollment, independent

study, internships, student-designed major, study abroad, teacher certification program. Special programs offered to physically disabled students include note-taking services, reader services, tutors. Career services highlights include: Most majors provide an opportunity for students to participate in an internship or practicum in the area of the major giving most graduates hand-on experience and an opportunity to experience a career in the major.

FACILITIES

Housing: Special housing for disabled students, men's dorms, women's dorms, apartments for married students 70% of campus accessible to physically disabled. **Computers:** 100% of classrooms, 100% of dorms, 100% of libraries, 100% of dining areas, 100% of student union, 100% of common outdoor areas have wireless network access. Administrative functions (other than registration) can be performed online.

CAMPUS LIFE

Environment: Metropolis. **Activities:** Choral groups, drama/theater, jazz band, literary magazine, music ensembles, musical theater, student government, yearbook. **Organizations:** 16 registered organizations, 2 honor societies. **Athletics (Intercollegiate):** *Men:* Basketball, cross-country, soccer, track/field (outdoor), track/field (indoor). *Women:* Basketball, cross-country, soccer, track/field (outdoor), track/field (indoor), volleyball. **On-Campus Highlights:** Classrooms, Student Center, The Cabin (coffee shop), Weight room, Womack and Hamstreet Fountains.

ADMISSIONS

Freshman Academic Profile: Average high school GPA 3. 85% from public high schools. Minimum paper TOEFL 500. Minimum computer TOEFL 173. **Basis for Candidate Selection:** *Other factors considered include:* Academic GPA, recommendation(s), standardized test scores. **Freshman Admission Requirements:** High school diploma is required and GED is accepted. *Academic units recommended:* 4 English, 3 mathematics, 2 science, (1 science labs), 2 foreign language, 4 social studies, 2 history, 1 computer science. **Freshman Admission Statistics: Transfer Admission Requirements:** High school transcript, college transcript(s), minimum college GPA of 2.0 required. Lowest grade transferable D. **General Admission Information:** Application fee $25. Nonfall registration accepted. Admission may be deferred for a maximum of 1 year. Credit offered for CEEB Advanced Placement tests.

COSTS AND FINANCIAL AID

Average book expense $900. **Required Forms and Deadlines:** FAFSA, institution's own financial aid form, Payment Plan Form, FERPA Release Form. Financial aid filing deadline 7/31. Priority financial aid filing date 5/1. **Notification of Awards:** Applicants will be notified of awards on a rolling basis beginning 2/15. **Types of Aid:** *Need-based scholarships/grants:* Federal Pell, SEOG, private scholarships, the school's own gift aid. *Loans:* FFEL Subsidized Stafford, FFEL Unsubsidized Stafford, FFEL PLUS, Private Loans. **Student Employment:** Federal Work-Study Program available. Institutional employment available. Highest amount earned per year from on-campus jobs $2,000. Off-campus job opportunities are excellent. **Financial Aid Statistics:** 79% freshmen, 51% undergrads receive need-based scholarship or grant aid. 15% freshmen, 74% undergrads receive non-need-based scholarship or grant aid. 69% freshmen, 68% undergrads receive need-based self-help aid. 48% freshmen, 36% undergrads receive athletic scholarships. 100% freshmen, 99% undergrads receive any aid. 84% undergrads borrow to pay for school. Average cumulative indebtedness $24,988. **Criteria for awarding institutional aid:** *Non-need-based:* Academics, athletics, leadership, music/drama, religious affiliation, state/district residency.

CASE WESTERN RESERVE UNIVERSITY

Wolstein Hall, 10900 Euclid Ave, Cleveland, OH 44106-7055
Phone: 216-368-4450 **Financial Aid Phone:** 216-368-4530
E-mail: admission@case.edu **CEEB Code:** 1105
Fax: 216-368-5111 **Website:** www.case.edu **ACT Code:** 3244

This private school was founded in 1826. It has a 155-acre campus.

RATINGS

Admissions Selectivity Rating: 92   **Fire Safety Rating:** 73   **Green Rating:** 81

STUDENTS AND FACULTY

Enrollment: 4,145. **Student Body:** 43% female, 57% male, 50% out-of-state, 5% international (22 countries represented). Asian 16%, African American 5%, Caucasian 55%, Hispanic 3%.

Retention and Graduation: 63% freshmen graduate within 4 years. 44% grads go on to further study within 1 year. 27% grads pursue arts and sciences degrees. 4% grads pursue law degrees. 3% grads pursue business degrees. 9% grads pursue medical degrees. **Faculty:** Student/faculty ratio 9.3:1. 746 full-time faculty, 90% hold PhDs, 18% are members of minority groups, 42% are women. 6% of classes are taught by teaching assistants.

ACADEMICS

Degrees: Bachelor's, doctoral, master's, post-bachelor's certificate. **Classes:** Most classes have 10–19 students. Most lab/discussion sessions have 20–29 students. **Majors with Highest Enrollment:** Biology/biological sciences; biomedical/medical engineering; psychology. **Special Study Options:** Accelerated program, cooperative education program, cross-registration, double major, dual enrollment, English as a Second Language (ESL), exchange student program (domestic), honors program, independent study, internships, liberal arts/career combination, student-designed major, study abroad, teacher certification program, Washington Semester. **Honors programs:** The College Scholars Program is a three-year honors program for a small group of students interested in exploring how academic learning can address larger world concerns. **Combined degree programs:** BA/MA, BA/DDS, BA/MEng, BS/MS, BS/MBA, BS/MAcc, BA/MPH, Sr Yr Prof Studies. Special programs offered to physically disabled students include note-taking services, reader services, tape recorders, tutors. **Career services:** Alumni network, alumni services, career/job search classes, career assessment, internships, regional alumni. **Career services highlights include:** Case's many experiential learning options. More than 83% of our undergraduate students participate in opportunities for research, cultural immersion through study abroad programs, clinical work in nursing, and internship and co-op programs, or garner valuable leadership experiences through campus, club, and community interactions.

FACILITIES

Housing: Coed dorms, fraternity/sorority housing, apartments for single students, wellness housing Secured women-only floor available. Special-interest housing available. Residential Colleges for first-year students. 90% of campus accessible to physically disabled. **Special Academic Facilities/Equipment:** Art, natural history, and auto-aviation museums, historical society, botanical garden, biology field stations, observatory. **Computers:** 100% of classrooms, 100% of dorms, 100% of libraries, 100% of dining areas, 100% of student union, 100% of common outdoor areas have wireless network access. Students can register for classes online. Administrative functions (other than registration) can be performed online.

CAMPUS LIFE

Environment: Metropolis. **Activities:** Choral groups, concert band, dance, drama/theater, jazz band, literary magazine, marching band, music ensembles, musical theater, pep band, radio station, student government, student newspaper, student-run film society, symphony orchestra, yearbook, campus ministries, international student organization, Model UN. **Organizations:** 150 registered organizations, 8 honor societies, 4 religious organizations. 16 fraternities, 8 sororities. **Athletics (Intercollegiate):** *Men:* Baseball, basketball, cross-country, football, soccer, swimming, tennis, track/field (outdoor), track/field (indoor), wrestling. *Women:* Basketball, cross-country, soccer, softball, swimming, tennis, track/field (outdoor), track/field (indoor), volleyball. **On-Campus Highlights:** North Residential Village, Peter B. Lewis Building, Kelvin Smith Library, Veale Convocation and Athletic Center, Turning Point Sculpture Garden. **Environmental Initiatives:** Signatory to the American College and University President's Climate Commitment. Ongoing comprehensive energy reduction program. Joined Ohio Solar Cooperative which will facilitate installation of PV arrays on campus buildings. Campus food service (Bon Appetit) purchasing bulk of fresh food and supplies from local farms and food producers. Organic, seasonal, local (low carbon footprint), and delicious!

ADMISSIONS

Freshman Academic Profile: 65% in top 10% of high school class, 87% in top 25% of high school class, 99% in top 50% of high school class. 70% from public high schools. SAT Math middle 50% range 650–740. SAT Critical Reading middle 50% range 590–700. SAT Writing middle 50% range 590–690. ACT middle 50% range 28–32. Minimum paper TOEFL 550. Minimum computer TOEFL 213. Minimum web-based TOEFL 80. **Basis for Candidate Selection:** *Very important factors considered include:* Class rank, academic GPA, rigor of secondary school record, standardized test scores, extracurricular activities. *Important factors considered include:* Application essay, recommendation(s), character/personal qualities, interview, level of applicant's interest, talent/ability, volunteer work, work experience. *Other factors considered include:* Alumni/ae relation, first generation, racial/ethnic status. **Freshman Admission Requirements:** High school diploma is required and GED is accepted. *Academic units required:* 4 English, 3 mathematics, 3 science, (2 science labs), 2 foreign language, 3 social studies. *Academic units recommended:* 4 mathematics, (3 science labs), 3 foreign language, 4 social studies. **Freshman Admission Statistics:** 7,998 applied, 70% admitted, 17% enrolled. **Transfer Admission**

Requirements: High school transcript, college transcript(s), essay or personal statement, statement of good standing from prior institution(s). Minimum college GPA of 3.2 required. Lowest grade transferable C. **General Admission Information:** Regular application deadline 1/15. Regular notification 4/1. Nonfall registration accepted. Admission may be deferred for a maximum of 1 year. Credit and/or placement offered for CEEB Advanced Placement tests.

COSTS AND FINANCIAL AID

Required Forms and Deadlines: FAFSA, institution's own financial aid form, business/farm supplement. Parent and student income tax returns and W-2 forms. Priority financial aid filing date 2/15. **Notification of Awards:** Applicants will be notified of awards on a rolling basis beginning 3/15. **Types of Aid:** *Need-based scholarships/grants:* Federal Pell, SEOG, state scholarships/grants, private scholarships, the school's own gift aid. *Loans:* FFEL Subsidized Stafford, FFEL Unsubsidized Stafford, FFEL PLUS, Federal Perkins, Federal Nursing, state loans, college/university loans from institutional funds, Alternative loans. **Student Employment:** Federal Work-Study Program available. Institutional employment available. Highest amount earned per year from on-campus jobs $3,200. Off-campus job opportunities are excellent. **Financial Aid Statistics:** 61% freshmen, 61% undergrads receive need-based scholarship or grant aid. 62% freshmen, 61% undergrads receive non-need-based scholarship or grant aid. 61% freshmen, 61% undergrads receive need-based self-help aid. 83% freshmen, 82% undergrads receive any aid. 61% undergrads borrow to pay for school. Average cumulative indebtedness $37,394. **Criteria for awarding institutional aid:** *Non-need-based:* Academics, art, leadership, music/drama.

CASTLETON STATE COLLEGE

Office of Admissions, Castleton, VT 05735
Phone: 802-468-1213 **Financial Aid Phone:** 802-468-6070
E-mail: info@castleton.edu **CEEB Code:** 3765
Fax: 802-468-1476 **ACT Code:** 4314

This public school was founded in 1787. It has a 165-acre campus.

RATINGS
Admissions Selectivity Rating: 71   **Fire Safety Rating:** 60*   **Green Rating:** 76

STUDENTS AND FACULTY
Enrollment: 1,891. **Student Body:** 54% female, 46% male, 37% out-of-state, international. Asian 1%, African American 1%, Caucasian 83%, Hispanic 2%. **Retention and Graduation:** 71% freshmen return for sophomore year. 31% freshmen graduate within 4 years. **Faculty:** Student/faculty ratio 14:1. 88 full-time faculty, 93% hold PhDs, 6% are members of minority groups, 45% are women.

ACADEMICS
Degrees: Associate, bachelor's, master's, post-bachelor's certificate, post-master's certificate. **Classes:** Most classes have 10–19 students. Most lab/discussion sessions have 10–19 students. **Majors with Highest Enrollment:** business/commerce; psychology **Special Study Options:** Cooperative education program, double major, dual enrollment, honors program, independent study, internships, liberal arts/career combination, student-designed major, study abroad, teacher certification program **Combined degree programs:** BA/MA, 4-1 MBA ; 4+3 Phys. Therapy; 4+2. Special programs offered to physically disabled students include note-taking services, reader services, tape recorders, tutors.

FACILITIES
Housing: Coed dorms 100% of campus accessible to physically disabled. **Special Academic Facilities/Equipment:** Historical/medical museum. **Computers:** 25% of classrooms, 100% of dorms, 100% of libraries, 100% of dining areas, 100% of student union, have wireless network access.

CAMPUS LIFE
Environment: Rural. **Activities:** Choral groups, dance, drama/theater, jazz band, literary magazine, music ensembles, musical theater, radio station, student government, student newspaper, student-run film society, television station, yearbook. **Organizations:** 40 registered organizations, 7 honor societies, 1 religious organizations. **Athletics (Intercollegiate):** *Men:* Baseball, basketball, cross-country, football, ice hockey, lacrosse, skiing (downhill/alpine), soccer, tennis. *Women:* Basketball, cross-country, field hockey, ice hockey, lacrosse, skiing (downhill/alpine), soccer, softball, tennis. **On-Campus Highlights:** Fireside Cafe, Coffee Cottage, fitness center, library. **Environmental Initiatives:** Student-driven recycling effort; new construction is significantly green; purchasing is significantly green

ADMISSIONS
Freshman Academic Profile: Average high school GPA 2.9. 3% in top 10% of high school class, 15% in top 25% of high school class, 53% in top 50% of high school class. SAT Math middle 50% range 440–550. SAT Critical Reading middle 50% range 440–530. SAT Writing middle 50% range 430–530. Minimum paper TOEFL 500. Minimum computer TOEFL 173. **Basis for Candidate Selection:** *Very important factors considered include:* Class rank, application essay, academic GPA, recommendation(s), rigor of secondary school record, character/personal qualities. *Important factors considered include:* Standardized test scores. *Other factors considered include:* Extracurricular activities, interview, level of applicant's interest, volunteer work, work experience. **Freshman Admission Requirements:** High school diploma is required and GED is accepted. *Academic units required:* 4 English, 3 mathematics, 2 science, (2 science labs), 3 social studies, 3 history. *Academic units recommended:* 4 English, 4 mathematics, 2 science, 2 foreign language, 4 social studies. **Freshman Admission Statistics:** 2,190 applied, 68% admitted, 32% enrolled. **Transfer Admission Requirements:** college transcript(s), essay or personal statement, minimum college GPA of 2.0 required. Lowest grade transferable C–. **General Admission Information:** Application fee $35. Notification on a rolling basis, beginning on or about 12/15. Nonfall registration accepted. Admission may be deferred for a maximum of 1 year. Credit and/or placement offered for CEEB Advanced Placement tests.

COSTS AND FINANCIAL AID
Annual in-state tuition $7,488. Annual out-of-state tuition $16,152. Room and board $7,509. Required fees $796. Average book expense $1,000. **Required Forms and Deadlines:** FAFSA. Priority financial aid filing date 2/15. **Notification of Awards:** Applicants will be notified of awards on a rolling basis beginning 2/15. **Types of Aid:** *Need-based scholarships/grants:* Federal Pell, SEOG, state scholarships/grants, private scholarships, the school's own gift aid. *Loans:* FFEL Subsidized Stafford, FFEL Unsubsidized Stafford, FFEL PLUS, Federal Perkins, Federal Nursing. **Student Employment:** Federal Work-Study Program available. Institutional employment available. Off-campus job opportunities are good. **Financial Aid Statistics:** 43% freshmen, 45% undergrads receive need-based scholarship or grant aid, 59% freshmen, 61% undergrads receive need-based self-help aid. 66% freshmen, 66% undergrads receive any aid. 84% undergrads borrow to pay for school. Average cumulative indebtedness $25,474. **Criteria for awarding institutional aid:** *Non-need-based:* Academics, alumni affiliation, art, leadership, music/drama, state/district residency.

See page 1048.

CATAWBA COLLEGE

2300 West Innes Street, Salisbury, NC 28144
Phone: 704-637-4402 **Financial Aid Phone:** 704-637-4416
E-mail: admission@catawba.edu **CEEB Code:** 5103
Fax: 704-637-4222 **Website:** www.catawba.edu **ACT Code:** 3080

This private school, affiliated with the United Church of Christ Church, was founded in 1851. It has a 276-acre campus.

RATINGS
Admissions Selectivity Rating: 77   **Fire Safety Rating:** 79   **Green Rating:** 78

STUDENTS AND FACULTY
Enrollment: 1,324. **Student Body:** 52% female, 48% male, 23% out-of-state, 2% international (12 countries represented). Asian 1%, African American 18%, Caucasian 77%, Hispanic 1%. **Retention and Graduation:** 42% freshmen graduate within 4 years. 13% grads go on to further study within 1 year. 4% grads pursue arts and sciences degrees. 2% grads pursue law degrees. 4% grads pursue business degrees. 1% grads pursue medical degrees. **Faculty:** Student/faculty ratio 15:1. 71 full-time faculty, 87% hold PhDs, 7% are members of minority groups, 42% are women.

ACADEMICS
Degrees: Bachelor's, master's. **Classes:** Most classes have 10–19 students. Most lab/discussion sessions have 20–29 students. **Majors with Highest Enrollment:** Business/commerce; drama and dramatics/theatre arts; elementary education and teaching. **Special Study Options:** Cross-registration, double major, dual enrollment, honors program, independent study, internships, liberal

arts/career combination, student-designed major, study abroad, teacher certification program. Special programs offered to physically disabled students include note-taking services, tape recorders, tutors. **Career services:** Career/job search classes, career assessment. **Career services highlights include:** Food Lion (Delhaize Group) offering limited internships in Brussels, Belgium.

FACILITIES

Housing: Coed dorms, men's dorms, women's dorms, Substance free housing. 90% of campus accessible to physically disabled. **Special Academic Facilities/Equipment:** Ecology preserve (183 acres). Wildlife preserve (300 acres) **Computers:** 90% of classrooms, 95% of dorms, 100% of libraries, 25% of dining areas, 80% of student union, 10% of common outdoor areas have wireless network access. Administrative functions (other than registration) can be performed online.

CAMPUS LIFE

Environment: Town. **Activities:** Choral groups, concert band, dance, drama/theater, jazz band, literary magazine, music ensembles, musical theater, pep band, student government, student newspaper, symphony orchestra, yearbook, campus ministries **Organizations:** 38 registered organizations, 9 honor societies, 4 religious organizations. **Athletics (Intercollegiate):** *Men:* Baseball, basketball, cheerleading, cross-country, football, golf, lacrosse, soccer, swimming, tennis. *Women:* Basketball, cheerleading, cross-country, golf, soccer, softball, swimming, tennis, volleyball. **On-Campus Highlights:** Center for the Environment, Cannon Field House, Robertson College Community Center, Ketner Hall, Cannon Student Center. **Environmental Initiatives:** Active re-cycling program; site of frequent regional and international environmental education forums through the campus Center for the Environment; LEED certified Center for the Environment Building and five new residence halls.

ADMISSIONS

Freshman Academic Profile: Average high school GPA 3.48. 17% in top 10% of high school class, 43% in top 25% of high school class, 82% in top 50% of high school class. 80% from public high schools. SAT Math middle 50% range 470–570. SAT Critical Reading middle 50% range 440–580. ACT middle 50% range 18–25. Minimum paper TOEFL 525. Minimum computer TOEFL 197. **Basis for Candidate Selection:** *Very important factors considered include:* Class rank, application essay, academic GPA, recommendation(s), standardized test scores. *Important factors considered include:* Rigor of secondary school record, character/personal qualities, extracurricular activities, interview, level of applicant's interest, talent/ability. *Other factors considered include:* Volunteer work. **Freshman Admission Requirements:** High school diploma is required and GED is accepted. *Academic units recommended:* 4 English, 3 mathematics, 3 science, (3 science labs), 2 foreign language, 3 social studies. **Freshman Admission Statistics:** 1,104 applied, 70% admitted, 40% enrolled. **Transfer Admission Requirements:** High school transcript, college transcript(s), essay or personal statement, statement of good standing from prior institution(s). Minimum college GPA of 2.0 required. Lowest grade transferable C. **General Admission Information:** Application fee $25. Notification on a rolling basis, beginning on or about 10/1. Nonfall registration accepted. Admission may be deferred for a maximum of 1 year. Credit and/or placement offered for CEEB Advanced Placement tests.

COSTS AND FINANCIAL AID

Required Forms and Deadlines: FAFSA, state aid form. Priority financial aid filing date 3/15. **Notification of Awards:** Applicants will be notified of awards on a rolling basis beginning 2/15. **Types of Aid:** *Need-based scholarships/grants:* Federal Pell, SEOG, state scholarships/grants, private scholarships, the school's own gift aid. *Loans:* FFEL Unsubsidized Stafford, FFEL PLUS, Federal Perkins, college/university loans from institutional funds, TERI Loans, Nellie Mae Loans, Advantage Loans, Alternative Loans. **Student Employment:** Federal Work-Study Program available. Institutional employment available. Highest amount earned per year from on-campus jobs $2,000. Off-campus job opportunities are good. **Financial Aid Statistics:** 44% freshmen, 46% undergrads receive need-based scholarship or grant aid. 69% freshmen, 69% undergrads receive non-need-based scholarship or grant aid. 48% freshmen, 51% undergrads receive need-based self-help aid. 33% freshmen, 25% undergrads receive athletic scholarships. 99% freshmen, 99% undergrads receive any aid. 77% undergrads borrow to pay for school. Average cumulative indebtedness $21,891. **Criteria for awarding institutional aid:** *Non-need-based:* Academics, athletics, leadership, music/drama, state/district residency.

THE CATHOLIC UNIVERSITY OF AMERICA

Office of Undergraduate Admissions, 620 Michigan Avenue, NE, Washington, DC, 20064
Phone: 202-319-5305 **Financial Aid Phone:** 202-319-5307
E-mail: cua-admissions@cua.edu **CEEB Code:** 5104
Fax: 202-319-6533 **Website:** www.cua.edu **ACT Code:** 654

This private school, affiliated with the Roman Catholic Church, was founded in 1887. It has a 193-acre campus.

RATINGS
Admissions Selectivity Rating: 84 **Fire Safety Rating:** 83 **Green Rating:** 87

STUDENTS AND FACULTY
Enrollment: 3,422. **Student Body:** 54% female, 46% male, 95% out-of-state, 3% international (80 countries represented). Asian 3%, African American 5%, Caucasian 64%, Hispanic 7%.
Retention and Graduation: 81% freshmen return for sophomore year. 38% grads go on to further study within 1 year. 31% grads pursue arts and sciences degrees. 13% grads pursue law degrees. 4% grads pursue business degrees. 4% grads pursue medical degrees. **Faculty:** Student/faculty ratio 10:1. 354 full-time faculty, 97% hold PhDs, 12% are members of minority groups, 39% are women. 11% of classes are taught by teaching assistants.

ACADEMICS
Degrees: Associate, bachelor's, doctoral, master's, post-bachelor's certificate, post-master's certificate. **Classes:** Most classes have 10–19 students. Most lab/discussion sessions have 10–19 students. **Majors with Highest Enrollment:** Architecture (BArch, BA/BS, MArch, MA/MS, PhD); nursing/registered nurse (RN, ASN, BSN, MSN); political science and government. **Special Study Options:** Accelerated program, cross-registration, distance learning, double major, dual enrollment, English as a Second Language (ESL), honors program, independent study, internships, study abroad, teacher certification program. **Honors programs:** The University Honors Program offers classes in the classical liberal arts and contemporary social and environmental sciences to compliment students' major studies. Students take small, rigorous, discussion-based courses from offerings in philosophy, theology, history and literature, social science, environmental science, and media studies. Students completing any of these six tracks receive distinction at graduation; students completing three tracks and a senior seminar are designated University Scholars. Special lectures, symposia, social events, and trips are organized for students in the program. **Combined degree programs:** BA/MA, BS/MS, BSN/MSN. Special programs offered to physically disabled students include note-taking services, reader services, tape recorders, tutors. **Career services:** Alumni network, alumni services, career assessment, internships, regional alumni. **Career services highlights include:** the Cardinal Connection (Jobs and Internships Online), through which we share with students the amazing variety and quality of experiential opportunities available to them. Each year hundreds of organizations in the Washington, DC, area and nationwide list internships that give students a chance to become involved in a range of responsibilities in politics, research, marketing, accounting, finance, public relations, computer science, engineering, architecture and arts management, to name a few. These experiences not only complement students' classroom education, they often lead to offers of full-time employment upon graduation from CUA.

FACILITIES
Housing: Coed dorms, special housing for disabled students, men's dorms, women's dorms, apartments for single students, wellness housing, theme housingResidential college, honors community, politics and current events community, living as leaders community and social justice community. 85% of campus accessible to physically disabled. **Special Academic Facilities/Equipment:** Facilities available on the university campus include an art department gallery; the John K. Mullen of Denver Memorial Library, which features a rare book collection containing 65,000 volumes that range from medieval documents to first editions of 20th-century authors; the university archives, which has nearly 9,000 feet of records and manuscripts; the Vitreous State Laboratory, which engages some of the world's leading glass scientists to help research and develop methods for safe containment of disposed radioactive materials, primarily by converting nuclear waste into solid glass using vitrification techniques. In 2008, the university dedicated Opus Hall, the first LEED (Leadership in Energy and Environmental Design)-compliant residence hall among colleges and universities in Washington, DC, The Edward J. Pryzbyla University Center

includes nine meeting spaces, two separate dining facilities, a convenience store, the campus bookstore, offices, various atrium and lounge spaces and a 7,500–square-foot great room, where Pope Benedict XVI delivered a speech in April 2008. Adjacent to the campus is the Roman Catholic Basilica of the National Shrine of the Immaculate Conception, the largest church in the Western hemisphere. University Masses and commencement are held every year at the National Shrine. Directly across the street from the university is the Pope John Paul II Cultural Center, a major Catholic museum. **Computers:** 40% of classrooms, 90% of dorms, 100% of libraries, 100% of dining areas, 100% of student union, 20% of common outdoor areas have wireless network access. Students can register for classes online. Administrative functions (other than registration) can be performed online.

CAMPUS LIFE

Environment: Metropolis. **Activities:** Choral groups, dance, drama/theater, jazz band, literary magazine, music ensembles, musical theater, opera, radio station, student government, student newspaper, student-run film society, symphony orchestra, yearbook, campus ministries, International student organization. **Organizations:** 87 registered organizations, 16 honor societies, 4 religious organizations. 1 fraternities, 1 sorority. **Athletics (Intercollegiate):** *Men:* Baseball, basketball, cross-country, football, lacrosse, soccer, swimming, tennis, track/field (outdoor), track/field (indoor). *Women:* Basketball, cross-country, field hockey, lacrosse, soccer, softball, swimming, tennis, track/field (outdoor), track/field (indoor), volleyball. **On-Campus Highlights:** Edward J. Pryzbyla University Center, Eugene I. Kane Fitness Center, St. Vincent de Paul Chapel, Raymond A. Dufour (athletic) Center, John K. Mullen of Denver Memorial Library, Catholic University's 193 acre campus is the largest among universities in Washington, DC, Its spacious campus setting is adjacent to a Washington Metrorail and has several campus malls for frisbee, football, softball, picnicking and sunning. **Environmental Initiatives:** LEED-NC Certified, 402 Bed Student Dormitory Alternative energy purchasing at 35% of consumption. The University just installed 1088 solar panels on 4 campus buildings. Thes solar panels will produce 350,000 kwh of "clean" electrical energy on an annual basis. (equaling 1% onsite renewable energy generation). CUA Beautification Day—On campus planting of 80 trees (large canopy type) donated by Casey Tree, Washington, DC, with continued collaboration.

ADMISSIONS

Freshman Academic Profile: Average high school GPA 3.25. 56% from public high schools. SAT Math middle 50% range 500–600. SAT Critical Reading middle 50% range 510–610. ACT middle 50% range 21–26. Minimum paper TOEFL 550. Minimum computer TOEFL 213. Minimum web-based TOEFL 80. **Basis for Candidate Selection:** *Very important factors considered include:* Academic GPA, recommendation(s), rigor of secondary school record, standardized test scores, character/personal qualities, level of applicant's interest, volunteer work. *Important factors considered include:* Application essay, extracurricular activities, first generation, interview, talent/ability. *Other factors considered include:* Class rank, alumni/ae relation, racial/ethnic status, work experience. **Freshman Admission Requirements:** High school diploma is required and GED is accepted. *Academic units recommended:* 4 English, 3 mathematics, 3 science, (1 science labs), 2 foreign language, 4 social studies, 1 fine arts or humanities. **Freshman Admission Statistics:** 5,044 applied, 86% admitted, 19% enrolled. **Transfer Admission Requirements:** High school transcript, college transcript(s), essay or personal statement, standardized test scores, minimum college GPA of 2.8 required. Lowest grade transferable C. **General Admission Information:** Application fee $55. Regular application deadline 2/15. Notification on a rolling basis, beginning on or about 3/15. Nonfall registration accepted. Admission may be deferred for a maximum of 1 year. Credit and/or placement offered for CEEB Advanced Placement tests.

COSTS AND FINANCIAL AID

Required Forms and Deadlines: FAFSA, Alumni and Parish Scholarship Applications if appropriate. Financial aid filing deadline 4/10. Priority financial aid filing date 2/15. **Notification of Awards:** Applicants will be notified of awards on a rolling basis beginning 4/1. **Types of Aid:** *Need-based scholarships/grants:* Federal Pell, SEOG, state scholarships/grants, private scholarships, the school's own gift aid. *Loans:* Direct Subsidized Stafford, Direct Unsubsidized Stafford, Direct PLUS, Commericial Loans. **Student Employment:** Federal Work-Study Program available. Institutional employment available. Off-campus job opportunities are good. **Financial Aid Statistics:** 64% freshmen, 56% undergrads receive need-based scholarship or grant aid. 59% freshmen, 54% undergrads receive need-based self-help aid. 93% freshmen, 89% undergrads receive any aid. **Criteria for awarding institutional aid:** *Non-need-based:* Academics, alumni affiliation, music/drama, religious affiliation.

CAZENOVIA COLLEGE

3 Sullivan Street, Cazenovia, NY 13035
Phone: 315-655-7208 **Financial Aid Phone:** 315-655-7887
E-mail: admission@cazenovia.edu
Fax: 315-655-4860

This private school was founded in 1824.

RATINGS

Admissions Selectivity Rating: 72   **Fire Safety Rating:** 98   **Green Rating:** 75

STUDENTS AND FACULTY

Enrollment: 1,073. **Student Body:** 73% female, 27% male, 18% out-of-state,. African American 4%, Caucasian 66%, Hispanic 3%.
Retention and Graduation: 72% freshmen return for sophomore year.
Faculty: Student/faculty ratio 12:1. 56 full-time faculty, 79% hold PhDs, 4% are members of minority groups, 61% are women.

ACADEMICS

Degrees: Associate, bachelor's, certificate. **Classes:** Most classes have 10–19 students. **Majors with Highest Enrollment:** Business administration, management and operations, other; fine/studio arts; interior design. **Special Study Options:** Accelerated program, double major, exchange student program (domestic), honors program, independent study, internships, student-designed major, study abroad, teacher certification program. **Honors programs:** The All-College Honors Program at Cazenovia College offers to outstanding students in all majors (in the liberal arts and in the professional studies) a stimulating learning environment beyond that found in standard classroom coursework, and fosters their exceptional academic talents and intellectual curiosity. Demanding curriculum, independent research opportunities and co-curricular activities challenge students to achieve their full educational potential not only through encouraging academic excellence but also through promoting social responsibilities in the global community. An honors degree certifies that students have produced academic work that meets the highest standards of academic rigor in both general education and in their career field. Special programs offered to physically disabled students include note-taking services, reader services, tape recorders, tutors. **Career services:** Alumni network, alumni services, career/job search classes, career assessment, internships, regional alumni. **Career services highlights include:** the College's academic programs provide students the opportunity to participate in off-campus internships, often as a graduation requirement. Internships generally provide students with one of three types of experience: A continuation of work in a familiar field to increase student knowledge by performing tasks beyond those already mastered in this career area; an experience intended to broaden student expertise within a career area by working in an area of that profession not previously experienced; and; a shadowing or observational experience of a professional in a specific career field as a means of exploring a possible new career interest. Regardless of the type of experience, internships make valuable connections between the world of work and the student's academic study. Each academic program has specific eligibility requirements for internships that can be checked in the College Catalog or by contacting either the Program Director or the Director of Career Services.

FACILITIES

Housing: Coed dorms, special housing for disabled students, women's dorms, Single room suites. **Special Academic Facilities/Equipment:** Reisman Hall is a state-of-the-art Art and Design facility and gallery; 243-acre Equine Education Center; historic Catherine Cummings Theatre. **Computers:** Administrative functions (other than registration) can be performed online.

CAMPUS LIFE

Environment: Rural. **Activities:** Choral groups, dance, drama/theater, jazz band, musical theater, radio station, student government, student newspaper, student-run film society, yearbook, campus ministries. **Organizations:** 54 registered organizations, 5 honor societies, 1 religious organizations. **Athletics (Intercollegiate):** *Men:* Baseball, basketball, cheerleading, crew/rowing, cross-country, equestrian sports, golf, horseback riding, lacrosse, soccer, swimming *Women:* Basketball, cheerleading, crew/rowing, cross-country, equestrian sports, horseback riding, lacrosse, soccer, softball, swimming, volleyball. **On-Campus Highlights:** Residence Halls, Academic Facilities—Art and Design Building, Equestrian Center, Athletic Facilities / Pool, Dining Hall. **Environmental Initiatives:** Environmental Studies education programs; Look Again program—sustainability in fashion. Sustainability is a goal in the institution's Strategic Plan and a study of our institutional carbon footprint is underway, use all biodegradable corn based products in place of foam and paper products in dining halls and kitchens, all green chemicals used in dining halls and kitchens, Apex system in use, and solar panels in use in two buildings on campus; contract with gas and electric energy providers that guarantee a minimum of 5% of energy comes from renewable sources. Cazenovia College hosts the Annual Symposium on Energy in the 21st Century: Seeking Environmental Solutions Through Partnerships www.cazenovia.edu/energy.

ADMISSIONS

Freshman Academic Profile: Average high school GPA 3.2. 12% in top 10% of high school class, 32% in top 25% of high school class, 77% in top 50% of high school class. SAT Math middle 50% range 440–550. SAT Critical Reading middle 50% range 440–540. ACT middle 50% range 17–24. Minimum paper TOEFL 550. Minimum computer TOEFL 213. **Basis for Candidate Selection:** *Very important factors considered include:* Rigor of secondary school record, extracurricular activities. *Important factors considered include:* Class rank, academic GPA, recommendation(s), standardized test scores, character/personal qualities, interview, talent/ability. *Other factors considered include:* Application essay, level of applicant's interest, volunteer work, work experience. **Freshman Admission Requirements:** High school diploma is required and GED is accepted. *Academic units recommended:* 4 English, 2 mathematics, 2 science, 4 social studies. **Freshman Admission Statistics:** 2,075 applied, 74% admitted, 18% enrolled. **Transfer Admission Requirements:** High school transcript, college transcript(s), minimum college GPA of 2.0 required. Lowest grade transferable C. **General Admission Information:** Application fee $30. Notification on a rolling basis, beginning on or about 11/1. Nonfall registration accepted. Admission may be deferred for a maximum of 1 year. Credit and/or placement offered for CEEB Advanced Placement tests.

COSTS AND FINANCIAL AID

Annual tuition $23,752. Room and board $10,476. Required fees $400. Average book expense $1,000. **Required Forms and Deadlines:** FAFSA, state aid form. Priority financial aid filing date 3/1. **Notification of Awards:** Applicants will be notified of awards on a rolling basis beginning 11/1. **Types of Aid:** *Need-based scholarships/grants:* Federal Pell, SEOG, state scholarships/grants, private scholarships, the school's own gift aid. *Loans:* Direct Subsidized Stafford, Direct Unsubsidized Stafford, Direct PLUS. **Student Employment:** Federal Work-Study Program available. **Financial Aid Statistics:** 83% freshmen, 85% undergrads receive need-based scholarship or grant aid. 9% freshmen, 8% undergrads receive non-need-based scholarship or grant aid. 67% freshmen, 71% undergrads receive need-based self-help aid. 86% freshmen, 85% undergrads receive any aid. 85% undergrads borrow to pay for school. **Criteria for awarding institutional aid:** *Non-need-based:* Academics.

CEDAR CREST COLLEGE

100 College Drive, Allentown, PA 18104
Phone: 610-740-3780 **Financial Aid Phone:** 610-606-4602
E-mail: cccadmis@cedarcrest.edu **CEEB Code:** 2079
Fax: 610-606-4647 **Website:** www.cedarcrest.edu **ACT Code:** 3536

This private school was founded in 1867. It has a 84-acre campus.

RATINGS

Admissions Selectivity Rating: 82   **Fire Safety Rating:** 74   **Green Rating:** 77

STUDENTS AND FACULTY

Enrollment: 1,653. **Student Body:** 95% female, 5% male, 19% out-of-state, 1% international (33 countries represented). Asian 3%, African American 8%, Caucasian 78%, Hispanic 7%.
Retention and Graduation: 79% freshmen return for sophomore year. 45% freshmen graduate within 4 years. 20% grads go on to further study within 1 year. 12% grads pursue arts and sciences degrees. 1% grads pursue law degrees. 3% grads pursue business degrees. 1% grads pursue medical degrees. **Faculty:** Student/faculty ratio 11:1. 90 full-time faculty, 72% hold PhDs, 4% are members of minority groups, 63% are women.

ACADEMICS

Degrees: Bachelor's, master's, post-bachelor's certificate, post-master's certificate. **Classes:** Most classes have 10–19 students. Most lab/discussion sessions have 10–19 students. **Majors with Highest Enrollment:** Nursing/registered nurse (RN, ASN, BSN, MSN); physical sciences, other; social work. **Special Study Options:** Cross-registration, distance learning, double major, honors program, independent study, internships, liberal arts/career combination, student-designed major, study abroad, teacher certification program, ethics. **Honors programs:** Special courses reserved for Honors Students, undergraduate research opportunities, including Honors Thesis. Special programs offered to physically disabled students include note-taking services, reader services, tape recorders, tutors. **Career services:** Alumni network, alumni services, career/job search classes, career assessment, internships, regional alumni. Career services highlights include: Our Marketing Practicum course has worked with employers such as Just Born, Crayola, and the PA Liquor Control Board to provide internship opportunities for students and hands-on experience.

FACILITIES

Housing: Special housing for disabled students, women's dorms 90% of campus accessible to physically disabled. **Special Academic Facilities/Equipment:**

Alumnae Museum **Computers:** 75% of classrooms, 85% of dorms, 100% of libraries, 85% of dining areas, 85% of student union, 50% of common outdoor areas have wireless network access. Students can register for classes online. Administrative functions (other than registration) can be performed online.

CAMPUS LIFE

Environment: City. **Activities:** Choral groups, dance, drama/theater, literary magazine, music ensembles, musical theater, radio station, student government, student newspaper, yearbook, campus ministries, international student organization. **Organizations:** 18 honor societies, 4 religious organizations. **Athletics (Intercollegiate):** *Women:* Basketball, cross-country, field hockey, lacrosse, soccer, softball, tennis, volleyball. **On-Campus Highlights:** Bistro, College Center, Fitness Center, Rodale Aquatic Center **Environmental Initiatives:** Recycling: participating in national RecycleMania. Decentralized heat plant

ADMISSIONS

Freshman Academic Profile: Average high school GPA 3.18. 26% in top 10% of high school class, 56% in top 25% of high school class, 89% in top 50% of high school class. 93% from public high schools. SAT Math middle 50% range 480–590. SAT Critical Reading middle 50% range 490–590. SAT Writing middle 50% range 480–570. ACT middle 50% range 20–26. Minimum paper TOEFL 500. Minimum computer TOEFL 173. Minimum web-based TOEFL 61. **Basis for Candidate Selection:** *Very important factors considered include:* Class rank, application essay, academic GPA, recommendation(s), rigor of secondary school record, standardized test scores. *Other factors considered include:* Alumni/ae relation, extracurricular activities, interview, volunteer work, work experience. **Freshman Admission Requirements:** High school diploma is required and GED is accepted. *Academic units required:* 4 English, 3 mathematics, 2 science, (2 science labs), 2 foreign language, 3 social studies. *Academic units recommended:* 3 academic electives. **Freshman Admission Statistics:** 1,583 applied, 63% admitted, 20% enrolled. **Transfer Admission Requirements:** High school transcript, college transcript(s), minimum college GPA of 2.00 required. Lowest grade transferable C. **General Admission Information:** Application fee $30. Notification on a rolling basis, beginning on or about 9/15. Nonfall registration accepted. Credit and/or placement offered for CEEB Advanced Placement tests.

COSTS AND FINANCIAL AID

Required Forms and Deadlines: FAFSA. Priority financial aid filing date 5/1. **Notification of Awards:** Applicants will be notified of awards on a rolling basis beginning 1/1. **Types of Aid:** *Need-based scholarships/grants:* Federal Pell, SEOG, state scholarships/grants, private scholarships, the school's own gift aid, Federal Nursing Scholarships. *Loans:* Direct Subsidized Stafford, Direct Unsubsidized Stafford, Direct PLUS, Federal Perkins, Federal Nursing. **Student Employment:** Federal Work-Study Program available. Institutional employment available. Highest amount earned per year from on-campus jobs $2,200. Off-campus job opportunities are fair. **Financial Aid Statistics:** 93% freshmen, 90% undergrads receive need-based scholarship or grant aid. 8% freshmen, 8% undergrads receive non-need-based scholarship or grant aid. 84% freshmen, 80% undergrads receive need-based self-help aid. 98% freshmen, 97% undergrads receive any aid. 92% undergrads borrow to pay for school. Average cumulative indebtedness $24,641. **Criteria for awarding institutional aid:** *Non-need-based:* Academics, alumni affiliation, art, leadership, music/drama.

CEDARVILLE UNIVERSITY

251 N.Main Street, Cedarville, OH 45314
Phone: 937-766-7700 **Financial Aid Phone:** 937-766-7866
E-mail: admissions@cedarville.edu
Fax: 937-766-7575 **Website:** www.cedarville.edu **ACT Code:** 3245

This private school, affiliated with the Baptist Church, was founded in 1887. It has a 400-acre campus.

RATINGS

Admissions Selectivity Rating: 88   **Fire Safety Rating:** 80   **Green Rating:** 60*

STUDENTS AND FACULTY

Enrollment: 2,951. **Student Body:** 55% female, 45% male, 64% out-of-state, 1% international (14 countries represented). Asian 1%, African American 1%, Caucasian 94%, Hispanic 2%.
Retention and Graduation: 85% freshmen return for sophomore year. 68% freshmen graduate within 4 years. 17% grads go on to further study within 1 year. 13% grads pursue arts and sciences degrees. 1% grads pursue law degrees. 1% grads pursue business degrees. 1% grads pursue medical degrees. **Faculty:** Student/faculty ratio 16:1. 185 full-time faculty, 62% hold PhDs, 6% are members of minority groups, 28% are women.

ACADEMICS

Degrees: Bachelor's, certificate, master's. **Classes:** Most classes have 10–19 students. Most lab/discussion sessions have 10–19 students. **Majors with Highest Enrollment:** Elementary education and teaching; mechanical engineering; nursing/registered nurse (RN, ASN, BSN, MSN). **Special Study Options:** Accelerated program, distance learning, double major, dual enrollment, honors program, independent study, internships, student-designed major, study abroad, teacher certification program. Special programs offered to physically disabled students include reader services, tape recorders, tutors. **Career services:** Alumni network, alumni services, career/job search classes, internships, regional alumni.

FACILITIES

Housing: Men's dorms, women's dorms, apartments for married students. **Computers:** 100% of classrooms, 100% of dorms, 100% of libraries, 100% of dining areas, 100% of student union, 80% of common outdoor areas have wireless network access. Students can register for classes online. Administrative functions (other than registration) can be performed online.

CAMPUS LIFE

Environment: Rural. **Activities:** Choral groups, concert band, drama/theater, jazz band, music ensembles, musical theater, pep band, radio station, student government, student newspaper, symphony orchestra, yearbook. **Organizations:** 74 registered organizations, 4 honor societies. **Athletics (Intercollegiate):** *Men:* Baseball, basketball, cheerleading, cross-country, golf, soccer, tennis, track/field (outdoor), track/field (indoor). *Women:* Basketball, cheerleading, cross-country, soccer, softball, tennis, track/field (outdoor), track/field (indoor), volleyball. **On-Campus Highlights:** Fitness and Recreation Center, The Hive—student snack shop, Dixon Ministry Center—daily chapel and concerts, Chucks—student cafeteria (popular hangout), Callan Athletic Center.

ADMISSIONS

Freshman Academic Profile: Average high school GPA 3.628. 37% in top 10% of high school class, 67% in top 25% of high school class, 91% in top 50% of high school class. 51% from public high schools. SAT Math middle 50% range 530–650. SAT Critical Reading middle 50% range 540–660. SAT Writing middle 50% range 520–640. ACT middle 50% range 23–29. Minimum paper TOEFL 550. Minimum computer TOEFL 213. **Basis for Candidate Selection:** *Very important factors considered include:* Application essay, academic GPA, rigor of secondary school record, standardized test scores, character/personal qualities, religious affiliation/commitment. *Important factors considered include:* Recommendation(s), racial/ethnic status. *Other factors considered include:* Class rank, alumni/ae relation, extracurricular activities, interview, talent/ability, volunteer work. **Freshman Admission Requirements:** High school diploma is required and GED is accepted. *Academic units recommended:* 4 English, 4 mathematics, 3 science, (3 science labs), 3 foreign language, 3 social studies. **Freshman Admission Statistics:** 2,654 applied, 76% admitted, 38% enrolled. **Transfer Admission Requirements:** High school transcript, college transcript(s), essay or personal statement, statement of good standing from prior institution(s). Minimum college GPA of 3.0 required. Lowest grade transferable C–. **General Admission Information:** Application fee $30. Notification on a rolling basis, beginning on or about 8/1. Nonfall registration accepted. Admission may be deferred for a maximum of 1 year/1 year. Credit and/or placement offered for CEEB Advanced Placement tests.

COSTS AND FINANCIAL AID

Annual tuition $19,680. Room and board $5,010. Average book expense $900. **Required Forms and Deadlines:** FAFSA. Priority financial aid filing date 3/1. **Notification of Awards:** Applicants will be notified of awards on a rolling basis beginning 3/1. **Types of Aid:** *Need-based scholarships/grants:* Federal Pell, SEOG, state scholarships/grants, private scholarships, the school's own gift aid. *Loans:* FFEL Subsidized Stafford, FFEL Unsubsidized Stafford, FFEL PLUS, Federal Perkins, Federal Nursing, state loans, college/university loans from institutional funds. **Student Employment:** Highest amount earned per year from on-campus jobs $5,238. **Financial Aid Statistics:** 41% freshmen, 43% undergrads receive need-based scholarship or grant aid. 52% freshmen, 46% undergrads receive non-need-based scholarship or grant aid. 51% freshmen, 51% undergrads receive need-based self-help aid. 6% freshmen, 6% undergrads receive athletic scholarships. 92.42% freshmen, 86.19% undergrads receive any aid. 69% undergrads borrow to pay for school. Average cumulative indebtedness $24,890. **Criteria for awarding institutional aid:** *Non-need-based:* Academics, alumni affiliation, athletics, leadership, minority status, music/drama, state/district residency.

CENTENARY COLLEGE

400 Jefferson Street, Hackettstown, NJ 07840
Phone: 800-236-8679 **Financial Aid Phone:** 18002368679
E-mail: admissions@centenarycollege.edu **CEEB Code:** 2080
Fax: 908-852-3454 **Website:** www.centenarycollege.edu **ACT Code:** 2544

This private school, affiliated with the Methodist Church, was founded in 1867. It has a 42-acre campus.

RATINGS

Admissions Selectivity Rating: 68   **Fire Safety Rating:** 60*   **Green Rating:** 60*

STUDENTS AND FACULTY

Enrollment: 2,140. **Student Body:** 63% female, 37% male, 14% out-of-state, 1% international (17 countries represented). Asian 4%, African American 4%, Caucasian 46%, Hispanic 3%.
Retention and Graduation: 24% grads go on to further study within 1 year. 16% grads pursue business degrees. **Faculty:** Student/faculty ratio 16:1. 69 full-time faculty, 57% hold PhDs, 7% are members of minority groups, 57% are women.

ACADEMICS

Degrees: Associate, bachelor's, master's, post-bachelor's certificate, terminal associate, transfer associate. **Classes:** Most classes have 10–19 students. Most lab/discussion sessions have 10–19 students. **Majors with Highest Enrollment:** Business administration and management; criminal justice/police science; elementary education and teaching. **Special Study Options:** Accelerated program, cross-registration, distance learning, double major, dual enrollment, English as a Second Language (ESL), exchange student program (domestic), honors program, independent study, internships, liberal arts/career combination, student-designed major, study abroad, teacher certification program, weekend college. Special programs offered to physically disabled students include note-taking services, reader services, tutors. **Career services:** Alumni network, alumni services, career/job search classes, career assessment, internships, regional alumni.

FACILITIES

Housing: Coed dorms, apartments for single students. 60% of campus accessible to physically disabled. **Special Academic Facilities/Equipment:** Art gallery, radio station WNTI 91.9FM, equity-status theater, equestrian center. **Computers:** 100% of classrooms, 100% of dorms, 100% of libraries, 100% of dining areas, 100% of student union, 100% of common outdoor areas have wireless network access. Students can register for classes online. Administrative functions (other than registration) can be performed online. Undergraduates are required to own a computer.

CAMPUS LIFE

Environment: Town. **Activities:** Choral groups, dance, drama/theater, literary magazine, music ensembles, musical theater, radio station, student government, student newspaper, student-run film society, television station, yearbook, campus ministries, international student organization, Model UN. **Organizations:** 30 registered organizations, 2 honor societies, 2 fraternities, 3 sororities. **Athletics (Intercollegiate):** *Men:* Baseball, basketball, cross-country, golf, lacrosse, soccer, wrestling. *Women:* Basketball, cross-country, golf, lacrosse, soccer, softball, volleyball. **On-Campus Highlights:** Reeves Athletic Facility, Bennett Smith Dormitory, Tilly's Cafe, Library Cyber Cafe

ADMISSIONS

Freshman Academic Profile: Average high school GPA 2.72. 14% in top 10% of high school class, 30% in top 25% of high school class, 69% in top 50% of high school class. 85% from public high schools. SAT Math middle 50% range 420–510. SAT Critical Reading middle 50% range 410–510. SAT Writing middle 50% range 410–510. ACT middle 50% range 16–20. Minimum paper TOEFL 450. Minimum computer TOEFL 200. **Basis for Candidate Selection:** *Very important factors considered include:* Application essay, academic GPA, standardized test scores, interview. *Important factors considered include:* Recommendation(s), rigor of secondary school record, character/personal qualities, extracurricular activities, talent/ability, volunteer work. *Other factors considered include:* Class rank, alumni/ae relation, level of applicant's interest, religious affiliation/commitment, work experience. **Freshman Admission Requirements:** High school diploma is required and GED is accepted. *Academic units required:* 4 English, 3 mathematics, 2 science, (1 science labs). *Academic units recommended:* 4 English, 4 mathematics, 4 science, (2 science labs), 2 foreign language, 4 social studies. **Freshman Admission Statistics:** 754 applied, 89% admitted, 40% enrolled. **Transfer Admission Requirements:** High school transcript, college transcript(s), essay or personal statement, minimum college GPA of 2.0 required. Lowest grade transferable C–. **General Admission Information:** Application fee $30. Notification on a rolling basis, beginning on or about 12/15. Nonfall registration accepted. Admission may be deferred for a maximum of 1 semester. Credit offered for CEEB Advanced Placement tests.

COSTS AND FINANCIAL AID
Annual tuition $15,700. Room and board $6,850. Required fees $1,100. Average book expense $666. **Required Forms and Deadlines:** FAFSA. Financial aid filing deadline 6/1. Priority financial aid filing date 4/1. **Notification of Awards:** Applicants will be notified of awards on a rolling basis beginning 3/15. **Types of Aid:** *Need-based scholarships/grants:* Federal Pell, SEOG, state scholarships/grants, private scholarships, the school's own gift aid. *Loans:* FFEL Subsidized Stafford, FFEL Unsubsidized Stafford, FFEL PLUS, Federal Perkins, state loans, Alternative. **Student Employment:** Off-campus job opportunities are excellent. **Financial Aid Statistics:** 72% freshmen, 47% undergrads receive need-based scholarship or grant aid. 8% freshmen, 4% undergrads receive non-need-based scholarship or grant aid. 60% freshmen, 41% undergrads receive need-based self-help aid. 83% freshmen, 86% undergrads receive any aid. 83% undergrads borrow to pay for school. Average cumulative indebtedness $28,104. **Criteria for awarding institutional aid:** *Non-need-based:* Academics, alumni affiliation, art, leadership, minority status, music/drama, religious affiliation, state/district residency.

CENTENARY COLLEGE OF LOUISIANA

P.O. Box 41188, 2911 Centenary Boulevard, Shreveport, LA 71134-1188
Phone: 318-869-5131 **Financial Aid Phone:** 318-869-5137
E-mail: admissions@centenary.edu **CEEB Code:** 6082
Fax: 318-869-5005 **Website:** www.centenary.edu **ACT Code:** 1576

This private school, affiliated with the Methodist Church, was founded in 1825. It has a 68-acre campus.

RATINGS
Admissions Selectivity Rating: 82   **Fire Safety Rating:** 76   **Green Rating:** 60*

STUDENTS AND FACULTY
Enrollment: 891. **Student Body:** 59% female, 41% male, 43% out-of-state, 2% international (12 countries represented). Asian 2%, African American 8%, Caucasian 82%, Hispanic 4%.
Retention and Graduation: 76% freshmen return for sophomore year. 43% freshmen graduate within 4 years. 50% grads go on to further study within 1 year. **Faculty:** Student/faculty ratio 12:1. 73 full-time faculty, 90% hold PhDs, 4% are members of minority groups, 37% are women.

ACADEMICS
Degrees: Bachelor's, master's. **Classes:** Most classes have 10–19 students. **Majors with Highest Enrollment:** Biology/biological sciences; business/commerce; mass communication/media studies. **Special Study Options:** Cross-registration, double major, dual enrollment, exchange student program (domestic), honors program, independent study, internships, liberal arts/career combination, student-designed major, study abroad, teacher certification program, weekend college, 3/2 Dual Degree (Liberal Arts/Engineering) program in cooperation with Case Western Reserve University, Columbia University, Texas A&M University, University of Southern California, and Washington University in St. Louis; Mathematics/Computer Science double degree program with Southern Methodist University; Semester in Washington, DC; British Studies at Oxford summer program. Special programs offered to physically disabled students include note-taking services, reader services, tape recorders, tutors. **Career services:** Alumni services, career/job search classes, career assessment, internships. Career services highlights include: Both Service Learning and Intercultural Experience expose students to people and places quite different from their own and help them appreciate and understand human diversity.

FACILITIES
Housing: Coed dorms, women's dorms, fraternity/sorority housing 95% of campus accessible to physically disabled. **Special Academic Facilities/Equipment:** Art museum, Art Center, art studios, theatre, performance and practice organs, piano lab, language lab, School of Music recording studio, Science Hall multimedia auditorium. **Computers:** 50% of classrooms, 25% of dorms, 50% of libraries, 100% of dining areas, 50% of student union, 10% of common outdoor areas have wireless network access. Students can register for classes online. Administrative functions (other than registration) can be performed online.

CAMPUS LIFE
Environment: Metropolis. **Activities:** Choral groups, concert band, dance, drama/theater, jazz band, literary magazine, music ensembles, musical theater, opera, radio station, student government, student newspaper, student-run film society, yearbook, campus ministries, international student organization. **Organizations:** 58 registered organizations, 15 honor societies, 8 religious organizations. 5 fraternities, 2 sororities. **Athletics (Intercollegiate):** *Men:* Baseball, basketball, cross-country, golf, soccer, swimming, tennis. *Women:* Basketball, cross-country, golf, gymnastics, soccer, softball, swimming, tennis, volleyball. **On-Campus Highlights:** Fitness Center, Jones-Rice Field, Student Union Building, Anderson Choral Building, Gold Dome, Peavy Climbing Tower Anderson Choral Building, Crumley Gardens Aboretum, Feazel Instrumental Hall.

ADMISSIONS
Freshman Academic Profile: 33% in top 10% of high school class, 63% in top 25% of high school class, 85% in top 50% of high school class. 70% from public high schools. SAT Math middle 50% range 520–620. SAT Critical Reading middle 50% range 520–630. ACT middle 50% range 24–28. Minimum paper TOEFL 550. Minimum computer TOEFL 213. **Basis for Candidate Selection:** *Very important factors considered include:* Academic GPA, rigor of secondary school record. *Important factors considered include:* Class rank, application essay, recommendation(s), standardized test scores, alumni/ae relation, character/personal qualities, extracurricular activities, interview, level of applicant's interest, talent/ability, volunteer work, work experience. *Other factors considered include:* First generation, geographical residence, racial/ethnic status, religious affiliation/commitment. **Freshman Admission Requirements:** High school diploma is required and GED is accepted. *Academic units recommended:* 4 English, 3 mathematics, 3 science, (2 science labs), 2 foreign language, 3 social studies. **Freshman Admission Statistics:** 1,076 applied, 69% admitted, 33% enrolled. **Transfer Admission Requirements:** High school transcript, college transcript(s), essay or personal statement, statement of good standing from prior institution(s). Minimum college GPA of 2.0 required. Lowest grade transferable C. **General Admission Information:** Application fee $30. Regular application deadline 8/1. Notification on a rolling basis, beginning on or about 10/1. Nonfall registration accepted. Admission may be deferred for a maximum of 1 year. Credit and/or placement offered for CEEB Advanced Placement tests.

COSTS AND FINANCIAL AID
Annual tuition $20,940. Room and board $7,000. Required fees $1,140. Average book expense $1,200. **Required Forms and Deadlines:** FAFSA, institution's own financial aid form. Priority financial aid filing date 2/15. **Notification of Awards:** Applicants will be notified of awards on or about 3/15. **Types of Aid:** *Need-based scholarships/grants:* Federal Pell, SEOG, state scholarships/grants, private scholarships, the school's own gift aid. *Loans:* FFEL Subsidized Stafford, FFEL Unsubsidized Stafford, FFEL PLUS, Federal Perkins. **Student Employment:** Federal Work-Study Program available. Institutional employment available. Highest amount earned per year from on-campus jobs $4,000. Off-campus job opportunities are good. **Financial Aid Statistics:** 67% freshmen, 56% undergrads receive need-based scholarship or grant aid. 15% freshmen, 16% undergrads receive non-need-based scholarship or grant aid. 46% freshmen, 34% undergrads receive need-based self-help aid. 13% freshmen, 14% undergrads receive athletic scholarships. 98% freshmen, 93% undergrads receive any aid. 64% undergrads borrow to pay for school. Average cumulative indebtedness $19,206. **Criteria for awarding institutional aid:** *Non-need-based:* Academics, art, athletics, music/drama, religious affiliation, state/district residency.

CENTRAL BAPTIST COLLEGE

1501 College Avenue, Conway, AR 72034
Phone: 501-329-6872
E-mail: ccalhoun@cbc.edu and lwatson@cbc.edu
Fax: 501-329-2941 **Website:** www.cbc.edu **ACT Code:** 119

This private school, affiliated with the Baptist Church, was founded in 1952. It has a 13-acre campus.

RATINGS
Admissions Selectivity Rating: 67   **Fire Safety Rating:** 60*   **Green Rating:** 60*

STUDENTS AND FACULTY
Enrollment: 394. **Student Body:** 46% female, 54% male, 11% out-of-state, 1% international. Asian 1%, African American 9%, Caucasian 92%, Hispanic 2%, Native American 1%.
Retention and Graduation: Faculty: Student/faculty ratio 17:1. 16 full-time faculty, 44% hold PhDs, 38% are women.

ACADEMICS

Degrees: Associate, bachelor's. **Majors with Highest Enrollment:** Elementary education and teaching; psychology; theology and religious vocations, other.

FACILITIES

Housing: Men's dorms, women's dorms

CAMPUS LIFE

Environment: Rural. **Activities:** Choral groups, music ensembles, musical theater, student government, yearbook. **Athletics (Intercollegiate):** *Men:* Baseball, basketball. *Women:* Basketball, volleyball.

ADMISSIONS

Freshman Academic Profile: Average high school GPA 3.08. 11% in top 10% of high school class, 29% in top 25% of high school class, 66% in top 50% of high school class. Minimum paper TOEFL 500. **Basis for Candidate Selection:** *Very important factors considered include:* Class rank, recommendation(s), rigor of secondary school record, standardized test scores, character/personal qualities. *Important factors considered include:* Religious affiliation/commitment. *Other factors considered include:* Extracurricular activities, talent/ability. **Freshman Admission Requirements:** High school diploma is required and GED is accepted. **Freshman Admission Statistics:** 164 applied, 84% admitted, 75% enrolled. **Transfer Admission Requirements:** College transcript(s), essay or personal statement, standardized test scores, minimum college GPA of 2.0 required. Lowest grade transferable C. **General Admission Information:** Application fee $25. Regular application deadline 8/15. Nonfall registration accepted. Admission may be deferred for a maximum of 12.

COSTS AND FINANCIAL AID

Average book expense $700. **Required Forms and Deadlines:** FAFSA. **Types of Aid:** *Need-based scholarships/grants:* Federal Pell, SEOG, state scholarships/grants, private scholarships *Loans:* FFEL Subsidized Stafford, FFEL Unsubsidized Stafford, FFEL PLUS. **Student Employment:** Federal Work-Study Program available. Off-campus job opportunities are good. **Criteria for awarding institutional aid:** *Non-need-based:* Academics, alumni affiliation, leadership, music/drama, religious affiliation.

CENTRAL COLLEGE

812 University Street, Pella, IA 50219-1999
Phone: 877-462-3687 **Financial Aid Phone:** 641-628-5336
E-mail: admission@central.edu **CEEB Code:** 6087
Fax: 641-628-5316 **Website:** www.central.edu **ACT Code:** 1284

This private school, affiliated with the Reformed Church Church, was founded in 1853. It has a 133-acre campus.

RATINGS
Admissions Selectivity Rating: 78   **Fire Safety Rating:** 60*   **Green Rating:** 60*

STUDENTS AND FACULTY

Enrollment: 1,606. **Student Body:** 55% female, 45% male, 17% out-of-state, (18 countries represented).
Retention and Graduation: 79% freshmen return for sophomore year. 63% freshmen graduate within 4 years. 15% grads go on to further study within 1 year. 9% grads pursue arts and sciences degrees. 1% grads pursue law degrees. 1% grads pursue business degrees. 4% grads pursue medical degrees. **Faculty:** Student/faculty ratio 13:1. 94 full-time faculty, 97% hold PhDs, 10% are members of minority groups, 38% are women.

ACADEMICS

Degrees: Bachelor's. **Classes:** Most classes have 10–19 students. Most lab/discussion sessions have 10–19 students. **Majors with Highest Enrollment:** Business/commerce; education; kinesiology and exercise science. **Special Study Options:** Double major, English as a Second Language (ESL), honors program, independent study, internships, liberal arts/career combination, student-designed major, study abroad, teacher certification program, off-campus study: Washington, DC, Chicago Metro Program. Study abroad in nine countries. Exploring Student Program encourages two years of multidisciplinary study before selecting a major. **Honors programs:** The entire 4-year Honors program is outstanding. **Combined degree programs:** BA/MEng, 3-4 architecture program with Washington U. Special programs offered to physically disabled students include note-taking services, reader services, tape recorders, tutors.

FACILITIES

Housing: Coed dorms, special housing for disabled students, men's dorms, special housing for international students, women's dorms, fraternity/soror-

ity housing, apartments for married students, apartments for single students. 95% of campus accessible to physically disabled. **Special Academic Facilities/Equipment:** Art gallery, center for communication and theatre, music center, language lab, glass-blowing studio. **Computers:** Students can register for classes online. Administrative functions (other than registration) can be performed online.

CAMPUS LIFE

Environment: Village. **Activities:** Choral groups, concert band, drama/theater, jazz band, literary magazine, music ensembles, musical theater, radio station, student government, student newspaper, symphony orchestra, yearbook. **Organizations:** 50 registered organizations, 4 religious organizations. 4 fraternities, 2 sororities. **Athletics (Intercollegiate):** *Men:* Baseball, basketball, football, golf, soccer, tennis, track/field (outdoor), track/field (indoor), wrestling. *Women:* Basketball, cross-country, golf, softball, tennis, track/field (outdoor), track/field (indoor), volleyball.

ADMISSIONS

Freshman Academic Profile: Average high school GPA 3.49. 25% in top 10% of high school class, 54% in top 25% of high school class, 85% in top 50% of high school class. 98% from public high schools. SAT Math middle 50% range 410–610. SAT Critical Reading middle 50% range 440–600. ACT middle 50% range 21–25. Minimum paper TOEFL 530. Minimum computer TOEFL 197. **Basis for Candidate Selection:** *Very important factors considered include:* Academic GPA, rigor of secondary school record, standardized test scores. *Important factors considered include:* Class rank. *Other factors considered include:* Application essay, recommendation(s), alumni/ae relation, character/personal qualities, extracurricular activities, first generation, interview, talent/ability, volunteer work, work experience. **Freshman Admission Requirements:** High school diploma is required and GED is accepted. *Academic units required:* 4 English, 2 mathematics, 2 science, (2 science labs), 3 social studies, 2 history. *Academic units recommended:* 3 mathematics, 3 science, 2 foreign language. **Freshman Admission Statistics:** 1,797 applied, 80% admitted, 29% enrolled. **Transfer Admission Requirements:** High school transcript, college transcript(s), standardized test scores, statement of good standing from prior institution(s). Minimum college GPA of 2.5 required. Lowest grade transferable C–. **General Admission Information:** Application fee $25. Notification on a rolling basis, beginning on or about 9/15. Nonfall registration accepted. Admission may be deferred for a maximum of 1 year. Credit and/or placement offered for CEEB Advanced Placement tests.

COSTS AND FINANCIAL AID

Annual tuition $20,972. Room and board $7,224. Required fees $250. Average book expense $880. **Required Forms and Deadlines:** FAFSA. Priority financial aid filing date 3/15. **Notification of Awards:** Applicants will be notified of awards on a rolling basis beginning 3/15. **Types of Aid:** *Need-based scholarships/grants:* Federal Pell, SEOG, state scholarships/grants, private scholarships, the school's own gift aid. *Loans:* Direct Subsidized Stafford, Direct Unsubsidized Stafford, Direct PLUS, Federal Perkins, college/university loans from institutional funds, Private Alternative Loans. **Student Employment:** Highest amount earned per year from on-campus jobs $2,600. **Financial Aid Statistics:** 83% freshmen, 78% undergrads receive need-based scholarship or grant aid. 12% freshmen, 10% undergrads receive non-need-based scholarship or grant aid. 71% freshmen, 68% undergrads receive need-based self-help aid. 100% freshmen, 99% undergrads receive any aid. 87% undergrads borrow to pay for school. Average cumulative indebtedness $27,596. **Criteria for awarding institutional aid:** *Non-need-based:* Academics, alumni affiliation, art, minority status, music/drama, religious affiliation, state/district residency.

CENTRAL CONNECTICUT STATE UNIVERSITY

1615 Stanley Street, New Britain, CT 06050
Phone: 860-832-2278 **Financial Aid Phone:** 860-832-2200
E-mail: admissions@ccsu.edu **CEEB Code:** 3898
Fax: 862-832-2295 **Website:** www.ccsu.edu **ACT Code:** 596

This public school was founded in 1849. It has a 294-acre campus.

RATINGS
Admissions Selectivity Rating: 71   **Fire Safety Rating:** 77   **Green Rating:** 86

STUDENTS AND FACULTY

Enrollment: 9,570. **Student Body:** 49% female, 51% male, 5% out-of-state, 1% international (64 countries represented). Asian 3%, African American 8%, Caucasian 74%, Hispanic 7%.
Retention and Graduation: 79% freshmen return for sophomore year. 13% freshmen graduate within 4 years. **Faculty:** Student/faculty ratio 16:1. 433

full-time faculty, 82% hold PhDs, 17% are members of minority groups, 44% are women.

ACADEMICS

Degrees: Bachelor's, master's, post-bachelor's certificate, post-master's certificate. **Classes:** Most classes have 20–29 students. Most lab/discussion sessions have fewer than 10 students. **Majors with Highest Enrollment:** Accounting; criminology; psychology. **Special Study Options:** Cooperative education program, cross-registration, distance learning, double major, dual enrollment, English as a Second Language (ESL), exchange student program (domestic), honors program, independent study, internships, student-designed major, study abroad, teacher certification program, undergrads may take grad classes. Co-Op programs: Arts, Business,Computer Science,Education,Humanities,Natural Science, Social/Behavioral Science,Technologies. **Honors programs:** Interdisciplinary writing/reading program for undergraduates with strong academic skills. Areas of study: Western Culture, Science and Society, and World Culture, capstone honors thesis in junior year. Scholarship available. **Combined degree programs:** BA/MEng Special programs offered to physically disabled students include note-taking services, reader services, tape recorders, tutors. **Career services:** Alumni services, career/job search classes, career assessment, internships. **Career services highlights include:** cooperative learning in the form of cooperative education.

FACILITIES

Housing: Coed dorms, women's dorms 95% of campus accessible to physically disabled. **Special Academic Facilities/Equipment:** Art gallery, language lab, childhood center, planetarium and space science center, center for economic education, TV studio. **Computers:** 50% of classrooms, 100% of libraries, 100% of dining areas, 100% of student union, 50% of common outdoor areas have wireless network access. Students can register for classes online. Administrative functions (other than registration) can be performed online.

CAMPUS LIFE

Environment: Town. **Activities:** Choral groups, concert band, dance, drama/theater, jazz band, literary magazine, music ensembles, musical theater, radio station, student government, student newspaper, student-run film society, television station, yearbook, international student organization. **Organizations:** 101 registered organizations, 18 honor societies, 5 religious organizations. 1 sorority. **Athletics (Intercollegiate):** *Men:* Baseball, basketball, cross-country, football, golf, soccer, track/field (outdoor), track/field (indoor). *Women:* Basketball, cross-country, diving, golf, lacrosse, soccer, softball, swimming, track/field (outdoor), track/field (indoor), volleyball. **On-Campus Highlights:** Student Center, Cafeteria, Memorial Hall, Torp Theatre, Davidson Hall, Vance Academic Center, Vance Hall, James Hall (Residence Hall), Semesters, Student Center. **Environmental Initiatives:** Emissions reduction energy conservation On-campus education and programs for more sustainable practices providing non-fosill fuel programs for campus stakeholders to change practices. Reducing solid waste production and promoting recycling.

ADMISSIONS

Freshman Academic Profile: 8% in top 10% of high school class, 30% in top 25% of high school class, 72% in top 50% of high school class. 93% from public high schools. SAT Math middle 50% range 470–550. SAT Critical Reading middle 50% range 470–550. SAT Writing middle 50% range 460–550. Minimum paper TOEFL 500. **Basis for Candidate Selection:** *Very important factors considered include:* Rigor of secondary school record. *Important factors considered include:* Class rank, academic GPA, standardized test scores. *Other factors considered include:* Application essay, recommendation(s), extracurricular activities, geographical residence, interview, racial/ethnic status, talent/ability. **Freshman Admission Requirements:** High school diploma is required and GED is accepted. *Academic units required:* 4 English, 3 mathematics, 2 science, (1 science labs), 2 social studies, 1 history. *Academic units recommended:* 3 foreign language. **Freshman Admission Statistics:** 6,791 applied, 54% admitted, 35% enrolled. **Transfer Admission Requirements:** High school transcript, college transcript(s), statement of good standing from prior institution(s). Minimum college GPA of 2.0 required. Lowest grade transferable C. **General Admission Information:** Application fee $50. Regular application deadline 6/1. Notification on a rolling basis, beginning on or about 12/1. Nonfall registration accepted. Admission may be deferred for a maximum of n/a. Credit offered for CEEB Advanced Placement tests.

COSTS AND FINANCIAL AID

Annual in-state tuition $3,742. Annual out-of-state tuition $12,112. Room and board $9,122. Required fees $3,672. Average book expense $1,100. **Required Forms and Deadlines:** FAFSA, business/farm supplement. Financial aid filing deadline 9/15. Priority financial aid filing date 3/1. **Notification of Awards:** Applicants will be notified of awards on a rolling basis beginning 3/15. **Types of Aid:** *Need-based scholarships/grants:* Federal Pell, SEOG, state scholarships/grants, the school's own gift aid. *Loans:* Direct Subsidized Stafford, Direct Unsubsidized Stafford, Direct PLUS, FFEL PLUS, Federal Perkins. **Student Employment:** Federal Work-Study Program available. Institutional

employment available. Highest amount earned per year from on-campus jobs $5,000. Off-campus job opportunities are good. **Financial Aid Statistics:** 44% freshmen, 47% undergrads receive need-based scholarship or grant aid. 7% freshmen, 5% undergrads receive non-need-based scholarship or grant aid. 43% freshmen, 49% undergrads receive need-based self-help aid. 1% freshmen, 2% undergrads receive athletic scholarships. 63% freshmen, 63% undergrads receive any aid. 48% undergrads borrow to pay for school. Average cumulative indebtedness $19,205. **Criteria for awarding institutional aid:** *Non-need-based:* Academics, athletics, minority status.

See page 1050.

CENTRAL METHODIST UNIVERSITY

411 CMC Square, Fayette, MO 65248
Phone: 660-248-6251
E-mail: admissions@cmc.edu **CEEB Code:** 6089
Fax: 660-248-1872 **Website:** www.cmc.edu **ACT Code:** 2270

This private school, affiliated with the Methodist Church, was founded in 1854. It has a 90-acre campus.

RATINGS
Admissions Selectivity Rating: 72   **Fire Safety Rating:** 60*   **Green Rating:** 60*

STUDENTS AND FACULTY
Enrollment: 829. **Student Body:** 52% female, 48% male, 10% out-of-state, 2% international (15 countries represented). African American 7%, Caucasian 85%, Hispanic 1%. **Retention and Graduation:** 57% freshmen return for sophomore year. 30% freshmen graduate within 4 years. 15% grads go on to further study within 1 year. 15% grads pursue arts and sciences degrees. 5% grads pursue law degrees. 5% grads pursue business degrees. 4% grads pursue medical degrees. **Faculty:** Student/faculty ratio 14:1. 54 full-time faculty, 65% hold PhDs, 4% are members of minority groups, 43% are women.

ACADEMICS
Degrees: Associate, bachelor's, master's. **Classes:** Most classes have fewer than 10 students. **Majors with Highest Enrollment:** Business/commerce; early childhood education; elementary education and teaching. **Special Study Options:** Accelerated program, distance learning, double major, dual enrollment, honors program, independent study, internships, liberal arts/career combination, student-designed major, study abroad, teacher certification program. **Career services:** Career/job search classes, career assessment, internships.

FACILITIES
Housing: Coed dorms, men's dorms, women's dorms, apartments for married students, apartments for single students. 39% of campus accessible to physically disabled. **Special Academic Facilities/Equipment:** 2 museums. Telecommunity Technology Center, computer lab in residence halls.

CAMPUS LIFE
Environment: Rural. **Activities:** Choral groups, concert band, drama/theater, jazz band, literary magazine, marching band, music ensembles, musical theater, radio station, student government, student newspaper, symphony orchestra, television station, yearbook. **Organizations:** 41 registered organizations, 13 honor societies, 2 religious organizations. 6 fraternities, 4 sororities. **Athletics (Intercollegiate):** *Men:* Baseball, basketball, cheerleading, cross-country, football, golf, soccer, track/field (outdoor). *Women:* Basketball, cheerleading, cross-country, golf, soccer, softball, track/field (outdoor), volleyball.

ADMISSIONS
Freshman Academic Profile: Average high school GPA 3.21. 7% in top 10% of high school class, 34% in top 25% of high school class, 70% in top 50% of high school class. ACT middle 50% range 19-23. Minimum paper TOEFL 500. Minimum computer TOEFL 173. **Basis for Candidate Selection:** *Very important factors considered include:* Class rank, rigor of secondary school record, standardized test scores, extracurricular activities. *Important factors considered include:* Alumni/ae relation, character/personal qualities, racial/ethnic status, religious affiliation/commitment, talent/ability, volunteer work, work experience. *Other factors considered include:* Recommendation(s), geographical residence, interview, state residency. **Freshman Admission Requirements:** High school diploma is required and GED is accepted. *Academic units recommended:* 4 English, 4 mathematics, 5 science, 2 foreign language, 3 social studies. **Freshman Admission Statistics:** 1,033 applied, 73% admitted, 30% enrolled. **Transfer Admission Requirements:** High school transcript, college transcript(s), standardized test scores, statement of good standing from prior institution(s). Minimum college GPA of 2.0 required. Lowest grade transferable D. **General**

Admission Information: Regular application deadline 8/1. Nonfall registration accepted. Admission may be deferred for a maximum of None. Credit offered for CEEB Advanced Placement tests.

COSTS AND FINANCIAL AID
Required Forms and Deadlines: FAFSA. Priority financial aid filing date 3/15. **Notification of Awards:** Applicants will be notified of awards on a rolling basis beginning 1/30. **Types of Aid:** *Need-based scholarships/grants:* Federal Pell, SEOG, state scholarships/grants, private scholarships, the school's own gift aid. *Loans:* FFEL Subsidized Stafford, FFEL Unsubsidized Stafford, FFEL PLUS, Federal Perkins, college/university loans from institutional funds. **Student Employment:** Federal Work-Study Program available. Off-campus job opportunities are good. **Financial Aid Statistics:** 75% freshmen, 80% undergrads receive need-based scholarship or grant aid. 75% freshmen, 80% undergrads receive non-need-based scholarship or grant aid. 67% freshmen, 65% undergrads receive need-based self-help aid. 2% freshmen, 1% undergrads receive athletic scholarships. 66% undergrads borrow to pay for school. Average cumulative indebtedness $17,037. **Criteria for awarding institutional aid:** *Non-need-based:* Academics, alumni affiliation, athletics, leadership, music/drama, religious affiliation.

CENTRAL MICHIGAN UNIVERSITY

105 Warriner Hall, Mount Pleasant, MI 48859
Phone: 989-774-3076 **Financial Aid Phone:** 888-392-0007
E-mail: cmuadmit@cmich.edu **CEEB Code:** 1106
Fax: 989-774-7267 **Website:** www.cmich.edu **ACT Code:** 1972

This public school was founded in 1892. It has a 854-acre campus.

RATINGS
Admissions Selectivity Rating: 78   **Fire Safety Rating:** 88   **Green Rating:** 77

STUDENTS AND FACULTY
Enrollment: 20,141. **Student Body:** 55% female, 45% male, 2% out-of-state, 1% international (64 countries represented). Asian 1%, African American 6%, Caucasian 82%, Hispanic 2%, Native American 1%.
Retention and Graduation: 21% freshmen graduate within 4 years. 16% grads go on to further study within 1 year. **Faculty:** Student/faculty ratio 21:1. 752 full-time faculty, 81% hold PhDs, 17% are members of minority groups, 40% are women. 6% of classes are taught by teaching assistants.

ACADEMICS
Degrees: Bachelor's, doctoral, master's, post-bachelor's certificate, post-master's certificate. **Classes:** Most classes have 20–29 students. Most lab/discussion sessions have 10–19 students. **Majors with Highest Enrollment:** Accounting; kinesiology and exercise science; psychology. **Special Study Options:** Accelerated program, distance learning, double major, dual enrollment, English as a Second Language (ESL), honors program, independent study, internships, student-designed major, study abroad, teacher certification program, Leadership Institute: The Central Michigan University Leadership Institute, which features a four-year leadership development program, an academic minor, and a scholarship cohort that includes a residential experience, s the premier center for leadership education, training, and development in the Midwest. **Honors programs:** The Honors Program, Centralis Program. **Combined degree programs:** BA/MA, 8 Accelerated Masters Degree Programs. Special programs offered to physically disabled students include note-taking services, reader services, tape recorders, tutors. **Career services:** Alumni network, alumni services, career/job search classes, career assessment, internships, regional alumni. **Career services highlights include:** 100% of undergraduates complete internships.

FACILITIES
Housing: Coed dorms, special housing for disabled students, men's dorms, special housing for international students, women's dorms, fraternity/sorority housing, apartments for married students, apartments for single students, theme housingResidential Colleges: Areas of residence halls designated for students with the same majors or academic interests. 95% of campus accessible to physically disabled. **Special Academic Facilities/Equipment:** Clarke Historical Library, Central Michigan University Museum of Cultural and Natural History, Gerald L. Poor School Museum, Brooks Astronomical Observatory, University Art Gallery, University Theater, Public Broadcasting, Student Activity Center, Charles V. Park Library, body scanner. **Computers:** 100% of classrooms, 100% of dorms, 100% of libraries, 100% of dining areas, 100% of student union, have wireless network access. Students can register for classes online. Administrative functions (other than registration) can be performed online.

CAMPUS LIFE
Environment: Town. **Activities:** Choral groups, concert band, dance, drama/theater, jazz band, literary magazine, marching band, music ensembles, musical theater, pep band, radio station, student government, student newspaper, student-run film society, television station, yearbook, campus ministries, international student organization. **Organizations:** 150 registered organizations, 6 honor societies, 12 religious organizations. 15 fraternities, 15 sororities. **Athletics (Intercollegiate):** *Men:* Baseball, basketball, cross-country, football, track/field (outdoor), track/field (indoor), wrestling. *Women:* Basketball, cross-country, field hockey, gymnastics, soccer, softball, track/field (outdoor), track/field (indoor), volleyball. **On-Campus Highlights:** Education Building (2009), Student Activity Center, Bovee University Center, Park Library, Academic Buildings. **Environmental Initiatives:** RecycleMania, Campus Sustainability Advisory Committee, achieving LEED certification on all new buildings, addition and major renovations.

ADMISSIONS
Freshman Academic Profile: Average high school GPA 3.3. 15.8% in top 10% of high school class, 40.5% in top 25% of high school class, 77.2% in top 50% of high school class. 88% from public high schools. SAT Math middle 50% range 450–570. SAT Critical Reading middle 50% range 438–560. ACT middle 50% range 20–25. Minimum paper TOEFL 550. Minimum computer TOEFL 213. Minimum web-based TOEFL 79. **Basis for Candidate Selection:** *Very important factors considered include:* Academic GPA, rigor of secondary school record, standardized test scores. *Important factors considered include:* Class rank, talent/ability. *Other factors considered include:* Application essay, recommendation(s), alumni/ae relation, character/personal qualities, extracurricular activities, geographical residence, interview, level of applicant's interest, volunteer work, work experience. **Freshman Admission Requirements:** High school diploma is required and GED is accepted. *Academic units recommended:* 4 English, 4 mathematics, 4 science, (1 science labs), 2 foreign language, 2 social studies, 2 history, 1 visual/performing arts, 1 computer science. **Freshman Admission Statistics:** 16,859 applied, 73% admitted, 30% enrolled. **Transfer Admission Requirements:** College transcript(s), statement of good standing from prior institution(s). Minimum college GPA of 2.00 required. Lowest grade transferable C–. **General Admission Information:** Application fee $35. Regular application deadline 7/1. Nonfall registration accepted. Admission may be deferred for a maximum of 1 semester. Credit and/or placement offered for CEEB Advanced Placement tests.

COSTS AND FINANCIAL AID
Average book expense $1,000. **Required Forms and Deadlines:** FAFSA. Priority financial aid filing date 3/1. **Notification of Awards:** Applicants will be notified of awards on a rolling basis beginning 4/1. **Types of Aid:** *Need-based scholarships/grants:* Federal Pell, SEOG, state scholarships/grants, private scholarships, the school's own gift aid. *Loans:* Direct Subsidized Stafford, Direct Unsubsidized Stafford, Direct PLUS, Federal Perkins, state loans, alternative loans. **Student Employment:** Federal Work-Study Program available. Institutional employment available. Highest amount earned per year from on-campus jobs $3,500. Off-campus job opportunities are good. **Financial Aid Statistics:** 49% freshmen, 43% undergrads receive need-based scholarship or grant aid. 6% freshmen, 3% undergrads receive non-need-based scholarship or grant aid. 45% freshmen, 48% undergrads receive need-based self-help aid. 1% freshmen, 1% undergrads receive athletic scholarships. 56% freshmen, 54% undergrads receive any aid. 71% undergrads borrow to pay for school. Average cumulative indebtedness $26,615. **Criteria for awarding institutional aid:** *Non-need-based:* Academics, alumni affiliation, art, athletics, leadership, minority status, music/drama, state/district residency.

CENTRAL STATE UNIVERSITY

PO Box 1004, Wilberforce, OH 45384
Phone: 937-376-6348
E-mail: admissions@centralstate.edu **CEEB Code:** 1107
Fax: 937-376-6648 **Website:** www.centralstate.edu **ACT Code:** 3246

This public school was founded in 1887. It has a 60-acre campus.

RATINGS
Admissions Selectivity Rating: 71   **Fire Safety Rating:** 60*   **Green Rating:** 60*

STUDENTS AND FACULTY
Enrollment: 2,362. **Student Body:** 49% female, 51% male, 39% out-of-state, international. African American 96%, Caucasian 1%, Hispanic 1%.
Retention and Graduation: 58% freshmen return for sophomore year. 8% freshmen graduate within 4 years. 32% grads go on to further study within 1 year. 50% grads pursue arts and sciences degrees. 7% grads pursue law degrees.

29% grads pursue business degrees. **Faculty:** Student/faculty ratio 16:1. 113 full-time faculty, 69% hold PhDs, 68% are members of minority groups, 34% are women.

ACADEMICS

Degrees: Bachelor's, master's. **Classes:** Most classes have 20–29 students. Most lab/discussion sessions have 10–19 students. **Majors with Highest Enrollment:** Biology; business/commerce; early childhood education. **Special Study Options:** Cooperative education program, cross-registration, double major, honors program, independent study, internships, study abroad, teacher certification program. Special programs offered to physically disabled students include note-taking services, reader services, tape recorders, tutors. **Career services:** Alumni services, career/job search classes, career assessment, internships, regional alumni.

FACILITIES

Housing: Coed dorms, men's dorms, women's dorms. 1% of campus accessible to physically disabled. **Special Academic Facilities/Equipment:** National Afro-American Museum and Cultural Center; CJ McLin International Center for Water Resources Management; Center for Integrated Manufacturing Protocols Architectures and Logistics Laboratory; Biology Technique Laboratory; Electrochemistry Research Laboratory; Cosby Mass Communication Center; Paul Robeson Cultural and Performing Arts Center. **Computers:** Administrative functions (other than registration) can be performed online.

CAMPUS LIFE

Environment: Rural. **Activities:** Choral groups, concert band, dance, drama/theater, jazz band, marching band, music ensembles, pep band, radio station, student government, student newspaper, television station, campus ministries **Organizations:** 30 registered organizations, 3 honor societies, 4 religious organizations. 1 fraternities, 3 sororities. **Athletics (Intercollegiate):** *Men:* Basketball, cheerleading, cross-country, golf, track/field (outdoor). *Women:* Basketball, cheerleading, cross-country, golf, track/field (outdoor), volleyball.

ADMISSIONS

Freshman Academic Profile: Average high school GPA 2.4. 7% in top 10% of high school class, 23% in top 25% of high school class, 57% in top 50% of high school class. SAT Math middle 50% range 320–420. SAT Critical Reading middle 50% range 340–430. ACT middle 50% range 14–17. Minimum paper TOEFL 500. **Basis for Candidate Selection:** *Very important factors considered include:* Academic GPA, rigor of secondary school record, standardized test scores. *Important factors considered include:* Class rank, application essay, character/personal qualities, geographical residence, state residency. *Other factors considered include:* Recommendation(s), extracurricular activities, interview, talent/ability. **Freshman Admission Requirements:** High school diploma is required and GED is accepted. *Academic units recommended:* 4 English, 3 mathematics, 3 science, 2 foreign language, 3 social studies, 1 art. **Freshman Admission Statistics:** 6,948 applied, 39% admitted, 26% enrolled. **Transfer Admission Requirements:** College transcript(s), statement of good standing from prior institution(s). Minimum college GPA of 2.0 required. Lowest grade transferable D. **General Admission Information:** Application fee $20. Nonfall registration accepted. Admission may be deferred for a maximum of none. Credit and/or placement offered for CEEB Advanced Placement tests.

COSTS AND FINANCIAL AID

Average book expense $1,200. **Required Forms and Deadlines:** FAFSA, institution's own financial aid form. Priority financial aid filing date 2/15. **Notification of Awards:** Applicants will be notified of awards on a rolling basis beginning 5/1. **Types of Aid:** *Need-based scholarships/grants:* Federal Pell, SEOG, state scholarships/grants, private scholarships, the school's own gift aid, United Negro College Fund. *Loans:* Direct Subsidized Stafford, Direct Unsubsidized Stafford, Direct PLUS, college/university loans from institutional funds. **Student Employment:** Federal Work-Study Program available. Institutional employment available. Off-campus job opportunities are fair. **Financial Aid Statistics:** 76% freshmen, 72% undergrads receive need-based scholarship or grant aid. 25% freshmen, 23% undergrads receive non-need-based scholarship or grant aid. 83% freshmen, 79% undergrads receive need-based self-help aid. 1% freshmen, 3% undergrads receive athletic scholarships. 85% undergrads borrow to pay for school. Average cumulative indebtedness $23,880. **Criteria for awarding institutional aid:** *Non-need-based:* Academics, alumni affiliation, art, athletics, leadership, music/drama, religious affiliation, state/district residency.

CENTRAL WASHINGTON UNIVERSITY

Admissions Office, 400 E. University Way, Ellensburg, WA 98926-7463
Phone: 509-963-1211 **Financial Aid Phone:** 509-963-1611
E-mail: cwuadmis@cwu.edu **CEEB Code:** 4044
Fax: 509-963-3022 **Website:** www.cwu.edu **ACT Code:** 4444

This public school was founded in 1891. It has a 350-acre campus.

RATINGS
Admissions Selectivity Rating: 73   **Fire Safety Rating:** 62   **Green Rating:** 89

STUDENTS AND FACULTY
Enrollment: 9,688. **Student Body:** 51% female, 49% male, 2% out-of-state, 2% international (60 countries represented). Asian 7%, African American 3%, Caucasian 75%, Hispanic 8%, Native American 3%. **Retention and Graduation:** 26% freshmen graduate within 4 years. **Faculty:** Student/faculty ratio 20:1. 432 full-time faculty, 12% are members of minority groups, 39% are women. 3% of classes are taught by teaching assistants.

ACADEMICS
Degrees: Bachelor's, master's, post-bachelor's certificate. **Classes:** Most classes have 20–29 students. Most lab/discussion sessions have 10–19 students. **Majors with Highest Enrollment:** Business/commerce; elementary education and teaching; social sciences. **Special Study Options:** Cooperative education program, distance learning, double major, dual enrollment, English as a Second Language (ESL), exchange student program (domestic), honors program, independent study, internships, liberal arts/career combination, student-designed major, study abroad, teacher certification program. **Honors programs:** The Douglas Honors College student is expected to maintain a grade point average above 3.0. A student will be placed on probation if the grade point average falls below 3.0, and will be dismissed from the Douglas Honors College if the cumulative grade point average is below 3.0 for two consecutive quarters. This policy does not affect academic standing as a student of Central Washington University. Special programs offered to physically disabled students include note-taking services, reader services, tape recorders, tutors. **Career services:** Alumni network, alumni services, career/job search classes, career assessment, internships, regional alumni.

FACILITIES
Housing: Coed dorms, special housing for disabled students, special housing for international students, women's dorms, apartments for married students, apartments for single students, theme housing, upperclassmen and 21 years and older. 100% of campus accessible to physically disabled. **Special Academic Facilities/Equipment:** Chimpanzee and Human Communication Institute; Geodesy Laboratory, a data analysis facility of the Pacific Northwest Geodetic Array; Educational Technology Center; Museum collection of NW Native and Circum-Pacific artifacts for teaching and research. Regional site of the National Consortium for Rural Geospatial Innovations; Sarah Spurgeon Art Gallery; Science Facility Building. **Computers:** 100% of libraries, 100% of dining areas, 100% of student union, 100% of common outdoor areas have wireless network access. Students can register for classes online. Administrative functions (other than registration) can be performed online.

CAMPUS LIFE
Environment: Village. **Activities:** Choral groups, concert band, dance, drama/theater, jazz band, literary magazine, marching band, music ensembles, musical theater, opera, pep band, radio station, student government, student newspaper, student-run film society, symphony orchestra, television station, campus ministries, international student organization. **Organizations:** 96 registered organizations, 3 honor societies, 9 religious organizations. **Athletics (Intercollegiate):** *Men:* Baseball, basketball, cheerleading, cross-country, football, track/field (outdoor), track/field (indoor). *Women:* Basketball, cheerleading, cross-country, soccer, softball, track/field (outdoor), track/field (indoor), volleyball. **On-Campus Highlights:** Award-winning Student Union Recreation Center, Japanese Garden, Nicholson Pavilion Athletic Facilities, Chimpanzee and Human Communication Institute, Performing Arts Center, Presidential Speaker Series. **Environmental Initiatives:** Carbon Reduction; Sustainability as defined by our "Sphere of Distinction;" Energy Conservation.

ADMISSIONS
Freshman Academic Profile: Average high school GPA 3.2. 4% in top 10% of high school class, 23% in top 25% of high school class, 65% in top 50% of high school class. SAT Math middle 50% range 440–550. SAT Critical Reading middle 50% range 440–540. ACT middle 50% range 18–23. Minimum paper TOEFL 525. Minimum computer TOEFL 195. **Basis for Candidate Selection:** *Very important factors considered include:* Academic GPA, rigor of secondary school record. *Important factors considered include:* Application essay, standardized test scores. *Other factors considered include:* Class rank, recommendation(s), character/personal qualities, extracurricular activities,

first generation, interview, level of applicant's interest, talent/ability, volunteer work, work experience. **Freshman Admission Requirements:** High school diploma is required and GED is accepted. *Academic units required:* 4 English, 3 mathematics, 2 science, (1 science labs), 2 foreign language, 3 social studies. *Academic units recommended:* 4 English, 4 mathematics, 3 science, (2 science labs), 2 foreign language, 3 social studies. **Freshman Admission Statistics:** 5,013 applied, 79% admitted, 40% enrolled. **Transfer Admission Requirements:** College transcript(s), statement of good standing from prior institution(s). Minimum college GPA of 2.5 required. Lowest grade transferable D–. **General Admission Information:** Application fee $55. Regular application deadline 4/1. Notification on a rolling basis, beginning on or about 11/1. Nonfall registration accepted. Credit and/or placement offered for CEEB Advanced Placement tests.

COSTS AND FINANCIAL AID

Annual in-state tuition $4,842. Annual out-of-state tuition $14,013. Room and board $8,052. Required fees $882. Average book expense $924. **Required Forms and Deadlines:** FAFSA. Priority financial aid filing date 3/1. **Notification of Awards:** Applicants will be notified of awards on a rolling basis beginning 4/15. **Types of Aid:** *Need-based scholarships/grants:* Federal Pell, SEOG, state scholarships/grants, private scholarships, the school's own gift aid. *Loans:* Direct Subsidized Stafford, Direct Unsubsidized Stafford, Direct PLUS, Federal Perkins, state loans, college/university loans from institutional funds. **Student Employment:** Highest amount earned per year from on-campus jobs $10,166. **Financial Aid Statistics:** 68% freshmen, 68% undergrads receive any aid. **Criteria for awarding institutional aid:** *Non-need-based:* Academics, alumni affiliation, art, athletics, job skills, leadership, minority status, music/drama, religious affiliation, state/district residency.

CENTRAL WYOMING COLLEGE

2660 Peck Avenue, Riverton, WY 82501
Phone: 307-855-2119 **Financial Aid Phone:** 307-855-2150
E-mail: admit@cwc.edu **CEEB Code:** 4115
Fax: 307-855-2093 **Website:** www.cwc.edu **ACT Code:** 514999

This public school was founded in 1966. It has a 200-acre campus.

RATINGS
Admissions Selectivity Rating: 64   **Fire Safety Rating:** 72   **Green Rating:** 65

STUDENTS AND FACULTY
Enrollment: 1,371. **Student Body:** 61% female, 39% male, 14% out-of-state, 1% international (17 countries represented). African American 1%, Caucasian 55%, Hispanic 4%, Native American 13%.
Retention and Graduation: 52% freshmen return for sophomore year.
Faculty: Student/faculty ratio 8:1. 138 full-time faculty, 32% hold PhDs, 5% are members of minority groups, 51% are women.

ACADEMICS
Degrees: Associate, certificate, diploma, terminal associate, transfer associate. **Classes:** Most classes have fewer than 10 students. **Majors with Highest Enrollment:** General studies; nursing/registered nurse (RN, ASN, BSN, MSN); parks, recreation and leisure facilities management. **Special Study Options:** cooperative education program, cross-registration, distance learning, double major, dual enrollment, external degree program, honors program, independent study, student-designed major, teacher certification program. Special programs offered to physically disabled students include note-taking services, reader services, tape recorders, tutors. **Career services:** Career/job search classes, career assessment, internships. **Career services highlights include:** Experiential Learning.

FACILITIES
Housing: Coed dorms, apartments for married students, apartments for single students 100% of campus accessible to physically disabled. **Special Academic Facilities/Equipment:** Fine Arts Center, Microsoft training lab, Cisco training lab, Wyoming Public Television Station and Radio station, Stewart Collection (Native American Artifacts), Sinks Canyon Center, Rodeo Arena, Library, Arts Gallery. **Computers:** Students can register for classes online. Administrative functions (other than registration) can be performed online.

CAMPUS LIFE
Environment: Village. **Activities:** Choral groups, concert band, dance, drama/theater, jazz band, music ensembles, musical theater, radio station, student government, television station, international student organization. **Organizations:** 16 registered organizations, 2 honor societies, 2 religious organizations. **Athletics (Intercollegiate):** *Men:* Basketball, rodeo. *Women:* Basketball, rodeo, volleyball. **On-Campus Highlights:** Arts Center, Stewart Collection,

Student Center, Food Court, The Underground. Others depend on the students interests. For instance, if they are interested in our equine program we would take them to our equine facilities.

ADMISSIONS
Freshman Academic Profile: Average high school GPA 2.97. 10% in top 10% of high school class, 26% in top 25% of high school class, 53% in top 50% of high school class. 89% from public high schools. SAT Math middle 50% range 390–550. SAT Critical Reading middle 50% range 420–590. ACT middle 50% range 17–23. Minimum paper TOEFL 500. Minimum computer TOEFL 175. **Basis for Candidate Selection: Freshman Admission Requirements:** High school diploma or equivalent is not required. **Freshman Admission Statistics:** 572 applied, 100% admitted, 81% enrolled. **Transfer Admission Requirements:** college transcript(s), Lowest grade transferable c. **General Admission Information:** Notification on a rolling basis, beginning on or about 1/1. Nonfall registration accepted. Admission may be deferred for a maximum of aslongasneed. Credit offered for CEEB Advanced Placement tests.

COSTS AND FINANCIAL AID
Average book expense $1,000. **Required Forms and Deadlines:** FAFSA, institution's own financial aid form. Priority financial aid filing date 4/15. **Notification of Awards:** Applicants will be notified of awards on a rolling basis beginning 5/1. **Types of Aid:** *Need-based scholarships/grants:* Federal Pell, SEOG, state scholarships/grants, private scholarships, the school's own gift aid. *Loans:* FFEL Subsidized Stafford, FFEL Unsubsidized Stafford, FFEL PLUS, state loans. **Student Employment:** Federal Work-Study Program available. Institutional employment available. Highest amount earned per year from on-campus jobs $3,000. Off-campus job opportunities are excellent. **Financial Aid Statistics:** 48% freshmen, 48% undergrads receive need-based scholarship or grant aid. 44% freshmen, 39% undergrads receive non-need-based scholarship or grant aid. 30% freshmen, 32% undergrads receive need-based self-help aid. 42% freshmen, 52% undergrads receive any aid. 30% undergrads borrow to pay for school. Average cumulative indebtedness $6,625. **Criteria for awarding institutional aid:** *Non-need-based:* Academics, alumni affiliation, art, athletics, leadership, minority status, music/drama, state/district residency.

CENTRE COLLEGE

600 West Walnut Street, 600 West Walnut, Danville, KY 40422
Phone: 859-238-5350
E-mail: admission@centre.edu **CEEB Code:** 1109
Fax: 859-238-5373 **Website:** www.centre.edu **ACT Code:** 1506

This private school, affiliated with the Presbyterian Church, was founded in 1819. It has a 115-acre campus.

RATINGS
Admissions Selectivity Rating: 91   **Fire Safety Rating:** 60*   **Green Rating:** 83

STUDENTS AND FACULTY
Enrollment: 1,214. **Student Body:** 55% female, 45% male, 39% out-of-state, 2% international (12 countries represented). Asian 3%, African American 4%, Caucasian 88%, Hispanic 2%.
Retention and Graduation: 91% freshmen return for sophomore year. 79% freshmen graduate within 4 years. 41% grads go on to further study within 1 year. 35% grads pursue arts and sciences degrees. 21% grads pursue law degrees. 3% grads pursue business degrees. 13% grads pursue medical degrees. **Faculty:** Student/faculty ratio 11:1. 103 full-time faculty, 92% hold PhDs, 11% are members of minority groups, 42% are women.

ACADEMICS
Degrees: Bachelor's. **Classes:** Most classes have 10–19 students. Most lab/discussion sessions have 10–19 students. **Majors with Highest Enrollment:** Economics; English language and literature; history. **Special Study Options:** Cross-registration, double major, honors program, independent study, internships, student-designed major, study abroad, teacher certification program. Special programs offered to physically disabled students include note-taking services, reader services, tape recorders, tutors. **Career services:** Alumni network, alumni services, career/job search classes, career assessment, internships, regional alumni. Career services highlights include: We provide a college-wide comprehensive internship program. We also provide a unique program of career counseling called "Centre Futures."

FACILITIES

Housing: Coed dorms, special housing for disabled students, men's dorms, fraternity/sorority housing, apartments for single students, wellness housing, theme housing. 80% of campus accessible to physically disabled. **Special Academic Facilities/Equipment:** Arts center, physical science and math facility, electron microscope, visible and infrared mass spectroscopy equipment, visual arts center. **Computers:** Administrative functions (other than registration) can be performed online.

CAMPUS LIFE

Environment: Village. **Activities:** Choral groups, dance, drama/theater, jazz band, literary magazine, music ensembles, musical theater, opera, pep band, radio station, student government, student newspaper, symphony orchestra, television station, campus ministries, international student organization. **Organizations:** 70 registered organizations, 12 honor societies, 6 religious organizations, 4 fraternities, 4 sororities. **Athletics (Intercollegiate):** *Men:* Baseball, basketball, cheerleading, cross-country, diving, football, golf, soccer, swimming, tennis, track/field (outdoor). *Women:* Basketball, cheerleading, cross-country, diving, field hockey, golf, soccer, softball, swimming, tennis, track/field (outdoor), volleyball. **On-Campus Highlights:** Norton Center for the Arts, College Centre, athletic and library, Combs Center, student center, 21 campus buildings on National Register, Jazzman's Cafe. **Environmental Initiatives:** All new buildings and major renovations will be designed and built to conserve energy and enhance the human environment as evaluated by LEED Silver standards or equivalent. Certification through U.S.G.B.C. will be pursued as appropriate. Energy consumption and life-cycle costs will be considered in purchases of all equipment and appliances. The intention will be to purchase E.P.A. Energy Star products in all areas for which such ratings exist. Waste minimization will be promoted and pursued by policy and practice. Specific activities will depend upon technical and economic opportunities. Current efforts include participation in the Waste minimization component of the RecycleMania competition.

ADMISSIONS

Freshman Academic Profile: Average high school GPA 3.58. 59% in top 10% of high school class, 84% in top 25% of high school class, 98% in top 50% of high school class. 79% from public high schools. SAT Math middle 50% range 570–670. SAT Critical Reading middle 50% range 550–670. SAT Writing middle 50% range 530–670. ACT middle 50% range 26–30. Minimum paper TOEFL 580. **Basis for Candidate Selection:** *Very important factors considered include:* Academic GPA, rigor of secondary school record. *Important factors considered include:* Class rank, application essay, recommendation(s), standardized test scores. *Other factors considered include:* Alumni/ae relation, character/personal qualities, extracurricular activities, first generation, geographical residence, interview, racial/ethnic status, talent/ability, volunteer work, work experience. **Freshman Admission Requirements:** High school diploma or equivalent is not required. *Academic units required:* 4 English, 3 mathematics, 2 science, (2 science labs), 2 foreign language, 1 social studies, 1 history. *Academic units recommended:* 4 mathematics, 4 science, 4 foreign language, 2 social studies, 2 history, 1 visual/performing arts. **Freshman Admission Statistics:** 2,056 applied, 69% admitted, 23% enrolled. **Transfer Admission Requirements:** High school transcript, college transcript(s), essay or personal statement, standardized test scores, statement of good standing from prior institution(s). Lowest grade transferable C. **General Admission Information:** Application fee $40. Regular application deadline 2/1. Regular notification 3/15. Nonfall registration not accepted. Admission may be deferred for a maximum of 1 year. Credit and/or placement offered for CEEB Advanced Placement tests.

COSTS AND FINANCIAL AID

Comprehensive fee $39,000. Average book expense $1,200. **Required Forms and Deadlines:** FAFSA, institution's own financial aid form Financial aid filing deadline 3/1. Priority financial aid filing date 3/1. **Notification of Awards:** Applicants will be notified of awards on or about 4/1. **Types of Aid:** *Need-based -scholarships/grants:* Federal Pell, SEOG, state scholarships/grants, private scholarships, the school's own gift aid, Federal ACG Federal SMART + Federal TEACH. *Loans:* FFEL Subsidized Stafford, FFEL Unsubsidized Stafford, FFEL PLUS, Federal Perkins, college/university loans from institutional funds. **Student Employment:** Federal Work-Study Program available. Institutional employment available. Off-campus job opportunities are fair. **Financial Aid Statistics:** 64% freshmen, 59% undergrads receive need-based scholarship or grant aid. 39% freshmen, 42% undergrads receive need-based self-help aid. 53% undergrads borrow to pay for school. Average cumulative indebtedness $17,190. **Criteria for awarding institutional aid:** *Non-need-based:* Academics, alumni affiliation, music/drama.

CHADRON STATE COLLEGE

1000 Main Street, Chadron, NE 69337
Phone: 308-432-6263 **Financial Aid Phone:** 308-432-6230
E-mail: inquire@csc.edu **CEEB Code:** 6466
Fax: 308-432-6229 **Website:** www.csc.edu **ACT Code:** 2466

This public school was founded in 1911. It has a 281-acre campus.

RATINGS

Admissions Selectivity Rating: 75   **Fire Safety Rating:** 60*   **Green Rating:** 60*

STUDENTS AND FACULTY

Enrollment: 2,152. **Student Body:** 57% female, 43% male, 32% out-of-state, 1% international (16 countries represented). Asian 1%, African American 1%, Caucasian 73%, Hispanic 2%, Native American 2%.
Retention and Graduation: 70% freshmen return for sophomore year. 17% freshmen graduate within 4 years. 41% grads go on to further study within 1 year. 25% grads pursue arts and sciences degrees. 3% grads pursue law degrees. 10% grads pursue business degrees. 3% grads pursue medical degrees. **Faculty:** Student/faculty ratio 19:1. 101 full-time faculty, 57% hold PhDs, 4% are members of minority groups, 36% are women.

ACADEMICS

Degrees: Bachelor's, master's, post-master's certificate. **Classes:** Most classes have fewer than 10 students. **Majors with Highest Enrollment:** Business/commerce; criminal justice/law enforcement administration; elementary education and teaching. **Special Study Options:** Accelerated program, cooperative education program, cross-registration, distance learning, double major, dual enrollment, honors program, independent study, internships, student-designed major, study abroad, teacher certification program. Special programs offered to physically disabled students include note-taking services, tape recorders, tutors. **Career services:** Career/job search classes.

FACILITIES

Housing: Coed dorms, men's dorms, women's dorms, apartments for married students, apartments for single students 100% of campus accessible to physically disabled. **Special Academic Facilities/Equipment:** Planetarium, herbarium, geology museum, Mari Sandoz Center. **Computers:** Students can register for classes online. Administrative functions (other than registration) can be performed online.

CAMPUS LIFE

Environment: Rural. **Activities:** Choral groups, concert band, dance, drama/theater, jazz band, literary magazine, music ensembles, musical theater, pep band, radio station, student government, student newspaper, yearbook. **Organizations:** 65 registered organizations, 14 honor societies, 5 religious organizations. **Athletics (Intercollegiate):** *Men:* Basketball, football, track/field (outdoor), track/field (indoor), wrestling. *Women:* Basketball, golf, track/field (outdoor), track/field (indoor), volleyball. **On-Campus Highlights:** Mari Sandoz Heritage Center, Educatiional Facility, Laboratories, Student Center.

ADMISSIONS

Freshman Academic Profile: Average high school GPA 3.13. 11% in top 10% of high school class, 33% in top 25% of high school class, 65% in top 50% of high school class. 83% from public high schools. Minimum paper TOEFL 550. Minimum computer TOEFL 213. **Basis for Candidate Selection:** *Other factors considered include:* Academic GPA. **Freshman Admission Requirements:** High school diploma is required and GED is accepted. *Academic units recommended:* 4 English, 3 mathematics, 2 science, (2 science labs), 3 social studies. **Freshman Admission Statistics: Transfer Admission Requirements:** college transcript(s), minimum college GPA of 2.0 required. Lowest grade transferable D. **General Admission Information:** Application fee $15. Nonfall registration accepted. Credit and/or placement offered for CEEB Advanced Placement tests.

COSTS AND FINANCIAL AID

Annual in-state tuition $2,933. Annual out-of-state tuition $5,865. Room and board $4,074. Required fees $730. **Required Forms and Deadlines:** FAFSA, institution's own financial aid form. Priority financial aid filing date 6/1. **Notification of Awards:** Applicants will be notified of awards on a rolling basis beginning 4/1. **Types of Aid:** *Need-based scholarships/grants:* Federal Pell, SEOG, state scholarships/grants, private scholarships, the school's own gift aid. *Loans:* Direct Subsidized Stafford, Direct Unsubsidized Stafford, Direct PLUS, FFEL Subsidized Stafford, FFEL Unsubsidized Stafford, FFEL PLUS, Federal Perkins. **Student Employment:** Federal Work-Study Program available. Institutional employment available. **Financial Aid Statistics:** 50% freshmen, 48% undergrads receive need-based scholarship or grant aid. 36% freshmen, 41% undergrads receive need-based self-help aid. **Criteria for awarding institutional aid:** *Non-need-based:* Academics, alumni affiliation, art, athletics, leadership, minority status, music/drama, state/district residency.

CHAMINADE UNIVERSITY OF HONOLULU

3140 Waialae Avenue, Honolulu, HI 96816-1578
Phone: 808-735-4735 **Financial Aid Phone:** 808-735-4780
E-mail: admissions@chaminade.edu **CEEB Code:** 4105
Fax: 808-739-4647 **Website:** www.chaminade.edu **ACT Code:** 898

This private school, affiliated with the Roman Catholic Church, was founded in 1955. It has a 67-acre campus.

RATINGS
Admissions Selectivity Rating: 70   **Fire Safety Rating:** 60*   **Green Rating:** 60*

STUDENTS AND FACULTY
Enrollment: 1,013. **Student Body:** 66% female, 34% male, 41% out-of-state, 3% international (12 countries represented). Asian 68%, African American 3%, Caucasian 18%, Hispanic 7%, Native American 1%.
Retention and Graduation: 20% freshmen graduate within 4 years. **Faculty:** Student/faculty ratio 12:1. 70 full-time faculty, 71% hold PhDs, 40% are members of minority groups, 37% are women.

ACADEMICS
Degrees: Associate, bachelor's, master's, post-bachelor's certificate, post-master's certificate. **Classes:** Most classes have 10–19 students. Most lab/discussion sessions have 10–19 students. **Majors with Highest Enrollment:** Business/commerce; criminal justice/safety studies; psychology. **Special Study Options:** Accelerated program, distance learning, double major, exchange student program (domestic), independent study, internships, student-designed major, study abroad, teacher certification program. Special programs offered to physically disabled students include note-taking services, reader services, tape recorders. **Career services:** Career/job search classes, career assessment, internships.

FACILITIES
Housing: Coed dorms, women's dorms, apartments for single students 75% of campus accessible to physically disabled. **Special Academic Facilities/Equipment:** Montessori lab school, observatory, black box theatre. **Computers:** Students can register for classes online. Administrative functions (other than registration) can be performed online.

CAMPUS LIFE
Environment: Metropolis. **Activities:** Choral groups, drama/theater, literary magazine, musical theater, student government, student newspaper, symphony orchestra, yearbook, campus ministries. **Organizations:** 38 registered organizations, 7 honor societies, 1 religious organizations. **Athletics (Intercollegiate):** *Men:* Basketball, cross-country, golf, tennis, water polo. *Women:* Cross-country, golf, softball, tennis, volleyball. **On-Campus Highlights:** Jean E. Rolles Sculoture Center, Henry Hall Courtyard Cafe, Brother's Brew Cafe, Weigand Observatory, Vi and Paul Loo Student Center.

ADMISSIONS
Freshman Academic Profile: Average high school GPA 3.17. 9% in top 10% of high school class, 34% in top 25% of high school class, 75% in top 50% of high school class. SAT Math middle 50% range 420–520. SAT Critical Reading middle 50% range 420–520. SAT Writing middle 50% range 410–510. ACT middle 50% range 18–22. Minimum paper TOEFL 450. Minimum computer TOEFL 133. **Basis for Candidate Selection:** *Very important factors considered include:* Academic GPA, standardized test scores. *Important factors considered include:* Application essay, character/personal qualities, extracurricular activities, interview, talent/ability, volunteer work. *Other factors considered include:* Recommendation(s), rigor of secondary school record, work experience. **Freshman Admission Requirements:** High school diploma is required and GED is accepted. *Academic units recommended:* 4 English, 3 mathematics, 2 science, 3 social studies, 4 academic electives. **Freshman Admission Statistics:** 1,037 applied, 95% admitted, 27% enrolled. **Transfer Admission Requirements:** College transcript(s), essay or personal statement, statement of good standing from prior institution(s). Minimum college GPA of 2.0 required. Lowest grade transferable C. **General Admission Information:** Application fee $50. Nonfall registration accepted. Admission may be deferred for a maximum of 1 year. Credit and/or placement offered for CEEB Advanced Placement tests.

COSTS AND FINANCIAL AID
Annual tuition $17,600. Required fees $140. Average book expense $1,200. **Required Forms and Deadlines:** FAFSA. Priority financial aid filing date 3/1. **Notification of Awards:** Applicants will be notified of awards on a rolling basis beginning 3/1. **Types of Aid:** *Need-based scholarships/grants:* Federal Pell, SEOG, private scholarships, the school's own gift aid, LEAP, ASG, SMART, TEACH. *Loans:* FFEL Subsidized Stafford, FFEL Unsubsidized Stafford, FFEL PLUS, Federal Perkins, CitiAssist Loans, Sallie Mae Signature Education Loan Program. **Student Employment:** Federal Work-Study Program available. Institutional employment available. Highest amount earned per year

from on-campus jobs $8,056. Off-campus job opportunities are fair. **Financial Aid Statistics:** 67% freshmen, 73% undergrads receive need-based scholarship or grant aid. 7% freshmen, 7% undergrads receive non-need-based scholarship or grant aid. 59% freshmen, 65% undergrads receive need-based self-help aid. 1% freshmen, 2% undergrads receive athletic scholarships. 99% freshmen, 96% undergrads receive any aid. 56% undergrads borrow to pay for school. Average cumulative indebtedness $22,263. **Criteria for awarding institutional aid:** *Non-need-based:* Academics, art, athletics, leadership, religious affiliation.

CHAMPLAIN COLLEGE

163 South Willard Street Box 670, PO Box 670, Burlington, VT 05402-0670
Phone: 802-860-2727 **Financial Aid Phone:** 802-860-2730
E-mail: admission@champlain.edu **CEEB Code:** 3291
Fax: 802-860-2767 **Website:** www.champlain.edu/ **ACT Code:** 3291

This private school was founded in 1878. It has a 19-acre campus.

RATINGS
Admissions Selectivity Rating: 77   **Fire Safety Rating:** 70   **Green Rating:** 60*

STUDENTS AND FACULTY
Enrollment: 1,928. **Student Body:** 50% female, 50% male, 59% out-of-state, international (28 countries represented).
Retention and Graduation: 83% freshmen return for sophomore year. 72% freshmen graduate within 4 years. 10% grads go on to further study within 1 year. 3% grads pursue arts and sciences degrees. 1% grads pursue law degrees. 6% grads pursue business degrees. **Faculty:** Student/faculty ratio 16:1. 65 full-time faculty, 37% hold PhDs, 2% are members of minority groups, 38% are women.

ACADEMICS
Degrees: Associate, bachelor's, certificate, master's, terminal associate, transfer associate. **Classes:** Most classes have 10–19 students. Most lab/discussion sessions have fewer than 10 students. **Majors with Highest Enrollment:** Business/commerce; intermedia/multimedia; liberal arts and sciences/liberal studies. **Special Study Options:** Accelerated program, cross-registration, distance learning, double major, honors program, independent study, internships, liberal arts/career combination, study abroad, teacher certification program. **Honors programs:** Honors Program invitation based on high school GPA and SAT/ACT scores. **Combined degree programs:** 4+1 MBA offered with Clarkson and SNHU. Special programs offered to physically disabled students include note-taking services, reader services, tape recorders, tutors. **Career services:** Career/job search classes, internships.

FACILITIES
Housing: Coed dorms, special housing for international students, women's dorms, Wellness, Performing Arts, International dorm. Suites style singles with common living room and kitchenette for selected sophomores, juniors and seniors. 50% of campus accessible to physically disabled. **Computers:** Students can register for classes online. Administrative functions (other than registration) can be performed online.

CAMPUS LIFE
Environment: Town. **Activities:** Choral groups, dance, drama/theater, literary magazine, musical theater, radio station, student government, student newspaper, television station. **Organizations:** 40 registered organizations, 2 honor societies, 1 religious organizations. **On-Campus Highlights:** Center for Global Technology, The View, Hauke Family Center, Student Life Center, Main Street Suites, Miller Information Commons.

ADMISSIONS
Freshman Academic Profile: Average high school GPA 3. 10% in top 10% of high school class, 15% in top 25% of high school class, 85% in top 50% of high school class. 85% from public high schools. SAT Math middle 50% range 500–610. SAT Critical Reading middle 50% range 500–590. ACT middle 50% range 20–25. Minimum paper TOEFL 500. Minimum computer TOEFL 173. **Basis for Candidate Selection:** *Very important factors considered include:* Application essay, academic GPA, rigor of secondary school record. *Important factors considered include:* Class rank, recommendation(s), standardized test scores, first generation, interview. *Other factors considered include:* Alumni/ae relation, character/personal qualities, extracurricular activities, level of applicant's interest, talent/ability, volunteer work, work experience. **Freshman Admission Requirements:** High school diploma is required and GED is accepted. *Academic units required:* 4 English, 3 mathematics, 3 science, (2 science labs), 4 history, 4 academic electives. *Academic units recommended:* 4 mathematics, 4 science, (3 science labs), 2 foreign language, 2 social studies. **Freshman Admission Statistics:** 2,152 applied, 58% admitted, 43% enrolled. **Transfer Admission Requirements:** High school transcript, college transcript(s), essay or personal

statement, minimum college GPA of 2.0 required. Lowest grade transferable C. **General Admission Information:** Application fee $40. Early decision application deadline 11/15. Regular application deadline 1/31. Regular notification 3/25. Nonfall registration accepted. Admission may be deferred for a maximum of 1 year w no tr. Credit offered for CEEB Advanced Placement tests.

COSTS AND FINANCIAL AID
Annual tuition $22,550. Room and board $10,910. Average book expense $600. **Required Forms and Deadlines:** FAFSA, institution's own financial aid form, state aid form, noncustodial PROFILE. Priority financial aid filing date 5/1. **Notification of Awards:** Applicants will be notified of awards on a rolling basis beginning 3/1. **Types of Aid:** *Need-based scholarships/grants:* Federal Pell, SEOG, state scholarships/grants, private scholarships, the school's own gift aid. *Loans:* FFEL Subsidized Stafford, FFEL Unsubsidized Stafford, FFEL PLUS, Federal Perkins. **Student Employment:** Highest amount earned per year from on-campus jobs $2,211. **Financial Aid Statistics:** 51% freshmen, 44% undergrads receive need-based scholarship or grant aid. 1% freshmen, 1% undergrads receive non-need-based scholarship or grant aid. 63% freshmen, 55% undergrads receive need-based self-help aid. 60% freshmen, 55% undergrads receive any aid. **Criteria for awarding institutional aid:** *Non-need-based:* Academics, leadership.

CHAPMAN UNIVERSITY

One University Drive, Orange, CA 92866
Phone: 714-997-6711 **Financial Aid Phone:** 714-997-6741
E-mail: admit@chapman.edu **CEEB Code:** 4047
Fax: 714-997-6713 **Website:** www.chapman.edu **ACT Code:** 0210

This private school, affiliated with the Disciples of Christ Church, was founded in 1861. It has a 75-acre campus.

RATINGS
Admissions Selectivity Rating: 93   **Fire Safety Rating:** 60*   **Green Rating:** 73

STUDENTS AND FACULTY
Enrollment: 4,437. **Student Body:** 58% female, 42% male, 29% out-of-state, 3% international (60 countries represented). Asian 9%, African American 2%, Caucasian 62%, Hispanic 10%, Native American 1%.
Retention and Graduation: 87% freshmen return for sophomore year. 53% freshmen graduate within 4 years. **Faculty:** Student/faculty ratio 14:1. 349 full-time faculty, 91% hold PhDs, 15% are members of minority groups, 38% are women.

ACADEMICS
Degrees: Bachelor's, master's, post-bachelor's certificate. **Classes:** Most classes have 20–29 students. Most lab/discussion sessions have 10–19 students. **Majors with Highest Enrollment:** Business administration and management; cinematography and film/video production; public relations/image management. **Special Study Options:** Distance learning, double major, English as a Second Language (ESL), honors program, independent study, internships, liberal arts/career combination, student-designed major, study abroad, teacher certification program. **Honors programs:** University Honors Program. **Combined degree programs:** BS/MBA. Special programs offered to physically disabled students include note-taking services, reader services, tape recorders, tutors. **Career services:** Alumni services, career/job search classes, career assessment, internships. Career services highlights include: We are particularly proud of our Internship Program, which strengthens the link between classroom learning and the work world. Chapman's Program allows students to earn academic credit through faculty and site supervisor advisement. Internships offer students the opportunity to increase their understanding of career fields, gain hands-on work experience and learn job skills, build self-confidence, and gain a new perspective. This "real world" experience gives our graduates an edge when they join the work force.

FACILITIES
Housing: Coed dorms, special housing for disabled students, apartments for married students, apartments for single students, houses for married, single, and students with dependents. **Special Academic Facilities/Equipment:** Anderson Center for Economic Research, Leatherby Center for Entrepreneurship and Business Ethics, Schmid Center for International Business, Law and organizational Economics Center, Center for Cold War Studies, Henley Social Science Research Laboratory, Guggenhiem Art gallery, TV studio, film and television production and digital editing studios, Waltmer Theatre, Albert

Schweitzer Collection. **Computers:** 100% of classrooms, 100% of dorms, 100% of libraries, 100% of dining areas, 100% of common outdoor areas have wireless network access. Students can register for classes online. Administrative functions (other than registration) can be performed online.

CAMPUS LIFE
Environment: Metropolis. **Activities:** Choral groups, concert band, dance, drama/theater, jazz band, literary magazine, music ensembles, musical theater, opera, pep band, radio station, student government, student newspaper, student-run film society, symphony orchestra, yearbook, campus ministries, international student organization, Model UN. **Organizations:** 84 registered organizations, 8 honor societies, 8 religious organizations. 6 fraternities, 6 sororities. **Athletics (Intercollegiate):** *Men:* Baseball, basketball, cross-country, football, golf, soccer, tennis, water polo. *Women:* Basketball, crew/rowing, cross-country, soccer, softball, swimming, tennis, track/field (outdoor), volleyball, water polo. **On-Campus Highlights:** Marion Knott Film Studios, Leatherby Libraries, Liberty Plaza, Beckman Hall, All-Faiths Chapel. **Environmental Initiatives:** Adoption of LEED standards in new building projects. Expanded commitment to reduce use and increase recycling of paper. Investment in energy-saving devices and new requirement of Energy Star rating on newly purchased electronic devices and appliances.

ADMISSIONS
Freshman Academic Profile: Average high school GPA 3.67. 48% in top 10% of high school class, 90% in top 25% of high school class, 99% in top 50% of high school class. 70% from public high schools. SAT Math middle 50% range 568–678. SAT Critical Reading middle 50% range 547–661. SAT Writing middle 50% range 557–671. ACT middle 50% range 25–29. Minimum paper TOEFL 550. Minimum computer TOEFL 213. **Basis for Candidate Selection:** *Very important factors considered include:* Class rank, application essay, academic GPA, rigor of secondary school record, standardized test scores, character/personal qualities. *Important factors considered include:* Extracurricular activities, talent/ability, volunteer work. *Other factors considered include:* Recommendation(s), alumni/ae relation, first generation, geographical residence, racial/ethnic status, state residency, work experience. **Freshman Admission Requirements:** High school diploma is required and GED is accepted. *Academic units required:* 2 English, 2 mathematics, 2 science, (1 science labs), 2 foreign language, 3 social studies. *Academic units recommended:* 4 English, 3 mathematics, 3 science, (1 science labs), 3 foreign language, 4 social studies. **Freshman Admission Statistics:** 6,159 applied, 56% admitted, 30% enrolled. **Transfer Admission Requirements:** college transcript(s), essay or personal statement, minimum college GPA of 2.5 required. Lowest grade transferable C–. **General Admission Information:** Application fee $55. Regular application deadline 1/15. Notification on a rolling basis, beginning on or about 3/15. Nonfall registration accepted. Credit and/or placement offered for CEEB Advanced Placement tests.

COSTS AND FINANCIAL AID
Annual tuition $35,790. Room and board $12,832. Required fees $974. Average book expense $1,200. **Required Forms and Deadlines:** FAFSA, state aid form. Priority financial aid filing date 3/2. **Notification of Awards:** Applicants will be notified of awards on a rolling basis beginning 3/15. **Types of Aid:** *Need-based scholarships/grants:* Federal Pell, SEOG, state scholarships/grants, private scholarships, the school's own gift aid, Academic Competitiveness Grants. *Loans:* FFEL Subsidized Stafford, FFEL Unsubsidized Stafford, FFEL PLUS, Federal Perkins. **Student Employment:** Federal Work-Study Program available. Institutional employment available. Off-campus job opportunities are excellent. **Financial Aid Statistics:** 59% freshmen, 58% undergrads receive need-based scholarship or grant aid. 48% freshmen, 50% undergrads receive need-based self-help aid. 64% undergrads borrow to pay for school. Average cumulative indebtedness $23,917. **Criteria for awarding institutional aid:** *Non-need-based:* Academics, alumni affiliation, art, music/drama, religious affiliation.

See page 1052.

CHARLESTON SOUTHERN UNIVERSITY

Enrollment Services, PO Box 118087, Charleston, SC 29423
Phone: 843-863-7050 **Financial Aid Phone:** 843-863-7050
E-mail: enroll@csuniv.edu **CEEB Code:** 5079
Fax: 843-863-7070 **Website:** www.charlestonsouthern.edu **ACT Code:** 3833

This private school, affiliated with the Southern Baptist Church, was founded in 1964. It has a 300-acre campus.

RATINGS
Admissions Selectivity Rating: 77   **Fire Safety Rating:** 60*   **Green Rating:** 60*

STUDENTS AND FACULTY

Enrollment: 2,473. **Student Body:** 61% female, 39% male, 18% out-of-state, 2% international (30 countries represented). Asian 2%, African American 27%, Caucasian 55%, Hispanic 1%, Native American 1%.
Retention and Graduation: 60% freshmen return for sophomore year. 22% freshmen graduate within 4 years. 14% grads go on to further study within 1 year. **Faculty:** Student/faculty ratio 18:1. 107 full-time faculty, 63% hold PhDs, 2% are members of minority groups, 45% are women.

ACADEMICS

Degrees: Bachelor's, master's. **Classes:** Most classes have 20–29 students. Most lab/discussion sessions have 20–29 students. **Majors with Highest Enrollment:** Business/commerce; elementary education and teaching; psychology; **Special Study Options:** Accelerated program, cooperative education program, cross-registration, distance learning, double major, dual enrollment, honors program, internships, study abroad, teacher certification program, other special programs: Evening Division. **Honors programs:** SAT 1200 or higher or ACT 27 or higher and high school GPA of 3.50 or higher. **Combined degree programs:** BA/MD, Allied health tech with Medical U of S. Carolina. Special programs offered to physically disabled students include note-taking services, reader services, tape recorders, tutors. **Career services:** Career assessment, internships. **Career services highlights include:** Applied Learning internships for credit.

FACILITIES

Housing: Men's dorms, women's dorms. 80% of campus accessible to physically disabled. **Special Academic Facilities/Equipment:** Earthquake Education Center; computer labs w/ wireless Internet; nursing clinical lab, specialized music rehearsal modules and advanced music keyboard technology. **Computers:** Students can register for classes online. Administrative functions (other than registration) can be performed online.

CAMPUS LIFE

Environment: Metropolis. **Activities:** Choral groups, concert band, dance, drama/theater, jazz band, literary magazine, marching band, music ensembles, musical theater, pep band, student government, student newspaper, yearbook. **Organizations:** 22 registered organizations, 3 honor societies, 4 religious organizations. **Athletics (Intercollegiate):** *Men:* Baseball, basketball, cross-country, football, golf, tennis, track/field (outdoor), track/field (indoor). *Women:* Basketball, cross-country, golf, soccer, softball, tennis, track/field (outdoor), track/field (indoor), volleyball.

ADMISSIONS

Freshman Academic Profile: Average high school GPA 3.3. 18% in top 10% of high school class, 47% in top 25% of high school class, 80% in top 50% of high school class. 81% from public high schools. SAT Math middle 50% range 480–570. SAT Critical Reading middle 50% range 490–570. ACT middle 50% range 20–24. Minimum paper TOEFL 550. Minimum computer TOEFL 213. **Basis for Candidate Selection:** *Very important factors considered include:* Rigor of secondary school record, standardized test scores. *Important factors considered include:* Class rank. *Other factors considered include:* Application essay, recommendation(s), character/personal qualities, extracurricular activities, interview, religious affiliation/commitment, talent/ability, work experience. **Freshman Admission Requirements:** High school diploma is required and GED is accepted. *Academic units required:* 4 English, 3 mathematics, 3 science, (2 science labs), 3 history, 3 academic electives. *Academic units recommended:* 4 English, 4 mathematics, 3 science, (2 science labs), 2 foreign language. **Freshman Admission Statistics:** 2,283 applied, 72% admitted, 47% enrolled. **Transfer Admission Requirements:** college transcript(s), statement of good standing from prior institution(s). Minimum college GPA of 2.0 required. Lowest grade transferable C. **General Admission Information:** Application fee $30. Nonfall registration accepted. Credit and/or placement offered for CEEB Advanced Placement tests.

COSTS AND FINANCIAL AID

Average book expense $1,000. **Required Forms and Deadlines:** FAFSA. Priority financial aid filing date 4/15. **Notification of Awards:** Applicants will be notified of awards on a rolling basis beginning 2/1. **Types of Aid:** *Need-based scholarships/grants:* Federal Pell, SEOG, state scholarships/grants, private scholarships, the school's own gift aid. *Loans:* Direct Subsidized Stafford, Direct Unsubsidized Stafford, Direct PLUS, FFEL Subsidized Stafford, FFEL PLUS, Federal Perkins, state loans. **Student Employment:** Highest amount earned per year from on-campus jobs $2,000. **Financial Aid Statistics:** 85% freshmen, 79% undergrads receive need-based scholarship or grant aid. 12% freshmen, 11% undergrads receive non-need-based scholarship or grant aid. 69% freshmen, 63% undergrads receive need-based self-help aid. 4% freshmen, 4% undergrads receive athletic scholarships. **Criteria for awarding institutional aid:** *Non-need-based:* Academics, alumni affiliation, art, athletics, leadership, music/drama, religious affiliation, state/district residency.

CHARTER OAK STATE COLLEGE

55 Paul J. Manafort Drive, New Britain, CT 06053-2142
Phone: 860-832-3800 **Financial Aid Phone:** 860-832-3872
E-mail: info@charteroak.edu
Fax: 860-832-3800

This public school was founded in 1973.

RATINGS

Admissions Selectivity Rating: 60* **Fire Safety Rating:** 60* **Green Rating:** 60*

STUDENTS AND FACULTY

Enrollment: 1,557. **Student Body:** 60% female, 40% male, 53% out-of-state, international (4 countries represented). Asian 1%, African American 12%, Caucasian 64%, Hispanic 6%, Native American 1%.
Retention and Graduation: Faculty: Student/faculty ratio 11:1.

ACADEMICS

Degrees: Associate, bachelor's, transfer associate. **Special Study Options:** Distance learning, external degree program, independent study, liberal arts/career combination, student-designed major .

FACILITIES

Housing: 100% of campus accessible to physically disabled. **Computers:** Students can register for classes online. Administrative functions (other than registration) can be performed online.

CAMPUS LIFE

Environment: Village.

ADMISSIONS

Freshman Admission Requirements: High school diploma is required and GED is accepted. **Transfer Admission Requirements:** College transcript(s), lowest grade transferable D. **General Admission Information:** Application fee $75. Nonfall registration not accepted. Admission may be deferred for a maximum of 1 year. Credit offered for CEEB Advanced Placement tests.

COSTS AND FINANCIAL AID

Required Forms and Deadlines: FAFSA, institution's own financial aid form, Contractual Consortium Agreement form and course approval form, if applicable. **Notification of Awards:** Applicants will be notified of awards on a rolling basis beginning 8/15. **Types of Aid:** *Need-based scholarships/grants:* Federal Pell, state scholarships/grants, private scholarships, the school's own gift aid. *Loans:* FFEL Subsidized Stafford, FFEL Unsubsidized Stafford, FFEL PLUS.

CHATHAM UNIVERSITY

Woodland Road, Pittsburgh, PA 15232
Phone: 412-365-1290 **Financial Aid Phone:** 412-365-2797
E-mail: admissions@chatham.edu **CEEB Code:** 2081
Fax: 412-365-1609 **Website:** www.chatham.edu **ACT Code:** 3538

This private school was founded in 1869. It has a 39388-acre campus.

RATINGS

Admissions Selectivity Rating: 77 **Fire Safety Rating:** 67 **Green Rating:** 98

STUDENTS AND FACULTY

Enrollment: 771. **Student Body:** 99% female, 1% male, 19% out-of-state, 6% international (26 countries represented). Asian 2%, African American 12%, Caucasian 67%, Hispanic 2%.
Retention and Graduation: 71% freshmen return for sophomore year. 51% freshmen graduate within 4 years. **Faculty:** Student/faculty ratio 9:1. 88 full-time faculty, 97% hold PhDs, 5% are members of minority groups, 64% are women.

ACADEMICS

Degrees: Bachelor's, master's, post-bachelor's certificate, post-master's certificate. **Classes:** Most classes have 10–19 students. Most lab/discussion sessions have 10–19 students. **Majors with Highest Enrollment:** Biology/biological sciences; English language and literature; psychology. **Special Study Options:** Accelerated program, cooperative education program, cross-registration, distance learning, double major, dual enrollment, English as a Second Language (ESL), exchange student program (domestic), honors program, independent study, internships, liberal arts/career combination, student-designed major, study abroad, teacher certification program, five-year bachelors/masters programs, five-year bachelors/masters programs also available with Carnegie Mellon (e.g, engineering, public policy) and other institutions. **Honors programs:** The Chatham Scholars Program offers students a challenging, integrated curriculum with special opportunities for enrichment, mentoring, and networking. **Combined degree programs:** BA/MA, 3-2 b/m in 9 fields and 4-2 b/doctorate in phys therapy. Special programs offered to physically disabled students include note-taking services, reader services, tape recorders, tutors. **Career services:** Alumni network, alumni services, career/job search classes, career assessment, internships.

FACILITIES

Housing: women's dorms, apartments for married students, apartments for single students, theme housing 75% of campus accessible to physically disabled. **Special Academic Facilities/Equipment:** Athletic and Fitness Center; Art and Design Center; broadcast studio; art gallery, classroom space, and coffee shop; campus arboretum and greenhouse; proscenium theater. **Computers:** 100% of classrooms, 20% of dorms, 100% of libraries, 100% of dining areas, 100% of student union, 75% of common outdoor areas have wireless network access. Students can register for classes online. Administrative functions (other than registration) can be performed online. Undergraduates are required to own a computer.

CAMPUS LIFE

Environment: Metropolis. **Activities:** Choral groups, dance, drama/theater, literary magazine, music ensembles, musical theater, student government, student newspaper, yearbook. **Organizations:** 25 registered organizations, 10 honor societies, 6 religious organizations. **Athletics (Intercollegiate):** *Women:* Basketball, cross-country, ice hockey, soccer, softball, swimming, tennis, volleyball, water polo **On-Campus Highlights:** New coffee shop and art gallery, Athletic and Fitness Center, Art and Design Center, Science Complex, Campus Arboretum, many of the campus residence halls are renovated historic mansions. The campus also features an outdoor meditation labyrinth, the largest in Pittsburgh. The Shadyside Campus on Woodland Road is a registered arboretum, with over 120 distinct tree species. **Environmental Initiatives:** The creation of the School of Sustainability and the Environment. The new School will provide innovative, interdisciplinary education and research opportunities for undergraduate, graduate and professional students to better prepare them to identify and solve challenges related to the environment and sustainability. Sustainable dining initiatives, including composting of pre- and post-consumer food waste, trayless dining, compostable serveware at all dining locations, vegan and vegetarian selections at all meals, no bovine growth hormone, locally-sourced food whenever possible, CSA for campus community, organic on-campus garden. Environmentally-friendly transportation initiatives, including public transit pass full subsidy, biofuel shuttle fleet for inter-campus travel, and bicycle support services that include a bike repair shop.

ADMISSIONS

Freshman Academic Profile: Average high school GPA 3.35. 14.6% in top 10% of high school class, 35.4% in top 25% of high school class, 73.2% in top 50% of high school class. SAT Math middle 50% range 458–583. SAT Critical Reading middle 50% range 478–600. SAT Writing middle 50% range 470–603. ACT middle 50% range 22–25. Minimum paper TOEFL 550. Minimum computer TOEFL 210. Minimum web-based TOEFL 79. **Basis for Candidate Selection:** *Very important factors considered include:* Rigor of secondary school record. *Important factors considered include:* Application essay, academic GPA. *Other factors considered include:* Class rank, recommendation(s), standardized test scores, alumni/ae relation, character/personal qualities, extracurricular activities, interview, level of applicant's interest, talent/ability, volunteer work, work experience. **Freshman Admission Requirements:** High school diploma is required and GED is accepted. *Academic units required:* 4 English, 2 mathematics, 2 science, 3 social science. *Academic units recommended:* 4 English, 3 mathematics, 3 science, 2 foreign language, 3 social science. **Freshman Admission Statistics:** 641 applied, 68% admitted, 30% enrolled. **Transfer Admission Requirements:** College transcript(s), essay or personal statement, minimum college GPA of 2.0 required. Lowest grade transferable C–. **General Admission Information:** Application fee $35. Regular application deadline 8/1. Notification on a rolling basis, beginning on or about 10/15. Nonfall registration accepted. Admission may be deferred for a maximum of 1 year. Credit offered for CEEB Advanced Placement tests.

COSTS AND FINANCIAL AID

Annual tuition $27,006. Room and board $8,700. Required fees $1,020. Average book expense $860. **Required Forms and Deadlines:** FAFSA. Priority financial aid filing date 5/1. **Notification of Awards:** Applicants will be notified of awards on a rolling basis beginning 2/15. **Types of Aid:** *Need-based scholarships/grants:* Federal Pell, SEOG, state scholarships/grants, private scholarships, the school's own gift aid, United Negro College Fund. *Loans:* FFEL Subsidized Stafford, FFEL Unsubsidized Stafford, FFEL PLUS, Federal Perkins. **Student Employment:** Federal Work-Study Program available. Institutional employment available. Highest amount earned per year from on-campus jobs

$2,200. Off-campus job opportunities are good. **Financial Aid Statistics:** 67% freshmen, 64% undergrads receive need-based scholarship or grant aid. 84% freshmen, 75% undergrads receive non-need-based scholarship or grant aid. 76% freshmen, 73% undergrads receive need-based self-help aid. 98% freshmen, 98% undergrads receive any aid. **Criteria for awarding institutional aid:** *Non-need-based:* Academics, alumni affiliation, leadership, minority status.

CHESTNUT HILL COLLEGE

9601 Germantown Avenue, Philadelphia, PA 19118-2693
Phone: 215-248-7001 **Financial Aid Phone:** 215-248-7182
E-mail: chcapply@chc.edu **CEEB Code:** 2082
Fax: 215-248-7082 **Website:** www.chc.edu **ACT Code:** 3540

This private school, affiliated with the Roman Catholic Church, was founded in 1924. It has a 75-acre campus.

RATINGS

Admissions Selectivity Rating: 72   **Fire Safety Rating:** 86   **Green Rating:** 65

STUDENTS AND FACULTY

Enrollment: 1,277. **Student Body:** 70% female, 30% male, 32% out-of-state, 1% international (24 countries represented). Asian 2%, African American 39%, Caucasian 49%, Hispanic 5%.
Retention and Graduation: 70% freshmen return for sophomore year. 40% grads go on to further study within 1 year. 30% grads pursue arts and sciences degrees. 2% grads pursue law degrees. 6% grads pursue business degrees. 3% grads pursue medical degrees. **Faculty:** Student/faculty ratio 10:1. 76 full-time faculty, 82% hold PhDs, 8% are members of minority groups, 68% are women.

ACADEMICS

Degrees: Associate, bachelor's, certificate, master's, post-bachelor's certificate, post-master's certificate, transfer associate. **Classes:** Most classes have 10–19 students. Most lab/discussion sessions have 10–19 students. **Majors with Highest Enrollment:** Business administration and management; elementary education and teaching; human services. **Special Study Options:** Cooperative education program, cross-registration, double major, dual enrollment, English as a Second Language (ESL), exchange student program (domestic), honors program, independent study, internships, student-designed major, study abroad, teacher certification program, upperclass undergraduates may take graduate classes. **Honors programs:** Interdisciplinary Honors Program for outstanding incoming first year students offers team-taught interdisciplinary seminars emphaisizing discussion and writing which satisfy general education requirements. Departmental Honors challenges students in the junior and senior year to complete an independent research project in their major field. **Combined degree programs:** BA/MA, BS/MEd, MA/PsyD, BS/DPM, BS/BS med tech, BS/MS Human Services. Special programs offered to physically disabled students include reader services, tutors. **Career services:** Alumni network, career/job search classes, career assessment, internships. Career services highlights include: Chestnut Hill College encourages all students to participate in some form of experiential learning. Internships are available in a large number of majors and work areas.

FACILITIES

Housing: Coed dorms. On-campus housing includes singles, doubles, suites, and apartment-like units. A new main campus residence hall opened in Fall 2006 and a renovated building opened as a residence hall on the SugarLoaf Hill campus in 2008. 80% of campus accessible to physically disabled. **Special Academic Facilities/Equipment:** Rare book collection, Irish literature collection, observatory, planetarium. **Computers:** 40% of classrooms, 100% of dorms, 100% of libraries, have wireless network access. Students can register for classes online. Undergraduates are required to own a computer.

CAMPUS LIFE

Environment: Metropolis. **Activities:** Choral groups, drama/theater, jazz band, literary magazine, music ensembles, musical theater, opera, student government, student newspaper, symphony orchestra, television station, yearbook, campus ministries, international student organization. **Organizations:** 19 registered organizations, 14 honor societies, 1 religious organizations. **Athletics (Intercollegiate):** *Men:* Baseball, basketball, cross-country, golf, lacrosse, soccer, tennis. *Women:* Basketball, cross-country, golf, lacrosse, soccer, softball, tennis, volleyball. **On-Campus Highlights:** Martino Hall (smart classrooms, gym), Griffin's Den, Fitzsimmons Hall (new residence hall), Dining Hall, Rotunda of Saint Joseph Hall, SugarLoaf Hill, a 32-acre recent addition to campus, will soon provide additional space for many campus activities. **Environmental Initiatives:** Recycling program; Go Green Committee.

ADMISSIONS

Freshman Academic Profile: Average high school GPA 3.02. 9% in top 10% of high school class, 29% in top 25% of high school class, 67% in top 50% of high school class. 50% from public high schools. SAT Math middle 50% range 470–540. SAT Critical Reading middle 50% range 460–540. SAT Writing middle 50% range 440–530. ACT middle 50% range 19–20. Minimum paper TOEFL 500. **Basis for Candidate Selection:** *Very important factors considered include:* Application essay, rigor of secondary school record. *Important factors considered include:* Academic GPA, recommendation(s), standardized test scores, character/personal qualities, extracurricular activities, interview. *Other factors considered include:* Class rank, alumni/ae relation, level of applicant's interest, talent/ability, volunteer work, work experience. **Freshman Admission Requirements:** High school diploma is required and GED is accepted. *Academic units recommended:* 4 English, 3 mathematics, 3 science, 2 foreign language, 4 social studies. **Freshman Admission Statistics:** 1,589 applied, 72% admitted, 17% enrolled. **Transfer Admission Requirements:** College transcript(s), essay or personal statement, minimum college GPA of 2.0 required. Lowest grade transferable C. **General Admission Information:** Application fee $35. Early decision application deadline 12/10. Notification on a rolling basis, beginning on or about 9/1. Nonfall registration accepted. Admission may be deferred for a maximum of 1 year. Credit and/or placement offered for CEEB Advanced Placement tests.

COSTS AND FINANCIAL AID

Annual tuition $27,000. Room and board $8,800. Required fees $100. Average book expense $1,100. **Required Forms and Deadlines:** FAFSA. Financial aid filing deadline 4/15. Priority financial aid filing date 4/15. **Notification of Awards:** Applicants will be notified of awards on a rolling basis beginning 1/31. **Types of Aid:** *Need-based scholarships/grants:* Federal Pell, SEOG, state scholarships/grants, private scholarships, the school's own gift aid. *Loans:* FFEL Subsidized Stafford, FFEL Unsubsidized Stafford, FFEL PLUS, Federal Perkins. **Student Employment:** Federal Work-Study Program available. Highest amount earned per year from on-campus jobs $1,500. Off-campus job opportunities are good. **Financial Aid Statistics:** 80% freshmen, 59% undergrads receive need-based scholarship or grant aid. 12% freshmen, 8% undergrads receive non-need-based scholarship or grant aid. 68% freshmen, 50% undergrads receive need-based self-help aid. 7% freshmen, 4% undergrads receive athletic scholarships. 80% freshmen, 60% undergrads receive any aid. **Criteria for awarding institutional aid:** *Non-need-based:* Academics, alumni affiliation, athletics, leadership, religious affiliation.

CHEYNEY UNIVERSITY OF PENNSYLVANIA

1837 University Circle, Cheyney, PA 19319
Phone: 610-399-2275 **Financial Aid Phone:** 610- 399-2302
E-mail: abrown@cheyney.edu **CEEB Code:** 2648
Fax: 610-399-2099 **Website:** www.cheyney.edu

This public school was founded in 1837. It has a 275-acre campus.

RATINGS

Admissions Selectivity Rating: 68   **Fire Safety Rating:** 92   **Green Rating:** 92

STUDENTS AND FACULTY

Enrollment: 1,339. **Student Body:** 53% female, 47% male, 22% out-of-state, international (4 countries represented). African American 92%, Caucasian 1%, Hispanic 1%.
Retention and Graduation: 60% freshmen return for sophomore year.
Faculty: Student/faculty ratio 15:1. 75 full-time faculty, 79% are members of minority groups, 48% are women.

ACADEMICS

Degrees: Associate, bachelor's, master's, post-bachelor's certificate. **Majors with Highest Enrollment:** Business administration and management; communication studies/speech communication and rhetoric; social sciences. **Special Study Options:** Cooperative education program, cross-registration, distance learning, double major, honors program, independent study, internships, study abroad, teacher certification program. **Honors programs:** Keystone Honors Program. Special programs offered to physically disabled students include note-taking services, tape recorders, tutors. **Career services:** Alumni services, career/job search classes, internships.

FACILITIES

Housing: Coed dorms, men's dorms, women's dorms, Honors dorm. 60% of campus accessible to physically disabled. **Special Academic Facilities/Equipment:** Afro-American history/culture collection, planetarium, weather station, satellite communication network. **Computers:** 60% of classrooms, 100% of libraries, 100% of student union, 20% of common outdoor areas have wireless network access. Students can register for classes online. Administrative functions (other than registration) can be performed online.

CAMPUS LIFE

Environment: Village. **Activities:** Choral groups, drama/theater, jazz band, marching band, music ensembles, radio station, student government, student newspaper, student-run film society, television station, yearbook. **Organizations:** 30 registered organizations, 12 honor societies, 1 religious organizations. 5 fraternities, 4 sororities. **Athletics (Intercollegiate):** *Men:* Basketball, cross-country, football, tennis, track/field (outdoor), wrestling. *Women:* Basketball, bowling, cross-country, tennis, track/field (outdoor), volleyball. **On-Campus Highlights:** Athletics, Culinary Arts, Communication Arts, dorms, bookstore. **Environmental Initiatives:** Recycling Oils Conversion-Biofuels Energy Conservation-Electric Power.

ADMISSIONS

Freshman Academic Profile: Average high school GPA 2.4. 6% in top 10% of high school class, 15% in top 25% of high school class, 46% in top 50% of high school class. SAT Math middle 50% range 320–410. SAT Critical Reading middle 50% range 330–420. SAT Writing middle 50% range 320–405. ACT middle 50% range 14–21. Minimum paper TOEFL 500. **Basis for Candidate Selection:** *Very important factors considered include:* Recommendation(s), rigor of secondary school record. *Important factors considered include:* Class rank, application essay, standardized test scores, extracurricular activities, interview, state residency. *Other factors considered include:* Racial/ethnic status, talent/ability. **Freshman Admission Requirements:** High school diploma is required and GED is accepted. *Academic units required:* 4 English, 3 mathematics, 2 science, 2 foreign language, 2 history. **Freshman Admission Statistics:** 3,298 applied, 50% admitted, 37% enrolled. **Transfer Admission Requirements:** college transcript(s), interview, statement of good standing from prior institution(s). Minimum college GPA of 2.0 required. Lowest grade transferable C. **General Admission Information:** Application fee $20. Regular application deadline 3/31. Nonfall registration accepted. Admission may be deferred for a maximum of 1 year. Placement offered for CEEB Advanced Placement tests.

COSTS AND FINANCIAL AID

Required Forms and Deadlines: FAFSA. Priority financial aid filing date 4/1. **Notification of Awards:** Applicants will be notified of awards on a rolling basis beginning 3/15. **Types of Aid:** *Need-based scholarships/grants:* Federal Pell, SEOG, state scholarships/grants, private scholarships, the school's own gift aid. *Loans:* FFEL Subsidized Stafford, FFEL Unsubsidized Stafford, FFEL PLUS, Federal Perkins. **Student Employment:** Federal Work-Study Program available. Institutional employment available. Off-campus job opportunities are good. **Financial Aid Statistics:** 71% freshmen, 71% undergrads receive need-based scholarship or grant aid. 26% freshmen, 28% undergrads receive non-need-based scholarship or grant aid. 68% freshmen, 71% undergrads receive need-based self-help aid. 96% undergrads borrow to pay for school. Average cumulative indebtedness $27,000. **Criteria for awarding institutional aid:** *Non-need-based:* Academics, alumni affiliation, athletics, minority status.

CHICAGO STATE UNIVERSITY

9501 South Street King Drive, ADM-200, Chicago, IL 60628
Phone: 773-995-2513 **Financial Aid Phone:**
E-mail: ug-Admissions@csu.edu
Fax: 773-995-3820 **Website:** www.csu.edu **ACT Code:** 1694

This public school was founded in 1867. It has a 161-acre campus.

RATINGS

Admissions Selectivity Rating: 71   **Fire Safety Rating:** 60*   **Green Rating:** 60*

STUDENTS AND FACULTY

Enrollment: 4,818. **Student Body:** 73% female, 27% male, 2% out-of-state, international. Asian 1%, African American 87%, Caucasian 3%, Hispanic 6%.
Retention and Graduation: Faculty: Student/faculty ratio 13:1. 322 full-time faculty, 61% are members of minority groups, 51% are women.

ACADEMICS

Degrees: Bachelor's, master's, post-bachelor's certificate. **Classes:** Most classes have 20–29 students. **Majors with Highest Enrollment:** Elementary education and teaching; liberal arts and sciences/liberal studies; nursing/registered nurse (RN, ASN, BSN, MSN). **Special Study Options:** Cooperative education program, distance learning, double major, English as a Second Language (ESL), honors program, independent study, internships, student-designed major, study abroad, teacher certification program, programs for mature adults (University Without Walls, Individual Curriculum, and Board of Governors degree program). Special programs offered to physically disabled students include note-taking services, reader services, tape recorders, tutors. **Career services:** Alumni services, career/job search classes, career assessment, internships.

FACILITIES
Housing: Coed dorms. 51% of campus accessible to physically disabled. **Special Academic Facilities/Equipment:** Art gallery; electron microscopes; greenhouse. **Computers:** Students can register for classes online.

CAMPUS LIFE
Activities: Choral groups, concert band, dance, drama/theater, jazz band, literary magazine, music ensembles, radio station, student government, student newspaper, television station. **Organizations:** 47 registered organizations, 30 honor societies, 4 religious organizations. 4 fraternities, 4 sororities. **Athletics (Intercollegiate):** *Men:* Baseball, basketball, cross-country, golf, tennis, track/field (outdoor), track/field (indoor). *Women:* Basketball, cross-country, golf, tennis, track/field (outdoor), track/field (indoor), volleyball.

ADMISSIONS
Freshman Academic Profile: Average high school GPA 2.69. 13% in top 10% of high school class, 35% in top 25% of high school class, 64% in top 50% of high school class. 80% from public high schools. ACT middle 50% range 16–19. Minimum paper TOEFL 500. **Basis for Candidate Selection:** *Very important factors considered include:* Rigor of secondary school record, standardized test scores. **Freshman Admission Requirements:** High school diploma is required and GED is accepted. *Academic units required:* 4 English, 3 mathematics, 3 science, 3 social studies, 2 academic electives. **Freshman Admission Statistics:** 3,949 applied, 56% admitted, 25% enrolled. **Transfer Admission Requirements:** college transcript(s), minimum college GPA of 2.0 required. Lowest grade transferable D. **General Admission Information:** Application fee $25. Regular application deadline 7/15. Nonfall registration accepted. Admission may be deferred for a maximum of 1 semester. Credit and/or placement offered for CEEB Advanced Placement tests.

COSTS AND FINANCIAL AID
Annual in-state tuition $3,762. Annual out-of-state tuition $8,448. Room and board $5,700. Required fees $1,060. Average book expense $1,400. **Required Forms and Deadlines:** FAFSA, institution's own financial aid form. **Notification of Awards:** Applicants will be notified of awards on a rolling basis beginning 3/1. **Types of Aid:** *Need-based scholarships/grants:* Federal Pell, SEOG, state scholarships/grants, private scholarships, the school's own gift aid. *Loans:* FFEL Subsidized Stafford, FFEL Unsubsidized Stafford, FFEL PLUS, Federal Perkins. **Student Employment:** Federal Work-Study Program available. Institutional employment available. Highest amount earned per year from on-campus jobs $2,000. Off-campus job opportunities are good. **Financial Aid Statistics:** 73% freshmen, 82% undergrads receive need-based scholarship or grant aid. 2% undergrads receive non-need-based scholarship or grant aid. 26% freshmen, 45% undergrads receive need-based self-help aid. **Criteria for awarding institutional aid:** *Non-need-based:* Academics, athletics, state/district residency.

CHOWAN UNIVERSITY

One University Place, Murfreesboro, NC 27855
Phone: 252-398-1236 **Financial Aid Phone:** 252-398-6513
E-mail: admissions@chowan.edu
Fax: 252-398-1190 **Website:** www.chowan.edu

This is a private school.

RATINGS
Admissions Selectivity Rating: 73   **Fire Safety Rating:** 61   **Green Rating:** 60*

STUDENTS AND FACULTY
Enrollment: 886. **Student Body:** 46% female, 54% male, 48% out-of-state. **Retention and Graduation:** 54% freshmen return for sophomore year. 18% freshmen graduate within 4 years. 5% grads go on to further study within 1 year. 2% grads pursue arts and sciences degrees. 1% grads pursue law degrees. 1% grads pursue business degrees. 1% grads pursue medical degrees. **Faculty:** Student/faculty ratio 16:1. 47 full-time faculty, 64% hold PhDs, 11% are members of minority groups, 43% are women.

ACADEMICS
Degrees: Associate, bachelor's, terminal associate. **Classes:** Most classes have fewer than 10 students. **Majors with Highest Enrollment:** Business/commerce; graphic communications; health services/allied health/health sciences. **Special Study Options:** Distance learning, double major, dual enrollment, honors program, independent study, internships, liberal arts/career combination, study abroad, teacher certification program. **Honors programs:** Honors

College Special programs offered to physically disabled students include note-taking services, reader services, tape recorders, tutors. **Career services:** Internships. **Career services highlights include:** Business Administration internships.

FACILITIES
Housing: Special housing for disabled students, men's dorms, women's dorms 80% of campus accessible to physically disabled. **Special Academic Facilities/Equipment:** Antiquities Room in Whitaker Library Ward Parlor in McDowell Columns Building, Green Hall Art Gallery, Daniel Hall Recital Hall. **Computers:** Students can register for classes online. Administrative functions (other than registration) can be performed online.

CAMPUS LIFE
Activities: Choral groups, concert band, drama/theater, jazz band, literary magazine, music ensembles, pep band, student government, yearbook. **Organizations:** 52 registered organizations, 5 honor societies, 2 religious organizations. 2 fraternities, 2 sororities. **Athletics (Intercollegiate):** *Men:* Baseball, basketball, cheerleading, football, golf, soccer, tennis. *Women:* Basketball, cheerleading, cross-country, golf, soccer, softball, tennis, volleyball. **On-Campus Highlights:** McDowell Columns Building (historic landmark), Jesse Helms Athletic Center, Jenkins Center for Health, Whitaker Library, McSweeney Computer Center.

ADMISSIONS
Freshman Academic Profile: Average high school GPA 2.6. 4% in top 10% of high school class, 35% in top 50% of high school class. 95% from public high schools. SAT Math middle 50% range 380–490. SAT Critical Reading middle 50% range 380–480. ACT middle 50% range 15–19. Minimum paper TOEFL 450. Minimum computer TOEFL 133. **Basis for Candidate Selection:** *Very important factors considered include:* Academic GPA, rigor of secondary school record, standardized test scores. *Other factors considered include:* Class rank, application essay, recommendation(s), alumni/ae relation, character/personal qualities, extracurricular activities, interview, level of applicant's interest, talent/ability, volunteer work, work experience. **Freshman Admission Requirements:** High school diploma is required and GED is accepted. *Academic units recommended:* 4 English, 3 mathematics, 2 science, (2 science labs), 3 social studies, 7 academic electives. **Freshman Admission Statistics:** 2,385 applied, 61% admitted, 24% enrolled. **Transfer Admission Requirements:** High school transcript, college transcript(s), statement of good standing from prior institution(s). Minimum college GPA of 2.0 required. Lowest grade transferable C. **General Admission Information:** Application fee $20. Notification on a rolling basis, beginning on or about 3/1. Nonfall registration accepted. Admission may be deferred for a maximum of 1 year. Credit and/or placement offered for CEEB Advanced Placement tests.

COSTS AND FINANCIAL AID
Annual tuition $15,800. Room and board $6,800. Required fees $240. Average book expense $885. **Required Forms and Deadlines:** FAFSA. Financial aid filing deadline 8/1. Priority financial aid filing date 5/1. **Notification of Awards:** Applicants will be notified of awards on a rolling basis beginning 3/1. **Types of Aid:** *Need-based scholarships/grants:* SEOG, state scholarships/grants, private scholarships, the school's own gift aid. *Loans:* FFEL Unsubsidized Stafford, FFEL PLUS, college/university loans from institutional funds, Alternative Loans. **Student Employment:** Federal Work-Study Program available. Institutional employment available. Highest amount earned per year from on-campus jobs $700. Off-campus job opportunities are fair. **Financial Aid Statistics:** 80% freshmen, 83% undergrads receive need-based scholarship or grant aid. 6% freshmen, 7% undergrads receive non-need-based scholarship or grant aid. 75% freshmen, 76% undergrads receive need-based self-help aid. 86% freshmen, 86% undergrads receive any aid. 80% undergrads borrow to pay for school. Average cumulative indebtedness $17,275. **Criteria for awarding institutional aid:** *Non-need-based:* Academics, leadership, music/drama, religious affiliation, state/district residency.

CHRISTENDOM COLLEGE

134 Christendom Drive, Front Royal, VA 22630
Phone: 540-636-2900 **Financial Aid Phone:** 800-877-5456
E-mail: admissions@christendom.edu **CEEB Code:** 5691
Fax: 540-636-1655 **Website:** www.christendom.edu **ACT Code:** 4339

This private school, affiliated with the Roman Catholic Church, was founded in 1977. It has a 100-acre campus.

RATINGS
Admissions Selectivity Rating: 87   **Fire Safety Rating:** 60*   **Green Rating:** 60*

STUDENTS AND FACULTY

Enrollment: 421. **Student Body:** 54% female, 46% male, 78% out-of-state, 4% international (3 countries represented). Asian 2%, Caucasian 92%, Hispanic 2%.

Retention and Graduation: 91% freshmen return for sophomore year. 74% freshmen graduate within 4 years. 25% grads go on to further study within 1 year. 15% grads pursue arts and sciences degrees. 5% grads pursue law degrees. 5% grads pursue business degrees. **Faculty:** Student/faculty ratio 12:1. 23 full-time faculty, 78% hold PhDs, 9% are women.

ACADEMICS

Degrees: Associate, bachelor's, master's. **Classes:** Most classes have 10–19 students. **Majors with Highest Enrollment:** History; philosophy; political science and government. **Special Study Options:** double major, honors program, independent study, internships, study abroad, Semester in Rome.

FACILITIES

Housing: Men's dorms, women's dorms.

CAMPUS LIFE

Environment: Rural. **Activities:** Choral groups, dance, drama/theater, literary magazine, musical theater, student government, student newspaper, student-run film society, yearbook. **Organizations:** 5 registered organizations, 4 religious organizations. **Athletics (Intercollegiate):** *Men:* Baseball, basketball, soccer. *Women:* Basketball, soccer, softball, volleyball. **On-Campus Highlights:** St. John the Evangelist Library, Chapel of Christ the King, Regina Coeli Building, John Paul II Student Center

ADMISSIONS

Freshman Academic Profile: Average high school GPA 3.5. 40% in top 10% of high school class, 63% in top 25% of high school class, 100% in top 50% of high school class. 20% from public high schools. SAT Math middle 50% range 520–630. SAT Critical Reading middle 50% range 570–700. SAT Writing middle 50% range 560–690. ACT middle 50% range 23–28. Minimum paper TOEFL 550. Minimum computer TOEFL 250. **Basis for Candidate Selection:** *Very important factors considered include:* Application essay, standardized test scores, character/personal qualities, level of applicant's interest, religious affiliation/commitment. *Important factors considered include:* Recommendation(s), rigor of secondary school record, interview. *Other factors considered include:* Class rank, academic GPA, alumni/ae relation, extracurricular activities, first generation, talent/ability, volunteer work, work experience. **Freshman Admission Requirements:** High school diploma or equivalent is not required. *Academic units recommended:* 4 English, 2 mathematics, 2 science, 2 foreign language, 1 social studies, 2 history, 1 academic electives. **Freshman Admission Statistics:** 271 applied, 88% admitted, 52% enrolled. **Transfer Admission Requirements:** College transcript(s), essay or personal statement, minimum college GPA of 2.8 required. Lowest grade transferable C. **General Admission Information:** Application fee $25. Regular application deadline 3/1. Regular notification 4/1. Nonfall registration not accepted. Credit offered for CEEB Advanced Placement tests.

COSTS AND FINANCIAL AID

Annual tuition $16,290. Room and board $6,066. Required fees $540. Average book expense $450. **Required Forms and Deadlines:** Institution's own financial aid form. Priority financial aid filing date 3/1. **Notification of Awards:** Applicants will be notified of awards on a rolling basis beginning 2/1. **Types of Aid:** *Need-based scholarships/grants:* Private scholarships, the school's own gift aid. *Loans:* College/university loans from institutional funds. **Student Employment:** Institutional employment available. Highest amount earned per year from on-campus jobs $1,850. Off-campus job opportunities are fair. **Financial Aid Statistics:** 47% freshmen, 47% undergrads receive need-based scholarship or grant aid. 15% freshmen, 12% undergrads receive non-need-based scholarship or grant aid. 50% freshmen, 48% undergrads receive need-based self-help aid. 80% freshmen, 65% undergrads receive any aid. 60% undergrads borrow to pay for school. Average cumulative indebtedness $22,000. **Criteria for awarding institutional aid:** *Non-need-based:* Academics.

CHRISTIAN BROTHERS UNIVERSITY

Admissions, Box T-6, 650 East Parkway South, Memphis, TN 38104-5519
Phone: 901-321-3205 **Financial Aid Phone:** 901-321-3306
E-mail: admissions@cbu.edu **CEEB Code:** 1121
Fax: 901-321-3202 **Website:** www.cbu.edu **ACT Code:** 3952

This private school, affiliated with the Roman Catholic Church, was founded in 1871. It has a 75-acre campus.

RATINGS

Admissions Selectivity Rating: 89   **Fire Safety Rating:** 60*   **Green Rating:** 60*

STUDENTS AND FACULTY

Enrollment: 1,413. **Student Body:** 56% female, 44% male, 17% out-of-state, 2% international (18 countries represented). Asian 5%, African American 27%, Caucasian 47%, Hispanic 2%.

Retention and Graduation: 77% freshmen return for sophomore year. 39% freshmen graduate within 4 years. **Faculty:** Student/faculty ratio 13:1. 99 full-time faculty, 87% hold PhDs, 16% are members of minority groups, 30% are women.

ACADEMICS

Degrees: Bachelor's, master's, post-bachelor's certificate. **Classes:** Most classes have 10–19 students. **Majors with Highest Enrollment:** Biology/biological sciences; business/commerce; psychology. **Special Study Options:** Accelerated program, distance learning, double major, dual enrollment, honors program, independent study, internships, liberal arts/career combination, study abroad, teacher certification program. **Honors programs:** The Honors Program at Christian Brothers University is designed to serve the capacities and needs of students with proven academic abilities who seek a more intensive and challenging educational experience. Students accepted into the Honors Program will be allowed each semester to take at least one special-topics course offered only to a limited number of Honors students by an instructor carefully chosen for his or her teaching expertise. These Honors courses will explore important topics in depth, often through a multi-disciplinary approach, and while the pace and the workload will demand self-motivated students, the small size of each Honors class will insure ample group discussion and individual interaction with the instructor. Besides taking honors classes, members of the Honors Program will participate in various extra-curricular activities, including outings to cultural events and regional honors conferences. Special programs offered to physically disabled students include note-taking services, reader services, tape recorders, tutors. **Career services:** Alumni services, career assessment, internships. **Career services highlights include:** internships.

FACILITIES

Housing: Men's dorms, women's dorms, apartments for single students, theme housing. Juniors and seniors may live in on-campus apartments. All freshmen and sophomores whose permanent address is beyond a 30 mile radius are required to live on campus. Some houses are available. A private quiet study facility is available. **Special Academic Facilities/Equipment:** Art exhibits, audiovisual lab, MAC graphics lab, engineering graphics lab, Ghandi institute for nonviolence, Facing History. **Computers:** 90% of classrooms, 100% of libraries, 100% of dining areas, 25% of common outdoor areas have wireless network access. Students can register for classes online. Administrative functions (other than registration) can be performed online.

CAMPUS LIFE

Environment: Metropolis. **Activities:** Choral groups, drama/theater, literary magazine, radio station, student government, yearbook, campus ministries **Organizations:** 37 registered organizations, 10 honor societies, 3 religious organizations. 5 fraternities, 6 sororities. **Athletics (Intercollegiate):** *Men:* Baseball, basketball, cross-country, golf, soccer, tennis. *Women:* Basketball, cross-country, golf, soccer, softball, tennis, volleyball. **On-Campus Highlights:** Thomas Center (cafeteria, coffee shop/grill gather, Canale Arena Gymnasium, Computer Center, Canale Outdoor Pool, Art Gallery in library.

ADMISSIONS

Freshman Academic Profile: Average high school GPA 3.56. 39% in top 10% of high school class, 73% in top 25% of high school class, 91% in top 50% of high school class. 73% from public high schools. ACT middle 50% range 21–26. Minimum paper TOEFL 500. Minimum computer TOEFL 173. **Basis for Candidate Selection:** *Very important factors considered include:* Academic GPA, rigor of secondary school record, standardized test scores. *Important factors considered include:* Class rank, application essay, recommendation(s), alumni/ae relation, extracurricular activities, interview, talent/ability, volunteer work, work experience. **Freshman Admission Requirements:** High school diploma is required and GED is accepted. *Academic units recommended:* 4 English, 4 mathematics, 4 science. **Freshman Admission Statistics:** 1,912 applied, 49% admitted, 32% enrolled. **Transfer Admission Requirements:** college transcript(s), minimum college GPA of 2.5 required. Lowest grade transferable C. **General Admission Information:** Application fee $25. Regular application deadline 8/1. Notification on a rolling basis, beginning on or about 12/1. Nonfall registration accepted. Admission may be deferred for a maximum of 1 year. Credit and/or placement offered for CEEB Advanced Placement tests.

COSTS AND FINANCIAL AID

Required Forms and Deadlines: FAFSA. Priority financial aid filing date 2/15. **Notification of Awards:** Applicants will be notified of awards on a rolling basis beginning 3/1. **Types of Aid:** *Need-based scholarships/grants:* Federal Pell, SEOG, state scholarships/grants, private scholarships, the school's own gift aid. *Loans:* FFEL Subsidized Stafford, FFEL Unsubsidized Stafford, FFEL PLUS, Federal Perkins, state loans **Student Employment:** Federal Work-Study Program available. Off-campus job opportunities are good. **Financial Aid Statistics:** 45% freshmen, 44% undergrads receive need-based scholarship or grant aid. 77% freshmen, 63% undergrads receive non-need-based scholarship or grant aid. 53% freshmen, 50% undergrads receive need-based self-help aid. 16% freshmen, 13% undergrads receive athletic scholarships. 94% freshmen, 77% undergrads receive any aid. 69% undergrads borrow to pay for school. Average cumulative indebtedness $28,259. **Criteria for awarding institutional aid:** *Non-need-based:* Academics, alumni affiliation, athletics, leadership, music/drama, religious affiliation, state/district residency.

CHRISTOPHER NEWPORT UNIVERSITY

1 University Place, Newport News, VA 23606-2998
Phone: 757-594-7015 **Financial Aid Phone:** 757-594-7170
E-mail: admit@cnu.edu **CEEB Code:** 5128
Fax: 757-594-7333 **Website:** www.cnu.edu **ACT Code:** 4345

This public school was founded in 1960. It has a 260-acre campus.

RATINGS
Admissions Selectivity Rating: 83   **Fire Safety Rating:** 85   **Green Rating:** 78

STUDENTS AND FACULTY
Enrollment: 4,771. **Student Body:** 56% female, 44% male, 7% out-of-state, international (35 countries represented). Asian 3%, African American 8%, Caucasian 81%, Hispanic 3%, Native American 1%.
Retention and Graduation: 80% freshmen return for sophomore year. 39% freshmen graduate within 4 years. **Faculty:** Student/faculty ratio 18:1. 236 full-time faculty, 86% hold PhDs, 11% are members of minority groups, 45% are women.

ACADEMICS
Degrees: Bachelor's, master's. **Classes:** Most classes have 20–29 students. **Majors with Highest Enrollment:** Biology/biological sciences; business administration and management; communication studies/speech communication and rhetoric. **Special Study Options:** Cross-registration, double major, dual enrollment, honors program, independent study, internships, student-designed major, study abroad, Member of the Virginia Tidewater Consortium, Freshman Learning Communities. **Honors programs:** CNU Honors Program provides enriched educational experience for academically talented students motivated to participate in challenging courses and cultural and intellectual activities. Special programs offered to physically disabled students include note-taking services, tape recorders. **Career services:** Career/job search classes, career assessment, internships **Career services highlights include:** A new initiative—Freshman Academic Success Program (incorporation of study skills, major choices, and career opportunities).

FACILITIES
Housing: Coed dorms, fraternity/sorority housing, apartments for single students, theme housing. 96% of campus accessible to physically disabled. **Special Academic Facilities/Equipment:** Falk Art Gallery, The Freeman Center, The Ferguson Center for the Arts, Trible Library houses the Mariners Museum Collection. **Computers:** 10% of classrooms, 10% of dorms, 100% of libraries, 100% of dining areas, 100% of student union, 100% of common outdoor areas have wireless network access. Students can register for classes online. Administrative functions (other than registration) can be performed online.

CAMPUS LIFE
Environment: City. **Activities:** Choral groups, concert band, dance, drama/theater, jazz band, literary magazine, marching band, music ensembles, musical theater, opera, pep band, radio station, student government, student newspaper, student-run film society, symphony orchestra, television station, campus ministries, international student organization, Model UN. **Organizations:** 139 registered organizations, 23 honor societies, 12 religious organizations. 7 fraternities, 7 sororities. **Athletics (Intercollegiate):** *Men:* Baseball, basketball, cheerleading, cross-country, football, golf, lacrosse, sailing, soccer, tennis, track/field (outdoor), track/field (indoor). *Women:* Basketball, cheerleading, cross-country, field hockey, lacrosse, sailing, soccer, softball, tennis, track/field (outdoor), track/field (indoor), volleyball. **On-Campus Highlights:** Trible Library, Freeman Athletic Center, Ferguson Center for the Arts, McMurran Classroom Building, David Student Union, CNU Village for upper class students.

ADMISSIONS
Freshman Academic Profile: Average high school GPA 3.62. 19% in top 10% of high school class, 57% in top 25% of high school class, 95% in top 50% of high school class. SAT Math middle 50% range 560–640. SAT Critical Reading middle 50% range 560–640. ACT middle 50% range 22–27. Minimum paper TOEFL 530. Minimum computer TOEFL 197. Minimum web-based TOEFL 71. **Basis for Candidate Selection:** *Very important factors considered include:* Academic GPA, rigor of secondary school record. *Important factors considered include:* Recommendation(s), alumni/ae relation, first generation. *Other factors considered include:* Application essay, standardized test scores, character/per-

sonal qualities, extracurricular activities, level of applicant's interest, talent/ability, volunteer work, work experience. **Freshman Admission Requirements:** High school diploma is required and GED is accepted. *Academic units required:* 4 English, 4 mathematics, 3 science, 3 foreign language, 3 history. *Academic units recommended:* 4 English, 4 mathematics, 4 science, 4 foreign language, 4 history, 4 academic electives. **Freshman Admission Statistics:** 7,317 applied, 60% admitted, 27% enrolled. **Transfer Admission Requirements:** High school transcript, college transcript(s), statement of good standing from prior institution(s). Minimum college GPA of 3.0 required. Lowest grade transferable C. **General Admission Information:** Application fee $45. Regular application deadline 3/1. Notification on a rolling basis, beginning on or about 12/1. Nonfall registration accepted. Admission may be deferred for a maximum of 1 year. Credit and/or placement offered for CEEB Advanced Placement tests.

COSTS AND FINANCIAL AID
Required Forms and Deadlines: FAFSA. Priority financial aid filing date 3/1. **Notification of Awards:** Applicants will be notified of awards on a rolling basis beginning 2/21. **Types of Aid:** *Need-based scholarships/grants:* Federal Pell, SEOG, state scholarships/grants, private scholarships, the school's own gift aid. *Loans:* FFEL Subsidized Stafford, FFEL Unsubsidized Stafford, FFEL PLUS **Student Employment:** Federal Work-Study Program available. Institutional employment available. Off-campus job opportunities are good. **Financial Aid Statistics:** 30% freshmen, 29% undergrads receive need-based scholarship or grant aid. 19% freshmen, 10% undergrads receive non-need-based scholarship or grant aid. 33% freshmen, 34% undergrads receive need-based self-help aid. 62% freshmen, 58% undergrads receive any aid. 53% undergrads borrow to pay for school. Average cumulative indebtedness $19,103. **Criteria for awarding institutional aid:** *Non-need-based:* Academics, art, leadership, music/drama, state/district residency.

CIRCLEVILLE BIBLE COLLEGE

1476 Lancaster Pike, PO Box 458, Circleville, OH 43113-9487
Phone: 740-477-7701
E-mail: enroll@biblecollege.edu
Fax: 740-477-7755 **Website:** www.biblecollege.edu **ACT Code:** 3030

This private school was founded in 1948.

RATINGS
Admissions Selectivity Rating: 72   **Fire Safety Rating:** 60*   **Green Rating:** 60*

STUDENTS AND FACULTY
Enrollment: 349. **Student Body:** 51% female, 49% male, 24% out-of-state. Asian 1%, African American 6%, Caucasian 91%, Hispanic 2%, Native American 1%.
Retention and Graduation: 58% freshmen return for sophomore year. **Faculty:** Student/faculty ratio 13:1. 14 full-time faculty, 64% hold PhDs, 14% are women.

ACADEMICS
Degrees: Associate, bachelor's, terminal associate, transfer associate. **Classes:** Most classes have 10–19 students. **Special Study Options:** Double major, independent study, internships, liberal arts/career combination, student-designed major. Special programs offered to physically disabled students include note-taking services, reader services, tape recorders, tutors.

FACILITIES
Housing: Men's dorms, special housing for international students, women's dorms, apartments for married students.

CAMPUS LIFE
Environment: Rural. **Activities:** Choral groups, drama/theater, music ensembles, student government, yearbook. **Athletics (Intercollegiate):** *Men:* Baseball, basketball. *Women:* Basketball, volleyball.

ADMISSIONS
Freshman Academic Profile: Average high school GPA 2.93. 21% in top 10% of high school class, 24% in top 25% of high school class, 32% in top 50% of high school class. ACT middle 50% range 17–23. **Basis for Candidate Selection:** *Very important factors considered include:* Class rank, recommendation(s), rigor of secondary school record, standardized test scores, religious affiliation/commitment. *Important factors considered include:* Application essay, character/personal qualities. *Other factors considered include:* interview. **Freshman Admission Requirements:** High school diploma is required and GED is accepted. *Academic units recommended:* 4 English, 3 mathematics, 3 science, 2 foreign language, 3 social studies. **Freshman Admission Statistics:** 138 applied, 69% admitted, 75% enrolled. **Transfer Admission**

Requirements: High school transcript, college transcript(s), essay or personal statement, standardized test scores, statement of good standing from prior institution(s). Minimum college GPA of 2.0 required. Lowest grade transferable C. **General Admission Information:** Application fee $25. Nonfall registration accepted. Admission may be deferred for a maximum of 1 year.

COSTS AND FINANCIAL AID

Annual tuition $7,950. Room and board $5,200. Required fees $850. Average book expense $500. **Required Forms and Deadlines:** FAFSA, institution's own financial aid form, CSS/Financial Aid PROFILE. Priority financial aid filing date 4/1. **Notification of Awards:** Applicants will be notified of awards on or about 6/1. **Student Employment:** Federal Work-Study Program available. Off-campus job opportunities are excellent. **Financial Aid Statistics:** 27% freshmen, 31% undergrads receive need-based scholarship or grant aid. 27% freshmen, 31% undergrads receive non-need-based scholarship or grant aid. 27% freshmen, 31% undergrads receive need-based self-help aid.

THE CITADEL, THE MILITARY COLLEGE OF SOUTH CAROLINA

171 Moultrie Street, Charleston, SC 29409
Phone: 843-953-5230 **Financial Aid Phone:** 843-953-5187
E-mail: admissions@citadel.edu
Fax: 843-953-7036 **Website:** www.citadel.edu **ACT Code:** 3838

This public school was founded in 1842. It has a 300-acre campus.

RATINGS

Admissions Selectivity Rating: 77   **Fire Safety Rating:** 95   **Green Rating:** 60*

STUDENTS AND FACULTY

Enrollment: 2,311. **Student Body:** 6% female, 94% male, 51% out-of-state, 1% international (17 countries represented). Asian 3%, African American 7%, Caucasian 82%, Hispanic 5%.
Retention and Graduation: 83% freshmen return for sophomore year. 17% grads go on to further study within 1 year. 6% grads pursue arts and sciences degrees. 4% grads pursue law degrees. 5% grads pursue business degrees. 2% grads pursue medical degrees. **Faculty:** Student/faculty ratio 16:1. 172 full-time faculty, 95% hold PhDs, 12% are members of minority groups, 30% are women.

ACADEMICS

Degrees: Bachelor's, master's, post-master's certificate. **Classes:** Most classes have 20–29 students. Most lab/discussion sessions have 10–19 students. **Majors with Highest Enrollment:** Business administration and management; civil engineering; criminal justice/law enforcement administration. **Special Study Options:** Cooperative education program, distance learning, double major, English as a Second Language (ESL), honors program, independent study, internships, study abroad, teacher certification program. **Honors programs:** The Citadel's Honors Program is a specially designed educational experience meeting the needs of students with an outstanding record of academic achievement and a sense of intellectual adventure. While pursuing any one of seventeen degree programs offered by The Citadel, Honors Students take a series of Core Curriculum Honors courses—for example, studies based in literature and writing, history, and mathematics—concentrated in their first two years, and an occasional Honors Seminar in their third and fourth years. For the qualified student, advantages of the Honors Program are clear: special program of pre-professional counseling, small classes, discussion-style teaching, tutorial session, special curriculum, fellow honors students, student advisory committee, honors faculty, special diploma seal and transcript, and emphasis on leadership. **Career services:** Alumni network, alumni services, career/job search classes, career assessment, internships.

FACILITIES

Housing: Coed dorms **Special Academic Facilities/Equipment:** Archives and Museum **Computers:** 5% of classrooms, 20% of dorms, 100% of libraries, 75% of student union, 10% of common outdoor areas have wireless network access. Students can register for classes online. Administrative functions (other than registration) can be performed online.

CAMPUS LIFE

Environment: City. **Activities:** Choral groups, concert band, jazz band, literary magazine, marching band, pep band, student government, student newspaper, yearbook, campus ministries. **Organizations:** 79 registered organizations, 12 honor societies, 16 religious organizations. **Athletics (Intercollegiate):** *Men:* Baseball, basketball, cross-country, football, riflery, tennis, track/field (outdoor), track/field (indoor), wrestling. *Women:* Cross-country, golf, riflery, soccer, track/field (outdoor), track/field (indoor), volleyball. **On-Campus Highlights:** Summerall Chapel, Mark Clark Hall, Daniel Library, Citadel Museum, McAlister Field House.

ADMISSIONS

Freshman Academic Profile: Average high school GPA 3.37. 12% in top 10% of high school class, 33% in top 25% of high school class, 70% in top 50% of high school class. SAT Math middle 50% range 510–600. SAT Critical Reading middle 50% range 480–580. ACT middle 50% range 19–23. Minimum paper TOEFL 550. Minimum web-based TOEFL 79. **Basis for Candidate Selection:** *Very important factors considered include:* Academic GPA, standardized test scores, level of applicant's interest. *Important factors considered include:* Rigor of secondary school record, character/personal qualities, extracurricular activities, state residency, talent/ability. *Other factors considered include:* Class rank, recommendation(s), alumni/ae relation, first generation, geographical residence, interview, volunteer work. **Freshman Admission Requirements:** High school diploma is required and GED is accepted. *Academic units required:* 4 English, 3 mathematics, 3 science, (3 science labs), 2 foreign language, 2 social studies, 1 history, 4 academic electives, 1 PE or ROTC. *Academic units recommended:* 4 mathematics. **Freshman Admission Statistics:** 2,165 applied, 79% admitted, 34% enrolled. **Transfer Admission Requirements:** High school transcript, college transcript(s), standardized test scores, statement of good standing from prior institution(s). Minimum college GPA of 2.0 required. Lowest grade transferable C. **General Admission Information:** Application fee $40. Early decision application deadline 10/26. Notification on a rolling basis, beginning on or about 7/15. Nonfall registration not accepted. Credit and/or placement offered for CEEB Advanced Placement tests.

COSTS AND FINANCIAL AID

Required Forms and Deadlines: FAFSA, institution's own financial aid form. Priority financial aid filing date 3/1. **Notification of Awards:** Applicants will be notified of awards on a rolling basis beginning 4/1. **Types of Aid:** *Need-based scholarships/grants:* Federal Pell, SEOG, state scholarships/grants, the school's own gift aid. *Loans:* Direct Subsidized Stafford, Direct Unsubsidized Stafford, Direct PLUS, Federal Perkins. **Student Employment:** Federal Work-Study Program available. **Financial Aid Statistics:** 50% freshmen, 41% undergrads receive need-based scholarship or grant aid. 27% freshmen, 27% undergrads receive non-need-based scholarship or grant aid. 42% freshmen, 35% undergrads receive need-based self-help aid. 4% freshmen, 5% undergrads receive athletic scholarships. 87% freshmen, 84% undergrads receive any aid. 73% undergrads borrow to pay for school. Average cumulative indebtedness $25,817. **Criteria for awarding institutional aid:** *Non-need-based:* Academics, alumni affiliation, athletics, leadership, state/district residency.

CITY UNIVERSITY

11900 NE First Street, Bellevue, WA 98005
Phone: 425-637-1010 **Financial Aid Phone:** 425-709-5251
E-mail: info@cityu.edu
Fax: 425-709-5361 **Website:** www.cityu.edu

This private school was founded in 1973. It has a 5-acre campus.

RATINGS

Admissions Selectivity Rating: 60*   **Fire Safety Rating:** 60*   **Green Rating:** 60*

STUDENTS AND FACULTY

Enrollment: 1,848. **Student Body:** 55% female, 45% male, 1% out-of-state, 5% international. Asian 6%, African American 5%, Caucasian 66%, Hispanic 3%, Native American 1%.
Retention and Graduation: Faculty: Student/faculty ratio 20:1. 36 full-time faculty, 25% hold PhDs, 19% are members of minority groups, 47% are women.

ACADEMICS

Degrees: Associate, bachelor's, certificate, master's, transfer associate. **Majors with Highest Enrollment:** Business administration and management; computer and information sciences and support services, other; elementary education and teaching. **Special Study Options:** Accelerated program, distance learning, double major, dual enrollment, English as a Second Language (ESL), internships, student-designed major, teacher certification program, weekend college.

FACILITIES

Housing: Computers: Students can register for classes online. Administrative functions (other than registration) can be performed online.

CAMPUS LIFE

Environment: Metropolis. **Activities:** Choral groups, drama/theater, music ensembles, student government, student newspaper **Organizations:**

ADMISSIONS

Freshman Academic Profile: Minimum paper TOEFL 540. Minimum computer TOEFL 207. **Freshman Admission Requirements:** High school diploma is required and GED is accepted. **Freshman Admission Statistics:** 15 applied, 100% admitted, 307% enrolled. **Transfer Admission Requirements:** High school transcript, college transcript(s), Lowest grade transferable C. **General Admission Information:** Application fee $80. Nonfall registration accepted. Admission may be deferred for a maximum of Undetermined.

COSTS AND FINANCIAL AID

Annual tuition $9,320. Required fees $120. Average book expense $500. **Student Employment:** Federal Work-Study Program available. **Financial Aid Statistics:** 27% freshmen, 29% undergrads receive any aid.

CITY UNIVERSITY OF NEW YORK— BARUCH COLLEGE

Undergraduate Admissions, 151 E 25th St, Room 720, New York, NY 10010
Phone: 646-312-1400 **Financial Aid Phone:** 646-312-1360
E-mail: admissions@baruch.cuny.edu **CEEB Code:** 2034
Fax: 646-312-1363 **Website:** www.baruch.cuny.edu

This public school was founded in 1968.

RATINGS
Admissions Selectivity Rating: 90   **Fire Safety Rating:** 60*   **Green Rating:** 64

STUDENTS AND FACULTY
Enrollment: 12,080. **Student Body:** 51% female, 49% male, 4% out-of-state, 13% international (115 countries represented). Asian 32%, African American 11%, Caucasian 31%, Hispanic 17%.
Retention and Graduation: 88% freshmen return for sophomore year. 33% freshmen graduate within 4 years. **Faculty:** Student/faculty ratio 18:1. 509 full-time faculty, 84% hold PhDs, 21% are members of minority groups, 37% are women. 1% of classes are taught by teaching assistants.

ACADEMICS
Degrees: Bachelor's, master's, post-master's certificate. **Classes:** Most classes have 20–29 students. Most lab/discussion sessions have 20–29 students. **Majors with Highest Enrollment:** Accounting; finance. **Special Study Options:** Accelerated program, cross-registration, distance learning, double major, English as a Second Language (ESL), exchange student program (domestic), honors program, independent study, internships, liberal arts/career combination, student-designed major, study abroad. **Honors programs:** CUNY Honors Program. **Combined degree programs:** BA/MA Special programs offered to physically disabled students include note-taking services, reader services, tape recorders, tutors. **Career services:** Alumni network, alumni services, career/job search classes, career assessment, internships.

FACILITIES
Housing: 100% of campus accessible to physically disabled. **Special Academic Facilities/Equipment:** Art gallery, Subotnik Financial Services Center, and Wasserman Trading Floor. **Computers:** 25% of classrooms, 100% of libraries, 100% of dining areas, 100% of student union, 100% of common outdoor areas have wireless network access. Students can register for classes online. Administrative functions (other than registration) can be performed online.

CAMPUS LIFE
Environment: Metropolis. **Activities:** Choral groups, dance, drama/theater, literary magazine, musical theater, radio station, student government, student newspaper, yearbook, campus ministries, Model UN. **Organizations:** 172 registered organizations, 9 honor societies, 7 religious organizations. 9 fraternities, 7 sororities. **Athletics (Intercollegiate):** *Men:* Baseball, basketball, crosscountry, soccer, swimming, tennis, volleyball. *Women:* Basketball, cheerleading, cross-country, softball, swimming, tennis, volleyball. **On-Campus Highlights:** Student Club Area- Vertical Campus Build, NewMan Library, Lobby- 23 St. Building, Food Court- Vertical Campus Building, College Fitness Center-Vertical Campus.

ADMISSIONS
Freshman Academic Profile: Average high school GPA 3.13. 37% in top 10% of high school class, 66% in top 25% of high school class, 90% in top 50% of high school class. 72% from public high schools. SAT Math middle 50% range 560–670. SAT Critical Reading middle 50% range 490–590. Minimum paper TOEFL 620. Minimum computer TOEFL 260. **Basis for Candidate Selection:** *Very important factors considered include:* Academic GPA, rigor of

secondary school record, standardized test scores. *Important factors considered include:* Application essay, recommendation(s). *Other factors considered include:* Class rank, alumni/ae relation, character/personal qualities, extracurricular activities, interview, talent/ability, work experience. **Freshman Admission Requirements:** High school diploma is required and GED is accepted. *Academic units required:* 4 English, 3 mathematics, 2 science, (2 science labs), 2 foreign language, 4 social studies. *Academic units recommended:* 4 mathematics, 2 foreign language, 1 academic electives. **Freshman Admission Statistics:** 19,775 applied, 23% admitted, 32% enrolled. **Transfer Admission Requirements:** High school transcript, college transcript(s), statement of good standing from prior institution(s). Minimum college GPA of 2.7 required. Lowest grade transferable C. **General Admission Information:** Application fee $65. Early decision application deadline 12/13. Regular application deadline 2/1. Regular notification 5/15. Notification on a rolling basis, beginning on or about 2/1. Nonfall registration accepted. Admission may be deferred for a maximum of Six months. Credit and/or placement offered for CEEB Advanced Placement tests.

COSTS AND FINANCIAL AID
Annual in-state tuition $4,600. Annual out-of-state tuition $12,450. Required fees $340. **Required Forms and Deadlines:** FAFSA, state aid form. Financial aid filing deadline 4/30. Priority financial aid filing date 3/15. **Notification of Awards:** Applicants will be notified of awards on a rolling basis beginning 4/1. **Types of Aid:** *Need-based scholarships/grants:* Federal Pell, SEOG, state scholarships/grants, the school's own gift aid, City merit scholarships. *Loans:* Direct Subsidized Stafford, Direct Unsubsidized Stafford, Direct PLUS, Federal Perkins. **Student Employment:** Federal Work-Study Program available. Institutional employment available. Off-campus job opportunities are excellent. **Financial Aid Statistics:** 58% freshmen, 35% undergrads receive need-based scholarship or grant aid. 1% freshmen, 1% undergrads receive non-need-based scholarship or grant aid. 46% freshmen, 28% undergrads receive need-based self-help aid. 72% freshmen, 57% undergrads receive any aid. 22% undergrads borrow to pay for school. Average cumulative indebtedness $14,737. **Criteria for awarding institutional aid:** *Non-need-based:* Academics, alumni affiliation, state/district residency.

CITY UNIVERSITY OF NEW YORK—BOROUGH OF MANHATTAN COMMUNITY COLLEGE

199 Chambers Street, New York, NY 10007-1097
Phone: 212-220-1265
E-mail: ebarrios@bmcc.cuny.edu
Fax: 212-346-8110

This public school was founded in 1964. It has a 5-acre campus.

RATINGS
Admissions Selectivity Rating: 60*   **Fire Safety Rating:** 60*   **Green Rating:** 60*

STUDENTS AND FACULTY
Enrollment: 16,732. **Student Body:** 64% female, 36% male, 12% international. Asian 10%, African American 37%, Caucasian 11%, Hispanic 30%.
Retention and Graduation: 40% grads go on to further study within 1 year. **Faculty:** Student/faculty ratio 21:1. 315 full-time faculty,

ACADEMICS
Degrees: Associate, certificate, terminal associate, transfer associate. **Special Study Options:** Cooperative education program, distance learning, English as a Second Language (ESL), honors program, independent study, internships, study abroad, weekend college. Special programs offered to physically disabled students include note-taking services, reader services, tape recorders, tutors. **Career services:** Alumni services, career/job search classes, career assessment, internships.

FACILITIES
Housing: Special housing for disabled students, men's dorms, special housing for international students, women's dorms, apartments for single students 100% of campus accessible to physically disabled. **Computers:** Students can register for classes online.

CAMPUS LIFE
Activities: Choral groups, concert band, dance, drama/theater, jazz band, music ensembles, pep band, student government, student newspaper, yearbook.

ADMISSIONS
Freshman Admission Requirements: High school diploma is required and GED is accepted. *Academic units recommended:* 4 English, 3 mathematics, (2 science labs), 2 foreign language, 4 social studies, 1 fine arts **Freshman Admission Statistics:** 6,374 applied, 85% admitted, 60% enrolled. **Transfer Admis-**

COSTS AND FINANCIAL AID

Annual in-state tuition $2,500. Annual out-of-state tuition $3,076. Required fees $80. Average book expense $350. **Student Employment:** Federal Work-Study Program available. Institutional employment available. Off-campus job opportunities are good.

CITY UNIVERSITY OF NEW YORK— BROOKLYN COLLEGE

2900 Bedford Avenue, Brooklyn, NY 11210
Phone: 718-951-5001 **Financial Aid Phone:** 718-951-5045
E-mail:
Fax: 718-951-4506 **Website:** www.brooklyn.cuny.edu **ACT Code:** 20169

This public school was founded in 1930. It has a 26-acre campus.

RATINGS

Admissions Selectivity Rating: 88 **Fire Safety Rating:** 60* **Green Rating:** 92

STUDENTS AND FACULTY

Enrollment: 12,021. **Student Body:** 59% female, 41% male, 2% out-of-state, 6% international. Asian 15%, African American 27%, Caucasian 41%, Hispanic 13%.
Retention and Graduation: 78% freshmen return for sophomore year. 17% freshmen graduate within 4 years. **Faculty:** Student/faculty ratio 15:1. 533 full-time faculty, 93% hold PhDs, 23% are members of minority groups, 44% are women.

ACADEMICS

Degrees: Bachelor's, certificate, master's, post-bachelor's certificate, post-master's certificate. **Classes:** Most classes have 20–29 students. **Special Study Options:** Distance learning, double major, dual enrollment, English as a Second Language (ESL), honors program, independent study, internships, study abroad, teacher certification program, weekend college. **Honors programs:** See the URL below for more information: www.brooklyn.edu/pub/1654. htm. **Combined degree programs:** BA/MD. Special programs offered to physically disabled students include note-taking services, reader services, tutors. **Career services:** Alumni network, alumni services, career/job search classes, career assessment, internships.

FACILITIES

Housing: 100% of campus accessible to physically disabled. **Special Academic Facilities/Equipment:** Art museum. language lab, TV studios, speech clinic, research centers and institutes, paricle accelerator. **Computers:** 2% of classrooms, 90% of libraries, 100% of dining areas, 75% of student union, 75% of common outdoor areas have wireless network access. Students can register for classes online. Administrative functions (other than registration) can be performed online.

CAMPUS LIFE

Environment: Metropolis. **Activities:** dance, drama/theater, literary magazine, music ensembles, musical theater, radio station, student government, student newspaper, television station, yearbook, international student organization. **Organizations:** 171 registered organizations, 7 honor societies, 7 fraternities, 9 sororities. **Athletics (Intercollegiate):** *Men:* Basketball, cross-country, soccer, tennis, track/field (outdoor), track/field (indoor), volleyball. *Women:* Basketball, cross-country, softball, tennis, track/field (outdoor), track/field (indoor), volleyball. **On-Campus Highlights:** Library, Student Center, Lily Pond, Library Cafe, Cafeteria, Dining Hall, Magner Center, James Hall. **Environmental Initiatives:** Reduce comsumption; awareness.

ADMISSIONS

Freshman Academic Profile: Average high school GPA 3.3. 14% in top 10% of high school class, 49% in top 25% of high school class, 79% in top 50% of high school class. SAT Math middle 50% range 480–590. SAT Critical Reading middle 50% range 450–570. Minimum paper TOEFL 500. Minimum computer TOEFL 173. **Basis for Candidate Selection:** *Very important factors considered include:* Academic GPA, rigor of secondary school record, standardized test scores. **Freshman Admission Requirements:** High school diploma is required and GED is accepted. *Academic units recommended:* 4 English, 3 mathematics, 3 science, 3 foreign language, 4 social studies, 4 academic elec-

tives. **Freshman Admission Statistics:** 17,497 applied, 28% admitted, 20% enrolled. **Transfer Admission Requirements:** college transcript(s), minimum college GPA of 2.3 required. Lowest grade transferable C–. **General Admission Information:** Application fee $65. Notification on a rolling basis, beginning on or about 2/1. Nonfall registration accepted. Credit and/or placement offered for CEEB Advanced Placement tests.

COSTS AND FINANCIAL AID

Annual in-state tuition $4,000. Annual out-of-state tuition $10,800. Required fees $431. **Required Forms and Deadlines:** FAFSA, state aid form. Priority financial aid filing date 4/1. **Notification of Awards:** Applicants will be notified of awards on a rolling basis beginning 5/1. **Types of Aid:** *Need-based scholarships/grants:* Federal Pell, SEOG, state scholarships/grants, private scholarships, the school's own gift aid. *Loans:* Direct Subsidized Stafford, Direct Unsubsidized Stafford, Direct PLUS, Federal Perkins. **Student Employment:** Federal Work-Study Program available. Institutional employment available. Off-campus job opportunities are excellent. **Financial Aid Statistics:** 74% freshmen, 66% undergrads receive need-based scholarship or grant aid. 24% freshmen, 20% undergrads receive non-need-based scholarship or grant aid. 72% freshmen, 69% undergrads receive need-based self-help aid. 74% freshmen, 70% undergrads receive any aid. 45% undergrads borrow to pay for school. Average cumulative indebtedness $16,600. **Criteria for awarding institutional aid:** *Non-need-based:* Academics, art, leadership, music/drama, state/district residency.

CITY UNIVERSITY OF NEW YORK—THE CITY COLLEGE OF NEW YORK

160 Convent Avenue, Wille Admin. Bldg, Room 101, New York, NY 10031
Phone: 212 650 6977 **Financial Aid Phone:** 212 650 5819
E-mail: admissions@ccny.cuny.edu **CEEB Code:** 2083
Fax: 212 650 6417 **Website:** www.ccny.cuny.edu **ACT Code:** 2950

This public school was founded in 1847. It has a 36-acre campus.

RATINGS

Admissions Selectivity Rating: 78 **Fire Safety Rating:** 93 **Green Rating:** 88

STUDENTS AND FACULTY

Enrollment: 12,340. **Student Body:** 51% female, 49% male, 4% out-of-state, 9% international (100 countries represented). Asian 17%, African American 20%, Caucasian 9%, Hispanic 30%.
Retention and Graduation: 4% freshmen graduate within 4 years. **Faculty:** Student/faculty ratio 11.3:1. 573 full-time faculty, 99% hold PhDs, 18% are members of minority groups, 39% are women.

ACADEMICS

Degrees: Bachelor's, master's, post-master's certificate. **Classes:** Most classes have 20–29 students. **Majors with Highest Enrollment:** Communication and media studies, other; electrical, electronics and communications engineering; psychology. **Special Study Options:** Accelerated program, cross-registration, double major, English as a Second Language (ESL), honors program, independent study, internships, study abroad, teacher certification program, Adult program called The Center for Worker Education which offers a evening and weekend program in liberal arts. **Honors programs:** CUNY Macauley College and City College Honors Program. **Combined degree programs:** BA/MD, BA/MA. Special programs offered to physically disabled students include note-taking services, reader services, tape recorders, tutors. **Career services:** Alumni network, alumni services, career/job search classes, career assessment, internships.

FACILITIES

Housing: The Towers new residence hall with apartment style quarter. **Special Academic Facilities/Equipment:** Planetarium, NYC Structural Biological Center, Aaron Davis Hall/Harlem Stage Gatehouse, Landmarked Gothic orignial campus buildings. **Computers:** 100% of classrooms, 100% of libraries, 100% of dining areas, 100% of common outdoor areas have wireless network access. Students can register for classes online. Administrative functions (other than registration) can be performed online.

CAMPUS LIFE

Environment: Metropolis. **Activities:** Choral groups, concert band, dance, drama/theater, jazz band, literary magazine, radio station, student government, student newspaper, student-run film society, yearbook, International student organization, Model UN. **Organizations:** 145 registered organizations, 8 religious organizations. 2 fraternities, 1 sorority. **Athletics (Intercollegiate):** *Men:* Baseball, basketball, cross-country, soccer, tennis, track/field (outdoor), track/field (indoor), volleyball. *Women:* Basketball, fencing, soccer, tennis, track/field (outdoor), track/field (indoor), volleyball. **On-Campus Highlights:** NAC Rotunda and Plaza, Spitzer School of Architecture, Wingate Hall Athletic Center, North Campus Quad in warm weather, The Towers residence hall. **Environmental Initiatives:** Signed on to ACUPCC and NYC Mayor's Campus 30in10 Challenge to reduce GHG emissions. Task Force to place sustainability at forefront in all operations, outreach and educational mission. Undergraduate and Graduate programs in sustainability, interdisciplinary with Science, Engineering, Architecture and Economics

ADMISSIONS

Freshman Academic Profile: 30% in top 10% of high school class, 36% in top 25% of high school class, 91% in top 50% of high school class. 85% from public high schools. SAT Math middle 50% range 470–600. SAT Critical Reading middle 50% range 440–550. Minimum paper TOEFL 500. Minimum computer TOEFL 173. Minimum web-based TOEFL 61. **Basis for Candidate Selection:** *Very important factors considered include:* Academic GPA, rigor of secondary school record. *Important factors considered include:* Standardized test scores. *Other factors considered include:* Application essay, recommendation(s). **Freshman Admission Requirements:** High school diploma is required and GED is accepted. *Academic units recommended:* 4 English, 2 mathematics, 2 science, (2 science labs), 2 foreign language, 4 social studies, 1 visual/performing arts. **Freshman Admission Statistics:** 22,159 applied, 38% admitted, 21% enrolled. **Transfer Admission Requirements:** college transcript(s), minimum college GPA of 2.0 required. Lowest grade transferable c. **General Admission Information:** Application fee $65. Notification on a rolling basis, beginning on or about 2/1. Nonfall registration accepted. Credit offered for CEEB Advanced Placement tests.

COSTS AND FINANCIAL AID

Annual in-state tuition $4,600. Annual out-of-state tuition $12,450. Room and board $12,207. Required fees $329. **Required Forms and Deadlines:** FAFSA. Priority financial aid filing date 4/1. **Notification of Awards:** Applicants will be notified of awards on a rolling basis beginning 4/1. **Types of Aid:** *Need-based scholarships/grants:* Federal Pell, SEOG, state scholarships/grants, the school's own gift aid, *Loans:* Direct Subsidized Stafford, Direct Unsubsidized Stafford, Direct PLUS **Student Employment:** Federal Work-Study Program available. Institutional employment available. Highest amount earned per year from on-campus jobs $7,200. Off-campus job opportunities are fair. **Financial Aid Statistics:** 86% freshmen, 77% undergrads receive need-based scholarship or grant aid. 35% freshmen, 14% undergrads receive non-need-based scholarship or grant aid. 52% freshmen, 68% undergrads receive need-based self-help aid. 70% freshmen, 71% undergrads receive any aid. 26% undergrads borrow to pay for school. **Criteria for awarding institutional aid:** *Non-need-based:* Academics, alumni affiliation, art, leadership, minority status, music/drama.

CITY UNIVERSITY OF NEW YORK— HUNTER COLLEGE

695 Park Ave, Room N203, New York, NY 10065
Phone: 212-772-4490 **Financial Aid Phone:** 212-772-4820
E-mail: admissions@hunter.cuny.edu **CEEB Code:** 2301
Fax: 212-650-3472 **Website:** www.hunter.cuny.edu

This public school was founded in 1870.

RATINGS
Admissions Selectivity Rating: 85   **Fire Safety Rating:** 93   **Green Rating:** 84

STUDENTS AND FACULTY
Enrollment: 14,806. **Student Body:** 67% female, 33% male, 4% out-of-state, 9% international. Asian 21%, African American 12%, Caucasian 39%, Hispanic 19%.
Retention and Graduation: 17% freshmen graduate within 4 years. **Faculty:** Student/faculty ratio 15:1. 694 full-time faculty, 82% hold PhDs, 19% are members of minority groups, 50% are women.

ACADEMICS
Degrees: Bachelor's, master's, post-master's certificate. **Classes:** Most classes have 20–29 students. **Majors with Highest Enrollment:** Accounting; English literature (British and commonwealth); psychology. **Special Study Options:** Accelerated program, cross-registration, distance learning, double major, dual

enrollment, exchange student program (domestic), honors program, independent study, internships, liberal arts/career combination, student-designed major, study abroad, teacher certification program. **Combined degree programs:** BA/MA, BA/MS. Special programs offered to physically disabled students include note-taking services, reader services, tape recorders, tutors. **Career services:** Alumni network, alumni services, career/job search classes, internships.

FACILITIES
Housing: Coed dorms. 100% of campus accessible to physically disabled. **Special Academic Facilities/Equipment:** Art Gallery, theatre, geology club, on-campus elementary and secondary schools. **Computers:** 70% of classrooms, have wireless network access. Students can register for classes online.

CAMPUS LIFE
Environment: Metropolis. **Activities:** Choral groups, concert band, dance, drama/theater, jazz band, literary magazine, music ensembles, musical theater, radio station, student government, student newspaper, student-run film society, symphony orchestra, television station, yearbook. **Organizations:** 150 registered organizations, 20 honor societies, 2 fraternities, 2 sororities. **Athletics (Intercollegiate):** *Men:* Basketball, cross-country, fencing, soccer, tennis, track/field (outdoor), track/field (indoor), volleyball, wrestling. *Women:* Basketball, cross-country, diving, fencing, softball, swimming, tennis, track/field (outdoor), track/field (indoor), volleyball. **On-Campus Highlights:** Over 100 Campus Clubs, CARSI Geography Lab, Television Studio, Learning Center and Computer Lab, Sports Complex. **Environmental Initiatives:** Hunter has an extensive program for recycling paper, metal, glass, plastic, e-waste, and household batteries. Hunter has installed occupancy sensors in nearly all of its rooms. Lights turn off automatically in unoccupied rooms. Nearly all campus computers are installed with software that turns the computers and monitors off if they are inactive for a certain amount of time. Hunter has installed modern, dual-fuel boilers. The boilers rely primarily on cleaner-burning natural gas, thus reducing greenhouse gas emissions.

ADMISSIONS
Freshman Academic Profile: 70% from public high schools. SAT Math middle 50% range 520–620. SAT Critical Reading middle 50% range 510–610. Minimum paper TOEFL 500. Minimum computer TOEFL 173. **Basis for Candidate Selection:** *Very important factors considered include:* Application essay, academic GPA, rigor of secondary school record, standardized test scores, **Freshman Admission Requirements:** High school diploma is required and GED is accepted. *Academic units required:* 2 English, 2 mathematics, 1 science, (1 science labs). *Academic units recommended:* 4 English, 3 mathematics, 2 science, 2 foreign language, 4 social studies, 1 visual/performing arts, 1 academic electives. **Freshman Admission Statistics:** 30,528 applied, 26% admitted, 26% enrolled. **Transfer Admission Requirements:** college transcript(s), minimum college GPA of 2.3 required. Lowest grade transferable C. **General Admission Information:** Application Fee $65. Regular application deadline 3/15. Notification on a rolling basis, beginning on or about 1/15. Nonfall registration accepted. Credit and/or placement offered for CEEB Advanced Placement tests.

COSTS AND FINANCIAL AID
Annual in-state tuition $4,600. Annual out-of-state tuition $12,450. Room and board $3,726. Required fees $399. **Required Forms and Deadlines:** FAFSA, state aid form. Priority financial aid filing date 5/1. **Notification of Awards:** Applicants will be notified of awards on a rolling basis beginning 5/15. **Types of Aid:** *Need-based scholarships/grants:* Federal Pell, state scholarships/grants, the school's own gift aid. *Loans:* Direct Subsidized Stafford, Direct Unsubsidized Stafford, Direct PLUS, Federal Perkins, state loans, college/university loans from institutional funds, CUNY Student Assistance Program(CUSTA), Aide for Part-Time-Study (APTS), SEEK. **Student Employment:** Federal Work-Study Program available. Institutional employment available. Off-campus job opportunities are fair. **Financial Aid Statistics:** 61% freshmen, 57% undergrads receive need-based scholarship or grant aid. 45% freshmen, 21% undergrads receive non-need-based scholarship or grant aid. 8% freshmen, 18% undergrads receive need-based self-help aid. 91% freshmen, 94% undergrads receive any aid. 48% undergrads borrow to pay for school. Average cumulative indebtedness $7,125. **Criteria for awarding institutional aid:** *Non-need-based:* Academics.

CITY UNIVERSITY OF NEW YORK—JOHN JAY COLLEGE OF CRIMINAL JUSTICE

899 Tenth Avenue, New York, NY 10019
Phone: 212-237-8869
E-mail: admissions@jjay.cuny.edu **CEEB Code:** 2115
Fax: 212-237-8777 **Website:** www.jjay.cuny.edu

This public school was founded in 1964.

RATINGS
Admissions Selectivity Rating: 60*   **Fire Safety Rating:** 60*   **Green Rating:** 60*

STUDENTS AND FACULTY
Student Body: 150 countries represented.

ACADEMICS
Degrees: Associate, bachelor's, certificate, master's, transfer associate. **Special Study Options:** Cooperative education program, distance learning, English as a Second Language (ESL), exchange student program (domestic), study abroad, weekend college, undergrads may take grad level classes. **Off-Campus Study:** Albany Internship Program. **Co-Op Programs:** Public Service. **Combined degree programs:** BA/MA. Special programs offered to physically disabled students include note-taking services, reader services, tape recorders, tutors. **Career services:** Alumni services, career/job search classes, career assessment.

FACILITIES
Housing: List of possible housing arrangements can be obtained from Student Activities 212-237-8698. **Special Academic Facilities/Equipment:** Criminal justice center, center for violence/human survival, toxicology research/training center, fire science institute, institute for criminal justice ethics, institute for the study of genocide, and institute on alcohol/substance abuse. **Computers:** Students can register for classes online.

CAMPUS LIFE
Environment: Metropolis. **Activities:** Choral groups, dance, drama/theater, musical theater, radio station, student government, student newspaper, yearbook. **Athletics (Intercollegiate):** *Men:* Basketball, cross-country, riflery, soccer. *Women:* Cross-country, riflery, softball, tennis, volleyball.

ADMISSIONS
Freshman Academic Profile: 63% from public high schools. Minimum paper TOEFL 500. Minimum computer TOEFL 173. **Freshman Admission Requirements:** High school diploma is required and GED is accepted.High school diploma is required and GED is not accepted. *Academic units recommended:* 4 English, 3 mathematics, 2 science, 2 social studies, 4 academic electives. **Freshman Admission Statistics:** Minimum college GPA of 2.0 required. Lowest grade transferable C. **General Admission Information:** Application fee $50. Regular application deadline 3/15. Nonfall registration accepted. Credit offered for CEEB Advanced Placement tests.

COSTS AND FINANCIAL AID
Annual in-state tuition $4,000. Annual out-of-state tuition $5,440. Room and board $1,802. Required fees $100. Average book expense $500. **Required Forms and Deadlines:** FAFSA **Types of Aid:** *Need-based scholarships/grants:* Federal Pell, SEOG, state scholarships/grants, private scholarships, the school's own gift aid. *Loans:* FFEL Subsidized Stafford, FFEL Unsubsidized Stafford, FFEL PLUS, Federal Perkins, college/university loans from institutional funds. **Student Employment:** Federal Work-Study Program available. Institutional employment available. Highest amount earned per year from on-campus jobs $2,500. Off-campus job opportunities are good.

CITY UNIVERSITY OF NEW YORK—KINGSBOROUGH COMMUNITY COLLEGE

2001 Oriental Blvd, Brooklyn, NY 11235
Phone: 718)368-4600
E-mail: info@kbcc.cuny.edu
Fax: 718-368-5356

This is a public school.

RATINGS
Admissions Selectivity Rating: 60*   **Fire Safety Rating:** 60*   **Green Rating:** 60*

STUDENTS AND FACULTY
Enrollment: 11,870. **Student Body:** 57% female, 43% male, % out-of-state, 6% international . Asian 12%, African American 33%, Caucasian 36%, Hispanic 14%.
Retention and Graduation: Faculty: Student/faculty ratio 25:1. 305 full-time faculty, 65% hold PhDs, 22% are members of minority groups, 51% are women.

ACADEMICS
Degrees: Associate, certificate, terminal associate, transfer associate. **Classes:** Most classes have 20–29 students. **Special Study Options:** Accelerated program, cross-registration, dual enrollment, English as a Second Language (ESL), honors program, independent study, internships, My Turn Program for senior citizens. New Start Program for students academically dismissed from 4-year institutions.

ADMISSIONS
Freshman Admission Requirements: High school diploma is required and GED is accepted. *Academic units recommended:* 4 English, 3 mathematics, 2 science, 2 foreign language, 4 social studies, 1 fine arts. **Transfer Admission Requirements:** College transcript(s), Lowest grade transferable C. **General Admission Information:** Application fee $65. Regular application deadline 8/15. Notification on a rolling basis, beginning on or about 3/31. Nonfall registration accepted.

CITY UNIVERSITY OF NEW YORK—LEHMAN COLLEGE

250 Bedford Park Boulevard West, Bronx, NY 10468
Phone: 718-960-8000 **Financial Aid Phone:** 718-960-8545
E-mail: wilkes@alpha.lehman.cuny.edu **CEEB Code:** 2950
Fax: 718-960-8712

This public school was founded in 1968. It has a 38-acre campus.

RATINGS
Admissions Selectivity Rating: 78   **Fire Safety Rating:** 60*   **Green Rating:** 60*

STUDENTS AND FACULTY
Enrollment: 8,236. **Student Body:** 71% female, 29% male, 1% out-of-state, 5% international (123 countries represented). Asian 4%, African American 32%, Caucasian 10%, Hispanic 49%.
Retention and Graduation: 77% freshmen return for sophomore year. 12% freshmen graduate within 4 years. **Faculty:** Student/faculty ratio 15:1. 368 full-time faculty, 75% hold PhDs, 27% are members of minority groups, 52% are women.

ACADEMICS
Degrees: Bachelor's, certificate, diploma, master's. **Classes:** Most classes have 20–29 students. **Majors with Highest Enrollment:** Nursing/registered nurse (RN, ASN, BSN, MSN); social work; sociology. **Special Study Options:** Accelerated program, cooperative education program, cross-registration, distance learning, double major, dual enrollment, English as a Second Language (ESL), exchange student program (domestic), honors program, independent study, internships, student-designed major, study abroad, teacher certification program, weekend college, bilingual liberal arts (first 2 years may be taken in Spanish), professional writing concentration, 3-2 engineering program with City College. **Honors programs:** Lehman Scholars Program. Students receive full tuition, stipends, an expense account to use for academically enriching experiences and a laptop computer. **Combined degree programs:** BA/MA Special programs offered to physically disabled students include note-taking services, reader services, tape recorders, tutors.

FACILITIES
Housing: 80% of campus accessible to physically disabled. **Special Academic Facilities/Equipment:** Art gallery, concert hall, sports complex. **Computers:** Students can register for classes online. Administrative functions (other than registration) can be performed online.

CAMPUS LIFE
Environment: Metropolis. **Activities:** Choral groups, concert band, dance, drama/theater, jazz band, literary magazine, music ensembles, musical theater, opera, radio station, student government, student newspaper, student-run film society, symphony orchestra, television station, yearbook, international student organization. **Organizations:** 3 honor societies, 1 religious organizations. 1 fraternities, 1 sorority. **Athletics (Intercollegiate):** *Men:* Badminton, baseball, basketball, cross-country, diving, swimming, tennis, track/field (outdoor), volleyball. *Women:* Badminton, basketball, cross-country, diving, softball, swimming, tennis, track/field (outdoor), volleyball. **On-Campus Highlights:** APEX athletic facility, cyber cafe, art gallery, concert hall, information technology center.

ADMISSIONS

Freshman Academic Profile: Average high school GPA 2.7. 74% from public high schools. SAT Math middle 50% range 400–500. SAT Critical Reading middle 50% range 400–490. Minimum paper TOEFL 500. Minimum computer TOEFL 173. **Basis for Candidate Selection:** *Very important factors considered include:* Rigor of secondary school record, standardized test scores. *Important factors considered include:* Academic GPA. *Other factors considered include:* Application essay, recommendation(s), extracurricular activities, interview, talent/ability. **Freshman Admission Requirements:** High school diploma is required and GED is accepted. *Academic units required:* 4 English, 2 mathematics, 2 science, (1 science labs), 2 foreign language, 1 social studies, 1 history. *Academic units recommended:* 4 English, 3 mathematics, 3 science, 2 foreign language, 2 social studies, 2 history, 1 visual/performing arts. **Freshman Admission Statistics:** 14,155 applied, 32% admitted, 58% enrolled. **Transfer Admission Requirements:** College transcript(s), minimum college GPA of 2 required. Lowest grade transferable C. **General Admission Information:** Application fee $65. Regular application deadline 8/15. Nonfall registration accepted. Admission may be deferred for a maximum of 1 semester. Credit offered for CEEB Advanced Placement tests.

COSTS AND FINANCIAL AID

Annual in-state tuition $4,000. Annual out-of-state tuition $10,800. Required fees $290. Average book expense $938. **Required Forms and Deadlines:** FAFSA, state aid form. **Notification of Awards:** Applicants will be notified of awards on a rolling basis beginning 3/1. **Types of Aid:** *Need-based scholarships/grants:* Federal Pell, SEOG, state scholarships/grants, private scholarships, the school's own gift aid, MARC, NBRS. *Loans:* Direct Subsidized Stafford, Direct Unsubsidized Stafford, Direct PLUS, Federal Perkins, state loans, college/university loans from institutional funds. **Student Employment:** Federal Work-Study Program available. Institutional employment available. Off-campus job opportunities are excellent. **Financial Aid Statistics:** 79% freshmen, 74% undergrads receive need-based scholarship or grant aid. 38% freshmen, 12% undergrads receive non-need-based scholarship or grant aid. 17% freshmen, 36% undergrads receive need-based self-help aid. 83% freshmen, 80% undergrads receive any aid. 34% undergrads borrow to pay for school. Average cumulative indebtedness $11,500. **Criteria for awarding institutional aid:** *Non-need-based:* Academics.

CITY UNIVERSITY OF NEW YORK— MEDGAR EVERS COLLEGE

1665 Bedford Avenue, Brooklyn, NY 11225
Phone: 718-270-6024 **Financial Aid Phone:** 718-270-6139
E-mail: applytomec@mec.cuny.edu
Fax: 718-270-6411 **Website:**

This public school was founded in 1969. It has a 7-acre campus.

RATINGS
Admissions Selectivity Rating: 60*   **Fire Safety Rating:** 60*   **Green Rating:** 60*

STUDENTS AND FACULTY

Enrollment: 6,757. **Student Body:** 75% female, 25% male, 0.2% out-of-state, 2% international . Asian 1%, African American 88%, Caucasian 1%, Hispanic 6%.
Retention and Graduation: Faculty: Student/faculty ratio 19:1. 189 full-time faculty, 52% hold PhDs, 89% are members of minority groups, 47% are women.

ACADEMICS

Degrees: Associate, bachelor's, certificate. **Classes:** Most classes have 30–39 students. Most lab/discussion sessions have 10–19 students. **Majors with Highest Enrollment:** Biology/biological sciences; business administration and management; liberal arts and sciences/liberal studies. **Special Study Options:** Cross-registration, distance learning, English as a Second Language (ESL), honors program, independent study, internships, study abroad, teacher certification program. Special programs offered to physically disabled students include note-taking services, reader services, tape recorders, tutors. **Career services:** Alumni services, career/job search classes, career assessment, internships. **Career services highlights include:** Career Job Search, classes: Business Etiquette Series Interviewing Skills.

FACILITIES

Housing: 100% of campus accessible to physically disabled. **Computers:** 90% of classrooms, 100% of libraries, have wireless network access. Students can register for classes online. Administrative functions (other than registration) can be performed online.

CAMPUS LIFE

Environment: Metropolis. **Activities:** Choral groups, dance, drama/theater, jazz band, literary magazine, musical theater, radio station, student government, student newspaper, television station, yearbook, international student organization. **Organizations:** 32 registered organizations, 4 honor societies, 2 religious organizations. **Athletics (Intercollegiate):** *Men:* Basketball, cross-country, soccer, swimming, track/field (outdoor), track/field (indoor), volleyball. *Women:* Basketball, cheerleading, cross-country, soccer, softball, swimming, tennis, track/field (outdoor), track/field (indoor), volleyball. **On-Campus Highlights:** Amphitheater, NASA Space Center Lab, library, departments, new building.

ADMISSIONS

Freshman Academic Profile: Average high school GPA 72.8. SAT Math middle 50% range 330–430. SAT Critical Reading middle 50% range 340–440. SAT Writing middle 50% range 340–430. Minimum paper TOEFL 475. **Basis for Candidate Selection:** *Other factors considered include:* Academic GPA, rigor of secondary school record, standardized test scores. **Freshman Admission Requirements:** High school diploma is required and GED is accepted. *Academic units recommended:* 4 English, 3 mathematics, (2 science labs), 2 foreign language, 2 social studies, 2 history, 1 visual/performing arts. **Freshman Admission Statistics:** 7,178 applied, 20% admitted, 95% enrolled. **Transfer Admission Requirements:** College transcript(s), minimum college GPA of 2.0 required. Lowest grade transferable C. **General Admission Information:** Application fee $65. Nonfall registration accepted. Admission may be deferred for a maximum of one semester.

COSTS AND FINANCIAL AID

Annual in-state tuition $4,600. Annual out-of-state tuition $9,960. Required fees $302. Average book expense $1,070. **Required Forms and Deadlines:** FAFSA, state aid form. Financial aid filing deadline 6/1. Priority financial aid filing date 1/2. **Notification of Awards:** Applicants will be notified of awards on a rolling basis beginning 5/1. **Types of Aid:** *Need-based scholarships/grants:* Federal Pell, SEOG, state scholarships/grants. *Loans:* Direct Subsidized Stafford, Direct Unsubsidized Stafford, Direct PLUS, Federal Perkins. **Student Employment:** Federal Work-Study Program available. Institutional employment available. Highest amount earned per year from on-campus jobs $1,300. Off-campus job opportunities are good. **Financial Aid Statistics:** 85% freshmen, 82% undergrads receive need-based scholarship or grant aid. 12% freshmen, 19% undergrads receive need-based self-help aid. **Criteria for awarding institutional aid:** *Non-need-based:* Academics, leadership.

CITY UNIVERSITY OF NEW YORK—NEW YORK CITY COLLEGE OF TECHNOLOGY

300 Jay Street, NG17, Brooklyn, NY 11201
Phone: 718-260-5500 **Financial Aid Phone:** 718-260-5700
E-mail: admissions@citytech.cuny.edu **CEEB Code:** 2550
Fax: 718-260-5504 **Website:** www.citytech.cuny.edu/ **ACT Code:** 2950

This public school was founded in 1946. It has a 3-acre campus.

RATINGS
Admissions Selectivity Rating: 60*   **Fire Safety Rating:** 60*   **Green Rating:** 60*

STUDENTS AND FACULTY

Enrollment: 14,366. **Student Body:** 47% female, 53% male, 1% out-of-state, 6% international (140 countries represented). Asian 16%, African American 37%, Caucasian 14%, Hispanic 27%.
Retention and Graduation: 6% freshmen graduate within 4 years. **Faculty:** Student/faculty ratio 17:1. 411 full-time faculty, 64% hold PhDs, 33% are members of minority groups, 45% are women.

ACADEMICS

Degrees: Associate, bachelor's, certificate. **Classes:** Most classes have 20–29 students. Most lab/discussion sessions have 20–29 students. **Majors with Highest Enrollment:** Computer technology/computer systems technology; hospitality administration/management; human services. **Special Study Options:** Distance learning, dual enrollment, English as a Second Language (ESL), honors program, independent study, internships, study abroad, teacher certification program, Bridge programs to higher education or careers in engineering technology, alternate format program for those out of high school 5 years with or without diploma. Special programs offered to physically disabled students include note-taking services, reader services, tape recorders, tutors. **Career services:** Career assessment, internships.

FACILITIES

Housing: Some housing avilable at nearby university. 100% of campus accessible to physically disabled. **Computers:** Students can register for classes online. Administrative functions (other than registration) can be performed online.

CAMPUS LIFE

Environment: Metropolis. **Activities:** Dance, drama/theater, musical theater, student government, student newspaper. **Organizations:** 60 registered organizations. **Athletics (Intercollegiate):** *Men:* Basketball, tennis, track/field (outdoor). *Women:* Basketball, tennis, track/field (outdoor).

ADMISSIONS

Freshman Academic Profile: Minimum paper TOEFL 500. Minimum computer TOEFL 173. Minimum web-based TOEFL 61. **Basis for Candidate Selection:** *Important factors considered include:* Academic GPA, rigor of secondary school record. *Other factors considered include:* Class rank, application essay, recommendation(s), standardized test scores. **Freshman Admission Requirements:** High school diploma is required and GED is accepted. *Academic units required:* 4 English, 3 mathematics, 2 science, (2 science labs), 2 foreign language, 3 social studies, 1 academic electives, 1 fine arts. *Academic units recommended:* 4 English, 4 mathematics, 3 science, (3 science labs), 2 foreign language, 4 social studies, 2 academic electives, 1 fine arts. **Freshman Admission Statistics:** 14,419 applied, 84% admitted, 27% enrolled. **Transfer Admission Requirements:** High school transcript, college transcript(s), statement of good standing from prior institution(s). Minimum college GPA of 2.0 required. Lowest grade transferable C. **General Admission Information:** Application fee $65. Notification on a rolling basis, beginning on or about 1/15. Nonfall registration accepted. Admission may be deferred for a maximum of 1 semester. Credit and/or placement offered for CEEB Advanced Placement tests.

COSTS AND FINANCIAL AID

Annual in-state tuition $4,000. Annual out-of-state tuition $12,450. Required fees $339. **Required Forms and Deadlines:** FAFSA. Priority financial aid filing date 3/31. **Types of Aid:** *Need-based scholarships/grants:* Federal Pell, SEOG, state scholarships/grants, Federal Nursing Scholarships. *Loans:* Direct Subsidized Stafford, Direct Unsubsidized Stafford, Direct PLUS, Federal Perkins. **Student Employment:** Federal Work-Study Program available. Institutional employment available. Off-campus job opportunities are fair. **Financial Aid Statistics:** 80% freshmen, 76% undergrads receive need-based scholarship or grant aid. 22% freshmen, 12% undergrads receive non-need-based scholarship or grant aid. 13% freshmen, 19% undergrads receive need-based self-help aid. 78% freshmen, 66% undergrads receive any aid. **Criteria for awarding institutional aid:** *Non-need-based:* State/district residency.

CITY UNIVERSITY OF NEW YORK— QUEENS COLLEGE

6530 Kissena Blvd, Jefferson 117, Flushing, NY 11367
Phone: 7189975600 **Financial Aid Phone:** 7189975123
E-mail: vincent.angrisani@qc.cuny.edu **CEEB Code:** 2750
Fax: 7189975617 **Website:** www.qc.cuny.edu **ACT Code:** 20173

This public school was founded in 1937. It has a 76-acre campus.

RATINGS

Admissions Selectivity Rating: 60*   **Fire Safety Rating:** 79   **Green Rating:** 60*

STUDENTS AND FACULTY

Enrollment: 15,270. **Student Body:** 59% female, 41% male, 1% out-of-state, international (140 countries represented).
Retention and Graduation: 84% freshmen return for sophomore year. **Faculty:** Student/faculty ratio 16:1. 630 full-time faculty, 86% hold PhDs, 19% are are members of minority groups, 43% are women. 1% of classes are taught by teaching assistants.

ACADEMICS

Degrees: Bachelor's, master's, post-bachelor's certificate, post-master's certificate. **Classes:** Most classes have 20–29 students. **Majors with Highest Enrollment:** Accounting; psychology; sociology. **Special Study Options:** Accelerated program, cross-registration, double major, dual enrollment, English as a Second Language (ESL), honors program, independent study, internships, liberal arts/career combination, student-designed major, study abroad, teacher

certification program, weekend college, Courses offered through Blackboard. **Honors programs:** Queens College participates in the CUNY Honors College—a highly selective program that offers a challenging curriculum and a full tuition scholarship PLUS. other financial support. The program accepts first-time freshmen in the fall semester only. **Combined degree programs:** BA/MA Special programs offered to physically disabled students include note-taking services, reader services, tape recorders, tutors. **Career services:** Career/job search classes, career assessment, internships. **Career services highlights include:** Career Fair—over 70 employers from various fields (accounting, banking, finance, human services, publishing, media, covernment, technology, etc) come to the campus to interview and meet with students.

FACILITIES

Housing: Coed dorms. 100% of campus accessible to physically disabled. **Special Academic Facilities/Equipment:** Godwin-Ternbach Museum, Louis Armstrong House Museum & Archieves, Colden Auditorium, Kupferberg Center for the Performing Arts, Art Library **Computers:** 100% of classrooms, 100% of dorms, 100% of libraries, 100% of dining areas, 100% of student union, 100% of common outdoor areas have wireless network access. Students can register for classes online. Administrative functions (other than registration) can be performed online.

CAMPUS LIFE

Environment: Metropolis. **Activities:** Choral groups, concert band, dance, drama/theater, jazz band, literary magazine, music ensembles, musical theater, radio station, student government, student newspaper, student-run film society, symphony orchestra, television station, yearbook, international student organization. **Organizations:** 114 registered organizations, 5 honor societies, 12 religious organizations. 4 fraternities, 3 sororities. **Athletics (Intercollegiate):** *Men:* Baseball, basketball, cross-country, diving, soccer, swimming, tennis, track/field (outdoor), water polo. *Women:* Basketball, cross-country, diving, fencing, lacrosse, soccer, softball, swimming, tennis, track/field (outdoor), volleyball, water polo. **On-Campus Highlights:** Rosenthal Library, Student Union, Athletic Center, Dining Hall, Classrooms and Laboratory Facilities, cafes around campus.

ADMISSIONS

Freshman Academic Profile: SAT Math middle 50% range 490–580. SAT Critical Reading middle 50% range 490–550. SAT Writing middle 50% range 490–550. Minimum paper TOEFL 500. Minimum computer TOEFL 173. Minimum web-based TOEFL 62. **Basis for Candidate Selection:** *Very important factors considered include:* Academic GPA, rigor of secondary school record, standardized test scores. **Freshman Admission Requirements:** High school diploma is required and GED is accepted. *Academic units required:* 4 English, 3 mathematics, 2 science, (2 science labs), 3 foreign language, 4 social studies. *Academic units recommended:* 3 science, (3 science labs). **Freshman Admission Statistics:** 18,028 applied, 33% admitted, 29% enrolled. **Transfer Admission Requirements:** High school transcript, college transcript(s), standardized test scores, minimum college GPA of 2.25 required. Lowest grade transferable C. **General Admission Information:** Application fee $65. Notification on a rolling basis, beginning on or about 1/15. Nonfall registration accepted. Admission may be deferred for a maximum of 1 semester. Credit offered for CEEB Advanced Placement tests.

COSTS AND FINANCIAL AID

Annual in-state tuition $4,600. Required fees $447. **Required Forms and Deadlines:** FAFSA, institution's own financial aid form, state aid form. Priority financial aid filing date 2/1. **Notification of Awards:** Applicants will be notified of awards on a rolling basis beginning 3/1. **Types of Aid:** *Need-based scholarships/grants:* Federal Pell, SEOG, state scholarships/grants, private scholarships, the school's own gift aid. *Loans:* Direct Subsidized Stafford, Direct Unsubsidized Stafford, Direct PLUS, Federal Perkins. *Student Employment:* Federal Work-Study Program available. Institutional employment available. Off-campus job opportunities are good. **Financial Aid Statistics:** 36% freshmen, 46% undergrads receive need-based scholarship or grant aid. 27% freshmen, 10% undergrads receive non-need-based scholarship or grant aid. 22% freshmen, 15% undergrads receive need-based self-help aid. 2% freshmen, 1% undergrads receive athletic scholarships. 52% freshmen, 46% undergrads receive any aid. 41% undergrads borrow to pay for school. Average cumulative indebtedness $14,000. **Criteria for awarding institutional aid:** *Non-need-based:* Academics, athletics.

CITY UNIVERSITY OF NEW YORK— QUEENSBOROUGH COMMUNITY COLLEGE

222-05 56th Ave, A-210, Queens, NY 11364
Phone: 718-631-6236
E-mail: wyarde@qcc.cuny.edu **CEEB Code:** 2751
Fax: 718-281-5208 **Website:**

This public school was founded in 1967. It has a 34-acre campus.

RATINGS
Admissions Selectivity Rating: 60*   **Fire Safety Rating:** 60*   **Green Rating:** 60*

STUDENTS AND FACULTY
Enrollment: 10,955. **Student Body:** 57% female, 43% male, 1% out-of-state, 12% international (132 countries represented). Asian 18%, African American 25%, Caucasian 24%, Hispanic 21%.
Retention and Graduation: Faculty: Student/faculty ratio 15:1. 289 full-time faculty.

ACADEMICS
Degrees: Associate, certificate, terminal associate, transfer associate. **Special Study Options:** Cooperative education program, distance learning, double major, dual enrollment, English as a Second Language (ESL), honors program, independent study, internships, liberal arts/career combination, study abroad, weekend college, external education for homebound students, honors program for high school seniors. **Honors programs:** Honors program that has smaller class size and enriched course material and activities. Special programs offered to physically disabled students include note-taking services, reader services, tape recorders, tutors. **Career services:** Alumni services, career/job search classes, career assessment, internships.

FACILITIES
Housing: Coed dorms, special housing for disabled students, men's dorms, special housing for international students, women's dorms, fraternity/sorority housing, apartments for married students, cooperative housing, apartments for single students. 85% of campus accessible to physically disabled. **Special Academic Facilities/Equipment:** Oakland Art Gallery, Performing Arts Center, The Holocaust Center. **Computers:** Students can register for classes online. Administrative functions (other than registration) can be performed online.

CAMPUS LIFE
Environment: Metropolis. **Organizations:** 37 registered organizations, 3 honor societies, **Athletics (Intercollegiate):** *Men:* Baseball, basketball, cross-country, soccer, swimming, tennis, track/field (indoor), volleyball, *Women:* Basketball, cross-country, softball, swimming, tennis, volleyball. **On-Campus Highlights:** Holocaust Resources Center and Archives, Student Union, Instructional Support Services Center, Registration Center, Library.

ADMISSIONS
Freshman Academic Profile: 10% in top 50% of high school class. 80% from public high schools. Minimum paper TOEFL 475. Minimum computer TOEFL 163. **Basis for Candidate Selection:** *Other factors considered include:* Academic GPA, standardized test scores. **Freshman Admission Requirements:** High school diploma is required and GED is accepted. **Freshman Admission Statistics:** 7,471 applied, 99% admitted, 35% enrolled. **Transfer Admission Requirements:** High school transcript, college transcript(s), minimum college GPA of 2.0 required. Lowest grade transferable D. **General Admission Information:** Application fee $50. Notification on a rolling basis, beginning on or about 12/1. Nonfall registration accepted. Credit offered for CEEB Advanced Placement tests.

COSTS AND FINANCIAL AID
Annual in-state tuition $2,800. Annual out-of-state tuition $4,560. Required fees $284. **Required Forms and Deadlines:** FAFSA, institution's own financial aid form. **Notification of Awards:** Applicants will be notified of awards on a rolling basis beginning 7/15. **Types of Aid:** *Need-based scholarships/grants:* Federal Pell, SEOG, state scholarships/grants, the school's own gift aid. *Loans:* Direct Subsidized Stafford, Direct Unsubsidized Stafford, Direct PLUS. **Student Employment:** Federal Work-Study Program available. Institutional employment available. Off-campus job opportunities are good.

CITY UNIVERSITY OF NEW YORK— THE COLLEGE OF STATEN ISLAND

2800 Victory Boulevard, Bldg 2A Room 103, Staten Island, NY 10314
Phone: 718-982-2010 **Financial Aid Phone:** 718-982-2030
E-mail: admissions@mail.csi.cuny.edu **CEEB Code:** 2778
Fax: 718-982-2500 **Website:** www.csi.cuny.edu **ACT Code:** 2950

This public school was founded in 1955. It has a 204-acre campus.

RATINGS
Admissions Selectivity Rating: 66   **Fire Safety Rating:** 60*   **Green Rating:** 77

STUDENTS AND FACULTY
Enrollment: 12,578. **Student Body:** 58% female, 42% male, 0.61% out-of-state, 3% international (102 countries represented). Asian 6%, African American 6%, Caucasian 33%, Hispanic 8%.
Retention and Graduation: 23% freshmen graduate within 4 years. **Faculty:** Student/faculty ratio 17.5:1. 319 full-time faculty, 85% hold PhDs, 20% are members of minority groups, 44% are women.

ACADEMICS
Degrees: Associate, bachelor's, certificate, master's, post-master's certificate, terminal associate. **Classes:** Most classes have 30–39 students. Most lab/discussion sessions have 30–39 students. **Majors with Highest Enrollment:** Business/commerce; liberal arts and sciences/liberal studies; psychology. **Special Study Options:** Accelerated program, cooperative education program, cross-registration, distance learning, double major, dual enrollment, English as a Second Language (ESL), exchange student program (domestic), honors program, independent study, internships, liberal arts/career combination, study abroad, teacher certification program, weekend college. **Honors programs:** CSI is one of seven campuses within CUNY that participates in the William E. Macaulay Honors College. Special programs offered to physically disabled students include note-taking services, reader services, tape recorders, tutors. **Career services:** Alumni services, career/job search classes, career assessment, internships. **Career services highlights include:** Internships, On Campus Recruitment Program.

FACILITIES
Housing: 95% of campus accessible to physically disabled. **Special Academic Facilities/Equipment:** Astrophysical Observatory, Archives and Special Collections, Center for the Arts, Center for Engineered Polymeric Materials, Center for Environmental Science, Center for Developmental Neuroscience and Developmental Disabilities, and the CSI Art Gallery. **Computers:** 97% of classrooms, 100% of libraries, 100% of dining areas, 100% of student union, 100% of common outdoor areas have wireless network access. Students can register for classes online. Administrative functions (other than registration) can be performed online.

CAMPUS LIFE
Environment: Metropolis. **Activities:** Choral groups, dance, drama/theater, jazz band, literary magazine, music ensembles, radio station, student government, student newspaper, student-run film society, yearbook, campus ministries, international student organization. **Organizations:** 47 registered organizations, 2 honor societies, 4 religious organizations. **Athletics (Intercollegiate):** *Men:* Baseball, basketball, cross-country, diving, soccer, swimming, tennis. *Women:* Basketball, cross-country, diving, soccer, softball, swimming, tennis, volleyball. **On-Campus Highlights:** Campus Center Rotunda, Center for the Performing Arts, library, sports and recreation center, Campus Center Game Room; the student lounges are also a popular site on campus for students. **Environmental Initiatives:** Developed paper/cans, bottles, glass/waste minirecycling deposit centers on all floors of all buildings on campus. Experimenting with a biodiesel kit to convert used cooking oil from our cafeteria to biodiesel fuel for equipment. Recently registered to participate in RecycleMania. We are currently recruiting student ambassadors.

ADMISSIONS
Freshman Academic Profile: Average high school GPA 2.96. 70% from public high schools. SAT Math middle 50% range 455–550. SAT Critical Reading middle 50% range 440–530. SAT Writing middle 50% range 450–520. Minimum paper TOEFL 450. Minimum computer TOEFL 133. **Basis for Candidate Selection:** *Very important factors considered include:* Rigor of secondary school record. *Important factors considered include:* Academic GPA, standardized test scores. **Freshman Admission Requirements:** High school diploma is required and GED is accepted. *Academic units required:* 4 English, 2 mathematics, 2 science, 2 foreign language, 4 social studies. *Academic units recommended:* 4 English, 3 mathematics, 3 science, 3 foreign language, 4 social studies. **Freshman Admission Statistics:** 9,730 applied, 100% admitted, 28%

enrolled. **Transfer Admission Requirements:** College transcript(s), minimum college GPA of 2.0 required. Lowest grade transferable C. **General Admission Information:** Application fee $65. Notification on a rolling basis, beginning on or about 12/15. Nonfall registration accepted. Admission may be deferred for a maximum of 1 semester. Credit and/or placement offered for CEEB Advanced Placement tests.

COSTS AND FINANCIAL AID

Required Forms and Deadlines: FAFSA. Priority financial aid filing date 3/31. **Types of Aid:** *Need-based scholarships/grants:* Federal Pell, SEOG, state scholarships/grants, private scholarships, the school's own gift aid. *Loans:* Direct Subsidized Stafford, Direct Unsubsidized Stafford, Direct PLUS, Federal Perkins, alternative proprietary loans. **Student Employment:** Federal Work-Study Program available. Institutional employment available. Off-campus job opportunities are good. **Financial Aid Statistics:** 59% freshmen, 56% undergrads receive need-based scholarship or grant aid. 16% freshmen, 8% undergrads receive non-need-based scholarship or grant aid. 13% freshmen, 17% undergrads receive need-based self-help aid. 58% freshmen, 57% undergrads receive any aid. **Criteria for awarding institutional aid:** *Non-need-based:* Academics, art, leadership, minority status, music/drama, state/district residency.

CITY UNIVERSITY OF NEW YORK— YORK COLLEGE

94-20 Guy R Brewer Boulevard, Jamaica, NY 11451
Phone: 718-262-2165
E-mail: admissions@york.cuny.edu **CEEB Code:** 2992
Fax: 718-262-2601 **Website:** www.york.cuny.edu **ACT Code:** 20175

This public school was founded in 1968. It has a 50-acre campus.

RATINGS
Admissions Selectivity Rating: 60*   **Fire Safety Rating:** 60*   **Green Rating:** 60*

STUDENTS AND FACULTY
Enrollment: 5,311. **Student Body:** 71% female, 29% male, 7% international (113 countries represented). Asian 8%, African American 44%, Caucasian 4%, Hispanic 14%.
Retention and Graduation: 77% freshmen return for sophomore year. 9% freshmen graduate within 4 years. **Faculty:** Student/faculty ratio 15:1. 166 full-time faculty, 73% hold PhDs, 39% are members of minority groups, 46% are women.

ACADEMICS
Degrees: Bachelor's. **Majors with Highest Enrollment:** Accounting; psychology; sociology. **Special Study Options:** Cooperative education program, double major, dual enrollment, English as a Second Language (ESL), honors program, independent study, internships, teacher certification program. **Co-Op Programs:** Business, Computer Science, Health Professions. Special programs offered to physically disabled students include note-taking services, reader services, tape recorders, tutors. **Career services:** Alumni services, career/job search classes, internships.

FACILITIES
Housing: 100% of campus accessible to physically disabled. **Special Academic Facilities/Equipment:** Center for educational technology. State-of-the-art cardio-pneumo-simulator. **Computers:** Students can register for classes online. Administrative functions (other than registration) can be performed online.

CAMPUS LIFE
Activities: Choral groups, drama/theater, jazz band, literary magazine, student government, student newspaper, student-run film society, television station, yearbook. **Organizations:** 50 registered organizations, 1 honor societies, 2 religious organizations. **Athletics (Intercollegiate):** *Men:* Basketball, cheerleading, cross-country, soccer, swimming, tennis, track/field (outdoor), volleyball. *Women:* Basketball, cheerleading, cross-country, softball, swimming, track/field (outdoor), volleyball.

ADMISSIONS
Freshman Academic Profile: 68% from public high schools. SAT Math middle 50% range 390–470. SAT Critical Reading middle 50% range 363–460. Minimum paper TOEFL 470. **Basis for Candidate Selection:** *Very important factors considered include:* Rigor of secondary school record, standardized test scores. **Freshman Admission Requirements:** High school diploma is required and GED is accepted. *Academic units required:* 3 English, 2 mathematics, 10 academic electives. *Academic units recommended:* 2 science, (2 science labs), 1 foreign language, 1 social studies, 2 history, 2 academic

electives. **Freshman Admission Statistics:** 2,389 applied, 31% admitted, 80% enrolled. **Transfer Admission Requirements:** High school transcript, college transcript(s), standardized test scores, minimum college GPA of 2.0 required. Lowest grade transferable C. **General Admission Information:** Application fee $40. Notification on a rolling basis, beginning on or about 2/16. Nonfall registration accepted. Admission may be deferred for a maximum of 1 semester. Placement offered for CEEB Advanced Placement tests.

COSTS AND FINANCIAL AID
Annual in-state tuition $3,200. Annual out-of-state tuition $6,800. Required fees $242. Average book expense $692. **Required Forms and Deadlines:** FAFSA, state aid form. **Notification of Awards:** Applicants will be notified of awards on a rolling basis beginning 3/1. **Types of Aid:** *Need-based scholarships/grants:* Federal Pell, SEOG, state scholarships/grants, private scholarships. *Loans:* Direct Subsidized Stafford, Direct Unsubsidized Stafford, Direct PLUS, Federal Perkins, college/university loans from institutional funds. **Student Employment:** Federal Work-Study Program available.

CLAFLIN UNIVERSITY

400 Magnolia Street, Orangeburg, SC 29115
Phone: 803-535-5340 **Financial Aid Phone:** 803-535-5720
E-mail: admissions@claflin.edu **CEEB Code:** 5109
Fax: 803-535-5387 **Website: ACT Code:** 3840

This private school, affiliated with the Methodist Church, was founded in 1869. It has a 43-acre campus.

RATINGS
Admissions Selectivity Rating: 79   **Fire Safety Rating:** 91   **Green Rating:** 67

STUDENTS AND FACULTY
Enrollment: 1,735. **Student Body:** 66% female, 34% male, 17% out-of-state, 2% international (11 countries represented). African American 95%, Caucasian 1%.
Retention and Graduation: 72% freshmen return for sophomore year. 29% freshmen graduate within 4 years. **Faculty:** Student/faculty ratio 14:1. 109 full-time faculty, 77% hold PhDs, 71% are members of minority groups, 46% are women.

ACADEMICS
Degrees: Bachelor's, master's. **Classes:** Most classes have 20–29 students. Most lab/discussion sessions have 10–19 students. **Majors with Highest Enrollment:** Biology/biological sciences; business administration and management; sociology. **Special Study Options:** Accelerated program, cooperative education program, cross-registration, double major, dual enrollment, English as a Second Language (ESL), honors program, independent study, internships, study abroad, teacher certification program, weekend college, (3+2) BS Mathematics(Applied Mathematics Track)/Claflin + BS Engineering/Clemson (3+2) BS Mathematics(Applied Mathematics Track)/Claflin + BS Engineering Technology/South Carolina State University (2+2) Associates Degree/ Orangeburg-Calhoun Technical College + BS Biotechnology/Claflin University. **Honors programs:** The Alice Carson Tisdale Honors College **Combined degree programs:** Dual-degree (2+2) in biotechnology. Special programs offered to physically disabled students include note-taking services. **Career services:** Career/job search classes, career assessment, internships.

FACILITIES
Housing: Men's dorms, women's dorms 90% of campus accessible to physically disabled. **Special Academic Facilities/Equipment:** TV studio, NMR Wilbur R. Gregg collection, Aruther Rose Museum. **Computers:** 33% of classrooms, 100% of libraries, 100% of dining areas have wireless network access. Students can register for classes online. Administrative functions (other than registration) can be performed online.

CAMPUS LIFE
Environment: Village. **Activities:** Choral groups, concert band, dance, drama/theater, jazz band, literary magazine, music ensembles, radio station, student government, student newspaper, student-run film society, television station, yearbook, international student organization. **Organizations:** 3 honor societies, 4 fraternities, 4 sororities. **Athletics (Intercollegiate):** *Men:* Baseball, basketball, cross-country, track/field (outdoor), track/field (indoor). *Women:* Basketball, cross-country, softball, track/field (outdoor), track/field (indoor), volleyball. **On-Campus Highlights:** Student Life Center, Computer Labs, SOAR Center, Center for Vocational Reflections, Arthur Rose Museum, Jonas T. Kennedy Health and Physical Education Center.

ADMISSIONS

Freshman Academic Profile: Average high school GPA 3. 9% in top 10% of high school class, 45% in top 25% of high school class, 59% in top 50% of high school class. 100% from public high schools. SAT Math middle 50% range 390–490. SAT Critical Reading middle 50% range 410–500. Minimum paper TOEFL 500. Minimum computer TOEFL 213. **Basis for Candidate Selection:** *Very important factors considered include:* Class rank, academic GPA, rigor of secondary school record, standardized test scores, character/personal qualities, first generation. *Important factors considered include:* Application essay, alumni/ae relation, extracurricular activities, level of applicant's interest, talent/ability. *Other factors considered include:* Recommendation(s), state residency, volunteer work, work experience. **Freshman Admission Requirements:** High school diploma is required and GED is accepted. *Academic units required:* 4 English, 3 mathematics, 2 science, (1 science labs), 2 social studies, 1 history, 7 academic electives. **Freshman Admission Statistics:** 4,092 applied, 35% admitted, 33% enrolled. **Transfer Admission Requirements:** College transcript(s), statement of good standing from prior institution(s). Minimum college GPA of 2.0 required. Lowest grade transferable C. **General Admission Information:** Application fee $20. Regular application deadline 7/15. Notification on a rolling basis, beginning on or about 10/1. Nonfall registration accepted. Admission may be deferred for a maximum of 12. Credit and/or placement offered for CEEB Advanced Placement tests.

COSTS AND FINANCIAL AID

Annual tuition $10,368. Room and board $6,806. Required fees $2,038. Average book expense $1,500. **Required Forms and Deadlines:** FAFSA, institution's own financial aid form. Priority financial aid filing date 4/15. **Notification of Awards:** Applicants will be notified of awards on a rolling basis beginning 5/15. **Types of Aid:** *Need-based scholarships/grants:* Federal Pell, SEOG, state scholarships/grants, private scholarships, the school's own gift aid, United Negro College Fund. *Loans:* FFEL Subsidized Stafford, FFEL Unsubsidized Stafford, FFEL PLUS, Federal Perkins. **Student Employment:** Federal Work-Study Program available. Institutional employment available. Highest amount earned per year from on-campus jobs $1,600. **Financial Aid Statistics:** 97% freshmen, 86% undergrads receive need-based scholarship or grant aid. 60% freshmen, 54% undergrads receive non-need-based scholarship or grant aid. 84% freshmen, 86% undergrads receive need-based self-help aid. 88% freshmen, 98% undergrads receive any aid. 89% undergrads borrow to pay for school. Average cumulative indebtedness $3,403.

CLAREMONT MCKENNA COLLEGE

890 Columbia Avenue, Claremont, CA 91711
Phone: 909-621-8088 **Financial Aid Phone:** 909-621-8356
E-mail: admission@claremontmckenna.edu **CEEB Code:** 4054
Fax: 909-621-8516 **Website:** www.claremontmckenna.edu **ACT Code:** 224

This private school was founded in 1946. It has a 56-acre campus.

RATINGS

Admissions Selectivity Rating: 97   **Fire Safety Rating:** 88   **Green Rating:** 86

STUDENTS AND FACULTY

Enrollment: 1,210. **Student Body:** 45% female, 55% male, 6% international (24 countries represented). Asian 12%, African American 3%, Caucasian 49%, Hispanic 9%.

Retention and Graduation: 94% freshmen return for sophomore year. 87% freshmen graduate within 4 years. 17% grads go on to further study within 1 year. 5% grads pursue arts and sciences degrees. 6% grads pursue law degrees. 1% grads pursue business degrees. 4% grads pursue medical degrees. **Faculty:** Student/faculty ratio 9:1. 128 full-time faculty, 98% hold PhDs, 21% are members of minority groups, 30% are women.

ACADEMICS

Degrees: Bachelor's, master's. **Classes:** Most classes have 10–19 students. **Majors with Highest Enrollment:** Economics; international relations and affairs; political science and government. **Special Study Options:** Cross-registration, double major, English as a Second Language (ESL), exchange student program (domestic), independent study, internships, student-designed major, study abroad. **Combined degree programs:** BA/JD, BA/MA, BA/MEng, BA/MBA. Special programs offered to physically disabled students include note-taking services, reader services, tape recorders, tutors. **Career services:**

Alumni network, alumni services, career/job search classes, career assessment, internships, regional alumni. **Career services highlights include:** School sponsored grants to cover political, community service, and international-based internships.

FACILITIES

Housing: Coed dorms, special housing for disabled students, apartments for single students 95% of campus accessible to physically disabled. **Special Academic Facilities/Equipment:** Art galleries, athenaeum complex, centers for Black and Chicano studies, computer lab, leadership lab, science center. **Computers:** 100% of classrooms, 100% of dorms, 100% of libraries, 100% of dining areas, 100% of student union, 100% of common outdoor areas have wireless network access. Administrative functions (other than registration) can be performed online.

CAMPUS LIFE

Environment: Town. **Activities:** Choral groups, dance, drama/theater, music ensembles, pep band, radio station, student government, student newspaper, symphony orchestra, yearbook, campus ministries, international student organization, Model UN. **Organizations:** 280 registered organizations, 7 honor societies, 5 religious organizations. **Athletics (Intercollegiate):** *Men:* Baseball, basketball, cross-country, diving, football, golf, soccer, swimming, tennis, track/field (outdoor), water polo. *Women:* Basketball, cross-country, diving, golf, lacrosse, soccer, softball, swimming, tennis, track/field (outdoor), volleyball, water polo. **On-Campus Highlights:** Marian Miner Cook Athenaeum, Athletic/Aquatics Center, Emett Student Center/The Hub, The Research Institutes, Keck Science Center, 11 of our 13 dorms have either been recently built or remodeled. Our newest dorm, Claremont Hall, finished construction last summer and is LEED-certified Silver. **Environmental Initiatives:** Building a LEED-certified new academic building. Completed construction of a LEED-certified dormitory. Initiated water saving measures using new sprinklers and water detection devices.

ADMISSIONS

Freshman Academic Profile: 85% in top 10% of high school class, 98% in top 25% of high school class, 100% in top 50% of high school class. 70% from public high schools. SAT Math middle 50% range 660–750. SAT Critical Reading middle 50% range 630–730. Minimum paper TOEFL 600. Minimum computer TOEFL 250. Minimum web-based TOEFL 100. **Basis for Candidate Selection:** *Very important factors considered include:* Rigor of secondary school record, standardized test scores, extracurricular activities. *Important factors considered include:* Application essay, recommendation(s). *Other factors considered include:* Academic GPA, alumni/ae relation, character/personal qualities, first generation, geographical residence, interview, racial/ethnic status, talent/ability, volunteer work, work experience. **Freshman Admission Requirements:** High school diploma is required and GED is accepted. *Academic units required:* 4 English, 3 mathematics, 2 science, (2 science labs), 3 foreign language, 1 social studies, 1 history. *Academic units recommended:* 4 mathematics, 3 science. **Freshman Admission Statistics:** 3,856 applied, 18% admitted, 40% enrolled. **Transfer Admission Requirements:** High school transcript, college transcript(s), essay or personal statement, statement of good standing from prior institution(s). Lowest grade transferable C. **General Admission Information:** Application fee $60. Early decision application deadline 11/15. Regular application deadline 1/2. Regular notification 4/1. Nonfall registration not accepted. Admission may be deferred for a maximum of 1 year. Credit and/or placement offered for CEEB Advanced Placement tests.

COSTS AND FINANCIAL AID

Annual tuition $38,510. Room and board $12,525. Required fees $235. Average book expense $2,000. **Required Forms and Deadlines:** FAFSA, CSS/Financial Aid PROFILE, noncustodial PROFILE, business/farm supplement. Financial aid filing deadline 2/1. Priority financial aid filing date 2/1. **Types of Aid:** *Need-based scholarships/grants:* Federal Pell, SEOG, state scholarships/grants, private scholarships, the school's own gift aid, United Negro College Fund. *Loans:* Direct Subsidized Stafford, Direct Unsubsidized Stafford, Direct PLUS, FFEL Subsidized Stafford, FFEL Unsubsidized Stafford, FFEL PLUS, Federal Perkins, college/university loans from institutional funds. **Student Employment:** Federal Work-Study Program available. Institutional employment available. Off-campus job opportunities are excellent. **Financial Aid Statistics:** 42% freshmen, 44% undergrads receive need-based scholarship or grant aid. 6% freshmen, 15% undergrads receive non-need-based scholarship or grant aid. 42% freshmen, 44% undergrads receive need-based self-help aid. 45% freshmen, 51% undergrads receive any aid. 30% undergrads borrow to pay for school. Average cumulative indebtedness $9,779. **Criteria for awarding institutional aid:** *Non-need-based:* Academics, leadership.

CLARION UNIVERSITY OF PENNSYLVANIA

Admissions Office, 840 Wood Street, Clarion, PA 16214
Phone: 814-393-2306 **Financial Aid Phone:** 814-393-2315
E-mail: admissions@clarion.edu **CEEB Code:** 2649
Fax: 814-393-2030 **Website:** www.clarion.edu **ACT Code:** 3698

This public school was founded in 1867. It has a 192-acre campus.

RATINGS
Admissions Selectivity Rating: 70   **Fire Safety Rating:** 85   **Green Rating:** 76

STUDENTS AND FACULTY
Enrollment: 5,929. **Student Body:** 60% female, 40% male, 4% out-of-state, 1% international (35 countries represented). Asian 1%, African American 6%, Caucasian 89%, Hispanic 1%.
Retention and Graduation: 71% freshmen return for sophomore year. 40% freshmen graduate within 4 years. **Faculty:** Student/faculty ratio 19:1. 256 full-time faculty, 11% are members of minority groups, 49% are women.

ACADEMICS
Degrees: Associate, bachelor's, certificate, master's, post-bachelor's certificate, post-master's certificate. **Classes:** Most classes have 20–29 students. Most lab/discussion sessions have 10–19 students. **Majors with Highest Enrollment:** Business administration and management; elementary education and teaching. **Special Study Options:** Accelerated program, cooperative education program, distance learning, double major, dual enrollment, honors program, independent study, internships, liberal arts/career combination, student-designed major, study abroad, teacher certification program, weekend college. **Honors programs:** Clarion University's Honors Program is a close-knit group of talented students preparing for the future. Honors courses satisfy general educational requirements and include field experiences. The 21-credit curriculum promotes development of essential life skills targeted for successful career outcomes. The Honors experience extends beyond the walls of the traditional classroom. Students may spend time with archaeologists in Italy, with anthropologists at a primate center, with large corporate firms and in small businesses, and with molecular biologists in laboratories. Studies have included 20th-century music, learning the art of problem solving, and pondered the ethical implications of research. Co-curricular themes prepare Honors Program students to assume leadership roles. The Honors Program is not for all students—only those individuals who desire professional success, demand academic excellence, and expect to create the future. Each year 50 freshmen are selected for the Honors Program. Courses are taught as special topics and faculty instructors are recruited for their scholarly expertise. Honors students major in every department within the university and receive pre-professional advisement. Students take a six-credit linked English and Speech class and a three-credit Humanities course in the Freshman year. In the sophomore year, students take a three-credit mathematics or science class and a three-credit social sciences course. As juniors, students take a Junior Seminar that culminates in a project prospectus for the capstone experience. Honors 450 is the Senior Presentation delivered in a university-wide presentation. The following program standards must be maintained at the end of each academic year: Freshman Year 3.0 GPA 9 program credits Sophomore Year 3.25 GPA 15 program credits Junior Year 3.4 GPA 18 program credits Senior Year 3.4 GPA 21 program credits To be considered for Honors Program admission, entering freshman must have a minimum SAT score of 1150 or equivalent ACT scores, graduate in the top 15 percent of high school class, and successful completion of an interview. Undergraduate students already enrolled or transfer students may also apply. If a student should fail to residence at Clarion University. Candidates for graduation with an associate degree must complete a minimum of 30 credit hours in residence at the Venango Campus in Oil City, Pennsylvania. maintain the required GPA and course progression, the student will be placed on probation and have one semester to meet the requirements. A student who fails to achieve the required GPA and course progression by the end of the probationary semester will not be allowed to continue in the Honors Program or to continue to receive an Honors scholarship. Special programs offered to physically disabled students include note-taking services, reader services, tape recorders, tutors. **Career services:** Career/job search classes, career assessment, internships.

FACILITIES
Housing: Coed dorms, men's dorms, women's dorms, fraternity/sorority housing, apartments for single students. Sororities occupy floors of residence halls. 98% of campus accessible to physically disabled. **Special Academic Facilities/Equipment:** Planetarium. Art Gallery. **Computers:** 40% of classrooms, 100% of libraries, 50% of dining areas, 90% of student union, 10% of common outdoor areas have wireless network access. Students can register for classes online. Administrative functions (other than registration) can be performed online.

CAMPUS LIFE
Environment: Village. **Activities:** Choral groups, concert band, dance, drama/theater, jazz band, literary magazine, marching band, music ensembles, musical theater, pep band, radio station, student government, student newspaper, television station, campus ministries, international student organization. **Organizations:** 150 registered organizations, 17 honor societies, 4 religious organizations. 5 fraternities, 8 sororities. **Athletics (Intercollegiate):** *Men:* Baseball, basketball, diving, football, golf, swimming, wrestling. *Women:* Basketball, cross-country, diving, soccer, softball, swimming, tennis, track/field (outdoor), volleyball. **On-Campus Highlights:** Recreation Center, Carlson Library/Art Gallery, student center, athletic field, Tippin Gymnasium.

ADMISSIONS
Freshman Academic Profile: Average high school GPA 3.2. 6% in top 10% of high school class, 22% in top 25% of high school class, 52% in top 50% of high school class. 87% from public high schools. SAT Math middle 50% range 420–530. SAT Critical Reading middle 50% range 410–520. SAT Writing middle 50% range 400–500. Minimum paper TOEFL 500. Minimum computer TOEFL 173. **Basis for Candidate Selection:** *Very important factors considered include:* Class rank, academic GPA, rigor of secondary school record, standardized test scores. *Important factors considered include:* Application essay, recommendation(s). *Other factors considered include:* Character/personal qualities, extracurricular activities, interview, level of applicant's interest, talent/ability, volunteer work, work experience. **Freshman Admission Requirements:** High school diploma is required and GED is accepted. *Academic units required:* 4 English, 3 mathematics, 3 science, 3 social studies. *Academic units recommended:* 4 English, 4 mathematics, 4 science, (1 science labs), 2 foreign language, 4 social studies. **Freshman Admission Statistics:** 4,777 applied, 68% admitted, 44% enrolled. **Transfer Admission Requirements:** High school transcript, college transcript(s), statement of good standing from prior institution(s). Minimum college GPA of 2.0 required. Lowest grade transferable C. **General Admission Information:** Notification on a rolling basis, beginning on or about 9/1. Nonfall registration accepted. Credit offered for CEEB Advanced Placement tests.

COSTS AND FINANCIAL AID
Annual in-state tuition $5,554. Annual out-of-state tuition $11,108. Room and board $6,390. Required fees $1,826. Average book expense $900. **Required Forms and Deadlines:** FAFSA. Financial aid filing deadline 4/15. Priority financial aid filing date 4/15. **Notification of Awards:** Applicants will be notified of awards on a rolling basis beginning 3/1. **Types of Aid:** *Need-based scholarships/grants:* Federal Pell, SEOG, state scholarships/grants, private scholarships, the school's own gift aid, United Negro College Fund, Federal Nursing Scholarships. *Loans:* Direct Subsidized Stafford, Direct Unsubsidized Stafford, Direct PLUS, FFEL PLUS. **Student Employment:** Federal Work-Study Program available. Institutional employment available. Highest amount earned per year from on-campus jobs $12,000. Off-campus job opportunities are fair. **Financial Aid Statistics:** 56% freshmen, 52% undergrads receive need-based scholarship or grant aid. 20% freshmen, 19% undergrads receive non-need-based scholarship or grant aid. 59% freshmen, 61% undergrads receive need-based self-help aid. 7% freshmen, 5% undergrads receive athletic scholarships. 78% freshmen, 75% undergrads receive any aid. **Criteria for awarding institutional aid:** *Non-need-based:* Academics, art, athletics, leadership, minority status, music/drama, state/district residency.

CLARK ATLANTA UNIVERSITY

223 James P. Brawley Dr, SW, Atlanta, GA 30314-4391
Phone: 404-880-8784 **Financial Aid Phone:** 404-880-8992
E-mail: cauadmissions@cau.edu **CEEB Code:** 5110
Fax: 404-880-6605 **Website:** www.cau.edu **ACT Code:** 804

This private school, affiliated with the Methodist Church, was founded in 1988. It has a 126-acre campus.

RATINGS
Admissions Selectivity Rating: 73   **Fire Safety Rating:** 90   **Green Rating:** 81

STUDENTS AND FACULTY
Enrollment: 3,202. **Student Body:** 73% female, 27% male, 65% out-of-state, 1% international (10 countries represented). African American 90%.
Retention and Graduation: 65% freshmen return for sophomore year. 30% freshmen graduate within 4 years. 26% grads go on to further study within 1 year. 19% grads pursue arts and sciences degrees. 1% grads pursue law degrees. 3% grads pursue business degrees. 1% grads pursue medical degrees. **Faculty:** Student/faculty ratio 17:1. 178 full-time faculty, 77% hold PhDs, 90% are members of minority groups, 38% are women.

ACADEMICS

Degrees: Cachelor's, master's, post-bachelor's certificate, post-master's certificate. **Classes:** Most classes have 20–29 students. Most lab/discussion sessions have fewer than 10 students. **Majors with Highest Enrollment:** Biology/biological sciences; business administration and management; radio, television, and digital communication, other. **Special Study Options:** Accelerated program, cooperative education program, cross-registration, double major, dual enrollment, exchange student program (domestic), honors program, independent study, internships, study abroad, teacher certification program, weekend college. **Combined degree programs:** BA/MA, BA/MEng. Special programs offered to physically disabled students include note-taking services, reader services, tape recorders, tutors. **Career services:** Career/job search classes, career assessment, internships.

FACILITIES

Housing: Coed dorms, men's dorms, women's dorms, apartments for single students 80% of campus accessible to physically disabled. **Computers:** 100% of classrooms, 5% of dorms, 100% of libraries, 100% of dining areas, 100% of student union, 80% of common outdoor areas have wireless network access. Students can register for classes online. Administrative functions (other than registration) can be performed online.

CAMPUS LIFE

Environment: Metropolis. **Activities:** Choral groups, concert band, dance, drama/theater, marching band, music ensembles, musical theater, opera, pep band, radio station, student government, student newspaper, student-run film society, symphony orchestra, television station, yearbook, campus ministries, international student organization. **Organizations:** 80 registered organizations, 12 honor societies, 5 religious organizations. 4 fraternities, 4 sororities. **Athletics (Intercollegiate):** *Men:* Baseball, basketball, cross-country, football, track/field (outdoor). *Women:* Basketball, cross-country, softball, tennis, track/field (outdoor), volleyball. **On-Campus Highlights:** Robert W. Woodruff Library, CAU Radio & Television Station, CAU Art Galleries, Heritage Commons Residence Hall, Henderson Student Center.

ADMISSIONS

Freshman Academic Profile: Average high school GPA 3.02. 8% in top 10% of high school class, 23% in top 25% of high school class, 46% in top 50% of high school class. 90% from public high schools. SAT Math middle 50% range 400–470. SAT Critical Reading middle 50% range 410–480. ACT middle 50% range 18–20. Minimum paper TOEFL 500. Minimum computer TOEFL 173. **Basis for Candidate Selection:** *Very important factors considered include:* Academic GPA, rigor of secondary school record, standardized test scores, character/personal qualities. *Important factors considered include:* Application essay, recommendation(s), talent/ability. *Other factors considered include:* Alumni/ae relation, level of applicant's interest, work experience. **Freshman Admission Requirements:** High school diploma is required and GED is accepted. *Academic units required:* 4 English, 3 mathematics, 3 science, (1 science labs), 2 foreign language, 3 social studies, 3 academic electives. **Freshman Admission Statistics:** 6,681 applied, 61% admitted, 17% enrolled. **Transfer Admission Requirements:** College transcript(s), statement of good standing from prior institution(s). Minimum college GPA of 2.5 required. Lowest grade transferable C. **General Admission Information:** Application fee $35. Regular application deadline 6/1. Notification on a rolling basis, beginning on or about 1/1. Nonfall registration accepted. Admission may be deferred for a maximum of 1 year. Credit and/or placement offered for CEEB Advanced Placement tests.

COSTS AND FINANCIAL AID

Annual tuition $16,328. Room and board $7,620. Required fees $710. Average book expense $2,200. **Required Forms and Deadlines:** FAFSA, state aid form. Financial aid filing deadline 3/1. Priority financial aid filing date 3/1. **Notification of Awards:** Applicants will be notified of awards on a rolling basis beginning 4/1. **Types of Aid:** *Need-based scholarships/grants:* Federal Pell, SEOG, state scholarships/grants, private scholarships, the school's own gift aid, United Negro College Fund. *Loans:* FFEL Subsidized Stafford, FFEL Unsubsidized Stafford, FFEL PLUS, Federal Perkins, state loans, Private Loans. **Student Employment:** Federal Work-Study Program available. Institutional employment available. Highest amount earned per year from on-campus jobs $8,500. Off-campus job opportunities are fair. **Financial Aid Statistics:** 76% freshmen, 76% undergrads receive need-based scholarship or grant aid. 21% freshmen, 20% undergrads receive non-need-based scholarship or grant aid. 90% freshmen, 87% undergrads receive need-based self-help aid. 80% freshmen, 98% undergrads receive any aid. 94% undergrads borrow to pay for school. Average cumulative indebtedness $51,979. **Criteria for awarding institutional aid:** *Non-need-based:* Academics, art, athletics, leadership, minority status, music/drama, religious affiliation, state/district residency.

CLARK UNIVERSITY

950 Main Street, Worcester, MA 01610-1477
Phone: 508-793-7431 **Financial Aid Phone:** 508-793-7478
E-mail: admissions@clarku.edu **CEEB Code:** 3279
Fax: 508-793-8821 **Website:** www.clarku.edu **ACT Code:** 1808

This private school was founded in 1887. It has a 50-acre campus.

RATINGS
Admissions Selectivity Rating: 91   **Fire Safety Rating:** 95   **Green Rating:** 85

STUDENTS AND FACULTY

Enrollment: 2,293. **Student Body:** 60% female, 40% male, 64% out-of-state, 8% international (72 countries represented). Asian 4%, African American 2%, Caucasian 68%, Hispanic 2%. **Retention and Graduation:** 91% freshmen return for sophomore year. 67% freshmen graduate within 4 years. 31% grads go on to further study within 1 year. 23% grads pursue arts and sciences degrees. 3% grads pursue law degrees. 4% grads pursue business degrees. 1% grads pursue medical degrees. **Faculty:** Student/faculty ratio 10:1. 184 full-time faculty, 97% hold PhDs, 16% are members of minority groups, 42% are women.

ACADEMICS

Degrees: Bachelor's, master's, post-bachelor's certificate, post-master's certificate. **Classes:** Most classes have 10–19 students. Most lab/discussion sessions have 10–19 students. **Majors with Highest Enrollment:** Biology/biological sciences; political science and government; psychology. **Special Study Options:** Cross-registration, double major, English as a Second Language (ESL), independent study, internships, liberal arts/career combination, student-designed major, study abroad, teacher certification program. **Combined degree programs:** BA/MA, BA/MA, BAMAT, BA/MBA, BA/MSF, BA/MSPC. Special programs offered to physically disabled students include note-taking services, tutors. **Career services:** Alumni network, alumni services, career/job search classes, career assessment, internships, regional alumni.

FACILITIES

Housing: Coed dorms, special housing for disabled students, women's dorms, apartments for single students, wellness housing. 95% of campus accessible to physically disabled. **Special Academic Facilities/Equipment:** Galleries, theatres, Robert H. Goddard historical exhibition, rare book room, craft center, music center, map library, arboretum, herbarium, extensive darkroom facilities, satellite dish for international program reception, electron microscope, nuclear magnetic resonance spectrometer. **Computers:** 100% of classrooms, 15% of dorms, 100% of libraries, 100% of dining areas, 100% of student union, 15% of common outdoor areas have wireless network access. Students can register for classes online. Administrative functions (other than registration) can be performed online.

CAMPUS LIFE

Environment: City. **Activities:** Choral groups, concert band, dance, drama/theater, jazz band, literary magazine, marching band, music ensembles, musical theater, pep band, radio station, student government, student newspaper, student-run film society, symphony orchestra, television station, yearbook, campus ministries, international student organization, Model UN. **Organizations:** 110 registered organizations, 10 honor societies, 7 religious organizations. **Athletics (Intercollegiate):** *Men:* Baseball, basketball; crew/rowing, cross-country, diving, lacrosse, soccer, swimming, tennis. *Women:* Basketball, crew/rowing, cross-country, diving, field hockey, soccer, softball, swimming, tennis, volleyball. **On-Campus Highlights:** Larger than life statue of Freud, rare book room, Goddard Library, Traina Center for the Arts, New: Dolan Field House and updated fields, The Green on a warm spring day. **Environmental Initiatives:** Becoming climate neutral; Clark University has operated an on-campus cogeneration facility since 1982; formation of the Clark University Environmental Sustainability Task Force (CUES).

ADMISSIONS

Freshman Academic Profile: Average high school GPA 3.47. 39% in top 10% of high school class, 76% in top 25% of high school class, 97% in top 50% of high school class. 70% from public high schools. SAT Math middle 50% range 540–650. SAT Critical Reading middle 50% range 550–660. SAT Writing middle 50% range 550–660. ACT middle 50% range 24–28. Minimum paper TOEFL 550. Minimum computer TOEFL 213. **Basis for Candidate Selection:** *Very important factors considered include:* Academic GPA, recommendation(s), rigor of secondary school record, standardized test scores, character/personal qualities. *Important factors considered include:* Application essay, extracurricular activities, talent/ability, volunteer work. *Other factors considered include:* Class rank, alumni/ae relation, first generation, geographical residence, interview, level of applicant's interest, racial/ethnic status, work experience. **Freshman Admission Requirements:** High school diploma is required and GED is accepted. *Academic units recommended:* 4 English, 3 mathematics, 3 science, (2 science labs), 2 foreign language, 2 social studies, 2 history. **Freshman Admission Statistics:** 5,299 applied, 56% admitted, 20% enrolled. **Transfer Admission Requirements:** High school transcript, college transcript(s), essay or personal statement, standardized test scores, statement of good standing from prior institution(s). Minimum college GPA of 2.8 required. **General Admission Information:** Application fee $55. Early decision application deadline 11/15. Regular application deadline 1/15. Regular notification 4/1. Nonfall registration accepted. Admission may be deferred for a maximum of 1 year. Credit and/or placement offered for CEEB Advanced Placement tests.

COSTS AND FINANCIAL AID

Annual tuition $34,900. Room and board $6,750. Required fees $320. Average book expense $800. **Required Forms and Deadlines:** FAFSA, CSS/Financial Aid PROFILE, noncustodial PROFILE Financial aid filing deadline 1/15. Priority financial aid filing date 1/15. **Notification of Awards:** Applicants will be notified of awards on or about 3/31. **Types of Aid:** *Need-based scholarships/grants:* Federal Pell, SEOG, state scholarships/grants, the school's own gift aid. *Loans:* Direct Subsidized Stafford, Direct Unsubsidized Stafford, Direct PLUS, Federal Perkins, state loans. **Student Employment:** Federal Work-Study Program available. Institutional employment available. Highest amount earned per year from on-campus jobs $2,500. Off-campus job opportunities are good. **Financial Aid Statistics:** 51% freshmen, 51% undergrads receive need-based scholarship or grant aid. 30% freshmen, 30% undergrads receive non-need-based scholarship or grant aid. 45% freshmen, 45% undergrads receive need-based self-help aid. 82% freshmen, 79% undergrads receive any aid. 90% undergrads borrow to pay for school. Average cumulative indebtedness $22,250. **Criteria for awarding institutional aid:** *Non-need-based:* Academics, leadership.

CLARKE COLLEGE

1550 Clarke Drive, Dubuque, IA 52001-3198
Phone: 563-588-6316
E-mail: admissions@clarke.edu **CEEB Code:** 6099
Fax: 563-588-6789 **Website:** www.clarke.edu **ACT Code:** 1290

This private school, affiliated with the Roman Catholic Church, was founded in 1843. It has a 55-acre campus.

RATINGS
Admissions Selectivity Rating: 79   **Fire Safety Rating:** 60*   **Green Rating:** 60*

STUDENTS AND FACULTY
Enrollment: 938. **Student Body:** 68% female, 32% male, 37% out-of-state, 1% international (8 countries represented). Asian 1%, African American 1%, Caucasian 63%, Hispanic 2%.
Retention and Graduation: 78% freshmen return for sophomore year. 48% freshmen graduate within 4 years. 25% grads go on to further study within 1 year. 23% grads pursue arts and sciences degrees. 2% grads pursue business degrees. **Faculty:** Student/faculty ratio 11:1. 75 full-time faculty, 68% hold PhDs, 63% are women.

ACADEMICS
Degrees: Associate, bachelor's, master's, terminal associate. **Classes:** Most classes have fewer than 10 students. Most lab/discussion sessions have fewer than 10 students. **Majors with Highest Enrollment:** Business/commerce; nursing/registered nurse (RN, ASN, BSN, MSN); psychology. **Special Study Options:** Accelerated program, cross-registration, distance learning, double major, honors program, independent study, internships, student-designed major, study abroad, teacher certification program. **Combined degree programs:** BS/MS in Physical Therapy. Special programs offered to physically disabled students include note-taking services, reader services, tape recorders, tutors. **Career services:** Alumni services, career/job search classes, career assessment, internships.

FACILITIES
Housing: Coed dorms, men's dorms, women's dorms, apartments for single students. 90% of campus accessible to physically disabled. **Special Academic Facilities/Equipment:** Art gallery, computer classrooms for math, biology, and computer science, computer-interfaced chemistry lab, human gross anatomy and nursing labs, electron microscope, music performance hall, foreign language lab, distance learning classroom. **Computers:** Students can register

for classes online. Administrative functions (other than registration) can be performed online.

CAMPUS LIFE
Environment: Town. **Activities:** Choral groups, concert band, dance, drama/theater, jazz band, literary magazine, music ensembles, musical theater, radio station, student government, student newspaper, yearbook. **Organizations:** 48 registered organizations, 5 honor societies, 1 religious organizations. **Athletics (Intercollegiate):** *Men:* Baseball, basketball, cheerleading, cross-country, golf, soccer, tennis, volleyball. *Women:* Basketball, cheerleading, cross-country, golf, soccer, softball, tennis, volleyball.

ADMISSIONS
Freshman Academic Profile: Average high school GPA 3.63. 23% in top 10% of high school class, 47% in top 25% of high school class, 76% in top 50% of high school class. 81% from public high schools. SAT Math middle 50% range 460–538. SAT Critical Reading middle 50% range 468–580. SAT Writing middle 50% range 510–560. ACT middle 50% range 21–26. Minimum paper TOEFL 527. Minimum computer TOEFL 197. **Basis for Candidate Selection:** *Very important factors considered include:* Academic GPA, rigor of secondary school record, standardized test scores, talent/ability. *Important factors considered include:* Class rank. *Other factors considered include:* Extracurricular activities, interview, racial/ethnic status, volunteer work. **Freshman Admission Requirements:** High school diploma is required and GED is accepted. *Academic units required:* 4 English, 3 mathematics, 3 science, (2 science labs), 2 foreign language, 2 social studies, 4 academic electives. *Academic units recommended:* 4 mathematics, 4 science. **Freshman Admission Statistics:** 823 applied, 77% admitted, 23% enrolled. **Transfer Admission Requirements:** High school transcript, college transcript(s), standardized test scores, statement of good standing from prior institution(s). Minimum college GPA of 2.0 required. Lowest grade transferable C. **General Admission Information:** Application fee $25. Notification on a rolling basis, beginning on or about 1/15. Nonfall registration accepted. Admission may be deferred for a maximum of 1 year. Credit and/or placement offered for CEEB Advanced Placement tests.

COSTS AND FINANCIAL AID
Annual tuition $22,800. Room and board $6,840. Required fees $720. Average book expense $700. **Required Forms and Deadlines:** Verification worksheets, if required. Priority financial aid filing date 4/15. **Notification of Awards:** Applicants will be notified of awards on a rolling basis beginning 3/1. **Types of Aid:** *Need-based scholarships/grants:* Federal Pell, SEOG, state scholarships/grants, private scholarships, the school's own gift aid. *Loans:* FFEL Subsidized Stafford, FFEL Unsubsidized Stafford, FFEL PLUS, Federal Perkins, Federal Nursing, state loans, college/university loans from institutional funds, alternative and private loans. **Student Employment:** Federal Work-Study Program available. Institutional employment available. Highest amount earned per year from on-campus jobs $1,422. Off-campus job opportunities are excellent. **Financial Aid Statistics:** 80% freshmen, 81% undergrads receive need-based scholarship or grant aid. 78% freshmen, 74% undergrads receive non-need-based scholarship or grant aid. 66% freshmen, 74% undergrads receive need-based self-help aid. 47% freshmen, 13% undergrads receive athletic scholarships. 85.2% undergrads borrow to pay for school. Average cumulative indebtedness $28,649. **Criteria for awarding institutional aid:** *Non-need-based:* Academics, alumni affiliation, art, athletics, leadership, minority status, music/drama, religious affiliation, state/district residency.

CLARKSON UNIVERSITY

Box 5605, Potsdam, NY 13699
Phone: 315-268-6480 **Financial Aid Phone:** 315-268-6413
E-mail: admission@clarkson.edu **CEEB Code:** 2084
Fax: 315-268-7647 **Website:** htttp://www.clarkson.edu

This private school was founded in 1896. It has a 640-acre campus.

RATINGS
Admissions Selectivity Rating: 86   **Fire Safety Rating:** 80   **Green Rating:** 88

STUDENTS AND FACULTY
Enrollment: 2,717. **Student Body:** 27% female, 73% male, 29% out-of-state, 3% international (44 countries represented). Asian 4%, African American 3%, Caucasian 84%, Hispanic 3%, Native American 1%.

Retention and Graduation: 54% freshmen graduate within 4 years. 23% grads go on to further study within 1 year. 10% grads pursue arts and sciences degrees. 1% grads pursue law degrees. 4% grads pursue business degrees. **Faculty:** Student/faculty ratio 14.9:1. 204 full-time faculty, 86% hold PhDs, 21% are members of minority groups, 26% are women.

ACADEMICS

Degrees: Bachelor's, master's. **Classes:** Most classes have 10–19 students. Most lab/discussion sessions have 20–29 students. **Majors with Highest Enrollment:** Business/commerce; civil engineering; mechanical engineering. **Special Study Options:** Accelerated program, cooperative education program, cross-registration, distance learning, double major, dual enrollment, English as a Second Language (ESL), honors program, independent study, liberal arts/career combination, student-designed major, study abroad, Women In Science and Engineering (WISE) Living/Learning Community; interdisciplinary degree programs that combine Engineering and Business, Business and Liberal Arts, and Environmental Science and Policy; a large number of 3+2 and 2+2 articulation agreements that facilitate transfer to Clarkson from community colleges and other baccalaureate institutions; business students experience a unique introduction to entrepreneurship through working with the Shipley Center for Innovation, the Clarkson Entrepreneurs Organization (CEO) and the Clarkson Center for Global Competitiveness. **Honors programs:** Built upon current and emerging problems in science, technology and society, the Clarkson University Honors Program offers unique academic challenges and opportunities for Clarkson's most promising students. The program is a gateway to a multitude of opportunities that include internships, research experience, fellowships, graduate schools, study abroad, and jobs. **Combined degree programs:** Business/Liberal Studies. Special programs offered to physically disabled students include note-taking services, reader services, tape recorders, tutors. **Career services:** Alumni network, alumni services, career/job search classes, career assessment, internships, regional alumni. **Career services highlights include:** The Clarkson University School of Business requires that all students complete an internship as part of their degree requirements. The commitment form the University to coordinate and facilitate placement of all students has resulted in tremendous placement outcomes a well as increased experiential application in the classroom.

FACILITIES

Housing: Coed dorms, special housing for disabled students, men's dorms, special housing for international students, women's dorms, fraternity/sorority housing, apartments for single students, wellness housing, theme housing. 85% of campus accessible to physically disabled. **Special Academic Facilities/Equipment:** The Center for Advanced Materials Processing (CAMP) is dedicated to developing innovations in advanced materials processing and to transfer this technology to business and industry, and is built on Clarkson's recognized expertise in colloid and surface science and fine particle technology. The Center for the Environment facilitates the development, promotion and operation of environmental activities within the University and among its partners. The Center for Rehabilitative Science and Technology (CREST). **Computers:** 100% of classrooms, 100% of libraries, 100% of dining areas, 100% of student union, 20% of common outdoor areas have wireless network access. Students can register for classes online. Administrative functions (other than registration) can be performed online.

CAMPUS LIFE

Environment: Village. **Activities:** Choral groups, drama/theater, jazz band, literary magazine, musical theater, pep band, radio station, student government, student newspaper, symphony orchestra, television station, yearbook, international student organization. **Organizations:** 117 registered organizations, 7 honor societies, 3 religious organizations. 11 fraternities, 3 sororities. **Athletics (Intercollegiate):** *Men:* Baseball, basketball, cross-country, diving, golf, ice hockey, lacrosse, skiing (downhill/alpine), skiing (nordic/cross-country), soccer, swimming. *Women:* Basketball, cross-country, diving, ice hockey, lacrosse, skiing (downhill/alpine), skiing (nordic/cross-country), soccer, swimming, volleyball. **On-Campus Highlights:** Snell Hall Shipley Center for Innovation, Adirondack Lodge, Cheel Campus Center Club 99, CAMP Building SPEED Labs, Java City/Library, Fitness Center. **Environmental Initiatives:** Elimination of all polystyrene product purchases. Recommitment to divert more waste from trash to recycling wastestream. Lighting upgrades in older facilities to energy efficient fixtures.

ADMISSIONS

Freshman Academic Profile: Average high school GPA 3.47. 34% in top 10% of high school class, 67% in top 25% of high school class, 94% in top 50% of high school class. 88% from public high schools. SAT Math middle 50% range 560–660. SAT Critical Reading middle 50% range 500–610. SAT Writing middle 50% range 490–580. ACT middle 50% range 23–27. Minimum paper TOEFL 550. Minimum computer TOEFL 213. **Basis for Candidate Selection:** *Very important factors considered include:* Academic GPA, rigor of secondary school record. *Important factors include:* Class rank, recommendation(s), standardized test scores, extracurricular activities, volunteer work. *Other factors considered include:* Application essay, alumni/ae relation, character/personal

qualities, first generation, level of applicant's interest, talent/ability, work experience. **Freshman Admission Requirements:** High school diploma is required and GED is accepted. *Academic units required:* 4 English, 3 mathematics, 3 science. *Academic units recommended:* 4 mathematics, 4 science. **Freshman Admission Statistics:** 4,125 applied, 73% admitted, 26% enrolled. **Transfer Admission Requirements:** College transcript(s), minimum college GPA of 2.75 required. Lowest grade transferable 2. **General Admission Information:** Application fee $50. Early decision application deadline 12/1. Regular application deadline 1/15. Notification on a rolling basis, beginning on or about 2/1. Nonfall registration accepted. Admission may be deferred for a maximum of 1 year. Credit offered for CEEB Advanced Placement tests.

COSTS AND FINANCIAL AID

Annual tuition $32,220. Room and board $11,518. Required fees $690. Average book expense $1,100. **Required Forms and Deadlines:** FAFSA, state aid form. Priority financial aid filing date 2/15. **Notification of Awards:** Applicants will be notified of awards on a rolling basis beginning 3/19. **Types of Aid:** *Need-based scholarships/grants:* Federal Pell, SEOG, state scholarships/grants, private scholarships, the school's own gift aid, HEOP. *Loans:* Direct Subsidized Stafford, Direct Unsubsidized Stafford, Direct PLUS, FFEL Subsidized Stafford, FFEL Unsubsidized Stafford, FFEL PLUS, Federal Perkins, college/university loans from institutional funds, private/alternative loans. **Student Employment:** Federal Work-Study Program available. Institutional employment available. Off-campus job opportunities are excellent. **Financial Aid Statistics:** 82% freshmen, 79% undergrads receive need-based scholarship or grant aid. 22% freshmen, 17% undergrads receive non-need-based scholarship or grant aid. 64% freshmen, 67% undergrads receive need-based self-help aid. 1% freshmen, 1% undergrads receive athletic scholarships. 95% freshmen, 92% undergrads receive any aid. 84.9% undergrads borrow to pay for school. Average cumulative indebtedness $32,125. **Criteria for awarding institutional aid:** *Non-need-based:* Academics, alumni affiliation, leadership, minority status.

CLAYTON STATE UNIVERSITY

2000 Clayton State Blvd, Morrow, GA 30206-0285
Phone: 678-466-4115
E-mail: ccsu-info@mail.clayton.edu
Fax: 678-466-4149 **Website:** www.clayton.edu

This is a public school.

RATINGS

Admissions Selectivity Rating: 70   **Fire Safety Rating:** 60*   **Green Rating:** 60*

STUDENTS AND FACULTY

Enrollment: 5,661. **Student Body:** 69% female, 31% male, 5% out-of-state, 2% international. Asian 4%, African American 48%, Caucasian 43%, Hispanic 3%, Native American 1%.
Retention and Graduation: 61% freshmen return for sophomore year. **Faculty:** Student/faculty ratio 28:1. 157 full-time faculty, 57% hold PhDs, 15% are members of minority groups, 59% are women.

ACADEMICS

Degrees: Associate, bachelor's, certificate, master's, terminal associate, transfer associate. **Classes:** Most classes have 20–29 students. Most lab/discussion sessions have fewer than 10 students. **Special Study Options:** Cooperative education program, cross-registration, distance learning, double major, dual enrollment, exchange student program (domestic), honors program, independent study, internships, liberal arts/career combination, study abroad, teacher certification program.

FACILITIES

Housing: Apartments for single students, local private apartment living.

CAMPUS LIFE

Activities: Choral groups, drama/theater, jazz band, literary magazine, music ensembles, musical theater, opera, pep band, student government, student newspaper.

ADMISSIONS

Freshman Academic Profile: Average high school GPA 2.88. SAT Math middle 50% range 440–550. SAT Critical Reading middle 50% range 450–550. ACT middle 50% range 17–21. **Basis for Candidate Selection:** *Very important factors considered include:* Academic GPA, rigor of secondary school record, standardized test scores. *Other factors considered include:* Class rank, extracurricular activities, talent/ability. **Freshman Admission Requirements:** High school diploma is required and GED is not accepted. *Academic units required:* 4 English, 4 mathematics, 3 science, 2 foreign language, 3 social studies. **Freshman Admission Statistics:** 2,920 applied, 71% admitted, 63% enrolled.

Transfer Admission Requirements: College transcript(s), statement of good standing from prior institution(s). Minimum college GPA of 2.0 required. Lowest grade transferable D. **General Admission Information:** Application fee $40. Regular application deadline 7/1. Notification on a rolling basis, beginning on or about 1/1. Nonfall registration accepted.

COSTS AND FINANCIAL AID

Annual in-state tuition $2,212. Annual out-of-state tuition $8,848. Average book expense $1,000. **Required Forms and Deadlines:** FAFSA, state aid form. Priority financial aid filing date 7/23. **Types of Aid:** *Need-based scholarships/ grants:* Federal Pell, SEOG, state scholarships/grants, private scholarships, the school's own gift aid, Federal Nursing Scholarships. *Loans:* FFEL Subsidized Stafford, FFEL Unsubsidized Stafford, FFEL PLUS, state loans. **Financial Aid Statistics:** 33% freshmen, 36% undergrads receive need-based scholarship or grant aid. 38% freshmen, 23% undergrads receive non-need-based scholarship or grant aid. 23% freshmen, 33% undergrads receive need-based self-help aid. 1% freshmen, 3% undergrads receive athletic scholarships. **Criteria for awarding institutional aid:** *Non-need-based:* Academics.

CLEAR CREEK BAPTIST BIBLE COLLEGE

300 Clear Creek Road, Pineville, KY 40977-9754
Phone: 606-337-3196 **Financial Aid Phone:** 606-337-1457
E-mail: ccbbc@ccbbc.edu
Fax: 606-337-2372 **Website:** www.ccbbc.edu

This private school, affiliated with the Southern Baptist Church, was founded in 1926. It has a 700-acre campus.

RATINGS
Admissions Selectivity Rating: 60*   **Fire Safety Rating:** 62   **Green Rating:** 60*

STUDENTS AND FACULTY
Enrollment: 168. **Student Body:** 21% female, 79% male, 47% out-of-state. African American 1%, Caucasian 95%.
Retention and Graduation: 77% freshmen return for sophomore year. 35% freshmen graduate within 4 years. 30% grads go on to further study within 1 year. **Faculty:** Student/faculty ratio 12:1. 6 full-time faculty, 83% hold PhDs.

ACADEMICS
Degrees: Associate, bachelor's, certificate, diploma. **Classes:** Most classes have 10–19 students. Most lab/discussion sessions have 10–19 students. **Majors with Highest Enrollment:** Bible/biblical studies. **Special Study Options:** Distance learning, double major, independent study, internships. **Career services:** Alumni network.

FACILITIES
Housing: Men's dorms, women's dorms, apartments for married students, apartments for single students, wellness housing. 95% of campus accessible to physically disabled. **Special Academic Facilities/Equipment:** Jerusalem model. **Computers:** 10% of dorms, 100% of libraries, 5% of common outdoor areas have wireless network access. Students can register for classes online.

CAMPUS LIFE
Environment: Rural. **Activities:** Choral groups, music ensembles, radio station, student government, student newspaper, campus ministries. **On-Campus Highlights:** Kelly Hall, Jerusalem model, Family Life Center, Creek and walking trails, Carolyn Boatman Brooks Memorial Library.

ADMISSIONS
Freshman Academic Profile: 95% from public high schools. Minimum paper TOEFL 550. **Basis for Candidate Selection:** *Very important factors considered include:* Application essay, recommendation(s), character/personal qualities, religious affiliation/commitment. *Other factors considered include:* Alumni/ae relation, interview, level of applicant's interest, talent/ability. **Freshman Admission Requirements:** High school diploma is required and GED is accepted. **Freshman Admission Statistics:** 20 applied, 100% admitted, 100% enrolled. **Transfer Admission Requirements:** High school transcript, college transcript(s), essay or personal statement, interview, minimum college GPA of 2.0 required. Lowest grade transferable C. **General Admission Information:** Application fee $40. Regular application deadline 8/2. Notification on a rolling basis, beginning on or about 4/1. Nonfall registration accepted. Admission may be deferred for a maximum of 2 years. Neither credit nor placement offered for CEEB Advanced Placement tests.

COSTS AND FINANCIAL AID
Annual tuition $4,972. Room and board $3,750. Required fees $350. Average book expense $800. **Required Forms and Deadlines:** FAFSA, institution's own financial aid form. Priority financial aid filing date 6/30. **Notification of Awards:** Applicants will be notified of awards on a rolling basis beginning 5/1.

Types of Aid: *Need-based scholarships/grants:* Federal Pell, SEOG, private scholarships, the school's own gift aid. **Student Employment:** Federal Work-Study Program available. Institutional employment available. Highest amount earned per year from on-campus jobs $7,000. Off-campus job opportunities are fair. **Financial Aid Statistics:** 75% freshmen, 89% undergrads receive need-based scholarship or grant aid. 63% freshmen, 14% undergrads receive non-need-based scholarship or grant aid. 19% freshmen, 22% undergrads receive need-based self-help aid. 81% freshmen, 75% undergrads receive any aid. 0.01% undergrads borrow to pay for school. **Criteria for awarding institutional aid:** *Non-need-based:* Academics, leadership, religious affiliation, state/district residency.

CLEARWATER CHRISTIAN COLLEGE

3400 Gulf-to-Bay Boulevard, Clearwater, FL 33759-4595
Phone: 727-726-1153 **Financial Aid Phone:** 727-726-1153
E-mail: admissions@clearwater.edu
Fax: 727-726-8597 **Website:** www.clearwater.edu **ACT Code:** 715

This private school, affiliated with the Christian (Nondenominational) Church, was founded in 1966. It has a 138-acre campus.

RATINGS
Admissions Selectivity Rating: 66   **Fire Safety Rating:** 94   **Green Rating:** 60*

STUDENTS AND FACULTY
Enrollment: 561. **Student Body:** 49% female, 51% male, 52% out-of-state, 1% international (5 countries represented). Asian 2%, African American 5%, Caucasian 87%, Hispanic 4%.
Retention and Graduation: 68% freshmen return for sophomore year. 20% grads go on to further study within 1 year. 10% grads pursue arts and sciences degrees. 2% grads pursue law degrees. 5% grads pursue business degrees. 1% grads pursue medical degrees. **Faculty:** Student/faculty ratio 15:1. 32 full-time faculty, 78% hold PhDs, 3% are members of minority groups, 34% are women.

ACADEMICS
Degrees: Associate, bachelor's, certificate, master's. **Classes:** Most classes have fewer than 10 students. **Majors with Highest Enrollment:** Business administration and management; elementary education and teaching; general studies. **Special Study Options:** Cooperative education program, distance learning, double major, dual enrollment, honors program, independent study, internships, liberal arts/career combination, student-designed major, study abroad, teacher certification program, Semester in Washington, DC. **Honors programs:** Interdisciplinary studies, a self-designed multidisciplinary program for students with exceptional ability and focus. Special programs offered to physically disabled students include tape recorders, tutors. **Career services:** Alumni services, career/job search classes, internships **Career services highlights include:** During an education student's last semester, the director of clinical field experiences places the student in Hillsborough and Pinellas County public and private schools for a 14-week teaching internship.

FACILITIES
Housing: Men's dorms, women's dorms. **Computers:** 100% of classrooms, 100% of dorms, 100% of libraries, 100% of dining areas, have wireless network access. Administrative functions (other than registration) can be performed online.

CAMPUS LIFE
Environment: City. **Activities:** Choral groups, concert band, drama/theater, music ensembles, pep band, student government, student newspaper, student-run film society, symphony orchestra, yearbook, campus ministries. **Organizations:** 17 registered organizations, 1 honor societies, 1 religious organizations. 5 fraternities, 6 sororities. **Athletics (Intercollegiate):** *Men:* Baseball, basketball, golf, soccer. *Women:* Basketball, golf, soccer, softball, volleyball. **On-Campus Highlights:** Centre Court Cafe, gymnasium, Cathcart Hall Cafeteria, Easter Library.

ADMISSIONS
Freshman Academic Profile: 10% in top 10% of high school class, 36% in top 25% of high school class, 64% in top 50% of high school class. 30% from public high schools. SAT Math middle 50% range 450–560. SAT Critical Reading middle 50% range 470–600. ACT middle 50% range 19–25. Minimum paper TOEFL 500. Minimum computer TOEFL 173. **Basis for Candidate Selection:** *Very important factors considered include:* Application essay, recommendation(s), standardized test scores, character/personal qualities, religious affiliation/commitment. *Important factors considered include:* Academic GPA, rigor of secondary school record, interview. *Other factors considered include:* Alumni/ae relation, level of applicant's interest, volunteer work. **Fresh-**

man **Admission Requirements:** High school diploma is required and GED is accepted. *Academic units required:* 4 English, 3 mathematics, 3 science, 2 foreign language, 3 social studies. **Freshman Admission Statistics:** 278 applied, 89% admitted, 64% enrolled. **Transfer Admission Requirements:** High school transcript, college transcript(s), essay or personal statement, standardized test scores, statement of good standing from prior institution(s). Minimum college GPA of 2.0 required. Lowest grade transferable C–. **General Admission Information:** Application fee $35. Regular application deadline 8/1. Nonfall registration not accepted. Admission may be deferred for a maximum of 1 year. Credit offered for CEEB Advanced Placement tests.

COSTS AND FINANCIAL AID

Annual tuition $14,710. Room and board $6,740. Average book expense $1,000. **Required Forms and Deadlines:** FAFSA, institution's own financial aid form, state aid form. **Types of Aid:** *Need-based scholarships/grants:* Federal Pell, SEOG, state scholarships/grants, private scholarships, the school's own gift aid, Additional scholarships available for students who are considered first generation, international, or whose parents are involved in Christian ministry. *Loans:* Direct Subsidized Stafford, Direct Unsubsidized Stafford, Direct PLUS, FFEL Subsidized Stafford, FFEL Unsubsidized Stafford, FFEL PLUS, state loans. **Student Employment:** Federal Work-Study Program available. Institutional employment available. Off-campus job opportunities are excellent. **Financial Aid Statistics:** 90% freshmen, 85% undergrads receive any aid. **Criteria for awarding institutional aid:** *Non-need-based:* Academics, alumni affiliation, leadership, music/drama, religious affiliation.

CLEARY UNIVERSITY

3750 Cleary Drive, Howell, MI 48843
Phone: 517-548-3670
E-mail: admissions@cleary.edu **CEEB Code:** 1123
Fax: 517-552-7805 **Website:** www.cleary.edu **ACT Code:** 1974

This private school was founded in 1883. It has a 32-acre campus.

RATINGS
Admissions Selectivity Rating: 60*   **Fire Safety Rating:** 60*   **Green Rating:** 60*

STUDENTS AND FACULTY
Enrollment: 626. **Student Body:** 54% female, 46% male, 1% international (5 countries represented). Asian 1%, African American 6%, Caucasian 77%, Hispanic 1%, Native American 1%.
Retention and Graduation: 75% freshmen return for sophomore year.
Faculty: Student/faculty ratio 10:1. 8 full-time faculty, 25% hold PhDs, 13% are members of minority groups, 63% are women.

ACADEMICS
Degrees: Associate, bachelor's, certificate, master's, terminal associate, transfer associate. **Classes:** Most classes have 10–19 students. Most lab/discussion sessions have 10–19 students. **Majors with Highest Enrollment:** Accounting; business/commerce; management information systems. **Special Study Options:** Accelerated program, cooperative education program, distance learning, dual enrollment, independent study, internships. Special programs offered to physically disabled students include tutors. **Career services:** Alumni network, alumni services, career/job search classes, internships.

FACILITIES
Housing: 90% of campus accessible to physically disabled. **Special Academic Facilities/Equipment:** Center for Quality, Quality Resource Collection, Center for Business Ethics and Leadership. **Computers:** Administrative functions (other than registration) can be performed online. Undergraduates are required to own a computer.

CAMPUS LIFE
Environment: Town. **Organizations:** 1 registered organization. **On-Campus Highlights:** Internet cafe, nature trail, computer lab.

ADMISSIONS
Freshman Academic Profile: Average high school GPA 2.97. 85% from public high schools. Minimum paper TOEFL 600. Minimum computer TOEFL 250. **Basis for Candidate Selection:** *Very important factors considered include:* Rigor of secondary school record. *Important factors considered include:* Standardized test scores, interview. *Other factors considered include:* Application essay, recommendation(s). **Freshman Admission Requirements:** High school diploma is required and GED is accepted. *Academic units recommended:* 4 English, 2 mathematics, 2 science, 2 social studies, 2 history, 12 academic electives. **Transfer Admission Requirements:** High school transcript, college transcript(s), statement of good standing from prior institution(s). Minimum

---

college GPA of 2.5 required. Lowest grade transferable D. **General Admission Information:** Application fee $25. Regular application deadline 8/15. Nonfall registration not accepted. Admission may be deferred for a maximum of 1 year. Credit and/or placement offered for CEEB Advanced Placement tests.

COSTS AND FINANCIAL AID

Annual tuition $13,680. **Required Forms and Deadlines:** FAFSA, institution's own financial aid form. Financial aid filing deadline 6/15. Priority financial aid filing date 3/15. **Types of Aid:** *Need-based scholarships/grants:* Federal Pell, SEOG, state scholarships/grants, private scholarships, the school's own gift aid. *Loans:* FFEL Subsidized Stafford, FFEL Unsubsidized Stafford, FFEL PLUS. **Financial Aid Statistics:** 54% freshmen, 37% undergrads receive need-based scholarship or grant aid. 10% freshmen, 2% undergrads receive non-need-based scholarship or grant aid. 54% freshmen, 50% undergrads receive need-based self-help aid. 75% freshmen, 48% undergrads receive any aid. 36% undergrads borrow to pay for school. Average cumulative indebtedness $10,500. **Criteria for awarding institutional aid:** *Non-need-based:* Academics.

CLEMSON UNIVERSITY

Best 373

105 Sikes Hall, Box 345124, Clemson, SC 29634-5124
Phone: 864-656-2287 **Financial Aid Phone:** 864-656-2280
E-mail: cuadmissions@clemson.edu **CEEB Code:** 5111
Fax: 864-656-2464 **Website:** www.clemson.edu **ACT Code:** 3842

This public school was founded in 1889.

RATINGS
Admissions Selectivity Rating: 91   **Fire Safety Rating:** 92   **Green Rating:** 89

STUDENTS AND FACULTY
Enrollment: 15,247. **Student Body:** 46% female, 54% male, 29% out-of-state, 1% international (84 countries represented). Asian 2%, African American 7%, Caucasian 83%, Hispanic 1%.
Retention and Graduation: 50% freshmen graduate within 4 years. 28% grads go on to further study within 1 year. 25% grads pursue arts and sciences degrees. 5% grads pursue law degrees. 21% grads pursue business degrees. 8% grads pursue medical degrees. **Faculty:** Student/faculty ratio 16:1. 1052 full-time faculty, 88% hold PhDs, 15% are members of minority groups, 33% are women. 7% of classes are taught by teaching assistants.

ACADEMICS
Degrees: Bachelor's, master's, post-master's certificate. **Classes:** Most classes have 10–19 students. Most lab/discussion sessions have 20–29 students. **Majors with Highest Enrollment:** Biology/biological sciences; business/commerce; engineering. **Special Study Options:** Cooperative education program, distance learning, double major, exchange student program (domestic), honors program, independent study, internships, study abroad, teacher certification program, We have an RN to BSN program located in Greenville, South Carolina. This is an off-campus degree program for students that have a 2-year degree in nursing and an RN. **Honors programs:** The National Scholars Program. Please visit: www.clemson.edu/national_scholars/. **Combined degree programs:** BA/MEng, RN to BSN program. Special programs offered to physically disabled students include note-taking services, reader services, tape recorders, tutors. **Career services:** Alumni network, alumni services, career/job search classes, career assessment, internships. **Career services highlights include:** Our alumni network has grown in both strength and number over the past few years. Current alumni recognize that today's Clemson graduates are significantly better prepared to enter the job market, if they choose to delay graduate school. Assisting other members of the "Clemson Family" is a natural bond ingrained as one prepares to leave the campus—as hard as that may be!.

FACILITIES
Housing: Coed dorms, men's dorms, special housing for international students, women's dorms, fraternity/sorority housing, apartments for single students, wellness housing, theme housing, learning-living communities. **Special Academic Facilities/Equipment:** The South Carolina Botanical Gardens, the Campbell Geology Museum, the Brooks Center for the Performing Arts, the Rudolph Lee Art Gallery, the Garrison Livestock Arena, the John C. Calhoun Home. **Computers:** 75% of classrooms, 25% of dorms, 100% of libraries, 100% of dining areas, 100% of student union, 40% of common outdoor areas have wireless network access. Students can register for classes online. Administrative functions (other than registration) can be performed online. Undergraduates are required to own a computer.

CAMPUS LIFE

Environment: Village. **Activities:** Choral groups, concert band, dance, drama/theater, jazz band, literary magazine, marching band, music ensembles, pep band, radio station, student government, student newspaper, television station, yearbook. **Organizations:** 292 registered organizations, 23 honor societies, 24 religious organizations. 26 fraternities, 17 sororities. **Athletics (Intercollegiate):** *Men:* Baseball, basketball, cheerleading, cross-country, diving, football, golf, soccer, swimming, tennis, track/field (outdoor), track/field (indoor). *Women:* Basketball, cheerleading, crew/rowing, cross-country, diving, soccer, swimming, tennis, track/field (outdoor), track/field (indoor), volleyball. **On-Campus Highlights:** SC Botanical Garden/Discovery Center/Geology Muse, Hendrix Student Center—Clemson Ice Cream, Conference Center and Inn at Clemson/Walker Golf Course, Fort Hill—John C. Calhoun House, Lee Art Gallery. Please visit: www.clemson.edu/visitors/index.html. **Environmental Initiatives:** LEED, Energy conservation policy, President's Commission on Sustainability.

ADMISSIONS

Freshman Academic Profile: Average high school GPA 4.1. 45% in top 10% of high school class, 78% in top 25% of high school class, 97% in top 50% of high school class. 89% from public high schools. SAT Math middle 50% range 580–670. SAT Critical Reading middle 50% range 550–640. SAT Writing middle 50% range 490–590. ACT middle 50% range 25–30. Minimum paper TOEFL 550. Minimum computer TOEFL 213. **Basis for Candidate Selection:** *Very important factors considered include:* Class rank, academic GPA, rigor of secondary school record, standardized test scores, state residency. *Important factors considered include:* Alumni/ae relation. *Other factors considered include:* Application essay, recommendation(s), extracurricular activities, talent/ability. **Freshman Admission Requirements:** High school diploma is required and GED is accepted. *Academic units required:* 4 English, 3 mathematics, 3 science, (3 science labs), 3 foreign language, 3 social studies, 1 history, 2 academic electives, 1 PE or ROTC. *Academic units recommended:* 4 mathematics, (4 science labs). **Freshman Admission Statistics:** 16,282 applied, 63% admitted, 33% enrolled. **Transfer Admission Requirements:** College transcript(s), minimum college GPA of 2.5 required. Lowest grade transferable C. **General Admission Information:** Application fee $60. Regular application deadline 5/1. Notification on a rolling basis, beginning on or about 2/15. Nonfall registration accepted. Credit and/or placement offered for CEEB Advanced Placement tests.

COSTS AND FINANCIAL AID

Annual in-state tuition $11,478. Annual out-of-state tuition $25,788. Room and board $6,774. Required fees $500. Average book expense $922. **Required Forms and Deadlines:** FAFSA. Priority financial aid filing date 4/1. **Notification of Awards:** Applicants will be notified of awards on a rolling basis beginning 4/1. **Types of Aid:** *Need-based scholarships/grants:* Federal Pell, SEOG, state scholarships/grants, private scholarships, the school's own gift aid, Federal Nursing Scholarships. *Loans:* Direct Subsidized Stafford, Direct Unsubsidized Stafford, Direct PLUS, FFEL Subsidized Stafford, FFEL Unsubsidized Stafford, FFEL PLUS, Federal Perkins, state loans, college/university loans from institutional funds. **Student Employment:** Federal Work-Study Program available. Institutional employment available. Highest amount earned per year from on-campus jobs $3,500. Off-campus job opportunities are fair. **Financial Aid Statistics:** 15% freshmen, 18% undergrads receive need-based scholarship or grant aid. 38% freshmen, 22% undergrads receive non-need-based scholarship or grant aid. 24% freshmen, 28% undergrads receive need-based self-help aid. 3% freshmen, 3% undergrads receive athletic scholarships. 87% freshmen, 71% undergrads receive any aid. 44% undergrads borrow to pay for school. Average cumulative indebtedness $17,882. **Criteria for awarding institutional aid:** *Non-need-based:* Academics, art, athletics, leadership, minority status, music/drama, state/district residency.

See page 1054.

THE CLEVELAND INSTITUTE OF ART

11141 East Boulevard, Cleveland, OH 44106
Phone: 216-421-7418 **Financial Aid Phone:** 216-421-7425
E-mail: admissions@cia.edu **CEEB Code:** 1152
Fax: 216-754-3634 **Website:** www.cia.edu **ACT Code:** 3243

This private school was founded in 1882. It has a 488-acre campus.

RATINGS

Admissions Selectivity Rating: 78   **Fire Safety Rating:** 74   **Green Rating:** 60*

STUDENTS AND FACULTY

Enrollment: 495. **Student Body:** 52% female, 48% male, 34% out-of-state, 2% international. Asian 5%, African American 6%, Caucasian 80%, Hispanic 5%.

Retention and Graduation: 81% freshmen return for sophomore year.
Faculty: Student/faculty ratio 8:1. 47 full-time faculty, 85% hold PhDs, 9% are members of minority groups, 45% are women.

ACADEMICS

Degrees: Bachelor's. **Classes:** Most classes have 10–19 students. Most lab/discussion sessions have 10–19 students. **Majors with Highest Enrollment:** Illustration; industrial design; intermedia/multimedia. **Special Study Options:** Cooperative education program, cross-registration, exchange student program (domestic), honors program, independent study, internships, study abroad, Study for up to 2 semesters at an Alliance of Independent Colleges of Art and Design. Special programs offered to physically disabled students include note-taking services, tape recorders, tutors. **Career services:** Alumni network, alumni services, career/job search classes, career assessment, internships.

FACILITIES

Housing: Coed dorms, fraternity/sorority housing, apartments for single students. **Special Academic Facilities/Equipment:** The Reinberger Galleries. **Computers:** 40% of classrooms, 100% of dorms, 100% of libraries, have wireless network access. Students can register for classes online. Administrative functions (other than registration) can be performed online.

CAMPUS LIFE

Environment: Metropolis. **Activities:** Marching band, student government, student newspaper, student-run film society, campus ministries. **Organizations:** 7 registered organizations, 2 religious organizations. **On-Campus Highlights:** Arabica Coffee Shop, Frank Gehry and Peter B. Lewis Building, Live music at Barking Spider, Cleveland Museum of Art, Reinberger Galleries.

ADMISSIONS

Freshman Academic Profile: Average high school GPA 3.18. 18% in top 10% of high school class, 32% in top 25% of high school class, 72% in top 50% of high school class. SAT Math middle 50% range 440–570. SAT Critical Reading middle 50% range 490–600. ACT middle 50% range 20–26. Minimum paper TOEFL 525. Minimum computer TOEFL 190. **Basis for Candidate Selection:** *Very important factors considered include:* Rigor of secondary school record, talent/ability. *Important factors considered include:* Application essay, academic GPA, recommendation(s), standardized test scores, character/personal qualities, interview. *Other factors considered include:* Extracurricular activities, level of applicant's interest. **Freshman Admission Requirements:** High school diploma is required and GED is accepted. *Academic units recommended:* 4 English, 3 mathematics, 3 science, 3 social studies, 6 academic electives, 3 Art 2 years recommended. **Freshman Admission Statistics:** 457 applied, 79% admitted, 31% enrolled. **Transfer Admission Requirements:** College transcript(s), essay or personal statement, minimum college GPA of 2.0 required. Lowest grade transferable C. **General Admission Information:** Application fee $30. Notification on a rolling basis, beginning on or about 10/1. Nonfall registration not accepted. Admission may be deferred for a maximum of 1 year. Credit offered for CEEB Advanced Placement tests.

COSTS AND FINANCIAL AID

Annual tuition $29,870. Room and board $10,536. Required fees $2,034. Average book expense $2,000. **Required Forms and Deadlines:** FAFSA, institution's own financial aid form. Priority financial aid filing date 3/15. **Notification of Awards:** Applicants will be notified of awards on a rolling basis beginning 3/15. **Types of Aid:** *Need-based scholarships/grants:* Federal Pell, SEOG, state scholarships/grants, private scholarships, the school's own gift aid, Academic Merit scholarships/grants (institutional funds). *Loans:* FFEL Subsidized Stafford, FFEL Unsubsidized Stafford, FFEL PLUS, Federal Perkins. **Student Employment:** Federal Work-Study Program available. Off-campus job opportunities are good. **Financial Aid Statistics:** 93% freshmen, 88% undergrads receive need-based scholarship or grant aid. 11% freshmen, 6% undergrads receive non-need-based scholarship or grant aid. 82% freshmen, 82% undergrads receive need-based self-help aid. 100% freshmen, 96% undergrads receive any aid. 81% undergrads borrow to pay for school. Average cumulative indebtedness $61,270. **Criteria for awarding institutional aid:** *Non-need-based:* Academics, art.

CLEVELAND STATE UNIVERSITY

2121 Euclid Avenue, RW 204, Cleveland, OH 44115
Phone: 216-687-5411 **Financial Aid Phone:** 216-687-5411
E-mail: admissions@csuohio.edu **CEEB Code:** 3032
Fax: 216-687-5501 **Website:** www.csuohio.edu **ACT Code:** 1221

This public school was founded in 1964. It has a 82-acre campus.

RATINGS

Admissions Selectivity Rating: 73   **Fire Safety Rating:** 60*   **Green Rating:** 60*

STUDENTS AND FACULTY

Enrollment: 9,805. **Student Body:** 55% female, 45% male, 2% out-of-state, 2% international (85 countries represented). Asian 3%, African American 21%, Caucasian 61%, Hispanic 4%.
Retention and Graduation: 66% freshmen return for sophomore year. 9% freshmen graduate within 4 years. **Faculty:** Student/faculty ratio 17.64:1. 537 full-time faculty, 91% hold PhDs, 22% are members of minority groups, 40% are women. 1% of classes are taught by teaching assistants.

ACADEMICS

Degrees: Bachelor's, doctoral, master's, post-bachelor's certificate, post-master's certificate. **Classes:** Most classes have 20–29 students. **Majors with Highest Enrollment:** Accounting; business administration, management and operations, other; psychology. **Special Study Options:** Accelerated program, cooperative education program, cross-registration, distance learning, double major, dual enrollment, English as a Second Language (ESL), exchange student program (domestic), honors program, independent study, internships, liberal arts/career combination, student-designed major, study abroad, teacher certification program, weekend college. **Honors programs:** CSU's Honors Program was established in 2004 to serve the needs of academically talented students. Each year, it accepts approximately 40 first-year students and 20–25 juniors who have demonstrated superior academic achievement through their coursework and results on tests such as the ACT and SAT. Honors students at CSU receive a scholarship that covers full tuition as well as all academic fees and the cost of books required for their classes. Honors students in good standing receive this support throughout their four-year undergraduate academic career. **Combined degree programs:** JD/MBA. Special programs offered to physically disabled students include note-taking services, reader services, tape recorders, tutors. **Career services:** Alumni services, career/job search classes, career assessment, internships.

FACILITIES

Housing: Coed dorms, special housing for disabled students, fraternity/sorority housing 90% of campus accessible to physically disabled. **Computers:** Students can register for classes online. Administrative functions (other than registration) can be performed online.

CAMPUS LIFE

Environment: Metropolis. **Activities:** Choral groups, concert band, dance, drama/theater, jazz band, literary magazine, musical theater, opera, pep band, radio station, student government, student newspaper, student-run film society, symphony orchestra, international student organization. **Organizations:** 10 religious organizations. 8 fraternities, 7 sororities. **Athletics (Intercollegiate):** *Men:* Baseball, basketball, fencing, golf, soccer, swimming, wrestling. *Women:* Basketball, cross-country, fencing, softball, swimming, tennis, track/field (outdoor), track/field (indoor), volleyball. **On-Campus Highlights:** Recreation Center, Main Classroom Atrium, Michael Schwartz Library, The Green Room, Farmer's Market.

ADMISSIONS

Freshman Academic Profile: Average high school GPA 3.09. 12% in top 10% of high school class, 33% in top 25% of high school class, 67% in top 50% of high school class. SAT Math middle 50% range 420–550. SAT Critical Reading middle 50% range 420–540. ACT middle 50% range 18–23. Minimum paper TOEFL 525. **Basis for Candidate Selection:** *Very important factors considered include:* Academic GPA, rigor of secondary school record, standardized test scores. *Important factors considered include:* Class rank. **Freshman Admission Requirements:** High school diploma is required and GED is accepted. *Academic units required:* 4 English, 3 mathematics, 3 science, 3 social studies. *Academic units recommended:* 2 foreign language, 1 visual/performing arts. **Freshman Admission Statistics:** 4,584 applied, 64% admitted, 40% enrolled. **Transfer Admission Requirements:** College transcript(s), minimum college GPA of 2.0 required. Lowest grade transferable D. **General Admission Information:** Application fee $30. Regular application deadline 8/15. Notification on a rolling basis, beginning on or about 9/1. Nonfall registration accepted. Admission may be deferred for a maximum of 1 year. Credit and/or placement offered for CEEB Advanced Placement tests.

COSTS AND FINANCIAL AID

Annual in-state tuition $8,196. Annual out-of-state tuition $11,026. Room and board $10,250. Average book expense $800. **Required Forms and Deadlines:** FAFSA, tax forms(for base tax year),if selected for verification by Department of Education or the institution; verification documents. Priority financial aid filing date 2/15. **Notification of Awards:** Applicants will be notified of awards on a rolling basis beginning 3/15. **Types of Aid:** *Need-based scholarships/grants:* Federal Pell, SEOG, state scholarships/grants, private scholarships, the school's own gift aid. *Loans:* FFEL Subsidized Stafford, FFEL Unsubsidized Stafford, FFEL PLUS, Federal Perkins, state loans, alternative. **Student Employment:** Federal Work-Study Program available. Institutional employment available. Off-campus job opportunities are excellent. **Financial Aid Statistics:** 56% freshmen, 59% undergrads receive need-based scholarship or grant aid. 2% freshmen, 3% undergrads receive non-need-based scholarship or grant aid. 52%

---

freshmen, 66% undergrads receive need-based self-help aid. 2% freshmen, 2% undergrads receive athletic scholarships. **Criteria for awarding institutional aid:** *Non-need-based:* Academics, alumni affiliation, art, athletics, leadership, minority status, music/drama, religious affiliation.

COASTAL CAROLINA UNIVERSITY

PO Box 261954, Conway, SC 29528-6054
Phone: 843-349-2170 **Financial Aid Phone:** 843-349-2325
E-mail: admissions@coastal.edu **CEEB Code:** 5837
Fax: 843-349-2127 **Website:** **ACT Code:** 5837

This public school was founded in 1954. It has a 302-acre campus.

RATINGS

Admissions Selectivity Rating: 78   **Fire Safety Rating:** 70   **Green Rating:** 84

STUDENTS AND FACULTY

Enrollment: 7,544. **Student Body:** 53% female, 47% male, 49% out-of-state, 1% international (38 countries represented). Asian 1%, African American 15%, Caucasian 78%, Hispanic 3%.
Retention and Graduation: 66% freshmen return for sophomore year. 22% freshmen graduate within 4 years. **Faculty:** Student/faculty ratio 18:1. 315 full-time faculty, 82% hold PhDs, 10% are members of minority groups, 41% are women.

ACADEMICS

Degrees: Bachelor's, master's, post-bachelor's certificate. **Classes:** Most classes have 20–29 students. Most lab/discussion sessions have 10–19 students. **Majors with Highest Enrollment:** Biology/biological sciences; business administration and management; marine biology and biological oceanography. **Special Study Options:** Accelerated program, cooperative education program, distance learning, double major, dual enrollment, honors program, independent study, internships, student-designed major, study abroad, teacher certification program Special programs offered to physically disabled students include note-taking services, reader services, tape recorders, tutors. **Career services:** Alumni network, alumni services, career/job search classes, career assessment, internships. **Career services highlights include:** Career Assessment Program which is an integral part of University 110 and is required of all freshmen.

FACILITIES

Housing: Coed dorms, special housing for disabled students 98% of campus accessible to physically disabled. **Computers:** 100% of classrooms, 100% of libraries, 100% of dining areas, 100% of student union, 83% of common outdoor areas have wireless network access. Students can register for classes online. Administrative functions (other than registration) can be performed online.

CAMPUS LIFE

Environment: Town. **Activities:** Choral groups, concert band, dance, drama/theater, jazz band, literary magazine, marching band, music ensembles, musical theater, pep band, radio station, student government, student newspaper, campus ministries, international student organization. **Organizations:** 91 registered organizations, 32 honor societies, 13 religious organizations. 9 fraternities, 7 sororities. **Athletics (Intercollegiate):** *Men:* Baseball, basketball, cheerleading, cross-country, football, golf, soccer, tennis, track/field (outdoor). *Women:* Basketball, cheerleading, cross-country, golf, soccer, softball, tennis, track/field (outdoor), volleyball. **On-Campus Highlights:** Humanities and fine arts building, Brooks Stadium, CINO Grille/Student Center, recreation center, Java City Cafe. **Environmental Initiatives:** Energy efficiency upgrades to 2 renovations; green power, including on-site solar, establishment of Sustainability Initiative.

ADMISSIONS

Freshman Academic Profile: Average high school GPA 3.31. 9% in top 10% of high school class, 32% in top 25% of high school class, 71% in top 50% of high school class. 95% from public high schools. SAT Math middle 50% range 470–570. SAT Critical Reading middle 50% range 460–550. ACT middle 50% range 19–22. Minimum paper TOEFL 550. Minimum computer TOEFL 213. Minimum web-based TOEFL 79. **Basis for Candidate Selection:** *Very important factors considered include:* Academic GPA, rigor of secondary school record, standardized test scores. *Important factors considered include:* Class rank. *Other factors considered include:* Application essay, recommendation(s), character/personal qualities, extracurricular activities, first generation, geographical residence, interview, level of applicant's interest, state residency, talent/ability, work experience. **Freshman Admission Requirements:** High school diploma is required and GED is accepted. *Academic units required:* 4 English, 3 mathematics, 3 science, (3 science labs), 2 foreign language, 2 social studies, 1 history, 4 academic electives, 1 PE or ROTC. *Academic units recommended:* 1 visual/performing arts, 1 computer science. **Freshman Admission Statistics:** 8,706 applied, 74% admitted, 28% enrolled. **Transfer Admission**

Requirements: College transcript(s), statement of good standing from prior institution(s). Minimum college GPA of 2.0 required. Lowest grade transferable C–. **General Admission Information:** Application fee $45. Regular application deadline 8/15. Notification on a rolling basis, beginning on or about 9/15. Nonfall registration accepted. Admission may be deferred for a maximum of 1 year. Credit and/or placement offered for CEEB Advanced Placement tests.

COSTS AND FINANCIAL AID

Required Forms and Deadlines: FAFSA. Priority financial aid filing date 3/1. **Notification of Awards:** Applicants will be notified of awards on a rolling basis beginning 3/1. **Types of Aid:** *Need-based scholarships/grants:* Federal Pell, SEOG, state scholarships/grants, private scholarships, the school's own gift aid, ACG/SMART. *Loans:* FFEL Subsidized Stafford, FFEL Unsubsidized Stafford, FFEL PLUS, Federal Perkins, state loans. **Student Employment:** Federal Work-Study Program available. Institutional employment available. Highest amount earned per year from on-campus jobs $20,030. Off-campus job opportunities are excellent. **Financial Aid Statistics:** 25% freshmen, 26% undergrads receive need-based scholarship or grant aid. 29% freshmen, 16% undergrads receive non-need-based scholarship or grant aid. 52% freshmen, 51% undergrads receive need-based self-help aid. 4% freshmen, 5% undergrads receive athletic scholarships. 84% freshmen, 84% undergrads receive any aid. 71% undergrads borrow to pay for school. Average cumulative indebtedness $26,646. **Criteria for awarding institutional aid:** *Non-need-based:* Academics, art, athletics, leadership, music/drama, state/district residency.

COE COLLEGE

1220 First Avenue NE, Cedar Rapids, IA 52402
Phone: 319-399-8500 **Financial Aid Phone:** 319-399-8540
E-mail: admission@coe.edu **CEEB Code:** 6101
Fax: 319-399-8816 **Website:** www.coe.edu **ACT Code:** 1294

This private school, affiliated with the Presbyterian Church, was founded in 1851. It has a 53-acre campus.

RATINGS
Admissions Selectivity Rating: 88 **Fire Safety Rating:** 60* **Green Rating:** 60*

STUDENTS AND FACULTY
Enrollment: 1,269. **Student Body:** 55% female, 45% male, 36% out-of-state, (15 countries represented).
Retention and Graduation: 80% freshmen return for sophomore year. 64% freshmen graduate within 4 years. 28% grads go on to further study within 1 year. 18% grads pursue arts and sciences degrees. 3% grads pursue law degrees. 2% grads pursue business degrees. 3% grads pursue medical degrees. **Faculty:** Student/faculty ratio 11:1. 88 full-time faculty, 84% hold PhDs, 9% are members of minority groups, 35% are women.

ACADEMICS
Degrees: Bachelor's, master's. **Classes:** Most classes have 10–19 students. Most lab/discussion sessions have 10–19 students. **Majors with Highest Enrollment:** Biology/biological sciences; business administration and management; psychology. **Special Study Options:** Accelerated program, cross-registration, double major, dual enrollment, English as a Second Language (ESL), exchange student program (domestic), honors program, independent study, internships, student-designed major, study abroad, teacher certification program. **Honors programs:** College honors program consisting of five honors seminars and an honors project or thesis. **Combined degree programs:** BA/MArch Washington University. Special programs offered to physically disabled students include note-taking services, tape recorders, tutors. **Career services:** Alumni network, career/job search classes, career assessment, internships, regional alumni. **Career services highlights include:** The Coe Plan requires all students to complete an internship, research, study abroad, or other "out of the classroom" experience during their junior year.

FACILITIES
Housing: Coed dorms, men's dorms, women's dorms, fraternity/sorority housing, apartments for single students, wellness housing, theme housing. 70% of campus accessible to physically disabled. **Special Academic Facilities/Equipment:** Ornithological museum, writing lab, theatre. **Computers:** 70% of classrooms, 10% of dorms, 100% of libraries, 100% of dining areas, 100% of student union, 80% of common outdoor areas have wireless network access. Students can register for classes online.

CAMPUS LIFE
Environment: City. **Activities:** Choral groups, concert band, dance, drama/theater, jazz band, literary magazine, music ensembles, musical theater, pep band, radio station, student government, student newspaper, symphony orchestra, television station, yearbook, campus ministries, international student organization. **Organizations:** 60 registered organizations, 8 honor societies, 4 religious organizations, 5 fraternities, 3 sororities. **Athletics (Intercollegiate):** *Men:* Baseball, basketball, cross-country, diving, football, golf, soccer, swimming, tennis, track/field (outdoor), track/field (indoor), wrestling. *Women:* Basketball, cheerleading, cross-country, diving, golf, soccer, softball, swimming, tennis, track/field (outdoor), track/field (indoor), volleyball. **On-Campus Highlights:** Student union/coffee shop, Dows Theatre, library/art galleries, fitness center, racquet center.

ADMISSIONS
Freshman Academic Profile: Average high school GPA 3.66. 30% in top 10% of high school class, 66% in top 25% of high school class, 94% in top 50% of high school class. 90% from public high schools. SAT Math middle 50% range 550–670. SAT Critical Reading middle 50% range 560–680. SAT Writing middle 50% range 540–650. ACT middle 50% range 23–28. Minimum paper TOEFL 500. Minimum computer TOEFL 173. **Basis for Candidate Selection:** *Very important factors considered include:* Academic GPA, standardized test scores. *Important factors considered include:* Class rank, application essay, recommendation(s). *Other factors considered include:* Rigor of secondary school record, alumni/ae relation, character/personal qualities, extracurricular activities, first generation, interview, level of applicant's interest, racial/ethnic status, talent/ability, volunteer work. **Freshman Admission Requirements:** High school diploma is required and GED is accepted. *Academic units recommended:* 4 English, 3 mathematics, 3 science, (1 science labs), 2 foreign language, 3 social studies, 2 academic electives. **Freshman Admission Statistics:** 1,943 applied, 63% admitted, 28% enrolled. **Transfer Admission Requirements:** High school transcript, college transcript(s), essay or personal statement, statement of good standing from prior institution(s). Minimum college GPA of 2.5 required. Lowest grade transferable C. **General Admission Information:** Application fee $30. Regular application deadline 3/1. Regular notification 3/15. Notification on a rolling basis, beginning on or about 10/1. Nonfall registration accepted. Admission may be deferred for a maximum of 2 years. Credit and/or placement offered for CEEB Advanced Placement tests.

COSTS AND FINANCIAL AID
Annual tuition $28,950. Room and board $7,150. Required fees $320. Average book expense $1,000. **Required Forms and Deadlines:** FAFSA. Priority financial aid filing date 3/1. **Notification of Awards:** Applicants will be notified of awards on a rolling basis beginning 3/15. **Types of Aid:** *Need-based scholarships/grants:* Federal Pell, SEOG, state scholarships/grants, private scholarships, the school's own gift aid. *Loans:* Direct Subsidized Stafford, Direct Unsubsidized Stafford, Direct PLUS, Federal Perkins, college/university loans from institutional funds. **Student Employment:** Federal Work-Study Program available. Institutional employment available. Highest amount earned per year from on-campus jobs $500. Off-campus job opportunities are excellent. **Financial Aid Statistics:** 73% freshmen, 72% undergrads receive need-based scholarship or grant aid. 19% freshmen, 13% undergrads receive non-need-based scholarship or grant aid. 58% freshmen, 62% undergrads receive need-based self-help aid. 98% freshmen, 96% undergrads receive any aid. 81% undergrads borrow to pay for school. Average cumulative indebtedness $30,385. **Criteria for awarding institutional aid:** *Non-need-based:* Academics, alumni affiliation, art, music/drama.

COGSWELL POLYTECHNICAL COLLEGE

1175 Bordeaux Drive, Sunnyvale, CA 94089-1299
Phone: 408-541-0100
E-mail: admissions@cogswell.edu **CEEB Code:** 1177
Fax: 408-747-0764 **Website:** **ACT Code:** 1177

This private school was founded in 1887. It has a 5-acre campus.

RATINGS
Admissions Selectivity Rating: 60* **Fire Safety Rating:** 60* **Green Rating:** 61

STUDENTS AND FACULTY
Enrollment: 199. **Student Body:** 16% female, 84% male, 13% out-of-state, 4% international (13 countries represented). Asian 11%, African American 4%, Caucasian 57%, Hispanic 12%.
Retention and Graduation: 57% freshmen return for sophomore year. 17% freshmen graduate within 4 years. **Faculty:** Student/faculty ratio 6:1. 10 full-time faculty, 60% hold PhDs, 20% are women.

ACADEMICS

Degrees: Bachelor's. **Classes:** Most classes have fewer than 10 students. **Majors with Highest Enrollment:** Animation, interactive technology, video graphics and special effects; fire protection and safety technology/technician; recording arts technology/technician. **Special Study Options:** Cooperative education program, distance learning, double major, exchange student program (domestic), internships, student-designed major, study abroad. **Combined degree programs:** Digital art and animation, digital audio technology. **Career services:** Alumni network, career/job search classes.

FACILITIES

Housing: Apartments for single students 100% of campus accessible to physically disabled. **Special Academic Facilities/Equipment:** The Gallery at Cogswell. **Computers:** 100% of classrooms, 100% of libraries, 100% of dining areas, 100% of student union, have wireless network access. Students can register for classes online. Administrative functions (other than registration) can be performed online. Undergraduates are required to own a computer.

CAMPUS LIFE

Environment: Village. **Activities:** Drama/theater, radio station, student government **Organizations:** 5 registered organizations. **On-Campus Highlights:** Gallery, library, Smart Lab, Dragon's Den, audio recording studio. **Environmental Initiatives:** Saving energy, recycling, saving water.

ADMISSIONS

Freshman Academic Profile: SAT Math middle 50% range 420–660. SAT Critical Reading middle 50% range 550–650. SAT Writing middle 50% range 450–640. ACT middle 50% range 21–32. Minimum paper TOEFL 525. Minimum computer TOEFL 197. **Basis for Candidate Selection:** *Very important factors considered include:* Academic GPA, talent/ability. *Important factors considered include:* Application essay, recommendation(s). *Other factors considered include:* Extracurricular activities, interview, level of applicant's interest, volunteer work. **Freshman Admission Requirements:** High school diploma is required and GED is accepted. *Academic units required:* 3 English, 3 mathematics, 1 science, (1 science labs). *Academic units recommended:* 1 visual/performing arts, 1 computer science. **Freshman Admission Statistics:** 32 applied, 94% admitted, 70% enrolled. **Transfer Admission Requirements:** High school transcript, college transcript(s), essay or personal statement, minimum college GPA of 2.5 required. Lowest grade transferable C. **General Admission Information:** Application fee $55. Regular application deadline 3/1. Nonfall registration accepted. Admission may be deferred for a maximum of 1 year. Credit and/or placement offered for CEEB Advanced Placement tests.

COSTS AND FINANCIAL AID

Required Forms and Deadlines: FAFSA, state aid form. Priority financial aid filing date 3/2. **Notification of Awards:** Applicants will be notified of awards on a rolling basis beginning 3/15. **Types of Aid:** *Need-based scholarships/grants:* Federal Pell, SEOG, state scholarships/grants, private scholarships, the school's own gift aid. *Loans:* FFEL Subsidized Stafford, FFEL Unsubsidized Stafford, FFEL PLUS. **Student Employment:** Federal Work-Study Program available. Institutional employment available. Off-campus job opportunities are good. **Financial Aid Statistics:** 63% freshmen, 30% undergrads receive need-based scholarship or grant aid. 69% freshmen, 58% undergrads receive non-need-based scholarship or grant aid. 19% freshmen, 10% undergrads receive need-based self-help aid. **Criteria for awarding institutional aid:** *Non-need-based:* Academics, art, music/drama.

COKER COLLEGE

300 East College Avenue, Hartsville, SC 29550
Phone: 843-383-8050
E-mail: admissions@coker.edu
Fax: 843-383-8056 **Website:** www.coker.edu

This is a private school.

RATINGS

Admissions Selectivity Rating: 79   **Fire Safety Rating:** 60*   **Green Rating:** 60*

STUDENTS AND FACULTY

Enrollment: 590. **Student Body:** 61% female, 39% male, 19% out-of-state, 2% international . Asian 1%, African American 23%, Caucasian 72%, Hispanic 2%, Native American 1%.

Retention and Graduation: 64% freshmen return for sophomore year. 22% freshmen graduate within 4 years. **Faculty:** Student/faculty ratio 10:1. 58 full-time faculty, 81% hold PhDs, 12% are members of minority groups, 47% are women.

ACADEMICS

Degrees: Bachelor's. **Classes:** Most classes have 10–19 students. Most lab/discussion sessions have 10–19 students. **Majors with Highest Enrollment:** Business/commerce; graphic design; psychology. **Special Study Options:** Double major, dual enrollment, honors program, independent study, internships, student-designed major, study abroad, teacher certification program. Special programs offered to physically disabled students include tape recorders, tutors. **Career services:** Career/job search classes, career assessment, internships. **Career services highlights include:** With our internships students have the opportunity to receive hands-on experience in their field, which gives them a competitive edge in today's job market.

FACILITIES

Housing: Coed dorms, special housing for international students 80% of campus accessible to physically disabled. **Special Academic Facilities/Equipment:** Art gallery, state-of-the-art performing arts center, dark rooms, botanical gardens, graduate-level science equipment. **Computers:** Administrative functions (other than registration) can be performed online.

CAMPUS LIFE

Activities: Choral groups, dance, drama/theater, literary magazine, music ensembles, musical theater, student government, student newspaper, campus ministries, international student organization. **Organizations:** 27 registered organizations, 4 honor societies, 2 religious organizations. **Athletics (Intercollegiate):** *Men:* Baseball, basketball, cheerleading, cross-country, golf, soccer, tennis. *Women:* Basketball, cheerleading, cross-country, soccer, softball, tennis, volleyball. **On-Campus Highlights:** The Cobra Den, The Cobra Caf, The Student Center, The Performing Arts Center, Outdoor Volleyball Courts, The Cobra Den includes a coffee area, dance floor, and a game room.

ADMISSIONS

Freshman Academic Profile: Average high school GPA 3.36. 1% in top 10% of high school class, 47% in top 25% of high school class, 80% in top 50% of high school class. SAT Math middle 50% range 440–570. SAT Critical Reading middle 50% range 420–570. ACT middle 50% range 17–22. Minimum paper TOEFL 500. Minimum computer TOEFL 173. **Basis for Candidate Selection:** *Very important factors considered include:* Academic GPA, standardized test scores. *Important factors considered include:* Class rank, rigor of secondary school record, level of applicant's interest. *Other factors considered include:* Application essay, recommendation(s), alumni/ae relation, character/personal qualities, extracurricular activities, interview, talent/ability, volunteer work, work experience. **Freshman Admission Requirements:** High school diploma is required and GED is accepted. *Academic units required:* 4 English, 3 mathematics, 3 science, (1 science labs), 2 foreign language, 3 social studies. **Freshman Admission Statistics:** 1,112 applied, 56% admitted, 25% enrolled. **Transfer Admission Requirements:** High school transcript, college transcript(s), statement of good standing from prior institution(s). Minimum college GPA of 2.0 required. Lowest grade transferable C. **General Admission Information:** Application fee $15. Regular application deadline 8/1. Notification on a rolling basis, beginning on or about 9/1. Nonfall registration accepted. Admission may be deferred for a maximum of 1 year. Credit and/or placement offered for CEEB Advanced Placement tests.

COSTS AND FINANCIAL AID

Annual tuition $19,368. Room and board $6,240. Required fees $490. Average book expense $1,200. **Required Forms and Deadlines:** FAFSA. Financial aid filing deadline 6/1. Priority financial aid filing date 4/1. **Notification of Awards:** Applicants will be notified of awards on a rolling basis beginning 3/1. **Types of Aid:** *Need-based scholarships/grants:* Federal Pell, SEOG, state scholarships/grants, private scholarships, the school's own gift aid. *Loans:* FFEL Subsidized Stafford, FFEL Unsubsidized Stafford, FFEL PLUS, Federal Perkins, state loans, private source loans. **Student Employment:** Federal Work-Study Program available. Institutional employment available. Highest amount earned per year from on-campus jobs $1,072. Off-campus job opportunities are good. **Financial Aid Statistics:** 81% freshmen, 77% undergrads receive need-based scholarship or grant aid. 88% freshmen, 78% undergrads receive non-need-based scholarship or grant aid. 81% freshmen, 74% undergrads receive need-based self-help aid. 5% freshmen, 7% undergrads receive athletic scholarships. 100% freshmen, 100% undergrads receive any aid. 85% undergrads borrow to pay for school. Average cumulative indebtedness $22,508. **Criteria for awarding institutional aid:** *Non-need-based:* Academics, alumni affiliation, art, athletics, job skills, leadership, minority status, music/drama, religious affiliation, state/district residency.

COLBY COLLEGE

Best 373

4000 Mayflower Hill, Waterville, ME 04901-8848
Phone: 207-859-4800 **Financial Aid Phone:** 207-859-4832
E-mail: admissions@colby.edu **CEEB Code:** 3280
Fax: 207-859-4828 **Website:** www.colby.edu **ACT Code:** 1638

This private school was founded in 1813. It has a 714-acre campus.

RATINGS

Admissions Selectivity Rating: 95   Fire Safety Rating: 92   Green Rating: 87

STUDENTS AND FACULTY

Enrollment: 1,838. **Student Body:** 54% female, 46% male, 87% out-of-state, 5% international (64 countries represented). Asian 8%, African American 3%, Caucasian 62%, Hispanic 3%, Native American 1%.
Retention and Graduation: 94% freshmen return for sophomore year. 82% freshmen graduate within 4 years. 23% grads go on to further study within 1 year. 15% grads pursue arts and sciences degrees. 4% grads pursue law degrees. 1% grads pursue business degrees. 3% grads pursue medical degrees. **Faculty:** Student/faculty ratio 10:1. 165 full-time faculty, 95% hold PhDs, 14% are members of minority groups, 44% are women.

ACADEMICS

Degrees: Bachelor's. **Classes:** Most classes have 10–19 students. Most lab/discussion sessions have 10–19 students. **Majors with Highest Enrollment:** Biology/biological sciences; economics; political science and government. **Special Study Options:** Cross-registration, double major, exchange student program (domestic), honors program, independent study, internships, student-designed major, study abroad, teacher certification program, Summer research assistantships; Colby has coordinated 3-2 engineering programs with Dartmouth; Colby offers junior-year abroad programs in France, Spain, and Russia. Special programs offered to physically disabled students include note-taking services, reader services, tape recorders, tutors. **Career services:** Alumni network, alumni services, career/job search classes, career assessment, internships, regional alumni. **Career services highlights include:** Colby Connect (see website for details www.colby.edu/academics_cs/resources/offices/careerservices/index.cfm).

FACILITIES

Housing: Coed dorms, wellness housing, theme housingQuiet halls, chem-free halls, apartments for seniors only, student interest halls. 92% of campus accessible to physically disabled. **Special Academic Facilities/Equipment:** 28,000 square foot art museum, completely renovated student center (Pulver Pavilion), arboretum, electronic microscopes, greenhouse, astronomical observatory, writer's center, cross-country ski trails, Goldfarb Center for Public Affairs and Civic Engagement, multicultural center, rare books and archives library, computer research classroom, language lab. **Computers:** 100% of classrooms, 100% of dorms, 100% of libraries, 100% of dining areas, 100% of student union, 10% of common outdoor areas have wireless network access. Students can register for classes online. Administrative functions (other than registration) can be performed online.

CAMPUS LIFE

Environment: Village. **Activities:** Choral groups, concert band, dance, drama/theater, jazz band, literary magazine, music ensembles, musical theater, radio station, student government, student newspaper, student-run film society, symphony orchestra, yearbook, international student organization. **Organizations:** 91 registered organizations, 9 honor societies, 6 religious organizations. **Athletics (Intercollegiate):** *Men:* Baseball, basketball, crew/rowing, cross-country, diving, football, golf, ice hockey, lacrosse, skiing (downhill/alpine), skiing (nordic/cross-country), soccer, squash, swimming, tennis, track/field (outdoor), track/field (indoor). *Women:* Basketball, crew/rowing, cross-country, diving, field hockey, golf, ice hockey, lacrosse, skiing (downhill/alpine), skiing (nordic/cross-country), soccer, softball, squash, swimming, tennis, track/field (outdoor), track/field (indoor), volleyball. **On-Campus Highlights:** Pulver Pavillion, Colby College Museum of Art, Johnson Pond, Perkins Arboretum trails (running, cross-country skiing). **Environmental Initiatives:** Beginning in October, 2003 Colby has consumed 100–percent renewable electricity. A co-generation turbine in the college's steam plant produces about 13 percent of the electricity used at the college. Colby is committed to seeking LEED certification for a new construction and has achieved it in its two newest buildings. To date, we have five buildings (2 Silver, 2 Gold, 1 standard) that meet LEED standards.

ADMISSIONS

Freshman Academic Profile: 59% in top 10% of high school class, 89% in top 25% of high school class, 97% in top 50% of high school class. 54% from public high schools. SAT Math middle 50% range 640–720. SAT Critical Reading middle 50% range 630–720. SAT Writing middle 50% range 630–710. ACT middle 50% range 28–31. Minimum web-based TOEFL 100. **Basis for Candidate Selection:** *Very important factors considered include:* Rigor of secondary school record, character/personal qualities. *Important factors considered include:* Class rank, application essay, academic GPA, recommendation(s), standardized test scores, extracurricular activities, racial/ethnic status, talent/ability. *Other factors considered include:* Alumni/ae relation, first generation, geographical residence, interview, level of applicant's interest, state residency, volunteer work, work experience. **Freshman Admission Requirements:** High school diploma or equivalent is not required. *Academic units recommended:* 4 English, 3 mathematics, 2 science, (2 science labs), 3 foreign language, 2 social studies or history. **Freshman Admission Statistics:** 4,520 applied, 34% admitted, 31% enrolled. **Transfer Admission Requirements:** High school transcript, college transcript(s), essay or personal statement, standardized test scores, statement of good standing from prior institution(s). Minimum college GPA of 3.0 required. Lowest grade transferable C. **General Admission Information:** Application fee $65. Early decision application deadline 11/15. Regular application deadline 1/1. Regular notification 4/1. Nonfall registration accepted. Admission may be deferred for a maximum of 1 year. Credit and/or placement offered for CEEB Advanced Placement tests.

COSTS AND FINANCIAL AID

Comprehensive fee $50,320. Average book expense $700. **Required Forms and Deadlines:** FAFSA, CSS/Financial Aid PROFILE, business/farm supplement. Either CSS Profile or institutional application, and tax returns to finalize aid offers. Financial aid filing deadline 2/1. **Notification of Awards:** Applicants will be notified of awards on or about 4/1. **Types of Aid:** *Need-based scholarships/grants:* Federal Pell, SEOG, state scholarships/grants, private scholarships, the school's own gift aid. *Loans:* Direct Subsidized Stafford, Direct Unsubsidized Stafford, Direct PLUS, FFEL Subsidized Stafford, FFEL Unsubsidized Stafford, FFEL PLUS, Federal Perkins, state loans, college/university loans from institutional funds, alternative loans. **Student Employment:** Federal Work-Study Program available. Institutional employment available. Highest amount earned per year from on-campus jobs $5,600. Off-campus job opportunities are poor. **Financial Aid Statistics:** 41% freshmen, 38% undergrads receive need-based scholarship or grant aid. 1% freshmen, 1% undergrads receive non-need-based scholarship or grant aid. 32% freshmen, 31% undergrads receive need-based self-help aid. 46% freshmen, 43% undergrads receive any aid. 41% undergrads borrow to pay for school. Average cumulative indebtedness $21,697.

COLBY-SAWYER COLLEGE

541Main Street, New London, NH 03257-7835
Phone: 603-526-3700 **Financial Aid Phone:** 603-526-3717
E-mail: admissions@colbysawyer.edu **CEEB Code:** 3281
Fax: 603-526-3452 **Website:** www.colby-sawyer.edu **ACT Code:** 2506

This private school was founded in 1837. It has a 200-acre campus.

RATINGS

Admissions Selectivity Rating: 71   Fire Safety Rating: 60*   Green Rating: 60*

STUDENTS AND FACULTY

Enrollment: 942. **Student Body:** 65% female, 35% male, 68% out-of-state, 1% international (11 countries represented). Asian 1%, African American 1%, Caucasian 90%, Hispanic 1%.
Retention and Graduation: 51% freshmen graduate within 4 years. **Faculty:** Student/faculty ratio 11:1. 60 full-time faculty, 73% hold PhDs, 2% are members of minority groups, 52% are women.

ACADEMICS

Degrees: Associate, bachelor's, transfer associate. **Classes:** Most classes have 10–19 students. Most lab/discussion sessions have 10–19 students. **Majors with Highest Enrollment:** Business administration and management; nursing/registered nurse (RN, ASN, BSN, MSN); sport and fitness administration/management. **Special Study Options:** Accelerated program, cross-registration, double major, dual enrollment, English as a Second Language (ESL), exchange student program (domestic), honors program, independent study, internships, student-designed major, study abroad, teacher certification program. **Honors programs:** The Wesson Honors Program is designed to provide highly motivated students with an optional intensive experience in the liberal arts. By creating academic, cultural, and social opportunities for integrative and interdisciplinary intellectual discovery, the program challenges students not only to widen their own avenues of intellectual exploration, but to take leadership in a community of scholars and participate as catalysts for inquiry and discussion across the college. Special programs offered to physically disabled students include tape recorders, tutors.

FACILITIES

Housing: Coed dorms, special housing for disabled students, women's dorms, Substance-free Residence Hall. 50% of campus accessible to physically disabled. **Special Academic Facilities/Equipment:** Sawyer Fine Arts Center, Windy Hill School (pre-school–grade 3 laboratory school), Ivey Science Center, Hogan Sports Center, video studio and editing room, radio station (WSCS 90.9 FM).

CAMPUS LIFE

Environment: Rural. **Activities:** Choral groups, dance, drama/theater, literary magazine, musical theater, radio station, student government, student newspaper, yearbook. **Organizations:** 40 registered organizations, 5 honor societies, 1 religious organizations. **Athletics (Intercollegiate):** *Men:* Baseball, basketball, diving, equestrian sports, skiing (downhill/alpine), soccer, swimming, tennis, track/field (outdoor). *Women:* Basketball, diving, equestrian sports, lacrosse, skiing (downhill/alpine), soccer, swimming, tennis, track/field (outdoor), volleyball. **On-Campus Highlights:** Dan and Kathleen Hogan Sports Center, Susan Colgate Cleveland Library/Learning Center, Lethbridge Lodge, Thornton Livingroom, Rooke Hall.

ADMISSIONS

Freshman Academic Profile: Average high school GPA 3. 83% from public high schools. SAT Math middle 50% range 440–530. SAT Critical Reading middle 50% range 440–540. ACT middle 50% range 18–22. Minimum paper TOEFL 500. Minimum computer TOEFL 173. **Basis for Candidate Selection:** *Very important factors considered include:* Academic GPA, rigor of secondary school record, interview. *Important factors considered include:* Class rank, application essay, recommendation(s), standardized test scores, alumni/ae relation, extracurricular activities, level of applicant's interest, talent/ability, volunteer work, work experience. *Other factors considered include:* First generation, geographical residence, state residency. **Freshman Admission Requirements:** High school diploma is required and GED is accepted. *Academic units recommended:* 4 English, 3 mathematics, 3 science, (3 science labs), 2 foreign language, 3 social studies. **Freshman Admission Statistics:** 1,672 applied, 87% admitted, 24% enrolled. **Transfer Admission Requirements:** College transcript(s), essay or personal statement, minimum college GPA of 2.0 required. Lowest grade transferable C. **General Admission Information:** Application fee $45. Early decision application deadline 12/1. Regular application deadline 4/1. Notification on a rolling basis, beginning on or about 1/1. Nonfall registration accepted. Admission may be deferred for a maximum of 1 year. Credit and/or placement offered for CEEB Advanced Placement tests.

COSTS AND FINANCIAL AID

Annual tuition $29,620. Room and board $10,340. Average book expense $750. **Required Forms and Deadlines:** FAFSA. Priority financial aid filing date 3/1. **Notification of Awards:** Applicants will be notified of awards on a rolling basis beginning 3/1. **Types of Aid:** *Need-based scholarships/grants:* Federal Pell, SEOG, state scholarships/grants, private scholarships, the school's own gift aid. *Loans:* FFEL Subsidized Stafford, FFEL Unsubsidized Stafford, FFEL PLUS, Federal Perkins, state loans, college/university loans from institutional funds. **Student Employment:** Federal Work-Study Program available. Institutional employment available. Off-campus job opportunities are good. **Financial Aid Statistics:** 67% freshmen, 68% undergrads receive need-based scholarship or grant aid. 3% freshmen, 4% undergrads receive non-need-based scholarship or grant aid. 63% freshmen, 68% undergrads receive need-based self-help aid. 83% freshmen, 83% undergrads receive any aid. 77% undergrads borrow to pay for school. Average cumulative indebtedness $18,306. **Criteria for awarding institutional aid:** *Non-need-based:* Academics, alumni affiliation, art, leadership, music/drama.

COLGATE UNIVERSITY

13 Oak Drive, Hamilton, NY 13346
Phone: 315-228-7401 **Financial Aid Phone:** 315-228-7431
E-mail: admission@mail.colgate.edu **CEEB Code:** 2086
Fax: 315-228-7544 **Website:** www.colgate.edu **ACT Code:** 2702

This private school was founded in 1819. It has a 515-acre campus.

RATINGS
Admissions Selectivity Rating: 97   **Fire Safety Rating:** 86   **Green Rating:** 85

STUDENTS AND FACULTY

Enrollment: 2,799. **Student Body:** 53% female, 47% male, 72% out-of-state, 5% international (36 countries represented). Asian 5%, African American 6%, Caucasian 74%, Hispanic 6%, Native American 1%.
Retention and Graduation: 95% freshmen return for sophomore year. 85% freshmen graduate within 4 years. 19% grads go on to further study within 1 year. 10% grads pursue arts and sciences degrees. 6% grads pursue law degrees. 1% grads pursue business degrees. 3% grads pursue medical degrees. **Faculty:** Student/faculty ratio 9.7:1. 266 full-time faculty, 96% hold PhDs, 21% are members of minority groups, 39% are women.

ACADEMICS

Degrees: Bachelor's, master's. **Classes:** Most classes have 10–19 students. Most lab/discussion sessions have 10–19 students. **Majors with Highest Enrollment:** Economics; English language and literature; history. **Special Study Options:** Cross-registration, double major, honors program, independent study, internships, liberal arts/career combination, student-designed major, study abroad, teacher certification program, Extended study program allows students to further academic work with a 3–5 week off campus experience during the winter or summer break. Recent trips have travelled to 13 locations around the world including South Africa, Ireland, and China. **Honors programs:** Each year, Colgate honors its top (approximately) 200 accepted students as Alumni Memorial Scholars. This recognition is the highest honor within the admission process, and an indication of an excellent match, both academically and personally, with Colgate. **Combined degree programs:** Pre-engineering: BA/MS in Architecture. Special programs offered to physically disabled students include note-taking services, reader services, tape recorders, tutors. **Career services:** Alumni network, alumni services, career assessment, internships. **Career services highlights include:** Colgate alumni are a valuable resource for students who are exploring their career options. Recently, more than 350 alumni helped currenst students in career exploration. Approximately 4,000 alumni are registered with Career Services to aid students in internship and job searches.

FACILITIES

Housing: Coed dorms, special housing for disabled students, fraternity/sorority housing, cooperative housing, apartments for single students, wellness housing, theme **Housing:** Peace Studies, La Casa Pan Latina, Harlem Reniassance Center, French-Italian House, etc. Accomodations for students with special needs. Townhouses for small groups of students. 20% of campus accessible to physically disabled. **Special Academic Facilities/Equipment:** Art galleries, anthropology museum, language lab, cable TV station, life sciences complex, geology/fossil collection, observatory, electron microscopes, laser lab, weather lab. **Computers:** Students can register for classes online. Administrative functions (other than registration) can be performed online.

CAMPUS LIFE

Environment: Rural. **Activities:** Choral groups, concert band, dance, drama/theater, jazz band, literary magazine, music ensembles, musical theater, pep band, radio station, student government, student newspaper, student-run film society, symphony orchestra, television station, yearbook, campus ministries, international student organization, Model UN. **Organizations:** 160 registered organizations, 4 honor societies, 8 religious organizations. 6 fraternities, 3 sororities. **Athletics (Intercollegiate):** *Men:* Basketball, crew/rowing, cross-country, diving, football, golf, ice hockey, lacrosse, soccer, swimming, tennis, track/field (outdoor). *Women:* Basketball, crew/rowing, cross-country, diving, field hockey, ice hockey, lacrosse, soccer, softball, swimming, tennis, track/field (outdoor), volleyball. **On-Campus Highlights:** Picker Art Gallery, Case-Geyer Library, ALANA Culture Center, Ho Science Center, O'Connor Campus Center (The Coop), two recently completed building projects: $52 million renovation to the Case Library and The Robert H.N. Ho Science Center. **Environmental Initiatives:** All electricity used on campus is hydroelectric, with some supplemental nuclear power. Colgate's wood-chip-burning heating plant utilizes a renewable energy source to provide about 70 percent of our total requirement. Colgate signed an agreement with Clean Air-Cool Planet in 2004, agreeing to complete a campuswide greenhouse gas emissions inventory, raise awareness about the importance of addressing climate change within the campus community, adopt a greenhouse gas emissions reduction target, and develop and implement a strategic plan to meet established targets and monitor progress over time. Colgate routinely builds and renovates to LEED Silver standards. Architectural consultants are required to be LEED-certified and to provide a rigorous analysis of sustainable features for each major design and construction project.

ADMISSIONS

Freshman Academic Profile: Average high school GPA 3.62. 68% in top 10% of high school class, 91% in top 25% of high school class, 100% in top 50% of high school class. 62% from public high schools. SAT Math middle 50% range 640–730. SAT Critical Reading middle 50% range 630–710. ACT middle 50% range 29–32. **Basis for Candidate Selection:** *Very important factors considered include:* Class rank, academic GPA, rigor of secondary school record. *Important factors considered include:* Application essay, recommendation(s), standardized test scores, character/personal qualities, extracurricular activities, talent/ability. *Other factors considered include:* Alumni/ae relation, first generation, geographical residence, racial/ethnic status, volunteer work, work experience. **Freshman Admission Requirements:** High school diploma is required and GED is accepted. *Academic units required:* 4 English, 3 mathematics, 3 science, (2 science labs), 3 foreign language, 3 social studies. *Academic units recommended:* 4 English, 4 mathematics, 4 science, (3 science labs), 4 foreign language, 4 social studies. **Freshman Admission Statistics:** 7,816 applied, 32% admitted, 30% enrolled. **Transfer Admission Requirements:** High school transcript, college transcript(s), essay or personal statement, standardized test scores, statement of good standing from prior institution(s). Minimum college GPA of 3.00 required. Lowest grade transferable C. **General Admission Information:** Application fee $55. Early decision application deadline 11/15. Regular application deadline 1/15. Regular notification 4/1. Nonfall registration not accepted. Admission may be deferred for a maximum of 1 year. Credit and/or placement offered for CEEB Advanced Placement tests.

COSTS AND FINANCIAL AID

Annual tuition $40,690. Room and board $9,970. Required fees $280. **Required Forms and Deadlines:** CSS/Financial Aid PROFILE, noncustodial PROFILE Financial aid filing deadline 1/15. **Notification of Awards:** Applicants will be notified of awards on or about 4/1. **Types of Aid:** *Need-based scholarships/grants:* Federal Pell, SEOG, state scholarships/grants, private scholarships, the school's own gift aid. *Loans:* FFEL Subsidized Stafford, FFEL Unsubsidized Stafford, FFEL PLUS, Federal Perkins. **Student Employment:** Federal Work-Study Program available. Institutional employment available. Highest amount earned per year from on-campus jobs $1,600. Off-campus job opportunities are fair. **Financial Aid Statistics:** 34% freshmen, 35% undergrads receive need-based scholarship or grant aid. 26% freshmen, 28% undergrads receive need-based self-help aid. 6% freshmen, 6% undergrads receive athletic scholarships. 34% freshmen, 35% undergrads receive any aid. 30% undergrads borrow to pay for school. Average cumulative indebtedness $19,202. **Criteria for awarding institutional aid:** *Non-need-based:* Athletics.

COLLEGE FOR CREATIVE STUDIES

201 East Kirby, Detroit, MI 48202
Phone: 313-664-7425 **Financial Aid Phone:** 313-664-7495
E-mail: admissions@ccscad.edu
Fax: 313-872-2739 **Website:** www.ccscad.edu

This private school was founded in 1906. It has a 11-acre campus.

RATINGS
Admissions Selectivity Rating: 60*　　**Fire Safety Rating:** 60*　　**Green Rating:** 60*

STUDENTS AND FACULTY
Student Body: 17% out-of-state.
Retention and Graduation: 73% freshmen return for sophomore year.
Faculty: Student/faculty ratio 8:1. 51 full-time faculty, 61% hold PhDs, 14% are members of minority groups, 31% are women.

ACADEMICS
Degrees: Bachelor's, post-bachelor's certificate. **Majors with Highest Enrollment:** Commercial and advertising art; film/video and photographic arts, other; industrial design. **Special Study Options:** Cooperative education program, double major, dual enrollment, English as a Second Language (ESL), exchange student program (domestic), independent study, internships, study abroad, teacher certification program Special programs offered to physically disabled students include reader services, tape recorders, tutors. **Career services:**

Alumni network, alumni services, career/job search classes, career assessment, internships, regional alumni. **Career services highlights include:** All seniors take part in a practicum class that allows students to work with and for outside companies, such as Ford Motor Company, Pixar, DaimlerChrysler and various companies.

FACILITIES
Housing: Coed dorms. 95% of campus accessible to physically disabled. **Special Academic Facilities/Equipment:** Top-of-the-line technology for design, animation and audiovisual editing. Wood and Metal shops, hot glass studio, gallery, private studios.

CAMPUS LIFE
Environment: Metropolis. **Activities:** Student government. **Organizations:** 5 registered organizations. **On-Campus Highlights:** Center Galleries, U245 Student Art Gallery, Jazzman's Café.

ADMISSIONS
Freshman Academic Profile: ACT middle 50% range 18–23. Minimum paper TOEFL 525. Minimum computer TOEFL 197. **Basis for Candidate Selection:** *Very important factors considered include:* Talent/ability. *Important factors considered include:* Academic GPA, standardized test scores. *Other factors considered include:* Level of applicant's interest. **Freshman Admission Requirements:** High school diploma is required and GED is accepted. **Freshman Admission Statistics:** 1,260 applied, 39% admitted, 51% enrolled. **Transfer Admission Requirements:** High school transcript, college transcript(s), minimum college GPA of 2.0 required. Lowest grade transferable C. **General Admission Information:** Application fee $35. Regular application deadline 8/1. Notification on a rolling basis, beginning on or about 9/15. Nonfall registration accepted. Admission may be deferred for a maximum of 4 semesters. Credit offered for CEEB Advanced Placement tests.

COSTS AND FINANCIAL AID
Annual tuition $27,090. Room and board $4,300. Required fees $1,185. Average book expense $2,500. **Required Forms and Deadlines:** FAFSA. Priority financial aid filing date 7/1. **Notification of Awards:** Applicants will be notified of awards on a rolling basis beginning 3/15. **Types of Aid:** *Need-based scholarships/grants:* Federal Pell, SEOG, state scholarships/grants, private scholarships, the school's own gift aid. *Loans:* FFEL Subsidized Stafford, FFEL Unsubsidized Stafford, FFEL PLUS, Alternative loans. **Student Employment:** Highest amount earned per year from on-campus jobs $1,000. **Financial Aid Statistics:** 74% undergrads borrow to pay for school. Average cumulative indebtedness $57,980. **Criteria for awarding institutional aid:** *Non-need-based:* Academics, art, minority status.

COLLEGE OF THE ATLANTIC

105 Eden Street, Admission Office, Bar Harbor, ME 04609
Phone: 207-288-5015 **Financial Aid Phone:** 207-288-5015
E-mail: inquiry@coa.edu **CEEB Code:** 3305
Fax: 207-288-4126 **Website:** www.coa.edu **ACT Code:** 1637

This private school was founded in 1969. It has a 35-acre campus.

RATINGS
Admissions Selectivity Rating: 87　　**Fire Safety Rating:** 95　　**Green Rating:** 99

STUDENTS AND FACULTY
Enrollment: 321. **Student Body:** 69% female, 31% male, 80% out-of-state, 15% international (37 countries represented). Asian 2%, African American 1%, Caucasian 32%, Hispanic 1%, Native American 1%.
Retention and Graduation: 81% freshmen return for sophomore year. 48% freshmen graduate within 4 years. 20% grads go on to further study within 1 year. 10% grads pursue arts and sciences degrees. 1% grads pursue law degrees. 4% grads pursue business degrees. 3% grads pursue medical degrees. **Faculty:** Student/faculty ratio 11:1. 24 full-time faculty, 79% hold PhDs, 4% are members of minority groups, 29% are women.

ACADEMICS
Degrees: Bachelor's, master's. **Classes:** Most classes have 10–19 students. Most lab/discussion sessions have 10–19 students. **Majors with Highest Enrollment:** Biology/biological sciences; ecology; education. **Special Study Options:** Cross-registration, exchange student program (domestic), independent study, internships, liberal arts/career combination, student-designed major,

study abroad, teacher certification program, Winter term program in Yucatan, Mexico. EcoLeague—consortium agreement with five other colleges for student exchanges (Alaska Pacific University, Antioch College, Green Mountain College, Northland College, Prescott College. Exchange program with Olin College of Engineering and University of Maine at Orono. **Honors programs:** We consider all our students to be capable of honors work, which is why all students finish their time at COA with a term-long capstone, or senior project. Special programs offered to physically disabled students include note-taking services, reader services, tape recorders, tutors. **Career services:** Alumni network, alumni services, career assessment, internships, regional alumni. **Career services highlights include:** Internships are required for graduation and allow students to apply their classroom knowledge to the world of work over ten weeks and 400 hours.

FACILITIES

Housing: Coed dorms, special housing for disabled students, Substance-free housing; green (environmentally conscious)housing. 70% of campus accessible to physically disabled. **Special Academic Facilities/Equipment:** Natural history museum, pottery studio, greenhouse, Geographic Information Systems lab, Green Graphics Studio, Deering Common Campus Center, organic community garden, Blum Gallery, outdoor equipment, two boats: Indigo and Borealis, off-site organic farm and two island research stations. **Computers:** 100% of classrooms, 100% of dorms, 100% of libraries, 100% of dining areas, 100% of student union, 25% of common outdoor areas have wireless network access. Students can register for classes online. Administrative functions (other than registration) can be performed online.

CAMPUS LIFE

Environment: Rural. **Activities:** Choral groups, dance, drama/theater, jazz band, literary magazine, music ensembles, student government, student newspaper, yearbook. **On-Campus Highlights:** George B. Dorr Museum of Natural History, Blum Art Gallery, the pier, Turrets, Take-A-Break. College of the Atlantic has recently completed state-of-the-art sustainable dorms and a creative restoration of an historic building into a similarly sustainable campus center. These are also very popular places to visit. **Environmental Initiatives:** Carbon NetZero Initiative—COA set as its goal to be carbon net zero by the end of 2007 and achieved this goal by offsetting all of its carbon emissions that it could not avoid or reduce. Energy conservation through renewables and campus audits: COA's new student dorms have space heating and hot water provided by wood pellet boilers, the buildings are super-insulated, have triple-pane windows and composting toilets. The building renovated to serve as the campus center received numerous energy efficient improvements and is also heated by the same wood pellet boiler system. Working with an energy services company, COA has completed an energy audit of the campus and implemented recommendations to make existing buildings more energy efficient. Retrofits and upgrades to buildings were completed in 2008. Local and organic food: COA has its own organic farm and hosts an organic community garden on its campus. Both sites helps supply the college cafeteria with local, organic food when possible given the northern growing season. A good percentage of what the farm can't supply is still local and organic. ALL food waste is composted, with composting bins in all dorms as well as the cafeteria. COA alumni, working with the organic farm, have been instrumental in creating a farm to school program for local elementary schools. The college has now initiated a Sustainable Food Systems Program to tie together its work in organic agriculture and larger food systems issues.

ADMISSIONS

Freshman Academic Profile: 26% in top 10% of high school class, 63% in top 25% of high school class, 93% in top 50% of high school class. 71% from public high schools. SAT Math middle 50% range 510–620. SAT Critical Reading middle 50% range 620–690. SAT Writing middle 50% range 570–670. ACT middle 50% range 21–27. Minimum paper TOEFL 567. Minimum computer TOEFL 227. Minimum web-based TOEFL 86. **Basis for Candidate Selection:** *Very important factors considered include:* Application essay, recommendation(s), rigor of secondary school record. *Important factors considered include:* Class rank, academic GPA, character/personal qualities, extracurricular activities, interview, talent/ability, volunteer work, work experience. *Other factors considered include:* Standardized test scores, alumni/ae relation, first generation, geographical residence, level of applicant's interest, racial/ethnic status, state residency. **Freshman Admission Requirements:** High school diploma is required and GED is accepted. *Academic units required:* 4 English, 3 mathematics, 2 science, (2 science labs), 2 social studies. *Academic units recommended:* 4 mathematics, 3 science, 2 foreign language, 2 history, 1 academic electives. **Freshman Admission Statistics:** 322 applied, 75% admitted, 32% enrolled. **Transfer Admission Requirements:** High school transcript, college transcript(s), essay or personal statement, minimum college GPA of 3.0 required. Lowest grade transferable C. **General Admission Information:** Application fee $45. Early decision application deadline 12/1. Regular application deadline 2/15. Regular notification 4/1. Nonfall registration accepted. Admission may be deferred for a maximum of 1 year. Credit and/or placement offered for CEEB Advanced Placement tests.

COSTS AND FINANCIAL AID

Annual tuition $32,580. Room and board $8,490. Required fees $480. Average book expense $600. **Required Forms and Deadlines:** FAFSA, institution's own financial aid form, noncustodial PROFILE, business/farm supplement. Financial aid filing deadline 2/15. Priority financial aid filing date 2/15. **Notification of Awards:** Applicants will be notified of awards on or about 4/1. **Types of Aid:** *Need-based scholarships/grants:* Federal Pell, SEOG, state scholarships/grants, private scholarships, the school's own gift aid. *Loans:* FFEL Subsidized Stafford, FFEL Unsubsidized Stafford, FFEL PLUS, Federal Perkins. **Student Employment:** Federal Work-Study Program available. Off-campus job opportunities are good. **Financial Aid Statistics:** 80% freshmen, 82% undergrads receive need-based scholarship or grant aid. 80% freshmen, 79% undergrads receive need-based self-help aid. 80% freshmen, 82% undergrads receive any aid. 56% undergrads borrow to pay for school. Average cumulative indebtedness $23,762. **Criteria for awarding institutional aid:** *Non-need-based:* Academics.

COLLEGE OF CHARLESTON

66 George Street, Charleston, SC 29424
Phone: 843-953-5670 **Financial Aid Phone:** 843-953-5540
E-mail: admissions@cofc.edu **CEEB Code:** 5113
Fax: 843-953-6322 **Website:** www.cofc.edu **ACT Code:** 3846

This public school was founded in 1770. It has a 52-acre campus.

RATINGS
Admissions Selectivity Rating: 87   **Fire Safety Rating:** 92   **Green Rating:** 80

STUDENTS AND FACULTY
Enrollment: 9,736. **Student Body:** 64% female, 36% male, 35.7% out-of-state, 1% international (71 countries represented). Asian 2%, African American 5%, Caucasian 83%, Hispanic 2%.
Retention and Graduation: 48% freshmen graduate within 4 years. 48.5% grads go on to further study within 1 year. 17.8% grads pursue arts and sciences degrees. 13.9% grads pursue law degrees. 17.8% grads pursue business degrees. 13.9% grads pursue medical degrees. **Faculty:** Student/faculty ratio 16.16:1. 523 full-time faculty, 87% hold PhDs, 10% are members of minority groups, 43% are women. 3.9% of classes are taught by teaching assistants.

ACADEMICS
Degrees: Bachelor's, master's, post-bachelor's certificate. **Classes:** Most classes have 20–29 students. Most lab/discussion sessions have 20–29 students. **Majors with Highest Enrollment:** Biology/biological sciences; business administration and management; communication studies/speech communication and rhetoric. **Special Study Options:** Accelerated program, cooperative education program, cross-registration, distance learning, double major, dual enrollment, English as a Second Language (ESL), exchange student program (domestic), honors program, independent study, internships, liberal arts/career combination, study abroad, teacher certification program, Semester at Sea. **Honors programs:** The Honors College at the College of Charleston began as an Honors Program in 1978 to provide a program and a community for talented and motivated students who enjoy active participation in small stimulating classes and want to be involved in a meaningful way in undergraduate research. In order to better serve the needs of the students, it became an Honors College in 2005, with new positions to provide academic advising and assistance in applying for postgraduate fellowships and additional funding to support its mission. The Honors College is dedicated to providing these students with a place where they can flourish and grow, a true learning community of teachers and students. In addition to receiving exciting and unique educational experiences, students can participate with their fellow Honors students in social, cultural, and intellectual events on the campus and in historic Charleston, SC. The Honors College challenges intellectually talented students to make the most of the opportunities available to them, to become actively involved in their own education, and to prepare themselves to excel in graduate programs, medical or law school, or in whatever comes after they complete their undergraduate education. In Honors classes, students take responsibility for their own learning through class discussions, through interaction with faculty and fellow students, and through independent research. Honors students are advised by a full time Honors academic advisor and specially chosen faculty mentors, receive priority registration, and have the opportunity to room with other Honors students in special Honors residence halls. Classes, seminars, and student gatherings are

held in the Honors Center, the historic William Aiken House built by Governor William Aiken in 1839. Special programs offered to physically disabled students include note-taking services, reader services, tape recorders, tutors. **Career services:** Alumni network, alumni services, career/job search classes, career assessment, internships, regional alumni. **Career services highlights include:** Internships. Most academic departments offer internships for credit and the career center offers a certificate/no-credit option. A large number of students do these each year.

FACILITIES

Housing: Coed dorms, men's dorms, women's dorms, fraternity/sorority housing, apartments for single students, theme housing. Restored old Charleston houses used as residence halls, some with kitchen facilities in suites. 80% of campus accessible to physically disabled. **Special Academic Facilities/Equipment:** Halsey Institute of Contemporary Art, sculpture facility, Rivers Communications Museum, Miles Early Childhood Development Center, Avery Institute for African-American History and Culture, physics and astronomy observatory, Grice Marine Laboratory, Patriots Point Athletics Complex (includes softball, baseball, tennis, soccer and sailing). **Computers:** 75% of classrooms, 100% of dorms, 100% of libraries, 100% of dining areas, 100% of student union, 80% of common outdoor areas have wireless network access. Students can register for classes online. Administrative functions (other than registration) can be performed online.

CAMPUS LIFE

Environment: City. **Activities:** Choral groups, dance, drama/theater, jazz band, literary magazine, music ensembles, musical theater, pep band, radio station, student government, student newspaper, symphony orchestra, yearbook, campus ministries, international student organization. **Organizations:** 120 registered organizations, 19 honor societies, 16 religious organizations. 13 fraternities, 12 sororities. **Athletics (Intercollegiate):** *Men:* Baseball, basketball, cross-country, diving, golf, sailing, soccer, swimming, tennis. *Women:* Basketball, cross-country, diving, equestrian sports, golf, sailing, soccer, softball, swimming, tennis, track/field (outdoor), track/field (indoor), volleyball. **On-Campus Highlights:** The Cistern Yard, Carolina First Arena, Fresh Food Company, Addleston Library, Cougar Plaza. The College opened two new facilities in January 2010: The The Marion and Wayland H. Cato Jr. Center for the Arts and a second building for the School of Sciences and Mathematics. Their completion is part of a significant transformation of the college's facilities, providing students with the best and most effective learning and recreational opportunities. Six new facilities were completed in 2007, and several others were finished in 2008. Patriots Point Athletics Complex is located just across the Ravenel Bridge in Mt. Pleasant. Recently renovated, this 35-acre complex is home to baseball, soccer, softball, sailing and tennis. **Environmental Initiatives:** Convened a Sustainability Committee, signed the ACUPCC, participate in RecycleMania.

ADMISSIONS

Freshman Academic Profile: Average high school GPA 3.89. 30.56% in top 10% of high school class, 67.68% in top 25% of high school class, 94.4% in top 50% of high school class. 80.8% from public high schools. SAT Math middle 50% range 560–640. SAT Critical Reading middle 50% range 560–650. ACT middle 50% range 23–27. Minimum paper TOEFL 570. Minimum computer TOEFL 230. Minimum web-based TOEFL 88. **Basis for Candidate Selection:** *Very important factors considered include:* Academic GPA, rigor of secondary school record, standardized test scores, state residency. *Important factors considered include:* Class rank, character/personal qualities, first generation, talent/ability. *Other factors considered include:* Application essay, recommendation(s), extracurricular activities, racial/ethnic status, volunteer work, work experience. **Freshman Admission Requirements:** High school diploma is required and GED is accepted. *Academic units required:* 4 English, 3 mathematics, 3 science, (3 science labs), 3 foreign language, 3 social studies, 4 academic electives. *Academic units recommended:* 4 English, 4 mathematics, 2 history. **Freshman Admission Statistics:** 11,083 applied, 70% admitted, 28% enrolled. **Transfer Admission Requirements:** College transcript(s), minimum college GPA of 2.6 required. Lowest grade transferable C. **General Admission Information:** Application fee $50. Regular application deadline 2/1. Nonfall registration accepted. Admission may be deferred for a maximum of 2 semesters. Credit and/or placement offered for CEEB Advanced Placement tests.

COSTS AND FINANCIAL AID

Annual in-state tuition $8,988. Annual out-of-state tuition $21,846. Room and board $9,411. Average book expense $1,170. **Required Forms and Deadlines:** FAFSA. Priority financial aid filing date 3/15. **Notification of Awards:** Applicants will be notified of awards on a rolling basis beginning 4/10. **Types of Aid:** *Need-based scholarships/grants:* Federal Pell, SEOG, state scholarships/grants, private scholarships, the school's own gift aid. *Loans:* Direct Subsidized Stafford, Direct Unsubsidized Stafford, Direct PLUS, Federal Perkins. **Student Employment:** Federal Work-Study Program available. Institutional employment available. Highest amount earned per year from on-campus jobs $9,400. Off-campus job opportunities are fair. **Financial Aid Statistics:** 27% freshmen, 24% undergrads receive need-based scholarship or grant aid. 30%

freshmen, 17% undergrads receive non-need-based scholarship or grant aid. 28% freshmen, 31% undergrads receive need-based self-help aid. 2% freshmen, 2% undergrads receive athletic scholarships. 37% freshmen, 37% undergrads receive any aid. 44.2% undergrads borrow to pay for school. Average cumulative indebtedness $17,139. **Criteria for awarding institutional aid:** *Non-need-based:* Academics, alumni affiliation, art, athletics, music/drama.

COLLEGE OF THE HOLY CROSS

Admissions Office, 1 College Street, Worcester, MA 01610-2395
Phone: 508-793-2443 **Financial Aid Phone:** 508-793-2265
E-mail: admissions@holycross.edu **CEEB Code:** 3282
Fax: 508-793-3888 **Website:** www.holycross.edu **ACT Code:** 1810

This private school, affiliated with the Roman Catholic Church, was founded in 1843. It has a 174-acre campus.

RATINGS

Admissions Selectivity Rating: 96   **Fire Safety Rating:** 97   **Green Rating:** 87

STUDENTS AND FACULTY

Enrollment: 2,897. **Student Body:** 55% female, 45% male, 63% out-of-state, 1% international (18 countries represented). Asian 6%, African American 4%, Caucasian 68%, Hispanic 8%.
Retention and Graduation: 96% freshmen return for sophomore year. 87% freshmen graduate within 4 years. 24% grads go on to further study within 1 year. 6% grads pursue arts and sciences degrees. 7% grads pursue law degrees. 1% grads pursue business degrees. 3% grads pursue medical degrees. **Faculty:** Student/faculty ratio 11:1. 244 full-time faculty, 98% hold PhDs, 13% are members of minority groups, 45% are women.

ACADEMICS

Degrees: Bachelor's. **Classes:** Most classes have 10–19 students. Most lab/discussion sessions have 10–19 students. **Majors with Highest Enrollment:** Economics; English language and literature; political science and government. **Special Study Options:** Accelerated program, cross-registration, double major, dual enrollment, exchange student program (domestic), honors program, independent study, internships, liberal arts/career combination, student-designed major, study abroad, teacher certification program, first-year integrated living and learning program ("Montserrat"). **Honors programs:** Fenwick Scholar Program. Special programs offered to physically disabled students include note-taking services, reader services, tutors. **Career services:** Alumni network, career/job search classes, internships, regional alumni. **Career services highlights include:** Summer Internship Program.

FACILITIES

Housing: Coed dorms, special housing for disabled students, apartments for single students, suites on campus available for juniors and seniors. Substance-free housing also available. 85% of campus accessible to physically disabled. **Special Academic Facilities/Equipment:** Art gallery, Concert Hall, Taylor and Boody tracker organ, O'Callahan Science Library, Rehm Library, Multimedia Resource Center, Wellness Center; scientific equipment on par with the best research universities. **Computers:** 100% of classrooms, 100% of dorms, 100% of libraries, 100% of dining areas, 100% of student union, 60% of common outdoor areas have wireless network access. Students can register for classes online. Administrative functions (other than registration) can be performed online.

CAMPUS LIFE

Environment: City. **Activities:** Choral groups, concert band, dance, drama/theater, jazz band, literary magazine, marching band, music ensembles, musical theater, pep band, radio station, student government, student newspaper, yearbook, campus ministries, international student organization. **Organizations:** 105 registered organizations, 20 honor societies, 4 religious organizations. **Athletics (Intercollegiate):** *Men:* Baseball, basketball, crew/rowing, cross-country, diving, football, golf, ice hockey, lacrosse, soccer, swimming, tennis, track/field (outdoor), track/field (indoor). *Women:* Basketball, crew/rowing, cross-country, diving, field hockey, golf, ice hockey, lacrosse, soccer, softball, swimming, tennis, track/field (outdoor), track/field (indoor), volleyball. **On-Campus Highlights:** Library, Smith Hall, St. Joseph Chapel, Hart Recreation Center, Hogan Campus Center. **Environmental Initiatives:** College has a four-year commitment with Trans-Canada to supply electric power will reduce the school's carbon footprint by 30%. College has committed to a 20% carbon reduction by 2015. College is continuously updating HVAC controls, installing windows, and replacing light fixtures to reduce overall energy consumption.

ADMISSIONS

Freshman Academic Profile: Average high school GPA 3.79. 66% in top 10% of high school class, 93% in top 25% of high school class, 99% in top 50% of high school class. 47% from public high schools. SAT Math middle 50% range 610–690. SAT Critical Reading middle 50% range 600–680. SAT Writing middle 50% range 600–690. ACT middle 50% range 26–30. Minimum paper TOEFL 550. Minimum computer TOEFL 213. Minimum web-based TOEFL 79. **Basis for Candidate Selection:** *Very important factors considered include:* Class rank, academic GPA, recommendation(s), rigor of secondary school record, interview. *Important factors considered include:* Application essay, character/personal qualities, extracurricular activities, level of applicant's interest. *Other factors considered include:* Standardized test scores, alumni/ae relation, first generation, geographical residence, racial/ethnic status, talent/ability, volunteer work, work experience. **Freshman Admission Requirements:** High school diploma is required and GED is accepted. *Academic units recommended:* 4 English, 4 mathematics, 4 science, (2 science labs), 4 foreign language, 2 social studies, 2 history. **Freshman Admission Statistics:** 6,652 applied, 36% admitted, 31% enrolled. **Transfer Admission Requirements:** High school transcript, college transcript(s), essay or personal statement, statement of good standing from prior institution(s). Lowest grade transferable C. **General Admission Information:** Application fee $60. Early decision application deadline 12/15. Regular application deadline 1/15. Nonfall registration not accepted. Admission may be deferred for a maximum of 1 year. Credit offered for CEEB Advanced Placement tests.

COSTS AND FINANCIAL AID

Annual tuition $39,330. Room and board $10,940. Required fees $562. Average book expense $700. **Required Forms and Deadlines:** FAFSA, CSS/Financial Aid PROFILE, noncustodial PROFILE, business/farm supplement. Parent and student federal tax returns. Financial aid filing deadline 2/1. Priority financial aid filing date 2/1. **Notification of Awards:** Applicants will be notified of awards on or about 4/1. **Types of Aid:** *Need-based scholarships/grants:* Federal Pell, SEOG, state scholarships/grants, private scholarships, the school's own gift aid. *Loans:* Direct Subsidized Stafford, Direct Unsubsidized Stafford, Direct PLUS, Federal Perkins, MEFA. **Student Employment:** Federal Work-Study Program available. Institutional employment available. Highest amount earned per year from on-campus jobs $1,604. Off-campus job opportunities are fair. **Financial Aid Statistics:** 45% freshmen, 43% undergrads receive need-based scholarship or grant aid. 2% freshmen, 1% undergrads receive non-need-based scholarship or grant aid. 41% freshmen, 41% undergrads receive need-based self-help aid. 4% freshmen, 2% undergrads receive athletic scholarships. 63% freshmen, 60% undergrads receive any aid. 57% undergrads borrow to pay for school. Average cumulative indebtedness $23,785. **Criteria for awarding institutional aid:** *Non-need-based:* Academics, athletics.

THE COLLEGE OF IDAHO

2112 Cleveland Boulevard, Caldwell, ID 83605
Phone: 208-459-5305 **Financial Aid Phone:** 208-459-5380
E-mail: admission@collegeofidaho.edu **CEEB Code:** 4060
Fax: 208-459-5757 **Website:** www.collegeofidaho.edu **ACT Code:** 916

This private school was founded in 1891. It has a 50-acre campus.

RATINGS
Admissions Selectivity Rating: 87   **Fire Safety Rating:** 66   **Green Rating:** 79

STUDENTS AND FACULTY

Enrollment: 920. **Student Body:** 60% female, 40% male, 24% out-of-state, 5% international (28 countries represented). Asian 2%, African American 1%, Caucasian 60%, Hispanic 8%.
Retention and Graduation: 80% freshmen return for sophomore year. 50% freshmen graduate within 4 years. **Faculty:** Student/faculty ratio 11:1. 65 full-time faculty, 82% hold PhDs, 3% are members of minority groups, 42% are women.

ACADEMICS

Degrees: Bachelor's, master's. **Classes:** Most classes have fewer than 10 students. **Majors with Highest Enrollment:** Biology/biological sciences;

business/commerce; psychology. **Special Study Options:** Cross-registration, double major, dual enrollment, exchange student program (domestic), honors program, independent study, internships, liberal arts/career combination, student-designed major, study abroad, teacher certification program. **Honors programs:** Heritage Scholars Program, Gipson Honors Program; Kathryn Albertson Scholars Program; Davis United World Scholars. **Combined degree programs:** BA/JD, MBA (Gonzaga, BSU), MNR (U of ID), Nursing (ISU). Special programs offered to physically disabled students include note-taking services, reader services, tape recorders. **Career services:** Alumni network, alumni services, career assessment, internships, regional alumni. **Career services highlights include:** Internship program—students are required to connect their internship with the academic coursework though writing.

FACILITIES

Housing: Coed dorms, special housing for disabled students, fraternity/sorority housing, apartments for single students, college-owned houses; dorms for healthy/quiet lifestyle, academic honor, first year community, honor code. 80% of campus accessible to physically disabled. **Special Academic Facilities/Equipment:** Art and natural history museums, gem and mineral collections, observatory, planetarium, nuclear magnetic resonance spectrometer, gas chromatograph, gamma camera, graphic computer, art gallery, Robert E. Smylie Archives. **Computers:** 100% of classrooms, 100% of dorms, 100% of libraries, 100% of dining areas, 100% of student union, 100% of common outdoor areas have wireless network access. Administrative functions (other than registration) can be performed online.

CAMPUS LIFE

Environment: Town. **Activities:** Choral groups, concert band, dance, drama/theater, jazz band, literary magazine, music ensembles, musical theater, opera, pep band, radio station, student government, student newspaper, student-run film society, symphony orchestra, yearbook, campus ministries, international student organization, Model UN. **Organizations:** 55 registered organizations, 4 honor societies, 3 religious organizations. 3 fraternities, 4 sororities. **Athletics (Intercollegiate):** *Men:* Baseball, cheerleading, cross-country, golf, skiing (downhill/alpine), skiing (nordic/cross-country), snowboarding, soccer, swimming, tennis, track/field (outdoor). *Women:* Basketball, cheerleading, cross-country, golf, skiing (downhill/alpine), skiing (nordic/cross-country), snowboarding, soccer, softball, swimming, tennis, track/field (outdoor), volleyball. **On-Campus Highlights:** J.A. Albertson Activity Center, McCain Student Center, Langroise Center for Performing and fine arts, Centennial Amphitheater, Dorms. **Environmental Initiatives:** Creating a campus sustainability council, environmental studies major.

ADMISSIONS

Freshman Academic Profile: Average high school GPA 3.63. 29% in top 10% of high school class, 68% in top 25% of high school class, 91% in top 50% of high school class. SAT Math middle 50% range 490–630. SAT Critical Reading middle 50% range 470–623. SAT Writing middle 50% range 460–570. ACT middle 50% range 22–27. Minimum paper TOEFL 550. Minimum computer TOEFL 213. Minimum web-based TOEFL 79. **Basis for Candidate Selection:** *Very important factors considered include:* Application essay, academic GPA, recommendation(s), rigor of secondary school record, standardized test scores, character/personal qualities, extracurricular activities, level of applicant's interest. *Important factors considered include:* Class rank, interview. *Other factors considered include:* Alumni/ae relation, first generation, geographical residence, talent/ability, volunteer work. **Freshman Admission Requirements:** High school diploma is required and GED is accepted. *Academic units required:* 3 English, 2 mathematics, 3 social studies, 3 history, 3 academic electives. *Academic units recommended:* 4 English, 4 mathematics, 3 science, (3 science labs), 3 foreign language, 3 social studies, 3 history, 3 academic electives. **Freshman Admission Statistics:** 1,275 applied, 59% admitted, 37% enrolled. **Transfer Admission Requirements:** College transcript(s), essay or personal statement, minimum college GPA of 2.2 required. Lowest grade transferable D–. **General Admission Information:** Regular application deadline 8/1. Notification on a rolling basis, beginning on or about 10/15. Nonfall registration accepted. Admission may be deferred for a maximum of 1 year. Credit and/or placement offered for CEEB Advanced Placement tests.

COSTS AND FINANCIAL AID

Annual tuition $19,300. Room and board $7,478. Required fees $735. Average book expense $900. **Required Forms and Deadlines:** FAFSA, institution's own financial aid form. Priority financial aid filing date 2/15. **Notification of Awards:** Applicants will be notified of awards on a rolling basis beginning 2/1. **Types of Aid:** *Need-based scholarships/grants:* Federal Pell, SEOG, state scholarships/grants, private scholarships, the school's own gift aid. *Loans:* FFEL Subsidized Stafford, FFEL Unsubsidized Stafford, FFEL PLUS, Federal Perkins, Alternative Education Loans. **Student Employment:** Federal Work-Study Program available. Highest amount earned per year from on-campus jobs $77,073. Off-campus job opportunities are good. **Financial Aid Statistics:** 45% freshmen, 39% undergrads receive need-based scholarship or grant aid. 66% freshmen, 59% undergrads receive non-need-based scholarship or grant aid. 49% freshmen, 44% undergrads receive need-based self-help aid. 21%

freshmen, 26% undergrads receive athletic scholarships. 99% freshmen, 98% undergrads receive any aid. 76% undergrads borrow to pay for school. Average cumulative indebtedness $24,919. **Criteria for awarding institutional aid:** *Non-need-based:* Academics, alumni affiliation, art, athletics, leadership, minority status, music/drama, religious affiliation, state/district residency.

COLLEGE OF MOUNT SAINT VINCENT

6301 Riverdale Avenue, Riverdale, NY 10471
Phone: 718-405-3267 **Financial Aid Phone:** 718-405-3349
E-mail: admissions@mountsaintvincent.edu **CEEB Code:** 2088
Fax: 718-549-7945 **Website:** www.mountsaintvincent.edu

This private school, affiliated with the Roman Catholic Church, was founded in 1847. It has a 70-acre campus.

RATINGS
Admissions Selectivity Rating: 71 **Fire Safety Rating:** 60* **Green Rating:** 60*

STUDENTS AND FACULTY
Enrollment: 1,448. **Student Body:** 74% female, 26% male, 13% out-of-state, 1% international (8 countries represented). Asian 11%, African American 13%, Caucasian 39%, Hispanic 29%.
Retention and Graduation: 70% freshmen return for sophomore year. 39% freshmen graduate within 4 years. 25% grads go on to further study within 1 year. 9% grads pursue arts and sciences degrees. 3% grads pursue law degrees. 7% grads pursue business degrees. 2% grads pursue medical degrees. **Faculty:** Student/faculty ratio 12:1. 73 full-time faculty, 93% hold PhDs, 8% are members of minority groups, 62% are women.

ACADEMICS
Degrees: Associate, bachelor's, master's, post-master's certificate. **Classes:** Most classes have 20–29 students. Most lab/discussion sessions have 10–19 students. **Majors with Highest Enrollment:** Business/commerce; nursing/registered nurse (RN, ASN, BSN, MSN); psychology. **Special Study Options:** Accelerated program, double major, honors program, independent study, internships, liberal arts/career combination, study abroad, teacher certification program. **Honors programs:** At present, the Honors Program reflects several distinctive dimensions and provides gifted students with the opportunity to develop critical thinking skills, an affirmative acknowledgement of the human dignity of self and others, and a commitment to realize one's intellectual potential, through participation in enhanced learning experiences both in and out of the classroom. Freshman and sophomore honors students are required to complete six of eight paired Honors Sections of the college's Core Curriculum courses. Specifically, in freshman year, literature is paired with psychology and fine arts with history; sociology is paired with economics and philosophy with religious studies in sophomore year. Juniors and seniors are challenged to enrich themselves through involvement in research projects that are faculty-mentored and through engaging themselves in reflective extra-curricular events (e.g, attending lectures, conferences, or cultural event) with faculty assistance and support. At the same time, the college has initiated a process to further develop and restructure the honors experience by the development of courses that are more inter-disciplinary in nature, utilize more diversified pedagogical styles, and, consistent with the college's mission, provide the opportunity for community service and learning. Through its honors program, the college seeks to develop informed, critically reflective, and value-oriented young men and women who will successfully pursue higher educational opportunities and make meaningful contributions to society both professionally and in their personal lives. Special programs offered to physically disabled students include note-taking services, tape recorders, tutors. **Career services:** Career/job search classes, career assessment, internships, regional alumni.

FACILITIES
Housing: Coed dorms, special housing for disabled students, women's dorms. 90% of campus accessible to physically disabled. **Special Academic Facilities/Equipment:** Newly renovated Maryvale Hall, with newly constructed wing, for communications and fine arts eepartments; nursing lab; TV studio, radio station; Elizabeth Seton Traveling Museum; forensic laboratory equipment. **Computers:** Students can register for classes online. Administrative functions (other than registration) can be performed online.

CAMPUS LIFE
Environment: Metropolis. **Activities:** Dance, drama/theater, literary magazine, musical theater, radio station, student government, student newspaper, television station, yearbook, campus ministries. **Organizations:** 30 registered organizations, 15 honor societies, 2 religious organizations. **Athletics (Intercollegiate):** *Men:* Baseball, basketball, cross-country, lacrosse, soccer, swimming,

tennis, volleyball. *Women:* Basketball, cross-country, lacrosse, soccer, softball, swimming, tennis, track/field (outdoor), volleyball. **On-Campus Highlights:** Crossroads (student lounge), Maryvale(new communication/srt building), fitness center (includes swimming pool), Benedict's Cafe. **Environmental Initiatives:** Recycling, green cleaning products, green construction.

ADMISSIONS
Freshman Academic Profile: Average high school GPA 2.8. 46% from public high schools. SAT Math middle 50% range 430–520. SAT Critical Reading middle 50% range 440–530. Minimum paper TOEFL 550. Minimum computer TOEFL 213. **Basis for Candidate Selection:** *Very important factors considered include:* Academic GPA, rigor of secondary school record. *Important factors considered include:* Application essay, recommendation(s), standardized test scores, character/personal qualities, extracurricular activities, interview. *Other factors considered include:* Class rank, alumni/ae relation, first generation, geographical residence, religious affiliation/commitment, state residency, volunteer work, work experience. **Freshman Admission Requirements:** High school diploma is required and GED is accepted. *Academic units required:* 4 English, 2 mathematics, 2 science, 2 foreign language, 3 social studies, 3 academic electives. *Academic units recommended:* 4 English, 4 mathematics, 3 science, (3 science labs), 3 foreign language, 4 social studies, 3 academic electives. **Freshman Admission Statistics:** 2,224 applied, 67% admitted, 25% enrolled. **Transfer Admission Requirements:** College transcript(s), essay or personal statement, minimum college GPA of 2.0 required. Lowest grade transferable C. **General Admission Information:** Application fee $35. Notification on a rolling basis, beginning on or about 2/1. Nonfall registration accepted. Admission may be deferred for a maximum of 1 year. Credit and/or placement offered for CEEB Advanced Placement tests.

COSTS AND FINANCIAL AID
Required Forms and Deadlines: FAFSA, state aid form. Priority financial aid filing date 2/15. **Notification of Awards:** Applicants will be notified of awards on a rolling basis beginning 3/1. **Types of Aid:** *Need-based scholarships/grants:* Federal Pell, SEOG, state scholarships/grants, private scholarships, the school's own gift aid. *Loans:* FFEL Subsidized Stafford, FFEL Unsubsidized Stafford, FFEL PLUS, Federal Perkins. **Student Employment:** Federal Work-Study Program available. Institutional employment available. Off-campus job opportunities are good. **Financial Aid Statistics:** 78% freshmen, 75% undergrads receive need-based scholarship or grant aid. 78% freshmen, 75% undergrads receive need-based self-help aid. 87% freshmen, 86% undergrads receive any aid. 80% undergrads borrow to pay for school. Average cumulative indebtedness $17,000. **Criteria for awarding institutional aid:** *Non-need-based:* Academics, alumni affiliation, leadership.

COLLEGE OF MOUNT ST. JOSEPH

5701 Delhi Road, Cincinnati, OH 45233
Phone: 513-244-4531 **Financial Aid Phone:** 513-244-4418
E-mail: admissions@mail.msj.edu **CEEB Code:** 1129
Fax: 513-244-4629 **Website:** www.msj.edu **ACT Code:** 3254

This private school, affiliated with the Roman Catholic Church, was founded in 1920. It has a 92-acre campus.

RATINGS
Admissions Selectivity Rating: 73 **Fire Safety Rating:** 98 **Green Rating:** 63

STUDENTS AND FACULTY
Enrollment: 1,860. **Student Body:** 63% female, 37% male, 15% out-of-state, international (3 countries represented). African American 10%, Caucasian 83%, Hispanic 1%.
Retention and Graduation: 72% freshmen return for sophomore year. 36% freshmen graduate within 4 years. 11.8% grads go on to further study within 1 year. 9.8% grads pursue arts and sciences degrees. 0.4% grads pursue business degrees. **Faculty:** Student/faculty ratio 11.5:1. 117 full-time faculty, 74% hold PhDs, 3% are members of minority groups, 59% are women.

ACADEMICS
Degrees: Associate, bachelor's, certificate, master's, post-bachelor's certificate. **Classes:** Most classes have 10–19 students. Most lab/discussion sessions have 10–19 students. **Majors with Highest Enrollment:** Business administration and management; nursing/registered nurse (RN, ASN, BSN, MSN); sport and fitness administration/management. **Special Study Options:** Accelerated program, cooperative education program, cross-registration, distance learning, double major, dual enrollment, honors program, independent study, internships, liberal arts/career combination, study abroad, teacher certification program. **Honors programs:** Honors program—designed to meet the interests of highly

motivated students who are able to take responsibility for their own learning under the guidance of experienced faculty members. Special programs offered to physically disabled students include note-taking services, reader services, tape recorders, tutors. **Career services:** Alumni services, career/job search classes, career assessment, internships. **Career services highlights include:** Qualified students have the opportunity to gain career-related, paid work experience. Co-ops earn academic credit that will complement classroom training by integrating theory and practice.

FACILITIES

Housing: Coed dorms, special housing for disabled students 95% of campus accessible to physically disabled. **Special Academic Facilities/Equipment:** Art studio/gallery, Student Scholar Center, computer labs, theatre. **Computers:** 100% of classrooms, 100% of dorms, 100% of libraries, 100% of dining areas, 100% of common outdoor areas have wireless network access. Students can register for classes online. Administrative functions (other than registration) can be performed online.

CAMPUS LIFE

Environment: Metropolis. **Activities:** Choral groups, concert band, dance, drama/theater, jazz band, literary magazine, music ensembles, musical theater, pep band, student government, student newspaper, campus ministries, international student organization. **Organizations:** 35 registered organizations, 10 honor societies, 1 religious organizations. **Athletics (Intercollegiate):** *Men:* Baseball, basketball, cross-country, football, golf, lacrosse, soccer, tennis, track/field (outdoor), track/field (indoor), volleyball, wrestling. *Women:* Basketball, cheerleading, cross-country, golf, lacrosse, soccer, softball, tennis, track/field (outdoor), track/field (indoor), volleyball. **On-Campus Highlights:** Harrington Student Center/Sports Complex, Starbucks Gallery, residential suites, computer learning center, Project EXCEL. **Environmental Initiatives:** New green roof installed on library (2008); switch to trayless dining in cafeteria (2008)—less food waste (450 lbs/day); water conservation (250 gallons/day); recycling across campus and increased amounts/types of materials.

ADMISSIONS

Freshman Academic Profile: Average high school GPA 3.19. 11% in top 10% of high school class, 35% in top 25% of high school class, 69% in top 50% of high school class. 71% from public high schools. SAT Math middle 50% range 430–540. SAT Critical Reading middle 50% range 430–520. ACT middle 50% range 19–24. Minimum paper TOEFL 510. Minimum computer TOEFL 180. Minimum web-based TOEFL 64. **Basis for Candidate Selection:** *Very important factors considered include:* Academic GPA, rigor of secondary school record, standardized test scores. *Other factors considered include:* Application essay, recommendation(s), alumni/ae relation, character/personal qualities, extracurricular activities, first generation, geographical residence, interview, level of applicant's interest, racial/ethnic status, religious affiliation/commitment, state residency, talent/ability, volunteer work, work experience. **Freshman Admission Requirements:** High school diploma is required and GED is accepted. *Academic units required:* 4 English, 3 mathematics, 3 science, (1 science labs), 2 foreign language, 1 social studies, 1 history, 1 visual/performing arts, 1 academic electives, 1 academic elective. *Academic units recommended:* 4 English, 4 mathematics, 4 science, (2 science labs), 2 foreign language, 2 social studies, 2 history, 1 visual/performing arts, 2 academic electives, 2 academic elective. **Freshman Admission Statistics:** 1,417 applied, 70% admitted, 37% enrolled. **Transfer Admission Requirements:** College transcript(s), minimum college GPA of 2.0 required. Lowest grade transferable C. **General Admission Information:** Application fee $25. Regular application deadline 8/15. Notification on a rolling basis, beginning on or about 10/1. Nonfall registration accepted. Admission may be deferred for a maximum of 1 year. Credit and/or placement offered for CEEB Advanced Placement tests.

COSTS AND FINANCIAL AID

Annual tuition $22,000. Room and board $7,152. Required fees $800. Average book expense $800. **Required Forms and Deadlines:** FAFSA. Priority financial aid filing date 3/1. **Notification of Awards:** Applicants will be notified of awards on a rolling basis beginning 1/31. **Types of Aid:** *Need-based scholarships/grants:* Federal Pell, SEOG, state scholarships/grants, private scholarships, the school's own gift aid. *Loans:* FFEL Subsidized Stafford, FFEL Unsubsidized Stafford, FFEL PLUS, Federal Perkins, Federal Nursing, state loans. **Student Employment:** Federal Work-Study Program available. Institutional employment available. Highest amount earned per year from on-campus jobs $1,500. Off-campus job opportunities are good. **Financial Aid Statistics:** 84% freshmen, 80% undergrads receive need-based scholarship or grant aid. 9% freshmen, 8% undergrads receive non-need-based scholarship or grant aid. 73% freshmen, 69% undergrads receive need-based self-help aid. 99% freshmen, 82% undergrads receive any aid. 86% undergrads borrow to pay for school. Average cumulative indebtedness $33,646. **Criteria for awarding institutional aid:** *Non-need-based:* Academics, alumni affiliation, art, leadership, music/drama, state/district residency.

THE COLLEGE OF NEW JERSEY

PO Box 7718, Ewing, NJ 08628-0718
Phone: 609-771-2131 **Financial Aid Phone:** 609-771-2211
E-mail: tcnjinfo@tcnj.edu **CEEB Code:** 2519
Fax: 609-637-5174 **Website:** www.tcnj.edu **ACT Code:** 2614

This public school was founded in 1855. It has a 289-acre campus.

RATINGS

Admissions Selectivity Rating: 93   **Fire Safety Rating:** 94   **Green Rating:** 88

STUDENTS AND FACULTY

Enrollment: 6,197. **Student Body:** 59% female, 41% male, 6% out-of-state, 1% international (17 countries represented). Asian 6%, African American 6%, Caucasian 65%, Hispanic 9%.
Retention and Graduation: 95% freshmen return for sophomore year. 73% freshmen graduate within 4 years. 27% grads go on to further study within 1 year. 12% grads pursue arts and sciences degrees. 3% grads pursue law degrees. 3% grads pursue business degrees. 3% grads pursue medical degrees. **Faculty:** Student/faculty ratio 13:1. 348 full-time faculty, 89% hold PhDs, 22% are members of minority groups, 50% are women.

ACADEMICS

Degrees: Bachelor's, master's, post-bachelor's certificate, post-master's certificate. **Classes:** Most classes have 20–29 students. Most lab/discussion sessions have 10–19 students. **Majors with Highest Enrollment:** Biology/biological sciences; business administration and management; psychology. **Special Study Options:** Accelerated program, double major, dual enrollment, exchange student program (domestic), honors program, independent study, internships, liberal arts/career combination, student-designed major, study abroad, teacher certification program, 7-year medical program with UMDNJ, 7-year BS/OD program with SUNY, mentored undergraduate summer research program. **Combined degree programs:** BA/MD, BS/MD, BS/OD, BS/MAT. Special programs offered to physically disabled students include note-taking services, reader services, tape recorders, tutors. **Career services:** Alumni services, career/job search classes, career assessment, internships. **Career services highlights include:** Education Interview Days Each Spring TCNJ hosts up to 150 school district interview visits. The districts send administrators to conduct 30 minute interviews on-campus. Over the four days the visits are scheduled more than 1500 first-round interviews are conducted. Though the school districts are primarily from New Jersey and the surrounding area, we attract school districts from throughout the nation, including as far away as Hawaii. Students and employers both report that this is a highly successful program for meeting their recruitment needs.

FACILITIES

Housing: Coed dorms, special housing for disabled students, special housing for international students, women's dorms, apartments for single students, wellness housingFaculty and students have the opportunity to develop their own special interest learning communities on campus. 90% of campus accessible to physically disabled. **Special Academic Facilities/Equipment:** Art gallery, concert hall, greenhouse, observatory, planetarium, nuclear magnetic resonance lab, optical spectroscopy lab, scanning and transmission electron microscopes. **Computers:** 22% of classrooms, 5% of dorms, 100% of libraries, 85% of dining areas, 70% of student union, 5% of common outdoor areas have wireless network access. Students can register for classes online. Administrative functions (other than registration) can be performed online.

CAMPUS LIFE

Environment: Village. **Activities:** Choral groups, concert band, dance, drama/theater, jazz band, literary magazine, music ensembles, musical theater, opera, pep band, radio station, student government, student newspaper, symphony orchestra, television station, yearbook, campus ministries, international student organization, Model UN. **Organizations:** 205 registered organizations, 16 honor societies, 11 religious organizations. 12 fraternities, 16 sororities. **Athletics (Intercollegiate):** *Men:* Baseball, basketball, cross-country, diving, football, soccer, swimming, tennis, track/field (outdoor), track/field (indoor). *Women:* Basketball, cross-country, diving, field hockey, lacrosse, soccer, softball, swimming, tennis, track/field (outdoor), track/field (indoor). **On-Campus Highlights:** New library, new science complex, new arts and multimedia building, student center, athletic center. **Environmental Initiatives:** Commitment to sustainability being incorporated into the curriculum at TCNJ. This may include Freshman seminars, liberal learning programs, research and possible new minor or major degrees. The college's Municipal Land Use Center is authoring the State's sustainability and climate neutrality plans. Development of a plan to achieve climate neutrality. Consultant was hired to prepare a comprehensive sustainability and climate neutrality plan for the college. That plan outlines potential projects and initiatives to bring the college to neutrality by 2040. The College has committed to offsetting greenhouse gas produced by faculty and staff travel on an annual basis through the purchase of carbon offsets.

ADMISSIONS

Freshman Academic Profile: 61% in top 10% of high school class, 92% in top 25% of high school class, 99% in top 50% of high school class. 70% from public high schools. SAT Math middle 50% range 590–690. SAT Critical Reading middle 50% range 560–660. SAT Writing middle 50% range 570–670. Minimum paper TOEFL 550. Minimum computer TOEFL 213. Minimum web-based TOEFL 90. **Basis for Candidate Selection:** *Very important factors considered include:* Class rank, rigor of secondary school record, standardized test scores, extracurricular activities, volunteer work. *Important factors considered include:* Application essay, recommendation(s), character/personal qualities, geographical residence, state residency, talent/ability. *Other factors considered include:* Academic GPA, alumni/ae relation, first generation, level of applicant's interest, racial/ethnic status, work experience. **Freshman Admission Requirements:** High school diploma is required and GED is accepted. *Academic units required:* 4 English, 3 mathematics, 3 science, (2 science labs), 2 foreign language, 2 social studies. *Academic units recommended:* 4 English, 3 mathematics, 3 science, (3 science labs), 3 foreign language, 3 social studies. **Freshman Admission Statistics:** 9,283 applied, 46% admitted, 30% enrolled. **Transfer Admission Requirements:** High school transcript, college transcript(s), essay or personal statement, standardized test scores, statement of good standing from prior institution(s). Minimum college GPA of 2.5 required. Lowest grade transferable C. **General Admission Information:** Application fee $70. Early decision application deadline 11/15. Regular application deadline 1/15. Notification on a rolling basis, beginning on or about 1/15. Nonfall registration accepted. Admission may be deferred for a maximum of 2 semesters. Credit and/or placement offered for CEEB Advanced Placement tests.

COSTS AND FINANCIAL AID

Annual in-state tuition $8,980. Annual out-of-state tuition $17,666. Room and board $9,612. Required fees $3,742. Average book expense $1,000. **Required Forms and Deadlines:** FAFSA. Financial aid filing deadline 10/1. Priority financial aid filing date 3/1. **Notification of Awards:** Applicants will be notified of awards on a rolling basis beginning 6/1. **Types of Aid:** *Need-based scholarships/grants:* Federal Pell, SEOG, state scholarships/grants, private scholarships, the school's own gift aid. *Loans:* FFEL Subsidized Stafford, FFEL Unsubsidized Stafford, FFEL PLUS, Federal Perkins, Federal Nursing. **Student Employment:** Federal Work-Study Program available. Institutional employment available. Highest amount earned per year from on-campus jobs $9,329. Off-campus job opportunities are excellent. **Financial Aid Statistics:** 22% freshmen, 19% undergrads receive need-based scholarship or grant aid. 33% freshmen, 19% undergrads receive non-need-based scholarship or grant aid. 29% freshmen, 34% undergrads receive need-based self-help aid. 86% freshmen, 72% undergrads receive any aid. 58% undergrads borrow to pay for school. Average cumulative indebtedness $24,801. **Criteria for awarding institutional aid:** *Non-need-based:* Academics.

See page 1056.

THE COLLEGE OF NEW ROCHELLE

29 Castle Place, New Rochelle, NY 10805-2339
Phone: 914-654-5452
E-mail: admission@cnr.edu **CEEB Code:** 2089
Fax: 914-654-5464 **Website: ACT Code:** 2712

This private school, affiliated with the Roman Catholic Church, was founded in 1904. It has a 20-acre campus.

RATINGS
Admissions Selectivity Rating: 77   **Fire Safety Rating:** 60*   **Green Rating:** 60*

STUDENTS AND FACULTY
Enrollment: 1,003. **Student Body:** 95% female, 5% male, 10% out-of-state, 1% international (6 countries represented). Asian 6%, African American 39%, Caucasian 14%, Hispanic 13%.
Retention and Graduation: 70% freshmen return for sophomore year. 41% freshmen graduate within 4 years. 15% grads go on to further study within 1 year. **Faculty:** 85 full-time faculty, 84% hold PhDs, 12% are members of minority groups, 71% are women.

ACADEMICS
Degrees: Bachelor's, master's, post-bachelor's certificate, post-master's certificate. **Classes:** Most classes have 10–19 students. Most lab/discussion sessions have fewer than 10 students. **Majors with Highest Enrollment:** Mass communication/media studies; nursing/registered nurse (RN, ASN, BSN, MSN); psychology. **Special Study Options:** Accelerated program, cooperative education program, cross-registration, double major, exchange student program (domestic), honors program, independent study, internships, liberal arts/career combination, student-designed major, study abroad, teacher certification program. **Combined degree programs:** BA/MA Special programs offered to physically disabled students include tape recorders, tutors. **Career services:** Alumni services, career/job search classes, career assessment, internships.

FACILITIES
Housing: Women's dorms 25% of campus accessible to physically disabled. **Special Academic Facilities/Equipment:** Art gallery, multimedia theatre/teleconference center, language lab, centers for media, computer studies, TV studio, Learning Center for Women, Learning Center for Nursing. **Computers:** Students can register for classes online. Administrative functions (other than registration) can be performed online.

CAMPUS LIFE
Environment: Village. **Activities:** Choral groups, dance, drama/theater, literary magazine, musical theater, student government, student newspaper, yearbook. **Organizations:** 26 registered organizations, 2 honor societies, 1 religious organizations. **Athletics (Intercollegiate):** *Women:* Basketball, cross-country, softball, swimming, tennis, volleyball.

ADMISSIONS
Freshman Academic Profile: 15% in top 10% of high school class, 46% in top 25% of high school class, 82% in top 50% of high school class. 76% from public high schools. SAT Math middle 50% range 440–530. SAT Critical Reading middle 50% range 440–530. ACT middle 50% range 16–22. Minimum paper TOEFL 550. **Basis for Candidate Selection:** *Very important factors considered include:* Rigor of secondary school record. *Important factors considered include:* Class rank, application essay, standardized test scores. *Other factors considered include:* Recommendation(s), alumni/ae relation, character/personal qualities, extracurricular activities, interview, talent/ability, volunteer work, work experience. **Freshman Admission Requirements:** High school diploma is required and GED is accepted. *Academic units recommended:* 4 English, 3 mathematics, 3 science, (2 science labs), 2 foreign language, 2 social studies. **Transfer Admission Requirements:** High school transcript, college transcript(s), Lowest grade transferable C–. **General Admission Information:** Application fee $20. Early decision application deadline 11/1. Notification on a rolling basis, beginning on or about 11/1. Nonfall registration accepted. Admission may be deferred for a maximum of 1 year. Credit and/or placement offered for CEEB Advanced Placement tests.

COSTS AND FINANCIAL AID
Annual tuition $23,200. Room and board $9,700. Required fees $500. Average book expense $600. **Required Forms and Deadlines:** FAFSA, institution's own financial aid formfederal income tax form(s). **Notification of Awards:** Applicants will be notified of awards on a rolling basis beginning 1/1. **Types of Aid:** *Need-based scholarships/grants:* Federal Pell, SEOG, state scholarships/grants, private scholarships, the school's own gift aid. *Loans:* Direct Subsidized Stafford, Direct Unsubsidized Stafford, FFEL PLUS, Federal Perkins, Federal Nursing **Student Employment:** Federal Work-Study Program available. Institutional employment available. Highest amount earned per year from on-campus jobs $1,500. Off-campus job opportunities are excellent. **Financial Aid Statistics:** 91% freshmen, 82% undergrads receive need-based scholarship or grant aid. 51% freshmen, 50% undergrads receive non-need-based scholarship or grant aid. 78% freshmen, 75% undergrads receive need-based self-help aid. **Criteria for awarding institutional aid:** *Non-need-based:* Academics, art, leadership.

COLLEGE OF NOTRE DAME OF MARYLAND

4701 North Charles Street, Baltimore, MD 21210
Phone: 410-532-5330 **Financial Aid Phone:** 410-532-5369
E-mail: admiss@ndm.edu **CEEB Code:** 5114
Fax: 410-532-6287 **Website:** www.ndm.edu **ACT Code:** 1727

This private school, affiliated with the Roman Catholic Church, was founded in 1896. It has a 58-acre campus.

RATINGS
Admissions Selectivity Rating: 81   **Fire Safety Rating:** 60*   **Green Rating:** 60*

STUDENTS AND FACULTY

Enrollment: 1,686. **Student Body:** 94% female, 6% male, % out-of-state, 2% international . Asian 3%, African American 26%, Caucasian 66%, Hispanic 3%. **Retention and Graduation:** 87% freshmen return for sophomore year. 49% freshmen graduate within 4 years. **Faculty:** Student/faculty ratio 13:1. 83 full-time faculty, 78% hold PhDs, 4% are members of minority groups, 65% are women.

ACADEMICS

Degrees: Bachelor's, master's, post-master's certificate. **Classes:** Most classes have 20–29 students. **Majors with Highest Enrollment:** Business, management, marketing, and related support services, other; liberal arts and sciences/liberal studies; nursing/registered nurse (RN, ASN, BSN, MSN). **Special Study Options:** Accelerated program, cross-registration, double major, dual enrollment, English as a Second Language (ESL), exchange student program (domestic), honors program, independent study, internships, liberal arts/career combination, student-designed major, study abroad, teacher certification program, weekend college, Orientation program for all new students to college which includes a first semester seminar course for entering freshman. Also a Career Action Plan for all students and an academic consortium with seven local colleges and universities. **Honors programs:** Exceptionally motivated students with outstanding academic ability may be invited to become a Morrissy Scholar. Students take selected interdisciplinary courses throughout their academic program and must complete 18 credits in the program to graduate as a Morrissy Scholar. The students are engaged in various activities on campus, off campus—nationally and internationally. The group selected each year to join the program is approximately 10–12% of the entering class. **Combined degree programs:** BA/MA, BA/MAT; dual degree BA/BS; BA/MA in Business. Special programs offered to physically disabled students include note-taking services, reader services, tutors. **Career services:** Alumni network, alumni services, career/job search classes, career assessment, internships, regional alumni, **Career services highlights include:** Approximately 90% or more of all graduating students from the women's College have at least one internship experience upon graduating. This takes the liberal arts in-classroom learning and ties it directly to practical experience—best of all worlds.

FACILITIES

Housing: Women's dorms. **Special Academic Facilities/Equipment:** Art gallery, photo labs, language labs, child care center, fitness center, television and radio studios, music practice labs, planetarium. **Computers:** Administrative functions (other than registration) can be performed online.

CAMPUS LIFE

Environment: Metropolis. **Activities:** Choral groups, dance, drama/theater, literary magazine, music ensembles, radio station, student government, student newspaper, student-run film society, television station, yearbook. **Organizations:** 24 registered organizations, 7 honor societies, **Athletics (Intercollegiate):** *Women:* Basketball, field hockey, lacrosse, soccer, swimming, tennis, volleyball. **On-Campus Highlights:** Gator Alley—pub-like eatery, MBK Sports and Activities center (fitness center), Loyola/Notre Dame library, Doyle Hall—residence hall, student activity area, Marikle Chapel.

ADMISSIONS

Freshman Academic Profile: Average high school GPA 3.35. 15% in top 10% of high school class, 43% in top 25% of high school class, 80% in top 50% of high school class. 71% from public high schools. SAT Math middle 50% range 450–560. SAT Critical Reading middle 50% range 490–580. **Basis for Candidate Selection:** *Very important factors considered include:* Application essay, recommendation(s), rigor of secondary school record, standardized test scores, interview. *Important factors considered include:* Extracurricular activities, volunteer work. *Other factors considered include:* Class rank, alumni/ae relation, character/personal qualities, talent/ability, work experience. **Freshman Admission Requirements:** High school diploma is required and GED is accepted. *Academic units required:* 4 English, 3 mathematics, 2 science, (2 science labs), 3 foreign language, 2 history, 4 academic electives. **Freshman Admission Statistics:** 450 applied; 72% admitted, 46% enrolled. **Transfer Admission Requirements:** College transcript(s), essay or personal statement, minimum college GPA of 2.5 required. Lowest grade transferable C. **General Admission Information:** Application fee $40. Notification on a rolling basis, beginning on or about 10/1. Nonfall registration accepted. Admission may be deferred for a maximum of 1 year. Credit and/or placement offered for CEEB Advanced Placement tests.

COSTS AND FINANCIAL AID

Annual tuition $19,900. . Room and board $7,800. Required fees $400. Average book expense $800. **Required Forms and Deadlines:** FAFSA. Priority financial aid filing date 2/15. **Notification of Awards:** Applicants will be notified of awards on a rolling basis beginning 3/1. **Types of Aid:** *Need-based scholarships/grants:* Federal Pell, SEOG, state scholarships/grants. *Loans:* Direct Subsidized Stafford, Direct Unsubsidized Stafford, Direct PLUS, Federal Perkins. **Student Employment:** Federal Work-Study Program available. Institutional

employment available. Off-campus job opportunities are good. **Financial Aid Statistics:** 85% freshmen, 65% undergrads receive need-based scholarship or grant aid. 76% freshmen, 65% undergrads receive non-need-based scholarship or grant aid. 65% freshmen, 60% undergrads receive need-based self-help aid. Average cumulative indebtedness $16,000. **Criteria for awarding institutional aid:** *Non-need-based:* Academics, alumni affiliation, art, leadership, music/drama.

COLLEGE OF THE OZARKS

Office of Admissions, P.O. Box 17, Point Lookout, MO 65726
Phone: 417-690-2636 **Financial Aid Phone:** 417-690-3292
E-mail: admiss4@cofo.edu **CEEB Code:** 6713
Fax: 417-335-2618 **Website:** www.cofo.edu **ACT Code:** 2364

This private school was founded in 1906. It has a 1000-acre campus.

RATINGS

Admissions Selectivity Rating: 90   **Fire Safety Rating:** 65   **Green Rating:** 72

STUDENTS AND FACULTY

Enrollment: 1,350. **Student Body:** 57% female, 43% male, 18% out-of-state, 1% international (13 countries represented). Asian 1%, African American 1%, Caucasian 95%, Hispanic 1%, Native American 1%. **Retention and Graduation:** 82% freshmen return for sophomore year. 16% grads go on to further study within 1 year. 8% grads pursue arts and sciences degrees. 1% grads pursue law degrees. 5% grads pursue business degrees. 1% grads pursue medical degrees. **Faculty:** Student/faculty ratio 13:1. 95 full-time faculty, 57% hold PhDs, 2% are members of minority groups, 35% are women.

ACADEMICS

Degrees: Bachelor's. **Classes:** Most classes have 10–19 students. Most lab/discussion sessions have 10–19 students. **Majors with Highest Enrollment:** Business administration and management; communication studies/speech communication and rhetoric; elementary education and teaching. **Special Study Options:** Accelerated program, double major, dual enrollment, independent study, internships, student-designed major, teacher certification program. **Combined degree programs:** BA/JD, BA/MEng. Special programs offered to physically disabled students include note-taking services, reader services, tape recorders, tutors. **Career services:** Alumni network, alumni services, career/job search classes, career assessment, internships. **Career services highlights include:** Outstanding internships that offer graduates opportunities for phenomenal careers.

FACILITIES

Housing: Men's dorms, women's dorms, wellness housing. All full-time students must live in residence halls unless they meet one of the following criteria: 21 years of age or older, married, living with parents, or veteran of the armed forces. 75% of campus accessible to physically disabled. **Special Academic Facilities/Equipment:** Ralph Foster Museum, Edwards Mill, The Keeter Center, Fruitcake and Jelly Kitchen Greenhouses. **Computers:** 100% of dorms, 100% of libraries, 100% of dining areas, 100% of student union, have wireless network access. Students can register for classes online. Administrative functions (other than registration) can be performed online.

CAMPUS LIFE

Environment: Rural. **Activities:** Choral groups, concert band, drama/theater, jazz band, literary magazine, music ensembles, musical theater, pep band, radio station, student government, student newspaper, student-run film society, yearbook, campus ministries. **Organizations:** 45 registered organizations, 6 honor societies, 10 religious organizations. **Athletics (Intercollegiate):** *Men:* Baseball, basketball, cheerleading. *Women:* Basketball, cheerleading, volleyball. **On-Campus Highlights:** Memorial Fieldhouse and Keeter Gymnasium, Ralph Foster Museum, Williams Memorial Chapel, The Keeter Center, Agriculture, Edwards Mill, Fruitcake and Jelly Kitchen. **Environmental Initiatives:** The College ensures proper management of hazardous, special and universal waste. There is campus-wide recycling: plastic bottles, corrugated cardboard, aluminum cans, tin cans, batteries, tires, light bulbs and electronic products. Light bulb reclamation (recycle of bulbs) and energy efficient lights. Agricultural Livestock Waste Containment program (protects area lakes). Lake water cools many buildings.

ADMISSIONS

Freshman Academic Profile: Average high school GPA 3.53. 22% in top 10% of high school class, 59% in top 25% of high school class, 91% in top 50% of high school class. 82% from public high schools. ACT middle 50% range 20–25. Minimum paper TOEFL 550. Minimum computer TOEFL 213. Minimum web-based TOEFL 79. **Basis for Candidate Selection:** *Very important factors considered include:* Class rank, rigor of secondary school record, character/personal qualities, interview. *Important factors considered include:* Academic GPA, recommendation(s), standardized test scores, geographical residence, level of applicant's interest, volunteer work, work experience. *Other factors considered include:* Alumni/ae relation, extracurricular activities, first generation, religious affiliation/commitment, state residency, talent/ability. **Freshman Admission Requirements:** High school diploma is required and GED is accepted. *Academic units recommended:* 4 English, 3 mathematics, 2 science, (1 science labs), 2 foreign language, 3 social studies, 1 visual/performing arts/public speaking. **Freshman Admission Statistics:** 3,025 applied, 9% admitted, 93% enrolled. **Transfer Admission Requirements:** College transcript(s), interview, statement of good standing from prior institution(s). Minimum college GPA of 3.0 required. Lowest grade transferable D–. **General Admission Information:** Regular application deadline 2/15. Notification on a rolling basis, beginning on or about 3/1. Nonfall registration accepted. Credit offered for CEEB Advanced Placement tests.

COSTS AND FINANCIAL AID

Room and board $5,300. Required fees $410. Average book expense $800. **Required Forms and Deadlines:** FAFSA. Priority financial aid filing date 2/15. **Notification of Awards:** Applicants will be notified of awards on or about 7/1. **Types of Aid:** *Need-based scholarships/grants:* Federal Pell, SEOG, state scholarships/grants, private scholarships, the school's own gift aid. **Student Employment:** Federal Work-Study Program available. Off-campus job opportunities are excellent. **Financial Aid Statistics:** 74% freshmen, 75% undergrads receive need-based scholarship or grant aid. 9% freshmen, 16% undergrads receive non-need-based scholarship or grant aid. 74% freshmen, 75% undergrads receive need-based self-help aid. 4% freshmen, 3% undergrads receive athletic scholarships. 100% freshmen, 100% undergrads receive any aid. 7.03% undergrads borrow to pay for school. Average cumulative indebtedness $6,029. **Criteria for awarding institutional aid:** *Non-need-based:* Academics, art, athletics, leadership, minority status, music/drama, state/district residency.

COLLEGE OF SAINT BENEDICT/ SAINT JOHN'S UNIVERSITY

PO Box 7155, Collegeville, MN 56321-7155
Phone: 320-363-2196 **Financial Aid Phone:** 320-363-5452
E-mail: admissions@csbsju.edu **CEEB Code:** 6624
Fax: 320-363-2750 **Website:** www.csbsju.edu **ACT Code:** 2140

This private school, affiliated with the Roman Catholic Church, was founded in 1857. It has a 2400-acre campus.

RATINGS
Admissions Selectivity Rating: 85   **Fire Safety Rating:** 89   **Green Rating:** 84

STUDENTS AND FACULTY
Enrollment: 3,966. **Student Body:** 52% female, 48% male, 16% out-of-state, 5% international (38 countries represented). Asian 2%, African American 1%, Caucasian 91%, Hispanic 1%.
Retention and Graduation: 90% freshmen return for sophomore year. 74% freshmen graduate within 4 years. 18% grads go on to further study within 1 year. 4% grads pursue arts and sciences degrees. 1% grads pursue law degrees. 1% grads pursue medical degrees. **Faculty:** Student/faculty ratio 13:1. 288 full-time faculty, 83% hold PhDs, 7% are members of minority groups, 43% are women.

ACADEMICS
Degrees: Bachelor's, first professional, master's. **Classes:** Most classes have 20–29 students. Most lab/discussion sessions have 10–19 students. **Majors with Highest Enrollment:** Biology/biological sciences; business administration and management; speech and rhetorical studies. **Special Study Options:** Cross-registration, double major, dual enrollment, English as a Second Language (ESL), exchange student program (domestic), honors program, independent study, internships, student-designed major, study abroad, teacher certification program. **Honors programs:** All departments may contribute courses to our honors program. Students in all majors may participate in the Honors Program and receive honors distinction inside the major. **Combined degree programs:** 3-2 program in engineering with U of MN–TC. Special programs offered to

physically disabled students include note-taking services, tape recorders, tutors. **Career services:** Alumni network, alumni services, career/job search classes, career assessment, internships, regional alumni. **Career services highlights include:** At CSB/SJU academic internships have tripled in the last decade. Currently 8% of our total student body engage in internships with a credit requirement attached. In any given semester students in 20 different majors receive individual guidance from faculty, so that intentional learning and reflection are integrated into the experience. Internship opportunities exist, not only for business-related majors in the private sector, but also for a variety of humanities and social science majors (Communication, Psychology, Political Science, Environmental Studies, Peace Studies to name a few) in government, education and the non profit sector. Within the last three years 53% of the total internships at CSB/SJU were completed in the private sector by business majors while 47% were service-related internships completed by non business majors.

FACILITIES

Housing: Special housing for disabled students, men's dorms, special housing for international students, women's dorms, apartments for single students, health and wellness floor, Global Initiative Group house, ROTC housing. 90% of campus accessible to physically disabled. **Special Academic Facilities/Equipment:** Hill Museum and Manuscript Library, art galleries, natural science museum, arboretum, Benedicta Arts Center, Sommers Digital Lab. **Computers:** 100% of classrooms, 20% of dorms, 100% of libraries, 100% of dining areas, 100% of student union, 100% of common outdoor areas have wireless network access. Students can register for classes online. Administrative functions (other than registration) can be performed online.

CAMPUS LIFE

Environment: Village. **Activities:** Choral groups, concert band, dance, drama/theater, jazz band, literary magazine, music ensembles, musical theater, opera, pep band, radio station, student government, student newspaper, symphony orchestra, campus ministries, international student organization, Model UN. **Organizations:** 85 registered organizations, 3 honor societies, 4 religious organizations. **Athletics (Intercollegiate):** *Men:* Baseball, basketball, cross-country, diving, football, golf, ice hockey, skiing (nordic/cross-country), soccer, swimming, tennis, track/field (outdoor), track/field (indoor), wrestling. *Women:* Basketball, cross-country, diving, golf, ice hockey, skiing (nordic/cross-country), Soccer, softball, swimming, tennis, track/field (outdoor), track/field (indoor), volleyball. **On-Campus Highlights:** Gorecki Dining Center, Benedicta Ars Center, Warner Palaestra/Clemens Field House, Lake Sagatagan/Stell Maris Chapel, Brother Willie's Pub/O'Connell's Coffee, Abbey Church/Sacred Heart Chapel; Hill Museum and Manuscript Library; 15 km hiking trails. **Environmental Initiatives:** ACUPCC signatory process, SJU arboretum, CSB Green building policy.

ADMISSIONS

Freshman Academic Profile: Average high school GPA 3.66. 34% in top 10% of high school class, 66% in top 25% of high school class, 93% in top 50% of high school class. 70% from public high schools. SAT Math middle 50% range 540–660. SAT Critical Reading middle 50% range 500–633. ACT middle 50% range 23–28. Minimum paper TOEFL 550. Minimum computer TOEFL 213. Minimum web-based TOEFL 80. **Basis for Candidate Selection:** *Very important factors considered include:* Application essay, academic GPA, rigor of secondary school record, standardized test scores. *Important factors considered include:* Recommendation(s), extracurricular activities. *Other factors considered include:* Class rank, alumni/ae relation, character/personal qualities, first generation, geographical residence, interview, racial/ethnic status, talent/ability, volunteer work, work experience. **Freshman Admission Requirements:** High school diploma is required and GED is accepted. *Academic units required:* 4 English, 3 mathematics, 2 science, (2 science labs), 2 social studies, 4 academic electives. *Academic units recommended:* 2 foreign language. **Freshman Admission Statistics:** 3,204 applied, 74% admitted, 44% enrolled. **Transfer Admission Requirements:** High school transcript, college transcript(s), essay or personal statement, statement of good standing from prior institution(s). Minimum college GPA of 2.75 required. Lowest grade transferable C. **General Admission Information:** Nonfall registration accepted. Admission may be deferred for a maximum of 1 year. Credit and/or placement offered for CEEB Advanced Placement tests.

COSTS AND FINANCIAL AID

Average book expense $800. **Required Forms and Deadlines:** FAFSA, institution's own financial aid form. Priority financial aid filing date 3/15. **Notification of Awards:** Applicants will be notified of awards on a rolling basis beginning 3/15. **Types of Aid:** *Need-based scholarships/grants:* Federal Pell, SEOG, state scholarships/grants, private scholarships, the school's own gift aid. *Loans:* FFEL Subsidized Stafford, FFEL Unsubsidized Stafford, FFEL PLUS, Federal Perkins, state loans, various private education loans. **Student Employment:** Federal Work-Study Program available. Institutional employment available. Highest amount earned per year from on-campus jobs $6,870. Off-campus job opportunities are fair. **Financial Aid Statistics:** 60% freshmen, 59% undergrads receive need-based scholarship or grant aid. 59% freshmen,

56% undergrads receive non-need-based scholarship or grant aid. 55% freshmen, 56% undergrads receive need-based self-help aid. 97% freshmen, 94% undergrads receive any aid. **Criteria for awarding institutional aid:** *Non-need-based:* Academics, art, leadership, music/drama.

COLLEGE OF SAINT ELIZABETH

Admissions Office, 2 Convent Road, Morristown, NJ 07960-6989
Phone: 973-290-4700 **Financial Aid Phone:** 973-290-4445
E-mail: apply@cse.edu **CEEB Code:** 2090
Fax: 973-290-4710

This private school, affiliated with the Roman Catholic Church, was founded in 1899. It has a 200-acre campus.

RATINGS
Admissions Selectivity Rating: 63   **Fire Safety Rating:** 93   **Green Rating:** 60*

STUDENTS AND FACULTY
Enrollment: 1,216. **Student Body:** 89% female, 11% male, 7% out-of-state, 5% international (57 countries represented). Asian 4%, African American 18%, Caucasian 42%, Hispanic 16%.
Retention and Graduation: 72% freshmen return for sophomore year. 56% freshmen graduate within 4 years. **Faculty:** Student/faculty ratio 11:1. 72 full-time faculty, 86% hold PhDs, 4% are members of minority groups, 67% are women.

ACADEMICS
Degrees: Bachelor's, certificate, master's, post-bachelor's certificate, post-master's certificate. **Classes:** Most classes have 10–19 students. **Majors with Highest Enrollment:** Business/commerce; nursing/registered nurse (RN, ASN, BSN, MSN); teacher education, multiple levels. **Special Study Options:** Accelerated program, cross-registration, distance learning, double major, dual enrollment, English as a Second Language (ESL), exchange student program (domestic), honors program, independent study, internships, student-designed major, study abroad, teacher certification program, weekend college. **Combined degree programs:** BA/MA, BS/MS. Special programs offered to physically disabled students include note-taking services, reader services, tape recorders, tutors. **Career services:** Alumni network, career/job search classes, career assessment, internships. **Career services highlights include:** Partnerships with employers such as American Red Cross, MEDCO Solutions, Verizon Wireless & the Department of Human Services have fortified our students with practical opportunities for development. An example of this is a collaborative venture between Career Services, the Communications and Business departments and the Business Club. Students are scheduled to spend a half day at Verizon, experiencing corporate culture and attend workshops lead by Verizon Human Resources staff on topics such as "Group Interviewing."

FACILITIES
Housing: Women's dorms. 85% of campus accessible to physically disabled. **Computers:** 100% of classrooms, 100% of dorms, 100% of libraries, 100% of dining areas, 100% of student union, 5% of common outdoor areas have wireless network access.

CAMPUS LIFE
Environment: Village. **Activities:** Choral groups, dance, drama/theater, literary magazine, music ensembles, student government, student newspaper, yearbook, campus ministries, international student organization. **Organizations:** 28 registered organizations, 9 honor societies, 1 religious organizations. **Athletics (Intercollegiate):** *Women:* Basketball, equestrian sports, soccer, softball, swimming, tennis. **On-Campus Highlights:** St. Joesph's Hall—student xenter, Henderson Hall—classroom building, O'Connor Hall—residence hall, Santa Rita Hall—administration building, Mahoney Library.

ADMISSIONS
Freshman Academic Profile: 15% in top 10% of high school class, 34% in top 25% of high school class, 70% in top 50% of high school class. 74% from public high schools. SAT Math middle 50% range 370–490. SAT Critical Reading middle 50% range 385–500. SAT Writing middle 50% range 380–510. Minimum paper TOEFL 500. Minimum computer TOEFL 173. **Basis for Candidate Selection:** *Very important factors considered include:* Class rank, academic GPA, recommendation(s), rigor of secondary school record, standardized test scores. *Important factors considered include:* Application essay, character/personal qualities. *Other factors considered include:* Alumni/ae relation, extracurricular activities, first generation, geographical residence, interview, level of applicant's interest, talent/ability, volunteer work, work experience. **Freshman Admission Requirements:** High school diploma is required and GED is accepted. *Academic units required:* 3 English, 2 mathematics, 1 science, (1 science labs), 2 foreign language, 1 history, 7 academic electives. *Academic units*

recommended: 4 English, 3 mathematics, 2 science, (2 science labs), 2 foreign language, 3 history, 7 academic electives. **Freshman Admission Statistics:** 509 applied, 83% admitted, 42% enrolled. **Transfer Admission Requirements:** College transcript(s), essay or personal statement, minimum college GPA of 2.0 required. Lowest grade transferable C. **General Admission Information:** Application fee $35. Regular application deadline 8/15. Notification on a rolling basis, beginning on or about 11/15. Nonfall registration accepted. Admission may be deferred for a maximum of 1 year. Credit and/or placement offered for CEEB Advanced Placement tests.

COSTS AND FINANCIAL AID
Required Forms and Deadlines: FAFSA. Priority financial aid filing date 3/1. **Notification of Awards:** Applicants will be notified of awards on a rolling basis beginning 11/15. **Types of Aid:** *Need-based scholarships/grants:* Federal Pell, SEOG, state scholarships/grants, private scholarships, the school's own gift aid. *Loans:* FFEL Subsidized Stafford, FFEL Unsubsidized Stafford, FFEL PLUS, Federal Perkins, state loans. **Student Employment:** Federal Work-Study Program available. Institutional employment available. Highest amount earned per year from on-campus jobs $4,350. Off-campus job opportunities are good. **Financial Aid Statistics:** 95% freshmen, 69% undergrads receive any aid. **Criteria for awarding institutional aid:** *Non-need-based:* Academics, alumni affiliation, art, leadership, religious affiliation, state/district residency.

COLLEGE OF SAINT MARY

7000 Mercy Rd, Omaha, NE 68106
Phone: 402-399-2355 **Financial Aid Phone:** 402-399-2415
E-mail: enroll@csm.edu **CEEB Code:** 6106
Fax: 402-399-2412 **Website:** www.csm.edu **ACT Code:** 2440

This private school, affiliated with the Roman Catholic Church, was founded in 1923. It has a 25-acre campus.

RATINGS
Admissions Selectivity Rating: 79   **Fire Safety Rating:** 94   **Green Rating:** 63

STUDENTS AND FACULTY
Enrollment: 816. **Student Body:** 100% female, 10% out-of-state, 1% international . Asian 1%, African American 12%, Caucasian 75%, Hispanic 9%, Native American 1%.
Retention and Graduation: 64% freshmen return for sophomore year. 42% freshmen graduate within 4 years. 50.5% grads go on to further study within 1 year. **Faculty:** Student/faculty ratio 9:1. 54 full-time faculty, 59% hold PhDs, 13% are members of minority groups, 83% are women.

ACADEMICS
Degrees: Associate, bachelor's, certificate, doctoral, master's, post-bachelor's certificate, terminal associate. **Classes:** Most classes have fewer than 10 students. Most lab/discussion sessions have fewer than 10 students. **Majors with Highest Enrollment:** Business, management, marketing, and related support services, other; elementary education and teaching; nursing/registered nurse (RN, ASN, BSN, MSN). **Special Study Options:** Accelerated program, cooperative education program, distance learning, double major, dual enrollment, honors program, independent study, internships, study abroad, teacher certification program, weekend college. **Honors programs:** Honors Program. **Combined degree programs:** BS/Eng. Special programs offered to physically disabled students include note-taking services, reader services, tape recorders, tutors. **Career services:** Alumni services, career/job search classes, career assessment, internships. **Career services highlights include:** Service learning projects are an integral part of classes.

FACILITIES
Housing: Special housing for disabled students, women's dorms, women with children housing. 100% of campus accessible to physically disabled. **Special Academic Facilities/Equipment:** Hillmer Art Gallery, Gross Auditorium. **Computers:** 100% of classrooms, 100% of dorms, 100% of libraries, 100% of dining areas, 100% of student union, 100% of common outdoor areas have wireless network access. Students can register for classes online. Administrative functions (other than registration) can be performed online.

CAMPUS LIFE
Environment: Metropolis. **Activities:** Choral groups, music ensembles, student government, campus ministries. **Organizations:** 20 registered organizations, 2 honor societies, 1 religious organizations. **Athletics (Intercollegiate):** *Women:* Basketball, cross-country, soccer, softball, swimming, volleyball. **On-Campus Highlights:** Hillmer Art Gallery—year round exhibits, Gross Theater, Hixson-Lied Commons—Student Center, Library, Lied Fitness Center—gym, weight room, pool, tennis, Our Lady of Mercy Chapel—daily mass offered. Our

residence halls include computer labs, lounge areas, a prayer and reflection room, and study area/small group meeting rooms. **Environmental Initiatives:** Reuseable to-go containers in dining hall. Going trayless in the dining hall. Recycle receptacles located across campus.

ADMISSIONS

Freshman Academic Profile: Average high school GPA 3.41. 14% in top 10% of high school class, 42% in top 25% of high school class, 76% in top 50% of high school class. 86% from public high schools. ACT middle 50% range 18–23. Minimum paper TOEFL 550. Minimum computer TOEFL 213. Minimum web-based TOEFL 79. **Basis for Candidate Selection:** *Very important factors considered include:* Class rank, academic GPA, standardized test scores. *Other factors considered include:* Application essay, recommendation(s), rigor of secondary school record, alumni/ae relation, character/personal qualities, extracurricular activities, interview, level of applicant's interest, talent/ability. **Freshman Admission Requirements:** High school diploma is required and GED is accepted. *Academic units required:* 4 English, 2 mathematics, 2 science, 2 social studies. *Academic units recommended:* 3 mathematics, 3 science, 1 history. **Freshman Admission Statistics:** 510 applied, 42% admitted, 50% enrolled. **Transfer Admission Requirements:** High school transcript, college transcript(s), minimum college GPA of 2.0 required. Lowest grade transferable C. **General Admission Information:** Application fee $30. Nonfall registration accepted. Admission may be deferred for a maximum of 1 year. Credit and/or placement offered for CEEB Advanced Placement tests.

COSTS AND FINANCIAL AID

Annual tuition $21,780. Room and board $6,400. Required fees $384. Average book expense $1,200. **Required Forms and Deadlines:** FAFSA. Priority financial aid filing date 3/15. **Notification of Awards:** Applicants will be notified of awards on a rolling basis beginning 3/15. **Types of Aid:** *Need-based scholarships/grants:* Federal Pell, SEOG, state scholarships/grants, private scholarships, the school's own gift aid, Federal Nursing Scholarships. *Loans:* Direct Subsidized Stafford, Direct Unsubsidized Stafford, Direct PLUS, Federal Perkins, Federal Nursing. **Student Employment:** Federal Work-Study Program available. Highest amount earned per year from on-campus jobs $1,800. Off-campus job opportunities are fair. **Financial Aid Statistics:** 94% freshmen, 90% undergrads receive need-based scholarship or grant aid. 8% freshmen, 4% undergrads receive non-need-based scholarship or grant aid. 86% freshmen, 89% undergrads receive need-based self-help aid. 4% freshmen, 3% undergrads receive athletic scholarships. 95% freshmen, 94% undergrads receive any aid. 75% undergrads borrow to pay for school. Average cumulative indebtedness $37,408. **Criteria for awarding institutional aid:** *Non-need-based:* Academics, art, athletics, leadership, music/drama.

THE COLLEGE OF SAINT ROSE

432 Western Avenue, Albany, NY 12203
Phone: 800-637-8556
E-mail: admit@strose.edu **CEEB Code:** 2091
Fax: 518-454-2013 **Website:** www.strose.edu **ACT Code:** 2714

This private school, affiliated with the Roman Catholic Church, was founded in 1920. It has a 28-acre campus.

RATINGS

Admissions Selectivity Rating: 84   **Fire Safety Rating:** 99   **Green Rating:** 60*

STUDENTS AND FACULTY

Enrollment: 3,165. **Student Body:** 71% female, 29% male, 7% out-of-state, (20 countries represented). Asian 1%, African American 3%, Caucasian 78%, Hispanic 4%.
Retention and Graduation: 82% freshmen return for sophomore year. 49% freshmen graduate within 4 years. **Faculty:** Student/faculty ratio 14:1. 198 full-time faculty, 82% hold PhDs, 11% are members of minority groups, 55% are women.

ACADEMICS

Degrees: Bachelor's, master's, post-bachelor's certificate, post-master's certificate. **Classes:** Most classes have 20–29 students. Most lab/discussion sessions have 10–19 students. **Special Study Options:** Accelerated program, cross-registration, double major, exchange student program (domestic), independent study, internships, liberal arts/career combination, student-designed major, study abroad, teacher certification program. **Combined degree programs:** BA/JD, BA/MA, MBA/JD graduate degree. Special programs offered to physically disabled students include note-taking services, reader services, tape recorders, tutors.

FACILITIES

Housing: Coed dorms, men's dorms, women's dorms, apartments for single students. 90% of campus accessible to physically disabled. **Special Academic Facilities/Equipment:** The Center for Art and Design houses the Saint Rose Art Gallery, the venue for student art shows and exhibits by acclaimed visiting artists, in addition to one of the largest screen printing facilities in the state of New York. The college's full-scale television studio is where communications students produce three 30-minute weekly television shows aired on Time Warner Cable. The Music Center features the Saints and Sinners Sound Studio, a 16-track professional recording studio, in addition to a music library. Athletic Facilities include the college's new Fitness Center, competition-size pool, weight room, and regulation NCAA basketball court. The Hubbard Interfaith Sanctuary is home to Campus Ministry and hosts a variety of interfaith lectures, concerts and poetry readings. With private meditation rooms and an indoor garden, this interreligious space provides a place to escape for a few minutes of quiet prayer. The Center for Cultural Diversity provides academic, social, and cultural support in an effort to enhance the quality of experiences for our diverse student population. **Computers:** 98% of classrooms, 90% of dorms, 100% of libraries, 100% of dining areas, 100% of student union, 80% of common outdoor areas have wireless network access. Students can register for classes online. Administrative functions (other than registration) can be performed online.

CAMPUS LIFE

Environment: City. **Activities:** Choral groups, concert band, dance, drama/theater, jazz band, literary magazine, music ensembles, musical theater, radio station, student government, student newspaper, symphony orchestra, television station, yearbook, campus ministries, international student organization. **Organizations:** 38 registered organizations, 6 honor societies, 2 religious organizations. **Athletics (Intercollegiate):** *Men:* Baseball, basketball, cross-country, golf, soccer, swimming, track/field (outdoor). *Women:* Basketball, cross-country, soccer, softball, swimming, tennis, track/field (outdoor), volleyball. **On-Campus Highlights:** Lally School of Education, Massry Center for the Fine Arts/Center for Art and Design, events and athletic center, Quiznos and Starbucks, Student Solution Center, completely renovated (all) classrooms.

ADMISSIONS

Freshman Academic Profile: Average high school GPA 3.6. 19% in top 10% of high school class, 48% in top 25% of high school class, 86% in top 50% of high school class. 82% from public high schools. SAT Math middle 50% range 480–580. SAT Critical Reading middle 50% range 480–580. ACT middle 50% range 21–27. Minimum paper TOEFL 500. Minimum computer TOEFL 175. Minimum web-based TOEFL 83. **Basis for Candidate Selection:** *Very important factors considered include:* Academic GPA, rigor of secondary school record, interview, level of applicant's interest, talent/ability, work experience. *Important factors considered include:* Standardized test scores, extracurricular activities, geographical residence, volunteer work. *Other factors considered include:* Class rank, application essay, alumni/ae relation, racial/ethnic status, state residency. **Freshman Admission Requirements:** High school diploma is required and GED is accepted. *Academic units required:* 4 English, 4 mathematics, 4 science, (2 science labs), 3 foreign language, 4 social studies, 4 history, 22 *Academic units recommended:* 4 English, 4 mathematics, 4 science, (2 science labs), 4 foreign language, 4 social studies, 4 history, 4 academic electives, 27 **Freshman Admission Statistics:** 3,842 applied, 67% admitted, 24% enrolled. **Transfer Admission Requirements:** High school transcript, college transcript(s), statement of good standing from prior institution(s). Minimum college GPA of 2.5 required. Lowest grade transferable C–. **General Admission Information:** Application fee $35. Regular application deadline 2/1. Notification on a rolling basis, beginning on or about 12/1. Nonfall registration accepted. Admission may be deferred for a maximum of 1 year. Credit and/or placement offered for CEEB Advanced Placement tests.

COSTS AND FINANCIAL AID

Required Forms and Deadlines: FAFSA. Priority financial aid filing date 3/1. **Notification of Awards:** Applicants will be notified of awards on a rolling basis beginning 3/15. **Types of Aid:** *Need-based scholarships/grants:* Federal Pell, SEOG, state scholarships/grants, private scholarships, the school's own gift aid. *Loans:* FFEL Subsidized Stafford, FFEL Unsubsidized Stafford, FFEL PLUS, Federal Perkins. **Financial Aid Statistics:** 73% freshmen, 76% undergrads receive need-based scholarship or grant aid. 80% freshmen, 79% undergrads receive need-based self-help aid. 2% freshmen, 2% undergrads receive athletic scholarships. 85% undergrads borrow to pay for school. Average cumulative indebtedness $24,920. **Criteria for awarding institutional aid:** *Non-need-based:* Academics, alumni affiliation, art, athletics, minority status, music/drama.

See page 1058.

THE COLLEGE OF SAINT SCHOLASTICA

1200 Kenwood Avenue, Duluth, MN 55811-4199
Phone: 218-723-6046 **Financial Aid Phone:** 218-723-6047
E-mail: admissions@css.edu **CEEB Code:** 6107
Fax: 218-723-5991 **Website:** www.css.edu **ACT Code:** 2098

This private school, affiliated with the Roman Catholic Church, was founded in 1912. It has a 186-acre campus.

RATINGS
Admissions Selectivity Rating: 78 **Fire Safety Rating:** 61 **Green Rating:** 60*

STUDENTS AND FACULTY
Enrollment: 2,144. **Student Body:** 68% female, 32% male, 12% out-of-state, 4% international (19 countries represented). Asian 1%, African American 2%, Caucasian 84%, Hispanic 1%, Native American 3%.
Retention and Graduation: 77% freshmen return for sophomore year. 57% freshmen graduate within 4 years. 29% grads go on to further study within 1 year. **Faculty:** Student/faculty ratio 14:1. 166 full-time faculty, 58% hold PhDs, 8% are members of minority groups, 60% are women.

ACADEMICS
Degrees: Bachelor's, certificate, master's, post-bachelor's certificate, post-master's certificate. **Classes:** Most classes have 20–29 students. Most lab/discussion sessions have 20–29 students. **Majors with Highest Enrollment:** Business administration and management; computer and information sciences; nursing/registered nurse (RN, ASN, BSN, MSN). **Special Study Options:** Accelerated program, cross-registration, distance learning, double major, dual enrollment, external degree program, honors program, independent study, internships, liberal arts/career combination, student-designed major, study abroad, teacher certification program. **Honors programs:** The Honors Program at The College of St. Scholastica was created to give honors students enriched learning experiences and to provide a community of support for learners devoted to a vigorous life of the mind. **Combined degree programs:** BA/MA, BA/Doctor of Physical Therapy. Special programs offered to physically disabled students include note-taking services, reader services, tape recorders, tutors. **Career services:** Alumni network, alumni services, career/job search classes, career assessment, internships. **Career services highlights include:** Semester abroad in Mexico: An international service learning program devoted to educating students about social justice issues and the life of the poor in Mexico.

FACILITIES
Housing: Coed dorms, special housing for disabled students, special housing for international students, apartments for single students, wellness housing, apartments for students with dependent children. Quiet or study wings available. 95% of campus accessible to physically disabled. **Computers:** Students can register for classes online. Administrative functions (other than registration) can be performed online.

CAMPUS LIFE
Environment: City. **Activities:** Choral groups, concert band, dance, drama/theater, jazz band, literary magazine, music ensembles, pep band, student government, student newspaper, television station, campus ministries, international student organization. **Organizations:** 67 registered organizations, 2 honor societies, 7 religious organizations. **Athletics (Intercollegiate):** *Men:* Baseball, basketball, cross-country, ice hockey, skiing (nordic/cross-country), soccer, tennis, track/field (outdoor), track/field (indoor). *Women:* Basketball, cross-country, skiing (nordic/cross-country), soccer, softball, tennis, track/field (outdoor), track/field (indoor), volleyball. **On-Campus Highlights:** Wellness Center, Student Union, Storm's Den, Cedar Hall.

ADMISSIONS
Freshman Academic Profile: Average high school GPA 3.49. 23% in top 10% of high school class, 54% in top 25% of high school class, 85% in top 50% of high school class. SAT Math middle 50% range 490–670. SAT Critical Reading middle 50% range 460–610. SAT Writing middle 50% range 450–640. ACT middle 50% range 21–26. Minimum paper TOEFL 550. Minimum computer TOEFL 213. **Basis for Candidate Selection:** *Very important factors considered include:* Academic GPA, standardized test scores. *Important factors considered include:* Class rank, rigor of secondary school record. *Other factors considered include:* Application essay, recommendation(s), interview. **Freshman Admission Requirements:** High school diploma is required and GED is accepted. *Academic units recommended:* 4 English, 2 mathematics, 3 science, 3 foreign language, 3 social studies, 3 history. **Freshman Admission Statistics:** 1,864 applied, 85% admitted, 34% enrolled. **Transfer Admission Requirements:** College transcript(s), minimum college GPA of 1.5 required. Lowest grade transferable C. **General Admission Information:** Application fee $25. Notification on a rolling basis, beginning on or about 9/1. Nonfall registration

accepted. Admission may be deferred for a maximum of 1 year. Credit and/or placement offered for CEEB Advanced Placement tests.

COSTS AND FINANCIAL AID
Annual tuition $27,114. Room and board $7,278. Required fees $170. Average book expense $1,000. **Required Forms and Deadlines:** FAFSA. Priority financial aid filing date 3/1. **Notification of Awards:** Applicants will be notified of awards on a rolling basis beginning 3/1. **Types of Aid:** *Need-based scholarships/grants:* Federal Pell, SEOG, state scholarships/grants, private scholarships, the school's own gift aid. *Loans:* Direct Subsidized Stafford, Direct Unsubsidized Stafford, Direct PLUS, Federal Perkins, Federal Nursing, state loans, Private supplemental loans. **Student Employment:** Federal Work-Study Program available. Institutional employment available. Highest amount earned per year from on-campus jobs $4,688. Off-campus job opportunities are good. **Financial Aid Statistics:** 66% freshmen, 65% undergrads receive need-based scholarship or grant aid. 76% freshmen, 74% undergrads receive non-need-based scholarship or grant aid. 61% freshmen, 61% undergrads receive need-based self-help aid. 79% freshmen, 98% undergrads receive any aid. 81% undergrads borrow to pay for school. Average cumulative indebtedness $40,401. **Criteria for awarding institutional aid:** *Non-need-based:* Academics, alumni affiliation, music/drama, religious affiliation, state/district residency.

COLLEGE OF SANTA FE

1600 St. Michaels Drive, Santa Fe, NM 87505-7634
Phone: 505-473-6133 **Financial Aid Phone:** 505-473-6454
E-mail: admissions@csf.edu **CEEB Code:** 4676
Fax: 505-473-6129 **Website:** www.csf.edu **ACT Code:** 2648

This private school was founded in 1874. It has a 100-acre campus.

RATINGS
Admissions Selectivity Rating: 76 **Fire Safety Rating:** 60* **Green Rating:** 60*

STUDENTS AND FACULTY
Enrollment: 1,225. **Student Body:** 58% female, 42% male, 73% out-of-state, 1% international . Asian 1%, African American 3%, Caucasian 55%, Hispanic 26%, Native American 3%.
Retention and Graduation: 75% freshmen return for sophomore year. 21% freshmen graduate within 4 years. **Faculty:** Student/faculty ratio 7:1. 76 full-time faculty, 79% hold PhDs, 14% are members of minority groups, 36% are women.

ACADEMICS
Degrees: Associate, bachelor's, master's, terminal associate. **Classes:** Most classes have 10–19 students. Most lab/discussion sessions have 40–49 students. **Majors with Highest Enrollment:** Creative writing; drama and dramatics/theatre arts; film/cinema studies. **Special Study Options:** Accelerated program, cooperative education program, distance learning, double major, dual enrollment, exchange student program (domestic), independent study, internships, student-designed major, study abroad, teacher certification program Special programs offered to physically disabled students include note-taking services, reader services, tape recorders, tutors. **Career services:** Career assessment, internships, regional alumni.

FACILITIES
Housing: Coed dorms, special housing for disabled students, men's dorms, women's dorms, apartments for single students, substance-free floors, quiet floors, smoking floors. 95% of campus accessible to physically disabled. **Special Academic Facilities/Equipment:** Thaw Art History Library, Marion Center Photographic Library, Garson Studios, Visual Art Center, Greer Garson Theatre Centre. **Computers:** Administrative functions (other than registration) can be performed online.

CAMPUS LIFE
Environment: Town. **Activities:** Choral groups, dance, drama/theater, literary magazine, music ensembles, musical theater, student government, student newspaper, television station **Organizations:** 14 registered organizations, 1 honor societies. **Athletics (Intercollegiate):** *Men:* Tennis. *Women:* Tennis. **On-Campus Highlights:** Visual Arts Center, Garson Studios, Driscoll Fitness Center, Greer Garson Theatre Center, Fogelson Library.

ADMISSIONS
Freshman Academic Profile: Average high school GPA 3.09. 7% in top 10% of high school class, 30% in top 25% of high school class, 63% in top 50% of high school class. SAT Math middle 50% range 460–590. SAT Critical Reading middle 50% range 520–640. ACT middle 50% range 20–25. Minimum paper TOEFL 550. Minimum computer TOEFL 213. **Basis for Candidate Selection:** *Very important factors considered include:* Rigor of secondary

school record, character/personal qualities, interview, talent/ability. *Important factors considered include:* Class rank, application essay, academic GPA, recommendation(s), standardized test scores, extracurricular activities, volunteer work. *Other factors considered include:* Alumni/ae relation, geographical residence, racial/ethnic status, state residency, work experience. **Freshman Admission Requirements:** High school diploma is required and GED is accepted. *Academic units required:* 4 English, 2 mathematics, 2 science, (2 science labs), 2 social studies, 6 academic electives. *Academic units recommended:* 4 English, 3 mathematics, 3 science, (2 science labs), 2 foreign language, 2 social studies, 2 history, 4 academic electives. **Freshman Admission Statistics:** 750 applied, 78% admitted, 27% enrolled. **Transfer Admission Requirements:** High school transcript, college transcript(s), essay or personal statement, lowest grade transferable C–. **General Admission Information:** Application fee $35. Notification on a rolling basis, beginning on or about 1/15. Nonfall registration accepted. Admission may be deferred for a maximum of 1 year. Credit and/or placement offered for CEEB Advanced Placement tests.

COSTS AND FINANCIAL AID

Annual tuition $21,530. Room and board $6,702. Required fees $746. Average book expense $840. **Required Forms and Deadlines:** FAFSA. Priority financial aid filing date 3/15. **Notification of Awards:** Applicants will be notified of awards on a rolling basis beginning 3/1. **Types of Aid:** *Need-based scholarships/grants:* Federal Pell, SEOG, state scholarships/grants, private scholarships, the school's own gift aid. *Loans:* FFEL Subsidized Stafford, FFEL Unsubsidized Stafford, FFEL PLUS, Federal Perkins, state loans, college/university loans from institutional funds. **Student Employment:** Federal Work-Study Program available. Institutional employment available. Off-campus job opportunities are excellent. **Financial Aid Statistics:** 55% freshmen, 60% undergrads receive need-based scholarship or grant aid. 61% freshmen, 33% undergrads receive non-need-based scholarship or grant aid. 58% freshmen, 62% undergrads receive need-based self-help aid. 1% undergrads receive athletic scholarships. 63% undergrads borrow to pay for school. Average cumulative indebtedness $17,540. **Criteria for awarding institutional aid:** *Non-need-based:* Academics, alumni affiliation, art, athletics, leadership, minority status, music/drama.

COLLEGE OF ST. JOSEPH IN VERMONT

71 Clement Road, Rutland, VT 05701
Phone: 802-776-5286 **Financial Aid Phone:** 802-776-5218
E-mail: admissions@csj.edu **CEEB Code:** 3297
Fax: 802-776-5258 **Website:** www.csj.edu

This private school, affiliated with the Roman Catholic Church, was founded in 1956. It has a 116-acre campus.

RATINGS

Admissions Selectivity Rating: 70 **Fire Safety Rating:** 61 **Green Rating:** 60*

STUDENTS AND FACULTY

Enrollment: 208. **Student Body:** 55% female, 45% male, 42% out-of-state, (6 countries represented). Asian 1%, African American 4%, Caucasian 89%, Hispanic 5%, Native American 1%.
Retention and Graduation: 83% freshmen return for sophomore year. 40% freshmen graduate within 4 years. **Faculty:** Student/faculty ratio 11:1. 15 full-time faculty, 47% hold PhDs, 40% are women.

ACADEMICS

Degrees: Associate, bachelor's, master's. **Classes:** Most classes have fewer than 10 students. **Majors with Highest Enrollment:** Business, management, marketing, and related support services, other; elementary education and teaching; psychology. **Special Study Options:** Accelerated program, double major, dual enrollment, independent study, internships, liberal arts/career combination, teacher certification program Special programs offered to physically disabled students include note-taking services, reader services, tape recorders, tutors. **Career services:** Alumni services, career/job search classes, career assessment, internships. **Career services highlights include:** Variety of internships available.

FACILITIES

Housing: Men's dorms, women's dorms. 100% of campus accessible to physically disabled. **Special Academic Facilities/Equipment:** Theater and athletic center. **Computers:** 100% of libraries, have wireless network access.

CAMPUS LIFE

Environment: Village. **Activities:** Choral groups, drama/theater, literary magazine, student government, campus ministries. **Organizations:** 20 registered organizations, 6 honor societies, 1 religious organizations. **Athletics (Intercollegiate):** *Men:* Baseball, basketball, soccer. *Women:* Basketball, soccer, softball.

On-Campus Highlights: Tuttle Hall-Student Center, Athletic Center, Theater, Giorgetti Library, St. Joseph Hall.

ADMISSIONS

Freshman Academic Profile: Average high school GPA 2.63. 3% in top 25% of high school class, 36% in top 50% of high school class. 75% from public high schools. SAT Math middle 50% range 390–490. SAT Critical Reading middle 50% range 410–530. ACT middle 50% range 17–23. Minimum paper TOEFL 550. Minimum computer TOEFL 213. Minimum web-based TOEFL 79.
Basis for Candidate Selection: *Very important factors considered include:* Academic GPA, recommendation(s), rigor of secondary school record. *Important factors considered include:* Application essay, standardized test scores, character/personal qualities, interview. *Other factors considered include:* Class rank, alumni/ae relation, extracurricular activities, level of applicant's interest, talent/ability, volunteer work. **Freshman Admission Requirements:** High school diploma is required and GED is not accepted. *Academic units required:* 4 English, 3 mathematics, 2 science, 2 social studies, 2 history, 5 academic electives. *Academic units recommended:* 2 foreign language. **Freshman Admission Statistics:** 101 applied, 88% admitted, 37% enrolled. **Transfer Admission Requirements:** High school transcript, college transcript(s), essay or personal statement, minimum college GPA of 2.0 required. Lowest grade transferable C. **General Admission Information:** Application fee $25. Notification on a rolling basis, beginning on or about 10/1. Nonfall registration accepted. Admission may be deferred for a maximum of 1 year. Credit and/or placement offered for CEEB Advanced Placement tests.

COSTS AND FINANCIAL AID

Annual tuition $15,500. Room and board $7,600. Required fees $260. Average book expense $1,000. **Required Forms and Deadlines:** FAFSA, institution's own financial aid form. Priority financial aid filing date 3/1. **Notification of Awards:** Applicants will be notified of awards on a rolling basis beginning 3/15. **Types of Aid:** *Need-based scholarships/grants:* Federal Pell, SEOG, state scholarships/grants, private scholarships, the school's own gift aid. *Loans:* FFEL Subsidized Stafford, FFEL Unsubsidized Stafford, FFEL PLUS, Federal Perkins. **Student Employment:** Federal Work-Study Program available. Institutional employment available. Highest amount earned per year from on-campus jobs $1,317. Off-campus job opportunities are good. **Financial Aid Statistics:** 90% freshmen, 86% undergrads receive need-based scholarship or grant aid. 2% undergrads receive non-need-based scholarship or grant aid. 87% freshmen, 83% undergrads receive need-based self-help aid. 91% freshmen, 88% undergrads receive any aid. 100% undergrads borrow to pay for school. Average cumulative indebtedness $24,402. **Criteria for awarding institutional aid:** *Non-need-based:* Academics, music/drama.

COLLEGE OF WILLIAM AND MARY

Office of Admissions, P.O. Box 8795, Williamsburg, VA 23187-8795
Phone: 757-221-4223 **Financial Aid Phone:** 757-221-2420
E-mail: admission@wm.edu **CEEB Code:** 5115
Fax: 757-221-1242 **Website:** www.wm.edu **ACT Code:** 4344

This public school was founded in 1693. It has a 1200-acre campus.

RATINGS

Admissions Selectivity Rating: 97 **Fire Safety Rating:** 76 **Green Rating:** 93

STUDENTS AND FACULTY

Enrollment: 5,790. **Student Body:** 54% female, 46% male, 32% out-of-state, 3% international (52 countries represented). Asian 8%, African American 7%, Caucasian 54%, Hispanic 7%, Native American 1%.
Retention and Graduation: **Faculty:** Student/faculty ratio 11:1. 601 full-time faculty, 91% hold PhDs, 10% are members of minority groups, 37% are women. 1% of classes are taught by teaching assistants.

ACADEMICS

Degrees: Bachelor's, doctoral, master's, post-master's certificate. **Classes:** Most classes have 10–19 students. Most lab/discussion sessions have 10–19 students. **Special Study Options:** Accelerated program, double major, dual enrollment, honors program, independent study, internships, student-designed major, study abroad, teacher certification program. **Honors programs:** Monroe Scholars; Sharpe Scholars; Murray Scholars; William and Mary Scholar Award; Alpha Lambda Delta and Phi Eta Sigma Honor Societies for freshmen. **Combined**

degree programs: BA/MEng, Bachelor's/Master of Forestry or Master of Env. Management from Duke Univ. Special programs offered to physically disabled students include note-taking services, reader services, tape recorders, tutors. **Career services:** Alumni network, alumni services, career/job search classes, career assessment, internships. **Career services highlights include:** The Alumni Mentoring Program provides valuable and searchable information for students and alumni alike to connect for the purposes of seeking career advice, support, and referral. The synergy of this networking program simultaneously strengthens the College community.

FACILITIES

Housing: Coed dorms, special housing for disabled students, special housing for international students, fraternity/sorority housing, apartments for single students, wellness housing, theme housing, International Studies hall, Eco-House, Community Scholars House, Africana House, Multicultural Unit, and 8 language houses (Arabic, Chinese, French, German, Italian, Japanese, Russian, Spanish). 80% of campus accessible to physically disabled. **Special Academic Facilities/Equipment:** Observatory, continuous beam accelerator, 3 interdisciplinary centers in humanities, international studies, writing resources, marine science institute, materials processes research center,public policy research center. **Computers:** 100% of classrooms, 100% of dorms, 100% of libraries, 100% of dining areas, 100% of student union, 33% of common outdoor areas have wireless network access. Students can register for classes online. Administrative functions (other than registration) can be performed online. Undergraduates are required to own a computer.

CAMPUS LIFE

Environment: Village. **Activities:** Choral groups, concert band, dance, drama/theater, jazz band, literary magazine, music ensembles, musical theater, opera, pep band, radio station, student government, student newspaper, student-run film society, symphony orchestra, television station, yearbook, campus ministries, international student organization, Model UN. **Organizations:** 375 registered organizations, 32 honor societies, 32 religious organizations. 18 fraternities, 11 sorority. **Athletics (Intercollegiate):** *Men:* Baseball, basketball, cheerleading, cross-country, diving, football, golf, gymnastics, soccer, swimming, tennis, track/field (outdoor), track/field (indoor). *Women:* Basketball, cheerleading, cross-country, diving, field hockey, golf, gymnastics, lacrosse, soccer, swimming, tennis, track/field (outdoor), track/field (indoor), volleyball. **On-Campus Highlights:** Wren Building (oldest academic building), Muscarelle Museum of Art, Lake Matoaka/College Woods, Crim Dell Bridge, Sunken Garden. **Environmental Initiatives:** Adhere to LEED construction guidelines in all new construction and renovations. Three buildings have been LEED-certified to date and two are in progress. Retrofit of systems to improve energy consumption and reduce consumption. Participated in major ESCO contract for Athletic Center. Purchase of environmentally sustainable materials.Develop a sustainable procurement manual. Provide leadership in providing state-wide sustainable procurement guidelines in higher education.

ADMISSIONS

Freshman Academic Profile: Average high school GPA 4. 79% in top 10% of high school class, 98% in top 25% of high school class, 100% in top 50% of high school class. ~70% from public high schools. SAT Math middle 50% range 620–720. SAT Critical Reading middle 50% range 620–730. SAT Writing middle 50% range 610–710. ACT middle 50% range 27–32. Minimum paper TOEFL 600. Minimum computer TOEFL 250. Minimum web-based TOEFL 100. **Basis for Candidate Selection:** *Very important factors considered include:* Class rank, application essay, academic GPA, recommendation(s), rigor of secondary school record, standardized test scores, character/personal qualities, extracurricular activities, state residency, talent/ability, volunteer work, work experience. *Other factors considered include:* Alumni/ae relation, first generation, geographical residence, interview, racial/ethnic status. **Freshman Admission Requirements:** High school diploma or equivalent is not required. *Academic units recommended:* 4 English, 4 mathematics, 4 science, (3 science labs), 4 foreign language, 4 social studies. **Freshman Admission Statistics:** 12,109 applied, 34% admitted, 34% enrolled. **Transfer Admission Requirements:** High school transcript, college transcript(s), essay or personal statement, statement of good standing from prior institution(s). Minimum college GPA of 3.00 required. Lowest grade transferable C. **General Admission Information:** Application fee $60. Early decision application deadline 11/1. Regular application deadline 1/1. Regular notification 4/1. Nonfall registration not accepted. Admission may be deferred for a maximum of 1 year. Credit and/or placement offered for CEEB Advanced Placement tests.

COSTS AND FINANCIAL AID

Required Forms and Deadlines: FAFSA. Priority financial aid filing date 2/15. **Notification of Awards:** Applicants will be notified of awards on a rolling basis beginning 3/15. **Types of Aid:** *Need-based scholarships/grants:* Federal Pell, SEOG, state scholarships/grants, private scholarships, the school's own gift aid. *Loans:* FFEL Subsidized Stafford, FFEL Unsubsidized Stafford, FFEL PLUS, Federal Perkins. **Student Employment:** Federal Work-Study Program available. Institutional employment available. Highest amount earned per

year from on-campus jobs $1,400. Off-campus job opportunities are excellent. **Financial Aid Statistics:** 21% freshmen, 23% undergrads receive need-based scholarship or grant aid. 14% freshmen, 11% undergrads receive non-need-based scholarship or grant aid. 23% freshmen, 24% undergrads receive need-based self-help aid. 4% freshmen, 5% undergrads receive athletic scholarships. 67% freshmen, 58% undergrads receive any aid. 40% undergrads borrow to pay for school. Average cumulative indebtedness $18,410. **Criteria for awarding institutional aid:** *Non-need-based:* Academics, art, athletics, leadership, music/drama, state/district residency.

THE COLLEGE OF WOOSTER

Best 373

847 College Avenue, Wooster, OH 44691
Phone: 330-263-2322 **Financial Aid Phone:** 800-877-3688
E-mail: admissions@wooster.edu **CEEB Code:** 1134
Fax: 330-263-2621 **Website:** www.wooster.edu **ACT Code:** 3260

This private school was founded in 1866. It has a 240-acre campus.

RATINGS

Admissions Selectivity Rating: 90   **Fire Safety Rating:** 70   **Green Rating:** 73

STUDENTS AND FACULTY

Enrollment: 1,868. **Student Body:** 53% female, 47% male, 60% out-of-state, 5% international (30 countries represented). Asian 2%, African American 5%, Caucasian 73%, Hispanic 2%. **Retention and Graduation:** 70% freshmen graduate within 4 years. 40% grads go on to further study within 1 year. 16% grads pursue arts and sciences degrees. 4% grads pursue law degrees. 2% grads pursue business degrees. 4% grads pursue medical degrees. **Faculty:** Student/faculty ratio 11.48:1. 162 full-time faculty, 91% hold PhDs, 8% are members of minority groups, 51% are women.

ACADEMICS

Degrees: Bachelor's. **Classes:** Most classes have 10–19 students. Most lab/discussion sessions have 10–19 students. **Majors with Highest Enrollment:** English language and literature; history; psychology. **Special Study Options:** Cooperative education program, double major, dual enrollment, exchange student program (domestic), independent study, internships, student-designed major, study abroad, teacher certification program. **Combined degree programs:** BA/MA, BA/DDS, BA/MEng, many combined programs with other institutions. Special programs offered to physically disabled students include note-taking services, reader services, tape recorders, tutors. **Career services:** Alumni network, alumni services, career/job search classes, career assessment, internships, regional alumni.

FACILITIES

Housing: Coed dorms, special housing for international students, women's dorms, fraternity/sorority housing, apartments for single students, theme housingSpecial housing for students participating in volunteer programs. 95% of campus accessible to physically disabled. **Special Academic Facilities/Equipment:** Art museum, language lab, on-campus nursery school, science library. **Computers:** 100% of classrooms, 95% of dorms, 100% of libraries, 100% of dining areas, 100% of student union, 50% of common outdoor areas have wireless network access. Students can register for classes online. Administrative functions (other than registration) can be performed online.

CAMPUS LIFE

Environment: Town. **Activities:** Choral groups, concert band, dance, drama/theater, jazz band, literary magazine, marching band, music ensembles, musical theater, pep band, radio station, student government, student newspaper, student-run film society, symphony orchestra, yearbook, campus ministries, international student organization, Model UN. **Organizations:** 100 registered organizations, 6 honor societies, 9 religious organizations. 5 fraternities, 6 sororities. **Athletics (Intercollegiate):** *Men:* Baseball, basketball, cross-country, diving, football, golf, lacrosse, soccer, swimming, tennis, track/field (outdoor), track/field (indoor). *Women:* Basketball, cross-country, diving, field hockey, lacrosse, soccer, softball, swimming, tennis, track/field (outdoor), track/field (indoor), volleyball. **On-Campus Highlights:** Kauke Hall, Severance Hall Chemistry Bldg, Timken Science Library, Ebert Art Center, Burton D. Morgan Hall, Gault Manor (residence hall). **Environmental Initiatives:** Reusable coffee mugs: To cut down on disposable cups, each student is issued a mug.

Whenever the student buys a new beverage on campus, he or she turns in the mug for cleaning and gets a clean one plus a discount on the beverage. Local foods initiative. We buy locally grown, seasonal produce as well as baked goods, dairy, eggs, and other food items that are locally produced. Recently we started purchasing biodegradable containers (Stalkmarket brand) and cutlery (Jaya brand) made from sustainable crops such as sugar cane stalks and corn. We have a longstanding and comprehensive recycling policy, which includes not only the usual paper etc. but also recycling computers (through Apple) and recycling yard waste (to use as mulch). Building debris is recycled wherever possible. Parking blocks are made of recycled materials.

ADMISSIONS

Freshman Academic Profile: Average high school GPA 3.51. 25% in top 10% of high school class, 63% in top 25% of high school class, 89% in top 50% of high school class. 65% from public high schools. SAT Math middle 50% range 540–660. SAT Critical Reading middle 50% range 540–670. SAT Writing middle 50% range 540–660. ACT middle 50% range 23–29. Minimum paper TOEFL 550. Minimum computer TOEFL 213. Minimum web-based TOEFL 80. **Basis for Candidate Selection:** *Very important factors considered include:* Class rank, academic GPA, rigor of secondary school record. *Important factors considered include:* Application essay, recommendation(s), standardized test scores, character/personal qualities, talent/ability. *Other factors considered include:* Alumni/ae relation, extracurricular activities, geographical residence, interview, racial/ethnic status, state residency, volunteer work, work experience. **Freshman Admission Requirements:** High school diploma is required and GED is accepted. *Academic units required:* 4 English, 3 mathematics, 3 science, 2 foreign language, 3 social studies, 2 academic electives. *Academic units recommended:* 4 mathematics, 4 science, 3 foreign language, 4 social studies. **Freshman Admission Statistics:** 3,445 applied, 81% admitted, 19% enrolled. **Transfer Admission Requirements:** High school transcript, college transcript(s), essay or personal statement, standardized test scores, statement of good standing from prior institution(s). Minimum college GPA of 2.5 required. Lowest grade transferable C. **General Admission Information:** Application fee $40. Early decision application deadline 12/1. Regular application deadline 2/15. Nonfall registration accepted. Admission may be deferred for a maximum of 1 year. Credit and/or placement offered for CEEB Advanced Placement tests.

COSTS AND FINANCIAL AID

Annual tuition $34,950. Room and board $8,950. Average book expense $1,000. **Required Forms and Deadlines:** FAFSA, institution's own financial aid form, CSS/Financial Aid PROFILE. Financial aid filing deadline 9/1. Priority financial aid filing date 2/15. **Notification of Awards:** Applicants will be notified of awards on or about 4/1. **Types of Aid:** *Need-based scholarships/grants:* Federal Pell, SEOG, state scholarships/grants, private scholarships, the school's own gift aid. *Loans:* Direct Subsidized Stafford, Direct Unsubsidized Stafford, Direct PLUS, Federal Perkins, college/university loans from institutional funds. **Student Employment:** Federal Work-Study Program available. Institutional employment available. Off-campus job opportunities are good. **Financial Aid Statistics:** 62% freshmen, 55% undergrads receive need-based scholarship or grant aid. 11% freshmen, 7% undergrads receive non-need-based scholarship or grant aid. 46% freshmen, 42% undergrads receive need-based self-help aid. 100% freshmen, 100% undergrads receive any aid. 63% undergrads borrow to pay for school. Average cumulative indebtedness $29,815. **Criteria for awarding institutional aid:** *Non-need-based:* Academics, leadership, minority status, music/drama, religious affiliation, state/district residency.

COLORADO CHRISTIAN UNIVERSITY

8787 W. Alameda Ave, Lakewood, CO 80226
Phone: 303-963-3200 **Financial Aid Phone:** 303-963-3233
E-mail: ccuadmissions@ccu.edu **CEEB Code:** 4659
Fax: 303-963-3201 **Website:** www.ccu.edu **ACT Code:** 523

This private school, affiliated with the Christian (Nondenominational) Church, was founded in 1914. It has a 26-acre campus.

RATINGS

Admissions Selectivity Rating: 79   **Fire Safety Rating:** 60*   **Green Rating:** 60*

STUDENTS AND FACULTY

Enrollment: 1,849. **Student Body:** 60% female, 40% male, 56% out-of-state, international . Asian 1%, African American 3%, Caucasian 69%, Hispanic 8%, Native American 1%.
Retention and Graduation: 86% freshmen return for sophomore year. 34% freshmen graduate within 4 years. **Faculty:** Student/faculty ratio 21:1. 41 full-time faculty, 68% hold PhDs, 5% are members of minority groups, 46% are women.

ACADEMICS

Degrees: Associate, bachelor's, master's. **Classes:** Most classes have fewer than 10 students. Most lab/discussion sessions have 10–19 students. **Majors with Highest Enrollment:** Computer/information technology services administration and management, other; liberal arts and sciences/liberal studies; management information systems. **Special Study Options:** Accelerated program, cooperative education program, distance learning, double major, honors program, independent study, internships, student-designed major, study abroad, teacher certification program, weekend college, American Studies Program (Washington, DC); Host University for Institute for Family Studies; China Studies Program (various sites in China); Latin American Studies Program (Costa Rica); Los Angeles Film Studies Center; Middle East Studies (Cairo, Egypt); Oxford Honors Program (University of Oxford, England); Russian Studies Program (various sites in Russia); Summer Institute of Journalism (Washington, DC). Special programs offered to physically disabled students include tutors. **Career services:** Alumni services, career/job search classes, career assessment, internships.

FACILITIES

Housing: Coed dorms, special housing for disabled students, men's dorms, women's dorms, apartments for single students, theme housing. 85% of campus accessible to physically disabled. **Special Academic Facilities/Equipment:** Music recording studio, electron microscope. **Computers:** 100% of classrooms, 100% of dorms, 100% of student union, have wireless network access. Students can register for classes online. Administrative functions (other than registration) can be performed online.

CAMPUS LIFE

Activities: Choral groups, concert band, drama/theater, jazz band, literary magazine, music ensembles, musical theater, student government, student newspaper, symphony orchestra **Organizations:** 21 registered organizations, 3 honor societies, 14 religious organizations. **Athletics (Intercollegiate):** *Men:* Basketball, cross-country, golf, soccer, tennis. *Women:* Basketball, cross-country, soccer, tennis, volleyball.

ADMISSIONS

Freshman Academic Profile: Average high school GPA 3.44. 22% in top 10% of high school class, 46% in top 25% of high school class, 79% in top 50% of high school class. SAT Math middle 50% range 480–590. SAT Critical Reading middle 50% range 510–630. ACT middle 50% range 20–26. Minimum paper TOEFL 500. Minimum computer TOEFL 150. **Basis for Candidate Selection:** *Very important factors considered include:* Application essay, rigor of secondary school record, standardized test scores, character/personal qualities, first generation, religious affiliation/commitment, talent/ability. *Important factors considered include:* Class rank, academic GPA, recommendation(s), extracurricular activities, level of applicant's interest, racial/ethnic status, volunteer work. *Other factors considered include:* Alumni/ae relation, interview, work experience. **Freshman Admission Requirements:** High school diploma is required and GED is accepted. *Academic units recommended:* 4 English, 3 mathematics, 3 science, (2 science labs), 3 foreign language, 1 social studies, 2 history, 1 computer science. **Freshman Admission Statistics:** 946 applied, 77% admitted, 33% enrolled. **Transfer Admission Requirements:** College transcript(s), essay or personal statement, statement of good standing from prior institution(s). Minimum college GPA of 2.0 required. Lowest grade transferable C. **General Admission Information:** Application fee $50. Regular application deadline 8/21. Notification on a rolling basis, beginning on or about 11/1. Nonfall registration accepted. Admission may be deferred for a maximum of 1 YEAR. Credit and/or placement offered for CEEB Advanced Placement tests.

COSTS AND FINANCIAL AID

Annual tuition $18,850. Room and board $6,682. Required fees $150. Average book expense $1,188. **Required Forms and Deadlines:** FAFSA. **Notification of Awards:** Applicants will be notified of awards on a rolling basis beginning 4/1. **Types of Aid:** *Need-based scholarships/grants:* Federal Pell, SEOG, private scholarships, the school's own gift aid. *Loans:* FFEL Subsidized Stafford, FFEL Unsubsidized Stafford, FFEL PLUS, Federal Perkins. **Student Employment:** Federal Work-Study Program available. Institutional employment available. Off-campus job opportunities are good. **Financial Aid Statistics:** 75% freshmen, 59% undergrads receive need-based scholarship or grant aid. 66% freshmen, 49% undergrads receive non-need-based scholarship or grant aid. 75% freshmen, 59% undergrads receive need-based self-help aid. 14% freshmen, 7% undergrads receive athletic scholarships. 61% undergrads borrow to pay for school. Average cumulative indebtedness $17,275. **Criteria for awarding institutional aid:** *Non-need-based:* Academics, athletics, leadership, minority status.

COLORADO COLLEGE

Best 373

14 East Cache la Poudre Street, Colorado Springs, CO 80903
Phone: 719-389-6344 **Financial Aid Phone:** 719-389-6651
E-mail: admission@coloradocollege.edu **CEEB Code:** 4072
Fax: 719-389-6816 **Website:** www.coloradocollege.edu **ACT Code:** 498

This private school was founded in 1874. It has a 90-acre campus.

RATINGS
Admissions Selectivity Rating: 95   **Fire Safety Rating:** 60*   **Green Rating:** 96

STUDENTS AND FACULTY
Enrollment: 1,966. **Student Body:** 53% female, 47% male, 76% out-of-state, 4% international (40 countries represented). Asian 6%, African American 2%, Caucasian 77%, Hispanic 7%, Native American 1%.
Retention and Graduation: 94% freshmen return for sophomore year. 78% freshmen graduate within 4 years. **Faculty:** Student/faculty ratio 10:1. 164 full-time faculty, 98% hold PhDs, 20% are members of minority groups, 42% are women.

ACADEMICS
Degrees: Bachelor's, master's. **Classes:** Most classes have 20–29 students. **Majors with Highest Enrollment:** Biology/biological sciences; economics; political science and government. **Special Study Options:** Double major, English as a Second Language (ESL), independent study, internships, liberal arts/career combination, student-designed major, study abroad, teacher licensure program; Cooperative 3/2 program. **Combined degree programs:** BA/JD, BA/MEng, Columbia University School of Law. Special programs offered to physically disabled students include note-taking services, tutors. **Career services:** Alumni network, alumni services, career assessment, internships.

FACILITIES
Housing: Coed dorms, men's dorms, women's dorms, fraternity/sorority housing, apartments for single students, theme housing. **Special Academic Facilities/Equipment:** Electronic music studio; telescope dome; multimedia computer laboratory; Balinese orchestras; the Colorado Electronic music studio; observatory; extensive herbarium collection; 4 greenhouses; environmental science van equipped for field research; Fourier transform nuclear magnetic resonance spectrometer; Packard Hall, 300 seat concert/lecture hall; photography darkrooms. Drama/Dance: Armstrong Theatre, 740–seat proscenium theatre; Armstrong 32, a 100–seat experimental theatre; 4 dance studios w/Marley, variable speed cd players; drama computer lab. Geology: petrographic microscopes X-ray diffractometer; sedimentology lab; El Pomar Sports Center: metabolic equipment, (COSMED Quark PFT Ergo), hydrostatic weighing equipment; cadaver study in sports science; biology: Scanning electron microscope, transmission electron microscope. **Computers:** 100% of classrooms, 100% of dorms, 100% of libraries, 100% of dining areas, 100% of student union, 80% of common outdoor areas have wireless network access. Students can register for classes online. Administrative functions (other than registration) can be performed online.

CAMPUS LIFE
Environment: Metropolis. **Activities:** Choral groups, concert band, dance, drama/theater, jazz band, literary magazine, music ensembles, musical theater, radio station, student government, student newspaper, student-run film society, yearbook, campus ministries, international student organization. **Organizations:** 147 registered organizations, 13 honor societies, 20 religious organizations. 1 fraternities, 3 sororities. **Athletics (Intercollegiate): Men:** Basketball, cross-country, ice hockey, lacrosse, soccer, swimming, tennis, track/field (outdoor). *Women:* Basketball, cross-country, lacrosse, soccer, swimming, tennis, track/field (outdoor), track/field (indoor), volleyball. **On-Campus Highlights:** Worner Student Center, Palmer Hall, Shove Chapel, Cutler Hall—Admission, View of Pikes Peak. **Environmental Initiatives:** Campus-wide, semester-long resource conservation and waste reduction campaign, "aCClimate14," which challenges campus community to adapt to shifting environmental and economic conditions. The campaign is supported by a UN Climate Crews Fellowship. Installation of a 25kW solar PV array on-campus, with feasibility studies underway for large-scale wind or solar projects in the region. College radio station will become the first National Public Radio station housed in an Earthship building and completely powered by renewable energy.

ADMISSIONS
Freshman Academic Profile: 63% in top 10% of high school class, 87% in top 25% of high school class, 99% in top 50% of high school class. 55% from public high schools. SAT Math middle 50% range 620–710. SAT Critical Reading middle 50% range 620–710. SAT Writing middle 50% range 610–710. ACT middle 50% range 28–31. Minimum paper TOEFL 550. Minimum computer TOEFL 213. Minimum web-based TOEFL 79. **Basis for Candidate Selection:** *Very important factors considered include:* Rigor of secondary school record. *Important factors considered include:* Class rank, application essay, academic GPA, recommendation(s), standardized test scores, extracurricular activities, interview. *Other factors considered include:* Alumni/ae relation, character/personal qualities, first generation, level of applicant's interest, racial/ethnic status, religious affiliation/commitment, talent/ability, volunteer work, work experience. **Freshman Admission Requirements:** High school diploma or equivalent is not required. *Academic units required:* 4 English. *Academic units recommended:* 4 English. **Freshman Admission Statistics:** 4,941 applied, 32% admitted, 33% enrolled. **Transfer Admission Requirements:** High school transcript, college transcript(s), essay or personal statement, standardized test scores, statement of good standing from prior institution(s). Lowest grade transferable C. **General Admission Information:** Application fee $50. Early decision application deadline 11/15. Regular application deadline 1/15. Regular notification 4/1. Nonfall registration accepted. Admission may be deferred for a maximum of 1 year. Credit and/or placement offered for CEEB Advanced Placement tests.

COSTS AND FINANCIAL AID
Required Forms and Deadlines: FAFSA, CSS/Financial Aid PROFILE, noncustodial PROFILE, Federal 1040 parent and student tax returns and parent W-2 forms. Financial aid filing deadline 2/15. Priority financial aid filing date 2/15. **Notification of Awards:** Applicants will be notified of awards on or about 3/20. **Types of Aid:** *Need-based scholarships/grants:* Federal Pell, SEOG, state scholarships/grants, private scholarships, Federal ACG and SMART grants. *Loans:* Direct Subsidized Stafford, Direct Unsubsidized Stafford, Direct PLUS, Federal Perkins. **Student Employment:** Federal Work-Study Program available. Institutional employment available. Off-campus job opportunities are good. **Financial Aid Statistics:** 33% freshmen, 36% undergrads receive need-based scholarship or grant aid. 10% freshmen, 11% undergrads receive non-need-based scholarship or grant aid. 23% freshmen, 24% undergrads receive need-based self-help aid. 2% freshmen, 2% undergrads receive athletic scholarships. 35% freshmen, 37% undergrads receive any aid. 35% undergrads borrow to pay for school. Average cumulative indebtedness $16,172. **Criteria for awarding institutional aid:** *Non-need-based:* Academics, athletics.

COLORADO SCHOOL OF MINES

1600 Maple Street, Golden, CO 80401
Phone: 303-273-3220 **Financial Aid Phone:** 3032733220
E-mail: admit@mines.edu **CEEB Code:** 4073
Fax: 303-273-3509 **Website:** www.mines.edu **ACT Code:** 500

This public school was founded in 1874. It has a 373-acre campus.

RATINGS
Admissions Selectivity Rating: 92   **Fire Safety Rating:** 60*   **Green Rating:** 60*

STUDENTS AND FACULTY
Enrollment: 3,605. **Student Body:** 25% female, 75% male, 22% out-of-state, 6% international (66 countries represented). Asian 6%, African American 2%, Caucasian 71%, Hispanic 7%, Native American 1%.
Retention and Graduation: 90% freshmen return for sophomore year. 41% freshmen graduate within 4 years. 14% grads go on to further study within 1 year. 4% grads pursue arts and sciences degrees. 1% grads pursue law degrees. 2% grads pursue business degrees. 1% grads pursue medical degrees. **Faculty:** Student/faculty ratio 15:1. 235 full-time faculty, 88% hold PhDs, 19% are members of minority groups, 19% are women.

ACADEMICS
Degrees: Bachelor's, master's, post-master's certificate. **Classes:** Most classes have 10–19 students. Most lab/discussion sessions have 20–29 students. **Majors with Highest Enrollment:** Chemical engineering; mechanical engineering; petroleum engineering. **Special Study Options:** Accelerated program, cooperative education program, double major, dual enrollment, English as a Second Language (ESL), exchange student program (domestic), honors program, independent study, internships, study abroad. **Honors programs:** McBride Honors Program—The McBride Honors Program, instituted in 1978 through a grant from the National Endowment for the Humanities, is a 24 semester-hour program of seminars and off-campus activities that has as its primary goal: To provide a select community of CSM students the enhanced opportunity to explore the interfaces between their areas of technical expertise and the humanities and social sciences; to gain the sensitivity to project and test the moral and social implications of their future professional judgments and activities; and

to foster their leadership abilities in preparation for managing change and promoting the general welfare in an evolving technological and global context. To achieve this goal, the program seeks to bring themes from the humanities and the social sciences into the engineering curriculum that will encourage in students the habits of thought necessary for effective management and enlightened leadership. **Combined degree programs:** BS/MS. Special programs offered to physically disabled students include note-taking services, reader services, tape recorders, tutors. **Career services:** Alumni services, career/job search classes, career assessment, internships. **Career services highlights include:** One of the newest opportunities is through the Renewable Energy Materials Research Science and Engineering Center: The Center focuses on preparing undergraduate and graduate students to embark on careers in renewable fields by providing a multitude of research and classroom experiences in renewable energy. REMRSEC offers a coordinated approach from K to gray in renewable energy education, outreach, and work force development founded on research proven best practices. National Renewable Energy Laboratory(NREL) NREL will be a principle partner in the Colorado School of Mines (CSM) Renewable Energy Materials Research Science and Engineering Center (REMRSEC), building upon and strengthening the existing relationship between CSM and NREL. The goals of this partnership are to provide a convenient avenue to transition basic research and engineering discoveries into more applied projects and ultimately into the market place using NREL's strengths, to facilitate the training of future scientists and engineers by providing access to world class researchers and equipment at NREL, and to greatly augment the outreach efforts of the Center by coupling with the superb outreach efforts at NREL. http://remrsec.mines.edu/educationoutreach.htm.

FACILITIES

Housing: Coed dorms, fraternity/sorority housing, apartments for married students, apartments for single students. 100% of campus accessible to physically disabled. **Special Academic Facilities/Equipment:** Geology Museum, US Geological Survey & Earthquake Center, Edgar Experimental Mine, Graduate Research Laboratory (GRL), Center for Technology & Learning Media which houses supercomputer "Ra,"—high performance computing (HPC) cluster that aims to be a national hub for computational inquiries aimed at the discovery of new ways to meet the world's energy demands. Estimated peak performance will be approximately 20 teraflops—this places the machine well within the top-100 fastest computers in the world. The new facility, administered by the Golden Energy Computing Organization (GECO), is dedicated to advancing energy-related science. **Computers:** 100% of classrooms, 100% of dorms, 100% of libraries, 100% of dining areas, 100% of student union, 80% of common outdoor areas have wireless network access. Students can register for classes online. Administrative functions (other than registration) can be performed online.

CAMPUS LIFE

Environment: Metropolis. **Activities:** Choral groups, concert band, dance, drama/theater, jazz band, literary magazine, marching band, music ensembles, musical theater, pep band, radio station, student government, student newspaper, symphony orchestra, yearbook, campus ministries, international student organization. **Organizations:** 148 registered organizations, 9 honor societies, 7 religious organizations. 7 fraternities, 3 sororities. **Athletics (Intercollegiate):** *Men:* Baseball, basketball, cross-country, diving, football, golf, soccer, swimming, track/field (outdoor), track/field (indoor), wrestling. *Women:* Basketball, cross-country, diving, soccer, softball, swimming, track/field (outdoor), track/field (indoor), volleyball. **On-Campus Highlights:** Student recreation center, outdoor recreation center, Geology Museum, National Earthquake Center, Computer Commons at the CTLM.

ADMISSIONS

Freshman Academic Profile: Average high school GPA 3.7. 52% in top 10% of high school class, 85% in top 25% of high school class, 99% in top 50% of high school class. 90% from public high schools. SAT Math middle 50% range 620–700. SAT Critical Reading middle 50% range 550–650. ACT middle 50% range 26–30. Minimum paper TOEFL 550. Minimum computer TOEFL 213. Minimum web-based TOEFL 79. **Basis for Candidate Selection:** *Very important factors considered include:* Class rank, academic GPA, rigor of secondary school record. *Important factors considered include:* Standardized test scores. *Other factors considered include:* Application essay, recommendation(s), alumni/ae relation, character/personal qualities, extracurricular activities, geographical residence, interview, level of applicant's interest, state residency, talent/ability. **Freshman Admission Requirements:** High school diploma is required and GED is accepted. *Academic units required:* 4 English, 4 mathematics, 3 science, (3 science labs), 3 social studies, 2 academic electives. *Academic units recommended:* 1 foreign language. **Freshman Admission Statistics:** 7,190 applied, 63% admitted, 19% enrolled. **Transfer Admission Requirements:** High school transcript, college transcript(s), statement of good standing from prior institution(s). Minimum college GPA of 2.75 required. Lowest grade transferable C. **General Admission Information:** Application fee $45. Regular application deadline 5/1. Notification on a rolling basis,

beginning on or about 10/1. Nonfall registration accepted. Admission may be deferred for a maximum of 1 year. Credit and/or placement offered for CEEB Advanced Placement tests.

COSTS AND FINANCIAL AID

Annual in-state tuition $10,590. Annual out-of-state tuition $24,750. Room and board $8,120. Required fees $1,654. Average book expense $1,300. **Required Forms and Deadlines:** FAFSA. Priority financial aid filing date 2/15. **Notification of Awards:** Applicants will be notified of awards on a rolling basis beginning 3/15. *Types of Aid:* *Need-based scholarships/grants:* Federal Pell, SEOG, state scholarships/grants, private scholarships, the school's own gift aid. *Loans:* FFEL Subsidized Stafford, FFEL Unsubsidized Stafford, FFEL PLUS, Federal Perkins, college/university loans from institutional funds. **Student Employment:** Federal Work-Study Program available. Institutional employment available. Highest amount earned per year from on-campus jobs $3,000. Off-campus job opportunities are good. **Financial Aid Statistics:** 38% freshmen, 30% undergrads receive need-based scholarship or grant aid. 23% freshmen, 8% undergrads receive non-need-based scholarship or grant aid. 49% freshmen, 42% undergrads receive need-based self-help aid. 11% freshmen, 9% undergrads receive athletic scholarships. 85% freshmen, 85% undergrads receive any aid. 62% undergrads borrow to pay for school. Average cumulative indebtedness $22,500. **Criteria for awarding institutional aid:** *Non-need-based:* Academics, athletics, music/drama.

COLORADO STATE UNIVERSITY

1062 campus Delivery, Ammons Hall, Fort Collins, CO 80523-1062
Phone: 970-491-6909 **Financial Aid Phone:** 970-491-6321
E-mail: admissions@colostate.edu **CEEB Code:** 4075
Fax: 970-491-7799 **Website:** www.colostate.edu **ACT Code:** 504

This public school was founded in 1870. It has a 582-acre campus.

RATINGS

Admissions Selectivity Rating: 81   **Fire Safety Rating:** 70   **Green Rating:** 93

STUDENTS AND FACULTY

Enrollment: 21,204. **Student Body:** 51% female, 49% male, 15.9% out-of-state, 2% international (82 countries represented). Asian 3%, African American 3%, Caucasian 79%, Hispanic 7%, Native American 2%.
Retention and Graduation: 83% freshmen return for sophomore year. 35% freshmen graduate within 4 years. **Faculty:** Student/faculty ratio 16.5:1. 944 full-time faculty, 99% hold PhDs, 13% are members of minority groups, 32% are women. 9.5% of classes are taught by teaching assistants.

ACADEMICS

Degrees: Bachelor's, doctoral, master's. **Classes:** Most classes have 10–19 students. Most lab/discussion sessions have 20–29 students. **Majors with Highest Enrollment:** Construction management; human development and family studies; psychology. **Special Study Options:** Accelerated program, cooperative education program, cross-registration, distance learning, double major, dual enrollment, English as a Second Language (ESL), exchange student program (domestic), honors program, independent study, internships, liberal arts/career combination, study abroad, teacher certification program. **Honors programs:** University Honors Program. **Combined degree programs:** MS/DVM. MBA/DVM, PhD/DVM, MS of Public Health/DVM, BS/MS. Special programs offered to physically disabled students include note-taking services, reader services, tape recorders, tutors. **Career services:** Alumni network, alumni services, career/job search classes, career assessment, internships.

FACILITIES

Housing: Coed dorms, special housing for disabled students, apartments for married students, apartments for single students, wellness housing, theme housing, non college-owned fraternity/sorority housing is available. Also available are living-learning communities and special interest floors. 97% of campus accessible to physically disabled. **Special Academic Facilities/Equipment:** International Poster collection, Gustafson Gallery—historic clothing, Curfman Gallery— Art, Student Recreation Center, Ropes Course, University Center for the Arts (performance hall, thrust theater, art museum) Avenir Museum of Design and Merchandising (Costumes, Textiles, Interior Artifacts). **Computers:** 100% of classrooms, 100% of dorms, 100% of libraries, 100% of dining areas, 100% of student union, 60% of common outdoor areas have wireless network access. Students can register for classes online. Administrative functions (other than registration) can be performed online.

CAMPUS LIFE

Environment: City. **Activities:** Choral groups, concert band, dance, drama/theater, jazz band, literary magazine, marching band, music ensembles, musical theater, opera, pep band, radio station, student government, student newspaper, symphony orchestra, television station, campus ministries, international student organization. **Organizations:** 350 registered organizations, 35 honor societies, 28 religious organizations. 21 fraternities, 14 sororities. **Athletics (Intercollegiate):** *Men:* Basketball, cross-country, football, golf, track/field (outdoor), track/field (indoor). *Women:* Basketball, cross-country, diving, golf, softball, swimming, tennis, track/field (outdoor), track/field (indoor), volleyball, water polo. **On-Campus Highlights:** Lory Student Center, Student Recreation Center, Library, University Center For the Arts, Moby Arena, The University Center for the Arts is complete, featuring the newly-constructed University Art Museum. Also housed at the UCA is the Griffin Concert Hall, Bohemian Complex with 317 seat thrust theatre, Casavant Organ Recital Hall, and other world-class student resources. **Environmental Initiatives:** Several renewable energy sources went live in the year 2009 including: A two megawatt solar array on the Foothills Campus, an 18.9 kW solar array on the roof of the Engineering building, and a 12.6 kW solar array at the Academic Village residence hall. The two smaller arrays are owned and operated by the university, the larger array is owned by a third party and Colorado State serves as a site host. In addition to solar power, CSU's Foothills Campus is also home to a biomass heating plant on the Foothills Campus. This plant burns wood chips to produce hot water for building heat and displaces natural gas use. Campaigns to engage campus faculty staff and students have launched in 2009 to advance sustainability efforts on campus. The faculty campaign, "Green is Gold" is intended to encourage environmentally friendly habits in the workplace. More information can be found at www.green.colostate.edu/gold/. The student campaign provides incentives for students to live more sustainably. More information can be found at www.green.colostate.edu/greenwarrior/ Colorado State is in the middle of constructing eight new buildings on campus. All of these buildings are pursuing LEED Gold certification. The university has embraced the green building concept and is getting creative on how to build and renovate buildings more sustainability. Some of the green features on these buildings involve collaboration with researchers on campus in order to further the value of the green buildings. For example, a greywater research project at the new residence hall will study the effects and feasibility of using greywater for irrigation on campus.

ADMISSIONS

Freshman Academic Profile: Average high school GPA 3.56. 21.5% in top 10% of high school class, 50.1% in top 25% of high school class, 87.4% in top 50% of high school class. SAT Math middle 50% range 510–640. SAT Critical Reading middle 50% range 500–610. SAT Writing middle 50% range 490–600. ACT middle 50% range 22–27. Minimum paper TOEFL 450. Minimum computer TOEFL 130. Minimum web-based TOEFL 45. **Basis for Candidate Selection:** *Very important factors considered include:* Class rank, academic GPA, rigor of secondary school record. *Important factors considered include:* Application essay, recommendation(s), standardized test scores, character/personal qualities, extracurricular activities, talent/ability, volunteer work. *Other factors considered include:* Alumni/ae relation, first generation, geographical residence, interview, level of applicant's interest, state residency, work experience. **Freshman Admission Requirements:** High school diploma is required and GED is accepted. *Academic units required:* 4 English, 4 mathematics, 3 science, (2 science labs), 1 foreign language, 2 social studies, 1 history, 2 academic electives. *Academic units recommended:* 4 English, 4 mathematics, 3 science, (2 science labs), 2 foreign language, 2 social studies, 1 history, 2 academic electives. **Freshman Admission Statistics:** 15,253 applied, 72% admitted, 39% enrolled. **Transfer Admission Requirements:** College transcript(s), essay or personal statement, minimum college GPA of 2.0 required. Lowest grade transferable C–. **General Admission Information:** Application fee $50. Regular application deadline 2/1. Notification on a rolling basis, beginning on or about 10/1. Nonfall registration accepted. Admission may be deferred for a maximum of 1 year. Credit and/or placement offered for CEEB Advanced Placement tests.

COSTS AND FINANCIAL AID

Annual in-state tuition $4,822. Annual out-of-state tuition $20,744. Room and board $8,378. Required fees $1,496. Average book expense $1,126. **Required Forms and Deadlines:** FAFSA. Priority financial aid filing date 3/1. **Notification of Awards:** Applicants will be notified of awards on a rolling basis beginning 3/1. **Types of Aid:** *Need-based scholarships/grants:* Federal Pell, SEOG, state scholarships/grants, private scholarships, the school's own gift aid. *Loans:* Direct Subsidized Stafford, Direct Unsubsidized Stafford, Direct PLUS, Federal Perkins, college/university loans from institutional funds, alternative loans. **Student Employment:** Federal Work-Study Program available. Institutional employment available. Highest amount earned per year from on-campus jobs $2,500. Off-campus job opportunities are excellent. **Financial Aid Statistics:** 37% freshmen, 37% undergrads receive need-based scholarship or grant aid. 26% freshmen, 32% undergrads receive need-based self-help aid. 1% freshmen, 1% undergrads receive athletic scholarships. 67% freshmen, 66%

undergrads receive any aid. 57% undergrads borrow to pay for school. Average cumulative indebtedness $20,432. **Criteria for awarding institutional aid:** *Non-need-based:* Academics, art, athletics, leadership, music/drama, state/district residency.

COLORADO STATE UNIVERSITY—PUEBLO

Admissions, 2200 Bonforte Blvd, Pueblo, CO 81001
Phone: 719-549-2461 **Financial Aid Phone:** 719-549-2178
E-mail: info@colostate-pueblo.edu **CEEB Code:** 4611
Fax: 719-549-2419 **Website:** www.colostate-pueblo.edu **ACT Code:** 524

This public school was founded in 1933. It has a 275-acre campus.

RATINGS
Admissions Selectivity Rating: 63   **Fire Safety Rating:** 60*   **Green Rating:** 60*

STUDENTS AND FACULTY

Enrollment: 3,947. **Student Body:** 57% female, 43% male, 7% out-of-state, 2% international (27 countries represented). Asian 3%, African American 6%, Caucasian 55%, Hispanic 25%, Native American 2%.
Retention and Graduation: 63% freshmen return for sophomore year.
Faculty: Student/faculty ratio 17:1. 155 full-time faculty, 17% are members of minority groups, 47% are women.

ACADEMICS

Degrees: Bachelor's, master's. **Classes:** Most classes have 10–19 students. Most lab/discussion sessions have 10–19 students. **Majors with Highest Enrollment:** Biology/biological sciences; liberal arts and sciences/liberal studies; mass communication/media studies. **Special Study Options:** Accelerated program, cooperative education program, distance learning, double major, dual enrollment, English as a Second Language (ESL), external degree program, independent study, internships, liberal arts/career combination, study abroad, teacher certification program, weekend college. **Honors programs:** We do not have an Honor Program, however, we offer several undergraduate honor courses. **Combined degree programs:** BSBA/MBA, BS/MS. Special programs offered to physically disabled students include note-taking services, reader services, tape recorders, tutors.

FACILITIES

Housing: Coed dorms, special housing for disabled students, apartments for single students. 100% of campus accessible to physically disabled. **Special Academic Facilities/Equipment:** Recital hall, public television and radio station. **Computers:** Students can register for classes online. Administrative functions (other than registration) can be performed online.

CAMPUS LIFE

Environment: City. **Activities:** Choral groups, concert band, dance, jazz band, literary magazine, music ensembles, pep band, student government, student newspaper, symphony orchestra, television station. **Organizations:** 24 registered organizations, 6 honor societies, 4 religious organizations. 2 fraternities, 1 sorority. **Athletics (Intercollegiate):** *Men:* Baseball, basketball, golf, soccer, tennis. *Women:* Basketball, cross-country, golf, soccer, softball, tennis, volleyball. **On-Campus Highlights:** University Library, Occhiato University Center—La Cantina, Occhiato University Center—The Underground, The Pavillion, The Wall.

ADMISSIONS

Freshman Academic Profile: Average high school GPA 3.1. 2% in top 10% of high school class, 8% in top 25% of high school class, 36% in top 50% of high school class. 85% from public high schools. SAT Math middle 50% range 420–550. SAT Critical Reading middle 50% range 420–530. ACT middle 50% range 18–22. Minimum paper TOEFL 500. Minimum computer TOEFL 173. **Basis for Candidate Selection:** *Very important factors considered include:* Academic GPA, rigor of secondary school record, standardized test scores. *Important factors considered include:* Class rank. *Other factors considered include:* Application essay, recommendation(s), character/personal qualities, interview, level of applicant's interest, talent/ability, volunteer work, work experience. **Freshman Admission Requirements:** High school diploma is required and GED is accepted. *Academic units required:* 4 English, 3 mathematics, 3 science, (2 science labs), 2 foreign language, 2 social studies, 1 history. *Academic units recommended:* 4 English, 3 mathematics, 3 science, (2 science labs), 2 foreign language, 2 social studies, 1 history. **Freshman Admission Statistics:** 1,485 applied, 94% admitted, 46% enrolled. **Transfer Admission Requirements:** College transcript(s), minimum college GPA of 2.3 required. Lowest grade transferable C–. **General Admission Information:** Application fee $25. Regular application deadline 8/1. Notification on a rolling basis, beginning on or about 8/1. Nonfall registration accepted. Admission may be deferred for a maximum of 1 semester. Credit offered for CEEB Advanced Placement tests.

COSTS AND FINANCIAL AID

Annual in-state tuition $3,422. Annual out-of-state tuition $13,543. Room and board $6,300. Required fees $996. Average book expense $1,698. **Required Forms and Deadlines:** FAFSA, institution's own financial aid form. Priority financial aid filing date 3/1. **Notification of Awards:** Applicants will be notified of awards on a rolling basis beginning 3/15. **Types of Aid:** *Need-based scholarships/grants:* Federal Pell, SEOG, state scholarships/grants, private scholarships, the school's own gift aid, Academic Competitiveness Grant and National SMART Grant. *Loans:* FFEL Subsidized Stafford, FFEL Unsubsidized Stafford, FFEL PLUS, Federal Perkins. **Student Employment:** Highest amount earned per year from on-campus jobs $8,000. **Financial Aid Statistics:** 61% freshmen, 54% undergrads receive need-based scholarship or grant aid. 5% freshmen, 2% undergrads receive non-need-based scholarship or grant aid. 58% freshmen, 58% undergrads receive need-based self-help aid. 3% freshmen, 4% undergrads receive athletic scholarships. 81% freshmen, 86% undergrads receive any aid. 54% undergrads borrow to pay for school. Average cumulative indebtedness $16,481. **Criteria for awarding institutional aid:** *Non-need-based:* Academics, alumni affiliation, art, athletics, leadership, minority status, music/drama, state/district residency.

COLORADO TECHNICAL UNIVERSITY

4435 North Chestnut Street, Colorado Springs, CO 80907-3740
Phone: 719-598-0200
E-mail: cosadmissions@coloradotech.edu
Fax: Website: www.coloradotech.edu

This is a proprietary school.

RATINGS

Admissions Selectivity Rating: 60*   **Fire Safety Rating:** 60*   **Green Rating:** 60*

STUDENTS AND FACULTY

Faculty: Student/faculty ratio 25:1. 31 full-time faculty, 52% hold PhDs, 13% are members of minority groups, 35% are women.

ACADEMICS

Degrees: Associate, bachelor's, certificate, master's, transfer associate. **Classes:** Most classes have 10–19 students. **Special Study Options:** Accelerated program, double major, independent study, internships, weekend college, 16.5 month MS degree programs and 2-year doctoral programs.

CAMPUS LIFE

Activities: Student government.

ADMISSIONS

Other factors considered include: Class rank, recommendation(s), rigor of secondary school record, standardized test scores, alumni/ae relation, character/personal qualities, interview, work experience. **Freshman Admission Requirements:** *Academic units required:* 1 English, 1 mathematics, 1 science, (1 science labs). *Academic units recommended:* 2 English, 2 mathematics, 2 science, (1 science labs). **Transfer Admission Requirements:** College transcript(s), statement of good standing from prior institution(s). Lowest grade transferable C. **General Admission Information:** Application fee $50. Regular application deadline 10/2. Nonfall registration accepted.

COSTS AND FINANCIAL AID

Annual tuition $4,650. Required fees $171. Average book expense $1,000. **Required Forms and Deadlines:** FAFSA, institution's own financial aid form, state aid form. **Notification of Awards:** Applicants will be notified of awards on a rolling basis beginning 2/1. **Types of Aid:** *Loans:* FFEL Subsidized Stafford, FFEL Unsubsidized Stafford, FFEL PLUS, Federal Perkins.

COLUMBIA COLLEGE (MO)

1001 Rogers St, Columbia, MO 65216
Phone: 573-875-7352 **Financial Aid Phone:** 573-875-7390
E-mail: admissions@ccis.edu **CEEB Code:** 6095
Fax: 573-875-7506 **Website:** www.ccis.edu **ACT Code:** 2276

This private school, affiliated with the Disciples of Christ Church, was founded in 1851. It has a 33-acre campus.

RATINGS

Admissions Selectivity Rating: 84   **Fire Safety Rating:** 84   **Green Rating:** 75

STUDENTS AND FACULTY

Enrollment: 1,038. **Student Body:** 59% female, 41% male, 8% out-of-state, 9% international (20 countries represented). Asian 1%, African American 6%, Caucasian 74%, Hispanic 2%, Native American 1%.
Retention and Graduation: 60% freshmen return for sophomore year. 32% freshmen graduate within 4 years. 18% grads go on to further study within 1 year. 21% grads pursue arts and sciences degrees. 3% grads pursue law degrees. 2% grads pursue business degrees. 2% grads pursue medical degrees. **Faculty:** Student/faculty ratio 14:1. 66 full-time faculty, 79% hold PhDs, 6% are members of minority groups, 45% are women.

ACADEMICS

Degrees: Associate, bachelor's, certificate, master's, post-bachelor's certificate. **Classes:** Most classes have 10–19 students. Most lab/discussion sessions have 10–19 students. **Majors with Highest Enrollment:** Biology/biological sciences; business administration and management; psychology. **Special Study Options:** Cross-registration, distance learning, double major, dual enrollment, English as a Second Language (ESL), honors program, independent study, internships, student-designed major, study abroad, teacher certification program. **Honors programs:** The Honors Program is designed for high achieving students who are philosophers in the literal sense, i.e., lovers of wisdom. The goal of the program is to promote genuine inquiry and collaborative learning, emphasizing the dialogic nature of academic work and intellectual discovery. Special programs offered to physically disabled students include note-taking services, tutors. **Career services:** Alumni network, alumni services, career/job search classes, internships, regional alumni. **Career services highlights include:** All of our Career Services that are offered to our regular students are offered to alumni and they are FREE.

FACILITIES

Housing: Coed dorms, special housing for disabled students, special housing for international students, women's dorms, apartments for single students, wellness housing 97% of campus accessible to physically disabled. **Special Academic Facilities/Equipment:** Most classrooms are multimedia with SmartBoards, new student commons building, arts center, Larson Gallery, Jane Froman Archive. **Computers:** 100% of classrooms, 100% of dorms, 100% of libraries, 100% of dining areas, 100% of student union, have wireless network access. Students can register for classes online. Administrative functions (other than registration) can be performed online.

CAMPUS LIFE

Environment: City. **Activities:** Choral groups, dance, drama/theater, literary magazine, music ensembles, musical theater, student government, student newspaper, campus ministries, international student organization, Model UN. **Organizations:** 42 registered organizations, 16 honor societies, 2 religious organizations. **Athletics (Intercollegiate):** *Men:* Basketball, soccer. *Women:* Basketball, softball, volleyball. **On-Campus Highlights:** Larson Art Gallery, the newly expanded Southwell Athletic Complex, new Atkins-Holman Student Commons building, Stafford Library. **Environmental Initiatives:** 77% of campus building square footage is on highly efficient ground source water heat pump system. We have in place a fairly substantial recycling program. We have in place a lighting retrofit program replacing ineffient lights with more efficient ones.

ADMISSIONS

Freshman Academic Profile: Average high school GPA 3.38. 24% in top 10% of high school class, 50% in top 25% of high school class, 71% in top 50% of high school class. 93.3% from public high schools. SAT Math middle 50% range 550–680. SAT Critical Reading middle 50% range 430–570. ACT middle 50% range 20–26. Minimum paper TOEFL 500. Minimum computer TOEFL 173. Minimum web-based TOEFL 61. **Basis for Candidate Selection:** *Very important factors considered include:* Class rank, academic GPA, standardized test scores. *Other factors considered include:* Rigor of secondary school record, character/personal qualities. **Freshman Admission Requirements:** High school diploma is required and GED is accepted. *Academic units recommended:* 4 English, 3 mathematics, 3 science, 2 foreign language, 2 social studies. **Freshman Admission Statistics:** 1,137 applied, 47% admitted, 32% enrolled. **Transfer Admission Requirements:** College transcript(s), statement of good standing from prior institution(s). Minimum college GPA of 2.0 required. Lowest grade transferable 2. **General Admission Information:** Regular application deadline 8/14. Notification on a rolling basis, beginning on or about 9/15. Nonfall registration accepted. Admission may be deferred for a maximum of 1 year. Credit and/or placement offered for CEEB Advanced Placement tests.

COSTS AND FINANCIAL AID

Annual tuition $15,596. Room and board $6,074. Average book expense $800. **Required Forms and Deadlines:** FAFSA. Priority financial aid filing date 3/1. **Notification of Awards:** Applicants will be notified of awards on a rolling basis beginning 3/1. **Types of Aid:** *Need-based scholarships/grants:* Federal Pell, SEOG, state scholarships/grants, private scholarships. *Loans:* Direct Subsidized Stafford, Direct Unsubsidized Stafford, Direct PLUS. **Student Employment:** Federal Work-Study Program available. Institutional employment available.

Highest amount earned per year from on-campus jobs $5,982. Off-campus job opportunities are excellent. **Financial Aid Statistics:** 44% freshmen, 42% undergrads receive need-based scholarship or grant aid. 35% freshmen, 31% undergrads receive non-need-based scholarship or grant aid. 44% freshmen, 45% undergrads receive need-based self-help aid. 6% freshmen, 4% undergrads receive athletic scholarships. 94% freshmen, 81% undergrads receive any aid. 63% undergrads borrow to pay for school. Average cumulative indebtedness $13,948. **Criteria for awarding institutional aid:** *Non-need-based:* Academics, alumni affiliation, art, athletics, job skills, leadership, music/drama, religious affiliation, state/district residency.

See page 1060.

COLUMBIA COLLEGE (SC)

1301 Columbia College Drive, Columbia, SC 29203
Phone: 803-786-3871 **Financial Aid Phone:** 803-786-3612
E-mail: admissions@columbiasc.edu **CEEB Code:** 5117
Fax: 803-786-3674 **Website:** www.columbiacollegesc.edu **ACT Code:** 3850

This private school, affiliated with the Methodist Church, was founded in 1854. It has a 33-acre campus.

RATINGS
Admissions Selectivity Rating: 76 **Fire Safety Rating:** 75 **Green Rating:** 60*

STUDENTS AND FACULTY
Enrollment: 1,225. **Student Body:** 97% female, 3% male, 6% out-of-state, international (14 countries represented). Asian 1%, African American 44%, Caucasian 47%, Hispanic 2%, Native American 2%. **Retention and Graduation:** 62% freshmen return for sophomore year. 39% freshmen graduate within 4 years. **Faculty:** Student/faculty ratio 10:1. 87 full-time faculty, 75% hold PhDs, 11% are members of minority groups, 68% are women.

ACADEMICS
Degrees: Bachelor's, master's, post-bachelor's certificate. **Classes:** Most classes have 10–19 students. **Majors with Highest Enrollment:** Business administration and management; elementary education and teaching; human development, family studies, and related services, other. **Special Study Options:** Distance learning, double major, dual enrollment, honors program, independent study, internships, student-designed major, study abroad, teacher certification program. **Honors programs:** The Columbia College Honors Program provides enriched academic and co-curricular experiences for outstanding, motivated students committed to excellence. Offering a variety of opportunities for superior, engaged learning both within and outside the classroom, honors challenges students to reach their highest potential as scholars, individual thinkers, and leaders by emphasizing rigorous intellectual standards, risk, creativity, integrity, and dedication to service and leadership. The program is deeply active in the National Collegiate Honors Council and its regional association, regularly sponsoring numerous faculty and students at annual conferences and in executive leadership positions; honors has also earned special recognition through national and regional awards for honors faculty and students. To complete honors, students take 24 semester hours across disciplines in honors courses, including the 3 hour interdisciplinary senior seminar and the 3–4 hour mentored independent project. Students must maintain at least a 3.4 cumulative GPA to remain in honors. **Career services:** Career/job search classes, career assessment, internships.

FACILITIES
Housing: Women's dorms, special programs: Leadership; Honors Program. 75% of campus accessible to physically disabled. **Special Academic Facilities/Equipment:** Language lab, Alumnae Hall, Barbara Bush Center for Science and Technology, Breed Leadership Center for Women. **Computers:** 50% of libraries, 100% of dining areas, 100% of student union, 30% of common outdoor areas have wireless network access. Students can register for classes online. Administrative functions (other than registration) can be performed online.

CAMPUS LIFE
Environment: Metropolis. **Activities:** Choral groups, concert band, dance, drama/theater, literary magazine, music ensembles, musical theater, opera, student government, student newspaper, yearbook, campus ministries, international student organization. **Organizations:** 53 registered organizations, 10 honor societies, 7 religious organizations. **Athletics (Intercollegiate):** *Women:* Basketball, soccer, softball, tennis, volleyball. **On-Campus Highlights:** Leadership Center, Terrace Cafe, Student Union, Cottingham Performance Theatre, Bush Science Center. **Environmental Initiatives:** Student-sponsored and initiated recycling program.

ADMISSIONS
Freshman Academic Profile: Average high school GPA 3.47. 19% in top 10% of high school class, 45% in top 25% of high school class, 78% in top 50% of high school class. SAT Math middle 50% range 450–550. SAT Critical Reading middle 50% range 450–570. SAT Writing middle 50% range 440–560. ACT middle 50% range 18–24. Minimum paper TOEFL 550. Minimum computer TOEFL 213. **Basis for Candidate Selection:** *Very important factors considered include:* Recommendation(s), rigor of secondary school record, standardized test scores. *Important factors considered include:* Class rank, character/personal qualities. *Other factors considered include:* Application essay, alumni/ae relation, extracurricular activities, talent/ability, volunteer work. **Freshman Admission Requirements:** High school diploma is required and GED is accepted. *Academic units recommended:* 4 English, 3 mathematics, 2 science, (2 science labs), 2 foreign language, 2 social studies, 1 history, 2 academic electives. **Freshman Admission Statistics:** 1,078 applied, 76% admitted, 34% enrolled. **Transfer Admission Requirements:** High school transcript, college transcript(s), standardized test scores, statement of good standing from prior institution(s). Minimum college GPA of 2.0 required. Lowest grade transferable C. **General Admission Information:** Application fee $25. Regular application deadline 8/1. Notification on a rolling basis, beginning on or about 10/1. Nonfall registration accepted. Admission may be deferred for a maximum of 1 year. Credit offered for CEEB Advanced Placement tests.

COSTS AND FINANCIAL AID
Annual tuition $22,580. Room and board $6,450. Required fees $450. **Required Forms and Deadlines:** FAFSA. Priority financial aid filing date 4/1. **Notification of Awards:** Applicants will be notified of awards on a rolling basis beginning 3/1. **Types of Aid:** *Need-based scholarships/grants:* Federal Pell, SEOG, state scholarships/grants, private scholarships, the school's own gift aid, United Negro College Fund. *Loans:* FFEL Subsidized Stafford, FFEL Unsubsidized Stafford, FFEL PLUS, Federal Perkins, state loans, signature student loan. **Student Employment:** Federal Work-Study Program available. Institutional employment available. Highest amount earned per year from on-campus jobs $1,000. Off-campus job opportunities are excellent. **Financial Aid Statistics:** 82% freshmen, 81% undergrads receive need-based scholarship or grant aid. 71% freshmen, 65% undergrads receive non-need-based scholarship or grant aid. 70% freshmen, 73% undergrads receive need-based self-help aid. 2% freshmen, 3% undergrads receive athletic scholarships. 99% freshmen, 92% undergrads receive any aid. 94% undergrads borrow to pay for school. Average cumulative indebtedness $16,976. **Criteria for awarding institutional aid:** *Non-need-based:* Academics, alumni affiliation, art, athletics, leadership, music/drama.

COLUMBIA COLLEGE CHICAGO (IL)

600 South Michigan Avenue, Chicago, IL 60605-1996
Phone: 312-369-7130 **Financial Aid Phone:** 312-369-7140
E-mail: admissions@colum.edu **CEEB Code:** 1135
Fax: 312-369-8024 **Website:** www.colum.edu **ACT Code:** 1002

This private school was founded in 1890.

RATINGS
Admissions Selectivity Rating: 71 **Fire Safety Rating:** 60* **Green Rating:** 70

STUDENTS AND FACULTY
Enrollment: 11,749. **Student Body:** 51% female, 49% male, 34% out-of-state, 1% international (61 countries represented). Asian 4%, African American 14%, Caucasian 63%, Hispanic 10%, Native American 1%. **Retention and Graduation:** 65% freshmen return for sophomore year. 26% freshmen graduate within 4 years. 9% grads go on to further study within 1 year. 10% grads pursue arts and sciences degrees. **Faculty:** Student/faculty ratio 11:1. 321 full-time faculty, 16% are members of minority groups.

ACADEMICS
Degrees: Bachelor's, master's, post-bachelor's certificate, post-master's certificate. **Classes:** Most classes have 10–19 students. **Majors with Highest Enrollment:** Arts management; cinematography and film/video production; fine/studio arts. **Special Study Options:** Cross-registration, exchange student program (domestic), honors program, independent study, internships, student-designed major, study abroad, teacher certification program. Special programs offered to physically disabled students include note-taking services, reader services, tape recorders, tutors.

FACILITIES
Housing: Coed dorms, apartments for single students. 90% of campus accessible to physically disabled. **Special Academic Facilities/Equipment:** Art gal-

leries, Center for Black Music Research, contemporary photography museum, dance center. **Computers:** Students can register for classes online. Administrative functions (other than registration) can be performed online.

CAMPUS LIFE

Environment: Metropolis. **Activities:** Choral groups, concert band, dance, drama/theater, jazz band, literary magazine, music ensembles, musical theater, opera, radio station, student government, student newspaper, student-run film society, television station, campus ministries, international student organization. **Organizations:** 64 registered organizations. **On-Campus Highlights:** Museum of Contemporary Photography, Center for Black Music Research, Hokin Annex and Gallery. **Environmental Initiatives:** Campus-wide recycling, sustainable materials in capital construction projects, LEED cerfitication in capital construction projects.

ADMISSIONS

Freshman Academic Profile: Average high school GPA 2.996. SAT Math middle 50% range 430–540. SAT Critical Reading middle 50% range 450–570. ACT middle 50% range 18–24. Minimum paper TOEFL 533. Minimum computer TOEFL 200. **Basis for Candidate Selection:** *Important factors considered include:* Application essay, Academic GPA, recommendation(s), character/personal qualities, talent/ability. *Other factors considered include:* Rigor of secondary school record, standardized test scores, extracurricular activities, interview, volunteer work, work experience. **Freshman Admission Requirements:** High school diploma is required and GED is accepted. **Freshman Admission Statistics:** 5,581 applied, 85% admitted, 50% enrolled. **Transfer Admission Requirements:** High school transcript, college transcript(s), essay or personal statement, Lowest grade transferable C. **General Admission Information:** Application fee $35. Nonfall registration accepted. Admission may be deferred for a maximum of 1 year. Credit and/or placement offered for CEEB Advanced Placement tests.

COSTS AND FINANCIAL AID

Annual tuition $17,950. Room and board $12,000. Required fees $990. Average book expense $1,400. **Required Forms and Deadlines:** FAFSA. Priority financial aid filing date 5/1. **Types of Aid:** *Need-based scholarships/grants:* Federal Pell, SEOG, state scholarships/grants, private scholarships, the school's own gift aid. *Loans:* Direct Subsidized Stafford, Direct Unsubsidized Stafford, Direct PLUS. **Student Employment:** Federal Work-Study Program available. **Financial Aid Statistics:** 34% freshmen, 32% undergrads receive need-based scholarship or grant aid. 19% freshmen, 11% undergrads receive non-need-based scholarship or grant aid. 61% freshmen, 58% undergrads receive need-based self-help aid. 72% freshmen, 71% undergrads receive any aid.

COLUMBIA COLLEGE—HOLLYWOOD

18618 Oxnard St, Tarzana, CA 91356
Phone: 818-345-8414
E-mail: admissions@columbiacollege.edu **CEEB Code:** 7213
Fax: 818-345-9053 **Website:** www.columbiacollege.edu

This private school was founded in 1952.

RATINGS

Admissions Selectivity Rating: 60*   **Fire Safety Rating:** 60*   **Green Rating:** 60*

STUDENTS AND FACULTY

Enrollment: 150. **Student Body:** 31% female, 69% male, 10% international (24 countries represented). Asian 5%, African American 9%, Caucasian 60%, Hispanic 14%, Native American 1%.
Retention and Graduation: 47% freshmen return for sophomore year. 36% freshmen graduate within 4 years. 5% grads go on to further study within 1 year. **Faculty:** Student/faculty ratio 6:1.

ACADEMICS

Degrees: Associate, bachelor's. **Majors with Highest Enrollment:** Cinematography and film/video production; film/cinema studies. **Special Study Options:** Accelerated program, double major, internships, liberal arts/career combination. **Combined degree programs:** Combined BA degree in cinema and video/TV. **Career services:** Alumni network, career assessment, internships. **Career services highlights include:** All students are strongly encouraged to meet with the Placement Advisor upon enrollment. Employment is not guaranteed but CCH offers career counseling and guidance that prepares students to meet the challenges of the highly competitive entertainment industry. For-pay and for-college credit internships at entertainment production companies are available year round. The Placement Advisor assists students in selecting internships, drafting resumes, and preparing for interviews. In addition, the Faculty Association mentors students with senior status. Each student is matched with a

faculty advisor in his or her chosen field of study. The advisor offers one-on-one counseling. Many faculty members are industry insiders with invaluable insight into the craft and the business of movie and television production.

FACILITIES

Housing: CCH does not offer housing, but our staff does assist students in trying to find apartments and potential roommates.

CAMPUS LIFE

Environment: Metropolis. **Activities:** Student government **Organizations:** 1 registered organizations, 3 honor societies.

ADMISSIONS

Freshman Academic Profile: Average high school GPA 3.3. 50% from public high schools. Minimum paper TOEFL 550. Minimum computer TOEFL 213. **Basis for Candidate Selection:** *Very important factors considered include:* Application essay, recommendation(s), rigor of secondary school record. *Other factors considered include:* Standardized test scores, character/personal qualities, extracurricular activities, interview, talent/ability. **Freshman Admission Requirements:** High school diploma is required and GED is accepted. **Freshman Admission Statistics:** 87 applied, 77% admitted, 90% enrolled. **Transfer Admission Requirements:** High school transcript, college transcript(s), essay or personal statement, minimum college GPA of 2.0 required. Lowest grade transferable C. **General Admission Information:** Application fee $50. Nonfall registration accepted. Admission may be deferred for a maximum of 1 year. Neither credit nor placement offered for CEEB Advanced Placement tests.

COSTS AND FINANCIAL AID

Annual tuition $11,400. Required fees $225. Average book expense $400. **Required Forms and Deadlines:** FAFSA, institution's own financial aid form. **Types of Aid:** *Need-based scholarships/grants:* Federal Pell, SEOG, state scholarships/grants. *Loans:* FFEL Subsidized Stafford, FFEL Unsubsidized Stafford, FFEL PLUS. **Student Employment:** Federal Work-Study Program available. Off-campus job opportunities are excellent. **Financial Aid Statistics:** 48% freshmen, 50% undergrads receive need-based scholarship or grant aid. 78% freshmen, 75% undergrads receive any aid. 95% undergrads borrow to pay for school. Average cumulative indebtedness $35,125.

COLUMBIA INTERNATIONAL UNIVERSITY

PO Box 3122, Columbia, SC 29230-3122
Phone: 803-754-4100
E-mail: yesciu@ciu.edu
Fax: 803-786-4041 **Website:** www.ciu.edu **ACT Code:** 5016

This private school was founded in 1923. It has a 400-acre campus.

RATINGS

Admissions Selectivity Rating: 76   **Fire Safety Rating:** 60*   **Green Rating:** 60*

STUDENTS AND FACULTY

Enrollment: 568. **Student Body:** 54% female, 46% male, 56% out-of-state. **Retention and Graduation:** 77% freshmen return for sophomore year. 35% freshmen graduate within 4 years. **Faculty:** Student/faculty ratio 19:1. 19 full-time faculty, 58% hold PhDs, 11% are members of minority groups, 21% are women.

ACADEMICS

Degrees: Associate, bachelor's, certificate, first professional, master's, post-bachelor's certificate, terminal associate, transfer associate. **Special Study Options:** Cross-registration, distance learning, double major, dual enrollment, English as a Second Language (ESL), independent study, internships, liberal arts/career combination, study abroad, cooperative studies with Midlands Technical College. Special programs offered to physically disabled students include note-taking services, reader services, tape recorders, tutors. **Career services:** Alumni services.

FACILITIES

Housing: Men's dorms, women's dorms, apartments for single students, mobile home park for married students.

CAMPUS LIFE

Environment: Village. **Activities:** Choral groups, concert band, drama/theater, music ensembles, student government, symphony orchestra, yearbook. **Organizations:** 4 religious organizations.

ADMISSIONS

Freshman Academic Profile: Minimum paper TOEFL 525. **Basis for Candidate Selection:** *Very important factors considered include:* Rigor of secondary school record, character/personal qualities, religious affiliation/commitment. *Important factors considered include:* Application essay, recommendation(s), standardized test scores, volunteer work. *Other factors considered include:* Class rank, extracurricular activities, interview, talent/ability. **Freshman Admission Requirements:** High school diploma is required and GED is accepted. *Academic units recommended:* 2 mathematics, 1 science, 2 foreign language, 2 social studies. **Freshman Admission Statistics:** 323 applied, 56% admitted, 62% enrolled. **Transfer Admission Requirements:** College transcript(s), essay or personal statement, statement of good standing from prior institution(s). Minimum college GPA of 2.0 required. Lowest grade transferable C. **General Admission Information:** Application fee $25. Notification on a rolling basis, beginning on or about 9/1. Nonfall registration accepted. Admission may be deferred for a maximum of n/a.

COSTS AND FINANCIAL AID
Annual tuition $8,980. . Room and board $4,520. Required fees $160. Average book expense $800. **Required Forms and Deadlines:** FAFSA. Financial aid filing deadline 8/1. Priority financial aid filing date 3/1. **Types of Aid:** *Need-based scholarships/grants:* Federal Pell, SEOG, state scholarships/grants, private scholarships, the school's own gift aid. *Loans:* FFEL Subsidized Stafford, FFEL Unsubsidized Stafford, FFEL PLUS, college/university loans from institutional funds. **Student Employment:** Federal Work-Study Program available. Highest amount earned per year from on-campus jobs $1,200. Off-campus job opportunities are good. **Financial Aid Statistics:** 55% freshmen, 58% undergrads receive need-based scholarship or grant aid. 13% freshmen, 17% undergrads receive non-need-based scholarship or grant aid. 72% freshmen, 73% undergrads receive need-based self-help aid. 58% undergrads borrow to pay for school. Average cumulative indebtedness $12,400.

COLUMBIA UNION COLLEGE

7600 Flower Avenue, Takoma Park, MD 20912
Phone: 301-891-4080 **Financial Aid Phone:** 301-891-4005
E-mail: enroll@cuc.edu **CEEB Code:** 5890
Fax: 301-891-4230 **ACT Code:** 1687

This private school, affiliated with the Seventh Day Adventist Church, was founded in 1904. It has a 19-acre campus.

RATINGS
Admissions Selectivity Rating: 60*   **Fire Safety Rating:** 60*   **Green Rating:** 60*

STUDENTS AND FACULTY
Enrollment: 893. **Student Body:** 62% female, 38% male, 43% out-of-state, 4% international (47 countries represented). Asian 6%, African American 54%, Caucasian 15%, Hispanic 9%.
Retention and Graduation: 59% freshmen return for sophomore year. 14% freshmen graduate within 4 years. **Faculty:** Student/faculty ratio 12:1. 50 full-time faculty, 48% hold PhDs, 36% are members of minority groups, 44% are women.

ACADEMICS
Degrees: Associate, bachelor's, master's. **Classes:** Most classes have fewer than 10 students. **Majors with Highest Enrollment:** Business/commerce; communication and media studies, other; nursing/registered nurse (RN, ASN, BSN, MSN). **Special Study Options:** Accelerated program, cooperative education program, cross-registration, distance learning, double major, dual enrollment, English as a Second Language (ESL), external degree program, honors program, independent study, internships, student-designed major, study abroad, teacher certification program. **Co-Op Programs:** Business, biochemistry, communication/journalism, computer science, english. Other special programs: Adult education and external degree programs. **Honors programs:** The Honors Program at CUC strives to provide academically talented students the opportunity to engage and explore subject material in greater depth. This does not mean more work, it means a different kind of work, with more individual attention. The honors classes are different in design as each class explores the topic from an interdisciplinary perspective, where areas of study are combined into one course. **Combined degree programs:** Liberal Studies—Combination of bachelor's programs designed by students. Special programs offered to physically disabled students include reader services, tutors. **Career services:** Career assessment, internships. **Career services highlights include:** Internships on Capitol Hill, NASA Cooperative Learning Experiences, White House Internships NOAA Internships.

FACILITIES
Housing: Men's dorms, women's dorms, apartments for married students, apartments for single students. 30% of campus accessible to physically disabled.

Special Academic Facilities/Equipment: Hospital adjacent to campus for students in health fields, performing arts at adjacent large church auditorium, learning center, radio station, playing fields and gymnasium. **Computers:** 100% of classrooms, 100% of dorms, 100% of libraries, 100% of dining areas, 100% of student union, 100% of common outdoor areas have wireless network access. Students can register for classes online. Administrative functions (other than registration) can be performed online.

CAMPUS LIFE
Environment: Metropolis. **Activities:** Choral groups, concert band, literary magazine, music ensembles, musical theater, radio station, student government, student newspaper, symphony orchestra, yearbook, campus ministries, international student organization. **Organizations:** 6 honor societies, **Athletics (Intercollegiate): Men:** Baseball, basketball, cross-country, soccer, track/field (outdoor). *Women:* Basketball, cross-country, soccer, softball, track/field (outdoor).

ADMISSIONS
Freshman Academic Profile: Average high school GPA 3.02. 53% from public high schools. SAT Math middle 50% range 340–478. SAT Critical Reading middle 50% range 386–508. ACT middle 50% range 14–22. Minimum paper TOEFL 550. Minimum computer TOEFL 213. **Basis for Candidate Selection:** *Very important factors considered include:* Academic GPA, rigor of secondary school record, standardized test scores. *Important factors considered include:* Recommendation(s), character/personal qualities, religious affiliation/commitment, talent/ability. *Other factors considered include:* Application essay, extracurricular activities, volunteer work, work experience. **Freshman Admission Requirements:** High school diploma is required and GED is accepted. *Academic units required:* 4 English, 2 mathematics, 2 science, (2 science labs), 2 history, 4 academic electives. **Freshman Admission Statistics:** 1,435 applied, 42% admitted, 24% enrolled. **Transfer Admission Requirements:** College transcript(s), minimum college GPA of 2.0 required. Lowest grade transferable C. **General Admission Information:** Application fee $25. Regular application deadline 8/1. Nonfall registration accepted. Admission may be deferred for a maximum of 1 year. Credit and/or placement offered for CEEB Advanced Placement tests.

COSTS AND FINANCIAL AID
Average book expense $945. **Required Forms and Deadlines:** FAFSA, state aid form. Priority financial aid filing date 3/1. **Notification of Awards:** Applicants will be notified of awards on a rolling basis beginning 5/1. **Types of Aid:** *Need-based scholarships/grants:* Federal Pell, SEOG, state scholarships/grants, private scholarships. *Loans:* Direct Subsidized Stafford, Direct Unsubsidized Stafford, Direct PLUS, FFEL Subsidized Stafford, FFEL PLUS, Federal Perkins. **Student Employment:** Federal Work-Study Program available. Institutional employment available. Off-campus job opportunities are excellent. **Financial Aid Statistics: Criteria for awarding institutional aid:** *Non-need-based:* Academics, athletics, music/drama.

COLUMBIA UNIVERSITY—COLUMBIA COLLEGE AND FU FOUNDATION SCHOOL OF ENGINEERING

212 Hamilton Hall MC 2807, 1130 Amsterdam A, New York, NY 10027
Phone: 212-854-2522
E-mail: CEEB Code: 2116 **Fax:** 212-894-1209
Website: http://studentaffairs.columbia.edu/admissions **ACT Code:** 2717

This private school was founded in 1754. It has a 36-acre campus.

RATINGS
Admissions Selectivity Rating: 99   **Fire Safety Rating:** 60*   **Green Rating:** 60*

STUDENTS AND FACULTY
Enrollment: 5,602. **Student Body:** 46% female, 54% male, 75% out-of-state, 9% international (87 countries represented). Asian 18%, African American 9%, Caucasian 42%, Hispanic 10%, Native American 1%.
Retention and Graduation: 97% freshmen return for sophomore year. 85% freshmen graduate within 4 years. **Faculty:** Student/faculty ratio 6:1. 864 full-time faculty, 16% are members of minority groups, 29% are women.

ACADEMICS

Degrees: Bachelor's, master's. **Classes:** Most classes have 10–19 students. **Majors with Highest Enrollment:** Engineering; English language and literature; political science and government. **Special Study Options:** Accelerated program, cooperative education program, cross-registration, double major, dual enrollment, English as a Second Language (ESL), exchange student program (domestic), independent study, internships, liberal arts/career combination, student-designed major, study abroad, teacher certification program, Combined 3-2 program. **Combined degree programs:** BA/JD, BA/MIA and BA/MPA (programs with SIPA). Special programs offered to physically disabled students include note-taking services, reader services, tape recorders, tutors. **Career services:** Alumni network, alumni services, career/job search classes, career assessment, internships.

FACILITIES

Housing: Coed dorms, special housing for disabled students, fraternity/sorority housing, special interest housing: Single-sex first-year floor available. 95% of campus accessible to physically disabled. **Special Academic Facilities/Equipment:** Art and Architecture Galleries, theatres, cinema, observatory. **Computers:** Students can register for classes online. Administrative functions (other than registration) can be performed online.

CAMPUS LIFE

Environment: Metropolis. **Activities:** Choral groups, concert band, dance, drama/theater, jazz band, literary magazine, marching band, music ensembles, musical theater, opera, pep band, radio station, student government, student newspaper, student-run film society, symphony orchestra, television station, yearbook, campus ministries, international student organization, Model UN. **Organizations:** 300 registered organizations, 17 religious organizations. 17 fraternities, 11 sorority. **Athletics (Intercollegiate):** *Men:* Baseball, basketball, crew/rowing, cross-country, diving, fencing, football, golf, soccer, swimming, tennis, track/field (outdoor), track/field (indoor), wrestling. *Women:* Archery, basketball, crew/rowing, cross-country, diving, fencing, field hockey, golf, lacrosse, soccer, softball, swimming, tennis, track/field (outdoor), track/field (indoor), volleyball. **On-Campus Highlights:** Low Library and Plaza, Butler Library, Postcrypt Coffee House, Ferris Booth Commons, Levian Gym.

ADMISSIONS

Freshman Academic Profile: Average high school GPA 3.9. 94% in top 10% of high school class, 98% in top 25% of high school class, 99% in top 50% of high school class. 59% from public high schools. SAT Math middle 50% range 680–780. SAT Critical Reading middle 50% range 680–770. SAT Writing middle 50% range 690–770. ACT middle 50% range 29–34. Minimum paper TOEFL 600. Minimum computer TOEFL 250. **Basis for Candidate Selection:** *Very important factors considered include:* Class rank, application essay, academic GPA, recommendation(s), rigor of secondary school record, standardized test scores, character/personal qualities. *Important factors considered include:* Extracurricular activities, talent/ability. *Other factors considered include:* Alumni/ae relation, geographical residence, interview, racial/ethnic status, volunteer work, work experience. **Freshman Admission Requirements:** High school diploma is required and GED is accepted. *Academic units recommended:* 4 English, 4 mathematics, 4 science, (4 science labs), 4 foreign language, 4 history, 4 academic electives. **Freshman Admission Statistics:** 21,342 applied, 10% admitted, 64% enrolled. **Transfer Admission Requirements:** High school transcript, college transcript(s), essay or personal statement, standardized test scores, statement of good standing from prior institution(s). Lowest grade transferable C. **General Admission Information:** Application fee $70. Early decision application deadline 11/1. Regular application deadline 1/2. Regular notification 4/1. Nonfall registration not accepted. Admission may be deferred for a maximum of 2 years. Credit and/or placement offered for CEEB Advanced Placement tests.

COSTS AND FINANCIAL AID

Annual tuition $37,470. **Required Forms and Deadlines:** FAFSA, CSS/Financial Aid PROFILE, noncustodial PROFILE, parent and student income tax forms. Financial aid filing deadline 3/1. **Notification of Awards:** Applicants will be notified of awards on or about 4/1. **Types of Aid:** *Need-based scholarships/grants:* Federal Pell, SEOG, state scholarships/grants, private scholarships, the school's own gift aid. *Loans:* FFEL Subsidized Stafford, FFEL Unsubsidized Stafford, FFEL PLUS, Federal Perkins, Alternative loans. **Student Employment:** Federal Work-Study Program available. Institutional employment available. Off-campus job opportunities are excellent. **Financial Aid Statistics:** 49% freshmen, 46% undergrads receive need-based scholarship or grant aid. 43% freshmen, 43% undergrads receive need-based self-help aid. 61% freshmen, 56% undergrads receive any aid.

COLUMBIA UNIVERSITY
SCHOOL OF GENERAL STUDIES

408 Lewisohn Hall, Mail Code 4101, 2970 Broadway, New York, NY 10027
Phone: 212)854-2772 **Financial Aid Phone:** 212-854-2772
E-mail: gs-admit@columbia.edu **CEEB Code:** 2095
Fax: 212-854-6316 **Website:** www.gs.columbia.edu **ACT Code:** 2716

This private school was founded in 1947. It has a 36-acre campus.

RATINGS

Admissions Selectivity Rating: 60*   **Fire Safety Rating:** 72   **Green Rating:** 94

STUDENTS AND FACULTY

Enrollment: 1,351. **Student Body:** 50% female, 50% male, % out-of-state, international (76 countries represented).
Retention and Graduation: Faculty: Student/faculty ratio 7.67:1. 777 full-time faculty, 100% hold PhDs, 23% are members of minority groups, 36% are women.

ACADEMICS

Degrees: Bachelor's, post-bachelor's certificate. **Majors with Highest Enrollment:** Economics; English language and literature; political science and government. **Special Study Options:** Accelerated program, cross-registration, double major, dual enrollment, exchange student program (domestic), honors program, independent study, internships, student-designed major, study abroad, teacher certification program. **Honors programs:** Honor Society of School of General Studies. **Combined degree programs:** BA/JD, BA/MA, BA/DDS, BA/MEng, Joint Programs. Special programs offered to physically disabled students include note-taking services, reader services, tape recorders, tutors. **Career services:** Alumni network, alumni services, career/job search classes, career assessment, internships, regional alumni.

FACILITIES

Housing: Coed dorms, special housing for international students, fraternity/sorority housing, apartments for married students, cooperative housing, apartments for single students, theme housing. 100% of campus accessible to physically disabled. **Special Academic Facilities/Equipment:** Earth Institute, Lamont-Doherty Earth Observatory, University Art Collection, Miller Theatre, Low Memorial Library Rotunda, LeRoy Neiman Center for Print Studies, music at St. Paul's Postcrypt Coffeehouse, Miriam and Ira D. Wallach Art Gallery Language Houses. **Computers:** 50% of classrooms, 10% of dorms, 64% of libraries, 50% of dining areas, 90% of student union, 25% of common outdoor areas have wireless network access. Students can register for classes online. Administrative functions (other than registration) can be performed online.

CAMPUS LIFE

Environment: Metropolis. **Activities:** Choral groups, concert band, dance, drama/theater, jazz band, literary magazine, marching band, music ensembles, musical theater, opera, radio station, student government, student newspaper, student-run film society, symphony orchestra, television station, yearbook, campus ministries, international student organization, Model UN. **Organizations:** 250 registered organizations, 2 honor societies, 21 religious organizations. **Athletics (Intercollegiate):** *Men:* Baseball, basketball, crew/rowing, cross-country, diving, fencing, football, golf, soccer, swimming, track/field (outdoor), track/field (indoor). *Women:* Archery, basketball, crew/rowing, cross-country, diving, fencing, field hockey, golf, lacrosse, soccer, softball, swimming, track/field (outdoor), track/field (indoor), volleyball. **On-Campus Highlights:** Low Library, Lerner Hall, Butler Library, Miller Theater, College Walk, Low Plaza. **Environmental Initiatives:** Greenhouse gas reduction program targeted to meet 30% reduction by 2017; LEED Silver base commitment for all new construction; LEED for Neighborhood Development pilot program for campus expansion; twenty-three environmental degrees granted; home of the Earth Institute and the Lamont Doherty Earth Observatory, also NASA/GIS—Columbia University is one of the world's leading research institutions on climate and earth systems.

ADMISSIONS

Freshman Academic Profile: Minimum paper TOEFL 600. Minimum computer TOEFL 250. **Basis for Candidate Selection:** *Very important factors considered include:* Application essay, academic GPA, recommendation(s), rigor of secondary school record, standardized test scores, character/personal qualities, first generation, interview, level of applicant's interest, talent/ability, work experience. *Important factors considered include:* Class rank, extracurricular activities, racial/ethnic status. *Other factors considered include:* Alumni/ae relation, geographical residence, state residency, volunteer work. **Freshman Admission Requirements:** High school diploma is required and GED is accepted. **Freshman Admission Statistics:** 249 applied, 37% admitted, 61% enrolled. **Transfer Admission Requirements:** High school transcript, college transcript(s), essay or personal statement, standardized test scores, lowest grade transferable C. **General Admission Information:** Application fee $65. Regular application deadline 6/1. Notification on a rolling basis, beginning on or about 2/1. Nonfall registration accepted. Admission may be deferred for a maximum of 2 semesters. Credit and/or placement offered for CEEB Advanced Placement tests.

COSTS AND FINANCIAL AID

Required Forms and Deadlines: FAFSA, institution's own financial aid form. Financial aid filing deadline 6/1. Priority financial aid filing date 6/1. **Types of Aid:** *Need-based scholarships/grants:* Federal Pell, SEOG, state scholarships/grants, private scholarships, the school's own gift aid. *Loans:* FFEL Subsidized Stafford, FFEL Unsubsidized Stafford, Federal Perkins, college/university loans from institutional funds. **Student Employment:** Federal Work-Study Program available. Institutional employment available. Off-campus job opportunities are excellent. **Financial Aid Statistics:** 70% undergrads receive any aid. **Criteria for awarding institutional aid:** *Non-need-based:* Academics.

See page 1062.

COLUMBUS COLLEGE OF ART AND DESIGN

107 North Ninth Street, Columbus, OH 43215-3875
Phone: 614-222-3261
E-mail: admissions@ccad.edu **CEEB Code:** 1085
Fax: 614-232-8344 **Website:** www.ccad.edu **ACT Code:** 3281

This private school was founded in 1879. It has a 17-acre campus.

RATINGS
Admissions Selectivity Rating: 74   **Fire Safety Rating:** 60*   **Green Rating:** 60*

STUDENTS AND FACULTY
Enrollment: 1,359. **Student Body:** 48% female, 52% male, 28% out-of-state, 5% international (29 countries represented). Asian 4%, African American 6%, Caucasian 83%, Hispanic 2%.
Retention and Graduation: 79% freshmen return for sophomore year. 32% freshmen graduate within 4 years. 12% grads go on to further study within 1 year. 12% grads pursue arts and sciences degrees. **Faculty:** Student/faculty ratio 12:1. 72 full-time faculty, 56% hold PhDs, 8% are members of minority groups, 29% are women.

ACADEMICS
Degrees: Bachelor's. **Special Study Options:** Cooperative education program, cross-registration, internships, study abroad, undergrads may take grad level classes. Other special programs: Evening classes for credit. Saturday school (ages 6–18). **Career services:** Career/job search classes, internships.

FACILITIES
Housing: Coed dorms **Special Academic Facilities/Equipment:** Student art exhibition hall, gallery, auditorium, recreation center.

CAMPUS LIFE
Activities: Literary magazine, student government, student newspaper. **Organizations:** 2 registered organizations, 1 religious organizations.

ADMISSIONS
Freshman Academic Profile: Average high school GPA 2.93. 10% in top 10% of high school class, 30% in top 25% of high school class, 61% in top 50% of high school class. SAT Math middle 50% range 433–550. SAT Critical Reading middle 50% range 433–580. ACT middle 50% range 18–23. Minimum paper TOEFL 500. Minimum computer TOEFL 173. **Basis for Candidate Selection:** *Very important factors considered include:* Rigor of secondary school record, talent/ability. *Important factors considered include:* Application essay, recommendation(s), standardized test scores, character/personal qualities, interview. *Other factors considered include:* Class rank, extracurricular activities. **Freshman Admission Requirements:** High school diploma is required and GED is accepted. *Academic units recommended:* 4 English, 4 mathematics, 4 science, 2 foreign language. **Transfer Admission Requirements:** High school transcript, college transcript(s), essay or personal statement, minimum college GPA of 2.0 required. Lowest grade transferable C. **General Admission Information:** Application fee $25. Nonfall registration accepted. Admission may be deferred for a maximum of 1 year. Credit and/or placement offered for CEEB Advanced Placement tests.

COSTS AND FINANCIAL AID
Annual tuition $17,880. . Room and board $6,300. Required fees $390. Average book expense $1,800. **Required Forms and Deadlines:** FAFSA Financial aid filing deadline 6/2. Priority financial aid filing date 3/3. **Notification of Awards:** Applicants will be notified of awards on or about 6/15. **Types of Aid:**

Need-based scholarships/grants: Federal Pell, SEOG, state scholarships/grants, private scholarships, the school's own gift aid. *Loans:* FFEL Subsidized Stafford, FFEL Unsubsidized Stafford, FFEL PLUS, Federal Perkins, state loans. **Student Employment:** Federal Work-Study Program available. Institutional employment available. Highest amount earned per year from on-campus jobs $2,500. Off-campus job opportunities are excellent. **Financial Aid Statistics:** 77% freshmen, 73% undergrads receive need-based scholarship or grant aid. 8% freshmen, 7% undergrads receive non-need-based scholarship or grant aid. 59% freshmen, 60% undergrads receive need-based self-help aid. 86% undergrads borrow to pay for school. Average cumulative indebtedness $21,700. **Criteria for awarding institutional aid:** *Non-need-based:* Academics, art.

COLUMBUS STATE UNIVERSITY

4225 University Avenue, Columbus, GA 31907-5645
Phone: 706-568-2035 **Financial Aid Phone:** 706-507-8800
E-mail: admissions@colstate.edu
Fax: 706-568-5091 **Website:** www.colstate.edu

This public school was founded in 1958. It has a 150-acre campus.

RATINGS
Admissions Selectivity Rating: 72   **Fire Safety Rating:** 76   **Green Rating:** 72

STUDENTS AND FACULTY
Enrollment: 6,760. **Student Body:** 60% female, 40% male, 14% out-of-state, 1% international (67 countries represented). Asian 2%, African American 33%, Caucasian 56%, Hispanic 5%, Native American 1%.
Retention and Graduation: 66% freshmen return for sophomore year. 11% freshmen graduate within 4 years. **Faculty:** Student/faculty ratio 18:1. 276 full-time faculty, 78% hold PhDs, 21% are members of minority groups, 44% are women.

ACADEMICS
Degrees: Bachelor's, certificate, doctoral, master's, post-master's certificate, terminal associate, transfer associate. **Classes:** Most classes have 20–29 students. Most lab/discussion sessions have 10–19 students. **Majors with Highest Enrollment:** Business/commerce; early childhood education and teaching; nursing/registered nurse (RN, ASN, BSN, MSN). **Special Study Options:** Accelerated program, cooperative education program, distance learning, double major, dual enrollment, English as a Second Language (ESL), honors program, independent study, internships, liberal arts/career combination, study abroad, teacher certification program. **Honors programs:** Honors Program Servant Leadership Program Special programs offered to physically disabled students include note-taking services, reader services, tape recorders, tutors. **Career services:** Alumni network, alumni services, career/job search classes, career assessment, internships, regional alumni. **Career services highlights include:** Internships and experiential learning via volunteer placements in the community.

FACILITIES
Housing: Special housing for disabled students, special housing for international students, apartments for married students, apartments for single students, theme housing. 100% of campus accessible to physically disabled. **Computers:** 80% of classrooms, 100% of libraries, 100% of dining areas, 100% of student union, 25% of common outdoor areas have wireless network access. Students can register for classes online. Administrative functions (other than registration) can be performed online.

CAMPUS LIFE
Environment: City. **Activities:** Choral groups, concert band, dance, drama/theater, jazz band, literary magazine, music ensembles, musical theater, pep band, student government, student newspaper, symphony orchestra, campus ministries, international student organization, Model UN. **Organizations:** 90 registered organizations, 22 honor societies, 10 religious organizations. 7 fraternities, 6 sororities. **Athletics (Intercollegiate):** *Men:* Baseball, basketball, cheerleading, cross-country, golf, riflery, tennis. *Women:* Basketball, cheerleading, cross-country, golf, riflery, soccer, softball, tennis. **On-Campus Highlights:** Einstein Bos. Bagels, RiverPark Campus, Davidson Student Center, Lumpkin Center, Coca Cola Space Science Center. **Environmental Initiatives:** Green Seal cleaning products; recycling of paper, plastic, and aluminum cans; energy efficient equipment upgrades throughout campus.

ADMISSIONS
Freshman Academic Profile: Average high school GPA 3.01. SAT Math middle 50% range 420–540. SAT Critical Reading middle 50% range 430–550. ACT middle 50% range 17–22. Minimum paper TOEFL 550. Minimum computer TOEFL 213. Minimum web-based TOEFL 79. **Basis for Candidate Selection:** *Very important factors considered include:* Rigor of secondary school

record. *Important factors considered include:* Academic GPA, standardized test scores. *Other factors considered include:* Extracurricular activities, geographical residence, interview, talent/ability. **Freshman Admission Requirements:** High school diploma is required and GED is not accepted. *Academic units required:* 4 English, 4 mathematics, 3 science, (2 science labs), 2 foreign language, 3 social studies. **Freshman Admission Statistics:** 3,445 applied, 64% admitted, 60% enrolled. **Transfer Admission Requirements:** College transcript(s), statement of good standing from prior institution(s). Minimum college GPA of 2.00 required. Lowest grade transferable D. **General Admission Information:** Application fee $30. Regular application deadline 6/30. Notification on a rolling basis, beginning on or about 9/1. Nonfall registration accepted. Admission may be deferred for a maximum of 1 year. Credit and/or placement offered for CEEB Advanced Placement tests.

COSTS AND FINANCIAL AID

Annual in-state tuition $3,100. Annual out-of-state tuition $12,398. Room and board $7,800. Required fees $1,150. Average book expense $974. **Required Forms and Deadlines:** FAFSA. Priority financial aid filing date 5/1. **Notification of Awards:** Applicants will be notified of awards on a rolling basis beginning 5/15. **Types of Aid:** *Need-based scholarships/grants:* Federal Pell, SEOG, state scholarships/grants, private scholarships, the school's own gift aid. *Loans:* Direct Subsidized Stafford, Direct Unsubsidized Stafford, Direct PLUS, Federal Perkins, Federal Nursing, state loans, college/university loans from institutional funds. **Student Employment:** Federal Work-Study Program available. Institutional employment available. Off-campus job opportunities are good. **Financial Aid Statistics:** 44% freshmen, 41% undergrads receive need-based scholarship or grant aid. 36% freshmen, 21% undergrads receive non-need-based scholarship or grant aid. 47% freshmen, 46% undergrads receive need-based self-help aid. 3% freshmen, 4% undergrads receive athletic scholarships. 87.3% freshmen, 75.6% undergrads receive any aid. 64% undergrads borrow to pay for school. Average cumulative indebtedness $21,538. **Criteria for awarding institutional aid:** *Non-need-based:* Academics, alumni affiliation, art, athletics, job skills, leadership, minority status, music/drama.

CONCEPTION SEMINARY COLLEGE

P.O. Box 502, 37174 State Highway W, Conception, MO 64433
Phone: 660-944-2886
E-mail: vocations@conception.edu
Fax: 660-944-2829 **Website:** www.conception.edu **ACT Code:** 2280

This private school, affiliated with the Roman Catholic Church, was founded in 1886. It has a 30-acre campus.

RATINGS

Admissions Selectivity Rating: 60*   **Fire Safety Rating:** 60*   **Green Rating:** 60*

STUDENTS AND FACULTY

Enrollment: 96. **Student Body:** 100% male, 73% out-of-state, 5% international . Asian 10%, Caucasian 56%, Hispanic 2%.
Retention and Graduation: 50% freshmen return for sophomore year. 60% grads go on to further study within 1 year. **Faculty:** Student/faculty ratio 4:1. 20 full-time faculty, 85% hold PhDs, 10% are members of minority groups, 15% are women.

ACADEMICS

Degrees: Bachelor's, certificate. **Special Study Options:** Double major, English as a Second Language (ESL), independent study.

FACILITIES

Housing: Men's dorms. **Computers:** Administrative functions (other than registration) can be performed online.

CAMPUS LIFE

Environment: Rural. **Activities:** Drama/theater, music ensembles, student government, student newspaper, yearbook. **Organizations:** 12 registered organizations, **Athletics (Intercollegiate):** *Men:* Soccer, volleyball.

ADMISSIONS

Freshman Academic Profile: ACT middle 50% range 12–29. Minimum computer TOEFL 173. **Basis for Candidate Selection:** *Very important factors considered include:* Application essay, recommendation(s), religious affiliation/commitment. *Important factors considered include:* Rigor of secondary school record, standardized test scores, character/personal qualities, talent/ability. *Other factors considered include:* Class rank, extracurricular activities, interview, volunteer work, work experience. **Freshman Admission Requirements:** High school diploma is required and GED is accepted. *Academic units required:* 4 English, 4 science, 4 social studies. **Freshman Admission Statistics:** 17 ap-

plied, 100% admitted, 100% enrolled. **Transfer Admission Requirements:** College transcript(s), essay or personal statement, minimum college GPA of 2.0 required. Lowest grade transferable C. **General Admission Information:** Regular application deadline 8/15. Notification on a rolling basis, beginning on or about 1/1. Nonfall registration accepted. Admission may be deferred for a maximum of 1 year.

COSTS AND FINANCIAL AID

Required Forms and Deadlines: FAFSA. **Financial Aid Statistics:** 53% freshmen, 51% undergrads receive need-based scholarship or grant aid. 20% freshmen, 30% undergrads receive non-need-based scholarship or grant aid. 20% freshmen, 31% undergrads receive need-based self-help aid. 33% undergrads borrow to pay for school. Average cumulative indebtedness $11,302. **Criteria for awarding institutional aid:** *Non-need-based:* Academics.

CONCORD UNIVERSITY

1000 Vermillion Street, P.O. Box 1000, Athens, WV 24712
Phone: 304-384-5248 **Financial Aid Phone:** 304-384-6069
E-mail: admissions@concord.edu **CEEB Code:** 5120
Fax: 304-384-9044 **Website:** www.concord.edu **ACT Code:** 003810

This public school was founded in 1872. It has a 123-acre campus.

RATINGS

Admissions Selectivity Rating: 78   **Fire Safety Rating:** 81   **Green Rating:** 60*

STUDENTS AND FACULTY

Enrollment: 3,023. **Student Body:** 57% female, 43% male, 18% out-of-state, (16 countries represented). Asian 1%, African American 3%, Caucasian 76%.
Retention and Graduation: 64% freshmen return for sophomore year. 33% grads go on to further study within 1 year. 8% grads pursue arts and sciences degrees. 2% grads pursue law degrees. 10% grads pursue business degrees. 3% grads pursue medical degrees. **Faculty:** Student/faculty ratio 24:1. 84 full-time faculty, 69% hold PhDs, 2% are members of minority groups, 38% are women.

ACADEMICS

Degrees: Associate, bachelor's, master's, terminal associate. **Classes:** Most classes have fewer than 10 students. Most lab/discussion sessions have 10–19 students. **Majors with Highest Enrollment:** Business administration and management; education; social sciences. **Special Study Options:** Cooperative education program, double major, dual enrollment, English as a Second Language (ESL), honors program, student-designed major, teacher certification program. **Career services:** Alumni services, career/job search classes, career assessment, internships.

FACILITIES

Housing: Coed dorms, special housing for disabled students, men's dorms, special housing for international students, women's dorms, apartments for married students. 100% of campus accessible to physically disabled. **Computers:** 50% of classrooms, 20% of dorms, 100% of libraries, 100% of dining areas, 100% of student union, 50% of common outdoor areas have wireless network access. Students can register for classes online. Administrative functions (other than registration) can be performed online.

CAMPUS LIFE

Environment: Rural. **Activities:** Choral groups, concert band, drama/theater, jazz band, pep band, radio station, student government, student newspaper, student-run film society, television station, yearbook. **Organizations:** 57 registered organizations, 1 honor societies, 2 religious organizations. 6 fraternities, 4 sororities. **Athletics (Intercollegiate):** *Men:* Baseball, basketball, cheerleading, cross-country, football, golf, soccer, tennis, track/field (outdoor). *Women:* Basketball, cheerleading, cross-country, golf, soccer, softball, tennis, track/field (outdoor), volleyball. **On-Campus Highlights:** Rahall Technology Ctr, 48 Bell Carillon, University Point, Beasley Student Ctr, Callaghan Stadium.

ADMISSIONS

Freshman Academic Profile: 95% from public high schools. SAT Math middle 50% range 410–560. SAT Critical Reading middle 50% range 390–560. ACT middle 50% range 23–27. Minimum paper TOEFL 500. **Basis for Candidate Selection:** *Very important factors considered include:* Rigor of secondary school record. *Important factors considered include:* Class rank, standardized test scores, extracurricular activities. *Other factors considered include:* Application essay, recommendation(s), alumni/ae relation, character/personal qualities, geographical residence, interview, racial/ethnic status, talent/ability, volunteer work, work experience. **Freshman Admission Requirements:** High school diploma is required and GED is accepted. *Academic units required:* 4 English, 2 mathematics, 2 science, (2 science labs), 2 social studies, 1 history, 6 academic electives. *Academic units recommended:* 3 mathematics, 2 foreign language. **Freshman Admission Statistics:** 2,330 applied, 65% admitted, 42% enrolled. **Transfer Admission Requirements:** College transcript(s), Lowest grade transferable D. **General Admission Information:** Notification on a rolling basis, beginning on or about 9/1. Nonfall registration accepted. Admission may be deferred for a maximum of 1 year. Credit and/or placement offered for CEEB Advanced Placement tests.

COSTS AND FINANCIAL AID
Annual in-state tuition $4,974. Annual out-of-state tuition $11,050. Room and board $6,796. Average book expense $650. **Required Forms and Deadlines:** FAFSA, institution's own financial aid form, verification worksheet. Priority financial aid filing date 3/1. **Notification of Awards:** Applicants will be notified of awards on a rolling basis beginning 3/1. **Types of Aid:** *Need-based scholarships/grants:* Federal Pell, SEOG, state scholarships/grants, the school's own gift aid. *Loans:* FFEL Subsidized Stafford, FFEL Unsubsidized Stafford, FFEL PLUS, Federal Perkins. **Student Employment:** Federal Work-Study Program available. Institutional employment available. Highest amount earned per year from on-campus jobs $1,343. Off-campus job opportunities are excellent. **Financial Aid Statistics:** 53% freshmen, 68% undergrads receive need-based scholarship or grant aid. 55% freshmen, 38% undergrads receive non-need-based scholarship or grant aid. 46% freshmen, 48% undergrads receive need-based self-help aid. 7% freshmen, 7% undergrads receive athletic scholarships. 90% freshmen, 77% undergrads receive any aid. 86% undergrads borrow to pay for school. Average cumulative indebtedness $13,716. **Criteria for awarding institutional aid:** *Non-need-based:* Academics, alumni affiliation, art, athletics, job skills, leadership, minority status, music/drama, state/district residency.

CONCORDIA COLLEGE (MOORHEAD, MN)

901 Eighth Street South, Moorhead, MN 56562
Phone: 218-299-3004
E-mail: admissions@cord.edu **CEEB Code:** 6113
Fax: 218-299-4720 **Website:** www.goconcordia.com **ACT Code:** 2104

This private school, affiliated with the Lutheran Church, was founded in 1891. It has a 120-acre campus.

RATINGS
Admissions Selectivity Rating: 75   **Fire Safety Rating:** 60*   **Green Rating:** 60*

STUDENTS AND FACULTY
Enrollment: 2,793. **Student Body:** 63% female, 37% male, 33% out-of-state, 6% international (42 countries represented). Asian 2%, African American 1%, Caucasian 92%, Hispanic 1%.
Retention and Graduation: 80% freshmen return for sophomore year. 57% freshmen graduate within 4 years. 20% grads go on to further study within 1 year. 9% grads pursue arts and sciences degrees. 4% grads pursue law degrees. 3% grads pursue business degrees. 4% grads pursue medical degrees. **Faculty:** Student/faculty ratio 14:1. 175 full-time faculty, 78% hold PhDs, 3% are members of minority groups, 45% are women.

ACADEMICS
Degrees: Bachelor's, master's. **Classes:** Most classes have 20–29 students. **Special Study Options:** Cooperative education program, double major, exchange student program (domestic), honors program, independent study, internships, liberal arts/career combination, study abroad, teacher certification program. **Combined degree programs:** BA/BS engineering NOSU, U of Minnesota Institute. Special programs offered to physically disabled students include note-taking services, reader services, tape recorders, tutors. **Career services:** Alumni network, alumni services, career/job search classes, career assessment, internships.

FACILITIES
Housing: Coed dorms, special housing for disabled students, men's dorms, women's dorms, apartments for single students, French, German, and Spanish language houses. 95% of campus accessible to physically disabled. **Special Academic Facilities/Equipment:** Cyrus M. Running Gallery. **Computers:** Administrative functions (other than registration) can be performed online.

CAMPUS LIFE
Environment: City. **Activities:** Choral groups, concert band, dance, drama/theater, jazz band, literary magazine, music ensembles, musical theater, pep band, radio station, student government, student newspaper, symphony orchestra, television station, yearbook. **Organizations:** 80 registered organizations, 22 honor societies, 12 religious organizations. 2 fraternities, 2 sororities. **Athletics (Intercollegiate):** *Men:* Baseball, basketball, cross-country, football, golf, ice hockey, soccer, tennis, track/field (outdoor), track/field (indoor), wrestling.

Women: Basketball, cross-country, diving, golf, ice hockey, soccer, softball, swimming, tennis, track/field (outdoor), track/field (indoor), volleyball.

ADMISSIONS
Freshman Academic Profile: 31% in top 10% of high school class, 62% in top 25% of high school class, 89% in top 50% of high school class. SAT Math middle 50% range 520–630. SAT Critical Reading middle 50% range 530–650. ACT middle 50% range 21–27. Minimum paper TOEFL 550. Minimum computer TOEFL 200. **Basis for Candidate Selection:** *Very important factors considered include:* Rigor of secondary school record. *Important factors considered include:* Class rank, recommendation(s). *Other factors considered include:* Standardized test scores, alumni/ae relation, character/personal qualities, extracurricular activities, racial/ethnic status, talent/ability, volunteer work. **Freshman Admission Requirements:** High school diploma is required and GED is accepted. *Academic units recommended:* 4 English, 3 mathematics, 3 science, 2 foreign language, 3 social studies. **Freshman Admission Statistics:** 2,444 applied, 86% admitted, 37% enrolled. **Transfer Admission Requirements:** College transcript(s), minimum college GPA of 2.0 required. Lowest grade transferable C–. **General Admission Information:** Application fee $20. Nonfall registration accepted. Admission may be deferred for a maximum of 1. Credit and/or placement offered for CEEB Advanced Placement tests.

COSTS AND FINANCIAL AID
Annual tuition $17,620. Room and board $4,690. Required fees $150. Average book expense $700. **Student Employment:** Federal Work-Study Program available. Institutional employment available. Off-campus job opportunities are excellent. **Financial Aid Statistics:** 97% freshmen, 94% undergrads receive any aid.

CONCORDIA COLLEGE (NY)

171 White Plains Road, Bronxville, NY 10708
Phone: 914-337-9300
E-mail: admission@concordia-ny.edu **CEEB Code:** 2096
Fax: 914-395-4636 **Website:** www.concordia-ny.edu **ACT Code:** 2722

This private school, affiliated with the Lutheran Church, was founded in 1881. It has a 33-acre campus.

RATINGS
Admissions Selectivity Rating: 70   **Fire Safety Rating:** 60*   **Green Rating:** 60*

STUDENTS AND FACULTY
Enrollment: 587. **Student Body:** 58% female, 42% male, 27% out-of-state, (36 countries represented). Asian 7%, African American 14%, Caucasian 63%, Hispanic 10%, Native American 1%.
Retention and Graduation: 76% freshmen return for sophomore year. 23% freshmen graduate within 4 years. 40% grads go on to further study within 1 year. 30% grads pursue arts and sciences degrees. 2% grads pursue law degrees. 30% grads pursue business degrees. 10% grads pursue medical degrees. **Faculty:** Student/faculty ratio 16:1. 33 full-time faculty, 67% hold PhDs, 18% are members of minority groups, 45% are women.

ACADEMICS
Degrees: Associate, bachelor's. **Classes:** Most classes have 10–19 students. Most lab/discussion sessions have 10–19 students. **Majors with Highest Enrollment:** Business/commerce; education; social sciences. **Special Study Options:** Accelerated program, cooperative education program, cross-registration, double major, English as a Second Language (ESL), exchange student program (domestic), honors program, independent study, internships, liberal arts/career combination, student-designed major, study abroad, teacher certification program. Special programs offered to physically disabled students include reader services, tutors. **Career services:** Career/job search classes, career assessment, internships.

FACILITIES
Housing: Men's dorms, women's dorms. 50% of campus accessible to physically disabled. **Special Academic Facilities/Equipment:** Art gallery, center for worship and performing arts, English language center, distance learning classroom.

CAMPUS LIFE
Environment: Village. **Activities:** Choral groups, concert band, drama/theater, jazz band, literary magazine, music ensembles, musical theater, student government, student newspaper, yearbook. **Organizations:** 35 registered organizations, 1 honor societies, 3 religious organizations. **Athletics (Intercollegiate):** *Men:* Baseball, basketball, soccer, tennis, volleyball. *Women:* Basketball, soccer, softball, tennis, volleyball.

ADMISSIONS

Freshman Academic Profile: Average high school GPA 2.7. 9% in top 10% of high school class, 20% in top 25% of high school class, 59% in top 50% of high school class. 60% from public high schools. SAT Math middle 50% range 410–530. SAT Critical Reading middle 50% range 420–520. ACT middle 50% range 17–22. Minimum paper TOEFL 550. Minimum computer TOEFL 213. **Basis for Candidate Selection:** *Very important factors considered include:* Rigor of secondary school record. *Important factors considered include:* Class rank, standardized test scores, character/personal qualities, interview. *Other factors considered include:* Application essay, recommendation(s), alumni/ae relation, extracurricular activities, religious affiliation/commitment, talent/ability, volunteer work, work experience. **Freshman Admission Requirements:** High school diploma is required and GED is accepted. *Academic units required:* 4 English, 3 mathematics, 2 science, (2 science labs), 2 foreign language, 2 social studies, 2 history. **Freshman Admission Statistics:** 684 applied, 70% admitted, 37% enrolled. **Transfer Admission Requirements:** High school transcript, college transcript(s), statement of good standing from prior institution(s). Minimum college GPA of 2.0 required. Lowest grade transferable C. **General Admission Information:** Application fee $40. Regular application deadline 3/15. Notification on a rolling basis, beginning on or about 1/15. Nonfall registration accepted. Admission may be deferred for a maximum of 12. Credit and/or placement offered for CEEB Advanced Placement tests.

COSTS AND FINANCIAL AID

Annual tuition $20,700. Room and board $8,230. Required fees $150. Average book expense $750. **Student Employment:** Federal Work-Study Program available. Institutional employment available. Highest amount earned per year from on-campus jobs $2,000. Off-campus job opportunities are excellent.

CONCORDIA UNIVERSITY AT AUSTIN

3400 I-35 N, Austin, TX 78705
Phone: 512-486-1106 **Financial Aid Phone:** 512-486-2000
E-mail: admissions@concordia.edu **CEEB Code:** 6127
Fax: 512-486-1350 **Website:** www.concordia.edu **ACT Code:** 4124

This private school, affiliated with the Lutheran Church, was founded in 1926. It has a 23-acre campus.

RATINGS
Admissions Selectivity Rating: 70   **Fire Safety Rating:** 60*   **Green Rating:** 60*

STUDENTS AND FACULTY
Enrollment: 966. **Student Body:** 56% female, 44% male, 7% out-of-state, 1% international (10 countries represented). Asian 2%, African American 9%, Caucasian 67%, Hispanic 14%, Native American 1%.
Retention and Graduation: 56% freshmen return for sophomore year. 12% freshmen graduate within 4 years. 12% grads go on to further study within 1 year. 9% grads pursue arts and sciences degrees. 1% grads pursue law degrees. 2% grads pursue business degrees. **Faculty:** Student/faculty ratio 19:1. 33 full-time faculty, 70% hold PhDs, 6% are members of minority groups, 36% are women.

ACADEMICS
Degrees: Associate, bachelor's, certificate, diploma, master's, post-bachelor's certificate. **Classes:** Most classes have 10–19 students. Most lab/discussion sessions have 20–29 students. **Majors with Highest Enrollment:** Biology; elementary education and teaching. **Special Study Options:** Accelerated program, cooperative education program, cross-registration, distance learning, double major, dual enrollment, exchange student program (domestic), external degree program, honors program, independent study, internships, study abroad, teacher certification program. **Honors programs:** Honors Program.

FACILITIES
Housing: Coed dorms, men's dorms, women's dorms 95% of campus accessible to physically disabled.

CAMPUS LIFE
Environment: Metropolis. **Activities:** Choral groups, drama/theater, jazz band, literary magazine, music ensembles, student government, yearbook. **Organizations:** 20 registered organizations, 4 honor societies, 5 religious organizations. **Athletics (Intercollegiate):** *Men:* Baseball, basketball, cross-country, golf, rugby, soccer, tennis. *Women:* Basketball, cross-country, golf, soccer, softball, tennis, volleyball. **On-Campus Highlights:** Oliver R. Harms Residential Suites (opened in 2001), Bokenkamp Student Center, Louise T Peter Center—communication and fine arts, Woltman Activity Center—Gymnasium, Texas Hall—dining facility.

ADMISSIONS

Freshman Academic Profile: Average high school GPA 3.14. 8% in top 10% of high school class, 26% in top 25% of high school class, 60% in top 50% of high school class. 86% from public high schools. SAT Math middle 50% range 450–550. SAT Critical Reading middle 50% range 430–500. ACT middle 50% range 18–24. **Basis for Candidate Selection:** *Very important factors considered include:* Rigor of secondary school record, standardized test scores. *Other factors considered include:* Class rank, application essay, recommendation(s). **Freshman Admission Requirements:** High school diploma is required and GED is accepted. *Academic units recommended:* 4 English, 3 mathematics, 3 science. **Freshman Admission Statistics:** 523 applied, 76% admitted, 40% enrolled. **Transfer Admission Requirements:** College transcript(s), minimum college GPA of 2.0 required. Lowest grade transferable C. **General Admission Information:** Application fee $25. Nonfall registration accepted. Credit offered for CEEB Advanced Placement tests.

COSTS AND FINANCIAL AID

Required Forms and Deadlines: FAFSA, institution's own financial aid form. Financial aid filing deadline 7/1. Priority financial aid filing date 4/1. **Notification of Awards:** Applicants will be notified of awards on a rolling basis beginning 2/1. **Types of Aid:** *Need-based scholarships/grants:* Federal Pell, SEOG, state scholarships/grants, the school's own gift aid. *Loans:* FFEL Subsidized Stafford, FFEL Unsubsidized Stafford, FFEL PLUS, state loans. **Student Employment:** Federal Work-Study Program available. Highest amount earned per year from on-campus jobs $1,000. Off-campus job opportunities are excellent. **Financial Aid Statistics:** 61% freshmen, 55% undergrads receive need-based scholarship or grant aid. 59% freshmen, 38% undergrads receive non-need-based scholarship or grant aid. 55% freshmen, 50% undergrads receive need-based self-help aid. 85% undergrads receive any aid. 54% undergrads borrow to pay for school. Average cumulative indebtedness $29,449. **Criteria for awarding institutional aid:** *Non-need-based:* Academics, leadership, music/drama, religious affiliation.

CONCORDIA UNIVERSITY—CHICAGO

7400 Augusta Street, River Forest, IL 60305-1499
Phone: 708-209-3100 **Financial Aid Phone:** 708-209-3113
E-mail: admission@cuchicago.edu **CEEB Code:** 1140
Fax: 708-209-3473 **Website:** www.cuchicago.edu **ACT Code:** 1004

This private school, affiliated with the Lutheran Church, was founded in 1864. It has a 40-acre campus.

RATINGS
Admissions Selectivity Rating: 78   **Fire Safety Rating:** 63   **Green Rating:** 60*

STUDENTS AND FACULTY
Enrollment: 1,011. **Student Body:** 62% female, 38% male, % out-of-state, (1 countries represented). Asian 1%, African American 13%, Caucasian 70%, Hispanic 9%.
Retention and Graduation: 79% freshmen return for sophomore year. 23% grads go on to further study within 1 year. **Faculty:** Student/faculty ratio 17:1. 99 full-time faculty.

ACADEMICS
Degrees: Bachelor's, master's, post-master's certificate. **Classes:** Most classes have 10–19 students. **Majors with Highest Enrollment:** Business/commerce; elementary education and teaching; kinesiology and exercise science. **Special Study Options:** Double major, exchange student program (domestic), honors program, independent study, internships, study abroad, teacher certification program. **Honors programs:** Honors Program Special programs offered to physically disabled students include note-taking services, reader services, tape recorders, tutors. **Career services:** Alumni services, career/job search classes, career assessment, internships.

FACILITIES
Housing: Coed dorms, special housing for disabled students, men's dorms, women's dorms 74% of campus accessible to physically disabled. **Special Academic Facilities/Equipment:** Art museum, zoology exhibit, human performance lab, early childhood education lab school, TV studio, weather station, radio station. **Computers:** Students can register for classes online. Administrative functions (other than registration) can be performed online.

CAMPUS LIFE
Environment: Metropolis. **Activities:** Choral groups, concert band, dance, drama/theater, jazz band, literary magazine, music ensembles, musical theater, pep band, radio station, student government, student newspaper, television sta-

tion, yearbook. **Organizations:** 15 registered organizations, 3 honor societies, 5 religious organizations. **Athletics (Intercollegiate):** *Men:* Baseball, basketball, cheerleading, cross-country, football, soccer, tennis, track/field (outdoor). *Women:* Basketball, cheerleading, cross-country, soccer, softball, tennis, track/field (outdoor), volleyball. **On-Campus Highlights:** Fitness center; soccer, football, and track stadium; library cafe, Triangle, Chapel of our Lord.

ADMISSIONS

Freshman Academic Profile: Average high school GPA 3.12. 18% in top 10% of high school class, 41% in top 25% of high school class, 67% in top 50% of high school class. ACT middle 50% range 19–26. Minimum paper TOEFL 500. Minimum computer TOEFL 173. **Basis for Candidate Selection:** *Important factors considered include:* Class rank, academic GPA, rigor of secondary school record, standardized test scores. *Other factors considered include:* Application essay, recommendation(s), character/personal qualities, extracurricular activities, interview. **Freshman Admission Requirements:** High school diploma is required and GED is accepted. *Academic units required:* 4 English, 3 mathematics, 2 science, (1 science labs), 2 social studies. *Academic units recommended:* 4 science, 2 foreign language, 1 history. **Freshman Admission Statistics:** 1,092 applied, 65% admitted, 30% enrolled. **Transfer Admission Requirements:** College transcript(s), statement of good standing from prior institution(s). Minimum college GPA of 2.0 required. Lowest grade transferable C. **General Admission Information:** Notification on a rolling basis, beginning on or about 9/4. Nonfall registration accepted. Admission may be deferred for a maximum of 1. Credit and/or placement offered for CEEB Advanced Placement tests.

COSTS AND FINANCIAL AID

Annual tuition $20,900. Room and board $6,992. Required fees $420. Average book expense $600. **Student Employment:** Federal Work-Study Program available. Institutional employment available. Highest amount earned per year from on-campus jobs $17,000. Off-campus job opportunities are good. **Financial Aid Statistics:** 81% freshmen, 77% undergrads receive any aid.

CONCORDIA UNIVERSITY—IRVINE

1530 Concordia West, Irvine, CA 92612-3299
Phone: 949-854-8002 **Financial Aid Phone:** 949-854-8002
E-mail: admission@cui.edu
Fax: 949-854-6894 **Website:** www.cui.edu **ACT Code:** 227

This private school, affiliated with the Lutheran Church, was founded in 1976. It has a 70-acre campus.

RATINGS

Admissions Selectivity Rating: 79   **Fire Safety Rating:** 82   **Green Rating:** 60*

STUDENTS AND FACULTY

Enrollment: 1,203. **Student Body:** 61% female, 39% male, 17% out-of-state, 2% international (18 countries represented). Asian 4%, African American 4%, Caucasian 68%, Hispanic 13%, Native American 1%. **Retention and Graduation:** 73% freshmen return for sophomore year. 56% freshmen graduate within 4 years. **Faculty:** Student/faculty ratio 14:1. 91 full-time faculty, 67% hold PhDs, 37% are women.

ACADEMICS

Degrees: Associate, bachelor's, master's, post-bachelor's certificate. **Classes:** Most classes have 10–19 students. **Majors with Highest Enrollment:** Business/commerce; liberal arts and sciences/liberal studies; psychology. **Special Study Options:** Accelerated program, cross-registration, distance learning, double major, dual enrollment, English as a Second Language (ESL), exchange student program (domestic), honors program, independent study, internships, liberal arts/career combination, student-designed major, study abroad, teacher certification program. **Honors programs:** General Education Honor Programs. **Combined degree programs:** BA/MA. Special programs offered to physically disabled students include tutors. **Career services highlights include:** We are proud of all the programs offered by Concordia University.

FACILITIES

Housing: Special housing for disabled students, men's dorms, women's dorms 75% of campus accessible to physically disabled. **Special Academic Facilities/ Equipment:** A high-tech educational/business/technology building, which was recently completed, also houses an art gallery. **Computers:** 60% of classrooms, 100% of dorms, 95% of libraries, 70% of dining areas, 100% of student union, 10% of common outdoor areas have wireless network access. Students can register for classes online.

CAMPUS LIFE

Environment: City. **Activities:** Choral groups, concert band, dance, drama/theater, literary magazine, music ensembles, musical theater, pep band, radio station, student government, student newspaper, student-run film society, yearbook, campus ministries. **Organizations:** 18 registered organizations, 5 honor societies, 8 religious organizations. **Athletics (Intercollegiate):** *Men:* Baseball, basketball, cross-country, golf, soccer, swimming, tennis, track/field (outdoor), water polo. *Women:* Basketball, cross-country, golf, soccer, softball, swimming, tennis, track/field (outdoor), volleyball, water polo. **On-Campus Highlights:** Gym, Student Life Center (lounge and computer resource), library, CU Center (Worship Center), Student Union (cafeteria).

ADMISSIONS

Freshman Academic Profile: Average high school GPA 3.51. 20% in top 10% of high school class, 54% in top 25% of high school class, 84% in top 50% of high school class. SAT Math middle 50% range 450–570. SAT Critical Reading middle 50% range 450–570. ACT middle 50% range 20–24. Minimum paper TOEFL 550. Minimum computer TOEFL 213. **Basis for Candidate Selection:** *Very important factors considered include:* Class rank, academic GPA, rigor of secondary school record, standardized test scores, character/personal qualities. *Important factors considered include:* Recommendation(s), religious affiliation/commitment. *Other factors considered include:* Application essay, alumni/ae relation, extracurricular activities, interview, level of applicant's interest, racial/ethnic status, talent/ability, volunteer work, work experience. **Freshman Admission Requirements:** High school diploma is required and GED is accepted. *Academic units required:* 4 English, 3 mathematics, 3 science, 2 foreign language, 2 social studies. **Freshman Admission Statistics:** 827 applied, 67% admitted, 41% enrolled. **Transfer Admission Requirements:** High school transcript, college transcript(s), statement of good standing from prior institution(s). Minimum college GPA of 2.3 required. Lowest grade transferable D. **General Admission Information:** Application fee $50. Nonfall registration accepted. Admission may be deferred for a maximum of 1 year. Credit and/or placement offered for CEEB Advanced Placement tests.

COSTS AND FINANCIAL AID

Annual tuition $23,400. Room and board $7,650. Required fees $300. **Required Forms and Deadlines:** FAFSA, institution's own financial aid form, state aid form, State aid form: GPA Verification Form. Financial aid filing deadline 4/1. Priority financial aid filing date 3/2. **Notification of Awards:** Applicants will be notified of awards on a rolling basis beginning 2/1. **Types of Aid:** *Need-based scholarships/grants:* Federal Pell, SEOG, state scholarships/grants, private scholarships, the school's own gift aid. *Loans:* FFEL Subsidized Stafford, FFEL Unsubsidized Stafford, FFEL PLUS. **Student Employment:** Highest amount earned per year from on-campus jobs $2,000. Off-campus job opportunities are good. **Financial Aid Statistics:** 69% freshmen, 61% undergrads receive need-based scholarship or grant aid. 13% freshmen, 9% undergrads receive non-need-based scholarship or grant aid. 51% freshmen, 50% undergrads receive need-based self-help aid. 10% freshmen, 7% undergrads receive athletic scholarships. 74.09% freshmen, 71.46% undergrads receive any aid. 67.19% undergrads borrow to pay for school. Average cumulative indebtedness $20,254. **Criteria for awarding institutional aid:** *Non-need-based:* Academics, art, athletics, leadership, music/drama, religious affiliation.

CONCORDIA UNIVERSITY—NEBRASKA

800 North Columbia Avenue, Seward, NE 68434-1556
Phone: 800-535-5494 **Financial Aid Phone:** 800 535-5494
E-mail: admiss@cune.edu **CEEB Code:** 6116
Fax: 402-643-4073 **Website:** www.cune.edu **ACT Code:** 2442

This private school, affiliated with the Lutheran Church, was founded in 1894. It has a 120-acre campus.

RATINGS

Admissions Selectivity Rating: 82   **Fire Safety Rating:** 65   **Green Rating:** 63

STUDENTS AND FACULTY

Enrollment: 1,076. **Student Body:** 52% female, 48% male, 59% out-of-state, international (5 countries represented). Asian 1%, African American 2%, Caucasian 88%, Hispanic 1%. **Retention and Graduation:** 81% freshmen return for sophomore year. 41% freshmen graduate within 4 years. 27% grads go on to further study within 1 year. 13% grads pursue arts and sciences degrees. 2% grads pursue law degrees. 2% grads pursue business degrees. 5% grads pursue medical degrees. **Faculty:** Student/faculty ratio 14:1. 58 full-time faculty, 69% hold PhDs, 2% are members of minority groups, 31% are women.

ACADEMICS

Degrees: Bachelor's, master's, post-bachelor's certificate. **Classes:** Most classes have 20–29 students. Most lab/discussion sessions have 10–19 students. **Majors with Highest Enrollment:** Biology/biological sciences; business/commerce; education. **Special Study Options:** Accelerated program, distance learning, double major, dual enrollment, English as a Second Language (ESL), exchange student program (domestic), independent study, internships, study abroad, teacher certification program, undergradate students may take graduate level classes. Special programs offered to physically disabled students include note-taking services, reader services, tape recorders, tutors. **Career services:** Alumni network, alumni services, career/job search classes, career assessment, internships, regional alumni. **Career services highlights include:** Intentional "4 year plan" to serve students prior to graduation.

FACILITIES

Housing: Special housing for disabled students, men's dorms, women's dorms, apartments for married students, apartments for single students 60% of campus accessible to physically disabled. **Special Academic Facilities/Equipment:** Art gallery, Bartels rock museum, observatory, arboretum. **Computers:** 40% of classrooms, 100% of dorms, 100% of libraries, 100% of student union, have wireless network access. Students can register for classes online. Administrative functions (other than registration) can be performed online.

CAMPUS LIFE

Environment: Village. **Activities:** Choral groups, concert band, dance, drama/theater, jazz band, literary magazine, music ensembles, musical theater, pep band, student government, student newspaper, symphony orchestra, yearbook, campus ministries. **Organizations:** 33 registered organizations, 1 honor societies, 5 religious organizations. **Athletics (Intercollegiate):** *Men:* Baseball, basketball, cross-country, football, golf, soccer, tennis, track/field (outdoor), track/field (indoor), wrestling. *Women:* Basketball, cross-country, golf, soccer, softball, tennis, track/field (outdoor), track/field (indoor), volleyball. **On-Campus Highlights:** Student Center / Game Room, Coffee Shop, Marxhausen Art Gallery, Osten Observatory, Physical Education Building. **Environmental Initiatives:** The committee is charged with outlining short-term and long-term plans that will render the university carbon neutral as soon as is feasible and to report progress periodically. Specific plans have not yet been formulated. Purchasing Energy Star equipment. Incorporating sustainability in new construction and renovation projects.

ADMISSIONS

Freshman Academic Profile: Average high school GPA 3.49. 22% in top 10% of high school class, 45% in top 25% of high school class, 74% in top 50% of high school class. SAT Math middle 50% range 460–570. SAT Critical Reading middle 50% range 440–590. ACT middle 50% range 21–27. Minimum paper TOEFL 500. Minimum computer TOEFL 173. **Basis for Candidate Selection:** *Very important factors considered include:* Academic GPA, standardized test scores. *Important factors considered include:* Class rank, rigor of secondary school record, character/personal qualities. *Other factors considered include:* Recommendation(s), alumni/ae relation, extracurricular activities, interview, religious affiliation/commitment. **Freshman Admission Requirements:** High school diploma is required and GED is accepted. *Academic units recommended:* 4 English, 3 mathematics, 2 science, 1 foreign language, 3 social studies, 3 One unit in music, art, physical education. **Freshman Admission Statistics:** 1,224 applied, 68% admitted, 33% enrolled. **Transfer Admission Requirements:** High school transcript, college transcript(s), minimum college GPA of 2.0 required. Lowest grade transferable D. **General Admission Information:** Regular application deadline 8/1. Notification on a rolling basis, beginning on or about 9/1. Nonfall registration accepted. Admission may be deferred for a maximum of 1 year. Credit and/or placement offered for CEEB Advanced Placement tests.

COSTS AND FINANCIAL AID

Annual tuition $21,100. Room and board $5,520. Required fees $150. Average book expense $750. **Required Forms and Deadlines:** FAFSA. Priority financial aid filing date 3/1. **Notification of Awards:** Applicants will be notified of awards on a rolling basis beginning 3/1. **Types of Aid:** *Need-based scholarships/grants:* Federal Pell, SEOG, state scholarships/grants, private scholarships, the school's own gift aid. *Loans:* FFEL Subsidized Stafford, FFEL Unsubsidized Stafford, FFEL PLUS, Federal Perkins. **Student Employment:** Federal Work-Study Program available. Institutional employment available. Highest amount earned per year from on-campus jobs $3,500. Off-campus job opportunities are good. **Financial Aid Statistics:** 76% freshmen, 76% undergrads receive need-based scholarship or grant aid. 13% freshmen, 11% undergrads receive non-need-based scholarship or grant aid. 55% freshmen, 57% undergrads receive need-based self-help aid. 12% freshmen, 9% undergrads receive athletic scholarships. 99% freshmen, 99% undergrads receive any aid. 76% undergrads borrow to pay for school. Average cumulative indebtedness $20,393. **Criteria for awarding institutional aid:** *Non-need-based:* Academics, alumni affiliation, art, athletics, leadership, music/drama, religious affiliation.

CONCORDIA UNIVERSITY—PORTLAND

2811 NE Holman St, Portland, OR 97211-6099
Phone: 503-280-8501 **Financial Aid Phone:** 800-321-9371
E-mail: admissions@cu-portland.edu **CEEB Code:** 4078
Fax: 503-280-8531 **Website:** www.cu-portland.edu **ACT Code:** 3458

This private school, affiliated with the Lutheran Church, was founded in 1905. It has a 12-acre campus.

RATINGS

Admissions Selectivity Rating: 84   **Fire Safety Rating:** 60*   **Green Rating:** 60*

STUDENTS AND FACULTY

Enrollment: 1,073. **Student Body:** 64% female, 36% male, 41% out-of-state, 1% international . Asian 6%, African American 7%, Caucasian 65%, Hispanic 6%, Native American 1%.
Retention and Graduation: 74% freshmen return for sophomore year.
Faculty: Student/faculty ratio 18:1. 52 full-time faculty, 67% hold PhDs, 4% are members of minority groups, 48% are women.

ACADEMICS

Degrees: Bachelor's, certificate, master's, post-bachelor's certificate, terminal associate. **Classes:** Most classes have 10–19 students. **Special Study Options:** Accelerated program, cross-registration, distance learning, dual enrollment, English as a Second Language (ESL), honors program, independent study, internships, study abroad, teacher certification program. **Honors programs:** Honors program features limited enrollment to 25 students create greater intellectual opportunity. **Career services:** Alumni services, career assessment, internships, regional alumni. **Career services highlights include:** Concordia Committment offers students who complete the 4-year program partial tuition reimbursement if they are not employed in the field of their choice 6 months after graduation.

FACILITIES

Housing: Coed dorms, apartments for single students. **Computers:** Administrative functions (other than registration) can be performed online.

CAMPUS LIFE

Environment: Metropolis. **Activities:** Choral groups, drama/theater, literary magazine, music ensembles, student government, student newspaper, campus ministries, international student organization. **Organizations:** 10 registered organizations, 2 honor societies, 1 religious organizations. **Athletics (Intercollegiate):** *Men:* Baseball, basketball, cross-country, golf, soccer, track/field (outdoor), track/field (indoor). *Women:* Basketball, cross-country, golf, soccer, softball, track/field (outdoor), track/field (indoor), volleyball.

ADMISSIONS

Freshman Academic Profile: Average high school GPA 3.4. 19% in top 10% of high school class, 45% in top 25% of high school class, 76% in top 50% of high school class. SAT Math middle 50% range 460–560. SAT Critical Reading middle 50% range 450–570. ACT middle 50% range 18–24. Minimum paper TOEFL 500. **Basis for Candidate Selection:** *Very important factors considered include:* Recommendation(s), rigor of secondary school record, standardized test scores. *Other factors considered include:* Class rank, application essay, academic GPA, character/personal qualities, interview. **Freshman Admission Requirements:** High school diploma is required and GED is accepted. *Academic units recommended:* 4 English, 3 mathematics, 3 science, 2 foreign language, 3 social studies, 3 academic electives, 1 computer/keyboard. **Freshman Admission Statistics:** 1,002 applied, 59% admitted, 32% enrolled. **Transfer Admission Requirements:** College transcript(s), statement of good standing from prior institution(s). Minimum college GPA of 2.0 required. Lowest grade transferable D. **General Admission Information:** Application fee $20. Regular application deadline 7/1. Notification on a rolling basis, beginning on or about 1/1. Nonfall registration accepted. Admission may be deferred for a maximum of 1.

COSTS AND FINANCIAL AID

Annual tuition $20,900. Room and board $6,270. Required fees $210. Average book expense $800. **Required Forms and Deadlines:** FAFSA. **Notification of Awards:** Applicants will be notified of awards on a rolling basis beginning 3/15. **Types of Aid:** *Need-based scholarships/grants:* Federal Pell, SEOG, state scholarships/grants, the school's own gift aid. *Loans:* FFEL Subsidized Stafford, FFEL Unsubsidized Stafford, FFEL PLUS, Federal Perkins. **Student Employment:** Federal Work-Study Program available. Institutional employment available. Off-campus job opportunities are good. **Financial Aid Statistics:** 66% freshmen, 63% undergrads receive need-based scholarship or grant aid. 73% freshmen, 69% undergrads receive non-need-based scholarship or grant aid. 62% freshmen, 61% undergrads receive need-based self-help aid. 28% freshmen, 27% undergrads receive athletic scholarships. 95% freshmen receive any aid. 78% undergrads borrow to pay for school. Average cumulative indebtedness $23,966. **Criteria for awarding institutional aid:** *Non-need-based:* Academics, athletics, leadership, music/drama, religious affiliation.

CONCORDIA UNIVERSITY—ST. PAUL

275 Syndicate Street N, Saint Paul, MN 55104-5494
Phone: 651-641-8230 **Financial Aid Phone:** 651-603-6300
E-mail: admission@csp.edu **CEEB Code:** 6114
Fax: 651-603-6320 **ACT Code:** 2106

This private school, affiliated with the Lutheran Church, was founded in 1893. It has a 37-acre campus.

RATINGS
Admissions Selectivity Rating: 73   **Fire Safety Rating:** 60*   **Green Rating:** 73

STUDENTS AND FACULTY
Enrollment: 1,471. **Student Body:** 57% female, 43% male, 18% out-of-state, international (4 countries represented). Asian 7%, African American 10%, Caucasian 56%, Hispanic 2%, Native American 1%.
Retention and Graduation: 72% freshmen return for sophomore year. 35% freshmen graduate within 4 years. **Faculty:** Student/faculty ratio 17:1. 70 full-time faculty, 67% hold PhDs, 7% are members of minority groups, 50% are women.

ACADEMICS
Degrees: Associate, bachelor's, certificate, master's, post-bachelor's certificate. **Classes:** Most classes have 10–19 students. **Special Study Options:** Accelerated program, cross-registration, distance learning, double major, dual enrollment, exchange student program (domestic), honors program, independent study, internships, student-designed major, study abroad, teacher certification program. Special programs offered to physically disabled students include note-taking services, reader services, tape recorders, tutors. **Career services:** Career assessment, internships.

FACILITIES
Housing: Coed dorms, men's dorms, women's dorms, apartments for married students, apartments for single students. 75% of campus accessible to physically disabled. **Computers:** Students can register for classes online. Administrative functions (other than registration) can be performed online.

CAMPUS LIFE
Environment: Metropolis. **Activities:** Choral groups, concert band, drama/theater, jazz band, music ensembles, musical theater, student government, student newspaper, television station, campus ministries. **Organizations:** Athletics (Intercollegiate): *Men:* Baseball, basketball, cross-country, football, golf, track/field (outdoor), track/field (indoor). *Women:* Basketball, cross-country, golf, soccer, softball, track/field (outdoor), track/field (indoor), volleyball. **On-Campus Highlights:** Residence Life Center, Library Technology Center, Graebner Memorial Chapel, Gangelhoff Athletic Center, Pearson Theater.

ADMISSIONS
Freshman Academic Profile: Average high school GPA 3.06. 6% in top 10% of high school class, 24% in top 25% of high school class, 56% in top 50% of high school class. 85% from public high schools. ACT middle 50% range 18–24. Minimum paper TOEFL 500. Minimum computer TOEFL 173. **Basis for Candidate Selection:** *Very important factors considered include:* Academic GPA, recommendation(s), standardized test scores. *Important factors considered include:* Rigor of secondary school record, character/personal qualities, talent/ability. *Other factors considered include:* Application essay, extracurricular activities, level of applicant's interest. **Freshman Admission Requirements:** High school diploma is required and GED is accepted. *Academic units required:* 4 English, 2 mathematics, 2 science, (2 science labs), 1 social studies, 1 history, 3 2 fine arts and 1 health/P.E. *Academic units recommended:* 1 foreign language. **Freshman Admission Statistics:** 1,106 applied, 56% admitted, 30% enrolled. **Transfer Admission Requirements:** College transcript(s), statement of good standing from prior institution(s). Minimum college GPA of 2.0 required. Lowest grade transferable D. **General Admission Information:** Application fee $30. Regular application deadline 8/1. Nonfall registration accepted. Admission may be deferred for a maximum of 1 year. Credit and/or placement offered for CEEB Advanced Placement tests.

COSTS AND FINANCIAL AID
Annual tuition $27,400. Room and board $7,500. Average book expense $740. **Required Forms and Deadlines:** FAFSA, institution's own financial aid form. Priority financial aid filing date 5/1. **Notification of Awards:** Applicants will be notified of awards on a rolling basis beginning 3/15. **Types of Aid:** *Need-based scholarships/grants:* Federal Pell, SEOG, state scholarships/grants, private scholarships, the school's own gift aid. *Loans:* FFEL Subsidized Stafford, FFEL

Unsubsidized Stafford, FFEL PLUS, Federal Perkins, state loans. **Student Employment:** Federal Work-Study Program available. Institutional employment available. Off-campus job opportunities are fair. **Financial Aid Statistics:** 88% freshmen, 61% undergrads receive need-based scholarship or grant aid. 74% freshmen, 60% undergrads receive need-based self-help aid. 3% freshmen, 3% undergrads receive athletic scholarships. 99% freshmen receive any aid. 85% undergrads borrow to pay for school. Average cumulative indebtedness $32,444. **Criteria for awarding institutional aid:** *Non-need-based:* Academics, art, athletics, minority status, music/drama, religious affiliation.

CONCORDIA UNIVERSITY—WISCONSIN

12800 North Lake Shore Drive, Mequon, WI 53097
Phone: 262-243-5700 **Financial Aid Phone:** 262-243-4392
E-mail: admissions@cuw.edu **CEEB Code:** 1139
Fax: 262-243-4545 **Website:** www.cuw.edu **ACT Code:** 4574

This private school, affiliated with the Lutheran Church, was founded in 1881. It has a 192-acre campus.

RATINGS
Admissions Selectivity Rating: 75   **Fire Safety Rating:** 60*   **Green Rating:** 60*

STUDENTS AND FACULTY
Enrollment: 3,790. **Student Body:** 65% female, 35% male, 27% out-of-state, 1% international (23 countries represented). Asian 1%, African American 14%, Caucasian 59%, Hispanic 2%, Native American 1%.
Retention and Graduation: 83% freshmen return for sophomore year. 29% grads go on to further study within 1 year. **Faculty:** Student/faculty ratio 12:1. 109 full-time faculty, 68% hold PhDs, 4% are members of minority groups, 45% are women.

ACADEMICS
Degrees: Associate, bachelor's, certificate, master's, post-bachelor's certificate. **Classes:** Most classes have 10–19 students. Most lab/discussion sessions have 10–19 students. **Majors with Highest Enrollment:** Business/commerce; education; health services/allied health/health sciences. **Special Study Options:** Accelerated program, cross-registration, distance learning, double major, dual enrollment, English as a Second Language (ESL), exchange student program (domestic), independent study, internships, liberal arts/career combination, student-designed major, study abroad, teacher certification program, CUW offers cooperative programs with Cardinal Stritch University, Marquette University, Milwaukee Institute of Art and Design, and Alverno College. **Combined degree programs:** 2-2 interior design program. Special programs offered to physically disabled students include note-taking services, reader services, tape recorders, tutors. **Career services:** Alumni network, alumni services, career/job search classes, career assessment, internships, regional alumni.

FACILITIES
Housing: Men's dorms, women's dorms.

CAMPUS LIFE
Environment: Village. **Activities:** Choral groups, concert band, dance, drama/theater, jazz band, music ensembles, musical theater, pep band, radio station, student government, student newspaper, campus ministries, international student organization. **Organizations: Athletics (Intercollegiate):** *Men:* Baseball, basketball, cross-country, football, ice hockey, soccer, tennis, track/field (outdoor), volleyball, wrestling. *Women:* Basketball, cross-country, ice hockey, soccer, softball, tennis, track/field (outdoor), volleyball. **On-Campus Highlights:** Coberg Residence Hall—new, Sports and Fitness Center, Field House. **Environmental Initiatives:** Construction of environmental education center with LEED status.

ADMISSIONS
Freshman Academic Profile: Average high school GPA 3.36. 15% in top 10% of high school class, 23% in top 25% of high school class, 71% in top 50% of high school class. ACT middle 50% range 19–25. Minimum paper TOEFL 500. Minimum computer TOEFL 173. **Basis for Candidate Selection:** *Very important factors considered include:* Application essay, academic GPA, rigor of secondary school record. *Important factors considered include:* Character/personal qualities, work experience. *Other factors considered include:* Class rank, recommendation(s), standardized test scores, alumni/ae relation, extracurricular activities, interview, racial/ethnic status, religious affiliation/commitment, state residency, talent/ability, volunteer work. **Freshman Admission Requirements:** High school diploma is required and GED is accepted. *Academic units required:* 3 English, 2 mathematics, 2 science, 2 social studies, 5 academic electives. *Academic units recommended:* 4 English, 3 mathematics, 2 foreign language, 5 academic electives. **Freshman Admission Statistics:** 2,538 applied,

64% admitted, 29% enrolled. **Transfer Admission Requirements:** College transcript(s), statement of good standing from prior institution(s). Minimum college GPA of 2.0 required. Lowest grade transferable C. **General Admission Information:** Application fee $35. Regular application deadline 8/15. Notification on a rolling basis, beginning on or about 10/15. Nonfall registration accepted.

COSTS AND FINANCIAL AID
Annual tuition $20,900. Room and board $7,990. Required fees $90. Average book expense $1,212. **Required Forms and Deadlines:** FAFSA. Priority financial aid filing date 4/1. **Notification of Awards:** Applicants will be notified of awards on a rolling basis beginning 2/1. **Types of Aid:** *Need-based scholarships/grants:* Federal Pell, SEOG, state scholarships/grants, private scholarships, the school's own gift aid. *Loans:* Direct Subsidized Stafford, Direct Unsubsidized Stafford, Direct PLUS. **Student Employment:** Off-campus job opportunities are excellent. **Financial Aid Statistics:** 77% freshmen, 74% undergrads receive need-based scholarship or grant aid. 25% freshmen, 21% undergrads receive non-need-based scholarship or grant aid. 77% freshmen, 74% undergrads receive need-based self-help aid. 95% freshmen receive any aid. 75% undergrads borrow to pay for school. Average cumulative indebtedness $25,179.

CONNECTICUT COLLEGE

270 Mohegan Avenue, New London, CT 06320
Phone: 860-439-2200 **Financial Aid Phone:** 860-439-2058
E-mail: admission@conncoll.edu **CEEB Code:** 3284
Fax: 860-439-4301 **Website:** www.conncoll.edu **ACT Code:** 556

This private school was founded in 1911. It has a 750-acre campus.

RATINGS
Admissions Selectivity Rating: 95   **Fire Safety Rating:** 78   **Green Rating:** 83

STUDENTS AND FACULTY
Enrollment: 1,777. **Student Body:** 61% female, 39% male, 85% out-of-state, 4% international (74 countries represented). Asian 5%, African American 4%, Caucasian 75%, Hispanic 6%.
Retention and Graduation: 90% freshmen return for sophomore year. 83% freshmen graduate within 4 years. 25% grads go on to further study within 1 year. **Faculty:** Student/faculty ratio 9:1. 177 full-time faculty, 91% hold PhDs, 23% are members of minority groups, 46% are women.

ACADEMICS
Degrees: Bachelor's, master's. **Classes:** Most classes have 10–19 students. Most lab/discussion sessions have 10–19 students. **Majors with Highest Enrollment:** Economics; English language and literature; political science and government. **Special Study Options:** Cross-registration, double major, exchange student program (domestic), independent study, internships, student-designed major, study abroad, teacher certification program, cross-registration with the U.S. Coast Guard Academy, Trinity College, and Wesleyan University; 3-2 Program with Washington University or Boston University for a five-year BA/BS degree; Exchange Student Program; 12 exchanges. **Combined degree programs:** BA/MA. Special programs offered to physically disabled students include note-taking services, reader services, tape recorders, tutors. **Career services:** Alumni network, alumni services, career/job search classes, career assessment, internships, regional alumni. **Career services highlights include:** Our Career-Enhancing Life Skills (CELS) office administers a program that facilitates college-funded internships for students who complete a series of preparatory seminars and workshops.

FACILITIES
Housing: Coed dorms, special housing for disabled students, wellness housing, theme housing, thematic housing (environmentalism, foreign language, substance-free housing, etc.), men's floors, women's floors; living and learning arrangements. **Special Academic Facilities/Equipment:** Children's Program used as "lab school" for human development program, language lab, 750–acre arboretum, botanic garden, greenhouse, environment control labs, transmission and scanning electron microscope, ion accelerator, GIS lab, refracting telescope, observatory. **Computers:** 75% of classrooms, 100% of dorms, 100% of libraries, 100% of dining areas, 100% of student union, 70% of common outdoor areas have wireless network access. Students can register for classes online. Administrative functions (other than registration) can be performed online.

CAMPUS LIFE
Environment: Town. **Activities:** Choral groups, concert band, dance, drama/theater, jazz band, literary magazine, music ensembles, radio station, student government, student newspaper, student-run film society, symphony orchestra, yearbook, campus ministries, international student organization. **Organizations:** 60 registered organizations, 5 honor societies, 6 religious organizations. **Athletics (Intercollegiate):** *Men:* Basketball, crew/rowing, cross-country, diving, ice hockey, lacrosse, sailing, soccer, squash, swimming, tennis, track/field (outdoor), track/field (indoor), water polo. *Women:* Basketball, crew/rowing, cross-country, diving, field hockey, ice hockey, lacrosse, sailing, soccer, squash, swimming, tennis, track/field (outdoor), track/field (indoor), volleyball, water polo. **On-Campus Highlights:** College Center (Crozier-Williams), Connecticut College Arboretum, Blue Camel Cafe (in library), Athletics Center, Coffee Grounds. **Environmental Initiatives:** Signatory of the American College and University President's Climate Commitment; signatory of the Talloires Declaration; U.S. Environmental Protection Agency green power partner.

ADMISSIONS
Freshman Academic Profile: 56% in top 10% of high school class, 93% in top 25% of high school class, 100% in top 50% of high school class. 55% from public high schools. SAT Math middle 50% range 610–690. SAT Critical Reading middle 50% range 610–700. SAT Writing middle 50% range 620–710. ACT middle 50% range 25–30. Minimum paper TOEFL 600. Minimum computer TOEFL 250. Minimum web-based TOEFL 100. **Basis for Candidate Selection:** *Very important factors considered include:* Class rank, academic GPA, rigor of secondary school record, character/personal qualities. *Important factors considered include:* Application essay, recommendation(s), extracurricular activities, interview, racial/ethnic status, talent/ability, volunteer work, work experience. *Other factors considered include:* Standardized test scores, alumni/ae relation, first generation, geographical residence, level of applicant's interest, religious affiliation/commitment, state residency. **Freshman Admission Requirements:** High school diploma is required and GED is accepted. **Freshman Admission Statistics:** 4,733 applied, 37% admitted, 29% enrolled. **Transfer Admission Requirements:** High school transcript, college transcript(s), essay or personal statement, statement of good standing from prior institution(s). Lowest grade transferable C. **General Admission Information:** Application fee $60. Early decision application deadline 11/15. Regular application deadline 1/1. Regular notification 3/31. Nonfall registration not accepted. Admission may be deferred for a maximum of 1 year. Credit and/or placement offered for CEEB Advanced Placement tests.

COSTS AND FINANCIAL AID
Average book expense $1,000. **Required Forms and Deadlines:** FAFSA, CSS/Financial Aid PROFILE, noncustodial PROFILE, business/farm supplement. Federal tax returns; personal, partnership, and Federal W2 statements. Financial aid filing deadline 2/1. **Notification of Awards:** Applicants will be notified of awards on or about 4/1. **Types of Aid:** *Need-based scholarships/grants:* Federal Pell, SEOG, state scholarships/grants, the school's own gift aid. *Loans:* Direct Subsidized Stafford, Direct Unsubsidized Stafford, Direct PLUS, FFEL Subsidized Stafford, FFEL Unsubsidized Stafford, FFEL PLUS, Federal Perkins. **Student Employment:** Federal Work-Study Program available. Institutional employment available. Off-campus job opportunities are good. **Financial Aid Statistics:** 43% freshmen, 42% undergrads receive need-based scholarship or grant aid. 42% freshmen, 41% undergrads receive need-based self-help aid. 41% freshmen receive any aid. 34% undergrads borrow to pay for school. Average cumulative indebtedness $22,038.

See page 1064.

CONVERSE COLLEGE

580 East Main Street, Spartanburg, SC 29302
Phone: 864-596-9040 **Financial Aid Phone:** 864-596-9019
E-mail: admissions@converse.edu **CEEB Code:** 5121
Fax: 864-596-9225 **ACT Code:** 3852

This private school was founded in 1889. It has a 70-acre campus.

RATINGS
Admissions Selectivity Rating: 89   **Fire Safety Rating:** 60*   **Green Rating:** 71

STUDENTS AND FACULTY
Enrollment: 746. **Student Body:** 100% female, 28% out-of-state, 4% international . Asian 1%, African American 12%, Caucasian 74%, Hispanic 2%.
Retention and Graduation: 79% freshmen return for sophomore year. 53% freshmen graduate within 4 years. 20% grads go on to further study within 1 year. 12% grads pursue arts and sciences degrees. 2% grads pursue law degrees.

4% grads pursue business degrees. 2% grads pursue medical degrees. **Faculty:** Student/faculty ratio 11:1. 84 full-time faculty, 89% hold PhDs, 6% are members of minority groups, 46% are women.

ACADEMICS

Degrees: Bachelor's, master's, post-master's certificate. **Classes:** Most classes have fewer than 10 students. Most lab/discussion sessions have fewer than 10 students. **Majors with Highest Enrollment:** Business/commerce; education; psychology. **Special Study Options:** Cross-registration, double major, English as a Second Language (ESL), honors program, independent study, internships, liberal arts/career combination, student-designed major, study abroad, teacher certification program, undergrads may take grad level classes. **Honors programs:** Nisbet Honors Program. Special programs offered to physically disabled students include note-taking services, tape recorders, tutors. **Career services:** Alumni network, alumni services, career/job search classes, career assessment, internships, regional alumni. **Career services highlights include:** Every undergraduate student at Converse is guaranteed an internship.

FACILITIES

Housing: Women's dorms. **Special Academic Facilities/Equipment:** Language lab, Phifer Science Building, Blackman Auditorium (Music), DNA sequencer and lab. **Computers:** Students can register for classes online. Administrative functions (other than registration) can be performed online.

CAMPUS LIFE

Environment: City. **Activities:** Choral groups, concert band, dance, drama/ theater, literary magazine, music ensembles, musical theater, opera, student government, student newspaper, symphony orchestra, yearbook. **Organizations:** 60 registered organizations, 16 honor societies, 7 religious organizations. **Athletics (Intercollegiate):** *Women:* Basketball, cross-country, lacrosse, soccer, swimming, tennis, volleyball. **On-Campus Highlights:** Montgomery Student Life Center, Weisiger Physical Activity Complex, Phifer Science Complex, Petrie School of Music—Twichell Auditorium, outdoor quad area for studying and relaxing. **Environmental Initiatives:** LEED-certified new construction; sustainable foodstuffs bought and used by Dining Services; student environmental group—WISE.

ADMISSIONS

Freshman Academic Profile: Average high school GPA 3.91. 22% in top 10% of high school class, 60% in top 25% of high school class, 91% in top 50% of high school class. 80% from public high schools. SAT Math middle 50% range 480–590. SAT Critical Reading middle 50% range 510–610. SAT Writing middle 50% range 480–580. ACT middle 50% range 20–26. Minimum paper TOEFL 550. Minimum computer TOEFL 213. Minimum web-based TOEFL 79. **Basis for Candidate Selection:** *Very important factors considered include:* Academic GPA, rigor of secondary school record. *Important factors considered include:* Class rank, application essay, recommendation(s), standardized test scores, character/personal qualities, extracurricular activities, talent/ability. *Other factors considered include:* Alumni/ae relation, first generation, interview, level of applicant's interest, racial/ethnic status, volunteer work, work experience. **Freshman Admission Requirements:** High school diploma is required and GED is accepted. *Academic units recommended:* 4 English, 3 mathematics, 2 science, (2 science labs), 2 foreign language, 1 social studies, 1 history. **Freshman Admission Statistics:** 1,299 applied, 57% admitted, 20% enrolled. **Transfer Admission Requirements:** College transcript(s), statement of good standing from prior institution(s). Minimum college GPA of 2.0 required. Lowest grade transferable C. **General Admission Information:** Notification on a rolling basis, beginning on or about 10/1. Nonfall registration accepted. Admission may be deferred for a maximum of 1 year. Credit offered for CEEB Advanced Placement tests.

COSTS AND FINANCIAL AID

Annual tuition $24,500. Room and board $7,550. Average book expense $850. **Required Forms and Deadlines:** FAFSA. **Notification of Awards:** Applicants will be notified of awards on a rolling basis beginning 3/1. **Types of Aid:** *Need-based scholarships/grants:* Federal Pell, SEOG, state scholarships/grants, private scholarships, the school's own gift aid. *Loans:* FFEL Subsidized Stafford, FFEL Unsubsidized Stafford, FFEL PLUS, Federal Perkins, state loans. **Student Employment:** Federal Work-Study Program available. Institutional employment available. Off-campus job opportunities are good. **Financial Aid Statistics:** 69% freshmen, 68% undergrads receive need-based scholarship or grant aid. 22% freshmen, 20% undergrads receive non-need-based scholarship or grant aid. 45% freshmen, 43% undergrads receive need-based self-help aid. 5% freshmen, 5% undergrads receive athletic scholarships. 95% freshmen, 93% undergrads receive any aid. 71.5% undergrads borrow to pay for school. Average cumulative indebtedness $20,861. **Criteria for awarding institutional aid:** *Non-need-based:* Academics, alumni affiliation, art, athletics, leadership, music/drama, state/district residency.

THE COOPER UNION FOR THE ADVANCEMENT OF SCIENCE AND ART

30 Cooper Square, Office of Admiss, New York, NY 10003
Phone: 212-353-4120 **Financial Aid Phone:** 212-353-4130
E-mail: admissions@cooper.edu **CEEB Code:** 2097
Fax: 212-353-4342 **Website:** www.cooper.edu **ACT Code:** 2724

This private school was founded in 1859.

RATINGS
Admissions Selectivity Rating: 99   **Fire Safety Rating:** 97   **Green Rating:** 79

STUDENTS AND FACULTY
Enrollment: 880. **Student Body:** 38% female, 63% male, 40% out-of-state, 15% international . Asian 19%, African American 5%, Caucasian 39%, Hispanic 8%, Native American 1%.
Retention and Graduation: 94% freshmen return for sophomore year. 75% freshmen graduate within 4 years. 60% grads go on to further study within 1 year. 15% grads pursue arts and sciences degrees. 6% grads pursue law degrees. 10% grads pursue business degrees. 3% grads pursue medical degrees. **Faculty:** Student/faculty ratio 8.7:1. 55 full-time faculty, 87% hold PhDs, 13% are members of minority groups, 25% are women.

ACADEMICS
Degrees: Bachelor's, certificate, master's. **Classes:** Most classes have 10–19 students. Most lab/discussion sessions have greater than 100 students. **Majors with Highest Enrollment:** Electrical, electronics and communications engineering; fine arts and art studies, other; mechanical engineering. **Special Study Options:** Cross-registration, exchange student program (domestic), independent study, internships, student-designed major, study abroad, Cooper Union is indeed an all-honors college. Research opportunities available. Students may take up to one year off during their studies with us to pursue other interests. **Honors programs:** Cooper Union is an all-honors college. **Combined degree programs:** MEng/MD. Special programs offered to physically disabled students include reader services, tape recorders, tutors. **Career services:** Alumni network, alumni services, career/job search classes, career assessment, internships, regional alumni. **Career services highlights include:** The Cooper Union Professional Internship Program provides funding for students to learn through an internship that normally doesn't pay.

FACILITIES
Housing: Coed dorms. 75% of campus accessible to physically disabled. **Special Academic Facilities/Equipment:** The Great Hall; Houghton Gallery; The Brooks Lab, Prototyping Lab, Bio-Medical Engineering Lab, Tissue Engineering Lab, Center for Sustainable Design, Center for Infrastructure and Urban Systems, Center for Signal Processing Communications and Computer Engineering Research. **Computers:** 85% of classrooms, have wireless network access. Administrative functions (other than registration) can be performed online.

CAMPUS LIFE
Environment: Metropolis. **Activities:** Choral groups, concert band, dance, drama/theater, jazz band, literary magazine, music ensembles, student government, student newspaper, student-run film society, symphony orchestra, yearbook. **Organizations:** 90 registered organizations, 18 honor societies, 8 religious organizations. 2 fraternities, 1 sorority. **Athletics (Intercollegiate):** *Men:* Baseball, basketball, cross-country, soccer, tennis, volleyball. *Women:* Basketball, cross-country, soccer, tennis, volleyball. **On-Campus Highlights:** Great Hall, 41 Cooper Square, Foundation Building, Houghton Gallery, 41 Cooper Square Gallery, 41 Cooper Square—our newest building, opened in September of 2009 to critical acclaim. Designed by Pritzker Prize winning architect, Thom Mayne, this building has many green features and is targeted to earn Platinum LEED certification. **Environmental Initiatives:** New academic building. Please see: www.cooper.edu/cubuilds/index.html and www.cooper.edu/cubuilds/green.html for more information.

ADMISSIONS
Freshman Academic Profile: Average high school GPA 3.6. 93% in top 10% of high school class, 98% in top 25% of high school class, 99% in top 50% of high school class. 65% from public high schools. SAT Math middle 50% range 600–770. SAT Critical Reading middle 50% range 590–710. SAT Writing middle 50% range 600–770. ACT middle 50% range 29–33. Minimum paper TOEFL 600. Minimum computer TOEFL 250. Minimum web-based TOEFL 100.

Basis for Candidate Selection: *Very important factors considered include:* Academic GPA, rigor of secondary school record, standardized test scores, level of applicant's interest, talent/ability. *Important factors considered include:* Application essay, character/personal qualities, extracurricular activities. *Other factors considered include:* Class rank, recommendation(s), first generation, interview, racial/ethnic status, volunteer work, work experience. **Freshman Admission Requirements:** High school diploma is required and GED is accepted. *Academic units required:* 4 English, 1 mathematics, 1 science, 1 social studies, 1 history, 8 academic electives. *Academic units recommended:* 4 English, 4 mathematics, 4 science, (3 science labs), 2 foreign language, 4 social studies. **Freshman Admission Statistics:** 3,387 applied, 7% admitted, 78% enrolled. **Transfer Admission Requirements:** High school transcript, college transcript(s), essay or personal statement, standardized test scores, statement of good standing from prior institution(s). Minimum college GPA of 3.0 required. Lowest grade transferable B. **General Admission Information:** Application fee $65. Early decision application deadline 12/1. Regular application deadline 1/1. Regular notification 4/1. Nonfall registration not accepted. Admission may be deferred for a maximum of 1 year. Credit and/or placement offered for CEEB Advanced Placement tests.

COSTS AND FINANCIAL AID

Annual tuition $35,000. Room and board $13,700. Required fees $1,650. Average book expense $1,800. **Required Forms and Deadlines:** FAFSA, CSS/Financial Aid PROFILE Financial aid filing deadline 6/1. Priority financial aid filing date 4/15. **Notification of Awards:** Applicants will be notified of awards on or about 6/1. **Types of Aid:** *Need-based scholarships/grants:* Federal Pell, SEOG, state scholarships/grants, private scholarships, the school's own gift aid. *Loans:* FFEL Subsidized Stafford, FFEL Unsubsidized Stafford, FFEL PLUS, Federal Perkins, college/university loans from institutional funds. **Student Employment:** Federal Work-Study Program available. Institutional employment available. Off-campus job opportunities are excellent. **Financial Aid Statistics:** 37% freshmen, 25% undergrads receive need-based scholarship or grant aid. 37% freshmen, 25% undergrads receive non-need-based scholarship or grant aid. 22% freshmen, 20% undergrads receive need-based self-help aid. 100% freshmen, 100% undergrads receive any aid. 27% undergrads borrow to pay for school. Average cumulative indebtedness $12,717. **Criteria for awarding institutional aid:** *Non-need-based:* Academics.

COPPIN STATE UNIVERSITY

2500 West North Avenue, Baltimore, MD 21216
Phone: 410-951-3600 **Financial Aid Phone:** 410-951-3636
E-mail: admissions@coppin.edu **CEEB Code:** 5122
Fax: 410-523-7351 **Website:** www.coppin.edu **ACT Code:** 1688

This public school was founded in 1900. It has a 52-acre campus.

RATINGS
Admissions Selectivity Rating: 74 **Fire Safety Rating:** 60* **Green Rating:** 60*

STUDENTS AND FACULTY
Enrollment: 3,185. **Student Body:** 77% female, 23% male, 8% out-of-state, 3% international . African American 95%, Caucasian 2%.
Retention and Graduation: 65% freshmen return for sophomore year. 7% freshmen graduate within 4 years. **Faculty:** Student/faculty ratio 19:1. 130 full-time faculty, 59% hold PhDs, 82% are members of minority groups, 49% are women.

ACADEMICS
Degrees: Bachelor's, master's, post-master's certificate. **Majors with Highest Enrollment:** Criminal justice/law enforcement administration; management science; nursing/registered nurse (RN, ASN, BSN, MSN). **Special Study Options:** Accelerated program, cooperative education program, distance learning, double major, dual enrollment, external degree program, honors program, independent study, internships, liberal arts/career combination, study abroad, teacher certification program, weekend college, 3-2 programs in Engineering; Pharmacy; Denistry; Physical Therapy. **Honors programs:** Honors Program and McNair Program **Combined degree programs:** BA/MA, dental and pharmacy. Special programs offered to physically disabled students include reader services, tutors. **Career services:** Alumni services, career/job search classes, career assessment, internships. **Career services highlights include:** Cooperative Education Program.

FACILITIES
Housing: Coed dorms, special housing for disabled students. 75% of campus accessible to physically disabled. **Special Academic Facilities/Equipment:** Language lab, school of special education, TV studio. **Computers:** Students can register for classes online. Administrative functions (other than registration) can be performed online.

CAMPUS LIFE
Environment: City. **Activities:** Choral groups, concert band, dance, drama/theater, music ensembles, radio station, student government, student newspaper, student-run film society, television station, yearbook. **Organizations:** 28 registered organizations, 1 honor societies, 1 religious organizations. 3 fraternities, 4 sororities. **Athletics (Intercollegiate):** *Men:* Baseball, basketball, cross-country, tennis, track/field (outdoor), track/field (indoor). *Women:* Basketball, bowling, cheerleading, cross-country, golf, softball, tennis, track/field (outdoor), track/field (indoor), volleyball. **On-Campus Highlights:** New dining facility (no official naming), Tawes Building (student building), Greek Row (located in front of dorms), Coppin Center (athletic facility).

ADMISSIONS
Freshman Academic Profile: Average high school GPA 2.83. SAT Math middle 50% range 370–450. SAT Critical Reading middle 50% range 380–460. Minimum paper TOEFL 500. Minimum computer TOEFL 173. **Basis for Candidate Selection:** *Very important factors considered include:* Rigor of secondary school record. *Important factors considered include:* Recommendation(s), standardized test scores, talent/ability. *Other factors considered include:* Class rank, application essay, alumni/ae relation, character/personal qualities, extracurricular activities, geographical residence, interview, racial/ethnic status, state residency, volunteer work, work experience. **Freshman Admission Requirements:** High school diploma is required and GED is accepted. *Academic units required:* 4 English, 3 mathematics, 2 science, (2 science labs), 2 foreign language, 3 social studies, 2 Advanced Tech Prep (alternative to Foreign language requirement). **Freshman Admission Statistics:** 3,075 applied, 46% admitted, 44% enrolled. **Transfer Admission Requirements:** College transcript(s), minimum college GPA of 2.0 required. Lowest grade transferable C. **General Admission Information:** Application fee $35. Regular application deadline 7/15. Notification on a rolling basis, beginning on or about 3/15. Nonfall registration accepted. Admission may be deferred for a maximum of 1 semester. Credit and/or placement offered for CEEB Advanced Placement tests.

COSTS AND FINANCIAL AID
Required Forms and Deadlines: FAFSA. Priority financial aid filing date 3/1. **Notification of Awards:** Applicants will be notified of awards on a rolling basis beginning 4/15. **Types of Aid:** *Need-based scholarships/grants:* Federal Pell, SEOG, state scholarships/grants, private scholarships, the school's own gift aid, United Negro College Fund, Federal Nursing Scholarships. *Loans:* Direct Subsidized Stafford, Direct Unsubsidized Stafford, Direct PLUS, FFEL PLUS, Federal Perkins, college/university loans from institutional funds, Sallie Mae's Signature Loans and Key Alternative Loan. **Student Employment:** Federal Work-Study Program available. Institutional employment available. Off-campus job opportunities are excellent. **Financial Aid Statistics:** 55% freshmen, 67% undergrads receive need-based scholarship or grant aid. 12% freshmen, 16% undergrads receive non-need-based scholarship or grant aid. 61% freshmen, 66% undergrads receive need-based self-help aid. 5% freshmen, 5% undergrads receive athletic scholarships. 90% undergrads borrow to pay for school. Average cumulative indebtedness $17,844. **Criteria for awarding institutional aid:** *Non-need-based:* Academics, alumni affiliation, athletics, state/district residency.

CORBAN UNIVERSITY

5000 Deer Park Drive Southeast, Salem, OR 97317
Phone: 503-375-7005 **Financial Aid Phone:** 503-375-7007
E-mail: admissions@wbc.edu
Fax: 503-585-4316 **Website:** www.corban.edu **ACT Code:** 477

This private school, affiliated with the Baptist Church, was founded in 1935. It has a 145-acre campus.

RATINGS
Admissions Selectivity Rating: 88 **Fire Safety Rating:** 82 **Green Rating:** 60*

STUDENTS AND FACULTY
Enrollment: 820. **Student Body:** 60% female, 40% male, 47% out-of-state, (4 countries represented). Asian 3%, African American 1%, Caucasian 72%, Hispanic 3%.
Retention and Graduation: 46% freshmen graduate within 4 years. **Faculty:** Student/faculty ratio 14:1. 45 full-time faculty, 56% hold PhDs, 2% are members of minority groups, 24% are women.

ACADEMICS
Degrees: Associate, bachelor's, master's. **Classes:** Most classes have 10–19 students. Most lab/discussion sessions have 10–19 students. **Majors with High-**

est Enrollment: Business/commerce; education; psychology. **Special Study Options:** Accelerated program, cross-registration, distance learning, double major, dual enrollment, honors program, independent study, internships, liberal arts/career combination, study abroad, teacher certification program, weekend college. **Combined degree programs:** BA/MA, Education. Special programs offered to physically disabled students include note-taking services, reader services, tape recorders, tutors. **Career services highlights include:** Students in business program work with local business and agencies on various projects beneficial to both.

FACILITIES

Housing: Men's dorms, women's dorms, apartments for married students, apartments for single students. 80% of campus accessible to physically disabled. **Special Academic Facilities/Equipment:** Prewitt-Allen Archeological Museum. Psalms Performing Arts Center. **Computers:** Students can register for classes online.

CAMPUS LIFE

Environment: City. **Activities:** Choral groups, concert band, drama/theater, jazz band, music ensembles, student government, student newspaper, yearbook, campus ministries. **Organizations:** 1 honor societies, 10 religious organizations. **Athletics (Intercollegiate):** *Men:* Baseball, basketball, cross-country, golf, soccer, track/field (outdoor). *Women:* Basketball, cross-country, golf, soccer, softball, track/field (outdoor), volleyball. **On-Campus Highlights:** Common Grounds Coffee Shop, Dining Hall, Gymnasium and Athletic Fields, Computer Lab, Book Store, Archaeological Museum, Psalms Performing Arts Center.

ADMISSIONS

Freshman Academic Profile: Average high school GPA 3.58. 31% in top 10% of high school class, 61% in top 25% of high school class, 87% in top 50% of high school class. 60% from public high schools. SAT Math middle 50% range 490–610. SAT Critical Reading middle 50% range 500–630. SAT Writing middle 50% range 470–590. ACT middle 50% range 20–26. Minimum paper TOEFL 500. Minimum computer TOEFL 250. **Basis for Candidate Selection:** *Very important factors considered include:* Application essay, academic GPA, recommendation(s), religious affiliation/commitment. *Important factors considered include:* Rigor of secondary school record, standardized test scores, character/personal qualities, level of applicant's interest. *Other factors considered include:* Class rank, alumni/ae relation, extracurricular activities, interview. **Freshman Admission Requirements:** High school diploma is required and GED is accepted. *Academic units recommended:* 4 English, 3 mathematics, 2 science, 2 foreign language, 3 social studies. **Freshman Admission Statistics:** 907 applied, 57% admitted, 42% enrolled. **Transfer Admission Requirements:** High school transcript, college transcript(s), essay or personal statement, minimum college GPA of 2.00 required. Lowest grade transferable C–. **General Admission Information:** Application fee $40. Regular application deadline 8/1. Notification on a rolling basis, beginning on or about 12/1. Nonfall registration accepted. Credit offered for CEEB Advanced Placement tests.

COSTS AND FINANCIAL AID

Annual tuition $22,932. Room and board $8,068. Required fees $270. Average book expense $900. **Required Forms and Deadlines:** FAFSA. Priority financial aid filing date 2/15. **Notification of Awards:** Applicants will be notified of awards on a rolling basis beginning 3/1. **Types of Aid:** *Need-based scholarships/grants:* Federal Pell, SEOG, state scholarships/grants, private scholarships, the school's own gift aid. *Loans:* Direct Subsidized Stafford, Direct Unsubsidized Stafford, Direct PLUS, Federal Perkins, state loans. **Student Employment:** Federal Work-Study Program available. Institutional employment available. Highest amount earned per year from on-campus jobs $1,000. Off-campus job opportunities are fair. **Financial Aid Statistics:** 83% freshmen, 83% undergrads receive need-based scholarship or grant aid. 7% freshmen, 7% undergrads receive non-need-based scholarship or grant aid. 59% freshmen, 64% undergrads receive need-based self-help aid. 8% freshmen, 6% undergrads receive athletic scholarships. 97% freshmen, 97% undergrads receive any aid. 91% undergrads borrow to pay for school. Average cumulative indebtedness $28,537. **Criteria for awarding institutional aid:** *Non-need-based:* Academics, alumni affiliation, athletics, leadership, music/drama.

CORCORAN COLLEGE OF ART AND DESIGN

500 17th Street NW, Washington, DC 20006-4804
Phone: 202-639-1814 **Financial Aid Phone:** 202-639-1816
E-mail: admissions@corcoran.org **CEEB Code:** 5705
Fax: 202-639-1830 **Website:** www.corcoran.edu **ACT Code:** 671

This private school was founded in 1890. It has a 7-acre campus.

RATINGS

Admissions Selectivity Rating: 75   Fire Safety Rating: 60*   Green Rating: 60*

STUDENTS AND FACULTY

Enrollment: 352. **Student Body:** 64% female, 36% male, 73% out-of-state, 11% international (20 countries represented). Asian 6%, African American 7%, Caucasian 51%, Hispanic 5%. **Retention and Graduation:** 64% freshmen return for sophomore year. **Faculty:** Student/faculty ratio 4:1. 31 full-time faculty, 42% hold PhDs, 48% are women.

ACADEMICS

Degrees: Associate, bachelor's, certificate, master's. **Classes:** Most classes have fewer than 10 students. **Majors with Highest Enrollment:** Fine/studio arts; graphic design; photography. **Special Study Options:** Cross-registration, exchange student program (domestic), internships, study abroad. **Combined degree programs:** BA/MA. Special programs offered to physically disabled students include note-taking services, reader services, tape recorders, tutors. **Career services:** Alumni network, alumni services, career/job search classes, internships.

FACILITIES

Housing: Corcoran Leased Apartments and assistance in finding area housing. 70% of campus accessible to physically disabled. **Special Academic Facilities/Equipment:** Art gallery, student exhibition spaces. **Computers:** Administrative functions (other than registration) can be performed online. Undergraduates are required to own a computer.

CAMPUS LIFE

Environment: Metropolis. **Activities:** Student government, student-run film society. **On-Campus Highlights:** Corcoran Gallery, Corcoran Studios, Corcoran Cafe des Artistes.

ADMISSIONS

Freshman Academic Profile: Average high school GPA 3.2. 11% in top 10% of high school class, 50% in top 25% of high school class, 83% in top 50% of high school class. SAT Math middle 50% range 410–530. SAT Critical Reading middle 50% range 460–585. SAT Writing middle 50% range 430–540. ACT middle 50% range 16–28. Minimum paper TOEFL 550. Minimum computer TOEFL 213. **Basis for Candidate Selection:** *Very important factors considered include:* Academic GPA, rigor of secondary school record, interview, talent/ability. *Important factors considered include:* Class rank, application essay, recommendation(s), standardized test scores. *Other factors considered include:* Alumni/ae relation, character/personal qualities, extracurricular activities, volunteer work, work experience. **Freshman Admission Requirements:** High school diploma is required and GED is accepted. *Academic units recommended:* 4 English, 4 history, 2 art courses. **Freshman Admission Statistics:** 167 applied, 90% admitted, 26% enrolled. **Transfer Admission Requirements:** High school transcript, college transcript(s), minimum college GPA of 2.5 required. Lowest grade transferable C. **General Admission Information:** Application fee $40. Notification on a rolling basis, beginning on or about 1/1. Nonfall registration accepted. Admission may be deferred for a maximum of 1 year. Credit and/or placement offered for CEEB Advanced Placement tests.

COSTS AND FINANCIAL AID

Annual tuition $24,289. . Room and board $10,795. Required fees $200. Average book expense $2,500. **Required Forms and Deadlines:** FAFSA, institution's own financial aid form. Priority financial aid filing date 3/1. **Notification of Awards:** Applicants will be notified of awards on a rolling basis beginning 4/1. **Types of Aid:** *Need-based scholarships/grants:* Federal Pell, SEOG, state scholarships/grants, the school's own gift aid. *Loans:* Direct Subsidized Stafford, Direct Unsubsidized Stafford, Direct PLUS, FFEL Subsidized Stafford, FFEL Unsubsidized Stafford, FFEL PLUS, Federal Perkins, alternative loans, i.e., PLATO, Signature Loans. **Student Employment:** Federal Work-Study Program available. Institutional employment available. Off-campus job opportunities are excellent. **Financial Aid Statistics:** 51% freshmen, 50% undergrads receive need-based scholarship or grant aid. 53% freshmen, 35% undergrads receive non-need-based scholarship or grant aid. 58% freshmen, 61% undergrads receive need-based self-help aid. 76% undergrads borrow to pay for school. Average cumulative indebtedness $31,541. **Criteria for awarding institutional aid:** *Non-need-based:* Academics, art.

See page 1066.

CORNELL COLLEGE

600 First Street South West, Mount Vernon, IA 52314-1098
Phone: 319-895-4477 **Financial Aid Phone:** 319-895-4216
E-mail: admissions@cornellcollege.edu **CEEB Code:** 6119
Fax: 319-895-4451 **Website:** www.cornellcollege.edu **ACT Code:** 1296

This private school, affiliated with the Methodist Church, was founded in 1853. It has a 129-acre campus.

RATINGS
Admissions Selectivity Rating: 91   **Fire Safety Rating:** 68   **Green Rating:** 76

STUDENTS AND FACULTY
Enrollment: 1,125. **Student Body:** 52% female, 48% male, 77% out-of-state, 4% international (19 countries represented). Asian 3%, African American 3%, Caucasian 75%, Hispanic 4%, Native American 1%.
Retention and Graduation: 79% freshmen return for sophomore year. 65% freshmen graduate within 4 years. **Faculty:** Student/faculty ratio 12:1. 87 full-time faculty, 93% hold PhDs, 9% are members of minority groups, 53% are women.

ACADEMICS
Degrees: Bachelor's. **Classes:** Most classes have 10–19 students. **Majors with Highest Enrollment:** Economics; history; psychology. **Special Study Options:** Accelerated program, double major, English as a Second Language (ESL), exchange student program (domestic), independent study, internships, liberal arts/career combination, student-designed major, study abroad, teacher certification program. **Combined degree programs:** BA/MA, engineering; forestry and environmental management, Duke University. Special programs offered to physically disabled students include tape recorders, tutors. **Career services:** Alumni network, alumni services, career/job search classes, career assessment, internships, regional alumni. **Career services highlights include:** Fellowships with premier internship programs. Externship Program, 3-5 day job shadowing opportunites.

FACILITIES
Housing: Coed dorms, men's dorms, women's dorms, apartments for single students. Our first year students live on first-year only floors and/or in first-year only residence halls. 47% of campus accessible to physically disabled. **Special Academic Facilities/Equipment:** Geology center and museum, MNR machine in West Sc. Building, Luce Art Gallery. **Computers:** 100% of classrooms, 20% of dorms, 100% of libraries, 100% of dining areas, 100% of student union, 10% of common outdoor areas have wireless network access. Administrative functions (other than registration) can be performed online.

CAMPUS LIFE
Environment: Rural. **Activities:** Choral groups, concert band, dance, drama/theater, jazz band, literary magazine, music ensembles, musical theater, opera, radio station, student government, student newspaper, symphony orchestra, yearbook, campus ministries, international student organization. **Organizations:** 90 registered organizations, 11 honor societies, 11 religious organizations. 8 fraternities, 7 sororities. **Athletics (Intercollegiate): Men:** Baseball, basketball, cross-country, football, golf, soccer, tennis, track/field (outdoor), track/field (indoor), wrestling. *Women:* Basketball, cross-country, golf, soccer, softball, tennis, track/field (outdoor), track/field (indoor), volleyball. **On-Campus Highlights:** Commons—Orange Carpet—student center, Cole Library, Small Multi—sports center, Kimmel Theatre—new state-of-the-art theatre, McWethy Hall—newly renovated art building. Most prodominant features on campus are our beautiful King Chapel. A newly renovated Armstrong Hall of fine arts. A new pedestrian mall (with outdoor ampitheatre) that connects the entire campus. **Environmental Initiatives:** Engineering study on costs of replacing current campus-side steam heat network, including specific costs and energy savings payback times for each building. Implementation of plan in two building remodels and designed into two upcoming remodel projects. Wrote and received grant for recycling facility construction and negotiating contract with cleaning service for nightly collection of recyclable categories possible in our area. Currently spec'ing biodiesel refinery to convert food service discarded oils into fuel for college equipment.

ADMISSIONS
Freshman Academic Profile: Average high school GPA 3.5. 35% in top 10% of high school class, 58% in top 25% of high school class, 87% in top 50% of high school class. 79% from public high schools. SAT Math middle 50% range 550–680. SAT Critical Reading middle 50% range 550–680. SAT Writing middle 50% range 530–650. ACT middle 50% range 24–29. Minimum paper TOEFL 550. Minimum computer TOEFL 213. **Basis for Candidate Selection:** *Very important factors considered include:* Application essay, academic GPA, recommendation(s), rigor of secondary school record. *Important factors considered include:* Class rank, standardized test scores, character/personal qualities, extracurricular activities, first generation, interview, level of applicant's interest, talent/ability, volunteer work, work experience. *Other factors considered include:* Alumni/ae relation, geographical residence, racial/ethnic status, state residency. **Freshman Admission Requirements:** High school diploma is required and GED is accepted. *Academic units recommended:* 4 English, 3 mathematics, 3 science, 2 foreign language, 3 social studies. **Freshman Admission Statistics:** 3,208 applied, 44% admitted, 24% enrolled. **Transfer Admission Requirements:** College transcript(s), essay or personal statement, statement of good standing from prior institution(s). Lowest grade transferable C. **General Admission Information:** Application fee $30. Regular application deadline 2/1. Regular notification 3/20. Nonfall registration accepted. Admission may be deferred for a maximum of 1 year. Credit and/or placement offered for CEEB Advanced Placement tests.

COSTS AND FINANCIAL AID
Average book expense $810. **Required Forms and Deadlines:** FAFSA, institution's own financial aid form, Noncustodial (Divorced/Separated) Parent's Statement. Financial aid filing deadline 3/1. Priority financial aid filing date 3/1. **Notification of Awards:** Applicants will be notified of awards on a rolling basis beginning 3/1. **Types of Aid:** *Need-based scholarships/grants:* Federal Pell, SEOG, state scholarships/grants, private scholarships, the school's own gift aid, AC, SMART, and TEACH Grants. *Loans:* Direct Subsidized Stafford, Direct Unsubsidized Stafford, Direct PLUS, Sherman Loan, United Methodist Loan. **Student Employment:** Federal Work-Study Program available. Institutional employment available. Highest amount earned per year from on-campus jobs $350. Off-campus job opportunities are fair. **Financial Aid Statistics:** 72% freshmen, 74% undergrads receive need-based scholarship or grant aid. 69% freshmen, 62% undergrads receive non-need-based scholarship or grant aid. 69% freshmen, 60% undergrads receive need-based self-help aid. 95% freshmen, 95% undergrads receive any aid. 72% undergrads borrow to pay for school. Average cumulative indebtedness $27,990. **Criteria for awarding institutional aid:** *Non-need-based:* Academics, art, leadership, minority status, music/drama, religious affiliation, state/district residency.

CORNELL UNIVERSITY

Undergraduate Admissions, 410 Thurston Ave, Ithaca, NY 14850
Phone: 607-255-5241 **Financial Aid Phone:** 607-255-5147
E-mail: admissions@cornell.edu **CEEB Code:** 2098
Fax: 607-255-0659 **Website:** www.cornell.edu **ACT Code:** 2726

This private school was founded in 1865. It has a 745-acre campus.

RATINGS
Admissions Selectivity Rating: 98   **Fire Safety Rating:** 70   **Green Rating:** 97

STUDENTS AND FACULTY
Enrollment: 13,882. **Student Body:** 49% female, 51% male, 64% out-of-state, 8% international (77 countries represented). Asian 17%, African American 5%, Caucasian 46%, Hispanic 6%.
Retention and Graduation: 96% freshmen return for sophomore year. 85% freshmen graduate within 4 years. 32% grads go on to further study within 1 year. 4% grads pursue law degrees. 1% grads pursue business degrees. 6% grads pursue medical degrees. **Faculty:** Student/faculty ratio 9:1. 1685 full-time faculty, 93% hold PhDs, 17% are members of minority groups, 31% are women.

ACADEMICS
Degrees: Bachelor's, master's. **Classes:** Most classes have 10–19 students. Most lab/discussion sessions have 10–19 students. **Majors with Highest Enrollment:** Biology/biological sciences; hotel/motel administration/management; labor and industrial relations. **Special Study Options:** Accelerated program, cooperative education program, cross-registration, distance learning, double major, English as a Second Language (ESL), exchange student program (domestic), honors program, independent study, internships, liberal arts/career combination, student-designed major, study abroad, teacher certification program. Special programs offered to physically disabled students include note-taking services, reader services, tape recorders, tutors. **Career services:** Alumni network, alumni services, career/job search classes, career assessment, internships, regional alumni. **Career services highlights include:** Two of our stellar programs, the Extern Program and FRESH, provide students the opportunity to shadow and work with alumni. This gives students a chance to broaden their horizons by exploring unfamiliar career fields or to deepen their

knowledge of a career field through hands-on exposure. Either way, the programs build networking skills in students and foster positive alumni connections with the university.

FACILITIES

Housing: Coed dorms, special housing for disabled students, men's dorms, special housing for international students, women's dorms, fraternity/sorority housing, apartments for married students, cooperative housing, apartments for single students, theme housing. See www.campuslife.cornell.edu/campuslife/housing. **Special Academic Facilities/Equipment:** Biotechnology institute, a woods sanctuary, 4 designated national resource centers, 2 local optical observatories, Africana studies and research center, arboretum, particle accelerator, supercomputer, national research centers, performing arts center, art museum, lab of ornithology, vertebrates museum, living and learning communities, campus orchard, dairy pilot plant, mineralogical museum, animal teaching hospital, 2 agricultural experiment stations, and marine laboratory. **Computers:** 20% of classrooms, 100% of dorms, 100% of libraries, 100% of dining areas, 75% of student union, 20% of common outdoor areas have wireless network access. Students can register for classes online. Administrative functions (other than registration) can be performed online.

CAMPUS LIFE

Environment: Town. **Activities:** Choral groups, concert band, dance, drama/theater, jazz band, literary magazine, marching band, music ensembles, musical theater, pep band, radio station, student government, student newspaper, student-run film society, symphony orchestra, television station, yearbook, campus ministries, international student organization, Model UN. **Organizations:** 841 registered organizations, 22 honor societies, 61 religious organizations. 50 fraternities, 19 sororities. **Athletics (Intercollegiate):** *Men:* Baseball, basketball, crew/rowing, cross-country, diving, football, golf, ice hockey, lacrosse, polo, soccer, squash, swimming, tennis, track/field (outdoor), track/field (indoor), wrestling. *Women:* Basketball, crew/rowing, cross-country, diving, equestrian sports, fencing, field hockey, gymnastics, ice hockey, lacrosse, polo, soccer, softball, squash, swimming, tennis, track/field (outdoor), track/field (indoor), volleyball. **On-Campus Highlights:** Johnson Art Museum, Gorges and waterfalls bordering campus, Center for Theater Arts, Cornell Plantations, including Beebe Lak, Willard Straight Hall, http://explore.cornell.edu/. **Environmental Initiatives:** Climate Neutrality by 2050. (www.sustainablecampus.cornell.edu/climate) Creation of Cornell Center for a Sustainable Future. (www.sustainablefuture.cornell.edu) Eliminate use of coal by 2011. (www.news.cornell.edu/stories/Jan10/CHPopening.html)

ADMISSIONS

Freshman Academic Profile: 86% in top 10% of high school class, 98% in top 25% of high school class, 100% in top 50% of high school class. 66% from public high schools. SAT Math middle 50% range 660–770. SAT Critical Reading middle 50% range 630–730. ACT middle 50% range 29–33. Minimum paper TOEFL 600. Minimum web-based TOEFL 100. **Basis for Candidate Selection:** *Very important factors considered include:* Application essay, academic GPA, recommendation(s), rigor of secondary school record, standardized test scores, extracurricular activities, talent/ability. *Important factors considered include:* Class rank. *Other factors considered include:* Alumni/ae relation, character/personal qualities, first generation, geographical residence, interview, racial/ethnic status, state residency, volunteer work, work experience. **Freshman Admission Requirements:** High school diploma or equivalent is not required. *Academic units required:* 4 English, 3 mathematics. *Academic units recommended:* 3 science, (3 science labs), 3 foreign language, 3 social studies, 3 history. **Freshman Admission Statistics:** 34,371 applied, 19% admitted, 48% enrolled. **Transfer Admission Requirements:** High school transcript, college transcript(s), essay or personal statement, statement of good standing from prior institution(s). Lowest grade transferable C. **General Admission Information:** Application fee $70. Early decision application deadline 11/1. Regular application deadline 1/2. Regular notification 4/1. Nonfall registration not accepted. Credit and/or placement offered for CEEB Advanced Placement tests.

COSTS AND FINANCIAL AID

Required Forms and Deadlines: FAFSA, institution's own financial aid form, CSS/Financial Aid PROFILE, noncustodial PROFILE, business/farm supplement. Prior year tax forms. Financial aid filing deadline 1/2. **Notification of Awards:** Applicants will be notified of awards on or about 4/1. **Types of Aid:** *Need-based scholarships/grants:* Federal Pell, SEOG, state scholarships/grants, private scholarships, the school's own gift aid. *Loans:* Direct Subsidized Stafford, Direct Unsubsidized Stafford, Direct PLUS, FFEL Subsidized Stafford, FFEL Unsubsidized Stafford, FFEL PLUS, Federal Perkins, college/university loans from institutional funds. **Student Employment:** Federal Work-Study Program available. Institutional employment available. Highest amount earned per year from on-campus jobs $2,500. Off-campus job opportunities are fair. **Financial Aid Statistics:** 51% freshmen, 46% undergrads receive need-based scholarship or grant aid. 46% freshmen, 43% undergrads receive need-based self-help aid. 51.8% freshmen, 46.4% undergrads receive any aid. 53% undergrads borrow to pay for school. Average cumulative indebtedness $21,549.

CORNERSTONE UNIVERSITY

1001 East Beltline Avenue, NE, Grand Rapids, MI 49525-5897
Phone: 616-222-1418 **Financial Aid Phone:** 616-949-5300
E-mail: admissions@cornerstone.edu
Fax: 616-222-1418 **Website:** www.cornerstone.edu **ACT Code:** 2002

This private school, affiliated with the Christian (Nondenominational) Church, was founded in 1941. It has a 130-acre campus.

RATINGS

Admissions Selectivity Rating: 77　　　**Fire Safety Rating:** 94　　　**Green Rating:** 71

STUDENTS AND FACULTY

Enrollment: 1,741. **Student Body:** 59% female, 41% male, 16% out-of-state, 1% international (15 countries represented). Asian 1%, African American 11%, Caucasian 83%, Hispanic 4%.
Retention and Graduation: 69% freshmen return for sophomore year. 15% grads go on to further study within 1 year. 10% grads pursue arts and sciences degrees. 1% grads pursue law degrees. 3% grads pursue business degrees. 1% grads pursue medical degrees. **Faculty:** Student/faculty ratio 13:1. 62 full-time faculty, 50% hold PhDs, 5% are members of minority groups, 32% are women.

ACADEMICS

Degrees: Associate, bachelor's, certificate, diploma, first professional, master's, terminal associate. **Classes:** Most classes have 10–19 students. **Majors with Highest Enrollment:** Elementary education and teaching; mass communication/media studies; youth ministry. **Special Study Options:** Accelerated program, distance learning, double major, dual enrollment, English as a Second Language (ESL), honors program, independent study, internships, liberal arts/career combination, study abroad, teacher certification program, weekend college. **Honors programs:** Honors Program based on a "great books" curriculum Special programs offered to physically disabled students include note-taking services, reader services, tape recorders, tutors. **Career services:** Career/job search classes, career assessment, internships **Career services highlights include:** The required internship of all students as part of the graduation requirements.

FACILITIES

Housing: Special housing for disabled students, men's dorms, women's dorms, apartments for married students, apartments for single students, theme housing 100% of campus accessible to physically disabled. **Computers:** 100% of classrooms, 100% of dorms, 100% of libraries, 100% of dining areas, 100% of student union, 100% of common outdoor areas have wireless network access. Students can register for classes online. Administrative functions (other than registration) can be performed online.

CAMPUS LIFE

Environment: City. **Activities:** Choral groups, concert band, dance, drama/theater, jazz band, literary magazine, music ensembles, musical theater, opera, pep band, radio station, student government, student newspaper, student-run film society, campus ministries, international student organization. **Organizations:** 11 registered organizations, 2 honor societies, 1 religious organizations. **Athletics (Intercollegiate):** *Men:* Basketball, cross-country, golf, soccer, track/field (outdoor), track/field (indoor). *Women:* Basketball, cross-country, golf, soccer, softball, track/field (outdoor), track/field (indoor), volleyball. **On-Campus Highlights:** Corum Student Union, Bernice Hansen Athletic Center, Campus Bookstore Atrium, Faber Hall Seating Area, Gordon Music Hall. **Environmental Initiatives:** On campus dialogue and focus on sustainability issues. Joining a community organization.

ADMISSIONS

Freshman Academic Profile: Average high school GPA 3.3. 60% from public high schools. SAT Math middle 50% range 440–540. SAT Critical Reading middle 50% range 360–580. SAT Writing middle 50% range 480–500. ACT middle 50% range 20–25. Minimum paper TOEFL 500. Minimum computer TOEFL 173. **Basis for Candidate Selection:** *Very important factors considered include:* Application essay, academic GPA, recommendation(s), standardized test scores, character/personal qualities, religious affiliation/commitment. *Important factors considered include:* Class rank, rigor of secondary school record. *Other factors considered include:* Level of applicant's interest. **Freshman Admission Requirements:** High school diploma is required and GED is accepted. *Academic units recommended:* 4 English, 3 mathematics, 2 science, (1 science labs), 2 foreign language, 3 social studies, 2 history, 4 academic electives. **Freshman Admission Statistics:** 939 applied, 75% admitted, 31% enrolled. **Transfer Admission Requirements:** High school transcript, college transcript(s), essay or personal statement, minimum college GPA of 2.0 required. Lowest grade transferable C–. **General Admission Information:** Application fee $25. Nonfall registration accepted. Credit and/or placement offered for CEEB Advanced Placement tests.

COSTS AND FINANCIAL AID

Annual tuition $19,190. Room and board $6,500. Required fees $340. Average book expense $1,000. **Required Forms and Deadlines:** FAFSA. Priority financial aid filing date 3/1. **Notification of Awards:** Applicants will be notified of awards on a rolling basis beginning 2/15. **Types of Aid:** *Need-based scholarships/grants:* Federal Pell, SEOG, state scholarships/grants, private scholarships, the school's own gift aid. *Loans:* FFEL Subsidized Stafford, FFEL Unsubsidized Stafford, FFEL PLUS, Federal Perkins. **Student Employment:** Federal Work-Study Program available. Highest amount earned per year from on-campus jobs $5,500. Off-campus job opportunities are good. **Financial Aid Statistics:** 83% freshmen, 81% undergrads receive need-based scholarship or grant aid. 83% freshmen, 77% undergrads receive non-need-based scholarship or grant aid. 67% freshmen, 65% undergrads receive need-based self-help aid. 23% freshmen, 15% undergrads receive athletic scholarships. 100% freshmen, 98% undergrads receive any aid. 77% undergrads borrow to pay for school. Average cumulative indebtedness $28,074. **Criteria for awarding institutional aid:** *Non-need-based:* Academics, athletics, leadership, music/drama, state/district residency.

CORNISH COLLEGE OF THE ARTS

1000 Lenora Street, Seattle, WA 98121
Phone: 206-726-5016 **Financial Aid Phone:** 206-726-5013
E-mail: admissions@cornish.edu **CEEB Code:** 58
Fax: 206-720-1011 **Website:** www.cornish.edu **ACT Code:** 4801

This private school was founded in 1914. It has a 4-acre campus.

RATINGS

Admissions Selectivity Rating: 60*   **Fire Safety Rating:** 60*   **Green Rating:** 60*

STUDENTS AND FACULTY

Enrollment: 649. **Student Body:** 61% female, 39% male, 35% out-of-state, 5% international (6 countries represented). Asian 5%, African American 2%, Caucasian 69%, Hispanic 4%, Native American 1%.
Retention and Graduation: 72% freshmen return for sophomore year. 12% grads go on to further study within 1 year. 5% grads pursue arts and sciences degrees. **Faculty:** Student/faculty ratio 9:1. 51 full-time faculty, 59% hold PhDs, 10% are members of minority groups, 47% are women.

ACADEMICS

Degrees: Bachelor's. **Classes:** Most classes have 10–19 students. **Majors with Highest Enrollment:** Design and visual communications; drama and dramatics/theatre arts; fine/studio arts. **Special Study Options:** Cooperative education program, independent study, internships, study abroad Special programs offered to physically disabled students include note-taking services, tape recorders. **Career services:** Internships

FACILITIES

Housing: 50% of campus accessible to physically disabled. **Special Academic Facilities/Equipment:** Art galleries, extensive art studio space, theatres, electronic music studio, dance studio, concert hall.

CAMPUS LIFE

Environment: Metropolis. **Activities:** Choral groups, concert band, dance, drama/theater, jazz band, literary magazine, music ensembles, musical theater, opera, student government, student newspaper, student-run film society. **Organizations:** 18 registered organizations, 6 honor societies, 1 religious organizations. **On-Campus Highlights:** Raisbeck Performance Hall, Cornsh Gallery, Nellie's Café.

ADMISSIONS

Freshman Academic Profile: Average high school GPA 3.1. 75% from public high schools. ACT middle 50% range 122–999. Minimum paper TOEFL 525. Minimum computer TOEFL 195. **Basis for Candidate Selection:** *Very important factors considered include:* Talent/ability. *Important factors considered include:* Application essay, rigor of secondary school record. *Other factors considered include:* Recommendation(s), standardized test scores, extracurricular activities, interview. **Freshman Admission Requirements:** High school diploma is required and GED is accepted. **Freshman Admission Statistics:** 602 applied, 81% admitted, 51% enrolled. **Transfer Admission Requirements:** High school transcript, college transcript(s), essay or personal statement, interview, minimum college GPA of 2.0 required. Lowest grade transferable C. **General Admission Information:** Application fee $35. Regular application deadline 2/15. Notification on a rolling basis, beginning on or about 1/1. Nonfall registration not accepted. Admission may be deferred for a maximum of 1 year. Credit offered for CEEB Advanced Placement tests.

COSTS AND FINANCIAL AID

Annual tuition $14,900. Room and board $11,000. Required fees $300. Average book expense $1,600. **Required Forms and Deadlines:** FAFSA, institution's own financial aid form Financial aid filing deadline 3/1. Priority financial aid filing date 2/1. **Notification of Awards:** Applicants will be notified of awards on or about 5/15. **Types of Aid:** *Need-based scholarships/grants:* Federal Pell, SEOG, state scholarships/grants, Merit scholarships based on artistic merit and merit w/need scholarships Both are insitutional money. *Loans:* FFEL Subsidized Stafford, FFEL Unsubsidized Stafford, FFEL PLUS, Federal Perkins. **Student Employment:** Federal Work-Study Program available. Highest amount earned per year from on-campus jobs $3,000. Off-campus job opportunities are excellent. **Financial Aid Statistics:** 66% undergrads receive need-based scholarship or grant aid. 78% undergrads receive non-need-based scholarship or grant aid. 66% undergrads receive need-based self-help aid. Average cumulative indebtedness $23,000. **Criteria for awarding institutional aid:** *Non-need-based:* Academics, art, music/drama.

COTTEY COLLEGE

1000 West Austin Blvd, Nevada, MO 64772
Phone: 417-667-8181
E-mail: enrollmgmt@cottey.edu
Fax: 417-667-8103

This is a private school.

RATINGS

Admissions Selectivity Rating: 67   **Fire Safety Rating:** 60*   **Green Rating:** 60*

STUDENTS AND FACULTY

Enrollment: 309. **Student Body:** 100% male, 89% out-of-state **Faculty:** Student/faculty ratio 9:1.

ACADEMICS

Degrees: Associate, transfer associate. **Special Study Options:** Distance learning, double major, independent study, internships.

CAMPUS LIFE

Activities: Choral groups, concert band, dance, drama/theater, jazz band, literary magazine, music ensembles, musical theater, student government, student newspaper, yearbook.

ADMISSIONS

Freshman Academic Profile: Average high school GPA 3.42. 16% in top 10% of high school class, 37% in top 25% of high school class. **Basis for Candidate Selection:** *Very important factors considered include:* Class rank, academic GPA, rigor of secondary school record, standardized test scores. *Important factors considered include:* Application essay, recommendation(s). *Other factors considered include:* Alumni/ae relation, extracurricular activities, talent/ability. **Freshman Admission Requirements:** High school diploma is required and GED is accepted. *Academic units required:* 4 English, 3 mathematics, 2 science, (2 science labs), 2 foreign language, 2 history, 1 academic electives. **Transfer Admission Requirements:** High school transcript, college transcript(s), Lowest grade transferable C. **General Admission Information:** Application fee $20. Nonfall registration accepted.

COSTS AND FINANCIAL AID

Notification of Awards: Applicants will be notified of awards on a rolling basis beginning 5/1. **Types of Aid:** *Need-based scholarships/grants:* Federal Pell, SEOG, state scholarships/grants, private scholarships. *Loans:* Direct Subsidized Stafford, Direct Unsubsidized Stafford, Direct PLUS, FFEL Subsidized Stafford, FFEL Unsubsidized Stafford, FFEL PLUS, Federal Perkins. **Criteria for awarding institutional aid:** *Non-need-based:* Academics, alumni affiliation, art, athletics, leadership, music/drama, state/district residency.

See page 1068.

COVENANT COLLEGE

14049 Scenic Highway, Lookout Mtn, GA 30750
Phone: 706-820-2398 **Financial Aid Phone:** 706-419-1126
E-mail: admissions@covenant.edu **CEEB Code:** 6124
Fax: 706-820-0893 **Website:** www.covenant.edu **ACT Code:** 3951

This private school was founded in 1955. It has a 300-acre campus.

RATINGS
Admissions Selectivity Rating: 88   **Fire Safety Rating:** 77   **Green Rating:** 60*

STUDENTS AND FACULTY
Enrollment: 976. **Student Body:** 56% female, 44% male, 75% out-of-state, 1% international (15 countries represented). Asian 2%, African American 2%, Caucasian 91%, Hispanic 2%.
Retention and Graduation: 75% freshmen return for sophomore year. 47% freshmen graduate within 4 years. 25% grads go on to further study within 1 year. 10% grads pursue arts and sciences degrees. 1% grads pursue law degrees. 2% grads pursue business degrees. 1% grads pursue medical degrees. **Faculty:** Student/faculty ratio 14:1. 58 full-time faculty, 88% hold PhDs, 7% are members of minority groups, 19% are women.

ACADEMICS
Degrees: Associate, bachelor's, master's. **Classes:** Most classes have 10–19 students. Most lab/discussion sessions have 20–29 students. **Majors with Highest Enrollment:** Elementary education and teaching; English language and literature; sociology. **Special Study Options:** Double major, dual enrollment, exchange student program (domestic), independent study, internships, student-designed major, study abroad, teacher certification program, dual-engineering degree with Georgia Tech; cooperative nursing program with Emory University and Chattanooga State; bridge program for MSN with Vanderbilt University. Special programs offered to physically disabled students include note-taking services, tape recorders. **Career services:** Alumni network, alumni services, career assessment, internships. **Career services highlights include:** Internship program.

FACILITIES
Housing: Men's dorms, women's dorms, apartments for single students 95% of campus accessible to physically disabled. **Computers:** 100% of classrooms, 100% of dorms, 100% of libraries, 100% of dining areas, 100% of common outdoor areas have wireless network access. Students can register for classes online. Administrative functions (other than registration) can be performed online.

CAMPUS LIFE
Environment: City. **Activities:** Choral groups, concert band, drama/theater, jazz band, literary magazine, music ensembles, radio station, student government, student newspaper, yearbook. **Organizations:** 40 registered organizations, 4 honor societies, 1 religious organization. **Athletics (Intercollegiate):** *Men:* Baseball, basketball, cross-country, golf, soccer, tennis. *Women:* Basketball, cross-country, golf, soccer, softball, tennis, volleyball. **On-Campus Highlights:** Probasco Visitor's Center, Carter Hall, The Overlook, The Chapel, Ashe Gym. The campus is located on top of Lookout Mountain in Georgia, providing a backdrop of scenic beauty.

ADMISSIONS
Freshman Academic Profile: Average high school GPA 3.7. 31% in top 10% of high school class, 56% in top 25% of high school class, 76% in top 50% of high school class. 31% from public high schools. SAT Math middle 50% range 510–620. SAT Critical Reading middle 50% range 540–660. SAT Writing middle 50% range 520–660. ACT middle 50% range 22–28. **Basis for Candidate Selection:** *Very important factors considered include:* Application essay, academic GPA, recommendation(s), rigor of secondary school record, standardized test scores, character/personal qualities. *Important factors considered include:* Interview. *Other factors considered include:* Class rank, alumni/ae relation, extracurricular activities, first generation, level of applicant's interest, racial/ethnic status, religious affiliation/commitment, volunteer work. **Freshman Admission Requirements:** High school diploma is required and GED is accepted. *Academic units required:* 4 English, 3 mathematics, 2 science, 2 social studies, 3 academic electives. *Academic units recommended:* 4 English, 3 mathematics, 2 science, 2 foreign language, 2 social studies, 3 academic electives. **Freshman Admission Statistics:** 1,078 applied, 60% admitted, 43% enrolled. **Transfer Admission Requirements:** High school transcript, college transcript(s), essay or personal statement, interview, standardized test scores, statement of good standing from prior institution(s). Minimum college GPA of 2.0 required. Lowest grade transferable C–. **General Admission Information:** Application fee $35. Notification on a rolling basis, beginning on or about 8/1. Nonfall registration accepted. Admission may be deferred for a maximum of 1 year. Credit offered for CEEB Advanced Placement tests.

COSTS AND FINANCIAL AID
Annual tuition $24,520. Room and board $7,170. Required fees $750. Average book expense $1,000. **Required Forms and Deadlines:** FAFSA, state aid form. **Notification of Awards:** Applicants will be notified of awards on a rolling basis beginning 2/1. **Types of Aid:** *Need-based scholarships/grants:* Federal Pell, SEOG, state scholarships/grants, private scholarships, the school's own gift aid. *Loans:* FFEL Subsidized Stafford, FFEL Unsubsidized Stafford, FFEL PLUS, Federal Perkins, state loans, college/university loans from institutional funds. **Student Employment:** Federal Work-Study Program available. Institutional employment available. Highest amount earned per year from on-campus jobs $3,840. Off-campus job opportunities are good. **Financial Aid Statistics:** 64% freshmen, 60% undergrads receive need-based scholarship or grant aid. 59% freshmen, 54% undergrads receive need-based self-help aid. 10% freshmen, 9% undergrads receive athletic scholarships. 99.3% freshmen, 98.6% undergrads receive any aid. 64.1% undergrads borrow to pay for school. Average cumulative indebtedness $17,824. **Criteria for awarding institutional aid:** *Non-need-based:* Academics, alumni affiliation, art, athletics, job skills, leadership, minority status, music/drama, religious affiliation, state/district residency.

CREIGHTON UNIVERSITY

2500 California Plaza, Omaha, NE 68178
Phone: 402-280-2703 **Financial Aid Phone:** 402-280-2731
E-mail: admissions@creighton.edu **CEEB Code:** 6121
Fax: 402-280-2685 **Website:** www.creighton.edu **ACT Code:** 2444

This private school, affiliated with the Roman Catholic Church, was founded in 1878. It has a 130-acre campus.

RATINGS
Admissions Selectivity Rating: 88   **Fire Safety Rating:** 89   **Green Rating:** 80

STUDENTS AND FACULTY
Enrollment: 4,133. **Student Body:** 59% female, 41% male, 63% out-of-state, 2% international (41 countries represented). Asian 10%, African American 3%, Caucasian 77%, Hispanic 4%, Native American 1%.
Retention and Graduation: 89% freshmen return for sophomore year. 64% freshmen graduate within 4 years. 40% grads go on to further study within 1 year. 10% grads pursue arts and sciences degrees. 9% grads pursue law degrees. 9% grads pursue business degrees. 12% grads pursue medical degrees. **Faculty:** Student/faculty ratio 11:1. 532 full-time faculty, 83% hold PhDs, 12% are members of minority groups, 42% are women.

ACADEMICS
Degrees: Associate, bachelor's, certificate, master's. **Classes:** Most classes have 20–29 students. Most lab/discussion sessions have 10–19 students. **Majors with Highest Enrollment:** Business/commerce; health/medical preparatory programs, other; psychology. **Special Study Options:** Accelerated program, cross-registration, distance learning, double major, dual enrollment, English as a Second Language (ESL), exchange student program (domestic), honors program, independent study, internships, liberal arts/career combination, study abroad, teacher certification program, 3-3 engineering program with University of Detroit Mercy; 3-3 law program within Creighton University. **Honors programs:** Designed for talented, imaginative students desirous of participation in small, iscussion-oriented classes and in courses on interdisciplinary and topical issues. **Combined degree programs:** BA/JD, BA/DDS, BA/MEng. Special programs offered to physically disabled students include note-taking services, reader services, tape recorders, tutors. **Career services:** Alumni network, alumni services, career/job search classes, career assessment, internships, regional alumni. **Career services highlights include:** Intership website: www2.creighton.edu/careercenter/internships/index.php.

FACILITIES
Housing: Coed dorms, special housing for disabled students, women's dorms, apartments for married students, apartments for single students, honors, Freshman Leadership. 97% of campus accessible to physically disabled. **Special Academic Facilities/Equipment:** Fine arts/performing center, health science and research complex, hospital. **Computers:** 100% of classrooms, 100% of dorms, 100% of libraries, 100% of dining areas, 100% of student union, 100% of common outdoor areas have wireless network access. Students can register for classes online. Administrative functions (other than registration) can be performed online.

CAMPUS LIFE

Environment: Metropolis. **Activities:** Choral groups, concert band, dance, drama/theater, jazz band, literary magazine, music ensembles, musical theater, pep band, student government, student newspaper, symphony orchestra, television station, yearbook, campus ministries, international student organization, Model UN. **Organizations:** 182 registered organizations, 11 honor societies, 6 religious organizations. 5 fraternities, 8 sororities. **Athletics (Intercollegiate):** *Men:* Baseball, basketball, cross-country, golf, soccer, tennis. *Women:* Basketball, crew/rowing, cross-country, golf, soccer, softball, tennis, volleyball. **On-Campus Highlights:** Harper Living Learning Center, Campus Mall and green in front of Studen, Hixson-Lied Science Building, Morrison Soccer stadium, Jesuit Gardens, Ryan Athletics Center and D.J. Sokol Auditorium completed fall 2009. **Environmental Initiatives:** The university is collaborating with local utilities to create a beta site for solar collection of ample size to generate electricity that can be sold on the grid. This site will be used to educate both our students and the community on solar panels and how they work. The enhanced recycling program is directed toward a single stream of recycle commodity collection. This includes entry in RecycleMania. We are actively involved in promoting sustainability in our community. The university started a forum of like-minded universities across the region; we hold these meetings quarterly. We organized a convocation for area businesses to learn more about how they can be more sustainable. We offer land to a local neighborhood association to host a community garden.

ADMISSIONS

Freshman Academic Profile: Average high school GPA 3.75. 41% in top 10% of high school class, 73% in top 25% of high school class, 93% in top 50% of high school class. 53% from public high schools. SAT Math middle 50% range 540–650. SAT Critical Reading middle 50% range 520–640. ACT middle 50% range 24–29. Minimum paper TOEFL 550. Minimum computer TOEFL 213. **Basis for Candidate Selection:** *Very important factors considered include:* Academic GPA, rigor of secondary school record. *Important factors considered include:* Application essay, standardized test scores. *Other factors considered include:* Class rank, recommendation(s), character/personal qualities, extracurricular activities, first generation, level of applicant's interest, racial/ethnic status, talent/ability, volunteer work. **Freshman Admission Requirements:** High school diploma is required and GED is accepted. *Academic units required:* 4 English, 3 mathematics, 2 science, 2 foreign language, 2 social studies, 0 history, 3 academic electives. *Academic units recommended:* 4 English, 4 mathematics, 3 science, 3 foreign language, 3 social studies, 1 history, 3 academic electives. **Freshman Admission Statistics:** 4,752 applied, 82% admitted, 27% enrolled. **Transfer Admission Requirements:** High school transcript, college transcript(s), statement of good standing from prior institution(s). Minimum college GPA of 2.50 required. Lowest grade transferable C. **General Admission Information:** Application fee $40. Regular application deadline 2/15. Notification on a rolling basis, beginning on or about 12/15. Nonfall registration accepted. Admission may be deferred for a maximum of 1 year. Credit and/or placement offered for CEEB Advanced Placement tests.

COSTS AND FINANCIAL AID

Required Forms and Deadlines: FAFSA, institution's own financial aid form. Priority financial aid filing date 3/1. **Notification of Awards:** Applicants will be notified of awards on a rolling basis beginning 3/15. **Types of Aid:** *Need-based scholarships/grants:* Federal Pell, SEOG, state scholarships/grants, private scholarships, the school's own gift aid. *Loans:* FFEL Subsidized Stafford, FFEL Unsubsidized Stafford, FFEL PLUS, Federal Perkins, Federal Nursing. **Student Employment:** Federal Work-Study Program available. Institutional employment available. Highest amount earned per year from on-campus jobs $1,400. Off-campus job opportunities are excellent. **Financial Aid Statistics:** 62% freshmen, 49% undergrads receive need-based scholarship or grant aid. 47% freshmen, 38% undergrads receive non-need-based scholarship or grant aid. 44% freshmen, 37% undergrads receive need-based self-help aid. 3% freshmen, 4% undergrads receive athletic scholarships. 98% freshmen, 96% undergrads receive any aid. 70% undergrads borrow to pay for school. Average cumulative indebtedness $32,888. **Criteria for awarding institutional aid:** *Non-need-based:* Academics, alumni affiliation, art, athletics, leadership, minority status, music/drama.

CROWN COLLEGE

8700 College View Drive, St. Bonifacius, MN 55375-9001
Phone: 952-446-4142 **Financial Aid Phone:** 952-446-4177
E-mail: info@crown.edu
Fax: 952-446-4149 **Website:** www.crown.edu **ACT Code:** 2152

This private school, affiliated with the Christian & Missionary Allianc Church, was founded in 1916. It has a 215-acre campus.

RATINGS

Admissions Selectivity Rating: 77   **Fire Safety Rating:** 63   **Green Rating:** 60*

STUDENTS AND FACULTY

Enrollment: 936. **Student Body:** 56% female, 44% male, 34% out-of-state, international (14 countries represented). Asian 8%, African American 4%, Caucasian 82%, Hispanic 3%, Native American 1%.
Retention and Graduation: 73% freshmen return for sophomore year. 32% freshmen graduate within 4 years. **Faculty:** Student/faculty ratio 11:1. 35 full-time faculty, 29% are women.

ACADEMICS

Degrees: Associate, bachelor's, certificate, master's, post-bachelor's certificate. **Classes:** Most classes have 10–19 students. Most lab/discussion sessions have 20–39 students. **Majors with Highest Enrollment:** Elementary education and teaching; nursing/registered nurse (RN, ASN, BSN, MSN); religious education. **Special Study Options:** Accelerated program, distance learning, double major, dual enrollment, English as a Second Language (ESL), honors program, independent study, internships, study abroad, teacher certification program, weekend college, 2-2 with non-accredited Bible colleges. **Honors programs:** The Honors Program Special programs offered to physically disabled students include note-taking services, reader services, tape recorders, tutors. **Career services:** Alumni services, career/job search classes, career assessment, internships. **Career services highlights include:** We are very excited about the number of opportunities that students have to engage in practical hands-on learning activities through the SIFE and practicum programs.

FACILITIES

Housing: Special housing for disabled students, men's dorms, women's dorms, apartments for married students, apartments for single students, apartments for students with dependent children. 95% of campus accessible to physically disabled. **Special Academic Facilities/Equipment:** Peter Watne Memorial Library. **Computers:** 100% of classrooms, 20% of dorms, 100% of libraries, 100% of dining areas, 100% of student union, 10% of common outdoor areas have wireless network access. Administrative functions (other than registration) can be performed online.

CAMPUS LIFE

Environment: Rural. **Activities:** Choral groups, concert band, drama/theater, jazz band, literary magazine, music ensembles, musical theater, pep band, radio station, student government, student newspaper, student-run film society, yearbook, campus ministries, international student organization. **Organizations:** 19 registered organizations, 1 honor societies, 6 religious organizations. **Athletics (Intercollegiate):** *Men:* Baseball, basketball, cross-country, football, golf, soccer. *Women:* Basketball, cross-country, golf, soccer, softball, volleyball. **On-Campus Highlights:** Student Center, Coffee Shoppe and Climbing Wall, Storm Cafe/student union, Wild Athletic Center/Weight Room, Life Fitness Center. **Environmental Initiatives:** Recycling bins at each employee's desk. Can, bottle and newspaper recycling bins throughout campus. Signs throughout main building on how "trees and oil are saved by recycling paper," how much "aluminum is saved by recycling pop cans," etc.

ADMISSIONS

Freshman Academic Profile: Average high school GPA 3.23. 11% in top 10% of high school class, 44% in top 25% of high school class, 68% in top 50% of high school class. SAT Math middle 50% range 470–635. SAT Critical Reading middle 50% range 500–655. ACT middle 50% range 20–24. Minimum paper TOEFL 450. Minimum computer TOEFL 130. **Basis for Candidate Selection:** *Very important factors considered include:* Application essay, academic GPA, recommendation(s), rigor of secondary school record, standardized test scores, religious affiliation/commitment. *Important factors considered include:* Class rank, character/personal qualities. *Other factors considered include:* Extracurricular activities, interview, level of applicant's interest, talent/ability, volunteer work, work experience. **Freshman Admission Requirements:** High school diploma is required and GED is accepted. *Academic units recommended:* 4 English, 3 mathematics, 3 science, 2 foreign language, 3 social studies. **Freshman Admission Statistics:** 457 applied, 66% admitted, 49% enrolled. **Transfer Admission Requirements:** High school transcript, college transcript(s), essay or personal statement, minimum college GPA of 2.0

required. Lowest grade transferable C. **General Admission Information:** Application fee $35. Regular application deadline 8/20. Nonfall registration accepted. Admission may be deferred for a maximum of 1 year. Credit offered for CEEB Advanced Placement tests.

COSTS AND FINANCIAL AID
Required Forms and Deadlines: FAFSA, institution's own financial aid form Financial aid filing deadline 8/1. Priority financial aid filing date 4/15. **Notification of Awards:** Applicants will be notified of awards on a rolling basis beginning 4/1. **Types of Aid:** *Need-based scholarships/grants:* Federal Pell, SEOG, state scholarships/grants, private scholarships, the school's own gift aid. *Loans:* FFEL Subsidized Stafford, FFEL Unsubsidized Stafford, FFEL PLUS, Federal Perkins, state loans, US Bank No-Fee Education loans, CitiAssist loans, Signature loans, Wells Fargo Collegiate Loan. **Student Employment:** Federal Work-Study Program available. Off-campus job opportunities are good. **Financial Aid Statistics:** 84% freshmen, 83% undergrads receive any aid. 88% undergrads borrow to pay for school. Average cumulative indebtedness $31,804. **Criteria for awarding institutional aid:** *Non-need-based:* Academics, alumni affiliation, leadership, minority status, music/drama, religious affiliation.

CULVER-STOCKTON COLLEGE

One College Hill, Canton, MO 63435
Phone: 573-288-6331 **Financial Aid Phone:** 573-288-6307
E-mail: admissions@culver.edu **CEEB Code:** 6123
Fax: 573-288-6618 **Website: ACT Code:** 2290

This private school, affiliated with the Disciples of Christ Church, was founded in 1853. It has a 139-acre campus.

RATINGS
Admissions Selectivity Rating: 77   **Fire Safety Rating:** 61   **Green Rating:** 60*

STUDENTS AND FACULTY
Enrollment: 723. **Student Body:** 55% female, 45% male, 48% out-of-state, 3% international (13 countries represented). Asian 1%, African American 10%, Caucasian 87%, Hispanic 2%, Native American 1%. **Retention and Graduation:** 59% freshmen return for sophomore year. 43% freshmen graduate within 4 years. 20% grads go on to further study within 1 year. 8% grads pursue arts and sciences degrees. 3% grads pursue law degrees. 5% grads pursue business degrees. 3% grads pursue medical degrees. **Faculty:** Student/faculty ratio 13:1. 45 full-time faculty, 76% hold PhDs, 9% are members of minority groups, 36% are women.

ACADEMICS
Degrees: Bachelor's. **Classes:** Most classes have 10–19 students. Most lab/discussion sessions have 10–19 students. **Majors with Highest Enrollment:** Business administration and management; elementary education and teaching; nursing/registered nurse (RN, ASN, BSN, MSN). **Special Study Options:** Accelerated program, distance learning, double major, dual enrollment, honors program, independent study, internships, liberal arts/career combination, student-designed major, study abroad, teacher certification program. **Honors programs:** Honors Scholars are expected to complete both an academic and enrichment requirement. **Combined degree programs:** BA/MA, Washington University OT program. Special programs offered to physically disabled students include note-taking services, reader services, tape recorders, tutors. **Career services:** Alumni network, alumni services, career/job search classes, career assessment, internships, regional alumni. **Career services highlights include:** All students participate in experiential learning since fall 2008 as part of the new CSC@EXP curriculum.

FACILITIES
Housing: Coed dorms, fraternity/sorority housing. 40% of campus accessible to physically disabled. **Special Academic Facilities/Equipment:** Art gallery, performing arts center. **Computers:** 100% of classrooms, 100% of dorms, 100% of libraries, 100% of dining areas, 100% of student union, 100% of common outdoor areas have wireless network access. Students can register for classes online. Administrative functions (other than registration) can be performed online.

CAMPUS LIFE
Environment: Rural. **Activities:** Choral groups, concert band, dance, drama/theater, jazz band, literary magazine, music ensembles, musical theater, pep band, radio station, student government, student newspaper, campus ministries, international student organization, Model UN. **Organizations:** 44 registered organizations, 11 honor societies, 4 religious organizations, 4 fraternities, 3 sororities. **Athletics (Intercollegiate):** *Men:* Baseball, basketball, cheerleading, cross-country, football, golf, soccer, track/field (outdoor), track/field (indoor). *Women:* Basketball, cheerleading, cross-country, golf, soccer, softball, track/field

(outdoor), track/field (indoor), volleyball. **On-Campus Highlights:** Computer labs, Cat's 'Pause', Cafeteria, Joe Charles Field House, Activity & Recreation Center. **Environmental Initiatives:** Thermostat control, recycling focus group, limited use of disposable containers.

ADMISSIONS
Freshman Academic Profile: Average high school GPA 3.27. 14% in top 10% of high school class, 36% in top 25% of high school class, 72% in top 50% of high school class. 93% from public high schools. SAT Math middle 50% range 460–700. SAT Critical Reading middle 50% range 410–750. ACT middle 50% range 19–24. Minimum paper TOEFL 500. Minimum computer TOEFL 176. Minimum web-based TOEFL 61. **Basis for Candidate Selection:** *Very important factors considered include:* Academic GPA, standardized test scores. *Important factors considered include:* Rigor of secondary school record. *Other factors considered include:* Application essay, recommendation(s), alumni/ae relation. **Freshman Admission Requirements:** High school diploma is required and GED is accepted. *Academic units recommended:* 4 English, 2 mathematics, 2 science, 3 social studies. **Freshman Admission Statistics:** 1,263 applied, 60% admitted, 19% enrolled. **Transfer Admission Requirements:** College transcript(s), minimum college GPA of 2.0 required. Lowest grade transferable C–. **General Admission Information:** Notification on a rolling basis, beginning on or about 10/15. Nonfall registration accepted. Admission may be deferred for a maximum of 1 year. Credit and/or placement offered for CEEB Advanced Placement tests.

COSTS AND FINANCIAL AID
Annual tuition $22,250. Room and board $7,400. Required fees $300. Average book expense $1,000. **Required Forms and Deadlines:** FAFSA Financial aid filing deadline 6/1. Priority financial aid filing date 3/1. **Notification of Awards:** Applicants will be notified of awards on a rolling basis beginning 2/15. **Types of Aid:** *Need-based scholarships/grants:* Federal Pell, SEOG, state scholarships/grants, private scholarships, the school's own gift aid. *Loans:* Direct Subsidized Stafford, Direct Unsubsidized Stafford, Direct PLUS, FFEL PLUS, Federal Perkins, state loans, college/university loans from institutional funds. **Student Employment:** Federal Work-Study Program available. Institutional employment available. Highest amount earned per year from on-campus jobs $4,954. Off-campus job opportunities are fair. **Financial Aid Statistics:** 89% freshmen, 87% undergrads receive need-based scholarship or grant aid. 16% freshmen, 13% undergrads receive non-need-based scholarship or grant aid. 76% freshmen, 76% undergrads receive need-based self-help aid. 7% freshmen, 10% undergrads receive athletic scholarships. 99.3% freshmen, 99.2% undergrads receive any aid. 90.3% undergrads borrow to pay for school. Average cumulative indebtedness $23,761. **Criteria for awarding institutional aid:** *Non-need-based:* Academics, alumni affiliation, art, athletics, job skills, leadership, music/drama, religious affiliation, state/district residency.

CUMBERLAND UNIVERSITY

Cumberland University, One Cumberland Square, Lebanon, TN 37087-3408
Phone: 615-444-2562
E-mail: admissions@cumberland.edu **CEEB Code:** 1146
Fax: 615-444-2569 **Website:** www.cumberland.edu **ACT Code:** 3954

This private school was founded in 1842. It has a 40-acre campus.

RATINGS
Admissions Selectivity Rating: 75   **Fire Safety Rating:** 60*   **Green Rating:** 60*

STUDENTS AND FACULTY
Enrollment: 921. **Student Body:** 57% female, 43% male, 15% out-of-state, 3% international (27 countries represented). Asian 2%, African American 14%, Caucasian 77%, Hispanic 1%. **Retention and Graduation:** 69% freshmen return for sophomore year. 23% freshmen graduate within 4 years. 15% grads go on to further study within 1 year. 5% grads pursue arts and sciences degrees. 3% grads pursue law degrees. 5% grads pursue business degrees. 1% grads pursue medical degrees. **Faculty:** Student/faculty ratio 13:1. 79 full-time faculty, 57% hold PhDs, 5% are members of minority groups, 38% are women.

ACADEMICS
Degrees: Associate, bachelor's, master's. **Classes:** Most classes have fewer than 10 students. Most lab/discussion sessions have fewer than 10 students. **Majors with Highest Enrollment:** Elementary education and teaching; nursing/registered nurse (RN, ASN, BSN, MSN). **Special Study Options:** Accelerated program, distance learning, double major, dual enrollment, honors program, independent study, internships, teacher certification program Special programs offered to physically disabled students include tutors. **Career services:** Career/job search classes, career assessment.

FACILITIES

Housing: Special housing for disabled students, men's dorms, women's dorms. 100% of campus accessible to physically disabled. **Special Academic Facilities/Equipment:** Cavett Wild Game Collection.

CAMPUS LIFE

Environment: Town. **Activities:** Choral groups, dance, drama/theater, jazz band, marching band, music ensembles, musical theater, radio station, student government, student newspaper, yearbook. **Organizations:** 15 registered organizations, 13 honor societies, 2 religious organizations. 3 fraternities, 2 sororities. **Athletics (Intercollegiate):** *Men:* Baseball, basketball, cheerleading, cross-country, football, golf, soccer, tennis, wrestling. *Women:* Basketball, cheerleading, cross-country, golf, soccer, softball, tennis, volleyball. **On-Campus Highlights:** Labry Hall Atrium, Memorial Hall Student Lounge, Mitchell Student Center, Phillips Dining Hall Patio.

ADMISSIONS

Freshman Academic Profile: Average high school GPA 3.03. 12% in top 10% of high school class, 32% in top 25% of high school class, 70% in top 50% of high school class. 89% from public high schools. SAT Math middle 50% range 380–510. SAT Critical Reading middle 50% range 410–530. ACT middle 50% range 17–22. Minimum paper TOEFL 500. Minimum computer TOEFL 173. **Basis for Candidate Selection:** *Very important factors considered include:* Class rank, rigor of secondary school record, standardized test scores. *Other factors considered include:* Application essay, recommendation(s), alumni/ae relation. **Freshman Admission Requirements:** High school diploma is required and GED is accepted. *Academic units recommended:* 4 English, 3 mathematics, 3 science, (1 science labs), 2 foreign language, 2 social studies, 1 history, 12 academic electives. **Freshman Admission Statistics:** 532 applied, 66% admitted, 59% enrolled. **Transfer Admission Requirements:** College transcript(s), minimum college GPA of 2.0 required. Lowest grade transferable C. **General Admission Information:** Application fee $25. Nonfall registration accepted. Admission may be deferred for a maximum of 1 year. Credit offered for CEEB Advanced Placement tests.

COSTS AND FINANCIAL AID

Annual tuition $12,130. Room and board $4,680. Required fees $100. Average book expense $1,040. **Required Forms and Deadlines:** FAFSA, institution's own financial aid form. Financial aid filing deadline 5/1. Priority financial aid filing date 2/15. **Notification of Awards:** Applicants will be notified of awards on or about 5/1. **Types of Aid:** *Need-based scholarships/grants:* Federal Pell, SEOG, state scholarships/grants, private scholarships, the school's own gift aid. *Loans:* FFEL Subsidized Stafford, FFEL Unsubsidized Stafford, FFEL PLUS, Federal Perkins, state loans. **Student Employment:** Federal Work-Study Program available. Off-campus job opportunities are excellent. **Financial Aid Statistics:** 48% freshmen, 43% undergrads receive need-based scholarship or grant aid. 91% freshmen, 76% undergrads receive non-need-based scholarship or grant aid. 58% freshmen, 52% undergrads receive need-based self-help aid. 85% freshmen, 96% undergrads receive athletic scholarships. 85% freshmen, 85% undergrads receive any aid. 70% undergrads borrow to pay for school. Average cumulative indebtedness $7,596.

CURRY COLLEGE

1071 Blue Hill Avenue, Milton, MA 02186
Phone: 617-333-2210
E-mail: curryadm@curry.edu **CEEB Code:** 3285
Fax: 617-333-2114 **Website:** www.curry.edu **ACT Code:** 1814

This private school was founded in 1879. It has a 137-acre campus.

RATINGS

Admissions Selectivity Rating: 63   **Fire Safety Rating:** 60*   **Green Rating:** 60*

STUDENTS AND FACULTY

Enrollment: 1,709. **Student Body:** 53% female, 47% male, 40% out-of-state, 1% international (20 countries represented). Asian 1%, African American 4%, Caucasian 48%, Hispanic 2%. **Retention and Graduation:** 68% freshmen return for sophomore year. 44% freshmen graduate within 4 years. 17% grads go on to further study within 1 year. 10% grads pursue arts and sciences degrees. 1% grads pursue law degrees. 2% grads pursue business degrees. **Faculty:** Student/faculty ratio 12:1.

ACADEMICS

Degrees: Bachelor's, master's. **Special Study Options:** Accelerated program, double major, honors program, independent study, internships, liberal arts/career combination, student-designed major, study abroad, teacher certification program, weekend college. Special programs offered to physically disabled students include tape recorders, tutors.

FACILITIES

Housing: Coed dorms, special housing for international students, women's dorms. **Special Academic Facilities/Equipment:** On-campus preschool, nursing lab, psychology lab. **Computers:** Students can register for classes online.

CAMPUS LIFE

Environment: Village. **Activities:** Choral groups, dance, drama/theater, literary magazine, music ensembles, radio station, student government, student newspaper, television station, yearbook. **Organizations:** 1 honor societies, 2 religious organizations. **Athletics (Intercollegiate):** *Men:* Baseball, basketball, cheerleading, football, ice hockey, lacrosse, soccer, tennis. *Women:* Basketball, cheerleading, cross-country, lacrosse, soccer, softball, tennis. **On-Campus Highlights:** Drapkin Student Center, Levin Library, WMLN Campus Radio Station, The Suites- New Residence Hall, Hafer Academic Center.

ADMISSIONS

Freshman Academic Profile: Average high school GPA 2.3. 5% in top 10% of high school class, 22% in top 25% of high school class, 65% in top 50% of high school class. 76% from public high schools. Minimum paper TOEFL 500. Minimum computer TOEFL 173. **Basis for Candidate Selection:** *Important factors considered include:* Class rank, academic GPA, recommendation(s), rigor of secondary school record. *Other factors considered include:* Application essay, standardized test scores, alumni/ae relation, character/personal qualities, extracurricular activities, interview, volunteer work, work experience. **Freshman Admission Requirements:** High school diploma is required and GED is accepted. *Academic units required:* 4 English, 3 mathematics, 2 science, (2 science labs), 1 social studies, 1 history, 5 academic electives. **Freshman Admission Statistics:** 3,509 applied, 66% admitted, 30% enrolled. **Transfer Admission Requirements:** College transcript(s), essay or personal statement, minimum college GPA of 2.0 required. Lowest grade transferable C–. **General Admission Information:** Application fee $40. Early decision application deadline 12/1. Regular application deadline 4/1. Notification on a rolling basis, beginning on or about 1/15. Nonfall registration accepted. Admission may be deferred for a maximum of 12. Credit and/or placement offered for CEEB Advanced Placement tests.

COSTS AND FINANCIAL AID

Annual tuition $17,160. Room and board $6,870. Required fees $755. Average book expense $700. **Required Forms and Deadlines:** FAFSA, institution's own financial aid form. Priority financial aid filing date 3/1. **Notification of Awards:** Applicants will be notified of awards on a rolling basis beginning 3/1. **Types of Aid:** *Need-based scholarships/grants:* Federal Pell, SEOG, state scholarships/grants, private scholarships, the school's own gift aid. *Loans:* FFEL Subsidized Stafford, FFEL Unsubsidized Stafford, FFEL PLUS, Federal Perkins, state loans. **Student Employment: Financial Aid Statistics:** 45% freshmen, 38% undergrads receive need-based scholarship or grant aid. 50% freshmen, 47% undergrads receive need-based self-help aid. 65% undergrads borrow to pay for school. Average cumulative indebtedness $19,125.

See page 1070.

D'YOUVILLE COLLEGE

One D'Youville Square, 320 Porter Avenue, Buffalo, NY 14201
Phone: 716-829-7600 **Financial Aid Phone:** 716-829-7500
E-mail: admiss@dyc.edu **CEEB Code:** 2197
Fax: 716-829-7790 **Website:** www.dyc.edu **ACT Code:** 2732

This private school was founded in 1908. It has a 7-acre campus.

RATINGS

Admissions Selectivity Rating: 69   **Fire Safety Rating:** 60*   **Green Rating:** 60*

STUDENTS AND FACULTY

Enrollment: 1,136. **Student Body:** 76% female, 24% male, 26% out-of-state, international (55 countries represented). Asian 3%, African American 23%, Caucasian 70%, Hispanic 5%, Native American 1%. **Retention and Graduation:** 72% freshmen return for sophomore year. 13% freshmen graduate within 4 years. **Faculty:** Student/faculty ratio 13:1. 105 full-time faculty, 64% hold PhDs, 10% are members of minority groups, 57% are women.

ACADEMICS

Degrees: Bachelor's, first professional, master's, post-bachelor's certificate, post-master's certificate. **Classes:** Most classes have 10–19 students. Most lab/discussion sessions have 10–19 students. **Majors with Highest Enrollment:** Business/commerce; education; nursing/registered nurse (RN, ASN, BSN,

MSN). **Special Study Options:** Accelerated program, cooperative education program, cross-registration, distance learning, double major, dual enrollment, exchange student program (domestic), independent study, internships, liberal arts/career combination, study abroad, teacher certification program, weekend college. **Combined degree programs:** BS/MS. Special programs offered to physically disabled students include note-taking services, reader services, tape recorders, tutors.

FACILITIES

Housing: Coed dorms, special housing for disabled students, apartments for married students, apartments for single students, quiet floors for 3rd–5th year students. Separate male and female floors available. New apartment style housing opened 1/05. 100% of campus accessible to physically disabled. **Special Academic Facilities/Equipment:** Kavinoky Theatre (professional theatre). **Computers:** Students can register for classes online. Administrative functions (other than registration) can be performed online.

CAMPUS LIFE

Environment: City. **Activities:** Choral groups, drama/theater, literary magazine, student government, student newspaper, yearbook. **Organizations:** 25 registered organizations, 3 honor societies, 1 religious organizations. **Athletics (Intercollegiate):** *Men:* Baseball, basketball, golf, soccer, volleyball. *Women:* Basketball, crew/rowing, golf, soccer, softball, volleyball. **On-Campus Highlights:** New academic center, new sym, Spot Spartian Cafe, weight room, gross anatomy lab, new apartment-style housing for junior level and up.

ADMISSIONS

Freshman Academic Profile: Average high school GPA 2.88. 10% in top 10% of high school class, 9% in top 25% of high school class, 81% in top 50% of high school class. 75% from public high schools. SAT Math middle 50% range 433–540. SAT Critical Reading middle 50% range 430–540. ACT middle 50% range 18–23. Minimum paper TOEFL 500. Minimum computer TOEFL 173. **Basis for Candidate Selection:** *Very important factors considered include:* Rigor of secondary school record, standardized test scores. *Important factors considered include:* Class rank. *Other factors considered include:* Recommendation(s), alumni/ae relation, character/personal qualities, extracurricular activities, interview, talent/ability, volunteer work, work experience. **Freshman Admission Requirements:** High school diploma is required and GED is accepted. *Academic units recommended:* 4 English, 3 mathematics, 3 science, 3 foreign language, 3 social studies. **Freshman Admission Statistics:** 1,242 applied, 72% admitted, 26% enrolled. **Transfer Admission Requirements:** High school transcript, college transcript(s), minimum college GPA of 2.0 required. Lowest grade transferable C. **General Admission Information:** Application fee $25. Nonfall registration accepted. Admission may be deferred for a maximum of 1 year. Credit offered for CEEB Advanced Placement tests.

COSTS AND FINANCIAL AID

Annual tuition $14,690. Room and board $7,340. Required fees $200. Average book expense $850. **Required Forms and Deadlines:** FAFSA, institution's own financial aid form, state aid form. Priority financial aid filing date 3/1. **Notification of Awards:** Applicants will be notified of awards on a rolling basis beginning 4/15. **Types of Aid:** *Need-based scholarships/grants:* Federal Pell, SEOG, state scholarships/grants, private scholarships, the school's own gift aid, Federal Nursing Scholarships. *Loans:* FFEL Subsidized Stafford, FFEL Unsubsidized Stafford, FFEL PLUS, Federal Perkins, Federal Nursing, college/university loans from institutional funds. **Student Employment:** Federal Work-Study Program available. Institutional employment available. Highest amount earned per year from on-campus jobs $2,000. Off-campus job opportunities are excellent. **Financial Aid Statistics:** 93% freshmen, 93% undergrads receive need-based scholarship or grant aid. 65% freshmen, 34% undergrads receive non-need-based scholarship or grant aid. 92% freshmen, 60% undergrads receive need-based self-help aid. 167% freshmen, 941% undergrads receive any aid. **Criteria for awarding institutional aid:** *Non-need-based:* Academics, alumni affiliation.

See page 1072.

DAEMEN COLLEGE

4380 Main Street, Amherst, NY 14226-3592
Phone: 716-839-8225 **Financial Aid Phone:** 716-839-8254
E-mail: admissions@daemen.edu **CEEB Code:** 2762
Fax: 716-839-8229 **Website:** www.daemen.edu **ACT Code:** 2874

This private school was founded in 1947. It has a 35-acre campus.

RATINGS

Admissions Selectivity Rating: 77   **Fire Safety Rating:** 80   **Green Rating:** 73

STUDENTS AND FACULTY

Enrollment: 1,650. **Student Body:** 75% female, 25% male, 3% out-of-state, 1% international (9 countries represented). Asian 1%, African American 10%, Caucasian 83%, Hispanic 4%, Native American 1%. **Retention and Graduation:** 30% freshmen graduate within 4 years. 39.5% grads go on to further study within 1 year. 2% grads pursue arts and sciences degrees. 2% grads pursue business degrees. 1% grads pursue medical degrees. **Faculty:** Student/faculty ratio 13.4:1. 99 full-time faculty, 77% hold PhDs, 8% are members of minority groups, 55% are women.

ACADEMICS

Degrees: Bachelor's, certificate, master's, post-master's certificate. **Classes:** Most classes have 10–19 students. Most lab/discussion sessions have 10–19 students. **Majors with Highest Enrollment:** Elementary education and teaching; health/medical preparatory programs, other; nursing/registered nurse (RN, ASN, BSN, MSN). **Special Study Options:** Accelerated program, cross-registration, distance learning, double major, dual enrollment, English as a Second Language (ESL), exchange student program (domestic), honors program, independent study, internships, liberal arts/career combination, student-designed major, study abroad, teacher certification program, weekend college, Washington semester through the Washington Internship Institute. Dual degree (BS/MS) awarded at the completion of the program in physician assistant studies and professional accountancy. **Honors programs:** The Honors Program provides an enriched curriculum relying upon multiple perspectives and using primary sources rather than textbooks. Honors program students enjoy special residential accommodations, priority registration by class rank, opportunities for domestic and international travel, and unique offerings such as field trips, access to campus speakers, and research and publication opportunities. **Combined degree programs:** BS/MS health sci./phys. asst.; BS/MS accountancy; BS nursing 1-2-1. Special programs offered to physically disabled students include note-taking services, tape recorders, tutors. **Career services:** Alumni network, alumni services, career/job search classes, career assessment, internships, regional alumni.

FACILITIES

Housing: Coed dorms, coed apartment-style residence halls for single students; some apartments are handicapped accessible. 92% of campus accessible to physically disabled. **Special Academic Facilities/Equipment:** Teaching Resource Center; Franette Goldman/Carolyn Greenfield Art Gallery; Natural and Health Sciences Research Center; video conferencing center; Research & Information Commons (new). **Computers:** 60% of classrooms, 100% of dorms, 100% of libraries, 75% of dining areas, 50% of student union, 10% of common outdoor areas have wireless network access. Students can register for classes online. Administrative functions (other than registration) can be performed online.

CAMPUS LIFE

Environment: City. **Activities:** Choral groups, dance, drama/theater, literary magazine, student government, student newspaper, yearbook, campus ministries. **Organizations:** 45 registered organizations, 8 honor societies, 1 fraternities, 4 sororities. **Athletics (Intercollegiate):** *Men:* Basketball, cross-country, golf, soccer. *Women:* Basketball, cross-country, soccer, volleyball. **On-Campus Highlights:** Research and Information Commons, Modern Apartment-Style Residence Halls, Wick Student Center, Academic Computing Facilities, Athletic Facilities. **Environmental Initiatives:** College has hosted conferences and symposia on campus: Annual Environmental Summit; Green Jobs Workshop; World on Your Plate Symposium, Focus the Nation Teach-In. College offers sustainability-focused courses and undergraduate majors On 1/27/2009 opened new building on campus registered for LEED certification.

ADMISSIONS

Freshman Academic Profile: Average high school GPA 3.53. SAT Math middle 50% range 460–570. SAT Critical Reading middle 50% range 450–540. SAT Writing middle 50% range 440–550. ACT middle 50% range 20–25. Minimum paper TOEFL 500. Minimum computer TOEFL 173. Minimum web-based TOEFL 61. **Basis for Candidate Selection:** *Very important factors considered include:* Academic GPA, rigor of secondary school record. *Important factors considered include:* Class rank, application essay, recommendation(s), interview. *Other factors considered include:* Standardized test scores, alumni/ae relation, character/personal qualities, extracurricular activities, level of applicant's interest, talent/ability, volunteer work, work experience. **Freshman Admission Requirements:** High school diploma is required and GED is accepted. *Academic units recommended:* 4 English, 4 mathematics, 4 science, (1 science labs), 4 social studies. **Freshman Admission Statistics:** 1,988 applied, 66% admitted, 31% enrolled. **Transfer Admission Requirements:** College transcript(s), statement of good standing from prior institution(s). Minimum college GPA of 2.0 required. Lowest grade transferable C. **General Admission Information:** Application fee $25. Notification on a rolling basis, beginning on or about 10/15. Nonfall registration accepted. Admission may be deferred for a maximum of 1 year. Credit offered for CEEB Advanced Placement tests.

COSTS AND FINANCIAL AID

Annual tuition $19,400. Room and board $9,050. Required fees $470. Average book expense $800. **Required Forms and Deadlines:** FAFSA, state aid form. Priority financial aid filing date 2/15. **Notification of Awards:** Applicants will be notified of awards on a rolling basis beginning 2/15. **Types of Aid:** *Need-based scholarships/grants:* Federal Pell, SEOG, state scholarships/grants, private scholarships, the school's own gift aid. *Loans:* FFEL Subsidized Stafford, FFEL Unsubsidized Stafford, FFEL PLUS, Federal Perkins, college/university loans from institutional funds, Alternative Loans through private lenders. **Student Employment:** Federal Work-Study Program available. Institutional employment available. Highest amount earned per year from on-campus jobs $800. Off-campus job opportunities are fair. **Financial Aid Statistics:** 80% freshmen, 79% undergrads receive need-based scholarship or grant aid. 74% freshmen, 73% undergrads receive non-need-based scholarship or grant aid. 70% freshmen, 73% undergrads receive need-based self-help aid. 4% freshmen, 6% undergrads receive athletic scholarships. 85% freshmen, 86% undergrads receive any aid. 87% undergrads borrow to pay for school. Average cumulative indebtedness $20,465. **Criteria for awarding institutional aid:** *Non-need-based:* Academics, art, athletics.

See page 1074.

DAKOTA STATE UNIVERSITY

820 North Washington Ave, Admissions, Madison, SD 57042
Phone: 605-256-5139 **Financial Aid Phone:** 605-256-5152
E-mail: admissions@dsu.edu **CEEB Code:** 6247
Fax: 605-256-5020 **Website:** www.dsu.edu **ACT Code:** 3910

This public school was founded in 1881. It has a 20-acre campus.

RATINGS
Admissions Selectivity Rating: 68   **Fire Safety Rating:** 60*   **Green Rating:** 63

STUDENTS AND FACULTY
Enrollment: 1,450. **Student Body:** 49% female, 51% male, 22.7% out-of-state, 1% international (13 countries represented). Asian 1%, African American 2%, Caucasian 86%, Hispanic 1%, Native American 1%. **Retention and Graduation:** 76% freshmen return for sophomore year. **Faculty:** 94 full-time faculty, 69% hold PhDs, 10% are members of minority groups, 33% are women. 1.4% of classes are taught by teaching assistants.

ACADEMICS
Degrees: Associate, bachelor's, certificate, master's. **Classes:** Most classes have 20–29 students. Most lab/discussion sessions have 10–19 students. **Majors with Highest Enrollment:** Business administration and management; elementary education and teaching; information science/studies. **Special Study Options:** Cooperative education program, cross-registration, distance learning, double major, dual enrollment, English as a Second Language (ESL), honors program, independent study, internships, teacher certification program. **Honors programs:** Center of Excellence(CEX), Honors Special programs offered to physically disabled students include note-taking services, reader services, tape recorders, tutors. **Career services:** Alumni services, career/job search classes, career assessment, internships **Career services highlights include:** On-campus interviews.

FACILITIES
Housing: Coed dorms, men's dorms, special housing for international students, women's dorms, apartments for single students. 80% of campus accessible to physically disabled. **Special Academic Facilities/Equipment:** Smith Zimmerman Museum. **Computers:** 100% of classrooms, 100% of dorms, 100% of libraries, 100% of dining areas, 100% of student union, 100% of common outdoor areas have wireless network access. Students can register for classes online. Administrative functions (other than registration) can be performed online. Undergraduates are required to own a computer.

CAMPUS LIFE
Environment: Rural. **Activities:** Choral groups, dance, drama/theater, literary magazine, music ensembles, musical theater, pep band, radio station, student government, student newspaper, international student organization. **Organizations:** 33 registered organizations, 3 honor societies, 2 religious organizations. **Athletics (Intercollegiate):** *Men:* Baseball, basketball, cheerleading, cross-country, football, track/field (outdoor), track/field (indoor). *Women:* Basketball, cheerleading, cross-country, softball, track/field (outdoor), track/field (indoor), volleyball. **On-Campus Highlights:** Tunheim Classroom Building, Community Center, Trojan Center, Myxers Coffee Shop, The Marketplace. **Environmental Initiatives:** LEED Silver project in progress; paper recycling; energy conservation measures.

ADMISSIONS
Freshman Academic Profile: Average high school GPA 3.06. 6.8% in top 10% of high school class, 23.8% in top 25% of high school class, 55.2% in top 50% of high school class. ACT middle 50% range 19–25. Minimum paper TOEFL 550. Minimum computer TOEFL 213. Minimum web-based TOEFL 80. **Basis for Candidate Selection:** *Important factors considered include:* Class rank, academic GPA, rigor of secondary school record, standardized test scores, level of applicant's interest. **Freshman Admission Requirements:** High school diploma is required and GED is accepted. *Academic units recommended:* 4 English, 3 mathematics, 3 science, (3 science labs), 3 social studies. **Freshman Admission Statistics:** 672 applied, 94% admitted, 51% enrolled. **Transfer Admission Requirements:** High school transcript, college transcript(s), minimum college GPA of 2.0 required. Lowest grade transferable D. **General Admission Information:** Application fee $20. Nonfall registration accepted. Credit and/or placement offered for CEEB Advanced Placement tests.

COSTS AND FINANCIAL AID
Annual in-state tuition $2,751. Annual out-of-state tuition $4,124. Room and board $4,818. Required fees $4,121. Average book expense $950. **Required Forms and Deadlines:** FAFSA, Institutional Scholarship Application Form. Priority financial aid filing date 3/1. **Notification of Awards:** Applicants will be notified of awards on a rolling basis beginning 4/1. **Types of Aid:** *Need-based scholarships/grants:* Federal Pell, SEOG, state scholarships/grants, private scholarships, the school's own gift aid, Agency Assistance (Veteran Benefits/Department of Labor). *Loans:* FFEL Subsidized Stafford, FFEL Unsubsidized Stafford, FFEL PLUS, Federal Perkins, alternative commercial loans. **Student Employment:** Federal Work-Study Program available. Institutional employment available. Highest amount earned per year from on-campus jobs $5,637. Off-campus job opportunities are good. **Financial Aid Statistics:** 31% freshmen, 31% undergrads receive need-based scholarship or grant aid. 43% freshmen, 27% undergrads receive non-need-based scholarship or grant aid. 61% freshmen, 60% undergrads receive need-based self-help aid. 14% freshmen, 12% undergrads receive athletic scholarships. 84% freshmen, 84% undergrads receive any aid. 92% undergrads borrow to pay for school. Average cumulative indebtedness $21,189. **Criteria for awarding institutional aid:** *Non-need-based:* Academics, alumni affiliation, art, athletics, leadership, minority status, music/drama, state/district residency.

DAKOTA WESLEYAN UNIVERSITY

1200 West University Avenue, Mitchell, SD 57301-4398
Phone: 605-995-2650 **Financial Aid Phone:** 605-995-2656
E-mail: admissions@dwu.edu **CEEB Code:** 6155
Fax: 605-995-2699 **Website:** www.dwu.edu **ACT Code:** 3906

This private school, affiliated with the Methodist Church, was founded in 1885. It has a 50-acre campus.

RATINGS
Admissions Selectivity Rating: 74   **Fire Safety Rating:** 60*   **Green Rating:** 60*

STUDENTS AND FACULTY
Enrollment: 654. **Student Body:** 59% female, 41% male, 24% out-of-state, 1% international (5 countries represented). Asian 1%, African American 4%, Caucasian 90%, Hispanic 2%, Native American 2%. **Retention and Graduation:** 58% freshmen return for sophomore year. 23% freshmen graduate within 4 years. 10% grads go on to further study within 1 year. **Faculty:** Student/faculty ratio 11:1. 45 full-time faculty, 64% hold PhDs, 2% are members of minority groups, 47% are women.

ACADEMICS
Degrees: Associate, bachelor's, master's, terminal associate. **Classes:** Most classes have 10–19 students. Most lab/discussion sessions have 10–19 students. **Majors with Highest Enrollment:** Business/commerce; elementary education and teaching; human services. **Special Study Options:** Distance learning, double major, dual enrollment, honors program, independent study, internships, liberal arts/career combination, student-designed major, study abroad, teacher certification program **Honors programs:** University Scholars Program, students take at least three USP courses, have a 3.5 GPA, and present original scholarship at the USP Symposium **Combined degree programs:** BA, M.Div. Special programs offered to physically disabled students include note-taking services, reader services, tape recorders, tutors.

FACILITIES
Housing: Coed dorms, men's dorms, women's dorms, apartments for married students, apartments for single students, Koka "honor housing" for upper class women; ADA rooms, apartments available. 100% of campus accessible to physically disabled. **Special Academic Facilities/Equipment:** Friends of the

Middle Border Museum and Grounds. **Computers:** Administrative functions (other than registration) can be performed online. Undergraduates are required to own a computer.

CAMPUS LIFE
Environment: Village. **Activities:** Choral groups, concert band, drama/theater, literary magazine, music ensembles, student government, student newspaper, yearbook. **Organizations:** 5 registered organizations, 6 honor societies, 3 religious organizations. **Athletics (Intercollegiate):** *Men:* Baseball, basketball, cheerleading, cross-country, football, golf, track/field (outdoor), track/field (indoor), wrestling. *Women:* Basketball, cheerleading, cross-country, golf, softball, track/field (outdoor), track/field (indoor), volleyball. **On-Campus Highlights:** Athletic Department/gym/wellness center, cafeteria/coffee shop, student lounge, residence halls common lounge, residence hall computer-labs.

ADMISSIONS
Freshman Academic Profile: Average high school GPA 3.01. 10% in top 10% of high school class, 35% in top 25% of high school class, 75% in top 50% of high school class. 98% from public high schools. ACT middle 50% range 22–28. Minimum paper TOEFL 500. Minimum computer TOEFL 200. **Basis for Candidate Selection:** *Very important factors considered include:* Class rank, rigor of secondary school record, standardized test scores. *Important factors considered include:* Application essay. *Other factors considered include:* Recommendation(s). **Freshman Admission Requirements:** High school diploma is required and GED is accepted. *Academic units recommended:* 4 English, 4 mathematics, 4 social studies. **Freshman Admission Statistics:** 423 applied, 79% admitted, 41% enrolled. **Transfer Admission Requirements:** College transcript(s), minimum college GPA of 2.0 required. Lowest grade transferable D–. **General Admission Information:** Application fee $25. Regular application deadline 8/29. Notification on a rolling basis, beginning on or about 9/1. Nonfall registration accepted. Admission may be deferred for a maximum of no set date. Credit and/or placement offered for CEEB Advanced Placement tests.

COSTS AND FINANCIAL AID
Annual tuition $15,600. Room and board $4,744. Average book expense $900. **Required Forms and Deadlines:** FAFSA. Priority financial aid filing date 4/1. **Notification of Awards:** Applicants will be notified of awards on a rolling basis beginning 3/1. **Types of Aid:** *Need-based scholarships/grants:* Federal Pell, SEOG, private scholarships, the school's own gift aid, Federal Nursing Scholarships. South Dakota Board of Nursing Scholarships / Loans. *Loans:* FFEL Subsidized Stafford, FFEL Unsubsidized Stafford, FFEL PLUS, Federal Perkins, Methodist Loans, and Private Alternative Student Loans. **Student Employment:** Highest amount earned per year from on-campus jobs $3,300. **Financial Aid Statistics:** 85% freshmen, 100% undergrads receive need-based scholarship or grant aid. 57% freshmen, 41% undergrads receive non-need-based scholarship or grant aid. 85% freshmen, 97% undergrads receive need-based self-help aid. 65% freshmen, 41% undergrads receive athletic scholarships. 98% freshmen, 98% undergrads receive any aid. 98% undergrads borrow to pay for school. Average cumulative indebtedness $13,925. **Criteria for awarding institutional aid:** *Non-need-based:* Academics, alumni affiliation, art, athletics, leadership, minority status, music/drama, religious affiliation.

DALLAS BAPTIST UNIVERSITY

3000 Mountain Creek Parkway, Dallas, TX 75211-9299
Phone: 214-333-5360 **Financial Aid Phone:** 214-333-5363
E-mail: admiss@dbu.edu **CEEB Code:** 6159
Fax: 214-333-5447 **Website:** www.dbu.edu/ **ACT Code:** 4080

This private school, affiliated with the Baptist Church, was founded in 1898. It has a 293-acre campus.

RATINGS
Admissions Selectivity Rating: 82   **Fire Safety Rating:** 60*   **Green Rating:** 60*

STUDENTS AND FACULTY
Enrollment: 3,533. **Student Body:** 59% female, 41% male, 5% out-of-state, 8% international (56 countries represented). Asian 2%, African American 19%, Caucasian 62%, Hispanic 9%, Native American 1%.
Retention and Graduation: 70% freshmen return for sophomore year. **Faculty:** Student/faculty ratio 14:1. 123 full-time faculty, 72% hold PhDs, 14% are members of minority groups, 39% are women.

ACADEMICS
Degrees: Associate, bachelor's, certificate, master's, post-bachelor's certificate, post-master's certificate, transfer associate. **Classes:** Most classes have 10–19 students. Most lab/discussion sessions have 10–19 students. **Majors with High-**

est Enrollment: Business/commerce; general studies; psychology. **Special Study Options:** Accelerated program, distance learning, double major, dual enrollment, English as a Second Language (ESL), honors program, independent study, internships, study abroad, teacher certification program, weekend college. **Honors programs:** www.dbu.edu/honors/ Special programs offered to physically disabled students include note-taking services, reader services, tape recorders, tutors. **Career services:** Alumni services, career/job search classes, career assessment, internships. **Career services highlights include:** Online job search engine—CareerBridge.

FACILITIES
Housing: Special housing for disabled students, men's dorms, women's dorms, apartments for married students, apartments for single students, wellness housing townhomes. 75% of campus accessible to physically disabled. **Special Academic Facilities/Equipment:** Corrie Ten Boom Collection. **Computers:** Students can register for classes online.

CAMPUS LIFE
Environment: Metropolis. **Activities:** Choral groups, dance, drama/theater, music ensembles, musical theater, opera, student government, yearbook, campus ministries, international student organization. **Organizations:** 36 registered organizations, 4 honor societies, 3 religious organizations. **Athletics (Intercollegiate):** *Men:* Baseball, cross-country, golf, soccer, tennis, track/field (outdoor). *Women:* Cross-country, golf, soccer, tennis, track/field (outdoor), volleyball. **On-Campus Highlights:** Mahler Student Center, Burg Center, Coffee House, Collins Learning Center, Crowley Co-Ed.

ADMISSIONS
Freshman Academic Profile: Average high school GPA 3.54. 19% in top 10% of high school class, 39% in top 25% of high school class, 61% in top 50% of high school class. SAT Math middle 50% range 499–637. SAT Critical Reading middle 50% range 478–643. ACT middle 50% range 18–22. Minimum paper TOEFL 525. Minimum computer TOEFL 197. **Basis for Candidate Selection:** *Very important factors considered include:* Class rank, application essay, academic GPA, rigor of secondary school record, standardized test scores, character/personal qualities, religious affiliation/commitment, talent/ability. *Important factors considered include:* Extracurricular activities, first generation, interview. *Other factors considered include:* Recommendation(s), alumni/ae relation, volunteer work, work experience. **Freshman Admission Requirements:** High school diploma is required and GED is accepted. *Academic units recommended:* 4 English, 3 mathematics, 2 science, 2 foreign language, 3 social studies, 2 history. **Freshman Admission Statistics:** 1,601 applied, 46% admitted, 48% enrolled. **Transfer Admission Requirements:** College transcript(s), essay or personal statement, minimum college GPA of 2.5 required. Lowest grade transferable C. **General Admission Information:** Application fee $25. Nonfall registration accepted. Credit offered for CEEB Advanced Placement tests.

COSTS AND FINANCIAL AID
Annual tuition $17,490. Room and board $5,636. Average book expense $1,950. **Required Forms and Deadlines:** FAFSA, institution's own financial aid form. **Types of Aid:** *Need-based scholarships/grants:* Federal Pell, SEOG, state scholarships/grants, private scholarships, the school's own gift aid. *Loans:* FFEL Subsidized Stafford, FFEL Unsubsidized Stafford, FFEL PLUS, Federal Perkins, state loans, college/university loans from institutional funds. **Student Employment:** Federal Work-Study Program available. Institutional employment available. Highest amount earned per year from on-campus jobs $2,880. Off-campus job opportunities are good. **Financial Aid Statistics:** 43% freshmen, 42% undergrads receive need-based scholarship or grant aid. 64% freshmen, 50% undergrads receive non-need-based scholarship or grant aid. 50% freshmen, 47% undergrads receive need-based self-help aid. 6% freshmen, 5% undergrads receive athletic scholarships. 79% undergrads borrow to pay for school. Average cumulative indebtedness $17,214. **Criteria for awarding institutional aid:** *Non-need-based:* Academics, athletics, job skills, leadership, music/drama, religious affiliation.

DANA COLLEGE

2848 College Drive, Blair, NE 68008-1099
Phone: 402-426-7222 **Financial Aid Phone:** 402-426-7226
E-mail: admissions@dana.edu
Fax: 402-426-7386 **Website:** www.dana.edu **ACT Code:** 2446

This private school, affiliated with the Lutheran Church, was founded in 1884. It has a 150-acre campus.

RATINGS
Admissions Selectivity Rating: 76   **Fire Safety Rating:** 80   **Green Rating:** 60*

STUDENTS AND FACULTY

Enrollment: 595. **Student Body:** 47% female, 53% male, 42% out-of-state, 1% international (3 countries represented). Asian 1%, African American 3%, Caucasian 91%, Hispanic 4%, Native American 1%.
Retention and Graduation: 60% freshmen return for sophomore year. 33% freshmen graduate within 4 years. 13% grads go on to further study within 1 year. 5% grads pursue arts and sciences degrees. 1% grads pursue law degrees. 1% grads pursue business degrees. 1% grads pursue medical degrees. **Faculty:** Student/faculty ratio 13:1. 31 full-time faculty, 81% hold PhDs, 3% are members of minority groups, 58% are women.

ACADEMICS

Degrees: Bachelor's. **Classes:** Most classes have fewer than 10 students. Most lab/discussion sessions have fewer than 10 students. **Majors with Highest Enrollment:** Business/commerce; criminal justice/law enforcement administration; education. **Special Study Options:** Accelerated program, cross-registration, double major, dual enrollment, English as a Second Language (ESL), honors program, independent study, internships, liberal arts/career combination, student-designed major, study abroad, teacher certification program. Special programs offered to physically disabled students include note-taking services, reader services, tutors. **Career services:** Career/job search classes, career assessment, internships.

FACILITIES

Housing: Coed dorms, women's dorms, apartments for married students, apartments for single students. 80% of campus accessible to physically disabled. **Special Academic Facilities/Equipment:** Danish Archives. **Computers:** Administrative functions (other than registration) can be performed online.

CAMPUS LIFE

Environment: Rural. **Activities:** Choral groups, concert band, dance, drama/theater, jazz band, literary magazine, music ensembles, musical theater, radio station, student government, student newspaper, television station, yearbook. **Organizations:** 25 registered organizations, 3 honor societies, 3 religious organizations. **Athletics (Intercollegiate):** *Men:* Baseball, basketball, cross-country, football, soccer, track/field (outdoor), wrestling. *Women:* Basketball, cheerleading, cross-country, golf, soccer, softball, track/field (outdoor), volleyball. **On-Campus Highlights:** Gardner-Hawks Center, Dragon's Head.

ADMISSIONS

Freshman Academic Profile: Average high school GPA 3.24. 16% in top 10% of high school class, 37% in top 25% of high school class, 62% in top 50% of high school class. SAT Math middle 50% range 420–550. SAT Critical Reading middle 50% range 480–560. ACT middle 50% range 20–25. Minimum paper TOEFL 500. Minimum computer TOEFL 173. **Basis for Candidate Selection:** *Very important factors considered include:* Academic GPA, rigor of secondary school record, standardized test scores. *Other factors considered include:* Application essay, recommendation(s), extracurricular activities, interview, level of applicant's interest, volunteer work, work experience. **Freshman Admission Requirements:** High school diploma is required and GED is accepted. *Academic units recommended:* 4 English, 3 mathematics, 3 science, (2 science labs), 2 foreign language, 4 social studies. **Freshman Admission Statistics:** 830 applied, 72% admitted, 24% enrolled. **Transfer Admission Requirements:** College transcript(s), minimum college GPA of 2.0 required. Lowest grade transferable C. **General Admission Information:** Notification on a rolling basis, beginning on or about 9/1. Nonfall registration accepted. Admission may be deferred for a maximum of 2 years. Credit offered for CEEB Advanced Placement tests.

COSTS AND FINANCIAL AID

Average book expense $900. **Required Forms and Deadlines:** FAFSA, institution's own financial aid form. Priority financial aid filing date 3/15. **Notification of Awards:** Applicants will be notified of awards on a rolling basis beginning 3/4. **Types of Aid:** *Need-based scholarships/grants:* Federal Pell, SEOG, state scholarships/grants, private scholarships, the school's own gift aid. *Loans:* FFEL Subsidized Stafford, FFEL Unsubsidized Stafford, FFEL PLUS, Federal Perkins. **Student Employment:** Federal Work-Study Program available. Institutional employment available. Highest amount earned per year from on-campus jobs $1,500. Off-campus job opportunities are good. **Financial Aid Statistics:** 39% freshmen, 48% undergrads receive need-based scholarship or grant aid. 62% freshmen, 59% undergrads receive non-need-based scholarship or grant aid. 65% freshmen, 64% undergrads receive need-based self-help aid. 68% freshmen, 59% undergrads receive athletic scholarships. 123% freshmen, 478% undergrads receive any aid. 85.5% undergrads borrow to pay for school. Average cumulative indebtedness $17,029. **Criteria for awarding institutional aid:** *Non-need-based:* Academics, alumni affiliation, art, athletics, leadership, music/drama, religious affiliation, state/district residency.

DANIEL WEBSTER COLLEGE

20 University Drive, Nashua, NH 03063-1300
Phone: 603-577-6600
E-mail: admissions@dwc.edu **CEEB Code:** 3648
Fax: 603-577-6001 **Website:** www.dwc.edu **ACT Code:** 2525

This private school was founded in 1965. It has a 50-acre campus.

RATINGS

Admissions Selectivity Rating: 76   **Fire Safety Rating:** 60*   **Green Rating:** 60*

STUDENTS AND FACULTY

Enrollment: 785. **Student Body:** 25% female, 75% male, 72% out-of-state, international (11 countries represented). Asian 1%, African American 4%, Hispanic 3%.
Retention and Graduation: 64% freshmen return for sophomore year. 40% freshmen graduate within 4 years. 8% grads go on to further study within 1 year. 8% grads pursue arts and sciences degrees. **Faculty:** Student/faculty ratio 14:1. 39 full-time faculty, 54% hold PhDs, 23% are women.

ACADEMICS

Degrees: Associate, bachelor's, master's, transfer associate. **Classes:** Most classes have 10–19 students. Most lab/discussion sessions have fewer than 10 students. **Majors with Highest Enrollment:** Airline/commercial/professional pilot and flight crew; business/commerce; computer and information sciences. **Special Study Options:** Accelerated program, cooperative education program, cross-registration, distance learning, double major, dual enrollment, independent study, internships, study abroad. **Combined degree programs:** 2-2 aeronautical enginering and engineering scienc. Special programs offered to physically disabled students include tutors. **Career services:** Alumni network, alumni services, career/job search classes, career assessment, internships.

FACILITIES

Housing: Coed dorms, men's dorms, women's dorms, Men's Townhouses, Women's Townhouses Suites. 80% of campus accessible to physically disabled. **Special Academic Facilities/Equipment:** Campus is adjacent to municipal airport; over 35 aircraft are available for flight training. Three flight simulators, aviation center.

CAMPUS LIFE

Environment: Village. **Activities:** Choral groups, drama/theater, jazz band, musical theater, student government, student newspaper, student-run film society, yearbook. **Organizations:** 17 registered organizations, 2 honor societies, 1 religious organizations. **Athletics (Intercollegiate):** *Men:* Baseball, basketball, cross-country, lacrosse, soccer. *Women:* Basketball, cross-country, soccer, softball, volleyball.

ADMISSIONS

Freshman Academic Profile: Average high school GPA 3.06. 7% in top 10% of high school class, 21% in top 25% of high school class, 52% in top 50% of high school class. 83% from public high schools. SAT Math middle 50% range 480–610. SAT Critical Reading middle 50% range 470–570. ACT middle 50% range 19–24. Minimum paper TOEFL 520. Minimum computer TOEFL 190. **Basis for Candidate Selection:** *Very important factors considered include:* Rigor of secondary school record. *Important factors considered include:* Class rank, recommendation(s), standardized test scores, extracurricular activities, interview. *Other factors considered include:* Application essay, character/personal qualities, level of applicant's interest, talent/ability, volunteer work, work experience. **Freshman Admission Requirements:** High school diploma is required and GED is accepted. *Academic units required:* 4 English, 3 mathematics, 3 science, (2 science labs), 2 social studies, 2 history, 2 academic electives. *Academic units recommended:* 4 mathematics, 2 foreign language. **Freshman Admission Statistics:** 823 applied, **Transfer Admission Requirements:** High school transcript, college transcript(s), minimum college GPA of 2.5 required. Lowest grade transferable C. **General Admission Information:** Application fee $35. Nonfall registration accepted. Admission may be deferred for a maximum of 1 year. Credit and/or placement offered for CEEB Advanced Placement tests.

COSTS AND FINANCIAL AID

Average book expense $750. **Required Forms and Deadlines:** FAFSA, institution's own financial aid form. Priority financial aid filing date 3/1. **Notification of Awards:** Applicants will be notified of awards on a rolling basis beginning 3/15. **Types of Aid:** *Need-based scholarships/grants:* Federal Pell, SEOG, state scholarships/grants, the school's own gift aid. *Loans:* Direct Subsidized Stafford, Direct Unsubsidized Stafford, Direct PLUS, Federal Perkins. **Student Employment:** Federal Work-Study Program available. Institutional employment available. Highest amount earned per year from on-campus jobs $2,000. Off-campus job opportunities are excellent. **Financial Aid Statistics:** 93% freshmen, 79% undergrads receive need-based scholarship or grant aid.

83% freshmen, 79% undergrads receive non-need-based scholarship or grant aid. 100% freshmen, 81% undergrads receive need-based self-help aid. 83% undergrads borrow to pay for school. Average cumulative indebtedness $48,000. **Criteria for awarding institutional aid:** *Non-need-based:* Academics, leadership.

DARTMOUTH COLLEGE

6016 McNutt Hall, Hanover, NH 03755
Phone: 603-646-2875 **Financial Aid Phone:** 603-646-2451
E-mail: admissions.office@dartmouth.edu **CEEB Code:** 3351
Fax: 603-646-1216 **Website:** www.dartmouth.edu

This private school was founded in 1769. It has a 265-acre campus.

RATINGS
Admissions Selectivity Rating: 99   **Fire Safety Rating:** 60*   **Green Rating:** 95

STUDENTS AND FACULTY
Enrollment: 4,090. **Student Body:** 50% female, 50% male, 95% out-of-state, 7% international . Asian 15%, African American 8%, Caucasian 54%, Hispanic 7%, Native American 4%.
Retention and Graduation: 98% freshmen return for sophomore year. 85% freshmen graduate within 4 years. **Faculty:** Student/faculty ratio 8:1. 533 full-time faculty, 95% hold PhDs, 17% are members of minority groups, 36% are women.

ACADEMICS
Degrees: Bachelor's, doctoral, master's. **Classes:** Most classes have 10–19 students. **Majors with Highest Enrollment:** Economics; political science and government; psychology. **Special Study Options:** Double major, exchange student program (domestic), honors program, independent study, internships, student-designed major, study abroad, teacher certification program. **Honors programs:** Presidential Scholarship Research Program; Senior Honors Thesis; Senior Fellowship. **Combined degree programs:** BA/BENG—5 year program. Special programs offered to physically disabled students include note-taking services, tape recorders, tutors. **Career services:** Alumni network, alumni services, career/job search classes, career assessment, internships, regional alumni. **Career services highlights include:** Unpaid internships are financially supported through the Rockefeller Center (public policy or political internships), the Dickey Center for International Understanding (overseas opportunities), the Tucker Foundation (religious or community service organizations), and through other sources on campus.

FACILITIES
Housing: Coed dorms, special housing for international students, fraternity/sorority housing, apartments for married students, cooperative housing, apartments for single students, theme housing, Academic Affinity Housing, Faculty-In-Residence Programs, Sustainable Living Center, Interfaith Living, Special Interest Housing. 75% of campus accessible to physically disabled. **Special Academic Facilities/Equipment:** Hood Museum of Art, Hopkins Center for Performing Arts, Tucker Foundation for volunteer services, observatory, centers for humanities, social science, and science. **Computers:** 100% of classrooms, 100% of dorms, 100% of libraries, 100% of dining areas, 100% of student union, 100% of common outdoor areas have wireless network access. Students can register for classes online. Administrative functions (other than registration) can be performed online. Undergraduates are required to own a computer.

CAMPUS LIFE
Environment: Village. **Activities:** Choral groups, concert band, dance, drama/theater, jazz band, literary magazine, marching band, music ensembles, musical theater, opera, pep band, radio station, student government, student newspaper, student-run film society, symphony orchestra, television station, yearbook, campus ministries, international student organization, Model UN. **Organizations:** 330 registered organizations, 26 religious organizations. 14 fraternities, 6 sororities. **Athletics (Intercollegiate):** *Men:* Baseball, basketball, crew/rowing, cross-country, diving, equestrian sports, fencing, football, golf, ice hockey, lacrosse, sailing, skiing (downhill/alpine), skiing (nordic/cross-country), soccer, squash, swimming, tennis, track/field (outdoor), track/field. *Women:* Basketball, crew/rowing, cross-country, diving, equestrian sports, fencing, field hockey, golf, ice hockey, lacrosse, sailing, skiing (downhill/alpine), skiing (nordic/cross-country), soccer, softball, squash, swimming, tennis, track/field

(outdoor), track/fi. **On-Campus Highlights:** Hopkins Center for Creative and Performing Arts, Hood Museum of Art, Murals by Jose Clemente Orozco, Ten library system, all open to visitors, Ledyard Canoe Club, oldest in the country. **Environmental Initiatives:** As part of our commitment to reduce greenhouse gas emissions, Dartmouth commissioned an energy audit for the buildings that collectively use 75% of the energy on campus. Based on the results of this audit, the Trustees invested $12.5 million in 250 energy conservation and efficiency projects in existing buildings, which are now underway. Dartmouth established a Sustainable Living Center and is working with students to develop it as a model green dormitory and center. As part of this effort we are working on plans to push the building toward zero net energy and developing a sustainable food system for the students who live there. (See www.dartmouth.edu/~slc). Building energy metering equipment has been upgraded and the innovative Green Lite Dartmouth feedback displays will be used to provide occupants with real-time resource use information. (See greenlite.dartmouth.edu). In the first term of operation, the students reduced electricity use by 58% below past years through behavioral change alone. Dartmouth established a new tenured faculty position in Sustainability Sciences. The position has been filled and new courses in sustainability will be added in fall of 2009.

ADMISSIONS
Freshman Academic Profile: 91% in top 10% of high school class, 99% in top 25% of high school class, 100% in top 50% of high school class. 60% from public high schools. SAT Math middle 50% range 680–780. SAT Critical Reading middle 50% range 660–770. SAT Writing middle 50% range 670–780. ACT middle 50% range 30–34. **Basis for Candidate Selection:** *Very important factors considered include:* Class rank, application essay, academic GPA, recommendation(s), rigor of secondary school record, standardized test scores, character/personal qualities, extracurricular activities. *Important factors considered include:* talent/ability, volunteer work. *Other factors considered include:* Alumni/ae relation, first generation, geographical residence, interview, racial/ethnic status. **Freshman Admission Requirements:** High school diploma or equivalent is not required. *Academic units recommended:* 4 English, 4 mathematics, 4 science, 3 social studies, 3 history. **Freshman Admission Statistics:** 18,132 applied, 13% admitted, 48% enrolled. **Transfer Admission Requirements:** High school transcript, college transcript(s), essay or personal statement, standardized test scores, statement of good standing from prior institution(s). Lowest grade transferable B. **General Admission Information:** Application fee $70. Early decision application deadline 11/1. Regular application deadline 1/1. Regular notification 4/1. Nonfall registration not accepted. Admission may be deferred for a maximum of 2 years. Credit and/or placement offered for CEEB Advanced Placement tests.

COSTS AND FINANCIAL AID
Annual tuition $38,445. Room and board $11,295. Required fees $234. Average book expense $1,618. **Required Forms and Deadlines:** FAFSA, CSS/Financial Aid PROFILE, noncustodial PROFILE, business/farm supplement, current W-2 or Federal Tax Returns. Financial aid filing deadline 2/1. **Notification of Awards:** Applicants will be notified of awards on or about 4/2. **Types of Aid:** *Need-based scholarships/grants:* Federal Pell, SEOG, state scholarships/grants, private scholarships, the school's own gift aid. *Loans:* FFEL Subsidized Stafford, FFEL Unsubsidized Stafford, FFEL PLUS, Federal Perkins, college/university loans from institutional funds. **Student Employment:** Federal Work-Study Program available. Institutional employment available. Off-campus job opportunities are excellent. **Financial Aid Statistics:** 48% freshmen, 51% undergrads receive need-based scholarship or grant aid. 40% freshmen, 47% undergrads receive need-based self-help aid. 50% freshmen, 52% undergrads receive any aid. 48% undergrads borrow to pay for school. Average cumulative indebtedness $19,051.

DAVENPORT UNIVERSITY

6191 Kraft Avenue S.E, Grand Rapids, MI 49512
Phone: 616-698-7111 **Financial Aid Phone:** 313-581-4400
E-mail: gradmiss@davenport.edu
Fax: 616-698-0333 **Website:** www.davenport.edu

This private school was founded in 1866. It has a 43-acre campus.

RATINGS
Admissions Selectivity Rating: 60*   **Fire Safety Rating:** 60*   **Green Rating:** 60*

STUDENTS AND FACULTY
Enrollment: 11,736. **Student Body:** 76% female, 24% male, 2% out-of-state, international (29 countries represented). Asian 1%, African American 24%, Caucasian 58%, Hispanic 4%.

Retention and Graduation: 61% freshmen return for sophomore year. **Faculty:** Student/faculty ratio 14:1. 130 full-time faculty, 24% hold PhDs, 54% are women.

ACADEMICS

Degrees: Associate, bachelor's, diploma, master's, post-bachelor's certificate. **Classes:** Most classes have fewer than 10 students. **Special Study Options:** Accelerated program, distance learning, dual enrollment, English as a Second Language (ESL), independent study, internships, student-designed major, study abroad. **Combined degree programs:** BA/MA. Special programs offered to physically disabled students include tutors.

ADMISSIONS

Freshman Academic Profile: Minimum paper TOEFL 500. Minimum computer TOEFL 180. **Basis for Candidate Selection: Freshman Admission Requirements:** High school diploma is required and GED is accepted. *Academic units required:* 6 English, 6 mathematics, 9 social studies, 31 academic electives, 10 interdisciplinary. *Academic units recommended:* 9 mathematics, 9 social studies, 47 academic electives, 10 interdisciplinary. **Freshman Admission Statistics:** 1,231 applied, 100% admitted, 100% enrolled. **Transfer Admission Requirements:** High school transcript, college transcript(s), minimum college GPA of 2 required. Lowest grade transferable C. **General Admission Information:** Application fee $25. Notification on a rolling basis, beginning on or about 9/1. Nonfall registration accepted. Admission may be deferred for a maximum of ongoing. Neither credit nor placement offered for CEEB Advanced Placement tests.

COSTS AND FINANCIAL AID

Annual tuition $8,760. Room and board $4,200. Required fees $120. Average book expense $1,000. **Required Forms and Deadlines:** FAFSA, scholarship application, if applicable. Priority financial aid filing date 3/15. **Notification of Awards:** Applicants will be notified of awards on a rolling basis beginning 3/1. **Types of Aid:** *Need-based scholarships/grants:* Federal Pell, SEOG, state scholarships/grants, private scholarships, the school's own gift aid, State of MI Nursing Scholarships. *Loans:* FFEL Subsidized Stafford, FFEL Unsubsidized Stafford, FFEL PLUS, state loans **Student Employment: Financial Aid Statistics:** 79% freshmen, 76% undergrads receive need-based scholarship or grant aid. 55% freshmen, 29% undergrads receive non-need-based scholarship or grant aid. 72% freshmen, 78% undergrads receive need-based self-help aid. 2% freshmen, 2% undergrads receive athletic scholarships. 75% undergrads borrow to pay for school. Average cumulative indebtedness $8,439. **Criteria for awarding institutional aid:** *Non-need-based:* Academics, alumni affiliation, athletics, leadership.

DAVIDSON COLLEGE

PO Box 7156, Davidson, NC 28035-7156
Phone: 704-894-2230
E-mail: admission@davidson.edu **CEEB Code:** 5150
Fax: 704-894-2016 **Website:** www.davidson.edu **ACT Code:** 3086

This private school, affiliated with the Presbyterian Church, was founded in 1837. It has a 556-acre campus.

RATINGS

Admissions Selectivity Rating: 98   **Fire Safety Rating:** 60*   **Green Rating:** 60*

STUDENTS AND FACULTY

Enrollment: 1,661. **Student Body:** 51% female, 49% male, 80% out-of-state, 4% international (36 countries represented). Asian 4%, African American 6%, Caucasian 74%, Hispanic 4%, Native American 1%.
Retention and Graduation: 96% freshmen return for sophomore year. 92% freshmen graduate within 4 years. 25% grads go on to further study within 1 year. **Faculty:** Student/faculty ratio 10:1. 168 full-time faculty, 97% hold PhDs, 15% are members of minority groups, 37% are women.

ACADEMICS

Degrees: Bachelor's. **Classes:** Most classes have 10–19 students. Most lab/discussion sessions have 10–19 students. **Majors with Highest Enrollment:** Biology/biological sciences; English language and literature; history. **Special Study Options:** Cross-registration, double major, exchange student program (domestic), honors program, independent study, student-designed major, study abroad, teacher certification program. Special programs offered to physically

disabled students include note-taking services, reader services, tape recorders, tutors. **Career services:** Alumni network, alumni services, career/job search classes, career assessment, internships.

FACILITIES

Housing: Coed dorms, cooperative housing, apartments for single students, wellness housing, theme housing. 90% of campus accessible to physically disabled. **Special Academic Facilities/Equipment:** Art gallery, scanning electron microscopes, UV-visible spectrometer, laser systems, Baker sports complex, Visual Arts building. **Computers:** Students can register for classes online.

CAMPUS LIFE

Environment: Village. **Activities:** Choral groups, concert band, dance, drama/theater, jazz band, literary magazine, music ensembles, musical theater, pep band, radio station, student government, student newspaper, symphony orchestra, yearbook, campus ministries, international student organization. **Organizations:** 151 registered organizations, 15 honor societies, 16 religious organizations. 8 fraternities. **Athletics (Intercollegiate):** *Men:* Baseball, basketball, cross-country, diving, football, golf, soccer, swimming, tennis, track/field (outdoor), wrestling. *Women:* Basketball, cross-country, diving, field hockey, lacrosse, soccer, swimming, tennis, track/field (outdoor), volleyball. **On-Campus Highlights:** Belk Visual Arts Center, Baker-Watt Science Complex, Baker Sports Complex, Campus Center, Lake Campus.

ADMISSIONS

Freshman Academic Profile: Average high school GPA 3.85. 81% in top 10% of high school class, 97% in top 25% of high school class, 100% in top 50% of high school class. 51% from public high schools. SAT Math middle 50% range 640–730. SAT Critical Reading middle 50% range 630–730. SAT Writing middle 50% range 630–730. ACT middle 50% range 28–32. Minimum paper TOEFL 600. Minimum computer TOEFL 250. **Basis for Candidate Selection:** *Very important factors considered include:* Recommendation(s), rigor of secondary school record, character/personal qualities, volunteer work. *Important factors considered include:* Application essay, standardized test scores, extracurricular activities, interview, talent/ability. *Other factors considered include:* Class rank, alumni/ae relation. **Freshman Admission Requirements:** High school diploma is required and GED is not accepted. *Academic units required:* 4 English, 3 mathematics, 2 science, 2 foreign language, 2 social studies or history. *Academic units recommended:* 4 mathematics, 4 science, 4 foreign language, 4 social studies or history. **Freshman Admission Statistics:** 4,412 applied, 26% admitted, 43% enrolled. **Transfer Admission Requirements:** High school transcript, college transcript(s), essay or personal statement, standardized test scores, statement of good standing from prior institution(s). Minimum college GPA of 3.0 required. Lowest grade transferable C. **General Admission Information:** Application fee $50. Early decision application deadline 11/15. Regular application deadline 1/2. Regular notification 4/1. Nonfall registration not accepted. Admission may be deferred for a maximum of 1 year. Credit and/or placement offered for CEEB Advanced Placement tests.

COSTS AND FINANCIAL AID

Annual tuition $34,776. Room and board $9,906. Required fees $348. Average book expense $1,000. **Required Forms and Deadlines:** FAFSA, CSS/Financial Aid PROFILE, noncustodial PROFILE, business/farm supplement, Noncustodial(Divorced/Separated)Parent's Statement; corporate tax return and/or noncustodial parent tax return(if applicable); parent and student tax returns and W-2 forms. Financial aid filing deadline 2/15. **Notification of Awards:** Applicants will be notified of awards on or about 4/1. **Types of Aid:** *Need-based scholarships/grants:* Federal Pell, SEOG, state scholarships/grants, private scholarships, the school's own gift aid. *Loans:* FFEL Subsidized Stafford, FFEL Unsubsidized Stafford, FFEL PLUS, Federal Perkins, alternative loans. **Student Employment:** Federal Work-Study Program available. Institutional employment available. Off-campus job opportunities are excellent. **Financial Aid Statistics:** 33% freshmen, 33% undergrads receive need-based scholarship or grant aid. 12% freshmen, 13% undergrads receive non-need-based scholarship or grant aid. 19% freshmen, 22% undergrads receive need-based self-help aid. 11% freshmen, 11% undergrads receive athletic scholarships. 35% freshmen, 35% undergrads receive any aid. 33.1% undergrads borrow to pay for school. Average cumulative indebtedness $25,025. **Criteria for awarding institutional aid:** *Non-need-based:* Academics, art, athletics, leadership, minority status, music/drama.

DAVIS AND ELKINS COLLEGE

100 Campus Drive, Elkins, WV 26241
Phone: 304-637-1230 **Financial Aid Phone:** 304-637-1373
E-mail: admiss@davisandelkins.edu **CEEB Code:** 5151
Fax: 304-637-1800 **Website:** www.davisandelkins.edu **ACT Code:** 4518

This private school, affiliated with the Presbyterian Church, was founded in 1904. It has a 170-acre campus.

RATINGS
Admissions Selectivity Rating: 74   **Fire Safety Rating:** 61   **Green Rating:** 60*

STUDENTS AND FACULTY
Enrollment: 624. **Student Body:** 63% female, 37% male, 23% out-of-state, international (15 countries represented). Asian 4%, African American 2%, Caucasian 98%, Hispanic 1%.
Retention and Graduation: 64% freshmen return for sophomore year. 29% freshmen graduate within 4 years. 13% grads go on to further study within 1 year. 2% grads pursue law degrees. 11% grads pursue business degrees. **Faculty:** Student/faculty ratio 11:1. 44 full-time faculty, 84% hold PhDs, 11% are members of minority groups, 50% are women.

ACADEMICS
Degrees: Associate, bachelor's, terminal associate, transfer associate. **Classes:** Most classes have fewer than 10 students. Most lab/discussion sessions have 20–29 students. **Majors with Highest Enrollment:** Business administration and management; marketing/marketing management; nursing/registered nurse (RN, ASN, BSN, MSN). **Special Study Options:** Cooperative education program, cross-registration, double major, dual enrollment, external degree program, honors program, independent study, internships, student-designed major, study abroad, teacher certification program Special programs offered to physically disabled students include note-taking services, reader services, tape recorders, tutors. **Career services:** Alumni services, career assessment, internships, regional alumni.

FACILITIES
Housing: Coed dorms, men's dorms, women's dorms 80% of campus accessible to physically disabled. **Special Academic Facilities/Equipment:** Planetarium, Graceland Inn and Conference Center(19th century Victorian mansion)—now used as training center for the hospitality program, Darby Collection—Civil War collection, Comstock collection, Pearl S. Buck collection. **Computers:** Administrative functions (other than registration) can be performed online.

CAMPUS LIFE
Environment: Village. **Activities:** Choral groups, concert band, drama/theater, jazz band, literary magazine, music ensembles, musical theater, radio station, student government, student newspaper, yearbook. **Organizations:** 39 registered organizations, 7 honor societies, 1 religious organizations. 2 fraternities, 2 sororities. **Athletics (Intercollegiate):** *Men:* Baseball, basketball, cross-country, golf, skiing (downhill/alpine), soccer. *Women:* Basketball, cross-country, skiing (downhill/alpine), soccer, softball, volleyball. **On-Campus Highlights:** Mansions/ Halliehurst and Graceland, Icehouse, Chapel, Madden Student Center, library. The 170-acre campus offers an historic district and newly renovated student center.

ADMISSIONS
Freshman Academic Profile: Average high school GPA 3.06. 12% in top 10% of high school class, 33% in top 25% of high school class, 71% in top 50% of high school class. 91% from public high schools. SAT Math middle 50% range 420–510. SAT Critical Reading middle 50% range 420–530. ACT middle 50% range 18–22. Minimum paper TOEFL 450. Minimum computer TOEFL 133. **Basis for Candidate Selection:** *Very important factors considered include:* Rigor of secondary school record, level of applicant's interest. *Important factors considered include:* Class rank, academic GPA, recommendation(s), standardized test scores, character/personal qualities, extracurricular activities, talent/ability. *Other factors considered include:* Application essay, alumni/ae relation, first generation, interview, volunteer work, work experience. **Freshman Admission Requirements:** High school diploma is required and GED is accepted. *Academic units required:* 4 English, 1 mathematics, 3 science, (1 science labs), 1 foreign language, 3 social studies, 2 mathematics units must include algebra I or II and geometry. *Academic units recommended:* 4 English, 1 mathematics, 3 science, (1 science labs), 1 foreign language, 3 social studies, 2 mathematics units must include algebra I or II and geometry. **Freshman Admission Statistics:** 563 applied, 55% admitted, 34% enrolled. **Transfer Admission Requirements:** High school transcript, college transcript(s), minimum college GPA of 2.0 required. Lowest grade transferable D. **General Admission Information:** Application fee $35. Notification on a rolling basis, beginning on or about 9/30. Nonfall registration accepted. Admission may be deferred for a maximum of 1 year. Credit and/or placement offered for CEEB Advanced Placement tests.

COSTS AND FINANCIAL AID
Average book expense $800. **Required Forms and Deadlines:** FAFSA. Priority financial aid filing date 3/1. **Notification of Awards:** Applicants will be notified of awards on or about 5/1. **Types of Aid:** *Need-based scholarships/grants:* Federal Pell, SEOG, state scholarships/grants, private scholarships, the school's own gift aid. *Loans:* FFEL Subsidized Stafford, FFEL Unsubsidized Stafford, FFEL PLUS, Federal Perkins, state loans. **Student Employment:** Federal Work-Study Program available. Institutional employment available. Highest amount earned per year from on-campus jobs $1,000. Off-campus job opportunities are good. **Financial Aid Statistics:** 32% freshmen, 48% undergrads receive need-based scholarship or grant aid. 72% freshmen, 79% undergrads receive non-need-based scholarship or grant aid. 47% freshmen, 63% undergrads receive need-based self-help aid. 44% freshmen, 24% undergrads receive athletic scholarships. 98% freshmen, 98% undergrads receive any aid. 76% undergrads borrow to pay for school. Average cumulative indebtedness $13,380. **Criteria for awarding institutional aid:** *Non-need-based:* Academics, alumni affiliation, art, athletics, leadership, minority status, music/drama, religious affiliation.

DE SALES UNIVERSITY

2755 Station Ave, 18, Center Valley, PA 18034
Phone: 610-282-4443 **Financial Aid Phone:** 610-282-4443
E-mail: admiss@desales.edu **CEEB Code:** 2021
Fax: 610-282-0131 **Website:** www.desales.edu

This private school, affiliated with the Roman Catholic Church, was founded in 1964. It has a 400-acre campus.

RATINGS
Admissions Selectivity Rating: 73   **Fire Safety Rating:** 78   **Green Rating:** 82

STUDENTS AND FACULTY
Enrollment: 2,333. **Student Body:** 59% female, 41% male, 17% out-of-state. Asian 1%, African American 2%, Caucasian 60%, Hispanic 3%.
Retention and Graduation: 63% freshmen graduate within 4 years. 25% grads go on to further study within 1 year. 20% grads pursue arts and sciences degrees. 3% grads pursue business degrees. 1% grads pursue medical degrees. **Faculty:** Student/faculty ratio 13:1. 104 full-time faculty, 69% hold PhDs, 5% are members of minority groups, 49% are women.

ACADEMICS
Degrees: Bachelor's, certificate, master's, post-bachelor's certificate, post-master's certificate. **Classes:** Most classes have 20–29 students. Most lab/discussion sessions have fewer than 10 students. **Majors with Highest Enrollment:** Drama and dramatics/theatre arts; nursing/registered nurse (RN, ASN, BSN, MSN); physician assistant. **Special Study Options:** Accelerated program, cross-registration, distance learning, double major, dual enrollment, English as a Second Language (ESL), exchange student program (domestic), honors program, independent study, internships, liberal arts/career combination, student-designed major, study abroad, teacher certification program, weekend college, online degrees. **Honors programs:** Faith and Reason Honors Program is competive and is limited to fifteen (15) students in each academic class. **Combined degree programs:** BS/MSPAS; BSN/MSN; MBA/MNS. Special programs offered to physically disabled students include note-taking services, reader services, tape recorders, tutors. **Career services:** Alumni network, alumni services, career/job search classes, career assessment, internships.

FACILITIES
Housing: Men's dorms, women's dorms, cooperative housing, theme housing 98% of campus accessible to physically disabled. **Computers:** 100% of classrooms, 5% of dorms, 100% of libraries, 100% of dining areas, 5% of student union, 20% of common outdoor areas have wireless network access. Students can register for classes online. Administrative functions (other than registration) can be performed online.

CAMPUS LIFE
Environment: Town. **Activities:** Choral groups, dance, drama/theater, musical theater, pep band, radio station, student government, student newspaper, television station, yearbook, campus ministries, international student organization, Model UN. **Organizations:** 42 registered organizations, 12 honor societies, 1 religious organizations. **Athletics (Intercollegiate):** *Men:* Baseball, basketball, cross-country, golf, lacrosse, soccer, tennis, track/field (outdoor), track/field (indoor). *Women:* Basketball, cross-country, field hockey, soccer, softball, tennis, track/field (outdoor), track/field (indoor), volleyball. **On-Campus Highlights:** Billera Athletics and Recreation Center, Hurd Science Center, Dog Pound in McShea Student Center, University Center, Labuda Center for the Performing

Arts. Summer brings the Pennsylvania Shakespeare Festival to campus at the Labuda Center for the Performing Arts. **Environmental Initiatives:** Water reduction program—after adding one new residence hall we still reduced our water usage by 10% from 2008 to 2009. Open Space Land preservation recently obtained over 80 acres for campus open space and for land preservation. DeSales Dining Services Sustainability Program.

ADMISSIONS

Freshman Academic Profile: 22% in top 10% of high school class, 49% in top 25% of high school class, 82% in top 50% of high school class. 59% from public high schools. SAT Math middle 50% range 490–600. SAT Critical Reading middle 50% range 490–600. SAT Writing middle 50% range 480–590. ACT middle 50% range 19–25. Minimum paper TOEFL 550. Minimum computer TOEFL 213. **Basis for Candidate Selection:** *Very important factors considered include:* Class rank, academic GPA, recommendation(s), rigor of secondary school record. *Important factors considered include:* Standardized test scores, extracurricular activities, interview, talent/ability. *Other factors considered include:* Application essay, geographical residence, racial/ethnic status, state residency, volunteer work, work experience. **Freshman Admission Requirements:** High school diploma is required and GED is accepted. *Academic units required:* 4 English, 3 mathematics, 2 science, (2 science labs), 2 foreign language, 3 social studies, 9 history, 19 academic electives. *Academic units recommended:* 4 mathematics, 4 social studies. **Freshman Admission Statistics:** 1,998 applied, 73% admitted, 26% enrolled. **Transfer Admission Requirements:** High school transcript, college transcript(s), statement of good standing from prior institution(s). Minimum college GPA of 2.00 required. Lowest grade transferable 2. **General Admission Information:** Regular application deadline 8/1. Notification on a rolling basis, beginning on or about 11/1. Nonfall registration accepted. Credit offered for CEEB Advanced Placement tests.

COSTS AND FINANCIAL AID

Annual tuition $26,000. Room and board $9,750. Required fees $1,000. Average book expense $1,200. **Required Forms and Deadlines:** FAFSA, institution's own financial aid form, state aid form. Financial aid filing deadline 5/1. Priority financial aid filing date 2/1. **Notification of Awards:** Applicants will be notified of awards on a rolling basis beginning 2/15. **Types of Aid:** *Need-based scholarships/grants:* Federal Pell, SEOG, state scholarships/grants, private scholarships, the school's own gift aid, Federal Nursing Scholarships. *Loans:* FFEL Subsidized Stafford, FFEL Unsubsidized Stafford, FFEL PLUS, Federal Perkins, Federal Nursing, state loans. **Student Employment:** Federal Work-Study Program available. Institutional employment available. Off-campus job opportunities are good. **Financial Aid Statistics:** 77% freshmen, 68% undergrads receive need-based scholarship or grant aid. 61% freshmen, 50% undergrads receive non-need-based scholarship or grant aid. 65% freshmen, 63% undergrads receive need-based self-help aid. 78% freshmen, 74% undergrads receive any aid. 76% undergrads borrow to pay for school. Average cumulative indebtedness $31,077. **Criteria for awarding institutional aid:** *Non-need-based:* Academics, leadership, music/drama.

See page 1076.

DEAN COLLEGE

Office of Admission, 99 Main Street, Franklin, MA 02038-1994
Phone: 508-541-1508
E-mail: admission@dean.edu
Fax: 508-541-8726 **Website:** www.dean.edu

This is a private school.

RATINGS
Admissions Selectivity Rating: 69   Fire Safety Rating: 60*   Green Rating: 60*

STUDENTS AND FACULTY
Enrollment: 1,106. **Student Body:** 48% female, 52% male, 53% out-of-state, 10% international . Asian 1%, African American 7%, Caucasian 50%, Hispanic 3%, Native American 1%.
Retention and Graduation: 62% freshmen return for sophomore year.
Faculty: Student/faculty ratio 19:1. 33 full-time faculty, 36% hold PhDs, 9% are members of minority groups, 55% are women.

ACADEMICS
Degrees: Associate, bachelor's, certificate. **Classes:** Most classes have 10–19 students. Most lab/discussion sessions have fewer than 10 students. **Special Study Options:** Accelerated program, double major, English as a Second Language (ESL), honors program, independent study, internships, liberal arts/career combination, study abroad.

FACILITIES
Housing: Coed dorms, women's dorms.

CAMPUS LIFE
Activities: Dance, drama/theater, literary magazine, musical theater, radio station, student government, yearbook.

ADMISSIONS
Freshman Academic Profile: Average high school GPA 2.2. SAT Math middle 50% range 380–490. SAT Critical Reading middle 50% range 390–490. ACT middle 50% range 15–20. **Basis for Candidate Selection:** *Other factors considered include:* Class rank, application essay, academic GPA, recommendation(s), rigor of secondary school record, standardized test scores, alumni/ae relation, character/personal qualities, extracurricular activities, interview, level of applicant's interest, talent/ability, volunteer work, work experience. **Freshman Admission Requirements:** High school diploma is required and GED is accepted. *Academic units required:* 3 English, 1 mathematics, 1 science, (1 science labs), 1 social studies, 1 history. *Academic units recommended:* 4 English, 2 mathematics, 2 science, (1 science labs), 1 foreign language, 2 social studies, 2 history, 1 academic electives. **Freshman Admission Statistics:** 1,910 applied, 73% admitted, 39% enrolled. **Transfer Admission Requirements:** High school transcript, college transcript(s), essay or personal statement, Lowest grade transferable C–. **General Admission Information:** Application fee $35. Notification on a rolling basis, beginning on or about 12/1. Nonfall registration accepted. Admission may be deferred for a maximum of 1 year.

COSTS AND FINANCIAL AID
Required Forms and Deadlines: FAFSA. Priority financial aid filing date 3/1. **Notification of Awards:** Applicants will be notified of awards on a rolling basis beginning 3/1. **Types of Aid:** *Need-based scholarships/grants:* Federal Pell, SEOG, state scholarships/grants, private scholarships, the school's own gift aid. *Loans:* FFEL Subsidized Stafford, FFEL Unsubsidized Stafford, FFEL PLUS, Federal Perkins. **Student Employment:** Financial Aid Statistics: 61% freshmen, 60% undergrads receive need-based scholarship or grant aid. 8% freshmen, 8% undergrads receive non-need-based scholarship or grant aid. 56% freshmen, 57% undergrads receive need-based self-help aid. 2% freshmen, 3% undergrads receive athletic scholarships. 72.5% undergrads borrow to pay for school. Average cumulative indebtedness $14,531. **Criteria for awarding institutional aid:** *Non-need-based:* Academics, athletics, leadership, music/drama.

DEEP SPRINGS COLLEGE

Applications Committee, HC 72 Box 45001, Dyer, NV 89010
Phone: 760-872-2000
E-mail: apcom@deepsprings.edu **CEEB Code:** 4281
Fax: 760-872-4466 **Website:** www.deepsprings.edu

This private school was founded in 1917. It has a 30000-acre campus.

RATINGS
Admissions Selectivity Rating: 99   Fire Safety Rating: 79   Green Rating: 60*

STUDENTS AND FACULTY
Enrollment: 26. **Student Body:** 100% male, 80% out-of-state, (3 countries represented).
Retention and Graduation: 100% freshmen return for sophomore year. 96% grads go on to further study within 1 year. 26% grads pursue arts and sciences degrees. 11% grads pursue law degrees. 3% grads pursue business degrees. 10% grads pursue medical degrees. **Faculty:** Student/faculty ratio 4:1. 3 full-time faculty, 67% hold PhDs, 33% are women.

ACADEMICS
Degrees: Associate. **Classes:** Most classes have fewer than 10 students. **Majors with Highest Enrollment:** Liberal arts and sciences studies and humanities, other. **Special Study Options:** Independent study, internships.

FACILITIES
Housing: Men's dorms. 100% of campus accessible to physically disabled. **Special Academic Facilities/Equipment:** Ranch—300 cattle, 20 horses, organic farm growing hay and produce; thousands of acres of wilderness surround the college.

CAMPUS LIFE

Environment: Rural. **Activities:** Student government. **Organizations:** 1 registered organizations. **On-Campus Highlights:** Boarding House, Dairy Barn, Horse Stables, The Upper Reservoir, The Druid.

ADMISSIONS

Freshman Academic Profile: 86% in top 10% of high school class, 93% in top 25% of high school class, 100% in top 50% of high school class. 50% from public high schools. SAT Math middle 50% range 700–800. SAT Critical Reading middle 50% range 750–800. **Basis for Candidate Selection:** *Very important factors considered include:* Application essay, character/personal qualities, interview, level of applicant's interest. *Important factors considered include:* Academic GPA, rigor of secondary school record, extracurricular activities, volunteer work, work experience. *Other factors considered include:* Class rank, recommendation(s), standardized test scores, racial/ethnic status, talent/ability. **Freshman Admission Requirements:** High school diploma or equivalent is not required. **Freshman Admission Statistics:** 170 applied, 7% admitted, 92% enrolled. **Transfer Admission Requirements:** High school transcript, college transcript(s), essay or personal statement, interview, standardized test scores, **General Admission Information:** Regular application deadline 11/15. Regular notification 4/15. Nonfall registration not accepted. Neither credit nor placement offered for CEEB Advanced Placement tests.

COSTS AND FINANCIAL AID

Average book expense $1,200. **Notification of Awards:** Applicants will be notified of awards on or about 4/15. **Financial Aid Statistics:** 100% freshmen, 100% undergrads receive any aid.

DEFIANCE COLLEGE

701 North Clinton Street, Defiance, OH 43512-1695
Phone: 419-783-2359 **Financial Aid Phone:** 419-783-2376
E-mail: admissions@defiance.edu **CEEB Code:** 1162
Fax: 419-783-2468 **Website:** www.defiance.edu **ACT Code:** 3264

This private school, affiliated with the United Church of Christ Church, was founded in 1850. It has a 150-acre campus.

RATINGS
Admissions Selectivity Rating: 74   **Fire Safety Rating:** 81   **Green Rating:** 72

STUDENTS AND FACULTY
Enrollment: 944. **Student Body:** 52% female, 48% male, 18% out-of-state, international (2 countries represented). Asian 1%, African American 7%, Caucasian 86%, Hispanic 4%, Native American 1%.
Retention and Graduation: 65% freshmen return for sophomore year. 38% freshmen graduate within 4 years. 18% grads go on to further study within 1 year. 2% grads pursue law degrees. 1% grads pursue business degrees. 1% grads pursue medical degrees. **Faculty:** Student/faculty ratio 13:1. 45 full-time faculty, 60% hold PhDs, 11% are members of minority groups, 40% are women.

ACADEMICS
Degrees: Associate, bachelor's, certificate, master's. **Classes:** Most classes have 10–19 students. Most lab/discussion sessions have 10–19 students. **Majors with Highest Enrollment:** Business administration, management and operations, other; education; forensic science and technology. **Special Study Options:** Cooperative education program, distance learning, double major, dual enrollment, honors program, independent study, internships, student-designed major, study abroad, teacher certification program, weekend college. **Career services:** Alumni network, alumni services, career/job search classes, career assessment, internships **Career services highlights include:** Cooperative Learning.

FACILITIES
Housing: Coed dorms, apartments for single students 100% of campus accessible to physically disabled. **Special Academic Facilities/Equipment:** Art gallery, media center, Eisenhower archives room, curriculum resource center, Cultural Arts Center, Indian wars collection. **Computers:** 100% of classrooms, 30% of dorms, 100% of libraries, 100% of dining areas, 100% of student union, 100% of common outdoor areas have wireless network access.

CAMPUS LIFE
Environment: Rural. **Activities:** Choral groups, concert band, drama/theater, literary magazine, musical theater, pep band, student government, student newspaper, yearbook, campus ministries. **Organizations:** 30 registered organizations, 1 honor societies, 2 religious organizations. 1 fraternities, 2 sororities. **Athletics (Intercollegiate):** *Men:* Baseball, basketball, cross-country, football, golf, soccer, tennis, track/field (outdoor), track/field (indoor). *Women:* Basketball, cross-country, golf, soccer, softball, tennis, track/field (outdoor), track/field

(indoor), volleyball. **On-Campus Highlights:** Smart Fitness Center, Tenzer Hall, Serrick Center, Hubbard Hall, Weaner/McMaster Center.

ADMISSIONS
Freshman Academic Profile: Average high school GPA 3.09. 9% in top 10% of high school class, 29% in top 25% of high school class, 67% in top 50% of high school class. 97% from public high schools. SAT Math middle 50% range 460–550. SAT Critical Reading middle 50% range 400–540. SAT Writing middle 50% range 380–510. ACT middle 50% range 19–24. Minimum paper TOEFL 550. Minimum computer TOEFL 213. **Basis for Candidate Selection:** *Very important factors considered include:* Academic GPA, rigor of secondary school record, standardized test scores. *Other factors considered include:* Class rank, character/personal qualities, extracurricular activities, interview, volunteer work. **Freshman Admission Requirements:** High school diploma is required and GED is accepted. *Academic units recommended:* 4 English, 3 mathematics, 3 science, (2 science labs), 2 foreign language, 2 social studies, 2 visual/performing arts, 1 visual and/or performing arts. **Freshman Admission Statistics:** 1,258 applied, 74% admitted, 23% enrolled. **Transfer Admission Requirements:** High school transcript, college transcript(s), essay or personal statement, statement of good standing from prior institution(s). Minimum college GPA of 2.0 required. Lowest grade transferable C. **General Admission Information:** Application fee $25. Notification on a rolling basis, beginning on or about 9/1. Nonfall registration accepted. Admission may be deferred for a maximum of 1 year. Credit and/or placement offered for CEEB Advanced Placement tests.

COSTS AND FINANCIAL AID
Annual tuition $22,375. Room and board $7,750. Required fees $520. Average book expense $1,350. **Required Forms and Deadlines:** FAFSA. **Types of Aid:** *Need-based scholarships/grants:* Federal Pell, SEOG, state scholarships/grants, private scholarships, the school's own gift aid. *Loans:* FFEL Subsidized Stafford, FFEL Unsubsidized Stafford, FFEL PLUS, Federal Perkins, ALTERNATIVE LOANS. **Student Employment:** Federal Work-Study Program available. Institutional employment available. Off-campus job opportunities are good. **Financial Aid Statistics: Criteria for awarding institutional aid:** *Non-need-based:* Academics, leadership.

DELAWARE VALLEY COLLEGE

700 East Butler Avenue, Doylestown, PA 18901-2697
Phone: 215-489-2211 **Financial Aid Phone:** 215-489-2272
E-mail: ADMITME@delval.edu **CEEB Code:** 2510
Fax: 215-230-2968 **Website:** www.delval.edu **ACT Code:** 3551

This private school was founded in 1896. It has a 600-acre campus.

RATINGS
Admissions Selectivity Rating: 77   **Fire Safety Rating:** 74   **Green Rating:** 76

STUDENTS AND FACULTY
Enrollment: 1,798. **Student Body:** 60% female, 40% male, 38% out-of-state, international (4 countries represented). Asian 1%, African American 3%, Caucasian 90%, Hispanic 2%.
Retention and Graduation: 74% freshmen return for sophomore year. 51% grads go on to further study within 1 year. 1% grads pursue law degrees. 9% grads pursue business degrees. 10% grads pursue medical degrees. **Faculty:** Student/faculty ratio 15:1. 84 full-time faculty, 61% hold PhDs, 8% are members of minority groups, 40% are women.

ACADEMICS
Degrees: Associate, bachelor's, certificate, master's, terminal associate, transfer associate. **Classes:** Most classes have 10–19 students. Most lab/discussion sessions have 10–19 students. **Majors with Highest Enrollment:** Animal sciences; animal sciences, other; business administration and management. **Special Study Options:** Accelerated program, cross-registration, distance learning, double major, honors program, independent study, internships, study abroad, teacher certification program, weekend college. **Honors programs:** The DVC Honors Program is an educational enrichment program designed to enhance the eductional opportunities and experiences of students admitted to the program. The programs consists of an Honors Colloquium followed by independent study programs in the 3rd and 4th years. It features guest lecturers, field trips and both faculty and student-led discussions. Special programs offered to physically disabled students include note-taking services, reader services, tape recorders **Career services:** Alumni services, career/job search classes, career assessment, internships **Career services highlights include:** Our required employment program requires students to work 500 hours in their field before they graduate. Delaware Valley College's Employment Program,

an experience-based graduation requirement, fosters the integration of theory and practice throughout the educational continuum, and helps students develop linkages with professionals in their fields of study. The Employment Program empowers students by equipping them with the skills and abilities necessary for success as they transition from college to career. Because of the college's commitment to career-oriented education, students graduate with a level of skill and experience that far exceeds that of the average entry-level candidate. Delaware Valley College is one of only 3% of colleges nationwide with a mandatory experiential-learning requirement, making it one of the most important and unique aspects of the DelVal educational experience.

FACILITIES

Housing: Coed dorms, women's dorms **Special Academic Facilities/Equipment:** Dairy processing plant, greenhouse and nursery lab complex, small animal science labs, poultry diagnostic lab, arboretum, equine facilities, 500+-acre farm, tissue culture lab. **Computers:** 25% of classrooms, 100% of dorms, 100% of libraries, 80% of student union, 20% of common outdoor areas have wireless network access. Students can register for classes online. Administrative functions (other than registration) can be performed online.

CAMPUS LIFE

Environment: Village. **Activities:** Choral groups, concert band, drama/theater, literary magazine, music ensembles, radio station, student government, student newspaper, yearbook. **Organizations:** 62 registered organizations, 2 honor societies, 2 religious organizations. 5 fraternities, 3 sororities. **Athletics (Intercollegiate):** *Men:* Baseball, basketball, cross-country, football, golf, soccer, track/field (outdoor), track/field (indoor), wrestling. *Women:* Basketball, cheerleading, cross-country, field hockey, soccer, softball, track/field (outdoor); track/field (indoor), volleyball. **On-Campus Highlights:** Smart Classroom, Small Animal Facility, Athletic Complex, Student Center, Equine center, The campus has many unique areas that are of specific interest depending on a student's major field of study (i.e. dairy barn, equine center, etc.). **Environmental Initiatives:** Recycling Wind Energy Bio-Diesel Fuel

ADMISSIONS

Freshman Academic Profile: Average high school GPA 3.47. 13% in top 10% of high school class, 37% in top 25% of high school class, 81% in top 50% of high school class. 85% from public high schools. SAT Math middle 50% range 470–560. SAT Critical Reading middle 50% range 460–550. SAT Writing middle 50% range 440–540. ACT middle 50% range 20–23. Minimum paper TOEFL 500. Minimum computer TOEFL 173. **Basis for Candidate Selection:** *Very important factors considered include:* Academic GPA, standardized test scores. *Important factors considered include:* Class rank, rigor of secondary school record, interview. *Other factors considered include:* Application essay, recommendation(s), alumni/ae relation, character/personal qualities, extracurricular activities, level of applicant's interest, talent/ability, volunteer work, work experience. **Freshman Admission Requirements:** High school diploma is required and GED is accepted. *Academic units required:* 3 English, 2 mathematics, 2 science, (1 science labs), 2 social studies, 6 academic electives. **Freshman Admission Statistics:** 1,847 applied, 71% admitted, 33% enrolled. **Transfer Admission Requirements:** High school transcript, college transcript(s), statement of good standing from prior institution(s). Minimum college GPA of 2.0 required. Lowest grade transferable C. **General Admission Information:** Application fee $35. Notification on a rolling basis, beginning on or about 10/31. Nonfall registration accepted. Admission may be deferred for a maximum of 1 year. Credit and/or placement offered for CEEB Advanced Placement tests.

COSTS AND FINANCIAL AID

Average book expense $1,000. **Required Forms and Deadlines:** FAFSA, state aid form Financial aid filing deadline 4/1. Priority financial aid filing date 4/1. **Notification of Awards:** Applicants will be notified of awards on a rolling basis beginning 2/1. **Types of Aid:** *Need-based scholarships/grants:* Federal Pell, SEOG, state scholarships/grants, private scholarships, the school's own gift aid. *Loans:* FFEL Subsidized Stafford, FFEL Unsubsidized Stafford, FFEL PLUS, Federal Perkins, Alternative Loans. **Student Employment:** Federal Work-Study Program available. Institutional employment available. Highest amount earned per year from on-campus jobs $2,200. **Financial Aid Statistics:** 77% freshmen, 77% undergrads receive need-based scholarship or grant aid. 20% freshmen, 16% undergrads receive non-need-based scholarship or grant aid. 70% freshmen, 62% undergrads receive need-based self-help aid. 98% freshmen, 91% undergrads receive any aid. 56% undergrads borrow to pay for school. Average cumulative indebtedness $28,929. **Criteria for awarding institutional aid:** *Non-need-based:* Academics, alumni affiliation, music/drama

DELTA STATE UNIVERSITY

Highway 8 West, Cleveland, MS 38733
Phone: 662-846-4018
E-mail: dheslep@deltastate.edu
Fax: 662-846-4683 **Website:** www.deltastate.edu **ACT Code:** 2190

This public school was founded in 1924. It has a 332-acre campus.

RATINGS
Admissions Selectivity Rating: 67   **Fire Safety Rating:** 60*   **Green Rating:** 60*

STUDENTS AND FACULTY
Enrollment: 3,156. **Student Body:** 62% female, 38% male, 10% out-of-state, (3 countries represented). Asian 1%, African American 33%, Caucasian 66%, Hispanic 1%.
Retention and Graduation: 68% freshmen return for sophomore year. 24% freshmen graduate within 4 years. **Faculty:** Student/faculty ratio 16:1. 162 full-time faculty, 60% hold PhDs, 7% are members of minority groups, 49% are women.

ACADEMICS
Degrees: Bachelor's, master's, post-master's certificate. **Majors with Highest Enrollment:** Business/commerce; elementary education and teaching; management information systems. **Special Study Options:** Cooperative education program, distance learning, double major, dual enrollment, honors program, independent study, internships, teacher certification program, weekend college. Special programs offered to physically disabled students include note-taking services, reader services, tape recorders, tutors.

FACILITIES
Housing: men's dorms, women's dorms, apartments for married students, Apartments for students with dependent children. 65% of campus accessible to physically disabled. **Special Academic Facilities/Equipment:** Art museum, performing arts center, natural history museum, language lab, airport facility with 12 airplanes, flight simulator, planetarium, art museum, Performing Arts Center, Natural History Museum, Language Lab, Airport facility, flight simulation, planetarium **Computers:** Students can register for classes online. Administrative functions (other than registration) can be performed online.

CAMPUS LIFE
Environment: Village. **Activities:** Choral groups, concert band, drama/theater, jazz band, literary magazine, marching band, music ensembles, musical theater, opera, student government, student newspaper, symphony orchestra, yearbook. **Organizations:** 46 registered organizations, 27 honor societies, 11 religious organizations. 8 fraternities, 6 sororities. **Athletics (Intercollegiate):** *Men:* Baseball, basketball, diving, football, golf, soccer, swimming, tennis. *Women:* Basketball, cross-country, diving, soccer, softball, swimming, tennis

ADMISSIONS
Freshman Academic Profile: 4% in top 25% of high school class, 57% in top 50% of high school class. ACT middle 50% range 17-21. Minimum paper TOEFL 525. Minimum computer TOEFL 196. **Basis for Candidate Selection:** *Very important factors considered include:* Class rank, rigor of secondary school record, standardized test scores. *Other factors considered include:* Recommendation(s), interview. **Freshman Admission Requirements:** High school diploma is required and GED is accepted. *Academic units required:* 4 English, 3 mathematics, 3 science, (2 science labs), 1 foreign language, 3 social studies, 1 academic electives. **Freshman Admission Statistics:** 1,289 applied, 32% admitted, 79% enrolled. **Transfer Admission Requirements:** College transcript(s), minimum college GPA of 2.0 required. Lowest grade transferable D. **General Admission Information:** Application fee $15. Regular application deadline 8/1. Notification on a rolling basis, beginning on or about 5/15. Nonfall registration accepted. Admission may be deferred for a maximum of N/A. Credit and/or placement offered for CEEB Advanced Placement tests.

COSTS AND FINANCIAL AID
Average book expense $700. **Required Forms and Deadlines:** FAFSA, institution's own financial aid form. Priority financial aid filing date 4/1. **Notification of Awards:** Applicants will be notified of awards on a rolling basis beginning 5/1. **Types of Aid:** *Need-based scholarships/grants:* Federal Pell, SEOG, private scholarships, the school's own gift aid. *Loans:* FFEL Subsidized Stafford, FFEL Unsubsidized Stafford, FFEL PLUS, Federal Perkins, college/university loans from institutional funds. **Student Employment:** Federal Work-Study Program available. Institutional employment available. Highest amount earned per year from on-campus jobs $1,200. Off-campus job opportunities are fair. **Financial Aid Statistics: Criteria for awarding institutional aid:** *Non-need-based:* Academics, alumni affiliation, art, athletics, leadership, music/drama, religious affiliation, state/district residency.

DENISON UNIVERSITY

Box H, Granville, OH 43023
Phone: 740-587-6276 **Financial Aid Phone:** 800-336-4766
E-mail: admissions@denison.edu **CEEB Code:** 1164
Fax: 740-587-6306 **Website:** www.denison.edu **ACT Code:** 3266

This private school was founded in 1831. It has a 900-acre campus.

RATINGS
Admissions Selectivity Rating: 94   **Fire Safety Rating:** 89   **Green Rating:** 87

STUDENTS AND FACULTY
Enrollment: 2,240. **Student Body:** 56% female, 44% male, 66% out-of-state, 6% international (25 countries represented). Asian 2%, African American 6%, Caucasian 79%, Hispanic 3%.
Retention and Graduation: 90% freshmen return for sophomore year. 80% freshmen graduate within 4 years. 23% grads go on to further study within 1 year. 15% grads pursue arts and sciences degrees. 2% grads pursue law degrees. 1% grads pursue business degrees. 2% grads pursue medical degrees. **Faculty:** Student/faculty ratio 10:1. 197 full-time faculty, 98% hold PhDs, 16% are members of minority groups, 44% are women.

ACADEMICS
Degrees: Bachelor's. **Classes:** Most classes have 10–19 students. **Majors with Highest Enrollment:** Economics; English language and literature; psychology. **Special Study Options:** Double major, honors program, independent study, internships, student-designed major, study abroad, teacher certification program, 3-2 Duke U Environmental Management; 3-2 U. of Michigan Natural Resources, 3-4 Case Western Reserve Dental; 3-2 Rensselaer Poly, Washington U. (St. Louis), Case Western Reserve, Columbia U. Engineering; Washington U. (St. Louis) Occupational Therapy. Special programs offered to physically disabled students include note-taking services, reader services, tape recorders, tutors. **Career services:** Alumni network, alumni services, career assessment, internships, regional alumni. **Career services highlights include:** We are proud of all of our programs.

FACILITIES
Housing: Coed dorms, men's dorms, women's dorms, cooperative housing, apartments for single students, wellness housing, theme housing 66% of campus accessible to physically disabled. **Special Academic Facilities/Equipment:** Burmese art collection in the Denison Museum, language lab, research station in 350–acre biological reserve, observatory, high resolution spectrometer lab, nuclear magnetic resonance spectrometer, planetarium, Economics computer laboratories. **Computers:** 100% of classrooms, 100% of dorms, 100% of libraries, 100% of dining areas, 100% of student union, 100% of common outdoor areas have wireless network access. Administrative functions (other than registration) can be performed online.

CAMPUS LIFE
Environment: Village. **Activities:** Choral groups, dance, drama/theater, jazz band, music ensembles, musical theater, radio station, student government, student newspaper, student-run film society, television station, yearbook, campus ministries, international student organization. **Organizations:** 160 registered organizations, 15 honor societies, 7 religious organizations, 8 fraternities, 6 sororities. **Athletics (Intercollegiate):** *Men:* Baseball, basketball, cross-country, diving, football, golf, lacrosse, soccer, swimming, tennis, track/field (outdoor), track/field (indoor). *Women:* Basketball, cross-country, diving, field hockey, golf, lacrosse, soccer, softball, swimming, tennis, track/field (outdoor), track/field (indoor), volleyball. **On-Campus Highlights:** Samson Talbot Hall of Biological Science, Mitchell Recreation and Athletics Center, Swasey Chapel, Biological Reserve and Polly Anderson Fi, Burke Hall Art Gallery, Burton D. Morgan Center. **Environmental Initiatives:** Campus recycling program takes paper, cardboard, aluminum, bi-metal, paper, magazines, books, glass, year end move out materials, construction/maintenance metal, wood, debris—community has access to drop of materials too. Have begun composting operaitons for yard wastes and kitchen food scraps. Operations department collects recyclables from all construction and maintenance operations, chemicals in cleaning and grounds are 90% 'green', incandescent bulbs are no longer used (except where reuired), lamp and balasts are recycled, inventory of mercury lamps identified—replace fixture rather than relamp. Currently establishing a systematic energy conservation/retrofit program for existing buildings—anticipate going through all campus buildings in the next 3-5 years. All new construction/major renovation projects currently under way and planned future projects to be LEED Sil-

ver certified, smaller renovations and projects to follow guidelines to the extent possible, exploring LEED-EB certification for some buildings on campus.

ADMISSIONS
Freshman Academic Profile: Average high school GPA 3.5. 54% in top 10% of high school class, 85% in top 25% of high school class, 97% in top 50% of high school class. 70% from public high schools. SAT Math middle 50% range 600–680. SAT Critical Reading middle 50% range 600–700. ACT middle 50% range 27–30. Minimum paper TOEFL 550. Minimum computer TOEFL 213. **Basis for Candidate Selection:** *Very important factors considered include:* Application essay, academic GPA, recommendation(s), rigor of secondary school record. *Important factors considered include:* Extracurricular activities, interview, level of applicant's interest, talent/ability. *Other factors considered include:* Class rank, standardized test scores, alumni/ae relation, character/personal qualities, first generation, geographical residence, racial/ethnic status, state residency, volunteer work, work experience. **Freshman Admission Requirements:** High school diploma is required and GED is accepted. *Academic units required:* 4 English, 4 mathematics, 4 science, 3 foreign language, 2 social studies, 1 history, 1 academic electives. **Freshman Admission Statistics:** 5,002 applied, 50% admitted, 26% enrolled. **Transfer Admission Requirements:** High school transcript, college transcript(s), essay or personal statement, statement of good standing from prior institution(s). Minimum college GPA of 3.0 required. Lowest grade transferable C–. **General Admission Information:** Application fee $40. Early decision application deadline 11/15. Regular application deadline 1/15. Regular notification 4/1. Nonfall registration not accepted. Admission may be deferred for a maximum of 1 year. Credit and/or placement offered for CEEB Advanced Placement tests.

COSTS AND FINANCIAL AID
Required Forms and Deadlines: FAFSA. Priority financial aid filing date 2/15. **Notification of Awards:** Applicants will be notified of awards on or about 3/28. **Types of Aid:** *Need-based scholarships/grants:* Federal Pell, SEOG, state scholarships/grants, private scholarships, the school's own gift aid. *Loans:* Direct Subsidized Stafford, Direct Unsubsidized Stafford, Direct PLUS, Federal Perkins, college/university loans from institutional funds. **Student Employment:** Federal Work-Study Program available. Institutional employment available. Highest amount earned per year from on-campus jobs $2,530. Off-campus job opportunities are fair. **Financial Aid Statistics:** 53% freshmen, 46% undergrads receive need-based scholarship or grant aid. 45% freshmen, 40% undergrads receive non-need-based scholarship or grant aid. 40% freshmen, 35% undergrads receive need-based self-help aid. 93% freshmen, 93% undergrads receive any aid. **Criteria for awarding institutional aid:** *Non-need-based:* Academics, alumni affiliation, art, leadership, minority status, music/drama, state/district residency.

DEPAUL UNIVERSITY

1 East Jackson Boulevard, Suite 9000, Chicago, IL 60604-2287
Phone: 312-362-8300 **Financial Aid Phone:** 312-362-8091
E-mail: admission@depaul.edu **CEEB Code:** 001671-00
Fax: 312-362-5749 **Website:** www.depaul.edu **ACT Code:** 1012

This private school, affiliated with the Roman Catholic Church, was founded in 1898. It has a 36-acre campus.

RATINGS
Admissions Selectivity Rating: 82   **Fire Safety Rating:** 82   **Green Rating:** 86

STUDENTS AND FACULTY
Enrollment: 15,821. **Student Body:** 55% female, 45% male, 17.9% out-of-state, 1% international (108 countries represented). Asian 7%, African American 7%, Caucasian 47%, Hispanic 11%.
Retention and Graduation: 43% freshmen graduate within 4 years. 15.8% grads go on to further study within 1 year. **Faculty:** Student/faculty ratio 16:1. 919 full-time faculty, 88% hold PhDs, 24% are members of minority groups, 45% are women. 1.64% of classes are taught by teaching assistants.

ACADEMICS
Degrees: Bachelor's, certificate, master's, post-bachelor's certificate, post-master's certificate. **Classes:** Most classes have 20–29 students. Most lab/discussion sessions have 10–19 students. **Majors with Highest Enrollment:** Accounting; communication studies/speech communication and rhetoric; psychology.

Special Study Options: Accelerated program, cooperative education program, distance learning, double major, dual enrollment, English as a Second Language (ESL), honors program, independent study, internships, student-designed major, study abroad, teacher certification program, weekend college. **Honors programs:** DePaul's honors program offers small classes organized in a seminar format and taught by faculty committed to academic excellence and the attainment of lifelong learning strategies. Benefits of our scholarly community include academic advising, an Honors Lounge, a student government, peer mentoring, student-faculty dinners, newsletters, cultural outings, service activities, and many other experiences that enrich the Honors community while extending the Honors experience beyond the classroom. **Combined degree programs:** BA/MA, BS/MS. Special programs offered to physically disabled students include note-taking services, reader services, tape recorders, tutors. **Career services:** Alumni network, alumni services, career/job search classes, career assessment, internships, regional alumni. **Career services highlights include:** In response to a mandated experiential learning requirement, we set up an university wide internship program that places 1,020 students a year in internships that meet the requirements.

FACILITIES

Housing: Coed dorms, special housing for disabled students, special housing for international students, apartments for single students, theme housing 95% of campus accessible to physically disabled. **Special Academic Facilities/Equipment:** Monsignor Andrew J. McGowan Environmental Science & Chemistry building (gold LEED-certified, 2009), Digital Cinema laboratory with motion-capture system, Green-screen studio, converged newsroom, Merle Reskin Theatre, Art Museum, William G. McGowan Biological & Environmental Science Building (1998), Ray Meyer Fitness & Recreational Center (1999), and three-level student center (2002). **Computers:** 60% of classrooms, 100% of dorms, 100% of libraries, 100% of dining areas, 75% of student union, 25% of common outdoor areas have wireless network access. Students can register for classes online. Administrative functions (other than registration) can be performed online.

CAMPUS LIFE

Environment: Metropolis. **Activities:** Choral groups, concert band, dance, drama/theater, jazz band, literary magazine, marching band, music ensembles, musical theater, opera, pep band, radio station, student government, student newspaper, student-run film society, symphony orchestra, yearbook, campus ministries, international student organization, Model UN. **Organizations:** 311 registered organizations, 9 honor societies, 19 religious organizations. 9 fraternities, 13 sororities. **Athletics (Intercollegiate):** *Men:* Basketball, cross-country, golf, soccer, tennis, track/field (outdoor), track/field (indoor). *Women:* Basketball, cross-country, soccer, softball, tennis, track/field (outdoor), track/field (indoor), volleyball. **On-Campus Highlights:** Quad (outside center of campus), Ray Meyer Fitness Center, Student Center, Student Lounge in DePaul Center, The Bean Cafe in the Schmitt Acad. Cntr. **Environmental Initiatives:** Designing all new construction to be LEED-certified. The signature activity related to campus sustainability is the construction of the Monsignor Andrew J. McGowan Science Center ("McGowan South"). McGowan South reflects DePaul's commitment to science education, research and sustainable practices. The facility was built following the standards of the U.S. Green Building Council's Leadership in Energy and Environmental Design (LEED) Rating System. Notable features of McGowan South include a rooftop garden, native plant landscaping, occupancy sensors and timers on interior lights, dual-flush toilets, a state-of-the-art energy recovery system and carbon dioxide (CO2) sensors throughout the building. It also houses state-of-the-art lecture halls and teaching and research laboratories. DePaul continues to implement and use alternative energy sources on campus. This past summer, 34 solar light poles were installed to reduce electricity usage and illuminate the campus using the power of the sun. The solar light poles, which have been placed on the east end of the campus, just south of Concert Hall. In addition, solar light poles and new power panels were installed in the Quad area of the Lincoln Park Campus. A "green roof" is planned for the DePaul Center on the Loop Campus. Materials used in its landscape maintenance operation to more organic products that are free of toxic pesticides. Document Services has switched to Domtar Earth Choice paper, which has been endorsed by The Rainforest Alliance, the Sustainable Forest Initiative and the Forest Stewardship Council. DePaul is constantly assessing the responsibilities to the development of academic programming to further research and learning associated with sustainability and the environment.

ADMISSIONS

Freshman Academic Profile: Average high school GPA 3.36. 21.6% in top 10% of high school class, 29.4% in top 25% of high school class, 84.6% in top 50% of high school class. 76.2% from public high schools. SAT Math middle 50% range 520–620. SAT Critical Reading middle 50% range 520–640. SAT Writing middle 50% range 520–630. ACT middle 50% range 22–27. Minimum paper TOEFL 550. Minimum computer TOEFL 213. Minimum web-based TOEFL 80. **Basis for Candidate Selection:** *Very important factors considered include:* Application essay, academic GPA, rigor of secondary school re-

cord, standardized test scores. *Important factors considered include:* Class rank, recommendation(s), character/personal qualities, extracurricular activities, level of applicant's interest, talent/ability, volunteer work, work experience. *Other factors considered include:* Alumni/ae relation, first generation, geographical residence, interview, racial/ethnic status, religious affiliation/commitment, state residency. **Freshman Admission Requirements:** High school diploma is required and GED is accepted. *Academic units required:* 4 English, 3 mathematics, 3 science, (2 science labs), 2 social science/history. *Academic units recommended:* 2 foreign language. **Freshman Admission Statistics:** 11,564 applied, 74% admitted, 29% enrolled. **Transfer Admission Requirements:** College transcript(s), minimum college GPA of 2.0 required. Lowest grade transferable D. **General Admission Information:** Application fee $40. Regular application deadline 2/1. Regular notification 3/15. Nonfall registration accepted. Admission may be deferred for a maximum of 1 year. Credit and/or placement offered for CEEB Advanced Placement tests.

COSTS AND FINANCIAL AID

Annual tuition $26,765. . Room and board $10,617. Required fees $577. Average book expense $1,005. **Required Forms and Deadlines:** FAFSA. Priority financial aid filing date 3/1. **Notification of Awards:** Applicants will be notified of awards on a rolling basis beginning 3/15. **Types of Aid:** *Need-based scholarships/grants:* Federal Pell, SEOG, state scholarships/grants, private scholarships, the school's own gift aid, Federal Academic Competitiveness Grant, Federal SMART Grant, and Federal TEACH Grant. *Loans:* Direct Subsidized Stafford, Direct Unsubsidized Stafford, Direct PLUS, Federal Perkins, Private Loans. **Student Employment:** Federal Work-Study Program available. Institutional employment available. Highest amount earned per year from on-campus jobs $14,000. Off-campus job opportunities are excellent. **Financial Aid Statistics:** 59% freshmen, 51% undergrads receive need-based scholarship or grant aid. 36% freshmen, 22% undergrads receive non-need-based scholarship or grant aid. 56% freshmen, 54% undergrads receive need-based self-help aid. 2% freshmen, 2% undergrads receive athletic scholarships. 88% freshmen, 90% undergrads receive any aid. 64% undergrads borrow to pay for school. Average cumulative indebtedness $19,072. **Criteria for awarding institutional aid:** *Non-need-based:* Academics, art, athletics, leadership, music/drama, state/district residency.

DEPAUW UNIVERSITY

101 E. Seminary, Greencastle, IN 46135
Phone: 765-658-4006 **Financial Aid Phone:** 765-658-4030
E-mail: admission@depauw.edu **CEEB Code:** 1166
Fax: 765-658-4007 **Website:** www.depauw.edu **ACT Code:** 1184

This private school, affiliated with the Methodist Church, was founded in 1837. It has a 1100-acre campus.

RATINGS

Admissions Selectivity Rating: 91   **Fire Safety Rating:** 60*   **Green Rating:** 65

STUDENTS AND FACULTY

Enrollment: 2,354. **Student Body:** 57% female, 43% male, 59% out-of-state, 7% international (32 countries represented). Asian 3%, African American 6%, Caucasian 76%, Hispanic 4%.
Retention and Graduation: 90% freshmen return for sophomore year. 79% freshmen graduate within 4 years. 23% grads go on to further study within 1 year. 15% grads pursue arts and sciences degrees. 5% grads pursue law degrees. 1% grads pursue business degrees. 2% grads pursue medical degrees. **Faculty:** Student/faculty ratio 10:1. 224 full-time faculty, 98% hold PhDs, 21% are members of minority groups, 43% are women.

ACADEMICS

Degrees: Bachelor's. **Classes:** Most classes have 10–19 students. Most lab/discussion sessions have 10–19 students. **Majors with Highest Enrollment:** Communication studies/speech communication and rhetoric; economics; English composition. **Special Study Options:** Double major, dual enrollment, exchange student program (domestic), honors program, independent study, internships, student-designed major, study abroad, teacher certification program. **Honors programs:** Please visit the following website for information about DePauw's **Honors programs:** www.depauw.edu/honors/index.asp. Special programs offered to physically disabled students include note-taking services, reader services, tape recorders, tutors. **Career services:** Alumni network, alumni services, career/job search classes, career assessment, internships, regional alumni. **Career services highlights include:** www.depauw.edu/admin/acadaffairs/studentprograms/internship.asp.

FACILITIES
Housing: Coed dorms, special housing for disabled students, special housing for international students, fraternity/sorority housing, apartments for single students 85% of campus accessible to physically disabled. **Special Academic Facilities/Equipment:** Recently opened Peeler Art Center housing gallery and studio space; Center for Contemporary Media; Performing Arts Center; Anthropology Museum; Shidzuo Iikudo Museum. **Computers:** Students can register for classes online. Administrative functions (other than registration) can be performed online. Undergraduates are required to own a computer.

CAMPUS LIFE
Environment: Village. **Activities:** Choral groups, concert band, dance, drama/theater, jazz band, literary magazine, music ensembles, musical theater, opera, pep band, radio station, student government, student newspaper, student-run film society, symphony orchestra, television station, campus ministries, international student organization. **Organizations:** 119 registered organizations, 13 honor societies, 10 religious organizations. 13 fraternities, 11 sorority. **Athletics (Intercollegiate):** *Men:* Baseball, basketball, cross-country, diving, football, golf, soccer, swimming, tennis, track/field (outdoor), track/field (indoor). *Women:* Basketball, cross-country, diving, field hockey, golf, soccer, softball, swimming, tennis, track/field (outdoor), track/field (indoor), volleyball. **On-Campus Highlights:** DePauw University School of Music, Roy O. West Library, Music Library, and the Prevo Science Library, Cafe Roy coffee shop, Memorial Student Union, Bowman Park. **Environmental Initiatives:** LEED-certified construction of the Janet Prindle Institute for Ethics. 2007-08 full year of campus programming, speakers, and colloquia on sustainability: Boswell Symposium on environmental justice, featuring Majora Carter (www.depauw.edu/admin/acadaffairs/Boswell/Symposium_2007.asp) Ubben Lecture by Ralph Nader (www.depauw.edu/news/index.asp?id=20101) Arts Fest 2007 on Art and the Environment (www.depauw.edu/arts/artsfest/) DePauw Discourse on Sustainability and Global Citizenship, featuring Bill McKibben and Robert Kennedy, Jr. (www.depauw.edu/discourse/) Focus the Nation teach-in on global warming (www.depauw.edu/univ/sustain/ftn/index.asp) DePauw Colloquium on the Liberal Arts: Liberal Education in a Time of Climate Crisis (www.depauw.edu/admin/acadaffairs/facdev/Events/DePauwColloquium2008.asp) Earth Week events currently in planning stages. Significant investment in/upgrades to campus utilities/infrastructure, including an HVAC audit, upgraded steam pipes, chiller planet water system replacement, lightbulb replacement, and a bike-share program, among other changes.

ADMISSIONS
Freshman Academic Profile: Average high school GPA 3.6. 51% in top 10% of high school class, 82% in top 25% of high school class, 100% in top 50% of high school class. 83% from public high schools. SAT Math middle 50% range 550–670. SAT Critical Reading middle 50% range 530–650. SAT Writing middle 50% range 530–640. ACT middle 50% range 24–29. Minimum paper TOEFL 560. Minimum computer TOEFL 225. **Basis for Candidate Selection:** *Very important factors considered include:* Academic GPA, rigor of secondary school record, standardized test scores. *Important factors considered include:* Class rank, application essay, recommendation(s). *Other factors considered include:* Alumni/ae relation, character/personal qualities, extracurricular activities, first generation, geographical residence, interview, level of applicant's interest, state residency, talent/ability, volunteer work, work experience. **Freshman Admission Requirements:** High school diploma is required and GED is accepted. *Academic units recommended:* 4 English, 4 mathematics, (2 science labs). **Freshman Admission Statistics:** 4,347 applied, 66% admitted, 25% enrolled. **Transfer Admission Requirements:** High school transcript, college transcript(s), essay or personal statement, statement of good standing from prior institution(s). Minimum college GPA of 3.0 required. Lowest grade transferable C. **General Admission Information:** Application fee $40. Early decision application deadline 11/1. Regular application deadline 2/1. Regular notification 4/1. Nonfall registration accepted. Admission may be deferred for a maximum of 1 year. Credit and/or placement offered for CEEB Advanced Placement tests.

COSTS AND FINANCIAL AID
Annual tuition $32,800. Room and board $8,740. Required fees $450. Average book expense $750. **Required Forms and Deadlines:** FAFSA, institution's own financial aid form. Priority financial aid filing date 2/15. **Notification of Awards:** Applicants will be notified of awards on or about 4/1. **Types of Aid:** *Need-based scholarships/grants:* Federal Pell, SEOG, state scholarships/grants, private scholarships, the school's own gift aid, United Negro College Fund. *Loans:* Direct Subsidized Stafford, Direct Unsubsidized Stafford, Direct PLUS, FFEL Subsidized Stafford, FFEL Unsubsidized Stafford, FFEL PLUS, Federal Perkins, state loans, college/university loans from institutional funds. **Student Employment:** Federal Work-Study Program available. Institutional employment available. Off-campus job opportunities are fair. **Financial Aid Statistics:** 57% freshmen, 53% undergrads receive need-based scholarship or

grant aid. 13% freshmen, 11% undergrads receive non-need-based scholarship or grant aid. 43% freshmen, 41% undergrads receive need-based self-help aid. 48% undergrads borrow to pay for school. Average cumulative indebtedness $24,210. **Criteria for awarding institutional aid:** *Non-need-based:* Academics, alumni affiliation, art, leadership, minority status, music/drama, religious affiliation, state/district residency.

DEVRY INSTITUTE OF TECHNOLOGY (LONG ISLAND CITY, NY)

3020 Thomson Avenue, Long Island City, NY 11101-3051
Phone: 718-472-2728
E-mail: nyemailleads@ny.devry.edu
Fax: 718-361-0004 **Website:** www.devry.edu

This proprietary school was founded in 1931. It has a 4-acre campus.

RATINGS
Admissions Selectivity Rating: 60* **Fire Safety Rating:** 60* **Green Rating:** 60*

STUDENTS AND FACULTY
Enrollment: 1,839. **Student Body:** 24% female, 76% male, 3% international (17 countries represented). Asian 8%, African American 40%, Caucasian 10%, Hispanic 23%, Native American 1%. **Retention and Graduation:** 36% freshmen return for sophomore year. **Faculty:** Student/faculty ratio 16:1. 60 full-time faculty.

ACADEMICS
Degrees: Associate, bachelor's, master's, post-bachelor's certificate, terminal associate. **Majors with Highest Enrollment:** Electrical, electronic and communications engineering technology/technician. **Special Study Options:** Accelerated program, cooperative education program, distance learning, double major, weekend college. Special programs offered to physically disabled students include note-taking services, reader services, tape recorders, tutors. **Career services:** Alumni services, career/job search classes.

FACILITIES
Housing: Private apartments;student plan housing, private rooms. 100% of campus accessible to physically disabled. **Computers:** Administrative functions (other than registration) can be performed online.

CAMPUS LIFE
Organizations: 4 registered organizations, 1 honor societies.

ADMISSIONS
Freshman Academic Profile: Minimum paper TOEFL 500. Minimum computer TOEFL 173. **Basis for Candidate Selection:** *Important factors considered include:* Interview. *Other factors considered include:* Standardized test scores. **Freshman Admission Requirements:** High school diploma is required and GED is accepted. *Academic units required:* 1 mathematics. **Transfer Admission Requirements:** College transcript(s), standardized test scores, minimum college GPA of 2.0 required. Lowest grade transferable C. **General Admission Information:** Application fee $50. Notification on a rolling basis, beginning on or about 11/2. Nonfall registration accepted. Admission may be deferred for a maximum of 1 year. Credit offered for CEEB Advanced Placement tests.

COSTS AND FINANCIAL AID
Annual tuition $12,450. Required fees $250. Average book expense $1,200. **Required Forms and Deadlines:** FAFSA **Types of Aid:** *Need-based scholarships/grants:* Federal Pell, SEOG, private scholarships, the school's own gift aid. *Loans:* FFEL Subsidized Stafford, FFEL Unsubsidized Stafford, FFEL PLUS, Federal Perkins, college/university loans from institutional funds. **Student Employment:** Federal Work-Study Program available. Institutional employment available. Highest amount earned per year from on-campus jobs $5,994. Off-campus job opportunities are good. **Financial Aid Statistics:** 60% freshmen, 66% undergrads receive need-based scholarship or grant aid. 64% freshmen, 74% undergrads receive need-based self-help aid.

DEVRY UNIVERSITY (ADDISON, IL)

1221 North Swift Road, Addision, IL 60101
Phone: 630-953-2000
E-mail: info@devry.edu
Fax: 630-953-1236 **Website:** www.devry.edu

This proprietary school was founded in 1931. It has a 13-acre campus.

RATINGS
Admissions Selectivity Rating: 60*   **Fire Safety Rating:** 60*   **Green Rating:** 60*

STUDENTS AND FACULTY
Enrollment: 4,827. **Student Body:** 34% female, 66% male, 1% international (23 countries represented). Asian 8%, African American 13%, Caucasian 52%, Hispanic 8%, Native American 1%.
Retention and Graduation: 51% freshmen return for sophomore year. **Faculty:** Student/faculty ratio 19:1. 69 full-time faculty.

ACADEMICS
Degrees: Associate, bachelor's, terminal associate. **Majors with Highest Enrollment:** Electrical, electronic and communications engineering technology/technician. **Special Study Options:** Accelerated program, cooperative education program, distance learning, double major, weekend college. Special programs offered to physically disabled students include note-taking services, reader services, tape recorders, tutors. **Career services:** Alumni services, career/job search classes.

FACILITIES
Housing: Concord Residence. 100% of campus accessible to physically disabled. **Computers:** Students can register for classes online. Administrative functions (other than registration) can be performed online.

CAMPUS LIFE
Environment: Village. **Activities:** Student government **Organizations:** 11 registered organizations, 3 honor societies, 1 religious organizations.

ADMISSIONS
Freshman Academic Profile: Minimum paper TOEFL 500. Minimum computer TOEFL 173. **Basis for Candidate Selection:** *Important factors considered include:* Interview. *Other factors considered include:* Standardized test scores. **Freshman Admission Requirements:** High school diploma is required and GED is accepted. *Academic units required:* 1 mathematics. **Transfer Admission Requirements:** College transcript(s), standardized test scores, minimum college GPA of 2.0 required. Lowest grade transferable C. **General Admission Information:** Application fee $50. Notification on a rolling basis, beginning on or about 11/2. Nonfall registration accepted. Admission may be deferred for a maximum of 1 year. Credit offered for CEEB Advanced Placement tests.

COSTS AND FINANCIAL AID
Annual tuition $11,330. Required fees $250. Average book expense $1,200. **Required Forms and Deadlines:** FAFSA. *Types of Aid: Need-based scholarships/grants:* Federal Pell, SEOG, private scholarships, the school's own gift aid. *Loans:* FFEL Subsidized Stafford, FFEL Unsubsidized Stafford, FFEL PLUS, Federal Perkins, college/university loans from institutional funds. **Student Employment:** Federal Work-Study Program available. Institutional employment available. Highest amount earned per year from on-campus jobs $6,750. Off-campus job opportunities are excellent. **Financial Aid Statistics:** 15% freshmen, 29% undergrads receive need-based scholarship or grant aid. 24% freshmen, 48% undergrads receive need-based self-help aid.

DEVRY UNIVERSITY (ALPHARETTA, GA)

2555 Northwinds Parkway, Alpharetta, GA 30004
Phone: 770-664-9520
E-mail: admissions@devry.com
Fax: 770-664-8824 **Website:** www.devry.edu

This proprietary school was founded in 1931. It has a 21-acre campus.

RATINGS
Admissions Selectivity Rating: 60*   **Fire Safety Rating:** 60*   **Green Rating:** 60*

STUDENTS AND FACULTY
Enrollment: 1,286. **Student Body:** 34% female, 66% male, % out-of-state, 2% international (17 countries represented). Asian 3%, African American 32%,

Caucasian 28%, Hispanic 3%, Native American 1%.
Retention and Graduation: 40% freshmen return for sophomore year. **Faculty:** Student/faculty ratio 36:1. 38 full-time faculty.

ACADEMICS
Degrees: Associate, bachelor's, master's, post-bachelor's certificate, terminal associate. **Special Study Options:** Accelerated program, cooperative education program, distance learning, double major, weekend college. Special programs offered to physically disabled students include note-taking services, reader services, tape recorders, tutors. **Career services:** Alumni services, career/job search classes.

FACILITIES
Housing: Private apartments. Student plan housing and private rooms. 98% of campus accessible to physically disabled. **Computers:** Students can register for classes online. Administrative functions (other than registration) can be performed online.

CAMPUS LIFE
Environment: City. **Activities:** Student government. **Organizations:** 12 registered organizations, 4 honor societies.

ADMISSIONS
Freshman Academic Profile: Minimum paper TOEFL 500. Minimum computer TOEFL 173. **Basis for Candidate Selection:** *Important factors considered include:* Interview. *Other factors considered include:* Standardized test scores. **Freshman Admission Requirements:** High school diploma is required and GED is accepted. *Academic units required:* 1 mathematics. **Transfer Admission Requirements:** College transcript(s), standardized test scores, minimum college GPA of 2.0 required. Lowest grade transferable C. **General Admission Information:** Application fee $50. Nonfall registration accepted. Admission may be deferred for a maximum of 12. Credit offered for CEEB Advanced Placement tests.

COSTS AND FINANCIAL AID
Annual tuition $11,240. Required fees $250. Average book expense $1,200. **Required Forms and Deadlines:** FAFSA **Types of Aid:** *Need-based scholarships/grants:* Federal Pell, SEOG, private scholarships, the school's own gift aid. *Loans:* FFEL Subsidized Stafford, FFEL Unsubsidized Stafford, FFEL PLUS, Federal Perkins, college/university loans from institutional funds. **Financial Aid Statistics:** 48% freshmen, 66% undergrads receive need-based scholarship or grant aid. 1% undergrads receive non-need-based scholarship or grant aid. 49% freshmen, 68% undergrads receive need-based self-help aid.

DEVRY UNIVERSITY (CHICAGO, IL)

3300 North Cambell Avenue, Chicago, IL 60618
Phone: 773-697-2155
E-mail: keaster@chi.devry.edu
Fax: 773-697-2710 **Website:** www.devry.edu

This proprietary school was founded in 1931. It has a 16-acre campus.

RATINGS
Admissions Selectivity Rating: 60*   **Fire Safety Rating:** 60*   **Green Rating:** 60*

STUDENTS AND FACULTY
Enrollment: 2,896. **Student Body:** 36% female, 64% male, 2% international (26 countries represented). Asian 11%, African American 69%, Caucasian 22%, Hispanic 31%.
Retention and Graduation: 46% freshmen return for sophomore year. **Faculty:** Student/faculty ratio 50:1. 74 full-time faculty.

ACADEMICS
Degrees: Associate, bachelor's, terminal associate. **Majors with Highest Enrollment:** Electrical, electronic and communications engineering technology/technician. **Special Study Options:** Accelerated program, cooperative education program, distance learning, double major, dual enrollment, English as a Second Language (ESL), weekend college. Special programs offered to physically disabled students include note-taking services, reader services, tape recorders, tutors. **Career services:** Alumni services, career/job search classes.

FACILITIES
Housing: Men's dorms, women's dorms, apartments for married students, apartments for single students. 100% of campus accessible to physically disabled. **Computers:** Students can register for classes online. Administrative functions (other than registration) can be performed online.

CAMPUS LIFE

Environment: Metropolis. **Activities:** Choral groups, drama/theater, music ensembles, yearbook. **Organizations:** 16 registered organizations, 3 honor societies, 2 religious organizations.

ADMISSIONS

Freshman Academic Profile: Minimum paper TOEFL 500. Minimum computer TOEFL 173. **Basis for Candidate Selection:** *Important factors considered include:* Interview. *Other factors considered include:* Standardized test scores. **Freshman Admission Requirements:** High school diploma is required and GED is accepted. *Academic units required:* 1 mathematics. **Transfer Admission Requirements:** College transcript(s), standardized test scores, minimum college GPA of 2.0 required. Lowest grade transferable C. **General Admission Information:** Application fee $50. Notification on a rolling basis, beginning on or about 11/2. Nonfall registration accepted. Admission may be deferred for a maximum of 1 year. Credit offered for CEEB Advanced Placement tests.

COSTS AND FINANCIAL AID

Annual tuition $11,330. Required fees $250. Average book expense $1,200. **Required Forms and Deadlines:** FAFSA. **Types of Aid:** *Need-based scholarships/grants:* Federal Pell, SEOG, private scholarships, the school's own gift aid. *Loans:* FFEL Subsidized Stafford, FFEL Unsubsidized Stafford, FFEL PLUS, Federal Perkins, college/university loans from institutional funds. **Student Employment:** Federal Work-Study Program available. Institutional employment available. Highest amount earned per year from on-campus jobs $9,000. Off-campus job opportunities are good. **Financial Aid Statistics:** 30% freshmen, 52% undergrads receive need-based scholarship or grant aid. 34% freshmen, 63% undergrads receive need-based self-help aid.

DEVRY UNIVERSITY (COLUMBUS, OH)

1350 Alum Creek Drive, Columbus, OH 43209-2705
Phone: 614-253-1525
E-mail: admissions@devry.edu
Fax: 614-253-0843 **Website:** www.devry.edu

This proprietary school was founded in 1931. It has a 13-acre campus.

RATINGS

Admissions Selectivity Rating: 60*   **Fire Safety Rating:** 60*   **Green Rating:** 60*

STUDENTS AND FACULTY

Enrollment: 3,145. **Student Body:** 25% female, 75% male, 12% out-of-state, 1% international (3 countries represented). Asian 3%, African American 20%, Caucasian 73%, Hispanic 1%.
Retention and Graduation: 40% freshmen return for sophomore year. **Faculty:** Student/faculty ratio 39:1. 83 full-time faculty.

ACADEMICS

Degrees: Associate, bachelor's, master's, post-bachelor's certificate, terminal associate. **Majors with Highest Enrollment:** Electrical, electronic and communications engineering technology/technician. **Special Study Options:** Accelerated program, cooperative education program, distance learning, double major, weekend college. Special programs offered to physically disabled students include note-taking services, reader services, tape recorders, tutors. **Career services:** Alumni services, career/job search classes.

FACILITIES

Housing: Private apartments Student plan housing and private rooms. 90% of campus accessible to physically disabled. **Computers:** Students can register for classes online. Administrative functions (other than registration) can be performed online.

CAMPUS LIFE

Environment: Metropolis. **Activities:** Student government, student newspaper. **Organizations:** 13 registered organizations, 2 honor societies,

ADMISSIONS

Freshman Academic Profile: Minimum paper TOEFL 500. Minimum computer TOEFL 173. **Basis for Candidate Selection:** *Important factors considered include:* Interview. *Other factors considered include:* Standardized test scores. **Freshman Admission Requirements:** High school diploma is required and GED is accepted. *Academic units required:* 1 mathematics. **Transfer Admission Requirements:** College transcript(s), standardized test scores, minimum college GPA of 2.0 required. Lowest grade transferable C. **General Admission Information:** Application fee $50. Notification on a rolling basis, beginning on or about 11/2. Nonfall registration accepted. Admission

may be deferred for a maximum of 1 year. Credit offered for CEEB Advanced Placement tests.

COSTS AND FINANCIAL AID

Annual tuition $11,240. Required fees $250. Average book expense $1,200. **Required Forms and Deadlines:** FAFSA **Types of Aid:** *Need-based scholarships/grants:* Federal Pell, SEOG, private scholarships, the school's own gift aid. *Loans:* FFEL Subsidized Stafford, FFEL Unsubsidized Stafford, FFEL PLUS, Federal Perkins, college/university loans from institutional funds. **Student Employment:** Federal Work-Study Program available. Institutional employment available. Highest amount earned per year from on-campus jobs $12,000. Off-campus job opportunities are excellent. **Financial Aid Statistics:** 46% freshmen, 54% undergrads receive need-based scholarship or grant aid. 1% freshmen, 1% undergrads receive non-need-based scholarship or grant aid. 50% freshmen, 72% undergrads receive need-based self-help aid.

DEVRY UNIVERSITY (DECATUR, GA)

250 N. Arcadia Avenue, Decatur, GA 30030
Phone: 404-292-2645
E-mail: dsilva@admin.atl.devry.edu
Fax: 404-292-7011 **Website:** www.atl.devry.edu

This proprietary school was founded in 1931. It has a 23-acre campus.

RATINGS

Admissions Selectivity Rating: 60*   **Fire Safety Rating:** 60*   **Green Rating:** 60*

STUDENTS AND FACULTY

Enrollment: 1,550. **Student Body:** 44% female, 56% male, 17% out-of-state, 3% international (8 countries represented). Asian 3%, African American 84%, Caucasian 15%, Hispanic 3%.
Retention and Graduation: 41% freshmen return for sophomore year. **Faculty:** Student/faculty ratio 36:1. 63 full-time faculty.

ACADEMICS

Degrees: Associate, bachelor's, master's, post-bachelor's certificate, terminal associate. **Majors with Highest Enrollment:** Business administration, management and operations, other. **Special Study Options:** Accelerated program, cooperative education program, distance learning, double major, weekend college. Special programs offered to physically disabled students include note-taking services, reader services, tape recorders, tutors. **Career services:** Alumni services, career/job search classes.

FACILITIES

Housing: Private apartments, student paln housing, private rooms. 100% of campus accessible to physically disabled. **Computers:** Students can register for classes online. Administrative functions (other than registration) can be performed online.

CAMPUS LIFE

Environment: City. **Activities:** **Organizations:** 10 registered organizations, 4 honor societies,

ADMISSIONS

Freshman Academic Profile: Minimum paper TOEFL 500. Minimum computer TOEFL 173. **Basis for Candidate Selection:** *Important factors considered include:* Interview. *Other factors considered include:* Standardized test scores. **Freshman Admission Requirements:** High school diploma is required and GED is accepted. *Academic units required:* 1 mathematics. **Transfer Admission Requirements:** College transcript(s), standardized test scores, minimum college GPA of 2.0 required. Lowest grade transferable C. **General Admission Information:** Application fee $50. Notification on a rolling basis, beginning on or about 11/2. Nonfall registration accepted. Admission may be deferred for a maximum of 1 year. Credit offered for CEEB Advanced Placement tests.

COSTS AND FINANCIAL AID

Annual tuition $17,104. Room and board $12,018. Required fees $250. Average book expense $1,346. **Required Forms and Deadlines:** FAFSA. **Types of Aid:** *Need-based scholarships/grants:* Federal Pell, SEOG, private scholarships, the school's own gift aid. *Loans:* FFEL Subsidized Stafford, FFEL Unsubsidized Stafford, FFEL PLUS, Federal Perkins, college/university loans from institutional funds. **Student Employment:** Federal Work-Study Program available. Institutional employment available. Highest amount earned per year from on-campus jobs $6,743. Off-campus job opportunities are good. **Financial Aid Statistics:** 72% freshmen, 79% undergrads receive need-based scholarship or grant aid. 1% undergrads receive non-need-based scholarship or grant aid. 74% freshmen, 83% undergrads receive need-based self-help aid.

DEVRY UNIVERSITY (DENVER)

Office of Admissions, 1870 W. 122nd Avenue, Denver, CO 80234-2010
Phone: 303-280-7400
E-mail: info@devry.edu
Fax: 303-280-7606 **Website:** www.devry.edu/denver

This proprietary school was founded in 1931. It has a 13-acre campus.

RATINGS
Admissions Selectivity Rating: 60*   **Fire Safety Rating:** 60*   **Green Rating:** 60*

ACADEMICS
Degrees: Associate, bachelor's, terminal associate. **Special Study Options:** Accelerated program, cooperative education program, distance learning, double major, dual enrollment, weekend college. Special programs offered to physically disabled students include note-taking services, reader services, tape recorders, tutors. **Career services:** Alumni services, career/job search classes.

FACILITIES
Housing: 100% of campus accessible to physically disabled. **Computers:** Students can register for classes online. Administrative functions (other than registration) can be performed online.

CAMPUS LIFE
Environment: City. **Organizations:** 3 registered organizations,

ADMISSIONS
Freshman Academic Profile: Minimum paper TOEFL 500. Minimum computer TOEFL 173. **General Admission Information:** Credit offered for CEEB Advanced Placement tests.

COSTS AND FINANCIAL AID
Annual tuition $11,870. Required fees $250. Average book expense $1,200. **Student Employment:** Federal Work-Study Program available. Institutional employment available. Off-campus job opportunities are good.

DEVRY UNIVERSITY (FREMONT, CA)

6600 Dumbarton Circle, Fremont, CA 94555
Phone: 510-574-1200
E-mail: info@devry.edu
Fax: 510-742-0868 **Website:** www.fre.devry.edu

This proprietary school was founded in 1931. It has a 17-acre campus.

RATINGS
Admissions Selectivity Rating: 60*   **Fire Safety Rating:** 60*   **Green Rating:** 60*

STUDENTS AND FACULTY
Enrollment: 1,477. **Student Body:** 26% female, 74% male, % out-of-state, 1% international (9 countries represented). Asian 28%, African American 4%, Caucasian 15%, Hispanic 15%, Native American 1%.
Faculty: Student/faculty ratio 29:1. 51 full-time faculty.

ACADEMICS
Degrees: Associate, bachelor's, master's, post-bachelor's certificate, terminal associate. **Special Study Options:** Accelerated program, cooperative education program, distance learning, double major, weekend college. Special programs offered to physically disabled students include note-taking services, reader services, tape recorders, tutors. **Career services:** Alumni services, career/job search classes.

FACILITIES
Housing: There is no on campus housing. 90% of campus accessible to physically disabled. **Computers:** Students can register for classes online. Administrative functions (other than registration) can be performed online.

CAMPUS LIFE
Environment: City. **Activities:** Student government. **Organizations:** 10 registered organizations, 2 honor societies.

ADMISSIONS
Freshman Academic Profile: Minimum paper TOEFL 500. Minimum computer TOEFL 173. **Basis for Candidate Selection:** *Important factors considered include:* Interview. *Other factors considered include:* Standardized test scores. **Freshman Admission Requirements:** High school diploma is required and GED is accepted. *Academic units required:* 1 mathematics.

Transfer Admission Requirements: College transcript(s), standardized test scores, minimum college GPA of 2.0 required. Lowest grade transferable C.
General Admission Information: Application fee $50. Notification on a rolling basis, beginning on or about 11/2. Nonfall registration accepted. Admission may be deferred for a maximum of 1 year. Credit offered for CEEB Advanced Placement tests.

COSTS AND FINANCIAL AID
Annual tuition $12,450. Required fees $250. Average book expense $1,200. **Required Forms and Deadlines:** FAFSA. **Types of Aid:** *Need-based scholarships/grants:* Federal Pell, SEOG, state scholarships/grants, private scholarships, the school's own gift aid. *Loans:* FFEL Subsidized Stafford, FFEL Unsubsidized Stafford, FFEL PLUS, Federal Perkins, college/university loans from institutional funds. **Student Employment:** Federal Work-Study Program available. Institutional employment available. Highest amount earned per year from on-campus jobs $2,700. Off-campus job opportunities are good. **Financial Aid Statistics:** 48% freshmen, 54% undergrads receive need-based scholarship or grant aid. 1% freshmen, 1% undergrads receive non-need-based scholarship or grant aid. 64% freshmen, 78% undergrads receive need-based self-help aid. 91% undergrads borrow to pay for school. Average cumulative indebtedness $29,198. **Criteria for awarding institutional aid:** *Non-need-based:* Academics.

DEVRY UNIVERSITY (IRVING, TX)

4800 Regent Boulevard, Irving, TX 75063-2439
Phone: 972-929-5777
E-mail: cwilliams@mail.dal.devry.edu
Fax: 972-929-2860 **Website:** www.devry.edu

This proprietary school was founded in 1931. It has a 9-acre campus.

RATINGS
Admissions Selectivity Rating: 60*   **Fire Safety Rating:** 60*   **Green Rating:** 60*

STUDENTS AND FACULTY
Enrollment: 2,500. **Student Body:** 29% female, 71% male, 1% international (5 countries represented). Asian 5%, African American 32%, Caucasian 42%, Hispanic 19%.
Retention and Graduation: 36% freshmen return for sophomore year. **Faculty:** Student/faculty ratio 16:1. 77 full-time faculty.

ACADEMICS
Degrees: Associate, bachelor's, master's, post-bachelor's certificate, terminal associate. **Majors with Highest Enrollment:** Computer systems networking and telecommunications; electrical, electronic and communications engineering technology/technician. **Special Study Options:** Accelerated program, cooperative education program, distance learning, double major, weekend college. Special programs offered to physically disabled students include note-taking services, reader services, tape recorders, tutors. **Career services:** Alumni services, career/job search classes.

FACILITIES
Housing: Private apartments, student plan housing, private rooms. 100% of campus accessible to physically disabled. **Computers:** Students can register for classes online. Administrative functions (other than registration) can be performed online.

CAMPUS LIFE
Environment: Metropolis. **Activities:** Student newspaper. **Organizations:** 15 registered organizations.

ADMISSIONS
Freshman Academic Profile: Minimum paper TOEFL 500. Minimum computer TOEFL 173. **Basis for Candidate Selection:** *Important factors considered include:* Interview. *Other factors considered include:* Standardized test scores. **Freshman Admission Requirements:** High school diploma is required and GED is accepted. *Academic units required:* 1 mathematics. **Transfer Admission Requirements:** College transcript(s), standardized test scores, statement of good standing from prior institution(s). Minimum college GPA of 2.0 required. Lowest grade transferable C. **General Admission Information:** Application fee $50. Notification on a rolling basis, beginning on or about 11/2. Nonfall registration accepted. Admission may be deferred for a maximum of 1 year. Credit offered for CEEB Advanced Placement tests.

COSTS AND FINANCIAL AID
Annual tuition $11,240. Required fees $250. Average book expense $1,200. **Required Forms and Deadlines:** FAFSA. **Types of Aid:** *Need-based scholarships/grants:* Federal Pell, SEOG, private scholarships, the school's

own gift aid. *Loans:* FFEL Subsidized Stafford, FFEL Unsubsidized Stafford, FFEL PLUS, Federal Perkins, college/university loans from institutional funds. **Student Employment:** Federal Work-Study Program available. Institutional employment available. Highest amount earned per year from on-campus jobs $7,500. Off-campus job opportunities are good. **Financial Aid Statistics:** 33% freshmen, 43% undergrads receive need-based scholarship or grant aid. 50% freshmen, 72% undergrads receive need-based self-help aid.

DEVRY UNIVERSITY (KANSAS CITY, MO)

11224 Holmes Street, Kansas City, MO 64131
Phone: 816-941-2810
E-mail: ssmeed@kc.devry.edu
Fax: 816-941-0896 **Website:** www.devry.edu

This proprietary school was founded in 1931. It has a 8-acre campus.

RATINGS
Admissions Selectivity Rating: 60*   **Fire Safety Rating:** 60*   **Green Rating:** 60*

STUDENTS AND FACULTY
Enrollment: 1,927. **Student Body:** 26% female, 74% male, % out-of-state, 1% international (8 countries represented). Asian 3%, African American 16%, Caucasian 76%, Hispanic 4%, Native American 1%.
Retention and Graduation: 51% freshmen return for sophomore year. **Faculty:** Student/faculty ratio 23:1. 69 full-time faculty.

ACADEMICS
Degrees: Associate, bachelor's, master's, post-bachelor's certificate, terminal associate. **Majors with Highest Enrollment:** Computer systems networking and telecommunications; electrical, electronic and communications engineering technology/technician. **Special Study Options:** Accelerated program, cooperative education program, distance learning, double major, weekend college. Special programs offered to physically disabled students include note-taking services, reader services, tape recorders, tutors. **Career services:** Alumni services, career/job search classes.

FACILITIES
Housing: Private apartments, student plan housing, private rooms. 100% of campus accessible to physically disabled. **Computers:** Students can register for classes online. Administrative functions (other than registration) can be performed online.

CAMPUS LIFE
Environment: Metropolis. **Activities:** Student newspaper **Organizations:** 8 registered organizations, 1 honor societies,

ADMISSIONS
Freshman Academic Profile: Minimum paper TOEFL 500. Minimum computer TOEFL 173. **Basis for Candidate Selection:** *Important factors considered include:* Interview. *Other factors considered include:* Standardized test scores. **Freshman Admission Requirements:** High school diploma is required and GED is accepted. *Academic units required:* 1 mathematics. **Transfer Admission Requirements:** College transcript(s), standardized test scores, minimum college GPA of 2.0 required. Lowest grade transferable C. **General Admission Information:** Application fee $50. Notification on a rolling basis, beginning on or about 11/2. Nonfall registration accepted. Admission may be deferred for a maximum of 1 year. Credit offered for CEEB Advanced Placement tests.

COSTS AND FINANCIAL AID
Annual tuition $11,240. Required fees $250. Average book expense $1,200. **Required Forms and Deadlines:** FAFSA **Types of Aid:** *Need-based scholarships/grants:* Federal Pell, SEOG, private scholarships, the school's own gift aid. *Loans:* FFEL Subsidized Stafford, FFEL Unsubsidized Stafford, FFEL PLUS **Student Employment:** Federal Work-Study Program available. Institutional employment available. Highest amount earned per year from on-campus jobs $5,625. Off-campus job opportunities are excellent. **Financial Aid Statistics:** 33% freshmen, 42% undergrads receive need-based scholarship or grant aid. 1% freshmen, 1% undergrads receive non-need-based scholarship or grant aid. 49% freshmen, 72% undergrads receive need-based self-help aid.

DEVRY UNIVERSITY (LONG BEACH, CA)

3880 Kilroy Airport Way, Long Beach, CA 90806-2449
Phone: 562-427-4162
E-mail: cblas@socal.devry.edu
Fax: 562-997-5371 **Website:** www.devry.edu

This proprietary school was founded in 1931. It has a 25-acre campus.

RATINGS
Admissions Selectivity Rating: 60*   **Fire Safety Rating:** 60*   **Green Rating:** 60*

STUDENTS AND FACULTY
Enrollment: 1,928. **Student Body:** 26% female, 74% male, % out-of-state, 2% international (11 countries represented). Asian 27%, African American 13%, Caucasian 19%, Hispanic 33%, Native American 1%.
Retention and Graduation: 51% freshmen return for sophomore year. **Faculty:** Student/faculty ratio 44:1. 40 full-time faculty.

ACADEMICS
Degrees: Associate, bachelor's, master's, post-bachelor's certificate, terminal associate. **Majors with Highest Enrollment:** Business administration, management and operations, other. **Special Study Options:** Accelerated program, cooperative education program, distance learning, double major, weekend college. Special programs offered to physically disabled students include note-taking services, reader services, tape recorders, tutors. **Career services:** Alumni services, career/job search classes.

FACILITIES
Housing: Men's dorms, women's dorms. 90% of campus accessible to physically disabled. **Computers:** Students can register for classes online. Administrative functions (other than registration) can be performed online.

CAMPUS LIFE
Environment: Metropolis. **Activities:** Choral groups, concert band, music ensembles, student government, student newspaper, symphony orchestra, yearbook. **Organizations:** 13 registered organizations, 5 honor societies,

ADMISSIONS
Freshman Academic Profile: Minimum paper TOEFL 500. Minimum computer TOEFL 173. **Basis for Candidate Selection:** *Important factors considered include:* Interview. *Other factors considered include:* Standardized test scores. **Freshman Admission Requirements:** High school diploma is required and GED is accepted. *Academic units required:* 1 mathematics. **Transfer Admission Requirements:** College transcript(s), standardized test scores, minimum college GPA of 2.0 required. Lowest grade transferable C. **General Admission Information:** Application fee $50. Notification on a rolling basis, beginning on or about 11/2. Nonfall registration accepted. Admission may be deferred for a maximum of 1 year. Credit offered for CEEB Advanced Placement tests.

COSTS AND FINANCIAL AID
Annual tuition $11,870. Required fees $250. Average book expense $1,200. **Required Forms and Deadlines:** FAFSA **Types of Aid:** *Need-based scholarships/grants:* Federal Pell, SEOG, state scholarships/grants, private scholarships, the school's own gift aid. *Loans:* FFEL Subsidized Stafford, FFEL Unsubsidized Stafford, FFEL PLUS, Federal Perkins, college/university loans from institutional funds. **Student Employment:** Federal Work-Study Program available. Institutional employment available. Highest amount earned per year from on-campus jobs $6,500. Off-campus job opportunities are good. **Financial Aid Statistics:** 35% freshmen, 50% undergrads receive need-based scholarship or grant aid. 48% freshmen, 71% undergrads receive need-based self-help aid.

DEVRY UNIVERSITY (NORTH BRUNSWICK, NJ)

630 US Highway One, N. Brunswick, NJ 08902-3362
Phone: 732-435-4850
E-mail: admissions@devry.edu
Fax: 732-435-4850 **Website:** www.devry.edu

This proprietary school was founded in 1931. It has a 15-acre campus.

RATINGS
Admissions Selectivity Rating: 60*   **Fire Safety Rating:** 60*   **Green Rating:** 60*

STUDENTS AND FACULTY

Enrollment: 2,517. **Student Body:** 21% female, 79% male, 1% international (23 countries represented). Asian 8%, African American 13%, Caucasian 43%, Hispanic 19%.
Retention and Graduation: 45% freshmen return for sophomore year. **Faculty:** Student/faculty ratio 19:1. 78 full-time faculty.

ACADEMICS

Degrees: Associate, bachelor's, diploma, terminal associate. **Special Study Options:** Accelerated program, cooperative education program, distance learning, double major, weekend college. Special programs offered to physically disabled students include note-taking services, reader services, tape recorders, tutors. **Career services:** Alumni services, career/job search classes.

FACILITIES

Housing: 90% of campus accessible to physically disabled. **Computers:** Students can register for classes online. Administrative functions (other than registration) can be performed online.

CAMPUS LIFE

Environment: Town. **Activities: Organizations:** 13 registered organizations, 2 honor societies,

ADMISSIONS

Freshman Academic Profile: Minimum paper TOEFL 500. Minimum computer TOEFL 173. **Basis for Candidate Selection:** *Important factors considered include:* Interview. *Other factors considered include:* Standardized test scores. **Freshman Admission Requirements:** High school diploma is required and GED is accepted. *Academic units required:* 1 mathematics. **Transfer Admission Requirements:** College transcript(s), standardized test scores, minimum college GPA of 2.0 required. Lowest grade transferable C. **General Admission Information:** Application fee $50. Notification on a rolling basis, beginning on or about 11/2. Nonfall registration accepted. Admission may be deferred for a maximum of 12. Credit offered for CEEB Advanced Placement tests.

COSTS AND FINANCIAL AID

Annual tuition $11,330. Required fees $250. Average book expense $1,200. **Required Forms and Deadlines:** FAFSA **Types of Aid:** *Need-based scholarships/grants:* Federal Pell, SEOG, private scholarships, the school's own gift aid. *Loans:* FFEL Subsidized Stafford, FFEL Unsubsidized Stafford, FFEL PLUS, Federal Perkins, college/university loans from institutional funds. **Student Employment:** Federal Work-Study Program available. Institutional employment available. Off-campus job opportunities are good. **Financial Aid Statistics:** 32% freshmen, 39% undergrads receive need-based scholarship or grant aid. 48% freshmen, 61% undergrads receive need-based self-help aid.

DEVRY UNIVERSITY (ORLANDO,FL)

4000 Millenia Blvd, Orlando, FL 32839
Phone: 407-370-3131
E-mail: krochford@orl.devry.edu
Fax: 407-370-3198 **Website:** www.devry.edu

This proprietary school was founded in 1931. It has a 11-acre campus.

RATINGS

Admissions Selectivity Rating: 60*   **Fire Safety Rating:** 60*   **Green Rating:** 60*

STUDENTS AND FACULTY

Enrollment: 1,346. **Student Body:** 29% female, 71% male, 3% international (13 countries represented). Asian 2%, African American 26%, Caucasian 30%, Hispanic 16%.
Retention and Graduation: 46% freshmen return for sophomore year. **Faculty:** Student/faculty ratio 32:1. 43 full-time faculty.

ACADEMICS

Degrees: Associate, bachelor's, master's, post-bachelor's certificate, terminal associate. **Majors with Highest Enrollment:** Business, management, marketing, and related support services, other; communication, journalism, and related programs, other; computer and information sciences and support services, other. **Special Study Options:** Accelerated program, cooperative education program, distance learning, double major, weekend college. Special programs offered to physically disabled students include note-taking services, reader services, tape recorders, tutors. **Career services:** Alumni services, career/job search classes.

FACILITIES

Housing: Men's dorms, women's dorms, apartments for married students 95% of campus accessible to physically disabled. **Computers:** Students can register

---

for classes online. Administrative functions (other than registration) can be performed online.

CAMPUS LIFE

Environment: Metropolis. **Activities:** Choral groups, music ensembles, student government, yearbook. **Organizations:** 6 registered organizations, 2 honor societies.

ADMISSIONS

Freshman Academic Profile: Minimum paper TOEFL 500. Minimum computer TOEFL 173. **Basis for Candidate Selection:** *Important factors considered include:* Interview. *Other factors considered include:* Standardized test scores. **Freshman Admission Requirements:** High school diploma is required and GED is accepted. *Academic units required:* 1 mathematics. **Transfer Admission Requirements:** College transcript(s), standardized test scores, minimum college GPA of 2.0 required. Lowest grade transferable C. **General Admission Information:** Application fee $50. Notification on a rolling basis, beginning on or about 11/2. Nonfall registration accepted. Admission may be deferred for a maximum of 1 year. Credit offered for CEEB Advanced Placement tests.

COSTS AND FINANCIAL AID

Annual tuition $11,870. Required fees $250. Average book expense $1,200. **Required Forms and Deadlines:** FAFSA. **Types of Aid:** *Need-based scholarships/grants:* Federal Pell, SEOG, private scholarships, the school's own gift aid. *Loans:* FFEL Subsidized Stafford, FFEL Unsubsidized Stafford, FFEL PLUS, Federal Perkins, college/university loans from institutional funds. **Student Employment:** Federal Work-Study Program available. Institutional employment available. Highest amount earned per year from on-campus jobs $6,916. Off-campus job opportunities are fair. **Financial Aid Statistics:** 49% freshmen, 52% undergrads receive need-based scholarship or grant aid. 67% freshmen, 77% undergrads receive need-based self-help aid.

DEVRY UNIVERSITY (PHOENIX, AZ)

2149 West Dunlap, Phoenix, AZ 85021
Phone: 602-870-9222
E-mail: admissions@phx.devry.edu
Fax: 602-331-1494 **Website:** www.devry.edu

This proprietary school was founded in 1931. It has a 12-acre campus.

RATINGS

Admissions Selectivity Rating: 60*   **Fire Safety Rating:** 60*   **Green Rating:** 60*

STUDENTS AND FACULTY

Enrollment: 1,496. **Student Body:** 24% female, 76% male, (4 countries represented). Asian 7%, African American 7%, Caucasian 58%, Hispanic 18%, Native American 6%.
Faculty: Student/faculty ratio 24:1. 73 full-time faculty.

ACADEMICS

Degrees: Associate, bachelor's, master's, post-bachelor's certificate, terminal associate. **Majors with Highest Enrollment:** Electrical, electronic and communications engineering technology/technician. **Special Study Options:** Accelerated program, cooperative education program, distance learning, double major, weekend college. Special programs offered to physically disabled students include note-taking services, reader services, tape recorders, tutors. **Career services:** Alumni services, career/job search classes.

FACILITIES

Housing: 100% of campus accessible to physically disabled. **Computers:** Students can register for classes online. Administrative functions (other than registration) can be performed online,

CAMPUS LIFE

Environment: Metropolis. **Activities:** Student government. **Organizations:** 19 registered organizations, 2 honor societies.

ADMISSIONS

Freshman Academic Profile: Minimum paper TOEFL 500. Minimum computer TOEFL 173. **Basis for Candidate Selection:** *Important factors considered include:* Interview. *Other factors considered include:* Standardized test scores. **Freshman Admission Requirements:** High school diploma is required and GED is accepted. **Transfer Admission Requirements:** College transcript(s), standardized test scores, minimum college GPA of 2.0 required. Lowest grade transferable C. **General Admission Information:** Application fee $50. Nonfall registration accepted. Admission may be deferred for a maximum of 1 year. Credit offered for CEEB Advanced Placement tests.

COSTS AND FINANCIAL AID

Annual tuition $11,240. Required fees $250. Average book expense $1,200. **Required Forms and Deadlines:** FAFSA. **Types of Aid:** *Need-based scholarships/grants:* Federal Pell, SEOG, private scholarships, the school's own gift aid. *Loans:* FFEL Subsidized Stafford, FFEL Unsubsidized Stafford, FFEL PLUS, Federal Perkins, college/university loans from institutional funds. **Student Employment:** Federal Work-Study Program available. Institutional employment available. Highest amount earned per year from on-campus jobs $6,500. Off-campus job opportunities are excellent. **Financial Aid Statistics:** 44% freshmen, 53% undergrads receive need-based scholarship or grant aid. 1% undergrads receive non-need-based scholarship or grant aid. 55% freshmen, 74% undergrads receive need-based self-help aid. 94% undergrads borrow to pay for school. Average cumulative indebtedness $29,684. **Criteria for awarding institutional aid:** *Non-need-based:* Academics.

DEVRY UNIVERSITY (POMONA, CA)

901 Corporate Center Drive, Pomona, CA 91768
Phone: 909-622-9800
E-mail: bchung@admin.pom.devry.edu
Fax: 909-868-4165 **Website:** www.pom.devry.edu

This proprietary school was founded in 1931. It has a 13-acre campus.

RATINGS

Admissions Selectivity Rating: 60*   **Fire Safety Rating:** 60*   **Green Rating:** 60*

STUDENTS AND FACULTY

Enrollment: 1,491. **Student Body:** 23% female, 77% male, 4% international (19 countries represented). Asian 41%, African American 12%, Caucasian 33%, Hispanic 64%, Native American 1%.
Retention and Graduation: 49% freshmen return for sophomore year. **Faculty:** Student/faculty ratio 34:1. 49 full-time faculty.

ACADEMICS

Degrees: Associate, bachelor's, master's, post-bachelor's certificate, terminal associate. **Majors with Highest Enrollment:** Electrical, electronic and communications engineering technology/technician. **Special Study Options:** Accelerated program, cooperative education program, distance learning, double major, weekend college. Special programs offered to physically disabled students include note-taking services, reader services, tape recorders, tutors. **Career services:** Alumni services, career/job search classes.

FACILITIES

Housing: Private apartments, student plan housing, private rooms. 100% of campus accessible to physically disabled. **Computers:** Students can register for classes online. Administrative functions (other than registration) can be performed online.

CAMPUS LIFE

Environment: City. **Organizations:** 15 registered organizations, 4 honor societies,

ADMISSIONS

Freshman Academic Profile: Minimum paper TOEFL 500. Minimum computer TOEFL 173. **Basis for Candidate Selection:** *Important factors considered include:* Interview. *Other factors considered include:* Standardized test scores. **Freshman Admission Requirements:** High school diploma is required and GED is accepted. *Academic units required:* 1 mathematics. **Transfer Admission Requirements:** High school transcript, standardized test scores, minimum college GPA of 2.0 required. Lowest grade transferable C. **General Admission Information:** Application fee $50. Notification on a rolling basis, beginning on or about 11/2. Nonfall registration accepted. Admission may be deferred for a maximum of 1 year. Credit offered for CEEB Advanced Placement tests.

COSTS AND FINANCIAL AID

Annual tuition $11,870. Required fees $250. Average book expense $1,200. **Types of Aid:** *Need-based scholarships/grants:* Federal Pell, SEOG, state scholarships/grants, private scholarships. *Loans:* FFEL Subsidized Stafford, FFEL Unsubsidized Stafford, FFEL PLUS, Federal Perkins. **Student Employment:** Federal Work-Study Program available. Institutional employment available. Highest amount earned per year from on-campus jobs $6,500. Off-campus job opportunities are good. **Financial Aid Statistics:** 37% freshmen, 50% undergrads receive need-based scholarship or grant aid. 52% freshmen, 74% undergrads receive need-based self-help aid.

DEVRY UNIVERSITY (WEST HILLS, CA)

22801 Roscoe Boulevard, West Hills, CA 91304
Phone: 818-932-3001
E-mail: admissions@devry.com
Fax: 909-868-4165 **Website:** www.devry.edu

This proprietary school was founded in 1931. It has a 20-acre campus.

RATINGS

Admissions Selectivity Rating: 60*   **Fire Safety Rating:** 60*   **Green Rating:** 60*

STUDENTS AND FACULTY

Enrollment: 1,161. **Student Body:** 26% female, 74% male, 3% international (13 countries represented). Asian 26%, African American 7%, Caucasian 32%, Hispanic 26%, Native American 1%.
Retention and Graduation: 46% freshmen return for sophomore year. **Faculty:** Student/faculty ratio 15:1. 19 full-time faculty.

ACADEMICS

Degrees: Associate, bachelor's, master's, post-bachelor's certificate, terminal associate. **Majors with Highest Enrollment:** General studies; psychology; youth ministry. **Special Study Options:** Accelerated program, cooperative education program, distance learning, double major, weekend college. Special programs offered to physically disabled students include note-taking services, reader services, tape recorders, tutors. **Career services:** Alumni services, career/job search classes.

FACILITIES

Housing: Special housing for disabled students, men's dorms, women's dorms 100% of campus accessible to physically disabled. **Computers:** Students can register for classes online. Administrative functions (other than registration) can be performed online.

CAMPUS LIFE

Environment: Metropolis. **Activities:** Dance, drama/theater, student government, student newspaper, yearbook. **Organizations:** 14 registered organizations, 3 honor societies.

ADMISSIONS

Freshman Academic Profile: Minimum paper TOEFL 500. Minimum computer TOEFL 173. **Basis for Candidate Selection:** *Important factors considered include:* Interview. *Other factors considered include:* Standardized test scores. **Freshman Admission Requirements:** High school diploma is required and GED is accepted. *Academic units required:* 1 mathematics. **Transfer Admission Requirements:** College transcript(s), standardized test scores, minimum college GPA of 4.0 required. Lowest grade transferable C. **General Admission Information:** Application fee $50. Notification on a rolling basis, beginning on or about 11/2. Nonfall registration accepted. Admission may be deferred for a maximum of 12. Credit offered for CEEB Advanced Placement tests.

COSTS AND FINANCIAL AID

Annual tuition $11,870. Required fees $250. Average book expense $1,200. **Required Forms and Deadlines:** FAFSA **Types of Aid:** *Need-based scholarships/grants:* Federal Pell, SEOG, private scholarships, the school's own gift aid. *Loans:* FFEL Subsidized Stafford, FFEL Unsubsidized Stafford, FFEL PLUS, Federal Perkins, college/university loans from institutional funds. **Student Employment:** Federal Work-Study Program available. Institutional employment available. Highest amount earned per year from on-campus jobs $6,075. Off-campus job opportunities are good. **Financial Aid Statistics:** 29% freshmen, 45% undergrads receive need-based scholarship or grant aid. 44% freshmen, 72% undergrads receive need-based self-help aid.

DICKINSON COLLEGE

Best 373

P.O. Box 1773, Carlisle, PA 17013-2896
Phone: 717-245-1231 **Financial Aid Phone:** 717-245-1308
E-mail: admit@dickinson.edu **CEEB Code:** 2186
Fax: 717-245-1442 **Website:** www.dickinson.edu **ACT Code:** 3550

This private school was founded in 1783. It has a 308-acre campus.

RATINGS
Admissions Selectivity Rating: 93   **Fire Safety Rating:** 77   **Green Rating:** 98

STUDENTS AND FACULTY
Enrollment: 2,330. **Student Body:** 56% female, 44% male, 75% out-of-state, 6% international (40 countries represented). Asian 4%, African American 4%, Caucasian 77%, Hispanic 5%.
Retention and Graduation: 92% freshmen return for sophomore year. 81% freshmen graduate within 4 years. 36.7% grads go on to further study within 1 year. 21.9% grads pursue arts and sciences degrees. 4.1% grads pursue law degrees. 1.2% grads pursue business degrees. 5.4% grads pursue medical degrees. **Faculty:** Student/faculty ratio 10:1. 193 full-time faculty, 93% hold PhDs, 10% are members of minority groups, 44% are women.

ACADEMICS
Degrees: Bachelor's. **Classes:** Most classes have 10–19 students. **Majors with Highest Enrollment:** International business/trade/commerce; political science and government; psychology. **Special Study Options:** Accelerated program, cross-registration, double major, English as a Second Language (ESL), exchange student program (domestic), independent study, internships, liberal arts/career combination, student-designed major, study abroad, teacher certification program. **Combined degree programs:** BA/JD, BA/MEng, 3-3 Dickinson School of Law (Penn State). Special programs offered to physically disabled students include note-taking services, reader services, tape recorders, tutors. **Career services:** Alumni network, alumni services, career/job search classes, career assessment, internships, regional alumni. **Career services highlights include:** Dickinson College believes in the power of experiential education. We maintain a database of over 1,200 business, government and social service internships for students to apply their education in a work setting. Internships can be done for credit. Over half of Dickinson College students do at least one internship during their four years. Over one quarter of our students who go overseas perform internships while in other countries. We have a rotational program set-up with local healthcare facilities for students to explore the medical fields. For those interested in law and government, we have many opportunities available in the county court, with local law firms and in the Pennsylvania state legislature.

FACILITIES
Housing: Coed dorms, special housing for disabled students, fraternity/sorority housing, apartments for single students, theme housing. foreign languages, arts, environmental, multicultural, etc. 67% of campus accessible to physically disabled. **Special Academic Facilities/Equipment:** Art gallery, center for the arts, planetarium, observatory, scanning electron microscope, archeology. **Computers:** 10% of classrooms, 100% of dorms, 100% of libraries, 100% of dining areas, 100% of student union, 5% of common outdoor areas have wireless network access. Students can register for classes online. Administrative functions (other than registration) can be performed online.

CAMPUS LIFE
Environment: City. **Activities:** Choral groups, concert band, dance, drama/theater, jazz band, literary magazine, music ensembles, musical theater, radio station, student government, student newspaper, student-run film society, symphony orchestra, yearbook, international student organization, Model UN. **Organizations:** 112 registered organizations, 15 honor societies, 11 religious organizations. 6 fraternities, 6 sororities. **Athletics (Intercollegiate):** *Men:* Baseball, basketball, cross-country, football, golf, lacrosse, soccer, swimming, tennis, track/field (outdoor), track/field (indoor). *Women:* Basketball, cross-country, field hockey, golf, lacrosse, soccer, softball, swimming, tennis, track/field (outdoor), track/field (indoor), volleyball. **On-Campus Highlights:** Old West, designed by Benjamin Latrobe, Rector Science Complex, Waidner Spahr Library, Stern Center for Global Education, Kline Athletic Center, The Quarry (coffee shop and late night party/gathering space),Weiss Center for the Arts, and the Trout Gallery. **Environmental Initiatives:** The Center for Environmental & Sustainable Education; LEED Silver certification (or comparable) for major projects; President's Climate Committee—moving towards climate neutrality and commitment to sustainable energy management and renewable energy

ADMISSIONS
Freshman Academic Profile: 37% in top 10% of high school class, 71% in top 25% of high school class, 95% in top 50% of high school class. 59% from public high schools. SAT Math middle 50% range 590–680. SAT Critical Reading middle 50% range 600–690. SAT Writing middle 50% range 590–690. ACT middle 50% range 26–30. Minimum paper TOEFL 600. Minimum computer TOEFL 250. Minimum web-based TOEFL 100. **Basis for Candidate Selection:** *Very important factors considered include:* Academic GPA, rigor of secondary school record, extracurricular activities, talent/ability, volunteer work. *Important factors considered include:* Class rank, recommendation(s), standardized test scores, alumni/ae relation, work experience. *Other factors considered include:* Application essay, character/personal qualities, first generation, geographical residence, interview, level of applicant's interest, racial/ethnic status, state residency. **Freshman Admission Requirements:** High school diploma is required and GED is accepted. *Academic units required:* 4 English, 3 mathematics, 3 science, (2 science labs), 2 foreign language, 2 social studies, 2 academic electives. *Academic units recommended:* 3 foreign language. **Freshman Admission Statistics:** 5,026 applied, 49% admitted, 24% enrolled. **Transfer Admission Requirements:** High school transcript, college transcript(s), essay or personal statement, statement of good standing from prior institution(s). Minimum college GPA of 2 required. Lowest grade transferable C. **General Admission Information:** Application fee $65. Early decision application deadline 11/15. Regular application deadline 2/1. Regular notification 3/31. Nonfall registration not accepted. Admission may be deferred for a maximum of 2 years. Credit and/or placement offered for CEEB Advanced Placement tests.

COSTS AND FINANCIAL AID
Annual tuition $39,780. Room and board $10,080. Required fees $334. Average book expense $1,000. **Required Forms and Deadlines:** FAFSA, CSS/Financial Aid PROFILE, state aid form, noncustodial PROFILE. Financial aid filing deadline 2/1. Priority financial aid filing date 11/15. **Notification of Awards:** Applicants will be notified of awards on or about 3/20. **Types of Aid:** *Need-based scholarships/grants:* Federal Pell, SEOG, state scholarships/grants, private scholarships, the school's own gift aid. *Loans:* FFEL Subsidized Stafford, FFEL Unsubsidized Stafford, FFEL PLUS, Federal Perkins, college/university loans from institutional funds. **Student Employment:** Federal Work-Study Program available. Institutional employment available. Off-campus job opportunities are good. **Financial Aid Statistics:** 54% freshmen, 50% undergrads receive need-based scholarship or grant aid. 5% freshmen, 3% undergrads receive non-need-based scholarship or grant aid. 48% freshmen, 47% undergrads receive need-based self-help aid. 59% freshmen, 57% undergrads receive any aid. 55% undergrads borrow to pay for school. Average cumulative indebtedness $23,224. **Criteria for awarding institutional aid:** *Non-need-based:* Academics, leadership.

DICKINSON STATE UNIVERSITY

Office of Enrollment Services, Box 173, Dickinson, ND 58601-4896
Phone: 701-483-2175 **Financial Aid Phone:** 701-483-2371
E-mail: dsu.hawks@dsu.nodak.edu
Fax: 701-483-2409 **Website:** www.dickinsonstate.com **ACT Code:** 3210

This public school was founded in 1918. It has a 137-acre campus.

RATINGS
Admissions Selectivity Rating: 70   **Fire Safety Rating:** 60*   **Green Rating:** 60*

STUDENTS AND FACULTY
Enrollment: 2,669. **Student Body:** 59% female, 41% male, 34% out-of-state, 12% international (30 countries represented). African American 1%, Caucasian 71%, Hispanic 1%, Native American 2%.
Retention and Graduation: 60% freshmen return for sophomore year. 9% freshmen graduate within 4 years. **Faculty:** Student/faculty ratio 19:1. 86 full-time faculty, 52% hold PhDs, 6% are members of minority groups, 43% are women.

ACADEMICS
Degrees: Associate, bachelor's, certificate, terminal associate, transfer associate. **Classes:** Most classes have 10–19 students. **Majors with Highest Enrollment:** Business/commerce; nursing/registered nurse (RN, ASN, BSN, MSN); teacher education, multiple levels. **Special Study Options:** Accelerated program, distance learning, double major, dual enrollment, honors program, independent study, internships, liberal arts/career combination, student-designed major, study abroad, teacher certification program. **Career services:** Alumni network, alumni services, career/job search classes, career assessment, internships.

FACILITIES

Housing: Coed dorms, special housing for disabled students, men's dorms, women's dorms, apartments for married students, apartments for single students, apartments for upperclassmen; apartments for scholars. **Special Academic Facilities/Equipment:** Art gallery, smart classrooms. **Computers:** Students can register for classes online.

CAMPUS LIFE

Environment: Rural. **Activities:** Choral groups, concert band, dance, drama/theater, jazz band, literary magazine, marching band, music ensembles, musical theater, pep band, student government, student newspaper, student-run film society, yearbook, international student organization. **Organizations:** 51 registered organizations, 7 honor societies, 6 religious organizations. **Athletics (Intercollegiate):** *Men:* Baseball, basketball, cheerleading, cross-country, football, golf, rodeo, track/field (outdoor), track/field (indoor), wrestling. *Women:* Basketball, cheerleading, cross-country, golf, rodeo, softball, track/field (outdoor), track/field (indoor), volleyball. **On-Campus Highlights:** Murphy Hall, Student Center, Common Grounds Coffee Shop, Whitney Stadium.

ADMISSIONS

Freshman Academic Profile: Average high school GPA 3.24. 6% in top 10% of high school class, 19% in top 25% of high school class, 53% in top 50% of high school class. 98% from public high schools. SAT Math middle 50% range 470–590. SAT Critical Reading middle 50% range 430–530. ACT middle 50% range 18–23. Minimum paper TOEFL 525. Minimum computer TOEFL 195. **Freshman Admission Requirements:** High school diploma is required and GED is accepted. *Academic units required:* 4 English, 3 mathematics, 3 science, 3 history and/or social studies. **Freshman Admission Statistics:** 627 applied, 80% admitted, 75% enrolled. **Transfer Admission Requirements:** College transcript(s), minimum college GPA of 2.0 required. Lowest grade transferable D. **General Admission Information:** Application fee $35. Non-fall registration accepted. Admission may be deferred for a maximum of none. Neither credit nor placement offered for CEEB Advanced Placement tests.

COSTS AND FINANCIAL AID

Annual in-state tuition $3,828. Annual out-of-state tuition $10,222. Room and board $4,076. Required fees $945. Average book expense $900. **Required Forms and Deadlines:** FAFSA. Priority financial aid filing date 3/15. **Notification of Awards:** Applicants will be notified of awards on a rolling basis beginning 4/30. **Types of Aid:** *Need-based scholarships/grants:* Federal Pell, SEOG, state scholarships/grants, private scholarships, the school's own gift aid. *Loans:* FFEL Subsidized Stafford, FFEL Unsubsidized Stafford, FFEL PLUS, Federal Perkins, Federal Nursing. **Student Employment:** Federal Work-Study Program available. Institutional employment available. Highest amount earned per year from on-campus jobs $1,304. Off-campus job opportunities are excellent. **Financial Aid Statistics: Criteria for awarding institutional aid:** *Non-need-based:* Academics, alumni affiliation, art, athletics, job skills, leadership, minority status, music/drama, state/district residency.

DILLARD UNIVERSITY

2601 Gentilly Boulevard, New Orleans, LA 70122
Phone: 504-816-4670 **Financial Aid Phone:** 504-816-4677
E-mail: admissions@dillard.edu **CEEB Code:** 6164
Fax: 504-816-4895 **Website:** www.dillard.edu **ACT Code:** 1578

This private school, affiliated with the United Church of Christ Church, was founded in 1869. It has a 55-acre campus.

RATINGS
Admissions Selectivity Rating: 79 **Fire Safety Rating:** 60* **Green Rating:** 60*

STUDENTS AND FACULTY
Enrollment: 2,155. **Student Body:** 78% female, 22% male, 54% out-of-state, international (12 countries represented). African American 99%.
Retention and Graduation: 78% freshmen return for sophomore year. 36% freshmen graduate within 4 years. 39% grads go on to further study within 1 year. 34% grads pursue arts and sciences degrees. 1% grads pursue law degrees. 1% grads pursue business degrees. 3% grads pursue medical degrees. **Faculty:** Student/faculty ratio 12:1. 145 full-time faculty, 68% hold PhDs, 91% are members of minority groups, 57% are women.

ACADEMICS
Degrees: Bachelor's, terminal associate. **Classes:** Most classes have 10–19 students. Most lab/discussion sessions have 20–29 students. **Special Study Options:** Double major, dual enrollment, honors program, independent study, internships, liberal arts/career combination, study abroad, teacher certification program. **Career services:** Alumni network, internships.

FACILITIES

Housing: Coed dorms, men's dorms, women's dorms, apartments for single students 60% of campus accessible to physically disabled. **Special Academic Facilities/Equipment:** Art gallery, language lab, communication studies facilities, electron microscope, observatory, outdoor challenge course. **Computers:** Administrative functions (other than registration) can be performed online.

CAMPUS LIFE

Environment: Metropolis. **Activities:** Choral groups, dance, drama/theater, music ensembles, radio station, student government, student newspaper, yearbook. **Organizations:** 67 registered organizations, 6 honor societies, 3 religious organizations. 4 fraternities, 4 sororities. **Athletics (Intercollegiate):** *Men:* Basketball, cross-country, tennis. *Women:* Basketball, cross-country, tennis, volleyball. **On-Campus Highlights:** Avenue of the Oaks, Lawless Memorial Chapel, Samuel DuBois Cook, Dent Hall.

ADMISSIONS

Freshman Academic Profile: Average high school GPA 3.2. 2% in top 10% of high school class, 44% in top 25% of high school class, 74% in top 50% of high school class. SAT Math middle 50% range 440–520. SAT Critical Reading middle 50% range 450–530. ACT middle 50% range 19–22. Minimum paper TOEFL 550. Minimum computer TOEFL 230. **Basis for Candidate Selection:** *Very important factors considered include:* Application essay, recommendation(s), rigor of secondary school record, standardized test scores. *Other factors considered include:* Class rank, alumni/ae relation, extracurricular activities, interview. **Freshman Admission Requirements:** High school diploma is required and GED is accepted. *Academic units required:* 4 English, 3 mathematics, 3 science, 3 social studies, 6 academic electives. *Academic units recommended:* 2 foreign language. **Freshman Admission Statistics:** 3,106 applied, 47% admitted, 35% enrolled. **Transfer Admission Requirements:** College transcript(s), statement of good standing from prior institution(s). Minimum college GPA of 2.0 required. Lowest grade transferable C. **General Admission Information:** Application fee $20. Regular application deadline 7/1. Nonfall registration accepted. Credit and/or placement offered for CEEB Advanced Placement tests.

COSTS AND FINANCIAL AID

Average book expense $1,000. **Required Forms and Deadlines:** FAFSA, institution's own financial aid form Financial aid filing deadline 5/1. Priority financial aid filing date 3/1. **Notification of Awards:** Applicants will be notified of awards on a rolling basis beginning 3/1. **Types of Aid:** *Need-based scholarships/grants:* Federal Pell, SEOG, state scholarships/grants, private scholarships, the school's own gift aid, United Negro College Fund, Federal Nursing Scholarships. *Loans:* Direct Subsidized Stafford, Direct Unsubsidized Stafford, Direct PLUS, FFEL Subsidized Stafford, FFEL Unsubsidized Stafford, FFEL PLUS, Federal Perkins, Federal Nursing. **Student Employment:** Federal Work-Study Program available. Highest amount earned per year from on-campus jobs $2,000. Off-campus job opportunities are good. **Financial Aid Statistics:** 76% freshmen, 58% undergrads receive need-based scholarship or grant aid. 100% freshmen, 99% undergrads receive need-based self-help aid. 3% freshmen, 2% undergrads receive athletic scholarships. 98% freshmen, 98% undergrads receive any aid. 90% undergrads borrow to pay for school. Average cumulative indebtedness $23,585. **Criteria for awarding institutional aid:** *Non-need-based:* Academics, alumni affiliation, art, athletics, music/drama, religious affiliation.

DIVINE WORD COLLEGE

Office of Admissions, PO Box 380, Epworth, IA 52045
Phone: 563-876-3332
E-mail: svdvocations@dwci.edu **CEEB Code:** 6174
Fax: 563-876-5515

This private school, affiliated with the Roman Catholic Church, was founded in 1964. It has a 30-acre campus.

RATINGS
Admissions Selectivity Rating: 60* **Fire Safety Rating:** 60* **Green Rating:** 60*

STUDENTS AND FACULTY
Student Body: 100% out-of-state, (12 countries represented).
Faculty: Student/faculty ratio 3:1. 16 full-time faculty, 56% hold PhDs, 25% are members of minority groups, 56% are women.

ACADEMICS
Degrees: Associate, bachelor's. **Special Study Options:** Double major, English as a Second Language (ESL), independent study, liberal arts/career combination.

FACILITIES

Housing: Men's dorms.

CAMPUS LIFE

Environment: Rural. **Activities:** Choral groups, student government, yearbook, campus ministries, international student organization. **Athletics (Intercollegiate):** *Men:* Soccer.

ADMISSIONS

Freshman Academic Profile: Minimum paper TOEFL 550. **Basis for Candidate Selection:** *Very important factors considered include:* Character/personal qualities, interview, level of applicant's interest, religious affiliation/commitment. *Important factors considered include:* Application essay, academic GPA, recommendation(s). *Other factors considered include:* Class rank, rigor of secondary school record, standardized test scores, extracurricular activities, geographical residence, talent/ability, volunteer work, work experience. **Freshman Admission Requirements:** High school diploma is required and GED is accepted. **Freshman Admission Statistics:** 3 applied, 67% admitted, **Transfer Admission Requirements:** High school transcript, college transcript(s), essay or personal statement, interview, statement of good standing from prior institution(s). **General Admission Information:** Application fee $25. Nonfall registration accepted. Admission may be deferred for a maximum of one semester. Credit and/or placement offered for CEEB Advanced Placement tests.

COSTS AND FINANCIAL AID

Annual tuition $10,400. Room and board $2,700. Required fees $120. Average book expense $500. **Types of Aid:** *Need-based scholarships/grants:* Federal Pell, SEOG, state scholarships/grants, private scholarships, the school's own gift aid. *Loans:* Direct Subsidized Stafford, Direct Unsubsidized Stafford, FFEL Subsidized Stafford, FFEL PLUS, Federal Perkins, state loans **Student Employment:** Federal Work-Study Program available.

DOANE COLLEGE

1014 Boswell Avenue, Crete, NE 68333
Phone: 402-826-8222 **Financial Aid Phone:** 402-826-8260
E-mail: admissions@doane.edu **CEEB Code:** 6165
Fax: 402-826-8600 **Website:** www.doane.edu **ACT Code:** 2448

This private school, affiliated with the United Church of Christ Church, was founded in 1872. It has a 300-acre campus.

RATINGS

Admissions Selectivity Rating: 76   **Fire Safety Rating:** 96   **Green Rating:** 67

STUDENTS AND FACULTY

Enrollment: 1,585. **Student Body:** 53% female, 47% male, 20% out-of-state, international (3 countries represented). Asian 1%, African American 4%, Caucasian 85%, Hispanic 4%.
Retention and Graduation: 77% freshmen return for sophomore year. 60% freshmen graduate within 4 years. 29% grads go on to further study within 1 year. 13% grads pursue arts and sciences degrees. 1% grads pursue law degrees. 1% grads pursue business degrees. 7% grads pursue medical degrees. **Faculty:** Student/faculty ratio 11:1. 70 full-time faculty, 79% hold PhDs, 6% are members of minority groups, 49% are women.

ACADEMICS

Degrees: Bachelor's, master's. **Classes:** Most classes have fewer than 10 students. Most lab/discussion sessions have fewer than 10 students. **Majors with Highest Enrollment:** Biological and physical sciences; business administration and management; elementary education and teaching. **Special Study Options:** Double major, English as a Second Language (ESL), honors program, independent study, internships, student-designed major, study abroad, teacher certification program. **Honors programs:** The Honors Program is designed to enrich, in a variety of ways, the educational experience of selected Doane students. Specialized, interdisciplinary, one-credit honors seminars form the intellectual core of the program. Another component is the study abroad experience undertaken during the junior or senior year. The culminating experience is a collaborative research project. **Combined degree programs:** BA/MEng. Special programs offered to physically disabled students include tutors. **Career services:** Alumni network, career assessment, internships. **Career services highlights include:** The intenship program at Doane offers students quality internship that build upon their academic coursework. up to 12 credit hours can apply toward graduation, giving students an edge in the job market and on graduate school acceptance.

FACILITIES

Housing: Coed dorms, men's dorms, women's dorms, theme housing. 60% of campus accessible to physically disabled. **Special Academic Facilities/Equip-**

ment: Art gallery, language lab, communication studies facilities, electron microscope, observatory, outdoor challenge course. **Computers:** 90% of classrooms, 100% of dorms, 100% of libraries, 100% of dining areas, 100% of student union, 10% of common outdoor areas have wireless network access. Students can register for classes online. Administrative functions (other than registration) can be performed online.

CAMPUS LIFE

Environment: Rural. **Activities:** Choral groups, concert band, dance, drama/theater, jazz band, literary magazine, marching band, music ensembles, musical theater, pep band, radio station, student government, student newspaper, television station, yearbook, campus ministries. **Organizations:** 50 registered organizations, 8 honor societies, 2 religious organizations. 5 fraternities, 4 sororities. **Athletics (Intercollegiate):** *Men:* Baseball, basketball, cross-country, football, golf, soccer, tennis, track/field (outdoor), track/field (indoor). *Women:* Basketball, cheerleading, cross-country, golf, soccer, softball, tennis, track/field (outdoor), track/field (indoor), volleyball. **On-Campus Highlights:** Tiger Inn, Perkins. Library, The Quads, Fuhrer Field House, Heckman Auditorium. **Environmental Initiatives:** Recycling.

ADMISSIONS

Freshman Academic Profile: Average high school GPA 3.42. 15% in top 10% of high school class, 42% in top 25% of high school class, 74% in top 50% of high school class. 89% from public high schools. ACT middle 50% range 20–26. Minimum paper TOEFL 525. Minimum computer TOEFL 195. **Basis for Candidate Selection:** *Very important factors considered include:* Academic GPA, standardized test scores. *Important factors considered include:* Rigor of secondary school record, alumni/ae relation, character/personal qualities, level of applicant's interest. *Other factors considered include:* Class rank, recommendation(s), extracurricular activities, interview, racial/ethnic status, talent/ability, volunteer work, work experience. **Freshman Admission Requirements:** High school diploma is required and GED is accepted. *Academic units recommended:* 4 English, 3 mathematics, 3 science, 2 social studies. **Freshman Admission Statistics:** 1,379 applied, 76% admitted, 30% enrolled. **Transfer Admission Requirements:** High school transcript, college transcript(s), statement of good standing from prior institution(s). Minimum college GPA of 2.0 required. Lowest grade transferable C–. **General Admission Information:** Notification on a rolling basis, beginning on or about 10/1. Nonfall registration accepted. Admission may be deferred for a maximum of 1 year. Credit offered for CEEB Advanced Placement tests.

COSTS AND FINANCIAL AID

Annual tuition $20,540. Room and board $5,970. Required fees $500. Average book expense $800. **Required Forms and Deadlines:** FAFSA. Financial aid filing deadline 3/1. Priority financial aid filing date 3/1. **Notification of Awards:** Applicants will be notified of awards on a rolling basis beginning 3/1. **Types of Aid:** *Need-based scholarships/grants:* Federal Pell, SEOG, state scholarships/grants, private scholarships, the school's own gift aid. *Loans:* FFEL Subsidized Stafford, FFEL Unsubsidized Stafford, FFEL PLUS, Federal Perkins. **Student Employment:** Federal Work-Study Program available. Institutional employment available. Highest amount earned per year from on-campus jobs $1,100. Off-campus job opportunities are fair. **Financial Aid Statistics:** 85% freshmen, 78% undergrads receive need-based scholarship or grant aid. 73% freshmen, 65% undergrads receive need-based self-help aid. 96% freshmen, 91% undergrads receive any aid. 81% undergrads borrow to pay for school. Average cumulative indebtedness $19,196. **Criteria for awarding institutional aid:** *Non-need-based:* Academics, art, athletics, leadership, music/drama.

DOMINICAN COLLEGE

470 Western Highway, Orangeburg, NY 10962-1210
Phone: 845-848-7900 **Financial Aid Phone:** 845-848-7822
E-mail: admissions@dc.edu **CEEB Code:** 2190
Fax: 845-365-3150 **Website:** www.dc.edu **ACT Code:** 2730

This private school was founded in 1952. It has a 70-acre campus.

RATINGS

Admissions Selectivity Rating: 71   **Fire Safety Rating:** 89   **Green Rating:** 69

STUDENTS AND FACULTY

Enrollment: 1,637. **Student Body:** 68% female, 32% male, 25% out-of-state, 1% international (7 countries represented). Asian 9%, African American 11%, Caucasian 44%, Hispanic 20%.
Retention and Graduation: 65% freshmen return for sophomore year. 19% freshmen graduate within 4 years. **Faculty:** Student/faculty ratio 15:1. 72 full-time faculty, 56% hold PhDs, 6% are members of minority groups, 74% are women.

ACADEMICS

Degrees: Associate, bachelor's, doctoral, master's. **Classes:** Most classes have 20–29 students. **Majors with Highest Enrollment:** Business/commerce; nursing/registered nurse (RN, ASN, BSN, MSN); social sciences. **Special Study Options:** Accelerated program, cooperative education program, distance learning, dual enrollment, honors program, independent study, internships, liberal arts/career combination, teacher certification program, weekend college, Independent study. **Combined degree programs:** BS/MS Occupational Therapy. Special programs offered to physically disabled students include note-taking services, reader services, tutors. **Career services:** Career/job search classes, career assessment, internships, regional alumni.

FACILITIES

Housing: Coed dorms. 100% of campus accessible to physically disabled. **Special Academic Facilities/Equipment:** New state-of-the-art Prusmack Center for Health Care Programs and Science Education. **Computers:** 100% of classrooms, 100% of dorms, 100% of libraries, 100% of dining areas, have wireless network access.

CAMPUS LIFE

Environment: Metropolis. **Activities:** Choral groups, dance, drama/theater, literary magazine, musical theater, student government, student newspaper, yearbook, campus ministries, Model UN. **Organizations:** 26 registered organizations, 8 honor societies, 1 religious organizations. **Athletics (Intercollegiate):** *Men:* Baseball, basketball, golf, lacrosse, soccer. *Women:* Basketball, cross-country, lacrosse, soccer, softball, track/field (outdoor), volleyball. **On-Campus Highlights:** Prusmack Center for Health and Science Education, Granito Center: Book Store, Health Services, Hennessy Athletic Center, Sullivan Library, Rosary Hall Lounge, Wild Onion Lounge/Cafeteria in Casey Hall. **Environmental Initiatives:** Geothermal HVAC system installed in most recently constructed academic building. Campus-wide recycling program. Use of environmentally safe cleaning products throughout the campus. All new construction projects incorporate as many green elements as possible

ADMISSIONS

Freshman Academic Profile: Average high school GPA 2.73. 69% from public high schools. SAT Math middle 50% range 400–500. SAT Critical Reading middle 50% range 390–490. SAT Writing middle 50% range 400–490. ACT middle 50% range 17–20. Minimum paper TOEFL 550. Minimum computer TOEFL 213. **Basis for Candidate Selection:** *Important factors considered include:* Academic GPA, recommendation(s), standardized test scores. *Other factors considered include:* Application essay, rigor of secondary school record, character/personal qualities, extracurricular activities, interview, level of applicant's interest, talent/ability, volunteer work, work experience. **Freshman Admission Requirements:** High school diploma is required and GED is accepted. *Academic units required:* 4 English, 3 mathematics, 3 science, (1 science labs), 1 foreign language, 3 social studies, 3 history, 2 academic electives. *Academic units recommended:* 4 English, 3 mathematics, 3 science, (1 science labs), 2 foreign language, 4 social studies, 4 history, 2 academic electives. **Freshman Admission Statistics:** 1,474 applied, 73% admitted, 35% enrolled. **Transfer Admission Requirements:** College transcript(s), minimum college GPA of 2.0 required. Lowest grade transferable C. **General Admission Information:** Application fee $35. Nonfall registration accepted. Admission may be deferred for a maximum of 1 year. Credit offered for CEEB Advanced Placement tests.

COSTS AND FINANCIAL AID

Average book expense $1,500. **Required Forms and Deadlines:** FAFSA, state aid form. Priority financial aid filing date 2/15. **Notification of Awards:** Applicants will be notified of awards on a rolling basis beginning 2/1. **Types of Aid:** *Need-based scholarships/grants:* Federal Pell, SEOG, state scholarships/grants, private scholarships, the school's own gift aid. *Loans:* FFEL Subsidized Stafford, FFEL Unsubsidized Stafford, FFEL PLUS, Federal Perkins, Federal Nursing **Student Employment:** Federal Work-Study Program available. Institutional employment available. Highest amount earned per year from on-campus jobs $2,000. Off-campus job opportunities are fair. **Financial Aid Statistics:** 76% freshmen, 80% undergrads receive need-based scholarship or grant aid. 13% freshmen, 8% undergrads receive non-need-based scholarship or grant aid. 80% freshmen, 81% undergrads receive need-based self-help aid. 8% freshmen, 4% undergrads receive athletic scholarships. 97% freshmen, 95% undergrads receive any aid. 97% undergrads borrow to pay for school. Average cumulative indebtedness $18,398. **Criteria for awarding institutional aid:** *Non-need-based:* Academics, athletics.

DOMINICAN SCHOOL OF PHILOSOPHY AND THEOLOGY

2301 Vine Street, Berkeley, CA 94708
Phone: 510-883-2073
E-mail: admissions@dspt.edu
Fax: 510-849-1372 **Website:** www.dspt.edu

This private school, affiliated with the Roman Catholic Church, was founded in 1932. It has a -1-acre campus.

RATINGS
Admissions Selectivity Rating: 60* **Fire Safety Rating:** 60* **Green Rating:** 60*

STUDENTS AND FACULTY

Enrollment: 5. **Student Body:** 40% female, 60% male, (6 countries represented). Asian 40%, Caucasian 20%, Hispanic 40%. **Retention and Graduation:** 100% freshmen return for sophomore year. 50% grads go on to further study within 1 year. 60% grads pursue arts and sciences degrees. 10% grads pursue law degrees. 50% grads pursue medical degrees. **Faculty:** Student/faculty ratio 4:1. 12 full-time faculty, 100% hold PhDs, 17% are women. 10% of classes are taught by teaching assistants.

ACADEMICS

Degrees: Bachelor's, certificate, first professional, master's. **Classes:** Most classes have 10–19 students. **Special Study Options:** Cross-registration, independent study, study abroad, select graduate level courses available to undergradute students.

FACILITIES

Housing: Men's dorms, women's dorms, apartments for married students, apartments for single students. 50% of campus accessible to physically disabled. **Computers:** Administrative functions (other than registration) can be performed online.

CAMPUS LIFE

Environment: City. **Activities:** Choral groups, concert band, music ensembles, student government, yearbook.

ADMISSIONS

Freshman Academic Profile: Minimum paper TOEFL 550. Minimum computer TOEFL 68. **Freshman Admission Requirements:** High school diploma is required and GED is accepted. **Transfer Admission Requirements:** College transcript(s), essay or personal statement, minimum college GPA of 2.3 required. Lowest grade transferable C. **General Admission Information:** Application fee $40. Nonfall registration not accepted. Admission may be deferred for a maximum of 1 year.

COSTS AND FINANCIAL AID

Annual tuition $11,880. Required fees $100. Average book expense $1,113. **Student Employment:** Highest amount earned per year from on-campus jobs $3,500.

DOMINICAN UNIVERSITY

7900 West Division, River Forest, IL 60305
Phone: 708-524-6800 **Financial Aid Phone:** 708-524-6809
E-mail: domadmis@dom.edu **CEEB Code:** 1667
Fax: 708-524-6864 **Website:** www.dom.edu **ACT Code:** 1126

This private school, affiliated with the Roman Catholic Church, was founded in 1901. It has a 37-acre campus.

RATINGS
Admissions Selectivity Rating: 77 **Fire Safety Rating:** 83 **Green Rating:** 71

STUDENTS AND FACULTY

Enrollment: 1,608. **Student Body:** 69% female, 31% male, 7.9% out-of-state, 2% international (32 countries represented). Asian 3%, African American 7%, Caucasian 58%, Hispanic 25%. **Retention and Graduation:** 79% freshmen return for sophomore year. 57% freshmen graduate within 4 years. 40% grads go on to further study within 1 year. 1% grads pursue law degrees. 12% grads pursue business degrees. 2% grads pursue medical degrees. **Faculty:** Student/faculty ratio 11.4:1. 132 full-time faculty, 86% hold PhDs, 12% are members of minority groups, 58% are women.

ACADEMICS

Degrees: Bachelor's, certificate, master's, post-bachelor's certificate, post-master's certificate. **Classes:** Most classes have 10–19 students. Most lab/discussion sessions have 10–19 students. **Majors with Highest Enrollment:** Business/commerce; English language and literature; psychology. **Special Study Options:** Accelerated program, cross-registration, distance learning, double major, dual enrollment, English as a Second Language (ESL), honors program, independent study, internships, liberal arts/career combination, student-designed major, study abroad, teacher certification program **Honors programs:** Honors seminars for high ability students **Combined degree programs:** BA/MA, BA/MBA; BA/MSLIS; BA/MSSPED; 5 yr. pr. w/ Rush U. Special programs offered to physically disabled students include note-taking services, reader services, tape recorders, tutors. **Career services:** Career/job search classes, career assessment, internships. **Career services highlights include:** We have an excellent Chicago internship program.

FACILITIES

Housing: Coed dorms, special housing for disabled students, co-ed by floor. 100% of campus accessible to physically disabled. **Special Academic Facilities/Equipment:** Art gallery, Technology Center, language lab, Recital Hall. **Computers:** 70% of classrooms, 100% of libraries, 75% of dining areas, 100% of student union, have wireless network access. Students can register for classes online. Administrative functions (other than registration) can be performed online.

CAMPUS LIFE

Environment: Metropolis. **Activities:** Choral groups, dance, drama/theater, literary magazine, musical theater, student government, student newspaper, campus ministries, international student organization. **Organizations:** 76 registered organizations, 14 honor societies, 2 religious organizations. **Athletics (Intercollegiate):** *Men:* Baseball, basketball, cross-country, soccer, tennis. *Women:* Basketball, cross-country, soccer, softball, tennis, volleyball. **On-Campus Highlights:** Cybercafe, New science building (Parmer Hall), Reading Room, Centennial Hall (residence hall), new parking pavillion. **Environmental Initiatives:** Over half the surface parking lots have permeable pavers. Newest building built to Silver LEED standards. Have replaced most lighting with flourescent bulbs, have retrofitted most original windows with energy saving windows.

ADMISSIONS

Freshman Academic Profile: Average high school GPA 3.36. 18% in top 10% of high school class, 49% in top 25% of high school class, 82% in top 50% of high school class. 60% from public high schools. SAT Math middle 50% range 410–560. SAT Critical Reading middle 50% range 450–580. SAT Writing middle 50% range 440–580. ACT middle 50% range 20–25. Minimum paper TOEFL 550. Minimum computer TOEFL 213. Minimum web-based TOEFL 79. **Basis for Candidate Selection:** *Very important factors considered include:* Academic GPA. *Important factors considered include:* Class rank, rigor of secondary school record, standardized test scores. *Other factors considered include:* Application essay, recommendation(s), alumni/ae relation, character/personal qualities, extracurricular activities, first generation, interview, talent/ability, volunteer work. **Freshman Admission Requirements:** High school diploma is required and GED is accepted. *Academic units required:* 4 English, 2 academic electives. *Academic units recommended:* 3 mathematics, 2 science, (2 science labs), 2 foreign language, 1 social studies, 2 history. **Freshman Admission Statistics:** 1,723 applied, 71% admitted, 34% enrolled. **Transfer Admission Requirements:** College transcript(s), essay or personal statement, minimum college GPA of 2.5 required. Lowest grade transferable C–. **General Admission Information:** Application fee $25. Notification on a rolling basis, beginning on or about 10/15. Nonfall registration accepted. Admission may be deferred for a maximum of 1 semester. Credit offered for CEEB Advanced Placement tests.

COSTS AND FINANCIAL AID

Required Forms and Deadlines: FAFSA, parent and student tax forms. Priority financial aid filing date 4/15. **Notification of Awards:** Applicants will be notified of awards on a rolling basis beginning 3/15. **Types of Aid:** *Need-based scholarships/grants:* Federal Pell, SEOG, state scholarships/grants, private scholarships, the school's own gift aid. *Loans:* FFEL Subsidized Stafford, FFEL Unsubsidized Stafford, FFEL PLUS, Federal Perkins, state loans. **Student Employment:** Federal Work-Study Program available. Institutional employment available. Highest amount earned per year from on-campus jobs $7,730. Off-campus job opportunities are good. **Financial Aid Statistics:** 85% freshmen, 71% undergrads receive need-based scholarship or grant aid. 13% freshmen, 8% undergrads receive non-need-based scholarship or grant aid. 73% freshmen, 57% undergrads receive need-based self-help aid. 97% freshmen, 92% undergrads receive any aid. 90% undergrads borrow to pay for school. Average cumulative indebtedness $18,233. **Criteria for awarding institutional aid:** *Non-need-based:* Academics, alumni affiliation, leadership, music/drama, religious affiliation.

DOMINICAN UNIVERSITY OF CALIFORNIA

Admissions, 50 Acacia Avenue, San Rafael, CA 94901-2298
Phone: 415-485-3204 **Financial Aid Phone:** 415-257-1302
E-mail: enroll@dominican.edu **CEEB Code:** 4284
Fax: 415-485-3204 **Website:** www.dominican.edu

This private school was founded in 1890. It has a 80-acre campus.

RATINGS

Admissions Selectivity Rating: 81   **Fire Safety Rating:** 98   **Green Rating:** 78

STUDENTS AND FACULTY

Enrollment: 1,426. **Student Body:** 75% female, 25% male, 6% out-of-state, 2% international (20 countries represented). Asian 23%, African American 6%, Caucasian 38%, Hispanic 16%, Native American 1%.
Retention and Graduation: 69% freshmen return for sophomore year. 31% freshmen graduate within 4 years. **Faculty:** Student/faculty ratio 11:1. 76 full-time faculty, 80% hold PhDs, 14% are members of minority groups, 64% are women.

ACADEMICS

Degrees: Bachelor's, master's, post-bachelor's certificate. **Classes:** Most classes have 10–19 students. Most lab/discussion sessions have fewer than 10 students. **Majors with Highest Enrollment:** Business administration and management; nursing/registered nurse (RN, ASN, BSN, MSN); psychology. **Special Study Options:** Accelerated program, cross-registration, distance learning, double major, dual enrollment, English as a Second Language (ESL), exchange student program (domestic), honors program, independent study, internships, study abroad, teacher certification program, weekend college. **Honors programs:** Honors Program Scholar in the World Special programs offered to physically disabled students include note-taking services, reader services, tape recorders, tutors. **Career services:** Alumni network, alumni services, career/job search classes, career assessment, internships, regional alumni. **Career services highlights include:** Internship Program: Most programs at Dominican University of California require an internship of 45–135 hours, undertaken after completing some coursework in the major. The internship helps students clarify and test their career goals, obtain hands-on work experience related to their major, gain professional contacts, and develop self-confidence. In addition to the completion of the internship hours, students must maintain a journal, submit a paper or give an oral presentation, and evaluate the internship at midterm and upon completion.

FACILITIES

Housing: Coed dorms, wellness housing. 65% of campus accessible to physically disabled. **Special Academic Facilities/Equipment:** Art gallery, science lab, computer labs, nursing skills lab. **Computers:** 10% of classrooms, 5% of dorms, 100% of libraries, 100% of dining areas, 100% of student union, have wireless network access. Administrative functions (other than registration) can be performed online.

CAMPUS LIFE

Environment: Town. **Activities:** Choral groups, dance, drama/theater, jazz band, literary magazine, music ensembles, musical theater, radio station, student government, student newspaper, yearbook, campus ministries. **Organizations:** 19 registered organizations, 7 honor societies, 4 religious organizations. **Athletics (Intercollegiate):** *Men:* Basketball, golf, lacrosse, soccer. *Women:* Basketball, golf, soccer, softball, tennis, volleyball. **On-Campus Highlights:** Conlan Recreation Center, Caleruega Dining Hall, Guzman Lecture Hall, Alemany Library, Science Center. **Environmental Initiatives:** We established the Dominican Center for Sustainability. The Center serves as ground central for Dominican University's numerous green activities, including educational programs, scholarships, community outreach, and national and international partnerships. We created the Center to tap the wealth of intellectual capital in place at Dominican in order to support existing and emerging "green" programs. The Center identifies and promotes economically viable green business practices and serves as a think-tank for ongoing green projects on a community, regional, and global level. Dominican greatly expanded its academic programs focused on sustainability. We introduced a certificate program that enables non-profit and corporate executives, as well as others who already hold an MBA, the Sustainable Enterprise Certificate provides individuals with the knowledge and tools to green their current workplaces while also advancing their careers. We also introduced a certificate program, offered through Dominican's Department of Professional and Continuing Education (PACE), designed for non-degree-seeking adults wanting to take positive steps to enhance their communities. The program offers three areas of concentration: Sustainable Careers and Advocacy, Sustainable Education, and Sustainable Lifestyles. Students will gain a high level of knowledge about sustainability issues as well as specific and practical skills to apply this knowledge to a particular area of specialization. The Institution formally adopted a "Green Statement" to signal its ongoing commitment to sustainability: Dominican University of California will model and instill the values, theories and practices of reverence, interdependence, sustainability, social justice and stewardship into the entirety of its learning environment. The Dominican learning environment encompasses the education programs as well as maintaining green working and living spaces, and adopting policies and business practices that minimize our environmental footprint. Dominican University strives to increase the awareness, knowledge, skills and sense of purpose within our students, faculty, staff and community to best meet the needs of the present, while creating a future that is just and sustainable for all.

ADMISSIONS

Freshman Academic Profile: Average high school GPA 3.35. 19% in top 10% of high school class, 50% in top 25% of high school class, 80% in top 50% of high school class. SAT Math middle 50% range 470–560. SAT Critical Reading middle 50% range 460–560. SAT Writing middle 50% range 460–560. ACT middle 50% range 20–25. Minimum paper TOEFL 550. Minimum computer TOEFL 213. **Basis for Candidate Selection:** *Very important factors considered include:* Application essay, academic GPA, recommendation(s), rigor of secondary school record, standardized test scores, character/personal qualities, first generation. *Important factors considered include:* Class rank, extracurricular activities, interview, talent/ability, volunteer work, work experience. *Other factors considered include:* Alumni/ae relation. **Freshman Admission Requirements:** High school diploma is required and GED is accepted. *Academic units required:* 4 English, 2 mathematics, 2 foreign language, 1 history. *Academic units recommended:* 34 mathematics, 2 history. **Freshman Admission Statistics:** 2,819 applied, 53% admitted, 18% enrolled. **Transfer Admission Requirements:** College transcript(s), essay or personal statement, minimum college GPA of 2.0 required. Lowest grade transferable C. **General Admission Information:** Application fee $40. Notification on a rolling basis, beginning on or about 10/15. Nonfall registration accepted. Admission may be deferred for a maximum of one term. Credit and/or placement offered for CEEB Advanced Placement tests.

COSTS AND FINANCIAL AID

Annual tuition $32,090. Room and board $12,560. Required fees $300. Average book expense $1,566. **Required Forms and Deadlines:** FAFSA, institution's own financial aid form. Priority financial aid filing date 3/2. **Notification of Awards:** Applicants will be notified of awards on a rolling basis beginning 3/15. **Types of Aid:** *Need-based scholarships/grants:* Federal Pell, SEOG, state scholarships/grants, private scholarships, the school's own gift aid. *Loans:* FFEL Subsidized Stafford, FFEL Unsubsidized Stafford, FFEL PLUS, Federal Perkins, Private Loans. **Student Employment:** Federal Work-Study Program available. Institutional employment available. Highest amount earned per year from on-campus jobs $3,834. Off-campus job opportunities are good. **Financial Aid Statistics:** 76% freshmen, 71% undergrads receive need-based scholarship or grant aid. 5% freshmen, 5% undergrads receive non-need-based scholarship or grant aid. 56% freshmen, 59% undergrads receive need-based self-help aid. 3% freshmen, 2% undergrads receive athletic scholarships. 98% freshmen, 84% undergrads receive any aid. 93% undergrads borrow to pay for school. Average cumulative indebtedness $19,806. **Criteria for awarding institutional aid:** *Non-need-based:* Academics, alumni affiliation, athletics, leadership, minority status, music/drama.

DORDT COLLEGE

498 4th Avenue Northeast, Sioux Center, IA 51250
Phone: 712-722-6080 **Financial Aid Phone:** 712-722-6087
E-mail: admissions@dordt.edu **CEEB Code:** 6171
Fax: 712-722-6035 **Website:** www.dordt.edu **ACT Code:** 1301

This private school was founded in 1955. It has a 150-acre campus.

RATINGS

Admissions Selectivity Rating: 81   **Fire Safety Rating:** 60*   **Green Rating:** 60*

STUDENTS AND FACULTY

Enrollment: 1,314. **Student Body:** 50% female, 50% male, 61% out-of-state, 17% international (19 countries represented). Caucasian 81%, Hispanic 1%. **Retention and Graduation:** 75% freshmen return for sophomore year. 65% freshmen graduate within 4 years. 15% grads go on to further study within 1 year. 9% grads pursue arts and sciences degrees. 1% grads pursue law degrees. 3% grads pursue business degrees. 2% grads pursue medical degrees. **Faculty:** Student/faculty ratio 15:1. 78 full-time faculty, 63% hold PhDs, 4% are members of minority groups, 23% are women.

ACADEMICS

Degrees: Associate, bachelor's, master's, terminal associate. **Classes:** Most classes have 10–19 students. Most lab/discussion sessions have 10–19 students. **Majors with Highest Enrollment:** Engineering. **Special Study Options:** Cooperative education program, double major, English as a Second Language (ESL), honors program, independent study, internships, liberal arts/career combination, student-designed major, study abroad, teacher certification program Special programs offered to physically disabled students include note-taking services, reader services, tape recorders, tutors. **Career services:** Alumni network, alumni services, career/job search classes, career assessment, internships, regional alumni.

FACILITIES

Housing: Special housing for disabled students, men's dorms, women's dorms, apartments for married students, apartments for single students 100% of campus accessible to physically disabled. **Special Academic Facilities/Equipment:** Observatories, 160 acre research farm for Ag program, modern recreation facilities which include indoor track, swimming and ice arena. **Computers:** 100% of classrooms, 100% of dorms, 100% of libraries, 100% of dining areas, 100% of student union, 100% of common outdoor areas have wireless network access. Students can register for classes online. Administrative functions (other than registration) can be performed online.

CAMPUS LIFE

Environment: Village. **Activities:** Choral groups, concert band, dance, drama/theater, jazz band, literary magazine, music ensembles, musical theater, opera, pep band, radio station, student government, student newspaper, student-run film society, symphony orchestra, yearbook, campus ministries, international student organization. **Organizations:** 40 registered organizations, 4 honor societies, 6 religious organizations. **Athletics (Intercollegiate):** *Men:* Baseball, basketball, cross-country, football, golf, ice hockey, soccer, tennis, track/field (outdoor), track/field (indoor). *Women:* Basketball, cross-country, soccer, softball, tennis, track/field (outdoor), track/field (indoor), volleyball. **On-Campus Highlights:** Campus Center, Recreation Center and De Wit Gymnasium, B J Haan Auditorium, Southview apartments, Covenant Hall.

ADMISSIONS

Freshman Academic Profile: Average high school GPA 3.5. 31% in top 10% of high school class, 52% in top 25% of high school class, 75% in top 50% of high school class. 30% from public high schools. SAT Math middle 50% range 500–640. SAT Critical Reading middle 50% range 480–600. SAT Writing middle 50% range 460–590. ACT middle 50% range 22–27. Minimum paper TOEFL 550. Minimum computer TOEFL 213. Minimum web-based TOEFL 80. **Basis for Candidate Selection:** *Very important factors considered include:* Rigor of secondary school record, standardized test scores, religious affiliation/commitment. *Other factors considered include:* Class rank, character/personal qualities, extracurricular activities, talent/ability. **Freshman Admission Requirements:** High school diploma is required and GED is accepted. *Academic units required:* 3 English, 2 mathematics, 2 science, 2 foreign language, 2 history, 6 academic electives. *Academic units recommended:* 4 English, 3 mathematics, 4 science, 3 foreign language, 1 social studies. **Freshman Admission Statistics:** 988 applied, 87% admitted, 47% enrolled. **Transfer Admission Requirements:** High school transcript, college transcript(s), standardized test scores, minimum college GPA of 2.0 required. Lowest grade transferable C. **General Admission Information:** Application fee $25. Regular application deadline 8/1. Notification on a rolling basis, beginning on or about 10/1. Nonfall registration accepted. Credit offered for CEEB Advanced Placement tests.

COSTS AND FINANCIAL AID

Annual tuition $21,720. Room and board $6,010. Required fees $360. Average book expense $850. **Required Forms and Deadlines:** FAFSA, institution's own financial aid form. Priority financial aid filing date 4/1. **Notification of Awards:** Applicants will be notified of awards on a rolling basis beginning 3/15. **Types of Aid:** *Need-based scholarships/grants:* Federal Pell, SEOG, state scholarships/grants, private scholarships, the school's own gift aid. *Loans:* Direct Subsidized Stafford, Direct Unsubsidized Stafford, Direct PLUS, FFEL Subsidized Stafford, FFEL Unsubsidized Stafford, FFEL PLUS, Federal Perkins, college/university loans from institutional fund,. Alternate Loans. **Student Employment:** Highest amount earned per year from on-campus jobs $1,500. Off-campus job opportunities are good. **Financial Aid Statistics:** 76% freshmen, 76% undergrads receive need-based scholarship or grant aid. 76% freshmen, 76% undergrads receive need-based self-help aid. 5% freshmen, 5% undergrads receive athletic scholarships. 98% freshmen, 98% undergrads receive any aid. 87% undergrads borrow to pay for school. Average cumulative indebtedness $18,120. **Criteria for awarding institutional aid:** *Non-need-based:* Academics, alumni affiliation, athletics, job skills, leadership, minority status, music/drama, religious affiliation, state/district residency.

DOWLING COLLEGE

Idle Hour Boulevard, Oakdale, NY 11769-1999
Phone: 800-369-5464 **Financial Aid Phone:** 631-244-3303
E-mail: admissions@dowling.edu **CEEB Code:** 2011
Fax: 631-563-3827 **Website:** www.dowling.edu **ACT Code:** 2665

This private school was founded in 1959. It has a 157-acre campus.

RATINGS
Admissions Selectivity Rating: 65   **Fire Safety Rating:** 60*   **Green Rating:** 60*

STUDENTS AND FACULTY
Enrollment: 3,627. **Student Body:** 61% female, 39% male, 10% out-of-state, 4% international (53 countries represented). Asian 2%, African American 9%, Caucasian 59%, Hispanic 9%.
Retention and Graduation: 66% freshmen return for sophomore year. 17% freshmen graduate within 4 years. **Faculty:** Student/faculty ratio 17:1. 124 full-time faculty, 90% hold PhDs, 9% are members of minority groups, 34% are women.

ACADEMICS
Degrees: Bachelor's, master's, post-bachelor's certificate, post-master's certificate. **Classes:** Most classes have 10–19 students. **Majors with Highest Enrollment:** Business/commerce; elementary education and teaching; special education and teaching. **Special Study Options:** Accelerated program, double major, English as a Second Language (ESL), honors program, independent study, internships, liberal arts/career combination, student-designed major, study abroad, teacher certification program, weekend college. **Honors programs:** The honor programs are for highly motivated, academically superior, and creative students. Special programs offered to physically disabled students include note-taking services, reader services, tape recorders, tutors.

FACILITIES
Housing: Coed dorms 100% of campus accessible to physically disabled. **Special Academic Facilities/Equipment:** Art gallery, cultural study center, media center, human factors lab, meteorology lab. **Computers:** Students can register for classes online. Administrative functions (other than registration) can be performed online.

CAMPUS LIFE
Environment: Town. **Activities:** Choral groups, drama/theater, jazz band, literary magazine, music ensembles, musical theater, student government, student newspaper, symphony orchestra, yearbook. **Organizations:** 29 registered organizations, 10 honor societies, 1 religious organizations. **Athletics (Intercollegiate):** *Men:* Baseball, basketball, crew/rowing, golf, lacrosse, soccer, tennis. *Women:* Basketball, crew/rowing, cross-country, equestrian sports, soccer, softball, tennis, volleyball. **On-Campus Highlights:** Riverside Cafe, Giordano Gallery, Loft Theatre, Connetuot River, Henry Building Atrium.

ADMISSIONS
Freshman Academic Profile: Average high school GPA 2.8. 6% in top 10% of high school class, 19% in top 25% of high school class, 50% in top 50% of high school class. 89% from public high schools. SAT Math middle 50% range 410–520. SAT Critical Reading middle 50% range 410–520. **Basis for Candidate Selection:** *Very important factors considered include:* Rigor of secondary school record. *Other factors considered include:* Class rank, application essay, academic GPA, recommendation(s), standardized test scores, alumni/ae relation, character/personal qualities, extracurricular activities, talent/ability. **Freshman Admission Requirements:** High school diploma is required and GED is accepted. *Academic units recommended:* 4 English, 3 mathematics, 2 science, 3 social studies, 4 **Freshman Admission Statistics:** 2,399 applied, 87% admitted, 22% enrolled. **Transfer Admission Requirements:** College transcript(s), minimum college GPA of 2.0 required. Lowest grade transferable C. **General Admission Information:** Application fee $25. Nonfall registration accepted. Admission may be deferred for a maximum of 1 year. Credit and/or placement offered for CEEB Advanced Placement tests.

COSTS AND FINANCIAL AID
Average book expense $1,000. **Required Forms and Deadlines:** FAFSA, state aid form. Priority financial aid filing date 4/30. **Notification of Awards:** Applicants will be notified of awards on a rolling basis beginning 2/1. **Types of Aid:** *Need-based scholarships/grants:* Federal Pell, SEOG, state scholarships/grants, private scholarships, the school's own gift aid. *Loans:* Direct Subsidized Stafford, Direct Unsubsidized Stafford, Direct PLUS, Federal Perkins, Alternative Loans. **Student Employment:** Federal Work-Study Program available. Off-campus job opportunities are good. **Financial Aid Statistics:** 69% freshmen, 65% undergrads receive need-based scholarship or grant aid. 64% freshmen, 57% undergrads receive need-based self-help aid. 2% freshmen, 3% undergrads receive athletic scholarships. 87% freshmen, 87% undergrads

receive any aid. 81% undergrads borrow to pay for school. Average cumulative indebtedness $5,091. **Criteria for awarding institutional aid:** *Non-need-based:* Academics, alumni affiliation, athletics.

DRAKE UNIVERSITY

2507 University Avenue, Des Moines, IA 50311-4505
Phone: 515-271-3181 **Financial Aid Phone:** 515-271-2905
E-mail: admission@drake.edu **CEEB Code:** 6168
Fax: 515-271-2831 **Website:** www.drake.edu **ACT Code:** 1302

This private school was founded in 1881. It has a 150-acre campus.

RATINGS
Admissions Selectivity Rating: 89   **Fire Safety Rating:** 89   **Green Rating:** 77

STUDENTS AND FACULTY
Enrollment: 3,465. **Student Body:** 57% female, 43% male, 62% out-of-state, 7% international (46 countries represented). Asian 4%, African American 3%, Caucasian 78%, Hispanic 2%.
Retention and Graduation: 86% freshmen return for sophomore year. 59% freshmen graduate within 4 years. 22% grads go on to further study within 1 year. 9% grads pursue arts and sciences degrees. 4% grads pursue law degrees. 3% grads pursue business degrees. 4% grads pursue medical degrees. **Faculty:** Student/faculty ratio 14:1. 270 full-time faculty, 95% hold PhDs, 14% are members of minority groups, 46% are women.

ACADEMICS
Degrees: Bachelor's, certificate, first professional, first professional certificate, master's, post-bachelor's certificate. **Classes:** Most classes have 10–19 students. Most lab/discussion sessions have 10–19 students. **Majors with Highest Enrollment:** Biology/biological sciences; journalism; marketing/marketing management. **Special Study Options:** Accelerated program, cooperative education program, distance learning, double major, dual enrollment, English as a Second Language (ESL), honors program, independent study, internships, liberal arts/career combination, student-designed major, study abroad, teacher certification program. **Honors programs:** The Honors Program is designed for motivated students who want to participate in challenging, discussion-based courses on interdisciplinary and topical issues. The program provides a unique opportunity for intellectual enrichment both in and out of the classroom. **Combined degree programs:** BA/JD, PharmD/MBA; PharmD/MPA; PharmD/JD; AandS/JD. Special programs offered to physically disabled students include note-taking services, reader services, tape recorders, tutors. **Career services:** Alumni network, alumni services, career/job search classes, career assessment, internships, regional alumni. **Career services highlights include:** Our Professional and Career Development Services does exemplary programming that empowers students to pursue their professional objectives.

FACILITIES
Housing: Coed dorms, special housing for disabled students, fraternity/sorority housing, apartments for single students, theme housing. There are a total of 261 undergrad students and 58 Grad students residing in DWV Drake Realty houses 152 undergraduates and 46 graduate students Greek Life 324 undergraduate students Residence Life 831 EFR and 1795 undergraduate students. 93% of campus accessible to physically disabled. **Special Academic Facilities/Equipment:** Language lab, observatory, media service center, Anderson art gallery, Oreon E. Scott Chapel. **Computers:** 100% of classrooms, 100% of dorms, 100% of libraries, 100% of dining areas, 100% of student union, have wireless network access. Students can register for classes online. Administrative functions (other than registration) can be performed online.

CAMPUS LIFE
Environment: Metropolis. **Activities:** Choral groups, concert band, drama/theater, jazz band, literary magazine, marching band, music ensembles, musical theater, pep band, radio station, student government, student newspaper, symphony orchestra, campus ministries, international student organization, Model UN. **Organizations:** 160 registered organizations, 24 honor societies, 10 religious organizations. 7 fraternities, 6 sororities. **Athletics (Intercollegiate):** *Men:* Basketball, cheerleading, cross-country, football, golf, soccer, tennis, track/field (outdoor), track/field (indoor). *Women:* Basketball, cheerleading, crew/rowing, cross-country, golf, soccer, softball, tennis, track/field (outdoor), track/field (indoor), volleyball. **On-Campus Highlights:** Athletic Facilities, Olmsted Center, Anderson Gallery, Helmick Commons, Residence Halls / Residence Life. **Environmental Initiatives:** Sustainable building practices. Employees and students receive unlimited, free bus transportation on Des Moines public transportation (DART) buses. Several academic programs include strong emphasis on environmental issues and long-term sustainability.

ADMISSIONS

Freshman Academic Profile: Average high school GPA 3.67. 41% in top 10% of high school class, 73% in top 25% of high school class, 94% in top 50% of high school class. 82% from public high schools. SAT Math middle 50% range 550–660. SAT Critical Reading middle 50% range 520–640. ACT middle 50% range 24–29. Minimum paper TOEFL 545. Minimum computer TOEFL 252. **Basis for Candidate Selection:** *Very important factors considered include:* Application essay, academic GPA, standardized test scores. *Important factors considered include:* Recommendation(s), rigor of secondary school record, interview. *Other factors considered include:* Class rank, character/personal qualities, extracurricular activities, level of applicant's interest, talent/ability, volunteer work, work experience. **Freshman Admission Requirements:** High school diploma is required and GED is accepted. *Academic units recommended:* 4 English, 3 mathematics, 2 science, (1 science labs), 2 foreign language, 4 social studies. **Freshman Admission Statistics:** 4,786 applied, 69% admitted, 27% enrolled. **Transfer Admission Requirements:** College transcript(s), minimum college GPA of 2.0 required. Lowest grade transferable C. **General Admission Information:** Application fee $25. Notification on a rolling basis, beginning on or about 10/1. Nonfall registration accepted. Admission may be deferred for a maximum of 1 year. Credit and/or placement offered for CEEB Advanced Placement tests.

COSTS AND FINANCIAL AID

Required Forms and Deadlines: FAFSA. Priority financial aid filing date 3/1. **Notification of Awards:** Applicants will be notified of awards on a rolling basis beginning 3/1. **Types of Aid:** *Need-based scholarships/grants:* Federal Pell, SEOG, state scholarships/grants, private scholarships, the school's own gift aid. *Loans:* FFEL Subsidized Stafford, FFEL Unsubsidized Stafford, FFEL PLUS, Federal Perkins, college/university loans from institutional funds, Federal Health Professional Loans. **Student Employment:** Federal Work-Study Program available. Institutional employment available. Off-campus job opportunities are good. **Financial Aid Statistics:** 58% freshmen, 57% undergrads receive need-based scholarship or grant aid. 15% freshmen, 13% undergrads receive non-need-based scholarship or grant aid. 48% freshmen, 49% undergrads receive need-based self-help aid. 2% freshmen, 3% undergrads receive athletic scholarships. 99% freshmen, 99% undergrads receive any aid. 64% undergrads borrow to pay for school. Average cumulative indebtedness $32,318. **Criteria for awarding institutional aid:** *Non-need-based:* Academics, alumni affiliation, art, athletics, music/drama, state/district residency.

See page 1078.

DREW UNIVERSITY

Office of College Admissions, Madison, NJ 07940-1493
Phone: 973-408-3739 **Financial Aid Phone:** 973-408-3112
E-mail: cadm@drew.edu **CEEB Code:** 2193
Fax: 973-408-3068 **Website:** www.drew.edu **ACT Code:** 2550

This private school, affiliated with the Methodist Church, was founded in 1868. It has a 186-acre campus.

RATINGS
Admissions Selectivity Rating: 86 **Fire Safety Rating:** 97 **Green Rating:** 84

STUDENTS AND FACULTY
Enrollment: 1,575. **Student Body:** 62% female, 38% male, 41% out-of-state, 2% international (19 countries represented). Asian 5%, African American 7%, Caucasian 61%, Hispanic 9%.
Retention and Graduation: 22% grads go on to further study within 1 year. 16% grads pursue arts and sciences degrees. 3% grads pursue law degrees. 2% grads pursue medical degrees. **Faculty:** Student/faculty ratio 11:1. 159 full-time faculty, 98% hold PhDs, 19% are members of minority groups, 46% are women.

ACADEMICS
Degrees: Bachelor's, first professional, master's, post-bachelor's certificate, post-master's certificate. **Classes:** Most classes have 10–19 students. Most lab/discussion sessions have 10–19 students. **Majors with Highest Enrollment:** Economics; political science and government; psychology. **Special Study Options:** Accelerated program, cross-registration, double major, exchange student program (domestic), independent study, internships, student-designed major, study abroad, teacher certification program, Seven-year dual degree BA/MD

program with UMDNJ-New Jersey Medical school. Five-year dual degree (BA/BS or BEng) programs in engineering and technologies with Columbia University, Stevens Institute of Technology, and Washington University. Five-year dual degree (B.A./Master of Forestry or Master of Environmental Management)program with Duke University. **Honors programs:** Phi Beta Kappa; Beta Beta Beta (biology), Delta Phi Alpha (German), Omicron Delta Epsilon (economics), Phi Alpha Theta (history), Pi Sigma Alpha (political science), Psi Chi (psychology), Dobro Slovo (Russian), Sigma Delta Pi (Spanish), Sigma Pi Sigma (physics), Pi Mu Epsilon (mathematics), Pi Delta Phi (French), Alpha Kappa Delta (sociology), Pinnacle (nontraditional continuing education students), and Epsilon Omega Psi (Educational Opportunity Scholars). Specialized Honors. **Combined degree programs:** BA/MD, Dual Degree Program with Columbia and Stevens Institute of Technology. Special programs offered to physically disabled students include note-taking services, tape recorders, tutors. **Career services:** Alumni network, alumni services, career/job search classes, internships.

FACILITIES
Housing: Coed dorms, special housing for disabled students, wellness housing, theme housing. **Special Academic Facilities/Equipment:** Art gallery, photography gallery, multimedia language lab, child development center, research greenhouse, arboretum, observatory, laser holography lab, nuclear magnetic resonator, electron microscope, optical and radio telescopes, computer graphics laboratory, New Jersey Shakespeare Festival (professional acting company). **Computers:** 90% of classrooms, 20% of dorms, 100% of libraries, 100% of dining areas, 100% of student union, 25% of common outdoor areas have wireless network access. Students can register for classes online. Administrative functions (other than registration) can be performed online. Undergraduates are required to own a computer.

CAMPUS LIFE
Environment: Village. **Activities:** Choral groups, dance, drama/theater, literary magazine, music ensembles, radio station, student government, student newspaper, student-run film society, symphony orchestra, television station, yearbook, campus ministries. **Organizations:** 80 registered organizations, 17 honor societies, 9 religious organizations. **Athletics (Intercollegiate):** *Men:* Baseball, basketball, cross-country, fencing, lacrosse, soccer, swimming, tennis. *Women:* Basketball, cross-country, fencing, field hockey, lacrosse, soccer, softball, swimming, tennis. **On-Campus Highlights:** Dorothy Young Center for the Arts, Simon Forum, Rose Memorial Library, University Center, Commons. **Environmental Initiatives:** New residence hall, McLendon Hall, meets USGBC Leadership in Energy and Environmental Design (LEED) Silver certification Commitment to planting only native tree and plant species on campus grounds. Restoration of forest floor through annual fern planting (Fern Fest) in sections of campus and removal of turf to create "no-mow zones." 100% composting/recycling of landscape waste

ADMISSIONS
Freshman Academic Profile: Average high school GPA 3.33. 36% in top 10% of high school class, 68% in top 25% of high school class, 90% in top 50% of high school class. 65% from public high schools. SAT Math middle 50% range 510–620. SAT Critical Reading middle 50% range 520–650. SAT Writing middle 50% range 510–640. ACT middle 50% range 23–28. Minimum paper TOEFL 550. Minimum computer TOEFL 213. **Basis for Candidate Selection:** *Very important factors considered include:* Academic GPA, rigor of secondary school record, talent/ability. *Important factors considered include:* Application essay, recommendation(s), extracurricular activities, interview, level of applicant's interest. *Other factors considered include:* Class rank, standardized test scores, alumni/ae relation, character/personal qualities, first generation, geographical residence, racial/ethnic status, volunteer work, work experience. **Freshman Admission Requirements:** High school diploma or equivalent is not required. *Academic units recommended:* 4 English, 3 mathematics, 2 science, 2 foreign language, 2 social studies, 2 history, 3 academic electives. **Freshman Admission Statistics:** 5,219 applied, 68% admitted, 11% enrolled. **Transfer Admission Requirements:** High school transcript, college transcript(s), essay or personal statement, statement of good standing from prior institution(s). Lowest grade transferable C. **General Admission Information:** Application fee $50. Early decision application deadline 12/1. Regular application deadline 2/15. Regular notification 3/21. Nonfall registration accepted. Admission may be deferred for a maximum of 1 year. Credit and/or placement offered for CEEB Advanced Placement tests.

COSTS AND FINANCIAL AID
Annual tuition $37,310. Room and board $10,368. Required fees $707. **Required Forms and Deadlines:** FAFSA, CSS/Financial Aid PROFILE. Financial aid filing deadline 2/15. **Notification of Awards:** Applicants will be notified of awards on or about 4/1. **Types of Aid:** *Need-based scholarships/grants:* Federal Pell, SEOG, state scholarships/grants, private scholarships, the school's own gift aid. *Loans:* FFEL Subsidized Stafford, FFEL Unsubsidized Stafford, FFEL PLUS, Federal Perkins, state loans. **Student Employment:** Federal Work-Study Program available. Institutional employment available.

Highest amount earned per year from on-campus jobs $5,800. Off-campus job opportunities are fair. **Financial Aid Statistics:** 53% undergrads receive need-based scholarship or grant aid. 8% undergrads receive non-need-based scholarship or grant aid. 44% undergrads receive need-based self-help aid. 97% freshmen, 88% undergrads receive any aid. 61.3% undergrads borrow to pay for school. Average cumulative indebtedness $16,640. **Criteria for awarding institutional aid:** *Non-need-based:* Academics, art, minority status, music/drama, state/district residency.

DREXEL UNIVERSITY

3141 Chestnut Street, Philadelphia, PA 19104
Phone: 215-895-2400 **Financial Aid Phone:** 215-895-2537
E-mail: enroll@drexel.edu **CEEB Code:** 2194
Fax: 215-895-5939 **Website:** www.drexel.edu **ACT Code:** 3556

This private school was founded in 1891. It has a 40-acre campus.

RATINGS

Admissions Selectivity Rating: 87   Fire Safety Rating: 75   Green Rating: 94

STUDENTS AND FACULTY

Enrollment: 13,069. **Student Body:** 45% female, 55% male, 48% out-of-state, 6% international (104 countries represented). Asian 12%, African American 8%, Caucasian 63%, Hispanic 3%.
Retention and Graduation: 80% freshmen return for sophomore year. 13% grads go on to further study within 1 year. 3% grads pursue arts and sciences degrees. 1% grads pursue law degrees. 3% grads pursue business degrees. 1% grads pursue medical degrees. **Faculty:** 928 full-time faculty, 80% hold PhDs, 17% are members of minority groups, 42% are women.

ACADEMICS

Degrees: Associate, bachelor's, certificate, doctoral, master's, post-bachelor's certificate, post-master's certificate. **Classes:** Most classes have 10–19 students. **Majors with Highest Enrollment:** Biology/biological sciences; information science/studies; mechanical engineering. **Special Study Options:** Accelerated program, cooperative education program, distance learning, double major, dual enrollment, English as a Second Language (ESL), honors program, independent study, internships, study abroad, teacher certification program, weekend college, 3-3 programs in engineering with Lincoln University, Indiana Univ. of Penn. **Honors programs:** The Pennoni Honors College enriches the University experience for students from all majors with demonstrated academic achievement and broad intellectual interests. Consider the benefits: ° Individual attention paid to your academic progress. ° A variety of small group courses with Drexel's best faculty. ° The experience of being in a small college while enjoying the diverse academic opportunities offered by a major medical and technological research University. ° Opportunities to meet students from a variety of fields who share many of your interests. ° Preparation assistance for admission to graduate or professional school, and for fellowships to further your education at home or abroad. ° Social and cultural events. ° The option of taking part in a true living-learning community in the residence halls, which have locations set aside specifically for Honors students. **Combined degree programs:** BA/MD, BA/MA, Engineering BS/PhD, BS/DPT, BSN/MSN, BS/MBA, BS/MS. Special programs offered to physically disabled students include note-taking services, reader services, tape recorders, tutors. **Career services:** Alumni services, career/job search classes, career assessment, internships. **Career services highlights include:** A pioneer in co-operative education since 1919, Drexel operates one of the largest co-operative education programs in the nation (in students placed annually). Over 1,500 business, industrial, governmental, and other institutions located in 27 states and 12 foreign countries "cooperate" with Drexel in offering students the opportunity to acquire practical experience in employment related to college studies.

FACILITIES

Housing: Coed dorms, special housing for disabled students, special housing for international students, fraternity/sorority housing, apartments for single students, freshmen required to live on campus unless living with parents. 80% of campus accessible to physically disabled. **Special Academic Facilities/Equipment:** Art museum, theatre, audiovisual center, TV studio, recreational center, center for automation technology, engineering center. **Computers:** 100% of classrooms, 100% of dorms, 100% of libraries, 100% of dining areas, 100% of student union, 100% of common outdoor areas have wireless network access. Students can register for classes online. Administrative functions (other than

registration) can be performed online. Undergraduates are required to own a computer.

CAMPUS LIFE

Environment: Metropolis. **Activities:** Choral groups, concert band, dance, drama/theater, jazz band, literary magazine, music ensembles, musical theater, pep band, radio station, student government, student newspaper, student-run film society, television station, yearbook, campus ministries. **Organizations:** 136 registered organizations, 8 honor societies, 8 religious organizations. 12 fraternities, 11 sorority. **Athletics (Intercollegiate): Men:** Basketball, cheerleading, crew/rowing, diving, golf, lacrosse, soccer, swimming, tennis, wrestling. *Women:* Basketball, cheerleading, crew/rowing, diving, field hockey, lacrosse, soccer, softball, swimming, tennis, volleyball. **On-Campus Highlights:** Ross Commons, University Bookstore, Creese Caf, Crossroads at the Handschumacher Dining Hall, The Quad. **Environmental Initiatives:** Construction of a $69.5 million five story Integrated Sciences Building. 140,000 sq. ft. teaching facility, will be the first academic building in the U.S. to have a 30– to 40–ft, four-story biofilter wall. This feature will be part of the HVAC system—air intakes and outputs will be filtered through the living wall of vegetation that will upgrade energy efficiency and indoor air quality, along with controlled humidity in dry weather. The building will be the Universities first LEED-certified building. A new $41.6 million Recreation Center, 84,000 sq. ft, addition will be the first building in the City of Philadelphia in 2008 to have total storm water management. The design of a cistern and rain water reuse system is being implemented to achieve a 20% reduction of post-development impervious cover. The storm water will be collected in a cistern, treated and used for toilet flushing in the new building. Construction of a $42 million, 140,000 sq. ft. Residence Hall with 17-stories, housing 482 students, will incorporate many environmental sustainable features including a green roof.

ADMISSIONS

Freshman Academic Profile: Average high school GPA 3.47. 30% in top 10% of high school class, 60% in top 25% of high school class, 86% in top 50% of high school class. 70% from public high schools. SAT Math middle 50% range 560–670. SAT Critical Reading middle 50% range 530–630. ACT middle 50% range 23–28. Minimum paper TOEFL 550. Minimum computer TOEFL 213. **Basis for Candidate Selection:** *Very important factors considered include:* Class rank, academic GPA, rigor of secondary school record, standardized test scores. *Important factors considered include:* Application essay, recommendation(s), character/personal qualities. *Other factors considered include:* Alumni/ae relation, extracurricular activities, first generation, interview, level of applicant's interest, talent/ability, volunteer work, work experience. **Freshman Admission Requirements:** High school diploma is required and GED is accepted. *Academic units required:* 3 mathematics, 1 science, (1 science labs). *Academic units recommended:* 1 foreign language. **Freshman Admission Statistics:** 16,867 applied, 72% admitted, 20% enrolled. **Transfer Admission Requirements:** College transcript(s), minimum college GPA of 2.5 required. Lowest grade transferable C. **General Admission Information:** Application fee $75. Regular application deadline 3/1. Nonfall registration accepted. Admission may be deferred for a maximum of 1 year. Credit and/or placement offered for CEEB Advanced Placement tests.

COSTS AND FINANCIAL AID

Annual tuition $29,800. Room and board $12,680. Required fees $2,035. Average book expense $1,875. **Required Forms and Deadlines:** FAFSA. Priority financial aid filing date 3/1. **Notification of Awards:** Applicants will be notified of awards on a rolling basis beginning 3/15. **Types of Aid:** *Need-based scholarships/grants:* Federal Pell, SEOG, state scholarships/grants, private scholarships, the school's own gift aid, United Negro College Fund. *Loans:* FFEL Subsidized Stafford, FFEL Unsubsidized Stafford, FFEL PLUS, Federal Perkins, Federal Nursing, college/university loans from institutional funds. **Student Employment:** Federal Work-Study Program available. **Financial Aid Statistics:** 64% freshmen, 61% undergrads receive need-based scholarship or grant aid. 10% freshmen, 5% undergrads receive non-need-based scholarship or grant aid. 52% freshmen, 59% undergrads receive need-based self-help aid. 1% freshmen, 2% undergrads receive athletic scholarships. 94% freshmen, 89% undergrads receive any aid. 73% undergrads borrow to pay for school. Average cumulative indebtedness $35,082. **Criteria for awarding institutional aid:** *Non-need-based:* Academics, alumni affiliation, art, athletics, leadership, music/drama.

DRURY UNIVERSITY

900 North Benton Avenue, Springfield, MO 65802-3712
Phone: 417-873-7205 **Financial Aid Phone:** 417-873-7312
E-mail: druryad@drury.edu **CEEB Code:** 6169
Fax: 417-866-3873 **Website:** www.drury.edu **ACT Code:** 2292

This private school was founded in 1873. It has a 84-acre campus.

RATINGS
Admissions Selectivity Rating: 86   **Fire Safety Rating:** 63   **Green Rating:** 89

STUDENTS AND FACULTY
Enrollment: 1,542. **Student Body:** 53% female, 47% male, 19% out-of-state, 5% international (37 countries represented). Asian 2%, African American 1%, Caucasian 70%, Hispanic 1%, Native American 1%.
Retention and Graduation: 82% freshmen return for sophomore year. 50% freshmen graduate within 4 years. 35% grads go on to further study within 1 year. 5% grads pursue arts and sciences degrees. 5% grads pursue law degrees. 9% grads pursue business degrees. 15% grads pursue medical degrees. **Faculty:** Student/faculty ratio 12:1. 127 full-time faculty, 91% hold PhDs, 7% are members of minority groups, 38% are women.

ACADEMICS
Degrees: Associate, bachelor's, master's. **Classes:** Most classes have 10–19 students. Most lab/discussion sessions have 20–29 students. **Majors with Highest Enrollment:** Biology/biological sciences; business/commerce; communication studies/speech communication and rhetoric. **Special Study Options:** Accelerated program, cooperative education program, distance learning, double major, dual enrollment, English as a Second Language (ESL), honors program, independent study, internships, liberal arts/career combination, student-designed major, study abroad, teacher certification program, Drury Center in Volos, Greece; Living-Learning Communities; Washington Semester. **Honors programs:** Drury Honors Program. **Combined degree programs:** BA/MEng, 3+2 Occupational therapy with Washington Univ. Special programs offered to physically disabled students include note-taking services, reader services, tape recorders, tutors. **Career services:** Alumni network, alumni services, career/job search classes, career assessment, internships, regional alumni. **Career services highlights include:** 75% of students complete at least one internship. Recent locations include National Public Radio in Washington, DC; state and federal legislators' offices, McSweeney's magazine, San Francisco; Fleishman-Hillard public relations, numerous not-for-profit organizations. Myriad opportunities are available thanks to Drury's widespread alumni base.

FACILITIES
Housing: Coed dorms, special housing for disabled students, fraternity/sorority housing, apartments for married students, apartments for single students, living-learning communities, leadership/community service. 97% of campus accessible to physically disabled. **Special Academic Facilities/Equipment:** Science center with greenhouse and astronomical observaton station, new visual art center with two galleries, TV studio, radio station, teleconference facility, language lab, electronic music lab, laser lab. **Computers:** 100% of classrooms, 30% of dorms, 100% of libraries, 100% of dining areas, 75% of student union, 20% of common outdoor areas have wireless network access. Students can register for classes online. Administrative functions (other than registration) can be performed online.

CAMPUS LIFE
Environment: City. **Activities:** Choral groups, concert band, dance, drama/theater, jazz band, literary magazine, music ensembles, musical theater, opera, pep band, radio station, student government, student newspaper, student-run film society, symphony orchestra, television station, campus ministries, international student organization. **Organizations:** 90 registered organizations, 11 honor societies, 7 religious organizations. 4 fraternities, 4 sororities. **Athletics (Intercollegiate):** *Men:* Baseball, basketball, cheerleading, cross-country, diving, golf, soccer, softball, swimming, tennis. *Women:* Basketball, cheerleading, cross-country, diving, golf, soccer, softball, swimming, tennis, volleyball. **On-Campus Highlights:** Trustee Science Center, Sunderland Hall (new student housing), Olin Library, Pool Art Center, College Park student housing, The Drury campus is impeccably maintained and is a registered tree farm; its overall appearance is the greatest highlight of a tour. **Environmental Initiatives:** Energy Management strategies on buildings (upgrading lighting, HVAC systems). Expanded recycling program and partnership with neighbor institutions. Sustainability across the curriculum developments.

ADMISSIONS
Freshman Academic Profile: Average high school GPA 3.83. 35% in top 10% of high school class, 67% in top 25% of high school class, 89% in top 50% of high school class. 85% from public high schools. ACT middle 50% range 22–28. Minimum paper TOEFL 530. Minimum computer TOEFL 197. **Basis for Candidate Selection:** *Very important factors considered include:*

Academic GPA. *Important factors considered include:* Class rank, application essay, recommendation(s), standardized test scores, character/personal qualities, interview. *Other factors considered include:* Rigor of secondary school record, alumni/ae relation, extracurricular activities, geographical residence, level of applicant's interest, racial/ethnic status, talent/ability, volunteer work, work experience. **Freshman Admission Requirements:** High school diploma is required and GED is accepted. *Academic units required:* 4 English, 3 mathematics, 3 science, 2 foreign language, 3 social studies. *Academic units recommended:* 4 English, 4 mathematics, 3 science, 2 foreign language, 3 social studies. **Freshman Admission Statistics:** 1,108 applied, 72% admitted, 42% enrolled. **Transfer Admission Requirements:** High school transcript, college transcript(s), essay or personal statement, minimum college GPA of 2.0 required. Lowest grade transferable C. **General Admission Information:** Application fee $25. Regular application deadline 8/1. Notification on a rolling basis, beginning on or about 10/1. Nonfall registration accepted. Admission may be deferred for a maximum of 1 semester. Credit and/or placement offered for CEEB Advanced Placement tests.

COSTS AND FINANCIAL AID
Annual tuition $18,598. Room and board $6,703. Required fees $415. Average book expense $1,500. **Required Forms and Deadlines:** FAFSA, institution's own financial aid form. Priority financial aid filing date 3/15. **Notification of Awards:** Applicants will be notified of awards on a rolling basis beginning 3/15. **Types of Aid:** *Need-based scholarships/grants:* Federal Pell, SEOG, state scholarships/grants, private scholarships, the school's own gift aid. *Loans:* FFEL Subsidized Stafford, FFEL Unsubsidized Stafford, FFEL PLUS, Federal Perkins. **Student Employment:** Federal Work-Study Program available. Institutional employment available. Highest amount earned per year from on-campus jobs $5,993. Off-campus job opportunities are good. **Financial Aid Statistics:** 84% freshmen, 88% undergrads receive need-based scholarship or grant aid. 86% freshmen, 88% undergrads receive non-need-based scholarship or grant aid. 75% freshmen, 86% undergrads receive need-based self-help aid. 10% freshmen, 6% undergrads receive athletic scholarships. 83% freshmen, 83.2% undergrads receive any aid. 61% undergrads borrow to pay for school. Average cumulative indebtedness $18,384. **Criteria for awarding institutional aid:** *Non-need-based:* Academics, alumni affiliation, art, athletics, job skills, leadership, minority status, music/drama, religious affiliation.

DUKE UNIVERSITY

2138 Campus Drive, Box 90586, Durham, NC 27708-0586
Phone: 919-684-3214
E-mail: CEEB Code: 5156
Fax: Website: www.duke.edu **ACT Code:** 3088

This private school, affiliated with the Methodist Church, was founded in 1838. It has a 8500-acre campus.

RATINGS
Admissions Selectivity Rating: 98   **Fire Safety Rating:** 60*   **Green Rating:** 95

STUDENTS AND FACULTY
Enrollment: 6,259. **Student Body:** 48% female, 52% male, 85% out-of-state, 5% international (89 countries represented). Asian 14%, African American 10%, Caucasian 56%, Hispanic 7%.
Retention and Graduation: 96% freshmen return for sophomore year. 86% freshmen graduate within 4 years. 38% grads go on to further study within 1 year. 14% grads pursue arts and sciences degrees. 11% grads pursue law degrees. 1% grads pursue business degrees. 12% grads pursue medical degrees. **Faculty:** Student/faculty ratio 11:1. 901 full-time faculty, 91% hold PhDs, 18% are members of minority groups, 27% are women. 4% of classes are taught by teaching assistants.

ACADEMICS
Degrees: Associate, bachelor's. **Classes:** Most classes have 10–19 students. Most lab/discussion sessions have 10–19 students. **Majors with Highest Enrollment:** Economics; psychology; public policy analysis. **Special Study Options:** Accelerated program, cross-registration, distance learning, double major, exchange student program (domestic), honors program, independent study, internships, student-designed major, study abroad, teacher certification program, undergrads may take grad level classes. **Off-Campus Study:** New York Arts Program. Other special programs: Semester and summer programs

The Princeton Review's Complete Book of Colleges

in ecology, geology, oceanography, physiology, and zoology at marine laboratory in Beaufort. **Combined degree programs:** BA/MA, BA/MEng, 3-2 and 4-1 med-tech programs. Special programs offered to physically disabled students include note-taking services, reader services, tape recorders, tutors. **Career services:** Alumni services, career/job search classes, career assessment, internships.

FACILITIES

Housing: Coed dorms, men's dorms, women's dorms, fraternity/sorority housing, apartments for single students, theme houses. **Special Academic Facilities/Equipment:** Art museum, language lab, university forest, primate center, phytotron, electron laser, nuclear magnetic resonance machine, nuclear lab. **Computers:** Students can register for classes online.

CAMPUS LIFE

Environment: City. **Activities:** Choral groups, concert band, dance, drama/theater, jazz band, literary magazine, marching band, music ensembles, musical theater, opera, pep band, radio station, student government, student newspaper, student-run film society, symphony orchestra, television station, yearbook. **Organizations:** 200 registered organizations, 10 honor societies, 25 religious organizations. 21 fraternities, 14 sororities. **Athletics (Intercollegiate):** *Men:* Baseball, basketball, cross-country, diving, fencing, football, golf, lacrosse, soccer, swimming, tennis, track/field (outdoor), track/field (indoor), volleyball, wrestling. *Women:* Basketball, crew/rowing, cross-country, diving, fencing, field hockey, golf, lacrosse, soccer, swimming, tennis, track/field (outdoor), track/field (indoor), volleyball. **On-Campus Highlights:** Duke Chapel, Primate Center, Sarah P. Duke Gardens, Duke Forest, Levine Science Research Center. **Environmental Initiatives:** Duke has signed the ACUPCC and made a commitment to make Duke a climate neutral institution. Duke signed a LEED building policy in 2003. The university now has 19 buildings that are certified or in the process of being certified. Sustainability has been a part of Duke's mission long before the word became fashionable. The Campus Master Plan, which guides all campus development, defines eight key principles including several that are related to the tenets of sustainability. Two of the most important of these principles are the commitment for Duke to be a "university in the forest" and a "citizen of Durham and the region." Campus development is shaped by these goals of preserving our community within the forest while being a leader in environmental stewardship for our region. The current Strategic Plan highlights the university's efforts to employ "knowledge in service to society" and to make Duke a leader in addressing pressing, global issues. The sustainability principles of environment, economy and society are embedded in these guiding documents of the university.

ADMISSIONS

Freshman Academic Profile: 90% in top 10% of high school class, 98% in top 25% of high school class, 100% in top 50% of high school class. 65% from public high schools. SAT Math middle 50% range 690–800. SAT Critical Reading middle 50% range 690–770. ACT middle 50% range 29–34. **Basis for Candidate Selection:** *Very important factors considered include:* Application essay, recommendation(s), rigor of secondary school record, standardized test scores, extracurricular activities, talent/ability. *Important factors considered include:* Character/personal qualities. *Other factors considered include:* Class rank, academic GPA, alumni/ae relation, geographical residence, interview, racial/ethnic status, state residency, volunteer work, work experience. **Freshman Admission Requirements:** High school diploma is required and GED is not accepted. *Academic units recommended:* 4 English, 4 mathematics, 4 science, 4 foreign language, 4 social studies. **Freshman Admission Statistics:** 18,090 applied, 22% admitted, 43% enrolled. **Transfer Admission Requirements:** High school transcript, college transcript(s), essay or personal statement, standardized test scores, Lowest grade transferable C. **General Admission Information:** Application fee $65. Early decision application deadline 11/1. Regular application deadline 1/2. Regular notification 4/1. Nonfall registration not accepted. Admission may be deferred for a maximum of 1. Credit and/or placement offered for CEEB Advanced Placement tests.

COSTS AND FINANCIAL AID

Annual tuition $31,420. Room and board $8,950. Required fees $1,180. Average book expense $970. **Required Forms and Deadlines:** FAFSA, CSS/Financial Aid PROFILE, noncustodial PROFILE, business/farm supplement, parent and student income tax returns. Financial aid filing deadline 3/1. **Notification of Awards:** Applicants will be notified of awards on or about 4/1. **Types of Aid:** *Need-based scholarships/grants:* Federal Pell, SEOG, state scholarships/grants, private scholarships, the school's own gift aid, ROTC. *Loans:* FFEL Subsidized Stafford, FFEL Unsubsidized Stafford, FFEL PLUS, Federal Perkins, college/university loans from institutional funds, Private loans. **Student Employment:** Federal Work-Study Program available. Institutional employment available. Highest amount earned per year from on-campus jobs $1,400. Off-campus job opportunities are good. **Financial Aid Statistics:** 38% freshmen, 37% undergrads receive need-based scholarship or grant aid. 1% freshmen, 1% undergrads receive non-need-based scholarship or grant aid. 35% freshmen, 35% undergrads receive need-based self-help aid. 40% undergrads borrow to pay

for school. Average cumulative indebtedness $16,502. **Criteria for awarding institutional aid:** *Non-need-based:* Academics, alumni affiliation, art, athletics, leadership, minority status, religious affiliation, state/district residency.

DUQUESNE UNIVERSITY

600 Forbes Avenue, Pittsburgh, PA 15282
Phone: 412-396-6222 **Financial Aid Phone:** 412-396-6607
E-mail: admissions@duq.edu
Fax: 412-396-6223 **Website:** www.duq.edu

This private school, affiliated with the Roman Catholic Church, was founded in 1878. It has a 49-acre campus.

RATINGS

Admissions Selectivity Rating: 82   **Fire Safety Rating:** 94   **Green Rating:** 88

STUDENTS AND FACULTY

Enrollment: 5,735. **Student Body:** 57% female, 43% male, 22% out-of-state, 2% international (80 countries represented). Asian 2%, African American 4%, Caucasian 83%, Hispanic 2%.
Retention and Graduation: 88% freshmen return for sophomore year. 36% grads go on to further study within 1 year. 25% grads pursue arts and sciences degrees. 4% grads pursue law degrees. 1% grads pursue business degrees. 1% grads pursue medical degrees. **Faculty:** Student/faculty ratio 14:1. 472 full-time faculty, 87% hold PhDs, 6% are members of minority groups, 43% are women.

ACADEMICS

Degrees: Bachelor's, master's, post-bachelor's certificate, post-master's certificate. **Classes:** Most classes have 10–19 students. Most lab/discussion sessions have fewer than 10 students. **Majors with Highest Enrollment:** Accounting; nursing/registered nurse (RN, ASN, BSN, MSN); Pharmacy (PharmD [USA], PharmD or BS/Bpharm [Canada]). **Special Study Options:** Accelerated program, cross-registration, distance learning, double major, dual enrollment, English as a Second Language (ESL), exchange student program (domestic), external degree program, honors program, independent study, internships, liberal arts/career combination, student-designed major, study abroad, teacher certification program, weekend college, Students have the opportunity to study abroad on our Italian campus in Rome, Italy. **Honors programs:** Duquesne University offers it's most qualified and outstanding freshmen the opportunity to participate in the Honors College. This selective and intellectually challenging program is available by invitation only after review of the applicant's academic record. The Honors College combines liberal arts, with opportunities for professional studies while providing the thinking, writing, and speaking skill necessary for continuing success. The foundation of Duquesne's Honors College is the Integrated Honors Program, an enhanced track of the University Core Curriculum. Special honors sections of the core courses feature some of the University's most distinguished faculty. Integrated Honors Program courses focus on our essential human heritage and on the major ideas and issues forming the background and direction of modern life. They are taught in small class sections allowing for close interaction between students and teachers and encouraging individual initiative as well as collaborative learning. **Combined degree programs:** BA/JD, BA/MA, BS/MSEd, BSBA/JD, BSN/MSN, BS/MS, BSBA/MBA, BA/MBA, BS/MBA, BA/BS, BS/MA. Special programs offered to physically disabled students include note-taking services, reader services, tape recorders, tutors. **Career services:** Alumni network, alumni services, career/job search classes, career assessment, internships, regional alumni. **Career services highlights include:** Duquesne University's Internship Program is designed to provide students with a professional, entry-level work experience as a valuable element of their academic curriculum. The Internship Program is open to all current students. Available internship positions are posted through the DuqConnection website on an on-going basis. In addition, companies seeking interns may participate in the On-Campus Recruiting Program. It is the responsibility of the student to apply for these positions according to the posted deadline dates. Students may also seek internship opportunities through other means, such as networking and application process.

FACILITIES

Housing: Coed dorms, special housing for disabled students, fraternity/sorority housing, apartments for married students, apartments for single students, wellness housingSorority and fraternity wings; club wings; international wings. 95% of campus accessible to physically disabled. **Special Academic Facilities/**

Equipment: Student Art Gallery. **Computers:** 10% of classrooms, 100% of libraries, 85% of dining areas, 100% of student union, 100% of common outdoor areas have wireless network access. Students can register for classes online. Administrative functions (other than registration) can be performed online.

CAMPUS LIFE

Environment: Metropolis. **Activities:** Choral groups, concert band, dance, drama/theater, jazz band, literary magazine, marching band, music ensembles, musical theater, opera, pep band, radio station, student government, student newspaper, student-run film society, symphony orchestra, television station, yearbook, campus ministries, international student organization, Model UN. **Organizations:** 160 registered organizations, 34 honor societies, 7 religious organizations. 10 fraternities, 7 sororities. **Athletics (Intercollegiate):** *Men:* Basketball, cross-country, football, soccer, tennis, track/field (outdoor). *Women:* Basketball, crew/rowing, cross-country, lacrosse, soccer, swimming, tennis, track/field (outdoor), track/field (indoor), volleyball. **On-Campus Highlights:** Power Recreation Center, Starbucks, The Red Ring, Academic Walk, The Night Spot, The Power Recreation Center is a newly opened recreation and fitness center. Starbucks is a popular coffeehouse located in the Duquesne Union. The Red Ring is a new, full service restaurant/bar with nightly musical entertainment. Academic Walk is the main walkway through campus where many activities are held. There is also a new quiet Study Lounge located on the second floor of the Union. **Environmental Initiatives:** Duquesne University relies 100 percent on clean energy. For over a decade, the University has produced the bulk of its own electricity with a clean-burning natural gas turbine located at the heart of campus. This co-generation plant produces approximately 85 percent of the power used to light, heat and cool the campus with overall efficiency greater than 70 percent. It is Pennsylvania's first approved generation system for creating Alternative Energy Credits. Sustainable initiatives reached an exceptional level with the purchase of more than 13 million kilowatt hours of renewable energy credits. This combination of energy generation and renewable energy purchase led Duquesne University to rely 100 percent on clean energy. A highly efficient cooling system that relies on ice – the first of its kind in a Pittsburgh academic institution— has bolstered the University's efforts in responsible energy consumption. Last year's greenhouse gas emissions inventory showed that, while the student population and campus physical size increased, greenhouse gas emissions decreased. Duquesne University has pledged to seek LEED certication for all future construction projects and to observe LEED principles in all major renovations. In the past year, the University has earned LEED Silver rating for new construction and LEED Gold Rating for commercial interiors. Duquesne University is committed to the continual assessment and betterment of its daily operations' environmental quality. Significant progress has been made in the areas of green cleaning, waste diversion, VOC–free products usage, "green" purchasing and other operational efforts.

ADMISSIONS

Freshman Academic Profile: Average high school GPA 3.57. 24% in top 10% of high school class, 55% in top 25% of high school class, 87% in top 50% of high school class. SAT Math middle 50% range 520–610. SAT Critical Reading middle 50% range 510–600. SAT Writing middle 50% range 510–600. ACT middle 50% range 23–28. Minimum paper TOEFL 575. Minimum computer TOEFL 230. Minimum web-based TOEFL 90. **Basis for Candidate Selection:** *Very important factors considered include:* Application essay, academic GPA, recommendation(s), rigor of secondary school record, standardized test scores. *Important factors considered include:* Class rank, character/personal qualities, extracurricular activities, interview, talent/ability, volunteer work. *Other factors considered include:* Alumni/ae relation, first generation, level of applicant's interest, racial/ethnic status, work experience. **Freshman Admission Requirements:** High school diploma is required and GED is accepted. *Academic units recommended:* 4 English, 2 mathematics, 2 science, 2 foreign language, 2 social studies, 4 academic electives. **Freshman Admission Statistics:** 6,626 applied, 76% admitted, 28% enrolled. **Transfer Admission Requirements:** High school transcript, college transcript(s), essay or personal statement, statement of good standing from prior institution(s). Minimum college GPA of 2.5 required. Lowest grade transferable C. **General Admission Information:** Application fee $50. Early decision application deadline 11/1. Regular application deadline 7/1. Notification on a rolling basis, beginning on or about 9/15. Nonfall registration accepted. Admission may be deferred for a maximum of One academic year. Credit and/or placement offered for CEEB Advanced Placement tests.

COSTS AND FINANCIAL AID

Annual tuition $24,385. Room and board $9,200. Required fees $2,083. Average book expense $1,000. **Required Forms and Deadlines:** FAFSA, institution's own financial aid form. Financial aid filing deadline 5/1. **Notification of Awards:** Applicants will be notified of awards on a rolling basis beginning 3/1. **Types of Aid:** *Need-based scholarships/grants:* Federal Pell, SEOG, state scholarships/grants, private scholarships, the school's own gift aid, United Negro College Fund. *Loans:* FFEL Subsidized Stafford, FFEL Unsubsidized Stafford, FFEL PLUS, Federal Perkins, Federal Nursing, Private Alternative Loans.

Student Employment: Federal Work-Study Program available. Institutional employment available. Off-campus job opportunities are good. **Financial Aid Statistics:** 67% freshmen, 67% undergrads receive need-based scholarship or grant aid. 66% freshmen, 59% undergrads receive non-need-based scholarship or grant aid. 58% freshmen, 58% undergrads receive need-based self-help aid. 7% freshmen, 6% undergrads receive athletic scholarships. 100% freshmen, 96% undergrads receive any aid. **Criteria for awarding institutional aid:** *Non-need-based:* Academics, athletics, music/drama.

EARLHAM COLLEGE

801 National Road West, Richmond, IN 47374-4095
Phone: 765-983-1600 **Financial Aid Phone:** 765-983-1217
E-mail: admissions@earlham.edu **CEEB Code:** 1195
Fax: 765-983-1560 **Website:** www.earlham.edu **ACT Code:** 1186

This private school, affiliated with the Quaker Church, was founded in 1847. It has a 800-acre campus.

RATINGS

Admissions Selectivity Rating: 87   **Fire Safety Rating:** 78   **Green Rating:** 60*

STUDENTS AND FACULTY

Enrollment: 1,097. **Student Body:** 55% female, 45% male, 77% out-of-state, 14% international (61 countries represented). Asian 3%, African American 6%, Caucasian 64%, Hispanic 2%, Native American 1%. **Retention and Graduation:** 81% freshmen return for sophomore year. 60% freshmen graduate within 4 years. 21% grads go on to further study within 1 year. 17% grads pursue arts and sciences degrees. 1% grads pursue medical degrees. **Faculty:** Student/faculty ratio 12:1. 89 full-time faculty, 98% hold PhDs, 22% are members of minority groups, 45% are women.

ACADEMICS

Degrees: Bachelor's, first professional, master's. **Classes:** Most classes have 10–19 students. Most lab/discussion sessions have 20–29 students. **Majors with Highest Enrollment:** Biology/biological sciences; history; psychology. **Special Study Options:** Accelerated program, cross-registration, double major, dual enrollment, English as a Second Language (ESL), independent study, internships, student-designed major, study abroad, teacher certification program, Teacher certification at Master's Degree level only. **Combined degree programs:** 3-2 in Architecture. Special programs offered to physically disabled students include note-taking services, reader services, tape recorders, tutors.

FACILITIES

Housing: Coed dorms, special housing for disabled students, men's dorms, special housing for international students, women's dorms, wellness housing, theme housing, Friendship houses. 80% of campus accessible to physically disabled. **Special Academic Facilities/Equipment:** Major academic building Landrum Bolling Center for Interdisciplinary and Social Studies opened, natural history museum, cultural centers, language labs, greenhouse, observatory, planetarium. **Computers:** 95% of classrooms, have wireless network access. Administrative functions (other than registration) can be performed online.

CAMPUS LIFE

Environment: Town. **Activities:** Choral groups, concert band, dance, drama/theater, jazz band, literary magazine, music ensembles, radio station, student government, student newspaper, student-run film society, symphony orchestra, yearbook, campus ministries, international student organization, Model UN. **Organizations:** 70 registered organizations, 1 honor societies, 15 religious organizations. **Athletics (Intercollegiate):** *Men:* Baseball, basketball, cross-country, football, soccer, tennis, track/field (outdoor), track/field (indoor). *Women:* Basketball, cross-country, field hockey, soccer, tennis, track/field (outdoor), track/field (indoor), volleyball. **On-Campus Highlights:** Landrum Bolling Center—Interdisciplinary Studies, Athletics and Wellness Center, Runyan Center, Natural History Museum, Coffee Shop.

ADMISSIONS

Freshman Academic Profile: Average high school GPA 3.53. 31% in top 10% of high school class, 59% in top 25% of high school class, 92% in top 50% of high school class. 68% from public high schools. SAT Math middle 50% range 530–640. SAT Critical Reading middle 50% range 560–690. SAT Writing middle 50% range 550–660. ACT middle 50% range 24–29. Minimum paper TOEFL 550. Minimum computer TOEFL 213. **Basis for Candidate Selection:** *Very important factors considered include:* Class rank, academic GPA, rigor of secondary school record, character/personal qualities. *Important factors considered include:* Application essay, recommendation(s), standardized test scores, extracurricular activities, talent/ability, volunteer work. *Other factors considered include:* Interview, work experience. **Freshman Admis-**

sion Requirements: High school diploma is required and GED is accepted. *Academic units required:* 4 English, 3 mathematics, 3 science, (2 science labs), 2 foreign language, 4 social studies, 2 history, 1 visual/performing arts. *Academic units recommended:* 4 English, 4 mathematics, 4 science, (2 science labs), 4 foreign language, 4 social studies, 2 history, 1 visual/performing arts. **Freshman Admission Statistics:** 1,668 applied, 76% admitted, 23% enrolled. **Transfer Admission Requirements:** High school transcript, college transcript(s), essay or personal statement, standardized test scores, statement of good standing from prior institution(s). Minimum college GPA of 2.7 required. Lowest grade transferable C. **General Admission Information:** Early decision application deadline 12/1. Regular application deadline 2/15. Regular notification 3/15. Nonfall registration accepted. Admission may be deferred for a maximum of 1 year. Credit offered for CEEB Advanced Placement tests.

COSTS AND FINANCIAL AID

Average book expense $850. **Required Forms and Deadlines:** FAFSA. Priority financial aid filing date 3/1. **Notification of Awards:** Applicants will be notified of awards on a rolling basis beginning 2/15. **Types of Aid:** *Need-based scholarships/grants:* Federal Pell, SEOG, state scholarships/grants, private scholarships, the school's own gift aid. *Loans:* Direct Subsidized Stafford, Direct Unsubsidized Stafford, Direct PLUS, Federal Perkins, college/university loans from institutional funds. **Student Employment:** Highest amount earned per year from on-campus jobs $2,259. **Financial Aid Statistics:** 44% freshmen, 45% undergrads receive need-based scholarship or grant aid. 30% freshmen, 28% undergrads receive non-need-based scholarship or grant aid. 45% freshmen, 44% undergrads receive need-based self-help aid. 93% freshmen, 92% undergrads receive any aid. 56% undergrads borrow to pay for school. Average cumulative indebtedness $23,270. **Criteria for awarding institutional aid:** *Non-need-based:* Academics, minority status, religious affiliation.

EAST CAROLINA UNIVERSITY

Office of Undergraduate Admissions, 106 Whichard Building, Greenville, NC 27858-4353

Phone: 252-328-6640 **Financial Aid Phone:** 252-328-9379
E-mail: admis@ecu.edu **CEEB Code:** 5180
Fax: 252-328-6945 **Website:** www.ecu.edu **ACT Code:** 3094

This public school was founded in 1907. It has a 1379-acre campus.

RATINGS
Admissions Selectivity Rating: 76   Fire Safety Rating: 60*   Green Rating: 60*

STUDENTS AND FACULTY
Enrollment: 19,651. **Student Body:** 59% female, 41% male, 10% out-of-state, international (40 countries represented). Asian 2%, African American 16%, Caucasian 75%, Hispanic 2%, Native American 1%.
Retention and Graduation: 26% freshmen graduate within 4 years. **Faculty:** Student/faculty ratio 20:1. 1058 full-time faculty, 81% hold PhDs, 11% are members of minority groups, 41% are women.

ACADEMICS
Degrees: Bachelor's, first professional, master's, post-bachelor's certificate, post-master's certificate. **Classes:** Most classes have fewer than 10 students. Most lab/discussion sessions have fewer than 10 students. **Majors with Highest Enrollment:** Construction engineering technology/technician; elementary education and teaching; nursing/registered nurse (RN, ASN, BSN, MSN). **Special Study Options:** Accelerated program, cooperative education program, distance learning, double major, dual enrollment, exchange student program (domestic), honors program, independent study, internships, student-designed major, study abroad, teacher certification program. **Combined degree programs:** BSA/MSA Accounting; MA/CAS in School Psychology. Special programs offered to physically disabled students include note-taking services, reader services, tape recorders, tutors. **Career services:** Alumni services, career/job search classes, career assessment, internships.

FACILITIES
Housing: Coed dorms, men's dorms, women's dorms, fraternity/sorority housing, First-year students floor, leadership hall, extended quiet study hours floor, upper division, academic year residence halls, music student communities, service community, engineering. 94% of campus accessible to physically disabled. **Special Academic Facilities/Equipment:** Wellington B. Gray Gallery, Museum Without Walls, Ledonia Wright Cultural Center, A.J. Fletcher Recital Hall, Hendrix Theatre, Jenkins fine arts Center, McGinnis Theatre, and Mendenhall Student Center. **Computers:** 68% of classrooms, 20% of dorms, 100% of libraries, 100% of dining areas, 100% of student union, 25% of common outdoor areas have wireless network access. Students can register for classes online. Administrative functions (other than registration) can be performed online.

CAMPUS LIFE
Environment: Town. **Activities:** Choral groups, concert band, dance, drama/theater, jazz band, literary magazine, marching band, music ensembles, musical theater, radio station, student government, student newspaper, student-run film society, symphony orchestra, television station, yearbook, campus ministries, international student organization, Model UN. **Organizations:** 297 registered organizations, 11 honor societies, 27 religious organizations. 20 fraternities, 13 sororities. **Athletics (Intercollegiate):** *Men:* Baseball, basketball, cheerleading, cross-country, diving, football, golf, swimming, tennis, track/field (outdoor). *Women:* Basketball, cheerleading, cross-country, diving, golf, soccer, softball, swimming, tennis, track/field (outdoor), volleyball. **On-Campus Highlights:** Student Recreation Center, Wright Plaza, Mendenhall Student Center, Blounts Sports Complex, Science and Technology Building. Athletic facilities include: Dowdy-Ficklen Stadium, Williams Arena in Minges Coliseum and Harrington Field.

ADMISSIONS
Freshman Academic Profile: Average high school GPA 3.45. 13% in top 10% of high school class, 40% in top 25% of high school class, 80% in top 50% of high school class. 90% from public high schools. SAT Math middle 50% range 470–560. SAT Critical Reading middle 50% range 450–540. SAT Writing middle 50% range 440–530. ACT middle 50% range 19–23. Minimum paper TOEFL 550, Minimum computer TOEFL 213. **Basis for Candidate Selection:** *Very important factors considered include:* Class rank, rigor of secondary school record, standardized test scores. *Other factors considered include:* Recommendation(s), alumni/ae relation, character/personal qualities, extracurricular activities, geographical residence, interview, state residency, talent/ability. **Freshman Admission Requirements:** High school diploma is required and GED is accepted. *Academic units required:* 4 English, 4 mathematics, 3 science, (1 science labs), 2 foreign language, 2 social studies. *Academic units recommended:* 1 visual/performing arts, 1 social studies must include one unit of US history. **Freshman Admission Statistics:** 14,653 applied, 84% admitted, 34% enrolled. **Transfer Admission Requirements:** High school transcript, college transcript(s), minimum college GPA of 2.0 required. Lowest grade transferable C. **General Admission Information:** Application fee $60. Regular application deadline 3/15. Notification on a rolling basis, beginning on or about 10/1. Nonfall registration accepted. Admission may be deferred for a maximum of 1 semester. Credit and/or placement offered for CEEB Advanced Placement tests.

COSTS AND FINANCIAL AID
Required Forms and Deadlines: FAFSA. Priority financial aid filing date 4/15. **Notification of Awards:** Applicants will be notified of awards on a rolling basis beginning 3/15. **Types of Aid:** *Need-based scholarships/grants:* Federal Pell, SEOG, state scholarships/grants, private scholarships, the school's own gift aid. *Loans:* FFEL Subsidized Stafford, FFEL Unsubsidized Stafford, FFEL PLUS, Federal Perkins, Federal Nursing. **Student Employment:** Federal Work-Study Program available. Institutional employment available. **Financial Aid Statistics:** 31% freshmen, 33% undergrads receive need-based scholarship or grant aid. 16% freshmen, 11% undergrads receive non-need-based scholarship or grant aid. 39% freshmen, 41% undergrads receive need-based self-help aid. 2% freshmen, 2% undergrads receive athletic scholarships. **Criteria for awarding institutional aid:** *Non-need-based:* Academics, alumni affiliation, art, athletics.

EAST STROUDSBURG UNIVERSITY OF PENNSYLVANIA

200 Prospect Street, East Stroudsburg, PA 18301-2999
Phone: 570-422-3542 **Financial Aid Phone:** 570-422-2800
E-mail: adm@esu.edu **CEEB Code:** 2650
Fax: 570-422-3933 **Website:** www4.esu.edu **ACT Code:** 3700

This public school was founded in 1893. It has a 213-acre campus.

RATINGS
Admissions Selectivity Rating: 72   Fire Safety Rating: 98   Green Rating: 60*

STUDENTS AND FACULTY
Enrollment: 6,288. **Student Body:** 54% female, 46% male, 25.5% out-of-state, 1% international (24 countries represented). Asian 2%, African American 6%, Caucasian 75%, Hispanic 6%.
Retention and Graduation: 36% freshmen graduate within 4 years. **Faculty:** Student/faculty ratio 18:1. 311 full-time faculty, 77% hold PhDs, 13% are members of minority groups, 47% are women.

ACADEMICS

Degrees: Associate, bachelor's, master's. **Classes:** Most classes have 20–29 students. Most lab/discussion sessions have 10–19 students. **Majors with Highest Enrollment:** Business administration and management; elementary education and teaching; physical education teaching and coaching. **Special Study Options:** Accelerated program, cross-registration, distance learning, double major, dual enrollment, exchange student program (domestic), honors program, independent study, internships, student-designed major, study abroad, teacher certification program. **Honors programs:** The Honors Program at ESU offers academically superior students an opportunity to challenge themselves intellectually both within and beyond the classroom setting. The focus of the Program was, and is, located in the area of the liberal arts general education curriculum. The goal of the program is to foster in the students an appreciation of the liberal arts perspective and a commitment to lifelong learning. Special programs offered to physically disabled students include note-taking services, reader services, tape recorders, tutors. **Career services:** Career assessment. **Career services highlights include:** We have had several interns placed at Sanofi Pasteur, a major parmaceutical company. Our individual career counseling services are rated very highly.

FACILITIES

Housing: Coed dorms. 95% of campus accessible to physically disabled. **Special Academic Facilities/Equipment:** Natural history museum, human performance lab, TV production studios, 119-acre student-owned/operated recreation area and wildlife sanctuary, observatory, electron microscopes. **Computers:** 50% of classrooms, 100% of dorms, 100% of libraries, 100% of student union, 10% of common outdoor areas have wireless network access. Students can register for classes online. Administrative functions (other than registration) can be performed online.

CAMPUS LIFE

Environment: Village. **Activities:** Choral groups, concert band, dance, drama/theater, jazz band, literary magazine, marching band, music ensembles, musical theater, pep band, radio station, student government, student newspaper, symphony orchestra, campus ministries, international student organization. **Organizations:** 110 registered organizations, 28 honor societies, 3 religious organizations. 5 fraternities, 5 sororities. **Athletics (Intercollegiate): Men:** Baseball, basketball, cross-country, football, soccer, tennis, track/field (outdoor), track/field (indoor), wrestling. **Women:** Basketball, cross-country, field hockey, golf, lacrosse, soccer, softball, swimming, tennis, track/field (outdoor), track/field (indoor), volleyball. **On-Campus Highlights:** Recreation Center, Java City, University Center, Stoney Acres, The Quad.

ADMISSIONS

Freshman Academic Profile: Average high school GPA 3.18. 6.3% in top 10% of high school class, 27.09% in top 25% of high school class, 66.8% in top 50% of high school class. 90% from public high schools. SAT Math middle 50% range 450–540. SAT Critical Reading middle 50% range 440–520. SAT Writing middle 50% range 430–520. Minimum paper TOEFL 560. Minimum computer TOEFL 220. Minimum web-based TOEFL 83. **Basis for Candidate Selection:** *Very important factors considered include:* Class rank, academic GPA, rigor of secondary school record, standardized test scores. **Freshman Admission Requirements:** High school diploma is required and GED is accepted. *Academic units recommended:* 4 English, 3 mathematics, 3 science, (2 science labs), 3 foreign language, 3 social studies, 3 history. **Freshman Admission Statistics:** 6,960 applied, 69% admitted, 28% enrolled. **Transfer Admission Requirements:** College transcript(s), minimum college GPA of 2.0 required. Lowest grade transferable C. **General Admission Information:** Application fee $35. Regular application deadline 4/1. Notification on a rolling basis, beginning on or about 12/1. Nonfall registration accepted. Credit and/or placement offered for CEEB Advanced Placement tests.

COSTS AND FINANCIAL AID

Annual in-state tuition $5,554. Annual out-of-state tuition $13,886. Room and board $6,418. Required fees $1,840. Average book expense $1,000. **Required Forms and Deadlines:** FAFSA. Financial aid filing deadline 3/1. Priority financial aid filing date 3/1. **Notification of Awards:** Applicants will be notified of awards on or about 4/1. **Types of Aid:** *Need-based scholarships/grants:* Federal Pell, SEOG, state scholarships/grants, private scholarships, the school's own gift aid. *Loans:* FFEL Subsidized Stafford, FFEL Unsubsidized Stafford, FFEL PLUS, Federal Perkins. **Student Employment:** Federal Work-Study Program available. Institutional employment available. Highest amount earned per year from on-campus jobs $2,145. Off-campus job opportunities are fair. **Financial Aid Statistics:** 27% freshmen, 27% undergrads receive need-based scholarship or grant aid. 3% freshmen, 2% undergrads receive non-need-based scholarship or grant aid. 40% freshmen, 37% undergrads receive need-based self-help aid. 3% freshmen, 4% undergrads receive athletic scholarships. 75% freshmen, 84% undergrads receive any aid. 73% undergrads borrow to pay for school. Average cumulative indebtedness $25,887. **Criteria for awarding institutional aid:** *Non-need-based:* Academics, alumni affiliation, art, athletics, leadership, minority status, music/drama, religious affiliation, state/district residency.

EAST TENNESSEE STATE UNIVERSITY

ETSU Box 70731, Johnson City, TN 37614-0731
Phone: 423-439-4213 **Financial Aid Phone:** 423-439-4300
E-mail: go2etsu@etsu.edu **CEEB Code:** 1198
Fax: 423-439-4630 **Website:** www.etsu.edu **ACT Code:** 3958

This public school was founded in 1911. It has a 366-acre campus.

RATINGS
Admissions Selectivity Rating: 73   **Fire Safety Rating:** 60*   **Green Rating:** 60*

STUDENTS AND FACULTY
Enrollment: 10,654. **Student Body:** 57% female, 43% male, 11% out-of-state, 1% international (63 countries represented). Asian 2%, African American 5%, Caucasian 87%, Hispanic 2%.
Retention and Graduation: 18% freshmen graduate within 4 years. **Faculty:** Student/faculty ratio 18:1. 529 full-time faculty, 71% hold PhDs, 12% are members of minority groups, 44% are women.

ACADEMICS
Degrees: Bachelor's, first professional, master's, post-bachelor's certificate, post-master's certificate. **Classes:** Most classes have 20–29 students. Most lab/discussion sessions have 20–29 students. **Majors with Highest Enrollment:** Business administration and management; multi-/interdisciplinary studies, other; nursing/registered nurse (RN, ASN, BSN, MSN). **Special Study Options:** Cooperative education program, distance learning, double major, dual enrollment, exchange student program (domestic), external degree program, honors program, independent study, internships, student-designed major, study abroad, teacher certification program. **Honors programs:** University Honors Program, Honors-in-Discipline Programs. Special programs offered to physically disabled students include note-taking services, reader services, tape recorders, tutors. **Career services:** Alumni network, alumni services, career/job search classes, career assessment, internships, regional alumni.

FACILITIES
Housing: Coed dorms, special housing for disabled students, men's dorms, women's dorms, fraternity/sorority housing, apartments for married students, apartments for single students. 75% of campus accessible to physically disabled. **Special Academic Facilities/Equipment:** Regional history museum, art gallery, archives of Appalachia, planetarium. **Computers:** Students can register for classes online. Administrative functions (other than registration) can be performed online.

CAMPUS LIFE
Environment: Town. **Activities:** Choral groups, concert band, drama/theater, jazz band, literary magazine, music ensembles, pep band, radio station, student government, student newspaper, television station, campus ministries, international student organization. **Organizations:** 200 registered organizations, 19 honor societies, 13 religious organizations. 9 fraternities, 7 sororities. **Athletics (Intercollegiate): Men:** Baseball, basketball, cheerleading, cross-country, golf, soccer, tennis, track/field (outdoor), track/field (indoor). **Women:** Basketball, cheerleading, cross-country, golf, soccer, softball, tennis, track/field (outdoor), track/field (indoor), volleyball. **On-Campus Highlights:** Memorial Center, New Sherrod Library, New Physical Activities Center, The Cave—a unique pizza pub located in the DP Culp Center. Built around a huge rock formation, indoors, Amphitheater—natural stone + earth outdoor theater.

ADMISSIONS
Freshman Academic Profile: Average high school GPA 3.27. 18.83% in top 10% of high school class, 44.76% in top 25% of high school class, 76.18% in top 50% of high school class. 90% from public high schools. SAT Math middle 50% range 440–560. SAT Critical Reading middle 50% range 440–555. SAT Writing middle 50% range 420–550. ACT middle 50% range 20–25. Minimum paper TOEFL 500. Minimum computer TOEFL 173. **Basis for Candidate Selection:** *Very important factors considered include:* Academic GPA, standardized test scores. *Important factors considered include:* Rigor of secondary school record. *Other factors considered include:* Class rank, geographical residence, state residency. **Freshman Admission Requirements:** High school diploma is required and GED is accepted. *Academic units required:* 4 English, 3 mathematics, 2 science, (1 science labs), 2 foreign language, 1 social studies, 1 history, 1 visual/performing arts. *Academic units recommended:* 4 mathematics, 3 science. **Transfer Admission Requirements:** High school transcript, college transcript(s), minimum college GPA of 2.0 required. Lowest grade transferable D. **General Admission Information:** Application fee $15. Nonfall registration accepted. Credit and/or placement offered for CEEB Advanced Placement tests.

COSTS AND FINANCIAL AID
Annual in-state tuition $4,584. Annual out-of-state tuition $16,512. Room and board $5,500. Required fees $949. Average book expense $1,090. **Required**

Forms and Deadlines: FAFSA. Priority financial aid filing date 4/15. Notification of Awards: Applicants will be notified of awards on a rolling basis beginning 4/15. Types of Aid: *Need-based scholarships/grants:* Federal Pell, SEOG, state scholarships/grants, private scholarships, the school's own gift aid, Federal Nursing Scholarships. *Loans:* Direct Subsidized Stafford, Direct Unsubsidized Stafford, Direct PLUS, Federal Perkins, Federal Nursing, state loans, college/university loans from institutional funds. Student Employment: Federal Work-Study Program available. Institutional employment available. Off-campus job opportunities are excellent. Financial Aid Statistics: 52% freshmen, 44% undergrads receive need-based scholarship or grant aid. 19% freshmen, 17% undergrads receive non-need-based scholarship or grant aid. 34% freshmen, 37% undergrads receive need-based self-help aid. 1% freshmen, 2% undergrads receive athletic scholarships. 84% freshmen receive any aid. 59% undergrads borrow to pay for school. Average cumulative indebtedness $16,635. Criteria for awarding institutional aid: *Non-need-based:* Academics, alumni affiliation, art, athletics, leadership, minority status, music/drama, religious affiliation, state/district residency.

EAST TEXAS BAPTIST UNIVERSITY

1209 North Grove, Marshall, TX 75670-1498
Phone: 903-923-2000 **Financial Aid Phone:** 903-923-2137
E-mail: admissions@etbu.edu **CEEB Code:** 6187
Fax: 903-923-2001 **Website:** www.etbu.edu **ACT Code:** 4086

This private school, affiliated with the Baptist Church, was founded in 1912. It has a 200-acre campus.

RATINGS
Admissions Selectivity Rating: 78   **Fire Safety Rating:** 61   **Green Rating:** 66

STUDENTS AND FACULTY
Enrollment: 1,116. **Student Body:** 51% female, 49% male, 10% out-of-state, 1% international (19 countries represented). Asian 1%, African American 15%, Caucasian 73%, Hispanic 8%, Native American 2%.
Retention and Graduation: 61% freshmen return for sophomore year. 27% freshmen graduate within 4 years. **Faculty:** Student/faculty ratio 15:1. 64 full-time faculty, 89% hold PhDs, 8% are members of minority groups, 38% are women.

ACADEMICS
Degrees: Bachelor's, certificate. **Classes:** Most classes have 10–19 students. Most lab/discussion sessions have 10–19 students. **Majors with Highest Enrollment:** Business/commerce; elementary education and teaching; nursing/registered nurse (RN, ASN, BSN, MSN). **Special Study Options:** Accelerated program, cross-registration, distance learning, double major, dual enrollment, exchange student program (domestic), honors program, independent study, internships, liberal arts/career combination, student-designed major, study abroad, teacher certification program Special programs offered to physically disabled students include reader services, tutors. **Career services:** Alumni services, career assessment, internships. **Career services highlights include:** Internships.

FACILITIES
Housing: Men's dorms, women's dorms, apartments for married students, Campus houses for married students. 95% of campus accessible to physically disabled. **Computers:** 100% of classrooms, 100% of dorms, 100% of libraries, 100% of dining areas, 100% of student union, 100% of common outdoor areas have wireless network access. Students can register for classes online. Administrative functions (other than registration) can be performed online.

CAMPUS LIFE
Environment: Village. **Activities:** Choral groups, concert band, drama/theater, jazz band, literary magazine, marching band, music ensembles, musical theater, pep band, radio station, student government, student newspaper, symphony orchestra, yearbook, campus ministries, international student organization, Model UN. **Organizations:** 38 registered organizations, 7 honor societies, 3 religious organizations. 2 fraternities, 2 sororities. **Athletics (Intercollegiate):** *Men:* Baseball, basketball, cross-country, football, soccer. *Women:* Basketball, cross-country, soccer, softball, volleyball. **On-Campus Highlights:** Scarborough Hall, The Quad, Bennett Student Center, Dean Healthplex, Tiger Grrill.

ADMISSIONS
Freshman Academic Profile: Average high school GPA 3.34. 13% in top 10% of high school class, 45% in top 25% of high school class, 81% in top 50% of high school class. 95% from public high schools. SAT Math middle 50% range 450–540. SAT Critical Reading middle 50% range 420–510. ACT middle 50% range 19–23. Minimum paper TOEFL 500. Minimum computer TOEFL

173. Minimum web-based TOEFL 61. **Basis for Candidate Selection:** *Very important factors considered include:* Class rank, standardized test scores. *Important factors considered include:* Academic GPA. *Other factors considered include:* Character/personal qualities. **Freshman Admission Requirements:** High school diploma is required and GED is accepted. *Academic units recommended:* 4 English, 3 mathematics, 2 science, 1 academic electives, 0.5 economics, 1.5 physical ed, 0.5 health ed, 1 technology applications, 0.5 speech. **Freshman Admission Statistics:** 1,038 applied, 53% admitted, 51% enrolled. **Transfer Admission Requirements:** College transcript(s), statement of good standing from prior institution(s). Minimum college GPA of 2.00 required. Lowest grade transferable D. **General Admission Information:** Application fee $25. Notification on a rolling basis, beginning on or about 9/1. Nonfall registration accepted. Admission may be deferred for a maximum of 1 year. Credit and/or placement offered for CEEB Advanced Placement tests.

COSTS AND FINANCIAL AID
Required Forms and Deadlines: FAFSA, institution's own financial aid form. Priority financial aid filing date 6/1. **Notification of Awards:** Applicants will be notified of awards on a rolling basis beginning 1/1. **Types of Aid:** *Need-based scholarships/grants:* Federal Pell, SEOG, state scholarships/grants, private scholarships, the school's own gift aid, Federal Nursing Scholarships. *Loans:* FFEL Subsidized Stafford, FFEL Unsubsidized Stafford, FFEL PLUS, Federal Perkins, state loans. **Student Employment:** Federal Work-Study Program available. Institutional employment available. Highest amount earned per year from on-campus jobs $2,096. Off-campus job opportunities are fair. **Financial Aid Statistics:** 66% freshmen, 66% undergrads receive need-based scholarship or grant aid. 82% freshmen, 69% undergrads receive non-need-based scholarship or grant aid. 59% freshmen, 58% undergrads receive need-based self-help aid. 99% freshmen, 98% undergrads receive any aid. 77% undergrads borrow to pay for school. Average cumulative indebtedness $21,380. **Criteria for awarding institutional aid:** *Non-need-based:* Academics, alumni affiliation, leadership, music/drama, religious affiliation.

EASTERN CONNECTICUT STATE UNIVERSITY

83 Windham Street, Willimantic, CT 06226
Phone: 860-465-5286 **Financial Aid Phone:** 860-365-5205
E-mail: admissions@easternct.edu **CEEB Code:** 3966
Fax: 860-465-5286 **Website:** www.easternct.edu

This public school was founded in 1889. It has a 182-acre campus.

RATINGS
Admissions Selectivity Rating: 69   **Fire Safety Rating:** 84   **Green Rating:** 90

STUDENTS AND FACULTY
Enrollment: 5,025. **Student Body:** 54% female, 46% male, 8% out-of-state, 1% international (34 countries represented). Asian 2%, African American 6%, Caucasian 64%, Hispanic 5%, Native American 1%.
Retention and Graduation: 78% freshmen return for sophomore year. 32% freshmen graduate within 4 years. 25% grads go on to further study within 1 year. **Faculty:** Student/faculty ratio 16:1. 202 full-time faculty, 92% hold PhDs, 26% are members of minority groups, 43% are women.

ACADEMICS
Degrees: Associate, bachelor's, master's. **Classes:** Most classes have 20–29 students. Most lab/discussion sessions have 10–19 students. **Majors with Highest Enrollment:** Business/commerce; communication and media studies; other; psychology. **Special Study Options:** Accelerated program, cooperative education program, cross-registration, distance learning, double major, dual enrollment, exchange student program (domestic), honors program, independent study, internships, student-designed major, study abroad, teacher certification program, weekend college. **Honors programs:** University Honor Scholars Program offers interdisciplinary and independent study opportunities. Special programs offered to physically disabled students include note-taking services, reader services, tape recorders, tutors. **Career services:** Alumni network, alumni services, career/job search classes, career assessment, internships, regional alumni. **Career services highlights include:** Internships that lead to permanent employment.

FACILITIES
Housing: Coed dorms, apartments for single students 95% of campus accessible to physically disabled. Art Gallery, Arboretum, Church Farm, Family/Child Development Center(2007), Green science bldg/labs(2008), electron microscope, planetarium, Media center with TV and radio station, Sports/Fitness Center and Studios, Center for Connecticut studies. **Computers:** 100% of libraries, 100% of dining areas, 100% of student union, 100% of common

outdoor areas have wireless network access. Students can register for classes on-line. Administrative functions (other than registration) can be performed online.

CAMPUS LIFE

Environment: Village. **Activities:** Choral groups, concert band, dance, drama/theater, jazz band, literary magazine, music ensembles, musical theater, radio station, student government, student newspaper, television station, yearbook, international student organization. **Organizations:** 68 registered organizations, 17 honor societies, 3 religious organizations. **Athletics (Intercollegiate):** *Men:* Baseball, basketball, cross-country, golf, lacrosse, soccer, track/field (outdoor), track/field (indoor). *Women:* Basketball, cross-country, diving, field hockey, lacrosse, soccer, softball, swimming, track/field (outdoor), track/field (indoor), volleyball. **On-Campus Highlights:** Library, Student Center, Sports Center, Church Farm, Planetarium. **Environmental Initiatives:** Education Project www.ctenergyeducation.com; Energy Solutions www.easternct.edu/depts/sustainenergy/energy_solutions/benchmarking.html; Green Campus Initiative www.easternct.edu/depts/sustainenergy/colleges_n_uni/home_colleges_n_uni.html.

ADMISSIONS

Freshman Academic Profile: SAT Math middle 50% range 480–560. SAT Critical Reading middle 50% range 470–550. Minimum paper TOEFL 550. Minimum computer TOEFL 213. **Basis for Candidate Selection:** *Very important factors considered include:* Class rank, standardized test scores, talent/ability. *Important factors considered include:* Academic GPA, recommendation(s), rigor of secondary school record, level of applicant's interest. *Other factors considered include:* Application essay, character/personal qualities, extracurricular activities, interview, volunteer work, work experience. **Freshman Admission Requirements:** High school diploma is required and GED is accepted. *Academic units required:* 4 English, 3 mathematics, 2 science, (1 science labs), 2 foreign language, 2 social studies, 3 history. **Freshman Admission Statistics:** 3,785 applied, 62% admitted, 42% enrolled. **Transfer Admission Requirements:** High school transcript, college transcript(s), minimum college GPA of 2.0 required. Lowest grade transferable C–. **General Admission Information:** Application fee $50. Notification on a rolling basis, beginning on or about 12/1. Nonfall registration accepted. Credit offered for CEEB Advanced Placement tests.

COSTS AND FINANCIAL AID

Annual in-state tuition $3,742. Annual out-of-state tuition $12,112. Room and board $13,340. Required fees $3,901. Average book expense $1,412. **Required Forms and Deadlines:** FAFSA. Priority financial aid filing date 3/15. **Types of Aid:** *Need-based scholarships/grants:* Federal Pell, SEOG, state scholarships/grants, private scholarships, the school's own gift aid. *Loans:* FFEL Subsidized Stafford, FFEL Unsubsidized Stafford, FFEL PLUS, Federal Perkins. **Student Employment:** Federal Work-Study Program available. Institutional employment available. Highest amount earned per year from on-campus jobs $5,500. Off-campus job opportunities are excellent. **Financial Aid Statistics:** 40% freshmen, 39% undergrads receive need-based scholarship or grant aid. 19% freshmen, 7% undergrads receive non-need-based scholarship or grant aid. 47% freshmen, 42% undergrads receive need-based self-help aid. 56% freshmen, 75% undergrads receive any aid. 57% undergrads borrow to pay for school. Average cumulative indebtedness $14,829. **Criteria for awarding institutional aid:** *Non-need-based:* Academics.

EASTERN ILLINOIS UNIVERSITY

600 Lincoln Avenue, Charleston, IL 61920
Phone: 217-581-2223 **Financial Aid Phone:** 217-581-7812
E-mail: admissions@eiu.edu **CEEB Code:** 1199
Fax: 217-581-7060 **Website:** www.eiu.edu **ACT Code:** 1016

This public school was founded in 1895. It has a 320-acre campus.

RATINGS

Admissions Selectivity Rating: 70 **Fire Safety Rating:** 74 **Green Rating:** 73

STUDENTS AND FACULTY

Enrollment: 10,055. **Student Body:** 58% female, 42% male, 2% out-of-state, international (41 countries represented). Asian 1%, African American 12%, Caucasian 77%, Hispanic 3%, Native American 1%.
Retention and Graduation: 79% freshmen return for sophomore year. **Faculty:** Student/faculty ratio 16:1. 629 full-time faculty, 70% hold PhDs, 10% are members of minority groups, 46% are women.

ACADEMICS

Degrees: Bachelor's, master's, post-bachelor's certificate, post-master's certificate. **Classes:** Most classes have 20–29 students. **Majors with Highest**

Enrollment: Biology/biological sciences; elementary education and teaching; physical education teaching and coaching. **Special Study Options:** Distance learning, double major, dual enrollment, exchange student program (domestic), external degree program, honors program, independent study, internships, study abroad, teacher certification program. **Honors programs:** Honors College Special programs offered to physically disabled students include note-taking services, reader services, tape recorders, tutors. **Career services:** Alumni network, alumni services, career/job search classes, career assessment, internships, regional alumni. **Career services highlights include:** The externship program provides early professional direction and networking to students who are narrowing their major and career choices for further development, academically and experientially.

FACILITIES

Housing: Coed dorms, special housing for disabled students, men's dorms, women's dorms, fraternity/sorority housing, apartments for married students, apartments for single students. 80% of campus accessible to physically disabled. **Special Academic Facilities/Equipment:** Arts center, electron microscope. **Computers:** 100% of classrooms, 50% of dorms, 100% of libraries, 100% of dining areas, 100% of student union, have wireless network access. Students can register for classes online. Administrative functions (other than registration) can be performed online.

CAMPUS LIFE

Environment: Village. **Activities:** Choral groups, concert band, dance, drama/theater, jazz band, literary magazine, marching band, music ensembles, musical theater, opera, pep band, radio station, student government, student newspaper, symphony orchestra, television station, yearbook, campus ministries, international student organization. **Organizations:** 232 registered organizations, 19 honor societies, 16 religious organizations. 15 fraternities, 11 sorority. **Athletics (Intercollegiate):** *Men:* Baseball, basketball, cross-country, football, golf, soccer, swimming, tennis, track/field (outdoor), track/field (indoor). *Women:* Basketball, cross-country, golf, rugby, soccer, softball, swimming, tennis, track/field (outdoor), track/field (indoor), volleyball. **On-Campus Highlights:** Doudna fine arts Building, Old Main, Martin Luther King Jr. University Union, Pemberton Hall, Student Recreation Center. **Environmental Initiatives:** Performance contracts have cut 30% off our total energy consumption. Performance contracts have cut 50% off our potable water consumption. Installing a new biomass gassification combined heat and power plant reducing CO_2 by over 15,000 mte.

ADMISSIONS

Freshman Academic Profile: Average high school GPA 3.23. 3% in top 10% of high school class, 12% in top 25% of high school class, 43% in top 50% of high school class. ACT middle 50% range 19–24. Minimum paper TOEFL 500. Minimum web-based TOEFL 61. **Basis for Candidate Selection:** *Very important factors considered include:* Academic GPA, rigor of secondary school record, standardized test scores, character/personal qualities. *Important factors considered include:* Class rank, extracurricular activities. *Other factors considered include:* Application essay, recommendation(s). **Freshman Admission Requirements:** High school diploma is required and GED is accepted. *Academic units required:* 4 English, 3 mathematics, 3 science, (3 science labs), 3 social studies, 2 academic electives. *Academic units recommended:* 2 foreign language. **Freshman Admission Statistics:** 7,563 applied, 68% admitted, 32% enrolled. **Transfer Admission Requirements:** High school transcript, college transcript(s), standardized test scores, minimum college GPA of 2.0 required. **General Admission Information:** Application fee $30. Nonfall registration accepted. Admission may be deferred for a maximum of 1 year. Credit offered for CEEB Advanced Placement tests.

COSTS AND FINANCIAL AID

Annual in-state tuition $7,170. Annual out-of-state tuition $21,510. Room and board $8,078. Required fees $2,259. Average book expense $120. **Required Forms and Deadlines:** FAFSA. Priority financial aid filing date 3/1. **Notification of Awards:** Applicants will be notified of awards on a rolling basis beginning 3/1. **Types of Aid:** *Need-based scholarships/grants:* Federal Pell, SEOG, state scholarships/grants, private scholarships, the school's own gift aid. *Loans:* Direct Subsidized Stafford, Direct Unsubsidized Stafford, Direct PLUS, Federal Perkins, college/university loans from institutional funds. **Student Employment:** Federal Work-Study Program available. Institutional employment available. Off-campus job opportunities are fair. **Financial Aid Statistics:** 29% freshmen, 28% undergrads receive need-based scholarship or grant aid. 12% freshmen, 10% undergrads receive non-need-based scholarship or grant aid. 45% freshmen, 41% undergrads receive need-based self-help aid. 3% freshmen, 2% undergrads receive athletic scholarships. 53% freshmen, 49% undergrads receive any aid. 53% undergrads borrow to pay for school. Average cumulative indebtedness $11,547. **Criteria for awarding institutional aid:** *Non-need-based:* Academics, art, athletics, leadership, music/drama.

EASTERN KENTUCKY UNIVERSITY

SSB CPO 54, 521 Lancaster Ave, Richmond, KY 40475
Phone: 859-622-2106 **Financial Aid Phone:** 859-622-2361
E-mail: admissions@eku.edu **CEEB Code:** 1200
Fax: 859-622-8024 **Website:** www.eku.edu **ACT Code:** 1512

This public school was founded in 1906. It has a 675-acre campus.

RATINGS
Admissions Selectivity Rating: 60* **Fire Safety Rating:** 81 **Green Rating:** 60*

STUDENTS AND FACULTY
Enrollment: 12,710. **Student Body:** 58% female, 42% male, 13% out-of-state, 1% international (36 countries represented). Asian 1%, African American 5%, Caucasian 99%, Hispanic 1%.
Retention and Graduation: Faculty: Student/faculty ratio 17:1. 599 full-time faculty, 69% hold PhDs, 11% are members of minority groups, 48% are women.

ACADEMICS
Degrees: Associate, bachelor's, certificate, master's, post-bachelor's certificate.
Classes: Most classes have 10–19 students. **Majors with Highest Enrollment:** Criminal justice/law enforcement administration; elementary education and teaching; nursing/registered nurse (RN, ASN, BSN, MSN). **Special Study Options:** Cooperative education program, distance learning, double major, English as a Second Language (ESL), honors program, independent study, internships, study abroad, teacher certification program. **Honors programs:** Honors Program: www.honors.eku.edu. Special programs offered to physically disabled students include note-taking services, reader services, tape recorders, tutors. **Career services:** Alumni network, alumni services, career/job search classes, career assessment, internships, regional alumni.

FACILITIES
Housing: Coed dorms, men's dorms, special housing for international students, women's dorms, fraternity/sorority housing, apartments for married students. 90% of campus accessible to physically disabled. **Special Academic Facilities/Equipment:** Hummel Planetarium, Giles Gallery. **Computers:** Students can register for classes online. Administrative functions (other than registration) can be performed online.

CAMPUS LIFE
Environment: Town. **Activities:** Choral groups, concert band, dance, drama/theater, jazz band, literary magazine, marching band, music ensembles, musical theater, pep band, radio station, student government, student newspaper, symphony orchestra. **Organizations:** 178 registered organizations, 30 honor societies, 11 religious organizations. 16 fraternities, 13 sororities. **Athletics (Intercollegiate):** *Men:* Baseball, basketball, cheerleading, cross-country, football, golf, tennis, track/field (outdoor), track/field (indoor). *Women:* Basketball, cheerleading, cross-country, golf, soccer, softball, tennis, track/field (outdoor), track/field (indoor), volleyball. **On-Campus Highlights:** Student Wellness Center (New), Library Cafe (New), Student Services Building (New), First Weekend Events.

ADMISSIONS
Freshman Academic Profile: SAT Math middle 50% range 440–450. SAT Critical Reading middle 50% range 440–450. SAT Writing middle 50% range 420–430. ACT middle 50% range 18–24. Minimum paper TOEFL 500. Minimum computer TOEFL 173. **Basis for Candidate Selection:** *Very important factors considered include:* Academic GPA, standardized test scores. *Other factors considered include:* Talent/ability. **Freshman Admission Requirements:** High school diploma is required and GED is accepted. *Academic units required:* 4 English, 3 mathematics, 3 science, (1 science labs), 2 foreign language, 3 social studies, 7 academic electives, 3 health, 0.5 physical ed. and 1 art. **Freshman Admission Statistics:** 6,928 applied, 69% admitted, 52% enrolled. **Transfer Admission Requirements:** College transcript(s), minimum college GPA of 2.0 required. Lowest grade transferable D. **General Admission Information:** Application fee $30. Regular application deadline 8/1. Notification on a rolling basis, beginning on or about 9/1. Nonfall registration accepted. Admission may be deferred for a maximum of 1 semester. Credit offered for CEEB Advanced Placement tests.

COSTS AND FINANCIAL AID
Annual in-state tuition $6,080. Annual out-of-state tuition $16,612. Room and board $5,288. Required fees $460. Average book expense $800. **Required Forms and Deadlines:** FAFSA. Priority financial aid filing date 3/15. **Notification of Awards:** Applicants will be notified of awards on a rolling basis beginning 4/1. **Types of Aid:** *Need-based scholarships/grants:* Federal Pell, SEOG, state scholarships/grants, private scholarships, the school's own gift aid. *Loans:* FFEL Subsidized Stafford, FFEL Unsubsidized Stafford, FFEL PLUS, Federal Perkins, college/university loans from institutional funds.

Student Employment: Federal Work-Study Program available. Institutional employment available. Highest amount earned per year from on-campus jobs $1,800. Off-campus job opportunities are good. **Financial Aid Statistics:** 38% freshmen, 35% undergrads receive need-based scholarship or grant aid. 51% freshmen, 31% undergrads receive non-need-based scholarship or grant aid. 47% freshmen, 49% undergrads receive need-based self-help aid. 2% freshmen, 1% undergrads receive athletic scholarships. 94% freshmen, 86% undergrads receive any aid. 69% undergrads borrow to pay for school. Average cumulative indebtedness $14,976. **Criteria for awarding institutional aid:** *Non-need-based:* Academics, alumni affiliation, art, athletics, job skills, leadership, minority status, music/drama.

EASTERN MENNONITE UNIVERSITY

1200 Park Rd, Harrisonburg, VA 22802
Phone: 540-432-4118 **Financial Aid Phone:** 540-432-4137
E-mail: CEEB Code: 5181
Fax: 540-432-4444 **Website:** www.emu.edu **ACT Code:** 3708

This school, affiliated with the Mennonite Church, was founded in 1917. It has a 93-acre campus.

RATINGS
Admissions Selectivity Rating: 60* **Fire Safety Rating:** 60* **Green Rating:** 60*

STUDENTS AND FACULTY
Student Body: International (20 countries represented).
Retention and Graduation: 5% grads go on to further study within 1 year. 1% grads pursue arts and sciences degrees. 2% grads pursue medical degrees.
Faculty:

ACADEMICS
Majors with Highest Enrollment: Business administration and management; nursing/registered nurse (RN, ASN, BSN, MSN); psychology. **Honors programs:** EMU's Honors Program accepts 10–14 academically-gifted first-year students into the selective Honors Program. Participation is renewable for up to 3 years. Honors students must maintain a 3.5 GPA and complete 9 SH of Honors Program Courses. Honors students gain access to many special educational opportunities and meet monthly for fellowship and discussion. Special programs offered to physically disabled students include note-taking services, reader services, tape recorders, tutors. **Career services:** Alumni services, career/job search classes, career assessment, internships, regional alumni.

FACILITIES
Housing: 75% of campus accessible to physically disabled. **Special Academic Facilities/Equipment:** D. Ralph Hostetter Museum of Natural History, M. T. Brackbill Planetarium, arboretum, Menno Simons Historical Library. **Computers:** Administrative functions (other than registration) can be performed online.

CAMPUS LIFE
Environment: Town. **Activities: Organizations:** 37 registered organizations, 2 honor societies, 4 religious organizations. **Athletics (Intercollegiate):** *Men:* Baseball, basketball, cross-country, soccer, tennis, track/field (outdoor), track/field (indoor), volleyball. *Women:* Basketball, cross-country, field hockey, soccer, softball, tennis, track/field (outdoor), track/field (indoor), volleyball. **On-Campus Highlights:** University Commons, Royals Den snack shop, Common Grounds coffeehouse, Campus Center Greeting Hall, Wood's Residence Halls, Park Woods.

ADMISSIONS
Freshman Academic Profile: 64% from public high schools. Minimum paper TOEFL 550. Minimum computer TOEFL 213. **General Admission Information:** Credit and/or placement offered for CEEB Advanced Placement tests.

COSTS AND FINANCIAL AID
Student Employment: Federal Work-Study Program available. Institutional employment available. Highest amount earned per year from on-campus jobs $3,500. Off-campus job opportunities are good. **Financial Aid Statistics:** 91% freshmen, 93% undergrads receive any aid.

EASTERN MICHIGAN UNIVERSITY

Eastern Michigan University, 400 Pierce Hall, Ypsilanti, MI 48197
Phone: 734-487-3060 **Financial Aid Phone:** 734-487-0455
E-mail: admissions@emich.edu **CEEB Code:** 1201
Fax: 734-487-1484 **Website:** www.emich.edu **ACT Code:** 1990

This public school was founded in 1849. It has a 460-acre campus.

RATINGS
Admissions Selectivity Rating: 73   **Fire Safety Rating:** 64   **Green Rating:** 82

STUDENTS AND FACULTY
Enrollment: 16,937. **Student Body:** 58% female, 42% male, 7% out-of-state, 1% international (70 countries represented). Asian 3%, African American 20%, Caucasian 66%, Hispanic 3%, Native American 1%.
Retention and Graduation: 79% freshmen return for sophomore year. 10% freshmen graduate within 4 years. **Faculty:** Student/faculty ratio 18:1. 738 full-time faculty, 81% hold PhDs, 17% are members of minority groups, 48% are women. 3% of classes are taught by teaching assistants.

ACADEMICS
Degrees: Bachelor's, doctoral, master's, post-bachelor's certificate, post-master's certificate. **Classes:** Most classes have 20–29 students. Most lab/discussion sessions have 20–29 students. **Majors with Highest Enrollment:** Business administration and management; nursing/registered nurse (RN, ASN, BSN, MSN); psychology. **Special Study Options:** Accelerated program, cooperative education program, distance learning, double major, dual enrollment, English as a Second Language (ESL), external degree program, honors program, independent study, internships, student-designed major, study abroad, teacher certification program, weekend college, Dual enrollment note: High school students may enroll in college courses while still enrolled in high school, but are required to apply for admission to Eastern. **Combined degree programs:** BA/MA, BA/BBA, BA/MSA, BS/MA, BS/MOT. Special programs offered to physically disabled students include note-taking services, reader services, tape recorders, tutors. **Career services:** Alumni network, alumni services, career/job search classes, career assessment, internships. **Career services highlights include:** We connect with area businesses to provide hands-on learning opportunities for our students. All three of the programs above work hand-in-hand toward helping students gain experience in their field of study (number one attributes employers look for in job candidates).

FACILITIES
Housing: Coed dorms, special housing for disabled students, special housing for international students, fraternity/sorority housing, apartments for married students, cooperative housing, apartments for single students, theme housinghouse rental to sorority house. 80% of campus accessible to physically disabled. **Special Academic Facilities/Equipment:** Intermedia art gallery, paint research center, Sherzer observatory, Bruce T. Halle Library, Terrestrial and Aquatics Ecology Research Facility, Coatings Research Institute, the John W. Porter Building housing the College of Education and the Marshall Building housing the College of Health and Human Services. **Computers:** 100% of classrooms, 25% of dorms, 100% of libraries, 100% of dining areas, 100% of student union, 15% of common outdoor areas have wireless network access. Students can register for classes online. Administrative functions (other than registration) can be performed online.

CAMPUS LIFE
Environment: City. **Activities:** Choral groups, concert band, dance, literary magazine, marching band, music ensembles, musical theater, pep band, radio station, student government, student newspaper, student-run film society, symphony orchestra, television station, campus ministries, international student organization. **Organizations:** 220 registered organizations, 14 honor societies, 24 religious organizations. 11 fraternities, 13 sororities. **Athletics (Intercollegiate):** *Men:* Basketball, diving, football, golf, swimming, track/field (outdoor), track/field (indoor), wrestling. *Women:* Basketball, crew/rowing, diving, golf, gymnastics, soccer, softball, swimming, tennis, track/field (outdoor), track/field (indoor), volleyball. **On-Campus Highlights:** New Student Center, Recreations and Intramurals Building, The Lakehouse, Halle Library, Athletic Campus. **Environmental Initiatives:** Energy performance contract, hiring an Energy & Sustainability Manager in March, Recycling initiative.

ADMISSIONS
Freshman Academic Profile: Average high school GPA 3.04. 12% in top 10% of high school class, 34% in top 25% of high school class, 67% in top 50% of high school class. 85% from public high schools. SAT Math middle 50% range 450–580. SAT Critical Reading middle 50% range 450–570. SAT Writing middle 50% range 440–570. ACT middle 50% range 18–23. Minimum paper TOEFL 500. Minimum computer TOEFL 173. **Basis for Candidate Selection:**

Very important factors considered include: Academic GPA, standardized test scores. *Important factors considered include:* Rigor of secondary school record, character/personal qualities. *Other factors considered include:* Application essay, recommendation(s), extracurricular activities, interview, talent/ability. **Freshman Admission Requirements:** High school diploma is required and GED is accepted. *Academic units recommended:* 4 English, 4 mathematics, 4 science, (1 science labs), 2 foreign language, 2 social studies, 1 history, 4 academic electives, 2 traditional college preparatory classes. **Freshman Admission Statistics:** 9,754 applied, 73% admitted, 32% enrolled. **Transfer Admission Requirements:** College transcript(s), minimum college GPA of 2.0 required. Lowest grade transferable C. **General Admission Information:** Application fee $30. Notification on a rolling basis, beginning on or about 10/1. Nonfall registration accepted. Admission may be deferred for a maximum of 1 year. Credit and/or placement offered for CEEB Advanced Placement tests.

COSTS AND FINANCIAL AID
Annual in-state tuition $7,148. Annual out-of-state tuition $21,053. Room and board $7,785. Required fees $1,230. Average book expense $900. **Required Forms and Deadlines:** FAFSA. **Notification of Awards:** Applicants will be notified of awards on a rolling basis beginning 3/1. **Types of Aid:** *Need-based scholarships/grants:* Federal Pell, SEOG, state scholarships/grants, private scholarships, the school's own gift aid. *Loans:* FFEL Subsidized Stafford, FFEL Unsubsidized Stafford, FFEL PLUS, Federal Perkins, state loans, college/university loans from institutional funds, Alternative (Private) Loans. **Student Employment:** Federal Work-Study Program available. Institutional employment available. Highest amount earned per year from on-campus jobs $13,375. Off-campus job opportunities are excellent. **Financial Aid Statistics:** 36% freshmen, 27% undergrads receive need-based scholarship or grant aid. 38% freshmen, 12% undergrads receive non-need-based scholarship or grant aid. 41% freshmen, 37% undergrads receive need-based self-help aid. 4% freshmen, 2% undergrads receive athletic scholarships. 91% freshmen, 80% undergrads receive any aid. 62% undergrads borrow to pay for school. Average cumulative indebtedness $20,940. **Criteria for awarding institutional aid:** *Non-need-based:* Academics, alumni affiliation, art, athletics, leadership, minority status, music/drama, state/district residency.

EASTERN NAZARENE COLLEGE

23 East Elm Avenue, Quincy, MA 02170-2999
Phone: 617-745-3711
E-mail: admissions@enc.edu **CEEB Code:** 3365
Fax: 617-745-3992 **Website:** www.enc.edu

This private school, affiliated with the Nazarene Church, was founded in 1918. It has a 19-acre campus.

RATINGS
Admissions Selectivity Rating: 75   **Fire Safety Rating:** 60*   **Green Rating:** 60*

STUDENTS AND FACULTY
Student Body: 58% out-of-state.
Retention and Graduation: 22% grads go on to further study within 1 year. 17% grads pursue arts and sciences degrees. 1% grads pursue law degrees. 2% grads pursue business degrees. 2% grads pursue medical degrees. **Faculty:** Student/faculty ratio 15:1.

ACADEMICS
Degrees: Associate, bachelor's, diploma, first professional certificate, master's. **Majors with Highest Enrollment:** Biology; business/commerce; communication studies/speech communication and rhetoric. **Special Study Options:** Accelerated program, cooperative education program, double major, honors program, independent study, internships, study abroad, teacher certification program Special programs offered to physically disabled students include note-taking services, reader services, tape recorders, tutors. **Career services:** Career assessment, internships.

FACILITIES
Housing: Special housing for disabled students, men's dorms, women's dorms, apartments for married students, suites-men's and women's.

CAMPUS LIFE
Environment: Village. **Activities:** Choral groups, drama/theater, music ensembles, musical theater, radio station, student government, student newspaper, yearbook. **Organizations:** 1 religious organizations. **Athletics (Intercollegiate):** *Men:* Baseball, basketball, cross-country, soccer, tennis. *Women:* Basketball, cross-country, soccer, softball, tennis, volleyball.

ADMISSIONS

Freshman Academic Profile: Minimum paper TOEFL 600. Minimum computer TOEFL 250. **Basis for Candidate Selection:** *Very important factors considered include:* Application essay, recommendation(s), rigor of secondary school record, standardized test scores, interview. *Other factors considered include:* Class rank, character/personal qualities, extracurricular activities, religious affiliation/commitment, talent/ability, volunteer work, work experience. **Freshman Admission Requirements:** High school diploma is required and GED is accepted. *Academic units required:* 4 English, 2 mathematics, 1 science, 2 foreign language, 1 social studies, 1 history. *Academic units recommended:* 4 mathematics, 4 science, 4 foreign language, 2 social studies, 2 history. **Transfer Admission Requirements:** High school transcript, college transcript(s), essay or personal statement, interview, standardized test scores, minimum college GPA of 2.0 required. Lowest grade transferable c. **General Admission Information:** Application fee $25. Nonfall registration accepted.

COSTS AND FINANCIAL AID

Annual tuition $17,700. Room and board $6,590. Required fees $610. Average book expense $500. **Required Forms and Deadlines:** FAFSA, institution's own financial aid form. **Types of Aid:** *Need-based scholarships/grants:* Federal Pell, SEOG, state scholarships/grants, private scholarships, the school's own gift aid, Church Scholarships. *Loans:* FFEL Subsidized Stafford, FFEL Unsubsidized Stafford, FFEL PLUS, Federal Perkins, state loans **Student Employment:** Federal Work-Study Program available. Highest amount earned per year from on-campus jobs $3,000. **Financial Aid Statistics:** 30% freshmen, 20% undergrads receive need-based scholarship or grant aid. 85% freshmen, 89% undergrads receive non-need-based scholarship or grant aid. 75% freshmen, 68% undergrads receive need-based self-help aid. **Criteria for awarding institutional aid:** *Non-need-based:* Academics, alumni affiliation, leadership, minority status, music/drama, religious affiliation, state/district residency.

EASTERN NEW MEXICO UNIVERSITY

Station #7, ENMU, Portales, NM 88130
Phone: 575-562-2178 **Financial Aid Phone:** 575-562-2194
E-mail: admissions@enmu.edu **CEEB Code:** 4299
Fax: 575-562-2118 **Website: ACT Code:** 2636

This public school was founded in 1934. It has a 400-acre campus.

RATINGS

Admissions Selectivity Rating: 73   **Fire Safety Rating:** 84   **Green Rating:** 63

STUDENTS AND FACULTY

Enrollment: 3,442. **Student Body:** 56% female, 44% male, 21% out-of-state, 3% international (20 countries represented). Asian 1%, African American 7%, Caucasian 53%, Hispanic 29%, Native American 3%.
Retention and Graduation: 61% freshmen return for sophomore year. 10% freshmen graduate within 4 years. **Faculty:** Student/faculty ratio 18:1. 148 full-time faculty, 76% hold PhDs, 11% are members of minority groups, 47% are women. 3.4% of classes are taught by teaching assistants.

ACADEMICS

Degrees: Associate, bachelor's, master's, terminal associate, transfer associate. **Classes:** Most classes have 10–19 students. Most lab/discussion sessions have 10–19 students. **Majors with Highest Enrollment:** Business administration and management; elementary education and teaching; general studies. **Special Study Options:** Accelerated program, distance learning, double major, dual enrollment, English as a Second Language (ESL), exchange student program (domestic), independent study, internships, student-designed major, teacher certification program Special programs offered to physically disabled students include note-taking services, reader services, tape recorders, tutors. **Career services:** Career assessment, internships.

FACILITIES

Housing: Coed dorms, special housing for disabled students, women's dorms, fraternity/sorority housing, apartments for married students, apartments for single students 100% of campus accessible to physically disabled. **Special Academic Facilities/Equipment:** Natural history and historical museums, theatre, child development center, audiovisual center, electron microscopes, laser, KNEW Broadcast Center. **Computers:** Students can register for classes online. Administrative functions (other than registration) can be performed online.

CAMPUS LIFE

Environment: Village. **Activities:** Choral groups, concert band, dance, drama/theater, jazz band, literary magazine, marching band, music ensembles, radio station, student government, student newspaper, student-run film society,

symphony orchestra, television station, campus ministries, international student organization. **Organizations:** 55 registered organizations, 2 honor societies, 4 religious organizations. 4 fraternities, 2 sororities. **Athletics (Intercollegiate):** *Men:* Baseball, basketball, cross-country, football, rodeo, soccer, track/field (outdoor). *Women:* Basketball, cross-country, rodeo, soccer, softball, track/field (outdoor), volleyball. **On-Campus Highlights:** New Science facilities/Natural History Museum, Campus Union Building, Communications-Broadcast Center, Library, University Theatre Center. **Environmental Initiatives:** Water savings project; energy management project; development of solar energy project.

ADMISSIONS

Freshman Academic Profile: Average high school GPA 3.22. 11% in top 10% of high school class, 34% in top 25% of high school class, 67% in top 50% of high school class. SAT Math middle 50% range 420–540. SAT Critical Reading middle 50% range 410–540. ACT middle 50% range 17–23. Minimum paper TOEFL 500. Minimum computer TOEFL 79. **Basis for Candidate Selection:** *Very important factors considered include:* Academic GPA, standardized test scores. **Freshman Admission Requirements:** High school diploma is required and GED is accepted. *Academic units recommended:* 4 English, 4 mathematics, 2 science, 2 social studies. **Freshman Admission Statistics:** 1,176 applied, 65% admitted, 83% enrolled. **Transfer Admission Requirements:** College transcript(s), statement of good standing from prior institution(s). Minimum college GPA of 2.0 required. Lowest grade transferable D. **General Admission Information:** Nonfall registration accepted. Admission may be deferred for a maximum of 0. Credit and/or placement offered for CEEB Advanced Placement tests.

COSTS AND FINANCIAL AID

Required Forms and Deadlines: FAFSA. Financial aid filing deadline 3/30. Priority financial aid filing date 3/1. **Notification of Awards:** Applicants will be notified of awards on a rolling basis beginning 4/15. **Types of Aid:** *Need-based scholarships/grants:* Federal Pell, SEOG, state scholarships/grants, the school's own gift aid. *Loans:* FFEL Subsidized Stafford, FFEL Unsubsidized Stafford, FFEL PLUS, Federal Perkins. **Student Employment:** Federal Work-Study Program available. Institutional employment available. **Financial Aid Statistics:** 58% freshmen, 56% undergrads receive need-based scholarship or grant aid. 57% freshmen, 36% undergrads receive non-need-based scholarship or grant aid. 34% freshmen, 41% undergrads receive need-based self-help aid. 15% freshmen, 10% undergrads receive athletic scholarships. 98.87% freshmen, 90.79% undergrads receive any aid. 1.19% undergrads borrow to pay for school. Average cumulative indebtedness $11,769. **Criteria for awarding institutional aid:** *Non-need-based:* Academics, alumni affiliation, art, athletics, leadership, music/drama, state/district residency.

EASTERN OREGON UNIVERSITY

One University Blvd, La Grande, OR 97850
Phone: 1-541-962-3393 **Financial Aid Phone:** 541-962-3550
E-mail: admissions@eou.edu **CEEB Code:** 4300
Fax: 541-962-3418 **Website:** www.eou.edu **ACT Code:** 3460

This public school was founded in 1929. It has a 121-acre campus.

RATINGS

Admissions Selectivity Rating: 84   **Fire Safety Rating:** 60*   **Green Rating:** 63

STUDENTS AND FACULTY

Enrollment: 2,823. **Student Body:** 62% female, 38% male, 27.94% out-of-state, 1% international (23 countries represented). Asian 2%, African American 2%, Caucasian 81%, Hispanic 4%, Native American 3%.
Retention and Graduation: 58% freshmen return for sophomore year. **Faculty:** Student/faculty ratio 22.7:1. 99 full-time faculty, 86% hold PhDs, 12% are members of minority groups, 39% are women.

ACADEMICS

Degrees: Bachelor's, master's. **Classes:** Most classes have 10–19 students. Most lab/discussion sessions have 10–19 students. **Majors with Highest Enrollment:** Business administration, management and operations, other; education, other; liberal arts and sciences/liberal studies. **Special Study Options:** Cooperative education program, cross-registration, distance learning, double major, dual enrollment, exchange student program (domestic), external degree program, honors program, independent study, internships, liberal arts/career combination, student-designed major, study abroad, teacher certification program, weekend college. Special programs offered to physically disabled students include note-taking services, reader services, tape recorders, tutors. **Career services:** Alumni services, career/job search classes, career assessment, internships.

FACILITIES

Housing: Coed dorms, apartments for married students 95% of campus accessible to physically disabled. **Special Academic Facilities/Equipment:** Art gallery, archaeological museum. **Computers:** 40% of classrooms, 80% of libraries, 90% of dining areas, 90% of student union, 50% of common outdoor areas have wireless network access. Students can register for classes online.

CAMPUS LIFE

Environment: Village. **Activities:** Choral groups, concert band, dance, drama/theater, jazz band, literary magazine, music ensembles, musical theater, radio station, student government, student newspaper, symphony orchestra. **Organizations:** 57 registered organizations, 2 honor societies, 4 religious organizations. **Athletics (Intercollegiate):** *Men:* Basketball, cross-country, football, track/field (outdoor), track/field (indoor). *Women:* Basketball, cross-country, soccer, softball, track/field (outdoor), track/field (indoor), volleyball. **On-Campus Highlights:** Loso Hall, Hoke Union, Community Stadium, Quinn Coliseum, sports practice fields.

ADMISSIONS

Freshman Academic Profile: Average high school GPA 3.15. 12.1% in top 10% of high school class, 33.8% in top 25% of high school class, 64.52% in top 50% of high school class. 98% from public high schools. SAT Math middle 50% range 410–510. SAT Critical Reading middle 50% range 410–530. SAT Writing middle 50% range 390–510. ACT middle 50% range 19–22. Minimum paper TOEFL 520. Minimum computer TOEFL 190. **Basis for Candidate Selection:** *Very important factors considered include:* Academic GPA, rigor of secondary school record. *Important factors considered include:* Recommendation(s), talent/ability. *Other factors considered include:* Class rank, application essay, standardized test scores, extracurricular activities, first generation, geographical residence, level of applicant's interest, volunteer work, work experience. **Freshman Admission Requirements:** High school diploma is required and GED is accepted. *Academic units required:* 4 English, 3 mathematics, 2 science, 2 foreign language. *Academic units recommended:* (1 science labs). **Freshman Admission Statistics:** 932 applied, 39% admitted, 95% enrolled. **Transfer Admission Requirements:** College transcript(s), minimum college GPA of 2.2 required. Lowest grade transferable D–. **General Admission Information:** Application fee $50. Regular application deadline 9/1. Notification on a rolling basis, beginning on or about 10/1. Nonfall registration accepted. Admission may be deferred for a maximum of 1 year. Credit offered for CEEB Advanced Placement tests.

COSTS AND FINANCIAL AID

Annual in-state tuition $4,929. Annual out-of-state tuition $4,929. Room and board $8,800. Required fees $1,296. Average book expense $1,152. **Required Forms and Deadlines:** FAFSA. Priority financial aid filing date 3/1. **Notification of Awards:** Applicants will be notified of awards on a rolling basis beginning 4/1. **Types of Aid:** *Need-based scholarships/grants:* Federal Pell, SEOG, state scholarships/grants, private scholarships, the school's own gift aid. *Loans:* FFEL Subsidized Stafford, FFEL Unsubsidized Stafford, FFEL PLUS, Federal Perkins. **Student Employment:** Federal Work-Study Program available. Institutional employment available. Off-campus job opportunities are good. **Financial Aid Statistics:** 48% freshmen, 51% undergrads receive need-based scholarship or grant aid. 47% freshmen, 30% undergrads receive non-need-based scholarship or grant aid. 69% freshmen, 71% undergrads receive need-based self-help aid. 21% freshmen, 11% undergrads receive athletic scholarships. 77% freshmen, 75% undergrads receive any aid. 75% undergrads borrow to pay for school. Average cumulative indebtedness $21,415. **Criteria for awarding institutional aid:** *Non-need-based:* Academics, art, leadership, minority status, music/drama, state/district residency.

EASTERN UNIVERSITY

1300 Eagle Road, St. Davids, PA 19087-3696
Phone: 610-341-5967 **Financial Aid Phone:** 610-341-5842
E-mail: ugadm@eastern.edu **CEEB Code:** 2220
Fax: 610-341-1723 **Website:** www.eastern.edu **ACT Code:** 3562

This private school, affiliated with the American Baptist Church, was founded in 1952. It has a 107-acre campus.

RATINGS

Admissions Selectivity Rating: 79   **Fire Safety Rating:** 60*   **Green Rating:** 60*

STUDENTS AND FACULTY

Enrollment: 2,054. **Student Body:** 65% female, 35% male, 52% out-of-state, 1% international . Asian 1%, African American 12%, Caucasian 77%, Hispanic 5%.

Retention and Graduation: 77% freshmen return for sophomore year. 56% freshmen graduate within 4 years. 19% grads go on to further study within 1 year. 24% grads pursue arts and sciences degrees. 4% grads pursue law degrees. 4% grads pursue business degrees. **Faculty:** Student/faculty ratio 13:1. 79 full-time faculty, 78% hold PhDs, 16% are members of minority groups, 42% are women.

ACADEMICS

Degrees: Associate, bachelor's, master's, post-bachelor's certificate, post-master's certificate, transfer associate. **Classes:** Most classes have fewer than 10 students. Most lab/discussion sessions have 10–19 students. **Majors with Highest Enrollment:** Business, management, marketing, and related support services, other; elementary education and teaching; social work. **Special Study Options:** Accelerated program, cross-registration, double major, honors program, independent study, internships, student-designed major, study abroad, teacher certification program. Special programs offered to physically disabled students include note-taking services, reader services, tape recorders, tutors.

FACILITIES

Housing: Coed dorms, apartments for single students. 75% of campus accessible to physically disabled. **Special Academic Facilities/Equipment:** Planetarium. **Computers:** Students can register for classes online. Administrative functions (other than registration) can be performed online.

CAMPUS LIFE

Environment: Town. **Activities:** Choral groups, concert band, dance, drama/theater, jazz band, literary magazine, music ensembles, musical theater, pep band, student government, student newspaper, yearbook. **Organizations:** 94 registered organizations, 10 honor societies, 20 religious organizations. **Athletics (Intercollegiate):** *Men:* Baseball, basketball, golf, soccer, tennis. *Women:* Basketball, field hockey, lacrosse, soccer, softball, tennis, volleyball.

ADMISSIONS

Freshman Academic Profile: Average high school GPA 3.34. 19% in top 10% of high school class, 47% in top 25% of high school class, 79% in top 50% of high school class. 75% from public high schools. SAT Math middle 50% range 490–590. SAT Critical Reading middle 50% range 510–610. ACT middle 50% range 19–31. Minimum paper TOEFL 213. Minimum computer TOEFL 213. **Basis for Candidate Selection:** *Very important factors considered include:* Class rank, rigor of secondary school record, standardized test scores. *Important factors considered include:* Application essay, recommendation(s), character/personal qualities, extracurricular activities, volunteer work. *Other factors considered include:* Alumni/ae relation, interview, religious affiliation/commitment, talent/ability, work experience. **Freshman Admission Requirements:** High school diploma is required and GED is accepted. **Freshman Admission Statistics:** 1,174 applied, 77% admitted, 43% enrolled. **Transfer Admission Requirements:** High school transcript, college transcript(s), essay or personal statement, minimum college GPA of 2.0 required. Lowest grade transferable C. **General Admission Information:** Application fee $25. Nonfall registration accepted. Admission may be deferred for a maximum of 1 year. Credit and/or placement offered for CEEB Advanced Placement tests.

COSTS AND FINANCIAL AID

Annual tuition $17,700. Room and board $7,600. Required fees $40. Average book expense $830. **Required Forms and Deadlines:** FAFSA **Types of Aid:** *Need-based scholarships/grants:* Federal Pell, SEOG, state scholarships/grants, private scholarships, the school's own gift aid. *Loans:* FFEL Subsidized Stafford, FFEL Unsubsidized Stafford, FFEL PLUS, Federal Perkins, alternative loans. **Student Employment:** Highest amount earned per year from on-campus jobs $1,200. **Financial Aid Statistics:** 64% freshmen receive need-based scholarship or grant aid. 22% freshmen receive non-need-based scholarship or grant aid. 57% freshmen receive need-based self-help aid. **Criteria for awarding institutional aid:** *Non-need-based:* Academics, leadership, music/drama, religious affiliation, state/district residency.

EASTERN WASHINGTON UNIVERSITY

101 Sutton Hall, Cheney, WA 99004
Phone: 509-359-2397
E-mail: admissions@ewu.edu **CEEB Code:** 4301
Fax: 509-359-6692 **Website:** www.ewu.edu **ACT Code:** 4454

This public school was founded in 1882. It has a 335-acre campus.

RATINGS

Admissions Selectivity Rating: 71   **Fire Safety Rating:** 60*   **Green Rating:** 60*

STUDENTS AND FACULTY

Enrollment: 9,919. **Student Body:** 55% female, 45% male, 6% out-of-state, 2% international (35 countries represented). Asian 4%, African American 4%, Caucasian 62%, Hispanic 9%, Native American 2%.
Retention and Graduation: 72% freshmen return for sophomore year. **Faculty:** Student/faculty ratio 21:1. 412 full-time faculty, 97% hold PhDs, 11% are members of minority groups, 45% are women.

ACADEMICS

Degrees: Bachelor's, certificate, master's, post-master's certificate. **Classes:** Most classes have 20–29 students. Most lab/discussion sessions have 20–29 students. **Special Study Options:** Distance learning, double major, English as a Second Language (ESL), honors program, independent study, internships, student-designed major, study abroad, teacher certification program. **Honors programs:** EWU Honors. **Combined degree programs:** BA/MA Special programs offered to physically disabled students include note-taking services, reader services, tape recorders.

FACILITIES

Housing: Coed dorms, special housing for disabled students, fraternity/sorority housing, apartments for married students, wellness housing, theme housing. 77% of campus accessible to physically disabled. **Special Academic Facilities/Equipment:** Anthropology museum, on-campus elementary school, education lab, primate research center, marine biology lab, ecological studies lab, wildlife refuge, planetarium. **Computers:** Students can register for classes online. Administrative functions (other than registration) can be performed online.

CAMPUS LIFE

Environment: Town. **Activities:** Choral groups, concert band, dance, drama/theater, jazz band, literary magazine, marching band, music ensembles, musical theater, pep band, radio station, student government, student newspaper, student-run film society, symphony orchestra, campus ministries, international student organization, Model UN. **Organizations:** 100 registered organizations, 14 honor societies, 10 religious organizations. 5 fraternities, 5 sororities. **Athletics (Intercollegiate):** *Men:* Basketball, cross-country, football, golf, tennis, track/field (outdoor), track/field (indoor). *Women:* Basketball, cross-country, golf, soccer, tennis, track/field (outdoor), track/field (indoor), volleyball. **On-Campus Highlights:** Pence Union Building, CyberCafe, Phase Athletic Facilities, Woodward Stadium, Central campus mall, EWU Gallery of Art.

ADMISSIONS

Freshman Academic Profile: Average high school GPA 3.18. 95% from public high schools. SAT Math middle 50% range 430–540. SAT Critical Reading middle 50% range 420–530. SAT Writing middle 50% range 410–520. ACT middle 50% range 17–23. Minimum paper TOEFL 525. Minimum computer TOEFL 195. **Basis for Candidate Selection:** *Very important factors considered include:* Academic GPA, standardized test scores. *Important factors considered include:* Application essay, rigor of secondary school record. *Other factors considered include:* Character/personal qualities, extracurricular activities, interview, talent/ability, volunteer work, work experience. **Freshman Admission Requirements:** High school diploma or equivalent is not required. *Academic units required:* 4 English, 3 mathematics, 2 science, (1 science labs), 2 foreign language, 3 social studies, 1 visual/performing arts. **Freshman Admission Statistics:** 3,728 applied, 82% admitted, 41% enrolled. **Transfer Admission Requirements:** College transcript(s), essay or personal statement, minimum college GPA of 2.0 required. Lowest grade transferable D–. **General Admission Information:** Application fee $50. Regular application deadline 8/15. Notification on a rolling basis, beginning on or about 11/1. Nonfall registration accepted. Admission may be deferred for a maximum of 1 year. Credit and/or placement offered for CEEB Advanced Placement tests.

COSTS AND FINANCIAL AID

Annual in-state tuition $6,088. Annual out-of-state tuition $14,761. Room and board $7,425. Required fees $512. Average book expense $1,035. **Required Forms and Deadlines:** FAFSA. Priority financial aid filing date 2/15. **Notification of Awards:** Applicants will be notified of awards on a rolling basis beginning 4/1. **Types of Aid:** *Need-based scholarships/grants:* Federal Pell, SEOG, state scholarships/grants, private scholarships, the school's own gift aid. *Loans:* FFEL Subsidized Stafford, FFEL Unsubsidized Stafford, FFEL PLUS, Federal Perkins. **Student Employment:** Highest amount earned per year from on-campus jobs $2,457. **Financial Aid Statistics:** 43% freshmen, 45% undergrads receive need-based scholarship or grant aid. 18% freshmen, 9% undergrads receive non-need-based scholarship or grant aid. 37% freshmen, 31% undergrads receive need-based self-help aid. 3% freshmen, 2% undergrads receive athletic scholarships. 68% undergrads borrow to pay for school. Average cumulative indebtedness $18,435. **Criteria for awarding institutional aid:** *Non-need-based:* Academics, alumni affiliation, athletics, state/district residency.

ECKERD COLLEGE

4200 54th Avenue South, St.Petersburg, FL 33711
Phone: 727-864-8331 **Financial Aid Phone:** 727-864-8334
E-mail: admissions@eckerd.edu **CEEB Code:** 5223
Fax: 727-866-2304 **Website:** www.eckerd.edu **ACT Code:** 731

This private school, affiliated with the Presbyterian Church, was founded in 1958. It has a 188-acre campus.

RATINGS

Admissions Selectivity Rating: 81 **Fire Safety Rating:** 65 **Green Rating:** 88

STUDENTS AND FACULTY

Enrollment: 1,847. **Student Body:** 58% female, 42% male, 76% out-of-state, 3% international (35 countries represented). Asian 2%, African American 4%, Caucasian 75%, Hispanic 4%.
Retention and Graduation: 80% freshmen return for sophomore year. 58% freshmen graduate within 4 years. **Faculty:** Student/faculty ratio 14:1. 110 full-time faculty, 95% hold PhDs, 11% are members of minority groups, 41% are women.

ACADEMICS

Degrees: Bachelor's. **Classes:** Most classes have 20–29 students. Most lab/discussion sessions have 10–19 students. **Majors with Highest Enrollment:** Business administration and management; environmental studies; marine biology and biological oceanography. **Special Study Options:** Accelerated program, double major, honors program, independent study, internships, liberal arts/career combination, student-designed major, study abroad. **Honors programs:** Ford Apprentice Scholar Program, The Honors Program at Eckerd College. **Combined degree programs:** BA/MEng. Special programs offered to physically disabled students include reader services, tape recorders, tutors. **Career services:** Alumni network, alumni services, career assessment, internships, regional alumni. **Career services highlights include:** We are 90% successful with placing students in internship experiences.

FACILITIES

Housing: Coed dorms, women's dorms, suite-style dorms wellness housing pet dorms community service dorms. 95% of campus accessible to physically disabled. **Special Academic Facilities/Equipment:** Language lab, oral communications lab, marine science center. **Computers:** 100% of classrooms, 100% of dorms, 100% of libraries, 100% of dining areas, 100% of student union, 90% of common outdoor areas have wireless network access. Students can register for classes online. Administrative functions (other than registration) can be performed online.

CAMPUS LIFE

Environment: City. **Activities:** Choral groups, concert band, dance, drama/theater, literary magazine, music ensembles, radio station, student government, student newspaper, television station, campus ministries, international student organization, Model UN. **Organizations:** 74 registered organizations, 8 honor societies, 3 religious organizations. **Athletics (Intercollegiate):** *Men:* Baseball, basketball, golf, sailing, soccer, tennis. *Women:* Basketball, golf, sailing, soccer, softball, tennis, volleyball. **On-Campus Highlights:** Peter Armacost Library, Turley Athletic Complex, Gailbraith Marine Science Lab, Hough Campus Center/Campus Pub, Eckerd Waterfront/Wallace Boathouse, awarded Phi Beta Kappa Chapter in summer 2003. **Environmental Initiatives:** All students are required to take an "Environmental Perspective" course in order to graduate. We signed the Climate Commitment in May 2007. We have a campus community "Yellow Bikes" program for free campus transportation.

ADMISSIONS

Freshman Academic Profile: Average high school GPA 3.27. 15% in top 10% of high school class, 45% in top 25% of high school class, 85% in top 50% of high school class. SAT Math middle 50% range 500–610. SAT Critical Reading middle 50% range 520–630. SAT Writing middle 50% range 500–615. ACT middle 50% range 22–27. Minimum paper TOEFL 550. Minimum computer TOEFL 213. Minimum web-based TOEFL 79. **Basis for Candidate Selection:** *Very important factors considered include:* Academic GPA, rigor of secondary school record. *Important factors considered include:* Application essay, recommendation(s), standardized test scores, character/personal qualities, extracurricular activities, interview, talent/ability. *Other factors considered include:* Class rank, alumni/ae relation, first generation, level of applicant's interest, volunteer work, work experience. **Freshman Admission Require-**

ments: High school diploma is required and GED is accepted. *Academic units recommended:* 4 English, 3 mathematics, 3 science, (2 science labs), 2 foreign language, 2 social studies, 1 history, 3 academic electives. **Freshman Admission Statistics:** 3,200 applied, 72% admitted, 22% enrolled. **Transfer Admission Requirements:** College transcript(s), essay or personal statement, statement of good standing from prior institution(s). Minimum college GPA of 2.5 required. Lowest grade transferable C. **General Admission Information:** Application fee $35. Notification on a rolling basis, beginning on or about 10/1. Nonfall registration accepted. Admission may be deferred for a maximum of 1 year. Credit and/or placement offered for CEEB Advanced Placement tests.

COSTS AND FINANCIAL AID

Annual tuition $31,818. Room and board $9,058. Required fees $286. Average book expense $1,000. **Required Forms and Deadlines:** FAFSA. Priority financial aid filing date 3/1. **Notification of Awards:** Applicants will be notified of awards on a rolling basis beginning 2/15. **Types of Aid:** *Need-based scholarships/grants:* Federal Pell, SEOG, state scholarships/grants, private scholarships, the school's own gift aid. *Loans:* Direct Subsidized Stafford, Direct Unsubsidized Stafford, Direct PLUS, Federal Perkins, college/university loans from institutional funds. **Student Employment:** Federal Work-Study Program available. Institutional employment available. Highest amount earned per year from on-campus jobs $2,500. Off-campus job opportunities are excellent. **Financial Aid Statistics:** 96.7% freshmen, 94.4% undergrads receive any aid. 63% undergrads borrow to pay for school. Average cumulative indebtedness $30,494. **Criteria for awarding institutional aid:** *Non-need-based:* Academics, art, athletics, music/drama, religious affiliation, state/district residency.

EDGEWOOD COLLEGE

1000 Edgewood College Drive, Madison, WI 53711-1997
Phone: 608-663-2294 **Financial Aid Phone:** 608-663-2206
E-mail: admissions@edgewood.edu **CEEB Code:** 1202
Fax: 608-663-2214 **Website:** www.edgewood.edu **ACT Code:** 4582

This private school, affiliated with the Roman Catholic Church, was founded in 1927. It has a 55-acre campus.

RATINGS
Admissions Selectivity Rating: 74   **Fire Safety Rating:** 60*   **Green Rating:** 74

STUDENTS AND FACULTY
Enrollment: 1,779. **Student Body:** 71% female, 29% male, 6.3% out-of-state, 2% international (23 countries represented). Asian 2%, African American 4%, Caucasian 84%, Hispanic 4%, Native American 1%.
Retention and Graduation: 76% freshmen return for sophomore year. 27% freshmen graduate within 4 years. **Faculty:** Student/faculty ratio 11:1. 108 full-time faculty, 89% hold PhDs, 9% are members of minority groups, 51% are women.

ACADEMICS
Degrees: Associate, bachelor's, master's. **Classes:** Most classes have 10–19 students. **Majors with Highest Enrollment:** Business/commerce; elementary education and teaching; nursing/registered nurse (RN, ASN, BSN, MSN). **Special Study Options:** Accelerated program, double major, dual enrollment, honors program, independent study, internships, liberal arts/career combination, student-designed major, study abroad, teacher certification program. **Honors programs:** We have an Honors Program for undergraduates. **Combined degree programs:** Undergraduate degrees from Edgewood and UW/Madison or Marquette. Special programs offered to physically disabled students include note-taking services, reader services, tape recorders, tutors. **Career services:** Alumni network, alumni services, career/job search classes, career assessment, internships, regional alumni. **Career services highlights include:** Career assessment is providing to all incoming students. Career services are available at no charge to alumni. Provide alumni mentor program.

FACILITIES
Housing: Coed dorms, special housing for disabled students, women's dorms, theme housing. **Special Academic Facilities/Equipment:** DeRicci Art Gallery, Science Exploration Center. **Computers:** 90% of classrooms, 100% of dorms, 100% of libraries, 100% of dining areas, 100% of student union, 80% of common outdoor areas have wireless network access. Students can register for classes online. Administrative functions (other than registration) can be performed online.

CAMPUS LIFE
Environment: City. **Activities:** Choral groups, concert band, dance, drama/theater, jazz band, literary magazine, marching band, music ensembles, musical theater, pep band, student government, student newspaper, symphony orches-

tra, campus ministries, international student organization. **Organizations:** 45 registered organizations, 4 honor societies, 1 religious organizations. **Athletics (Intercollegiate):** *Men:* Baseball, basketball, cross-country, golf, soccer, tennis, track/field (outdoor), track/field (indoor). *Women:* Basketball, cross-country, golf, soccer, softball, tennis, track/field (outdoor), track/field (indoor), volleyball. **On-Campus Highlights:** Dominican Hall, Mazzuchelli Hall, Lake Wingra Boardwalk, Predolin Humanities Center, SondeRegger Science Center. **Environmental Initiatives:** Dominican Hall.

ADMISSIONS
Freshman Academic Profile: Average high school GPA 3.3. 12% in top 10% of high school class, 36% in top 25% of high school class, 79% in top 50% of high school class. 93% from public high schools. SAT Math middle 50% range 430–580. SAT Critical Reading middle 50% range 440–570. ACT middle 50% range 20–25. Minimum paper TOEFL 525. Minimum computer TOEFL 197. Minimum web-based TOEFL 72. **Basis for Candidate Selection:** *Very important factors considered include:* Class rank, academic GPA, standardized test scores. *Other factors considered include:* Application essay, recommendation(s). **Freshman Admission Requirements:** High school diploma is required and GED is accepted. *Academic units required:* 4 English, 2 mathematics, 2 science, (1 science labs), 2 foreign language, 2 social studies, 1 history. *Academic units recommended:* 4 English, 2 mathematics, 2 science, (1 science labs), 2 foreign language, 2 social studies, 1 history. **Freshman Admission Statistics:** 1,210 applied, 72% admitted, 33% enrolled. **Transfer Admission Requirements:** High school transcript, college transcript(s), minimum college GPA of 2.0 required. Lowest grade transferable C–. **General Admission Information:** Application fee $25. Regular application deadline 8/14. Notification on a rolling basis, beginning on or about 9/15. Nonfall registration accepted. Admission may be deferred for a maximum of 1 year. Credit and/or placement offered for CEEB Advanced Placement tests.

COSTS AND FINANCIAL AID
Annual tuition $21,042. Room and board $7,101. Average book expense $800. **Required Forms and Deadlines:** FAFSA, institution's own financial aid form. Priority financial aid filing date 3/1. **Notification of Awards:** Applicants will be notified of awards on a rolling basis beginning 3/15. **Types of Aid:** *Need-based scholarships/grants:* Federal Pell, SEOG, state scholarships/grants, private scholarships, the school's own gift aid. *Loans:* FFEL Subsidized Stafford, FFEL Unsubsidized Stafford, FFEL PLUS, Federal Perkins, state loans, college/university loans from institutional funds. **Student Employment:** Federal Work-Study Program available. Institutional employment available. Highest amount earned per year from on-campus jobs $2,000. Off-campus job opportunities are good. **Financial Aid Statistics:** 73% freshmen, 64% undergrads receive need-based scholarship or grant aid. 8% freshmen, 4% undergrads receive non-need-based scholarship or grant aid. 67% freshmen, 66% undergrads receive need-based self-help aid. 95% freshmen, 86% undergrads receive any aid. 76.1% undergrads borrow to pay for school. Average cumulative indebtedness $28,982. **Criteria for awarding institutional aid:** *Non-need-based:* Academics, alumni affiliation, art, leadership, music/drama, religious affiliation.

EDINBORO UNIVERSITY OF PENNSYLVANIA

200 East Normal Street, Edinboro, PA 16444
Phone: 814-732-2761 **Financial Aid Phone:** 814-732-5555
E-mail: eup_admissions@edinboro.edu **CEEB Code:** 2651
Fax: 814-732-2420 **Website:** www.edinboro.edu **ACT Code:** 3702

This public school was founded in 1857. It has a 585-acre campus.

RATINGS
Admissions Selectivity Rating: 70   **Fire Safety Rating:** 98   **Green Rating:** 79

STUDENTS AND FACULTY
Enrollment: 6,301. **Student Body:** 56% female, 44% male, 11% out-of-state, 1% international (28 countries represented). Asian 1%, African American 9%, Caucasian 87%, Hispanic 2%.
Retention and Graduation: 75% freshmen return for sophomore year. 24% freshmen graduate within 4 years. **Faculty:** 346 full-time faculty, 7% are members of minority groups, 46% are women.

ACADEMICS
Degrees: Associate, bachelor's, master's, post-bachelor's certificate, post-master's certificate. **Classes:** Most classes have 20–29 students. **Majors with Highest Enrollment:** Art/art studies; elementary education and teaching; political science and government. **Special Study Options:** Cooperative education program, cross-registration, distance learning, double major, dual enrollment, honors program, independent study, internships, liberal arts/career combination,

student-designed major, study abroad, teacher certification program. **Honors programs:** Admission to the Upper Division Honors Program, may be made by any full time EUP student who has completed 63 credit hours with an overall GPA of 3.4 or higher. They must also provide letters of support from two faculty members, secure approval of their academic advisor, and complete a proposal for the Senior Project in consultation with the Honors Director, Academic Advisor and and Faculty Member who will supervise the Senior Project. **Combined degree programs:** BA/MEng. Special programs offered to physically disabled students include note-taking services, reader services, tape recorders, tutors. **Career services:** Alumni network, alumni services, career/job search classes, career assessment, internships, regional alumni. **Career services highlights include:** We offer our students extensive internship opportunities.

FACILITIES

Housing: Coed dorms, special housing for disabled students, living-learning and suite style housing. Choosing to become part of a living-learning community is a unique opportunity for any student to live on the same floor with others who share the same major, filed of study, or interest area. Participants will interact with faculty and staff outside of the classroom through programs, activities, and events. Residents are able to gain assistance and ideas from peers who share their strong commitment to the living-learning experience. 98% of campus accessible to physically disabled. **Special Academic Facilities/Equipment:** Planetarium, Solar Observatory, Governor George Leader Speech and Hearing Center, Bates Art Gallery, Bruce Gallery. **Computers:** 90% of classrooms, 30% of dorms, 100% of libraries, 100% of dining areas, 75% of student union, 40% of common outdoor areas have wireless network access. Students can register for classes online. Administrative functions (other than registration) can be performed online.

CAMPUS LIFE

Environment: Rural. **Activities:** Choral groups, dance, drama/theater, jazz band, literary magazine, marching band, music ensembles, opera, radio station, student government, student newspaper, student-run film society, television station, campus ministries, international student organization. **Organizations:** 157 registered organizations, 13 honor societies, 4 religious organizations. 10 fraternities, 7 sororities. **Athletics (Intercollegiate):** *Men:* Basketball, cross-country, football, swimming, track/field (outdoor), track/field (indoor), wheel-chair basketball, wrestling. *Women:* Basketball, cross-country, lacrosse, soccer, softball, swimming, track/field (outdoor), track/field (indoor), volleyball. **On-Campus Highlights:** Frank G. Pogue Student Center, Baron-Forness Library, R. Benjamin Wiley Arts & Sciences Center, Louis J. Cole Memorial Auditorium, McComb Fieldhouse, Planetarium. **Environmental Initiatives:** LEED Certification for all new building projects. Use of geothermal heat pumps in new construction and HVAC renovations. Energy conservation programs include lighting retrofits, fuel switch, use of variable speed drives.

ADMISSIONS

Freshman Academic Profile: Average high school GPA 3.15. 5% in top 10% of high school class, 20% in top 25% of high school class, 51% in top 50% of high school class. N/A% from public high schools. SAT Math middle 50% range 410–520. SAT Critical Reading middle 50% range 415–520. ACT middle 50% range 17–223. Minimum paper TOEFL 500. Minimum computer TOEFL 173. Minimum web-based TOEFL 61. **Basis for Candidate Selection:** *Very important factors considered include:* Class rank, academic GPA, rigor of secondary school record, standardized test scores. *Other factors considered include:* Application essay, recommendation(s), character/personal qualities, extracurricular activities, interview, talent/ability, volunteer work, work experience. **Freshman Admission Requirements:** High school diploma is required and GED is accepted. *Academic units recommended:* 4 English, 3 mathematics, 3 science, 2 foreign language, 4 social studies, 1 computer science. **Freshman Admission Statistics:** 4,411 applied, 73% admitted, 44% enrolled. **Transfer Admission Requirements:** High school transcript, college transcript(s), statement of good standing from prior institution(s). Minimum college GPA of 2.0 required. Lowest grade transferable C–. **General Admission Information:** Application fee $30. Notification on a rolling basis, beginning on or about 9/15. Nonfall registration accepted. Admission may be deferred for a maximum of 1 year. Credit and/or placement offered for CEEB Advanced Placement tests.

COSTS AND FINANCIAL AID

Annual in-state tuition $5,554. Annual out-of-state tuition $8,332. Room and board $7,130. Average book expense $900. **Required Forms and Deadlines:** FAFSA. Financial aid filing deadline 5/1. Priority financial aid filing date 3/15. **Notification of Awards:** Applicants will be notified of awards on a rolling basis beginning 3/22. **Types of Aid:** *Need-based scholarships/grants:* Federal Pell, SEOG, state scholarships/grants, private scholarships, the school's own gift aid. *Loans:* Direct Subsidized Stafford, Direct Unsubsidized Stafford, FFEL Subsidized Stafford, FFEL Unsubsidized Stafford, FFEL PLUS, Federal Perkins, Federal Nursing. **Student Employment:** Federal Work-Study Program available. Institutional employment available. Highest amount earned per year from on-campus jobs $7,233. Off-campus job opportunities are good. **Financial Aid Statistics:** 70% freshmen, 70% undergrads receive need-based scholarship or

grant aid. 74% freshmen, 72% undergrads receive non-need-based scholarship or grant aid. 64% freshmen, 66% undergrads receive need-based self-help aid. 3% freshmen, 2% undergrads receive athletic scholarships. 79% freshmen, 84% undergrads receive any aid. 46% undergrads borrow to pay for school. Average cumulative indebtedness $21,518. **Criteria for awarding institutional aid:** *Non-need-based:* Academics, alumni affiliation, art, athletics, job skills, leadership, minority status, music/drama, religious affiliation, state/district residency.

ELIZABETH CITY STATE UNIVERSITY

1704 Weeksville Road, Elizabeth City, NC 27909
Phone: 252-335-3305
E-mail: admissions@mail.ecsu.edu **CEEB Code:** 5629
Fax: 252-335-3537 **Website:** www.ecsu.edu **ACT Code:** 3095

This public school was founded in 1891. It has a 114-acre campus.

RATINGS

Admissions Selectivity Rating: 66   **Fire Safety Rating:** 60*   **Green Rating:** 60*

STUDENTS AND FACULTY

Enrollment: 2,015. **Student Body:** 62% female, 38% male, 12% out-of-state. African American 77%, Caucasian 22%, Hispanic 1%.
Retention and Graduation: 39% freshmen graduate within 4 years. 20% grads go on to further study within 1 year. 20% grads pursue arts and sciences degrees. **Faculty:** Student/faculty ratio 12:1. 114 full-time faculty, 70% hold PhDs, 80% are members of minority groups, 27% are women.

ACADEMICS

Degrees: Bachelor's, master's. **Classes:** Most classes have fewer than 10 students. **Special Study Options:** Cooperative education program, distance learning, double major, honors program, independent study, internships, liberal arts/career combination, teacher certification program, weekend college. **Career services:** Alumni services, career/job search classes, career assessment, internships.

FACILITIES

Housing: Coed dorms, men's dorms, women's dorms, apartments for single students, college-leased housing available. **Special Academic Facilities/Equipment:** Lab school, planetarium, science complex, music engineering station. **Computers:** Students can register for classes online. Administrative functions (other than registration) can be performed online.

CAMPUS LIFE

Environment: Village. **Activities:** Choral groups, concert band, dance, drama/theater, jazz band, literary magazine, marching band, music ensembles, musical theater, pep band, radio station, student government, student newspaper, symphony orchestra, television station, yearbook. **Organizations:** 46 registered organizations, 3 honor societies, 4 religious organizations. 4 fraternities, 4 sororities. **Athletics (Intercollegiate):** *Men:* Baseball, basketball, cheerleading, cross-country, football, golf, softball, tennis, track/field (outdoor), volleyball. *Women:* Baseball, basketball, cheerleading, cross-country, golf, softball, tennis, track/field (outdoor), volleyball

ADMISSIONS

Freshman Academic Profile: 99% from public high schools. SAT Math middle 50% range 360–450. SAT Critical Reading middle 50% range 360–450. Minimum paper TOEFL 550. **Basis for Candidate Selection:** *Very important factors considered include:* Rigor of secondary school record, standardized test scores, character/personal qualities, geographical residence, state residency. *Important factors considered include:* Class rank, racial/ethnic status, talent/ability. *Other factors considered include:* Application essay, recommendation(s), alumni/ae relation, extracurricular activities, interview, religious affiliation/commitment, work experience. **Freshman Admission Requirements:** High school diploma is required and GED is accepted. *Academic units required:* 4 English, 3 mathematics, 3 science, 1 social studies, 1 history, 8 academic electives. *Academic units recommended:* 2 foreign language. **Freshman Admission Statistics:** 1,262 applied, 77% admitted, 48% enrolled. **Transfer Admission Requirements:** High school transcript, college transcript(s), statement of good standing from prior institution(s). Minimum college GPA of 2.0 required. Lowest grade transferable C. **General Admission Information:** Application fee $30. Regular application deadline 8/1. Nonfall registration accepted. Admission may be deferred for a maximum of 1 year. Credit and/or placement offered for CEEB Advanced Placement tests.

COSTS AND FINANCIAL AID

Required Forms and Deadlines: FAFSA, institution's own financial aid form. **Notification of Awards:** Applicants will be notified of awards on or about

4/1. **Types of Aid:** *Need-based scholarships/grants:* Federal Pell, SEOG, state scholarships/grants, private scholarships, the school's own gift aid. *Loans:* FFEL Subsidized Stafford, FFEL Unsubsidized Stafford, FFEL PLUS, Federal Perkins, college/university loans from institutional funds. **Student Employment:** Federal Work-Study Program available. Highest amount earned per year from on-campus jobs $643. Off-campus job opportunities are fair.

ELIZABETHTOWN COLLEGE

Leffler House, One Alpha Drive, Elizabethtown, PA 17022
Phone: 717-361-1400 **Financial Aid Phone:** 717-361-1404
E-mail: admissions@etown.edu **CEEB Code:** 2225
Fax: 717-361-1365 **Website:** www.etown.edu **ACT Code:** 3568

This private school, affiliated with the Church of Brethren Church, was founded in 1899. It has a 193-acre campus.

RATINGS
Admissions Selectivity Rating: 86   **Fire Safety Rating:** 60*   **Green Rating:** 60*

STUDENTS AND FACULTY
Enrollment: 2,096. **Student Body:** 65% female, 35% male, 34% out-of-state, 2% international (17 countries represented). Asian 2%, African American 1%, Caucasian 82%, Hispanic 1%.
Retention and Graduation: 84% freshmen return for sophomore year. 64% freshmen graduate within 4 years. 20% grads go on to further study within 1 year. **Faculty:** Student/faculty ratio 13:1. 125 full-time faculty, 82% hold PhDs, 9% are members of minority groups, 40% are women.

ACADEMICS
Degrees: Associate, bachelor's, certificate, diploma, master's, post-bachelor's certificate. **Classes:** Most classes have 10–19 students. Most lab/discussion sessions have 10–19 students. **Majors with Highest Enrollment:** Biology; business/commerce; communication, journalism, and related programs, other. **Special Study Options:** Accelerated program, cooperative education program, distance learning, double major, dual enrollment, English as a Second Language (ESL), exchange student program (domestic), honors program, independent study, internships, liberal arts/career combination, study abroad, teacher certification program, 2+2, 3+3 and 4+2 (PT docotorate) programs with Thomas Jefferson University in nursing, physical therapy, labratory sceinces, diagnostic imaging, 3+2 in engineering with Penn State University, 3+2 with Duke University in Forestry, 3+3 in physical therapy with Widener University and University of Maryland, Baltimore County, 3+1 in Invasive Cardiovascular Technology with Lancaster Institute for Health Education,articulation agreements with Lehigh Unversity, Rutgers Univesity, Loyola College (MD) and Penn State University, Harrisburg to satisfy 150–hour requirement in Accounting. **Combined degree programs:** BA/MD, BA/MA, 3+3 physical therapy with Thomas Jefferson Univers. Special programs offered to physically disabled students include tape recorders, tutors.

FACILITIES
Housing: Coed dorms, special housing for disabled students, special housing for international students, women's dorms, apartments for single students, Off-campus houses for student service-learning groups. 75% of campus accessible to physically disabled. **Special Academic Facilities/Equipment:** Art gallery, Meetinghouse/center for Anabaptist and Pietist studies, chapel/performance center, Fourier transform multinuclear NMR spectrometer, blood gas analyzer, scanning densitometer, PCR machine, radiometer/data logger, automated ion analyzer, computerized language lab. **Computers:** Students can register for classes online. Administrative functions (other than registration) can be performed online.

CAMPUS LIFE
Environment: Village. **Activities:** Choral groups, concert band, dance, drama/theater, jazz band, literary magazine, music ensembles, musical theater, pep band, radio station, student government, student newspaper, student-run film society, symphony orchestra, television station, yearbook. **Organizations:** 80 registered organizations, 16 honor societies, 6 religious organizations. **Athletics (Intercollegiate):** *Men:* Baseball, basketball, cross-country, diving, golf, lacrosse, soccer, swimming, tennis, track/field (outdoor), track/field (indoor), wrestling. *Women:* Basketball, cross-country, diving, field hockey, lacrosse, soccer, softball, swimming, tennis, track/field (outdoor), track/field (indoor), volleyball. **On-Campus Highlights:** Brossman Commons Students Center, The Jay's Nest Snack Bar, The Dell, The Blue Bean Cafe, The Ira R Herr Soccer Complex, During the academic year it is great to hang out in The Dell, located in the middle of campus, on a hot day for frisbee or just soaking up the sun. The Ira R Herr Soccer Complex is the place to be to see the Blue Jays men's or

women's soccer team in action—either day or night—the stadium is one of the finest soccer venues in the East.

ADMISSIONS
Freshman Academic Profile: Average high school GPA 3.64. 30% in top 10% of high school class, 65% in top 25% of high school class, 93% in top 50% of high school class. 80% from public high schools. SAT Math middle 50% range 510–630. SAT Critical Reading middle 50% range 510–610. ACT middle 50% range 21–26. Minimum paper TOEFL 525. Minimum computer TOEFL 200. **Basis for Candidate Selection:** *Very important factors considered include:* Rigor of secondary school record. *Important factors considered include:* Class rank, recommendation(s), standardized test scores, interview, racial/ethnic status, volunteer work. *Other factors considered include:* Application essay, alumni/ae relation, character/personal qualities, extracurricular activities, geographical residence, religious affiliation/commitment, state residency, talent/ability, work experience. **Freshman Admission Requirements:** High school diploma is required and GED is accepted. *Academic units required:* 4 English, 3 mathematics, 2 science, (2 science labs), 2 foreign language, 2 social studies, 2 history. *Academic units recommended:* 4 English, 4 mathematics, 4 science, (3 science labs), 2 foreign language, 2 social studies, 2 history, 2 academic electives. **Freshman Admission Statistics:** 2,923 applied, 64% admitted, 29% enrolled. **Transfer Admission Requirements:** High school transcript, college transcript(s), essay or personal statement, standardized test scores, statement of good standing from prior institution(s). Minimum college GPA of 2.5 required. Lowest grade transferable C. **General Admission Information:** Application fee $30. Notification on a rolling basis, beginning on or about 11/15. Nonfall registration accepted. Admission may be deferred for a maximum of 1 year. Credit and/or placement offered for CEEB Advanced Placement tests.

COSTS AND FINANCIAL AID
Annual tuition $26,950. Room and board $7,300. Average book expense $700. **Required Forms and Deadlines:** FAFSA, institution's own financial aid form, Federal Tax Records. Priority financial aid filing date 3/15. **Notification of Awards:** Applicants will be notified of awards on a rolling basis beginning 3/1. **Types of Aid:** *Need-based scholarships/grants:* Federal Pell, SEOG, state scholarships/grants, private scholarships, the school's own gift aid. *Loans:* FFEL Subsidized Stafford, FFEL Unsubsidized Stafford, FFEL PLUS, Federal Perkins, state loans. **Student Employment: Financial Aid Statistics:** 71% freshmen, 71% undergrads receive need-based scholarship or grant aid. 14% freshmen, 9% undergrads receive non-need-based scholarship or grant aid. 59% freshmen, 61% undergrads receive need-based self-help aid. 96% freshmen, 94% undergrads receive any aid. 78% undergrads borrow to pay for school. Average cumulative indebtedness $25,545. **Criteria for awarding institutional aid:** *Non-need-based:* Academics, art, music/drama, religious affiliation.

ELMHURST COLLEGE

190 S Prospect Avenue, Elmhurst, IL 60126
Phone: 630-617-3400 **Financial Aid Phone:** 630-617-3075
E-mail: admit@elmhurst.edu **CEEB Code:** 1204
Fax: 630-617-5501 **Website:** public.elmhurst.edu **ACT Code:** 1020

This private school, affiliated with the United Church of Christ Church, was founded in 1871. It has a 38-acre campus.

RATINGS
Admissions Selectivity Rating: 80   **Fire Safety Rating:** 60*   **Green Rating:** 60*

STUDENTS AND FACULTY
Enrollment: 2,960. **Student Body:** 64% female, 36% male, 12% out-of-state, 1% international (29 countries represented). Asian 4%, African American 3%, Caucasian 72%, Hispanic 7%.
Retention and Graduation: 87% freshmen return for sophomore year. 53% freshmen graduate within 4 years. 17% grads go on to further study within 1 year. 1% grads pursue law degrees. 8% grads pursue business degrees. 2% grads pursue medical degrees. **Faculty:** Student/faculty ratio 14:1. 131 full-time faculty, 85% hold PhDs, 10% are members of minority groups, 53% are women.

ACADEMICS
Degrees: Bachelor's, master's. **Classes:** Most classes have 20–29 students. **Majors with Highest Enrollment:** Business administration and management; elementary education and teaching; nursing/registered nurse (RN, ASN, BSN, MSN). **Special Study Options:** Accelerated program, double major, dual enrollment, honors program, independent study, internships, liberal arts/career combination, student-designed major, study abroad, teacher certification program. **Honors programs:** The Elmhurst College Honors program provides a challenging set of educational experiences for the most academically students

featuring small, stimulating seminar courses where class discussions are lively and engaging; opportunities to conduct and present professional-level research; private receptions with distinguished guest speakers; trips to theatre and dance performances, social events, and more. **Combined degree programs:** BA/MEng. Special programs offered to physically disabled students include note-taking services, reader services, tape recorders, tutors. **Career services:** Alumni network, career/job search classes, career assessment, internships **Career services highlights include:** Elmhurst College's Center for Professional Excellence provides a comprehensive suite of services to link students' academic expereinces with opportunities to explore career options and to prepare for future careers.

FACILITIES

Housing: Coed dorms, apartments for single students. 95% of campus accessible to physically disabled. **Special Academic Facilities/Equipment:** Accelerator/art space, language lab, recording studio, computer science/technology center, four electron microscopes. **Computers:** Students can register for classes online. Administrative functions (other than registration) can be performed online.

CAMPUS LIFE

Environment: Town. **Activities:** Choral groups, concert band, dance, drama/theater, jazz band, literary magazine, music ensembles, musical theater, radio station, student government, student newspaper, symphony orchestra, yearbook, campus ministries, international student organization, Model UN. **Organizations:** 106 registered organizations, 15 honor societies, 6 religious organizations. 3 fraternities, 6 sororities. **Athletics (Intercollegiate):** *Men:* Baseball, basketball, cross-country, football, golf, soccer, tennis, track/field (outdoor), wrestling. *Women:* Basketball, bowling, cross-country, golf, soccer, softball, tennis, track/field (outdoor), volleyball. **On-Campus Highlights:** Alumni Circle, Frick Center, Library, Tyrrell Fitness Center, Circle Hall.

ADMISSIONS

Freshman Academic Profile: Average high school GPA 3.4. 23% in top 10% of high school class, 52% in top 25% of high school class, 86% in top 50% of high school class. 92% from public high schools. SAT Math middle 50% range 490–590. SAT Critical Reading middle 50% range 490–630. SAT Writing middle 50% range 490–590. ACT middle 50% range 21–26. Minimum paper TOEFL 550. Minimum computer TOEFL 213. **Basis for Candidate Selection:** *Very important factors considered include:* Class rank, academic GPA, rigor of secondary school record, standardized test scores. *Important factors considered include:* Application essay, recommendation(s), interview. *Other factors considered include:* Alumni/ae relation, character/personal qualities, extracurricular activities, talent/ability. **Freshman Admission Requirements:** High school diploma is required and GED is accepted. *Academic units required:* 4 English, 2 mathematics, 2 science, (2 science labs), 0 foreign language, 2 social studies, 1 history, 4 academic electives. *Academic units recommended:* 4 English, 3 mathematics, 3 science, (3 science labs), 1 foreign language, 3 social studies, 2 history, 4 academic electives. **Freshman Admission Statistics:** 2,773 applied, 69% admitted, 30% enrolled. **Transfer Admission Requirements:** High school transcript, college transcript(s), statement of good standing from prior institution(s). Minimum college GPA of 2.6 required. Lowest grade transferable C. **General Admission Information:** Regular application deadline 7/15. Notification on a rolling basis, beginning on or about 11/1. Nonfall registration accepted. Admission may be deferred for a maximum of 2 years. Credit offered for CEEB Advanced Placement tests.

COSTS AND FINANCIAL AID

Annual tuition $27,270. Room and board $7,874. Required fees $60. Average book expense $1,000. **Required Forms and Deadlines:** FAFSA. Priority financial aid filing date 4/15. **Notification of Awards:** Applicants will be notified of awards on a rolling basis beginning 2/21. **Types of Aid:** *Need-based scholarships/grants:* Federal Pell, SEOG, state scholarships/grants, private scholarships, the school's own gift aid. *Loans:* Direct Subsidized Stafford, Direct Unsubsidized Stafford, Direct PLUS, Federal Perkins, Private alternative student loans. **Student Employment:** Federal Work-Study Program available. Institutional employment available. Highest amount earned per year from on-campus jobs $3,000. Off-campus job opportunities are excellent. **Financial Aid Statistics:** 65% freshmen, 69% undergrads receive need-based scholarship or grant aid. 26% freshmen, 8% undergrads receive non-need-based scholarship or grant aid. 62% freshmen, 52% undergrads receive need-based self-help aid. 95% freshmen, 87% undergrads receive any aid. 69% undergrads borrow to pay for school. Average cumulative indebtedness $20,675. **Criteria for awarding institutional aid:** *Non-need-based:* Academics, alumni affiliation, art, minority status, music/drama, religious affiliation, state/district residency.

See page 1080.

ELMIRA COLLEGE

One Park Place, Elmira, NY 14901
Phone: 607-735-1724
E-mail: admissions@elmira.edu **CEEB Code:** 2226
Fax: 607-735-1718 **Website:** www.elmira.edu **ACT Code:** 2736

This private school was founded in 1855. It has a 50-acre campus.

RATINGS

Admissions Selectivity Rating: 84   **Fire Safety Rating:** 60*   **Green Rating:** 60*

STUDENTS AND FACULTY

Enrollment: 1,363. **Student Body:** 71% female, 29% male, 51% out-of-state, 5% international (20 countries represented). Asian 1%, African American 1%, Caucasian 67%, Hispanic 1%.
Retention and Graduation: 84% freshmen return for sophomore year. 55% freshmen graduate within 4 years. 47% grads go on to further study within 1 year. 35% grads pursue arts and sciences degrees. 2% grads pursue law degrees. 9% grads pursue business degrees. 1% grads pursue medical degrees. **Faculty:** Student/faculty ratio 12:1. 81 full-time faculty, 63% hold PhDs, 4% are members of minority groups, 44% are women.

ACADEMICS

Degrees: Bachelor's, master's. **Classes:** Most classes have 10–19 students. Most lab/discussion sessions have 10–19 students. **Majors with Highest Enrollment:** Business/commerce; elementary education and teaching; psychology. **Special Study Options:** Accelerated program, double major, English as a Second Language (ESL), exchange student program (domestic), independent study, internships, liberal arts/career combination, student-designed major, study abroad, teacher certification program. **Combined degree programs:** 3-2 Chemical Engineering with Clarkson University.

FACILITIES

Housing: Coed dorms, special housing for disabled students, women's dorms, apartments for single students. 25% of campus accessible to physically disabled. **Special Academic Facilities/Equipment:** Center for Mark Twain studies, American studies center.

CAMPUS LIFE

Environment: Town. **Activities:** Choral groups, concert band, dance, drama/theater, literary magazine, music ensembles, musical theater, pep band, radio station, student government, student newspaper, yearbook. **Organizations:** 85 registered organizations, 13 honor societies, 3 religious organizations. **Athletics (Intercollegiate):** *Men:* Basketball, cheerleading, golf, ice hockey, lacrosse, soccer, tennis. *Women:* Basketball, cheerleading, field hockey, golf, ice hockey, lacrosse, soccer, softball, tennis, volleyball. **On-Campus Highlights:** Emerson Hall, Mark Twain Study, Towers, Campus Center, The Puddle.

ADMISSIONS

Freshman Academic Profile: Average high school GPA 3.4. 30% in top 10% of high school class, 65% in top 25% of high school class, 98% in top 50% of high school class. 65% from public high schools. SAT Math middle 50% range 480–590. SAT Critical Reading middle 50% range 480–600. ACT middle 50% range 19–26. Minimum paper TOEFL 500. Minimum computer TOEFL 173. **Basis for Candidate Selection:** *Very important factors considered include:* Class rank, academic GPA, rigor of secondary school record, character/personal qualities. *Important factors considered include:* Application essay, recommendation(s), standardized test scores, extracurricular activities. *Other factors considered include:* Alumni/ae relation, first generation, geographical residence, interview, level of applicant's interest, racial/ethnic status, talent/ability, volunteer work, work experience. **Freshman Admission Requirements:** High school diploma is required and GED is accepted. *Academic units required:* 4 English, 3 mathematics, 3 science, (2 science labs), 3 social studies, 1 history, 2 academic electives. *Academic units recommended:* 2 foreign language. **Freshman Admission Statistics:** 2,118 applied, 68% admitted, 25% enrolled. **Transfer Admission Requirements:** College transcript(s), essay or personal statement, statement of good standing from prior institution(s). Minimum college GPA of 2.0 required. Lowest grade transferable C–. **General Admission Information:** Application fee $50. Early decision application deadline 11/15. Regular application deadline 3/1. Notification on a rolling basis, beginning on or about 10/15. Nonfall registration accepted. Admission may be deferred for a maximum of 1 year. Credit and/or placement offered for CEEB Advanced Placement tests.

COSTS AND FINANCIAL AID

Annual tuition $29,000. Room and board $9,100. Required fees $1,050. Average book expense $450. **Required Forms and Deadlines:** FAFSA, state aid form if applicable (NY, VT, RI). Financial aid filing deadline 6/30. Priority financial aid filing date 2/1. **Notification of Awards:** Applicants will be notified of awards on a rolling basis beginning 2/1. **Types of Aid:** *Need-based scholarships/grants:* Federal Pell, SEOG, state scholarships/grants, private scholarships, the school's own gift aid. *Loans:* FFEL Subsidized Stafford, FFEL Unsubsidized Stafford, FFEL PLUS, Federal Perkins, college/university loans from institutional funds, GATE Student Loan; Private Alternative Loans. **Student Employment:** Federal Work-Study Program available. Institutional employment available. Highest amount earned per year from on-campus jobs $1,000. Off-campus job opportunities are good. **Financial Aid Statistics:** 82% freshmen, 78% undergrads receive need-based scholarship or grant aid. 10% freshmen, 9% undergrads receive non-need-based scholarship or grant aid. 69% freshmen, 65% undergrads receive need-based self-help aid. 80% freshmen, 80% undergrads receive any aid. 69% undergrads borrow to pay for school. Average cumulative indebtedness $25,347. **Criteria for awarding institutional aid:** *Non-need-based:* Academics, leadership.

See page 1082.

ELON UNIVERSITY

100 Campus Drive, 2700 Campus Box, Elon, NC 27244-2010
Phone: 336-278-3566 **Financial Aid Phone:** 336-278-7640
E-mail: admissions@elon.edu **CEEB Code:** 5183
Fax: 336-278-7699 **Website:** www.elon.edu **ACT Code:** 3096

This private school, affiliated with the United Church of Christ Church, was founded in 1889. It has a 575-acre campus.

RATINGS
Admissions Selectivity Rating: 92   **Fire Safety Rating:** 80   **Green Rating:** 88

STUDENTS AND FACULTY
Enrollment: 4,995. **Student Body:** 59% female, 41% male, 72% out-of-state, 2% international (49 countries represented). Asian 1%, African American 6%, Caucasian 81%, Hispanic 2%.
Retention and Graduation: 71% freshmen graduate within 4 years. 20% grads go on to further study within 1 year. 15% grads pursue arts and sciences degrees. 4% grads pursue law degrees. 2% grads pursue business degrees. 2% grads pursue medical degrees. **Faculty:** Student/faculty ratio 13.4:1. 343 full-time faculty, 87% hold PhDs, 9% are members of minority groups, 45% are women.

ACADEMICS
Degrees: Bachelor's, master's. **Classes:** Most classes have 10–19 students. Most lab/discussion sessions have 10–19 students. **Majors with Highest Enrollment:** Business/commerce; communication studies/speech communication and rhetoric; education. **Special Study Options:** Accelerated program, cross-registration, distance learning, double major, dual enrollment, English as a Second Language (ESL), exchange student program (domestic), honors program, independent study, internships, liberal arts/career combination, student-designed major, study abroad, teacher certification program **Honors programs:** Forty freshmen are selected for the Honors Fellows program, which has benefits of specialized courses, $2,500–$10,000 scholarship renewable annually based on academic performance and participation in the program, $1,000 study abroad, development and presentation of their honors thesis, and housing options such as a living-learning community for Fellows. **Combined degree programs:** BS/BS (3-2) Engineering. Special programs offered to physically disabled students include note-taking services, reader services, tape recorders, tutors. **Career services:** Alumni network, alumni services, career/job search classes, career assessment, internships, regional alumni. **Career services highlights include:** All students are required to particpate in an experiential learning experience and most Elon students particpate in internship/coop.

FACILITIES
Housing: Coed dorms, men's dorms, special housing for international students, women's dorms, fraternity/sorority housing, apartments for single students, wellness housing, theme housing. 80% of campus accessible to physically disabled. **Special Academic Facilities/Equipment:** Resource center, fine arts center with recital hall, theatre, television studios, music rooms, campus center, athletic center, art gallery. **Computers:** 100% of classrooms, 100% of dorms, 100% of libraries, 100% of dining areas, 100% of student union, 25% of common outdoor areas have wireless network access. Students can register for classes online. Administrative functions (other than registration) can be performed online.

CAMPUS LIFE
Environment: Town. **Activities:** Choral groups, concert band, dance, drama/theater, jazz band, literary magazine, marching band, music ensembles, musical theater, pep band, radio station, student government, student newspaper, student-run film society, symphony orchestra, television station, yearbook, campus ministries, international student organization, Model UN. **Organizations:** 150 registered organizations, 27 honor societies, 10 religious organizations. 11 fraternities, 12 sororities. **Athletics (Intercollegiate):** *Men:* Baseball, basketball, cheerleading, cross-country, football, golf, soccer, tennis. *Women:* Basketball, cheerleading, cross-country, golf, soccer, softball, tennis, track/field (outdoor), track/field (indoor), volleyball. **On-Campus Highlights:** Belk Library, Rhodes Football Stadium, Koury Business Center, Moseley Student Center, Koury Athletic Center, Lindner Hall, Academic Village. **Environmental Initiatives:** Reducing greenhouse gas emissions; conserving resources; educating the community.

ADMISSIONS
Freshman Academic Profile: Average high school GPA 3.97. 32% in top 10% of high school class, 70% in top 25% of high school class, 92% in top 50% of high school class. 67% from public high schools. SAT Math middle 50% range 570–660. SAT Critical Reading middle 50% range 570–660. SAT Writing middle 50% range 570–670. ACT middle 50% range 25–29. Minimum paper TOEFL 550. Minimum computer TOEFL 213. Minimum web-based TOEFL 79. **Basis for Candidate Selection:** *Very important factors considered include:* Academic GPA, rigor of secondary school record, standardized test scores. *Important factors considered include:* Application essay, recommendation(s), alumni/ae relation, extracurricular activities, talent/ability, volunteer work, work experience. *Other factors considered include:* Class rank, character/personal qualities, first generation, geographical residence, level of applicant's interest, racial/ethnic status, state residency. **Freshman Admission Requirements:** High school diploma is required and GED is accepted. *Academic units required:* 4 English, 3 mathematics, 3 science, (1 science labs), 2 foreign language, 1 social studies, 2 history. *Academic units recommended:* 4 English, 4 mathematics, 3 science, (1 science labs), 3 foreign language, 1 social studies, 2 history. **Freshman Admission Statistics:** 9,041 applied, 48% admitted, 30% enrolled. **Transfer Admission Requirements:** High school transcript, college transcript(s), standardized test scores, statement of good standing from prior institution(s). Minimum college GPA of 2.7 required. Lowest grade transferable C–. **General Admission Information:** Application fee $50. Early decision application deadline 11/1. Regular application deadline 1/10. Regular notification 3/15. Nonfall registration not accepted. Admission may be deferred for a maximum of 1 year. Credit and/or placement offered for CEEB Advanced Placement tests.

COSTS AND FINANCIAL AID
Annual tuition $25,159. Room and board $8,236. Required fees $330. Average book expense $900. **Required Forms and Deadlines:** FAFSA, institution's own financial aid form, CSS/Financial Aid PROFILE. Priority financial aid filing date 2/15. **Notification of Awards:** Applicants will be notified of awards on a rolling basis beginning 3/30. **Types of Aid:** *Need-based scholarships/grants:* Federal Pell, SEOG, state scholarships/grants, private scholarships, the school's own gift aid. *Loans:* FFEL Subsidized Stafford, FFEL Unsubsidized Stafford, FFEL PLUS, Federal Perkins, state loans, privately funded alternative loans. **Student Employment:** Federal Work-Study Program available. Institutional employment available. Highest amount earned per year from on-campus jobs $2,500. Off-campus job opportunities are good. **Financial Aid Statistics:** 32% freshmen, 31% undergrads receive need-based scholarship or grant aid. 5% freshmen, 3% undergrads receive non-need-based scholarship or grant aid. 28% freshmen, 28% undergrads receive need-based self-help aid. 5% freshmen, 6% undergrads receive athletic scholarships. 77% freshmen, 73% undergrads receive any aid. 45% undergrads borrow to pay for school. Average cumulative indebtedness $22,939. **Criteria for awarding institutional aid:** *Non-need-based:* Academics, art, athletics, leadership, music/drama, state/district residency.

EMBRY RIDDLE AERONAUTICAL UNIVERSITY (FL)

600 South Clyde Morris Boulevard, Daytona Beach, FL 32114-3900
Phone: 386-226-6100 **Financial Aid Phone:** 800-226-6307
E-mail: dbadmit@erau.edu **CEEB Code:** 5190
Fax: 386-226-7070 **Website:** www.embryriddle.edu **ACT Code:** 725

This private school was founded in 1926. It has a 185-acre campus.

RATINGS
Admissions Selectivity Rating: 79   **Fire Safety Rating:** 60*   **Green Rating:** 60*

STUDENTS AND FACULTY

Enrollment: 4,430. **Student Body:** 17% female, 83% male, 69% out-of-state, 13% international (96 countries represented). Asian 6%, African American 6%, Caucasian 58%, Hispanic 8%.
Retention and Graduation: 71% freshmen return for sophomore year. 29% freshmen graduate within 4 years. **Faculty:** Student/faculty ratio 17:1. 240 full-time faculty, 66% hold PhDs, 14% are members of minority groups, 18% are women.

ACADEMICS

Degrees: Associate, bachelor's, master's. **Classes:** Most classes have 20–29 students. Most lab/discussion sessions have 10–19 students. **Majors with Highest Enrollment:** Aeronautics/aviation/aerospace science and technology; aerospace, aeronautical and astronautical engineering; airline/commercial/professional pilot and flight crew. **Special Study Options:** Accelerated program, cooperative education program, distance learning, double major, dual enrollment, English as a Second Language (ESL), honors program, independent study, internships, student-designed major, study abroad. **Honors programs:** The Embry-Riddle Honors Program is highly selective, offering its student members enriched educational experiences. Emphasizing Honors course work in General Education and in the majors, the Program involves selected faculty who develop innovative courses and establish mentoring relationships with students. The Program is designed to attract and retain top students and to develop their communicative, analytical, critical, and research skills, nurturing a love of life-long learning, leadership, and service. Special programs offered to physically disabled students include reader services, tape recorders, tutors. **Career services:** Alumni network, alumni services, career/job search classes, career assessment, internships, regional alumni. **Career services highlights include:** Cooperative Education/Internship Program: The Co-op/Internship program provides students with practical experience which reinforces the theoretical concepts learned in the classroom. The Co-op/Internship program aids in bridging the gap between student life and the world of work. This program combines students' academic and career interests with work experience in business, industry, government, or service organizations. Key elements of the Co-op/Internship program experience are: Professional level work assignments in areas related to the student's academic major. Supervision and evaluation of performance by professionals in a chosen career field. Completion of learning objectives designed to relate academic studies to the work world.

FACILITIES

Housing: Coed dorms, apartments for married students, apartments for single students. 80% of campus accessible to physically disabled. **Special Academic Facilities/Equipment:** Fully equipped aircraft, training simulators, airway science simulation lab, wind tunnel. **Computers:** 100% of classrooms, 100% of dorms, 100% of libraries, 100% of dining areas, 100% of student union, 15% of common outdoor areas have wireless network access. Students can register for classes online. Administrative functions (other than registration) can be performed online.

CAMPUS LIFE

Environment: Town. **Activities:** Choral groups, dance, drama/theater, music ensembles, pep band, radio station, student government, student newspaper, yearbook, campus ministries, international student organization, Model UN. **Organizations:** 140 registered organizations, 12 honor societies, 5 religious organizations. 12 fraternities, 4 sororities. **Athletics (Intercollegiate):** *Men:* Baseball, basketball, cheerleading, cross-country, golf, soccer, softball, tennis, track/field (outdoor), volleyball. *Women:* Basketball, cheerleading, cross-country, golf, soccer, softball, tennis, track/field (outdoor), volleyball. **On-Campus Highlights:** Lehman Engineering and Technology Center, College of Aviation, Simulator Building, ICI Center (fieldhouse), The Green Garage—EcoCAR Challenge, The College of Aviation tour is a brief look at the Air Traffic Management Laboratory and its Pseudo-Pilots' Lab, the Aircraft Performance Lab, the Computer Flight Simulation Lab, the College of Aviation Student Success Center (Tutor Lab), and the Flight Tutor Lab. The COA building also contains a Weather Center and two Meteorology Labs, Basic and Advanced. **Environmental Initiatives:** Embry-Riddle Opens 'Green Garage' Doors: EcoCAR Project Advances University's Environmental Commitment Daytona Beach, Fla, Dec. 10, 2009—Embry-Riddle Aeronautical University has opened the doors of a new "green garage," where engineering students are using aerospace techniques to develop the car of tomorrow. The garage includes a rotary vehicle lift, dedicated high-voltage room, and integrated hardware-in-the-loop laboratory donated by National Instruments. It also showcases an environmental focus at Embry-Riddle's College of Engineering. Every component in the lab was chosen to reduce environmental impact, including the floor covering, which is made from recycled tires. Interior design students from Daytona State College assisted in designing the new facility. http://givingto.erau.edu/givingnews/09releases/ecocar.html The Green Flight Challenge is a competition that is sponsored by NASA and run by the CAFE Foundation, and involves helping General Aviation move toward a "greener" way of travel. The main requirements state that a new or modified aircraft must travel 200

miles while averaging 100 mph and obtaining at least 200 passenger-mpg. Embry Riddle was accepted into the competition several weeks ago as one of the 18 teams which will compete for the $1.5 million prize in July of 2011. The following was submitted to the CAFE Foundation in the Design Proposal that was accepted: "While winning the competition is the current goal, it is neither the primary objective nor the long term goal for participating in the Green Flight Challenge. The environment is an extremely important consideration that has been disregarded in the aviation industry for years. Embry Riddle Aeronautical University specializes in all aspects of the aviation industry and would like to put forth what knowledge and resources are available to the school in order to further the 'green' movement. This competition would not be the first environmentally friendly project to have been undertaken at the University, but unlike the others it would not stop with the completion of the competition. While it is most unlikely that the short time span of the competition will allow for the discovery of the most efficient and green aircraft propulsion system, the competition will pinpoint the direction in which Embry Riddle should head. The University hopes to use what knowledge it gathers from this competition to continue research into healthier, more 'green' technologies. This competition is a stepping stone to a smarter, more environmentally friendly way to travel, one that hopefully will lead to reductions in all aircraft's carbon flight plans."

ADMISSIONS

Freshman Academic Profile: Average high school GPA 3.26. 21% in top 10% of high school class, 48% in top 25% of high school class, 79% in top 50% of high school class. SAT Math middle 50% range 490–620. SAT Critical Reading middle 50% range 450–580. ACT middle 50% range 21-27. Minimum paper TOEFL 550. Minimum computer TOEFL 213. Minimum web-based TOEFL 79. **Basis for Candidate Selection:** *Very important factors considered include:* Class rank, academic GPA, recommendation(s), standardized test scores. *Other factors considered include:* Application essay, rigor of secondary school record, alumni/ae relation, character/personal qualities, extracurricular activities, interview, level of applicant's interest, volunteer work, work experience. **Freshman Admission Requirements:** High school diploma is required and GED is accepted. *Academic units required:* 4 English, 3 mathematics, 2 science, (2 science labs), 0 foreign language, 2 social studies, 1 history, 3 academic electives. *Academic units recommended:* 4 English, 4 mathematics, 3 science, (2 science labs), 1 foreign language, 2 social studies, 2 history, 3 academic electives. **Freshman Admission Statistics:** 3,524 applied, 80% admitted, 38% enrolled. **Transfer Admission Requirements:** College transcript(s), minimum college GPA of 2.0 required. Lowest grade transferable C. **General Admission Information:** Application fee $50. Notification on a rolling basis, beginning on or about 11/1. Nonfall registration accepted. Admission may be deferred for a maximum of 1 year. Credit and/or placement offered for CEEB Advanced Placement tests.

COSTS AND FINANCIAL AID

Annual tuition $26,950. Room and board $9,964. Required fees $1,164.
Required Forms and Deadlines: FAFSA. Priority financial aid filing date 3/1. **Types of Aid:** *Need-based scholarships/grants:* Federal Pell, SEOG, state scholarships/grants, private scholarships, the school's own gift aid. *Loans:* Direct Subsidized Stafford, Direct Unsubsidized Stafford, Direct PLUS, FFEL Subsidized Stafford. **Student Employment:** Federal Work-Study Program available. Institutional employment available. Off-campus job opportunities are good. **Financial Aid Statistics:** 70% freshmen, 57% undergrads receive need-based scholarship or grant aid. 57% freshmen, 49% undergrads receive need-based self-help aid. 3% freshmen, 3% undergrads receive athletic scholarships. 70% freshmen, 59% undergrads receive any aid. 68% undergrads borrow to pay for school. **Criteria for awarding institutional aid:** *Non-need-based:* Academics, alumni affiliation, athletics, leadership

EMBRY RIDDLE AERONAUTICAL UNIVERSITY—PRESCOTT

3700 Willow Creek, Prescott, AZ 86301
Phone: 928-777-6600 **Financial Aid Phone:** 800-888-3728
E-mail: pradmit@erau.edu **CEEB Code:** 4305
Fax: 928-777-6606 **Website:** www.embryriddle.edu **ACT Code:** 725

This private school was founded in 1926. It has a 539-acre campus.

RATINGS

Admissions Selectivity Rating: 82   **Fire Safety Rating:** 60*   **Green Rating:** 60*

STUDENTS AND FACULTY

Enrollment: 1,672. **Student Body:** 18% female, 82% male, 79% out-of-state, 4% international (26 countries represented). Asian 7%, African American 2%,

Caucasian 67%, Hispanic 8%, Native American 1%.
Retention and Graduation: 79% freshmen return for sophomore year. 31% freshmen graduate within 4 years. **Faculty:** Student/faculty ratio 15:1. 98 full-time faculty, 70% hold PhDs, 8% are members of minority groups, 18% are women.

ACADEMICS

Degrees: Bachelor's, master's. **Classes:** Most classes have 10–19 students. Most lab/discussion sessions have 10–19 students. **Majors with Highest Enrollment:** Aeronautics/aviation/aerospace science and technology; aerospace, aeronautical and astronautical engineering; airline/commercial/professional pilot and flight crew. **Special Study Options:** Accelerated program, cooperative education program, distance learning, double major, dual enrollment, English as a Second Language (ESL), exchange student program (domestic), honors program, independent study, internships, Flight Training. Special programs offered to physically disabled students include note-taking services, reader services, tape recorders, tutors. **Career services:** Alumni network, alumni services, career/job search classes, career assessment, internships, regional alumni.

FACILITIES

Housing: Coed dorms, apartments for single students 50% of campus accessible to physically disabled. **Computers:** 100% of classrooms, 100% of dorms, 100% of libraries, 100% of dining areas, 100% of student union, 80% of common outdoor areas have wireless network access. Administrative functions (other than registration) can be performed online.

CAMPUS LIFE

Environment: Town. **Activities:** Dance, literary magazine, music ensembles, radio station, student government, student newspaper **Organizations:** 85 registered organizations, 5 honor societies, 2 religious organizations. 5 fraternities, 3 sororities. **Athletics (Intercollegiate):** *Men:* wrestling. **On-Campus Highlights:** Flight Line Facilities, Wind Tunnel Labs, Outdoor Pool and Racquetball, Tennis Area, The Hangar—Cafeteria, Two athletic facilities and weight room, Embry-Riddle Prescott is culturally diverse with students representing 49 states and 24 countries for a combined total of approximately 1700 students. Embry-Riddle Prescott is home to the Golden Eagles Flight Team, a nationally ranked flight team. In the last 22 years, the Golden Eagles are undefeated at the regional level, and the National Championship has been secured six times.

ADMISSIONS

Freshman Academic Profile: Average high school GPA 3.45. 25% in top 10% of high school class, 52% in top 25% of high school class, 82% in top 50% of high school class. SAT Math middle 50% range 500–640. SAT Critical Reading middle 50% range 470–600. ACT middle 50% range 22-28. Minimum paper TOEFL 550. Minimum computer TOEFL 213. Minimum web-based TOEFL 79. **Basis for Candidate Selection:** *Very important factors considered include:* Class rank, academic GPA, standardized test scores. *Important factors considered include:* Recommendation(s). *Other factors considered include:* Application essay, rigor of secondary school record, alumni/ae relation, character/personal qualities, extracurricular activities, interview, level of applicant's interest, volunteer work, work experience. **Freshman Admission Requirements:** High school diploma is required and GED is accepted. *Academic units required:* 4 English, 3 mathematics, 2 science, (2 science labs), 0 foreign language, 2 social studies, 1 history, 4 academic electives. *Academic units recommended:* 4 English, 4 mathematics, 3 science, (3 science labs), 2 foreign language, 2 social studies, 1 history, 2 academic electives. **Freshman Admission Statistics:** 1,148 applied, 86% admitted, 42% enrolled. **Transfer Admission Requirements:** College transcript(s), minimum college GPA of 2.00 required. Lowest grade transferable C. **General Admission Information:** Application fee $50. Notification on a rolling basis, beginning on or about 11/1. Nonfall registration accepted. Admission may be deferred for a maximum of 1 year. Credit and/or placement offered for CEEB Advanced Placement tests.

COSTS AND FINANCIAL AID

Annual tuition $26,950. Room and board $8,008. Required fees $800. **Required Forms and Deadlines:** FAFSA. **Types of Aid:** *Need-based scholarships/grants:* Federal Pell, SEOG, state scholarships/grants, private scholarships, the school's own gift aid. *Loans:* FFEL Subsidized Stafford, FFEL Unsubsidized Stafford, FFEL PLUS, Federal Perkins. **Student Employment:** Federal Work-Study Program available. Institutional employment available. Off-campus job opportunities are good. **Financial Aid Statistics:** 70% freshmen, 63% undergrads receive need-based scholarship or grant aid. 54% freshmen, 53% undergrads receive need-based self-help aid. 4% freshmen, 4% undergrads receive athletic scholarships. 77% freshmen, 65% undergrads receive any aid. 75% undergrads borrow to pay for school. **Criteria for awarding institutional aid:** *Non-need-based:* Academics, alumni affiliation, athletics, leadership.

EMERSON COLLEGE

120 Boylston Street, Boston, MA 02116-4624
Phone: 617-824-8600 **Financial Aid Phone:** 617-824-8655
E-mail: admission@emerson.edu **CEEB Code:** 3367
Fax: 617-824-8609 **Website:** www.emerson.edu **ACT Code:** 1820

This private school was founded in 1880. It has a 10-acre campus.

RATINGS
Admissions Selectivity Rating: 94   **Fire Safety Rating:** 71   **Green Rating:** 73

STUDENTS AND FACULTY
Enrollment: 3,454. **Student Body:** 59% female, 41% male, 75% out-of-state, 3% international (48 countries represented). Asian 5%, African American 3%, Caucasian 62%, Hispanic 8%.
Retention and Graduation: 88% freshmen return for sophomore year. 74% freshmen graduate within 4 years. 12% grads go on to further study within 1 year. **Faculty:** Student/faculty ratio 13:1. 177 full-time faculty, 71% hold PhDs, 18% are members of minority groups, 44% are women. 3% of classes are taught by teaching assistants.

ACADEMICS
Degrees: Bachelor's, certificate, master's. **Classes:** Most classes have 10–19 students. Most lab/discussion sessions have 10–19 students. **Majors with Highest Enrollment:** Cinematography and film/video production; creative writing; theatre/theater. **Special Study Options:** Cross-registration, double major, honors program, independent study, internships, liberal arts/career combination, student-designed major, study abroad, teacher certification program. **Combined degree programs:** BS/MSSp in Communication Disorders. Special programs offered to physically disabled students include note-taking services, reader services, tape recorders, tutors. **Career services:** Alumni network, alumni services, career/job search classes, career assessment, internships, regional alumni.

FACILITIES
Housing: Coed dorms, Optional Learning Communities, such as the Writers' Block, Film Immersion Community, and Digital Culture Floor. 80% of campus accessible to physically disabled. **Special Academic Facilities/Equipment:** Emerson is home to the historic 1,200–seat Cutler Majestic Theatre and WERS-FM, Boston's oldest noncommercial broadcaster. The College has an 11-story performance and production center, housing rehearsal space, a costume shop, makeup lab, theatre design/tech center, and sound-treated TV studios. There are also digital and audio post-production labs, recording studios, a film equipment distribution center, seven clinics/programs to observe speech and hearing therapy, an integrated digital newsroom, and marketing research suite. A new 14-story campus center and residence hall houses a gymnasium and space for student organizations. Current campus construction projects include new student residences in the renovated Colonial Building and a sound stage, scene shop, black box, and cinema in the refurbished Paramount Theatre complex. **Computers:** 100% of classrooms, 100% of dorms, 100% of libraries, 100% of dining areas, 100% of student union, 100% of common outdoor areas have wireless network access. Students can register for classes online. Administrative functions (other than registration) can be performed online.

CAMPUS LIFE
Environment: Metropolis. **Activities:** Choral groups, dance, drama/theater, literary magazine, music ensembles, musical theater, radio station, student government, student newspaper, student-run film society, television station, yearbook, campus ministries, international student organization. **Organizations:** 60 registered organizations, 4 honor societies, 4 religious organizations. 4 fraternities, 3 sororities. **Athletics (Intercollegiate):** *Men:* Baseball, basketball, cross-country, golf, lacrosse, soccer, tennis, track/field (indoor), volleyball. *Women:* Basketball, cross-country, golf, lacrosse, soccer, softball, tennis, track/field (indoor), volleyball. **On-Campus Highlights:** WERS-FM (Boston's oldest public radio), Historic Cutler Majestic Theatre, Tufte Performance and Production Center, Journalism's Integrated Digital Newsroom, Piano Row Residence Hall/College Center, Emerson is currently remodeling the Colonial Building into student residences and renovating the Paramount Theater complex to house a sound stage, scene shop, rehearsal space, and a student residence. **Environmental Initiatives:** LEED-certified residence hall (one of only two in the city of Boston), campus center, and gymnasium. Alternative energy sources. Major recycling programs

ADMISSIONS

Freshman Academic Profile: Average high school GPA 3.59. 42.4% in top 10% of high school class, 76.6% in top 25% of high school class, 98% in top 50% of high school class. 70% from public high schools. SAT Math middle 50% range 540–640. SAT Critical Reading middle 50% range 570–670. SAT Writing middle 50% range 580–670. ACT middle 50% range 24–29. Minimum paper TOEFL 550. Minimum computer TOEFL 213. Minimum web-based TOEFL 80. **Basis for Candidate Selection:** *Very important factors considered include:* Academic GPA, standardized test scores. *Important factors considered include:* Class rank, application essay, recommendation(s), rigor of secondary school record, character/personal qualities, extracurricular activities, talent/ability. *Other factors considered include:* Alumni/ae relation, first generation, geographical residence, racial/ethnic status, volunteer work, work experience. **Freshman Admission Requirements:** High school diploma is required and GED is accepted. *Academic units required:* 4 English, 3 mathematics, 3 science, 3 foreign language, 3 social studies. *Academic units recommended:* 4 English, 3 mathematics, 3 science, 3 foreign language, 3 social studies, 4 academic electives. **Freshman Admission Statistics:** 6,943 applied, 42% admitted, 26% enrolled. **Transfer Admission Requirements:** High school transcript, college transcript(s), essay or personal statement, statement of good standing from prior institution(s). Minimum college GPA of 3.0 required. Lowest grade transferable C. **General Admission Information:** Application fee $65. Regular application deadline 1/5. Regular notification 4/1. Nonfall registration accepted. Admission may be deferred for a maximum of 1 year. Credit and/or placement offered for CEEB Advanced Placement tests.

COSTS AND FINANCIAL AID

Annual tuition $29,408. Room and board $12,280. Required fees $532. Average book expense $800. **Required Forms and Deadlines:** FAFSA, CSS/Financial Aid PROFILE, noncustodial PROFILE, business/farm supplement, Tax Returns. Priority financial aid filing date 3/1. **Notification of Awards:** Applicants will be notified of awards on or about 4/1. **Types of Aid:** *Need-based scholarships/grants:* Federal Pell, SEOG, state scholarships/grants, private scholarships, the school's own gift aid. *Loans:* FFEL Subsidized Stafford, FFEL Unsubsidized Stafford, FFEL PLUS, Federal Perkins, state loans. **Student Employment:** Federal Work-Study Program available. Institutional employment available. Highest amount earned per year from on-campus jobs $2,400. Off-campus job opportunities are excellent. **Financial Aid Statistics:** 53% freshmen, 43% undergrads receive need-based scholarship or grant aid. 3% freshmen, 1% undergrads receive non-need-based scholarship or grant aid. 53% freshmen, 52% undergrads receive need-based self-help aid. 85.3% freshmen, 70.6% undergrads receive any aid. 59% undergrads borrow to pay for school. Average cumulative indebtedness $15,262. **Criteria for awarding institutional aid:** *Non-need-based:* Academics, leadership, music/drama, state/district residency.

EMILY CARR UNIVERSITY OF ART & DESIGN

1399 Johnston Street, Granville Island, Vancouver, BC V6H 3R9 Canada
Phone: 604-844-3897
E-mail: admissions@ecuad.ca
Fax: 604-844-3089 **Website:** www.ecuad.ca

This public school was founded in 1925. It has a 80-acre campus.

RATINGS

Admissions Selectivity Rating: 79   **Fire Safety Rating:** 60*   **Green Rating:** 60*

STUDENTS AND FACULTY

Student Body: 32% out-of-state..
Retention and Graduation: 85% freshmen return for sophomore year. 20% grads go on to further study within 1 year. 15% grads pursue arts and sciences degrees.

ACADEMICS

Degrees: Bachelor's, master's. **Special Study Options:** Cooperative education program, cross-registration, distance learning, exchange student program (domestic), external degree program, independent study, internships, liberal arts/career combination, student-designed major, study abroad. Special programs offered to physically disabled students include note-taking services, reader services, tape recorders, tutors. **Career services:** Alumni network, alumni services, career/job search classes, career assessment, internships, regional alumni.

FACILITIES

Housing: Off campus housing assistance. 85% of campus accessible to physically disabled. **Special Academic Facilities/Equipment:** Two galleries, aCentre for Art and Technolog.

CAMPUS LIFE

Activities: Student government, student newspaper, yearbook. **Organizations:** 12 registered organizations.

ADMISSIONS

Freshman Academic Profile: 35% from public high schools. Minimum paper TOEFL 570. Minimum computer TOEFL 230. **Basis for Candidate Selection:** *Very important factors considered include:* Character/personal qualities, level of applicant's interest, talent/ability. *Important factors considered include:* Academic GPA, rigor of secondary school record. *Other factors considered include:* Extracurricular activities, volunteer work, work experience. **Freshman Admission Requirements:** High school diploma is required and GED is not accepted. *Academic units required:* 3 English, 6 visual/performing arts, 6 academic electives. **Transfer Admission Requirements:** College transcript(s), essay or personal statement, statement of good standing from prior institution(s). Minimum college GPA of 2.0 required. Lowest grade transferable C. **General Admission Information:** Application fee $40. Early decision application deadline 1/30. Regular application deadline 2/1. Regular notification 4/1. Nonfall registration accepted. Admission may be deferred for a maximum of 1 year. Credit and/or placement offered for CEEB Advanced Placement tests.

COSTS AND FINANCIAL AID

Annual in-state tuition $3,658. Average book expense $2,500. **Student Employment:** Institutional employment available. Highest amount earned per year from on-campus jobs $1,200. Off-campus job opportunities are good.

EMMANUEL COLLEGE

400 The Fenway, Boston, MA 02115
Phone: 617-735-9715 **Financial Aid Phone:** 617-735-9938
E-mail: enroll@emmanuel.edu **CEEB Code:** 3368
Fax: 617-735-9801 **Website:** www.emmanuel.edu **ACT Code:** 1822

This private school, affiliated with the Roman Catholic Church, was founded in 1919. It has a 17-acre campus.

RATINGS

Admissions Selectivity Rating: 81   **Fire Safety Rating:** 60*   **Green Rating:** 60*

STUDENTS AND FACULTY

Enrollment: 1,997. **Student Body:** 74% female, 26% male, 38% out-of-state, 1% international (34 countries represented). Asian 3%, African American 7%, Caucasian 64%, Hispanic 5%.
Retention and Graduation: 79% freshmen return for sophomore year. 55% freshmen graduate within 4 years. **Faculty:** Student/faculty ratio 16:1. 82 full-time faculty, 84% hold PhDs, 15% are members of minority groups, 62% are women.

ACADEMICS

Degrees: Bachelor's, master's, post-bachelor's certificate, post-master's certificate. **Classes:** Most classes have 10–19 students. Most lab/discussion sessions have 10–19 students. **Majors with Highest Enrollment:** Biology/biological sciences; business administration and management; psychology. **Special Study Options:** Accelerated program, cross-registration, distance learning, double major, exchange student program (domestic), honors program, independent study, internships, liberal arts/career combination, student-designed major, study abroad, teacher certification program. **Honors programs:** Emmanuel College's Honors Program is a four-year academic and co-curricular program that combines rigorous, discussion-based course work with special complementary opportunities such as cultural activities, faculty-directed research projects, and service in the community. The program begins with the yearlong Honors Colloquium, a forum for students to engage in an active and open dialogue with their peers and members of the College's faculty from across the disciplines. Students also participate in four interdisciplinary writing-intensive seminars over the course of their studies, as well as a research and presentation skills seminar in preparation for independent study as an upperclassman, and ultimately the opportunity to achieve Distinction in the Field. Special programs offered to physically disabled students include note-taking services, reader services, tape recorders, tutors. **Career services:** Alumni network, alumni services, career/job search classes, career assessment, internships, regional alumni. **Career services highlights include:** Part-time Job Fair the first week of school in September.

FACILITIES

Housing: Coed dorms, special housing for disabled students, theme housing 90% of campus accessible to physically disabled. **Special Academic Facilities/Equipment:** Academic Science Center, Lillian Immig Gallery, Academic

Resource Center, Jean Yawkey Center. **Computers:** Students can register for classes online. Administrative functions (other than registration) can be performed online.

CAMPUS LIFE
Environment: Metropolis. **Activities:** Choral groups, dance, drama/theater, jazz band, literary magazine, music ensembles, musical theater, pep band, radio station, student government, student newspaper, student-run film society, symphony orchestra, yearbook, campus ministries, international student organization, Model UN. **Organizations:** 48 registered organizations, 11 honor societies. **Athletics (Intercollegiate):** *Men:* Basketball, cross-country, golf, soccer, track/field (outdoor), track/field (indoor), volleyball. *Women:* Basketball, cross-country, lacrosse, soccer, softball, tennis, track/field (outdoor), track/field (indoor), volleyball. **On-Campus Highlights:** Jean Yawkey Center, Residence Halls, Academic Science Center, Chapel.

ADMISSIONS
Freshman Academic Profile: Average high school GPA 3.44. 12% in top 10% of high school class, 41% in top 25% of high school class, 83% in top 50% of high school class. SAT Math middle 50% range 480–570. SAT Critical Reading middle 50% range 510–590. SAT Writing middle 50% range 500–590. ACT middle 50% range 20–24. Minimum paper TOEFL 550. Minimum computer TOEFL 213. Minimum web-based TOEFL 80. **Basis for Candidate Selection:** *Very important factors considered include:* Application essay, academic GPA, recommendation(s), rigor of secondary school record. *Important factors considered include:* Standardized test scores, character/personal qualities, extracurricular activities, level of applicant's interest, volunteer work. *Other factors considered include:* Class rank, alumni/ae relation, first generation, geographical residence, interview, religious affiliation/commitment, talent/ability, work experience. **Freshman Admission Requirements:** High school diploma is required and GED is accepted. *Academic units required:* 4 English, 3 mathematics, 2 science, (2 science labs), 2 foreign language, 2 social studies. **Freshman Admission Statistics:** 5,518 applied, 56% admitted, 14% enrolled. **Transfer Admission Requirements:** High school transcript, college transcript(s), essay or personal statement, standardized test scores, statement of good standing from prior institution(s). Minimum college GPA of n/a required. Lowest grade transferable C. **General Admission Information:** Application fee $40. Early decision application deadline 11/1. Regular application deadline 3/1. Notification on a rolling basis, beginning on or about 12/1. Nonfall registration accepted. Admission may be deferred for a maximum of 1 year. Credit and/or placement offered for CEEB Advanced Placement tests.

COSTS AND FINANCIAL AID
Annual tuition $29,200. Room and board $11,950. Required fees $165. Average book expense $880. **Required Forms and Deadlines:** FAFSA, institution's own financial aid form. Priority financial aid filing date 4/1. **Notification of Awards:** Applicants will be notified of awards on a rolling basis beginning 3/15. **Types of Aid:** *Need-based scholarships/grants:* Federal Pell, SEOG, state scholarships/grants, private scholarships, the school's own gift aid. *Loans:* Direct Subsidized Stafford, Direct Unsubsidized Stafford, Direct PLUS, Federal Perkins, state loans. **Student Employment:** Federal Work-Study Program available. Institutional employment available. Highest amount earned per year from on-campus jobs $7,581. Off-campus job opportunities are excellent. **Financial Aid Statistics:** 76% freshmen, 77% undergrads receive need-based scholarship or grant aid. 70% freshmen, 42% undergrads receive non-need-based scholarship or grant aid. 81% freshmen, 77% undergrads receive need-based self-help aid. 94% freshmen, 88% undergrads receive any aid. **Criteria for awarding institutional aid:** *Non-need-based:* Academics, alumni affiliation, leadership.

See page 1084.

See page 1084.

EMMANUEL COLLEGE (GA)

P.O. Box 129, Franklin Springs, GA 30639-0129
Phone: 706-245-7226 **Financial Aid Phone:** 706-245-2844
E-mail: admissions@emmanuelcollege.edu **CEEB Code:** 5184
Fax: 706-245-2876 **Website:** www.ec.edu

This private school, affiliated with the Pentecostal Church, was founded in 1919. It has a 150-acre campus.

RATINGS
Admissions Selectivity Rating: 78   **Fire Safety Rating:** 60*   **Green Rating:** 60*

STUDENTS AND FACULTY
Enrollment: 613. **Student Body:** 54% female, 46% male, 22% out-of-state, 1% international (4 countries represented). Asian 1%, African American 16%, Caucasian 80%, Hispanic 2%.

RETENTION AND GRADUATION
Retention and Graduation: 61% freshmen return for sophomore year. 18% freshmen graduate within 4 years. **Faculty:** Student/faculty ratio 13:1. 40 full-time faculty, 65% hold PhDs, 3% are members of minority groups, 40% are women.

ACADEMICS
Degrees: Associate, bachelor's, terminal associate, transfer associate. **Classes:** Most classes have fewer than 10 students. **Special Study Options:** Dual enrollment, honors program, independent study, internships, teacher certification program. Special programs offered to physically disabled students include note-taking services, tutors.

FACILITIES
Housing: Men's dorms, women's dorms, apartments for married students. 75% of campus accessible to physically disabled. **Computers:** Students can register for classes online.

CAMPUS LIFE
Environment: Rural. **Activities:** Choral groups, drama/theater, jazz band, literary magazine, music ensembles, musical theater, student government, student newspaper, yearbook. **Organizations:** 25 registered organizations, 3 honor societies, 15 religious organizations. **Athletics (Intercollegiate):** *Men:* Baseball, basketball, soccer, tennis. *Women:* Basketball, soccer, softball, tennis. **On-Campus Highlights:** EC Cafe, Student Activities Center.

ADMISSIONS
Freshman Academic Profile: 10% in top 10% of high school class, 50% in top 25% of high school class, 60% in top 50% of high school class. 85% from public high schools. SAT Math middle 50% range 400–550. SAT Critical Reading middle 50% range 430–570. Minimum paper TOEFL 550. Minimum computer TOEFL 213. **Basis for Candidate Selection:** *Very important factors considered include:* Academic GPA, standardized test scores. *Important factors considered include:* Level of applicant's interest. *Other factors considered include:* Recommendation(s). **Freshman Admission Requirements:** High school diploma is required and GED is accepted. **Freshman Admission Statistics:** 1,661 applied, 35% admitted, 45% enrolled. **Transfer Admission Requirements:** College transcript(s), standardized test scores, Lowest grade transferable D. **General Admission Information:** Application fee $25. Regular application deadline 8/1. Notification on a rolling basis, beginning on or about 9/1. Nonfall registration accepted. Admission may be deferred for a maximum of 1 year. Credit offered for CEEB Advanced Placement tests.

COSTS AND FINANCIAL AID
Average book expense $600. **Required Forms and Deadlines:** FAFSA, institution's own financial aid form, state aid form. Financial aid filing deadline 8/1. Priority financial aid filing date 3/1. **Notification of Awards:** Applicants will be notified of awards on a rolling basis beginning 3/1. **Types of Aid:** *Need-based scholarships/grants:* Federal Pell, SEOG, state scholarships/grants. *Loans:* FFEL Subsidized Stafford, FFEL Unsubsidized Stafford, FFEL PLUS. **Student Employment:** Federal Work-Study Program available. Institutional employment available. Off-campus job opportunities are good. **Criteria for awarding institutional aid:** *Non-need-based:* Academics, alumni affiliation, athletics, leadership, music/drama, religious affiliation.

EMORY AND HENRY COLLEGE

PO Box 10, Emory, VA 24327
Phone: 276-944-6133 **Financial Aid Phone:** 866-794-0010
E-mail: ehadmiss@ehc.edu **CEEB Code:** 5185
Fax: 276-944-6935 **Website:** www.ehc.edu **ACT Code:** 4350

This private school, affiliated with the Methodist Church, was founded in 1836. It has a 331-acre campus.

RATINGS
Admissions Selectivity Rating: 79   **Fire Safety Rating:** 60*   **Green Rating:** 78

STUDENTS AND FACULTY
Enrollment: 886. **Student Body:** 48% female, 52% male, 30% out-of-state, 1% international (3 countries represented). Asian 1%, African American 6%, Caucasian 85%, Hispanic 1%, Native American 1%.
Retention and Graduation: 68% freshmen return for sophomore year. 50% freshmen graduate within 4 years. 37% grads go on to further study within 1 year. 24% grads pursue arts and sciences degrees. 31% grads pursue law degrees. 23% grads pursue business degrees. 12% grads pursue medical degrees. **Faculty:** Student/faculty ratio 10:1. 76 full-time faculty, 82% hold PhDs, 5% are members of minority groups, 39% are women.

ACADEMICS

Degrees: Bachelor's, diploma, master's. **Classes:** Most classes have 10–19 students. **Majors with Highest Enrollment:** Business administration and management; education; pre-medicine/pre-medical studies. **Special Study Options:** Cooperative education program, distance learning, double major, dual enrollment, honors program, independent study, internships, liberal arts/career combination, student-designed major, study abroad, teacher certification program. **Combined degree programs:** BA/MA. Special programs offered to physically disabled students include reader services, tape recorders, tutors. **Career services:** Career/job search classes, career assessment, internships.

FACILITIES

Housing: Coed dorms, special housing for disabled students, men's dorms, women's dorms, theme housing. **Special Academic Facilities/Equipment:** Language lab, capillary gas chromatograph, DNA vertical slab gel electrophoretic equipment, infrared spectrophotometer. Theatre Studio, Art gallery. **Computers:** 100% of classrooms, 100% of dorms, 100% of libraries, 100% of dining areas, 100% of student union, 100% of common outdoor areas have wireless network access.

CAMPUS LIFE

Environment: Rural. **Activities:** Choral groups, drama/theater, literary magazine, music ensembles, musical theater, opera, pep band, radio station, student government, student newspaper, television station, yearbook, campus ministries, international student organization. **Organizations:** 53 registered organizations, 7 honor societies, 4 religious organizations. 7 fraternities, 6 sororities. **Athletics (Intercollegiate):** *Men:* Baseball, basketball, cross-country, football, golf, soccer, tennis. *Women:* Basketball, cross-country, soccer, softball, swimming, tennis, volleyball. **On-Campus Highlights:** McGlothlin-Street Hall (new science buil, Memorial Chapel, Byars Hall (Arts, Music, and Theatre), King Athletic Center, Emory Mercantile (campus bookstore). **Environmental Initiatives:** Recycling is now in full swing, with a widespread distribution of recycling bins for paper, cardboard, aluminum, plastics and steel. There are thirty bins specially made for the college from sustainably-harvested local poplar. We have already reduced our trash volume significantly. We are a participant in the national RecycleMania competition, in the waste minimization category. All new campus construction will be LEED silver certified, including the use of local, sustainably harvested wood. The college food service has committed to buying a significant amount of local organic produce, eggs and meat from Appalachian Harvest, a cooperative of farmers in our region. This is for the fall semester of 2008. This is one of our most effective ways of reducing our college's environmental footprint.

ADMISSIONS

Freshman Academic Profile: Average high school GPA 3.38. 14% in top 10% of high school class, 41% in top 25% of high school class, 78% in top 50% of high school class. 92% from public high schools. SAT Math middle 50% range 430–560. SAT Critical Reading middle 50% range 450–580. SAT Writing middle 50% range 430–540. ACT middle 50% range 19–25. Minimum paper TOEFL 550. **Basis for Candidate Selection:** *Very important factors considered include:* Academic GPA, recommendation(s), rigor of secondary school record, character/personal qualities, level of applicant's interest. *Important factors considered include:* Application essay, standardized test scores, extracurricular activities, geographical residence, interview, state residency, talent/ability, volunteer work. *Other factors considered include:* Class rank, alumni/ae relation, first generation, racial/ethnic status, religious affiliation/commitment, work experience. **Freshman Admission Requirements:** High school diploma is required and GED is accepted. *Academic units required:* 4 English, 3 mathematics, 2 science, (2 science labs), 2 foreign language, 2 social studies. *Academic units recommended:* 1 visual/performing arts. **Freshman Admission Statistics:** 1,131 applied, 72% admitted, 37% enrolled. **Transfer Admission Requirements:** High school transcript, college transcript(s), statement of good standing from prior institution(s). Minimum college GPA of 2.5 required. Lowest grade transferable C. **General Admission Information:** Application fee $30. Notification on a rolling basis, beginning on or about 8/1. Nonfall registration accepted. Admission may be deferred for a maximum of 1 year. Credit and/or placement offered for CEEB Advanced Placement tests.

COSTS AND FINANCIAL AID

Annual tuition $23,860. Room and board $7,980. Average book expense $800. **Required Forms and Deadlines:** FAFSA, state aid form. Priority financial aid filing date 4/15. **Notification of Awards:** Applicants will be notified of awards on a rolling basis beginning 3/1. **Types of Aid:** *Need-based scholarships/grants:* Federal Pell, SEOG, state scholarships/grants, private scholarships, the school's own gift aid. *Loans:* FFEL Subsidized Stafford, FFEL Unsubsidized Stafford, FFEL PLUS, Federal Perkins. **Student Employment: Financial Aid Statistics:** 71% freshmen, 69% undergrads receive need-based scholarship or grant aid. 11% freshmen, 8% undergrads receive non-need-based scholarship or grant aid. 71% freshmen, 69% undergrads receive need-based self-help aid. 61% undergrads borrow to pay for school. Average cumulative indebtedness $19,744.

Criteria for awarding institutional aid: *Non-need-based:* Academics, art, music/drama, religious affiliation, state/district residency.

See page 1086.

EMORY UNIVERSITY

Emory University, Boiseuillet Jones Ctr, Atlanta, GA 30322
Phone: 404-727-6036 **Financial Aid Phone:** 404-727-6039
E-mail: admiss@emory.edu **CEEB Code:** 5186
Fax: 404-727-4303 **Website:** www.emory.edu **ACT Code:** 851

This private school, affiliated with the Methodist Church, was founded in 1836. It has a 56-acre campus.

RATINGS

Admissions Selectivity Rating: 98   **Fire Safety Rating:** 66   **Green Rating:** 91

STUDENTS AND FACULTY

Enrollment: 6,868. **Student Body:** 55% female, 45% male, 70% out-of-state, 8% international (40 countries represented). Asian 22%, African American 10%, Caucasian 47%, Hispanic 4%.
Retention and Graduation: 96% freshmen return for sophomore year. 84% freshmen graduate within 4 years. 37% grads go on to further study within 1 year. 21% grads pursue arts and sciences degrees. 21% grads pursue law degrees. 2% grads pursue business degrees. 30% grads pursue medical degrees. **Faculty:** Student/faculty ratio 7:1. 1229 full-time faculty, 99% hold PhDs, 17% are members of minority groups, 41% are women. 10% of classes are taught by teaching assistants.

ACADEMICS

Degrees: Associate, bachelor's, first professional, master's. **Classes:** Most classes have 10–19 students. Most lab/discussion sessions have 10–19 students. **Majors with Highest Enrollment:** Business/commerce; economics; English language and literature. **Special Study Options:** Cooperative education program, cross-registration, double major, dual enrollment, English as a Second Language (ESL), honors program, independent study, internships, liberal arts/career combination, study abroad, teacher certification program, Qualified undergraduates may take a semester of off-campus study in Washington, DC. **Combined degree programs:** BA/MA, 4 year BA/MA or BS/MS program. Special programs offered to physically disabled students include note-taking services, reader services, tape recorders, tutors. **Career services:** Alumni network, alumni services, career/job search classes, career assessment, internships, regional alumni.

FACILITIES

Housing: Coed dorms, special housing for disabled students, special housing for international students, women's dorms, fraternity/sorority housing, apartments for married students, apartments for single students, theme housing. **Computers:** Students can register for classes online. Administrative functions (other than registration) can be performed online.

CAMPUS LIFE

Environment: Town. **Activities:** Choral groups, concert band, dance, drama/theater, jazz band, literary magazine, marching band, music ensembles, musical theater, opera, pep band, radio station, student government, student newspaper, student-run film society, symphony orchestra, television station, campus ministries, international student organization. **Organizations:** 51 registered organizations, 30 honor societies, 27 religious organizations. 14 fraternities, 12 sororities. **Athletics (Intercollegiate):** *Men:* Baseball, basketball, cross-country, diving, golf, soccer, swimming, tennis, track/field (outdoor). *Women:* Basketball, cross-country, diving, soccer, softball, swimming, tennis, track/field (outdoor), volleyball. **On-Campus Highlights:** Michael C. Carlos Museum, Lullwater Park, Clifton Health Sciences Corridor, Top of Woodruff Library, Dooley's Den at the Depot, 6) Candler Library Reading Room. **Environmental Initiatives:** Emory has among the highest number of square feet of LEED-certified space of any campus in America (we're #2 nationally as of the time of this writing). Emory constructed the first LEED-certified building in the Southeast in the 1990's, and all new and future construction must be LEED Silver. We also are auditing and retrofitting 1 million square feet of existing building space to achieve LEED standards—the auditing is completed and the retrofitting work will begin this summer. We plan to continue this renovation effort with another 1 million square feet at the end of the summer. Emory has set the goal of serving 75% local or sustainable ingredients in our campus and hospital cafeterias by 2015. To reach this ambitious target, we have hired a local farmer as Emory's Farm Liaison who is building a network of other local farmers to expand production. We are also working closely with the non-profit Georgia Organics and our vendor, Sodexho, to overcome barriers to distribution from farm to plate. Finally, we've started an on-campus Farmers' Market and have 5 educational food gardens on campus to allow students and staff the experience of growing their own local food. Emory has a robust alternative transportation program with one of the largest bus fleets in the state of Georgia which is 100% alternatively fueled, with half the fleet running on a biodiesel blend made from the used cooking oil from our campus cafeterias and hospitals. Emory has also been named by global bike manufacturer, Fuji, as its first "Fuji University" and has a bike share program with free fleets of bikes at check-out locations around campus, discounted bikes for students and staff, and other incentives for biking (see www.bike.emory.edu). We give staff free public transit passes, and incentives for carpooling, walking, and vanpooling. We also have three park-n-ride facilities at shopping centers around Atlanta's perimeter highway so that staff can take our free shuttle into work instead of driving into the heart of the city.

ADMISSIONS

Freshman Academic Profile: Average high school GPA 3.84. 85% in top 10% of high school class, 98% in top 25% of high school class, 100% in top 50% of high school class. SAT Math middle 50% range 660–750. SAT Critical Reading middle 50% range 640–730. SAT Writing middle 50% range 650–740. ACT middle 50% range 29–33. Minimum paper TOEFL 600. Minimum computer TOEFL 250. **Basis for Candidate Selection:** *Very important factors considered include:* Application essay, academic GPA, recommendation(s), rigor of secondary school record, standardized test scores, character/personal qualities, extracurricular activities, first generation, talent/ability. *Important factors considered include:* Alumni/ae relation, geographical residence, level of applicant's interest, racial/ethnic status, volunteer work, work experience. *Other factors considered include:* Class rank, interview. **Freshman Admission Requirements:** High school diploma is required and GED is not accepted. *Academic units required:* 4 English, 3 mathematics, 2 science, (2 science labs), 2 foreign language, 2 social studies, 2 history, 1 visual/performing arts, 2 academic electives. *Academic units recommended:* 4 mathematics, 3 science, 3 foreign language. **Freshman Admission Statistics:** 15,599 applied, 30% admitted, 28% enrolled. **Transfer Admission Requirements:** High school transcript, college transcript(s), essay or personal statement, standardized test scores, statement of good standing from prior institution(s). Minimum college GPA of 3.00 required. Lowest grade transferable C. **General Admission Information:** Application fee $50. Early decision application deadline 11/1. Regular application deadline 1/15. Regular notification 4/1. Nonfall registration not accepted. Admission may be deferred for a maximum of 1 year. Credit and/or placement offered for CEEB Advanced Placement tests.

COSTS AND FINANCIAL AID

Annual tuition $37,500. Room and board $10,896. Required fees $536. Average book expense $1,100. **Required Forms and Deadlines:** FAFSA, CSS/Financial Aid PROFILE, noncustodial PROFILE. Financial aid filing deadline 3/1. Priority financial aid filing date 2/15. **Notification of Awards:** Applicants will be notified of awards on or about 4/1. *Types of Aid: Need-based scholarships/grants:* Federal Pell, SEOG, state scholarships/grants, private scholarships, the school's own gift aid. *Loans:* FFEL Subsidized Stafford, FFEL Unsubsidized Stafford, FFEL PLUS, Federal Perkins, Federal Nursing, state loans, college/university loans from institutional funds. **Student Employment: Financial Aid Statistics:** 46% freshmen, 43% undergrads receive need-based scholarship or grant aid. 7% freshmen, 4% undergrads receive non-need-based scholarship or grant aid. 41% freshmen, 39% undergrads receive need-based self-help aid. 78% freshmen, 42% undergrads receive any aid. 42% undergrads borrow to pay for school. Average cumulative indebtedness $25,865. **Criteria for awarding institutional aid:** *Non-need-based:* Academics, art, leadership, music/drama, religious affiliation, state/district residency.

See page 1088.

EMPORIA STATE UNIVERSITY

1200 Commercial, Emporia, KS 66801-5087
Phone: 620-341-5465 **Financial Aid Phone:** 620-341-5457
E-mail: go2esu@emporia.edu **CEEB Code:** 6335
Fax: 620-341-5599 **Website:** www.emporia.edu **ACT Code:** 1430

This public school was founded in 1863. It has a 212-acre campus.

RATINGS
Admissions Selectivity Rating: 70   **Fire Safety Rating:** 63   **Green Rating:** 67

STUDENTS AND FACULTY

Enrollment: 4,148. **Student Body:** 59% female, 41% male, 10% out-of-state, 6% international (40 countries represented). Asian 1%, African American 5%, Caucasian 79%, Hispanic 5%, Native American 1%.
Retention and Graduation: 22% freshmen graduate within 4 years. 20% grads go on to further study within 1 year. **Faculty:** Student/faculty ratio 18:1. 260 full-time faculty, 81% hold PhDs, 9% are members of minority groups, 46% are women. 9% of classes are taught by teaching assistants.

ACADEMICS

Degrees: Bachelor's, master's, post-bachelor's certificate, post-master's certificate. **Classes:** Most classes have 20–29 students. Most lab/discussion sessions have 20–29 students. **Majors with Highest Enrollment:** Business/commerce; elementary education and teaching; nursing/registered nurse (RN, ASN, BSN, MSN). **Special Study Options:** Distance learning, double major, dual enrollment, honors program, independent study, internships, student-designed major, study abroad, teacher certification program, continuing education courses, evening courses, interdisciplinary or interdepartmental course of study, learning assistance program, Pass-Fail grading option, Student Exchange program, summer sessions, tutorial programs, Trio programs, Service members Opportunity College, undergrads may take grad level classes, except 800 level. **Honors programs:** Honors Programs **Combined degree programs:** MLS Legal studies with KU. Special programs offered to physically disabled students include note-taking services, reader services, tape recorders, tutors. **Career services:** Alumni network, alumni services, career assessment, internships. **Career services highlights include:** Formal, for-credit internship program available to any student, any major.

FACILITIES

Housing: Coed dorms, special housing for disabled students, special housing for international students, fraternity/sorority housing, apartments for married students, apartments for single students, wellness housing, theme housing. 100% of campus accessible to physically disabled. **Special Academic Facilities/Equipment:** Art gallery, geology and natural history museums, Great Plains study center, planetarium. **Computers:** 25% of classrooms, 100% of libraries, 50% of student union, have wireless network access. Students can register for classes online. Administrative functions (other than registration) can be performed online.

CAMPUS LIFE

Environment: Town. **Activities:** Choral groups, concert band, dance, drama/theater, jazz band, literary magazine, marching band, music ensembles, musical theater, opera, pep band, student government, student newspaper, student-run film society, symphony orchestra, yearbook, campus ministries, international student organization. **Organizations:** 141 registered organizations, 15 honor societies, 11 religious organizations. 6 fraternities, 4 sororities. **Athletics (Intercollegiate):** *Men:* Baseball, basketball, cheerleading, cross-country, football, tennis, track/field (outdoor), track/field (indoor). *Women:* Basketball, cheerleading, cross-country, soccer, softball, tennis, track/field (outdoor), track/field (indoor), volleyball. **On-Campus Highlights:** Student Recreation Center, The Memorial Student Union, Beach Music Hall, Wooster Lake, William Allen White Library.

ADMISSIONS

Freshman Academic Profile: Average high school GPA 3.28. 10% in top 10% of high school class, 34% in top 25% of high school class, 67% in top 50% of high school class. 96% from public high schools. ACT middle 50% range 19–25. Minimum paper TOEFL 450. Minimum computer TOEFL 133. **Basis for Candidate Selection:** *Very important factors considered include:* Class rank, academic GPA, standardized test scores. *Important factors considered include:* Talent/ability. *Other factors considered include:* Application essay, extracurricular activities. **Freshman Admission Requirements:** High school diploma is required and GED is accepted. *Academic units required:* 4 English, 3 mathematics, 3 science, 3 social studies, 1 computer science. *Academic units recommended:* 4 English, 3 mathematics, 3 science, 3 social studies, 1 computer science. **Freshman Admission Statistics:** 1,229 applied, 92% admitted, 61% enrolled. **Transfer Admission Requirements:** College transcript(s), minimum college GPA of 2.0 required. Lowest grade transferable D. **General Admission Information:** Application fee $30. Nonfall registration accepted. Admission may be deferred for a maximum of 1 year. Credit and/or placement offered for CEEB Advanced Placement tests.

COSTS AND FINANCIAL AID

Annual in-state tuition $3,426. Annual out-of-state tuition $12,630. Room and board $6,146. Required fees $948. **Required Forms and Deadlines:** FAFSA, state aid form. Priority financial aid filing date 3/15. **Notification of Awards:** Applicants will be notified of awards on a rolling basis beginning 2/2. *Types of Aid: Need-based scholarships/grants:* Federal Pell, SEOG, state scholarships/grants, private scholarships, the school's own gift aid, Jones Foundation Grants. *Loans:* FFEL Subsidized Stafford, FFEL Unsubsidized Stafford, FFEL PLUS, Federal Perkins, Alaska Loans, alternative loans. **Student Employment:** Federal Work-Study Program available. Institutional employment available. Highest amount earned per year from on-campus jobs $3,500. Off-campus job opportunities are good. **Financial Aid Statistics:** 37% freshmen, 23% undergrads receive need-based scholarship or grant aid. 25% freshmen, 14% undergrads receive non-need-based scholarship or grant aid. 4% freshmen, 5% undergrads receive need-based self-help aid. 7% freshmen, 4% undergrads receive athletic scholarships. 61% freshmen, 57% undergrads receive any aid. 70% undergrads borrow to pay for school. Average cumulative indebtedness $17,520. **Criteria for awarding institutional aid:** *Non-need-based:* Academics, alumni affiliation, art, athletics, job skills, leadership, minority status, music/drama, religious affiliation, state/district residency.

ENDICOTT COLLEGE

376 Hale Street, Beverly, MA 01915
Phone: 978-921-1000 **Financial Aid Phone:** 978-232-2060
E-mail: admissio@endicott.edu **CEEB Code:** 3369
Fax: 978-232-2520 **Website:** www.endicott.edu **ACT Code:** 1824

This private school was founded in 1939. It has a 231-acre campus.

RATINGS
Admissions Selectivity Rating: 76   **Fire Safety Rating:** 90   **Green Rating:** 75

STUDENTS AND FACULTY
Enrollment: 2,273. **Student Body:** 58% female, 42% male, 52% out-of-state, 2% international (26 countries represented). Asian 1%, African American 1%, Caucasian 77%, Hispanic 2%.
Retention and Graduation: 83% freshmen return for sophomore year. 68% freshmen graduate within 4 years. 26% grads go on to further study within 1 year. **Faculty:** Student/faculty ratio 16:1. 77 full-time faculty, 66% hold PhDs, 6% are members of minority groups, 53% are women.

ACADEMICS
Degrees: Associate, bachelor's, master's, post-bachelor's certificate, terminal associate. **Classes:** Most classes have 10–19 students. Most lab/discussion sessions have 10–19 students. **Majors with Highest Enrollment:** Business administration and management; mass communication/media studies; sport and fitness administration/management. **Special Study Options:** Accelerated program, cross-registration, distance learning, dual enrollment, honors program, independent study, internships, liberal arts/career combination, student-designed major, study abroad, teacher certification program **Honors programs:** Alpha Phi Sigma, Eta Sigma Delta, Kappa Delta Pi, Lambda Pi Eta, Communications Mortar Board, Psi Chi, Sigma Beta Delta, National Honor Society for Criminal Justice Students, Endicott College Honors Program, International Hospitality Management Society, National Honor Society for students in Senior Year. Special programs offered to physically disabled students include note-taking services, reader services, tape recorders, tutors. **Career services:** Alumni network, alumni services, career/job search classes, career assessment, internships, regional alumni, **Career services highlights include:** Internships are required for all traditional undergraduate students.

FACILITIES
Housing: Coed dorms, special housing for disabled students, special housing for international students, women's dorms, apartments for single students, theme housingSingle parent housing, suites, healthy living, academic. 80% of campus accessible to physically disabled. **Special Academic Facilities/Equipment:** Center for the Arts (galleries, theaters) www.endicott.edu/centerfortheearts, Endicott Archives Museum www.endicott.edu/archives, La Chanterelle, a student-run restaraunt www.endicott.edu/lachanterelle **Computers:** 100% of classrooms, 96% of dorms, 100% of libraries, 100% of dining areas, 100% of student union, have wireless network access. Students can register for classes online. Administrative functions (other than registration) can be performed online.

CAMPUS LIFE
Environment: Town. **Activities:** Choral groups, concert band, dance, drama/theater, jazz band, literary magazine, music ensembles, musical theater, student government, student newspaper, student-run film society, television station, yearbook, campus ministries, international student organization, Model UN. **Organizations:** 47 registered organizations, 7 honor societies, 1 religious organizations. **Athletics (Intercollegiate):** *Men:* Baseball, basketball, cross-country, equestrian sports, football, golf, lacrosse, soccer, tennis, volleyball. *Women:* Basketball, cross-country, equestrian sports, field hockey, lacrosse, soccer, softball, tennis, volleyball. **On-Campus Highlights:** Center for the Arts, The Lodge, Post Center—Sports Complex, Callahan Center, Endicott Beaches. **Environmental Initiatives:** Wind turbine research project Energy efficient

replacements for boilers and temperature control systems Waste reduction plan—increased recycling and composting

ADMISSIONS
Freshman Academic Profile: 10% in top 10% of high school class, 41% in top 25% of high school class, 80% in top 50% of high school class. 74% from public high schools. SAT Math middle 50% range 500–590. SAT Critical Reading middle 50% range 490–580. SAT Writing middle 50% range 480–580. ACT middle 50% range 20–25. Minimum paper TOEFL 550. Minimum computer TOEFL 213. Minimum web-based TOEFL 79. **Basis for Candidate Selection:** *Very important factors considered include:* Academic GPA, rigor of secondary school record, character/personal qualities. *Important factors considered include:* Class rank, application essay, standardized test scores, alumni/ae relation, extracurricular activities, geographical residence, talent/ability, volunteer work, work experience. *Other factors considered include:* Recommendation(s), first generation, interview, level of applicant's interest, racial/ethnic status, state residency. **Freshman Admission Requirements:** High school diploma is required and GED is accepted. *Academic units recommended:* 4 English, 3 mathematics, 2 science, 2 social studies, 1 history, 4 academic electives. **Freshman Admission Statistics:** 3,885 applied, 53% admitted, 27% enrolled. **Transfer Admission Requirements:** High school transcript, college transcript(s), essay or personal statement, standardized test scores, statement of good standing from prior institution(s). Minimum college GPA of 2.5 required. Lowest grade transferable C. **General Admission Information:** Application fee $40. Regular application deadline 2/15. Notification on a rolling basis, beginning on or about 11/1. Non-fall registration accepted. Credit offered for CEEB Advanced Placement tests.

COSTS AND FINANCIAL AID
Annual tuition $24,976. Room and board $11,836. Required fees $400. Average book expense $1,000. **Required Forms and Deadlines:** FAFSA, institution's own financial aid form. Priority financial aid filing date 3/15. **Notification of Awards:** Applicants will be notified of awards on a rolling basis beginning 3/15. **Types of Aid:** *Loans:* FFEL Subsidized Stafford, FFEL Unsubsidized Stafford, FFEL PLUS, Federal Perkins, college/university loans from institutional funds. **Student Employment:** Federal Work-Study Program available. Institutional employment available. Highest amount earned per year from on-campus jobs $1,500. Off-campus job opportunities are good. **Financial Aid Statistics:** 49% freshmen, 45% undergrads receive need-based scholarship or grant aid. 44% freshmen, 35% undergrads receive non-need-based scholarship or grant aid. 62% freshmen, 57% undergrads receive need-based self-help aid. 86% freshmen, 83% undergrads receive any aid. 69% undergrads borrow to pay for school. Average cumulative indebtedness $33,783. **Criteria for awarding institutional aid:** *Non-need-based:* Academics, alumni affiliation, art, job skills, leadership, music/drama, religious affiliation, state/district residency.

ERSKINE COLLEGE

Erskine College, P.O. Box 338, Due West, SC 29639
Phone: 864-379-8838 **Financial Aid Phone:** 864-379-8832
E-mail: admissions@erskine.edu
Fax: 864-379-2167 **Website:** www.erskine.edu

This private school, affiliated with the Presbyterian Church, was founded in 1839. It has a 85-acre campus.

RATINGS
Admissions Selectivity Rating: 86   **Fire Safety Rating:** 60*   **Green Rating:** 60*

STUDENTS AND FACULTY
Enrollment: 578. **Student Body:** 55% female, 45% male, 23% out-of-state, 3% international (10 countries represented). Asian 1%, African American 7%, Caucasian 71%, Hispanic 1%.
Retention and Graduation: 63% freshmen return for sophomore year. 63% freshmen graduate within 4 years. 29% grads go on to further study within 1 year. **Faculty:** Student/faculty ratio 11:1. 42 full-time faculty, 86% hold PhDs, 7% are members of minority groups, 38% are women.

ACADEMICS
Degrees: Bachelor's, certificate, master's. **Classes:** Most classes have 10–19 students. Most lab/discussion sessions have 20–29 students. **Majors with Highest Enrollment:** Biology/biological sciences; business/commerce; elementary education and teaching. **Special Study Options:** Double major, independent study, internships, study abroad, teacher certification program **Combined degree programs:** Medical Technology w/Medical Univ. of S. Carolina. Special programs offered to physically disabled students include tutors. **Career services:** Career/job search classes.

FACILITIES

Housing: Men's dorms, women's dorms 75% of campus accessible to physically disabled. **Special Academic Facilities/Equipment:** Bowie Arts Center.

CAMPUS LIFE

Environment: Rural. **Activities:** Choral groups, concert band, dance, drama/theater, jazz band, literary magazine, music ensembles, musical theater, radio station, student government, student newspaper, yearbook, campus ministries. **Organizations:** 51 registered organizations, 6 honor societies. **Athletics (Intercollegiate):** *Men:* Baseball, basketball, cross-country, golf, soccer, tennis. *Women:* Basketball, cross-country, golf, lacrosse, soccer, softball, tennis, volleyball. **On-Campus Highlights:** Java City, The Phoenix, Watkins Student Center, Bowie Arts Center.

ADMISSIONS

Freshman Academic Profile: Average high school GPA 3.83. 31% in top 10% of high school class, 67% in top 25% of high school class, 88% in top 50% of high school class. 85% from public high schools. SAT Math middle 50% range 490–610. SAT Critical Reading middle 50% range 471–580. ACT middle 50% range 23–27. Minimum paper TOEFL 550. **Basis for Candidate Selection:** *Very important factors considered include:* Application essay, academic GPA, recommendation(s), rigor of secondary school record, standardized test scores, alumni/ae relation. *Important factors considered include:* Character/personal qualities, extracurricular activities, talent/ability. *Other factors considered include:* Class rank, first generation, geographical residence, interview, level of applicant's interest, racial/ethnic status, religious affiliation/commitment, state residency, volunteer work, work experience. **Freshman Admission Requirements:** High school diploma is required and GED is accepted. *Academic units required:* 4 English, 2 mathematics, 2 science, (2 science labs). **Freshman Admission Statistics:** 589 applied, 70% admitted, 44% enrolled. **Transfer Admission Requirements:** College transcript(s), essay or personal statement, statement of good standing from prior institution(s). Minimum college GPA of 2.0 required. Lowest grade transferable C. **General Admission Information:** Application fee $25. Notification on a rolling basis, beginning on or about 11/15. Nonfall registration accepted. Credit and/or placement offered for CEEB Advanced Placement tests.

COSTS AND FINANCIAL AID

Annual tuition $23,000. Room and board $8,325. Required fees $1,645. Average book expense $1,500. **Required Forms and Deadlines:** FAFSA, institution's own financial aid form, state aid form. Priority financial aid filing date 4/1. **Notification of Awards:** Applicants will be notified of awards on a rolling basis beginning 12/15. **Types of Aid:** *Need-based scholarships/grants:* Federal Pell, SEOG, state scholarships/grants, private scholarships, the school's own gift aid Federal ACG, Smart & Teach Grants. *Loans:* FFEL Subsidized Stafford, FFEL Unsubsidized Stafford, FFEL PLUS, Federal Perkins, college/university loans from institutional funds, Alternative Loans. **Student Employment:** Federal Work-Study Program available. Institutional employment available. **Financial Aid Statistics:** 81% freshmen, 90% undergrads receive need-based scholarship or grant aid. 81% freshmen, 90% undergrads receive non-need-based scholarship or grant aid. 65% undergrads receive athletic scholarships. 82% undergrads borrow to pay for school. Average cumulative indebtedness $14,756. **Criteria for awarding institutional aid:** *Non-need-based:* Academics, alumni affiliation, athletics, leadership, minority status, music/drama, religious affiliation, state/district residency.

EUGENE BIBLE COLLEGE

2155 Bailey Hill Road, Eugene, OR 97405-1194
Phone: 800-322-2638 **Financial Aid Phone:** 800-322-2638
E-mail: admissions@ebc.edu **CEEB Code:** 4274
Fax: 541-343-5801 **Website:** www.ebc.edu **ACT Code:** 3468

This private school was founded in 1925. It has a 33-acre campus.

RATINGS
Admissions Selectivity Rating: 78   **Fire Safety Rating:** 60*   **Green Rating:** 60*

STUDENTS AND FACULTY
Enrollment: 180. **Student Body:** 44% female, 56% male, 54% out-of-state, international (5 countries represented).
Retention and Graduation: 68% freshmen return for sophomore year. 31% freshmen graduate within 4 years. 35% grads go on to further study within 1 year. **Faculty:** Student/faculty ratio 10:1. 10 full-time faculty, 30% hold PhDs, 20% are members of minority groups, 40% are women.

ACADEMICS
Degrees: Bachelor's, certificate. **Classes:** Most classes have 10–19 students. Most lab/discussion sessions have 10–19 students. **Majors with Highest**

Enrollment: Bible/biblical studies; pastoral studies/counseling; youth ministry. **Special Study Options:** Cooperative education program, distance learning, double major, dual enrollment, independent study, internships, liberal arts/career combination, one year Bible Certificate obtainable by external studies program.

FACILITIES

Housing: Men's dorms, women's dorms, apartments for married students, apartments for single students. 75% of campus accessible to physically disabled. **Special Academic Facilities/Equipment:** Music lab, computer lab.

CAMPUS LIFE

Environment: City. **Activities:** Choral groups, drama/theater, music ensembles, student government, yearbook. **Organizations: Athletics (Intercollegiate):** *Men:* Basketball, soccer. *Women:* Soccer, volleyball. **On-Campus Highlights:** Student Center, cafeteria, dorm lounges, computer lab, workout room.

ADMISSIONS

Freshman Academic Profile: Average high school GPA 3.1. 8% in top 10% of high school class, 29% in top 25% of high school class, 67% in top 50% of high school class. 90% from public high schools. SAT Math middle 50% range 430–610. SAT Critical Reading middle 50% range 450–580. ACT middle 50% range 19–24. Minimum paper TOEFL 500. Minimum computer TOEFL 200. **Basis for Candidate Selection:** *Very important factors considered include:* Application essay, recommendation(s), character/personal qualities, religious affiliation/commitment. *Important factors considered include:* Rigor of secondary school record. *Other factors considered include:* Class rank, standardized test scores, extracurricular activities, talent/ability, volunteer work, work experience. **Freshman Admission Requirements:** High school diploma is required and GED is accepted. **Freshman Admission Statistics:** 217 applied, 47% admitted, 63% enrolled. **Transfer Admission Requirements:** College transcript(s), essay or personal statement, minimum college GPA of 2.0 required. Lowest grade transferable C. **General Admission Information:** Application fee $30. Regular application deadline 9/1. Notification on a rolling basis, beginning on or about 10/1. Nonfall registration accepted. Admission may be deferred for a maximum of 24 months. Credit offered for CEEB Advanced Placement tests.

COSTS AND FINANCIAL AID

Annual tuition $7,500. . Room and board $4,575. Required fees $801. Average book expense $800. **Required Forms and Deadlines:** FAFSA. Financial aid filing deadline 9/1. Priority financial aid filing date 3/1. **Notification of Awards:** Applicants will be notified of awards on a rolling basis beginning 7/15. **Types of Aid:** *Need-based scholarships/grants:* Federal Pell, SEOG, the school's own gift aid. *Loans:* Direct Subsidized Stafford, Direct Unsubsidized Stafford, Direct PLUS, FFEL PLUS. **Student Employment: Financial Aid Statistics:** 73% freshmen, 73% undergrads receive need-based scholarship or grant aid. 12% freshmen, 9% undergrads receive non-need-based scholarship or grant aid. 73% freshmen, 73% undergrads receive need-based self-help aid. 1% freshmen receive athletic scholarships. 90% undergrads borrow to pay for school. Average cumulative indebtedness $25,000. **Criteria for awarding institutional aid:** *Non-need-based:* Academics, alumni affiliation, athletics, leadership, music/drama.

EUGENE LANG COLLEGE THE NEW SCHOOL FOR LIBERAL ARTS

72 5th Avenue, 2nd Floor, New York, NY 10011
Phone: 212-229-5665 **Financial Aid Phone:** 212-229-8930
E-mail: lang@newschool.edu **CEEB Code:** 2521
Fax: 212-229-5355 **Website:** www.newschool.edu/lang **ACT Code:** 9384

This private school was founded in 1978.

RATINGS
Admissions Selectivity Rating: 85   **Fire Safety Rating:** 73   **Green Rating:** 91

STUDENTS AND FACULTY
Enrollment: 1,439. **Student Body:** 67% female, 33% male, 71% out-of-state, 4% international (35 countries represented). Asian 5%, African American 5%, Caucasian 58%, Hispanic 9%.
Retention and Graduation: 67% freshmen return for sophomore year. 48% freshmen graduate within 4 years. **Faculty:** Student/faculty ratio 15:1. 70 full-

time faculty, 79% hold PhDs, 24% are members of minority groups, 53% are women.

ACADEMICS

Degrees: Bachelor's. **Classes:** Most classes have 10–19 students. Most lab/discussion sessions have 10–19 students. **Special Study Options:** Accelerated program, cross-registration, distance learning, double major, dual enrollment, English as a Second Language (ESL), exchange student program (domestic), independent study, internships, liberal arts/career combination, student-designed major, study abroad, five year combined BA/BFA program. **Combined degree programs:** BA/BFA. Special programs offered to physically disabled students include note-taking services, reader services, tape recorders. **Career services:** Alumni network, alumni services, career/job search classes, career assessment, internships, regional alumni.

FACILITIES

Housing: Coed dorms, special housing for disabled students, apartments for single students. 99% of campus accessible to physically disabled. **Special Academic Facilities/Equipment:** Art gallery, photography gallery, extensive collections of contemporary art, concert hall, public lectures, conferences, cultural and intellectual events. **Computers:** 95% of classrooms, 100% of libraries, 100% of dining areas, na% of student union, 100% of common outdoor areas have wireless network access. Students can register for classes online. Administrative functions (other than registration) can be performed online.

CAMPUS LIFE

Environment: Metropolis. **Activities:** Choral groups, dance, drama/theater, jazz band, literary magazine, music ensembles, opera, radio station, student government, student newspaper, symphony orchestra, international student organization. **Organizations:** 34 registered organizations. **On-Campus Highlights:** Harry Scherman Library, Raymond Fogelman Library, Lang Courtyard, University Welcome Center, Sheila C. Johnson Design Center. **Environmental Initiatives:** The New School composts all behind the counter organic wastes and has begun a post-consumer pilot program. Waste Reduction and Recycling The New School has established a comprehensive waste management and recycling program that includes glass, metal, plastic, paper, cardboard, electronic waste, ink jet cartridges, and compost. These recycling initiatives significantly reduce the amount of trash sent to landfills and/or incinerators by the university. Sustainable Product Procurement The New School currently purchases copy and printer paper composed of 100% post-consumer recycled content. Similarly, all promotional materials are printed on Forest Stewardship Council Certified paper. An Energy Star purchasing policy is in place for all computers and appliances; further all computers are EPEAT gold rated. "Green" cleaning products are in use across campus, and low-VOC paints are used in high-sensitivity areas. Recent major renovations have featured rapidly renewable or recycled building materials, including linoleum flooring, bamboo flooring, and composite countertops made from post-industrial content. Compostable plates and cutlery are in use in all cafeterias, and locally produced/organic foods are offered in increasing volumes. "green cleaning products and low VOC paints are in use across the campus. Energy Management and Carbon Emission Reductions In 2007, The New School signed on to the NYC Mayoral Challenge to Universities to reduce carbon emissions by 30% by 2017. The New School began the challenge with the lowest CO_2 footprint of all participating schools, and is already taking steps to further minimize its impact on global climate change. 100% of electricity directly paid for by the university is offset with Renewable Energy Credits from wind power. The New School has conducted a lighting retrofit in its five largest buildings and is in the process of conducting an investment grade audit of its mechanical system, an in further exploring opportunities to increase energy efficiency through HVAC commissioning, and other projects.

ADMISSIONS

Freshman Academic Profile: Average high school GPA 3.2. 22.5% in top 10% of high school class, 62.5% in top 25% of high school class, 92.5% in top 50% of high school class. SAT Math middle 50% range 480–580. SAT Critical Reading middle 50% range 530–640. SAT Writing middle 50% range 540–640. ACT middle 50% range 22–27. Minimum paper TOEFL 600. Minimum computer TOEFL 250. Minimum web-based TOEFL 100. **Basis for Candidate Selection:** *Very important factors considered include:* Application essay, academic GPA, recommendation(s), rigor of secondary school record. *Important factors considered include:* Standardized test scores, character/personal qualities, interview, level of applicant's interest, volunteer work. *Other factors considered include:* Class rank, alumni/ae relation, extracurricular activities, first generation, geographical residence, talent/ability, work experience. **Freshman Admission Requirements:** High school diploma is required and GED is accepted. *Academic units required:* 4 English. *Academic units recommended:* 3 mathematics, 3 science, 2 foreign language, 3 social studies, 2 history. **Freshman Admission Statistics:** 1,682 applied, 68% admitted, 26% enrolled. **Transfer Admission Requirements:** High school transcript, college transcript(s), essay or personal statement, standardized test scores, minimum college GPA of 3.0 required. Lowest grade transferable C. **General Admission Information:** Application fee $50. Early decision application deadline 11/15. Regular application deadline

2/1. Notification on a rolling basis, beginning on or about 3/25. Nonfall registration accepted. Admission may be deferred for a maximum of 1 year. Neither credit nor placement offered for CEEB Advanced Placement tests.

COSTS AND FINANCIAL AID

Required Forms and Deadlines: FAFSA, state aid form. **Notification of Awards:** Applicants will be notified of awards on a rolling basis beginning 3/1. **Types of Aid:** *Need-based scholarships/grants:* Federal Pell, SEOG, state scholarships/grants, private scholarships, the school's own gift aid. *Loans:* FFEL Subsidized Stafford, FFEL Unsubsidized Stafford, FFEL PLUS, Federal Perkins. **Student Employment:** Federal Work-Study Program available. Institutional employment available. Off-campus job opportunities are excellent. **Financial Aid Statistics:** 56% freshmen, 54% undergrads receive need-based scholarship or grant aid. 7% freshmen, 1% undergrads receive non-need-based scholarship or grant aid. 59% freshmen, 55% undergrads receive need-based self-help aid. 70% freshmen, 70% undergrads receive any aid. 62% undergrads borrow to pay for school. Average cumulative indebtedness $25,348. **Criteria for awarding institutional aid:** *Non-need-based:* Academics, leadership.

EUREKA COLLEGE

300 East College Avenue, Eureka, IL 61530-1500
Phone: 309-467-6350 **Financial Aid Phone:** 309-467-6311
E-mail: admissions@eureka.edu **CEEB Code:** 1206
Fax: 309-467-6576 **Website:** www.eureka.edu/index.html **ACT Code:** 1022

This private school, affiliated with the Disciples of Christ Church, was founded in 1855. It has a 112-acre campus.

RATINGS

Admissions Selectivity Rating: 74   **Fire Safety Rating:** 73   **Green Rating:** 60*

STUDENTS AND FACULTY

Enrollment: 654. **Student Body:** 56% female, 44% male, 10% out-of-state, international (5 countries represented). Asian 1%, African American 3%, Caucasian 73%, Hispanic 2%.
Retention and Graduation: 74% freshmen return for sophomore year. 41% freshmen graduate within 4 years. 24% grads go on to further study within 1 year. 8% grads pursue arts and sciences degrees. 6% grads pursue law degrees. 2% grads pursue business degrees. 3% grads pursue medical degrees. **Faculty:** Student/faculty ratio 16:1. 35 full-time faculty, 80% hold PhDs, 3% are members of minority groups, 34% are women.

ACADEMICS

Degrees: Bachelor's, certificate. **Classes:** Most classes have 10–19 students. Most lab/discussion sessions have fewer than 10 students. **Majors with Highest Enrollment:** Business/commerce; elementary education and teaching; psychology. **Special Study Options:** Double major, dual enrollment, honors program, independent study, internships, liberal arts/career combination, student-designed major, study abroad, teacher certification program, weekend college, Weekend Degree Completion Cohort Program in Organizational Leadership Weekend Degree Certification in Special Education. **Honors programs:** Academic Honors Program, Reagan Leadership Program, Sandifer Mentorship Program. **Combined degree programs:** BA/MEng, 2-2 nursing prog with Mennonite Coll of Nursing. Special programs offered to physically disabled students include tutors.

FACILITIES

Housing: Coed dorms, special housing for disabled students, men's dorms, women's dorms, fraternity/sorority housing 60% of campus accessible to physically disabled. **Special Academic Facilities/Equipment:** Ronald Reagan Museum, electron microscope, Peace Garden. **Computers:** Administrative functions (other than registration) can be performed online.

CAMPUS LIFE

Environment: Village. **Activities:** Choral groups, concert band, dance, drama/theater, jazz band, literary magazine, musical theater, pep band, student government, student newspaper, student-run film society, yearbook. **Organizations:** 41 registered organizations, 15 honor societies, 4 religious organizations. 3 fraternities, 3 sororities. **Athletics (Intercollegiate):** *Men:* Baseball, basketball, cross-country, football, golf, soccer, swimming, tennis, track/field (outdoor). *Women:* Basketball, cross-country, golf, soccer, softball, swimming, tennis, track/field (outdoor), volleyball. **On-Campus Highlights:** Ronald Reagan Museum and Peace Garden, Cerf College Center, National Historic Site: Administration Building, National Historic Site: The Chapel, Lilac Arboretum, Founded in 1855 by abolitionists, Eureka College is located on 130 acres of trees and gardens. 1st college in Illinois to accept men and women on an equal basis. Small town setting located between two midsize cities—the best of both worlds! Personal. Faith-based. Liberal Arts. Pillow to Port Internet access for all!.

ADMISSIONS

Freshman Academic Profile: Average high school GPA 3.2. 17% in top 10% of high school class, 44% in top 25% of high school class, 96% in top 50% of high school class. 87% from public high schools. ACT middle 50% range 18–24. Minimum paper TOEFL 500. Minimum computer TOEFL 173. **Basis for Candidate Selection:** *Very important factors considered include:* Class rank, recommendation(s), rigor of secondary school record, standardized test scores, character/personal qualities, extracurricular activities, volunteer work. *Important factors considered include:* talent/ability. *Other factors considered include:* Application essay, alumni/ae relation, interview, work experience. **Freshman Admission Requirements:** High school diploma is required and GED is accepted.High school diploma is required and GED is not accepted. *Academic units recommended:* 4 English, 3 mathematics, 3 science, 2 foreign language, 3 social studies, 2 history. **Freshman Admission Statistics:** 635 applied, 75% admitted, 31% enrolled. **Transfer Admission Requirements:** College transcript(s), statement of good standing from prior institution(s). Minimum college GPA of 2.0 required. Lowest grade transferable C. **General Admission Information:** Regular application deadline 8/1. Nonfall registration accepted. Admission may be deferred for a maximum of 1 year. Credit offered for CEEB Advanced Placement tests.

COSTS AND FINANCIAL AID

Annual tuition $15,673. Room and board $7,130. Required fees $580. Average book expense $1,000. **Required Forms and Deadlines:** FAFSA. Priority financial aid filing date 4/15. **Notification of Awards:** Applicants will be notified of awards on or about 5/1. **Types of Aid:** *Need-based scholarships/grants:* Federal Pell, SEOG, state scholarships/grants, private scholarships, the school's own gift aid. *Loans:* Direct Subsidized Stafford, Direct Unsubsidized Stafford, Direct PLUS, FFEL Subsidized Stafford, FFEL Unsubsidized Stafford, FFEL PLUS, Federal Perkins, college/university loans from institutional funds, alternative loans. **Student Employment:** Federal Work-Study Program available. Institutional employment available. Highest amount earned per year from on-campus jobs $1,000. Off-campus job opportunities are excellent. **Financial Aid Statistics:** 66% freshmen, 70% undergrads receive need-based scholarship or grant aid. 60% freshmen, 63% undergrads receive need-based self-help aid. 100% freshmen, 94% undergrads receive any aid. 86% undergrads borrow to pay for school. Average cumulative indebtedness $14,727. **Criteria for awarding institutional aid:** *Non-need-based:* Academics, alumni affiliation, art, leadership, music/drama, religious affiliation.

EVANGEL UNIVERSITY

111 North Glenstone, Springfield, MO 65802
Phone: 417-865-2811
E-mail: admissions@evangel.edu **CEEB Code:** 6198
Fax: 417-520-0545 **Website:** www.evangel.edu **ACT Code:** 2296

This private school was founded in 1955. It has a 80-acre campus.

RATINGS

Admissions Selectivity Rating: 60*   **Fire Safety Rating:** 60*   **Green Rating:** 60*

STUDENTS AND FACULTY

Enrollment: 1,616. **Student Body:** 56% female, 44% male, 60% out-of-state, 1% international (13 countries represented). African American 2%, Caucasian 64%.
Retention and Graduation: 77% freshmen return for sophomore year.

ACADEMICS

Degrees: Associate, bachelor's, master's. **Special Study Options:** Cooperative education program, double major, dual enrollment, independent study, internships, teacher certification program. **Career services:** Career/job search classes, career assessment, internships.

FACILITIES

Housing: Men's dorms, women's dorms, apartments for married students, Co-occupancy dorm with men and women in separate wings.

CAMPUS LIFE

Activities: Choral groups, concert band, drama/theater, jazz band, music ensembles, pep band, radio station, student government, student newspaper, television station, yearbook. **Organizations:** 14 registered organizations, 10 honor societies, 3 religious organizations. **Athletics (Intercollegiate):** *Men:* Baseball, basketball, cheerleading, cross-country, football, golf, track/field (outdoor), track/field (indoor). *Women:* Basketball, cheerleading, cross-country, golf, softball, track/field (outdoor), track/field (indoor), volleyball.

ADMISSIONS

Freshman Academic Profile: 76% from public high schools. Minimum paper TOEFL 490. **Basis for Candidate Selection:** *Very important factors considered include:* Class rank, recommendation(s), rigor of secondary school record, standardized test scores, religious affiliation/commitment. *Important factors considered include:* Character/personal qualities. **Freshman Admission Requirements:** High school diploma is required and GED is accepted. *Academic units recommended:* 3 English, 2 mathematics, 1 science, (1 science labs), 2 foreign language, 2 social studies, 3 academic electives. **Freshman Admission Statistics:** 1,254 applied, 78% admitted, **Transfer Admission Requirements:** College transcript(s), statement of good standing from prior institution(s). Minimum college GPA of 2.0 required. Lowest grade transferable C. **General Admission Information:** Application fee $35. Regular application deadline 8/15. Notification on a rolling basis, beginning on or about 9/1. Nonfall registration accepted. Admission may be deferred for a maximum of 1. Credit offered for CEEB Advanced Placement tests.

COSTS AND FINANCIAL AID

Annual tuition $13,530. Room and board $5,120. Required fees $660. Average book expense $800. **Required Forms and Deadlines:** FAFSA. **Notification of Awards:** Applicants will be notified of awards on a rolling basis beginning 4/1. **Types of Aid:** *Need-based scholarships/grants:* Federal Pell, SEOG, private scholarships. *Loans:* Direct Subsidized Stafford, Direct Unsubsidized Stafford, Direct PLUS, FFEL Subsidized Stafford, FFEL Unsubsidized Stafford, FFEL PLUS, Federal Perkins, college/university loans from institutional funds. **Student Employment:** Federal Work-Study Program available. Institutional employment available. Off-campus job opportunities are excellent. **Financial Aid Statistics:** 121% undergrads receive need-based scholarship or grant aid. 26% undergrads receive non-need-based scholarship or grant aid.

THE EVERGREEN STATE COLLEGE

2700 Evergreen Pkwy NW, Office of Admissions, Olympia, WA 98505
Phone: 360-867-6170 **Financial Aid Phone:** 360-867-6205
E-mail: admissions@evergreen.edu **CEEB Code:** 4292
Fax: 360-867-5114 **Website:** www.evergreen.edu **ACT Code:** 4457

This public school was founded in 1967. It has a 1000-acre campus.

RATINGS

Admissions Selectivity Rating: 71   **Fire Safety Rating:** 81   **Green Rating:** 99

STUDENTS AND FACULTY

Enrollment: 4,385. **Student Body:** 54% female, 46% male, 27% out-of-state, 1% international (23 countries represented). Asian 5%, African American 5%, Caucasian 69%, Hispanic 5%, Native American 4%.
Retention and Graduation: 72% freshmen return for sophomore year. 43% freshmen graduate within 4 years. 24% grads go on to further study within 1 year. 15% grads pursue arts and sciences degrees. 1% grads pursue law degrees. 1% grads pursue business degrees. 2% grads pursue medical degrees. **Faculty:** Student/faculty ratio 23:1. 169 full-time faculty. 86% hold PhDs, 25% are members of minority groups, 49% are women.

ACADEMICS

Degrees: Bachelor's, certificate, master's. **Classes:** Most classes have 20–29 students. **Majors with Highest Enrollment:** Environmental studies; liberal arts and sciences/liberal studies; social sciences, other. **Special Study Options:** Accelerated program, double major, exchange student program (domestic), independent study, internships, student-designed major, study abroad, teacher certification program, weekend college, Learning disabilities services, summer session for credit, off-campus study. **Combined degree programs:** BA/BS Lib Arts; Master Environ Stud/Pub Admin. Special programs offered to physically disabled students include note-taking services, tape recorders, tutors. **Career services:** Alumni network, alumni services, career/job search classes, career assessment, internships. **Career services highlights include:** Community Opportunities & Internship Fair (COIF) www.evergreen.edu/advising/coif.

FACILITIES

Housing: Coed dorms, special housing for disabled students, special housing for international students, apartments for married students, apartments for single students, wellness housing, theme housing, First-Year/Freshman residence halls, quiet housing, substance-free housing, Gender Neutral Housing,

Community Action House, Sustainability House. 85% of campus accessible to physically disabled. **Special Academic Facilities/Equipment:** Longhouse Cultural Center, 4 computer music labs, 3 digital studio production studios, 4 analog audio recording studio/control room clusters, digital still imaging lab, multimedia lab, 3 nonlinear video editing suites, 4 linear analog video editing suites, color and BandW photography labs, animation stand, 2 digital animation suites, film mixing studio with 5 editing suites, 2 flatbed film edit rooms, 3 A/V classrooms, 5 A/V lecture halls, Media Loan equipment checkout facility, academic sailing fleet (two 40' wooden sailboats), organic farm, scanning electron microscope, gas chromatography mass spectrometer, FTNMR, FTIR, scientific computing laboratory, printmaking studio, ceramics studio, academic wood and metal shops, weaving studio, fine metal studio, two art galleries. **Computers:** 100% of classrooms, 95% of dorms, 100% of libraries, 100% of dining areas, 100% of student union, 80% of common outdoor areas have wireless network access. Students can register for classes online. Administrative functions (other than registration) can be performed online.

CAMPUS LIFE

Environment: City. **Activities:** Choral groups, dance, drama/theater, literary magazine, music ensembles, pep band, radio station, student government, student newspaper, student-run film society, television station, campus ministries, Model UN. **Organizations:** 61 registered organizations, 3 religious organizations. **Athletics (Intercollegiate):** *Men:* Basketball, cross-country, soccer, track/field (outdoor), track/field (indoor). *Women:* Basketball, cross-country, soccer, track/field (outdoor), track/field (indoor), volleyball. **On-Campus Highlights:** Longhouse Cultural and Education Center, Organic Farm, College Library, College Activities Building, New Seminar II Building, The Flaming Eggplant, a student-run cafe featuring organic, local, and vegan food. **Environmental Initiatives:** We have completed the planning and begun implementation of our Climate Action Plan—Carbon Neutrality by 2020. Integrating sustainability across the curriculum begins; Free bus passes for all faculty/staff/students; first publicly funded LEED Gold building in the state of Washington; 32% of food purchases from local/organic sources; campus waste diversion and composting programs; annual carbon inventory.

ADMISSIONS

Freshman Academic Profile: Average high school GPA 3.01. 12% in top 10% of high school class, 29% in top 25% of high school class, 62% in top 50% of high school class. SAT Math middle 50% range 460–590. SAT Critical Reading middle 50% range 500–640. SAT Writing middle 50% range 480–600. ACT middle 50% range 20–26. Minimum paper TOEFL 550. Minimum computer TOEFL 213. Minimum web-based TOEFL 79. **Basis for Candidate Selection:** *Very important factors considered include:* Application essay, academic GPA, rigor of secondary school record. *Important factors considered include:* Standardized test scores, first generation, level of applicant's interest. *Other factors considered include:* Recommendation(s), extracurricular activities, interview, volunteer work, work experience. **Freshman Admission Requirements:** High school diploma is required and GED is accepted. *Academic units required:* 4 English, 3 mathematics, 2 science, (1 science labs), 2 foreign language, 3 social studies, 1 academic electives, 1 fine, visual or performing arts elective or other college prep elective from the areas above. **Freshman Admission Statistics:** 1,769 applied, 95% admitted, 34% enrolled. **Transfer Admission Requirements:** College transcript(s), minimum college GPA of 2 required. Lowest grade transferable C. **General Admission Information:** Application fee $50. Notification on a rolling basis, beginning on or about 11/1. Nonfall registration accepted. Admission may be deferred for a maximum of One quarter. Credit offered for CEEB Advanced Placement tests.

COSTS AND FINANCIAL AID

Annual in-state tuition $5,412. Annual out-of-state tuition $16,440. Room and board $8,052. Required fees $547. Average book expense $924. **Required Forms and Deadlines:** FAFSA, institution's own financial aid form. Priority financial aid filing date 3/15. **Notification of Awards:** Applicants will be notified of awards on a rolling basis beginning 4/1. **Types of Aid:** *Need-based scholarships/grants:* Federal Pell, SEOG, state scholarships/grants, private scholarships, the school's own gift aid, Federal Academic Competitiveness Grant (ACG); National Science and Mathematics Access to Retain Talent Grant(SMART Grant). *Loans:* FFEL Subsidized Stafford, FFEL Unsubsidized Stafford, FFEL PLUS, Federal Perkins, Private Alternative Loans. **Student Employment:** Federal Work-Study Program available. Institutional employment available. Highest amount earned per year from on-campus jobs $9,975. Off-campus job opportunities are good. **Financial Aid Statistics:** 39% freshmen, 46% undergrads receive need-based scholarship or grant aid. 26% freshmen, 10% undergrads receive non-need-based scholarship or grant aid. 31% freshmen, 43% undergrads receive need-based self-help aid. 1% freshmen, 47% freshmen, 55% undergrads receive any aid. 51% undergrads borrow to pay for school. Average cumulative indebtedness $14,310. **Criteria for awarding institutional aid:** *Non-need-based:* Academics, art, athletics, state/district residency.

EXCELSIOR COLLEGE

7 Columbia Circle, Albany, NY 12203-5159
Phone: 518-464-8500 **Financial Aid Phone:** 518-464-8500
E-mail: admissions@excelsior.edu **CEEB Code:** 759
Fax: 518-464-8777 **Website:** www.excelsior.edu **ACT Code:** 20214

This private school was founded in 1970.

RATINGS

Admissions Selectivity Rating: 60* **Fire Safety Rating:** 60* **Green Rating:** 60*

STUDENTS AND FACULTY

Enrollment: 32,133. **Student Body:** 58% female, 42% male, 90% out-of-state, international (56 countries represented). Asian 4%, African American 17%, Caucasian 58%, Hispanic 5%, Native American 1%.

ACADEMICS

Degrees: Associate, bachelor's, master's, post-bachelor's certificate, post-master's certificate. **Classes:** Most classes have 10–19 students. **Majors with Highest Enrollment:** Business administration and management; liberal arts and sciences/liberal studies; nursing/registered nurse (RN, ASN, BSN, MSN). **Special Study Options:** Accelerated program, distance learning, external degree program, honors program, independent study. **Combined degree programs:** RN/MSN. **Career services:** Alumni network, alumni services, career assessment.

FACILITIES

Housing: No housing available on campus. **Computers:** Students can register for classes online. Administrative functions (other than registration) can be performed online.

CAMPUS LIFE

Environment: City. **Activities: Organizations:** 1 honor societies. **Environmental Initiatives:** EC has a staff created and led committee that looks for opportunites to create a more green environment.

ADMISSIONS

Freshman Admission Requirements: High school diploma is required and GED is accepted. **Freshman Admission Statistics:** Lowest grade transferable C. **General Admission Information:** Application fee $75. Nonfall registration accepted.

COSTS AND FINANCIAL AID

Required Forms and Deadlines: FAFSA, institution's own financial aid form. **Notification of Awards:** Applicants will be notified of awards on a rolling basis beginning 8/1. **Types of Aid:** *Need-based scholarships/grants:* Federal Pell, state scholarships/grants, private scholarships, the school's own gift aid. *Loans:* Direct Subsidized Stafford, Direct Unsubsidized Stafford, Direct PLUS. **Financial Aid Statistics:** 3% undergrads receive any aid.

FAIRFIELD UNIVERSITY

1073 North Benson Road, Fairfield, CT 06824-5195
Phone: 203-254-4100 **Financial Aid Phone:** 203-254-4125
E-mail: admis@fairfield.edu **CEEB Code:** 3390
Fax: 203-254-4199 **Website:** www.fairfield.edu **ACT Code:** 560

This private school, affiliated with the Roman CatholiC–Jesuit Church, was founded in 1942. It has a 200-acre campus.

RATINGS

Admissions Selectivity Rating: 89 **Fire Safety Rating:** 91 **Green Rating:** 82

STUDENTS AND FACULTY

Enrollment: 3,623. **Student Body:** 58% female, 42% male, 73% out-of-state, 1% international (58 countries represented). Asian 3%, African American 4%, Caucasian 60%, Hispanic 8%.
Retention and Graduation: 88% freshmen return for sophomore year. 83% freshmen graduate within 4 years. 21% grads go on to further study within 1 year. 5% grads pursue arts and sciences degrees. 4% grads pursue law degrees.

5% grads pursue business degrees. 3% grads pursue medical degrees. **Faculty:** Student/faculty ratio 13:1. 253 full-time faculty, 92% hold PhDs, 49% are women.

ACADEMICS

Degrees: Associate, bachelor's, master's, post-master's certificate. **Classes:** Most classes have 20–29 students. **Majors with Highest Enrollment:** Finance; nursing/registered nurse (RN, ASN, BSN, MSN); psychology. **Special Study Options:** Cross-registration, double major, exchange student program (domestic), honors program, independent study, internships, liberal arts/career combination, student-designed major, study abroad, teacher certification program, 3/2 Program with UCONN, Rensselaer Polytechnic Institute of Technology, Columbia and Stevens Institute of Technology. **Honors programs:** Magis Scholars, Four year Honors Program, Corrigan Research Scholars. **Combined degree programs:** BA/MEng, BS/MS Software Engineering. Special programs offered to physically disabled students include note-taking services, reader services, tape recorders, tutors. **Career services:** Alumni network, alumni services, career/job search classes, career assessment, internships. **Career services highlights include:** Fairfield's proximity to NYC, Stamford, and Bridgeport maximizes student opportunities for internships in all majors from finance to psychology.

FACILITIES

Housing: Coed dorms, special housing for disabled students, apartments for single students, Wellness Floor, Sophomore College, Women in Math & Science, Freshmen Residence Halls, Diversity & Social Justice Floor (for Sophomores), Leadership House, Community Service House, The Green House, Empowering Women House; Extensive theme based living-learning options for sophomores. 70% of campus accessible to physically disabled. **Special Academic Facilities/Equipment:** Quick Center for the arts, 2 art galleries, media center, TV studio, language labs, computer center for teacher education, Business Experiential, Simulation & Trading Floor (BEST) at the School of Business. School of Nursing Learning Resouce center is a simulated hospital environment with a Human Patient Simulator (SimMan) for simulation based learning. **Computers:** 50% of classrooms, 100% of dorms, 100% of libraries, 100% of dining areas, 100% of student union, 5% of common outdoor areas have wireless network access. Students can register for classes online. Administrative functions (other than registration) can be performed online.

CAMPUS LIFE

Environment: Town. **Activities:** Choral groups, concert band, dance, drama/theater, jazz band, literary magazine, music ensembles, pep band, radio station, student government, student newspaper, student-run film society, television station, yearbook, campus ministries, international student organization, Model UN. **Organizations:** 110 registered organizations, 21 honor societies, 3 religious organizations. **Athletics (Intercollegiate):** *Men:* Baseball, basketball, crew/rowing, cross-country, diving, golf, lacrosse, soccer, swimming, tennis. *Women:* Basketball, crew/rowing, cross-country, diving, field hockey, golf, lacrosse, soccer, softball, swimming, tennis, volleyball. **On-Campus Highlights:** Quick Center for the Arts(includes Walsh Art Gallery, Kelley Theatre and Wien Theatre, Egan/Loyola Chapel, DiMenna-Nyselius Library, Leslie C. Quick, Jr. Recreation Complex, Barone Campus Center (Student Center), Jazzman's Coffee Bar. **Environmental Initiatives:** We have joined Campus Climate Pact. Built a Co-generation facility providing 90% of campus electricity; 60% campus heating. Large scale recycling and composting/biofuels initiative. While there is no Full-time dedicated staff person, sustainability efforts are performed by several folk and overseen by the Environmental Steering Committees that was convened in 2006–07 and meets quarterly.

ADMISSIONS

Freshman Academic Profile: Average high school GPA 3.4. 41% in top 10% of high school class, 78% in top 25% of high school class, 95% in top 50% of high school class. 55% from public high schools. SAT Math middle 50% range 530–630. SAT Critical Reading middle 50% range 520–610. SAT Writing middle 50% range 530–630. Minimum paper TOEFL 550. Minimum computer TOEFL 213. Minimum web-based TOEFL 80. **Basis for Candidate Selection:** *Very important factors considered include:* Application essay, academic GPA, recommendation(s), rigor of secondary school record. *Important factors considered include:* Character/personal qualities, extracurricular activities, first generation, interview, talent/ability, volunteer work, work experience. *Other factors considered include:* Class rank, standardized test scores, alumni/ae relation, geographical residence, racial/ethnic status. **Freshman Admission Requirements:** High school diploma is required and GED is not accepted. *Academic units required:* 4 English, 3 mathematics, 2 science, (2 science labs), 2 foreign language, 2 social studies, 2 history, 1 academic electives. *Academic units recommended:* 4 English, 4 mathematics, 3 science, (2 science labs), 4 foreign language, 2 social studies, 2 history, 1 academic electives. **Freshman Admission Statistics:** 8,316 applied, 65% admitted, 26% enrolled. **Transfer Admission Requirements:** High school transcript, college transcript(s), essay or personal statement, statement of good standing from prior institution(s). Minimum college GPA of .03 required. Lowest grade transferable C. **General**

Admission Information: Application fee $60. Regular application deadline 1/15. Regular notification 4/1. Nonfall registration not accepted. Admission may be deferred for a maximum of 1 year. Credit and/or placement offered for CEEB Advanced Placement tests.

COSTS AND FINANCIAL AID

Annual tuition $36,900. Room and board $11,270. Required fees $590. Average book expense $900. **Required Forms and Deadlines:** FAFSA, CSS/Financial Aid PROFILE, noncustodial PROFILE, business/farm supplement. Financial aid filing deadline 2/15. Priority financial aid filing date 2/15. **Notification of Awards:** Applicants will be notified of awards on or about 4/1. **Types of Aid:** *Need-based scholarships/grants:* Federal Pell, SEOG, state scholarships/grants, private scholarships, the school's own gift aid, Federal Nursing Scholarships. *Loans:* FFEL Subsidized Stafford, FFEL Unsubsidized Stafford, FFEL PLUS, Federal Perkins, Federal Nursing, Alternative Loans. **Student Employment:** Federal Work-Study Program available. Institutional employment available. Highest amount earned per year from on-campus jobs $1,500. Off-campus job opportunities are good. **Financial Aid Statistics:** 49% freshmen, 49% undergrads receive need-based scholarship or grant aid. 17% freshmen, 15% undergrads receive non-need-based scholarship or grant aid. 48% freshmen, 46% undergrads receive need-based self-help aid. 6% freshmen, 7% undergrads receive athletic scholarships. 68% freshmen, 63% undergrads receive any aid. 60% undergrads borrow to pay for school. Average cumulative indebtedness $35,161. **Criteria for awarding institutional aid:** *Non-need-based:* Academics, alumni affiliation, art, athletics, leadership, music/drama.

FAIRLEIGH DICKINSON UNIVERSITY, COLLEGE AT FLORHAM

285 Madison Ave, Madison, NJ 07940
Phone: 800-338-8803
E-mail: globaleducation@fdu.edu **CEEB Code:** 226241
Fax: 973-443-8088 **Website:** www.fdu.edu **ACT Code:** 2554

This private school was founded in 1942. It has a 178-acre campus.

RATINGS

Admissions Selectivity Rating: 77   **Fire Safety Rating:** 60*   **Green Rating:** 72

STUDENTS AND FACULTY

Enrollment: 2,419. **Student Body:** 53% female, 47% male, 15% out-of-state, 1% international (12 countries represented). Asian 3%, African American 8%, Caucasian 68%, Hispanic 8%.
Retention and Graduation: 75% freshmen return for sophomore year. 35% freshmen graduate within 4 years.

ACADEMICS

Degrees: Bachelor's, master's, post-bachelor's certificate, post-master's certificate. **Majors with Highest Enrollment:** Business administration and management; communication studies/speech communication and rhetoric; psychology. **Special Study Options:** Accelerated program, cooperative education program, cross-registration, distance learning, double major, external degree program, honors program, independent study, internships, liberal arts/career combination, student-designed major, teacher certification program, weekend college. **Combined degree programs:** BA/MD, BA/MA, BA/DDS, BA or BS/MAT, BA or BS/MBA, BA/MPA. Special programs offered to physically disabled students include note-taking services, reader services, tape recorders, tutors. **Career services:** Alumni network, alumni services, career/job search classes, career assessment, internships. **Career services highlights include:** Experiential learning.

FACILITIES

Housing: Coed dorms, special housing for disabled students 34% of campus accessible to physically disabled. **Computers:** 100% of classrooms, 100% of libraries, 100% of dining areas, 100% of student union, have wireless network access. Students can register for classes online. Administrative functions (other than registration) can be performed online.

CAMPUS LIFE

Environment: Village. **Activities:** Choral groups, dance, drama/theater, literary magazine, musical theater, radio station, student government, student newspaper, student-run film society, yearbook, campus ministries, international student organization. **Organizations:** 44 registered organizations, 9 honor societies, 3 religious organizations. 6 fraternities, 4 sororities. **Athletics (Intercollegiate):** *Men:* Baseball, basketball, cross-country, football, golf, lacrosse, soccer, swimming, tennis. *Women:* Basketball, cross-country, field hockey, lacrosse, soccer, softball, swimming, tennis, volleyball. **On-Campus Highlights:**

Recreation Center, Bottle Hill Pub, Florham Perks, L'Orangerie of Library, Mansion gardens. **Environmental Initiatives:** RecycleMania, recycling bins, new contruction LEED certification, HVAC upgrades will be energy efficient.

ADMISSIONS

Freshman Academic Profile: Average high school GPA 3.17. 16% in top 10% of high school class, 43% in top 25% of high school class, 75% in top 50% of high school class. SAT Math middle 50% range 470–570. SAT Critical Reading middle 50% range 460–550. SAT Writing middle 50% range 450–560. Minimum paper TOEFL 550. Minimum computer TOEFL 213. Minimum web-based TOEFL 79. **Basis for Candidate Selection:** *Very important factors considered include:* Academic GPA, rigor of secondary school record. *Important factors considered include:* Standardized test scores. *Other factors considered include:* Class rank, recommendation(s), extracurricular activities, interview, volunteer work, work experience. **Freshman Admission Requirements:** High school diploma is required and GED is accepted. *Academic units required:* 4 English, 3 mathematics, 2 science, (2 science labs), 2 foreign language, 2 social studies, 2 history, 3 academic electives. *Academic units recommended:* 3 mathematics, 3 science, (3 science labs), 2 foreign language, 2 social studies, 2 history, 3 academic electives. **Freshman Admission Statistics:** 3,907 applied, 67% admitted, 25% enrolled. **Transfer Admission Requirements:** College transcript(s), minimum college GPA of 2.0 required. Lowest grade transferable C. **General Admission Information:** Application fee $40. Notification on a rolling basis, beginning on or about 11/15. Nonfall registration accepted. Admission may be deferred for a maximum of 1 year. Credit offered for CEEB Advanced Placement tests.

COSTS AND FINANCIAL AID

Student Employment: Federal Work-Study Program available. Institutional employment available. Off-campus job opportunities are good.

FAIRLEIGH DICKINSON UNIVERSITY, METROPOLITAN CAMPUS

1000 River Road, H-DH3-10, Teaneck, NJ 07666-1966
Phone: 201-692-2553
E-mail: globaleducation@fdu.edu **CEEB Code:** 226341
Fax: 201-692-7319 **Website:** www.fdu.edu **ACT Code:** 2552

This private school was founded in 1942. It has a 68-acre campus.

RATINGS

Admissions Selectivity Rating: 77   **Fire Safety Rating:** 60*   **Green Rating:** 71

STUDENTS AND FACULTY

Enrollment: 3,672. **Student Body:** 57% female, 43% male, 14% out-of-state, 7% international (64 countries represented). Asian 6%, African American 14%, Caucasian 34%, Hispanic 26%.
Retention and Graduation: 21% freshmen graduate within 4 years.

ACADEMICS

Degrees: Associate, bachelor's, certificate, master's, post-bachelor's certificate, post-master's certificate, terminal associate. **Majors with Highest Enrollment:** Business administration and management; nursing/registered nurse (RN, ASN, BSN, MSN); psychology. **Special Study Options:** Accelerated program, cooperative education program, cross-registration, distance learning, English as a Second Language (ESL), external degree program, honors program, independent study, internships, liberal arts/career combination, student-designed major, study abroad, teacher certification program, weekend college. **Combined degree programs:** BA/MD, BA/MA, BA/DDS, BA/MPA, BA/BS-MAT, BA/MBA, BS/DMD,BS/DC, BSEE/MSEE, BSEE/MSCE. Special programs offered to physically disabled students include note-taking services, reader services, tape recorders, tutors. **Career services:** Alumni network, alumni services, career/job search classes, career assessment, internships. **Career services highlights include:** Experiential Learning.

FACILITIES

Housing: Coed dorms, special housing for disabled students, °LIFE House—Substance Free Living °Global Scholars Hall °Honor's House °Academic Year Round Housing. 41% of campus accessible to physically disabled. **Computers:** 90% of classrooms, 100% of libraries, 100% of dining areas, 100% of student union, have wireless network access. Students can register for classes online. Administrative functions (other than registration) can be performed online.

CAMPUS LIFE

Environment: Town. **Activities:** Choral groups, dance, drama/theater, literary magazine, pep band, radio station, student government, student newspaper,

student-run film society, yearbook, campus ministries, international student organization, Model UN. **Organizations:** 72 registered organizations, 10 honor societies, 4 religious organizations, 5 fraternities, 7 sororities. **Athletics (Intercollegiate):** *Men:* Baseball, basketball, cross-country, golf, soccer, tennis, track/field (indoor). *Women:* Basketball, bowling, cross-country, fencing, golf, soccer, softball, tennis, track/field (indoor), volleyball. **On-Campus Highlights:** Weiner Library, Fitness Center, Jeepers (Wireless Cafe), Knight Club, Hackensack River. **Environmental Initiatives:** RecycleMania, recycling bins, new construction LEED certification, HVAC upgrades will be energy efficient.

ADMISSIONS

Freshman Academic Profile: Average high school GPA 3.05. 17% in top 10% of high school class, 39% in top 25% of high school class, 81% in top 50% of high school class. SAT Math middle 50% range 450–560. SAT Critical Reading middle 50% range 440–530. SAT Writing middle 50% range 430–530. Minimum paper TOEFL 550. Minimum computer TOEFL 213. Minimum web-based TOEFL 79. **Basis for Candidate Selection:** *Very important factors considered include:* Academic GPA, rigor of secondary school record. *Important factors considered include:* Standardized test scores. *Other factors considered include:* Class rank, recommendation(s), extracurricular activities, interview, volunteer work, work experience. **Freshman Admission Requirements:** High school diploma is required and GED is accepted. *Academic units required:* 4 English, 3 mathematics, 2 science, (2 science labs), 2 foreign language, 2 social studies, 2 history, 3 academic electives. *Academic units recommended:* 3 mathematics, 3 science, (3 science labs), 2 foreign language, 2 social studies, 2 history, 3 academic electives. **Freshman Admission Statistics:** 5,108 applied, 57% admitted, 24% enrolled. **Transfer Admission Requirements:** College transcript(s), minimum college GPA of 2.0 required. Lowest grade transferable C. **General Admission Information:** Application fee $40. Notification on a rolling basis, beginning on or about 11/15. Nonfall registration accepted. Admission may be deferred for a maximum of 1 year. Credit offered for CEEB Advanced Placement tests.

COSTS AND FINANCIAL AID

Student Employment: Federal Work-Study Program available. Off-campus job opportunities are good.

FAIRMONT STATE UNIVERSITY, INCLUDING PIERPONT COMMUNITY & TECHNICAL COLLEGE

Office of Admissions, Fairmont State, 1201 Locust Ave, Fairmont, WV 26554
Phone: 304-367-4892 **Financial Aid Phone:** 304-367-4813
E-mail: admit@fairmontstate.edu **CEEB Code:** 4520
Website: www.fairmontstate.edu **ACT Code:** 4520

This public school was founded in 1865.

RATINGS

Admissions Selectivity Rating: 67   **Fire Safety Rating:** 60*   **Green Rating:** 60*

STUDENTS AND FACULTY

Enrollment: 6,227. **Student Body:** 57% female, 43% male, 4% out-of-state, 1% international . African American 4%, Caucasian 91%, Hispanic 1%.
Retention and Graduation: 70% freshmen return for sophomore year. 11% freshmen graduate within 4 years. **Faculty:** Student/faculty ratio 18:1. 232 full-time faculty, 48% hold PhDs, 6% are members of minority groups, 45% are women.

ACADEMICS

Degrees: Associate, bachelor's, certificate, master's, terminal associate, transfer associate. **Classes:** Most classes have 10–19 students. Most lab/discussion sessions have fewer than 10 students. **Majors with Highest Enrollment:** Business administration and management; criminal justice/safety studies; teacher education and professional development, specific levels and methods, other. **Special Study Options:** Accelerated program, cooperative education program, cross-registration, distance learning, double major, dual enrollment, English as a Second Language (ESL), honors program, independent study, internships, liberal arts/career combination, study abroad, teacher certification program, weekend college. Special programs offered to physically disabled students include note-taking services, reader services, tutors. **Career services:** Career/job search classes, career assessment.

FACILITIES

Housing: Coed dorms, men's dorms, women's dorms, apartments for married students, apartments for single students. 100% of campus accessible to physically disabled. **Special Academic Facilities/Equipment:** Folk Life Center. **Computers:** Students can register for classes online. Administrative functions (other than registration) can be performed online.

CAMPUS LIFE

Environment: Town. **Activities:** Choral groups, concert band, dance, drama/theater, jazz band, literary magazine, marching band, music ensembles, musical theater, student government, student newspaper, symphony orchestra, yearbook, campus ministries, international student organization. **Organizations:** 90 registered organizations, 4 religious organizations. 4 fraternities, 3 sororities. **Athletics (Intercollegiate):** *Men:* Baseball, basketball, cross-country, football, golf, swimming, tennis. *Women:* Basketball, cheerleading, cross-country, golf, softball, tennis, volleyball.

ADMISSIONS

Freshman Academic Profile: Average high school GPA 3. 7% in top 10% of high school class, 24% in top 25% of high school class, 57% in top 50% of high school class. SAT Math middle 50% range 390–500. SAT Critical Reading middle 50% range 400–507.5. ACT middle 50% range 17–22. Minimum paper TOEFL 500. Minimum computer TOEFL 173. **Basis for Candidate Selection:** *Very important factors considered include:* Academic GPA, standardized test scores. **Freshman Admission Requirements:** High school diploma is required and GED is accepted. *Academic units required:* 4 English, 3 mathematics, 3 science, (2 science labs), 3 social studies, 1 history. *Academic units recommended:* 2 foreign language. **Freshman Admission Statistics:** 3,400 applied, 79% admitted, 45% enrolled. **Transfer Admission Requirements:** College transcript(s), minimum college GPA of 2.00 required. Lowest grade transferable D. **General Admission Information:** Notification on a rolling basis, beginning on or about 10/1. Nonfall registration accepted. Credit and/or placement offered for CEEB Advanced Placement tests.

COSTS AND FINANCIAL AID

Annual in-state tuition $4,656. Annual out-of-state tuition $9,956. Room and board $5,990. Average book expense $900. **Student Employment:** Federal Work-Study Program available. Institutional employment available. Off-campus job opportunities are good. **Financial Aid Statistics:** 85% freshmen, 80% undergrads receive any aid.

FAITH BAPTIST BIBLE COLLEGE AND THEOLOGICAL SEMINARY

1900 NW 4th Street, Ankeny, IA 50023
Phone: 1.888.faith.4.u **Financial Aid Phone:** 515-964-0601
E-mail: admissions@faith.edu **CEEB Code:** 6214
Fax: 515-964-1638 **Website:** www.faith.edu **ACT Code:** 1315

This private school, affiliated with the Baptist Church, was founded in 1921. It has a 52-acre campus.

RATINGS

Admissions Selectivity Rating: 84   **Fire Safety Rating:** 60*   **Green Rating:** 60*

STUDENTS AND FACULTY

Enrollment: 340. **Student Body:** 59% female, 41% male, 50% out-of-state, 1% international . Asian 1%, African American 1%, Caucasian 94%, Hispanic 2%, Native American 1%.
Retention and Graduation: 79% freshmen return for sophomore year. 21% freshmen graduate within 4 years. 28% grads go on to further study within 1 year. **Faculty:** Student/faculty ratio 12:1. 21 full-time faculty, 62% hold PhDs, 10% are members of minority groups, 14% are women.

ACADEMICS

Degrees: Associate, bachelor's, certificate, master's. **Classes:** Most classes have fewer than 10 students. **Majors with Highest Enrollment:** Bible/biblical studies; elementary education and teaching; religious education. **Special Study Options:** Independent study, internships, teacher certification program.

FACILITIES

Housing: Special housing for disabled students, men's dorms, women's dorms, apartments for married students, apartments for single students **Computers:** 75% of classrooms, 100% of dorms, 100% of libraries, 100% of dining areas, 100% of student union, 60% of common outdoor areas have wireless network access.

CAMPUS LIFE

Environment: Town. **Activities:** Choral groups, concert band, dance, drama/theater, music ensembles, student government, symphony orchestra, yearbook, campus ministries, international student organization. **Organizations:** 1 registered organizations, 1 religious organization. **Athletics (Intercollegiate):** *Men:* Basketball, soccer. *Women:* Basketball, soccer, volleyball. **On-Campus Highlights:** Convocation Building, Benson Hall, Library, Gray Hall, Residence Halls.

ADMISSIONS

Freshman Academic Profile: Average high school GPA 3.38. 16% in top 10% of high school class, 42% in top 25% of high school class, 65% in top 50% of high school class. SAT Math middle 50% range 540–570. SAT Critical Reading middle 50% range 570–630. SAT Writing middle 50% range 580–620. ACT middle 50% range 20–25. Minimum paper TOEFL 500. Minimum web-based TOEFL 173. **Basis for Candidate Selection:** *Very important factors considered include:* Religious affiliation/commitment. *Important factors considered include:* Application essay. *Other factors considered include:* Class rank, academic GPA, recommendation(s), standardized test scores, character/personal qualities, extracurricular activities, interview, level of applicant's interest, talent/ability, volunteer work. **Freshman Admission Requirements:** High school diploma is required and GED is accepted. *Academic units recommended:* 4 English, 4 mathematics, 2 science, 2 social studies, 2 history. **Freshman Admission Statistics:** 179 applied, 57% admitted, 89% enrolled. **Transfer Admission Requirements:** College transcript(s), essay or personal statement, statement of good standing from prior institution(s). Minimum college GPA of 2.0 required. Lowest grade transferable C. **General Admission Information:** Application fee $25. Regular application deadline 8/1. Notification on a rolling basis, beginning on or about 9/1. Nonfall registration accepted. Admission may be deferred for a maximum of 1 year. Credit offered for CEEB Advanced Placement tests.

COSTS AND FINANCIAL AID

Required Forms and Deadlines: FAFSA. **Types of Aid:** *Need-based scholarships/grants:* Federal Pell, state scholarships/grants, private scholarships, the school's own gift aid. *Loans:* FFEL Subsidized Stafford, FFEL Unsubsidized Stafford, FFEL PLUS **Student Employment:** Institutional employment available. Off-campus job opportunities are excellent. **Financial Aid Statistics:** 70% freshmen, 95% undergrads receive any aid. **Criteria for awarding institutional aid:** *Non-need-based:* Academics, leadership, music/drama, state/district residency.

FAULKNER UNIVERSITY

5345 Atlanta Highway, Montgomery, AL 36109-3398
Phone: 334-386-7200 **Financial Aid Phone:** 334-386-7195
E-mail: admissions@faulkner.edu **CEEB Code:** 1034
Fax: 334-386-7137 **Website:** www.faulkner.edu **ACT Code:** 3

This private school, affiliated with the Church of Christ Church, was founded in 1942. It has a 78-acre campus.

RATINGS

Admissions Selectivity Rating: 70   **Fire Safety Rating:** 64   **Green Rating:** 60*

STUDENTS AND FACULTY

Enrollment: 2,032. **Student Body:** 63% female, 37% male, 12% out-of-state, 1% international (15 countries represented). Asian 1%, African American 57%, Caucasian 63%, Hispanic 1%, Native American 1%.
Retention and Graduation: 59% freshmen return for sophomore year. 8% freshmen graduate within 4 years. 80% grads go on to further study within 1 year. 35% grads pursue arts and sciences degrees. 12% grads pursue law degrees. 32% grads pursue business degrees, 19% grads pursue medical degrees. **Faculty:** Student/faculty ratio 19:1. 105 full-time faculty, 67% hold PhDs, 10% are members of minority groups, 32% are women.

ACADEMICS

Degrees: Associate, bachelor's, first professional, master's. **Classes:** Most classes have fewer than 10 students. Most lab/discussion sessions have fewer than 10 students. **Majors with Highest Enrollment:** Business/commerce; management information systems. **Special Study Options:** Accelerated program, cooperative education program, cross-registration, distance learning, double major, dual enrollment, honors program, independent study, internships, liberal arts/career combination, study abroad, teacher certification program, weekend college. **Honors programs:** Great Books Honors College. Special programs offered to physically disabled students include note-taking services, reader services, tape recorders, tutors. **Career services:** Alumni services, career/job search classes, career assessment, internships. **Career services highlights include:** All undergraduate programs have an internship. In fall 2009 the University is starting a Spiritual Formation Program with a service-learning component.

FACILITIES

Housing: Special housing for disabled students, men's dorms, women's dorms, apartments for single students. 75% of campus accessible to physically disabled. **Computers:** 100% of classrooms, 100% of dorms, 100% of libraries, 100% of dining areas, 100% of student union, 100% of common outdoor areas have wireless network access. Administrative functions (other than registration) can be performed online.

CAMPUS LIFE
Environment: City. **Activities:** Choral groups, drama/theater, music ensembles, musical theater, pep band, student government, student newspaper, yearbook, campus ministries. **Organizations:** 12 registered organizations, 5 honor societies, 3 religious organizations. 5 fraternities, 5 sororities. **Athletics (Intercollegiate):** *Men:* Baseball, basketball, cheerleading, fishing, football, golf, soccer. *Women:* Cheerleading, fishing, soccer, softball, volleyball. **On-Campus Highlights:** Cafe Sienna, Student Multiplex, Dorm Lobbies, Perry Cafeteria, Dinner Theatre.

ADMISSIONS
Freshman Academic Profile: Average high school GPA 3.08. 8% in top 10% of high school class, 10% in top 25% of high school class, 40% in top 50% of high school class. 75% from public high schools. SAT Math middle 50% range 430–550. SAT Critical Reading middle 50% range 440–560. ACT middle 50% range 18–22. Minimum paper TOEFL 450. Minimum computer TOEFL 133. **Basis for Candidate Selection:** *Very important factors considered include:* Class rank, recommendation(s), rigor of secondary school record, standardized test scores, character/personal qualities, extracurricular activities, interview. *Important factors considered include:* Application essay, alumni/ae relation, religious affiliation/commitment, talent/ability. *Other factors considered include:* volunteer work, work experience. **Freshman Admission Requirements:** High school diploma is required and GED is accepted. *Academic units recommended:* 12 academic electives. **Freshman Admission Statistics:** 982 applied, 59% admitted, 48% enrolled. **Transfer Admission Requirements:** High school transcript, college transcript(s), standardized test scores, statement of good standing from prior institution(s). Minimum college GPA of 2.0 required. Lowest grade transferable C. **General Admission Information:** Application fee $10. Notification on a rolling basis, beginning on or about 8/1. Nonfall registration accepted. Admission may be deferred for a maximum of 12. Credit and/or placement offered for CEEB Advanced Placement tests.

COSTS AND FINANCIAL AID
Annual tuition $12,720. Room and board $6,320. Required fees $1,170. Average book expense $1,200. **Required Forms and Deadlines:** FAFSA, institution's own financial aid form, state aid form. Priority financial aid filing date 5/1. **Notification of Awards:** Applicants will be notified of awards on a rolling basis beginning 6/1. **Types of Aid:** *Need-based scholarships/grants:* Federal Pell, SEOG, state scholarships/grants, private scholarships, the school's own gift aid. *Loans:* FFEL Subsidized Stafford, FFEL Unsubsidized Stafford, FFEL PLUS, Federal Perkins. **Student Employment:** Federal Work-Study Program available. Institutional employment available. Highest amount earned per year from on-campus jobs $1,250. **Financial Aid Statistics:** 53% freshmen, 53% undergrads receive need-based scholarship or grant aid. 43% freshmen, 42% undergrads receive non-need-based scholarship or grant aid. 62% freshmen, 62% undergrads receive need-based self-help aid. 12% freshmen, 11% undergrads receive athletic scholarships. 95% freshmen, 93% undergrads receive any aid. 87% undergrads borrow to pay for school. Average cumulative indebtedness $19,300. **Criteria for awarding institutional aid:** *Non-need-based:* Academics, alumni affiliation, art, athletics, job skills, leadership, minority status, music/drama, religious affiliation, state/district residency.

ACADEMICS
Degrees: Bachelor's, master's. **Classes:** Most classes have 20–29 students. Most lab/discussion sessions have 20–29 students. **Majors with Highest Enrollment:** Business/commerce; criminal justice/police science; elementary education and teaching. **Special Study Options:** Cooperative education program, distance learning, double major, honors program, independent study, internships, liberal arts/career combination, study abroad, teacher certification program, weekend college. **Career services:** Alumni services, career/job search classes, career assessment, internships.

FACILITIES
Housing: Special housing for disabled students, men's dorms, women's dorms, apartments for married students, apartments for single students. 100% of campus accessible to physically disabled. **Special Academic Facilities/Equipment:** Planetarium; Observatory; Distance Learning Center; Science Labs; Health, Physical Education, and Recreation Complex; Art Gallery.

CAMPUS LIFE
Activities: Choral groups, concert band, dance, drama/theater, jazz band, marching band, music ensembles, musical theater, opera, pep band, radio station, student government, student newspaper, student-run film society, television station, yearbook. **Organizations:** 56 registered organizations, 7 honor societies, 3 religious organizations. 4 fraternities, 4 sororities. **Athletics (Intercollegiate):** *Men:* Basketball, cheerleading, cross-country, football, golf. *Women:* Basketball, cheerleading, cross-country, softball, tennis, volleyball.

ADMISSIONS
Freshman Academic Profile: SAT Math middle 50% range 360–470. SAT Critical Reading middle 50% range 380–470. **Basis for Candidate Selection:** *Important factors considered include:* Class rank, rigor of secondary school record, standardized test scores, character/personal qualities, extracurricular activities, talent/ability. **Freshman Admission Requirements:** High school diploma is required and GED is accepted. High school diploma is required and GED is not accepted. *Academic units required:* 4 English, 3 mathematics, 3 science, 1 social studies, 1 history, 6 academic electives. *Academic units recommended:* 2 foreign language. **Freshman Admission Statistics:** 1,570 applied, 85% admitted, 58% enrolled. **Transfer Admission Requirements:** College transcript(s), statement of good standing from prior institution(s). Lowest grade transferable C. **General Admission Information:** Application fee $25. Regular application deadline 8/15. Notification on a rolling basis, beginning on or about 11/1. Nonfall registration accepted. Credit and/or placement offered for CEEB Advanced Placement tests.

COSTS AND FINANCIAL AID
Annual in-state tuition $1,258. Annual out-of-state tuition $10,173. Room and board $3,820. Required fees $437. Average book expense $160. **Required Forms and Deadlines:** FAFSA, institution's own financial aid form. **Notification of Awards:** Applicants will be notified of awards on or about 7/15. **Types of Aid:** *Need-based scholarships/grants:* Federal Pell, SEOG, state scholarships/grants, private scholarships, the school's own gift aid. *Loans:* Direct Subsidized Stafford, Direct Unsubsidized Stafford, Direct PLUS, FFEL Subsidized Stafford, FFEL Unsubsidized Stafford, FFEL PLUS, Federal Perkins, Federal Nursing, state loans **Student Employment:** Federal Work-Study Program available. Off-campus job opportunities are excellent.

FAYETTEVILLE STATE UNIVERSITY

Newbold Station, Fayetteville, NC 28301
Phone: 910-672-1371
E-mail: admissions@uncfsu.edu **CEEB Code:** 5212
Fax: 910-672-1414 **Website:** www.uncfsu.edu **ACT Code:** 3098

This public school was founded in 1867. It has a 136-acre campus.

RATINGS
Admissions Selectivity Rating: 65   **Fire Safety Rating:** 60*   **Green Rating:** 60*

STUDENTS AND FACULTY
Enrollment: 3,660. **Student Body:** 64% female, 36% male, 11% out-of-state. Asian 1%, African American 80%, Caucasian 14%, Hispanic 4%, Native American 1%. **Retention and Graduation:** 74% freshmen return for sophomore year. 14% freshmen graduate within 4 years. 11% grads go on to further study within 1 year. 10% grads pursue arts and sciences degrees. 1% grads pursue business degrees. **Faculty:** Student/faculty ratio 20:1. 202 full-time faculty, 70% hold PhDs, 77% are members of minority groups, 41% are women.

FELICIAN COLLEGE

262 South Main Street, Lodi, NJ 07644
Phone: 201-559-6131
E-mail: admissions@felician.edu **CEEB Code:** 2321
Fax: 201-559-6138 **Website:** www.felician.edu **ACT Code:** 2559

This private school, affiliated with the Roman Catholic Church, was founded in 1942. It has a 27-acre campus.

RATINGS
Admissions Selectivity Rating: 66   **Fire Safety Rating:** 60*   **Green Rating:** 60*

STUDENTS AND FACULTY
Enrollment: 1,761. **Student Body:** 78% female, 22% male, 5% out-of-state, international . Asian 8%, African American 13%, Caucasian 43%, Hispanic 14%. **Retention and Graduation:** 60% freshmen return for sophomore year. 17% freshmen graduate within 4 years. 20% grads go on to further study within 1 year. 40% grads pursue arts and sciences degrees. 10% grads pursue law degrees. 12% grads pursue business degrees. 5% grads pursue medical degrees. **Faculty:** Student/faculty ratio 9:1. 81 full-time faculty, 57% are women.

ACADEMICS

Degrees: Associate, bachelor's, certificate, master's, post-bachelor's certificate. **Classes:** Most classes have greater than 100 students. **Majors with Highest Enrollment:** Business/commerce; nursing/registered nurse (RN, ASN, BSN, MSN); psychology. **Special Study Options:** Accelerated program, cooperative education program, cross-registration, distance learning, double major, dual enrollment, English as a Second Language (ESL), honors program, independent study, internships, liberal arts/career combination, student-designed major, study abroad, teacher certification program, weekend college. **Combined degree programs:** 3-2 Clinical lab science prog w/ U of Medicine NJ. Special programs offered to physically disabled students include note-taking services, reader services, tape recorders, tutors. **Career services:** Alumni services, career/job search classes, internships.

FACILITIES

Housing: Coed dorms, special housing for disabled students, men's dorms, women's dorms. 90% of campus accessible to physically disabled. **Special Academic Facilities/Equipment:** On-campus elementary school for exceptional children.

CAMPUS LIFE

Activities: Choral groups, drama/theater, literary magazine, student government **Organizations:** 25 registered organizations, 2 honor societies, 3 religious organizations. 1 fraternities, 2 sororities. **Athletics (Intercollegiate):** *Men:* Baseball, basketball, cheerleading, cross-country, soccer, track/field (outdoor). *Women:* Basketball, cheerleading, cross-country, soccer, softball, track/field (outdoor).

ADMISSIONS

Freshman Academic Profile: 70% from public high schools. SAT Math middle 50% range 400–500. SAT Writing middle 50% range 390–490. **Basis for Candidate Selection:** *Very important factors considered include:* Academic GPA, standardized test scores. *Important factors considered include:* Application essay, rigor of secondary school record. *Other factors considered include:* Class rank, recommendation(s), character/personal qualities, extracurricular activities, interview, volunteer work, work experience. **Freshman Admission Requirements:** High school diploma is required and GED is accepted. *Academic units recommended:* 4 English, 3 mathematics, 3 science, 3 social studies, 6 academic electives. **Freshman Admission Statistics:** 1,479 applied, 64% admitted, 28% enrolled. **Transfer Admission Requirements:** College transcript(s), essay or personal statement, Lowest grade transferable C. **General Admission Information:** Application fee $30. Notification on a rolling basis, beginning on or about 3/15. Nonfall registration accepted. Admission may be deferred for a maximum of 1 year. Credit and/or placement offered for CEEB Advanced Placement tests.

COSTS AND FINANCIAL AID

Annual tuition $18,900. Room and board $7,432. Required fees $1,050. Average book expense $2,163. **Required Forms and Deadlines:** FAFSA. **Notification of Awards:** Applicants will be notified of awards on a rolling basis beginning 4/1. **Types of Aid:** *Need-based scholarships/grants:* Federal Pell, SEOG, state scholarships/grants, private scholarships, the school's own gift aid. *Loans:* FFEL Subsidized Stafford, FFEL Unsubsidized Stafford, FFEL PLUS, state loans. **Student Employment:** Federal Work-Study Program available. Off-campus job opportunities are good. **Financial Aid Statistics:** 31% freshmen, 50% undergrads receive need-based scholarship or grant aid. 9% freshmen, 15% undergrads receive non-need-based scholarship or grant aid. 31% freshmen, 50% undergrads receive need-based self-help aid. 13% freshmen, 7% undergrads receive athletic scholarships. 57% undergrads borrow to pay for school. Average cumulative indebtedness $19,500. **Criteria for awarding institutional aid:** *Non-need-based:* Academics, alumni affiliation, athletics.

See page 1090.

FERRIS STATE UNIVERSITY

1201 South State Street, Center fo Student Services, Big Rapids, MI 49307
Phone: 231-591-2100 **Financial Aid Phone:** 231-591-2110
E-mail: admissions@ferris.edu **CEEB Code:** 1222
Fax: 231-591-3944 **Website:** www.ferris.edu **ACT Code:** 1994

This public school was founded in 1884. It has a 880-acre campus.

RATINGS

Admissions Selectivity Rating: 71   **Fire Safety Rating:** 60*   **Green Rating:** 60*

STUDENTS AND FACULTY

Enrollment: 11,030. **Student Body:** 47% female, 53% male, 5% out-of-state, 1% international . Asian 2%, African American 6%, Caucasian 78%, Hispanic 1%, Native American 1%.
Retention and Graduation: 69% freshmen return for sophomore year. 18% freshmen graduate within 4 years. 11% grads go on to further study within 1 year. **Faculty:** Student/faculty ratio 16:1. 537 full-time faculty, 51% hold PhDs, 8% are members of minority groups, 36% are women.

ACADEMICS

Degrees: Associate, bachelor's, certificate, first professional, master's, terminal associate, transfer associate. **Classes:** Most classes have 20–29 students. Most lab/discussion sessions have 10–19 students. **Majors with Highest Enrollment:** Elementary education and teaching; pharmacy (pharmd [usa], pharmd or bs/bpharm [canada]); pre-pharmacy studies. **Special Study Options:** Accelerated program, cooperative education program, cross-registration, distance learning, double major, dual enrollment, exchange student program (domestic), external degree program, honors program, independent study, internships, liberal arts/career combination, study abroad, teacher certification program, weekend college. Special programs offered to physically disabled students include note-taking services, reader services, tape recorders, tutors.

FACILITIES

Housing: Coed dorms, special housing for disabled students, special housing for international students, apartments for married students, apartments for single students, Honors, smoke-free, alcohol-free, quiet residence halls, living/earning communities. 98% of campus accessible to physically disabled. **Special Academic Facilities/Equipment:** Rankin Art Gallery, Student Recreation Center, Card Wildlife Museum, Jim Crowe Museum, Elastomer Center, FLITE. **Computers:** Students can register for classes online. Administrative functions (other than registration) can be performed online.

CAMPUS LIFE

Environment: Village. **Activities:** Choral groups, concert band, dance, drama/theater, jazz band, literary magazine, music ensembles, pep band, radio station, student government, student newspaper, symphony orchestra, television station. **Organizations:** 180 registered organizations, 11 honor societies, 14 religious organizations. 8 fraternities, 6 sororities. **Athletics (Intercollegiate):** *Men:* Basketball, cheerleading, cross-country, football, golf, ice hockey, tennis, track/field (outdoor). *Women:* Basketball, cheerleading, cross-country, golf, soccer, softball, tennis, track/field (outdoor), volleyball. **On-Campus Highlights:** FLITE Library, Student Recreation Center, Card Wildlife Center, Center for Student Services, Ewigleben Ice Arena.

ADMISSIONS

Freshman Academic Profile: Average high school GPA 3.18. 90% from public high schools. ACT middle 50% range 18–23. Minimum paper TOEFL 500. Minimum computer TOEFL 173. **Basis for Candidate Selection:** *Very important factors considered include:* Academic GPA, standardized test scores. *Important factors considered include:* Character/personal qualities. *Other factors considered include:* Recommendation(s), rigor of secondary school record, alumni/ae relation, extracurricular activities, volunteer work. **Freshman Admission Requirements:** High school diploma is required and GED is accepted. *Academic units recommended:* 4 English, 4 mathematics, 3 science, (1 science labs), 2 foreign language, 2 social studies, 2 history, 3 academic electives. **Freshman Admission Statistics:** 8,623 applied, 76% admitted, 34% enrolled. **Transfer Admission Requirements:** College transcript(s), statement of good standing from prior institution(s). Minimum college GPA of 2.0 required. Lowest grade transferable C. **General Admission Information:** Application fee $30. Regular application deadline 8/4. Notification on a rolling basis, beginning on or about 7/1. Nonfall registration accepted. Credit and/or placement offered for CEEB Advanced Placement tests.

COSTS AND FINANCIAL AID

Annual in-state tuition $7,200. Annual out-of-state tuition $14,640. Room and board $7,220. Required fees $142. Average book expense $1,000. **Required Forms and Deadlines:** FAFSA. Financial aid filing deadline 8/3. Priority financial aid filing date 3/1. **Notification of Awards:** Applicants will be notified of awards on a rolling basis beginning 4/1. **Types of Aid:** *Need-based scholarships/grants:* Federal Pell, SEOG, state scholarships/grants, private scholarships, the school's own gift aid. *Loans:* Direct Subsidized Stafford, Direct Unsubsidized Stafford, Direct PLUS, Federal Perkins, Federal Nursing, college/university loans from institutional funds, Key Loan, MI-Loan, Citi Assist. **Student Employment:** Highest amount earned per year from on-campus jobs $4,992. **Financial Aid Statistics:** 36% freshmen, 40% undergrads receive need-based scholarship or grant aid. 14% freshmen, 8% undergrads receive non-need-based scholarship or grant aid. 51% freshmen, 57% undergrads receive need-based self-help aid. 30% freshmen, 19% undergrads receive athletic scholarships. 68% freshmen, 86% undergrads receive any aid. 85% undergrads borrow to pay for school. Average cumulative indebtedness $15,000. **Criteria for awarding institutional aid:** *Non-need-based:* Academics, alumni affiliation, art, athletics, leadership, minority status, music/drama, religious affiliation.

FISK UNIVERSITY

1000 17th Avenue N, Nasville, TN, 37208,
Phone: 1-800-443-3475
Fax: Website: www.fisk.edu

RATINGS
Admissions Selectivity Rating: 83   **Fire Safety Rating:** 60*   **Green Rating:** 60*

ACADEMICS
Special Study Options: Cross-registration, double major, exchange student program (domestic), honors program, independent study, internships, student-designed major, study abroad, teacher certification program.

ADMISSIONS
Freshman Academic Profile: Average high school GPA 3.33. 10% in top 10% of high school class, 30% in top 25% of high school class, 75% in top 50% of high school class. 92% from public high schools. SAT Math middle 50% range 455–540. SAT Critical Reading middle 50% range 467–546. SAT Writing middle 50% range 447–547. ACT middle 50% range 18–23. Minimum paper TOEFL 550. **Basis for Candidate Selection:** *Very important factors considered include:* Rigor of secondary school record. *Important factors considered include:* Class rank, application essay, academic GPA, standardized test scores, character/personal qualities, extracurricular activities, interview. *Other factors considered include:* Recommendation(s), alumni/ae relation, geographical residence, level of applicant's interest, talent/ability, volunteer work. **Freshman Admission Requirements:** High school diploma is required and GED is accepted. *Academic units required:* 4 English, 4 mathematics, 3 science, (2 science labs), 1 foreign language, 1 history. *Academic units recommended:* 4 English, 4 mathematics, 3 science, (2 science labs), 2 foreign language, 1 history. **Freshman Admission Statistics:** 2,700 applied, 45% admitted, 51% enrolled. **Transfer Admission Requirements:** College transcript(s), essay or personal statement, statement of good standing from prior institution(s). Minimum college GPA of 2.5 required. Lowest grade transferable C. **General Admission Information:** Application fee $50. Regular application deadline 3/1. Notification on a rolling basis, beginning on or about 9/1. Admission may be deferred for a maximum of 1 year. Credit and/or placement offered for CEEB Advanced Placement tests.

COSTS AND FINANCIAL AID
Comprehensive fee $15,140. Room and board $7,730. Required fees $1,100. Average book expense $1,500.

FITCHBURG STATE COLLEGE

160 Pearl Street, Fitchburg, MA 01420-2697
Phone: 978-665-3144 **Financial Aid Phone:** 978-665-3156
E-mail: admissions@fsc.edu **CEEB Code:** 3518
Fax: 978-665-4540 **Website:** www.fsc.edu **ACT Code:** 1902

This public school was founded in 1894. It has a 78-acre campus.

RATINGS
Admissions Selectivity Rating: 75   **Fire Safety Rating:** 86   **Green Rating:** 72

STUDENTS AND FACULTY
Enrollment: 3,987. **Student Body:** 53% female, 47% male, 9% out-of-state, international (6 countries represented).
Retention and Graduation: 77% freshmen return for sophomore year. 24% freshmen graduate within 4 years. 10% grads go on to further study within 1 year. **Faculty:** Student/faculty ratio 17:1. 179 full-time faculty, 91% hold PhDs, 13% are members of minority groups, 46% are women.

ACADEMICS
Degrees: Bachelor's, certificate, master's, post-bachelor's certificate, post-master's certificate. **Classes:** Most classes have 20–29 students. **Majors with Highest Enrollment:** Business administration and management; communication studies/speech communication and rhetoric; liberal arts and sciences/liberal studies. **Special Study Options:** Cross-registration, distance learning, double major, dual enrollment, honors program, independent study, internships, liberal arts/career combination, student-designed major, study abroad, teacher certification program. **Honors programs:** Leadership Academy Honors Program Special programs offered to physically disabled students include note-taking

---

services, reader services, tape recorders, tutors. **Career services:** Alumni network, alumni services, career/job search classes, career assessment, internships

FACILITIES
Housing: Coed dorms, special housing for disabled students, apartments for single students, alcohol and tobacco free housing. 80% of campus accessible to physically disabled. **Special Academic Facilities/Equipment:** Art gallery, on-campus teacher education school, 120–acre conservation area. **Computers:** 100% of classrooms, 10% of dorms, 100% of libraries, 40% of dining areas, 100% of student union, 90% of common outdoor areas have wireless network access. Students can register for classes online. Administrative functions (other than registration) can be performed online. Undergraduates are required to own a computer.

CAMPUS LIFE
Environment: Town. **Activities:** Choral groups, concert band, dance, drama/theater, jazz band, radio station, student government, student newspaper, student-run film society, campus ministries, international student organization, Model UN. **Organizations:** 60 registered organizations, 8 honor societies, 1 religious organizations. 2 fraternities, 3 sororities. **Athletics (Intercollegiate):** *Men:* Baseball, basketball, cross-country, football, ice hockey, soccer, track/field (outdoor), track/field (indoor). *Women:* Basketball, cross-country, field hockey, lacrosse, soccer, softball, track/field (outdoor), track/field (indoor). **On-Campus Highlights:** Campus Recreation Center, Student Center Lounge, Campus Dining Hall, Commuter Cafe, Computer Labs. **Environmental Initiatives:** Single stream recycling program Seeking LEED certification of newest residence hall

ADMISSIONS
Freshman Academic Profile: Average high school GPA 3.03. 90% from public high schools. SAT Math middle 50% range 460–560. SAT Critical Reading middle 50% range 460–560. SAT Writing middle 50% range 450–550. ACT middle 50% range 19–23. Minimum paper TOEFL 550. Minimum computer TOEFL 213. **Basis for Candidate Selection:** *Very important factors considered include:* Rigor of secondary school record. *Important factors considered include:* Application essay, academic GPA, standardized test scores. *Other factors considered include:* Recommendation(s), alumni/ae relation, character/personal qualities, extracurricular activities, level of applicant's interest, talent/ability, volunteer work, work experience. **Freshman Admission Requirements:** High school diploma is required and GED is accepted. *Academic units required:* 4 English, 3 mathematics, 3 science, (2 science labs), 2 foreign language, 1 social studies, 1 history, 2 academic electives. **Freshman Admission Statistics:** 3,809 applied, 64% admitted, 32% enrolled. **Transfer Admission Requirements:** College transcript(s), essay or personal statement, minimum college GPA of 2.0 required. Lowest grade transferable C. **General Admission Information:** Application fee $25. Notification on a rolling basis, beginning on or about 12/1. Nonfall registration accepted. Admission may be deferred for a maximum of 1 year. Credit and/or placement offered for CEEB Advanced Placement tests.

COSTS AND FINANCIAL AID
Average book expense $800. **Required Forms and Deadlines:** FAFSA. Priority financial aid filing date 3/1. **Notification of Awards:** Applicants will be notified of awards on a rolling basis beginning 3/15. **Types of Aid:** *Need-based scholarships/grants:* Federal Pell, SEOG, state scholarships/grants, private scholarships, the school's own gift aid. *Loans:* Direct Subsidized Stafford, Direct Unsubsidized Stafford, Direct PLUS, Federal Perkins, Federal Nursing, state loans **Student Employment:** Federal Work-Study Program available. Institutional employment available. Off-campus job opportunities are good. **Financial Aid Statistics:** 45% freshmen, 39% undergrads receive need-based scholarship or grant aid. 10% freshmen, 4% undergrads receive non-need-based scholarship or grant aid. 50% freshmen, 47% undergrads receive need-based self-help aid. 55% freshmen, 47% undergrads receive any aid. 68% undergrads borrow to pay for school. Average cumulative indebtedness $18,177. **Criteria for awarding institutional aid:** *Non-need-based:* Academics, alumni affiliation, job skills, leadership.

FIVE TOWNS COLLEGE

Five Towns College, 305 North Service Road, Dix Hills, NY 11746
Phone: 631-656-2110 **Financial Aid Phone:** 631-656-2164
E-mail: admissions@ftc.edu **CEEB Code:** 3142
Fax: 631-656-2172 **Website:** www.ftc.edu

This proprietary school was founded in 1972. It has a 35-acre campus.

RATINGS
Admissions Selectivity Rating: 60*   **Fire Safety Rating:** 60*   **Green Rating:** 60*

STUDENTS AND FACULTY

Enrollment: 997. **Student Body:** 36% female, 64% male, 11% out-of-state. **Faculty:** 33 full-time faculty.

ACADEMICS

Degrees: Associate, bachelor's, doctoral, master's. **Classes:** Most classes have 20–29 students. **Majors with Highest Enrollment:** Film/cinema studies; music; recording arts technology/technician. **Special Study Options:** Distance learning, dual enrollment, internships, liberal arts/career combination, teacher certification program. Special programs offered to physically disabled students include note-taking services, reader services, tape recorders, tutors. **Career services:** Career/job search classes, career assessment, internships.

FACILITIES

Housing: Coed dorms, wellness housing. **Computers:** 100% of classrooms, 100% of dorms, 100% of libraries, 100% of dining areas, 100% of common outdoor areas have wireless network access. Administrative functions (other than registration) can be performed online.

CAMPUS LIFE

Environment: Village. **Activities:** Choral groups, concert band, dance, drama/theater, jazz band, music ensembles, musical theater, radio station, student government, student newspaper, student-run film society, symphony orchestra, television station, yearbook. **On-Campus Highlights:** Student Center, Audio Studios, Film Video Studios, Radio Station, Court Yard.

ADMISSIONS

Freshman Academic Profile: 80% from public high schools. SAT Math middle 50% range 390–520. SAT Critical Reading middle 50% range 400–510. SAT Writing middle 50% range 400–510. ACT middle 50% range 18–22. Minimum paper TOEFL 520. Minimum computer TOEFL 213. Minimum web-based TOEFL 80. **Basis for Candidate Selection:** *Very important factors considered include:* Application essay, academic GPA, recommendation(s), rigor of secondary school record, standardized test scores, character/personal qualities, talent/ability. *Important factors considered include:* Class rank, interview, level of applicant's interest. *Other factors considered include:* Extracurricular activities, volunteer work, work experience. **Freshman Admission Requirements:** High school diploma is required and GED is accepted. *Academic units recommended:* 4 English, 3 mathematics, 3 science, 2 foreign language, 4 social studies. **Transfer Admission Requirements:** High school transcript, college transcript(s), essay or personal statement, statement of good standing from prior institution(s). Minimum college GPA of 2.5 required. Lowest grade transferable C. **General Admission Information:** Application fee $35. Early decision application deadline 12/1. Notification on a rolling basis, beginning on or about 11/1. Nonfall registration accepted. Admission may be deferred for a maximum of 1 year. Placement offered for CEEB Advanced Placement tests.

COSTS AND FINANCIAL AID

Annual tuition $17,400. Room and board $12,650. Average book expense $1,200. **Required Forms and Deadlines:** FAFSA, institution's own financial aid form, state aid form. Priority financial aid filing date 3/31. **Notification of Awards:** Applicants will be notified of awards on a rolling basis beginning 3/31. **Types of Aid:** *Need-based scholarships/grants:* Federal Pell, SEOG, state scholarships/grants, private scholarships, the school's own gift aid. *Loans:* Direct Subsidized Stafford, Direct Unsubsidized Stafford, Direct PLUS. **Student Employment:** Federal Work-Study Program available. Institutional employment available. **Financial Aid Statistics:** 65% freshmen, 66% undergrads receive need-based scholarship or grant aid. 41% freshmen, 41% undergrads receive non-need-based scholarship or grant aid. 73% freshmen, 74% undergrads receive need-based self-help aid. 73% freshmen, 75% undergrads receive any aid. 80% undergrads borrow to pay for school. Average cumulative indebtedness $19,000. **Criteria for awarding institutional aid:** *Non-need-based:* Academics, music/drama.

FLAGLER COLLEGE

74 King Street, St. Augustine, FL 32085-1027
Phone: 800-304-4208 **Financial Aid Phone:** 904-819-6225
E-mail: admiss@flagler.edu **CEEB Code:** 5235
Fax: 904-826-0094 **Website:** www.flagler.edu **ACT Code:** 772

This private school was founded in 1968. It has a 42-acre campus.

RATINGS

Admissions Selectivity Rating: 86   **Fire Safety Rating:** 87   **Green Rating:** 70

STUDENTS AND FACULTY

Enrollment: 2,706. **Student Body:** 60% female, 40% male, 31% out-of-state, 2% international (25 countries represented). African American 2%, Caucasian 87%, Hispanic 4%.
Retention and Graduation: 49% freshmen graduate within 4 years. 24% grads go on to further study within 1 year. 1% grads pursue arts and sciences degrees. 2% grads pursue law degrees. 3% grads pursue business degrees. **Faculty:** Student/faculty ratio 20.2:1. 95 full-time faculty, 57% hold PhDs, 4% are members of minority groups, 46% are women.

ACADEMICS

Degrees: Bachelor's. **Classes:** Most classes have 20–29 students. **Majors with Highest Enrollment:** Business/commerce; communication, journalism, and related programs, other; elementary education and teaching. **Special Study Options:** Double major, external degree program, independent study, internships, liberal arts/career combination, study abroad, teacher certification program **Combined degree programs:** none. Special programs offered to physically disabled students include note-taking services, reader services, tape recorders, tutors. **Career services:** Alumni network, alumni services, career/job search classes, career assessment **Career services highlights include:** Most majors require students to gain internship experience.

FACILITIES

Housing: Men's dorms, women's dorms. 95% of campus accessible to physically disabled. **Special Academic Facilities/Equipment:** Museum/theatre; learning disabilities clinic for student teachers; NorthEast Florida Archeological Association; Crisp-Ellert Art Gallery. **Computers:** 30% of classrooms, 100% of dorms, 100% of libraries, 100% of dining areas, 100% of student union, 80% of common outdoor areas have wireless network access. Students can register for classes online. Administrative functions (other than registration) can be performed online.

CAMPUS LIFE

Environment: Town. **Activities:** Choral groups, drama/theater, literary magazine, radio station, student government, student newspaper, campus ministries. **Organizations:** 7 honor societies, 3 religious organizations. **Athletics (Intercollegiate):** *Men:* Baseball, basketball, cross-country, golf, soccer, tennis. *Women:* Basketball, cross-country, golf, soccer, softball, tennis, volleyball. **On-Campus Highlights:** The Student Center, Proctor Library, Campus Courtyard, Flagler College Tennis Complex, Flagler College Sports Complex. **Environmental Initiatives:** Chiller upgrades, compact flourescents, green cleaning supplies.

ADMISSIONS

Freshman Academic Profile: Average high school GPA 3.35. 18% in top 10% of high school class, 56% in top 25% of high school class, 95% in top 50% of high school class. 78% from public high schools. SAT Math middle 50% range 510–590. SAT Critical Reading middle 50% range 520–590. SAT Writing middle 50% range 500–570. ACT middle 50% range 21–24. Minimum paper TOEFL 550. Minimum computer TOEFL 213. **Basis for Candidate Selection:** *Very important factors considered include:* Rigor of secondary school record. *Important factors considered include:* Application essay, academic GPA, standardized test scores, alumni/ae relation, extracurricular activities. *Other factors considered include:* Class rank, recommendation(s), character/personal qualities, first generation, interview, level of applicant's interest, talent/ability, volunteer work. **Freshman Admission Requirements:** High school diploma is required and GED is accepted. *Academic units required:* 4 English, 3 mathematics, 2 science, (1 science labs), 3 social studies, 1 history, 2 academic electives. *Academic units recommended:* 4 English, 4 mathematics, 3 science, (2 science labs), 2 foreign language, 3 social studies, 2 history, 1 visual/performing arts, 1 computer science, 2 academic electives. **Freshman Admission Statistics:** 2,585 applied, 44% admitted, 49% enrolled. **Transfer Admission Requirements:** College transcript(s), essay or personal statement, minimum college GPA of 2.0 required. Lowest grade transferable C. **General Admission Information:** Application fee $40. Early decision application deadline 12/1. Regular application deadline 3/1. Regular notification 3/30. Nonfall registration accepted. Admission may be deferred for a maximum of 1 year. Credit and/or placement offered for CEEB Advanced Placement tests.

COSTS AND FINANCIAL AID

Annual tuition $13,300. Room and board $7,190. Average book expense $1,000. **Required Forms and Deadlines:** FAFSA, institution's own financial aid form, state aid form. Priority financial aid filing date 4/1. **Notification of Awards:** Applicants will be notified of awards on a rolling basis beginning 4/1. **Types of Aid:** *Need-based scholarships/grants:* Federal Pell, SEOG, state scholarships/grants, private scholarships, the school's own gift aid. *Loans:* Direct Subsidized Stafford, Direct Unsubsidized Stafford, Direct PLUS, Federal Perkins, Private Alternative Loans. **Student Employment:** Federal Work-Study Program available. Institutional employment available. Highest amount earned per year from on-campus jobs $1,400. Off-campus job opportunities are excellent. **Financial Aid Statistics:** 50% freshmen, 39% undergrads receive need-based scholarship or grant aid. 43% freshmen, 38% undergrads receive non-need-based scholarship or grant aid. 52% freshmen, 45% undergrads receive need-based self-help aid. 6% freshmen, 6% undergrads receive athletic scholarships. 90% freshmen, 90% undergrads receive any aid. 55% undergrads borrow to pay for school. Average cumulative indebtedness $18,190. **Criteria for awarding institutional aid:** *Non-need-based:* Academics, art, athletics, job skills, leadership, minority status, music/drama, state/district residency.

FLORIDA A&M UNIVERSITY

Suite G-9, Foote-Hilyer Administration Center, Tallahassee, FL 32307
Phone: 850-599-3796 **Financial Aid Phone:** 850-599-3730
E-mail: admission@famu.edu **CEEB Code:** 5215
Fax: 850-599-3069 **Website:** www.famu.edu **ACT Code:** 726

This public school was founded in 1887. It has a 419-acre campus.

RATINGS

Admissions Selectivity Rating: 74   Fire Safety Rating: 91   Green Rating: 85

STUDENTS AND FACULTY

Enrollment: 9,967. **Student Body:** 58% female, 42% male, 27% out-of-state, 1% international (71 countries represented). Asian 1%, African American 95%, Caucasian 3%, Hispanic 1%.
Retention and Graduation: 35.5% grads go on to further study within 1 year. 3.4% grads pursue law degrees. 8.2% grads pursue business degrees. 1.6% grads pursue medical degrees. **Faculty:** Student/faculty ratio 17:1. 610 full-time faculty, 73% hold PhDs, 78% are members of minority groups, 41% are women. 1.8% of classes are taught by teaching assistants.

ACADEMICS

Degrees: Associate, bachelor's, first professional, master's. **Classes:** Most classes have fewer than 10 students. **Majors with Highest Enrollment:** Business administration and management; nursing/registered nurse (RN, ASN, BSN, MSN); pharmacy (pharmd [usa], pharmd or bs/bpharm [canada]). **Special Study Options:** Accelerated program, cooperative education program, distance learning, double major, dual enrollment, honors program, independent study, internships, study abroad, teacher certification program, weekend college. **Honors programs:** Florida Agricultural and Mechanical University Honors Program provides a series of challenging courses and academic enhancement experiences for undergraduate students who excel. Enhancement of academic performance in critical thinking skills, in essence, will lead to consummate intellectual engagement and strong research orientation as a launch to both graduate and professional schools, as well as career paths. The program stresses four major areas of concentration: Academic achievement, development of leadership potential, community service and cultural enrichment. **Combined degree programs:** BA/JD, BA/MA, Pharmacy, Architecture, Occupational Therapy. Special programs offered to physically disabled students include note-taking services, reader services, tape recorders, tutors. **Career services:** Alumni network, alumni services, career/job search classes, career assessment, internships. **Career services highlights include:** Wonderful and successfull interns.

FACILITIES

Housing: Coed dorms, men's dorms, women's dorms, apartments for married students, outside housing (apartment complexes) agreement through the university. 100% of campus accessible to physically disabled. **Special Academic Facilities/Equipment:** Black Archives and Resource Ctr. Coleman Memorial Library Foster Tanner Music/Art Bldg. **Computers:** 90% of classrooms, 100% of dorms, 100% of libraries, 100% of dining areas, 100% of student union, 60% of common outdoor areas have wireless network access. Students can register for classes online. Administrative functions (other than registration) can be performed online.

CAMPUS LIFE

Environment: City. **Activities:** Choral groups, concert band, dance, drama/theater, jazz band, marching band, music ensembles, pep band, radio station, student government, student newspaper, symphony orchestra, television station, yearbook. **Organizations:** 145 registered organizations, 16 honor societies, 11 religious organizations. 4 fraternities, 4 sororities. **Athletics (Intercollegiate):** *Men:* Baseball, basketball, cheerleading, cross-country, football, golf, swimming, tennis, track/field (outdoor), track/field (indoor). *Women:* Basketball, bowling, cheerleading, cross-country, golf, softball, swimming, tennis, track/field (outdoor), track/field (indoor), volleyball. **On-Campus Highlights:** The Black Archives, FAMU/FSU College of Engineering, Athletic Department, Army/Navy ROTC, Alfred Lawson Jr. Multipurpose Center and Teaching Gymnasium. **Environmental Initiatives:** Establishment of an advisory body—the Enviroment & Sustainability Council to design and oversee the implementation of a sustainability strategic plan which informs and guides the various operatives on campus of the principles of sustainability as they apply specifically to the respective facets of the University—Administrative, Academic, Operations and Community Development of a comprehensive Recycling Program to facilite the recyling needs of the faculty, staff, and students on campus. The recycling program engages collaborations with various external groups in the community including City and County Divisions with "green" student groups on campus. FAMU co-hosts the local staging of the annual National Conference of Mayoers/Keep America Beautiful Cash for Cans Recycling Day. This is a major recycling event in Tallahassee, also co-hosted by both the City and County Recycling Divisions. FAMU's facilities planning and construction team has made the commitment to design and build all new renovation and construction projects to LEED standards.

ADMISSIONS

Freshman Academic Profile: Average high school GPA 3. 85% from public high schools. SAT Math middle 50% range 440–550. SAT Critical Reading middle 50% range 440–550. ACT middle 50% range 19–22. Minimum paper TOEFL 500. Minimum computer TOEFL 173. Minimum web-based TOEFL 80. **Basis for Candidate Selection:** *Very important factors considered include:* Application essay, academic GPA, rigor of secondary school record, standardized test scores. *Other factors considered include:* Class rank, alumni/ae relation, character/personal qualities, extracurricular activities, racial/ethnic status, state residency, talent/ability, volunteer work, work experience. **Freshman Admission Requirements:** High school diploma is required and GED is accepted. *Academic units required:* 4 English, 3 mathematics, 3 science, (1 science labs), 2 foreign language, 3 social studies, 3 academic electives. *Academic units recommended:* 4 English, 3 mathematics, 3 science, 2 foreign language, 3 social studies, 3 academic electives. **Freshman Admission Statistics:** 4,708 applied, 61% admitted, 61% enrolled. **Transfer Admission Requirements:** College transcript(s), minimum college GPA of 2.0 required. Lowest grade transferable C. **General Admission Information:** Application fee $20. Regular application deadline 5/9. Nonfall registration accepted. Credit offered for CEEB Advanced Placement tests.

COSTS AND FINANCIAL AID

Annual in-state tuition $3,047. Annual out-of-state tuition $14,243. Room and board $5,492. Required fees $222. Average book expense $700. **Required Forms and Deadlines:** FAFSA. Financial aid filing deadline 6/30. Priority financial aid filing date 3/1. **Notification of Awards:** Applicants will be notified of awards on a rolling basis beginning 3/1. **Types of Aid:** *Need-based scholarships/grants:* Federal Pell, SEOG, state scholarships/grants, private scholarships, the school's own gift aid, United Negro College Fund, Federal Nursing Scholarships. *Loans:* Direct Subsidized Stafford, Direct Unsubsidized Stafford, Direct PLUS, Federal Perkins. **Student Employment:** Federal Work-Study Program available. Institutional employment available. Highest amount earned per year from on-campus jobs $9,800. Off-campus job opportunities are good. **Financial Aid Statistics:** 57% freshmen, 61% undergrads receive need-based scholarship or grant aid. 68% freshmen, 57% undergrads receive non-need-based scholarship or grant aid. 44% freshmen, 60% undergrads receive need-based self-help aid. 3% freshmen, 3% undergrads receive athletic scholarships. 93% freshmen, 85% undergrads receive any aid. 82% undergrads borrow to pay for school. Average cumulative indebtedness $27,641. **Criteria for awarding institutional aid:** *Non-need-based:* Academics, art, leadership.

FLORIDA ATLANTIC UNIVERSITY

777 Glades Road, PO Box 3091, Boca Raton, FL 33431-0991
Phone: 561-297-3040 **Financial Aid Phone:** 561-297-3530
E-mail: UGrecruitment@fau.edu **CEEB Code:** 5229
Fax: 561-297-2758 **Website:** www.fau.edu **ACT Code:** 729

This public school was founded in 1961. It has a 860-acre campus.

RATINGS
Admissions Selectivity Rating: 82   **Fire Safety Rating:** 60*   **Green Rating:** 60*

STUDENTS AND FACULTY
Enrollment: 20,525. **Student Body:** 59% female, 41% male, 6% out-of-state, 3% international . Asian 5%, African American 18%, Caucasian 55%, Hispanic 19%.
Retention and Graduation: 74% freshmen return for sophomore year. 15% freshmen graduate within 4 years. **Faculty:** Student/faculty ratio 19:1. 783 full-time faculty, 85% hold PhDs, 19% are members of minority groups, 40% are women. 15% of classes are taught by teaching assistants.

ACADEMICS
Degrees: Associate, bachelor's, certificate, master's, post-master's certificate. **Classes:** Most classes have 20–29 students. Most lab/discussion sessions have 20–29 students. **Majors with Highest Enrollment:** Accounting; education; nursing/registered nurse (RN, ASN, BSN, MSN). **Special Study Options:** Accelerated program, cooperative education program, cross-registration, distance learning, double major, dual enrollment, English as a Second Language (ESL), honors program, independent study, internships, liberal arts/career combination, study abroad, teacher certification program, weekend college. **Honors programs:** The Harriet L. Wilkes Honors College of Florida Atlantic University, which opened in the fall of 1999, is the first public honors institution to be built from the ground up in the United States. Its intellectual foundation is a belief in liberal arts education as the best preparation for a full and productive life. The University Scholars Program is the honors program located on the Boca Raton campus. It is for freshman and sophomore students. The historical mission of a liberal arts education has been to develop the qualities of a free and responsible citizen, one who can reason clearly, read analytically, argue persuasively in speech and in writing, and contribute in fundamental and innovative ways to a chosen field of study or work. **Combined degree programs:** BA/MEng. Special programs offered to physically disabled students include note-taking services, reader services, tape recorders, tutors. **Career services:** Alumni network, alumni services, career/job search classes, career assessment, internships, regional alumni.

FACILITIES
Housing: Coed dorms, apartments for married students, apartments for single students. 100% of campus accessible to physically disabled. **Special Academic Facilities/Equipment:** Art gallery, on-campus elementary school, robotics lab, marine research facilities. **Computers:** Students can register for classes online. Administrative functions (other than registration) can be performed online.

CAMPUS LIFE
Environment: City. **Activities:** Choral groups, dance, drama/theater, jazz band, literary magazine, marching band, music ensembles, musical theater, opera, radio station, student government, student newspaper, television station **Organizations:** 150 registered organizations, 11 honor societies, 6 religious organizations. 9 fraternities, 4 sororities. **Athletics (Intercollegiate):** *Men:* Baseball, basketball, cheerleading, cross-country, diving, football, golf, soccer, swimming, tennis. *Women:* Basketball, cheerleading, cross-country, diving, golf, soccer, softball, swimming, tennis, track/field (outdoor), volleyball. **On-Campus Highlights:** Student Services Building, Student Union, Dining Hall, Breezeway, Residence Halls.

ADMISSIONS
Freshman Academic Profile: Average high school GPA 3.4. 9% in top 10% of high school class, 35% in top 25% of high school class, 74% in top 50% of high school class. SAT Math middle 50% range 470–560. SAT Critical Reading middle 50% range 260–550. SAT Writing middle 50% range 450–540. ACT middle 50% range 19–23. Minimum paper TOEFL 550. Minimum web-based TOEFL 80. **Basis for Candidate Selection:** *Very important factors considered include:* Academic GPA, standardized test scores. *Important factors considered include:* Class rank, rigor of secondary school record. *Other factors considered include:* Application essay, recommendation(s), alumni/ae relation, character/personal qualities, extracurricular activities, first generation, level of applicant's interest, talent/ability, volunteer work. **Freshman Admission Requirements:** High school diploma is required and GED is accepted. *Academic units required:* 4 English, 3 mathematics, 3 science, (2 science labs), 2 foreign language, 3 social studies, 3 academic electives. *Academic units recommended:* 4

English, 4 mathematics, 3 science, (2 science labs), 2 foreign language, 3 social studies, 3 academic electives. **Freshman Admission Statistics:** 11,822 applied, 26% admitted, 167% enrolled. **Transfer Admission Requirements:** College transcript(s), minimum college GPA of 3.0 required. Lowest grade transferable D–. **General Admission Information:** Application fee $30. Regular application deadline 6/1. Notification on a rolling basis, beginning on or about 9/1. Nonfall registration accepted. Admission may be deferred for a maximum of 2 semesters. Credit offered for CEEB Advanced Placement tests.

COSTS AND FINANCIAL AID
Annual in-state tuition $3,367. Annual out-of-state tuition $16,431. Room and board $8,610. Average book expense $748. **Required Forms and Deadlines:** FAFSA. Priority financial aid filing date 3/1. **Notification of Awards:** Applicants will be notified of awards on a rolling basis beginning 4/1. **Types of Aid:** *Need-based scholarships/grants:* Federal Pell, SEOG, state scholarships/grants, private scholarships, the school's own gift aid, Federal Nursing Scholarships. *Loans:* FFEL Subsidized Stafford, FFEL Unsubsidized Stafford, FFEL PLUS, Federal Perkins, college/university loans from institutional funds. **Student Employment:** Federal Work-Study Program available. Institutional employment available. Highest amount earned per year from on-campus jobs $1,500. Off-campus job opportunities are excellent. **Financial Aid Statistics:** 40% freshmen, 37% undergrads receive need-based scholarship or grant aid. 26% freshmen, 30% undergrads receive need-based self-help aid. 2% freshmen, 2% undergrads receive athletic scholarships. **Criteria for awarding institutional aid:** *Non-need-based:* Academics, athletics, music/drama, state/district residency.

See page 1092.

FLORIDA COLLEGE

Admissions Office, 119 North Glen Arven Avenue, Temple Terrace, FL 33617-5578
Phone: 813-899-6716 **Financial Aid Phone:** 813-899-6720
E-mail: Admissions@FloridaCollege.edu **CEEB Code:** 1562
Fax: 813-899-6722 **Website:** www.floridacollege.edu **ACT Code:** 1482

This private school was founded in 1946.

RATINGS
Admissions Selectivity Rating: 60*   **Fire Safety Rating:** 60*   **Green Rating:** 60*

STUDENTS AND FACULTY
Enrollment: 467. **Student Body:** 53% female, 47% male, 63% out-of-state, 2% international (6 countries represented). Asian 1%, African American 4%, Caucasian 84%, Hispanic 6%, Native American 1%.
Retention and Graduation: 75% freshmen return for sophomore year. **Faculty:** 37 full-time faculty, 38% hold PhDs, 22% are women.

ACADEMICS
Degrees: Associate, bachelor's, transfer associate. **Classes:** Most classes have fewer than 10 students. Most lab/discussion sessions have 10–19 students. **Special Study Options:** Cross-registration, double major, independent study, teacher certification program Special programs offered to physically disabled students include tape recorders, tutors.

FACILITIES
Housing: Special housing for disabled students, men's dorms, women's dorms

CAMPUS LIFE
Environment: Town. **Activities:** Choral groups, concert band, drama/theater, jazz band, literary magazine, music ensembles, musical theater, pep band, student government, yearbook. **Organizations: Athletics (Intercollegiate):** *Men:* Basketball, cross-country, soccer. *Women:* Cheerleading, cross-country, soccer, volleyball. **On-Campus Highlights:** Riverwalk, Student Center.

ADMISSIONS
Freshman Academic Profile: SAT Math middle 50% range 440–570. SAT Critical Reading middle 50% range 460–570. SAT Writing middle 50% range 440–580. ACT middle 50% range 20–25. Minimum paper TOEFL 550. Minimum computer TOEFL 213. **Basis for Candidate Selection:** *Very important factors considered include:* Academic GPA, recommendation(s), rigor of secondary school record, standardized test scores, character/personal qualities, religious affiliation/commitment. *Important factors considered include:* Class rank, level of applicant's interest. *Other factors considered include:* Alumni/ae relation, talent/ability. **Freshman Admission Requirements:** High school diploma is required and GED is accepted. *Academic units required:* 4 English, 3 mathematics, 2 science, (2 science labs), 2 social studies. *Academic units recommended:* 2 foreign language, 3 social studies. **Freshman Admission Statistics:** 349 applied, **Transfer Admission Requirements:** High school transcript,

college transcript(s), standardized test scores, statement of good standing from prior institution(s). Minimum college GPA of 2.0 required. Lowest grade transferable C. **General Admission Information:** Application fee $30. Regular application deadline 8/1. Nonfall registration accepted. Placement offered for CEEB Advanced Placement tests.

COSTS AND FINANCIAL AID

Annual tuition $11,400. Room and board $7,040. Required fees $750. Average book expense $1,300. **Required Forms and Deadlines:** FAFSA, institution's own financial aid form, state aid form. Financial aid filing deadline 6/1. Priority financial aid filing date 4/1. **Notification of Awards:** Applicants will be notified of awards on a rolling basis beginning 3/1. **Types of Aid:** *Need-based scholarships/grants:* Federal Pell, SEOG, state scholarships/grants, private scholarships, the school's own gift aid. *Loans:* FFEL Subsidized Stafford, FFEL Unsubsidized Stafford, FFEL PLUS, Federal Perkins, Alternative Loans. **Financial Aid Statistics:** 40% freshmen, 45% undergrads receive need-based scholarship or grant aid. 49% freshmen, 41% undergrads receive non-need-based scholarship or grant aid. 36% freshmen, 39% undergrads receive need-based self-help aid. 5% freshmen, 4% undergrads receive athletic scholarships. **Criteria for awarding institutional aid:** *Non-need-based:* Academics, athletics, music/drama, state/district residency.

FLORIDA GULF COAST UNIVERSITY

10501 FGCU Blvd. South, Fort Myers, FL 33965-6565
Phone: 239-590-7878 **Financial Aid Phone:** 239-590-7920
E-mail: admissions@fgcu.edu **CEEB Code:** 5221
Fax: 239-590-7894 **Website: ACT Code:** 733

This public school was founded in 1991. It has a 760-acre campus.

RATINGS
Admissions Selectivity Rating: 76   **Fire Safety Rating:** 90   **Green Rating:** 60*

STUDENTS AND FACULTY
Enrollment: 9,493. **Student Body:** 56% female, 44% male, 8% out-of-state, 2% international (89 countries represented). Asian 2%, African American 5%, Caucasian 76%, Hispanic 14%, Native American 1%.
Retention and Graduation: 76% freshmen return for sophomore year. **Faculty:** Student/faculty ratio 22:1. 348 full-time faculty, 76% hold PhDs, 17% are members of minority groups, 47% are women.

ACADEMICS
Degrees: Associate, bachelor's, certificate, master's, transfer associate. **Classes:** Most classes have 20–29 students. **Majors with Highest Enrollment:** Business/commerce; elementary education and teaching; liberal arts and sciences/liberal studies. **Special Study Options:** Accelerated program, cross-registration, distance learning, double major, dual enrollment, honors program, independent study, internships, student-designed major, study abroad, teacher certification program. **Honors programs:** The University Honors Program at Florida Gulf Coast University offers special opportunities for superior students to pursue academic work that challenges their interests and abilities. The program is university-wide, which gives students full access to the faculty and the entire range of programs at FGCU. Since the honors program at Florida Gulf Coast University is exclusive, we have the ability to design a unique program for each individual student. Scholarship opportunities and special programs that support the honors student's educational, intellectual, and personal goals will be designed individually with the student and his or her faculty mentor. **Combined degree programs:** Nursing, BS/MS. Special programs offered to physically disabled students include note-taking services, reader services, tape recorders, tutors. **Career services:** Alumni network, alumni services, career/job search classes, career assessment, internships.

FACILITIES
Housing: Coed dorms, special housing for disabled students, apartments for single students. 100% of campus accessible to physically disabled. **Special Academic Facilities/Equipment:** Art gallery, observatory. **Computers:** Students can register for classes online. Administrative functions (other than registration) can be performed online.

CAMPUS LIFE
Environment: City. **Activities:** Choral groups, dance, drama/theater, literary magazine, radio station, student government, student newspaper. **Organizations:** 105 registered organizations, 7 honor societies, 8 religious organizations. 4 fraternities, 4 sororities. **Athletics (Intercollegiate):** *Men:* Baseball, basketball, cross-country, golf, soccer, tennis. *Women:* Basketball, cross-country, diving, golf, soccer, softball, swimming, tennis, volleyball. **On-Campus Highlights:** Alico Arena, Student Union, the Quad, the library, baseball/softball fields.

ADMISSIONS
Freshman Academic Profile: Average high school GPA 3.34. 13% in top 10% of high school class, 39% in top 25% of high school class, 81% in top 50% of high school class. SAT Math middle 50% range 470–550. SAT Critical Reading middle 50% range 480–560. SAT Writing middle 50% range 460–540. ACT middle 50% range 20–23. Minimum paper TOEFL 550. Minimum computer TOEFL 213. Minimum web-based TOEFL 79. **Basis for Candidate Selection:** *Very important factors considered include:* Academic GPA, standardized test scores. *Important factors considered include:* Rigor of secondary school record. *Other factors considered include:* Class rank, recommendation(s). **Freshman Admission Requirements:** High school diploma is required and GED is accepted. *Academic units required:* 4 English, 3 mathematics, 3 science, (2 science labs), 2 foreign language, 3 social studies, 3 academic electives. **Freshman Admission Statistics:** 8,298 applied, 66% admitted, 37% enrolled. **Transfer Admission Requirements:** College transcript(s), minimum college GPA of 2.0 required. Lowest grade transferable D. **General Admission Information:** Application fee $30. Regular application deadline 5/1. Nonfall registration accepted. Admission may be deferred for a maximum of 2 semesters. Credit and/or placement offered for CEEB Advanced Placement tests.

COSTS AND FINANCIAL AID
Average book expense $1,200. **Required Forms and Deadlines:** FAFSA. Financial aid filing deadline 6/30. Priority financial aid filing date 3/1. **Types of Aid:** *Need-based scholarships/grants:* Federal Pell, SEOG, state scholarships/grants, private scholarships, the school's own gift aid. *Loans:* FFEL Subsidized Stafford, FFEL Unsubsidized Stafford, FFEL PLUS **Financial Aid Statistics:** 17% freshmen, 19% undergrads receive need-based scholarship or grant aid. 25% freshmen, 37% undergrads receive non-need-based scholarship or grant aid. 18% freshmen, 21% undergrads receive need-based self-help aid. 2% freshmen, 2% undergrads receive athletic scholarships. 88% freshmen, 35% undergrads receive any aid. 35% undergrads borrow to pay for school. Average cumulative indebtedness $9,449. **Criteria for awarding institutional aid:** *Non-need-based:* Academics, alumni affiliation, athletics, leadership, minority status, music/drama, religious affiliation, state/district residency.

FLORIDA INSTITUTE OF TECHNOLOGY

150 West University Boulevard, Melbourne, FL 32901-6975
Phone: 321-674-8030 **Financial Aid Phone:** 800-666-4348
E-mail: admission@fit.edu **CEEB Code:** 5080
Fax: 321-674-8004 **Website:** www.fit.edu **ACT Code:** 716

This private school was founded in 1958. It has a 130-acre campus.

RATINGS
Admissions Selectivity Rating: 84   **Fire Safety Rating:** 83   **Green Rating:** 75

STUDENTS AND FACULTY
Enrollment: 4,839. **Student Body:** 45% female, 55% male, 56% out-of-state, 14% international (104 countries represented). Asian 2%, African American 14%, Caucasian 52%, Hispanic 7%, Native American 1%.
Retention and Graduation: 75% freshmen return for sophomore year. 39% freshmen graduate within 4 years. 28% grads go on to further study within 1 year. 7% grads pursue arts and sciences degrees. 1% grads pursue law degrees. 2% grads pursue business degrees. 2% grads pursue medical degrees. **Faculty:** Student/faculty ratio 17:1. 240 full-time faculty, 89% hold PhDs, 14% are members of minority groups, 23% are women. 5% of classes are taught by teaching assistants.

ACADEMICS
Degrees: Associate, bachelor's, master's, post-master's certificate. **Classes:** Most classes have 10–19 students. Most lab/discussion sessions have 10–19 students. **Majors with Highest Enrollment:** Aerospace, aeronautical and astronautical engineering; marine biology and biological oceanography; mechanical engineering. **Special Study Options:** Accelerated program, cooperative education program, cross-registration, distance learning, double major, dual enrollment, English as a Second Language (ESL), independent study, internships, study abroad, teacher certification program, Dual degrees in computer engineering/electrical engineering, chemical engineering/chemistry, molecular/marine biology. Special programs offered to physically disabled students include note-taking services, reader services, tutors. **Career services:** Alumni services, career/job search classes, internships. **Career services highlights include:** Internships.

FACILITIES
Housing: Coed dorms, apartments for single students, wellness housing. 90% of campus accessible to physically disabled. **Special Academic Facilities/**

Equipment: New facility openings have been the highlight of 2009, beginning in February with the dedication of the Emil Buehler Center for Aviation Training and Research at Melbourne International Airport. The center, valued at $5.1 million, consists of a main building and 17,600–square-foot hanger, located on eight acres at the airport. The new building houses the operations of F.I.T. Aviation. In August, the university's Department of Humanities got a boost with the opening of the 3,000–square-foot Ruth Funk Center for Textile Arts. The only textiles center in the state of Florida, the facility is dedicated to furthering the understanding of cultural and creative achievements in the textile and fine arts. October gave another boost to the College of Psychology and Liberal Arts with the opening of the Scott Center for Autism Treatment. The 18,000–square-foot center provides services for individuals with autism spectrum disorder, training for parents, teachers and other professionals and research on effective treatments for autism. The College of Engineering and College of Science also gained a new building in October with the opening of the Harris Center for Science and Engineering. While computer science and marine biology laboratories fill two-thirds of the building, the rest is dedicated to the Harris Institute for Assured Information. The institute is already recognized for its work and numerous government and national foundation contracts. The College of Business received a tremendous boost in 2009 with a $5 million gift from Nathan M. Bisk, a leader in continuing education and online learning. The gift enhances business programs offerings and strengthens online education and marks the start of fund-raising for a new building, to be named the Nathan M. Bisk College of Business. **Computers:** 100% of classrooms, 30% of dorms, 100% of libraries, 100% of dining areas, 100% of student union, 5% of common outdoor areas have wireless network access. Students can register for classes online. Administrative functions (other than registration) can be performed online.

CAMPUS LIFE

Environment: Town. **Activities:** Choral groups, dance, drama/theater, literary magazine, pep band, radio station, student government, student newspaper, television station, campus ministries, international student organization. **Organizations:** 106 registered organizations, 8 honor societies, 3 religious organizations. 7 fraternities, 3 sororities. **Athletics (Intercollegiate):** *Men:* Baseball, basketball, cross-country, golf, soccer, tennis. *Women:* Basketball, crew/rowing, cross-country, golf, soccer, softball, tennis, volleyball. **On-Campus Highlights:** Student Union Building, Clemente Center for Sports & Recreation, Olin Engineering Complex, Harris Village, Botanical Gardens. **Environmental Initiatives:** All new construction to be LEED Silver equivalent. Comprehensive campus-wide recycling program. Green procurement program (2010–11).

ADMISSIONS

Freshman Academic Profile: Average high school GPA 3.5. 27% in top 10% of high school class, 52% in top 25% of high school class, 88% in top 50% of high school class. 63% from public high schools. SAT Math middle 50% range 540–660. SAT Critical Reading middle 50% range 500–610. ACT middle 50% range 23–28. Minimum paper TOEFL 550. Minimum computer TOEFL 213. **Basis for Candidate Selection:** *Very important factors considered include:* Rigor of secondary school record. *Important factors considered include:* Academic GPA, standardized test scores, level of applicant's interest. *Other factors considered include:* Class rank, application essay, recommendation(s), alumni/ae relation, character/personal qualities, extracurricular activities, interview, work experience. **Freshman Admission Requirements:** High school diploma is required and GED is accepted. *Academic units required:* 4 English, 3 mathematics, 3 science, (3 science labs), 1 social studies, 2 history, 7 academic electives. *Academic units recommended:* 4 English, 4 mathematics, 4 science, (4 science labs), 2 foreign language, 3 social studies, 2 history, 2 computer science, 5 academic electives. **Freshman Admission Statistics:** 3,340 applied, 74% admitted, 22% enrolled. **Transfer Admission Requirements:** College transcript(s), minimum college GPA of 2.5 required. Lowest grade transferable C. **General Admission Information:** Application fee $50. Notification on a rolling basis, beginning on or about 7/1. Nonfall registration accepted. Admission may be deferred for a maximum of 12 month. Credit and/or placement offered for CEEB Advanced Placement tests.

COSTS AND FINANCIAL AID

Required Forms and Deadlines: FAFSA, state aid form. Priority financial aid filing date 3/1. **Notification of Awards:** Applicants will be notified of awards on a rolling basis beginning 2/15. **Types of Aid:** *Need-based scholarships/grants:* Federal Pell, SEOG, state scholarships/grants, private scholarships, the school's own gift aid. *Loans:* FFEL Subsidized Stafford, FFEL Unsubsidized Stafford, FFEL PLUS, Federal Perkins, state loans, college/university loans from institutional funds. **Student Employment:** Federal Work-Study Program available. Institutional employment available. Highest amount earned per year from on-campus jobs $15,715. Off-campus job opportunities are fair. **Financial Aid Statistics:** 69% freshmen, 60% undergrads receive need-based scholarship or grant aid. 69% freshmen, 55% undergrads receive non-need-based scholarship or grant aid. 52% freshmen, 48% undergrads receive need-based self-help aid. 2% freshmen, 3% undergrads receive athletic scholarships. 97% freshmen, 91% undergrads receive any aid. 69% undergrads borrow to pay for school. Average cumulative indebtedness $40,630. **Criteria for awarding institutional aid:** *Non-need-based:* Academics, alumni affiliation, athletics, state/district residency.

FLORIDA INTERNATIONAL UNIVERSITY

University Park, PC 140, Miami, FL 33199
Phone: 305-348-2363 **Financial Aid Phone:** 305-348-7272
E-mail: admiss@fiu.edu **CEEB Code:** 5206
Fax: 305-348-3648 **Website:** www.fiu.edu **ACT Code:** 776

This public school was founded in 1965. It has a 573-acre campus.

RATINGS
Admissions Selectivity Rating: 91   **Fire Safety Rating:** 79   **Green Rating:** 60*

STUDENTS AND FACULTY
Enrollment: 30,936. **Student Body:** 56% female, 44% male, 2% out-of-state, 5% international (148 countries represented). Asian 3%, African American 12%, Caucasian 14%, Hispanic 65%.
Retention and Graduation: 81% freshmen return for sophomore year. 20% freshmen graduate within 4 years. **Faculty:** Student/faculty ratio 27:1. 871 full-time faculty, 87% hold PhDs, 34% are members of minority groups, 37% are women.

ACADEMICS
Degrees: Associate, bachelor's, certificate, master's, post-master's certificate. **Classes:** Most classes have 20–29 students. Most lab/discussion sessions have 20–29 students. **Majors with Highest Enrollment:** Business administration and management; economics; psychology. **Special Study Options:** Accelerated program, cooperative education program, distance learning, double major, dual enrollment, exchange student program (domestic), honors program, independent study, internships, study abroad, teacher certification program, weekend college. **Combined degree programs:** BA/MA, BA/MEng, economics, Asian studies, international relations, liberal studies. Special programs offered to physically disabled students include note-taking services, reader services, tape recorders, tutors. **Career services:** Alumni services, career/job search classes, career assessment, internships, regional alumni. **Career services highlights include:** We are particularly proud of our Executive Protege Initiative that is designed for students who commit quality time to attend career readiness presentations and professional development actitivies. We are also proud of our yearly Federal Government Statewide Conference that brings together FIU students and federal agencies to help students freshman-graduate learn about internship and full-time opportunities in the federal government.

FACILITIES
Housing: Coed dorms, fraternity/sorority housing, apartments for married students, apartments for single students. 100% of campus accessible to physically disabled. **Special Academic Facilities/Equipment:** The Frost Art Museum, The Wolfsonian Art Museum, Natural Preserve, Biscayne Bay Preserve. **Computers:** 100% of classrooms, 100% of dorms, 1000% of libraries, 100% of dining areas, 100% of student union, 100% of common outdoor areas have wireless network access. Students can register for classes online. Administrative functions (other than registration) can be performed online.

CAMPUS LIFE
Environment: Metropolis. **Activities:** Choral groups, drama/theater, jazz band, music ensembles, opera, radio station, student government, student newspaper, symphony orchestra, yearbook, campus ministries, international student organization, Model UN. **Organizations:** 250 registered organizations, 40 honor societies, 5 religious organizations. 21 fraternities, 17 sororities. **Athletics (Intercollegiate):** *Men:* Baseball, basketball, cross-country, football, soccer, track/field (outdoor), track/field (indoor). *Women:* Basketball, cross-country, diving, golf, soccer, softball, swimming, tennis, track/field (outdoor), track/field (indoor), volleyball. **On-Campus Highlights:** The Frost Museum, The Wolfsonian Museum, Steven and Dorothea Green Library, Graham University Center, Biscayne Bay Campus Library, The Recreational Center. **Environmental Initiatives:** The latest initiative in FIU's commitment to going green, the web-based carpool program features award-winning software that makes signing up hassle-free and completely safe. Open to all FIU students, faculty and staff, university leaders are hoping the program will save money for participants, reduce traffic and relieve parking congestion, and help improve air quality and conserve energy. FIU organic market Began to install sensor monitor for office light and installed new xerox machines which are energy efficient and are setfor double-sided copying

ADMISSIONS
Freshman Academic Profile: Average high school GPA 3.7. 72% from public high schools. SAT Math middle 50% range 530–610. SAT Critical Reading middle 50% range 540–620. SAT Writing middle 50% range 530–610. ACT middle 50% range 24–27. Minimum paper TOEFL 500. Minimum computer TOEFL 173. Minimum web-based TOEFL 63. **Basis for Candidate Selection:** *Very important factors considered include:* Class rank, academic GPA, rigor

of secondary school record, standardized test scores; first generation. *Other factors considered include:* Application essay, recommendation(s), alumni/ae relation, character/personal qualities, extracurricular activities, geographical residence, interview, level of applicant's interest, state residency, talent/ability, volunteer work, work experience. **Freshman Admission Requirements:** High school diploma is required and GED is accepted. *Academic units required:* 4 English, 3 mathematics, 3 science, (2 science labs), 2 foreign language, 3 social studies, 3 academic electives. **Freshman Admission Statistics:** 12,978 applied, 43% admitted, 36% enrolled. **Transfer Admission Requirements:** College transcript(s), statement of good standing from prior institution(s). Minimum college GPA of 2.0 required. Lowest grade transferable D. **General Admission Information:** Application fee $30. Regular application deadline 5/1. Notification on a rolling basis, beginning on or about 12/1. Nonfall registration accepted. Credit offered for CEEB Advanced Placement tests.

COSTS AND FINANCIAL AID
Student Employment: Federal Work-Study Program available. Institutional employment available. Off-campus job opportunities are good.

FLORIDA SOUTHERN COLLEGE

111 Lake Hollingworth Drive, Lakeland, FL 33801
Phone: 863-680-4131 **Financial Aid Phone:** 863-680-4140
E-mail: fscadm@flsouthern.edu **CEEB Code:** 5218
Fax: 863-680-4120 **Website:** www.flsouthern.edu **ACT Code:** 732

This private school, affiliated with the Methodist Church, was founded in 1883. It has a 100-acre campus.

RATINGS
Admissions Selectivity Rating: 83   **Fire Safety Rating:** 79   **Green Rating:** 69

STUDENTS AND FACULTY
Enrollment: 1,881. **Student Body:** 58% female, 42% male; 25% out-of-state, 3% international (31 countries represented). Asian 2%, African American 6%, Caucasian 80%, Hispanic 8%, Native American 1%.
Retention and Graduation: 79% freshmen return for sophomore year. 38% freshmen graduate within 4 years. 27% grads go on to further study within 1 year. **Faculty:** Student/faculty ratio 13:1. 109 full-time faculty, 87% hold PhDs, 9% are members of minority groups, 38% are women.

ACADEMICS
Degrees: Bachelor's, master's. **Classes:** Most classes have 20–29 students. Most lab/discussion sessions have 10–19 students. **Majors with Highest Enrollment:** Biology/biological sciences; business administration and management; nursing/registered nurse (RN, ASN, BSN, MSN). **Special Study Options:** Double major, dual enrollment, honors program, independent study, internships, liberal arts/career combination, student-designed major, study abroad, teacher certification program, FSC Honors Program—USF College of Medicine Medical Education Program. **Honors programs:** The mission of the Florida Southern College Honors Program is to offer academically talented and highly motivated students opportunities to explore special topics through carefully constructed courses. Professors employ innovative teaching techniques that challenge students to explore subjects through multiple perspectives. The Honors Program fosters an interactive learning environment within a community of scholars. **Combined degree programs:** BA/MD, Priority admittance to USF School of Medicine. **Career services:** Alumni network, alumni services, career/job search classes, career assessment, internships, regional alumni. **Career services highlights include:** Florida Southern College guarantees meaningful, real-world engaged learning experiences, including internships, to every student.

FACILITIES
Housing: Coed dorms, special housing for disabled students, men's dorms, women's dorms, fraternity/sorority housing, apartments for married students, apartments for single students, theme housing. 70% of campus accessible to physically disabled. **Special Academic Facilities/Equipment:** Campus designed by Frank Lloyd Wright; contains world's largest collection of Wright-designed structures at a single site. Also home to three buildings designed by world renowned architect Robert A.M. Stern: 2 residence halls and 1 classroom building, which includes an art gallery and film studies center. The science building features a planetarium; the communication building features a television studio. The latest two building additions are 1) a 24-hour, state-of-the-art

Technology and Learning Center; and 2) a high-tech nursing building featuring virtual patient simulators. The college houses two newly renovated art galleries—the Melvin and Burke Galleries. Also of note, FSC has a world-class performing arts venue seating 2200. Students enjoy a Wellness Center accompanied by an outdoor pool and a boathouse for water-skiing, sailing, and kayaking. At the center of campus is a spectacular, 50-foot high Water Dome, which is next to the library's Cyber Café, which serves Starbuck's products. A spectacular Archives Center, also adjacent to the library, was completed within the past year. **Computers:** 20% of classrooms, 20% of dorms, 100% of libraries, 100% of dining areas, 50% of student union, 50% of common outdoor areas have wireless network access. Students can register for classes online. Administrative functions (other than registration) can be performed online.

CAMPUS LIFE
Environment: City. **Activities:** Choral groups, concert band, dance, drama/theater, jazz band, literary magazine, music ensembles, musical theater, opera, pep band, student government, student newspaper, symphony orchestra, television station, yearbook, campus ministries, international student organization. **Organizations:** 70 registered organizations, 22 honor societies, 9 religious organizations. 7 fraternities, 7 sororities. **Athletics (Intercollegiate):** *Men:* Baseball, basketball, cross-country, golf, lacrosse, soccer, swimming, tennis, track/field (outdoor). *Women:* Basketball, cross-country, golf, soccer, softball, swimming, tennis, track/field (outdoor), volleyball. **On-Campus Highlights:** Tutu's Cyber Cafe, Wellness Center and Pool, Badcock Garden's "outdoor living room", The Terrace Cafe, Field House, Our sunny campus offers something for everyone, including more than 70 clubs and organizations that cater to every interest. On beautiful Lake Hollingsworth, students enjoy free kayaking, sailing, and canoeing. Our state-of-the-art Wellness Center offers classes in everything from yoga to Pilates to water aerobics in our OlympiC–sized pool. If the arts are more your speed, visit the Melvin Art Gallery, which exhibits the works of students and internationally recognized artists. Take in an opera, play, or concert through the renowned Festival of fine arts series, or catch a movie on the Badcock Garden lawn. Our championship Division II NCAA sports programs mean there's always something to cheer about, and intramural sports such as flag football, tennis, and soccer give you a chance to get in the game. And if you've worked up an appetite, grab lunch from the Grillmaster in the Badcock Garden or enjoy a cup of Starbuck's coffee and a bagel on the patio overlooking the Water Dome at TéTé's Cyber Café. **Environmental Initiatives:** Florida Southern built its first LEED approved garden this past year, Lynn's Garden, which uses sustainable designs, recycled materials, and native plant species. Trayless cafeteria initiative Cycling Initiative Explanation: In an effort to encourage members of the campus community to ride bikes on short trips, we make bikes available for students, faculty, and staffers to check out at no charge at the Wellness Center.

ADMISSIONS
Freshman Academic Profile: Average high school GPA 3.4. 21% in top 10% of high school class, 48% in top 25% of high school class, 80% in top 50% of high school class. 77% from public high schools. SAT Math middle 50% range 480–580. SAT Critical Reading middle 50% range 480–580. SAT Writing middle 50% range 470–570. ACT middle 50% range 21–25. Minimum paper TOEFL 550. Minimum computer TOEFL 213. **Basis for Candidate Selection:** *Very important factors considered include:* Academic GPA, rigor of secondary school record. *Important factors considered include:* Application essay, recommendation(s), standardized test scores, character/personal qualities, extracurricular activities, level of applicant's interest, talent/ability. *Other factors considered include:* Class rank, alumni/ae relation, first generation, interview, racial/ethnic status, religious affiliation/commitment, volunteer work, work experience. **Freshman Admission Requirements:** High school diploma is required and GED is accepted. *Academic units required:* 4 English, 3 mathematics, 2 science, (2 science labs), 3 social studies, 3 history, 2 academic electives. *Academic units recommended:* 2 foreign language. **Freshman Admission Statistics:** 2,437 applied, 69% admitted, 33% enrolled. **Transfer Admission Requirements:** College transcript(s), essay or personal statement, statement of good standing from prior institution(s). Minimum college GPA of 2.0 required. Lowest grade transferable C. **General Admission Information:** Application fee $30. Early decision application deadline 12/1. Regular application deadline 3/1. Notification on a rolling basis, beginning on or about 1/15. Nonfall registration accepted. Admission may be deferred for a maximum of 1 year. Credit offered for CEEB Advanced Placement tests.

COSTS AND FINANCIAL AID
Annual tuition $21,620. Room and board $7,850. Required fees $525. Average book expense $1,150. **Required Forms and Deadlines:** FAFSA, institution's own financial aid form. Financial aid filing deadline 7/1. Priority financial aid filing date 3/1. **Notification of Awards:** Applicants will be notified of awards on a rolling basis beginning 3/1. **Types of Aid:** *Need-based scholarships/grants:* Federal Pell, SEOG, state scholarships/grants, private scholarships, the school's own gift aid, Federal Nursing Scholarships. *Loans:* FFEL Subsidized Stafford, FFEL Unsubsidized Stafford, FFEL PLUS, Federal Perkins. **Student Employment:** Federal Work-Study Program available. Institutional employment available. Highest amount earned per year from on-campus jobs $1,500. Off-

campus job opportunities are good. **Financial Aid Statistics:** 53% freshmen, 47% undergrads receive need-based scholarship or grant aid. 74% freshmen, 63% undergrads receive non-need-based scholarship or grant aid. 51% freshmen, 48% undergrads receive need-based self-help aid. 10% freshmen, 13% undergrads receive athletic scholarships. 99% freshmen, 97% undergrads receive any aid. 64% undergrads borrow to pay for school. Average cumulative indebtedness $23,182. **Criteria for awarding institutional aid:** *Non-need-based:* Academics, alumni affiliation, art, athletics, job skills, leadership, minority status, music/drama, religious affiliation, state/district residency.

FLORIDA STATE UNIVERSITY

PO Box 3062400, Tallahassee, FL 32306-2400
Phone: 850-644-6200 **Financial Aid Phone:** 850-644-5716
E-mail: admissions@admin.fsu.edu **CEEB Code:** 5219
Fax: 850-644-0197 **Website:** www.fsu.edu **ACT Code:** 734

This public school was founded in 1851. It has a 452-acre campus.

RATINGS
Admissions Selectivity Rating: 88   **Fire Safety Rating:** 83   **Green Rating:** 86

STUDENTS AND FACULTY
Enrollment: 30,474. **Student Body:** 55% female, 45% male, 10.1% out-of-state, 1% international (128 countries represented). Asian 4%, African American 10%, Caucasian 71%, Hispanic 13%, Native American 1%. **Retention and Graduation:** 91% freshmen return for sophomore year. 42% grads go on to further study within 1 year. **Faculty:** Student/faculty ratio 20.5:1. 1298 full-time faculty, 92% hold PhDs, 15% are members of minority groups, 38% are women. 28% of classes are taught by teaching assistants.

ACADEMICS
Degrees: Associate, bachelor's, certificate, master's, post-bachelor's certificate, post-master's certificate, transfer associate. **Classes:** Most classes have 20–29 students. **Majors with Highest Enrollment:** English language and literature; finance; political science and government. **Special Study Options:** Accelerated program, cooperative education program, cross-registration, distance learning, double major, dual enrollment, English as a Second Language (ESL), honors program, independent study, internships, study abroad, teacher certification program. **Honors programs:** The Florida State University Honors Program provides an enriched curriculum and special opportunities for exceptional, high-achieving students who are entering college for the first time. Each fall, freshmen who are admitted into this program attend the University Honors Colloquium, a weekly forum that features stimulating lectures by distinguished faculty as well as informative presentations from directors of academic programs. As they work to meet their liberal study requirements, University Honors students then have the chance to take small, honors-only courses and special topic seminars with some of the university's best researchers and teachers. With its emphasis on small classes taught by top faculty, this program provides the atmosphere of a small liberal arts college within a large research university. **Combined degree programs:** BA/MA. Special programs offered to physically disabled students include note-taking services, reader services, tape recorders, tutors. **Career services:** Alumni network, alumni services, career/job search classes, career assessment, internships, regional alumni.

FACILITIES
Housing: Coed dorms, special housing for disabled students, women's dorms, fraternity/sorority housing, apartments for married students, apartments for single students. On-campus: Honors Residences; Living Learning Communities. Off-campus: Cooperative housing through Southern Scholarship Foundation; off-campus private residence halls. 99% of campus accessible to physically disabled. **Special Academic Facilities/Equipment:** Art gallery, museum, developmental research school, marine lab, oceanographic institute, tandem Van de Graaff accelerator, national high magnetic field lab. **Computers:** 50% of classrooms, 25% of dorms, 90% of libraries, 100% of dining areas, 90% of student union, 70% of common outdoor areas have wireless network access. Students can register for classes online. Administrative functions (other than registration) can be performed online. Undergraduates are required to own a computer.

CAMPUS LIFE
Environment: City. **Activities:** Choral groups, concert band, dance, drama/theater, jazz band, literary magazine, marching band, music ensembles, musical theater, opera, pep band, radio station, student government, student newspaper, student-run film society, symphony orchestra, television station, yearbook, campus ministries, international student organization, Model UN. **Organizations:** 520 registered organizations, 23 honor societies, 30 religious organizations. 32 fraternities, 28 sororities. **Athletics (Intercollegiate):** *Men:* Baseball, basketball, cheerleading, cross-country, diving, football, golf, swimming, tennis, track/field (outdoor), track/field (indoor). *Women:* Basketball, cheerleading, cross-country, diving, golf, soccer, softball, swimming, tennis, track/field (outdoor), track/field (indoor), volleyball. **On-Campus Highlights:** Suwannee Dining Hall, Bobby E. Leach Student Recreation Center, Bobby Bowden Field at Doak Campbell Stadium, National High Magnetic Field Laboratory, FSU Reservation. **Environmental Initiatives:** The revised FSU Design Guidelines and Specifications require that all new construction and major renovations be designed and built to LEED certification levels and to achieve Silver whenever practical. To date, there are 3 certified buildings, 4 buildings awaiting certification, 2 buildings under construction, and 2 buildings designed and registered with USGBC. A campus-wide energy conservation program including increased building monitoring, energy conservation competitions between buildings, a Vice President appointed energy task force, and a commitment to monitor and certify campus buildings through the EPA Energy Star Rating program. Last year, energy conservation programs on campus saved $3.3 million. Longevity of the Strategic Planning Group. Members of the SPG have committed over 3 years of service to continuing campus sustainability efforts. In lieu of a campus sustainability office and/or coordinator this group of staff, faculty, and students are responsible for all major outreach, education, and programming efforts.

ADMISSIONS
Freshman Academic Profile: Average high school GPA 3.71. 31% in top 10% of high school class; 71% in top 25% of high school class, 96% in top 50% of high school class. 84% from public high schools. SAT Math middle 50% range 560–650. SAT Critical Reading middle 50% range 550–640. ACT middle 50% range 24–28. Minimum paper TOEFL 550. Minimum computer TOEFL 213. **Basis for Candidate Selection:** *Very important factors considered include:* Academic GPA, rigor of secondary school record. *Important factors considered include:* Standardized test scores, state residency, talent/ability. *Other factors considered include:* Class rank, application essay, recommendation(s), alumni/ae relation, character/personal qualities, extracurricular activities, first generation, geographical residence, volunteer work, work experience. **Freshman Admission Requirements:** High school diploma is required and GED is accepted. *Academic units required:* 4 English, 4 mathematics, 3 science, (2 science labs), 2 foreign language, 1 social studies, 2 history, 3 academic electives. *Academic units recommended:* 4 English, 4 mathematics, 4 science, (2 science labs), 4 foreign language, 2 social studies, 2 history, 3 academic electives. **Freshman Admission Statistics:** 23,439 applied, 61% admitted, 42% enrolled. **Transfer Admission Requirements:** College transcript(s), minimum college GPA of 3.0 required. Lowest grade transferable D–. **General Admission Information:** Application fee $30. Regular application deadline 1/21. Nonfall registration accepted. Credit and/or placement offered for CEEB Advanced Placement tests.

COSTS AND FINANCIAL AID
Annual in-state tuition $2,933. Annual out-of-state tuition $17,171. Room and board $8,000. Required fees $1,633. Average book expense $1,000. **Required Forms and Deadlines:** FAFSA. **Notification of Awards:** Applicants will be notified of awards on a rolling basis beginning 3/15. **Types of Aid:** *Need-based scholarships/grants:* Federal Pell, SEOG, state scholarships/grants, private scholarships, the school's own gift aid. *Loans:* FFEL Subsidized Stafford, FFEL Unsubsidized Stafford, FFEL PLUS, Federal Perkins. **Student Employment:** Federal Work-Study Program available. Institutional employment available. Highest amount earned per year from on-campus jobs $10,000. Off-campus job opportunities are good. **Financial Aid Statistics:** 20% freshmen, 21% undergrads receive need-based scholarship or grant aid. 32% freshmen, 26% undergrads receive non-need-based scholarship or grant aid. 22% freshmen, 27% undergrads receive need-based self-help aid. 1% freshmen, 1% undergrads receive athletic scholarships. 98% freshmen, 88% undergrads receive any aid. 48% undergrads borrow to pay for school. Average cumulative indebtedness $16,927. **Criteria for awarding institutional aid:** *Non-need-based:* Academics, athletics, state/district residency.

FONTBONNE UNIVERSITY

6800 Wydown Boulevard, St. Louis, MO 63105
Phone: 314-889-1400 **Financial Aid Phone:** 314-889-1414
E-mail: fcadmis@fontbonne.edu **CEEB Code:** 6216
Fax: 314-889-1451 **Website:** www.fontbonne.edu **ACT Code:** 2298

This private school, affiliated with the Roman Catholic Church, was founded in 1917. It has a 13-acre campus.

RATINGS
Admissions Selectivity Rating: 73   **Fire Safety Rating:** 78   **Green Rating:** 60*

STUDENTS AND FACULTY
Enrollment: 1,993. **Student Body:** 72% female, 28% male, 12% out-of-state, 1% international (23 countries represented). Asian 1%, African American 34%, Caucasian 62%, Hispanic 1%.
Retention and Graduation: 58% freshmen return for sophomore year. 33% freshmen graduate within 4 years. 25% grads go on to further study within 1 year. **Faculty:** Student/faculty ratio 16:1. 73 full-time faculty, 71% hold PhDs, 10% are members of minority groups, 68% are women.

ACADEMICS
Degrees: Bachelor's, certificate, master's, post-bachelor's certificate. **Classes:** Most classes have 10–19 students. Most lab/discussion sessions have 10–19 students. **Majors with Highest Enrollment:** Business administration and management; elementary education and teaching; special education and teaching. **Special Study Options:** Accelerated program, cooperative education program, cross-registration, distance learning, double major, English as a Second Language (ESL), exchange student program (domestic), honors program, independent study, internships, liberal arts/career combination, student-designed major, study abroad, teacher certification program, weekend college. **Combined degree programs:** BA/MEng, BS/MS with Washington University. Special programs offered to physically disabled students include note-taking services, reader services, tape recorders, tutors. **Career services:** Alumni services, career/job search classes, career assessment, internships.

FACILITIES
Housing: Coed dorms, special housing for international students, apartments for single students, off campus house holds 13 females. 85% of campus accessible to physically disabled. **Special Academic Facilities/Equipment:** Art gallery. **Computers:** 75% of classrooms, 100% of dorms, 100% of libraries, 100% of dining areas, 100% of student union, 100% of common outdoor areas have wireless network access. Students can register for classes online. Administrative functions (other than registration) can be performed online.

CAMPUS LIFE
Environment: Metropolis. **Activities:** Choral groups, dance, drama/theater, literary magazine, music ensembles, radio station, student government, student newspaper, campus ministries. **Organizations:** 34 registered organizations, 7 honor societies, 4 religious organizations. **Athletics (Intercollegiate):** *Men:* Baseball, basketball, cross-country, field hockey, golf, lacrosse, soccer, tennis. *Women:* Basketball, bowling, cross-country, field hockey, golf, lacrosse, soccer, softball, tennis, volleyball. **On-Campus Highlights:** Ryan Hall, Dunham Student Activity Center, Library, Medaille Hall, fine arts Center, Message from the President. On behalf of the entire Fontbonne University family, I am pleased to welcome you to our web site. As you navigate these electronic pages, I trust that you will find whatever information you seek about our University. When you explore the Fontbonne University campus, either in person or on a virtual visit like this, you will learn that Fontbonne has certain advantages that are evidenced in the following ways: Location Our campus is located in the heart of Clayton, Missouri, which is one of the most beautiful suburbs in the United States. There is easy access from our campus to Forest Park, the St. Louis Zoo, the Art Museum and the History Museum. In addition, you are approximately fifteen minutes from downtown St. Louis, home of the St. Louis Cardinals, NFL Rams and NHL Blues. Academics The academic programs are excellent, and they are taught in a values-based, student-centered context. Because of our student-faculty ratio, the faculty know you as an individual and will help you incorporate experiential learning in your academic program. Focus The individual student is the primary focus at Fontbonne University. You are the central focus of the administration, faculty and staff. We are dedicated to your academic, moral, emotional, spiritual, social, cultural, career and co-curricular development. Ultimate Goal At Fontbonne, we strive to achieve strength of curriculum and strength of character. Therefore, we will teach you not only how to make a living but also how to live a life so that you are prepared to face the challenges of the 21st century and to prevail. Fontbonne is a Catholic University sponsored by the Sisters of St. Joseph of Carondelet. We are co-educational with 2,800 students, and a student body comprised of both traditional-aged undergraduate students as well as adult learners. All of our students are taught to think

critically, to act ethically and to assume responsibility as citizens and leaders for a world in need. If you are seeking a university education where the individual student is at the epicenter of all activity, then Fontbonne is for you. I invite you to visit our campus in person and come to know and value, as we do, the advantage that is a Fontbonne University education. Dennis C. Golden President.

ADMISSIONS
Freshman Academic Profile: Average high school GPA 3.05. 7% in top 10% of high school class, 28% in top 25% of high school class, 61% in top 50% of high school class. 56% from public high schools. SAT Math middle 50% range 470–625. SAT Critical Reading middle 50% range 500–625. ACT middle 50% range 18–24. Minimum paper TOEFL 525. Minimum computer TOEFL 193. **Basis for Candidate Selection:** *Very important factors considered include:* Class rank, academic GPA, rigor of secondary school record, standardized test scores, character/personal qualities. *Other factors considered include:* Application essay, recommendation(s), alumni/ae relation, extracurricular activities, first generation, interview, level of applicant's interest, talent/ability, volunteer work, work experience. **Freshman Admission Requirements:** High school diploma is required and GED is accepted. *Academic units required:* 4 English, 3 mathematics, 3 science, (1 science labs), 3 social studies, 3 academic electives. **Freshman Admission Statistics:** 600 applied, 75% admitted, 42% enrolled. **Transfer Admission Requirements:** College transcript(s), essay or personal statement, minimum college GPA of 2.0 required. Lowest grade transferable D. **General Admission Information:** Application fee $25. Regular application deadline 8/1. Notification on a rolling basis, beginning on or about 8/15. Nonfall registration accepted. Admission may be deferred for a maximum of 1year. Credit and/or placement offered for CEEB Advanced Placement tests.

COSTS AND FINANCIAL AID
Annual tuition $19,000. Room and board $6,739. Required fees $320. Average book expense $650. **Required Forms and Deadlines:** FAFSA, institution's own financial aid form. Financial aid filing deadline 7/1. Priority financial aid filing date 4/1. **Types of Aid:** *Need-based scholarships/grants:* Federal Pell, SEOG, state scholarships/grants, private scholarships, the school's own gift aid. *Loans:* FFEL Subsidized Stafford, FFEL Unsubsidized Stafford, FFEL PLUS, Federal Perkins, state loans, college/university loans from institutional funds. **Student Employment:** Federal Work-Study Program available. **Financial Aid Statistics:** 55% freshmen, 66% undergrads receive need-based scholarship or grant aid. 40% freshmen, 42% undergrads receive non-need-based scholarship or grant aid. 55% freshmen, 66% undergrads receive need-based self-help aid. 85% undergrads borrow to pay for school. Average cumulative indebtedness $17,500. **Criteria for awarding institutional aid:** *Non-need-based:* Academics, alumni affiliation, art, job skills, leadership, minority status, religious affiliation.

FORDHAM UNIVERSITY

441 East Fordham Road, Duane Library, New York, NY 10458
Phone: 718-817-4000 **Financial Aid Phone:** 718-817-3800
E-mail: enroll@fordham.edu **CEEB Code:** 2259
Fax: 718-367-9404 **Website:** www.fordham.edu **ACT Code:** 2748

This private school, affiliated with the Roman Catholic Church, was founded in 1841. It has a 93-acre campus.

RATINGS
Admissions Selectivity Rating: 92   **Fire Safety Rating:** 60*   **Green Rating:** 60*

STUDENTS AND FACULTY
Enrollment: 7,451. **Student Body:** 58% female, 42% male, 46% out-of-state, 2% international (58 countries represented). Asian 7%, African American 6%, Caucasian 58%, Hispanic 13%.
Retention and Graduation: 90% freshmen return for sophomore year. 72% freshmen graduate within 4 years. 25% grads go on to further study within 1 year. 10% grads pursue arts and sciences degrees. 5% grads pursue law degrees. 1% grads pursue business degrees. 2% grads pursue medical degrees. **Faculty:** Student/faculty ratio 12:1. 645 full-time faculty, 96% hold PhDs, 16% are members of minority groups, 38% are women.

ACADEMICS
Degrees: Bachelor's, first professional, master's, post-master's certificate. **Classes:** Most classes have 10–19 students. Most lab/discussion sessions have

10–19 students. **Majors with Highest Enrollment:** Business/commerce; communication and media studies, other; social sciences. **Special Study Options:** Double major, English as a Second Language (ESL), exchange student program (domestic), honors program, independent study, internships, student-designed major, study abroad, teacher certification program, Globe Program in International Business. 3:2 Engineering Cooperative with Columbia University or Case Western Reserve University. **Honors programs:** Each undergraduate college has its own Honors Program. All four programs offer enriched academic opportunity for qualified and interested students. Additionally, there are major programs of study designated as selective. Students must be invited into those programs and meet minimum GPA requirements for consideration. Many more majors offer Honors designation at graduation usually based upon completion of a thesis or senior project. **Combined degree programs:** BA/JD, BA/MA, BS/MSW, BS/MBA, 3:2 Engineering. Special programs offered to physically disabled students include note-taking services, reader services, tape recorders, tutors.

FACILITIES

Housing: Coed dorms, special housing for disabled students, apartments for single students, Residential Colleges. 80% of campus accessible to physically disabled. **Special Academic Facilities/Equipment:** Television station, radio station, theaters, white and black box studio spaces, media and visual arts labs and design space, art gallery, University Church, seismic station, 113 biological field station The Louis Calder Center, in Armonk, NY. **Computers:** 90% of classrooms, 98% of dorms, 95% of libraries, 100% of dining areas, 80% of common outdoor areas have wireless network access. Students can register for classes online. Administrative functions (other than registration) can be performed online.

CAMPUS LIFE

Environment: Metropolis. **Activities:** Choral groups, concert band, dance, drama/theater, jazz band, literary magazine, music ensembles, musical theater, pep band, radio station, student government, student newspaper, student-run film society, symphony orchestra, television station, yearbook. **Organizations:** 133 registered organizations, 12 honor societies, 3 religious organizations. **Athletics (Intercollegiate):** *Men:* Baseball, basketball, cross-country, diving, football, golf, soccer, squash, swimming, tennis, track/field (outdoor), track/field (indoor), water polo. *Women:* Basketball, cheerleading, crew/rowing, cross-country, diving, soccer, softball, swimming, tennis, track/field (outdoor), track/field (indoor), volleyball. **On-Campus Highlights:** William D. Walsh Family Library (Rose Hill), O'Hare Hall (Residential College at Rose Hill), Edwards Parade/Keating Hall (Rose Hill), McMahon Hall (Lincoln Center), Pope Auditorium (Lincoln Center), With three distinct campuses, there are numerous noteworthy buildings including new and recently renovated academic and extracurricular space, residence halls and athletic centers/fields. Additional space to note includes student-run coffee houses, white and black box studio spaces and historic buildings designated as NYC landmarks.

ADMISSIONS

Freshman Academic Profile: Average high school GPA 3.7. 42.5% in top 10% of high school class, 73% in top 25% of high school class, 96% in top 50% of high school class. 47% from public high schools. SAT Math middle 50% range 560–660. SAT Critical Reading middle 50% range 570–670. SAT Writing middle 50% range 560–660. ACT middle 50% range 25–29. Minimum paper TOEFL 575. Minimum computer TOEFL 231. **Basis for Candidate Selection:** *Very important factors considered include:* Class rank, rigor of secondary school record, standardized test scores. *Important factors considered include:* Application essay, recommendation(s), character/personal qualities, extracurricular activities, talent/ability. *Other factors considered include:* Alumni/ae relation, first generation, geographical residence, racial/ethnic status, volunteer work, work experience. **Freshman Admission Requirements:** High school diploma is required and GED is accepted. *Academic units required:* 4 English, 3 mathematics, 3 science, 2 foreign language, 2 social studies, 2 history, 6 academic electives. *Academic units recommended:* 4 English, 4 mathematics, 4 science, 3 foreign language, 2 social studies, 2 history, 6 academic electives. **Freshman Admission Statistics:** 18,161 applied, 47% admitted, 20% enrolled. **Transfer Admission Requirements:** High school transcript, college transcript(s), essay or personal statement, statement of good standing from prior institution(s). Minimum college GPA of 3.0 required. Lowest grade transferable C. **General Admission Information:** Application fee $50. Regular application deadline 1/15. Regular notification 4/1. Nonfall registration accepted. Admission may be deferred for a maximum of 1 year. Credit and/or placement offered for CEEB Advanced Placement tests.

COSTS AND FINANCIAL AID

Annual tuition $34,200. Room and board $12,980. Required fees $1,057. Average book expense $800. **Required Forms and Deadlines:** FAFSA, CSS/Financial Aid PROFILE, noncustodial PROFILE, business/farm supplement. Financial aid filing deadline 2/1. Priority financial aid filing date 2/1. **Notification of Awards:** Applicants will be notified of awards on or about 4/1. **Types of Aid:** *Need-based scholarships/grants:* Federal Pell, SEOG, state scholarships/grants, private scholarships, the school's own gift aid. *Loans:* FFEL Subsidized Stafford, FFEL Unsubsidized Stafford, FFEL PLUS, Federal Perkins. **Financial Aid Statistics:** 66% freshmen, 62% undergrads receive need-based scholarship or grant aid. 8% freshmen, 5% undergrads receive non-need-based scholarship or grant aid. 51% freshmen, 52% undergrads receive need-based self-help aid. 2% freshmen, 2% undergrads receive athletic scholarships. 67% freshmen, 62% undergrads receive any aid. **Criteria for awarding institutional aid:** *Non-need-based:* Academics, athletics.

See page 1094.

FORT HAYS STATE UNIVERSITY

600 Park Street, Hays, KS 67601-4099
Phone: 785-628-5666 **Financial Aid Phone:** 785-628-4408
E-mail: tigers@fhsu.edu **CEEB Code:** 6218
Fax: 785-628-4187 **Website: ACT Code:** 1408

This public school was founded in 1902. It has a 4160-acre campus.

RATINGS

Admissions Selectivity Rating: 70   **Fire Safety Rating:** 60*   **Green Rating:** 70

STUDENTS AND FACULTY

Enrollment: 7,926. **Student Body:** 51% female, 49% male, 11% out-of-state, 30% international . Asian 1%, African American 2%, Caucasian 61%, Hispanic 3%.
Retention and Graduation: 21% freshmen graduate within 4 years. 20% grads go on to further study within 1 year. **Faculty:** Student/faculty ratio 17:1. 268 full-time faculty, 67% hold PhDs, 6% are members of minority groups, 40% are women. 1% of classes are taught by teaching assistants.

ACADEMICS

Degrees: Associate, bachelor's, certificate, master's, post-master's certificate. **Classes:** Most classes have 10–19 students. Most lab/discussion sessions have fewer than 10 students. **Majors with Highest Enrollment:** Business/commerce; elementary education and teaching; health and physical education. **Special Study Options:** Distance learning, double major, dual enrollment, English as a Second Language (ESL), exchange student program (domestic), external degree program, independent study, internships, liberal arts/career combination, student-designed major, study abroad, teacher certification program. **Combined degree programs:** BA/MEng, 3-1 progs in allied health, dentistry, and eng. Special programs offered to physically disabled students include note-taking services, reader services, tutors. **Career services:** Alumni network, alumni services, career/job search classes, career assessment, internships.

FACILITIES

Housing: Coed dorms, men's dorms, women's dorms, fraternity/sorority housing, apartments for married students, apartments for single students 100% of campus accessible to physically disabled. **Special Academic Facilities/Equipment:** Paleontology, natural history, visual arts and media center, farm, NMR gas analyzer, telescope (HG). **Computers:** 100% of classrooms, 100% of dorms, 100% of libraries, 100% of dining areas, 100% of student union, 100% of common outdoor areas have wireless network access.

CAMPUS LIFE

Environment: Village. **Activities:** Choral groups, concert band, dance, drama/theater, jazz band, marching band, music ensembles, musical theater, pep band, radio station, student government, student newspaper, symphony orchestra, television station, yearbook. **Organizations:** 103 registered organizations, 20 honor societies, 2 religious organizations. 3 fraternities, 3 sororities. **Athletics (Intercollegiate):** *Men:* Baseball, basketball, cheerleading, cross-country, football, golf, track/field (outdoor), track/field (indoor), wrestling. *Women:* Basketball, cheerleading, cross-country, golf, softball, tennis, track/field (outdoor), track/field (indoor), volleyball. **On-Campus Highlights:** www.tigersportszone.com, www.fhsu.edu/sternberg/, www.fhsu.edu/int/kfhsradio/, www.fhsu.edu/int/kfhstv/, www.fhsu.edu/leader. **Environmental Initiatives:** Clean up of Big Creek; clean up of area neighborhoods; recycling of paper, newspapers and aluminum all over campus.

ADMISSIONS

Freshman Academic Profile: Average high school GPA 3.28. 9.85% in top 10% of high school class, 31.49% in top 25% of high school class, 63.28% in top 50% of high school class. 95% from public high schools. Minimum paper TOEFL 500. Minimum computer TOEFL 173. Minimum web-based TOEFL 61. **Basis for Candidate Selection:** *Other factors considered include:* Class rank, academic GPA, rigor of secondary school record, standardized test scores. **Freshman Admission Requirements:** High school diploma is required and GED is accepted. *Academic units recommended:* 4 English, 3 mathematics, 3 science, 2 social studies, 1 history, 1 computer science. **Freshman Admission Statistics:** 1,477 applied, 88% admitted, 62% enrolled. **Transfer Admission Requirements:** College transcript(s), minimum college GPA of 2.0 required. Lowest grade transferable D. **General Admission Information:** Application fee $30. Nonfall registration accepted. Admission may be deferred for a maximum of 1 year. Credit offered for CEEB Advanced Placement tests.

COSTS AND FINANCIAL AID
Annual in-state tuition $3,051. Annual out-of-state tuition $9,575. Room and board $5,450. Average book expense $800. **Required Forms and Deadlines:** FAFSA. **Types of Aid:** *Need-based scholarships/grants:* Federal Pell, SEOG, state scholarships/grants, private scholarships, the school's own gift aid. *Loans:* FFEL Subsidized Stafford, FFEL Unsubsidized Stafford, FFEL PLUS, Federal Perkins, college/university loans from institutional funds. **Student Employment:** Federal Work-Study Program available. Highest amount earned per year from on-campus jobs $2,000. Off-campus job opportunities are fair. **Financial Aid Statistics:** 56% freshmen, 53% undergrads receive need-based scholarship or grant aid. 5% freshmen, 3% undergrads receive non-need-based scholarship or grant aid. 47% freshmen, 60% undergrads receive need-based self-help aid. 6% freshmen, 4% undergrads receive athletic scholarships. 42.5% undergrads borrow to pay for school. Average cumulative indebtedness $15,077. **Criteria for awarding institutional aid:** *Non-need-based:* Academics, alumni affiliation, art, athletics, job skills, leadership, minority status, music/drama, religious affiliation, state/district residency.

FORT LEWIS COLLEGE

1000 Rim Drive, Durango, CO 81301
Phone: 970-247-7184 **Financial Aid Phone:** 970-247-7142
E-mail: admisson@fortlewis.edu **CEEB Code:** 4310
Fax: 970-247-7179 **Website:** www.fortlewis.edu **ACT Code:** 510

This public school was founded in 1911. It has a 362-acre campus.

RATINGS
Admissions Selectivity Rating: 75   **Fire Safety Rating:** 78   **Green Rating:** 83

STUDENTS AND FACULTY
Enrollment: 3,571. **Student Body:** 48% female, 52% male, 34% out-of-state, 1% international (18 countries represented). Asian 1%, African American 1%, Caucasian 64%, Hispanic 5%, Native American 21%.
Retention and Graduation: 60% freshmen return for sophomore year. 15% freshmen graduate within 4 years. 14% grads go on to further study within 1 year. **Faculty:** Student/faculty ratio 17:1. 171 full-time faculty, 83% hold PhDs, 11% are members of minority groups, 45% are women.

ACADEMICS
Degrees: Bachelor's. **Classes:** Most classes have 10–19 students. Most lab/discussion sessions have 10–19 students. **Majors with Highest Enrollment:** Biology/biological sciences; business administration and management; psychology. **Special Study Options:** Accelerated program, cooperative education program, distance learning, double major, dual enrollment, English as a Second Language (ESL), exchange student program (domestic), honors program, independent study, internships, liberal arts/career combination, student-designed major, study abroad, teacher certification program. **Honors programs:** The John F. Reed honors program selects outstanding first and second-year students who demonstrate ability and interest in pursuing additional academic achievements and challenges. The program requires honors courses called forums which ask students to study innovative thinkers, intellectual foundations, and multidisciplinary perspectives. All of the student's work culminates in an honors thesis presented in a public forum. Students in the honors program also benefit from the honors lounge (computers, tv, fridge, reference materials, etc.), free tickets to events and mentoring by professional associates. Upon graduation, the students receive a minor in Honors called "Rhetoric of Inquiry". Special programs offered to physically disabled students include note-taking services, reader services, tape recorders, tutors. **Career services:** Alumni network, alumni services, career/job search classes, career assessment, internships, regional alumni. **Career services highlights include:** The Skyhawks Job Source: Our new on-line, web-based system allows students to search for positions, post resumes and cover letters for employers to view. The system also allows students to apply for positions on-line. Students who up-load a resume to the site will be included in candidate searches by employers and by the Career Services Office. Students can keep track of and manage their job search activities as well.

FACILITIES
Housing: Coed dorms, special housing for disabled students, apartments for married students, apartments for single students, wellness housing, theme hous-

ing 100% of campus accessible to physically disabled. **Special Academic Facilities/Equipment:** Center of Southwest Studies, Community Concert Hall. **Computers:** 100% of classrooms, 100% of dorms, 100% of libraries, 100% of dining areas, 100% of student union, 10% of common outdoor areas have wireless network access. Students can register for classes online. Administrative functions (other than registration) can be performed online.

CAMPUS LIFE
Environment: Town. **Activities:** Choral groups, concert band, drama/theater, jazz band, literary magazine, musical theater, pep band, radio station, student government, student newspaper, campus ministries. **Organizations:** 65 registered organizations, 5 honor societies, 3 religious organizations. **Athletics (Intercollegiate):** *Men:* Basketball, cross-country, football, golf, soccer. *Women:* Basketball, cross-country, lacrosse, soccer, softball, volleyball. **On-Campus Highlights:** Center of Southwest Studies, Student Life Center, College Union Building, Residence Halls, Academic buildings, Highly qualified, committed faculty who are available, helpful, and engaged. Emphasis on active, experiential learning through community service, undergraduate research, study abroad, and internships. Student-faculty ratio of 17:1. Collaborative campus culture where student voices are heard and respected. Graduates who are twice as likely as those other schools to say their education was "excellent." Cultural diversity is a core value and key feature of Fort Lewis College. Approximately 28% of our students are from ethnic minority backgrounds. **Environmental Initiatives:** President's Climate Commitment, three LEED-certified buildings under construction, drafting of the sustainability action plan

ADMISSIONS
Freshman Academic Profile: Average high school GPA 3.13. 11% in top 10% of high school class, 30% in top 25% of high school class, 64% in top 50% of high school class. SAT Math middle 50% range 460–570. SAT Critical Reading middle 50% range 470–575. SAT Writing middle 50% range 450–570. ACT middle 50% range 20–24. Minimum paper TOEFL 500. Minimum computer TOEFL 173. Minimum web-based TOEFL 61. **Basis for Candidate Selection:** *Very important factors considered include:* Class rank, academic GPA, rigor of secondary school record, standardized test scores. *Other factors considered include:* Application essay, recommendation(s), alumni/ae relation, character/personal qualities, extracurricular activities, first generation, interview, level of applicant's interest, talent/ability, volunteer work, work experience. **Freshman Admission Requirements:** High school diploma is required and GED is accepted. *Academic units required:* 4 English, 4 mathematics, 3 science, (2 science labs), 1 foreign language, 2 social studies, 1 history, 2 academic electives. **Freshman Admission Statistics:** 2,722 applied, 68% admitted, 43% enrolled. **Transfer Admission Requirements:** College transcript(s), minimum college GPA of 2.40 required. Lowest grade transferable C–. **General Admission Information:** Application fee $40. Regular application deadline 8/10. Notification on a rolling basis, beginning on or about 10/10. Nonfall registration accepted. Admission may be deferred for a maximum of 1 semester. Credit and/or placement offered for CEEB Advanced Placement tests.

COSTS AND FINANCIAL AID
Annual in-state tuition $3,102. Annual out-of-state tuition $16,072. Room and board $7,444. Required fees $1,544. Average book expense $1,698. **Required Forms and Deadlines:** FAFSA. Priority financial aid filing date 2/15. **Notification of Awards:** Applicants will be notified of awards on a rolling basis beginning 3/15. **Types of Aid:** *Need-based scholarships/grants:* Federal Pell, SEOG, state scholarships/grants, private scholarships, the school's own gift aid. *Loans:* FFEL Subsidized Stafford, FFEL Unsubsidized Stafford, FFEL PLUS, Federal Perkins, college/university loans from institutional funds. **Student Employment:** Federal Work-Study Program available. Institutional employment available. Highest amount earned per year from on-campus jobs $6,905. Off-campus job opportunities are good. **Financial Aid Statistics:** 34% freshmen, 41% undergrads receive need-based scholarship or grant aid. 38% freshmen, 25% undergrads receive non-need-based scholarship or grant aid. 35% freshmen, 42% undergrads receive need-based self-help aid. 7% freshmen, 6% undergrads receive athletic scholarships. 82% freshmen, 68% undergrads receive any aid. 54% undergrads borrow to pay for school. Average cumulative indebtedness $15,962. **Criteria for awarding institutional aid:** *Non-need-based:* Academics, alumni affiliation, art, athletics, leadership, minority status, music/drama, state/district residency.

FRAMINGHAM STATE COLLEGE

100 State Street, PO Box 9101, Framingham, MA 01701-9101
Phone: 508-626-4500 **Financial Aid Phone:** 508-626-4534
E-mail: admissions@framingham.edu **CEEB Code:** 3519
Fax: 508-626-4017 **Website:** www.framingham.edu **ACT Code:** 1904

This public school was founded in 1839. It has a 73-acre campus.

RATINGS
Admissions Selectivity Rating: 74   **Fire Safety Rating:** 88   **Green Rating:** 83

STUDENTS AND FACULTY
Enrollment: 3,485. **Student Body:** 66% female, 34% male, 5% out-of-state, 1% international (12 countries represented). Asian 2%, African American 5%, Caucasian 83%, Hispanic 4%.
Retention and Graduation: 73% freshmen return for sophomore year. 33% freshmen graduate within 4 years. 11% grads go on to further study within 1 year. **Faculty:** Student/faculty ratio 17:1. 164 full-time faculty, 77% hold PhDs, 5% are members of minority groups, 57% are women.

ACADEMICS
Degrees: Bachelor's, master's, post-bachelor's certificate. **Classes:** Most classes have 20–29 students. **Majors with Highest Enrollment:** Business/commerce; family and consumer sciences/human sciences; sociology. **Special Study Options:** Cross-registration, distance learning, double major, honors program, independent study, internships, liberal arts/career combination, study abroad, teacher certification program, pre-engineering program in conjunction with University of Massachusetts Amherst, University of Massachusetts Dartmouth, and University of Massachusetts Lowell. **Honors programs:** The Honors Program offers challenging courses and projects for qualified students, and sponsors events which contribute to the intellectual life of the college community. Special programs offered to physically disabled students include note-taking services, reader services, tape recorders, tutors. **Career services:** Alumni network, alumni services, career/job search classes, career assessment, internships **Career services highlights include:** Current working relationships with key employers in the MetroWest area with plans to expand in MetroWest, Boston and Worcester.

FACILITIES
Housing: Coed dorms, women's dorms, wellness housing, theme housing 95% of campus accessible to physically disabled. **Special Academic Facilities/Equipment:** Mazmanian Art Gallery, McAuliffe Challenger Learning Center, Greenhouse, Early Childhood Development Lab, Education Curriculum Library, Planetarium. **Computers:** 100% of classrooms, 100% of dorms, 100% of libraries, 100% of dining areas, 100% of student union, have wireless network access. Students can register for classes online. Administrative functions (other than registration) can be performed online. Undergraduates are required to own a computer.

CAMPUS LIFE
Environment: City. **Activities:** Choral groups, dance, drama/theater, literary magazine, musical theater, radio station, student government, student newspaper, campus ministries, international student organization. **Organizations:** 55 registered organizations, 11 honor societies, 4 religious organizations. **Athletics (Intercollegiate):** *Men:* Baseball, basketball, cross-country, football, ice hockey, soccer. *Women:* Basketball, cross-country, field hockey, lacrosse, soccer, softball, volleyball. **On-Campus Highlights:** Residence Halls, Athletic Facility, College Center, Academic Buildings, Library. **Environmental Initiatives:** Developing a Climate Action Plan. Increasing recycling program in residence halls and classromms. Completing capital improvements including re-lighting project in gymnasium to reduce electrical requirement for lighting by 50%.

ADMISSIONS
Freshman Academic Profile: Average high school GPA 3.18. 9% in top 10% of high school class, 32% in top 25% of high school class, 79% in top 50% of high school class. 93% from public high schools. SAT Math middle 50% range 480–560. SAT Critical Reading middle 50% range 460–560. SAT Writing middle 50% range 470–560. ACT middle 50% range 20–21. Minimum paper TOEFL 550. Minimum computer TOEFL 213. Minimum web-based TOEFL 80. **Basis for Candidate Selection:** *Very important factors considered include:* Academic GPA, rigor of secondary school record, standardized test scores. *Important factors considered include:* Class rank, application essay, recommendation(s). *Other factors considered include:* Alumni/ae relation, character/personal qualities, extracurricular activities, first generation, level of applicant's interest, state residency, talent/ability, volunteer work, work experience. **Freshman Admission Requirements:** High school diploma is required and GED is accepted. *Academic units required:* 4 English, 3 mathematics, 3 science, (2 science labs), 2 foreign language, 1 social studies, 1 history, 2 academic electives. *Academic units recommended:* 4 mathematics, 4 science, (3 science labs), 4 foreign language, 2 history. **Freshman Admission Statistics:** 3,384

applied, 63% admitted, 34% enrolled. **Transfer Admission Requirements:** High school transcript, college transcript(s), essay or personal statement, minimum college GPA of 2.5 required. Lowest grade transferable C–. **General Admission Information:** Application fee $50. Notification on a rolling basis, beginning on or about 1/15. Nonfall registration accepted. Admission may be deferred for a maximum of 1 year. Credit and/or placement offered for CEEB Advanced Placement tests.

COSTS AND FINANCIAL AID
Annual in-state tuition $970. Annual out-of-state tuition $7,050. Room and board $8,148. Required fees $5,570. Average book expense $900. **Required Forms and Deadlines:** FAFSA. Priority financial aid filing date 3/1. **Notification of Awards:** Applicants will be notified of awards on a rolling basis beginning 3/15. **Types of Aid:** *Need-based scholarships/grants:* Federal Pell, SEOG, state scholarships/grants, private scholarships, the school's own gift aid. *Loans:* FFEL Subsidized Stafford, FFEL Unsubsidized Stafford, FFEL PLUS, Federal Perkins, state loans. **Student Employment:** Federal Work-Study Program available. Institutional employment available. Highest amount earned per year from on-campus jobs $1,000. Off-campus job opportunities are excellent. **Financial Aid Statistics:** 46% freshmen, 41% undergrads receive need-based scholarship or grant aid. 12% freshmen, 7% undergrads receive non-need-based scholarship or grant aid. 56% freshmen, 49% undergrads receive need-based self-help aid. 43% freshmen, 36% undergrads receive any aid. 65% undergrads borrow to pay for school. Average cumulative indebtedness $19,000. **Criteria for awarding institutional aid:** *Non-need-based:* Academics.

FRANCIS MARION UNIVERSITY

Office of Admissions, PO Box 100547, Florence, SC 29501-0547
Phone: 843-661-1231 **Financial Aid Phone:** 843-661-1190
E-mail: admissions@fmarion.edu **CEEB Code:** 5442
Fax: 843-661-4635 **Website:** www.fmarion.edu **ACT Code:** 3856

This public school was founded in 1970. It has a 300-acre campus.

RATINGS
Admissions Selectivity Rating: 73   **Fire Safety Rating:** 60*   **Green Rating:** 60*

STUDENTS AND FACULTY
Enrollment: 3,068. **Student Body:** 62% female, 38% male, 4% out-of-state, 1% international (24 countries represented). Asian 1%, African American 40%, Caucasian 54%, Hispanic 1%, Native American 1%.
Retention and Graduation: 65% freshmen return for sophomore year. 29% freshmen graduate within 4 years. **Faculty:** Student/faculty ratio 17:1. 170 full-time faculty, 83% hold PhDs, 5% are members of minority groups, 32% are women.

ACADEMICS
Degrees: Bachelor's, master's. **Classes:** Most classes have 20–29 students. **Majors with Highest Enrollment:** Biology; business/commerce; elementary education and teaching. **Special Study Options:** Accelerated program, cross-registration, distance learning, double major, dual enrollment, honors program, independent study, internships, study abroad, teacher certification program **Combined degree programs:** 2-2 Forestry prog with Clemson U.; engineering, BSN. Special programs offered to physically disabled students include note-taking services, reader services, tape recorders, tutors.

FACILITIES
Housing: Special housing for disabled students, men's dorms, women's dorms, apartments for single students. 100% of campus accessible to physically disabled. **Special Academic Facilities/Equipment:** Media center, planetarium, observatory. **Computers:** Students can register for classes online.

CAMPUS LIFE
Environment: Rural. **Activities:** Choral groups, drama/theater, jazz band, literary magazine, music ensembles, student government, student newspaper, television station **Organizations:** 56 registered organizations, 13 honor societies, 5 religious organizations. 7 fraternities, 7 sororities. **Athletics (Intercollegiate):** *Men:* Baseball, basketball, cross-country, golf, soccer, tennis, track/field (outdoor). *Women:* Basketball, cross-country, soccer, softball, tennis, track/field (outdoor), volleyball. **On-Campus Highlights:** The Cottage, The Smith University Center, The Dooley Planetarium, The Hyman fine arts Center, The Hewn Timber Cabins.

ADMISSIONS
Freshman Academic Profile: Average high school GPA 3.34. 12% in top 10% of high school class, 34% in top 25% of high school class, 72% in top 50% of high school class. 88% from public high schools. SAT Math middle 50% range 420–520. SAT Critical Reading middle 50% range 420–510. ACT middle 50%

range 17–20. Minimum paper TOEFL 500. Minimum computer TOEFL 173. **Basis for Candidate Selection:** *Very important factors considered include:* Rigor of secondary school record, standardized test scores. *Important factors considered include:* Class rank. *Other factors considered include:* Recommendation(s). **Freshman Admission Requirements:** High school diploma is required and GED is accepted. *Academic units required:* 4 English, 3 mathematics, 3 science, (3 science labs), 2 foreign language, 2 social studies, 1 history, 4 academic electives, 1 PE or ROTC. *Academic units recommended:* 4 mathematics, 4 science. **Freshman Admission Statistics:** 2,179 applied, 76% admitted, 45% enrolled. **Transfer Admission Requirements:** High school transcript, college transcript(s), statement of good standing from prior institution(s). Minimum college GPA of 2.0 required. Lowest grade transferable C. **General Admission Information:** Application fee $30. Notification on a rolling basis, beginning on or about 9/1. Nonfall registration accepted. Admission may be deferred for a maximum of 1 semester. Credit offered for CEEB Advanced Placement tests.

COSTS AND FINANCIAL AID

Annual in-state tuition $5,849. Annual out-of-state tuition $11,698. Room and board $5,130. Required fees $135. Average book expense $796. **Required Forms and Deadlines:** FAFSA, institution's own financial aid form. Financial aid filing deadline 6/15. Priority financial aid filing date 3/1. **Notification of Awards:** Applicants will be notified of awards on a rolling basis beginning 4/15. **Types of Aid:** *Need-based scholarships/grants:* Federal Pell, SEOG, state scholarships/grants, private scholarships, the school's own gift aid. *Loans:* FFEL Subsidized Stafford, FFEL Unsubsidized Stafford, FFEL PLUS, Federal Perkins, state loans, college/university loans from institutional funds. **Financial Aid Statistics:** Average cumulative indebtedness $18,094. **Criteria for awarding institutional aid:** *Non-need-based:* Academics.

THE FRANCISCAN UNIVERSITY

400 North Bluff Blvd, PO Box 2967, Clinton, IA 52733-2967
Phone: 563-242-4153
E-mail: admissns@tfu.edu **CEEB Code:** 6418
Fax: 563-243-6102 **Website:** www.tfu.edu **ACT Code:** 1342

This private school was founded in 1918. It has a 25-acre campus.

RATINGS

Admissions Selectivity Rating: 72   **Fire Safety Rating:** 60*   **Green Rating:** 60*

STUDENTS AND FACULTY

Enrollment: 416. **Student Body:** 56% female, 44% male, 46% out-of-state, 3% international (10 countries represented). Asian 1%, African American 6%, Caucasian 87%, Hispanic 3%.
Retention and Graduation: 69% freshmen return for sophomore year. 25% freshmen graduate within 4 years. 25% grads go on to further study within 1 year. **Faculty:** Student/faculty ratio 12:1. 27 full-time faculty, 48% hold PhDs, 4% are members of minority groups, 44% are women.

ACADEMICS

Degrees: Associate, bachelor's, master's, transfer associate. **Classes:** Most classes have 10–19 students. Most lab/discussion sessions have fewer than 10 students. **Majors with Highest Enrollment:** Education; liberal arts and sciences studies and humanities, other; social sciences. **Special Study Options:** Distance learning, double major, dual enrollment, honors program, independent study, internships, student-designed major, study abroad, teacher certification program, Advanced Placement Program Summer School, off-campus study senior capstone or culminating academic experiences, undergraduate research/creative projects writing in the disciplines. Special programs offered to physically disabled students include tutors.

FACILITIES

Housing: Coed dorms: Durham Hall = 2 bedroom suites (one side floors are designated for men and one side designated for women. Sides of building joined by common lounge area); Regis Hall = single bedrooms (1 floor for women and 1 floor for men). 95% of campus accessible to physically disabled. **Special Academic Facilities/Equipment:** On-campus preschool. Indoor swimming pool, multipurpose educ. center, resident halls, 1 bedroom suites or 2 single rooms. **Computers:** Administrative functions (other than registration) can be performed online.

CAMPUS LIFE

Environment: Town. **Activities:** Choral groups, music ensembles, student government, student newspaper **Organizations:** 20 registered organizations, 2 honor societies. **Athletics (Intercollegiate):** *Men:* Baseball, basketball, cross-country, golf, soccer, track/field (outdoor). *Women:* Basketball, cross-country, soccer, softball, track/field (outdoor), volleyball.

ADMISSIONS

Freshman Academic Profile: Average high school GPA 2.84. 8% in top 10% of high school class, 16% in top 25% of high school class, 50% in top 50% of high school class. ACT middle 50% range 16–22. Minimum paper TOEFL 430. Minimum computer TOEFL 213. **Basis for Candidate Selection:** *Very important factors considered include:* Class rank, rigor of secondary school record, standardized test scores. *Other factors considered include:* Recommendation(s). **Freshman Admission Requirements:** High school diploma is required and GED is accepted. *Academic units recommended:* 4 English, 3 mathematics, 3 science, (2 science labs), 2 foreign language, 3 social studies, 3 history. **Freshman Admission Statistics:** 246 applied, 77% admitted, 28% enrolled. **Transfer Admission Requirements:** College transcript(s), statement of good standing from prior institution(s). Minimum college GPA of 2.0 required. Lowest grade transferable C. **General Admission Information:** Application fee $20. Regular application deadline 8/15. Nonfall registration accepted. Admission may be deferred for a maximum of 1 academic year. Credit and/or placement offered for CEEB Advanced Placement tests.

COSTS AND FINANCIAL AID

Annual tuition $13,800. Room and board $5,250. Required fees $250. Average book expense $600. **Required Forms and Deadlines:** FAFSA. Financial aid filing deadline 8/1. Priority financial aid filing date 4/1. **Notification of Awards:** Applicants will be notified of awards on a rolling basis beginning 3/15. **Types of Aid:** *Need-based scholarships/grants:* Federal Pell, SEOG, state scholarships/grants, private scholarships, the school's own gift aid. *Loans:* FFEL Subsidized Stafford, FFEL Unsubsidized Stafford, FFEL PLUS, Federal Perkins, Private Loan Company. **Financial Aid Statistics:** 87% freshmen, 89% undergrads receive need-based scholarship or grant aid. 11% freshmen, 12% undergrads receive non-need-based scholarship or grant aid. 68% freshmen, 72% undergrads receive need-based self-help aid. 23% freshmen, 12% undergrads receive athletic scholarships. 88% undergrads borrow to pay for school. Average cumulative indebtedness $15,868. **Criteria for awarding institutional aid:** *Non-need-based:* Academics, alumni affiliation, art, athletics, job skills, leadership, minority status, music/drama, religious affiliation.

FRANCISCAN UNIVERSITY OF STEUBENVILLE

1235 University Boulevard, Steubenville, OH 43952-1763
Phone: 740-283-6226 **Financial Aid Phone:** 740-283-6226
E-mail: admissions@franciscan.edu **CEEB Code:** 1133
Fax: 740-284-5456 **Website:** www.franciscan.edu **ACT Code:** 3258

This private school, affiliated with the Roman Catholic Church, was founded in 1946. It has a 124-acre campus.

RATINGS

Admissions Selectivity Rating: 88   **Fire Safety Rating:** 60*   **Green Rating:** 60*

STUDENTS AND FACULTY

Enrollment: 2,034. **Student Body:** 61% female, 39% male, 80% out-of-state, 1% international (20 countries represented). Asian 2%, Caucasian 80%, Hispanic 3%.
Retention and Graduation: 84% freshmen return for sophomore year. 63% freshmen graduate within 4 years. 13% grads go on to further study within 1 year. 9% grads pursue arts and sciences degrees. 1% grads pursue business degrees. 1% grads pursue medical degrees. **Faculty:** Student/faculty ratio 15:1. 112 full-time faculty, 79% hold PhDs, 1% are members of minority groups, 26% are women.

ACADEMICS

Degrees: Associate, bachelor's, master's. **Classes:** Most classes have 10–19 students. Most lab/discussion sessions have 10–19 students. **Majors with Highest Enrollment:** Business/commerce; elementary education and teaching; theology/theological studies. **Special Study Options:** Accelerated program, distance learning, double major, dual enrollment, honors program, independent study, internships, liberal arts/career combination, study abroad, teacher certification program **Honors programs:** We have a Great Books program. **Combined degree programs:** BA/MA, 4+1 in business and philosophy. Special programs offered to physically disabled students include note-taking services, reader services, tape recorders, tutors. **Career services:** Career/job search classes, career assessment, internships.

FACILITIES

Housing: Men's dorms, women's dorms, apartments for single students 75% of campus accessible to physically disabled. **Special Academic Facilities/Equipment:** Art gallery. **Computers:** Students can register for classes online. Administrative functions (other than registration) can be performed online.

CAMPUS LIFE

Environment: Village. **Activities:** Choral groups, drama/theater, literary magazine, music ensembles, radio station, student government, student newspaper, yearbook, campus ministries, international student organization. **Organizations:** 31 registered organizations, 3 honor societies, 6 religious organizations. 1 fraternities, 1 sorority. **On-Campus Highlights:** Heavenly Grounds Coffee Shop, Sts. Cosmas and Damian Hall-Science Building, Finnegan Fieldhouse, Christ The King Chapel, Portiuncula Chapel.

ADMISSIONS

Freshman Academic Profile: Average high school GPA 3.66. 31% in top 10% of high school class, 60% in top 25% of high school class, 84% in top 50% of high school class. 42% from public high schools. SAT Math middle 50% range 500–630. SAT Critical Reading middle 50% range 540–650. SAT Writing middle 50% range 510–630. ACT middle 50% range 23–28. Minimum paper TOEFL 550. Minimum computer TOEFL 213. **Basis for Candidate Selection:** *Very important factors considered include:* Application essay, academic GPA, rigor of secondary school record, standardized test scores, character/personal qualities, interview. *Important factors considered include:* Extracurricular activities, level of applicant's interest, talent/ability. *Other factors considered include:* Recommendation(s). **Freshman Admission Requirements:** High school diploma is required and GED is accepted. *Academic units recommended:* 4 English, 3 mathematics, 3 science, (3 science labs), 2 foreign language, 2 social studies, 1 history, 1 academic electives. **Freshman Admission Statistics:** 1,450 applied, 72% admitted, 43% enrolled. **Transfer Admission Requirements:** High school transcript, college transcript(s), essay or personal statement, minimum college GPA of 2.2 required. Lowest grade transferable C. **General Admission Information:** Application fee $20. Regular application deadline 5/1. Notification on a rolling basis, beginning on or about 9/1. Nonfall registration accepted. Admission may be deferred for a maximum of 1 year. Credit and/or placement offered for CEEB Advanced Placement tests.

COSTS AND FINANCIAL AID

Average book expense $800. **Required Forms and Deadlines:** FAFSA. Priority financial aid filing date 4/15. **Notification of Awards:** Applicants will be notified of awards on a rolling basis beginning 3/15. **Types of Aid:** *Need-based scholarships/grants:* Federal Pell, SEOG, state scholarships/grants, private scholarships, the school's own gift aid. *Loans:* FFEL Subsidized Stafford, FFEL Unsubsidized Stafford, FFEL PLUS, Federal Perkins, Alternative Loans. **Student Employment:** Federal Work-Study Program available. Institutional employment available. Highest amount earned per year from on-campus jobs $3,090. Off-campus job opportunities are good. **Financial Aid Statistics:** 60% freshmen, 62% undergrads receive need-based scholarship or grant aid. 5% freshmen, 4% undergrads receive non-need-based scholarship or grant aid. 61% freshmen, 63% undergrads receive need-based self-help aid. 63% freshmen, 62% undergrads receive any aid. 77% undergrads borrow to pay for school. Average cumulative indebtedness $21,616. **Criteria for awarding institutional aid:** *Non-need-based:* Academics, leadership, religious affiliation.

FRANKLIN AND MARSHALL COLLEGE

P.O. Box 3003, PO Box 3003, Lancaster, PA 17604-3003
Phone: 717-291-3953 **Financial Aid Phone:** 717-291-3991
E-mail: admission@fandm.edu **CEEB Code:** 2261
Fax: 717-291-4389 **Website:** www.fandm.edu **ACT Code:** 3574

This private school was founded in 1787. It has a 180-acre campus.

RATINGS

Admissions Selectivity Rating: 94   **Fire Safety Rating:** 93   **Green Rating:** 97

STUDENTS AND FACULTY

Enrollment: 2,137. **Student Body:** 51% female, 49% male, 70% out-of-state, 8% international (41 countries represented). Asian 4%, African American 4%, Caucasian 67%, Hispanic 5%, Native American 1%. **Retention and Graduation:** 92% freshmen return for sophomore year. 79% freshmen graduate within 4 years. 25% grads go on to further study within 1 year. 10% grads pursue arts and sciences degrees. 6% grads pursue law degrees. 1% grads pursue business degrees. 8% grads pursue medical degrees. **Faculty:** Student/faculty ratio 10:1. 201 full-time faculty, 94% hold PhDs, 12% are members of minority groups, 38% are women.

ACADEMICS

Degrees: Bachelor's. **Classes:** Most classes have 10–19 students. Most lab/discussion sessions have 10–19 students. **Majors with Highest Enrollment:** Business/commerce; political science and government; psychology. **Special Study Options:** Accelerated program, cross-registration, double major, dual enrollment, exchange student program (domestic), honors program, independent study, internships, student-designed major, study abroad, teacher certification program. Special programs offered to physically disabled students include note-taking services, tutors. **Career services:** Alumni network, alumni services, career/job search classes, career assessment, internships, regional alumni.

FACILITIES

Housing: Coed dorms, special housing for disabled students, men's dorms, special housing for international students, women's dorms, fraternity/sorority housing, apartments for single students, Arts House, French House, Community Outreach House, Sustainability House. 80% of campus accessible to physically disabled. **Special Academic Facilities/Equipment:** Art gallery, associated with natural history museums, bronze casting foundry, retail sales complex, psychology and language labs, TV and radio station, observatory/planetarium, Writers House **Computers:** 100% of classrooms, 100% of dorms, 100% of libraries, 100% of dining areas, 100% of student union, 100% of common outdoor areas have wireless network access. Students can register for classes online. Administrative functions (other than registration) can be performed online.

CAMPUS LIFE

Environment: Town. **Activities:** Choral groups, concert band, dance, drama/theater, jazz band, literary magazine, music ensembles, musical theater, radio station, student government, student newspaper, symphony orchestra, yearbook, campus ministries, international student organization, Model UN. **Organizations:** 90 registered organizations, 13 honor societies, 8 religious organizations. 7 fraternities, 3 sororities. **Athletics (Intercollegiate):** *Men:* Baseball, basketball, crew/rowing, cross-country, football, golf, lacrosse, soccer, squash, swimming, tennis, track/field (outdoor), track/field (indoor), wrestling. *Women:* Basketball, crew/rowing, cross-country, field hockey, golf, lacrosse, soccer, softball, squash, swimming, tennis, track/field (outdoor), track/field (indoor), volleyball. **On-Campus Highlights:** Alumni Sport and Fitness Center, Barshinger Center in Hensel Hall, Barnes and Noble Bookstore and Jazzman's Cafe, Roschel Performing Arts Center, Writers House. **Environmental Initiatives:** We have established the Wohlsen Center for the Sustainable Environment, including a Director, student staff member, and Artist-in-Residence, and partnership with the Millport Conservancy. We have a Student Sustainability House, are incorporating sustainability into 1st year orientation and support very active clubs: The Environmental Action Alliance, Fair Trade Cafe, and Dirt Army (organic garden). We have majors in Environmental Studies and Environmental Science and integrate interdisciplinary collaboration in sustainability across the curriculum.

ADMISSIONS

Freshman Academic Profile: 63% in top 10% of high school class, 86% in top 25% of high school class, 99% in top 50% of high school class. 62% from public high schools. SAT Math middle 50% range 630–700. SAT Critical Reading middle 50% range 600–690. ACT middle 50% range 28–31. Minimum paper TOEFL 600. Minimum computer TOEFL 250. **Basis for Candidate Selection:** *Very important factors considered include:* Class rank, academic GPA, rigor of secondary school record, character/personal qualities. *Important factors considered include:* Application essay, recommendation(s), standardized test scores, extracurricular activities, interview, talent/ability, volunteer work. *Other factors considered include:* Alumni/ae relation, geographical residence, level of applicant's interest, racial/ethnic status, work experience. **Freshman Admission Requirements:** High school diploma is required and GED is accepted. *Academic units required:* 4 English, 3 mathematics, 2 science, (2 science labs), 2 foreign language, 1 social studies, 2 history, 1 visual/performing arts. *Academic units recommended:* 4 mathematics, 3 science, (3 science labs), 4 foreign language, 3 social studies, 3 history. **Freshman Admission Statistics:** 5,256 applied, 48% admitted, 25% enrolled. **Transfer Admission Requirements:** High school transcript, college transcript(s), essay or personal statement, interview, standardized test scores, statement of good standing from prior institution(s). Lowest grade transferable C–. **General Admission Information:** Application fee $60. Early decision application deadline 11/15. Regular application deadline 2/1. Regular notification 4/1. Nonfall registration accepted. Admission may be deferred for a maximum of 1 year. Credit and/or placement offered for CEEB Advanced Placement tests.

COSTS AND FINANCIAL AID

Annual tuition $39,930. Room and board $10,430. Required fees $50. Average book expense $700. **Required Forms and Deadlines:** FAFSA, CSS/Financial Aid PROFILE, noncustodial PROFILE, business/farm supplement. Financial aid filing deadline 2/15. Priority financial aid filing date 2/15. **Notification of Awards:** Applicants will be notified of awards on or about 4/1. **Types of Aid:** *Need-based scholarships/grants:* Federal Pell, SEOG, state scholarships/grants, private scholarships, the school's own gift aid. *Loans:* FFEL Subsidized Stafford, FFEL Unsubsidized Stafford, FFEL PLUS, Federal Perkins, college/university loans from institutional funds. **Student Employment:** Federal Work-Study Program available. Highest amount earned per year from on-campus jobs $2,175. **Financial Aid Statistics:** 45% freshmen, 41% undergrads receive need-based scholarship or grant aid. 3% freshmen, 2% undergrads receive non-need-based scholarship or grant aid. 42% freshmen, 41% undergrads receive need-based self-help aid. 56% freshmen, 56% undergrads receive any aid. 52% undergrads borrow to pay for school. Average cumulative indebtedness $27,162. **Criteria for awarding institutional aid:** *Non-need-based:* Academics, art, leadership, minority status.

FRANKLIN COLLEGE

101 Branigin Blvd, Franklin, IN 46131-2623
Phone: 317-738-8062 **Financial Aid Phone:** 317-738-8075
E-mail: admissions@franklincollege.edu **CEEB Code:** 1228
Fax: 317-738-8274 **Website:** www.franklincollege.edu **ACT Code:** 1194

This private school, affiliated with the American Baptist Church, was founded in 1834. It has a 156-acre campus.

RATINGS
Admissions Selectivity Rating: 79   **Fire Safety Rating:** 72   **Green Rating:** 70

STUDENTS AND FACULTY
Enrollment: 1,153. **Student Body:** 50% female, 50% male, 3% out-of-state, (3 countries represented). Asian 1%, African American 2%, Caucasian 59%, Hispanic 1%.
Retention and Graduation: 71% freshmen return for sophomore year. 50% freshmen graduate within 4 years. 15% grads go on to further study within 1 year. 12% grads pursue arts and sciences degrees. 2% grads pursue law degrees. 1% grads pursue medical degrees. **Faculty:** Student/faculty ratio 12.3:1. 67 full-time faculty, 90% hold PhDs, 6% are members of minority groups, 45% are women.

ACADEMICS
Degrees: Bachelor's. **Classes:** Most classes have 10–19 students. **Majors with Highest Enrollment:** Biology/biological sciences; elementary education and teaching; psychology. **Special Study Options:** Double major, dual enrollment, exchange student program (domestic), independent study, internships, study abroad, teacher certification program. **Honors programs:** The intercultural Honors Experience is a freshman-year program designed to attract and retain superior students and faculty to FC while internationalizing the FC community. The program is designed to help students build a solid intercultural foundation, introduce them to interdisciplinary learning, and provide them with opportunities and incentives to study abroad. Faculty development is an integral part of the project. Special programs offered to physically disabled students include note-taking services, reader services, tape recorders, tutors. **Career services:** Alumni services, career/job search classes, career assessment.

FACILITIES
Housing: Coed dorms, special housing for disabled students, men's dorms, women's dorms, fraternity/sorority housing 100% of campus accessible to physically disabled. **Special Academic Facilities/Equipment:** Pulliam School of Journalism, Dietz Center for Professional Development, Leadership Center. **Computers:** 100% of classrooms, 100% of libraries, 100% of dining areas, 100% of student union, have wireless network access. Students can register for classes online. Administrative functions (other than registration) can be performed online.

CAMPUS LIFE
Environment: Village. **Activities:** Choral groups, dance, drama/theater, literary magazine, musical theater, pep band, radio station, student government, student newspaper, yearbook. **Organizations:** 66 registered organizations, 13 honor societies, 3 religious organizations. 5 fraternities, 4 sororities. **Athletics (Intercollegiate):** *Men:* Baseball, basketball, cross-country, diving, football, golf, soccer, swimming, tennis, track/field (outdoor). *Women:* Basketball, cheerleading, cross-country, diving, golf, soccer, softball, swimming, tennis, track/field (outdoor), volleyball. **On-Campus Highlights:** Student Center, Spurlock Center (athletic facility), library, residence hall, fraternity houses. **Environmental Initiatives:** Completing green house car emissions inventory; Star purchase policy; recycling, composting program.

ADMISSIONS
Freshman Academic Profile: Average high school GPA 3.42. 21% in top 10% of high school class, 56% in top 25% of high school class, 92% in top 50% of high school class. 92% from public high schools. SAT Math middle 50% range 460–570. SAT Critical Reading middle 50% range 420–520. SAT Writing middle

50% range 440–540. ACT middle 50% range 19–24. Minimum paper TOEFL 550. Minimum computer TOEFL 213. **Basis for Candidate Selection:** *Very important factors considered include:* Class rank, academic GPA, rigor of secondary school record, standardized test scores. *Important factors considered include:* Application essay, alumni/ae relation, character/personal qualities, extracurricular activities. *Other factors considered include:* Recommendation(s), first generation, geographical residence, interview, level of applicant's interest, racial/ethnic status, religious affiliation/commitment, state residency, talent/ability, volunteer work, work experience. **Freshman Admission Requirements:** High school diploma is required and GED is accepted. *Academic units required:* 4 English, 4 mathematics, 2 science, 3 social studies. **Freshman Admission Statistics:** 1,734 applied, 67% admitted, 28% enrolled. **Transfer Admission Requirements:** High school transcript, college transcript(s), essay or personal statement, statement of good standing from prior institution(s). Minimum college GPA of 2.0 required. Lowest grade transferable C–. **General Admission Information:** Application fee $30. Regular notification 9/1. Nonfall registration accepted. Admission may be deferred for a maximum of 1 year. Credit and/or placement offered for CEEB Advanced Placement tests.

COSTS AND FINANCIAL AID
Required Forms and Deadlines: FAFSA, institution's own financial aid form Financial aid filing deadline 3/1. Priority financial aid filing date 3/1. **Notification of Awards:** Applicants will be notified of awards on or about 4/1. **Types of Aid:** *Need-based scholarships/grants:* Federal Pell, SEOG, state scholarships/grants, private scholarships, the school's own gift aid. *Loans:* FFEL Subsidized Stafford, FFEL Unsubsidized Stafford, FFEL PLUS, Federal Perkins, college/university loans from institutional funds. **Student Employment:** Federal Work-Study Program available. Institutional employment available. Highest amount earned per year from on-campus jobs $2,000. Off-campus job opportunities are good. **Financial Aid Statistics:** 78% freshmen, 80% undergrads receive need-based scholarship or grant aid. 13% freshmen, 11% undergrads receive non-need-based scholarship or grant aid. 60% freshmen, 65% undergrads receive need-based self-help aid. 84% freshmen, 85% undergrads receive any aid. 85% undergrads borrow to pay for school. Average cumulative indebtedness $26,903. **Criteria for awarding institutional aid:** *Non-need-based:* Academics, alumni affiliation, leadership, minority status, religious affiliation, state/district residency.

FRANKLIN PIERCE UNIVERSITY

Admissions Office, 40 University Dr, Rindge, NH 03461
Phone: 603-899-4050 **Financial Aid Phone:** 603-899-4180
E-mail: admissions@franklinpierce.edu **CEEB Code:** 3395
Fax: 603-889-4394 **Website:** www.franklinpierce.edu **ACT Code:** 2509

This private school was founded in 1962. It has a 1200-acre campus.

RATINGS
Admissions Selectivity Rating: 75   **Fire Safety Rating:** 84   **Green Rating:** 79

STUDENTS AND FACULTY
Enrollment: 2,061. **Student Body:** 49% female, 51% male, 78% out-of-state. **Retention and Graduation:** 26% grads go on to further study within 1 year. 5% grads pursue arts and sciences degrees. 3% grads pursue law degrees. 7% grads pursue business degrees. 1% grads pursue medical degrees. **Faculty:** Student/faculty ratio 18:1. 100 full-time faculty, 68% hold PhDs, 1% are members of minority groups, 45% are women.

ACADEMICS
Degrees: Associate, bachelor's, certificate, first professional, master's, post-master's certificate. **Classes:** Most classes have 10–19 students. Most lab/discussion sessions have fewer than 10 students. **Majors with Highest Enrollment:** Accounting and business/management; criminal justice/safety studies; education; mass communication/media studies. **Special Study Options:** Distance learning, double major, dual enrollment, English as a Second Language (ESL), exchange student program (domestic), honors program, independent study, internships, liberal arts/career combination, student-designed major, study abroad, teacher certification program, Walk Across Europe Program, Washington Semester, Arcadia Study Abroad. **Honors programs:** Honors Program Special programs offered to physically disabled students include note-taking services, reader services, tape recorders, tutors. **Career services:** Alumni network, alumni services, career/job search classes, career assessment, internships, regional alumni. **Career services highlights include:** Http://franklinpierce.edu/academics/career/ugrad_rindge_cpp.htm.

FACILITIES
Housing: Coed dorms, special housing for disabled students, apartments for single students, wellness housing, condominiums (townhouses). 67% of

campus accessible to physically disabled. **Special Academic Facilities/Equipment:** Thoreau Art Gallery; Flynt Center; Fitzwater Communications Center; Dance Studio; Pottery Kiln; Glass Blowing Studio; TV Station; Radio Station; Grimshaw-Gudewicz Activities Center: Lakeside Activity Center. **Computers:** 20% of classrooms, 20% of dorms, 100% of libraries, 80% of dining areas, 100% of student union, 50% of common outdoor areas have wireless network access. Administrative functions (other than registration) can be performed online.

CAMPUS LIFE

Environment: Rural. **Activities:** Choral groups, dance, drama/theater, literary magazine, music ensembles, musical theater, radio station, student government, student newspaper, television station, yearbook, campus ministries. **Organizations:** 35 registered organizations, 8 honor societies, 3 religious organizations. **Athletics (Intercollegiate):** *Men:* Baseball, basketball, crew/rowing, golf, ice hockey, rugby, soccer, tennis. *Women:* Basketball, crew/rowing, cross-country, field hockey, lacrosse, soccer, softball, volleyball. **On-Campus Highlights:** Peterson Hall, The Campus Center, The Northfields Activity Center, The Fitzwater Center for Communications, The Pub. **Environmental Initiatives:** Development of on enhanced on-campus recycling program. Conversion to online format materials, reducing paper waste (online catalogue, billing, forms, etc). Conversion of incandescent lighting to compact flourescent throughout campus.

ADMISSIONS

Freshman Academic Profile: Average high school GPA 2.78. 7% in top 10% of high school class, 20% in top 25% of high school class, 54% in top 50% of high school class. 89% from public high schools. SAT Math middle 50% range 430–540. SAT Critical Reading middle 50% range 440–550. SAT Writing middle 50% range 420–520. Minimum paper TOEFL 500. Minimum computer TOEFL 173. Minimum web-based TOEFL 61. **Basis for Candidate Selection:** *Very important factors considered include:* Academic GPA, recommendation(s), character/personal qualities. *Important factors considered include:* Application essay, rigor of secondary school record, standardized test scores. *Other factors considered include:* Class rank, extracurricular activities, interview, talent/ability, volunteer work, work experience. **Freshman Admission Requirements:** High school diploma is required and GED is accepted. *Academic units required:* 4 English, 3 mathematics, 2 science, (2 science labs), 3 social studies, 4 academic electives. **Transfer Admission Requirements:** College transcript(s), essay or personal statement, minimum college GPA of 2.0 required. Lowest grade transferable C–. **General Admission Information:** Application fee $40. Notification on a rolling basis, beginning on or about 10/15. Nonfall registration accepted. Admission may be deferred for a maximum of 1 year. Credit and/or placement offered for CEEB Advanced Placement tests.

COSTS AND FINANCIAL AID

Annual tuition $27,700. Room and board $9,800. Required fees $1,300. Average book expense $1,000. **Required Forms and Deadlines:** FAFSA. **Notification of Awards:** Applicants will be notified of awards on a rolling basis beginning 2/1. **Types of Aid:** *Need-based scholarships/grants:* Federal Pell, SEOG, state scholarships/grants, private scholarships, the school's own gift aid. *Loans:* FFEL Subsidized Stafford, FFEL Unsubsidized Stafford, FFEL PLUS, Federal Perkins. **Student Employment:** Federal Work-Study Program available. Institutional employment available. Highest amount earned per year from on-campus jobs $2,200. Off-campus job opportunities are fair. **Financial Aid Statistics:** 75% freshmen, 77% undergrads receive need-based scholarship or grant aid. 7% freshmen, 7% undergrads receive non-need-based scholarship or grant aid. 68% freshmen, 70% undergrads receive need-based self-help aid. 4% freshmen, 5% undergrads receive athletic scholarships. 99% freshmen, 87% undergrads receive any aid. 67% undergrads borrow to pay for school. Average cumulative indebtedness $28,750. **Criteria for awarding institutional aid:** *Non-need-based:* Academics, alumni affiliation, athletics, leadership, minority status, music/drama.

FRANKLIN UNIVERSITY

201 S Grant Ave, Columbus, OH 43215
Phone: 614-797-4700
E-mail: info@franklin.edu **CEEB Code:** 1229
Fax: 614-224-8027 **Website:** 201 S Grant Ave **ACT Code:** 3275

This private school was founded in 1902. It has a 14-acre campus.

RATINGS
Admissions Selectivity Rating: 60*   **Fire Safety Rating:** 60*   **Green Rating:** 60*

STUDENTS AND FACULTY
Enrollment: 5,682. **Student Body:** 55% female, 45% male, 26% out-of-state, 5% international . Asian 3%, African American 19%, Caucasian 66%, Hispanic 2%.

Retention and Graduation: 72% freshmen return for sophomore year. **Faculty:** Student/faculty ratio 19:1. 36 full-time faculty, 64% hold PhDs, 6% are members of minority groups, 44% are women.

ACADEMICS

Degrees: Associate, bachelor's, master's. **Classes:** Most classes have 10–19 students. **Majors with Highest Enrollment:** Accounting; business/commerce; computer and information science. **Special Study Options:** Accelerated program, cooperative education program, cross-registration, distance learning, double major, dual enrollment, English as a Second Language (ESL), independent study, internships, study abroad, weekend college. **Combined degree programs:** BS/MBA. Special programs offered to physically disabled students include note-taking services, reader services, tape recorders, tutors. **Career services:** Alumni network, alumni services, internships.

FACILITIES

Housing: 100% of campus accessible to physically disabled. **Computers:** Students can register for classes online.

CAMPUS LIFE

Organizations: 6 registered organizations,

ADMISSIONS

Freshman Academic Profile: Minimum paper TOEFL 430. Minimum computer TOEFL 117. **Freshman Admission Requirements:** High school diploma is required and GED is accepted. *Academic units recommended:* 3 mathematics. **Freshman Admission Statistics:** 262 applied, 100% admitted, 47% enrolled. **Transfer Admission Requirements:** College transcript(s), lowest grade transferable C–. **General Admission Information:** Nonfall registration accepted. Admission may be deferred for a maximum of indefinite. Credit and/or placement offered for CEEB Advanced Placement tests.

COSTS AND FINANCIAL AID

Annual tuition $6,990. . **Required Forms and Deadlines:** FAFSA. Priority financial aid filing date 6/15. **Types of Aid:** *Need-based scholarships/grants:* Federal Pell, SEOG, state scholarships/grants, private scholarships, the school's own gift aid. *Loans:* FFEL Subsidized Stafford, FFEL Unsubsidized Stafford, FFEL PLUS, college/university loans from institutional funds. **Student Employment:** Federal Work-Study Program available. Institutional employment available. Off-campus job opportunities are good. **Financial Aid Statistics:** 61% freshmen, 40% undergrads receive need-based scholarship or grant aid. 72% freshmen, 51% undergrads receive non-need-based scholarship or grant aid. 78% freshmen, 59% undergrads receive need-based self-help aid. **Criteria for awarding institutional aid:** *Non-need-based:* Academics, leadership, minority status.

FRANKLIN W. OLIN COLLEGE OF ENGINEERING

Olin Way, Needham, MA 02492-1245
Phone: 781-292-2222 **Financial Aid Phone:** 781 292 2343
E-mail: info@olin.edu **CEEB Code:** 2824
Fax: 781-292-2210 **Website:** www.olin.edu **ACT Code:** 1883

This private school was founded in 1997.

RATINGS
Admissions Selectivity Rating: 99   **Fire Safety Rating:** 98   **Green Rating:** 70

STUDENTS AND FACULTY
Enrollment: 330. **Student Body:** 45% female, 55% male, 90% out-of-state, 4% international (14 countries represented). Asian 6%, African American 2%, Caucasian 37%, Hispanic 3%.
Retention and Graduation: 100% freshmen return for sophomore year. 85% freshmen graduate within 4 years. 27% grads go on to further study within 1 year. 20% grads pursue arts and sciences degrees. 2% grads pursue law degrees. 2% grads pursue business degrees. 2% grads pursue medical degrees. **Faculty:** Student/faculty ratio 8:1. 37 full-time faculty, 95% hold PhDs, 16% are members of minority groups, 32% are women.

ACADEMICS

Degrees: Bachelor's. **Classes:** Most classes have 20–29 students. **Majors with Highest Enrollment:** Electrical, electronics and communications engineering; engineering; mechanical engineering. **Special Study Options:** Cross-registration, exchange student program (domestic), independent study, internships, liberal arts/career combination, student-designed major, study abroad, Passionate Pursuits program. **Career services:** Alumni network, alumni services, career/job search classes, internships, regional alumni. **Career services highlights include:** Because we are a fairly new school, our network of alumni remains small but powerful. Many are now at prestigious companies or graduate school programs, and they often return to campus to talk about their company, career, grad school experience, or they perform mock interviews and/or provide advice to our current students. Due to our young age, our students are especially interested in hearing of our alumni's tales of continued development and success.

FACILITIES

Housing: Coed dorms, special housing for disabled students **Computers:** 100% of classrooms, 100% of dorms, 100% of libraries, 100% of dining areas, 100% of student union, 100% of common outdoor areas have wireless network access. Students can register for classes online. Administrative functions (other than registration) can be performed online. Undergraduates are required to own a computer.

CAMPUS LIFE

Environment: Town. **Activities:** Choral groups, dance, drama/theater, jazz band, music ensembles, musical theater, student government, student-run film society, symphony orchestra, yearbook. **Organizations:** 55 registered organizations. **Environmental Initiatives:** Hiring an energy manager. Registered Milas Hall with the USGBC for LEED-EB certification. Class of 2007 established a "Green Initiatives" fund for sustainability efforts.

ADMISSIONS

Freshman Academic Profile: Average high school GPA 3.9. 95% in top 10% of high school class, 100% in top 25% of high school class, SAT Math middle 50% range 740–800. SAT Critical Reading middle 50% range 700–790. SAT Writing middle 50% range 670–770. ACT middle 50% range 32–35. **Basis for Candidate Selection:** *Very important factors considered include:* Application essay, academic GPA, recommendation(s), rigor of secondary school record, character/personal qualities, extracurricular activities, level of applicant's interest, talent/ability. *Important factors considered include:* Class rank, standardized test scores, racial/ethnic status, volunteer work. *Other factors considered include:* First generation, geographical residence, interview, state residency, work experience. **Freshman Admission Requirements:** High school diploma or equivalent is not required. *Academic units recommended:* 4 English, 4 mathematics, 3 science, (3 science labs), 2 foreign language, 2 social studies, 2 history, 2 Require at least one year of calculusa nd one year of physics prior to high school graduation. **Freshman Admission Statistics:** 874 applied, 16% admitted, 60% enrolled. **General Admission Information:** Application fee $80. Regular application deadline 1/1. Regular notification 3/22. Nonfall registration not accepted. Admission may be deferred for a maximum of 1 year.

COSTS AND FINANCIAL AID

Annual tuition $36,400. Room and board $13,230. Required fees $1,645. Average book expense $750. **Required Forms and Deadlines:** FAFSA. Priority financial aid filing date 2/15. **Notification of Awards:** Applicants will be notified of awards on a rolling basis beginning 4/1. **Types of Aid:** *Need-based scholarships/grants:* Federal Pell, SEOG, private scholarships, the school's own gift aid. *Loans:* FFEL Subsidized Stafford, FFEL Unsubsidized Stafford, FFEL PLUS **Student Employment:** Institutional employment available. **Financial Aid Statistics:** 100% freshmen, 100% undergrads receive any aid. **Criteria for awarding institutional aid:** *Non-need-based:* Academics, leadership.

FREED-HARDEMAN UNIVERSITY

158 East Main Street, Henderson, TN 38340
Phone: 731-989-6651 **Financial Aid Phone:** 731-989-6662
E-mail: jathoms1@yahoo.com **CEEB Code:** 1230
Fax: 731-989-6047 **Website:** web.fhu.edu **ACT Code:** 3962

This private school, affiliated with the Church of Christ Church, was founded in 1869. It has a 122-acre campus.

RATINGS

Admissions Selectivity Rating: 84   **Fire Safety Rating:** 60*   **Green Rating:** 66

STUDENTS AND FACULTY

Enrollment: 1,428. **Student Body:** 55% female, 45% male, 50% out-of-state, 3% international (26 countries represented). African American 4%, Caucasian 91%, Hispanic 1%.
Retention and Graduation: 74% freshmen return for sophomore year. 41% freshmen graduate within 4 years. 40% grads go on to further study within 1 year. **Faculty:** Student/faculty ratio 14:1. 108 full-time faculty, 69% hold PhDs, 5% are members of minority groups, 31% are women.

ACADEMICS

Degrees: Bachelor's, first professional, master's, post-bachelor's certificate, post-master's certificate, terminal associate. **Classes:** Most classes have 10–19 students. Most lab/discussion sessions have 10–19 students. **Majors with Highest Enrollment:** Bible/biblical studies; biology/biological sciences; liberal arts and sciences studies and humanities, other. **Special Study Options:** Accelerated program, cooperative education program, cross-registration, distance learning, double major, dual enrollment, honors program, independent study, internships, liberal arts/career combination, student-designed major, study abroad, teacher certification program, 3-2 engineering, Honors College, study abroad in Belgium and Italy. **Honors programs:** Exceptional students may be admitted to the Honors College, where he or she may graduate as an Honors College Scholar, or as an Honors College Scholar with University Honors. **Combined degree programs:** BBA/MBA. Special programs offered to physically disabled students include note-taking services, reader services, tutors. **Career services:** Alumni network, career assessment, internships.

FACILITIES

Housing: Men's dorms, women's dorms, apartments for single students, Some student teacher housing is available. 70% of campus accessible to physically disabled. **Special Academic Facilities/Equipment:** Child development lab, nursery school. **Computers:** Students can register for classes online. Administrative functions (other than registration) can be performed online.

CAMPUS LIFE

Environment: Rural. **Activities:** Choral groups, concert band, drama/theater, jazz band, music ensembles, musical theater, pep band, radio station, student government, student newspaper, television station, yearbook. **Organizations:** 52 registered organizations, 4 honor societies, 5 religious organizations. 6 fraternities, 6 sororities. **Athletics (Intercollegiate):** *Men:* Baseball, basketball, cheerleading, soccer. *Women:* Basketball, cheerleading, soccer, softball, volleyball. **On-Campus Highlights:** The Commons, The Student Center, The Sports Center, Brown-Kopel Business Center, The Library.

ADMISSIONS

Freshman Academic Profile: Average high school GPA 3.37. 25% in top 10% of high school class, 51% in top 25% of high school class, 79% in top 50% of high school class. SAT Math middle 50% range 480–600. SAT Critical Reading middle 50% range 480–640. ACT middle 50% range 20–26. **Basis for Candidate Selection:** *Very important factors considered include:* Academic GPA, rigor of secondary school record, standardized test scores. *Other factors considered include:* Recommendation(s), alumni/ae relation, character/personal qualities, extracurricular activities, racial/ethnic status, religious affiliation/commitment, volunteer work, work experience. **Freshman Admission Requirements:** High school diploma is required and GED is accepted. *Academic units recommended:* 4 English, 2 mathematics, 2 science, 2 social studies, 10 academic electives. **Freshman Admission Statistics:** 1,326 applied, 55% admitted, 53% enrolled. **Transfer Admission Requirements:** College transcript(s), statement of good standing from prior institution(s). Lowest grade transferable D. **General Admission Information:** Notification on a rolling basis, beginning on or about 5/2. Nonfall registration accepted. Admission may be deferred for a maximum of 2 years. Credit and/or placement offered for CEEB Advanced Placement tests.

COSTS AND FINANCIAL AID

Annual tuition $13,192. Room and board $6,560. Average book expense $1,710. **Required Forms and Deadlines:** FAFSA. Priority financial aid filing date 3/1. **Notification of Awards:** Applicants will be notified of awards on a rolling basis beginning 3/1. **Types of Aid:** *Need-based scholarships/grants:* Federal Pell, SEOG, state scholarships/grants, private scholarships, the school's own gift aid. *Loans:* FFEL Subsidized Stafford, FFEL Unsubsidized Stafford, FFEL PLUS, Federal Perkins, Alternative loan programs. **Student Employment:** Federal Work-Study Program available. Institutional employment available. Off-campus job opportunities are fair. **Financial Aid Statistics:** 69% freshmen, 60% undergrads receive need-based scholarship or grant aid. 14% freshmen, 11% undergrads receive non-need-based scholarship or grant aid. 52% freshmen, 51% undergrads receive need-based self-help aid. 4% freshmen, 4% undergrads receive athletic scholarships. 86% freshmen receive any aid. 76% undergrads borrow to pay for school. Average cumulative indebtedness $34,216. **Criteria for awarding institutional aid:** *Non-need-based:* Academics, art, athletics, leadership, minority status, music/drama, state/district residency.

FRESNO PACIFIC UNIVERSITY

1717 S. Chestnut Ave, Fresno, CA 93702
Phone: 559-453-2039 **Financial Aid Phone:** 559-453-2041
E-mail: ugadmis@fresno.edu
Fax: 559-453-2007 **Website:** www.fresno.edu

This private school, affiliated with the Mennonite Church, was founded in 1944. It has a 42-acre campus.

RATINGS
Admissions Selectivity Rating: 80   **Fire Safety Rating:** 60*   **Green Rating:** 60*

STUDENTS AND FACULTY
Enrollment: 1,459. **Student Body:** 68% female, 32% male, 4% out-of-state, 2% international . Asian 4%, African American 4%, Caucasian 53%, Hispanic 26%, Native American 1%.
Retention and Graduation: 70% freshmen return for sophomore year. 48% freshmen graduate within 4 years. **Faculty:** Student/faculty ratio 16:1. 84 full-time faculty, 61% hold PhDs, 12% are members of minority groups, 37% are women.

ACADEMICS
Degrees: Associate, bachelor's, certificate, master's, post-bachelor's certificate. **Classes:** Most classes have fewer than 10 students. Most lab/discussion sessions have fewer than 10 students. **Majors with Highest Enrollment:** Bible/biblical studies; business/commerce; education. **Special Study Options:** Accelerated program, cooperative education program, cross-registration, distance learning, double major, English as a Second Language (ESL), independent study, internships, liberal arts/career combination, student-designed major, study abroad, teacher certification program Special programs offered to physically disabled students include note-taking services, reader services, tutors. **Career services:** Alumni services, career/job search classes, career assessment, internships.

FACILITIES
Housing: Special housing for disabled students, men's dorms, women's dorms, apartments for single students, houses. 100% of campus accessible to physically disabled. **Special Academic Facilities/Equipment:** English Language Training Institute.

CAMPUS LIFE
Environment: Metropolis. **Activities:** Choral groups, concert band, dance, drama/theater, jazz band, music ensembles, pep band, student government, student newspaper, yearbook. **Organizations:** 36 registered organizations, 1 honor societies, 11 religious organizations. **Athletics (Intercollegiate):** *Men:* Baseball, basketball, cross-country, soccer, tennis, track/field (outdoor). *Women:* Basketball, cross-country, soccer, tennis, track/field (outdoor), volleyball. **On-Campus Highlights:** Special Events Center (Gym), Steinert Campus Center, The Green (students hang out there), Bookshop, New AIMS Building.

ADMISSIONS
Freshman Academic Profile: Average high school GPA 3.54. 27% in top 10% of high school class, 58% in top 25% of high school class, 85% in top 50% of high school class. SAT Math middle 50% range 420–560. SAT Critical Reading middle 50% range 430–580. SAT Writing middle 50% range 410–570. ACT middle 50% range 16–24. **Basis for Candidate Selection:** *Very important factors considered include:* Rigor of secondary school record, standardized test scores. *Important factors considered include:* Class rank, application essay, academic GPA, recommendation(s), religious affiliation/commitment. *Other factors considered include:* Character/personal qualities. **Freshman Admission Requirements:** High school diploma is required and GED is accepted. *Academic units required:* 4 English, 3 mathematics, 1 science, (1 science labs), 2 foreign language, 2 social studies. *Academic units recommended:* 1 visual/performing arts. **Freshman Admission Statistics:** 672 applied, 68% admitted, 46% enrolled. **Transfer Admission Requirements:** High school transcript, college transcript(s), essay or personal statement, minimum college GPA of 2.4 required. Lowest grade transferable C. **General Admission Information:** Application fee $40. Regular application deadline 7/31. Notification on a rolling basis, beginning on or about 12/1. Nonfall registration accepted. Admission may be deferred for a maximum of NA. Credit offered for CEEB Advanced Placement tests.

COSTS AND FINANCIAL AID
Average book expense $1,314. **Required Forms and Deadlines:** FAFSA, institution's own financial aid form. Priority financial aid filing date 3/2. **Notification of Awards:** Applicants will be notified of awards on a rolling basis beginning 3/2. **Types of Aid:** *Need-based scholarships/grants:* Federal Pell, SEOG, state scholarships/grants, private scholarships, the school's own gift aid. *Loans:* FFEL Subsidized Stafford, FFEL Unsubsidized Stafford, FFEL PLUS, Federal Perkins. **Student Employment:** Federal Work-Study Program available. Institutional employment available. Off-campus job opportunities

---

are good. **Financial Aid Statistics:** 80% freshmen, 65% undergrads receive need-based scholarship or grant aid. 35% freshmen, 25% undergrads receive non-need-based scholarship or grant aid. 62% freshmen, 65% undergrads receive need-based self-help aid. 20% freshmen, 12% undergrads receive athletic scholarships. 99% undergrads borrow to pay for school. Average cumulative indebtedness $15,588. **Criteria for awarding institutional aid:** *Non-need-based:* Academics, alumni affiliation, art, athletics, leadership, minority status, music/drama, religious affiliation, state/district residency.

FRIENDS UNIVERSITY

2100 University Street, Wichita, KS 67213
Phone: 316-295-5100
E-mail: learn@friends.edu
Fax: 316-295-5101 **Website:** www.friends.edu **ACT Code:** 1918

This private school, affiliated with the Quaker Church, was founded in 1898. It has a 45-acre campus.

RATINGS
Admissions Selectivity Rating: 60*   **Fire Safety Rating:** 60*   **Green Rating:** 60*

STUDENTS AND FACULTY
Student Body: 13% out-of-state, (20 countries represented).
Retention and Graduation: 63% freshmen return for sophomore year. 33% grads go on to further study within 1 year. **Faculty:** Student/faculty ratio 10:1. 72 full-time faculty, 43% hold PhDs, 4% are members of minority groups, 29% are women.

ACADEMICS
Degrees: Bachelor's, master's, terminal associate, transfer associate. **Special Study Options:** Cooperative education program, cross-registration, double major, dual enrollment, external degree program, honors program, independent study, internships, student-designed major, study abroad, teacher certification program, Degree completion program for working adults. **Career services:** Career/job search classes, internships.

FACILITIES
Housing: Men's dorms, women's dorms, apartments for married students, apartments for single students, university-owned houses.

CAMPUS LIFE
Activities: Choral groups, concert band, dance, drama/theater, jazz band, literary magazine, music ensembles, musical theater, pep band, student government, symphony orchestra, yearbook. **Organizations:** 32 registered organizations, 4 honor societies, 3 religious organizations. 2 fraternities, 1 sorority. **Athletics (Intercollegiate):** *Men:* Baseball, basketball, cheerleading, cross-country, football, golf, soccer, tennis, track/field (outdoor). *Women:* Basketball, cheerleading, cross-country, soccer, softball, tennis, track/field (outdoor), volleyball.

ADMISSIONS
Freshman Academic Profile: ACT middle 50% range 17–26. Minimum paper TOEFL 500. **Basis for Candidate Selection:** *Very important factors considered include:* Rigor of secondary school record, standardized test scores. *Important factors considered include:* Recommendation(s), interview. *Other factors considered include:* Alumni/ae relation, extracurricular activities, racial/ethnic status, religious affiliation/commitment, talent/ability. **Freshman Admission Requirements:** High school diploma is required and GED is accepted. *Academic units recommended:* 3 mathematics, 3 science. **Freshman Admission Statistics:** 668 applied, 93% admitted. **Transfer Admission Requirements:** College transcript(s), statement of good standing from prior institution(s). Minimum college GPA of 2.0 required. Lowest grade transferable C. **General Admission Information:** Application fee $15. Nonfall registration accepted. Credit and/or placement offered for CEEB Advanced Placement tests.

COSTS AND FINANCIAL AID
Annual tuition $11,050. Room and board $3,420. Required fees $90. Average book expense $750. **Required Forms and Deadlines:** FAFSA, institution's own financial aid form. Priority financial aid filing date 4/1. **Types of Aid:** *Need-based scholarships/grants:* Federal Pell, SEOG, private scholarships. *Loans:* Direct Subsidized Stafford, Direct Unsubsidized Stafford, Direct PLUS, Federal Perkins. **Student Employment:** Federal Work-Study Program available. Institutional employment available. Off-campus job opportunities are excellent. **Criteria for awarding institutional aid:** *Non-need-based:* Academics, alumni affiliation, athletics, leadership, minority status, music/drama, religious affiliation.

FROSTBURG STATE UNIVERSITY

FSU, 101 Braddock Road, Frostburg, MD 21532
Phone: 301-687-4201 **Financial Aid Phone:** 301-687-4301
E-mail: fsuadmissions@frostburg.edu **CEEB Code:** 5402
Fax: 301-687-7074 **Website:** www.frostburg.edu **ACT Code:** 1714

This public school was founded in 1898. It has a 260-acre campus.

RATINGS
Admissions Selectivity Rating: 71 **Fire Safety Rating:** 60* **Green Rating:** 77

STUDENTS AND FACULTY
Enrollment: 4,187. **Student Body:** 48% female, 52% male, 10% out-of-state, 1% international (25 countries represented). Asian 2%, African American 17%, Caucasian 76%, Hispanic 2%.
Retention and Graduation: 72% freshmen return for sophomore year. 22% freshmen graduate within 4 years. **Faculty:** Student/faculty ratio 16:1. 240 full-time faculty, 84% hold PhDs, 13% are members of minority groups, 38% are women.

ACADEMICS
Degrees: Bachelor's, certificate, master's, post-bachelor's certificate, post-master's certificate. **Classes:** Most classes have 20–29 students. Most lab/discussion sessions have 10–19 students. **Majors with Highest Enrollment:** Business/commerce; elementary education and teaching; psychology. **Special Study Options:** Accelerated program, distance learning, double major, dual enrollment, honors program, independent study, internships, liberal arts/career combination, study abroad, teacher certification program, Learning Communities, Dual Degree Program. **Combined degree programs:** MBA/BS in Accounting. Special programs offered to physically disabled students include note-taking services, reader services, tape recorders, tutors.

FACILITIES
Housing: Coed dorms, women's dorms, special interest housing: Leadership Hall Honors Housing Community Service. 100% of campus accessible to physically disabled. **Special Academic Facilities/Equipment:** Art gallery, planetarium, electron microscope. **Computers:** Students can register for classes online. Administrative functions (other than registration) can be performed online.

CAMPUS LIFE
Environment: Rural. **Activities:** Choral groups, concert band, dance, drama/theater, jazz band, literary magazine, marching band, music ensembles, musical theater, pep band, radio station, student government, student newspaper, symphony orchestra, television station. **Organizations:** 95 registered organizations, 18 honor societies, 6 religious organizations. 9 fraternities, 6 sororities. **Athletics (Intercollegiate):** *Men:* Baseball, basketball, cross-country, diving, football, golf, soccer, swimming, tennis, track/field (outdoor), track/field (indoor). *Women:* Basketball, cross-country, diving, field hockey, lacrosse, soccer, softball, swimming, tennis, track/field (outdoor), track/field (indoor), volleyball. **On-Campus Highlights:** Lane University Center, Cordts PE Center, Performing Arts Center, Stephanie Roper Art Gallery, Compton Science Center. **Environmental Initiatives:** Adopt an energy-efficient appliance purchasing policy requiring purchase of Energy Star-certified products in all areas for which such ratings exist. Begin purchasing or producing at least 15 percent of our institutions electricity consumption from renewable sources within one year of signing the ACUPCC. Participate in the Waste Minimization component of the national RecycleMania competition, and adopt three or more associated measures to reduce waste.

ADMISSIONS
Freshman Academic Profile: Average high school GPA 3.04. 10% in top 10% of high school class, 27% in top 25% of high school class, 62% in top 50% of high school class. SAT Math middle 50% range 430–540. SAT Critical Reading middle 50% range 430–530. SAT Writing middle 50% range 420–520. ACT middle 50% range 17–22. Minimum paper TOEFL 550. Minimum computer TOEFL 213. **Basis for Candidate Selection:** *Very important factors considered include:* Academic GPA, rigor of secondary school record, standardized test scores. *Important factors considered include:* Recommendation(s), interview. *Other factors considered include:* Alumni/ae relation, character/personal qualities, extracurricular activities, talent/ability. **Freshman Admission Requirements:** High school diploma is required and GED is accepted. *Academic units required:* 4 English, 3 mathematics, 3 science, (2 science labs), 2 foreign language, 3 social studies. **Freshman Admission Statistics:** 3,810 applied, 70% admitted, 39% enrolled. **Transfer Admission Requirements:** College transcript(s), minimum college GPA of 2.0 required. Lowest grade transferable C. **General Admission Information:** Application fee $30. Early decision application deadline 12/15. Notification on a rolling basis, beginning on or about 11/1. Nonfall registration accepted. Credit and/or placement offered for CEEB Advanced Placement tests.

COSTS AND FINANCIAL AID
Annual in-state tuition $5,000. Annual out-of-state tuition $14,612. Room and board $6,746. Required fees $1,550. Average book expense $750. **Required Forms and Deadlines:** FAFSA. Priority financial aid filing date 3/1. **Notification of Awards:** Applicants will be notified of awards on a rolling basis beginning 3/15. **Types of Aid:** *Need-based scholarships/grants:* Federal Pell, SEOG, state scholarships/grants, private scholarships, the school's own gift aid. *Loans:* Direct Subsidized Stafford, Direct Unsubsidized Stafford, Direct PLUS, FFEL PLUS, Federal Perkins, college/university loans from institutional funds. **Student Employment:** Highest amount earned per year from on-campus jobs $1,000. **Financial Aid Statistics:** 42% freshmen, 36% undergrads receive need-based scholarship or grant aid. 20% freshmen, 13% undergrads receive non-need-based scholarship or grant aid. 36% freshmen, 37% undergrads receive need-based self-help aid. 72% freshmen, 65% undergrads receive any aid. 61% undergrads borrow to pay for school. Average cumulative indebtedness $15,678. **Criteria for awarding institutional aid:** *Non-need-based:* Academics, alumni affiliation, art, leadership, music/drama, state/district residency.

See page 1096.

FURMAN UNIVERSITY

Best 373

3300 Poinsett Highway, Greenville, SC 29613
Phone: 864-294-2034 **Financial Aid Phone:** 864-294-2204
E-mail: admissions@furman.edu **CEEB Code:** 5222
Fax: 864-294-2018 **Website:** www.furman.edu **ACT Code:** 3858

This private school was founded in 1826. It has a 800-acre campus.

RATINGS
Admissions Selectivity Rating: 94 **Fire Safety Rating:** 83 **Green Rating:** 98

STUDENTS AND FACULTY
Enrollment: 2,724. **Student Body:** 57% female, 43% male, 69% out-of-state, 1% international (47 countries represented). Asian 2%, African American 7%, Caucasian 81%, Hispanic 2%.
Retention and Graduation: 81% freshmen graduate within 4 years. 40% grads go on to further study within 1 year. 30% grads pursue arts and sciences degrees. 4% grads pursue law degrees. 2% grads pursue business degrees. 4% grads pursue medical degrees. **Faculty:** Student/faculty ratio 11:1. 234 full-time faculty, 96% hold PhDs, 12% are members of minority groups, 32% are women.

ACADEMICS
Degrees: Bachelor's, master's, post-bachelor's certificate. **Classes:** Most classes have 10–19 students. **Majors with Highest Enrollment:** Communication studies/speech communication and rhetoric; history; political science and government. **Special Study Options:** Double major, independent study, internships, student-designed major, study abroad, teacher certification program. **Combined degree programs:** BA/MD, BA/MA, BA/DDS, Environmental Studies, Pharmacy, Nursing. Special programs offered to physically disabled students include note-taking services, reader services, tape recorders, tutors. **Career services:** Alumni network, career/job search classes, career assessment, internships. **Career services highlights include:** Furman's internships, both paid and unpaid, are available to virtually every student. They run the gamut from medical research to international business opportunities.

FACILITIES
Housing: Coed dorms, men's dorms, special housing for international students, women's dorms, apartments for single students, wellness housing, theme housing lakeside cottages, language houses, eco-cottage. 98% of campus accessible to physically disabled. **Special Academic Facilities/Equipment:** Visual arts gallery and teaching facility, language lab. Astronomical lab; Center for Engaged Learning; and Center for Collaborative Learning and Communication. **Computers:** 100% of classrooms, 100% of libraries, 100% of dining areas, 100% of student union, have wireless network access. Students can register for classes online. Administrative functions (other than registration) can be performed online.

CAMPUS LIFE
Environment: City. **Activities:** Choral groups, concert band, dance, drama/theater, jazz band, literary magazine, marching band, music ensembles, musical theater, opera, pep band, radio station, student government, student newspaper, student-run film society, symphony orchestra, television station, yearbook, campus ministries, international student organization. **Organizations:** 143 regis-

tered organizations, 29 honor societies, 17 religious organizations. 7 fraternities, 7 sororities. **Athletics (Intercollegiate): Men:** Baseball, basketball, cheerleading, cross-country, football, golf, soccer, tennis, track/field (outdoor), track/field (indoor). **Women:** Basketball, cheerleading, cross-country, golf, soccer, softball, tennis, track/field (outdoor), track/field (indoor), volleyball. **On-Campus Highlights:** Charles Townes Science Center, Timmons Arena, Library, 18-hole Golf Course, Physical Activities Center, Place of Peace, David Shi Center for Sustainability. **Environmental Initiatives:** Sustainable Furman: The approval of Sustainable Furman, the university's comprehensive sustainability master plan. The plan covers all aspects of the university; the 8 goals of Sustainable Furman address sustainability in the curriculum, co-curricular activities, campus culture, renewable energy, efficiency in operations and maintenance, transportation, sustainability service, and continuing national leadership in the sustainability arena. In addition, the plan sets out a path for the university to reach carbon neutrality by 2026. Sustainability curriculum development: In recent years Furman has sought to infuse sustainability and environmental issues across the curriculum. The university offers a wide range of sustainability-related courses at all levels. The new university-wide curriculum, inaugurated in the fall of 2008, requires all students to take at least one course that focuses on the relationship between "Humans and the Natural Environment." In 2009–2010, 31 courses in 11 departments were offered to fulfill the Humans and the Natural Environment credit. Nine departments in the natural sciences, social sciences, and humanities contribute faculty members to a multi-disciplinary Concentration in Environmental Studies. Students in the capstone course for the concentration are also involved in service learning projects in the community. The most recent new courses in sustainability have included several first-year seminars and an environmental policy course that focuses on campus/community connections. Creation of the David E. Shi Center for Sustainability

ADMISSIONS

Freshman Academic Profile: Average high school GPA 3.83. 61% in top 10% of high school class, 86% in top 25% of high school class, 98% in top 50% of high school class. 63% from public high schools. SAT Math middle 50% range 600–680. SAT Critical Reading middle 50% range 580–690. SAT Writing middle 50% range 580–680. ACT middle 50% range 25–30. Minimum paper TOEFL 570. Minimum computer TOEFL 230. **Basis for Candidate Selection:** *Very important factors considered include:* Rigor of secondary school record. *Important factors considered include:* Class rank, application essay, academic GPA, standardized test scores, character/personal qualities, extracurricular activities. *Other factors considered include:* Recommendation(s), alumni/ae relation, first generation, level of applicant's interest, racial/ethnic status, talent/ability, volunteer work, work experience. **Freshman Admission Requirements:** High school diploma is required and GED is accepted. *Academic units required:* 4 English, 3 mathematics, 2 science, (2 science labs), 2 foreign language, 3 social studies. *Academic units recommended:* 4 English, 4 mathematics, 3 science, (2 science labs), 3 foreign language, 4 social studies. **Freshman Admission Statistics:** 4,538 applied, 68% admitted, 21% enrolled. **Transfer Admission Requirements:** High school transcript, college transcript(s), essay or personal statement, standardized test scores, statement of good standing from prior institution(s). Minimum college GPA of 3.0 required. Lowest grade transferable C. **General Admission Information:** Application fee $50. Early decision application deadline 11/15. Regular application deadline 1/15. Regular notification 3/15. Nonfall registration not accepted. Credit and/or placement offered for CEEB Advanced Placement tests.

COSTS AND FINANCIAL AID

Annual tuition $36,296. Room and board $9,170. Required fees $360. Average book expense $1,110. **Required Forms and Deadlines:** FAFSA, institution's own financial aid form, CSS/Financial Aid PROFILE, state aid form, South Carolina residents must complete required state forms for South Carolina. Financial aid filing deadline 1/15. **Notification of Awards:** Applicants will be notified of awards on or about 3/15. **Types of Aid:** *Need-based scholarships/ grants:* Federal Pell, SEOG, state scholarships/grants, private scholarships, the school's own gift aid, Donor sponsored loans for study abroad. *Loans:* FFEL Subsidized Stafford, FFEL Unsubsidized Stafford, FFEL PLUS, Federal Perkins, state loans, Federal SMART and ACG grants. **Student Employment:** Federal Work-Study Program available. Institutional employment available. Highest amount earned per year from on-campus jobs $1,500. Off-campus job opportunities are excellent. **Financial Aid Statistics:** 53% freshmen, 47% undergrads receive need-based scholarship or grant aid. 48% freshmen, 37% undergrads receive non-need-based scholarship or grant aid. 38% freshmen, 35% undergrads receive need-based self-help aid. 11% freshmen, 9% undergrads receive athletic scholarships. 85% freshmen, 83% undergrads receive any aid. 40% undergrads borrow to pay for school. Average cumulative indebtedness $27,373. **Criteria for awarding institutional aid:** *Non-need-based:* Academics, alumni affiliation, art, athletics, leadership, music/drama, religious affiliation, state/district residency.

GALLAUDET UNIVERSITY

800 Florida Avenue NE, Washington DC, DC 20002
Phone: 202-651-5750 **Financial Aid Phone:** 202-651-5290
E-mail: admissions.office@gallaudet.edu **CEEB Code:** 5240
Fax: 202-651-5744 **Website:** www.gallaudet.edu **ACT Code:** 662

This private school was founded in 1864. It has a 99-acre campus.

RATINGS
Admissions Selectivity Rating: 60*   **Fire Safety Rating:** 60*   **Green Rating:** 60*

STUDENTS AND FACULTY
Enrollment: 1,053. **Student Body:** 53% female, 47% male, 95% out-of-state, 5% international (27 countries represented). Asian 4%, African American 11%, Caucasian 68%, Hispanic 9%, Native American 2%.
Retention and Graduation: 75% freshmen return for sophomore year. 11% freshmen graduate within 4 years.

ACADEMICS
Degrees: Bachelor's, master's, post-bachelor's certificate. **Classes:** Most classes have 10–19 students. Most lab/discussion sessions have fewer than 10 students. **Majors with Highest Enrollment:** Business/commerce; psychology. **Special Study Options:** Accelerated program, cross-registration, distance learning, double major, English as a Second Language (ESL), exchange student program (domestic), honors program, independent study, internships, student-designed major, study abroad, teacher certification program, Experiential programs off-campus including orientation program for employers of deaf students and paraprofessional jobs on campus, programs for interpreter-assisted mainstreaming of students into area colleges such as Georgetown University, George Mason University, Catholic University, and Howard University. **Honors programs:** The Gallaudet Honors Program is a Learning Community for the most academically capable and motivated students. The overall goal is to foster skills, work habits, and attitudes conducive to future achievement and lifelong learning. To this end, the Program focuses on linking rigorous, challenging, and innovative curricular offerings with co-curricular activities. It also serves as a leader in and test laboratory of curricular, co-curricular, and extracurricular innovations; successes may then be replicated for all students. **Combined degree programs:** BA/MA, BA or BS (Education) with MA in Teaching. Special programs offered to physically disabled students include tutors. **Career services:** Alumni network, alumni services, career/job search classes, career assessment, internships. **Career services highlights include:** Internship program.

FACILITIES
Housing: Coed dorms, special housing for disabled students, apartments for married students, theme housing 100% of campus accessible to physically disabled. **Special Academic Facilities/Equipment:** Kendall Demonstration Elementary School and Model Secondary School for the Deaf. **Computers:** 100% of classrooms, 100% of dorms, 100% of libraries, 100% of dining areas, 100% of student union, 20% of common outdoor areas have wireless network access. Students can register for classes online. Administrative functions (other than registration) can be performed online.

CAMPUS LIFE
Environment: Metropolis. **Activities:** Dance, drama/theater, literary magazine, student government, student newspaper, student-run film society, yearbook, campus ministries, international student organization. **Organizations:** 25 registered organizations, 1 honor societies, 1 religious organizations. 5 fraternities, 4 sororities. **Athletics (Intercollegiate): Men:** Baseball, basketball, cross-country, diving, football, soccer, swimming, tennis, track/field (outdoor), wrestling. **Women:** Basketball, cross-country, diving, soccer, softball, swimming, tennis, track/field (outdoor), volleyball. **On-Campus Highlights:** Rathskellar, Cafeteria, Bison Shop, Starbucks, Student Academic Center.

ADMISSIONS
Freshman Academic Profile: ACT middle 50% range 15–20. **Basis for Candidate Selection:** *Very important factors considered include:* Application essay, academic GPA, recommendation(s), rigor of secondary school record, standardized test scores. *Important factors considered include:* Class rank, first generation. *Other factors considered include:* Alumni/ae relation, extracurricular activities, talent/ability. **Freshman Admission Requirements:** High school diploma is required and GED is accepted. *Academic units recommended:* 4 English, 4 mathematics, 4 science, (2 science labs), 4 social studies, 4 history. **Freshman Admission Statistics:** 413 applied, 68% admitted, 75% enrolled. **Transfer Admission Requirements:** College transcript(s), essay or personal statement, Lowest grade transferable C–. **General Admission Information:** Application fee $50. Nonfall registration accepted. Credit and/or placement offered for CEEB Advanced Placement tests.

COSTS AND FINANCIAL AID

Annual tuition $10,850. Room and board $9,660. Required fees $376. Average book expense $942. **Required Forms and Deadlines:** FAFSA, institution's own financial aid form. Priority financial aid filing date 7/1. **Notification of Awards:** Applicants will be notified of awards on a rolling basis beginning 3/1. **Types of Aid:** *Need-based scholarships/grants:* Federal Pell, SEOG, state scholarships/grants, private scholarships, the school's own gift aid. *Loans:* FFEL Subsidized Stafford, FFEL Unsubsidized Stafford, FFEL PLUS, Federal Perkins. **Student Employment:** Federal Work-Study Program available. Institutional employment available. **Financial Aid Statistics:** 76% freshmen, 72% undergrads receive need-based scholarship or grant aid. 27% freshmen, 26% undergrads receive non-need-based scholarship or grant aid. 33% freshmen, 35% undergrads receive need-based self-help aid. 54% undergrads borrow to pay for school. Average cumulative indebtedness $13,484. **Criteria for awarding institutional aid:** *Non-need-based:* Academics, leadership, minority status.

GANNON UNIVERSITY

University Square, Erie, PA 16541
Phone: 814-871-7240 **Financial Aid Phone:** 814-871-7337
E-mail: CEEB Code: 2270
Fax: 814-871-5803 **Website:** www.gannon.edu **ACT Code:** 3576

This private school, affiliated with the Roman Catholic Church, was founded in 1925. It has a 13-acre campus.

RATINGS

Admissions Selectivity Rating: 77   **Fire Safety Rating:** 92   **Green Rating:** 75

STUDENTS AND FACULTY

Enrollment: 2,593. **Student Body:** 59% female, 41% male, 23.3% out-of-state, 2% international (22 countries represented). Asian 2%, African American 6%, Caucasian 84%, Hispanic 2%.
Retention and Graduation: 41% grads go on to further study within 1 year. 32% grads pursue arts and sciences degrees. 2% grads pursue law degrees. 3% grads pursue business degrees. 3% grads pursue medical degrees. **Faculty:** Student/faculty ratio 13:1. 200 full-time faculty, 72% hold PhDs, 13% are members of minority groups, 45% are women. 1% of classes are taught by teaching assistants.

ACADEMICS

Degrees: Associate, bachelor's, certificate, master's, post-bachelor's certificate, post-master's certificate. **Classes:** Most classes have 10–19 students. Most lab/discussion sessions have 10–19 students. **Majors with Highest Enrollment:** kinesiology and exercise science; nursing/registered nurse (RN, ASN, BSN, MSN); physician assistant. **Special Study Options:** Accelerated program, distance learning, double major, dual enrollment, honors program, independent study, internships, liberal arts/career combination, study abroad, teacher certification program. **Honors programs:** Gannon offers an honors program for the academically talented and highly motivated students. Last year, 246 students participated in honors classes that were small in size and staffed by Gannon's best teachers. **Combined degree programs:** BA/MD, BA/JD, BA/MA, BS/MBA. Special programs offered to physically disabled students include note-taking services, reader services, tape recorders, tutors. **Career services:** Alumni network, alumni services, career/job search classes, career assessment, internships, regional alumni. **Career services highlights include:** The Career Road Show program we offer—it has the Career Development staff making over 55 in-class career and job search presentations each year. The program continues to grow and students benefit from learning valuable career information taught in classes within their major.

FACILITIES

Housing: Coed dorms, special housing for disabled students, apartments for single students. 85% of campus accessible to physically disabled. **Special Academic Facilities/Equipment:** Laser and spectrographic labs, Patient Simulation Center, metallurgy institute, computer-integrated manufacturing facilities, Schuster Art Gallery, Schuster Theatres, Erie Technology Incubator. **Computers:** 100% of classrooms, 100% of dorms, 100% of libraries, 100% of dining areas, 100% of student union, 100% of common outdoor areas have wireless network access. Students can register for classes online. Administrative functions (other than registration) can be performed online.

CAMPUS LIFE

Environment: City. **Activities:** Choral groups, concert band, dance, drama/theater, literary magazine, music ensembles, musical theater, pep band, radio station, student government, student newspaper, yearbook, campus ministries, international student organization, Model UN. **Organizations:** 71 registered organizations, 11 honor societies, 6 religious organizations. 5 fraternities, 5 sororities. **Athletics (Intercollegiate):** *Men:* Baseball, basketball, cheerleading, cross-country, football, golf, soccer, swimming, water polo, wrestling. *Women:* Basketball, cheerleading, cross-country, golf, lacrosse, soccer, softball, swimming, volleyball, water polo. **On-Campus Highlights:** Multi-purpose Athletic Field, Waldron Campus Center, A.J. Palumbo Academic Center, Carnaval Athletic Pavilion, Zurn Science Center, Schuster Art Gallery Morosky College of Health Professions and Science. **Environmental Initiatives:** Switching out all campus light fixtures to compact flourescent. Purchasing 15% of energy from wind power. Experimenting with and switching to green cleaning products.

ADMISSIONS

Freshman Academic Profile: Average high school GPA 3.42. 27.6% in top 10% of high school class, 49.9% in top 25% of high school class, 77.6% in top 50% of high school class. 84% from public high schools. SAT Math middle 50% range 450–590. SAT Critical Reading middle 50% range 440–560. ACT middle 50% range 19–26. Minimum paper TOEFL 550. Minimum computer TOEFL 213. Minimum web-based TOEFL 79. **Basis for Candidate Selection:** *Very important factors considered include:* Class rank, academic GPA, rigor of secondary school record, standardized test scores. *Important factors considered include:* Recommendation(s), level of applicant's interest. *Other factors considered include:* Application essay, extracurricular activities, interview, talent/ability, volunteer work. **Freshman Admission Requirements:** High school diploma is required and GED is accepted. *Academic units required:* 4 English, 2 social studies, 1 history, 3 academic electives. *Academic units recommended:* 4 English, 4 mathematics, 4 science, (3 science labs), 2 foreign language, 2 social studies, 1 history, 3 academic electives. **Freshman Admission Statistics:** 3,019 applied, 84% admitted, 26% enrolled. **Transfer Admission Requirements:** College transcript(s), statement of good standing from prior institution(s). Minimum college GPA of 2.0 required. Lowest grade transferable C. **General Admission Information:** Application fee $25. Notification on a rolling basis, beginning on or about 9/15. Nonfall registration accepted. Admission may be deferred for a maximum of 1 year. Credit and/or placement offered for CEEB Advanced Placement tests.

COSTS AND FINANCIAL AID

Required Forms and Deadlines: FAFSA, institution's own financial aid form. Priority financial aid filing date 3/15. **Notification of Awards:** Applicants will be notified of awards on a rolling basis beginning 11/1. **Types of Aid:** *Need-based scholarships/grants:* Federal Pell, SEOG, state scholarships/grants, private scholarships, the school's own gift aid. *Loans:* Direct Subsidized Stafford, Direct Unsubsidized Stafford, Direct PLUS, FFEL Subsidized Stafford, FFEL Unsubsidized Stafford, FFEL PLUS, Federal Perkins. **Student Employment:** Federal Work-Study Program available. Institutional employment available. Highest amount earned per year from on-campus jobs $2,300. Off-campus job opportunities are good. **Financial Aid Statistics:** 87% freshmen, 84% undergrads receive need-based scholarship or grant aid. 12% freshmen, 11% undergrads receive non-need-based scholarship or grant aid. 79% freshmen, 81% undergrads receive need-based self-help aid. 3% freshmen, 3% undergrads receive athletic scholarships. 97.8% freshmen, 93.1% undergrads receive any aid. 86.4% undergrads borrow to pay for school. Average cumulative indebtedness $31,234. **Criteria for awarding institutional aid:** *Non-need-based:* Academics, athletics, leadership, music/drama, religious affiliation.

GARDNER-WEBB UNIVERSITY

PO Box 817, Boiling Springs, NC 28017
Phone: 704-406-4498 **Financial Aid Phone:** 704-406-4243
E-mail: admissions@gardner-webb.edu **CEEB Code:** 5242
Fax: 704-406-4488 **Website:** www.gardner-webb.edu **ACT Code:** 3102

This private school, affiliated with the Baptist Church, was founded in 1905. It has a 250-acre campus.

RATINGS

Admissions Selectivity Rating: 80   **Fire Safety Rating:** 60*   **Green Rating:** 66

STUDENTS AND FACULTY

Enrollment: 2,640. **Student Body:** 65% female, 35% male, 21% out-of-state, (22 countries represented). African American 19%, Caucasian 73%, Hispanic 2%, Native American 1%.
Retention and Graduation: 36% freshmen graduate within 4 years. **Faculty:** Student/faculty ratio 13:1. 140 full-time faculty, 80% hold PhDs, 4% are members of minority groups, 46% are women.

ACADEMICS

Degrees: Associate, bachelor's, doctoral, master's. **Classes:** Most classes have fewer than 10 students. **Majors with Highest Enrollment:** Business/commerce; religion/religious studies; social sciences, other. **Special Study Options:**

Accelerated program, distance learning, double major, dual enrollment, English as a Second Language (ESL), honors program, independent study, internships, liberal arts/career combination, study abroad, teacher certification program **Honors programs:** Alpha Chi Honors Program, Beta Beta Beta, Delta Mu, Delta Sigma, Delta Pi, Sigma Tau, Delta Theta, Alpha Kappa Pi, Delta Phi Psi, Chi Sigma, Zeta Sigma, Theta Tau, Who's Who. **Combined degree programs:** MusiC–Business—BM/MBA. Special programs offered to physically disabled students include note-taking services, reader services, tape recorders, tutors. **Career services:** Alumni network, career/job search classes, career assessment, internships. **Career services highlights include:** Our Career Services office organizes a mock formal dinner interview and sponsors the Metrolina Career Fair and a Nursing Career Fair.

FACILITIES

Housing: Special housing for disabled students, men's dorms, women's dorms, apartments for single students, wellness housing. Housing for Honor Students. 100% of campus accessible to physically disabled. **Special Academic Facilities/Equipment:** Williams Observatory, Millennium Playhouse, Broyhill Adventure Course, Lake Hollifield Complex and Carillon. **Computers:** 100% of classrooms, 100% of dorms, 100% of libraries, 100% of dining areas, 100% of student union, 100% of common outdoor areas have wireless network access. Students can register for classes online. Administrative functions (other than registration) can be performed online.

CAMPUS LIFE

Environment: Rural. **Activities:** Choral groups, concert band, dance, drama/theater, jazz band, literary magazine, marching band, music ensembles, musical theater, opera, pep band, radio station, student government, student newspaper, symphony orchestra, yearbook, campus ministries, international student organization. **Organizations:** 65 registered organizations, 12 honor societies, 11 religious organizations. **Athletics (Intercollegiate):** *Men:* Baseball, basketball, cheerleading, cross-country, football, golf, soccer, swimming, tennis, track/field (outdoor), track/field (indoor), wrestling. *Women:* Basketball, cheerleading, cross-country, golf, soccer, softball, swimming, tennis, track/field (outdoor), track/field (indoor), volleyball. **On-Campus Highlights:** Dover Campus Center, Suttle Wellness Center, Cafeteria, Lutz-Yelton Convocation Center, Kennel Snack Bar. **Environmental Initiatives:** Recycling programs environmental science major with student projects.

ADMISSIONS

Freshman Academic Profile: Average high school GPA 3.47. 32% in top 10% of high school class, 49% in top 25% of high school class, 72% in top 50% of high school class. 84% from public high schools. SAT Math middle 50% range 420–550. SAT Critical Reading middle 50% range 440–560. ACT middle 50% range 18–23. Minimum paper TOEFL 500. Minimum computer TOEFL 173. Minimum web-based TOEFL 61. **Basis for Candidate Selection:** *Very important factors considered include:* Academic GPA, rigor of secondary school record, standardized test scores, level of applicant's interest. *Important factors considered include:* Class rank, recommendation(s), character/personal qualities, extracurricular activities. *Other factors considered include:* Application essay, interview, talent/ability, volunteer work. **Freshman Admission Requirements:** High school diploma is required and GED is accepted. *Academic units recommended:* 4 English, 3 mathematics, 3 science, (2 science labs), 2 foreign language, 1 social studies, 1 history. **Freshman Admission Statistics:** 3,277 applied, 62% admitted, 22% enrolled. **Transfer Admission Requirements:** College transcript(s), statement of good standing from prior institution(s). Minimum college GPA of 2.25 required. Lowest grade transferable C. **General Admission Information:** Application fee $40. Notification on a rolling basis, beginning on or about 9/1. Nonfall registration accepted. Admission may be deferred for a maximum of 2 Semesters. Credit and/or placement offered for CEEB Advanced Placement tests.

COSTS AND FINANCIAL AID

Annual tuition $22,050. Room and board $7,195. Required fees $390. Average book expense $1,000. **Required Forms and Deadlines:** FAFSA, state aid form. Priority financial aid filing date 3/15. **Notification of Awards:** Applicants will be notified of awards on a rolling basis beginning 3/1. **Types of Aid:** *Need-based scholarships/grants:* Federal Pell, SEOG, state scholarships/grants, private scholarships, the school's own gift aid. *Loans:* FFEL Subsidized Stafford, FFEL Unsubsidized Stafford, FFEL PLUS, Federal Perkins, Federal Nursing, state loans. **Student Employment:** Federal Work-Study Program available. Institutional employment available. Off-campus job opportunities are good. **Financial Aid Statistics:** 100% freshmen receive any aid. **Criteria for awarding institutional aid:** *Non-need-based:* Academics, athletics, leadership, music/drama, state/district residency.

GENEVA COLLEGE

3200 College Avenue, Beaver Falls, PA 15010
Phone: 724-847-6500 **Financial Aid Phone:** 724-847-6530
E-mail: admissions@geneva.edu **CEEB Code:** 2273
Fax: 724-847-6776 **Website:** www.geneva.edu/ **ACT Code:** 33578

This private school was founded in 1848. It has a 55-acre campus.

RATINGS
Admissions Selectivity Rating: 77   **Fire Safety Rating:** 62   **Green Rating:** 60*

STUDENTS AND FACULTY
Enrollment: 1,340. **Student Body:** 54% female, 46% male, 26% out-of-state, 1% international (7 countries represented). Asian 1%, African American 15%, Caucasian 105%, Hispanic 1%.
Retention and Graduation: 78% freshmen return for sophomore year. 45% freshmen graduate within 4 years. 32% grads go on to further study within 1 year. **Faculty:** Student/faculty ratio 13:1. 84 full-time faculty, 76% hold PhDs, 8% are members of minority groups, 35% are women.

ACADEMICS
Degrees: Associate, bachelor's, master's. **Classes:** Most classes have 10–19 students. **Majors with Highest Enrollment:** Bible/biblical studies; business/commerce; elementary education and teaching. **Special Study Options:** Accelerated program, cooperative education program, cross-registration, double major, dual enrollment, honors program, independent study, internships, student-designed major, study abroad, teacher certification program. **Honors programs:** Freshmen Honors Program. **Combined degree programs:** BA/MA, psychology and business. Special programs offered to physically disabled students include note-taking services, reader services, tape recorders, tutors. **Career services:** Alumni network, alumni services, career/job search classes, career assessment, internships.

FACILITIES
Housing: Men's dorms, women's dorms, apartments for single students. 85% of campus accessible to physically disabled. **Special Academic Facilities/Equipment:** Center for Technology Development. **Computers:** Students can register for classes online. Administrative functions (other than registration) can be performed online.

CAMPUS LIFE
Environment: Village. **Activities:** Choral groups, concert band, dance, drama/theater, jazz band, literary magazine, marching band, music ensembles, pep band, radio station, student government, student newspaper, yearbook. **Organizations:** 56 registered organizations, 5 honor societies, 11 religious organizations. **Athletics (Intercollegiate):** *Men:* Baseball, basketball, cross-country, football, soccer, track/field (outdoor), track/field (indoor). *Women:* Basketball, cheerleading, cross-country, soccer, softball, tennis, track/field (outdoor), track/field (indoor), volleyball. **On-Campus Highlights:** The Riverview Cafe (Coffee Shop), The Briagadoon (Cafe-Casual Dining), The Fitness Center, Track/Soccer Field, Skye Lounge—Student Center.

ADMISSIONS
Freshman Academic Profile: Average high school GPA 3.4. 16% in top 10% of high school class, 37% in top 25% of high school class, 71% in top 50% of high school class. 72% from public high schools. SAT Math middle 50% range 480–590. SAT Critical Reading middle 50% range 490–610. ACT middle 50% range 20–25. Minimum paper TOEFL 480. Minimum computer TOEFL 157. **Basis for Candidate Selection:** *Very important factors considered include:* Application essay, academic GPA, rigor of secondary school record, standardized test scores. *Other factors considered include:* Class rank, recommendation(s), alumni/ae relation, character/personal qualities, extracurricular activities, interview. **Freshman Admission Requirements:** High school diploma is required and GED is accepted. *Academic units required:* 4 English, 2 mathematics, 1 science, 2 foreign language, 3 social studies, 4 academic electives. **Freshman Admission Statistics:** 1,329 applied, 64% admitted, 35% enrolled. **Transfer Admission Requirements:** High school transcript, college transcript(s), essay or personal statement, minimum college GPA of 2.0 required. Lowest grade transferable C–. **General Admission Information:** Application fee $40. Notification on a rolling basis, beginning on or about 9/1. Nonfall registration accepted. Admission may be deferred for a maximum of 3 years. Credit and/or placement offered for CEEB Advanced Placement tests.

COSTS AND FINANCIAL AID
Annual tuition $19,430. Room and board $7,200. Average book expense $800. **Required Forms and Deadlines:** FAFSA. Priority financial aid filing date 3/15. **Notification of Awards:** Applicants will be notified of awards on a rolling basis beginning 3/15. **Types of Aid:** *Need-based scholarships/grants:* Federal

Pell, SEOG, state scholarships/grants, private scholarships, the school's own gift aid, FSEOG. *Loans:* FFEL Subsidized Stafford, FFEL Unsubsidized Stafford, FFEL PLUS, Federal Perkins. **Student Employment:** Federal Work-Study Program available. Institutional employment available. Highest amount earned per year from on-campus jobs $2,000. Off-campus job opportunities are fair. **Financial Aid Statistics:** 83% freshmen, 79% undergrads receive need-based scholarship or grant aid. 10% freshmen, 9% undergrads receive non-need-based scholarship or grant aid. 70% freshmen, 68% undergrads receive need-based self-help aid. 3% undergrads receive athletic scholarships. 95% freshmen, 92% undergrads receive any aid. 95.9% undergrads borrow to pay for school. Average cumulative indebtedness $26,034. **Criteria for awarding institutional aid:** *Non-need-based:* Academics, athletics, music/drama, religious affiliation.

GEORGE FOX UNIVERSITY

414 N. Meridian St, Newberg, OR 97132
Phone: 503-554-2240 **Financial Aid Phone:** 503-554-2290
E-mail: admissions@georgefox.edu **CEEB Code:** 4325
Fax: 503-554-3110 **Website:** www.georgefox.edu **ACT Code:** 3462

This private school was founded in 1891. It has a 85-acre campus.

RATINGS
Admissions Selectivity Rating: 85   **Fire Safety Rating:** 70   **Green Rating:** 62

STUDENTS AND FACULTY
Enrollment: 1,949. **Student Body:** 60% female, 40% male, 33% out-of-state, 5% international (34 countries represented). Asian 5%, African American 2%, Caucasian 72%, Hispanic 5%, Native American 2%.
Retention and Graduation: 54% freshmen graduate within 4 years. 16% grads go on to further study within 1 year. 10% grads pursue arts and sciences degrees. 1% grads pursue law degrees. 1% grads pursue medical degrees. **Faculty:** Student/faculty ratio 11:1. 165 full-time faculty, 67% hold PhDs, 7% are members of minority groups, 39% are women.

ACADEMICS
Degrees: Bachelor's, master's, post-bachelor's certificate, post-master's certificate. **Classes:** Most classes have 10–19 students. Most lab/discussion sessions have 10–19 students. **Majors with Highest Enrollment:** Business administration and management; elementary education and teaching; nursing/registered nurse (RN, ASN, BSN, MSN). **Special Study Options:** Accelerated program, cross-registration, double major, dual enrollment, English as a Second Language (ESL), exchange student program (domestic), honors program, independent study, internships, student-designed major, study abroad, teacher certification program. **Honors programs:** University Scholars, Richter Scholars, Honors Scholarships, Advance Leadership Development Program. **Combined degree programs:** 3-1 coop. program in design and merchandising. Special programs offered to physically disabled students include note-taking services, reader services, tape recorders, tutors. **Career services:** Alumni network, alumni services, career/job search classes, career assessment, internships, regional alumni. **Career services highlights include:** All.

FACILITIES
Housing: Special housing for disabled students, men's dorms, women's dorms, apartments for single students, wellness housing, theme housing, houses. 98% of campus accessible to physically disabled. **Special Academic Facilities/ Equipment:** Nuclear magnetic resonance spectrometer, Providence Nursing Learning Lab, language lab, electron microscope. **Computers:** 100% of classrooms, 90% of dorms, 100% of libraries, 100% of dining areas, 100% of student union, 50% of common outdoor areas have wireless network access. Students can register for classes online. Administrative functions (other than registration) can be performed online.

CAMPUS LIFE
Environment: Village. **Activities:** Choral groups, concert band, drama/theater, jazz band, literary magazine, music ensembles, musical theater, pep band, radio station, student government, student newspaper, symphony orchestra, yearbook, campus ministries, international student organization. **Organizations:** 20 registered organizations, 3 honor societies, 3 religious organizations. **Athletics (Intercollegiate):** *Men:* Baseball, basketball, cross-country, golf, soccer, tennis, track/field (outdoor). *Women:* Basketball, cross-country, golf, soccer, softball, tennis, track/field (outdoor), volleyball. **On-Campus Highlights:** Bruin Den-Cafe in the Student Union Bldg, The Foxhole-Student-run coffee house, Dorm Movie Rooms-most have movie areas, Wheeler Sports Center. **Environmental Initiatives:** LEED-certified residence hall, fleet vehicle hybrid purchases, progressive recycling program.

ADMISSIONS
Freshman Academic Profile: Average high school GPA 3.65. 29% in top 10% of high school class, 60% in top 25% of high school class, 87% in top 50% of high school class. 75% from public high schools. SAT Math middle 50% range 480–610. SAT Critical Reading middle 50% range 490–610. SAT Writing middle 50% range 480–590. ACT middle 50% range 21–26. Minimum paper TOEFL 550. Minimum computer TOEFL 213. Minimum web-based TOEFL 80. **Basis for Candidate Selection:** *Very important factors considered include:* Rigor of secondary school record. *Important factors considered include:* Application essay, academic GPA, recommendation(s), standardized test scores. *Other factors considered include:* Character/personal qualities, extracurricular activities, interview, religious affiliation/commitment, talent/ability, volunteer work, work experience. **Freshman Admission Requirements:** High school diploma is required and GED is accepted. *Academic units recommended:* 4 English, 2 mathematics, 2 science, (2 science labs), 2 foreign language, 3 social studies, 2 history, 1 health and physical education. **Freshman Admission Statistics:** 1,528 applied, 69% admitted, 39% enrolled. **Transfer Admission Requirements:** College transcript(s), essay or personal statement, statement of good standing from prior institution(s). Minimum college GPA of 2.6 required. Lowest grade transferable C–. **General Admission Information:** Application fee $40. Notification on a rolling basis, beginning on or about 10/1. Nonfall registration accepted. Admission may be deferred for a maximum of 1 year. Credit and/or placement offered for CEEB Advanced Placement tests.

COSTS AND FINANCIAL AID
Required Forms and Deadlines: FAFSA, state aid form. Priority financial aid filing date 2/1. **Notification of Awards:** Applicants will be notified of awards on a rolling basis beginning 3/1. **Types of Aid:** *Need-based scholarships/grants:* Federal Pell, SEOG, state scholarships/grants, private scholarships, the school's own gift aid, ACG & SMART, TEACH Grants. *Loans:* Direct Subsidized Stafford, Direct Unsubsidized Stafford, Direct PLUS, Federal Perkins, alternative loans. **Student Employment:** Federal Work-Study Program available. Institutional employment available. Highest amount earned per year from on-campus jobs $3,715. Off-campus job opportunities are good. **Financial Aid Statistics:** 74% freshmen, 68% undergrads receive need-based scholarship or grant aid. 67% freshmen, 60% undergrads receive non-need-based scholarship or grant aid. 78% freshmen, 74% undergrads receive need-based self-help aid. 99% freshmen, 96% undergrads receive any aid. **Criteria for awarding institutional aid:** *Non-need-based:* Academics, alumni affiliation, art, job skills, leadership, minority status, music/drama, religious affiliation.

GEORGE MASON UNIVERSITY

Undergraduate Admissions Office, 4400 Univ. Drive, Fairfax, VA 22030-4444
Phone: 703-993-2400 **Financial Aid Phone:** 703-993-2353
E-mail: admissions@gmu.edu **CEEB Code:** 5827
Fax: 703-993-4622 **Website:** www.gmu.edu **ACT Code:** 4357

This public school was founded in 1972. It has a 806-acre campus.

RATINGS
Admissions Selectivity Rating: 83   **Fire Safety Rating:** 75   **Green Rating:** 92

STUDENTS AND FACULTY
Enrollment: 18,240. **Student Body:** 53% female, 47% male, 10% out-of-state, 3% international (131 countries represented). Asian 16%, African American 7%, Caucasian 43%, Hispanic 6%.
Retention and Graduation: 84% freshmen return for sophomore year. 42% freshmen graduate within 4 years. **Faculty:** Student/faculty ratio 15:1. 1123 full-time faculty, 92% hold PhDs, 18% are members of minority groups, 41% are women. 9.9% of classes are taught by teaching assistants.

ACADEMICS
Degrees: Bachelor's, first professional, master's, post-bachelor's certificate, post-master's certificate. **Classes:** Most classes have 20–29 students. Most lab/discussion sessions have 20–29 students. **Majors with Highest Enrollment:** Biology/biological sciences; political science and government; psychology. **Special Study Options:** Accelerated program, cooperative education program, cross-registration, distance learning, double major, dual enrollment, English as a Second Language (ESL), exchange student program (domestic), external degree program, honors program, independent study, internships, liberal arts/career combination, student-designed major, study abroad, teacher certification

program. **Honors programs:** Honors Program in General Education provides small courses with outstanding faculty. The University Scholars program provides an elite group of students with exceptional academic and research opportunities in a dynamic community of learners. **Combined degree programs:** BS/MS. Special programs offered to physically disabled students include note-taking services, reader services, tape recorders **Career services:** Alumni network, alumni services, career/job search classes, career assessment, internships, regional alumni. **Career services highlights include:** Current initiative to increase student uptake of federal government internship opportunities (Federal Student Career Experience Program—SCEP). Students enroll for SCEP positions through Mason's Cooperative Education program. Cooperative Education employs students in the DC metro area and adds value to student degree. Internships can be taken in concert with Co-op or stand alone.

FACILITIES

Housing: Coed dorms, special housing for disabled students, men's dorms, women's dorms, apartments for single students. 95% of campus accessible to physically disabled. **Special Academic Facilities/Equipment:** Center for the Arts, science/technology building, television studio, art galleries in Mason Hall and Johnson Center, astronomy observatory, Smithsonian Conservation and Research Center. **Computers:** 30% of classrooms, 100% of dorms, 100% of libraries, 100% of dining areas, 100% of student union, 5% of common outdoor areas have wireless network access. Students can register for classes online. Administrative functions (other than registration) can be performed online.

CAMPUS LIFE

Environment: City. **Activities:** Choral groups, concert band, dance, drama/theater, jazz band, literary magazine, music ensembles, musical theater, opera, pep band, radio station, student government, student newspaper, student-run film society, symphony orchestra, television station, yearbook, campus ministries, international student organization. **Organizations:** 250 registered organizations, 7 honor societies, 29 religious organizations. 22 fraternities, 13 sororities. **Athletics (Intercollegiate):** *Men:* Baseball, basketball, cheerleading, cross-country, diving, golf, soccer, swimming, tennis, track/field (outdoor), track/field (indoor), volleyball, wrestling. *Women:* Basketball, cheerleading, crew/rowing, cross-country, diving, lacrosse, soccer, softball, swimming, tennis, track/field (outdoor), track/field (indoor), volleyball. **On-Campus Highlights:** Johnson Center, Aquatic and Fitness Center, Center for the Arts, Patriot Center, Freedom Aquatic Center at Prince William. **Environmental Initiatives:** Climate neutrality: Have committed to the American College and University Presidents Climate Commitment. A team is currently working on producing a baseline emissions inventory for all campuses, and will produce a climate action plan by September 2009 for our approach and timeline to climate neutrality. Currently examining various interim options for reducing emissions through energy service company contracts, building contracts, and through student research. Built **Environment:** Have committed all new buildings to be built to the USGBC LEED Silver standard, and have 6 registered projects in the queue for certification at this time. LEED standards are being worked into our Design Manual guidelines for all contractors. Transportation: Have put in place multiple shuttles to the metro and to off-campus lots; provide transportation credits to employees; free local bus rides to all Mason ID holders; bike committee examining ways to increase cycling accessibility on campus; Bike to Mason day on Earth Day being planned; van pool is offered to employees coming in from far away at a reduced monthly cost versus driving and parking; rideshare and carpooling is being promoted. Mason also offers Gunston's Go-Bus, a social shuttle service provided free to all Mason community members who travel to local establishments.

ADMISSIONS

Freshman Academic Profile: Average high school GPA 3.48. 18% in top 10% of high school class, 52% in top 25% of high school class, 93% in top 50% of high school class. 86% from public high schools. SAT Math middle 50% range 520–610. SAT Critical Reading middle 50% range 500–600. ACT middle 50% range 22–26. Minimum paper TOEFL 570. Minimum computer TOEFL 230. Minimum web-based TOEFL 88. **Basis for Candidate Selection:** *Very important factors considered include:* Academic GPA, rigor of secondary school record. *Important factors considered include:* Class rank, application essay, recommendation(s), alumni/ae relation, character/personal qualities, talent/ability. *Other factors considered include:* Standardized test scores, extracurricular activities, first generation, level of applicant's interest, volunteer work, work experience. **Freshman Admission Requirements:** High school diploma is required and GED is accepted. *Academic units required:* 4 English, 3 mathematics, 3 science, (3 science labs), 2 foreign language, 3 social studies, 3 academic electives. *Academic units recommended:* 4 English, 4 mathematics, 4 science, (4 science labs), 3 foreign language, 4 social studies, 5 academic electives. **Freshman Admission Statistics:** 12,943 applied, 63% admitted, 32% enrolled. **Transfer Admission Requirements:** College transcript(s), minimum college GPA of 2.0 required. Lowest grade transferable C. **General Admission Information:** Application fee $70. Regular application deadline 1/15. Regular notification 4/1. Nonfall registration accepted. Admission may be deferred

for a maximum of one semester. Credit and/or placement offered for CEEB Advanced Placement tests.

COSTS AND FINANCIAL AID

Annual in-state tuition $5,640. Annual out-of-state tuition $20,736. Room and board $7,700. Required fees $2,384. Average book expense $900. **Required Forms and Deadlines:** FAFSA. Priority financial aid filing date 3/1. **Notification of Awards:** Applicants will be notified of awards on a rolling basis beginning 4/1. **Types of Aid:** *Need-based scholarships/grants:* Federal Pell, SEOG, state scholarships/grants, private scholarships, the school's own gift aid, Federal ACG and SMART Grants. *Loans:* FFEL Subsidized Stafford, FFEL Unsubsidized Stafford, FFEL PLUS, Federal Perkins, Federal Nursing **Student Employment:** Federal Work-Study Program available. Institutional employment available. Highest amount earned per year from on-campus jobs $7,200. Off-campus job opportunities are excellent. **Financial Aid Statistics:** 32% freshmen, 29% undergrads receive need-based scholarship or grant aid. 12% freshmen, 6% undergrads receive non-need-based scholarship or grant aid. 32% freshmen, 31% undergrads receive need-based self-help aid. 2% freshmen, 2% undergrads receive athletic scholarships. 63.9% freshmen, 51.6% undergrads receive any aid. 54% undergrads borrow to pay for school. Average cumulative indebtedness $18,547. **Criteria for awarding institutional aid:** *Non-need-based:* Academics, athletics, minority status, music/drama, state/district residency.

THE GEORGE WASHINGTON UNIVERSITY

2121 Eye Street NW, Suite 201, Washington, DC 20052
Phone: 202-994-6040
E-mail: gwadm@gwu.edu **CEEB Code:** 5246
Fax: 202-994-0325 **Website:** www.gwu.edu **ACT Code:** 664

This private school was founded in 1821. It has a 45-acre campus.

RATINGS
Admissions Selectivity Rating: 96   **Fire Safety Rating:** 60*   **Green Rating:** 90

STUDENTS AND FACULTY
Enrollment: 10,225. **Student Body:** 56% female, 44% male, 99% out-of-state, 6% international (101 countries represented). Asian 11%, African American 7%, Caucasian 55%, Hispanic 7%, Native American 1%.
Retention and Graduation: 76% freshmen graduate within 4 years. 19% grads go on to further study within 1 year. 7% grads pursue arts and sciences degrees. 6% grads pursue law degrees. 2% grads pursue business degrees. 4% grads pursue medical degrees. **Faculty:** Student/faculty ratio 12:1. 903 full-time faculty, 92% hold PhDs, 20% are members of minority groups, 37% are women. 3% of classes are taught by teaching assistants.

ACADEMICS
Degrees: Associate, bachelor's, certificate, master's, post-bachelor's certificate, post-master's certificate. **Classes:** Most classes have 10–19 students. Most lab/discussion sessions have 20–29 students. **Majors with Highest Enrollment:** Business administration and management; international relations and affairs; liberal arts and sciences/liberal studies. **Special Study Options:** Accelerated program, cooperative education program, cross-registration, distance learning, double major, dual enrollment, honors program, independent study, internships, liberal arts/career combination, student-designed major, study abroad. **Combined degree programs:** BA/MD, BA/JD, BA/MA. Special programs offered to physically disabled students include note-taking services, reader services, tape recorders, tutors.

FACILITIES
Housing: Coed dorms, fraternity/sorority housing, apartments for single students, theme housing. **Special Academic Facilities/Equipment:** Art gallery, language lab, word processing center. **Computers:** Students can register for classes online. Administrative functions (other than registration) can be performed online.

CAMPUS LIFE
Environment: Metropolis. **Activities:** Choral groups, concert band, dance, drama/theater, jazz band, literary magazine, marching band, music ensembles, musical theater, pep band, radio station, student government, student newspaper, student-run film society, television station, yearbook, international student organization, Model UN. **Organizations:** 220 registered organizations, 3

honor societies, 5 religious organizations. 12 fraternities, 9 sororities. **Athletics (Intercollegiate): Men:** Baseball, basketball, crew/rowing, cross-country, diving, fencing, golf, rugby, soccer, squash, swimming, tennis, water polo. **Women:** Basketball, crew/rowing, cross-country, fencing, gymnastics, soccer, swimming, tennis, volleyball. **On-Campus Highlights:** The Smith Center, The Hippo, Media and Public Affairs Building, Kogan Plaza, Gelman Library.

ADMISSIONS

Freshman Academic Profile: 67% in top 10% of high school class, 93% in top 25% of high school class, 100% in top 50% of high school class. 70% from public high schools. SAT Math middle 50% range 600–690. SAT Critical Reading middle 50% range 600–690. SAT Writing middle 50% range 600–690. ACT middle 50% range 27–30. Minimum paper TOEFL 550. Minimum computer TOEFL 300. **Basis for Candidate Selection:** *Very important factors considered include:* Academic GPA, rigor of secondary school record. *Important factors considered include:* Class rank, application essay, recommendation(s), standardized test scores, extracurricular activities, interview, talent/ability, volunteer work. *Other factors considered include:* Alumni/ae relation, character/personal qualities, first generation, geographical residence, level of applicant's interest, racial/ethnic status, work experience. **Freshman Admission Requirements:** High school diploma is required and GED is not accepted. *Academic units required:* 4 English, 2 mathematics, 2 science, (1 science labs), 2 foreign language, 2 social studies. *Academic units recommended:* 4 English, 4 mathematics, 4 science, 4 foreign language, 4 social studies. **Freshman Admission Statistics:** 19,842 applied, 37% admitted, 36% enrolled. **Transfer Admission Requirements:** High school transcript, college transcript(s), essay or personal statement, standardized test scores, Lowest grade transferable C. **General Admission Information:** Application fee $65. Early decision application deadline 11/10. Regular application deadline 1/10. Regular notification 4/1. Nonfall registration accepted. Credit and/or placement offered for CEEB Advanced Placement tests.

COSTS AND FINANCIAL AID

Required Forms and Deadlines: FAFSA, CSS/Financial Aid PROFILE Financial aid filing deadline 2/1. Priority financial aid filing date 2/1. **Notification of Awards:** Applicants will be notified of awards on a rolling basis beginning 3/24. **Types of Aid:** *Need-based scholarships/grants:* Federal Pell, SEOG, state scholarships/grants, the school's own gift aid. *Loans:* FFEL Subsidized Stafford, FFEL Unsubsidized Stafford, FFEL PLUS, Federal Perkins. **Student Employment:** Federal Work-Study Program available. Institutional employment available. Highest amount earned per year from on-campus jobs $3,160. Off-campus job opportunities are excellent. **Financial Aid Statistics:** 38% freshmen, 38% undergrads receive need-based scholarship or grant aid. 11% freshmen, 9% undergrads receive non-need-based scholarship or grant aid. 33% freshmen, 33% undergrads receive need-based self-help aid. 2% freshmen, 2% undergrads receive athletic scholarships. 47% undergrads borrow to pay for school. Average cumulative indebtedness $31,299. **Criteria for awarding institutional aid:** *Non-need-based:* Academics, art, athletics, music/drama.

GEORGETOWN COLLEGE

400 East College Street, Georgetown, KY 40324
Phone: 502-863-8009 **Financial Aid Phone:** 502-863-8027
E-mail: admissions@georgetowncollege.edu **CEEB Code:** 1249
Fax: 502-868-7733 **Website:** www.georgetowncollege.edu **ACT Code:** 1514

This private school was founded in 1787. It has a 104-acre campus.

RATINGS
Admissions Selectivity Rating: 80   **Fire Safety Rating:** 70   **Green Rating:** 71

STUDENTS AND FACULTY
Enrollment: 1,297. **Student Body:** 56% female, 44% male, 15% out-of-state, 1% international (11 countries represented). African American 7%, Caucasian 90%, Hispanic 1%.
Retention and Graduation: 79% freshmen return for sophomore year. 49% freshmen graduate within 4 years. 79% grads go on to further study within 1 year. **Faculty:** Student/faculty ratio 11:1. 110 full-time faculty, 95% hold PhDs, 6% are members of minority groups, 42% are women.

ACADEMICS
Degrees: Bachelor's, master's. **Classes:** Most classes have 20–29 students. Most lab/discussion sessions have 10–19 students. **Majors with Highest Enrollment:** Business/commerce; communication and media studies, other; psychology. **Special Study Options:** Accelerated program, cooperative education program, double major, dual enrollment, honors program, independent study, internships, liberal arts/career combination, student-designed major, study abroad, teacher certification program. **Honors programs:** Georgetown

College Academic Honors Program. Special programs offered to physically disabled students include note-taking services, reader services, tape recorders, tutors. **Career services:** Alumni network, alumni services, career/job search classes, career assessment, internships, regional alumni.

FACILITIES

Housing: Men's dorms, women's dorms, fraternity/sorority housing, Apartments for upper classmen. **Special Academic Facilities/Equipment:** To name only some: the Anna Ashcraft Ensor Learning Resource Center, an arboretum, three antebellum buildings, the Asher Science Center, the Anne Wright Wilson fine arts Building, and the Wilson Laboratory Theatre. **Computers:** 10% of classrooms, 60% of dorms, 90% of libraries, 100% of dining areas, 100% of student union, have wireless network access. Students can register for classes online. Administrative functions (other than registration) can be performed online.

CAMPUS LIFE

Environment: Town. **Activities:** Choral groups, concert band, dance, drama/theater, literary magazine, music ensembles, musical theater, pep band, radio station, student government, student newspaper, yearbook, campus ministries. **Organizations:** 110 registered organizations, 20 honor societies, 8 religious organizations. 5 fraternities, 4 sororities. **Athletics (Intercollegiate): Men:** Baseball, basketball, cross-country, football, golf, soccer, tennis, track/field (outdoor), track/field (indoor). **Women:** Basketball, cheerleading, cross-country, golf, soccer, softball, tennis, track/field (outdoor), track/field (indoor), volleyball. **On-Campus Highlights:** The Ensor Learning Resource Center, Starbucks—in the Learning Resource Center, The Grille. **Environmental Initiatives:** Student led "Green Team:" sustainability themed student activities.

ADMISSIONS

Freshman Academic Profile: Average high school GPA 3.48. 31% in top 10% of high school class, 60% in top 25% of high school class, 93% in top 50% of high school class. 88% from public high schools. SAT Math middle 50% range 480–560. SAT Critical Reading middle 50% range 430–570. ACT middle 50% range 21–26. Minimum paper TOEFL 520. Minimum computer TOEFL 190. Minimum web-based TOEFL 68. **Basis for Candidate Selection:** *Very important factors considered include:* Academic GPA, rigor of secondary school record. *Important factors considered include:* Class rank, recommendation(s), standardized test scores, character/personal qualities, extracurricular activities, talent/ability. *Other factors considered include:* Application essay, alumni/ae relation, geographical residence, interview, level of applicant's interest, religious affiliation/commitment, state residency, volunteer work. **Freshman Admission Requirements:** High school diploma is required and GED is accepted. *Academic units recommended:* 4 English, 3 mathematics, 3 science, 2 foreign language, 2 social studies. **Freshman Admission Statistics:** 1,720 applied, 79% admitted, 28% enrolled. **Transfer Admission Requirements:** High school transcript, college transcript(s), statement of good standing from prior institution(s). Minimum college GPA of 2.5 required. Lowest grade transferable C. **General Admission Information:** Application fee $30. Regular application deadline 8/1. Notification on a rolling basis, beginning on or about 10/1. Nonfall registration accepted. Admission may be deferred for a maximum of 1 year. Credit and/or placement offered for CEEB Advanced Placement tests.

COSTS AND FINANCIAL AID

Annual tuition $26,080. Room and board $7,030. Average book expense $1,250. **Required Forms and Deadlines:** FAFSA, institution's own financial aid form. Financial aid filing deadline 3/15. Priority financial aid filing date 2/15. **Notification of Awards:** Applicants will be notified of awards on a rolling basis beginning 3/15. **Types of Aid:** *Need-based scholarships/grants:* Federal Pell, SEOG, state scholarships/grants, private scholarships, the school's own gift aid. *Loans:* FFEL Subsidized Stafford, FFEL Unsubsidized Stafford, FFEL PLUS, Federal Perkins, college/university loans from institutional funds. **Student Employment:** Federal Work-Study Program available. Institutional employment available. Highest amount earned per year from on-campus jobs $2,500. Off-campus job opportunities are good. **Financial Aid Statistics:** 82% freshmen, 77% undergrads receive need-based scholarship or grant aid. 17% freshmen, 12% undergrads receive non-need-based scholarship or grant aid. 59% freshmen, 56% undergrads receive need-based self-help aid. 6% freshmen, 7% undergrads receive athletic scholarships. 100% freshmen, 99% undergrads receive any aid. 76% undergrads borrow to pay for school. Average cumulative indebtedness $24,462. **Criteria for awarding institutional aid:** *Non-need-based:* Academics, alumni affiliation, art, athletics, leadership, minority status, music/drama, religious affiliation, state/district residency.

GEORGETOWN UNIVERSITY

Best 373

37th and O Streets, NW, 103 White-Graven, Washington, DC 20057
Phone: 202-687-3600 **Financial Aid Phone:** 202-687-4547
CEEB Code: 5244
Fax: 202-687-5084 **Website:** www.georgetown.edu **ACT Code:** 668

This private school, affiliated with the Roman Catholic Church, was founded in 1789. It has a 104-acre campus.

RATINGS
Admissions Selectivity Rating: 98   **Fire Safety Rating:** 91   **Green Rating:** 90

STUDENTS AND FACULTY
Enrollment: 6,692. **Student Body:** 54% female, 46% male, 97% out-of-state, 5% international (138 countries represented). Asian 10%, African American 7%, Caucasian 68%, Hispanic 7%.
Retention and Graduation: 90% freshmen graduate within 4 years. **Faculty:** Student/faculty ratio 11:1. 845 full-time faculty, 89% hold PhDs, 15% are members of minority groups, 38% are women. 8% of classes are taught by teaching assistants.

ACADEMICS
Degrees: Bachelor's, certificate, first professional, master's. **Majors with Highest Enrollment:** English language and literature; international relations and affairs; political science and government. **Special Study Options:** Cross-registration, double major, English as a Second Language (ESL), honors program, independent study, internships, student-designed major, study abroad **Honors programs:** The John Carroll Programs guide and support a highly selective group of academically talented and ambitious students from around the world. The Programs seek individuals who desire to make a lasting difference in the fields and communities they touch. For these young men and women, the Programs provide models and skills to help them make the most effective use of their undergraduate years, and to assists them in moving from the undergraduate experience to their post-graduate academic and professional lives. The Programs invite students to take as their own the Carroll motto, mentis vita pro vita mundi: the life of the mind for the life of the world. **Combined degree programs:** BA/MA. Special programs offered to physically disabled students include note-taking services, reader services, tape recorders, tutors. **Career services:** Alumni network, alumni services, career/job search classes, career assessment, internships, regional alumni.

FACILITIES
Housing: Coed dorms, special housing for disabled students, apartments for single students, freshmen and sophomores are required to live on campus. 92% of campus accessible to physically disabled. **Special Academic Facilities/Equipment:** Language lab, seismological observatory. **Computers:** Students can register for classes online. Administrative functions (other than registration) can be performed online.

CAMPUS LIFE
Environment: Metropolis. **Activities:** Choral groups, concert band, dance, drama/theater, jazz band, literary magazine, music ensembles, musical theater, pep band, radio station, student government, student newspaper, student-run film society, symphony orchestra, television station, yearbook. **Organizations:** 139 registered organizations, 14 honor societies, 20 religious organizations. **Athletics (Intercollegiate):** *Men:* Baseball, basketball, crew/rowing, cross-country, diving, football, golf, lacrosse, sailing, soccer, swimming, tennis, track/field (outdoor), track/field (indoor). *Women:* Basketball, crew/rowing, cross-country, diving, field hockey, golf, lacrosse, sailing, soccer, softball, swimming, tennis, track/field (outdoor), track/field (indoor), volleyball. **On-Campus Highlights:** Yates Field House, Uncommon Grounds, The Observatory, The Quadrangle, Healy Hall. **Environmental Initiatives:** Set LEED certification as the standard for new constructions & major renovations. Implemented energy construction programs in utility operations. Expanded recycling program to include construction waste

ADMISSIONS
Freshman Academic Profile: 45.5% from public high schools. SAT Math middle 50% range 660–750. SAT Critical Reading middle 50% range 650–740. ACT middle 50% range 26–33. Minimum paper TOEFL 200. **Basis for Candidate Selection:** *Very important factors considered include:* Class rank, application essay, academic GPA, recommendation(s), rigor of secondary school record, standardized test scores, character/personal qualities, talent/ability. *Important factors considered include:* Extracurricular activities, interview, volunteer work. *Other factors considered include:* Alumni/ae relation, geographical residence, racial/ethnic status, state residency, work experience. **Freshman Admission Requirements:** High school diploma is required and GED is accepted. *Academic units recommended:* 4 English, 2 mathematics, 1 science, 2 foreign language, 2 social studies, 2 history. **Freshman Admission Statistics:** 18,696 applied, 19% admitted, 45% enrolled. **Transfer Admission Requirements:** High school transcript, college transcript(s), essay or personal statement, standardized test scores, statement of good standing from prior institution(s). Minimum college GPA of 3.0 required. Lowest grade transferable C. **General Admission Information:** Application fee $65. Regular application deadline 1/10. Regular notification 4/1. Nonfall registration not accepted. Admission may be deferred for a maximum of 1 year. Credit and/or placement offered for CEEB Advanced Placement tests.

COSTS AND FINANCIAL AID
Annual tuition $38,616. Room and board $13,125. Required fees $420. Average book expense $1,160. **Required Forms and Deadlines:** FAFSA, CSS/Financial Aid PROFILE, noncustodial PROFILE, business/farm supplement, tax returns. Financial aid filing deadline 2/1. Priority financial aid filing date 2/1. **Notification of Awards:** Applicants will be notified of awards on or about 4/1. **Types of Aid:** *Need-based scholarships/grants:* Federal Pell, SEOG, state scholarships/grants, private scholarships, the school's own gift aid. *Loans:* FFEL Subsidized Stafford, FFEL Unsubsidized Stafford, FFEL PLUS, Federal Perkins, Federal Nursing, alternative loans. **Student Employment:** Federal Work-Study Program available. Institutional employment available. Off-campus job opportunities are excellent. **Financial Aid Statistics:** 40% freshmen, 37% undergrads receive need-based scholarship or grant aid. 8% freshmen, 7% undergrads receive non-need-based scholarship or grant aid. 38% freshmen, 36% undergrads receive need-based self-help aid. 5% freshmen, 4% undergrads receive athletic scholarships. 40.22% freshmen, 38.55% undergrads receive any aid. 44% undergrads borrow to pay for school. Average cumulative indebtedness $23,333. **Criteria for awarding institutional aid:** *Non-need-based:* Athletics.

GEORGIA COLLEGE & STATE UNIVERSITY

Campus Box 23, Milledgeville, GA 31061
Phone: 478-445-1283 **Financial Aid Phone:** 478-445-5149
E-mail: admissions@gcsu.edu **CEEB Code:** 5252
Fax: 478-445-1914 **Website:** www.gcsu.edu **ACT Code:** 828

This public school was founded in 1889. It has a 590-acre campus.

RATINGS
Admissions Selectivity Rating: 82   **Fire Safety Rating:** 96   **Green Rating:** 71

STUDENTS AND FACULTY
Enrollment: 5,603. **Student Body:** 60% female, 40% male, 2% out-of-state, 2% international (53 countries represented). Asian 1%, African American 6%, Caucasian 86%, Hispanic 3%.
Retention and Graduation: 84% freshmen return for sophomore year. 25% freshmen graduate within 4 years. **Faculty:** Student/faculty ratio 17:1. 301 full-time faculty.

ACADEMICS
Degrees: Bachelor's, master's, post-master's certificate. **Classes:** Most classes have 20–29 students. Most lab/discussion sessions have 20–29 students. **Majors with Highest Enrollment:** Business/commerce; marketing/marketing management; psychology. **Special Study Options:** Accelerated program, distance learning, double major, English as a Second Language (ESL), honors program, independent study, internships, study abroad, teacher certification program **Honors programs:** Honors and/or Scholars Program. Special programs offered to physically disabled students include note-taking services, reader services, tape recorders, tutors. **Career services:** Alumni network, career/job search classes, career assessment, internships

FACILITIES
Housing: Coed dorms, special housing for international students, apartments for single students, theme housing. 90% of campus accessible to physically disabled. **Special Academic Facilities/Equipment:** Education archives museum, old governor's mansion, Museum of fine arts, Natural History Museum and Planetarium. **Computers:** 98% of classrooms, 98% of dorms, 100% of libraries, 98% of dining areas, 100% of student union, 100% of common outdoor areas have wireless network access. Students can register for classes online. Administrative functions (other than registration) can be performed online.

CAMPUS LIFE
Environment: Town. **Activities:** Choral groups, concert band, dance, drama/theater, jazz band, literary magazine, music ensembles, musical theater, radio

station, student government, student newspaper, television station, campus ministries, international student organization. **Organizations:** 238 registered organizations, 8 religious organizations. 8 fraternities, 6 sororities. **Athletics (Intercollegiate):** *Men:* Baseball, basketball, cross-country, golf, tennis. *Women:* Basketball, cross-country, softball, speed skating, tennis. **On-Campus Highlights:** The Depot (Wellness Center), The Centennial Center (Gymnasium), Cafeteria, Library and Information Technology Center.

ADMISSIONS

Freshman Academic Profile: Average high school GPA 3.31. SAT Math middle 50% range 520–600. SAT Critical Reading middle 50% range 520–600. SAT Writing middle 50% range 510–600. ACT middle 50% range 22–25. Minimum paper TOEFL 500. Minimum computer TOEFL 173. Minimum web-based TOEFL 61. **Basis for Candidate Selection:** *Very important factors considered include:* Academic GPA, rigor of secondary school record, standardized test scores. *Important factors considered include:* Class rank, application essay, recommendation(s), extracurricular activities, talent/ability. *Other factors considered include:* Alumni/ae relation, character/personal qualities, first generation, geographical residence, level of applicant's interest, racial/ethnic status, state residency, volunteer work, work experience. **Freshman Admission Requirements:** High school diploma is required and GED is accepted. *Academic units required:* 4 English, 4 mathematics, 3 science, (2 science labs), 2 foreign language, 3 social studies. **Freshman Admission Statistics:** 4,080 applied, 62% admitted, 48% enrolled. **Transfer Admission Requirements:** College transcript(s), statement of good standing from prior institution(s). Minimum college GPA of 2.0 required. **General Admission Information:** Application fee $40. Regular application deadline 4/1. Nonfall registration accepted. Admission may be deferred for a maximum of 1 year. Credit offered for CEEB Advanced Placement tests.

COSTS AND FINANCIAL AID

Annual in-state tuition $4,520. Annual out-of-state tuition $18,076. Room and board $8,228. Required fees $1,218. Average book expense $1,100. **Required Forms and Deadlines:** FAFSA. Priority financial aid filing date 3/1. **Notification of Awards:** Applicants will be notified of awards on a rolling basis beginning 3/1. **Types of Aid:** *Need-based scholarships/grants:* Federal Pell, SEOG, state scholarships/grants, private scholarships, the school's own gift aid. *Loans:* Direct PLUS, FFEL Subsidized Stafford, FFEL Unsubsidized Stafford, FFEL PLUS, Federal Perkins, state loans. **Student Employment:** Federal Work-Study Program available. Institutional employment available. Highest amount earned per year from on-campus jobs $6,812. Off-campus job opportunities are good. **Financial Aid Statistics:** 11% freshmen, 15% undergrads receive need-based scholarship or grant aid. 34% freshmen, 35% undergrads receive non-need-based scholarship or grant aid. 18% freshmen, 24% undergrads receive need-based self-help aid. 3% freshmen, 3% undergrads receive athletic scholarships. 52% undergrads borrow to pay for school. Average cumulative indebtedness $14,312. **Criteria for awarding institutional aid:** *Non-need-based:* Academics, alumni affiliation, art, athletics, leadership, music/drama, state/district residency.

See page 1098.

GEORGIA INSTITUTE OF TECHNOLOGY

Georgia Institute of Technology, Atlanta, GA 30332-0320
Phone: 404-894-4154 **Financial Aid Phone:** 404-894-4160
E-mail: admission@gatech.edu **CEEB Code:** 5248
Fax: 404-894-9511 **Website:** www.gatech.edu **ACT Code:** 818

This public school was founded in 1885. It has a 450-acre campus.

RATINGS

Admissions Selectivity Rating: 95   **Fire Safety Rating:** 87   **Green Rating:** 99

STUDENTS AND FACULTY

Enrollment: 12,942. **Student Body:** 30% female, 70% male, 27% out-of-state, 6% international (68 countries represented). Asian 17%, African American 6%, Caucasian 63%, Hispanic 4%.
Retention and Graduation: 93% freshmen return for sophomore year. 31% freshmen graduate within 4 years. 23.1% grads go on to further study within 1 year. 13.7% grads pursue arts and sciences degrees. 1.7% grads pursue law degrees. 0.5% grads pursue business degrees. 4% grads pursue medical degrees.
Faculty: Student/faculty ratio 20:1. 939 full-time faculty, 97% hold PhDs, 27%

are members of minority groups, 20% are women. 3% of classes are taught by teaching assistants.

ACADEMICS

Degrees: Bachelor's, master's. **Classes:** Most classes have 20–29 students. Most lab/discussion sessions have 20–29 students. **Majors with Highest Enrollment:** Business administration and management; industrial engineering; mechanical engineering. **Special Study Options:** Accelerated program, cooperative education program, cross-registration, distance learning, double major, dual enrollment, English as a Second Language (ESL), honors program, independent study, internships, student-designed major, study abroad, Dual degree program (3-2); Regent's Engineering Transfer Program with 14 colleges in the University System of Georgia; Georgia Tech Regional Engineering Program (GTREP) offers undergraduate and graduate Engineering degrees in collaboration with Armstrong Atlantic state University, Georgia Southern University, and Savannah State University. **Honors programs:** The Georgia Tech Honors Program combines the challenging academic standards of one of the finest technological universities in the world with the closer connections between students and faculty that one might expect to find in a smaller college. Our mission is to create a lively environment in which students and faculty members learn from each other through a common commitment to intellectual inquiry, careful analysis, and energetic exchange of ideas. To promote and sustain this close engagement between students and faculty, the Honors Program will offer unique opportunities to students in the first two years of their studies at Georgia Tech: 1) An Honors Program Residence where first-year students can find a supportive community of interesting people, continue their conversations beyond the classroom, and develop connections to Georgia Tech and the surrounding community; 2) Small sections of introductory core courses designed to emphasize not just mastery of the material, but innovative inquiry and exploration within the discipline and often beyond; 3) A selection of small special topics courses, each with an enrollment limit of twenty HP students, that encourage critical thinking and an interdisciplinary approach to some of the most significant issues facing the world today; 4) A program of well-coordinated advising that will help students build upon their first two years in the Honors Program as they move into their chosen undergraduate majors in the third and fourth years. **Combined degree programs:** BS/MS, BS/MCRP. Special programs offered to physically disabled students include note-taking services, reader services, tape recorders, tutors. **Career services:** Alumni network, alumni services, career/job search classes, career assessment, internships, regional alumni. **Career services highlights include:** With more than 2,700 students participating, Georgia Tech's co-op program is currently the largest optional co-op program in the United States and has perennially been listed in *U.S. News & World Report* as one of the "Top Ten" co-op programs in America.

FACILITIES

Housing: Coed dorms, special housing for disabled students, men's dorms, special housing for international students, women's dorms, fraternity/sorority housing, apartments for married students, apartments for single students, theme housing. First Year housing is guaranteed to all new freshman and transfer students who submit an application by May 1. 75% of campus accessible to physically disabled. **Special Academic Facilities/Equipment:** Nuclear Magnetic Resonance Spectroscopy Center, Georgia Tech Research Institute, Ovarian Cancer Institute, Paper Museum, Mechanical Properties Research Laboratory with scanning electron microscope, Virtual Factory Laboratory, Ferris-Goldsmith Trading Floor, Advanced Technology Development Center, Klaus Advanced Computing Building, Electron Microscope, Marcus Nanotechnology Research Center, Solar Decathlon House at College of Architecture, Wind Tunnel, GT Smart House, Clough Undergraduates Learning Commons (under construction). **Computers:** 100% of classrooms, 100% of dorms, 100% of libraries, 100% of dining areas, 100% of student union, 65% of common outdoor areas have wireless network access. Students can register for classes online. Administrative functions (other than registration) can be performed online. Undergraduates are required to own a computer.

CAMPUS LIFE

Environment: Metropolis. **Activities:** Choral groups, concert band, dance, drama/theater, jazz band, literary magazine, marching band, music ensembles, musical theater, pep band, radio station, student government, student newspaper, student-run film society, symphony orchestra, television station, yearbook, campus ministries, international student organization, Model UN. **Organizations:** 429 registered organizations, 24 honor societies, 39 religious organizations. 38 fraternities, 14 sororities. **Athletics (Intercollegiate):** *Men:* Baseball, basketball, cheerleading, cross-country, diving, football, golf, swimming, tennis, track/field (outdoor), track/field (indoor). *Women:* Basketball, cheerleading, cross-country, diving, softball, swimming, tennis, track/field (outdoor), track/field (indoor), volleyball. **On-Campus Highlights:** Tech Square—Bookstore/Hotel/College of, Olympic Aquatic Center/Campus Recreation, The Hill/Tech Tower, Student Center Commons and the Library W, Ferst Center for the Arts. **Environmental Initiatives:** Education: Over 260 courses across all colleges with a goal of having every student who graduates have at least one sustainability course(23 degree programs in the undergraduate and graduate levels, many continuing eduation and certificate programs also focus on sustainability and major areas of sustainability). Research: Institute of Sustainable Systems Strategic Energy Institute—alternative energy and energy efficiency focus Sustainable Design and Manufacturing Center—21 Endowed Chairs and 23 Research Centers that include significant components or a sustainability focus. Green Campus as Role model: 1. Recycling 2. Transportation 3. Green building (new & renovations/retrofits).

ADMISSIONS

Freshman Academic Profile: Average high school GPA 3.81. 80.55% in top 10% of high school class, 95.18% in top 25% of high school class, 99.65% in top 50% of high school class. 86.4% from public high schools. SAT Math middle 50% range 650–750. SAT Critical Reading middle 50% range 580–680. SAT Writing middle 50% range 580–670. ACT middle 50% range 27–31. **Basis for Candidate Selection:** *Very important factors considered include:* Academic GPA, rigor of secondary school record, extracurricular activities. *Important factors considered include:* Application essay, standardized test scores, character/personal qualities, geographical residence, state residency, talent/ability, volunteer work, work experience. *Other factors considered include:* Alumni/ae relation, racial/ethnic status. **Freshman Admission Requirements:** High school diploma is required and GED is accepted. *Academic units required:* 4 English, 4 mathematics, 3 science, (3 science labs), 2 foreign language, 3 social studies. **Freshman Admission Statistics:** 11,432 applied, 59% admitted, 40% enrolled. **Transfer Admission Requirements:** College transcript(s), statement of good standing from prior institution(s). Minimum college GPA of 2.7 required. Lowest grade transferable C. **General Admission Information:** Application fee $65. Regular application deadline 1/15. Regular notification 3/15. Nonfall registration accepted. Credit and/or placement offered for CEEB Advanced Placement tests.

COSTS AND FINANCIAL AID

Required Forms and Deadlines: FAFSA, institution's own financial aid form. Financial aid filing deadline 3/1. Priority financial aid filing date 3/1. **Notification of Awards:** Applicants will be notified of awards on or about 4/1. **Types of Aid:** *Need-based scholarships/grants:* Federal Pell, SEOG, state scholarships/grants, private scholarships, the school's own gift aid. *Loans:* Direct Subsidized Stafford, Direct Unsubsidized Stafford, Direct PLUS, Federal Perkins, college/university loans from institutional funds. **Student Employment:** Federal Work-Study Program available. Institutional employment available. Off-campus job opportunities are excellent. **Financial Aid Statistics:** 31% freshmen, 28% undergrads receive need-based scholarship or grant aid. 26% freshmen, 19% undergrads receive non-need-based scholarship or grant aid. 19% freshmen, 24% undergrads receive need-based self-help aid. 2% freshmen, 2% undergrads receive athletic scholarships. 79% freshmen, 71% undergrads receive any aid. 72% undergrads borrow to pay for school. Average cumulative indebtedness $13,445. **Criteria for awarding institutional aid:** *Non-need-based:* Academics, athletics, leadership, music/drama, state/district residency.

GEORGIA SOUTHERN UNIVERSITY

P.O. Box 8024, Statesboro, GA 30460
Phone: 912-478-5391 **Financial Aid Phone:** 912-478-5413
E-mail: admissions@georgiasouthern.edu **CEEB Code:** 5253
Fax: 912-478-7240 **Website:** www.georgiasouthern.edu **ACT Code:** 830

This public school was founded in 1906. It has a 700-acre campus.

RATINGS
Admissions Selectivity Rating: 79　　**Fire Safety Rating:** 88　　**Green Rating:** 91

STUDENTS AND FACULTY
Enrollment: 15,626. **Student Body:** 48% female, 52% male, 4% out-of-state, 1% international (83 countries represented). Asian 1%, African American 22%, Caucasian 70%, Hispanic 3%.
Retention and Graduation: 81% freshmen return for sophomore year. 17% freshmen graduate within 4 years. 15% grads go on to further study within 1 year. 2% grads pursue law degrees. 12% grads pursue business degrees. 2% grads pursue medical degrees. **Faculty:** Student/faculty ratio 22:1. 728 full-time faculty, 80% hold PhDs, 17% are members of minority groups, 48% are women. 3.9% of classes are taught by teaching assistants.

ACADEMICS
Degrees: Bachelor's, master's, post-master's certificate. **Classes:** Most classes have 20–29 students. Most lab/discussion sessions have 20–29 students. **Majors with Highest Enrollment:** Biology/biological sciences; elementary education and teaching; nursing/registered nurse (RN, ASN, BSN, MSN). **Special Study Options:** Accelerated program, cooperative education program, distance

learning, double major, English as a Second Language (ESL), honors program, independent study, internships, student-designed major, study abroad, teacher certification program. **Honors programs:** Georgia Southern offers University Honors Program (UHP) and 1906 Scholars. The UHP is designed to offer exceptionally able and diligent students the opportunity to enroll in particularly stimulating classes and to integrate their classroom learning with the needs of the community in which they live. The 1906 Scholars, a selective group within the UHP, accepts 15–18 freshmen from the pool of approximately 400 UHP applicants. The program offers interdisciplinary course options. Weekly seminars and colloquia emphasize discussion and independent endeavor, and nurture curiosity and the sharing of ideas among students and faculty. Selected students receive a full tuition scholarship, including out-of-state fees. **Combined degree programs:** Bachelor's/Graduate in accounting and nursing. Special programs offered to physically disabled students include note-taking services, reader services, tape recorders, tutors. **Career services:** Alumni network, alumni services, career/job search classes, career assessment, internships, regional alumni. **Career services highlights include:** Cooperative Education Program.

FACILITIES

Housing: Coed dorms, special housing for disabled students, special housing for international students, apartments for single students, theme housing 97% of campus accessible to physically disabled. **Special Academic Facilities/ Equipment:** Art galleries, teaching museum, performing arts center, wildlife education center, eagle cinema, broadcasting studios, planetarium, botanical garden, radio station, black box theatre, and Recreation Activity Center. **Computers:** 80% of classrooms, 45% of dorms, 100% of libraries, 100% of dining areas, 100% of student union, 20% of common outdoor areas have wireless network access. Students can register for classes online. Administrative functions (other than registration) can be performed online.

CAMPUS LIFE

Environment: Village. **Activities:** Choral groups, concert band, dance, drama/theater, jazz band, literary magazine, marching band, music ensembles, musical theater, pep band, radio station, student government, student newspaper, student-run film society, symphony orchestra, television station, campus ministries, international student organization. **Organizations:** 235 registered organizations, 17 honor societies, 20 religious organizations. 20 fraternities, 9 sororities. **Athletics (Intercollegiate):** *Men:* Baseball, basketball, cheerleading, football, golf, soccer, tennis. *Women:* Basketball, cheerleading, cross-country, diving, soccer, softball, swimming, tennis, track/field (outdoor), volleyball. **On-Campus Highlights:** Russell Union, Recreation Activity Center, Center for Wildlife Education, Georgia Southern Museum, Paulson Stadium, Performing Arts Center, Lamar Q. Ball Raptor Center, Georgia Southern Planetarium, Gallery 303, the Georgia Southern Botanical Gardens, Eagle Cinema, College of Information Technology and Eagle Village. **Environmental Initiatives:** 4 Credit Enviromental science courses requirement for all graduates, Academic and Operations commitment to sustainability with new Academic Center for Sustainablitiy and operations/Enviromental Sustainability Coordinator. LEED-certified building.

ADMISSIONS

Freshman Academic Profile: Average high school GPA 3.15. 14% in top 10% of high school class, 42% in top 25% of high school class, 74% in top 50% of high school class. SAT Math middle 50% range 510–590. SAT Critical Reading middle 50% range 510–580. SAT Writing middle 50% range 480–570. ACT middle 50% range 21–25. Minimum paper TOEFL 523. Minimum computer TOEFL 193. Minimum web-based TOEFL 69. **Basis for Candidate Selection:** *Very important factors considered include:* Academic GPA, rigor of secondary school record, standardized test scores. *Other factors considered include:* Class rank. **Freshman Admission Requirements:** High school diploma is required and GED is not accepted. *Academic units required:* 4 English, 4 mathematics, 3 science, (2 science labs), 2 foreign language, 3 social studies. **Freshman Admission Statistics:** 9,214 applied, 56% admitted, 69% enrolled. **Transfer Admission Requirements:** College transcript(s), statement of good standing from prior institution(s). Minimum college GPA of 2.0 required. Lowest grade transferable D. **General Admission Information:** Application fee $30. Regular application deadline 5/1. Nonfall registration accepted. Admission may be deferred for a maximum of circumstantial. Placement offered for CEEB Advanced Placement tests.

COSTS AND FINANCIAL AID

Annual in-state tuition $3,996. Annual out-of-state tuition $15,972. Room and board $7,900. Required fees $1,644. Average book expense $1,200. **Required Forms and Deadlines:** FAFSA. Priority financial aid filing date 4/20. **Notification of Awards:** Applicants will be notified of awards on a rolling basis beginning 4/20. **Types of Aid:** *Need-based scholarships/grants:* Federal Pell, SEOG, state scholarships/grants, private scholarships, the school's own gift aid, Hope Scholarships, Federal Work Study, TEACH Grant, ACG, SMART Grant. *Loans:* Direct Subsidized Stafford, Direct Unsubsidized Stafford, Direct PLUS, Federal Perkins, state loans, Service-Cancelable State Direct Student Loans,

External Alternative Loans. **Student Employment:** Federal Work-Study Program available. Institutional employment available. Highest amount earned per year from on-campus jobs $2,142. Off-campus job opportunities are excellent. **Financial Aid Statistics:** 44% freshmen, 42% undergrads receive need-based scholarship or grant aid. 5% freshmen, 3% undergrads receive non-need-based scholarship or grant aid. 36% freshmen, 43% undergrads receive need-based self-help aid. 1% freshmen, 1% undergrads receive athletic scholarships. 87% freshmen, 82% undergrads receive any aid. 65% undergrads borrow to pay for school. Average cumulative indebtedness $18,618. **Criteria for awarding institutional aid:** *Non-need-based:* Academics, alumni affiliation, art, athletics, leadership, minority status, music/drama, state/district residency.

GEORGIA SOUTHWESTERN STATE UNIVERSITY

800 Georgia Southwestern State University Dr, Americus, GA 31709-4693
Phone: 912-928-1273 **Financial Aid Phone:** 229-928-1378
E-mail: gswapps@canes.gsw.edu **CEEB Code:** 5250
Fax: 912-931-2983 **Website:** www.gsw.edu **ACT Code:** 824

This public school was founded in 1906. It has a 325-acre campus.

RATINGS
Admissions Selectivity Rating: 72   Fire Safety Rating: 60*   Green Rating: 60*

STUDENTS AND FACULTY
Enrollment: 2,209. **Student Body:** 65% female, 35% male, 4% out-of-state, 2% international (34 countries represented). Asian 1%, African American 31%, Caucasian 62%, Hispanic 1%.
Retention and Graduation: 12% freshmen graduate within 4 years. **Faculty:** Student/faculty ratio 17:1. 92 full-time faculty, 73% hold PhDs, 20% are members of minority groups, 53% are women.

ACADEMICS
Degrees: Bachelor's, master's, post-bachelor's certificate, post-master's certificate. **Classes:** Most classes have 20–29 students. **Majors with Highest Enrollment:** Accounting; business administration and management; elementary education and teaching. **Special Study Options:** Accelerated program, cooperative education program, distance learning, double major, dual enrollment, English as a Second Language (ESL), honors program, internships, study abroad, teacher certification program, Special programs offered to physically disabled students include note-taking services, reader services, tape recorders, tutors.

FACILITIES
Housing: Coed dorms, apartment housing for upperclassmen. 100% of campus accessible to physically disabled. **Special Academic Facilities/Equipment:** Observatory, glass-blowing studio. **Computers:** Students can register for classes online. Administrative functions (other than registration) can be performed online.

CAMPUS LIFE
Environment: Village. **Activities:** Choral groups, concert band, drama/theater, jazz band, literary magazine, music ensembles, musical theater, student government, student newspaper, television station, international student organization. **Organizations:** 12 honor societies, 7 fraternities, 6 sororities. **Athletics (Intercollegiate):** *Men:* Baseball, basketball, golf, soccer, tennis. *Women:* Basketball, cross-country, soccer, softball, tennis.

ADMISSIONS
Freshman Academic Profile: Average high school GPA 3.14. 19% in top 10% of high school class, 46% in top 25% of high school class, 77% in top 50% of high school class. SAT Math middle 50% range 430–530. SAT Critical Reading middle 50% range 440–530. ACT middle 50% range 18–21. Minimum paper TOEFL 523. Minimum computer TOEFL 193. **Basis for Candidate Selection:** *Very important factors considered include:* Academic GPA, rigor of secondary school record, standardized test scores. *Important factors considered include:* Class rank. *Other factors considered include:* Application essay, recommendation(s), extracurricular activities, interview, talent/ability. **Freshman Admission Requirements:** High school diploma is required and GED is accepted. *Academic units required:* 4 English, 4 mathematics, 3 science, (2 science labs), 2 foreign language, 1 social studies, 2 history, 2 academic electives. *Academic units recommended:* 2 academic electives. **Freshman Admission Statistics:** 1,050 applied, 78% admitted, 52% enrolled. **Transfer Admission Requirements:** College transcript(s), minimum college GPA of 2.0 required. Lowest grade transferable D. **General Admission Information:** Application fee $25. Early decision application deadline 12/15. Notification on a rolling basis, beginning on or about 8/1. Nonfall registration accepted. Admission may be deferred for a maximum of 1 year. Credit and/or placement offered for CEEB Advanced Placement tests.

COSTS AND FINANCIAL AID
Average book expense $1,000. **Required Forms and Deadlines:** FAFSA, institution's own financial aid form, state aid form. Financial aid filing deadline 6/1. Priority financial aid filing date 4/1. **Notification of Awards:** Applicants will be notified of awards on a rolling basis beginning 3/1. **Types of Aid:** *Need-based scholarships/grants:* Federal Pell, SEOG, state scholarships/grants, the school's own gift aid. *Loans:* FFEL Subsidized Stafford, FFEL Unsubsidized Stafford, FFEL PLUS, Federal Perkins. **Student Employment:** Federal Work-Study Program available. Institutional employment available. Off-campus job opportunities are fair. **Financial Aid Statistics:** 64% freshmen, 59% undergrads receive any aid. **Criteria for awarding institutional aid:** *Non-need-based:* Academics, athletics, leadership.

GEORGIA STATE UNIVERSITY

PO Box 4009, Atlanta, GA 30302-4009
Phone: 404-651-2365 **Financial Aid Phone:** 404-651-2223
E-mail: admissions@gsu.edu **CEEB Code:** 5251
Fax: 404-651-4811 **Website:** www.gsu.edu **ACT Code:** 826

This public school was founded in 1913. It has a 33-acre campus.

RATINGS
Admissions Selectivity Rating: 79   Fire Safety Rating: 87   Green Rating: 60*

STUDENTS AND FACULTY
Enrollment: 18,478. **Student Body:** 61% female, 39% male, 7% out-of-state, 3% international (159 countries represented). Asian 10%, African American 30%, Caucasian 36%, Hispanic 4%.
Retention and Graduation: 80% freshmen return for sophomore year. 15% freshmen graduate within 4 years. **Faculty:** Student/faculty ratio 17:1. 1046 full-time faculty, 85% hold PhDs, 20% are members of minority groups, 45% are women.

ACADEMICS
Degrees: Bachelor's, certificate, first professional, master's, post-bachelor's certificate, post-master's certificate. **Classes:** Most classes have 20–29 students. **Majors with Highest Enrollment:** Finance; journalism; marketing/marketing management. **Special Study Options:** Accelerated program, cooperative education program, cross-registration, distance learning, double major, dual enrollment, English as a Second Language (ESL), honors program, independent study, internships, student-designed major, study abroad, teacher certification program, Freshman Learning Communities. **Honors programs:** Students have the advantage of small classes and close contact with faculty members. **Combined degree programs:** BA/MA, BA/MIB in French, German or Spanish. Special programs offered to physically disabled students include note-taking services, reader services, tape recorders, tutors.

FACILITIES
Housing: Coed dorms, special housing for disabled students, special housing for international students, apartments for married students, apartments for single students, some arrangments for visiting faculty/scholars. 100% of campus accessible to physically disabled. **Special Academic Facilities/Equipment:** Cartography Production Laboratory, Commuter Student Services, Cooperative Learning Laboratory, Economic Forecasting Center, Ernest G. Welch School of Art and Design Gallery, Instructional Technology Center, James M. Cox, Jr. Multi-Media Instructional Lab and Satellite Downlink Facility, Kopleff Recital Hall,Lanette L. Suttles Child Development Center, Language Acquisition and Resource Center, Mathematics Assistance Complex, Mathematics Interactive Learning Environment, Music Media Center, Rialto Center for the Performing Arts, Small Business Development Center, Visual Resource Center, Writing Studio. **Computers:** Students can register for classes online. Administrative functions (other than registration) can be performed online.

CAMPUS LIFE
Environment: Metropolis. **Activities:** Choral groups, concert band, dance, drama/theater, jazz band, literary magazine, music ensembles, pep band, radio station, student government, student newspaper, student-run film society, television station **Organizations:** 201 registered organizations, 19 honor societies, 21 religious organizations. 9 fraternities, 15 sororities. **Athletics (Intercollegiate):** *Men:* Baseball, basketball, cross-country, golf, soccer, tennis, track/field (outdoor), volleyball. *Women:* Basketball, cross-country, golf, soccer, softball, tennis, track/field (outdoor), volleyball. **On-Campus Highlights:** Recreatoin Center, Student Housing, Aderhold Learning Center, The Rialto Center for the Performing Arts, The Student Center.

ADMISSIONS
Freshman Academic Profile: Average high school GPA 3.33. 93% from public high schools. SAT Math middle 50% range 500–600. SAT Critical Read-

ing middle 50% range 490–590. ACT middle 50% range 20–25. Minimum paper TOEFL 525. Minimum computer TOEFL 213. **Basis for Candidate Selection:** *Very important factors considered include:* Academic GPA, rigor of secondary school record, standardized test scores. *Other factors considered include:* Application essay, recommendation(s), alumni/ae relation, character/personal qualities, extracurricular activities, first generation, geographical residence, interview, level of applicant's interest, state residency, talent/ability, volunteer work, work experience. **Freshman Admission Requirements:** High school diploma is required and GED is not accepted. *Academic units required:* 4 English, 4 mathematics, 3 science, (2 science labs), 2 foreign language, 2 social studies, 1 history. **Freshman Admission Statistics:** 8,346 applied, 52% admitted, 50% enrolled. **Transfer Admission Requirements:** College transcript(s), minimum college GPA of 2.5 required. Lowest grade transferable D. **General Admission Information:** Application fee $50. Regular application deadline 3/1. Notification on a rolling basis, beginning on or about 10/1. Nonfall registration accepted. Admission may be deferred for a maximum of 2 terms. Credit offered for CEEB Advanced Placement tests.

COSTS AND FINANCIAL AID

Required Forms and Deadlines: FAFSA. Financial aid filing deadline 11/1. Priority financial aid filing date 4/1. **Notification of Awards:** Applicants will be notified of awards on a rolling basis beginning 3/30. **Types of Aid:** *Need-based scholarships/grants:* Federal Pell, SEOG, state scholarships/grants, private scholarships, the school's own gift aid. *Loans:* Direct Subsidized Stafford, Direct Unsubsidized Stafford, Direct PLUS, FFEL PLUS, Federal Perkins, state loans **Student Employment:** Federal Work-Study Program available. Institutional employment available. Off-campus job opportunities are good. **Financial Aid Statistics:** 34% freshmen, 39% undergrads receive need-based scholarship or grant aid. 59% freshmen, 60% undergrads receive non-need-based scholarship or grant aid. 9% freshmen, 24% undergrads receive need-based self-help aid. 1% freshmen, 66% freshmen, 42% undergrads receive any aid. **Criteria for awarding institutional aid:** *Non-need-based:* Academics, alumni affiliation, art, athletics, minority status, music/drama, state/district residency.

GEORGIAN COURT UNIVERSITY

900 Lakewood Avenue, Lakewood, NJ 08701-2697
Phone: 732-987-2200 **Financial Aid Phone:** 732-987-2109
E-mail: admissions@georgian.edu **CEEB Code:** 2274
Fax: 732-987-2000 **Website:** www.georgian.edu **ACT Code:** 2562

This private school, affiliated with the Roman Catholic Church, was founded in 1908. It has a 156-acre campus.

RATINGS
Admissions Selectivity Rating: 70　　　**Fire Safety Rating:** 99　　　**Green Rating:** 76

STUDENTS AND FACULTY
Enrollment: 1,736. **Student Body:** 94% female, 6% male, 3% out-of-state, international (10 countries represented). Asian 2%, African American 11%, Caucasian 63%, Hispanic 8%.
Retention and Graduation: 78% freshmen return for sophomore year. 24% freshmen graduate within 4 years. **Faculty:** Student/faculty ratio 15:1. 103 full-time faculty, 87% hold PhDs, 16% are members of minority groups, 62% are women.

ACADEMICS
Degrees: Bachelor's, certificate, master's, post-bachelor's certificate, post-master's certificate. **Classes:** Most classes have 10–19 students. **Majors with Highest Enrollment:** Elementary education and teaching; English language and literature; psychology. **Special Study Options:** Accelerated program, distance learning, double major, dual enrollment, English as a Second Language (ESL), honors program, independent study, internships, liberal arts/career combination, study abroad, teacher certification program, undergrads may take grad level classes. **Co-Op Programs:** Arts, business, health professions, natural science, social/behavioral science. **Honors programs:** Members of the University Honors Program receive an enriched academic curriculum featuring: ° Faculty chosen for their excellence as teaching-scholars ° Challenging interactive classroom format ° Emphasis on primary texts and sources ° Rigorous scholarly writing assignments and oral presentations ° Close faculty mentoring ° Preference in academic advisement and course registration ° A strong sense of belonging to a community of scholars ° Sponsorship in funding presentations at regional and national conferences ° Special advisement by faculty regarding graduate and professional school applications and prestigious fellowship opportunities ° Special recognition at commencement ceremonies. **Combined degree programs:** BS/MBA. Special programs offered to physically disabled students include note-taking services, reader services, tape recorders, tutors. **Career services:** Alumni network, alumni services, career/job search classes,

career assessment, internships **Career services highlights include:** Career Connections, GCU's new online job board with research tools for students and alumni. Members can search for jobs, view the calendar of events and register for them, network with alumni, and upload their resumes. Employers can post jobs and internships directly online and search through resumes.

FACILITIES
Housing: women's dorms, wellness housing 77% of campus accessible to physically disabled. **Special Academic Facilities/Equipment:** Art gallery, arboretum, Wellness Center, NASA ERC. **Computers:** 98% of classrooms, 77% of dorms, 100% of libraries, 50% of dining areas, 100% of student union, have wireless network access. Students can register for classes online. Administrative functions (other than registration) can be performed online.

CAMPUS LIFE
Environment: Town. **Activities:** Choral groups, concert band, dance, jazz band, literary magazine, music ensembles, student government, student newspaper, yearbook, campus ministries, international student organization, Model UN. **Organizations:** 48 registered organizations, 18 honor societies, 1 religious organizations. **Athletics (Intercollegiate):.** *Women:* Basketball, cross-country, lacrosse, soccer, softball, tennis, track/field (outdoor), volleyball. **On-Campus Highlights:** Arboretum, NASA Educational Resource Center, Art Gallery, Library, Wellness Center. **Environmental Initiatives:** We have included a sustainability commitment in our strategic plan. Our president was the 8th signatory of ACUPCC in New Jersey. GCU purchased Green-E certified renewable energy certificates equivalent to 100% of our projected campus electrical usage for 2009–10.

ADMISSIONS
Freshman Academic Profile: Average high school GPA 3.1. 16% in top 10% of high school class, 41% in top 25% of high school class, 79% in top 50% of high school class. 80% from public high schools. Minimum paper TOEFL 550. Minimum computer TOEFL 213. Minimum web-based TOEFL 79. **Basis for Candidate Selection:** *Very important factors considered include:* Academic GPA, rigor of secondary school record. *Important factors considered include:* Standardized test scores. *Other factors considered include:* Class rank, application essay, recommendation(s), alumni/ae relation, character/personal qualities, extracurricular activities, first generation, interview, level of applicant's interest, talent/ability, volunteer work, work experience. **Freshman Admission Requirements:** High school diploma is required and GED is accepted. *Academic units required:* 4 English, 2 mathematics, (1 science labs), 2 foreign language, 1 history, 6 academic electives. **Freshman Admission Statistics:** 1,008 applied, 62% admitted, 41% enrolled. **Transfer Admission Requirements:** College transcript(s), minimum college GPA of 2.0 required. Lowest grade transferable c. **General Admission Information:** Application fee $40. Regular application deadline 8/1. Notification on a rolling basis, beginning on or about 10/1. Nonfall registration accepted. Credit and/or placement offered for CEEB Advanced Placement tests.

COSTS AND FINANCIAL AID
Required Forms and Deadlines: FAFSA, institution's own financial aid form. **Notification of Awards:** Applicants will be notified of awards on a rolling basis beginning 2/1. **Types of Aid:** *Need-based scholarships/grants:* Federal Pell, SEOG, state scholarships/grants, private scholarships, the school's own gift aid. *Loans:* FFEL Subsidized Stafford, FFEL Unsubsidized Stafford, FFEL PLUS, Federal Perkins, state loans. **Student Employment:** Federal Work-Study Program available. Institutional employment available. Highest amount earned per year from on-campus jobs $2,000. Off-campus job opportunities are good. **Financial Aid Statistics:** 89% freshmen, 82% undergrads receive need-based scholarship or grant aid. 7% freshmen, 7% undergrads receive non-need-based scholarship or grant aid. 73% freshmen, 71% undergrads receive need-based self-help aid. 3% freshmen, 2% undergrads receive athletic scholarships. 99% freshmen, 96% undergrads receive any aid. 85% undergrads borrow to pay for school. Average cumulative indebtedness $33,729. **Criteria for awarding institutional aid:** *Non-need-based:* Academics, alumni affiliation, art, athletics, leadership, minority status, music/drama, religious affiliation.

See page 1100.

GETTYSBURG COLLEGE

Best 373

Admissions Office, Eisenhower House, Gettysburg, PA 17325-1484
Phone: 717-337-6100 **Financial Aid Phone:** 717-337-6611
E-mail: admiss@gettysburg.edu **CEEB Code:** 2275
Fax: 717-337-6145 **Website:** www.gettysburg.edu **ACT Code:** 3580

This private school, affiliated with the Lutheran Church, was founded in 1832. It has a 200-acre campus.

RATINGS
Admissions Selectivity Rating: 95   **Fire Safety Rating:** 88   **Green Rating:** 88

STUDENTS AND FACULTY
Enrollment: 2,516. **Student Body:** 51% female, 49% male, 75% out-of-state, 2% international (27 countries represented). Asian 2%, African American 5%, Caucasian 88%, Hispanic 3%.
Retention and Graduation: 90% freshmen return for sophomore year. 78% freshmen graduate within 4 years. 40% grads go on to further study within 1 year. **Faculty:** Student/faculty ratio 10.7:1. 209 full-time faculty, 91% hold PhDs, 13% are members of minority groups, 43% are women.

ACADEMICS
Degrees: Bachelor's. **Classes:** Most classes have 10–19 students. **Majors with Highest Enrollment:** Business/commerce; political science and government; psychology. **Special Study Options:** Double major, independent study, internships, student-designed major, study abroad, teacher certification program **Combined degree programs:** Optometry, Physical Therapy, Nursing. Special programs offered to physically disabled students include tape recorders. **Career services:** Alumni network, alumni services, career/job search classes, career assessment, internships, regional alumni.

FACILITIES
Housing: Coed dorms, women's dorms, fraternity/sorority housing, apartments for single students, theme housing, special interest and theme housing. **Special Academic Facilities/Equipment:** Art gallery, language lab, Child Study lab, Majestic Theatre, Sunderman Conservatory, planetarium, observatory, electron microscopes, NMR spectrometer, greenhouse, digital classrooms, wireless network, Plasma Physics labs, Science Center. **Computers:** 100% of classrooms, 100% of dorms, 100% of libraries, 100% of dining areas, 100% of student union, 90% of common outdoor areas have wireless network access. Students can register for classes online. Administrative functions (other than registration) can be performed online.

CAMPUS LIFE
Environment: Village. **Activities:** Choral groups, concert band, dance, drama/theater, jazz band, literary magazine, marching band, music ensembles, radio station, student government, student newspaper, student-run film society, symphony orchestra, television station, yearbook, campus ministries, international student organization, Model UN. **Organizations:** 120 registered organizations, 16 honor societies, 7 religious organizations. 10 fraternities, 6 sororities. **Athletics (Intercollegiate):** *Men:* Baseball, basketball, cheerleading, cross-country, football, golf, lacrosse, soccer, swimming, tennis, track/field (outdoor), track/field (indoor), wrestling. *Women:* Basketball, cheerleading, cross-country, field hockey, golf, lacrosse, soccer, softball, swimming, tennis, track/field (outdoor), track/field (indoor), volleyball. **On-Campus Highlights:** Beautiful 200–acre campus, Musselman Library, Science Center, Center for Athletics, Recreation, and Fitness, College Union Building. **Environmental Initiatives:** The Center—a new althetic building which is designed to be LEED-certified. Painted Turtle—an organic garden on campus. Move-Out Day—each May, our students donate unwanted clothing, furniture, etc., to the United Way, thus reducing the amount of garbage.

ADMISSIONS
Freshman Academic Profile: 68% in top 10% of high school class, 86% in top 25% of high school class, 99% in top 50% of high school class. 70% from public high schools. SAT Math middle 50% range 610–690. SAT Critical Reading middle 50% range 610–690. Minimum paper TOEFL 570. Minimum computer TOEFL 230. **Basis for Candidate Selection:** *Very important factors considered include:* Class rank, academic GPA; recommendation(s), rigor of secondary school record. *Important factors considered include:* Application essay, standardized test scores, character/personal qualities, extracurricular activities, interview, talent/ability, volunteer work. *Other factors considered include:* Alumni/ae relation, first generation, geographical residence, level of applicant's interest, racial/ethnic status, work experience. **Freshman Admission Requirements:** High school diploma is required and GED is accepted. *Academic*

units required: 4 English, 3 mathematics, 3 science, (3 science labs), 3 foreign language, 3 social studies, 3 history. *Academic units recommended:* 4 English, 4 mathematics, 4 science, (4 science labs), 4 foreign language, 4 social studies, 4 history. **Freshman Admission Statistics:** 5,448 applied, 40% admitted, 34% enrolled. **Transfer Admission Requirements:** High school transcript, college transcript(s), essay or personal statement, standardized test scores, statement of good standing from prior institution(s). Minimum college GPA of 2.5 required. Lowest grade transferable C. **General Admission Information:** Application fee $55. Early decision application deadline 11/15. Regular application deadline 2/1. Regular notification 4/1. Nonfall registration accepted. Admission may be deferred for a maximum of 1 year. Credit and/or placement offered for CEEB Advanced Placement tests.

COSTS AND FINANCIAL AID
Annual tuition $38,690. Room and board $9,360. Required fees $410. Average book expense $500. **Required Forms and Deadlines:** FAFSA, CSS/Financial Aid PROFILE, business/farm supplement. Financial aid filing deadline 2/15. **Notification of Awards:** Applicants will be notified of awards on or about 3/26. **Types of Aid:** *Need-based scholarships/grants:* Federal Pell, SEOG, state scholarships/grants, private scholarships, the school's own gift aid. *Loans:* FFEL Subsidized Stafford, FFEL Unsubsidized Stafford, FFEL PLUS, Federal Perkins, college/university loans from institutional funds. **Student Employment:** Federal Work-Study Program available. Institutional employment available. Highest amount earned per year from on-campus jobs $1,500. Off-campus job opportunities are excellent. **Financial Aid Statistics:** 58% freshmen, 52% undergrads receive need-based scholarship or grant aid. 31% freshmen, 26% undergrads receive non-need-based scholarship or grant aid. 55% freshmen, 47% undergrads receive need-based self-help aid. 70% freshmen, 70% undergrads receive any aid. 61% undergrads borrow to pay for school. Average cumulative indebtedness $23,258. **Criteria for awarding institutional aid:** *Non-need-based:* Academics, music/drama.

GIBBS COLLEGE

85 Garfield Ave, Cranston, RI 02920
Phone: 401-824-5300 **Financial Aid Phone:** 401-824-5327
E-mail: psimonin@gbbsRI.edu
Fax: 401-824-5376 **Website:** www.gibbsri.edu

This proprietary school was founded in 1911. It has a 30-acre campus.

RATINGS
Admissions Selectivity Rating: 60*   **Fire Safety Rating:** 60*   **Green Rating:** 60*

STUDENTS AND FACULTY
Enrollment: 613. **Student Body:** 72% female, 28% male, Asian 5%, African American 6%, Caucasian 57%, Hispanic 22%.
Retention and Graduation: Faculty: Student/faculty ratio 11:1. 17 full-time faculty, 47% hold PhDs, 12% are members of minority groups, 41% are women.

ACADEMICS
Degrees: Associate, certificate, terminal associate, transfer associate. **Majors with Highest Enrollment:** Computer and information systems security; criminal justice/law enforcement administration; medical/clinical assistant. **Special Study Options:** Internships, liberal arts/career combination Special programs offered to physically disabled students include tape recorders, tutors. **Career services:** Alumni network, alumni services, career/job search classes, career assessment.

FACILITIES
Housing: None. 100% of campus accessible to physically disabled.

CAMPUS LIFE
Environment: City. **Activities:** Student government.

ADMISSIONS
Very important factors considered include: Interview, level of applicant's interest. *Important factors considered include:* Character/personal qualities. *Other factors considered include:* Recommendation(s), talent/ability. **Freshman Admission Requirements:** High school diploma is required and GED is accepted. **Transfer Admission Requirements:** High school transcript, college transcript(s), interview, Lowest grade transferable C. **General Admission Information:** Application fee $50. Nonfall registration accepted. Admission may be deferred for a maximum of 1 year. Credit and/or placement offered for CEEB Advanced Placement tests.

COSTS AND FINANCIAL AID
Annual tuition $11,250. Required fees $450.

GLENVILLE STATE COLLEGE

200 High Street, Glenville, WV 26351
Phone: 304-462-4128
E-mail: admissions@glenville.edu
Fax: 304-462-8619 **Website:** www.glenville.edu **ACT Code:** 4522

This public school was founded in 1872.

RATINGS
Admissions Selectivity Rating: 60*   **Fire Safety Rating:** 60*   **Green Rating:** 60*

STUDENTS AND FACULTY
Enrollment: 1,374. **Student Body:** 54% female, 46% male.
Retention and Graduation: 49% freshmen return for sophomore year.
Faculty: Student/faculty ratio 20:1. 53 full-time faculty, 30% hold PhDs, 6% are
members of minority groups, 36% are women.

ACADEMICS
Degrees: Associate, bachelor's, certificate. **Special Study Options:** Cooperative education program, double major, honors program, internships, student-
designed major, teacher certification program. Special programs offered to
physically disabled students include reader services, tape recorders, tutors.

FACILITIES
Housing: Coed dorms, special housing for disabled students, men's dorms,
women's dorms, apartments for married students, apartments for single students.

CAMPUS LIFE
Environment: Rural. **Activities:** Choral groups, concert band, drama/theater,
jazz band, marching band, music ensembles, student government, student
newspaper, yearbook. **Organizations:** 30 registered organizations, 2 religious
organizations. 2 fraternities, 2 sororities. **Athletics (Intercollegiate):** *Men:*
Basketball, cross-country, football, golf, track/field (outdoor). *Women:* Basketball, cross-country, golf, softball, track/field (outdoor), volleyball. **On-Campus
Highlights:** High Adventure, GSC Fitness Center, fine arts Building, PG's
Snack Bar, Pioneer Village.

ADMISSIONS
Freshman Academic Profile: Minimum paper TOEFL 550. **Basis for
Candidate Selection:** *Very important factors considered include:* Rigor of
secondary school record, standardized test scores. *Other factors considered
include:* Class rank, academic GPA, recommendation(s), talent/ability. **Freshman Admission Requirements:** High school diploma is required and GED
is accepted. *Academic units required:* 4 English, 3 mathematics, 3 science, (2
science labs), 3 social studies. **Freshman Admission Statistics:** 1,132 applied,
100% admitted, 41% enrolled. **Transfer Admission Requirements:** College
transcript(s), minimum college GPA of 2.0 required. Lowest grade transferable
C. **General Admission Information:** Nonfall registration accepted. Admission
may be deferred for a maximum of 1 year. Credit offered for CEEB Advanced
Placement tests.

COSTS AND FINANCIAL AID
Comprehensive fee $4,810. Room and board $3,480. Average book expense
$350. **Required Forms and Deadlines:** FAFSA. **Types of Aid:** *Need-based
scholarships/grants:* Federal Pell, SEOG, state scholarships/grants, private
scholarships, the school's own gift aid. *Loans:* Direct Subsidized Stafford, Direct
Unsubsidized Stafford, Direct PLUS, Federal Perkins. **Student Employment:**
Federal Work-Study Program available. Highest amount earned per year from
on-campus jobs $900. Off-campus job opportunities are fair. **Financial Aid
Statistics:** 64% freshmen, 59% undergrads receive need-based scholarship or
grant aid. 16% freshmen, 14% undergrads receive non-need-based scholarship
or grant aid. 48% freshmen, 51% undergrads receive need-based self-help aid.
1% freshmen, 3% undergrads receive athletic scholarships. 71% undergrads
borrow to pay for school. Average cumulative indebtedness $12,117. **Criteria
for awarding institutional aid:** *Non-need-based:* Academics, art, athletics,
music/drama.

GLOBAL UNIVERSITY

1211 S. Glenstone Ave, Springfield, MO 65804
Phone: 800-443-1083
E-mail: studentinfo@globaluniversity.edu
Fax: 417-862-0863 **Website:** www.globaluniversity.edu

This is a private school.

RATINGS
Admissions Selectivity Rating: 60*   **Fire Safety Rating:** 60*   **Green Rating:** 60*

STUDENTS AND FACULTY
Faculty: Student/faculty ratio 29:1. 49 full-time faculty, 27% are women.

ACADEMICS
Degrees: Associate, bachelor's, diploma, first professional, master's. **Special
Study Options:** Distance learning, dual enrollment, external degree program,
honors program, independent study.

ADMISSIONS
Basis for Candidate Selection: *Very important factors considered include:*
Character/personal qualities. *Important factors considered include:* Religious
affiliation/commitment. *Other factors considered include:* Volunteer work, work
experience. **Freshman Admission Requirements:** High school diploma is
required and GED is accepted. **Transfer Admission Requirements:** High
school transcript, college transcript(s), Lowest grade transferable C. **General
Admission Information:** Application fee $35. Nonfall registration accepted.
Admission may be deferred for a maximum of 3 months.

COSTS AND FINANCIAL AID
Annual tuition $2,160. **Types of Aid:** *Loans:* Aid provided from Veterans and
DANTES.

GOLDEN GATE UNIVERSITY

536 Mission Street, San Francisco, CA 94105
Phone: 415-442-7800
E-mail: info@ggu.edu **CEEB Code:** 4329
Fax: 415-442-7807 **Website:** www.ggu.edu **ACT Code:** 278

This private school was founded in 1901.

RATINGS
Admissions Selectivity Rating: 60*   **Fire Safety Rating:** 60*   **Green Rating:** 60*

STUDENTS AND FACULTY
Enrollment: 393. **Student Body:** 57% female, 43% male, (61 countries
represented).
Retention and Graduation: 67% freshmen return for sophomore year. 15%
grads go on to further study within 1 year. 30% grads pursue business degrees.
Faculty: Student/faculty ratio 11:1. 71 full-time faculty, 35% are women.

ACADEMICS
Degrees: Bachelor's, certificate, first professional, master's, post-bachelor's
certificate, post-master's certificate. **Classes:** Most classes have 10–19 students.
Special Study Options: Accelerated program, cooperative education program,
distance learning, dual enrollment, English as a Second Language (ESL),
independent study, internships, weekend college. Special programs offered to
physically disabled students include tape recorders. **Career services:** Alumni
network, alumni services, career/job search classes, career assessment, internships. **Career services highlights include:** Virtual career center—ggucareer.
com. 24/7 access to career management tools and resources including self assessment, company contact databases, industry reports and job board.

FACILITIES
Housing: 100% of campus accessible to physically disabled. **Computers:**
Students can register for classes online. Administrative functions (other than
registration) can be performed online.

CAMPUS LIFE
Activities: Student government, student newspaper. **Organizations:** 16 registered organizations, 5 honor societies.

ADMISSIONS
Freshman Academic Profile: Average high school GPA 2.7. Minimum
paper TOEFL 525. Minimum computer TOEFL 197. **Basis for Candidate
Selection:** *Very important factors considered include:* Rigor of secondary

school record. *Other factors considered include:* Class rank, application essay, recommendation(s), standardized test scores. **Freshman Admission Requirements:** High school diploma is required and GED is accepted. *Academic units recommended:* 4 English, 3 mathematics, 2 science, (1 science labs), 2 foreign language, 1 social studies, 1 history. **Freshman Admission Statistics:** 8 applied, 88% admitted, 71% enrolled. **Transfer Admission Requirements:** College transcript(s), minimum college GPA of 2.0 required. Lowest grade transferable C–. **General Admission Information:** Application fee $55. Notification on a rolling basis, beginning on or about 1/15. Nonfall registration accepted. Admission may be deferred for a maximum of 1 year. Credit offered for CEEB Advanced Placement tests.

COSTS AND FINANCIAL AID

Annual tuition $16,200. Average book expense $1,200. **Required Forms and Deadlines:** FAFSA, institution's own financial aid form. **Types of Aid:** *Need-based scholarships/grants:* Federal Pell, SEOG, the school's own gift aid. *Loans:* Direct Subsidized Stafford, Direct Unsubsidized Stafford, Federal Perkins, state loans. **Student Employment:** Federal Work-Study Program available. Institutional employment available. Highest amount earned per year from on-campus jobs $2,480. Off-campus job opportunities are good. **Criteria for awarding institutional aid:** *Non-need-based:* Academics, alumni affiliation, leadership.

GOLDEY-BEACOM COLLEGE

4701 Limestone Road, Wilmington, DE 19808
Phone: 302-998-8814
E-mail: admissions@gbc.edu **CEEB Code:** 5255
Fax: 302-996-5408 **Website:** www.goldey.gbc.edu

This private school was founded in 1886. It has a 27-acre campus.

RATINGS

Admissions Selectivity Rating: 72   **Fire Safety Rating:** 60*   **Green Rating:** 60*

STUDENTS AND FACULTY

Enrollment: 385. **Student Body:** 100% female, 50% out-of-state, 8% international (60 countries represented). Asian 2%, African American 6%, Caucasian 64%, Hispanic 2%.
Retention and Graduation: 5% grads go on to further study within 1 year. 1% grads pursue law degrees. 4% grads pursue business degrees.

ACADEMICS

Degrees: Associate, bachelor's, master's. **Special Study Options:** Accelerated program, cooperative education program, distance learning, independent study, internships.

FACILITIES

Housing: Coed dorms, fraternity/sorority housing, apartments for single students.

CAMPUS LIFE

Environment: Village. **Activities:** Drama/theater, student government, student newspaper. **Organizations:** 4 religious organizations. **Athletics (Intercollegiate):** *Men:* Soccer, softball. *Women:* Softball.

ADMISSIONS

Freshman Academic Profile: 90% from public high schools. SAT Math middle 50% range 440–593. SAT Critical Reading middle 50% range 400–512. Minimum paper TOEFL 500. **Basis for Candidate Selection:** *Very important factors considered include:* Rigor of secondary school record, standardized test scores. *Important factors considered include:* Class rank, recommendation(s). *Other factors considered include:* Character/personal qualities, interview. **Freshman Admission Requirements:** High school diploma is required and GED is accepted. *Academic units required:* 4 English, 3 mathematics, 3 science. *Academic units recommended:* 4 English, 3 mathematics, 3 science. **Freshman Admission Statistics:** 689 applied, 77% admitted, 56% enrolled. **Transfer Admission Requirements:** High school transcript, college transcript(s), minimum college GPA of 2.0 required. Lowest grade transferable 2. **General Admission Information:** Application fee $30. Regular application deadline 8/15. Notification on a rolling basis, beginning on or about 10/1. Nonfall registration accepted. Admission may be deferred for a maximum of 12. Credit and/or placement offered for CEEB Advanced Placement tests.

COSTS AND FINANCIAL AID

Annual tuition $12,928. Room and board $4,240. Required fees $120. Average book expense $700. **Types of Aid:** *Need-based scholarships/grants:* Federal Pell, SEOG, state scholarships/grants, private scholarships, the school's own gift aid. *Loans:* FFEL Subsidized Stafford, FFEL Unsubsidized Stafford, FFEL

PLUS, Federal Perkins, state loans, college/university loans from institutional funds. **Student Employment:** Federal Work-Study Program available. Off-campus job opportunities are excellent.

GONZAGA UNIVERSITY

502 E. Boone Avenue, Spokane, WA 99258
Phone: 509-313-6572 **Financial Aid Phone:** 509-323-6582
E-mail: admissions@gonzaga.edu **CEEB Code:** 4330
Fax: 509-324-5780 **Website:** www.gonzaga.edu **ACT Code:** 4458

This private school, affiliated with the Roman Catholic Church,, affiliated with the CatholiC–Jesuit Church, was founded in 1887. It has a 108-acre campus.

RATINGS

Admissions Selectivity Rating: 88   **Fire Safety Rating:** 89   **Green Rating:** 60*

STUDENTS AND FACULTY

Enrollment: 4,655. **Student Body:** 53% female, 47% male, 50.7% out-of-state, 2% international (36 countries represented). Asian 5%, African American 1%, Caucasian 76%, Hispanic 5%, Native American 1%.
Retention and Graduation: 92% freshmen return for sophomore year. 68% freshmen graduate within 4 years. 30% grads go on to further study within 1 year. 20% grads pursue arts and sciences degrees. 5% grads pursue law degrees. 15% grads pursue business degrees. 1% grads pursue medical degrees. **Faculty:** Student/faculty ratio 10.4:1. 393 full-time faculty, 83% hold PhDs, 14% are members of minority groups, 39% are women.

ACADEMICS

Degrees: Bachelor's, master's. **Classes:** Most classes have 20–29 students. Most lab/discussion sessions have 10–19 students. **Majors with Highest Enrollment:** Political science and government; psychology. **Special Study Options:** Accelerated program, double major, dual enrollment, English as a Second Language (ESL), exchange student program (domestic), honors program, independent study, internships, study abroad, teacher certification program. **Honors programs:** Hogan Entrepreneurial Leadership Program—Immerses students in the fundamentals of creating and managing new ventures in the public and private sectors. **Combined degree programs:** MAcc/JD, MBA/JD, BSN/MSN. Special programs offered to physically disabled students include note-taking services, reader services, tape recorders. **Career services:** Alumni network, alumni services, career/job search classes, career assessment, internships, regional alumni.

FACILITIES

Housing: Coed dorms, special housing for disabled students, men's dorms, special housing for international students, women's dorms, apartments for married students, apartments for single students, theme housing. 90% of campus accessible to physically disabled. **Special Academic Facilities/Equipment:** Art center, museum, language lab, TV production center, educational center, two electron microscopes. **Computers:** 75% of classrooms, 90% of dorms, 100% of libraries, 100% of student union, 75% of common outdoor areas have wireless network access. Students can register for classes online. Administrative functions (other than registration) can be performed online.

CAMPUS LIFE

Environment: City. **Activities:** Choral groups, concert band, dance, drama/theater, jazz band, literary magazine, music ensembles, pep band, radio station, student government, student newspaper, symphony orchestra, television station, yearbook, campus ministries. **Organizations:** 86 registered organizations, 10 honor societies, 4 religious organizations. **Athletics (Intercollegiate):** *Men:* Baseball, basketball, crew/rowing, cross-country, golf, soccer, tennis, track/field (outdoor). *Women:* Basketball, crew/rowing, cross-country, golf, soccer, tennis, track/field (outdoor), volleyball. **On-Campus Highlights:** St Aloysius Cathedral, McCarthy Athletic Center, Jundt Art Museum, Bing Crosby Museum in the Crosby Student Center, The Gonzaga University Bookstore.

ADMISSIONS

Freshman Academic Profile: Average high school GPA 3.66. 38% in top 10% of high school class, 72% in top 25% of high school class, 93% in top 50% of high school class. 71% from public high schools. SAT Math middle 50% range 550–650. SAT Critical Reading middle 50% range 530–640. ACT middle 50% range 24–29. Minimum paper TOEFL 550. Minimum computer TOEFL 213. **Basis for Candidate Selection:** *Very important factors considered include:* Academic

GPA, rigor of secondary school record, character/personal qualities, first generation. *Important factors considered include:* Application essay, recommendation(s), standardized test scores, extracurricular activities, talent/ability. *Other factors considered include:* Class rank, alumni/ae relation, interview, level of applicant's interest, racial/ethnic status, volunteer work, work experience. **Freshman Admission Requirements:** High school diploma is required and GED is not accepted. *Academic units required:* 4 English, 3 mathematics, 3 science, (3 science labs), 3 foreign language, 2 social studies, 2 history, 2 academic electives. *Academic units recommended:* 4 English, 4 mathematics, 4 science, (4 science labs), 4 foreign language, 3 social studies, 3 history, 3 academic electives. **Freshman Admission Statistics:** 5,042 applied, 78% admitted, 31% enrolled. **Transfer Admission Requirements:** College transcript(s), essay or personal statement, statement of good standing from prior institution(s). Minimum college GPA of 2.7 required. Lowest grade transferable C. **General Admission Information:** Application fee $50. Regular application deadline 2/1. Regular notification 3/15. Nonfall registration accepted. Admission may be deferred for a maximum of 1 year. Credit and/or placement offered for CEEB Advanced Placement tests.

COSTS AND FINANCIAL AID

Annual tuition $26,120. Room and board $7,520. Required fees $438. Average book expense $900. **Required Forms and Deadlines:** FAFSA. Priority financial aid filing date 2/1. **Notification of Awards:** Applicants will be notified of awards on a rolling basis beginning 3/1. **Types of Aid:** *Need-based scholarships/grants:* Federal Pell, SEOG, state scholarships/grants, private scholarships, the school's own gift aid, United Negro College Fund, Federal Nursing Scholarships. *Loans:* FFEL Subsidized Stafford, FFEL Unsubsidized Stafford, FFEL PLUS, Federal Perkins, Federal Nursing, state loans, college/university loans from institutional funds. **Student Employment:** Federal Work-Study Program available. Institutional employment available. Off-campus job opportunities are excellent. **Financial Aid Statistics:** 54% freshmen, 56% undergrads receive need-based scholarship or grant aid. 21% freshmen, 24% undergrads receive non-need-based scholarship or grant aid. 32% freshmen, 41% undergrads receive need-based self-help aid. 3% freshmen, 3% undergrads receive athletic scholarships. 97% freshmen, 95% undergrads receive any aid. 64% undergrads borrow to pay for school. Average cumulative indebtedness $19,735. **Criteria for awarding institutional aid:** *Non-need-based:* Academics, alumni affiliation, athletics, leadership, minority status, music/drama.

See page 1102.

GORDON COLLEGE

255 Grapevine Road, Wenham, MA 01984-1899
Phone: 978-867-4218 **Financial Aid Phone:** 978-867-4246
E-mail: admissions@gordon.edu **CEEB Code:** 3417
Fax: 978-867-4682 **Website:** www.gordon.edu **ACT Code:** 1838

This private school, affiliated with the Protestant Church, was founded in 1889. It has a 500-acre campus.

RATINGS

Admissions Selectivity Rating: 84   **Fire Safety Rating:** 84   **Green Rating:** 60*

STUDENTS AND FACULTY

Enrollment: 1,572. **Student Body:** 62% female, 38% male, 71% out-of-state, 4% international (23 countries represented). Asian 2%, African American 2%, Caucasian 84%, Hispanic 3%.
Retention and Graduation: 90% freshmen return for sophomore year. 64% freshmen graduate within 4 years. **Faculty:** Student/faculty ratio 14:1. 97 full-time faculty, 77% hold PhDs, 10% are members of minority groups, 29% are women.

ACADEMICS

Degrees: Bachelor's, master's. **Classes:** Most classes have 10–19 students. Most lab/discussion sessions have 10–19 students. **Majors with Highest Enrollment:** Business/commerce; English language and literature; psychology. **Special Study Options:** Cooperative education program, cross-registration, double major, honors program, independent study, internships, liberal arts/career combination, student-designed major, study abroad, teacher certification program, Gordon-in-Boston Urban Semester; Gordon-in-France; Italian Semester in Orvieto, Italy; Oregon Extension; Outdoor Education Immersion Semester; LaVida Wilderness Expedition. **Co-Op Programs:** Arts, Business, Computer Science, Education, Engineering, Health Professions, Humanities, Natural Science, Social/Behavioral Science. **Honors programs:** The Jerusalem and Athens Forum is a new interdisciplinary honors program at Gordon College, beginning in the academic year 2004–05. Through a variety of program components, but principally a great books course in the history of Christian thought and literature, the program strives to help students reflect on the relationship between faith and intellect, deepen their own sense of vocation, and awaken their capacities

for intellectual and moral leadership. (Description taken from www.gordon.edu/jaf) The Kenneth L. Pike Honors Program provides exceptional students with an opportunity to meet unique academic goals not possible under existing Gordon programs by designing individualized, disciplined and chalenging interdisciplinary academic experiences. (Description taken from the Gordon College Academic Catalog). **Combined degree programs:** BA/MA, 2-2 allied health sciences prog with Thomas Jeffer. Special programs offered to physically disabled students include tape recorders, tutors. **Career services:** Alumni network, career/job search classes, career assessment, internships. **Career services highlights include:** Harmeling Physical Therapy Clinic located on campus provides Movement Science students hands-on experience.

FACILITIES

Housing: Coed dorms, special housing for disabled students, men's dorms, apartments for married students, apartments for single students, theme housingInternational hall, mentoring hall, theme houses. Also Gordon's dorms are coed by floors and/or wings. Men and women do not live together or share facilities. 99% of campus accessible to physically disabled. **Special Academic Facilities/Equipment:** Barrington Center for the Arts; Phillips Music Center; Center for Balance and Mobility; an electron microscope; a gene sequencer; papers of British Statesman/Reformer, William Wilberforce; East-West Institute; Center for Student Leadership; Center for Christian Studies; international office for Christians in the Visual Arts (CIVA). **Computers:** Administrative functions (other than registration) can be performed online.

CAMPUS LIFE

Environment: Village. **Activities:** Choral groups, concert band, drama/theater, jazz band, literary magazine, music ensembles, musical theater, student government, student newspaper, student-run film society, symphony orchestra, yearbook, campus ministries, international student organization, Model UN. **Organizations:** 35 registered organizations, 17 honor societies, 15 religious organizations. **Athletics (Intercollegiate):** *Men:* Baseball, basketball, cross-country, lacrosse, soccer, swimming, tennis, track/field (outdoor), track/field (indoor). *Women:* Basketball, cross-country, field hockey, lacrosse, soccer, softball, swimming, tennis, track/field (outdoor), track/field (indoor), volleyball. **On-Campus Highlights:** Gillies Lounge/Claymore Cafe, hiking/biking/cross country ski trails, Bennett Athletic and Recreation Center, Barrington Center for the Arts, canoeing/swimming ponds, Gordon's campus had many lakes and trails for use by the student body. On campus recreational activities are regularly planned and/or available.

ADMISSIONS

Freshman Academic Profile: 32% in top 10% of high school class, 58% in top 25% of high school class, 86% in top 50% of high school class. 70% from public high schools. SAT Math middle 50% range 500–640. SAT Critical Reading middle 50% range 520–650. SAT Writing middle 50% range 560–640. ACT middle 50% range 24–28. Minimum paper TOEFL 550. Minimum computer TOEFL 213. **Basis for Candidate Selection:** *Very important factors considered include:* Application essay, academic GPA, recommendation(s), rigor of secondary school record, standardized test scores, character/personal qualities, extracurricular activities, interview, religious affiliation/commitment. *Important factors considered include:* Class rank, talent/ability. *Other factors considered include:* Alumni/ae relation, racial/ethnic status, volunteer work, work experience. **Freshman Admission Requirements:** High school diploma is required and GED is accepted. *Academic units required:* 4 English, 2 mathematics, 2 science, (1 science labs), 2 foreign language, 2 social studies, 5 academic electives. *Academic units recommended:* 3 mathematics, 3 science, (3 science labs), 4 foreign language, 3 social studies. **Freshman Admission Statistics:** 1,664 applied, 66% admitted, 35% enrolled. **Transfer Admission Requirements:** College transcript(s), essay or personal statement, interview, statement of good standing from prior institution(s). Minimum college GPA of 2.0 required. Lowest grade transferable C. **General Admission Information:** Application fee $50. Early decision application deadline 11/15. Notification on a rolling basis, beginning on or about 12/15. Nonfall registration accepted. Admission may be deferred for a maximum of 1 year. Credit offered for CEEB Advanced Placement tests.

COSTS AND FINANCIAL AID

Annual tuition $27,152. Room and board $7,720. Required fees $1,200. Average book expense $800. **Required Forms and Deadlines:** FAFSA. Financial aid filing deadline 3/1. **Notification of Awards:** Applicants will be notified of awards on a rolling basis beginning 4/15. **Types of Aid:** *Need-based scholarships/grants:* Federal Pell, SEOG, state scholarships/grants, private scholarships, the school's own gift aid. *Loans:* FFEL Subsidized Stafford, FFEL Unsubsidized Stafford, FFEL PLUS, Federal Perkins, state loans, college/university loans from institutional funds. **Student Employment:** Federal Work-Study Program available. Highest amount earned per year from on-campus jobs $1,500. Off-campus job opportunities are good. **Financial Aid Statistics:** 63% freshmen, 65% undergrads receive need-based scholarship or grant aid. 9% freshmen, 7% undergrads receive non-need-based scholarship or grant aid. 53% freshmen, 57% undergrads receive need-based self-help aid. 96% freshmen, 90.5% undergrads receive any aid. 81.37% undergrads borrow to pay for school. Average cumulative indebtedness $33,332. **Criteria for awarding institutional aid:** *Non-need-based:* Academics, alumni affiliation, art, leadership, minority status, music/drama, religious affiliation.

The Princeton Review's Complete Book of Colleges

GOSHEN COLLEGE

1700 South Main Street, Goshen, IN 46526-4794
Phone: 574-535-7535 **Financial Aid Phone:** 574-535-7525
E-mail: admission@goshen.edu **CEEB Code:** 1251
Fax: 574-535-7609 **Website:** www.goshen.edu **ACT Code:** 1196

This private school, affiliated with the Mennonite Church, was founded in 1894. It has a 135-acre campus.

RATINGS

Admissions Selectivity Rating: 85   **Fire Safety Rating:** 97   **Green Rating:** 73

STUDENTS AND FACULTY

Enrollment: 951. **Student Body:** 60% female, 40% male, 49% out-of-state, 4% international (25 countries represented). Asian 2%, African American 4%, Caucasian 82%, Hispanic 7%.
Retention and Graduation: 84% freshmen return for sophomore year. 56% freshmen graduate within 4 years. 13.4% grads go on to further study within 1 year. 10.2% grads pursue arts and sciences degrees. 0.8% grads pursue business degrees. 1.6% grads pursue medical degrees. **Faculty:** Student/faculty ratio 10.1:1. 68 full-time faculty, 68% hold PhDs, 6% are members of minority groups, 47% are women.

ACADEMICS

Degrees: Bachelor's, certificate, master's. **Classes:** Most classes have 10–19 students. Most lab/discussion sessions have 10–19 students. **Majors with Highest Enrollment:** Business/commerce; elementary education and teaching; nursing/registered nurse (RN, ASN, BSN, MSN). **Special Study Options:** Cross-registration, double major, dual enrollment, independent study, internships, liberal arts/career combination, student-designed major, study abroad, teacher certification program, adult degree completion program (one evening per week, concentrated study). **Combined degree programs:** BA/BS Eng. Special programs offered to physically disabled students include note-taking services, reader services, tape recorders, tutors. **Career services:** Alumni network, career/job search classes, internships, regional alumni.

FACILITIES

Housing: Coed dorms, special housing for disabled students, men's dorms, women's dorms, apartments for married students, apartments for single students, wellness housing. 88% of campus accessible to physically disabled. **Special Academic Facilities/Equipment:** X-ray precision lab, lab kindergarten, Mennonite Historical Library. **Computers:** 100% of classrooms, 25% of dorms, 80% of libraries, 75% of dining areas, 100% of student union, have wireless network access. Students can register for classes online. Administrative functions (other than registration) can be performed online.

CAMPUS LIFE

Environment: Town. **Activities:** Choral groups, concert band, drama/theater, jazz band, music ensembles, musical theater, opera, radio station, student government, student newspaper, student-run film society, symphony orchestra, yearbook, campus ministries, international student organization. **Organizations:** 21 registered organizations, 4 religious organizations. **Athletics (Intercollegiate):** *Men:* Baseball, basketball, cross-country, golf, soccer, tennis, track/field (outdoor), track/field (indoor). *Women:* Basketball, cross-country, soccer, softball, tennis, track/field (outdoor), track/field (indoor), volleyball. **On-Campus Highlights:** Music Center, Gingerich ReC–Fitness Center, Science Building, Residential Halls Connector, Good Library. **Environmental Initiatives:** Built the first Platinum LEED-certified facility in Indiana at our Merry Lea Environmental Center www.goshen.edu/merrylea. Signing the President's Climate Commitment and the formation of the Ecological Stewardship Committee. Have reduced campus wide gas use by 31% and electric use by 17% over the last six years during a time when actual square footage of buildings increased by 20%.

ADMISSIONS

Freshman Academic Profile: Average high school GPA 3.59. 30% in top 10% of high school class, 58% in top 25% of high school class, 82% in top 50% of high school class. 78% from public high schools. SAT Math middle 50% range 490–630. SAT Critical Reading middle 50% range 470–640. SAT Writing middle 50% range 450–620. ACT middle 50% range 21-29. Minimum paper TOEFL 550. Minimum computer TOEFL 213. **Basis for Candidate Selection:** *Very important factors considered include:* Academic GPA, rigor of secondary school record, standardized test scores. *Important factors considered include:* Class rank, recommendation(s), character/personal qualities, interview. *Other factors considered include:* Application essay, alumni/ae relation, extracurricular activities, level of applicant's interest, religious affiliation/commitment, talent/ability, volunteer work, work experience. **Freshman Admission Requirements:** High school diploma is required and GED is accepted. *Academic units required:* 4 English, 2 mathematics, 2 science, 2 foreign language, 2 social studies, 2 history.

Academic units recommended: 4 English, 3 mathematics, 3 science, 2 foreign language, 2 social studies, 2 history. **Freshman Admission Statistics:** 788 applied, 68% admitted, 45% enrolled. **Transfer Admission Requirements:** College transcript(s), essay or personal statement, statement of good standing from prior institution(s). Lowest grade transferable C. **General Admission Information:** Application fee $25. Regular application deadline 8/1. Notification on a rolling basis, beginning on or about 9/15. Nonfall registration accepted. Admission may be deferred for a maximum of 1 year. Credit and/or placement offered for CEEB Advanced Placement tests.

COSTS AND FINANCIAL AID

Annual tuition $23,400. Room and board $7,900. Average book expense $890. **Required Forms and Deadlines:** FAFSA, institution's own financial aid form. Priority financial aid filing date 2/1. **Notification of Awards:** Applicants will be notified of awards on a rolling basis beginning 3/1. **Types of Aid:** *Need-based scholarships/grants:* Federal Pell, SEOG, state scholarships/grants, private scholarships, the school's own gift aid. *Loans:* Direct Subsidized Stafford, Direct Unsubsidized Stafford, Direct PLUS, Federal Perkins, Federal Nursing, college/university loans from institutional funds. **Student Employment:** Federal Work-Study Program available. Institutional employment available. Highest amount earned per year from on-campus jobs $1,001. Off-campus job opportunities are poor. **Financial Aid Statistics:** 84% freshmen, 82% undergrads receive need-based scholarship or grant aid. 12% freshmen, 12% undergrads receive non-need-based scholarship or grant aid. 66% freshmen, 66% undergrads receive need-based self-help aid. 8% freshmen, 7% undergrads receive athletic scholarships. 100% freshmen, 99% undergrads receive any aid. 76.7% undergrads borrow to pay for school. Average cumulative indebtedness $20,857. **Criteria for awarding institutional aid:** *Non-need-based:* Academics, art, athletics, leadership, music/drama.

GOUCHER COLLEGE

1021 Dulaney Valley Road, Baltimore, MD 21204-2794
Phone: 410-337-6100 **Financial Aid Phone:** 410-337-6141
E-mail: admissions@goucher.edu **CEEB Code:** 5257
Fax: 410-337-6354 **Website:** www.goucher.edu **ACT Code:** 1696

This private school was founded in 1885. It has a 287-acre campus.

RATINGS

Admissions Selectivity Rating: 84   **Fire Safety Rating:** 86   **Green Rating:** 94

STUDENTS AND FACULTY

Enrollment: 1,464. **Student Body:** 69% female, 31% male, 72% out-of-state, 1% international (30 countries represented). Asian 3%, African American 8%, Caucasian 66%, Hispanic 5%, Native American 1%.
Retention and Graduation: 75% freshmen return for sophomore year. 60% freshmen graduate within 4 years. 34% grads go on to further study within 1 year. **Faculty:** Student/faculty ratio 9:1. 130 full-time faculty, 88% hold PhDs, 15% are members of minority groups, 65% are women.

ACADEMICS

Degrees: Bachelor's, master's, post-bachelor's certificate. **Classes:** Most classes have 10–19 students. **Majors with Highest Enrollment:** Biology/biological sciences; business administration and management; elementary education and teaching. **Special Study Options:** Cross-registration, distance learning, double major, dual enrollment, independent study, internships, student-designed major, study abroad, teacher certification program. **Combined degree programs:** BA/MEng **Career services:** Alumni network, alumni services, career assessment, internships. **Career services highlights include:** Goucher has been linking liberal arts education with internships for more than 75 years. Through our internship program, we help students explore career paths, enhance skills, and experience the world of work.

FACILITIES

Housing: Coed dorms, special housing for disabled students, women's dorms, apartments for single students, wellness housing, theme housing. **Special Academic Facilities/Equipment:** The Athenaeum is a 103,000–square-foot building which is open 24 hours a day and features a new, technologically superior library; a spacious open forum for performances, public discussions, and other events; a cafe, art gallery; a center for community service and multicultural affairs programming; and spaces for exercise, conversation, and quiet reflection and relaxation. Goucher, in collaboration with the architecture firm RMJM, approached every aspect of the Athenaeum project with an eye toward sustainable design strategies, and the project is in the process of applying for Silver certification from the Leadership in Energy and Environmental Design (LEED) Green-Building Rating System. The Silber Art Gallery in the Athenaeum provides a suitably secure gallery dedicated solely to the exhibition of art, both from the Goucher collection and from contemporary artists and collectors outside the campus. The 1,000–square-foot gallery is the new home to Goucher's permanent collection and its critically acclaimed program of contemporary art exhibitions. In addition to enabling us to display selections from the college's permanent collection, the gallery hosts a range of programming, from the traditional to the experimental, featuring the work of students, emerging artists, and established names alike. Additionally, Goucher has the Rosenberg Art Gallery and the Scientific Visualization Lab. **Computers:** 95% of classrooms, 40% of dorms, 100% of libraries, 100% of dining areas, 100% of student union, 80% of common outdoor areas have wireless network access. Students can register for classes online. Administrative functions (other than registration) can be performed online.

CAMPUS LIFE

Environment: City. **Activities:** Choral groups, dance, drama/theater, jazz band, literary magazine, music ensembles, musical theater, opera, radio station, student government, student newspaper, student-run film society, symphony orchestra, television station, yearbook, campus ministries, international student organization, Model UN. **Organizations:** 60 registered organizations, 1 honor societies, 8 religious organizations. **Athletics (Intercollegiate):** *Men:* Basketball, cross-country, lacrosse, soccer, swimming, tennis, track/field (outdoor), track/field (indoor). *Women:* Basketball, cross-country, equestrian sports, field hockey, lacrosse, soccer, swimming, tennis, track/field (outdoor), track/field (indoor), volleyball. **On-Campus Highlights:** The Library at the Athenaeum, Alice's Cafe, Sports and Recreation Center, Pearlstone Cafe, Gopher Hole. **Environmental Initiatives:** Building our newest building, the Athenaeum, to be LEED-certified, and committing that future buildings and renovations will also be LEED-certified. Signing the American College and University Presidents' Climate Commitment which requires a comprehensive inventory of all greenhouse gas emissions and developing an institutional action plan to become climate neutral. Creating the Goucher Environmental sustainability Advisory Council. The council will research and explore solutions to the environmental issues raised by members of the Goucher community and report its findings to the president. It will help implement campus environmental programs and monitor the college's progress in fulfilling the requirements of the climate commitment.

ADMISSIONS

Freshman Academic Profile: Average high school GPA 3.17. 26% in top 10% of high school class, 52% in top 25% of high school class, 89% in top 50% of high school class. 63% from public high schools. SAT Math middle 50% range 510–630. SAT Critical Reading middle 50% range 550–670. SAT Writing middle 50% range 540–650. ACT middle 50% range 23–29. Minimum paper TOEFL 550. Minimum computer TOEFL 213. **Basis for Candidate Selection:** *Very important factors considered include:* Academic GPA, rigor of secondary school record. *Important factors considered include:* Application essay, recommendation(s), talent/ability. *Other factors considered include:* Class rank, standardized test scores, alumni/ae relation, character/personal qualities, extracurricular activities, first generation, geographical residence, interview, level of applicant's interest, racial/ethnic status, state residency, volunteer work, work experience. **Freshman Admission Requirements:** High school diploma is required and GED is accepted. *Academic units required:* 4 English, 3 mathematics, 2 science, 2 foreign language, 3 social studies, 2 academic electives. *Academic units recommended:* 4 English, 4 mathematics, 3 science, 4 foreign language, 3 social studies, 2 academic electives. **Freshman Admission Statistics:** 3,651 applied, 73% admitted, 15% enrolled. **Transfer Admission Requirements:** College transcript(s), essay or personal statement, Lowest grade transferable C. **General Admission Information:** Application fee $55. Regular application deadline 2/1. Regular notification 4/1. Nonfall registration accepted. Admission may be deferred for a maximum of 1 year. Credit and/or placement offered for CEEB Advanced Placement tests.

COSTS AND FINANCIAL AID

Required Forms and Deadlines: FAFSA, CSS/Financial Aid PROFILE, noncustodial PROFILE, business/farm supplement. Financial aid filing deadline 2/1. Priority financial aid filing date 2/1. **Notification of Awards:** Applicants will be notified of awards on a rolling basis beginning 4/1. **Types of Aid:** *Need-based scholarships/grants:* Federal Pell, SEOG, state scholarships/grants, private scholarships, the school's own gift aid. *Loans:* FFEL Subsidized Stafford, FFEL Unsubsidized Stafford, FFEL PLUS, Federal Perkins, college/university loans from institutional funds. **Student Employment:** Federal Work-Study Program available. Institutional employment available. Highest amount earned per year from on-campus jobs $8,356. Off-campus job opportunities are excellent. **Financial Aid Statistics:** 60% freshmen, 55% undergrads receive need-based scholarship or grant aid. 5% freshmen, 6% undergrads receive non-need-based scholarship or grant aid. 56% freshmen, 51% undergrads

receive need-based self-help aid. 82% freshmen, 80.2% undergrads receive any aid. 65% undergrads borrow to pay for school. Average cumulative indebtedness $14,783. **Criteria for awarding institutional aid:** *Non-need-based:* Academics, art, leadership, music/drama.

GOVERNORS STATE UNIVERSITY

1 University Parkway, Admission Proces, University Park, IL 60484
Phone: 708-534-4490 **Financial Aid Phone:** 708-534-4480
E-mail: gsunow@govst.edu
Fax: 708-534-1640 **Website:** www.govst.edu

This public school was founded in 1969. It has a 720-acre campus.

RATINGS
Admissions Selectivity Rating: 60*   **Fire Safety Rating:** 60*   **Green Rating:** 60*

STUDENTS AND FACULTY
Student Body: 3% out-of-state, international (17 countries represented). **Retention and Graduation:** 34% grads go on to further study within 1 year. 17% grads pursue arts and sciences degrees. 1% grads pursue law degrees. 16% grads pursue business degrees. **Faculty:** Student/faculty ratio 16:1. 203 full-time faculty, 80% hold PhDs, 25% are members of minority groups, 40% are women.

ACADEMICS
Degrees: Bachelor's, master's, post-master's certificate. **Majors with Highest Enrollment:** Business/commerce; communication and media studies, other; elementary education and teaching. **Special Study Options:** Cross-registration, distance learning, dual enrollment, external degree program, honors program, independent study, internships, student-designed major, study abroad, teacher certification program. Special programs offered to physically disabled students include note-taking services, reader services, tape recorders, tutors. **Career services:** Alumni network, alumni services, career/job search classes, career assessment, internships.

FACILITIES
Housing: 99% of campus accessible to physically disabled. **Special Academic Facilities/Equipment:** Manilow Sculpture Park. **Computers:** Students can register for classes online. Administrative functions (other than registration) can be performed online.

CAMPUS LIFE
Environment: Village. **Activities:** Drama/theater, literary magazine, student government, student newspaper, student-run film society. **Organizations:** 7 honor societies.

ADMISSIONS
Transfer Admission Requirements: College transcript(s), statement of good standing from prior institution(s). Minimum college GPA of 2.0 required. Lowest grade transferable C. **General Admission Information:** Nonfall registration not accepted.

COSTS AND FINANCIAL AID
Annual in-state tuition $4,470. Annual out-of-state tuition $13,410. Required fees $480. **Types of Aid:** *Need-based scholarships/grants:* Federal Pell, SEOG, state scholarships/grants, private scholarships, the school's own gift aid, Federal Nursing Scholarships. *Loans:* Direct Subsidized Stafford, Federal Perkins, Federal Nursing, state loans, college/university loans from institutional funds. **Student Employment:** Federal Work-Study Program available. Institutional employment available. **Criteria for awarding institutional aid:** *Non-need-based:* Academics.

GRACE BIBLE COLLEGE

1011 Aldon Street SW, PO Box 910, Grand Rapids, MI 49509-1921
Phone: 616-538-2330
E-mail: enrollment@gbcol.edu
Fax: 616-538-0599 **Website:** www.gbcol.edu

This is a private school.

RATINGS
Admissions Selectivity Rating: 60*   **Fire Safety Rating:** 60*   **Green Rating:** 60*

STUDENTS AND FACULTY

Enrollment: 153. **Student Body:** 52% female, 48% male, % out-of-state. **Retention and Graduation:** 45% freshmen return for sophomore year. 13% freshmen graduate within 4 years.

ACADEMICS

Degrees: Associate, bachelor's.

CAMPUS LIFE

Environment: Village.

ADMISSIONS

Freshman Academic Profile: Basis for Candidate Selection: *Very important factors considered include:* Application essay, rigor of secondary school record, standardized test scores. *Important factors considered include:* Class rank, recommendation(s), character/personal qualities, religious affiliation/commitment. *Other factors considered include:* Extracurricular activities, talent/ability, volunteer work, work experience. **Freshman Admission Requirements:** High school diploma is required and GED is accepted. **Freshman Admission Statistics:** 166 applied, 43% admitted, 56% enrolled.

COSTS AND FINANCIAL AID

Annual tuition $11,120. Room and board $6,400. Required fees $520. **Types of Aid:** *Need-based scholarships/grants:* Federal Pell, SEOG, state scholarships/grants, private scholarships, the school's own gift aid. *Loans:* FFEL Subsidized Stafford, FFEL Unsubsidized Stafford, FFEL PLUS, state loans. **Criteria for awarding institutional aid:** *Non-need-based:* Academics.

GRACE COLLEGE AND SEMINARY

200 Seminary Drive, Winona Lake, IN 46590
Phone: 800-544-7223 **Financial Aid Phone:** 574-372-5100
E-mail: enroll@grace.edu **CEEB Code:** 1252
Fax: 574-372-5120 **Website:** www.grace.edu **ACT Code:** 1198

This private school was founded in 1948. It has a 150-acre campus.

RATINGS

Admissions Selectivity Rating: 83   **Fire Safety Rating:** 60*   **Green Rating:** 60*

STUDENTS AND FACULTY

Enrollment: 1,383. **Student Body:** 47% female, 53% male, 53% out-of-state, 1% international (6 countries represented). Asian 1%, African American 11%, Caucasian 84%, Hispanic 2%, Native American 1%.
Retention and Graduation: 80% freshmen return for sophomore year. 50% freshmen graduate within 4 years. **Faculty:** Student/faculty ratio 18:1. 57 full-time faculty, 65% hold PhDs, 2% are members of minority groups, 16% are women.

ACADEMICS

Degrees: Associate, bachelor's, certificate, diploma, master's. **Classes:** Most classes have 10–19 students. Most lab/discussion sessions have 10–19 students. **Majors with Highest Enrollment:** Business/commerce; counseling psychology; elementary education and teaching. **Special Study Options:** Cooperative education program, cross-registration, distance learning, double major, dual enrollment, exchange student program (domestic), honors program, independent study, internships, liberal arts/career combination, study abroad, teacher certification program, degree completion. Special programs offered to physically disabled students include note-taking services, reader services, tape recorders, tutors. **Career services:** Career assessment.

FACILITIES

Housing: Men's dorms, women's dorms, apartments for single students. 85% of campus accessible to physically disabled. **Special Academic Facilities/Equipment:** Reneker Museum of Winona History. **Computers:** 100% of classrooms, 100% of dorms, 100% of libraries, 100% of dining areas, 100% of student union, 33% of common outdoor areas have wireless network access. Students can register for classes online. Administrative functions (other than registration) can be performed online.

CAMPUS LIFE

Environment: Village. **Activities:** Choral groups, concert band, drama/theater, music ensembles, musical theater, opera, pep band, student government, student newspaper, symphony orchestra, yearbook, campus ministries. **Organizations:** 9 registered organizations, 1 honor societies, 8 religious organizations. **Athletics (Intercollegiate):** *Men:* Baseball, basketball, cheerleading, cross-country, golf, soccer, tennis, track/field (outdoor). *Women:* Basketball, cheerleading, cross-country, soccer, softball, tennis, track/field (outdoor), volleyball. **On-Campus Highlights:** Gordon Recreation Center, Tree of Life Coffee shop, Westminster Grille, Orthopedic Capital Center.

ADMISSIONS

Freshman Academic Profile: Average high school GPA 3.463. 28% in top 10% of high school class, 57% in top 25% of high school class, 85% in top 50% of high school class. 71% from public high schools. SAT Math middle 50% range 470–590. SAT Critical Reading middle 50% range 460–590. ACT middle 50% range 21-28. **Basis for Candidate Selection:** *Very important factors considered include:* Application essay, recommendation(s), rigor of secondary school record, standardized test scores, religious affiliation/commitment. *Important factors considered include:* Academic GPA, character/personal qualities. *Other factors considered include:* Class rank, alumni/ae relation, extracurricular activities, interview, talent/ability. **Freshman Admission Requirements:** High school diploma is required and GED is accepted. *Academic units recommended:* 4 English, 2 mathematics, 2 science, (1 science labs), 2 foreign language, 2 social studies, 1 history. **Freshman Admission Statistics:** 1,027 applied, 97% admitted, 23% enrolled. **Transfer Admission Requirements:** College transcript(s), essay or personal statement, standardized test scores, minimum college GPA of 2.0 required. Lowest grade transferable C–. **General Admission Information:** Application fee $20. Regular application deadline 8/15. Notification on a rolling basis, beginning on or about 9/1. Nonfall registration accepted. Admission may be deferred for a maximum of 1 semester. Credit offered for CEEB Advanced Placement tests.

COSTS AND FINANCIAL AID

Annual tuition $21,100. Room and board $6,880. Average book expense $800. **Required Forms and Deadlines:** FAFSA. Priority financial aid filing date 3/10. **Notification of Awards:** Applicants will be notified of awards on a rolling basis beginning 3/1. **Types of Aid:** *Need-based scholarships/grants:* Federal Pell, SEOG, state scholarships/grants, private scholarships, the school's own gift aid. *Loans:* FFEL Subsidized Stafford, FFEL Unsubsidized Stafford, FFEL PLUS, Federal Perkins, Alternative Educational Loan Program. **Student Employment:** Federal Work-Study Program available. Institutional employment available. Off-campus job opportunities are good. **Financial Aid Statistics: Criteria for awarding institutional aid:** *Non-need-based:* Academics, art, athletics, leadership, music/drama.

GRACE UNIVERSITY

1311 S 9th St, Omaha, NE 68108
Phone: 402-449-2831
E-mail: admissions@graceu.com
Fax: 402-341-9587 **Website:** www.graceuniversity.com **ACT Code:** 2454

This private school, affiliated with the Christian (Nondenominational) Church, was founded in 1943. It has a 20-acre campus.

RATINGS

Admissions Selectivity Rating: 60*   **Fire Safety Rating:** 60*   **Green Rating:** 60*

STUDENTS AND FACULTY

Enrollment: 427. **Student Body:** 57% female, 43% male, 60% out-of-state, 1% international (7 countries represented). African American 5%, Caucasian 99%, Hispanic 2%.
Faculty: Student/faculty ratio 18:1. 25 full-time faculty, 100% hold PhDs, 8% are members of minority groups, 28% are women.

ACADEMICS

Degrees: Associate, bachelor's, certificate, master's, terminal associate, transfer associate. **Majors with Highest Enrollment:** Bible/biblical studies; education; youth ministry. **Special Study Options:** Accelerated program, cooperative education program, distance learning, double major, dual enrollment, independent study, student-designed major, study abroad, teacher certification program. Special programs offered to physically disabled students include note-taking services, tape recorders. **Career services:** Career assessment, internships.

FACILITIES

Housing: Men's dorms, women's dorms, apartments for married students 100% of campus accessible to physically disabled. **Computers:** Administrative functions (other than registration) can be performed online.

CAMPUS LIFE

Environment: Metropolis. **Activities:** Choral groups, concert band, drama/theater, music ensembles, musical theater, pep band, radio station, student government, student newspaper, yearbook. **Organizations:** 6 registered organizations, 1 religious organizations. **Athletics (Intercollegiate):** *Men:* Basketball, soccer. *Women:* Basketball, volleyball. **On-Campus Highlights:** Dirk Lounge, Health and Fitness Center, Dorms, Dining Commons, Royal's Court.

ADMISSIONS

Freshman Academic Profile: Minimum paper TOEFL 550. Minimum computer TOEFL 213. **Basis for Candidate Selection:** *Very important factors considered include:* Application essay, recommendation(s), rigor of secondary school record, religious affiliation/commitment. *Important factors considered include:* Class rank, standardized test scores, character/personal qualities. *Other factors considered include:* Alumni/ae relation, extracurricular activities, interview, talent/ability, volunteer work, work experience. **Freshman Admission Requirements:** High school diploma is required and GED is accepted. *Academic units recommended:* 4 English, 4 mathematics, 4 science, 2 foreign language, 4 social studies, 4 history. **Freshman Admission Statistics: Transfer Admission Requirements:** High school transcript, college transcript(s), essay or personal statement, minimum college GPA of 2.0 required. Lowest grade transferable C. **General Admission Information:** Application fee $35. Nonfall registration accepted. Admission may be deferred for a maximum of 1 year. Credit offered for CEEB Advanced Placement tests.

COSTS AND FINANCIAL AID

Required Forms and Deadlines: FAFSA, institution's own financial aid form. Priority financial aid filing date 1/31. **Notification of Awards:** Applicants will be notified of awards on or about 4/1. **Types of Aid:** *Need-based scholarships/grants:* Federal Pell, SEOG, state scholarships/grants, private scholarships, the school's own gift aid, United Negro College Fund. *Loans:* FFEL Subsidized Stafford, FFEL Unsubsidized Stafford, FFEL PLUS, alternative loans. **Student Employment:** Federal Work-Study Program available. Institutional employment available. Highest amount earned per year from on-campus jobs $3,750. Off-campus job opportunities are excellent. **Financial Aid Statistics:** 57% freshmen, 70% undergrads receive need-based scholarship or grant aid. 5% freshmen, 7% undergrads receive non-need-based scholarship or grant aid. 50% freshmen, 62% undergrads receive need-based self-help aid. 77% freshmen, 78% undergrads receive any aid. 72% undergrads borrow to pay for school. Average cumulative indebtedness $11,282. **Criteria for awarding institutional aid:** *Non-need-based:* Academics, alumni affiliation, leadership, music/drama, religious affiliation.

GRACELAND UNIVERSITY

1 University Place, Lamoni, IA 50140
Phone: 6417845196 **Financial Aid Phone:** 641 784 5140
E-mail: admissions@graceland.edu/apply-now **CEEB Code:** 6249
Fax: 6417845480 **Website:** www.graceland.edu **ACT Code:** 1314

This private school was founded in 1895. It has a 170-acre campus.

RATINGS

Admissions Selectivity Rating: 78   **Fire Safety Rating:** 67   **Green Rating:** 75

STUDENTS AND FACULTY

Enrollment: 1,330. **Student Body:** 60% female, 40% male, 37% out-of-state, 9% international (49 countries represented). Asian 2%, African American 10%, Caucasian 69%, Hispanic 3%, Native American 1%. **Retention and Graduation:** 68% freshmen return for sophomore year. 34% freshmen graduate within 4 years. 28% grads go on to further study within 1 year. **Faculty:** Student/faculty ratio 15.5:1. 85 full-time faculty, 68% hold PhDs, 16% are members of minority groups, 56% are women.

ACADEMICS

Degrees: Bachelor's, master's, post-bachelor's certificate, post-master's certificate. **Classes:** Most classes have 10–19 students. Most lab/discussion sessions have 20–29 students. **Majors with Highest Enrollment:** Business administration and management; elementary education and teaching; nursing/registered nurse (RN, ASN, BSN, MSN). **Special Study Options:** Accelerated program, distance learning, double major, dual enrollment, English as a Second Language (ESL), honors program, independent study, internships, liberal arts/career combination, student-designed major, study abroad, teacher certification program. **Honors programs:** The Graceland University Honors Program includes courses in Honors English, Honors Humanities, Honors Advanced Composition, the combined Jr. and Sr. Honors Seminar, a Sr. Honors Thesis, and Honors Contracts to be created with instructors in any academic course the students choose. Completion of the Honors Program requires 21 hours of honors credit, completion of the Jr. and Sr. Honors Seminars, a Sr. Honors Thesis, and a minimum 3.5 gpa overall and in their honors work. Honors Students with a 3.75 gpa or higher are eligible for an Honors Scholarship. Incoming students with a 3.75 gap and an ACT of 27 or higher may apply for full tuition Prestigious Honors Scholarship, which are available on a competitive basis, and require an interview. Graceland University offers an Excellent Education in a caring community. So we believe the best reason to participate in the Honors Program

is the people in it, and to participate in the Honors community. **Combined degree programs:** BSN/MSN. Special programs offered to physically disabled students include note-taking services, reader services, tape recorders, tutors. **Career services:** Alumni network, alumni services, career/job search classes, career assessment, internships. **Career services highlights include:** We have our own job posting site for students and alumni. We offer our career exploration and job search classes online each semester.

FACILITIES

Housing: Men's dorms, women's dorms, apartments for married students 95% of campus accessible to physically disabled. **Computers:** 100% of classrooms, 91% of dorms, 100% of libraries, 100% of dining areas, 100% of student union, 30% of common outdoor areas have wireless network access. Students can register for classes online. Administrative functions (other than registration) can be performed online.

CAMPUS LIFE

Environment: Rural. **Activities:** Choral groups, concert band, dance, drama/theater, jazz band, music ensembles, musical theater, pep band, radio station, student government, student newspaper, symphony orchestra, yearbook, campus ministries, international student organization. **Organizations:** 54 registered organizations, 1 religious organizations. **Athletics (Intercollegiate):** *Men:* Baseball, basketball, cross-country, football, golf, soccer, tennis, track/field (outdoor), track/field (indoor), volleyball. *Women:* Basketball, cross-country, golf, soccer, softball, tennis, track/field (outdoor), track/field (indoor), volleyball. **On-Campus Highlights:** Resch Science & Technology Hall, The Helene Center for Visual Arts, The Closson Center, The Shaw Center for Performing Arts, The Higdon Administration Building. **Environmental Initiatives:** Paper, plastic, and aluminium recycling; as much as possible, all building materials are green-labeled; Campus Committee made up of students/staff/faculty to develop a realistic sustainability plan

ADMISSIONS

Freshman Academic Profile: Average high school GPA 3.44. 11% in top 10% of high school class, 30% in top 25% of high school class, 60% in top 50% of high school class. 99% from public high schools. SAT Math middle 50% range 420–550. SAT Critical Reading middle 50% range 420–530. ACT middle 50% range 16–23. Minimum paper TOEFL 450. Minimum computer TOEFL 133. Minimum web-based TOEFL 45. **Basis for Candidate Selection:** *Very important factors considered include:* Class rank, academic GPA, rigor of secondary school record, standardized test scores, character/personal qualities, talent/ability. *Important factors considered include:* Extracurricular activities, interview. *Other factors considered include:* Application essay, recommendation(s), alumni/ae relation, religious affiliation/commitment. **Freshman Admission Requirements:** High school diploma is required and GED is accepted. *Academic units recommended:* 4 English, 4 mathematics, 4 science, 4 social studies. **Freshman Admission Statistics:** 598 applied, 88% admitted, 42% enrolled. **Transfer Admission Requirements:** College transcript(s), minimum college GPA of 2.0 required. Lowest grade transferable D. **General Admission Information:** Application fee $50. Nonfall registration accepted. Credit and/or placement offered for CEEB Advanced Placement tests.

COSTS AND FINANCIAL AID

Annual tuition $20,680. Room and board $7,040. Required fees $300. Average book expense $1,000. **Required Forms and Deadlines:** FAFSA. **Notification of Awards:** Applicants will be notified of awards on a rolling basis beginning 3/1. **Types of Aid:** *Need-based scholarships/grants:* Federal Pell, SEOG, state scholarships/grants, private scholarships, the school's own gift aid. *Loans:* Direct Subsidized Stafford, Direct Unsubsidized Stafford, Direct PLUS, Federal Perkins, state loans, college/university loans from institutional funds, Alternative loans. **Student Employment:** Federal Work-Study Program available. Institutional employment available. Highest amount earned per year from on-campus jobs $6,062. Off-campus job opportunities are poor. **Financial Aid Statistics:** 81% freshmen, 66% undergrads receive need-based scholarship or grant aid. 44% freshmen, 30% undergrads receive non-need-based scholarship or grant aid. 70% freshmen, 62% undergrads receive need-based self-help aid. 17% freshmen, 14% undergrads receive athletic scholarships. 96% freshmen, 88% undergrads receive any aid. 89% undergrads borrow to pay for school. Average cumulative indebtedness $29,934. **Criteria for awarding institutional aid:** *Non-need-based:* Academics, alumni affiliation, art, athletics, job skills, leadership, music/drama, religious affiliation.

See page 1104.

GRAMBLING STATE UNIVERSITY

P. O. Box 864, Grambling, LA 71245
Phone: 318-274-6423
E-mail: taylorn@gram.edu **CEEB Code:** 6250
Fax: 318-274-3292 **Website:** www.gram.edu **ACT Code:** 1582

This public school was founded in 1901. It has a 340-acre campus.

RATINGS
Admissions Selectivity Rating: 60*   **Fire Safety Rating:** 60*   **Green Rating:** 60*

STUDENTS AND FACULTY
Enrollment: 4,171. **Student Body:** 57% female, 43% male, 34% out-of-state, 2% international (21 countries represented). African American 105%, Caucasian 4%.
Retention and Graduation: 68% freshmen return for sophomore year. 20% freshmen graduate within 4 years. 33% grads go on to further study within 1 year. 33% grads pursue arts and sciences degrees. **Faculty:** Student/faculty ratio 17:1. 243 full-time faculty, 57% hold PhDs, 78% are members of minority groups, 42% are women.

ACADEMICS
Degrees: Associate, bachelor's, master's. **Special Study Options:** Accelerated program, cooperative education program, distance learning, double major, exchange student program (domestic), honors program, independent study, internships, study abroad, teacher certification program. **Career services:** Career assessment.

FACILITIES
Housing: Men's dorms, women's dorms, fraternity/sorority housing, graduate dorm. **Special Academic Facilities/Equipment:** Audiovisual and TV center, lab schools.

CAMPUS LIFE
Environment: Village. **Activities:** Choral groups, dance, drama/theater, jazz band, marching band, music ensembles, radio station, student government, student newspaper, television station, yearbook. **Organizations:** 50 registered organizations, 11 honor societies, 3 religious organizations. 4 fraternities, 5 sororities. **Athletics (Intercollegiate):** *Men:* Baseball, basketball, cross-country, football, golf, tennis, track/field (outdoor), track/field (indoor). *Women:* Basketball, cross-country, golf, soccer, softball, tennis, track/field (outdoor), track/field (indoor).

ADMISSIONS
Freshman Academic Profile: Average high school GPA 2.65. **Basis for Candidate Selection:** *Very important factors considered include:* standardized test scores. *Other factors considered include:* Recommendation(s), alumni/ae relation, extracurricular activities, talent/ability. **Freshman Admission Requirements:** High school diploma is required and GED is accepted. *Academic units required:* 4 English, 3 mathematics, 3 science, 3 social studies, 8 academic electives, 2 health and P.E. **Freshman Admission Statistics:** 2,923 applied, 62% admitted, 57% enrolled. **Transfer Admission Requirements:** College transcript(s), statement of good standing from prior institution(s). Minimum college GPA of 2.0 required. Lowest grade transferable C. **General Admission Information:** Application fee $20. Early decision application deadline 4/15. Regular application deadline 8/1. Nonfall registration accepted. Admission may be deferred for a maximum of 6 months.

COSTS AND FINANCIAL AID
Annual in-state tuition $5,652. Annual out-of-state tuition $8,327. Room and board $2,912. Required fees $60. Average book expense $600. **Required Forms and Deadlines:** FAFSA, Institutional Scholarship Application. Financial aid filing deadline 6/1. Priority financial aid filing date 6/1. **Notification of Awards:** Applicants will be notified of awards on a rolling basis beginning 3/1. **Types of Aid:** *Need-based scholarships/grants:* Federal Pell, SEOG, state scholarships/grants. *Loans:* Direct Subsidized Stafford, Direct Unsubsidized Stafford, Direct PLUS, FFEL Subsidized Stafford, FFEL Unsubsidized Stafford, FFEL PLUS, Federal Perkins, college/university loans from institutional funds, non-federal alternative/private loans. **Student Employment:** Federal Work-Study Program available. Institutional employment available. Highest amount earned per year from on-campus jobs $4,648. Off-campus job opportunities are good. **Financial Aid Statistics:** 73% freshmen, 68% undergrads receive need-based scholarship or grant aid. 24% freshmen, 19% undergrads receive non-need-based scholarship or grant aid. 78% freshmen, 69% undergrads receive need-based self-help aid. 4% freshmen, 5% undergrads receive athletic scholarships. 90% freshmen, 92% undergrads receive any aid. 90% undergrads borrow to pay for school. Average cumulative indebtedness $25,000. **Criteria for awarding institutional aid:** *Non-need-based:* Academics, alumni affiliation, athletics, leadership, minority status, music/drama, state/district residency.

GRAND CANYON UNIVERSITY

3300 W Camelback Road, 3300 W Camelback Road, Phoenix, AZ 85061-0197
Phone: 602-589-2855
E-mail: admissions@grand-canyon.edu **CEEB Code:** 4331
Fax: 602-589-2580 **Website:** www.grand-canyon.edu **ACT Code:** 92

This private school was founded in 1949. It has a 90-acre campus.

RATINGS
Admissions Selectivity Rating: 60*   **Fire Safety Rating:** 60*   **Green Rating:** 60*

STUDENTS AND FACULTY
Enrollment: 1,609. **Student Body:** 64% female, 36% male, 19% out-of-state, 3% international. Asian 2%, African American 3%, Caucasian 56%, Hispanic 7%, Native American 1%.
Retention and Graduation: 76% freshmen return for sophomore year. 32% freshmen graduate within 4 years. **Faculty:** Student/faculty ratio 16:1. 97 full-time faculty, 58% hold PhDs, 3% are members of minority groups, 52% are women.

ACADEMICS
Degrees: Bachelor's, diploma, master's. **Classes:** Most classes have fewer than 10 students. Most lab/discussion sessions have 10–19 students. **Special Study Options:** Accelerated program, cooperative education program, distance learning, double major, dual enrollment, English as a Second Language (ESL), exchange student program (domestic), honors program, independent study, internships, study abroad, teacher certification program Special programs offered to physically disabled students include note-taking services, reader services, tape recorders, tutors. **Career services:** Alumni services, career assessment, internships.

FACILITIES
Housing: Men's dorms, women's dorms, apartments for married students, apartments for single students. 99% of campus accessible to physically disabled. **Special Academic Facilities/Equipment:** Art gallery, dynamical systems laboratory.

CAMPUS LIFE
Activities: Choral groups, concert band, drama/theater, jazz band, literary magazine, music ensembles, musical theater, opera, student government, student newspaper. **Organizations:** 20 registered organizations, 3 honor societies, 4 religious organizations. **Athletics (Intercollegiate):** *Men:* Baseball, basketball, golf, soccer. *Women:* Basketball, soccer, tennis, volleyball. **On-Campus Highlights:** New student union, new student suites, sthletic facilities, Ethington Theatre, medical cadaver lab.

ADMISSIONS
Freshman Academic Profile: Minimum paper TOEFL 500. **Basis for Candidate Selection:** *Very important factors considered include:* Rigor of secondary school record, standardized test scores. *Important factors considered include:* Class rank. *Other factors considered include:* Application essay, recommendation(s), character/personal qualities, extracurricular activities, interview, talent/ability. **Freshman Admission Requirements:** High school diploma is required and GED is accepted. *Academic units required:* 4 English, 3 mathematics, 2 science, (2 science labs), 2 social studies. *Academic units recommended:* 4 English, 3 mathematics, 2 science, (2 science labs), 2 social studies. **Freshman Admission Statistics:** 823 applied, 69% admitted, 44% enrolled. **Transfer Admission Requirements:** College transcript(s), minimum college GPA of 2.0 required. Lowest grade transferable C. **General Admission Information:** Application fee $50. Nonfall registration accepted. Credit offered for CEEB Advanced Placement tests.

COSTS AND FINANCIAL AID
Annual tuition $9,750. Room and board $7,130. Average book expense $780. **Required Forms and Deadlines:** FAFSA. **Notification of Awards:** Applicants will be notified of awards on a rolling basis beginning 3/15. **Types of Aid:** *Need-based scholarships/grants:* Federal Pell, SEOG, state scholarships/grants, private scholarships, the school's own gift aid, Bureau of Indian Affairs Grant. *Loans:* FFEL Subsidized Stafford, FFEL Unsubsidized Stafford, FFEL PLUS, Federal Perkins, state loans, Alternative loans. **Student Employment:** Federal Work-Study Program available. Institutional employment available. Highest amount earned per year from on-campus jobs $1,500. Off-campus job opportunities are excellent. **Financial Aid Statistics:** 23% freshmen, 29% undergrads receive need-based scholarship or grant aid. 59% freshmen, 46% undergrads receive non-need-based scholarship or grant aid. 39% freshmen, 49% undergrads receive need-based self-help aid. 4% freshmen, 5% undergrads receive athletic scholarships. 61% undergrads borrow to pay for school. Average cumulative indebtedness $46,640. **Criteria for awarding institutional aid:** *Non-need-based:* Academics, alumni affiliation, art, athletics, job skills, leadership, minority status, music/drama, religious affiliation, state/district residency.

GRAND RAPIDS THEOLOGICAL SEMINARY

1001 E Beltline Ave. NE, Grand Rapids, MI 49525
Phone: 1-800-697-1133 **Financial Aid Phone:** 616-949-5300
E-mail: grts@cornerstone.edu
Fax: 616-254-1623 **Website:** http://grts.cornerstone.edu

This is a private school.

RATINGS
Admissions Selectivity Rating: 60*   **Fire Safety Rating:** 60*   **Green Rating:** 70

STUDENTS AND FACULTY
Retention and Graduation: 15% grads go on to further study within 1 year. 10% grads pursue arts and sciences degrees. 1% grads pursue law degrees. 3% grads pursue business degrees. 1% grads pursue medical degrees. **Faculty:** Student/faculty ratio 17:1. 9 full-time faculty, 300% hold PhDs, 56% are women.

ACADEMICS
Degrees: Certificate, master's. **Majors with Highest Enrollment:** Business/commerce; education; psychology. **Special Study Options:** Distance learning, double major, dual enrollment, honors program, independent study, internships, study abroad. **Honors programs:** Honors Program based on a "great books" curriculum. Special programs offered to physically disabled students include note-taking services, reader services, tape recorders, tutors. **Career services:** Career/job search classes, career assessment, internships. **Career services highlights include:** The required internship of all students as part of the graduation requirements.

FACILITIES
Housing: Special housing for disabled students, men's dorms, women's dorms, apartments for married students, apartments for single students 100% of campus accessible to physically disabled. **Computers:** Students can register for classes online. Administrative functions (other than registration) can be performed online. Undergraduates are required to own a computer.

CAMPUS LIFE
Activities: Student government, campus ministries, international student organization. **Organizations:** 11 registered organizations, 2 honor societies, 1 religious organizations. **Athletics (Intercollegiate):** *Men:* Basketball, cross-country, golf, soccer, track/field (outdoor), track/field (indoor). *Women:* Basketball, cross-country, golf, soccer, softball, track/field (outdoor), track/field (indoor), volleyball. **On-Campus Highlights:** Corum Student Union, Bernice Hansen Athletic Center, Campus Bookstore Atrium, Faber Hall Seating Area, Gordon Music Hall. **Environmental Initiatives:** On campus dialogue and focus on sustainability issues. Joining a community organization.

ADMISSIONS
Freshman Academic Profile: 60% from public high schools. Minimum paper TOEFL 500. Minimum computer TOEFL 173. **Basis for Candidate Selection:** *Very important factors considered include:* Application essay, academic GPA, recommendation(s), religious affiliation/commitment. *Important factors considered include:* Standardized test scores, character/personal qualities, extracurricular activities, level of applicant's interest, volunteer work. *Other factors considered include:* Rigor of secondary school record, talent/ability, work experience. **Freshman Admission Requirements:** High school diploma is required and GED is accepted. **Transfer Admission Requirements:** College transcript(s), essay or personal statement, minimum college GPA of 2.5 required. Lowest grade transferable C. **General Admission Information:** Credit and/or placement offered for CEEB Advanced Placement tests.

COSTS AND FINANCIAL AID
Types of Aid: *Need-based scholarships/grants:* state scholarships/grants, private scholarships, the school's own gift aid. *Loans:* Direct Subsidized Stafford, Direct Unsubsidized Stafford. **Student Employment:** Federal Work-Study Program available. Highest amount earned per year from on-campus jobs $5,500. Off-campus job opportunities are good. **Financial Aid Statistics:** 100% freshmen, 98% undergrads receive any aid. **Criteria for awarding institutional aid:** *Non-need-based:* Academics, job skills, leadership, minority status, religious affiliation.

GRAND VALLEY STATE UNIVERSITY

1 Campus Drive, Allendale, MI 49401
Phone: 616-331-2025 **Financial Aid Phone:** 616-331-3234
E-mail: admissions@gvsu.edu **CEEB Code:** 1258
Fax: 616-331-2000 **Website:** www.gvsu.edu **ACT Code:** 2005

This public school was founded in 1960. It has a 1275-acre campus.

RATINGS
Admissions Selectivity Rating: 78   **Fire Safety Rating:** 82   **Green Rating:** 98

STUDENTS AND FACULTY
Enrollment: 20,731. **Student Body:** 59% female, 41% male, 4% out-of-state, 1% international (59 countries represented). Asian 3%, African American 9%, Caucasian 86%, Hispanic 3%, Native American 1%.
Retention and Graduation: 83% freshmen return for sophomore year. **Faculty:** Student/faculty ratio 17:1. 1051 full-time faculty, 54% hold PhDs, 16% are members of minority groups, 46% are women.

ACADEMICS
Degrees: Bachelor's, certificate, master's, post-bachelor's certificate, post-master's certificate. **Classes:** Most classes have 20–29 students. Most lab/discussion sessions have 20–29 students. **Majors with Highest Enrollment:** Business/commerce; health services/allied health/health sciences; psychology. **Special Study Options:** Distance learning, double major, dual enrollment, English as a Second Language (ESL), honors program, independent study, internships, student-designed major, study abroad, teacher certification program. **Honors programs:** Honor's College. **Combined degree programs:** BA/JD, BA/MEng, Physical therapy program; Occupational Therapy; Ph. Special programs offered to physically disabled students include reader services, tape recorders, tutors. **Career services:** Alumni network, alumni services, career/job search classes, career assessment, internships, regional alumni. **Career services highlights include:** We have a very strong cooperative education program in engineering that is mature and provides one year of full-time work for students. We also have very strong internship programs in the following departments: computer science, hospitality, communications, education, health majors, and social work.

FACILITIES
Housing: Coed dorms, fraternity/sorority housing, apartments for married students, apartments for single students, theme housing. 99% of campus accessible to physically disabled. **Special Academic Facilities/Equipment:** Two Great Lakes research vessels, audio-visual center, performance/recital hall, pipe organ, physical therapy/human performance lab. **Computers:** 100% of classrooms, 63% of dorms, 100% of libraries, 100% of dining areas, 100% of student union, have wireless network access. Students can register for classes online. Administrative functions (other than registration) can be performed online.

CAMPUS LIFE
Environment: City. **Activities:** Choral groups, concert band, dance, drama/theater, jazz band, literary magazine, marching band, music ensembles, musical theater, pep band, radio station, student government, student newspaper, symphony orchestra, television station, campus ministries, international student organization. **Organizations:** 301 registered organizations, 20 honor societies, 20 religious organizations. 11 fraternities, 11 sorority. **Athletics (Intercollegiate):** *Men:* Baseball, basketball, cross-country, diving, football, golf, swimming, tennis, track/field (outdoor), track/field (indoor). *Women:* Basketball, cross-country, diving, golf, soccer, softball, swimming, tennis, track/field (outdoor), track/field (indoor), volleyball. **On-Campus Highlights:** Living Centers, Cook DeVos Center for Health Sciences, Recreation Center and Fieldhouse, Laker Turf Building, Kirkhof Center. **Environmental Initiatives:** Climate Mitigation: GVSU is a signatory to American College and University Presidents' Climate Commitment and has recently completed its Climate Action Plan and set a goal of climate neutrality by 2037. The climate action plan is available online. Currently there are over 650 colleges and universities that have signed on to this agreement. LEED construction projects and bus transportation are both important climate mitigation strategies. GVSU has completed and certified 10 LEED projects with 2 more LEED projects under construction. These 12 LEED projects represent over 925,000 square feet and ~19% of total square footage. Annual bus ridership is over ~ 2MM bus rides per year for faculty and students and saves millions of dollars in annual fuel purchases and vehicle maintenance costs while reducing our carbon footprint. Waste Minimization: GVSU's currently diverts over 600 TPY of waste on our main campus from the landfill. Our recycling rate is over 30% and we have entered the national Recylemania competition again this year in a number of waste categories. We have also begun to divert waste from the landfill by composting our campus food waste. In a pilot project at a few locations, we have been able to compost ~50 tons of food waste per month. Local, fair trade, organic food purchases continue to track at a 25% + annualized rate with additional healthy, nutritional and local food options

being offered. A Farmers Market is available on campus during the growing season as well as the development of a campus community garden.

ADMISSIONS

Freshman Academic Profile: Average high school GPA 3.53. 21% in top 10% of high school class, 55% in top 25% of high school class, 91% in top 50% of high school class. 84% from public high schools. SAT Math middle 50% range 520–640. SAT Critical Reading middle 50% range 480–610. SAT Writing middle 50% range 470–580. ACT middle 50% range 22–26. Minimum paper TOEFL 550. Minimum computer TOEFL 213. **Basis for Candidate Selection:** *Very important factors considered include:* Academic GPA, rigor of secondary school record. *Important factors considered include:* Standardized test scores. *Other factors considered include:* Class rank, application essay, recommendation(s), alumni/ae relation, extracurricular activities, first generation, talent/ability, volunteer work, work experience. **Freshman Admission Requirements:** High school diploma is required and GED is accepted. *Academic units required:* 4 English, 3 mathematics, 3 science, (1 science labs), 2 foreign language, 3 social studies. **Freshman Admission Statistics:** 13,051 applied, 81% admitted, 35% enrolled. **Transfer Admission Requirements:** College transcript(s), statement of good standing from prior institution(s). Minimum college GPA of 2.5 required. Lowest grade transferable D. **General Admission Information:** Application fee $30. Nonfall registration accepted. Credit and/or placement offered for CEEB Advanced Placement tests.

COSTS AND FINANCIAL AID

Annual in-state tuition $8,630. Annual out-of-state tuition $12,944. Room and board $7,478. Average book expense $1,000. **Required Forms and Deadlines:** FAFSA. Priority financial aid filing date 3/1. **Notification of Awards:** Applicants will be notified of awards on a rolling basis beginning 3/10. **Types of Aid:** *Need-based scholarships/grants:* Federal Pell, SEOG, state scholarships/grants, private scholarships, the school's own gift aid. *Loans:* Direct Subsidized Stafford, Direct Unsubsidized Stafford, Direct PLUS, Federal Perkins, Federal Nursing. **Student Employment:** Federal Work-Study Program available. Institutional employment available. Highest amount earned per year from on-campus jobs $5,200. Off-campus job opportunities are good. **Financial Aid Statistics:** 50% freshmen, 42% undergrads receive need-based scholarship or grant aid. 4% freshmen, 3% undergrads receive non-need-based scholarship or grant aid. 45% freshmen receive need-based self-help aid. 1% freshmen, 1% undergrads receive athletic scholarships. 68% freshmen, 65% undergrads receive any aid. 70% undergrads borrow to pay for school. Average cumulative indebtedness $21,475. **Criteria for awarding institutional aid:** *Non-need-based:* Academics, alumni affiliation, art, athletics, music/drama, state/district residency.

GRAND VIEW UNIVERSITY

1200 Grandview Avenue, Des Moines, IA 50316-1599
Phone: 515-263-2810 **Financial Aid Phone:** 515-263-2963
E-mail: admissions@GrandView.edu **CEEB Code:** 6251
Fax: 515-263-2974 **Website:** www.admissions.grandview.edu **ACT Code:** 1316

This private school, affiliated with the Lutheran Church, was founded in 1896. It has a 35-acre campus.

RATINGS

Admissions Selectivity Rating: 70   **Fire Safety Rating:** 60*   **Green Rating:** 60*

STUDENTS AND FACULTY

Enrollment: 1,921. **Student Body:** 62% female, 38% male, 8% out-of-state, 1% international (16 countries represented). Asian 3%, African American 7%, Caucasian 75%, Hispanic 3%.
Retention and Graduation: 70% freshmen return for sophomore year. 27% freshmen graduate within 4 years. **Faculty:** Student/faculty ratio 16:1. 87 full-time faculty, 60% hold PhDs, 7% are members of minority groups, 62% are women.

ACADEMICS

Degrees: Associate, bachelor's, certificate, master's, post-bachelor's certificate, terminal associate, transfer associate. **Classes:** Most classes have 10–19 students. Most lab/discussion sessions have 10–19 students. **Majors with Highest Enrollment:** Business/commerce; education; nursing/registered nurse (RN, ASN, BSN, MSN). **Special Study Options:** Accelerated program, cooperative education program, cross-registration, distance learning, double major, dual enrollment, honors program, independent study, internships, liberal arts/career combination, student-designed major, study abroad, teacher certification program, weekend college. **Honors programs:** Logos Honors Program. **Combined degree programs:** Dual degrees.

FACILITIES

Housing: Coed dorms, apartments for single students **Special Academic Facilities/Equipment:** Danish American Archives. **Computers:** Administrative functions (other than registration) can be performed online.

CAMPUS LIFE

Activities: Choral groups, concert band, dance, drama/theater, literary magazine, music ensembles, radio station, student government, student newspaper, television station, campus ministries, international student organization. **Organizations:** 28 registered organizations, 1 religious organizations. **Athletics (Intercollegiate):** *Men:* Baseball, basketball, cross-country, golf, soccer. *Women:* Basketball, cross-country, golf, soccer, softball, volleyball.

ADMISSIONS

Freshman Academic Profile: Average high school GPA 3.22. 16% in top 10% of high school class, 36% in top 25% of high school class, 78% in top 50% of high school class. SAT Math middle 50% range 380–500. SAT Critical Reading middle 50% range 410–500. SAT Writing middle 50% range 410–480. ACT middle 50% range 18–23. Minimum paper TOEFL 550. Minimum computer TOEFL 210. **Basis for Candidate Selection:** *Very important factors considered include:* Class rank, academic GPA, rigor of secondary school record, character/personal qualities. *Important factors considered include:* standardized test scores. *Other factors considered include:* Alumni/ae relation, extracurricular activities, talent/ability, volunteer work, work experience. **Freshman Admission Requirements:** High school diploma is required and GED is accepted. *Academic units recommended:* 4 English, 3 mathematics, 3 science, 2 foreign language, 3 social studies. **Freshman Admission Statistics:** 689 applied, 95% admitted, 36% enrolled. **Transfer Admission Requirements:** College transcript(s), minimum college GPA of 2.0 required. Lowest grade transferable D. **General Admission Information:** Application fee $35. Regular application deadline 8/15. Notification on a rolling basis, beginning on or about 9/15. Nonfall registration accepted. Admission may be deferred for a maximum of 1 semester. Credit and/or placement offered for CEEB Advanced Placement tests.

COSTS AND FINANCIAL AID

Annual tuition $18,944. Room and board $6,442. Required fees $380. Average book expense $900. **Required Forms and Deadlines:** FAFSA. Priority financial aid filing date 3/1. **Notification of Awards:** Applicants will be notified of awards on a rolling basis beginning 3/1. **Types of Aid:** *Need-based scholarships/grants:* Federal Pell, SEOG, state scholarships/grants, private scholarships, the school's own gift aid. *Loans:* FFEL Subsidized Stafford, FFEL Unsubsidized Stafford, FFEL PLUS, Federal Perkins, Federal Nursing. **Student Employment:** Federal Work-Study Program available. Institutional employment available. Highest amount earned per year from on-campus jobs $1,500. Off-campus job opportunities are excellent. **Financial Aid Statistics:** 66% freshmen, 73% undergrads receive need-based scholarship or grant aid. 13% freshmen, 9% undergrads receive non-need-based scholarship or grant aid. 66% freshmen, 69% undergrads receive need-based self-help aid. 10% freshmen, 5% undergrads receive athletic scholarships. 97% freshmen, 99% undergrads receive any aid. 83% undergrads borrow to pay for school. Average cumulative indebtedness $27,337. **Criteria for awarding institutional aid:** *Non-need-based:* Academics, alumni affiliation, art, athletics, leadership, music/drama.

GRANTHAM UNIVERSITY

7200 NW Eighty-sixth Street, Kansas City, MO 64153
E-mail: admissions@grantham.edu
Fax: 816-595-5757

This is a proprietary school.

RATINGS

Admissions Selectivity Rating: 60*   **Fire Safety Rating:** 60*   **Green Rating:** 60*

ACADEMICS

Degrees: Associate, bachelor's, master's. **Special Study Options:** Accelerated program, distance learning, external degree program, independent study.

ADMISSIONS

Freshman Admission Requirements: High school diploma is required, and GED is accepted. **Transfer Admission Requirements:** High school transcript, college transcript(s). Minimum college GPA of 2.0 required. Lowest grade transferable C. **General Admission Information:** Nonfall registration accepted.

COSTS AND FINANCIAL AID

Annual tuition $7,500.

See page 1106.

GRATZ COLLEGE

7605 Old York Road, Melrose Park, PA 19027
Phone: 215-635-7300
E-mail: admissions@gratz.edu
Fax: 215-635-7399 **Website:** www.gratzcollege.edu

This is a private school.

RATINGS
Admissions Selectivity Rating: 60* **Fire Safety Rating:** 60* **Green Rating:** 60*

STUDENTS AND FACULTY
Enrollment: 12. **Student Body:** 92% female, 8% male, 25% out-of-state,. Asian 8%, Caucasian 100%.
Retention and Graduation: 88% freshmen return for sophomore year.
Faculty: Student/faculty ratio 12:1. 8 full-time faculty, 100% hold PhDs, 50% are women.

ACADEMICS
Degrees: Bachelor's, master's, post-bachelor's certificate. **Classes:** Most classes have fewer than 10 students. Most lab/discussion sessions have fewer than 10 students. **Special Study Options:** Cross-registration, double major, dual enrollment, independent study, internships, liberal arts/career combination, study abroad, teacher certification program, joint programs with area colleges and universities are offered only at the master's level. **Career services:** Alumni services, career/job search classes, internships.

FACILITIES
Housing: The college does not offer housing. All students live off campus. 100% of campus accessible to physically disabled.

CAMPUS LIFE
Activities: Choral groups, music ensembles.

ADMISSIONS
Freshman Academic Profile: Minimum paper TOEFL 450. Minimum computer TOEFL 133. **Basis for Candidate Selection:** *Very important factors considered include:* Application essay, recommendation(s), character/personal qualities, religious affiliation/commitment, talent/ability. *Important factors considered include:* Rigor of secondary school record, interview, volunteer work. *Other factors considered include:* Class rank, standardized test scores, alumni/ae relation, extracurricular activities, racial/ethnic status, work experience. **Freshman Admission Requirements:** High school diploma is required and GED is accepted. *Academic units required:* 3 English, 2 mathematics, 2 science, (1 science labs), 2 foreign language, 3 social studies, 3 history, 2 academic electives. *Academic units recommended:* 4 English, 2 mathematics, 2 science, (1 science labs), 4 foreign language, 4 social studies, 4 history, 2 academic electives. **Freshman Admission Statistics:** 7 applied, 71% admitted, 100% enrolled. **Transfer Admission Requirements:** High school transcript, college transcript(s), essay or personal statement. Lowest grade transferable C. **General Admission Information:** Application fee $50. Nonfall registration accepted. Admission may be deferred for a maximum of 2 years. Neither credit nor placement offered for CEEB Advanced Placement tests.

COSTS AND FINANCIAL AID
Annual tuition $9,500. Required fees $400. Average book expense $550. **Required Forms and Deadlines:** FAFSA, institution's own financial aid form. **Types of Aid:** *Need-based scholarships/grants:* Federal Pell, private scholarships. *Loans:* FFEL Subsidized Stafford, FFEL Unsubsidized Stafford, FFEL PLUS. **Student Employment:** Institutional employment available. Off-campus job opportunities are good.

GREEN MOUNTAIN COLLEGE

One College Circle, Poultney, VT 05764-1199
Phone: 802-287-8000 **Financial Aid Phone:** 802-287-8210
E-mail: admiss@greenmtn.edu **CEEB Code:** 3418
Fax: 802-287-8099 **Website:** www.greenmtn.edu **ACT Code:** 4302

This private school, affiliated with the Methodist Church, was founded in 1834. It has a 155-acre campus.

RATINGS
Admissions Selectivity Rating: 74 **Fire Safety Rating:** 60* **Green Rating:** 98

STUDENTS AND FACULTY
Enrollment: 759. **Student Body:** 48% female, 52% male, 85% out-of-state, international (7 countries represented). Asian 1%, African American 3%, Caucasian 72%, Hispanic 2%, Native American 1%.
Retention and Graduation: 62% freshmen return for sophomore year. 25% freshmen graduate within 4 years. 17% grads go on to further study within 1 year. **Faculty:** Student/faculty ratio 14:1. 43 full-time faculty, 84% hold PhDs, 2% are members of minority groups, 30% are women.

ACADEMICS
Degrees: Bachelor's, certificate, master's. **Classes:** Most classes have 10–19 students. Most lab/discussion sessions have 10–19 students. **Majors with Highest Enrollment:** Environmental studies; parks, recreation and leisure studies; psychology. **Special Study Options:** Cooperative education program, distance learning, double major, exchange student program (domestic), honors program, independent study, internships, liberal arts/career combination, student-designed major, study abroad, teacher certification program. **Honors programs:** College Honors Program. Special programs offered to physically disabled students include note-taking services, tape recorders, tutors. **Career services highlights include:** All resort management students participate in two co-ops. Last year, 384 students completed 5,829 hours of service with 54 community partners. GMC has an active internship program and requires many students to complete an internship within their chosen field.

FACILITIES
Housing: Coed dorms, special housing for disabled students, substance free theme floors—recreation, education, community, Honors. **Special Academic Facilities/Equipment:** Welsh Heritage Collection, Rare Books Room, Feick Arts Center. **Computers:** Students can register for classes online. Administrative functions (other than registration) can be performed online.

CAMPUS LIFE
Environment: Rural. **Activities:** Choral groups, concert band, drama/theater, jazz band, literary magazine, music ensembles, radio station, student government, student newspaper, student-run film society, yearbook. **Organizations:** 25 registered organizations, 2 honor societies, 2 religious organizations. **Athletics (Intercollegiate):** *Men:* Basketball, cross-country, golf, lacrosse, skiing (downhill/alpine), soccer, tennis. *Women:* Basketball, cross-country, lacrosse, skiing (downhill/alpine), soccer, softball, tennis, volleyball. **On-Campus Highlights:** Withey Student Center, Moses Coffeehouse, Surdam Art Building, Griswold Library, The Farm.

ADMISSIONS
Freshman Academic Profile: Average high school GPA 3.1. 10.6% in top 10% of high school class, 24.7% in top 25% of high school class, 57.6% in top 50% of high school class. 86% from public high schools. SAT Math middle 50% range 450–560. SAT Critical Reading middle 50% range 470–600. SAT Writing middle 50% range 460–580. ACT middle 50% range 17–23. Minimum paper TOEFL 500. Minimum computer TOEFL 173. **Basis for Candidate Selection:** *Very important factors considered include:* Application essay, academic GPA, rigor of secondary school record, character/personal qualities. *Important factors considered include:* Class rank, recommendation(s), extracurricular activities, interview, volunteer work. *Other factors considered include:* standardized test scores, level of applicant's interest, talent/ability, work experience. **Freshman Admission Requirements:** High school diploma is required and GED is accepted. *Academic units required:* 4 English, 3 mathematics, 3 science, (2 science labs), 2 foreign language, 3 social studies, 1 history, 5 academic electives. *Academic units recommended:* 4 mathematics, 4 science, 3 foreign language, 3 social studies, 2 history. **Freshman Admission Statistics:** 1,290 applied, 79% admitted, 25% enrolled. **Transfer Admission Requirements:** High school transcript, college transcript(s), essay or personal statement, statement of good standing from prior institution(s). Minimum college GPA of 2.0 required. Low-

est grade transferable C–. **General Admission Information:** Application fee $30. Notification on a rolling basis, beginning on or about 9/1. Nonfall registration accepted. Admission may be deferred for a maximum of 1 year. Credit and/or placement offered for CEEB Advanced Placement tests.

COSTS AND FINANCIAL AID

Annual tuition $24,938. Room and board $9,522. Required fees $900. Average book expense $1,100. **Required Forms and Deadlines:** FAFSA, CSS/Financial Aid PROFILE, noncustodial PROFILE. Priority financial aid filing date 3/1. **Notification of Awards:** Applicants will be notified of awards on a rolling basis beginning 1/1. *Types of Aid: Need-based scholarships/grants:* Federal Pell, SEOG, state scholarships/grants, private scholarships, the school's own gift aid. *Loans:* FFEL Subsidized Stafford, FFEL Unsubsidized Stafford, FFEL PLUS, state loans, alternative loans. **Financial Aid Statistics:** 77% freshmen, 83% undergrads receive need-based scholarship or grant aid. 6% freshmen, 6% undergrads receive non-need-based scholarship or grant aid. 69% freshmen, 78% undergrads receive need-based self-help aid. 80% freshmen, 84% undergrads receive any aid. 78% undergrads borrow to pay for school. **Criteria for awarding institutional aid:** *Non-need-based:* Academics, alumni affiliation, art, leadership, music/drama, religious affiliation.

GREENVILLE COLLEGE

315 East College Avenue, Greenville, IL 62246-0159
Phone: 618-664-7100 **Financial Aid Phone:** 618-664-7110
E-mail: admissions@greenville.edu **CEEB Code:** 1256
Fax: 618-664-9841 **Website:** www.greenville.edu **ACT Code:** 1032

This private school, affiliated with the Free Methodist Church, was founded in 1892. It has a 40-acre campus.

RATINGS

Admissions Selectivity Rating: 75   **Fire Safety Rating:** 89   **Green Rating:** 60*

STUDENTS AND FACULTY

Enrollment: 1,307. **Student Body:** 55% female, 45% male, 29% out-of-state, 1% international (14 countries represented). Asian 1%, African American 7%, Caucasian 83%, Hispanic 2%, Native American 1%.
Retention and Graduation: 67% freshmen return for sophomore year. 39% freshmen graduate within 4 years. **Faculty:** Student/faculty ratio 16:1. 54 full-time faculty, 70% hold PhDs, 7% are members of minority groups, 31% are women.

ACADEMICS

Degrees: Bachelor's, master's. **Classes:** Most classes have 10–19 students. **Majors with Highest Enrollment:** Elementary education and teaching; organizational behavior studies; visual and performing arts, other. **Special Study Options:** Accelerated program, cooperative education program, cross-registration, double major, external degree program, honors program, independent study, internships, liberal arts/career combination, student-designed major, study abroad, teacher certification program. **Honors programs:** Greenville College's Honors Program is an academic program that was established in 1995 to provide a "value-added" dimension to the excellent, Christ-centered education students regularly receive at Greenville College. The Honors Program consists of a blend of enriched sections of several general education classes special honors seminars, and experiential learning opportunities offered in an enhanced educational environment that strives for small class sizes to encourage total student participation, facilitate spirited discussions and promote greater student-faculty interaction. Outside the classroom, the Honors Programs offers a co-curricular program consisting of diversified cultural, social and educationally-oriented activities and events developed especially for program members. The Honors Program encourages its members to be persons with multi-dimensional interests who participate in a wide range of College sponsored events, activities, and organizations. Students admitted to The Honors Program automatically become members of The Honors Society, the student organization within the program which elects officers who assist with the planning and implementation of the aforementioned activities and other community building opportunities. The Greenville College Honors Program strives to emulate the guidelines, "Basic Characteristics of a Fully-Developed Honors Program," developed by the National Collegiate Honors Council. It, also, cooperates with member institutions of the Council of Christian Colleges and Universities by encouraging GC students to participate in one of the nearly twenty semester-long academic programs coordinated and promoted by CCCU that are offered at off-campus sites, both domestic and abroad. Locally, The Honors Program is administered by a director who is assisted by an Honors Council composed of faculty and students. To graduate with Honors Program recognition, students must fulfill the requirements of their academic major, earn a minimum of 25 credit hours of honors work, maintain a cumulative grade point average of 3.50

and complete a Departmental Honors Thesis under the supervision of a three-person faculty thesis committee. Graduates of the Honors Program are awarded a special medallion and receive special recognition at commencement. For additional information about The Honors Program, contact the director at (618) 664-6610. Special programs offered to physically disabled students include note-taking services, reader services, tutors.

FACILITIES

Housing: Men's dorms, women's dorms, apartments for single students, All single students not living at home must live in college approved housing. 40% of campus accessible to physically disabled. **Special Academic Facilities/Equipment:** Sculpture museum, sports training annex. **Computers:** Administrative functions (other than registration) can be performed online.

CAMPUS LIFE

Environment: Village. **Activities:** Choral groups, concert band, drama/theater, jazz band, music ensembles, musical theater, pep band, radio station, student government, student newspaper, yearbook. **Organizations:** 25 registered organizations, 6 honor societies, 2 religious organizations. **Athletics (Intercollegiate):** *Men:* Baseball, basketball, cross-country, football, soccer, tennis, track/field (outdoor), track/field (indoor). *Women:* Basketball, cross-country, soccer, softball, tennis, track/field (outdoor), track/field (indoor), volleyball. **On-Campus Highlights:** Hogue Hall, Family Christian Bookstore, Jo's Java, Maves Art Center, Fitness Center.

ADMISSIONS

Freshman Academic Profile: Average high school GPA 3.38. 17% in top 10% of high school class, 48% in top 25% of high school class, 74% in top 50% of high school class. SAT Math middle 50% range 460–570. SAT Critical Reading middle 50% range 480–580. ACT middle 50% range 19–25. Minimum paper TOEFL 500. Minimum computer TOEFL 173. **Basis for Candidate Selection:** *Very important factors considered include:* Class rank, application essay, academic GPA, rigor of secondary school record, character/personal qualities, religious affiliation/commitment, talent/ability. *Important factors considered include:* Recommendation(s), standardized test scores. *Other factors considered include:* Alumni/ae relation, extracurricular activities, first generation, geographical residence, interview, level of applicant's interest, racial/ethnic status, volunteer work, work experience. **Freshman Admission Requirements:** High school diploma is required and GED is accepted. *Academic units recommended:* 4 English, 2 mathematics, 1 science, (1 science labs), 2 foreign language, 1 history. **Freshman Admission Statistics:** 879 applied, 82% admitted, 42% enrolled. **Transfer Admission Requirements:** High school transcript, college transcript(s), essay or personal statement, minimum college GPA of 2.0 required. Lowest grade transferable C. **General Admission Information:** Application fee $25. Regular application deadline 8/1. Notification on a rolling basis, beginning on or about 10/15. Nonfall registration accepted. Admission may be deferred for a maximum of 1 year. Credit and/or placement offered for CEEB Advanced Placement tests.

COSTS AND FINANCIAL AID

Average book expense $900. **Required Forms and Deadlines:** FAFSA. **Notification of Awards:** Applicants will be notified of awards on a rolling basis beginning 3/15. *Types of Aid: Need-based scholarships/grants:* Federal Pell, SEOG, state scholarships/grants, private scholarships, the school's own gift aid. *Loans:* Direct Subsidized Stafford, Direct Unsubsidized Stafford, Direct PLUS, FFEL Subsidized Stafford, FFEL Unsubsidized Stafford, FFEL PLUS, Federal Perkins, college/university loans from institutional funds. **Student Employment:** Federal Work-Study Program available. Institutional employment available. Highest amount earned per year from on-campus jobs $2,407. Off-campus job opportunities are fair. **Financial Aid Statistics:** 82% freshmen, 85% undergrads receive need-based scholarship or grant aid. 7% freshmen, 6% undergrads receive non-need-based scholarship or grant aid. 74% freshmen, 77% undergrads receive need-based self-help aid. 94% freshmen, 92% undergrads receive any aid. 85% undergrads borrow to pay for school. Average cumulative indebtedness $19,820. **Criteria for awarding institutional aid:** *Non-need-based:* Academics, alumni, affiliation, art, leadership, minority status, music/drama, religious affiliation, state/district residency.

GRIGGS UNIVERSITY

PO Box 4437, Silver Spring, MD 20914-4437
Phone: 301-680-6579
E-mail: enrollmentservices@griggs.edu
Fax: 301-680-6526 **Website:** www.griggs.edu

This private school, affiliated with the Seventh Day Adventist Church, was founded in 1909.

RATINGS
Admissions Selectivity Rating: 60*   **Fire Safety Rating:** 60*   **Green Rating:** 60*

STUDENTS AND FACULTY
Enrollment: 1,076. **Student Body:** 50% female, 50% male, % out-of-state,. **Faculty:** Student/faculty ratio 3:1.

ACADEMICS
Degrees: Associate, bachelor's. **Majors with Highest Enrollment:** accounting and business/management; business/commerce; computer and information sciences. **Special Study Options:** Accelerated program, distance learning, independent study.

ADMISSIONS
Basis for Candidate Selection: *Very important factors considered include:* Rigor of secondary school record. *Important factors considered include:* Application essay, religious affiliation/commitment, work experience. *Other factors considered include:* Recommendation(s), standardized test scores, alumni/ae relation, character/personal qualities, extracurricular activities, interview, talent/ability, volunteer work. **Freshman Admission Requirements:** *Academic units required:* 4 English, 3 mathematics, 2 science, 3 social studies, 3 academic electives, 7 Bible, health, word processing. **Transfer Admission Requirements:** College transcript(s), essay or personal statement, minimum college GPA of 2.0 required. Lowest grade transferable C. **General Admission Information:** Application fee $60. Nonfall registration accepted.

COSTS AND FINANCIAL AID
Annual tuition $6,400. Required fees $120. Average book expense $1,000. **Types of Aid:** *Need-based scholarships/grants:* The school's own gift aid.

GRINNELL COLLEGE

1103 Park Street, Grinnell, IA 50112-1690
Phone: 641-269-3600 **Financial Aid Phone:** 641-269-3250
E-mail: askgrin@grinnell.edu **CEEB Code:** 6252
Fax: 641-269-4800 **Website:** www.grinnell.edu **ACT Code:** 1318

This private school was founded in 1846. It has a 120-acre campus.

RATINGS
Admissions Selectivity Rating: 96   **Fire Safety Rating:** 85   **Green Rating:** 82

STUDENTS AND FACULTY
Enrollment: 1,630. **Student Body:** 53% female, 47% male, 86% out-of-state, 11% international (54 countries represented). Asian 8%, African American 6%, Caucasian 59%, Hispanic 7%, Native American 1%.
Retention and Graduation: 95% freshmen return for sophomore year. 78% freshmen graduate within 4 years. 33% grads go on to further study within 1 year. 25% grads pursue arts and sciences degrees. 3% grads pursue law degrees. 1% grads pursue business degrees. 3% grads pursue medical degrees. **Faculty:** Student/faculty ratio 9:1. 157 full-time faculty, 97% hold PhDs, 16% are members of minority groups, 41% are women.

ACADEMICS
Degrees: Bachelor's. **Classes:** Most classes have 10–19 students. Most lab/discussion sessions have 10–19 students. **Majors with Highest Enrollment:** Economics; political science and government; psychology. **Special Study Options:** Accelerated program, double major, independent study, internships, liberal arts/career combination, student-designed major, study abroad, teacher certification program; study abroad available in 32 countries, including Grinnell-in-London, Grinnell-in-Washington program, 3-2 programs available in engineering, architecture, and law. **Combined degree programs:** Architec-

ture With Washington Univ, St.Louis Law Col. Special programs offered to physically disabled students include note-taking services, reader services, tape recorders, tutors. **Career services:** Alumni network, alumni services, career assessment, internships, regional alumni. **Career services highlights include:** Support 12+ funded internships each summer.

FACILITIES
Housing: Coed dorms, special housing for disabled students, cooperative housing, wellness housing, theme housing. 67% of campus accessible to physically disabled. **Special Academic Facilities/Equipment:** Art galleries, language lab, nuclear magnetic resonance spectrometer, electron microscope, 24-inch reflecting telescope, 365-acre environmental research area. **Computers:** 100% of classrooms, 100% of dorms, 100% of libraries, 100% of dining areas, 100% of student union, 100% of common outdoor areas have wireless network access. Administrative functions (other than registration) can be performed online.

CAMPUS LIFE
Environment: Village. **Activities:** Choral groups, concert band, dance, drama/theater, jazz band, literary magazine, music ensembles, musical theater, pep band, radio station, student government, student newspaper, student-run film society, symphony orchestra, yearbook, campus ministries, international student organization, Model UN. **Organizations:** 240 registered organizations, 2 honor societies, 12 religious organizations. **Athletics (Intercollegiate):** *Men:* Baseball, basketball, cross-country, diving, football, golf, soccer, swimming, tennis, track/field (outdoor), track/field (indoor). *Women:* Basketball, cross-country, diving, golf, soccer, softball, swimming, tennis, track/field (outdoor), track/field (indoor), volleyball. **On-Campus Highlights:** Two building on campus are listed on the National Register of Historic Places: Mears Cottage and Goodnow Hall, Faulconer Gallery, Burling Library, Joe Rosenfield '25 Center, Bucksbaum Center for the Arts, Robert N. Noyce '49 Science Center; Athletic Center. **Environmental Initiatives:** All new buildings are LEED-certified. Once our new Athletics Facility is complete, 33% of the college's building square footage will be LEED-certified. The college has committed to building a wind farm near campus which will provide 50% of the campus' electricity. The college has dedicated one of its student houses as an Ecohouse and will use that house to demonstrate green technologies, energy conservation, water conservation, and local foods to the Grinnell community.

ADMISSIONS
Freshman Academic Profile: 65% in top 10% of high school class, 93% in top 25% of high school class, 98% in top 50% of high school class. 62% from public high schools. SAT Math middle 50% range 620–730. SAT Critical Reading middle 50% range 600–730. ACT middle 50% range 28–32. Minimum paper TOEFL 550. Minimum computer TOEFL 220. Minimum web-based TOEFL 80. **Basis for Candidate Selection:** *Very important factors considered include:* Class rank, academic GPA, recommendation(s), rigor of secondary school record, standardized test scores, extracurricular activities, talent/ability. *Important factors considered include:* Application essay, interview, racial/ethnic status. *Other factors considered include:* Alumni/ae relation, character/personal qualities, first generation, geographical residence, level of applicant's interest, state residency, volunteer work, work experience. **Freshman Admission Requirements:** High school diploma is required and GED is accepted. *Academic units recommended:* 4 English, 4 mathematics, 4 science, (3 science labs), 4 foreign language, 4 social studies. **Freshman Admission Statistics:** 3,291 applied, 34% admitted, 34% enrolled. **Transfer Admission Requirements:** High school transcript, college transcript(s), essay or personal statement, standardized test scores, statement of good standing from prior institution(s). Lowest grade transferable C. **General Admission Information:** Application fee $30. Early decision application deadline 11/15. Regular application deadline 1/2. Regular notification 4/1. Nonfall registration not accepted. Admission may be deferred for a maximum of 1 year. Credit offered for CEEB Advanced Placement tests.

COSTS AND FINANCIAL AID
Average book expense $900. **Required Forms and Deadlines:** FAFSA, institution's own financial aid form, noncustodial PROFILE. Financial aid filing deadline 2/1. Priority financial aid filing date 2/1. **Notification of Awards:** Applicants will be notified of awards on or about 4/1. **Types of Aid:** *Need-based scholarships/grants:* Federal Pell, SEOG, state scholarships/grants, private scholarships, the school's own gift aid. *Loans:* FFEL Subsidized Stafford, FFEL Unsubsidized Stafford, FFEL PLUS, Federal Perkins, college/university loans from institutional funds. **Student Employment:** Federal Work-Study Program available. Institutional employment available. Highest amount earned per year from on-campus jobs $2,500. Off-campus job opportunities are excellent. **Financial Aid Statistics:** 71% freshmen, 63% undergrads receive need-based scholarship or grant aid. 8% freshmen, 6% undergrads receive non-need-based scholarship or grant aid. 61% freshmen, 55% undergrads receive need-based self-help aid. 84% freshmen, 85% undergrads receive any aid. 54% undergrads borrow to pay for school. Average cumulative indebtedness $19,540. **Criteria for awarding institutional aid:** *Non-need-based:* Academics.

GROVE CITY COLLEGE

100 Campus Drive, Grove City, PA 16127-2104
Phone: 724-458-2100 **Financial Aid Phone:** 724-458-3300
E-mail: admissions@gcc.edu **CEEB Code:** 2277
Fax: 724-458-3395 **Website:** www.gcc.edu **ACT Code:** 3582

This private school, affiliated with the Presbyterian Church, was founded in 1876. It has a 150-acre campus.

RATINGS
Admissions Selectivity Rating: 92   **Fire Safety Rating:** 82   **Green Rating:** 61

STUDENTS AND FACULTY
Enrollment: 2,504. **Student Body:** 50% female, 50% male, 53% out-of-state, international (9 countries represented). Asian 2%, African American 1%, Caucasian 94%, Hispanic 2%.
Retention and Graduation: 93% freshmen return for sophomore year. 78% freshmen graduate within 4 years. 23% grads go on to further study within 1 year. 17% grads pursue arts and sciences degrees. 2% grads pursue law degrees. 2% grads pursue business degrees. 2% grads pursue medical degrees. **Faculty:** Student/faculty ratio 16:1. 128 full-time faculty, 92% hold PhDs, 2% are members of minority groups, 26% are women.

ACADEMICS
Degrees: Bachelor's. **Classes:** Most classes have 20–29 students. Most lab/discussion sessions have 20–29 students. **Majors with Highest Enrollment:** Elementary education and teaching; English language and literature; mechanical engineering. **Special Study Options:** Accelerated program, double major, independent study, internships, study abroad, teacher certification program Special programs offered to physically disabled students include tutors. **Career services:** Alumni network, alumni services, career/job search classes, career assessment, internships, regional alumni. **Career services highlights include:** Entrepreneurship-Internships are required of most majors.

FACILITIES
Housing: Men's dorms, women's dorms, fraternity/sorority housing, apartments for single students, theme housing. 100% of campus accessible to physically disabled. **Special Academic Facilities/Equipment:** Fine arts center, language lab, on-campus preschool, technological learning center. **Computers:** 100% of classrooms, 15% of dorms, 100% of libraries, 33% of dining areas, 100% of student union, 10% of common outdoor areas have wireless network access. Students can register for classes online. Administrative functions (other than registration) can be performed online. Undergraduates are required to own a computer.

CAMPUS LIFE
Environment: Rural. **Activities:** Choral groups, concert band, dance, drama/theater, jazz band, literary magazine, marching band, music ensembles, musical theater, opera, pep band, radio station, student government, student newspaper, symphony orchestra, television station, yearbook, campus ministries, international student organization. **Organizations:** 130 registered organizations, 19 honor societies, 22 religious organizations. 8 fraternities, 8 sororities. **Athletics (Intercollegiate):** *Men:* Baseball, basketball, cross-country, diving, football, golf, soccer, swimming, tennis, track/field (outdoor). *Women:* Basketball, cheerleading, cross-country, diving, golf, soccer, softball, swimming, tennis, track/field (outdoor), volleyball, water polo. **On-Campus Highlights:** Student union, chapel, Hall of Arts and Letters, fitness center, Ketler Recreation Room.

ADMISSIONS
Freshman Academic Profile: Average high school GPA 3.8. 51% in top 10% of high school class, 85% in top 25% of high school class, 97% in top 50% of high school class. 74% from public high schools. SAT Math middle 50% range 568–682. SAT Critical Reading middle 50% range 563–685. ACT middle 50% range 25–30. Minimum paper TOEFL 550. Minimum computer TOEFL 213. Minimum web-based TOEFL 79. **Basis for Candidate Selection:** *Very important factors considered include:* Application essay, academic GPA, rigor of secondary school record, standardized test scores, character/personal qualities, interview, level of applicant's interest, religious affiliation/commitment. *Important factors considered include:* Recommendation(s), extracurricular activities, geographical residence. *Other factors considered include:* Class rank, alumni/ae relation, first generation, racial/ethnic status, state residency, talent/ability, volunteer work, work experience. **Freshman Admission Requirements:** High school diploma is required and GED is accepted. *Academic units recommended:* 4 English, 3 mathematics, 3 science, (2 science labs), 3 foreign language, 2 social studies, 2 history. **Freshman Admission Statistics:** 1,764 applied, 64%

admitted, 56% enrolled. **Transfer Admission Requirements:** High school transcript, college transcript(s), essay or personal statement, standardized test scores, statement of good standing from prior institution(s). Minimum college GPA of 2.0 required. Lowest grade transferable C. **General Admission Information:** Application fee $50. Early decision application deadline 11/15. Regular application deadline 2/1. Regular notification 3/15. Nonfall registration accepted. Admission may be deferred for a maximum of 1 year. Credit offered for CEEB Advanced Placement tests.

COSTS AND FINANCIAL AID
Annual tuition $12,590. Room and board $6,824. Average book expense $1,000. **Required Forms and Deadlines:** Institution's own financial aid form Financial aid filing deadline 4/15. Priority financial aid filing date 4/15. **Notification of Awards:** Applicants will be notified of awards on or about 3/26. **Types of Aid:** *Need-based scholarships/grants:* state scholarships/grants, private scholarships, the school's own gift aid. *Loans:* State loans, private loans. **Student Employment:** Institutional employment available. Highest amount earned per year from on-campus jobs $1,500. Off-campus job opportunities are good. **Financial Aid Statistics:** 42% freshmen, 36% undergrads receive need-based scholarship or grant aid. 5% freshmen, 3% undergrads receive non-need-based scholarship or grant aid. 20% freshmen, 22% undergrads receive need-based self-help aid. 42% freshmen, 38% undergrads receive any aid. 45% undergrads borrow to pay for school. Average cumulative indebtedness $24,895. **Criteria for awarding institutional aid:** *Non-need-based:* Academics, leadership, minority status.

GUILFORD COLLEGE

5800 West Friendly Avenue, Greensboro, NC 27410
Phone: 336-316-2100 **Financial Aid Phone:** 336-316-2354
E-mail: admission@guilford.edu **CEEB Code:** 5261
Fax: 336-316-2954 **Website:** www.guilford.edu **ACT Code:** 3106

This private school, affiliated with the Quaker Church, was founded in 1837. It has a 340-acre campus.

RATINGS
Admissions Selectivity Rating: 78   **Fire Safety Rating:** 73   **Green Rating:** 94

STUDENTS AND FACULTY
Enrollment: 2,681. **Student Body:** 59% female, 41% male, 34% out-of-state, 1% international (13 countries represented). Asian 1%, African American 25%, Caucasian 64%, Hispanic 3%, Native American 1%.
Retention and Graduation: 80% freshmen return for sophomore year. 48% freshmen graduate within 4 years. 25% grads go on to further study within 1 year. 13% grads pursue arts and sciences degrees. 2% grads pursue law degrees. 5% grads pursue business degrees. **Faculty:** Student/faculty ratio 15:1. 126 full-time faculty, 86% hold PhDs, 16% are members of minority groups, 48% are women.

ACADEMICS
Degrees: Bachelor's, certificate. **Classes:** Most classes have 10–19 students. Most lab/discussion sessions have 10–19 students. **Majors with Highest Enrollment:** Business/commerce; criminal justice/safety studies; psychology. **Special Study Options:** Accelerated program, cooperative education program, cross-registration, double major, honors program, independent study, internships, liberal arts/career combination, student-designed major, study abroad, teacher certification program, weekend college, There are 3-2 degree programs available in forestry and environmental studies with Duke University, and in physician assistant training with Bowman Gray School of Medicine at Wake Forest University. Guilford also offers many internships, a Washington semester, work-study programs, accelerated degree programs in business management, computer information systems, psychology, and biology, dual majors, student-designed majors, study abroad in 9 countries, and cross-registration with members of the Greater Greensboro Consortium (8 colleges/universities). **Honors programs:** Guilford College is a participating member of the National Collegiate Honors Council. Membership in the NCHC means that students in the Guilford College Honors Program can participate in the NCHC Honors Semesters. These semester programs are regularly offered in different sites around the world and enable Honors students from across the country to meet and learn in unique settings. In recent years, Guilford College students have participated in the Study Abroad programs sponsored by Honors Programs at other colleges and universities. The University of North Carolina at Wilming-

ton offers an Honors Semester Program at the University of Wales Swansea. For more information visit the following site: www.swan.ac.uk. Eastern Illinois University offers a n Honors Summer Program at the Universite Catholique de Louvain in Belgium that features archaeological study of historic sites. For more information, one can visit: www.eiu.edu/~honprog/abroad.htm. Both these programs offer college credit courses that are transferable. **Combined degree programs:** 3-1 Physician's asst program, 3-2 Forestry/environ. Special programs offered to physically disabled students include note-taking services, reader services, tape recorders, tutors. **Career services:** Alumni network, alumni services, career/job search classes, career assessment, internships. **Career services highlights include:** Internships offer students up top 12 credit hours. Local, national, and international opportunities are available. Program is centralized and provides a coordinator to assist students with the process and reflection.

FACILITIES

Housing: Coed dorms, special housing for disabled students, men's dorms, special housing for international students, women's dorms, cooperative housing, apartments for single students, theme housingSpecial interest housing available. Alternative houses with themes and community service project requirements. 97% of campus accessible to physically disabled. Friends Historical Collection, Frank Family Science Center, art gallery, language lab, research-grade observatory and planetarium. **Computers:** 15% of classrooms, 10% of dorms, 100% of libraries, 100% of dining areas, 50% of student union, 10% of common outdoor areas have wireless network access. Students can register for classes online. Administrative functions (other than registration) can be performed online.

CAMPUS LIFE

Environment: City. **Activities:** Choral groups, concert band, dance, drama/theater, jazz band, literary magazine, music ensembles, musical theater, pep band, radio station, student government, student newspaper, student-run film society, yearbook, campus ministries. **Organizations:** 47 registered organizations, 1 honor societies, 8 religious organizations. **Athletics (Intercollegiate):** *Men:* Baseball, basketball, cross-country, football, golf, lacrosse, rugby, soccer, tennis. *Women:* Basketball, cross-country, lacrosse, rugby, soccer, softball, swimming, tennis, volleyball. **On-Campus Highlights:** Hege Library and Art Gallery, Community Center, Frank Family Science Center, Founders Student Center and the new Grill 155, The Greenleaf Café—coffee co-op. The Guilford College campus is a beautiful 340 acre campus situated in the western residential area of Greensboro, North Carolina. The college is bordered by woods on one end and easy access to stores on the other. **Environmental Initiatives:** Becoming signatories of the American College and Universities Presidents' Climate Commitment; composting program for the on-campus dining service; substantial commitment to local food procurement for the dining services.

ADMISSIONS

Freshman Academic Profile: Average high school GPA 3.12. 16% in top 10% of high school class, 39% in top 25% of high school class, 82% in top 50% of high school class. 78% from public high schools. SAT Math middle 50% range 590–460. SAT Critical Reading middle 50% range 600–460. SAT Writing middle 50% range 590–440. ACT middle 50% range 26–20. Minimum paper TOEFL 550. Minimum computer TOEFL 213. **Basis for Candidate Selection:** *Very important factors considered include:* Application essay, academic GPA, rigor of secondary school record, character/personal qualities. *Important factors considered include:* Class rank, recommendation(s), standardized test scores, extracurricular activities, interview, level of applicant's interest, talent/ability, volunteer work, work experience. *Other factors considered include:* Alumni/ae relation, first generation, geographical residence, racial/ethnic status, state residency. **Freshman Admission Requirements:** High school diploma is required and GED is accepted. *Academic units recommended:* 4 English, 3 mathematics, 3 science, 2 foreign language, 3 social studies, 3 history. **Freshman Admission Statistics:** 3,780 applied, 62% admitted, 19% enrolled. **Transfer Admission Requirements:** High school transcript, college transcript(s), essay or personal statement, standardized test scores, statement of good standing from prior institution(s). Minimum college GPA of 2.5 required. Lowest grade transferable C. **General Admission Information:** Application fee $25. Regular application deadline 8/10. Notification on a rolling basis, beginning on or about 10/1. Non-fall registration accepted. Admission may be deferred for a maximum of 1 year. Credit and/or placement offered for CEEB Advanced Placement tests.

COSTS AND FINANCIAL AID

Annual tuition $27,120. Required fees $330. Average book expense $1,150. **Required Forms and Deadlines:** FAFSA. Priority financial aid filing date 3/1. **Notification of Awards:** Applicants will be notified of awards on a rolling basis beginning 2/15. **Types of Aid:** *Need-based scholarships/grants:* Federal Pell, SEOG, state scholarships/grants, private scholarships, the school's own gift aid. *Loans:* FFEL Subsidized Stafford, FFEL Unsubsidized Stafford, FFEL PLUS, Federal Perkins, college/university loans from institutional funds. **Student Employment:** Federal Work-Study Program available. Institutional employment available. Highest amount earned per year from on-campus jobs $6,911. Off-campus job opportunities are fair. **Financial Aid Statistics:** 73% freshmen,

72% undergrads receive need-based scholarship or grant aid. 68% freshmen, 60% undergrads receive need-based self-help aid. 79% freshmen, 89% undergrads receive any aid. 69% undergrads borrow to pay for school. Average cumulative indebtedness $24,500. **Criteria for awarding institutional aid:** *Non-need-based:* Academics.

GUSTAVUS ADOLPHUS COLLEGE

800 West College Avenue, Saint Peter, MN 56082
Phone: 507-933-7676 **Financial Aid Phone:** 507-933-7527
E-mail: admission@gustavus.edu **CEEB Code:** 6253
Fax: 507-933-7474 **Website:** www.gustavus.edu **ACT Code:** 2112

This private school, affiliated with the Lutheran Church, was founded in 1862. It has a 340-acre campus.

RATINGS
Admissions Selectivity Rating: 86 **Fire Safety Rating:** 88 **Green Rating:** 88

STUDENTS AND FACULTY
Enrollment: 2,515. **Student Body:** 57% female, 43% male, 18% out-of-state, international (15 countries represented).
Retention and Graduation: 91% freshmen return for sophomore year. 79% freshmen graduate within 4 years. 19% grads go on to further study within 1 year. 5% grads pursue arts and sciences degrees. 3% grads pursue law degrees. 1% grads pursue business degrees. 2% grads pursue medical degrees. **Faculty:** Student/faculty ratio 12:1. 200 full-time faculty, 85% hold PhDs, 13% are members of minority groups, 46% are women.

ACADEMICS
Degrees: Bachelor's. **Classes:** Most classes have 10–19 students. Most lab/discussion sessions have 10–19 students. **Majors with Highest Enrollment:** Biology/biological sciences; business/commerce; psychology. **Special Study Options:** Cooperative education program, cross-registration, double major, dual enrollment, exchange student program (domestic), honors program, independent study, internships, liberal arts/career combination, student-designed major, study abroad, teacher certification program. **Honors programs:** Curriculum II. Special programs offered to physically disabled students include note-taking services, reader services, tape recorders, tutors. **Career services:** Alumni network, alumni services, career assessment, internships. **Career services highlights include:** We have a well developed internship program offering month-long career explorations as well as full-semester and summer full-time and part-time internships for academic credit. Forty-eight percent of our graduates participate in an internship for academic credit and 93.4% participated in some type of experiential learning during their college experience.

FACILITIES
Housing: Coed dorms, special housing for disabled students, special housing for international students, apartments for single students, wellness housing, theme housing 95% of campus accessible to physically disabled. **Special Academic Facilities/Equipment:** Art gallery, mineral museum, electron microscopes, arboretum, 14-inch computer-guided Celestron telescope, artificial intelligence laboratory, materials science laboratory, 300–MHz NMR spectrometer, five-section greenhouse. **Computers:** 100% of dorms, 100% of libraries, 100% of dining areas, 100% of student union, 50% of common outdoor areas have wireless network access. Students can register for classes online. Administrative functions (other than registration) can be performed online.

CAMPUS LIFE
Environment: Village. **Activities:** Choral groups, concert band, dance, drama/theater, jazz band, literary magazine, music ensembles, musical theater, pep band, radio station, student government, student newspaper, symphony orchestra, television station, yearbook. **Organizations:** 120 registered organizations, 11 honor societies, 8 religious organizations. 5 fraternities, 5 sororities. **Athletics (Intercollegiate):** *Men:* Baseball, basketball, cross-country, diving, football, golf, ice hockey, skiing (nordic & cross-country), soccer, swimming, tennis, track/field (outdoor), track/field (indoor). *Women:* Basketball, cross-country, diving, golf, gymnastics, ice hockey, skiing (nordic & cross-country), soccer, softball, swimming, tennis, track/field (outdoor), track/field (indoor), volleyball. **On-Campus Highlights:** Campus Center, Courtyard Cafe, Lund Athletic Center, Christ Chapel, Linnaeus Arboretum. With over 75% of students remaining on campus during a typical weekend (according to our Dining Service), our students actively use the entire campus. As there are no city streets intersecting

our campus, Gusties enjoy their home on the hill. **Environmental Initiatives:** Seeking to acquire 5 MW of wind generator capacity Established the Johnson Center for Environmental Innovation Strong institutional commitment to recycling & energy conservation

ADMISSIONS

Freshman Academic Profile: Average high school GPA 3.64. 34% in top 10% of high school class, 69% in top 25% of high school class, 97% in top 50% of high school class. 92% from public high schools. SAT Math middle 50% range 580–690. ACT middle 50% range 24–29. Minimum paper TOEFL 550. Minimum computer TOEFL 213. Minimum web-based TOEFL 80. **Basis for Candidate Selection:** *Very important factors considered include:* Rigor of secondary school record. *Important factors considered include:* Application essay, academic GPA, recommendation(s), standardized test scores. *Other factors considered include:* Alumni/ae relation, extracurricular activities, first generation, geographical residence, interview, level of applicant's interest, racial/ethnic status, religious affiliation/commitment, state residency, talent/ability, volunteer work, work experience. **Freshman Admission Requirements:** High school diploma is required and GED is accepted. *Academic units required:* 4 English, 3 mathematics, 2 science, (2 science labs), 2 foreign language, 2 social studies, 2 history. *Academic units recommended:* 4 mathematics, 3 science, (3 science labs), 3 foreign language, 2 academic electives. **Freshman Admission Statistics:** 3,128 applied, 75% admitted, 27% enrolled. **Transfer Admission Requirements:** High school transcript, college transcript(s), essay or personal statement, standardized test scores, statement of good standing from prior institution(s). Minimum college GPA of 2.4 required. Lowest grade transferable 2. **General Admission Information:** Notification on a rolling basis, beginning on or about 11/20. Nonfall registration accepted. Admission may be deferred for a maximum of 1 year. Credit and/or placement offered for CEEB Advanced Placement tests.

COSTS AND FINANCIAL AID

Annual tuition $29,990. Room and board $7,460. Required fees $140. Average book expense $750. **Required Forms and Deadlines:** FAFSA, CSS/Financial Aid PROFILE, CSS Profile required of all students applying for need-based assistance. Financial aid filing deadline 4/15. Priority financial aid filing date 2/15. **Notification of Awards:** Applicants will be notified of awards on a rolling basis beginning 1/20. **Types of Aid:** *Need-based scholarships/grants:* Federal Pell, SEOG, state scholarships/grants, private scholarships, the school's own gift aid. *Loans:* Direct Subsidized Stafford, Direct Unsubsidized Stafford, Direct PLUS, Federal Perkins, state loans, alternative loans from private lenders. **Student Employment:** Federal Work-Study Program available. Institutional employment available. Highest amount earned per year from on-campus jobs $1,800. Off-campus job opportunities are good. **Financial Aid Statistics:** 70% freshmen, 65% undergrads receive need-based scholarship or grant aid. 35% freshmen, 39% undergrads receive non-need-based scholarship or grant aid. 70% freshmen, 65% undergrads receive need-based self-help aid. 96% freshmen, 95% undergrads receive any aid. 70% undergrads borrow to pay for school. Average cumulative indebtedness $24,297. **Criteria for awarding institutional aid:** *Non-need-based:* Academics, alumni affiliation, art, music/drama, religious affiliation.

GWYNEDD-MERCY COLLEGE

1325 Sumneytown Pike, PO Box 901, Gwynedd Valley, PA 19437-0901
Phone: 215-641-5510 **Financial Aid Phone:** 215-646-7300
E-mail: admissions@gmc.edu **CEEB Code:** 2278
Fax: 215-641-5556 **Website:** www.gmc.edu

This private school, affiliated with the Roman Catholic Church, was founded in 1948. It has a 160-acre campus.

RATINGS

Admissions Selectivity Rating: 64　　**Fire Safety Rating:** 60*　　**Green Rating:** 60*

STUDENTS AND FACULTY

Enrollment: 2,130. **Student Body:** 74% female, 26% male, 8% out-of-state, international (28 countries represented). Asian 2%, African American 21%, Caucasian 69%, Hispanic 1%.
Retention and Graduation: 76% freshmen return for sophomore year. 50% freshmen graduate within 4 years. **Faculty:** Student/faculty ratio 13:1. 75 full-time faculty, 63% hold PhDs, 71% are women.

ACADEMICS

Degrees: Associate, bachelor's, certificate, master's, post-bachelor's certificate, post-master's certificate. **Classes:** Most classes have 10–19 students. Most lab/discussion sessions have 10–19 students. **Majors with Highest Enrollment:** Business administration and management; education; nursing/registered nurse (RN, ASN, BSN, MSN). **Special Study Options:** Accelerated program,

cross-registration, double major, English as a Second Language (ESL), honors program, independent study, internships, liberal arts/career combination, study abroad, teacher certification program, weekend college. **Honors programs:** The Honors Program in Liberal Studies consists of six interdisciplinary, team-taught courses developing the theme of "The Quest for Community and Freedom: The Individual and Society." **Combined degree programs:** BSN/MSN. Special programs offered to physically disabled students include reader services, tutors. **Career services:** Alumni services, career assessment, internships.

FACILITIES

Housing: Coed dorms, special housing for international students. 95% of campus accessible to physically disabled. **Special Academic Facilities/Equipment:** Keiss Hall (Health and Science Center), television production room and small theater, computer labs. **Computers:** Students can register for classes online.

CAMPUS LIFE

Environment: City. **Activities:** Choral groups, literary magazine, student government, student newspaper, yearbook, campus ministries. **Organizations:** 22 registered organizations, 10 honor societies, 1 religious organizations. **Athletics (Intercollegiate):** *Men:* Baseball, basketball, cross-country, golf, soccer, tennis, track/field (outdoor), track/field (indoor). *Women:* Basketball, cross-country, field hockey, lacrosse, soccer, softball, tennis, track/field (outdoor), track/field (indoor), volleyball. **On-Campus Highlights:** Assumption Hall, The Sister Isabelle Keiss Center for Health and Sciences, The Griffin Complex Student Union and Athletic Facility, Saint Bernard Lobby and Snack Bar, Loyola Hall and Saint Brigid's Hall—residence halls.

ADMISSIONS

Freshman Academic Profile: 4% in top 10% of high school class, 14% in top 25% of high school class, 40% in top 50% of high school class. 57% from public high schools. SAT Math middle 50% range 430–530. SAT Critical Reading middle 50% range 440–530. Minimum paper TOEFL 525. Minimum computer TOEFL 195. **Basis for Candidate Selection:** *Very important factors considered include:* Rigor of secondary school record. *Important factors considered include:* Class rank, academic GPA, recommendation(s), standardized test scores, extracurricular activities. *Other factors considered include:* Application essay, alumni/ae relation, character/personal qualities, interview, volunteer work, work experience. **Freshman Admission Requirements:** High school diploma is required and GED is accepted. *Academic units required:* 4 English, 3 mathematics, 3 science, 1 history, 3 academic electives. **Freshman Admission Statistics:** 1,844 applied, 67% admitted, 25% enrolled. **Transfer Admission Requirements:** High school transcript, college transcript(s), minimum college GPA of 2.0 required. Lowest grade transferable C. **General Admission Information:** Application fee $25. Regular application deadline 8/20. Notification on a rolling basis, beginning on or about 9/20. Nonfall registration accepted. Admission may be deferred for a maximum of 1 year. Credit and/or placement offered for CEEB Advanced Placement tests.

COSTS AND FINANCIAL AID

Annual tuition $25,160. Room and board $9,760. Required fees $450. Average book expense $600. **Required Forms and Deadlines:** FAFSA, institution's own financial aid form. Financial aid filing deadline 7/15. Priority financial aid filing date 3/1. **Notification of Awards:** Applicants will be notified of awards on a rolling basis beginning 3/1. **Types of Aid:** *Need-based scholarships/grants:* Federal Pell, SEOG, state scholarships/grants, private scholarships, the school's own gift aid. *Loans:* Direct Subsidized Stafford, Direct Unsubsidized Stafford, Direct PLUS, FFEL Subsidized Stafford, FFEL Unsubsidized Stafford, FFEL PLUS, Federal Perkins, Federal Nursing, alternative loan through banks. **Student Employment:** Federal Work-Study Program available. Off-campus job opportunities are fair. **Financial Aid Statistics:** 71% freshmen, 72% undergrads receive need-based scholarship or grant aid. 57% freshmen, 57% undergrads receive non-need-based scholarship or grant aid. 67% freshmen, 61% undergrads receive need-based self-help aid. 97% freshmen, 92% undergrads receive any aid. 90% undergrads borrow to pay for school. Average cumulative indebtedness $36,255. **Criteria for awarding institutional aid:** *Non-need-based:* Academics, leadership.

HAMILTON COLLEGE

Best 373

Office of Admission, 198 College Hill Road, Clinton, NY 13323
Phone: 315-859-4421 **Financial Aid Phone:** 800-859-4413
E-mail: admission@hamilton.edu **CEEB Code:** 2286
Fax: 315-859-4457 **Website:** www.hamilton.edu **ACT Code:** 2754

This private school was founded in 1812. It has a 1300-acre campus.

RATINGS
Admissions Selectivity Rating: 97   **Fire Safety Rating:** 82   **Green Rating:** 95

STUDENTS AND FACULTY
Enrollment: 1,851. **Student Body:** 53% female, 47% male, 67% out-of-state, 5% international (40 countries represented). Asian 8%, African American 4%, Caucasian 68%, Hispanic 5%, Native American 1%.
Retention and Graduation: 96% freshmen return for sophomore year. 83% freshmen graduate within 4 years. 18% grads go on to further study within 1 year. 11% grads pursue arts and sciences degrees. 4% grads pursue law degrees. 1% grads pursue business degrees. 1% grads pursue medical degrees. **Faculty:** Student/faculty ratio 10:1. 177 full-time faculty, 97% hold PhDs, 16% are members of minority groups, 41% are women.

ACADEMICS
Degrees: Bachelor's. **Classes:** Most classes have 10–19 students. Most lab/discussion sessions have 10–19 students. **Majors with Highest Enrollment:** Economics; political science and government; psychology. **Special Study Options:** Accelerated program, cross-registration, double major, English as a Second Language (ESL), independent study, internships, student-designed major, study abroad, 3-2 program in Engineering with Columbia University, Rensselaer Polytechnic Institute, and Washington University (St. Louis); 3-3 program in Law with Columbia University. **Combined degree programs:** BA/JD, BA/MEng, Cooperative Program with Columbia University. Special programs offered to physically disabled students include note-taking services, reader services, tape recorders, tutors. **Career services:** Alumni network, alumni services, career/job search classes, career assessment, internships, regional alumni. **Career services highlights include:** The Summer Internship Fund, launched with a $1.6 million endowment in 2006, provides cost-of-living stipends each summer to a number of undergraduates who accept unpaid internships in any career field.

FACILITIES
Housing: Coed dorms, special housing for disabled students, apartments for married students, cooperative housing, apartments for single students, wellness housing. **Special Academic Facilities/Equipment:** Art gallery, language lab, fitness center, observatory, two electron microscopes. Arthur Levitt Public Affairs Center. **Computers:** 100% of classrooms, 100% of dorms, 100% of libraries, 100% of dining areas, 100% of student union, 100% of common outdoor areas have wireless network access. Students can register for classes online. Administrative functions (other than registration) can be performed online.

CAMPUS LIFE
Environment: Rural. **Activities:** Choral groups, concert band, dance, drama/theater, jazz band, literary magazine, music ensembles, musical theater, radio station, student government, student newspaper, student-run film society, symphony orchestra, yearbook, campus ministries, international student organization, Model UN. **Organizations:** 117 registered organizations, 8 honor societies, 4 religious organizations. 11 fraternities, 7 sororities. **Athletics (Intercollegiate):** *Men:* Baseball, basketball, crew/rowing, cross-country, diving, football, golf, ice hockey, lacrosse, soccer, squash, swimming, tennis, track/field (outdoor), track/field (indoor). *Women:* Basketball, crew/rowing, cross-country, diving, field hockey, ice hockey, lacrosse, soccer, softball, squash, swimming, tennis, track/field (outdoor), track/field (indoor), volleyball. **On-Campus Highlights:** Blood Fitness and Dance Center, Kirner-Johnson Commons, Outdoor Leadership Center/Root Glen, Science Center, Cafe Opus. **Environmental Initiatives:** Academic initiatives associated with Hamilton's new Environmental Studies major (2005), and various research related projects. Charter signatory to the President's Climate Commitment, which is actively implementing various administrative and logistical programs to meet and eventually go beyond the minimum participation requirements. Robust sustainable construction and renovation program that pursues LEED silver certification or comparable, including 3 on-campus renewable energy systems in 2008—2 photovoltaic solar arrays, and 1 wind turbine (46kw cumulative).

ADMISSIONS
Freshman Academic Profile: 80% in top 10% of high school class, 97% in top 25% of high school class, 100% in top 50% of high school class. 57%

from public high schools. SAT Math middle 50% range 650–730. SAT Critical Reading middle 50% range 660–740. SAT Writing middle 50% range 650–740. ACT middle 50% range 28–31. **Basis for Candidate Selection:** *Very important factors considered include:* Class rank, academic GPA, rigor of secondary school record. *Important factors considered include:* Application essay, recommendation(s), standardized test scores, character/personal qualities, extracurricular activities, interview. *Other factors considered include:* Alumni/ae relation, first generation, geographical residence, level of applicant's interest, racial/ethnic status, talent/ability, volunteer work, work experience. **Freshman Admission Requirements:** High school diploma is required and GED is accepted. *Academic units recommended:* 4 English, 3 mathematics, 3 science, 3 foreign language, 3 social studies. **Freshman Admission Statistics:** 4,661 applied, 30% admitted, 34% enrolled. **Transfer Admission Requirements:** High school transcript, college transcript(s), essay or personal statement, standardized test scores, statement of good standing from prior institution(s). Lowest grade transferable C. **General Admission Information:** Application fee $75. Early decision application deadline 11/15. Regular application deadline 1/1. Regular notification 4/1. Nonfall registration accepted. Admission may be deferred for a maximum of 2 years. Credit and/or placement offered for CEEB Advanced Placement tests.

COSTS AND FINANCIAL AID
Required Forms and Deadlines: FAFSA, institution's own financial aid form, CSS/Financial Aid PROFILE, state aid form, noncustodial PROFILE, business/farm supplement. Financial aid filing deadline 2/8. Priority financial aid filing date 2/8. **Notification of Awards:** Applicants will be notified of awards on or about 4/1. **Types of Aid:** *Need-based scholarships/grants:* Federal Pell, SEOG, state scholarships/grants, private scholarships, the school's own gift aid. *Loans:* FFEL Subsidized Stafford, FFEL Unsubsidized Stafford, FFEL PLUS, Federal Perkins, college/university loans from institutional funds. **Student Employment:** Federal Work-Study Program available. Institutional employment available. Highest amount earned per year from on-campus jobs $1,800. **Financial Aid Statistics:** 44% freshmen, 41% undergrads receive need-based scholarship or grant aid. 36% freshmen, 35% undergrads receive need-based self-help aid. 56.22% freshmen, 56.67% undergrads receive any aid. 46% undergrads borrow to pay for school. Average cumulative indebtedness $19,466. **Criteria for awarding institutional aid:** *Non-need-based:* State/district residency.

HAMLINE UNIVERSITY

1536 Hewitt Avenue, Saint Paul, MN 55104
Phone: 651-523-2207 **Financial Aid Phone:** 651-523-3000
E-mail: CLA-admis@hamline.edu **CEEB Code:** 6265
Fax: 651-523-2458 **Website:** www.hamline.edu **ACT Code:** 2114

This private school, affiliated with the Methodist Church, was founded in 1854. It has a 77-acre campus.

RATINGS
Admissions Selectivity Rating: 79   **Fire Safety Rating:** 80   **Green Rating:** 70

STUDENTS AND FACULTY
Enrollment: 1,986. **Student Body:** 58% female, 42% male, 15% out-of-state, 3% international (53 countries represented). Asian 6%, African American 5%, Caucasian 75%, Hispanic 2%, Native American 1%.
Retention and Graduation: 82% freshmen return for sophomore year. 61% freshmen graduate within 4 years. 27% grads go on to further study within 1 year. 17% grads pursue arts and sciences degrees. 4% grads pursue law degrees. 2% grads pursue business degrees. 1% grads pursue medical degrees. **Faculty:** Student/faculty ratio 14:1. 173 full-time faculty, 87% hold PhDs, 11% are members of minority groups, 49% are women.

ACADEMICS
Degrees: Bachelor's, first professional, master's, post-bachelor's certificate. **Classes:** Most classes have 10–19 students. Most lab/discussion sessions have 10–19 students. **Majors with Highest Enrollment:** Business/commerce; criminal justice/police science; psychology. **Special Study Options:** Cross-registration, double major, dual enrollment, English as a Second Language (ESL), exchange student program (domestic), honors program, independent study, internships, student-designed major, study abroad, teacher certification program **Combined degree programs:** BA/JD, BA/MEng, 3-3 prog with Hamline School of Law. Special programs offered to physically disabled students include note-taking services, reader services, tape recorders, tutors. **Career services:** Alumni network, alumni services, career/job search classes, career assessment, internships, regional alumni. **Career services highlights include:** All students must fulfill the Leadership, Education, and Development (LEAD) requirement which integrates the liberal arts with the world of work. Most students choose an internship to fulfill this requirement.

FACILITIES

Housing: Coed dorms, fraternity/sorority housing, apartments for married students, cooperative housing, apartments for single students, PRIDE (African-American), Spectrum (GLBT), Hmong, foreign language interest, theme housing (floors organized around areas like Arts, Weekends on Campus, GLBT, and Social Justice). 80% of campus accessible to physically disabled. **Special Academic Facilities/Equipment:** Theatre, music hall, art gallery, science center. **Computers:** 100% of classrooms, 100% of dorms, 100% of libraries, 100% of dining areas, 100% of student union, 100% of common outdoor areas have wireless network access. Students can register for classes online. Administrative functions (other than registration) can be performed online.

CAMPUS LIFE

Environment: Metropolis. **Activities:** Choral groups, concert band, dance, drama/theater, jazz band, literary magazine, music ensembles, musical theater, pep band, radio station, student government, student newspaper, symphony orchestra, television station, yearbook, campus ministries, international student organization, Model UN. **Organizations:** 77 registered organizations, 11 honor societies, 9 religious organizations. 1 fraternities, 2 sororities. **Athletics (Intercollegiate):** *Men:* Baseball, basketball, cross-country, diving, football, ice hockey, soccer, swimming, tennis, track/field (outdoor), track/field (indoor). *Women:* Basketball, cross-country, diving, gymnastics, ice hockey, soccer, softball, swimming, tennis, track/field (outdoor), track/field (indoor), volleyball. **On-Campus Highlights:** Klas Center (stadium and food service), Walker Field House, Sorin Dining Hall, Sundin Music Hall, Bush Student Center. **Environmental Initiatives:** Recycling program Energy saving projects such as chiller replacement, boiler burner replacement and lighting retrofits. Transportation initiatives (increases in bike parking and the use of electric vehicles in mail services and safety and security services, discounted transit pass).

ADMISSIONS

Freshman Academic Profile: Average high school GPA 3.4. 20% in top 10% of high school class, 49% in top 25% of high school class, 79% in top 50% of high school class. 90% from public high schools. SAT Math middle 50% range 540–640. SAT Critical Reading middle 50% range 512.5–645. SAT Writing middle 50% range 510–615. ACT middle 50% range 21–27. Minimum paper TOEFL 550. Minimum computer TOEFL 213. **Basis for Candidate Selection:** *Very important factors considered include:* Class rank, rigor of secondary school record. *Important factors considered include:* Application essay, academic GPA, recommendation(s), standardized test scores, extracurricular activities, interview, talent/ability. *Other factors considered include:* Alumni/ae relation, character/personal qualities, first generation, racial/ethnic status, volunteer work, work experience. **Freshman Admission Requirements:** High school diploma is required and GED is accepted. *Academic units recommended:* 4 English, 3 mathematics, 3 science, (3 science labs), 2 foreign language, 4 social studies, 0 history, 4 academic electives. **Freshman Admission Statistics:** 2,018 applied, 78% admitted, 29% enrolled. **Transfer Admission Requirements:** College transcript(s), essay or personal statement, minimum college GPA of 2.0 required. Lowest grade transferable C–. **General Admission Information:** Notification on a rolling basis, beginning on or about 12/20. Nonfall registration accepted. Admission may be deferred for a maximum of 2 years. Credit and/or placement offered for CEEB Advanced Placement tests.

COSTS AND FINANCIAL AID

Required Forms and Deadlines: FAFSA. Priority financial aid filing date 3/1. **Notification of Awards:** Applicants will be notified of awards on a rolling basis beginning 3/15. **Types of Aid:** *Need-based scholarships/grants:* Federal Pell, SEOG, state scholarships/grants, private scholarships, the school's own gift aid, Federal ACG and SMART grants. *Loans:* FFEL Subsidized Stafford, FFEL Unsubsidized Stafford, FFEL PLUS, Federal Perkins, state loans, Non-federal alternative loans. **Student Employment:** Federal Work-Study Program available. Institutional employment available. Highest amount earned per year from on-campus jobs $3,250. Off-campus job opportunities are excellent. **Financial Aid Statistics:** 74% freshmen, 72% undergrads receive need-based scholarship or grant aid. 8% freshmen, 7% undergrads receive non-need-based scholarship or grant aid. 66% freshmen, 65% undergrads receive need-based self-help aid. 98% freshmen, 95% undergrads receive any aid. 79% undergrads borrow to pay for school. Average cumulative indebtedness $30,518. **Criteria for awarding institutional aid:** *Non-need-based:* Academics, alumni affiliation, art, job skills, leadership, minority status, music/drama, religious affiliation, state/district residency.

HAMPDEN-SYDNEY COLLEGE

PO Box 667, Hampden-Sydney, VA 23943-0667
Phone: 434-223-6120 **Financial Aid Phone:** 434-223-6119
E-mail: hsapp@hsc.edu **CEEB Code:** 5291
Fax: 434-223-6346 **Website:** www.hsc.edu **ACT Code:** 4356

This private school, affiliated with the Presbyterian Church, was founded in 1775. It has a 1200-acre campus.

RATINGS

Admissions Selectivity Rating: 79   **Fire Safety Rating:** 73   **Green Rating:** 74

STUDENTS AND FACULTY

Enrollment: 1,068. **Student Body:** 100% male, 29% out-of-state, 1% international (18 countries represented). Asian 1%, African American 3%, Caucasian 63%, Hispanic 1%.
Retention and Graduation: 61% freshmen graduate within 4 years. 20% grads go on to further study within 1 year. 6.5% grads pursue arts and sciences degrees. 5.5% grads pursue law degrees. 3% grads pursue business degrees. 4% grads pursue medical degrees. **Faculty:** Student/faculty ratio 9:1. 96 full-time faculty, 89% hold PhDs, 7% are members of minority groups, 27% are women.

ACADEMICS

Degrees: Bachelor's. **Classes:** Most classes have 10–19 students. **Majors with Highest Enrollment:** Economics; history; political science and government. **Special Study Options:** Cooperative education program, cross-registration, double major, dual enrollment, exchange student program (domestic), honors program, independent study, internships, study abroad, Appalachian semester, junior year exchange with members of Virginia consortium. Semester at sea and Washington semester also available. **Honors programs:** Student Summer Research programs, Departmental Honors. Special programs offered to physically disabled students include note-taking services, reader services, tape recorders, tutors. **Career services:** Alumni network, alumni services, career/job search classes, career assessment, internships, regional alumni. **Career services highlights include:** Internships—our goal is to assist all of our students who want internships with finding them.

FACILITIES

Housing: Men's dorms, special housing for international students, fraternity/sorority housing, apartments for married students, apartments for single students, theme housing, Language Houses. 90% of campus accessible to physically disabled. **Special Academic Facilities/Equipment:** History museum, language lab, international communications center, observatory. **Computers:** 15% of classrooms, 100% of libraries, 100% of dining areas, 100% of student union, 20% of common outdoor areas have wireless network access. Students can register for classes online. Administrative functions (other than registration) can be performed online.

CAMPUS LIFE

Environment: Rural. **Activities:** Choral groups, drama/theater, literary magazine, music ensembles, pep band, radio station, student government, student newspaper, yearbook, campus ministries, international student organization. **Organizations:** 45 registered organizations, 14 honor societies, 6 religious organizations. 11 fraternities. **Athletics (Intercollegiate):** *Men:* Baseball, basketball, cross-country, football, golf, lacrosse, soccer, tennis. **On-Campus Highlights:** Bortz Library, Kirby Fieldhouse (athletic facility), Gammon gym/Hall of Fame, Tiger Inn, Campus Museum. **Environmental Initiatives:** Electrical energy conservation. Removal of all underground fossil fuel tanks. Conversion from heating oil to propane for improved air quality.

ADMISSIONS

Freshman Academic Profile: Average high school GPA 3.2. 15% in top 10% of high school class, 35% in top 25% of high school class, 63% in top 50% of high school class. 57% from public high schools. SAT Math middle 50% range 500–610. SAT Critical Reading middle 50% range 500–600. SAT Writing middle 50% range 460–580. ACT middle 50% range 21–26. Minimum paper TOEFL 600. Minimum computer TOEFL 250. Minimum web-based TOEFL 100. **Basis for Candidate Selection:** *Very important factors considered include:* Application essay, academic GPA, recommendation(s), rigor of secondary school record, standardized test scores, character/personal qualities. *Important factors considered include:* Class rank, extracurricular activities. *Other factors considered include:* First generation, interview, level of applicant's interest, talent/ability, volunteer work, work experience. **Freshman Admission Requirements:** High school diploma is required and GED is accepted.

Academic units required: 4 English, 3 mathematics, 2 science, (1 science labs), 2 foreign language, 1 social studies, 1 history, 3 academic electives. *Academic units recommended:* 4 mathematics, 3 science, 3 foreign language. **Freshman Admission Statistics:** 2,270 applied, 56% admitted, 23% enrolled. **Transfer Admission Requirements:** High school transcript, college transcript(s), essay or personal statement, standardized test scores, statement of good standing from prior institution(s). Minimum college GPA of 2.5 required. Lowest grade transferable C. **General Admission Information:** Application fee $30. Early decision application deadline 11/15. Regular application deadline 3/1. Regular notification 4/15. Nonfall registration accepted. Credit and/or placement offered for CEEB Advanced Placement tests.

COSTS AND FINANCIAL AID
Annual tuition $29,518. Room and board $9,690. Required fees $1,370. Average book expense $1,200. **Required Forms and Deadlines:** FAFSA, CSS/Financial Aid PROFILE, state aid form. Financial aid filing deadline 5/1. Priority financial aid filing date 11/15. **Notification of Awards:** Applicants will be notified of awards on or about 3/15. **Types of Aid:** *Need-based scholarships/grants:* Federal Pell, SEOG, state scholarships/grants, private scholarships, the school's own gift aid. *Loans:* FFEL Subsidized Stafford, FFEL Unsubsidized Stafford, FFEL PLUS, Federal Perkins, college/university loans from institutional funds. **Student Employment:** Federal Work-Study Program available. Institutional employment available. Highest amount earned per year from on-campus jobs $2,884. Off-campus job opportunities are fair. **Financial Aid Statistics:** 58% freshmen, 52% undergrads receive need-based scholarship or grant aid. 13% freshmen, 9% undergrads receive non-need-based scholarship or grant aid. 46% freshmen, 42% undergrads receive need-based self-help aid. 99.7% freshmen, 98.1% undergrads receive any aid. 54% undergrads borrow to pay for school. Average cumulative indebtedness $23,822. **Criteria for awarding institutional aid:** *Non-need-based:* Academics, leadership, minority status, religious affiliation, state/district residency.

HAMPSHIRE COLLEGE

Admissions Office, 893 West Street, Amherst, MA 01002
Phone: 413-559-5471 **Financial Aid Phone:** 413-559-5484
E-mail: admissions@hampshire.edu **CEEB Code:** 3447
Fax: 413-559-5631 **Website:** www.hampshire.edu **ACT Code:** 1842

This private school was founded in 1965. It has a 850-acre campus.

RATINGS
Admissions Selectivity Rating: 89   **Fire Safety Rating:** 60*   **Green Rating:** 82

STUDENTS AND FACULTY
Enrollment: 1,438. **Student Body:** 60% female, 40% male, 82% out-of-state, 4% international (31 countries represented). Asian 4%, African American 4%, Caucasian 68%, Hispanic 8%, Native American 1%.
Retention and Graduation: 87% freshmen return for sophomore year. 53% freshmen graduate within 4 years. 10% grads go on to further study within 1 year. 8% grads pursue arts and sciences degrees. 1% grads pursue law degrees. 1% grads pursue medical degrees. **Faculty:** Student/faculty ratio 12:1. 99 full-time faculty, 83% hold PhDs, 20% are members of minority groups, 54% are women.

ACADEMICS
Degrees: Bachelor's. **Classes:** Most classes have 10–19 students. Most lab/discussion sessions have 10–19 students. **Majors with Highest Enrollment:** Creative writing; drama and dramatics/theatre arts; film/video and photographic arts, other. **Special Study Options:** Exchange student program (domestic), independent study, internships, student-designed major, study abroad, teacher certification program. Special programs offered to physically disabled students include note-taking services, reader services, tape recorders. **Career services:** Alumni network, alumni services, career/job search classes, career assessment, internships.

FACILITIES
Housing: Coed dorms, special housing for disabled students, special housing for international students, women's dorms, apartments for single students, theme housing. 50% of campus accessible to physically disabled. **Special Academic Facilities/Equipment:** Performing and visual arts center, bioshelter (integrated greenhouse/aquaculture facility), farm center, electronic music and

TV production studios, extensive film and photography facilities, multimedia center. **Computers:** 100% of classrooms, 10% of dorms, 100% of libraries, 100% of dining areas, 50% of common outdoor areas have wireless network access. Students can register for classes online. Administrative functions (other than registration) can be performed online.

CAMPUS LIFE
Environment: Town. **Activities:** Choral groups, dance, drama/theater, jazz band, student newspaper, student-run film society, international student organization. **Organizations:** 94 registered organizations, 3 religious organizations. **On-Campus Highlights:** Bridge Cafe, Bookstore, Library, Eric Carle Museum of Picture Book Art, Liebling Center—Film/Photo. **Environmental Initiatives:** Constructing a new facility addition to LEED standards (minimum silver; hopefully gold); constructing a condominium community to be LEED-certified. ACUPCC signatory, establishing an environmental committee and mandating emissions inventory. Formed a committee on sustainability that will engage all administrative areas, including Facilities and Grounds, Purchasing, Environmental Health and Safety, Dining Services, Campus Planning, and Information Technology. The campus sustainability committment has also been re-emphasized at the trustee committee level.

ADMISSIONS
Freshman Academic Profile: Average high school GPA 3.49. 27% in top 10% of high school class, 69% in top 25% of high school class, 89% in top 50% of high school class. 44% from public high schools. SAT Math middle 50% range 530–660. SAT Critical Reading middle 50% range 600–710. SAT Writing middle 50% range 590–700. ACT middle 50% range 25–29. Minimum paper TOEFL 577. Minimum computer TOEFL 233. Minimum web-based TOEFL 91. **Basis for Candidate Selection:** *Very important factors considered include:* Application essay, character/personal qualities. *Important factors considered include:* Recommendation(s), rigor of secondary school record, extracurricular activities, level of applicant's interest, talent/ability. *Other factors considered include:* Class rank, academic GPA, standardized test scores, alumni/ae relation, interview, racial/ethnic status, volunteer work, work experience. **Freshman Admission Requirements:** High school diploma is required and GED is accepted. *Academic units required:* 4 English, 3 mathematics, 3 science, (2 science labs), 3 foreign language, 3 history. *Academic units recommended:* 4 English, 4 mathematics, 4 science, (2 science labs), 4 foreign language, 4 history. **Freshman Admission Statistics:** 2,515 applied, 63% admitted, 24% enrolled. **Transfer Admission Requirements:** High school transcript, college transcript(s), essay or personal statement, Lowest grade transferable C. **General Admission Information:** Application fee $60. Early decision application deadline 11/15. Regular application deadline 1/1. Regular notification 4/1. Nonfall registration accepted. Admission may be deferred for a maximum of 1 year. Placement offered for CEEB Advanced Placement tests.

COSTS AND FINANCIAL AID
Required Forms and Deadlines: FAFSA, CSS/Financial Aid PROFILE, noncustodial PROFILE. Priority financial aid filing date 2/1. **Notification of Awards:** Applicants will be notified of awards on or about 4/1. **Types of Aid:** *Need-based scholarships/grants:* Federal Pell, SEOG, state scholarships/grants, private scholarships, the school's own gift aid. *Loans:* Direct Subsidized Stafford, Direct Unsubsidized Stafford, Direct PLUS, FFEL PLUS, Federal Perkins. **Student Employment:** Federal Work-Study Program available. Highest amount earned per year from on-campus jobs $2,600. **Financial Aid Statistics:** 69% freshmen, 61% undergrads receive need-based scholarship or grant aid. 63% freshmen, 53% undergrads receive non-need-based scholarship or grant aid. 69% freshmen, 61% undergrads receive need-based self-help aid. 86% freshmen, 77% undergrads receive any aid. 51% undergrads borrow to pay for school. Average cumulative indebtedness $20,669. **Criteria for awarding institutional aid:** *Non-need-based:* Academics, leadership, minority status.

HAMPTON UNIVERSITY

Office of Admissions, Hampton University, Hampton, VA 23668
Phone: 757-727-5328 **Financial Aid Phone:** 757-727-5332
E-mail: admit@hamptonu.edu **CEEB Code:** 5292
Fax: 757-727-5095 **Website:** www.hamptonu.edu **ACT Code:** 4358

This private school was founded in 1868. It has a 255-acre campus.

RATINGS
Admissions Selectivity Rating: 85   **Fire Safety Rating:** 60*   **Green Rating:** 60*

STUDENTS AND FACULTY

Enrollment: 5,056. **Student Body:** 64% female, 36% male, 69% out-of-state, (33 countries represented). Asian 1%, African American 96%, Caucasian 12%, Hispanic 1%.

Retention and Graduation: 85% freshmen return for sophomore year. 40% grads go on to further study within 1 year. 40% grads pursue arts and sciences degrees. 2% grads pursue law degrees. 5% grads pursue business degrees. 10% grads pursue medical degrees. **Faculty:** Student/faculty ratio 16:1. 363 full-time faculty, 75% hold PhDs, 79% are members of minority groups, 58% are women.

ACADEMICS

Degrees: Associate, bachelor's, certificate, first professional, master's, post-master's certificate. **Classes:** Most classes have 20–29 students. Most lab/discussion sessions have 10–19 students. **Majors with Highest Enrollment:** Business/commerce; journalism; psychology. **Special Study Options:** Accelerated program, cooperative education program, cross-registration, distance learning, double major, dual enrollment, honors program, independent study, internships, study abroad, teacher certification program, Undergrads may take grad level programs. Co-Op Programs: arts, business, education, engineering, social/behavioral science, Pre-college, Army ROTC, Navy ROTC. Member Tidewater Consortium. **Honors programs:** Honors College—Designed to augment, enhance and extend the undergraduate academic experience through community, exposure and expectations. Leadership Institute—Offers the undergraduate student a curricular option that enhances the university experience. **Combined degree programs:** Bachelor of Arts/Master in Teaching. Special programs offered to physically disabled students include note-taking services, reader services, tape recorders, tutors. **Career services:** Alumni network, alumni services, career/job search classes, career assessment, internships. **Career services highlights include:** Students who experience jobs through Cooperative Education have a chance to determine their life's work while earning academic credit.

FACILITIES

Housing: Coed dorms, men's dorms, special housing for international students, women's dorms. 90% of campus accessible to physically disabled. **Special Academic Facilities/Equipment:** African, Native American, and Oceanic museums, and gallery. New Student Center. **Computers:** 100% of classrooms, 100% of dorms, 100% of libraries, 100% of dining areas, 100% of student union, 100% of common outdoor areas have wireless network access. Students can register for classes online. Administrative functions (other than registration) can be performed online.

CAMPUS LIFE

Environment: City. **Activities:** Choral groups, concert band, dance, drama/theater, jazz band, marching band, music ensembles, musical theater, opera, pep band, radio station, student government, student newspaper, symphony orchestra, television station, yearbook. **Organizations:** 85 registered organizations, 16 honor societies, 3 religious organizations. 6 fraternities, 3 sororities. **Athletics (Intercollegiate):** *Men:* Basketball, cross-country, football, golf, sailing, tennis, track/field (outdoor), track/field (indoor). *Women:* Basketball, bowling, cross-country, golf, sailing, softball, tennis, track/field (outdoor), track/field (indoor), volleyball. **On-Campus Highlights:** Emancipation Oak, Memorial Chapel, Huntington Memorial Museum, Booker T. Washington Monument, Student Center: bowling, fitness, and movie.

ADMISSIONS

Freshman Academic Profile: Average high school GPA 3.2. 20% in top 10% of high school class, 45% in top 25% of high school class, 90% in top 50% of high school class. 90% from public high schools. SAT Math middle 50% range 464–606. SAT Critical Reading middle 50% range 481–552. ACT middle 50% range 17–26. Minimum paper TOEFL 550. Minimum computer TOEFL 214. **Basis for Candidate Selection:** *Very important factors considered include:* Application essay, rigor of secondary school record, standardized test scores, character/personal qualities. *Important factors considered include:* Class rank, recommendation(s). *Other factors considered include:* Alumni/ae relation, extracurricular activities, talent/ability, volunteer work. **Freshman Admission Requirements:** High school diploma is required and GED is accepted. *Academic units required:* 4 English, 3 mathematics, 2 science, (2 science labs), 2 social studies, 6 academic electives. *Academic units recommended:* 2 foreign language. **Freshman Admission Statistics:** 7,120 applied, 37% admitted, 43% enrolled. **Transfer Admission Requirements:** College transcript(s), essay or personal statement, statement of good standing from prior institution(s). Minimum college GPA of 2.3 required. Lowest grade transferable C. **General Admission Information:** Application fee $35. Nonfall registration accepted. Admission may be deferred for a maximum of 1 year. Credit and/or placement offered for CEEB Advanced Placement tests.

COSTS AND FINANCIAL AID

Annual tuition $13,358. Room and board $6,746. Required fees $1,460. Average book expense $750. **Required Forms and Deadlines:** FAFSA. Priority financial aid filing date 3/1. **Notification of Awards:** Applicants will be noti-

fied of awards on a rolling basis beginning 4/15. **Types of Aid:** *Need-based scholarships/grants:* Federal Pell, SEOG, state scholarships/grants, private scholarships, the school's own gift aid, Federal Nursing Scholarships. *Loans:* Direct Subsidized Stafford, Direct Unsubsidized Stafford, Direct PLUS, FFEL Subsidized Stafford, FFEL Unsubsidized Stafford, FFEL PLUS, Federal Perkins, alternative loans. **Student Employment:** Federal Work-Study Program available. Off-campus job opportunities are excellent. **Financial Aid Statistics:** 96% freshmen, 44% undergrads receive need-based scholarship or grant aid. 23% freshmen, 13% undergrads receive non-need-based scholarship or grant aid. 79% freshmen, 44% undergrads receive need-based self-help aid. 44% freshmen, 100% undergrads receive any aid. 51% undergrads borrow to pay for school. Average cumulative indebtedness $17,125. **Criteria for awarding institutional aid:** *Non-need-based:* Academics, athletics, leadership, music/drama.

HANNIBAL-LAGRANGE COLLEGE

2800 Palmyra Road, Hannibal, MO 63401
Phone: 573-221-3113 **Financial Aid Phone:** 573-629-3280
E-mail: admissio@hlg.edu
Fax: 573-221-6594 **Website:** www.hlg.edu **ACT Code:** 2320

This private school, affiliated with the Southern Baptist Church, was founded in 1858. It has a 110-acre campus.

RATINGS

Admissions Selectivity Rating: 64   **Fire Safety Rating:** 60*   **Green Rating:** 60*

STUDENTS AND FACULTY

Enrollment: 902. **Student Body:** 63% female, 37% male, 26% out-of-state, 9% international (11 countries represented). Asian 1%, African American 3%, Caucasian 84%, Hispanic 2%.

Faculty: 63 full-time faculty, 27% hold PhDs, 2% are members of minority groups, 52% are women.

ACADEMICS

Degrees: Associate, bachelor's, master's. **Majors with Highest Enrollment:** Elementary education and teaching; non-profit/public/organizational management; secondary education and teaching. **Special Study Options:** Accelerated program, distance learning, dual enrollment, English as a Second Language (ESL), honors program, independent study, internships, liberal arts/career combination, student-designed major, study abroad, teacher certification program, weekend college, Adult Program. **Honors programs:** Honors Program qualifies a student for a semester of study at Harlaxton College, Grantham, England. Special programs offered to physically disabled students include tape recorders, tutors. **Career services:** Career assessment, internships. **Career services highlights include:** FOCUS online career exploration program.

FACILITIES

Housing: Special housing for disabled students, men's dorms, women's dorms, apartments for single students. 98% of campus accessible to physically disabled. **Special Academic Facilities/Equipment:** L.A. Foster Library, T.M. Matthews Science Building, Mary Wiehe Science Building, Partee Tech. Center, Roland Fine Arts Center. **Computers:** Students can register for classes online.

CAMPUS LIFE

Environment: Village. **Activities:** Choral groups, concert band, drama/theater, jazz band, music ensembles, musical theater, student government, student newspaper, yearbook, campus ministries, international student organization. **Organizations:** 22 registered organizations, 1 honor societies, 3 religious organizations. **Athletics (Intercollegiate):** *Men:* Baseball, basketball, cross-country, golf, soccer, swimming, track/field (outdoor), volleyball, wrestling. *Women:* Basketball, cheerleading, cross-country, golf, soccer, softball, swimming, track/field (outdoor), volleyball. **On-Campus Highlights:** Roland Fine Arts Center, Mabee Sports Complex, Common Grounds, Snack Shack, Carroll Mission Center.

ADMISSIONS

Freshman Academic Profile: 21% in top 10% of high school class, 37% in top 25% of high school class, 52% in top 50% of high school class. SAT Math middle 50% range 440–540. SAT Critical Reading middle 50% range 420–510. SAT Writing middle 50% range 420–480. ACT middle 50% range 19–24. Minimum paper TOEFL 520. Minimum computer TOEFL 190. **Basis for Candidate Selection:** *Very important factors considered include:* Academic GPA, standardized test scores. *Important factors considered include:* Rigor of secondary school record. *Other factors considered include:* Class rank, recommendation(s), character/personal qualities, level of applicant's interest, religious affiliation/commitment, talent/ability. **Freshman Admission Requirements:** High school diploma is required and GED is accepted. *Academic units recommended:* 4 English, 3 mathematics, 2 science, (1 science labs), 3 history. **Freshman Admission Statistics:** 646 applied, 94% admitted, 31% enrolled. **Transfer Admission Requirements:** College transcript(s), minimum college GPA of 2.0 required. Lowest grade transferable 1. **General Admission Information:** Application fee $25. Nonfall registration accepted. Admission may be deferred for a maximum of 1 semester. Neither credit nor placement offered for CEEB Advanced Placement tests.

COSTS AND FINANCIAL AID
Annual tuition $14,820. Room and board $6,000. Required fees $660. Average book expense $800. **Required Forms and Deadlines:** FAFSA, institution's own financial aid form. Financial aid filing deadline 7/1. Priority financial aid filing date 7/1. **Types of Aid:** *Need-based scholarships/grants:* Federal Pell, SEOG, state scholarships/grants, private scholarships, the school's own gift aid. *Loans:* FFEL Subsidized Stafford, FFEL Unsubsidized Stafford, FFEL PLUS, Federal Perkins. **Student Employment:** Federal Work-Study Program available. Institutional employment available. Off-campus job opportunities are fair. **Financial Aid Statistics:** 42% freshmen, 50% undergrads receive need-based scholarship or grant aid. 63% freshmen, 47% undergrads receive non-need-based scholarship or grant aid. 6% freshmen, 66% undergrads receive need-based self-help aid. 34% freshmen, 17% undergrads receive athletic scholarships. **Criteria for awarding institutional aid:** *Non-need-based:* Academics, art, athletics, music/drama, religious affiliation.

HANOVER COLLEGE

P.O. Box 108, Hanover, IN 47243-0108
Phone: 812-213-2178 **Financial Aid Phone:** 812-866-7029
E-mail: admission@hanover.edu **CEEB Code:** 1290
Fax: 812-866-7098 **Website:** www.hanover.edu **ACT Code:** 1200

This private school, affiliated with the Presbyterian Church, was founded in 1827. It has a 650-acre campus.

RATINGS
Admissions Selectivity Rating: 88 **Fire Safety Rating:** 72 **Green Rating:** 77

STUDENTS AND FACULTY
Enrollment: 932. **Student Body:** 54% female, 46% male, 32% out-of-state, 3% international (13 countries represented). Asian 1%, African American 2%, Caucasian 86%, Hispanic 2%.
Retention and Graduation: 80% freshmen return for sophomore year. 58% freshmen graduate within 4 years. 27% grads go on to further study within 1 year. 19% grads pursue arts and sciences degrees. 4% grads pursue law degrees. 1% grads pursue business degrees. 1% grads pursue medical degrees. **Faculty:** Student/faculty ratio 10:1. 91 full-time faculty, 100% hold PhDs, 8% are members of minority groups, 37% are women.

ACADEMICS
Degrees: Bachelor's. **Classes:** Most classes have 10–19 students. **Majors with Highest Enrollment:** Communication studies/speech communication and rhetoric; history; psychology. **Special Study Options:** Double major, dual enrollment, independent study, internships, student-designed major, study abroad, teacher certification program, CBP (Center for Business Preparation) Business Scholar Program, Philadelphia Center and Washington Center Internship Programs. Special programs offered to physically disabled students include note-taking services, tutors. **Career services:** Alumni network, alumni services, career/job search classes, career assessment, internships, regional alumni. **Career services highlights include:** Hanover College curriculum teaches students to communicate effectively, think critically, and solve problems creatively. Through a variety of experiential learning opportunities and networking events, the CBP builds upon the liberal arts foundation by emphasizing personal leadership development and team working skills.

FACILITIES
Housing: Coed dorms, men's dorms, women's dorms, fraternity/sorority housing, apartments for single students, wellness housing, theme housing. 50% of campus accessible to physically disabled. **Special Academic Facilities/Equipment:** Cadaver lab, geological museum, electronic language lab, observatory. **Computers:** 80% of classrooms, 100% of dorms, 50% of libraries, 100% of dining areas, 100% of student union, 20% of common outdoor areas have wireless network access. Students can register for classes online. Administrative functions (other than registration) can be performed online.

CAMPUS LIFE
Environment: Rural. **Activities:** Choral groups, concert band, dance, drama/theater, jazz band, literary magazine, music ensembles, musical theater, pep band, radio station, student government, student newspaper, student-run film society, symphony orchestra, television station, yearbook, campus ministries, international student organization. **Organizations:** 60 registered organizations, 8 honor societies, 4 religious organizations. 4 fraternities, 4 sororities. **Athletics (Intercollegiate):** *Men:* Baseball, basketball, cross-country, football, golf, lacrosse, soccer, tennis, track/field (outdoor). *Women:* Basketball, cross-country, golf, soccer, softball, tennis, track/field (outdoor), volleyball. **On-Campus Highlights:** Science Center, Horner Health and Recreation Center (Collier Arena), Campus Center, The Shoebox, The Point-River View, The Shoebox serves food and drinks, as does the new coffee house in Crowe Hall. **Environmental Initiatives:** Paint, Carpeting, and lighting in the newly renovated buildings are completed using environmental products or ideas. Housekeeping uses all green products and the landscaping is also environmentally friendly. A recycling program is in place for the campus.

ADMISSIONS
Freshman Academic Profile: Average high school GPA 3.63. 32% in top 10% of high school class, 71% in top 25% of high school class, 96% in top 50% of high school class. 82% from public high schools. SAT Math middle 50% range 500–620. SAT Critical Reading middle 50% range 490–600. SAT Writing middle 50% range 470–570. ACT middle 50% range 22–28. Minimum paper TOEFL 550. Minimum computer TOEFL 213. Minimum web-based TOEFL 120. **Basis for Candidate Selection:** *Very important factors considered include:* Class rank, academic GPA, rigor of secondary school record. *Important factors considered include:* Recommendation(s), standardized test scores, talent/ability. *Other factors considered include:* Application essay, alumni/ae relation, character/personal qualities, extracurricular activities, first generation, geographical residence, interview, level of applicant's interest, racial/ethnic status, state residency, volunteer work, work experience. **Freshman Admission Requirements:** High school diploma is required and GED is not accepted. *Academic units required:* 4 English, 3 mathematics, 3 science, (2 science labs), 2 foreign language, 2 social studies, 2 history, 2 academic electives. *Academic units recommended:* 4 English, 4 mathematics, 4 science, (3 science labs), 4 foreign language, 3 social studies, 3 history, 3 academic electives. **Freshman Admission Statistics:** 3,019 applied, 61% admitted, 16% enrolled. **Transfer Admission Requirements:** High school transcript, college transcript(s), essay or personal statement, standardized test scores, statement of good standing from prior institution(s). Minimum college GPA of 2.0 required. Lowest grade transferable C–. **General Admission Information:** Application fee $40. Regular application deadline 3/1. Notification on a rolling basis, beginning on or about 9/1. Nonfall registration accepted. Admission may be deferred for a maximum of 1 year. Credit and/or placement offered for CEEB Advanced Placement tests.

COSTS AND FINANCIAL AID
Annual tuition $25,800. Room and board $7,900. Required fees $550. Average book expense $900. **Required Forms and Deadlines:** FAFSA. Priority financial aid filing date 3/1. **Notification of Awards:** Applicants will be notified of awards on a rolling basis beginning 3/1. **Types of Aid:** *Need-based scholarships/grants:* Federal Pell, SEOG, state scholarships/grants, private scholarships, the school's own gift aid. *Loans:* FFEL Subsidized Stafford, FFEL Unsubsidized Stafford, FFEL PLUS, college/university loans from institutional funds. **Student Employment:** Institutional employment available. Highest amount earned per year from on-campus jobs $3,000. Off-campus job opportunities are fair. **Financial Aid Statistics:** 73% freshmen, 73% undergrads receive need-based scholarship or grant aid. 14% freshmen, 12% undergrads receive non-need-based scholarship or grant aid. 52% freshmen, 57% undergrads receive need-based self-help aid. 99% freshmen, 98% undergrads receive any aid. 60% undergrads borrow to pay for school. Average cumulative indebtedness $26,570. **Criteria for awarding institutional aid:** *Non-need-based:* Academics, alumni affiliation, art, leadership, minority status, music/drama, religious affiliation, state/district residency.

HARDIN-SIMMONS UNIVERSITY

Box 16050, Abilene, TX 79698
Phone: 325-670-1206 **Financial Aid Phone:** 325-670-1206
E-mail: enroll@hsutx.edu **CEEB Code:** 6268
Fax: 325-671-2115 **Website:** www.hsutx.edu **ACT Code:** 4096

This private school was founded in 1891. It has a 209-acre campus.

RATINGS
Admissions Selectivity Rating: 87 **Fire Safety Rating:** 67 **Green Rating:** 67

STUDENTS AND FACULTY

Enrollment: 1,882. **Student Body:** 56% female, 44% male, 4% out-of-state, 1% international (16 countries represented). Asian 1%, African American 6%, Caucasian 77%, Hispanic 10%, Native American 1%.
Retention and Graduation: 71% freshmen return for sophomore year. 29% freshmen graduate within 4 years. 44% grads go on to further study within 1 year. 25% grads pursue arts and sciences degrees. 1% grads pursue law degrees. 7% grads pursue business degrees. 3% grads pursue medical degrees. **Faculty:** Student/faculty ratio 13:1. 136 full-time faculty, 89% hold PhDs, 2% are members of minority groups, 33% are women. 1% of classes are taught by teaching assistants.

ACADEMICS

Degrees: Bachelor's, doctoral, master's, post-bachelor's certificate. **Classes:** Most classes have 10–19 students. Most lab/discussion sessions have 20–29 students. **Majors with Highest Enrollment:** Biology/biological sciences; business, management, marketing, and related support services; other; education. **Special Study Options:** Accelerated program, cross-registration, distance learning, double major, dual enrollment, honors program, independent study, internships, study abroad, teacher certification program. **Honors programs:** The Hardin-Simmons University Honors Program provides an enriched educational environment for undergraduate students of exceptional promise who have a wide variety of interests and seek an enhanced learning opportunity. The Honors Program promotes creative and critical thinking skills to equip individuals for success in today's world. The Program, which serves as an integral part of the academic community, includes courses taught by selected faculty members interested in working with highly motivated students. The Honors Program expects participants to strive for excellence and assume personal accountability for their intellectual growth. Special programs offered to physically disabled students include note-taking services, reader services, tape recorders, tutors. **Career services:** Alumni network, alumni services, career/job search classes, career assessment, internships, regional alumni. **Career services highlights include:** Internship program—the Office of Career Services at HSU hosts internship listings through our online service, Career Connection. In addition, many academic departments have a specific faculty person designated to help students find internship opportunities within their field of study.

FACILITIES

Housing: Special housing for disabled students, men's dorms, women's dorms, apartments for married students, apartments for single students, Single and Duplex housing with priority given to families. 100% of campus accessible to physically disabled. **Special Academic Facilities/Equipment:** Art center, observatory with 14-inch telescope, rare and fine book room, SIX WHITE HORSE facility, Holland Health Science Medical High School. **Computers:** 90% of classrooms, 100% of dorms, 80% of libraries, 100% of dining areas, 100% of student union, 50% of common outdoor areas have wireless network access.

CAMPUS LIFE

Environment: City. **Activities:** Choral groups, concert band, drama/theater, jazz band, literary magazine, marching band, music ensembles, musical theater, opera, student government, student newspaper, symphony orchestra, yearbook, campus ministries, international student organization, Model UN. **Organizations:** 15 honor societies, 1 religious organizations. 4 fraternities, 4 sororities. **Athletics (Intercollegiate):** *Men:* Baseball, basketball, cheerleading, cross-country, football, golf, soccer, tennis, track/field (outdoor). *Women:* Basketball, cheerleading, cross-country, golf, soccer, softball, tennis, track/field (outdoor), volleyball. **On-Campus Highlights:** Moody Center (Student Center), Java City Coffee House, The Pond/Gazebo, Dorm Lobbies, The Pool, Gym/Fitness Center; Connally Mission Center; Skiles Social Science Building.

ADMISSIONS

Freshman Academic Profile: Average high school GPA 3.56. 27% in top 10% of high school class, 59% in top 25% of high school class, 85% in top 50% of high school class. 90% from public high schools. SAT Math middle 50% range 480–600. SAT Critical Reading middle 50% range 450–560. SAT Writing middle 50% range 450–570. ACT middle 50% range 20–25. Minimum paper TOEFL 550. Minimum computer TOEFL 213. Minimum web-based TOEFL 75. **Basis for Candidate Selection:** *Very important factors considered include:* Class rank, academic GPA, standardized test scores. *Important factors considered include:* Recommendation(s), rigor of secondary school record, character/personal qualities, talent/ability. *Other factors considered include:* Alumni/ae relation, extracurricular activities, level of applicant's interest, religious affiliation/commitment. **Freshman Admission Requirements:** High school diploma is required and GED is accepted. *Academic units required:* 3 English, 2 mathematics, 2 science, 2 social studies, 7 academic electives. **Freshman Admission Statistics:** 1,677 applied, 38% admitted, 65% enrolled. **Transfer Admission Requirements:** College transcript(s), minimum college GPA of 2.0 required. Lowest grade transferable C. **General Admission Information:** Application fee $50. Notification on a rolling basis, beginning on or about 9/1. Nonfall registration accepted. Admission may be deferred for a maximum of 1 Year. Credit offered for CEEB Advanced Placement tests.

COSTS AND FINANCIAL AID

Annual tuition $19,950. Room and board $6,282. Required fees $1,040. Average book expense $800. **Required Forms and Deadlines:** FAFSA. Priority financial aid filing date 3/15. **Notification of Awards:** Applicants will be notified of awards on a rolling basis beginning 2/1. **Types of Aid:** *Need-based scholarships/grants:* Federal Pell, SEOG, state scholarships/grants, private scholarships, the school's own gift aid, ACG/SMART (federal grants). *Loans:* FFEL Subsidized Stafford, FFEL Unsubsidized Stafford, FFEL PLUS, Federal Perkins, state loans, college/university loans from institutional funds. **Student Employment:** Federal Work-Study Program available. Institutional employment available. Highest amount earned per year from on-campus jobs $2,400. Off-campus job opportunities are excellent. **Financial Aid Statistics:** 55% freshmen, 51% undergrads receive need-based scholarship or grant aid. 66% freshmen, 60% undergrads receive non-need-based scholarship or grant aid. 64% freshmen, 63% undergrads receive need-based self-help aid. 99% freshmen, 94% undergrads receive any aid. 73% undergrads borrow to pay for school. Average cumulative indebtedness $35,429. **Criteria for awarding institutional aid:** *Non-need-based:* Academics, art, job skills, music/drama, religious affiliation.

HARDING UNIVERSITY

Box 12255, Searcy, AR 72149
Phone: 501-279-4407 **Financial Aid Phone:** 501-279-4257
E-mail: admissions@harding.edu **CEEB Code:** 10311
Fax: 501-279-4129 **Website:** www.harding.edu **ACT Code:** 0124

This private school, affiliated with the Church of Christ Church, was founded in 1924. It has a 275-acre campus.

RATINGS

Admissions Selectivity Rating: 87   **Fire Safety Rating:** 74   **Green Rating:** 66

STUDENTS AND FACULTY

Enrollment: 4,052. **Student Body:** 53% female, 47% male, 72% out-of-state, 6% international (49 countries represented). Asian 1%, African American 4%, Caucasian 85%, Hispanic 2%, Native American 1%.
Retention and Graduation: 81% freshmen return for sophomore year. 38% freshmen graduate within 4 years. 36% grads go on to further study within 1 year. 2% grads pursue law degrees. 9% grads pursue business degrees. 2% grads pursue medical degrees. **Faculty:** Student/faculty ratio 17:1. 248 full-time faculty, 67% hold PhDs, 3% are members of minority groups, 31% are women.

ACADEMICS

Degrees: Bachelor's, master's, post-master's certificate. **Classes:** Most classes have 10–19 students. Most lab/discussion sessions have 10–19 students. **Majors with Highest Enrollment:** Business/commerce; early childhood education and teaching; nursing/registered nurse (RN, ASN, BSN, MSN). **Special Study Options:** Accelerated program, cooperative education program, distance learning, double major, dual enrollment, English as a Second Language (ESL), honors program, independent study, internships, liberal arts/career combination, study abroad, teacher certification program. **Combined degree programs:** BA/PharmD. Special programs offered to physically disabled students include note-taking services, reader services, tape recorders, tutors. **Career services:** Alumni services, career/job search classes, career assessment, internships.

FACILITIES

Housing: Special housing for disabled students, men's dorms, women's dorms, apartments for married students, apartments for single students, Approved Off-Campus Housing. 95% of campus accessible to physically disabled. **Special Academic Facilities/Equipment:** On-campus academy (prep school grades K–12). **Computers:** 95% of classrooms, 100% of libraries, 100% of dining areas, 100% of student union, 80% of common outdoor areas have wireless network access. Students can register for classes online. Administrative functions (other than registration) can be performed online.

CAMPUS LIFE

Environment: Village. **Activities:** Choral groups, concert band, drama/theater, jazz band, marching band, music ensembles, pep band, radio station, student government, student newspaper, symphony orchestra, television station, yearbook, campus ministries, international student organization. **Organizations:** 100 registered organizations, 12 honor societies, 10 religious organizations. 14 fraternities, 15 sororities. **Athletics (Intercollegiate):** *Men:* Baseball, basketball, cross-country, football, golf, soccer, tennis, track/field (outdoor). *Women:* Basketball, cheerleading, cross-country, golf, soccer, tennis, track/field (outdoor), volleyball. **On-Campus Highlights:** Cyber Cafe in Student Center, Front Lawn with Swings, Campus Dining until 9:00pm, Rhodes Memorial Field House, First Security Stadium. **Environmental Initiatives:** Recycling, composting, trayless dining.

ADMISSIONS

Freshman Academic Profile: Average high school GPA 3.49. 28% in top 10% of high school class, 50% in top 25% of high school class, 79% in top 50% of high school class. 70% from public high schools. SAT Math middle 50% range 490–640. SAT Critical Reading middle 50% range 490–630. ACT middle 50% range 21–28. Minimum paper TOEFL 550. Minimum web-based TOEFL 79. **Basis for Candidate Selection:** *Very important factors considered include:* Recommendation(s), rigor of secondary school record, standardized test scores, character/personal qualities, interview. *Important factors considered include:* Class rank, academic GPA, talent/ability. *Other factors considered include:* Application essay, alumni/ae relation, extracurricular activities, first generation, geographical residence, level of applicant's interest, state residency, volunteer work, work experience. **Freshman Admission Requirements:** High school diploma is required and GED is accepted. *Academic units required:* 4 English, 3 mathematics, 2 science, 3 social studies, 3 academic electives. *Academic units recommended:* 4 English, 4 mathematics, 4 science, 2 foreign language, 4 social studies, 2 academic electives. **Freshman Admission Statistics:** 1,970 applied, 73% admitted, 67% enrolled. **Transfer Admission Requirements:** College transcript(s), essay or personal statement, statement of good standing from prior institution(s). Minimum college GPA of 2 required. Lowest grade transferable C. **General Admission Information:** Application fee $40. Notification on a rolling basis, beginning on or about 5/1. Nonfall registration accepted. Admission may be deferred for a maximum of 1 year. Credit and/or placement offered for CEEB Advanced Placement tests.

COSTS AND FINANCIAL AID

Annual tuition $13,140. Room and board $5,814. Required fees $440. Average book expense $900. **Required Forms and Deadlines:** FAFSA. Priority financial aid filing date 4/15. **Notification of Awards:** Applicants will be notified of awards on a rolling basis beginning 2/15. *Types of Aid: Need-based scholarships/grants:* Federal Pell, SEOG, state scholarships/grants, private scholarships, the school's own gift aid, Stephens Scholars Program for African-American students. *Loans:* FFEL Subsidized Stafford, FFEL Unsubsidized Stafford, FFEL PLUS, Federal Perkins, Federal Nursing, college/university loans from institutional funds. **Student Employment:** Federal Work-Study Program available. Institutional employment available. **Financial Aid Statistics:** 50% freshmen, 47% undergrads receive need-based scholarship or grant aid. 11% freshmen, 7% undergrads receive non-need-based scholarship or grant aid. 37% freshmen, 46% undergrads receive need-based self-help aid. 4% freshmen, 4% undergrads receive athletic scholarships. 97% freshmen, 94% undergrads receive any aid. 70% undergrads borrow to pay for school. Average cumulative indebtedness $31,730. **Criteria for awarding institutional aid:** *Non-need-based:* Academics, alumni affiliation, art, athletics, leadership, music/drama, religious affiliation, state/district residency.

HARRINGTON COLLEGE OF DESIGN

200 West Madison, Suite 200, Chicago, IL 60606-3433
Phone: 877-939-4975
E-mail: hiid@interiordesign.edu
Fax: 312-697-8032 **Website:** www.harringtoncollege.com **ACT Code:** 6641

This proprietary school was founded in 1931.

RATINGS
Admissions Selectivity Rating: 60*   **Fire Safety Rating:** 60*   **Green Rating:** 60*

STUDENTS AND FACULTY
Student Body: 9% out-of-state.
Faculty: Student/faculty ratio 17:1.

ACADEMICS
Degrees: Associate, bachelor's, certificate, diploma. **Special Study Options:** Accelerated program, internships, study abroad.

FACILITIES
Housing: Apartments for single students, independent referral housing, shared apartment housing.

CAMPUS LIFE
Activities: Student government.

ADMISSIONS
Freshman Academic Profile: Minimum paper TOEFL 500. **Basis for Candidate Selection:** *Very important factors considered include:* Interview. *Important factors considered include:* Character/personal qualities, talent/ability. *Other factors considered include:* Class rank, application essay, recommendation(s), rigor of secondary school record, standardized test

---

scores, extracurricular activities, geographical residence, volunteer work, work experience. **Freshman Admission Requirements:** High school diploma is required and GED is accepted. **Freshman Admission Statistics:** 568 applied, 90% admitted, 7% enrolled. **Transfer Admission Requirements:** College transcript(s), interview, Lowest grade transferable C. **General Admission Information:** Application fee $60. Nonfall registration accepted.

COSTS AND FINANCIAL AID

Annual tuition $6,300. Average book expense $900. **Required Forms and Deadlines:** FAFSA. *Types of Aid: Need-based scholarships/grants:* Federal Pell, SEOG. *Loans:* FFEL Subsidized Stafford, FFEL Unsubsidized Stafford, FFEL PLUS. **Student Employment:** Off-campus job opportunities are excellent.

HARRISBURG UNIVERSITY OF SCIENCE AND TECHNOLOGY

326 Market Street, Harrisburg, PA 17101
Phone: 717-901-5101 **Financial Aid Phone:** 717-901-5115
E-mail: admissions@HarrisburgU.edu **CEEB Code:** 4511
Fax: 717-901-3101 **Website:** www.HarrisburgU.edu **ACT Code:** 3637

This private school was founded in 2001. It has a 2-acre campus.

RATINGS
Admissions Selectivity Rating: 60*   **Fire Safety Rating:** 60*   **Green Rating:** 60*

STUDENTS AND FACULTY
Enrollment: 145. **Student Body:** 46% female, 54% male, 10% out-of-state, 1% international (3 countries represented). Asian 6%, African American 40%, Caucasian 63%, Hispanic 16%.
Retention and Graduation: 40% freshmen return for sophomore year. 10% grads go on to further study within 1 year. 10% grads pursue arts and sciences degrees. **Faculty:** Student/faculty ratio 9:1. 10 full-time faculty, 100% hold PhDs, 40% are members of minority groups, 40% are women.

ACADEMICS
Degrees: Bachelor's, master's. **Majors with Highest Enrollment:** Biotechnology; computer and information sciences; physical sciences. **Special Study Options:** Dual enrollment, internships, student-designed major. **Career services:** Internships.

FACILITIES
Housing: 100% of campus accessible to physically disabled. **Computers:** 100% of classrooms, 100% of libraries, 100% of dining areas, 100% of student union, 100% of common outdoor areas have wireless network access. Students can register for classes online. Administrative functions (other than registration) can be performed online. Undergraduates are required to own a computer.

CAMPUS LIFE
Environment: City. **On-Campus Highlights:** Conference Center

ADMISSIONS
Freshman Academic Profile: 90% from public high schools. Minimum paper TOEFL 80. **Basis for Candidate Selection:** *Very important factors considered include:* Application essay, academic GPA. *Important factors considered include:* Interview. *Other factors considered include:* Recommendation(s), standardized test scores. **Freshman Admission Requirements:** High school diploma is required and GED is accepted. **Freshman Admission Statistics:** 203 applied, 56% admitted, 40% enrolled. **Transfer Admission Requirements:** High school transcript, essay or personal statement, lowest grade transferable C. **General Admission Information:** Notification on a rolling basis, beginning on or about 9/15. Neither credit nor placement offered for CEEB Advanced Placement tests.

COSTS AND FINANCIAL AID
Annual tuition $18,000. **Required Forms and Deadlines:** FAFSA. **Types of Aid:** *Need-based scholarships/grants:* Federal Pell, SEOG, state scholarships/grants, private scholarships, the school's own gift aid. *Loans:* FFEL Subsidized Stafford, FFEL Unsubsidized Stafford, FFEL PLUS. **Student Employment:** Federal Work-Study Program available. Institutional employment available. Highest amount earned per year from on-campus jobs $5,000. Off-campus job opportunities are excellent. **Financial Aid Statistics:** 55% freshmen, 74% undergrads receive need-based scholarship or grant aid. 1% undergrads receive non-need-based scholarship or grant aid. 48% freshmen, 66% undergrads receive need-based self-help aid. 98% freshmen, 94% undergrads receive any aid. 92% undergrads borrow to pay for school. Average cumulative indebtedness $21,936. **Criteria for awarding institutional aid:** *Non-need-based:* Academics.

HARTWICK COLLEGE

PO Box 4020, Oneonta, NY 13820-4020
Phone: 607-431-4154 **Financial Aid Phone:** 607-431-4130
E-mail: admissions@hartwick.edu **CEEB Code:** 2288
Fax: 607-431-4102 **Website:** www.hartwick.edu **ACT Code:** 2756

This private school was founded in 1797. It has a 425-acre campus.

RATINGS
Admissions Selectivity Rating: 70   **Fire Safety Rating:** 86   **Green Rating:** 71

STUDENTS AND FACULTY
Enrollment: 1,455. **Student Body:** 59% female, 41% male, 33% out-of-state, 3% international (22 countries represented). Asian 2%, African American 4%, Caucasian 61%, Hispanic 4%.
Retention and Graduation: 75% freshmen return for sophomore year. 44% freshmen graduate within 4 years. 23% grads go on to further study within 1 year. 19% grads pursue arts and sciences degrees. 2% grads pursue law degrees. 1% grads pursue business degrees. 1% grads pursue medical degrees. **Faculty:** Student/faculty ratio 10.8:1. 103 full-time faculty, 80% hold PhDs, 10% are members of minority groups, 41% are women.

ACADEMICS
Degrees: Bachelor's. **Classes:** Most classes have 10–19 students. Most lab/discussion sessions have 30–39 students. **Majors with Highest Enrollment:** Business/commerce; nursing/registered nurse (RN, ASN, BSN, MSN); psychology. **Special Study Options:** Accelerated program, cross-registration, double major, exchange student program (domestic), honors program, independent study, internships, student-designed major, study abroad, teacher certification program, January thematic term, study abroad/international internships. **Honors programs:** Requirements for the Honors Program are: Challenges—4 must be completed by graduation; Divisions—3 must be represented in Challenges; Honors Forum—a presentation of a project; Academic Excellence—a 3.50 Grade Point Average Also, students in the Honors program can choose to live on the Honors floor in a campus residence hall. **Combined degree programs:** BA/JD, BA/MEng, JD with Albany Law School. Special programs offered to physically disabled students include reader services, tape recorders, tutors. **Career services:** Career/job search classes, internships. **Career services highlights include:** Learning outside the classroom is an integral part of preparing our students for careers after graduation and why we've designed our curriculum and teaching approaches to break down the barriers that separate the classroom from the world. As a Hartwick student, you'll get to learn "out there" and bring that experience back, making your time in the classroom more engaging and effective.

FACILITIES
Housing: Coed dorms, women's dorms, fraternity/sorority housing, apartments for single students, housing at Pine Lake environmental campus (lodge and cabins) also available. 50% of campus accessible to physically disabled. **Special Academic Facilities/Equipment:** Art and history museums, Indian artifact collection, environmental center, observatory, electron microscope, tissue culture lab, spectrophotometers. **Computers:** 100% of classrooms, 100% of dorms, 100% of libraries, 50% of dining areas, 50% of student union, have wireless network access. Students can register for classes online. Administrative functions (other than registration) can be performed online.

CAMPUS LIFE
Environment: Village. **Activities:** Choral groups, dance, drama/theater, literary magazine, music ensembles, pep band, radio station, student government, student newspaper, yearbook, campus ministries. **Organizations:** 70 registered organizations, 30 honor societies, 3 religious organizations. 3 fraternities, 3 sororities. **Athletics (Intercollegiate):** *Men:* Basketball, cross-country, diving, football, lacrosse, soccer, swimming, tennis. *Women:* Basketball, cheerleading, cross-country, diving, equestrian sports, field hockey, lacrosse, soccer, swimming, tennis, volleyball, water polo. **On-Campus Highlights:** Yager Museum, Stevens-German Library, Johnstone Science Center, Binder Athletic Facility, Dewar Student Union. **Environmental Initiatives:** Hartwick is a signatory of the Talloires Declaration and is a member of the Association for the Advancement of Sustainability in Higher Education. In 2005, the College received a Kresge Green Building Iniative planning grant to partially fund green design of its first LEED-certified building, Golisano Hall. In keeping with Hartwick's emphasis on hands-on learning, the project provided the basis for a course entitled "Sustainable Design", taught by Richard Rittelman, FAIA principal architect and Karl Seeley, PhD. of Hartwick's economics department. The LEED-certification process for Golisano Hall is currently underway. The process involves commissioning the building's systems, which are estimated to use 75% less energy than the average building on Hartwick's campus. As an institution, Hartwick has a long history of environmental awareness and action. The 125 acre

Pine Lake Environmental Campus (which borders 3,000 acres of state park) was created in 1971, offering students a unique living laboratory for sustainability where ecological principles such as energy conservation, organic gardening, composting, waste reduction, and recycling are practiced every day. The lake, forests, trails, and mud bog have been the sites of more than 40 courses and 30 ongoing student/faculty research projects. Pine Lake is also a residence for 30–35 students. In 2002, students in the class "Architecture of the Sacred," finished construction on a 900–square foot strawbale house at the Lake. Built of compressed strawbale and finished with natural plaster, the house is economical and environmentally friendly and was the first green building constructed by Hartwick. Subsequently, students constructed a cob house, also at Pine Lake. Since 2002–03 Hartwick's academic year theme fas focused on sustainablilty, including annual themes on sustainable living, food in our lives, health and the human experience, globalization, water works, climate change and balance. Several leaders in the sustainability movement, including Vandura Shiva, Bill McKibben, Peter Finn, David Orr, Winona LaDuke, and Oren Lyons have spent time on campus, led college activities, and made public presentations. The Pine Lake Institute (PLI) for Environmental and Sustainability Studies sets an example for the College and community as to how to live sustainably.

ADMISSIONS
Freshman Academic Profile: Average high school GPA 86.3. 17% in top 10% of high school class, 42% in top 25% of high school class, 77% in top 50% of high school class. 84% from public high schools. SAT Math middle 50% range 490–600. SAT Critical Reading middle 50% range 480–598. SAT Writing middle 50% range 480–580. ACT middle 50% range 23–27. Minimum paper TOEFL 550. Minimum computer TOEFL 213. **Basis for Candidate Selection:** *Very important factors considered include:* Rigor of secondary school record. *Important factors considered include:* Class rank, academic GPA, recommendation(s). *Other factors considered include:* Application essay, standardized test scores, alumni/ae relation, character/personal qualities, extracurricular activities, first generation, geographical residence, interview, level of applicant's interest, racial/ethnic status, state residency, talent/ability, volunteer work, work experience. **Freshman Admission Requirements:** High school diploma is required and GED is accepted. *Academic units recommended:* 4 English, 3 mathematics, 3 science, (2 science labs), 3 foreign language, 2 social studies, 2 history. **Freshman Admission Statistics:** 2,385 applied, 91% admitted, 18% enrolled. **Transfer Admission Requirements:** College transcript(s), essay or personal statement, statement of good standing from prior institution(s). Minimum college GPA of 2.0 required. Lowest grade transferable C–. **General Admission Information:** Application fee $35. Early decision application deadline 11/15. Regular application deadline 2/15. Nonfall registration accepted. Admission may be deferred for a maximum of 1 year. Credit offered for CEEB Advanced Placement tests.

COSTS AND FINANCIAL AID
Average book expense $700. **Required Forms and Deadlines:** FAFSA. Priority financial aid filing date 2/15. **Notification of Awards:** Applicants will be notified of awards on or about 3/15. **Types of Aid:** *Need-based scholarships/grants:* Federal Pell, SEOG, state scholarships/grants, private scholarships, the school's own gift aid. *Loans:* FFEL Subsidized Stafford, FFEL Unsubsidized Stafford, FFEL PLUS, Federal Perkins, Federal Nursing. **Student Employment:** Federal Work-Study Program available. Institutional employment available. Highest amount earned per year from on-campus jobs $2,000. Off-campus job opportunities are good. **Criteria for awarding institutional aid:** *Non-need-based:* Academics, alumni affiliation, art, athletics, leadership, music/drama, state/district residency.

HARVARD COLLEGE

86 Brattle Street, Cambridge, MA 02138
Phone: 617-495-1551 **Financial Aid Phone:** 617-495-1581
E-mail: college@fas.harvard.edu **CEEB Code:** 3434
Fax: 617-495-8821 **Website:** www.college.harvard.edu **ACT Code:** 1840

This private school was founded in 1636. It has a 380-acre campus.

RATINGS
Admissions Selectivity Rating: 99   **Fire Safety Rating:** 60*   **Green Rating:** 99

STUDENTS AND FACULTY
Enrollment: 6,655. **Student Body:** 51% female, 49% male, 85% out-of-state, 11% international (114 countries represented). Asian 17%, African American

8%, Caucasian 42%, Hispanic 7%, Native American 1%.
Retention and Graduation: 98% freshmen return for sophomore year. 88% freshmen graduate within 4 years. **Faculty:** Student/faculty ratio 7:1. 1712 full-time faculty, 99% hold PhDs, 14% are members of minority groups, 32% are women.

ACADEMICS

Degrees: Bachelor's, master's, post-master's certificate. **Classes:** Most classes have fewer than 10 students. **Majors with Highest Enrollment:** Economics; political science and government; sociology. **Special Study Options:** Accelerated program, cross-registration, double major, exchange student program (domestic), honors program, independent study, internships, student-designed major, study abroad, teacher certification program. **Combined degree programs:** BA/MA, BA/MEng. Special programs offered to physically disabled students include note-taking services, reader services, tape recorders, tutors. **Career services:** Alumni network, alumni services.

FACILITIES

Housing: Coed dorms, special housing for disabled students, apartments for married students, cooperative housing. **Special Academic Facilities/Equipment:** Museums (University Arts Museums, Museums of Cultural History, many others), language labs, observatory, many science and research laboratories and facilities, new state-of-the-art computer science facility. **Computers:** 98% of classrooms, 100% of dorms, 100% of libraries, have wireless network access. Students can register for classes online. Administrative functions (other than registration) can be performed online.

CAMPUS LIFE

Environment: City. **Activities:** Choral groups, concert band, dance, drama/theater, jazz band, literary magazine, marching band, music ensembles, musical theater, opera, pep band, radio station, student government, student newspaper, student-run film society, symphony orchestra, television station, yearbook, campus ministries, international student organization, Model UN. **Organizations:** 393 registered organizations, 1 honor societies, 28 religious organizations. **Athletics (Intercollegiate):** *Men:* Baseball, basketball, crew/rowing, cross-country, diving, fencing, football, golf, ice hockey, lacrosse, sailing, skiing (downhill/alpine), skiing (nordic & cross-country), soccer, squash, swimming, tennis, track/field (outdoor), track/field (indoor), volleybal. *Women:* Basketball, crew/rowing, cross-country, diving, fencing, field hockey, golf, ice hockey, lacrosse, sailing, skiing (downhill/alpine), skiing (nordic & cross-country), soccer, softball, squash, swimming, tennis, track/field (outdoor), track/field (indoor), volle. **On-Campus Highlights:** Widener Library, Harvard Yard, Fogg Museum, Annenburg/Memorial Hall, Science Center. **Environmental Initiatives:** 1. Establishing a university-wide Office for Sustainability (www.green.harvard.edu) in 2008 based on 8 years of development of the Harvard Green Campus Initiative. 2. Adopting Campus wide Sustainability Principles and Green Building Standards (www.green.harvard.edu/green-building) 3. Committing to a 30% greenhouse gas reduction by FY16, inclusive of growth.

ADMISSIONS

Freshman Academic Profile: 95% in top 10% of high school class, 100% in top 25% of high school class, 100% in top 50% of high school class. SAT Math middle 50% range 690–790. SAT Critical Reading middle 50% range 690–780. SAT Writing middle 50% range 690–780. ACT middle 50% range 31–34. **Basis for Candidate Selection:** *Other factors considered include:* Application essay, academic GPA, recommendation(s), rigor of secondary school record, standardized test scores, alumni/ae relation, character/personal qualities, extracurricular activities, first generation, geographical residence, interview, racial/ethnic status, talent/ability, volunteer work, work experience. **Freshman Admission Requirements:** High school diploma or equivalent is not required. *Academic units recommended:* 4 English, 4 mathematics, 4 science, 4 foreign language, 3 social studies, 2 history. **Freshman Admission Statistics:** 29,114 applied, 7% admitted, 76% enrolled. **General Admission Information:** Application fee $75. Regular application deadline 1/1. Regular notification 4/1. Nonfall registration not accepted. Admission may be deferred for a maximum of 1 year. Credit and/or placement offered for CEEB Advanced Placement tests.

COSTS AND FINANCIAL AID

Required Forms and Deadlines: FAFSA, CSS/Financial Aid PROFILE, tax forms through IDOC. Financial aid filing deadline 2/1. **Notification of Awards:** Applicants will be notified of awards on or about 4/1. **Types of Aid:** *Need-based scholarships/grants:* Federal Pell, SEOG, state scholarships/grants, private scholarships, the school's own gift aid. *Loans:* Direct Subsidized Stafford, Direct Unsubsidized Stafford, Direct PLUS, Federal Perkins, college/university loans from institutional funds. **Student Employment:** Federal Work-Study Program available. Institutional employment available. Highest amount earned per year from on-campus jobs $19,967. Off-campus job opportunities are excellent. **Financial Aid Statistics:** 63% freshmen, 60% undergrads receive need-based scholarship or grant aid. 39% freshmen, 49% undergrads receive need-based self-help aid. 70% freshmen, 70% undergrads receive any aid. 38% undergrads borrow to pay for school. Average cumulative indebtedness $11,059.

HARVEY MUDD COLLEGE

301 Platt Boulevard, 301 Platt Blvd, Claremont, CA 91711-5990
Phone: 909-621-8011 **Financial Aid Phone:** 909-621-8055
E-mail: admission@hmc.edu **CEEB Code:** 4341
Fax: 909-621-8360 **Website:** www.hmc.edu

This private school was founded in 1955. It has a 33-acre campus.

RATINGS

Admissions Selectivity Rating: 98   **Fire Safety Rating:** 71   **Green Rating:** 80

STUDENTS AND FACULTY

Enrollment: 757. **Student Body:** 36% female, 64% male, 57% out-of-state, 3% international (15 countries represented). Asian 20%, African American 1%, Caucasian 58%, Hispanic 7%, Native American 1%.
Retention and Graduation: 91% freshmen return for sophomore year. 79% freshmen graduate within 4 years. 47% grads go on to further study within 1 year. 34% grads pursue arts and sciences degrees. **Faculty:** Student/faculty ratio 8.38:1. 81 full-time faculty, 100% hold PhDs, 15% are members of minority groups, 35% are women.

ACADEMICS

Degrees: Bachelor's. **Classes:** Most classes have 10–19 students. Most lab/discussion sessions have 10–19 students. **Majors with Highest Enrollment:** Computer and information sciences; engineering; mathematics. **Special Study Options:** Cross-registration, double major, dual enrollment, exchange student program (domestic), independent study, internships, liberal arts/career combination, student-designed major, study abroad, Innovative client-sponsored design projects. **Combined degree programs:** BS/MS math, BS/MBA, BS/MIS, BA/BS. **Career services:** Alumni network, alumni services, career assessment, internships. **Career services highlights include:** See www.hmc.edu/academicsclinicresearch/clinicprogram1/history.html.

FACILITIES

Housing: Coed dorms, apartments for married students, apartments for single students, housing exchange program w/ Pomona College, Pitzer College, Scripps College, and Claremont McKenna College. 80% of campus accessible to physically disabled. **Computers:** 100% of classrooms, 100% of dorms, 100% of libraries, 100% of dining areas, 100% of student union, 75% of common outdoor areas have wireless network access. Students can register for classes online. Administrative functions (other than registration) can be performed online.

CAMPUS LIFE

Environment: Town. **Activities:** Choral groups, concert band, dance, drama/theater, jazz band, literary magazine, music ensembles, musical theater, pep band, radio station, student government, student newspaper, student-run film society, symphony orchestra, yearbook, campus ministries, international student organization, Model UN. **Organizations:** 109 registered organizations, 4 honor societies, 6 religious organizations. **Athletics (Intercollegiate):** *Men:* Baseball, basketball, cross-country, diving, football, golf, soccer, swimming, tennis, track/field (outdoor), water polo. *Women:* Basketball, cross-country, diving, golf, lacrosse, soccer, softball, swimming, tennis, track/field (outdoor), volleyball, water polo. **On-Campus Highlights:** Dorm Lounges, Platt Campus Center Living Room, Liquidamber mall, Jay's Pizza Place, Linde Student Activities Center. **Environmental Initiatives:** In February 2008 Harvey Mudd College President Maria Klawe signed the American College & University Presidents Climate Commitment and Harvey Mudd College Board of Trustees adopted HMC Sustainability Policy Statement. Additionally, the Board of Trustees passed a resolution where the standard for new buildings will be at least U.S. Green Building Council LEED Silver standard or equivalent and premium rated or ENERGY STAR certified products are purchased for use on campus where possible. In 2007 a team of students lead by faculty advisers documented the historical usage of key resources and utilities—electricity, natural gas, and water for Harvey Mudd College and the other Claremont Colleges—in order to establish baselines against which to compare future usage, and to identify targets for conservation programs. The team also studied emissions, waste disposal, and recycling programs with the ultimate goal of assessing the feasibility of achieving carbon neutrality within the next decade or two. Finally the team developed recommendations for creating a more sustainable Claremont Colleges Community. The Center for Environmental Studies at Harvey Mudd College was created in May 1999 to create and coordinate interdepartmental programs related to environmental studies. The Center provides a framework through which students, faculty, and alumni can come together to identify critical issues in the relationship between human life and both natural and human-built environments, to investigate those issues, and to help articulate the important roles that science, mathematics, and engineering will take in addressing those issues. Through this framework, the Center seeks to perpetuate creative and responsible professional practices in an increasingly fragile world.

ADMISSIONS

Freshman Academic Profile: 94% in top 10% of high school class, 100% in top 25% of high school class, 100% in top 50% of high school class. 71.3% from public high schools. SAT Math middle 50% range 740–790. SAT Critical Reading middle 50% range 680–770. SAT Writing middle 50% range 663–750. ACT middle 50% range 32–35. Minimum paper TOEFL 600. Minimum computer TOEFL 250. Minimum web-based TOEFL 100. **Basis for Candidate Selection:** *Very important factors considered include:* Application essay, academic GPA, recommendation(s), rigor of secondary school record, character/personal qualities, talent/ability. *Important factors considered include:* Class rank, standardized test scores, extracurricular activities. *Other factors considered include:* Alumni/ae relation, first generation, geographical residence, interview, level of applicant's interest, racial/ethnic status, state residency, volunteer work, work experience. **Freshman Admission Requirements:** High school diploma is required and GED is accepted.High school diploma or equivalent is not required. *Academic units required:* 4 English, 3 mathematics, 3 science, 1 history. *Academic units recommended:* 4 mathematics, 4 science, (2 science labs), 2 foreign language, 2 social studies, 2 history. **Freshman Admission Statistics:** 2,205 applied, 34% admitted, 28% enrolled. **Transfer Admission Requirements:** High school transcript, college transcript(s), essay or personal statement, statement of good standing from prior institution(s). Minimum college GPA of 3.0 required. Lowest grade transferable C. **General Admission Information:** Application fee $60. Early decision application deadline 11/15. Regular application deadline 1/2. Regular notification 4/1. Nonfall registration not accepted. Admission may be deferred for a maximum of 1 year. Placement offered for CEEB Advanced Placement tests.

COSTS AND FINANCIAL AID

Annual tuition $38,222. Room and board $12,570. Required fees $245. Average book expense $800. **Required Forms and Deadlines:** FAFSA, CSS/Financial Aid PROFILE, state aid form, noncustodial PROFILE, business/farm supplement. Financial aid filing deadline 2/1. **Notification of Awards:** Applicants will be notified of awards on or about 4/1. **Types of Aid:** *Need-based scholarships/grants:* Federal Pell, SEOG, state scholarships/grants, private scholarships, the school's own gift aid. Federal ACG and SMART Grants. *Loans:* FFEL Subsidized Stafford, FFEL Unsubsidized Stafford, FFEL PLUS, Federal Perkins, college/university loans from institutional funds, alternative loans. **Student Employment:** Federal Work-Study Program available. Institutional employment available. Highest amount earned per year from on-campus jobs $11,776. Off-campus job opportunities are excellent. **Financial Aid Statistics:** 59% freshmen, 54% undergrads receive need-based scholarship or grant aid. 23% freshmen, 26% undergrads receive non-need-based scholarship or grant aid. 33% freshmen, 39% undergrads receive need-based self-help aid. 83.09% freshmen, 84.12% undergrads receive any aid. 59.12% undergrads borrow to pay for school. Average cumulative indebtedness $16,384. **Criteria for awarding institutional aid:** *Non-need-based:* Academics.

HASTINGS COLLEGE

Hastings College, 710 N. Turner Avenue, Hastings, NE 68901
Phone: 402-461-7403 **Financial Aid Phone:** 402-461-7431
E-mail: mmolliconi@hastings.edu **CEEB Code:** 6270
Fax: 402-461-7490 **Website:** www.hastings.edu **ACT Code:** 2456

This private school, affiliated with the Presbyterian Church, was founded in 1882. It has a 109-acre campus.

RATINGS

Admissions Selectivity Rating: 80   **Fire Safety Rating:** 64   **Green Rating:** 60*

STUDENTS AND FACULTY

Enrollment: 1,067. **Student Body:** 46% female, 54% male, 28% out-of-state, 1% international (7 countries represented). Asian 1%, African American 2%, Caucasian 91%, Hispanic 3%.
Retention and Graduation: 76% freshmen return for sophomore year. 52% freshmen graduate within 4 years. 24% grads go on to further study within 1 year. 16% grads pursue arts and sciences degrees. 2% grads pursue law degrees. 1% grads pursue business degrees. 1% grads pursue medical degrees. **Faculty:** Student/faculty ratio 11:1. 87 full-time faculty, 71% hold PhDs, 1% are members of minority groups, 34% are women.

ACADEMICS

Degrees: Bachelor's, master's. **Classes:** Most classes have 10–19 students. Most lab/discussion sessions have fewer than 10 students. **Majors with Highest Enrollment:** Business/commerce; education; psychology. **Special Study Options:** Double major, exchange student program (domestic), independent study, internships, student-designed major, study abroad, teacher certification program. **Combined degree programs:** BA/BM. Special programs offered to physically disabled students include note-taking services, reader services, tape recorders, tutors. **Career services:** Alumni network, alumni services, career/job search classes, career assessment, internships, regional alumni. **Career services highlights include:** Service Learning program.

FACILITIES

Housing: Coed dorms, men's dorms, women's dorms, apartments for single students, Honors housing, one apartment complex is for quiet and alcohol-free living. 90% of campus accessible to physically disabled. **Special Academic Facilities/Equipment:** Center for communication arts, glass-blowing studio, observatory, art gallery. **Computers:** 95% of classrooms, 100% of libraries, 100% of dining areas, 100% of student union, have wireless network access. Administrative functions (other than registration) can be performed online.

CAMPUS LIFE

Environment: Village. **Activities:** Choral groups, concert band, dance, drama/theater, jazz band, literary magazine, marching band, music ensembles, musical theater, pep band, radio station, student government, student newspaper, symphony orchestra, television station, yearbook, campus ministries. **Organizations:** 85 registered organizations, 13 honor societies, 10 religious organizations. 4 fraternities, 4 sororities. **Athletics (Intercollegiate):** *Men:* Baseball, basketball, cross-country, football, golf, soccer, tennis, track/field (outdoor), track/field (indoor), wrestling. *Women:* Basketball, cheerleading, cross-country, golf, soccer, softball, tennis, track/field (outdoor), track/field (indoor), volleyball. **On-Campus Highlights:** Fleharty Educational Center and weight room, Hazelrigg Student Union, Perkins Library, Gray Center of Communication Arts, dorm lounges.

ADMISSIONS

Freshman Academic Profile: Average high school GPA 3.2. 16% in top 10% of high school class, 40% in top 25% of high school class, 65% in top 50% of high school class. 88% from public high schools. SAT Math middle 50% range 490–605. SAT Critical Reading middle 50% range 500–600. ACT middle 50% range 20–26. Minimum paper TOEFL 600. Minimum computer TOEFL 250. **Basis for Candidate Selection:** *Very important factors considered include:* Class rank, academic GPA, recommendation(s), rigor of secondary school record, standardized test scores. *Important factors considered include:* Character/personal qualities, extracurricular activities, talent/ability. *Other factors considered include:* Application essay, alumni/ae relation, interview, level of applicant's interest, racial/ethnic status. **Freshman Admission Requirements:** High school diploma is required and GED is accepted. *Academic units required:* 3 English, 3 mathematics, 3 science, (3 science labs), 4 social studies, 3 history. *Academic units recommended:* 4 English, 4 mathematics, 4 science, (4 science labs), 2 foreign language, 4 social studies, 4 history. **Freshman Admission Statistics:** 597,501 applied, 25% enrolled. **Transfer Admission Requirements:** High school transcript, college transcript(s), statement of good standing from prior institution(s). Minimum college GPA of 2.0 required. Lowest grade transferable C. **General Admission Information:** Application fee $20. Notification on a rolling basis, beginning on or about 10/15. Nonfall registration accepted. Credit and/or placement offered for CEEB Advanced Placement tests.

COSTS AND FINANCIAL AID

Average book expense $730. **Required Forms and Deadlines:** FAFSA, institution's own financial aid form. Priority financial aid filing date 5/1. **Notification of Awards:** Applicants will be notified of awards on a rolling basis beginning 3/1. **Types of Aid:** *Need-based scholarships/grants:* Federal Pell, SEOG, state scholarships/grants, private scholarships, the school's own gift aid. *Loans:* FFEL Subsidized Stafford, FFEL Unsubsidized Stafford, FFEL PLUS, Federal Perkins. **Student Employment:** Federal Work-Study Program available. Institutional employment available. Highest amount earned per year from on-campus jobs $1,000. Off-campus job opportunities are good. **Financial Aid Statistics:** 77% freshmen, 71% undergrads receive need-based scholarship or grant aid. 15% freshmen, 12% undergrads receive non-need-based scholarship or grant aid. 56% freshmen, 57% undergrads receive need-based self-help aid. 23% freshmen, 16% undergrads receive athletic scholarships. 97% freshmen, 98% undergrads receive any aid. **Criteria for awarding institutional aid:** *Non-need-based:* Academics, art, athletics, leadership, music/drama.

HAVERFORD COLLEGE

370 Lancaster Avenue, Haverford, PA 19041
Phone: 610-896-1350 **Financial Aid Phone:** 610-896-1350
E-mail: admitme@haverford.edu **CEEB Code:** 2289
Fax: 610-896-1338 **Website:** www.haverford.edu **ACT Code:** 3409

This private school was founded in 1833. It has a 200-acre campus.

RATINGS
Admissions Selectivity Rating: 98   **Fire Safety Rating:** 73   **Green Rating:** 92

STUDENTS AND FACULTY
Enrollment: 1,190. **Student Body:** 55% female, 45% male, 86% out-of-state, 3% international (35 countries represented). Asian 9%, African American 8%, Caucasian 68%, Hispanic 8%.
Retention and Graduation: 95% freshmen return for sophomore year. 88% freshmen graduate within 4 years. 17% grads go on to further study within 1 year. 9% grads pursue arts and sciences degrees. 3% grads pursue law degrees. 3% grads pursue medical degrees. **Faculty:** Student/faculty ratio 8:1. 121 full-time faculty, 97% hold PhDs, 26% are members of minority groups, 46% are women.

ACADEMICS
Degrees: Bachelor's. **Classes:** Most classes have fewer than 10 students. Most lab/discussion sessions have fewer than 10 students. **Majors with Highest Enrollment:** Biology/biological sciences; economics; English language and literature. **Special Study Options:** Cross-registration, double major, exchange student program (domestic), independent study, internships, liberal arts/career combination, student-designed major, study abroad, teacher certification program. **Combined degree programs:** BA/MEng. Special programs offered to physically disabled students include note-taking services, tape recorders. **Career services:** Alumni network, alumni services, career assessment, internships, regional alumni.

FACILITIES
Housing: Coed dorms, men's dorms, women's dorms, apartments for single students, theme housingTheme houses. 60% of campus accessible to physically disabled. **Special Academic Facilities/Equipment:** Art gallery, center for cross-cultural study of religion, arboretum, observatory, foundry. **Computers:** 75% of classrooms, 75% of libraries, 100% of dining areas, 100% of student union, 80% of common outdoor areas have wireless network access. Students can register for classes online. Administrative functions (other than registration) can be performed online.

CAMPUS LIFE
Environment: Town. **Activities:** Choral groups, dance, drama/theater, literary magazine, music ensembles, musical theater, student government, student newspaper, yearbook, campus ministries, international student organization. **Organizations:** 144 registered organizations, 1 honor societies, 6 religious organizations. **Athletics (Intercollegiate):** *Men:* Baseball, basketball, cross-country, fencing, lacrosse, soccer, squash, tennis, track/field (outdoor), track/field (indoor). *Women:* Basketball, cross-country, fencing, field hockey, lacrosse, soccer, softball, squash, tennis, track/field (outdoor), track/field (indoor), volleyball. **On-Campus Highlights:** Integrated Natural Sciences Center, John Whitehead Campus Center, Cantor Fitzgerald Gallery, Arboretum, Douglas B. Gardner Athletic Center. **Environmental Initiatives:** Our athletic center is the 1st gold LEED-certified recreation center in the US (opened in 2005). We have reached 75–85% for grounds recycling. We have completed a master plan to identify utility and powerhouse improvements, and will commence work on these improvements immediately.

ADMISSIONS
Freshman Academic Profile: 94% in top 10% of high school class, 99% in top 25% of high school class, 100% in top 50% of high school class. 57% from public high schools. SAT Math middle 50% range 640–740. SAT Critical Reading middle 50% range 660–740. SAT Writing middle 50% range 660–750. Minimum paper TOEFL 600. Minimum computer TOEFL 250. **Basis for Candidate Selection:** *Very important factors considered include:* Application essay, academic GPA, recommendation(s), rigor of secondary school record, character/personal qualities, extracurricular activities. *Important factors considered include:* Class rank, standardized test scores, talent/ability, volunteer work, work experience. *Other factors considered include:* Alumni/ae relation, first generation, geographical residence, interview, level of applicant's interest, ra-

cial/ethnic status. **Freshman Admission Requirements:** High school diploma or equivalent is not required. **Freshman Admission Statistics:** 3,403 applied, 25% admitted, 37% enrolled. **Transfer Admission Requirements:** College transcript(s), essay or personal statement, standardized test scores, statement of good standing from prior institution(s). Minimum college GPA of 3.0 required. Lowest grade transferable C. **General Admission Information:** Application fee $60. Early decision application deadline 11/15. Regular application deadline 1/15. Regular notification 4/15. Nonfall registration not accepted. Admission may be deferred for a maximum of 1 year.

COSTS AND FINANCIAL AID
Annual tuition $38,735. Room and board $11,890. Required fees $350. Average book expense $1,194. **Required Forms and Deadlines:** FAFSA, CSS/Financial Aid PROFILE, noncustodial PROFILE, business/farm supplement. CSS College Board Noncustodial Parents' Statement is required—not the Noncustodial supplement. Financial aid filing deadline 1/31. **Notification of Awards:** Applicants will be notified of awards on or about 4/1. **Types of Aid:** *Need-based scholarships/grants:* Federal Pell, SEOG, state scholarships/grants, the school's own gift aid. *Loans:* FFEL Subsidized Stafford, FFEL Unsubsidized Stafford, FFEL PLUS, Federal Perkins. **Student Employment:** Federal Work-Study Program available. Institutional employment available. Highest amount earned per year from on-campus jobs $2,300. Off-campus job opportunities are good. **Financial Aid Statistics:** 47% freshmen, 46% undergrads receive need-based scholarship or grant aid. 46% freshmen, 44% undergrads receive need-based self-help aid. 59% freshmen, 58% undergrads receive any aid. 38% undergrads borrow to pay for school. Average cumulative indebtedness $16,500.

HAWAI'I PACIFIC UNIVERSITY

1164 Bishop Street, Suite 200, Honolulu, HI 96813
Phone: 808-544-0238 **Financial Aid Phone:** 808-544-0253
E-mail: admissions@hpu.edu **CEEB Code:** 4352
Fax: 808-544-1136 **Website:** www.hpu.edu **ACT Code:** 4352

This private school was founded in 1965. It has a 135-acre campus.

RATINGS
Admissions Selectivity Rating: 75   **Fire Safety Rating:** 74   **Green Rating:** 60*

STUDENTS AND FACULTY
Enrollment: 6,262. **Student Body:** 61% female, 39% male, 40% out-of-state, 10% international (102 countries represented). Asian 31%, African American 7%, Caucasian 34%, Hispanic 7%, Native American 1%.
Retention and Graduation: 66% freshmen return for sophomore year. 68% grads go on to further study within 1 year. 20% grads pursue arts and sciences degrees. 5% grads pursue law degrees. 45% grads pursue business degrees. 3% grads pursue medical degrees. **Faculty:** Student/faculty ratio 16:1. 264 full-time faculty, 66% hold PhDs, 25% are members of minority groups, 46% are women.

ACADEMICS
Degrees: Associate, bachelor's, certificate, master's, post-bachelor's certificate, post-master's certificate. **Classes:** Most classes have 10–19 students. Most lab/discussion sessions have fewer than 10 students. **Majors with Highest Enrollment:** Business, management, marketing, and related support services, other; management information systems; nursing/registered nurse (RN, ASN, BSN, MSN). **Special Study Options:** Accelerated program, cooperative education program, distance learning, double major, dual enrollment, English as a Second Language (ESL), honors program, independent study, internships, liberal arts/career combination, student-designed major, study abroad, weekend college. **Honors programs:** University Scholars Honors Program: During the freshman and sophomore years University Scholars enroll in honors sections of many courses required in the general education curriculum. Normally, University Scholars are required to complete at least six of these courses, but exceptions can be made for students who have completed certain requirements through AP courses in high school or for majors with different general education requirements. At the upper-division level, University Scholars enroll in three honors seminars. The Certificate of Merit is awarded at the time of graduation to students who fulfill the University Scholars requirements. **Combined degree programs:** BA/MA.

FACILITIES
Housing: Coed dorms, women's dorms, apartments for married students, apartments for single students, apartment search and referral service. 90% of campus accessible to physically disabled. **Special Academic Facilities/Equipment:** Hawaii Pacific University Art Gallery, Hawaii Pacific University Theatre. **Computers:** Students can register for classes online. Administrative functions (other than registration) can be performed online.

CAMPUS LIFE

Environment: Metropolis. **Activities:** Choral groups, dance, drama/theater, literary magazine, music ensembles, musical theater, pep band, student government, student newspaper, student-run film society. **Organizations:** 80 registered organizations, 18 honor societies, 3 religious organizations. **Athletics (Intercollegiate):** *Men:* Baseball, basketball, cheerleading, cross-country, golf, tennis. *Women:* cheerleading, cross-country, golf, softball, tennis, volleyball. **On-Campus Highlights:** Frear Center, Sea Warrior Center, Windward Campus, Art Gallery, Fort Street Mall.

ADMISSIONS

Freshman Academic Profile: Average high school GPA 3.26. 20% in top 10% of high school class, 45% in top 25% of high school class, 80% in top 50% of high school class. 60% from public high schools. SAT Math middle 50% range 430–560. SAT Critical Reading middle 50% range 420–550. SAT Writing middle 50% range 350–540. ACT middle 50% range 17–24. Minimum paper TOEFL 550. Minimum computer TOEFL 213. **Basis for Candidate Selection:** *Very important factors considered include:* Academic GPA, rigor of secondary school record. *Important factors considered include:* Standardized test scores, extracurricular activities, interview. *Other factors considered include:* Class rank, application essay, recommendation(s), character/personal qualities, first generation, talent/ability, volunteer work, work experience. **Freshman Admission Requirements:** High school diploma is required and GED is accepted. *Academic units recommended:* 4 English, 3 mathematics, 2 science, 1 foreign language, 4 history. **Freshman Admission Statistics:** 2,991 applied, 80% admitted, 29% enrolled. **Transfer Admission Requirements:** College transcript(s), minimum college GPA of 2.0 required. Lowest grade transferable C. **General Admission Information:** Application fee $50. Notification on a rolling basis, beginning on or about 1/1. Nonfall registration accepted. Admission may be deferred for a maximum of 24 months. Credit and/or placement offered for CEEB Advanced Placement tests.

COSTS AND FINANCIAL AID

Annual tuition $13,000. Room and board $10,560. Required fees $80. Average book expense $2,096. **Required Forms and Deadlines:** FAFSA. Priority financial aid filing date 3/1. **Notification of Awards:** Applicants will be notified of awards on a rolling basis beginning 4/1. **Types of Aid:** *Need-based scholarships/grants:* Federal Pell, SEOG, state scholarships/grants, the school's own gift aid, Federal Nursing Scholarships. *Loans:* FFEL Subsidized Stafford, FFEL Unsubsidized Stafford, FFEL PLUS, Federal Perkins, Federal Nursing, alternative loans. **Student Employment:** Highest amount earned per year from on-campus jobs $3,800. **Financial Aid Statistics:** 19% freshmen, 18% undergrads receive need-based scholarship or grant aid. 17% freshmen, 11% undergrads receive non-need-based scholarship or grant aid. 39% freshmen, 38% undergrads receive need-based self-help aid. 75% freshmen, 67% undergrads receive any aid. 36% undergrads borrow to pay for school. Average cumulative indebtedness $17,125. **Criteria for awarding institutional aid:** *Non-need-based:* Academics, alumni affiliation, athletics, job skills, leadership, music/drama, religious affiliation.

See page 1108.

HEBREW COLLEGE

160 Herrick Road, Newton Centre, MA 02459
Phone: 617-559-8610 **Financial Aid Phone:** 617-559-8642
E-mail: admissions@hebrewcollege.edu
Fax: 617-559-8601 **Website:** www.hebrewcollege.edu

This private school, affiliated with the Jewish Church, was founded in 1921.

RATINGS
Admissions Selectivity Rating: 60*   **Fire Safety Rating:** 60*   **Green Rating:** 60*

STUDENTS AND FACULTY
Enrollment: 4. **Student Body:** 50% female, 50% male, 1% out-of-state, 25% international, Caucasian 125%.
Retention and Graduation: 40% grads go on to further study within 1 year.

ACADEMICS
Degrees: Bachelor's, certificate, master's. **Majors with Highest Enrollment:** Business administration and management; education; psychology. **Special Study Options:** Cross-registration, distance learning, independent study, internships, student-designed major, Semester in Israel is encouraged.

CAMPUS LIFE
Environment: City. **Activities:** Choral groups. **On-Campus Highlights:** Library.

ADMISSIONS

Freshman Academic Profile: Minimum paper TOEFL 400. Minimum computer TOEFL 100. **Basis for Candidate Selection:** *Very important factors considered include:* Application essay, religious affiliation/commitment, talent/ability. *Important factors considered include:* Class rank, recommendation(s), rigor of secondary school record, standardized test scores, character/personal qualities, extracurricular activities, interview, volunteer work, work experience. *Other factors considered include:* Alumni/ae relation, geographical residence, state residency. **Transfer Admission Requirements:** College transcript(s), essay or personal statement, interview, Lowest grade transferable C. **General Admission Information:** Regular application deadline 4/15. Nonfall registration accepted.

COSTS AND FINANCIAL AID

Annual tuition $7,920. **Student Employment:** Off-campus job opportunities are good.

HEC MONTREAL

3000 chemin de la Cote Ste-Catherine, Montreal, QC Canada
Phone: 514-340-6151
E-mail: registraire.info@hec.ca
Fax: 514-340-6151 **Website:** www.hec.ca

This public school was founded in 1907.

RATINGS
Admissions Selectivity Rating: 60*   **Fire Safety Rating:** 60*   **Green Rating:** 60*

STUDENTS AND FACULTY
Student Body: 102 countries represented.

ACADEMICS
Degrees: Bachelor's, certificate, diploma, master's.

CAMPUS LIFE
Environment: Metropolis. **Activities:** radio station, student newspaper, yearbook, international student organization.

ADMISSIONS
General Admission Information: Application fee $62. Regular application deadline 2/15. Nonfall registration accepted.

COSTS AND FINANCIAL AID
Annual in-state tuition $2,120. Room and board $9,600. Required fees $2,700. Average book expense $800.

HEIDELBERG UNIVERSITY

310 East Market Street, Tiffin, OH 44883
Phone: 419-448-2330 **Financial Aid Phone:** 419-448-2293
E-mail: adminfo@heidelberg.edu **CEEB Code:** 1292
Fax: 419-448-2334 **Website:** www.heidelberg.edu **ACT Code:** 3278

This private school, affiliated with the United Church of Christ Church, was founded in 1850. It has a 120-acre campus.

RATINGS
Admissions Selectivity Rating: 73   **Fire Safety Rating:** 60*   **Green Rating:** 71

STUDENTS AND FACULTY
Enrollment: 1,255. **Student Body:** 46% female, 54% male, 8% out-of-state, 3% international. African American 8%, Caucasian 81%, Hispanic 2%.
Retention and Graduation: 66% freshmen return for sophomore year. 37% freshmen graduate within 4 years. 25% grads go on to further study within 1 year. 15% grads pursue arts and sciences degrees. 2% grads pursue law degrees. 5% grads pursue business degrees. 3% grads pursue medical degrees. **Faculty:** Student/faculty ratio 14:1. 62 full-time faculty, 85% hold PhDs, 10% are members of minority groups, 45% are women.

ACADEMICS
Degrees: Bachelor's, master's. **Classes:** Most classes have fewer than 10 students. Most lab/discussion sessions have 10–19 students. **Majors with Highest Enrollment:** Biological and physical sciences; business/commerce; education. **Special Study Options:** Cross-registration, double major, dual enrollment, English as a Second Language (ESL), exchange student program

(domestic), honors program, independent study, internships, liberal arts/career combination, study abroad, teacher certification program. **Honors programs:** The Honors Program, entitled "The Life of the Mind," integrates learning and life experiences, stems from the mission of the University. It features extensive contact with the fundamental values that underpin self-worth and integrity, free inquiry, and intellectual rigor, an understanding of other cultures and traditions, and a lifelong habit of commitment to the community and concern for social responsibility. Special programs offered to physically disabled students include tutors. **Career services:** Alumni network, career assessment, internships

FACILITIES

Housing: Coed dorms, special housing for disabled students, women's dorms, cooperative housing, apartments for single students, theme housing. 65% of campus accessible to physically disabled. **Special Academic Facilities/Equipment:** Forest research lots, water quality lab, Center for Historic and Military Archaeology. **Computers:** 80% of classrooms, 70% of dorms, 100% of libraries, 100% of dining areas, 100% of student union, have wireless network access. Students can register for classes online. Administrative functions (other than registration) can be performed online.

CAMPUS LIFE

Environment: Village. **Activities:** Choral groups, concert band, dance, drama/theater, jazz band, literary magazine, music ensembles, musical theater, opera, pep band, radio station, student government, student newspaper, student-run film society, symphony orchestra, television station, yearbook, campus ministries, international student organization, Model UN. **Organizations:** 75 registered organizations, 6 honor societies, 3 religious organizations. 5 fraternities, 4 sororities. **Athletics (Intercollegiate):** *Men:* Baseball, basketball, cheerleading, cross-country, football, golf, soccer, tennis, track/field (outdoor), track/field (indoor), wrestling. *Women:* Basketball, cheerleading, cross-country, golf, soccer, softball, tennis, track/field (outdoor), track/field (indoor), volleyball. **On-Campus Highlights:** Gillmor Science Center, Campus Center, Seiberling Gymnasium, Education Center.

ADMISSIONS

Freshman Academic Profile: Average high school GPA 3.14. 12% in top 10% of high school class, 37% in top 25% of high school class, 66% in top 50% of high school class. 61% from public high schools. SAT Math middle 50% range 440–590. SAT Critical Reading middle 50% range 440–580. SAT Writing middle 50% range 420–550. ACT middle 50% range 18–24. Minimum paper TOEFL 550. Minimum computer TOEFL 213. **Basis for Candidate Selection:** *Very important factors considered include:* Academic GPA, rigor of secondary school record, standardized test scores, character/personal qualities, talent/ability. *Important factors considered include:* Class rank, extracurricular activities, interview, level of applicant's interest. *Other factors considered include:* Application essay, recommendation(s), alumni/ae relation, first generation, geographical residence, religious affiliation/commitment, state residency, volunteer work, work experience. **Freshman Admission Requirements:** High school diploma is required and GED is accepted. *Academic units recommended:* 4 English, 3 mathematics, 3 science, (I science labs), 2 foreign language, 3 social studies, 2 history, 3 academic electives. **Freshman Admission Statistics:** 2,059 applied, 73% admitted, 26% enrolled. **Transfer Admission Requirements:** High school transcript, college transcript(s), standardized test scores, statement of good standing from prior institution(s). Minimum college GPA of 2.0 required. Lowest grade transferable C–. **General Admission Information:** Application fee $25. Regular application deadline 8/1. Notification on a rolling basis, beginning on or about 8/1. Nonfall registration accepted. Admission may be deferred for a maximum of 1 year. Credit and/or placement offered for CEEB Advanced Placement tests.

COSTS AND FINANCIAL AID

Annual tuition $20,826. Room and board $8,384. Required fees $504. Average book expense $600. **Required Forms and Deadlines:** FAFSA. Priority financial aid filing date 3/1. **Notification of Awards:** Applicants will be notified of awards on a rolling basis beginning 3/1. **Types of Aid:** *Need-based scholarships/grants:* Federal Pell, SEOG, state scholarships/grants, private scholarships, the school's own gift aid. *Loans:* FFEL Subsidized Stafford, FFEL Unsubsidized Stafford, FFEL PLUS, Federal Perkins. **Student Employment:** Federal Work-Study Program available. Institutional employment available. Highest amount earned per year from on-campus jobs $1,500. Off-campus job opportunities are good. **Financial Aid Statistics:** 84% freshmen, 81% undergrads receive need-based scholarship or grant aid. 10% freshmen, 9% undergrads receive non-need-based scholarship or grant aid. 84% freshmen, 73% undergrads receive need-based self-help aid. 99% freshmen, 97% undergrads receive any aid. 74% undergrads borrow to pay for school. Average cumulative indebtedness $30,589. **Criteria for awarding institutional aid:** *Non-need-based:* Academics, music/drama, religious affiliation, state/district residency.

HELLENIC COLLEGE

50 Goddard Avenue, Brookline, MA 02445
Phone: 617-850-1260 **Financial Aid Phone:** 617-850-1317
E-mail: admissions@hchc.edu
Fax: 617-850-1460 **Website:** www.hchc.edu **ACT Code:** 1843

This private school, affiliated with the Greek Orthodox Church, was founded in 1937. It has a 59-acre campus.

RATINGS

Admissions Selectivity Rating: 78 **Fire Safety Rating:** 80 **Green Rating:** 60*

STUDENTS AND FACULTY

Enrollment: 85. **Student Body:** 41% female, 59% male, 80% out-of-state, (9 countries represented).
Retention and Graduation: 50% grads go on to further study within 1 year.
Faculty: Student/faculty ratio 9:1. 13 full-time faculty, 54% are women.

ACADEMICS

Degrees: Bachelor's, master's. **Classes:** Most classes have 20–29 students. **Majors with Highest Enrollment:** Business/commerce. **Special Study Options:** Honors program, liberal arts/career combination. **Combined degree programs:** BA/MA. Special programs offered to physically disabled students include tutors. **Career services:** Alumni services, regional alumni.

FACILITIES

Housing: Coed dorms, apartments for married students 20% of campus accessible to physically disabled. **Computers:** 100% of dorms, have wireless network access.

CAMPUS LIFE

Environment: Village. **Activities:** Choral groups, student government, yearbook, campus ministries. **Athletics (Intercollegiate):** *Men:* Basketball. *Women:* Tennis.

ADMISSIONS

Freshman Academic Profile: Average high school GPA 2.978. 100% from public high schools. SAT Math middle 50% range 330–640. SAT Critical Reading middle 50% range 350–730. SAT Writing middle 50% range 360–730. ACT middle 50% range 20–21. Minimum paper TOEFL 500. Minimum computer TOEFL 173. Minimum web-based TOEFL 61. **Basis for Candidate Selection:** *Very important factors considered include:* Application essay, academic GPA, recommendation(s), rigor of secondary school record, standardized test scores, interview. *Important factors considered include:* Class rank. *Other factors considered include:* Alumni/ae relation, character/personal qualities, extracurricular activities. **Freshman Admission Requirements:** High school diploma is required and GED is accepted. *Academic units required:* 4 English, 2 mathematics, 2 science, 2 foreign language, 2 social studies, 2 history. **Freshman Admission Statistics:** 61 applied, 72% admitted, 80% enrolled. **Transfer Admission Requirements:** College transcript(s), essay or personal statement, interview, minimum college GPA of 2.0 required. Lowest grade transferable C+. **General Admission Information:** Application fee $50. Regular application deadline 8/15. Notification on a rolling basis, beginning on or about 9/1. Nonfall registration accepted. Admission may be deferred for a maximum of 2. Credit offered for CEEB Advanced Placement tests.

COSTS AND FINANCIAL AID

Annual tuition $18,400. . Room and board $11,780. Required fees $480. Average book expense $1,000. **Required Forms and Deadlines:** FAFSA, institution's own financial aid form. Financial aid filing deadline 4/1. Priority financial aid filing date 4/1. **Notification of Awards:** Applicants will be notified of awards on a rolling basis beginning 4/1. **Types of Aid:** *Need-based scholarships/grants:* Federal Pell, SEOG, state scholarships/grants, private scholarships, the school's own gift aid. *Loans:* FFEL Subsidized Stafford, FFEL Unsubsidized Stafford, FFEL PLUS. **Student Employment:** Highest amount earned per year from on-campus jobs $1,600. **Financial Aid Statistics:** 100% freshmen receive need-based scholarship or grant aid. 98% freshmen, 96% undergrads receive any aid. 67% undergrads borrow to pay for school. Average cumulative indebtedness $19,000. **Criteria for awarding institutional aid:** *Non-need-based:* Academics, alumni affiliation, religious affiliation.

HENDERSON STATE UNIVERSITY

1100 Henderson Street, HSU Box 7560, Arkadelphia, AR 71999-0001
Phone: 870-230-5028 **Financial Aid Phone:** 870-230-5148
E-mail: admissions@hsu.edu **CEEB Code:** 6272
Fax: 870-230-5066 **Website: ACT Code:** 126

This public school was founded in 1890. It has a 151-acre campus.

RATINGS

Admissions Selectivity Rating: 79   **Fire Safety Rating:** 77   **Green Rating:** 60*

STUDENTS AND FACULTY

Enrollment: 3,095. **Student Body:** 53% female, 47% male, 14% out-of-state, 3% international (24 countries represented). Asian 1%, African American 20%, Caucasian 72%, Hispanic 2%, Native American 1%.
Retention and Graduation: 55% freshmen return for sophomore year. 16% freshmen graduate within 4 years. **Faculty:** Student/faculty ratio 16:1. 168 full-time faculty, 65% hold PhDs, 11% are members of minority groups, 41% are women.

ACADEMICS

Degrees: Associate, bachelor's, master's. **Majors with Highest Enrollment:** Business/commerce; early childhood education and teaching; nursing/registered nurse (RN, ASN, BSN, MSN). **Special Study Options:** Cross-registration, distance learning, English as a Second Language (ESL), honors program, internships, liberal arts/career combination, teacher certification program. **Honors programs:** The overarching purpose of the Honors College is summed up in the single ancient Greek word, arete (highest excellence), which the students and faculty of the College have taken as their motto. In working to achieve this purpose, the Honors College shares the university's goal "to excel in undergraduate education, always striving to enrich the quality of learning and teaching." The program is directly involved in "actively recruiting, challenging, and supporting those students" who are among the most "highly motivated toward achieving academic success." Special programs offered to physically disabled students include note-taking services, tutors. **Career services:** Alumni services, career assessment, internships.

FACILITIES

Housing: Coed dorms, men's dorms, special housing for international students, women's dorms, cooperative housing, honors dorm. 72% of campus accessible to physically disabled. **Special Academic Facilities/Equipment:** Closed-circuit TV studio, planetarium. **Computers:** Students can register for classes online. Administrative functions (other than registration) can be performed online.

CAMPUS LIFE

Environment: Rural. **Activities:** Choral groups, concert band, dance, drama/theater, jazz band, literary magazine, marching band, music ensembles, radio station, student government, student newspaper, symphony orchestra, television station, yearbook, international student organization. **Organizations:** 80 registered organizations, 11 honor societies, 7 religious organizations. 9 fraternities, 6 sororities. **Athletics (Intercollegiate): Men:** Baseball, basketball, cross-country, football, golf, swimming. *Women:* Basketball, cross-country, golf, softball, swimming, tennis, volleyball. **On-Campus Highlights:** HSU Planetarium, New Reddie Athletic Center, Newly Renovated Arkansas Hall, Henderson House Bed and Breakfast, Java Spot Coffee House. **Environmental Initiatives:** Recycling paper, cans and bottles on campus. On-going "Green News" newsletter to faculty and staff that promotes living green and ways to do so.

ADMISSIONS

Freshman Academic Profile: Average high school GPA 3.23. 16% in top 10% of high school class, 44% in top 25% of high school class, 76% in top 50% of high school class. 92% from public high schools. SAT Math middle 50% range 460–610. SAT Writing middle 50% range 420–520. ACT middle 50% range 19–26. Minimum paper TOEFL 500. Minimum computer TOEFL 300. **Basis for Candidate Selection:** *Very important factors considered include:* Academic GPA, rigor of secondary school record, standardized test scores. *Other factors considered include:* Class rank, application essay, recommendation(s), character/personal qualities, interview. **Freshman Admission Requirements:** High school diploma is required and GED is accepted. *Academic units required:* 4 English, 2 mathematics, 2 science, 2 social studies, 1 history. *Academic units recommended:* 4 English, 4 mathematics, 3 science, 2 foreign language, 2 social studies, 2 history, 3 academic electives. **Freshman Admission Statistics:** 2,361 applied, 67% admitted, 47% enrolled. **Transfer Admission Requirements:** College transcript(s). Lowest grade transferable C. **General Admission Information:** Regular application deadline 7/15. Nonfall registration accepted. Admission may be deferred for a maximum of 1+. Neither credit nor placement offered for CEEB Advanced Placement tests.

COSTS AND FINANCIAL AID

Annual in-state tuition $2,520. Annual out-of-state tuition $5,040. Room and board $3,272. Required fees $275. Average book expense $800. **Required Forms and Deadlines:** FAFSA. Financial aid filing deadline 6/1. Priority financial aid filing date 6/1. **Notification of Awards:** Applicants will be notified of awards on a rolling basis beginning 3/1. **Types of Aid:** *Need-based scholarships/grants:* Federal Pell, SEOG, state scholarships/grants, private scholarships, the school's own gift aid. *Loans:* Direct Subsidized Stafford, Direct Unsubsidized Stafford, Direct PLUS, FFEL Subsidized Stafford, FFEL Unsubsidized Stafford, FFEL PLUS, Federal Perkins. **Student Employment:** Federal Work-Study Program available. Off-campus job opportunities are good. **Financial Aid Statistics:** 54% freshmen, 50% undergrads receive need-based scholarship or grant aid. 11% freshmen, 15% undergrads receive non-need-based scholarship or grant aid. 14% freshmen, 35% undergrads receive need-based self-help aid. 81% freshmen, 86% undergrads receive any aid. 37% undergrads borrow to pay for school. Average cumulative indebtedness $17,800. **Criteria for awarding institutional aid:** *Non-need-based:* Academics, alumni affiliation, art, athletics, leadership, minority status, music/drama.

HENDRIX COLLEGE

1600 Washington Avenue, Conway, AR 72032
Phone: 501-450-1362 **Financial Aid Phone:** 501-450-1368
E-mail: adm@hendrix.edu **CEEB Code:** 6273
Fax: 501-450-3843 **Website:** www.hendrix.edu **ACT Code:** 128

This private school, affiliated with the Methodist Church, was founded in 1876. It has a 160-acre campus.

RATINGS

Admissions Selectivity Rating: 91   **Fire Safety Rating:** 63   **Green Rating:** 79

STUDENTS AND FACULTY

Enrollment: 1,454. **Student Body:** 56% female, 44% male, 52% out-of-state, 3% international (13 countries represented). Asian 3%, African American 3%, Caucasian 79%, Hispanic 4%, Native American 1%.
Retention and Graduation: 88% freshmen return for sophomore year. 59% freshmen graduate within 4 years. 42% grads go on to further study within 1 year. 14% grads pursue arts and sciences degrees. 13% grads pursue law degrees. 6% grads pursue business degrees. 19% grads pursue medical degrees. **Faculty:** Student/faculty ratio 13:1. 102 full-time faculty, 95% hold PhDs, 10% are members of minority groups, 38% are women.

ACADEMICS

Degrees: Bachelor's, master's. **Classes:** Most classes have 10–19 students. Most lab/discussion sessions have 20–29 students. **Majors with Highest Enrollment:** Biochemistry/biophysics and molecular biology; biology/biological sciences; psychology. **Special Study Options:** Cooperative education program, double major, English as a Second Language (ESL), independent study, internships, student-designed major, study abroad, teacher certification program, Hendrix-in-Brussels (Belgium), Hendrix-in-Costa Rica, Hendrix-in-Heilongjiang (China), Hendrix-in-Graz (Austria), Hendrix-in-London (UK), Hendrix-in-Madrid (Spain), Hendrix-in-Oxford (UK), Accademia dell'Arte, other programs with 140 colleges and universities on 6 continents including countries such as Australia, Finland, France, Ghana, Japan etc. **Combined degree programs:** BA/MEng, 4-1 BA/MPH Program in Public Health with UAMS. Special programs offered to physically disabled students include note-taking services, reader services, tape recorders, tutors. **Career services:** Alumni network, alumni services, career/job search classes, career assessment, internships, regional alumni. **Career services highlights include:** ASK, The Alumni Sharing Knowledge Program, Internships, Grad Expo, Career Week/Fair.

FACILITIES

Housing: Coed dorms, special housing for disabled students, men's dorms, women's dorms, cooperative housing, apartments for single students, wellness housing, theme housing, co-educational foreign language house (Spanish, German, French alternating years) available; suite-style small houses; ecology house; Christian House. 49% of campus accessible to physically disabled. **Special Academic Facilities/Equipment:** Herbarium, Wilbur A. Mills Library. **Computers:** 100% of classrooms, 100% of dorms, 100% of libraries, 100% of dining areas, 100% of student union, 100% of common outdoor areas have wireless network access. Students can register for classes online. Administrative functions (other than registration) can be performed online.

CAMPUS LIFE

Environment: Town. **Activities:** Choral groups, concert band, dance, drama/theater, jazz band, literary magazine, music ensembles, musical theater, pep band, radio station, student government, student newspaper, student-run film society, symphony orchestra, yearbook, campus ministries, international student organization, Model UN. **Organizations:** 80 registered organizations, 6 honor societies, 5 religious organizations. **Athletics (Intercollegiate):** *Men:* Baseball, basketball, cross-country, diving, golf, lacrosse, soccer, swimming, tennis, track/field (outdoor). *Women:* Basketball, cross-country, diving, field hockey, golf, soccer, softball, swimming, tennis, track/field (outdoor), volleyball. **On-Campus Highlights:** Student Life & Technology Center, Village at Hendrix Apartments, Wellness & Athletic Center, Charles D. Morgan Center for Physical Sci, D.W. Reynolds building for the life sci, Art Complex, Butler Plaza Fountain, the Burrow (campus center). **Environmental Initiatives:** Reduction in paper utilization; maintaining and building environmentally sound buildings; recycling.

ADMISSIONS

Freshman Academic Profile: Average high school GPA 3.83. 49% in top 10% of high school class, 77% in top 25% of high school class, 95% in top 50% of high school class. 83% from public high schools. SAT Math middle 50% range 560–680. SAT Critical Reading middle 50% range 580–700. ACT middle 50% range 27–32. Minimum paper TOEFL 550. Minimum computer TOEFL 213. Minimum web-based TOEFL 79. **Basis for Candidate Selection:** *Very important factors considered include:* Application essay, academic GPA, rigor of secondary school record, standardized test scores. *Important factors considered include:* Class rank, recommendation(s), extracurricular activities, interview. *Other factors considered include:* Racial/ethnic status, talent/ability, volunteer work. **Freshman Admission Requirements:** High school diploma is required and GED is accepted. *Academic units recommended:* 4 English, 3 mathematics, 2 science, 2 foreign language, 3 social studies. **Freshman Admission Statistics:** 1,627 applied, 81% admitted, 31% enrolled. **Transfer Admission Requirements:** College transcript(s), essay or personal statement, statement of good standing from prior institution(s). Minimum college GPA of 2.5 required. Lowest grade transferable C. **General Admission Information:** Application fee $40. Regular application deadline 8/1. Notification on a rolling basis, beginning on or about 11/1. Nonfall registration accepted. Admission may be deferred for a maximum of 1 year. Credit and/or placement offered for CEEB Advanced Placement tests.

COSTS AND FINANCIAL AID

Annual tuition $29,970. Room and board $8,664. Required fees $300. Average book expense $900. **Required Forms and Deadlines:** FAFSA, application for admission serves as primary merit-based scholarship application. Priority financial aid filing date 2/15. **Notification of Awards:** Applicants will be notified of awards on a rolling basis beginning 2/15. **Types of Aid:** *Need-based scholarships/grants:* Federal Pell, SEOG, state scholarships/grants, private scholarships, the school's own gift aid. *Loans:* Direct Subsidized Stafford, Direct Unsubsidized Stafford, Direct PLUS, FFEL Subsidized Stafford, FFEL Unsubsidized Stafford, FFEL PLUS, Federal Perkins, Private alternative loans as selected by the student. **Student Employment:** Federal Work-Study Program available. Institutional employment available. Highest amount earned per year from on-campus jobs $1,500. Off-campus job opportunities are good. **Financial Aid Statistics:** 59% freshmen, 61% undergrads receive need-based scholarship or grant aid. 22% freshmen, 17% undergrads receive non-need-based scholarship or grant aid. 37% freshmen, 44% undergrads receive need-based self-help aid. 100% freshmen, 100% undergrads receive any aid. 87% undergrads borrow to pay for school. Average cumulative indebtedness $17,641. **Criteria for awarding institutional aid:** *Non-need-based:* Academics, art, leadership, music/drama, state/district residency.

HERITAGE UNIVERSITY

3240 Fort Road, Toppenish, WA 98948
Phone: 509-865-8508 **Financial Aid Phone:** 509-865-8502
E-mail: 3w_Admissions@heritage.edu **CEEB Code:** 3777
Fax: 509-865-8659 **Website:** www.heritage.edu

This private school was founded in 1982. It has a 20-acre campus.

RATINGS

Admissions Selectivity Rating: 60*   **Fire Safety Rating:** 60*   **Green Rating:** 60*

STUDENTS AND FACULTY

Enrollment: 756. **Student Body:** 73% female, 27% male,. Asian 1%, African American 1%, Caucasian 35%, Hispanic 56%, Native American 11%.

Retention and Graduation: 49% freshmen return for sophomore year. **Faculty:** Student/faculty ratio 10:1. 47 full-time faculty, 38% hold PhDs, 23% are members of minority groups, 49% are women.

ACADEMICS

Degrees: Associate, bachelor's, certificate, master's, post-bachelor's certificate, post-master's certificate, terminal associate, transfer associate. **Classes:** Most classes have fewer than 10 students. **Special Study Options:** Cooperative education program, distance learning, double major, English as a Second Language (ESL), honors program, independent study, internships, liberal arts/career combination, teacher certification program. **Honors programs:** Students take Honors seminar, Honors sections of general education requirements, and have frequent interactions with faculty, other scholars, and community leaders; develop and implement strategies for community improvement and participate in cultural events. Special programs offered to physically disabled students include note-taking services, reader services, tape recorders, tutors.

FACILITIES

Housing: 90% of campus accessible to physically disabled.

CAMPUS LIFE

Environment: Rural. **Activities:** drama/theater, literary magazine, music ensembles, student government, student newspaper **Organizations:**. **On-Campus Highlights:** Student Services Center, Jewett Center, Library, Academic Skills Center

ADMISSIONS

Freshman Academic Profile: 95% from public high schools. Minimum paper TOEFL 500. Minimum computer TOEFL 173. **Basis for Candidate Selection: Freshman Admission Requirements:** High school diploma is required and GED is accepted. *Academic units recommended:* 3 English, 2 mathematics, 1 science, (1 science labs), 3 history, 4 academic electives. **Freshman Admission Statistics:** 475 applied, 60% admitted, 31% enrolled. **Transfer Admission Requirements:** College transcript(s), Lowest grade transferable C–. **General Admission Information:** Regular application deadline 9/1. Nonfall registration accepted. Admission may be deferred for a maximum of 3. Credit and/or placement offered for CEEB Advanced Placement tests.

COSTS AND FINANCIAL AID

Annual tuition $9,600. Required fees $45. **Required Forms and Deadlines:** FAFSA, institution's own financial aid form. Priority financial aid filing date 2/10. **Types of Aid:** *Need-based scholarships/grants:* Federal Pell, SEOG, state scholarships/grants, private scholarships, the school's own gift aid. *Loans:* FFEL Subsidized Stafford, FFEL Unsubsidized Stafford, FFEL PLUS, Federal Perkins. **Financial Aid Statistics:** 92% undergrads borrow to pay for school. Average cumulative indebtedness $11,909.

HIGH POINT UNIVERSITY

University Station 3598, High Point, NC 27262-3598
Phone: 336-841-9216 **Financial Aid Phone:** 336-841-9128
E-mail: admiss@highpoint.edu **CEEB Code:** 5293
Fax: 336-888-6382 **Website:** www.highpoint.edu **ACT Code:** 3108

This private school, affiliated with the Methodist Church, was founded in 1924. It has a 135-acre campus.

RATINGS

Admissions Selectivity Rating: 77   **Fire Safety Rating:** 60*   **Green Rating:** 60*

STUDENTS AND FACULTY

Enrollment: 2,736. **Student Body:** 62% female, 38% male, 63% out-of-state, international (40 countries represented).
Retention and Graduation: 79% freshmen return for sophomore year. 46% freshmen graduate within 4 years. 31% grads go on to further study within 1 year. 21% grads pursue arts and sciences degrees. 1% grads pursue law degrees. 8% grads pursue business degrees. **Faculty:** Student/faculty ratio 15:1. 129 full-time faculty, 77% hold PhDs, 9% are members of minority groups, 40% are women.

ACADEMICS

Degrees: Bachelor's, master's, post-bachelor's certificate. **Classes:** Most classes have 10–19 students. **Majors with Highest Enrollment:** communication studies/speech communication and rhetoric; education; psychology. **Special Study Options:** Accelerated program, cooperative education program, cross-registration, double major, dual enrollment, English as a Second Language (ESL), honors program, independent study, internships, liberal arts/career combination, student-designed major, study abroad, teacher certification program. Joint degree programs in environmental science, forestry and medical technology.

Honors programs: More than 200 students are enrolled in the university's Honors Program. In addition to enrollment in honors courses, members of the Honors Program often present the results of their research at the Honors Symposium sponsored annually by the university's Odyssey Club, an organization of students enrolled in the Honors Program. In addition to activities for members of the Honors Program, the Odyssey Club sponsors a number of activities annually for the campus at large, including academic bowls and visiting lecturers. **Combined degree programs:** 3-2 programs: med tech; environ sci; forestry. Special programs offered to physically disabled students include tape recorders, tutors. **Career services:** career/job search classes, career assessment, internships. **Career services highlights include:** The mission of the civic engagement program is to increase students' understanding of their diverse responsibilities as stewards of their communities by: providing students with opportunities to participate in activities that contribute to the public good; encouraging students to reflect on their experiences as a means of making more permanent the practical lessons they learn in the field; instilling in students an awareness of the mutually beneficial relationship that exists between social institutions and centers of higher learning; teaching students to think critically, speak clearly, and write effectively as a means of becoming productive members of society.

FACILITIES

Housing: Coed dorms, special housing for disabled students, men's dorms, women's dorms, fraternity/sorority housing, apartments for married students, cooperative housing, apartments for single students. The number of apartments/houses are available for married students is limited. 98% of campus accessible to physically disabled. **Special Academic Facilities/Equipment:** Hayworth Chapel; Hayworth Fine Arts Center; Sechrest Gallery; Smith Library; Campus Television Studio; Radio Studio/Station (WHPU). Beginning a $100 million new-construction and renovation program, the campus of High Point University is currently experiencing the greatest period of growth in our 81-year history. Currently under construction are: Blessing Residence Hall is a $10–million facility which is made possible by the generous lead gift of one anonymous donor who requested we call it the "Blessing" residence hall. It will be loaded with amenities that make it a prototype for 21st Century college residence halls. It will offer 240 fully furnished, private bedrooms arranged in suites with living rooms, kitchens and dining areas. Residents will enjoy spacious common areas, computer lounges, conference areas, laundry rooms and elevators. Slane Student Life & Wellness Center will be a centerpiece of campus. This $6.5 million, 45,000–square-foot building will connect to the current Slane Student Center via a two-story atrium, and will feature a high-performance aerobics room, rock-climbing wall, indoor track, fully equipped weight room, food court, dramatic inside & outside basketball courts, outdoor swimming pool, sand volleyball.courts, and a grand student atrium with billiard tables and sitting areas. The Earl N. Phillips School of Business will be a new 27,000–square-foot building which will become the home for the more than 1,000 undergraduate students pursuing a degree in one of High Point University's 12 undergraduate majors and Master of Business Administration graduate degree. The facility will feature a 200–seat, tiered lecture hall, four smaller lecture rooms, as well as traditional classrooms, a spacious auditorium, private study rooms, computer labs and faculty offices. The Jerry & Kitty Steele Sports Center will be a $5 million, 2-story, 27,000–square-foot facility featuring training & weight rooms, a hospitality/conference room, locker rooms, and an academic services room. In addition, another $5 million is being invested to build a new soccer stadium, baseball stadium, and eight-lane track. University Park will be an extraordinary outdoor experience. Featuring a network of trails and bridges, spectacular waterfalls, a 15-foot overhead trellis, multi-level reflecting pools, 65' covered walkway, and an amphitheatre, this will be the perfect place for an outdoor class, receptions, plays and programs. **Computers:** 100% of classrooms, 100% of dorms, 100% of libraries, 100% of dining areas, 100% of student union, 100% of common outdoor areas have wireless network access. Students can register for classes online. Administrative functions (other than registration) can be performed online.

CAMPUS LIFE

Environment: City. **Activities:** Choral groups, concert band, dance, drama/theater, literary magazine, music ensembles, musical theater, pep band, radio station, student government, student newspaper, symphony orchestra, television station, yearbook, campus ministries, Model UN. **Organizations:** 109 registered organizations, 14 honor societies, 8 religious organizations. 4 fraternities, 5 sororities. **Athletics (Intercollegiate):** *Men:* Baseball, basketball, cheerleading, cross-country, golf, soccer, tennis, track/field (outdoor), track/field (indoor). *Women:* Basketball, cheerleading, cross-country, golf, soccer, tennis, track/field (outdoor), track/field (indoor), volleyball. **On-Campus Highlights:** Slane University Center, Hayworth Fine Arts Center, Millis Athletic/Convocation Center, Hayworth Chapel, The International Promenade, High Point University is in the midst of a 5-year, $250 million campus development plan that will result in the construction of a new building for the School of Business, a new Student Activity Center, a new soccer stadium and track, a new residence hall, a new Sports Center, a new University Park, and dozens of renovations across campus.

ADMISSIONS

Freshman Academic Profile: Average high school GPA 3.18. 17% in top 10% of high school class, 38% in top 25% of high school class, 70% in top 50% of high school class. 86% from public high schools. SAT Math middle 50% range 460–570. SAT Critical Reading middle 50% range 460–570. SAT Writing middle 50% range 460–560. ACT middle 50% range 19–24. Minimum paper TOEFL 500. Minimum computer TOEFL 150. **Basis for Candidate Selection:** *Very important factors considered include:* Rigor of secondary school record, standardized test scores. *Important factors considered include:* Class rank, academic GPA. *Other factors considered include:* Application essay, recommendation(s), extracurricular activities, interview, talent/ability, volunteer work, work experience. **Freshman Admission Requirements:** High school diploma is required and GED is accepted. *Academic units required:* 4 English, 3 mathematics, 2 science, (2 science labs), 2 social studies, 2 history, 1 academic electives. *Academic units recommended:* 2 foreign language, 2 academic electives. **Freshman Admission Statistics:** 2,546 applied, 73% admitted, 40% enrolled. **Transfer Admission Requirements:** High school transcript, college transcript(s), standardized test scores, statement of good standing from prior institution(s). Minimum college GPA of 2.0 required. Lowest grade transferable C. **General Admission Information:** Application fee $40. Early decision application deadline 11/7. Regular application deadline 8/15. Notification on a rolling basis, beginning on or about 11/6. Nonfall registration accepted. Admission may be deferred for a maximum of 1 year. Credit and/or placement offered for CEEB Advanced Placement tests.

COSTS AND FINANCIAL AID

Comprehensive fee $31,000. Average book expense $1,500. **Required Forms and Deadlines:** FAFSA, state aid form. Priority financial aid filing date 3/1. **Notification of Awards:** Applicants will be notified of awards on a rolling basis beginning 4/1. **Types of Aid:** *Need-based scholarships/grants:* Federal Pell, SEOG, state scholarships/grants, private scholarships, the school's own gift aid. *Loans:* Direct Subsidized Stafford, Direct Unsubsidized Stafford, Direct PLUS, FFEL Subsidized Stafford, FFEL Unsubsidized Stafford, FFEL PLUS, Federal Perkins. **Student Employment:** Federal Work-Study Program available. Institutional employment available. Off-campus job opportunities are good. **Financial Aid Statistics:** 55% freshmen, 51% undergrads receive need-based scholarship or grant aid. 41% freshmen, 59% undergrads receive non-need-based scholarship or grant aid. 60% freshmen, 62% undergrads receive need-based self-help aid. 6% freshmen, 4% undergrads receive athletic scholarships. 79% freshmen, 88% undergrads receive any aid. 58% undergrads borrow to pay for school. Average cumulative indebtedness $16,850. **Criteria for awarding institutional aid:** *Non-need-based:* Academics, alumni affiliation, art, athletics, leadership, music/drama, religious affiliation, state/district residency.

HILBERT COLLEGE

5200 South Park Avenue, Hamburg, NY 14075-1597
Phone: 716-649-7900 **Financial Aid Phone:** 716-649-7900
E-mail: admissions@hilbert.edu **CEEB Code:** 2334
Fax: 716-649-0702 **Website:** www.hilbert.edu **ACT Code:** 2759

This private school, affiliated with the Roman Catholic Church, was founded in 1957. It has a 40-acre campus.

RATINGS

Admissions Selectivity Rating: 64   **Fire Safety Rating:** 87   **Green Rating:** 60*

STUDENTS AND FACULTY

Enrollment: 998. **Student Body:** 60% female, 40% male, 10% out-of-state, international (4 countries represented). African American 6%, Caucasian 82%, Hispanic 2%, Native American 2%.
Retention and Graduation: 70% freshmen return for sophomore year. 49% freshmen graduate within 4 years. 15% grads go on to further study within 1 year. 4% grads pursue arts and sciences degrees. 4% grads pursue law degrees. 4% grads pursue business degrees. **Faculty:** Student/faculty ratio 13:1. 48 full-time faculty, 50% hold PhDs, 2% are members of minority groups, 48% are women.

ACADEMICS

Degrees: Associate, bachelor's, certificate, terminal associate. **Classes:** Most classes have 10–19 students. Most lab/discussion sessions have fewer than 10 students. **Majors with Highest Enrollment:** Business/commerce; criminal justice/law enforcement administration; forensic science and technology. **Special Study Options:** Cross-registration, distance learning, dual enrollment, honors program, independent study, internships, study abroad, Member of Western New York consortium of colleges. **Honors programs:** About the Honors Program: The Hilbert Honors Program will give you more from your college experience. You will enroll in regular classes and fulfill honors credit requirements by doing advanced work, or in lieu of projects. These special projects allow you to work one-on-one with Hilbert's outstanding honors faculty in your major and in other academic areas. As an honors student, you will also have a student mentor for your first semester and personal faculty advisement. Special programs offered to physically disabled students include note-taking services, reader services, tape recorders, tutors. **Career services:** Alumni network, alumni services, career assessment, internships. **Career services highlights include:** Internships are available with agencies in most majors.

FACILITIES

Housing: Coed dorms, apartments for single studentsCampus Apartments. 95% of campus accessible to physically disabled. **Special Academic Facilities/Equipment:** Honors Lounge, Institute for Law and Justice, Center for Creative Media. **Computers:** 100% of classrooms, 100% of dorms, 100% of libraries, 100% of dining areas, 100% of student union, 100% of common outdoor areas have wireless network access. Students can register for classes online. Administrative functions (other than registration) can be performed online.

CAMPUS LIFE

Environment: Village. **Activities:** Choral groups, drama/theater, literary magazine, student government, student newspaper, campus ministries. **Organizations:** 20 registered organizations, 5 honor societies, 1 religious organizations. **Athletics (Intercollegiate):** *Men:* Baseball, basketball, cross-country, golf, soccer, volleyball. *Women:* Basketball, cross-country, golf, soccer, softball, volleyball. **On-Campus Highlights:** Hafner Recreation Center, Franciscan Hall Atrium, Campus Apartments, Swan Auditorium, Paczesny Hall.

ADMISSIONS

Freshman Academic Profile: Average high school GPA 2.8. 2% in top 10% of high school class, 13% in top 25% of high school class, 40% in top 50% of high school class. 85% from public high schools. SAT Math middle 50% range 400–510. SAT Critical Reading middle 50% range 400–510. ACT middle 50% range 17–22. Minimum paper TOEFL 500. Minimum computer TOEFL 173. **Basis for Candidate Selection:** *Very important factors considered include:* Academic GPA, rigor of secondary school record. *Important factors considered include:* Recommendation(s). *Other factors considered include:* Application essay, character/personal qualities, extracurricular activities, interview, talent/ability, volunteer work, work experience. **Freshman Admission Requirements:** High school diploma is required and GED is accepted. *Academic units required:* 4 English, 2 mathematics, 2 science, (1 science labs), 2 social studies, 2 history, 4 academic electives. *Academic units recommended:* 4 English, 3 mathematics, 3 science, 1 foreign language, 3 social studies, 3 history, 3 academic electives. **Freshman Admission Statistics:** 726 applied, 85% admitted, 35% enrolled. **Transfer Admission Requirements:** High school transcript, college transcript(s), minimum college GPA of 2.0 required. Lowest grade transferable C. **General Admission Information:** Application fee $20. Regular application deadline 9/1. Nonfall registration accepted. Admission may be deferred for a maximum of 1 year. Credit offered for CEEB Advanced Placement tests.

COSTS AND FINANCIAL AID

Annual tuition $16,000. Room and board $6,600. Required fees $600. Average book expense $700. **Required Forms and Deadlines:** FAFSA, state aid form. Priority financial aid filing date 3/1. **Notification of Awards:** Applicants will be notified of awards on a rolling basis beginning 3/1. **Types of Aid:** *Need-based scholarships/grants:* Federal Pell, SEOG, state scholarships/grants, private scholarships, the school's own gift aid. *Loans:* FFEL Subsidized Stafford, FFEL Unsubsidized Stafford, FFEL PLUS, Federal Perkins. **Student Employment:** Federal Work-Study Program available. Institutional employment available. Highest amount earned per year from on-campus jobs $1,250. Off-campus job opportunities are excellent. **Financial Aid Statistics:** 91% freshmen, 85% undergrads receive need-based scholarship or grant aid. 4% freshmen, 5% undergrads receive non-need-based scholarship or grant aid. 82% freshmen, 77% undergrads receive need-based self-help aid. 92% freshmen, 87% undergrads receive any aid. 93% undergrads borrow to pay for school. Average cumulative indebtedness $26,583. **Criteria for awarding institutional aid:** *Non-need-based:* Academics, leadership, minority status.

HILLSDALE COLLEGE

33 East College Street, Hillsdale, MI 49242
Phone: 517-607-2327 **Financial Aid Phone:** 517-607-2350
E-mail: admissions@hillsdale.edu **CEEB Code:** 1295
Fax: 517-607-2223 **Website:** www.hillsdale.edu **ACT Code:** 2010

This private school was founded in 1844. It has a 200-acre campus.

RATINGS
Admissions Selectivity Rating: 92   **Fire Safety Rating:** 85   **Green Rating:** 60*

STUDENTS AND FACULTY

Enrollment: 1,326. **Student Body:** 52% female, 48% male, 59% out-of-state, 2% international (13 countries represented).
Retention and Graduation: 88% freshmen return for sophomore year. 67% freshmen graduate within 4 years. 46% grads go on to further study within 1 year. 11% grads pursue arts and sciences degrees. 5% grads pursue law degrees. 13% grads pursue business degrees. 4% grads pursue medical degrees. **Faculty:** Student/faculty ratio 10:1. 110 full-time faculty, 83% hold PhDs, 27% are women.

ACADEMICS

Degrees: Bachelor's. **Classes:** Most classes have fewer than 10 students. Most lab/discussion sessions have 20–29 students. **Majors with Highest Enrollment:** Biology/biological sciences; business administration and management; education. **Special Study Options:** Double major, dual enrollment, honors program, independent study, internships, student-designed major, study abroad, teacher certification program. **Honors programs:** Honors Program available. **Career services:** Alumni network, alumni services, career assessment, internships. **Career services highlights include:** National Professional Sales Internship Program.

FACILITIES

Housing: Men's dorms, women's dorms, fraternity/sorority housing, apartments for single students. **Special Academic Facilities/Equipment:** Early childhood education lab, media center, K–8 private academy, Slayton Arboretum, rare books library. **Computers:** 100% of classrooms, 85% of dorms, 100% of libraries, 100% of dining areas, 100% of student union, 100% of common outdoor areas have wireless network access.

CAMPUS LIFE

Environment: Village. **Activities:** Choral groups, concert band, dance, drama/theater, jazz band, literary magazine, music ensembles, musical theater, pep band, student government, student newspaper, symphony orchestra, yearbook, campus ministries, international student organization. **Organizations:** 50 registered organizations, 26 honor societies, 4 religious organizations. 3 fraternities, 3 sororities. **Athletics (Intercollegiate):** *Men:* Baseball, basketball, cheerleading, cross-country, football, track/field (outdoor), track/field (indoor). *Women:* Basketball, cheerleading, cross-country, diving, equestrian sports, softball, swimming, track/field (outdoor), track/field (indoor), volleyball. **On-Campus Highlights:** Student Union, Quad (outdoor quadrangle), Sage Center for the Arts, Howard Music Hall, Sports Complex. **Environmental Initiatives:** Central heating and cooling efficiency plan, high efficiency lighting in all new facilities; environmental controls in all buildings for energy management.

ADMISSIONS

Freshman Academic Profile: Average high school GPA 3.72. 47% in top 10% of high school class, 75% in top 25% of high school class, 98% in top 50% of high school class. 48% from public high schools. SAT Math middle 50% range 570–660. SAT Critical Reading middle 50% range 640–720. SAT Writing middle 50% range 610–690. ACT middle 50% range 25–30. Minimum paper TOEFL 570. Minimum computer TOEFL 210. **Basis for Candidate Selection:** *Very important factors considered include:* Academic GPA, rigor of secondary school record, standardized test scores, character/personal qualities, interview. *Important factors considered include:* Class rank, application essay, recommendation(s), extracurricular activities, level of applicant's interest, volunteer work, work experience. *Other factors considered include:* Alumni/ae relation, talent/ability. **Freshman Admission Requirements:** High school diploma is required and GED is accepted. *Academic units recommended:* 4 English, 4 mathematics, 3 science, (1 science labs), 2 foreign language, 1 social studies, 2 history. **Freshman Admission Statistics:** 1,401 applied, 64% admitted, 42% enrolled. **Transfer Admission Requirements:** High school transcript, college transcript(s), essay or personal statement, standardized test scores, statement of good standing from prior institution(s). Minimum college GPA of 3.25 required. Lowest grade transferable C. **General Admission**

Information: Application fee $35. Early decision application deadline 11/15. Regular application deadline 2/15. Nonfall registration accepted. Admission may be deferred for a maximum of 1 year. Credit and/or placement offered for CEEB Advanced Placement tests.

COSTS AND FINANCIAL AID

Annual tuition $18,650. Room and board $7,340. Required fees $490. Average book expense $850. **Required Forms and Deadlines:** Institution's own financial aid form, noncustodial PROFILE, business/farm supplement. Financial aid filing deadline 3/15. Priority financial aid filing date 2/15. **Notification of Awards:** Applicants will be notified of awards on a rolling basis beginning 2/15. **Types of Aid:** *Need-based scholarships/grants:* private scholarships, the school's own gift aid. *Loans:* college/university loans from institutional funds. **Student Employment:** Institutional employment available. Highest amount earned per year from on-campus jobs $1,300. Off-campus job opportunities are good. **Financial Aid Statistics:** 47% freshmen, 41% undergrads receive need-based scholarship or grant aid. 32% freshmen, 26% undergrads receive non-need-based scholarship or grant aid. 47% freshmen, 41% undergrads receive need-based self-help aid. 17% freshmen, 16% undergrads receive athletic scholarships. 83% freshmen, 86% undergrads receive any aid. 62% undergrads borrow to pay for school. Average cumulative indebtedness $14,500. **Criteria for awarding institutional aid:** *Non-need-based:* Academics, alumni affiliation, art, athletics, leadership, music/drama.

See page 1110.

HIRAM COLLEGE

PO Box 96, Hiram, OH 44234
Phone: 330-569-5169
E-mail: CEEB Code: 1297
Fax: Website: www.hiram.edu **ACT Code:** 3280

This private school, affiliated with the Disciples of Christ Church, was founded in 1850. It has a 110-acre campus.

RATINGS
Admissions Selectivity Rating: 76   **Fire Safety Rating:** 60*   **Green Rating:** 60*

STUDENTS AND FACULTY

Enrollment: 1,313. **Student Body:** 54% female, 46% male, 21% out-of-state, 5% international (17 countries represented). Asian 1%, African American 11%, Caucasian 66%, Hispanic 2%, Native American 1%.
Retention and Graduation: 80% freshmen return for sophomore year. 58% freshmen graduate within 4 years. 36% grads go on to further study within 1 year. 30% grads pursue arts and sciences degrees. 3% grads pursue law degrees. 1% grads pursue business degrees. 2% grads pursue medical degrees. **Faculty:** Student/faculty ratio 11.5:1. 74 full-time faculty, 93% hold PhDs, 3% are members of minority groups, 49% are women.

ACADEMICS

Degrees: Bachelor's, master's. **Classes:** Most classes have 10–19 students. Most lab/discussion sessions have 10–19 students. **Majors with Highest Enrollment:** Biology; education. **Special Study Options:** Accelerated program, cross-registration, double major, English as a Second Language (ESL), exchange student program (domestic), independent study, internships, student-designed major, study abroad, teacher certification program, weekend college. **Combined degree programs:** BA(Hiram)/BS(Engineering) 5 years. Special programs offered to physically disabled students include note-taking services, reader services, tape recorders, tutors. **Career services:** Alumni network, alumni services, career/job search classes, career assessment, internships. **Career services highlights include:** Internships including participation in the regional. ClevelandIntern.net, biomedical research, and virtual internships.

FACILITIES

Housing: Coed dorms, special housing for disabled students, women's dorms, theme housingsuite style housing. 55% of campus accessible to physically disabled. **Special Academic Facilities/Equipment:** Psychology lab, language lab, international center, center for literature and medicine, fitness center, health center, observatory, electron microscope, two field stations for study and research.

CAMPUS LIFE

Environment: Rural. **Activities:** Choral groups, concert band, dance, drama/theater, jazz band, literary magazine, marching band, music ensembles, opera, pep band, radio station, student government, student newspaper, symphony orchestra, yearbook, campus ministries, international student organization, Model UN. **Organizations:** 55 registered organizations, 7 honor societies, 6 religious organizations. 3 fraternities, 3 sororities. **Athletics (Intercollegiate):** *Men:* Baseball, basketball, cheerleading, cross-country, diving, football, golf, soccer, swimming, tennis, track/field (outdoor), track/field (indoor). *Women:* Basketball, cheerleading, cross-country, diving, golf, soccer, softball, swimming, tennis, track/field (outdoor), track/field (indoor), volleyball. **On-Campus Highlights:** James H. Barrow Field Station, The Hiram College Library, Kennedy Center(Food Court, Bookstore, ballroom,and other facilities), Hiram Church, Stevens Memorial Observatory.

ADMISSIONS

Freshman Academic Profile: Average high school GPA 3.3. 18% in top 10% of high school class, 42% in top 25% of high school class, 79% in top 50% of high school class. 86% from public high schools. SAT Math middle 50% range 470–590. SAT Critical Reading middle 50% range 480–610. ACT middle 50% range 20–26. Minimum paper TOEFL 550. **Basis for Candidate Selection: Freshman Admission Requirements: Freshman Admission Statistics:** 1,513 applied, 75% admitted, 29% enrolled. **General Admission Information:** Credit and/or placement offered for CEEB Advanced Placement tests.

COSTS AND FINANCIAL AID

Annual tuition $24,775. Room and board $9,010. Required fees $670. Average book expense $700. **Required Forms and Deadlines:** FAFSA. Priority financial aid filing date 2/15. **Notification of Awards:** Applicants will be notified of awards on a rolling basis beginning 3/1. **Types of Aid:** *Need-based scholarships/grants:* Federal Pell, SEOG, state scholarships/grants, private scholarships, the school's own gift aid, United Negro College Fund. *Loans:* FFEL Subsidized Stafford, FFEL Unsubsidized Stafford, FFEL PLUS, Federal Perkins, college/university loans from institutional funds. **Student Employment:** Highest amount earned per year from on-campus jobs $500. **Financial Aid Statistics:** 78% undergrads borrow to pay for school. Average cumulative indebtedness $21,247. **Criteria for awarding institutional aid:** *Non-need-based:* Academics, alumni affiliation, music/drama, religious affiliation, state/district residency.

HOBART AND WILLIAM SMITH COLLEGES

629 South Main Street, Geneva, NY 14456
Phone: 315-781-3622 **Financial Aid Phone:** 315-781-3315
E-mail: admissions@hws.edu **CEEB Code:** 2294
Fax: 315-781-3914 **Website:** www.hws.edu **ACT Code:** 2758

This private school was founded in 1822. It has a 170-acre campus.

RATINGS
Admissions Selectivity Rating: 87   **Fire Safety Rating:** 60*   **Green Rating:** 60*

STUDENTS AND FACULTY

Enrollment: 1,855. **Student Body:** 54% female, 46% male, 55% out-of-state, 2% international (18 countries represented). Asian 2%, African American 4%, Caucasian 88%, Hispanic 4%.
Retention and Graduation: 85% freshmen return for sophomore year. 30% grads go on to further study within 1 year. 20% grads pursue arts and sciences degrees. 7% grads pursue law degrees. 10% grads pursue business degrees. 4% grads pursue medical degrees. **Faculty:** Student/faculty ratio 11:1. 156 full-time faculty, 94% hold PhDs, 13% are members of minority groups, 41% are women.

ACADEMICS

Degrees: Bachelor's, master's. **Classes:** Most classes have 10–19 students. **Majors with Highest Enrollment:** Economics; English language and literature; history. **Special Study Options:** Cross-registration, double major, dual enrollment, English as a Second Language (ESL), exchange student program (domestic), honors program, independent study, internships, student-designed major, study abroad, teacher certification program. **Combined degree programs:** BA/MA, 3-2 Engineer; 3-4 Architect; 4-1 MBA; 4-1 MAT. Special programs offered to physically disabled students include note-taking services, reader services, tape recorders, tutors. **Career services:** Alumni network, alumni services, career/job search classes, career assessment, internships.

FACILITIES

Housing: Coed dorms, men's dorms, special housing for international students, women's dorms, fraternity/sorority housing, cooperative housing, apartments for single students, Upperclass townhouses; theme houses; Honors Houses. **Special Academic Facilities/Equipment:** Houghton Gallery, HWS Explorer (reesearch vessel), 100-acre nature preserve, Melly Academic Center, Rosenberg science center. **Computers:** Students can register for classes online. Administrative functions (other than registration) can be performed online.

CAMPUS LIFE

Environment: Village. **Activities:** Choral groups, dance, drama/theater, jazz band, literary magazine, music ensembles, radio station, student government, student newspaper, student-run film society, symphony orchestra, yearbook. **Organizations:** 77 registered organizations, 12 honor societies, 4 religious organizations. 5 fraternities, **Athletics (Intercollegiate):** *Men:* Basketball, crew/rowing, cross-country, football, golf, ice hockey, lacrosse, sailing, soccer, squash, tennis. *Women:* Basketball, crew/rowing, cross-country, diving, field hockey, golf, lacrosse, sailing, soccer, squash, swimming, tennis. **On-Campus Highlights:** Scandling Center, South Hall, Stern Hall, North Hall, Bristol Field House, Trinity Hall, with the newly remodeled Salisbury Center, houses the Offices of Career Development, Public Service and Global Education.

ADMISSIONS

Freshman Academic Profile: Average high school GPA 3.22. 33% in top 10% of high school class, 67% in top 25% of high school class, 95% in top 50% of high school class. 65% from public high schools. SAT Math middle 50% range 540–630. SAT Critical Reading middle 50% range 530–640. ACT middle 50% range 24–27. Minimum paper TOEFL 550. Minimum computer TOEFL 220. **Basis for Candidate Selection:** *Very important factors considered include:* Rigor of secondary school record. *Important factors considered include:* Class rank, application essay, academic GPA, recommendation(s), standardized test scores, character/personal qualities, extracurricular activities, volunteer work, work experience. *Other factors considered include:* Alumni/ae relation, first generation, geographical residence, interview, level of applicant's interest, racial/ethnic status, talent/ability. **Freshman Admission Requirements:** High school diploma is required and GED is accepted. *Academic units required:* 4 English, 3 mathematics, 3 science, (2 science labs), 2 foreign language, 2 social studies, 2 history, 2 academic electives. *Academic units recommended:* 3 foreign language, 3 social studies, 4 academic electives. **Freshman Admission Statistics:** 3,410 applied, 65% admitted, 25% enrolled. **Transfer Admission Requirements:** High school transcript, college transcript(s), essay or personal statement, standardized test scores, minimum college GPA of 2.5 required. Lowest grade transferable C. **General Admission Information:** Application fee $45. Early decision application deadline 11/15. Regular application deadline 2/1. Regular notification 4/1. Nonfall registration not accepted. Admission may be deferred for a maximum of 2 years. Credit offered for CEEB Advanced Placement tests.

COSTS AND FINANCIAL AID

Annual tuition $31,850. Room and board $8,386. Required fees $887. Average book expense $850. **Required Forms and Deadlines:** FAFSA, CSS/Financial Aid PROFILE, state aid form, noncustodial PROFILE, parent's and student's tax return. Financial aid filing deadline 2/1. Priority financial aid filing date 2/1. **Notification of Awards:** Applicants will be notified of awards on or about 4/1. **Types of Aid:** *Need-based scholarships/grants:* Federal Pell, SEOG, state scholarships/grants, private scholarships, the school's own gift aid. *Loans:* FFEL Subsidized Stafford, FFEL Unsubsidized Stafford, FFEL PLUS, Federal Perkins. **Student Employment:** Federal Work-Study Program available. Institutional employment available. Highest amount earned per year from on-campus jobs $600. Off-campus job opportunities are good. **Financial Aid Statistics:** 58% freshmen, 60% undergrads receive need-based scholarship or grant aid. 10% freshmen, 7% undergrads receive non-need-based scholarship or grant aid. 48% freshmen, 53% undergrads receive need-based self-help aid. 74% freshmen, 64% undergrads receive any aid. 65% undergrads borrow to pay for school. Average cumulative indebtedness $21,545. **Criteria for awarding institutional aid:** *Non-need-based:* Academics, art, leadership, music/drama.

HODGES UNIVERSITY

2655 Northbrooke Drive, Naples, FL 34119
Phone: 239-513-1122 **Financial Aid Phone:** 239-513-1122
E-mail: admit@internationalcollege.edu **CEEB Code:** 7113
Fax: 239-598-6254 **Website:** www.hodges.edu **ACT Code:** 4775

This private school was founded in 1990.

RATINGS
Admissions Selectivity Rating: 60*   **Fire Safety Rating:** 60*   **Green Rating:** 69

STUDENTS AND FACULTY

Enrollment: 1,475. **Student Body:** 68% female, 32% male, 1% out-of-state, international (40 countries represented). Asian 2%, African American 16%, Caucasian 55%, Hispanic 24%.
Faculty: Student/faculty ratio 17:1. 61 full-time faculty, 66% hold PhDs, 8% are members of minority groups, 33% are women.

ACADEMICS

Degrees: Associate, bachelor's, certificate, master's. **Classes:** Most classes have 10–19 students. **Majors with Highest Enrollment:** Business, management, marketing, and related support services, other; health professions and related clinical sciences, other; multi-/interdisciplinary studies, other. **Special Study Options:** Accelerated program, cooperative education program, distance learning, double major, English as a Second Language (ESL), independent study, internships, weekend college. **Career services:** Alumni services, career/job search classes, career assessment.

FACILITIES

Housing: 100% of campus accessible to physically disabled. **Computers:** 100% of classrooms, 100% of libraries, have wireless network access. Students can register for classes online. Administrative functions (other than registration) can be performed online.

CAMPUS LIFE

Environment: City. **Activities:** Literary magazine. **Organizations:** 1 honor societies. **Environmental Initiatives:** Reduction in energy usage; recycling programs.

ADMISSIONS

Freshman Academic Profile: Minimum paper TOEFL 500. Minimum computer TOEFL 173. **Basis for Candidate Selection:** *Important factors considered include:* Interview, level of applicant's interest. **Freshman Admission Requirements:** High school diploma is required and GED is accepted. **Freshman Admission Statistics:** 210 applied, 79% admitted, 94% enrolled. **Transfer Admission Requirements:** High school transcript, essay or personal statement, Lowest grade transferable C. **General Admission Information:** Application fee $20. Nonfall registration accepted. Admission may be deferred for a maximum of 1 year. Credit offered for CEEB Advanced Placement tests.

COSTS AND FINANCIAL AID

Required Forms and Deadlines: FAFSA. **Types of Aid:** *Need-based scholarships/grants:* Federal Pell, SEOG, state scholarships/grants, private scholarships, the school's own gift aid. *Loans:* FFEL Subsidized Stafford, FFEL Unsubsidized Stafford, FFEL PLUS. **Student Employment:** Federal Work-Study Program available. Institutional employment available. Off-campus job opportunities are good. **Financial Aid Statistics:** 72% freshmen, 78% undergrads receive need-based scholarship or grant aid. 33% freshmen, 55% undergrads receive non-need-based scholarship or grant aid. 69% freshmen, 76% undergrads receive need-based self-help aid. 81% undergrads borrow to pay for school. Average cumulative indebtedness $18,100. **Criteria for awarding institutional aid:** *Non-need-based:* Academics, leadership.

HOFSTRA UNIVERSITY

100 Hofstra University, Bernon Hall, Hempstead, NY 11549
Phone: 516-463-6700 **Financial Aid Phone:** 516-463-8000
E-mail: admission@hofstra.edu **CEEB Code:** 2295
Fax: 516-463-5100 **Website:** www.hofstra.edu/Admission/ **ACT Code:** 2760

This private school was founded in 1935. It has a 240-acre campus.

RATINGS
Admissions Selectivity Rating: 87   **Fire Safety Rating:** 92   **Green Rating:** 82

STUDENTS AND FACULTY

Enrollment: 7,756. **Student Body:** 52% female, 48% male, 36% out-of-state, 2% international (70 countries represented). Asian 5%, African American 9%, Caucasian 65%, Hispanic 9%.
Retention and Graduation: 76% freshmen return for sophomore year. 41% freshmen graduate within 4 years. 30% grads go on to further study within 1 year. 9% grads pursue arts and sciences degrees. 4% grads pursue law degrees. 4% grads pursue business degrees. 1% grads pursue medical degrees. **Faculty:** Student/faculty ratio 14:1. 544 full-time faculty, 91% hold PhDs, 17% are members of minority groups, 40% are women.

ACADEMICS

Degrees: Bachelor's, certificate, doctoral, master's, post-bachelor's certificate, post-master's certificate. **Classes:** Most classes have 10–19 students. Most lab/discussion sessions have 10–19 students. **Majors with Highest Enrollment:** Business administration and management; marketing/marketing management; psychology. **Special Study Options:** Accelerated program, cross-registration, distance learning, double major, dual enrollment, English as a Second Language (ESL), external degree program, honors program, independent study, internships, liberal arts/career combination, student-designed major, study abroad, teacher certification program. **Honors programs:** Hofstra University's Honors College (HUHC) is the leading edge of Hofstra University's pursuit of academic excellence. Serving the highly motivated, high achieving student, every aspect of its curriculum is designed to provide them with the resources they need to meet their academic objectives. Combining the support of a strong community with the freedom to pursue individual goals HUHC emphasizes student ownership and direction of their own education. At the same time, HUHC recognizes its responsibility to support students so that they can explore, reflect upon and achieve their educational objectives. HUHC is an intimate community of students, faculty and administrators committed to challenging and supporting one another in the pursuit of excellence at all levels. Its students are connected to every college, department, major and program on campus and engaged in every aspect of campus life. All entering HUHC students begin their Hofstra careers with Culture and Expression (C&E) a four-course, year-long sequence designed specifically for the honors college community. C&E is our primary tool for establishing a community among the students of each entering class. Together, they follow a common reading list, attend common lectures and take ownership of the materials via small group discussions with some of Hofstra's best faculty. C&E addresses life's biggest questions with rigor. Most importantly, it provides a broad foundation for a lifetime of learning in college and beyond. After the first year, Honors College students pursue honors work in those Hofstra courses that they find most exciting. Each semester HUHC offers an array of small, discussion based seminars, taught by professors from around the university, who are invited to offer their dream course. In addition, HUHC's Honors Option program allows students to enrich regular courses that align with their personal and intellectual passions. These honors experiences are all recognized on the transcript and count toward completion of an HUHC designation which is applied to both the student's transcript and diploma. Thus, HUHC students may choose from among any of Hofstra's more than 145 undergraduate majors and upon graduation receive a bachelor's degree with a special designation marking it as having been achieved with an extraordinary level of distinction. HUHC sponsors a rich array of cultural and social experiences, including trips to New York City to visit museums, Broadway shows, concerts, and major league sporting events. Given our location, HUHC faculty mentors regularly organize outdoor adventures, such as sea kayaking, hiking and visits to ocean beaches. A significant percentage of HUHC students participate in a variety of HUHC-based social service programs, including those focused on serving the homeless, promoting early literacy and working toward environmental responsibility. HUHC students can be found in leadership roles in virtually every club and activity on the Hofstra campus. They are student government leaders, newspaper editors, and champions of social and political causes. They are committed to the arts and to sports (including Division I) and can be found in just about every form of meaningful activity imaginable. They come from across the United States, and increasingly from abroad. Most of all, they are curious about one another and the wider world. Many HUHC students opt to live in honors housing, where they enjoy an even greater sense of community and an exceptional level of support from a professional staff and specially selected student leaders. HUHC graduates have won prestigious grants and fellowships such as the Fulbright, the National Science Fellowship, and the Jack Kent Cooke fellowship. They've also been admitted to the most prestigious graduate and professional schools. Hofstra University also recognizes high-achieving students in many other ways, including Dean's List, Provost's Scholars, Phi Beta Kappa, Phi Eta Sigma, Golden Key, and the chance to earn baccalaureate degrees with distinction and departmental honors. **Combined degree programs:** BA/JD, BBA/MS, BBA/MBA. Special programs offered to physically disabled students include note-taking services, reader services, tape recorders, tutors. **Career services:** Alumni network, alumni services, career/job search classes, career assessment, internships. **Career services highlights include:** Comprehensive on-campus job fairs and recruiting program including internship opportunities for all majors with Fortune 500, media outlets, government, law, not-for-profit, and education, many of which lead to job opportunities for graduates.

FACILITIES

Housing: Coed dorms, special housing for disabled students, apartments for single students, theme housing, living-learning center, honors housing, quiet floors, and women's floors. 100% of campus accessible to physically disabled. **Special Academic Facilities/Equipment:** New state-of-the-art medical school, financial trading room, multi-media converged news room, comprehensive media production facility including a 24 hour radio station, linux beowolf cluster, digital language lab, technology, science and engineering labs, a rooftop observatory, 6 theaters including a black box teaching theater, assessment centers for client observation and counseling, child care institute, cultural center,

museum, arboretum, and bird sanctuary. **Computers:** 57% of classrooms, 100% of dorms, 100% of libraries, 100% of dining areas, 100% of student union, 60% of common outdoor areas have wireless network access. Students can register for classes online. Administrative functions (other than registration) can be performed online.

CAMPUS LIFE

Environment: City. **Activities:** Choral groups, concert band, dance, drama/theater, jazz band, literary magazine, music ensembles, musical theater, opera, pep band, radio station, student government, student newspaper, student-run film society, symphony orchestra, television station, yearbook, campus ministries, international student organization. **Organizations:** 135 registered organizations, 32 honor societies, 9 religious organizations. 13 fraternities, 12 sororities. **Athletics (Intercollegiate):** *Men:* Baseball, basketball, cross-country, golf, lacrosse, soccer, tennis, wrestling. *Women:* Basketball, cross-country, field hockey, golf, lacrosse, soccer, softball, tennis, volleyball. **Environmental Initiatives:** Use of green power/products—The university increased its purchase of green power to 6% of campus load and has recently undertaken the purchasing of green products that consider environmental impacts. The university uses only Green Seal-certified custodial supplies, and purchases Energy Star qualified Products including computers, monitors, copy machines, air conditioners and other appliances. The university no longer purchases/uses polystyrene products (Styrofoam), instead choosing products that may be recycled. The University Senate's Environmental Priorities Committee has undertaken to promote sustainability in all sectors of the university–from governance and operations to curriculum and outreach–through education, communication, research and professional development. A recent recommendation by this committee resulted in Hofstra University becoming a charter member of the Association for the Advancement of Sustainability in Higher Education (AASHE), an organization of colleges and universities in the United States and Canada working to create a sustainable future. The university's cogeneration plant provides the simultaneous energy-efficient generation of both electricity and useful heat for campus services. The university cogeneration engines produce 2,300 kilowatts of electricity per hour (equivalent to the electrical needs for 2,064 average residential customers annually). The corresponding residual heat from these engines is efficiently used to support campus heating. In 2007, the cogeneration plant supplied over 27% of the university's energy demand.

ADMISSIONS

Freshman Academic Profile: Average high school GPA 3.4. 31% in top 10% of high school class, 59% in top 25% of high school class, 87% in top 50% of high school class. SAT Math middle 50% range 560–640. SAT Critical Reading middle 50% range 540–630. ACT middle 50% range 24–28. Minimum paper TOEFL 550. Minimum computer TOEFL 213. Minimum web-based TOEFL 80. **Basis for Candidate Selection:** *Very important factors considered include:* Class rank, application essay, academic GPA, recommendation(s), rigor of secondary school record, standardized test scores. *Important factors considered include:* Character/personal qualities, extracurricular activities, interview, talent/ability. *Other factors considered include:* Alumni/ae relation, geographical residence, level of applicant's interest, racial/ethnic status, volunteer work, work experience. **Freshman Admission Requirements:** High school diploma is required and GED is accepted. *Academic units required:* 4 English, 3 mathematics, 3 science, (1 science labs), 2 foreign language, 3 social studies. *Academic units recommended:* 4 mathematics, 4 science, (2 science labs), 3 foreign language, 4 social studies. **Freshman Admission Statistics:** 20,829 applied, 57% admitted, 13% enrolled. **Transfer Admission Requirements:** College transcript(s), statement of good standing from prior institution(s). Lowest grade transferable C–. **General Admission Information:** Application fee $70. Notification on a rolling basis, beginning on or about 2/1. Nonfall registration accepted. Admission may be deferred for a maximum of 1 year. Credit and/or placement offered for CEEB Advanced Placement tests.

COSTS AND FINANCIAL AID

Annual tuition $29,080. Room and board $11,330. Required fees $1,050. Average book expense $1,000. **Required Forms and Deadlines:** FAFSA, state aid form. Priority financial aid filing date 2/15. **Notification of Awards:** Applicants will be notified of awards on a rolling basis beginning 3/1. **Types of Aid:** *Need-based scholarships/grants:* Federal Pell, SEOG, state scholarships/grants, private scholarships, the school's own gift aid, ACG & SMART. *Loans:* FFEL Subsidized Stafford, FFEL Unsubsidized Stafford, FFEL PLUS, Federal Perkins, college/university loans from institutional funds. **Student Employment:** Federal Work-Study Program available. Institutional employment available. Highest amount earned per year from on-campus jobs $22,795. Off-campus job opportunities are excellent. **Financial Aid Statistics:** 56% freshmen, 49% undergrads receive need-based scholarship or grant aid. 7% freshmen, 5% undergrads receive non-need-based scholarship or grant aid. 52% freshmen, 49% undergrads receive need-based self-help aid. 1% freshmen, 1% undergrads receive athletic scholarships. 91% freshmen, 84% undergrads receive any aid. 64% undergrads borrow to pay for school. **Criteria for awarding institutional aid:** *Non-need-based:* Academics, alumni affiliation, art, athletics, leadership, music/drama, state/district residency.

See page 1112.

HOLLINS UNIVERSITY

PO Box 9707, Roanoke, VA 24020-1707
Phone: 540-362-6401 **Financial Aid Phone:** 540-362-6332
E-mail: huadm@hollins.edu **CEEB Code:** 5294
Fax: 540-362-6218 **Website:** www.hollins.edu **ACT Code:** 4360

This private school was founded in 1842. It has a 475-acre campus.

RATINGS
Admissions Selectivity Rating: 83 **Fire Safety Rating:** 71 **Green Rating:** 84

STUDENTS AND FACULTY
Enrollment: 775. **Student Body:** 100% female, 44% out-of-state, 4% international (22 countries represented). Asian 2%, African American 8%, Caucasian 82%, Hispanic 4%, Native American 1%.
Retention and Graduation: 76% freshmen return for sophomore year. 60% freshmen graduate within 4 years. 25% grads go on to further study within 1 year. 1% grads pursue law degrees. 2% grads pursue medical degrees. **Faculty:** Student/faculty ratio 11:1. 72 full-time faculty, 97% hold PhDs, 10% are members of minority groups, 46% are women.

ACADEMICS
Degrees: Bachelor's, master's, post-bachelor's certificate, post-master's certificate. **Classes:** Most classes have 10–19 students. Most lab/discussion sessions have 10–19 students. **Majors with Highest Enrollment:** Business/commerce; English language and literature; psychology. **Special Study Options:** Accelerated program, cross-registration, double major, dual enrollment, exchange student program (domestic), independent study, internships, student-designed major, study abroad, teacher certification program. **Honors programs:** A number of university departments offer honors programs. The specific nature of departmental honors varies from department to department. The programs, which are undertaken for at least the full senior year, may involve research, theses, oral or written examinations, seminars, reading programs, or any combination thereof. Special programs offered to physically disabled students include tape recorders. **Career services:** Alumni network, alumni services, career/job search classes, career assessment, internships, regional alumni.

FACILITIES
Housing: Special housing for disabled students, women's dorms, apartments for single students, wellness housing, theme housing. 38% of campus accessible to physically disabled. **Special Academic Facilities/Equipment:** Athletic complex, a writing center, language labs, campus-wide computer network, scientific equipment and instrumentation, art museum, and a state-of-the-art library. **Computers:** 90% of classrooms, 100% of dorms, 100% of libraries, 100% of dining areas, 100% of student union, 100% of common outdoor areas have wireless network access. Students can register for classes online. Administrative functions (other than registration) can be performed online.

CAMPUS LIFE
Environment: City. **Activities:** Choral groups, dance, drama/theater, literary magazine, music ensembles, musical theater, student government, student newspaper, student-run film society, television station, yearbook, campus ministries, international student organization, Model UN. **Organizations:** 28 registered organizations, 15 honor societies, 5 religious organizations. **Athletics (Intercollegiate):** *Women:* Basketball, equestrian sports, golf, lacrosse, soccer, swimming, tennis. **On-Campus Highlights:** Front Quadrangle, Wetherill Visual Arts Center and Wilson Museum, Wyndham Robertson Library, Moody Center, Gymnasium, Northen Swim Center, Tayloe Fitness Center. **Environmental Initiatives:** Signing the President's Climate Agreement; campus-wide recycling program; completed a strategic plan (April 2009) with target of 3% annual reduction of green gasses for 5 years.

ADMISSIONS
Freshman Academic Profile: Average high school GPA 3.5. 23% in top 10% of high school class, 55% in top 25% of high school class, 73% in top 50% of high school class. 85% from public high schools. SAT Math middle 50% range 450–570. SAT Critical Reading middle 50% range 510–660. SAT Writing middle 50% range 500–620. ACT middle 50% range 22–28. Minimum paper TOEFL 550. Minimum computer TOEFL 213. Minimum web-based TOEFL 79. **Basis for Candidate Selection:** *Very important factors considered include:* Academic GPA, standardized test scores. *Important factors considered include:* Application essay, recommendation(s), talent/ability. *Other factors considered include:* Class rank, rigor of secondary school record, alumni/ae relation, charac-

ter/personal qualities, extracurricular activities, first generation, interview, level of applicant's interest, volunteer work, work experience. **Freshman Admission Requirements:** High school diploma is required and GED is accepted. *Academic units required:* 4 English, 3 mathematics, 3 science, 3 foreign language, 3 social studies. **Freshman Admission Statistics:** 693 applied, 90% admitted, 32% enrolled. **Transfer Admission Requirements:** High school transcript, college transcript(s), essay or personal statement, minimum college GPA of 2.5 required. Lowest grade transferable C. **General Admission Information:** Application fee $40. Early decision application deadline 12/1. Notification on a rolling basis, beginning on or about 12/15. Nonfall registration accepted. Admission may be deferred for a maximum of usually one year. Credit and/or placement offered for CEEB Advanced Placement tests.

COSTS AND FINANCIAL AID
Required Forms and Deadlines: FAFSA, state aid form. Priority financial aid filing date 2/15. **Notification of Awards:** Applicants will be notified of awards on a rolling basis beginning 3/1. **Types of Aid:** *Need-based scholarships/grants:* Federal Pell, SEOG, state scholarships/grants, private scholarships, the school's own gift aid. *Loans:* Direct Subsidized Stafford, Direct Unsubsidized Stafford, Direct PLUS, Federal Perkins, college/university loans from institutional funds, PLATO, CitiAssist, SallieMae, Nelnet, Campus Door. **Student Employment:** Federal Work-Study Program available. Institutional employment available. Highest amount earned per year from on-campus jobs $3,067. Off-campus job opportunities are good. **Financial Aid Statistics:** 76% freshmen, 79% undergrads receive need-based scholarship or grant aid. 55% freshmen, 43% undergrads receive non-need-based scholarship or grant aid. 71% freshmen, 74% undergrads receive need-based self-help aid. 99% freshmen, 94% undergrads receive any aid. 83% undergrads borrow to pay for school. Average cumulative indebtedness $24,002. **Criteria for awarding institutional aid:** *Non-need-based:* Academics, alumni affiliation, art, leadership, music/drama, state/district residency.

HOLY FAMILY UNIVERSITY

9801 Frankford Avenue, Philadephia, PA 19114-2009
Phone: 215-637-3050 **Financial Aid Phone:** 215-637-5538
E-mail: admissions@holyfamily.edu gradstudy@holyfamily.edu **CEEB Code:** 2297
Fax: 215-281-1022 **Website:** www.holyfamily.edu **ACT Code:** 3592

This private school, affiliated with the Roman Catholic Church, was founded in 1954. It has a 46-acre campus.

RATINGS
Admissions Selectivity Rating: 72 **Fire Safety Rating:** 86 **Green Rating:** 60*

STUDENTS AND FACULTY
Enrollment: 2,123. **Student Body:** 76% female, 24% male, 6% out-of-state, 1% international (9 countries represented). Asian 5%, African American 8%, Caucasian 73%, Hispanic 3%.
Retention and Graduation: 85% freshmen return for sophomore year. 52% freshmen graduate within 4 years. 9% grads go on to further study within 1 year. 3% grads pursue arts and sciences degrees. 2% grads pursue business degrees. **Faculty:** Student/faculty ratio 15:1. 99 full-time faculty, 69% hold PhDs, 12% are members of minority groups, 65% are women.

ACADEMICS
Degrees: Associate, bachelor's, certificate, master's, post-bachelor's certificate. **Classes:** Most classes have 10–19 students. **Majors with Highest Enrollment:** Business administration and management; elementary education and teaching; nursing/registered nurse (RN, ASN, BSN, MSN). **Special Study Options:** Accelerated program, cooperative education program, double major, dual enrollment, English as a Second Language (ESL), independent study, internships, study abroad, teacher certification program Special programs offered to physically disabled students include note-taking services, reader services, tape recorders, tutors. **Career services:** Alumni services, career/job search classes, career assessment, internships. **Career services highlights include:** Our Co-op Program. Refer to website for more details.

FACILITIES
Housing: Coed dorms, 100% of campus accessible to physically disabled. **Special Academic Facilities/Equipment:** On-campus nursery school, art gallery. **Computers:** 100% of classrooms, 100% of dorms, 100% of libraries, 100% of dining areas, 100% of student union, 100% of common outdoor areas have wireless network access. Students can register for classes online. Administrative functions (other than registration) can be performed online.

CAMPUS LIFE
Environment: Metropolis. **Activities:** Choral groups, drama/theater, literary magazine, radio station, student government, student newspaper, television

The Princeton Review's Complete Book of Colleges

station, yearbook, campus ministries, international student organization. **Organizations:** 15 registered organizations, 14 honor societies, 1 religious organizations. **Athletics (Intercollegiate):** *Men:* Basketball, cross-country, golf, soccer, track/field (outdoor), track/field (indoor). *Women:* Basketball, cross-country, lacrosse, soccer, softball, tennis, track/field (outdoor), track/field (indoor), volleyball. **On-Campus Highlights:** Campus Center, Education/Technology Center, Library, Student Residence Halls, Nurse Education Building.

ADMISSIONS

Freshman Academic Profile: Average high school GPA 3.01. 11% in top 10% of high school class, 33% in top 25% of high school class, 95% in top 50% of high school class. 39% from public high schools. SAT Math middle 50% range 420–510. SAT Critical Reading middle 50% range 430–510. ACT middle 50% range 19–20. Minimum paper TOEFL 550. **Basis for Candidate Selection:** *Very important factors considered include:* Class rank, rigor of secondary school record, interview. *Important factors considered include:* Academic GPA, standardized test scores, alumni/ae relation, character/personal qualities, level of applicant's interest. *Other factors considered include:* Application essay, recommendation(s), extracurricular activities, talent/ability, volunteer work, work experience. **Freshman Admission Requirements:** High school diploma is required and GED is accepted. *Academic units required:* 4 English, 3 mathematics, 2 science, 2 history, 3 academic electives. *Academic units recommended:* 2 foreign language. **Freshman Admission Statistics:** 1,097 applied, 63% admitted, 43% enrolled. **Transfer Admission Requirements:** High school transcript, college transcript(s), essay or personal statement, statement of good standing from prior institution(s). Minimum college GPA of 2.5 required. Lowest grade transferable C. **General Admission Information:** Application fee $25. Nonfall registration not accepted. Admission may be deferred for a maximum of 1 year. Neither credit nor placement offered for CEEB Advanced Placement tests.

COSTS AND FINANCIAL AID

Annual tuition $20,990. Room and board $9,400. Required fees $600. Average book expense $972. **Required Forms and Deadlines:** FAFSA, institution's own financial aid form. Priority financial aid filing date 3/1. **Notification of Awards:** Applicants will be notified of awards on a rolling basis beginning 4/1. **Types of Aid:** *Need-based scholarships/grants:* Federal Pell, SEOG, state scholarships/grants, private scholarships, the school's own gift aid. *Loans:* FFEL Subsidized Stafford, FFEL Unsubsidized Stafford, FFEL PLUS, Federal Perkins, Federal Nursing, college/university loans from institutional funds. **Student Employment:** Federal Work-Study Program available. Off-campus job opportunities are excellent. **Financial Aid Statistics:** 83% freshmen, 79% undergrads receive need-based scholarship or grant aid. 12% freshmen, 9% undergrads receive non-need-based scholarship or grant aid. 67% freshmen, 67% undergrads receive need-based self-help aid. 2% freshmen, 3% undergrads receive athletic scholarships. 99% freshmen, 86% undergrads receive any aid. 70% undergrads borrow to pay for school. Average cumulative indebtedness $10,023. **Criteria for awarding institutional aid:** *Non-need-based:* Academics, alumni affiliation, athletics.

HOLY NAMES UNIVERSITY

3500 Mountain Boulevard, Oakland, CA 94619-1699
Phone: 510-436-1351
E-mail: admissions@hnu.edu **CEEB Code:** 4059
Fax: 510-436-1325 **Website:** www.hnu.edu **ACT Code:** 230

This private school, affiliated with the Roman Catholic Church, was founded in 1868. It has a 60-acre campus.

RATINGS

Admissions Selectivity Rating: 76   **Fire Safety Rating:** 60*   **Green Rating:** 60*

STUDENTS AND FACULTY

Enrollment: 592. **Student Body:** 78% female, 22% male, 4% out-of-state, 3% international (25 countries represented). Asian 6%, African American 32%, Caucasian 28%, Hispanic 16%, Native American 1%.
Retention and Graduation: 62% freshmen return for sophomore year. 30% freshmen graduate within 4 years. **Faculty:** Student/faculty ratio 12:1. 31 full-time faculty, 90% hold PhDs, 23% are members of minority groups, 68% are women.

ACADEMICS

Degrees: Bachelor's, master's, post-bachelor's certificate. **Classes:** Most classes have 10–19 students. Most lab/discussion sessions have 10–19 students. **Majors with Highest Enrollment:** Business/commerce; nursing/registered nurse (RN, ASN, BSN, MSN); psychology. **Special Study Options:** Accelerated program, cross-registration, distance learning, double major, English as a Second Language (ESL), exchange student program (domestic), independent study, internships, liberal arts/career combination, student-designed major, study abroad, teacher certification program, weekend college, academic remediating, independent study, learning disabled services, off campus study. **Combined degree programs:** BA/MA. Special programs offered to physically disabled students include note-taking services, tape recorders, tutors. **Career services:** Alumni network, alumni services, career/job search classes, career assessment, internships, regional alumni. **Career services highlights include:** Assistance is available for researching and obtaining positions in business, government, education and non- profits All students are encouraged to enhance their professional development. They can earn a maximum of 6 units for internship credit.

FACILITIES

Housing: Coed dorms, Single sex floor and wings. 30% of campus accessible to physically disabled. **Special Academic Facilities/Equipment:** Valley Center for the Performing Arts and the J.D. Kennedy Arts Center Gallery.

CAMPUS LIFE

Environment: Metropolis. **Activities:** Choral groups, drama/theater, music ensembles, student government, symphony orchestra. **Organizations:** 16 registered organizations, 11 honor societies, 1 religious organizations. **Athletics (Intercollegiate):** *Men:* Basketball, cross-country, golf, soccer. *Women:* Basketball, cross-country, soccer, volleyball. **On-Campus Highlights:** Green Banana Cafe, Gym, Soda Commons, Cafeteria, Valley Center for Performing Arts.

ADMISSIONS

Freshman Academic Profile: Average high school GPA 3.22. 12% in top 10% of high school class, 40% in top 25% of high school class, 79% in top 50% of high school class. 62% from public high schools. SAT Math middle 50% range 440–540. SAT Critical Reading middle 50% range 450–510. ACT middle 50% range 16–23. Minimum paper TOEFL 490. Minimum computer TOEFL 163. **Basis for Candidate Selection:** *Very important factors considered include:* Rigor of secondary school record. *Important factors considered include:* Application essay, recommendation(s), standardized test scores. *Other factors considered include:* Class rank, alumni/ae relation, character/personal qualities, extracurricular activities, interview, talent/ability, volunteer work, work experience. **Freshman Admission Requirements:** High school diploma is required and GED is accepted. *Academic units required:* 4 English, 3 mathematics, 1 science, (1 science labs), 2 foreign language, 1 history, 4 academic electives. *Academic units recommended:* 3 foreign language. **Freshman Admission Statistics:** 211 applied, 62% admitted, 44% enrolled. **Transfer Admission Requirements:** College transcript(s), essay or personal statement, statement of good standing from prior institution(s). Minimum college GPA of 2.2 required. Lowest grade transferable C–. **General Admission Information:** Application fee $35. Regular application deadline 8/1. Notification on a rolling basis, beginning on or about 10/1. Nonfall registration accepted. Admission may be deferred for a maximum of 1 year. Credit offered for CEEB Advanced Placement tests.

COSTS AND FINANCIAL AID

Annual tuition $19,970. . Room and board $7,800. Required fees $210. Average book expense $946. **Required Forms and Deadlines:** FAFSA, institution's own financial aid form, state aid form. Priority financial aid filing date 3/2. **Notification of Awards:** Applicants will be notified of awards on a rolling basis beginning 4/1. **Types of Aid:** *Need-based scholarships/grants:* Federal Pell, SEOG, state scholarships/grants, private scholarships, the school's own gift aid. *Loans:* FFEL Subsidized Stafford, FFEL Unsubsidized Stafford, FFEL PLUS, Federal Perkins, alternative loans. **Student Employment:** Federal Work-Study Program available. Institutional employment available. Off-campus job opportunities are good. **Financial Aid Statistics:** 74% freshmen, 66% undergrads receive need-based scholarship or grant aid. 79% freshmen, 54% undergrads receive non-need-based scholarship or grant aid. 79% freshmen, 66% undergrads receive need-based self-help aid. 42% freshmen, 20% undergrads receive athletic scholarships. 79% freshmen, 57% undergrads receive any aid. 95% undergrads borrow to pay for school. Average cumulative indebtedness $21,000. **Criteria for awarding institutional aid:** *Non-need-based:* Academics, alumni affiliation, athletics, leadership, music/drama, religious affiliation.

HOOD COLLEGE

401 Rosemont Avenue, Frederick, MD 21701
Phone: 301-696-3400 **Financial Aid Phone:** 301-696-3411
E-mail: admissions@hood.edu **CEEB Code:** 5296
Fax: 301-696-3819 **Website:** www.hood.edu **ACT Code:** 1702

This private school, affiliated with the United Church of Christ Church, was founded in 1893. It has a 50-acre campus.

RATINGS
Admissions Selectivity Rating: 80   **Fire Safety Rating:** 82   **Green Rating:** 67

STUDENTS AND FACULTY
Enrollment: 1,363. **Student Body:** 68% female, 32% male, 19% out-of-state, 2% international (40 countries represented). Asian 2%, African American 11%, Caucasian 73%, Hispanic 4%.
Retention and Graduation: 85% freshmen return for sophomore year. 61% freshmen graduate within 4 years. 40% grads go on to further study within 1 year. 25% grads pursue arts and sciences degrees. 2% grads pursue law degrees. 9% grads pursue business degrees. 1% grads pursue medical degrees. **Faculty:** Student/faculty ratio 12:1. 80 full-time faculty, 98% hold PhDs, 13% are members of minority groups, 59% are women.

ACADEMICS
Degrees: Bachelor's, master's, post-bachelor's certificate. **Classes:** Most classes have 10–19 students. Most lab/discussion sessions have 10–19 students. **Majors with Highest Enrollment:** Biology/biological sciences; business administration and management; psychology. **Special Study Options:** Double major, dual enrollment, honors program, independent study, internships, liberal arts/career combination, student-designed major, study abroad, teacher certification program. **Honors programs:** Our award-winning program offers exceptional undergraduate students four years of exciting coursework and co-curriucular activities. Classes are small, discussion oriented, and enhanced by guest speakers and field trips. Interdisciplinary in approach, students are encouraged to engage in personal and intellectual development in the context of community memebership and service. **Combined degree programs:** BA biology/MS biomed sci with Montgomery CC. Special programs offered to physically disabled students include note-taking services, reader services, tape recorders, tutors. **Career services:** Alumni network, alumni services, career assessment, internships, regional alumni. **Career services highlights include:** Hood College has a very active internship program. In 2008–2009,more than 100 students completed internships at a variety of sites throughout the Baltimore/Washington/Frederick area.,

FACILITIES
Housing: Coed dorms, women's dorms, theme housing 30% of campus accessible to physically disabled. **Special Academic Facilities/Equipment:** Art gallery, child development lab, language lab, observatory, science labs. **Computers:** 100% of classrooms, 100% of dorms, 100% of libraries, 100% of dining areas, 100% of student union, 100% of common outdoor areas have wireless network access. Students can register for classes online. Administrative functions (other than registration) can be performed online.

CAMPUS LIFE
Environment: Town. **Activities:** Choral groups, dance, drama/theater, jazz band, literary magazine, music ensembles, musical theater, radio station, student government, student newspaper, student-run film society, campus ministries, international student organization, Model UN. **Organizations:** 92 registered organizations, 14 honor societies, 6 religious organizations. **Athletics (Intercollegiate):** *Men:* Basketball, cross-country, golf, lacrosse, soccer, swimming, tennis, track/field (outdoor). *Women:* Basketball, cross-country, field hockey, golf, lacrosse, soccer, softball, swimming, tennis, track/field (outdoor), volleyball. **On-Campus Highlights:** Whitaker Campus Center, Hodson Science and Technology Building, Coblentz Dining Hall, Beneficial-Hodson Library, The Residence Halls.

ADMISSIONS
Freshman Academic Profile: Average high school GPA 3.52. 20% in top 10% of high school class, 51% in top 25% of high school class, 85% in top 50% of high school class. 79% from public high schools. SAT Math middle 50% range 570–590. SAT Critical Reading middle 50% range 490–600. SAT Writing middle 50% range 480–600. ACT middle 50% range 20–25. Minimum paper TOEFL 550. Minimum computer TOEFL 213. Minimum web-based TOEFL 79. **Basis for Candidate Selection:** *Very important factors considered include:* Academic GPA, rigor of secondary school record. *Important factors considered include:* Standardized test scores. *Other factors considered include:* Class rank, application essay, recommendation(s), alumni/ae relation, extracurricular activities, first generation, interview, level of applicant's interest. **Freshman Admission Requirements:** High school diploma is required and GED is accepted. *Academic units required:* 4 English, 3 mathematics, 3 science, (2 science labs), 2 foreign language, 2 social studies, 1 history, 1 academic electives. *Academic units recommended:* 4 mathematics. **Freshman Admission Statistics:** 1,622 applied, 72% admitted, 22% enrolled. **Transfer Admission Requirements:** College transcript(s), minimum college GPA of 2.5 required. Lowest grade transferable C–. **General Admission Information:** Application fee $35. Notification on a rolling basis, beginning on or about 12/1. Nonfall registration accepted. Admission may be deferred for a maximum of 1 year. Credit and/or placement offered for CEEB Advanced Placement tests.

COSTS AND FINANCIAL AID
Required Forms and Deadlines: FAFSA. Priority financial aid filing date 2/15. **Notification of Awards:** Applicants will be notified of awards on a rolling basis beginning 2/15. **Types of Aid:** *Need-based scholarships/grants:* Federal Pell, SEOG, state scholarships/grants, private scholarships, the school's own gift aid. *Loans:* Direct Subsidized Stafford, Direct Unsubsidized Stafford, Direct PLUS, FFEL Subsidized Stafford, FFEL Unsubsidized Stafford, FFEL PLUS, Federal Perkins. **Student Employment:** Federal Work-Study Program available. Institutional employment available. Highest amount earned per year from on-campus jobs $1,800. Off-campus job opportunities are good. **Financial Aid Statistics:** 76% freshmen, 81% undergrads receive need-based scholarship or grant aid. 19% freshmen, 15% undergrads receive non-need-based scholarship or grant aid. 58% freshmen, 64% undergrads receive need-based self-help aid. 96% freshmen, 94% undergrads receive any aid. 64% undergrads borrow to pay for school. Average cumulative indebtedness $17,382. **Criteria for awarding institutional aid:** *Non-need-based:* Academics, alumni affiliation, music/drama.

HOPE COLLEGE

69 East 10th, Holland, MI 49422-9000
Phone: 616-395-7850 **Financial Aid Phone:** 616-395-7765
E-mail: admissions@hope.edu **CEEB Code:** 1301
Fax: 616-395-7130 **Website:** www.hope.edu **ACT Code:** 2012

This private school, affiliated with the Reformed Church Church, was founded in 1862. It has a 120-acre campus.

RATINGS
Admissions Selectivity Rating: 84   **Fire Safety Rating:** 76   **Green Rating:** 78

STUDENTS AND FACULTY
Enrollment: 3,153. **Student Body:** 60% female, 40% male, 31% out-of-state, 1% international (28 countries represented). Asian 2%, African American 2%, Caucasian 89%, Hispanic 4%.
Retention and Graduation: 88% freshmen return for sophomore year. 66% freshmen graduate within 4 years. 33.3% grads go on to further study within 1 year. 17.7% grads pursue arts and sciences degrees. 0.3% grads pursue law degrees. 1.7% grads pursue business degrees. 11.6% grads pursue medical degrees. **Faculty:** Student/faculty ratio 12:1. 230 full-time faculty, 78% hold PhDs, 10% are members of minority groups, 45% are women.

ACADEMICS
Degrees: Bachelor's. **Classes:** Most classes have 10–19 students. Most lab/discussion sessions have 20–29 students. **Majors with Highest Enrollment:** Business/commerce; communication studies/speech communication and rhetoric; English language and literature. **Special Study Options:** Distance learning, double major, English as a Second Language (ESL), independent study, internships, student-designed major, study abroad, teacher certification program Special programs offered to physically disabled students include note-taking services, reader services, tape recorders, tutors. **Career services:** Alumni network, alumni services, career/job search classes, career assessment, internships, regional alumni. **Career services highlights include:** Hope has an extensive undergraduate research program engaging more than 200 students each summer.

FACILITIES
Housing: Coed dorms, special housing for disabled students, men's dorms, special housing for international students, women's dorms, fraternity/sorority housing, apartments for single students, wellness housing, theme housing. 95% of campus accessible to physically disabled. **Special Academic Facilities/Equipment:** Art gallery, particle accelerator, computational chemistry lab, electron microscopes, spectrometers, ultracentrifuge, observatory, new $38M science building. **Computers:** 70% of classrooms, 100% of libraries, 34% of dining areas, 100% of student union, 40% of common outdoor areas have wireless network access. Students can register for classes online. Administrative functions (other than registration) can be performed online.

CAMPUS LIFE
Environment: Town. **Activities:** Choral groups, concert band, dance, drama/theater, jazz band, literary magazine, music ensembles, radio station,

student government, student newspaper, symphony orchestra, television station, yearbook, campus ministries, international student organization, Model UN. **Organizations:** 67 registered organizations, 22 honor societies, 6 religious organizations. 6 fraternities, 7 sororities. **Athletics (Intercollegiate):** *Men:* Baseball, basketball, cheerleading, cross-country, diving, football, golf, soccer, swimming, tennis, track/field (outdoor), track/field (indoor). *Women:* Basketball, cheerleading, cross-country, diving, golf, soccer, softball, swimming, tennis, track/field (outdoor), track/field (indoor), volleyball. **On-Campus Highlights:** DeWitt Student Center, Martha Miller Center for Global Communic, Library, Paul A Schaap Science Center, DeVos Fieldhouse, Kletz—student grill. **Environmental Initiatives:** Electrical use reduction, water use reduction, expanded recycling.

ADMISSIONS

Freshman Academic Profile: Average high school GPA 3.72. 34% in top 10% of high school class, 63% in top 25% of high school class, 91% in top 50% of high school class. 88% from public high schools. SAT Math middle 50% range 520–660. SAT Writing middle 50% range 540–670. ACT middle 50% range 23–29. Minimum paper TOEFL 550. Minimum computer TOEFL 213. Minimum web-based TOEFL 79. **Basis for Candidate Selection:** *Very important factors considered include:* Academic GPA, rigor of secondary school record, standardized test scores. *Important factors considered include:* Class rank, application essay. *Other factors considered include:* Recommendation(s), alumni/ae relation, character/personal qualities, extracurricular activities, first generation, geographical residence, interview, racial/ethnic status, religious affiliation/commitment, state residency, talent/ability, volunteer work, work experience. **Freshman Admission Requirements:** High school diploma is required and GED is accepted. *Academic units recommended:* 4 English, 3 mathematics, 2 science, (2 science labs), 2 foreign language, 5 academic electives. **Freshman Admission Statistics:** 2,941 applied, 84% admitted, 32% enrolled. **Transfer Admission Requirements:** High school transcript, college transcript(s), essay or personal statement, standardized test scores, statement of good standing from prior institution(s). Minimum college GPA of 2.5 required. Lowest grade transferable C. **General Admission Information:** Application fee $35. Notification on a rolling basis, beginning on or about 12/15. Nonfall registration accepted. Admission may be deferred for a maximum of 1 year. Credit offered for CEEB Advanced Placement tests.

COSTS AND FINANCIAL AID

Annual tuition $26,350. Room and board $8,110. Required fees $160. Average book expense $800. **Required Forms and Deadlines:** FAFSA, institution's own financial aid form, business/farm supplement. Priority financial aid filing date 3/1. **Notification of Awards:** Applicants will be notified of awards on a rolling basis beginning 3/15. **Types of Aid:** *Need-based scholarships/grants:* Federal Pell, SEOG, state scholarships/grants, private scholarships, the school's own gift aid. *Loans:* Direct Subsidized Stafford, Direct Unsubsidized Stafford, Direct PLUS, Federal Perkins, college/university loans from institutional funds. **Student Employment:** Federal Work-Study Program available. Institutional employment available. Highest amount earned per year from on-campus jobs $7,455. Off-campus job opportunities are good. **Financial Aid Statistics:** 56% freshmen, 53% undergrads receive need-based scholarship or grant aid. 51% freshmen, 44% undergrads receive non-need-based scholarship or grant aid. 54% freshmen, 51% undergrads receive need-based self-help aid. 95% freshmen, 92% undergrads receive any aid. 64% undergrads borrow to pay for school. Average cumulative indebtedness $28,682. **Criteria for awarding institutional aid:** *Non-need-based:* Academics, art, minority status, music/drama, religious affiliation.

HOPE INTERNATIONAL UNIVERSITY

Undergraduate Admissions, 2500 East Nutwoo, Fullerton, CA 92831
Phone: 866-722-4673 **Financial Aid Phone:** 714-879-3901
E-mail: pccadmissions@hiu.edu
Fax: 714-681-7423 **Website:** www.hiu.edu **ACT Code:** 356

This private school, affiliated with the Church of Christ Church, was founded in 1928. It has a 18-acre campus.

RATINGS

Admissions Selectivity Rating: 75 **Fire Safety Rating:** 61 **Green Rating:** 60*

STUDENTS AND FACULTY

Enrollment: 521. **Student Body:** 60% female, 40% male, 24% out-of-state, 2% international. Asian 5%, African American 5%, Caucasian 61%, Hispanic 16%, Native American 1%.
Retention and Graduation: 71% freshmen return for sophomore year. 1% freshmen graduate within 4 years. **Faculty:** Student/faculty ratio 15:1. 32 full-time faculty, 59% hold PhDs, 6% are members of minority groups, 25% are women.

ACADEMICS

Degrees: Associate, bachelor's, certificate, master's, post-bachelor's certificate. **Classes:** Most classes have fewer than 10 students. Most lab/discussion sessions have fewer than 10 students. **Majors with Highest Enrollment:** Psychology; teacher education, multiple levels; youth ministry. **Special Study Options:** Accelerated program, cross-registration, distance learning, double major, dual enrollment, English as a Second Language (ESL), independent study, internships, liberal arts/career combination, student-designed major, study abroad, teacher certification program Special programs offered to physically disabled students include note-taking services, tape recorders, tutors.

FACILITIES

Housing: Men's dorms, women's dorms. 95% of campus accessible to physically disabled.

CAMPUS LIFE

Environment: City. **Activities:** Choral groups, drama/theater, jazz band, music ensembles, musical theater, student government, student newspaper, yearbook. **Organizations:** **Athletics (Intercollegiate):** *Men:* Basketball, soccer, tennis, volleyball. *Women:* Basketball, soccer, softball, tennis, volleyball. **On-Campus Highlights:** Lawson-Fulton Student Center, Darling Library, Lambda Lounge, Auditorium, The Commons.

ADMISSIONS

Freshman Academic Profile: Average high school GPA 3.3. 20% in top 10% of high school class, 37% in top 25% of high school class, 77% in top 50% of high school class. 95% from public high schools. SAT Math middle 50% range 420–530. SAT Critical Reading middle 50% range 440–540. SAT Writing middle 50% range 420–520. ACT middle 50% range 18–21. Minimum paper TOEFL 500. Minimum computer TOEFL 173. **Basis for Candidate Selection:** *Very important factors considered include:* Class rank, application essay, academic GPA, recommendation(s), rigor of secondary school record, standardized test scores. *Important factors considered include:* level of applicant's interest. *Other factors considered include:* character/personal qualities, extracurricular activities, interview, religious affiliation/commitment, talent/ability, volunteer work. **Freshman Admission Requirements:** High school diploma is required and GED is accepted. *Academic units recommended:* 4 English, 2 mathematics, 1 science, (1 science labs), 1 foreign language, 1 social studies, 1 history, 3 academic electives. **Freshman Admission Statistics:** 413 applied, 71% admitted, 59% enrolled. **Transfer Admission Requirements:** College transcript(s), essay or personal statement, statement of good standing from prior institution(s). Minimum college GPA of 2.5 required. Lowest grade transferable C. **General Admission Information:** Application fee $40. Notification on a rolling basis, beginning on or about 8/1. Nonfall registration accepted. Credit and/or placement offered for CEEB Advanced Placement tests.

COSTS AND FINANCIAL AID

Annual tuition $21,560. Room and board $6,940. Required fees $325. Average book expense $1,386. **Required Forms and Deadlines:** FAFSA, institution's own financial aid form. Financial aid filing deadline 3/2. Priority financial aid filing date 3/2. **Notification of Awards:** Applicants will be notified of awards on a rolling basis beginning 3/15. **Types of Aid:** *Need-based scholarships/grants:* Federal Pell, SEOG, state scholarships/grants, private scholarships, the school's own gift aid. *Loans:* Direct Subsidized Stafford, Direct Unsubsidized Stafford, Direct PLUS, FFEL Subsidized Stafford, FFEL Unsubsidized Stafford, FFEL PLUS, Federal Perkins, state loans, college/university loans from institutional funds. **Student Employment:** Federal Work-Study Program available. Institutional employment available. Off-campus job opportunities are good. **Financial Aid Statistics:** 77% freshmen, 80% undergrads receive need-based scholarship or grant aid. 15% freshmen, 12% undergrads receive non-need-based scholarship or grant aid. 58% freshmen, 64% undergrads receive need-based self-help aid. 67% freshmen, 73% undergrads receive any aid. 92% undergrads borrow to pay for school. Average cumulative indebtedness $18,627. **Criteria for awarding institutional aid:** *Non-need-based:* Academics, alumni affiliation, athletics, leadership, music/drama, religious affiliation.

HOUGHTON COLLEGE

PO Box 128, Houghton, NY 14744
Phone: 585-567-9353 **Financial Aid Phone:** 585-567-9328
E-mail: admission@houghton.edu **CEEB Code:** 2299
Fax: 716-567-9522 **Website:** www.houghton.edu **ACT Code:** 2766

This private school, affiliated with the Wesleyan Church, was founded in 1883. It has a 1300-acre campus.

RATINGS
Admissions Selectivity Rating: 85   **Fire Safety Rating:** 66   **Green Rating:** 85

STUDENTS AND FACULTY
Enrollment: 1,270. **Student Body:** 66% female, 34% male, 40% out-of-state, 4% international (20 countries represented). Asian 2%, African American 2%, Caucasian 89%, Hispanic 1%.
Retention and Graduation: 61% freshmen graduate within 4 years. 43.8% grads go on to further study within 1 year. 25.3% grads pursue arts and sciences degrees. 1.1% grads pursue law degrees. 2.8% grads pursue business degrees. 3.4% grads pursue medical degrees. **Faculty:** 88 full-time faculty, 88% hold PhDs, 6% are members of minority groups, 31% are women.

ACADEMICS
Degrees: Associate, bachelor's, master's. **Classes:** Most classes have 10–19 students. Most lab/discussion sessions have 10–19 students. **Majors with Highest Enrollment:** Biology/biological sciences; business administration and management; elementary education and teaching. **Special Study Options:** Cross-registration, double major, exchange student program (domestic), honors program, independent study, internships, liberal arts/career combination, study abroad, teacher certification program **Honors programs:** First-year honors program in London, England; first-year honors program in Eastern Europe; first-year honors program in math and science Special programs offered to physically disabled students include note-taking services, tape recorders, tutors. **Career services:** Alumni network, alumni services, career/job search classes, career assessment, internships.

FACILITIES
Housing: Men's dorms, special housing for international students, women's dorms, apartments for married students, apartments for single students. 80% of campus accessible to physically disabled. **Special Academic Facilities/Equipment:** Electron microscope, art gallery, greenhouse. **Computers:** 100% of classrooms, 100% of dorms, 100% of libraries, 100% of dining areas, 100% of student union, 50% of common outdoor areas have wireless network access. Students can register for classes online. Administrative functions (other than registration) can be performed online.

CAMPUS LIFE
Environment: Rural. **Activities:** Choral groups, concert band, dance, drama/theater, jazz band, literary magazine, music ensembles, musical theater, opera, student government, student newspaper, symphony orchestra, yearbook, campus ministries, international student organization. **Organizations:** 34 registered organizations, 2 honor societies, 9 religious organizations. **Athletics (Intercollegiate):** *Men:* Basketball, cross-country, soccer, track/field (outdoor), track/field (indoor). *Women:* Basketball, cross-country, field hockey, soccer, track/field (outdoor), track/field (indoor), volleyball. **On-Campus Highlights:** Center for the Arts, Nielsen P.E. Center, Wesley Chapel, Campus Center, Library. **Environmental Initiatives:** Decreasing electricity usage through fluorescent and LED lighting and electronic ballasts for all lighting. Forest maintenance and expansion through tree planting. Created Sustainability Coordinator position to oversee environmental issues on campus.

ADMISSIONS
Freshman Academic Profile: Average high school GPA 3.56. 36% in top 10% of high school class, 62% in top 25% of high school class, 89% in top 50% of high school class. 67% from public high schools. SAT Math middle 50% range 510–640. SAT Critical Reading middle 50% range 520–660. SAT Writing middle 50% range 510–640. ACT middle 50% range 22–29. Minimum paper TOEFL 550. Minimum computer TOEFL 213. Minimum web-based TOEFL 80. **Basis for Candidate Selection:** *Very important factors considered include:* Academic GPA, religious affiliation/commitment. *Important factors considered include:* Class rank, application essay, recommendation(s), rigor of secondary school record, standardized test scores, character/personal qualities. *Other factors considered include:* Alumni/ae relation, extracurricular activities, interview, level of applicant's interest, racial/ethnic status, talent/ability, volunteer work, work experience. **Freshman Admission Requirements:** High school diploma is required and GED is accepted. *Academic units recommended:* 4 English, 3 mathematics, 2 science, (2 science labs), 2 foreign language, 1 social studies, 2 history. **Freshman Admission Statistics:** 1,080 applied, 82% admitted, 32%

enrolled. **Transfer Admission Requirements:** College transcript(s), essay or personal statement, lowest grade transferable C–. **General Admission Information:** Application fee $40. Notification on a rolling basis, beginning on or about 1/1. Nonfall registration accepted. Admission may be deferred for a maximum of 2 years. Credit and/or placement offered for CEEB Advanced Placement tests.

COSTS AND FINANCIAL AID
Annual tuition $24,440. Room and board $7,000. Average book expense $900. **Required Forms and Deadlines:** FAFSA. Priority financial aid filing date 3/1. **Notification of Awards:** Applicants will be notified of awards on a rolling basis beginning 3/15. **Types of Aid:** *Need-based scholarships/grants:* Federal Pell, SEOG, state scholarships/grants, private scholarships, the school's own gift aid. *Loans:* FFEL Subsidized Stafford, FFEL Unsubsidized Stafford, FFEL PLUS, Federal Perkins. **Student Employment:** Federal Work-Study Program available. Institutional employment available. Highest amount earned per year from on-campus jobs $4,283. Off-campus job opportunities are poor. **Financial Aid Statistics:** 81% freshmen, 81% undergrads receive need-based scholarship or grant aid. 12% freshmen, 9% undergrads receive non-need-based scholarship or grant aid. 71% freshmen, 73% undergrads receive need-based self-help aid. 1% freshmen, 2% undergrads receive athletic scholarships. 100% freshmen, 99% undergrads receive any aid. 81% undergrads borrow to pay for school. Average cumulative indebtedness $28,334. **Criteria for awarding institutional aid:** *Non-need-based:* Academics, alumni affiliation, art, athletics, music/drama, religious affiliation.

HOUSTON BAPTIST UNIVERSITY

7502 Fondren Road, Houston, TX 77074
Phone: 281-649-3211 **Financial Aid Phone:** 281-649-3471
E-mail: unadm@hbu.edu **CEEB Code:** 6282
Fax: 281-649-3217 **Website:** www.hbu.edu **ACT Code:** 4101

This private school, affiliated with the Southern Baptist Church, was founded in 1960. It has a 100-acre campus.

RATINGS
Admissions Selectivity Rating: 75   **Fire Safety Rating:** 76   **Green Rating:** 60*

STUDENTS AND FACULTY
Enrollment: 1,916. **Student Body:** 67% female, 33% male, 3% out-of-state, 6% international (36 countries represented). Asian 13%, African American 20%, Caucasian 46%, Hispanic 14%.
Retention and Graduation: 74% freshmen return for sophomore year. 32% freshmen graduate within 4 years. **Faculty:** Student/faculty ratio 14:1. 103 full-time faculty, 81% hold PhDs, 10% are members of minority groups, 48% are women.

ACADEMICS
Degrees: Associate, bachelor's, master's. **Classes:** Most classes have 10–19 students. Most lab/discussion sessions have fewer than 10 students. **Majors with Highest Enrollment:** Biology/biological sciences; business/commerce; psychology. **Special Study Options:** Accelerated program, double major, dual enrollment, English as a Second Language (ESL), independent study, internships, liberal arts/career combination, teacher certification program. **Combined degree programs:** Accelerated MATS degree program (with BA or BS). **Career services:** Alumni network, alumni services, career/job search classes, career assessment, internships, regional alumni. **Career services highlights include:** Our internship program provides opportunities for student to work with early stage companies at the BU incubators, as well as in the community. One particularly unusual aspect of the program is that we provide opportunities for non-business students to "intern" with startups our business students are creating. One such program this year had Graphic Design students working with MBA student entrepreneurs to develop corporate identity programs for them.

FACILITIES
Housing: Men's dorms, women's dorms, apartments for single students 90% of campus accessible to physically disabled. **Special Academic Facilities/Equipment:** Museum of architecture/decorative arts, language lab, research center. **Computers:** Students can register for classes online.

CAMPUS LIFE
Environment: Metropolis. **Activities:** Choral groups, concert band, drama/theater, music ensembles, pep band, student government, student newspaper, yearbook. **Organizations:** 36 registered organizations, 9 honor societies, 3 religious organizations. 2 fraternities, 2 sororities. **Athletics (Intercollegiate):** *Men:* Baseball, basketball, cheerleading. *Women:* Basketball, cheerleading, soft-

ball, volleyball. **On-Campus Highlights:** Hinton Center, Baugh Center and the Bone Appetit Cafe, Bible Museum, Wellness Center, Admissions Office.

ADMISSIONS

Freshman Academic Profile: 24% in top 10% of high school class, 44% in top 25% of high school class, 79% in top 50% of high school class. 79% from public high schools. SAT Math middle 50% range 500–620. SAT Critical Reading middle 50% range 500–610. ACT middle 50% range 19–25. Minimum paper TOEFL 550. Minimum computer TOEFL 213. **Basis for Candidate Selection:** *Very important factors considered include:* Application essay, recommendation(s), rigor of secondary school record, standardized test scores. *Important factors considered include:* Class rank, extracurricular activities, geographical residence, religious affiliation/commitment, talent/ability, volunteer work. *Other factors considered include:* Alumni/ae relation, character/personal qualities, interview. **Freshman Admission Requirements:** High school diploma is required and GED is accepted. *Academic units recommended:* 4 English, 3 mathematics, 3 science, (1 science labs), 2 foreign language, 2 social studies, 2 history, 2 academic electives. **Freshman Admission Statistics:** 867 applied, 65% admitted, 55% enrolled. **Transfer Admission Requirements:** College transcript(s), essay or personal statement, statement of good standing from prior institution(s). Minimum college GPA of 2.0 required. Lowest grade transferable C. **General Admission Information:** Application fee $25. Nonfall registration accepted. Admission may be deferred for a maximum of None. Credit offered for CEEB Advanced Placement tests.

COSTS AND FINANCIAL AID

Required Forms and Deadlines: FAFSA. Financial aid filing deadline 4/15. Priority financial aid filing date 3/1. **Notification of Awards:** Applicants will be notified of awards on a rolling basis beginning 3/10. **Types of Aid:** *Need-based scholarships/grants:* Federal Pell, SEOG, state scholarships/grants, private scholarships, the school's own gift aid. *Loans:* FFEL Subsidized Stafford, FFEL Unsubsidized Stafford, FFEL PLUS, state loans, Private, non federal. **Student Employment:** Federal Work-Study Program available. Highest amount earned per year from on-campus jobs $1,800. **Financial Aid Statistics:** 78% freshmen, 84% undergrads receive need-based scholarship or grant aid. 11% freshmen, 6% undergrads receive non-need-based scholarship or grant aid. 58% freshmen, 72% undergrads receive need-based self-help aid. 3% freshmen, 1% undergrads receive athletic scholarships. 64% freshmen, 85% undergrads receive any aid. **Criteria for awarding institutional aid:** *Non-need-based:* Academics, alumni affiliation, art, athletics, leadership, music/drama, religious affiliation.

HOWARD PAYNE UNIVERSITY

Howard Payne Station, Brownwood, TX 76801
Phone: 325-649-8027 **Financial Aid Phone:** 325-649-8015
E-mail: enroll@hputx.edu
Fax: 325-649-8901 **Website:** www.hputx.edu **ACT Code:** 4102

This private school, affiliated with the Baptist Church, was founded in 1889. It has a 30-acre campus.

RATINGS

Admissions Selectivity Rating: 72   **Fire Safety Rating:** 60*   **Green Rating:** 60*

STUDENTS AND FACULTY

Enrollment: 1,303. **Student Body:** 50% female, 50% male, 3% out-of-state, 1% international (6 countries represented). Asian 1%, African American 8%, Caucasian 75%, Hispanic 12%, Native American 1%.
Retention and Graduation: 61% freshmen return for sophomore year. 21% freshmen graduate within 4 years. 15% grads go on to further study within 1 year. 2% grads pursue law degrees. 2% grads pursue business degrees. 2% grads pursue medical degrees. **Faculty:** Student/faculty ratio 11:1. 75 full-time faculty, 59% hold PhDs, 5% are members of minority groups, 36% are women.

ACADEMICS

Degrees: Associate, bachelor's, certificate. **Classes:** Most classes have fewer than 10 students. **Majors with Highest Enrollment:** Bible/biblical studies; business/commerce; education. **Special Study Options:** Accelerated program, cooperative education program, distance learning, double major, dual enrollment, English as a Second Language (ESL), honors program, independent study, internships, liberal arts/career combination, study abroad, teacher certification program, Extension campuses are located in El Paso, Corpus Christi, Weatherford, and Harlingen, Texas. **Honors programs:** The Douglas MacArthur Academy of Freedom is designed for academically gifted students who aspire to leadership roles in a variety of careers. The Academy program prepares students to read critically, think analytically, and communicate ideas effectively. Through a broad-based liberal arts education that emphasizes Ju-

deo-Christian values, western civilization, free enterprise principles, and political awareness, the Academy explores the meaning and significance of traditional American values and seeks to understand the problems of contemporary society. Students develop critical thinking skills by analyzing current issues through the multidisciplinary Academy major, which includes courses from the School of Humanities, the School of Christian Studies, and the School of Business. Special programs offered to physically disabled students include tutors. **Career services:** Alumni network, career assessment.

FACILITIES

Housing: Men's dorms, women's dorms, apartments for single students. 95% of campus accessible to physically disabled. **Special Academic Facilities/Equipment:** Douglas MacArthur Academy of Freedom and Museum. **Computers:** Administrative functions (other than registration) can be performed online.

CAMPUS LIFE

Environment: Rural. **Activities:** Choral groups, concert band, drama/theater, jazz band, literary magazine, marching band, music ensembles, musical theater, opera, radio station, student government, student newspaper, yearbook. **Organizations:** 32 registered organizations, 3 honor societies, 4 religious organizations. 5 fraternities, 5 sororities. **Athletics (Intercollegiate):** *Men:* Baseball, basketball, cheerleading, cross-country, football, tennis, track/field (outdoor). *Women:* Basketball, cheerleading, cross-country, softball, tennis, track/field (outdoor), volleyball. **On-Campus Highlights:** Elliston-Cassle Wellness Center, Mabee University Center, Douglas MacArther Academy of Freedom, Muse Mall and Plaza, Old Main Park.

ADMISSIONS

Freshman Academic Profile: Average high school GPA 3.3. 15% in top 10% of high school class, 39% in top 25% of high school class, 71% in top 50% of high school class. 94% from public high schools. SAT Math middle 50% range 440–550. SAT Critical Reading middle 50% range 440–570. ACT middle 50% range 17–23. Minimum paper TOEFL 550. Minimum computer TOEFL 213. **Basis for Candidate Selection:** *Very important factors considered include:* Rigor of secondary school record, standardized test scores. *Important factors considered include:* Recommendation(s), interview. *Other factors considered include:* Class rank, character/personal qualities, work experience. **Freshman Admission Requirements:** High school diploma is required and GED is accepted. *Academic units recommended:* 4 English, 3 mathematics, 2 science, (1 science labs), 3 social studies, 10 academic electives. **Freshman Admission Statistics:** 640 applied, 78% admitted, 62% enrolled. **Transfer Admission Requirements:** College transcript(s), minimum college GPA of 2.0 required. Lowest grade transferable D. **General Admission Information:** Application fee $25. Regular application deadline 8/31. Nonfall registration accepted. Admission may be deferred for a maximum of 1 year. Credit and/or placement offered for CEEB Advanced Placement tests.

COSTS AND FINANCIAL AID

Annual tuition $11,500. Room and board $4,615. Required fees $1,000. Average book expense $1,000. **Required Forms and Deadlines:** FAFSA, institution's own financial aid form. Priority financial aid filing date 3/15. **Notification of Awards:** Applicants will be notified of awards on a rolling basis beginning 3/1. **Types of Aid:** *Need-based scholarships/grants:* Federal Pell, SEOG, state scholarships/grants, private scholarships, the school's own gift aid. *Loans:* FFEL Subsidized Stafford, FFEL Unsubsidized Stafford, FFEL PLUS, Federal Perkins, state loans **Student Employment:** Federal Work-Study Program available. Institutional employment available. Off-campus job opportunities are good. **Financial Aid Statistics:** 79% freshmen, 76% undergrads receive need-based scholarship or grant aid. 8% freshmen, 8% undergrads receive non-need-based scholarship or grant aid. 58% freshmen, 59% undergrads receive need-based self-help aid. 69% undergrads borrow to pay for school. Average cumulative indebtedness $18,960. **Criteria for awarding institutional aid:** *Non-need-based:* Academics, alumni affiliation, art, leadership, music/drama, religious affiliation.

HOWARD UNIVERSITY

Best 373

2400 Sixth Street, NW, Washington, DC 20059
Phone: 202-806-2700 **Financial Aid Phone:** 202-806-2840
E-mail: admission@howard.edu **CEEB Code:** 5297
Fax: 202-806-4467 **Website:** www.howard.edu **ACT Code:** 4102

This private school was founded in 1867. It has a 258-acre campus.

RATINGS
Admissions Selectivity Rating: 88 **Fire Safety Rating:** 96 **Green Rating:** 60*

STUDENTS AND FACULTY
Enrollment: 7,086. **Student Body:** 66% female, 34% male, 97% out-of-state, 4% international (86 countries represented). African American 49%, Hispanic 1%.
Retention and Graduation: 85% freshmen return for sophomore year. 46% freshmen graduate within 4 years. 60% grads go on to further study within 1 year. 42% grads pursue arts and sciences degrees. 12% grads pursue law degrees. 15% grads pursue business degrees. 11% grads pursue medical degrees. **Faculty:** Student/faculty ratio 8:1. 1064 full-time faculty, 91% hold PhDs, 81% are members of minority groups, 42% are women.

ACADEMICS
Degrees: Bachelor's, certificate, first professional, first professional certificate, master's, post-master's certificate. **Classes:** Most classes have fewer than 10 students. Most lab/discussion sessions have 10–19 students. **Majors with Highest Enrollment:** Biology/biological sciences; journalism; radio and television. **Special Study Options:** Accelerated program, cooperative education program, distance learning, double major, English as a Second Language (ESL), exchange student program (domestic), honors program, independent study, internships, study abroad, teacher certification program, Tutorial program, advanced placement, continuing education. **Combined degree programs:** BA/MD, BA/DDS, MBA/JD, MD/PhD. Special programs offered to physically disabled students include note-taking services, reader services. **Career services:** Career/job search classes, career assessment, internships. **Career services highlights include:** Rangel Scholars Program Internships offer exposure to Capital Hii and countries abroad. Students get personal experiences regarding the working of our political system and those of other countries from experienced state department professionals and elected government officials.

FACILITIES
Housing: Coed dorms, men's dorms, women's dorms, apartments for married students, apartments for single students. 100% of campus accessible to physically disabled. **Special Academic Facilities/Equipment:** Three art galleries, language labs, hospital. Research center with comprehensive collection on Africa and persons of African descent. **Computers:** 10% of classrooms, 100% of dorms, 100% of libraries, 10% of dining areas, 50% of student union, 10% of common outdoor areas have wireless network access. Students can register for classes online. Administrative functions (other than registration) can be performed online.

CAMPUS LIFE
Environment: Metropolis. **Activities:** Choral groups, concert band, dance, drama/theater, jazz band, literary magazine, marching band, music ensembles, musical theater, opera, pep band, radio station, student government, student newspaper, student-run film society, symphony orchestra, television station, yearbook, campus ministries, international student organization. **Organizations:** 150 registered organizations, 15 honor societies, 3 religious organizations. 10 fraternities, 8 sororities. **Athletics (Intercollegiate):** *Men:* Basketball, cheerleading, cross-country, diving, football, soccer, swimming, tennis, track/field (outdoor). *Women:* Basketball, bowling, boxing, cheerleading, cross-country, diving, lacrosse, soccer, softball, swimming, tennis, track/field (outdoor), volleyball. **On-Campus Highlights:** Founders Library, Rankin Chapel, Punchout, Ira Aldridge Theatre, Burr Gymnasium.

ADMISSIONS
Freshman Academic Profile: Average high school GPA 3.2. 26% in top 10% of high school class, 55% in top 25% of high school class, 84% in top 50% of high school class. 80% from public high schools. SAT Math middle 50% range 460–680. SAT Critical Reading middle 50% range 470–670. SAT Writing middle 50% range 430–670. ACT middle 50% range 19–29. Minimum paper TOEFL 550. Minimum computer TOEFL 213. **Basis for Candidate Selection:** *Very important factors considered:* Class rank, rigor of secondary school record, standardized test scores. *Important factors considered include:* Recommendation(s), character/personal qualities. *Other factors considered include:* Application essay, alumni/ae relation, extracurricular activities, talent/ability, volunteer work, work experience. **Freshman Admission Requirements:** High school diploma is required and GED is accepted. *Academic units required:* 4 English, 2 mathematics, 2 science, 2 foreign language, 2 social studies, 2 history. *Academic units recommended:* 4 English, 3 mathematics, 4 science, (2 science labs), 2 foreign language, 2 social studies, 2 history, 4 any other academic courses counted towards graduation. **Freshman Admission Statistics:** 9,750 applied, 49% admitted, 31% enrolled. **Transfer Admission Requirements:** College transcript(s), statement of good standing from prior institution(s). Minimum college GPA of 2.5 required. Lowest grade transferable C. **General Admission Information:** Application fee $45. Early decision application deadline 11/1. Regular application deadline 2/15. Nonfall registration accepted. Admission may be deferred for a maximum of 1. Credit and/or placement offered for CEEB Advanced Placement tests.

COSTS AND FINANCIAL AID
Annual tuition $15,270. . Room and board $7,966. Required fees $805. Average book expense $2,000. **Required Forms and Deadlines:** FAFSA. Financial aid filing deadline 8/15. Priority financial aid filing date 2/15. **Notification of Awards:** Applicants will be notified of awards on a rolling basis beginning 4/1. **Types of Aid:** *Need-based scholarships/grants:* Federal Pell, SEOG, state scholarships/grants, private scholarships, the school's own gift aid, Federal Nursing Scholarships. *Loans:* Direct Subsidized Stafford, Direct Unsubsidized Stafford, Direct PLUS, Federal Perkins, Federal Nursing. **Student Employment:** Federal Work-Study Program available. Institutional employment available. Highest amount earned per year from on-campus jobs $3,500. Off-campus job opportunities are excellent. **Financial Aid Statistics:** 32% freshmen, 38% undergrads receive need-based scholarship or grant aid. 40% freshmen, 15% undergrads receive non-need-based scholarship or grant aid. 24% freshmen, 21% undergrads receive need-based self-help aid. 5% freshmen, 3% undergrads receive athletic scholarships. 96% freshmen, 96% undergrads receive any aid. 80% undergrads borrow to pay for school. Average cumulative indebtedness $16,473. **Criteria for awarding institutional aid:** *Non-need-based:* Academics, art, athletics, job skills, music/drama, state/district residency.

HUMBOLDT STATE UNIVERSITY

1 Harpst Street, Arcata, CA 95521-8299
Phone: 707-826-4402 **Financial Aid Phone:** 707-826-4321
E-mail: hsuinfo@humboldt.edu **CEEB Code:** 4345
Fax: 707-826-6190 **Website:** www.humboldt.edu **ACT Code:** 286

This public school was founded in 1913. It has a 161-acre campus.

RATINGS
Admissions Selectivity Rating: 83 **Fire Safety Rating:** 88 **Green Rating:** 94

STUDENTS AND FACULTY
Enrollment: 7,093. **Student Body:** 54% female, 46% male, 12% out-of-state, 1% international (40 countries represented). Asian 4%, African American 3%, Caucasian 56%, Hispanic 13%, Native American 2%.
Retention and Graduation: 75% freshmen return for sophomore year. 11% freshmen graduate within 4 years. **Faculty:** Student/faculty ratio 22:1. 254 full-time faculty, 99% hold PhDs, 11% are members of minority groups, 36% are women.

ACADEMICS
Degrees: Bachelor's, master's, post-bachelor's certificate. **Classes:** Most classes have 20–29 students. Most lab/discussion sessions have 20–29 students. **Majors with Highest Enrollment:** Liberal arts and sciences/liberal studies; social sciences. **Special Study Options:** Double major, English as a Second Language (ESL), exchange student program (domestic), student-designed major, study abroad, teacher certification program Special programs offered to physically disabled students include note-taking services, reader services, tape recorders, tutors. **Career services:** Alumni services, career/job search classes, career assessment, internships, regional alumni. **Career services highlights include:** Internships allow students to get jobs in their fields after they graduate. The Career Center connects students with the internships that work best for them.

FACILITIES
Housing: Coed dorms. 75% of campus accessible to physically disabled. **Special Academic Facilities/Equipment:** Art and geology museums, marine research lab, fish hatchery, wildlife game pen, observatory, First Street Gallery **Computers:** 85% of classrooms, 100% of dorms, 100% of libraries, 100% of dining areas, 100% of student union, 80% of common outdoor areas have

wireless network access. Students can register for classes online. Administrative functions (other than registration) can be performed online.

CAMPUS LIFE

Environment: Village. **Activities:** Choral groups, concert band, dance, drama/theater, jazz band, literary magazine, music ensembles, pep band, radio station, student government, student newspaper, symphony orchestra, international student organization, Model UN. **Organizations:** 160 registered organizations, 6 honor societies, 8 religious organizations. 2 fraternities, 4 sororities. **Athletics (Intercollegiate):** *Men:* Basketball, cross-country, football, soccer, track/field (outdoor). *Women:* Basketball, crew/rowing, cross-country, soccer, softball, track/field (outdoor), volleyball. **On-Campus Highlights:** Founders Hall, Campus Center for Appropriate Technology, University Center, Redwood Bowl, University Library. **Environmental Initiatives:** Campus Center for Appropriate Technology (CCAT): For 30 years, the Campus Center for Appropriate Technology's live-in demonstration home for sustainability annually exposes over 2,000 students, faculty, staff, and visitors through tours, student-taught courses, workshops, presentations and hands-on projects. The first of its kind, CCAT has been the inspiration for similar projects on college campuses across the nation (www.humboldt.edu/~ccat/). For the past 15 years, Humboldt State's Schatz Energy Research Center has been an international leader in the development of clean and renewable energy. Most recently, the Center unveiled a hydrogen fueling station that powers a hydrogen fueled Toyota Prius (www.schatzlab.org). Humbodlt Energy Independent Fund (HEIF): The Humboldt State Energy Independence Fund (HEIF) seeks to reduce the environmental impacts of energy use at HSU through student created, designed, and implemented projects. The funds for these projects come from a $10 per semester student fee (students approved the fee via a university-wide vote). Projects educate about energy, save energy or generate energy. So far, $100,000 has been commissioned towards two HEIF projects: a solar monitoring station on campus and a 10.5 kW solar installation along with a student-designed interpretive sign and energy-themed art project (www.humboldt.edu/~heif/).

ADMISSIONS

Freshman Academic Profile: Average high school GPA 3.17. 15% in top 10% of high school class, 38% in top 25% of high school class, 82% in top 50% of high school class. 90% from public high schools. SAT Math middle 50% range 460–570. SAT Critical Reading middle 50% range 470–590. SAT Writing middle 50% range 450–570. ACT middle 50% range 19–25. Minimum paper TOEFL 500. Minimum computer TOEFL 173. **Basis for Candidate Selection:** *Very important factors considered include:* Academic GPA, standardized test scores. *Important factors considered include:* Rigor of secondary school record. *Other factors considered include:* State residency. **Freshman Admission Requirements:** High school diploma is required and GED is accepted. *Academic units required:* 4 English, 3 mathematics, 2 science, (1 science labs), 2 foreign language, 1 social studies, 1 history, 1 visual/performing arts, 1 academic electives. **Freshman Admission Statistics:** 9,379 applied, 31% admitted, 48% enrolled. **Transfer Admission Requirements:** College transcript(s), statement of good standing from prior institution(s). Minimum college GPA of 2.00 required. Lowest grade transferable D–. **General Admission Information:** Application fee $55. Regular application deadline 11/30. Notification on a rolling basis, beginning on or about 12/1. Nonfall registration not accepted. Credit and/or placement offered for CEEB Advanced Placement tests.

COSTS AND FINANCIAL AID

Annual in-state tuition $5,166. Annual out-of-state tuition $14,094. Room and board $9,510. Average book expense $1,528. **Required Forms and Deadlines:** FAFSA. Priority financial aid filing date 3/2. **Notification of Awards:** Applicants will be notified of awards on a rolling basis beginning 4/1. **Types of Aid:** *Need-based scholarships/grants:* Federal Pell, SEOG, state scholarships/grants, private scholarships, the school's own gift aid. *Loans:* Direct Subsidized Stafford, Direct Unsubsidized Stafford, Direct PLUS, Federal Perkins. **Student Employment:** Federal Work-Study Program available. Institutional employment available. Off-campus job opportunities are good. **Financial Aid Statistics:** 51% freshmen, 57% undergrads receive need-based scholarship or grant aid. 39% freshmen, 45% undergrads receive need-based self-help aid. 2% freshmen, 1% undergrads receive athletic scholarships. 43% freshmen, 52% undergrads receive any aid. 50% undergrads borrow to pay for school. Average cumulative indebtedness $17,302. **Criteria for awarding institutional aid:** *Non-need-based:* Academics, alumni affiliation, athletics, leadership, minority status, music/drama, religious affiliation.

HUMPHREYS COLLEGE

6650 Inglewood Avenue, Stockton, CA 95207
Phone: 209-478-0800 **Financial Aid Phone:** 209-478-0800
E-mail: slopez@humphreys.edu
Fax: 209-478-0800 **Website:** www.humphreys.edu

This private school was founded in 1896. It has a 10-acre campus.

RATINGS

Admissions Selectivity Rating: 65   **Fire Safety Rating:** 60*   **Green Rating:** 60*

STUDENTS AND FACULTY

Enrollment: 692. **Student Body:** 85% female, 15% male, international. Asian 12%, African American 15%, Caucasian 25%, Hispanic 33%, Native American 1%.
Retention and Graduation: 64% freshmen return for sophomore year. 100% freshmen graduate within 4 years. 54% grads go on to further study within 1 year. 20% grads pursue arts and sciences degrees. 30% grads pursue law degrees. 40% grads pursue business degrees. 1% grads pursue medical degrees. **Faculty:** Student/faculty ratio 18:1. 18 full-time faculty, 17% hold PhDs, 6% are members of minority groups, 67% are women.

ACADEMICS

Degrees: Associate, bachelor's, certificate, first professional. **Classes:** Most classes have greater than 100 students. **Special Study Options:** Distance learning, double major, dual enrollment, independent study, internships. Career services : alumni services, internships. **Career services highlights include:** Internships.

FACILITIES

Housing: Apartments for single students. 100% of campus accessible to physically disabled.

CAMPUS LIFE

Environment: Village. **Activities:** Literary magazine, student newspaper. **Organizations:** 3 registered organizations.

ADMISSIONS

Freshman Academic Profile: Average high school GPA 3. 15% in top 50% of high school class. 95% from public high schools. Minimum paper TOEFL 450. Minimum computer TOEFL 300. **Basis for Candidate Selection:** *Very important factors considered include:* Interview. *Important factors considered include:* Character/personal qualities. *Other factors considered include:* Level of applicant's interest. **Freshman Admission Requirements:** High school diploma is required and GED is accepted. **Freshman Admission Statistics:** 143 applied, 81% admitted, 100% enrolled. **Transfer Admission Requirements:** High school transcript, college transcript(s), interview, minimum college GPA of 2.0 required. Lowest grade transferable C–. **General Admission Information:** Application fee $35. Nonfall registration accepted. Admission may be deferred for a maximum of 5. Placement offered for CEEB Advanced Placement tests.

COSTS AND FINANCIAL AID

Required Forms and Deadlines: FAFSA **Types of Aid:** *Need-based scholarships/grants:* Federal Pell, SEOG, state scholarships/grants, private scholarships. *Loans:* FFEL Subsidized Stafford, FFEL Unsubsidized Stafford, FFEL PLUS. **Student Employment:** Highest amount earned per year from on-campus jobs $1,603. Off-campus job opportunities are fair. **Financial Aid Statistics:** 81% freshmen, 67% undergrads receive need-based scholarship or grant aid. 18% freshmen, 5% undergrads receive need-based self-help aid. 98% freshmen, 98% undergrads receive any aid. 8% undergrads borrow to pay for school. Average cumulative indebtedness $28,000.

HUNTINGDON COLLEGE

1500 East Fairview Avenue, Montgomery, AL 36106-2148
Phone: 334-833-4497 **Financial Aid Phone:** 334-833-4519
E-mail: admiss@huntingdon.edu **CEEB Code:** 1303
Fax: 334-833-4347 **Website:** www.huntingdon.edu **ACT Code:** 0018

This private school, affiliated with the Methodist Church, was founded in 1854. It has a 71-acre campus.

RATINGS

Admissions Selectivity Rating: 82   **Fire Safety Rating:** 91   **Green Rating:** 67

STUDENTS AND FACULTY

Enrollment: 1,067. **Student Body:** 52% female, 48% male, 13% out-of-state, 1% international (8 countries represented). Asian 1%, African American 16%, Caucasian 60%, Hispanic 1%.
Retention and Graduation: 63% freshmen return for sophomore year. 35% freshmen graduate within 4 years. **Faculty:** Student/faculty ratio 13:1. 45 full-time faculty, 89% hold PhDs, 7% are members of minority groups, 40% are women.

ACADEMICS

Degrees: Bachelor's. **Classes:** Most classes have fewer than 10 students. Most lab/discussion sessions have 10–19 students. **Majors with Highest Enrollment:** Accounting; business/commerce; kinesiology and exercise science. **Special Study Options:** Cross-registration, double major, honors program, independent study, internships, liberal arts/career combination, student-designed major, study abroad, teacher certification program, Adult Degree Completion Program in which students take classes only in the evening all year long, dual engineering degree with Auburn University and exchange student program with universities Ireland; travel opportunities to all full-time junior and seniors within regular educational costs or for nominal additional fees. **Honors programs:** Program Honors—An outstanding student in a particular major has the opportunity to create an individualized honors project within the major to meet a particular need and interest. Special programs offered to physically disabled students include note-taking services, reader services, tape recorders, tutors. **Career services:** Alumni network, alumni services, career/job search classes, career assessment, internships. **Career services highlights include:** The Internship program is exceptional. The Center for Career and Vocation currently has more internships and jobs than there are students and alumni needing such opportunities. Huntingdon College's partnership with the community and local business and industry is paying huge dividends for Huntingdon students, alumni and the college.

FACILITIES

Housing: Coed dorms, men's dorms, women's dorms 85% of campus accessible to physically disabled. **Special Academic Facilities/Equipment:** 1. The Bowman Ecological Center is a protected area in Prattville, AL that provides space for students to collect and study samples of plants, trees, and aquatic life. 2. Sybil Smith Hall is a fully equipped music facility housing the Lucile Crowell Delchamps Recital Hall, the Julia Lightfoot Sellers Reception Hall, faculty offices and studios, rehersal rooms, classrooms, a modern electronic music laboratory, and one of the most extensive music collections in the South, with more than 10,000 records, CDs and tapes. 3. The Staton Center for Learning Enrichment Center oversees the Academic Success Centers, advises students who have not declared majors, provides academic counseling for students with provisional enrollment, serves as a resource for study halls as related to study skills and time management skills, and advises staff and faculty serving the First Year Experience (FYEx) program. 4. Leon and Myra Allman Ligon Chapel contains the newly expanded and installed Bellingrath Memorial Organ, which Dr. Harold Rohlig, professor of music, designed. The Bellingrath Memorial Organ is one of the largest of its kind among private colleges in the Southeast, with 141 ranks and a four-manual keyboard. The Chapel's Green Window, revered by alumni as a symbol of the Huntingdon experience, is framed by the new organ pipes, some of which are 32 feet in length. Ligon Chapel is the site of pageants, performances, lectures, convocations, concerts, and countless traditions at Huntingdon College. **Computers:** 40% of classrooms, 33% of dorms, 100% of libraries, 100% of dining areas, 100% of student union, have wireless network access. Administrative functions (other than registration) can be performed online. Undergraduates are required to own a computer.

CAMPUS LIFE

Environment: City. **Activities:** Choral groups, concert band, dance, drama/theater, literary magazine, marching band, music ensembles, pep band, student government, student newspaper, yearbook, campus ministries, international student organization, Model UN. **Organizations:** 50 registered organizations, 15 honor societies, 3 religious organizations. 4 fraternities, 4 sororities. **Athletics (Intercollegiate):** *Men:* Baseball, basketball, cross-country, football, golf, soccer, tennis. *Women:* Basketball, cross-country, golf, soccer, softball, tennis, volleyball. **On-Campus Highlights:** Flowers Hall, Houghton Memorial Library, Wilson Center, Carolyn & Wynton Blount (Residence) Hall, Julia Walker Russell Dining Hall.

ADMISSIONS

Freshman Academic Profile: Average high school GPA 3.31. 14% in top 10% of high school class, 36% in top 25% of high school class, 75% in top 50% of high school class. 73% from public high schools. SAT Math middle 50% range 430–560. SAT Critical Reading middle 50% range 450–610. SAT Writing middle 50% range 450–560. ACT middle 50% range 19–24. Minimum paper TOEFL 500. Minimum computer TOEFL 173. Minimum web-based TOEFL 45. **Basis for Candidate Selection:** *Very important factors considered include:* Academic GPA, standardized test scores. *Important factors considered include:* Rigor of secondary school record. *Other factors considered include:* Class rank, application essay, recommendation(s), interview. **Freshman Admission Re-**

quirements: High school diploma is required and GED is accepted. *Academic units recommended:* 4 English, 3 mathematics, 2 science, 2 foreign language, 3 social studies. **Freshman Admission Statistics:** 1,138 applied, 67% admitted, 31% enrolled. **Transfer Admission Requirements:** High school transcript, college transcript(s), statement of good standing from prior institution(s). Minimum college GPA of 2.25 required. Lowest grade transferable C. **General Admission Information:** Regular application deadline 8/15. Notification on a rolling basis, beginning on or about 9/7. Nonfall registration accepted. Admission may be deferred for a maximum of 2 semesters. Credit and/or placement offered for CEEB Advanced Placement tests.

COSTS AND FINANCIAL AID

Required Forms and Deadlines: Institution's own financial aid form. Priority financial aid filing date 4/15. **Notification of Awards:** Applicants will be notified of awards on a rolling basis beginning 3/1. **Types of Aid:** *Need-based scholarships/grants:* Federal Pell, SEOG, state scholarships/grants, private scholarships, the school's own gift aid. *Loans:* FFEL Subsidized Stafford, FFEL Unsubsidized Stafford, FFEL PLUS, Federal Perkins. **Student Employment:** Federal Work-Study Program available. Institutional employment available. Off-campus job opportunities are excellent. **Financial Aid Statistics:** 81% freshmen, 69% undergrads receive need-based scholarship or grant aid. 10% freshmen, 10% undergrads receive non-need-based scholarship or grant aid. 64% freshmen, 55% undergrads receive need-based self-help aid. 58% undergrads borrow to pay for school. Average cumulative indebtedness $14,034. **Criteria for awarding institutional aid:** *Non-need-based:* Academics, alumni affiliation, leadership, music/drama, religious affiliation, state/district residency.

HUNTINGTON UNIVERSITY

2303 College Avenue, Huntington, IN 46750
Phone: 260-359-4000 **Financial Aid Phone:** 260-359-4015
E-mail: admissions@huntington.edu **CEEB Code:** 1304
Fax: 260-358-3699 **Website:** www.huntington.edu **ACT Code:** 1202

This private school, affiliated with the Protestant Church, was founded in 1897. It has a 170-acre campus.

RATINGS
Admissions Selectivity Rating: 75   **Fire Safety Rating:** 64   **Green Rating:** 68

STUDENTS AND FACULTY

Enrollment: 973. **Student Body:** 55% female, 45% male, 43% out-of-state, 3% international (16 countries represented). Asian 1%, African American 1%, Caucasian 98%, Hispanic 2%.
Retention and Graduation: 73% freshmen return for sophomore year. 54% freshmen graduate within 4 years. 10% grads go on to further study within 1 year. 2.5% grads pursue arts and sciences degrees. 0.6% grads pursue law degrees. 3.1% grads pursue business degrees. 2.5% grads pursue medical degrees. **Faculty:** Student/faculty ratio 13:1. 62 full-time faculty, 76% hold PhDs, 6% are members of minority groups, 37% are women.

ACADEMICS

Degrees: Associate, bachelor's, diploma, master's, terminal associate, transfer associate. **Classes:** Most classes have 10–19 students. Most lab/discussion sessions have 10–19 students. **Majors with Highest Enrollment:** Animation, interactive technology, video graphics and special effects; elementary education and teaching; nursing/registered nurse (RN, ASN, BSN, MSN). **Special Study Options:** Accelerated program, double major, independent study, internships, study abroad, teacher certification program, Bible and religion. Special programs offered to physically disabled students include note-taking services, reader services, tutors. **Career services:** Alumni network, alumni services, career/job search classes, career assessment, internships, regional alumni. **Career services highlights include:** www.huntington.edu/erc/.

FACILITIES

Housing: Special housing for disabled students, men's dorms, women's dorms, apartments for single students, college-owned houses. 62% of campus accessible to physically disabled. **Special Academic Facilities/Equipment:** Thornhill Nature Preserve **Computers:** 100% of classrooms, 100% of dorms, 100% of libraries, 100% of dining areas, 100% of student union, have wireless network access. Students can register for classes online. Administrative functions (other than registration) can be performed online.

CAMPUS LIFE

Environment: Town. **Activities:** Choral groups, concert band, dance, drama/theater, jazz band, literary magazine, music ensembles, musical theater, pep band, radio station, student government, student newspaper, student-run film society, television station, yearbook, campus ministries, international student organization. **Organizations:** 6 honor societies, 4 religious organizations.

Athletics (Intercollegiate): *Men:* Baseball, basketball, cheerleading, cross-country, golf, soccer, tennis, track/field (outdoor), track/field (indoor). *Women:* Basketball, cheerleading, cross-country, golf, soccer, softball, tennis, track/field (outdoor), track/field (indoor), volleyball. **On-Campus Highlights:** Residence Halls-lounges, Habecker Dining Commons, Norm's Place-snack lounge, Merillat Complex for P.E.and Recreation, Merillat Centre for the Arts. **Environmental Initiatives:** We are working with our contracted custodial service vendor to secure a Green Cleaning certification. Campus recycling program

ADMISSIONS

Freshman Academic Profile: Average high school GPA 3.39. 18% in top 10% of high school class, 46% in top 25% of high school class, 82% in top 50% of high school class. 84% from public high schools. SAT Math middle 50% range 480–560. SAT Critical Reading middle 50% range 480–580. SAT Writing middle 50% range 440–580. ACT middle 50% range 20–26. Minimum paper TOEFL 530. Minimum computer TOEFL 210. Minimum web-based TOEFL 75. **Basis for Candidate Selection:** *Very important factors considered include:* Academic GPA, rigor of secondary school record, standardized test scores, religious affiliation/commitment. *Important factors considered include:* Class rank, application essay, character/personal qualities, extracurricular activities. *Other factors considered include:* Recommendation(s), alumni/ae relation, first generation, interview, level of applicant's interest, racial/ethnic status, talent/ability, volunteer work, work experience. **Freshman Admission Requirements:** High school diploma is required and GED is accepted. *Academic units required:* 4 English, 3 mathematics, 2 science, (1 science labs), 2 social studies, 2 history. *Academic units recommended:* 2 foreign language, 2 visual/performing arts, 1 computer science, 2 academic electives. **Freshman Admission Statistics:** 897 applied, 89% admitted, 32% enrolled. **Transfer Admission Requirements:** College transcript(s), essay or personal statement, minimum college GPA of 2.0 required. Lowest grade transferable C. **General Admission Information:** Application fee $20. Regular application deadline 8/1. Notification on a rolling basis, beginning on or about 10/1. Nonfall registration accepted. Admission may be deferred for a maximum of 1 year. Credit and/or placement offered for CEEB Advanced Placement tests.

COSTS AND FINANCIAL AID

Annual tuition $20,820. Room and board $7,180. Required fees $470. Average book expense $900. **Required Forms and Deadlines:** FAFSA. Priority financial aid filing date 3/1. **Notification of Awards:** Applicants will be notified of awards on a rolling basis beginning 3/1. **Types of Aid:** *Need-based scholarships/grants:* Federal Pell, SEOG, state scholarships/grants, private scholarships, the school's own gift aid. *Loans:* FFEL Subsidized Stafford, FFEL Unsubsidized Stafford, FFEL PLUS, Federal Perkins. **Student Employment:** Federal Work-Study Program available. Institutional employment available. Highest amount earned per year from on-campus jobs $3,500. Off-campus job opportunities are good. **Financial Aid Statistics:** 83% freshmen, 70% undergrads receive need-based scholarship or grant aid. 27% freshmen, 25% undergrads receive non-need-based scholarship or grant aid. 77% freshmen, 68% undergrads receive need-based self-help aid. 4% freshmen, 4% undergrads receive athletic scholarships. 90% freshmen, 81% undergrads receive any aid. 55% undergrads borrow to pay for school. Average cumulative indebtedness $27,541. **Criteria for awarding institutional aid:** *Non-need-based:* Academics, alumni affiliation, art, athletics, leadership, music/drama, religious affiliation.

HUSSON UNIVERSITY

One College Circle, Bangor, ME 04401
Phone: 207-941-7100 **Financial Aid Phone:** 207-941-7156
E-mail: admit@husson.edu **CEEB Code:** 3440
Fax: 207-941-7935 **Website:** www.husson.edu **ACT Code:** 1646

This private school was founded in 1898. It has a 170-acre campus.

RATINGS
Admissions Selectivity Rating: 72   **Fire Safety Rating:** 93   **Green Rating:** 60*

STUDENTS AND FACULTY
Enrollment: 2,383. **Student Body:** 58% female, 42% male, 14% out-of-state, 1% international (9 countries represented). Asian 1%, African American 5%, Caucasian 91%, Hispanic 1%.
Retention and Graduation: 67% freshmen return for sophomore year. 3% grads go on to further study within 1 year. 1% grads pursue arts and sciences degrees. 1% grads pursue law degrees. 2% grads pursue business degrees.
Faculty: Student/faculty ratio 18:1. 101 full-time faculty, 67% hold PhDs, 5% are members of minority groups, 44% are women.

ACADEMICS
Degrees: Associate, bachelor's, certificate, diploma, master's, post-master's certificate, terminal associate. **Classes:** Most classes have 20–29 students. Most lab/discussion sessions have fewer than 10 students. **Majors with Highest Enrollment:** Business/commerce; nursing/registered nurse (RN, ASN, BSN, MSN); physical therapy/therapist. **Special Study Options:** Accelerated program, cooperative education program, distance learning, double major, dual enrollment, independent study, internships, liberal arts/career combination, student-designed major, teacher certification program, weekend college. **Combined degree programs:** BS/BS, BS/MS, DPT/BS. Special programs offered to physically disabled students include note-taking services, tape recorders, tutors. **Career services:** Alumni network, career/job search classes, internships.

FACILITIES
Housing: Coed dorms, special housing for disabled students 85% of campus accessible to physically disabled. **Special Academic Facilities/Equipment:** White Art Gallery, Dahl Anatomy Lab, Kenduskeag Research Institute, Gracie Theater. **Computers:** 100% of classrooms, 100% of dorms, 100% of libraries, 100% of student union, have wireless network access. Students can register for classes online. Administrative functions (other than registration) can be performed online.

CAMPUS LIFE
Environment: City. **Activities:** Drama/theater, literary magazine, pep band, radio station, student government, student newspaper, television station, yearbook, campus ministries, international student organization. **Organizations:** 30 registered organizations, 1 honor societies, 2 religious organizations. 2 fraternities, 3 sororities. **Athletics (Intercollegiate):** *Men:* Baseball, basketball, football, golf, lacrosse, soccer. *Women:* Basketball, field hockey, lacrosse, soccer, softball, swimming, tennis, volleyball. **On-Campus Highlights:** Swan Fitness Center, Campus Center, Student Lounge, Newman Gym, Library, The Meeting House, a new academic building, opened in the fall of 2008. The attached 500–seat balconied, performing arts center opened in the fall of 2009. **Environmental Initiatives:** Green cleaning supplies, recycle paper

ADMISSIONS
Freshman Academic Profile: Average high school GPA 3.03. 11% in top 10% of high school class, 30% in top 25% of high school class, 61% in top 50% of high school class. 92% from public high schools. SAT Math middle 50% range 420–510. SAT Critical Reading middle 50% range 410–510. SAT Writing middle 50% range 390–500. ACT middle 50% range 16–22. Minimum paper TOEFL 500. Minimum computer TOEFL 173. **Basis for Candidate Selection:** *Very important factors considered include:* Recommendation(s), rigor of secondary school record, interview. *Important factors considered include:* Class rank, application essay, academic GPA, standardized test scores, character/personal qualities, extracurricular activities. *Other factors considered include:* Alumni/ae relation, first generation, level of applicant's interest, volunteer work, work experience. **Freshman Admission Requirements:** High school diploma is required and GED is accepted. *Academic units recommended:* 4 English, 3 mathematics, 3 science, (2 science labs), 1 social studies, 1 history. **Freshman Admission Statistics:** 1,280 applied, 64% admitted, 65% enrolled. **Transfer Admission Requirements:** High school transcript, college transcript(s), essay or personal statement, minimum college GPA of 2.0 required. Lowest grade transferable C. **General Admission Information:** Application fee $25. Notification on a rolling basis, beginning on or about 12/1. Nonfall registration accepted. Admission may be deferred for a maximum of 1 year. Credit and/or placement offered for CEEB Advanced Placement tests.

COSTS AND FINANCIAL AID
Annual tuition $12,690. Room and board $6,994. Required fees $300. Average book expense $970. **Required Forms and Deadlines:** FAFSA. Priority financial aid filing date 4/15. **Notification of Awards:** Applicants will be notified of awards on a rolling basis beginning 3/1. **Types of Aid:** *Need-based scholarships/grants:* Federal Pell, SEOG, state scholarships/grants, private scholarships, the school's own gift aid. *Loans:* FFEL Subsidized Stafford, FFEL Unsubsidized Stafford, FFEL PLUS, Federal Perkins, state loans. **Student Employment:** Federal Work-Study Program available. Institutional employment available. Highest amount earned per year from on-campus jobs $1,600. Off-campus job opportunities are good. **Financial Aid Statistics:** 97% freshmen, 75% undergrads receive need-based scholarship or grant aid. 2% freshmen, 3% undergrads receive non-need-based scholarship or grant aid. 78% freshmen, 79% undergrads receive need-based self-help aid. 92% freshmen, 87% undergrads receive any aid. 80% undergrads borrow to pay for school. Average cumulative indebtedness $33,010. **Criteria for awarding institutional aid:** *Non-need-based:* Academics, leadership.

HUSTON-TILLOTSON UNIVERSITY

900 Chicon Street, Austin, TX 78702
Phone: 512-505-3028
E-mail: admission@htu.edu **CEEB Code:** 6280
Fax: 512-505-3192 **Website:** www.htu.edu. **ACT Code:** 4104

This private school was founded in 1875. It has a 35-acre campus.

RATINGS
Admissions Selectivity Rating: 70　　**Fire Safety Rating:** 60*　　**Green Rating:** 60*

STUDENTS AND FACULTY
Enrollment: 843. **Student Body:** 52% female, 48% male, 6% out-of-state, 3% international (13 countries represented). African American 77%, Caucasian 6%, Hispanic 13%.
Retention and Graduation: 55% freshmen return for sophomore year. 15% freshmen graduate within 4 years. **Faculty:** Student/faculty ratio 16:1. 40 full-time faculty, 75% hold PhDs, 63% are members of minority groups, 58% are women.

ACADEMICS
Degrees: Bachelor's, post-bachelor's certificate. **Classes:** Most classes have fewer than 10 students. Most lab/discussion sessions have fewer than 10 students. **Majors with Highest Enrollment:** Computer and information science; education. **Special Study Options:** cross-registration, distance learning, double major, dual enrollment, external degree program, honors program, independent study, internships, liberal arts/career combination, study abroad, teacher certification program, 3-2 Engineering Program with Prairie View A&M University.

FACILITIES
Housing: Men's dorms, women's dorms.

CAMPUS LIFE
Activities: Choral groups, dance, jazz band, literary magazine, music ensembles, student government, student-run film society, campus ministries, international student organization. **Organizations:** 17 registered organizations, 5 honor societies, 5 religious organizations. **Athletics (Intercollegiate):** *Men:* Baseball, basketball, soccer, track/field (outdoor). *Women:* Basketball, track/field (outdoor), volleyball.

ADMISSIONS
Freshman Academic Profile: Average high school GPA 2.83. 6% in top 10% of high school class, 29% in top 25% of high school class, 47% in top 50% of high school class. 91% from public high schools. SAT Math middle 50% range 360–460. SAT Critical Reading middle 50% range 350–460. ACT middle 50% range 14–18. Minimum paper TOEFL 500. Minimum computer TOEFL 173.
Basis for Candidate Selection: *Very important factors considered include:* Rigor of secondary school record, standardized test scores. *Important factors considered include:* Application essay, academic GPA, interview, religious affiliation/commitment. *Other factors considered include:* Recommendation(s), alumni/ae relation, extracurricular activities, talent/ability. **Freshman Admission Requirements:** High school diploma is required and GED is accepted. *Academic units required:* 4 English, 3 mathematics, 2 science, 3 social studies, 1 computer science, 2 health/P.E. *Academic units recommended:* 2 foreign language. **Freshman Admission Statistics:** 1,422 applied, 48% admitted, 36% enrolled. **Transfer Admission Requirements:** College transcript(s), essay or personal statement, minimum college GPA of 2.0 required. Lowest grade transferable C. **General Admission Information:** Application fee $25. Regular application deadline 7/1. Notification on a rolling basis, beginning on or about 1/1. Nonfall registration accepted. Admission may be deferred for a maximum of 1 Year. Credit and/or placement offered for CEEB Advanced Placement tests.

COSTS AND FINANCIAL AID
Annual tuition $9,450. Room and board $6,690. Required fees $1,734. Average book expense $800. **Required Forms and Deadlines:** FAFSA, institution's own financial aid form. Priority financial aid filing date 3/15. **Notification of Awards:** Applicants will be notified of awards on a rolling basis beginning 4/1. **Types of Aid:** *Need-based scholarships/grants:* Federal Pell, SEOG, state scholarships/grants, private scholarships, the school's own gift aid, United Negro College Fund. *Loans:* Direct Subsidized Stafford, Direct Unsubsidized Stafford, Direct PLUS, FFEL Subsidized Stafford, FFEL Unsubsidized Stafford, FFEL PLUS, state loans, private loans. **Student Employment:** Federal Work-Study Program available. Off-campus job opportunities are good. **Financial Aid Statistics:** 75% freshmen, 74% undergrads receive need-based scholarship or grant aid. 3% freshmen, 3% undergrads receive non-need-based scholarship or grant aid. 89% freshmen, 78% undergrads receive need-based self-help aid. 1% freshmen, 1% undergrads receive athletic scholarships. 87% undergrads borrow to pay for school. Average cumulative indebtedness $12,200. **Criteria**

for awarding institutional aid: *Non-need-based:* Academics, alumni affiliation, art, athletics, job skills, leadership, minority status, music/drama, religious affiliation, state/district residency.

IDAHO STATE UNIVERSITY

Museum of National History 319, Stop 8270, Pocatello, ID 83209-8270
Phone: 208-282-2475 **Financial Aid Phone:** 208-282-2981
E-mail: info@isu.edu **CEEB Code:** 4355
Fax: 208-282-4231 **Website:** www.isu.edu **ACT Code:** 918

This public school was founded in 1901. It has a 1100-acre campus.

RATINGS
Admissions Selectivity Rating: 72　　**Fire Safety Rating:** 60*　　**Green Rating:** 66

STUDENTS AND FACULTY
Enrollment: 10,034. **Student Body:** 54% female, 46% male, 6% out-of-state, 1% international (65 countries represented). Asian 2%, African American 1%, Caucasian 82%, Hispanic 6%, Native American 2%.
Retention and Graduation: 60% freshmen return for sophomore year. 4% freshmen graduate within 4 years. **Faculty:** Student/faculty ratio 16:1. 602 full-time faculty, 76% hold PhDs, 7% are members of minority groups, 43% are women.

ACADEMICS
Degrees: Associate, bachelor's, certificate, doctoral, master's, post-bachelor's certificate, post-master's certificate. **Classes:** Most classes have 10–19 students. Most lab/discussion sessions have 20–29 students. **Special Study Options:** Accelerated program, cooperative education program, cross-registration, distance learning, double major, dual enrollment, English as a Second Language (ESL), exchange student program (domestic), honors program, independent study, internships, liberal arts/career combination, student-designed major, study abroad, teacher certification program, weekend college. **Honors programs:** Honors courses are offered in small classes and deal with interdisciplinary issues and confront some aspect of the human condition. Innovative teaching and assignments are encourages and interaction with faculty and class members is lively. **Combined degree programs:** BA/MA, BS/MS in chemistry. Special programs offered to physically disabled students include note-taking services, reader services, tape recorders, tutors.

FACILITIES
Housing: Coed dorms, special housing for disabled students, men's dorms, women's dorms, fraternity/sorority housing, apartments for married students, apartments for single students, graduate student housing. 100% of campus accessible to physically disabled. **Special Academic Facilities/Equipment:** Museum of Natural History, Idaho Accelerator Center, Rendezvous Center. **Computers:** Students can register for classes online. Administrative functions (other than registration) can be performed online.

CAMPUS LIFE
Environment: Town. **Activities:** Choral groups, concert band, dance, drama/theater, jazz band, marching band, music ensembles, musical theater, opera, pep band, radio station, student government, student newspaper, symphony orchestra, television station, yearbook, campus ministries, international student organization. **Organizations:** 134 registered organizations, 8 honor societies, 7 religious organizations. 2 fraternities, 3 sororities. **Athletics (Intercollegiate):** *Men:* Basketball, cheerleading, cross-country, football, golf, tennis, track/field (outdoor). *Women:* Basketball, cheerleading, cross-country, golf, soccer, softball, tennis, track/field (outdoor), volleyball. **On-Campus Highlights:** Idaho Museum of Natural History, Rock Climbing Wall at Reed Gym, L.E. and Thelma E Stephens Performing Arts, Rendezvous Center, Particle Accelerator.

ADMISSIONS
Freshman Academic Profile: Average high school GPA 3.21. 13% in top 10% of high school class, 31% in top 25% of high school class, 61% in top 50% of high school class. 91% from public high schools. SAT Math middle 50% range 470–570. SAT Writing middle 50% range 460–600. ACT middle 50% range 18–24. Minimum paper TOEFL 500. Minimum computer TOEFL 173. **Basis for Candidate Selection:** *Other factors considered include:* Academic GPA, standardized test scores. **Freshman Admission Requirements:** High school diploma is required and GED is accepted. *Academic units required:* 4 English, 3 mathematics, 3 science, (1 science labs), 1 foreign language. *Academic units recommended:* 4 mathematics. **Freshman Admission Statistics:** 3,889 applied, 73% admitted, 67% enrolled. **Transfer Admission Requirements:** High school transcript, college transcript(s), standardized test scores, minimum college GPA of 2.0 required. Lowest grade transferable D. **General Admission Information:** Application fee $40. Notification on a rolling basis, beginning

on or about 3/1. Nonfall registration accepted. Admission may be deferred for a maximum of 3 years. Credit and/or placement offered for CEEB Advanced Placement tests.

COSTS AND FINANCIAL AID

Annual in-state tuition $3,318. Annual out-of-state tuition $13,120. Room and board $5,050. Required fees $1,650. Average book expense $900. **Required Forms and Deadlines:** FAFSA. Priority financial aid filing date 3/1. **Notification of Awards:** Applicants will be notified of awards on a rolling basis beginning 4/1. **Types of Aid:** *Need-based scholarships/grants:* Federal Pell, SEOG, state scholarships/grants, private scholarships, the school's own gift aid, Federal Nursing Scholarships. *Loans:* Direct Subsidized Stafford, Direct Unsubsidized Stafford, Direct PLUS, Federal Perkins. **Student Employment:** Off-campus job opportunities are good. **Financial Aid Statistics:** 36% freshmen, 48% undergrads receive need-based scholarship or grant aid. 42% freshmen, 26% undergrads receive non-need-based scholarship or grant aid. 34% freshmen, 56% undergrads receive need-based self-help aid. 5% freshmen, 4% undergrads receive athletic scholarships. 68% freshmen, 70% undergrads receive any aid. 72% undergrads borrow to pay for school. Average cumulative indebtedness $21,862. **Criteria for awarding institutional aid:** *Non-need-based:* Academics, alumni affiliation, art, athletics, leadership, minority status, music/drama, state/district residency.

ILLINOIS COLLEGE

1101 West College, Jacksonville, IL 62650
Phone: 217-245-3030
E-mail: admissions@ic.edu **CEEB Code:** 1315
Fax: 217-245-3034 **Website:** www.ic.edu **ACT Code:** 1034

This private school, affiliated with the Presbyterian Church, was founded in 1829. It has a 62-acre campus.

RATINGS
Admissions Selectivity Rating: 84   **Fire Safety Rating:** 60*   **Green Rating:** 60*

STUDENTS AND FACULTY
Enrollment: 854. **Student Body:** 50% female, 50% male, 10% out-of-state, 3% international. Asian 1%, African American 5%, Caucasian 82%, Hispanic 2%, Native American 1%.
Retention and Graduation: 83% freshmen return for sophomore year. 50% freshmen graduate within 4 years. 22% grads go on to further study within 1 year. 13% grads pursue arts and sciences degrees. 5% grads pursue law degrees. 2% grads pursue business degrees. 4% grads pursue medical degrees. **Faculty:** Student/faculty ratio 11:1. 74 full-time faculty, 84% hold PhDs, 9% are members of minority groups, 50% are women.

ACADEMICS
Degrees: Bachelor's. **Classes:** Most classes have 10–19 students. Most lab/discussion sessions have 10–19 students. **Special Study Options:** Cross-registration, double major, dual enrollment, independent study, internships, liberal arts/career combination, student-designed major, study abroad, teacher certification program. **Combined degree programs:** 3-2 nursing, 3-2 occupational ther and 3-1 med-tech. **Career services:** Career/job search classes, career assessment, internships.

FACILITIES
Housing: Coed dorms, men's dorms, women's dorms, apartments for single students. **Special Academic Facilities/Equipment:** Art gallery, language lab.

CAMPUS LIFE
Environment: Rural. **Activities:** Choral groups, concert band, drama/theater, literary magazine, music ensembles, student government, student newspaper, yearbook, campus ministries, international student organization, Model UN. **Organizations:** 72 registered organizations, 12 honor societies, 3 religious organizations. 4 fraternities, 3 sororities. **Athletics (Intercollegiate):** *Men:* Baseball, basketball, cross-country, football, golf, soccer, tennis, track/field (outdoor), track/field (indoor), wrestling. *Women:* Basketball, cheerleading, cross-country, golf, soccer, softball, tennis, track/field (outdoor), track/field (indoor), volleyball.

ADMISSIONS
Freshman Academic Profile: Average high school GPA 3.39. 26% in top 10% of high school class, 56% in top 25% of high school class, 85% in top 50% of high school class. 80% from public high schools. ACT middle 50% range 21–27. Minimum paper TOEFL 550. **Basis for Candidate Selection:** *Very important factors considered include:* Academic GPA, rigor of secondary school record, character/personal qualities. *Important factors considered include:* Class rank, application essay, recommendation(s), extracurricular activities, interview,

state residency, talent/ability. *Other factors considered include:* Standardized test scores, alumni/ae relation, first generation, geographical residence, level of applicant's interest, racial/ethnic status, volunteer work, work experience. **Freshman Admission Requirements:** High school diploma is required and GED is accepted. *Academic units required:* 4 English, 3 mathematics, 2 science, (2 science labs), 1 social studies, 1 history, 3 academic electives. *Academic units recommended:* 4 English, 3 mathematics, 3 science, (3 science labs), 2 foreign language, 1 social studies, 1 history, 3 academic electives. **Freshman Admission Statistics:** 1,313 applied, 55% admitted, 31% enrolled. **Transfer Admission Requirements:** High school transcript, college transcript(s), minimum college GPA of 2.50 required. Lowest grade transferable C. **General Admission Information:** Notification on a rolling basis, beginning on or about 11/15. Nonfall registration accepted. Admission may be deferred for a maximum of 1 year. Credit and/or placement offered for CEEB Advanced Placement tests.

COSTS AND FINANCIAL AID
Annual tuition $20,900, Room and board $7,600. Required fees $400. Average book expense $900. **Required Forms and Deadlines:** FAFSA. Priority financial aid filing date 3/1. **Notification of Awards:** Applicants will be notified of awards on a rolling basis beginning 3/1. **Types of Aid:** *Need-based scholarships/grants:* Federal Pell, SEOG, state scholarships/grants, private scholarships, the school's own gift aid. *Loans:* Direct Subsidized Stafford, Direct Unsubsidized Stafford, Direct PLUS, Federal Perkins. **Student Employment:** Federal Work-Study Program available. Institutional employment available. Highest amount earned per year from on-campus jobs $800. Off-campus job opportunities are good. **Financial Aid Statistics:** 80% freshmen, 81% undergrads receive need-based scholarship or grant aid. 14% freshmen, 12% undergrads receive non-need-based scholarship or grant aid. 65% freshmen, 68% undergrads receive need-based self-help aid. 76% undergrads borrow to pay for school. Average cumulative indebtedness $21,258. **Criteria for awarding institutional aid:** *Non-need-based:* Academics, art, minority status, music/drama.

ILLINOIS INSTITUTE OF TECHNOLOGY

Best 373

10 West 33rd Street, PH 101, Chicago, IL 60616
Phone: 312-567-3025 **Financial Aid Phone:** 312-567-7219
E-mail: admission@iit.edu **CEEB Code:** 1318
Fax: 312-567-6939 **Website:** www.iit.edu **ACT Code:** 1040

This private school was founded in 1892. It has a 120-acre campus.

RATINGS
Admissions Selectivity Rating: 92   **Fire Safety Rating:** 70   **Green Rating:** 86

STUDENTS AND FACULTY
Enrollment: 2,618. **Student Body:** 29% female, 71% male, 82% out-of-state, 17% international (103 countries represented). Asian 13%, African American 4%, Caucasian 46%, Hispanic 8%, Native American 1%.
Retention and Graduation: 89% freshmen return for sophomore year. 35% freshmen graduate within 4 years. **Faculty:** Student/faculty ratio 10:1. 385 full-time faculty, 89% hold PhDs, 3% are members of minority groups, 21% are women.

ACADEMICS
Degrees: Bachelor's, master's. **Classes:** Most classes have 10–19 students. Most lab/discussion sessions have 20–29 students. **Majors with Highest Enrollment:** Architecture (BArch, BA/BS, MArch, MA/MS, PhD); electrical, electronics and communications engineering; mechanical engineering. **Special Study Options:** Cooperative education program, cross-registration, distance learning, double major, English as a Second Language (ESL), independent study, liberal arts/career combination, study abroad, teacher certification program, Joint Enrollment: Enrollment at 2 institutions for 2 degrees. **Honors programs:** Honors Pharmacy Program, and Honors Medical Program, Honors Law Program, Business Honors Law Program. **Combined degree programs:** BS/MBA; BS/JD; BArch/MS; BArch/MBA; BS/MS; BS/MPA. Special programs offered to physically disabled students include note-taking services, reader services, tape recorders, tutors. **Career services:** Alumni network, alumni services, career/job search classes, career assessment, internships, regional alumni. **Career services highlights include:** Co-operative Education.

FACILITIES

Housing: Coed dorms, fraternity/sorority housing, men's/women's floors in residence halls, university apartments, arrangements for disabled students. 90% of campus accessible to physically disabled. **Special Academic Facilities/Equipment:** The Center for Accelerator and Particle Physics (CAPP), The Center for Complex Systems and Dynamics (CCSD), The Center for Digital Design and Manufacturing (CDDM), The Center for Electrochemical Science and Engineering, The Center for Excellence in Polymer Science and Engineering, The Center for Integrative Neuroscience and Neuroengineering Research, The Center for the Management of Medical Technology (CMMT), The Center for Molecular Study of Soft Condensed Matter (CMS2), The Center for Strategic Competitiveness (CSC), The Center for the Study of Ethics in the Professions (CSEP), The Center for Synchrotron Radiation Research and Instrumentation, The Center for Work Zone Safety and Mobility (CWZSM), Electric Power and Power Electronics Center (EPPEC), Energy + Power Center, Energy and Sustainability Institute, The Engineering Center For Diabetes Research and Education (ECDRE), The Fluid Dynamics Research Center, The High Performance Computing Center (HPCC), IIT Research Institute (IITRI), The International Center for Sensor Science and Engineering (ICSSE), The International Center for Sustainable New Cities (ICSNC), The Medical Imaging Research Center (MIRC), The National Center for Food Safety and Technology (NCFST), The Particle Technology and Crystallization Center (PTCC), The Pritzker Institute of Biomedical Science and Engineering, The Thermal Processing Technology Center (TPTC), The Wireless Network and Communications Research Center (WiNCom), Main Campus design by Ludwig Mies van der Rohe, McCormick Tribune Campus Center (MTCC) design by Rem Koolhaas, residence hall designed by Helmut Jahn, IIT Research Institute (IITRI), University Technology Park At IIT (UTP), Kemper Room Art Gallery, Illinois Tech Model Railroad (ITMR). **Computers:** 100% of classrooms, 100% of dorms, 100% of libraries, 100% of dining areas, 100% of student union, have wireless network access. Students can register for classes online. Administrative functions (other than registration) can be performed online.

CAMPUS LIFE

Environment: Metropolis. **Activities:** Choral groups, concert band, dance, drama/theater, literary magazine, music ensembles, musical theater, radio station, student government, student newspaper, student-run film society, television station, yearbook, campus ministries, international student organization. **Organizations:** 100 registered organizations, 4 honor societies, 10 religious organizations. 7 fraternities, 3 sororities. **Athletics (Intercollegiate):** *Men:* Baseball, cross-country, diving, soccer, swimming. *Women:* cross-country, diving, soccer, swimming, volleyball. **On-Campus Highlights:** S.R. Crown Hall (Architecture Building), McCormick Tribune Center, Keating Athletic Center, Hermann Hall, State Street Village. **Environmental Initiatives:** Creation of an Office of Campus Energy and Sustainability and the Wanger Institute of Sustainable Energy Research bringing students, faculty, staff, and alumni together to address complex sustainability issues. Energy Efficiency through Retro-Commissioning, System Improvements, and LEED: University Sustainability Policies: Recognizing that human behavior represents the largest obstacle and opportunity related to implementing sustainability on campus, IIT adopted seven Campus Sustainability Policies in April 2009. These include some related to university operations, but most related to the actions of the occupants. Students, faculty and staff commit to turn off electricity consuming equipment when not in use, reduce printing use, and actively recycle. Campus operations is developing a comprehensive energy policy to create reductions in demand and consumption, revise landscape management practices to reduce water and fuel consumption, and eliminate the purchase of bottled water throughout campus. Information Management: The Office of Campus Energy and Sustainability (OCES) in cooperation with the Facilities Maintenance Department will upgrade all campus meters to a real-time, digital system to allow for better communication of resource use patterns. This information will help decision makers get better data in a more useful format, and allow end-users to see the impact of their actions in a real-time fashion. With this system, OCES will implement competitions and education initiatives that will drive down the base-load of the campus. LEED: All new buildings on campus will be designed to achieve LEED certification. OCES is working with Facilities Maintenance at the Main Campus, Downtown Campus and Rice Campus to implement LEED for Existing Buildings: Operations and Maintenance 2009 in five campus buildings in 2010. This April, IIT will announce plans to expand that throughout all campus buildings. Recycling Expansion: In 2008, IIT re-invigorated its recycling program under the banner of "IIT Hawk Recycling" and expanded into other areas to include other recyclables such as glass, cans, and batteries in addition to the paper and e-waste programs already in existence. In 2009, the program was expanded to include all campus academic, support and residence buildings and is anticipated to include all research buildings by May 2010. IIT projects an annual improvement between 5-10% in recycling rates due to the expanded program. The recycling effort will avoid approximately 750 cubic yards of landfill waste per year. Recycling reports are available to the campus community, as well as details on where recycled material ends up, at www.iit.edu/recycling. In addition, IIT has collaborated with the government of Cook County to implement an organic waste recycling program on campus that is targeted to begin in spring 2010.

ADMISSIONS

Freshman Academic Profile: Average high school GPA 3.42. 41% in top 10% of high school class, 72% in top 25% of high school class, 96% in top 50% of high school class. 75% from public high schools. SAT Math middle 50% range 630–723. SAT Critical Reading middle 50% range 540–670. SAT Writing middle 50% range 528–640. ACT middle 50% range 25–31. Minimum paper TOEFL 550. Minimum computer TOEFL 213. Minimum web-based TOEFL 80. **Basis for Candidate Selection:** *Very important factors considered include:* Academic GPA, rigor of secondary school record. *Important factors considered include:* Class rank, application essay, recommendation(s), standardized test scores. *Other factors considered include:* Alumni/ae relation, character/personal qualities, extracurricular activities, first generation, interview, level of applicant's interest, talent/ability, volunteer work, work experience. **Freshman Admission Requirements:** High school diploma is required and GED is accepted. *Academic units required:* 4 English, 4 mathematics, 3 science, (2 science labs), 2 foreign language, 2 social studies. *Academic units recommended:* 4 English, 4 mathematics, 3 science, (2 science labs), 2 foreign language, 2 social studies, 2 history, 1 visual/performing arts, 1 computer science. **Freshman Admission Statistics:** 2,918 applied, 60% admitted, 45% enrolled. **Transfer Admission Requirements:** College transcript(s), essay or personal statement, statement of good standing from prior institution(s). Minimum college GPA of 3.0 required. Lowest grade transferable C. **General Admission Information:** Early decision application deadline 11/9. Notification on a rolling basis, beginning on or about 10/10. Nonfall registration accepted. Admission may be deferred for a maximum of 1 Year. Credit and/or placement offered for CEEB Advanced Placement tests.

COSTS AND FINANCIAL AID

Average book expense $1,000. **Required Forms and Deadlines:** FAFSA. Priority financial aid filing date 4/15. **Notification of Awards:** Applicants will be notified of awards on a rolling basis beginning 3/1. **Types of Aid:** *Need-based scholarships/grants:* Federal Pell, SEOG, state scholarships/grants, private scholarships, the school's own gift aid. *Loans:* FFEL Subsidized Stafford, FFEL Unsubsidized Stafford, FFEL PLUS, Federal Perkins, college/university loans from institutional funds. **Student Employment:** Federal Work-Study Program available. Institutional employment available. Off-campus job opportunities are good. **Financial Aid Statistics:** 70% freshmen, 60% undergrads receive need-based scholarship or grant aid. 17% freshmen, 8% undergrads receive non-need-based scholarship or grant aid. 45% freshmen, 47% undergrads receive need-based self-help aid. 3% freshmen, 4% undergrads receive athletic scholarships. 98% freshmen, 95% undergrads receive any aid. 61% undergrads borrow to pay for school. Average cumulative indebtedness $21,326. **Criteria for awarding institutional aid:** *Non-need-based:* Academics, alumni affiliation, athletics, leadership, minority status.

See page 1114.

ILLINOIS STATE UNIVERSITY

Admissions Office, Campus Box 2200, Normal, IL 61790-2200
Phone: 309-438-2181 **Financial Aid Phone:** 309-438-2231
E-mail: admissions@ilstu.edu **CEEB Code:** 1319
Fax: 309-438-3932 **Website:** www.ilstu.edu **ACT Code:** 1042

This public school was founded in 1857. It has a 850-acre campus.

RATINGS

Admissions Selectivity Rating: 78   **Fire Safety Rating:** 60*   **Green Rating:** 88

STUDENTS AND FACULTY

Enrollment: 18,325. **Student Body:** 56% female, 44% male, 1% out-of-state, international (56 countries represented). Asian 2%, African American 6%, Caucasian 83%, Hispanic 5%.
Retention and Graduation: 85% freshmen return for sophomore year. 42% freshmen graduate within 4 years. **Faculty:** Student/faculty ratio 19:1. 876 full-time faculty, 83% hold PhDs, 13% are members of minority groups, 48% are women. 7% of classes are taught by teaching assistants.

ACADEMICS

Degrees: Bachelor's, master's, post-bachelor's certificate, post-master's certificate. **Classes:** Most classes have 20–29 students. Most lab/discussion sessions have 20–29 students. **Majors with Highest Enrollment:** Business administration and management; elementary education and teaching; special education and teaching. **Special Study Options:** Accelerated program, cooperative education program, distance learning, double major, dual enrollment, English as a Second Language (ESL), exchange student program (domestic), honors program, independent study, internships, student-designed major, study abroad, teacher certification program. **Combined degree programs:** BS/MPA. Special programs offered to physically disabled students include note-taking services, reader services, tape recorders, tutors. **Career services:** Alumni services, internships.

FACILITIES

Housing: Coed dorms, special housing for disabled students, special housing for international students, women's dorms, fraternity/sorority housing, apartments for married students, apartments for single students 100% of campus accessible to physically disabled. **Special Academic Facilities/Equipment:** Art gallery, cultural museums, on-campus elementary and secondary schools, greenhouse, farm, planetarium. **Computers:** 100% of classrooms, 100% of dorms, 100% of libraries, 100% of dining areas, 100% of student union, have wireless network access. Students can register for classes online. Administrative functions (other than registration) can be performed online. Undergraduates are required to own a computer.

CAMPUS LIFE

Environment: City. **Activities:** Choral groups, concert band, dance, drama/theater, jazz band, literary magazine, marching band, music ensembles, musical theater, pep band, radio station, student government, student newspaper, student-run film society, symphony orchestra, television station. **Organizations:** 270 registered organizations, 23 honor societies, 22 religious organizations. 21 fraternities, 17 sororities. **Athletics (Intercollegiate):** *Men:* Baseball, basketball, cheerleading, cross-country, football, golf, tennis, track/field (outdoor), track/field (indoor). *Women:* Basketball, cheerleading, cross-country, diving, golf, gymnastics, soccer, softball, swimming, tennis, track/field (outdoor), track/field (indoor), volleyball. **On-Campus Highlights:** College of Business Building, Science Laboratory Building, Redbird Arena. **Environmental Initiatives:** Becoming a signatory of the American College and University Presidents' Climate Commitment. The creation of a Renewable Energy major and Center for Renewable Energy. Releasing a formal, campus-wide sustainability report—www.greenteam.ilstu.edu/about/reporting.shtml

ADMISSIONS

Freshman Academic Profile: Average high school GPA 3.4. 88% from public high schools. ACT middle 50% range 22–26. Minimum paper TOEFL 550. Minimum computer TOEFL 213. **Basis for Candidate Selection:** *Very important factors considered include:* Academic GPA, rigor of secondary school record, standardized test scores. *Important factors considered include:* Application essay. *Other factors considered include:* Class rank, character/personal qualities, first generation, talent/ability. **Freshman Admission Requirements:** High school diploma is required and GED is accepted. *Academic units required:* 4 English, 3 mathematics, 2 science, (2 science labs), 2 foreign language, 2 social studies, 2 academic electives. **Freshman Admission Statistics:** 14,114 applied, 62% admitted, 70% enrolled. **Transfer Admission Requirements:** College transcript(s), essay or personal statement, minimum college GPA of 3.0 required. Lowest grade transferable D. **General Admission Information:** Application fee $40. Regular application deadline 3/1. Notification on a rolling basis, beginning on or about 9/1. Nonfall registration accepted. Credit and/or placement offered for CEEB Advanced Placement tests.

COSTS AND FINANCIAL AID

Annual in-state tuition $8,280. Annual out-of-state tuition $14,310. Room and board $7,882. Required fees $2,251. Average book expense $1,084. **Required Forms and Deadlines:** FAFSA. Priority financial aid filing date 3/1. **Notification of Awards:** Applicants will be notified of awards on a rolling basis beginning 4/1. **Types of Aid:** *Need-based scholarships/grants:* Federal Pell, SEOG, state scholarships/grants, private scholarships, the school's own gift aid, Federal Nursing Scholarships. *Loans:* Direct Subsidized Stafford, Direct Unsubsidized Stafford, Direct PLUS, Federal Perkins, Federal Nursing, college/university loans from institutional funds. **Student Employment:** Off-campus job opportunities are excellent. **Financial Aid Statistics:** 34% freshmen, 31% undergrads receive need-based scholarship or grant aid. 31% freshmen, 16% undergrads receive non-need-based scholarship or grant aid. 45% freshmen, 46% undergrads receive need-based self-help aid. 1% freshmen, 1% undergrads receive athletic scholarships. 61% undergrads borrow to pay for school. Average cumulative indebtedness $20,105. **Criteria for awarding institutional aid:** *Non-need-based:* Academics, art, athletics, music/drama.

ILLINOIS WESLEYAN UNIVERSITY

P.O. Box 2900, Bloomington, IL 61702-2900
Phone: 309-556-3031 **Financial Aid Phone:** 309-556-3096
E-mail: iwuadmit@iwu.edu **CEEB Code:** 1320
Fax: 309-556-3820 **Website:** www.iwu.edu **ACT Code:** 1044

This private school was founded in 1850. It has a 80-acre campus.

RATINGS
Admissions Selectivity Rating: 92   **Fire Safety Rating:** 78   **Green Rating:** 73

STUDENTS AND FACULTY
Enrollment: 2,059. **Student Body:** 59% female, 41% male, 12% out-of-state, 4% international (22 countries represented). Asian 5%, African American 5%, Caucasian 75%, Hispanic 3%.
Retention and Graduation: 93% freshmen return for sophomore year. 80% freshmen graduate within 4 years. 35% grads go on to further study within 1 year. **Faculty:** Student/faculty ratio 11:1. 162 full-time faculty, 92% hold PhDs, 13% are members of minority groups, 40% are women.

ACADEMICS
Degrees: Bachelor's. **Classes:** Most classes have 10–19 students. Most lab/discussion sessions have 10–19 students. **Majors with Highest Enrollment:** Biology/biological sciences; business/commerce; psychology. **Special Study Options:** Double major, exchange student program (domestic), honors program, independent study, internships, student-designed major, study abroad, teacher certification program. **Honors programs:** IWU offers a research honors designation to eligible senior students who successfully complete and defend an intensive, advanced research or creative project under the direction of an interdisciplinary faculty committee. Performance Honors designations are also available in the Art, Music, and Theatre Arts. **Combined degree programs:** 3-2 prgrms—Engrng, Forestry, or Environ. Special programs offered to physically disabled students include note-taking services, reader services, tape recorders, tutors. **Career services:** Alumni network, alumni services, career/job search classes, career assessment, internships, regional alumni. **Career services highlights include:** The Action Research Center links students in seminar and internships classes with community partners, such as social service and non-profit agencies. Students in these classes work with the partners on major projects intended to have a lasting, positive impact on the community. Projects have been as varied as those on environmental issues, historic preservation, pre-school education, crisis intervention, mentoring troubled youth, drug courts, living wage legislation, and ESL tutoring. See www2.iwu.edu/action/ for more details.

FACILITIES
Housing: Coed dorms, special housing for disabled students, special housing for international students, fraternity/sorority housing, apartments for single students. Groups of students with common curricular or cocurricular interests can propose and implement theme housing consistent with their educational goals in a limited number of residential buildings. Examples of past and current interest areas include the arts, languages, environmentalism, multi-faith issues, wellness, culinary arts, and internationalism. 80% of campus accessible to physically disabled. **Special Academic Facilities/Equipment:** Observatory, computerized music lab, graphic design studio, Ames Library archives and special collections, visual anthropology lab, social science lab. **Computers:** 60% of classrooms, 100% of libraries, 100% of dining areas, 100% of student union, have wireless network access. Students can register for classes online. Administrative functions (other than registration) can be performed online.

CAMPUS LIFE
Environment: City. **Activities:** Choral groups, concert band, dance, drama/theater, jazz band, literary magazine, music ensembles, musical theater, opera, pep band, radio station, student government, student newspaper, student-run film society, symphony orchestra, television station, yearbook, campus ministries, international student organization, Model UN. **Organizations:** 165 registered organizations, 29 honor societies, 15 religious organizations. 6 fraternities, 5 sororities. **Athletics (Intercollegiate):** *Men:* Baseball, basketball, cross-country, diving, football, golf, soccer, swimming, tennis, track/field (outdoor), track/field (indoor). *Women:* Basketball, cross-country, diving, golf, soccer, softball, swimming, tennis, track/field (outdoor), track/field (indoor), volleyball. **On-Campus Highlights:** Ames Library, Hansen Student Center, Shirk Center for Athletics and Wellness, Center for Natural Science, The Dugout (snack bar and coffee shop). **Environmental Initiatives:** IWU has a commitment to

environmental sustainability in its mission statement. IWU signed the Talloires Declaration. IWU signed the Illinois Sustainability Compact—July 22, 2009. Our new Welcome Center is LEED-certified.

ADMISSIONS

Freshman Academic Profile: Average high school GPA 3.91. 45% in top 10% of high school class, 81% in top 25% of high school class, 99% in top 50% of high school class. 81% from public high schools. SAT Math middle 50% range 600–720. SAT Critical Reading middle 50% range 570–680. ACT middle 50% range 26–30. Minimum paper TOEFL 550. Minimum computer TOEFL 213. **Basis for Candidate Selection:** *Very important factors considered include:* Academic GPA, rigor of secondary school record, interview. *Important factors considered include:* Class rank, application essay, standardized test scores, character/personal qualities, extracurricular activities, talent/ability. *Other factors considered include:* Recommendation(s), alumni/ae relation, first generation, geographical residence, level of applicant's interest, racial/ethnic status, state residency, volunteer work, work experience. **Freshman Admission Requirements:** High school diploma is required and GED is accepted. *Academic units recommended:* 4 English, 3 mathematics, 3 science, (2 science labs), 3 foreign language, 2 social studies. **Freshman Admission Statistics:** 3,321 applied, 54% admitted, 29% enrolled. **Transfer Admission Requirements:** High school transcript, college transcript(s), essay or personal statement, standardized test scores, minimum college GPA of 2.0 required. Lowest grade transferable C–. **General Admission Information:** Notification on a rolling basis, beginning on or about 12/15. Nonfall registration accepted. Admission may be deferred for a maximum of 1 year. Credit and/or placement offered for CEEB Advanced Placement tests.

COSTS AND FINANCIAL AID

Required Forms and Deadlines: FAFSA, institution's own financial aid form, CSS/Financial Aid PROFILE. Financial aid filing deadline 3/1. Priority financial aid filing date 3/1. **Notification of Awards:** Applicants will be notified of awards on a rolling basis beginning 2/15. **Types of Aid:** *Need-based scholarships/grants:* Federal Pell, SEOG, state scholarships/grants, private scholarships, the school's own gift aid. *Loans:* FFEL Subsidized Stafford, FFEL Unsubsidized Stafford, FFEL PLUS, Federal Perkins, Federal Nursing, college/university loans from institutional funds. **Student Employment:** Federal Work-Study Program available. Institutional employment available. Off-campus job opportunities are good. **Financial Aid Statistics:** 67% freshmen, 59% undergrads receive need-based scholarship or grant aid. 14% freshmen, 8% undergrads receive non-need-based scholarship or grant aid. 59% freshmen, 55% undergrads receive need-based self-help aid. 95% freshmen, 89% undergrads receive any aid. 58% undergrads borrow to pay for school. Average cumulative indebtedness $26,458. **Criteria for awarding institutional aid:** *Non-need-based:* Academics, art, music/drama.

IMMACULATA UNIVERSITY COLLEGE OF LIFE-LONG LEARNING

1145 King Road, P, Immaculata, PA 19345-0642
Phone: 610)647-4400 ext. 3238 **Financial Aid Phone:** 877-428-6329
E-mail: cll@immaculata.edu **CEEB Code:** 2320
Fax: 610-647-0215 **Website:** www.immaculata.edu/CLL/home.htm **ACT Code:** 3596

This private school, affiliated with the Roman Catholic Church, was founded in 2000. It has a 400-acre campus.

RATINGS
Admissions Selectivity Rating: 60*   **Fire Safety Rating:** 60*   **Green Rating:** 60*

STUDENTS AND FACULTY
Student Body: 19% out-of-state, (8 countries represented).

ACADEMICS

Degrees: Associate, bachelor's, certificate, post-bachelor's certificate. **Majors with Highest Enrollment:** Business administration and management; human resources management and services, other; nursing/registered nurse (RN, ASN, BSN, MSN). **Special Study Options:** Accelerated program, cooperative education program, cross-registration, distance learning, double major, dual enrollment, external degree program, honors program, independent study, internships, liberal arts/career combination, study abroad, teacher certification program. Special programs offered to physically disabled students include note-taking services, reader services, tape recorders, tutors. **Career services:** Career assessment, internships.

FACILITIES

Housing: No housing is available for CLL students. 100% of campus accessible to physically disabled. **Special Academic Facilities/Equipment:** Annual art show on-campus. **Computers:** Administrative functions (other than registration) can be performed online.

CAMPUS LIFE

Environment: Town. **Activities:** Choral groups, dance, drama/theater, literary magazine, music ensembles, musical theater, student government, student newspaper, symphony orchestra, yearbook. **Organizations:** 28 registered organizations, 14 honor societies, 1 religious organizations. **Athletics (Intercollegiate)** *Men:* Basketball, golf, soccer, tennis. *Women:* Basketball, cross-country, field hockey, golf, lacrosse, soccer, softball, tennis, volleyball. **On-Campus Highlights:** Java Hut, pool, weight room.

ADMISSIONS

Freshman Academic Profile: Minimum paper TOEFL 500. Minimum computer TOEFL 200. **Basis for Candidate Selection:** *Important factors considered include:* Level of applicant's interest. *Other factors considered include:* Character/personal qualities, interview, work experience. **Freshman Admission Requirements:** High school diploma is required and GED is accepted. **Freshman Admission Statistics: Transfer Admission Requirements:** High school transcript, college transcript(s), minimum college GPA of 2.0 required. Lowest grade transferable C. **General Admission Information:** Application fee $50. Nonfall registration accepted. Admission may be deferred for a maximum of 1 year. Credit and/or placement offered for CEEB Advanced Placement tests.

COSTS AND FINANCIAL AID

Annual tuition $10,050. **Required Forms and Deadlines:** FAFSA. **Notification of Awards:** Applicants will be notified of awards on a rolling basis beginning 2/1. **Types of Aid:** *Need-based scholarships/grants:* Federal Pell, state scholarships/grants, private scholarships, United Negro College Fund. *Loans:* FFEL Subsidized Stafford, FFEL Unsubsidized Stafford, FFEL PLUS, Federal Perkins. **Student Employment:** Federal Work-Study Program available. Institutional employment available. Highest amount earned per year from on-campus jobs $1,053. Off-campus job opportunities are good. **Financial Aid Statistics:** 16% undergrads receive need-based scholarship or grant aid. 2% undergrads receive non-need-based scholarship or grant aid. 33% undergrads receive need-based self-help aid. 34% undergrads receive any aid. 80% undergrads borrow to pay for school. Average cumulative indebtedness $12,000.

See page 1116.

INDIANA INSTITUTE OF TECHNOLOGY

1600 East Washington Blvd, Fort Wayne, IN 46803
Phone: 260-422-5561
E-mail: admissions@indtech.edu **CEEB Code:** 1805
Fax: 260-422-7696 **Website:** www.indianatech.edu **ACT Code:** 1208

This private school was founded in 1930. It has a 57-acre campus.

RATINGS
Admissions Selectivity Rating: 61   **Fire Safety Rating:** 60*   **Green Rating:** 60*

STUDENTS AND FACULTY

Enrollment: 2,985. **Student Body:** 56% female, 44% male, 13% out-of-state, 1% international (14 countries represented). Asian 1%, African American 17%, Caucasian 63%, Hispanic 2%, Native American 1%.
Retention and Graduation: 56% freshmen return for sophomore year. 11% freshmen graduate within 4 years. **Faculty:** Student/faculty ratio 17:1. 40 full-time faculty, 38% hold PhDs, 15% are members of minority groups, 30% are women.

ACADEMICS

Degrees: Associate, bachelor's, master's. **Classes:** Most classes have 10–19 students. **Majors with Highest Enrollment:** Business/commerce; electrical, electronics and communications engineering; engineering, other. **Special Study Options:** Accelerated program, cooperative education program, distance learning, double major, external degree program, independent study, internships. **Career services:** Alumni services, career assessment, internships.

FACILITIES

Housing: Coed dorms, fraternity/sorority housing, apartments for single students. **Computers:** Students can register for classes online. Undergraduates are required to own a computer.

CAMPUS LIFE

Activities: Choral groups, dance, pep band, student government, student newspaper. **Organizations:** 14 registered organizations, 1 honor societies, 3 fraternities, 1 sorority. **Athletics (Intercollegiate):** *Men:* Baseball, basketball, soccer. *Women:* Basketball, soccer, softball.

ADMISSIONS

Freshman Academic Profile: Average high school GPA 2.93. 8% in top 10% of high school class, 27% in top 25% of high school class, 57% in top 50% of high school class. 80% from public high schools. Minimum paper TOEFL 500. **Basis for Candidate Selection:** *Very important factors considered include:* Rigor of secondary school record, alumni/ae relation. *Important factors considered include:* Class rank, standardized test scores, interview, racial/ethnic status. *Other factors considered include:* Application essay, recommendation(s), character/personal qualities, extracurricular activities, talent/ability, volunteer work, work experience. **Freshman Admission Requirements:** High school diploma is required and GED is accepted. *Academic units required:* 4 English, 3 mathematics, 2 science. *Academic units recommended:* 4 English, 4 mathematics, 3 science. **Freshman Admission Statistics:** 1,989 applied, 92% admitted, 13% enrolled. **Transfer Admission Requirements:** College transcript(s), minimum college GPA of 2.0 required. Lowest grade transferable C. **General Admission Information:** Application fee $50. Regular application deadline 9/1. Notification on a rolling basis, beginning on or about 10/15. Nonfall registration accepted. Admission may be deferred for a maximum of 2 years. Credit and/or placement offered for CEEB Advanced Placement tests.

COSTS AND FINANCIAL AID

Annual tuition $16,680. Room and board $6,272. **Required Forms and Deadlines:** FAFSA, institution's own financial aid form. Financial aid filing deadline 3/10. Priority financial aid filing date 3/10. **Notification of Awards:** Applicants will be notified of awards on a rolling basis beginning 2/2. **Types of Aid:** *Need-based scholarships/grants:* Federal Pell, SEOG, state scholarships/grants, private scholarships, the school's own gift aid, United Negro College Fund. *Loans:* FFEL Subsidized Stafford, FFEL Unsubsidized Stafford, FFEL PLUS, Federal Perkins. **Student Employment:** Federal Work-Study Program available. Institutional employment available. Off-campus job opportunities are good. **Financial Aid Statistics:** 64% freshmen, 62% undergrads receive need-based scholarship or grant aid. 6% freshmen, 4% undergrads receive non-need-based scholarship or grant aid. 62% freshmen, 65% undergrads receive need-based self-help aid. 6% freshmen, 4% undergrads receive athletic scholarships. 73% undergrads borrow to pay for school. Average cumulative indebtedness $15,020. **Criteria for awarding institutional aid:** *Non-need-based:* Academics, alumni affiliation, athletics, leadership, minority status, music/drama, state/district residency.

INDIANA STATE UNIVERSITY

Office of Admissions, 218 N 6th Street, Erickson H. 114, Terre Haute, IN 47809
Phone: 812-237-2121 **Financial Aid Phone:** 812-237-2215
E-mail: ADMISU@isugw.indstate.edu **CEEB Code:** 1322
Fax: 812-237-8023 **Website:** www.indstate.edu **ACT Code:** 1206

This public school was founded in 1865. It has a 92-acre campus.

RATINGS

Admissions Selectivity Rating: 71   **Fire Safety Rating:** 67   **Green Rating:** 76

STUDENTS AND FACULTY

Enrollment: 8,405. **Student Body:** 51% female, 49% male, 13% out-of-state, 3% international (56 countries represented). Asian 1%, African American 15%, Caucasian 76%, Hispanic 2%.
Retention and Graduation: 64% freshmen return for sophomore year. 17% grads go on to further study within 1 year. **Faculty:** Student/faculty ratio 17.8:1. 430 full-time faculty, 85% hold PhDs, 14% are members of minority groups, 41% are women. 4% of classes are taught by teaching assistants.

ACADEMICS

Degrees: Associate, bachelor's, certificate, master's, post-bachelor's certificate, post-master's certificate, terminal associate, transfer associate. **Classes:** Most classes have 20–29 students. **Majors with Highest Enrollment:** Business administration and management; criminology; nursing/registered nurse (RN, ASN, BSN, MSN). **Special Study Options:** Accelerated program, cooperative education program, distance learning, double major, dual enrollment, English as a Second Language (ESL), honors program, independent study, internships, study abroad, teacher certification program. **Honors programs:** University Honors Program Special programs offered to physically disabled students include note-taking services, tape recorders, tutors. **Career services:** Alumni services, career assessment, internships. **Career services highlights include:**

At Indiana State, students from every discipline are able to apply what they are learning through hands-on inquiry and research, and life-changing field experiences. Our students program robots, conduct research alongside expert faculty, assist K–12 teachers in the classroom, analyze artifacts from a major archaeological dig, compose, dance, write and perform. They assist non-profit organizations, sample deep-ocean sediments off the California coast, and care for patients at our community health education center. Experiential learning brings knowledge to life and gives student the kind of real-world understanding that sets you apart from students at other institutions.

FACILITIES

Housing: Coed dorms, special housing for disabled students, men's dorms, women's dorms, fraternity/sorority housing, apartments for married students, apartments for single students, theme housing, special housing for freshmen, and apartments for students with dependent children. 98% of campus accessible to physically disabled. **Special Academic Facilities/Equipment:** Music hall, art gallery, civic center, museum, flight simulator, audio-visual center, observatory, theaters. **Computers:** 100% of classrooms, 100% of dorms, 100% of libraries, 100% of dining areas, 100% of student union, have wireless network access. Students can register for classes online. Administrative functions (other than registration) can be performed online. Undergraduates are required to own a computer.

CAMPUS LIFE

Environment: Town. **Activities:** Choral groups, concert band, dance, drama/theater, jazz band, literary magazine, marching band, music ensembles, musical theater, pep band, radio station, student government, student newspaper, student-run film society, symphony orchestra, yearbook, campus ministries, international student organization. **Organizations:** 130 registered organizations, 19 honor societies, 13 religious organizations. 11 fraternities, 10 sororities. **Athletics (Intercollegiate):** *Men:* Baseball, basketball, cross-country, football, track/field (outdoor), track/field (indoor). *Women:* Basketball, cross-country, golf, soccer, softball, track/field (outdoor), track/field (indoor), volleyball. **On-Campus Highlights:** Hulman Memorial Student Union, Student Recreation Center, John C. Hook's Memorial Observatory, Cunningham Memorial Library, Three Art Galleries, The Hulman Memorial Student Union Building contains the University Bookstore, The Commons(food court), Le Club(exercise club),etc. Various Libraries = Cunningham Memorial (main), Women Study, Arts and Science, etc. **Environmental Initiatives:** Signing of the ACUPPC Agreement. Policy development that will eventually be spelled out in the Climate Action Plan. President's development of an organizational structure to guide the university through the development of a campus sustainability planning document. Public and Campus Recycling efforts since 1989.

ADMISSIONS

Freshman Academic Profile: Average high school GPA 3. 9.3% in top 10% of high school class, 28.7% in top 25% of high school class, 64% in top 50% of high school class. SAT Math middle 50% range 420–520. SAT Critical Reading middle 50% range 410–510. SAT Writing middle 50% range 390–500. ACT middle 50% range 17–22. Minimum paper TOEFL 500. Minimum computer TOEFL 173. Minimum web-based TOEFL 61. **Basis for Candidate Selection:** *Very important factors considered include:* Class rank, academic GPA, rigor of secondary school record. *Important factors considered include:* Application essay, recommendation(s), standardized test scores. *Other factors considered include:* character/personal qualities, extracurricular activities, interview, talent/ability. **Freshman Admission Requirements:** High school diploma is required and GED is accepted. *Academic units recommended:* 8 English, 7 mathematics, 6 science, (6 science labs), 2 foreign language, 4 social studies, 2 history, 3 academic electives, 2 electives: 2 health and safety/P.E., 6+ career area. **Freshman Admission Statistics:** 8,154 applied, 68% admitted, 36% enrolled. **Transfer Admission Requirements:** College transcript(s), minimum college GPA of 2.0 required. Lowest grade transferable C. **General Admission Information:** Application fee $25. Regular application deadline 8/15. Nonfall registration accepted. Admission may be deferred for a maximum of 1 year. Credit offered for CEEB Advanced Placement tests.

COSTS AND FINANCIAL AID

Annual in-state tuition $7,226. Annual out-of-state tuition $15,802. Room and board $7,463. Required fees $200. Average book expense $1,170. **Required Forms and Deadlines:** FAFSA. Financial aid filing deadline 3/1. Priority financial aid filing date 3/1. **Notification of Awards:** Applicants will be notified of awards on a rolling basis beginning 4/15. **Types of Aid:** *Need-based scholarships/grants:* Federal Pell, SEOG, state scholarships/grants, private scholarships, the school's own gift aid. *Loans:* FFEL Subsidized Stafford, FFEL Unsubsidized Stafford, FFEL PLUS, Federal Perkins, alternative loans. **Student Employment:** Federal Work-Study Program available. Institutional employment available. Highest amount earned per year from on-campus jobs $13,370. Off-campus job opportunities are good. **Financial Aid Statistics:** 44% freshmen, 41% undergrads receive need-based scholarship or grant aid. 43% freshmen, 28% undergrads receive non-need-based scholarship or grant aid. 50% freshmen, 48% undergrads receive need-based self-help aid. 4% freshmen, need-based self-help aid. 78% undergrads borrow to pay for school. Average cumulative indebtedness $27,300. **Criteria for awarding institutional aid:** *Non-need-based:* Academics, alumni affiliation, leadership.

4% undergrads receive athletic scholarships. 69% freshmen, 61% undergrads receive any aid. 66% undergrads borrow to pay for school. Average cumulative indebtedness $22,944. **Criteria for awarding institutional aid:** *Non-need-based:* Academics, alumni affiliation, art, athletics, minority status, music/drama, state/district residency.

INDIANA UNIVERSITY EAST

2325 Chester Boulevard, Whitewater 151, Richmond, IN 47374-1289
Phone: 765-973-8208 **Financial Aid Phone:** 765-973-8206
E-mail: eaadmit@indiana.edu
Fax: 765-973-8288 **Website:** www.iue.edu

This public school was founded in 1971. It has a 182-acre campus.

RATINGS
Admissions Selectivity Rating: 70 **Fire Safety Rating:** 60* **Green Rating:** 60*

STUDENTS AND FACULTY
Enrollment: 2,444. **Student Body:** 68% female, 32% male, 15% out-of-state, international (11 countries represented). Asian 1%, African American 4%, Caucasian 89%, Hispanic 1%.
Retention and Graduation: 60% freshmen return for sophomore year. 9% freshmen graduate within 4 years. **Faculty:** Student/faculty ratio 16:1. 86 full-time faculty, 56% hold PhDs, 13% are members of minority groups, 58% are women.

ACADEMICS
Degrees: Associate, bachelor's, master's, post-bachelor's certificate. **Classes:** Most classes have 10–19 students. **Majors with Highest Enrollment:** Business/commerce; elementary education and teaching; nursing/registered nurse (RN, ASN, BSN, MSN). **Special Study Options:** cooperative education program, cross-registration, distance learning, double major, dual enrollment, external degree program, honors program, independent study, internships, teacher certification program, weekend college, State-wide technology program with Purdue University. Special programs offered to physically disabled students include note-taking services, reader services, tape recorders, tutors.

FACILITIES
Housing: Computers: Students can register for classes online. Administrative functions (other than registration) can be performed online.

CAMPUS LIFE
Environment: Town. **Activities:** Drama/theater, literary magazine, student government, student newspaper, television station. **Organizations: Athletics (Intercollegiate):** *Men:* Basketball, golf. *Women:* Volleyball.

ADMISSIONS
Freshman Academic Profile: Average high school GPA 2.99. 5% in top 10% of high school class, 24% in top 25% of high school class, 62% in top 50% of high school class. SAT Math middle 50% range 420–510. SAT Critical Reading middle 50% range 400–510. ACT middle 50% range 17–22. **Basis for Candidate Selection:** *Very important factors considered include:* Rigor of secondary school record, standardized test scores. *Important factors considered include:* Class rank, academic GPA. *Other factors considered include:* Geographical residence, state residency. **Freshman Admission Requirements:** High school diploma is required and GED is accepted. *Academic units required:* 4 English, 3 mathematics, 1 science, (1 science labs), 2 social studies. *Academic units recommended:* 3 mathematics, 4 academic electives. **Freshman Admission Statistics:** 861 applied, 74% admitted, 63% enrolled. **Transfer Admission Requirements:** College transcript(s), minimum college GPA of 2.0 required. Lowest grade transferable C. **General Admission Information:** Application fee $35. Notification on a rolling basis, beginning on or about 9/1. Nonfall registration accepted. Admission may be deferred for a maximum of Contact campus.

COSTS AND FINANCIAL AID
Annual in-state tuition $5,416. Annual out-of-state tuition $14,572. Required fees $385. Average book expense $1,076. **Required Forms and Deadlines:** FAFSA, institution's own financial aid form. Priority financial aid filing date 3/1. **Notification of Awards:** Applicants will be notified of awards on a rolling basis beginning 5/1. **Types of Aid:** *Need-based scholarships/grants:* Federal Pell, SEOG, state scholarships/grants, private scholarships, the school's own gift aid. *Loans:* Direct Subsidized Stafford, Direct Unsubsidized Stafford, Direct PLUS, Federal Perkins, college/university loans from institutional funds. **Student Employment: Financial Aid Statistics:** 68% freshmen, 65% undergrads receive need-based scholarship or grant aid. 8% freshmen, 3% undergrads receive non-need-based scholarship or grant aid. 48% freshmen, 59% undergrads receive

INDIANA UNIVERSITY NORTHWEST

3400 Broadway, Hawthorn 100, Gary, IN 46408-1197
Phone: 219-980-6991
E-mail: admit@iun.edu
Fax: 219-981-4219 **Website:** www.iun.edu

This public school was founded in 1948. It has a 38-acre campus.

RATINGS
Admissions Selectivity Rating: 70 **Fire Safety Rating:** 60* **Green Rating:** 60*

STUDENTS AND FACULTY
Enrollment: 4,531. **Student Body:** 69% female, 31% male, 1% out-of-state, international (23 countries represented). Asian 2%, African American 21%, Caucasian 57%, Hispanic 13%.
Retention and Graduation: 69% freshmen return for sophomore year. 9% freshmen graduate within 4 years. **Faculty:** Student/faculty ratio 16:1. 177 full-time faculty, 72% hold PhDs, 23% are members of minority groups, 50% are women.

ACADEMICS
Degrees: Associate, bachelor's, certificate, master's, post-bachelor's certificate. **Classes:** Most classes have 20–29 students. Most lab/discussion sessions have 20–29 students. **Majors with Highest Enrollment:** Business/commerce; criminal justice/safety studies; nursing/registered nurse (RN, ASN, BSN, MSN). **Special Study Options:** Accelerated program, cooperative education program, distance learning, double major, dual enrollment, external degree program, independent study, internships, liberal arts/career combination, student-designed major, study abroad, teacher certification program, weekend college. Special programs offered to physically disabled students include reader services, tape recorders, tutors. **Career services:** Alumni services, career/job search classes, career assessment, internships.

FACILITIES
Housing: Computers: Students can register for classes online. Administrative functions (other than registration) can be performed online.

CAMPUS LIFE
Activities: Choral groups, dance, drama/theater, literary magazine, musical theater, radio station, student government, student newspaper, international student organization. **Organizations:** 60 registered organizations, 4 honor societies, 2 religious organizations. 2 fraternities, 3 sororities. **Athletics (Intercollegiate):** *Men:* Baseball, basketball, cheerleading, golf. *Women:* Basketball, cheerleading, volleyball.

ADMISSIONS
Freshman Academic Profile: Average high school GPA 2.62. 7% in top 10% of high school class, 22% in top 25% of high school class, 53% in top 50% of high school class. SAT Math middle 50% range 390–500. SAT Critical Reading middle 50% range 400–500. ACT middle 50% range 16–22. **Basis for Candidate Selection:** *Very important factors considered include:* Class rank, academic GPA, rigor of secondary school record, standardized test scores. *Other factors considered include:* Recommendation(s). **Freshman Admission Requirements:** High school diploma is required and GED is accepted. *Academic units required:* 4 English, 3 mathematics, 2 science, 2 social studies, 4 academic electives. *Academic units recommended:* (1 science labs), 2 foreign language. **Freshman Admission Statistics:** 1,707 applied, 79% admitted, 71% enrolled. **Transfer Admission Requirements:** High school transcript, college transcript(s), minimum college GPA of 2.0 required. Lowest grade transferable C. **General Admission Information:** Application fee $25. Nonfall registration accepted. Admission may be deferred for a maximum of 2 years. Credit offered for CEEB Advanced Placement tests.

COSTS AND FINANCIAL AID
Annual in-state tuition $5,478. Annual out-of-state tuition $14,583. Required fees $441. Average book expense $1,100. **Required Forms and Deadlines:** FAFSA, institution's own financial aid form. Priority financial aid filing date 3/1. **Notification of Awards:** Applicants will be notified of awards on a rolling basis beginning 5/1. **Types of Aid:** *Need-based scholarships/grants:* Federal Pell, SEOG, state scholarships/grants, private scholarships, the school's own gift aid, Federal Nursing Scholarships. *Loans:* Direct Subsidized Stafford, Direct Unsubsidized Stafford, Direct PLUS, Federal Perkins, college/university loans from institutional funds. **Student Employment:** Federal Work-Study Program available. Off-campus job opportunities are good. **Financial Aid Statistics:**

45% freshmen, 50% undergrads receive need-based scholarship or grant aid. 2% freshmen, 1% undergrads receive non-need-based scholarship or grant aid. 40% freshmen, 50% undergrads receive need-based self-help aid. 1% freshmen, 68% undergrads borrow to pay for school. Average cumulative indebtedness $28,403. **Criteria for awarding institutional aid:** *Non-need-based:* Academics, athletics.

INDIANA UNIVERSITY OF PENNSYLVANIA

1011 South Drive, Suite 117 Sutton Hall, Indiana, PA 15705
Phone: 724-357-2230 **Financial Aid Phone:** 724-357-2218
E-mail: admissions-inquiry@iup.edu **CEEB Code:** 2652
Fax: 724-357-6281 **Website:** www.iup.edu **ACT Code:** 3704

This public school was founded in 1875. It has a 342-acre campus.

RATINGS
Admissions Selectivity Rating: 69   **Fire Safety Rating:** 88   **Green Rating:** 60*

STUDENTS AND FACULTY
Enrollment: 11,821. **Student Body:** 56% female, 44% male, 6% out-of-state, 1% international (56 countries represented). Asian 1%, African American 11%, Caucasian 80%, Hispanic 2%.
Retention and Graduation: 74% freshmen return for sophomore year.
Faculty: Student/faculty ratio 18:1. 611 full-time faculty, 13% are members of minority groups, 49% are women.

ACADEMICS
Degrees: Associate, bachelor's, certificate, master's, post-bachelor's certificate, post-master's certificate. **Classes:** Most classes have 20–29 students. Most lab/discussion sessions have 10–19 students. **Majors with Highest Enrollment:** Criminology; management information systems; nursing/registered nurse (RN, ASN, BSN, MSN). **Special Study Options:** Accelerated program, cooperative education program, cross-registration, distance learning, double major, dual enrollment, English as a Second Language (ESL), exchange student program (domestic), external degree program, honors program, independent study, internships, liberal arts/career combination, student-designed major, study abroad, teacher certification program, weekend college. **Honors programs:** Robert E. Cook Honors College. Special programs offered to physically disabled students include note-taking services, reader services, tape recorders. **Career services:** Alumni network, alumni services, internships. **Career services highlights include:** Mock Interview Simulation Program—800 participants each year.

FACILITIES
Housing: Coed dorms, special housing for disabled students, special housing for international students, apartments for married students, apartments for single students, wellness housing, theme housing, living learning communities. 98% of campus accessible to physically disabled. **Special Academic Facilities/Equipment:** Art museum, natural history museum, on-campus elementary school, lodge, farm, co-generation plant, ski slope, sailing base. **Computers:** 90% of classrooms, 60% of dorms, 100% of libraries, 100% of dining areas, 80% of student union, 100% of common outdoor areas have wireless network access. Students can register for classes online. Administrative functions (other than registration) can be performed online.

CAMPUS LIFE
Environment: Village. **Activities:** Choral groups, concert band, dance, drama/theater, jazz band, marching band, music ensembles, musical theater, radio station, student government, student newspaper, symphony orchestra, television station, campus ministries, international student organization. **Organizations:** 210 registered organizations, 23 honor societies, 18 religious organizations. 18 fraternities, 14 sororities. **Athletics (Intercollegiate):** *Men:* Baseball, basketball, cross-country, diving, football, golf, swimming, track/field (outdoor), track/field (indoor). *Women:* Basketball, cross-country, diving, field hockey, lacrosse, soccer, softball, swimming, tennis, track/field (outdoor), track/field (indoor), volleyball. **On-Campus Highlights:** Suites on Grant, Oak Grove, Hadley Union Building Fitness Center/Foo, Stapleton Library, Miller Stadium.

ADMISSIONS
Freshman Academic Profile: 7% in top 10% of high school class, 26% in top 25% of high school class, 61% in top 50% of high school class. SAT Math middle 50% range 450–540. SAT Critical Reading middle 50% range 450–530. SAT Writing middle 50% range 440–530. Minimum paper TOEFL 500. Minimum

computer TOEFL 173. **Basis for Candidate Selection:** *Very important factors considered include:* Academic GPA, standardized test scores. *Important factors considered include:* Rigor of secondary school record. *Other factors considered include:* Class rank, application essay, recommendation(s), extracurricular activities. **Freshman Admission Requirements:** High school diploma is required and GED is accepted. *Academic units recommended:* 3 English, 3 mathematics, 3 science, 2 foreign language, 3 social studies. **Freshman Admission Statistics:** 11,669 applied, 60% admitted, 60% enrolled. **Transfer Admission Requirements:** High school transcript, college transcript(s), statement of good standing from prior institution(s). Minimum college GPA of 2.0 required. Lowest grade transferable C–. **General Admission Information:** Application fee $35. Notification on a rolling basis, beginning on or about 9/15. Nonfall registration accepted. Admission may be deferred for a maximum of 1 year. Credit offered for CEEB Advanced Placement tests.

COSTS AND FINANCIAL AID
Annual in-state tuition $5,554. Annual out-of-state tuition $13,886. Room and board $8,558. Required fees $1,655. Average book expense $1,100. **Required Forms and Deadlines:** FAFSA. Priority financial aid filing date 4/15. **Notification of Awards:** Applicants will be notified of awards on a rolling basis beginning 3/15. **Types of Aid:** *Need-based scholarships/grants:* Federal Pell, SEOG, state scholarships/grants, private scholarships, the school's own gift aid, United Negro College Fund. *Loans:* FFEL Subsidized Stafford, FFEL Unsubsidized Stafford, FFEL PLUS, Federal Perkins, private alternative loans. **Student Employment:** Federal Work-Study Program available. Institutional employment available. Highest amount earned per year from on-campus jobs $8,043. Off-campus job opportunities are good. **Financial Aid Statistics:** 47% freshmen, 46% undergrads receive need-based scholarship or grant aid. 25% freshmen, 15% undergrads receive non-need-based scholarship or grant aid. 65% freshmen, 61% undergrads receive need-based self-help aid. 2% freshmen, 2% undergrads receive athletic scholarships. 82% freshmen, 82% undergrads receive any aid. 84% undergrads borrow to pay for school. Average cumulative indebtedness $25,224. **Criteria for awarding institutional aid:** *Non-need-based:* Academics, alumni affiliation, art, athletics, job skills, leadership, music/drama, state/district residency.

INDIANA UNIVERSITY SOUTH BEND

1700 Mishawaka Avenue, P.O. Box 7111, A169, South Bend, IN 46634-7111
Phone: 574-520-4839
E-mail: admissio@iusb.edu **CEEB Code:** 1339
Fax: 574-520-4834 **Website:** www.iusb.edu

This public school was founded in 1922. It has a 80-acre campus.

RATINGS
Admissions Selectivity Rating: 67   **Fire Safety Rating:** 60*   **Green Rating:** 60*

STUDENTS AND FACULTY
Enrollment: 6,360. **Student Body:** 62% female, 38% male, 4% out-of-state, 2% international (75 countries represented). Asian 1%, African American 8%, Caucasian 78%, Hispanic 5%.
Retention and Graduation: 67% freshmen return for sophomore year. 7% freshmen graduate within 4 years. **Faculty:** Student/faculty ratio 15:1. 292 full-time faculty, 63% hold PhDs, 20% are members of minority groups, 51% are women.

ACADEMICS
Degrees: Associate, bachelor's, certificate, diploma, master's, post-bachelor's certificate. **Classes:** Most classes have 20–29 students. Most lab/discussion sessions have 20–29 students. **Special Study Options:** Accelerated program, cross-registration, distance learning, double major, English as a Second Language (ESL), external degree program, honors program, internships, liberal arts/career combination, study abroad, teacher certification program, weekend college, electrical, mechanical engineering, computer technology with Purdue University on Indiana University South Bend Campus. Northern Indiana Consortium for Education (NICE)—IUSB is one of six member institutions sharing library resources, faculty expertise, and academic strengths resulting in broadened course opportunities to students. Special programs offered to physically disabled students include note-taking services, reader services, tape recorders, tutors. **Career services:** Alumni services, career/job search classes, career assessment, internships.

FACILITIES
Housing: Coed dorms, special housing for international students, apartments for single students. **Computers:** Students can register for classes online. Administrative functions (other than registration) can be performed online.

CAMPUS LIFE

Activities: Choral groups, drama/theater, jazz band, literary magazine, music ensembles, musical theater, opera, student government, student newspaper, student-run film society, symphony orchestra. **Organizations:** 30 registered organizations, 1 religious organizations. 2 fraternities, 1 sorority. **Athletics (Intercollegiate):** *Men:* Basketball. *Women:* Basketball.

ADMISSIONS

Freshman Academic Profile: Average high school GPA 2.84. 7% in top 10% of high school class, 22% in top 25% of high school class, 60% in top 50% of high school class. SAT Math middle 50% range 420–530. SAT Critical Reading middle 50% range 420–520. ACT middle 50% range 17–23. Minimum paper TOEFL 550. **Basis for Candidate Selection:** *Very important factors considered include:* Rigor of secondary school record. *Important factors considered include:* Class rank, academic GPA. *Other factors considered include:* Recommendation(s), standardized test scores, extracurricular activities, interview, state residency. **Freshman Admission Requirements:** High school diploma is required and GED is accepted. *Academic units required:* 4 English, 3 mathematics, 1 science, (1 science labs), 2 social studies. *Academic units recommended:* 2 foreign language. **Freshman Admission Statistics:** 2,272 applied, 80% admitted, 66% enrolled. **Transfer Admission Requirements:** College transcript(s), minimum college GPA of 2.0 required. Lowest grade transferable C. **General Admission Information:** Application fee $45. Nonfall registration accepted. Admission may be deferred for a maximum of Contact admissions. Neither credit nor placement offered for CEEB Advanced Placement tests.

COSTS AND FINANCIAL AID

Annual in-state tuition $5,573. Annual out-of-state tuition $15,270. Room and board $6,796. Required fees $442. Average book expense $1,200. **Required Forms and Deadlines:** FAFSA, institution's own financial aid form. Priority financial aid filing date 3/1. **Notification of Awards:** Applicants will be notified of awards on a rolling basis beginning 5/1. **Types of Aid:** *Need-based scholarships/grants:* Federal Pell, SEOG, state scholarships/grants, private scholarships, the school's own gift aid. *Loans:* Direct Subsidized Stafford, Direct Unsubsidized Stafford, Direct PLUS, Federal Perkins, college/university loans from institutional funds. **Student Employment:** Federal Work-Study Program available. Off-campus job opportunities are good. **Financial Aid Statistics:** 50% freshmen, 49% undergrads receive need-based scholarship or grant aid. 1% freshmen, 2% undergrads receive non-need-based scholarship or grant aid. 38% freshmen, 45% undergrads receive need-based self-help aid. 71% undergrads borrow to pay for school. Average cumulative indebtedness $25,384. **Criteria for awarding institutional aid:** *Non-need-based:* Academics, athletics.

INDIANA UNIVERSITY SOUTHEAST

4201 Grant Line Road, UC–100, New Albany, IN 47150
Phone: 812-941-2212
E-mail: admissions@ius.edu **CEEB Code:** 1314
Fax: 812-941-2595 **Website:** www.ius.edu **ACT Code:** 1229

This public school was founded in 1941. It has a 177-acre campus.

RATINGS

Admissions Selectivity Rating: 68　　**Fire Safety Rating:** 60*　　**Green Rating:** 60*

STUDENTS AND FACULTY

Enrollment: 5,716. **Student Body:** 60% female, 40% male, 28% out-of-state, international (35 countries represented). Asian 2%, African American 6%, Caucasian 86%, Hispanic 2%.
Retention and Graduation: 63% freshmen return for sophomore year. 8% freshmen graduate within 4 years. **Faculty:** Student/faculty ratio 17:1. 200 full-time faculty, 72% hold PhDs, 16% are members of minority groups, 48% are women.

ACADEMICS

Degrees: Associate, bachelor's, certificate, master's, post-bachelor's certificate. **Classes:** Most classes have 20–29 students. Most lab/discussion sessions have 10–19 students. **Special Study Options:** Accelerated program, cross-registration, distance learning, double major, dual enrollment, external degree program, honors program, independent study, internships, student-designed major, study abroad, teacher certification program, weekend college. Special programs offered to physically disabled students include note-taking services, reader services, tutors. **Career services:** Alumni services, career/job search classes, career assessment, internships.

FACILITIES

Housing: Coed dorms 95% of campus accessible to physically disabled. **Special Academic Facilities/Equipment:** Paul W. Ogle Center, Concert Hall,

---

Theatre, Recital Hall, Japanese Cultural Center, Ronald L. Barr Art Gallery.
Computers: Students can register for classes online. Administrative functions (other than registration) can be performed online.

CAMPUS LIFE

Environment: Village. **Activities:** Choral groups, concert band, drama/theater, literary magazine, music ensembles, student government, student newspaper, symphony orchestra. **Organizations:** 76 registered organizations, 1 religious organizations. 2 fraternities, 4 sororities. **Athletics (Intercollegiate):** *Men:* Baseball, basketball, cross-country, tennis. *Women:* Basketball, cross-country, softball, tennis, volleyball.

ADMISSIONS

Freshman Academic Profile: Average high school GPA 2.95. 6% in top 10% of high school class, 27% in top 25% of high school class, 64% in top 50% of high school class. SAT Math middle 50% range 420–520. SAT Critical Reading middle 50% range 420–520. ACT middle 50% range 17–22. **Basis for Candidate Selection:** *Very important factors considered include:* Class rank, rigor of secondary school record. *Important factors considered include:* Academic GPA, standardized test scores. *Other factors considered include:* Recommendation(s), interview. **Freshman Admission Requirements:** High school diploma is required and GED is accepted. *Academic units required:* 4 English, 3 mathematics, 1 science, (1 science labs), 2 social studies, 4 academic electives. *Academic units recommended:* 4 mathematics, 2 science, (2 science labs), 2 foreign language, 1 history. **Freshman Admission Statistics:** 1,985 applied, 85% admitted, 65% enrolled. **Transfer Admission Requirements:** College transcript(s), lowest grade transferable C. **General Admission Information:** Application fee $30. Nonfall registration accepted. Admission may be deferred for a maximum of: Contact admissions. Credit offered for CEEB Advanced Placement tests.

COSTS AND FINANCIAL AID

Annual in-state tuition $5,417. Annual out-of-state tuition $14,105. Room and board $8,860. Required fees $473. Average book expense $880. **Required Forms and Deadlines:** FAFSA. Priority financial aid filing date 3/1. **Notification of Awards:** Applicants will be notified of awards on a rolling basis beginning 5/1. **Types of Aid:** *Need-based scholarships/grants:* Federal Pell, SEOG, state scholarships/grants, private scholarships, the school's own gift aid. *Loans:* Direct Subsidized Stafford, Direct Unsubsidized Stafford, Direct PLUS, Federal Perkins, Federal Nursing, college/university loans from institutional funds. **Student Employment:** Federal Work-Study Program available. Institutional employment available. Off-campus job opportunities are excellent. **Financial Aid Statistics:** 47% freshmen, 44% undergrads receive need-based scholarship or grant aid. 3% freshmen, 2% undergrads receive non-need-based scholarship or grant aid. 33% freshmen, 38% undergrads receive need-based self-help aid. 1% freshmen, 1% undergrads receive athletic scholarships. 60% undergrads borrow to pay for school. Average cumulative indebtedness $22,649. **Criteria for awarding institutional aid:** *Non-need-based:* Academics, art, athletics, leadership, minority status, music/drama.

INDIANA UNIVERSITY—BLOOMINGTON

Best 373

300 North Jordan Avenue, Bloomington, IN 47405-1106
Phone: 812-855-0661 **Financial Aid Phone:** 812-855-0321
E-mail: iuadmit@indiana.edu **CEEB Code:** 1324
Fax: 812-855-5102 **Website:** www.indiana.edu **ACT Code:** 1210

This public school was founded in 1820. It has a 1937-acre campus.

RATINGS

Admissions Selectivity Rating: 87　　**Fire Safety Rating:** 76　　**Green Rating:** 60*

STUDENTS AND FACULTY

Enrollment: 32,000. **Student Body:** 50% female, 50% male, 33% out-of-state, 6% international (136 countries represented). Asian 4%, African American 5%, Caucasian 81%, Hispanic 3%.
Retention and Graduation: 89% freshmen return for sophomore year. 53% freshmen graduate within 4 years. **Faculty:** Student/faculty ratio 19:1. 1917 full-time faculty, 78% hold PhDs, 17% are members of minority groups, 38% are women.

ACADEMICS

Degrees: Bachelor's, certificate, diploma, doctoral, master's, post-bachelor's certificate, post-master's certificate. **Classes:** Most classes have 20–29 students.

Most lab/discussion sessions have 20–29 students. **Majors with Highest Enrollment:** Business/commerce; communication, journalism, and related programs, other; education. **Special Study Options:** Accelerated program, cooperative education program, distance learning, double major, dual enrollment, English as a Second Language (ESL), external degree program, honors program, independent study, internships, liberal arts/career combination, student-designed major, study abroad, teacher certification program **Honors programs:** Hutton Honors College and the Hudson/Holland Scholar Programs Special programs offered to physically disabled students include note-taking services, reader services, tape recorders, tutors. **Career services:** Alumni network, career/job search classes, career assessment, internships. **Career services highlights include:** The New IU Alumni Connections Program that we initated this year which brings back successful alumni to work with current students.

FACILITIES

Housing: Coed dorms, special housing for disabled students, men's dorms, special housing for international students, women's dorms, fraternity/sorority housing, apartments for married students, cooperative housing, apartments for single students, apartments for students with dependent children, residential language houses and living/learning centers available, wellness center, African-American living/learning. Honor College floors, First-Year Academic Interest Group Housing; suites for 2–3 students. 95% of campus accessible to physically disabled. **Special Academic Facilities/Equipment:** Art Gallery, folklore, radio station, natural history museum, TV station, art museum, Mathers Museum of World Cultures, Kirkwood Observatory, Hilltop Garden and Nature Center, Arboretum, Student Recreational Sports and Aquatic Center, Auditorium, Beck Chapel, Golf Driving Range, Musical Arts Center, Health P.E. and Recreation facilities (HPER), indoor swimming, outdoor swimming, Wildermuth Intramural Center (in HPER complex), cyclotron, Lilly Library, and more than 70 research centers. **Computers:** Students can register for classes online. Administrative functions (other than registration) can be performed online.

CAMPUS LIFE

Environment: City. **Activities:** Choral groups, concert band, dance, drama/theater, jazz band, literary magazine, marching band, music ensembles, musical theater, opera, radio station, student government, student newspaper, symphony orchestra, television station, yearbook, campus ministries, international student organization. **Organizations:** 9 religious organizations. **Athletics (Intercollegiate):** *Men:* Baseball, basketball, cheerleading, cross-country, diving, football, golf, soccer, swimming, tennis, track/field (outdoor), wrestling. *Women:* Basketball, cheerleading, cross-country, diving, field hockey, golf, soccer, softball, swimming, tennis, track/field (outdoor), volleyball, water polo. **On-Campus Highlights:** Indiana Memorial Union, Art Museum, Lilly Library, Assembly Hall, Student Recreational Sports Center.

ADMISSIONS

Freshman Academic Profile: Average high school GPA 3.6. 34% in top 10% of high school class, 71% in top 25% of high school class, 96% in top 50% of high school class. SAT Math middle 50% range 540–660. SAT Critical Reading middle 50% range 520–630. ACT middle 50% range 24–29. **Basis for Candidate Selection:** *Very important factors considered include:* Class rank, academic GPA, rigor of secondary school record. *Important factors considered include:* Standardized test scores. *Other factors considered include:* Application essay, recommendation(s), alumni/ae relation, character/personal qualities, extracurricular activities, first generation, geographical residence, interview, level of applicant's interest, racial/ethnic status, state residency, talent/ability, volunteer work, work experience. **Freshman Admission Requirements:** High school diploma is required and GED is accepted. *Academic units required:* 4 English, 3 mathematics, 1 science, (1 science labs), 2 social studies, 4 academic electives. *Academic units recommended:* 4 mathematics, 3 science, 3 foreign language, 3 social studies. **Freshman Admission Statistics:** 33,011 applied, 73% admitted, 31% enrolled. **Transfer Admission Requirements:** College transcript(s), minimum college GPA of 2.0 required. Lowest grade transferable C. **General Admission Information:** Application fee $55. Nonfall registration accepted. Admission may be deferred for a maximum of 1 year. Credit and/or placement offered for CEEB Advanced Placement tests.

COSTS AND FINANCIAL AID

Annual in-state tuition $7,722. Annual out-of-state tuition $25,269. Room and board $7,546. Required fees $891. Average book expense $792. **Required Forms and Deadlines:** FAFSA. Priority financial aid filing date 3/1. **Notification of Awards:** Applicants will be notified of awards on a rolling basis beginning 4/1. **Types of Aid:** *Need-based scholarships/grants:* Federal Pell, SEOG, state scholarships/grants, private scholarships, the school's own gift aid. *Loans:* Direct Subsidized Stafford, Direct Unsubsidized Stafford, Direct PLUS, Federal Perkins, college/university loans from institutional funds. **Student Employment:** Federal Work-Study Program available. Institutional employment available. Off-campus job opportunities are good. **Financial Aid Statistics:** 34% freshmen, 29% undergrads receive need-based scholarship or grant aid. 6% freshmen, 4% undergrads receive non-need-based scholarship or grant aid.

26% freshmen, 28% undergrads receive need-based self-help aid. 1% freshmen, 1% undergrads receive athletic scholarships. 54% undergrads borrow to pay for school. Average cumulative indebtedness $25,522. **Criteria for awarding institutional aid:** *Non-need-based:* Academics, art, athletics, leadership, minority status, music/drama, religious affiliation.

INDIANA UNIVERSITY—KOKOMO

Office of Admissions, P.O. Box 9003, KC 230A, Kokomo, IN 46904-9003
Phone: 765-455-9217
E-mail: iuadmis@iuk.edu **CEEB Code:** 1337
Fax: 765-455-9537 **Website:** www.iuk.edu **ACT Code:** 1219

This public school was founded in 1945. It has a 51-acre campus.

RATINGS
Admissions Selectivity Rating: 69   **Fire Safety Rating:** 60*   **Green Rating:** 60*

STUDENTS AND FACULTY
Enrollment: 2,350. **Student Body:** 67% female, 33% male, 1% out-of-state, international (19 countries represented). Asian 1%, African American 5%, Caucasian 86%, Hispanic 2%.
Retention and Graduation: 58% freshmen return for sophomore year. 9% freshmen graduate within 4 years. **Faculty:** Student/faculty ratio 17:1. 89 full-time faculty, 63% hold PhDs, 16% are members of minority groups, 57% are women.

ACADEMICS
Degrees: Associate, bachelor's, certificate, master's, post-bachelor's certificate. **Classes:** Most classes have 20–29 students. Most lab/discussion sessions have 20–29 students. **Special Study Options:** Accelerated program, cross-registration, distance learning, double major, dual enrollment, external degree program, honors program, independent study, internships, liberal arts/career combination, study abroad, teacher certification program. Special programs offered to physically disabled students include note-taking services, reader services, tutors. **Career services:** Alumni services, career/job search classes, career assessment, internships.

FACILITIES
Housing: Special Academic Facilities/Equipment: Observatory, Art Gallery. **Computers:** Students can register for classes online. Administrative functions (other than registration) can be performed online.

CAMPUS LIFE
Environment: Village. **Activities:** Choral groups, drama/theater, music ensembles, student government, student newspaper **Organizations:**

ADMISSIONS
Freshman Academic Profile: Average high school GPA 2.93. 9% in top 10% of high school class, 32% in top 25% of high school class, 66% in top 50% of high school class. SAT Math middle 50% range 430–530. SAT Critical Reading middle 50% range 420–520. ACT middle 50% range 17–22. **Basis for Candidate Selection:** *Very important factors considered include:* Class rank, rigor of secondary school record. *Important factors considered include:* Standardized test scores. *Other factors considered include:* Recommendation(s). **Freshman Admission Requirements:** High school diploma is required and GED is accepted. *Academic units required:* 4 English, 3 mathematics, 1 science, 2 social studies. *Academic units recommended:* 2 foreign language, 2 history. **Freshman Admission Statistics:** 758 applied, 81% admitted, 71% enrolled. **Transfer Admission Requirements:** College transcript(s), minimum college GPA of 2.0 required. Lowest grade transferable C. **General Admission Information:** Application fee $45. Nonfall registration accepted. Admission may be deferred for a maximum of Contact admissions. Credit and/or placement offered for CEEB Advanced Placement tests.

COSTS AND FINANCIAL AID
Annual in-state tuition $5,408. Annual out-of-state tuition $14,097. Required fees $430. Average book expense $858. **Required Forms and Deadlines:** FAFSA, institution's own financial aid form. Priority financial aid filing date 3/1. **Notification of Awards:** Applicants will be notified of awards on a rolling basis beginning 5/1. **Types of Aid:** *Need-based scholarships/grants:* Federal Pell, SEOG, state scholarships/grants, private scholarships, the school's own gift aid. *Loans:* Direct Subsidized Stafford, Direct Unsubsidized Stafford, Direct PLUS, Federal Perkins, Federal Nursing, college/university loans from institutional funds. **Student Employment:** Federal Work-Study Program available. Institutional employment available. **Financial Aid Statistics:** 48% freshmen, 48% undergrads receive need-based scholarship or grant aid. 4% freshmen, 3% undergrads receive non-need-based scholarship or grant aid. 33% freshmen, 43% undergrads receive need-based self-help aid. 65% undergrads borrow to

pay for school. Average cumulative indebtedness $24,788. **Criteria for awarding institutional aid:** *Non-need-based:* Academics.

INDIANA UNIVERSITY— PURDUE UNIV. FORT WAYNE

2101 East Coliseum Boulevard, Fort Wayne, IN 46805-1499
Phone: 260-481-6812
E-mail: ipfwadms@ipfw.edu **CEEB Code:** 1336
Fax: 260-481-6880 **Website:** www.ipfw.edu **ACT Code:** 1217

This public school was founded in 1917. It has a 565-acre campus.

RATINGS
Admissions Selectivity Rating: 63   **Fire Safety Rating:** 60*   **Green Rating:** 60*

STUDENTS AND FACULTY
Enrollment: 10,587. **Student Body:** 58% female, 42% male, 5% out-of-state, 2% international (71 countries represented). Asian 2%, African American 5%, Caucasian 87%, Hispanic 2%.
Retention and Graduation: 60% freshmen return for sophomore year.
Faculty: Student/faculty ratio 19:1. 329 full-time faculty, 83% hold PhDs, 13% are members of minority groups, 37% are women. 1% of classes are taught by teaching assistants.

ACADEMICS
Degrees: Associate, bachelor's, certificate, master's, post-bachelor's certificate, post-master's certificate, terminal associate, transfer associate. **Classes:** Most classes have 20–29 students. Most lab/discussion sessions have 20–29 students. **Majors with Highest Enrollment:** Business/commerce; elementary education and teaching; nursing/registered nurse (RN, ASN, BSN, MSN). **Special Study Options:** Cooperative education program, distance learning, double major, English as a Second Language (ESL), exchange student program (domestic), honors program, independent study, internships, liberal arts/career combination, student-designed major, study abroad, teacher certification program, weekend college. Special programs offered to physically disabled students include note-taking services, reader services, tape recorders, tutors. **Career services:** Alumni network, alumni services, career/job search classes, career assessment, internships, regional alumni.

FACILITIES
Housing: Coed dorms. 100% of campus accessible to physically disabled. **Special Academic Facilities/Equipment:** Williams Theatre, recital hall, anthropology and geology exhibits, art gallery. **Computers:** Students can register for classes online. Administrative functions (other than registration) can be performed online.

CAMPUS LIFE
Environment: Village. **Activities:** Choral groups, concert band, dance, drama/theater, jazz band, literary magazine, music ensembles, musical theater, opera, pep band, student government, student newspaper, symphony orchestra, television station **Organizations:** 65 registered organizations, 7 honor societies, 3 religious organizations. 2 fraternities, 3 sororities. **Athletics (Intercollegiate):** *Men:* Baseball, basketball, cross-country, soccer, tennis, track/field (outdoor), volleyball. *Women:* Basketball, cross-country, soccer, softball, tennis, track/field (outdoor), volleyball.

ADMISSIONS
Freshman Academic Profile: Average high school GPA 2.59. 7% in top 10% of high school class, 24% in top 25% of high school class, 57% in top 50% of high school class. 84% from public high schools. SAT Math middle 50% range 430–550. SAT Critical Reading middle 50% range 420–540. ACT middle 50% range 17–23. Minimum paper TOEFL 550. Minimum computer TOEFL 213. **Basis for Candidate Selection:** *Very important factors considered include:* Class rank, rigor of secondary school record, standardized test scores. *Other factors considered include:* Recommendation(s), state residency. **Freshman Admission Requirements:** High school diploma is required and GED is accepted. *Academic units required:* 4 English, 3 mathematics, 1 science, 1 foreign language, 1 social studies. *Academic units recommended:* 3 science, (1 science labs), 3 foreign language, 3 social studies. **Freshman Admission Statistics:** 2,471 applied, 97% admitted, 71% enrolled. **Transfer Admission Requirements:** High school transcript, college transcript(s), minimum college GPA of 2.0 required. Lowest grade transferable C–. **General Admission Information:** Application fee $30. Regular application deadline 8/1. Notification on a rolling basis, beginning on or about 12/1. Nonfall registration accepted. Credit and/or placement offered for CEEB Advanced Placement tests.

COSTS AND FINANCIAL AID
Annual in-state tuition $3,100. Annual out-of-state tuition $7,728. Required fees $384. Average book expense $800. **Required Forms and Deadlines:** FAFSA. Priority financial aid filing date 3/1. **Notification of Awards:** Applicants will be notified of awards on or about 4/30. **Types of Aid:** *Need-based scholarships/grants:* Federal Pell, SEOG, state scholarships/grants, private scholarships, Federal Nursing Scholarships. *Loans:* FFEL Subsidized Stafford, FFEL Unsubsidized Stafford, FFEL PLUS, Federal Perkins, Federal Nursing. **Student Employment:** Federal Work-Study Program available. Institutional employment available. Highest amount earned per year from on-campus jobs $1,200. Off-campus job opportunities are excellent. **Financial Aid Statistics:** 35% freshmen, 57% undergrads receive need-based scholarship or grant aid. 14% freshmen, 16% undergrads receive non-need-based scholarship or grant aid. 23% freshmen, 33% undergrads receive need-based self-help aid. 3% freshmen, 3% undergrads receive athletic scholarships. 59% undergrads borrow to pay for school. Average cumulative indebtedness $13,764. **Criteria for awarding institutional aid:** *Non-need-based:* Academics, alumni affiliation, art, athletics.

INDIANA UNIVERSITY— PURDUE UNIVERSITY INDIANAPOLIS

420 University Blvd, Indianapolis, IN 46202
Phone: 317-274-4591 **Financial Aid Phone:** 317-274-4162
E-mail: apply@iupui.edu
Fax: 317-278-1862 **Website:** www.iupui.edu **ACT Code:** 1214

This public school was founded in 1969. It has a 509-acre campus.

RATINGS
Admissions Selectivity Rating: 75   **Fire Safety Rating:** 60*   **Green Rating:** 60*

STUDENTS AND FACULTY
Enrollment: 20,926. **Student Body:** 58% female, 42% male, 2% out-of-state, 3% international (138 countries represented). Asian 3%, African American 10%, Caucasian 77%, Hispanic 3%.
Retention and Graduation: 72% freshmen return for sophomore year. 10% freshmen graduate within 4 years. **Faculty:** Student/faculty ratio 16:1. 2116 full-time faculty, 83% hold PhDs, 22% are members of minority groups, 38% are women.

ACADEMICS
Degrees: Associate, bachelor's, certificate, doctoral, master's, post-bachelor's certificate. **Classes:** Most classes have 20–29 students. Most lab/discussion sessions have 10–19 students. **Majors with Highest Enrollment:** Business/commerce; elementary education and teaching; nursing/registered nurse (RN, ASN, BSN, MSN). **Special Study Options:** Accelerated program, cooperative education program, cross-registration, distance learning, double major, dual enrollment, English as a Second Language (ESL), exchange student program (domestic), external degree program, honors program, independent study, internships, student-designed major, study abroad, teacher certification program, weekend college. **Honors programs:** The Honors Program provides a challenging campus-wide program for high achieving students from all academic disciplines. Honors Program students have the opportunity to enroll in smaller dynamic classes and to collaborate with faculty in independent study and research projects. Participants in the IUPUI Honors Program will be required to complete at least three credit hours of honors course work each semester. **Combined degree programs:** BA/MEng; BS /MS; MD/PhD; MA/MPA; MBA/JD. Special programs offered to physically disabled students include note-taking services, reader services, tape recorders, tutors.

FACILITIES
Housing: Coed dorms, special housing for international students, apartments for married students, apartments for single students. 90% of campus accessible to physically disabled. **Special Academic Facilities/Equipment:** Inlow Hall-Law School; Eskenazi Hall—Herron School of Art and Design; Cavanaugh Hall—School of Liberal Arts and IUPUI Enrollment Center; University Library—most high tech library in North America; IUPUI Sport Complex—host of 11 Olympic Team Trials; White River State Park—Indianapolis' version of the mall in Washington, DC. **Computers:** 100% of classrooms, 100% of dorms, 100% of libraries, 100% of dining areas, 100% of student union, 100% of common outdoor areas have wireless network access. Students can register for classes online. Administrative functions (other than registration) can be performed online.

CAMPUS LIFE
Environment: Metropolis. **Activities:** Choral groups, concert band, dance, drama/theater, jazz band, literary magazine, music ensembles, pep band, stu-

dent government, student newspaper, campus ministries, international student organization. **Organizations:** 154 registered organizations, 9 honor societies, 10 religious organizations. 2 fraternities, 1 sorority. **Athletics (Intercollegiate):** *Men:* Basketball, cross-country, diving, golf, soccer, swimming, tennis. *Women:* Basketball, cross-country, diving, golf, soccer, softball, swimming, tennis, volleyball. **On-Campus Highlights:** IUPUI Sport Complex, University College, Cavanaugh Hall, University Library, Eskenazi Hall, IU Medical Center.

ADMISSIONS

Freshman Academic Profile: Average high school GPA 3.27. 15% in top 10% of high school class, 44% in top 25% of high school class, 87% in top 50% of high school class. SAT Math middle 50% range 450–560. SAT Critical Reading middle 50% range 440–550. ACT middle 50% range 19–24. Minimum paper TOEFL 550. Minimum computer TOEFL 213. **Basis for Candidate Selection:** *Very important factors considered include:* Rigor of secondary school record. *Important factors considered include:* Academic GPA. *Other factors considered include:* Class rank, application essay, recommendation(s), standardized test scores, character/personal qualities, first generation, volunteer work, work experience. **Freshman Admission Requirements:** High school diploma is required and GED is accepted. *Academic units required:* 4 English, 3 mathematics, 3 science, (3 science labs), 2 social studies, 2 history, 4 academic electives. *Academic units recommended:* 4 mathematics, 4 science, 3 foreign language. **Freshman Admission Statistics:** 9,641 applied, 67% admitted, 47% enrolled. **Transfer Admission Requirements:** College transcript(s), minimum college GPA of 2.0 required. Lowest grade transferable C. **General Admission Information:** Application fee $50. Nonfall registration accepted. Admission may be deferred for a maximum of 1 year. Credit and/or placement offered for CEEB Advanced Placement tests.

COSTS AND FINANCIAL AID

Annual in-state tuition $6,923. Annual out-of-state tuition $21,820. Room and board $7,944. Required fees $600. Average book expense $672. **Required Forms and Deadlines:** FAFSA. Priority financial aid filing date 3/1. **Notification of Awards:** Applicants will be notified of awards on a rolling basis beginning 4/1. *Types of Aid: Need-based scholarships/grants:* Federal Pell, SEOG, state scholarships/grants, private scholarships, the school's own gift aid. *Loans:* Direct Subsidized Stafford, Direct Unsubsidized Stafford, Direct PLUS, Federal Perkins, Federal Nursing, college/university loans from institutional funds. **Student Employment:** Federal Work-Study Program available. Institutional employment available. **Financial Aid Statistics:** 50% freshmen, 46% undergrads receive need-based scholarship or grant aid. 4% freshmen, 3% undergrads receive non-need-based scholarship or grant aid. 41% freshmen, 48% undergrads receive need-based self-help aid. 1% freshmen, 1% undergrads receive athletic scholarships. 72% undergrads borrow to pay for school. Average cumulative indebtedness $27,062. **Criteria for awarding institutional aid:** *Non-need-based:* Academics.

INDIANA WESLEYAN UNIVERSITY

4201 South Washington Street, Marion, IN 46953-4974
Phone: 765-677-2138 **Financial Aid Phone:** 765-677-2137
E-mail: admissions@indwes.edu **CEEB Code:** 1446
Fax: 317-677-2333 **Website:** www.indwes.edu **ACT Code:** 1226

This private school, affiliated with the Wesleyan Church, was founded in 1920. It has a 220-acre campus.

RATINGS

Admissions Selectivity Rating: 81   **Fire Safety Rating:** 94   **Green Rating:** 69

STUDENTS AND FACULTY

Enrollment: 3,109. **Student Body:** 63% female, 37% male, 46% out-of-state, (14 countries represented). Asian 1%, African American 1%, Caucasian 92%, Hispanic 1%.
Retention and Graduation: 55% freshmen graduate within 4 years. **Faculty:** Student/faculty ratio 14:1. 165 full-time faculty, 55% hold PhDs, 6% are members of minority groups, 38% are women.

ACADEMICS

Degrees: Associate, bachelor's. **Classes:** Most classes have 10–19 students. Most lab/discussion sessions have 10–19 students. **Majors with Highest Enrollment:** Business administration and management; elementary education and teaching; nursing/registered nurse (RN, ASN, BSN, MSN). **Special Study Options:** Double major, dual enrollment, honors program, independent study, internships, study abroad, teacher certification program. **Honors programs:** John Wesley Honors College. **Combined degree programs:** BA/MA, MA/Ed.D. in Leadership. Special programs offered to physically disabled students include note-taking services, reader services, tape recorders, tutors. **Career services:** Alumni network, alumni services, career/job search classes, career

assessment, internships, regional alumni. **Career services highlights include:** The Center for Life Calling and Leadership enables individuals to find an overriding purpose for their lives, equips them to make life decisions based on this purpose, and empowers them to develop this purpose into world changing leadership.

FACILITIES

Housing: Men's dorms, women's dorms, apartments for married students, apartments for single students 99% of campus accessible to physically disabled. **Special Academic Facilities/Equipment:** Lee Howard art collection (European artists); Lewis Jackson Library (2003); Tom and Joanne Phillippe Performing Arts Center (1998); Bronze statues from Israel (1998-2002); Williams chapel—medieval replica (2001); Burns Hall of Science and Nursing (2000); Luckey Recreation and Wellness Center (2001); John Maxwell Business Center (1999). **Computers:** 100% of classrooms, 100% of dorms, 100% of libraries, 100% of dining areas, 100% of student union, 100% of common outdoor areas have wireless network access. Students can register for classes online. Administrative functions (other than registration) can be performed online.

CAMPUS LIFE

Environment: Town. **Activities:** Choral groups, concert band, drama/theater, jazz band, literary magazine, music ensembles, musical theater, pep band, radio station, student government, student newspaper, symphony orchestra, television station, yearbook, campus ministries, international student organization. **Organizations:** 35 registered organizations, 1 honor societies, 5 religious organizations. **Athletics (Intercollegiate):** *Men:* Baseball, basketball, cheerleading, cross-country, golf, soccer, tennis, track/field (outdoor), track/field (indoor). *Women:* Basketball, cheerleading, cross-country, soccer, softball, tennis, track/field (outdoor), track/field (indoor), volleyball. **On-Campus Highlights:** McConn Coffee Shop, Recreation and Wellness Center, Globe Theater, The 1920 Art Gallery, Williams Chapel, The McCoon Coffee Shop is one of the more striking facilities on any college campus—situated in a long indoor mall area of the student center—and includes a fireplace and numerous seating configurations. **Environmental Initiatives:** Creation of a multi-disciplinary Task Force for Campus Sustainabilty; researching grant opportunities for alternative energy projects; currently developing an RFP to calculate our carbon footprint.

ADMISSIONS

Freshman Academic Profile: Average high school GPA 3.63. 28% in top 10% of high school class, 55% in top 25% of high school class, 82% in top 50% of high school class. SAT Math middle 50% range 480–600. SAT Critical Reading middle 50% range 480–600. ACT middle 50% range 21–27. Minimum paper TOEFL 550. Minimum computer TOEFL 213. Minimum web-based TOEFL 79. **Basis for Candidate Selection:** *Very important factors considered include:* Academic GPA, recommendation(s), standardized test scores, character/personal qualities. *Important factors considered include:* Class rank, rigor of secondary school record. *Other factors considered include:* Application essay, alumni/ae relation, extracurricular activities, first generation, interview, level of applicant's interest, religious affiliation/commitment, talent/ability, volunteer work, work experience. **Freshman Admission Requirements:** High school diploma is required and GED is accepted. *Academic units recommended:* 4 English, 3 mathematics, 3 science, 2 foreign language, 3 social studies, 5 academic electives, 1 health/PE. **Freshman Admission Statistics:** 2,588 applied, 85% admitted, 40% enrolled. **Transfer Admission Requirements:** College transcript(s), statement of good standing from prior institution(s). Minimum college GPA of 2.0 required. Lowest grade transferable C. **General Admission Information:** Application fee $25. Regular application deadline 8/1. Notification on a rolling basis, beginning on or about 10/1. Nonfall registration accepted. Admission may be deferred for a maximum of 1 year. Credit offered for CEEB Advanced Placement tests.

COSTS AND FINANCIAL AID

Annual tuition $20,496. Room and board $6,770. Average book expense $800. **Required Forms and Deadlines:** FAFSA. Financial aid filing deadline 3/1. **Notification of Awards:** Applicants will be notified of awards on or about 4/1. *Types of Aid: Need-based scholarships/grants:* Federal Pell, SEOG, state scholarships/grants, private scholarships, the school's own gift aid. *Loans:* FFEL Subsidized Stafford, FFEL Unsubsidized Stafford, FFEL PLUS, Federal Perkins, Federal Nursing, college/university loans from institutional funds. **Student Employment:** Federal Work-Study Program available. Institutional employment available. Off-campus job opportunities are good. **Financial Aid Statistics:** 73% freshmen, 72% undergrads receive need-based scholarship or grant aid. 7% freshmen, 8% undergrads receive non-need-based scholarship or grant aid. 61% freshmen, 61% undergrads receive need-based self-help aid. 5% freshmen, 5% undergrads receive athletic scholarships. 92% undergrads receive any aid. **Criteria for awarding institutional aid:** *Non-need-based:* Academics, alumni affiliation, art, athletics, leadership, music/drama.

IONA COLLEGE

715 North Avenue, New Rochelle, NY 10801
Phone: 914-633-2502 **Financial Aid Phone:** 914-633-2497
E-mail: icad@iona.edu **CEEB Code:** 2324
Fax: 914-633-2642 **Website:** www.iona.edu **ACT Code:** 2770

This private school, affiliated with the Roman Catholic Church, was founded in 1940. It has a 35-acre campus.

RATINGS
Admissions Selectivity Rating: 87   **Fire Safety Rating:** 91   **Green Rating:** 82

STUDENTS AND FACULTY
Enrollment: 3,314. **Student Body:** 56% female, 44% male, 22% out-of-state, 1% international (35 countries represented). Asian 2%, African American 5%, Caucasian 67%, Hispanic 12%.
Retention and Graduation: 85% freshmen return for sophomore year. 50% freshmen graduate within 4 years. 70% grads go on to further study within 1 year. 36% grads pursue arts and sciences degrees. 6% grads pursue law degrees. 25% grads pursue business degrees. 3% grads pursue medical degrees. **Faculty:** Student/faculty ratio 13:1. 183 full-time faculty, 92% hold PhDs, 14% are members of minority groups, 34% are women.

ACADEMICS
Degrees: Bachelor's, master's, post-bachelor's certificate, post-master's certificate. **Classes:** Most classes have 20–29 students. Most lab/discussion sessions have 10–19 students. **Majors with Highest Enrollment:** finance; mass communication/media studies; psychology. **Special Study Options:** Accelerated program, distance learning, double major, honors program, independent study, internships, liberal arts/career combination, study abroad, teacher certification program, weekend college. **Honors programs:** The Iona College Honors Degree Program is designed to meet the educational needs of the ablest and most highly motivated students at Iona. Grounded in a challenging curriculum, the program offers gifted students the resources and opportunities to develop their talents and to perform at the peak of their capabilities. The course of study is designed to develop intellectual curiosity, analytic abilities, and awareness of ethical and civic responsibilities. The program encourages the development of a nucleus of independent learners able to inspire each other academically and fosters a sense of self-respect in students, encouraging them to stretch their abilities in pursuit of lifelong learning, independent thinking, and personal fulfillment. The Honors Degree Program seeks to establish a core academic community that enriches and serves the wider college community. The program endeavors to create an intellectual atmosphere to attract and challenge superior students and faculty and to enhance the public image of the College by promoting the concept of excellence in education. The curriculum promotes an appreciation and understanding of the interrelatedness of knowledge and culture by providing a wide range of interdisciplinary courses and opportunities to study abroad. Students in the program take specially designed honors courses and advanced courses in other areas, and engage in independent research under the guidance of faculty mentors. Small class sizes encourage student participation and promote a close student-faculty relationship. Students are offered close individual guidance, both academically and in terms of career preparation. There is a faculty committee that works with students interested in applying for competitive grants and fellowships and advises them regarding graduate and professional studies. A career mentoring program affords students a unique chance to explore career opportunities by matching them with an appropriate alumnus/alumna or corporate liaison. **Combined degree programs:** BA/MA. Special programs offered to physically disabled students include note-taking services, reader services, tape recorders, tutors. **Career services:** Alumni network, alumni services, career/job search classes, career assessment, internships, regional alumni.

FACILITIES
Housing: Coed dorms, special housing for disabled students, apartments for single students, living-learning communities in science, education, wellness housing to Honors Program Students. 100% of campus accessible to physically disabled. **Special Academic Facilities/Equipment:** Iona College Art Center, Br. Kenneth Chapman Public Art Gallary, Murphy Science Technology Center, Hynes Natural Science Center, Advanced Computer Laboratory, TV Production Studio, LaPenta Student Union, Hynes Athletic Center, Rowing tank, Arrigoni center. **Computers:** 100% of classrooms, 100% of dorms, 100% of libraries, 100% of dining areas, 100% of student union, 100% of common outdoor areas have wireless network access. Students can register for classes online. Administrative functions (other than registration) can be performed online.

CAMPUS LIFE
Environment: City. **Activities:** Choral groups, dance, drama/theater, literary magazine, musical theater, pep band, radio station, student government, student newspaper, student-run film society, television station, yearbook, campus ministries, international student organization, Model UN. **Organizations:** 65 registered organizations, 9 honor societies, 4 religious organizations. 4 fraternities, 6 sororities. **Athletics (Intercollegiate):** *Men:* Baseball, basketball, crew/rowing, cross-country, diving, golf, soccer, swimming, track/field (outdoor), track/field (indoor), water polo. *Women:* Basketball, crew/rowing, cross-country, diving, lacrosse, soccer, softball, swimming, track/field (outdoor), track/field (indoor), volleyball, water polo. **On-Campus Highlights:** Lapenta Student Union, Hynes Athletics Center, Ryan Library, North Residence Hall, Loftus Courtyard. **Environmental Initiatives:** Recycling, green cleaning, lowering of emissions.

ADMISSIONS
Freshman Academic Profile: Average high school GPA 3.5. 31% in top 10% of high school class, 54% in top 25% of high school class, 93% in top 50% of high school class. 55% from public high schools. SAT Math middle 50% range 553–651. SAT Critical Reading middle 50% range 541–642. Minimum paper TOEFL 550. Minimum computer TOEFL 213. **Basis for Candidate Selection:** *Very important factors considered include:* Academic GPA, rigor of secondary school record. *Important factors considered include:* Class rank, application essay, standardized test scores, character/personal qualities, interview. *Other factors considered include:* Recommendation(s), alumni/ae relation, extracurricular activities, first generation, geographical residence, level of applicant's interest, talent/ability, volunteer work, work experience. **Freshman Admission Requirements:** High school diploma is required and GED is accepted. *Academic units required:* 4 English, 3 mathematics, 2 science, (2 science labs), 2 foreign language, 1 social studies, 1 history, 1 academic electives. *Academic units recommended:* 4 mathematics, 3 science, 2 social studies, 2 history, 3 academic electives. **Freshman Admission Statistics:** 7,313 applied, 58% admitted, 19% enrolled. **Transfer Admission Requirements:** High school transcript, college transcript(s), essay or personal statement, minimum college GPA of 2.5 required. Lowest grade transferable C. **General Admission Information:** Application fee $50. Regular application deadline 2/15. Regular notification 3/20. Nonfall registration accepted. Admission may be deferred for a maximum of 1 year. Credit and/or placement offered for CEEB Advanced Placement tests.

COSTS AND FINANCIAL AID
Annual tuition $26,850. . Room and board $11,800. Required fees $2,000. Average book expense $1,800. **Required Forms and Deadlines:** FAFSA, institution's own financial aid form, state aid form. Financial aid filing deadline 4/15. Priority financial aid filing date 2/15. **Notification of Awards:** Applicants will be notified of awards on a rolling basis beginning 12/20. **Types of Aid:** *Need-based scholarships/grants:* Federal Pell, SEOG, state scholarships/grants, private scholarships, the school's own gift aid. *Loans:* FFEL Subsidized Stafford, FFEL Unsubsidized Stafford, FFEL PLUS, Federal Perkins, alternative loans. **Student Employment:** Federal Work-Study Program available. Institutional employment available. Highest amount earned per year from on-campus jobs $9,729. Off-campus job opportunities are good. **Financial Aid Statistics:** 67% freshmen, 49% undergrads receive need-based scholarship or grant aid. 77% freshmen, 72% undergrads receive non-need-based scholarship or grant aid. 62% freshmen, 58% undergrads receive need-based self-help aid. 8% freshmen, 7% undergrads receive athletic scholarships. 98% freshmen, 94% undergrads receive any aid. 68% undergrads borrow to pay for school. Average cumulative indebtedness $24,213. **Criteria for awarding institutional aid:** *Non-need-based:* Academics, alumni affiliation, athletics.

See page 1118.

IOWA STATE UNIVERSITY

100 Enrollment Services Center, Ames, IA 50011-2011
Phone: 515-294-5836 **Financial Aid Phone:** 515-294-2223
E-mail: admissions@iastate.edu **CEEB Code:** 6306
Fax: 515-294-2592 **Website:** www.iastate.edu **ACT Code:** 1320

This public school was founded in 1858. It has a 1794-acre campus.

RATINGS
Admissions Selectivity Rating: 81   **Fire Safety Rating:** 72   **Green Rating:** 87

STUDENTS AND FACULTY
Enrollment: 21,959. **Student Body:** 43% female, 57% male, 24% out-of-state, 5% international (105 countries represented). Asian 3%, African American 3%, Caucasian 82%, Hispanic 3%.

Retention and Graduation: 84% freshmen return for sophomore year. 35% freshmen graduate within 4 years. 17% grads go on to further study within 1 year. 6% grads pursue arts and sciences degrees. 2% grads pursue law degrees. 4% grads pursue business degrees. 2% grads pursue medical degrees. **Faculty:** Student/faculty ratio 16.3:1. 1435 full-time faculty, 92% hold PhDs, 20% are members of minority groups, 32% are women. 13% of classes are taught by teaching assistants.

ACADEMICS

Degrees: Bachelor's, master's. **Classes:** Most classes have 20–29 students. Most lab/discussion sessions have 20–29 students. **Majors with Highest Enrollment:** Finance; marketing/marketing management; mechanical engineering. **Special Study Options:** Accelerated program, cooperative education program, cross-registration, distance learning, double major, dual enrollment, English as a Second Language (ESL), exchange student program (domestic), external degree program, honors program, independent study, internships, liberal arts/career combination, student-designed major, study abroad, teacher certification program, weekend college. **Honors programs:** ISU offers both a University Honors Program and a Freshman Honors Program. Each program promotes an enhanced academic environment for students of high ability and emphasizes the development of an enriched, individualized program study that meets each student's particular needs, interests and abilities. Honors gives students a supportive community in which to pursue their goals and stretch their horizons. Benefits include uniques courses, small class sizes, research opportunities and funding, access to graduate-level courses, and priority registration. **Combined degree programs:** BA/MEng, BS/MS. Special programs offered to physically disabled students include note-taking services, reader services, tape recorders, tutors. **Career services:** Alumni network, alumni services, career/job search classes, career assessment, internships. **Career services highlights include:** Our Learning Communities, in which students who have similar career goals live together and share academic courses, are ranked high nationally.

FACILITIES

Housing: Coed dorms, special housing for disabled students, men's dorms, special housing for international students, women's dorms, fraternity/sorority housing, apartments for married students, apartments for single students, theme housing: Learning Communities; family housing; quiet, non-smoking, or alcohol-free floors; graduate/adult undergraduate housing. 95% of campus accessible to physically disabled. **Special Academic Facilities/Equipment:** Brunnier art museum, Farm House museum, observatory, numerous institutes, research centers, College of Design Gallery, Virtual Reality Application Center, Pappajohn Center for Entrepreneurship. **Computers:** 100% of classrooms, 75% of dorms, 100% of libraries, 100% of dining areas, 100% of student union, 40% of common outdoor areas have wireless network access. Students can register for classes online. Administrative functions (other than registration) can be performed online.

CAMPUS LIFE

Environment: Town. **Activities:** Choral groups, concert band, dance, drama/theater, jazz band, literary magazine, marching band, music ensembles, musical theater, opera, pep band, radio station, student government, student newspaper, student-run film society, symphony orchestra, television station **Organizations:** 799 registered organizations, 43 honor societies, 34 religious organizations. 34 fraternities, 19 sororities. **Athletics (Intercollegiate):** *Men:* Basketball, cross-country, football, golf, track/field (outdoor), track/field (indoor), wrestling. *Women:* Basketball, cross-country, diving, golf, gymnastics, soccer, softball, swimming, tennis, track/field (outdoor), track/field (indoor), volleyball. **On-Campus Highlights:** Union Drive Community Center (dining center), Reiman Gardens, Lied Recreation Center, Memorial Union, Virtual Reality Lab (available to visitors also), Campanile. **Environmental Initiatives:** Establishment of the Live Green Initiative (www.livegreen.iastate.edu/about/) that has included: 1. Hiring of a Director of Sustainability (www.iastate.edu/Inside/2008/1212/rankin.shtml) 2. Creation of a 13-member (students, staff, and faculty) President's Advisory Committee on Energy Conservation and Global Climate Change (www.committees.iastate.edu/comm-info.php?id=136) 3. Creation of a Live Green Loan Fund for energy conservation and sustainability projects (www.livegreen.iastate.edu/loan/) 4. Completion of an annual Symposium on Sustainability (www.livegreen.iastate.edu/symposium/) Commitment to Sustainable Operations highlighted by: 1. Energy—through a joint contract with the City of Ames, 10% of Iowa State University's energy is derived from wind. In addition, there is ongoing evaluation and testing of renewable fuel sources. 2. Building and Construction—LEED Gold Certification Requirement for all new construction and major renovation projects. Specific Iowa State University required LEED credits have also been designated. In addition, for all other campus projects the incorporation of sustainable design standards is required. 3. Dining Services—10% of purchases are local, organic, or environmentally-preferable. Trayless dining in two dining centers has reduced food waste by 50%. Food waste is composted at the university's compost facility and utilized for on-campus projects. Prepared leftover food is donated to a free meal program in the Ames community. 4. Campus Green Teams—Development of campus green teams dedicated to increasing sustainability efforts as related to a specific

campus building, college, department, or operation. To date, there are 25 Iowa State University Green Teams. Student Engagement highlighted by: 1. Solar Decathlon—multi-disciplinary, internationally recognized team (www.solard.iastate.edu/)taking part in a competition to design, build, and operate the most attractive, effective, and energy-efficient solar-powered home. 2. Greenhouse Group—residence hall team committed to greening Iowa State University through student initiatives and activities—including the establishment of a residence hall multi-commodity recycling program(http://sodb.stuorg.iastate.edu/view.php?id=1603) 3. Green Umbrella Group—founded by the Government of the Student Body Sustainability Director for the purpose of offering a collective representation and collaboration opportunity for all student organizations (~25) that support sustainability at Iowa State University (http://sodb.stuorg.iastate.edu/view.php?id=1586)

ADMISSIONS

Freshman Academic Profile: Average high school GPA 3.53. 28% in top 10% of high school class, 62% in top 25% of high school class, 93% in top 50% of high school class. 91% from public high schools. SAT Math middle 50% range 540–690. SAT Critical Reading middle 50% range 490–640. ACT middle 50% range 22–28. Minimum paper TOEFL 530. Minimum web-based TOEFL 71. **Basis for Candidate Selection:** *Very important factors considered include:* Class rank, academic GPA, rigor of secondary school record, standardized test scores. *Other factors considered include:* Application essay, recommendation(s), character/personal qualities, extracurricular activities, geographical residence, interview, state residency, talent/ability, volunteer work, work experience. **Freshman Admission Requirements:** High school diploma is required and GED is accepted. *Academic units required:* 4 English, 3 mathematics, 3 science, (2 science labs), 2 foreign language, 2 social studies. *Academic units recommended:* 4 English, 4 mathematics, 4 science, (3 science labs), 3 foreign language, 4 social studies. **Freshman Admission Statistics:** 12,536 applied, 85% admitted, 41% enrolled. **Transfer Admission Requirements:** College transcript(s), statement of good standing from prior institution(s). Minimum college GPA of 2.0 required. Lowest grade transferable D. **General Admission Information:** Application fee $30. Regular application deadline 7/1. Notification on a rolling basis, beginning on or about 7/1. Nonfall registration accepted. Admission may be deferred for a maximum of 1 year. Credit and/or placement offered for CEEB Advanced Placement tests.

COSTS AND FINANCIAL AID

Annual in-state tuition $6,102. Annual out-of-state tuition $17,668. Room and board $7,277. Required fees $895. Average book expense $1,000. **Required Forms and Deadlines:** FAFSA. Priority financial aid filing date 3/1. **Notification of Awards:** Applicants will be notified of awards on a rolling basis beginning 4/1. **Types of Aid:** *Need-based scholarships/grants:* Federal Pell, SEOG, state scholarships/grants, the school's own gift aid. *Loans:* Direct Subsidized Stafford, Direct Unsubsidized Stafford, Direct PLUS, Federal Perkins, state loans, college/university loans from institutional funds, private alternative loans. **Student Employment:** Federal Work-Study Program available. Institutional employment available. Highest amount earned per year from on-campus jobs $1,877. Off-campus job opportunities are excellent. **Financial Aid Statistics:** 51% freshmen, 52% undergrads receive need-based scholarship or grant aid. 25% freshmen, 26% undergrads receive non-need-based scholarship or grant aid. 38% freshmen, 43% undergrads receive need-based self-help aid. 2% freshmen, 2% undergrads receive athletic scholarships. 83.7% freshmen, 79.1% undergrads receive any aid. 71.2% undergrads borrow to pay for school. Average cumulative indebtedness $30,411. **Criteria for awarding institutional aid:** *Non-need-based:* Academics, art, athletics, leadership, minority status, music/drama, state/district residency.

ITHACA COLLEGE

Ithaca College—Office of Admissions, Ithaca, NY 14850-7020
Phone: 607-274-3124 **Financial Aid Phone:** 607-274-3131
E-mail: admission@ithaca.edu **CEEB Code:** 2325
Fax: 607-274-1900 **Website:** www.ithaca.edu **ACT Code:** 2772

This private school was founded in 1892. It has a 650-acre campus.

RATINGS
Admissions Selectivity Rating: 83   **Fire Safety Rating:** 75   **Green Rating:** 98

STUDENTS AND FACULTY

Enrollment: 6,400. **Student Body:** 57% female, 43% male, 55.2% out-of-state, 2% international (80 countries represented). Asian 4%, African American 3%, Caucasian 69%, Hispanic 4%, Native American 1%.
Retention and Graduation: 71% freshmen graduate within 4 years. 40% grads go on to further study within 1 year. 36% grads pursue arts and sciences degrees. 1% grads pursue law degrees. 2% grads pursue business degrees. 1% grads pursue medical degrees. **Faculty:** Student/faculty ratio 12.4:1. 461 full-time faculty, 95% hold PhDs, 8% are members of minority groups, 46% are women. 1% of classes are taught by teaching assistants.

ACADEMICS

Degrees: Bachelor's, certificate, master's. **Classes:** Most classes have fewer than 10 students. Most lab/discussion sessions have 10–19 students. **Majors with Highest Enrollment:** Business/commerce; music; radio and television. **Special Study Options:** Accelerated program, cross-registration, distance learning, double major, dual enrollment, honors program, independent study, internships, liberal arts/career combination, student-designed major, study abroad, teacher certification program, London Center (London, England), Los Angeles Program, Washington, DC semester program, Walkabout Down Under Program(Australia), opportunities to study in over 50 countries around the world. **Honors programs:** Students in the Humanities and Sciences Honors Program participate in a series of special intensive seminars complemented by an array of out-of-class activities. Starting in the fall of the first year, honors students begin a sequence of eight honors seminar courses that help them meet general requirements of the school. The sequence includes: a first-year seminar taken in the first semester, four intermediate seminars normally taken in the second, third and fourth semesters, a seminar on cultural themes taken in the junior year, and a capstone seminar on contemporary issues, taken in the senior year. **Combined degree programs:** BS/MS-Occup. Therapy and BS/DPT in Physical Therapy. Special programs offered to physically disabled students include note-taking services, reader services, tape recorders. **Career services:** Alumni network, alumni services, career/job search classes, career assessment, internships, regional alumni. **Career services highlights include:** Park School of Communication Internships are normally taken during a students senior year. Sponsors include local, regional, national, and international TV, radio, advertising, public relations, motion picture, education and corporate media organizations and many corporations and non-profit organizations.

FACILITIES

Housing: Coed dorms, special housing for disabled students, women's dorms, fraternity/sorority housing, apartments for single students, theme housing. **Special Academic Facilities/Equipment:** Two newly-constructed Platinum LEED-certified buildings (the Business School and the Peggy Williams Center, Art Gallery, Radio and TV stations, digital technology throughout Communications building, Observatory, Wellness Clinic, Fitness Center, Trading Room, Speech and Hearing Handicapped Clinic, Physical Therapy Clinic, Performing Arts Centers (Music And Theater), Music Recording Facility. **Computers:** 50% of classrooms, 100% of dorms, 100% of libraries, 100% of dining areas, 100% of student union, have wireless network access. Students can register for classes online. Administrative functions (other than registration) can be performed online.

CAMPUS LIFE

Environment: Town. **Activities:** Choral groups, concert band, dance, drama/theater, jazz band, literary magazine, music ensembles, musical theater, opera, pep band, radio station, student government, student newspaper, student-run film society, symphony orchestra, television station, yearbook, campus ministries, international student organization. **Organizations:** 180 registered organizations, 28 honor organizations, 8 religious organizations. 3 fraternities, 1 sorority. **Athletics (Intercollegiate):** *Men:* Baseball, basketball, crew/rowing, cross-country, diving, football, lacrosse, soccer, swimming, tennis, track/field (outdoor), wrestling. *Women:* Basketball, crew/rowing, cross-country, diving, field hockey, golf, gymnastics, lacrosse, soccer, softball, swimming, tennis, track/field (outdoor), volleyball. **On-Campus Highlights:** IC Square and Food Court, Handwerker Gallery, Fitness Center, Business School Atrium, Library. **Environmental Initiatives:** 1. Sustainability Initiative that spurs and chronicles progress in three separate but highly inter-related areas: development of curriculum to infuse considerations of sustainability and applied research opportunities to study and solve sustainability challenges; modification of campus operations to incorporate more sustainable decision-making; and campus in-reach and community outreach to share our experiences as a learning organization seeking to become more sustainable. 2. Achieving LEED Platinum certification for our School of Business, and modifying business school curriculum to incorporate sustainability principles and to use the building as a "teaching tool" to model sustainable operations. The new Peggy R. Williams Center is also designed to achieve LEED Platinum certification (application on file); when certified, this may make Ithaca the first institution in the world to have two LEED Platinum facilities on its campus. 3. We have collaborated with our regional Sodexho Facilities Management group to pilot a comprehensive energy and resource audit and sustainability assessment of all of our dining services-related facilities including board dining halls and retail operations.

ADMISSIONS

Freshman Academic Profile: 27.4% in top 10% of high school class, 67.2% in top 25% of high school class, 93% in top 50% of high school class. 83% from public high schools. SAT Math middle 50% range 530–640. SAT Critical Reading middle 50% range 530–630. SAT Writing middle 50% range 525–630. Minimum paper TOEFL 550. Minimum computer TOEFL 213. Minimum web-based TOEFL 80. **Basis for Candidate Selection:** *Very important factors considered include:* Academic GPA, rigor of secondary school record, standardized test scores. *Important factors considered include:* Class rank, application essay, recommendation(s), character/personal qualities, extracurricular activities, talent/ability. *Other factors considered include:* Alumni/ae relation, first generation, level of applicant's interest, volunteer work, work experience. **Freshman Admission Requirements:** High school diploma is required and GED is accepted. *Academic units required:* 4 English, 3 mathematics, 3 science, 2 foreign language, 4 social studies, 1 academic electives. **Freshman Admission Statistics:** 11,916 applied, 79% admitted, 21% enrolled. **Transfer Admission Requirements:** High school transcript, college transcript(s), essay or personal statement, statement of good standing from prior institution(s). Minimum college GPA of 2.75 required. Lowest grade transferable C–. **General Admission Information:** Application fee $60. Early decision application deadline 11/1. Regular application deadline 2/1. Regular notification 4/15. Notification on a rolling basis, beginning on or about 11/15. Nonfall registration accepted. Admission may be deferred for a maximum of 1 year. Credit and/or placement offered for CEEB Advanced Placement tests.

COSTS AND FINANCIAL AID

Annual tuition $32,060. Room and board $11,780. Average book expense $1,200. **Required Forms and Deadlines:** FAFSA, CSS/Financial Aid PROFILE. Priority financial aid filing date 2/1. **Notification of Awards:** Applicants will be notified of awards on a rolling basis beginning 2/15. **Types of Aid:** *Need-based scholarships/grants:* Federal Pell, SEOG, state scholarships/grants, private scholarships, the school's own gift aid. *Loans:* FFEL Subsidized Stafford, FFEL Unsubsidized Stafford, FFEL PLUS, Federal Perkins, alternative loans. **Student Employment:** Federal Work-Study Program available. Institutional employment available. Highest amount earned per year from on-campus jobs $2,400. Off-campus job opportunities are good. **Financial Aid Statistics:** 73% freshmen, 67% undergrads receive need-based scholarship or grant aid. 23% freshmen, 17% undergrads receive non-need-based scholarship or grant aid. 68% freshmen, 64% undergrads receive need-based self-help aid. 96.2% freshmen, 90.5% undergrads receive any aid. **Criteria for awarding institutional aid:** *Non-need-based:* Academics, alumni affiliation, leadership, minority status, music/drama.

See page 1120.

JACKSON STATE UNIVERSITY

1400 J. R. Lynch Street, P. O. Box 17330, Jackson, MS 39217
Phone: 601-979-2100 **Financial Aid Phone:** 601-979-2227
E-mail: schatman@ccaix.jsums.edu **CEEB Code:** 1341
Fax: 601-979-3445 **Website:** www.jsums.edu **ACT Code:** 2204

This public school was founded in 1877. It has a 150-acre campus.

RATINGS

Admissions Selectivity Rating: 82   **Fire Safety Rating:** 64   **Green Rating:** 60*

STUDENTS AND FACULTY

Enrollment: 6,509. **Student Body:** 62% female, 38% male, 18% out-of-state, 1% international. African American 87%, Caucasian 2%.
Retention and Graduation: 66% freshmen return for sophomore year. 14% freshmen graduate within 4 years. 13% grads go on to further study within 1 year. 6% grads pursue law degrees. 7% grads pursue medical degrees. **Faculty:** Student/faculty ratio 18:1. 354 full-time faculty, 76% hold PhDs, 82% are members of minority groups, 46% are women.

ACADEMICS

Degrees: Bachelor's, master's, post-master's certificate. **Majors with Highest Enrollment:** Education, other; elementary education and teaching; social work. **Special Study Options:** Cooperative education program, distance learning, double major, dual enrollment, English as a Second Language (ESL), honors program, independent study, internships, study abroad, teacher certification program, weekend college, Undergrads may take grad level classes. Off-Campus Programs: Research semester at Lawrence Berkeley Lab. Co-Op Programs: Business, Computer Science, Natural Science. **Honors programs:** Honors College Special programs offered to physically disabled students include note-taking services, tape recorders, tutors. **Career services:** Career/job search classes, career assessment. **Career services highlights include:** They both are important in assisting students for job placement after graduation.

FACILITIES
Housing: Men's dorms, women's dorms 100% of campus accessible to physically disabled. **Special Academic Facilities/Equipment:** Research center. **Computers:** Students can register for classes online. Administrative functions (other than registration) can be performed online.

CAMPUS LIFE
Environment: Metropolis. **Activities:** Choral groups, concert band, dance, drama/theater, jazz band, literary magazine, marching band, music ensembles, opera, pep band, radio station, student government, student newspaper, student-run film society, symphony orchestra, television station, yearbook. **Organizations:** 150 registered organizations, 20 honor societies, 11 religious organizations. 4 fraternities, 4 sororities. **Athletics (Intercollegiate):** *Men:* Baseball, basketball, cross-country, football, golf, soccer, tennis, track/field (outdoor), track/field (indoor), volleyball. *Women:* Basketball, cross-country, golf, soccer, softball, tennis, track/field (outdoor), track/field (indoor), volleyball.

ADMISSIONS
Freshman Academic Profile: Average high school GPA 2.9. 31% in top 25% of high school class, 58% in top 50% of high school class. 85% from public high schools. ACT middle 50% range 16–20. Minimum paper TOEFL 525. Minimum computer TOEFL 300. **Basis for Candidate Selection:** *Very important factors considered include:* Academic GPA, rigor of secondary school record, standardized test scores. *Important factors considered include:* level of applicant's interest. **Freshman Admission Requirements:** High school diploma is required and GED is accepted. *Academic units required:* 4 English, 3 mathematics, 3 science, 3 social studies, 2 academic electives. **Freshman Admission Statistics:** 8,052 applied, 39% admitted, 29% enrolled. **Transfer Admission Requirements:** High school transcript, college transcript(s), minimum college GPA of 2.0 required. Lowest grade transferable C. **General Admission Information:** Nonfall registration accepted.

COSTS AND FINANCIAL AID
Average book expense $800. **Required Forms and Deadlines:** FAFSA, institution's own financial aid form, state aid form **Notification of Awards:** Applicants will be notified of awards on a rolling basis beginning 2/15. **Types of Aid:** *Need-based scholarships/grants:* Federal Pell, SEOG, state scholarships/grants, private scholarships, the school's own gift aid. *Loans:* FFEL Subsidized Stafford, FFEL Unsubsidized Stafford, FFEL PLUS, Federal Perkins, college/university loans from institutional funds. **Student Employment:** Federal Work-Study Program available. Institutional employment available. Highest amount earned per year from on-campus jobs $2,200. Off-campus job opportunities are good.

FACILITIES
Housing: Coed dorms, men's dorms, special housing for international students, women's dorms, fraternity/sorority housing, apartments for married students, apartments for single students, apartments for students with dependent children. 90% of campus accessible to physically disabled. **Computers:** Students can register for classes online.

CAMPUS LIFE
Environment: Village. **Activities:** Choral groups, concert band, dance, drama/theater, jazz band, marching band, music ensembles, musical theater, pep band, radio station, student government, student newspaper, symphony orchestra, yearbook. **Organizations:** 100 registered organizations, 13 honor societies, 8 religious organizations. 11 fraternities, 9 sororities. **Athletics (Intercollegiate):** *Men:* Baseball, basketball, cheerleading, football, golf, riflery, tennis. *Women:* Basketball, cheerleading, cross-country, golf, riflery, soccer, softball, tennis, track/field (outdoor), volleyball. **On-Campus Highlights:** Houston Cole Library, Theron Montgomery Bldg—Student Life, Stephenson Gym, Bibb Graves—Adm Bldg, Paul Snow Stadium.

ADMISSIONS
Freshman Academic Profile: Average high school GPA 2.99. 3% in top 10% of high school class, 13% in top 25% of high school class, 34% in top 50% of high school class. 99% from public high schools. SAT Math middle 50% range 400–530. SAT Critical Reading middle 50% range 420–530. ACT middle 50% range 17–23. Minimum paper TOEFL 500. Minimum computer TOEFL 173. **Basis for Candidate Selection:** *Very important factors considered include:* Rigor of secondary school record, standardized test scores. **Freshman Admission Requirements:** High school diploma is required and GED is accepted. *Academic units required:* 3 English, 4 academic electives. **Freshman Admission Statistics:** 2,419 applied, 88% admitted, 50% enrolled. **Transfer Admission Requirements:** College transcript(s), Lowest grade transferable D. **General Admission Information:** Application fee $20. Nonfall registration accepted. Admission may be deferred for a maximum of 4. Credit and/or placement offered for CEEB Advanced Placement tests.

COSTS AND FINANCIAL AID
Annual in-state tuition $4,040. Annual out-of-state tuition $8,080. Room and board $3,312. Required fees $20. Average book expense $1,008. **Required Forms and Deadlines:** FAFSA, institution's own financial aid form. Priority financial aid filing date 3/15. **Notification of Awards:** Applicants will be notified of awards on a rolling basis beginning 5/15. **Types of Aid:** *Need-based scholarships/grants:* Federal Pell, SEOG, state scholarships/grants, private scholarships, Federal Nursing Scholarships. *Loans:* Direct Subsidized Stafford, Direct Unsubsidized Stafford, Direct PLUS, college/university loans from institutional funds.

JACKSONVILLE STATE UNIVERSITY

700 Pelham Road North, Jacksonville, AL 36265
Phone: 256-782-5268 **Financial Aid Phone:** 256-782-5006
E-mail: info@jsu.edu
Fax: 256-782-5953 **Website:** www.jsu.edu **ACT Code:** 20

This public school was founded in 1883. It has a 459-acre campus.

RATINGS
Admissions Selectivity Rating: 64   **Fire Safety Rating:** 60*   **Green Rating:** 60*

STUDENTS AND FACULTY
Enrollment: 7,096. **Student Body:** 58% female, 42% male, 12% out-of-state, 1% international (73 countries represented). Asian 1%, African American 22%, Caucasian 71%, Hispanic 1%, Native American 1%.
Retention and Graduation: 63% freshmen return for sophomore year. 15% freshmen graduate within 4 years. **Faculty:** Student/faculty ratio 21:1. 300 full-time faculty, 66% hold PhDs, 11% are members of minority groups, 44% are women.

ACADEMICS
Degrees: Bachelor's, master's, post-master's certificate. **Classes:** Most classes have 20–29 students. **Majors with Highest Enrollment:** Criminal justice/safety studies; elementary education and teaching; nursing/registered nurse (RN, ASN, BSN, MSN). **Special Study Options:** Accelerated program, cooperative education program, distance learning, double major, dual enrollment, honors program, independent study, internships, teacher certification program Special programs offered to physically disabled students include note-taking services, reader services, tape recorders, tutors.

JACKSONVILLE UNIVERSITY

Office of Admissions, 2800 University Boulevard North, Jacksonville, FL 32211
Phone: 904-256-7000 **Financial Aid Phone:** 800-558-3467
E-mail: admissions@ju.edu **CEEB Code:** 5331
Fax: Website: www.ju.edu **ACT Code:** 740

This private school was founded in 1934. It has a 198-acre campus.

RATINGS
Admissions Selectivity Rating: 80   **Fire Safety Rating:** 69   **Green Rating:** 60*

STUDENTS AND FACULTY
Enrollment: 3,084. **Student Body:** 60% female, 40% male, 36% out-of-state, 2% international (50 countries represented). Asian 3%, African American 19%, Caucasian 58%, Hispanic 6%, Native American 1%.
Retention and Graduation: 63% freshmen return for sophomore year. 29% freshmen graduate within 4 years. 22% grads go on to further study within 1 year. **Faculty:** Student/faculty ratio 14:1. 166 full-time faculty, 81% hold PhDs, 10% are members of minority groups, 45% are women.

ACADEMICS
Degrees: Bachelor's, master's. **Classes:** Most classes have 10–19 students. **Majors with Highest Enrollment:** aviation/airway management and operations; business/commerce; nursing/registered nurse (RN, ASN, BSN, MSN). **Special Study Options:** Accelerated program, cooperative education program, distance learning, double major, dual enrollment, honors program, independent study, internships, liberal arts/career combination, student-designed major, study abroad, teacher certification program. **Honors programs:** University Honors Program. Special programs offered to physically disabled students include note-taking services, reader services, tutors.

FACILITIES

Housing: Coed dorms, special housing for disabled students, men's dorms, women's dorms, fraternity/sorority housing, apartments for single students. **Special Academic Facilities/Equipment:** Art museum, dance pavilion, concert hall, on-campus pre-school. **Computers:** Students can register for classes online. Administrative functions (other than registration) can be performed online.

CAMPUS LIFE

Environment: Metropolis. **Activities:** Choral groups, concert band, dance, drama/theater, jazz band, literary magazine, music ensembles, musical theater, pep band, radio station, student government, student newspaper, symphony orchestra, television station, yearbook, campus ministries, international student organization. **Organizations:** 60 registered organizations, 16 honor societies, 9 fraternities, 6 sororities. **Athletics (Intercollegiate):** *Men:* Baseball, basketball, crew/rowing, cross-country, football, golf, soccer, tennis. *Women:* Basketball, crew/rowing, cross-country, golf, soccer, softball, tennis, track/field (outdoor), track/field (indoor), volleyball. **On-Campus Highlights:** Alexander Brest Fine Arts Museum, Davis College of Business/ Jazzman's Cafe (New), JU Baseball Complex, Lazzara Health Sciences Center (New), Residential Apartment Village (New).

ADMISSIONS

Freshman Academic Profile: Average high school GPA 3.41. SAT Math middle 50% range 470–560. SAT Critical Reading middle 50% range 470–560. ACT middle 50% range 19–25. Minimum paper TOEFL 540. Minimum computer TOEFL 207. **Basis for Candidate Selection:** *Very important factors considered include:* Academic GPA, standardized test scores. *Important factors considered include:* Rigor of secondary school record, talent/ability. *Other factors considered include:* Application essay, recommendation(s), character/personal qualities, extracurricular activities, interview, volunteer work, work experience. **Freshman Admission Requirements:** High school diploma is required and GED is accepted. *Academic units required:* 4 English, 3 mathematics, 3 science, (2 science labs), 3 social studies. **Freshman Admission Statistics:** 6,854 applied, 54% admitted, 18% enrolled. **Transfer Admission Requirements:** College transcript(s), essay or personal statement, statement of good standing from prior institution(s). Minimum college GPA of 2.0 required. Lowest grade transferable C. **General Admission Information:** Notification on a rolling basis, beginning on or about 10/1. Nonfall registration accepted. Admission may be deferred for a maximum of NA. Credit and/or placement offered for CEEB Advanced Placement tests.

COSTS AND FINANCIAL AID

Required Forms and Deadlines: FAFSA, institution's own financial aid form, state aid form. Priority financial aid filing date 3/15. Applicants will be notified of awards on a rolling basis beginning 2/15. **Types of Aid:** *Need-based scholarships/grants:* Federal Pell, SEOG, state scholarships/grants, private scholarships, the school's own gift aid, ACG/SMART. *Loans:* FFEL Subsidized Stafford, FFEL Unsubsidized Stafford, FFEL PLUS, Federal Perkins, state loans, college/university loans from institutional funds. **Student Employment:** Highest amount earned per year from on-campus jobs $4,677. **Financial Aid Statistics:** 72% freshmen, 76% undergrads receive need-based scholarship or grant aid. 1% freshmen, 1% undergrads receive non-need-based scholarship or grant aid. 45% freshmen, 53% undergrads receive need-based self-help aid. 2% freshmen, 4% undergrads receive athletic scholarships. 97% freshmen, 87% undergrads receive any aid. **Criteria for awarding institutional aid:** *Non-need-based:* Academics, art, athletics, job skills, leadership, music/drama, state/district residency.

JAMES MADISON UNIVERSITY

Best 373

Sonner Hall, MSC 0101, Harrisonburg, VA 22807
Phone: 540-568-5681 **Financial Aid Phone:** 540-568-7820
E-mail: admissions@jmu.edu **CEEB Code:** 5392
Fax: 540-568-3332 **Website:** www.jmu.edu **ACT Code:** 4370

This public school was founded in 1908. It has a 712-acre campus.

RATINGS

Admissions Selectivity Rating: 88　　**Fire Safety Rating:** 68　　**Green Rating:** 90

STUDENTS AND FACULTY

Enrollment: 16,979. **Student Body:** 60% female, 40% male, 29% out-of-state, 1% international (69 countries represented). Asian 5%, African American 4%, Caucasian 81%, Hispanic 3%.

Retention and Graduation: 64% freshmen graduate within 4 years. 40% grads go on to further study within 1 year. **Faculty:** Student/faculty ratio 16:1. 906 full-time faculty, 78% hold PhDs, 8% are members of minority groups, 45% are women. 1% of classes are taught by teaching assistants.

ACADEMICS

Degrees: Bachelor's, master's, post-master's certificate. **Classes:** Most classes have 20–29 students. Most lab/discussion sessions have 20–29 students. **Majors with Highest Enrollment:** Community health services/liaison/counseling; marketing/marketing management; psychology. **Special Study Options:** Accelerated program, distance learning, double major, English as a Second Language (ESL), honors program, independent study, internships, study abroad, teacher certification program, continuing education programs offered on campus. **Honors programs:** Academic honors program, honors scholars (3.25 or above), honors courses, and senior honors project (3.25). **Combined degree programs:** BS in Bio. JMU/Master of Forestry VA Tech 3-2. Special programs offered to physically disabled students include note-taking services, reader services, tape recorders. **Career services:** Alumni network, alumni services, career/job search classes, career assessment, internships. **Career services highlights include:** We offer a course designed for first and second year students who have not selected a major called Life and Career Planning. It is offered for academic credit and serves over 10% of the freshman class. Our assessment data has demonstrated the effectiveness of this course in enhancing students' understanding of career decision-makinng processes, career decisiveness and career decision-making self-efficacy.

FACILITIES

Housing: Coed dorms, special housing for disabled students, fraternity/sorority housing, apartments for single students, wellness housing, theme housing 90% of campus accessible to physically disabled. **Special Academic Facilities/Equipment:** Language lab, music and fine arts buildings, herbarium, university farm, planetarium, arboretum, mineral museum, Science on a Sphere. **Computers:** 25% of classrooms, 100% of dorms, 100% of libraries, 50% of dining areas, 100% of student union, 25% of common outdoor areas have wireless network access. Students can register for classes online. Administrative functions (other than registration) can be performed online.

CAMPUS LIFE

Environment: Town. **Activities:** Choral groups, concert band, dance, drama/theater, jazz band, literary magazine, marching band, music ensembles, musical theater, opera, pep band, radio station, student government, student newspaper, student-run film society, symphony orchestra, yearbook, campus ministries, international student organization. **Organizations:** 298 registered organizations, 28 honor societies, 28 religious organizations. 15 fraternities, 9 sororities. **Athletics (Intercollegiate):** *Men:* Baseball, basketball, cheerleading, football, golf, soccer, tennis. *Women:* Basketball, cheerleading, cross-country, diving, field hockey, golf, lacrosse, soccer, softball, swimming, tennis, track/field (outdoor), volleyball. **On-Campus Highlights:** Quad, Taylor Down Under, UREC, East Campus Library, Festival Student Center. **Environmental Initiatives:** JMU's President formed a Commission on Environmental Stewardship and Sustainability and later created an Institute and five supporting committees to coordinate campus environmental stewardship efforts. JMU's recycling program is award-winning. They employ six full time and four wage employees. JMU offers extensive academic and co-curricular experiences that allow students hands-on exploration of sustainability.

ADMISSIONS

Freshman Academic Profile: Average high school GPA 3.8. 28% in top 10% of high school class, 72% in top 25% of high school class, 98% in top 50% of high school class. SAT Math middle 50% range 530–630. SAT Critical Reading middle 50% range 520–610. ACT middle 50% range 22–27. Minimum paper TOEFL 550. Minimum computer TOEFL 213. **Basis for Candidate Selection:** *Very important factors considered include:* Academic GPA, rigor of secondary school record. *Important factors considered include:* standardized test scores. *Other factors considered include:* Class rank, application essay, recommendation(s), alumni/ae relation, character/personal qualities, extracurricular activities, geographical residence, state residency, talent/ability, volunteer work, work experience. **Freshman Admission Requirements:** High school diploma is required and GED is accepted. *Academic units required:* 4 English, 4 mathematics, 3 science, (3 science labs), 2 foreign language, 3 social studies. *Academic units recommended:* 4 English, 4 mathematics, 4 science, (4 science labs), 3 foreign language, 4 social studies. **Freshman Admission Statistics:** 20,963 applied, 61% admitted, 31% enrolled. **Transfer Admission Requirements:** High school transcript, college transcript(s), minimum college GPA of 2.0 required. Lowest grade transferable C. **General Admission Information:** Application fee $50. Regular application deadline 1/15. Regular notification 4/1. Nonfall registration not accepted. Admission may be deferred for a maximum of 1 year with. Credit offered for CEEB Advanced Placement tests.

COSTS AND FINANCIAL AID

Annual in-state tuition $3,734. Annual out-of-state tuition $15,866. Room and board $7,690. Required fees $3,510. Average book expense $876. **Required**

Forms and Deadlines: FAFSA. Priority financial aid filing date 3/1. **Notification of Awards:** Applicants will be notified of awards on a rolling basis beginning 4/1. **Types of Aid:** *Need-based scholarships/grants:* Federal Pell, SEOG, state scholarships/grants, private scholarships, the school's own gift aid. *Loans:* Direct Subsidized Stafford, Direct Unsubsidized Stafford, Direct PLUS, Federal Perkins, Federal Nursing. **Student Employment:** Federal Work-Study Program available. Institutional employment available. Highest amount earned per year from on-campus jobs $3,640. Off-campus job opportunities are good. **Financial Aid Statistics:** 17% freshmen, 15% undergrads receive need-based scholarship or grant aid. 2% freshmen, 2% undergrads receive non-need-based scholarship or grant aid. 31% freshmen, 26% undergrads receive need-based self-help aid. 2% freshmen, 2% undergrads receive athletic scholarships. 58% freshmen, 53% undergrads receive any aid. 51% undergrads borrow to pay for school. Average cumulative indebtedness $18,183. **Criteria for awarding institutional aid:** *Non-need-based:* Academics, alumni affiliation, art, athletics, leadership, minority status, music/drama, state/district residency.

JAMESTOWN COLLEGE

6081 College Lane, Jamestown, ND 58405-0001
Phone: 701-252-3467 **Financial Aid Phone:** 701-252-3467
E-mail: admissions@jc.edu
Fax: 701-253-4318 **Website:** www.jc.edu **ACT Code:** 3200

This private school, affiliated with the Presbyterian Church, was founded in 1883. It has a 110-acre campus.

RATINGS
Admissions Selectivity Rating: 82   **Fire Safety Rating:** 65   **Green Rating:** 60*

STUDENTS AND FACULTY
Enrollment: 965. **Student Body:** 53% female, 47% male, 44% out-of-state, 4% international (12 countries represented). Asian 2%, African American 1%, Caucasian 90%, Hispanic 2%, Native American 1%.
Retention and Graduation: 70% freshmen return for sophomore year. 31% freshmen graduate within 4 years. 20% grads go on to further study within 1 year. 9% grads pursue arts and sciences degrees. 2% grads pursue law degrees. 2% grads pursue medical degrees. **Faculty:** Student/faculty ratio 14.53:1. 57 full-time faculty, 54% hold PhDs, 7% are members of minority groups, 46% are women.

ACADEMICS
Degrees: Bachelor's. **Classes:** Most classes have 10–19 students. Most lab/discussion sessions have fewer than 10 students. **Majors with Highest Enrollment:** Business/commerce; elementary education and teaching; nursing/registered nurse (RN, ASN, BSN, MSN). **Special Study Options:** Cooperative education program, double major, dual enrollment, English as a Second Language (ESL), exchange student program (domestic), honors program, independent study, internships, liberal arts/career combination, student-designed major, study abroad, teacher certification program. **Honors programs:** Character and Leadership Program. The heart of the Character in Leadership program is its academic core. Each student who participates will receive a minor in leadership. Jamestown College values its reputation for quality education and therefore is committed through its Character in Leadership Program to providing a broad and sound intellectual foundation that will enable its students to provide ethical leadership in an ever-changing world. Special programs offered to physically disabled students include note-taking services, reader services, tape recorders, tutors. **Career services:** Alumni network, alumni services, career/job search classes, internships.

FACILITIES
Housing: Coed dorms, special housing for disabled students, apartments for married students, apartments for single students 80% of campus accessible to physically disabled. **Computers:** 95% of classrooms, 100% of dorms, 100% of libraries, 100% of dining areas, 100% of student union, 50% of common outdoor areas have wireless network access. Students can register for classes online. Administrative functions (other than registration) can be performed online.

CAMPUS LIFE
Environment: Village. **Activities:** Choral groups, concert band, dance, drama/theater, jazz band, literary magazine, music ensembles, musical theater, pep band, student government, student newspaper, television station, campus ministries, international student organization. **Organizations:** 35 registered organizations, 6 honor societies, 5 religious organizations. **Athletics (Intercollegiate):** *Men:* Baseball, basketball, cross-country, football, golf, track/field (outdoor), track/field (indoor), wrestling. *Women:* Basketball, cross-country, golf, soccer, softball, track/field (outdoor), track/field (indoor), volleyball, wrestling.

On-Campus Highlights: Library lobby, lounge/tv room outside of cafeteria, Larson Center (athletic center)/Foss Wellness Center, Residence Hall lounges, Level 2 (campus nightclub).

ADMISSIONS
Freshman Academic Profile: Average high school GPA 3.34. 13% in top 10% of high school class, 37% in top 25% of high school class, 73% in top 50% of high school class. SAT Math middle 50% range 400–570. SAT Critical Reading middle 50% range 400–520. ACT middle 50% range 20–25. Minimum paper TOEFL 525. Minimum computer TOEFL 195. **Basis for Candidate Selection:** *Important factors considered include:* Academic GPA, recommendation(s), standardized test scores. *Other factors considered include:* Rigor of secondary school record, character/personal qualities, extracurricular activities, level of applicant's interest, talent/ability, volunteer work, work experience. **Freshman Admission Requirements:** High school diploma is required and GED is accepted. *Academic units recommended:* 4 English, 3 mathematics, 4 science, 2 foreign language, 3 social studies. **Freshman Admission Statistics:** 898 applied, 43% admitted, 30% enrolled. **Transfer Admission Requirements:** High school transcript, college transcript(s), statement of good standing from prior institution(s). Minimum college GPA of 2.5 required. Lowest grade transferable C. **General Admission Information:** Application fee $35. Notification on a rolling basis, beginning on or about 7/1. Nonfall registration accepted. Admission may be deferred for a maximum of 1. Credit offered for CEEB Advanced Placement tests.

COSTS AND FINANCIAL AID
Annual tuition $13,450. Room and board $5,536. Required fees $420. Average book expense $1,000. **Required Forms and Deadlines:** FAFSA. Priority financial aid filing date 3/1. **Notification of Awards:** Applicants will be notified of awards on a rolling basis beginning 2/1. **Types of Aid:** *Need-based scholarships/grants:* Federal Pell, SEOG, state scholarships/grants, private scholarships, the school's own gift aid, Federal Nursing Scholarships. *Loans:* FFEL Subsidized Stafford, FFEL Unsubsidized Stafford, FFEL PLUS, Federal Perkins, college/university loans from institutional funds, alternative loans (private). **Student Employment:** Federal Work-Study Program available. Institutional employment available. Highest amount earned per year from on-campus jobs $2,262. Off-campus job opportunities are good. **Financial Aid Statistics:** 66% freshmen, 61% undergrads receive need-based scholarship or grant aid. 15% freshmen, 10% undergrads receive non-need-based scholarship or grant aid. 51% freshmen, 51% undergrads receive need-based self-help aid. 26% freshmen, 21% undergrads receive athletic scholarships. 99% freshmen, 99% undergrads receive any aid. 84% undergrads borrow to pay for school. Average cumulative indebtedness $25,612. **Criteria for awarding institutional aid:** *Non-need-based:* Academics, alumni affiliation, art, athletics, job skills, leadership, music/drama, religious affiliation.

JARVIS CHRISTIAN COLLEGE

P.O. BOX 1470, Hawkins, TX 75765-1470
Phone: 903-769-5730 **Financial Aid Phone:** 903-769-5740
E-mail: felecia_tyiska@jarvis.edu
Fax: 903-769-1282 **Website:** www.jarvis.edu **ACT Code:** 4110

This private school, affiliated with the Disciples of Christ Church, was founded in 1912. It has a 243-acre campus.

RATINGS
Admissions Selectivity Rating: 61   **Fire Safety Rating:** 85   **Green Rating:** 60*

STUDENTS AND FACULTY
Enrollment: 547. **Student Body:** 60% female, 40% male, 15% out-of-state, international (2 countries represented). African American 107%, Caucasian 2%, Hispanic 4%.
Retention and Graduation: 41% freshmen return for sophomore year. 17% freshmen graduate within 4 years. 2% grads go on to further study within 1 year. 1% grads pursue business degrees. **Faculty:** Student/faculty ratio 13:1. 35 full-time faculty, 46% hold PhDs, 63% are members of minority groups, 49% are women.

ACADEMICS
Degrees: Bachelor's. **Classes:** Most classes have fewer than 10 students. Most lab/discussion sessions have 10–19 students. **Majors with Highest Enrollment:** Biology/biological sciences; criminal justice/law enforcement administration; health and P.E.. **Special Study Options:** cross-registration, distance learning, double major, dual enrollment, English as a Second Language (ESL), honors program, independent study, internships, liberal arts/career combination, student-designed major, teacher certification program. **Honors programs:** JETS Honors Program Special programs offered to physically disabled

students include reader services, tutors. **Career services:** Alumni network, alumni services.

FACILITIES

Housing: Special housing for disabled students, men's dorms, women's dorms, apartments for married students, apartments for single students. 95% of campus accessible to physically disabled. **Special Academic Facilities/Equipment:** Archives. **Computers:** 100% of classrooms, 100% of dorms, 100% of libraries, 100% of dining areas, 100% of student union, 20% of common outdoor areas have wireless network access. Students can register for classes online.

CAMPUS LIFE

Environment: Rural. **Activities:** Choral groups, drama/theater, music ensembles, pep band, student government, international student organization. **Organizations:** 33 registered organizations, 6 honor societies, 5 religious organizations. 4 fraternities, 4 sororities. **Athletics (Intercollegiate):** *Men:* Baseball, basketball. *Women:* Basketball, volleyball. **On-Campus Highlights:** E. W. Rand Health, P.E., and Recreat, J. N. Ervin Religion Center, Walk of Fame, Community and Technology Center, Meyer Science and Mathematics Center, Archives of the Texas Christian Missionary Fellowship of the Christian Church (Disciples of Christ).

ADMISSIONS

Freshman Academic Profile: Average high school GPA 2.63. 6% in top 25% of high school class, 23% in top 50% of high school class. 99% from public high schools. Minimum paper TOEFL 500. Minimum computer TOEFL 173. **Basis for Candidate Selection:** *Other factors considered include:* Class rank, academic GPA, rigor of secondary school record, standardized test scores, character/personal qualities, extracurricular activities, talent/ability. **Freshman Admission Requirements:** High school diploma is required and GED is accepted. *Academic units required:* 3 English, 2 mathematics, 1 science, 3 social studies, 7 academic electives. *Academic units recommended:* 3 English, 2 mathematics, 1 science, 3 social studies, 7 academic electives. **Freshman Admission Statistics:** 525 applied, 92% admitted, 25% enrolled. **Transfer Admission Requirements:** High school transcript, college transcript(s), standardized test scores, Lowest grade transferable F. **General Admission Information:** Application fee $50. Notification on a rolling basis, beginning on or about 8/1. Nonfall registration accepted. Admission may be deferred for a maximum of 1 year. Neither credit nor placement offered for CEEB Advanced Placement tests.

COSTS AND FINANCIAL AID

Annual tuition $8,528. Room and board $6,715. Required fees $1,080. Average book expense $1,000. **Required Forms and Deadlines:** FAFSA, institution's own financial aid form, state aid form Financial aid filing deadline 4/15. Priority financial aid filing date 3/1. **Notification of Awards:** Applicants will be notified of awards on a rolling basis beginning 5/1. **Types of Aid:** *Need-based scholarships/grants:* Federal Pell, SEOG, state scholarships/grants, private scholarships, the school's own gift aid, United Negro College Fund. *Loans:* Direct Subsidized Stafford, Direct Unsubsidized Stafford, Direct PLUS, FFEL Subsidized Stafford, FFEL Unsubsidized Stafford, FFEL PLUS, Federal Perkins, UNCF institutional. **Student Employment:** Federal Work-Study Program available. Highest amount earned per year from on-campus jobs $1,729. Off-campus job opportunities are fair. **Financial Aid Statistics:** 75% freshmen, 100% undergrads receive need-based scholarship or grant aid. 33% freshmen, 23% undergrads receive non-need-based scholarship or grant aid. 63% freshmen, 89% undergrads receive need-based self-help aid. 3% freshmen, 6% undergrads receive athletic scholarships. 98% freshmen, 98% undergrads receive any aid. 93% undergrads borrow to pay for school. Average cumulative indebtedness $20,000. **Criteria for awarding institutional aid:** *Non-need-based:* Academics, athletics, religious affiliation, state/district residency.

JEWISH THEOLOGICAL SEMINARY, ALBERT A. LIST COLLEGE

3080 Broadway, Box 32, New York, NY 10027
Phone: 212-678-8832 **Financial Aid Phone:** 212-678-8007
E-mail: lcadmissions@jtsa.edu **CEEB Code:** 2339
Fax: 212-280-6022 **Website:** www.jtsa.edu **ACT Code:** 2776

This private school, affiliated with the Jewish Church, was founded in 1886. It has a 1-acre campus.

RATINGS

Admissions Selectivity Rating: 89   **Fire Safety Rating:** 60*   **Green Rating:** 63

STUDENTS AND FACULTY

Enrollment: 177. **Student Body:** 54% female, 46% male, 84% out-of-state, 3% international (10 countries represented). Caucasian 94%, Hispanic 1%. **Retention and Graduation:** 89% freshmen return for sophomore year. 15% grads go on to further study within 1 year. 6% grads pursue arts and sciences degrees. 6% grads pursue law degrees. 3% grads pursue medical degrees. **Faculty:** Student/faculty ratio 6:1. 52 full-time faculty, 113% hold PhDs, 29% are women.

ACADEMICS

Degrees: Bachelor's, master's. **Classes:** Most classes have fewer than 10 students. **Majors with Highest Enrollment:** Bible/biblical studies; Jewish/Judaic studies; talmudic studies. **Special Study Options:** Cross-registration, distance learning, double major, exchange student program (domestic), honors program, independent study, internships, liberal arts/career combination, student-designed major, study abroad, BA/MA program with JTS Graduate School or William Davidson School of Jewish Education. **Combined degree programs:** BA/MA, BA/BA and BA/BS programs with Columbia University and Barnard College. Special programs offered to physically disabled students include tape recorders, tutors. **Career services:** Alumni network, alumni services, career/job search classes, internships. **Career services highlights include:** career/job search classes and alumni network.

FACILITIES

Housing: Coed dorms, apartments for married students, apartments for single students **Special Academic Facilities/Equipment:** The Jewish Museum and the Rare Book Room of the Library. **Computers:** 100% of classrooms, 100% of dorms, 80% of libraries, 100% of dining areas, 50% of common outdoor areas have wireless network access. Students can register for classes online. Administrative functions (other than registration) can be performed online.

CAMPUS LIFE

Environment: Metropolis. **Activities:** Choral groups, concert band, dance, drama/theater, jazz band, literary magazine, music ensembles, musical theater, radio station, student government, student newspaper, yearbook. **Organizations:** 1 religious organizations. **Athletics (Intercollegiate):** *Men:* Baseball, basketball, crew/rowing, soccer, tennis, track/field (outdoor), volleyball. *Women:* Baseball, basketball, crew/rowing, soccer, tennis, track/field (outdoor), volleyball. **On-Campus Highlights:** The Library of the Jewish Theological Seminary. **Environmental Initiatives:** 4-Day work week to save on electricity The cafeteria has replaced styrofoam products with paper products and promotes the use of reusable plates, bowls and utensils. Energy saving film applied to all windows

ADMISSIONS

Freshman Academic Profile: Average high school GPA 3.7. SAT Math middle 50% range 620–660. SAT Critical Reading middle 50% range 640–700. SAT Writing middle 50% range 620–720. ACT middle 50% range 30–32. Minimum paper TOEFL 600. **Basis for Candidate Selection:** *Very important factors considered include:* Academic GPA, rigor of secondary school record, standardized test scores. *Important factors considered include:* Class rank, application essay, recommendation(s), interview. *Other factors considered include:* Alumni/ae relation, character/personal qualities, extracurricular activities, first generation, level of applicant's interest, religious affiliation/commitment, talent/ability, volunteer work. **Freshman Admission Requirements:** High school diploma is required and GED is not accepted. *Academic units recommended:* 4 English, 4 mathematics, 4 science, 4 foreign language, 1 social studies, 3 history, 4 academic electives. **Freshman Admission Statistics:** 102 applied, 62% admitted, 65% enrolled. **Transfer Admission Requirements:** High school transcript, college transcript(s), essay or personal statement, standardized test scores, statement of good standing from prior institution(s). **General Admission Information:** Application fee $65. Early decision application deadline 11/15. Regular application deadline 2/15. Regular notification 4/1. Nonfall registration accepted. Admission may be deferred for a maximum of 1. Credit and/or placement offered for CEEB Advanced Placement tests.

COSTS AND FINANCIAL AID

Annual tuition $14,200. Room and board $9,200. Required fees $800. Average book expense $500. **Required Forms and Deadlines:** FAFSA, institution's own financial aid form, CSS/Financial Aid PROFILE, state aid form, noncustodial PROFILE, business/farm supplement. Financial aid filing deadline 3/1. Priority financial aid filing date 2/1. **Notification of Awards:** Applicants will be notified of awards on a rolling basis beginning 4/1. **Types of Aid:** *Need-based scholarships/grants:* Private scholarships, the school's own gift aid. *Loans:* Direct Subsidized Stafford, Direct Unsubsidized Stafford, college/university loans from institutional funds. **Student Employment:** Federal Work-Study Program available. Institutional employment available. Off-campus job opportunities are excellent. **Financial Aid Statistics:** 35% freshmen, 42% undergrads receive need-based scholarship or grant aid. 18% freshmen, 17% undergrads receive non-need-based scholarship or grant aid. 30% freshmen, 40% undergrads receive need-based self-help aid. 42% undergrads borrow to pay for school. Average cumulative indebtedness $16,892. **Criteria for awarding institutional aid:** *Non-need-based:* Academics, alumni affiliation, leadership.

JOHN BROWN UNIVERSITY

2000 West University Street, Siloam Springs, AR 72761
Phone: 479-524-7157 **Financial Aid Phone:** 479-524-7424
E-mail: jbuinfo@jbu.edu **CEEB Code:** 6321
Fax: 479-524-4196 **Website:** www.jbu.edu **ACT Code:** 130

This private school was founded in 1919. It has a 200-acre campus.

RATINGS
Admissions Selectivity Rating: 87 **Fire Safety Rating:** 60* **Green Rating:** 65

STUDENTS AND FACULTY
Enrollment: 1,691. **Student Body:** 56% female, 44% male, 68% out-of-state, 7% international (49 countries represented). Asian 1%, African American 1%, Caucasian 61%, Hispanic 2%, Native American 1%.
Retention and Graduation: 77% freshmen return for sophomore year. 53% freshmen graduate within 4 years. 34% grads go on to further study within 1 year. **Faculty:** Student/faculty ratio 13:1. 80 full-time faculty, 74% hold PhDs, 4% are members of minority groups, 25% are women.

ACADEMICS
Degrees: Bachelor's, master's. **Classes:** Most classes have 10–19 students. Most lab/discussion sessions have 10–19 students. **Majors with Highest Enrollment:** Business administration and management; digital communication and media/multimedia; graphic design. **Special Study Options:** Accelerated program, distance learning, double major, dual enrollment, English as a Second Language (ESL), honors program, independent study, internships, liberal arts/career combination, student-designed major, study abroad, teacher certification program. **Honors programs:** The Honors Scholars Program consists of enriched Core Curriculum courses developed especially for gifted and highly motivated students. Emphasizing the use of primary texts, instructors challenge students through individual research, critical reflection, incisive discussion, interactive projects, and professional presentations. Special programs offered to physically disabled students include note-taking services, reader services, tutors. **Career services:** Alumni network, career/job search classes, career assessment

FACILITIES
Housing: Coed dorms, men's dorms, women's dorms, apartments for married students, apartments for single students 80% of campus accessible to physically disabled. **Special Academic Facilities/Equipment:** Art gallery, human anatomy lab, TV studio, radio station, Outdoor Learning Center, Center for Relationship Enrichment, Soderquist Center for Business and Ethics. **Computers:** 100% of classrooms, 100% of dorms, 100% of libraries, 100% of dining areas, 100% of student union, 30% of common outdoor areas have wireless network access. Students can register for classes online. Administrative functions (other than registration) can be performed online.

CAMPUS LIFE
Environment: Village. **Activities:** Choral groups, dance, drama/theater, jazz band, literary magazine, music ensembles, musical theater, pep band, radio station, student government, student newspaper, student-run film society, yearbook, campus ministries, international student organization. **Organizations:** 20 registered organizations, 3 honor societies, **Athletics (Intercollegiate):** *Men:* Basketball, golf, soccer, tennis. *Women:* Basketball, soccer, swimming, tennis, volleyball. **On-Campus Highlights:** Walker Student Center, California Cafe, Chapel, Walton Lifetime Health Complex, Intramural Sports. **Environmental Initiatives:** New major in Renewable Energy

ADMISSIONS
Freshman Academic Profile: Average high school GPA 3.58. 32% in top 10% of high school class, 60% in top 25% of high school class, 83% in top 50% of high school class. 65% from public high schools. SAT Math middle 50% range 510–640. SAT Critical Reading middle 50% range 520–660. SAT Writing middle 50% range 510–640. ACT middle 50% range 22–28. Minimum paper TOEFL 500. Minimum computer TOEFL 173. Minimum web-based TOEFL 61. **Basis for Candidate Selection:** *Very important factors considered include:* Academic GPA, recommendation(s), standardized test scores. *Important factors considered include:* Class rank, application essay, character/personal qualities, interview, religious affiliation/commitment. *Other factors considered include:* Rigor of secondary school record, alumni/ae relation, extracurricular activities, first generation, level of applicant's interest, talent/ability. **Freshman Admission Requirements:** High school diploma is required and GED is accepted. *Academic units recommended:* 4 English, 3 mathematics, 2 science, (1 science labs), 2 foreign language, 2 social studies, 1 history. **Freshman Admission**

Statistics: 846 applied, 73% admitted, 50% enrolled. **Transfer Admission Requirements:** High school transcript, college transcript(s), essay or personal statement, minimum college GPA of 2.5 required. Lowest grade transferable C. **General Admission Information:** Application fee $25. Notification on a rolling basis, beginning on or about 11/1. Nonfall registration accepted. Admission may be deferred for a maximum of 1 year. Neither credit nor placement offered for CEEB Advanced Placement tests.

COSTS AND FINANCIAL AID
Annual tuition $18,032. Room and board $6,876. Required fees $848. Average book expense $600. **Required Forms and Deadlines:** FAFSA. Priority financial aid filing date 3/1. **Notification of Awards:** Applicants will be notified of awards on or about 3/1. **Types of Aid:** *Need-based scholarships/grants:* Federal Pell, SEOG, state scholarships/grants, private scholarships, the school's own gift aid. *Loans:* Direct Subsidized Stafford, Direct Unsubsidized Stafford, Direct PLUS, FFEL Subsidized Stafford, FFEL Unsubsidized Stafford, FFEL PLUS, Federal Perkins, college/university loans from institutional funds. **Student Employment:** Federal Work-Study Program available. Institutional employment available. Highest amount earned per year from on-campus jobs $1,415. Off-campus job opportunities are fair. **Financial Aid Statistics:** 36% freshmen, 58% undergrads receive need-based scholarship or grant aid. 24% freshmen, 35% undergrads receive non-need-based scholarship or grant aid. 32% freshmen, 52% undergrads receive need-based self-help aid. 3% freshmen, 4% undergrads receive athletic scholarships. 90% freshmen, 87% undergrads receive any aid. 60% undergrads borrow to pay for school. Average cumulative indebtedness $19,991. **Criteria for awarding institutional aid:** *Non-need-based:* Academics, alumni affiliation, art, athletics, leadership, music/drama.

JOHN CARROLL UNIVERSITY

20700 North Park Boulevard, University Heights, OH 44118-4581
Phone: 216-397-4294 **Financial Aid Phone:** 216-397-4248
E-mail: admission@jcu.edu **CEEB Code:** 1342
Fax: 216-397-3098 **Website:** www.jcu.edu **ACT Code:** 3282

This private school, affiliated with the Roman Catholic Church, was founded in 1886. It has a 60-acre campus.

RATINGS
Admissions Selectivity Rating: 81 **Fire Safety Rating:** 63 **Green Rating:** 73

STUDENTS AND FACULTY
Enrollment: 3,081. **Student Body:** 51% female, 49% male, 28% out-of-state, (18 countries represented). Asian 2%, African American 6%, Caucasian 79%, Hispanic 3%.
Retention and Graduation: 90% freshmen return for sophomore year. 77% freshmen graduate within 4 years. 29% grads go on to further study within 1 year. 26% grads pursue arts and sciences degrees. 10% grads pursue law degrees. 22% grads pursue business degrees. 23% grads pursue medical degrees. **Faculty:** Student/faculty ratio 15:1. 210 full-time faculty, 89% hold PhDs, 11% are members of minority groups, 43% are women. 1.2% of classes are taught by teaching assistants.

ACADEMICS
Degrees: Bachelor's, master's, post-bachelor's certificate. **Classes:** Most classes have 20–29 students. Most lab/discussion sessions have 10–19 students. **Majors with Highest Enrollment:** Biology/biological sciences; communication studies/speech communication and rhetoric; marketing/marketing management. **Special Study Options:** Accelerated program, cooperative education program, cross-registration, double major, dual enrollment, exchange student program (domestic), honors program, independent study, internships, liberal arts/career combination, student-designed major, study abroad, teacher certification program, undergrads may take grad level classes. Co-Op Programs: All majors. **Combined degree programs:** 3-4 Doctor of nursing program with Case Western Reserve U. Special programs offered to physically disabled students include note-taking services, reader services, tape recorders. **Career services:** Alumni network, alumni services, career/job search classes, career assessment, internships, regional alumni. **Career services highlights include:** Internships are available to our students for 0–3 credits and they can be paid or unpaid. We have a large number of students working at non-profits who are eligible for scholarships.

FACILITIES
Housing: Coed dorms, special housing for disabled students, women's dorms, fraternity/sorority housing, apartments for single students, theme housing. 94% of campus accessible to physically disabled. **Computers:** 100% of classrooms, 100% of dorms, 100% of libraries, 100% of dining areas, 100% of student union,

100% of common outdoor areas have wireless network access. Students can register for classes online. Administrative functions (other than registration) can be performed online.

CAMPUS LIFE

Environment: Metropolis. **Activities:** Choral groups, dance, drama/theater, literary magazine, music ensembles, pep band, radio station, student government, student newspaper, television station, yearbook, campus ministries. **Organizations:** 95 registered organizations, 12 honor societies, 2 religious organizations. 4 fraternities, 5 sororities. **Athletics (Intercollegiate):** *Men:* Baseball, basketball, cross-country, diving, football, golf, soccer, swimming, tennis, track/field (outdoor), track/field (indoor), wrestling. *Women:* Basketball, cheerleading, cross-country, diving, golf, soccer, softball, swimming, tennis, track/field (outdoor), track/field (indoor), volleyball. **On-Campus Highlights:** Einstein Bagel Bros, Dolan Center for Science and Technology, Inn-Between Cafe, Grasselli Library, Student Center Atrium. **Environmental Initiatives:** Lighting efficiency improvements HVAC system efficiency improvements comingled recycling program.

ADMISSIONS

Freshman Academic Profile: Average high school GPA 3.34. 19.6% in top 10% of high school class, 48.6% in top 25% of high school class, 83% in top 50% of high school class. 61% from public high schools. SAT Math middle 50% range 490–600. SAT Critical Reading middle 50% range 490–590. SAT Writing middle 50% range 480–590. ACT middle 50% range 21–26. Minimum paper TOEFL 550. Minimum computer TOEFL 213. **Basis for Candidate Selection:** *Very important factors considered include:* Academic GPA, rigor of secondary school record. *Important factors considered include:* Application essay, standardized test scores, character/personal qualities, extracurricular activities, talent/ability, volunteer work, work experience. *Other factors considered include:* Class rank, recommendation(s), alumni/ae relation, first generation, geographical residence, interview. **Freshman Admission Requirements:** High school diploma is required and GED is accepted. *Academic units required:* 4 English, 3 mathematics, 2 science, (2 science labs), 2 foreign language, 2 social studies, 3 academic electives, 2 2 units must be distributed between social studies and/or history; 4 recommended *Academic units recommended:* 4 English, 4 mathematics, 3 science, (3 science labs), 3 foreign language, 4 social studies, 4 2 units must be distributed between social studies and/or history; 4 recommended. **Freshman Admission Statistics:** 3,481 applied, 80% admitted, 29% enrolled. **Transfer Admission Requirements:** High school transcript, college transcript(s), essay or personal statement, standardized test scores, statement of good standing from prior institution(s). Lowest grade transferable 2. **General Admission Information:** Regular application deadline 2/1. Notification on a rolling basis, beginning on or about 12/15. Nonfall registration accepted. Admission may be deferred for a maximum of 1-2 terms. Credit and/or placement offered for CEEB Advanced Placement tests.

COSTS AND FINANCIAL AID

Annual tuition $27,940. Room and board $8,330. Required fees $900. Average book expense $1,200. **Required Forms and Deadlines:** FAFSA. Financial aid filing deadline 3/15. Priority financial aid filing date 2/15. **Notification of Awards:** Applicants will be notified of awards on a rolling basis beginning 2/15. **Types of Aid:** *Need-based scholarships/grants:* Federal Pell, SEOG, state scholarships/grants, private scholarships, the school's own gift aid. *Loans:* FFEL Subsidized Stafford, FFEL Unsubsidized Stafford, FFEL PLUS, Federal Perkins. **Student Employment:** Federal Work-Study Program available. Institutional employment available. Highest amount earned per year from on-campus jobs $2,747. Off-campus job opportunities are good. **Financial Aid Statistics:** 74% freshmen, 68% undergrads receive need-based scholarship or grant aid. 11% freshmen, 9% undergrads receive non-need-based scholarship or grant aid. 64% freshmen, 60% undergrads receive need-based self-help aid. 74.8% freshmen, 67.3% undergrads receive any aid. 75% undergrads borrow to pay for school. Average cumulative indebtedness $19,079. **Criteria for awarding institutional aid:** *Non-need-based:* Academics, alumni affiliation, leadership, minority status, state/district residency.

JOHNS HOPKINS UNIVERSITY

3400 North Charles Street, Mason Hall, Baltimore, MD 21218
Phone: 410-516-8171 **Financial Aid Phone:** 410-516-8028
E-mail: gotojhu@jhu.edu **CEEB Code:** 5332
Fax: 410-516-6025 **Website:** www.jhu.edu

This private school was founded in 1876. It has a 140-acre campus.

RATINGS
Admissions Selectivity Rating: 98   **Fire Safety Rating:** 74   **Green Rating:** 95

STUDENTS AND FACULTY
Enrollment: 4,970. **Student Body:** 47% female, 53% male, 86% out-of-state, 7% international (71 countries represented). Asian 23%, African American 7%, Caucasian 47%, Hispanic 7%.
Retention and Graduation: 83% freshmen graduate within 4 years. 45% grads go on to further study within 1 year. 30% grads pursue arts and sciences degrees. 4% grads pursue law degrees. 14% grads pursue medical degrees. **Faculty:** Student/faculty ratio 12:1. 519 full-time faculty, 87% hold PhDs, 12% are members of minority groups, 30% are women.

ACADEMICS
Degrees: Bachelor's, certificate, diploma, master's, post-bachelor's certificate, post-master's certificate. **Classes:** Most classes have 10–19 students. Most lab/discussion sessions have 20–29 students. **Majors with Highest Enrollment:** International relations and affairs; neuroscience; public health, other. **Special Study Options:** Cross-registration, double major, dual enrollment, independent study, internships, student-designed major, study abroad, combined bachelor's/master's programs. **Combined degree programs:** BA/MA, BA/MEng, accelerated bachelor's/master's programs. Special programs offered to physically disabled students include note-taking services, reader services, tape recorders, tutors. **Career services:** Alumni network, alumni services, career/job search classes, career assessment, internships, regional alumni. **Career services highlights include:** Second Decade Society summer internship grants; medical tutorial program, wherein students shadow physicians.

FACILITIES
Housing: Coed dorms, men's dorms, women's dorms, fraternity/sorority housing, apartments for single students. **Special Academic Facilities/Equipment:** Baltimore Museum of Art, on-campus Digital Media Center, art gallery, electron microscope, Space Telescope Science Institute, four major research centers. **Computers:** 95% of classrooms, 100% of dorms, 100% of libraries, 90% of dining areas, 100% of student union, 50% of common outdoor areas have wireless network access. Students can register for classes online. Administrative functions (other than registration) can be performed online.

CAMPUS LIFE
Environment: Metropolis. **Activities:** Choral groups, concert band, dance, drama/theater, jazz band, literary magazine, music ensembles, musical theater, pep band, radio station, student government, student newspaper, student-run film society, symphony orchestra, yearbook, campus ministries, Model UN. **Organizations:** 250 registered organizations, 17 honor societies, 20 religious organizations. 12 fraternities, 7 sororities. **Athletics (Intercollegiate):** *Men:* Baseball, basketball, cross-country, diving, fencing, football, lacrosse, soccer, swimming, tennis, track/field (outdoor), track/field (indoor), water polo, wrestling. *Women:* Basketball, cross-country, diving, fencing, field hockey, lacrosse, soccer, swimming, tennis, track/field (outdoor), track/field (indoor), volleyball. **On-Campus Highlights:** Mason Hall—new Visitor's Center, Mattin Student Arts Center, Homewood House Museum, Lacrosse Hall of Fame and Museum, Ralph S. O'Connor Recreation Center, Also, Charles Commons, a new building that houses 618 upperclassmen, as well as a new dining facility and retail spaces, opened in the fall of 2007. **Environmental Initiatives:** Commitment to reduce greenhouse gas emissions by 51% by 2025 Integrate the skills, experience, and creativity of our students and faculty into each project to the greatest extent possible. Develop and nurture strong relationships with state, city and community groups within Baltimore to promote and develop sustainable practices across the region.

ADMISSIONS
Freshman Academic Profile: Average high school GPA 3.68. 80.2% in top 10% of high school class, 95.3% in top 25% of high school class, 99.6% in top 50% of high school class. 69% from public high schools. SAT Math middle 50% range 670–770. SAT Critical Reading middle 50% range 630–730. SAT Writing

middle 50% range 650–730. ACT middle 50% range 29–33. Minimum paper TOEFL 600. **Basis for Candidate Selection:** *Very important factors considered include:* Academic GPA, recommendation(s), rigor of secondary school record, character/personal qualities. *Important factors considered include:* Class rank, application essay, standardized test scores, extracurricular activities, talent/ability, volunteer work, work experience. *Other factors considered include:* Alumni/ae relation, first generation, geographical residence, interview, racial/ethnic status, state residency. **Freshman Admission Requirements:** High school diploma or equivalent is not required. *Academic units recommended:* 4 English, 4 mathematics, 4 science, 4 foreign language, 2 social studies, 2 history. **Freshman Admission Statistics:** 16,122 applied, 27% admitted, 31% enrolled. **Transfer Admission Requirements:** High school transcript, college transcript(s), essay or personal statement, statement of good standing from prior institution(s). Minimum college GPA of 3.0 required. Lowest grade transferable C. **General Admission Information:** Application fee $70. Early decision application deadline 11/1. Regular application deadline 1/1. Regular notification 4/1. Nonfall registration not accepted. Admission may be deferred for a maximum of 2 Years. Credit offered for CEEB Advanced Placement tests.

COSTS AND FINANCIAL AID
Annual tuition $39,150. Room and board $12,040. Average book expense $1,200. **Required Forms and Deadlines:** FAFSA, CSS/Financial Aid PROFILE, noncustodial PROFILE, business/farm supplement. current year federal tax returns. Financial aid filing deadline 3/1. Priority financial aid filing date 3/1. **Notification of Awards:** Applicants will be notified of awards on or about 4/1. **Types of Aid:** *Need-based scholarships/grants:* Federal Pell, SEOG, state scholarships/grants, private scholarships, the school's own gift aid. *Loans:* Direct Subsidized Stafford, Direct Unsubsidized Stafford, Direct PLUS, Federal Perkins, college/university loans from institutional funds. **Student Employment:** Federal Work-Study Program available. Institutional employment available. Off-campus job opportunities are good. **Financial Aid Statistics:** 34% freshmen, 40% undergrads receive need-based scholarship or grant aid. 5% freshmen, 5% undergrads receive non-need-based scholarship or grant aid. 40% freshmen, 44% undergrads receive need-based self-help aid. 1% freshmen, 1% undergrads receive athletic scholarships. 47% freshmen, 45% undergrads receive any aid. 46% undergrads borrow to pay for school. Average cumulative indebtedness $21,859. **Criteria for awarding institutional aid:** *Non-need-based:* Academics, athletics, leadership, state/district residency.

See page 1122.

JOHNSON AND WALES UNIVERSITY

8 Abbott Park Place, Providence, RI 02903-3703
Phone: 401-598-2310
E-mail: admissions.pvd@jwu.edu
Fax: 401-598-2948 **Website:** www.jwu.edu **ACT Code:** 3804

This private school was founded in 1914. It has a 50-acre campus.

RATINGS
Admissions Selectivity Rating: 60*　**Fire Safety Rating:** 60*　**Green Rating:** 60*

STUDENTS AND FACULTY
Enrollment: 9,053. **Student Body:** 53% female, 47% male, 86% out-of-state, 5% international. Asian 3%, African American 8%, Caucasian 58%, Hispanic 7%.
Retention and Graduation: 69% freshmen return for sophomore year. **Faculty:** Student/faculty ratio 28:1. 287 full-time faculty, 43% are women.

ACADEMICS
Degrees: Associate, bachelor's, certificate, master's, post-master's certificate. **Classes:** Most classes have 10–19 students. Most lab/discussion sessions have 10–19 students. **Special Study Options:** Accelerated program, cooperative education program, English as a Second Language (ESL), exchange student program (domestic), external degree program, honors program, independent study, study abroad, weekend college.

FACILITIES
Housing: Coed dorms, special housing for disabled students, special housing for international students, Technology Living/Learning Community at Snowden Hall—A wing for first-year technology majors (among other upperclassman technology majors) interested in living with other students in the same academic program. The floor Resident Assistant is an upperclassman Technology Major. Faculty from the School of Technology will be involved in programming and mentorship in this community, providing out of classroom contact with instructors and academic program content. **Special Academic Facilities/Equipment:** Culinary Archives and Museum. **Computers:** Students can register for classes online. Administrative functions (other than registration) can be performed online.

CAMPUS LIFE
Environment: City. **Activities:** Choral groups, dance, drama/theater, pep band, student government, student newspaper, yearbook. **Organizations: Athletics (Intercollegiate):** *Men:* Baseball, basketball, cheerleading, cross-country, equestrian sports, golf, ice hockey, soccer, tennis, volleyball, wrestling. *Women:* Basketball, cheerleading, cross-country, equestrian sports, golf, ice hockey, soccer, softball, tennis, volleyball.

ADMISSIONS
Freshman Academic Profile: Average high school GPA 2. **Basis for Candidate Selection:** *Very important factors considered include:* Class rank, rigor of secondary school record, interview. *Important factors considered include:* extracurricular activities, work experience. *Other factors considered include:* Academic GPA, recommendation(s), standardized test scores, level of applicant's interest, volunteer work. **Freshman Admission Requirements:** High school diploma is required and GED is accepted. *Academic units recommended:* 4 English, 3 mathematics, 3 science, 2 social studies. **Freshman Admission Statistics:** 13,617 applied, 72% admitted, 23% enrolled. **Transfer Admission Requirements:** High school transcript, college transcript(s), minimum college GPA of 2.0 required. Lowest grade transferable C. **General Admission Information:** Notification on a rolling basis, beginning on or about 11/1. Nonfall registration accepted. Admission may be deferred for a maximum of 1 year.

COSTS AND FINANCIAL AID
Annual tuition $23,034. Room and board $8,892. Required fees $1,023. Average book expense $1,000. **Required Forms and Deadlines:** FAFSA **Notification of Awards:** Applicants will be notified of awards on a rolling basis beginning 3/1. **Types of Aid:** *Need-based scholarships/grants:* Federal Pell, SEOG, state scholarships/grants, private scholarships, the school's own gift aid. *Loans:* FFEL Subsidized Stafford, FFEL Unsubsidized Stafford, FFEL PLUS, Federal Perkins, state loans, college/university loans from institutional funds. **Financial Aid Statistics:** 60% freshmen, 82% undergrads receive need-based scholarship or grant aid. 47% freshmen, 58% undergrads receive non-need-based scholarship or grant aid. 62% freshmen, 93% undergrads receive need-based self-help aid. 77% undergrads borrow to pay for school. Average cumulative indebtedness $26,193. **Criteria for awarding institutional aid:** *Non-need-based:* Academics, alumni affiliation, job skills, leadership, state/district residency.

JOHNSON AND WALES UNIVERSITY—DENVER

7150 Montview Boulevard, Denver, CO 80220
Phone: 303-256-9300
Fax: 303-256-9333 **Website:** www.jwu.edu

This private school was founded in 1914.

RATINGS
Admissions Selectivity Rating: 60*　**Fire Safety Rating:** 60*　**Green Rating:** 60*

STUDENTS AND FACULTY
Enrollment: 1,466. **Student Body:** 52% female, 48% male, 46% out-of-state, 2% international. Asian 4%, African American 5%, Caucasian 59%, Hispanic 11%, Native American 1%.
Retention and Graduation: 64% freshmen return for sophomore year. **Faculty:** Student/faculty ratio 19:1. 47 full-time faculty, 30% are women.

ACADEMICS
Degrees: Associate, bachelor's. **Classes:** Most classes have 10–19 students. Most lab/discussion sessions have 20–29 students. **Majors with Highest Enrollment:** Business/commerce; hotel/motel administration/management; restaurant/food services management. **Special Study Options:** Cooperative education program, double major, honors program, independent study, internships, study abroad.

FACILITIES
Housing: Coed dorms, Living-Learning Communities (LLCs) and Theme Floors, are an exciting approach to combining residential and academic life at Johnson and Wales University, Denver. LLCs and theme floors provide students with an opportunity to interact with faculty, staff, and other students around a theme or academic discipline in an active and collaborative program that enhances the teaching and learning process by incorporating all aspects of a Student's collegiate experience.

CAMPUS LIFE
Activities: Choral groups, dance, literary magazine, student government, yearbook.

ADMISSIONS

Freshman Academic Profile: Average high school GPA 3.05. **Basis for Candidate Selection:** *Very important factors considered include:* Class rank, rigor of secondary school record, interview. *Important factors considered include:* extracurricular activities, work experience. *Other factors considered include:* Academic GPA, recommendation(s), standardized test scores, alumni/ae relation, level of applicant's interest, volunteer work. **Freshman Admission Requirements:** High school diploma is required and GED is accepted. *Academic units recommended:* 4 English, 3 mathematics, 3 science, 2 social studies. **Freshman Admission Statistics:** 2,217 applied, 76% admitted, 22% enrolled. **Transfer Admission Requirements:** High school transcript, college transcript(s), minimum college GPA of 2.0 required. Lowest grade transferable C. **General Admission Information:** Notification on a rolling basis, beginning on or about 11/1. Nonfall registration accepted. Admission may be deferred for a maximum of 1 year.

COSTS AND FINANCIAL AID

Annual tuition $21,297. Room and board $7,956. Required fees $1,023. Average book expense $1,000. **Required Forms and Deadlines:** FAFSA. **Notification of Awards:** Applicants will be notified of awards on a rolling basis beginning 3/1. **Types of Aid:** *Need-based scholarships/grants:* Federal Pell, SEOG, state scholarships/grants, private scholarships, the school's own gift aid. *Loans:* FFEL Subsidized Stafford, FFEL Unsubsidized Stafford, FFEL PLUS, Federal Perkins, state loans, college/university loans from institutional funds. **Financial Aid Statistics:** 62% freshmen, 54% undergrads receive need-based scholarship or grant aid. 58% freshmen, 48% undergrads receive non-need-based scholarship or grant aid. 62% freshmen, 60% undergrads receive need-based self-help aid. 74% undergrads borrow to pay for school. Average cumulative indebtedness $24,664. **Criteria for awarding institutional aid:** *Non-need-based:* Academics, alumni affiliation, job skills, leadership, state/district residency.

See page 1124.

JOHNSON AND WALES UNIVERSITY—NORTH MIAMI

1701 NE 127th Street, North Miami, FL 33181
Phone: 305-892-7600
E-mail: admissions.mia@jwu.edu
Fax: 305-892-7020 **Website:** www.jwu.edu

This is a private school.

RATINGS
Admissions Selectivity Rating: 60*   **Fire Safety Rating:** 60*   **Green Rating:** 60*

STUDENTS AND FACULTY
Enrollment: 1,955. **Student Body:** 54% female, 46% male, 47% out-of-state, 9% international. Asian 1%, African American 27%, Caucasian 23%, Hispanic 21%.
Retention and Graduation: 59% freshmen return for sophomore year. **Faculty:** Student/faculty ratio 28:1. 57 full-time faculty, 35% are women.

ACADEMICS
Degrees: Associate, bachelor's. **Classes:** Most classes have 10–19 students. Most lab/discussion sessions have 20–29 students. **Special Study Options:** Accelerated program, cooperative education program, honors program, independent study, internships, study abroad, weekend college.

FACILITIES
Housing: Coed dorms, special housing for disabled students.

CAMPUS LIFE
Activities: Dance, drama/theater, student government, student newspaper, yearbook.

ADMISSIONS
Freshman Academic Profile: Average high school GPA 2.96. **Basis for Candidate Selection:** *Very important factors considered include:* Class rank, rigor of secondary school record, interview. *Important factors considered include:* Extracurricular activities, work experience. *Other factors considered include:* Academic GPA, recommendation(s), standardized test scores, alumni/ae relation; volunteer work. **Freshman Admission Requirements:** High school diploma is required and GED is accepted. *Academic units recommended:* 4 English, 3 mathematics, 3 science, 2 social studies. **Freshman Admission Statistics:** 5,954 applied, 63% admitted, 14% enrolled. **Transfer Admission Requirements:** High school transcript, college transcript(s), minimum college GPA of 2.0 required. Lowest grade transferable C. **General Admission Information:**

Notification on a rolling basis, beginning on or about 11/1. Nonfall registration accepted. Admission may be deferred for a maximum of 1 year.

COSTS AND FINANCIAL AID

Annual tuition $21,297. Room and board $7,956. Required fees $1,023. **Required Forms and Deadlines:** FAFSA. **Notification of Awards:** Applicants will be notified of awards on a rolling basis beginning 3/1. **Types of Aid:** *Need-based scholarships/grants:* Federal Pell, SEOG, state scholarships/grants, private scholarships, the school's own gift aid. *Loans:* FFEL Subsidized Stafford, FFEL Unsubsidized Stafford, FFEL PLUS, Federal Perkins, state loans, college/university loans from institutional funds. **Student Employment:** Financial Aid Statistics:** 187% freshmen, 64% undergrads receive need-based scholarship or grant aid. 54% freshmen, 43% undergrads receive non-need-based scholarship or grant aid. 75% freshmen, 66% undergrads receive need-based self-help aid. 82% undergrads borrow to pay for school. Average cumulative indebtedness $31,737. **Criteria for awarding institutional aid:** *Non-need-based:* Academics, alumni affiliation, job skills, leadership, state/district residency.

JOHNSON BIBLE COLLEGE

7900 Johnson Drive, Knoxville, TN 37998
Phone: 800-827-2122 **Financial Aid Phone:** 865-251-2303
E-mail: jbc@jbc.edu **CEEB Code:** 1345
Fax: 865-251-2336 **Website:** www.jbc.edu **ACT Code:** 3968

This private school, affiliated with the Christian (Nondenominational) Church, was founded in 1893. It has a 350-acre campus.

RATINGS
Admissions Selectivity Rating: 76   **Fire Safety Rating:** 60*   **Green Rating:** 60*

STUDENTS AND FACULTY
Enrollment: 680. **Student Body:** 49% female, 51% male, 78% out-of-state, 1% international (12 countries represented). Caucasian 67%, Hispanic 2%. **Faculty:** Student/faculty ratio 21:1. 30 full-time faculty, 63% hold PhDs, 17% are women.

ACADEMICS
Degrees: Associate, bachelor's, certificate, master's. **Special Study Options:** Accelerated program, cooperative education program, distance learning, double major, English as a Second Language (ESL), honors program, independent study, internships, teacher certification program Special programs offered to physically disabled students include reader services, tape recorders

FACILITIES
Housing: Men's dorms, women's dorms, apartments for married students. **Computers:** Students can register for classes online. Administrative functions (other than registration) can be performed online.

CAMPUS LIFE
Environment: Rural. **Activities:** Choral groups, music ensembles, musical theater, radio station, student government, yearbook. **Organizations:** 3 honor societies, 3 religious organizations. **Athletics (Intercollegiate):** *Men:* Baseball, basketball, cheerleading, soccer. *Women:* Basketball, cheerleading, volleyball. **On-Campus Highlights:** Women's residence hall, men's residence hall, global-education-tech building.

ADMISSIONS
Freshman Academic Profile: Average high school GPA 3. 21% in top 10% of high school class, 48% in top 25% of high school class, 78% in top 50% of high school class. SAT Math middle 50% range 470–560. SAT Critical Reading middle 50% range 480–612. SAT Writing middle 50% range 487–562. ACT middle 50% range 20–26. Minimum paper TOEFL 500. Minimum computer TOEFL 173. **Basis for Candidate Selection:** *Very important factors considered include:* Class rank, recommendation(s), rigor of secondary school record, standardized test scores, character/personal qualities, religious affiliation/commitment. *Important factors considered include:* Application essay, interview. *Other factors considered include:* Alumni/ae relation, extracurricular activities, talent/ability, volunteer work. **Freshman Admission Requirements:** High school diploma is required and GED is accepted. **Freshman Admission Statistics:** 213 applied, 95% admitted, 58% enrolled. **Transfer Admission Requirements:** High school transcript, college transcript(s), essay or personal statement, statement of good standing from prior institution(s). Lowest grade transferable C. **General Admission Information:** Application fee $35. Regular application deadline 7/1. Regular notification 9/1. Nonfall registration accepted. Admission may be deferred for a maximum of 1 year.

COSTS AND FINANCIAL AID

Annual tuition $7,000. Room and board $4,890. Required fees $770. Average book expense $1,300. **Required Forms and Deadlines:** FAFSA, institution's own financial aid form. Financial aid filing deadline 3/1. Priority financial aid filing date 3/1. **Notification of Awards:** Applicants will be notified of awards on or about 3/30. **Types of Aid:** *Need-based scholarships/grants:* Federal Pell, SEOG, state scholarships/grants, private scholarships, the school's own gift aid. *Loans:* FFEL Subsidized Stafford, FFEL Unsubsidized Stafford, FFEL PLUS. **Student Employment:** Federal Work-Study Program available. Institutional employment available. Highest amount earned per year from on-campus jobs $1,240. **Financial Aid Statistics:** 79% freshmen, 79% undergrads receive need-based scholarship or grant aid. 19% freshmen, 21% undergrads receive non-need-based scholarship or grant aid. 49% freshmen, 47% undergrads receive need-based self-help aid. 97% undergrads receive any aid. 63% undergrads borrow to pay for school. Average cumulative indebtedness $17,487. **Criteria for awarding institutional aid:** *Non-need-based:* Academics, minority status, music/drama, religious affiliation, state/district residency.

JOHNSON STATE COLLEGE

337 College Hill, Johnson, VT 05656-9408
Phone: 802-635-1219 **Financial Aid Phone:** 802-635-1380
E-mail: jscadmissions@jsc.edu **CEEB Code:** 3766
Fax: 802-635-1230 **Website:** www.jsc.edu **ACT Code:** 4316

This public school was founded in 1828. It has a 350-acre campus.

RATINGS

Admissions Selectivity Rating: 75   **Fire Safety Rating:** 60*   **Green Rating:** 60*

STUDENTS AND FACULTY

Enrollment: 1,564. **Student Body:** 60% female, 40% male, 28% out-of-state, international (11 countries represented). Asian 1%, African American 2%, Caucasian 94%, Hispanic 2%, Native American 1%.
Retention and Graduation: 68% freshmen return for sophomore year.
Faculty: Student/faculty ratio 17:1. 53 full-time faculty, 94% hold PhDs, 2% are members of minority groups, 36% are women.

ACADEMICS

Degrees: Associate, bachelor's, master's, post-bachelor's certificate, terminal associate. **Classes:** Most classes have 10–19 students. **Majors with Highest Enrollment:** Elementary education and teaching; tourism and travel services management; visual and performing arts, other. **Special Study Options:** Cross-registration, double major, dual enrollment, English as a Second Language (ESL), exchange student program (domestic), external degree program, honors program, independent study, internships, study abroad, teacher certification program Special programs offered to physically disabled students include note-taking services, reader services, tape recorders, tutors. **Career services:** Alumni network, alumni services, career/job search classes, career assessment, internships, regional alumni. **Career services highlights include:** Internships.

FACILITIES

Housing: Coed dorms, apartments for married students, apartments for single students, Apartments for students who have 60 credits and a 3.0 average GPA. 65% of campus accessible to physically disabled. **Special Academic Facilities/Equipment:** Art gallery, visual arts center, child development center, human performance lab, 1,000–acre nature preserve, snowboard terrain park, dance studio **Computers:** Students can register for classes online. Administrative functions (other than registration) can be performed online.

CAMPUS LIFE

Environment: Rural. **Activities:** Choral groups, concert band, dance, drama/theater, jazz band, literary magazine, music ensembles, musical theater, pep band, radio station, student government, student newspaper, yearbook, international student organization. **Organizations:** 30 registered organizations, 1 honor societies, 4 religious organizations. **Athletics (Intercollegiate):** *Men:* Basketball, cross-country, golf, lacrosse, soccer, tennis. *Women:* Basketball, cross-country, soccer, softball, tennis, volleyball. **On-Campus Highlights:** Dibden Center For the Arts, Snowboarding Hill, Baselodge, Disc Golf Course, SHAPE Athletic Facility, Located in the heart of the Green Mountains, 1 hour from Vermont largest city, Burlington. JSC has 14 buildings on 1,350 acres (including our nature preserve). **Environmental Initiatives:** We compost. We own a 1,000–acre land preserve. Bio-diesel school bus for students' transportation.

ADMISSIONS

Freshman Academic Profile: 34% in top 10% of high school class, 66% in top 25% of high school class, 68% in top 50% of high school class. SAT Math middle 50% range 430–550. SAT Critical Reading middle 50% range 430–550. ACT middle 50% range 20–28. Minimum paper TOEFL 500. Minimum computer TOEFL 173. Minimum web-based TOEFL 61. **Basis for Candidate Selection:** *Very important factors considered include:* Rigor of secondary school record, standardized test scores. *Important factors considered include:* Class rank, application essay, academic GPA, recommendation(s), character/personal qualities, talent/ability. *Other factors considered include:* Extracurricular activities, interview, volunteer work, work experience. **Freshman Admission Requirements:** High school diploma is required and GED is accepted. *Academic units required:* 4 English, 2 mathematics, 2 science, (1 science labs), 3 social studies, 2 history. *Academic units recommended:* 4 English, 3 mathematics, 3 science, (2 science labs), 1 foreign language, 3 social studies, 3 history. **Freshman Admission Statistics: Transfer Admission Requirements:** High school transcript, college transcript(s), essay or personal statement, statement of good standing from prior institution(s). Minimum college GPA of 2.0 required. Lowest grade transferable C–. **General Admission Information:** Application fee $39. Notification on a rolling basis, beginning on or about 12/1. Nonfall registration accepted. Admission may be deferred for a maximum of 1 year. Credit and/or placement offered for CEEB Advanced Placement tests.

COSTS AND FINANCIAL AID

Annual in-state tuition $7,992. Annual out-of-state tuition $17,232. Room and board $7,808. Required fees $921. Average book expense $1,000. **Required Forms and Deadlines:** FAFSA, state aid form. Priority financial aid filing date 3/1. **Notification of Awards:** Applicants will be notified of awards on a rolling basis beginning 4/1. **Types of Aid:** *Need-based scholarships/grants:* Federal Pell, SEOG, state scholarships/grants, private scholarships, the school's own gift aid. *Loans:* FFEL Subsidized Stafford, FFEL Unsubsidized Stafford, FFEL PLUS, Federal Perkins. **Student Employment:** Federal Work-Study Program available. Institutional employment available. Off-campus job opportunities are good. **Financial Aid Statistics:** 69% freshmen, 67% undergrads receive need-based scholarship or grant aid. 71% freshmen, 72% undergrads receive need-based self-help aid. 92% freshmen, 90% undergrads receive any aid. **Criteria for awarding institutional aid:** *Non-need-based:* Academics, art, leadership, music/drama, state/district residency.

JONES INTERNATIONAL UNIVERSITY

9697 E. Mineral Avenue, Centennial, CO 80112
Phone: 800-811-5663
E-mail: admissions@international.edu
Fax: 303-799-0966 **Website:** www.jonesinternational.edu

This is a private school.

RATINGS

Admissions Selectivity Rating: 60*   **Fire Safety Rating:** 60*   **Green Rating:** 60*

STUDENTS AND FACULTY

Enrollment: 22. **Student Body:** 50% female, 50% male.
Retention and Graduation: 97% freshmen return for sophomore year.

ACADEMICS

Degrees: Bachelor's, certificate, master's. **Special Study Options:** Accelerated program, distance learning, external degree program.

ADMISSIONS

Freshman Admission Requirements: High school diploma is required and GED is accepted. **Freshman Admission Statistics:** 22 applied, 100% admitted, 86% enrolled. **General Admission Information:** Application fee $75. Nonfall registration accepted. Admission may be deferred for a maximum of 1 year.

COSTS AND FINANCIAL AID

Annual tuition $835. Required fees $75. Average book expense $100.

JUDSON COLLEGE (AL)

302 Bibb Street, Marion, AL 36756
Phone: 334-683-5110 **Financial Aid Phone:** 334-683-5157
E-mail: admissions@judson.edu **CEEB Code:** 1349
Fax: 334-683-5282 **Website:** www.judson.edu **ACT Code:** 22

This private school, affiliated with the Baptist Church, was founded in 1838. It has a 80-acre campus.

RATINGS
Admissions Selectivity Rating: 76 **Fire Safety Rating:** 63 **Green Rating:** 60*

STUDENTS AND FACULTY
Enrollment: 315. **Student Body:** 97% female, 3% male, 29% out-of-state, 1% international (3 countries represented). African American 12%, Caucasian 83%, Hispanic 1%, Native American 1%.
Retention and Graduation: 61% freshmen return for sophomore year. 49% freshmen graduate within 4 years. 15% grads go on to further study within 1 year. 83% grads pursue arts and sciences degrees. 17% grads pursue medical degrees. **Faculty:** Student/faculty ratio 11:1. 18 full-time faculty, 83% hold PhDs, 39% are women.

ACADEMICS
Degrees: Bachelor's. **Classes:** Most classes have fewer than 10 students. Most lab/discussion sessions have fewer than 10 students. **Majors with Highest Enrollment:** Biology/biological sciences; elementary education and teaching; psychology. **Special Study Options:** Accelerated program, cross-registration, distance learning, double major, dual enrollment, independent study, internships, student-designed major, study abroad, teacher certification program Special programs offered to physically disabled students include tutors. **Career services:** Alumni services, career assessment, internships.

FACILITIES
Housing: Women's dorms. 50% of campus accessible to physically disabled. **Special Academic Facilities/Equipment:** Alabama Women's Hall of Fame. **Computers:** 50% of classrooms, 100% of dorms, 100% of libraries, 100% of student union, have wireless network access.

CAMPUS LIFE
Environment: Rural. **Activities:** Choral groups, drama/theater, literary magazine, marching band, music ensembles, student government, student newspaper, yearbook, campus ministries. **Organizations:** 23 registered organizations, 8 honor societies, 1 religious organizations. **Athletics (Intercollegiate):** *Women:* Basketball, equestrian sports, soccer, softball, volleyball. **On-Campus Highlights:** Residence Hall Lobbies, Gym, Computer Labs, Club House, Student Center.

ADMISSIONS
Freshman Academic Profile: Average high school GPA 3.41. 32% in top 10% of high school class, 22% in top 25% of high school class, 84% in top 50% of high school class. 78% from public high schools. SAT Math middle 50% range 470–590. SAT Critical Reading middle 50% range 540–590. SAT Writing middle 50% range 520–630. ACT middle 50% range 19–26. Minimum paper TOEFL 500. Minimum computer TOEFL 173. **Basis for Candidate Selection:** *Very important factors considered include:* Class rank, academic GPA, standardized test scores. *Other factors considered include:* Recommendation(s), rigor of secondary school record, alumni/ae relation, character/personal qualities, extracurricular activities, level of applicant's interest, talent/ability. **Freshman Admission Requirements:** High school diploma is required and GED is accepted. *Academic units required:* 4 English, 2 mathematics, 2 science, 3 social studies, 5 academic electives. *Academic units recommended:* 4 English, 4 mathematics, 4 science, 2 foreign language, 4 social studies, 2 history. **Freshman Admission Statistics:** 306 applied, 84% admitted, 38% enrolled. **Transfer Admission Requirements:** College transcript(s), minimum college GPA of 2.0 required. Lowest grade transferable C–. **General Admission Information:** Application fee $35. Notification on a rolling basis, beginning on or about 8/1. Nonfall registration accepted. Admission may be deferred for a maximum of 1 Year. Credit and/or placement offered for CEEB Advanced Placement tests.

COSTS AND FINANCIAL AID
Annual tuition $12,327. Room and board $7,969. Required fees $220. Average book expense $1,200. **Required Forms and Deadlines:** FAFSA, institution's own financial aid form, state aid form. Priority financial aid filing date 3/1. **Notification of Awards:** Applicants will be notified of awards on a rolling basis beginning 11/15. **Types of Aid:** *Need-based scholarships/grants:* Federal Pell, SEOG, state scholarships/grants, private scholarships, the school's own gift aid. *Loans:* FFEL Subsidized Stafford, FFEL Unsubsidized Stafford, FFEL PLUS, Federal Perkins, college/university loans from institutional funds. **Student Employment:** Federal Work-Study Program available. Institutional employ-

ment available. Highest amount earned per year from on-campus jobs $1,750. Off-campus job opportunities are poor. **Financial Aid Statistics:** 76% freshmen, 77% undergrads receive need-based scholarship or grant aid. 9% freshmen, 10% undergrads receive non-need-based scholarship or grant aid. 59% freshmen, 68% undergrads receive need-based self-help aid. 12% freshmen, 12% undergrads receive athletic scholarships. 99% freshmen, 96% undergrads receive any aid. 74% undergrads borrow to pay for school. Average cumulative indebtedness $17,185. **Criteria for awarding institutional aid:** *Non-need-based:* Academics, alumni affiliation, art, athletics, music/drama, religious affiliation, state/district residency.

JUDSON UNIVERSITY (IL)

1151 North State Street, Elgin, IL 60123
Phone: 847-628-2510 **Financial Aid Phone:** 847-628-2530
E-mail: admission@JudsonU.edu **CEEB Code:** 1700
Fax: 847-628-2526 **Website:** www.JudsonU.edu **ACT Code:** 1101

This private school, affiliated with the Baptist Church, was founded in 1963. It has a 84-acre campus.

RATINGS
Admissions Selectivity Rating: 74 **Fire Safety Rating:** 71 **Green Rating:** 60*

STUDENTS AND FACULTY
Enrollment: 1,132. **Student Body:** 58% female, 42% male, 35% out-of-state, 3% international (25 countries represented). Asian 1%, African American 4%, Caucasian 69%, Hispanic 5%.
Retention and Graduation: 72% freshmen return for sophomore year. **Faculty:** Student/faculty ratio 16:1. 54 full-time faculty, 74% hold PhDs, 13% are members of minority groups, 30% are women.

ACADEMICS
Degrees: Bachelor's, certificate, master's. **Classes:** Most classes have 10–19 students. Most lab/discussion sessions have fewer than 10 students. **Majors with Highest Enrollment:** Architecture (BArch, BA/BS, MArch, MA/MS, PhD); business/commerce; elementary education and teaching. **Special Study Options:** Accelerated program, distance learning, double major, English as a Second Language (ESL), honors program, independent study, internships, study abroad, teacher certification program. **Honors programs:** GEN101H Faith and Learning: The Consecrated Genius; MAT 211H Functions and Calculus. **Combined degree programs:** BA/MA, Architecture. Special programs offered to physically disabled students include tutors. **Career services:** Alumni network, alumni services, career/job search classes, career assessment, internships. **Career services highlights include:** Internships in the following areas: architecture, business, education, worship arts, youth ministry.

FACILITIES
Housing: Coed dorms, special housing for disabled students, men's dorms, women's dorms, apartments for married students. **Computers:** Students can register for classes online. Administrative functions (other than registration) can be performed online.

CAMPUS LIFE
Environment: City. **Activities:** Choral groups, drama/theater, music ensembles, student government **Organizations:** 23 registered organizations, 1 honor societies. **Athletics (Intercollegiate):** *Men:* Baseball, basketball, cheerleading, soccer. *Women:* Basketball, cheerleading, soccer, softball, volleyball. **On-Campus Highlights:** Harm A. Weber Academic Center, Lindner Fitness Center, Lindner Commons, Eyrie Coffee House.

ADMISSIONS
Freshman Academic Profile: Average high school GPA 3.27. 7% in top 10% of high school class, 35% in top 25% of high school class, 59% in top 50% of high school class. SAT Math middle 50% range 440–660. SAT Critical Reading middle 50% range 430–600. ACT middle 50% range 20–26. Minimum paper TOEFL 550. Minimum computer TOEFL 213. **Basis for Candidate Selection:** *Very important factors considered include:* Rigor of secondary school record, standardized test scores. *Important factors considered include:* Character/personal qualities. *Other factors considered include:* Class rank, recommendation(s), talent/ability. **Freshman Admission Requirements:** High school diploma is required and GED is accepted. *Academic units recommended:* 4 English, 3 mathematics, 2 science, (2 science labs), 2 social studies. **Freshman Admission Statistics:** 520 applied, 73% admitted, 44% enrolled. **Transfer Admission Requirements:** College transcript(s), minimum college GPA of 2.0 required. Lowest grade transferable C–. **General Admission Information:** Application fee $30. Notification on a rolling basis, beginning on or about 7/1. Nonfall registration accepted. Admission may be deferred for a

maximum of 1semester. Credit and/or placement offered for CEEB Advanced Placement tests.

COSTS AND FINANCIAL AID

Annual tuition $13,872. Room and board $5,570. Required fees $550. Average book expense $680. **Required Forms and Deadlines:** FAFSA. **Types of Aid:** *Need-based scholarships/grants:* Federal Pell, SEOG, state scholarships/grants, private scholarships, the school's own gift aid. *Loans:* Direct Subsidized Stafford, Direct Unsubsidized Stafford, Direct PLUS, Federal Perkins. **Student Employment:** Federal Work-Study Program available. Institutional employment available. Highest amount earned per year from on-campus jobs $1,200. Off-campus job opportunities are excellent. **Financial Aid Statistics:** 90% freshmen, 90% undergrads receive any aid. **Criteria for awarding institutional aid:** *Non-need-based:* Academics, art, athletics, music/drama.

THE JUILLIARD SCHOOL

60 Lincoln Center Plaza, New York, NY 10023-6588
Phone: 212-799-2000 ext.223 **Financial Aid Phone:** 212-799-5000
E-mail: admissions@juilliard.edu **CEEB Code:** 2340
Fax: 212-769-6420 **Website:** www.juilliard.edu

This private school was founded in 1905.

RATINGS

Admissions Selectivity Rating: 60*   **Fire Safety Rating:** 60*   **Green Rating:** 60*

STUDENTS AND FACULTY

Enrollment: 489. **Student Body:** 48% female, 52% male, 80% out-of-state, 5% international (40 countries represented). Asian 4%, African American 1%, Caucasian 11%, Hispanic 1%.
Retention and Graduation: 93% freshmen return for sophomore year. 74% freshmen graduate within 4 years. **Faculty:** Student/faculty ratio 3:1. 116 full-time faculty, 10% are members of minority groups, 37% are women.

ACADEMICS

Degrees: Bachelor's, diploma, master's, post-master's certificate. **Classes:** Most classes have fewer than 10 students. **Majors with Highest Enrollment:** Piano and organ; violin, viola, guitar and other stringed instruments; voice and opera.

FACILITIES

Housing: Coed dorms **Special Academic Facilities/Equipment:** 2 recital halls, 1 theater (1000 ppl), 1 drama theater (200 ppl), 15 two-story studios, 35 private teaching studios, 106 practice rooms, organ studios, 200+ pianos, recording studio, The Peter Jay Sharp Special Collections Room. **Computers:** Students can register for classes online. Administrative functions (other than registration) can be performed online.

CAMPUS LIFE

Environment: Metropolis. **Activities:** Student government. **Organizations:** 5 registered organizations, 2 religious organizations. **On-Campus Highlights:** Lila Acheson Wallace Library, Lincoln Center, Rose Building—cafeteria, Juilliard Bookstore.

ADMISSIONS

Freshman Academic Profile: Minimum paper TOEFL 533. Minimum computer TOEFL 200. **Basis for Candidate Selection:** *Very important factors considered include:* interview, talent/ability. *Other factors considered include:* Application essay, academic GPA, recommendation(s). **Freshman Admission Requirements:** High school diploma is required and GED is accepted. **Freshman Admission Statistics:** 2,151 applied, 7% admitted, 71% enrolled. **Transfer Admission Requirements:** College transcript(s), essay or personal statement, interview, Lowest grade transferable C. **General Admission Information:** Application fee $100. Regular application deadline 12/1. Regular notification 4/1. Nonfall registration not accepted. Neither credit nor placement offered for CEEB Advanced Placement tests.

COSTS AND FINANCIAL AID

Annual tuition $28,640. Room and board $11,250. Average book expense $700. **Required Forms and Deadlines:** FAFSA, institution's own financial aid form. Financial aid filing deadline 3/1. Priority financial aid filing date 3/1. **Notification of Awards:** Applicants will be notified of awards on or about 4/1. **Types of Aid:** *Need-based scholarships/grants:* Federal Pell, SEOG, state scholarships/grants, private scholarships, the school's own gift aid. *Loans:* Direct Subsidized Stafford, Direct Unsubsidized Stafford, Direct PLUS, FFEL PLUS, Federal Perkins. **Student Employment:** Highest amount earned per year from on-campus jobs $4,500. **Financial Aid Statistics:** 69% freshmen, 75% undergrads receive need-based scholarship or grant aid. 69% freshmen, 75%

undergrads receive need-based self-help aid. 108% freshmen, 481% undergrads receive any aid. 64% undergrads borrow to pay for school. Average cumulative indebtedness $26,780. **Criteria for awarding institutional aid:** *Non-need-based:* Music/drama.

JUNIATA COLLEGE

1700 Moore Street, Huntingdon, PA 16652
Phone: 814-641-3420 **Financial Aid Phone:** 814-641-3141
E-mail: admissions@juniata.edu **CEEB Code:** 2341
Fax: 814-641-3100 **Website:** www.juniata.edu **ACT Code:** 3600

This private school was founded in 1876. It has a 800-acre campus.

RATINGS

Admissions Selectivity Rating: 89   **Fire Safety Rating:** 75   **Green Rating:** 76

STUDENTS AND FACULTY

Enrollment: 1,360. **Student Body:** 56% female, 44% male, 32% out-of-state, 7% international (32 countries represented). Asian 2%, African American 2%, Caucasian 87%, Hispanic 2%.
Retention and Graduation: 85% freshmen return for sophomore year. 75% freshmen graduate within 4 years. 39% grads go on to further study within 1 year. 19% grads pursue arts and sciences degrees. 1% grads pursue law degrees. 1% grads pursue business degrees. 6% grads pursue medical degrees. **Faculty:** Student/faculty ratio 12:1. 100 full-time faculty, 94% hold PhDs, 6% are members of minority groups, 39% are women.

ACADEMICS

Degrees: Bachelor's. **Classes:** Most classes have 10–19 students. Most lab/discussion sessions have 10–19 students. **Majors with Highest Enrollment:** Biology/biological sciences; business/commerce; education. **Special Study Options:** Double major, dual enrollment, English as a Second Language (ESL), exchange student program (domestic), honors program, independent study, internships, student-designed major, study abroad, teacher certification program, Philadelphia Urban Semester, Marine Science Semester, Washington Semester, Cooperative Degree Programs (3-1, 3-2, etc.). **Honors programs:** Entire college is considered to be an honors program. **Combined degree programs:** BA/MD, BA/JD, BA/MA, BA/DDS, BA/MEng, dentistry, optometry, podiatry, allied health, nursing. Special programs offered to physically disabled students include reader services, tape recorders, tutors. **Career services:** Alumni network, alumni services, career/job search classes, career assessment, internships. **Career services highlights include:** At Juniata, countless opportunities abound to learn by doing. Whether students are participating in internships, studying abroad, volunteering for local charities, leading student organizations, starting their own business, designing a play, or working on individual research, Juniata students learn early in their education how to make things happen.

FACILITIES

Housing: Coed dorms, special housing for international students, women's dorms, apartments for single students, substance-free housing. 75% of campus accessible to physically disabled. **Special Academic Facilities/Equipment:** Environmental Studies Field Station, Juniata Museum of Art, Early Childhood Education Center, Ceramics studio and Anagama Kiln, Nature preserve and Peace Chapel, observatory, electron microscopes, nuclear magnetic resonance spectrometers, Human Interaction Lab. Three story, free form theater. **Computers:** 100% of classrooms, 100% of dorms, 100% of libraries, 100% of dining areas, 100% of student union, 100% of common outdoor areas have wireless network access. Students can register for classes online. Administrative functions (other than registration) can be performed online. Undergraduates are required to own a computer.

CAMPUS LIFE

Environment: Village. **Activities:** Choral groups, concert band, dance, drama/theater, jazz band, literary magazine, music ensembles, musical theater, radio station, student government, student newspaper, symphony orchestra, television station, campus ministries, international student organization, Model UN. **Organizations:** 94 registered organizations, 12 honor societies, 7 religious organizations. **Athletics (Intercollegiate):** *Men:* Baseball, basketball, cross-country, football, soccer, tennis, track/field (outdoor), track/field (indoor), volleyball. *Women:* Basketball, cross-country, field hockey, soccer, softball, swimming, tennis, track/field (outdoor), track/field (indoor), volleyball. **On-Campus High-**

lights: von Liebig Science Center, Juniata College Museum of Art, Ceramics Studio w/Anagama Kiln, Sill Business Incubator and Juniata College Center, Suzanne von Liebig Theatre. **Environmental Initiatives:** 40% today and 75% by 2012; Electric in Wind RECS; 2 LEED-certified Buildings, one Gold with Geothermal Goals part of campus strategic plan.

ADMISSIONS

Freshman Academic Profile: Average high school GPA 3.75. 41% in top 10% of high school class, 74% in top 25% of high school class, 96% in top 50% of high school class. 83% from public high schools. SAT Math middle 50% range 550–660. SAT Critical Reading middle 50% range 550–650. Minimum paper TOEFL 550. Minimum computer TOEFL 213. **Basis for Candidate Selection:** *Very important factors considered include:* Application essay, academic GPA, recommendation(s), rigor of secondary school record, standardized test scores, character/personal qualities. *Important factors considered include:* Extracurricular activities, first generation, interview, talent/ability, volunteer work. *Other factors considered include:* Alumni/ae relation, geographical residence, level of applicant's interest, racial/ethnic status, state residency. **Freshman Admission Requirements:** High school diploma is required and GED is accepted. *Academic units required:* 4 English, 3 mathematics, 3 science, (2 science labs), 2 foreign language, 1 social studies, 3 history. *Academic units recommended:* 4 English, 4 mathematics, 4 science, 2 foreign language, 1 social studies, 3 history. **Freshman Admission Statistics:** 1,964 applied, 72% admitted, 26% enrolled. **Transfer Admission Requirements:** High school transcript, college transcript(s), essay or personal statement, minimum college GPA of 2.5 required. Lowest grade transferable C–. **General Admission Information:** Application fee $30. Early decision application deadline 12/1. Regular application deadline 3/15. Notification on a rolling basis, beginning on or about 2/28. Nonfall registration accepted. Admission may be deferred for a maximum of 1 year. Credit and/or placement offered for CEEB Advanced Placement tests.

COSTS AND FINANCIAL AID

Annual tuition $32,120. Room and board $8,980. Required fees $700. Average book expense $600. **Required Forms and Deadlines:** FAFSA. Financial aid filing deadline 3/1. Priority financial aid filing date 3/1. **Notification of Awards:** Applicants will be notified of awards on a rolling basis beginning 2/28. **Types of Aid:** *Need-based scholarships/grants:* Federal Pell, SEOG, state scholarships/grants, private scholarships, the school's own gift aid. *Loans:* FFEL Subsidized Stafford, FFEL Unsubsidized Stafford, FFEL PLUS, Federal Perkins, college/university loans from institutional funds. **Student Employment:** Federal Work-Study Program available. Institutional employment available. Highest amount earned per year from on-campus jobs $4,596. Off-campus job opportunities are good. **Financial Aid Statistics:** 72% freshmen, 71% undergrads receive need-based scholarship or grant aid. 10% freshmen, 10% undergrads receive non-need-based scholarship or grant aid. 63% freshmen, 60% undergrads receive need-based self-help aid. 100% freshmen, 100% undergrads receive any aid. 89% undergrads borrow to pay for school. Average cumulative indebtedness $23,618. **Criteria for awarding institutional aid:** *Non-need-based:* Academics, art, leadership.

KALAMAZOO COLLEGE

1200 Academy Street, Kalamazoo, MI 49006
Phone: 269-337-7166 **Financial Aid Phone:** 269-337-7192
E-mail: admission@kzoo.edu **CEEB Code:** 1365
Fax: 269-337-7390 **Website:** www.kzoo.edu **ACT Code:** 2018

This private school was founded in 1833. It has a 60-acre campus.

RATINGS

Admissions Selectivity Rating: 90   **Fire Safety Rating:** 60*   **Green Rating:** 82

STUDENTS AND FACULTY

Enrollment: 1,356. **Student Body:** 57% female, 43% male, 31% out-of-state, 3% international (20 countries represented). Asian 5%, African American 4%, Caucasian 68%, Hispanic 4%.
Retention and Graduation: 89% freshmen return for sophomore year. 71% freshmen graduate within 4 years. **Faculty:** Student/faculty ratio 14:1. 93 full-time faculty, 86% hold PhDs, 18% are members of minority groups, 48% are women.

ACADEMICS

Degrees: Bachelor's. **Classes:** Most classes have 10–19 students. Most lab/discussion sessions have fewer than 10 students. **Majors with Highest Enrollment:** Economics; English language and literature; psychology. **Special Study Options:** Cross-registration, double major, dual enrollment, English as a Second Language (ESL), exchange student program (domestic), independent study, internships, student-designed major, study abroad Special programs offered to physically disabled students include note-taking services, tape recorders, tutors. **Career services:** Alumni network, alumni services, career/job search classes, career assessment, internships, regional alumni. **Career services highlights include:** See website: www.kzoo.edu/careerdevelopment/.

FACILITIES

Housing: Coed dorms, wellness housing, theme housing 25% of campus accessible to physically disabled. **Special Academic Facilities/Equipment:** Science center, rare book room. **Computers:** 100% of classrooms, 70% of dorms, 100% of libraries, 100% of dining areas, 100% of student union, have wireless network access. Students can register for classes online. Administrative functions (other than registration) can be performed online.

CAMPUS LIFE

Environment: City. **Activities:** Choral groups, concert band, dance, drama/theater, jazz band, literary magazine, music ensembles, musical theater, pep band, radio station, student government, student newspaper, symphony orchestra, yearbook, campus ministries, international student organization, Model UN. **Organizations:** 50 registered organizations, 3 honor societies, 5 religious organizations. **Athletics (Intercollegiate):** *Men:* Baseball, basketball, cross-country, diving, football, golf, soccer, swimming, tennis. *Women:* Basketball, cross-country, diving, golf, soccer, softball, swimming, tennis, volleyball. **On-Campus Highlights:** Upjohn Library Commons, The Quad, Biggby Coffee Shop, Hicks Student Center, Anderson Athletic Center. **Environmental Initiatives:** The college is currently involved in a LEED registered expansion and renovation of Hicks Student Center. The project is expected to receive Silver certification when completed in summer 2008. The college has had an active recycling operation since 1988 and is participating in RecycleMania 2008 for the fourth consecutive year. In RecycleMania 2007, Kalamazoo College placed in the top 10 in 5 of the 8 RecycleMania categories, with a first place finish in "Bottles and Cans." Kalamazoo College has formed a Sustainability Guild which is overseen by full-time staff and will link students with College alumni who have chosen green career paths.

ADMISSIONS

Freshman Academic Profile: Average high school GPA 3.6. 46% in top 10% of high school class, 84% in top 25% of high school class, 98% in top 50% of high school class. 85% from public high schools. SAT Math middle 50% range 560–680. SAT Critical Reading middle 50% range 570–690. SAT Writing middle 50% range 550–680. ACT middle 50% range 26–30. Minimum paper TOEFL 550. Minimum computer TOEFL 213. Minimum web-based TOEFL 80. **Basis for Candidate Selection:** *Very important factors considered include:* Academic GPA, rigor of secondary school record, extracurricular activities, volunteer work, work experience. *Important factors considered include:* Application essay, recommendation(s), standardized test scores. *Other factors considered include:* Alumni/ae relation, character/personal qualities, first generation, geographical residence, interview, level of applicant's interest, racial/ethnic status, talent/ability. **Freshman Admission Requirements:** High school diploma is required and GED is accepted. *Academic units required:* 4 English, 3 mathematics, 3 science, 3 foreign language, 2 social studies, 2 history. *Academic units recommended:* 4 English, 4 mathematics, 4 science, 4 foreign language, 2 social studies, 2 history. **Freshman Admission Statistics:** 1,979 applied, 73% admitted, 27% enrolled. **Transfer Admission Requirements:** High school transcript, college transcript(s), essay or personal statement, standardized test scores, statement of good standing from prior institution(s). Lowest grade transferable C. **General Admission Information:** Application fee $40. Early decision application deadline 11/10. Regular application deadline 2/1. Regular notification 4/1. Nonfall registration not accepted. Admission may be deferred for a maximum of 1 year. Credit and/or placement offered for CEEB Advanced Placement tests.

COSTS AND FINANCIAL AID

Required Forms and Deadlines: FAFSA, CSS/Financial Aid PROFILE. Priority financial aid filing date 2/15. **Notification of Awards:** Applicants will be notified of awards on a rolling basis beginning 3/21. **Types of Aid:** *Need-based scholarships/grants:* Federal Pell, SEOG, state scholarships/grants, private scholarships, the school's own gift aid. *Loans:* Direct Subsidized Stafford, Direct Unsubsidized Stafford, Direct PLUS, Federal Perkins. **Student Employment:** Federal Work-Study Program available. Institutional employment available. Off-campus job opportunities are good. **Financial Aid Statistics:** 50% freshmen, 52% undergrads receive need-based scholarship or grant aid. 50% freshmen, 50% undergrads receive non-need-based scholarship or grant aid. 41% freshmen, 42% undergrads receive need-based self-help aid. 98% freshmen, 98% undergrads receive any aid.

KANSAS CITY ART INSTITUTE

4415 Warwick Boulevard, Kansas City, MO 64111
Phone: 800-522-5224 **Financial Aid Phone:** 816-802-3337
E-mail: admiss@kcai.edu **CEEB Code:** 6330
Fax: 816-802-3309 **Website:** www.kcai.edu **ACT Code:** 2277

This private school was founded in 1885. It has a 15-acre campus.

RATINGS
Admissions Selectivity Rating: 78   **Fire Safety Rating:** 60*   **Green Rating:** 60*

STUDENTS AND FACULTY
Enrollment: 671. **Student Body:** 55% female, 45% male, 62% out-of-state, 1% international (6 countries represented). Asian 4%, African American 3%, Caucasian 80%, Hispanic 6%, Native American 1%.
Retention and Graduation: 78% freshmen return for sophomore year. 43% freshmen graduate within 4 years. 40% grads go on to further study within 1 year. **Faculty:** Student/faculty ratio 12:1. 51 full-time faculty, 84% hold PhDs, 2% are members of minority groups, 37% are women.

ACADEMICS
Degrees: Bachelor's. **Classes:** Most classes have 20–29 students. **Majors with Highest Enrollment:** Design and visual communications; film/video and photographic arts, other; painting. **Special Study Options:** Cross-registration, double major, exchange student program (domestic), independent study, internships, student-designed major, study abroad. Special programs offered to physically disabled students include tape recorders, tutors. **Career services:** Alumni network, alumni services, career/job search classes, career assessment, internships, regional alumni, **Career services highlights include:** Community Arts and Service Learning program (CASL).

FACILITIES
Housing: Coed dorms, apartments for single students. **Special Academic Facilities/Equipment:** H and R Block Art Space. **Computers:** Students can register for classes online. Administrative functions (other than registration) can be performed online.

CAMPUS LIFE
Environment: Metropolis. **Activities:** Student government. **On-Campus Highlights:** Dodge Painting Building, Cafe Nerman, Jannes Library-Learning Center, H&R Block Artspace, green space in center of campus.

ADMISSIONS
Freshman Academic Profile: Average high school GPA 3.2. 11% in top 10% of high school class, 39% in top 25% of high school class, 73% in top 50% of high school class. 80% from public high schools. SAT Math middle 50% range 430–590. SAT Critical Reading middle 50% range 430–580. SAT Writing middle 50% range 420–570. ACT middle 50% range 20–25. Minimum paper TOEFL 550. Minimum computer TOEFL 213. Minimum web-based TOEFL 79.
Basis for Candidate Selection: *Very important factors considered include:* Recommendation(s). *Important factors considered include:* Application essay, academic GPA, rigor of secondary school record, standardized test scores. *Other factors considered include:* Character/personal qualities, extracurricular activities, first generation, interview, level of applicant's interest, talent/ability, volunteer work, work experience. **Freshman Admission Requirements:** High school diploma is required and GED is accepted. *Academic units recommended:* 4 English, 3 mathematics, 3 science, 3 social studies, 3 academic electives, 4 fine art. **Freshman Admission Statistics:** 537 applied, 63% admitted, 41% enrolled. **Transfer Admission Requirements:** High school transcript, college transcript(s), essay or personal statement, statement of good standing from prior institution(s). Minimum college GPA of 2.5 required. Lowest grade transferable C. **General Admission Information:** Application fee $35. Notification on a rolling basis, beginning on or about 9/1. Nonfall registration accepted. Admission may be deferred for a maximum of 12. Credit offered for CEEB Advanced Placement tests.

COSTS AND FINANCIAL AID
Annual tuition $27,220. Room and board $8,294. Average book expense $1,500. **Required Forms and Deadlines:** FAFSA. Priority financial aid filing date 3/15. **Notification of Awards:** Applicants will be notified of awards on a rolling basis beginning 4/1. **Types of Aid:** *Need-based scholarships/grants:* Federal Pell, SEOG, state scholarships/grants, the school's own gift aid. *Loans:* FFEL Subsidized Stafford, FFEL Unsubsidized Stafford, FFEL PLUS, Federal Perkins, alternative loans. **Student Employment:** Federal Work-Study Program available. Institutional employment available. Highest amount earned per year from on-campus jobs $1,000. Off-campus job opportunities are good. **Financial Aid Statistics:** 79% freshmen, 80% undergrads receive need-based scholarship or grant aid. 12% freshmen, 7% undergrads receive non-need-based scholarship or grant aid. 62% freshmen, 70% undergrads receive need-based self-help aid.

99% freshmen, 95% undergrads receive any aid. 84% undergrads borrow to pay for school. Average cumulative indebtedness $34,559. **Criteria for awarding institutional aid:** *Non-need-based:* Academics, art,

KANSAS STATE UNIVERSITY

119 Anderson Hall, Manhattan, KS 66506
Phone: 785-532-6250 **Financial Aid Phone:** 785-532-6420
E-mail: k-state@k-state.edu **CEEB Code:** 6334
Fax: 785-532-6393 **Website:** www.k-state.edu **ACT Code:** 1428

This public school was founded in 1863. It has a 668-acre campus.

RATINGS
Admissions Selectivity Rating: 83   **Fire Safety Rating:** 60*   **Green Rating:** 82

STUDENTS AND FACULTY
Enrollment: 18,230. **Student Body:** 48% female, 52% male, 15% out-of-state, 5% international (102 countries represented). Asian 1%, African American 4%, Caucasian 82%, Hispanic 4%, Native American 1%.
Retention and Graduation: 79% freshmen return for sophomore year. 26% freshmen graduate within 4 years. 18% grads go on to further study within 1 year. **Faculty:** Student/faculty ratio 20:1. 973 full-time faculty, 81% hold PhDs, 18% are members of minority groups, 37% are women. 17% of classes are taught by teaching assistants.

ACADEMICS
Degrees: Associate, bachelor's, master's, post-bachelor's certificate. **Classes:** Most classes have fewer than 10 students. **Majors with Highest Enrollment:** Animal sciences; business administration and management; elementary education and teaching. **Special Study Options:** Accelerated program, cooperative education program, distance learning, double major, English as a Second Language (ESL), exchange student program (domestic), honors program, independent study, internships, study abroad, teacher certification program, Minors. **Honors programs:** The University Honors Program is an opportunity for undergraduate students from all colleges to enhance their education with special classes and opportunities for personal growth. **Combined degree programs:** BS/MS Architectural Engineering, BS/MS Industrial Engineering. Special programs offered to physically disabled students include note-taking services, reader services, tape recorders, tutors. **Career services:** career/job search classes, career assessment **Career services highlights include:** Alumni career services partnership with the K-State Alumni Association provides life-long career services.

FACILITIES
Housing: Coed dorms, men's dorms, women's dorms, fraternity/sorority housing, apartments for married students, cooperative housing, apartments for single students. 100% of campus accessible to physically disabled. **Special Academic Facilities/Equipment:** South Asian area study center, education communications center, center for cancer research, planetarium, nuclear reactor/accelerator, Beach Art museum. **Computers:** 85% of classrooms, 100% of dorms, 100% of libraries, 100% of dining areas, 100% of student union, 10% of common outdoor areas have wireless network access. Students can register for classes online. Administrative functions (other than registration) can be performed online.

CAMPUS LIFE
Environment: Town. **Activities:** Choral groups, concert band, dance, drama/theater, jazz band, marching band, music ensembles, musical theater, pep band, radio station, student government, student newspaper, symphony orchestra, television station, yearbook, campus ministries, international student organization, Model UN. **Organizations:** 594 registered organizations, 36 honor societies, 37 religious organizations. 28 fraternities, 16 sororities. **Athletics (Intercollegiate):** *Men:* Baseball, basketball, cheerleading, cross-country, football, golf, track/field (outdoor), track/field (indoor). *Women:* Basketball, cheerleading, crew/rowing, cross-country, equestrian sports, golf, tennis, track/field (outdoor), track/field (indoor), volleyball. **On-Campus Highlights:** Peters Recreation Complex, Sports Complexes: Wagner Field, Bramlage Coliseum, K-State Student Union, Ahearn Fieldhouse, Beach Museum of Art. **Environmental Initiatives:** A university-wide task force for long-term visioning and planning in all areas of the university, including campus operations, curriculum, research, and external relations/outreach. Development of a new 10,000 square foot recycling facility on campus. Planning to install a used functional 750kW

wind turbine donated by our local utility for research and education as well as feeding renewable energy into our campus grid.

ADMISSIONS

Freshman Academic Profile: Average high school GPA 3.4. 22% in top 10% of high school class, 49% in top 25% of high school class, 79% in top 50% of high school class. 81% from public high schools. ACT middle 50% range 20–27. **Basis for Candidate Selection:** *Very important factors considered include:* Class rank, academic GPA, rigor of secondary school record, standardized test scores. *Other factors considered include:* Recommendation(s). **Freshman Admission Requirements:** High school diploma is required and GED is accepted. *Academic units recommended:* 4 English, 3 mathematics, 3 science, 3 social studies, 1 computer technology **Freshman Admission Statistics:** 10,003 applied, 55% admitted, 72% enrolled. **Transfer Admission Requirements:** College transcript(s), minimum college GPA of 2.0 required. Lowest grade transferable C. **General Admission Information:** Application fee $30. Nonfall registration accepted. Credit and/or placement offered for CEEB Advanced Placement tests.

COSTS AND FINANCIAL AID

Annual in-state tuition $6,186. Annual out-of-state tuition $16,893. Room and board $6,752. Required fees $684. Average book expense $1,100. **Required Forms and Deadlines:** FAFSA. Priority financial aid filing date 3/1. **Notification of Awards:** Applicants will be notified of awards on a rolling basis beginning 4/1. **Types of Aid:** *Need-based scholarships/grants:* Federal Pell, SEOG, state scholarships/grants, private scholarships, the school's own gift aid. *Loans:* Direct Subsidized Stafford, Direct Unsubsidized Stafford, Direct PLUS, FFEL Subsidized Stafford, FFEL Unsubsidized Stafford, FFEL PLUS, Federal Perkins, college/university loans from institutional funds, Alternative Student Loans. **Student Employment:** Federal Work-Study Program available. Institutional employment available. Off-campus job opportunities are good. **Financial Aid Statistics:** 30% freshmen, 28% undergrads receive need-based scholarship or grant aid. 32% freshmen, 21% undergrads receive non-need-based scholarship or grant aid. 36% freshmen, 41% undergrads receive need-based self-help aid. 1% freshmen, 47% freshmen, 49% undergrads receive any aid. 57% undergrads borrow to pay for school. Average cumulative indebtedness $19,281. **Criteria for awarding institutional aid:** *Non-need-based:* Academics, alumni affiliation, art, athletics, leadership, music/drama, state/district residency.

KANSAS WESLEYAN UNIVERSITY

100 E. Claflin, Box 20, Salina, KS 67401
Phone: ext 1285 **Financial Aid Phone:** 785-827-5541
Fax: 785-827-0927 **Website:** www.kwu.edu **ACT Code:** 1434

This private school, affiliated with the Methodist Church, was founded in 1886. It has a 28-acre campus.

RATINGS

Admissions Selectivity Rating: 76   **Fire Safety Rating:** 60*   **Green Rating:** 60*

STUDENTS AND FACULTY

Enrollment: 742. **Student Body:** 57% female, 43% male, 29% out-of-state, 2% international (8 countries represented). Asian 1%, African American 7%, Caucasian 58%, Hispanic 7%, Native American 1%.
Retention and Graduation: 30% grads go on to further study within 1 year. 24% grads pursue arts and sciences degrees. **Faculty:** Student/faculty ratio 15:1. 42 full-time faculty, 67% hold PhDs, 38% are women.

ACADEMICS

Degrees: Associate, bachelor's, master's. **Classes:** Most classes have 10–19 students. **Special Study Options:** Cross-registration, double major, honors program, independent study, internships, student-designed major, study abroad, teacher certification program. **Honors programs:** Alpha Chi, Beta Beta Beta, Sigma Pi Sigma, Alpha Psi Omega, Phi Alpha Theta. **Career services:** Alumni services, career assessment, internships, regional alumni.

FACILITIES

Housing: Coed dorms, special housing for disabled students, men's dorms, women's dorms, apartments for married students, apartments for single students. 95% of campus accessible to physically disabled.

CAMPUS LIFE

Environment: Town. **Activities:** Choral groups, concert band, dance, drama/theater, jazz band, literary magazine, music ensembles, musical theater, pep band, student government, student newspaper, symphony orchestra, yearbook, campus ministries, international student organization, Model UN. **Organizations:** 20 registered organizations, 5 honor societies, 3 religious organizations.
Athletics (Intercollegiate): *Men:* Baseball, basketball, cheerleading, cross-

country, football, golf, racquetball, soccer, tennis, track/field (outdoor). *Women:* Basketball, cheerleading, cross-country, golf, racquetball, soccer, softball, tennis, track/field (outdoor), volleyball. **On-Campus Highlights:** NEW Student Center & Gym, Sam's Chapel, dorms, library, Science Hall.

ADMISSIONS

Freshman Academic Profile: Average high school GPA 3.207. 9.3% in top 10% of high school class, 32% in top 25% of high school class, 62% in top 50% of high school class. SAT Math middle 50% range 500–590. SAT Critical Reading middle 50% range 420–520. **Basis for Candidate Selection:** *Very important factors considered include:* Academic GPA, standardized test scores. **Freshman Admission Requirements:** High school diploma is required and GED is accepted. **Freshman Admission Statistics:** 442 applied, 61% admitted, 43% enrolled. **Transfer Admission Requirements:** College transcript(s), minimum college GPA of 2.0 required. Lowest grade transferable D. **General Admission Information:** Application fee $20. Nonfall registration accepted.

COSTS AND FINANCIAL AID

Annual tuition $18,200. Room and board $6,400. Average book expense $800. **Required Forms and Deadlines:** FAFSA. **Types of Aid:** *Need-based scholarships/grants:* Federal Pell, SEOG, state scholarships/grants, private scholarships, the school's own gift aid. *Loans:* Direct Subsidized Stafford, Direct Unsubsidized Stafford, Direct PLUS, Federal Perkins. **Student Employment:** Federal Work-Study Program available. Off-campus job opportunities are excellent. **Financial Aid Statistics:** 75% undergrads receive any aid. 75% undergrads borrow to pay for school. Average cumulative indebtedness $16,769. **Criteria for awarding institutional aid:** *Non-need-based:* Academics, alumni affiliation, art, athletics, music/drama.

KEAN UNIVERSITY

PO Box 411, 1000 Morris Avenue, Union, NJ 07083-0411
Phone: 908-737-7100 **Financial Aid Phone:** 908-737-3190
E-mail: admitme@kean.edu **CEEB Code:** 2517
Fax: 908-737-7105 **Website:** www.kean.edu **ACT Code:** 2582

This public school was founded in 1855. It has a 186-acre campus.

RATINGS

Admissions Selectivity Rating: 71   **Fire Safety Rating:** 96   **Green Rating:** 75

STUDENTS AND FACULTY

Enrollment: 11,730. **Student Body:** 62% female, 38% male, 2% out-of-state, 2% international (67 countries represented). Asian 7%, African American 19%, Caucasian 46%, Hispanic 21%.
Retention and Graduation: 81% freshmen return for sophomore year. 19% freshmen graduate within 4 years. **Faculty:** Student/faculty ratio 17:1. 352 full-time faculty, 91% hold PhDs, 28% are members of minority groups, 46% are women.

ACADEMICS

Degrees: Bachelor's, master's, post-master's certificate. **Classes:** Most classes have 20–29 students. **Majors with Highest Enrollment:** accounting; business administration and management; psychology. **Special Study Options:** Accelerated program, cooperative education program, distance learning, double major, dual enrollment, English as a Second Language (ESL), honors program, independent study, internships, liberal arts/career combination, study abroad, teacher certification program, weekend college, 2-year bachelor's degree program for RNs, Foreign Transfer Programs, Travelearn. **Honors programs:** NJCSTME—The New Jersey Center for Science, Technology and Mathematics Education: 5 year BS/MS—BS/MA Scholars programs—There is a critical and immediate need for highly qualified Science and mathematics teachers in New Jersey, especially in urban school districts. There is also a need for highly trained research technicians to work in the pharmaceutical and biotechnology industries in New Jersey. Kean University created The New Jersey Center for Science, Technology and Mathematics Education (NJCSTME) to respond to both these needs. Through NJCSTME, Kean University offers an innovative and rigorous five year combined bachelor/master degree program to qualified students who are interested either in teaching science or mathematics (teacher track) or in a career in biotechnology or computational mathematics (research track). This program prepares graduates for immediate, well paid employment, and helps future generations of New Jersey students by putting highly qualified science and math teachers in the classroom and researchers in industry laboratories. These are some of the programs important features: It is the only program in New Jersey that offers a core curriculum that links science and math laboratory courses with a team teaching approach. This program is a great opportunity for any student interested in both mathematics and science.

Each student has both an academic advisor and a career mentor. The progress of every student in the program is closely tracked by dedicated faculty who offer personal attention and support. It is a rigorous but highly structured and very supportive program that is designed for ensuring student success. -Students participate in research seminars and presentations, team research projects under faculty leadership, and educational outreach enrichment programs at area schools to help them appreciate the career choice between teaching and research. 4+4 BS/MD Scholars Program—Kean University's NJ Center for Science, Technology and Mathematics Education (NJCSTME), Drexel University College of Medicine and St. Peter's University Hospital have partnered to offer a 4+4 BS/MD Scholars Program to highly qualified incoming freshmen. Students who meet all the requirements of this joint program while in college are awarded the BS in science and technology degree from NJCSTME at the end of their fourth year, then proceed to enter the first year medical school class at DCOM. **Combined degree programs:** BA/MA, BA/MPA, BA/MS, BS/MS, BS/MA, BS/DPT, BS/MD, BA/DPM, MSN/MPA. Special programs offered to physically disabled students include note-taking services, reader services, tape recorders, tutors. **Career services:** Alumni services, career/job search classes, career assessment, internships. **Career services highlights include:** Interviewing Workshop.

FACILITIES

Housing: Coed dorms, special housing for disabled students, apartments for single students, freshmen housing, floor for women-only housing. 100% of campus accessible to physically disabled. **Special Academic Facilities/Equipment:** Liberty Hall Museum, Holocaust Resource Center, Center for Academic Success, Harwood Arena, Human Rights Institute, Wynona Moore Lipman Ethnic Studies Center. **Computers:** 100% of classrooms, 100% of dorms, 100% of libraries, 100% of dining areas, 100% of student union, 100% of common outdoor areas have wireless network access. Students can register for classes online. Administrative functions (other than registration) can be performed online.

CAMPUS LIFE

Environment: City. **Activities:** Choral groups, concert band, dance, drama/theater, jazz band, literary magazine, music ensembles, musical theater, pep band, radio station, student government, student newspaper, student-run film society, symphony orchestra, television station, yearbook, campus ministries, international student organization. **Organizations:** 143 registered organizations, 23 honor societies, 6 religious organizations. 16 fraternities, 17 sororities. **Athletics (Intercollegiate):** *Men:* Baseball, basketball, football, lacrosse, soccer, track/field (outdoor). *Women:* Basketball, field hockey, lacrosse, soccer, softball, tennis, track/field (outdoor), volleyball. **On-Campus Highlights:** University Center, Harwood Arena and Football Field, Center for Academic Success (CAS), Kean Hall, One Stop Service Center, Liberty Hall Museum, Weather Station, Holocaust Resource Center, Wynona Moore Lipman Ethnic Studies Center, planetarium, CAS and Vaughn Eames—art galleries. **Environmental Initiatives:** Construction of a LEED Gold-certified Center for Science and Technology which is powered by geothermal energy Composting all of our food waste, plates, and compostable utensils on campus starting in winter 2009–2010 LEED-certified renovation of our Center for Academic Success building

ADMISSIONS

Freshman Academic Profile: Average high school GPA 2.96. 8% in top 10% of high school class, 26% in top 25% of high school class, 66% in top 50% of high school class. 80% from public high schools. SAT Math middle 50% range 420–510. SAT Critical Reading middle 50% range 410–500. **Basis for Candidate Selection:** *Very important factors considered include:* Academic GPA, rigor of secondary school record. *Important factors considered include:* Standardized test scores. *Other factors considered include:* Class rank, application essay, recommendation(s), alumni/ae relation, character/personal qualities, extracurricular activities, interview, talent/ability, volunteer work, work experience. **Freshman Admission Requirements:** High school diploma is required and GED is accepted. *Academic units required:* 4 English, 3 mathematics, 2 science, (2 science labs), 2 history, 5 academic electives. *Academic units recommended:* 2 foreign language, 2 social studies. **Freshman Admission Statistics:** 5,955 applied, 62% admitted, 42% enrolled. **Transfer Admission Requirements:** College transcript(s), statement of good standing from prior institution(s). Minimum college GPA of 2.0 required. Lowest grade transferable C. **General Admission Information:** Application fee $50. Regular application deadline 5/31. Notification on a rolling basis, beginning on or about 11/1. Non-fall registration accepted. Credit and/or placement offered for CEEB Advanced Placement tests.

COSTS AND FINANCIAL AID

Required Forms and Deadlines: FAFSA. Priority financial aid filing date 3/15. **Notification of Awards:** Applicants will be notified of awards on a rolling basis beginning 3/15. **Types of Aid:** *Need-based scholarships/grants:* Federal Pell, SEOG, state scholarships/grants, private scholarships, the school's own gift aid. *Loans:* Direct Subsidized Stafford, Direct Unsubsidized Stafford, Direct PLUS, Federal Perkins. **Student Employment:** Federal Work-Study Program available. Institutional employment available. Highest amount earned per year from on-campus jobs $6,290. Off-campus job opportunities are excellent.

Financial Aid Statistics: 66% freshmen, 62% undergrads receive need-based scholarship or grant aid. 9% freshmen, 8% undergrads receive non-need-based scholarship or grant aid. 66% freshmen, 61% undergrads receive need-based self-help aid. 78% freshmen, 74% undergrads receive any aid. 68% undergrads borrow to pay for school. Average cumulative indebtedness $19,698. **Criteria for awarding institutional aid:** *Non-need-based:* Academics, alumni affiliation, art, leadership, music/drama.

KEENE STATE COLLEGE

229 Main Street, Keene, NH 03435-2604
Phone: 603-358-2276 **Financial Aid Phone:** 603-358-2280
E-mail: admissions@keene.edu **CEEB Code:** 3472
Fax: 603-358-2767 **Website:** www.keene.edu **ACT Code:** 2510

This public school was founded in 1909. It has a 150-acre campus.

RATINGS
Admissions Selectivity Rating: 72   **Fire Safety Rating:** 95   **Green Rating:** 83

STUDENTS AND FACULTY
Enrollment: 4,990. **Student Body:** 57% female, 43% male, 47% out-of-state, international (4 countries represented). Caucasian 94%, Hispanic 1%. **Retention and Graduation:** 79% freshmen return for sophomore year. 36% freshmen graduate within 4 years. **Faculty:** Student/faculty ratio 18:1. 194 full-time faculty, 85% hold PhDs, 4% are members of minority groups, 47% are women.

ACADEMICS
Degrees: Associate, bachelor's, certificate, master's, post-bachelor's certificate, post-master's certificate. **Classes:** Most classes have 10–19 students. **Majors with Highest Enrollment:** Business administration and management; elementary education and teaching; occupational safety and health technology/technician. **Special Study Options:** Cooperative education program, double major, English as a Second Language (ESL), exchange student program (domestic), honors program, independent study, internships, liberal arts/career combination, student-designed major, study abroad, teacher certification program. **Honors programs:** The Keene State College Honors Program; National Society of Collegiate Scholars in addition to Honors Programs in: psychology, safety studies. Special programs offered to physically disabled students include note-taking services, reader services, tape recorders, tutors. **Career services:** Alumni services, career/job search classes, career assessment, internships. **Career services highlights include:** Experiential learning/service learning and commitment to the community. Students apply what they learn from their course work by working in the local community. These real-life working situations enhance student learning and help students meet their course goals.

FACILITIES
Housing: Coed dorms, women's dorms, fraternity/sorority housing, apartments for married students, apartments for single students, wellness housing, theme housing: honors, language/culture, leadership, quiet study, substance-free. 98% of campus accessible to physically disabled. **Special Academic Facilities/Equipment:** Thorne-Sagendorph Art gallery, Redfern Arts Center, Recreational Center, Science Center, Mason Library, Media Arts Center, Cohen Center for Holocaust Studies, Center for Writing, Child Development Center. **Computers:** 10% of classrooms, 100% of libraries, 50% of dining areas, 80% of student union, have wireless network access. Students can register for classes online. Administrative functions (other than registration) can be performed online.

CAMPUS LIFE
Environment: Village. **Activities:** Choral groups, concert band, dance, drama/theater, jazz band, literary magazine, music ensembles, musical theater, radio station, student government, student newspaper, student-run film society, television station, yearbook, campus ministries, international student organization. **Organizations:** 100 registered organizations, 21 honor societies, 4 religious organizations. 4 fraternities, 5 sororities. **Athletics (Intercollegiate):** *Men:* Baseball, basketball, cheerleading, cross-country, diving, lacrosse, soccer, swimming, track/field (outdoor), track/field (indoor). *Women:* Basketball, cheerleading, cross-country, diving, field hockey, lacrosse, soccer, softball, swimming, track/field (outdoor), track/field (indoor), volleyball. **On-Campus Highlights:** Science Building, Mason Library, Young Student Center, Night Owl Cafe, Arts Center on Brickyard Pond, Spaulding Gymnasium, Zorn Dining Commons new facility, New Pondside residence hall, Bodyworks Fitness Center, New Alumni Center in progress. **Environmental Initiatives:** LEED Silver residence hall (awarded 2008); development of cogeneration capability in steam heat plant (combined heat and power); President's Council for a Sustainable Future.

ADMISSIONS

Freshman Academic Profile: Average high school GPA 3.03. 5% in top 10% of high school class, 22% in top 25% of high school class, 67% in top 50% of high school class. SAT Math middle 50% range 450–550. SAT Critical Reading middle 50% range 450–550. SAT Writing middle 50% range 450–540. Minimum paper TOEFL 550. Minimum computer TOEFL 173. Minimum web-based TOEFL 61. **Basis for Candidate Selection:** *Very important factors considered include:* Rigor of secondary school record. *Important factors considered include:* Application essay, academic GPA, recommendation(s), standardized test scores. *Other factors considered include:* Class rank, alumni/ae relation, character/personal qualities, extracurricular activities, first generation, level of applicant's interest, racial/ethnic status, talent/ability, volunteer work, work experience. **Freshman Admission Requirements:** High school diploma is required and GED is accepted. *Academic units required:* 4 English, 3 mathematics, 3 science, 2 social studies, 2 academic electives. **Freshman Admission Statistics:** 4,997 applied, 71% admitted, 34% enrolled. **Transfer Admission Requirements:** High school transcript, college transcript(s), essay or personal statement, statement of good standing from prior institution(s). Minimum college GPA of 2.0 required. Lowest grade transferable C. **General Admission Information:** Application fee $40. Regular application deadline 4/1. Nonfall registration accepted. Admission may be deferred for a maximum of 1 year. Credit and/or placement offered for CEEB Advanced Placement tests.

COSTS AND FINANCIAL AID

Annual in-state tuition $7,000. Annual out-of-state tuition $15,170. Room and board $8,444. Required fees $2,334. Average book expense $800. **Required Forms and Deadlines:** FAFSA. Financial aid filing deadline 3/1. **Types of Aid:** *Need-based scholarships/grants:* Federal Pell, SEOG, state scholarships/grants, private scholarships, the school's own gift aid. *Loans:* FFEL Subsidized Stafford, FFEL Unsubsidized Stafford, FFEL PLUS, Federal Perkins, college/university loans from institutional funds. **Student Employment:** Federal Work-Study Program available. Institutional employment available. Off-campus job opportunities are excellent. **Financial Aid Statistics:** 34% freshmen, 32% undergrads receive need-based scholarship or grant aid. 13% freshmen, 12% undergrads receive non-need-based scholarship or grant aid. 53% freshmen, 49% undergrads receive need-based self-help aid. 78% undergrads borrow to pay for school. Average cumulative indebtedness $27,785. **Criteria for awarding institutional aid:** *Non-need-based:* Academics, alumni affiliation, art, music/drama.

KENDALL COLLEGE

900 N. North Branch Street, Chicago, IL 60622
Phone: 877-588-8860 **Financial Aid Phone:** 866-803-9988
E-mail: admissions@kendall.edu
Fax: 312-752-2021 **Website:** www.kendall.edu **ACT Code:** 1703

This private school, affiliated with the Methodist Church, was founded in 1934.

RATINGS
Admissions Selectivity Rating: 60*   **Fire Safety Rating:** 60*   **Green Rating:** 60*

STUDENTS AND FACULTY
Student Body: 12% out-of-state, international (19 countries represented).
Faculty: Student/faculty ratio 19:1. 37 full-time faculty, 14% are members of minority groups, 38% are women.

ACADEMICS
Degrees: Associate, bachelor's, certificate. **Majors with Highest Enrollment:** Culinary arts and related services, other; hospitality administration/management; hospitality administration/management, other. **Special Study Options:** Accelerated program, cooperative education program, distance learning, double major, internships, student-designed major, study abroad, teacher certification program Special programs offered to physically disabled students include tutors. **Career services:** Alumni network, alumni services, career/job search classes, career assessment, internships, regional alumni.

FACILITIES
Housing: Coed dorms, special housing for disabled students.

CAMPUS LIFE
Environment: Metropolis. **Activities:** Student government, student newspaper **On-Campus Highlights:** Kitchens, Hyatt Suite, formal dining room, student-run cafeteria.

ADMISSIONS
Freshman Academic Profile: Average high school GPA 3.2. Minimum paper TOEFL 525. Minimum computer TOEFL 200. **Basis for Candidate Selec-**

tion: Very important factors considered include: Class rank, academic GPA, recommendation(s), rigor of secondary school record, standardized test scores. *Important factors considered include:* Character/personal qualities. *Other factors considered include:* Application essay, extracurricular activities, geographical residence, interview, talent/ability, work experience. **Freshman Admission Requirements:** High school diploma is required and GED is accepted. *Academic units required:* 4 English, 2 mathematics, 2 science, 2 foreign language, 2 social studies. **Freshman Admission Statistics: Transfer Admission Requirements:** College transcript(s), statement of good standing from prior institution(s). Minimum college GPA of 2.0 required. Lowest grade transferable C. **General Admission Information:** Application fee $50. Nonfall registration accepted. Admission may be deferred for a maximum of 2 years. Credit and/or placement offered for CEEB Advanced Placement tests.

COSTS AND FINANCIAL AID

Annual tuition $21,510. Room and board $10,200. Required fees $440. **Required Forms and Deadlines:** FAFSA, institution's own financial aid form, verification form, federal tax return. Financial aid filing deadline 5/1. Priority financial aid filing date 3/1. **Notification of Awards:** Applicants will be notified of awards on or about 4/1. **Types of Aid:** *Need-based scholarships/grants:* Federal Pell, SEOG, state scholarships/grants, private scholarships, the school's own gift aid. *Loans:* Direct Subsidized Stafford, Direct Unsubsidized Stafford, Direct PLUS, FFEL Subsidized Stafford, FFEL Unsubsidized Stafford, FFEL PLUS, Federal Perkins, college/university loans from institutional funds. **Student Employment:** Federal Work-Study Program available. Institutional employment available. Off-campus job opportunities are excellent. **Financial Aid Statistics:** 87% undergrads receive any aid. **Criteria for awarding institutional aid:** *Non-need-based:* Academics, athletics, leadership, religious affiliation.

KENDALL COLLEGE OF ART AND DESIGN OF FERRIS STATE UNIVERSITY

17 Fountain Street NW, Grand Rapids, MI 49503-3002
Phone: 616-451-2787 **Financial Aid Phone:** 616-451-2787
E-mail: brittons@ferris.edu **CEEB Code:** 1983
Fax: 616-831-9689 **Website:** www.kcad.edu **ACT Code:** 1983

This public school was founded in 1928. It has a 2-acre campus.

RATINGS
Admissions Selectivity Rating: 61   **Fire Safety Rating:** 60*   **Green Rating:** 60*

STUDENTS AND FACULTY
Student Body: 13% out-of-state, (15 countries represented).
Retention and Graduation: 12% grads go on to further study within 1 year. 12% grads pursue arts and sciences degrees. **Faculty:** Student/faculty ratio 15:1. 50 full-time faculty, 6% hold PhDs, 4% are members of minority groups.

ACADEMICS
Degrees: Bachelor's, master's. **Majors with Highest Enrollment:** Graphic design; illustration; interior design. **Special Study Options:** Cooperative education program, double major, dual enrollment, independent study, internships, liberal arts/career combination, study abroad, teacher certification program. Special programs offered to physically disabled students include note-taking services, reader services, tape recorders, tutors. **Career services:** Alumni network, alumni services, career/job search classes, internships, regional alumni.

FACILITIES
Housing: Apartments for married students, apartments for single students, Fabulous historic district with rental apartments nearby. 100% of campus accessible to physically disabled. **Computers:** 100% of classrooms, 100% of libraries, 100% of student union, have wireless network access. Students can register for classes online. Administrative functions (other than registration) can be performed online. Undergraduates are required to own a computer.

CAMPUS LIFE
Environment: Metropolis. **Activities: Organizations:** 12 registered organizations, 1 religious organizations. **On-Campus Highlights:** Studio Spaces, Studio Class Rooms, Library, Student Commons, Labs.

ADMISSIONS
Freshman Academic Profile: Average high school GPA 3.1. 10% in top 10% of high school class, 20% in top 25% of high school class, 75% in top 50% of high school class. Minimum paper TOEFL 500. Minimum computer TOEFL 173. Minimum web-based TOEFL 61. **Basis for Candidate Selection:** *Very important factors considered include:* Application essay, academic GPA, rigor of secondary school record, standardized test scores, talent/ability. *Important fac-*

tors considered include: Character/personal qualities, interview. *Other factors considered include:* Class rank, recommendation(s), extracurricular activities. **Freshman Admission Requirements:** High school diploma is required and GED is accepted. **Freshman Admission Statistics: Transfer Admission Requirements:** High school transcript, college transcript(s), essay or personal statement, Lowest grade transferable C. **General Admission Information:** Application fee $30. Nonfall registration accepted. Admission may be deferred for a maximum of one semester. Credit offered for CEEB Advanced Placement tests.

COSTS AND FINANCIAL AID

Annual in-state tuition $12,674. Annual out-of-state tuition $19,220. Required fees $420. Average book expense $3,604. **Required Forms and Deadlines:** FAFSA. Financial aid filing deadline 2/15. Priority financial aid filing date 2/15. **Notification of Awards:** Applicants will be notified of awards on a rolling basis beginning 4/1. **Types of Aid:** *Need-based scholarships/grants:* Federal Pell, SEOG, state scholarships/grants, private scholarships, the school's own gift aid. *Loans:* Direct Subsidized Stafford, Direct Unsubsidized Stafford, Direct PLUS, Federal Perkins, Key Alternative Loan, CitiAssist Student Loan, Michigan Alternative Loan. **Student Employment:** Federal Work-Study Program available. Institutional employment available. Highest amount earned per year from on-campus jobs $2,000. **Financial Aid Statistics: Criteria for awarding institutional aid:** *Non-need-based:* Academics, alumni affiliation, art.

KENNESAW STATE UNIVERSITY

1000 Chastain Road, Campus Box 0115, Kennesaw, GA 30144-5591
Phone: 770-423-6300 **Financial Aid Phone:** 770-423-6074
E-mail: ksuadmit@kennesaw.edu **CEEB Code:** 5359
Fax: 770-420-4435 **Website:** www.kennesaw.edu **ACT Code:** 833

This public school was founded in 1963. It has a 384-acre campus.

RATINGS

Admissions Selectivity Rating: 84 **Fire Safety Rating:** 99 **Green Rating:** 87

STUDENTS AND FACULTY

Enrollment: 20,237. **Student Body:** 59% female, 41% male, 6% out-of-state, 2% international (136 countries represented). Asian 3%, African American 13%, Caucasian 70%, Hispanic 5%.
Retention and Graduation: 75% freshmen return for sophomore year. 10% freshmen graduate within 4 years. **Faculty:** Student/faculty ratio 21:1. 703 full-time faculty, 75% hold PhDs, 23% are members of minority groups, 51% are women.

ACADEMICS

Degrees: Bachelor's, doctoral, master's. **Classes:** Most classes have 20–29 students. Most lab/discussion sessions have 20–29 students. **Majors with Highest Enrollment:** Business administration and management; elementary education and teaching; nursing/registered nurse (RN, ASN, BSN, MSN). **Special Study Options:** Cooperative education program, cross-registration, distance learning, double major, English as a Second Language (ESL), honors program, internships, study abroad, teacher certification program, weekend college. **Honors programs:** The Honors Program at KSU provides a unique opportunity for exceptional students to customize their college experience. Through colloquia, seminars and directed studies, honor students can tailor their experience to meet their needs and interest. Instead of being restricted to the guidelines of a course catalog, students are encouraged to think outside the box and stretch themselves in academic directions that appeal to them. To guide them in their journey, a faculty mentor is assigned to each student. Most students only know faculty in a classroom setting, but honor students develop a one-on-one relationship designed to enhance their collegiate experience. Special programs offered to physically disabled students include note-taking services, reader services, tape recorders, tutors. **Career services:** Alumni network, alumni services, internships. **Career services highlights include:** Internships at KSU are on the rise and fully supported by campus administration. The president of KSU has expressed he wants to see a 10% annual increase in the number of students participating in this program from now on.

FACILITIES

Housing: Apartments for single students. 100% of campus accessible to physically disabled. **Computers:** 100% of classrooms, 100% of libraries, 100% of dining areas, 100% of student union, 5% of common outdoor areas have wireless network access. Students can register for classes online. Administrative functions (other than registration) can be performed online.

CAMPUS LIFE

Environment: Town. **Activities:** Choral groups, concert band, dance, drama/theater, jazz band, music ensembles, musical theater, radio station, student

government, student newspaper, symphony orchestra, campus ministries, international student organization, Model UN. **Organizations:** 151 registered organizations, 20 honor societies, 18 religious organizations. 10 fraternities, 8 sororities. **Athletics (Intercollegiate):** *Men:* Baseball, basketball, cross-country, golf, tennis, track/field (outdoor), track/field (indoor). *Women:* Basketball, cheerleading, cross-country, golf, soccer, softball, tennis, track/field (outdoor), track/field (indoor), volleyball. **On-Campus Highlights:** Student Dining Hall, Lounge in Student Center, Game Room in Student Center, Student Recreation Center, Campus Green. **Environmental Initiatives:** Commitment by KSU President Daniel S. Papp to reduce the university's carbon footprint, in line with a national coalition of college and university presidents. Naming of a campus Director of Sustainability who will oversee the university's green initiatives and teach students as a member of the faculty. Launching a new undergraduate degree program with emphases in environmental science or environmental polity within KSU's existing Interdisciplinary Studies program.

ADMISSIONS

Freshman Academic Profile: Average high school GPA 3018. 21% in top 10% of high school class, 53% in top 25% of high school class, 81% in top 50% of high school class. 90% from public high schools. SAT Math middle 50% range 490–580. SAT Critical Reading middle 50% range 500–580. SAT Writing middle 50% range 470–560. ACT middle 50% range 20–24. Minimum paper TOEFL 527. Minimum computer TOEFL 197. Minimum web-based TOEFL 75. **Basis for Candidate Selection:** *Very important factors considered include:* Academic GPA, standardized test scores. **Freshman Admission Requirements:** High school diploma is required and GED is not accepted. *Academic units required:* 4 English, 4 mathematics, 3 science, (3 science labs), 2 foreign language, 3 social studies. **Freshman Admission Statistics:** 7,877 applied, 64% admitted, 55% enrolled. **Transfer Admission Requirements:** College transcript(s), minimum college GPA of 2.0 required. Lowest grade transferable D. **General Admission Information:** Application fee $40. Regular application deadline 5/14. Notification on a rolling basis, beginning on or about 1/1. Nonfall registration accepted. Admission may be deferred for a maximum of 1 year. Credit offered for CEEB Advanced Placement tests.

COSTS AND FINANCIAL AID

Annual in-state tuition $4,196. Annual out-of-state tuition $16,172. Room and board $6,593. Required fees $948. Average book expense $1,250. **Required Forms and Deadlines:** FAFSA. Priority financial aid filing date 4/1. **Notification of Awards:** Applicants will be notified of awards on a rolling basis beginning 4/1. **Types of Aid:** *Need-based scholarships/grants:* Federal Pell, SEOG, state scholarships/grants, private scholarships *Loans:* FFEL Subsidized Stafford, FFEL. Unsubsidized Stafford, FFEL PLUS, Federal Perkins, Federal Nursing, state loans. **Student Employment:** Federal Work-Study Program available. Institutional employment available. Highest amount earned per year from on-campus jobs $15,732. Off-campus job opportunities are good. **Financial Aid Statistics:** 28% freshmen, 29% undergrads receive need-based scholarship or grant aid. 37% freshmen, 22% undergrads receive non-need-based scholarship or grant aid. 41% freshmen, 45% undergrads receive need-based self-help aid. 5% freshmen, 4% undergrads receive athletic scholarships. 73% freshmen, 65% undergrads receive any aid. 75% undergrads borrow to pay for school. Average cumulative indebtedness $13,500. **Criteria for awarding institutional aid:** *Non-need-based:* Academics, alumni affiliation, art, athletics, job skills, leadership, minority status, music/drama, state/district residency.

KENT STATE UNIVERSITY—KENT CAMPUS

161 Michael Schwartz Center, Kent, OH 44242-0001
Phone: 330-672-2444 **Financial Aid Phone:** 330-672-2972
E-mail: admissions@kent.edu **CEEB Code:** 1367
Fax: 330-672-2499 **Website:** www.kent.edu **ACT Code:** 3284

This public school was founded in 1910. It has a 1200-acre campus.

RATINGS

Admissions Selectivity Rating: 74 **Fire Safety Rating:** 83 **Green Rating:** 79

STUDENTS AND FACULTY

Enrollment: 19,337. **Student Body:** 58% female, 42% male, 12% out-of-state, 2% international (81 countries represented). Asian 2%, African American 9%, Caucasian 82%, Hispanic 2%, Native American 1%.
Retention and Graduation: 78% freshmen return for sophomore year. 25% freshmen graduate within 4 years. **Faculty:** Student/faculty ratio 20:1. 888 full-time faculty, 17% are members of minority groups, 49% are women. 4% of classes are taught by teaching assistants.

ACADEMICS

Degrees: Associate, bachelor's, certificate, doctoral, master's, post-bachelor's certificate, post-master's certificate, terminal associate, transfer associate.

Classes: Most classes have 20–29 students. **Majors with Highest Enrollment:** Business administration and management; nursing/registered nurse (RN, ASN, BSN, MSN); psychology. **Special Study Options:** Accelerated program, cooperative education program, cross-registration, distance learning, double major, dual enrollment, English as a Second Language (ESL), exchange student program (domestic), external degree program, honors program, independent study, internships, liberal arts/career combination, student-designed major, study abroad, teacher certification program, weekend college. **Honors programs:** Honors College membership at Kent State University is open to all majors and hosts approximately 1,350 students at the Kent Campus and five Regional Campuses. Honors College classes emphasize the intellectual value in the pursuit of knowledge. Every effort is made to show students the connections between disciplines. Honors College classes are small, taught by carefully chosen faculty, and emphasize students' active involvement in their learning. Plentiful opportunities for individual study, including the Senior Honors Thesis/Project give students exciting experiences in following their intellectual curiosity. An Honors College residence complex, state-of-the-art facilities, experiences including study abroad/away opportunities and cultural programming all support bright and motivated students seeking an intellectual home within the larger university. **Combined degree programs:** BA/MD, BA/MA. Special programs offered to physically disabled students include note-taking services, reader services, tape recorders, tutors. **Career services:** Alumni network, alumni services, career/job search classes, career assessment, internships, regional alumni. **Career services highlights include:** Kent State University is home to the first academic trading floor with live derivatives exchange data. The Olga A. Mural Financial Engineering Trading Floor cost $2.2M to build and has an annual operating budget of $450,000. The Kent State Financial Engineering students are provided experience through industry-based projects (internships). Internships are 10 weeks in length and begin in May.

FACILITIES

Housing: Coed dorms, special housing for disabled students, men's dorms, special housing for international students, women's dorms, fraternity/sorority housing, apartments for married students, apartments for single students. 95% of campus accessible to physically disabled. **Special Academic Facilities/Equipment:** Fashion museum, herbarium, liquid crystal institute, planetarium, airport. **Computers:** 90% of classrooms, 20% of dorms, 40% of libraries, 70% of dining areas, 100% of student union, 10% of common outdoor areas have wireless network access. Students can register for classes online. Administrative functions (other than registration) can be performed online.

CAMPUS LIFE

Environment: Town. **Activities:** Choral groups, concert band, dance, drama/theater, jazz band, literary magazine, marching band, music ensembles, pep band, radio station, student government, student newspaper, television station, campus ministries, international student organization. **Organizations:** 214 registered organizations, 10 honor societies, 15 religious organizations. 17 fraternities, 6 sororities. **Athletics (Intercollegiate):** *Men:* Baseball, basketball, cheerleading, cross-country, football, golf, track/field (outdoor), track/field (indoor), wrestling. *Women:* Basketball, cheerleading, cross-country, field hockey, football, golf, gymnastics, soccer, softball, track/field (outdoor), track/field (indoor), volleyball. **On-Campus Highlights:** Student Recreation and Wellness Center, Kent State University Museum, Kent Student Center Plaza, Pan African Center Gallery, May 4 Memorial. **Environmental Initiatives:** The construction of a combined heat and power plant on campus. Ongoing energy efficiency improvement. Creating a more walkable campus through the construction of the Esplanade walking and biking path through campus.

ADMISSIONS

Freshman Academic Profile: Average high school GPA 3.19. 13% in top 10% of high school class, 37% in top 25% of high school class, 70% in top 50% of high school class. SAT Math middle 50% range 460–580. SAT Critical Reading middle 50% range 460–560. SAT Writing middle 50% range 440–560. ACT middle 50% range 20–25. Minimum paper TOEFL 525. Minimum computer TOEFL 197. **Basis for Candidate Selection:** *Very important factors considered include:* Academic GPA, rigor of secondary school record, standardized test scores. *Other factors considered include:* Class rank, recommendation(s). **Freshman Admission Requirements:** High school diploma is required and GED is accepted. *Academic units recommended:* 4 English, 3 mathematics, 3 science, (2 science labs), 3 foreign language, 3 social studies, 1 visual/performing arts. **Freshman Admission Statistics:** 14,933 applied, 72% admitted, 39% enrolled. **Transfer Admission Requirements:** College transcript(s), minimum college GPA of 2.0 required. Lowest grade transferable C. **General Admission Information:** Application fee $40. Regular application deadline 8/1. Notification on a rolling basis, beginning on or about 10/1. Nonfall registration accepted. Admission may be deferred for a maximum of 1 year. Credit and/or placement offered for CEEB Advanced Placement tests.

COSTS AND FINANCIAL AID

Required Forms and Deadlines: FAFSA. Priority financial aid filing date 3/1. **Notification of Awards:** Applicants will be notified of awards on or about

3/15. **Types of Aid:** *Need-based scholarships/grants:* Federal Pell, SEOG, state scholarships/grants, private scholarships, the school's own gift aid. *Loans:* Direct Subsidized Stafford, Direct Unsubsidized Stafford, Direct PLUS, Federal Perkins, Federal Nursing, state loans, college/university loans from institutional funds, alternative loans. **Student Employment:** Federal Work-Study Program available. Institutional employment available. Highest amount earned per year from on-campus jobs $14,000. Off-campus job opportunities are excellent. **Financial Aid Statistics:** 52% freshmen, 45% undergrads receive need-based scholarship or grant aid. 16% freshmen, 8% undergrads receive non-need-based scholarship or grant aid. 62% freshmen, 59% undergrads receive need-based self-help aid. 1% freshmen, 1% undergrads receive athletic scholarships. 88% freshmen, 81% undergrads receive any aid. 75% undergrads borrow to pay for school. Average cumulative indebtedness $26,698. **Criteria for awarding institutional aid:** *Non-need-based:* Academics, alumni affiliation, art, athletics, leadership, minority status, music/drama, state/district residency.

KENTUCKY STATE UNIVERSITY

400 East Main Street, suite 312, Frankfort, KY 40601
Phone: 502-597-6813 **Financial Aid Phone:** 502-597-6033
E-mail: admissions@kysu.edu **CEEB Code:** 1368
Fax: 502-597-5814 **Website:** www.kysu.edu **ACT Code:** 1516

This public school was founded in 1886. It has a 915-acre campus.

RATINGS

Admissions Selectivity Rating: 60* **Fire Safety Rating:** 90 **Green Rating:** 65

STUDENTS AND FACULTY

Enrollment: 2,326. **Student Body:** 58% female, 42% male, 41% out-of-state, 1% international (23 countries represented). African American 64%, Caucasian 21%, Hispanic 1%.
Retention and Graduation: 51% freshmen return for sophomore year. 8% freshmen graduate within 4 years. 50% grads go on to further study within 1 year. 20% grads pursue arts and sciences degrees. 2% grads pursue law degrees. 10% grads pursue business degrees. 2% grads pursue medical degrees. **Faculty:** Student/faculty ratio 15:1. 128 full-time faculty, 68% hold PhDs, 34% are members of minority groups, 44% are women.

ACADEMICS

Degrees: Associate, bachelor's, master's. **Classes:** Most classes have 20–29 students. Most lab/discussion sessions have fewer than 10 students. **Majors with Highest Enrollment:** Business/commerce; criminal justice/safety studies; elementary education and teaching. **Special Study Options:** Cooperative education program, distance learning, double major, dual enrollment, English as a Second Language (ESL), honors program, independent study, internships, liberal arts/career combination, student-designed major, study abroad, teacher certification program. **Honors programs:** The Whitney Young School of Honors and Liberal Studies. The Honors Program is an integrated liberal arts program that emphasizes student discussion of excellent books. Special programs offered to physically disabled students include note-taking services, reader services, tape recorders, tutors. **Career services:** Alumni network, alumni services, career assessment, internships, regional alumni. **Career services highlights include:** KSU Intern and Cooperative Education program. The students gain hands on experience and 85% are offered positions after graduation.

FACILITIES

Housing: Coed dorms, men's dorms, women's dorms 100% of campus accessible to physically disabled. **Special Academic Facilities/Equipment:** Art gallery, nutrition lab, agriculture research building, research farm, fish hatchery, electron microscope. **Computers:** 100% of classrooms, 100% of dorms, 100% of libraries, 100% of dining areas, 100% of student union, 60% of common outdoor areas have wireless network access. Students can register for classes online. Administrative functions (other than registration) can be performed online.

CAMPUS LIFE

Environment: Town. **Activities:** Choral groups, concert band, dance, drama/theater, jazz band, marching band, music ensembles, musical theater, opera, pep band, student government, student newspaper, campus ministries, international student organization. **Organizations:** 30 registered organizations, 5 honor societies, 4 religious organizations. 6 fraternities, 5 sororities. **Athletics (Intercollegiate):** *Men:* Baseball, basketball, cross-country, football, golf, track/field (outdoor), track/field (indoor). *Women:* Basketball, cross-country, softball, track/field (outdoor), track/field (indoor), volleyball. **On-Campus Highlights:** Jackson Hall, Carl Hill Student Center, William Exum Building, Whitney Young Residence Hall, Hume Hall. **Environmental Initiatives:** Recycling of paper and plastic products, recycling cardboard, recycling metal.

ADMISSIONS

Freshman Academic Profile: Average high school GPA 2.58. SAT Math middle 50% range 340–460. SAT Critical Reading middle 50% range 360–460. SAT Writing middle 50% range 350–440. ACT middle 50% range 15–19. Minimum paper TOEFL 525. **Basis for Candidate Selection:** *Very important factors considered include:* Academic GPA, standardized test scores. *Important factors considered include:* Rigor of secondary school record, first generation, level of applicant's interest, state residency. *Other factors considered include:* Application essay, recommendation(s), alumni/ae relation, character/personal qualities, extracurricular activities, geographical residence, interview. **Freshman Admission Requirements:** High school diploma is required and GED is accepted. *Academic units required:* 4 English, 3 mathematics, 3 science, 2 foreign language, 3 social studies, 1 visual/performing arts, 1 0.5 P.E. and 0.5 Health Education. **Transfer Admission Requirements:** College transcript(s), minimum college GPA of 2.0 required. Lowest grade transferable C. **General Admission Information:** Application fee $30. Nonfall registration accepted. Credit and/or placement offered for CEEB Advanced Placement tests.

COSTS AND FINANCIAL AID

Annual in-state tuition $5,086. Annual out-of-state tuition $13,458. Room and board $6,480. Required fees $600. Average book expense $1,300. **Required Forms and Deadlines:** FAFSA. Priority financial aid filing date 4/15. **Notification of Awards:** Applicants will be notified of awards on or about 4/1. **Types of Aid:** *Need-based scholarships/grants:* Federal Pell, SEOG, state scholarships/grants, private scholarships, the school's own gift aid, United Negro College Fund, Federal Nursing Scholarships. *Loans:* Direct Subsidized Stafford, Direct Unsubsidized Stafford, Direct PLUS. **Student Employment:** Federal Work-Study Program available. Institutional employment available. Highest amount earned per year from on-campus jobs $2,500. Off-campus job opportunities are good. **Financial Aid Statistics:** 64% freshmen, 62% undergrads receive need-based scholarship or grant aid. 40% freshmen, 38% undergrads receive non-need-based scholarship or grant aid. 75% freshmen, 72% undergrads receive need-based self-help aid. 6% freshmen, 7% undergrads receive athletic scholarships. 87% freshmen, 81% undergrads receive any aid. 76% undergrads borrow to pay for school. Average cumulative indebtedness $35,552. **Criteria for awarding institutional aid:** *Non-need-based:* Academics, alumni affiliation, art, athletics, minority status, music/drama.

KENTUCKY WESLEYAN COLLEGE

3000 Frederica Street, Owensboro, KY 42301
Phone: 270-852-3120 **Financial Aid Phone:** 270-852-3130
E-mail: www.kwc.edu/admission/index.aspx **CEEB Code:** 1369
Fax: 270-852-3133 **Website:** www.kwc.edu **ACT Code:** 1518

This private school, affiliated with the Methodist Church, was founded in 1858. It has a 52-acre campus.

RATINGS

Admissions Selectivity Rating: 75 **Fire Safety Rating:** 61 **Green Rating:** 60*

STUDENTS AND FACULTY

Enrollment: 862. **Student Body:** 47% female, 53% male, 21% out-of-state, 1% international (8 countries represented). African American 9%, Caucasian 76%, Hispanic 1%.
Retention and Graduation: 63% freshmen return for sophomore year. 35% freshmen graduate within 4 years. **Faculty:** Student/faculty ratio 15:1. 43 full-time faculty, 84% hold PhDs, 9% are members of minority groups, 40% are women.

ACADEMICS

Degrees: Bachelor's. **Classes:** Most classes have 10–19 students. Most lab/discussion sessions have 10–19 students. **Majors with Highest Enrollment:** Biology/biological sciences; business/commerce; criminal justice/safety studies. **Special Study Options:** Double major, independent study, internships, liberal arts/career combination, student-designed major, study abroad, teacher certification program, Online Program. **Combined degree programs:** University of Louisville and Auburn University. Special programs offered to physically disabled students include note-taking services, tutors. **Career services:** Alumni network, career/job search classes, career assessment, internships.

FACILITIES

Housing: Coed dorms, special housing for disabled students, men's dorms, women's dorms, fraternity/sorority housing, apartments for married students, apartments for single students 100% of campus accessible to physically disabled. **Special Academic Facilities/Equipment:** President's Hall/Library Learning Center Ralph Center for Fine Arts. Woodward Health and Recreation Center.

Yu Hak Hahn Center for the Sciences. **Computers:** 100% of classrooms, 100% of dorms, 100% of libraries, 100% of dining areas, 100% of student union, have wireless network access. Students can register for classes online. Administrative functions (other than registration) can be performed online.

CAMPUS LIFE

Environment: Town. **Activities:** Choral groups, dance, drama/theater, literary magazine, music ensembles, pep band, radio station, student government, student newspaper, yearbook, campus ministries. **Organizations:** 42 registered organizations, 6 honor societies, 6 religious organizations. 3 fraternities, 2 sororities. **Athletics (Intercollegiate): Men:** Baseball, basketball, cheerleading, cross-country, football, golf, soccer. **Women:** Basketball, cheerleading, cross-country, golf, soccer, softball, tennis, volleyball. **On-Campus Highlights:** Winchester Center-New Campus Center, Ralph Fine Arts Center, Yu Hak Hahn Center for the Sciences, Woodward Health and Recreation Center, The Quad, for virtual tours, visit www.kwc.edu.

ADMISSIONS

Freshman Academic Profile: Average high school GPA 3.18. 18% in top 10% of high school class, 36% in top 25% of high school class, 68% in top 50% of high school class. 90% from public high schools. SAT Math middle 50% range 430–520. SAT Critical Reading middle 50% range 450–550. SAT Writing middle 50% range 390–490. ACT middle 50% range 19–24. Minimum paper TOEFL 500. Minimum computer TOEFL 173. **Basis for Candidate Selection:** *Very important factors considered include:* Academic GPA, standardized test scores. *Important factors considered include:* Rigor of secondary school record, extracurricular activities, interview. *Other factors considered include:* Class rank, recommendation(s), alumni/ae relation, character/personal qualities, level of applicant's interest, talent/ability, volunteer work, work experience. **Freshman Admission Requirements:** High school diploma is required and GED is accepted. *Academic units required:* 4 English, 3 mathematics, 3 science, 3 social studies. *Academic units recommended:* 2 foreign language. **Freshman Admission Statistics:** 1,240 applied, 67% admitted, 27% enrolled. **Transfer Admission Requirements:** College transcript(s), minimum college GPA of 2.0 required. Lowest grade transferable C. **General Admission Information:** Notification on a rolling basis, beginning on or about 9/1. Nonfall registration accepted. Admission may be deferred for a maximum of 12 mo. Credit and/or placement offered for CEEB Advanced Placement tests.

COSTS AND FINANCIAL AID

Annual tuition $16,870. Room and board $6,440. Average book expense $1,200. **Required Forms and Deadlines:** FAFSA. Financial aid filing deadline 3/15. Priority financial aid filing date 3/15. **Notification of Awards:** Applicants will be notified of awards on a rolling basis beginning 2/15. **Types of Aid:** *Need-based scholarships/grants:* Federal Pell, SEOG, state scholarships/grants, private scholarships, the school's own gift aid. *Loans:* FFEL Subsidized Stafford, FFEL Unsubsidized Stafford, FFEL PLUS, Federal Perkins, college/university loans from institutional funds, Alternative Education Loans. **Student Employment:** Federal Work-Study Program available. Institutional employment available. Off-campus job opportunities are good. **Financial Aid Statistics:** 89% freshmen, 82% undergrads receive need-based scholarship or grant aid. 11% freshmen, 12% undergrads receive non-need-based scholarship or grant aid. 63% freshmen, 60% undergrads receive need-based self-help aid. 98% freshmen, 85% undergrads receive any aid. 89% undergrads borrow to pay for school. Average cumulative indebtedness $20,906. **Criteria for awarding institutional aid:** *Non-need-based:* Academics, alumni affiliation, art, athletics, leadership, music/drama, religious affiliation, state/district residency.

KENYON COLLEGE

Admissions Office, Ransom Hall, Gambier, OH 43022-9623
Phone: 740-427-5776 **Financial Aid Phone:** 740-427-5240
E-mail: admissions@kenyon.edu **CEEB Code:** 1370
Fax: 740-427-5770 **Website:** www.kenyon.edu **ACT Code:** 3286

This private school was founded in 1824. It has a 1200-acre campus.

RATINGS

Admissions Selectivity Rating: 96 **Fire Safety Rating:** 63 **Green Rating:** 92

STUDENTS AND FACULTY

Enrollment: 1,616. **Student Body:** 52% female, 48% male, 83% out-of-state, 4% international (35 countries represented). Asian 6%, African American 4%,

Caucasian 79%, Hispanic 3%, Native American 1%.
Retention and Graduation: 91% freshmen return for sophomore year. 85% freshmen graduate within 4 years. 25% grads go on to further study within 1 year. 7% grads pursue arts and sciences degrees. 3% grads pursue law degrees. 3% grads pursue business degrees. 2% grads pursue medical degrees. **Faculty:** Student/faculty ratio 9.5:1. 156 full-time faculty, 99% hold PhDs, 13% are members of minority groups, 44% are women.

ACADEMICS

Degrees: Bachelor's. **Classes:** Most classes have 10–19 students. **Majors with Highest Enrollment:** Economics; English language and literature; political science and government. **Special Study Options:** Accelerated program, double major, exchange student program (domestic), honors program, independent study, internships, liberal arts/career combination, student-designed major, study abroad **Honors programs:** Honors programs are offered by all departmental and interdepartmental majors. **Combined degree programs:** Education, Environmental Studies. Special programs offered to physically disabled students include note-taking services, reader services, tape recorders, tutors. **Career services:** Alumni network, alumni services, career/job search classes, career assessment, internships, regional alumni. **Career services highlights include:** Our Extern program enables students to explore career options through an experiential week of job-showing during winter or spring breaks. This often helps students decide what internships and/or career paths they'd like to pursue while building a network of contacts.

FACILITIES

Housing: Coed dorms, special housing for disabled students, women's dorms, fraternity/sorority housing, apartments for single students, wellness housing, theme housinghousing options for community service, substance-free, wellness, international wing, Kosher, twp. fire dept. groups. 41% of campus accessible to physically disabled. **Special Academic Facilities/Equipment:** Horn and Olin art galleries; Bolton and Hill theaters; Black Box Theater; Rosse and Storer halls for music; new sciences quadrangle; greenhouse and observatory; environmental center; $70–million fitness, recreation, and athletics facility. new art history building under construction. **Computers:** 100% of classrooms, 100% of dorms, 100% of libraries, 100% of dining areas, 33% of common outdoor areas have wireless network access. Administrative functions (other than registration) can be performed online.

CAMPUS LIFE

Environment: Rural. **Activities:** Choral groups, concert band, dance, drama/theater, jazz band, literary magazine, music ensembles, musical theater, opera, pep band, radio station, student government, student newspaper, student-run film society, symphony orchestra, yearbook, campus ministries, international student organization, Model UN. **Organizations:** 140 registered organizations, 5 honor societies, 6 religious organizations. 8 fraternities, 4 sororities. **Athletics (Intercollegiate):** *Men:* Baseball, basketball, cross-country, diving, football, golf, lacrosse, soccer, swimming, tennis, track/field (outdoor), track/field (indoor). *Women:* Basketball, cross-country, diving, field hockey, lacrosse, soccer, softball, swimming, tennis, track/field (outdoor), track/field (indoor), volleyball. **On-Campus Highlights:** Kenyon College Bookstore, Fitness./Recreation, Athletic Facility, Middle Ground Coffee Shop, Brown Family Environmental Center, Horn Gallery. **Environmental Initiatives:** 1. Food for Thought (purchase of local foods for dining hall and building a county-wide sustainable food system) http://rurallife.kenyon.edu/FFT/index.html. 2. Brown Family Environmental Center (academic and public sustainability programs). 3. Kenyon Environmental Sustainability Council www.kenyon.edu/sustainability.xml. 4. Paper/can/bottle recycling program campus-wide.

ADMISSIONS

Freshman Academic Profile: Average high school GPA 3.82. 56% in top 10% of high school class, 87% in top 25% of high school class, 99% in top 50% of high school class. 54% from public high schools. SAT Math middle 50% range 600–680. SAT Critical Reading middle 50% range 630–720. SAT Writing middle 50% range 620–730. ACT middle 50% range 28–32. Minimum paper TOEFL 600. Minimum web-based TOEFL 100. **Basis for Candidate Selection:** *Very important factors considered include:* Application essay, academic GPA, recommendation(s), rigor of secondary school record, character/personal qualities. *Important factors considered include:* Class rank, standardized test scores, extracurricular activities, interview, level of applicant's interest, talent/ability. *Other factors considered include:* Alumni/ae relation, first generation, geographical residence, racial/ethnic status, state residency, volunteer work, work experience. **Freshman Admission Requirements:** High school diploma is required and GED is accepted. *Academic units required:* 4 English, 3 mathematics, 3 science, (3 science labs), 3 foreign language, 1 social studies, 2 history, 3 academic electives. *Academic units recommended:* 4 English, 4 mathematics, 4 science, (3 science labs), 4 foreign language, 1 social studies, 3 history, 3 academic electives. **Freshman Admission Statistics:** 3,992 applied, 39% admitted, 30% enrolled. **Transfer Admission Requirements:** High school transcript, college transcript(s), essay or personal statement, standardized test scores, statement of good standing from prior institution(s). Minimum college GPA of 3.0 required.

Lowest grade transferable C. **General Admission Information:** Application fee $45. Early decision application deadline 11/15. Regular application deadline 1/15. Regular notification 4/1. Nonfall registration not accepted. Admission may be deferred for a maximum of 1 year. Credit and/or placement offered for CEEB Advanced Placement tests.

COSTS AND FINANCIAL AID

Annual tuition $39,420. Room and board $9,500. Required fees $1,480. Average book expense $1,800. **Required Forms and Deadlines:** FAFSA, CSS/Financial Aid PROFILE, noncustodial PROFILE. Financial aid filing deadline 2/15. Priority financial aid filing date 2/15. **Notification of Awards:** Applicants will be notified of awards on or about 4/1. *Types of Aid: Need-based scholarships/ grants:* Federal Pell, SEOG, state scholarships/grants, private scholarships, the school's own gift aid. *Loans:* FFEL Subsidized Stafford, FFEL Unsubsidized Stafford, FFEL PLUS, Federal Perkins, college/university loans from institutional funds. **Student Employment:** Federal Work-Study Program available. Institutional employment available. Highest amount earned per year from on-campus jobs $1,255. Off-campus job opportunities are poor. **Financial Aid Statistics:** 43% freshmen, 41% undergrads receive need-based scholarship or grant aid. 15% freshmen, 10% undergrads receive non-need-based scholarship or grant aid. 31% freshmen, 33% undergrads receive need-based self-help aid. 54.7% freshmen, 51.2% undergrads receive any aid. 58% undergrads borrow to pay for school. Average cumulative indebtedness $19,934. **Criteria for awarding institutional aid:** *Non-need-based:* Academics, minority status.

KETTERING UNIVERSITY

1700 University Ave, Flint, MI 48504-6214
Phone: 810-762-7865 **Financial Aid Phone:** 810-762-7859
E-mail: admissions@kettering.edu **CEEB Code:** 1246
Fax: 810-762-9837 **Website:** www.kettering.edu **ACT Code:** 1998

This private school was founded in 1919. It has a 85-acre campus.

RATINGS
Admissions Selectivity Rating: 88 | **Fire Safety Rating:** 63 | **Green Rating:** 60*

STUDENTS AND FACULTY
Enrollment: 2,009. **Student Body:** 17% female, 83% male, 30% out-of-state, 4% international (22 countries represented). Asian 3%, African American 3%, Caucasian 60%, Hispanic 2%.
Retention and Graduation: 86% freshmen return for sophomore year. 8% freshmen graduate within 4 years. 23% grads go on to further study within 1 year. 23% grads pursue arts and sciences degrees. 6% grads pursue law degrees. 9% grads pursue business degrees. 2% grads pursue medical degrees. **Faculty:** Student/faculty ratio 10:1. 120 full-time faculty, 87% hold PhDs, 10% are members of minority groups, 18% are women.

ACADEMICS
Degrees: Bachelor's, master's. **Classes:** Most classes have 20–29 students. Most lab/discussion sessions have 10–19 students. **Majors with Highest Enrollment:** Computer engineering; electrical, electronics and communications engineering; mechanical engineering. **Special Study Options:** Accelerated program, cooperative education program, distance learning, double major, dual enrollment, independent study, study abroad, co-op is required of all undergraduate students and typically begins in the first year. Each 24 week semester is divided into 11-weeks of classes and 12–13 weeks of paid professional co-op experience in industry. Students co-op with employers in 43 states and several countries. Income from co-op is a major resource for Kettering students whose total co-op income over their 4.5-year program typically ranges between $40,000 and $65,000. In addition to study abroad some Kettering students also gain experience in foreign locations for their co-op employer. Accelerated program, cooperative (work-study) program, distance learning, double major, independent study. Distance learing is for graduate students only. **Combined degree programs:** BS/MS engineering. Special programs offered to physically disabled students include note-taking services, reader services, tape recorders, tutors. **Career services highlights include:** Kettering University is a preimere cooperative education program. All students are required to complete a specified number of co-op terms to graduate. Students may start their co-op experience as early as their freshmen year.

FACILITIES
Housing: Coed dorms, fraternity/sorority housing, apartments for single students. 100% of campus accessible to physically disabled. **Special Academic Facilities/Equipment:** Art museum, Scharschburg Archieves and Industrial History Museum (principal repository for SAE Patents and Technical Papers). Kettering is renown for the variety and quality of its laboratories for student

use and teaching. Labs are required in nearly all science and engineering courses. Of special note are the Bosch Automotive Electronics Systems Lab, Ford Design Simulation Studio, the GM/PACE e-Design and e-Manufacturing Studio, Center for Fuel Cell Systems and Powertrain Integration, the Crash Test Safety, Computer Intergrated Manufacturing (CIM), Polymer Processing, and Mechatronics Labs, the Lubrizol Engine Test Center, SAE Project Vehicle facilities, Biomedical, and the Environmental Scanning Electron Microscopy Lab. The Connie and Jim John Recreation Center and Kettering Park (outdoor recreation). **Computers:** 100% of classrooms, 100% of libraries, 100% of dining areas, have wireless network access. Students can register for classes online. Administrative functions (other than registration) can be performed online.

CAMPUS LIFE

Environment: City. **Activities:** Drama/theater, music ensembles, radio station, student government, student newspaper, yearbook. **Organizations:** 43 registered organizations, 13 honor societies, 1 religious organizations. 13 fraternities, 6 sororities. **On-Campus Highlights:** CS Mott Engineering and Science Center, Connie and Jim John Recreation Center, Frances Willson Thompson Residence Hall, Cemistry and Physics Laboratories, Engineering Laboratories, Kettering University takes great pride in our TOP ranked programs and one-of-a kind co-op program. Kettering students earn on average $40,000–$65,000 and up to 2 1/2 years of relevant work experience while working for one of our 600+ co-op employers. Prospective students are encouraged to visit campus to learn more about our academic programs, one-of-a-kind co-op program and to meet our faculty, students and staff.

ADMISSIONS

Freshman Academic Profile: Average high school GPA 3.58. 32.6% in top 10% of high school class, 68.2% in top 25% of high school class, 94.8% in top 50% of high school class. SAT Math middle 50% range 590–670. SAT Critical Reading middle 50% range 530–630. ACT middle 50% range 24–29. Minimum paper TOEFL 550. Minimum computer TOEFL 213. Minimum web-based TOEFL 79. **Basis for Candidate Selection:** *Very important factors considered include:* Academic GPA, rigor of secondary school record, standardized test scores. *Important factors considered include:* Class rank, extracurricular activities. *Other factors considered include:* Application essay, recommendation(s), interview, racial/ethnic status, volunteer work, work experience. **Freshman Admission Requirements:** High school diploma is required and GED is not accepted. *Academic units required:* 3 English, 4 mathematics, 2 science, (2 science labs). *Academic units recommended:* 4 English, 4 mathematics, 3 science, (3 science labs), 2 foreign language, 2 social studies, 2 history, 1 computer science. **Freshman Admission Statistics:** 2,529 applied, 67% admitted, 26% enrolled. **Transfer Admission Requirements:** College transcript(s), minimum college GPA of 3.0 required. Lowest grade transferable C. **General Admission Information:** Application fee $35. Notification on a rolling basis, beginning on or about 10/15. Nonfall registration accepted. Admission may be deferred for a maximum of 1 year. Credit offered for CEEB Advanced Placement tests.

COSTS AND FINANCIAL AID

Annual tuition $26,336. Room and board $5,662. Required fees $448. **Required Forms and Deadlines:** FAFSA. Priority financial aid filing date 2/14. **Notification of Awards:** Applicants will be notified of awards on a rolling basis beginning 1/15. **Types of Aid:** *Need-based scholarships/grants:* Federal Pell, SEOG, state scholarships/grants, private scholarships, the school's own gift aid. *Loans:* Direct Subsidized Stafford, Direct Unsubsidized Stafford, Direct PLUS, FFEL Subsidized Stafford, FFEL Unsubsidized Stafford, FFEL PLUS. **Student Employment:** Federal Work-Study Program available. Institutional employment available. Highest amount earned per year from on-campus jobs $1,200. Off-campus job opportunities are fair. **Financial Aid Statistics:** 71% freshmen, 53% undergrads receive need-based scholarship or grant aid. 13% freshmen, 7% undergrads receive non-need-based scholarship or grant aid. 72% freshmen, 55% undergrads receive need-based self-help aid. 98% freshmen, 88% undergrads receive any aid. 81% undergrads borrow to pay for school. Average cumulative indebtedness $48,767. **Criteria for awarding institutional aid:** *Non-need-based:* Academics, alumni affiliation, leadership, state/district residency.

See page 1126.

KEUKA COLLEGE

Office of Admissions, Keuka Park, NY 14478-0098
Phone: 315-279-5254 **Financial Aid Phone:** 315-279-5646
E-mail: admissions@mail.keuka.edu **CEEB Code:** 2744
Fax: 315-536-5386 **Website:** www.keuka.edu **ACT Code:** 2782

This private school, affiliated with the American Baptist Church, was founded in 1890. It has a 203-acre campus.

RATINGS
Admissions Selectivity Rating: 72   **Fire Safety Rating:** 60*   **Green Rating:** 60*

STUDENTS AND FACULTY
Enrollment: 1,522. **Student Body:** 75% female, 25% male, 6% out-of-state, international (3 countries represented). Asian 2%, African American 7%, Caucasian 77%, Hispanic 3%, Native American 1%.
Retention and Graduation: 64% freshmen return for sophomore year. 42% freshmen graduate within 4 years. 28% grads go on to further study within 1 year. **Faculty:** Student/faculty ratio 14:1. 74 full-time faculty, 84% hold PhDs, 3% are members of minority groups, 62% are women.

ACADEMICS
Degrees: Bachelor's, master's. **Classes:** Most classes have 20–29 students. Most lab/discussion sessions have 10–19 students. **Majors with Highest Enrollment:** Business administration and management; occupational therapy/therapist; special education and teaching. **Special Study Options:** Accelerated program, cooperative education program, cross-registration, double major, dual enrollment, independent study, internships, student-designed major, study abroad, teacher certification program. **Combined degree programs:** Clinical Science to Chiropractic with NY Chiroprac. Special programs offered to physically disabled students include note-taking services, reader services, tape recorders, tutors. **Career services:** Alumni network, alumni services, career/job search classes, career assessment, internships, regional alumni. **Career services highlights include:** Experiential learning—national leader in experiential, hands-on learning.

FACILITIES
Housing: Coed dorms, special housing for disabled students, men's dorms, women's dorms, cooperative housing, theme housing. 61% of campus accessible to physically disabled. **Special Academic Facilities/Equipment:** Bird Museum, Lightner Gallery.

CAMPUS LIFE
Environment: Rural. **Activities:** Choral groups, concert band, dance, drama/theater, literary magazine, musical theater, radio station, student government, student newspaper, student-run film society, yearbook. **Organizations:** 32 registered organizations, 7 honor societies, 2 religious organizations. **Athletics (Intercollegiate):** *Men:* Baseball, basketball, cross-country, golf, lacrosse, soccer, tennis. *Women:* Basketball, cross-country, golf, lacrosse, soccer, softball, synchronized swimming, tennis, volleyball. **On-Campus Highlights:** The Weed Physical Arts Center (gym, pool, fitness rooms, coaches offices), Dahstrom Student Center (bookstore, club offices, student affairs), Ostrander Field (soccer, lacrosse games), Hegeman Hall (classes, faculty offices), Jephson Hall (sciences, greenhouse, labs, electronic classroom).

ADMISSIONS
Freshman Academic Profile: Average high school GPA 3.12. 11.44% in top 10% of high school class, 38.31% in top 25% of high school class, 10.65% in top 50% of high school class. 96% from public high schools. SAT Math middle 50% range 430–510. SAT Critical Reading middle 50% range 410–550. SAT Writing middle 50% range 410–515. ACT middle 50% range 18–24. Minimum paper TOEFL 500. Minimum computer TOEFL 300. **Basis for Candidate Selection:** *Very important factors considered include:* Rigor of secondary school record. *Important factors considered include:* Class rank, application essay, academic GPA, recommendation(s), character/personal qualities, extracurricular activities, interview. *Other factors considered include:* standardized test scores, alumni/ae relation, level of applicant's interest, talent/ability, volunteer work, work experience. **Freshman Admission Requirements:** High school diploma is required and GED is accepted. *Academic units recommended:* 4 English, 3 mathematics, 3 science, (2 science labs), 3 foreign language, 3 social studies, 2 history. **Freshman Admission Statistics:** 867 applied, 77% admitted, 38% enrolled. **Transfer Admission Requirements:** College transcript(s), essay or personal statement, minimum college GPA of 2.0 required. Lowest grade transferable C. **General Admission Information:** Application fee $30. Notification on a rolling basis, beginning on or about 9/1. Nonfall registration accepted. Admission may be deferred for a maximum of 12. Credit and/or placement offered for CEEB Advanced Placement tests.

COSTS AND FINANCIAL AID

Annual tuition $22,040. Room and board $9,160. Required fees $790. Average book expense $1,000. **Required Forms and Deadlines:** FAFSA. **Notification of Awards:** Applicants will be notified of awards on a rolling basis beginning 3/1. **Types of Aid:** *Need-based scholarships/grants:* Federal Pell, SEOG, state scholarships/grants, the school's own gift aid. *Loans:* FFEL Subsidized Stafford, FFEL Unsubsidized Stafford, FFEL PLUS, Federal Perkins. **Student Employment:** Highest amount earned per year from on-campus jobs $1,800. Off-campus job opportunities are good. **Financial Aid Statistics:** 91% freshmen, 85% undergrads receive need-based scholarship or grant aid. 6% freshmen, 7% undergrads receive non-need-based scholarship or grant aid. 80% freshmen, 80% undergrads receive need-based self-help aid. 92% freshmen, 93% undergrads receive any aid. 95% undergrads borrow to pay for school. Average cumulative indebtedness $16,119. **Criteria for awarding institutional aid:** *Non-need-based:* Academics, alumni affiliation, leadership, minority status, religious affiliation.

KEYSTONE COLLEGE

One College Green, La Plume, PA 18440
Phone: 570-945-8111 **Financial Aid Phone:** 570-945-8132
E-mail: admissions@keystone.edu **CEEB Code:** 2351
Fax: 570-945-7916 **Website:** www.keystone.edu **ACT Code:** 2602

This private school was founded in 1868. It has a 270-acre campus.

RATINGS
Admissions Selectivity Rating: 61   **Fire Safety Rating:** 94   **Green Rating:** 87

STUDENTS AND FACULTY

Enrollment: 1,612. **Student Body:** 60% female, 40% male, 11% out-of-state, international (10 countries represented). Asian 1%, African American 2%, Caucasian 57%, Hispanic 2%.
Retention and Graduation: 61% freshmen return for sophomore year. 46% grads go on to further study within 1 year. **Faculty:** Student/faculty ratio 10:1. 71 full-time faculty, 41% hold PhDs, 4% are members of minority groups, 63% are women.

ACADEMICS

Degrees: Associate, bachelor's, certificate, post-bachelor's certificate, terminal associate, transfer associate. **Classes:** Most classes have 10–19 students. Most lab/discussion sessions have fewer than 10 students. **Majors with Highest Enrollment:** Business administration and management; education; security and protective services, other. **Special Study Options:** Cooperative education program, cross-registration, distance learning, double major, dual enrollment, English as a Second Language (ESL), honors program, independent study, internships, study abroad, teacher certification program, weekend college. **Honors programs:** Freshmen Honor's Program Special programs offered to physically disabled students include note-taking services, reader services, tutors. **Career services:** Alumni network, alumni services, career/job search classes, career assessment, internships, regional alumni. **Career services highlights include:** Student internship placements have included NBC Dateline, Late Night with Conan O'Brien, U.S. Olympic Training Committee, US Secret Service, ESPN Radio, Atlantic Records, and placements abroad in several countries.

FACILITIES

Housing: Coed dorms, special housing for disabled students, women's dorms 80% of campus accessible to physically disabled. **Special Academic Facilities/Equipment:** Linder Art Gallery; Cupillari Astronomical Observatory; Willary Water Resource Center. **Computers:** 100% of classrooms, 50% of dorms, 100% of libraries, 100% of dining areas, 100% of student union, 50% of common outdoor areas have wireless network access. Students can register for classes online. Administrative functions (other than registration) can be performed online.

CAMPUS LIFE

Environment: Rural. **Activities:** Choral groups, drama/theater, literary magazine, musical theater, radio station, student government, student newspaper, yearbook, campus ministries, international student organization. **Organizations:** 22 registered organizations, 1 religious organizations. **Athletics (Intercollegiate):** *Men:* Baseball, basketball, cross-country, golf, soccer, tennis, track/field (outdoor), track/field (indoor). *Women:* Basketball, cross-country, field hockey, soccer, softball, tennis, track/field (outdoor), track/field (indoor), volleyball. **On-Campus Highlights:** Linder Art Gallery, 270 acre woodlands campus (trail system), Astronomical Observatory, Giants' Den, Keystone Commons. **Environmental Initiatives:** A recycling program; a policy for purchasing Energy Star compliant products; purchase of wind derived electricity(10%), and erection of a test tower on campus to determine if the campus is suitable for windmills.

ADMISSIONS

Freshman Academic Profile: 3% in top 10% of high school class, 11% in top 25% of high school class, 45% in top 50% of high school class. SAT Math middle 50% range 380–480. SAT Critical Reading middle 50% range 390–480. SAT Writing middle 50% range 380–470. ACT middle 50% range 15.5–18. Minimum paper TOEFL 550. Minimum computer TOEFL 213. Minimum web-based TOEFL 80. **Basis for Candidate Selection:** *Very important factors considered include:* Academic GPA, rigor of secondary school record, interview, talent/ability. *Important factors considered include:* standardized test scores, character/personal qualities, extracurricular activities. *Other factors considered include:* Class rank, application essay, recommendation(s), alumni/ae relation, level of applicant's interest, volunteer work, work experience. **Freshman Admission Requirements:** High school diploma is required and GED is accepted. *Academic units required:* 4 English, 3 mathematics, 2 science, (1 science labs), 2 social studies, 1 history, 4 academic electives, 2 years of algebra recommended. *Academic units recommended:* 4 English, 3 mathematics, 3 science, (1 science labs), 2 foreign language, 2 social studies, 1 history, 1 visual/performing arts, 1 computer science, 3 academic electives, 2 years of algebra recommended. **Freshman Admission Statistics:** 778 applied, 95% admitted, 45% enrolled. **Transfer Admission Requirements:** College transcript(s), minimum college GPA of 2.0 required. Lowest grade transferable C. **General Admission Information:** Application fee $30. Regular application deadline 7/15. Notification on a rolling basis, beginning on or about 10/1. Nonfall registration accepted. Admission may be deferred for a maximum of 1 year. Credit and/or placement offered for CEEB Advanced Placement tests.

COSTS AND FINANCIAL AID

Annual tuition $17,570. Room and board $8,760. Required fees $2,025. Average book expense $1,600. **Required Forms and Deadlines:** FAFSA, state aid form Financial aid filing deadline 5/1. Priority financial aid filing date 4/26. **Notification of Awards:** Applicants will be notified of awards on a rolling basis beginning 2/1. **Types of Aid:** *Need-based scholarships/grants:* Federal Pell, SEOG, state scholarships/grants, private scholarships, the school's own gift aid. *Loans:* FFEL Subsidized Stafford, FFEL Unsubsidized Stafford, FFEL PLUS, Federal Perkins. **Student Employment:** Federal Work-Study Program available. Institutional employment available. Highest amount earned per year from on-campus jobs $1,450. Off-campus job opportunities are good. **Financial Aid Statistics:** 90% freshmen, 89% undergrads receive need-based scholarship or grant aid. 94% freshmen, 91% undergrads receive non-need-based scholarship or grant aid. 90% freshmen, 89% undergrads receive need-based self-help aid. 88.7% freshmen, 89.1% undergrads receive any aid. 84% undergrads borrow to pay for school. Average cumulative indebtedness $23,479. **Criteria for awarding institutional aid:** *Non-need-based:* Academics, alumni affiliation, leadership.

See page 1128.

KING COLLEGE

1350 King College Road, Bristol, TN 37620-2699
Phone: 423-652-4861 **Financial Aid Phone:** 423-652-4728
E-mail: admissions@king.edu **CEEB Code:** 1371
Fax: 423-652-4727 **Website:** www.king.edu **ACT Code:** 3970

This private school, affiliated with the Presbyterian Church, was founded in 1867. It has a 135-acre campus.

RATINGS
Admissions Selectivity Rating: 82   **Fire Safety Rating:** 60*   **Green Rating:** 60*

STUDENTS AND FACULTY

Enrollment: 1,320. **Student Body:** 65% female, 35% male, 46% out-of-state, 3% international (21 countries represented). African American 2%, Caucasian 70%, Hispanic 2%.
Retention and Graduation: 43% freshmen graduate within 4 years. 25% grads go on to further study within 1 year. 21% grads pursue arts and sciences degrees. 1% grads pursue law degrees. 3% grads pursue business degrees. 2% grads pursue medical degrees. **Faculty:** Student/faculty ratio 14:1. 67 full-time faculty, 76% hold PhDs, 3% are members of minority groups, 51% are women.

ACADEMICS

Degrees: Bachelor's, master's. **Classes:** Most classes have 10–19 students. Most lab/discussion sessions have fewer than 10 students. **Majors with Highest Enrollment:** Business/commerce; nursing/registered nurse (RN, ASN, BSN, MSN); religion/religious studies. **Special Study Options:** Accelerated program, cross-registration, double major, dual enrollment, exchange student program (domestic), honors program, independent study, internships, student-designed major, study abroad, teacher certification program. **Honors programs:** The Jack E. Snider Honors Center allows students to interact with other students and faculty of diverse interests. Participants take selected courses that stimulate thinking and allow for creative response while engaging in special opportunities such as meeting with faculty members and outside guests. Other courses may allow honors students, for extra credit, to develop more extensive research projects. The honors seminars also examine ideas from a variety of academic disciplines. Participants serve both the campus and the larger community by tutoring and mentoring and are encouraged to explore other perspectives through study abroad experiences. **Combined degree programs:** BA/MEng, 3-1 pharmacyprogram, 3-1 medical technology program. Special programs offered to physically disabled students include tutors. **Career services:** Alumni network, alumni services, career assessment, internships.

FACILITIES

Housing: Special housing for disabled students, men's dorms, women's dorms. 80% of campus accessible to physically disabled, **Special Academic Facilities/ Equipment:** Electron microscope, observatory with two reflecting telescopes, solar telescope.

CAMPUS LIFE

Environment: Town. **Activities:** Choral groups, concert band, dance, drama/ theater, literary magazine, music ensembles, musical theater, pep band, student government, student newspaper, yearbook, campus ministries, international student organization. **Organizations:** 35 registered organizations, 5 honor societies, 9 religious organizations. **Athletics (Intercollegiate):** *Men:* Baseball, basketball, bowling, cheerleading, cross-country, cycling, diving, golf, soccer, swimming, tennis, track/field (outdoor), track/field (indoor), wrestling. *Women:* Basketball, bowling, cheerleading, cross-country, cycling, diving, golf, soccer, softball, swimming, tennis, track/field (outdoor), track/field (indoor), volleyball, wrestling. **On-Campus Highlights:** New student center/athletic complex, campus oval, library, residence hall lobbies, entrance way and sporting fields.

ADMISSIONS

Freshman Academic Profile: Average high school GPA 3.37. 28% in top 10% of high school class, 49% in top 25% of high school class, 79% in top 50% of high school class. 88% from public high schools. SAT Math middle 50% range 440–550. SAT Critical Reading middle 50% range 450–540. SAT Writing middle 50% range 440–553. ACT middle 50% range 19–24. Minimum paper TOEFL 563. Minimum computer TOEFL 223. **Basis for Candidate Selection:** *Very important factors considered include:* Academic GPA, standardized test scores. *Other factors considered include:* Class rank, application essay, recommendation(s), rigor of secondary school record, character/personal qualities, extracurricular activities, interview, level of applicant's interest. **Freshman Admission Requirements:** High school diploma is required and GED is accepted. *Academic units required:* 4 English, 3 mathematics, 1 science, (1 science labs), 2 foreign language, 2 history, 4 academic electives. **Freshman Admission Statistics:** 898 applied, 63% admitted, 33% enrolled. **Transfer Admission Requirements:** College transcript(s), minimum college GPA of 2.0 required. Lowest grade transferable C–. **General Admission Information:** Application fee $20. Nonfall registration accepted. Admission may be deferred for a maximum of 1 semester. Credit and/or placement offered for CEEB Advanced Placement tests.

COSTS AND FINANCIAL AID

Annual tuition $20,592. Room and board $7,418. Required fees $1,288. Average book expense $900. **Required Forms and Deadlines:** FAFSA. Priority financial aid filing date 3/1. **Notification of Awards:** Applicants will be notified of awards on a rolling basis beginning 3/1. **Types of Aid:** *Need-based scholarships/ grants:* Federal Pell, SEOG, state scholarships/grants, the school's own gift aid. *Loans:* FFEL Subsidized Stafford, FFEL Unsubsidized Stafford, FFEL PLUS, Federal Perkins, state loans, college/university loans from institutional funds. **Student Employment:** Federal Work-Study Program available. Institutional employment available. Highest amount earned per year from on-campus jobs $1,236. Off-campus job opportunities are good. **Financial Aid Statistics:** 79% freshmen, 60% undergrads receive need-based scholarship or grant aid. 14% freshmen, 9% undergrads receive non-need-based scholarship or grant aid. 56% freshmen, 52% undergrads receive need-based self-help aid. 14% freshmen, 9% undergrads receive athletic scholarships. 98% freshmen, 98% undergrads receive any aid. 97.52% undergrads borrow to pay for school. Average cumulative indebtedness $15,019. **Criteria for awarding institutional aid:** *Non-need-based:* Academics, athletics, music/drama.

KING'S COLLEGE (PA)

133 North River Street, Wilkes-Barre, PA 18711
Phone: 570-208-5858 **Financial Aid Phone:** 570-208-5868
E-mail: admissions@kings.edu **CEEB Code:** 2353
Fax: 570-208-5971 **Website:** www.kings.edu **ACT Code:** 3604

This private school, affiliated with the Roman Catholic Church, was founded in 1946. It has a 48-acre campus.

RATINGS

Admissions Selectivity Rating: 75 **Fire Safety Rating:** 85 **Green Rating:** 75

STUDENTS AND FACULTY

Enrollment: 2,042. **Student Body:** 49% female, 51% male, 28.4% out-of-state, international (5 countries represented). Asian 1%, African American 2%, Caucasian 79%, Hispanic 4%.
Retention and Graduation: 63% freshmen graduate within 4 years. 27% grads go on to further study within 1 year. 14% grads pursue arts and sciences degrees. 3% grads pursue law degrees. 2% grads pursue business degrees. 8% grads pursue medical degrees. **Faculty:** Student/faculty ratio 13:1. 124 full-time faculty, 85% hold PhDs, 5% are members of minority groups, 40% are women.

ACADEMICS

Degrees: Associate, bachelor's, certificate, master's, post-bachelor's certificate. **Classes:** Most classes have 10–19 students. Most lab/discussion sessions have 10–19 students. **Majors with Highest Enrollment:** Accounting; business administration and management; elementary education and teaching. **Special Study Options:** Accelerated program, cross-registration, distance learning, double major, dual enrollment, English as a Second Language (ESL), honors program, independent study, internships, student-designed major, study abroad, teacher certification program, weekend college. **Combined degree programs:** BS medical studies/MS physician's assistant. Special programs offered to physically disabled students include note-taking services, reader services, tape recorders, tutors. **Career services:** Alumni network, alumni services, career assessment, internships, regional alumni.

FACILITIES

Housing: Coed dorms, special housing for disabled students, men's dorms, women's dorms, apartments for single students, wellness housing, theme housing 99% of campus accessible to physically disabled. **Special Academic Facilities/Equipment:** Electron microscope, rooftop greenhouse, molecular biology lab, computer graphics lab **Computers:** 50% of classrooms, 25% of dorms, 100% of libraries, 100% of dining areas, 100% of student union, 100% of common outdoor areas have wireless network access. Students can register for classes online. Administrative functions (other than registration) can be performed online.

CAMPUS LIFE

Environment: City. **Activities:** Choral groups, dance, drama/theater, literary magazine, music ensembles, pep band, radio station, student government, student newspaper, yearbook, campus ministries. **Organizations:** 50 registered organizations, 15 honor societies, 2 religious organizations. **Athletics (Intercollegiate):** *Men:* Baseball, basketball, cheerleading, cross-country, football, golf, lacrosse, soccer, swimming, tennis, wrestling. *Women:* Basketball, cheerleading, cross-country, field hockey, lacrosse, soccer, softball, swimming, tennis, volleyball. **On-Campus Highlights:** Sheehy-Farmer Campus Center, McGowan School of Business, Scandlon P.E. Center, Betzler Fields (Athletic Complex), Gateway Corners.

ADMISSIONS

Freshman Academic Profile: Average high school GPA 3.3. 15% in top 10% of high school class, 40% in top 25% of high school class, 75% in top 50% of high school class. 78% from public high schools. SAT Math middle 50% range 470–560. SAT Critical Reading middle 50% range 460–550. SAT Writing middle 50% range 450–550. Minimum paper TOEFL 530. Minimum computer TOEFL 197. Minimum web-based TOEFL 71. **Basis for Candidate Selection:** *Very important factors considered include:* Class rank, academic GPA, rigor of secondary school record. *Important factors considered include:* Application essay, standardized test scores, character/personal qualities. *Other factors considered include:* Recommendation(s), alumni/ae relation, extracurricular activities, interview, volunteer work, work experience. **Freshman Admission Requirements:** High school diploma is required and GED is accepted. *Academic units required:* 4 English, 3 mathematics, 3 science, (2 science labs), 2 foreign language, 3 social studies, 1 history. *Academic units recommended:* 4 English, 4 mathematics, 4 science, (2 science labs), 4 foreign language, 3 social studies, 1 history, 2 computer science, 2 academic electives. **Freshman Admission Statistics:** 2,172 applied, 75% admitted, 30% enrolled. **Transfer Admission Requirements:** High school transcript, college transcript(s), essay or personal statement, minimum college GPA of 2.0 required. Lowest grade transferable C. **General Admission Information:** Application fee $30. Notification on a rolling basis, beginning on or about 10/1. Nonfall registration accepted. Admission may be deferred for a maximum of 1 year. Neither credit nor placement offered for CEEB Advanced Placement tests.

COSTS AND FINANCIAL AID

Annual tuition $25,644. Room and board $9,838. Average book expense $1,220. **Required Forms and Deadlines:** FAFSA, institution's own financial aid form. Priority financial aid filing date 2/15. **Notification of Awards:** Applicants will be notified of awards on a rolling basis beginning 3/1. **Types of Aid:** *Need-based scholarships/grants:* Federal Pell, SEOG, state scholarships/grants, private scholarships, the school's own gift aid. *Loans:* FFEL Subsidized Stafford, FFEL Unsubsidized Stafford, FFEL PLUS, Federal Perkins, Private Loans. **Student Employment:** Federal Work-Study Program available. Institutional employment available. Highest amount earned per year from on-campus jobs $2,000. Off-campus job opportunities are fair. **Financial Aid Statistics:** 86% freshmen, 80% undergrads receive need-based scholarship or grant aid. 10% freshmen, 8% undergrads receive non-need-based scholarship or grant aid. 76% freshmen, 70% undergrads receive need-based self-help aid. 97% freshmen, 95% undergrads receive any aid. 84% undergrads borrow to pay for school. Average cumulative indebtedness $30,843. **Criteria for awarding institutional aid:** *Non-need-based:* Academics, leadership.

See page 1130.

KNOX COLLEGE

2 East South Street, Box K-148, Galesburg, IL 61401
Phone: 309-341-7100 **Financial Aid Phone:** 309-341-7149
E-mail: admission@knox.edu **CEEB Code:** 1372
Fax: 309-341-7070 **Website:** www.knox.edu **ACT Code:** 1052

This private school was founded in 1837. It has a 82-acre campus.

RATINGS

Admissions Selectivity Rating: 88   **Fire Safety Rating:** 82   **Green Rating:** 78

STUDENTS AND FACULTY

Enrollment: 1,384. **Student Body:** 60% female, 40% male, 47% out-of-state, 7% international (33 countries represented). Asian 7%, African American 5%, Caucasian 69%, Hispanic 5%, Native American 1%. **Retention and Graduation:** 90% freshmen return for sophomore year. 66% freshmen graduate within 4 years. 21% grads go on to further study within 1 year. 10% grads pursue arts and sciences degrees. 2% grads pursue law degrees. 1% grads pursue business degrees. 2% grads pursue medical degrees. **Faculty:** Student/faculty ratio 12:1. 108 full-time faculty, 94% hold PhDs, 14% are members of minority groups, 40% are women.

ACADEMICS

Degrees: Bachelor's. **Classes:** Most classes have 10–19 students. Most lab/discussion sessions have 10–19 students. **Majors with Highest Enrollment:** Economics; education; political science and government. **Special Study Options:** double major, dual enrollment, honors program, independent study, internships, student-designed major, study abroad, teacher certification program **Honors programs:** Knox College is an "honors college." If you compare Knox's academic requirements, student profile, educational opportunities, and student experiences with those of an honors program at a university, Knox provides comparable and often much richer opportunities for its students. **Combined degree programs:** BA/JD, BA/MEng, architecture, environment, medical tech. Special programs offered to physically disabled students include note-taking services, tape recorders, tutors. **Career services:** Career assessment, internships. **Career services highlights include:** Kemper Scholars Program.

FACILITIES

Housing: Coed dorms, special housing for disabled students, men's dorms, special housing for international students, women's dorms, fraternity/sorority housing, apartments for single students, wellness housing, theme housing 60% of campus accessible to physically disabled. **Special Academic Facilities/Equipment:** Anthropology, art, and field museums, theatre with revolving stage and computerized lighting, ceramics, sculpture, painting, and printmaking studios, 760–acre biological field station, environmental climate chambers, electron microscope. **Computers:** 100% of classrooms, 100% of dorms, 100% of libraries, 100% of dining areas, 100% of student union, 90% of common outdoor areas

have wireless network access. Students can register for classes online. Administrative functions (other than registration) can be performed online.

CAMPUS LIFE

Environment: Town. **Activities:** Choral groups, dance, drama/theater, jazz band, literary magazine, music ensembles, radio station, student government, student newspaper, symphony orchestra, campus ministries, international student organization, Model UN. **Organizations:** 102 registered organizations, 8 honor societies, 6 religious organizations. 5 fraternities, 3 sororities. **Athletics (Intercollegiate): Men:** Baseball, basketball, cross-country, football, golf, soccer, swimming, tennis, track/field (outdoor), track/field (indoor), wrestling. *Women:* Basketball, cross-country, golf, soccer, softball, swimming, tennis, track/field (outdoor), track/field (indoor), volleyball. **On-Campus Highlights:** Gizmo Snack Bar, Andrew Fitness Center, Hard Knox Cafe, Gizmo Patio, Seymour Library.

ADMISSIONS

Freshman Academic Profile: Average high school GPA 3.32. 37% in top 10% of high school class, 67% in top 25% of high school class, 97% in top 50% of high school class. SAT Math middle 50% range 560–690. SAT Critical Reading middle 50% range 600–730. SAT Writing middle 50% range 560–680. ACT middle 50% range 26–31. Minimum paper TOEFL 550. Minimum computer TOEFL 213. Minimum web-based TOEFL 80. **Basis for Candidate Selection:** *Very important factors considered include:* Academic GPA, rigor of secondary school record. *Important factors considered include:* Class rank, application essay, recommendation(s), character/personal qualities. *Other factors considered include:* Standardized test scores, alumni/ae relation, extracurricular activities, first generation, geographical residence, interview, level of applicant's interest, racial/ethnic status, state residency, talent/ability, volunteer work. **Freshman Admission Requirements:** High school diploma is required and GED is accepted. *Academic units recommended:* 4 English, 4 mathematics, 4 science, (3 science labs), 3 foreign language, 2 social studies, 2 history. **Freshman Admission Statistics:** 2,427 applied, 74% admitted, 20% enrolled. **Transfer Admission Requirements:** High school transcript, college transcript(s), essay or personal statement, statement of good standing from prior institution(s). Minimum college GPA of 3.0 required. Lowest grade transferable C. **General Admission Information:** Application fee $40. Regular application deadline 2/1. Regular notification 3/31. Admission may be deferred for a maximum of 1 year. Credit and/or placement offered for CEEB Advanced Placement tests.

COSTS AND FINANCIAL AID

Average book expense $900. **Required Forms and Deadlines:** FAFSA, institution's own financial aid form. Priority financial aid filing date 2/15. **Notification of Awards:** Applicants will be notified of awards on a rolling basis beginning 3/15. **Types of Aid:** *Need-based scholarships/grants:* Federal Pell, SEOG, state scholarships/grants, private scholarships, the school's own gift aid. *Loans:* Direct Subsidized Stafford, Direct Unsubsidized Stafford, Direct PLUS, Federal Perkins, college/university loans from institutional funds. **Student Employment:** Federal Work-Study Program available. Institutional employment available. Highest amount earned per year from on-campus jobs $5,479. Off-campus job opportunities are fair. **Financial Aid Statistics:** 74% freshmen, 69% undergrads receive need-based scholarship or grant aid. 13% freshmen, 8% undergrads receive non-need-based scholarship or grant aid. 63% freshmen, 63% undergrads receive need-based self-help aid. 98% freshmen, 97% undergrads receive any aid. 73% undergrads borrow to pay for school. Average cumulative indebtedness $24,018. **Criteria for awarding institutional aid:** *Non-need-based:* Academics, art, music/drama.

KUTZTOWN UNIVERSITY OF PENNSYLVANIA

Admissions Office, PO Box 730, Kutztown, PA 19530-0730
Phone: 610-683-4060 **Financial Aid Phone:** 610-683-4032
E-mail: admission@kutztown.edu **CEEB Code:** 2653
Fax: 610-683-1375 **Website:** www.kutztown.edu **ACT Code:** 3706

This public school was founded in 1866. It has a 325-acre campus.

RATINGS

Admissions Selectivity Rating: 71   **Fire Safety Rating:** 60*   **Green Rating:** 60*

STUDENTS AND FACULTY

Enrollment: 9,181. **Student Body:** 57% female, 43% male, 9.6% out-of-state, 1% international (32 countries represented). Asian 1%, African American 6%, Caucasian 86%, Hispanic 5%. **Retention and Graduation:** 78% freshmen return for sophomore year. 30% freshmen graduate within 4 years. 25% grads go on to further study within 1 year. 18% grads pursue arts and sciences degrees. 2% grads pursue law degrees. 7% grads pursue business degrees. 13% grads pursue medical degrees. **Fac-**

ulty: Student/faculty ratio 19:1. 461 full-time faculty, 77% hold PhDs, 15% are members of minority groups, 46% are women.

ACADEMICS

Degrees: Bachelor's, master's, post-bachelor's certificate. **Classes:** Most classes have 20–29 students. Most lab/discussion sessions have 20–29 students. **Majors with Highest Enrollment:** Business administration and management; criminal justice/safety studies; psychology. **Special Study Options:** Cross-registration, distance learning, double major, dual enrollment, honors program, independent study, internships, liberal arts/career combination, student-designed major, study abroad, teacher certification program. **Honors programs:** 1)University Honors Program 2)Various Honor Societies. **Combined degree programs:** BS/MS Computer Information Science. Special programs offered to physically disabled students include note-taking services, reader services, tape recorders, tutors. **Career services:** Alumni network, alumni services, career/job search classes, career assessment, internships, regional alumni. **Career services highlights include:** Proudest of the wide array of services and events for Kutztown University students.

FACILITIES

Housing: Coed dorms, women's dorms, cooperative housing, apartments for single students, Apartment Units. 90% of campus accessible to physically disabled. **Special Academic Facilities/Equipment:** Art gallery, German Cultural Heritage Center, Early Childhood Learning Center, cartography lab, observatory, planetarium, daycare center. **Computers:** 25% of classrooms, 95% of dorms, 100% of libraries, 75% of dining areas, 100% of student union, 65% of common outdoor areas have wireless network access. Students can register for classes online. Administrative functions (other than registration) can be performed online.

CAMPUS LIFE

Environment: Rural. **Activities:** Choral groups, concert band, dance, drama/theater, jazz band, literary magazine, marching band, music ensembles, musical theater, radio station, student government, student newspaper, student-run film society, symphony orchestra, television station, yearbook, campus ministries, international student organization, Model UN. **Organizations:** 218 registered organizations, 15 honor societies, 11 religious organizations. 9 fraternities, 8 sororities. **Athletics (Intercollegiate):** *Men:* Baseball, basketball, cross-country, football, tennis, track/field (outdoor), track/field (indoor), wrestling. *Women:* Basketball, bowling, cross-country, field hockey, golf, lacrosse, soccer, softball, swimming, tennis, track/field (outdoor), track/field (indoor), volleyball. **On-Campus Highlights:** Taylor and Burnes Gourmet Coffee, Student Rec Center, Alumni Plaza-new walkway with outdoor amphitheater, Pennsylvania German Cultural Heritage Center, Academic Forum.

ADMISSIONS

Freshman Academic Profile: Average high school GPA 3.03. 5.6% in top 10% of high school class, 22.4% in top 25% of high school class, 62.7% in top 50% of high school class. 99% from public high schools. SAT Math middle 50% range 430–530. SAT Critical Reading middle 50% range 440–530. SAT Writing middle 50% range 430–520. ACT middle 50% range 17–22. Minimum paper TOEFL 550. Minimum web-based TOEFL 79. **Basis for Candidate Selection:** *Very important factors considered include:* Class rank, rigor of secondary school record, standardized test scores. *Other factors considered include:* Academic GPA, recommendation(s), character/personal qualities, extracurricular activities, geographical residence, interview, racial/ethnic status, state residency, talent/ability, volunteer work, work experience. **Freshman Admission Requirements:** High school diploma is required and GED is accepted. *Academic units recommended:* 4 English, 4 mathematics, 4 science, 2 foreign language, 4 social studies. **Freshman Admission Statistics:** 9,540 applied, 66% admitted, 32% enrolled. **Transfer Admission Requirements:** College transcript(s), statement of good standing from prior institution(s). Minimum college GPA of 2.0 required. Lowest grade transferable C–. **General Admission Information:** Application fee $35. Notification on a rolling basis, beginning on or about 10/1. Nonfall registration accepted. Admission may be deferred for a maximum of 1 year. Credit and/or placement offered for CEEB Advanced Placement tests.

COSTS AND FINANCIAL AID

Annual in-state tuition $5,554. Annual out-of-state tuition $13,886. Room and board $7,698. Required fees $1,843. Average book expense $1,100. **Required Forms and Deadlines:** FAFSA. Priority financial aid filing date 3/1. **Notification of Awards:** Applicants will be notified of awards on a rolling basis beginning 3/30. **Types of Aid:** *Need-based scholarships/grants:* Federal Pell, SEOG, state scholarships/grants, private scholarships, the school's own gift aid. *Loans:* FFEL Subsidized Stafford, FFEL Unsubsidized Stafford, FFEL PLUS, Federal Perkins. **Student Employment:** Federal Work-Study Program available. Institutional employment available. Highest amount earned per year from on-campus jobs $9,899. Off-campus job opportunities are fair. **Financial Aid Statistics:** 42% freshmen, 39% undergrads receive need-based scholarship or grant aid. 2% freshmen, 2% undergrads receive non-need-based scholarship or grant aid. 53% freshmen, 50% undergrads receive need-based self-help aid. 2% freshmen, 2% undergrads receive athletic scholarships. 82% freshmen, 76% undergrads receive any aid. 86% undergrads borrow to pay for school. Aver-

age cumulative indebtedness $20,707. **Criteria for awarding institutional aid:** *Non-need-based:* Academics, art, athletics, leadership, minority status, music/drama.

LA ROCHE COLLEGE

9000 Babcock Boulevard, Pittsburgh, PA 15237
Phone: 412-536-1271 **Financial Aid Phone:** 412-536-1120
E-mail: admissions@laroche.edu **CEEB Code:** 2379
Fax: 412-536-1048 **Website:** www.laroche.edu **ACT Code:** 3607

This private school, affiliated with the Roman Catholic Church, was founded in 1963. It has a 43-acre campus.

RATINGS

Admissions Selectivity Rating: 70   **Fire Safety Rating:** 90   **Green Rating:** 60*

STUDENTS AND FACULTY

Enrollment: 1,181. **Student Body:** 64% female, 36% male, 7% out-of-state, 11% international (39 countries represented). Asian 1%, African American 6%, Caucasian 66%, Hispanic 1%.
Retention and Graduation: 60% freshmen return for sophomore year. 34% freshmen graduate within 4 years. **Faculty:** Student/faculty ratio 12:1. 63 full-time faculty, 76% hold PhDs, 8% are members of minority groups, 51% are women.

ACADEMICS

Degrees: Associate, bachelor's, certificate, master's, post-bachelor's certificate, terminal associate. **Classes:** Most classes have 10–19 students. Most lab/discussion sessions have 10–19 students. **Majors with Highest Enrollment:** design and visual communications; elementary education and teaching; interior architecture. **Special Study Options:** Accelerated program, cross-registration, distance learning, double major, English as a Second Language (ESL), honors program, independent study, internships, student-designed major, study abroad, teacher certification program. **Combined degree programs:** BA/MA. Special programs offered to physically disabled students include note-taking services, reader services, tutors. **Career services:** career/job search classes, career assessment, internships, regional alumni.

FACILITIES

Housing: Coed dorms 100% of campus accessible to physically disabled. **Special Academic Facilities/Equipment:** Cantellopes Art Gallery; College Center extension has state of the art smart classrooms. **Computers:** 100% of classrooms, 10% of dorms, 100% of libraries, 100% of dining areas, 100% of student union, 25% of common outdoor areas have wireless network access. Students can register for classes online. Administrative functions (other than registration) can be performed online.

CAMPUS LIFE

Environment: City. **Activities:** Choral groups, dance, drama/theater, literary magazine, musical theater, radio station, student government, student newspaper, campus ministries, international student organization. **Organizations:** 40 registered organizations, 4 honor societies, 2 religious organizations. **Athletics (Intercollegiate):** *Men:* Baseball, basketball, cross-country, golf, lacrosse, soccer. *Women:* Basketball, cheerleading, cross-country, soccer, softball, tennis, volleyball. **On-Campus Highlights:** Sports and Fitness Center, College bookstore, Magdalen Chapel, College Center Annex.

ADMISSIONS

Freshman Academic Profile: Average high school GPA 3.084. 3% in top 10% of high school class, 21% in top 25% of high school class, 53% in top 50% of high school class. 88% from public high schools. SAT Math middle 50% range 390–500. SAT Critical Reading middle 50% range 380–500. SAT Writing middle 50% range 400–510. ACT middle 50% range 17–22. **Basis for Candidate Selection:** *Very important factors considered include:* Academic GPA, standardized test scores. *Important factors considered include:* level of applicant's interest. *Other factors considered include:* Application essay, recommendation(s), rigor of secondary school record, character/personal qualities, interview, talent/ability, volunteer work. **Freshman Admission Requirements:** High school diploma is required and GED is accepted. *Academic units required:* 4 English, 3 mathematics, 3 science, (2 science labs), 3 social studies, 3 history. *Academic units recommended:* 4 English, 3 mathematics, 3 science, 1 foreign language, 3 social studies. **Freshman Admission Statistics:** 859 applied, 68% admitted, 33% enrolled. **Transfer Admission Requirements:** College transcript(s), essay or personal statement, minimum college GPA of 2.0 required. Lowest grade transferable C. **General Admission Information:** Application fee $50. Notification on a rolling basis, beginning on or about 9/15. Nonfall registration accepted. Admission may be deferred for a maximum of 1 year. Credit offered for CEEB Advanced Placement tests.

COSTS AND FINANCIAL AID

Annual tuition $20,938. . Room and board $8,756. Required fees $700. Average book expense $1,000. **Required Forms and Deadlines:** FAFSA. Financial aid filing deadline 5/1. Priority financial aid filing date 2/15. **Notification of Awards:** Applicants will be notified of awards on a rolling basis beginning 3/1. **Types of Aid:** *Need-based scholarships/grants:* Federal Pell, SEOG, state scholarships/grants, private scholarships, the school's own gift aid. *Loans:* FFEL Subsidized Stafford, FFEL Unsubsidized Stafford, FFEL PLUS, Federal Perkins, private loans. **Student Employment:** Federal Work-Study Program available. Institutional employment available. Off-campus job opportunities are excellent. **Financial Aid Statistics:** 59% freshmen, 53% undergrads receive need-based scholarship or grant aid. 77% freshmen, 70% undergrads receive non-need-based scholarship or grant aid. 64% freshmen, 62% undergrads receive need-based self-help aid. 92% freshmen, 90% undergrads receive any aid. 78% undergrads borrow to pay for school. Average cumulative indebtedness $69,494. **Criteria for awarding institutional aid:** *Non-need-based:* Academics.

LAFAYETTE COLLEGE

118 Markle Hall, Easton, PA 18042
Phone: 610-330-5100
E-mail: admissions@lafayette.edu **CEEB Code:** 2361
Fax: 610-330-5355 **Website:** www.lafayette.edu

This private school, affiliated with the Presbyterian Church, was founded in 1826. It has a 340-acre campus.

RATINGS

Admissions Selectivity Rating: 94   **Fire Safety Rating:** 60*   **Green Rating:** 98

STUDENTS AND FACULTY

Enrollment: 2,378. **Student Body:** 47% female, 53% male, 76% out-of-state, 7% international (46 countries represented). Asian 4%, African American 5%, Caucasian 66%, Hispanic 5%.
Retention and Graduation: 95% freshmen return for sophomore year. 86% freshmen graduate within 4 years. 29% grads go on to further study within 1 year. 12% grads pursue arts and sciences degrees. 7% grads pursue law degrees. 5% grads pursue business degrees. 3% grads pursue medical degrees. **Faculty:** Student/faculty ratio 11:1. 208 full-time faculty, 100% hold PhDs, 13% are members of minority groups, 35% are women.

ACADEMICS

Degrees: Bachelor's. **Classes:** Most classes have 10–19 students. Most lab/discussion sessions have 10–19 students. **Special Study Options:** cross-registration, double major, dual enrollment, exchange student program (domestic), honors program, independent study, internships, student-designed major, study abroad, interim sessions here and abroad. Special programs offered to physically disabled students include tutors. **Career services:** Alumni services, career/job search classes, career assessment, internships.

FACILITIES

Housing: Coed dorms, special housing for disabled students, men's dorms, women's dorms, fraternity/sorority housing, apartments for single students, wellness housing, theme housing, scholars houses, Hillel House, arts houses. 100% of campus accessible to physically disabled. **Special Academic Facilities/Equipment:** Art and geological museums, center for the arts, engineering labs, INSTRON materials testing machine, electron microscopes, transform nuclear magnetic resonance spectrometer, computerized gas chromatograph/mass spectrometer. **Computers:** Students can register for classes online. Administrative functions (other than registration) can be performed online.

CAMPUS LIFE

Environment: Village. **Activities:** Choral groups, concert band, dance, drama/theater, jazz band, literary magazine, music ensembles, musical theater, pep band, radio station, student government, student newspaper, student-run film society, symphony orchestra, yearbook, campus ministries, international student organization. **Organizations:** 250 registered organizations, 14 honor societies, 7 religious organizations. 7 fraternities, 6 sororities. **Athletics (Intercollegiate):** *Men:* Baseball, basketball, cheerleading, crew/rowing, cross-country, diving, equestrian sports, fencing, football, golf, gymnastics, ice hockey, lacrosse, soccer, softball, swimming, tennis, track/field (outdoor), track/field

(indoor), volleyball, wrestling. *Women:* Basketball, cheerleading, crew/rowing, cross-country, diving, equestrian sports, fencing, field hockey, golf, gymnastics, softball, swimming, tennis, track/field (outdoor), track/field (indoor), volleyball. **On-Campus Highlights:** Skillman and Kirby Libraries, Farinon College Center, Williams Center for the Arts. **Environmental Initiatives:** In addition to signing American College and University Presidents' Climate Commitment, three undertakings summarize the college's efforts towards responsible stewardship of the environment: Waste Reduction—Recycling, including composting. Purchases of materials/goods made from recycled materials and/or virgin material that is recyclable and produced from renewable sources. Resource Conservation—Seeking to enhance our energy use portfolio's renewable energy sources (i.e., electric power suppliers with more sustainable product offerings). Installation of conservation/efficiency technology to reduce consumption of water, electric power, and natural gas. Purchases of materials/goods made from recycled materials and/or virgin material that is recyclable and produced from renewable sources. Commitment to education and information dissemination of sustainable practices. Information dissemination through College website, public discussions, and campus publications. Inclusion of "sustainability" in our curriculum offerings (i.e., Environmental Engineering's composting initiative) and as a cornerstone of orientation week for new students. New curriculum initiative at Metzgar property involving the growing of vegetables through sustainable and organic methods.

ADMISSIONS

Freshman Academic Profile: Average high school GPA 3.46. 59% in top 10% of high school class, 87% in top 25% of high school class, 99% in top 50% of high school class. 68% from public high schools. SAT Math middle 50% range 600–710. SAT Critical Reading middle 50% range 570–670. SAT Writing middle 50% range 580–680. ACT middle 50% range 26–30. Minimum paper TOEFL 550. **Basis for Candidate Selection:** *Very important factors considered include:* Academic GPA, rigor of secondary school record. *Important factors considered include:* Class rank, application essay, recommendation(s), standardized test scores, character/personal qualities, extracurricular activities, talent/ability. *Other factors considered include:* Alumni/ae relation, first generation, geographical residence, interview, level of applicant's interest, racial/ethnic status, volunteer work, work experience. **Freshman Admission Requirements:** High school diploma or equivalent is not required. *Academic units recommended:* 4 English, 3 mathematics, 2 science, (2 science labs), 2 foreign language, 5 academic electives. **Freshman Admission Statistics:** 5,635 applied, 42% admitted, 26% enrolled. **Transfer Admission Requirements:** High school transcript, college transcript(s), essay or personal statement, statement of good standing from prior institution(s). Lowest grade transferable C. **General Admission Information:** Application fee $60. Early decision application deadline 2/15. Regular application deadline 1/1. Regular notification 4/1. Nonfall registration accepted. Admission may be deferred for a maximum of 1 year. Credit and/or placement offered for CEEB Advanced Placement tests.

COSTS AND FINANCIAL AID

Annual tuition $37,520. Room and board $11,799. Required fees $295. Average book expense $1,000. **Required Forms and Deadlines:** FAFSA, CSS/Financial Aid PROFILE, noncustodial PROFILE, business/farm supplement. Financial aid filing deadline 3/15. Priority financial aid filing date 2/1. **Notification of Awards:** Applicants will be notified of awards on or about 4/1. **Types of Aid:** *Need-based scholarships/grants:* Federal Pell, SEOG, state scholarships/grants, private scholarships, the school's own gift aid. *Loans:* FFEL Subsidized Stafford, FFEL Unsubsidized Stafford, FFEL PLUS, Federal Perkins, college/university loans from institutional funds, HELP loan to parents (Lafayette Loan Program). **Student Employment:** Federal Work-Study Program available. Institutional employment available. Highest amount earned per year from on-campus jobs $1,000. Off-campus job opportunities are good. **Financial Aid Statistics:** 41% freshmen, 45% undergrads receive need-based scholarship or grant aid. 11% freshmen, 13% undergrads receive non-need-based scholarship or grant aid. 36% freshmen, 38% undergrads receive need-based self-help aid. 2% freshmen, 1% undergrads receive athletic scholarships. 47% undergrads borrow to pay for school. Average cumulative indebtedness $20,745. **Criteria for awarding institutional aid:** *Non-need-based:* Academics, athletics, leadership.

LAGRANGE COLLEGE

Office of Admission, 601 Broad Street, LaGrange, GA 30240
Phone: 706-880-8005 **Financial Aid Phone:** 888-253-9918
E-mail: lgcadmis@lagrange.edu **CEEB Code:** 5362
Fax: 706-880-8010 **Website:** www.lagrange.edu **ACT Code:** 834

This private school, affiliated with the Methodist Church, was founded in 1831. It has a 120-acre campus.

RATINGS

Admissions Selectivity Rating: 80   **Fire Safety Rating:** 60*   **Green Rating:** 79

STUDENTS AND FACULTY

Enrollment: 860. **Student Body:** 55% female, 45% male, 11% out-of-state, 2% international (10 countries represented). Asian 1%, African American 22%, Caucasian 72%, Hispanic 2%.
Retention and Graduation: 71% freshmen return for sophomore year. 39% freshmen graduate within 4 years. **Faculty:** Student/faculty ratio 10:1. 65 full-time faculty, 83% hold PhDs, 48% are women.

ACADEMICS

Degrees: Associate, bachelor's, master's. **Classes:** Most classes have 10–19 students. Most lab/discussion sessions have 10–19 students. **Majors with Highest Enrollment:** Business administration and management; organizational behavior studies; teacher education, multiple levels. **Special Study Options:** Double major, dual enrollment, independent study, internships, liberal arts/career combination, study abroad, teacher certification program. **Career services:** Alumni network, alumni services, career/job search classes, career assessment, internships.

FACILITIES

Housing: Coed dorms, men's dorms, women's dorms, fraternity/sorority housing, apartments for single students, theme housing 75% of campus accessible to physically disabled. **Special Academic Facilities/Equipment:** Lamar Dodd Art Center, Price Theater, Callaway Auditorium. **Computers:** Students can register for classes online. Administrative functions (other than registration) can be performed online.

CAMPUS LIFE

Environment: Village. **Activities:** Choral groups, drama/theater, literary magazine, music ensembles, musical theater, pep band, student government, student newspaper, symphony orchestra, yearbook, campus ministries, international student organization. **Organizations:** 49 registered organizations, 11 honor societies, 8 religious organizations. 3 fraternities, 6 sororities. **Athletics (Intercollegiate):** *Men:* Baseball, basketball, cross-country, football, golf, soccer, swimming, tennis. *Women:* Basketball, cheerleading, cross-country, soccer, softball, swimming, tennis, volleyball. **On-Campus Highlights:** Turner Student Center, Smith Hall, Academic Quadrangle, Smith Patio, Callaway Sports Facilities. **Environmental Initiatives:** Building a LEED library Conserving water Relamped buildings along with HVAC retrofitting.

ADMISSIONS

Freshman Academic Profile: Average high school GPA 3.47. 25% in top 10% of high school class, 54% in top 25% of high school class, 92% in top 50% of high school class. SAT Math middle 50% range 460–570. SAT Critical Reading middle 50% range 460–570. ACT middle 50% range 20–25. Minimum paper TOEFL 500. Minimum computer TOEFL 173. **Basis for Candidate Selection:** *Very important factors considered include:* Academic GPA, standardized test scores, character/personal qualities. *Important factors considered include:* Class rank, recommendation(s), extracurricular activities, level of applicant's interest. *Other factors considered include:* Application essay, rigor of secondary school record, alumni/ae relation, geographical residence, interview, talent/ability, volunteer work. **Freshman Admission Requirements:** High school diploma is required and GED is accepted. *Academic units required:* 4 English, 4 mathematics, 3 science, 3 social studies. *Academic units recommended:* 4 English, 4 mathematics, 3 science, 2 foreign language, 3 social studies. **Freshman Admission Statistics:** 1,342 applied, 65% admitted, 27% enrolled. **Transfer Admission Requirements:** College transcript(s), statement of good standing from prior institution(s). Minimum college GPA of 2.0 required. Lowest grade transferable 1. **General Admission Information:** Application fee $30. Notification on a rolling basis, beginning on or about 9/15. Nonfall registration accepted. Admission may be deferred for a maximum of one term. Credit and/or placement offered for CEEB Advanced Placement tests.

COSTS AND FINANCIAL AID

Annual tuition $19,900. Room and board $8,168. **Required Forms and Deadlines:** FAFSA, state aid form. Financial aid filing deadline 3/1. **Notification of Awards:** Applicants will be notified of awards on a rolling basis beginning 3/15. **Types of Aid:** *Need-based scholarships/grants:* Federal Pell, SEOG, state

scholarships/grants, private scholarships, the school's own gift aid. *Loans:* FFEL Subsidized Stafford, FFEL Unsubsidized Stafford, FFEL PLUS, Federal Perkins, state loans **Student Employment:** Federal Work-Study Program available. Institutional employment available. Off-campus job opportunities are excellent. **Financial Aid Statistics:** 75% freshmen, 75% undergrads receive need-based scholarship or grant aid. 18% freshmen, 13% undergrads receive non-need-based scholarship or grant aid. 52% freshmen, 58% undergrads receive need-based self-help aid. 75% undergrads borrow to pay for school. Average cumulative indebtedness $23,106. **Criteria for awarding institutional aid:** *Non-need-based:* Academics, art, leadership, music/drama, religious affiliation, state/district residency.

LAKE ERIE COLLEGE

391 West Washington Street, Painesville, OH 44077-3389
Phone: 440-375-7050 **Financial Aid Phone:** 440-375-7100
E-mail: admissions@lec.edu
Fax: 440-375-7005 **Website:** www.lec.edu

This is a private school.

RATINGS

Admissions Selectivity Rating: 75   **Fire Safety Rating:** 60*   **Green Rating:** 60*

STUDENTS AND FACULTY

Enrollment: 903. **Student Body:** 71% female, 29% male, 22% out-of-state, international. Asian 1%, African American 5%, Caucasian 58%, Hispanic 1%.
Retention and Graduation: 64% freshmen return for sophomore year. 32% freshmen graduate within 4 years. **Faculty:** Student/faculty ratio 12:1. 34 full-time faculty, 76% hold PhDs, 6% are members of minority groups, 50% are women.

ACADEMICS

Degrees: Bachelor's, certificate, master's, post-bachelor's certificate. **Classes:** Most classes have fewer than 10 students. **Special Study Options:** Accelerated program, cross-registration, double major, dual enrollment, honors program, independent study, internships, liberal arts/career combination, student-designed major, study abroad, teacher certification program, weekend college. **Honors programs:** LEC Scholars Program Special programs offered to physically disabled students include note-taking services, reader services, tape recorders, tutors. **Career services:** Alumni network, alumni services, career/job search classes, career assessment, internships.

FACILITIES

Housing: Coed dorms, women's dorms, apartments for single students, Theme Housing. 90% of campus accessible to physically disabled. **Computers:** Students can register for classes online. Administrative functions (other than registration) can be performed online.

CAMPUS LIFE

Activities: Choral groups, dance, drama/theater, pep band, student government, student newspaper, yearbook, international student organization. **Organizations:** 15 registered organizations, 3 honor societies, 1 sorority. **Athletics (Intercollegiate):** *Men:* Baseball, basketball, cross-country, equestrian sports, football, golf, soccer. *Women:* Basketball, cross-country, equestrian sports, soccer, softball, volleyball.

ADMISSIONS

Freshman Academic Profile: Average high school GPA 3.07. 15% in top 10% of high school class, 29% in top 25% of high school class, 59% in top 50% of high school class. 83% from public high schools. SAT Math middle 50% range 420–530. SAT Critical Reading middle 50% range 430–550. SAT Writing middle 50% range 420–550. ACT middle 50% range 17–24. Minimum paper TOEFL 550. Minimum computer TOEFL 213. **Basis for Candidate Selection:** *Very important factors considered include:* Application essay, academic GPA, recommendation(s), rigor of secondary school record, standardized test scores, character/personal qualities, level of applicant's interest. *Important factors considered include:* Class rank, interview, talent/ability. *Other factors considered include:* Alumni/ae relation, extracurricular activities, first generation, geographical residence, religious affiliation/commitment, state residency, volunteer work, work experience. **Freshman Admission Requirements:** High school diploma is required and GED is accepted. *Academic units required:* 4 English, 3 mathematics, 3 science, (2 science labs), 2 foreign language, 3 social studies. *Academic units recommended:* 4 English, 4 mathematics, 3 science, (2 science labs), 3 foreign language, 3 social studies. **Freshman Admission Statistics:** 1,130 applied, 60% admitted, 35% enrolled. **Transfer Admission Requirements:** High school transcript, college transcript(s), statement of good standing from prior institution(s). Minimum college GPA of 2.0 required. Lowest grade transferable C. **General Admission Information:** Application fee $30. Notification on a rolling basis, beginning on or about 7/1. Nonfall registration accepted. Admission may be deferred for a maximum of 1 year. Credit and/or placement offered for CEEB Advanced Placement tests.

COSTS AND FINANCIAL AID
Annual tuition $23,950. Room and board $7,650. Required fees $1,270. Average book expense $900. **Required Forms and Deadlines:** FAFSA. **Notification of Awards:** Applicants will be notified of awards on a rolling basis beginning 1/20. **Types of Aid:** *Need-based scholarships/grants:* Federal Pell, SEOG, state scholarships/grants, private scholarships, the school's own gift aid. *Loans:* FFEL Subsidized Stafford, FFEL Unsubsidized Stafford, FFEL PLUS, Federal Perkins, Payment plans. **Student Employment:** Federal Work-Study Program available. Institutional employment available. Highest amount earned per year from on-campus jobs $1,200. Off-campus job opportunities are good. **Financial Aid Statistics:** 100% freshmen, 90% undergrads receive non-need-based scholarship or grant aid. 100% freshmen, 90% undergrads receive need-based self-help aid. 100% freshmen, 99% undergrads receive any aid. Average cumulative indebtedness $17,125. **Criteria for awarding institutional aid:** *Non-need-based:* Academics, art, leadership, music/drama, state/district residency.

See page 1132.

LAKE FOREST COLLEGE

555 North Sheridan Road, Lake Forest, IL 60045
Phone: 847-735-5000 **Financial Aid Phone:** 847-725-5103
E-mail: admissions@lakeforest.edu **CEEB Code:** 1392
Fax: 847-735-6291 **Website:** www.lakeforest.edu **ACT Code:** 1054

This private school was founded in 1857. It has a 107-acre campus.

RATINGS
Admissions Selectivity Rating: 87   **Fire Safety Rating:** 60*   **Green Rating:** 60*

STUDENTS AND FACULTY
Enrollment: 1,375. **Student Body:** 59% female, 41% male, 50% out-of-state, 11% international (71 countries represented). Asian 4%, African American 5%, Caucasian 73%, Hispanic 7%.
Retention and Graduation: 83% freshmen return for sophomore year. 59% freshmen graduate within 4 years. 35% grads go on to further study within 1 year. 55% grads pursue arts and sciences degrees. 19% grads pursue law degrees. 7% grads pursue business degrees. 14% grads pursue medical degrees. **Faculty:** Student/faculty ratio 12:1. 95 full-time faculty, 98% hold PhDs, 12% are members of minority groups, 40% are women.

ACADEMICS
Degrees: Bachelor's, master's. **Classes:** Most classes have 10–19 students. Most lab/discussion sessions have 10–19 students. **Majors with Highest Enrollment:** Business/commerce; communication studies/speech communication and rhetoric; English language and literature. **Special Study Options:** Accelerated program, double major, honors program, independent study, internships, liberal arts/career combination, student-designed major, study abroad, teacher certification program. **Honors programs:** The Honors Fellows program recognizes those students admitted to Lake Forest College with exemplary high school careers and high promise for independent study and research at the College. Fellows are expected to think deeply and broadly, and to join their teachers and fellow students in serious intellectual inquiry and debate. They will produce independent work, research, Student Symposium presentations, Independent Scholar majors, distinguished senior theses, and provide intellectual leadership. The Richter Apprentice Scholars Program provides students, early in their academic careers, with the opportunity to conduct independent, individual research with Lake Forest College faculty. In the summer between their first and second year, each student in the Richter Program is employed for a ten week period and works one-on-one with a faculty member, doing independent research in a particular field. As the Richter Apprentice Scholars live and work together and participate in a weekly colloquium, they become a community of peers providing encouragement and support for each other's present and future intellectual and research endeavors. **Combined degree programs:** BA/JD, BA/MA, accelerated BA/JD with select law schools—Acc. BA/MA with Monterey Inst. Special programs offered to physically disabled students include note-taking services, reader services, tape recorders, tutors. **Career services:** Alumni network, alumni services, career/job search classes, career assessment,

internships, regional alumni. **Career services highlights include:** Internships—Due to our location near Chicago and the many partnerships Lake Forest College has developed with Chicago institutions over the years, there are a myriad of internship opportunities available to our students. Experiential learning—Again, due to our location near Chicago and the relationships with area insitutions we offer dozens of courses that have been developed to utilize the rich resources of Chicago to enhance the curriculum. Beginning with our innovative First-Year Studies program students travel downtown to Chicago with professors and take advantage of the many resources.

FACILITIES
Housing: Coed dorms, special housing for disabled students, women's dorms, apartments for single students, wellness housing 80% of campus accessible to physically disabled. **Special Academic Facilities/Equipment:** Center for Chicago Programs, art galleries, language labs, technology resource center, speech and video production room, "smart" classrooms, music/recording studio with synthesizers, public access computer labs, electron microscope, computer molecular modeling equipment, high-resolution FT-IR, NMR spectrometer, neutron howitzer, digital storage oscilloscopes, flourescence microscope. **Computers:** 90% of classrooms, 100% of dorms, 100% of libraries, 75% of dining areas, 100% of student union, 10% of common outdoor areas have wireless network access. Administrative functions (other than registration) can be performed online.

CAMPUS LIFE
Environment: Village. **Activities:** Choral groups, concert band, dance, drama/theater, jazz band, literary magazine, music ensembles, musical theater, radio station, student government, student newspaper, symphony orchestra, campus ministries, international student organization, Model UN. **Organizations:** 80 registered organizations, 12 honor societies, 6 religious organizations. 2 fraternities, 4 sororities. **Athletics (Intercollegiate):** *Men:* Basketball, cross-country, diving, football, handball, ice hockey, soccer, swimming, tennis. *Women:* Basketball, cross-country, diving, handball, ice hockey, soccer, softball, swimming, tennis, volleyball. **On-Campus Highlights:** Donnelley and Lee Library, Mohr Student Center, Sports Center, Center for Chicago Programs, Career Advancement Center.

ADMISSIONS
Freshman Academic Profile: Average high school GPA 3.48. 38% in top 10% of high school class, 62% in top 25% of high school class, 92% in top 50% of high school class. 64% from public high schools. SAT Math middle 50% range 530–640. SAT Critical Reading middle 50% range 520–630. SAT Writing middle 50% range 530–640. ACT middle 50% range 23–28. Minimum paper TOEFL 550. Minimum computer TOEFL 220. **Basis for Candidate Selection:** *Very important factors considered include:* Academic GPA, recommendation(s), rigor of secondary school record, interview. *Important factors considered include:* Application essay, character/personal qualities, extracurricular activities, level of applicant's interest, talent/ability. *Other factors considered include:* Class rank, standardized test scores, alumni/ae relation, first generation, geographical residence, volunteer work, work experience. **Freshman Admission Requirements:** High school diploma is required and GED is accepted. *Academic units required:* 4 English, 3 mathematics, 3 science, (3 science labs), 2 foreign language, 2 social studies, 2 history, 3 academic electives. *Academic units recommended:* 4 English, 4 mathematics, 4 science, (4 science labs), 4 foreign language, 2 social studies, 2 history, 3 academic electives, 1 honors or AP course. **Freshman Admission Statistics:** 2,026 applied, 69% admitted, 25% enrolled. **Transfer Admission Requirements:** High school transcript, college transcript(s), essay or personal statement, minimum college GPA of 2.5 required. Lowest grade transferable C–. **General Admission Information:** Application fee $40. Early decision application deadline 12/1. Regular notification 3/20. Nonfall registration accepted. Admission may be deferred for a maximum of 1 year. Credit and/or placement offered for CEEB Advanced Placement tests.

COSTS AND FINANCIAL AID
Annual tuition $33,576. Room and board $8,006. Required fees $630. Average book expense $1,000. **Required Forms and Deadlines:** FAFSA, institution's own financial aid form, federal income tax return. Financial aid filing deadline 5/1. Priority financial aid filing date 2/15. **Notification of Awards:** Applicants will be notified of awards on a rolling basis beginning 2/1. **Types of Aid:** *Need-based scholarships/grants:* Federal Pell, SEOG, state scholarships/grants, private scholarships, the school's own gift aid. *Loans:* FFEL Subsidized Stafford, FFEL Unsubsidized Stafford, FFEL PLUS, Federal Perkins, private loans. **Student Employment:** Federal Work-Study Program available. Institutional employment available. Off-campus job opportunities are good. **Financial Aid Statistics:** 79% freshmen, 76% undergrads receive need-based scholarship or grant aid. 65% freshmen, 44% undergrads receive need-based self-help aid. 94% freshmen, 94% undergrads receive any aid. 74% undergrads borrow to pay for school. Average cumulative indebtedness $29,279. **Criteria for awarding institutional aid:** *Non-need-based:* Academics, alumni affiliation, art, leadership, music/drama, state/district residency.

See page 1134.

LAKE REGION STATE COLLEGE

1801 College Drive N, Devils Lake, ND 58301-1598
Phone: 701-662-1514 **Financial Aid Phone:** 701-662-1516
E-mail: lrsc.admissions@lrsc.edu
Fax: 701-662-1581 **Website:** www.lrsc.edu **ACT Code:** 3198

This public school was founded in 1941. It has a 120-acre campus.

RATINGS
Admissions Selectivity Rating: 60*   **Fire Safety Rating:** 93   **Green Rating:** 60*

STUDENTS AND FACULTY
Enrollment: 696. **Student Body:** 53% female, 47% male, 12% out-of-state, 3% international (14 countries represented). Asian 2%, African American 4%, Caucasian 82%, Hispanic 2%, Native American 5%.
Faculty: Student/faculty ratio 12.8:1. 35 full-time faculty, 14% hold PhDs, 3% are members of minority groups, 51% are women.

ACADEMICS
Degrees: Associate, certificate, diploma, terminal associate, transfer associate. **Classes:** Most classes have fewer than 10 students. **Majors with Highest Enrollment:** Business administration and management; criminal justice/police science; liberal arts and sciences/liberal studies. **Special Study Options:** Cooperative education program, cross-registration, distance learning, dual enrollment, English as a Second Language (ESL), internships, liberal arts/career combination Special programs offered to physically disabled students include note-taking services, reader services, tape recorders, tutors. **Career services:** Career/job search classes, internships.

FACILITIES
Housing: Special housing for disabled students, men's dorms, women's dorms, apartments for married students, apartments for single students, coed dorms for adult students. 100% of campus accessible to physically disabled. **Special Academic Facilities/Equipment:** Paul Hoghaug Library and Law Library **Computers:** 100% of classrooms, 100% of dorms, 100% of libraries, 100% of dining areas, 100% of student union, have wireless network access. Students can register for classes online. Administrative functions (other than registration) can be performed online.

CAMPUS LIFE
Environment: Village. **Activities:** Drama/theater, literary magazine, musical theater, student government, symphony orchestra. **Organizations:** 12 registered organizations, 1 religious organizations. **Athletics (Intercollegiate):** *Men:* Basketball. *Women:* Basketball. **On-Campus Highlights:** Student union, computer lab, recreational area, library, gymnasium.

ADMISSIONS
Freshman Academic Profile: 98% from public high schools. ACT middle 50% range 18–25. Minimum paper TOEFL 510. Minimum computer TOEFL 185. Minimum web-based TOEFL 65. **Basis for Candidate Selection: Freshman Admission Requirements:** High school diploma is required and GED is accepted. *Academic units recommended:* 4 English, 3 mathematics, 3 science, (2 science labs), 2 foreign language, 3 social studies. **Freshman Admission Statistics:** 233 applied, 99% admitted, 95% enrolled. **Transfer Admission Requirements:** High school transcript, college transcript(s), statement of good standing from prior institution(s). Minimum college GPA of 2.0 required. Lowest grade transferable D. **General Admission Information:** Application fee $35. Nonfall registration accepted. Admission may be deferred for a maximum of one semester. Credit offered for CEEB Advanced Placement tests.

COSTS AND FINANCIAL AID
Annual in-state tuition $3,065. Annual out-of-state tuition $3,065. Room and board $5,230. Required fees $843. Average book expense $900. **Required Forms and Deadlines:** FAFSA. Priority financial aid filing date 3/15. **Notification of Awards:** Applicants will be notified of awards on a rolling basis beginning 5/15. **Types of Aid:** *Need-based scholarships/grants:* Federal Pell, SEOG, state scholarships/grants, private scholarships, the school's own gift aid, Academic Competitiveness Grant. *Loans:* FFEL Subsidized Stafford, FFEL Unsubsidized Stafford, FFEL PLUS, Federal Perkins, state loans **Student Employment:** Federal Work-Study Program available. Institutional employment available. Off-campus job opportunities are good. **Financial Aid Statistics:** 58% freshmen, 53% undergrads receive need-based scholarship or grant aid. 1% freshmen, 54% freshmen, 54% undergrads receive need-based self-help aid. 6% freshmen, 6% undergrads receive athletic scholarships. 80% undergrads receive any aid. 71.05% undergrads borrow to pay for school. Average cumulative indebtedness $9,392. **Criteria for awarding institutional aid:** *Non-need-based:* Academics, athletics, leadership, minority status, music/drama.

LAKE SUPERIOR STATE UNIVERSITY

650 W. Easterday Avenue, Sault Ste. Marie, MI 49783-1699
Phone: 906-635-2231 **Financial Aid Phone:** 906-635-2678
E-mail: admissions@lssu.edu **CEEB Code:** 1421
Fax: 906-635-6669 **Website:** **ACT Code:** 2031

This public school was founded in 1946. It has a 115-acre campus.

RATINGS
Admissions Selectivity Rating: 69   **Fire Safety Rating:** 60*   **Green Rating:** 76

STUDENTS AND FACULTY
Enrollment: 2,753. **Student Body:** 51% female, 49% male, 4% out-of-state, 11% international. Asian 1%, African American 1%, Caucasian 78%, Hispanic 1%, Native American 9%.
Retention and Graduation: 61% freshmen return for sophomore year. 18% freshmen graduate within 4 years. **Faculty:** Student/faculty ratio 17:1. 112 full-time faculty, 65% hold PhDs, 5% are members of minority groups, 42% are women.

ACADEMICS
Degrees: Associate, bachelor's, certificate, master's. **Classes:** Most classes have 20–29 students. Most lab/discussion sessions have 10–19 students. **Special Study Options:** Cooperative education program, cross-registration, distance learning, double major, dual enrollment, honors program, independent study, internships, student-designed major, teacher certification program, weekend college. Special programs offered to physically disabled students include note-taking services, reader services, tape recorders, tutors.

FACILITIES
Housing: Coed dorms, men's dorms, women's dorms, fraternity/sorority housing, apartments for married students, apartments for single students. 90% of campus accessible to physically disabled. **Special Academic Facilities/Equipment:** Natural science, Michigan history, and Great Lakes shipping museums, planetarium, industrial robots, atomic absorption/flame emission spectrophotometer. **Computers:** Students can register for classes online.

CAMPUS LIFE
Environment: City. **Activities:** Choral groups, concert band, dance, drama/theater, jazz band, literary magazine, music ensembles, pep band, radio station, student government, student newspaper, symphony orchestra **Organizations:** 60 registered organizations, 4 fraternities, 4 sororities. **Athletics (Intercollegiate):** *Men:* Basketball, cross-country, ice hockey, tennis, track/field (outdoor), track/field (indoor). *Women:* Basketball, cross-country, softball, tennis, track/field (outdoor), track/field (indoor), volleyball.

ADMISSIONS
Freshman Academic Profile: Average high school GPA 3.01. 9% in top 10% of high school class, 28% in top 25% of high school class, 60% in top 50% of high school class. ACT middle 50% range 18–23. Minimum paper TOEFL 550. Minimum computer TOEFL 213. **Basis for Candidate Selection:** *Very important factors considered include:* Academic GPA, rigor of secondary school record, standardized test scores. *Other factors considered include:* Class rank, recommendation(s), geographical residence, interview. **Freshman Admission Requirements:** High school diploma is required and GED is accepted. *Academic units recommended:* 4 English, 3 mathematics, 3 science, (3 science labs), 2 foreign language, 2 social studies, 1 history. **Freshman Admission Statistics:** 1,566 applied, 85% admitted, 41% enrolled. **Transfer Admission Requirements:** College transcript(s), minimum college GPA of 2.0 required. Lowest grade transferable C–. **General Admission Information:** Application fee $20. Regular application deadline 8/15. Notification on a rolling basis, beginning on or about 9/15. Nonfall registration accepted. Admission may be deferred for a maximum of 1 Year. Credit offered for CEEB Advanced Placement tests.

COSTS AND FINANCIAL AID
Annual in-state tuition $5,988. Annual out-of-state tuition $11,976. Room and board $6,536. Required fees $318. Average book expense $750. **Required Forms and Deadlines:** FAFSA. Priority financial aid filing date 2/21. **Notification of Awards:** Applicants will be notified of awards on a rolling basis beginning 11/1. **Types of Aid:** *Need-based scholarships/grants:* Federal Pell, SEOG, state scholarships/grants, private scholarships, the school's own gift aid, Federal Nursing Scholarships. third party payments. *Loans:* Direct Subsidized Stafford, Direct Unsubsidized Stafford, Direct PLUS, Federal Perkins, Federal Nursing, state loans. **Student Employment:** Highest amount earned per year from on-campus jobs $2,400. Off-campus job opportunities are good. **Financial Aid Statistics:** 44% freshmen, 39% undergrads receive need-based scholarship or grant aid. 72% freshmen, 50% undergrads receive non-need-based scholarship or grant aid. 70% freshmen, 64% undergrads receive need-based self-help aid. 5% freshmen, 6% undergrads receive athletic scholarships. 83% undergrads receive any aid. 63% undergrads borrow to pay for school. Average cumulative indebtedness $17,458.

LAKEHEAD UNIVERSITY

955 Oliver Road, Thunder Bay, ON P7B 5E1 Canada
Phone: 807-343-8500 **Financial Aid Phone:** 807-343-8206
E-mail: admissions@lakeheadu.ca
Fax: 807-766-7209 **Website:** www.lakeheadu.ca

This public school was founded in 1965. It has a 288-acre campus.

RATINGS
Admissions Selectivity Rating: 60*   **Fire Safety Rating:** 60*   **Green Rating:** 60*

STUDENTS AND FACULTY

Retention and Graduation: 85% freshmen return for sophomore year. **Faculty:** Student/faculty ratio 24:1.

ACADEMICS
Degrees: Bachelor's, certificate, diploma, first professional, master's. **Classes:** Most classes have 30–39 students. **Majors with Highest Enrollment:** Business administration and management; engineering; forestry.

FACILITIES
Housing: Coed dorms, special housing for disabled students, apartments for single students, wellness housing. **Computers:** Students can register for classes online.

CAMPUS LIFE
Environment: City. **Activities:** Choral groups, concert band, dance, drama/theater, jazz band, literary magazine, music ensembles, musical theater, radio station, student government, student newspaper, campus ministries, international student organization, Model UN. **Organizations: Athletics (Intercollegiate):** *Men:* Basketball, cross-country, ice hockey, skiing (nordic & cross-country), track/field (outdoor), track/field (indoor), wrestling. *Women:* Basketball, cross-country, skiing (nordic & cross-country), track/field (outdoor), track/field (indoor), volleyball, wrestling.

ADMISSIONS
Freshman Admission Requirements: High school diploma is required and GED is accepted. **General Admission Information:** Application fee $105. Regular application deadline 9/24. Nonfall registration accepted. Admission may be deferred for a maximum of 1 year.

COSTS AND FINANCIAL AID
Annual in-state tuition $4,670. Annual out-of-state tuition $4,670. Room and board $3,098. Required fees $825.

LAMAR UNIVERSITY

P.O. Box 10009, Beaumont, TX 77710
Phone: 409-880-8888
E-mail: admissions@hal.lamar.edu **CEEB Code:** 6360
Fax: 409-880-8463 **Website:** www.lamar.edu **ACT Code:** 4114

This public school was founded in 1923. It has a 200-acre campus.

RATINGS
Admissions Selectivity Rating: 60*   **Fire Safety Rating:** 60*   **Green Rating:** 60*

STUDENTS AND FACULTY
Enrollment: 9,057. **Student Body:** 55% female, 45% male, 1% out-of-state, 1% international. Asian 3%, African American 22%, Caucasian 74%, Hispanic 5%, Native American 1%.
Faculty:

ACADEMICS
Degrees: Bachelor's, master's. **Special Study Options:** Cooperative education program, distance learning, double major, dual enrollment, English as a Second Language (ESL), honors program, internships, study abroad, teacher certification program, Texas Academy for Leadership in the Humanities, a two-year residential, early admission program for gifted high school students. Students are selected during the sophomore year of high school and enter the University at the end of their junior year. **Combined degree programs:** 3-1 program medicine/dentistry, 3-2 pharmacy program. Special programs offered to physically disabled students include note-taking services, reader services, tape recorders, tutors. **Career services:** Alumni services, career/job search classes, career assessment.

FACILITIES
Housing: Coed dorms, men's dorms, women's dorms, fraternity/sorority housing, apartments for single students. **Special Academic Facilities/Equipment:** Museum.

CAMPUS LIFE
Environment: Village. **Activities:** student government, student newspaper. **Organizations:** 145 registered organizations, 11 fraternities, 8 sororities. **Athletics (Intercollegiate):** *Men:* Baseball, basketball, cross-country, golf, tennis, track/field (outdoor). *Women:* Basketball, cross-country, golf, tennis, track/field (outdoor), volleyball.

ADMISSIONS
Freshman Academic Profile: 10% in top 10% of high school class, 27% in top 25% of high school class, 90% in top 50% of high school class. 96% from public high schools. Minimum paper TOEFL 500. **Basis for Candidate Selection: Freshman Admission Requirements:** High school diploma is required and GED is accepted. High school diploma is required and GED is not accepted. *Academic units recommended:* 4 English, 3 mathematics, 2 science, 2 social studies, 2 academic electives. **Freshman Admission Statistics:** Minimum college GPA of 2.0 required. Lowest grade transferable D. **General Admission Information:** Regular application deadline 8/1. Nonfall registration accepted. Credit and/or placement offered for CEEB Advanced Placement tests.

COSTS AND FINANCIAL AID
Annual in-state tuition $864. Annual out-of-state tuition $5,976. Room and board $3,040. Required fees $840. **Required Forms and Deadlines:** FAFSA, institution's own financial aid form, state aid form. **Types of Aid:** *Need-based scholarships/grants: Loans:* FFEL Subsidized Stafford, FFEL PLUS. **Student Employment:** Federal Work-Study Program available. Institutional employment available. Highest amount earned per year from on-campus jobs $1,200. Off-campus job opportunities are good.

LAMBUTH UNIVERSITY

705 Lambuth Boulevard, Jackson, TN 38301-5296
Phone: 731-425-3223 **Financial Aid Phone:** 731-425-3332
E-mail: admit@lambuth.edu **CEEB Code:** 1394
Fax: 731-425-3496 **Website:** www.lambuth.edu **ACT Code:** 3974

This private school, affiliated with the Methodist Church, was founded in 1843. It has a 50-acre campus.

RATINGS
Admissions Selectivity Rating: 86   **Fire Safety Rating:** 74   **Green Rating:** 60*

STUDENTS AND FACULTY
Enrollment: 765. **Student Body:** 47% female, 53% male, 21% out-of-state (9 countries represented).
Retention and Graduation: 60% freshmen return for sophomore year. 29% freshmen graduate within 4 years. 20% grads go on to further study within 1 year. 5% grads pursue arts and sciences degrees. 5% grads pursue law degrees. 5% grads pursue business degrees. 5% grads pursue medical degrees. **Faculty:** Student/faculty ratio 11.5:1. 51 full-time faculty, 78% hold PhDs, 2% are members of minority groups, 41% are women.

ACADEMICS
Degrees: Bachelor's. **Classes:** Most classes have fewer than 10 students. Most lab/discussion sessions have 20–29 students. **Majors with Highest Enrollment:** Business/commerce; health and P.E.; psychology. **Special Study Options:** Cross-registration, double major, honors program, independent study, internships, student-designed major, study abroad, teacher certification program, Washington Semester. Tennessee Legislative Internship. Interdisciplinary courses. Lambuth in London. **Honors programs:** University Honors is a 3-semester sequence of courses designed to offer more in-depth study of classic literature and themes. Various topics are considered including art, psychology, ecology, history, ethics, politics, science, sociology, business, religion, and literature. Honors study is available in most disciplines and consists of an 8-hour sequence of research over the last 3 semesters of study in a particular discipline. Special programs offered to physically disabled students include tape recorders, tutors. **Career services:** Alumni network, alumni services, career/job search classes, career assessment, internships, regional alumni. **Career services highlights include:** Excellent internships for business, communications, psychology, education and social science majors.

FACILITIES
Housing: Coed dorms, special housing for disabled students, men's dorms, women's dorms, fraternity/sorority housing, apartments for single students 80%

of campus accessible to physically disabled. **Special Academic Facilities/ Equipment:** Academic Support Center, Interior Design lab, M.D. Anderson Planetarium, Oxley Biological Field Station. **Computers:** 40% of classrooms, 10% of dorms, 100% of libraries, 100% of dining areas, 100% of student union, 50% of common outdoor areas have wireless network access.

CAMPUS LIFE

Environment: City. **Activities:** Choral groups, concert band, dance, drama/theater, jazz band, literary magazine, music ensembles, musical theater, student government, student newspaper, yearbook, campus ministries, international student organization, Model UN. **Organizations:** 41 registered organizations, 6 honor societies, 3 religious organizations. 3 fraternities, 3 sororities. **Athletics (Intercollegiate):** *Men:* Baseball, basketball, football, golf, soccer, tennis. *Women:* Basketball, golf, soccer, softball, tennis. **On-Campus Highlights:** Eagle's Nest Bistro, E/MI Studio, The Quadrangle, Eickoff Plaza, M.D. Anderson Planetarium, Oxley Square (apartment-style dorms), computer center, Hamilton Performing Arts Center, R. E. Womack Memorial Chapel, Greek houses, wellness center, athletic center/Olympic pool.

ADMISSIONS

Freshman Academic Profile: Average high school GPA 3.3. 21% in top 10% of high school class, 42% in top 25% of high school class, 71% in top 50% of high school class. 85% from public high schools. SAT Math middle 50% range 460–570. SAT Critical Reading middle 50% range 440–570. ACT middle 50% range 20–25. Minimum paper TOEFL 425. Minimum computer TOEFL 115. **Basis for Candidate Selection:** *Very important factors considered include:* Academic GPA, rigor of secondary school record, standardized test scores. *Important factors considered include:* Application essay, recommendation(s), extracurricular activities, interview, level of applicant's interest. *Other factors considered include:* Class rank, alumni/ae relation, first generation, geographical residence, religious affiliation/commitment, state residency, talent/ability, volunteer work, work experience. **Freshman Admission Requirements:** High school diploma is required and GED is accepted. *Academic units recommended:* 4 English, 3 mathematics, 3 science, 1 foreign language, 2 social studies, 1 history. **Freshman Admission Statistics:** 679 applied, 62% admitted, 49% enrolled. **Transfer Admission Requirements:** College transcript(s), essay or personal statement, statement of good standing from prior institution(s). Minimum college GPA of 2.0 required. Lowest grade transferable D. **General Admission Information:** Application fee $25. Notification on a rolling basis, beginning on or about 10/1. Nonfall registration accepted. Admission may be deferred for a maximum of 1 year. Credit and/or placement offered for CEEB Advanced Placement tests.

COSTS AND FINANCIAL AID

Annual tuition $17,000. Room and board $7,160. Required fees $400. Average book expense $1,200. **Required Forms and Deadlines:** FAFSA, institution's own financial aid form, admission application. Priority financial aid filing date 2/15. **Notification of Awards:** Applicants will be notified of awards on a rolling basis beginning 2/15. **Types of Aid:** *Need-based scholarships/grants:* Federal Pell, SEOG, state scholarships/grants, private scholarships, the school's own gift aid, Tennessee Hope Lottery Programs. *Loans:* FFEL Subsidized Stafford, FFEL Unsubsidized Stafford, FFEL PLUS, Federal Perkins. **Student Employment:** Federal Work-Study Program available. Institutional employment available. Highest amount earned per year from on-campus jobs $1,404. Off-campus job opportunities are excellent. **Financial Aid Statistics:** 80% freshmen, 80% undergrads receive need-based scholarship or grant aid. 19% freshmen, 18% undergrads receive non-need-based scholarship or grant aid. 53% freshmen, 56% undergrads receive need-based self-help aid. 9% freshmen, 9% undergrads receive athletic scholarships. 99% freshmen, 99% undergrads receive any aid. 64% undergrads borrow to pay for school. Average cumulative indebtedness $19,950. **Criteria for awarding institutional aid:** *Non-need-based:* Academics, alumni affiliation, art, athletics, job skills, leadership, music/drama, religious affiliation.

LANCASTER BIBLE COLLEGE & GRADUATE SCHOOL

901 Eden Rd, Lancaster, PA 17601-5036
Phone: 717-569-7071 **Financial Aid Phone:** 717-560-8254
E-mail: admissions@lbc.edu **CEEB Code:** 2388
Fax: 717-560-8213 **Website:** www.lbc.edu **ACT Code:** 3707

This private school was founded in 1933. It has a 100-acre campus.

RATINGS

Admissions Selectivity Rating: 77   **Fire Safety Rating:** 60*   **Green Rating:** 60*

STUDENTS AND FACULTY

Enrollment: 702. **Student Body:** 47% female, 53% male, 26% out-of-state, 1% international. Asian 1%, African American 3%, Caucasian 71%, Hispanic 1%.
Faculty: Student/faculty ratio 10:1. 48 full-time faculty, 52% hold PhDs, 2% are members of minority groups, 25% are women.

ACADEMICS

Degrees: Associate, bachelor's, certificate, master's, post-bachelor's certificate. **Classes:** Most classes have fewer than 10 students. Most lab/discussion sessions have 10–19 students. **Majors with Highest Enrollment:** Bible/biblical studies; elementary education and teaching; theology and religious vocations, other. **Special Study Options:** Accelerated program, double major, independent study, internships, study abroad, teacher certification program Special programs offered to physically disabled students include note-taking services, reader services, tape recorders, tutors. **Career services:** Alumni network, internships.

FACILITIES

Housing: Men's dorms, women's dorms. 80% of campus accessible to physically disabled.

CAMPUS LIFE

Environment: Village. **Activities:** Choral groups, concert band, drama/theater, music ensembles, musical theater, student government, student newspaper, yearbook. **Organizations:** 20 registered organizations. **Athletics (Intercollegiate):** *Men:* Baseball, basketball, cheerleading, soccer, volleyball. *Women:* Basketball, cheerleading, lacrosse, soccer, volleyball.

ADMISSIONS

Freshman Academic Profile: 60% from public high schools. Minimum paper TOEFL 550. Minimum computer TOEFL 213. **Basis for Candidate Selection:** *Very important factors considered include:* Application essay, recommendation(s), rigor of secondary school record, standardized test scores, character/personal qualities, religious affiliation/commitment. *Important factors considered include:* Extracurricular activities. *Other factors considered include:* Interview, talent/ability, volunteer work. **Freshman Admission Requirements:** High school diploma is required and GED is accepted. **Freshman Admission Statistics:** 314 applied, 97% admitted, 44% enrolled. **Transfer Admission Requirements:** High school transcript, college transcript(s), essay or personal statement, standardized test scores, statement of good standing from prior institution(s). Minimum college GPA of 2.0 required. Lowest grade transferable C. **General Admission Information:** Application fee $25. Notification on a rolling basis, beginning on or about 9/1. Nonfall registration accepted. Admission may be deferred for a maximum of 1 year.

COSTS AND FINANCIAL AID

Annual tuition $15,240. Room and board $6,780. Required fees $600. Average book expense $1,000. **Required Forms and Deadlines:** FAFSA, state aid form. Priority financial aid filing date 5/1. **Notification of Awards:** Applicants will be notified of awards on a rolling basis beginning 3/1. **Types of Aid:** *Need-based scholarships/grants:* Federal Pell, SEOG, state scholarships/grants, private scholarships, the school's own gift aid, Office of Vocational Rehabilitation Blindness and Visual Services Awards. *Loans:* FFEL Subsidized Stafford, FFEL Unsubsidized Stafford, FFEL PLUS, Federal Perkins, alternative loans. **Student Employment:** Federal Work-Study Program available. Institutional employment available. Highest amount earned per year from on-campus jobs $1,400. Off-campus job opportunities are good. **Financial Aid Statistics:** 77% freshmen, 74% undergrads receive need-based scholarship or grant aid. 75% freshmen, 62% undergrads receive non-need-based scholarship or grant aid. 64% freshmen, 70% undergrads receive need-based self-help aid. 27% undergrads borrow to pay for school. Average cumulative indebtedness $19,579. **Criteria for awarding institutional aid:** *Non-need-based:* Academics, alumni affiliation, leadership, music/drama.

LANDER UNIVERSITY

320 Stanley Avenue, Greenwood, SC 29649
Phone: 864-388-8307 **Financial Aid Phone:** 864-388-8340
E-mail: admissions@lander.edu **CEEB Code:** 5363
Fax: 864-388-8125 **Website:** www.lander.edu **ACT Code:** 3860

This public school was founded in 1872. It has a 100-acre campus.

RATINGS

Admissions Selectivity Rating: 70   **Fire Safety Rating:** 60*   **Green Rating:** 60*

STUDENTS AND FACULTY

Enrollment: 2,655. **Student Body:** 67% female, 33% male, 3% out-of-state, 2% international (21 countries represented). Asian 1%, African American 22%, Caucasian 74%, Hispanic 1%.
Retention and Graduation: 65% freshmen return for sophomore year. 28% freshmen graduate within 4 years. **Faculty:** Student/faculty ratio 20:1. 117 full-time faculty, 72% hold PhDs, 8% are members of minority groups, 44% are women.

ACADEMICS

Degrees: Bachelor's, certificate, master's. **Classes:** Most classes have 20–29 students. **Majors with Highest Enrollment:** Business/commerce; elementary education and teaching; nursing/registered nurse (RN, ASN, BSN, MSN). **Special Study Options:** Cooperative education program, distance learning, double major, dual enrollment, honors program, independent study, internships, liberal arts/career combination, student-designed major, study abroad, teacher certification program, nursing (RN to BSN completion) program courses now offered on the web. MBA from Clemson U. offered on campus. MEd counseling/school administration from Clemson U. offered on campus. MEd elementary education. MAT Master of Arts in Teaching. Dual degree in engineering offered in conjunction with Clemson University. **Combined degree programs:** BA/MEng. Special programs offered to physically disabled students include note-taking services, reader services, tape recorders, tutors. **Career services:** Internships.

FACILITIES

Housing: Coed dorms, women's dorms, apartments for single students. 100% of campus accessible to physically disabled. **Special Academic Facilities/ Equipment:** Art gallery, continuing education center, media center, electronic piano instruction facility, amphitheatre. **Computers:** Students can register for classes online. Administrative functions (other than registration) can be performed online.

CAMPUS LIFE

Environment: Village. **Activities:** Choral groups, concert band, dance, drama/ theater, jazz band, literary magazine, music ensembles, student government, student newspaper. **Organizations:** 65 registered organizations, 6 honor societies, 7 religious organizations. 6 fraternities, 6 sororities. **Athletics (Intercollegiate):** *Men:* Baseball, basketball, golf, soccer, tennis. *Women:* Basketball, cross-country, soccer, softball, tennis, volleyball. **On-Campus Highlights:** Student center, Grill Works, cafeteria, student atrium, library.

ADMISSIONS

Freshman Academic Profile: Average high school GPA 3.4. 8% in top 10% of high school class, 30% in top 25% of high school class, 68% in top 50% of high school class. SAT Math middle 50% range 440–540. SAT Critical Reading middle 50% range 430–530. ACT middle 50% range 17–22. Minimum paper TOEFL 550. Minimum computer TOEFL 213. **Basis for Candidate Selection:** *Very important factors considered include:* Class rank, rigor of secondary school record, standardized test scores. *Other factors considered include:* Application essay, recommendation(s), alumni/ae relation, character/ personal qualities, extracurricular activities, interview, talent/ability, volunteer work, work experience. **Freshman Admission Requirements:** High school diploma is required and GED is accepted. *Academic units required:* 4 English, 3 mathematics, 3 science, (3 science labs), 2 foreign language, 2 social studies, 1 history, 4 academic electives, 1 P.E./ROTC. *Academic units recommended:* 4 English, 3 mathematics, 3 science, (3 science labs), 2 foreign language, 2 social studies, 1 history, 4 academic electives, 1 P.E./ROTC. **Freshman Admission Statistics:** 1,750 applied, 85% admitted, 45% enrolled. **Transfer Admission Requirements:** College transcript(s), statement of good standing from prior institution(s). Minimum college GPA of 2.0 required. Lowest grade transferable C. **General Admission Information:** Application fee $35. Regular application deadline 8/5. Nonfall registration accepted. Admission may be deferred for a maximum of Individual. Credit and/or placement offered for CEEB Advanced Placement tests.

COSTS AND FINANCIAL AID

Annual in-state tuition $7,152. Annual out-of-state tuition $12,024. Room and board $5,176. Required fees $150. Average book expense $840. **Required Forms and Deadlines:** FAFSA. Priority financial aid filing date 4/15. **Notification of Awards:** Applicants will be notified of awards on or about 6/1. **Types of Aid:** *Need-based scholarships/grants:* Federal Pell, SEOG, state scholarships/grants, private scholarships, the school's own gift aid, Federal Nursing Scholarships. *Loans:* FFEL Subsidized Stafford, FFEL Unsubsidized Stafford, FFEL PLUS, Federal Perkins, state loans. **Student Employment:** Federal Work-Study Program available. Highest amount earned per year from on-campus jobs $4,500. Off-campus job opportunities are good. **Financial Aid Statistics:** 29% freshmen, 32% undergrads receive need-based scholarship or grant aid. 24% freshmen, 27% undergrads receive non-need-based scholarship or grant aid. 36% freshmen, 40% undergrads receive need-based self-help aid. 80% freshmen, 80% undergrads receive any aid. 49% undergrads borrow to pay

for school. Average cumulative indebtedness $13,500. **Criteria for awarding institutional aid:** *Non-need-based:* Academics, art, athletics, leadership, music/drama, state/district residency.

LANDMARK COLLEGE

P.O. Box 820, Putney, VT 05346-0820
Phone: 802-387-6718 **Financial Aid Phone:** 802-387-6736
E-mail: admissions@landmark.edu
Fax: 802-387-6868 **Website:** www.landmark.edu **ACT Code:** 4317

This private school was founded in 1984. It has a 128-acre campus.

RATINGS

Admissions Selectivity Rating: 60*   **Fire Safety Rating:** 68   **Green Rating:** 60*

STUDENTS AND FACULTY

Enrollment: 462. **Student Body:** 28% female, 72% male, 95% out-of-state, 5% international (14 countries represented). Asian 2%, African American 5%, Caucasian 65%, Hispanic 6%.
Retention and Graduation: 95% grads go on to further study within 1 year. **Faculty:** Student/faculty ratio 5:1. 93 full-time faculty, 12% hold PhDs, 1% are members of minority groups, 62% are women.

ACADEMICS

Degrees: Associate, terminal associate, transfer associate. **Classes:** Most classes have 10–19 students. **Special Study Options:** Internships, study abroad.

FACILITIES

Housing: Coed dorms, special housing for disabled students, wellness housing. 65% of campus accessible to physically disabled.

CAMPUS LIFE

Environment: Rural. **Activities:** Choral groups, dance, drama/theater, jazz band, literary magazine, music ensembles, radio station, student government.

ADMISSIONS

Freshman Academic Profile: 70% from public high schools. Minimum paper TOEFL 200. Minimum computer TOEFL 40. **Basis for Candidate Selection:** *Very important factors considered include:* Recommendation(s), interview. *Important factors considered include:* Character/personal qualities, level of applicant's interest. *Other factors considered include:* Class rank, application essay, academic GPA, rigor of secondary school record, standardized test scores, extracurricular activities, talent/ability. **Freshman Admission Requirements:** High school diploma is required and GED is accepted. *Academic units recommended:* 4 English, 3 mathematics, 3 science, 1 foreign language, 3 social studies, 3 history, 1 visual/performing arts, 1 academic electives. **Freshman Admission Statistics:** 242 applied, 79% admitted, 69% enrolled. **Transfer Admission Requirements:** High school transcript, college transcript(s), essay or personal statement, interview, Lowest grade transferable C–. **General Admission Information:** Application fee $75. Notification on a rolling basis, beginning on or about 12/1. Nonfall registration accepted. Admission may be deferred for a maximum of 1 calendar year.

COSTS AND FINANCIAL AID

Annual tuition $45,300. Room and board $8,100. Required fees $500. Average book expense $1,200. **Required Forms and Deadlines:** FAFSA, federal tax return—parent and student. Priority financial aid filing date 3/15. **Notification of Awards:** Applicants will be notified of awards on a rolling basis beginning 4/15. **Types of Aid:** *Need-based scholarships/grants:* Federal Pell, SEOG, state scholarships/grants, private scholarships, the school's own gift aid, Vocational Rehabilitation Grants. *Loans:* FFEL Subsidized Stafford, FFEL Unsubsidized Stafford, FFEL PLUS. **Student Employment:** Federal Work-Study Program available. Institutional employment available. Highest amount earned per year from on-campus jobs $1,500. Off-campus job opportunities are good. **Financial Aid Statistics:** 67% undergrads receive need-based scholarship or grant aid. 1% undergrads receive non-need-based scholarship or grant aid. 68% undergrads receive need-based self-help aid. 35% freshmen, 42% undergrads receive any aid. 75% undergrads borrow to pay for school. Average cumulative indebtedness $4,372. **Criteria for awarding institutional aid:** *Non-need-based:* Academics, art, athletics, leadership, minority status, music/drama.

See page 1136.

LANE COLLEGE

545 Lane Avenue, Jackson, TN 38301
Phone: 731-426-7532 **Financial Aid Phone:** 731-426-7536
E-mail: admissions@lanecollege.edu
Fax: 731-426-7559 **Website:** www.lanecollege.edu **ACT Code:** 3976

This private school, affiliated with the Methodist Church, was founded in 1882. It has a 25-acre campus.

RATINGS
Admissions Selectivity Rating: 82   **Fire Safety Rating:** 89   **Green Rating:** 60*

STUDENTS AND FACULTY
Enrollment: 2,146. **Student Body:** 53% female, 47% male, 36% out-of-state, international (3 countries represented). African American 100%.
Retention and Graduation: 62% freshmen return for sophomore year. 18% freshmen graduate within 4 years. 52% grads go on to further study within 1 year. 41% grads pursue arts and sciences degrees. 3% grads pursue law degrees. 2% grads pursue business degrees. 5% grads pursue medical degrees. **Faculty:** Student/faculty ratio 21:1. 94 full-time faculty.

ACADEMICS
Degrees: Bachelor's. **Classes:** Most classes have 20–29 students. **Majors with Highest Enrollment:** Business/commerce; criminal justice/law enforcement administration; multi-/interdisciplinary studies, other. **Special Study Options:** Accelerated program, independent study, internships, study abroad, teacher certification program. Special programs offered to physically disabled students include tutors. **Career services:** Alumni services, career/job search classes, career assessment, internships.

FACILITIES
Housing: Men's dorms, women's dorms. 98% of campus accessible to physically disabled. **Special Academic Facilities/Equipment:** The Grand Student Center, The Cyber Café. **Computers:** 50% of classrooms, 100% of libraries, 100% of student union, 25% of common outdoor areas have wireless network access.

CAMPUS LIFE
Environment: Town. **Activities:** Choral groups, concert band, dance, drama/theater, marching band, music ensembles, student government, student newspaper, yearbook, campus ministries. **Organizations:** 21 registered organizations, 6 honor societies, 4 religious organizations. 4 fraternities, 4 sororities. **Athletics (Intercollegiate):** *Men:* Baseball, basketball, cross-country, football, tennis, track/field (outdoor). *Women:* Basketball, cheerleading, cross-country, softball, tennis, track/field (outdoor), volleyball. **On-Campus Highlights:** Pond at the Plain, Williams/Boyd Campus Center, The Cyber Cafe, Phillips Dining Hall, The Grand. **Environmental Initiatives:** LEED, TP3-Pollution Tennessee Pollution Prevention Partnership, EPH Environmental Self-audit Program.

ADMISSIONS
Freshman Academic Profile: Average high school GPA 2.8. 4% in top 10% of high school class, 16% in top 25% of high school class, 38% in top 50% of high school class. 96% from public high schools. ACT middle 50% range 16–19. Minimum paper TOEFL 339. **Basis for Candidate Selection:** *Very important factors considered include:* Recommendation(s), rigor of secondary school record, character/personal qualities. *Important factors considered include:* standardized test scores. *Other factors considered include:* Academic GPA, interview, level of applicant's interest, talent/ability. **Freshman Admission Requirements:** High school diploma is required and GED is accepted. *Academic units recommended:* 4 English, 2 mathematics, 2 science, 2 foreign language, 2 social studies. **Freshman Admission Statistics:** 5,619 applied, 37% admitted, 34% enrolled. **Transfer Admission Requirements:** College transcript(s), standardized test scores, statement of good standing from prior institution(s). Lowest grade transferable C. **General Admission Information:** Regular application deadline 8/1. Notification on a rolling basis, beginning on or about 2/1. Nonfall registration accepted. Admission may be deferred for a maximum of one semester. Credit offered for CEEB Advanced Placement tests.

COSTS AND FINANCIAL AID
Annual tuition $7,330. Room and board $5,520. Required fees $670. Average book expense $1,000. **Required Forms and Deadlines:** FAFSA. Priority financial aid filing date 3/1. **Notification of Awards:** Applicants will be notified of awards on a rolling basis beginning 3/31. **Types of Aid:** *Need-based scholarships/grants:* Federal Pell, SEOG, state scholarships/grants, private scholarships, the school's own gift aid, United Negro College Fund *Loans:* Direct Subsidized Stafford, Direct Unsubsidized Stafford, Direct PLUS. **Student Employment:** Federal Work-Study Program available. Institutional employment available. Off-campus job opportunities are excellent. **Financial Aid Statistics:** 93% freshmen, 94% undergrads receive need-based scholarship or grant aid. 79% freshmen, 80% undergrads receive need-based self-help aid. 96% fresh-

men, 97% undergrads receive any aid. **Criteria for awarding institutional aid:** *Non-need-based:* Academics, athletics, religious affiliation.

LASALLE UNIVERSITY

1900 West Olney Avenue, Philadelphia, PA 19141-1199
Phone: 215-951-1500 **Financial Aid Phone:** 215-951-1070
E-mail: admiss@lasalle.edu **CEEB Code:** 2363
Fax: 215-951-1656 **Website:** www.lasalle.edu **ACT Code:** 3608

This private school, affiliated with the Roman Catholic Church, was founded in 1863. It has a 120-acre campus.

RATINGS
Admissions Selectivity Rating: 83   **Fire Safety Rating:** 66   **Green Rating:** 60*

STUDENTS AND FACULTY
Enrollment: 4,207. **Student Body:** 61% female, 39% male, 43% out-of-state, 1% international (13 countries represented). Asian 3%, African American 16%, Caucasian 63%, Hispanic 8%.
Retention and Graduation: 82% freshmen return for sophomore year. 63% freshmen graduate within 4 years. 20% grads go on to further study within 1 year. 15% grads pursue arts and sciences degrees. 5% grads pursue law degrees. 3% grads pursue business degrees. 3% grads pursue medical degrees. **Faculty:** Student/faculty ratio 15:1. 233 full-time faculty, 80% hold PhDs, 8% are members of minority groups, 47% are women.

ACADEMICS
Degrees: Associate, bachelor's, certificate, master's, post-bachelor's certificate, post-master's certificate. **Classes:** Most classes have 20–29 students. Most lab/discussion sessions have fewer than 10 students. **Majors with Highest Enrollment:** Communication, journalism, and related programs, other; education; public health/community nurse/nursing. **Special Study Options:** Accelerated program, cooperative education program, cross-registration, double major, dual enrollment, English as a Second Language (ESL), exchange student program (domestic), honors program, independent study, internships, student-designed major, study abroad, teacher certification program, 2+2 with Thomas Jefferson University. **Combined degree programs:** BS/MS (5-year) speech/language pathology and audiology. Special programs offered to physically disabled students include note-taking services, reader services, tape recorders, tutors.

FACILITIES
Housing: Coed dorms, special housing for disabled students, fraternity/sorority housing, apartments for single students. 95% of campus accessible to physically disabled. **Special Academic Facilities/Equipment:** Art museum, Japanese tea house, language lab, child development center. **Computers:** Students can register for classes online. Administrative functions (other than registration) can be performed online.

CAMPUS LIFE
Environment: Metropolis. **Activities:** Choral groups, concert band, drama/theater, jazz band, literary magazine, music ensembles, musical theater, pep band, radio station, student government, student newspaper, student-run film society, television station, yearbook. **Organizations:** 100 registered organizations, 10 honor societies, 4 religious organizations, 7 fraternities, 5 sororities. **Athletics (Intercollegiate):** *Men:* Baseball, basketball, cheerleading, crew/rowing, cross-country, diving, football, golf, soccer, swimming, tennis, track/field (outdoor), wrestling. *Women:* Basketball, cheerleading, crew/rowing, cross-country, diving, field hockey, golf, lacrosse, soccer, softball, swimming, tennis, track/field (outdoor), volleyball. **On-Campus Highlights:** Hayman Center (sports facility), Connelly Library, Student Union Building-food court, coffee house, restaurant, La Salle University Art Museum, Japanese Tea Ceremony House.

ADMISSIONS
Freshman Academic Profile: Average high school GPA 3.1. 25% in top 10% of high school class, 55% in top 25% of high school class, 86% in top 50% of high school class. 35% from public high schools. SAT Math middle 50% range 480–580. SAT Critical Reading middle 50% range 480–580. Minimum paper TOEFL 500. Minimum computer TOEFL 175. **Basis for Candidate Selection:** *Very important factors considered include:* Rigor of secondary school record. *Important factors considered include:* Class rank, application essay, standardized test scores. *Other factors considered include:* Recommendation(s), alumni/ae relation, character/personal qualities, extracurricular activities, interview, talent/ability, volunteer work, work experience. **Freshman Admission Requirements:** High school diploma is required and GED is accepted. *Academic units required:* 4 English, 3 mathematics, 1 science, (1 science labs), 2 foreign language, 1 history, 5 academic electives. **Freshman Admission**

Statistics: 5,205 applied, 64% admitted, 27% enrolled. **Transfer Admission Requirements:** High school transcript, college transcript(s), essay or personal statement, standardized test scores, statement of good standing from prior institution(s). Minimum college GPA of 2.5 required. Lowest grade transferable C. **General Admission Information:** Application fee $35. Notification on a rolling basis, beginning on or about 11/15. Nonfall registration accepted. Admission may be deferred for a maximum of info. not available.

COSTS AND FINANCIAL AID

Annual tuition $21,270. Room and board $7,810. Required fees $150. Average book expense $500. **Required Forms and Deadlines:** FAFSA. Priority financial aid filing date 2/15. **Notification of Awards:** Applicants will be notified of awards on a rolling basis beginning 3/15. **Types of Aid:** *Need-based scholarships/grants:* Federal Pell, SEOG, state scholarships/grants, private scholarships, the school's own gift aid. *Loans:* FFEL Subsidized Stafford, FFEL Unsubsidized Stafford, FFEL PLUS, Federal Perkins. **Financial Aid Statistics:** 76% freshmen, 70% undergrads receive need-based scholarship or grant aid. 7% freshmen, 7% undergrads receive non-need-based scholarship or grant aid. 65% freshmen, 61% undergrads receive need-based self-help aid. 5% freshmen, 5% undergrads receive athletic scholarships. 77% freshmen, 72% undergrads receive any aid. 76% undergrads borrow to pay for school. Average cumulative indebtedness $32,431. **Criteria for awarding institutional aid:** *Non-need-based:* Academics, athletics.

LASELL COLLEGE

Office of Undergraduate Admissions, 1844 Commonwealth Avenue, Newton, MA 02466
Phone: 617-243-2225 **Financial Aid Phone:** 617-243-2227
E-mail: info@lasell.edu **CEEB Code:** 3481
Fax: 617-243-2380 **Website:** www.lasell.edu **ACT Code:** 1848

This private school was founded in 1851. It has a 55-acre campus.

RATINGS
Admissions Selectivity Rating: 72　　　**Fire Safety Rating:** 60*　　　**Green Rating:** 60*

STUDENTS AND FACULTY
Enrollment: 1,154. **Student Body:** 71% female, 29% male, 4% international (15 countries represented). Asian 4%, African American 6%, Caucasian 75%, Hispanic 6%.
Retention and Graduation: 18% grads go on to further study within 1 year. 13% grads pursue arts and sciences degrees. 5% grads pursue business degrees. **Faculty:** Student/faculty ratio 13:1. 55 full-time faculty, 45% hold PhDs, 64% are women.

ACADEMICS
Degrees: Bachelor's, master's, post-bachelor's certificate. **Classes:** Most classes have 10–19 students. Most lab/discussion sessions have 10–19 students. **Majors with Highest Enrollment:** Criminology; fashion/apparel design; psychology. **Special Study Options:** Double major, honors program, internships, liberal arts/career combination, study abroad. **Honors programs:** Lasell College Honor's Program. **Career services:** Alumni services, career/job search classes, career assessment, internships.

FACILITIES
Housing: Coed dorms, women's dorms, Special interst (human services). Some houses Alcohol free. All houses smoke-free. 30% of campus accessible to physically disabled. **Special Academic Facilities/Equipment:** Center for Public Service, Yamawaki Art/Cultural Center.

CAMPUS LIFE
Environment: City. **Activities:** Choral groups, dance, drama/theater, literary magazine, music ensembles, musical theater, radio station, student government, student newspaper, television station, yearbook. **Organizations:** 30 registered organizations, 1 honor societies. **Athletics (Intercollegiate):** *Men:* Basketball, cross-country, lacrosse, soccer, volleyball. *Women:* Basketball, cross-country, field hockey, lacrosse, soccer, softball, volleyball. **On-Campus Highlights:** Yamawaki Art and Cultural Center, campus center, athletic center, Winslow Academic Center, Edwards Student Center.

ADMISSIONS
Freshman Academic Profile: Average high school GPA 2.7. 6% in top 10% of high school class, 32% in top 25% of high school class, 79% in top 50% of high school class. 85% from public high schools. SAT Math middle 50% range 510–420. SAT Critical Reading middle 50% range 520–430. ACT middle 50% range 21–20. Minimum paper TOEFL 500. Minimum computer TOEFL 173. **Basis for Candidate Selection:** *Very important factors considered include:*

Recommendation(s), rigor of secondary school record. *Important factors considered include:* Standardized test scores, extracurricular activities, interview. *Other factors considered include:* Class rank, application essay, alumni/ae relation, character/personal qualities, talent/ability, volunteer work, work experience. **Freshman Admission Requirements:** High school diploma is required and GED is accepted. *Academic units required:* 4 English, 3 mathematics, 2 science, (2 science labs), 2 social studies, 2 history. *Academic units recommended:* 4 English, 3 mathematics, 3 science, (2 science labs), 2 foreign language, 3 social studies, 3 history. **Freshman Admission Statistics:** 2,498 applied, 65% admitted, 24% enrolled. **Transfer Admission Requirements:** College transcript(s), standardized test scores, statement of good standing from prior institution(s). Minimum college GPA of 2.3 required. Lowest grade transferable C. **General Admission Information:** Application fee $40. Notification on a rolling basis, beginning on or about 12/15. Nonfall registration accepted. Admission may be deferred for a maximum of 1 year. Credit offered for CEEB Advanced Placement tests.

COSTS AND FINANCIAL AID

Annual tuition $18,700. Room and board $8,800. Required fees $1,000. Average book expense $1,000. **Required Forms and Deadlines:** FAFSA, institution's own financial aid form. Priority financial aid filing date 3/15. **Notification of Awards:** Applicants will be notified of awards on a rolling basis beginning 2/15. **Types of Aid:** *Need-based scholarships/grants:* Federal Pell, SEOG, state scholarships/grants, private scholarships, the school's own gift aid. *Loans:* FFEL Subsidized Stafford, FFEL Unsubsidized Stafford, FFEL PLUS, Federal Perkins, state loans. **Student Employment:** Federal Work-Study Program available. Institutional employment available. Off-campus job opportunities are excellent. **Financial Aid Statistics:** 81% freshmen, 81% undergrads receive need-based scholarship or grant aid. 6% freshmen, 10% undergrads receive non-need-based scholarship or grant aid. 72% freshmen, 72% undergrads receive need-based self-help aid. 87% freshmen, 85% undergrads receive any aid. 87% undergrads borrow to pay for school. Average cumulative indebtedness $20,500. **Criteria for awarding institutional aid:** *Non-need-based:* Academics, alumni affiliation.

LAURA AND ALVIN SIEGAL COLLEGE OF JUDAIC STUDIES

26500 Shaker Boulevard, Beachwood, OH 44122-7116
Phone: 216-464-4050 **Financial Aid Phone:** 216-464-4050
E-mail: admissions@siegalcollege.edu
Fax: 216-464-5827

This private school, affiliated with the Jewish Church, was founded in 1963.

RATINGS
Admissions Selectivity Rating: 60*　　　**Fire Safety Rating:** 60*　　　**Green Rating:** 60*

STUDENTS AND FACULTY
Enrollment: 12. **Student Body:** 67% female, 33% male, 90% out-of-state, (1 countries represented). Caucasian 100%.
Retention and Graduation: 100% freshmen return for sophomore year. **Faculty:** Student/faculty ratio 2:1. 11 full-time faculty, 82% hold PhDs, 36% are women.

ACADEMICS
Degrees: Bachelor's, certificate, master's. **Majors with Highest Enrollment:** Bible/biblical studies. **Special Study Options:** Distance learning, double major, independent study, internships.

FACILITIES
Housing: No housing available on campus. 100% of campus accessible to physically disabled. **Computers:** Students can register for classes online.

CAMPUS LIFE
Environment: Village. **Activities: Organizations:** 1 registered organizations. **On-Campus Highlights:** Library, video conferencing rooms, student lounge, language media center, professors offices.

ADMISSIONS
Freshman Academic Profile: Basis for Candidate Selection: *Very important factors considered include:* Application essay, recommendation(s), interview, level of applicant's interest. *Important factors considered include:* Academic GPA, rigor of secondary school record. *Other factors considered include:* Class rank, standardized test scores, character/personal qualities, extracurricular activities, talent/ability, work experience. **Freshman Admission Requirements:** High school diploma is required and GED is accepted. **Freshman**

Admission Statistics: 3 applied, 100% admitted, 100% enrolled. **Transfer Admission Requirements:** College transcript(s), essay or personal statement, interview, minimum college GPA of 2.7 required. Lowest grade transferable C. **General Admission Information:** Application fee $50. Nonfall registration accepted. Admission may be deferred for a maximum of 1 year.

COSTS AND FINANCIAL AID

Annual tuition $12,600. Required fees $25. **Required Forms and Deadlines:** institution's own financial aid form. **Notification of Awards:** Applicants will be notified of awards on a rolling basis beginning 9/5. **Types of Aid:** *Need-based scholarships/grants:* Federal Pell, the school's own gift aid. *Loans:* FFEL Subsidized Stafford, FFEL Unsubsidized Stafford, FFEL PLUS. **Student Employment:** Off-campus job opportunities are good. **Financial Aid Statistics:** 100% freshmen receive need-based scholarship or grant aid.

LAWRENCE TECHNOLOGICAL UNIVERSITY

21000 West Ten Mile Rd, Southfield, MI 48075-1058
Phone: 248-204-3160 **Financial Aid Phone:** 248-204-2120
E-mail: admissions@ltu.edu **CEEB Code:** 1399
Fax: 248-204-3188 **Website:** www.ltu.edu **ACT Code:** 2020

This private school was founded in 1932. It has a 102-acre campus.

RATINGS

Admissions Selectivity Rating: 85   Fire Safety Rating: 73   Green Rating: 74

STUDENTS AND FACULTY

Enrollment: 2,257. **Student Body:** 26% female, 74% male, 2% out-of-state, 7% international (40 countries represented). Asian 4%, African American 13%, Caucasian 63%, Hispanic 2%.
Retention and Graduation: 72% freshmen return for sophomore year. **Faculty:** Student/faculty ratio 11:1. 129 full-time faculty, 72% hold PhDs, 10% are members of minority groups, 26% are women.

ACADEMICS

Degrees: Associate, bachelor's, certificate, doctoral, master's, post-bachelor's certificate. **Classes:** Most classes have 10–19 students. Most lab/discussion sessions have fewer than 10 students. **Majors with Highest Enrollment:** Architecture (BArch, BA/BS, MArch, MA/MS, PhD); computer science; mechanical engineering. **Special Study Options:** Cooperative education program, cross-registration, distance learning, double major, dual enrollment, English as a Second Language (ESL), honors program, independent study, internships, liberal arts/career combination, study abroad, weekend college. **Honors programs:** The LTU Honors Program is designed for highly qualified students who want an educational experience that will take full advantage of the challenging curricula offered at Lawrence Tech. **Combined degree programs:** Many dual degree combinations. Special programs offered to physically disabled students include note-taking services, reader services, tape recorders, tutors. **Career services:** Alumni network, alumni services, career/job search classes, career assessment, internships, regional alumni. **Career services highlights include:** "Find Your First Professional Job," a 10–week program to develop student skills to locate and secure their career goals. Classes are taught by leading employers, and each student is assigned a career counselor to help develop an individualized approach to their quest.

FACILITIES

Housing: Special housing for disabled students, fraternity/sorority housing, apartments for married students, apartments for single students. 97% of campus accessible to physically disabled. **Special Academic Facilities/Equipment:** Albert Kahn Library, Center for Innovative Materials Research. **Computers:** 100% of classrooms, 100% of dorms, 100% of libraries, 100% of dining areas, 100% of student union, 75% of common outdoor areas have wireless network access. Students can register for classes online. Administrative functions (other than registration) can be performed online. Undergraduates are required to own a computer.

CAMPUS LIFE

Environment: City. **Activities:** Drama/theater, literary magazine, music ensembles, student government, student newspaper. **Organizations:** 54 registered organizations, 7 honor societies, 1 religious organizations. 6 fraternities, 3 sororities. **On-Campus Highlights:** Atrium, Field House, Engineering Lounge, Larry Joe Coffee Bar, Housing. **Environmental Initiatives:** A. Alfred Taubman Student Services Center is a green building including geothermal wells and a vegetated roof. It serves as a living laboratory for sustainability education of architects and engineers. Establishment of the Center for Sustainability including campus standards for sustainability, a speaker series, and recycling. Academic programming including participation in the Solar Decathlon and Formula Zero international competitions.

ADMISSIONS

Freshman Academic Profile: Average high school GPA 3.34. 26% in top 10% of high school class, 56% in top 25% of high school class, 85% in top 50% of high school class. ACT middle 50% range 21–27. Minimum paper TOEFL 550. Minimum computer TOEFL 213. Minimum web-based TOEFL 79. **Basis for Candidate Selection:** *Very important factors considered include:* Academic GPA, rigor of secondary school record, standardized test scores. *Other factors considered include:* Application essay, recommendation(s), interview. **Freshman Admission Requirements:** High school diploma is required and GED is accepted. *Academic units required:* 4 English, 3 mathematics, 2 science, 3 social studies. *Academic units recommended:* 4 mathematics, 4 science, (2 science labs), 2 history. **Freshman Admission Statistics:** 1,698 applied, 50% admitted, 41% enrolled. **Transfer Admission Requirements:** High school transcript, college transcript(s), minimum college GPA of 2.2 required. Lowest grade transferable C. **General Admission Information:** Application fee $30. Nonfall registration accepted. Credit and/or placement offered for CEEB Advanced Placement tests.

COSTS AND FINANCIAL AID

Annual tuition $22,638. Room and board $9,353. Required fees $370. Average book expense $1,319. **Required Forms and Deadlines:** FAFSA. Priority financial aid filing date 4/1. **Notification of Awards:** Applicants will be notified of awards on a rolling basis beginning 3/1. **Types of Aid:** *Need-based scholarships/grants:* Federal Pell, SEOG, state scholarships/grants, private scholarships, the school's own gift aid. *Loans:* Direct Subsidized Stafford, Direct Unsubsidized Stafford, Direct PLUS, Federal Perkins, state loans, college/university loans from institutional funds, Private alternative loans. **Student Employment:** Federal Work-Study Program available. Institutional employment available. Highest amount earned per year from on-campus jobs $13,110. Off-campus job opportunities are excellent. **Financial Aid Statistics:** 70% freshmen, 55% undergrads receive need-based scholarship or grant aid. 58% freshmen, 39% undergrads receive non-need-based scholarship or grant aid. 65% freshmen, 54% undergrads receive need-based self-help aid. 90% freshmen, 55% undergrads receive any aid. 73% undergrads borrow to pay for school. Average cumulative indebtedness $42,723. **Criteria for awarding institutional aid:** *Non-need-based:* Academics, alumni affiliation, art, job skills, leadership, minority status, state/district residency.

See page 1138.

LAWRENCE UNIVERSITY

PO Box 599, Appleton, WI 54912-0599
Phone: 920-832-6500 **Financial Aid Phone:** 920-832-6583
E-mail: excel@lawrence.edu **CEEB Code:** 1398
Fax: 920-832-6782 **Website:** www.lawrence.edu **ACT Code:** 4596

This private school was founded in 1847. It has a 84-acre campus.

RATINGS

Admissions Selectivity Rating: 90   Fire Safety Rating: 70   Green Rating: 81

STUDENTS AND FACULTY

Enrollment: 1,433. **Student Body:** 54% female, 46% male, 63% out-of-state, 8% international (48 countries represented). Asian 3%, African American 3%, Caucasian 70%, Hispanic 2%.
Retention and Graduation: 92% freshmen return for sophomore year. 60% freshmen graduate within 4 years. 18% grads go on to further study within 1 year. 14% grads pursue arts and sciences degrees. 2% grads pursue law degrees. 2% grads pursue medical degrees. **Faculty:** Student/faculty ratio 9:1. 157 full-time faculty, 89% hold PhDs, 11% are members of minority groups, 38% are women.

ACADEMICS

Degrees: Bachelor's. **Classes:** Most classes have 10–19 students. **Majors with Highest Enrollment:** Biology/biological sciences; psychology; visual and performing arts. **Special Study Options:** double major, independent study, internships, student-designed major, study abroad, teacher certification program. **Combined degree programs:** BA/B-MUS. Special programs offered to physically disabled students include note-taking services, reader services, tape recorders, tutors. **Career services:** Alumni network, alumni services, career assessment, internships, regional alumni.

FACILITIES

Housing: Coed dorms, special housing for disabled students, men's dorms, women's dorms, apartments for married students, theme housing theme/group houses available. 70% of campus accessible to physically disabled. **Special Academic Facilities/Equipment:** Art galleries, anthropology collection, 425-acre estate on Lake Michigan hosting retreats and seminars for students, new student center (Warch Center) electron microscope, laser physics lab, physics/computational graphics lab, nuclear magnetic resonance spectrometer. **Computers:** 100% of classrooms, 20% of dorms, 100% of libraries, 100% of dining areas, 100% of student union, have wireless network access. Students can register for classes online. Administrative functions (other than registration) can be performed online.

CAMPUS LIFE

Environment: City. **Activities:** Choral groups, concert band, dance, drama/theater, jazz band, literary magazine, music ensembles, musical theater, opera, pep band, radio station, student government, student newspaper, student-run film society, symphony orchestra, yearbook, campus ministries, international student organization, Model UN. **Organizations:** 90 registered organizations, 5 honor societies, 3 religious organizations. 5 fraternities, 3 sororities. **Athletics (Intercollegiate):** *Men:* Baseball, basketball, cross-country, diving, fencing, football, golf, ice hockey, soccer, swimming, tennis, track/field (outdoor), track/field (indoor), wrestling. *Women:* Basketball, cross-country, diving, fencing, soccer, softball, swimming, tennis, track/field (outdoor), track/field (indoor), volleyball. **On-Campus Highlights:** Wriston Art Gallery, Music Conservatory, new Warch Campus Center, new $18 million science building, Hiett Hall (new $8 million residence hall). **Environmental Initiatives:** Construction of LEED-certified Student Center—Gold! Campus Garden (SLUG) (http://blogs.lawrence.edu/SLUG/) which provides produce to the dining hall and composts all food prep waste. Also serves an educational garden for the Community Garden Partnership of the Fox Cities. Lawrence has a long standing environmental studies Program and offers majors and minors. www.lawrence.edu/academics/enst/

ADMISSIONS

Freshman Academic Profile: Average high school GPA 3.63. 38% in top 10% of high school class, 70% in top 25% of high school class, 97% in top 50% of high school class. 76% from public high schools. SAT Math middle 50% range 600–710. SAT Critical Reading middle 50% range 590–730. SAT Writing middle 50% range 590–680. ACT middle 50% range 27–31. Minimum paper TOEFL 577. Minimum computer TOEFL 233. Minimum web-based TOEFL 90. **Basis for Candidate Selection:** *Very important factors considered include:* Class rank, academic GPA, rigor of secondary school record. *Important factors considered include:* Application essay, recommendation(s), character/personal qualities, extracurricular activities, talent/ability. *Other factors considered include:* standardized test scores, alumni/ae relation, first generation, interview, racial/ethnic status, volunteer work, work experience. **Freshman Admission Requirements:** High school diploma is required and GED is not accepted. *Academic units required:* 4 English. *Academic units recommended:* 3 mathematics, 3 science, 2 foreign language, 2 social studies, 2 history. **Freshman Admission Statistics:** 2,516 applied, 69% admitted, 20% enrolled. **Transfer Admission Requirements:** High school transcript, college transcript(s), essay or personal statement, minimum college GPA of 2.75 required. Lowest grade transferable C–. **General Admission Information:** Application fee $40. Early decision application deadline 11/15. Regular application deadline 1/15. Regular notification 4/1. Nonfall registration not accepted. Admission may be deferred for a maximum of 12 months. Credit and/or placement offered for CEEB Advanced Placement tests.

COSTS AND FINANCIAL AID

Average book expense $750. **Required Forms and Deadlines:** FAFSA, institution's own financial aid form, copies of Federal Tax Returns & W-2 forms for parent and student; Non-custodial parent form. Priority financial aid filing date 3/1. **Notification of Awards:** Applicants will be notified of awards on a rolling basis beginning 3/1. **Types of Aid:** *Need-based scholarships/grants:* Federal Pell, SEOG, state scholarships/grants, private scholarships, the school's own gift aid. *Loans:* Direct Subsidized Stafford, Direct Unsubsidized Stafford, Direct PLUS, Federal Perkins. **Student Employment:** Federal Work-Study Program available. Institutional employment available. Highest amount earned per year from on-campus jobs $4,189. Off-campus job opportunities are good. **Financial Aid Statistics:** 64% freshmen, 62% undergrads receive need-based scholarship or grant aid. 53% freshmen, 56% undergrads receive need-based self-help aid. 92% freshmen, 91% undergrads receive any aid. 72% undergrads borrow to pay for school. Average cumulative indebtedness $25,049. **Criteria for awarding institutional aid:** *Non-need-based:* Academics, alumni affiliation, leadership, minority status, music/drama.

See page 1140.

LE MOYNE COLLEGE

1419 Salt Springs Rd, Syracuse, NY 13214-1301
Phone: 315-445-4300 **Financial Aid Phone:** 315-445-4400
E-mail: admission@lemoyne.edu **CEEB Code:** 2366
Fax: 315-445-4711 **Website:** www.lemoyne.edu **ACT Code:** 2790

This private school, affiliated with the Roman Catholic Church, was founded in 1946. It has a 161-acre campus.

RATINGS
Admissions Selectivity Rating: 80   **Fire Safety Rating:** 79   **Green Rating:** 79

STUDENTS AND FACULTY
Enrollment: 2,465. **Student Body:** 61% female, 39% male, 5% out-of-state, 1% international (33 countries represented). Asian 2%, African American 4%, Caucasian 82%, Hispanic 5%, Native American 1%. **Retention and Graduation:** 85% freshmen return for sophomore year. 61% freshmen graduate within 4 years. 40% grads go on to further study within 1 year. 22% grads pursue arts and sciences degrees. 2% grads pursue law degrees. 2% grads pursue business degrees. 3% grads pursue medical degrees. **Faculty:** Student/faculty ratio 13:1. 158 full-time faculty, 94% hold PhDs, 15% are members of minority groups, 43% are women.

ACADEMICS
Degrees: Bachelor's, master's, post-master's certificate. **Classes:** Most classes have 20–29 students. Most lab/discussion sessions have 10–19 students. **Majors with Highest Enrollment:** Accounting; biology/biological sciences; psychology. **Special Study Options:** Accelerated program, double major, dual enrollment, honors program, independent study, internships, study abroad, teacher certification program, Certificate of Advanced Studies in Educational Leadership and Certificate of Advanced Studies in Nursing. **Honors programs:** Students in the program complete a 21-hour sequence of interdisciplinary humanities courses that replaces the standard core requirements in English, history, philosophy, and religious studies. Seniors complete an honors project working in close collaboration with a faculty advisor. **Combined degree programs:** BA/MA, BA/DDS, BA/MEng; 3-4:pre-optometry (PA Coll), pre-podiatry (NY Coll); 3-3: Dr of Physical Therapy. Special programs offered to physically disabled students include note-taking services, reader services, tape recorders, tutors. **Career services:** Alumni network, alumni services, career/job search classes, career assessment, internships, regional alumni. **Career services highlights include:** Business and Science Internship Programs and Mock Interview week.

FACILITIES
Housing: Coed dorms, special housing for disabled students, men's dorms, women's dorms, apartments for single students, living/learning communities. 96% of campus accessible to physically disabled. **Special Academic Facilities/Equipment:** Art gallery, audiovisual center, electron microscopes, and Academic Support Center. **Computers:** 100% of classrooms, 75% of dorms, 100% of libraries, 100% of dining areas, 100% of student union, 100% of common outdoor areas have wireless network access. Students can register for classes online. Administrative functions (other than registration) can be performed online.

CAMPUS LIFE
Environment: City. **Activities:** Choral groups, concert band, dance, drama/theater, jazz band, literary magazine, music ensembles, musical theater, pep band, radio station, student government, student newspaper, student-run film society, television station, yearbook, campus ministries, international student organization, Model UN. **Organizations:** 70 registered organizations, 14 honor societies, 11 religious organizations. **Athletics (Intercollegiate):** *Men:* Baseball, basketball, cross-country, diving, golf, lacrosse, soccer, swimming, tennis. *Women:* Basketball, cross-country, diving, golf, lacrosse, soccer, softball, swimming, tennis, volleyball. **On-Campus Highlights:** The Thomas J. Niland Athletic Complex, Campus Center, The W. Carroll Coyne Center for the Performing Arts, Panasci Family Chapel, Noreen Reale Falcone Library. **Environmental Initiatives:** Student Environmental Coalition (SEC); College Committee on Environmental Sustainability (CCES); Center for the Study of Environmental Change.

ADMISSIONS
Freshman Academic Profile: Average high school GPA 3.34. 22% in top 10% of high school class, 58% in top 25% of high school class, 88% in top 50% of high school class. 82% from public high schools. SAT Math middle 50% range 505–610. SAT Critical Reading middle 50% range 490–580. ACT middle 50% range 20–26. Minimum paper TOEFL 550. Minimum computer TOEFL 213. Minimum web-based TOEFL 79. **Basis for Candidate Selection:** *Very important factors considered include:* Academic GPA, rigor of secondary school record. *Important factors considered include:* Class rank, application essay, recommendation(s), standardized test scores, extracurricular activities, interview, talent/ability, work experience. *Other factors considered include:*

Alumni/ae relation, character/personal qualities, geographical residence, level of applicant's interest, state residency, volunteer work. **Freshman Admission Requirements:** High school diploma is required and GED is accepted. *Academic units required:* 4 English, 3 mathematics, 3 science, 3 foreign language, 4 social studies. *Academic units recommended:* 4 mathematics, 4 science, (3 science labs). **Freshman Admission Statistics:** 4,526 applied, 67% admitted, 20% enrolled. **Transfer Admission Requirements:** College transcript(s), essay or personal statement, minimum college GPA of 2.6 required. Lowest grade transferable C–. **General Admission Information:** Application fee $35. Early decision application deadline 12/1. Notification on a rolling basis, beginning on or about 1/1. Nonfall registration accepted. Admission may be deferred for a maximum of 1 year. Credit and/or placement offered for CEEB Advanced Placement tests.

COSTS AND FINANCIAL AID

Annual tuition $25,110. Room and board $9,990. Required fees $670. Average book expense $1,230. **Required Forms and Deadlines:** FAFSA, institution's own financial aid form, state aid form. Priority financial aid filing date 2/1. **Notification of Awards:** Applicants will be notified of awards on or about 3/15. **Types of Aid:** *Need-based scholarships/grants:* Federal Pell, SEOG, state scholarships/grants, private scholarships, the school's own gift aid. *Loans:* FFEL Subsidized Stafford, FFEL Unsubsidized Stafford, FFEL PLUS, Federal Perkins. **Student Employment:** Federal Work-Study Program available. Institutional employment available. Highest amount earned per year from on-campus jobs $2,000. Off-campus job opportunities are excellent. **Financial Aid Statistics:** 76% freshmen, 76% undergrads receive need-based scholarship or grant aid. 24% freshmen, 19% undergrads receive non-need-based scholarship or grant aid. 67% freshmen, 69% undergrads receive need-based self-help aid. 8% freshmen, 7% undergrads receive athletic scholarships. 88% freshmen, 90% undergrads receive any aid. 84% undergrads borrow to pay for school. Average cumulative indebtedness $27,483. **Criteria for awarding institutional aid:** *Non-need-based:* Academics, alumni affiliation, athletics, leadership, minority status.

See page 1142.

LEBANON VALLEY COLLEGE

101 North College Avenue, Annville, PA 17003-1400
Phone: 717-867-6181 **Financial Aid Phone:** 717-867-6126
E-mail: admission@lvc.edu **CEEB Code:** 2364
Fax: 717-867-6026 **Website:** www.lvc.edu **ACT Code:** 3610

This private school, affiliated with the Methodist Church, was founded in 1866. It has a 340-acre campus.

RATINGS
Admissions Selectivity Rating: 81   **Fire Safety Rating:** 83   **Green Rating:** 70

STUDENTS AND FACULTY
Enrollment: 1,650. **Student Body:** 56% female, 44% male, 20% out-of-state, international (3 countries represented). Asian 2%, African American 2%, Caucasian 89%, Hispanic 2%.
Retention and Graduation: 86% freshmen return for sophomore year. 68% freshmen graduate within 4 years. 26% grads go on to further study within 1 year. 22% grads pursue arts and sciences degrees. 2% grads pursue business degrees. **Faculty:** Student/faculty ratio 13:1. 100 full-time faculty, 88% hold PhDs, 7% are members of minority groups, 37% are women.

ACADEMICS
Degrees: Associate, bachelor's, certificate, master's, post-bachelor's certificate, terminal associate. **Classes:** Most classes have 10–19 students. Most lab/discussion sessions have 10–19 students. **Majors with Highest Enrollment:** Business/commerce; elementary education and teaching; health services/allied health/health sciences. **Special Study Options:** Double major, dual enrollment, independent study, internships, liberal arts/career combination, student-designed major, study abroad, teacher certification program. **Combined degree programs:** Forestry/Environmental Studies—3+2 w/ Duke. Special programs offered to physically disabled students include note-taking services, reader services, tape recorders, tutors. **Career services:** Alumni network, alumni services, career assessment, internships. **Career services highlights include:** Career Connections is our on-line mentoring/networking system for connecting students with alumni who can assist in career planning and the job search.

FACILITIES
Housing: Coed dorms, special housing for disabled students, women's dorms, apartments for single students, theme housing, suites. 80% of campus ac-

cessible to physically disabled. **Special Academic Facilities/Equipment:** Electric pianos, sound recording studio, transmission electron microscope, scanning electron microscope, Fourier transform infrared spectrometer, atomic absorption spectrometer, nuclear magnetic resonance spectrometer, molecular modeling lab, campus Arboretum, art gallery, therapy pool. **Computers:** 100% of classrooms, 100% of dorms, 100% of libraries, 100% of dining areas, 100% of student union, 90% of common outdoor areas have wireless network access. Students can register for classes online. Administrative functions (other than registration) can be performed online.

CAMPUS LIFE
Environment: Rural. **Activities:** Choral groups, drama/theater, jazz band, literary magazine, marching band, music ensembles, musical theater, radio station, student government, student newspaper, symphony orchestra, yearbook, campus ministries. **Organizations:** 79 registered organizations, 6 honor societies, 14 religious organizations. 4 fraternities, 4 sororities. **Athletics (Intercollegiate):** *Men:* Baseball, basketball, cross-country, football, golf, ice hockey, lacrosse, soccer, swimming, tennis, track/field (outdoor), track/field (indoor). *Women:* Basketball, cross-country, field hockey, lacrosse, soccer, softball, swimming, tennis, track/field (outdoor), track/field (indoor), volleyball. **On-Campus Highlights:** Neidig Garber Science Center, Lynch Memorial—Synodinos Commons, The Peace Garden, Bishop Library, Suzanne Arnold Art Gallery and Zimmerman Recital Hall, Athletic fields are outstanding. Stanson Residence Hall, with 148 beds, was opened in fall 2009. **Environmental Initiatives:** Energy conservation, recycling, green products used in cleaning and grounds care.

ADMISSIONS
Freshman Academic Profile: 34% in top 10% of high school class, 71% in top 25% of high school class, 93% in top 50% of high school class. 95% from public high schools. SAT Math middle 50% range 500–620. SAT Critical Reading middle 50% range 480–590. SAT Writing middle 50% range 470–580. ACT middle 50% range 19–25. Minimum paper TOEFL 550. Minimum computer TOEFL 213. Minimum web-based TOEFL 80. **Basis for Candidate Selection:** *Very important factors considered include:* Class rank, rigor of secondary school record. *Important factors considered include:* Academic GPA, character/personal qualities, extracurricular activities, interview, level of applicant's interest, talent/ability. *Other factors considered include:* Application essay, recommendation(s), standardized test scores, alumni/ae relation, first generation, geographical residence, racial/ethnic status, state residency, volunteer work, work experience. **Freshman Admission Requirements:** High school diploma is required and GED is accepted. *Academic units required:* 4 English, 3 mathematics, 2 science, 2 foreign language, 1 social studies. *Academic units recommended:* 3 science, (2 science labs), 3 foreign language, 2 history. **Freshman Admission Statistics:** 1,698 applied, 81% admitted, 28% enrolled. **Transfer Admission Requirements:** High school transcript, college transcript(s), essay or personal statement, statement of good standing from prior institution(s). Minimum college GPA of 2.0 required. Lowest grade transferable C–. **General Admission Information:** Application fee $30. Notification on a rolling basis, beginning on or about 10/15. Nonfall registration accepted. Credit offered for CEEB Advanced Placement tests.

COSTS AND FINANCIAL AID
Annual tuition $29,780. Room and board $8,080. Required fees $710. Average book expense $1,000. **Required Forms and Deadlines:** FAFSA, institution's own financial aid form. Priority financial aid filing date 3/1. **Notification of Awards:** Applicants will be notified of awards on a rolling basis beginning 3/1. **Types of Aid:** *Need-based scholarships/grants:* Federal Pell, SEOG, state scholarships/grants, private scholarships, the school's own gift aid. *Loans:* FFEL Subsidized Stafford, FFEL Unsubsidized Stafford, FFEL PLUS, Federal Perkins. **Student Employment:** Federal Work-Study Program available. Institutional employment available. Highest amount earned per year from on-campus jobs $901. Off-campus job opportunities are good. **Financial Aid Statistics:** 85% freshmen, 80% undergrads receive need-based scholarship or grant aid. 10% freshmen, 8% undergrads receive non-need-based scholarship or grant aid. 74% freshmen, 69% undergrads receive need-based self-help aid. 99% freshmen, 99% undergrads receive any aid. 82% undergrads borrow to pay for school. Average cumulative indebtedness $33,348. **Criteria for awarding institutional aid:** *Non-need-based:* Academics, alumni affiliation, music/drama.

LEE UNIVERSITY

P.O. Box 3450, Cleveland, TN 37320-3450
Phone: 423-614-8500 **Financial Aid Phone:** 423-614-8300
E-mail: admissions@leeuniversity.edu **CEEB Code:** 1401
Fax: 423-614-8533 **Website:** www.leeuniversity.edu **ACT Code:** 3978

This private school, affiliated with the Church of God Church, was founded in 1918. It has a 115-acre campus.

RATINGS
Admissions Selectivity Rating: 83 **Fire Safety Rating:** 68 **Green Rating:** 60*

STUDENTS AND FACULTY
Enrollment: 3,602. **Student Body:** 56% female, 44% male, 57.33% out-of-state, 5% international (49 countries represented). Asian 1%, African American 4%, Caucasian 80%, Hispanic 3%.
Retention and Graduation: 73% freshmen return for sophomore year. 37% freshmen graduate within 4 years. 20% grads go on to further study within 1 year. **Faculty:** Student/faculty ratio 18:1. 149 full-time faculty, 76% hold PhDs, 15% are members of minority groups, 34% are women.

ACADEMICS
Degrees: Bachelor's, master's, post-master's certificate. **Classes:** Most classes have 20–29 students. Most lab/discussion sessions have fewer than 10 students. **Majors with Highest Enrollment:** Business administration and management; education, other; psychology. **Special Study Options:** Distance learning, double major, dual enrollment, English as a Second Language (ESL), exchange student program (domestic), external degree program, honors program, independent study, internships, liberal arts/career combination, study abroad, teacher certification program. **Honors programs:** The Kairos Scholars Honors Program. Also, several academic subject honors societies like Psychology, Business, Music and Pre-Med. Special programs offered to physically disabled students include reader services, tape recorders, tutors. **Career services:** Alumni services, career assessment, internships.

FACILITIES
Housing: Men's dorms, women's dorms, apartments for married students, apartments for single students, wellness housing. Lee University leases apartments and houses for students. 71% of campus accessible to physically disabled. **Special Academic Facilities/Equipment:** Curriculum Library in the College of Education. **Computers:** 80% of classrooms, 50% of dorms, 100% of libraries, 100% of dining areas, 100% of student union, 50% of common outdoor areas have wireless network access. Students can register for classes online. Administrative functions (other than registration) can be performed online.

CAMPUS LIFE
Environment: Town. **Activities:** Choral groups, concert band, drama/theater, jazz band, literary magazine, music ensembles, musical theater, opera, pep band, student government, student newspaper, symphony orchestra, yearbook, campus ministries, international student organization, Model UN. **Organizations:** 72 registered organizations, 16 honor societies, 10 religious organizations. 5 fraternities, 4 sororities. **Athletics (Intercollegiate):** *Men:* Baseball, basketball, cheerleading, cross-country, golf, soccer, tennis. *Women:* Basketball, cheerleading, cross-country, soccer, softball, tennis, volleyball. **On-Campus Highlights:** Paul Conn Student Union—bookstore; Pizza Hut; Chickfil; Conn Center—home of chapels, concerts, etc.; Dixon Center—plays, recitals, community events; De Vos Recreaction Cente;, The House—coffeehouse; and Jazzman's Cafe.

ADMISSIONS
Freshman Academic Profile: Average high school GPA 3.42. 25.05% in top 10% of high school class, 46.49% in top 25% of high school class, 71.54% in top 50% of high school class. 75% from public high schools. SAT Math middle 50% range 460–600. SAT Critical Reading middle 50% range 480–610. ACT middle 50% range 20–27. Minimum paper TOEFL 450. Minimum computer TOEFL 133. **Basis for Candidate Selection:** *Very important factors considered include:* Academic GPA, rigor of secondary school record, standardized test scores. *Important factors considered include:* Class rank, character/personal qualities, level of applicant's interest. *Other factors considered include:* Recommendation(s), alumni/ae relation, extracurricular activities, first generation, interview, talent/ability. **Freshman Admission Requirements:** High school diploma is required and GED is accepted. *Academic units required:* 4 English, 3 mathematics, 2 science, 1 foreign language, 2 social studies, 1 history. *Academic units recommended:* 4 English, 3 mathematics, 2 science, 1 foreign language, 2 social studies, 1 history, 1 computer science. **Freshman Admission Statistics:** 1,768 applied, 65% admitted, 73% enrolled. **Transfer Admission Requirements:** College transcript(s), minimum college GPA of 2.0 required. Lowest grade transferable D. **General Admission Information:** Application

fee $25. Regular application deadline 9/1. Notification on a rolling basis, beginning on or about 9/1. Nonfall registration accepted. Admission may be deferred for a maximum of 1 semester. Credit and/or placement offered for CEEB Advanced Placement tests.

COSTS AND FINANCIAL AID
Required Forms and Deadlines: FAFSA. Priority financial aid filing date 3/15. **Notification of Awards:** Applicants will be notified of awards on a rolling basis beginning 2/1. **Types of Aid:** *Need-based scholarships/grants:* Federal Pell, SEOG, state scholarships/grants, private scholarships, the school's own gift aid. *Loans:* FFEL Subsidized Stafford, FFEL Unsubsidized Stafford, FFEL PLUS, Federal Perkins, college/university loans from institutional funds. **Student Employment:** Federal Work-Study Program available. Institutional employment available. Off-campus job opportunities are good. **Financial Aid Statistics:** 59% freshmen, 56% undergrads receive need-based scholarship or grant aid. 14% freshmen, 7% undergrads receive non-need-based scholarship or grant aid. 38% freshmen, 48% undergrads receive need-based self-help aid. 4% freshmen, 4% undergrads receive athletic scholarships. 86% freshmen, 85% undergrads receive any aid. 64.13% undergrads borrow to pay for school. Average cumulative indebtedness $27,549. **Criteria for awarding institutional aid:** *Non-need-based:* Academics, alumni affiliation, athletics, leadership, minority status, music/drama, religious affiliation, state/district residency.

LEHIGH UNIVERSITY

27 Memorial Drive West, Bethlehem, PA 18015
Phone: 610-758-3100 **Financial Aid Phone:** 610-758-3181
E-mail: admissions@lehigh.edu **CEEB Code:** 2365
Fax: 610-758-4361 **Website:** www.lehigh.edu **ACT Code:** 3612

This private school was founded in 1865. It has a 1600-acre campus.

RATINGS
Admissions Selectivity Rating: 97 **Fire Safety Rating:** 92 **Green Rating:** 79

STUDENTS AND FACULTY
Enrollment: 4,792. **Student Body:** 41% female, 59% male, 75% out-of-state, 4% international (51 countries represented). Asian 6%, African American 4%, Caucasian 71%, Hispanic 6%.
Retention and Graduation: 76% freshmen graduate within 4 years. 31% grads go on to further study within 1 year. 37% grads pursue arts and sciences degrees. 6% grads pursue law degrees. 7% grads pursue business degrees. 15% grads pursue medical degrees. **Faculty:** Student/faculty ratio 10:1. 464 full-time faculty, 99% hold PhDs, 16% are members of minority groups, 28% are women.

ACADEMICS
Degrees: Bachelor's, doctoral, master's, post-bachelor's certificate, post-master's certificate. **Classes:** Most classes have 10–19 students. Most lab/discussion sessions have 10–19 students. **Majors with Highest Enrollment:** Accounting; finance; mechanical engineering. **Special Study Options:** Accelerated program, cooperative education program, cross-registration, distance learning, double major, English as a Second Language (ESL), exchange student program (domestic), external degree program, honors program, independent study, internships, liberal arts/career combination, study abroad. **Honors programs:** Integrated Business and Engineering (IBE) Honors Program, program description available at www.lehigh.edu/~inibep/. **Combined degree programs:** BA/MD, BA/DDS, 7-year BA/OD program with SUNY optometry. Special programs offered to physically disabled students include note-taking services, reader services, tape recorders, tutors. **Career services:** Alumni network, alumni services, career/job search classes, career assessment, internships, regional alumni. **Career services highlights include:** Lehigh University's Integrated Business and Engineering Honors Program infuses engineering thinking into the world of entrepreneurship and business. The interdisciplinary four-year program ends with a year-long experiential capstone project usually involving a high-tech startup. This senior project incorporates marketing, strategic planning and competitive analysis, along with product, process and system design issues.

FACILITIES
Housing: Coed dorms, special housing for disabled students, special housing for international students, fraternity/sorority housing, apartments for married students, apartments for single students, wellness housing, theme housing. **Special Academic Facilities/Equipment:** Art Museum, Zoellner Arts Center,

electron optical labs, civil engineering lab, particle accelerator. **Computers:** 70% of classrooms, 100% of dorms, 100% of libraries, 100% of dining areas, 75% of student union, 80% of common outdoor areas have wireless network access. Students can register for classes online. Administrative functions (other than registration) can be performed online.

CAMPUS LIFE

Environment: City. **Activities:** Choral groups, concert band, dance, drama/theater, jazz band, literary magazine, marching band, music ensembles, musical theater, pep band, radio station, student government, student newspaper, student-run film society, symphony orchestra, yearbook, campus ministries, international student organization, Model UN. **Organizations:** 18 honor societies, 10 religious organizations. 21 fraternities, 9 sororities. **Athletics (Intercollegiate):** *Men:* Baseball, basketball, cross-country, diving, football, golf, lacrosse, soccer, swimming, tennis, track/field (outdoor), track/field (indoor), wrestling. *Women:* Basketball, crew/rowing, cross-country, diving, field hockey, golf, lacrosse, soccer, softball, swimming, tennis, track/field (outdoor), track/field (indoor), volleyball. **On-Campus Highlights:** Zoellner Arts Center LU Art Galleries, Campus Square, Taylor Gymnasium, Ulrich Student Center, Goodman Campus. **Environmental Initiatives:** LEAG (Lehigh Environmental Advisory Group); Environmental Initiative Program, ECo (Environmental Coalition—Student Umbrella organization for all Lehigh Environmental Student Groups); new LEED building.

ADMISSIONS

Freshman Academic Profile: 93% in top 10% of high school class, 99% in top 25% of high school class, 100% in top 50% of high school class. SAT Math middle 50% range 630–710. SAT Critical Reading middle 50% range 590–630. Minimum paper TOEFL 570. Minimum computer TOEFL 230. Minimum web-based TOEFL 90. **Basis for Candidate Selection:** *Very important factors considered include:* Recommendation(s), rigor of secondary school record. *Important factors considered include:* Application essay, standardized test scores, character/personal qualities, extracurricular activities, level of applicant's interest, talent/ability, volunteer work. *Other factors considered include:* Class rank, academic GPA, alumni/ae relation, first generation, geographical residence, racial/ethnic status, work experience. **Freshman Admission Requirements:** High school diploma or equivalent is not required. *Academic units required:* 4 English, 3 mathematics, 2 science, (2 science labs), 2 foreign language, 2 social studies, 3 academic electives. **Freshman Admission Statistics:** 11,170 applied, 33% admitted, 33% enrolled. **Transfer Admission Requirements:** High school transcript, college transcript(s), essay or personal statement, statement of good standing from prior institution(s). Minimum college GPA of 3.25 required. **General Admission Information:** Application fee $70. Early decision application deadline 11/15. Regular application deadline 1/1. Regular notification 4/1. Nonfall registration accepted. Admission may be deferred for a maximum of 1 year. Credit and/or placement offered for CEEB Advanced Placement tests.

COSTS AND FINANCIAL AID

Required Forms and Deadlines: FAFSA, CSS/Financial Aid PROFILE, noncustodial PROFILE, business/farm supplement. Financial aid filing deadline 2/15. **Notification of Awards:** Applicants will be notified of awards on or about 3/30. **Types of Aid:** *Need-based scholarships/grants:* Federal Pell, SEOG, state scholarships/grants, private scholarships, the school's own gift aid, United Negro College Fund *Loans:* FFEL Subsidized Stafford, FFEL Unsubsidized Stafford, FFEL PLUS, Federal Perkins, college/university loans from institutional funds. **Student Employment:** Federal Work-Study Program available. Institutional employment available. Off-campus job opportunities are good. **Financial Aid Statistics:** 45% freshmen, 44% undergrads receive need-based scholarship or grant aid. 5% freshmen, 5% undergrads receive non-need-based scholarship or grant aid. 44% freshmen, 43% undergrads receive need-based self-help aid. 1% freshmen, 1% undergrads receive athletic scholarships. 59% freshmen, 58% undergrads receive any aid. 54% undergrads borrow to pay for school. Average cumulative indebtedness $31,123. **Criteria for awarding institutional aid:** *Non-need-based:* Academics, art, athletics, leadership, music/drama.

LEMOYNE-OWEN COLLEGE

807 Walker Avenue, Memphis, TN 38126
Phone: 901-942-7302 **Financial Aid Phone:** 901-942-7313
E-mail: admission@loc.edu **CEEB Code:** 1403
Fax: 901-942-6233 **Website:** www.loc.edu **ACT Code:** 3980

This private school was founded in 1862. It has a 15-acre campus.

RATINGS

Admissions Selectivity Rating: 60*   **Fire Safety Rating:** 60*   **Green Rating:** 60*

STUDENTS AND FACULTY

Enrollment: 720. **Student Body:** 100% male, 3% out-of-state, 2% international. African American 98%.
Retention and Graduation: 38% freshmen graduate within 4 years. **Faculty:** Student/faculty ratio 12:1. 54 full-time faculty, 80% hold PhDs, 89% are members of minority groups, 50% are women. 85% of classes are taught by teaching assistants.

ACADEMICS

Degrees: Bachelor's, post-bachelor's certificate. **Classes:** Most classes have 20–29 students. **Majors with Highest Enrollment:** Business/commerce; education. **Special Study Options:** Cross-registration, double major, honors program, independent study, internships, student-designed major, study abroad, teacher certification program, undergrads may take grad level courses. **Combined degree programs:** BA/MEng, dual degree program in English. **Career services:** Alumni network, alumni services, career/job search classes, career assessment, internships, regional alumni.

FACILITIES

Housing: Coed dorms, men's dorms, women's dorms. 85% of campus accessible to physically disabled. **Special Academic Facilities/Equipment:** Museum/gallery, language lab.

CAMPUS LIFE

Environment: Metropolis. **Activities:** Choral groups, drama/theater, jazz band, music ensembles, student government, student newspaper, yearbook. **Organizations:** 5 honor societies, 6 religious organizations. 4 fraternities, 3 sororities. **Athletics (Intercollegiate):** *Men:* Baseball, basketball, cross-country, tennis. *Women:* Basketball, cross-country, softball, tennis, volleyball.

ADMISSIONS

Freshman Academic Profile: 95% from public high schools. Minimum paper TOEFL 475. Minimum computer TOEFL 150. **Basis for Candidate Selection:** *Very important factors considered include:* standardized test scores. **Freshman Admission Requirements:** High school diploma is required and GED is accepted. **Freshman Admission Statistics:** 1,118 applied, 17% admitted, 63% enrolled. **Transfer Admission Requirements:** College transcript(s), standardized test scores, minimum college GPA of 2.0 required. Lowest grade transferable C. **General Admission Information:** Application fee $25. Regular application deadline 6/15. Nonfall registration accepted. Credit and/or placement offered for CEEB Advanced Placement tests.

COSTS AND FINANCIAL AID

Annual tuition $8,250. Room and board $4,620. Required fees $200. Average book expense $700. **Required Forms and Deadlines:** FAFSA. **Types of Aid:** *Need-based scholarships/grants:* United Negro College Fund. *Loans:* FFEL Subsidized Stafford, FFEL PLUS. **Student Employment:** Federal Work-Study Program available. Institutional employment available.

LENOIR-RHYNE COLLEGE

Admissions Office, LRC Box 7227, Hickory, NC 28603
Phone: 828-328-7300
E-mail: admission@lrc.edu **CEEB Code:** 5365
Fax: 828-328-7378 **Website:** www.lrc.edu **ACT Code:** 2941

This private school, affiliated with the Lutheran Church, was founded in 1891. It has a 100-acre campus.

RATINGS

Admissions Selectivity Rating: 77   **Fire Safety Rating:** 60*   **Green Rating:** 60*

STUDENTS AND FACULTY

Enrollment: 1,358. **Student Body:** 64% female, 36% male, 29% out-of-state, international. Asian 1%, African American 7%, Caucasian 91%, Hispanic 1%.
Retention and Graduation: 80% freshmen return for sophomore year. 40% grads go on to further study within 1 year. 1% grads pursue arts and sciences degrees. 4% grads pursue law degrees. 5% grads pursue business degrees. 4% grads pursue medical degrees. **Faculty:** Student/faculty ratio 12:1. 107 full-time faculty, 108% hold PhDs, 45% are women.

ACADEMICS

Degrees: Bachelor's, certificate, master's. **Special Study Options:** Accelerated program, double major, dual enrollment, English as a Second Language (ESL), honors program, independent study, internships, student-designed major, study abroad, teacher certification program. **Combined degree programs:** BA/MEng Special programs offered to physically disabled students include note-taking services, tutors. **Career services:** Alumni services, career/job search classes, career assessment, internships.

FACILITIES

Housing: Coed dorms, special housing for disabled students, men's dorms, women's dorms, fraternity/sorority housing, Honors, Hearing Impaired. 90% of campus accessible to physically disabled. **Special Academic Facilities/Equipment:** Language lab.

CAMPUS LIFE

Environment: Village. **Activities:** Choral groups, concert band, dance, drama/theater, jazz band, music ensembles, musical theater, pep band, radio station, student government, student newspaper, television station, yearbook. **Organizations:** 54 registered organizations, 10 honor societies, 6 religious organizations. 4 fraternities, 4 sororities. **Athletics (Intercollegiate):** *Men:* Baseball, basketball, cheerleading, cross-country, football, golf, soccer. *Women:* Basketball, cheerleading, cross-country, golf, soccer, softball, volleyball. **On-Campus Highlights:** McCrorie Center, Cromer College Center, Shuford Fitness Center, Living and Learning Center, Quad.

ADMISSIONS

Freshman Academic Profile: 90% from public high schools. SAT Math middle 50% range 470–580. SAT Critical Reading middle 50% range 460–570. ACT middle 50% range 17–24. Minimum paper TOEFL 500. **Basis for Candidate Selection:** *Very important factors considered include:* Rigor of secondary school record, standardized test scores. *Important factors considered include:* Class rank, interview. *Other factors considered include:* Application essay, recommendation(s), character/personal qualities, extracurricular activities, volunteer work, work experience. **Freshman Admission Requirements:** High school diploma is required and GED is accepted. *Academic units required:* 4 English, 3 mathematics, 1 science, (1 science labs), 2 foreign language, 1 social studies, 1 history. **Freshman Admission Statistics:** 915 applied, 85% admitted, 35% enrolled. **Transfer Admission Requirements:** College transcript(s), statement of good standing from prior institution(s). Minimum college GPA of 2.5 required. Lowest grade transferable C. **General Admission Information:** Application fee $25. Notification on a rolling basis, beginning on or about 9/1. Nonfall registration accepted. Admission may be deferred for a maximum of 1 year. Credit offered for CEEB Advanced Placement tests.

COSTS AND FINANCIAL AID

Annual tuition $12,870. Room and board $4,920. Required fees $486. Average book expense $700. **Required Forms and Deadlines:** FAFSA, institution's own financial aid form, state aid form. Priority financial aid filing date 3/1. **Types of Aid:** *Need-based scholarships/grants:* Federal Pell, SEOG, state scholarships/grants, the school's own gift aid. *Loans:* Direct Subsidized Stafford, Direct Unsubsidized Stafford, Direct PLUS, Federal Perkins. **Student Employment:** Federal Work-Study Program available. Institutional employment available. Highest amount earned per year from on-campus jobs $1,000. Off-campus job opportunities are excellent. **Financial Aid Statistics: Criteria for awarding institutional aid:** *Non-need-based:* Academics, alumni affiliation, athletics, leadership, minority status, music/drama, religious affiliation, state/district residency.

LESLEY COLLEGE AT LESLEY UNIVERSITY

Office of Admissions, 29 Everett St, Cambridge, MA 02138
Phone: 617-349-8800 **Financial Aid Phone:** 617-349-8710
E-mail: lcadmissions@lesley.edu **CEEB Code:** 3483
Fax: 617-349-8810 **Website:** web.lesley.edu **ACT Code:** 1850

This private school was founded in 1909. It has a 1-acre campus.

RATINGS

Admissions Selectivity Rating: 81   **Fire Safety Rating:** 85   **Green Rating:** 71

STUDENTS AND FACULTY

Enrollment: 1,261. **Student Body:** 75% female, 25% male, 44% out-of-state, 3% international (30 countries represented). Asian 3%, African American 4%, Caucasian 63%, Hispanic 5%.
Retention and Graduation: 66% freshmen return for sophomore year. 37% freshmen graduate within 4 years. **Faculty:** Student/faculty ratio 10:1. 73 full-time faculty, 68% hold PhDs, 12% are members of minority groups, 55% are women.

ACADEMICS

Degrees: Associate, bachelor's, certificate, diploma, master's, post-bachelor's certificate, post-master's certificate. **Classes:** Most classes have 10–19 students. **Majors with Highest Enrollment:** Counseling psychology; elementary education and teaching; marketing/marketing management. **Special Study Options:** Accelerated program, cross-registration, distance learning, double major, dual

enrollment, exchange student program (domestic), honors program, independent study, internships, liberal arts/career combination, student-designed major, study abroad, teacher certification program, studio courses. **Combined degree programs:** BA/MA, BS/MEd. Special programs offered to physically disabled students include note-taking services, reader services, tape recorders, tutors. **Career services:** Alumni network, alumni services, career/job search classes, career assessment, internships, regional alumni. **Career services highlights include:** Wellesley College funded at least one internship for more than half the class of 2009. This included grants of up $3,500 for what otherwise would have been unpaid internships over the summer.

FACILITIES

Housing: Coed dorms, women's dorms, Special Interest and themed housing. 85% of campus accessible to physically disabled. **Special Academic Facilities/Equipment:** Kresge Center for Teaching Resources and Educational Software Collection, Marran Art Gallery, Porter Exchange Gallery, AIB Main Gallery. **Computers:** 100% of classrooms, 100% of libraries, 100% of dining areas, 100% of student union, 20% of common outdoor areas have wireless network access. Students can register for classes online. Administrative functions (other than registration) can be performed online.

CAMPUS LIFE

Environment: Metropolis. **Activities:** Choral groups, dance, drama/theater, literary magazine, musical theater, student government, student newspaper, campus ministries, international student organization. **Organizations:** 25 registered organizations, 2 honor societies, 2 religious organizations. **Athletics (Intercollegiate):** *Men:* Basketball, cross-country, soccer, tennis, volleyball. *Women:* Basketball, crew/rowing, cross-country, soccer, softball, tennis, volleyball. **On-Campus Highlights:** Student Center, Ludke Library, Porter Exchange Building, Stebbins Fitness Room, Kresge Center for Teaching Resources. **Environmental Initiatives:** The continual enhancement of recycling, waste management and composting programs on campus. The formation of sustainability recommendations for faculty, staff and students. Student groups on campus are involved with and sponsor sustainability events.

ADMISSIONS

Freshman Academic Profile: Average high school GPA 3. 12% in top 10% of high school class, 38% in top 25% of high school class, 70% in top 50% of high school class. 83% from public high schools. SAT Math middle 50% range 460–560. SAT Critical Reading middle 50% range 490–600. SAT Writing middle 50% range 490–590. ACT middle 50% range 19–26. Minimum paper TOEFL 500. Minimum computer TOEFL 173. Minimum web-based TOEFL 61. **Basis for Candidate Selection:** *Very important factors considered include:* Academic GPA, rigor of secondary school record. *Important factors considered include:* Class rank, application essay, recommendation(s), standardized test scores, character/personal qualities, extracurricular activities, interview, talent/ability, volunteer work. *Other factors considered include:* Alumni/ae relation, first generation, geographical residence, level of applicant's interest, racial/ethnic status, work experience. **Freshman Admission Requirements:** High school diploma is required and GED is accepted. *Academic units required:* 4 English, 3 mathematics, 3 science, (2 science labs), 1 social studies, 1 history, 4 academic electives. *Academic units recommended:* 4 English, 4 mathematics, 4 science, (2 science labs), 2 foreign language, 2 social studies, 2 history, 2 visual/performing arts recommended for some programs in art or expressive therapies. **Freshman Admission Statistics:** 2,523 applied, 65% admitted, 20% enrolled. **Transfer Admission Requirements:** High school transcript, college transcript(s), essay or personal statement, statement of good standing from prior institution(s). Minimum college GPA of 2.5 required. Lowest grade transferable C. **General Admission Information:** Application fee $50. Notification on a rolling basis, beginning on or about 1/15. Nonfall registration accepted. Admission may be deferred for a maximum of 1 year. Credit and/or placement offered for CEEB Advanced Placement tests.

COSTS AND FINANCIAL AID

Annual tuition $28,150. Room and board $12,400. Required fees $310. Average book expense $700. **Required Forms and Deadlines:** FAFSA. Priority financial aid filing date 2/15. **Notification of Awards:** Applicants will be notified of awards on a rolling basis beginning 2/15. **Types of Aid:** *Need-based scholarships/grants:* Federal Pell, SEOG, state scholarships/grants, private scholarships, the school's own gift aid. *Loans:* Direct Subsidized Stafford, Direct Unsubsidized Stafford, Direct PLUS, Federal Perkins, state loans **Student Employment:** Federal Work-Study Program available. Institutional employment available. Highest amount earned per year from on-campus jobs $1,200. Off-campus job opportunities are excellent. **Financial Aid Statistics:** 73% freshmen, 51% undergrads receive need-based scholarship or grant aid. 18% freshmen, 34% undergrads receive non-need-based scholarship or grant aid. 69% freshmen, 63% undergrads receive need-based self-help aid. 70% freshmen, 70% undergrads receive any aid. 93% undergrads borrow to pay for school. Average cumulative indebtedness $17,000. **Criteria for awarding institutional aid:** *Non-need-based:* Academics, art, leadership, minority status, state/district residency.

LETOURNEAU UNIVERSITY

PO Box 7001, Longview, TX 75607
Phone: 903-233-3400
E-mail: admissions@letu.edu **CEEB Code:** 6365
Fax: 903-233-4301 **Website:** www.letu.edu **ACT Code:** 4120

This private school was founded in 1946. It has a 162-acre campus.

RATINGS
Admissions Selectivity Rating: 87   **Fire Safety Rating:** 60*   **Green Rating:** 60*

STUDENTS AND FACULTY
Enrollment: 3,296. **Student Body:** 56% female, 44% male, 52% out-of-state, 1% international (24 countries represented). Asian 1%, African American 20%, Caucasian 68%, Hispanic 8%.
Retention and Graduation: 75% freshmen return for sophomore year. 19% grads go on to further study within 1 year. **Faculty:** Student/faculty ratio 19:1. 74 full-time faculty, 74% hold PhDs, 11% are members of minority groups, 18% are women.

ACADEMICS
Degrees: Associate, bachelor's, master's. **Classes:** Most classes have fewer than 10 students. Most lab/discussion sessions have 10–19 students. **Majors with Highest Enrollment:** Aviation/airway management and operations; business/commerce; engineering. **Special Study Options:** Accelerated program, cooperative education program, distance learning, double major, dual enrollment, honors program, independent study, internships, study abroad, teacher certification program, weekend college. **Career services:** Alumni services, career/job search classes, career assessment, internships.

FACILITIES
Housing: Special housing for disabled students, men's dorms, special housing for international students, women's dorms, apartments for married students, apartments for single students, theme housingResidential societies available. **Special Academic Facilities/Equipment:** Longview Citizens Resource Center; R.G. LeTourneau Memorial Museum. **Computers:** Students can register for classes online. Administrative functions (other than registration) can be performed online.

CAMPUS LIFE
Environment: Town. **Activities:** Choral groups, drama/theater, jazz band, literary magazine, music ensembles, musical theater, student government, student newspaper, student-run film society, yearbook, campus ministries, international student organization. **Organizations:** 44 registered organizations, 4 honor societies, 10 religious organizations. **Athletics (Intercollegiate):** *Men:* Baseball, basketball, cross-country, golf, soccer, tennis. *Women:* Basketball, cross-country, golf, soccer, softball, tennis, volleyball.

ADMISSIONS
Freshman Academic Profile: Average high school GPA 3.58. 30% in top 10% of high school class, 59% in top 25% of high school class, 85% in top 50% of high school class. 56% from public high schools. SAT Math middle 50% range 540–660. SAT Critical Reading middle 50% range 520–650. SAT Writing middle 50% range 490–620. ACT middle 50% range 22–29. Minimum paper TOEFL 500. Minimum computer TOEFL 173. **Basis for Candidate Selection:** *Very important factors considered include:* Academic GPA, rigor of secondary school record, standardized test scores. *Important factors considered include:* Class rank, application essay, character/personal qualities, religious affiliation/commitment. *Other factors considered include:* Recommendation(s), alumni/ae relation, extracurricular activities, first generation, interview, racial/ethnic status, talent/ability, volunteer work. **Freshman Admission Requirements:** High school diploma is required and GED is accepted. *Academic units required:* 4 English, 3 mathematics, 3 science, (3 science labs), 2 social studies, 1 history. *Academic units recommended:* 1 foreign language, 2 academic electives. **Freshman Admission Statistics:** 970 applied, 66% admitted, 50% enrolled. **Transfer Admission Requirements:** College transcript(s), essay or personal statement, minimum college GPA of 2.0 required. Lowest grade transferable C. **General Admission Information:** Application fee $25. Regular notification 8/26. Notification on a rolling basis, beginning on or about 9/15. Nonfall registration accepted. Credit and/or placement offered for CEEB Advanced Placement tests.

COSTS AND FINANCIAL AID
Annual tuition $8,855. **Required Forms and Deadlines:** FAFSA. Priority financial aid filing date 2/15. **Notification of Awards:** Applicants will be notified of awards on a rolling basis beginning 3/1. **Types of Aid:** *Need-based scholarships/grants:* Federal Pell, SEOG, state scholarships/grants, private scholarships, the school's own gift aid. *Loans:* FFEL Subsidized Stafford, FFEL Unsubsidized Stafford, FFEL PLUS, Federal Perkins, state loans **Student Em-**

ployment: Federal Work-Study Program available. Institutional employment available. Off-campus job opportunities are excellent. **Financial Aid Statistics:** 96% undergrads receive any aid. **Criteria for awarding institutional aid:** *Non-need-based:* Academics, leadership.

LEWIS AND CLARK COLLEGE

0615 SW Palatine Hill Road, Portland, OR 97219-7899
Phone: 503-768-7040 **Financial Aid Phone:** 503-768-7090
E-mail: admissions@lclark.edu **CEEB Code:** 4384
Fax: 503-768-7055 **Website:** www.lclark.edu **ACT Code:** 3464

This private school was founded in 1867. It has a 137-acre campus.

RATINGS
Admissions Selectivity Rating: 93   **Fire Safety Rating:** 94   **Green Rating:** 76

STUDENTS AND FACULTY
Enrollment: 1,921. **Student Body:** 61% female, 39% male, 5% international (41 countries represented). Asian 6%, African American 2%, Caucasian 60%, Hispanic 5%, Native American 1%.
Retention and Graduation: 87% freshmen return for sophomore year. 64% freshmen graduate within 4 years. 17% grads go on to further study within 1 year. 14% grads pursue arts and sciences degrees. 1% grads pursue law degrees. 1% grads pursue business degrees. 2% grads pursue medical degrees. **Faculty:** Student/faculty ratio 12:1. 222 full-time faculty, 97% hold PhDs, 10% are members of minority groups, 45% are women.

ACADEMICS
Degrees: Bachelor's, first professional, master's, post-master's certificate. **Classes:** Most classes have 20–29 students. Most lab/discussion sessions have 20–29 students. **Majors with Highest Enrollment:** Biology/biological sciences; international relations and affairs; psychology. **Special Study Options:** Accelerated program, cross-registration, double major, dual enrollment, English as a Second Language (ESL), honors program, independent study, internships, student-designed major, study abroad, teacher certification program, Teacher certification is graduate level only. **Honors programs:** Honors are designated by each department **Combined degree programs:** BA/MA, BA/MAT, 4+1 year master's degree and credential. Special programs offered to physically disabled students include note-taking services, reader services, tape recorders, tutors. **Career services:** Alumni network, alumni services, career assessment, internships, regional alumni.

FACILITIES
Housing: Coed dorms, women's dorms, theme floors, apartment-style residence halls for upper-class students. 85% of campus accessible to physically disabled. **Special Academic Facilities/Equipment:** Art gallery, observatory, world music room, 85 Rank Casavant organ, renovated greenhouse. **Computers:** 50% of classrooms, 20% of dorms, 100% of libraries, 25% of common outdoor areas have wireless network access. Students can register for classes online. Administrative functions (other than registration) can be performed online.

CAMPUS LIFE
Environment: City. **Activities:** Choral groups, concert band, dance, drama/theater, jazz band, literary magazine, music ensembles, musical theater, radio station, student government, student newspaper, symphony orchestra, television station, yearbook, campus ministries, international student organization, Model UN. **Organizations:** 70 registered organizations, 5 honor societies, 9 religious organizations. **Athletics (Intercollegiate):** *Men:* Baseball, basketball, crew/rowing, cross-country, football, golf, swimming, tennis, track/field (outdoor). *Women:* Basketball, crew/rowing, cross-country, golf, soccer, softball, swimming, tennis, track/field (outdoor), volleyball. **On-Campus Highlights:** Gallery of Contemporary Art, New residence halls/Maggie's Cafe, Library, Templeton Student Center, Pamplin Sports Center, Howard Hall, newest academic building. **Environmental Initiatives:** Lewis & Clark provides students, faculty, and staff with a fare-free shuttle bus system that allows access to downtown Portland, local neighborhoods, and retail stores. We installed a 100kW photovoltaic system. Students funds are used to purchase green power. Lewis & Clark established an Environmental Council in the late 1990's that has since been renamed as the Sustainability Council. The trustee investment committee has made a $3 million commitment to fund sustainable energy development. Since 1991 Lewis & Clark has invested in energy conservation projects that have resulted

in a current annual reduction in use of 4,000,000 kWh of electricity and 230,000 Therms of natural gas with a corresponding decrease in carbon footprint.

ADMISSIONS

Freshman Academic Profile: Average high school GPA 3.7. 43% in top 10% of high school class, 83% in top 25% of high school class, 99% in top 50% of high school class. 74% from public high schools. SAT Math middle 50% range 590–680. SAT Critical Reading middle 50% range 630–720. SAT Writing middle 50% range 610–700. ACT middle 50% range 27–31. Minimum paper TOEFL 550. Minimum computer TOEFL 213. **Basis for Candidate Selection:** *Very important factors considered include:* Academic GPA, rigor of secondary school record, racial/ethnic status. *Important factors considered include:* Class rank, application essay, recommendation(s), standardized test scores, alumni/ae relation, character/personal qualities, extracurricular activities, first generation, talent/ability, volunteer work. *Other factors considered include:* Geographical residence, interview, level of applicant's interest, state residency, work experience. **Freshman Admission Requirements:** High school diploma is required and GED is accepted. *Academic units recommended:* 4 English, 4 mathematics, 3 science, (2 science labs), 3 foreign language, 4 social studies, 1 fine arts. **Freshman Admission Statistics:** 5,551 applied, 58% admitted, 17% enrolled. **Transfer Admission Requirements:** High school transcript, college transcript(s), essay or personal statement, statement of good standing from prior institution(s). Minimum college GPA of 2.0 required. Lowest grade transferable C. **General Admission Information:** Application fee $50. Regular application deadline 2/1. Regular notification 4/1. Nonfall registration accepted. Admission may be deferred for a maximum of 1 year. Credit and/or placement offered for CEEB Advanced Placement tests.

COSTS AND FINANCIAL AID

Annual tuition $35,283. . Room and board $9,242. Required fees $238. Average book expense $2,040. **Required Forms and Deadlines:** FAFSA, CSS/Financial Aid PROFILE. Priority financial aid filing date 2/15. **Notification of Awards:** Applicants will be notified of awards on a rolling basis beginning 3/1. **Types of Aid:** *Need-based scholarships/grants:* Federal Pell, SEOG, state scholarships/grants, private scholarships, the school's own gift aid. *Loans:* Direct Subsidized Stafford, Direct Unsubsidized Stafford, Direct PLUS, FFEL Subsidized Stafford, FFEL Unsubsidized Stafford, FFEL PLUS, Federal Perkins. **Student Employment:** Federal Work-Study Program available. Institutional employment available. Highest amount earned per year from on-campus jobs $1,800. Off-campus job opportunities are fair. **Financial Aid Statistics:** 51% freshmen, 52% undergrads receive need-based scholarship or grant aid. 3% freshmen, 4% undergrads receive non-need-based scholarship or grant aid. 46% freshmen, 43% undergrads receive need-based self-help aid. 78% freshmen, 80% undergrads receive any aid. 57% undergrads borrow to pay for school. Average cumulative indebtedness $20,611. **Criteria for awarding institutional aid:** *Non-need-based:* Academics, leadership, music/drama.

See page 1144.

LEWIS UNIVERSITY

One University Parkway, Box 297, Romeoville, IL 60446-2200
Phone: 815-836-5250 **Financial Aid Phone:** 815-836-5135
E-mail: admissions@lewisu.edu **CEEB Code:** 1404
Fax: 815-836-5002 **Website:** www.lewisu.edu **ACT Code:** 1058

This private school, affiliated with the Roman Catholic Church, was founded in 1932. It has a 375-acre campus.

RATINGS

Admissions Selectivity Rating: 76   **Fire Safety Rating:** 60*   **Green Rating:** 60*

STUDENTS AND FACULTY

Enrollment: 3,913. **Student Body:** 59% female, 41% male, 4.1% out-of-state, 3% international (31 countries represented). Asian 4%, African American 10%, Caucasian 69%, Hispanic 11%.
Retention and Graduation: 78% freshmen return for sophomore year. 37% freshmen graduate within 4 years. **Faculty:** Student/faculty ratio 13:1. 183 full-time faculty, 67% hold PhDs, 10% are members of minority groups, 53% are women.

ACADEMICS

Degrees: Associate, bachelor's, certificate, master's, post-master's certificate. **Classes:** Most classes have 10–19 students. Most lab/discussion sessions have 10–19 students. **Majors with Highest Enrollment:** Business/commerce; criminal justice/police science; nursing/registered nurse (RN, ASN, BSN, MSN). **Special Study Options:** Accelerated program, distance learning, double major, dual enrollment, English as a Second Language (ESL), exchange

student program (domestic), honors program, independent study, internships, liberal arts/career combination, student-designed major, study abroad, teacher certification program **Honors programs:** Honors Program offers academically motivated students opportunities for active and collaborative learning. Students have the opporuntiy to fulfill many of their general education requirements in a "paired course" arrangement that allows for greater integration of material and content. **Combined degree programs:** BA/MA, MSN-MBA/BS-MBA. Special programs offered to physically disabled students include note-taking services, tape recorders, tutors. **Career services:** Alumni network, alumni services, career/job search classes, career assessment, internships, regional alumni. **Career services highlights include:** Our Alumni Volunteer Network pairs current stduents with professionals active in their field of interest for mentoring and career search guidance.

FACILITIES

Housing: Coed dorms, special housing for disabled students, theme housing 95% of campus accessible to physically disabled. **Special Academic Facilities/Equipment:** Lewis University is located immediately adjacent to the Lewis University airport, and contains an aviation complex, which includes a Boeing 737 located on campus for use by students studying aviation maintenance. Special collections on campus include: Curriculum Collection, Eva White Memorial Aviation Collection, Library of American Civilization (ultrafiche), Library of English Literature (ultrafiche), ERIC fiche, Government Documents (Lewis University has housed a selective Federal Depository since 1952, and possesses a strong collection of the public documents generated during each decennial census), and Canal and Regional History Collection/I and M Canal Archives (one of the largest collections of documents, photographs, and artifacts pertaining to the canal era in the United States). **Computers:** 100% of classrooms, 100% of dorms, 100% of libraries, 100% of dining areas, 100% of student union, 100% of common outdoor areas have wireless network access. Students can register for classes online. Administrative functions (other than registration) can be performed online.

CAMPUS LIFE

Environment: Metropolis. **Activities:** Choral groups, dance, drama/theater, jazz band, literary magazine, music ensembles, musical theater, radio station, student government, student newspaper, television station, campus ministries, international student organization. **Organizations:** 45 registered organizations, 10 honor societies, 7 religious organizations. 7 fraternities, 6 sororities. **Athletics (Intercollegiate):** *Men:* Baseball, basketball, cheerleading, cross-country, golf, soccer, swimming, tennis, track/field (outdoor), track/field (indoor), volleyball. *Women:* Basketball, cheerleading, cross-country, golf, soccer, softball, swimming, tennis, track/field (outdoor), track/field (indoor), volleyball. **On-Campus Highlights:** Harold E. White Aviation Center, Student Recreation and Fitness Center, Philip Lynch Theatre, Student Union/Bookstore, Flyer's Den.

ADMISSIONS

Freshman Academic Profile: Average high school GPA 3.17. 11% in top 10% of high school class, 35% in top 25% of high school class, 73% in top 50% of high school class. 75% from public high schools. SAT Math middle 50% range 430–620. SAT Critical Reading middle 50% range 420–530. ACT middle 50% range 19–24. Minimum paper TOEFL 500. Minimum computer TOEFL 173. **Basis for Candidate Selection:** *Very important factors considered include:* Academic GPA, rigor of secondary school record, standardized test scores. *Important factors considered include:* Application essay. *Other factors considered include:* Class rank, recommendation(s), alumni/ae relation, character/personal qualities, extracurricular activities, first generation, geographical residence, interview, level of applicant's interest, racial/ethnic status, talent/ability, volunteer work, work experience. **Freshman Admission Requirements:** High school diploma is required and GED is accepted. *Academic units required:* 3 English. *Academic units recommended:* 4 English, 3 mathematics, 2 science, (1 science labs), 2 foreign language, 2 social studies, 1 history, 4 academic electives. **Freshman Admission Statistics:** 2,644 applied, 71% admitted, 35% enrolled. **Transfer Admission Requirements:** College transcript(s), minimum college GPA of 2.0 required. Lowest grade transferable D. **General Admission Information:** Application fee $40. Notification on a rolling basis, beginning on or about 10/1. Nonfall registration accepted. Admission may be deferred for a maximum of 1 year. Credit and/or placement offered for CEEB Advanced Placement tests.

COSTS AND FINANCIAL AID

Required Forms and Deadlines: FAFSA. Financial aid filing deadline 5/1. Priority financial aid filing date 5/1. **Notification of Awards:** Applicants will be notified of awards on a rolling basis beginning 2/1. **Types of Aid:** *Need-based scholarships/grants:* Federal Pell, SEOG, state scholarships/grants, private scholarships, the school's own gift aid, Federal Nursing Scholarships. *Loans:* FFEL Subsidized Stafford, FFEL Unsubsidized Stafford, FFEL PLUS, Federal Perkins. **Student Employment:** Federal Work-Study Program available. Institutional employment available. Highest amount earned per year from on-campus jobs $3,000. Off-campus job opportunities are good. **Financial Aid**

Statistics: 56% freshmen, 81% freshmen, 61% freshmen, 9% freshmen, 85% freshmen, 80% undergrads receive any aid. 23.8% undergrads borrow to pay for school. Average cumulative indebtedness $24,451. **Criteria for awarding institutional aid:** *Non-need-based:* Academics, alumni affiliation, art, athletics, leadership, music/drama, religious affiliation.

LEWIS-CLARK STATE COLLEGE

500 Eighth Avenue, Lewiston, ID 83501
Phone: 208-792-2210 **Financial Aid Phone:** 208-792-2224
E-mail: admissions@lcsc.edu **CEEB Code:** 4385
Fax: 208-792-2876 **Website:** www.lcsc.edu **ACT Code:** 920

This public school was founded in 1893. It has a 44-acre campus.

RATINGS
Admissions Selectivity Rating: 74   **Fire Safety Rating:** 60*   **Green Rating:** 60*

STUDENTS AND FACULTY
Enrollment: 3,027. **Student Body:** 61% female, 39% male, 14% out-of-state, 5% international (32 countries represented). Asian 2%, African American 1%, Caucasian 81%, Hispanic 4%, Native American 4%.
Retention and Graduation: 52% freshmen return for sophomore year. 7% grads go on to further study within 1 year. **Faculty:** Student/faculty ratio 18:1. 159 full-time faculty, 47% hold PhDs, 4% are members of minority groups, 53% are women.

ACADEMICS
Degrees: Associate, bachelor's, certificate, diploma, terminal associate, transfer associate. **Classes:** Most classes have fewer than 10 students. **Majors with Highest Enrollment:** Business/commerce; elementary education and teaching; nursing/registered nurse (RN, ASN, BSN, MSN). **Special Study Options:** Accelerated program, cooperative education program, distance learning, double major, dual enrollment, English as a Second Language (ESL), independent study, internships, study abroad, teacher certification program Special programs offered to physically disabled students include note-taking services, reader services, tape recorders, tutors.

FACILITIES
Housing: Coed dorms, apartments for married students, apartments for single students. 95% of campus accessible to physically disabled. **Special Academic Facilities/Equipment:** Museum/art gallery, Media Services **Computers:** Students can register for classes online. Administrative functions (other than registration) can be performed online.

CAMPUS LIFE
Environment: Town. **Activities:** Drama/theater, jazz band, literary magazine, radio station, student government, student newspaper, campus ministries, international student organization. **Organizations:** 52 registered organizations, 1 honor societies, 3 religious organizations. **Athletics (Intercollegiate):** *Men:* Baseball, basketball, cross-country, golf, tennis. *Women:* Basketball, cross-country, golf, tennis, volleyball. **On-Campus Highlights:** Information Commons in the library, Student Union Building, Athletic Center which is under construction, Centennial Mall, Yo Espresso or Jitterz.

ADMISSIONS
Freshman Academic Profile: Average high school GPA 3.01. 6.62% in top 10% of high school class, 23.29% in top 25% of high school class, 52.14% in top 50% of high school class. 99% from public high schools. SAT Math middle 50% range 440–550. SAT Critical Reading middle 50% range 420–520. ACT middle 50% range 17–23. Minimum paper TOEFL 500. Minimum computer TOEFL 173. **Basis for Candidate Selection:** *Very important factors considered include:* Academic GPA, rigor of secondary school record, standardized test scores. **Freshman Admission Requirements:** High school diploma is required and GED is accepted. *Academic units required:* 4 English, 3 mathematics, 3 science, (2 science labs). **Freshman Admission Statistics:** 1,434 applied, 59% admitted, 74% enrolled. **Transfer Admission Requirements:** College transcript(s), minimum college GPA of 2.0 required. Lowest grade transferable D. **General Admission Information:** Application fee $35. Nonfall registration accepted. Admission may be deferred for a maximum of 1 year. Credit and/or placement offered for CEEB Advanced Placement tests.

COSTS AND FINANCIAL AID
Annual in-state tuition $4,296. Annual out-of-state tuition $11,950. Room and board $5,400. Average book expense $1,500. **Required Forms and Deadlines:** FAFSA. Priority financial aid filing date 3/1. **Notification of Awards:** Applicants will be notified of awards on a rolling basis beginning 4/15. **Types of Aid:** *Need-based scholarships/grants:* Federal Pell, SEOG, state scholarships/

grants, private scholarships, the school's own gift aid. *Loans:* FFEL Subsidized Stafford, FFEL Unsubsidized Stafford, FFEL PLUS, Federal Perkins, Federal Nursing **Student Employment:** Federal Work-Study Program available. Institutional employment available. **Financial Aid Statistics:** 40% freshmen, 47% undergrads receive need-based scholarship or grant aid. 35% freshmen, 17% undergrads receive non-need-based scholarship or grant aid. 50% freshmen, 57% undergrads receive need-based self-help aid. 5% freshmen, 8% undergrads receive athletic scholarships. 85% freshmen, 76% undergrads receive any aid. 61% undergrads borrow to pay for school. **Criteria for awarding institutional aid:** *Non-need-based:* Academics, alumni affiliation, art, athletics, leadership, minority status, music/drama.

LIBERTY UNIVERSITY

1971 University Blvd, Lynchburg, VA 24502
Phone: 434-582-2000 **Financial Aid Phone:** 434-582-2270
E-mail: admissions@liberty.edu **CEEB Code:** 5385
Fax: 800-628-7977 **Website:** www.liberty.edu **ACT Code:** 4364

This private school, affiliated with the Baptist Church, was founded in 1971. It has a 4400-acre campus.

RATINGS
Admissions Selectivity Rating: 87   **Fire Safety Rating:** 71   **Green Rating:** 60*

STUDENTS AND FACULTY
Enrollment: 28,243. **Student Body:** 54% female, 46% male, 58.26% out-of-state, 2% international (63 countries represented). Asian 1%, African American 14%, Caucasian 59%, Hispanic 3%.
Retention and Graduation: 79% freshmen return for sophomore year. 30% freshmen graduate within 4 years. **Faculty:** Student/faculty ratio 45:1. 379 full-time faculty, 32% are women.

ACADEMICS
Degrees: Associate, bachelor's, certificate, doctoral, master's, post-master's certificate, terminal associate. **Classes:** Most classes have 20–29 students. **Majors with Highest Enrollment:** Business/commerce; psychology; religion/religious studies. **Special Study Options:** Accelerated program, cooperative education program, distance learning, double major, dual enrollment, English as a Second Language (ESL), external degree program, honors program, independent study, internships, student-designed major, teacher certification program, weekend college. **Honors programs:** An early class registration period, smaller class size (15:1) for general education Honors seminars, and a generous scholarship based on grade point average are just a few of the benefits enjoyed by our Honors students. Once Honors students reach junior status, they petition one Honors course per semester in their desired major field of study. Special programs offered to physically disabled students include tutors. **Career services:** Career assessment, internships. **Career services highlights include:** www.liberty.edu/academics/general/career/index.cfm?PID=6149.

FACILITIES
Housing: Special housing for disabled students, men's dorms, women's dorms, apartments for single students. 94% of campus accessible to physically disabled. **Special Academic Facilities/Equipment:** Displays from the Museum of Life and Earth History are located in the Library. The Jerry Falwell Museum located in the main lobby of DeMoss Hall. **Computers:** 90% of classrooms, have wireless network access. Students can register for classes online. Administrative functions (other than registration) can be performed online.

CAMPUS LIFE
Environment: Town. **Activities:** Choral groups, concert band, drama/theater, literary magazine, marching band, music ensembles, musical theater, pep band, radio station, student government, student newspaper, symphony orchestra, television station, yearbook, campus ministries. **Organizations:** 25 registered organizations, 8 honor societies, 10 religious organizations. **Athletics (Intercollegiate):** *Men:* Baseball, basketball, cheerleading, cross-country, football, golf, soccer, tennis, track/field (outdoor), track/field (indoor), wrestling. *Women:* Basketball, cheerleading, cross-country, soccer, softball, tennis, track/field (outdoor), track/field (indoor), volleyball. **On-Campus Highlights:** LaHaye Student Center, bookstore, Hangar (food court), ILRC Computer Lab, LaHaye Ice Center (ice arena).

ADMISSIONS
Freshman Academic Profile: Average high school GPA 3.23. SAT Math middle 50% range 430–550. SAT Critical Reading middle 50% range 440–570. ACT middle 50% range 18–24. Minimum paper TOEFL 500. Minimum computer TOEFL 173. **Basis for Candidate Selection:** *Very important factors considered include:* Rigor of secondary school record, standardized test scores.

Important factors considered include: Application essay, academic GPA. *Other factors considered include:* Class rank, recommendation(s), character/personal qualities, extracurricular activities, level of applicant's interest, talent/ability. **Freshman Admission Requirements:** High school diploma is required and GED is accepted. *Academic units recommended:* 4 English, 3 mathematics, 2 science, (2 science labs), 2 foreign language, 2 social studies, 4 academic electives. **Freshman Admission Statistics:** 38,097 applied, 20% admitted, 67% enrolled. **Transfer Admission Requirements:** High school transcript, college transcript(s), essay or personal statement, statement of good standing from prior institution(s). Minimum college GPA of 2.0 required. Lowest grade transferable C. **General Admission Information:** Application fee $40. Nonfall registration accepted. Admission may be deferred for a maximum of 1 year. Credit and/or placement offered for CEEB Advanced Placement tests.

COSTS AND FINANCIAL AID

Annual tuition $15,992. Room and board $5,996. Required fees $1,210. Average book expense $1,400. **Required Forms and Deadlines:** FAFSA, state aid form Financial aid filing deadline 3/1. Priority financial aid filing date 3/1. **Notification of Awards:** Applicants will be notified of awards on a rolling basis beginning 3/15. **Types of Aid:** *Need-based scholarships/grants:* Federal Pell, SEOG, state scholarships/grants, private scholarships, the school's own gift aid. *Loans:* FFEL Subsidized Stafford, FFEL Unsubsidized Stafford, FFEL PLUS. **Student Employment:** Off-campus job opportunities are good. **Financial Aid Statistics:** 95% freshmen, 87% undergrads receive any aid. **Criteria for awarding institutional aid:** *Non-need-based:* Academics, alumni affiliation, athletics, leadership, music/drama, religious affiliation, state/district residency.

See page 1146.

LIFE PACIFIC COLLEGE

1100 Covina Blvd, San Dimas, CA 91773
Phone: 909-599-5433 **Financial Aid Phone:** 909-599-5433
E-mail: adm@lifepacific.edu
Fax: 909-599-6690 **Website:** www.lifepacific.edu **ACT Code:** 489

This private school, affiliated with the Protestant Church, was founded in 1923. It has a 9-acre campus.

RATINGS
Admissions Selectivity Rating: 70   **Fire Safety Rating:** 60*   **Green Rating:** 60*

STUDENTS AND FACULTY
Enrollment: 528. **Student Body:** 46% female, 54% male, 48% out-of-state, (2 countries represented).
Retention and Graduation: 69% freshmen return for sophomore year. 18% freshmen graduate within 4 years. 48% grads go on to further study within 1 year. **Faculty:** Student/faculty ratio 17:1. 12 full-time faculty, 17% hold PhDs, 8% are members of minority groups, 17% are women.

ACADEMICS
Degrees: Associate, bachelor's. **Classes:** Most classes have 10–19 students. Most lab/discussion sessions have 20–29 students. **Special Study Options:** Accelerated program, distance learning, dual enrollment, external degree program, independent study, internships Special programs offered to physically disabled students include note-taking services, tape recorders, tutors. **Career services:** Alumni services, career/job search classes, internships. **Career services highlights include:** Our service learning program is required for all students.

FACILITIES
Housing: Men's dorms, women's dorms 100% of campus accessible to physically disabled. **Special Academic Facilities/Equipment:** New gymnasium and work out facilities; new computer lab; new student center; new music facilities. **Computers:** Students can register for classes online.

CAMPUS LIFE
Environment: Town. **Activities:** Choral groups, dance, drama/theater, music ensembles, student government, yearbook. **Athletics (Intercollegiate):** *Men:* Basketball. *Women:* Volleyball. **On-Campus Highlights:** The Cove Student Center, New Gymnasium, New Work-out room, Music Wing (new).

ADMISSIONS
Freshman Academic Profile: Average high school GPA 2.87. 5% in top 10% of high school class, 21% in top 25% of high school class, 38% in top 50% of high school class. SAT Math middle 50% range 410–510. SAT Critical Reading middle 50% range 430–540. ACT middle 50% range 14–23. Minimum paper TOEFL 550. Minimum computer TOEFL 213. **Basis for Candidate Selection:** *Very important factors considered include:* Application essay, academic

---

GPA, recommendation(s), standardized test scores, character/personal qualities, level of applicant's interest, religious affiliation/commitment. *Other factors considered include:* Alumni/ae relation, extracurricular activities, talent/ability. **Freshman Admission Requirements:** High school diploma is required and GED is accepted. **Freshman Admission Statistics:** 102 applied, 87% admitted, 70% enrolled. **Transfer Admission Requirements:** College transcript(s), essay or personal statement, statement of good standing from prior institution(s). Minimum college GPA of 2.0 required. Lowest grade transferable C. **General Admission Information:** Application fee $35. Regular application deadline 6/1. Nonfall registration accepted. Admission may be deferred for a maximum of 1 year. Credit and/or placement offered for CEEB Advanced Placement tests.

COSTS AND FINANCIAL AID
Annual tuition $9,750. Room and board $5,000. Required fees $350. Average book expense $1,242. **Required Forms and Deadlines:** FAFSA. Priority financial aid filing date 6/1. **Notification of Awards:** Applicants will be notified of awards on a rolling basis beginning 6/1. **Types of Aid:** *Need-based scholarships/grants:* Federal Pell, SEOG, state scholarships/grants, private scholarships, the school's own gift aid. *Loans:* FFEL Subsidized Stafford, FFEL Unsubsidized Stafford, FFEL PLUS. **Student Employment:** Federal Work-Study Program available. Institutional employment available. Off-campus job opportunities are excellent. **Financial Aid Statistics:** 55% freshmen, 51% undergrads receive need-based scholarship or grant aid. 13% freshmen, 2% undergrads receive non-need-based scholarship or grant aid. 56% freshmen, 49% undergrads receive need-based self-help aid. 70% undergrads borrow to pay for school. Average cumulative indebtedness $17,125. **Criteria for awarding institutional aid:** *Non-need-based:* Academics, alumni affiliation, leadership, religious affiliation.

LIM COLLEGE

12 East 53rd Street, New York, NY 10022
Phone: 212-752-1530 **Financial Aid Phone:** 212-752-1530
E-mail: admissions@limcollege.edu **CEEB Code:** 2380
Fax: 212-317-8602 **Website:** www.limcollege.edu **ACT Code:** 4807

This proprietary school was founded in 1939.

RATINGS
Admissions Selectivity Rating: 70   **Fire Safety Rating:** 60*   **Green Rating:** 60*

STUDENTS AND FACULTY
Enrollment: 1,308. **Student Body:** 94% female, 6% male, 57% out-of-state, 1% international (13 countries represented). Asian 6%, African American 11%, Caucasian 68%, Hispanic 14%.
Retention and Graduation: 64% freshmen return for sophomore year. 53% freshmen graduate within 4 years. **Faculty:** Student/faculty ratio 17:1. 26 full-time faculty, 38% hold PhDs, 31% are members of minority groups, 46% are women.

ACADEMICS
Degrees: Associate, bachelor's, master's. **Classes:** Most classes have 10–19 students. **Majors with Highest Enrollment:** Fashion merchandising; marketing/marketing management. **Special Study Options:** Cooperative education program, internships, study abroad, 3 credit trip in winter/summer to Europe. Special programs offered to physically disabled students include tape recorders, tutors. **Career services:** Alumni network, alumni services, career/job search classes, career assessment, internships. **Career services highlights include:** All first and second year students must participate in a 5 week internship between Thanksgiving and Christmas. All seniors must participate in a full-semester co-op.

FACILITIES
Housing: Coed dorms. 100% of campus accessible to physically disabled. **Computers:** 100% of classrooms, 100% of dorms, 100% of libraries, 100% of dining areas, 100% of student union, have wireless network access. Students can register for classes online. Administrative functions (other than registration) can be performed online.

CAMPUS LIFE
Environment: Metropolis. **Activities:** student government, yearbook. **Organizations:** 12 registered organizations, 1 honor societies. **On-Campus Highlights:** Library, Cafe 45, Cyber Lounge, 1760 Third Ave.

ADMISSIONS
Freshman Academic Profile: Average high school GPA 84.5. 3% in top 10% of high school class, 17% in top 25% of high school class, 55% in top 50% of

high school class. 73% from public high schools. SAT Math middle 50% range 420–510. SAT Critical Reading middle 50% range 440–520. SAT Writing middle 50% range 500–520..ACT middle 50% range 19–23. Minimum paper TOEFL 550. Minimum computer TOEFL 213. **Basis for Candidate Selection:** *Very important factors considered include:* Academic GPA, interview, level of applicant's interest. *Important factors considered include:* Class rank, application essay, recommendation(s), rigor of secondary school record, standardized test scores, alumni/ae relation, character/personal qualities, extracurricular activities, talent/ability, volunteer work, work experience. *Other factors considered include:* geographical residence, racial/ethnic status, state residency. **Freshman Admission Requirements:** High school diploma is required and GED is accepted. **Freshman Admission Statistics:** 1,069 applied, 56% admitted, 51% enrolled. **Transfer Admission Requirements:** High school transcript, college transcript(s), essay or personal statement, minimum college GPA of 2.0 required. Lowest grade transferable D–. **General Admission Information:** Application fee $40. Notification on a rolling basis, beginning on or about 12/15. Nonfall registration accepted. Admission may be deferred for a maximum of 1 Semester. Credit offered for CEEB Advanced Placement tests.

COSTS AND FINANCIAL AID

Annual tuition $19,900. Room and board $19,400. Required fees $525. **Required Forms and Deadlines:** FAFSA, institution's own financial aid form. Priority financial aid filing date 4/1. **Notification of Awards:** Applicants will be notified of awards on a rolling basis beginning 2/15. **Types of Aid:** *Need-based scholarships/grants:* Federal Pell, SEOG, state scholarships/grants, private scholarships, the school's own gift aid. *Loans:* Direct Subsidized Stafford, Direct Unsubsidized Stafford, Direct PLUS. **Student Employment:** Federal Work-Study Program available. Institutional employment available. Off-campus job opportunities are excellent. **Financial Aid Statistics:** 38% freshmen, 55% undergrads receive need-based scholarship or grant aid. 15% freshmen, 10% undergrads receive non-need-based scholarship or grant aid. 44% freshmen, 51% undergrads receive need-based self-help aid. 85% freshmen, 85% undergrads receive any aid. 68% undergrads borrow to pay for school. Average cumulative indebtedness $27,505. **Criteria for awarding institutional aid:** *Non-need-based:* Academics.

See page 1148.

LIMESTONE COLLEGE

1115 College Drive, Gaffney, SC 29340-3799
Phone: 864-488-4549 **Financial Aid Phone:** 864-488-8700
E-mail: admiss@limestone.edu **CEEB Code:** 5366
Fax: 864-487-8706 **Website:** www.limestone.edu **ACT Code:** 3862

This private school was founded in 1845. It has a 115-acre campus.

RATINGS

Admissions Selectivity Rating: 74   Fire Safety Rating: 69   Green Rating: 60*

STUDENTS AND FACULTY

Enrollment: 805. **Student Body:** 42% female, 58% male, 45% out-of-state, international. African American 20%, Caucasian 72%, Hispanic 3%. **Retention and Graduation:** 58% freshmen return for sophomore year. 21% freshmen graduate within 4 years. **Faculty:** Student/faculty ratio 11.7:1. 63 full-time faculty, 81% hold PhDs, 5% are members of minority groups, 44% are women.

ACADEMICS

Degrees: Bachelor's, transfer associate. **Classes:** Most classes have 20–29 students. Most lab/discussion sessions have fewer than 10 students. **Majors with Highest Enrollment:** Business/managerial economics; elementary education and teaching; health and P.E./fitness, other. **Special Study Options:** Accelerated program, distance learning, double major, honors program, independent study, internships, liberal arts/career combination, student-designed major, teacher certification program. **Honors programs:** The Honors Program was established at Limestone College in 1983 to create a challenging academic environment for gifted and special ability students. Special programs offered to physically disabled students include tape recorders, tutors. **Career services:** Alumni services, career assessment. **Career services highlights include:** The student is placed in a local private or public enterprise to gain work-related experience consistent with their field of study.

FACILITIES

Housing: Men's dorms, women's dorms, apartments for single students. 90% of campus accessible to physically disabled. **Special Academic Facilities/Equipment:** Computer graphic arts lab; museum of Southern history in Winnie Davis Hall. **Computers:** 20% of classrooms, 20% of dorms, 100% of libraries, 100%

of student union, 5% of common outdoor areas have wireless network access. Students can register for classes online. Administrative functions (other than registration) can be performed online.

CAMPUS LIFE

Environment: Town. **Activities:** Choral groups, concert band, drama/theater, jazz band, literary magazine, music ensembles, musical theater, pep band, student government, yearbook, campus ministries. **Organizations:** 2 religious organizations. **Athletics (Intercollegiate): Men:** Baseball, basketball, cross-country, golf, lacrosse, soccer, swimming, tennis, track/field (outdoor), volleyball, wrestling. **Women:** Basketball, cross-country, field hockey, golf, lacrosse, soccer, softball, swimming, tennis, track/field (outdoor), volleyball. **On-Campus Highlights:** Dixie Lodge, Stephenson Dining Hall, Timken Gym and Pool, Eastwood Library, Curtis Administration Building, The Walt Griffin P.E. Center, Limestone Learning Center, Winnie Davis Hall of History. **Environmental Initiatives:** Community Garden.

ADMISSIONS

Freshman Academic Profile: Average high school GPA 3.09. 3% in top 10% of high school class, 11.6% in top 25% of high school class, 43% in top 50% of high school class. 90% from public high schools. SAT Math middle 50% range 430–540. SAT Critical Reading middle 50% range 410–490. ACT middle 50% range 15–26. Minimum paper TOEFL 500. Minimum computer TOEFL 173. **Basis for Candidate Selection:** *Very important factors considered include:* Academic GPA, rigor of secondary school record, standardized test scores. *Important factors considered include:* Class rank. *Other factors considered include:* Recommendation(s), interview. **Freshman Admission Requirements:** High school diploma is required and GED is accepted. *Academic units required:* 4 English, 3 mathematics, 2 science, (2 science labs), 3 social studies. **Freshman Admission Statistics:** 1,236 applied, 71% admitted, 29% enrolled. **Transfer Admission Requirements:** College transcript(s), statement of good standing from prior institution(s). Minimum college GPA of 2.0 required. Lowest grade transferable C. **General Admission Information:** Application fee $25. Regular application deadline 8/26. Notification on a rolling basis, beginning on or about 6/1..Nonfall registration accepted. Admission may be deferred for a maximum of 18 months. Credit offered for CEEB Advanced Placement tests.

COSTS AND FINANCIAL AID

Annual tuition $19,200. Room and board $7,000. Average book expense $2,304. **Required Forms and Deadlines:** FAFSA. Priority financial aid filing date 2/1. **Notification of Awards:** Applicants will be notified of awards on a rolling basis beginning 1/15. **Types of Aid:** *Need-based scholarships/grants:* Federal Pell, SEOG, state scholarships/grants, private scholarships, the school's own gift aid. *Loans:* FFEL Subsidized Stafford, FFEL Unsubsidized Stafford, FFEL PLUS, Federal Perkins. **Student Employment:** Federal Work-Study Program available. Institutional employment available. Highest amount earned per year from on-campus jobs $8,300. Off-campus job opportunities are good. **Financial Aid Statistics:** 76% freshmen, 72% undergrads receive need-based scholarship or grant aid. 8% freshmen, 5% undergrads receive non-need-based scholarship or grant aid. 80% freshmen, 84% undergrads receive need-based self-help aid. 7% freshmen, 3% undergrads receive athletic scholarships. 98% freshmen, 95% undergrads receive any aid. 88.89% undergrads borrow to pay for school. Average cumulative indebtedness $20,701. **Criteria for awarding institutional aid:** *Non-need-based:* Academics, art, athletics, job skills, leadership, music/drama, state/district residency.

LINCOLN CHRISTIAN COLLEGE AND SEMINARY

100 Campus View Dr, Lincoln, IL 62656-2167
Phone: 2177323168 x:2251 **Financial Aid Phone:** 2177323168
E-mail: coladmis@lccs.edu
Fax: 217-732-4199 **Website:** www.lincolnchristian.edu **ACT Code:** 1060

This private school, affiliated with the Church of Christ Church, was founded in 1944. It has a 100-acre campus.

RATINGS

Admissions Selectivity Rating: 70   Fire Safety Rating: 74   Green Rating: 60*

STUDENTS AND FACULTY

Enrollment: 601. **Student Body:** 51% female, 49% male, 40% out-of-state, (19 countries represented). African American 5%, Caucasian 91%, Hispanic 2%. **Retention and Graduation:** 16.8% grads go on to further study within 1 year. **Faculty:** Student/faculty ratio 15:1. 44 full-time faculty, 45% hold PhDs, 5% are members of minority groups, 18% are women.

ACADEMICS

Degrees: Associate, bachelor's, certificate, first professional, master's. **Special Study Options:** Distance learning, double major, honors program, independent study, internships, study abroad, teacher certification program, weekend college, teacher preparatory program through University of Illinois at Springfield, Illinois State University, and Greenville College. **Honors programs:** Students with at least sophomore standing and a cumulative grade average of 3.5 or higher may apply for acceptance into an honors degree program. The honors degree requires 5 additional semester hours of study under a mentoring professor and the completion of a capstone project. The additional work may be completed in the area of the student's ministry specialization or in an area of interest outside the specialization. Since the program is funded by memorial gifts, honors degree students do not pay tuition for the additional 5 hours. For students who complet the honors degree requirements, special recognition will be given at the Commencement service, and an honors designation will be included on the academic transcript. Special programs offered to physically disabled students include reader services, tape recorders, tutors.

FACILITIES

Housing: Men's dorms, women's dorms, apartments for married students 80% of campus accessible to physically disabled. **Computers:** 90% of classrooms, 100% of dorms, 80% of libraries, have wireless network access. Students can register for classes online. Administrative functions (other than registration) can be performed online.

CAMPUS LIFE

Environment: Village. **Activities:** Choral groups, drama/theater, music ensembles, musical theater, student government, student newspaper, campus ministries, international student organization. **Organizations:** 7 registered organizations. **Athletics (Intercollegiate):** *Men:* Baseball, basketball, soccer. *Women:* Basketball, softball, volleyball. **On-Campus Highlights:** The Warehouse, The Coffee Shop.

ADMISSIONS

Freshman Academic Profile: 19% in top 10% of high school class, 45% in top 25% of high school class, 76% in top 50% of high school class. ACT middle 50% range 19–25. Minimum paper TOEFL 550. Minimum computer TOEFL 213. Minimum web-based TOEFL 75. **Basis for Candidate Selection:** *Very important factors considered include:* Application essay, rigor of secondary school record, standardized test scores, level of applicant's interest, religious affiliation/commitment, state residency. *Important factors considered include:* Class rank, academic GPA, alumni/ae relation, character/personal qualities, extracurricular activities, geographical residence, racial/ethnic status, volunteer work. *Other factors considered include:* Recommendation(s), interview, talent/ability, work experience. **Freshman Admission Requirements:** High school diploma is required and GED is accepted. *Academic units recommended:* 4 English, 3 mathematics, 2 science, 2 foreign language, 3 social studies, 3 history. **Freshman Admission Statistics:** 195 applied, 84% admitted, 65% enrolled. **Transfer Admission Requirements:** High school transcript, college transcript(s), essay or personal statement, minimum college GPA of 2.0 required. Lowest grade transferable C. **General Admission Information:** Application fee $25. Nonfall registration accepted. Admission may be deferred for a maximum of 1 semester. Credit offered for CEEB Advanced Placement tests.

COSTS AND FINANCIAL AID

Annual tuition $11,790. Room and board $5,355. **Required Forms and Deadlines:** FAFSA **Notification of Awards:** Applicants will be notified of awards on a rolling basis beginning 3/1. **Types of Aid:** *Need-based scholarships/grants:* Federal Pell, SEOG, state scholarships/grants. *Loans:* FFEL Subsidized Stafford, FFEL Unsubsidized Stafford, FFEL PLUS, Federal Perkins, college/university loans from institutional funds. **Student Employment:** Federal Work-Study Program available. Institutional employment available. Off-campus job opportunities are good. **Financial Aid Statistics:** 41% freshmen, 50% undergrads receive need-based scholarship or grant aid. 62% freshmen, 61% undergrads receive non-need-based scholarship or grant aid. 49% freshmen, 56% undergrads receive need-based self-help aid. 80% freshmen, 80% undergrads receive any aid. 71% undergrads borrow to pay for school. Average cumulative indebtedness $17,625. **Criteria for awarding institutional aid:** *Non-need-based:* Academics.

LINCOLN COLLEGE

300 Keokuk St, Lincoln, IL 62656
Phone: 800-569-0556
E-mail: admission@lincolncollege.com
Fax: 217-732-7715 **Website:** www.lincolncollege.edu **ACT Code:** 1062

This private school was founded in 1865. It has a 60-acre campus.

RATINGS
Admissions Selectivity Rating: 60*   **Fire Safety Rating:** 60*   **Green Rating:** 60*

ACADEMICS
Degrees: Associate, transfer associate. **Classes:** Special programs offered to physically disabled students include tape recorders, tutors.

FACILITIES
Housing: 90% of campus accessible to physically disabled. **Computers:** Students can register for classes online. Administrative functions (other than registration) can be performed online.

CAMPUS LIFE
Environment: Village. **Activities: Organizations:** 10 registered organizations, 1 honor societies. **Athletics (Intercollegiate):** *Men:* Baseball, basketball, cheerleading, cross-country, diving, golf, soccer, swimming, wrestling. *Women:* Basketball, cheerleading, cross-country, diving, golf, soccer, softball, swimming, volleyball. **On-Campus Highlights:** Meyer-Evans Student Center, Library-Museum, Heritage Resident Halls, Dooley Hall, University Hall, Johnston Center for Performing Arts.

ADMISSIONS
Freshman Academic Profile: 80% from public high schools. Minimum paper TOEFL 480. Minimum computer TOEFL 157. **General Admission Information:** Placement offered for CEEB Advanced Placement tests.

COSTS AND FINANCIAL AID
Student Employment: Federal Work-Study Program available. Institutional employment available. Highest amount earned per year from on-campus jobs $1,500. Off-campus job opportunities are fair. **Financial Aid Statistics:** 92% freshmen, 92% undergrads receive any aid.

LINCOLN MEMORIAL UNIVERSITY

6965 Cumberland Gap Parkway, Harrogate, TN 37752
Phone: 423-869-6280
E-mail: admissions@lmunet.edu **CEEB Code:** 1408
Fax: 423-869-6250 **Website:** www.lmunet.edu **ACT Code:** 3982

This private school was founded in 1897. It has a 1000-acre campus.

RATINGS
Admissions Selectivity Rating: 78   **Fire Safety Rating:** 60*   **Green Rating:** 60*

STUDENTS AND FACULTY
Enrollment: 1,464. **Student Body:** 72% female, 28% male, 36% out-of-state, 4% international (14 countries represented). Asian 1%, African American 5%, Caucasian 77%, Hispanic 1%.
Retention and Graduation: 65% freshmen return for sophomore year. 22% freshmen graduate within 4 years. **Faculty:** Student/faculty ratio 12:1.

ACADEMICS
Degrees: Associate, bachelor's, master's, post-bachelor's certificate, post-master's certificate. **Classes:** Most classes have fewer than 10 students. Most lab/discussion sessions have 10–19 students. **Special Study Options:** Accelerated program, distance learning, double major, dual enrollment, English as a Second Language (ESL), internships, teacher certification program. **Career services:** Alumni services.

FACILITIES
Housing: Coed dorms, special housing for disabled students, men's dorms, women's dorms, apartments for married students, apartments for single students. 60% of campus accessible to physically disabled. **Special Academic Facilities/Equipment:** Civil War museum, including Abraham Lincoln memorabilia collection of over 6,000 books, paintings, and manuscripts.

CAMPUS LIFE
Environment: Rural. **Activities:** Choral groups, dance, drama/theater, literary magazine, music ensembles, pep band, radio station, student government,

television station, yearbook, campus ministries, international student organization. **Organizations:** 26 registered organizations, 5 honor societies, 3 religious organizations. 3 fraternities, 3 sororities. **Athletics (Intercollegiate):** *Men:* Baseball, basketball, cross-country, golf, soccer, tennis. *Women:* Basketball, cross-country, golf, soccer, softball, tennis, volleyball.

ADMISSIONS

Freshman Academic Profile: Average high school GPA 3.35. 90% from public high schools. SAT Math middle 50% range 440–560. SAT Critical Reading middle 50% range 420–550. ACT middle 50% range 18–23. Minimum paper TOEFL 500. **Basis for Candidate Selection:** *Very important factors considered include:* Academic GPA, rigor of secondary school record, standardized test scores. *Important factors considered include:* Class rank, alumni/ae relation, character/personal qualities. *Other factors considered include:* Extracurricular activities, first generation, racial/ethnic status, religious affiliation/commitment, volunteer work. **Freshman Admission Requirements:** High school diploma is required and GED is accepted. *Academic units required:* 4 English, 3 mathematics, 2 science, 2 foreign language, 1 social studies, 1 history, 1 visual/performing arts. *Academic units recommended:* 4 English, 4 mathematics, (2 science labs), 2 social studies, 7 academic electives. **Freshman Admission Statistics:** 1,412 applied, 69% admitted, 33% enrolled. **Transfer Admission Requirements:** High school transcript, college transcript(s), standardized test scores, minimum college GPA of 2.0 required. Lowest grade transferable C. **General Admission Information:** Application fee $25. Notification on a rolling basis, beginning on or about 9/1. Nonfall registration accepted. Credit offered for CEEB Advanced Placement tests.

COSTS AND FINANCIAL AID

Average book expense $1,200. **Required Forms and Deadlines:** FAFSA. Priority financial aid filing date 4/1. **Notification of Awards:** Applicants will be notified of awards on a rolling basis beginning 4/15. **Types of Aid:** *Need-based scholarships/grants:* Federal Pell, SEOG, state scholarships/grants, private scholarships, the school's own gift aid. *Loans:* FFEL Subsidized Stafford, FFEL Unsubsidized Stafford, FFEL PLUS, Federal Perkins. **Student Employment:** Federal Work-Study Program available. Highest amount earned per year from on-campus jobs $1,500. Off-campus job opportunities are fair. **Financial Aid Statistics:** 90% freshmen, 83% undergrads receive need-based scholarship or grant aid. 3% freshmen, 10% undergrads receive non-need-based scholarship or grant aid. 42% freshmen, 51% undergrads receive need-based self-help aid. 13% freshmen, 5% undergrads receive athletic scholarships. 60% undergrads borrow to pay for school. Average cumulative indebtedness $10,623. **Criteria for awarding institutional aid:** *Non-need-based:* Academics, alumni affiliation, art, athletics, leadership, music/drama.

LINCOLN UNIVERSITY (CA)

401 15th Street, Oakland, CA 94612
Phone: 510-628-8010 **Financial Aid Phone:** 510-628-8023
E-mail: admissions@lincolnuca.edu
Fax: 510-628-8012 **Website:** www.lincolnuca.edu

This private school was founded in 1919.

RATINGS
Admissions Selectivity Rating: 60*   **Fire Safety Rating:** 60*   **Green Rating:** 60*

STUDENTS AND FACULTY
Enrollment: 114. **Student Body:** 65% female, 35% male. African American 2%.
Faculty: 6 full-time faculty, 100% hold PhDs, 50% are women.

ACADEMICS
Degrees: Associate, bachelor's, certificate, master's. **Majors with Highest Enrollment:** Bible/biblical studies; education; youth ministry. **Special Study Options:** Cross-registration, double major, English as a Second Language (ESL), internships, student-designed major. **Career services:** Alumni network, internships.

FACILITIES
Housing: Universal Student Housing Placement.

CAMPUS LIFE
Environment: Metropolis. **Activities:** student government.

ADMISSIONS
Freshman Academic Profile: Minimum paper TOEFL 500. Minimum computer TOEFL 173. **Basis for Candidate Selection:** *Very important factors considered include:* Rigor of secondary school record. *Important factors con-*

sidered include: Academic GPA. *Other factors considered include:* Class rank, standardized test scores. **Freshman Admission Requirements:** High school diploma is required and GED is accepted. **Freshman Admission Statistics:** 33 applied, 100% admitted, 52% enrolled. **Transfer Admission Requirements:** College transcript(s), minimum college GPA of 2.0 required. Lowest grade transferable C. **General Admission Information:** Application fee $75. Regular application deadline 8/15. Nonfall registration accepted. Admission may be deferred for a maximum of 3 semester.

COSTS AND FINANCIAL AID
Annual tuition $7,080. Required fees $400. Average book expense $400. **Types of Aid:** *Need-based scholarships/grants:* Federal Pell.

LINCOLN UNIVERSITY (MO)

820 Chestnut Street, B7 Young Hall, Jefferson City, MO 65102-0029
Phone: 573-681-5599 **Financial Aid Phone:** 573-681-6156
E-mail: enroll@lincolnu.edu **CEEB Code:** 177940
Fax: 573-681-5889 **Website:** www.lincolnu.edu **ACT Code:** 2322

This public school was founded in 1866. It has a 165-acre campus.

RATINGS
Admissions Selectivity Rating: 64   **Fire Safety Rating:** 60*   **Green Rating:** 71

STUDENTS AND FACULTY
Enrollment: 2,650. **Student Body:** 59% female, 41% male, 15% out-of-state, 2% international (29 countries represented). Asian 1%, African American 46%, Caucasian 47%, Hispanic 2%.
Retention and Graduation: 52% freshmen return for sophomore year. 11% freshmen graduate within 4 years. **Faculty:** Student/faculty ratio 15:1. 139 full-time faculty, 29% are members of minority groups, 50% are women.

ACADEMICS
Degrees: Associate, bachelor's, master's, post-master's certificate, terminal associate, transfer associate. **Classes:** Most classes have 20–29 students. **Majors with Highest Enrollment:** Business administration and management; computer and information sciences; criminal justice/law enforcement administration. **Special Study Options:** Accelerated program, distance learning, double major, dual enrollment, exchange student program (domestic), honors program, independent study, internships, study abroad, teacher certification program, Senior Citizen Program; Learning in Retirement, Inc.; Intersession courses. **Honors programs:** Lincoln University offers a 24-credit-hour Honors Program which features small classes, unique academic challenges, individual attention from Honors faculty, and association with other like-minded students. An Honors student has opportunities to compete for summer mentorships, work closely with a faculty member on a research or creative project; to do sustained research or creative work leading to a thesis in the student's major; and to present his/her work at regional, national, and international conferences. These students also qualify for Honors housing, certain restricted courses, and other activities. Special programs offered to physically disabled students include note-taking services, reader services, tape recorders, tutors. **Career services:** Alumni services, career assessment, internships. **Career services highlights include:** All of the above.

FACILITIES
Housing: Coed dorms, men's dorms, women's dorms, wellness housingHonors Student Housing. 100% of campus accessible to physically disabled. **Special Academic Facilities/Equipment:** University Archives/Ethnic Studies Center, Media Center, Student Support Services Center for Academic Enrichment, Agriculture and Extension Information Center, Education Curriculum Library. **Computers:** 100% of classrooms, 100% of dorms, 100% of libraries, 100% of dining areas, 100% of student union, have wireless network access. Students can register for classes online. Administrative functions (other than registration) can be performed online.

CAMPUS LIFE
Environment: Town. **Activities:** Choral groups, concert band, dance, drama/theater, jazz band, literary magazine, marching band, music ensembles, pep band, radio station, student government, student newspaper, television station, yearbook, campus ministries, international student organization. **Organizations:** 24 registered organizations, 6 honor societies, 2 religious organizations. 4 fraternities, 2 sororities. **Athletics (Intercollegiate):** *Men:* Baseball, basketball, football, golf, track/field (outdoor). *Women:* Basketball, cheerleading, cross-country, golf, softball, tennis, track/field (outdoor). **On-Campus Highlights:** Clifford G. Scruggs University Center (SUC), Inman E. Page Library, Stamper Hall (Business and Economics), Richardson Fine Arts Center, Dwight T. Reed Stadium, university farms used for agricultural research include: Busby

Research Farm (273 acres); Carver Research Farm (173 acres); and Freeman Research Farm (199 acres). **Environmental Initiatives:** Composting cafeteria food waste; built and are using a cardboard collection bin for recycling from the cafeteria; in the planning stages for developing an integrated and sustainable small farm operation (a microcommunity project).

ADMISSIONS
Freshman Academic Profile: Average high school GPA 2.6. 3% in top 10% of high school class, 16% in top 25% of high school class, 47% in top 50% of high school class. SAT Math middle 50% range 382.5–457.5. SAT Critical Reading middle 50% range 380–447.5. ACT middle 50% range 14–20. Minimum paper TOEFL 500. Minimum computer TOEFL 173. Minimum web-based TOEFL 61. **Basis for Candidate Selection:** *Other factors considered include:* Academic GPA, state residency. **Freshman Admission Requirements:** High school diploma is required and GED is accepted. *Academic units recommended:* 4 English, 3 mathematics, 2 science, (1 science labs), 2 foreign language, 3 social studies, 1 visual/performing arts, 1 academic electives. **Freshman Admission Statistics:** 2,769 applied, 68% admitted, 39% enrolled. **Transfer Admission Requirements:** College transcript(s), minimum college GPA of 2.0 required. Lowest grade transferable C. **General Admission Information:** Application fee $20. Regular application deadline 7/15. Nonfall registration accepted. Credit and/or placement offered for CEEB Advanced Placement tests.

COSTS AND FINANCIAL AID
Annual in-state tuition $5,685. Room and board $4,660. Required fees $490. Average book expense $950. **Required Forms and Deadlines:** FAFSA, institution's own financial aid form. Priority financial aid filing date 3/1. **Notification of Awards:** Applicants will be notified of awards on a rolling basis beginning 3/15. **Types of Aid:** *Need-based scholarships/grants:* Federal Pell, SEOG, state scholarships/grants, private scholarships, the school's own gift aid. *Loans:* FFEL Subsidized Stafford, FFEL Unsubsidized Stafford, FFEL PLUS. **Student Employment:** Federal Work-Study Program available. Institutional employment available. Off-campus job opportunities are fair. **Financial Aid Statistics:** 76% freshmen, 67% undergrads receive need-based scholarship or grant aid. 2% freshmen, 2% undergrads receive non-need-based scholarship or grant aid. 73% freshmen, 63% undergrads receive need-based self-help aid. 1% freshmen, 3% undergrads receive athletic scholarships. 86% freshmen, 77% undergrads receive any aid. 65.56% undergrads borrow to pay for school. Average cumulative indebtedness $26,114. **Criteria for awarding institutional aid:** *Non-need-based:* Academics, art, athletics, job skills, leadership, minority status, music/drama, state/district residency.

LINCOLN UNIVERSITY (PA)

1570 Balitmore Pike, P.O. Box 179, Lincoln University, PA 19352
Phone: 484-365-7206 **Financial Aid Phone:** 800-561-2606
E-mail: admiss@lincoln.edu **CEEB Code:** 2367
Fax: 484-365-8109 **Website:** www.lincoln.edu **ACT Code:** 3614

This public school was founded in 1854. It has a 422-acre campus.

RATINGS
Admissions Selectivity Rating: 75   **Fire Safety Rating:** 60*   **Green Rating:** 65

STUDENTS AND FACULTY
Enrollment: 1,898. **Student Body:** 60% female, 40% male, 57% out-of-state, 3% international (23 countries represented). African American 96%, Hispanic 1%.
Retention and Graduation: 66% freshmen return for sophomore year. 21% freshmen graduate within 4 years. **Faculty:** Student/faculty ratio 17:1. 99 full-time faculty, 71% hold PhDs, 71% are members of minority groups, 64% are women.

ACADEMICS
Degrees: Bachelor's, master's. **Classes:** Most classes have 20–29 students. Most lab/discussion sessions have 10–19 students. **Majors with Highest Enrollment:** Criminal justice/safety studies; elementary education and teaching. **Special Study Options:** Double major, exchange student program (domestic), honors program, independent study, internships, study abroad, teacher certification program, 3-2 in advanced science/egineering with Drexel University, Pennsylvania State University, Howard University, University of Delaware, Temple University, Widener University, and New Jersey Institute of Technology. **Combined degree programs:** 2-2 nursing program with West Chester U. Special programs offered to physically disabled students include reader services, tutors. **Career services:** Alumni services, internships.

FACILITIES
Housing: Coed dorms, men's dorms, women's dorms, apartments for single students. 90% of campus accessible to physically disabled. **Special Academic**

Facilities/Equipment: African museum, fine arts center, hall for life sciences, learning resource center.

CAMPUS LIFE
Environment: Rural. **Activities:** Choral groups, dance, drama/theater, jazz band, music ensembles, radio station, student government, student newspaper, television station, yearbook. **Organizations:** 30 registered organizations, 9 honor societies, 4 fraternities, 3 sororities. **Athletics (Intercollegiate):** *Men:* Baseball, basketball, cross-country, soccer, tennis, track/field (outdoor), track/field (indoor). *Women:* Basketball, cross-country, soccer, tennis, track/field (outdoor), track/field (indoor), volleyball. **On-Campus Highlights:** Langston Hughes Memorial Library, Thurgood Marshall Living and Learning Ce, John Miller Dickey Hall, Student Union Building, Fredrick Douglass Memorial statue area.

ADMISSIONS
Freshman Academic Profile: Average high school GPA 2.74. 5% in top 10% of high school class, 17% in top 25% of high school class, 45% in top 50% of high school class. SAT Math middle 50% range 360–450. SAT Critical Reading middle 50% range 370–450. ACT middle 50% range 14–18. Minimum paper TOEFL 500. **Basis for Candidate Selection:** *Very important factors considered include:* Class rank, rigor of secondary school record. *Important factors considered include:* Academic GPA, recommendation(s), standardized test scores, talent/ability. *Other factors considered include:* Application essay, alumni/ae relation, character/personal qualities, extracurricular activities, first generation, geographical residence, interview, level of applicant's interest, religious affiliation/commitment, state residency, volunteer work, work experience. **Freshman Admission Requirements:** High school diploma is required and GED is accepted. *Academic units required:* 4 English, 3 mathematics, 3 science, 3 social studies, 5 academic electives, 3 2 arts or humanities, and 1 health and P.E. is required. **Freshman Admission Statistics:** 5,488 applied, 38% admitted, 31% enrolled. **Transfer Admission Requirements:** College transcript(s), essay or personal statement, statement of good standing from prior institution(s). Minimum college GPA of 2.0 required. Lowest grade transferable C. **General Admission Information:** Application fee $20. Notification on a rolling basis, beginning on or about 2/15. Nonfall registration accepted. Admission may be deferred for a maximum of 1 year. Credit offered for CEEB Advanced Placement tests.

COSTS AND FINANCIAL AID
Annual in-state tuition $5,472. Annual out-of-state tuition $9,312. Room and board $7,278. Required fees $2,290. Average book expense $1,330. **Required Forms and Deadlines:** FAFSA. Financial aid filing deadline 5/1. Priority financial aid filing date 5/1. **Notification of Awards:** Applicants will be notified of awards on a rolling basis beginning 4/1. **Types of Aid:** *Need-based scholarships/grants:* Federal Pell, SEOG, state scholarships/grants, private scholarships, the school's own gift aid, United Negro College Fund. *Loans:* FFEL Subsidized Stafford, FFEL Unsubsidized Stafford, FFEL PLUS, Federal Perkins. **Student Employment:** Federal Work-Study Program available. Institutional employment available. Highest amount earned per year from on-campus jobs $3,500. Off-campus job opportunities are fair. **Financial Aid Statistics:** 68% freshmen, 66% undergrads receive need-based scholarship or grant aid. 36% freshmen, 36% undergrads receive non-need-based scholarship or grant aid. 82% freshmen, 82% undergrads receive need-based self-help aid. 94% freshmen, 93% undergrads receive any aid. 84% undergrads borrow to pay for school. Average cumulative indebtedness $28,582. **Criteria for awarding institutional aid:** *Non-need-based:* Academics, alumni affiliation, leadership, music/drama.

LINDENWOOD UNIVERSITY

209 South Kingshighway, Saint Charles, MO 63301-1695
Phone: 314-949-4949
E-mail: admissions@lindenwood.edu **CEEB Code:** 6367
Fax: 314-949-4989 **Website:** www.lindenwood.edu **ACT Code:** 2324

This private school, affiliated with the Presbyterian Church, was founded in 1827. It has a 172-acre campus.

RATINGS
Admissions Selectivity Rating: 78   **Fire Safety Rating:** 60*   **Green Rating:** 61

STUDENTS AND FACULTY
Enrollment: 6,330. **Student Body:** 56% female, 44% male, 20% out-of-state, 10% international. Asian 1%, African American 11%, Caucasian 62%, Hispanic 2%.
Retention and Graduation: 66% freshmen return for sophomore year. 26% freshmen graduate within 4 years. 20% grads go on to further study within 1

year. 8% grads pursue arts and sciences degrees. 1% grads pursue law degrees. 10% grads pursue business degrees. 1% grads pursue medical degrees. **Faculty:** Student/faculty ratio 13:1. 190 full-time faculty, 65% hold PhDs, 8% are members of minority groups, 40% are women.

ACADEMICS

Degrees: Bachelor's, certificate, master's, post-bachelor's certificate, post-master's certificate. **Classes:** Most classes have 10–19 students. Most lab/discussion sessions have 20–29 students. **Special Study Options:** Accelerated program, cross-registration, double major, dual enrollment, English as a Second Language (ESL), honors program, independent study, internships, student-designed major, study abroad, teacher certification program Special programs offered to physically disabled students include reader services, tutors. **Career services:** Alumni services, career assessment, internships.

FACILITIES

Housing: Men's dorms, women's dorms, apartments for married students, apartments for single students. **Special Academic Facilities/Equipment:** University archives. Daniel Boone Campus.

CAMPUS LIFE

Activities: Choral groups, concert band, dance, drama/theater, jazz band, literary magazine, marching band, music ensembles, musical theater, pep band, radio station, student government, student newspaper, symphony orchestra, television station, campus ministries, international student organization. **Organizations:** 72 registered organizations, 8 honor societies, 13 religious organizations. 1 fraternities, 1 sorority. **Athletics (Intercollegiate):** *Men:* Baseball, basketball, cheerleading, cross-country, diving, football, golf, ice hockey, lacrosse, riflery, soccer, swimming, tennis, track/field (outdoor), track/field (indoor), volleyball, water polo, wrestling. *Women:* Basketball, cheerleading, cross-country, diving, field hockey, golf, ice hockey, lacrosse, riflery, soccer, softball, swimming, tennis, track/field (outdoor), track/field (indoor), volleyball, water polo. **Environmental Initiatives:** Paper recycling, lighting.

ADMISSIONS

Freshman Academic Profile: Average high school GPA 3.12. 10% in top 10% of high school class, 30% in top 25% of high school class, 62% in top 50% of high school class. 75% from public high schools. SAT Math middle 50% range 480–560. SAT Critical Reading middle 50% range 410–490. ACT middle 50% range 20–24. Minimum paper TOEFL 500. Minimum computer TOEFL 173. **Basis for Candidate Selection:** *Very important factors considered include:* Academic GPA, standardized test scores. *Important factors considered include:* Class rank, rigor of secondary school record, character/personal qualities, extracurricular activities, interview, talent/ability. *Other factors considered include:* Application essay, recommendation(s), alumni/ae relation, first generation, level of applicant's interest, volunteer work. **Freshman Admission Requirements:** High school diploma is required and GED is accepted. *Academic units recommended:* 4 English, 3 mathematics, 3 science, (1 science labs), 2 foreign language, 3 social studies, 3 history, 1 visual/performing arts. **Freshman Admission Statistics:** 4,020 applied, 40% admitted, 69% enrolled. **Transfer Admission Requirements:** College transcript(s), minimum college GPA of 2.0 required. Lowest grade transferable D. **General Admission Information:** Application fee $30. Nonfall registration accepted. Admission may be deferred for a maximum of Eval Individually. Credit and/or placement offered for CEEB Advanced Placement tests.

COSTS AND FINANCIAL AID

Annual tuition $12,960. Room and board $6,700. Required fees $300. **Required Forms and Deadlines:** FAFSA. **Types of Aid:** *Need-based scholarships/grants:* Federal Pell, SEOG, state scholarships/grants, private scholarships, the school's own gift aid. *Loans:* FFEL Subsidized Stafford, FFEL Unsubsidized Stafford, FFEL PLUS, Federal Perkins. **Student Employment:** Federal Work-Study Program available. Institutional employment available. Off-campus job opportunities are good. **Financial Aid Statistics:** 33% freshmen, 37% undergrads receive need-based scholarship or grant aid. 13% freshmen, 17% undergrads receive non-need-based scholarship or grant aid. 45% freshmen, 52% undergrads receive need-based self-help aid. **Criteria for awarding institutional aid:** *Non-need-based:* Academics, alumni affiliation, art, job skills, leadership, music/drama.

LINDSEY WILSON COLLEGE

210 Lindsey Wilson Street, Columbia, KY 42728
Phone: 800-264-0138
E-mail: admissions@lindsey.edu **CEEB Code:** 1409
Fax: 270-384-8591 **Website:** www.lindsey.edu **ACT Code:** 1522

This private school, affiliated with the Methodist Church, was founded in 1903. It has a 43-acre campus.

RATINGS

Admissions Selectivity Rating: 60* **Fire Safety Rating:** 60* **Green Rating:** 60*

STUDENTS AND FACULTY

Student Body: 6% out-of-state.
Retention and Graduation: 49% freshmen return for sophomore year. **Faculty:** Student/faculty ratio 21:1.

ACADEMICS

Degrees: Associate, bachelor's, master's. **Majors with Highest Enrollment:** Biology; elementary education and teaching; social sciences. **Special Study Options:** Cooperative education program, English as a Second Language (ESL), internships, study abroad Special programs offered to physically disabled students include reader services, tutors. **Career services:** Alumni services, career assessment, internships.

FACILITIES

Housing: Men's dorms, women's dorms, apartments for single students. **Computers:** Students can register for classes online. Administrative functions (other than registration) can be performed online.

CAMPUS LIFE

Environment: Rural. **Activities:** Choral groups, literary magazine, student government, student newspaper, yearbook. **Organizations:** 28 registered organizations. **Athletics (Intercollegiate):** *Men:* Baseball, basketball, cross-country, golf, soccer, tennis, track/field (outdoor). *Women:* Basketball, cross-country, golf, soccer, softball, tennis, track/field (outdoor), volleyball.

ADMISSIONS

Freshman Academic Profile: Minimum paper TOEFL 490. **Freshman Admission Requirements:** High school diploma is required and GED is accepted. **Freshman Admission Statistics:** 1,335 applied, 57% admitted, 55% enrolled. **Transfer Admission Requirements:** College transcript(s), standardized test scores, statement of good standing from prior institution(s). Lowest grade transferable D. **General Admission Information:** Nonfall registration accepted. Placement offered for CEEB Advanced Placement tests.

COSTS AND FINANCIAL AID

Annual tuition $12,456. . Room and board $5,484. Required fees $146. Average book expense $350. **Required Forms and Deadlines:** FAFSA, institution's own financial aid form, state aid form. **Types of Aid:** *Need-based scholarships/grants:* Federal Pell, SEOG, state scholarships/grants, private scholarships, the school's own gift aid. *Loans:* FFEL Subsidized Stafford, FFEL PLUS, Federal Perkins, college/university loans from institutional funds. **Student Employment:** Federal Work-Study Program available. Institutional employment available. Off-campus job opportunities are good.

LINFIELD COLLEGE

900 South East Baker Street, McMinnville, OR 97128-6894
Phone: 503-883-2213 **Financial Aid Phone:** 503-883-2225
E-mail: admission@linfield.edu **CEEB Code:** 4387
Fax: 503-883-2472 **Website:** www.linfield.edu **ACT Code:** 3466

This private school, affiliated with the American Baptist Church, was founded in 1858. It has a 193-acre campus.

RATINGS

Admissions Selectivity Rating: 86 **Fire Safety Rating:** 86 **Green Rating:** 84

STUDENTS AND FACULTY

Enrollment: 1,625. **Student Body:** 57% female, 43% male, 45% out-of-state, 5% international (28 countries represented). Asian 9%, African American 2%, Caucasian 69%, Hispanic 5%, Native American 2%.
Retention and Graduation: 81% freshmen return for sophomore year. 64% freshmen graduate within 4 years. 22% grads go on to further study within 1

year. 10% grads pursue arts and sciences degrees. 2% grads pursue law degrees. 2% grads pursue business degrees. 2% grads pursue medical degrees. **Faculty:** Student/faculty ratio 12:1. 112 full-time faculty, 96% hold PhDs, 45% are women.

ACADEMICS

Degrees: Bachelor's. **Classes:** Most classes have 10–19 students. **Majors with Highest Enrollment:** Business/commerce; elementary education and teaching; kinesiology and exercise science. **Special Study Options:** Cross-registration, distance learning, double major, English as a Second Language (ESL), external degree program, independent study, internships, liberal arts/career combination, student-designed major, study abroad, teacher certification program, Unique January Term courses, widespread participation in off-campus international study. Special programs offered to physically disabled students include note-taking services, reader services, tape recorders, tutors. **Career services:** Alumni network, alumni services, career/job search classes, internships, regional alumni.

FACILITIES

Housing: Coed dorms, special housing for disabled students, men's dorms, women's dorms, fraternity/sorority housing, apartments for single students, wellness housing 80% of campus accessible to physically disabled. **Special Academic Facilities/Equipment:** New library, art gallery, anthropology museum, language classroom with murals, environmental field station, undergraduate research institute, electron microscope. **Computers:** 90% of classrooms, 90% of dorms, 100% of libraries, have wireless network access. Students can register for classes online. Administrative functions (other than registration) can be performed online.

CAMPUS LIFE

Environment: Town. **Activities:** Choral groups, concert band, dance, drama/theater, jazz band, literary magazine, music ensembles, musical theater, opera, pep band, radio station, student government, student newspaper, symphony orchestra, campus ministries, international student organization, Model UN. **Organizations:** 41 registered organizations, 18 honor societies, 5 religious organizations. 4 fraternities, 4 sororities. **Athletics (Intercollegiate):** *Men:* Baseball, basketball, cross-country, football, golf, soccer, swimming, tennis, track/field (outdoor). *Women:* Basketball, cross-country, golf, lacrosse, soccer, softball, swimming, tennis, track/field (outdoor), volleyball. **On-Campus Highlights:** Nicholson Library, modern language rooms (Walker Hall, 3rd floor), Elkington and Terrell Halls, food services and coffee shop, athletic complex. **Environmental Initiatives:** Signatory on ACUPCC; established sustainability committee; completed part I of carbon footprint survey.

ADMISSIONS

Freshman Academic Profile: Average high school GPA 3.55. 30% in top 10% of high school class, 67% in top 25% of high school class, 92% in top 50% of high school class. 85% from public high schools. SAT Math middle 50% range 490–600. SAT Critical Reading middle 50% range 480–600. SAT Writing middle 50% range 460–580. ACT middle 50% range 21–27. Minimum paper TOEFL 550. Minimum computer TOEFL 213. Minimum web-based TOEFL 79. **Basis for Candidate Selection:** *Very important factors considered include:* Academic GPA, rigor of secondary school record, standardized test scores. *Important factors considered include:* Class rank, application essay, recommendation(s). *Other factors considered include:* Alumni/ae relation, character/personal qualities, extracurricular activities, first generation, geographical residence, level of applicant's interest, racial/ethnic status, talent/ability, volunteer work, work experience. **Freshman Admission Requirements:** High school diploma is required and GED is accepted. *Academic units recommended:* 4 English, 4 mathematics. **Freshman Admission Statistics:** 1,692 applied, 82% admitted, 31% enrolled. **Transfer Admission Requirements:** College transcript(s), essay or personal statement, Lowest grade transferable C. **General Admission Information:** Application fee $40. Regular notification 4/1. Nonfall registration accepted. Admission may be deferred for a maximum of 1 year. Credit offered for CEEB Advanced Placement tests.

COSTS AND FINANCIAL AID

Annual tuition $28,760. Room and board $8,280. Required fees $294. Average book expense $750. **Required Forms and Deadlines:** FAFSA. Priority financial aid filing date 2/1. **Notification of Awards:** Applicants will be notified of awards on or about 4/1. **Types of Aid:** *Need-based scholarships/grants:* Federal Pell, SEOG, state scholarships/grants, private scholarships, the school's own gift aid. *Loans:* Direct Subsidized Stafford, Direct Unsubsidized Stafford, Direct PLUS, Federal Perkins, private loans from multiple lenders. **Student Employment:** Federal Work-Study Program available. Institutional employment available. Highest amount earned per year from on-campus jobs $2,250. Off-campus job opportunities are fair. **Financial Aid Statistics:** 60% freshmen, 60% undergrads receive need-based scholarship or grant aid. 40% freshmen, 41% undergrads receive non-need-based scholarship or grant aid. 49% freshmen, 58% undergrads receive need-based self-help aid. 99% freshmen, 96% undergrads receive any aid. 72% undergrads borrow to pay for school. Average

cumulative indebtedness $27,750. **Criteria for awarding institutional aid:** *Non-need-based:* Academics, minority status, music/drama.

LIPSCOMB UNIVERSITY

One University Park Dr, Nashville, TN 37204-3951
Phone: 615-966-1776 **Financial Aid Phone:** 615-966-1791
E-mail: admissions@lipscomb.edu **CEEB Code:** 1161
Fax: 615-966-1804 **Website:** www.lipscomb.edu **ACT Code:** 3956

This private school, affiliated with the Church of Christ Church, was founded in 1891. It has a 65-acre campus.

RATINGS
Admissions Selectivity Rating: 85   **Fire Safety Rating:** 93   **Green Rating:** 78

STUDENTS AND FACULTY

Enrollment: 2,319. **Student Body:** 57% female, 43% male, 35% out-of-state, 1% international (24 countries represented). Asian 2%, African American 5%, Caucasian 84%, Hispanic 2%.
Retention and Graduation: 76% freshmen return for sophomore year. 36% freshmen graduate within 4 years. **Faculty:** Student/faculty ratio 15:1. 110 full-time faculty, 85% hold PhDs, 2% are members of minority groups, 28% are women.

ACADEMICS

Degrees: Bachelor's, first professional, master's, post-bachelor's certificate. **Classes:** Most classes have 10–19 students. Most lab/discussion sessions have 20–29 students. **Majors with Highest Enrollment:** Business administration and management; elementary education and teaching; pre-nursing studies. **Special Study Options:** Cross-registration, distance learning, double major, dual enrollment, honors program, independent study, internships, study abroad, teacher certification program, weekend college. Special programs offered to physically disabled students include note-taking services, reader services, tape recorders, tutors. **Career services:** Alumni network, alumni services, career/job search classes, career assessment, internships.

FACILITIES

Housing: Men's dorms, women's dorms, out-of-town undergraduates required to live on campus except for seniors, students over 21, and married students. 100% of campus accessible to physically disabled. **Special Academic Facilities/Equipment:** On-campus elementary, middle, and secondary schools. **Computers:** 100% of classrooms, 100% of dorms, 100% of libraries, 100% of dining areas, 100% of student union, 100% of common outdoor areas have wireless network access. Students can register for classes online. Administrative functions (other than registration) can be performed online.

CAMPUS LIFE

Environment: Metropolis. **Activities:** Choral groups, concert band, drama/theater, jazz band, literary magazine, marching band, music ensembles, musical theater, pep band, radio station, student government, student newspaper, yearbook, campus ministries, international student organization. **Organizations:** 65 registered organizations, **Athletics (Intercollegiate):** *Men:* Baseball, basketball, cross-country, golf, soccer, tennis, track/field (outdoor). *Women:* Basketball, cheerleading, cross-country, soccer, softball, tennis, track/field (outdoor), track/field (indoor), volleyball. **On-Campus Highlights:** Student Center, SAC—Student Activity Center, Allen Arena, Willard Collins Alumni Auditorium, Bison Square. **Environmental Initiatives:** Internal Sustainability Practices: Geothermal heating and cooling in all new building and rennovation since 2005 (currently three buildings), hybrid cars for VP's, a green housekeeping program, internal sustainability audit and near completion of the state's first LEED-certified academic building. Established Sustainability Program: New Institute for Sustainable Practice, TN's first green MBA, TN's first sustainability undergrad degree and TN's first sustainability minor. Leading State and Local Dialogue and Awareness: Hosted Tennessee first state wide conference on sustainability and sponsored TN's first green business summit and expo.

ADMISSIONS

Freshman Academic Profile: Average high school GPA 3.49. 25% in top 10% of high school class, 52% in top 25% of high school class, 75% in top 50% of high school class. SAT Math middle 50% range 490–620. SAT Critical Reading middle 50% range 500–610. SAT Writing middle 50% range 490–593. ACT middle 50% range 21–27. Minimum paper TOEFL 550. Minimum computer TOEFL 213. **Basis for Candidate Selection:** *Very important factors considered include:* Class rank, standardized test scores, interview. *Important factors considered include:* Academic GPA, recommendation(s), rigor of secondary school record, character/personal qualities. *Other factors considered include:* Extracurricular activities, first generation, talent/ability, volunteer work, work experience. **Freshman Admission Requirements:** High school diploma is required and GED is accepted. *Academic units required:* 4 English, 2 mathematics, 2 science, 2 foreign language, 2 social studies, 2 academic electives. **Freshman Admission Statistics:** 2,240 applied, 57% admitted, 45% enrolled. **Transfer Admission Requirements:** College transcript(s), interview, statement of good standing from prior institution(s). Minimum college GPA of 2.0 required. Lowest grade transferable C. **General Admission Information:** Application fee $25. Nonfall registration accepted. Credit and/or placement offered for CEEB Advanced Placement tests.

COSTS AND FINANCIAL AID

Annual tuition $15,986. Room and board $7,070. Required fees $825. Average book expense $1,000. **Required Forms and Deadlines:** FAFSA. Priority financial aid filing date 3/1. **Notification of Awards:** Applicants will be notified of awards on a rolling basis beginning 2/15. **Types of Aid:** *Need-based scholarships/grants:* Federal Pell, SEOG, state scholarships/grants, private scholarships, the school's own gift aid. *Loans:* FFEL Subsidized Stafford, FFEL Unsubsidized Stafford, FFEL PLUS, Federal Perkins, Federal Nursing, alternative. **Financial Aid Statistics:** 24% freshmen, 24% undergrads receive need-based scholarship or grant aid. 52% freshmen, 40% undergrads receive non-need-based scholarship or grant aid. 43% freshmen, 45% undergrads receive need-based self-help aid. 4% freshmen, 5% undergrads receive athletic scholarships. 60% freshmen, 55% undergrads receive any aid. 65% undergrads borrow to pay for school. Average cumulative indebtedness $15,939. **Criteria for awarding institutional aid:** *Non-need-based:* Academics, alumni affiliation, art, athletics, leadership, minority status, music/drama, religious affiliation, state/district residency.

LIVINGSTONE COLLEGE

701 West Monroe Street, Salisbury, NC 28144-5213
Phone: 704-216-6001 **Financial Aid Phone:** 707-216-6273
E-mail: admissions@livingstone.edu
Fax: 704-216-6215 **Website:** www.livingstone.edu

This private school, affiliated with the African Methodist Episcopal Church, was founded in 1879. It has a 272-acre campus.

RATINGS
Admissions Selectivity Rating: 60*   **Fire Safety Rating:** 60*   **Green Rating:** 60*

STUDENTS AND FACULTY
Enrollment: 907. **Student Body:** 43% female, 57% male, 1% international (5 countries represented). African American 67%, Caucasian 1%.
Retention and Graduation: 61% freshmen return for sophomore year. 50% grads go on to further study within 1 year. 25% grads pursue arts and sciences degrees. 5% grads pursue law degrees. 15% grads pursue business degrees. 5% grads pursue medical degrees. **Faculty:** Student/faculty ratio 15:1. 54 full-time faculty, 50% hold PhDs, 33% are members of minority groups, 44% are women.

ACADEMICS
Degrees: Bachelor's. **Classes:** Most classes have fewer than 10 students. Most lab/discussion sessions have 10–19 students. **Majors with Highest Enrollment:** Business administration and management; computer and information sciences; criminal justice/safety studies. **Special Study Options:** Accelerated program, cross-registration, double major, independent study, internships, teacher certification program, community service.

FACILITIES
Housing: Special housing for disabled students, men's dorms, special housing for international students, women's dorms, apartments for married students, apartments for single students. 90% of campus accessible to physically disabled. **Special Academic Facilities/Equipment:** Heritage Hall; Poets and Dreamers Garden; NASA SEMAA Lab; and the Elizabeth Koontz Center. **Computers:** Students can register for classes online. Administrative functions (other than registration) can be performed online.

CAMPUS LIFE
Environment: Town. **Activities:** Choral groups, concert band, dance, drama/theater, jazz band, marching band, music ensembles, musical theater, pep band, radio station, student government, student-run film society, yearbook. **Organizations:** 16 registered organizations, 4 honor societies, 2 religious organizations. 4 fraternities, 4 sororities. **Athletics (Intercollegiate):** *Men:* Basketball, cross-country, football, track/field (outdoor). *Women:* Basketball, bowling, cheerleading, cross-country, softball, tennis, track/field (outdoor), volleyball.

ADMISSIONS
Freshman Academic Profile: SAT Math middle 50% range 320–430. SAT Critical Reading middle 50% range 323–420. SAT Writing middle 50% range

320–400. ACT middle 50% range 12–16. Minimum paper TOEFL 500. Minimum computer TOEFL 250. **Basis for Candidate Selection:** *Important factors considered include:* Academic GPA, recommendation(s). *Other factors considered include:* Class rank, application essay, rigor of secondary school record, alumni/ae relation, character/personal qualities, extracurricular activities, first generation, geographical residence, interview, level of applicant's interest, state residency, talent/ability, volunteer work, work experience. **Freshman Admission Requirements:** High school diploma is required and GED is accepted. *Academic units required:* 4 English, 3 mathematics, 2 science, 2 foreign language, 2 social studies, 1 history. **Freshman Admission Statistics:** 1,587 applied, 58% admitted, 28% enrolled. **Transfer Admission Requirements:** College transcript(s), statement of good standing from prior institution(s). Minimum college GPA of 2.0 required. Lowest grade transferable C. **General Admission Information:** Application fee $25. Nonfall registration accepted. Credit and/or placement offered for CEEB Advanced Placement tests.

COSTS AND FINANCIAL AID
Required Forms and Deadlines: FAFSA, institution's own financial aid form, state aid form. Priority financial aid filing date 3/15. **Types of Aid:** *Loans:* FFEL Subsidized Stafford, FFEL PLUS. **Student Employment:** Highest amount earned per year from on-campus jobs $1,200. **Financial Aid Statistics:** 88% freshmen, 89% undergrads receive need-based scholarship or grant aid. 8% freshmen, 6% undergrads receive non-need-based scholarship or grant aid. 70% freshmen, 79% undergrads receive need-based self-help aid. 97.1% undergrads borrow to pay for school. Average cumulative indebtedness $15,306.

LOCK HAVEN UNIVERSITY OF PENNSYLVANIA

Lock Haven University, Akeley Hall, Lock Haven, PA 17745
Phone: 570-484-2027
E-mail: admissions@lhup.edu **CEEB Code:** 2654
Fax: 570-484-2201 **Website:** www.lhup.edu **ACT Code:** 3708

This public school was founded in 1870. It has a 175-acre campus.

RATINGS
Admissions Selectivity Rating: 70   **Fire Safety Rating:** 60*   **Green Rating:** 60*

STUDENTS AND FACULTY
Enrollment: 4,874. **Student Body:** 57% female, 43% male, 8% out-of-state, 1% international (39 countries represented). Asian 1%, African American 7%, Caucasian 88%, Hispanic 2%.
Retention and Graduation: 29% freshmen graduate within 4 years. **Faculty:** Student/faculty ratio 21:1. 236 full-time faculty, 74% hold PhDs, 13% are members of minority groups, 46% are women.

ACADEMICS
Degrees: Associate, bachelor's, master's. **Classes:** Most classes have 20–29 students. Most lab/discussion sessions have 20–29 students. **Majors with Highest Enrollment:** Elementary education and teaching; health and P.E./fitness, other; health professions and related clinical sciences, other. **Special Study Options:** Cross-registration, distance learning, double major, dual enrollment, honors program, independent study, internships, student-designed major, study abroad, teacher certification program. **Honors programs:** The University Honors Program provides students and faculty opportunities for creative intellectual engagement through a mix of special curricular and co-curricular opportunities. Students may apply for entry as a first-year freshman or after completing 1-4 semesters of college-level work. Entry as a first-year freshman may be either directly into the University Honors or through the First Year Excellence Program. Students successfully completing the First Year Excellence Program receive certificate recognition. Students completing the University Honors Program receive recognition on their transcript, on their diploma and at commencement. Students in both the First Year Excellence and University Honors programs must participate in co-curricular activities and community service in addition to their curriculum. Engaging activity groups and Speaker Series allow students in the Honors Program to bond together and learn from each other, creating a community of both friends and scholars. Special programs offered to physically disabled students include note-taking services, reader services, tape recorders, tutors. **Career services:** Alumni network, alumni services, career/job search classes, career assessment, internships, regional alumni.

FACILITIES
Housing: Coed dorms, apartments for single students 98% of campus accessible to physically disabled. **Special Academic Facilities/Equipment:** Planetarium, Sloan Art Gallery, Library Archives. **Computers:** Students can register for classes online. Administrative functions (other than registration) can be performed online. Undergraduates are required to own a computer.

CAMPUS LIFE

Environment: Village. **Activities:** Choral groups, concert band, dance, drama/theater, jazz band, literary magazine, marching band, music ensembles, musical theater, pep band, radio station, student government, student newspaper, symphony orchestra, television station, yearbook, campus ministries, international student organization. **Organizations:** 96 registered organizations, 10 honor societies, 7 religious organizations, 6 fraternities, 4 sororities. **Athletics (Intercollegiate):** *Men:* Baseball, basketball, football, soccer, track/field (outdoor), track/field (indoor), wrestling. *Women:* Basketball, field hockey, lacrosse, soccer, softball, swimming, track/field (outdoor), track/field (indoor), volleyball. **On-Campus Highlights:** Student Recreation Center, Parsons Union Building, Library, Residence Halls, Bentley Dining Hall.

ADMISSIONS

Freshman Academic Profile: Average high school GPA 3.24. 7% in top 10% of high school class, 25% in top 25% of high school class, 62% in top 50% of high school class. SAT Math middle 50% range 420–520. SAT Critical Reading middle 50% range 410–510. SAT Writing middle 50% range 400–500. ACT middle 50% range 17–21. Minimum paper TOEFL 550. **Basis for Candidate Selection:** *Very important factors considered include:* Class rank, academic GPA, rigor of secondary school record, character/personal qualities, talent/ability. *Important factors considered include:* standardized test scores, racial/ethnic status. *Other factors considered include:* Application essay, recommendation(s), extracurricular activities, first generation, interview, level of applicant's interest, volunteer work, work experience. **Freshman Admission Requirements:** High school diploma is required and GED is accepted. *Academic units required:* 4 English, 3 mathematics, 3 science, (2 science labs), 2 social studies, 2 history. *Academic units recommended:* 4 English, 4 mathematics, 4 science, (3 science labs), 2 foreign language, 2 social studies, 2 history. **Freshman Admission Statistics:** 4,499 applied, 76% admitted, 35% enrolled. **Transfer Admission Requirements:** College transcript(s), statement of good standing from prior institution(s). Minimum college GPA of 2.0 required. Lowest grade transferable C. **General Admission Information:** Application fee $25. Notification on a rolling basis, beginning on or about 10/1. Nonfall registration accepted. Admission may be deferred for a maximum of 1 year. Credit and/or placement offered for CEEB Advanced Placement tests.

COSTS AND FINANCIAL AID

Annual in-state tuition $5,554. Annual out-of-state tuition $11,886. Room and board $6,736. Required fees $1,751. Average book expense $1,139. **Required Forms and Deadlines:** FAFSA. Financial aid filing deadline 3/15. Priority financial aid filing date 3/15. **Notification of Awards:** Applicants will be notified of awards on a rolling basis beginning 4/1. **Types of Aid:** *Need-based scholarships/grants:* Federal Pell, SEOG, state scholarships/grants, private scholarships, United Negro College Fund. *Loans:* FFEL Subsidized Stafford, FFEL Unsubsidized Stafford, FFEL PLUS, Federal Perkins, college/university loans from institutional funds. **Student Employment:** Federal Work-Study Program available. Institutional employment available. Off-campus job opportunities are good. **Financial Aid Statistics:** 49% freshmen, 48% undergrads receive need-based scholarship or grant aid. 4% freshmen, 5% undergrads receive non-need-based scholarship or grant aid. 57% freshmen, 56% undergrads receive need-based self-help aid. 4% freshmen, 5% undergrads receive athletic scholarships. 85% undergrads borrow to pay for school. Average cumulative indebtedness $22,585. **Criteria for awarding institutional aid:** *Non-need-based:* Academics, art, athletics, leadership, minority status, music/drama, state/district residency.

LOMA LINDA UNIVERSITY

Office of Admissions, Loma Linda, CA 92350
Phone: 909-824-4599
Fax: 909-824-4291 **Website:** www.llu.edu

This private school, affiliated with the Seventh Day Adventist Church, was founded in 1905.

RATINGS

Admissions Selectivity Rating: 60*   **Fire Safety Rating:** 60*   **Green Rating:** 60*

STUDENTS AND FACULTY

Student Body: 80 countries represented.

ACADEMICS

Degrees: Associate, bachelor's, certificate, master's, post-bachelor's certificate. **Special Study Options:** Distance learning, double major.

FACILITIES

Housing: Coed dorms, men's dorms, women's dorms, apartments for single students.

CAMPUS LIFE

Environment: Village. **Activities:** Student government, student newspaper, yearbook. **Organizations:** 1 honor societies, 1 religious organizations.

ADMISSIONS

Basis for Candidate Selection: *Very important factors considered include:* Application essay, recommendation(s), character/personal qualities, interview, religious affiliation/commitment. *Important factors considered include:* Talent/ability, volunteer work, work experience. *Other factors considered include:* Alumni/ae relation, extracurricular activities. **Freshman Admission Requirements:** High school diploma is required and GED is accepted. **Transfer Admission Requirements:** High school transcript, college transcript(s), essay or personal statement, interview, minimum college GPA of 2.0 required. Lowest grade transferable C. **General Admission Information:** Application fee $50. Nonfall registration not accepted. Admission may be deferred for a maximum of 1.

COSTS AND FINANCIAL AID

Types of Aid: *Loans:* FFEL Subsidized Stafford, FFEL PLUS.

LONGWOOD UNIVERSITY

Admissions Office, 201 High Street, Farmville, VA 23909
Phone: 434-395-2060 **Financial Aid Phone:** 800-281-4677
E-mail: admissions@longwood.edu **CEEB Code:** 5368
Fax: 434-395-2332 **Website:** www.whylongwood.com **ACT Code:** 4366

This public school was founded in 1839. It has a 160-acre campus.

RATINGS

Admissions Selectivity Rating: 74   **Fire Safety Rating:** 60*   **Green Rating:** 78

STUDENTS AND FACULTY

Enrollment: 4,021. **Student Body:** 66% female, 34% male, 4% out-of-state, international (20 countries represented). Asian 1%, African American 6%, Caucasian 85%, Hispanic 2%, Native American 1%. **Retention and Graduation:** 78% freshmen return for sophomore year. 49% freshmen graduate within 4 years. 15% grads go on to further study within 1 year. **Faculty:** Student/faculty ratio 18:1. 207 full-time faculty, 79% hold PhDs, 7% are members of minority groups, 48% are women.

ACADEMICS

Degrees: Bachelor's, master's. **Classes:** Most classes have 20–29 students. Most lab/discussion sessions have 20–29 students. **Majors with Highest Enrollment:** Business/commerce; elementary education and teaching; psychology. **Special Study Options:** Accelerated program, cross-registration, distance learning, double major, dual enrollment, English as a Second Language (ESL), honors program, independent study, internships, study abroad, teacher certification program. **Honors programs:** The Longwood University Honors Program is designed to meet the needs of academically gifted and talented undergraduate students. Challenging courses with high academic standards enable students to expand their intellectual and creative horizons. The Honors Program focuses on the exchange of ideas and the enrichment of students' educational and cultural experiences. Learning takes place not only in the classroom, but also through cultural events, conferences, field trips, and study abroad. In keeping with the university's mission, the Longwood Honors Program strives to develop citizens who are committed to using their learning to provide service to their local communities as well as to the larger national and global communities. The concept of linking learning with the practice of citizenship is the distinctive feature of our Program. **Combined degree programs:** BA/MA, Special Education BA/MS and BS/MS. Special programs offered to physically disabled students include note-taking services, reader services, tape recorders, tutors. **Career services:** career/job search classes, career assessment, internships. **Career services highlights include:** Students must complete either am internship, study abroad program or work on a research project to graduate.

FACILITIES

Housing: Coed dorms, special housing for disabled students, women's dorms, fraternity/sorority housing, apartments for single students, Honor Student Housing. 100% of campus accessible to physically disabled. **Special Academic Facilities/Equipment:** Longwood Center for the Visual Arts **Computers:** 100% of classrooms, 100% of libraries, 100% of dining areas, 100% of student union, have wireless network access. Students can register for classes online. Administrative functions (other than registration) can be performed online. Undergraduates are required to own a computer.

CAMPUS LIFE

Environment: Village. **Activities:** Choral groups, concert band, dance, drama/theater, jazz band, literary magazine, music ensembles, pep band, radio station, student government, student newspaper, yearbook, campus ministries, international student organization. **Organizations:** 129 registered organizations, 17 honor societies, 11 religious organizations. 9 fraternities, 12 sororities. **Athletics (Intercollegiate):** *Men:* Baseball, basketball, cheerleading, cross-country, golf, soccer, tennis. *Women:* Basketball, cheerleading, cross-country, field hockey, golf, lacrosse, soccer, softball, tennis. **On-Campus Highlights:** Brock Commons, Lankford Student Union, Health and Fitness Center, Greenwood Library, Dorrill Dining Hall, Science Building.

ADMISSIONS

Freshman Academic Profile: Average high school GPA 3.36. 12% in top 10% of high school class, 40% in top 25% of high school class, 84% in top 50% of high school class. 92% from public high schools. SAT Math middle 50% range 480–560. SAT Critical Reading middle 50% range 480–560. ACT middle 50% range 20–24. Minimum paper TOEFL 550. Minimum computer TOEFL 213. Minimum web-based TOEFL 79. **Basis for Candidate Selection:** *Very important factors considered include:* Application essay, academic GPA, rigor of secondary school record, standardized test scores. *Important factors considered include:* Class rank, alumni/ae relation, character/personal qualities, extracurricular activities, first generation, geographical residence, racial/ethnic status, talent/ability, volunteer work. *Other factors considered include:* Recommendation(s), state residency. **Freshman Admission Requirements:** High school diploma is required and GED is accepted. *Academic units required:* 4 English, 3 mathematics, 3 science, (2 science labs), 2 foreign language, 2 social studies, 2 history, 1 visual/performing arts. *Academic units recommended:* 4 English, 4 mathematics, 4 science, (3 science labs), 4 foreign language, 2 social studies, 2 history, 1 visual/performing arts. **Freshman Admission Statistics:** 4,301 applied, 70% admitted, 34% enrolled. **Transfer Admission Requirements:** High school transcript, college transcript(s), essay or personal statement, minimum college GPA of 2.50 required. Lowest grade transferable C–. **General Admission Information:** Application fee $40. Notification on a rolling basis, beginning on or about 1/15. Nonfall registration accepted. Admission may be deferred for a maximum of 1 year. Credit offered for CEEB Advanced Placement tests.

COSTS AND FINANCIAL AID

Annual in-state tuition $4,680. Annual out-of-state tuition $13,590. Room and board $7,596. Required fees $4,245. Average book expense $800. **Required Forms and Deadlines:** FAFSA. Priority financial aid filing date 3/1. **Notification of Awards:** Applicants will be notified of awards on or about 4/1. **Types of Aid:** *Need-based scholarships/grants:* Federal Pell, SEOG, state scholarships/grants, private scholarships, the school's own gift aid. *Loans:* Direct Subsidized Stafford, Direct Unsubsidized Stafford, Direct PLUS, Federal Perkins. **Student Employment:** Federal Work-Study Program available. Institutional employment available. Off-campus job opportunities are good. **Financial Aid Statistics:** 42% freshmen, 40% undergrads receive need-based scholarship or grant aid. 1% freshmen, 1% undergrads receive non-need-based scholarship or grant aid. 33% freshmen, 35% undergrads receive need-based self-help aid. 3% freshmen, 3% undergrads receive athletic scholarships. 60% freshmen receive any aid. 62% undergrads borrow to pay for school. Average cumulative indebtedness $12,915. **Criteria for awarding institutional aid:** *Non-need-based:* Academics, alumni affiliation, art, athletics, leadership, music/drama, state/district residency.

LORAS COLLEGE

1450 Alta Vista, Dubuque, IA 52004-0178
Phone: 800-245-6727 **Financial Aid Phone:** 563-588-7136
E-mail: admissions@loras.edu **CEEB Code:** 6370
Fax: 563-588-7119 **Website:** www.loras.edu **ACT Code:** 1328

This private school, affiliated with the Roman Catholic Church, was founded in 1839. It has a 60-acre campus.

RATINGS

Admissions Selectivity Rating: 73 **Fire Safety Rating:** 87 **Green Rating:** 60*

STUDENTS AND FACULTY

Enrollment: 1,565. **Student Body:** 50% female, 50% male, 45% out-of-state, 3% international (7 countries represented). Asian 1%, African American 1%, Caucasian 93%, Hispanic 1%.
Retention and Graduation: 78% freshmen return for sophomore year. 55% freshmen graduate within 4 years. 20% grads go on to further study within 1 year. 4% grads pursue arts and sciences degrees. 1% grads pursue law degrees.

2% grads pursue business degrees. 8% grads pursue medical degrees. **Faculty:** Student/faculty ratio 13:1. 111 full-time faculty, 95% hold PhDs, 5% are members of minority groups, 31% are women.

ACADEMICS

Degrees: Associate, bachelor's, master's. **Classes:** Most classes have 20–29 students. Most lab/discussion sessions have fewer than 10 students. **Majors with Highest Enrollment:** Business/commerce; elementary education and teaching; secondary education and teaching. **Special Study Options:** Cooperative education program, cross-registration, double major, dual enrollment, English as a Second Language (ESL), honors program, independent study, internships, liberal arts/career combination, student-designed major, study abroad, teacher certification program, Undergrads may take graduate level classes if certain qualifications are met. **Combined degree programs:** BA/MA, 2-2 nursing program with U of Iowa. Special programs offered to physically disabled students include note-taking services, reader services, tape recorders. **Career services:** Internships.

FACILITIES

Housing: Coed dorms, men's dorms, women's dorms, apartments for single students. 95% of campus accessible to physically disabled. **Special Academic Facilities/Equipment:** Language lab, television studio, observatory and planetarium. **Computers:** Students can register for classes online. Administrative functions (other than registration) can be performed online. Undergraduates are required to own a computer.

CAMPUS LIFE

Environment: Town. **Activities:** Choral groups, concert band, dance, drama/theater, jazz band, music ensembles, musical theater, radio station, student government, student newspaper, television station, yearbook. **Organizations:** 71 registered organizations, 710 honor societies, 5 religious organizations. 2 fraternities, 2 sororities. **Athletics (Intercollegiate):** *Men:* Baseball, basketball, cross-country, diving, football, golf, soccer, swimming, tennis, track/field (outdoor), track/field (indoor), wrestling. *Women:* Basketball, cross-country, diving, golf, soccer, softball, swimming, tennis, track/field (outdoor), track/field (indoor), volleyball. **On-Campus Highlights:** Academic Resource Center, Alumni Campus Center, The Pub and Cafeteria, The Grotto.

ADMISSIONS

Freshman Academic Profile: Average high school GPA 3.22. 13% in top 10% of high school class, 34% in top 25% of high school class, 65% in top 50% of high school class. 57% from public high schools. SAT Math middle 50% range 503–625. SAT Critical Reading middle 50% range 453–575. ACT middle 50% range 20–25. Minimum paper TOEFL 550. Minimum computer TOEFL 213. **Basis for Candidate Selection:** *Very important factors considered include:* Academic GPA, rigor of secondary school record, standardized test scores. *Important factors considered include:* Class rank. *Other factors considered include:* Application essay, recommendation(s), character/personal qualities, extracurricular activities, racial/ethnic status, volunteer work. **Freshman Admission Requirements:** High school diploma is required and GED is accepted. *Academic units recommended:* 4 English, 3 mathematics, 3 science, 3 social studies, 3 history. **Freshman Admission Statistics:** 1,402 applied, 82% admitted, 32% enrolled. **Transfer Admission Requirements:** High school transcript, college transcript(s), standardized test scores, minimum college GPA of 2.0 required. Lowest grade transferable C. **General Admission Information:** Application fee $25. Nonfall registration accepted. Admission may be deferred for a maximum of Two Terms. Credit offered for CEEB Advanced Placement tests.

COSTS AND FINANCIAL AID

Annual tuition $19,990. Room and board $6,095. Required fees $1,108. Average book expense $800. **Required Forms and Deadlines:** FAFSA. Priority financial aid filing date 4/15. **Notification of Awards:** Applicants will be notified of awards on a rolling basis beginning 3/1. **Types of Aid:** *Need-based scholarships/grants:* Federal Pell, SEOG, state scholarships/grants, private scholarships, the school's own gift aid. *Loans:* FFEL Subsidized Stafford, FFEL Unsubsidized Stafford, FFEL PLUS, Federal Perkins, college/university loans from institutional funds. **Student Employment:** Highest amount earned per year from on-campus jobs $1,500. **Financial Aid Statistics:** 76% freshmen, 68% undergrads receive need-based scholarship or grant aid. 88% freshmen, 66% undergrads receive non-need-based scholarship or grant aid. 76% freshmen, 68% undergrads receive need-based self-help aid. 99% freshmen, 86% undergrads receive any aid. 94% undergrads borrow to pay for school. Average cumulative indebtedness $24,320. **Criteria for awarding institutional aid:** *Non-need-based:* Academics, alumni affiliation, music/drama.

LOUISIANA COLLEGE

1140 College Drive, P.O. Box 560, Pineville, LA 71359-0560
Phone: 318-487-7259
E-mail: admissions@lacollege.edu **CEEB Code:** 6371
Fax: 318-487-7550 **Website:** www.lacollege.edu **ACT Code:** 1586

This private school, affiliated with the Baptist Church, was founded in 1906. It has a 81-acre campus.

RATINGS
Admissions Selectivity Rating: 78   **Fire Safety Rating:** 60*   **Green Rating:** 60*

STUDENTS AND FACULTY
Enrollment: 1,014. **Student Body:** 56% female, 44% male, 9% out-of-state, 1% international. Asian 1%, African American 7%, Caucasian 89%, Hispanic 2%.
Retention and Graduation: 59% freshmen return for sophomore year. 25% freshmen graduate within 4 years. **Faculty:** Student/faculty ratio 13:1. 68 full-time faculty, 60% hold PhDs, 46% are women.

ACADEMICS
Degrees: Bachelor's. **Classes:** Most classes have fewer than 10 students. Most lab/discussion sessions have 10–19 students. **Majors with Highest Enrollment:** Biology; elementary education and teaching; psychology. **Special Study Options:** Double major, honors program, independent study, internships, liberal arts/career combination, student-designed major, study abroad, teacher certification program. **Honors programs:** London Semester Special programs offered to physically disabled students include note-taking services, reader services, tutors. **Career services:** Career/job search classes, career assessment, internships, **Career services highlights include:** Several majors require internships to fulfill graduation requirements. Academic credit may be available to students who wish to pursue internship opportunities outside major requirements.

FACILITIES
Housing: Men's dorms, women's dorms, apartments for married students, apartments for single students. 95% of campus accessible to physically disabled. **Special Academic Facilities/Equipment:** Art gallery, radio station, performing arts center, theater.

CAMPUS LIFE
Environment: Village. **Activities:** Choral groups, concert band, drama/theater, jazz band, literary magazine, music ensembles, musical theater, opera, pep band, radio station, student government, student newspaper, symphony orchestra, yearbook. **Organizations:** 60 registered organizations, 13 honor societies, 8 religious organizations. 4 fraternities, 3 sororities. **Athletics (Intercollegiate):** *Men:* Baseball, basketball, cheerleading, football, golf, soccer. *Women:* Basketball, cheerleading, cross-country, soccer, softball, tennis. **On-Campus Highlights:** Healthplex/Wellness Center, Student Center, Martin Performing Arts Center, Weathersby Fine Arts Building, Alexandria Hall.

ADMISSIONS
Freshman Academic Profile: Average high school GPA 3.48. 29% in top 10% of high school class, 54% in top 25% of high school class, 87% in top 50% of high school class. 82% from public high schools. SAT Math middle 50% range 440–600. SAT Critical Reading middle 50% range 440–570. ACT middle 50% range 21–26. Minimum paper TOEFL 550. Minimum computer TOEFL 213. **Basis for Candidate Selection:** *Very important factors considered include:* Class rank, rigor of secondary school record, standardized test scores. *Other factors considered include:* Recommendation(s), alumni/ae relation, character/personal qualities, extracurricular activities, geographical residence, interview, racial/ethnic status, religious affiliation/commitment, state residency, talent/ability, volunteer work, work experience. **Freshman Admission Requirements:** High school diploma is required and GED is accepted. *Academic units required:* 4 English, 3 mathematics, 3 science, (2 science labs), 2 social studies, 1 history, 4 academic electives. *Academic units recommended:* 2 foreign language. **Freshman Admission Statistics:** 727 applied, 85% admitted, 43% enrolled. **Transfer Admission Requirements:** College transcript(s), minimum college GPA of 2.0 required. Lowest grade transferable D. **General Admission Information:** Application fee $25. Regular application deadline 8/15. Notification on a rolling basis, beginning on or about 1/1. Nonfall registration accepted. Admission may be deferred for a maximum of 1 year. Credit and/or placement offered for CEEB Advanced Placement tests.

COSTS AND FINANCIAL AID
Annual tuition $8,850. Room and board $3,740. Required fees $800. Average book expense $750. **Required Forms and Deadlines:** FAFSA, institution's own financial aid form. Priority financial aid filing date 3/31. **Notification of Awards:** Applicants will be notified of awards on a rolling basis beginning 3/1. **Types of Aid:** *Need-based scholarships/grants:* Federal Pell, SEOG, state

scholarships/grants, private scholarships, the school's own gift aid, LEAP. *Loans:* Direct Subsidized Stafford, Direct Unsubsidized Stafford, Direct PLUS, FFEL Subsidized Stafford, FFEL Unsubsidized Stafford, FFEL PLUS, college/university loans from institutional funds. **Student Employment:** Federal Work-Study Program available. Institutional employment available. Highest amount earned per year from on-campus jobs $400. Off-campus job opportunities are excellent. **Financial Aid Statistics:** 29% freshmen, 27% undergrads receive need-based scholarship or grant aid. 64% freshmen, 57% undergrads receive non-need-based scholarship or grant aid. 37% freshmen, 34% undergrads receive need-based self-help aid. 98% freshmen, 82% undergrads receive any aid. 54% undergrads borrow to pay for school. Average cumulative indebtedness $5,742. **Criteria for awarding institutional aid:** *Non-need-based:* Academics, art, leadership, music/drama.

LOUISIANA STATE UNIVERSITY

1146 Pleasant Hall, Baton Rouge, LA 70803
Phone: 225-578-1175 **Financial Aid Phone:** 225-578-3113
E-mail: admissions@lsu.edu **CEEB Code:** 6373
Fax: 225-578-4433 **Website:** www.lsu.edu **ACT Code:** 1590

This public school was founded in 1860. It has a 2000-acre campus.

RATINGS
Admissions Selectivity Rating: 82   **Fire Safety Rating:** 82   **Green Rating:** 90

STUDENTS AND FACULTY
Enrollment: 23,057. **Student Body:** 51% female, 49% male, 15% out-of-state, 1% international (117 countries represented). Asian 3%, African American 9%, Caucasian 80%, Hispanic 3%.
Retention and Graduation: 28% freshmen graduate within 4 years. **Faculty:** Student/faculty ratio 21:1. 1324 full-time faculty, 85% hold PhDs, 14% are members of minority groups, 34% are women. 11% of classes are taught by teaching assistants.

ACADEMICS
Degrees: Bachelor's, doctoral, master's, post-master's certificate. **Classes:** Most classes have 20–29 students. Most lab/discussion sessions have 20–29 students. **Majors with Highest Enrollment:** Biology/biological sciences; mass communication/media studies; P.E. teaching and coaching. **Special Study Options:** Accelerated program, cooperative education program, cross-registration, distance learning, double major, dual enrollment, English as a Second Language (ESL), exchange student program (domestic), honors program, independent study, internships, liberal arts/career combination, student-designed major, study abroad, teacher certification program. **Honors programs:** Admissions to the Honors College. **Combined degree programs:** BS/MED Elementary Education/Holmes. Special programs offered to physically disabled students include note-taking services, reader services, tape recorders **Career services:** Alumni network, alumni services, career/job search classes, career assessment, internships. **Career services highlights include:** We feel that the newly initiated Fellows Program will bring our Institute the creme of the crop in both students from around campus and in internships for those students. We are committed to teaching entrepreneurship to students in order that they are prepared to start new, innovative ventures sometime in their lives.

FACILITIES
Housing: Coed dorms, special housing for disabled students, men's dorms, women's dorms, fraternity/sorority housing, apartments for married students, apartments for single students, theme housing. 75% of campus accessible to physically disabled. **Special Academic Facilities/Equipment:** Art Museum, Natural Science Museum, Rural Life Museum, Lichen/Bryophyte Mycological and Vascular Plant herbariums, on-campus K–12 schools, geoscience and mycological museums, electron microscope, nuclear science center and civil war center. **Computers:** 100% of classrooms, 100% of dorms, 100% of libraries, 90% of dining areas, 100% of student union, 90% of common outdoor areas have wireless network access. Students can register for classes online. Administrative functions (other than registration) can be performed online.

CAMPUS LIFE
Environment: Metropolis. **Activities:** Choral groups, concert band, dance, drama/theater, jazz band, literary magazine, marching band, music ensembles, musical theater, opera, pep band, radio station, student government, student

newspaper, student-run film society, symphony orchestra, television station, yearbook, campus ministries, international student organization. **Organizations:** 300 registered organizations, 32 honor societies, 25 religious organizations. 23 fraternities, 15 sororities. **Athletics (Intercollegiate):** *Men:* Baseball, basketball, cheerleading, cross-country, diving, football, golf, swimming, tennis, track/field (outdoor), track/field (indoor). *Women:* Basketball, cheerleading, cross-country, diving, golf, gymnastics, soccer, softball, swimming, tennis, track/field (outdoor), track/field (indoor), volleyball. **On-Campus Highlights:** LSU Student Union, Mike VI Tiger Habitat, Indian Mounds, Tiger Stadium, Alex Box Stadium, FACES Laboratory. **Environmental Initiatives:** Energy efficiency programs including recommissioning; utility insulation; LED lighting; class utilization study and IT power management enforcement programs; reducing vehicles on campus by 60%, new bus service using low-sulphur diesel and increasing ridership; new bike facility master plan; Advanced Recycling Program, athletics in-stadium recycling increased by 77%; composting during fall festival events; sustainable Christmas tree.

ADMISSIONS

Freshman Academic Profile: Average high school GPA 3.49. 26% in top 10% of high school class, 53% in top 25% of high school class, 84% in top 50% of high school class. 54% from public high schools. SAT Math middle 50% range 550–650. SAT Critical Reading middle 50% range 520–630. SAT Writing middle 50% range 490–600. ACT middle 50% range 23–28. Minimum paper TOEFL 550. Minimum computer TOEFL 213. Minimum web-based TOEFL 79. **Basis for Candidate Selection:** *Very important factors considered include:* Academic GPA, rigor of secondary school record, standardized test scores. *Important factors considered include:* Class rank, talent/ability. *Other factors considered include:* Application essay, recommendation(s), extracurricular activities, first generation. **Freshman Admission Requirements:** High school diploma is required and GED is accepted. *Academic units required:* 4 English, 3 mathematics, 3 science, 2 foreign language, 1 social studies, 2 history. *Academic units recommended:* 4 mathematics. **Freshman Admission Statistics:** 15,093 applied, 73% admitted, 46% enrolled. **Transfer Admission Requirements:** College transcript(s), minimum college GPA of 2.5 required. Lowest grade transferable D. **General Admission Information:** Application fee $40. Regular application deadline 4/15. Nonfall registration accepted. Admission may be deferred for a maximum of 1 year. Credit offered for CEEB Advanced Placement tests.

COSTS AND FINANCIAL AID

Annual in-state tuition $3,469. Annual out-of-state tuition $12,619. Room and board $7,738. Required fees $1,764. Average book expense $1,500. **Required Forms and Deadlines:** FAFSA, institution's own financial aid form. **Notification of Awards:** Applicants will be notified of awards on a rolling basis beginning 3/1. **Types of Aid:** *Need-based scholarships/grants:* Federal Pell, SEOG, state scholarships/grants, private scholarships, the school's own gift aid, ACG/SMART. *Loans:* FFEL Subsidized Stafford, FFEL Unsubsidized Stafford, FFEL PLUS, Federal Perkins, Alternative/Grad Plus. **Student Employment:** Federal Work-Study Program available. Institutional employment available. Off-campus job opportunities are excellent. **Financial Aid Statistics:** 34% freshmen, 28% undergrads receive need-based scholarship or grant aid. 2% freshmen, 1% undergrads receive non-need-based scholarship or grant aid. 19% freshmen, 24% undergrads receive need-based self-help aid. 2% freshmen, 2% undergrads receive athletic scholarships. 95% freshmen, 76% undergrads receive any aid. 40% undergrads borrow to pay for school. Average cumulative indebtedness $17,060. **Criteria for awarding institutional aid:** *Non-need-based:* Academics, alumni affiliation, art, athletics, leadership, music/drama, state/district residency.

LOUISIANA STATE UNIVERSITY IN SHREVEPORT

One University Place, Shreveport, LA 71115-2399
Phone: 318-797-5061
E-mail: admissions@pilot.lsus.edu **CEEB Code:** 6355
Fax: 318-797-5204 **Website:** www.lsus.edu **ACT Code:** 1593

This public school was founded in 1965. It has a 200-acre campus.

RATINGS

Admissions Selectivity Rating: 73   **Fire Safety Rating:** 60*   **Green Rating:** 60*

STUDENTS AND FACULTY

Enrollment: 3,594. **Student Body:** 62% female, 38% male, 2% out-of-state, 1% international. Asian 2%, African American 22%, Caucasian 65%, Hispanic 2%, Native American 1%.
Retention and Graduation: 53% freshmen return for sophomore year. **Faculty:** Student/faculty ratio 16:1. 155 full-time faculty, 72% hold PhDs, 12% are members of minority groups, 39% are women.

ACADEMICS

Degrees: Bachelor's, master's, post-master's certificate. **Classes:** Most classes have 20–29 students. **Majors with Highest Enrollment:** Business/commerce; Elementary education and teaching; general studies. **Special Study Options:** Cooperative education program, study abroad, teacher certification program, undergrads may take grad level courses and evening courses. **Combined degree programs:** Combined social work program w/ Grambling State U. Special programs offered to physically disabled students include note-taking services, reader services, tape recorders, tutors. **Career services:** Alumni services, career/job search classes, career assessment, internships.

FACILITIES

Housing: Apartments for married students, apartments for single students. 100% of campus accessible to physically disabled. **Special Academic Facilities/Equipment:** Art center, life science museum, pioneer heritage center. **Computers:** Students can register for classes online. Administrative functions (other than registration) can be performed online.

CAMPUS LIFE

Activities: Student government, student newspaper **Organizations:** 52 registered organizations, 4 honor societies, 3 religious organizations. 5 fraternities, 3 sororities. **Athletics (Intercollegiate):** *Men:* Baseball.

ADMISSIONS

Freshman Academic Profile: Average high school GPA 3.06. 90% from public high schools. ACT middle 50% range 18–23. Minimum paper TOEFL 500. **Basis for Candidate Selection:** *Other factors considered include:* Rigor of secondary school record, standardized test scores. **Freshman Admission Requirements:** High school diploma is required and GED is accepted. *Academic units recommended:* 4 English, 3 mathematics, 3 science, 3 social studies. **Freshman Admission Statistics:** 848 applied, 65% admitted, 106% enrolled. **Transfer Admission Requirements:** College transcript(s), minimum college GPA of 2.0 required. Lowest grade transferable D. **General Admission Information:** Application fee $10. Regular application deadline 8/1. Nonfall registration accepted. Credit offered for CEEB Advanced Placement tests.

COSTS AND FINANCIAL AID

Required Forms and Deadlines: FAFSA, institution's own financial aid form. **Types of Aid:** *Need-based scholarships/grants:* state scholarships/grants *Loans:* FFEL Subsidized Stafford, FFEL PLUS. **Student Employment:** Federal Work-Study Program available. Institutional employment available. Highest amount earned per year from on-campus jobs $2,000. Off-campus job opportunities are good.

LOURDES COLLEGE

6832 Convent Road, Sylvania, OH 43560-2898
Phone: 419-885-5291 **Financial Aid Phone:** 419-824-3732
E-mail: lcadmits@lourdes.edu **CEEB Code:** 1427
Fax: 419-882-3987 **Website:** www.lourdes.edu **ACT Code:** 3598

This private school, affiliated with the Roman Catholic Church, was founded in 1958. It has a 94-acre campus.

RATINGS

Admissions Selectivity Rating: 70   **Fire Safety Rating:** 60*   **Green Rating:** 60*

STUDENTS AND FACULTY

Enrollment: 1,789. **Student Body:** 82% female, 18% male, 8% out-of-state, international. Asian 1%, African American 16%, Caucasian 73%, Hispanic 5%. **Retention and Graduation:** 58% freshmen return for sophomore year. **Faculty:** Student/faculty ratio 11:1. 80 full-time faculty, 51% hold PhDs, 10% are members of minority groups, 73% are women.

ACADEMICS

Degrees: Associate, bachelor's, certificate, master's, post-bachelor's certificate. **Classes:** Most classes have 10–19 students. Most lab/discussion sessions have fewer than 10 students. **Majors with Highest Enrollment:** Early childhood education and teaching; nursing/registered nurse (RN, ASN, BSN, MSN); social work. **Special Study Options:** Distance learning, double major, dual enrollment, independent study, internships, liberal arts/career combination, student-designed major, study abroad, teacher certification program Special programs offered to physically disabled students include note-taking services, reader services, tape recorders, tutors. **Career services:** Career/job search classes, career assessment.

FACILITIES

Housing: Special Academic Facilities/Equipment: Planetarium, Life Lab. **Computers:** 100% of classrooms, 100% of libraries; 100% of dining areas,

100% of student union, have wireless network access. Students can register for classes online. Administrative functions (other than registration) can be performed online.

CAMPUS LIFE

Environment: Village. **Activities:** Choral groups, drama/theater, literary magazine, student government, campus ministries. **Organizations:** 25 registered organizations, 2 honor societies, **Athletics (Intercollegiate): Men:** Basketball, golf. *Women:* Golf, volleyball. **On-Campus Highlights:** McAlear Hall, Ebied Center.

ADMISSIONS

Freshman Academic Profile: Average high school GPA 2.91. 7% in top 10% of high school class, 21% in top 25% of high school class, 53% in top 50% of high school class. SAT Math middle 50% range 420–570. SAT Critical Reading middle 50% range 370–530. ACT middle 50% range 17–21. Minimum paper TOEFL 500. Minimum computer TOEFL 173. **Basis for Candidate Selection:** *Very important factors considered include:* Academic GPA. *Other factors considered include:* interview. **Freshman Admission Requirements:** High school diploma is required and GED is accepted. *Academic units recommended:* 4 English, 3 mathematics, 3 science, (2 science labs), 2 foreign language, 3 social studies, 1 visual/performing arts, 1 P.E./health. **Freshman Admission Statistics:** 390 applied, 80% admitted, 41% enrolled. **Transfer Admission Requirements:** College transcript(s), minimum college GPA of 2.0 required. Lowest grade transferable C. **General Admission Information:** Application fee $25. Nonfall registration accepted. Admission may be deferred for a maximum of 4 years. Credit and/or placement offered for CEEB Advanced Placement tests.

COSTS AND FINANCIAL AID

Annual tuition $13,440. Required fees $1,860. **Required Forms and Deadlines:** FAFSA. Priority financial aid filing date 3/1. **Notification of Awards:** Applicants will be notified of awards on a rolling basis beginning 3/1. **Types of Aid:** *Need-based scholarships/grants:* Federal Pell, SEOG, state scholarships/grants, private scholarships, the school's own gift aid. *Loans:* Direct Subsidized Stafford, Direct Unsubsidized Stafford, Direct PLUS, Federal Perkins, state loans, college/university loans from institutional funds. **Student Employment:** Federal Work-Study Program available. Institutional employment available. Off-campus job opportunities are excellent. **Financial Aid Statistics:** 62% freshmen, 63% undergrads receive need-based scholarship or grant aid. 56% freshmen, 46% undergrads receive non-need-based scholarship or grant aid. 78% freshmen, 80% undergrads receive need-based self-help aid. 96% freshmen, 78% undergrads receive any aid. **Criteria for awarding institutional aid:** *Non-need-based:* Academics, art, minority status, state/district residency.

LOYOLA MARYMOUNT UNIVERSITY

One LMU Drive, Suite 100, Los Angeles, CA 90045
Phone: 310-338-2750 **Financial Aid Phone:** 3103382753
E-mail: admissions@lmu.edu **CEEB Code:** 4403
Fax: 310-338-2797 **Website:** www.lmu.edu **ACT Code:** 326

This private school, affiliated with the Roman Catholic Church, was founded in 1911. It has a 128-acre campus.

RATINGS

Admissions Selectivity Rating: 89   **Fire Safety Rating:** 60*   **Green Rating:** 74

STUDENTS AND FACULTY

Enrollment: 5,590. **Student Body:** 59% female, 41% male, 23% out-of-state, 1% international (50 countries represented). Asian 13%, African American 7%, Caucasian 56%, Hispanic 19%, Native American 1%. **Retention and Graduation:** 90% freshmen return for sophomore year. 62% freshmen graduate within 4 years. **Faculty:** Student/faculty ratio 13:1. 419 full-time faculty, 87% hold PhDs, 22% are members of minority groups, 35% are women.

ACADEMICS

Degrees: Bachelor's, first professional, first professional certificate, master's, post-bachelor's certificate, post-master's certificate. **Classes:** Most classes have 20–29 students. Most lab/discussion sessions have 10–19 students. **Majors with Highest Enrollment:** Business administration and management; communication studies/speech communication and rhetoric; psychology. **Special Study**

Options: Cross-registration, double major, dual enrollment, honors program, independent study, internships, liberal arts/career combination, student-designed major, study abroad, teacher certification program, Encore program for adult students. Special programs offered to physically disabled students include note-taking services, reader services, tape recorders, tutors. **Career services:** Alumni services, career assessment, internships.

FACILITIES

Housing: Coed dorms, special housing for disabled students, men's dorms, women's dorms, apartments for single students. 99% of campus accessible to physically disabled. **Special Academic Facilities/Equipment:** Art gallery, theater, TV production labs, computer graphics lab. **Computers:** Students can register for classes online. Administrative functions (other than registration) can be performed online.

CAMPUS LIFE

Environment: Metropolis. **Activities:** Choral groups, dance, drama/theater, literary magazine, music ensembles, musical theater, pep band, radio station, student government, student newspaper, student-run film society, television station, yearbook. **Organizations:** 120 registered organizations, 12 honor societies, 2 religious organizations. 6 fraternities, 8 sororities. **Athletics (Intercollegiate): Men:** Baseball, basketball, crew/rowing, cross-country, golf, soccer, tennis, water polo. *Women:* Basketball, crew/rowing, cross-country, soccer, softball, swimming, tennis, volleyball, water polo. **Environmental Initiatives:** LEED Building Program: LMU's new $64 million library—currently under construction—incorporates state-of-the-art technologies and energy efficiency features, complementing other LEED-certified campus buildings and signifying LMU's commitment ton continued leadership in environmental stewardship. The library will also act as a 'living lab' for students studying Information Systems and IT in the context of building automation systems applications. LMU's solar energy program is the largest of its kind in the entire City of Los Angeles. Integrating on-site renewable energy generation together with extensive retro-fitting and efficiency features is a natural extension of our commitment to reducing our carbon footprint. The creation of the Environmental Stewardship and Sustainability Committee represents a tremendous step in establishing comprehensive, campus-wide policies and governance over every aspect of campus operations by instituting sustainability considerations and decision variables to be used across the university, from purchasing and procurement to academics and student life. The committee seeks to emphasize the inextricable link between ecological justice and social justice within our mission as a Jesuit university.

ADMISSIONS

Freshman Academic Profile: Average high school GPA 3.6. 30% in top 10% of high school class, 66% in top 25% of high school class, 99% in top 50% of high school class. 47% from public high schools. SAT Math middle 50% range 540–640. SAT Critical Reading middle 50% range 530–630. Minimum paper TOEFL 550. Minimum computer TOEFL 213. **Basis for Candidate Selection:** *Very important factors considered include:* Academic GPA, rigor of secondary school record. *Important factors considered include:* Class rank, application essay, standardized test scores, character/personal qualities, talent/ability. *Other factors considered include:* Recommendation(s), alumni/ae relation, extracurricular activities, first generation, geographical residence, interview, volunteer work, work experience. **Freshman Admission Requirements:** High school diploma is required and GED is accepted. *Academic units recommended:* 4 English, 3 mathematics, 2 science, (2 science labs), 3 foreign language, 3 social studies, 1 academic electives. **Freshman Admission Statistics:** 8,533 applied, 51% admitted, 28% enrolled. **Transfer Admission Requirements:** College transcript(s), essay or personal statement, statement of good standing from prior institution(s). Minimum college GPA of 2.8 required. Lowest grade transferable C. **General Admission Information:** Application fee $50. Notification on a rolling basis, beginning on or about 1/1. Nonfall registration accepted. Admission may be deferred for a maximum of 12. Credit and/or placement offered for CEEB Advanced Placement tests.

COSTS AND FINANCIAL AID

Annual tuition $33,901. Room and board $11,808. Required fees $636. Average book expense $3,465. **Required Forms and Deadlines:** FAFSA, CSS/Financial Aid PROFILE, business/farm supplement. Financial aid filing deadline 4/1. Priority financial aid filing date 2/15. **Notification of Awards:** Applicants will be notified of awards on a rolling basis beginning 3/15. **Types of Aid:** *Need-based scholarships/grants:* Federal Pell, SEOG, state scholarships/grants, private scholarships, the school's own gift aid. *Loans:* FFEL Subsidized Stafford, FFEL Unsubsidized Stafford, FFEL PLUS, Federal Perkins, college/university loans from institutional funds. **Student Employment:** Federal Work-Study Program available. Institutional employment available. Off-campus job opportunities are excellent. **Financial Aid Statistics:** 46% freshmen, 47% undergrads receive need-based scholarship or grant aid. 6% freshmen, 8% undergrads receive non-need-based scholarship or grant aid. 42% freshmen, 44% undergrads receive need-based self-help aid. 7% freshmen, 4% undergrads receive athletic scholarships. 66% undergrads borrow to pay for school. Average cumulative indebtedness $28,548.

LOYOLA UNIVERSITY MARYLAND

4501 North Charles Street, Baltimore, MD 21210
Phone: 410-617-5012 **Financial Aid Phone:** 410-617-2576
E-mail: CEEB Code: 5370
Fax: 410-617-2176 **Website:** www.loyola.edu

This private school, affiliated with the Roman Catholic Church, was founded in 1852. It has a 89-acre campus.

RATINGS
Admissions Selectivity Rating: 88   **Fire Safety Rating:** 83   **Green Rating:** 76

STUDENTS AND FACULTY
Enrollment: 999. **Student Body:** 61% female, 39% male, 82% out-of-state, 2% international (60 countries represented). Asian 12%, African American 16%, Caucasian 319%, Hispanic 16%, Native American 1%. **Retention and Graduation:** 89% freshmen return for sophomore year. 77% freshmen graduate within 4 years. **Faculty:** Student/faculty ratio 12:1. 331 full-time faculty, 79% hold PhDs, 12% are members of minority groups, 46% are women.

ACADEMICS
Degrees: Bachelor's, master's, post-master's certificate. **Classes:** Most classes have 20–29 students. Most lab/discussion sessions have 10–19 students. **Majors with Highest Enrollment:** Business/commerce; communications technology/technician; psychology. **Special Study Options:** Cross-registration, double major, dual enrollment, exchange student program (domestic), honors program, independent study, internships, liberal arts/career combination, study abroad, teacher certification program. **Honors programs:** http://www.loyola.edu/Undergraduate/Become-a-Greyhound/Apply/honors-program-app-process.aspx. Special programs offered to physically disabled students include note-taking services, reader services, tape recorders, tutors. **Career services:** Alumni network, alumni services, career/job search classes, career assessment, internships.

FACILITIES
Housing: Coed dorms, cooperative housing, apartments for single students, wellness housing, theme housing. 100% of campus accessible to physically disabled. **Special Academic Facilities/Equipment:** Art gallery, advanced biology lab, humanities building, speech pathology lab and audiology center, black box theater. **Computers:** 75% of classrooms, 80% of dorms, 100% of libraries, 100% of dining areas, 50% of student union, 50% of common outdoor areas have wireless network access. Students can register for classes online. Administrative functions (other than registration) can be performed online.

CAMPUS LIFE
Environment: Village. **Activities:** Choral groups, dance, drama/theater, literary magazine, music ensembles, musical theater, radio station, student government, student newspaper, television station, yearbook, campus ministries, international student organization. **Organizations:** 185 registered organizations, 25 honor societies, 4 religious organizations. **Athletics (Intercollegiate):** *Men:* Basketball, crew/rowing, cross-country, diving, golf, lacrosse, soccer, swimming, tennis. *Women:* Basketball, crew/rowing, cross-country, diving, lacrosse, soccer, swimming, tennis, track/field (outdoor), track/field (indoor), volleyball. **On-Campus Highlights:** Loyola/Notre Dame Library, The Loyola University Art Gallery, Fitness and Aquatic Center, Boulder Garden Cafe, Primo's: The New Marketplace. **Environmental Initiatives:** Built a Green Residential Hall that is 100,000 square feet in fall of 2007. Single stream recycling 35% of waste. Implemented an energy management plan to reduce energy usage on campus.

ADMISSIONS
Freshman Academic Profile: Average high school GPA 3.41. 31% in top 10% of high school class, 65% in top 25% of high school class, 93% in top 50% of high school class. 50% from public high schools. SAT Math middle 50% range 540–640. SAT Critical Reading middle 50% range 530–630. SAT Writing middle 50% range 550–640. ACT middle 50% range 24–28. Minimum paper TOEFL 550. Minimum computer TOEFL 213. **Basis for Candidate Selection:** *Very important factors considered include:* Application essay, recommendation(s), rigor of secondary school record, character/personal qualities. *Important factors considered include:* Class rank, alumni/ae relation, extracurricular activities, first generation, talent/ability, volunteer work. *Other factors considered include:* Academic GPA, standardized test scores, geographical residence, interview, level of applicant's interest, racial/ethnic status, work experience. **Freshman Admission Requirements:** High school diploma is required and GED is accepted. *Academic units required:* 4 English, 3 mathematics, 3 science, 3 foreign language, 2 social studies, 2 history. *Academic units recommended:* 4 English, 4 mathematics, 4 science, 4 foreign language, 3 social studies, 3 history, 1 visual/performing arts, 1 computer science. **Freshman Admission Statistics:** 9,117 applied, 66% admitted, 16% enrolled. **Transfer Admission Requirements:** High school transcript, college transcript(s), essay or personal statement, statement of good standing from prior institution(s). Minimum college GPA of 2.7 required. Lowest grade transferable C. **General Admission Information:** Application fee $50. Regular application deadline 6/1. Nonfall registration accepted. Admission may be deferred for a maximum of 1. Credit and/or placement offered for CEEB Advanced Placement tests.

COSTS AND FINANCIAL AID
Required Forms and Deadlines: FAFSA, CSS/Financial Aid PROFILE, noncustodial PROFILE, business/farm supplement. Financial aid filing deadline 2/15. Priority financial aid filing date 2/15. **Notification of Awards:** Applicants will be notified of awards on or about 4/1. **Types of Aid:** *Need-based scholarships/grants:* Federal Pell, SEOG, state scholarships/grants, private scholarships, the school's own gift aid. *Loans:* Direct Subsidized Stafford, Direct Unsubsidized Stafford, Direct PLUS, Federal Perkins, college/university loans from institutional funds. **Student Employment:** Federal Work-Study Program available. Institutional employment available. Highest amount earned per year from on-campus jobs $2,420. Off-campus job opportunities are good. **Financial Aid Statistics:** 51% freshmen, 44% undergrads receive need-based scholarship or grant aid. 10% freshmen, 11% undergrads receive non-need-based scholarship or grant aid. 53% freshmen, 46% undergrads receive need-based self-help aid. 3% freshmen, 4% undergrads receive athletic scholarships. 72% freshmen, 70% undergrads receive any aid. 72% undergrads borrow to pay for school. Average cumulative indebtedness $26,855. **Criteria for awarding institutional aid:** *Non-need-based:* Academics, athletics, minority status.

LOYOLA UNIVERSITY NEW ORLEANS

6363 St. Charles Avenue, Box 18, New Orleans, LA 70118-6195
Phone: 504-865-3240 **Financial Aid Phone:** 504-865-3231
E-mail: admit@loyno.edu **CEEB Code:** 6374
Fax: 504-865-3383 **Website:** www.loyno.edu **ACT Code:** 1592

This private school, affiliated with the Roman Catholic Church,, affiliated with the Jesuit Church, was founded in 1912. It has a 26-acre campus.

RATINGS
Admissions Selectivity Rating: 89   **Fire Safety Rating:** 92   **Green Rating:** 81

STUDENTS AND FACULTY
Enrollment: 2,721. **Student Body:** 57% female, 43% male, 48% out-of-state, 3% international (44 countries represented). Asian 5%, African American 14%, Caucasian 58%, Hispanic 11%, Native American 1%. **Retention and Graduation:** 80% freshmen return for sophomore year. 64.4% grads go on to further study within 1 year. 22.1% grads pursue arts and sciences degrees. 31.8% grads pursue law degrees. 12.3% grads pursue business degrees. 29.7% grads pursue medical degrees. **Faculty:** Student/faculty ratio 11:1. 283 full-time faculty, 88% hold PhDs, 13% are members of minority groups, 43% are women.

ACADEMICS
Degrees: Bachelor's, master's, post-bachelor's certificate, post-master's certificate. **Classes:** Most classes have 10–19 students. Most lab/discussion sessions have fewer than 10 students. **Majors with Highest Enrollment:** Marketing/marketing management; mass communication/media studies; psychology. **Special Study Options:** Accelerated program, cross-registration, distance learning, double major, dual enrollment, English as a Second Language (ESL), exchange student program (domestic), honors program, independent study, internships, liberal arts/career combination, student-designed major, study abroad, teacher certification program, Advance placement credit. Limited weekend courses available. Evening Courses available. Also teacher certification program is available in music only. **Honors programs:** The Loyola University Honors Program offers the opportunity for academically superior, highly motivated students to take challenging Honors courses and to participate in special cultural and intellectual enrichment activities. The University Honors Program is open to qualified students of all undergraduate colleges and majors. The Honors courses replace other required courses, and therefore do not add to the number of requirements for graduation. **Combined degree programs:** RN/MSN/DNP,

JD/MBA, MPS/MS, Early Law Admission. Special programs offered to physically disabled students include note-taking services, reader services, tape recorders, tutors. **Career services:** Alumni network, alumni services, career/job search classes, career assessment, internships, regional alumni.

FACILITIES

Housing: Coed dorms, special housing for disabled students, apartments for single students, wellness housing, theme housingHonors floor available. 95% of campus accessible to physically disabled. **Special Academic Facilities/Equipment:** Collins C. Diboll Art Gallery, Humanities Lab with Perseus Project and TLG TV, Multimedia Classrooms, 24-hour Microcomputer Labs, Computer Science Lab, Graphics Lab, Visual Arts Lab, Ad Club/Communications Lab, RATHE Business Computer Lab, Multi-Media Training Center, Donnelley Center for Non-Profit Communications, Chemistry Wing, Television Broadcast Studio, Multimedia Studio, Audio Recording Studio, Editing Studio, Library Learning Commons, Multimedia Exhibit Room, Satchmo's Deli and Performance Area, Center for International Education, University Sports Complex with Suspended Pool, Career Development Center, Jesuit Social Research Institute, Learning Communities. **Computers:** 50% of classrooms, 100% of dorms, 100% of libraries, 100% of dining areas, 100% of student union, 100% of common outdoor areas have wireless network access. Students can register for classes online. Administrative functions (other than registration) can be performed online.

CAMPUS LIFE

Environment: City. **Activities:** Choral groups, concert band, dance, drama/theater, jazz band, literary magazine, music ensembles, musical theater, opera, pep band, radio station, student government, student newspaper, student-run film society, symphony orchestra, yearbook, campus ministries, international student organization. **Organizations:** 90 registered organizations, 13 honor societies, 4 religious organizations. 7 fraternities, 7 sororities. **Athletics (Intercollegiate): Men:** Baseball, basketball, cross-country, track/field (outdoor), track/field (indoor). **Women:** Basketball, cross-country, track/field (outdoor), track/field (indoor), volleyball. **On-Campus Highlights:** J. Edgar and Louise S. Monroe Library, Danna Student Center, Recreational Sports Complex, Peace Quad, Residential Quad, Collins C. Diboll Art Gallery, Humanities Lab with Perseus Project and TLG TV, Multimedia Classrooms, 24-hour Microcomputer Labs, Computer Science Lab, Graphics Lab, Visual Arts Lab, Ad Club/Communications Lab, RATHE Business Computer Lab, Multi-Media Training Center, Donnelley Center for Non-Profit Communications, Chemistry Wing, Television Broadcast Studio, Multimedia Studio, Audio Recording Studio, Editing Studio, Library Learning Commons, Multimedia Exhibit Room, Satchmo's Deli and Performance Area, Center for International Education, University Sports Complex with Suspended Pool, Career Development Center, Jesuit Social Research Institute, Learning Communities. **Environmental Initiatives:** Formation of a committee that has representatives from important units on campus, including SGA and other student organizations. Full support of the Administration, starting with the President and Provost. Have signed on to the leading sustainable action groups (Talloires Sustainability Declaration, EPA WasteWise Team, President's Climate Change, NWF Campus Ecology Program, etc.). Implemented major inventories of sustainable operations across campus.

ADMISSIONS

Freshman Academic Profile: Average high school GPA 3.72. 29% in top 10% of high school class, 60% in top 25% of high school class, 91% in top 50% of high school class. 40.3% from public high schools. SAT Math middle 50% range 550–660. SAT Critical Reading middle 50% range 570–670. SAT Writing middle 50% range 550–660. ACT middle 50% range 24–29. Minimum paper TOEFL 550. Minimum computer TOEFL 213. **Basis for Candidate Selection:** *Very important factors considered include:* Academic GPA, rigor of secondary school record, standardized test scores. *Important factors considered include:* Application essay, recommendation(s), extracurricular activities, talent/ability. *Other factors considered include:* Class rank, alumni/ae relation, character/personal qualities, geographical residence, interview, level of applicant's interest, state residency, volunteer work, work experience. **Freshman Admission Requirements:** High school diploma is required and GED is accepted. *Academic units required:* 4 English, 2 mathematics, 2 science, 2 social studies. *Academic units recommended:* 4 English, 3 mathematics, 3 science, (1 science labs), 2 foreign language, 2 social studies. **Freshman Admission Statistics:** 4,345 applied, 58% admitted, 45% enrolled. **Transfer Admission Requirements:** College transcript(s), essay or personal statement, statement of good standing from prior institution(s). Minimum college GPA of 2.25 required. Lowest grade transferable C. **General Admission Information:** Application fee $20. Notification on a rolling basis, beginning on or about 10/20. Nonfall registration accepted. Credit and/or placement offered for CEEB Advanced Placement tests.

COSTS AND FINANCIAL AID

Annual tuition $30,468. Room and board $7,160. Required fees $1,036. Average book expense $1,000. **Required Forms and Deadlines:** FAFSA. Financial aid filing deadline 6/1. Priority financial aid filing date 2/15. **Notification of Awards:** Applicants will be notified of awards on a rolling basis beginning 3/1.

Types of Aid: *Need-based scholarships/grants:* Federal Pell, SEOG, private scholarships, the school's own gift aid. *Loans:* FFEL Subsidized Stafford, FFEL Unsubsidized Stafford, FFEL PLUS, Federal Perkins. **Student Employment:** Federal Work-Study Program available. Institutional employment available. Highest amount earned per year from on-campus jobs $1,920. Off-campus job opportunities are excellent. **Financial Aid Statistics:** 69% freshmen, 63% undergrads receive need-based scholarship or grant aid. 68% freshmen, 49% undergrads receive non-need-based scholarship or grant aid. 49% freshmen, 47% undergrads receive need-based self-help aid. 1% freshmen, 1% undergrads receive athletic scholarships. 98% freshmen, 97% undergrads receive any aid. 64% undergrads borrow to pay for school. Average cumulative indebtedness $22,320. **Criteria for awarding institutional aid:** *Non-need-based:* Academics, alumni affiliation, art, leadership.

LOYOLA UNIVERSITY OF CHICAGO

820 North Michigan Avenue, Chicago, IL 60611
Phone: 312-915-6500 **Financial Aid Phone:** 773-508-7704
E-mail: admission@luc.edu **CEEB Code:** 1412
Fax: 312-915-7216 **Website:** www.luc.edu

This private school, affiliated with the Roman CatholiC–Jesuit Church, was founded in 1870. It has a 105-acre campus.

RATINGS
Admissions Selectivity Rating: 86   **Fire Safety Rating:** 74   **Green Rating:** 89

STUDENTS AND FACULTY
Enrollment: 9,602. **Student Body:** 65% female, 35% male, 35% out-of-state, 1% international (101 countries represented). Asian 12%, African American 5%, Caucasian 64%, Hispanic 10%.
Retention and Graduation: 48% freshmen graduate within 4 years. **Faculty:** Student/faculty ratio 15:1. 629 full-time faculty, 93% hold PhDs, 10% are members of minority groups, 45% are women.

ACADEMICS
Degrees: Bachelor's, certificate, master's, post-bachelor's certificate, post-master's certificate. **Classes:** Most classes have 10–19 students. Most lab/discussion sessions have 10–19 students. **Majors with Highest Enrollment:** Biology/biological sciences; nursing/registered nurse (RN, ASN, BSN, MSN); psychology. **Special Study Options:** Accelerated program, distance learning, double major, dual enrollment, English as a Second Language (ESL), exchange student program (domestic), honors program, independent study, internships, study abroad, teacher certification program. **Honors programs:** Loyola University Chicago offers an Interdisciplinary Honors Program that integrates a challenging academic program with service-learning opportunities. Taking a series of team-taught, interdisciplinary courses, students learn to perceive unexpected convergences among discrete facts, to synthesize information from many sources, and to use their knowledge to benefit society. **Combined degree programs:** BA/JD, BA/MA, BA/MEng, BBA/MBA business administration; BS biology/MBA; BBA/MSA Ac. Special programs offered to physically disabled students include note-taking services, reader services, tape recorders, tutors. **Career services:** Alumni network, alumni services, career/job search classes, career assessment, internships, regional alumni. **Career services highlights include:** The Career Development Center counselors teach 4 sections each semester of the "Career and Life Planning" course. This unique course takes students through a thorough self assessment, exploration of their passions and calling, and provides detailed information on job search skills. This self-reflective course encourages students to research and explore a variety of industries and employment options so they are more focused and confident in their internship choices and their future career goals.

FACILITIES
Housing: Coed dorms, special housing for disabled students, apartments for single students, Honors floors; living learning community floors. 90% of campus accessible to physically disabled. **Special Academic Facilities/Equipment:** Renaissance art gallery, Loyola University Museum of Art (LUMA), Madonna Della Strada Chapel, The Quinlin Life Sciences Building Bio Deisel Labs, Mock Trial Room, Mundelein Auditorium. **Computers:** 75% of classrooms, 60% of dorms, 95% of libraries, 50% of dining areas, 100% of student union, 40% of common outdoor areas have wireless network access. Students can register for classes online. Administrative functions (other than registration) can be performed online.

CAMPUS LIFE

Environment: Metropolis. **Activities:** Concert band, dance, drama/theater, jazz band, literary magazine, music ensembles, musical theater, pep band, radio station, student government, student newspaper, student-run film society, television station, campus ministries, international student organization, Model UN. **Organizations:** 185 registered organizations, 11 honor societies, 9 religious organizations. 6 fraternities, 9 sororities. **Athletics (Intercollegiate):** *Men:* Basketball, cheerleading, cross-country, golf, soccer, track/field (outdoor), track/field (indoor), volleyball. *Women:* Basketball, cheerleading, cross-country, golf, soccer, softball, track/field (outdoor), track/field (indoor), volleyball. **On-Campus Highlights:** Information Commons, Lake front Residence Halls, Joseph J. Gentile Center, Halas Athletic Center/Alumni Gym, Quinlan Life Sciences Center. LAKE SHORE CAMPUS: Loyola's main residential campus is located on Chicago's North Side, minutes from downtown Chicago and the Water Tower Campus, and is set along the shore of Lake Michigan. It's home to the College of Arts and Sciences, Graduate School and Marcella Niehoff School of Nursing. The School of Education offers academic courses, programs and student advising. More than 3,000 students live in residence halls. The Lake Shore Campus includes Cudahy Library, Madonna della Strada Chapel, Joseph J. Gentile Center and the Halas Sports Center. WATER TOWER CAMPUS: Loyola's downtown campus is located along Pearson Street, just off North Michigan Avenue, Chicago's "Magnificent Mile." Here, both residential and commuter students can complete one of many undergraduate degree programs, as well as take advantage of internships at many of Chicago's business and cultural institutions. The Water Tower Campus is home to the Schools of Business Administration, Education, Law and Social Work, and to selected programs in the College of Arts and Sciences. **Environmental Initiatives:** 1. Energy reduction and conservation: Adopt green building design standards for all new construction. Lighting, heating/cooling retrofits. Transportation: walk-to-work program, bicycle program, electric vehicles, biodiessel derived from dining waste cooking oil in shuttle buses, public transit passes for students, car sharing program. 2. Environmental awareness programs: Solutions to Environmental Problems (STEP) program, Green Living Learning Community, Natural Science sustainability, biodiesel courses, professional non-credit sustainability education courses/workshops, environmental education themes across the disciplines, design student environmental community engagement projects and outreach. 3. Consumption Reduction programs: rainwater cistern, permeable walkways, semi-permeable artificial turf and track walkway, expanded recycling to include batteries, inkjet/printer cartridges. Trayfree dining halls, nondisposable water bottle campaign, waste vegetable oil conversion to biodiesel production lab, and spring move-out landfill diversion program.

ADMISSIONS

Freshman Academic Profile: Average high school GPA 3.7. 32% in top 10% of high school class, 67% in top 25% of high school class, 96% in top 50% of high school class. 66.5% from public high schools. SAT Math middle 50% range 530–650. SAT Critical Reading middle 50% range 540–650. SAT Writing middle 50% range 540–640. ACT middle 50% range 24–29. Minimum paper TOEFL 550. Minimum web-based TOEFL 79. **Basis for Candidate Selection:** *Very important factors considered include:* Academic GPA, rigor of secondary school record, standardized test scores. *Important factors considered include:* Application essay, recommendation(s), character/personal qualities, extracurricular activities, level of applicant's interest, volunteer work. *Other factors considered include:* Class rank, alumni/ae relation, first generation, geographical residence, interview, state residency, talent/ability, work experience. **Freshman Admission Requirements:** High school diploma is required and GED is accepted. *Academic units required:* 4 English, 3 mathematics, 3 science, 2 foreign language, 2 social studies, 1 history. *Academic units recommended:* 4 English, 4 mathematics, 3 science, 2 foreign language, 2 social studies, 2 history, 3 academic electives. **Freshman Admission Statistics:** 17,383 applied, 78% admitted, 15% enrolled. **Transfer Admission Requirements:** College transcript(s), minimum college GPA of 2.0 required. Lowest grade transferable C. **General Admission Information:** Application fee $25. Notification on a rolling basis, beginning on or about 10/1. Nonfall registration accepted. Credit and/or placement offered for CEEB Advanced Placement tests.

COSTS AND FINANCIAL AID

Annual tuition $30,180. Room and board $11,220. Required fees $1,074. Average book expense $1,200. **Required Forms and Deadlines:** FAFSA. Priority financial aid filing date 3/1. **Notification of Awards:** Applicants will be notified of awards on a rolling basis beginning 2/15. **Types of Aid:** *Need-based scholarships/grants:* Federal Pell, SEOG, state scholarships/grants, private scholarships, the school's own gift aid. *Loans:* FFEL Subsidized Stafford, FFEL Unsubsidized Stafford, FFEL PLUS, Federal Perkins, Federal Nursing **Student Employment:** Federal Work-Study Program available. Institutional employment available. Highest amount earned per year from on-campus jobs $9,803. Off-campus job opportunities are good. **Financial Aid Statistics:** 69% freshmen, 67% undergrads receive need-based scholarship or grant aid. 6% freshmen, 4% undergrads receive non-need-based scholarship or grant aid. 61% freshmen, 61% undergrads receive need-based self-help aid. 1% freshmen, 1%

undergrads receive athletic scholarships. 94.5% freshmen, 90.7% undergrads receive any aid. 57.9% undergrads borrow to pay for school. **Criteria for awarding institutional aid:** *Non-need-based:* Academics, athletics, leadership, music/drama, religious affiliation.

LUBBOCK CHRISTIAN UNIVERSITY

5601 19th Street, Lubbock, TX 79407
Phone: 800-720-7151 **Financial Aid Phone:** 806-720-7176
E-mail: admissions@lcu.edu **CEEB Code:** 6378
Fax: 806-720-7162 **Website:** www.lcu.edu **ACT Code:** 4123

This private school, affiliated with the Church of Christ Church, was founded in 1957. It has a 120-acre campus.

RATINGS

Admissions Selectivity Rating: 77   **Fire Safety Rating:** 60*   **Green Rating:** 60*

STUDENTS AND FACULTY

Enrollment: 1,728. **Student Body:** 56% female, 44% male, 9% out-of-state, international. Asian 1%, African American 6%, Caucasian 79%, Hispanic 14%, Native American 1%.

Retention and Graduation: 67% freshmen return for sophomore year. 27% freshmen graduate within 4 years. **Faculty:** Student/faculty ratio 15:1. 79 full-time faculty, 59% hold PhDs, 39% are women.

ACADEMICS

Degrees: Bachelor's, master's. **Classes:** Most classes have 10–19 students. Most lab/discussion sessions have fewer than 10 students. **Majors with Highest Enrollment:** Elementary education and teaching; humanities/humanistic studies; small business administration/management. **Special Study Options:** distance learning, double major, dual enrollment, honors program, internships, liberal arts/career combination, student-designed major, study abroad, teacher certification program, weekend college. **Honors programs:** Honors program available to all majors Special programs offered to physically disabled students include tape recorders, tutors. **Career services:** Alumni services, career/job search classes, career assessment, internships. **Career services highlights include:** Education—experietial learning opportunities in local schools are required with each education course.

FACILITIES

Housing: Special housing for disabled students, men's dorms, women's dorms, apartments for married students, apartments for single students. 78% of campus accessible to physically disabled. **Computers:** Students can register for classes online.

CAMPUS LIFE

Environment: City. **Activities:** Choral groups, drama/theater, music ensembles, student government, student newspaper, yearbook. **Organizations:** 24 registered organizations, 3 honor societies, 4 fraternities, 4 sororities. **Athletics (Intercollegiate):** *Men:* Baseball, basketball, cheerleading, golf. *Women:* Basketball, cheerleading, golf, volleyball. **On-Campus Highlights:** Student Union Building, Ramona Perrin Fitness Center, Rip Griffin Athletic Center, library, snack bar.

ADMISSIONS

Freshman Academic Profile: Average high school GPA 3.48. 18% in top 10% of high school class, 44% in top 25% of high school class, 76% in top 50% of high school class. 76% from public high schools. SAT Math middle 50% range 440–572. SAT Critical Reading middle 50% range 450–582. ACT middle 50% range 18–24. Minimum paper TOEFL 500. Minimum computer TOEFL 173. **Basis for Candidate Selection:** *Very important factors considered include:* Standardized test scores. *Important factors considered include:* Rigor of secondary school record, character/personal qualities. *Other factors considered include:* Class rank, recommendation(s), alumni/ae relation, racial/ethnic status, religious affiliation/commitment, talent/ability, volunteer work. **Freshman Admission Requirements:** High school diploma is required and GED is accepted. *Academic units recommended:* 4 English, 3 mathematics, 3 science, (2 science labs), 2 foreign language, 2 social studies, 2 history, 4 academic electives. **Freshman Admission Statistics:** 771 applied, 77% admitted, 45% enrolled. **Transfer Admission Requirements:** College transcript(s), statement of good standing from prior institution(s). Lowest grade transferable C. **General Admission Information:** Application fee $20. Regular application deadline 8/15. Notification on a rolling basis, beginning on or about 9/1. Nonfall registration accepted. Credit and/or placement offered for CEEB Advanced Placement tests.

COSTS AND FINANCIAL AID

Annual tuition $11,644. Room and board $2,125. Required fees $916. Average book expense $832. **Required Forms and Deadlines:** FAFSA, institution's own financial aid form. Priority financial aid filing date 6/1. **Notification of Awards:** Applicants will be notified of awards on a rolling basis beginning 3/1. **Types of Aid:** *Need-based scholarships/grants:* Federal Pell, SEOG, state scholarships/grants *Loans:* FFEL Subsidized Stafford, FFEL Unsubsidized Stafford, FFEL PLUS, Federal Perkins. **Student Employment:** Federal Work-Study Program available. Off-campus job opportunities are excellent. **Financial Aid Statistics:** 80% freshmen, 670% undergrads receive need-based scholarship or grant aid. 10% freshmen, 43% undergrads receive non-need-based scholarship or grant aid. 68% freshmen, 634% undergrads receive need-based self-help aid. 5% freshmen, 36% undergrads receive athletic scholarships. 78% freshmen, 72% undergrads receive any aid. 76% undergrads borrow to pay for school. Average cumulative indebtedness $20,244. **Criteria for awarding institutional aid:** *Non-need-based:* Academics, athletics, leadership, music/drama.

LUTHER COLLEGE

700 College Drive, Decorah, IA 52101-1042
Phone: 563-387-1287 **Financial Aid Phone:** 563-387-1018
E-mail: admissions@luther.edu **CEEB Code:** 6375
Fax: 563-387-2159 **Website:** www.luther.edu **ACT Code:** 1330

This private school, affiliated with the Lutheran Church, was founded in 1861. It has a 175-acre campus.

RATINGS

Admissions Selectivity Rating: 88   Fire Safety Rating: 60*   Green Rating: 89

STUDENTS AND FACULTY

Enrollment: 2,450. **Student Body:** 57% female, 43% male, 67% out-of-state, 5% international (46 countries represented). Asian 2%, African American 2%, Caucasian 81%, Hispanic 2%.
Retention and Graduation: 65% freshmen graduate within 4 years. 22.9% grads go on to further study within 1 year. 16.3% grads pursue arts and sciences degrees. 2.3% grads pursue law degrees. 0.02% grads pursue business degrees. 3.1% grads pursue medical degrees. **Faculty:** Student/faculty ratio 12.3:1. 177 full-time faculty, 92% hold PhDs, 3% are members of minority groups, 39% are women.

ACADEMICS

Degrees: Bachelor's. **Classes:** Most classes have 10–19 students. Most lab/discussion sessions have 10–19 students. **Majors with Highest Enrollment:** Biology/biological sciences; business administration and management; music. **Special Study Options:** Double major, dual enrollment, honors program, independent study, internships, student-designed major, study abroad, teacher certification program Special programs offered to physically disabled students include note-taking services, reader services, tutors. **Career services:** Alumni network, career/job search classes, internships.

FACILITIES

Housing: Coed dorms, special housing for disabled students, apartments for married students, apartments for single students, wellness housing. 95% of campus accessible to physically disabled. **Special Academic Facilities/Equipment:** Natural history museum, Norwegian-American museum, five art galleries, planetarium, live animal center, archaeological research center, computer music lab, two electron microscopes. **Computers:** 90% of classrooms, 75% of dorms, 90% of libraries, 90% of dining areas, 90% of student union, 25% of common outdoor areas have wireless network access. Students can register for classes online. Administrative functions (other than registration) can be performed online.

CAMPUS LIFE

Environment: Village. **Activities:** Choral groups, concert band, dance, drama/theater, jazz band, literary magazine, music ensembles, musical theater, pep band, radio station, student government, student newspaper, symphony orchestra, yearbook, campus ministries, international student organization, Model UN. **Organizations:** 83 registered organizations, 13 honor societies, 8 religious organizations. 1 fraternities, 3 sororities. **Athletics (Intercollegiate): Men:** Baseball, basketball, cross-country, diving, football, golf, soccer, swimming, tennis, track/field (outdoor), track/field (indoor), wrestling. *Women:* Basketball, cross-country, diving, golf, soccer, softball, swimming, tennis, track/field (outdoor), track/field (indoor), volleyball. **On-Campus Highlights:** Marty's Cyber Cafe, Legends Fitness Center, The Cafeteria, Residence Hall Lounges, Sunnyside Cafe in the Center for the Arts. **Environmental Initiatives:** Energy

audit and efficiency upgrades totaling $1.5 million and has reduced campus carbon footprint by 15%; built new science facility to LEED Gold certification; geothermal energy heats and cools two of the facilities on campus reducing our need for fossil fuel heating and cooling

ADMISSIONS

Freshman Academic Profile: Average high school GPA 3.64. 35.2% in top 10% of high school class, 63.9% in top 25% of high school class, 91.2% in top 50% of high school class. 95% from public high schools. SAT Math middle 50% range 530–670. SAT Critical Reading middle 50% range 500–640. SAT Writing middle 50% range 490–640. ACT middle 50% range 23–29. Minimum paper TOEFL 589. Minimum computer TOEFL 223. **Basis for Candidate Selection:** *Very important factors considered include:* Class rank, academic GPA, recommendation(s), rigor of secondary school record, standardized test scores. *Important factors considered include:* Character/personal qualities, extracurricular activities, talent/ability. *Other factors considered include:* Application essay, alumni/ae relation, first generation, interview, level of applicant's interest, racial/ethnic status, volunteer work. **Freshman Admission Requirements:** High school diploma is required and GED is accepted. *Academic units recommended:* 4 English, 3 mathematics, 2 science, (1 science labs), 2 foreign language, 3 social studies. **Freshman Admission Statistics:** 3,445 applied, 70% admitted, 27% enrolled. **Transfer Admission Requirements:** High school transcript, college transcript(s), essay or personal statement, standardized test scores, minimum college GPA of 2.50 required. Lowest grade transferable C. **General Admission Information:** Application fee $25. Nonfall registration accepted. Admission may be deferred for a maximum of 1 year. Credit and/or placement offered for CEEB Advanced Placement tests.

COSTS AND FINANCIAL AID

Annual tuition $33,330. Room and board $5,800. Required fees $150. Average book expense $910. **Required Forms and Deadlines:** FAFSA, institution's own financial aid form. Priority financial aid filing date 3/1. **Notification of Awards:** Applicants will be notified of awards on a rolling basis beginning 3/15. **Types of Aid:** *Need-based scholarships/grants:* Federal Pell, SEOG, state scholarships/grants, private scholarships, the school's own gift aid. *Loans:* Direct Subsidized Stafford, Direct Unsubsidized Stafford, Direct PLUS, Federal Perkins, college/university loans from institutional funds. **Student Employment:** Federal Work-Study Program available. Institutional employment available. Highest amount earned per year from on-campus jobs $3,190. Off-campus job opportunities are good. **Financial Aid Statistics:** 73% freshmen, 68% undergrads receive need-based scholarship or grant aid. 13% freshmen, 9% undergrads receive non-need-based scholarship or grant aid. 57% freshmen, 58% undergrads receive need-based self-help aid. 98% freshmen, 97% undergrads receive any aid. 82% undergrads borrow to pay for school. Average cumulative indebtedness $34,101. **Criteria for awarding institutional aid:** *Non-need-based:* Academics, alumni affiliation, art, minority status, music/drama.

LYCOMING COLLEGE

700 College Place, Box 164, Williamsport, PA 17701
Phone: 570-321-4026 **Financial Aid Phone:** 570-433-3068
E-mail: admissions@lycoming.edu **CEEB Code:** 2372
Fax: 570-321-4317 **Website:** www.lycoming.edu **ACT Code:** 3622

This private school, affiliated with the Methodist Church, was founded in 1812. It has a 39-acre campus.

RATINGS

Admissions Selectivity Rating: 78   Fire Safety Rating: 72   Green Rating: 76

STUDENTS AND FACULTY

Enrollment: 1,347. **Student Body:** 52% female, 48% male, 35% out-of-state, 1% international (7 countries represented). Asian 1%, African American 3%, Caucasian 87%, Hispanic 2%, Native American 1%.
Retention and Graduation: 78% freshmen return for sophomore year. 67% freshmen graduate within 4 years. 20% grads go on to further study within 1 year. 10% grads pursue arts and sciences degrees. 1% grads pursue law degrees. 1% grads pursue business degrees. 6% grads pursue medical degrees. **Faculty:** Student/faculty ratio 13:1. 89 full-time faculty, 97% hold PhDs, 7% are members of minority groups, 37% are women.

ACADEMICS

Degrees: Bachelor's. **Classes:** Most classes have 10–19 students. Most lab/discussion sessions have 10–19 students. **Majors with Highest Enrollment:** Biology/biological sciences; business administration and management; psychology. **Special Study Options:** Accelerated program, cross-registration, double major, honors program, independent study, internships, student-designed major, study abroad, teacher certification program. **Honors programs:** Scholars Program offered to students through admissions process; each major also provides an Honors major option for students who wish to graduate with honors within their field of study. Special programs offered to physically disabled students include note-taking services, reader services, tape recorders, tutors. **Career services:** Alumni network, career/job search classes, career assessment, internships. **Career services highlights include:** Lycoming College has a successful internship program with local businesses. Williamsport, PA serves as the County Seat and offers a rich array of business and government opportunities for students. In addition, Lycoming has successfully placed students in nationally competitive internship programs with the FBI, top 5 accounting firms, Datatel, and the National Science Foundation.

FACILITIES

Housing: Coed dorms, special housing for disabled students, women's dorms, fraternity/sorority housing, apartments for single students, theme housingSubstance-free housing, Study-intensive housing, Creative Arts Society housing. 85% of campus accessible to physically disabled. **Special Academic Facilities/Equipment:** Language lab, tissue culture lab, TV studio, planetarium, video conferencing. **Computers:** 100% of classrooms, 100% of dorms, 100% of libraries, 100% of dining areas, 100% of student union, 100% of common outdoor areas have wireless network access. Students can register for classes online. Administrative functions (other than registration) can be performed online.

CAMPUS LIFE

Environment: Town. **Activities:** Choral groups, concert band, dance, drama/theater, jazz band, literary magazine, music ensembles, musical theater, pep band, radio station, student government, student newspaper, student-run film society, symphony orchestra, television station, yearbook, campus ministries, international student organization. **Organizations:** 78 registered organizations, 20 honor societies, 3 religious organizations. 5 fraternities, 5 sororities. **Athletics (Intercollegiate):** *Men:* Basketball, cross-country, football, golf, lacrosse, soccer, swimming, tennis, wrestling. *Women:* Basketball, cross-country, golf, lacrosse, soccer, softball, swimming, tennis, volleyball. **On-Campus Highlights:** Quad, Dining Hall, Jack's Place, Lamade Gymnasium, Recreation Center. **Environmental Initiatives:** The college has a Sustainability Committee that is comprised of faculty, administrators and students. Several initiatives have emerged from this group including using the grease waste from campus dining and converting it into biodiesel. The college has replaced older less efficient lighting systems on campus to more energy efficient systems. All residence halls and many of the other campus buildings have been retrofitted to include high EER rated lighting equipment. This has cut our energy costs in half for many buildings. New and renovated buildings are updated to include the latest technology in energy efficiency.

ADMISSIONS

Freshman Academic Profile: 19% in top 10% of high school class, 43% in top 25% of high school class, 80% in top 50% of high school class. 90% from public high schools. SAT Math middle 50% range 470–580. SAT Critical Reading middle 50% range 470–580. SAT Writing middle 50% range 460–570. ACT middle 50% range 20–27. Minimum paper TOEFL 500. Minimum computer TOEFL 173. **Basis for Candidate Selection:** *Very important factors considered include:* Rigor of secondary school record. *Important factors considered include:* Class rank, application essay, academic GPA, recommendation(s), standardized test scores, interview, racial/ethnic status. *Other factors considered include:* Alumni/ae relation, character/personal qualities, extracurricular activities, first generation, geographical residence, level of applicant's interest, talent/ability, volunteer work, work experience. **Freshman Admission Requirements:** High school diploma is required and GED is accepted. *Academic units required:* 4 English, 3 mathematics, 3 science, (2 science labs), 2 foreign language, 4 social studies, 3 history, 2 academic electives. *Academic units recommended:* 4 English, 4 mathematics, 4 science, (2 science labs), 4 foreign language, 4 social studies, 4 history, 2 academic electives. **Freshman Admission Statistics:** 1,601 applied, 69% admitted, 31% enrolled. **Transfer Admission Requirements:** College transcript(s), statement of good standing from prior institution(s). Minimum college GPA of 2.0 required. Lowest grade transferable C–. **General Admission Information:** Application fee $35. Regular application deadline 7/1. Notification on a rolling basis, beginning on or about 12/15. Nonfall registration accepted. Admission may be deferred for a maximum of 1 year. Credit offered for CEEB Advanced Placement tests.

COSTS AND FINANCIAL AID

Annual tuition $29,344. Room and board $8,134. Required fees $550. Average book expense $900. **Required Forms and Deadlines:** FAFSA, institution's own financial aid form. Priority financial aid filing date 3/1. **Notification of Awards:** Applicants will be notified of awards on a rolling basis beginning 3/1. **Types of Aid:** *Need-based scholarships/grants:* Federal Pell, SEOG, state scholarships/grants, private scholarships, the school's own gift aid. *Loans:* FFEL Subsidized Stafford, FFEL Unsubsidized Stafford, FFEL PLUS, Federal Perkins, college/university loans from institutional funds. **Student Employment:** Federal Work-Study Program available. Institutional employment available.

Highest amount earned per year from on-campus jobs $4,004. Off-campus job opportunities are good. **Financial Aid Statistics:** 90% freshmen, 85% undergrads receive need-based scholarship or grant aid. 8% freshmen, 7% undergrads receive non-need-based scholarship or grant aid. 74% freshmen, 73% undergrads receive need-based self-help aid. 95% freshmen, 95% undergrads receive any aid. 85% undergrads borrow to pay for school. Average cumulative indebtedness $29,478. **Criteria for awarding institutional aid:** *Non-need-based:* Academics, art, leadership, minority status, music/drama.

LYME ACADEMY COLLEGE OF FINE ARTS

84 Lyme St, Old Lyme, CT 06371
Phone: 860-434-3571 x118 **Financial Aid Phone:** 860-434-5232
E-mail: admissions@lymeacademy.edu **CEEB Code:** 1971
Fax: 860-434-8725 **Website:** www.lymeacademy.edu

This private school was founded in 1976. It has a 47-acre campus.

RATINGS

Admissions Selectivity Rating: 71   Fire Safety Rating: 60*   Green Rating: 60*

STUDENTS AND FACULTY

Enrollment: 96. **Student Body:** 57% female, 43% male, 47% out-of-state, Asian 1%, African American 2%, Caucasian 84%, Hispanic 1%, Native American 2%.

Retention and Graduation: 82% freshmen return for sophomore year. 11% freshmen graduate within 4 years. 10% grads go on to further study within 1 year. **Faculty:** Student/faculty ratio 14:1. 8 full-time faculty, 75% hold PhDs, 38% are women.

ACADEMICS

Degrees: Bachelor's, certificate, post-bachelor's certificate. **Classes:** Most classes have 10–19 students. **Majors with Highest Enrollment:** Illustration; painting; sculpture. **Special Study Options:** Independent study.

FACILITIES

Housing: Currently, all housing is off-campus. Students live in local homes as well as apartments. Contact Patti Broedlin in Student Services for assistance, lists and referrals. 95% of campus accessible to physically disabled. **Special Academic Facilities/Equipment:** Sill House Gallery, Chauncey Stillman Gallery, Academy Wood Shop, sculpture casting rooms. **Computers:** 20% of classrooms, 100% of libraries, 100% of dining areas, 100% of student union, 40% of common outdoor areas have wireless network access.

CAMPUS LIFE

Environment: Village. **Activities:** Literary magazine, student government, student-run film society. **Organizations:**. **On-Campus Highlights:** Chauncey Stillman Art Gallery, Cafe, Student Commons, Library, Sill House Art Gallery.

ADMISSIONS

Freshman Academic Profile: Average high school GPA 3.22. 85% from public high schools. SAT Math middle 50% range 450–590. SAT Critical Reading middle 50% range 515–615. SAT Writing middle 50% range 460–570. Minimum paper TOEFL 550. Minimum computer TOEFL 213. **Basis for Candidate Selection:** *Very important factors considered include:* Academic GPA, character/personal qualities, interview, level of applicant's interest, talent/ability. *Important factors considered include:* Application essay, recommendation(s), rigor of secondary school record. *Other factors considered include:* standardized test scores, racial/ethnic status. **Freshman Admission Requirements:** High school diploma is required and GED is accepted. **Freshman Admission Statistics:** 30 applied, 100% admitted, 37% enrolled. **Transfer Admission Requirements:** College transcript(s), essay or personal statement, interview, minimum college GPA of 2.0 required. Lowest grade transferable C. **General Admission Information:** Application fee $55. Notification on a rolling basis, beginning on or about 12/1. Nonfall registration accepted. Admission may be deferred for a maximum of 1 year. Credit and/or placement offered for CEEB Advanced Placement tests.

COSTS AND FINANCIAL AID

Annual tuition $21,792. . Required fees $1,300. Average book expense $1,500. **Required Forms and Deadlines:** FAFSA, CSS/Financial Aid PROFILE, business/farm supplement. Copies of previous year's Tax forms and W2's. Priority financial aid filing date 3/1. **Notification of Awards:** Applicants will be notified of awards on a rolling basis beginning 3/1. **Types of Aid:** *Need-based scholarships/grants:* Federal Pell, SEOG, state scholarships/grants, private scholarships, the school's own gift aid. *Loans:* FFEL Subsidized Stafford, FFEL Unsubsidized Stafford, FFEL PLUS. **Student Employment:** Federal Work-Study Program available. Institutional employment available. Off-campus job opportunities are good. **Financial Aid Statistics:** 73% freshmen receive need-based scholarship or grant aid. 9% freshmen receive non-need-based scholarship or grant aid. 73% freshmen receive need-based self-help aid. 88% freshmen, 84% undergrads receive any aid. **Criteria for awarding institutional aid:** *Non-need-based:* Academics, art, leadership.

LYNCHBURG COLLEGE

1501 Lakeside Drive, Lynchburg, VA 24501
Phone: 434-544-8300 **Financial Aid Phone:** 434-544-8229
E-mail: admissions@lynchburg.edu **CEEB Code:** 5372
Fax: 434-544-8653 **Website:** www.lynchburg.edu **ACT Code:** 4368

This private school, affiliated with the Disciples of Christ Church, was founded in 1903. It has a 214-acre campus.

RATINGS
Admissions Selectivity Rating: 77   **Fire Safety Rating:** 75   **Green Rating:** 78

STUDENTS AND FACULTY
Enrollment: 2,165. **Student Body:** 60% female, 40% male, 36% out-of-state, international (21 countries represented). Asian 1%, African American 8%, Caucasian 78%, Hispanic 2%, Native American 1%.
Retention and Graduation: 72% freshmen return for sophomore year. 54% freshmen graduate within 4 years. **Faculty:** Student/faculty ratio 12:1. 155 full-time faculty, 74% hold PhDs, 7% are members of minority groups, 50% are women.

ACADEMICS
Degrees: Bachelor's, master's, post-bachelor's certificate. **Classes:** Most classes have 10–19 students. Most lab/discussion sessions have 10–19 students. **Majors with Highest Enrollment:** Business administration and management; communication studies/speech communication and rhetoric; teacher education and professional development, specific levels and methods, other. **Special Study Options:** Accelerated program, cross-registration, double major, dual enrollment, honors program, independent study, internships, study abroad, teacher certification program. **Honors programs:** Westover Honors Program Special programs offered to physically disabled students include note-taking services, reader services, tape recorders, tutors. **Career services:** Alumni network, alumni services, career/job search classes, career assessment, internships, regional alumni. **Career services highlights include:** Experiential learning and internship programs are so numerous and diverse that it is impossible to select one that is most outstanding.

FACILITIES
Housing: Coed dorms, special housing for disabled students, men's dorms, special housing for international students, women's dorms, fraternity/sorority housing, apartments for single students, wellness housing, theme housing 83% of campus accessible to physically disabled. **Special Academic Facilities/Equipment:** Daura Art Gallery, Claytor Nature Study Center, Ramsey-Freer Herbarium, Forensics cadaver lab; Centennial Hall audio-visual and television studios, Dillard Fine Arts Center. **Computers:** 20% of dorms, 100% of libraries, 100% of dining areas, 100% of student union, have wireless network access. Students can register for classes online. Administrative functions (other than registration) can be performed online.

CAMPUS LIFE
Environment: City. **Activities:** Choral groups, concert band, dance, drama/theater, jazz band, literary magazine, music ensembles, musical theater, pep band, student government, student newspaper, student-run film society, symphony orchestra, yearbook, campus ministries, international student organization, Model UN. **Organizations:** 90 registered organizations, 14 honor societies, 10 religious organizations. 4 fraternities, 6 sororities. **Athletics (Intercollegiate):** *Men:* Baseball, basketball, cheerleading, cross-country, golf, lacrosse, soccer, tennis, track/field (outdoor), track/field (indoor). *Women:* Basketball, cheerleading, cross-country, equestrian sports, field hockey, lacrosse, soccer, softball, tennis, track/field (outdoor), track/field (indoor), volleyball. **On-Campus Highlights:** Shellenberger Field, Burton Student Center, Claytor Nature Study Center, Stingers Coffee House, Schewel Hall. **Environmental Initiatives:** Recovery of College Lake. Working with the Army Corp of Engineers, and the state of Virginia, Lynchburg College is attempting to restore College Lake. Dr. Garren (LC President) has signed the American College &

University Presidents Climate Commitment, a pledge to reverse the actions that lead to global warming. Signatories agree to develop a plan to reduce their use of greenhouse gases. Dr. Nancy Cowden, associate professor of biology, is leading the task force on LC's climate commitment. Development of Claytor Nature Study Center.

ADMISSIONS
Freshman Academic Profile: Average high school GPA 3.16. 12% in top 10% of high school class, 40% in top 25% of high school class, 77% in top 50% of high school class. 86% from public high schools. SAT Math middle 50% range 455–570. SAT Critical Reading middle 50% range 460–560. SAT Writing middle 50% range 450–550. ACT middle 50% range 19–24. Minimum paper TOEFL 525. Minimum computer TOEFL 197. **Basis for Candidate Selection:** *Very important factors considered include:* Academic GPA, rigor of secondary school record, standardized test scores. *Important factors considered include:* Class rank, interview. *Other factors considered include:* Application essay, recommendation(s), extracurricular activities, level of applicant's interest, talent/ability, volunteer work. **Freshman Admission Requirements:** High school diploma is required and GED is accepted. *Academic units required:* 4 English, 3 mathematics, 3 science, (2 science labs), 2 foreign language, 2 social studies, 2 history. *Academic units recommended:* 4 English, 4 mathematics, 4 science, (2 science labs), 3 foreign language, 2 social studies, 2 history, 1 academic electives. **Freshman Admission Statistics:** 4,571 applied, 66% admitted, 20% enrolled. **Transfer Admission Requirements:** College transcript(s), minimum college GPA of 2.0 required. Lowest grade transferable C. **General Admission Information:** Application fee $30. Early decision application deadline 11/15. Notification on a rolling basis, beginning on or about 9/1. Nonfall registration accepted. Admission may be deferred for a maximum of 1 year. Credit offered for CEEB Advanced Placement tests.

COSTS AND FINANCIAL AID
Annual tuition $27,980. Room and board $7,770. Required fees $945. Average book expense $750. **Required Forms and Deadlines:** FAFSA, state aid form. Priority financial aid filing date 3/1. **Notification of Awards:** Applicants will be notified of awards on a rolling basis beginning 3/5. **Types of Aid:** *Need-based scholarships/grants:* Federal Pell, SEOG, state scholarships/grants, private scholarships, the school's own gift aid. *Loans:* FFEL Subsidized Stafford, FFEL Unsubsidized Stafford, FFEL PLUS, Federal Perkins. **Student Employment:** Federal Work-Study Program available. Institutional employment available. Off-campus job opportunities are good. **Financial Aid Statistics:** 73% freshmen, 69% undergrads receive need-based scholarship or grant aid. 10% freshmen, 10% undergrads receive non-need-based scholarship or grant aid. 62% freshmen, 58% undergrads receive need-based self-help aid. 96% freshmen, 96% undergrads receive any aid. 67% undergrads borrow to pay for school. Average cumulative indebtedness $30,954. **Criteria for awarding institutional aid:** *Non-need-based:* Academics, leadership, music/drama, religious affiliation.

LYNDON STATE COLLEGE

P O Box 919, 1001 College Hill Rd, Lyndonville, VT 05851
Phone: 802-626-6413
E-mail: admissions@lyndonstate.edu **CEEB Code:** 3767
Fax: 802-626-6335 **Website:** www.lyndonstate.edu **ACT Code:** 4318

This public school was founded in 1911. It has a 175-acre campus.

RATINGS
Admissions Selectivity Rating: 66   **Fire Safety Rating:** 60*   **Green Rating:** 60*

STUDENTS AND FACULTY
Enrollment: 1,273. **Student Body:** 49% female, 51% male, 40% out-of-state, international. African American 1%, Caucasian 52%, Hispanic 1%.
Retention and Graduation: 67% freshmen return for sophomore year. 24% freshmen graduate within 4 years. 10% grads go on to further study within 1 year. **Faculty:** Student/faculty ratio 20:1. 59 full-time faculty, 90% hold PhDs, 34% are women.

ACADEMICS
Degrees: Associate, bachelor's, certificate, master's. **Classes:** Most classes have 10–19 students. Most lab/discussion sessions have 10–19 students. **Special Study Options:** Accelerated program, cooperative education program, double major, dual enrollment, exchange student program (domestic), independent study, internships, liberal arts/career combination, student-designed major, study abroad, teacher certification program Special programs offered to physically disabled students include note-taking services, tape recorders, tutors. **Career services:** Alumni network, alumni services, career/job search classes, career assessment, internships, regional alumni.

FACILITIES

Housing: Coed dorms, special housing for disabled students, women's dorms, Substance free dorms. 100% of campus accessible to physically disabled. **Special Academic Facilities/Equipment:** Museum of college history, weather satellite lab, television studio, radio station, science labs: geology, chemistry, physics; GIS/GPS lab.

CAMPUS LIFE

Environment: Rural. **Activities:** Choral groups, dance, drama/theater, literary magazine, musical theater, radio station, student government, student newspaper, television station. **Organizations:** 26 registered organizations, 1 honor societies, 1 religious organizations. **Athletics (Intercollegiate):** *Men:* Baseball, basketball, cross-country, soccer, tennis. *Women:* Basketball, cross-country, soccer, softball, tennis.

ADMISSIONS

Freshman Academic Profile: Average high school GPA 2.5. 12% in top 10% of high school class, 22% in top 25% of high school class, 69% in top 50% of high school class. SAT Math middle 50% range 410–530. SAT Critical Reading middle 50% range 418–520. Minimum paper TOEFL 500. Minimum computer TOEFL 173. **Basis for Candidate Selection:** *Very important factors considered include:* Rigor of secondary school record. *Important factors considered include:* Class rank, recommendation(s), character/personal qualities, interview, talent/ability. *Other factors considered include:* Application essay, standardized test scores, alumni/ae relation, extracurricular activities, volunteer work, work experience. **Freshman Admission Requirements:** High school diploma is required and GED is accepted. *Academic units required:* 4 English, 3 mathematics, 2 science, (2 science labs), 2 social studies, 2 history. *Academic units recommended:* 4 mathematics, 3 science, 2 foreign language. **Freshman Admission Statistics:** 994 applied, 94% admitted, 36% enrolled. **Transfer Admission Requirements:** College transcript(s), essay or personal statement, statement of good standing from prior institution(s). Minimum college GPA of 2.2 required. Lowest grade transferable C–. **General Admission Information:** Application fee $35. Notification on a rolling basis, beginning on or about 12/1. Nonfall registration accepted. Admission may be deferred for a maximum of 1 year. Credit and/or placement offered for CEEB Advanced Placement tests.

COSTS AND FINANCIAL AID

Average book expense $600. **Required Forms and Deadlines:** FAFSA. Priority financial aid filing date 2/13. **Notification of Awards:** Applicants will be notified of awards on a rolling basis beginning 4/1. **Types of Aid:** *Need-based scholarships/grants:* Federal Pell, SEOG, state scholarships/grants, private scholarships, the school's own gift aid. *Loans:* Direct Subsidized Stafford, Direct Unsubsidized Stafford, Direct PLUS, Federal Perkins, state loans. **Student Employment:** Federal Work-Study Program available. Institutional employment available. Highest amount earned per year from on-campus jobs $700. Off-campus job opportunities are good. **Financial Aid Statistics:** 41% freshmen, 39% undergrads receive need-based scholarship or grant aid. 17% freshmen, 6% undergrads receive non-need-based scholarship or grant aid. 76% freshmen, 74% undergrads receive need-based self-help aid. **Criteria for awarding institutional aid:** *Non-need-based:* Academics, leadership.

LYNN UNIVERSITY

3601 North Military Trail, Boca Raton, FL 33431-5598
Phone: 561-237-7900 **Financial Aid Phone:** 561-237-7186
E-mail: admission@lynn.edu **CEEB Code:** 5437
Fax: 561-237-7100 **Website:** www.lynn.edu **ACT Code:** 706

This private school was founded in 1962. It has a 123-acre campus.

RATINGS

Admissions Selectivity Rating: 69   **Fire Safety Rating:** 90   **Green Rating:** 64

STUDENTS AND FACULTY

Enrollment: 1,737. **Student Body:** 49% female, 51% male, 61% out-of-state, 15% international (82 countries represented). African American 3%, Caucasian 48%, Hispanic 7%.
Retention and Graduation: 58% freshmen return for sophomore year. 23% freshmen graduate within 4 years. **Faculty:** Student/faculty ratio 16:1. 103 full-time faculty, 69% hold PhDs, 23% are members of minority groups, 42% are women.

ACADEMICS

Degrees: Bachelor's, certificate, master's, post-bachelor's certificate, post-master's certificate. **Classes:** Most classes have 10–19 students. **Majors with Highest Enrollment:** Business/commerce; hospitality administration/manage-

ment; journalism. **Special Study Options:** Accelerated program, cooperative education program, distance learning, double major, dual enrollment, English as a Second Language (ESL), honors program, independent study, internships, liberal arts/career combination, study abroad, teacher certification program. **Honors programs:** Honors Program Special programs offered to physically disabled students include note-taking services, reader services, tape recorders. **Career services:** Alumni services, career/job search classes, career assessment, internships, regional alumni. **Career services highlights include:** Well developed internship program, with approximately 300 internship students for whom we provide services in all program areas, excluding education and aviation.

FACILITIES

Housing: Coed dorms, special housing for disabled students, special housing for international students, women's dorms 100% of campus accessible to physically disabled. **Computers:** Students can register for classes online. Administrative functions (other than registration) can be performed online.

CAMPUS LIFE

Environment: City. **Activities:** Choral groups, dance, drama/theater, literary magazine, music ensembles, radio station, student government, student newspaper, student-run film society, symphony orchestra, television station, yearbook, campus ministries, international student organization. **Organizations:** 25 registered organizations, 4 honor societies, 4 religious organizations. 2 fraternities, 1 sorority. **Athletics (Intercollegiate):** *Men:* Baseball, basketball, golf, soccer, tennis. *Women:* Basketball, golf, soccer, softball, tennis, volleyball. **On-Campus Highlights:** The de Hoernle Sports Complex, The de Hoernle Sports and Cultural Center, The Coleman Electronic Lab, The Lynn Student Center, The Eugene M. and Christine E. Lynn Library. **Environmental Initiatives:** On campsu recycling program (paper, glass and cans); recycling of flourescent light bulbs; use of re-claimed water for irrigation.

ADMISSIONS

Freshman Academic Profile: Average high school GPA 2.79. 7% in top 10% of high school class, 23% in top 25% of high school class, 51% in top 50% of high school class. SAT Math middle 50% range 420–530. SAT Critical Reading middle 50% range 420–520. ACT middle 50% range 17–22. Minimum paper TOEFL 525. Minimum computer TOEFL 197. Minimum web-based TOEFL 71. **Basis for Candidate Selection:** *Very important factors considered include:* Academic GPA, rigor of secondary school record, standardized test scores. *Important factors considered include:* Class rank, application essay, recommendation(s), character/personal qualities, work experience. *Other factors considered include:* Alumni/ae relation, extracurricular activities, first generation, interview, state residency, talent/ability, volunteer work. **Freshman Admission Requirements:** High school diploma is required and GED is accepted. *Academic units required:* 4 English, 4 mathematics, 4 science, 2 social studies, 2 history. **Freshman Admission Statistics:** 1,650 applied, 98% admitted, 21% enrolled. **Transfer Admission Requirements:** College transcript(s), essay or personal statement, statement of good standing from prior institution(s). Minimum college GPA of 2.0 required. Lowest grade transferable C. **General Admission Information:** Application fee $35. Nonfall registration accepted. Credit offered for CEEB Advanced Placement tests.

COSTS AND FINANCIAL AID

Annual tuition $28,600. Room and board $10,900. Required fees $1,500. Average book expense $1,200. **Required Forms and Deadlines:** FAFSA, institution's own financial aid form. Priority financial aid filing date 3/1. **Notification of Awards:** Applicants will be notified of awards on a rolling basis beginning 2/1. **Types of Aid:** *Need-based scholarships/grants:* Federal Pell, SEOG, state scholarships/grants, private scholarships, the school's own gift aid. *Loans:* Direct Subsidized Stafford, Direct Unsubsidized Stafford, Direct PLUS, FFEL Subsidized Stafford, FFEL Unsubsidized Stafford, FFEL PLUS, Federal Perkins, state loans, college/university loans from institutional funds. **Student Employment:** Federal Work-Study Program available. Institutional employment available. Highest amount earned per year from on-campus jobs $16,420. Off-campus job opportunities are excellent. **Financial Aid Statistics:** 40% freshmen, 36% undergrads receive need-based scholarship or grant aid. 43% freshmen, 39% undergrads receive non-need-based scholarship or grant aid. 31% freshmen, 30% undergrads receive need-based self-help aid. 12% freshmen, 12% undergrads receive athletic scholarships. 54% freshmen, 55% undergrads receive any aid. 42.6% undergrads borrow to pay for school. Average cumulative indebtedness $34,075. **Criteria for awarding institutional aid:** *Non-need-based:* Academics, athletics, leadership, music/drama, religious affiliation, state/district residency.

See page 1150.

LYON COLLEGE

P.O. Box 2317, Batesville, AR 72503-2317
Phone: 870-307-7250 **Financial Aid Phone:** 870-307-7257
E-mail: admissions@lyon.edu **CEEB Code:** 1088
Fax: 870-307-7542 **Website:** www.lyon.edu **ACT Code:** 112

This private school, affiliated with the Presbyterian Church, was founded in 1872. It has a 136-acre campus.

RATINGS
Admissions Selectivity Rating: 87   **Fire Safety Rating:** 70   **Green Rating:** 61

STUDENTS AND FACULTY
Enrollment: 453. **Student Body:** 54% female, 46% male, 30% out-of-state, 2% international (7 countries represented). Asian 1%, African American 4%, Caucasian 80%, Hispanic 2%, Native American 2%.
Retention and Graduation: 56% freshmen graduate within 4 years. 21% grads go on to further study within 1 year. 3% grads pursue arts and sciences degrees. 3% grads pursue law degrees. 1% grads pursue business degrees. 7% grads pursue medical degrees. **Faculty:** Student/faculty ratio 9:1. 44 full-time faculty, 91% hold PhDs, 9% are members of minority groups, 23% are women.

ACADEMICS
Degrees: Bachelor's. **Classes:** Most classes have 10–19 students. Most lab/discussion sessions have fewer than 10 students. **Majors with Highest Enrollment:** Biology/biological sciences; business/commerce; psychology. **Special Study Options:** Accelerated program, cross-registration, double major, dual enrollment, independent study, internships, liberal arts/career combination, student-designed major, study abroad, teacher certification program. **Combined degree programs:** BA/MEng, BS/BEng (with U. MO. Rolla). Special programs offered to physically disabled students include tape recorders. **Career services:** Alumni network, alumni services, career/job search classes, career assessment, internships, regional alumni.

FACILITIES
Housing: Coed dorms, special housing for disabled students, men's dorms, women's dorms, apartments for single students, limited college-owned off campus housing. 80% of campus accessible to physically disabled. **Special Academic Facilities/Equipment:** Ozark Regional Studies Center **Computers:** 100% of classrooms, 100% of dorms, 100% of libraries, 100% of dining areas, 100% of student union, 100% of common outdoor areas have wireless network access. Students can register for classes online. Administrative functions (other than registration) can be performed online.

CAMPUS LIFE
Environment: Village. **Activities:** Choral groups, concert band, drama/theater, literary magazine, music ensembles, student government, student newspaper, yearbook, campus ministries, Model UN. **Organizations:** 44 registered organizations, 9 honor societies, 7 religious organizations. 3 fraternities, 2 sororities. **Athletics (Intercollegiate):** *Men:* Baseball, basketball, cheerleading, cross-country, golf, soccer. *Women:* Basketball, cheerleading, cross-country, golf, soccer, softball, volleyball. **On-Campus Highlights:** Derby Center for Science and Mathematics, Becknell Gymnasium, Holloway Theater, Edwards Commons Bookstore, Mabee Simpson Library.

ADMISSIONS
Freshman Academic Profile: Average high school GPA 3.54. 26.5% in top 10% of high school class, 54.2% in top 25% of high school class, 86.7% in top 50% of high school class. 84% from public high schools. SAT Math middle 50% range 545–610. SAT Critical Reading middle 50% range 545–618. SAT Writing middle 50% range 525–580. ACT middle 50% range 22–27. Minimum paper TOEFL 550. Minimum computer TOEFL 213. Minimum web-based TOEFL 79. **Basis for Candidate Selection:** *Very important factors considered include:* Academic GPA, standardized test scores. *Important factors considered include:* Rigor of secondary school record. *Other factors considered include:* Class rank, application essay, recommendation(s), character/personal qualities, extracurricular activities, interview, level of applicant's interest, talent/ability, volunteer work, work experience. **Freshman Admission Requirements:** High school diploma is required and GED is accepted. *Academic units required:* 4 English, 3 mathematics, 3 science, (2 science labs), 2 foreign language, 1 social studies, 2 history, 1 academic electives. *Academic units recommended:* 4 English, 4 mathematics, 4 science, (2 science labs), 2 foreign language, 1 social studies, 2 history, 1 academic electives. **Freshman Admission Statistics:** 847 applied, 67% admitted, 19% enrolled. **Transfer Admission Requirements:** College transcript(s), statement of good standing from prior institution(s). Minimum college GPA of 2.75 required. Lowest grade transferable C. **General Admission Information:** Application fee $25. Nonfall registration accepted. Admission may be deferred for a maximum of 1 year. Credit and/or placement offered for CEEB Advanced Placement tests.

COSTS AND FINANCIAL AID
Annual tuition $17,534. Room and board $7,340. Required fees $544. Average book expense $1,000. **Required Forms and Deadlines:** FAFSA. Priority financial aid filing date 3/15. **Notification of Awards:** Applicants will be notified of awards on a rolling basis beginning 3/1. **Types of Aid:** *Need-based scholarships/grants:* Federal Pell, SEOG, state scholarships/grants, private scholarships, the school's own gift aid. *Loans:* FFEL Subsidized Stafford, FFEL Unsubsidized Stafford, FFEL PLUS, Federal Perkins. **Student Employment:** Highest amount earned per year from on-campus jobs $5,600. Off-campus job opportunities are good. **Financial Aid Statistics:** 72% freshmen, 79% undergrads receive need-based scholarship or grant aid. 71% freshmen, 78% undergrads receive non-need-based scholarship or grant aid. 61% freshmen, 78% undergrads receive need-based self-help aid. 20% freshmen, 18% undergrads receive athletic scholarships. 100% freshmen, 99% undergrads receive any aid. 64% undergrads borrow to pay for school. Average cumulative indebtedness $18,428. **Criteria for awarding institutional aid:** *Non-need-based:* Academics, art, athletics, job skills, leadership, music/drama, religious affiliation.

MACALESTER COLLEGE

1600 Grand Avenue, St. Paul, MN 55105
Phone: 651-696-6357 **Financial Aid Phone:** 651-696-6214
E-mail: admissions@macalester.edu **CEEB Code:** 6390
Fax: 651-696-6724 **Website:** www.macalester.edu **ACT Code:** 2122

This private school, affiliated with the Presbyterian Church, was founded in 1874. It has a 53-acre campus.

RATINGS
Admissions Selectivity Rating: 96   **Fire Safety Rating:** 86   **Green Rating:** 82

STUDENTS AND FACULTY
Enrollment: 1,871. **Student Body:** 58% female, 42% male, 80% out-of-state, 11% international (91 countries represented). Asian 9%, African American 4%, Caucasian 71%, Hispanic 4%, Native American 1%.
Retention and Graduation: 92% freshmen return for sophomore year. 84% freshmen graduate within 4 years. 28% grads go on to further study within 1 year. 22% grads pursue arts and sciences degrees. 3% grads pursue law degrees. 1% grads pursue business degrees. 2% grads pursue medical degrees. **Faculty:** Student/faculty ratio 10:1. 164 full-time faculty, 92% hold PhDs, 20% are members of minority groups, 48% are women.

ACADEMICS
Degrees: Bachelor's. **Classes:** Most classes have 10–19 students. Most lab/discussion sessions have 10–19 students. **Majors with Highest Enrollment:** Economics; English language and literature; political science and government. **Special Study Options:** Cross-registration, double major, honors program, independent study, internships, student-designed major, study abroad, Combined bachelors/graduate programs: BA/master's in architecture with Washington University, St. Louis, Missouri; BA/BS in engineering with Washington University, St. Louis or the University of Minnesota. **Combined degree programs:** 3/3 Architecture Washington U. Special programs offered to physically disabled students include note-taking services, reader services, tape recorders, tutors. **Career services:** Alumni network, alumni services, career assessment, internships, regional alumni. **Career services highlights include:** Students at Macalester are civically engaged through a broad range of experientially focused programs. Last year, 302 students did internships for academic credit, 22 classes were offered that included a significant civic engagement component, 42 students worked in non-profit settings through an off-campus student employment program, and students contributed almost 50,000 hours of volunteer service to the community. This is possible due to the college's vibrant urban location and the strongly held belief of faculty, staff, and administration that experiential education and civic engagement are vital elements in a quality liberal arts education.

FACILITIES
Housing: Coed dorms, cooperative housing, apartments for single students, theme housing, language houses, Kosher Residence, EcoHouse. 75% of campus accessible to physically disabled. **Special Academic Facilities/Equipment:** Humanities learning center, econometrics lab, cartography lab, 250-acre nature preserve, observatory and planetarium, two electron microscopes, nuclear magnetic resonance spectrometer, laser spectroscopy lab, X-ray diffractometer, International Center, Center for Scholarship and Teaching, Ethnographic lab,

GIS lab, State-of-the-Art science labs. **Computers:** 100% of classrooms, 98% of dorms, 100% of libraries, 100% of dining areas, 100% of student union, 90% of common outdoor areas have wireless network access. Students can register for classes online. Administrative functions (other than registration) can be performed online.

CAMPUS LIFE

Environment: Metropolis. **Activities:** Choral groups, concert band, dance, drama/theater, jazz band, literary magazine, music ensembles, radio station, student government, student newspaper, symphony orchestra, campus ministries, international student organization, Model UN. **Organizations:** 80 registered organizations, 15 honor societies, 10 religious organizations. **Athletics (Intercollegiate):** *Men:* Baseball, basketball, cross-country, diving, football, golf, soccer, swimming, tennis, track/field (outdoor), track/field (indoor). *Women:* Basketball, cross-country, diving, golf, soccer, softball, swimming, tennis, track/field (outdoor), track/field (indoor), volleyball, water polo. **On-Campus Highlights:** Second Floor Campus Center, Bateman Plaza (our front patio), The Quad (our front yard), Shaw Field, Smail Gallery in the Science Center. **Environmental Initiatives:** Signed President's Climate Commitment, hired a sustainability manager, building a LEED Platinum building.

ADMISSIONS

Freshman Academic Profile: 66% in top 10% of high school class, 96% in top 25% of high school class, 100% in top 50% of high school class. 63% from public high schools. SAT Math middle 50% range 630–710. SAT Critical Reading middle 50% range 640–740. SAT Writing middle 50% range 630–730. ACT middle 50% range 28–32. Minimum paper TOEFL 573. Minimum computer TOEFL 230. **Basis for Candidate Selection:** *Very important factors considered include:* Academic GPA, rigor of secondary school record. *Important factors considered include:* Application essay, recommendation(s), standardized test scores, character/personal qualities, extracurricular activities. *Other factors considered include:* Class rank, alumni/ae relation, first generation, interview, racial/ethnic status, talent/ability, volunteer work, work experience. **Freshman Admission Requirements:** High school diploma or equivalent is not required. *Academic units recommended:* 4 English, 3 mathematics, 3 science, (3 science labs), 3 foreign language, 3 social studies. **Freshman Admission Statistics:** 5,041 applied, 41% admitted, 23% enrolled. **Transfer Admission Requirements:** High school transcript, college transcript(s), essay or personal statement, standardized test scores, statement of good standing from prior institution(s). Lowest grade transferable C–. **General Admission Information:** Application fee $40. Early decision application deadline 11/15. Regular application deadline 1/15. Regular notification 3/30. Nonfall registration not accepted. Admission may be deferred for a maximum of 1 year. Credit and/or placement offered for CEEB Advanced Placement tests.

COSTS AND FINANCIAL AID

Annual tuition $37,947. Room and board $8,768. Required fees $200. Average book expense $925. **Required Forms and Deadlines:** FAFSA, CSS/Financial Aid PROFILE, noncustodial PROFILE Financial aid filing deadline 3/1. Priority financial aid filing date 2/8. **Notification of Awards:** Applicants will be notified of awards on or about 4/1. **Types of Aid:** *Need-based scholarships/grants:* Federal Pell, SEOG, state scholarships/grants, private scholarships, the school's own gift aid. *Loans:* Direct Subsidized Stafford, Direct Unsubsidized Stafford, Direct PLUS, Federal Perkins, state loans. **Student Employment:** Federal Work-Study Program available. Institutional employment available. Highest amount earned per year from on-campus jobs $2,800. Off-campus job opportunities are excellent. **Financial Aid Statistics:** 63% freshmen, 66% undergrads receive need-based scholarship or grant aid. 58% freshmen, 64% undergrads receive need-based self-help aid. 67.8% freshmen, 71.2% undergrads receive any aid. 72% undergrads borrow to pay for school. Average cumulative indebtedness $17,304. **Criteria for awarding institutional aid:** *Non-need-based:* Academics, minority status.

MACMURRAY COLLEGE

447 East College, Jacksonville, IL 62650
Phone: 217-479-7056 **Financial Aid Phone:** 217-479-7041
E-mail: admissions@mac.edu **CEEB Code:** 1435
Fax: 217-291-0702 **Website:** www.mac.edu **ACT Code:** 1068

This private school, affiliated with the Methodist Church, was founded in 1846. It has a 60-acre campus.

RATINGS
Admissions Selectivity Rating: 70   **Fire Safety Rating:** 60*   **Green Rating:** 60*

STUDENTS AND FACULTY
Enrollment: 581. **Student Body:** 66% female, 34% male, 11% out-of-state, international (2 countries represented). Asian 1%, African American 13%, Caucasian 73%, Hispanic 3%.
Retention and Graduation: 72% freshmen return for sophomore year. 26% freshmen graduate within 4 years. 25% grads go on to further study within 1 year. 9% grads pursue arts and sciences degrees. 1% grads pursue law degrees. 12% grads pursue business degrees. 1% grads pursue medical degrees. **Faculty:** Student/faculty ratio 14:1. 35 full-time faculty, 63% hold PhDs, 3% are members of minority groups, 74% are women.

ACADEMICS
Degrees: Associate, bachelor's. **Classes:** Most classes have 10–19 students. Most lab/discussion sessions have 10–19 students. **Majors with Highest Enrollment:** Nursing/registered nurse (RN, ASN, BSN, MSN); special education and teaching. **Special Study Options:** Cooperative education program, double major, dual enrollment, independent study, internships, liberal arts/career combination, student-designed major, study abroad, teacher certification program. **Combined degree programs:** BA/MEng, 3-2 Occupational Therapy prog. w/ Washington U. Special programs offered to physically disabled students include note-taking services, reader services, tape recorders, tutors. **Career services:** Alumni network, alumni services, career/job search classes, career assessment, internships, regional alumni.

FACILITIES
Housing: Coed dorms, special housing for disabled students, women's dorms. 50% of campus accessible to physically disabled. **Special Academic Facilities/Equipment:** Art gallery, language lab, music hall, nursing labs.

CAMPUS LIFE
Environment: Village. **Activities:** Choral groups, dance, drama/theater, literary magazine, student government, yearbook, campus ministries. **Organizations:** 37 registered organizations, 2 honor societies, 2 religious organizations. 2 fraternities, 1 sorority. **Athletics (Intercollegiate):** *Men:* Baseball, basketball, football, golf, soccer, wrestling. *Women:* Basketball, golf, soccer, softball, volleyball. **On-Campus Highlights:** Gamble Campus, Education Complex, Jane Hall, Putnam Center for the Arts, McClelland Dining Hall.

ADMISSIONS
Freshman Academic Profile: Average high school GPA 2.84. 4% in top 10% of high school class, 28% in top 25% of high school class, 55% in top 50% of high school class. 75% from public high schools. SAT Math middle 50% range 430–500. SAT Critical Reading middle 50% range 370–470. SAT Writing middle 50% range 340–430. ACT middle 50% range 17–23. Minimum paper TOEFL 550. Minimum computer TOEFL 213. **Basis for Candidate Selection:** *Very important factors considered include:* Academic GPA, rigor of secondary school record, standardized test scores. *Important factors considered include:* Class rank, character/personal qualities, extracurricular activities. *Other factors considered include:* Application essay, recommendation(s), interview, volunteer work, work experience. **Freshman Admission Requirements:** High school diploma is required and GED is accepted. *Academic units recommended:* 4 English, 3 mathematics, 3 science, (2 science labs), 2 foreign language, 2 social studies, 3 history. **Freshman Admission Statistics:** 800 applied, 61% admitted, 19% enrolled. **Transfer Admission Requirements:** College transcript(s), minimum college GPA of 2.0 required. Lowest grade transferable C. **General Admission Information:** Application fee $25. Notification on a rolling basis, beginning on or about 9/1. Nonfall registration accepted. Admission may be deferred for a maximum of 12. Credit and/or placement offered for CEEB Advanced Placement tests.

COSTS AND FINANCIAL AID
Annual tuition $15,500. Room and board $5,998. Required fees $250. Average book expense $775. **Required Forms and Deadlines:** FAFSA. Priority financial aid filing date 5/1. **Notification of Awards:** Applicants will be notified of awards on a rolling basis beginning 2/1. **Types of Aid:** *Need-based scholarships/grants:* Federal Pell, SEOG, state scholarships/grants, private scholarships, the school's own gift aid, Federal Nursing Scholarships. *Loans:* FFEL Subsidized Stafford, FFEL Unsubsidized Stafford, FFEL PLUS, Federal Perkins. **Student Employment:** Federal Work-Study Program available. Institutional employment available. Highest amount earned per year from on-campus jobs $945. **Financial Aid Statistics:** 90% freshmen, 91% undergrads receive need-based scholarship or grant aid. 8% freshmen, 7% undergrads receive non-need-based scholarship or grant aid. 71% freshmen, 78% undergrads receive need-based self-help aid. 95% freshmen, 97% undergrads receive any aid. 95% undergrads borrow to pay for school. Average cumulative indebtedness $22,469. **Criteria for awarding institutional aid:** *Non-need-based:* Academics, alumni affiliation, art, leadership, music/drama, religious affiliation.

MAHARISHI UNIVERSITY OF MANAGEMENT

1000 North Fourth Street, Fairfield, IA 52557
Phone: 641-472-1110 **Financial Aid Phone:** 641-472-1156
E-mail: admissions@mum.edu
Fax: 641-472-1179 **Website:** www.mum.edu **ACT Code:** 1317

This private school was founded in 1971. It has a 242-acre campus.

RATINGS
Admissions Selectivity Rating: 74   **Fire Safety Rating:** 60*   **Green Rating:** 90

STUDENTS AND FACULTY
Enrollment: 199. **Student Body:** 43% female, 57% male, 65% out-of-state, 17% international. Asian 4%, African American 2%, Caucasian 71%, Hispanic 7%.
Retention and Graduation: 84% grads go on to further study within 1 year. **Faculty:** Student/faculty ratio 16:1. 52 full-time faculty, 98% hold PhDs, 13% are members of minority groups, 21% are women.

ACADEMICS
Degrees: Associate, bachelor's, certificate, doctoral, master's. **Majors with Highest Enrollment:** Business/commerce; environmental studies; fine/studio arts. **Special Study Options:** double major, independent study, internships, study abroad, teacher certification program, Rotating University: several one-month blocks out of each academic year, a course is offered abroad-e.g., students spend a month with professor studying Art in Italy, Literature in Switzerland, or Business in Japan.

FACILITIES
Housing: Special housing for disabled students, men's dorms, women's dorms, apartments for married students, apartments for single students, Apartments for students with dependent children; "quiet" dorms. 80% of campus accessible to physically disabled. **Special Academic Facilities/Equipment:** art gallery; scanning electron microscope; real-time cell-imaging computer system; DNA synthesizer; rock-climbing wall.

CAMPUS LIFE
Environment: Village. **Activities:** Choral groups, dance, drama/theater, music ensembles, musical theater, radio station, student government, student newspaper, yearbook. **Organizations:** 25 registered organizations, 3 honor societies, 1 religious organizations. **Athletics (Intercollegiate):** *Men:* Golf. *Women:* golf. **On-Campus Highlights:** Golden Domes, Vedic Architecture, 60,000 sq. ft. Recreation Center, Student Cafe, Vedic Organic Greenhouses. **Environmental Initiatives:** Four-year bachelor's of science degree offered in sustainable living. Construction of new Sustainable Living Center. Implementation of Climate Action Plan.

ADMISSIONS
Freshman Academic Profile: Average high school GPA 3.61. 80% in top 50% of high school class. Minimum paper TOEFL 550. Minimum computer TOEFL 213. **Basis for Candidate Selection:** *Very important factors considered include:* Character/personal qualities, interview. *Important factors considered include:* Application essay, academic GPA, recommendation(s), rigor of secondary school record, extracurricular activities, level of applicant's interest, talent/ability. *Other factors considered include:* Standardized test scores, alumni/ae relation, volunteer work, work experience. **Freshman Admission Requirements:** High school diploma is required and GED is accepted. *Academic units recommended:* 4 English, 3 mathematics, 3 science, 2 foreign language, 3 social studies. **Freshman Admission Statistics:** 126 applied, 41% admitted, 87% enrolled. **Transfer Admission Requirements:** High school transcript, college transcript(s), essay or personal statement, interview, minimum college GPA of 2.5 required. Lowest grade transferable 2. **General Admission Information:** Application fee $30. Notification on a rolling basis, beginning on or about 12/1. Nonfall registration accepted. Admission may be deferred for a maximum of one semester. Credit offered for CEEB Advanced Placement tests.

COSTS AND FINANCIAL AID
Annual tuition $24,000. Room and board $6,000. Required fees $430. Average book expense $800. **Required Forms and Deadlines:** FAFSA. Priority financial aid filing date 4/15. **Notification of Awards:** Applicants will be notified of awards on a rolling basis beginning 3/1. **Types of Aid:** *Need-based scholarships/grants:* Federal Pell, SEOG, state scholarships/grants, private scholarships, the school's own gift aid, Federal Work Study, Veterans, Benefits. *Loans:* FFEL Subsidized Stafford, FFEL Unsubsidized Stafford, FFEL PLUS, Federal Perkins, college/university loans from institutional funds. **Student Employment:** Federal Work-Study Program available. Off-campus job opportunities are fair. **Financial Aid Statistics:** 93% freshmen, 93% undergrads receive need-based scholarship or grant aid. 7% undergrads receive non-need-based scholarship

or grant aid. 93% freshmen, 93% undergrads receive need-based self-help aid. 93% freshmen, 98% undergrads receive any aid. 83% undergrads borrow to pay for school. Average cumulative indebtedness $22,691. **Criteria for awarding institutional aid:** *Non-need-based:* Academics, alumni affiliation, music/drama, state/district residency.

MAINE COLLEGE OF ART

97 Spring Street, Portland, ME 04101
Phone: 207-775-3052 **Financial Aid Phone:** 207-775-5157
E-mail: admissions@meca.edu **CEEB Code:** 3701
Fax: 207-772-5069 **Website:** www.meca.edu **ACT Code:** 6908

This private school was founded in 1882.

RATINGS
Admissions Selectivity Rating: 75   **Fire Safety Rating:** 60*   **Green Rating:** 60*

STUDENTS AND FACULTY
Enrollment: 425. **Student Body:** 62% female, 38% male, 2% international (7 countries represented). Caucasian 49%, Hispanic 2%.
Retention and Graduation: 73% freshmen return for sophomore year. 32% freshmen graduate within 4 years. **Faculty:** Student/faculty ratio 10:1. 30 full-time faculty, 93% hold PhDs, 3% are members of minority groups, 63% are women.

ACADEMICS
Degrees: Bachelor's, master's. **Classes:** Most classes have 10–19 students. **Special Study Options:** Cross-registration, double major, exchange student program (domestic), independent study, internships, student-designed major, study abroad, teacher certification program, Mobility program with 36 AICAD (Associated Independent Colleges of Art and Design) institutions in USA and Canada; cross-registration program with 4 other colleges and universites in the greater Portland area; BFA credit available through Provincetown, MA, Fine Arts Work Center. Special programs offered to physically disabled students include note-taking services, reader services, tape recorders, tutors. **Career services:** Alumni network, alumni services, career/job search classes, career assessment, internships, regional alumni.

FACILITIES
Housing: Coed dorms, cooperative housing. 80% of campus accessible to physically disabled. **Special Academic Facilities/Equipment:** Institute of Contemporary Art at Maine College of Art, June Fitzpatrick Gallery, ArtMart (art supply store).

CAMPUS LIFE
Environment: City. **Activities:** Student government, student-run film society. **On-Campus Highlights:** The Gorman Student Center ("Living Room"), The Student Gallery, Individual Major Spaces, Institute of Contemporary Art at MECA, Computer Labs.

ADMISSIONS
Freshman Academic Profile: Average high school GPA 3.18. 8% in top 10% of high school class, 19% in top 25% of high school class, 48% in top 50% of high school class. SAT Math middle 50% range 440–560. SAT Critical Reading middle 50% range 480–610. ACT middle 50% range 17–23. Minimum paper TOEFL 500. Minimum computer TOEFL 173. **Basis for Candidate Selection:** *Very important factors considered include:* Rigor of secondary school record, talent/ability. *Important factors considered include:* Application essay, recommendation(s), character/personal qualities. *Other factors considered include:* Class rank, standardized test scores, alumni/ae relation, extracurricular activities, geographical residence, interview, racial/ethnic status, state residency, volunteer work, work experience. **Freshman Admission Requirements:** High school diploma is required and GED is accepted. *Academic units recommended:* 4 English, 3 mathematics, 3 science, 2 foreign language, 4 social studies, 4 history, 3 academic electives, 4 art. **Freshman Admission Statistics:** 440 applied, 64% admitted, 35% enrolled. **Transfer Admission Requirements:** College transcript(s), essay or personal statement, statement of good standing from prior institution(s). Lowest grade transferable C. **General Admission Information:** Application fee $40. Nonfall registration accepted. Admission may be deferred for a maximum of 1 year. Credit and/or placement offered for CEEB Advanced Placement tests.

COSTS AND FINANCIAL AID
Annual tuition $20,600. Room and board $8,550. Required fees $520. **Required Forms and Deadlines:** FAFSA. Financial aid filing deadline 4/15. Priority financial aid filing date 3/15. **Notification of Awards:** Applicants will be

notified of awards on a rolling basis beginning 2/15. **Types of Aid:** *Need-based scholarships/grants:* Federal Pell, SEOG, state scholarships/grants, the school's own gift aid. *Loans:* FFEL Subsidized Stafford, FFEL Unsubsidized Stafford, FFEL PLUS, Federal Perkins. **Financial Aid Statistics:** 82% freshmen, 81% undergrads receive need-based scholarship or grant aid. 4% freshmen, 3% undergrads receive non-need-based scholarship or grant aid. 76% freshmen, 74% undergrads receive need-based self-help aid. 79% undergrads borrow to pay for school. Average cumulative indebtedness $25,743. **Criteria for awarding institutional aid:** *Non-need-based:* Academics, art.

MAINE MARITIME ACADEMY

66 Pleasant Street, Castine, ME 04420
Phone: 207-326-2206
E-mail: admissions@mma.edu **CEEB Code:** 3505
Fax: 207-326-2515 **Website:** www.mainemaritime.edu **ACT Code:** 1648

This public school was founded in 1941. It has a 35-acre campus.

RATINGS
Admissions Selectivity Rating: 61 **Fire Safety Rating:** 60* **Green Rating:** 60*

STUDENTS AND FACULTY
Enrollment: 814. **Student Body:** 15% female, 85% male, 39% out-of-state, (10 countries represented). Asian 1%, Caucasian 95%, Hispanic 1%, Native American 1%.
Retention and Graduation: 75% freshmen return for sophomore year. 2% grads go on to further study within 1 year. 1% grads pursue arts and sciences degrees. 1% grads pursue law degrees. **Faculty:** Student/faculty ratio 12:1. 55 full-time faculty.

ACADEMICS
Degrees: Associate, bachelor's, master's. **Classes:** Most classes have 10–19 students. Most lab/discussion sessions have 10–19 students. **Special Study Options:** Cooperative education program, internships, annual training cruises. **Career services:** Alumni services, career/job search classes, internships.

FACILITIES
Housing: Coed dorms, apartments for single students. 90% of campus accessible to physically disabled. **Computers:** Administrative functions (other than registration) can be performed online. Undergraduates are required to own a computer.

CAMPUS LIFE
Environment: Rural. **Activities:** Concert band, drama/theater, jazz band, marching band, student government, yearbook. **Organizations:** 28 registered organizations. **Athletics (Intercollegiate):** *Men:* Basketball, cross-country, football, golf, lacrosse, sailing, soccer. *Women:* Basketball, cross-country, golf, sailing, soccer, softball.

ADMISSIONS
Freshman Academic Profile: 28% in top 10% of high school class, 48% in top 25% of high school class, 74% in top 50% of high school class. Minimum paper TOEFL 550. Minimum computer TOEFL 213. **Basis for Candidate Selection:** *Very important factors considered include:* Rigor of secondary school record, character/personal qualities. *Important factors considered include:* Interview. *Other factors considered include:* Class rank, recommendation(s), alumni/ae relation, extracurricular activities, talent/ability, volunteer work, work experience. **Freshman Admission Requirements:** High school diploma is required and GED is accepted. *Academic units required:* 4 English, 3 mathematics, 2 science, (2 science labs). *Academic units recommended:* 3 mathematics, 3 science, (3 science labs), 2 foreign language, 2 computer literacy. **Freshman Admission Statistics:** 613 applied, 76% admitted, 49% enrolled. **Transfer Admission Requirements:** High school transcript, college transcript(s), standardized test scores, statement of good standing from prior institution(s). Minimum college GPA of 2.0 required. Lowest grade transferable C. **General Admission Information:** Application fee $15. Early decision application deadline 12/20. Regular application deadline 7/1. Notification on a rolling basis, beginning on or about 10/1. Nonfall registration accepted. Admission may be deferred for a maximum of 1 year. Credit offered for CEEB Advanced Placement tests.

COSTS AND FINANCIAL AID
Annual in-state tuition $4,739. Annual out-of-state tuition $8,774. Room and board $5,227. Required fees $715. Average book expense $700. **Types of Aid:** *Loans:* FFEL Subsidized Stafford, FFEL PLUS. **Student Employment:** Federal Work-Study Program available. Institutional employment available. Highest amount earned per year from on-campus jobs $1,200. Off-campus job opportunities are fair.

MALONE UNIVERSITY

2600 Cleveland Avenue NW, Canton, OH 44709
Phone: 330-471-8145 **Financial Aid Phone:** 330-471-8162
E-mail: admissions@malone.edu **CEEB Code:** 1439
Fax: 330-471-8149 **Website:** www.malone.edu **ACT Code:** 3289

This private school was founded in 1892. It has a 87-acre campus.

RATINGS
Admissions Selectivity Rating: 78 **Fire Safety Rating:** 73 **Green Rating:** 60*

STUDENTS AND FACULTY
Enrollment: 2,097. **Student Body:** 59% female, 41% male, 13% out-of-state, 1% international (17 countries represented). Asian 1%, African American 8%, Caucasian 88%, Hispanic 1%.
Retention and Graduation: 44% freshmen graduate within 4 years. 20% grads go on to further study within 1 year. 6.2% grads pursue arts and sciences degrees. 5% grads pursue business degrees. **Faculty:** Student/faculty ratio 14.7:1. 110 full-time faculty, 69% hold PhDs, 4% are members of minority groups, 49% are women.

ACADEMICS
Degrees: Bachelor's, master's, post-bachelor's certificate. **Classes:** Most classes have 10–19 students. Most lab/discussion sessions have 10–19 students. **Majors with Highest Enrollment:** Business/commerce; early childhood education and teaching; nursing/registered nurse (RN, ASN, BSN, MSN). **Special Study Options:** Accelerated program, cross-registration, distance learning, double major, dual enrollment, exchange student program (domestic), honors program, independent study, internships, student-designed major, study abroad, teacher certification program, weekend college, 2 degree-completion programs for adults; management, nursing. NOTE: Weekend college is only for degree-completion programs and graduate programs. NOTE: Cooperative education credits are available; but not entire program. **Honors programs:** The purpose of the Malone University Honors Program is to support the university's intellectually gifted and highly motivated students, to create a community of students and faculty engaged in serious, substantive, and sustained critical inquiry, and to underscore the university's commitment to academic excellence. The Honors Program fulfills this purpose through pursuit of the following goals: 1. Challenging students to fulfill their intellectual and personal potential through enriching and stimulating experiences in and out of the classroom. 2. Cultivating an esprit de corps, committed to an earnest, cooperative, free, and open pursuit of truth. 3. Developing students' understanding of the unity of knowledge and the interrelationship of the academic disciplines. 4. Providing students the occasion for mentoring relationships with faculty. 5. Preparing students for the pursuit of original and advanced research, scholarship, and performance. 6. Equipping students for outstanding leadership in service to God, their communities, and the world. **Combined degree programs:** 3-1 Medical Technology program. Special programs offered to physically disabled students include note-taking services, reader services, tape recorders, tutors. **Career services:** Alumni services, career/job search classes, career assessment, internships. **Career services highlights include:** The highest number of graduates who are hired by the employer providing experiential learning is in nursing.

FACILITIES
Housing: Special housing for disabled students, men's dorms, women's dorms, theme housing. **Special Academic Facilities/Equipment:** Child development center. **Computers:** 100% of classrooms, 85% of dorms, 100% of libraries, 100% of dining areas, 100% of student union, 40% of common outdoor areas have wireless network access. Students can register for classes online. Administrative functions (other than registration) can be performed online.

CAMPUS LIFE
Environment: City. **Activities:** Choral groups, concert band, dance, drama/theater, jazz band, literary magazine, marching band, music ensembles, musical theater, radio station, student government, student newspaper, student-run film society, television station, yearbook, campus ministries, international student organization. **Organizations:** 53 registered organizations, 11 honor societies, 9 religious organizations. **Athletics (Intercollegiate):** *Men:* Baseball, basketball, cheerleading, cross-country, diving, football, golf, soccer, swimming, tennis, track/field (outdoor), track/field (indoor). *Women:* Basketball, cheerleading, cross-country, diving, golf, soccer, softball, swimming, tennis, track/field (outdoor), track/field (indoor), volleyball. **On-Campus Highlights:** Hoover Dining Commons—Brehme Centennial Center, Randall Campus Center, Wellness Center, Froggy's & Regula Cafe, Classrooms, Randall Campus Center houses the Office of Student Development; a game room, among other features. The Wellness Center houses equipment and laboratories to support the programs of the majors in the Health and Human Performance Department. Also, its aerobic exercise and weight room are available for all Malone University, students,

faculty, and staff. It was just opened in fall 2004. **Environmental Initiatives:** Recycling.

ADMISSIONS
Freshman Academic Profile: Average high school GPA 3.34. 23.1% in top 10% of high school class, 48.3% in top 25% of high school class, 75.6% in top 50% of high school class. 83% from public high schools. SAT Math middle 50% range 460–590. SAT Critical Reading middle 50% range 470–592.5. ACT middle 50% range 19–26. Minimum paper TOEFL 550. Minimum computer TOEFL 213. Minimum web-based TOEFL 79. **Basis for Candidate Selection:** *Very important factors considered include:* Academic GPA, rigor of secondary school record, standardized test scores, character/personal qualities. *Important factors considered include:* Class rank, level of applicant's interest, religious affiliation/commitment, talent/ability. *Other factors considered include:* Application essay, recommendation(s), alumni/ae relation, extracurricular activities, interview, racial/ethnic status, volunteer work. **Freshman Admission Requirements:** High school diploma is required and GED is accepted. *Academic units required:* 4 English, 3 mathematics, 3 science, (1 science labs), 2 foreign language, 2 social studies, 1 history, 1 visual/performing arts, 2 academic electives. **Freshman Admission Statistics:** 1,641 applied, 71% admitted, 42% enrolled. **Transfer Admission Requirements:** High school transcript, college transcript(s), statement of good standing from prior institution(s). Minimum college GPA of 2.0 required. **General Admission Information:** Application fee $20. Regular application deadline 7/1. Notification on a rolling basis, beginning on or about 9/1. Nonfall registration accepted. Admission may be deferred for a maximum of 2 years. Credit and/or placement offered for CEEB Advanced Placement tests.

COSTS AND FINANCIAL AID
Annual tuition $21,954. Room and board $7,348. Required fees $490. Average book expense $930. **Required Forms and Deadlines:** FAFSA, Verification worksheet and tax forms if chosen for verification. Financial aid filing deadline 7/31. Priority financial aid filing date 3/1. **Notification of Awards:** Applicants will be notified of awards on a rolling basis beginning 3/1. **Types of Aid:** *Need-based scholarships/grants:* Federal Pell, SEOG, state scholarships/grants, private scholarships, the school's own gift aid, Academic Competetiveness and Smart Grant. *Loans:* FFEL Subsidized Stafford, FFEL Unsubsidized Stafford, FFEL PLUS, Federal Perkins, state loans, college/university loans from institutional funds, Private Loans. **Student Employment:** Federal Work-Study Program available. Institutional employment available. Highest amount earned per year from on-campus jobs $2,500. Off-campus job opportunities are good. **Financial Aid Statistics:** 87% freshmen, 76% undergrads receive need-based scholarship or grant aid. 84% freshmen, 63% undergrads receive non-need-based scholarship or grant aid. 70% freshmen, 66% undergrads receive need-based self-help aid. 4% freshmen, 4% undergrads receive athletic scholarships. 99% freshmen, 93% undergrads receive any aid. 81% undergrads borrow to pay for school. Average cumulative indebtedness $25,655. **Criteria for awarding institutional aid:** *Non-need-based:* Academics, alumni affiliation, athletics, leadership, music/drama, religious affiliation.

MANCHESTER COLLEGE

604 E. College Avenue, N. Manchester, IN 46962
Phone: 260-982-5055 **Financial Aid Phone:** 260-982-5066
E-mail: admitinfo@manchester.edu **CEEB Code:** 1440
Fax: 260-982-5239 **Website:** www.manchester.edu **ACT Code:** 1222

This private school was founded in 1889. It has a 124-acre campus.

RATINGS
Admissions Selectivity Rating: 76   **Fire Safety Rating:** 70   **Green Rating:** 76

STUDENTS AND FACULTY
Enrollment: 1,187. **Student Body:** 50% female, 50% male, 10% out-of-state, 3% international (25 countries represented). Asian 1%, African American 2%, Caucasian 56%, Hispanic 1%.
Retention and Graduation: 66% freshmen return for sophomore year. 38% freshmen graduate within 4 years. 25% grads go on to further study within 1 year. 8% grads pursue arts and sciences degrees. 1% grads pursue law degrees. 11% grads pursue business degrees. 2% grads pursue medical degrees. **Faculty:** Student/faculty ratio 16:1. 67 full-time faculty, 82% hold PhDs, 9% are members of minority groups.

ACADEMICS
Degrees: Associate, bachelor's, master's. **Classes:** Most classes have 20–29 students. **Majors with Highest Enrollment:** Accounting and business/management; biochemistry; education. **Special Study Options:** Accelerated program, cross-registration, double major, dual enrollment, exchange student program

(domestic), honors program, independent study, internships, liberal arts/career combination, student-designed major, study abroad, teacher certification program. **Honors programs:** An Honors Program for top students Special programs offered to physically disabled students include reader services, tape recorders, tutors. **Career services:** Alumni network, alumni services, career/job search classes, career assessment, internships, regional alumni. **Career services highlights include:** College-paid internships in regional businesses.

FACILITIES
Housing: Coed dorms, special housing for disabled students, apartments for married students, apartments for single students. **Special Academic Facilities/Equipment:** Language lab, observatory, environmental center and labs. **Computers:** 50% of classrooms, 100% of libraries, 100% of dining areas, 100% of student union, 5% of common outdoor areas have wireless network access. Students can register for classes online. Administrative functions (other than registration) can be performed online.

CAMPUS LIFE
Environment: Rural. **Activities:** Choral groups, concert band, dance, drama/theater, jazz band, literary magazine, music ensembles, musical theater, opera, pep band, radio station, student government, student newspaper, symphony orchestra, yearbook, campus ministries, international student organization, Model UN. **Organizations:** 47 registered organizations, 3 honor societies, 5 religious organizations. **Athletics (Intercollegiate):** *Men:* Baseball, basketball, cheerleading, cross-country, football, golf, soccer, tennis, track/field (outdoor), wrestling. *Women:* Basketball, cheerleading, cross-country, golf, soccer, softball, tennis, track/field (outdoor), volleyball. **On-Campus Highlights:** Athletic Facilities, Residence Halls, College Union, Petersime Chapel, Science Center, The campus is located on a well maintained wooded 125 acres. **Environmental Initiatives:** Over 25 years of active recyling on campus. One of the oldest environmental studies majors in the country. Manchester College environmental studies program director Jerry Sweeten is 2009 Indiana Professor of the Year; see www.manchester.edu/OCA/PR/Files/News/SweetenPoY.htm. Over 25 years of dedication to reduction in energy consumption.

ADMISSIONS
Freshman Academic Profile: Average high school GPA 3.25. 20% in top 10% of high school class, 54% in top 25% of high school class, 85% in top 50% of high school class. 98% from public high schools. SAT Math middle 50% range 450–570. SAT Critical Reading middle 50% range 430–550. SAT Writing middle 50% range 410–535. ACT middle 50% range 18–25. Minimum paper TOEFL 550. Minimum computer TOEFL 213. **Basis for Candidate Selection:** *Very important factors considered include:* Rigor of secondary school record. *Important factors considered include:* Academic GPA, recommendation(s), standardized test scores. *Other factors considered include:* Class rank, alumni/ae relation, character/personal qualities, interview, religious affiliation/commitment, talent/ability. **Freshman Admission Requirements:** High school diploma is required and GED is accepted. *Academic units required:* 4 English, 2 mathematics, 2 science, (2 science labs), 2 foreign language, 2 social studies, 1 history, 1 academic electives. *Academic units recommended:* 4 English, 3 mathematics, 3 science, (3 science labs), 2 foreign language, 2 social studies, 2 history, 2 academic electives. **Freshman Admission Statistics:** 2,991 applied, 77% admitted, 19% enrolled. **Transfer Admission Requirements:** High school transcript, college transcript(s), statement of good standing from prior institution(s). Minimum college GPA of 2.0 required. **General Admission Information:** Application fee $25. Notification on a rolling basis, beginning on or about 9/1. Nonfall registration accepted. Admission may be deferred for a maximum of 1 year. Credit and/or placement offered for CEEB Advanced Placement tests.

COSTS AND FINANCIAL AID
Annual tuition $23,000. Room and board $8,050. Required fees $790. Average book expense $1,000. **Required Forms and Deadlines:** FAFSA. Priority financial aid filing date 3/10. **Notification of Awards:** Applicants will be notified of awards on a rolling basis beginning 3/30. **Types of Aid:** *Need-based scholarships/grants:* Federal Pell, SEOG, state scholarships/grants, private scholarships, the school's own gift aid. *Loans:* FFEL Subsidized Stafford, FFEL Unsubsidized Stafford, FFEL PLUS, Federal Perkins. **Student Employment:** Highest amount earned per year from on-campus jobs $2,000. Off-campus job opportunities are fair. **Financial Aid Statistics:** 76% freshmen, 78% undergrads receive need-based scholarship or grant aid. 84% freshmen, 75% undergrads receive non-need-based scholarship or grant aid. 69% freshmen, 73% undergrads receive need-based self-help aid. 100% freshmen, 98% undergrads receive any aid. **Criteria for awarding institutional aid:** *Non-need-based:* Academics, alumni affiliation, minority status, religious affiliation.

MANHATTAN CHRISTIAN COLLEGE

1415 Anderson, Manhattan, KS 66502-4081
Phone: 877-246-4622 **Financial Aid Phone:** 785-539-3571
E-mail: admit@mccks.edu
Fax: 785-776-9251 **Website:** www.mccks.edu **ACT Code:** 1436

This private school, affiliated with the Christian (Nondenominational) Church, was founded in 1927. It has a 1-acre campus.

RATINGS
Admissions Selectivity Rating: 77   **Fire Safety Rating:** 60*   **Green Rating:** 60*

STUDENTS AND FACULTY
Enrollment: 310. **Student Body:** 51% female, 49% male, 35% out-of-state, international. African American 4%, Caucasian 99%, Hispanic 2%.
Retention and Graduation: 51% freshmen return for sophomore year. 3% grads go on to further study within 1 year. **Faculty:** Student/faculty ratio 15:1. 10 full-time faculty, 40% hold PhDs, 10% are members of minority groups, 20% are women.

ACADEMICS
Degrees: Associate, bachelor's, certificate, post-bachelor's certificate, transfer associate. **Classes:** Most classes have 10–19 students. **Majors with Highest Enrollment:** Bible/biblical studies; management science; pastoral counseling and specialized ministries, other. **Special Study Options:** Double major, dual enrollment, internships. **Combined degree programs:** Dual-degree program with Kansas State University. Special programs offered to physically disabled students include tutors. **Career services:** Career assessment, internships. **Career services highlights include:** Internships are required as a Directed Field Experience that must be at least 10–weeks long.

FACILITIES
Housing: Men's dorms, women's dorms, apartments for married students, apartments for single students. 100% of campus accessible to physically disabled.

CAMPUS LIFE
Environment: Town. **Activities:** Dance, music ensembles, student government, yearbook. **Organizations:** 2 honor societies, 10 religious organizations. **Athletics (Intercollegiate):** *Men:* Baseball, basketball, soccer. *Women:* Basketball, soccer, volleyball. **On-Campus Highlights:** Coffin Memorial Hall, Campus Center, Residence Halls.

ADMISSIONS
Freshman Academic Profile: Average high school GPA 3.38. 30% in top 10% of high school class, 40% in top 25% of high school class, 70% in top 50% of high school class. 95% from public high schools. ACT middle 50% range 19–25. Minimum paper TOEFL 550. Minimum computer TOEFL 213. **Basis for Candidate Selection:** *Very important factors considered include:* Recommendation(s), character/personal qualities, religious affiliation/commitment. *Important factors considered include:* Application essay, rigor of secondary school record, standardized test scores, talent/ability. *Other factors considered include:* Extracurricular activities, interview, volunteer work. **Freshman Admission Requirements:** High school diploma is required and GED is accepted. *Academic units recommended:* 4 English, 2 mathematics, 2 science. **Freshman Admission Statistics:** 155 applied, 79% admitted, 66% enrolled. **Transfer Admission Requirements:** College transcript(s), essay or personal statement, minimum college GPA of 2.0 required. Lowest grade transferable C. **General Admission Information:** Application fee $25. Regular application deadline 8/1. Notification on a rolling basis, beginning on or about 10/1. Nonfall registration accepted. Admission may be deferred for a maximum of 1 year. Credit and/or placement offered for CEEB Advanced Placement tests.

COSTS AND FINANCIAL AID
Annual tuition $8,826. Room and board $5,224. Required fees $110. Average book expense $1,150. **Required Forms and Deadlines:** FAFSA. Priority financial aid filing date 4/1. **Notification of Awards:** Applicants will be notified of awards on a rolling basis beginning 5/1. **Types of Aid:** *Need-based scholarships/grants:* Federal Pell, SEOG, state scholarships/grants, private scholarships, the school's own gift aid. *Loans:* Direct Subsidized Stafford, Direct Unsubsidized Stafford, Direct PLUS, Federal Perkins. **Student Employment:** Federal Work-Study Program available. Off-campus job opportunities are good. **Financial Aid Statistics:** 33% freshmen, 70% undergrads receive need-based scholarship or grant aid. 59% freshmen, 66% undergrads receive non-need-based scholarship or grant aid. 48% freshmen, 76% undergrads receive need-based self-help aid. 55% undergrads borrow to pay for school. Average cumulative indebtedness $8,639. **Criteria for awarding institutional aid:** *Non-need-based:* Academics, alumni affiliation, leadership, music/drama, religious affiliation.

MANHATTAN COLLEGE

Manhattan College Parkway, Riverdale, NY 10471
Phone: 718-862-7200 **Financial Aid Phone:** 718-862-7100
E-mail: admit@manhattan.edu **CEEB Code:** 2395
Fax: 718-862-8019 **Website:** www.manhattan.edu

This private school, affiliated with the Roman Catholic Church, was founded in 1853. It has a 22-acre campus.

RATINGS
Admissions Selectivity Rating: 85   **Fire Safety Rating:** 71   **Green Rating:** 65

STUDENTS AND FACULTY
Enrollment: 3,049. **Student Body:** 47% female, 53% male, 28% out-of-state, international (39 countries represented). Asian 4%, African American 3%, Caucasian 70%, Hispanic 12%.
Retention and Graduation: 96% freshmen return for sophomore year. 15% grads go on to further study within 1 year. 15% grads pursue arts and sciences degrees. 2% grads pursue law degrees. 4% grads pursue business degrees. 4% grads pursue medical degrees. **Faculty:** Student/faculty ratio 12:1. 191 full-time faculty, 96% hold PhDs, 15% are members of minority groups, 36% are women.

ACADEMICS
Degrees: Bachelor's, master's. **Classes:** Most classes have 20–29 students. Most lab/discussion sessions have 10–19 students. **Majors with Highest Enrollment:** Civil engineering; marketing/marketing management; special education and teaching, other. **Special Study Options:** Accelerated program, cooperative education program, cross-registration, distance learning, double major, English as a Second Language (ESL), exchange student program (domestic), honors program, independent study, internships, liberal arts/career combination, student-designed major, study abroad, teacher certification program **Honors programs:** Honors Enrichment Program **Combined degree programs:** BA/MA, BA/MEng, Education. Special programs offered to physically disabled students include note-taking services, reader services, tape recorders, tutors. **Career services:** Alumni services, career/job search classes, career assessment, internships.

FACILITIES
Housing: Coed dorms 100% of campus accessible to physically disabled. **Special Academic Facilities/Equipment:** Research and learning center, 24-hour Internet cafe. **Computers:** 100% of classrooms, 50% of dorms, 100% of libraries, 100% of dining areas, 100% of student union, 100% of common outdoor areas have wireless network access. Students can register for classes online. Administrative functions (other than registration) can be performed online.

CAMPUS LIFE
Environment: Metropolis. **Activities:** Choral groups, concert band, dance, drama/theater, jazz band, literary magazine, music ensembles, musical theater, radio station, student government, student newspaper, symphony orchestra, television station, yearbook, campus ministries, international student organization, Model UN. **Organizations:** 64 registered organizations, 30 honor societies, 2 religious organizations. 2 fraternities, 2 sororities. **Athletics (Intercollegiate):** *Men:* Baseball, basketball, cross-country, golf, lacrosse, soccer, tennis, track/field (outdoor), track/field (indoor). *Women:* Basketball, cross-country, lacrosse, soccer, softball, swimming, tennis, track/field (outdoor), track/field (indoor), volleyball. **On-Campus Highlights:** Quadrangle, O'Malley Library, Internet Cafe, Galligan Exercise Center, Thomas Hall.

ADMISSIONS
Freshman Academic Profile: Average high school GPA 3.3. 60% from public high schools. SAT Math middle 50% range 500–615. SAT Critical Reading middle 50% range 490–580. ACT middle 50% range 21–25. Minimum paper TOEFL 550. Minimum computer TOEFL 213. **Basis for Candidate Selection:** *Very important factors considered include:* Academic GPA, rigor of secondary school record, standardized test scores. *Important factors considered include:* Class rank, application essay, recommendation(s), extracurricular activities, interview. *Other factors considered include:* Alumni/ae relation, character/personal qualities, talent/ability, volunteer work, work experience. **Freshman Admission Requirements:** High school diploma is required and GED is accepted. *Academic units required:* 4 English, 3 mathematics, 2 science, 2 foreign language, 3 social studies, 2 academic electives. *Academic units recommended:* 4 English, 4 mathematics, 3 science, 3 foreign language, 3 social studies. **Freshman Admission Statistics:** 5,055 applied, 65% admitted, 21% enrolled. **Transfer Admission Requirements:** High school transcript, college transcript(s), standardized test scores, statement of good standing from prior institution(s). Minimum college GPA of 2.5 required. Lowest grade transferable C. **General Admission Information:** Application fee $60. Early decision application deadline 11/15. Notification on a rolling basis, beginning on or about 12/15. Nonfall registration accepted. Admission may be deferred for a maximum of 1 year. Credit and/or placement offered for CEEB Advanced Placement tests.

COSTS AND FINANCIAL AID

Annual tuition $23,900. Room and board $10,520. Required fees $2,000. Average book expense $750. **Required Forms and Deadlines:** FAFSA. Financial aid filing deadline 4/1. Priority financial aid filing date 3/1. **Notification of Awards:** Applicants will be notified of awards on a rolling basis beginning 2/15. **Types of Aid:** *Need-based scholarships/grants:* Federal Pell, SEOG, state scholarships/grants, private scholarships, the school's own gift aid. *Loans:* Direct Subsidized Stafford, Direct Unsubsidized Stafford, Direct PLUS, FFEL. Subsidized Stafford, FFEL Unsubsidized Stafford, FFEL PLUS, Federal Perkins. **Student Employment:** Highest amount earned per year from on-campus jobs $1,500. **Financial Aid Statistics:** 59% freshmen, 54% undergrads receive need-based scholarship or grant aid. 4% freshmen, 5% undergrads receive non-need-based scholarship or grant aid. 50% freshmen, 48% undergrads receive need-based self-help aid. 3% freshmen, 3% undergrads receive athletic scholarships. 87% freshmen, 76% undergrads receive any aid. 72% undergrads borrow to pay for school. Average cumulative indebtedness $28,294. **Criteria for awarding institutional aid:** *Non-need-based:* Academics, athletics.

MANHATTAN SCHOOL OF MUSIC

120 Claremont Ave, New York, NY 10027
Phone: 212-749-2802 **Financial Aid Phone:** 917-493-4463
E-mail: admission@msmnyc.edu **CEEB Code:** 2396
Fax: 212-749-3025 **Website:** www.msmnyc.edu **ACT Code:** 2809

This private school was founded in 1917. It has a 1-acre campus.

RATINGS
Admissions Selectivity Rating: 60*   **Fire Safety Rating:** 60*   **Green Rating:** 60*

STUDENTS AND FACULTY
Enrollment: 408. **Student Body:** 48% female, 52% male, 69% out-of-state, 20% international (27 countries represented). Asian 9%, African American 3%, Caucasian 44%, Hispanic 4%.
Retention and Graduation: 82% freshmen return for sophomore year. 90% grads go on to further study within 1 year. 75% grads pursue arts and sciences degrees. 1% grads pursue law degrees. 1% grads pursue business degrees. 1% grads pursue medical degrees. **Faculty:** 1% of classes are taught by teaching assistants.

ACADEMICS
Degrees: Bachelor's, diploma, master's, post-master's certificate. **Special Study Options:** cross-registration, English as a Second Language (ESL), study abroad. Special programs offered to physically disabled students include note-taking services, reader services, tape recorders, tutors. **Career services:** Alumni network, alumni services, career/job search classes, **Career services highlights include:** Training in educational and community outreach.

FACILITIES
Housing: Apartments for married students, apartments for single students. 75% of campus accessible to physically disabled. **Special Academic Facilities/Equipment:** Electronic music studios, electronic piano lab, recording studio, practice rooms, 1,000–seat auditorium, 3 recital halls.

CAMPUS LIFE
Environment: Metropolis. **Activities:** Choral groups, dance, drama/theater, jazz band, literary magazine, music ensembles, student government, symphony orchestra. **Organizations:** 8 registered organizations. **On-Campus Highlights:** Library, residence hall, practice rooms, concert aalls, cafeteria.

ADMISSIONS
Freshman Academic Profile: 75% from public high schools. Minimum paper TOEFL 550. Minimum computer TOEFL 213. **Basis for Candidate Selection:** *Very important factors considered include:* Rigor of secondary school record, interview, talent/ability. *Important factors considered include:* Application essay, recommendation(s), character/personal qualities, extracurricular activities, volunteer work. *Other factors considered include:* Class rank, standardized test scores, alumni/ae relation, racial/ethnic status, work experience. **Freshman Admission Requirements:** High school diploma is required and GED is accepted. *Academic units required:* 2 English, 2 mathematics, 2 science, 3 social studies, 3 history. *Academic units recommended:* 4 English, 3 mathematics, 3 science, 4 foreign language, 4 social studies, 4 history. **Freshman Admission Statistics:** 794 applied, 40% admitted, 32% enrolled. **Transfer Admission Requirements:** College transcript(s), essay or personal statement, interview, minimum college GPA of 3 required. Lowest grade transferable C. **General Admission Information:** Application fee $100. Regular application deadline 12/1. Regular notification 4/1. Nonfall registration not accepted. Admission may

be deferred for a maximum of 2 semesters. Credit offered for CEEB Advanced Placement tests.

COSTS AND FINANCIAL AID
Annual tuition $26,000. Room and board $14,250. Required fees $460. Average book expense $850. **Required Forms and Deadlines:** FAFSA, institution's own financial aid form, CSS/Financial Aid PROFILE. Financial aid filing deadline 3/1. Priority financial aid filing date 3/1. **Notification of Awards:** Applicants will be notified of awards on or about 4/1. **Types of Aid:** *Need-based scholarships/grants:* Federal Pell, SEOG, state scholarships/grants, the school's own gift aid. *Loans:* FFEL Subsidized Stafford, FFEL Unsubsidized Stafford, FFEL PLUS, Federal Perkins. **Student Employment:** Federal Work-Study Program available. Institutional employment available. Highest amount earned per year from on-campus jobs $4,000. Off-campus job opportunities are excellent. **Financial Aid Statistics:** 30% freshmen, 39% undergrads receive need-based scholarship or grant aid. 2% freshmen, 5% undergrads receive non-need-based scholarship or grant aid. 26% freshmen, 44% undergrads receive need-based self-help aid. 66% freshmen, 75% undergrads receive any aid. 58% undergrads borrow to pay for school. Average cumulative indebtedness $14,100. **Criteria for awarding institutional aid:** *Non-need-based:* Academics, alumni affiliation, art, music/drama.

MANHATTANVILLE COLLEGE

Best 373

2900 Purchase Street, Admissions Office, Purchase, NY 10577
Phone: 914-323-5124 **Financial Aid Phone:** 914-323-5357
E-mail: admissions@mville.edu **CEEB Code:** 2397
Fax: 914-694-1732 **Website:** www.mville.edu **ACT Code:** 2800

This private school was founded in 1841. It has a 100-acre campus.

RATINGS
Admissions Selectivity Rating: 80   **Fire Safety Rating:** 95   **Green Rating:** 86

STUDENTS AND FACULTY
Enrollment: 1,771. **Student Body:** 66% female, 34% male, 47% out-of-state, 13% international (64 countries represented). Asian 2%, African American 8%, Caucasian 45%, Hispanic 17%.
Retention and Graduation: 75% freshmen return for sophomore year. 53% freshmen graduate within 4 years. **Faculty:** Student/faculty ratio 10:1. 101 full-time faculty, 100% hold PhDs, 11% are members of minority groups, 50% are women.

ACADEMICS
Degrees: Bachelor's, master's, post-bachelor's certificate, post-master's certificate. **Classes:** Most classes have 10–19 students. **Majors with Highest Enrollment:** Business/commerce; psychology; visual and performing arts, other. **Special Study Options:** Accelerated program, cross-registration, double major, dual enrollment, English as a Second Language (ESL), exchange student program (domestic), honors program, independent study, internships, student-designed major, study abroad, teacher certification program, weekend college. **Honors programs:** The Castle Scholars Program offers students of exceptional ability a broader and more intensive program of study than the usual college curriculum. It provides motivated students in any major field with challenging, cross-disciplinary courses that encourage their academic and personal growth. Participation in the Castle Scholars Program encourages intellectual exchange among students and faculty and fosters independent initiative in academic and creative realms. Advised and mentored by the Program Director, Castle Scholars are well prepared for success in graduate and professional schools, as well as in the professional world. Castle Scholars build relationships with each other and with the college's faculty in specially-designed Honors Seminars and other unique academic opportunities, as well as in a host of social events throughout the year. Through their studies, research, and service, the Scholars contribute to the intellectual and social life of the college. Studies are augmented by participation in the wider New York City community. The Castle Scholars Program complements a student's chosen major and minor and is distinct from honors options within the major. Castle Scholars are recognized annually at college-wide awards receptions, and honors courses are noted on student academic transcripts. Successful completion of the program will be noted on the final transcript as well as on printed graduation materials. **Combined degree programs:** BA/MA, Dual BS programs. Special programs offered to physically disabled students include note-taking services, reader services, tape recorders,

tutors. **Career services:** Alumni network, alumni services, career/job search classes, career assessment, internships, regional alumni. **Career services highlights include:** Internships involved career-related work that enhances a student's academic program.

FACILITIES
Housing: Coed dorms. 95% of campus accessible to physically disabled. **Special Academic Facilities/Equipment:** Art gallery, art and music studios, Environmental Park, English language institute, two electron microscopes, library. **Computers:** Students can register for classes online. Administrative functions (other than registration) can be performed online.

CAMPUS LIFE
Environment: Town. **Activities:** Choral groups, concert band, dance, drama/theater, jazz band, literary magazine, music ensembles, musical theater, opera, radio station, student government, student newspaper, student-run film society, symphony orchestra, television station, yearbook, campus ministries, international student organization. **Organizations:** 46 registered organizations, 2 honor societies, 5 religious organizations. **Athletics (Intercollegiate):** *Men:* Baseball, basketball, golf, ice hockey, lacrosse, soccer, tennis. *Women:* Basketball, cheerleading, field hockey, ice hockey, lacrosse, soccer, softball, tennis, volleyball. **On-Campus Highlights:** The Castle, Library Cafe, Richard Berman Student Center, Kennedy Gymnasium, Quad, New Student Center. **Environmental Initiatives:** Environmental classroom building's Platinum rating (LEED); new student center's Gold rating (LEED); green cleaning.

ADMISSIONS
Freshman Academic Profile: 22% in top 10% of high school class, 47% in top 25% of high school class, 80% in top 50% of high school class. Minimum paper TOEFL 550. Minimum computer TOEFL 217. **Basis for Candidate Selection:** *Very important factors considered include:* Rigor of secondary school record. *Important factors considered include:* Application essay, recommendation(s), extracurricular activities, interview. *Other factors considered include:* Alumni/ae relation, character/personal qualities, geographical residence, talent/ability, volunteer work, work experience. **Freshman Admission Requirements:** High school diploma is required and GED is accepted. *Academic units required:* 4 English, 3 mathematics, 2 science, 2 social studies, 5 academic electives. **Freshman Admission Statistics:** 4,502 applied, 53% admitted, 21% enrolled. **Transfer Admission Requirements:** College transcript(s), statement of good standing from prior institution(s). Minimum college GPA of 2.5 required. Lowest grade transferable C. **General Admission Information:** Application fee $70. Early decision application deadline 12/1. Regular application deadline 3/1. Notification on a rolling basis, beginning on or about 1/5. Nonfall registration accepted. Admission may be deferred for a maximum of 1 year. Credit and/or placement offered for CEEB Advanced Placement tests.

COSTS AND FINANCIAL AID
Annual tuition $33,030. Room and board $13,920. Required fees $1,320. Average book expense $800. **Required Forms and Deadlines:** FAFSA, state aid form. Financial aid filing deadline 3/1. Priority financial aid filing date 3/1. **Notification of Awards:** Applicants will be notified of awards on a rolling basis beginning 3/1. **Types of Aid:** *Need-based scholarships/grants:* Federal Pell, SEOG, state scholarships/grants, private scholarships, the school's own gift aid. *Loans:* Direct Subsidized Stafford, Direct Unsubsidized Stafford, Direct PLUS. **Student Employment:** Federal Work-Study Program available. Institutional employment available. Off-campus job opportunities are excellent. **Financial Aid Statistics:** 68% freshmen, 62% undergrads receive need-based scholarship or grant aid. 54% freshmen, 50% undergrads receive non-need-based scholarship or grant aid. 64% freshmen, 57% undergrads receive need-based self-help aid. 75% freshmen, 70% undergrads receive any aid. 53% undergrads borrow to pay for school. Average cumulative indebtedness $23,138. **Criteria for awarding institutional aid:** *Non-need-based:* Academics, alumni affiliation, art, leadership, music/drama.

MANNES COLLEGE— THE NEW SCHOOL FOR MUSIC

150 West 85th Street, New York, NY 10024
Phone: 212-580-0210-4862 **Financial Aid Phone:** 212-229-8930
E-mail: mannesadmissions@newschool.edu **CEEB Code:** 2398
Fax: 212-580-1738 **Website:** www.mannes.edu

This private school was founded in 1916.

RATINGS
Admissions Selectivity Rating: 60*   **Fire Safety Rating:** 73   **Green Rating:** 91

STUDENTS AND FACULTY
Enrollment: 207. **Student Body:** 57% female, 43% male, 62% out-of-state, 39% international (24 countries represented). Asian 11%, African American 4%, Caucasian 33%, Hispanic 3%.
Retention and Graduation: 86% freshmen return for sophomore year. 67% freshmen graduate within 4 years. **Faculty:** Student/faculty ratio 7:1. 6 full-time faculty, 17% hold PhDs, 17% are women.

ACADEMICS
Degrees: Bachelor's, diploma, master's, post-bachelor's certificate, post-master's certificate. **Classes:** Most classes have fewer than 10 students. **Special Study Options:** Accelerated program, double major, English as a Second Language (ESL), independent study, internships Special programs offered to physically disabled students include note-taking services, reader services, tape recorders. **Career services:** Alumni network, alumni services, career/job search classes, career assessment, internships, regional alumni.

FACILITIES
Housing: Coed dorms, special housing for disabled students, apartments for single students. 99% of campus accessible to physically disabled. **Special Academic Facilities/Equipment:** Art gallery, photography gallery, extensive collections of contemporary art, concert hall, public lectures, conferences, cultural and intellectual events. **Computers:** 95% of classrooms, 100% of libraries, 100% of dining areas, na% of student union, 100% of common outdoor areas have wireless network access. Students can register for classes online. Administrative functions (other than registration) can be performed online.

CAMPUS LIFE
Environment: Metropolis. **Activities:** Choral groups, dance, drama/theater, jazz band, literary magazine, music ensembles, opera, radio station, student government, student newspaper, symphony orchestra, international student organization. **Organizations:** 39 registered organizations. **On-Campus Highlights:** Mannes Concert Hall. **Environmental Initiatives:** The New School composts all behind the counter organic wastes and has begun a post-consumer pilot program. Waste Reduction and Recycling: The New School has established a comprehensive waste management and recycling program that includes glass, metal, plastic, paper, cardboard, electronic waste, ink jet cartridges, and compost. These recycling initiatives significantly reduce the amount of trash sent to landfills and/or incinerators by the university. Sustainable Product Procurement The New School currently purchases copy and printer paper composed of 100% post-consumer paper across campus. Energy Star purchasing policy is in place for all computers and appliances; further all computers are EPEAT gold Rated Green cleaning products and low-VOC paints are in use across campus; post-consumer recycled content. Similarly, all promotional materials are printed on Forest Stewardship Council Certified paper. An Energy Star purchasing policy is in place for all computers and appliances. Green cleaning products are in use across campus, and low-VOC paints are used in high-sensitivity areas. Recent major renovations have featured rapidly renewable or recycled building materials, including linoleum flooring, bamboo flooring, and composite countertops made from post-industrial content. Compostable plates and cutlery are in use in all cafeterias, and locally produced/organic foods are offered in increasing volumes. Energy Management and Carbon Emission Reductions In 2007, The New School signed on to the NYC Mayoral Challenge to Universities to reduce carbon emissions by 30% by 2017. The New School began the challenge with the lowest CO^2 footprint of all participating schools, and is already taking steps to further minimize its impact on global climate change. 100% of electricity directly paid for by the university is offset with Renewable Energy Credits from wind power. The New School has conducted a lighting retrofit in its five largest buildings, and is in the process of conducting an investment grade audit of its mechanical systems.

ADMISSIONS
Freshman Academic Profile: Average high school GPA 3.4. Minimum paper TOEFL 550. Minimum computer TOEFL 213. Minimum web-based TOEFL 92. **Basis for Candidate Selection:** *Very important factors considered include:* Level of applicant's interest, talent/ability. *Important factors considered include:* Academic GPA, recommendation(s), rigor of secondary school record. *Other factors considered include:* Class rank, application essay, character/personal qualities, extracurricular activities, interview. **Freshman Admission Requirements:** High school diploma is required and GED is accepted. *Academic units required:* 4 English, 4 mathematics, 4 science, (2 science labs), 2 social studies. *Academic units recommended:* 2 foreign language. **Freshman Admission Statistics:** 442 applied, 35% admitted, 34% enrolled. **Transfer Admission Requirements:** College transcript(s), essay or personal statement, minimum college GPA of 2.0 required. Lowest grade transferable C. **General Admission Information:** Application fee $100. Regular application deadline 12/1. Notification on a rolling basis, beginning on or about 4/1. Nonfall registration not accepted. Credit and/or placement offered for CEEB Advanced Placement tests.

COSTS AND FINANCIAL AID

Required Forms and Deadlines: FAFSA, state aid form. Priority financial aid filing date 3/1. **Notification of Awards:** Applicants will be notified of awards on a rolling basis beginning 3/1. **Types of Aid:** *Need-based scholarships/grants:* Federal Pell, SEOG, state scholarships/grants, private scholarships, the school's own gift aid. *Loans:* FFEL Subsidized Stafford, FFEL Unsubsidized Stafford, FFEL PLUS, Federal Perkins. **Student Employment:** Federal Work-Study Program available. Institutional employment available. Off-campus job opportunities are good. **Financial Aid Statistics:** 21% freshmen, 27% undergrads receive need-based scholarship or grant aid. 2% freshmen, 4% undergrads receive non-need-based scholarship or grant aid. 13% freshmen, 30% undergrads receive need-based self-help aid. 85% freshmen, 65% undergrads receive any aid. 71% undergrads borrow to pay for school. Average cumulative indebtedness $30,942. **Criteria for awarding institutional aid:** *Non-need-based:* Music/drama.

MANSFIELD UNIVERSITY

Academy Street, Mansfield, PA 16933
Phone: 570-662-4243
E-mail: admissions@mansfield.edu **CEEB Code:** 2655
Fax: 570-662-4121 **Website:** mansfield.edu **ACT Code:** 3710

This public school was founded in 1857. It has a 174-acre campus.

RATINGS
Admissions Selectivity Rating: 72   **Fire Safety Rating:** 60*   **Green Rating:** 60*

STUDENTS AND FACULTY
Enrollment: 2,921. **Student Body:** 62% female, 38% male, 21% out-of-state, 1% international (17 countries represented). Asian 1%, African American 5%, Caucasian 84%, Hispanic 2%, Native American 1%.
Retention and Graduation: 66% freshmen return for sophomore year. 33% freshmen graduate within 4 years. 23% grads go on to further study within 1 year. **Faculty:** Student/faculty ratio 16:1. 151 full-time faculty, 81% hold PhDs, 15% are members of minority groups, 44% are women.

ACADEMICS
Degrees: Associate, bachelor's, certificate, diploma, master's. **Classes:** Most classes have 20–29 students. Most lab/discussion sessions have 20–29 students. **Majors with Highest Enrollment:** Criminal justice/law enforcement administration; education; music teacher education. **Special Study Options:** Cross-registration, distance learning, double major, dual enrollment, exchange student program (domestic), honors program, independent study, internships, liberal arts/career combination, student-designed major, study abroad, teacher certification program Special programs offered to physically disabled students include note-taking services, reader services, tape recorders, tutors. **Career services:** Career/job search classes, career assessment, internships.

FACILITIES
Housing: Coed dorms, fraternity/sorority housing. 90% of campus accessible to physically disabled. **Special Academic Facilities/Equipment:** Science museum, two art galleries, animal collection, planetarium, solar collector. **Computers:** Students can register for classes online.

CAMPUS LIFE
Environment: Rural. **Activities:** Choral groups, concert band, dance, drama/theater, jazz band, literary magazine, marching band, music ensembles, musical theater, pep band, radio station, student government, student newspaper, symphony orchestra, television station. **Organizations:** 108 registered organizations, 10 honor societies, 4 religious organizations. 6 fraternities, 4 sororities. **Athletics (Intercollegiate):** *Men:* Baseball, basketball, cross-country, football, track/field (outdoor), track/field (indoor). *Women:* Basketball, cheerleading, cross-country, diving, field hockey, soccer, softball, swimming, track/field (outdoor), track/field (indoor). **On-Campus Highlights:** North Hall Library, fitness center, student union.

ADMISSIONS
Freshman Academic Profile: 8.7% in top 10% of high school class, 32.6% in top 25% of high school class, 70.7% in top 50% of high school class. SAT Math middle 50% range 430–540. SAT Critical Reading middle 50% range 430–530. SAT Writing middle 50% range 420–510. Minimum paper TOEFL 500. Minimum web-based TOEFL 61. **Basis for Candidate Selection:** *Very important factors considered include:* Class rank, academic GPA, rigor of secondary school record, standardized test scores. *Other factors considered include:* Application essay, recommendation(s), alumni/ae relation, character/personal qualities, extracurricular activities, first generation, geographical residence, interview, talent/ability, volunteer work, work experience. **Freshman Admission Requirements:** High school diploma is required and GED is accepted. *Academic*

units required: 4 English, 3 mathematics, 2 science, (2 science labs), 2 foreign language, 4 history, 6 academic electives. **Freshman Admission Statistics:** 3,367 applied, 70% admitted, 29% enrolled. **Transfer Admission Requirements:** College transcript(s), minimum college GPA of 2.0 required. Lowest grade transferable D. **General Admission Information:** Application fee $25. Notification on a rolling basis, beginning on or about 7/1. Nonfall registration accepted. Admission may be deferred for a maximum of 12. Credit offered for CEEB Advanced Placement tests.

COSTS AND FINANCIAL AID
Annual in-state tuition $5,177. Annual out-of-state tuition $12,944. Room and board $6,236. Required fees $1,827. Average book expense $1,200. **Required Forms and Deadlines:** FAFSA, institution's own financial aid form. Priority financial aid filing date 3/15. **Notification of Awards:** Applicants will be notified of awards on a rolling basis beginning 3/15. **Types of Aid:** *Need-based scholarships/grants:* Federal Pell, SEOG, state scholarships/grants, private scholarships, the school's own gift aid, United Negro College Fund, Federal Nursing Scholarships. *Loans:* FFEL Subsidized Stafford, FFEL Unsubsidized Stafford, FFEL PLUS, Federal Perkins, Federal Nursing, state loans **Student Employment:** Federal Work-Study Program available. Institutional employment available. Highest amount earned per year from on-campus jobs $1,236. Off-campus job opportunities are fair. **Financial Aid Statistics:** 47% freshmen, 49% undergrads receive need-based scholarship or grant aid. 19% freshmen, 12% undergrads receive non-need-based scholarship or grant aid. 3% freshmen, 4% undergrads receive need-based self-help aid. 2% freshmen, 2% undergrads receive athletic scholarships. 85% freshmen, 85% undergrads receive any aid. 74% undergrads borrow to pay for school. Average cumulative indebtedness $19,262. **Criteria for awarding institutional aid:** *Non-need-based:* Academics, art, athletics, leadership, music/drama, state/district residency.

MARIAN COLLEGE

3200 Cold Spring Rd, Indianapolis, IN 46222-1997
Phone: 317-955-6300 **Financial Aid Phone:** 317.955.6040
E-mail: admissions@marian.edu
Fax: 317-955-6401 **Website:** www.marian.edu

This private school is affiliated with the Roman Catholic Church.

RATINGS
Admissions Selectivity Rating: 75   **Fire Safety Rating:** 60*   **Green Rating:** 60*

STUDENTS AND FACULTY
Enrollment: 1,906. **Student Body:** 68% female, 32% male, 5% out-of-state, 1% international. Asian 1%, African American 16%, Caucasian 62%, Hispanic 1%.
Retention and Graduation: 76% freshmen return for sophomore year. **Faculty:** Student/faculty ratio 15:1. 82 full-time faculty, 43% hold PhDs, 6% are members of minority groups, 51% are women.

ACADEMICS
Degrees: Associate, bachelor's, certificate, master's, terminal associate, transfer associate. **Classes:** Most classes have fewer than 10 students. Most lab/discussion sessions have 10–19 students. **Majors with Highest Enrollment:** Business/commerce; elementary education and teaching; nursing/registered nurse (RN, ASN, BSN, MSN). **Special Study Options:** Accelerated program, cooperative education program, cross-registration, double major, dual enrollment, honors program, independent study, internships, liberal arts/career combination, study abroad, teacher certification program Special programs offered to physically disabled students include note-taking services, reader services, tape recorders, tutors. **Career services:** Alumni network, alumni services, career/job search classes, career assessment, internships.

FACILITIES
Housing: Coed dorms, cooperative housing, On-campus seminary, housing for Peace and Justice. **Computers:** 15% of classrooms, 100% of dorms, 100% of libraries, 100% of dining areas, 100% of student union, 50% of common outdoor areas have wireless network access. Administrative functions (other than registration) can be performed online.

CAMPUS LIFE
Environment: Metropolis. **Activities:** Choral groups, concert band, dance, drama/theater, marching band, music ensembles, musical theater, pep band, student government, student newspaper, yearbook, campus ministries, international student organization. **Organizations: Athletics (Intercollegiate):** *Men:* Baseball, basketball, cheerleading, cross-country, cycling, football, golf, tennis, track/field (outdoor), track/field (indoor). *Women:* Basketball, cheerleading, cross-country, cycling, golf, softball, tennis, track/field (outdoor), track/field (indoor), volleyball.

ADMISSIONS

Freshman Academic Profile: Average high school GPA 3.19. 13% in top 10% of high school class, 36% in top 25% of high school class, 69% in top 50% of high school class. SAT Math middle 50% range 430–610. SAT Critical Reading middle 50% range 440–550. ACT middle 50% range 19–25. Minimum paper TOEFL 550. Minimum computer TOEFL 213. **Basis for Candidate Selection:** *Very important factors considered include:* Academic GPA, rigor of secondary school record, standardized test scores. *Important factors considered include:* Class rank, recommendation(s). *Other factors considered include:* Application essay, alumni/ae relation, extracurricular activities, interview, level of applicant's interest, talent/ability. **Freshman Admission Requirements:** High school diploma is required and GED is accepted. *Academic units required:* 4 English, 2 mathematics, 2 science, (2 science labs), 1 foreign language, 2 social studies, 9 academic electives. *Academic units recommended:* 3 mathematics, 3 science, 2 foreign language, 1 social studies. **Freshman Admission Statistics:** 1,376 applied, 62% admitted, 36% enrolled. **Transfer Admission Requirements:** College transcript(s), minimum college GPA of 2 required. Lowest grade transferable C–. **General Admission Information:** Application fee $20. Regular application deadline 8/1. Notification on a rolling basis, beginning on or about 9/15. Nonfall registration accepted. Admission may be deferred for a maximum of 1 year. Credit and/or placement offered for CEEB Advanced Placement tests.

COSTS AND FINANCIAL AID

Average book expense $700. **Required Forms and Deadlines:** FAFSA, institution's own financial aid form. Financial aid filing deadline 3/10. Priority financial aid filing date 3/10. **Types of Aid:** *Need-based scholarships/grants:* Federal Pell, SEOG, state scholarships/grants, private scholarships, the school's own gift aid. *Loans:* Direct Subsidized Stafford, Direct Unsubsidized Stafford, Direct PLUS, FFEL Subsidized Stafford, FFEL Unsubsidized Stafford, FFEL PLUS, Federal Perkins, state loans **Student Employment:** Federal Work-Study Program available. **Financial Aid Statistics:** 52% freshmen, 53% undergrads receive need-based scholarship or grant aid. 67% freshmen, 72% undergrads receive non-need-based scholarship or grant aid. 68% freshmen, 66% undergrads receive need-based self-help aid. 7% freshmen, 6% undergrads receive athletic scholarships. 80.9% undergrads borrow to pay for school. Average cumulative indebtedness $25,107. **Criteria for awarding institutional aid:** *Non-need-based:* Academics, alumni affiliation, art, athletics, leadership, music/drama, religious affiliation.

MARIAN UNIVERSITY

45 South National Avenue, Fond du Lac, WI 54935
Phone: 920-923-7650 **Financial Aid Phone:** 920-923-7614
E-mail: admissions@marianuniversity.edu **CEEB Code:** 1443
Fax: 920-923-8755 **Website:** www.marianuniversity.edu **ACT Code:** 4606

This private school, affiliated with the Roman Catholic Church, was founded in 1936. It has a 100-acre campus.

RATINGS

Admissions Selectivity Rating: 68   **Fire Safety Rating:** 60*   **Green Rating:** 60*

STUDENTS AND FACULTY

Enrollment: 1,903. **Student Body:** 75% female, 25% male, 7% out-of-state, 1% international (13 countries represented). Asian 1%, African American 5%, Caucasian 88%, Hispanic 2%, Native American 1%.
Retention and Graduation: 21% freshmen graduate within 4 years. 16% grads go on to further study within 1 year. **Faculty:** Student/faculty ratio 12:1. 83 full-time faculty, 60% hold PhDs, 6% are members of minority groups, 55% are women.

ACADEMICS

Degrees: Bachelor's, master's. **Classes:** Most classes have 10–19 students. Most lab/discussion sessions have 10–19 students. **Majors with Highest Enrollment:** Business/commerce; nursing/registered nurse (RN, ASN, BSN, MSN); teacher education and professional development, specific levels and methods, other. **Special Study Options:** Accelerated program, cooperative education program, distance learning, double major, dual enrollment, honors program, independent study, internships, liberal arts/career combination, student-designed major, study abroad, teacher certification program, Accelerated programs for adults in business, criminal justice, nursing, operations management, and radiologic technology. **Honors programs:** Honors Special programs offered to physically disabled students include note-taking services, reader services, tape recorders, tutors. **Career services:** Career/job search classes, career assessment, internships. **Career services highlights include:** 97% of students receive field experience.

FACILITIES

Housing: Coed dorms, special housing for disabled students, fraternity/sorority housing, apartments for single students, townhouses, penthouses and suites. 95% of campus accessible to physically disabled. **Special Academic Facilities/Equipment:** On-campus child-care center, electron microscope. **Computers:** Students can register for classes online. Administrative functions (other than registration) can be performed online.

CAMPUS LIFE

Environment: Town. **Activities:** Choral groups, concert band, dance, drama/theater, jazz band, literary magazine, music ensembles, pep band, student government, student newspaper, symphony orchestra, campus ministries, Model UN. **Organizations:** 40 registered organizations, 6 honor societies, 1 religious organizations. 1 fraternities, 2 sororities. **Athletics (Intercollegiate):** *Men:* Baseball, basketball, cross-country, golf, ice hockey, soccer, tennis. *Women:* Basketball, cross-country, golf, ice hockey, soccer, softball, tennis, volleyball. **On-Campus Highlights:** Housing, Coffee House, Student Center, Stayer Center, library and academic buildings.

ADMISSIONS

Freshman Academic Profile: Average high school GPA 3.02. 9% in top 10% of high school class, 30% in top 25% of high school class, 66% in top 50% of high school class. 87% from public high schools. ACT middle 50% range 18–22. Minimum paper TOEFL 525. Minimum computer TOEFL 193. **Basis for Candidate Selection:** *Very important factors considered include:* Class rank, academic GPA, rigor of secondary school record, standardized test scores. *Important factors considered include:* character/personal qualities, interview, level of applicant's interest. *Other factors considered include:* Application essay, recommendation(s), alumni/ae relation, extracurricular activities, talent/ability, volunteer work, work experience. **Freshman Admission Requirements:** High school diploma is required and GED is accepted. *Academic units required:* 4 English, 2 mathematics, 1 science, (1 science labs), 1 history. *Academic units recommended:* 3 mathematics, 2 science, 2 foreign language. **Freshman Admission Statistics:** 843 applied, 86% admitted, 40% enrolled. **Transfer Admission Requirements:** High school transcript, college transcript(s), minimum college GPA of 2.0 required. Lowest grade transferable C. **General Admission Information:** Application fee $20. Notification on a rolling basis, beginning on or about 9/15. Nonfall registration accepted. Admission may be deferred for a maximum of case by case. Credit and/or placement offered for CEEB Advanced Placement tests.

COSTS AND FINANCIAL AID

Annual tuition $19,590. Room and board $5,380. Required fees $350. Average book expense $700. **Required Forms and Deadlines:** FAFSA, institution's own financial aid form. Priority financial aid filing date 3/1. **Notification of Awards:** Applicants will be notified of awards on a rolling basis beginning 3/1. **Types of Aid:** *Need-based scholarships/grants:* Federal Pell, SEOG, state scholarships/grants, private scholarships, the school's own gift aid. *Loans:* FFEL Subsidized Stafford, FFEL Unsubsidized Stafford, FFEL PLUS, Federal Perkins, Federal Nursing **Student Employment:** Federal Work-Study Program available. Institutional employment available. Highest amount earned per year from on-campus jobs $2,000. Off-campus job opportunities are fair. **Financial Aid Statistics:** 90% freshmen, 81% undergrads receive need-based scholarship or grant aid. 83% freshmen, 70% undergrads receive non-need-based scholarship or grant aid. 80% freshmen, 76% undergrads receive need-based self-help aid. 99% freshmen, 94% undergrads receive any aid. 90% undergrads borrow to pay for school. Average cumulative indebtedness $22,200. **Criteria for awarding institutional aid:** *Non-need-based:* Academics, state/district residency.

MARIETTA COLLEGE

215 Fifth Street, Marietta, OH 45750
Phone: 740-376-4600 **Financial Aid Phone:** 740-376-4712
E-mail: admit@marietta.edu **CEEB Code:** 1444
Fax: 740-376-8888 **Website:** www.marietta.edu **ACT Code:** 3290

This private school was founded in 1835. It has a 90-acre campus.

RATINGS

Admissions Selectivity Rating: 83   **Fire Safety Rating:** 64   **Green Rating:** 70

STUDENTS AND FACULTY

Enrollment: 1,470. **Student Body:** 49% female, 51% male, 31% out-of-state, 10% international (22 countries represented). Asian 1%, African American 4%, Caucasian 75%, Hispanic 1%.
Retention and Graduation: 77% freshmen return for sophomore year. 43% freshmen graduate within 4 years. 30% grads go on to further study within 1

year. 15% grads pursue arts and sciences degrees. 2% grads pursue law degrees. 5% grads pursue business degrees. 3% grads pursue medical degrees. **Faculty:** Student/faculty ratio 12:1. 105 full-time faculty, 82% hold PhDs, 7% are members of minority groups, 46% are women.

ACADEMICS
Degrees: Associate, bachelor's, certificate, master's. **Classes:** Most classes have 10–19 students. **Majors with Highest Enrollment:** Athletic training/trainer; education; petroleum engineering. **Special Study Options:** Double major, dual enrollment, English as a Second Language (ESL), exchange student program (domestic), honors program, independent study, internships, liberal arts/career combination, student-designed major, study abroad, teacher certification program **Honors programs:** Four-Year Program for top scholarship winners. **Combined degree programs:** BA/MA. Special programs offered to physically disabled students include note-taking services, reader services, tape recorders, tutors. **Career services:** Alumni network, alumni services, career/job search classes, career assessment, internships, regional alumni.

FACILITIES
Housing: Coed dorms, special housing for disabled students, men's dorms, women's dorms, fraternity/sorority housing, apartments for single students, wellness housing, theme housing is available. 90% of campus accessible to physically disabled. **Special Academic Facilities/Equipment:** Mass media building, fine arts center, natural science field camp, observatory, special collections in library. **Computers:** 100% of classrooms, 100% of dorms, 100% of libraries, 100% of dining areas, 100% of student union, have wireless network access. Students can register for classes online. Administrative functions (other than registration) can be performed online.

CAMPUS LIFE
Environment: Town. **Activities:** Choral groups, concert band, dance, drama/theater, jazz band, literary magazine, music ensembles, musical theater, radio station, student government, student newspaper, television station, yearbook, campus ministries, international student organization, Model UN. **Organizations:** 80 registered organizations, 23 honor societies, 2 religious organizations. 3 fraternities, 3 sororities. **Athletics (Intercollegiate):** *Men:* Baseball, basketball, crew/rowing, cross-country, football, soccer, tennis, track/field (outdoor), track/field (indoor). *Women:* Basketball, crew/rowing, cross-country, soccer, softball, tennis, track/field (outdoor), track/field (indoor), volleyball. **On-Campus Highlights:** Gathering Place, new Upper Class Residence Hall, Legacy Library, Hermann Fine Arts Center, Dyson Baudo Recreation Center. New Rickey Science Center , New Soccer and Softball Fields, Andrews Hall—Izzy's Snack Place. **Environmental Initiatives:** 1. (a) Recycling Club- students and faculty advisor, (b) regular recycling schedule: www.marietta.edu/employees/recycling.html 2. Dining Hall: (a) no trays twice a week. Has reduced waste by almost 30%, as well as cutting back on energy, water, and harmful detergents. (b) All deep fry oil is recycled as bio-diesel fuel for local sternwheeler. 3. Replacing incandescent light bulbs with energy-saving compact florescent.

ADMISSIONS
Freshman Academic Profile: Average high school GPA 3.45. 32% in top 10% of high school class, 58% in top 25% of high school class, 88% in top 50% of high school class. 89% from public high schools. SAT Math middle 50% range 490–610. SAT Critical Reading middle 50% range 480–600. ACT middle 50% range 21–27. Minimum paper TOEFL 550. Minimum computer TOEFL 213. Minimum web-based TOEFL 79. **Basis for Candidate Selection:** *Very important factors considered include:* Class rank, academic GPA, rigor of secondary school record, standardized test scores. *Important factors considered include:* Application essay, recommendation(s), character/personal qualities, interview. *Other factors considered include:* Alumni/ae relation, extracurricular activities, first generation, geographical residence, level of applicant's interest, racial/ethnic status, state residency, talent/ability, volunteer work, work experience. **Freshman Admission Requirements:** High school diploma is required and GED is accepted. *Academic units required:* 4 English, 3 mathematics, 3 science, (2 science labs), 2 foreign language, 2 social studies, 2 history. **Freshman Admission Statistics:** 2,521 applied, 76% admitted, 20% enrolled. **Transfer Admission Requirements:** College transcript(s), essay or personal statement, statement of good standing from prior institution(s). Minimum college GPA of 2.3 required. Lowest grade transferable C. **General Admission Information:** Application fee $25. Notification on a rolling basis, beginning on or about 9/1. Nonfall registration accepted. Admission may be deferred for a maximum of 1 year. Credit and/or placement offered for CEEB Advanced Placement tests.

COSTS AND FINANCIAL AID
Annual tuition $26,386. Room and board $8,046. Required fees $680. Average book expense $720. **Required Forms and Deadlines:** FAFSA. Financial aid filing deadline 4/15. Priority financial aid filing date 3/1. **Notification of Awards:** Applicants will be notified of awards on a rolling basis beginning 3/15. **Types of Aid:** *Need-based scholarships/grants:* Federal Pell, SEOG, state scholarships/grants, private scholarships, the school's own gift aid. *Loans:* Direct Subsidized Stafford, Direct Unsubsidized Stafford, Direct PLUS, FFEL Subsidized Stafford, FFEL Unsubsidized Stafford, FFEL PLUS, Federal Perkins, college/university loans from institutional funds. **Student Employ-**

ment: Federal Work-Study Program available. Institutional employment available. Highest amount earned per year from on-campus jobs $2,000. Off-campus job opportunities are good. **Financial Aid Statistics:** 80% freshmen, 74% undergrads receive need-based scholarship or grant aid. 53% freshmen, 52% undergrads receive non-need-based scholarship or grant aid. 67% freshmen, 65% undergrads receive need-based self-help aid. 96% freshmen, 95% undergrads receive any aid. 84% undergrads borrow to pay for school. Average cumulative indebtedness $22,623. **Criteria for awarding institutional aid:** *Non-need-based:* Academics, alumni affiliation, art, leadership, minority status, music/drama, state/district residency.

MARIST COLLEGE

Best 373

3399 North Road, Poughkeepsie, NY 12601-1387
Phone: 845-575-3226 **Financial Aid Phone:** 845-575-3230
E-mail: admission@marist.edu **CEEB Code:** 2400
Fax: 845-575-3215 **Website:** www.marist.edu **ACT Code:** 2804

This private school was founded in 1929. It has a 180-acre campus.

RATINGS
Admissions Selectivity Rating: 90   **Fire Safety Rating:** 88   **Green Rating:** 75

STUDENTS AND FACULTY
Enrollment: 4,837. **Student Body:** 58% female, 42% male, 43% out-of-state, international (11 countries represented). Asian 2%, African American 3%, Caucasian 73%, Hispanic 6%.
Retention and Graduation: 88% freshmen return for sophomore year. 76% freshmen graduate within 4 years. 20% grads go on to further study within 1 year. 9% grads pursue arts and sciences degrees. 3% grads pursue law degrees. 2% grads pursue business degrees. 4% grads pursue medical degrees. **Faculty:** Student/faculty ratio 15:1. 220 full-time faculty, 75% hold PhDs, 10% are members of minority groups, 44% are women.

ACADEMICS
Degrees: Bachelor's, certificate, master's, post-bachelor's certificate. **Classes:** Most classes have 20–29 students. Most lab/discussion sessions have 20–29 students. **Majors with Highest Enrollment:** Business administration and management; psychology; special education and teaching. **Special Study Options:** Accelerated program, cooperative education program, cross-registration, distance learning, double major, dual enrollment, English as a Second Language (ESL), honors program, independent study, internships, liberal arts/career combination, study abroad, teacher certification program, weekend college, undergrads may take grad level classes. Cooperative ed—arts, business, computer science, education, humanities, natural science, social/behavioral science, technologies. **Honors programs:** The Marist College Honors Program brings together talented students in honors-enriched classes that often coordinate with co-curricular activities such as field trips and lectures. The cultural enrichment exchange is a highlight of the Program. It encourages students to move beyond standard curricula and engage in a broader range of experience consonant with their interests. **Combined degree programs:** BA/MA, BS/MS. Special programs offered to physically disabled students include note-taking services, reader services, tape recorders, tutors. **Career services:** Alumni network, alumni services, career/job search classes, career assessment, internships, regional alumni. **Career services highlights include:** We have a very extensive internship program that provides students with practical work experience and reinforces the lessons from the classroom.

FACILITIES
Housing: Coed dorms, special housing for disabled students, apartments for single students, wellness housinggarden apartments, townhouses, suites. 88% of campus accessible to physically disabled. **Special Academic Facilities/Equipment:** Art gallery, language lab, estuarine and environmental studies lab, public opinion institute, audiovisual/TV center, communications center, high tech classroom,digital state of the art library. **Computers:** 100% of classrooms, 100% of dorms, 100% of libraries, 100% of dining areas, 100% of student union, 57% of common outdoor areas have wireless network access. Students can register for classes online. Administrative functions (other than registration) can be performed online.

CAMPUS LIFE
Environment: Town. **Activities:** Choral groups, concert band, dance, drama/theater, jazz band, literary magazine, marching band, music ensembles,

musical theater, pep band, radio station, student government, student newspaper, student-run film society, television station, yearbook, campus ministries. **Organizations:** 86 registered organizations, 16 honor societies, 6 religious organizations. 3 fraternities, 4 sororities. **Athletics (Intercollegiate):** *Men:* Baseball, basketball, crew/rowing, cross-country, diving, football, lacrosse, soccer, swimming, tennis, track/field (outdoor). *Women:* Basketball, crew/rowing, cross-country, diving, lacrosse, soccer, softball, swimming, tennis, track/field (outdoor), volleyball, water polo. **On-Campus Highlights:** James A Cannavino Library, James J McCann Recreation Center, Student Center, Newly Renovated Freshman Residence Halls, Tenney Stadium at Leonidoff Field. **Environmental Initiatives:** Sustainable food purchases; energy efficiency/reduction (electricity and heat); composting; recycling; green information technology initiatives.

ADMISSIONS

Freshman Academic Profile: Average high school GPA 3.2. 27% in top 10% of high school class, 70% in top 25% of high school class, 89% in top 50% of high school class. 72% from public high schools. SAT Math middle 50% range 540–640. SAT Critical Reading middle 50% range 520–620. SAT Writing middle 50% range 530–640. ACT middle 50% range 23–28. Minimum paper TOEFL 550. Minimum computer TOEFL 213. Minimum web-based TOEFL 80. **Basis for Candidate Selection:** *Very important factors considered include:* Academic GPA, rigor of secondary school record, standardized test scores. *Important factors considered include:* Class rank, application essay, recommendation(s), character/personal qualities, extracurricular activities, geographical residence, state residency, talent/ability, volunteer work, work experience. *Other factors considered include:* Alumni/ae relation, level of applicant's interest, racial/ethnic status. **Freshman Admission Requirements:** High school diploma is required and GED is accepted. *Academic units required:* 4 English, 3 mathematics, 3 science, (2 science labs), 2 foreign language, 2 social studies, 1 history, 2 academic electives. *Academic units recommended:* 4 mathematics, 4 science, (3 science labs), 3 foreign language. **Freshman Admission Statistics:** 10,004 applied, 36% admitted, 29% enrolled. **Transfer Admission Requirements:** High school transcript, college transcript(s), essay or personal statement, minimum college GPA of 2.8 required. Lowest grade transferable 2. **General Admission Information:** Application fee $50. Early decision application deadline 11/15. Regular application deadline 2/15. Regular notification 3/30. Nonfall registration accepted. Admission may be deferred for a maximum of 1 year. Credit and/or placement offered for CEEB Advanced Placement tests.

COSTS AND FINANCIAL AID

Required Forms and Deadlines: FAFSA, institution's own financial aid form. Financial aid filing deadline 5/1. Priority financial aid filing date 2/15. **Notification of Awards:** Applicants will be notified of awards on a rolling basis beginning 3/15. **Types of Aid:** *Need-based scholarships/grants:* Federal Pell, SEOG, state scholarships/grants, private scholarships, the school's own gift aid. *Loans:* FFEL Subsidized Stafford, FFEL Unsubsidized Stafford, FFEL PLUS, Federal Perkins, alternative loans. **Student Employment:** Federal Work-Study Program available. Institutional employment available. Highest amount earned per year from on-campus jobs $7,920. Off-campus job opportunities are excellent. **Financial Aid Statistics:** 60% freshmen, 57% undergrads receive need-based scholarship or grant aid. 39% freshmen, 29% undergrads receive non-need-based scholarship or grant aid. 47% freshmen, 52% undergrads receive need-based self-help aid. 8% freshmen, 6% undergrads receive athletic scholarships. 89% freshmen, 90% undergrads receive any aid. 76% undergrads borrow to pay for school. Average cumulative indebtedness $35,993. **Criteria for awarding institutional aid:** *Non-need-based:* Academics, athletics, music/drama, state/district residency.

MARLBORO COLLEGE

Best 373

PO Box A, 2582 South Road, Marlboro, VT 05344-0300
Phone: 802-258-9236 **Financial Aid Phone:** 802-258-9312
E-mail: admissions@marlboro.edu **CEEB Code:** 3509
Fax: 802-451-7555 **Website:** www.marlboro.edu **ACT Code:** 4304

This private school was founded in 1946. It has a 350-acre campus.

RATINGS
Admissions Selectivity Rating: 93   **Fire Safety Rating:** 67   **Green Rating:** 73

STUDENTS AND FACULTY
Enrollment: 311. **Student Body:** 48% female, 52% male, 88% out-of-state, 1% international (4 countries represented). Asian 3%, African American 1%, Caucasian 61%, Hispanic 3%.
Retention and Graduation: 75% freshmen return for sophomore year. 69% grads go on to further study within 1 year. **Faculty:** Student/faculty ratio 8:1. 39 full-time faculty, 87% hold PhDs, 5% are members of minority groups, 36% are women.

ACADEMICS
Degrees: Bachelor's, master's. **Classes:** Most classes have fewer than 10 students. Most lab/discussion sessions have fewer than 10 students. **Majors with Highest Enrollment:** English language and literature; social sciences; visual and performing arts, other. **Special Study Options:** Double major, dual enrollment, independent study, internships, student-designed major, study abroad, World Studies Program for students interested in international relations while also integrating an internship with study abroad opportunities. Special programs offered to physically disabled students include note-taking services, reader services, tape recorders, tutors. **Career services:** Alumni services, career/job search classes, career assessment.

FACILITIES
Housing: Coed dorms, special housing for disabled students, women's dorms, apartments for married students, cooperative housing, apartments for single students, Housing is to a human scale; the largest residence hall accommodates about 30 students. 80% of campus accessible to physically disabled. **Special Academic Facilities/Equipment:** Serkin Center for the Performing Arts, Drury art gallery, theater, dance studio, observatory, darkroom, art studios, music practice and performance spaces. **Computers:** 80% of classrooms, 85% of dorms, 100% of libraries, 100% of dining areas, 100% of student union, 80% of common outdoor areas have wireless network access. Students can register for classes online. Administrative functions (other than registration) can be performed online.

CAMPUS LIFE
Environment: Rural. **Activities:** Choral groups, dance, drama/theater, literary magazine, music ensembles, musical theater, radio station, student government, student newspaper, student-run film society. **Organizations:** 22 registered organizations. **On-Campus Highlights:** The Rice-Aron Library, Whittemore Theatre, Rod Gander World Studies Center, Serkin Center for the Performing Arts, Persons Auditorium. **Environmental Initiatives:** Energy audits of all campus buildings in preparation for efficiency upgrades. Solar-powered water heater in new Total Health Center facility. Recycling.

ADMISSIONS
Freshman Academic Profile: Average high school GPA 3.2. 40% in top 10% of high school class, 60% in top 25% of high school class, 95% in top 50% of high school class. 70% from public high schools. SAT Math middle 50% range 510–650. SAT Critical Reading middle 50% range 590–690. SAT Writing middle 50% range 640–720. ACT middle 50% range 24–32. Minimum paper TOEFL 550. Minimum computer TOEFL 213. Minimum web-based TOEFL 80. **Basis for Candidate Selection:** *Very important factors considered include:* Application essay, academic GPA, rigor of secondary school record, character/personal qualities. *Important factors considered include:* Extracurricular activities, interview. *Other factors considered include:* Class rank, recommendation(s), standardized test scores, alumni/ae relation, first generation, geographical residence, level of applicant's interest, state residency, talent/ability, volunteer work, work experience. **Freshman Admission Requirements:** High school diploma is required and GED is accepted. *Academic units recommended:* 4 English, 3 mathematics, 3 science, (1 science labs), 3 foreign language, 3 social studies, 3 history, 3 academic electives. **Freshman Admission Statistics: Transfer Admission Requirements:** High school transcript, college transcript(s), essay or personal statement, interview, minimum college GPA of 2.0 required. Lowest grade transferable C–. **General Admission Information:** Application fee $50. Early decision application deadline 12/1. Regular application deadline 3/1. Notification on a rolling basis, beginning on or about 12/1. Nonfall registration accepted. Admission may be deferred for a maximum of 1 year. Credit offered for CEEB Advanced Placement tests.

COSTS AND FINANCIAL AID
Annual tuition $32,550. Room and board $9,220. Required fees $1,110. Average book expense $1,000. **Required Forms and Deadlines:** FAFSA. Financial aid filing deadline 3/1. Priority financial aid filing date 3/1. **Notification of Awards:** Applicants will be notified of awards on a rolling basis beginning 3/15. **Types of Aid:** *Need-based scholarships/grants:* Federal Pell, SEOG, state scholarships/grants, private scholarships, the school's own gift aid. *Loans:* FFEL Subsidized Stafford, FFEL Unsubsidized Stafford, FFEL PLUS. **Student Employment:** Federal Work-Study Program available. Institutional employment available. Highest amount earned per year from on-campus jobs $2,050. Off-campus job opportunities are fair. **Financial Aid Statistics:** 62% freshmen, 63% undergrads receive need-based scholarship or grant aid. 73% freshmen, 54%

undergrads receive non-need-based scholarship or grant aid. 65% freshmen, 68% undergrads receive need-based self-help aid. 92.43% freshmen, 96.25% undergrads receive any aid. 93.94% undergrads borrow to pay for school. Average cumulative indebtedness $6,631. **Criteria for awarding institutional aid:** *Non-need-based:* Academics, leadership.

See page 1152.

MARQUETTE UNIVERSITY

PO Box 1881, Milwaukee, WI 53201-1881
Phone: 414-288-7302 **Financial Aid Phone:** 414-288-7390
E-mail: admissions@Marquette.edu **CEEB Code:** 1448
Fax: 414-288-3764 **Website:** www.marquette.edu **ACT Code:** 4610

This private school, affiliated with the Roman Catholic–Jesuit Church,, affiliated with the Jesuit Church, was founded in 1881. It has a 93-acre campus.

RATINGS
Admissions Selectivity Rating: 84   **Fire Safety Rating:** 70   **Green Rating:** 90

STUDENTS AND FACULTY
Enrollment: 7,857. **Student Body:** 53% female, 47% male, 57% out-of-state, 2% international (77 countries represented). Asian 4%, African American 5%, Caucasian 82%, Hispanic 6%.
Retention and Graduation: 89% freshmen return for sophomore year. 60% freshmen graduate within 4 years. **Faculty:** Student/faculty ratio 14.4:1. 627 full-time faculty, 94% hold PhDs, 15% are members of minority groups, 43% are women.

ACADEMICS
Degrees: Bachelor's, doctoral, master's, post-master's certificate. **Classes:** Most classes have 10–19 students. Most lab/discussion sessions have 20–29 students. **Majors with Highest Enrollment:** Nursing/registered nurse (RN, ASN, BSN, MSN). **Special Study Options:** Accelerated program, cooperative education program, cross-registration, double major, dual enrollment, honors program, independent study, internships, student-designed major, study abroad, teacher certification program, weekend college. **Honors programs:** Pre-Law Scholars Program Pre-Dental Scholars Program **Combined degree programs:** BA/JD, BA/MA, BA/DDS, physical therapy, physician assistant studies. Special programs offered to physically disabled students include note-taking services, reader services, tape recorders, tutors.

FACILITIES
Housing: Coed dorms, special housing for disabled students, men's dorms, special housing for international students, women's dorms, fraternity/sorority housing, apartments for married students, apartments for single students, Specialty housing for honor students, engineering students, nursing students. 90% of campus accessible to physically disabled. **Special Academic Facilities/Equipment:** Haggerty Museum of Art, Helfaer Theatre, Al McGuire Center Broadcast Facilities, Dental School/Clinic. **Computers:** 30% of classrooms, 100% of dorms, 100% of libraries, 100% of dining areas, 100% of student union, 10% of common outdoor areas have wireless network access. Students can register for classes online. Administrative functions (other than registration) can be performed online.

CAMPUS LIFE
Environment: Metropolis. **Activities:** Choral groups, concert band, dance, drama/theater, jazz band, literary magazine, music ensembles, musical theater, pep band, radio station, student government, student newspaper, symphony orchestra, television station, yearbook, campus ministries, international student organization, Model UN. **Organizations:** 230 registered organizations, 21 honor societies, 11 religious organizations. 11 fraternities, 11 sorority **Athletics (Intercollegiate):** *Men:* Basketball, cheerleading, cross-country, golf, soccer, tennis, track/field (outdoor), track/field (indoor). *Women:* Basketball, cheerleading, cross-country, soccer, tennis, track/field (outdoor), track/field (indoor), volleyball. **On-Campus Highlights:** The Raynor Memorial Library and the Law, Gesu Church, Haggerty Museum of Art, Al McGuire Center, Helfaer Recreation Center, Other places of interest Alumni Memorial Union and the Golden Eagle giftshop. (Located in the AMU). **Environmental Initiatives:** All full-time undergraduate students receive a UPASS (allows unlimited use of Milwaukee County Transit System Buses). Recycling garbage and electronic

equipment. Marquette uses steam from the power company (waste heat) for 75% of campus heating. Marquette participates in the state of Wisconsin's Focus on Energy Program

ADMISSIONS
Freshman Academic Profile: 33% in top 10% of high school class, 65% in top 25% of high school class, 92% in top 50% of high school class. 56% from public high schools. SAT Math middle 50% range 540–660. SAT Critical Reading middle 50% range 540–640. SAT Writing middle 50% range 530–640. ACT middle 50% range 24–29. Minimum paper TOEFL 520. Minimum computer TOEFL 190. **Basis for Candidate Selection:** *Very important factors considered include:* Academic GPA, rigor of secondary school record. *Important factors considered include:* Class rank, application essay, recommendation(s), standardized test scores. *Other factors considered include:* Alumni/ae relation, character/personal qualities, extracurricular activities, first generation, geographical residence, racial/ethnic status, state residency, talent/ability, volunteer work. **Freshman Admission Requirements:** High school diploma is required and GED is accepted. *Academic units required:* 4 English, 2 mathematics, 2 science, (2 science labs), 2 social studies, 2 academic electives. *Academic units recommended:* 4 English, 4 mathematics, 3 science, (3 science labs), 2 foreign language, 3 social studies, 5 academic electives. **Freshman Admission Statistics:** 17,825 applied, 66% admitted, 17% enrolled. **Transfer Admission Requirements:** High school transcript, college transcript(s), essay or personal statement, Lowest grade transferable C. **General Admission Information:** Application fee $30. Regular application deadline 12/1. Regular notification 1/31. Nonfall registration accepted. Admission may be deferred for a maximum of 1 year. Credit and/or placement offered for CEEB Advanced Placement tests.

COSTS AND FINANCIAL AID
Annual tuition $30,040. Room and board $9,680. Required fees $422. Average book expense $900. **Required Forms and Deadlines:** FAFSA, MU Admissions Application. **Notification of Awards:** Applicants will be notified of awards on a rolling basis beginning 3/20. **Types of Aid:** *Need-based scholarships/grants:* Federal Pell, SEOG, state scholarships/grants, private scholarships, the school's own gift aid, Marquette Merit Based aid is not based on need, but is used to cover need. *Loans:* Direct Subsidized Stafford, Direct Unsubsidized Stafford, Direct PLUS, Federal Perkins, Federal Nursing, state loans, college/university loans from institutional funds, private educational/alternative loans. **Student Employment:** Highest amount earned per year from on-campus jobs $2,500. Off-campus job opportunities are excellent. **Financial Aid Statistics:** 63% freshmen, 58% undergrads receive need-based scholarship or grant aid. 6% freshmen, 5% undergrads receive non-need-based scholarship or grant aid. 56% freshmen, 52% undergrads receive need-based self-help aid. 1% freshmen, 1% undergrads receive athletic scholarships. 65% undergrads borrow to pay for school. Average cumulative indebtedness $31,469. **Criteria for awarding institutional aid:** *Non-need-based:* Academics, athletics, leadership, music/drama.

See page 1154.

MARS HILL COLLEGE

PO Box 370, Mars Hill, NC 28754
Phone: 828-689-1201 **Financial Aid Phone:** 828-689-1123
E-mail: admissions@mhc.edu **CEEB Code:** 5395
Fax: 828-689-1473 **Website: ACT Code:** 3124

This private school, affiliated with the Baptist Church, was founded in 1856. It has a 180-acre campus.

RATINGS
Admissions Selectivity Rating: 60*   **Fire Safety Rating:** 60*   **Green Rating:** 60*

STUDENTS AND FACULTY
Enrollment: 1,177. **Student Body:** 56% female, 44% male, 35% out-of-state, 3% international (20 countries represented). African American 8%, Caucasian 99%, Hispanic 1%, Native American 1%.
Retention and Graduation: 71% freshmen return for sophomore year.
Faculty: Student/faculty ratio 14:1. 78 full-time faculty, 63% hold PhDs, 1% are members of minority groups, 36% are women.

ACADEMICS
Degrees: Bachelor's, diploma. **Majors with Highest Enrollment:** Biology/biological sciences; business/commerce; elementary education and teaching. **Special Study Options:** Accelerated program, cooperative education program, distance learning, double major, dual enrollment, English as a Second Language (ESL), honors program, independent study, internships, liberal arts/career com-

bination, study abroad, teacher certification program. **Honors programs:** www.mhc.edu/honors.asp Special programs offered to physically disabled students include note-taking services, reader services, tape recorders, tutors.

FACILITIES

Housing: Special housing for disabled students, men's dorms, women's dorms, apartments for married students, apartments for single students. **Special Academic Facilities/Equipment:** Language lab, Appalachian artifacts museum, rural life museum. **Computers:** Students can register for classes online. Administrative functions (other than registration) can be performed online.

CAMPUS LIFE

Environment: Rural. **Activities:** Choral groups, concert band, dance, drama/theater, jazz band, literary magazine, marching band, music ensembles, musical theater, radio station, student government, student newspaper, symphony orchestra, yearbook. **Organizations:** 45 registered organizations, 9 honor societies, 5 religious organizations. 6 fraternities, 5 sororities. **Athletics (Intercollegiate):** *Men:* Baseball, basketball, cheerleading, cross-country, football, golf, lacrosse, soccer, tennis, track/field (outdoor). *Women:* Basketball, cheerleading, cross-country, golf, soccer, softball, swimming, tennis, track/field (outdoor), volleyball. **On-Campus Highlights:** Wren Student Union, The Loft, The Ice Cream Shoppe, cafeteria, gym.

ADMISSIONS

Freshman Academic Profile: Average high school GPA 3.38. **Basis for Candidate Selection:** *Very important factors considered include:* Rigor of secondary school record, standardized test scores. *Important factors considered include:* Class rank, recommendation(s), character/personal qualities, extracurricular activities, interview, talent/ability. *Other factors considered include:* Alumni/ae relation, religious affiliation/commitment, volunteer work, work experience. **Freshman Admission Requirements:** High school diploma is required and GED is accepted. *Academic units required:* 4 English, 3 mathematics, 2 science, (1 science labs), 2 social studies, 2 history. *Academic units recommended:* 2 foreign language. **Freshman Admission Statistics: Transfer Admission Requirements:** College transcript(s), statement of good standing from prior institution(s). Minimum college GPA of 2.0 required. Lowest grade transferable C. **General Admission Information:** Application fee $25. Nonfall registration accepted.

COSTS AND FINANCIAL AID

Annual tuition $16,854. Room and board $5,900. Required fees $800. Average book expense $600. **Required Forms and Deadlines:** FAFSA, state aid form. **Types of Aid:** *Need-based scholarships/grants:* state scholarships/grants. *Loans:* FFEL Subsidized Stafford, FFEL PLUS. **Student Employment: Financial Aid Statistics:** 99% freshmen, 90% undergrads receive any aid.

MARSHALL UNIVERSITY

One John Marshall Drive, Huntington, WV 25755
Phone: 304-696-3160 **Financial Aid Phone:** 304-696-3162
E-mail: admissions@marshall.edu **CEEB Code:** 5396
Fax: 304-696-3135 **Website:** www.marshall.edu **ACT Code:** 4526

This public school was founded in 1837. It has a 70-acre campus.

RATINGS

Admissions Selectivity Rating: 72 **Fire Safety Rating:** 60* **Green Rating:** 60*

STUDENTS AND FACULTY

Enrollment: 9,051. **Student Body:** 56% female, 44% male, 23% out-of-state, 1% international. Asian 1%, African American 6%, Caucasian 87%, Hispanic 1%.
Retention and Graduation: 71% freshmen return for sophomore year. 27% grads go on to further study within 1 year. **Faculty:** Student/faculty ratio 19:1. 478 full-time faculty, 80% hold PhDs, 13% are members of minority groups, 41% are women.

ACADEMICS

Degrees: Associate, bachelor's, master's, post-bachelor's certificate, post-master's certificate. **Classes:** Most classes have 20–29 students. **Majors with Highest Enrollment:** Business/commerce; elementary education and teaching; psychology. **Special Study Options:** Accelerated program, cooperative education program, cross-registration, distance learning, double major, dual enrollment, English as a Second Language (ESL), exchange student program (domestic), honors program, independent study, internships, study abroad, teacher certification program. **Honors programs:** John Marshall Scholars, Society of Yeager Scholars. **Combined degree programs:** BS/MF Forestry (w/ Duke),BS/MEM Env Mgmt (w/ Duke). Special programs offered to physically disabled students

include note-taking services, reader services, tutors. **Career services:** Alumni network, alumni services, career/job search classes, career assessment, internships, regional alumni.

FACILITIES

Housing: Coed dorms, special housing for disabled students, women's dorms 100% of campus accessible to physically disabled. **Special Academic Facilities/Equipment:** Art gallery, audiovisual center, language lab, superconducting nuclear magnetic resonance spectrometer. **Computers:** Students can register for classes online. Administrative functions (other than registration) can be performed online.

CAMPUS LIFE

Environment: Town. **Activities:** Choral groups, concert band, dance, drama/theater, jazz band, literary magazine, marching band, music ensembles, musical theater, opera, pep band, radio station, student government, student newspaper, symphony orchestra, television station, campus ministries, international student organization, Model UN. **Organizations:** 100 registered organizations, 11 honor societies, 10 religious organizations. 12 fraternities, 7 sororities. **Athletics (Intercollegiate):** *Men:* Baseball, basketball, cross-country, football, golf, soccer, track/field (outdoor). *Women:* Basketball, cross-country, golf, soccer, softball, swimming, tennis, track/field (outdoor), volleyball. **On-Campus Highlights:** Memorial Student Center Plaza, Drinko Library, Marshall Stadium, Henderson Center, Buskirk Field.

ADMISSIONS

Freshman Academic Profile: Average high school GPA 3.3. SAT Math middle 50% range 430–550. SAT Critical Reading middle 50% range 440–560. SAT Writing middle 50% range 430–550. ACT middle 50% range 19–25. Minimum paper TOEFL 500. Minimum computer TOEFL 173. **Basis for Candidate Selection:** *Very important factors considered include:* Academic GPA, standardized test scores. *Other factors considered include:* Rigor of secondary school record. **Freshman Admission Requirements:** High school diploma is required and GED is accepted. *Academic units required:* 4 English, 4 mathematics, 3 science, (3 science labs), 2 foreign language, 3 social studies, 1 visual/performing arts. **Freshman Admission Statistics:** 2,577 applied, 86% admitted, 85% enrolled. **Transfer Admission Requirements:** College transcript(s). **General Admission Information:** Application fee $30. Notification on a rolling basis, beginning on or about 9/1. Nonfall registration accepted. Admission may be deferred for a maximum of 1 year. Credit offered for CEEB Advanced Placement tests.

COSTS AND FINANCIAL AID

Annual in-state tuition $4,319. Annual out-of-state tuition $11,565. Room and board $7,556. Required fees $917. Average book expense $1,100. **Required Forms and Deadlines:** FAFSA, state aid form. Priority financial aid filing date 3/1. **Notification of Awards:** Applicants will be notified of awards on a rolling basis beginning 5/1. **Types of Aid:** *Need-based scholarships/grants:* Federal Pell, SEOG, state scholarships/grants, private scholarships, the school's own gift aid. *Loans:* Direct Subsidized Stafford, Direct Unsubsidized Stafford, Direct PLUS, Federal Perkins. **Student Employment:** Off-campus job opportunities are good. **Financial Aid Statistics:** 33% freshmen, 39% undergrads receive need-based scholarship or grant aid. 28% freshmen, 21% undergrads receive non-need-based scholarship or grant aid. 34% freshmen, 43% undergrads receive need-based self-help aid. 3% freshmen, 5% undergrads receive athletic scholarships. 62% undergrads borrow to pay for school. Average cumulative indebtedness $19,562. **Criteria for awarding institutional aid:** *Non-need-based:* Academics, art, athletics, minority status, music/drama, state/district residency.

MARY BALDWIN COLLEGE

PO Box 1500, Staunton, VA 24402
Phone: 540-887-7019 **Financial Aid Phone:** 540-887-7019
E-mail: admit@mbc.edu **CEEB Code:** 5397
Fax: 540-887-7279 **Website:** www.mbc.edu **ACT Code:** 4374

This private school, affiliated with the Presbyterian Church, was founded in 1842. It has a 54-acre campus.

RATINGS

Admissions Selectivity Rating: 76 **Fire Safety Rating:** 60* **Green Rating:** 70

STUDENTS AND FACULTY

Enrollment: 1,390. **Student Body:** 95% female, 5% male, 16% out-of-state, 1% international (4 countries represented). Asian 2%, African American 19%, Caucasian 72%, Hispanic 4%, Native American 1%.

Retention and Graduation: 65% freshmen return for sophomore year. 51% freshmen graduate within 4 years. 20% grads go on to further study within 1 year. 5% grads pursue law degrees. 3% grads pursue business degrees. 3% grads pursue medical degrees. **Faculty:** Student/faculty ratio 10:1. 77 full-time faculty, 97% hold PhDs, 9% are members of minority groups, 51% are women.

ACADEMICS

Degrees: Bachelor's, certificate, master's. **Classes:** Most classes have 10–19 students. Most lab/discussion sessions have 10–19 students. **Majors with Highest Enrollment:** Business/commerce; psychology; sociology. **Special Study Options:** Accelerated program, cooperative education program, cross-registration, distance learning, double major, dual enrollment, English as a Second Language (ESL), exchange student program (domestic), external degree program, honors program, independent study, internships, liberal arts/career combination, student-designed major, study abroad, teacher certification program, Summer exchange program with Doshisha Women's College in Kyoto, Japan. Special programs offered to physically disabled students include tape recorders, tutors. **Career services:** Alumni services, career/job search classes, career assessment, internships.

FACILITIES

Housing: Special housing for international students, women's dorms, apartments for single students, Special interest (club) housing focuses on students,honors,leadership and community services available. 75% of campus accessible to physically disabled. **Special Academic Facilities/Equipment:** Audiovisual center, TV studio, communications lab, electron microscope, gas chromatoscope, greenhouse. **Computers:** 100% of classrooms, 100% of dorms, 100% of libraries, 100% of common outdoor areas have wireless network access. Students can register for classes online. Administrative functions (other than registration) can be performed online.

CAMPUS LIFE

Environment: Village. **Activities:** Choral groups, dance, drama/theater, literary magazine, marching band, music ensembles, musical theater, radio station, student government, student newspaper, student-run film society, television station, yearbook. **Organizations:** 34 registered organizations, 9 honor societies, 4 religious organizations. **Athletics (Intercollegiate):** *Women:* Basketball, field hockey, soccer, softball, swimming, tennis, volleyball. **On-Campus Highlights:** Coffee House (The Nut House), SMA (VWIL) Museum, the library, Spencer Center for Civic & Global Engage, computer center Llbs. **Environmental Initiatives:** Trayless dining hall; enhancing native landscaping.

ADMISSIONS

Freshman Academic Profile: Average high school GPA 3.3. 13% in top 10% of high school class, 39% in top 25% of high school class, 75% in top 50% of high school class. 75% from public high schools. SAT Math middle 50% range 430–560. SAT Critical Reading middle 50% range 460–600. SAT Writing middle 50% range 470–590. ACT middle 50% range 18–23. Minimum paper TOEFL 500. **Basis for Candidate Selection:** *Very important factors considered include:* Rigor of secondary school record, standardized test scores. *Important factors considered include:* character/personal qualities, extracurricular activities, interview. *Other factors considered include:* Class rank, application essay, recommendation(s), alumni/ae relation, talent/ability, volunteer work, work experience. **Freshman Admission Requirements:** High school diploma is required and GED is accepted. *Academic units required:* 4 English, 3 mathematics, 2 science, (1 science labs), 2 foreign language, 3 social studies. *Academic units recommended:* 3 foreign language, 2 academic electives. **Freshman Admission Statistics:** 1,784 applied, 70% admitted, 22% enrolled. **Transfer Admission Requirements:** High school transcript, college transcript(s), statement of good standing from prior institution(s). Minimum college GPA of 2.0 required. Lowest grade transferable C–. **General Admission Information:** Application fee $35. Early decision application deadline 11/8. Notification on a rolling basis, beginning on or about 9/8. Nonfall registration accepted. Admission may be deferred for a maximum of 1 semester. Credit offered for CEEB Advanced Placement tests.

COSTS AND FINANCIAL AID

Annual tuition $24,370. Room and board $7,070. Required fees $215. Average book expense $900. **Required Forms and Deadlines:** FAFSA, state aid form. Priority financial aid filing date 5/15. **Notification of Awards:** Applicants will be notified of awards on a rolling basis beginning 1/1. **Types of Aid:** *Need-based scholarships/grants:* Federal Pell, SEOG, state scholarships/grants, private scholarships, the school's own gift aid. *Loans:* FFEL Subsidized Stafford, FFEL Unsubsidized Stafford, FFEL PLUS, Federal Perkins, private alternative loans. **Student Employment:** Federal Work-Study Program available. Institutional employment available. Highest amount earned per year from on-campus jobs $1,356. Off-campus job opportunities are excellent. **Financial Aid Statistics:** 70% freshmen, 73% undergrads receive need-based scholarship or grant aid. 57% freshmen, 56% undergrads receive non-need-based scholarship or grant aid. 61% freshmen, 62% undergrads receive need-based self-help aid. 91% freshmen, 92% undergrads receive any aid. 79% undergrads borrow to pay for school. Average cumulative indebtedness $24,079. **Criteria for awarding institutional aid:** *Non-need-based:* Academics, leadership, state/district residency.

MARYGROVE COLLEGE

8425 West McNichols R, Detroit, MI 48221-2599
Phone: 313-927-1240
E-mail: info@marygrove.edu **CEEB Code:** 1452
Fax: 313-927-1345 **Website:** www.marygrove.edu **ACT Code:** 2024

This private school, affiliated with the Roman Catholic Church, was founded in 1927. It has a 50-acre campus.

RATINGS

Admissions Selectivity Rating: 80   **Fire Safety Rating:** 60*   **Green Rating:** 60*

STUDENTS AND FACULTY

Enrollment: 662. **Student Body:** 79% female, 21% male, 2% out-of-state, 1% international. African American 70%, Caucasian 5%, Hispanic 2%.
Retention and Graduation: 61% freshmen return for sophomore year. 30% grads go on to further study within 1 year. 30% grads pursue arts and sciences degrees. **Faculty:** Student/faculty ratio 16:1. 65 full-time faculty, 66% hold PhDs, 25% are members of minority groups, 65% are women.

ACADEMICS

Degrees: Associate, bachelor's, certificate, master's, post-bachelor's certificate. **Classes:** Most classes have fewer than 10 students. **Majors with Highest Enrollment:** Computer and information science; social work. **Special Study Options:** Cooperative education program, distance learning, double major, honors program, independent study, student-designed major, study abroad, teacher certification program. **Honors programs:** Honors program Special programs offered to physically disabled students include tutors. **Career services:** Alumni network, alumni services, career/job search classes, career assessment, internships, regional alumni.

FACILITIES

Housing: Coed dorms. 95% of campus accessible to physically disabled. **Special Academic Facilities/Equipment:** Conference center, chapel, theatre, art gallery **Computers:** Students can register for classes online. Administrative functions (other than registration) can be performed online.

CAMPUS LIFE

Environment: Metropolis. **Activities:** Choral groups, dance, music ensembles, student government **Organizations:** 17 registered organizations, 6 honor societies. **On-Campus Highlights:** Theater, chapel, conference center, art gallery.

ADMISSIONS

Freshman Academic Profile: Average high school GPA 2.87. 10% in top 10% of high school class, 75% in top 25% of high school class, 100% in top 50% of high school class. 80% from public high schools. ACT middle 50% range 16–21. Minimum paper TOEFL 520. **Basis for Candidate Selection:** *Important factors considered include:* Rigor of secondary school record, standardized test scores, character/personal qualities, interview, talent/ability. *Other factors considered include:* Recommendation(s), extracurricular activities, volunteer work, work experience. **Freshman Admission Requirements:** High school diploma is required and GED is accepted. *Academic units recommended:* 8 English, 4 mathematics, 1 science, 1 foreign language, 4 social studies, 5 history. **Freshman Admission Statistics:** 290 applied, 40% admitted, 36% enrolled. **Transfer Admission Requirements:** College transcript(s), statement of good standing from prior institution(s). Minimum college GPA of 2.7 required. Lowest grade transferable C. **General Admission Information:** Application fee $25. Regular application deadline 8/15. Regular notification 8/15. Nonfall registration accepted. Admission may be deferred for a maximum of 1 year. Credit and/or placement offered for CEEB Advanced Placement tests.

COSTS AND FINANCIAL AID

Annual tuition $12,190. Room and board $6,000. Required fees $250. Average book expense $1,180. **Required Forms and Deadlines:** FAFSA, institution's own financial aid form. Priority financial aid filing date 3/15. **Notification of Awards:** Applicants will be notified of awards on a rolling basis beginning 5/1. **Types of Aid:** *Need-based scholarships/grants:* Federal Pell, SEOG, state scholarships/grants, private scholarships, the school's own gift aid. *Loans:* Direct Subsidized Stafford, Direct Unsubsidized Stafford, Direct PLUS, FFEL Subsidized Stafford, FFEL Unsubsidized Stafford, FFEL PLUS, Federal Perkins, state loans. **Student Employment:** Federal Work-Study Program available. Highest amount earned per year from on-campus jobs $2,700. Off-campus job opportunities are good. **Financial Aid Statistics: Criteria for awarding institutional aid:** *Non-need-based:* Academics, art, leadership, music/drama.

MARYLAND INSTITUTE COLLEGE OF ART

1300 Mount Royal Avenue, Baltimore, MD 21217
Phone: 410-225-2222 **Financial Aid Phone:** 410-225-2285
E-mail: admissions@mica.edu **CEEB Code:** 5399
Fax: 410-225-2337 **Website:** www.mica.edu **ACT Code:** 1710

This private school was founded in 1826. It has a 12-acre campus.

RATINGS
Admissions Selectivity Rating: 91   **Fire Safety Rating:** 86   **Green Rating:** 64

STUDENTS AND FACULTY
Enrollment: 1,699. **Student Body:** 71% female, 29% male, 80% out-of-state, 4% international (49 countries represented). Asian 11%, African American 4%, Caucasian 63%, Hispanic 4%.
Retention and Graduation: 83% freshmen return for sophomore year. 61% freshmen graduate within 4 years. 23% grads go on to further study within 1 year. **Faculty:** Student/faculty ratio 10:1. 129 full-time faculty, 83% hold PhDs, 12% are members of minority groups, 54% are women.

ACADEMICS
Degrees: Bachelor's, master's, post-bachelor's certificate. **Classes:** Most classes have 10–19 students. **Majors with Highest Enrollment:** Graphic design; intermedia/multimedia; painting. **Special Study Options:** Accelerated program, cross-registration, distance learning, double major, dual enrollment, exchange student program (domestic), independent study, internships, student-designed major, study abroad, teacher certification program, cooperative exchange programs with Johns Hopkins University, Goucher College, The Peabody Conservatory of Music, University of Baltimore, Loyola College, Notre Dame College, University of Maryland Baltimore County, Morgan State University, and Towson University; 5-year BFA/MAT program is available. **Combined degree programs:** BA/MA, BFA/MAT. Special programs offered to physically disabled students include note-taking services, tape recorders, tutors. **Career services:** Alumni network, alumni services, career/job search classes, career assessment, internships, regional alumni.

FACILITIES
Housing: Coed dorms, special housing for disabled students, special housing for international students, apartments for single students 85% of campus accessible to physically disabled. **Special Academic Facilities/Equipment:** There are seven art galleries open to the public year-round featuring work by MICA faculty, students, and nationally/internationally known artists; a nature library; and an extensive slide library containing over 220,000 slides. **Computers:** 100% of libraries, 100% of dining areas, 80% of common outdoor areas have wireless network access. Students can register for classes online. Administrative functions (other than registration) can be performed online.

CAMPUS LIFE
Environment: Metropolis. **Activities:** Choral groups, dance, drama/theater, literary magazine, radio station, student government, student-run film society, international student organization. **Organizations:** 50 registered organizations, 3 religious organizations. **On-Campus Highlights:** The Gateway, our new dormitory, The Brown Center, our digital arts center, The Meyerhoff House dormitory & dining, Various on-campus galleries/exhibitions, Cafe Doris and Java Corner, two eateries. **Environmental Initiatives:** Single-stream recycling of recyclable waste. Using an independent auditor to track the college's energy for an energy-use audit. MICA does not use chemical drain cleaners and openers to unclog plumbing because these products are highly acidic and detrimental to the environment, persons handling the products, as well as the plumbing.

ADMISSIONS
Freshman Academic Profile: Average high school GPA 3.5. 30% in top 10% of high school class, 71% in top 25% of high school class, 93% in top 50% of high school class. 56% from public high schools. SAT Math middle 50% range 510–620. SAT Critical Reading middle 50% range 530–660. SAT Writing middle 50% range 530–650. Minimum paper TOEFL 550. Minimum computer TOEFL 213. **Basis for Candidate Selection:** *Very important factors considered include:* Academic GPA, rigor of secondary school record, level of applicant's interest, talent/ability. *Important factors considered include:* Class rank, application essay, standardized test scores, extracurricular activities, interview. *Other factors considered include:* Recommendation(s), alumni/ae relation, character/personal qualities, racial/ethnic status, volunteer work. **Freshman Admission Requirements:** High school diploma is required and GED is accepted. *Academic units required:* 4 English, 2 mathematics, 2 science, (1 science labs), 4 social studies, 3 history, 6 academic electives, 2 studio art, 4 studio art recommended, 1 art history recommended. *Academic units recommended:* 4 English, 3 mathematics, 3 science, 4 social studies, 4 history, 5 studio art, 4 studio art recommended, 1 art history recommended. **Freshman**

Admission Statistics: 2,892 applied, 47% admitted, 34% enrolled. **Transfer Admission Requirements:** High school transcript, college transcript(s), essay or personal statement, minimum college GPA of 2.8 required. Lowest grade transferable C. **General Admission Information:** Application fee $60. Early decision application deadline 11/14. Regular application deadline 2/13. Regular notification 3/13. Nonfall registration accepted. Admission may be deferred for a maximum of 1 year. Credit and/or placement offered for CEEB Advanced Placement tests.

COSTS AND FINANCIAL AID
Annual tuition $33,000. Room and board $9,450. Required fees $1,090. Average book expense $1,450. **Required Forms and Deadlines:** FAFSA, institution's own financial aid form Financial aid filing deadline 3/1. **Notification of Awards:** Applicants will be notified of awards on or about 4/10. **Types of Aid:** *Need-based scholarships/grants:* Federal Pell, SEOG, state scholarships/grants, private scholarships, the school's own gift aid. *Loans:* FFEL Subsidized Stafford, FFEL Unsubsidized Stafford, FFEL PLUS, Federal Perkins. **Student Employment:** Federal Work-Study Program available. Institutional employment available. Off-campus job opportunities are excellent. **Financial Aid Statistics: Criteria for awarding institutional aid:** *Non-need-based:* Academics, art.

MARYLHURST UNIVERSITY

PO Box 261, Marylhurst, OR 97036
Phone: 503-699-6268 **Financial Aid Phone:** 503-699-6253
E-mail: admissions@marylhurst.edu **CEEB Code:** 440
Fax: 503-636-9526 **Website:** www.marylhurst.edu **ACT Code:** 3470

This private school, affiliated with the Roman Catholic Church, was founded in 1893. It has a 68-acre campus.

RATINGS
Admissions Selectivity Rating: 60*   **Fire Safety Rating:** 60*   **Green Rating:** 60*

STUDENTS AND FACULTY
Enrollment: 775. **Student Body:** 72% female, 28% male, 2% international. Asian 1%, African American 1%, Caucasian 24%, Hispanic 1%.
Faculty: Student/faculty ratio 7:1.

ACADEMICS
Degrees: Bachelor's, certificate, first professional, master's, post-bachelor's certificate, post-master's certificate. **Classes:** Most classes have fewer than 10 students. **Majors with Highest Enrollment:** Business administration and management; interior design; multi-/interdisciplinary studies, other. **Special Study Options:** Accelerated program, cooperative education program, cross-registration, distance learning, double major, English as a Second Language (ESL), independent study, internships, student-designed major, study abroad, teacher certification program, weekend college, Special programs offered to physically disabled students include note-taking services, reader services, tape recorders, tutors.

FACILITIES
Housing: 90% of campus accessible to physically disabled. **Special Academic Facilities/Equipment:** Art Gym Art Gallery Streff Gallery **Computers:** Students can register for classes online. Administrative functions (other than registration) can be performed online.

CAMPUS LIFE
Environment: City. **Activities:** Choral groups, jazz band, literary magazine, music ensembles, symphony orchestra **Organizations:** 6 registered organizations, 1 honor societies.

ADMISSIONS
Freshman Academic Profile: Minimum paper TOEFL 550. Minimum computer TOEFL 213. Minimum web-based TOEFL 79. **Basis for Candidate Selection:** *Other factors considered include:* Academic GPA, recommendation(s), interview. **Freshman Admission Requirements:** High school diploma is required and GED is accepted. **Freshman Admission Statistics: Transfer Admission Requirements:** High school transcript, college transcript(s), minimum college GPA of 2.0 required. Lowest grade transferable C–. **General Admission Information:** Application fee $20. Nonfall registration accepted. Admission may be deferred for a maximum of 1 year. Credit and/or placement offered for CEEB Advanced Placement tests.

COSTS AND FINANCIAL AID
Annual tuition $15,120. Required fees $450. **Required Forms and Deadlines:** FAFSA, institution's own financial aid form. **Notification of Awards:**

Applicants will be notified of awards on a rolling basis beginning 4/15. **Types of Aid:** *Need-based scholarships/grants:* Federal Pell, SEOG, state scholarships/grants, private scholarships, the school's own gift aid. *Loans:* FFEL Subsidized Stafford, FFEL Unsubsidized Stafford, FFEL PLUS, Federal Perkins. **Student Employment: Financial Aid Statistics:** 56% freshmen, 64% undergrads receive need-based scholarship or grant aid. 6% freshmen, 2% undergrads receive non-need-based scholarship or grant aid. 44% freshmen, 66% undergrads receive need-based self-help aid. 67% undergrads borrow to pay for school. Average cumulative indebtedness $9,055. **Criteria for awarding institutional aid:** *Non-need-based:* Academics.

MARYMOUNT COLLEGE

Marymount College, 30800 Palos Verdes Drive East, CA 90275-6299
Phone: 310-377-5501 **Financial Aid Phone:** 310.303.7282
E-mail: admissions@marymountpv.edu **CEEB Code:** 4515
Fax: 310-265-0962 **Website:** www.marymountpv.edu **ACT Code:** 0316

This private school, affiliated with the Roman Catholic Church, was founded in 1932. It has a 22-acre campus.

RATINGS
Admissions Selectivity Rating: 80 **Fire Safety Rating:** 60* **Green Rating:** 72

STUDENTS AND FACULTY
Enrollment: 561. **Student Body:** 51% female, 49% male, 10% out-of-state, 6% international (13 countries represented). Asian 7%, African American 7%, Caucasian 36%, Hispanic 20%.
Retention and Graduation: 59% freshmen return for sophomore year. 90% grads go on to further study within 1 year. **Faculty:** Student/faculty ratio 15:1. 26 full-time faculty, 65% hold PhDs, 8% are members of minority groups, 42% are women.

ACADEMICS
Degrees: Associate, bachelor's. **Classes:** Most classes have 10–19 students. **Special Study Options:** Dual enrollment, English as a Second Language (ESL), honors program, internships, study abroad, weekend college. **Honors programs:** Marymount Honors Program, Phi Theta Kappa. Special programs offered to physically disabled students include note-taking services, reader services, tape recorders, tutors.

FACILITIES
Housing: Coed dorms, special housing for disabled students 100% of campus accessible to physically disabled. **Computers:** 100% of classrooms, 100% of dorms, 100% of libraries, 100% of dining areas, 100% of student union, 75% of common outdoor areas have wireless network access. Administrative functions (other than registration) can be performed online.

CAMPUS LIFE
Environment: Town. **Activities:** Choral groups, dance, drama/theater, jazz band, literary magazine, musical theater, radio station, student government, student newspaper, student-run film society, campus ministries, international student organization. **Organizations:** 2 honor societies, 2 religious organizations. **Athletics (Intercollegiate):** *Men:* Soccer. *Women:* Soccer.

ADMISSIONS
Freshman Academic Profile: Average high school GPA 2.69. 40% in top 25% of high school class, 40% in top 50% of high school class. SAT Math middle 50% range 409–552. SAT Critical Reading middle 50% range 429–541. SAT Writing middle 50% range 438–550. **Basis for Candidate Selection:** *Very important factors considered include:* Academic GPA, rigor of secondary school record. *Other factors considered include:* Class rank, application essay, recommendation(s), standardized test scores, alumni/ae relation, character/personal qualities, extracurricular activities, interview, level of applicant's interest, talent/ability, volunteer work. **Freshman Admission Requirements:** High school diploma is required and GED is accepted. *Academic units recommended:* 4 English, 3 mathematics, 2 science, 2 foreign language, 2 social studies, 2 history, 1 academic electives. **Freshman Admission Statistics:** 1,256 applied, 61% admitted, 39% enrolled. **Transfer Admission Requirements:** High school transcript, college transcript(s), Lowest grade transferable C–. **General Admission Information:** Application fee $40. Notification on a rolling basis, beginning on or about 12/1. Nonfall registration accepted. Admission may be deferred for a maximum of 1 year. Credit and/or placement offered for CEEB Advanced Placement tests.

COSTS AND FINANCIAL AID
Annual tuition $24,052. Room and board $10,600. Required fees $490. Average book expense $1,638. **Required Forms and Deadlines:** FAFSA. Priority financial aid filing date 3/1. **Notification of Awards:** Applicants will be noti-

fied of awards on or about 3/1. **Types of Aid:** *Need-based scholarships/grants:* Federal Pell, SEOG, state scholarships/grants, private scholarships, the school's own gift aid. *Loans:* FFEL Subsidized Stafford, FFEL Unsubsidized Stafford, FFEL PLUS. **Student Employment:** Federal Work-Study Program available. Institutional employment available. Highest amount earned per year from on-campus jobs $3,840. Off-campus job opportunities are good. **Financial Aid Statistics:** 46% freshmen, 50% undergrads receive need-based scholarship or grant aid. 24% freshmen, 19% undergrads receive non-need-based scholarship or grant aid. 38% freshmen, 41% undergrads receive need-based self-help aid. 62% freshmen, 71% undergrads receive any aid. 78.3% undergrads borrow to pay for school. Average cumulative indebtedness $17,227. **Criteria for awarding institutional aid:** *Non-need-based:* Academics, art, athletics, leadership.

MARYMOUNT MANHATTAN COLLEGE

221 East 71st Street, New York, NY, 10021,
Financial Aid Phone: 212-517-0500
CEEB Code: 2405
ACT Code: 2810

This private school was founded in 1936. It has a 1-acre campus.

RATINGS
Admissions Selectivity Rating: 77 **Fire Safety Rating:** 79 **Green Rating:** 82

STUDENTS AND FACULTY
Enrollment: 1,897. **Student Body:** 75% female, 25% male, 42% out-of-state, 3% international (24 countries represented). Asian 3%, African American 11%, Caucasian 71%, Hispanic 11%.
Retention and Graduation: 62% freshmen return for sophomore year. 41% freshmen graduate within 4 years. 33% grads go on to further study within 1 year. 9% grads pursue arts and sciences degrees. 7% grads pursue law degrees. 12% grads pursue business degrees. 5% grads pursue medical degrees. **Faculty:** Student/faculty ratio 12:1. 96 full-time faculty, 89% hold PhDs, 14% are members of minority groups, 55% are women.

ACADEMICS
Degrees: Associate, bachelor's, certificate. **Classes:** Most classes have 10–19 students. **Majors with Highest Enrollment:** Communication and media studies, other; dance; drama and dramatics/theatre arts. **Special Study Options:** Accelerated program, distance learning, double major, dual enrollment, exchange student program (domestic), independent study, internships, liberal arts/career combination, study abroad, teacher certification program Special programs offered to physically disabled students include note-taking services, reader services, tape recorders, tutors. **Career services:** Alumni network, alumni services, career assessment, internships.

FACILITIES
Housing: Coed dorms. 100% of campus accessible to physically disabled. **Special Academic Facilities/Equipment:** Gallery, communications and learning center, theatre, media center, college skills center, mathematics lab, Samuel Freeman science center,Comm Arts multimedia suite. **Computers:** 40% of classrooms, 100% of libraries, have wireless network access. Students can register for classes online. Administrative functions (other than registration) can be performed online.

CAMPUS LIFE
Environment: Metropolis. **Activities:** Choral groups, dance, drama/theater, literary magazine, musical theater, radio station, student government, student newspaper, yearbook, international student organization. **Organizations:** 30 registered organizations, 7 honor societies, 2 religious organizations. **On-Campus Highlights:** Theresa Lang Theatre, Hewitt Gallery of Art, Science Laboratories, 55th Street Residence Hall, Shanahan Library, student cafeterias. **Environmental Initiatives:** Purchase of renewable energy; recycling of paper and bottles; awareness campaigns to get students and faculty and staff moving in a green direction.

ADMISSIONS
Freshman Academic Profile: Average high school GPA 3.17. 70% from public high schools. SAT Math middle 50% range 460–560. SAT Critical Reading middle 50% range 500–600. ACT middle 50% range 21–25. Minimum paper TOEFL 550. Minimum computer TOEFL 213. Minimum web-based TOEFL 80. **Basis for Candidate Selection:** *Very important factors considered include:* Academic GPA, rigor of secondary school record, standardized test scores. *Important factors considered include:* Application essay, recommendation(s), character/personal qualities, extracurricular activities, talent/ability. *Other factors considered include:* Class rank, interview, volunteer work, work experience. **Freshman Admission Requirements:** High school diploma is required

and GED is accepted. *Academic units required:* 4 English, 3 mathematics, 3 science, 3 social studies, 4 academic electives. *Academic units recommended:* (2 science labs), 2 foreign language. **Freshman Admission Statistics:** 3,065 applied, 69% admitted, 26% enrolled. **Transfer Admission Requirements:** High school transcript, college transcript(s), essay or personal statement, statement of good standing from prior institution(s). Minimum college GPA of 2.5 required. Lowest grade transferable C–. **General Admission Information:** Application fee $60. Notification on a rolling basis, beginning on or about 9/1. Nonfall registration accepted. Admission may be deferred for a maximum of 1 Semester. Credit and/or placement offered for CEEB Advanced Placement tests.

COSTS AND FINANCIAL AID
Annual tuition $20,748. Room and board $12,660. Required fees $1,044. Average book expense $1,000. **Required Forms and Deadlines:** FAFSA. Priority financial aid filing date 3/15. **Notification of Awards:** Applicants will be notified of awards on a rolling basis beginning 3/15. **Types of Aid:** *Need-based scholarships/grants:* Federal Pell, SEOG, state scholarships/grants, private scholarships, the school's own gift aid. *Loans:* FFEL Subsidized Stafford, FFEL Unsubsidized Stafford, FFEL PLUS. **Student Employment:** Federal Work-Study Program available. Institutional employment available. Highest amount earned per year from on-campus jobs $2,000. Off-campus job opportunities are excellent. **Financial Aid Statistics:** 61% freshmen, 55% undergrads receive need-based scholarship or grant aid. 47% freshmen, 2% undergrads receive non-need-based scholarship or grant aid. 62% freshmen, 53% undergrads receive need-based self-help aid. 80% freshmen, 67% undergrads receive any aid. 41% undergrads borrow to pay for school. Average cumulative indebtedness $16,765.

See page 1156.

MARYMOUNT UNIVERSITY

2807 North Glebe Road, Arlington, VA 22207
Phone: 703-284-1500 **Financial Aid Phone:** 703-284-1530
E-mail: admissions@marymount.edu **CEEB Code:** 5405
Fax: 703-522-0349 **Website:** www.marymount.edu **ACT Code:** 4378

This private school, affiliated with the Roman Catholic Church, was founded in 1950. It has a 21-acre campus.

RATINGS
Admissions Selectivity Rating: 74   **Fire Safety Rating:** 60*   **Green Rating:** 60*

STUDENTS AND FACULTY
Enrollment: 2,199. **Student Body:** 75% female, 25% male, 42% out-of-state, 6% international (70 countries represented). Asian 8%, African American 15%, Caucasian 46%, Hispanic 12%, Native American 1%. **Retention and Graduation:** 71% freshmen return for sophomore year. **Faculty:** Student/faculty ratio 14:1. 138 full-time faculty, 89% hold PhDs, 5% are members of minority groups, 74% are women.

ACADEMICS
Degrees: Bachelor's, certificate, master's, post-bachelor's certificate, post-master's certificate. **Classes:** Most classes have 10–19 students. **Majors with Highest Enrollment:** Business administration and management; interior design; nursing/registered nurse (RN, ASN, BSN, MSN). **Special Study Options:** Accelerated program, cross-registration, distance learning, double major, English as a Second Language (ESL), honors program, independent study, internships, student-designed major, study abroad, teacher certification program. **Honors programs:** The Honors Program at Marymount University **Combined degree programs:** BBA/MBA, health promotion management. BS/MS. Special programs offered to physically disabled students include note-taking services, reader services, tape recorders, tutors. **Career services:** Alumni network, career/job search classes, internships.

FACILITIES
Housing: Coed dorms, men's dorms. women's dorms 75% of campus accessible to physically disabled. **Special Academic Facilities/Equipment:** Art gallery, learning resource center, audiovisual center, studio, and computer labs. **Computers:** Students can register for classes online. Administrative functions (other than registration) can be performed online.

CAMPUS LIFE
Environment: City. **Activities:** Choral groups, dance, drama/theater, literary magazine, student government, student newspaper, yearbook, campus ministries, international student organization. **Organizations:** 33 registered organizations, 11 honor societies, 2 religious organizations. **Athletics (Intercollegiate):** *Men:* Basketball, cross-country, golf, lacrosse, soccer, swimming.

Women: Basketball, cross-country, lacrosse, soccer, swimming, volleyball. **On-Campus Highlights:** Student Center, Gym, Bernie's Cafe, Turf field, Ballston campus. **Environmental Initiatives:** Recycling program, public transportation available, car pool incentives.

ADMISSIONS
Freshman Academic Profile: Average high school GPA 3.14. 15% in top 10% of high school class, 41% in top 25% of high school class, 81% in top 50% of high school class. 68% from public high schools. SAT Math middle 50% range 450–550. SAT Critical Reading middle 50% range 450–560. SAT Writing middle 50% range 450–550. ACT middle 50% range 18–24. Minimum paper TOEFL 550. Minimum computer TOEFL 213. Minimum web-based TOEFL 79. **Basis for Candidate Selection:** *Very important factors considered include:* Academic GPA, rigor of secondary school record, standardized test scores. *Important factors considered include:* Class rank, recommendation(s), interview, talent/ability. *Other factors considered include:* Application essay, alumni/ae relation, character/personal qualities, extracurricular activities, first generation, level of applicant's interest, volunteer work, work experience. **Freshman Admission Requirements:** High school diploma is required and GED is accepted. *Academic units recommended:* 4 English, 3 mathematics, 2 science, 3 foreign language, 3 social studies. **Freshman Admission Statistics:** 1,904 applied, 81% admitted, 26% enrolled. **Transfer Admission Requirements:** College transcript(s), statement of good standing from prior institution(s). Minimum college GPA of 2.0 required. Lowest grade transferable C. **General Admission Information:** Application fee $40. Nonfall registration accepted. Admission may be deferred for a maximum of 1 year. Credit offered for CEEB Advanced Placement tests.

COSTS AND FINANCIAL AID
Annual tuition $20,190. Room and board $8,705. Required fees $220. Average book expense $800. **Required Forms and Deadlines:** FAFSA. Priority financial aid filing date 3/1. **Notification of Awards:** Applicants will be notified of awards on a rolling basis beginning 3/15. **Types of Aid:** *Need-based scholarships/grants:* Federal Pell, SEOG, state scholarships/grants, private scholarships, the school's own gift aid. *Loans:* Direct Subsidized Stafford, Direct Unsubsidized Stafford, FFEL Subsidized Stafford, FFEL Unsubsidized Stafford, FFEL PLUS, Federal Perkins. **Student Employment:** Federal Work-Study Program available. Institutional employment available. Off-campus job opportunities are good. **Financial Aid Statistics:** 53% freshmen, 44% undergrads receive need-based scholarship or grant aid. 50% freshmen, 43% undergrads receive non-need-based scholarship or grant aid. 49% freshmen, 48% undergrads receive need-based self-help aid. 92% freshmen, 84% undergrads receive any aid. 70% undergrads borrow to pay for school. Average cumulative indebtedness $20,686. **Criteria for awarding institutional aid:** *Non-need-based:* Academics, alumni affiliation, leadership, state/district residency.

See page 1158.

MARYVILLE COLLEGE

502 East Lamar Alexander Parkway, Maryville, TN 37804-5907
Phone: 865-981-8092 **Financial Aid Phone:** 865-981-8100
E-mail: admissions@maryvillecollege.edu **CEEB Code:** 1454
Fax: 865-981-8005 **Website:** www.maryvillecollege.edu **ACT Code:** 3988

This private school, affiliated with the Presbyterian Church, was founded in 1819. It has a 370-acre campus.

RATINGS
Admissions Selectivity Rating: 84   **Fire Safety Rating:** 86   **Green Rating:** 77

STUDENTS AND FACULTY
Enrollment: 1,114. **Student Body:** 55% female, 45% male, 24% out-of-state, 4% international (20 countries represented). Asian 1%, African American 5%, Caucasian 86%, Hispanic 2%. **Retention and Graduation:** 67% freshmen return for sophomore year. 43% freshmen graduate within 4 years. 28% grads go on to further study within 1 year. **Faculty:** Student/faculty ratio 11.5:1. 79 full-time faculty, 76% hold PhDs, 4% are members of minority groups, 54% are women.

ACADEMICS
Degrees: Bachelor's. **Classes:** Most classes have 10–19 students. Most lab/discussion sessions have 10–19 students. **Majors with Highest Enrollment:** Biology/biological sciences; business/commerce; education. **Special Study Options:** Double major, English as a Second Language (ESL), honors program, independent study, internships, liberal arts/career combination, student-designed major, study abroad, teacher certification program. **Honors programs:** Presidential and Deans scholars participate in honors courses and honors tutorial practicum. Most courses may be taken with "honors" status. **Combined**

degree programs: BA/MSN. Special programs offered to physically disabled students include note-taking services, reader services, tape recorders, tutors. **Career services:** Alumni network, alumni services, career/job search classes, career assessment, internships, regional alumni. **Career services highlights include:** Internships and practica are available in almost all major fields.

FACILITIES

Housing: Coed dorms, special housing for disabled students, men's dorms, women's dorms, apartments for single students, Special Interest groups. 90% of campus accessible to physically disabled. **Special Academic Facilities/Equipment:** Art gallery, theatre, greenhouse, College Woods. **Computers:** 100% of classrooms, 100% of dorms, 100% of libraries, 100% of dining areas, 100% of student union, 50% of common outdoor areas have wireless network access. Students can register for classes online. Administrative functions (other than registration) can be performed online.

CAMPUS LIFE

Environment: Town. **Activities:** Choral groups, concert band, dance, drama/theater, jazz band, literary magazine, music ensembles, musical theater, student government, student newspaper, symphony orchestra, yearbook, campus ministries. **Organizations:** 63 registered organizations, 15 honor societies, 5 religious organizations. **Athletics (Intercollegiate):** *Men:* Baseball, basketball, cross-country, equestrian sports, football, soccer, tennis. *Women:* Basketball, cross-country, equestrian sports, soccer, softball, tennis, volleyball. **On-Campus Highlights:** Isaacs Student Center, Mountain Challenge, Lloyd Beach, New Lloyd Residence Hall, Center for Calling and Career, Mountain Challenge includes a 60' Alpine Tower, rock climbing wall, ropes course, and kayak roll sessions on campus. In addition there are trips offered every Saturday to nearby attractions, i.e., rock climbing, white water rafting, camping, and caving. **Environmental Initiatives:** Steam plant boiler is fueled by recycled wood products; campus-wide recycling program; purchase of green power for selected campus buildings.

ADMISSIONS

Freshman Academic Profile: Average high school GPA 3.59. 34% in top 10% of high school class, 65% in top 25% of high school class, 89% in top 50% of high school class. 91% from public high schools. SAT Math middle 50% range 480–610. SAT Critical Reading middle 50% range 470–630. SAT Writing middle 50% range 450–610. ACT middle 50% range 21–28. Minimum paper TOEFL 525. Minimum computer TOEFL 200. **Basis for Candidate Selection:** *Very important factors considered include:* Class rank, rigor of secondary school record, standardized test scores. *Important factors considered include:* Academic GPA, recommendation(s), extracurricular activities, interview. *Other factors considered include:* Application essay, alumni/ae relation, character/personal qualities, first generation, level of applicant's interest, talent/ability, volunteer work. **Freshman Admission Requirements:** High school diploma is required and GED is accepted. *Academic units required:* 4 English, 3 mathematics, 2 science, (1 science labs), 2 foreign language, 2 social studies, 1 academic electives. *Academic units recommended:* 1 history. **Freshman Admission Statistics:** 1,621 applied, 75% admitted, 24% enrolled. **Transfer Admission Requirements:** College transcript(s), statement of good standing from prior institution(s). Minimum college GPA of 2.0 required. Lowest grade transferable C. **General Admission Information:** Early decision application deadline 11/15. Notification on a rolling basis, beginning on or about 12/1. Nonfall registration accepted. Admission may be deferred for a maximum of 1 year. Credit and/or placement offered for CEEB Advanced Placement tests.

COSTS AND FINANCIAL AID

Annual tuition $26,272. Room and board $8,240. Required fees $675. Average book expense $880. **Required Forms and Deadlines:** FAFSA. Priority financial aid filing date 3/1. *Types of Aid: Need-based scholarships/grants:* Federal Pell, SEOG, state scholarships/grants, private scholarships, the school's own gift aid. *Loans:* Direct Subsidized Stafford, Direct Unsubsidized Stafford, Direct PLUS, FFEL Subsidized Stafford, FFEL Unsubsidized Stafford, FFEL PLUS, Federal Perkins, state loans, college/university loans from institutional funds. **Student Employment:** Federal Work-Study Program available. Highest amount earned per year from on-campus jobs $2,617. Off-campus job opportunities are good. **Financial Aid Statistics:** 65% freshmen, 78% undergrads receive need-based scholarship or grant aid. 27% freshmen, 20% undergrads receive non-need-based scholarship or grant aid. 68% freshmen, 48% undergrads receive need-based self-help aid. 100% freshmen, 98% undergrads receive any aid. 92% undergrads borrow to pay for school. Average cumulative indebtedness $13,929. **Criteria for awarding institutional aid:** *Non-need-based:* Academics, art, leadership, minority status, music/drama, religious affiliation, state/district residency.

MARYVILLE UNIVERSITY OF SAINT LOUIS

650 Maryville University Drive, St. Louis, MO 63141-7299
Phone: 314-529-9350 **Financial Aid Phone:** 314-529-9360
E-mail: admissions@maryville.edu **CEEB Code:** 6399
Fax: 314-529-9927 **Website: ACT Code:** 2326

This private school was founded in 1872. It has a 130-acre campus.

RATINGS
Admissions Selectivity Rating: 83   **Fire Safety Rating:** 85   **Green Rating:** 60*

STUDENTS AND FACULTY
Enrollment: 2,826. **Student Body:** 76% female, 24% male, 13% out-of-state, 1% international (14 countries represented). Asian 2%, African American 7%, Caucasian 80%, Hispanic 2%.
Retention and Graduation: 82% freshmen return for sophomore year. 54% freshmen graduate within 4 years. **Faculty:** Student/faculty ratio 12:1. 111 full-time faculty, 86% hold PhDs, 13% are members of minority groups, 59% are women.

ACADEMICS
Degrees: Bachelor's, certificate, master's. **Classes:** Most classes have 10–19 students. Most lab/discussion sessions have fewer than 10 students. **Majors with Highest Enrollment:** Business/commerce; nursing/registered nurse (RN, ASN, BSN, MSN); physical therapy/therapist. **Special Study Options:** Accelerated program, cooperative education program, cross-registration, distance learning, double major, dual enrollment, honors program, independent study, internships, liberal arts/career combination, student-designed major, study abroad, teacher certification program, weekend college, Washington Center, Semester at Sea. **Honors programs:** Bascom Honors Program. **Combined degree programs:** MU-St. Louis Univ. MSW joint degree Program. Special programs offered to physically disabled students include note-taking services, reader services, tape recorders, tutors. **Career services:** Career/job search classes, career assessment, internships. **Career services highlights include:** Cooperative Education—over 80 students per year participate in a co-op experience.

FACILITIES
Housing: Coed dorms, apartments for single students, wellness housing, theme housing. 90% of campus accessible to physically disabled. **Special Academic Facilities/Equipment:** University Center, art galleries, auditorium, chapel, observatory, teaching lab, clinical labs, art and design labs, videoconferencing facility with downlinking and electronic multi-media capability for presentations. **Computers:** 100% of classrooms, 100% of dorms, 100% of libraries, 100% of dining areas, 100% of student union, 100% of common outdoor areas have wireless network access. Students can register for classes online. Administrative functions (other than registration) can be performed online.

CAMPUS LIFE
Environment: Metropolis. **Activities:** Choral groups, dance, drama/theater, jazz band, literary magazine, music ensembles, pep band, student government, student newspaper, symphony orchestra, campus ministries. **Organizations:** 40 registered organizations, 3 honor societies, 4 religious organizations. **Athletics (Intercollegiate):** *Men:* Baseball, basketball, cheerleading, cross-country, golf, soccer, tennis. *Women:* Basketball, cheerleading, cross-country, golf, soccer, softball, tennis, volleyball.

ADMISSIONS
Freshman Academic Profile: Average high school GPA 3.53. 26% in top 10% of high school class, 56% in top 25% of high school class, 79% in top 50% of high school class. 77% from public high schools. SAT Math middle 50% range 490–520. SAT Critical Reading middle 50% range 450–570. ACT middle 50% range 22–27. Minimum paper TOEFL 500. Minimum computer TOEFL 173. **Basis for Candidate Selection:** *Very important factors considered include:* Academic GPA, standardized test scores. *Important factors considered include:* Rigor of secondary school record, extracurricular activities. *Other factors considered include:* Class rank, application essay, recommendation(s), character/personal qualities, interview, talent/ability. **Freshman Admission Requirements:** High school diploma is required and GED is accepted. *Academic units required:* 4 English, 3 mathematics, 2 science, 2 social studies, 8 academic electives. **Freshman Admission Statistics:** 1,154 applied, 66% admitted, 49% enrolled. **Transfer Admission Requirements:** College transcript(s), minimum college GPA of 2.0 required. Lowest grade transferable C–. **General Admission Information:** Application fee $30. Regular application deadline 8/15. Nonfall registration accepted. Admission may be deferred for a maximum of 1 year. Credit offered for CEEB Advanced Placement tests.

COSTS AND FINANCIAL AID
Annual tuition $20,384. Room and board $8,210. Required fees $610. Average book expense $1,600. **Required Forms and Deadlines:** FAFSA. Priority

financial aid filing date 3/1. **Notification of Awards:** Applicants will be notified of awards on a rolling basis beginning 3/1. **Types of Aid:** *Need-based scholarships/grants:* Federal Pell, SEOG, state scholarships/grants, private scholarships, the school's own gift aid, TEACH Grant, Academic Competiveness Grant, Smart Grant. *Loans:* Direct Subsidized Stafford, Direct Unsubsidized Stafford, Direct PLUS, Federal Perkins, Five Month Installment Deferred Payment Program. **Student Employment:** Federal Work-Study Program available. **Financial Aid Statistics:** 74% freshmen, 75% undergrads receive need-based scholarship or grant aid. 11% freshmen, 6% undergrads receive non-need-based scholarship or grant aid. 55% freshmen, 71% undergrads receive need-based self-help aid. 2% freshmen, 72% freshmen, 65% undergrads receive any aid. 73% undergrads borrow to pay for school. Average cumulative indebtedness $18,341. **Criteria for awarding institutional aid:** *Non-need-based:* Academics, alumni affiliation, art, athletics, leadership, minority status.

MARYWOOD UNIVERSITY

Office of Admissions, 2300 Adams Avenu, Scranton, PA 18509
Phone: 570-348-6234 **Financial Aid Phone:** 866-279-9663
E-mail: yourfuture@marywood.edu **CEEB Code:** 2407
Fax: 570-961-4763 **Website:** www.marywood.edu **ACT Code:** 3626

This private school, affiliated with the Roman Catholic Church, was founded in 1915. It has a 115-acre campus.

RATINGS
Admissions Selectivity Rating: 79   **Fire Safety Rating:** 90   **Green Rating:** 73

STUDENTS AND FACULTY
Enrollment: 2,147. **Student Body:** 70% female, 30% male, 26.5% out-of-state, 1% international (20 countries represented). Asian 2%, African American 1%, Caucasian 86%, Hispanic 3%.
Retention and Graduation: 55% freshmen graduate within 4 years. 35% grads go on to further study within 1 year. **Faculty:** Student/faculty ratio 12.8:1. 142 full-time faculty, 85% hold PhDs, 5% are members of minority groups, 56% are women.

ACADEMICS
Degrees: Bachelor's, master's, post-bachelor's certificate, post-master's certificate. **Classes:** Most classes have 10–19 students. **Majors with Highest Enrollment:** Elementary education and teaching; nursing/registered nurse (RN, ASN, BSN, MSN); psychology. **Special Study Options:** Cross-registration, double major, dual enrollment, English as a Second Language (ESL), honors program, independent study, internships, student-designed major, study abroad, teacher certification program. **Honors programs:** Open Door Honors program Special programs offered to physically disabled students include note-taking services, reader services, tape recorders, tutors. **Career services:** Alumni services, career/job search classes, career assessment, internships, regional alumni.

FACILITIES
Housing: Coed dorms, special housing for disabled students, men's dorms, women's dorms, apartments for single students, 100% of campus accessible to physically disabled. **Special Academic Facilities/Equipment:** Mellow Athletic and Fitness Center, Mahady Gallery, Suraci Gallery, The Maslow Study Gallery for Contemporary Art, Performing Arts Center, O'Neill Center for Healthy Families, Insalaco Studio Arts Center, Center for Architectural Studies, Marywood University Arboretum, Curriculum Lab, electronic learning labs, Broadcast Studios, instructional media lab, interactive video lab, computerized editing facility, center for natural and health sciences, psycho-physiology experimental lab, psychology/education research lab, science multi-media lab, language lab, center for justice and peace, on-campus preschool and day care, video tele-conferencing lab. **Computers:** 75% of classrooms, 75% of dorms, 100% of libraries, 100% of dining areas, 100% of student union, 75% of common outdoor areas have wireless network access. Students can register for classes online. Administrative functions (other than registration) can be performed online.

CAMPUS LIFE
Environment: City. **Activities:** Choral groups, concert band, dance, drama/theater, jazz band, literary magazine, music ensembles, musical theater, radio station, student government, student newspaper, television station, campus ministries, international student organization. **Organizations:** 43 registered

organizations, 31 honor societies, 1 religious organizations. 1 sorority. **Athletics (Intercollegiate):** *Men:* Baseball, basketball, cross-country, diving, lacrosse, soccer, swimming, tennis. *Women:* Basketball, cross-country, diving, field hockey, lacrosse, soccer, softball, swimming, tennis, volleyball. **On-Campus Highlights:** Mellow Center for Athletics and Wellness, Insalaco Center for Studio Arts, Liberal Arts Center Rotunda, Cafe Ritazza/Main Dining Room, Nazareth Student Center. **Environmental Initiatives:** Wind energy; daylight harvesting; increase in recycling efforts (5%).

ADMISSIONS
Freshman Academic Profile: Average high school GPA 3.19. 22.4% in top 10% of high school class, 56.3% in top 25% of high school class, 83.8% in top 50% of high school class. 78% from public high schools. SAT Math middle 50% range 480–570. SAT Critical Reading middle 50% range 480–570. SAT Writing middle 50% range 470–570. ACT middle 50% range 20–23. Minimum paper TOEFL 530. Minimum computer TOEFL 197. Minimum web-based TOEFL 71. **Basis for Candidate Selection:** *Very important factors considered include:* Class rank, academic GPA, rigor of secondary school record, standardized test scores, character/personal qualities. *Important factors considered include:* Application essay, recommendation(s), interview, talent/ability. *Other factors considered include:* Extracurricular activities, level of applicant's interest, volunteer work. **Freshman Admission Requirements:** High school diploma is required and GED is accepted. *Academic units required:* 4 English, 2 mathematics, 1 science, (1 science labs), 3 social studies, 6 academic electives. **Freshman Admission Statistics:** 1,923 applied, 72% admitted, 34% enrolled. **Transfer Admission Requirements:** High school transcript, college transcript(s), minimum college GPA of 2.25 required. Lowest grade transferable C. **General Admission Information:** Application fee $35. Notification on a rolling basis, beginning on or about 10/1. Nonfall registration accepted. Credit and/or placement offered for CEEB Advanced Placement tests.

COSTS AND FINANCIAL AID
Annual tuition $25,150. Room and board $11,498. Required fees $1,120. Average book expense $900. **Required Forms and Deadlines:** FAFSA. Priority financial aid filing date 2/15. **Notification of Awards:** Applicants will be notified of awards on a rolling basis beginning 2/15. **Types of Aid:** *Need-based scholarships/grants:* Federal Pell, SEOG, state scholarships/grants, private scholarships, the school's own gift aid, Federal Nursing Scholarships. *Loans:* FFEL Subsidized Stafford, FFEL Unsubsidized Stafford, FFEL PLUS, Federal Perkins, state loans, Private alternative loans. **Student Employment:** Federal Work-Study Program available. **Financial Aid Statistics:** 98% freshmen, 98% undergrads receive any aid. **Criteria for awarding institutional aid:** *Non-need-based:* Academics, art, leadership, music/drama, state/district residency.

MASSACHUSETTS COLLEGE OF ART AND DESIGN

621 Huntington Avenue, Boston, MA 02115
Phone: 617-879-7222 **Financial Aid Phone:** 617.879.7850
E-mail: admissions@massart.edu **CEEB Code:** 3516
Fax: 617-879-7250 **Website:** **ACT Code:** 1846

This public school was founded in 1873. It has a 5-acre campus.

RATINGS
Admissions Selectivity Rating: 84   **Fire Safety Rating:** 60*   **Green Rating:** 75

STUDENTS AND FACULTY
Enrollment: 1,772. **Student Body:** 67% female, 33% male, 29% out-of-state, 2% international. Asian 6%, African American 3%, Caucasian 70%, Hispanic 5%, Native American 1%.
Retention and Graduation: 88% freshmen return for sophomore year. 10% grads go on to further study within 1 year. 10% grads pursue arts and sciences degrees. **Faculty:** Student/faculty ratio 13:1. 101 full-time faculty, 78% hold PhDs, 13% are members of minority groups, 54% are women.

ACADEMICS
Degrees: Bachelor's, certificate, master's, post-bachelor's certificate. **Classes:** Most classes have 10–19 students. **Majors with Highest Enrollment:** Graphic design; illustration; painting. **Special Study Options:** cross-registration, double major, exchange student program (domestic), independent study, internships, liberal arts/career combination, student-designed major, study abroad, teacher certification program Special programs offered to physically disabled students include note-taking services, reader services, tutors. **Career services:** Alumni network, alumni services, career/job search classes, career assessment, internships.

FACILITIES

Housing: Coed dorms, apartments for single students, Off campus housing assistance from school. Additional housing available in Simmons College dorms. 95% of campus accessible to physically disabled. **Special Academic Facilities/Equipment:** Ten art galleries, foundry, glass furnaces, ceramic kilns, video and film studios, performance spaces, Polaroid 20x24 camera, individual studio spaces, design research unit, printmaking facilities, video and photography equipment and facilities, specialized computer labs, specialized equipment and facilities for all art and design programs and levels. **Computers:** 100% of classrooms, 100% of dorms, 100% of libraries, 100% of dining areas, 100% of student union, 100% of common outdoor areas have wireless network access. Students can register for classes online. Administrative functions (other than registration) can be performed online.

CAMPUS LIFE

Environment: Metropolis. **Activities:** Dance, drama/theater, music ensembles, radio station, student government, student newspaper, student-run film society, television station, yearbook. **Organizations:** 30 registered organizations, 1 honor societies, 3 religious organizations. **Athletics (Intercollegiate):** *Men:* Baseball, basketball, cross-country, golf, lacrosse, soccer, softball, tennis, volleyball. *Women:* Basketball, cross-country, golf, lacrosse, soccer, softball, tennis, volleyball. **On-Campus Highlights:** 10 art galleries, student studios, courtyard, cafes, student center, see http://inside.massart.edu/x942.xml for a description of student activites. **Environmental Initiatives:** MassArt is a leader in sustainability accomplishments. In 2008 MassArt won the Massachusetts Leading By Example(LBE) Award. See http://inside.massart.edu/Offices_and_Services/Facilities/Sustainability.html for more about MassArt's sustainability commitment.

ADMISSIONS

Freshman Academic Profile: Average high school GPA 3.32. 18% in top 10% of high school class, 51% in top 25% of high school class, 85% in top 50% of high school class. SAT Math middle 50% range 490–590. SAT Critical Reading middle 50% range 510–610. SAT Writing middle 50% range 500–500. Minimum paper TOEFL 530. Minimum computer TOEFL 213. Minimum web-based TOEFL 85. **Basis for Candidate Selection:** *Very important factors considered include:* Application essay, academic GPA, rigor of secondary school record, talent/ability. *Important factors considered include:* standardized test scores, state residency. *Other factors considered include:* Class rank, recommendation(s), character/personal qualities, extracurricular activities, geographical residence, volunteer work, work experience. **Freshman Admission Requirements:** High school diploma is required and GED is accepted. *Academic units required:* 4 English, 2 mathematics, 2 science, (2 science labs), 2 foreign language, 2 social studies, 2 academic electives, 2 Art electives *Academic units recommended:* 1 history. **Freshman Admission Statistics:** 1,631 applied, 51% admitted, 38% enrolled. **Transfer Admission Requirements:** College transcript(s), essay or personal statement, statement of good standing from prior institution(s). Minimum college GPA of 2.5 required. Lowest grade transferable C. **General Admission Information:** Application fee $65. Regular application deadline 2/1. Notification on a rolling basis, beginning on or about 2/1. Nonfall registration not accepted. Admission may be deferred for a maximum of 1 year. Credit and/or placement offered for CEEB Advanced Placement tests.

COSTS AND FINANCIAL AID

Annual in-state tuition $8,400. Annual out-of-state tuition $24,400. Room and board $11,288. Average book expense $2,100. **Required Forms and Deadlines:** FAFSA. Priority financial aid filing date 2/1. **Notification of Awards:** Applicants will be notified of awards on or about 2/1. **Types of Aid:** *Need-based scholarships/grants:* Federal Pell, SEOG, state scholarships/grants, private scholarships, the school's own gift aid. *Loans:* Direct Subsidized Stafford, Direct Unsubsidized Stafford, Direct PLUS, FFEL Subsidized Stafford, FFEL Unsubsidized Stafford, FFEL PLUS, Federal Perkins, state loans, college/university loans from institutional funds, alternative loans (credit Based). **Student Employment:** Federal Work-Study Program available. Institutional employment available. Highest amount earned per year from on-campus jobs $800. Off-campus job opportunities are good. **Financial Aid Statistics:** 35% freshmen, 37% undergrads receive need-based scholarship or grant aid. 17% freshmen, 8% undergrads receive non-need-based scholarship or grant aid. 61% freshmen, 57% undergrads receive need-based self-help aid. **Criteria for awarding institutional aid:** *Non-need-based:* Academics, art, leadership.

MASSACHUSETTS COLLEGE OF PHARMACY AND HEALTH SCIENCE

Office of Admissions, 179 Longwood Avenue, Boston, MA 02115
Phone: 617-732-2850 **Financial Aid Phone:** 617-732-2864
E-mail: admissions@mcphs.edu **CEEB Code:** 3512
Fax: 617-732-2118 **Website:** www.mcphs.edu **ACT Code:** 1860

This private school was founded in 1823. It has a 3-acre campus.

RATINGS
Admissions Selectivity Rating: 83   **Fire Safety Rating:** 97   **Green Rating:** 60*

STUDENTS AND FACULTY

Enrollment: 2,883. **Student Body:** 68% female, 32% male, 43.1% out-of-state, 3% international (32 countries represented). Asian 28%, African American 5%, Caucasian 53%, Hispanic 3%.
Retention and Graduation: 83% freshmen return for sophomore year. 59% freshmen graduate within 4 years. **Faculty:** Student/faculty ratio 18:1. 206 full-time faculty, 85% hold PhDs, 65% are women.

ACADEMICS

Degrees: Bachelor's, certificate, master's, post-bachelor's certificate. **Classes:** Most classes have 20–29 students. Most lab/discussion sessions have 10–19 students. **Majors with Highest Enrollment:** nursing/registered nurse (RN, ASN, BSN, MSN); pharmacy (PharmD [US], PharmD or BS/BPharm [Canada]); pre-medicine/pre-medical studies. **Special Study Options:** Accelerated program, cross-registration, distance learning, double major, independent study, internships, study abroad **Combined degree programs:** BS/MS Pharmaceutical Chemistry. Special programs offered to physically disabled students include note-taking services, reader services, tape recorders, tutors. **Career services:** Alumni network, alumni services, regional alumni. **Career services highlights include:** Students in most majors have "rotations" in hospitals, pharmacies, clinics.

FACILITIES

Housing: Coed dorms, wellness housing, separate all-women floors. 100% of campus accessible to physically disabled. **Special Academic Facilities/Equipment:** Museum of Fine Arts and Isabella Stewart Gardner museum next door. **Computers:** 100% of classrooms, 100% of dorms, 100% of libraries, 100% of dining areas, 100% of student union, 100% of common outdoor areas have wireless network access. Students can register for classes online. Administrative functions (other than registration) can be performed online.

CAMPUS LIFE

Environment: Metropolis. **Activities:** Choral groups, concert band, dance, drama/theater, literary magazine, music ensembles, musical theater, student government, student newspaper, yearbook, international student organization. **Organizations:** 66 registered organizations, 5 honor societies, 2 religious organizations. **On-Campus Highlights:** New building residence hall, labs, pharmacy laboratory, dental hygiene clinic, cafeteria (located in Mass. College of Art), student lounge. In addition to the Boston campus, there are campuses in Worcester and Manchester, New Hampshire, with expanding program offerings.

ADMISSIONS

Freshman Academic Profile: Average high school GPA 3.46. SAT Math middle 50% range 520–620. SAT Critical Reading middle 50% range 480–570. SAT Writing middle 50% range 490–590. ACT middle 50% range 21–26. Minimum paper TOEFL 550. Minimum computer TOEFL 213. Minimum web-based TOEFL 79. **Basis for Candidate Selection:** *Very important factors considered include:* Academic GPA, rigor of secondary school record, standardized test scores. *Other factors considered include:* Class rank, application essay, recommendation(s), alumni/ae relation, character/personal qualities, extracurricular activities, first generation, level of applicant's interest, talent/ability, volunteer work, work experience. **Freshman Admission Requirements:** High school diploma is required and GED is accepted. *Academic units required:* 4 English, 3 mathematics, 2 science, (2 science labs), 1 social studies, 5 academic electives. **Freshman Admission Statistics:** 3,011 applied, 55% admitted, 42% enrolled. **Transfer Admission Requirements:** College transcript(s), essay or personal statement, minimum college GPA of 2.5 required. Lowest grade transferable C. **General Admission Information:** Application fee $70. Regular notification 2/15. Nonfall registration not accepted. Admission may be deferred for a maximum of 1 year. Credit and/or placement offered for CEEB Advanced Placement tests.

COSTS AND FINANCIAL AID

Annual tuition $23,800. Room and board $11,900. Required fees $750. Average book expense $850. **Required Forms and Deadlines:** FAFSA. Priority financial aid filing date 3/15. **Notification of Awards:** Applicants will be notified of awards on a rolling basis beginning 2/1. **Types of Aid:** *Need-based scholarships/ grants:* Federal Pell, SEOG, state scholarships/grants, private scholarships, the school's own gift aid. *Loans:* Direct Subsidized Stafford, Direct Unsubsidized Stafford, Direct PLUS, FFEL Subsidized Stafford, FFEL Unsubsidized Stafford, FFEL PLUS, Federal Perkins, Health Professions Loans. **Student Employment:** Federal Work-Study Program available. Off-campus job opportunities are excellent. **Financial Aid Statistics:** 72% freshmen, 66% undergrads receive need-based scholarship or grant aid. 79% freshmen, 78% undergrads receive need-based self-help aid. 90% freshmen, 90% undergrads receive any aid. **Criteria for awarding institutional aid:** *Non-need-based:* Academics.

MASSACHUSETTS INSTITUTE OF TECHNOLOGY

77 Massachusetts Avenue, Room 3-108, Cambridge, MA 02139
Phone: 617-253-3400 **Financial Aid Phone:** 617-253-4971
E-mail: admissions@mit.edu **CEEB Code:** 3514
Fax: 617-258-8304 **Website:** web.mit.edu **ACT Code:** 1858

This private school was founded in 1861. It has a 168-acre campus.

RATINGS
Admissions Selectivity Rating: 99   **Fire Safety Rating:** 75   **Green Rating:** 90

STUDENTS AND FACULTY
Enrollment: 4,218. **Student Body:** 45% female, 55% male, 91% out-of-state, 9% international (93 countries represented). Asian 26%, African American 8%, Caucasian 36%, Hispanic 13%, Native American 1%.
Retention and Graduation: 97% freshmen return for sophomore year. 83% freshmen graduate within 4 years. 45% grads go on to further study within 1 year. 11% grads pursue arts and sciences degrees. 1% grads pursue law degrees. 1% grads pursue business degrees. 6% grads pursue medical degrees. **Faculty:** Student/faculty ratio 6.8:1. 1326 full-time faculty, 90% hold PhDs, 15% are members of minority groups, 22% are women.

ACADEMICS
Degrees: Bachelor's, master's. **Classes:** Most classes have fewer than 10 students. Most lab/discussion sessions have 10–19 students. **Majors with Highest Enrollment:** Business/commerce; computer science; mechanical engineering. **Special Study Options:** Cooperative education program, cross-registration, double major, internships, study abroad, teacher certification program, Undergraduate Research Opportunities Program (UROP); Independent Activities Period (IAP); freshman learning communities. **Combined degree programs:** Two bachelor's, SB/SM, SB/MEng, SB/MCP. Special programs offered to physically disabled students include note-taking services, reader services, tape recorders **Career services:** Alumni network, alumni services, career/job search classes, career assessment, internships, regional alumni. **Career services highlights include:** We have a very strong on-campus recruiting system, with over 397 employers who came to our Careers Office to interview students.

FACILITIES
Housing: Coed dorms, special housing for disabled students, women's dorms, fraternity/sorority housing, apartments for married students, cooperative housing, apartments for single students, theme housing, independent living group housing, apartments for students with dependent children, and living learning communities available. **Special Academic Facilities/Equipment:** List Visual Arts Center; MIT Museum; Ray and Maria Stata Center for Computer, Information and Intelligence Sciences; numerous labs and centers. **Computers:** 100% of classrooms, 100% of dorms, 100% of libraries, 100% of dining areas, 100% of student union, 80–98% of common outdoor areas have wireless network access. Administrative functions (other than registration) can be performed online.

CAMPUS LIFE
Environment: City. **Activities:** Choral groups, concert band, dance, drama/ theater, jazz band, literary magazine, marching band, music ensembles, musical theater, radio station, student government, student newspaper, student-run film society, symphony orchestra, television station, yearbook, campus ministries, international student organization, Model UN. **Organizations:** 400 registered organizations, 10 honor societies, 29 religious organizations, 27 fraternities, 6 sororities. **Athletics (Intercollegiate):** *Men:* Baseball, basketball, crew/rowing, cross-country, diving, fencing, football, golf, gymnastics, lacrosse, pistol, riflery,

sailing, skiing (downhill/alpine), skiing (nordic & cross-country), soccer, squash, swimming, tennis, track/field (outdoor), track/field (indoor). *Women:* Basketball, crew/rowing, cross-country, diving, fencing, field hockey, gymnastics, ice hockey, lacrosse, pistol, riflery, sailing, skiing (downhill/alpine), skiing (nordic & cross-country), soccer, softball, swimming, tennis, track/field (outdoor), track/field (indoor). **On-Campus Highlights:** Ray and Maria Stata Center, Zesiger Sports and Fitness Center, Killian Court, The Infinite Corridor, The Student Center (W20), Stata Center is a 720,000 square foot building designed by Frank Gehry. Zesiger Sports and Fitness Center is our state-of-the-art athletics facility. At 778.8 feet, the Infinite Corridor is reputed to be the longest straight hallway in the world—it connects many of the buildings on central campus and runs though two popular gathering spots: Lobbies 7 and 10. **Environmental Initiatives:** Campus energy management (co-generation, conservation, efficiency, renewables); recycling (40% recycling rate); green building (LEED) for new and existing buildings.

ADMISSIONS
Freshman Academic Profile: 95% in top 10% of high school class, 100% in top 25% of high school class, 100% in top 50% of high school class. 66% from public high schools. SAT Math middle 50% range 720–800. SAT Critical Reading middle 50% range 650–760. SAT Writing middle 50% range 660–760. ACT middle 50% range 32–35. Minimum paper TOEFL 577. Minimum computer TOEFL 233. Minimum web-based TOEFL 90. **Basis for Candidate Selection:** *Very important factors considered include:* Character/personal qualities. *Important factors considered include:* Class rank, academic GPA, recommendation(s), rigor of secondary school record, standardized test scores, extracurricular activities, interview, talent/ability. *Other factors considered include:* Application essay, alumni/ae relation, first generation, geographical residence, racial/ethnic status, volunteer work, work experience. **Freshman Admission Requirements:** High school diploma or equivalent is not required. *Academic units recommended:* 4 English, 4 mathematics, 4 science, 2 foreign language, 2 social studies. **Freshman Admission Statistics:** 15,663 applied, 11% admitted, 64% enrolled. **Transfer Admission Requirements:** High school transcript, college transcript(s), essay or personal statement, standardized test scores, statement of good standing from prior institution(s). Lowest grade transferable B. **General Admission Information:** Application fee $75. Regular application deadline 1/1. Regular notification 3/20. Nonfall registration not accepted. Admission may be deferred for a maximum of 2 years. Credit and/or placement offered for CEEB Advanced Placement tests.

COSTS AND FINANCIAL AID
Required Forms and Deadlines: FAFSA, CSS/Financial Aid PROFILE, noncustodial PROFILE, business/farm supplement. Parent's complete federal income tax returns from prior year and W2s. Financial aid filing deadline 2/15. Priority financial aid filing date 2/15. **Notification of Awards:** Applicants will be notified of awards on or about 4/1. **Types of Aid:** *Need-based scholarships/ grants:* Federal Pell, SEOG, state scholarships/grants, private scholarships, the school's own gift aid. *Loans:* Direct Subsidized Stafford, Direct Unsubsidized Stafford, Direct PLUS, Federal Perkins, college/university loans from institutional funds. **Student Employment:** Federal Work-Study Program available. Institutional employment available. Highest amount earned per year from on-campus jobs $25,990. Off-campus job opportunities are excellent. **Financial Aid Statistics:** 63% freshmen, 60% undergrads receive need-based scholarship or grant aid. 3% freshmen, 2% undergrads receive non-need-based scholarship or grant aid. 40% freshmen, 43% undergrads receive need-based self-help aid. 82% freshmen, 80% undergrads receive any aid. 45% undergrads borrow to pay for school. Average cumulative indebtedness $15,043.

MASSACHUSETTS MARITIME ACADEMY

101 Academy Drive, Buzzards Bay, MA 02532
Phone: 800-544-3411
E-mail: admissions@maritime.edu
Fax: 508-830-5077 **Website:** www.maritime.edu

This public school was founded in 1891. It has a 55-acre campus.

RATINGS
Admissions Selectivity Rating: 63   **Fire Safety Rating:** 60*   **Green Rating:** 60*

STUDENTS AND FACULTY
Enrollment: 923. **Student Body:** 12% female, 88% male, 28% out-of-state, (6 countries represented).
Retention and Graduation: 30% grads go on to further study within 1 year. 10% grads pursue arts and sciences degrees. 4% grads pursue law degrees. 15% grads pursue business degrees. 1% grads pursue medical degrees. **Faculty:** Student/faculty ratio 15:1.

ACADEMICS

Degrees: Bachelor's, first professional certificate, master's. **Majors with Highest Enrollment:** Environmental science; environmental/environmental health engineering; ocean engineering. **Special Study Options:** Cooperative education program, double major, internships, Semester-at-Sea. **Career services:** Alumni network, alumni services, career/job search classes, internships.

FACILITIES

Housing: Coed dorms. 80% of campus accessible to physically disabled. **Special Academic Facilities/Equipment:** Maritime Ship Model Museum Training Ship Enterprise. **Computers:** Undergraduates are required to own a computer.

CAMPUS LIFE

Environment: Village. **Activities:** Drama/theater, jazz band, marching band, music ensembles, student government, student newspaper, yearbook. **Organizations:** 12 registered organizations, 1 honor societies, 1 religious organizations. **Athletics (Intercollegiate):** *Men:* Baseball, crew/rowing, cross-country, football, lacrosse, riflery, rugby, sailing, soccer. *Women:* crew/rowing, cross-country, riflery, rugby, sailing, softball, volleyball.

ADMISSIONS

Freshman Academic Profile: Average high school GPA 2.8. 65% from public high schools. Minimum paper TOEFL 500. **Basis for Candidate Selection:** *Very important factors considered include:* Rigor of secondary school record, standardized test scores. *Important factors considered include:* Application essay, character/personal qualities. *Other factors considered include:* Recommendation(s), alumni/ae relation, extracurricular activities, interview, talent/ability, volunteer work, work experience. **Freshman Admission Requirements:** High school diploma is required and GED is accepted. *Academic units required:* 4 English, 3 mathematics, 3 science, (2 science labs), 2 foreign language, 2 history, 2 academic electives. **Freshman Admission Statistics:** 808 applied, 60% admitted, 56% enrolled. **Transfer Admission Requirements:** High school transcript, college transcript(s), essay or personal statement, minimum college GPA of 2.0 required. Lowest grade transferable C. **General Admission Information:** Application fee $50. Notification on a rolling basis, beginning on or about 12/15. Nonfall registration not accepted. Admission may be deferred for a maximum of 1. Credit and/or placement offered for CEEB Advanced Placement tests.

COSTS AND FINANCIAL AID

Annual in-state tuition $9,165. Annual out-of-state tuition $19,500. Room and board $5,500. Required fees $2,600. Average book expense $700. **Required Forms and Deadlines:** FAFSA, institution's own financial aid form. Priority financial aid filing date 4/30. **Notification of Awards:** Applicants will be notified of awards on a rolling basis beginning 3/1. **Types of Aid:** *Need-based scholarships/grants:* Federal Pell, SEOG, state scholarships/grants, private scholarships, the school's own gift aid. *Loans:* Direct Subsidized Stafford, Direct Unsubsidized Stafford, Direct PLUS. **Student Employment:** Federal Work-Study Program available. Highest amount earned per year from on-campus jobs $650. Off-campus job opportunities are good. **Financial Aid Statistics:** 8% freshmen, 8% undergrads receive need-based scholarship or grant aid. 5% freshmen, 16% undergrads receive non-need-based scholarship or grant aid. 35% freshmen, 26% undergrads receive need-based self-help aid. 82% undergrads borrow to pay for school. Average cumulative indebtedness $12,125. **Criteria for awarding institutional aid:** *Non-need-based:* Academics, leadership.

THE MASTER'S COLLEGE AND SEMINARY

21726 Placerita Canyon Road, Santa Clarita, CA 91321
Phone: 661-259-3540 **Financial Aid Phone:** 661-259-3540
E-mail: admissions@masters.edu **CEEB Code:** 4411
Fax: 661-288-1037 **Website:** www.masters.edu **ACT Code:** 303

This private school was founded in 1927. It has a 95-acre campus.

RATINGS

Admissions Selectivity Rating: 88 **Fire Safety Rating:** 84 **Green Rating:** 60*

STUDENTS AND FACULTY

Enrollment: 1,039. **Student Body:** 51% female, 49% male, 26% out-of-state, 4% international (36 countries represented). Asian 5%, African American 2%, Caucasian 67%, Hispanic 6%, Native American 1%. **Retention and Graduation:** 78% freshmen return for sophomore year. 48% freshmen graduate within 4 years. **Faculty:** Student/faculty ratio 10:1. 70 full-time faculty, 76% hold PhDs, 10% are members of minority groups, 13% are women.

ACADEMICS

Degrees: Bachelor's, certificate, first professional, first professional certificate, master's. **Classes:** Most classes have fewer than 10 students. **Majors with Highest Enrollment:** Bible/biblical studies; business/commerce; elementary education and teaching. **Special Study Options:** Accelerated program, cooperative education program, distance learning, double major, independent study, internships, liberal arts/career combination, study abroad, teacher certification program, Israel semester. Special programs offered to physically disabled students include note-taking services, reader services, tape recorders, tutors. **Career services:** Alumni network, alumni services, career/job search classes, career assessment, internships.

FACILITIES

Housing: Men's dorms, special housing for international students, women's dorms, wellness housing. 95% of campus accessible to physically disabled. **Computers:** 100% of classrooms, 100% of dorms, 100% of libraries, 100% of dining areas, 100% of student union, 95% of common outdoor areas have wireless network access. Students can register for classes online. Administrative functions (other than registration) can be performed online. Undergraduates are required to own a computer.

CAMPUS LIFE

Environment: City. **Activities:** Choral groups, concert band, drama/theater, jazz band, music ensembles, opera, pep band, student government, symphony orchestra **Organizations:** 15 registered organizations, 1 honor societies, 11 religious organizations. **Athletics (Intercollegiate):** *Men:* Baseball, basketball, cross-country, golf, soccer, track/field (outdoor). *Women:* Basketball, cross-country, soccer, tennis, track/field (outdoor), volleyball. **On-Campus Highlights:** New All-Weather Field (2005), Dining Center Remodeled (2005), Music Center, Smith Hall Dormitory, Canyon Cafe.

ADMISSIONS

Freshman Academic Profile: Average high school GPA 3.65. 33% in top 10% of high school class, 61% in top 25% of high school class, 86% in top 50% of high school class. 52% from public high schools. SAT Math middle 50% range 480–610. SAT Critical Reading middle 50% range 480–630. ACT middle 50% range 22–27. Minimum paper TOEFL 525. Minimum computer TOEFL 197. **Basis for Candidate Selection:** *Very important factors considered include:* Application essay, academic GPA, recommendation(s), rigor of secondary school record, standardized test scores, character/personal qualities, interview, religious affiliation/commitment. *Other factors considered include:* Alumni/ae relation, extracurricular activities, level of applicant's interest, talent/ability. **Freshman Admission Requirements:** High school diploma is required and GED is accepted. *Academic units required:* 4 English, 3 mathematics, 2 science, 2 history. *Academic units recommended:* 3 academic electives. **Freshman Admission Statistics:** 387 applied, 51% admitted, 97% enrolled. **Transfer Admission Requirements:** High school transcript, college transcript(s), essay or personal statement, interview, statement of good standing from prior institution(s). Minimum college GPA of 2.5 required. Lowest grade transferable C. **General Admission Information:** Application fee $40. Notification on a rolling basis, beginning on or about 3/15. Nonfall registration accepted. Admission may be deferred for a maximum of 2 semesters. Credit and/or placement offered for CEEB Advanced Placement tests.

COSTS AND FINANCIAL AID

Annual tuition $24,280. Room and board $8,000. Average book expense $1,638. **Required Forms and Deadlines:** FAFSA, institution's own financial aid form, state aid form. Priority financial aid filing date 3/2. **Notification of Awards:** Applicants will be notified of awards on a rolling basis beginning 2/18. **Types of Aid:** *Need-based scholarships/grants:* Federal Pell, SEOG, state scholarships/grants, private scholarships, the school's own gift aid. *Loans:* FFEL Subsidized Stafford, FFEL Unsubsidized Stafford, FFEL PLUS, Federal Perkins, Alternative private loans. **Student Employment:** Federal Work-Study Program available. Institutional employment available. Highest amount earned per year from on-campus jobs $5,000. Off-campus job opportunities are excellent. **Financial Aid Statistics:** 77% freshmen, 84% undergrads receive need-based scholarship or grant aid. 5% freshmen, 9% undergrads receive non-need-based scholarship or grant aid. 73% freshmen, 76% undergrads receive need-based self-help aid. 6% freshmen, 3% undergrads receive athletic scholarships. 71% freshmen, 72% undergrads receive any aid. 45.6% undergrads borrow to pay for school. Average cumulative indebtedness $18,994. **Criteria for awarding institutional aid:** *Non-need-based:* Academics, alumni affiliation, art, athletics, leadership, music/drama.

MAYVILLE STATE UNIVERSITY

330 Third Street Northeast, Mayville, ND 58257-1299
Phone: 701-788-4842 **Financial Aid Phone:** 701-788-4767
E-mail: admit@mayvillestate.edu **CEEB Code:** 6478
Fax: 701-788-4748 **Website:** www.mayvillestate.edu **ACT Code:** 3212

This public school was founded in 1889. It has a 55-acre campus.

RATINGS
Admissions Selectivity Rating: 82　　**Fire Safety Rating:** 61　　**Green Rating:** 60*

STUDENTS AND FACULTY
Enrollment: 789. **Student Body:** 62% female, 38% male, 32% out-of-state, 3% international (3 countries represented). Asian 1%, African American 5%, Caucasian 85%, Hispanic 2%, Native American 3%.
Retention and Graduation: 60% freshmen return for sophomore year. 24% freshmen graduate within 4 years. 6% grads go on to further study within 1 year. 3% grads pursue arts and sciences degrees. 1% grads pursue law degrees. 1% grads pursue business degrees. 1% grads pursue medical degrees. **Faculty:** Student/faculty ratio 12:1. 36 full-time faculty, 47% hold PhDs, 3% are members of minority groups, 36% are women.

ACADEMICS
Degrees: Bachelor's, transfer associate. **Classes:** Most classes have 10–19 students. **Majors with Highest Enrollment:** Business/commerce; elementary education and teaching; P.E. teaching and coaching. **Special Study Options:** Accelerated program, cooperative education program, distance learning, double major, dual enrollment, independent study, internships, student-designed major, teacher certification program Special programs offered to physically disabled students include note-taking services, tape recorders, tutors. **Career services:** Alumni network, alumni services, career/job search classes, career assessment, internships, regional alumni. **Career services highlights include:** The internship program provides opportunities for students to have related work experience with a variety of local, regional and national employers.

FACILITIES
Housing: men's dorms, women's dorms, apartments for married students, apartments for single students 80% of campus accessible to physically disabled. **Special Academic Facilities/Equipment:** Art gallery available in the Campus Center. **Computers:** 100% of classrooms, 25% of dorms, 100% of libraries, 100% of dining areas, 100% of student union, 25% of common outdoor areas have wireless network access. Students can register for classes online. Administrative functions (other than registration) can be performed online. Undergraduates are required to own a computer.

CAMPUS LIFE
Environment: Rural. **Activities:** Choral groups, concert band, drama/theater, jazz band, music ensembles, musical theater, radio station, student government, student newspaper. **Organizations:** 118 registered organizations, 1 honor societies, 2 religious organizations. **Athletics (Intercollegiate):** *Men:* Baseball, basketball, football. *Women:* Basketball, softball, volleyball. **On-Campus Highlights:** Lewy Lee Fieldhouse, Campus Center, Residence Halls, Library, West Hall.

ADMISSIONS
Freshman Academic Profile: Average high school GPA 3.2. 47% in top 25% of high school class, 76% in top 50% of high school class. 91% from public high schools. ACT middle 50% range 177–23. Minimum paper TOEFL 525. Minimum computer TOEFL 195. Minimum web-based TOEFL 70. **Basis for Candidate Selection:** *Very important factors considered include:* Academic GPA. *Important factors considered include:* Rigor of secondary school record, standardized test scores. *Other factors considered include:* Character/personal qualities, interview. **Freshman Admission Requirements:** High school diploma is required and GED is accepted. *Academic units required:* 4 English, 3 mathematics, 3 science, (3 science labs), 3 social studies. *Academic units recommended:* 2 foreign language. **Freshman Admission Statistics:** 204 applied, 87% admitted, 51% enrolled. **Transfer Admission Requirements:** College transcript(s), statement of good standing from prior institution(s). Minimum college GPA of 2.0 required. Lowest grade transferable D. **General Admission Information:** Application fee $35. Notification on a rolling basis, beginning on or about 1/1. Nonfall registration accepted. Admission may be deferred for a maximum of NA. Credit and/or placement offered for CEEB Advanced Placement tests.

COSTS AND FINANCIAL AID
Annual in-state tuition $4,124. Annual out-of-state tuition $6,180. Room and board $4,488. Required fees $1,669. Average book expense $900. **Required Forms and Deadlines:** FAFSA. Priority financial aid filing date 2/15. **Notification of Awards:** Applicants will be notified of awards on a rolling basis

beginning 5/1. **Types of Aid:** *Need-based scholarships/grants:* Federal Pell, SEOG, state scholarships/grants, private scholarships, the school's own gift aid. *Loans:* FFEL Subsidized Stafford, FFEL Unsubsidized Stafford, FFEL PLUS, Federal Perkins. **Student Employment:** Federal Work-Study Program available. Institutional employment available. Highest amount earned per year from on-campus jobs $1,500. Off-campus job opportunities are fair. **Financial Aid Statistics:** 79% freshmen, 64% undergrads receive need-based scholarship or grant aid. 5% freshmen, 1% undergrads receive non-need-based scholarship or grant aid. 84% freshmen, 78% undergrads receive need-based self-help aid. 22% freshmen, 21% undergrads receive athletic scholarships. 80% freshmen, 89% undergrads receive any aid. 84% undergrads borrow to pay for school. Average cumulative indebtedness $19,338. **Criteria for awarding institutional aid:** *Non-need-based:* Academics, athletics, leadership, minority status, music/drama, state/district residency.

MCGILL UNIVERSITY

845 Sherbrooke Street West, James Administration Building, Room 205, Montreal, QC H3A 2T5 Canada
Phone: 514-398-3910 **Financial Aid Phone:** 514-398-6013
E-mail: admissions@mcgill.ca **CEEB Code:** 935
Fax: 514-398-4193 **Website:** www.mcgill.ca **ACT Code:** 5231

This public school was founded in 1821. It has a 80-acre campus.

RATINGS
Admissions Selectivity Rating: 88　　**Fire Safety Rating:** 65　　**Green Rating:** 83

STUDENTS AND FACULTY
Enrollment: 20,831. **Student Body:** 59% female, 41% male, 37% out-of-state, 17% international (136 countries represented).
Retention and Graduation: 93% freshmen return for sophomore year. 67% freshmen graduate within 4 years. **Faculty:** Student/faculty ratio 16:1. 1689 full-time faculty, 95% hold PhDs, 29% are women.

ACADEMICS
Degrees: Bachelor's, certificate, diploma, first professional, master's, post-bachelor's certificate. **Classes:** Most classes have 10–19 students. Most lab/discussion sessions have 20–29 students. **Majors with Highest Enrollment:** Business/commerce; political science and government; psychology. **Special Study Options:** Accelerated program, cooperative education program, cross-registration, distance learning, double major, English as a Second Language (ESL), exchange student program (domestic), honors program, independent study, internships, study abroad, teacher certification program. **Honors programs:** McGill's Faculties of Arts, Science, and Engineering, the Desautels Faculty of Management, and the McGill School of Environment offer many outstanding honours and joint honours programs. Honours programs offer specialization and research in one academic discipline while joint honours programs offer specialization and research in a combination of disciplines. **Combined degree programs:** BSc/BEd; BMus/BEd; BCL/LLB; MSW/Law; MDCM/MBA; MDCM/PhD. Special programs offered to physically disabled students include note-taking services, reader services, tape recorders, tutors. **Career services:** Career/job search classes, career assessment. **Career services highlights include:** Bilingual Mining and Materials Co-op Program.

FACILITIES
Housing: Coed dorms, special housing for disabled students, women's dorms, apartments for single students, shared facilities housing: similar to cooperative housing but chores and costs are not shared amongst the students. 90% of campus accessible to physically disabled. **Special Academic Facilities/Equipment:** McCord Museum of Canadian History, Redpath Museum of Natural History, Lyman Entomological Museum and Research Laboratory, Ecomuseum, Rutherford Museum, Lawrence Lande Collection of Canadiana, Canadian Architecture Collection, Morgan Arboretum, Gault Nature Reserve, Herbarium, McGill Archives (Canadian History), Islamic Studies Library, Bellairs Research Institute, McConnell Brain Imaging Centre, McConnell Winter Arena, McGill Sports Centre Gymnasiums, Percival Molson Stadium, Memorial Pool, Richard Tomlinson Fieldhouse, Outdoor Tennis Courts, McGill Arctic Research Station, McGill Subarctic Research Station, Phytotron, Schulich School of Music (world-class sound stage, recording studio), McGill Centre for Interdisciplinary Research in Music, Media and Technology, Research Greenhouse, J. S. Marshall Weather Radar Observatory, Mountain and Glen Campuses (McGill University Health Centre Teaching Hospitals), McGill

Medical Simulation Centre, McGill Reproductive Centre, McGill University and Genome Quebec Innovation Centre. **Computers:** 100% of classrooms, 100% of dorms, 100% of libraries, 100% of dining areas, 100% of student union, 100% of common outdoor areas have wireless network access. Students can register for classes online. Administrative functions (other than registration) can be performed online.

CAMPUS LIFE

Environment: Metropolis. **Activities:** Choral groups, concert band, dance, drama/theater, jazz band, literary magazine, marching band, music ensembles, musical theater, opera, pep band, radio station, student government, student newspaper, student-run film society, symphony orchestra, television station, yearbook, international student organization. **Organizations:** 250 registered organizations, 2 honor societies, 10 religious organizations. 8 fraternities, 4 sororities. **Athletics (Intercollegiate):** *Men:* Badminton, baseball, basketball, cheerleading, crew/rowing, cross-country, curling, cycling, fencing, football, golf, ice hockey, lacrosse, rugby, sailing, skiing (downhill/alpine), skiing (nordic & cross-country), soccer, squash, swimming, tennis, track/field. *Women:* Badminton, basketball, cheerleading, crew/rowing, cross-country, curling, cycling, fencing, field hockey, golf, ice hockey, lacrosse, rugby, sailing, skiing (downhill/ alpine), skiing (nordic & cross-country), soccer, squash, swimming, synchronized swimming, ten. **On-Campus Highlights:** Arts Building, Schulich School of Music, McGill Bookstore, MacDonald Campus, Redpath Museum, To get a big-picture view of the entire campus, take a walk up Mont-Royal. From the Chateau look-out it is possible to see the entire downtown campus. **Environmental Initiatives:** Excellence in environmental research and teaching (e.g., School of Environment, GEC3, Brace, VERT, etc.) Continual investment in energy infrastructure improvements to efficiency and reduce resource consumption Conservation efforts (including Gault Reserve, Morgan Arboretum, EcoMuseum, etc.)

ADMISSIONS

Freshman Academic Profile: Average high school GPA 3.52. SAT Math middle 50% range 650–720. SAT Critical Reading middle 50% range 640–740. SAT Writing middle 50% range 650–730. ACT middle 50% range 29-32. Minimum paper TOEFL 577. Minimum computer TOEFL 233. Minimum web-based TOEFL 90. **Basis for Candidate Selection:** *Very important factors considered include:* Academic GPA, rigor of secondary school record, standardized test scores. *Important factors considered include:* Class rank. *Other factors considered include:* Recommendation(s). **Freshman Admission Requirements:** High school diploma is required and GED is not accepted. *Academic units recommended:* 4 English, 4 mathematics, 3 science, (3 science labs), 3 foreign language, 2 social studies, 2 history. **Freshman Admission Statistics:** 21,242 applied, 54% admitted, 44% enrolled. **Transfer Admission Requirements:** High school transcript, college transcript(s), minimum college GPA of 3.00 required. Lowest grade transferable C. **General Admission Information:** Application fee $85. Regular application deadline 1/15. Notification on a rolling basis, beginning on or about 1/30. Nonfall registration accepted. Admission may be deferred for a maximum of 1 year. Credit and/or placement offered for CEEB Advanced Placement tests.

COSTS AND FINANCIAL AID

Annual in-state tuition $1,968. Annual out-of-state tuition $5,500. Room and board $11,000. Required fees $1,500. Average book expense $1,000. **Required Forms and Deadlines:** institution's own financial aid formProvincial Government Loan Applications. Financial aid filing deadline 6/30. **Notification of Awards:** Applicants will be notified of awards on a rolling basis beginning 3/1. **Types of Aid:** *Need-based scholarships/grants:* private scholarships, the school's own gift aid, Canadian (Federal & Provincial) Student Assistance. *Loans:* FFEL Subsidized Stafford, FFEL Unsubsidized Stafford, FFEL PLUS, college/university loans from institutional funds. **Student Employment:** Institutional employment available. Off-campus job opportunities are fair. **Financial Aid Statistics:** 18% undergrads receive need-based scholarship or grant aid. 9% undergrads receive non-need-based scholarship or grant aid. 25% undergrads receive need-based self-help aid. 28% undergrads receive any aid. 24% undergrads borrow to pay for school. **Criteria for awarding institutional aid:** *Non-need-based:* Academics, art, athletics, leadership, music/drama, state/district residency.

See page 1160.

MCKENDREE COLLEGE

701 College Road, Lebanon, IL 62254
Phone: 618-537-6831 **Financial Aid Phone:** 618-537-6828
E-mail: inquiry@mckendree.edu **CEEB Code:** 1456
Fax: 618-537-6496 **Website:** www.mckendree.edu **ACT Code:** 1076

This private school, affiliated with the Methodist Church, was founded in 1828. It has a 100-acre campus.

RATINGS
Admissions Selectivity Rating: 81   **Fire Safety Rating:** 60*   **Green Rating:** 60*

STUDENTS AND FACULTY
Enrollment: 2,118. **Student Body:** 57% female, 43% male, 13% out-of-state, 2% international (24 countries represented). Asian 1%, African American 12%, Caucasian 81%, Hispanic 2%.
Retention and Graduation: 73% freshmen return for sophomore year. 37% freshmen graduate within 4 years. 14% grads go on to further study within 1 year. 5% grads pursue arts and sciences degrees. 3% grads pursue law degrees. 6% grads pursue business degrees. 1% grads pursue medical degrees. **Faculty:** Student/faculty ratio 15:1. 70 full-time faculty, 81% hold PhDs, 4% are members of minority groups, 51% are women.

ACADEMICS
Degrees: Associate, bachelor's, master's. **Classes:** Most classes have 10–19 students. Most lab/discussion sessions have 10–19 students. **Special Study Options:** Accelerated program, cooperative education program, double major, external degree program, honors program, independent study, internships, liberal arts/career combination, student-designed major, study abroad, teacher certification program, evening programs in accounting, business administration, organizational communication, 3-2 occupational therapy program with Washington University. Special programs offered to physically disabled students include note-taking services, reader services, tutors. **Career services:** Alumni services, career/job search classes, career assessment, internships. **Career services highlights include:** Internships.

FACILITIES
Housing: Coed dorms, special housing for disabled students, women's dorms, apartments for single students, suite-style apartments are available for both men and women. 80% of campus accessible to physically disabled. **Computers:** Students can register for classes online. Administrative functions (other than registration) can be performed online.

CAMPUS LIFE
Environment: Rural. **Activities:** Choral groups, concert band, dance, drama/ theater, jazz band, literary magazine, marching band, music ensembles, musical theater, pep band, student government, student newspaper, student-run film society, yearbook. **Organizations:** 59 registered organizations, 9 honor societies, 3 religious organizations. 4 fraternities, 3 sororities. **Athletics (Intercollegiate):** *Men:* Baseball, basketball, bowling, cheerleading, cross-country, football, golf, ice hockey, soccer, tennis, track/field (outdoor), track/field (indoor), wrestling. *Women:* Basketball, bowling, cheerleading, cross-country, golf, ice hockey, soccer, softball, tennis, track/field (outdoor), track/field (indoor), volleyball. **On-Campus Highlights:** Marion K. Piper Academic Center, Bothwell Chapel, Melvin Price Convocation Center, The Lair-student lounge and snack bar, McKendree West Clubhouse.

ADMISSIONS
Freshman Academic Profile: Average high school GPA 3.6. 25% in top 10% of high school class, 54% in top 25% of high school class, 91% in top 50% of high school class. SAT Math middle 50% range 430–630. SAT Critical Reading middle 50% range 420–530. ACT middle 50% range 20–27. Minimum paper TOEFL 500. Minimum computer TOEFL 173. **Basis for Candidate Selection:** *Very important factors considered include:* Rigor of secondary school record. *Important factors considered include:* Class rank, recommendation(s), standardized test scores, character/personal qualities. *Other factors considered include:* Application essay, alumni/ae relation, extracurricular activities, interview, talent/ability, volunteer work, work experience. **Freshman Admission Requirements:** High school diploma is required and GED is accepted. *Academic units recommended:* 4 English, 3 mathematics, 3 science, 2 social studies, 1 history. **Freshman Admission Statistics:** 1,150 applied, 69% admitted, 43% enrolled. **Transfer Admission Requirements:** High school transcript, college transcript(s), statement of good standing from prior institution(s). Minimum college GPA of 2.2 required. Lowest grade transferable C. **General Admission Information:** Application fee $40. Nonfall registration accepted. Admission may be deferred for a maximum of 6. Credit and/or placement offered for CEEB Advanced Placement tests.

COSTS AND FINANCIAL AID

Annual tuition $16,400. Room and board $6,480. Required fees $200. Average book expense $1,000. **Required Forms and Deadlines:** FAFSA, institution's own financial aid form. Priority financial aid filing date 5/31. **Notification of Awards:** Applicants will be notified of awards on a rolling basis beginning 3/1. **Types of Aid:** *Need-based scholarships/grants:* Federal Pell, SEOG, state scholarships/grants. *Loans:* FFEL Subsidized Stafford, FFEL Unsubsidized Stafford, FFEL PLUS, Federal Perkins, college/university loans from institutional funds. **Student Employment:** Federal Work-Study Program available. Institutional employment available. Highest amount earned per year from on-campus jobs $2,326. Off-campus job opportunities are good. **Financial Aid Statistics:** 78% freshmen, 78% undergrads receive need-based scholarship or grant aid. 15% freshmen, 14% undergrads receive non-need-based scholarship or grant aid. 58% freshmen, 59% undergrads receive need-based self-help aid. 12% freshmen, 12% undergrads receive athletic scholarships. 99% freshmen, 97% undergrads receive any aid. 58% undergrads borrow to pay for school. Average cumulative indebtedness $16,240. **Criteria for awarding institutional aid:** *Non-need-based:* Academics, art, athletics, leadership, minority status, music/drama, religious affiliation.

MCNEESE STATE UNIVERSITY

Box 91740 MSU, Lake Charles, LA 70609
Phone: 337-475-5356
Fax: 337-475-5151 **Website:** www.mcneese.edu

This is a public school.

RATINGS
Admissions Selectivity Rating: 76 **Fire Safety Rating:** 60* **Green Rating:** 60*

STUDENTS AND FACULTY
Enrollment: 7,041. **Student Body:** 61% female, 39% male, 7% out-of-state, 3% international. Asian 1%, African American 18%, Caucasian 72%, Hispanic 1%, Native American 1%.
Retention and Graduation: 64% freshmen return for sophomore year. **Faculty:** Student/faculty ratio 20:1. 316 full-time faculty, 66% hold PhDs, 15% are members of minority groups, 45% are women.

ACADEMICS
Degrees: Associate, bachelor's, master's, post-master's certificate. **Classes:** Most classes have 20–29 students. Most lab/discussion sessions have 10–19 students. **Special Study Options:** Accelerated program, cooperative education program, distance learning, double major, dual enrollment, English as a Second Language (ESL), honors program, independent study, internships, study abroad, teacher certification program.

FACILITIES
Housing: Coed dorms, apartments for married students, apartments for single students.

CAMPUS LIFE
Activities: Drama/theater, marching band, student government, student newspaper, yearbook.

ADMISSIONS
Freshman Academic Profile: Average high school GPA 3.16. 15% in top 10% of high school class, 35% in top 25% of high school class, 68% in top 50% of high school class. 82% from public high schools. ACT middle 50% range 19–23. Minimum paper TOEFL 550. Minimum computer TOEFL 213. **Basis for Candidate Selection:** *Very important factors considered include:* Rigor of secondary school record, standardized test scores. *Important factors considered include:* Class rank, academic GPA. *Other factors considered include:* Character/personal qualities, extracurricular activities, talent/ability, volunteer work, work experience. **Freshman Admission Requirements:** High school diploma is required and GED is accepted. *Academic units recommended:* 4 English, 3 mathematics, 3 science, 2 foreign language, 3 social studies, 1 fine arts. **Freshman Admission Statistics: Transfer Admission Requirements:** College transcript(s), statement of good standing from prior institution(s). Minimum college GPA of 2.00 required. Lowest grade transferable C. **General Admission Information:** Application fee $20. Nonfall registration accepted. Credit and/or placement offered for CEEB Advanced Placement tests.

COSTS AND FINANCIAL AID
Annual in-state tuition $2,226. Annual out-of-state tuition $8,292. Room and board $3,460. Required fees $1,036. Average book expense $1,200. **Required Forms and Deadlines:** FAFSA, institution's own financial aid form. Priority financial aid filing date 5/1. **Notification of Awards:** Applicants will be notified of awards on a rolling basis beginning 4/15. **Criteria for awarding institution-**

al aid: *Non-need-based:* Academics, alumni affiliation, art, athletics, leadership, minority status, music/drama, state/district residency.

MCPHERSON COLLEGE

P.O. Box 1402, 1600 E. Euclid, McPherson, KS 67460
Phone: 620-241-0731
E-mail: admiss@mcpherson.edu **CEEB Code:** 6404
Fax: 620-241-8443 **Website: ACT Code:** 1440

This private school, affiliated with the Church of Brethren Church, was founded in 1887. It has a 23-acre campus.

RATINGS
Admissions Selectivity Rating: 73 **Fire Safety Rating:** 60* **Green Rating:** 60*

STUDENTS AND FACULTY
Enrollment: 573. **Student Body:** 43% female, 57% male, 5% out-of-state, 1% international. Asian 2%, African American 9%, Caucasian 76%, Hispanic 7%, Native American 3%.
Retention and Graduation: 67% freshmen return for sophomore year. 36% freshmen graduate within 4 years. 9% grads go on to further study within 1 year. 9% grads pursue medical degrees. **Faculty:** Student/faculty ratio 15:1. 34 full-time faculty, 82% hold PhDs, 12% are members of minority groups, 32% are women.

ACADEMICS
Degrees: Bachelor's. **Classes:** Most classes have 10–19 students. Most lab/discussion sessions have 10–19 students. **Special Study Options:** Cross-registration, double major, dual enrollment, English as a Second Language (ESL), independent study, internships, student-designed major, study abroad, teacher certification program. **Combined degree programs:** 2-2 program with Hutchinson Com Col.

FACILITIES
Housing: Coed dorms, special housing for disabled students, men's dorms, women's dorms. **Special Academic Facilities/Equipment:** Natural history museum.

CAMPUS LIFE
Environment: Village. **Activities:** Choral groups, concert band, dance, drama/theater, jazz band, music ensembles, musical theater, pep band, student government, student newspaper, yearbook, campus ministries. **Organizations:** **Athletics (Intercollegiate):** *Women:* Basketball, cross-country, golf, tennis, track/field (outdoor), volleyball.

ADMISSIONS
Freshman Academic Profile: Average high school GPA 3.16. 9% in top 10% of high school class, 25% in top 25% of high school class, 60% in top 50% of high school class. 99% from public high schools. SAT Math middle 50% range 450–563. SAT Critical Reading middle 50% range 448–560. ACT middle 50% range 19–24. Minimum paper TOEFL 550. **Basis for Candidate Selection:** *Very important factors considered include:* Academic GPA, rigor of secondary school record, standardized test scores. *Other factors considered include:* Class rank, recommendation(s), character/personal qualities, extracurricular activities, first generation, interview, level of applicant's interest, talent/ability, volunteer work, work experience. **Freshman Admission Requirements:** High school diploma is required and GED is accepted. **Freshman Admission Statistics:** 474 applied, 87% admitted, 54% enrolled. **Transfer Admission Requirements:** High school transcript, college transcript(s), statement of good standing from prior institution(s). Minimum college GPA of 2.0 required. Lowest grade transferable C. **General Admission Information:** Application fee $25. Non-fall registration accepted. Admission may be deferred for a maximum of i year. Credit offered for CEEB Advanced Placement tests.

COSTS AND FINANCIAL AID
Annual tuition $17,900. Room and board $6,910. Required fees $500. Average book expense $1,170. **Required Forms and Deadlines:** FAFSA, state aid form Financial aid filing deadline 8/1. Priority financial aid filing date 3/1. **Notification of Awards:** Applicants will be notified of awards on a rolling basis beginning 3/1. **Types of Aid:** *Need-based scholarships/grants:* Federal Pell, SEOG, state scholarships/grants, private scholarships, the school's own gift aid, United Negro College Fund. *Loans:* FFEL Subsidized Stafford, FFEL Unsubsidized Stafford, FFEL PLUS, Federal Perkins. **Student Employment:** Federal Work-Study Program available. Institutional employment available. Highest amount earned per year from on-campus jobs $400. Off-campus job opportunities are good. **Financial Aid Statistics:** 72% freshmen, 71% undergrads receive need-based scholarship or grant aid. 81% freshmen, 82% undergrads receive non-need-based scholarship or grant aid. 74% freshmen, 74%

undergrads receive need-based self-help aid. 66% freshmen, 38% undergrads receive athletic scholarships. 91% undergrads borrow to pay for school. Average cumulative indebtedness $24,690. **Criteria for awarding institutional aid:** *Non-need-based:* Academics, alumni affiliation, art, athletics, music/drama, religious affiliation, state/district residency.

MEDAILLE COLLEGE

18 Agassiz Circle, Buffalo, NY 14214
Phone: 716-884-3281
E-mail: jmatheny@medaille.edu **CEEB Code:** 2422
Fax: 716-884-0291 **Website:** www.medaille.edu **ACT Code:** 2822

This private school was founded in 1937. It has a 13-acre campus.

RATINGS
Admissions Selectivity Rating: 72   **Fire Safety Rating:** 60*   **Green Rating:** 60*

STUDENTS AND FACULTY
Enrollment: 1,650. **Student Body:** 67% female, 33% male, 1% out-of-state, 3% international (2 countries represented). Asian 1%, African American 16%, Caucasian 65%, Hispanic 3%, Native American 1%.
Retention and Graduation: 70% freshmen return for sophomore year. 15% freshmen graduate within 4 years. 24% grads go on to further study within 1 year. 4% grads pursue arts and sciences degrees. 1% grads pursue law degrees. 5% grads pursue business degrees. 1% grads pursue medical degrees. **Faculty:** Student/faculty ratio 15:1. 70 full-time faculty, 56% hold PhDs, 7% are members of minority groups, 43% are women.

ACADEMICS
Degrees: Associate, bachelor's, certificate, master's. **Classes:** Most classes have 10–19 students. Most lab/discussion sessions have 10–19 students. **Special Study Options:** Accelerated program, cross-registration, double major, honors program, independent study, internships, liberal arts/career combination, student-designed major, teacher certification program, weekend college, Module system for full-time evening studies. **Honors programs:** Theodore Roosevelt Scholars Program. **Combined degree programs:** BS/MBA. Special programs offered to physically disabled students include note-taking services, reader services, tape recorders, tutors. **Career services:** Alumni services, career/job search classes, career assessment, internships, **Career services highlights include:** Internships available in each academic program, required for most academic programs.

FACILITIES
Housing: Coed dorms, men's dorms, women's dorms, apartments for married students, apartments for single students 100% of campus accessible to physically disabled. **Special Academic Facilities/Equipment:** Veterinary technology labs, New Media Institute, Childrens Literature Collection.

CAMPUS LIFE
Environment: City. **Activities:** Drama/theater, literary magazine, musical theater, radio station, student government, student newspaper, student-run film society, television station, yearbook. **Organizations:** 18 registered organizations, 2 honor societies. **Athletics (Intercollegiate):** *Men:* Baseball, basketball, cheerleading, lacrosse, soccer, volleyball. *Women:* Basketball, cheerleading, cross-country, lacrosse, soccer, softball, volleyball. **On-Campus Highlights:** Kevin I. Sullivan Campus Center, Cafeteria, New Media Laboratory, Computer Lab, Radio Station.

ADMISSIONS
Freshman Academic Profile: Average high school GPA 2.8. 14% in top 10% of high school class, 45% in top 25% of high school class, 75% in top 50% of high school class. 85% from public high schools. SAT Math middle 50% range 410–500. SAT Critical Reading middle 50% range 420–520. ACT middle 50% range 17–21. Minimum paper TOEFL 550. Minimum computer TOEFL 213. **Basis for Candidate Selection:** *Very important factors considered include:* Rigor of secondary school record, standardized test scores, interview. *Important factors considered include:* Application essay, recommendation(s), extracurricular activities. *Other factors considered include:* Class rank, alumni/ae relation, character/personal qualities, talent/ability, volunteer work, work experience. **Freshman Admission Requirements:** High school diploma is required and GED is accepted. *Academic units required:* 4 English, 2 mathematics, 2 science, 4 social studies. *Academic units recommended:* 4 English, 3 mathematics, 3 science, (2 science labs), 2 foreign language, 4 social studies, 2 history, 3 3 units mathematics, 3 units science recommended for veterinary technology. **Freshman Admission Statistics:** 763 applied, 68% admitted, 55% enrolled. **Transfer Admission Requirements:** High school transcript, college transcript(s), essay or personal statement, minimum college GPA of 2.0

required. Lowest grade transferable C. **General Admission Information:** Application fee $25. Notification on a rolling basis, beginning on or about 10/1. Nonfall registration accepted. Admission may be deferred for a maximum of 1year. Credit and/or placement offered for CEEB Advanced Placement tests.

COSTS AND FINANCIAL AID
Annual tuition $13,350. Room and board $6,400. Required fees $310. Average book expense $930. **Required Forms and Deadlines:** FAFSA, institution's own financial aid form, state aid form. Priority financial aid filing date 4/15. **Notification of Awards:** Applicants will be notified of awards on a rolling basis beginning 5/1. **Types of Aid:** *Need-based scholarships/grants:* Federal Pell, SEOG, state scholarships/grants, private scholarships, the school's own gift aid. *Loans:* FFEL Subsidized Stafford, FFEL Unsubsidized Stafford, FFEL PLUS. **Student Employment:** Federal Work-Study Program available. Institutional employment available. Highest amount earned per year from on-campus jobs $1,500. Off-campus job opportunities are good. **Financial Aid Statistics:** 84% freshmen, 67% undergrads receive need-based scholarship or grant aid. 32% freshmen, 10% undergrads receive non-need-based scholarship or grant aid. 87% freshmen, 73% undergrads receive need-based self-help aid. 85% freshmen, 85% undergrads receive any aid. 75% undergrads borrow to pay for school. Average cumulative indebtedness $18,000. **Criteria for awarding institutional aid:** *Non-need-based:* Academics.

MEDCENTER ONE COLLEGE OF NURSING

512 North 7th Street, Bismarck, ND 58501
Phone: 701-323-6271 **Financial Aid Phone:** 701-323-6270
E-mail: msmith@mohs.org
Fax: 701-323-6289 **Website:** www.medcenterone.com/collegeofnursing **ACT Code:** 3197

This private school was founded in 1988.

RATINGS
Admissions Selectivity Rating: 60*   **Fire Safety Rating:** 60*   **Green Rating:** 60*

STUDENTS AND FACULTY
Enrollment: 89. **Student Body:** 93% female, 7% male, 8% out-of-state, African American 2%, Caucasian 96%, Native American 2%.
Retention and Graduation: 88% freshmen graduate within 4 years. **Faculty:** Student/faculty ratio 8:1. 10 full-time faculty, 10% hold PhDs, 10% are members of minority groups, 100% are women.

ACADEMICS
Degrees: Bachelor's. **Classes:** Most classes have 40–49 students. Most lab/discussion sessions have fewer than 10 students. **Majors with Highest Enrollment:** Nursing/registered nurse (RN, ASN, BSN, MSN). **Special Study Options:** independent study, internships.

FACILITIES
Special Academic Facilities/Equipment: Alumni Corner. **Computers:** 100% of classrooms, 100% of libraries, 100% of common outdoor areas have wireless network access.

CAMPUS LIFE
Environment: Rural. **Activities:** Student government. **Organizations:** 2 registered organizations, 1 honor societies. **On-Campus Highlights:** Simulation lab.

ADMISSIONS
Freshman Admission Requirements: High school diploma is required and GED is accepted. **Transfer Admission Requirements:** High school transcript, college transcript(s), essay or personal statement, interview, minimum college GPA of 2.5 required. Lowest grade transferable C. **General Admission Information:** Application fee $40. Notification on a rolling basis, beginning on or about 11/4. Nonfall registration not accepted.

COSTS AND FINANCIAL AID
Annual tuition $9,720. Required fees $889. **Required Forms and Deadlines:** FAFSA, institution's own financial aid form. Priority financial aid filing date 3/15. **Notification of Awards:** Applicants will be notified of awards on a rolling basis beginning 6/1. **Types of Aid:** *Need-based scholarships/grants:* Federal Pell, SEOG, state scholarships/grants, private scholarships, the school's own gift aid. *Loans:* FFEL Subsidized Stafford, FFEL Unsubsidized Stafford, FFEL PLUS, Federal Perkins, Federal Nursing, college/university loans from institutional funds. **Student Employment:** Federal Work-Study Program available. Off-campus job opportunities are good. **Financial Aid Statistics:** 44% undergrads receive need-based scholarship or grant aid. 12% undergrads

receive non-need-based scholarship or grant aid. 47% undergrads receive need-based self-help aid. **Criteria for awarding institutional aid:** *Non-need-based:* Academics, alumni affiliation, leadership.

MEDICAL UNIVERSITY OF SOUTH CAROLINA

41 Bee Street, MSC 203, Charleston, SC 29425
Phone: 843-792-3281 **Financial Aid Phone:** 843-792-2536
E-mail: oesadmis@musc.edu
Fax: 843-792-6615 **Website:** www.musc.edu **ACT Code:** 6440

This public school was founded in 1824. It has a 80-acre campus.

RATINGS
Admissions Selectivity Rating: 60*　　　**Fire Safety Rating:** 60*　　　**Green Rating:** 84

STUDENTS AND FACULTY
Enrollment: 267. **Student Body:** 83% female, 17% male, 14% out-of-state, (29 countries represented). Asian 5%, African American 10%, Caucasian 71%, Hispanic 1%, Native American 1%.
Faculty: Student/faculty ratio 8:1. 133 full-time faculty, 87% hold PhDs, 7% are members of minority groups, 59% are women.

ACADEMICS
Degrees: Bachelor's, doctoral, master's, post-bachelor's certificate, post-master's certificate. **Classes:** Most classes have 50–59 students. **Majors with Highest Enrollment:** cardiovascular technology/technologist; nursing/registered nurse (RN, ASN, BSN, MSN). **Special Study Options:** Accelerated program, distance learning, varies with the academic program selected. Special programs offered to physically disabled students include note-taking services, reader services, tape recorders, tutors. **Career services:** Internships. **Career services highlights include:** We are an academic health science center and each specialty has various programs for placement of these highly specialized graduates. Internship refers to post-graduate programs and are not part of the degree curriculum.

FACILITIES
Housing: No on-campus housing available. Housing available in community and promoted to students via the Off-Campus Housing Service's website. 97% of campus accessible to physically disabled. **Special Academic Facilities/ Equipment:** Dental Museum, and Medical Museum, and Pharmacy Museum. **Computers:** 100% of classrooms, n/a% of dorms, 100% of libraries, 100% of dining areas, n/a% of student union, 100% of common outdoor areas have wireless network access. Students can register for classes online. Administrative functions (other than registration) can be performed online.

CAMPUS LIFE
Environment: City. **Activities:** Choral groups, dance, literary magazine, music ensembles, student government, campus ministries, international student organization. **Organizations:** 77 registered organizations, 4 honor societies. **On-Campus Highlights:** Student Activity and Fitness Center, library, various student lounges, classroom and laboratories. **Environmental Initiatives:** Installed ground source heat pump as first renewable energy project; recycling program since 1992. Green building projects include: energy performance contract (in progress from January 2009); constructing first LEED building (in progress July 2009).

ADMISSIONS
Freshman Academic Profile: Minimum paper TOEFL 600. Minimum computer TOEFL 250.

COSTS AND FINANCIAL AID
Annual in-state tuition $12,637. Annual out-of-state tuition $27,813. Required fees $995. **Required Forms and Deadlines:** FAFSA, institution's own financial aid form. Priority financial aid filing date 3/10. **Notification of Awards:** Applicants will be notified of awards on a rolling basis beginning 4/21. **Types of Aid:** *Need-based scholarships/grants:* Federal Pell, SEOG, state scholarships/grants, private scholarships, the school's own gift aid, Federal Nursing Scholarships. *Loans:* FFEL Subsidized Stafford, FFEL Unsubsidized Stafford, FFEL PLUS, Federal Perkins, Federal Nursing, college/university loans from institutional funds. **Student Employment:** Federal Work-Study Program available. Off-campus job opportunities are good. **Financial Aid Statistics:** 38% undergrads receive need-based scholarship or grant aid. 14% undergrads receive non-need-based scholarship or grant aid. 69% undergrads receive need-based self-help aid. 82% undergrads receive any aid. **Criteria for awarding institutional aid:** *Non-need-based:* Academics, alumni affiliation, minority status, state/district residency.

MEMORIAL UNIVERSITY OF NEWFOUNDLAND

Memorial University of Newfoundland, Admissions Office-Faculty of Medicine, St. Johns, NF A1B 3V6 Canada
Phone: 709-777-6615
E-mail: munmed@mun.ca
Fax: 709-777-6615 **Website:** www.med.mun.ca/admissions

This public school was founded in 1925. It has a 220-acre campus.

RATINGS
Admissions Selectivity Rating: 60*　　　**Fire Safety Rating:** 60*　　　**Green Rating:** 60*

STUDENTS AND FACULTY
Student Body: 40% out-of-state.
Faculty: Student/faculty ratio 16:1. 1012 full-time faculty, 26% are women. 3% of classes are taught by teaching assistants.

ACADEMICS
Degrees: Special Study Options: Accelerated program, cooperative education program, distance learning, double major, English as a Second Language (ESL), exchange student program (domestic), honors program, internships, liberal arts/career combination, study abroad, teacher certification program. **Combined degree programs:** BA/BBA, BM/BEd. Special programs offered to physically disabled students include note-taking services, reader services, tape recorders, tutors. **Career services:** Alumni services, career/job search classes, career assessment, internships.

FACILITIES
Special Academic Facilities/Equipment: Olympic sized swimming pool, complete fitness centre, student eating area, indoor aerobics, track and field, soccer field, basketball courts. **Computers:** Students can register for classes online. Administrative functions (other than registration) can be performed online.

CAMPUS LIFE
Activities: Student government. **Organizations:** 81 registered organizations. **Athletics (Intercollegiate):** *Men:* Basketball, fencing, ice hockey, riflery, rugby, skiing (downhill/alpine), soccer, softball, squash, swimming, track/field (outdoor), volleyball, wrestling. *Women:* Basketball, fencing, ice hockey, riflery, rugby, skiing (downhill/alpine), soccer, softball, squash, swimming, track/field (outdoor), volleyball, wrestling.

ADMISSIONS
Freshman Academic Profile: Minimum paper TOEFL 550. **Freshman Admission Requirements:** High school diploma is required and GED is accepted. *Academic units required:* 3 English, 4 mathematics, 4 science, (4 science labs), 2 social studies, 2 academic electives. **Freshman Admission Statistics:** 3,900 applied, 86% admitted, 116% enrolled. **Transfer Admission Requirements:** High school transcript, college transcript(s), standardized test scores. **General Admission Information:** Application fee $80. Regular application deadline 3/1. Notification on a rolling basis, beginning on or about 6/21. Nonfall registration accepted.

COSTS AND FINANCIAL AID
Required Forms and Deadlines: FAFSA. **Types of Aid:** *Need-based scholarships/grants:* Universities Scholarships awarded for academic excellence. *Loans:* Canada/Newfoundland Government Student Loans. **Student Employment:** Institutional employment available. Off-campus job opportunities are good. **Financial Aid Statistics:** 63% undergrads borrow to pay for school. Average cumulative indebtedness $15,167. **Criteria for awarding institutional aid:** *Non-need-based:* Academics, athletics, leadership, minority status, music/drama, state/district residency.

MEMPHIS COLLEGE OF ART

Overton Park, 1930 Poplar Avenue, Memphis, TN 38104-2764
Phone: 901-272-5151 **Financial Aid Phone:** 901-272-5136
E-mail: info@mca.edu **CEEB Code:** 1511
Fax: 901-272-5158 **Website:** www.mca.edu **ACT Code:** 3991

This private school was founded in 1936. It has a 340-acre campus.

RATINGS
Admissions Selectivity Rating: 82　　　**Fire Safety Rating:** 69　　　**Green Rating:** 71

STUDENTS AND FACULTY

Enrollment: 320. **Student Body:** 57% female, 43% male, 55% out-of-state, 2% international (5 countries represented). Asian 2%, African American 19%, Caucasian 73%, Hispanic 3%.
Retention and Graduation: 66% freshmen return for sophomore year. 18% freshmen graduate within 4 years. 10% grads go on to further study within 1 year. **Faculty:** Student/faculty ratio 10:1. 21 full-time faculty, 81% hold PhDs, 10% are members of minority groups, 48% are women. 1% of classes are taught by teaching assistants.

ACADEMICS

Degrees: Bachelor's, master's. **Classes:** Most classes have 10–19 students.
Special Study Options: Cross-registration, double major, exchange student program (domestic), independent study, internships, study abroad, teacher certification program, New York Studies Program. Arts Exchange possible with othe AICAD schools. Special programs offered to physically disabled students include note-taking services, reader services, tape recorders, tutors. **Career services:** Alumni network, alumni services, career/job search classes, internships, regional alumni.

FACILITIES

Housing: Coed dorms, apartments for single students. 100% of campus accessible to physically disabled. **Special Academic Facilities/Equipment:** Art museum, numerous galleries for student exhibition. Computer writing lab. **Computers:** 100% of classrooms, 100% of dorms, 100% of libraries, 100% of dining areas, have wireless network access.

CAMPUS LIFE

Environment: Metropolis. **Activities:** Student government, student newspaper.

ADMISSIONS

Freshman Academic Profile: Average high school GPA 3.22. 80% from public high schools. ACT middle 50% range 19–25. Minimum paper TOEFL 500. Minimum computer TOEFL 195. **Basis for Candidate Selection:** *Very important factors considered include:* Academic GPA, talent/ability. *Important factors considered include:* Rigor of secondary school record, standardized test scores, interview. *Other factors considered include:* Class rank, application essay, recommendation(s), character/personal qualities, extracurricular activities, level of applicant's interest, volunteer work, work experience. **Freshman Admission Requirements:** High school diploma is required and GED is accepted. **Freshman Admission Statistics:** 664 applied, 52% admitted, 30% enrolled. **Transfer Admission Requirements:** College transcript(s), minimum college GPA of 2.0 required. Lowest grade transferable C. **General Admission Information:** Application fee $25. Notification on a rolling basis, beginning on or about 12/1. Nonfall registration accepted. Admission may be deferred for a maximum of 1 year. Credit and/or placement offered for CEEB Advanced Placement tests.

COSTS AND FINANCIAL AID

Annual tuition $20,100. Room and board $7,960. Required fees $560. Average book expense $1,600. **Required Forms and Deadlines:** FAFSA. Priority financial aid filing date 3/1. **Notification of Awards:** Applicants will be notified of awards on a rolling basis beginning 1/15. **Types of Aid:** *Need-based scholarships/grants:* Federal Pell, SEOG, state scholarships/grants, private scholarships, the school's own gift aid. *Loans:* Direct Subsidized Stafford, Direct Unsubsidized Stafford, Direct PLUS, FFEL Subsidized Stafford, FFEL Unsubsidized Stafford, FFEL PLUS, Federal Perkins, college/university loans from institutional funds. **Student Employment:** Federal Work-Study Program available. Highest amount earned per year from on-campus jobs $1,000. Off-campus job opportunities are good. **Financial Aid Statistics:** 52% freshmen, 48% undergrads receive need-based scholarship or grant aid. 76% freshmen, 73% undergrads receive non-need-based scholarship or grant aid. 79% freshmen, 78% undergrads receive need-based self-help aid. 95% freshmen, 95% undergrads receive any aid. 90% undergrads borrow to pay for school. Average cumulative indebtedness $34,360. **Criteria for awarding institutional aid:** *Non-need-based:* Academics, art.

MENLO COLLEGE

1000 El Camino Real, Atherton, CA 94027
Phone: 650-543-3753 **Financial Aid Phone:** 650-543-3880
E-mail: admissions@menlo.edu **CEEB Code:** 4483
Fax: 650-543-4496 **Website:** www.menlo.edu **ACT Code:** 330

This private school was founded in 1927. It has a 45-acre campus.

RATINGS
Admissions Selectivity Rating: 78 **Fire Safety Rating:** 60* **Green Rating:** 66

STUDENTS AND FACULTY

Enrollment: 594. **Student Body:** 36% female, 64% male, 25% out-of-state, 12% international (25 countries represented). Asian 12%, African American 4%, Caucasian 43%, Hispanic 14%.
Retention and Graduation: 64% freshmen return for sophomore year. 30% freshmen graduate within 4 years. **Faculty:** Student/faculty ratio 14:1. 25 full-time faculty, 92% hold PhDs, 24% are members of minority groups, 40% are women.

ACADEMICS

Degrees: Bachelor's. **Classes:** Most classes have 20–29 students. Most lab/discussion sessions have 10–19 students. **Majors with Highest Enrollment:** Business/commerce; psychology; sport and fitness administration/management.
Special Study Options: Accelerated program, double major, independent study, internships, student-designed major, study abroad, Advanced Placement credit Learning disability services. Special programs offered to physically disabled students include note-taking services, reader services, tape recorders, tutors. **Career services:** Alumni network, alumni services, career/job search classes, career assessment, internships, regional alumni.

FACILITIES

Housing: Coed dorms, special housing for disabled students, men's dorms, women's dorms 95% of campus accessible to physically disabled. **Computers:** 33% of classrooms, 100% of libraries, 100% of dining areas, 100% of student union, have wireless network access. Students can register for classes online. Administrative functions (other than registration) can be performed online.

CAMPUS LIFE

Environment: Town. **Activities:** Radio station, student government, student newspaper, student-run film society, television station, yearbook, international student organization. **Organizations:** 30 registered organizations, 2 honor societies, **Athletics (Intercollegiate):** *Men:* Baseball, basketball, cross-country, football, golf, soccer, wrestling. *Women:* Basketball, cross-country, soccer, softball, volleyball, wrestling. **On-Campus Highlights:** Library, Student Union, Dining commons **Environmental Initiatives:** Menlo offers Principles of Environmental Resource Management and Management for Small Planets class.

ADMISSIONS

Freshman Academic Profile: Average high school GPA 3.13. 11.4% in top 10% of high school class, 40% in top 25% of high school class, 80% in top 50% of high school class. SAT Math middle 50% range 430–560. SAT Critical Reading middle 50% range 420–540. SAT Writing middle 50% range 420–520. ACT middle 50% range 17-23. Minimum paper TOEFL 500. Minimum computer TOEFL 173. **Basis for Candidate Selection:** *Very important factors considered include:* Rigor of secondary school record, character/personal qualities. *Important factors considered include:* Class rank, application essay, academic GPA, recommendation(s), standardized test scores, alumni/ae relation, extracurricular activities, level of applicant's interest, volunteer work. *Other factors considered include:* Interview, talent/ability, work experience. **Freshman Admission Requirements:** High school diploma is required and GED is accepted. *Academic units recommended:* 4 English, 3 mathematics, 3 science, (1 science labs), 2 foreign language, 3 social studies. **Freshman Admission Statistics:** 1,492 applied, 52% admitted, 17% enrolled. **Transfer Admission Requirements:** College transcript(s), essay or personal statement, statement of good standing from prior institution(s). Minimum college GPA of 2.0 required. Lowest grade transferable C–. **General Admission Information:** Application fee $40. Notification on a rolling basis, beginning on or about 12/1. Nonfall registration accepted. Admission may be deferred for a maximum of 2 semesters. Credit and/or placement offered for CEEB Advanced Placement tests.

COSTS AND FINANCIAL AID

Annual tuition $33,150. Room and board $11,330. Required fees $400. Average book expense $1,620. **Required Forms and Deadlines:** FAFSA, state aid form Financial aid filing deadline 8/1. Priority financial aid filing date 3/2. **Notification of Awards:** Applicants will be notified of awards on a rolling basis beginning 12/15. **Types of Aid:** *Need-based scholarships/grants:* Federal Pell, SEOG, state scholarships/grants, the school's own gift aid, Federal ACG Grant. *Loans:* Direct Subsidized Stafford, Direct Unsubsidized Stafford, Direct PLUS, FFEL Subsidized Stafford, FFEL Unsubsidized Stafford, FFEL PLUS. **Student Employment:** Federal Work-Study Program available. Institutional employment available. Highest amount earned per year from on-campus jobs $2,000. Off-campus job opportunities are excellent. **Financial Aid Statistics:** 59% freshmen, 58% undergrads receive need-based scholarship or grant aid. 7% freshmen, 3% undergrads receive non-need-based scholarship or grant aid. 55% freshmen, 54% undergrads receive need-based self-help aid. 88% freshmen, 89% undergrads receive any aid. 76.27% undergrads borrow to pay for school. Average cumulative indebtedness $25,696. **Criteria for awarding institutional aid:** *Non-need-based:* Academics.

MERCER UNIVERSITY—MACON

Admissions Office, 1400 Coleman Avenue, Macon, GA 31207-0001
Phone: 478-301-2650 **Financial Aid Phone:** 478-301-2670
E-mail: admissions@mercer.edu **CEEB Code:** 5409
Fax: 478-301-2828 **Website:** www.mercer.edu **ACT Code:** 838

This private school, affiliated with the Baptist Church, was founded in 1833. It has a 150-acre campus.

RATINGS

Admissions Selectivity Rating: 89   **Fire Safety Rating:** 76   **Green Rating:** 80

STUDENTS AND FACULTY

Enrollment: 2,295. **Student Body:** 53% female, 47% male, 20% out-of-state, 3% international (39 countries represented). Asian 6%, African American 16%, Caucasian 57%, Hispanic 3%.
Retention and Graduation: 85% freshmen return for sophomore year. 45% freshmen graduate within 4 years. 23% grads go on to further study within 1 year. **Faculty:** Student/faculty ratio 13.5:1. 370 full-time faculty, 88% hold PhDs, 19% are are members of minority groups, 45% are women.

ACADEMICS

Degrees: Bachelor's, master's, post-master's certificate. **Classes:** Most classes have 10–19 students. Most lab/discussion sessions have 20–29 students. **Majors with Highest Enrollment:** Biology/biological sciences; business/commerce; engineering. **Special Study Options:** Accelerated program, cooperative education program, cross-registration, double major, dual enrollment, honors program, independent study, internships, liberal arts/career combination, student-designed major, study abroad, teacher certification program, Great Books program. **Honors programs:** Qualified students may be admitted to the Honors Program in the College of Liberal Arts, the Stetson School of Business and Economics, the School of Engineering, and the Tift College of Education. The Honors Program includes honors courses, out of classroom activities, independent study, and other opportunities. **Combined degree programs:** BA/MEng, Pharmacy (D. Pharm), Medicine (MD), Law (JD). Special programs offered to physically disabled students include note-taking services, reader services, tape recorders, tutors. **Career services:** Alumni network, alumni services, career/job search classes, career assessment, internships. **Career services highlights include:** Aproximately 65% of undergraduate students participate in some form of structured experiential education prior to graduation. These experiences serve to enhance the students' academic and leadership skills and also prepares them well for their chosen career paths.

FACILITIES

Housing: Coed dorms, special housing for disabled students, men's dorms, special housing for international students, women's dorms, fraternity/sorority housing, apartments for married students, apartments for single students 85% of campus accessible to physically disabled. **Special Academic Facilities/Equipment:** McCorkle Music Building. **Computers:** 100% of classrooms, 100% of dorms, 100% of libraries, 100% of dining areas, 100% of student union, 100% of common outdoor areas have wireless network access. Students can register for classes online. Administrative functions (other than registration) can be performed online.

CAMPUS LIFE

Environment: City. **Activities:** Choral groups, concert band, dance, drama/theater, jazz band, literary magazine, music ensembles, musical theater, opera, pep band, student government, student newspaper, television station, campus ministries, international student organization. **Organizations:** 115 registered organizations, 18 honor societies, 7 religious organizations. 9 fraternities, 7 sororities. **Athletics (Intercollegiate):** *Men:* Baseball, basketball, cross-country, golf, riflery, soccer, tennis. *Women:* Basketball, cross-country, golf, soccer, softball, tennis, volleyball. **On-Campus Highlights:** University Center, Connell Student Center, Greek Village, Porter Patch, Jesse Mercer Plaza. **Environmental Initiatives:** We participate in the RecycleMania competition. We have an active mixed paper, aluminum can, and plastic recycling program. We provide subsidies for faculty and staff to purchase homes that are within walking distance of the university.

ADMISSIONS

Freshman Academic Profile: Average high school GPA 3.6. 42% in top 10% of high school class, 72% in top 25% of high school class, 80% in top 50% of high school class. SAT Math middle 50% range 550–640. SAT Critical Reading middle 50% range 530–630. SAT Writing middle 50% range 520–620. ACT middle 50% range 22–27. Minimum paper TOEFL 550. Minimum computer TOEFL 213. **Basis for Candidate Selection:** *Very important factors considered include:* Academic GPA, rigor of secondary school record, standardized test scores, level of applicant's interest. *Important factors considered include:* Character/personal qualities, extracurricular activities, talent/ability, volunteer work. *Other factors considered include:* Class rank, recommendation(s), alumni/ae relation, interview, work experience. **Freshman Admission Requirements:** High school diploma is required and GED is accepted. *Academic units required:* 4 English, 4 mathematics, 3 science, (2 science labs), 2 foreign language, 1 social studies, 2 history. **Freshman Admission Statistics:** 2,857 applied, 79% admitted, 25% enrolled. **Transfer Admission Requirements:** College transcript(s), statement of good standing from prior institution(s). Minimum college GPA of 2.5 required. Lowest grade transferable C. **General Admission Information:** Application fee $50. Regular application deadline 7/1. Notification on a rolling basis, beginning on or about 11/1. Nonfall registration not accepted. Admission may be deferred for a maximum of 1 year. Credit and/or placement offered for CEEB Advanced Placement tests.

COSTS AND FINANCIAL AID

Annual tuition $29. Room and board $8,788. Required fees $200. Average book expense $1,200. **Required Forms and Deadlines:** FAFSA, institution's own financial aid form, state aid form. Priority financial aid filing date 4/1. **Notification of Awards:** Applicants will be notified of awards on a rolling basis beginning 3/15. **Types of Aid:** *Need-based scholarships/grants:* Federal Pell, SEOG, state scholarships/grants, the school's own gift aid, Federal Nursing Scholarships. *Loans:* Direct Subsidized Stafford, Direct Unsubsidized Stafford, Direct PLUS, Federal Perkins, Federal Nursing, college/university loans from institutional funds. *Student Employment:* Federal Work-Study Program available. Institutional employment available. Off-campus job opportunities are good. **Financial Aid Statistics:** 77% freshmen, 71% undergrads receive need-based scholarship or grant aid. 25% freshmen, 19% undergrads receive non-need-based scholarship or grant aid. 48% freshmen, 47% undergrads receive need-based self-help aid. 5% freshmen, 6% undergrads receive athletic scholarships. 100% freshmen, 98% undergrads receive any aid. 58.4% undergrads borrow to pay for school. Average cumulative indebtedness $29,065. **Criteria for awarding institutional aid:** *Non-need-based:* Academics, art, athletics, job skills, leadership, music/drama, state/district residency.

MERCY COLLEGE

555 Broadway, Dobbs Ferry, NY 10522
Phone: 914-674-7324 **Financial Aid Phone:** 914-674-3027
E-mail: admissions@mercy.edu **CEEB Code:** 002409
Fax: 914-674-7608 **Website:** www.mercy.edu **ACT Code:** 2814

This private school was founded in 1950. It has a 90-acre campus.

RATINGS

Admissions Selectivity Rating: 60*   **Fire Safety Rating:** 99   **Green Rating:** 60*

STUDENTS AND FACULTY

Enrollment: 5,516. **Student Body:** 67% female, 33% male, 5% out-of-state, 1% international (39 countries represented). Asian 3%, African American 27%, Caucasian 27%, Hispanic 30%.
Retention and Graduation: 13% freshmen graduate within 4 years. **Faculty:** Student/faculty ratio 17:1. 193 full-time faculty, 79% hold PhDs, 21% are are members of minority groups, 56% are women.

ACADEMICS

Degrees: Associate, bachelor's, certificate, master's, post-bachelor's certificate, post-master's certificate, terminal associate, transfer associate. **Classes:** Most classes have 10–19 students. **Majors with Highest Enrollment:** Business administration and management; psychology; social sciences. **Special Study Options:** Accelerated program, cooperative education program, distance learning, double major, dual enrollment, honors program, internships, teacher certification program, weekend college, program for college students with learning disabilities. **Honors programs:** Admission criteria to the Honors Program is a 87 or above high school average. One hundred and thirty new and transfer students were admitted in 2009–2010. Students in the Honors Program take Honors versions of General Education courses (e.g. English, speech, and math) at the lower level and complete individualized Honors project in connection with their major for a total of 24 Honors credits. **Combined degree programs:** BA/MA, accounting, education, nursing. Special programs offered to physically disabled students include note-taking services, reader services, tape recorders, tutors. **Career services:** Alumni network, alumni services, career/job search classes, career assessment, internships. **Career services highlights include:** Cooperative Learning.

FACILITIES

Housing: Coed dorms. 100% of campus accessible to physically disabled. **Special Academic Facilities/Equipment:** Childcare center located at the Bronx campus. **Computers:** 40% of classrooms, 100% of dorms, 60% of libraries, 60% of dining areas, 60% of student union, have wireless network access. Students can register for classes online. Administrative functions (other than registration) can be performed online.

CAMPUS LIFE

Environment: Village. **Activities:** dance, student government, student newspaper, campus ministries, Model UN. **Organizations:** 20 registered organizations, 1 religious organizations. **Athletics (Intercollegiate):** *Men:* Baseball, basketball, cross-country, lacrosse, soccer, tennis, track/field (outdoor). *Women:* Basketball, cross-country, lacrosse, soccer, softball, track/field (outdoor), volleyball. **On-Campus Highlights:** Waterfront campus on the Hudson River, new state-of-the-art library, student cafe, music and recording studio, Roy Disney Center for Computer Animation. Mercy College offers the best value of a quality, award-winning, private education at an affordable price. Mercy College is a private institution in the New York metropolitan area with a unique combination of over 90 undergraduate and graduate programs within its five schools: Business, Education, Health and Natural Sciences, Liberal Arts, and Social and Behavioral Sciences. Nearly 10,000 students study at the main campus in Dobbs Ferry PLUS. additional campus locations in Bronx, Manhattan, White Plains, and Yorktown Heights. Mercy College tuition is nearly $10,000 less than the national average of 4-year private colleges. Mercy College was featured as a "Smart Choice" by Peterson's Honors Programs and Colleges publication. The Mercy College student PACT program is a national model for retention and career services and official Best Practice of the National Association of Colleges and Employers. Mercy College's School of Health and Sciences produces a 100% employment rate after graduation. Mercy College was named a Top Military-Friendly College in the nation by GI Jobs magazine and highlighted in the book, "Cool Colleges,' as one of the most exciting schools in America. Anthony Mullen ('02) was named the 2009 National Teacher of the Year by the President of the United States for his outstanding commitment to education.

ADMISSIONS

Freshman Academic Profile: Minimum paper TOEFL 550. Minimum computer TOEFL 213. Minimum web-based TOEFL 79. **Basis for Candidate Selection:** *Very important factors considered include:* Academic GPA, character/personal qualities, extracurricular activities, talent/ability. *Important factors considered include:* Class rank, application essay, recommendation(s), rigor of secondary school record, standardized test scores, interview, level of applicant's interest. *Other factors considered include:* Alumni/ae relation, volunteer work, work experience. **Freshman Admission Requirements:** High school diploma is required and GED is accepted. *Academic units required:* 4 English, 4 mathematics, 3 science, (1 science labs), 3 foreign language, 2 social studies, 2 history, 3 academic electives. **Freshman Admission Statistics:** 4,355 applied, 59% admitted, 36% enrolled. **Transfer Admission Requirements:** College transcript(s), minimum college GPA of 2.0 required. Lowest grade transferable C. **General Admission Information:** Application fee $40. Notification on a rolling basis, beginning on or about 12/1. Nonfall registration accepted. Credit offered for CEEB Advanced Placement tests.

COSTS AND FINANCIAL AID

Annual tuition $15,990. Room and board $10,812. Required fees $500. Average book expense $1,320. **Required Forms and Deadlines:** FAFSA, state aid form. Priority financial aid filing date 2/15. **Notification of Awards:** Applicants will be notified of awards on a rolling basis beginning 4/1. **Types of Aid:** *Need-based scholarships/grants:* Federal Pell, SEOG, state scholarships/grants, private scholarships, the school's own gift aid, Federal Nursing Scholarships. *Loans:* FFEL Subsidized Stafford, FFEL Unsubsidized Stafford, FFEL PLUS, Federal Nursing, private educational loans. *Student Employment:* Federal Work-Study Program available. Institutional employment available. Highest amount earned per year from on-campus jobs $5,342. Off-campus job opportunities are good. **Financial Aid Statistics:** 77% freshmen, 72% undergrads receive need-based scholarship or grant aid. 49% freshmen, 27% undergrads receive non-need-based scholarship or grant aid. 58% freshmen, 65% undergrads receive need-based self-help aid. 1% undergrads receive athletic scholarships. 94% freshmen, 83% undergrads receive any aid. 68% undergrads borrow to pay for school. Average cumulative indebtedness $15,481. **Criteria for awarding institutional aid:** *Non-need-based:* Academics, athletics.

MERCYHURST COLLEGE

Admissions, 501 E. 38th Street, Erie, PA 16546
Phone: 814-824-2202 **Financial Aid Phone:** 814-824-2000
E-mail: admissions@mercyhurst.edu **CEEB Code:** 2410
Fax: 814-824-2071 **Website:** admissions.mercyhurst.edu **ACT Code:** 3629

This private school, affiliated with the Roman Catholic Church, was founded in 1926. It has a 88-acre campus.

RATINGS

Admissions Selectivity Rating: 82   **Fire Safety Rating:** 60*   **Green Rating:** 60*

STUDENTS AND FACULTY

Student Body: 34% out-of-state.
Retention and Graduation: 79% freshmen return for sophomore year. 16% grads go on to further study within 1 year. 9% grads pursue arts and sciences degrees. 2% grads pursue law degrees. 9% grads pursue business degrees. 2% grads pursue medical degrees. **Faculty:** Student/faculty ratio 19:1. 151 full-time faculty, 41% hold PhDs, 3% are are members of minority groups, 44% are women.

ACADEMICS

Degrees: Associate, bachelor's, certificate, master's, post-bachelor's certificate, terminal associate, transfer associate. **Classes:** Most classes have fewer than 10 students. Most lab/discussion sessions have 10–19 students. **Special Study Options:** Accelerated program, cooperative education program, cross-registration, double major, exchange student program (domestic), honors program, independent study, internships, liberal arts/career combination, student-designed major, study abroad, teacher certification program, weekend college, arts, business, computer science, education, health professions, history, English, home economics, humanities, natural science, social/behavioral science. **Off campus study:** Washington, DC. Undergrads may take grad level classes. **Combined degree programs:** 3+4 Medical school program. Special programs offered to physically disabled students include note-taking services, reader services, tape recorders, tutors. **Career services:** Alumni network, alumni services, career/job search classes, career assessment, internships.

FACILITIES

Housing: Special housing for disabled students, men's dorms, women's dorms, apartments for single students. **Special Academic Facilities/Equipment:** Art gallery, college-owned restaurant for hotel/restaurant management department, observatory, archaeology lab. **Computers:** Students can register for classes online. Administrative functions (other than registration) can be performed online.

CAMPUS LIFE

Environment: Village. **Activities:** Choral groups, concert band, dance, drama/theater, literary magazine, music ensembles, musical theater, pep band, radio station, student government, student newspaper, television station, yearbook. **Organizations:** 9 honor societies, 2 religious organizations. **Athletics (Intercollegiate):** *Men:* Baseball, basketball, cheerleading, crew/rowing, cross-country, football, golf, ice hockey, lacrosse, soccer, tennis, volleyball, water polo, wrestling. *Women:* Basketball, cheerleading, crew/rowing, cross-country, field hockey, golf, ice hockey, lacrosse, soccer, softball, tennis, volleyball, water polo. **On-Campus Highlights:** Performing arts center, Mercyhurst Athletic Center, library, student union, ice rink.

ADMISSIONS

Freshman Academic Profile: Average high school GPA 3.4. 18% in top 10% of high school class, 43% in top 25% of high school class, 79% in top 50% of high school class. 78% from public high schools. SAT Math middle 50% range 490–590. SAT Critical Reading middle 50% range 480–590. ACT middle 50% range 19–25. Minimum paper TOEFL 550. Minimum computer TOEFL 300. **Basis for Candidate Selection:** *Very important factors considered include:* Rigor of secondary school record. *Important factors considered include:* Class rank, standardized test scores, character/personal qualities, interview, talent/ability. *Other factors considered include:* Application essay, recommendation(s), alumni/ae relation, extracurricular activities, geographical residence, racial/ethnic status, religious affiliation/commitment, state residency, volunteer work, work experience. **Freshman Admission Requirements:** High school diploma is required and GED is accepted. *Academic units recommended:* 4 English, 3 mathematics, 3 science, (1 science labs), 2 foreign language, 2 social studies, 2 history. **Transfer Admission Requirements:** High school transcript, college transcript(s), standardized test scores, minimum college GPA of 2.0 required. Lowest grade transferable C. **General Admission Information:** Application fee $30. Notification on a rolling basis, beginning on or about 11/15. Nonfall registration accepted. Admission may be deferred for a maximum of 1 year. Credit and/or placement offered for CEEB Advanced Placement tests.

COSTS AND FINANCIAL AID

Annual tuition $18,930. Room and board $3,700. Required fees $1,434. Average book expense $750. **Required Forms and Deadlines:** FAFSA, institution's own financial aid form. Financial aid filing deadline 5/1. Priority financial aid filing date 3/1. **Notification of Awards:** Applicants will be notified of awards on a rolling basis beginning 2/15. **Types of Aid:** *Need-based scholarships/grants:* Federal Pell, SEOG, state scholarships/grants, private scholarships, the school's own gift aid. *Loans:* FFEL Subsidized Stafford, FFEL Unsubsidized Stafford, FFEL PLUS, Federal Perkins. *Student Employment:* Federal Work-Study Program available. Institutional employment available. Highest amount earned per year from on-campus jobs $1,200. **Financial Aid Statistics:** 76% freshmen, 76% undergrads receive need-based scholarship or grant aid. 58% freshmen, 59% undergrads receive non-need-based scholarship or grant aid. 75% freshmen, 71% undergrads receive need-based self-help aid. 5% freshmen, 5% undergrads receive athletic scholarships. 93% freshmen receive any aid. 95% undergrads borrow to pay for school. Average cumulative indebtedness $22,000. **Criteria for awarding institutional aid:** *Non-need-based:* Academics, alumni affiliation, art, athletics, leadership, minority status, music/drama, religious affiliation.

MEREDITH COLLEGE

3800 Hillsborough Street, Raleigh, NC 27607
Phone: 919-760-8581 **Financial Aid Phone:** 919-760-8565
E-mail: admissions@meredith.edu **CEEB Code:** 5410
Fax: 919-760-2348 **Website:** www.meredith.edu **ACT Code:** 3126

This private school was founded in 1891. It has a 225-acre campus.

RATINGS
Admissions Selectivity Rating: 76   **Fire Safety Rating:** 77   **Green Rating:** 60*

STUDENTS AND FACULTY
Enrollment: 1,901. **Student Body:** 100% female, 10% out-of-state, 2% international (39 countries represented). Asian 2%, African American 11%, Caucasian 76%, Hispanic 2%.
Retention and Graduation: 74% freshmen return for sophomore year. **Faculty:** Student/faculty ratio 10:1. 147 full-time faculty, 10% are are members of minority groups, 67% are women.

ACADEMICS
Degrees: Bachelor's, master's, post-bachelor's certificate. **Classes:** Most classes have 10–19 students. Most lab/discussion sessions have fewer than 10 students. **Majors with Highest Enrollment:** Business/commerce; interior design; psychology. **Special Study Options:** Accelerated program, cooperative education program, cross-registration, double major, dual enrollment, honors program, independent study, internships, liberal arts/career combination, student-designed major, study abroad, teacher certification program, Semester Programs at American U, Drew U, Marymount Manhattan. **Honors programs:** Meredith offers an enriched academic and co-curricular Honors Program that spans the four years and involves honors courses in general education, in the major field, and a thesis or equivalent project. Interdisciplinary honors courses and weekend trips/programs enrich the experience, and a Focus on Excellence series offers a variety of outings to cultural/intellectual/entertainment venues. Scholarships are provided for Honors Program participants. **Combined degree programs:** BA/MEng, BS/MBA in accounting. Special programs offered to physically disabled students include note-taking services, reader services, tape recorders, tutors. **Career services:** Alumni network, alumni services, career/job search classes, career assessment, internships.

FACILITIES
Housing: women's dorms, apartments for married students, apartments for single students. 80% of campus accessible to physically disabled. **Special Academic Facilities/Equipment:** Art gallery, amphitheatre, child-care lab, learning center and fitness center. Experimental and clinical psychology labs including an autism lab. A new Science and Mathematics Building provides a roof-top telescope platform for astronomy observations, an electron microscope suite, greenhouse, and 15 student/faculty research labs. **Computers:** Students can register for classes online. Administrative functions (other than registration) can be performed online.

CAMPUS LIFE
Environment: Metropolis. **Activities:** Choral groups, concert band, dance, drama/theater, literary magazine, music ensembles, musical theater, student government, student newspaper, symphony orchestra, yearbook, Model UN. **Organizations:** 91 registered organizations, 22 honor societies, 7 religious organizations. **Athletics (Intercollegiate):** *Women:* Basketball, cross-country,

soccer, softball, tennis, volleyball. **On-Campus Highlights:** Science and Math Building, McIver Ampitheatre and Meredith Lake, Weatherspoon Physical Education -Dance Building, Belk Dining Hall, Cate Student Center/Bee Hive (snack bar).

ADMISSIONS
Freshman Academic Profile: Average high school GPA 3.21. 18% in top 10% of high school class, 48% in top 25% of high school class, 84% in top 50% of high school class. SAT Math middle 50% range 470–570. SAT Critical Reading middle 50% range 470–560. ACT middle 50% range 19–24. Minimum paper TOEFL 500. Minimum computer TOEFL 173. **Basis for Candidate Selection:** *Very important factors considered include:* Class rank, academic GPA, rigor of secondary school record. *Important factors considered include:* Recommendation(s), standardized test scores, character/personal qualities. *Other factors considered include:* Application essay, alumni/ae relation, extracurricular activities, interview, talent/ability, volunteer work, work experience. **Freshman Admission Requirements:** High school diploma is required and GED is not accepted. *Academic units required:* 4 English, 3 mathematics, 3 science, 2 foreign language. *Academic units recommended:* 1 academic electives. **Freshman Admission Statistics:** 1,557 applied, 69% admitted, 37% enrolled. **Transfer Admission Requirements:** High school transcript, college transcript(s), statement of good standing from prior institution(s). Minimum college GPA of 2.0 required. Lowest grade transferable C. **General Admission Information:** Application fee $40. Early decision application deadline 10/15. Notification on a rolling basis, beginning on or about 11/1. Nonfall registration accepted. Admission may be deferred for a maximum of 1 year. Credit offered for CEEB Advanced Placement tests.

COSTS AND FINANCIAL AID
Required Forms and Deadlines: FAFSA. Priority financial aid filing date 2/15. **Notification of Awards:** Applicants will be notified of awards on a rolling basis beginning 3/15. **Types of Aid:** *Need-based scholarships/grants:* Federal Pell, SEOG, state scholarships/grants, private scholarships, the school's own gift aid. *Loans:* FFEL Subsidized Stafford, FFEL Unsubsidized Stafford, FFEL PLUS, Federal Perkins, college/university loans from institutional funds. *Student Employment:* **Financial Aid Statistics:** 64% freshmen, 8% freshmen, 54% freshmen, 72.5% undergrads borrow to pay for school. Average cumulative indebtedness $29,193. **Criteria for awarding institutional aid:** *Non-need-based:* Academics, art, leadership, minority status, music/drama, religious affiliation, state/district residency.

See page 1162.

MERRIMACK COLLEGE

Office of Admission, Austin Hall, North Andover, MA 01845
Phone: 978-837-5100 **Financial Aid Phone:** 978-837-5186
E-mail: admission@merrimack.edu **CEEB Code:** 3525
Fax: 978-837-5133 **Website:** www.merrimack.edu

This private school, affiliated with the Roman Catholic Church, was founded in 1947. It has a 220-acre campus.

RATINGS
Admissions Selectivity Rating: 79   **Fire Safety Rating:** 60*   **Green Rating:** 60*

STUDENTS AND FACULTY
Enrollment: 2,057. **Student Body:** 50% female, 50% male, 35% out-of-state, 2% international (10 countries represented). Asian 2%, African American 2%, Caucasian 77%, Hispanic 3%.
Retention and Graduation: 71% freshmen return for sophomore year. 23% grads go on to further study within 1 year. 10% grads pursue arts and sciences degrees. 2% grads pursue law degrees. 5% grads pursue business degrees. 1% grads pursue medical degrees. **Faculty:** Student/faculty ratio 12:1. 126 full-time faculty, 84% hold PhDs, 7% are are members of minority groups, 42% are women.

ACADEMICS
Degrees: Associate, bachelor's, master's. **Classes:** Most classes have 10–19 students. **Majors with Highest Enrollment:** Business administration and management; marketing/marketing management; psychology. **Special Study Options:** Accelerated program, cooperative education program, cross-registration, double major, dual enrollment, English as a Second Language (ESL), independent study, internships, liberal arts/career combination, student-designed major, study abroad, teacher certification program, Five-year combined BA/BS program, continuing education program, center for corporate education. ESL available through Kaplan with offices on the college campus. Cross-registration available through college's membership in 10–college consortium. **Honors pro-**

grams: The Honors Program offers students with strong academic credentials, class standing, and leadership qualities the opportunity to study with other exceptional students in smaller classes. It is an innovative and exciting approach to fulfilling the college's general education requirements and includes a variety of social and co-curricular activities. Special programs offered to physically disabled students include note-taking services, reader services, tape recorders, tutors. **Career services:** Alumni network, alumni services, career/job search classes, career assessment, internships, regional alumni. **Career services highlights include:** At Merrimack College we offer experiential opportunities for students in each major: traditional 5-year cooperative education program; full-time paid summer internships; part-time paid internship opportunities during the academic year; in conjunction with academic departments, unpaid but for-academic credit internships; service learning volunteer opportunities with local non-profit agencies.

FACILITIES

Housing: Coed dorms, special housing for disabled students, apartments for single students, wellness house, theme housing, 90% of campus accessible to physically disabled. **Special Academic Facilities/Equipment:** Observatory, Rogers Center for the Arts. **Computers:** 100% of classrooms, 100% of libraries, 100% of dining areas, 100% of student union, have wireless network access. Students can register for classes online. Administrative functions (other than registration) can be performed online.

CAMPUS LIFE

Environment: Town. **Activities:** Choral groups, dance, drama/theater, jazz band, music ensembles, musical theater, pep band, student government, student newspaper, student-run film society, television station, yearbook, campus ministries, international student organization, Model UN. **Organizations:** 47 registered organizations, 3 honor societies, 5 religious organizations. 2 fraternities, 3 sororities. **Athletics (Intercollegiate):** *Men:* Baseball, basketball, cross-country, football, ice hockey, lacrosse, soccer, tennis. *Women:* Basketball, cross-country, field hockey, lacrosse, soccer, softball, tennis, volleyball. **On-Campus Highlights:** Sakowich Student Center, Rogers Center for the Arts, Santagati Hall, McQuade Library, Volpe Athletic Complex, Campus observatory open one night a week to the public. Rogers Center and the McQuade Library have art gallerys. McQuade Gallery frequently displays student art. **Environmental Initiatives:** Bio-diesel project. Merrimack College is embracing a new, comprehensive recycling program. **Food Service initiatives:** environmentally friendly paper products; tray-free in cafeteria.

ADMISSIONS

Freshman Academic Profile: Average high school GPA 3.2. 18% in top 10% of high school class, 24% in top 25% of high school class, 56% in top 50% of high school class. 65% from public high schools. Minimum paper TOEFL 550. Minimum computer TOEFL 230. **Basis for Candidate Selection:** *Very important factors considered include:* Application essay, academic GPA, rigor of secondary school record. *Important factors considered include:* Class rank, recommendation(s), character/personal qualities, talent/ability. *Other factors considered include:* Alumni/ae relation, extracurricular activities, interview, level of applicant's interest, volunteer work, work experience. **Freshman Admission Requirements:** High school diploma is required and GED is accepted. *Academic units required:* 4 English, 3 mathematics, 3 science, (3 science labs), 2 foreign language, 1 social studies, 1 history, 3 academic electives. *Academic units recommended:* 4 English, 4 mathematics, 4 science, (4 science labs), 3 foreign language, 2 social studies, 2 history, 3 academic electives. **Freshman Admission Statistics:** 3,915 applied, 79% admitted, 20% enrolled. **Transfer Admission Requirements:** College transcript(s), essay or personal statement, minimum college GPA of 2.5 required. Lowest grade transferable C. **General Admission Information:** Application fee $60. Regular application deadline 2/1. Regular notification 4/1. Nonfall registration accepted. Admission may be deferred for a maximum of 1 year. Credit and/or placement offered for CEEB Advanced Placement tests.

COSTS AND FINANCIAL AID

Annual tuition $29,310. Room and board $10,190. Required fees $500. Average book expense $800. **Required Forms and Deadlines:** FAFSA, noncustodial PROFILE, business/farm supplement. Sibling Verification. Financial aid filing deadline 2/1. Priority financial aid filing date 2/1. **Notification of Awards:** Applicants will be notified of awards on or about 3/15. **Types of Aid:** *Need-based scholarships/grants:* Federal Pell, SEOG, state scholarships/grants, private scholarships, the school's own gift aid. *Loans:* FFEL Subsidized Stafford, FFEL Unsubsidized Stafford, FFEL PLUS, Federal Perkins, state loans, college/university loans from institutional funds, alternative loans. *Student Employment:* Federal Work-Study Program available. Highest amount earned per year from on-campus jobs $1,500. Off-campus job opportunities are good. **Financial Aid Statistics:** 80% freshmen, 63% undergrads receive need-based scholarship or grant aid. 12% freshmen, 19% undergrads receive non-need-based scholarship or grant aid. 53% freshmen, 45% undergrads receive need-based self-help aid. 13% freshmen, 13% undergrads receive athletic scholarships. 95% freshmen, 80% undergrads receive any aid. 75% undergrads borrow to pay for school. Average cumulative indebtedness $42,000. **Criteria for awarding institutional**

aid: *Non-need-based:* Academics, athletics, leadership, minority status, religious affiliation.

MESSIAH COLLEGE

PO Box 3005, One College Avenue, Grantham, PA 17027
Phone: 717-691-6000 **Financial Aid Phone:** 717-766-2511 Ext 3630
E-mail: bwaltman@messiah.edu **CEEB Code:** 2411
Fax: 717-691-2307 **Website:** www.messiah.edu **ACT Code:** 3630

This private school was founded in 1909. It has a 471-acre campus.

RATINGS

Admissions Selectivity Rating: 88   **Fire Safety Rating:** 72   **Green Rating:** 76

STUDENTS AND FACULTY

Enrollment: 2,802. **Student Body:** 63% female, 37% male, 43% out-of-state, 2% international (25 countries represented). Asian 2%, African American 2%, Caucasian 84%, Hispanic 1%.
Retention and Graduation: 83% freshmen return for sophomore year. 68% freshmen graduate within 4 years. 16% grads go on to further study within 1 year. 4% grads pursue arts and sciences degrees. 1% grads pursue law degrees. 1% grads pursue business degrees. 9% grads pursue medical degrees. **Faculty:** Student/faculty ratio 13:1. 173 full-time faculty, 83% hold PhDs, 5% are are members of minority groups, 38% are women.

ACADEMICS

Degrees: Bachelor's. **Classes:** Most classes have 20–29 students. Most lab/discussion sessions have 10–19 students. **Majors with Highest Enrollment:** Elementary education and teaching; nursing/registered nurse (RN, ASN, BSN, MSN); psychology. **Special Study Options:** Accelerated program, double major, dual enrollment, English as a Second Language (ESL), exchange student program (domestic), honors program, independent study, internships, student-designed major, study abroad, teacher certification program, Pass/Fail option. **Honors programs:** The College Honors Program is designed for students who demonstrate high scholarly ability early in their academic career. The program provides a series of interdisciplinary honors courses which satisfy selected general education requirements. In addition, various campus activities are designed each semester for participants in the College Honors Program. Participation in the program culminates in an honors research project, typically during the senior year. Admission to the program is highly competitive and students selected for the College Honors Program receive either full tuition or partial tuition scholarships. Special programs offered to physically disabled students include note-taking services, reader services, tutors. **Career services:** Alumni network, alumni services, career assessment, internships. **Career services highlights include:** Internship program supports ~150 students each year.

FACILITIES

Housing: Coed dorms, special housing for disabled students, men's dorms, special housing for international students, women's dorms, apartments for single students 80% of campus accessible to physically disabled. **Special Academic Facilities/Equipment:** Boyer Center for Advanced Studies; Brethren in Christ Historical Society and Archives; Oakes Museum of Natural History. **Computers:** 100% of classrooms, 100% of dorms, 100% of libraries, 100% of dining areas, 100% of student union, have wireless network access. Students can register for classes online. Administrative functions (other than registration) can be performed online.

CAMPUS LIFE

Environment: Village. **Activities:** Choral groups, concert band, dance, drama/theater, jazz band, literary magazine, music ensembles, musical theater, pep band, radio station, student government, student newspaper, student-run film society, symphony orchestra, yearbook, campus ministries, international student organization. **Organizations:** 71 registered organizations, 7 honor societies, 10 religious organizations. **Athletics (Intercollegiate):** *Men:* Baseball, basketball, cross-country, golf, lacrosse, soccer, swimming, tennis, track/field (outdoor), track/field (indoor), ultimate frisbee, wrestling. *Women:* Basketball, cross-country, field hockey, lacrosse, soccer, softball, swimming, tennis, track/field (outdoor), track/field (indoor), volleyball. **On-Campus Highlights:** Boyer Hall (Schools of Humanities, Ed. and Soc. Sci, Eisenhower Campus Center/Sollenberger Sports Cent, Oakes Museum of Natural History, Stoner Covered Bridge, Starry Athletic Complex. The scenic Yellow Breeches Creek runs through the 471 acre campus. It is a nationally recognized trout fishing stream, complete with covered bridge and swinging foot bridge. **Environmental Initiatives:** Recycling and composting of wastes by Facilities Management and Conference Services. Creation Care Community Garden—Community-supported agriculture that is student run by the EarthKeepers Digital energy management system across campus buildings which is yielding solid energy savings.

ADMISSIONS

Freshman Academic Profile: Average high school GPA 3.71. 33% in top 10% of high school class, 70% in top 25% of high school class, 94% in top 50% of high school class. 75% from public high schools. SAT Math middle 50% range 520–640. SAT Critical Reading middle 50% range 520–630. SAT Writing middle 50% range 520–640. ACT middle 50% range 22–27. Minimum paper TOEFL 550. Minimum computer TOEFL 213. Minimum web-based TOEFL 80. **Basis for Candidate Selection:** *Very important factors considered include:* Class rank, academic GPA, recommendation(s), rigor of secondary school record, standardized test scores, character/personal qualities, extracurricular activities, religious affiliation/commitment, talent/ability. *Important factors considered include:* Application essay, volunteer work. *Other factors considered include:* Alumni/ae relation, interview, level of applicant's interest, racial/ethnic status, work experience. **Freshman Admission Requirements:** High school diploma is required and GED is accepted. *Academic units required:* 4 English, 2 mathematics, 2 science, (2 science labs), 2 foreign language, 2 social studies, 4 academic electives. *Academic units recommended:* 4 English, 3 mathematics, 3 science, (3 science labs), 2 foreign language, 2 social studies, 2 history, 4 academic electives. **Freshman Admission Statistics:** 2,844 applied, 70% admitted, 36% enrolled. **Transfer Admission Requirements:** College transcript(s), essay or personal statement, statement of good standing from prior institution(s). Minimum college GPA of 2.5 required. Lowest grade transferable C. **General Admission Information:** Application fee $30. Notification on a rolling basis, beginning on or about 7/1. Nonfall registration accepted. Admission may be deferred for a maximum of 2 years. Credit and/or placement offered for CEEB Advanced Placement tests.

COSTS AND FINANCIAL AID

Annual tuition $24,900. Room and board $7,610. Required fees $770. Average book expense $960. **Required Forms and Deadlines:** FAFSA. Priority financial aid filing date 4/1. **Notification of Awards:** Applicants will be notified of awards on a rolling basis beginning 3/15. *Types of Aid: Need-based scholarships/grants:* Federal Pell, SEOG, state scholarships/grants, private scholarships, the school's own gift aid. *Loans:* Direct Subsidized Stafford, Direct Unsubsidized Stafford, Direct PLUS, FFEL Subsidized Stafford, FFEL Unsubsidized Stafford, FFEL PLUS, Federal Perkins, Federal Nursing *Student Employment:* Federal Work-Study Program available. Institutional employment available. Highest amount earned per year from on-campus jobs $5,730. Off-campus job opportunities are good. **Financial Aid Statistics:** 71% freshmen, 68% undergrads receive need-based scholarship or grant aid. 9% freshmen, 6% undergrads receive non-need-based scholarship or grant aid. 57% freshmen, 57% undergrads receive need-based self-help aid. 97% freshmen, 97% undergrads receive any aid. 73% undergrads borrow to pay for school. Average cumulative indebtedness $34,871. **Criteria for awarding institutional aid:** *Non-need-based:* Academics, art, leadership, music/drama, religious affiliation.

See page 1164.

METHODIST UNIVERSITY

5400 Ramsey Street, Fayetteville, NC 28311
Phone: 910-630-7027 **Financial Aid Phone:** 910-630-7192
E-mail: admissions@methodist.edu **CEEB Code:** 5426
Fax: 910-630-7285 **Website:** www.methodist.edu **ACT Code:** 3127

This private school, affiliated with the Methodist Church, was founded in 1956. It has a 600-acre campus.

RATINGS

Admissions Selectivity Rating: 76   **Fire Safety Rating:** 60*   **Green Rating:** 60*

STUDENTS AND FACULTY

Enrollment: 1,929. **Student Body:** 44% female, 56% male, 48% out-of-state, 4% international (31 countries represented). Asian 1%, African American 19%, Caucasian 57%, Hispanic 6%, Native American 1%.
Retention and Graduation: 67% freshmen return for sophomore year. 16% freshmen graduate within 4 years. 38% grads go on to further study within 1 year. 8% grads pursue arts and sciences degrees. 1% grads pursue law degrees. 12% grads pursue business degrees. 7% grads pursue medical degrees. **Faculty:** Student/faculty ratio 12:1. 136 full-time faculty, 72% hold PhDs, 11% are are members of minority groups, 46% are women.

ACADEMICS

Degrees: Associate, bachelor's, master's, terminal associate. **Classes:** Most classes have fewer than 10 students. Most lab/discussion sessions have 20–29 students. **Majors with Highest Enrollment:** Business/commerce; cell/cellular and molecular biology; secondary education and teaching. **Special Study**

Options: Cooperative education program, distance learning, double major, dual enrollment, English as a Second Language (ESL), honors program, independent study, internships, liberal arts/career combination, student-designed major, study abroad, teacher certification program, weekend college, distance learning is on-line coursework available. **Honors programs:** The Methodist College Honors Program is based on the "Great Books" and is an outstanding opportunity for high acheiving students. Special programs offered to physically disabled students include note-taking services, reader services, tape recorders, tutors. **Career services:** Career/job search classes, career assessment, internships.

FACILITIES

Housing: Coed dorms, men's dorms, women's dorms, apartments for single students, first year experience hall. 80% of campus accessible to physically disabled. **Special Academic Facilities/Equipment:** Art gallery, Nature Trail, 18 hole golf course with practice facilities for PGM students, Academic Developement Center. **Computers:** Administrative functions (other than registration) can be performed online.

CAMPUS LIFE

Environment: City. **Activities:** Choral groups, concert band, dance, drama/theater, jazz band, literary magazine, marching band, music ensembles, musical theater, opera, pep band, radio station, student government, student newspaper, symphony orchestra, yearbook, campus ministries, Model UN. **Organizations:** 72 registered organizations, 15 honor societies, 8 religious organizations. 3 fraternities, 2 sororities. **Athletics (Intercollegiate):** *Men:* Baseball, basketball, cheerleading, cross-country, football, golf, soccer, tennis, track/field (outdoor). *Women:* Basketball, cheerleading, cross-country, golf, lacrosse, soccer, softball, tennis, track/field (outdoor), volleyball.

ADMISSIONS

Freshman Academic Profile: Average high school GPA 3.23. 12% in top 10% of high school class, 33% in top 25% of high school class, 72% in top 50% of high school class. 86% from public high schools. SAT Math middle 50% range 440–560. SAT Critical Reading middle 50% range 440–540. SAT Writing middle 50% range 410–510. ACT middle 50% range 18–23. Minimum paper TOEFL 500. Minimum computer TOEFL 173. **Basis for Candidate Selection:** *Very important factors considered include:* Academic GPA, rigor of secondary school record. *Important factors considered include:* Class rank, standardized test scores, interview. *Other factors considered include:* Application essay, recommendation(s), alumni/ae relation, character/personal qualities, extracurricular activities, first generation, talent/ability. **Freshman Admission Requirements:** High school diploma is required and GED is accepted. *Academic units required:* 4 English, 3 mathematics, 3 science, (1 science labs), 1 social studies, 2 history, 4 academic electives. *Academic units recommended:* 4 English, 4 mathematics, 4 science, (1 science labs), 2 foreign language, 2 social studies, 2 history. **Freshman Admission Statistics:** 2,937 applied, 66% admitted, 24% enrolled. **Transfer Admission Requirements:** High school transcript, college transcript(s), statement of good standing from prior institution(s). Minimum college GPA of 2.0 required. Lowest grade transferable C. **General Admission Information:** Application fee $25. Notification on a rolling basis, beginning on or about 9/1. Nonfall registration accepted. Admission may be deferred for a maximum of 1 academic year. Credit and/or placement offered for CEEB Advanced Placement tests.

COSTS AND FINANCIAL AID

Annual tuition $22,260. Room and board $8,400. Required fees $418. Average book expense $1,200. **Required Forms and Deadlines:** FAFSA **Notification of Awards:** Applicants will be notified of awards on a rolling basis beginning 3/1. *Types of Aid: Need-based scholarships/grants:* Federal Pell, SEOG, state scholarships/grants, private scholarships, the school's own gift aid. *Loans:* FFEL Subsidized Stafford, FFEL Unsubsidized Stafford, FFEL PLUS, Federal Perkins. *Student Employment:* Federal Work-Study Program available. Highest amount earned per year from on-campus jobs $1,600. Off-campus job opportunities are good. **Financial Aid Statistics:** 75% freshmen, 65% undergrads receive need-based scholarship or grant aid. 55% freshmen, 57% undergrads receive non-need-based scholarship or grant aid. 71% freshmen, 62% undergrads receive need-based self-help aid. 90% freshmen, 86% undergrads receive any aid. 81% undergrads borrow to pay for school. Average cumulative indebtedness $24,716. **Criteria for awarding institutional aid:** *Non-need-based:* Academics, alumni affiliation, leadership, music/drama, religious affiliation, state/district residency.

METROPOLITAN COLLEGE OF NEW YORK

75 Varick Street, New York, NY 10013
Phone: 212-343-1234
E-mail: admissions@metropolitan.edu **CEEB Code:** 4802
Fax: 212-343-8470 **Website:** www.metropolitan.edu

This private school was founded in 1964.

RATINGS
Admissions Selectivity Rating: 60*   **Fire Safety Rating:** 60*   **Green Rating:** 60*

STUDENTS AND FACULTY
Enrollment: 1,093. **Student Body:** 80% female, 20% male, 10% out-of-state, (12 countries represented). Asian 1%, African American 102%, Caucasian 5%, Hispanic 18%, Native American 1%.
Retention and Graduation: 72% freshmen return for sophomore year. 60% grads go on to further study within 1 year. 15% grads pursue law degrees. 24% grads pursue business degrees. **Faculty:** Student/faculty ratio 17:1. 26 full-time faculty.

ACADEMICS
Degrees: Associate, bachelor's, certificate, master's, transfer associate. **Classes:** Most classes have 10–19 students. **Special Study Options:** Accelerated program, cooperative education program, distance learning, honors program, internships, weekend college. **Combined degree programs:** MS/MBA. Special programs offered to physically disabled students include tutors. **Career services:** Alumni services, internships.

FACILITIES
Housing: 4% of campus accessible to physically disabled. **Computers:** Administrative functions (other than registration) can be performed online.

CAMPUS LIFE
Activities: Student government, student newspaper. **Organizations:** 10 registered organizations.

ADMISSIONS
Freshman Academic Profile: 70% from public high schools. Minimum paper TOEFL 550. **Basis for Candidate Selection:** *Very important factors considered include:* Interview. *Important factors considered include:* Extracurricular activities, talent/ability, volunteer work, work experience. *Other factors considered include:* Recommendation(s), character/personal qualities. **Freshman Admission Requirements:** High school diploma is required and GED is accepted. **Freshman Admission Statistics:** 399 applied, 78% admitted, 62% enrolled. **Transfer Admission Requirements:** High school transcript, essay or personal statement, interview, Lowest grade transferable C. **General Admission Information:** Application fee $30. Early decision application deadline 5/2. Nonfall registration accepted. Admission may be deferred for a maximum of 12. Neither credit nor placement offered for CEEB Advanced Placement tests.

COSTS AND FINANCIAL AID
Annual tuition $12,960. Required fees $400. Average book expense $1,500. **Required Forms and Deadlines:** FAFSA, state aid form, noncustodial PROFILE. **Types of Aid:** *Need-based scholarships/grants:* Federal Pell, SEOG, state scholarships/grants, private scholarships, the school's own gift aid. *Loans:* FFEL Subsidized Stafford, FFEL Unsubsidized Stafford, FFEL PLUS, signature loan. *Student Employment:* Federal Work-Study Program available. Off-campus job opportunities are good. **Financial Aid Statistics:** 62% freshmen, 68% undergrads receive need-based scholarship or grant aid. 12% freshmen, 12% undergrads receive non-need-based scholarship or grant aid. 62% freshmen, 65% undergrads receive need-based self-help aid. 80% undergrads borrow to pay for school. Average cumulative indebtedness $24,000. **Criteria for awarding institutional aid:** *Non-need-based:* Academics, leadership.

MIAMI UNIVERSITY

301 S. Campus Ave, Oxford, OH 45056
Phone: 513-529-2531 **Financial Aid Phone:** 513-529-8734
E-mail: admission@muohio.edu **CEEB Code:** 1463
Fax: 513-529-1550 **Website:** www.miami.muohio.edu **ACT Code:** 3294

This public school was founded in 1809. It has a 2000-acre campus.

RATINGS
Admissions Selectivity Rating: 87   **Fire Safety Rating:** 75   **Green Rating:** 77

STUDENTS AND FACULTY
Enrollment: 14,553. **Student Body:** 53% female, 47% male, 30% out-of-state, 3% international (49 countries represented). Asian 3%, African American 4%, Caucasian 84%, Hispanic 2%, Native American 1%.
Retention and Graduation: 89% freshmen return for sophomore year. 70% freshmen graduate within 4 years. **Faculty:** Student/faculty ratio 17:1. 827 full-time faculty, 89% hold PhDs, 17% are are members of minority groups, 41% are women. 6% of classes are taught by teaching assistants.

ACADEMICS
Degrees: Associate, bachelor's, certificate, doctoral, master's, post-master's certificate, terminal associate, transfer associate. **Classes:** Most classes have 20–29 students. Most lab/discussion sessions have 20–29 students. **Majors with Highest Enrollment:** Finance; marketing/marketing management; psychology. **Special Study Options:** Cooperative education program, cross-registration, distance learning, double major, exchange student program (domestic), honors program, independent study, internships, liberal arts/career combination, student-designed major, study abroad, teacher certification program. **Honors programs:** Miami has a University Honors Program. Students selected to participate receive a renewable scholarship, priority registration, and other special opportunities. **Combined degree programs:** 3-2 forestry/env. studies with Duke; 3-1 Arts/Prof. Degree, 3-2 engineering. Special programs offered to physically disabled students include note-taking services, reader services, tape recorders, tutors. **Career services:** Alumni network, alumni services, career/job search classes, career assessment, internships, regional alumni.

FACILITIES
Housing: Coed dorms, special housing for disabled students, men's dorms, special housing for international students, women's dorms, fraternity/sorority housing, apartments for married students, cooperative housing, apartments for single students, wellness house, theme housing. 100% of campus accessible to physically disabled. **Special Academic Facilities/Equipment:** Geology, art, anthropology, and zoology museums, performing arts center, herbarium, ecology research center, 400–acre nature preserve, electron microscope center. **Computers:** 100% of classrooms, 100% of dorms, 100% of libraries, 100% of dining areas, 100% of student union, 65% of common outdoor areas have wireless network access. Students can register for classes online. Administrative functions (other than registration) can be performed online.

CAMPUS LIFE
Environment: Village. **Activities:** Choral groups, concert band, dance, drama/theater, jazz band, literary magazine, marching band, music ensembles, musical theater, opera, pep band, radio station, student government, student newspaper, student-run film society, symphony orchestra, television station, yearbook, campus ministries, international student organization, Model UN. **Organizations:** 304 registered organizations, 38 honor societies, 22 religious organizations. 32 fraternities, 23 sororities. **Athletics (Intercollegiate):** *Men:* Baseball, basketball, cross-country, diving, football, golf, ice hockey, swimming, track/field (outdoor). *Women:* Basketball, cross-country, diving, field hockey, soccer, softball, swimming, tennis, track/field (outdoor), volleyball. **On-Campus Highlights:** Farmer School of Business, McGuffey Museum, Center for the Performing Arts, Recreational Sports Center, Peabody Hall (National Historical Landmark), Formal Gardens. **Environmental Initiatives:** Our focus currently is on making sustainability a central part of campus decision-making at Miami, including: administration, operations, academic affairs, student life, and community relations. The creation of a sustainability coordinator role and standing sustainability committee now enables Miami to systematically research sustainability-related issues, set goals, implement strategies, and track progress. Our efforts have previously been scattered and uncoordinated. Now they are an ongoing priority. The university is developing a set of public commitments to measurable sustainability progress, including but not limited to a CO_2 emissions reduction target. In future months these specific targets and actions will be

announced publicly, and a process of ongoing assessment of progress developed. Miami is committed to complying with Ohio House Bill 251, which mandates a 20% reduction in energy consumption by 2014. A set of energy efficiency and waste reduction strategies are underway. Miami continues to compete in RecycleMania, which now covers all campus buildings. Housing Dining and Guest Services has created a residence hall competition "Unplugged, Untapped, Game On!" to reduce resource consumption. An "energy point of contact" is now assigned in all state buildings to coordinate efficiency strategies. Building energy consumption is now metered and available publicly on-line, and will soon be communicated to building users by updated bulletin boards. Major new construction projects have been designed to LEED certification standards.

ADMISSIONS

Freshman Academic Profile: Average high school GPA 3.65. 39% in top 10% of high school class, 74% in top 25% of high school class, 97% in top 50% of high school class. 72% from public high schools. SAT Math middle 50% range 560–660. SAT Critical Reading middle 50% range 530–630. ACT middle 50% range 24–29. Minimum paper/TOEFL 533. Minimum computer TOEFL 200. Minimum web-based TOEFL 72. **Basis for Candidate Selection:** *Very important factors considered include:* Class rank, application essay, academic GPA, recommendation(s), rigor of secondary school record, standardized test scores, character/personal qualities, talent/ability. *Other factors considered include:* Alumni/ae relation, extracurricular activities, first generation, geographical residence, state residency, volunteer work, work experience. **Freshman Admission** diploma is required and GED is accepted. *Academic units recommended:* 4 English, 3 mathematics, 3 science, 2 foreign language, 2 social studies, 1 history, 1 visual/performing arts. **Freshman Admission Statistics:** 16,772 applied, 79% admitted, 24% enrolled. **Transfer Admission Requirements:** High school transcript, college transcript(s), essay or personal statement, statement of good standing from prior institution(s). Minimum college GPA of 2.0 required. Lowest grade transferable C. **General Admission Information:** Application fee $50. Early decision application deadline 11/1. Regular application deadline 2/1. Regular notification 3/15. Nonfall registration accepted. Admission may be deferred for a maximum of 1 year. Credit offered for CEEB Advanced Placement tests.

COSTS AND FINANCIAL AID

Required Forms and Deadlines: FAFSA. Priority financial aid filing date 2/15. **Notification of Awards:** Applicants will be notified of awards on a rolling basis beginning 3/20. **Types of Aid:** *Need-based scholarships/grants:* Federal Pell, SEOG, state scholarships/grants, private scholarships, the school's own gift aid. *Loans:* Direct Subsidized Stafford, Direct Unsubsidized Stafford, Direct PLUS, Federal Perkins, Federal Nursing, college/university loans from institutional funds, Bank Education Loans. *Student Employment:* Federal Work-Study Program available. Institutional employment available. Off-campus job opportunities are good. **Financial Aid Statistics:** 35% freshmen, 22% undergrads receive need-based scholarship or grant aid. 25% freshmen, 18% undergrads receive non-need-based scholarship or grant aid. 33% freshmen, 32% undergrads receive need-based self-help aid. 2% freshmen, 3% undergrads receive athletic scholarships. 51% undergrads borrow to pay for school. Average cumulative indebtedness $26,798. **Criteria for awarding institutional aid:** *Non-need-based:* Academics, art, athletics, leadership, minority status, music/drama, state/district residency.

MICHIGAN STATE UNIVERSITY

250 Administration Building, East Lansing, MI 48824-1046
Phone: 517-355-8332 **Financial Aid Phone:** 517-353-5940
E-mail: admis@msu.edu **CEEB Code:** 1465
Fax: 517-353-1647 **Website:** www.msu.edu **ACT Code:** 2032

This public school was founded in 1855. It has a 5200-acre campus.

RATINGS
Admissions Selectivity Rating: 85   **Fire Safety Rating:** 60*   **Green Rating:** 89

STUDENTS AND FACULTY
Enrollment: 36,224. **Student Body:** 52% female, 48% male, 8.9% out-of-state, 7% international (136 countries represented). Asian 5%, African American 8%, Caucasian 75%, Hispanic 3%, Native American 1%. **Retention and Graduation:** 91% freshmen return for sophomore year. 22% grads go on to further study within 1 year. **Faculty:** Student/faculty ratio 17:1.

2620 full-time faculty, 93% hold PhDs, 23% are are members of minority groups, 36% are women.

ACADEMICS
Degrees: Bachelor's, certificate, master's, post-master's certificate. **Classes:** Most classes have 20–29 students. Most lab/discussion sessions have 20–29 students. **Special Study Options:** Accelerated program, cooperative education program, distance learning, double major, dual enrollment, English as a Second Language (ESL), exchange student program (domestic), honors program, independent study, internships, liberal arts/career combination, student-designed major, study abroad, teacher certification program, weekend college. **Honors programs:** MSU's Honors College embodies MSU's long-standing commitment to provide programs of study that attract and challenge unusually talented undergraduates utilizing carefully planned, highly individualized programs of study that will meet the needs of academically talented students. **Combined degree programs:** BA/MA, computer science. Special programs offered to physically disabled students include note-taking services, reader services, tape recorders, tutors. **Career services:** Alumni network, alumni services, career/job search classes, career assessment, internships, regional alumni.

FACILITIES
Housing: Coed dorms, special housing for disabled students, special housing for international students, women's dorms, fraternity/sorority housing, apartments for married students, cooperative housing, apartments for single students, theme housing. **Special Academic Facilities/Equipment:** Art, natural history, Michigan history and anthropology museums, art center, on-campus preschool and elementary school, biological station, experimental farms, botanical garden, planetarium, two superconducting cyclotrons, observatory. **Computers:** Students can register for classes online. Administrative functions (other than registration) can be performed online. Undergraduates are required to own a computer.

CAMPUS LIFE
Environment: Town. **Activities:** Choral groups, concert band, dance, drama/theater, jazz band, literary magazine, marching band, music ensembles, musical theater, opera, pep band, radio station, student government, student newspaper, student-run film society, symphony orchestra, television station, yearbook, campus ministries, international student organization, Model UN. **Organizations:** 500 registered organizations, 47 honor societies, 50 religious organizations, 31 fraternity, 19 sororities. **Athletics (Intercollegiate):** *Men:* Baseball, basketball, cheerleading, cross-country, diving, football, golf, ice hockey, soccer, swimming, tennis, track/field (outdoor), track/field (indoor), wrestling. *Women:* Basketball, cheerleading, crew/rowing, cross-country, diving, field hockey, golf, gymnastics, soccer, softball, swimming, tennis, track/field (outdoor), track/field (indoor), volleyball. **On-Campus Highlights:** MSU Student Union, Jack Breslin Student Events Center, MSU Main Library and Cyber Caf, The International Center, Wharton Center for the Performing Arts. **Environmental Initiatives:** Chicago Climate Exchange; implementing an Office of Campus Sustainability; Fair Trade products preference.

ADMISSIONS
Freshman Academic Profile: Average high school GPA 3.6. 30.8% in top 10% of high school class, 69.9% in top 25% of high school class, 95.6% in top 50% of high school class. SAT Math middle 50% range 540–660. SAT Critical Reading middle 50% range 470–610. SAT Writing middle 50% range 480–610. ACT middle 50% range 23–27. Minimum paper TOEFL 550. Minimum computer TOEFL 213. Minimum web-based TOEFL 80. **Basis for Candidate Selection:** *Very important factors considered include:* Academic GPA, rigor of secondary school record, standardized test scores. *Important factors considered include:* Application essay, extracurricular activities, first generation, geographical residence. *Other factors considered include:* Class rank, recommendation(s), alumni/ae relation, character/personal qualities, level of applicant's interest, state residency, talent/ability, volunteer work, work experience. **Freshman Admission Requirements:** High school diploma is required and GED is accepted. *Academic units required:* 4 English, 3 mathematics, 2 science, 2 foreign language, 2 social studies, 1 history. *Academic units recommended:* (2 science labs), 2 foreign language, 2 social studies, 2 history. **Freshman Admission Statistics:** 25,349 applied, 73% admitted, 40% enrolled. **Transfer Admission Requirements:** College transcript(s), essay or personal statement, statement of good standing from prior institution(s). Minimum college GPA of 2.0 required. Lowest grade transferable C. **General Admission Information:** Application fee $35. Nonfall registration accepted. Credit and/or placement offered for CEEB Advanced Placement tests.

COSTS AND FINANCIAL AID
Annual in-state tuition $11,415. Annual out-of-state tuition $27,750. Room and board $7,394. Required fees $470. Average book expense $962. **Required Forms and Deadlines:** FAFSA. **Notification of Awards:** Applicants will be notified of awards on a rolling basis beginning 3/15. **Types of Aid:** *Need-based scholarships/grants:* Federal Pell, SEOG, state scholarships/grants, private scholarships, the school's own gift aid, United Negro College Fund *Loans:* Di-

rect Subsidized Stafford, Direct Unsubsidized Stafford, Direct PLUS, Federal Perkins, college/university loans from institutional funds. *Student Employment:* Federal Work-Study Program available. Institutional employment available. Off-campus job opportunities are excellent. **Financial Aid Statistics:** 29% freshmen, 28% undergrads receive need-based scholarship or grant aid. 33% freshmen, 20% undergrads receive non-need-based scholarship or grant aid. 45% freshmen, 43% undergrads receive need-based self-help aid. 1% freshmen, 1% undergrads receive athletic scholarships. 50% freshmen, 48% undergrads receive any aid. 44% undergrads borrow to pay for school. Average cumulative indebtedness $19,696. **Criteria for awarding institutional aid:** *Non-need-based:* Academics, alumni affiliation, art, athletics, leadership, music/drama, state/district residency.

MICHIGAN TECHNOLOGICAL UNIVERSITY

1400 Townsend Drive, Houghton, MI 49931
Phone: 906-487-2335 **Financial Aid Phone:** 906-487-2622
E-mail: mtu4u@mtu.edu **CEEB Code:** 1464
Fax: 906-487-2125 **Website:** www.mtu.edu **ACT Code:** 2030

This public school was founded in 1885. It has a 925-acre campus.

RATINGS
Admissions Selectivity Rating: 85   **Fire Safety Rating:** 97   **Green Rating:** 75

STUDENTS AND FACULTY
Enrollment: 5,835. **Student Body:** 24% female, 76% male, 23% out-of-state, 7% international (69 countries represented). Asian 1%, African American 2%, Caucasian 83%, Hispanic 2%, Native American 1%. **Retention and Graduation:** 83% freshmen return for sophomore year. 22% freshmen graduate within 4 years. 16.7% grads go on to further study within 1 year. 5% grads pursue arts and sciences degrees. 1% grads pursue law degrees. 5% grads pursue business degrees. 3% grads pursue medical degrees. **Faculty:** Student/faculty ratio 15:1. 379 full-time faculty, 86% hold PhDs, 14% are are members of minority groups, 29% are women. 3% of classes are taught by teaching assistants.

ACADEMICS
Degrees: Associate, bachelor's, certificate, master's, post-bachelor's certificate, terminal associate. **Classes:** Most classes have 10–19 students. Most lab/discussion sessions have 10–19 students. **Majors with Highest Enrollment:** Business administration and management; civil engineering; mechanical engineering. **Special Study Options:** Cooperative education program, distance learning, double major, dual enrollment, English as a Second Language (ESL), exchange student program (domestic), honors program, independent study, internships, study abroad, teacher certification program, Dual degrees with Northwestern MI College, Adrian College, Albion College, Augsburg College (MN), College of St. Scholastica (MN), Mount Senario College, Olivet College, Northland College, University of Wisconsin—Superior, St. Norbert College (WI), Northcentral Technical College (WI), College of Lake County (IL), and Macomb Community College (MI). **Honors programs:** Qualifying students are invited to apply to Michigan Tech's Honors Institute. Membership focuses on activities and enrichment for top scholars, rather than separate honors courses. More details are at http://honors.mtu.edu/. Special programs offered to physically disabled students include note-taking services, reader services, tape recorders, tutors. **Career services:** Alumni services, career/job search classes, career assessment, internships. **Career services highlights include:** The MTU Career Center is proud to be able to provide career advising. We want to have students focus on a career verses a job. Advising includes graduate school, military, and professional employment. 96% of the 2007–2008 graduates were placed either in a job relevant to their degree, graduate school, or military education.

FACILITIES
Housing: Coed dorms, special housing for disabled students, special housing for international students, fraternity/sorority housing, apartments for married students, apartments for single students, wellness house, theme housing, alcohol-free, Research Scholar Honors Housing, ROTC Learning Communities: Computer Science; First-year Experience; Health Summit; Forest Resources & Environmental Science; International House; Visual & Performing Arts; Leadership. 90% of campus accessible to physically disabled. **Special Academic Facilities/Equipment:** Mineralogical Museum, 4,700–acre research forest,

scanning electron microscope, PUMA Robots, X-ray fluorescence spectrometer, Process Simulation and Control Center, Rozsa Center for the Performing Arts, cleanrooms, MEMS Fabrication Facility, environmental scanning electron microscope, transmission electron microscope, radio-frequency plasma-assisted deposition chamber, electron lithography equipment. **Computers:** 93% of classrooms, 10% of dorms, 100% of libraries, 100% of dining areas, 100% of student union, 10% of common outdoor areas have wireless network access. Students can register for classes online. Administrative functions (other than registration) can be performed online.

CAMPUS LIFE
Environment: Village. **Activities:** Choral groups, concert band, dance, drama/theater, jazz band, literary magazine, music ensembles, musical theater, opera, pep band, radio station, student government, student newspaper, student-run film society, symphony orchestra, campus ministries, international student organization. **Organizations:** 210 registered organizations, 16 honor societies, 16 religious organizations. 13 fraternities, 8 sororities. **Athletics (Intercollegiate):** *Men:* Basketball, cross-country, football, ice hockey, skiing (nordic/cross-country), tennis, track/field (outdoor). *Women:* Basketball, cross-country, skiing (nordic/cross-country), tennis, track/field (outdoor), volleyball. **On-Campus Highlights:** Student Development Complex, Rozsa Center for the Performing Arts, Mont Ripley Ski Hill, Portage Lake Golf Course, Memorial Union Building. **Environmental Initiatives:** Emphasis on multidisciplinary sustainability research (www.mtu.edu/sfhi/initiatives/), education, and outreach (www.mtu.edu/sfhi/outreach/), such as Sustainable Futures Institute, Center for Water and Society, Environmentally Responsible Design and Manufacturing Research Group, National Institute for Climatic Change Research (Midwestern Region), Advanced Power Systems Research Center, Materials in Sustainable Transportation Infrastructure, Power and Energy Research Center, International Sustainable Engineering Initiative, IGERT for Sustainable Futures, Graduate Certificate in Sustainability, D80 Center, Peace Corps Masters International Program, International Sustainable Development Engineering Certificate, International Senior Design Programs, Sustainability Research Experience for Undergraduates, Wood-to-Wheels Graduate Enterprise, sustainability-based undergraduate Enterprise programs (Challenge X, Clean Snowmobile, Alternative Fuels Group, Aqua Terra Tech, Efficiency Through Engineering and Construction), Undergraduate and Graduate Colloquium in Sustainability, Sustainable Futures 1 and 2 courses Commitment of Administration to sustainability in strategic plan and NCA AQIP accreditation project to move toward a carbon-neutral campus (as referenced above). Sustainability Strategic Faculty Hiring Initiative (www.mtu.edu/sfhi) and other development efforts that are focused on strengthening Michigan Tech's sustainability infrastructure.

ADMISSIONS
Freshman Academic Profile: Average high school GPA 3.56. 28% in top 10% of high school class, 60% in top 25% of high school class, 90% in top 50% of high school class. 90% from public high schools. SAT Math middle 50% range 600–690. SAT Critical Reading middle 50% range 510–650. SAT Writing middle 50% range 510–630. ACT middle 50% range 23–29. Minimum paper TOEFL 550. Minimum computer TOEFL 213. Minimum web-based TOEFL 79. **Basis for Candidate Selection:** *Very important factors considered include:* Academic GPA, rigor of secondary school record, standardized test scores. *Important factors considered include:* Class rank. *Other factors considered include:* Application essay, recommendation(s), alumni/ae relation, character/personal qualities, extracurricular activities, interview, talent/ability, volunteer work, work experience. **Freshman Admission Requirements:** High school diploma is required and GED is accepted. *Academic units required:* 3 English, 3 mathematics, 2 science. *Academic units recommended:* 4 English, 4 mathematics, 3 science, 2 foreign language, 3 social studies, 1 history, 1 computer science, 2 academic electives. **Freshman Admission Statistics:** 4,719 applied, 73% admitted, 34% enrolled. **Transfer Admission Requirements:** College transcript(s), statement of good standing from prior institution(s). Minimum college GPA of 2.75 required. Lowest grade transferable C. **General Admission Information:** Notification on a rolling basis, beginning on or about 9/15. Nonfall registration accepted. Admission may be deferred for a maximum of 1 year. Credit and/or placement offered for CEEB Advanced Placement tests.

COSTS AND FINANCIAL AID
Required Forms and Deadlines: FAFSA. **Types of Aid:** *Need-based scholarships/grants:* Federal Pell, SEOG, state scholarships/grants, private scholarships, the school's own gift aid. *Loans:* Direct Subsidized Stafford, Direct Unsubsidized Stafford, Direct PLUS, Federal Perkins, college/university loans from institutional funds, External private loans. *Student Employment:* Federal Work-Study Program available. Institutional employment available. Highest amount earned per year from on-campus jobs $4,500. Off-campus job opportunities are excellent. **Financial Aid Statistics:** 94.9% freshmen, 88.3% undergrads receive any aid. **Criteria for awarding institutional aid:** *Non-need-based:* Academics, alumni affiliation, art, athletics, job skills, leadership, music/drama, state/district residency.

MID-AMERICA CHRISTIAN UNIVERSITY

3500 SW 119th Street, Oklahoma City, OK 73170
Phone: 405-691-3188
E-mail: info@macu.edu **CEEB Code:** 6942
Fax: 405-692-3165 **Website:** www.macu.edu **ACT Code:** 4097

This private school, affiliated with the Church of God Church, was founded in 1953.

RATINGS
Admissions Selectivity Rating: 60* **Fire Safety Rating:** 60* **Green Rating:** 60*

STUDENTS AND FACULTY
Student Body: 3 countries represented.

ACADEMICS
Degrees: Associate, bachelor's. **Majors with Highest Enrollment:** Business/commerce; pastoral studies/counseling; theology and religious vocations, other. **Special Study Options:** Accelerated program, distance learning, double major, external degree program, internships, liberal arts/career combination, student-designed major, teacher certification program **Combined degree programs:** Multidisciplinary. **Career services:** Internships.

FACILITIES
Housing: Special housing for disabled students, men's dorms, women's dorms. 100% of campus accessible to physically disabled.

CAMPUS LIFE
Environment: Metropolis. **Activities:** Choral groups, student government, student newspaper, yearbook. **Organizations:** 1 honor society, 5 religious organizations. **Athletics (Intercollegiate):** *Men:* Baseball, basketball, soccer. *Women:* Basketball, softball, volleyball. **On-Campus Highlights:** Gaulke Activity Center, President's Chapel, Fowler Student Center, Charles Ewing Brown Library.

ADMISSIONS
Freshman Academic Profile: Minimum paper TOEFL 500. **Transfer Admission Requirements:** College transcript(s), lowest grade transferable D. **General Admission Information:** Credit and/or placement offered for CEEB Advanced Placement tests.

COSTS AND FINANCIAL AID
Comprehensive fee $6,796. Room and board $2,896. Average book expense $500. **Types of Aid:** *Loans:* FFEL Subsidized Stafford, FFEL PLUS. *Student Employment:* Federal Work-Study Program available. Off-campus job opportunities are excellent.

MIDAMERICA NAZARENE UNIVERSITY

2030 College Way, Olathe, KS 66062
Phone: 913-791-3380 **Financial Aid Phone:** 913-971-3298
E-mail: admissions@mnu.edu **CEEB Code:** 6437
Fax: 913-791-3481 **Website:** www.mnu.edu **ACT Code:** 1445

This private school, affiliated with the Nazarene Church, was founded in 1966. It has a 105-acre campus.

RATINGS
Admissions Selectivity Rating: 84 **Fire Safety Rating:** 65 **Green Rating:** 60*

STUDENTS AND FACULTY
Enrollment: 1,283. **Student Body:** 56% female, 44% male, 33% out-of-state, 2% international (12 countries represented). Asian 1%, African American 7%, Caucasian 68%, Hispanic 3%, Native American 1%. **Retention and Graduation:** 70% freshmen return for sophomore year. 39% freshmen graduate within 4 years. **Faculty:** Student/faculty ratio 17:1. 86 full-time faculty, 41% hold PhDs, 5% are are members of minority groups.

ACADEMICS
Degrees: Associate, bachelor's, master's, post-master's certificate. **Classes:** Most classes have 10–19 students. Most lab/discussion sessions have 10–19 students. **Majors with Highest Enrollment:** Business/commerce; elementary education and teaching; nursing/registered nurse (RN, ASN, BSN, MSN). **Special Study Options:** Accelerated program, cross-registration, distance learning, double major, dual enrollment, independent study, internships, student-designed major, study abroad, teacher certification program, weekend

college. Special programs offered to physically disabled students include note-taking services, reader services, tape recorders, tutors. **Career services:** Career assessment.

FACILITIES
Housing: Special housing for disabled students, men's dorms, women's dorms, apartments for single students. 90% of campus accessible to physically disabled. **Computers:** Students can register for classes online. Administrative functions (other than registration) can be performed online.

CAMPUS LIFE
Environment: City. **Activities:** Choral groups, concert band, drama/theater, jazz band, literary magazine, music ensembles, musical theater, pep band, radio station, student government, student newspaper, television station, yearbook, campus ministries, international student organization. **Organizations:** 43 registered organizations, 6 honor societies, 4 religious organizations. **Athletics (Intercollegiate):** *Men:* Baseball, basketball, cheerleading, cross-country, football, soccer, track/field (outdoor), track/field (indoor). *Women:* Basketball, cheerleading, cross-country, soccer, softball, track/field (outdoor), track/field (indoor), volleyball. **On-Campus Highlights:** Cook Center, Land Memorial Gym, Fitness Center, Campus Center, Bell Cultural Events Center.

ADMISSIONS
Freshman Academic Profile: Average high school GPA 3.379. 20% in top 10% of high school class, 40% in top 25% of high school class, 70% in top 50% of high school class. 88% from public high schools. SAT Math middle 50% range 420–560. SAT Critical Reading middle 50% range 360–590. ACT middle 50% range 20–26. Minimum paper TOEFL 550. Minimum computer TOEFL 214. **Basis for Candidate Selection:** *Very important factors considered include:* Class rank, rigor of secondary school record, standardized test scores, character/personal qualities. *Important factors considered include:* Academic GPA, recommendation(s), level of applicant's interest. *Other factors considered include:* Application essay, extracurricular activities, interview, talent/ability. **Freshman Admission Requirements:** High school diploma is required and GED is accepted. *Academic units recommended:* 4 English, 3 mathematics, 3 science, 1 foreign language, 3 social studies. **Freshman Admission Statistics:** 535 applied, 41% admitted, 100% enrolled. **Transfer Admission Requirements:** College transcript(s), minimum college GPA of 2.0 required. Lowest grade transferable D. **General Admission Information:** Application fee $25. Regular application deadline 8/1. Nonfall registration not accepted. Admission may be deferred for a maximum of 2 years. Credit offered for CEEB Advanced Placement tests.

COSTS AND FINANCIAL AID
Annual tuition $17,216. Room and board $6,180. Required fees $1,000. Average book expense $1,180. **Required Forms and Deadlines:** FAFSA. Priority financial aid filing date 3/1. **Notification of Awards:** Applicants will be notified of awards on a rolling basis beginning 2/1. **Types of Aid:** *Need-based scholarships/grants:* Federal Pell, SEOG, state scholarships/grants, private scholarships, the school's own gift aid. *Loans:* FFEL Subsidized Stafford, FFEL Unsubsidized Stafford, FFEL PLUS, Federal Perkins. *Student Employment:* Off-campus job opportunities are good. **Financial Aid Statistics:** 63% freshmen, 71% undergrads receive need-based scholarship or grant aid. 44% freshmen, 31% undergrads receive non-need-based scholarship or grant aid. 61% freshmen, 60% undergrads receive need-based self-help aid. 46% freshmen, 36% undergrads receive athletic scholarships. 92% freshmen, 86% undergrads receive any aid. 77% undergrads borrow to pay for school. Average cumulative indebtedness $28,678. **Criteria for awarding institutional aid:** *Non-need-based:* Academics, athletics, leadership, minority status, music/drama, religious affiliation, state/district residency.

MIDDLE TENNESSEE STATE UNIVERSITY

Cope Administration Building 208, Murfreesboro, TN 37132
Phone: 615-898-2111
E-mail: admissions@mtsu.edu
Fax: 615-898-5478 **Website:** www.mtsu.edu

This is a public school.

RATINGS
Admissions Selectivity Rating: 60* **Fire Safety Rating:** 60* **Green Rating:** 60*

STUDENTS AND FACULTY
Enrollment: 21,252. **Student Body:** 52% female, 48% male, 5% out-of-state, international Asian 3%, African American 15%, Caucasian 78%, Hispanic 2%. **Retention and Graduation:** 71% freshmen return for sophomore year. 14% freshmen graduate within 4 years. **Faculty:** Student/faculty ratio 22:1. 828 full-time faculty, 16% are are members of minority groups, 44% are women.

ACADEMICS

Degrees: Bachelor's, master's, post-bachelor's certificate, post-master's certificate. **Classes:** Most classes have 20–29 students. Most lab/discussion sessions have fewer than 10 students. **Special Study Options:** Distance learning, double major, dual enrollment, honors program, independent study, internships, study abroad, teacher certification program.

FACILITIES

Housing: Coed dorms, special housing for disabled students, men's dorms, special housing for international students, women's dorms, fraternity/sorority housing, apartments for married students, cooperative housing, apartments for single students, wellness house, theme housing, wellness housing.

CAMPUS LIFE

Activities: Choral groups, concert band, dance, drama/theater, jazz band, literary magazine, marching band, music ensembles, musical theater, opera, pep band, radio station, student government, student newspaper, symphony orchestra, television station, campus ministries, international student organization, Model UN.

ADMISSIONS

Freshman Academic Profile: SAT Math middle 50% range 450–580. SAT Critical Reading middle 50% range 450–580. ACT middle 50% range 19–24. Minimum paper TOEFL 500. Minimum computer TOEFL 173. **Basis for Candidate Selection:** *Very important factors considered include:* Academic GPA, rigor of secondary school record, standardized test scores. *Important factors considered include:* Racial/ethnic status, talent/ability. *Other factors considered include:* Class rank, recommendation(s), character/personal qualities, extracurricular activities, first generation, level of applicant's interest, volunteer work, work experience. **Freshman Admission Requirements:** High school diploma is required and GED is accepted. *Academic units required:* 4 English, 3 mathematics, 2 science, 2 foreign language, 1 social studies, 1 history, 1 visual/performing arts. **Freshman Admission Statistics:** 9,583 applied, 65% admitted, 56% enrolled. **Transfer Admission Requirements:** College transcript(s), minimum college GPA of 2.0 required. Lowest grade transferable D. **General Admission Information:** Application fee $25. Nonfall registration accepted. Credit offered for CEEB Advanced Placement tests.

MIDDLEBURY COLLEGE

The Emma Willard House, Middlebury, VT 05753-6002
Phone: 802-443-3000
E-mail: admissions@middlebury.edu **CEEB Code:** 3526
Fax: 802-443-2056 **Website:** www.middlebury.edu **ACT Code:** 4306

This private school was founded in 1800. It has a 350-acre campus.

RATINGS

Admissions Selectivity Rating: 98   **Fire Safety Rating:** 89   **Green Rating:** 96

STUDENTS AND FACULTY

Enrollment: 2,455. **Student Body:** 51% female, 49% male, 94% out-of-state, 10% international (64 countries represented). Asian 9%, African American 4%, Caucasian 65%, Hispanic 5%.
Retention and Graduation: 97% freshmen return for sophomore year. 83% freshmen graduate within 4 years. **Faculty:** Student/faculty ratio 8.9:1. 260 full-time faculty, 95% hold PhDs, 11% are are members of minority groups, 41% are women.

ACADEMICS

Degrees: Bachelor's, master's. **Classes:** Most classes have 10–19 students. **Majors with Highest Enrollment:** Economics; English language and literature; psychology. **Special Study Options:** Accelerated program, double major, exchange student program (domestic), honors program, independent study, internships, student-designed major, study abroad, teacher certification program, Williams College-Mystic Seaport Program in American Maritime Studies, Oxford University summer Program,independent scholar programs with Berea College and Swarthmore College, 3-year international major. Special programs offered to physically disabled students include note-taking services, reader services, tape recorders, tutors. **Career services:** Alumni network, alumni services, career/job search classes, career assessment, internships, regional alumni.

FACILITIES

Housing: Coed dorms, special housing for disabled students, apartments for single students, multi-cultural house, environmental house, foreign language house, 5 co-ed social houses. Commons System organizes residence halls into 5 groups,each with its own budget, government, faculty, and staff associates. 60% of campus accessible to physically disabled. **Special Academic Facilities/Equipment:** Art museum, theatres, language lab, observatory, electron microscope, mountain campus, downhill and cross-country ski areas, golf course, Franklin Environmental Center, organic garden. **Computers:** Students can register for classes online. Administrative functions (other than registration) can be performed online.

CAMPUS LIFE

Environment: Village. **Activities:** Choral groups, dance, drama/theater, jazz band, literary magazine, music ensembles, musical theater, radio station, student government, student newspaper, student-run film society, symphony orchestra, yearbook. **Organizations:** 100 registered organizations, **Athletics (Intercollegiate):** *Men:* Baseball, basketball, cross-country, diving, football, golf, ice hockey, lacrosse, skiing (downhill/alpine), skiing (nordic/cross-country), soccer, swimming, tennis, track/field (outdoor), track/field (indoor). *Women:* Basketball, cross-country, diving, field hockey, golf, ice hockey, lacrosse, skiing (downhill/alpine), skiing (nordic/cross-country), soccer, softball, squash, swimming, tennis, track/field (outdoor), track/field (indoor), volleyball. **On-Campus Highlights:** Science—Bicentennial Hall, The Center for the Arts, Athletic Facilities, The Commons System, Middlebury College Snow Bowl (Ski Area). **Environmental Initiatives:** Trustees resolution in 2007 charging the entire college community to work together to achieve carbon neutrality by 2016. Completion of a $12 million biomass gasification system that burns renewable wood chips, reduces carbon emissions by 40% and fuel oil consumption by 1,000,000 gallons less, and shifts fuel dollars to the local region rather than overseas oil locales. Our Franklin Environmental Center at Hillcrest recently received LEED Platinum certification. The first in Vermont and only the seventh nationwide.

ADMISSIONS

Freshman Academic Profile: 87% in top 10% of high school class, 94% in top 25% of high school class, 100% in top 50% of high school class. 52% from public high schools. SAT Math middle 50% range 650–740. SAT Critical Reading middle 50% range 638–730. SAT Writing middle 50% range 650–740. ACT middle 50% range 30–33. **Basis for Candidate Selection:** *Very important factors considered include:* Class rank, academic GPA, rigor of secondary school record, character/personal qualities, extracurricular activities, talent/ability. *Important factors considered include:* Application essay, recommendation(s), standardized test scores, racial/ethnic status. *Other factors considered include:* Alumni/ae relation, first generation, geographical residence, interview, level of applicant's interest, volunteer work, work experience. **Freshman Admission Requirements:** High school diploma or equivalent is not required. *Academic units recommended:* 4 English, 4 mathematics, 3 science, (3 science labs), 4 foreign language, 3 social studies, 2 history, 1 academic electives, 1 fine arts, music, or drama courses recommended. **Freshman Admission Statistics:** 6,904 applied, 20% admitted, 43% enrolled. **Transfer Admission Requirements:** High school transcript, college transcript(s), essay or personal statement, statement of good standing from prior institution(s). Minimum college GPA of 3.0 required. Lowest grade transferable C–. **General Admission Information:** Application fee $65. Early decision application deadline 11/1. Regular application deadline 1/1. Regular notification 4/1. Nonfall registration accepted. Admission may be deferred for a maximum of 1 year. Credit and/or placement offered for CEEB Advanced Placement tests.

COSTS AND FINANCIAL AID

Comprehensive fee $50,780. Average book expense $1,000. **Required Forms and Deadlines:** FAFSA, CSS/Financial Aid PROFILE, noncustodial PROFILE. Financial aid filing deadline 2/1. Priority financial aid filing date 11/1. **Notification of Awards:** Applicants will be notified of awards on or about 4/1. **Types of Aid:** *Need-based scholarships/grants:* Federal Pell, SEOG, state scholarships/grants, private scholarships, the school's own gift aid. *Loans:* FFEL Subsidized Stafford, FFEL Unsubsidized Stafford, FFEL PLUS, Federal Perkins, college/university loans from institutional funds. *Student Employment:* **Financial Aid Statistics:** 43% freshmen, 49% undergrads receive need-based scholarship or grant aid. 35% freshmen, 42% undergrads receive need-based self-help aid. 43% freshmen, 49% undergrads receive any aid. 44% undergrads borrow to pay for school. Average cumulative indebtedness $21,458.

MIDWAY COLLEGE

512 East Stephen Street, Midway, KY 40347-1120
Phone: 859-846-5347 **Financial Aid Phone:** 859-846-5410
E-mail: admissions@midway.edu **CEEB Code:** 1975
Fax: 859-846-5787 **Website:** www.midway.edu **ACT Code:** 1528

This private school, affiliated with the Disciples of Christ Church, was founded in 1847. It has a 105-acre campus.

RATINGS
Admissions Selectivity Rating: 71 **Fire Safety Rating:** 60* **Green Rating:** 60*

STUDENTS AND FACULTY
Enrollment: 1,395. **Student Body:** 91% female, 9% male, 9% out-of-state, international (1 countries represented). African American 7%, Caucasian 86%, Hispanic 1%.
Retention and Graduation: 78% freshmen return for sophomore year. 26% freshmen graduate within 4 years. **Faculty:** Student/faculty ratio 15:1. 41 full-time faculty, 46% hold PhDs, 39% are women.

ACADEMICS
Degrees: Associate, bachelor's, master's. **Classes:** Most classes have 10–19 students. Most lab/discussion sessions have 10–19 students. **Majors with Highest Enrollment:** Elementary education and teaching; nursing/registered nurse (RN, ASN, BSN, MSN). **Special Study Options:** Accelerated program, distance learning, double major, dual enrollment, honors program, study abroad, teacher certification program, weekend college. **Honors programs:** Ruth Slack Roach Leadership, President's Ambassadors, Gamma Beta Phi, Tri Beta Special programs offered to physically disabled students include note-taking services, reader services, tape recorders, tutors.

FACILITIES
Housing: Women's dorms. 75% of campus accessible to physically disabled.

CAMPUS LIFE
Environment: Rural. **Activities:** Choral groups, music ensembles, student government, student newspaper, yearbook. **Athletics (Intercollegiate):** *Women:* Basketball, cross-country, equestrian sports, soccer, softball, tennis, volleyball. **On-Campus Highlights:** Anne Hart Raymond Center, Little Memorial Library, Equestrian Center, McManus Student Center, Piper Dining Hall.

ADMISSIONS
Freshman Academic Profile: Average high school GPA 3.15. 12% in top 10% of high school class, 25% in top 25% of high school class, 64% in top 50% of high school class. SAT Math middle 50% range 400–560. SAT Critical Reading middle 50% range 420–560. ACT middle 50% range 18–22. Minimum paper TOEFL 500. Minimum computer TOEFL 213. **Basis for Candidate Selection:** *Very important factors considered include:* Rigor of secondary school record, standardized test scores. *Important factors considered include:* Alumni/ae relation. *Other factors considered include:* Class rank, application essay, recommendation(s), character/personal qualities, extracurricular activities, interview, talent/ability, volunteer work, work experience. **Freshman Admission Requirements:** High school diploma is required and GED is accepted. *Academic units required:* 4 English. *Academic units recommended:* 3 mathematics, 2 science, 1 foreign language, 1 social studies. **Freshman Admission Statistics:** 456 applied, 71% admitted, 63% enrolled. **Transfer Admission Requirements:** High school transcript, college transcript(s), minimum college GPA of 2.0 required. Lowest grade transferable C. **General Admission Information:** Application fee $25. Notification on a rolling basis, beginning on or about 9/5. Nonfall registration accepted. Admission may be deferred for a maximum of 0. Credit and/or placement offered for CEEB Advanced Placement tests.

COSTS AND FINANCIAL AID
Annual tuition $15,750. Room and board $6,000. Required fees $150. Average book expense $1,200. **Required Forms and Deadlines:** FAFSA, institution's own financial aid form. Financial aid filing deadline 8/1. Priority financial aid filing date 4/1. **Types of Aid:** *Need-based scholarships/grants:* Federal Pell, SEOG, state scholarships/grants, private scholarships, the school's own gift aid. *Loans:* FFEL Subsidized Stafford, FFEL Unsubsidized Stafford, FFEL PLUS, Federal Perkins, college/university loans from institutional funds. *Student Employment:* Federal Work-Study Program available. Institutional employment available. Off-campus job opportunities are good. **Financial Aid Statistics:** 77% freshmen, 74% undergrads receive need-based scholarship or grant aid. 6% freshmen, 6% undergrads receive non-need-based scholarship or grant aid. 62% freshmen, 71% undergrads receive need-based self-help aid. 1% freshmen, 1% undergrads receive athletic scholarships. 85% freshmen, 81% undergrads receive any aid. 86% undergrads borrow to pay for school. Average cumulative indebtedness $18,223. **Criteria for awarding institutional aid:** *Non-need-based:* Academics, alumni affiliation, athletics, leadership, religious affiliation.

MIDWESTERN STATE UNIVERSITY

3410 Taft Blvd, Wichita Falls, TX 76308-2099
Phone: 940-397-4334 **Financial Aid Phone:** 940-397-4119
E-mail: admissions@mwsu.edu **CEEB Code:** 6408
Fax: 940-397-4672 **Website:** www.mwsu.edu **ACT Code:** 4132

This public school was founded in 1922. It has a 255-acre campus.

RATINGS
Admissions Selectivity Rating: 75 **Fire Safety Rating:** 99 **Green Rating:** 60*

STUDENTS AND FACULTY
Enrollment: 5,358. **Student Body:** 58% female, 42% male, 5% out-of-state, 5% international (41 countries represented). Asian 4%, African American 13%, Caucasian 67%, Hispanic 9%, Native American 1%.
Retention and Graduation: 66% freshmen return for sophomore year. 9% freshmen graduate within 4 years. **Faculty:** Student/faculty ratio 19:1. 206 full-time faculty, 68% hold PhDs, 11% are are members of minority groups, 47% are women. 2% of classes are taught by teaching assistants.

ACADEMICS
Degrees: Associate, bachelor's, master's, post-bachelor's certificate. **Classes:** Most classes have 20–29 students. Most lab/discussion sessions have 10–19 students. **Majors with Highest Enrollment:** journalism; marketing/marketing management; social sciences. **Special Study Options:** Distance learning, double major, dual enrollment, English as a Second Language (ESL), honors program, independent study, internships, liberal arts/career combination, study abroad, teacher certification program **Honors programs:** First established in 1964 and developed upon Midwestern State University's Tradition of Excellence, the University Honors Program offers high achieving MSU students a challenging premier undergraduate learning experience. From the Honors Introductory Seminar at the beginning, through Honors designated classes taught by outstanding faculty, to the Honors Capstone Course and Graduation with Honors at the end, the MSU Honors Program serves as a powerful program from start to finish. **Combined degree programs:** Accounting/MBA. Special programs offered to physically disabled students include note-taking services, reader services, tape recorders, tutors. **Career services:** Alumni network, alumni services, career/job search classes, internships. **Career services highlights include:** Career and job search.

FACILITIES
Housing: Coed dorms, special housing for disabled students, men's dorms, women's dorms, apartments for married students, apartments for single students, housing for Honor students, biology cooperative housing. 99% of campus accessible to physically disabled. **Special Academic Facilities/Equipment:** Language lab, technology lab, video lab, planetarium, art museum. **Computers:** Students can register for classes online. Administrative functions (other than registration) can be performed online.

CAMPUS LIFE
Environment: City. **Activities:** Choral groups, concert band, dance, drama/theater, jazz band, literary magazine, marching band, music ensembles, pep band, student government, student newspaper, student-run film society, television station, yearbook. **Organizations:** 145 registered organizations, 23 honor societies, 15 religious organizations. 8 fraternities, 8 sororities. **Athletics (Intercollegiate):** *Men:* Basketball, football, golf, soccer, tennis. *Women:* Basketball, cross-country, soccer, softball, tennis, volleyball. **On-Campus Highlights:** Clark Student Center, D.L. Ligon Coliseum, Corner Perk Coffee Shop, Wellness Center, Library, Sikes Lake, an art meuseum.

ADMISSIONS
Freshman Academic Profile: Average high school GPA 3.41. 12% in top 10% of high school class, 37% in top 25% of high school class, 73% in top 50% of high school class. 96% from public high schools. SAT Math middle 50% range 450–560. SAT Critical Reading middle 50% range 440–550. SAT Writing middle 50% range 440–540. ACT middle 50% range 18–23. Minimum paper TOEFL 550. Minimum computer TOEFL 213. **Basis for Candidate Selection:** *Very important factors considered include:* Class rank, academic GPA, rigor of secondary school record, standardized test scores. *Other factors considered include:* Application essay, alumni/ae relation, character/personal qualities, extracurricular activities, first generation, geographical residence, interview, level of applicant's interest, racial/ethnic status, state residency, talent/ability, volunteer work, work experience. **Freshman Admission Requirements:** High school diploma is required and GED is accepted. *Academic units required:* 4 English, 3 mathematics, 2 science, 6 academic electives. **Freshman Admission Statistics:** 1,407 applied, 69% admitted, 70% enrolled. **Transfer Admission Requirements:** College transcript(s), statement of good standing from prior institution(s). Minimum college GPA of 2.0 required. Lowest grade transferable D. **General Admission Information:** Application fee $25. Regular application

deadline 8/7. Notification on a rolling basis, beginning on or about 9/1. Nonfall registration accepted. Credit and/or placement offered for CEEB Advanced Placement tests.

COSTS AND FINANCIAL AID

Required Forms and Deadlines: FAFSA, institution's own financial aid form. Priority financial aid filing date 5/1. **Notification of Awards:** Applicants will be notified of awards on a rolling basis beginning 3/15. **Types of Aid:** *Need-based scholarships/grants:* Federal Pell, SEOG, state scholarships/grants, private scholarships, the school's own gift aid. *Loans:* FFEL Subsidized Stafford, FFEL Unsubsidized Stafford, FFEL PLUS, Federal Perkins, state loans, college/university loans from institutional funds, Alternative private loans. *Student Employment:* Federal Work-Study Program available. Institutional employment available. Highest amount earned per year from on-campus jobs $9,120. Off-campus job opportunities are good. **Financial Aid Statistics:** 37% freshmen, 40% undergrads receive need-based scholarship or grant aid. 1% freshmen, 1% undergrads receive non-need-based scholarship or grant aid. 34% freshmen, 40% undergrads receive need-based self-help aid. 5% freshmen, 3% undergrads receive athletic scholarships. 72% freshmen, 76% undergrads receive any aid. 54% undergrads borrow to pay for school. Average cumulative indebtedness $17,882. **Criteria for awarding institutional aid:** *Non-need-based:* Academics, alumni affiliation, art, athletics, leadership, minority status, music/drama.

MILES COLLEGE

5500 Myron Massey Blvd, ATTN: Admissions, Fairfield, AL 35064
Phone: 205-929-1656
E-mail: admissions@mail.miles.edu
Fax: 205-929-1627 **Website:** miles.edu

This private school, affiliated with the Episcopal Church, was founded in 1905. It has a 37-acre campus.

RATINGS
Admissions Selectivity Rating: 73   **Fire Safety Rating:** 60*   **Green Rating:** 60*

STUDENTS AND FACULTY
Enrollment: 1,660. **Student Body:** 57% female, 43% male, 33% out-of-state, international African American 98%, Caucasian 1%.
Retention and Graduation: 70% freshmen return for sophomore year. 26% freshmen graduate within 4 years. **Faculty:** Student/faculty ratio 20:1. 94 full-time faculty, 35% hold PhDs, 51% are women.

ACADEMICS
Degrees: Bachelor's. **Special Study Options:** Cooperative education program, double major, honors program, internships, study abroad, teacher certification program, weekend college.

FACILITIES
Housing: Coed dorms, men's dorms, women's dorms, apartments for single students.

CAMPUS LIFE
Activities: Choral groups, concert band, drama/theater, jazz band, marching band, music ensembles, pep band, student government, student newspaper, television station **Organizations:** 8 honor societies, 1 religious organizations. **Athletics (Intercollegiate):** *Men:* Baseball, basketball, cheerleading, football, tennis, track/field (outdoor). *Women:* Basketball, cheerleading, softball, tennis, track/field (outdoor), volleyball.

ADMISSIONS
Freshman Academic Profile: Average high school GPA 2.35. 15% in top 10% of high school class, 31% in top 25% of high school class, 48% in top 50% of high school class. Minimum paper TOEFL 450. **Basis for Candidate Selection:** *Other factors considered include:* Standardized test scores, alumni/ae relation. **Freshman Admission Requirements:** High school diploma is required and GED is accepted. *Academic units required:* 20 English, 20 mathematics, 20 science, 20 social studies, 20 history, 2 electives. **Freshman Admission Statistics:** Lowest grade transferable C. **General Admission Information:** Application fee $25. Regular application deadline 8/23. Nonfall registration accepted. Admission may be deferred for a maximum of 1 year.

COSTS AND FINANCIAL AID
Annual tuition $5,008. Room and board $2,950. Required fees $350. Average book expense $600. **Required Forms and Deadlines:** FAFSA, state aid form. **Types of Aid:** *Need-based scholarships/grants:* Federal Pell, SEOG, state scholarships/grants, private scholarships, the school's own gift aid, United Negro College Fund. *Loans:* Direct Subsidized Stafford, Direct Unsubsidized Staf-

ford, Direct PLUS, FFEL Subsidized Stafford, FFEL Unsubsidized Stafford, FFEL PLUS, Federal Perkins, state loans, college/university loans from institutional funds. *Student Employment:* Federal Work-Study Program available. Highest amount earned per year from on-campus jobs $1,000. **Criteria for awarding institutional aid:** *Non-need-based:* Academics, job skills, religious affiliation, state/district residency.

MILLERSVILLE UNIVERSITY OF PENNSYLVANIA

PO Box 1002, Millersville, PA 17551-0302
Phone: 717-872-3371 **Financial Aid Phone:** 717-872-3026
E-mail: admissions@millersville.edu **CEEB Code:** 2656
Fax: 717-871-2147 **Website:** www.millersville.edu **ACT Code:** 3712

This public school was founded in 1855. It has a 250-acre campus.

RATINGS
Admissions Selectivity Rating: 75   **Fire Safety Rating:** 60*   **Green Rating:** 90

STUDENTS AND FACULTY
Enrollment: 7,242. **Student Body:** 56% female, 44% male, 4.1% out-of-state, international (52 countries represented). Asian 1%, African American 7%, Caucasian 80%, Hispanic 4%.
Retention and Graduation: 36% freshmen graduate within 4 years. **Faculty:** Student/faculty ratio 21.4:1. 304 full-time faculty, 97% hold PhDs, 15% are are members of minority groups, 46% are women.

ACADEMICS
Degrees: Associate, bachelor's, master's, post-bachelor's certificate, post-master's certificate. **Classes:** Most classes have 30–39 students. Most lab/discussion sessions have 20–29 students. **Majors with Highest Enrollment:** Business administration and management; elementary education and teaching; psychology. **Special Study Options:** Accelerated program, cooperative education program, cross-registration, distance learning, double major, dual enrollment, honors program, independent study, internships, study abroad, teacher certification program, academic remediation; Advanced Placement credit; off-campus study; learning disabilities services; Adult and Continuing Education (ACE) Program; Internet courses; Summer Session for credit. **Honors programs:** Honors College. **Combined degree programs:** AS/pre-pharmacy; BS/pre-optometry; BS/pre-podiatry; BS/pre-athl. training. Special programs offered to physically disabled students include note-taking services, reader services, tape recorders, tutors. **Career services:** Alumni services, career/job search classes, career assessment. **Career services highlights include:** Internships and co-ops are a winning strategy for students, employers and the university. Students develop their professional proficiency and self-confidence and get a chance to "test drive" their career choice. Employers get a highly motivated employee for a specific amount of time. The university gains valuable feedback regarding its instruction, curriculum, and programs.

FACILITIES
Housing: Coed dorms, wellness house, theme housingAcademic Interest Housing for several subject areas. 85% of campus accessible to physically disabled. **Special Academic Facilities/Equipment:** Art galleries, foreign language lab, extensive inventory of scientific & technological instrumentation, weather station, TV studio, radio station, teleconferencing center, Distance Learning **Computers:** 100% of classrooms, 100% of dorms, 100% of libraries, 100% of dining areas, 100% of student union, 100% of common outdoor areas have wireless network access. Students can register for classes online. Administrative functions (other than registration) can be performed online.

CAMPUS LIFE
Environment: Village. **Activities:** Choral groups, concert band, dance, drama/theater, jazz band, literary magazine, marching band, music ensembles, musical theater, pep band, radio station, student government, student newspaper, symphony orchestra, television station, yearbook, campus ministries. **Organizations:** 120 registered organizations, 11 honor societies, 12 religious organizations. 9 fraternities, 10 sororities. **Athletics (Intercollegiate):** *Men:* Baseball, basketball, cross-country, football, golf, soccer, tennis, track/field (outdoor), track/field (indoor), wrestling. *Women:* Basketball, cheerleading, cross-country, field hockey, lacrosse, soccer, softball, swimming, tennis, track/field (outdoor), track/field (indoor), volleyball. **On-Campus Highlights:** Student Memorial Center, Ganser Library, Science and Technology Building, Biemesderfer Executive Center, Gordinier Dining Hall. **Environmental Initiatives:** Constructed a LEED-certified building; campus recycling program; use of bio-diesel fuel.

ADMISSIONS
Freshman Academic Profile: 16.4% in top 10% of high school class, 44.7% in top 25% of high school class, 81.2% in top 50% of high school class. SAT Math

middle 50% range 490–590. SAT Critical Reading middle 50% range 480–570. SAT Writing middle 50% range 460–560. ACT middle 50% range 20–24. Minimum paper TOEFL 500. Minimum computer TOEFL 183. Minimum web-based TOEFL 65. **Basis for Candidate Selection:** *Very important factors considered include:* Class rank, rigor of secondary school record, standardized test scores. *Important factors considered include:* character/personal qualities, extracurricular activities, talent/ability, volunteer work, work experience. *Other factors considered include:* Application essay, recommendation(s), alumni/ae relation, geographical residence, interview, racial/ethnic status, state residency. **Freshman Admission Requirements:** High school diploma is required and GED is accepted. *Academic units required:* 4 English, 3 mathematics, 3 science, (1 science labs), 3 social studies, 2 history. *Academic units recommended:* 2 foreign language, 4 academic electives. **Freshman Admission Statistics:** 7,241 applied, 53% admitted, 35% enrolled. **Transfer Admission Requirements:** High school transcript, college transcript(s), statement of good standing from prior institution(s). Minimum college GPA of 2.0 required. Lowest grade transferable C. **General Admission Information:** Application fee $50. Notification on a rolling basis, beginning on or about 9/15. Nonfall registration accepted. Admission may be deferred for a maximum of 1 semester. Credit and/or placement offered for CEEB Advanced Placement tests.

COSTS AND FINANCIAL AID
Annual in-state tuition $5,554. Annual out-of-state tuition $13,886. Room and board $7,766. Required fees $1,593. Average book expense $1,000. **Required Forms and Deadlines:** FAFSA. Financial aid filing deadline 3/15. **Notification of Awards:** Applicants will be notified of awards on a rolling basis beginning 3/19. **Types of Aid:** *Need-based scholarships/grants:* Federal Pell, SEOG, state scholarships/grants, private scholarships, the school's own gift aid, Shock Scholarship. *Loans:* FFEL Subsidized Stafford, FFEL Unsubsidized Stafford, FFEL PLUS, Federal Perkins, college/university loans from institutional funds. *Student Employment:* Federal Work-Study Program available. Institutional employment available. Highest amount earned per year from on-campus jobs $12,787. Off-campus job opportunities are excellent. **Financial Aid Statistics:** 39% freshmen, 34% undergrads receive need-based scholarship or grant aid. 12% freshmen, 7% undergrads receive non-need-based scholarship or grant aid. 50% freshmen, 47% undergrads receive need-based self-help aid. 1% freshmen, 1% undergrads receive athletic scholarships. 84% freshmen, 79% undergrads receive any aid. 64% undergrads borrow to pay for school. Average cumulative indebtedness $22,408. **Criteria for awarding institutional aid:** *Non-need-based:* Academics, athletics, minority status.

MILLIGAN COLLEGE

P.O. Box 210, Milligan College, TN 37682
Phone: 423-461-8730 **Financial Aid Phone:** 423-461-8968
E-mail: admissions@milligan.edu **CEEB Code:** 1469
Fax: 423-461-8982 **Website:** www.milligan.edu **ACT Code:** 3996

This private school was founded in 1866. It has a 181-acre campus.

RATINGS
Admissions Selectivity Rating: 87   **Fire Safety Rating:** 90   **Green Rating:** 64

STUDENTS AND FACULTY
Enrollment: 859. **Student Body:** 59% female, 41% male, 35% out-of-state, 3% international (14 countries represented). African American 7%, Caucasian 86%, Hispanic 3%.
Retention and Graduation: 71% freshmen return for sophomore year. 9% grads pursue arts and sciences degrees. 2% grads pursue law degrees. 2% grads pursue business degrees. 6% grads pursue medical degrees. **Faculty:** Student/faculty ratio 12.7:1. 67 full-time faculty, 76% hold PhDs, 3% are are members of minority groups, 51% are women.

ACADEMICS
Degrees: Bachelor's, master's. **Classes:** Most classes have fewer than 10 students. Most lab/discussion sessions have fewer than 10 students. **Majors with Highest Enrollment:** Bible/biblical studies; business/commerce; nursing/registered nurse (RN, ASN, BSN, MSN). **Special Study Options:** Cross-registration, double major, independent study, internships, study abroad, teacher certification program Special programs offered to physically disabled students include note-taking services, tape recorders, tutors. **Career services:** Alumni network, career/job search classes, career assessment, regional alumni.

FACILITIES
Housing: Men's dorms, women's dorms, apartments for married students, apartments for single students. 80% of campus accessible to physically disabled. **Computers:** 95% of classrooms, 95% of dorms, 100% of libraries, 100% of dining areas, 100% of student union, 25% of common outdoor areas have wireless

network access. Students can register for classes online. Administrative functions (other than registration) can be performed online.

CAMPUS LIFE
Environment: Town. **Activities:** Choral groups, concert band, drama/theater, jazz band, literary magazine, music ensembles, musical theater, pep band, radio station, student government, student newspaper, symphony orchestra, yearbook. **Organizations:** 36 registered organizations, 5 honor societies, 5 religious organizations. **Athletics (Intercollegiate):** *Men:* Baseball, basketball, cross-country, golf, mountain biking, soccer, swimming, tennis, track/field (outdoor), track/field (indoor). *Women:* Basketball, cross-country, soccer, softball, swimming, tennis, track/field (outdoor), track/field (indoor), volleyball. **On-Campus Highlights:** The Gregory Center, student center, residence halls/dining hall, Seeger Chapel, athletic facilities. **Environmental Initiatives:** Campus-wide recycling; construction of a new LEED-certified Wellness Center opening in March 2010; campus-wide energy audit.

ADMISSIONS
Freshman Academic Profile: Average high school GPA 3.58. 37% in top 10% of high school class, 65% in top 25% of high school class, 89% in top 50% of high school class. 80% from public high schools. SAT Math middle 50% range 460–570. SAT Critical Reading middle 50% range 480–580. SAT Writing middle 50% range 453–570. ACT middle 50% range 21–25.5. Minimum paper TOEFL 550. Minimum computer TOEFL 213. Minimum web-based TOEFL 79. **Basis for Candidate Selection:** *Very important factors considered include:* Application essay, academic GPA, rigor of secondary school record, standardized test scores, character/personal qualities, religious affiliation/commitment. *Important factors considered include:* Recommendation(s), extracurricular activities. *Other factors considered include:* Class rank, alumni/ae relation, interview, racial/ethnic status, talent/ability, volunteer work, work experience. **Freshman Admission Requirements:** High school diploma is required and GED is accepted. *Academic units recommended:* 4 English, 3 mathematics, 3 science, 2 foreign language, 2 social studies, 3 history. **Freshman Admission Statistics:** 643 applied, 57% admitted, 327% enrolled. **Transfer Admission Requirements:** College transcript(s), essay or personal statement, minimum college GPA of 2.0 required. Lowest grade transferable C–. **General Admission Information:** Application fee $30. Regular application deadline 8/1. Notification on a rolling basis, beginning on or about 10/1. Nonfall registration accepted. Admission may be deferred for a maximum of 1 year. Credit and/or placement offered for CEEB Advanced Placement tests.

COSTS AND FINANCIAL AID
Annual tuition $21,200. Room and board $5,850. Required fees $660. Average book expense $750. **Required Forms and Deadlines:** FAFSA. Financial aid filing deadline 3/1. **Notification of Awards:** Applicants will be notified of awards on a rolling basis beginning 3/15. **Types of Aid:** *Need-based scholarships/grants:* Federal Pell, SEOG, state scholarships/grants, private scholarships, the school's own gift aid. *Loans:* FFEL Subsidized Stafford, FFEL Unsubsidized Stafford, FFEL PLUS, Federal Perkins. *Student Employment:* Federal Work-Study Program available. Institutional employment available. Off-campus job opportunities are excellent. **Financial Aid Statistics:** 82% freshmen, 77% undergrads receive need-based scholarship or grant aid. 20% freshmen, 17% undergrads receive non-need-based scholarship or grant aid. 50% freshmen, 55% undergrads receive need-based self-help aid. 20% freshmen, 17% undergrads receive athletic scholarships. 99% freshmen, 90% undergrads receive any aid. 75.2% undergrads borrow to pay for school. Average cumulative indebtedness $19,803. **Criteria for awarding institutional aid:** *Non-need-based:* Academics, alumni affiliation, art, athletics, job skills, minority status, music/drama, religious affiliation, state/district residency.

MILLIKIN UNIVERSITY

1184 West Main Street, Decatur, IL 62522-2084
Phone: 217-424-6210 **Financial Aid Phone:** 217-424-6317
E-mail: admis@millikin.edu **CEEB Code:** 1470
Fax: 217-425-4669 **Website:** www.millikin.edu **ACT Code:** 1080

This private school, affiliated with the Presbyterian Church, was founded in 1901. It has a 75-acre campus.

RATINGS
Admissions Selectivity Rating: 78   **Fire Safety Rating:** 96   **Green Rating:** 60*

STUDENTS AND FACULTY
Enrollment: 2,214. **Student Body:** 60% female, 40% male, 12% out-of-state, 1% international (9 countries represented). Asian 1%, African American 10%, Caucasian 80%, Hispanic 3%.

Retention and Graduation: 53% freshmen graduate within 4 years. 24% grads go on to further study within 1 year. 13.8% grads pursue arts and sciences degrees. 1% grads pursue law degrees. 1% grads pursue business degrees. 2.4% grads pursue medical degrees. **Faculty:** Student/faculty ratio 11.4:1. 154 full-time faculty, 81% hold PhDs, 10% are are members of minority groups, 51% are women.

ACADEMICS

Degrees: Bachelor's, master's. **Classes:** Most classes have 10–19 students. Most lab/discussion sessions have 10–19 students. **Majors with Highest Enrollment:** Elementary education and teaching; music performance; nursing/registered nurse (RN, ASN, BSN, MSN). **Special Study Options:** Accelerated program, double major, exchange student program (domestic), honors program, independent study, internships, student-designed major, study abroad, teacher certification program. **Honors programs:** Presidential Scholars are Millikin's best and brightest students; selection is based upon outstanding academic performance and demonstrated leadership; they receive a full tuition scholarship, renewable for up to four years. Millikin's Honors Program introduces students to college-level scholarship, research, critical thinking, and writing during the freshman and sophomore years; classes are taught as seminars—sessions involving intense discussion and requiring active participation; Millikin's strongest juniors are invited to join the next phase of the Honors Program to become James Millikin Scholars. Special programs offered to physically disabled students include note-taking services, reader services, tape recorders, tutors. **Career services:** Alumni network, alumni services, career/job search classes, career assessment, internships. **Career services highlights include:** Millikin's Blue Connection, a retail art gallery, serves as the practical laboratory for Millikin's innovative Art of Entrepreneurship curriculum. This gallery sells, original art, produced by Millikin alumni, faculty, staff and students. The Blue Connection retail art store is fully operated by Millikin students, a majority of which are from art, business, and music programs. The talents of the various majors are integrated with the concept of business ownership. The success of the venture is in the hands of the Millikin students.

FACILITIES

Housing: Coed dorms, special housing for disabled students, men's dorms, special housing for international students, women's dorms, fraternity/sorority housing, apartments for married students, apartments for single students, wellness houseLearning Communities. 66% of campus accessible to physically disabled. **Special Academic Facilities/Equipment:** Art galleries, art museum, fitness/wellness center, recording studio, indoor sports center, greenhouse, observatory, 2 indoor sports centers, 2,000 seat performance center. **Computers:** 75% of classrooms, 75% of dorms, 100% of libraries, 100% of dining areas, 100% of student union, 5% of common outdoor areas have wireless network access. Students can register for classes online. Administrative functions (other than registration) can be performed online.

CAMPUS LIFE

Environment: City. **Activities:** Choral groups, concert band, dance, drama/theater, jazz band, literary magazine, music ensembles, musical theater, opera, pep band, radio station, student government, student newspaper, student-run film society, symphony orchestra, international student organization, Model UN. **Organizations:** 96 registered organizations, 7 honor societies, 2 religious organizations. 5 fraternities, 4 sororities. **Athletics (Intercollegiate):** *Men:* Baseball, basketball, cheerleading, cross-country, football, golf, soccer, swimming, track/field (outdoor), track/field (indoor). *Women:* Basketball, cheerleading, cross-country, golf, soccer, softball, swimming, tennis, track/field (outdoor), track/field (indoor), volleyball. **On-Campus Highlights:** ADM-Scovill Hall, Perkinson Music Center, Albert Taylor Theatre, Decatur Indoor Sports Center, Kirkland Fine Arts Center.

ADMISSIONS

Freshman Academic Profile: Average high school GPA 3.338. 17% in top 10% of high school class, 40% in top 25% of high school class, 76% in top 50% of high school class. 90% from public high schools. SAT Math middle 50% range 480–560. SAT Critical Reading middle 50% range 480–590. SAT Writing middle 50% range 460–560. ACT middle 50% range 20–25. Minimum paper TOEFL 550. Minimum computer TOEFL 213. Minimum web-based TOEFL 79. **Basis for Candidate Selection:** *Very important factors considered include:* Rigor of secondary school record. *Important factors considered include:* Class rank, academic GPA, recommendation(s), standardized test scores, interview. *Other factors considered include:* Alumni/ae relation, character/personal qualities, extracurricular activities, level of applicant's interest, talent/ability, volunteer work, work experience. **Freshman Admission Requirements:** High school diploma is required and GED is accepted. *Academic units recommended:* 4 English, 3 mathematics, 3 science, 2 foreign language, 2 social studies, 2 history. **Freshman Admission Statistics:** 3,167 applied, 60% admitted, 28% enrolled. **Transfer Admission Requirements:** High school transcript, college transcript(s), minimum college GPA of 2.0 required. Lowest grade transferable C–. **General Admission Information:** Notification on a rolling basis, beginning on or about 9/15. Nonfall registration accepted. Admission may be deferred for a maximum of 1 year. Credit and/or placement offered for CEEB Advanced Placement tests.

COSTS AND FINANCIAL AID

Required Forms and Deadlines: FAFSA. Priority financial aid filing date 3/15. **Notification of Awards:** Applicants will be notified of awards on a rolling basis beginning 3/15. **Types of Aid:** *Need-based scholarships/grants:* Federal Pell, SEOG, state scholarships/grants, private scholarships, the school's own gift aid. *Loans:* FFEL Subsidized Stafford, FFEL Unsubsidized Stafford, FFEL PLUS, Federal Perkins, state loans. *Student Employment:* Federal Work-Study Program available. Institutional employment available. Highest amount earned per year from on-campus jobs $4,285. Off-campus job opportunities are good. **Financial Aid Statistics:** 77% freshmen, 71% undergrads receive need-based scholarship or grant aid. 80% freshmen, 69% undergrads receive non-need-based scholarship or grant aid. 58% freshmen, 60% undergrads receive need-based self-help aid. 99% freshmen, 98% undergrads receive any aid. 82% undergrads borrow to pay for school. Average cumulative indebtedness $28,388. **Criteria for awarding institutional aid:** *Non-need-based:* Academics, alumni affiliation, art, leadership, minority status, music/drama.

MILLS COLLEGE

5000 MacArthur Boulevard, Oakland, CA 94613
Phone: 510-430-2135 **Financial Aid Phone:** 510-430-2000
E-mail: admission@mills.edu **CEEB Code:** 4485
Fax: 510-430-3314 **Website:** www.mills.edu **ACT Code:** 4485

This private school was founded in 1852. It has a 135-acre campus.

RATINGS

Admissions Selectivity Rating: 89   **Fire Safety Rating:** 64   **Green Rating:** 97

STUDENTS AND FACULTY

Enrollment: 914. **Student Body:** 100% female, 22% out-of-state, 3% international (15 countries represented). Asian 7%, African American 9%, Caucasian 39%, Hispanic 14%, Native American 1%.
Retention and Graduation: 77% freshmen return for sophomore year. 54% freshmen graduate within 4 years. 47% grads go on to further study within 1 year. 27% grads pursue arts and sciences degrees. 2% grads pursue law degrees. 4% grads pursue business degrees. 1% grads pursue medical degrees. **Faculty:** Student/faculty ratio 12:1. 93 full-time faculty, 88% hold PhDs, 25% are are members of minority groups, 62% are women.

ACADEMICS

Degrees: Bachelor's, certificate, master's, post-bachelor's certificate. **Classes:** Most classes have 10–19 students. Most lab/discussion sessions have 10–19 students. **Majors with Highest Enrollment:** English language and literature; political science and government; psychology. **Special Study Options:** Cooperative education program, cross-registration, double major, exchange student program (domestic), independent study, internships, liberal arts/career combination, student-designed major, study abroad, teacher certification program. **Combined degree programs:** BA/MA, BA/MEng, BA/MBA; BA/MPP; BA/MA/Teaching Credential. Special programs offered to physically disabled students include note-taking services, reader services, tape recorders, tutors. **Career services:** Alumni network, alumni services, career/job search classes, career assessment, internships, regional alumni. **Career services highlights include:** We are very proud of our expanding internship services program within career services. In 2006, we hired a dedicated internship coordinator for the campus and this position has focused on increasing access to local and national internships for our student population. We have also worked to track student success related to internship completion and to make the process more user friendly.

FACILITIES

Housing: Coed dorms, special housing for disabled students, women's dorms, apartments for married students, cooperative housing, apartments for single students, wellness house, theme housing, Resumer Student Housing. 90% of campus accessible to physically disabled. **Special Academic Facilities/Equipment:** Art Museum, Center for contemporary Music, on-campus elementary school, botanical gardens. **Computers:** 100% of classrooms, 100% of dorms, 100% of libraries, 100% of dining areas, 100% of student union, 100% of common outdoor areas have wireless network access. Students can register for classes online. Administrative functions (other than registration) can be performed online.

CAMPUS LIFE

Environment: Metropolis. **Activities:** Choral groups, dance, drama/theater, literary magazine, music ensembles, musical theater, radio station, student government, student newspaper, student-run film society, yearbook, campus ministries, international student organization, Model UN. **Organizations:** 47 registered organizations, 2 honor societies, 4 religious organizations. **Athletics (Intercollegiate):** *Women:* crew/rowing, cross-country, soccer, swimming, tennis, track/field (outdoor), volleyball. **On-Campus Highlights:** The Mills College Art Museum, Haas Pavilion & Trefethen Aquatic Center, Rothwell Student Center, Lorrie Lokey Graduate School of Business, Littlefield Concert Hall. **Environmental Initiatives:** Mills recycles, composts and reuses all consumer materials to the extent possible www.mills.edu/recycling. Mills students, staff and faculty participate in Recycle Mania. Mills builds to LEED standards of silver or higher. Mills has been awarded a LEED Platinum for new science building and has just broken ground on a business school designed to achieve LEED Gold. Mills encourages the use and provides access to public and shared transportation by offering a Mills Shuttle service, car share and web based carpool system. Public Transit passes available to all undergraduate students, funded through student fees.

ADMISSIONS

Freshman Academic Profile: Average high school GPA 3.7. 44% in top 10% of high school class, 76% in top 25% of high school class, 96% in top 50% of high school class. 80% from public high schools. SAT Math middle 50% range 500–600. SAT Critical Reading middle 50% range 530–650. SAT Writing middle 50% range 530–630. ACT middle 50% range 22–27. Minimum paper TOEFL 550. Minimum computer TOEFL 213. **Basis for Candidate Selection:** *Very important factors considered include:* Rigor of secondary school record. *Important factors considered include:* Class rank, application essay, academic GPA, recommendation(s), standardized test scores, character/personal qualities, extracurricular activities. *Other factors considered include:* Alumni/ae relation, first generation, interview, level of applicant's interest, talent/ability, volunteer work, work experience. **Freshman Admission Requirements:** High school diploma is required and GED is accepted. *Academic units required:* 4 English, 3 mathematics, 2 science, (2 science labs), 2 foreign language, 2 social studies, 2 history. *Academic units recommended:* 4 English, 4 mathematics, 4 science, (2 science labs), 4 foreign language, 4 social studies, 4 history, 2 visual/performing arts, 2 academic electives. **Freshman Admission Statistics:** 1,519 applied, 57% admitted, 19% enrolled. **Transfer Admission Requirements:** High school transcript, college transcript(s), essay or personal statement, Lowest grade transferable C–. **General Admission Information:** Application fee $50. Regular application deadline 8/1. Notification on a rolling basis, beginning on or about 11/1. Nonfall registration accepted. Admission may be deferred for a maximum of 1 year. Credit and/or placement offered for CEEB Advanced Placement tests.

COSTS AND FINANCIAL AID

Required Forms and Deadlines: FAFSA, institution's own financial aid form, Noncustodial Parent Statement, if applicable. Priority financial aid filing date 2/15. **Notification of Awards:** Applicants will be notified of awards on a rolling basis beginning 3/1. **Types of Aid:** *Need-based scholarships/grants:* Federal Pell, SEOG, state scholarships/grants, private scholarships, the school's own gift aid. *Loans:* FFEL Subsidized Stafford, FFEL Unsubsidized Stafford, FFEL PLUS, Federal Perkins, college/university loans from institutional funds. *Student Employment:* Federal Work-Study Program available. Institutional employment available. Highest amount earned per year from on-campus jobs $2,700. Off-campus job opportunities are excellent. **Financial Aid Statistics:** 91% freshmen, 84% undergrads receive need-based scholarship or grant aid. 76% freshmen, 71% undergrads receive non-need-based scholarship or grant aid. 91% freshmen, 84% undergrads receive need-based self-help aid. 91% freshmen, 84% undergrads receive any aid. 96% undergrads borrow to pay for school. Average cumulative indebtedness $24,255. **Criteria for awarding institutional aid:** *Non-need-based:* Academics, leadership, minority status, music/drama.

MILLSAPS COLLEGE

1701 North State Street, Jackson, MS 39210
Phone: 601-974-1050 **Financial Aid Phone:** 800-352-1050
E-mail: admissions@millsaps.edu **CEEB Code:** 1471
Fax: 601-974-1059 **Website:** www.millsaps.edu **ACT Code:** 2212

This private school, affiliated with the Methodist Church, was founded in 1890. It has a 100-acre campus.

RATINGS

Admissions Selectivity Rating: 85   **Fire Safety Rating:** 81   **Green Rating:** 60*

STUDENTS AND FACULTY

Enrollment: 1,002. **Student Body:** 50% female, 50% male, 52% out-of-state, 2% international (19 countries represented). Asian 4%, African American 11%, Caucasian 78%, Hispanic 2%.
Retention and Graduation: 78% freshmen return for sophomore year. 59% freshmen graduate within 4 years. 51% grads go on to further study within 1 year. 44% grads pursue arts and sciences degrees. 22% grads pursue law degrees. 15% grads pursue business degrees. 14% grads pursue medical degrees.
Faculty: Student/faculty ratio 10:1. 96 full-time faculty, 94% hold PhDs, 13% are are members of minority groups, 44% are women.

ACADEMICS

Degrees: Bachelor's, master's. **Classes:** Most classes have 10–19 students. Most lab/discussion sessions have 10–19 students. **Majors with Highest Enrollment:** Biology/biological sciences; business administration and management; English language and literature. **Special Study Options:** Accelerated program, double major, honors program, independent study, internships, liberal arts/career combination, student-designed major, study abroad, teacher certification program. The Millsaps FAITH & WORK INITIATIVE offers an array of curricular and extracurricular programs to help students discern their vocation or call in life and to pursue that call with passion, integrity and an eye toward the needs of the world. Faith & Work options include service-learning courses and the Meaning of Work course, immersion and service experiences, discussion programs with faculty and professionals, leadership and service clubs, internships, and public lecture series. Other INTERDISCIPLINARY PROGRAMS or concentrations are available in American studies, Christian education, environmental studies, film studies, human services, international studies, women's and gender studies, and church music. UNDERGRADUATE RESEARCH is available in most academic departments, including field research opportunities in the Pacific Northwest, Yellowstone, the Mexico, and Europe. Millsaps' nonprofit biocultural reserve on 4500 acres in the Yucatan Peninsula of Mexico offers multi-disciplinary options for study, including archaeology, business, ecology, education, geology, history, literature, math and socio-cultural anthropology. Students may also choose among other STUDY ABROAD programs developed by Millsaps faculty—in Albania, Belgium, China, Costa Rica, England, France, Germany, Ghana, Greece, Ireland, Israel, Italy, Japan, Mexico (Yucatan), and Tanzania. PRE-PROFESSIONAL programs include dentistry, engineering, law, medicine, ministry, and social work. Millsaps students may work towards DUAL DEGREES in engineering, applied science or nursing through agreements with Auburn University, Columbia University, Vanderbilt University, Washington University, and the University of Mississippi Medical Health Center. Other distinctive programs include the FORD TEACHING FELLOWS program (research and internships for students interested in college teaching), and the Weiner PRE-MEDICAL FELLOWS program (summer research). **Honors programs:** The Honors Program, Ford Teaching Fellows program (research and internships for students interested in college teaching), Weiner Pre-Medical Fellows Program (summer research), Lilly Fellows Faith and Work Initiative (connecting individual passions with learning, meaning, service, and career) **Combined degree programs:** BA/MBA-Millsaps, 3-2 BSN nursing-Univ.ofMiss, 4-2 MSN nursing-Vanderbilt. Special programs offered to physically disabled students include note-taking services, reader services, tutors. **Career services:** Alumni network, alumni services, career assessment, internships, regional alumni. **Career services highlights include:** The Millsaps Career Center sponsors an internship-for-credit program designed to assist students with career choices and relate student work experiences to their education. Initially, the Career Center offers orientation and internship search assistance. During the internships, students maintain work logs, write monthly journals of their work experiences, and receive monthly feedback from the Career Center. Interns also obtain written evaluations from their supervisors and write final reports, evaluating their work sites and relating their work experiences to their education and career objectives.

FACILITIES

Housing: Coed dorms, special housing for disabled students, women's dorms, fraternity/sorority housing, wellness house, theme housingOur theme housing is community service housing. 90% of campus accessible to physically disabled. **Special Academic Facilities/Equipment:** Millsaps' W.M. Keck Center for Instrumental and Biochemical Comparative Archaeology is the only undergraduate facility of its kind in the world. The new multi-disciplinary research laboratory provides undergraduate students with the opportunity to explore complex archeological questions using advanced bioanalytical and biochemical techniques. Four to six Keck Fellows assist each year in gathering the artifacts studied in the lab from the College's archaeological field programs in Yucatan, Mexico, and northern Albania. The lab houses an inductively-coupled plasma spectrometer with laser ablation, a gas-chromotography spectrometer, a liquid-chromotography spectrometer, and a portable x-ray fluorescence spectrometer. In addition, the college's other labs include a unique array of spectrometers for measuring atomic absorption, infrared transitional modes, nuclear magnetic resonance, and other forms of energy; high performance chromatographs for separation and identification of compounds; electrophoresis instruments for analyzing biomolecules and other biological materials; and an inert atmosphere reaction chamber. Other facilities include a state-of-the-art molecular biology/functional genomics research laboratory; a fluorescence microscopy suite and imaging facility; a GIS workstation with Rockware and Arcview 9.1 GIS Software; a specially-designed automated 24-hour food monitoring system for rats; a microsurgical lab for animal surgeries; an on-campus hydrogeologic monitoring station to measure the water table and water levels in four on-campus wells; and a computational modeling lab for math, chemistry and physics students which provides numerical and graphical solutions in three dimensions. The College Sorbent and Environmental Laboratory provides undergraduates with opportunities for oil spill and stormwater remediation research. Another unique facility is the college's 4,000–acre biocultural reserve and learning center in the state of Yucatan, Mexico. Here students excavate ancient Mayan archaeological sites, conduct environmental studies of the jungle, research the biology and geology of the area, and live in a sustainable solar-powered facility constructed of materials inspired by the native Mayan architecture. Millsaps' Yucatan program also includes a newly-renovated teaching and living facility for international business studies which is located in the large city of Merida. In addition, Millsaps' newly-renovated digital Language Resource Center has been equipped with 25 network computers and satellite connections for international programming. **Computers:** 100% of classrooms, 100% of dorms, 100% of libraries, 100% of dining areas, 100% of student union, 100% of common outdoor areas have wireless network access. Students can register for classes online. Administrative functions (other than registration) can be performed online.

CAMPUS LIFE

Environment: Metropolis. **Activities:** Choral groups, dance, drama/theater, literary magazine, music ensembles, musical theater, student government, student newspaper, yearbook, campus ministries, international student organization, Model UN. **Organizations:** 85 registered organizations, 28 honor societies, 12 religious organizations. 6 fraternities, 6 sororities. **Athletics (Intercollegiate):** *Men:* Baseball, basketball, cross-country, football, golf, lacrosse, soccer, tennis, track/field (outdoor). *Women:* Basketball, cross-country, golf, lacrosse, soccer, softball, tennis, track/field (outdoor), volleyball. **On-Campus Highlights:** Hall Activities Center (fitness/athletic facility), Campbell College Center (student activities), The Bowl (outdoor green space/campus center), Millsaps Wilson Library (study center), Fraternity Row, The Campbell College Center includes a cafeteria, a coffeehouse, live entertainment and game areas, and a bookstore. The Bowl is a natural, outdoor space in the heart of the campus where students congregate between classes to relax and to participate in outdoor activities.

ADMISSIONS

Freshman Academic Profile: Average high school GPA 3.51. 33% in top 10% of high school class, 50% in top 25% of high school class, 81% in top 50% of high school class. 62% from public high schools. SAT Math middle 50% range 520–640. SAT Critical Reading middle 50% range 510–640. ACT middle 50% range 23–29. Minimum paper TOEFL 550. Minimum computer TOEFL 220. Minimum web-based TOEFL 80. **Basis for Candidate Selection:** *Very important factors considered include:* Academic GPA, rigor of secondary school record, standardized test scores, character/personal qualities. *Important factors considered include:* Class rank, application essay, recommendation(s), extracurricular activities, interview, talent/ability, volunteer work. *Other factors considered include:* work experience. **Freshman Admission Requirements:** High school diploma is required and GED is accepted. *Academic units required:* 4 English, 3 mathematics, 3 science, (1 science labs), 2 social studies, 2 history. *Academic units recommended:* 4 English, 4 mathematics, 4 science, (1 science labs), 2 foreign language, 2 social studies, 2 history, 2 academic electives. **Freshman Admission Statistics:** 1,348 applied, 74% admitted, 29% enrolled. **Transfer Admission Requirements:** College transcript(s), essay or personal statement, standardized test scores, statement of good standing from prior institution(s). Minimum college GPA of 2.75 required. Lowest grade transferable C. **General Admission Information:** Notification on a rolling basis,

beginning on or about 10/1. Nonfall registration accepted. Admission may be deferred for a maximum of 1 year. Credit and/or placement offered for CEEB Advanced Placement tests.

COSTS AND FINANCIAL AID

Average book expense $1,050. **Required Forms and Deadlines:** FAFSA. Priority financial aid filing date 3/1. **Notification of Awards:** Applicants will be notified of awards on a rolling basis beginning 3/15. **Types of Aid:** *Need-based scholarships/grants:* Federal Pell, SEOG, state scholarships/grants, private scholarships, the school's own gift aid. *Loans:* FFEL Subsidized Stafford, FFEL Unsubsidized Stafford, FFEL PLUS, Federal Perkins, college/university loans from institutional funds. *Student Employment:* Federal Work-Study Program available. Institutional employment available. Highest amount earned per year from on-campus jobs $8,429. Off-campus job opportunities are good. **Financial Aid Statistics:** 66% freshmen, 57% undergrads receive need-based scholarship or grant aid. 19% freshmen, 14% undergrads receive non-need-based scholarship or grant aid. 45% freshmen, 41% undergrads receive need-based self-help aid. 100% freshmen, 96% undergrads receive any aid. 58.65% undergrads borrow to pay for school. Average cumulative indebtedness $31,304. **Criteria for awarding institutional aid:** *Non-need-based:* Academics, art, leadership, music/drama, religious affiliation.

MILWAUKEE INSTITUTE OF ART AND DESIGN

273 East Erie Street, 273 E. Erie Street, Milwaukee, WI 53202
Phone: 414-847-3200 **Financial Aid Phone:** 414-291-8272
E-mail: admissions@miad.edu **CEEB Code:** 1506
Fax: 414-291-8077 **Website:** 273 E. Erie Street **ACT Code:** 4701

This private school was founded in 1974. It has a 2-acre campus.

RATINGS

Admissions Selectivity Rating: 64   **Fire Safety Rating:** 60*   **Green Rating:** 60*

STUDENTS AND FACULTY

Enrollment: 643. **Student Body:** 50% female, 50% male, 37% out-of-state, 4% international (3 countries represented). Asian 3%, African American 3%, Caucasian 80%, Hispanic 9%, Native American 1%.
Retention and Graduation: 81% freshmen return for sophomore year. 38% freshmen graduate within 4 years. 6% grads go on to further study within 1 year. 4% grads pursue arts and sciences degrees. **Faculty:** Student/faculty ratio 9:1. 33 full-time faculty, 67% hold PhDs, 6% are are members of minority groups, 42% are women.

ACADEMICS

Degrees: Bachelor's. **Classes:** Most classes have 10–19 students. Most lab/discussion sessions have fewer than 10 students. **Majors with Highest Enrollment:** Graphic design; illustration; industrial design. **Special Study Options:** Double major, exchange student program (domestic), independent study, internships, study abroad. Special programs offered to physically disabled students include note-taking services, reader services, tape recorders, tutors. **Career services:** Alumni network, alumni services, career assessment, internships.

FACILITIES

Housing: Coed dorms. 100% of campus accessible to physically disabled. **Special Academic Facilities/Equipment:** Eisner Museum of Advertising and Design, Brook Stevens Gallery of Industrial Design, Frederick Layton Gallery.

CAMPUS LIFE

Environment: Metropolis. **Activities:** Drama/theater, literary magazine, student government, student newspaper. **Organizations:** 12 registered organizations, 2 honor societies, 1 religious organizations.

ADMISSIONS

Freshman Academic Profile: Average high school GPA 3.04. 6% in top 10% of high school class, 25% in top 25% of high school class, 56% in top 50% of high school class. Minimum paper TOEFL 550. Minimum computer TOEFL 213. **Basis for Candidate Selection:** *Very important factors considered include:* Application essay, academic GPA, character/personal qualities, interview, level of applicant's interest, talent/ability. *Other factors considered include:* Class rank, recommendation(s), rigor of secondary school record, standardized test scores, extracurricular activities, volunteer work, work experience. **Freshman Admission Requirements:** High school diploma is required and GED is accepted. **Freshman Admission Statistics:** 416 applied, 75% admitted, 62% enrolled. **Transfer Admission Requirements:** essay or personal statement, interview, minimum college GPA of 2.0 required. Lowest grade transferable C. **General Admission Information:** Application fee $25. Notification on a rolling basis, beginning on or about 9/1. Nonfall registration accepted. Admission may be deferred for a maximum of 2 years. Neither credit nor placement offered for CEEB Advanced Placement tests.

COSTS AND FINANCIAL AID

Required Forms and Deadlines: FAFSA. Priority financial aid filing date 3/1. **Notification of Awards:** Applicants will be notified of awards on a rolling basis beginning 4/1. **Types of Aid:** *Need-based scholarships/grants:* Federal Pell, SEOG, state scholarships/grants, private scholarships, the school's own gift aid. *Loans:* Direct Subsidized Stafford, Direct Unsubsidized Stafford, Direct PLUS. *Student Employment:* Federal Work-Study Program available. Institutional employment available. Highest amount earned per year from on-campus jobs $1,200. Off-campus job opportunities are good. **Financial Aid Statistics:** 64% freshmen, 80% undergrads receive need-based scholarship or grant aid. 6% freshmen, 5% undergrads receive non-need-based scholarship or grant aid. 59% freshmen, 76% undergrads receive need-based self-help aid. 95% freshmen, 92% undergrads receive any aid. 100% undergrads borrow to pay for school. **Criteria for awarding institutional aid:** *Non-need-based:* Academics, art.

MILWAUKEE SCHOOL OF ENGINEERING

1025 North Broadway, Milwaukee, WI 53202-3109
Phone: 414-277-6763 **Financial Aid Phone:** 800-778-7223
E-mail: explore@msoe.edu **CEEB Code:** 1476
Fax: 414-277-7475 **Website:** www.msoe.edu **ACT Code:** 4616

This private school was founded in 1903. It has a 15-acre campus.

RATINGS
Admissions Selectivity Rating: 82   **Fire Safety Rating:** 99   **Green Rating:** 86

STUDENTS AND FACULTY
Enrollment: 2,438. **Student Body:** 19% female, 81% male, 28% out-of-state, 3% international (15 countries represented). Asian 3%, African American 3%, Caucasian 84%, Hispanic 3%, Native American 1%.
Retention and Graduation: 75% freshmen return for sophomore year. 39% freshmen graduate within 4 years. 5.3% grads go on to further study within 1 year. 3% grads pursue business degrees. **Faculty:** Student/faculty ratio 14:1. 132 full-time faculty, 73% hold PhDs, 10% are are members of minority groups, 27% are women.

ACADEMICS
Degrees: Bachelor's, master's. **Classes:** Most classes have 20–29 students. Most lab/discussion sessions have 10–19 students. **Majors with Highest Enrollment:** architectural engineering; electrical, electronics and communications engineering; mechanical engineering. **Special Study Options:** Accelerated program, distance learning, double major, dual enrollment, English as a Second Language (ESL), independent study, internships, study abroad, BS in international business and in electrical and mechanical engineering with Fachhochschule Lubeck, Germany. All students may apply to study at Czech Technical University, Prague, Czech Republic. **Combined degree programs:** BA/MEng, architectural eng. and construction management. Special programs offered to physically disabled students include note-taking services, reader services, tape recorders, tutors. **Career services:** Alumni network, alumni services, career/job search classes, career assessment, internships, regional alumni. **Career services highlights include:** Approximatly 85% of gradates have had internship experience.

FACILITIES
Housing: Coed dorms, special housing for disabled students. 85% of campus accessible to physically disabled. **Special Academic Facilities/Equipment:** Grohmann Museum, Kern Center Health, Wellness and Recreation Facility, Rader School of Business, Johnson Controls Software Engineering Lab, Fluid Power Institute, Rapid Prototyping Center, Applied Technology Center, Center for BioMolecular Modeling, Warren P. Knowles Nursing Lab, Harley Davidson Design Lab, Johnson Controls Environmental Systems Lab. **Computers:** 100% of classrooms, 10% of dorms, 100% of libraries, 100% of dining areas, 100% of student union, 100% of common outdoor areas have wireless network access. Students can register for classes online. Administrative functions (other than registration) can be performed online. Undergraduates are required to own a computer.

CAMPUS LIFE
Environment: Metropolis. **Activities:** dance, drama/theater, jazz band, literary magazine, pep band, radio station, student government, symphony orchestra, campus ministries, international student organization. **Organizations:** 61 registered organizations, 6 honor societies, 4 religious organizations. 3 fraternities, 3 sororities. **Athletics (Intercollegiate):** *Men:* Baseball, basketball, cheerleading,

crew/rowing, cross-country, golf, ice hockey, lacrosse, soccer, tennis, track/field (outdoor), track/field (indoor), volleyball, wrestling. *Women:* Basketball, cheerleading, cross-country, golf, soccer, softball, tennis, track/field (outdoor), track/field (indoor), volleyball. **On-Campus Highlights:** Kern Center—Health and Wellness Center, Student Life and Campus Center (dining and game room), The Grohmann Museum, Rapid Prototyping Center, School of Nursing Simulation Lab. **Environmental Initiatives:** USEPA/Wisconsin Department of Natural Resources WAICU agreements to participate in self audit initiative. MSOE was one of the first institutions under this agreement to undergo the audit and satisfy the agreement. Interdisciplinary energy committee that provided the impetus for receiving state and local incentive funds to install a solar PV system on one building and participation in a City of Milwaukee Shines grant to support a solar thermal system on a dormitory. Both systems are integrated into the curriculum in a Mechanical Engineering Advanced Energy Technologies laboratory which will enable MSOE students to become leaders in renewable and advanced energy. Providing institutional and budget support for incorporating sustainable design and LEED into Architectural Engineering and Construction management curricula.

ADMISSIONS
Freshman Academic Profile: Average high school GPA 3.52. 87% from public high schools. SAT Math middle 50% range 530–590. SAT Critical Reading middle 50% range 500–640. ACT middle 50% range 24–29. Minimum paper TOEFL 550. Minimum computer TOEFL 213. Minimum web-based TOEFL 79. **Basis for Candidate Selection:** *Very important factors considered include:* Academic GPA, rigor of secondary school record, standardized test scores. *Other factors considered include:* Recommendation(s), character/personal qualities, extracurricular activities, level of applicant's interest, volunteer work, work experience. **Freshman Admission Requirements:** High school diploma is required and GED is accepted. *Academic units required:* 4 English, 4 mathematics, 2 science. *Academic units recommended:* 4 English, 4 mathematics, 2 science, (2 science labs). **Freshman Admission Statistics:** 2,126 applied, 67% admitted, 37% enrolled. **Transfer Admission Requirements:** College transcript(s), minimum college GPA of 2.5 required. Lowest grade transferable C. **General Admission Information:** Application fee $25. Notification on a rolling basis, beginning on or about 10/15. Nonfall registration accepted. Admission may be deferred for a maximum of 2 year. Placement offered for CEEB Advanced Placement tests.

COSTS AND FINANCIAL AID
Annual tuition $29,520. Room and board $7,431. Average book expense $1,500. **Required Forms and Deadlines:** FAFSA, Admission Application. Priority financial aid filing date 3/15. **Notification of Awards:** Applicants will be notified of awards on a rolling basis beginning 3/1. **Types of Aid:** *Need-based scholarships/grants:* Federal Pell, SEOG, state scholarships/grants, private scholarships, the school's own gift aid. *Loans:* FFEL Subsidized Stafford, FFEL Unsubsidized Stafford, FFEL PLUS, Federal Perkins, state loans *Student Employment:* Federal Work-Study Program available. Institutional employment available. Highest amount earned per year from on-campus jobs $14,141. Off-campus job opportunities are excellent. **Financial Aid Statistics:** 81% freshmen, 82% undergrads receive need-based scholarship or grant aid. 8% freshmen, 8% undergrads receive non-need-based scholarship or grant aid. 72% freshmen, 74% undergrads receive need-based self-help aid. 99% freshmen, 98% undergrads receive any aid. 94.18% undergrads borrow to pay for school. Average cumulative indebtedness $35,722. **Criteria for awarding institutional aid:** *Non-need-based:* Academics.

MINNEAPOLIS COLLEGE OF ART AND DESIGN

2501 Stevens Avenue, Minneapolis, MN 55404
Phone: 612-874-3760
E-mail: admissions@mcad.edu **CEEB Code:** 6411
Fax: 612-874-3701 **Website:** www.mcad.edu **ACT Code:** 2130

This private school was founded in 1886. It has a 3-acre campus.

RATINGS
Admissions Selectivity Rating: 79   **Fire Safety Rating:** 60*   **Green Rating:** 60*

STUDENTS AND FACULTY
Enrollment: 740. **Student Body:** 53% female, 47% male, 64% out-of-state, 1% international (10 countries represented). Asian 3%, African American 1%, Caucasian 76%, Hispanic 4%, Native American 1%.
Retention and Graduation: 80% freshmen return for sophomore year. 10% grads go on to further study within 1 year. 10% grads pursue arts and sciences degrees. **Faculty:** Student/faculty ratio 13:1. 41 full-time faculty, 98% hold PhDs, 2% are are members of minority groups, 41% are women.

ACADEMICS

Degrees: Bachelor's, master's, post-bachelor's certificate. **Classes:** Most classes have 10–19 students. **Special Study Options:** Cooperative education program, cross-registration, distance learning, independent study, internships, study abroad, off-campus study: arts program in New York. Co-op programs: arts. Special programs offered to physically disabled students include note-taking services, reader services, tape recorders, tutors. **Career services:** Alumni services, career assessment, internships.

FACILITIES

Housing: Coed dorms, apartments for single students. 95% of campus accessible to physically disabled. **Special Academic Facilities/Equipment:** Art gallery.

CAMPUS LIFE

Environment: Metropolis. **Activities:** Radio station, student government, student-run film society. **On-Campus Highlights:** Main gallery, Student Center.

ADMISSIONS

Freshman Academic Profile: Average high school GPA 3.2. 89% from public high schools. SAT Math middle 50% range 470–590. SAT Critical Reading middle 50% range 540–670. SAT Writing middle 50% range 480–600. ACT middle 50% range 21–27. Minimum paper TOEFL 550. Minimum computer TOEFL 550. **Basis for Candidate Selection:** *Very important factors considered include:* Application essay, academic GPA, recommendation(s), standardized test scores, talent/ability. *Important factors considered include:* Character/personal qualities, interview. **Freshman Admission Requirements:** High school diploma is required and GED is accepted. *Academic units recommended:* 4 English, 4 social studies, 4 history, 4 art. **Freshman Admission Statistics:** 506 applied, 56% admitted. **Transfer Admission Requirements:** High school transcript, college transcript(s), essay or personal statement, standardized test scores, minimum college GPA of 2.5 required. Lowest grade transferable C–. **General Admission Information:** Application fee $50. Regular application deadline 5/1. Nonfall registration accepted. Admission may be deferred for a maximum of 1 semester. Credit offered for CEEB Advanced Placement tests.

COSTS AND FINANCIAL AID

Annual tuition $28,200. Room and board $4,340. Required fees $200. Average book expense $2,400. **Required Forms and Deadlines:** FAFSA. Priority financial aid filing date 3/15. **Notification of Awards:** Applicants will be notified of awards on a rolling basis beginning 4/1. **Types of Aid:** *Need-based scholarships/grants:* Federal Pell, SEOG, state scholarships/grants, private scholarships, the school's own gift aid. *Loans:* FFEL Subsidized Stafford, FFEL Unsubsidized Stafford, FFEL PLUS, Federal Perkins, state loans *Student Employment:* Federal Work-Study Program available. Institutional employment available. Highest amount earned per year from on-campus jobs $1,656. Off-campus job opportunities are good. **Financial Aid Statistics:** 79% freshmen, 75% undergrads receive need-based scholarship or grant aid. 6% freshmen, 4% undergrads receive non-need-based scholarship or grant aid. 75% freshmen, 73% undergrads receive need-based self-help aid. 91% undergrads borrow to pay for school. Average cumulative indebtedness $48,163. **Criteria for awarding institutional aid:** *Non-need-based:* Academics, alumni affiliation, art, leadership.

MINNESOTA STATE UNIVERSITY MOORHEAD

Owens Hall, MSU Moorhead, Moorhead, MN 56563
Phone: 218-477-2161 **Financial Aid Phone:** 218-477-2251
E-mail: dragon@mnstate.edu **CEEB Code:** 6678
Fax: 218-477-4374 **Website:** www.mnstate.edu **ACT Code:** 2134

This public school was founded in 1887. It has a 140-acre campus.

RATINGS

Admissions Selectivity Rating: 66   **Fire Safety Rating:** 60*   **Green Rating:** 60*

STUDENTS AND FACULTY

Enrollment: 6,730. **Student Body:** 57% female, 43% male, 51% out-of-state, 5% international (56 countries represented). Asian 1%, African American 2%, Caucasian 81%, Hispanic 1%, Native American 1%.
Retention and Graduation: 71% freshmen return for sophomore year. 17% freshmen graduate within 4 years. 13% grads go on to further study within 1 year. **Faculty:** Student/faculty ratio 17:1. 304 full-time faculty, 69% hold PhDs, 7% are are members of minority groups, 45% are women. 0.8% of classes are taught by teaching assistants.

ACADEMICS

Degrees: Associate, bachelor's, certificate, master's, post-bachelor's certificate, post-master's certificate, transfer associate. **Classes:** Most classes have 20–29

students. Most lab/discussion sessions have 20–29 students. **Majors with Highest Enrollment:** Biology/biological sciences; elementary education and teaching; mass communication/media studies. **Special Study Options:** Cross-registration, distance learning, double major, dual enrollment, exchange student program (domestic), external degree program, honors program, independent study, internships, student-designed major, study abroad, teacher certification program **Honors programs:** Honors Program to reward and encourage superior academic achievement. **Combined degree programs:** Dual degree programs w/University of MN in depts of chemistry & physics. Special programs offered to physically disabled students include note-taking services, reader services, tape recorders, tutors. **Career services:** Career/job search classes, career assessment, internships.

FACILITIES

Housing: Coed dorms, special housing for disabled students, men's dorms, women's dorms, apartments for single students, theme housing, sorority housing. 95% of campus accessible to physically disabled. **Special Academic Facilities/Equipment:** Art and biology museums on-campus, planetarium, regional science center, Center for Business, new Science Building, Center for Business, Wellness Center. **Computers:** Students can register for classes online. Administrative functions (other than registration) can be performed online.

CAMPUS LIFE

Environment: City. **Activities:** Choral groups, concert band, dance, drama/theater, jazz band, literary magazine, music ensembles, musical theater, radio station, student government, student newspaper, student-run film society, symphony orchestra, television station, campus ministries, international student organization, Model UN. **Organizations:** 109 registered organizations, 6 honor societies, 11 religious organizations. 2 sororities. **Athletics (Intercollegiate):** *Men:* Basketball, cross-country, football, track/field (outdoor), track/field (indoor), wrestling. *Women:* Basketball, cross-country, golf, soccer, softball, swimming, tennis, track/field (outdoor), track/field (indoor), volleyball. **On-Campus Highlights:** Underground Nightclub, Comstock Memorial Student Union, regional science center, Nemzek Athletic Complex, planetarium, new science lab building, new wellness center.

ADMISSIONS

Freshman Academic Profile: Average high school GPA 3.1. 8% in top 10% of high school class, 26% in top 25% of high school class, 60% in top 50% of high school class. ACT middle 50% range 19–24. Minimum paper TOEFL 500. Minimum computer TOEFL 173. **Basis for Candidate Selection:** *Very important factors considered include:* Class rank, rigor of secondary school record, standardized test scores. **Freshman Admission Requirements:** High school diploma is required and GED is accepted. *Academic units required:* 4 English, 3 mathematics, 3 science, (1 science labs), 2 foreign language, 3 social studies, 1 world culture or the arts. **Freshman Admission Statistics:** 3,125 applied, 80% admitted, 49% enrolled. **Transfer Admission Requirements:** College transcript(s), statement of good standing from prior institution(s). Minimum college GPA of 2.0 required. Lowest grade transferable D. **General Admission Information:** Application fee $20. Regular application deadline 8/1. Notification on a rolling basis, beginning on or about 10/1. Nonfall registration accepted. Admission may be deferred for a maximum of case by case. Credit and/or placement offered for CEEB Advanced Placement tests.

COSTS AND FINANCIAL AID

Annual in-state tuition $5,236. Annual out-of-state tuition $5,236. Room and board $5,936. Required fees $908. Average book expense $800. **Required Forms and Deadlines:** FAFSA. Priority financial aid filing date 2/15. **Notification of Awards:** Applicants will be notified of awards on a rolling basis beginning 6/1. **Types of Aid:** *Need-based scholarships/grants:* Federal Pell, SEOG, state scholarships/grants, private scholarships, the school's own gift aid. *Loans:* Direct Subsidized Stafford, Direct Unsubsidized Stafford, Direct PLUS, Federal Perkins, state loans. *Student Employment:* Federal Work-Study Program available. Institutional employment available. Highest amount earned per year from on-campus jobs $2,200. Off-campus job opportunities are excellent. **Financial Aid Statistics:** 29% freshmen, 27% undergrads receive need-based scholarship or grant aid. 60% freshmen, 58% undergrads receive need-based self-help aid. 3% freshmen, 3% undergrads receive athletic scholarships. 88% freshmen, 70% undergrads receive any aid. 70% undergrads borrow to pay for school. Average cumulative indebtedness $24,493. **Criteria for awarding institutional aid:** *Non-need-based:* Academics, art, athletics, leadership, minority status, music/drama, state/district residency.

MINNESOTA STATE UNIVERSITY, MANKATO

Room 122, Taylor Center, Mankato, MN 56001
Phone: 507-389-1822 Financial Aid Phone: 507-389-1866
E-mail: admissions@mnsu.edu CEEB Code: 6677
Fax: 507-389-1511 Website: www.mnsu.edu ACT Code: 2126

This public school was founded in 1868. It has a 354-acre campus.

RATINGS
Admissions Selectivity Rating: 63   Fire Safety Rating: 60*   Green Rating: 77

STUDENTS AND FACULTY
Enrollment: 12,369. **Student Body:** 50% female, 50% male, 14% out-of-state, 3% international (76 countries represented). Asian 3%, African American 4%, Caucasian 85%, Hispanic 2%.
Retention and Graduation: 20% freshmen graduate within 4 years. 12.8% grads go on to further study within 1 year. 18% grads pursue arts and sciences degrees. 3.5% grads pursue business degrees. **Faculty:** Student/faculty ratio 23:1. 496 full-time faculty, 82% hold PhDs, 8% are are members of minority groups, 45% are women. 4% of classes are taught by teaching assistants.

ACADEMICS
Degrees: Associate, bachelor's, certificate, master's, post-master's certificate. **Classes:** Most classes have 20–29 students. Most lab/discussion sessions have 20–29 students. **Majors with Highest Enrollment:** Business administration and management; elementary education and teaching; nursing/registered nurse (RN, ASN, BSN, MSN). **Special Study Options:** Cross-registration, distance learning, double major, dual enrollment, English as a Second Language (ESL), exchange student program (domestic), external degree program, honors program, independent study, internships, student-designed major, study abroad, teacher certification program Special programs offered to physically disabled students include note-taking services, reader services, tape recorders. **Career services:** Alumni network, alumni services, career/job search classes, career assessment, internships. **Career services highlights include:** Walk-in hours for student resume review and other services.

FACILITIES
Housing: Coed dorms, special housing for disabled students 90% of campus accessible to physically disabled. **Special Academic Facilities/Equipment:** 2 art galleries, day care facility, two astronomy observatories, main stage and studio theatres. **Computers:** 100% of classrooms, 10% of dorms, 100% of libraries, 100% of dining areas, 100% of student union, 80% of common outdoor areas have wireless network access. Students can register for classes online. Administrative functions (other than registration) can be performed online.

CAMPUS LIFE
Environment: Town. **Activities:** Choral groups, concert band, dance, drama/theater, jazz band, literary magazine, music ensembles, musical theater, pep band, radio station, student government, student newspaper, symphony orchestra, campus ministries, international student organization. **Organizations:** 178 registered organizations, 18 honor societies, 15 religious organizations. 7 fraternities, 4 sororities. **Athletics (Intercollegiate):** *Men:* Baseball, basketball, cross-country, diving, football, golf, ice hockey, swimming, tennis, track/field (outdoor), track/field (indoor), wrestling. *Women:* Basketball, bowling, cross-country, diving, golf, ice hockey, soccer, softball, swimming, tennis, track/field (outdoor), track/field (indoor), volleyball. **On-Campus Highlights:** Student Union, Myers Field House, Campus Recreation Center, Julia Sears Residence Hall, Memorial Library. **Environmental Initiatives:** Energy retrofit of building for lighting and motors; all new buildings exceed LEED compliance; purchase of three electric cars for University Security and Environmental Health and Safety Offices.

ADMISSIONS
Freshman Academic Profile: 7% in top 10% of high school class, 29% in top 25% of high school class, 70% in top 50% of high school class. 95% from public high schools. ACT middle 50% range 20–24. Minimum paper TOEFL 500. Minimum computer TOEFL 173. Minimum web-based TOEFL 61. **Basis for Candidate Selection:** *Very important factors considered include:* Class rank, standardized test scores. *Other factors considered include:* Academic GPA, recommendation(s). **Freshman Admission Requirements:** High school diploma is required and GED is accepted. *Academic units required:* 4 English, 3 mathematics, 3 science, (3 science labs), 2 foreign language, 2 social studies, 1 history, 1 visual/performing arts. **Freshman Admission Statistics:** 6,196 applied, 89% admitted, 42% enrolled. **Transfer Admission Requirements:** College transcript(s), statement of good standing from prior institution(s). Minimum college GPA of 2.0 required. Lowest grade transferable D. **General Admission Information:** Application fee $20. Nonfall registration accepted. Admission may be deferred for a maximum of No set time frame. Credit offered for CEEB Advanced Placement tests.

COSTS AND FINANCIAL AID
Required Forms and Deadlines: FAFSA, SELF or Alternative Loan Application or PLUS Application. Priority financial aid filing date 3/15. **Notification of Awards:** Applicants will be notified of awards on a rolling basis beginning 3/30. **Types of Aid:** *Need-based scholarships/grants:* Federal Pell, SEOG, state scholarships/grants, private scholarships, the school's own gift aid, Federal ACG/SMART. *Loans:* FFEL Subsidized Stafford, FFEL Unsubsidized Stafford, FFEL PLUS, Federal Perkins, state loans, alternative loans. *Student Employment:* Federal Work-Study Program available. Institutional employment available. Off-campus job opportunities are fair. **Financial Aid Statistics:** 43% freshmen, 40% undergrads receive need-based scholarship or grant aid. 18% freshmen, 11% undergrads receive non-need-based scholarship or grant aid. 51% freshmen, 50% undergrads receive need-based self-help aid. 1% freshmen, 1% undergrads receive athletic scholarships. 63% freshmen, 66% undergrads receive any aid. 82% undergrads borrow to pay for school. Average cumulative indebtedness $25,667. **Criteria for awarding institutional aid:** *Non-need-based:* Academics, art, athletics, leadership, minority status, music/drama.

MISERICORDIA UNIVERSITY

301 Lake Street, Dallas, PA 18612
Phone: 570-674-6264 Financial Aid Phone: 570-674-6280
E-mail: admiss@misericordia.edu CEEB Code: 2087
Fax: 570-675-2441 Website: www.misericordia.edu ACT Code: 3539

This private school, affiliated with the Roman Catholic Church, was founded in 1924. It has a 120-acre campus.

RATINGS
Admissions Selectivity Rating: 77   Fire Safety Rating: 79   Green Rating: 60*

STUDENTS AND FACULTY
Enrollment: 2,315. **Student Body:** 71% female, 29% male, 16% out-of-state, international (1 countries represented). Asian 1%, African American 1%, Caucasian 95%, Hispanic 2%.
Retention and Graduation: 85% freshmen return for sophomore year. 66% freshmen graduate within 4 years. 16% grads go on to further study within 1 year. 3% grads pursue arts and sciences degrees. 4% grads pursue business degrees. 1% grads pursue medical degrees. **Faculty:** Student/faculty ratio 13:1. 96 full-time faculty, 79% hold PhDs, 8% are are members of minority groups, 54% are women.

ACADEMICS
Degrees: Bachelor's, certificate, master's, post-bachelor's certificate, post-master's certificate. **Classes:** Most classes have 10–19 students. Most lab/discussion sessions have 10–19 students. **Majors with Highest Enrollment:** Business/commerce; elementary education and teaching; nursing/registered nurse (RN, ASN, BSN, MSN). **Special Study Options:** Accelerated program, cross-registration, distance learning, double major, dual enrollment, honors program, independent study, internships, student-designed major, study abroad, teacher certification program, weekend college. **Honors programs:** The Honors Program is an interdisciplinary community of undergraduate students and faculty working together to create an intellectually stimulating and challenging environment for learning. Honors students take a common sequence of core curriculum courses in place of regular core offerings, participate each semester in our Honors Explorations Seminar, and procuce a professional quality paper or project as part of the Honors Capstone. **Combined degree programs:** BS/MSPT and BS/MSOT and BS/MSSLP. Special programs offered to physically disabled students include tape recorders, tutors. **Career services:** Alumni network, alumni services, career/job search classes, career assessment, internships.

FACILITIES
Housing: Coed dorms, Leadership House, Women with Children House. 100% of campus accessible to physically disabled. **Computers:** 5% of classrooms, 100% of libraries, 100% of dining areas, 100% of student union, 10% of common outdoor areas have wireless network access. Students can register for classes online. Administrative functions (other than registration) can be performed online.

CAMPUS LIFE
Environment: Town. **Activities:** Choral groups, dance, drama/theater, jazz band, literary magazine, music ensembles, radio station, student government, student newspaper, television station, yearbook, campus ministries. **Organizations:** 27 registered organizations, 1 honor societies, 1 religious organizations. **Athletics (Intercollegiate):** *Men:* Baseball, basketball, cross-country, golf, lacrosse, soccer, swimming, tennis, track/field (outdoor). *Women:* Basketball, cheerleading, cross-country, field hockey, lacrosse, soccer, softball, swimming, tennis, track/field (outdoor), volleyball. **On-Campus Highlights:** Anderson

Sports and Health Center, Banks Student Life Center, Mangelsdorf Field, Bevevino Library.

ADMISSIONS
Freshman Academic Profile: Average high school GPA 3.2. 15% in top 10% of high school class, 49% in top 25% of high school class, 79% in top 50% of high school class. 86% from public high schools. SAT Math middle 50% range 480–570. SAT Critical Reading middle 50% range 470–550. ACT middle 50% range 20–25. Minimum paper TOEFL 550. Minimum computer TOEFL 213. Minimum web-based TOEFL 79. **Basis for Candidate Selection:** *Very important factors considered include:* Academic GPA, rigor of secondary school record. *Important factors considered include:* Class rank, standardized test scores. *Other factors considered include:* Application essay, recommendation(s), character/personal qualities, extracurricular activities, interview, racial/ethnic status, volunteer work, work experience. **Freshman Admission Requirements:** High school diploma is required and GED is accepted. *Academic units required:* 4 English, 4 mathematics, 4 science, 4 social studies. **Freshman Admission Statistics:** 1,533 applied, 69% admitted, 36% enrolled. **Transfer Admission Requirements:** College transcript(s), minimum college GPA of 2.0 required. Lowest grade transferable C. **General Admission Information:** Application fee $25. Notification on a rolling basis, beginning on or about 10/1. Nonfall registration accepted. Admission may be deferred for a maximum of 1 year. Credit and/or placement offered for CEEB Advanced Placement tests.

COSTS AND FINANCIAL AID
Annual tuition $22,850. Room and board $10,050. Required fees $1,200. Average book expense $800. **Required Forms and Deadlines:** FAFSA, institution's own financial aid form. Financial aid filing deadline 5/1. Priority financial aid filing date 3/1. **Notification of Awards:** Applicants will be notified of awards on a rolling basis beginning 3/15. **Types of Aid:** *Need-based scholarships/grants:* Federal Pell, SEOG, state scholarships/grants, private scholarships, the school's own gift aid, Federal Nursing Scholarships. *Loans:* FFEL Subsidized Stafford, FFEL Unsubsidized Stafford, FFEL PLUS, Federal Perkins, Federal Nursing, state loans. *Student Employment:* Federal Work-Study Program available, Institutional employment available. Highest amount earned per year from on-campus jobs $1,600. Off-campus job opportunities are good. **Financial Aid Statistics:** 83% freshmen, 82% undergrads receive need-based scholarship or grant aid. 9% freshmen, 7% undergrads receive non-need-based scholarship or grant aid. 67% freshmen, 70% undergrads receive need-based self-help aid. 99% freshmen, 98% undergrads receive any aid. 78% undergrads borrow to pay for school. Average cumulative indebtedness $33,641. **Criteria for awarding institutional aid:** *Non-need-based:* Academics, alumni affiliation, leadership, minority status, state/district residency.

MISSISSIPPI COLLEGE

Box 4026, Clinton, MS 39058
Phone: 601-925-3800 **Financial Aid Phone:** 601-925-3212
E-mail: enrollment-services@mc.edu **CEEB Code:** 1477
Fax: 601-925-3950 **Website:** www.mc.edu **ACT Code:** 2214

This private school, affiliated with the Southern Baptist Church, was founded in 1826. It has a 320-acre campus.

RATINGS
Admissions Selectivity Rating: 85   **Fire Safety Rating:** 74   **Green Rating:** 60*

STUDENTS AND FACULTY
Enrollment: 3,084. **Student Body:** 60% female, 40% male, 18% out-of-state, 2% international (21 countries represented). Asian 1%, African American 25%, Caucasian 65%, Hispanic 1%.
Retention and Graduation: 67% freshmen return for sophomore year. 36% freshmen graduate within 4 years. 37% grads go on to further study within 1 year. **Faculty:** Student/faculty ratio 16:1. 180 full-time faculty, 77% hold PhDs, 5% are are members of minority groups, 48% are women. 1% of classes are taught by teaching assistants.

ACADEMICS
Degrees: Bachelor's, doctoral, master's, post-bachelor's certificate, post-master's certificate. **Classes:** Most classes have 10–19 students. Most lab/discussion sessions have fewer than 10 students. **Majors with Highest Enrollment:** Biology/biological sciences; business administration and management; nursing/registered nurse (RN, ASN, BSN, MSN). **Special Study Options:** Accelerated program, distance learning, double major, dual enrollment, English as a Second Language (ESL), honors program, independent study, internships, study abroad, teacher certification program, Academic remediation, Advance Placement credit, Work-Study program, Learning disabilities services. **Honors**

programs: Honors programs open to freshmen, sophomores, juniors, and seniors and administered by the Honors Council. Freshmen who have a high ACT score (established each year) are invited to participate in a program of study called Freshman Honors Seminar (IDS161), it is an interdisciplinary study dealing with contemporary issues and interests. Upperclassmen who maintain a high GPA may also participate in Sophomore and Senior Honors Seminars (IDS 261, 461). Successful completion of the Junior-Senior Honors Program leads to a degree "With Honors" or "With High Honors." **Combined degree programs:** BA/JD Special programs offered to physically disabled students include note-taking services, reader services, tape recorders, tutors. **Career services:** Alumni services, career/job search classes, career assessment, internships.

FACILITIES
Housing: Special housing for disabled students, men's dorms, women's dorms, apartments for single students. 90% of campus accessible to physically disabled. **Computers:** 60% of classrooms, 100% of dorms, 100% of libraries, 100% of dining areas, 60% of common outdoor areas have wireless network access. Students can register for classes online. Administrative functions (other than registration) can be performed online.

CAMPUS LIFE
Environment: Metropolis. **Activities:** Choral groups, concert band, dance, drama/theater, jazz band, literary magazine, marching band, music ensembles, musical theater, opera, radio station, student government, student newspaper, yearbook, campus ministries, international student organization. **Organizations:** 66 registered organizations, 22 honor societies, 6 religious organizations. 5 fraternities, 4 sororities. **Athletics (Intercollegiate):** *Men:* Baseball, basketball, cross-country, football, golf, soccer, tennis, track/field (outdoor). *Women:* Basketball, cheerleading, cross-country, equestrian sports, soccer, softball, tennis, track/field (outdoor), volleyball. **On-Campus Highlights:** Gore Gallery, Healthplex, Men's Rotunda and new Women's Residence Hall, Provine Chapel, Anderson Hall in BCR Student Center, Nelson Hall—administration building, Robinson-Wright Field House.

ADMISSIONS
Freshman Academic Profile: Average high school GPA 3.36. 24% in top 10% of high school class, 50% in top 25% of high school class, 77% in top 50% of high school class. SAT Math middle 50% range 470–600. SAT Critical Reading middle 50% range 450–600. ACT middle 50% range 20–27. **Basis for Candidate Selection:** *Very important factors considered include:* standardized test scores. *Important factors considered include:* Rigor of secondary school record, character/personal qualities, extracurricular activities, level of applicant's interest. *Other factors considered include:* Class rank, academic GPA, recommendation(s), alumni/ae relation, interview, talent/ability, volunteer work, work experience. **Freshman Admission Requirements:** High school diploma is required and GED is accepted. *Academic units recommended:* 4 English, 4 mathematics, 4 science, (2 science labs), 1 foreign language, 2 social studies, 2 history, 1 visual/performing arts, 1 computer science, 3 academic electives. **Freshman Admission Statistics:** 1,763 applied, 61% admitted, 43% enrolled. **Transfer Admission Requirements:** College transcript(s), essay or personal statement, statement of good standing from prior institution(s). Minimum college GPA of 2.0 required. Lowest grade transferable C. **General Admission Information:** Early decision application deadline 12/1. Nonfall registration accepted. Admission may be deferred for a maximum of 1 year. Credit offered for CEEB Advanced Placement tests.

COSTS AND FINANCIAL AID
Annual tuition $12,900. Room and board $6,150. Required fees $650. Average book expense $1,000. **Required Forms and Deadlines:** FAFSA, state aid form. Priority financial aid filing date 3/1. **Notification of Awards:** Applicants will be notified of awards on a rolling basis beginning 3/1. **Types of Aid:** *Need-based scholarships/grants:* Federal Pell, SEOG, state scholarships/grants, private scholarships, the school's own gift aid, Federal Nursing Scholarships. *Loans:* FFEL Subsidized Stafford, FFEL Unsubsidized Stafford, FFEL PLUS, Federal Perkins, Federal Nursing, college/university loans from institutional funds. *Student Employment:* Federal Work-Study Program available. Highest amount earned per year from on-campus jobs $3,000. Off-campus job opportunities are good. **Financial Aid Statistics:** 39% freshmen, 46% undergrads receive need-based scholarship or grant aid. 17% freshmen, 12% undergrads receive non-need-based scholarship or grant aid. 34% freshmen, 46% undergrads receive need-based self-help aid. 99% freshmen, 95% undergrads receive any aid. 72% undergrads borrow to pay for school. Average cumulative indebtedness $26,323. **Criteria for awarding institutional aid:** *Non-need-based:* Academics, alumni affiliation, art, leadership, music/drama, religious affiliation.

MISSISSIPPI STATE UNIVERSITY

P. O. Box 6334, Mississippi State, MS 39762
Phone: 662-325-2224 **Financial Aid Phone:** 662-325-2450
E-mail: admit@msstate.edu **CEEB Code:** 1480
Fax: 662-325-1678 **Website:** www.msstate.edu **ACT Code:** 2220

This public school was founded in 1878. It has a 4200-acre campus.

RATINGS
Admissions Selectivity Rating: 80   **Fire Safety Rating:** 60*   **Green Rating:** 74

STUDENTS AND FACULTY
Enrollment: 13,730. **Student Body:** 48% female, 52% male, 18% out-of-state, 2% international (72 countries represented). Asian 1%, African American 20%, Caucasian 74%, Hispanic 1%, Native American 1%.
Retention and Graduation: 82% freshmen return for sophomore year. 31% freshmen graduate within 4 years. **Faculty:** Student/faculty ratio 18:1. 844 full-time faculty, 80% hold PhDs, 14% are are members of minority groups, 34% are women. 8.8% of classes are taught by teaching assistants.

ACADEMICS
Degrees: Bachelor's, doctoral, master's. **Classes:** Most classes have 20–29 students. Most lab/discussion sessions have fewer than 10 students. **Majors with Highest Enrollment:** Business administration and management; elementary education and teaching; physical education teaching and coaching. **Special Study Options:** Cooperative education program, distance learning, double major, dual enrollment, English as a Second Language (ESL), exchange student program (domestic), external degree program, honors program, independent study, internships, liberal arts/career combination, student-designed major, study abroad, teacher certification program, weekend college. **Honors programs:** University Honors Program Special programs offered to physically disabled students include note-taking services, reader services, tape recorders, tutors. **Career services:** Alumni network, alumni services, career/job search classes, career assessment, internships, regional alumni. **Career services highlights include:** MSU offers a diversified co-op program. Students are participating from several colleges and schools at the university.

FACILITIES
Housing: Special housing for disabled students, men's dorms, women's dorms, fraternity/sorority housing, apartments for married students, apartments for single students, theme housingco-residential. 95% of campus accessible to physically disabled. **Special Academic Facilities/Equipment:** Geology, archeology, music, entomological museums; art gallery; flight research lab. **Computers:** 100% of classrooms, 100% of dorms, 100% of libraries, 100% of dining areas, 100% of student union, 100% of common outdoor areas have wireless network access. Students can register for classes online. Administrative functions (other than registration) can be performed online.

CAMPUS LIFE
Environment: Town. **Activities:** Choral groups, concert band, dance, drama/theater, jazz band, literary magazine, marching band, music ensembles, musical theater, pep band, radio station, student government, student newspaper, television station, yearbook, campus ministries, international student organization, Model UN. **Organizations:** 326 registered organizations, 42 honor societies, 30 religious organizations. 17 fraternities, 11 sorority. **Athletics (Intercollegiate):** *Men:* Baseball, basketball, cheerleading, cross-country, football, golf, tennis, track/field (outdoor). *Women:* Basketball, cheerleading, cross-country, golf, soccer, softball, tennis, track/field (outdoor), volleyball. **On-Campus Highlights:** Scott Field Stadium, Dudy Noble Field, Humphrey Coliseum, Barnes and Noble Campus Bookstore, Sanderson Student Recreation Center. **Environmental Initiatives:** Recycling; bicycle program; Environmental Sustainability Research Center.

ADMISSIONS
Freshman Academic Profile: Average high school GPA 3.17. 27% in top 10% of high school class, 27% in top 25% of high school class, 83% in top 50% of high school class. SAT Math middle 50% range 490–640. SAT Critical Reading middle 50% range 470–610. ACT middle 50% range 20–27. Minimum paper TOEFL 525. Minimum computer TOEFL 197. Minimum web-based TOEFL 71. *Basis for Candidate Selection: Very important factors considered include:* Academic GPA, standardized test scores. *Important factors considered include:* Class rank. *Other factors considered include:* Rigor of secondary school record, talent/ability. **Freshman Admission Requirements:** High school diploma is required and GED is accepted. *Academic units required:* 4 English, 3 mathematics, 3 science, (2 science labs), 1 social studies, 2 history, 2 academic electives. *Academic units recommended:* 4 English, 4 mathematics, 4 science, (2 science labs), 1 foreign language, 2 social studies, 2 history, 2 academic electives, 1 world geography. **Freshman Admission Statistics:** 7,839 applied,

65% admitted, 48% enrolled. **Transfer Admission Requirements:** College transcript(s), statement of good standing from prior institution(s). Minimum college GPA of 2.0 required. Lowest grade transferable D. **General Admission Information:** Application fee $35. Notification on a rolling basis, beginning on or about 9/1. Nonfall registration accepted. Credit offered for CEEB Advanced Placement tests.

COSTS AND FINANCIAL AID
Annual in-state tuition $5,151. Annual out-of-state tuition $13,021. Room and board $7,520. Average book expense $1,200. **Required Forms and Deadlines:** FAFSAState grant/scholarship application. Priority financial aid filing date 4/1. **Notification of Awards:** Applicants will be notified of awards on a rolling basis beginning 12/1. **Types of Aid:** *Need-based scholarships/grants:* Federal Pell, SEOG, state scholarships/grants, private scholarships, the school's own gift aid, United Negro College Fund. *Loans:* FFEL Subsidized Stafford, FFEL Unsubsidized Stafford, FFEL PLUS, Federal Perkins, college/university loans from institutional funds. *Student Employment:* Federal Work-Study Program available. Institutional employment available. Off-campus job opportunities are good. **Financial Aid Statistics:** 53% freshmen, 49% undergrads receive need-based scholarship or grant aid. 10% freshmen, 5% undergrads receive non-need-based scholarship or grant aid. 38% freshmen, 41% undergrads receive need-based self-help aid. 3% freshmen, 3% undergrads receive athletic scholarships. 56% freshmen, 54% undergrads receive any aid. 51% undergrads borrow to pay for school. Average cumulative indebtedness $23,413. **Criteria for awarding institutional aid:** *Non-need-based:* Academics, alumni affiliation, art, athletics, job skills, leadership, minority status, music/drama, state/district residency.

MISSISSIPPI VALLEY STATE UNIVERSITY

14000 Highway 82 West, #7222, Itta Bena, MS 38941-1400
Phone: 662-254-3344 **Financial Aid Phone:** 662-254-3338
E-mail: nbtaylor@mvsu.edu **CEEB Code:** 1482
Fax: 662-254-3759 **Website:** www.mvsu.edu **ACT Code:** 2224

This public school was founded in 1950. It has a 250-acre campus.

RATINGS
Admissions Selectivity Rating: 76   **Fire Safety Rating:** 70   **Green Rating:** 71

STUDENTS AND FACULTY
Enrollment: 2,357. **Student Body:** 62% female, 38% male, 11% out-of-state, (2 countries represented). African American 93%, Caucasian 4%, Hispanic 1%.
Retention and Graduation: 55% freshmen return for sophomore year. 18% freshmen graduate within 4 years. **Faculty:** Student/faculty ratio 21:1. 133 full-time faculty, 58% hold PhDs, 30% are are members of minority groups, 46% are women.

ACADEMICS
Degrees: Bachelor's, master's. **Classes:** Most classes have fewer than 10 students. Most lab/discussion sessions have 20–29 students. **Majors with Highest Enrollment:** Business, management, marketing, and related support services, other; kindergarten/preschool education and teaching; social work. **Special Study Options:** Cooperative education program, distance learning, double major, honors program, internships, teacher certification program, weekend college, co-op programs: business, computer science, natural science, social/behavioral science. Special programs offered to physically disabled students include tape recorders, tutors. **Career services:** Alumni services. **Career services highlights include:** Many of our students have received internships with the Environmental Protection Agency in Washington, DC.

FACILITIES
Housing: men's dorms, women's dorms, apartments for married students, apartments for single students. **Computers:** Students can register for classes online.

CAMPUS LIFE
Environment: Rural. **Activities:** Choral groups, concert band, drama/theater, marching band, radio station, student government, student newspaper, yearbook. **Organizations:** 35 registered organizations, 19 honor societies, 4 religious organizations. 4 fraternities, 2 sororities. **Athletics (Intercollegiate):** *Men:* Baseball, basketball, cross-country, football, golf, tennis, track/field (outdoor). *Women:* Basketball, cross-country, golf, soccer, softball, tennis, track/field (outdoor), volleyball. **On-Campus Highlights:** Student union, student pavillion, administration building, library.

ADMISSIONS
Freshman Academic Profile: Average high school GPA 2.58. 96% from public high schools. ACT middle 50% range 15–19. Minimum paper TOEFL

525. Minimum computer TOEFL 195. **Basis for Candidate Selection:** *Very important factors considered include:* Class rank, rigor of secondary school record, standardized test scores, state residency. *Other factors considered include:* Recommendation(s), extracurricular activities, interview, talent/ability. **Freshman Admission Requirements:** High school diploma is required and GED is accepted. *Academic units required:* 4 English, 3 mathematics, 3 science, (2 science labs), 1 foreign language, 3 social studies, 2 academic electives, 1 Computer Applications *Academic units recommended:* 1 foreign language. **Freshman Admission Statistics:** 6,086 applied, 30% admitted, 23% enrolled. **Transfer Admission Requirements:** College transcript(s), minimum college GPA of 2.0 required. Lowest grade transferable C. **General Admission Information:** Nonfall registration accepted.

COSTS AND FINANCIAL AID

Annual in-state tuition $4,575. Annual out-of-state tuition $11,410. Room and board $5,081. Required fees $25. Average book expense $1,400. **Required Forms and Deadlines:** FAFSA, institution's own financial aid form. Priority financial aid filing date 4/1. **Notification of Awards:** Applicants will be notified of awards on or about 7/15. **Types of Aid:** *Need-based scholarships/grants:* Federal Pell, SEOG, state scholarships/grants, private scholarships, the school's own gift aid. *Loans:* Direct Unsubsidized Stafford, Direct PLUS. *Student Employment:* Federal Work-Study Program available. **Financial Aid Statistics:** 95% freshmen, 95% undergrads receive any aid.

MISSOURI SOUTHERN STATE UNIVERSITY— JOPLIN

3950 E. Newman Road, Joplin, MO 64801-1595
Phone: 417-625-9378 **Financial Aid Phone:** 417-625-9325
E-mail: admissions@mssu.edu **CEEB Code:** 6322
Fax: 417-659-4429 **Website: ACT Code:** 2304

This public school was founded in 1937. It has a 365-acre campus.

RATINGS

Admissions Selectivity Rating: 62   **Fire Safety Rating:** 60*   **Green Rating:** 60*

STUDENTS AND FACULTY

Enrollment: 5,135. **Student Body:** 59% female, 41% male, 15% out-of-state, 1% international (31 countries represented). Asian 1%, African American 3%, Caucasian 89%, Hispanic 2%, Native American 3%.
Retention and Graduation: 63% freshmen return for sophomore year. 18% freshmen graduate within 4 years. **Faculty:** Student/faculty ratio 19:1. 208 full-time faculty, 64% hold PhDs, 9% are are members of minority groups, 37% are women.

ACADEMICS

Degrees: Associate, bachelor's, certificate, master's. **Classes:** Most classes have 20–29 students. Most lab/discussion sessions have fewer than 10 students. **Majors with Highest Enrollment:** Business/commerce; criminal justice/law enforcement administration; education. **Special Study Options:** Accelerated program, cooperative education program, distance learning, double major, dual enrollment, English as a Second Language (ESL), exchange student program (domestic), honors program, independent study, internships, liberal arts/career combination, study abroad, teacher certification program, weekend college. **Honors programs:** MSSU Honors Program. Special programs offered to physically disabled students include note-taking services, reader services, tape recorders, tutors.

FACILITIES

Housing: Coed dorms, special housing for disabled students, men's dorms, women's dorms, apartments for single students. 100% of campus accessible to physically disabled. **Special Academic Facilities/Equipment:** Spiva Art Gallery, biology pond, forensics laboratory, child development center, indoor "livefire" firearms range, green house, law library, Cyber Coffee Shop, International Trade and Quality Center, graduate center, tv station, radio station, small business development center, Thomas E. Taylor Performing Arts Center, health center. **Computers:** Administrative functions (other than registration) can be performed online.

CAMPUS LIFE

Environment: Town. **Activities:** Choral groups, concert band, dance, drama/theater, jazz band, literary magazine, marching band, music ensembles, musical theater, pep band, radio station, student government, student newspaper, student-run film society, symphony orchestra, television station. **Organizations:** 82 registered organizations, 12 honor societies, 9 religious organizations. 2 fraternities, 2 sororities. **Athletics (Intercollegiate):** *Men:* Baseball, basketball,

cheerleading, cross-country, football, golf, soccer, track/field (outdoor). *Women:* Basketball, cheerleading, cross-country, soccer, softball, tennis, track/field (outdoor), volleyball. **On-Campus Highlights:** Cyber Coffee Shop, Lion's Den, Student Life Activity Center, Leggett and Platt Athletic Center, Spiva Art Gallery. In addition to MSSU's campus facilities, Missouri Southern's low crime rate, well-lit campus, 24-hour security and emergency phones located in key spots help to ensure the safety of students as they enjoy Missouri Southern's campus.

ADMISSIONS

Freshman Academic Profile: 17% in top 10% of high school class, 40% in top 25% of high school class, 72% in top 50% of high school class. 98% from public high schools. ACT middle 50% range 17–19. Minimum paper TOEFL 535. Minimum computer TOEFL 200. **Basis for Candidate Selection:** *Very important factors considered include:* Class rank, academic GPA, rigor of secondary school record, standardized test scores. *Other factors considered include:* Recommendation(s). **Freshman Admission Requirements:** High school diploma is required and GED is accepted. *Academic units recommended:* 4 English, 3 mathematics, 2 science, (1 science labs), 2 foreign language, 3 social studies, 3 academic electives, 1 visual/performing arts. **Freshman Admission Statistics:** 2,669 applied, 98% admitted, 36% enrolled. **Transfer Admission Requirements:** College transcript(s), minimum college GPA of 2.0 required. Lowest grade transferable D. **General Admission Information:** Application fee $15. Notification on a rolling basis, beginning on or about 9/1. Nonfall registration accepted. Admission may be deferred for a maximum of 1 year. Credit and/or placement offered for CEEB Advanced Placement tests.

COSTS AND FINANCIAL AID

Average book expense $600. **Required Forms and Deadlines:** FAFSA. Priority financial aid filing date 2/15. **Notification of Awards:** Applicants will be notified of awards on a rolling basis beginning 2/15. **Types of Aid:** *Need-based scholarships/grants:* Federal Pell, SEOG, state scholarships/grants, private scholarships Loans:* Direct Subsidized Stafford, Direct Unsubsidized Stafford, Direct PLUS, Federal Perkins, state loans. **Criteria for awarding institutional aid:** *Non-need-based:* Academics, alumni affiliation, art, athletics, job skills, leadership, minority status, music/drama, state/district residency.

MISSOURI STATE UNIVERSITY

901 S. National, Springfield, MO 65897
Phone: 417-836-5517 **Financial Aid Phone:** 417-835-5262
E-mail: info@missouristate.edu **CEEB Code:** 6665
Fax: 417-836-6334 **Website:** www.missouristate.edu **ACT Code:** 2370

This public school was founded in 1905. It has a 450-acre campus.

RATINGS

Admissions Selectivity Rating: 78   **Fire Safety Rating:** 80   **Green Rating:** 60*

STUDENTS AND FACULTY

Enrollment: 14,463. **Student Body:** 56% female, 44% male, 7% out-of-state, 2% international Asian 1%, African American 2%, Caucasian 77%, Hispanic 1%, Native American 1%.
Retention and Graduation: 73% freshmen return for sophomore year. 20% grads go on to further study within 1 year. 2% grads pursue arts and sciences degrees. 2% grads pursue law degrees. 10% grads pursue business degrees. 2% grads pursue medical degrees. **Faculty:** Student/faculty ratio 18:1. 728 full-time faculty, 78% hold PhDs, 7% are are members of minority groups, 40% are women. 8% of classes are taught by teaching assistants.

ACADEMICS

Degrees: Bachelor's, master's, post-bachelor's certificate, post-master's certificate. **Classes:** Most classes have 20–29 students. Most lab/discussion sessions have 20–29 students. **Majors with Highest Enrollment:** Elementary education and teaching; management information systems; marketing/marketing management. **Special Study Options:** Accelerated program, cooperative education program, distance learning, double major, dual enrollment, English as a Second Language (ESL), exchange student program (domestic), honors program, independent study, internships, student-designed major, study abroad, teacher certification program. **Honors programs:** The Honors College is to provide a program of enhanced, advanced study and recognition for students of unusually strong academic achievement and motivation. The Honors College is to provide these students with intellectual opportunities beyond those generally found in the more traditional programs: smaller and enriched classes; direct contact with outstanding faculty members, and the option to pursue their own intellectual, research, and creative interests. The Honors College is to provide the means whereby individual departments may develop departmental honors opportunities. These opportunities will allow students with higher academic achievement and motivation to develop their individual interests more fully through contact with faculty and students of similar interests and abilities while maintaining involvement in the University community as a whole. Special programs offered to physically disabled students include note-taking services, reader services, tape recorders, tutors.

FACILITIES

Housing: Coed dorms, special housing for disabled students, special housing for international students, fraternity/sorority housing, apartments for married students, apartments for single students, graduate student housing, non-traditional student housing, upper-class student housing, honor student housing, transfer student housing and family housing. 95% of campus accessible to physically disabled. **Special Academic Facilities/Equipment:** On-campus laboratory school (K–12), 125-acre Darr Agricultrual Center, Baker Observatory, Bull Shoals Field Station, electron microscope, molecular beam epitaxy laboratory, Ion implantation laboratory, Art and Design Gallery, Student Exhibition Center, Coger Theatre, Ellis Recital Hall, instructional TV studio, computer animation studio, foundry, Wehr Band Hall, multimedia lab, language lab, Juanita K. Hammons Hall for the Performing Arts. **Computers:** Students can register for classes online. Administrative functions (other than registration) can be performed online.

CAMPUS LIFE

Environment: City. **Activities:** Choral groups, concert band, dance, drama/theater, jazz band, literary magazine, marching band, music ensembles, musical theater, pep band, radio station, student government, student newspaper, student-run film society, symphony orchestra, television station **Organizations:** 270 registered organizations, 26 honor societies, 28 religious organizations. 15 fraternities, 9 sororities. **Athletics (Intercollegiate):** *Men:* Baseball, basketball, cross-country, diving, football, golf, soccer, swimming, tennis, track/field (outdoor), track/field (indoor), volleyball. *Women:* Basketball, cross-country, diving, field hockey, golf, soccer, softball, swimming, tennis, track/field (outdoor), track/field (indoor), volleyball. **On-Campus Highlights:** Plaster Student Union, Meyer Library, Baker Bookstore, Hammons Fountains, Plaster Sports Complex.

ADMISSIONS

Freshman Academic Profile: Average high school GPA 3.57. 22% in top 10% of high school class, 49% in top 25% of high school class, 81% in top 50% of high school class. ACT middle 50% range 21–26. Minimum paper TOEFL 500. Minimum computer TOEFL 173. **Basis for Candidate Selection:** *Very important factors considered include:* Class rank, rigor of secondary school record, standardized test scores. *Other factors considered include:* Application essay, recommendation(s), alumni/ae relation, character/personal qualities, extracurricular activities, interview, racial/ethnic status, talent/ability, volunteer work, work experience. **Freshman Admission Requirements:** High school diploma is required and GED is accepted. *Academic units required:* 4 English, 3 mathematics, 2 science, (1 science labs), 3 social studies, 3 academic electives. **Freshman Admission Statistics:** 6,866 applied, 77% admitted, 50% enrolled. **Transfer Admission Requirements:** College transcript(s), minimum college GPA of 2.0 required. Lowest grade transferable D. **General Admission Information:** Application fee $30. Regular application deadline 7/20. Nonfall registration accepted. Credit and/or placement offered for CEEB Advanced Placement tests.

COSTS AND FINANCIAL AID

Annual in-state tuition $4,920. Annual out-of-state tuition $9,840. Room and board $5,294. Required fees $534. Average book expense $800. **Required Forms and Deadlines:** FAFSA. Priority financial aid filing date 3/30. **Notification of Awards:** Applicants will be notified of awards on a rolling basis beginning 4/1. **Types of Aid:** *Need-based scholarships/grants:* Federal Pell, SEOG, state scholarships/grants, private scholarships, the school's own gift aid. *Loans:* FFEL Subsidized Stafford, FFEL Unsubsidized Stafford, FFEL PLUS, Federal Perkins, college/university loans from institutional funds. *Student Employment:* **Financial Aid Statistics:** 42% freshmen, 41% undergrads receive need-based scholarship or grant aid. 8% freshmen, 4% undergrads receive non-need-based scholarship or grant aid. 40% freshmen, 48% undergrads receive need-based self-help aid. 3% freshmen, 3% undergrads receive athletic scholarships. 66% undergrads borrow to pay for school. Average cumulative indebtedness $16,003. **Criteria for awarding institutional aid:** *Non-need-based:* Academics, alumni affiliation, art, athletics, job skills, leadership, minority status, music/drama, state/district residency.

MISSOURI UNIVERSITY OF SCIENCE AND TECHNOLOGY

300 W. 13th Street; 106 Parker Hall, Rolla, MO 65409-1060
Phone: 573-341-4165 **Financial Aid Phone:** 573-341-4282
E-mail: admissions@mst.edu **CEEB Code:** 6876
Fax: 573-341-4082 **Website:** www.mst.edu **ACT Code:** 2398

This public school was founded in 1870. It has a 284-acre campus.

RATINGS
Admissions Selectivity Rating: 86 **Fire Safety Rating:** 76 **Green Rating:** 73

STUDENTS AND FACULTY
Enrollment: 5,145. **Student Body:** 22% female, 78% male, 19% out-of-state, 3% international (49 countries represented). Asian 2%, African American 5%, Caucasian 82%, Hispanic 2%, Native American 1%.
Retention and Graduation: 88% freshmen return for sophomore year. 25% freshmen graduate within 4 years. **Faculty:** Student/faculty ratio 16:1. 360 full-time faculty, 89% hold PhDs, 28% are are members of minority groups, 19% are women. 12% of classes are taught by teaching assistants.

ACADEMICS
Degrees: Bachelor's, certificate, master's, post-bachelor's certificate. **Classes:** Most classes have 20–29 students. Most lab/discussion sessions have 20–29 students. **Majors with Highest Enrollment:** Civil engineering; electrical, electronics and communications engineering; mechanical engineering. **Special Study Options:** Distance learning, double major, dual enrollment, English as a Second Language (ESL), honors program, independent study, internships, liberal arts/career combination, study abroad, teacher certification program **Honors programs:** Honors Academy and Master Student Fellowship Programs http://ugs.mst.edu/honors.html. **Combined degree programs:** BA/MEng. Special programs offered to physically disabled students include note-taking services, reader services, tape recorders, tutors. **Career services:** Alumni network, alumni services, career/job search classes, career assessment, internships, regional alumni.

FACILITIES
Housing: Coed dorms, special housing for disabled students, fraternity/sorority housing, apartments for married students, cooperative housing, apartments for single students, wellness house, theme housing. 95% of campus accessible to physically disabled. **Special Academic Facilities/Equipment:** Writing Center; Student Design Center; nuclear reactor; observatory; explosives testing lab; underground mine; Museum of Rocks, Minerals, and Gemstones; Centers for Environmental Research, Water Resources, Industrial Research, and Rock Mechanics Research; Geophysical Observatory, computerized manufacturing system, Millenium Arch, and Stonehenge. **Computers:** 100% of classrooms, 100% of dorms, 100% of libraries, 66% of dining areas, 100% of student union, 80% of common outdoor areas have wireless network access. Students can register for classes online. Administrative functions (other than registration) can be performed online.

CAMPUS LIFE
Environment: Village. **Activities:** Choral groups, concert band, dance, drama/theater, jazz band, literary magazine, marching band, music ensembles, musical theater, pep band, radio station, student government, student newspaper, symphony orchestra, yearbook, campus ministries, international student organization. **Organizations:** 202 registered organizations, 29 honor societies, 13 religious organizations. 21 fraternity, 4 sororities. **Athletics (Intercollegiate):** *Men:* Baseball, basketball, cross-country, football, soccer, swimming, track/field (outdoor), track/field (indoor). *Women:* Basketball, cross-country, soccer, softball, track/field (outdoor), track/field (indoor), volleyball. **On-Campus Highlights:** Havener Student Center, Residential College, Student Design Team Center, Castleman Performing Arts Center, Student Recreation Center. **Environmental Initiatives:** Reducing amount of paper being consumed. Reducing amount of energy being consumed. Reducing solid waste.

ADMISSIONS
Freshman Academic Profile: Average high school GPA 3.63. 43% in top 10% of high school class, 71% in top 25% of high school class, 94% in top 50% of high school class. 85% from public high schools. SAT Math middle 50% range 610–700. SAT Critical Reading middle 50% range 550–670. ACT middle 50% range 25–31. Minimum paper TOEFL 550. Minimum computer TOEFL

213. Minimum web-based TOEFL 79. **Basis for Candidate Selection:** *Very important factors considered include:* Class rank, academic GPA, rigor of secondary school record, standardized test scores. *Important factors considered include:* Recommendation(s). *Other factors considered include:* Application essay, character/personal qualities, extracurricular activities, interview, talent/ability, volunteer work, work experience. **Freshman Admission Requirements:** High school diploma is required and GED is accepted. *Academic units required:* 4 English, 4 mathematics, 3 science, (1 science labs), 2 foreign language, 3 social studies, 1 visual/performing arts. **Freshman Admission Statistics:** 2,620 applied, 93% admitted, 46% enrolled. **Transfer Admission Requirements:** College transcript(s), minimum college GPA of 2.5 required. **General Admission Information:** Application fee $45. Regular application deadline 7/1. Notification on a rolling basis, beginning on or about 10/1. Nonfall registration accepted. Admission may be deferred for a maximum of 2 year. Credit and/or placement offered for CEEB Advanced Placement tests.

COSTS AND FINANCIAL AID
Required Forms and Deadlines: FAFSA. Priority financial aid filing date 3/1. **Types of Aid:** *Need-based scholarships/grants:* Federal Pell, state scholarships/grants, private scholarships, the school's own gift aid. *Loans:* FFEL Subsidized Stafford, FFEL Unsubsidized Stafford, FFEL PLUS, Federal Perkins. *Student Employment:* Federal Work-Study Program available. Institutional employment available. Off-campus job opportunities are good. **Financial Aid Statistics:** 35% freshmen, 35% undergrads receive need-based scholarship or grant aid. 28% freshmen, 28% undergrads receive non-need-based scholarship or grant aid. 40% freshmen, 40% undergrads receive need-based self-help aid. 3% freshmen, 2% undergrads receive athletic scholarships. 81% undergrads borrow to pay for school. Average cumulative indebtedness $23,760. **Criteria for awarding institutional aid:** *Non-need-based:* Academics, alumni affiliation, athletics, job skills, leadership, minority status, music/drama, religious affiliation, state/district residency.

MISSOURI VALLEY COLLEGE

500 East College Street, Marshall, MO 65340
Phone: 660-831-4114
E-mail: admissions@moval.edu
Fax: 660-831-4233 **Website:** www.moval.edu **ACT Code:** 2330

This private school, affiliated with the Presbyterian Church, was founded in 1889. It has a 150-acre campus.

RATINGS
Admissions Selectivity Rating: 74   **Fire Safety Rating:** 60*   **Green Rating:** 60*

STUDENTS AND FACULTY
Enrollment: 1,425. **Student Body:** 43% female, 57% male, 34% out-of-state, 8% international (29 countries represented). Asian 4%, African American 13%, Caucasian 70%, Hispanic 4%, Native American 1%.
Retention and Graduation: 45% freshmen return for sophomore year. 11% freshmen graduate within 4 years. 20% grads go on to further study within 1 year. **Faculty:** Student/faculty ratio 18:1. 66 full-time faculty, 53% hold PhDs, 3% are are members of minority groups, 35% are women.

ACADEMICS
Degrees: Associate, bachelor's. **Classes:** Most classes have 20–29 students. Most lab/discussion sessions have 20–29 students. **Majors with Highest Enrollment:** Business/commerce; criminal justice/law enforcement administration; elementary education and teaching. **Special Study Options:** Double major, dual enrollment, internships, teacher certification program Special programs offered to physically disabled students include reader services, tutors. **Career services:** Internships. **Career services highlights include:** Many of our majors require the completion of an internship.

FACILITIES
Housing: Men's dorms, women's dorms, fraternity/sorority housing, apartments for married students, apartments for single students.

CAMPUS LIFE
Environment: Rural. **Activities:** Choral groups, dance, drama/theater, literary magazine, music ensembles, musical theater, pep band, radio station, student government, student newspaper, television station, yearbook. **Organizations:** 28 registered organizations, 8 honor societies, 7 religious organizations, 4 fraternities, 2 sororities. **Athletics (Intercollegiate):** *Men:* Baseball, basketball, cheerleading, cross-country, football, golf, rodeo, soccer, tennis, track/field (outdoor), track/field (indoor), volleyball, wrestling. *Women:* Basketball, cheerleading, cross-country, golf, rodeo, soccer, softball, tennis, track/field (outdoor), track/field (indoor), volleyball, wrestling. **On-Campus Highlights:** Burns

Gym, Eckilson-Mabee Theater, black box theater, student lounge (basement of MacDonald Hall), tech center computer lab.

ADMISSIONS
Freshman Academic Profile: Average high school GPA 2.9. 4% in top 10% of high school class, 38% in top 25% of high school class, 54% in top 50% of high school class. SAT Math middle 50% range 412–597. SAT Critical Reading middle 50% range 372–537. ACT middle 50% range 19–27. Minimum paper TOEFL 450. Minimum computer TOEFL 200. **Basis for Candidate Selection:** *Very important factors considered include:* Character/personal qualities, interview. *Important factors considered include:* Extracurricular activities, talent/ability, volunteer work. *Other factors considered include:* Class rank, recommendation(s), rigor of secondary school record, standardized test scores, alumni/ae relation, work experience. **Freshman Admission Requirements:** High school diploma is required and GED is accepted. *Academic units recommended:* 4 English, 3 mathematics, 2 science, (1 science labs), 2 social studies, 2 history, 3 academic electives. **Freshman Admission Statistics:** 1,345 applied, 67% admitted, 45% enrolled. **Transfer Admission Requirements:** High school transcript, college transcript(s), standardized test scores, minimum college GPA of 2.0 required. Lowest grade transferable C. **General Admission Information:** Application fee $15. Regular application deadline 9/1. Nonfall registration accepted.

COSTS AND FINANCIAL AID
Annual tuition $13,000. Room and board $5,200. Required fees $500. Average book expense $1,300. **Required Forms and Deadlines:** FAFSA, state aid form. Priority financial aid filing date 3/1. **Types of Aid:** *Need-based scholarships/grants:* Federal Pell, SEOG, state scholarships/grants, private scholarships, the school's own gift aid. *Loans:* FFEL Subsidized Stafford, FFEL Unsubsidized Stafford, FFEL PLUS, Federal Perkins. *Student Employment:* Federal Work-Study Program available. Institutional employment available. Off-campus job opportunities are excellent. **Financial Aid Statistics:** 95% freshmen, 96% undergrads receive need-based scholarship or grant aid. 95% freshmen, 96% undergrads receive non-need-based scholarship or grant aid. 83% freshmen, 83% undergrads receive need-based self-help aid. 98% freshmen, 92% undergrads receive any aid. 86% undergrads borrow to pay for school. Average cumulative indebtedness $12,000.

MISSOURI WESTERN STATE COLLEGE

4525 Downs Drive, Saint Joseph, MO 64507
Phone: 816-271-4266
E-mail: admissn@mwsc.edu
Fax: 816-271-5833 **Website:** www.mwsc.edu **ACT Code:** 2344

This public school was founded in 1969. It has a 740-acre campus.

RATINGS
Admissions Selectivity Rating: 61   **Fire Safety Rating:** 60*   **Green Rating:** 60*

STUDENTS AND FACULTY
Enrollment: 4,652. **Student Body:** 61% female, 39% male, 9% out-of-state, international (5 countries represented). Asian 1%, African American 11%, Caucasian 85%, Hispanic 2%, Native American 1%.
Retention and Graduation: 55% freshmen return for sophomore year. 16% freshmen graduate within 4 years. 20% grads go on to further study within 1 year. 11% grads pursue arts and sciences degrees. 1% grads pursue law degrees. 6% grads pursue business degrees. 2% grads pursue medical degrees. **Faculty:** Student/faculty ratio 18:1. 180 full-time faculty, 75% hold PhDs, 6% are are members of minority groups, 41% are women.

ACADEMICS
Degrees: Associate, bachelor's, certificate, terminal associate, transfer associate. **Classes:** Most classes have 20–29 students. Most lab/discussion sessions have 20–29 students. **Majors with Highest Enrollment:** Business/commerce; criminal justice/law enforcement administration; nursing/registered nurse (RN, ASN, BSN, MSN). **Special Study Options:** Distance learning, double major, dual enrollment, honors program, internships, liberal arts/career combination, teacher certification program, weekend college. Special programs offered to physically disabled students include note-taking services, reader services, tutors. **Career services:** Career/job search classes, career assessment.

FACILITIES
Housing: Coed dorms, fraternity/sorority housing, apartments for single students. 99% of campus accessible to physically disabled. **Special Academic Facilities/Equipment:** Multi-media classroom building, planetarium.

CAMPUS LIFE

Environment: Village. **Activities:** Choral groups, concert band, dance, drama/theater, jazz band, marching band, music ensembles, pep band, student government, student newspaper, yearbook. **Organizations:** 64 registered organizations, 5 honor societies, 7 religious organizations. 5 fraternities, 6 sororities. **Athletics (Intercollegiate):** *Men:* Baseball, basketball, football, golf. *Women:* Basketball, golf, softball, tennis, volleyball.

ADMISSIONS

Freshman Academic Profile: 8% in top 10% of high school class, 25% in top 25% of high school class, 55% in top 50% of high school class. 95% from public high schools. ACT middle 50% range 16–22. Minimum paper TOEFL 500. **Freshman Admission Requirements:** High school diploma is required and GED is accepted. *Academic units required:* 4 English, 3 mathematics, 2 science, (1 science labs), 3 social studies, 3 academic electives, 1 Visual/Perf Arts *Academic units recommended:* 2 foreign language. **Freshman Admission Statistics:** 2,421 applied, 100% admitted, 43% enrolled. **Transfer Admission Requirements:** College transcript(s), Lowest grade transferable D. **General Admission Information:** Application fee $15. Regular application deadline 8/15. Notification on a rolling basis, beginning on or about 10/1. Nonfall registration accepted. Credit offered for CEEB Advanced Placement tests.

COSTS AND FINANCIAL AID

Annual in-state tuition $4,098. Annual out-of-state tuition $7,674. Room and board $4,058. Required fees $366. Average book expense $700. **Required Forms and Deadlines:** FAFSA, institution's own financial aid form. Priority financial aid filing date 3/1. **Notification of Awards:** Applicants will be notified of awards on a rolling basis beginning 3/2. **Types of Aid:** *Need-based scholarships/grants:* Federal Pell, SEOG, state scholarships/grants, private scholarships, the school's own gift aid. *Loans:* FFEL Subsidized Stafford, FFEL Unsubsidized Stafford, FFEL PLUS, Federal Perkins, *Student Employment:* Federal Work-Study Program available. Institutional employment available. Highest amount earned per year from on-campus jobs $1,400. Off-campus job opportunities are good. **Financial Aid Statistics:** 39% freshmen, 38% undergrads receive need-based scholarship or grant aid. 29% freshmen, 21% undergrads receive non-need-based scholarship or grant aid. 39% freshmen, 44% undergrads receive need-based self-help aid. 3% freshmen, 5% undergrads receive athletic scholarships. 68% undergrads borrow to pay for school. Average cumulative indebtedness $15,100. **Criteria for awarding institutional aid:** *Non-need-based:* Academics, alumni affiliation, art, athletics, job skills, leadership, minority status, music/drama, state/district residency.

MITCHELL COLLEGE

437 Pequot Avenue, New London, CT 06320
Phone: 860-701-5011 **Financial Aid Phone:** 800-443-2811
E-mail: admissions@mitchell.edu **CEEB Code:** 3528
Fax: 860-444-1209 **Website:** www.mitchell.edu **ACT Code:** 572

This private school was founded in 1938. It has a 68-acre campus.

RATINGS

Admissions Selectivity Rating: 71   **Fire Safety Rating:** 60*   **Green Rating:** 60*

STUDENTS AND FACULTY

Enrollment: 762. **Student Body:** 54% female, 46% male, 36% out-of-state, 1% international Asian 1%, African American 8%, Caucasian 64%, Hispanic 6%, Native American 2%.
Retention and Graduation: 95% grads go on to further study within 1 year. **Faculty:** Student/faculty ratio 12:1. 27 full-time faculty, 48% hold PhDs, 56% are women.

ACADEMICS

Degrees: Associate, bachelor's, certificate. **Majors with Highest Enrollment:** Education, other; entrepreneurship/entrepreneurial studies; sport and fitness administration/management. **Special Study Options:** dual enrollment, English as a Second Language (ESL), internships, teacher certification program Special programs offered to physically disabled students include note-taking services, reader services, tape recorders, tutors.

FACILITIES

Housing: Coed dorms, special housing for disabled students. Four residence halls are Victorian and Colonial houses located on the waterfront. Three other residence halls are of traditional design. 50% of campus accessible to physically disabled. **Special Academic Facilities/Equipment:** Private dock w/fleet of sailboats, 2 private beaches, 26 acres of woods.

CAMPUS LIFE

Environment: Town. **Activities:** Choral groups, dance, drama/theater, literary magazine, student government, student newspaper, yearbook. **Organizations:** 30 registered organizations, 2 honor societies, 2 religious organizations. **Athletics (Intercollegiate):** *Men:* Baseball, basketball, cross-country, golf, lacrosse, soccer, tennis. *Women:* Basketball, cross-country, golf, soccer, softball, tennis, volleyball.

ADMISSIONS

Freshman Academic Profile: Average high school GPA 2.8. 3% in top 10% of high school class, 15% in top 25% of high school class, 35% in top 50% of high school class. 85% from public high schools. SAT Math middle 50% range 460–350. SAT Critical Reading middle 50% range 460–360. ACT middle 50% range 17–15. Minimum paper TOEFL 500. **Basis for Candidate Selection:** *Very important factors considered include:* Recommendation(s), rigor of secondary school record, interview. *Important factors considered include:* Application essay, standardized test scores, character/personal qualities, extracurricular activities, talent/ability. *Other factors considered include:* Class rank, alumni/ae relation, volunteer work, work experience. **Freshman Admission Requirements:** High school diploma is required and GED is accepted. *Academic units recommended:* 4 English, 3 mathematics, 3 science, 2 social studies, 2 history, 2 academic electives. **Freshman Admission Statistics: Transfer Admission Requirements:** High school transcript, college transcript(s), essay or personal statement, standardized test scores, minimum college GPA of 2.0 required. Lowest grade transferable C–. **General Admission Information:** Application fee $30. Early decision application deadline 11/15. Notification on a rolling basis, beginning on or about 12/15. Nonfall registration accepted. Admission may be deferred for a maximum of 1 year. Credit and/or placement offered for CEEB Advanced Placement tests.

COSTS AND FINANCIAL AID

Annual tuition $20,382. Room and board $9,795. Required fees $1,355. Average book expense $800. **Required Forms and Deadlines:** FAFSA. Priority financial aid filing date 3/1. **Notification of Awards:** Applicants will be notified of awards on a rolling basis beginning 3/1. **Types of Aid:** *Need-based scholarships/grants:* Federal Pell, SEOG, state scholarships/grants, private scholarships, the school's own gift aid. *Loans:* FFEL Subsidized Stafford, FFEL Unsubsidized Stafford, FFEL PLUS, Federal Perkins, Plato. *Student Employment:* **Financial Aid Statistics:** 65% freshmen receive need-based scholarship or grant aid. 65% freshmen receive non-need-based scholarship or grant aid. 65% freshmen receive need-based self-help aid. **Criteria for awarding institutional aid:** *Non-need-based:* Academics, alumni affiliation, art, leadership, state/district residency.

MOLLOY COLLEGE

1000 Hempstead Avenue, Rockville Centre, NY 11570
Phone: 516-678-5000
E-mail: admissions@molloy.edu **CEEB Code:** 2415
Fax: 516-256-2247 **Website:** www.molloy.edu **ACT Code:** 2820

This private school, affiliated with the Roman Catholic Church, was founded in 1955. It has a 35-acre campus.

RATINGS

Admissions Selectivity Rating: 79   **Fire Safety Rating:** 60*   **Green Rating:** 60*

STUDENTS AND FACULTY

Enrollment: 2,969. **Student Body:** 78% female, 22% male, 1% international Asian 7%, African American 15%, Caucasian 63%, Hispanic 11%.
Retention and Graduation: 87% freshmen return for sophomore year. **Faculty:** Student/faculty ratio 9:1. 169 full-time faculty, 67% hold PhDs, 14% are are members of minority groups, 73% are women.

ACADEMICS

Degrees: Associate, bachelor's, master's, post-master's certificate. **Classes:** Most classes have 10–19 students. Most lab/discussion sessions have 10–19 students. **Majors with Highest Enrollment:** Business/commerce; education; nursing/registered nurse (RN, ASN, BSN, MSN). **Special Study Options:** Double major, English as a Second Language (ESL), honors program, independent study, internships, liberal arts/career combination, student-designed major, study abroad, teacher certification program. **Combined degree programs:** BSW/MSW, BS/MS, BS/MBA. Special programs offered to physically disabled students include note-taking services, reader services, tape recorders, tutors. **Career services:** Alumni network, alumni services, internships, regional alumni.

FACILITIES

Housing: 100% of campus accessible to physically disabled. **Special Academic Facilities/Equipment:** Professional Repertory Theatre Company in residence, dance studio, institute of cross-cultural and cross-ethnic studies, institute of gerontology, cablevision studio. **Computers:** 100% of classrooms, 100% of libraries, 100% of dining areas, 100% of student union, 100% of common outdoor areas have wireless network access. Students can register for classes online. Administrative functions (other than registration) can be performed online.

CAMPUS LIFE

Environment: Village. **Activities:** Choral groups, dance, drama/theater, jazz band, literary magazine, music ensembles, student government, student newspaper, yearbook, campus ministries. **Organizations:** 21 registered organizations, 18 honor societies, 1 religious organizations. **Athletics (Intercollegiate):** *Men:* Baseball, basketball, cross-country, lacrosse, soccer, track/field (outdoor), track/field (indoor). *Women:* Basketball, cross-country, lacrosse, soccer, softball, tennis, track/field (outdoor), track/field (indoor), volleyball. **On-Campus Highlights:** The Anselma Room, the fitness center, Center for Social and Ethical Concerns, media center. **Environmental Initiatives:** The Sustainability Institute at Molloy College www.molloy.edu/si/index.asp.

ADMISSIONS

Freshman Academic Profile: Average high school GPA 2.9. 30% in top 10% of high school class, 50% in top 25% of high school class, 86% in top 50% of high school class. 70% from public high schools. SAT Math middle 50% range 480–570. SAT Critical Reading middle 50% range 460–560. SAT Writing middle 50% range 470–560. ACT middle 50% range 22–27. Minimum paper TOEFL 500. Minimum computer TOEFL 175. **Basis for Candidate Selection:** *Very important factors considered include:* Academic GPA, rigor of secondary school record, standardized test scores. *Other factors considered include:* Class rank, application essay, recommendation(s), extracurricular activities, interview, talent/ability, volunteer work, work experience. **Freshman Admission Requirements:** High school diploma is required and GED is accepted. *Academic units required:* 4 English, 3 mathematics, 3 science, 3 foreign language, 4 social studies. *Academic units recommended:* 4 English, 4 mathematics, 4 science, 3 foreign language, 4 social studies. **Freshman Admission Statistics:** 1,803 applied, 59% admitted, 39% enrolled. **Transfer Admission Requirements:** College transcript(s), minimum college GPA of 2.0 required. Lowest grade transferable C. **General Admission Information:** Application fee $30. Notification on a rolling basis, beginning on or about 10/15. Nonfall registration accepted. Admission may be deferred for a maximum of 1 year. Credit offered for CEEB Advanced Placement tests.

COSTS AND FINANCIAL AID

Required Forms and Deadlines: FAFSA, state aid form. Financial aid filing deadline 5/1. Priority financial aid filing date 4/15. **Notification of Awards:** Applicants will be notified of awards on a rolling basis beginning 2/1. **Types of Aid:** *Need-based scholarships/grants:* Federal Pell, SEOG, state scholarships/grants, private scholarships, the school's own gift aid, Federal Nursing Scholarships. *Loans:* FFEL Subsidized Stafford, FFEL Unsubsidized Stafford, FFEL PLUS, Federal Perkins, Federal Nursing *Student Employment:* Federal Work-Study Program available. Off-campus job opportunities are good. **Financial Aid Statistics:** 70% freshmen, 71% undergrads receive need-based scholarship or grant aid. 10% freshmen, 6% undergrads receive non-need-based scholarship or grant aid. 54% freshmen, 70% undergrads receive need-based self-help aid. 4% freshmen, 3% undergrads receive athletic scholarships. 94% freshmen, 75% undergrads receive any aid. 77% undergrads borrow to pay for school. Average cumulative indebtedness $29,823. **Criteria for awarding institutional aid:** *Non-need-based:* Academics, alumni affiliation, art, athletics, leadership, music/drama, religious affiliation.

MONMOUTH COLLEGE

700 East Broadway, Monmouth, IL 61462
Phone: 800-74-SCOTS **Financial Aid Phone:** 309-457-2129
E-mail: admit@monm.edu **CEEB Code:** 1484
Fax: 309-457-2141 **Website:** www.monm.edu **ACT Code:** 1084

This private school, affiliated with the Presbyterian Church, was founded in 1853. It has a 80-acre campus.

RATINGS

Admissions Selectivity Rating: 76   **Fire Safety Rating:** 60*   **Green Rating:** 76

STUDENTS AND FACULTY

Enrollment: 1,362. **Student Body:** 52% female, 48% male, 6% out-of-state, 1% international (11 countries represented). Asian 1%, African American 6%, Caucasian 86%, Hispanic 5%, Native American 1%.

Retention and Graduation: 77% freshmen return for sophomore year. 51% freshmen graduate within 4 years. 24% grads go on to further study within 1 year. 16% grads pursue arts and sciences degrees. 2% grads pursue law degrees. 1% grads pursue business degrees. 1% grads pursue medical degrees. **Faculty:** Student/faculty ratio 14:1. 83 full-time faculty, 83% hold PhDs, 8% are are members of minority groups, 42% are women.

ACADEMICS

Degrees: Bachelor's. **Classes:** Most classes have 20–29 students. Most lab/discussion sessions have 10–19 students. **Majors with Highest Enrollment:** Business administration and management; education; psychology. **Special Study Options:** Double major, English as a Second Language (ESL), exchange student program (domestic), honors program, independent study, internships, student-designed major, study abroad, teacher certification program. **Honors programs:** The Monmouth Coillege Honors Program is intended for a select group of academically well-prepared and intellectually ambitious students. Acceptance into the program is determined competitively, normally occurring at the end of the first semester of the freshman year. The program consists of three levels: exploration of the history of the liberal arts as a field of inquiry, in-depth seminars upon historically significant persons, events, movements and ideas, and a senior capstone course. **Combined degree programs:** 3/3 and 3/4 agreements in architecture, nursing, phys. therapy, med. tech. Special programs offered to physically disabled students include note-taking services, reader services, tape recorders, tutors. **Career services:** Alumni network, alumni services, career/job search classes, career assessment, internships, regional alumni. **Career services highlights include:** All Monmouth students are encouraged to seek out rigorous, academically-grounded internship opportunities. The Career Center provides pre-internship orientation to professional office conduct, placement advising, maintenance of contacts with internship sponsors, and quality-control oversight of internship experiences. The Career Center coordinates closely with academic departments in selecting internship opportunities and in assisting students with placements.

FACILITIES

Housing: Coed dorms, special housing for disabled students, men's dorms, special housing for international students, women's dorms, fraternity/sorority housing, apartments for single students, wellness house, theme housing. 70% of campus accessible to physically disabled. **Special Academic Facilities/Equipment:** Shields Art & Antiquities Collection, Wackerle Career & Leadership Center, Mellinger Teaching & Learning Center, MC–TV (student-run television station), WMCR (student-run radio station). **Computers:** 100% of classrooms, 100% of dorms, 100% of libraries, 100% of dining areas, 100% of student union, 80% of common outdoor areas have wireless network access. Students can register for classes online. Administrative functions (other than registration) can be performed online.

CAMPUS LIFE

Environment: Village. **Activities:** Choral groups, concert band, dance, drama/theater, jazz band, literary magazine, marching band, music ensembles, musical theater, radio station, student government, student newspaper, symphony orchestra, television station, campus ministries, international student organization. **Organizations:** 67 registered organizations, 16 honor societies, 6 religious organizations. 4 fraternities, 3 sororities. **Athletics (Intercollegiate):** *Men:* Baseball, basketball, cross-country, diving, football, golf, soccer, swimming, tennis, track/field (outdoor), track/field (indoor). *Women:* Basketball, cross-country, diving, golf, soccer, softball, swimming, tennis, track/field (outdoor), track/field (indoor), volleyball. **On-Campus Highlights:** Stockdale Student Center, Hewes Library (including coffee shop!), Huff Athletic Center, Mellinger Teaching and Learning Center, Wallace Hall—main floor coffee/study, The nature trail at LeSuer Nature Preserve offers many opportunities for recreation and scientific study. The new Monmouth College athletic fields are available for team practice, of course, but also open to ad hoc student groups and individuals. **Environmental Initiatives:** We provide recycling receptacles for paper, glass, plastic and aluminum in all academic buildings and residence halls, with a recycling center for electronics, flourescent lights and cell phones in the Stockdale Center (the student center). We recycle all cardboard generated at the dining service. We have a fleet of 5 hybrid cars for use by Monmouth faculty and staff for college purposes; Admissions and Advancement have priority, but any Monmouth employee has access to them. In 2007 we retrofitted light fixtures in all of our academic buildings, and, in 2008, placed energy-efficient boilers in five buildings. We are now engaged in the second phase of a feasibility study for the construction of a wind-turbine to generate power for the campus. We offer an increasingly popular organic-foods meal plan. We are implementing a trayless program in our dining areas this year.

ADMISSIONS

Freshman Academic Profile: Average high school GPA 3.2. 9% in top 10% of high school class, 32% in top 25% of high school class, 66% in top 50% of high school class. SAT Math middle 50% range 430–570. SAT Critical Reading middle 50% range 510–590. SAT Writing middle 50% range 440–520. ACT middle 50% range 20–25. Minimum paper TOEFL 550. Minimum computer TOEFL 213. Minimum web-based TOEFL 79. **Basis for Candidate Selection:** *Very important factors considered include:* Rigor of secondary school record. *Important factors considered include:* Class rank, academic GPA, standardized test scores, character/personal qualities, extracurricular activities, interview, talent/ability. *Other factors considered include:* Application essay, recommendation(s), alumni/ae relation, first generation, geographical residence, state residency, volunteer work, work experience. **Freshman Admission Requirements:** High school diploma is required and GED is accepted. *Academic units required:* 4 English, 3 mathematics, 2 science, (1 science labs), 2 foreign language, 2 social studies, 1 history. *Academic units recommended:* 4 English, 3 mathematics, 3 science, (2 science labs), 3 foreign language, 3 social studies, 2 history. **Freshman Admission Statistics:** 2,070 applied, 70% admitted, 30% enrolled. **Transfer Admission Requirements:** College transcript(s), minimum college GPA of 2.5 required. Lowest grade transferable C–. **General Admission Information:** Notification on a rolling basis, beginning on or about 9/15. Nonfall registration accepted. Admission may be deferred for a maximum of 1 year. Placement offered for CEEB Advanced Placement tests.

COSTS AND FINANCIAL AID
Average book expense $900. **Required Forms and Deadlines:** FAFSA. Priority financial aid filing date 3/1. **Notification of Awards:** Applicants will be notified of awards on a rolling basis beginning 3/1. **Types of Aid:** *Need-based scholarships/grants:* Federal Pell, SEOG, state scholarships/grants, private scholarships, the school's own gift aid. *Loans:* Direct Subsidized Stafford, Direct Unsubsidized Stafford, Direct PLUS, FFEL Subsidized Stafford, FFEL Unsubsidized Stafford, FFEL PLUS, Federal Perkins, college/university loans from institutional funds. *Student Employment:* Federal Work-Study Program available. Institutional employment available. Highest amount earned per year from on-campus jobs $2,325. Off-campus job opportunities are fair. **Financial Aid Statistics:** 89% freshmen, 84% undergrads receive need-based scholarship or grant aid. 13% freshmen, 11% undergrads receive non-need-based scholarship or grant aid. 71% freshmen, 67% undergrads receive need-based self-help aid. 100% freshmen, 99% undergrads receive any aid. 81% undergrads borrow to pay for school. Average cumulative indebtedness $24,476. **Criteria for awarding institutional aid:** *Non-need-based:* Academics, art, leadership, music/drama.

MONMOUTH UNIVERSITY (NJ)

Admission, Monmouth University, 400 Cedar Avenue, West Long Branch, NJ 07764-1898
Phone: 732-571-3456 **Financial Aid Phone:** 732-571-3463
E-mail: admission@monmouth.edu **CEEB Code:** 2416
Fax: 732-263-5166 **Website:** www.monmouth.edu **ACT Code:** 2571

This private school was founded in 1933. It has a 156-acre campus.

RATINGS
Admissions Selectivity Rating: 79   **Fire Safety Rating:** 95   **Green Rating:** 79

STUDENTS AND FACULTY
Enrollment: 4,633. **Student Body:** 58% female, 42% male, 12% out-of-state, 1% international (17 countries represented). Asian 2%; African American 4%, Caucasian 77%, Hispanic 6%.
Retention and Graduation: 78% freshmen return for sophomore year. 40% freshmen graduate within 4 years. **Faculty:** Student/faculty ratio 15:1. 248 full-time faculty, 83% hold PhDs, 15% are are members of minority groups, 53% are women.

ACADEMICS
Degrees: Associate, bachelor's, certificate, master's, post-bachelor's certificate, post-master's certificate. **Classes:** Most classes have 10–19 students. **Majors with Highest Enrollment:** Business administration and management; communication studies/speech communication and rhetoric; education. **Special Study Options:** Accelerated program, cooperative education program, cross-registration, distance learning, double major, dual enrollment, honors program, independent study, internships, liberal arts/career combination, student-designed major, study abroad, teacher certification program, Clinical Lab Science Program in collaboration with UMDNJ. Air Force ROTC at Rutgers University. Affiliated with Washington Center providing semester and summer internships and shorter symposia. Monmouth Medical Scholars Program allows five incoming freshmen to complete undergraduate degree at Monmouth, including nine credit clinical requirement at Monmouth Medical Center, and commence medical studies at Drexel University School of Medicine. Study Abroad in London at Regent's College and Sydney, Australia at Macquarie University. **Honors programs:** The Honors School is committed to providing motivated students with a unique learning environment in a community of scholars. By supporting both disciplinary and interdisciplinary approaches to education, the Honors School seeks to help students develop not only depth within their intended field of study, but also an appreciation for how that knowledge is embedded within a broader context of intellectual inquiry. The Honors School also is dedicated to raising students' level of cultural, ethical, and societal awareness as its participants develop into well-rounded scholars and citizens within a global community. **Combined degree programs:** BA/MD, BA/MA, 5-year programs BS/MBA, BS//MS, BA/MA, BSW/MSW, BA/MEd, BA/MSEd. Special programs offered to physically disabled students include note-taking services, reader services, tape recorders, tutors. **Career services:** Alumni network, alumni services, career/job search classes, career assessment, internships, regional alumni. **Career services highlights include:** Experiential Education graduation requirement.

FACILITIES
Housing: Coed dorms, apartments for single students, wellness house, theme housing, Honor Program housing, health & wellness housing, community service housing. 95% of campus accessible to physically disabled. **Special Academic Facilities/Equipment:** Art gallery, instructional media center with TV and Radio stations, theatre **Computers:** 100% of classrooms, 100% of dorms, 100% of libraries, 100% of dining areas, 100% of student union, 90% of common outdoor areas have wireless network access. Students can register for classes online. Administrative functions (other than registration) can be performed online.

CAMPUS LIFE
Environment: Village. **Activities:** Choral groups, concert band, dance, drama/theater, jazz band, literary magazine, music ensembles, musical theater, pep band, radio station, student government, student newspaper, television station, yearbook, campus ministries, international student organization, Model UN. **Organizations:** 67 registered organizations, 19 honor societies, 3 religious organizations. 7 fraternities, 6 sororities. **Athletics (Intercollegiate):** *Men:* Baseball, basketball, cross-country, football, golf, soccer, tennis, track/field (outdoor), track/field (indoor). *Women:* Basketball, cross-country, field hockey, golf, lacrosse, soccer, softball, tennis, track/field (outdoor), track/field (indoor). **On-Campus Highlights:** Woodrow Wilson Hall, Plangere Center for Communication, Rebecca Stafford Student Center, Multipurpose Activity Center. **Environmental Initiatives:** Solar power 454.5 kW solar installation on four university buildings; establishment of the Sustainability Advisory Council. The Monmouth University Sustainabiltiy Advisory Council (SAC) is an interdisciplinary work group comprised of students, faculty, staff and administrators that promotes environmental awareness and encourages the development of an environmentally responsible and sustainable campus community in its operations, education, research, outreach and services.

ADMISSIONS
Freshman Academic Profile: Average high school GPA 3.31. 18% in top 10% of high school class, 46% in top 25% of high school class, 83% in top 50% of high school class. 86% from public high schools. SAT Math middle 50% range 510–600. SAT Critical Reading middle 50% range 490–570. SAT Writing middle 50% range 490–570. ACT middle 50% range 22–26. Minimum paper TOEFL 550. Minimum computer TOEFL 213. Minimum web-based TOEFL 79. **Basis for Candidate Selection:** *Very important factors considered include:* Academic GPA, rigor of secondary school record, standardized test scores. *Important factors considered include:* extracurricular activities, volunteer work, work experience. *Other factors considered include:* Application essay, recommendation(s), alumni/ae relation, character/personal qualities. **Freshman Admission Requirements:** High school diploma is required and GED is accepted. *Academic units required:* 4 English, 3 mathematics, 2 science, (1 science labs), 2 history, 5 academic electives. *Academic units recommended:* 2 foreign language, 2 social studies. **Freshman Admission Statistics:** 6,738 applied, 62% admitted, 120% enrolled. **Transfer Admission Requirements:** College transcript(s), statement of good standing from prior institution(s). Minimum college GPA of 2.25 required. Lowest grade transferable C. **General Admission Information:** Application fee $50. Regular application deadline 3/1. Nonfall registration accepted. Admission may be deferred for a maximum of 2 semesters. Credit and/or placement offered for CEEB Advanced Placement tests.

COSTS AND FINANCIAL AID
Annual tuition $24,386. Room and board $9,554. Required fees $628. Average book expense $1,000. **Required Forms and Deadlines:** FAFSA. Financial aid filing deadline 6/30. Priority financial aid filing date 2/15. **Notification of Awards:** Applicants will be notified of awards on a rolling basis beginning 2/15. **Types of Aid:** *Need-based scholarships/grants:* Federal Pell, SEOG, state scholarships/grants, private scholarships, the school's own gift aid, Federal

Nursing Scholarships. *Loans:* Direct Subsidized Stafford, Direct Unsubsidized Stafford, Direct PLUS, FFEL PLUS, Federal Perkins, state loans, college/university loans from institutional funds, alternative loans. *Student Employment:* Federal Work-Study Program available. Institutional employment available. Highest amount earned per year from on-campus jobs $5,000. Off-campus job opportunities are good. **Financial Aid Statistics:** 30% freshmen, 26% undergrads receive need-based scholarship or grant aid. 70% freshmen, 61% undergrads receive non-need-based scholarship or grant aid. 56% freshmen, 53% undergrads receive need-based self-help aid. 3% freshmen, 2% undergrads receive athletic scholarships. 99.2% freshmen receive any aid. 73.3% undergrads borrow to pay for school. Average cumulative indebtedness $25,000. **Criteria for awarding institutional aid:** *Non-need-based:* Academics, alumni affiliation, art, athletics, leadership, religious affiliation, state/district residency.

MONROE COLLEGE

2501 Jerome Ave, Bronx, NY 10468
Phone: 718-933-6700
E-mail: ejerome@monroecollege.edu
Fax: 718-364-3552 **Website:** www.monroecollege.edu

This is a proprietary school.

RATINGS
Admissions Selectivity Rating: 60*   **Fire Safety Rating:** 60*   **Green Rating:** 60*

STUDENTS AND FACULTY
Enrollment: 6,674. **Student Body:** 71% female, 29% male, 2% out-of-state, 5% international Asian 1%, African American 46%, Caucasian 2%, Hispanic 42%.
Retention and Graduation: 75% freshmen return for sophomore year. **Faculty:** Student/faculty ratio 21:1. 70 full-time faculty, 40% hold PhDs, 57% are are members of minority groups, 44% are women.

ACADEMICS
Degrees: Associate, bachelor's, master's. **Classes:** Most classes have 20–29 students. **Special Study Options:** Distance learning, honors program, independent study, internships, weekend college.

FACILITIES
Housing: Coed dorms.

CAMPUS LIFE
Activities: Literary magazine.

ADMISSIONS
Basis for Candidate Selection: *Very important factors considered include:* interview. *Important factors considered include:* Application essay. *Other factors considered include:* Class rank, recommendation(s), rigor of secondary school record, standardized test scores, alumni/ae relation, character/personal qualities, extracurricular activities, geographical residence, racial/ethnic status, religious affiliation/commitment, state residency, talent/ability, volunteer work, work experience. **Freshman Admission Requirements:** High school diploma or equivalent is not required. **Freshman Admission Statistics:** 2,108 applied, 67% admitted, 95% enrolled. **Transfer Admission Requirements:** College transcript(s), essay or personal statement, interview, Lowest grade transferable C. **General Admission Information:** Application fee $35. Nonfall registration accepted.

COSTS AND FINANCIAL AID
Annual tuition $11,744. Room and board $11,660. Required fees $800. Average book expense $900. **Required Forms and Deadlines:** FAFSA. Financial aid filing deadline 3/31. **Notification of Awards:** Applicants will be notified of awards on or about 7/1. **Types of Aid:** *Need-based scholarships/grants:* Federal Pell, the school's own gift aid. *Loans:* Direct Subsidized Stafford, Direct Unsubsidized Stafford, Direct PLUS. **Financial Aid Statistics:** 96% freshmen, 96% undergrads receive need-based scholarship or grant aid. 1% freshmen, 1% undergrads receive non-need-based scholarship or grant aid. 41% freshmen, 41% undergrads receive need-based self-help aid. 1% freshmen, 27% undergrads borrow to pay for school. Average cumulative indebtedness $4,700.

MONTANA STATE UNIVERSITY—BILLINGS

1500 University Drive, Billings, MT 59101
Phone: 406-657-2158 **Financial Aid Phone:** 406-657-2288
E-mail: cjohannes@msubillings.edu **CEEB Code:** 4298
Fax: 406-657-2051 **Website:** www.msubillings.edu **ACT Code:** 2416

This public school was founded in 1927. It has a 92-acre campus.

RATINGS
Admissions Selectivity Rating: 69   **Fire Safety Rating:** 60*   **Green Rating:** 60*

STUDENTS AND FACULTY
Enrollment: 4,425. **Student Body:** 62% female, 38% male, 8% out-of-state, international (20 countries represented). Asian 1%, African American 1%, Caucasian 84%, Hispanic 4%, Native American 6%.
Retention and Graduation: 55% freshmen return for sophomore year. 7% grads go on to further study within 1 year. 80% grads pursue arts and sciences degrees. 13% grads pursue business degrees. **Faculty:** Student/faculty ratio 20:1. 154 full-time faculty, 65% hold PhDs, 4% are are members of minority groups, 40% are women.

ACADEMICS
Degrees: Associate, bachelor's, certificate, master's, post-bachelor's certificate, terminal associate, transfer associate. **Classes:** Most classes have 20–29 students. Most lab/discussion sessions have 10–19 students. **Majors with Highest Enrollment:** Business/commerce; elementary education and teaching; liberal arts and sciences/liberal studies. **Special Study Options:** Accelerated program, cooperative education program, cross-registration, distance learning, double major, dual enrollment, English as a Second Language (ESL), external degree program, honors program, independent study, internships, student-designed major, study abroad, teacher certification program, weekend college, On-line degrees and extensive on-line course offerings. Evening College. **Honors programs:** The MSU—Billings University Honors Program is designed for curious students who are eager to participate actively in their education. Classes in the University Honors Program tend to be smaller than other classes and emphasize class discussion. Often these classes are interdisciplinary in nature; this helps students study issues from several perspectives. Some classes are team-taught, which also enriches the discussion. Special programs offered to physically disabled students include note-taking services, reader services, tape recorders, tutors. **Career services:** Career/job search classes, career assessment, internships.

FACILITIES
Housing: Coed dorms, special housing for disabled students, men's dorms, women's dorms, apartments for married students, apartments for students with dependent children. 99% of campus accessible to physically disabled. **Special Academic Facilities/Equipment:** Montana Center for Disabilities, Business Enterprise, Small Business Institute, Urban Institute, Public Radio, Applied Economic Research, Biological Station, Northern Plains Studies Center, Montana Business Connections, Information Commons, Academic Support Center, Advising Center, TRIO Programs, SOS Programs, Northcutt Steele Gallery, Cisel Recital Hall, Petro Theatre, MSU—Billings Downtown. **Computers:** 30% of classrooms, 100% of dorms, 100% of libraries, 100% of dining areas, 100% of student union, have wireless network access. Students can register for classes online. Administrative functions (other than registration) can be performed online.

CAMPUS LIFE
Environment: City. **Activities:** Choral groups, concert band, drama/theater, jazz band, literary magazine, music ensembles, musical theater, pep band, radio station, student government, student newspaper, symphony orchestra, campus ministries, international student organization. **Organizations:** 53 registered organizations, 10 honor societies, 8 religious organizations. **Athletics (Intercollegiate):** *Men:* Baseball, basketball, cross-country, golf, soccer, tennis, track/field (outdoor), track/field (indoor). *Women:* Basketball, cross-country, golf, soccer, softball, tennis, track/field (outdoor), track/field (indoor), volleyball. **On-Campus Highlights:** Alterowitz Gym, MSU—Billings Downtown, SUB Coffee Shop, Liberal Arts Coffee Shop, library.

ADMISSIONS
Freshman Academic Profile: Average high school GPA 3. 11% in top 10% of high school class, 25% in top 25% of high school class, 59% in top 50% of high school class. 96% from public high schools. SAT Math middle 50% range 460–590. SAT Critical Reading middle 50% range 460–580. ACT middle 50% range 18–24. Minimum paper TOEFL 500. Minimum computer TOEFL 173. **Basis for Candidate Selection:** *Very important factors considered include:* Class rank, academic GPA, rigor of secondary school record, standardized test scores, level of applicant's interest. *Other factors considered include:* character/personal qualities. **Freshman Admission Requirements:** High school

diploma is required and GED is accepted. *Academic units required:* 4 English, 3 mathematics, 2 science, (2 science labs), 3 social studies, 2 foreign language, visual arts, or computer science. **Freshman Admission Statistics:** 1,384 applied, 100% admitted, 65% enrolled. **Transfer Admission Requirements:** College transcript(s), statement of good standing from prior institution(s). Minimum college GPA of 2.0 required. Lowest grade transferable C–. **General Admission Information:** Application fee $30. Regular application deadline 7/1. Notification on a rolling basis, beginning on or about 7/1. Nonfall registration accepted. Credit and/or placement offered for CEEB Advanced Placement tests.

COSTS AND FINANCIAL AID

Annual in-state tuition $3,988. Annual out-of-state tuition $14,648. Room and board $5,310. Required fees $1,219. Average book expense $1,000. **Required Forms and Deadlines:** FAFSA, institution's own financial aid form. Priority financial aid filing date 3/1. **Notification of Awards:** Applicants will be notified of awards on or about 5/1. **Types of Aid:** *Need-based scholarships/grants:* Federal Pell, SEOG, state scholarships/grants, private scholarships, the school's own gift aid, Montana State University-Billings Foundation. *Loans:* FFEL Subsidized Stafford, FFEL Unsubsidized Stafford, FFEL PLUS, Federal Perkins, college/university loans from institutional funds. *Student Employment:* Federal Work-Study Program available. Institutional employment available. Highest amount earned per year from on-campus jobs $2,000. Off-campus job opportunities are excellent. **Financial Aid Statistics:** 47% freshmen, 45% undergrads receive need-based scholarship or grant aid. 2% freshmen, 1% undergrads receive non-need-based scholarship or grant aid. 48% freshmen, 49% undergrads receive need-based self-help aid. 2% freshmen, 2% undergrads receive athletic scholarships. 74% freshmen, 80% undergrads receive any aid. 73% undergrads borrow to pay for school. Average cumulative indebtedness $23,189. **Criteria for awarding institutional aid:** *Non-need-based:* Academics, alumni affiliation, art, athletics, job skills, leadership, minority status, music/drama, state/district residency.

MONTANA STATE UNIVERSITY—BOZEMAN

New Student Services, PO Box 172190, Bozeman, MT 59717-2190
Phone: 406-994-2452 **Financial Aid Phone:** 406-994-2845
E-mail: admissions@montana.edu **CEEB Code:** 4488
Fax: 406-994-1923 **Website:** www.montana.edu **ACT Code:** 2420

This public school was founded in 1893. It has a 1780-acre campus.

RATINGS
Admissions Selectivity Rating: 79   **Fire Safety Rating:** 85   **Green Rating:** 77

STUDENTS AND FACULTY
Enrollment: 10,754. **Student Body:** 45% female, 55% male, 33% out-of-state, 2% international (69 countries represented). Asian 2%, African American 1%, Caucasian 88%, Hispanic 2%, Native American 3%.
Retention and Graduation: 72% freshmen return for sophomore year. 19% freshmen graduate within 4 years. 13% grads go on to further study within 1 year. **Faculty:** Student/faculty ratio 16:1. 569 full-time faculty, 78% hold PhDs, 3% are members of minority groups, 36% are women. 6% of classes are taught by teaching assistants.

ACADEMICS
Degrees: Bachelor's, certificate, doctoral, master's, post-master's certificate. **Classes:** Most classes have 10–19 students. Most lab/discussion sessions have 10–19 students. **Majors with Highest Enrollment:** Business/commerce; family and consumer sciences/human sciences; nursing/registered nurse (RN, ASN, BSN, MSN). **Special Study Options:** Cooperative education program, cross-registration, distance learning, double major, English as a Second Language (ESL), exchange student program (domestic), honors program, independent study, internships, student-designed major, study abroad, teacher certification program. **Honors programs:** www.montana.edu/wwwuhp/ **Combined degree programs:** BA/MEng, BA in environmental design/Master of Architecture. Special programs offered to physically disabled students include note-taking services, reader services, tape recorders, tutors. **Career services:** Alumni network, career/job search classes, career assessment, internships.

FACILITIES
Housing: Coed dorms, men's dorms, women's dorms, fraternity/sorority housing, apartments for married students, apartments for single students, wellness house, theme housing, wellness floors, non-smoking, older student floors. 90% of campus accessible to physically disabled. **Special Academic Facilities/Equipment:** Museum of the Rockies (history & paleontology museum), planetarium, Studio 1080 (multi-media, interactive learning center), Subzero Lab, wind tunnel, Clean Laboratory, nano laboratory, ion beam laboratory, electron microscopes, Center for Biofilm Engineering, Plant Growth Center (29 green houses), fitness center ($11.7 million student-funded renovation completed in 2008), chemistry & biochemistry research facility, Copeland Art Gallery, Exit Art Gallery (student art gallery), Wild Trout Research Laboratory, Burns Telecommunications Center, Plant and Animal Bioscience Research Facilities. **Computers:** Students can register for classes online. Administrative functions (other than registration) can be performed online.

CAMPUS LIFE
Environment: Town. **Activities:** Choral groups, concert band, dance, drama/theater, jazz band, literary magazine, marching band, music ensembles, musical theater, pep band, radio station, student newspaper, student-run film society, television station, campus ministries, international student organization. **Organizations:** 140 registered organizations, 18 honor societies, 12 religious organizations. 9 fraternities, 4 sororities. **Athletics (Intercollegiate):** *Men:* Basketball, cheerleading, cross-country, football, rodeo, skiing (downhill/alpine), skiing (nordic/cross-country), tennis, track/field (outdoor), track/field (indoor). *Women:* Basketball, cheerleading, cross-country, golf, rodeo, skiing (downhill/alpine), skiing (nordic/cross-country), tennis, track/field (outdoor), track/field (indoor), volleyball. **On-Campus Highlights:** Museum of the Rockies, Planetarium, Fitness Center ($11.7 million student-funded renovation completed in 2008), Burns Telecommunications Center, Chemistry & Biochemistry Research Facility, Blackbox Theatre Student Union Building Exit Art Gallery (student art gallery) Copeland Art Gallery (art gallery). **Environmental Initiatives:** 1) Building Lighting Retrofit projects; 2) Recycling to reduce waste stream; 3) Steam Go-Generation Turbine (generates ~1/7th of campus electrical power need).

ADMISSIONS
Freshman Academic Profile: Average high school GPA 3.28. 17% in top 10% of high school class, 41% in top 25% of high school class, 69% in top 50% of high school class. SAT Math middle 50% range 500–640. SAT Critical Reading middle 50% range 500–620. ACT middle 50% range 21–27. Minimum paper TOEFL 563. Minimum computer TOEFL 202. Minimum web-based TOEFL 90. **Basis for Candidate Selection:** *Very important factors considered include:* Class rank, rigor of secondary school record, standardized test scores. **Freshman Admission Requirements:** High school diploma is required and GED is accepted. *Academic units required:* 4 English, 3 mathematics, 2 science, (2 science labs), 3 social studies, 2 Two years chosen from the following: foreign language, computer science, visual/performing arts. **Freshman Admission Statistics:** 8,033 applied, 64% admitted, 45% enrolled. **Transfer Admission Requirements:** College transcript(s), standardized test scores, statement of good standing from prior institution(s). Minimum college GPA of 2.0 required. Lowest grade transferable D–. **General Admission Information:** Application fee $30. Nonfall registration accepted. Admission may be deferred for a maximum of 1 year. Credit and/or placement offered for CEEB Advanced Placement tests.

COSTS AND FINANCIAL AID
Annual in-state tuition $5,988. Annual out-of-state tuition $17,650. Room and board $7,578. Average book expense $1,100. **Required Forms and Deadlines:** FAFSA. Priority financial aid filing date 3/1. **Notification of Awards:** Applicants will be notified of awards on a rolling basis beginning 4/1. **Types of Aid:** *Need-based scholarships/grants:* Federal Pell, SEOG, state scholarships/grants, private scholarships, the school's own gift aid, Federal Nursing Scholarships. *Loans:* FFEL Subsidized Stafford, FFEL Unsubsidized Stafford, FFEL PLUS, Federal Perkins, Federal Nursing, college/university loans from institutional funds. *Student Employment:* Institutional employment available. Highest amount earned per year from on-campus jobs $11,700. Off-campus job opportunities are good. **Financial Aid Statistics:** 36% freshmen, 33% undergrads receive need-based scholarship or grant aid. 3% freshmen, 1% undergrads receive non-need-based scholarship or grant aid. 36% freshmen, 41% undergrads receive need-based self-help aid. 2% freshmen, 2% undergrads receive athletic scholarships. 48% freshmen, 48% undergrads receive any aid. 64% undergrads borrow to pay for school. Average cumulative indebtedness $21,571. **Criteria for awarding institutional aid:** *Non-need-based:* Academics, alumni affiliation, art, athletics, job skills, leadership, minority status, music/drama, state/district residency.

MONTANA TECH OF THE UNIVERSITY OF MONTANA

1300 West Park Street, Butte, MT 59701
Phone: 406-496-4256 **Financial Aid Phone:** 406-496-4212
E-mail: admissions@mtech.edu **CEEB Code:** 4487
Fax: 406-496-4710 **Website:** www.mtech.edu **ACT Code:** 24180

This public school was founded in 1893. It has a 113-acre campus.

RATINGS
Admissions Selectivity Rating: 72   **Fire Safety Rating:** 87   **Green Rating:** 60*

STUDENTS AND FACULTY
Enrollment: 2,236. **Student Body:** 41% female, 59% male, 12% out-of-state, 4% international (18 countries represented). Asian 1%, Caucasian 83%, Hispanic 2%, Native American 1%.
Retention and Graduation: 68% freshmen return for sophomore year. 5% freshmen graduate within 4 years. 14% grads go on to further study within 1 year. **Faculty:** Student/faculty ratio 16:1. 124 full-time faculty.

ACADEMICS
Degrees: Associate, bachelor's, certificate, master's, post-bachelor's certificate. **Classes:** Most classes have fewer than 10 students. Most lab/discussion sessions have 10–19 students. **Majors with Highest Enrollment:** Biology/biological sciences; mass communication/media studies; resort management. **Special Study Options:** Cooperative education program, distance learning, double major, dual enrollment, honors program, independent study, internships, teacher certification program. **Honors programs:** Honors program provided for all programs. Consists of honors seminar and a few extra courses. **Combined degree programs:** BA/MA. Special programs offered to physically disabled students include note-taking services, reader services, tape recorders, tutors. **Career services:** Alumni services, career/job search classes, career assessment, internships, regional alumni. **Career services highlights include:** Internships.

FACILITIES
Housing: Coed dorms, special housing for disabled students, special housing for international students, apartments for married students, apartments for single students, apartments for families (don't have to be married if have children). 75% of campus accessible to physically disabled. **Special Academic Facilities/Equipment:** Mineral Museum, World Museum of Mining. **Computers:** 30% of classrooms, 100% of libraries, 100% of dining areas, 100% of student union, have wireless network access. Students can register for classes online. Administrative functions (other than registration) can be performed online.

CAMPUS LIFE
Environment: Town. **Activities:** Concert band, pep band, radio station, student government, student newspaper, yearbook, campus ministries. **Organizations:** 58 registered organizations, 2 honor societies, 3 religious organizations. **Athletics (Intercollegiate):** *Men:* Basketball, football, golf. *Women:* Basketball, golf, volleyball. **On-Campus Highlights:** Mineral Museum, Mil Building (which houses Starbucks and HPER athletic facility), Student Union, Mall area (outdoor located in the center).

ADMISSIONS
Freshman Academic Profile: Average high school GPA 3.23. 17% in top 10% of high school class, 37% in top 25% of high school class, 70% in top 50% of high school class. 92% from public high schools. SAT Math middle 50% range 490–620. SAT Critical Reading middle 50% range 440–580. SAT Writing middle 50% range 430–560. ACT middle 50% range 20–25. Minimum paper TOEFL 525. Minimum computer TOEFL 195. **Basis for Candidate Selection:** *Other factors considered include:* Class rank, academic GPA, standardized test scores. **Freshman Admission Requirements:** High school diploma is required and GED is accepted. *Academic units required:* 4 English, 3 mathematics, 2 science, (2 science labs), 3 social studies, 2 Combined 2 years of foreign language, visual and performing arts, computer science, or vocational ed *Academic units recommended:* 4 English, 4 mathematics, 4 science, (2 science labs), 2 foreign language. **Freshman Admission Statistics:** 508 applied, 89% admitted, 98% enrolled. **Transfer Admission Requirements:** College transcript(s), minimum college GPA of 2.0 required. Lowest grade transferable C. **General Admission Information:** Application fee $30. Notification on a rolling basis, beginning on or about 8/30. Nonfall registration accepted. Admission may be deferred for a maximum of 1 year. Credit and/or placement offered for CEEB Advanced Placement tests.

COSTS AND FINANCIAL AID
Annual in-state tuition $5,714. Annual out-of-state tuition $15,425. Room and board $6,140. Average book expense $1,000. **Required Forms and Deadlines:** FAFSA, institution's own financial aid form. Priority financial aid filing date 2/8. **Notification of Awards:** Applicants will be notified of awards on a rolling basis beginning 3/15. **Types of Aid:** *Need-based scholarships/grants:* Federal Pell, SEOG, state scholarships/grants, private scholarships, the school's own gift aid. *Loans:* FFEL Subsidized Stafford, FFEL Unsubsidized Stafford, FFEL PLUS, Federal Perkins, college/university loans from institutional funds. *Student Employment:* Federal Work-Study Program available. Institutional employment available. Highest amount earned per year from on-campus jobs $4,200. Off-campus job opportunities are good. **Financial Aid Statistics:** 1% undergrads receive need-based scholarship or grant aid. 39% freshmen, 20% undergrads receive non-need-based scholarship or grant aid. 78% freshmen, 64% undergrads receive need-based self-help aid. 13% freshmen, 5% undergrads receive athletic scholarships. 80% freshmen, 68% undergrads receive any aid. 85% undergrads borrow to pay for school. Average cumulative indebtedness $20,000. **Criteria for awarding institutional aid:** *Non-need-based:* Academics, alumni affiliation, athletics, job skills, minority status, state/district residency.

MONTCLAIR STATE UNIVERSITY

One Normal Avenue, Montclair, NJ 07043-1624
Phone: 973-655-4444 **Financial Aid Phone:** 973-655-4461
E-mail: undergraduate.admissions@montclair.edu **CEEB Code:** 2520
Fax: 973-655-7700 **Website:** www.montclair.edu

This public school was founded in 1908. It has a 275-acre campus.

RATINGS
Admissions Selectivity Rating: 79   **Fire Safety Rating:** 84   **Green Rating:** 84

STUDENTS AND FACULTY
Enrollment: 13,542. **Student Body:** 61% female, 39% male, 3% out-of-state, 2% international (79 countries represented). Asian 6%, African American 9%, Caucasian 54%, Hispanic 20%.
Retention and Graduation: 82% freshmen return for sophomore year. **Faculty:** Student/faculty ratio 17:1. 553 full-time faculty, 92% hold PhDs, 25% are are members of minority groups, 48% are women.

ACADEMICS
Degrees: Bachelor's, certificate, master's, post-bachelor's certificate. **Majors with Highest Enrollment:** Business/commerce; family and consumer sciences/human sciences; psychology. **Special Study Options:** Cooperative education program, double major, English as a Second Language (ESL), honors program, independent study, internships, study abroad, teacher certification program. **Combined degree programs:** BA/MA, 5yr BA/MA, 5yr BA/M practical anthropolo. Special programs offered to physically disabled students include note-taking services, reader services, tape recorders, tutors. **Career services:** Alumni network, alumni services, career/job search classes, career assessment, internships, regional alumni. **Career services highlights include:** All of our programs are exceptional.

FACILITIES
Housing: Coed dorms, special housing for disabled students, special housing for international students, women's dorms, apartments for single students, theme housing. 90% of campus accessible to physically disabled. **Special Academic Facilities/Equipment:** The Dumont Television Center, Yogi Berra Museum and Stadium, Floyd Hall Arena. **Computers:** 70% of classrooms, 20% of dorms, 100% of libraries, 75% of dining areas, 50% of student union, 10% of common outdoor areas have wireless network access. Students can register for classes online. Administrative functions (other than registration) can be performed online.

CAMPUS LIFE
Environment: Town. **Activities:** Choral groups, concert band, dance, drama/theater, jazz band, literary magazine, marching band, music ensembles, musical theater, opera, pep band, radio station, student government, student newspaper, symphony orchestra, television station, yearbook, campus ministries, international student organization. **Organizations:** 121 registered organizations, 28 honor societies, 8 religious organizations. 13 fraternities, 16 sororities. **Athletics (Intercollegiate):** *Men:* Baseball, basketball, diving, football, lacrosse, soccer, swimming, track/field (outdoor). *Women:* Basketball, diving, field hockey, lacrosse, soccer, softball, swimming, track/field (outdoor), volleyball. **On-Campus Highlights:** Cafe Diem, University Hall, Student Center, Recreation Center,

Kasser Theater. **Environmental Initiatives:** Recycling Program—campuswide; green products used in housekeeping (This was built into the recent contract that was awarded); food waste composter (Transitions Dining Services food waste into compost that is used by Grounds Services in plantings around campus).

ADMISSIONS

Freshman Academic Profile: 10% in top 10% of high school class, 40% in top 25% of high school class, 83% in top 50% of high school class. SAT Math middle 50% range 460–550. SAT Critical Reading middle 50% range 440–540. SAT Writing middle 50% range 450–550. **Basis for Candidate Selection:** *Very important factors considered include:* Academic GPA, rigor of secondary school record. *Important factors considered include:* Class rank, standardized test scores. *Other factors considered include:* Recommendation(s), extracurricular activities, first generation, talent/ability, volunteer work, work experience. **Freshman Admission Requirements:** High school diploma is required and GED is accepted. *Academic units required:* 4 English, 3 mathematics, 2 science, (2 science labs), 2 foreign language, 2 social studies, 3 academic electives. **Freshman Admission Statistics:** 13,469 applied, 47% admitted, 33% enrolled. **Transfer Admission Requirements:** College transcript(s), statement of good standing from prior institution(s). Minimum college GPA of 2.0 required. Lowest grade transferable C–. **General Admission Information:** Application fee $60. Regular application deadline 3/1. Notification on a rolling basis, beginning on or about 10/1. Nonfall registration accepted. Admission may be deferred for a maximum of 1 semester. Credit offered for CEEB Advanced Placement tests.

COSTS AND FINANCIAL AID

Annual in-state tuition $7,042. Annual out-of-state tuition $15,053. Room and board $10,208. Required fees $2,730. Average book expense $1,200. **Required Forms and Deadlines:** FAFSA. Priority financial aid filing date 3/1. **Notification of Awards:** Applicants will be notified of awards on a rolling basis beginning 4/1. **Types of Aid:** *Need-based scholarships/grants:* Federal Pell, SEOG, state scholarships/grants, private scholarships, the school's own gift aid. *Loans:* FFEL Subsidized Stafford, FFEL Unsubsidized Stafford, FFEL PLUS, Federal Perkins, state loans *Student Employment:* Federal Work-Study Program available. Institutional employment available. Highest amount earned per year from on-campus jobs $2,297. Off-campus job opportunities are good. **Financial Aid Statistics:** 24% freshmen, 119% undergrads receive need-based scholarship or grant aid. 11% freshmen, 30% undergrads receive non-need-based scholarship or grant aid. 47% freshmen, 194% undergrads receive need-based self-help aid. 68% freshmen, 69% undergrads receive any aid. Average cumulative indebtedness $18,307. **Criteria for awarding institutional aid:** *Non-need-based:* Academics, alumni affiliation, art, leadership, minority status, music/drama, religious affiliation, state/district residency.

MONTREAT COLLEGE

310 Gaither Circle, Montreat, NC 28757-1267
Phone: 828-669-8011 **Financial Aid Phone:** 800-545-4656
E-mail: admissions@montreat.edu **CEEB Code:** 5423
Fax: 828-669-0120 **Website:** www.montreat.edu **ACT Code:** 3130

This private school, affiliated with the Christian (Nondenominational) Church, was founded in 1916. It has a 162-acre campus.

RATINGS

Admissions Selectivity Rating: 74   **Fire Safety Rating:** 60*   **Green Rating:** 60*

STUDENTS AND FACULTY

Enrollment: 937. **Student Body:** 60% female, 40% male, 20% out-of-state, international (12 countries represented).
Retention and Graduation: Faculty: Student/faculty ratio 22:1. 46 full-time faculty, 67% hold PhDs, 13% are are members of minority groups, 35% are women.

ACADEMICS

Degrees: Associate, bachelor's, master's. **Classes:** Most classes have 10–19 students. Most lab/discussion sessions have 10–19 students. **Majors with Highest Enrollment:** Bible/biblical studies; business administration and management; environmental studies. **Special Study Options:** Accelerated program, double major, dual enrollment, independent study, internships, student-designed major, study abroad, teacher certification program, American Studies Program (Washington, DC). L.A. Film Studies Center (Los Angeles, CA). Martha's Vineyard Semester. Special programs offered to physically disabled students include reader services, tutors.

FACILITIES

Housing: Men's dorms, women's dorms. 100% of campus accessible to physically disabled. **Special Academic Facilities/Equipment:** Hamilton Art Gal-

lery, Chapel of the Prodigal. **Computers:** Administrative functions (other than registration) can be performed online.

CAMPUS LIFE

Environment: Village. **Activities:** Choral groups, dance, drama/theater, music ensembles, musical theater, student government, student newspaper. **Organizations:** 11 registered organizations, **Athletics (Intercollegiate):** *Men:* Baseball, basketball, cross-country, golf, soccer. *Women:* Basketball, cross-country, golf, soccer, softball, volleyball. **On-Campus Highlights:** Gaither Chapel, Chapel of the Prodigal (contains original fresco), Student Game Area with LCD flat panel TV, Student Lounge Area with 24-hour Computer Access, Cavalier Grill—relaxing cafe-style eatery.

ADMISSIONS

Freshman Academic Profile: Average high school GPA 3.01. 7% in top 10% of high school class, 20% in top 25% of high school class, 59% in top 50% of high school class. SAT Math middle 50% range 430–540. SAT Critical Reading middle 50% range 410–560. ACT middle 50% range 18–22. Minimum paper TOEFL 500. Minimum computer TOEFL 173. **Basis for Candidate Selection:** *Very important factors considered include:* Application essay, academic GPA, rigor of secondary school record, standardized test scores. *Important factors considered include:* Recommendation(s), character/personal qualities, interview. *Other factors considered include:* Class rank, alumni/ae relation, extracurricular activities, first generation, level of applicant's interest, talent/ability, volunteer work, work experience. **Freshman Admission Requirements:** High school diploma is required and GED is accepted. *Academic units required:* 4 English, 3 mathematics, 3 science, 1 foreign language, 3 history. **Freshman Admission Statistics: Transfer Admission Requirements:** College transcript(s), essay or personal statement, statement of good standing from prior institution(s). Minimum college GPA of 2.5 required. Lowest grade transferable C. **General Admission Information:** Application fee $30. Regular application deadline 8/1. Notification on a rolling basis, beginning on or about 9/1. Nonfall registration accepted. Admission may be deferred for a maximum of 1 semester. Credit and/or placement offered for CEEB Advanced Placement tests.

COSTS AND FINANCIAL AID

Annual tuition $20,196. Room and board $6,540. Average book expense $1,000. **Required Forms and Deadlines:** FAFSA. Priority financial aid filing date 3/15. **Notification of Awards:** Applicants will be notified of awards on a rolling basis beginning 2/1. **Types of Aid:** *Need-based scholarships/grants:* Federal Pell, SEOG, state scholarships/grants, private scholarships, the school's own gift aid. *Loans:* FFEL Subsidized Stafford, FFEL Unsubsidized Stafford, FFEL PLUS, Federal Perkins. *Student Employment:* Highest amount earned per year from on-campus jobs $2,212. **Financial Aid Statistics:** 78% freshmen, 79% undergrads receive need-based scholarship or grant aid. 66% freshmen, 76% undergrads receive non-need-based scholarship or grant aid. 59% freshmen, 71% undergrads receive need-based self-help aid. 68% freshmen, 62% undergrads receive athletic scholarships. 98% freshmen, 98% undergrads receive any aid. 89% undergrads borrow to pay for school. Average cumulative indebtedness $18,005. **Criteria for awarding institutional aid:** *Non-need-based:* Academics, alumni affiliation, athletics, leadership, music/drama, state/district residency.

MONTSERRAT COLLEGE OF ART

23 Essex Street, P.O. Box 26, Beverly, MA 01915
Phone: 978-921-4242
E-mail: admiss@montserrat.edu **CEEB Code:** 9101
Fax: 978-921-4241 **Website:** www.montserrat.edu **ACT Code:** 1847

This private school was founded in 1970. It has a 12-acre campus.

RATINGS

Admissions Selectivity Rating: 70   **Fire Safety Rating:** 60*   **Green Rating:** 60*

STUDENTS AND FACULTY

Enrollment: 298. **Student Body:** 62% female, 38% male, 50% out-of-state. Asian 2%, African American 1%, Caucasian 76%, Hispanic 2%.
Retention and Graduation: 51% freshmen return for sophomore year. 45% freshmen graduate within 4 years. **Faculty:** Student/faculty ratio 7:1. 26 full-time faculty, 62% hold PhDs, 4% are are members of minority groups, 58% are women.

ACADEMICS

Degrees: Bachelor's, certificate, diploma. **Classes:** Most classes have 10–19 students. **Majors with Highest Enrollment:** graphic design; illustration; painting. **Special Study Options:** Cross-registration, dual enrollment, exchange student program (domestic), independent study, internships, student-designed major, study abroad, teacher certification program Special programs offered to physically disabled students include reader services, tape recorders. **Career services:** Career/job search classes, internships.

FACILITIES

Housing: Special housing for disabled students, apartment-style: coed buildings with single sex apartments. **Special Academic Facilities/Equipment:** Montserrat Gallery, 301 Gallery, Carol Schlosberg Alumni Gallery, 292 Gallery.

CAMPUS LIFE

Environment: Town. **Activities:** Literary magazine, student government. **Organizations:** 5 registered organizations. **On-Campus Highlights:** Student Lounge, Hardie Building, 292 Cabot, Montserrat Gallery, 301 Gallery.

ADMISSIONS

Freshman Academic Profile: Average high school GPA 2.8. SAT Math middle 50% range 372–589. SAT Critical Reading middle 50% range 416–642. ACT middle 50% range 18–22. Minimum paper TOEFL 550. Minimum computer TOEFL 213. **Basis for Candidate Selection:** *Very important factors considered include:* Application essay, recommendation(s), rigor of secondary school record, character/personal qualities, interview, talent/ability. *Important factors considered include:* standardized test scores. *Other factors considered include:* Class rank, extracurricular activities, volunteer work, work experience. **Freshman Admission Requirements:** High school diploma is required and GED is accepted. *Academic units recommended:* 4 English, 2 social studies, 2 history, 4 visual arts. **Freshman Admission Statistics:** 326 applied, 85% admitted, 27% enrolled. **Transfer Admission Requirements:** College transcript(s), essay or personal statement, minimum college GPA of 2.2 required. Lowest grade transferable C. **General Admission Information:** Application fee $40. Notification on a rolling basis, beginning on or about 12/20. Nonfall registration accepted. Admission may be deferred for a maximum of 1 year. Credit offered for CEEB Advanced Placement tests.

COSTS AND FINANCIAL AID

Required Forms and Deadlines: FAFSA, institution's own financial aid form, noncustodial PROFILE. Financial aid filing deadline 7/1. Priority financial aid filing date 3/2. **Notification of Awards:** Applicants will be notified of awards on a rolling basis beginning 3/1. **Types of Aid:** *Need-based scholarships/grants:* Federal Pell, SEOG, state scholarships/grants, private scholarships, the school's own gift aid. *Loans:* FFEL Subsidized Stafford, FFEL Unsubsidized Stafford, FFEL PLUS, state loans *Student Employment:* Federal Work-Study Program available. Institutional employment available. Highest amount earned per year from on-campus jobs $1,500. Off-campus job opportunities are good. **Financial Aid Statistics:** 71% freshmen, 69% undergrads receive need-based scholarship or grant aid. 68% freshmen, 59% undergrads receive non-need-based scholarship or grant aid. 73% freshmen, 76% undergrads receive need-based self-help aid. 96% freshmen, 79% undergrads receive any aid. 84% undergrads borrow to pay for school. Average cumulative indebtedness $24,006. **Criteria for awarding institutional aid:** *Non-need-based:* Academics, art.

MOORE COLLEGE OF ART AND DESIGN

20th Street and The Parkway, Philadelphia, PA 19103-1179
Phone: 215-965-4014 **Financial Aid Phone:** 215-965-4042
E-mail: enroll@moore.edu **CEEB Code:** 2417
Fax: 215-568-3547 **Website:** www.moore.edu **ACT Code:** 2417

This private school was founded in 1848.

RATINGS
Admissions Selectivity Rating: 77   **Fire Safety Rating:** 60*   **Green Rating:** 60*

STUDENTS AND FACULTY

Enrollment: 525. **Student Body:** 100% female, 41% out-of-state, 2% international (15 countries represented). Asian 2%, African American 12%, Caucasian 74%, Hispanic 6%, Native American 1%.
Retention and Graduation: 76% freshmen return for sophomore year. 57% freshmen graduate within 4 years. **Faculty:** Student/faculty ratio 8:1. 30 full-time faculty, 70% hold PhDs, 7% are are members of minority groups, 53% are women.

ACADEMICS

Degrees: Bachelor's, post-bachelor's certificate. **Classes:** Most classes have 10–19 students. **Majors with Highest Enrollment:** Fashion/apparel design; fine/studio arts; graphic design. **Special Study Options:** Double major, independent study, internships, study abroad, teacher certification program, arts, education student travel courses. Special programs offered to physically disabled students include tape recorders, tutors. **Career services:** Alumni services, internships, regional alumni. **Career services highlights include:** All majors require an internship before senior year.

FACILITIES

Housing: Women's dorms. **Special Academic Facilities/Equipment:** Paley, Graham, and Levy Galleries **Computers:** 100% of classrooms, 100% of dorms, 100% of libraries, 100% of dining areas, have wireless network access. Students can register for classes online. Administrative functions (other than registration) can be performed online. Undergraduates are required to own a computer.

CAMPUS LIFE

Environment: Metropolis. **Activities:** student government, yearbook. **Organizations:** 8 registered organizations, **On-Campus Highlights:** Three art galleries, Outdoor coffee shop, Internships, Leadership Fellowships, Locks Career Center for Women.

ADMISSIONS

Freshman Academic Profile: Average high school GPA 3.08. SAT Math middle 50% range 430–550. SAT Critical Reading middle 50% range 450–570. ACT middle 50% range 18–25. Minimum paper TOEFL 527. Minimum computer TOEFL 197. **Basis for Candidate Selection:** *Very important factors considered include:* Academic GPA, rigor of secondary school record, standardized test scores, character/personal qualities, interview, level of applicant's interest, talent/ability. *Important factors considered include:* Application essay, recommendation(s), extracurricular activities. *Other factors considered include:* Class rank, volunteer work, work experience. **Freshman Admission Requirements:** High school diploma is required and GED is accepted. **Freshman Admission Statistics:** 549 applied, 59% admitted, 33% enrolled. **Transfer Admission Requirements:** High school transcript, college transcript(s), essay or personal statement, statement of good standing from prior institution(s). Minimum college GPA of 2.5 required. Lowest grade transferable C. **General Admission Information:** Application fee $40. Early decision application deadline 11/15. Regular application deadline 8/15. Notification on a rolling basis, beginning on or about 11/15. Nonfall registration accepted. Admission may be deferred for a maximum of 1 year. Credit offered for CEEB Advanced Placement tests.

COSTS AND FINANCIAL AID

Annual tuition $26,800. Room and board $10,501. Required fees $918. Average book expense $2,060. **Required Forms and Deadlines:** FAFSA. Priority financial aid filing date 3/1. **Notification of Awards:** Applicants will be notified of awards on a rolling basis beginning 2/15. **Types of Aid:** *Need-based scholarships/grants:* Federal Pell, SEOG, state scholarships/grants, private scholarships, the school's own gift aid. *Loans:* FFEL Subsidized Stafford, FFEL Unsubsidized Stafford, FFEL PLUS, Federal Perkins, Alternative loans. *Student Employment:* Federal Work-Study Program available. Off-campus job opportunities are good. **Financial Aid Statistics:** 38% freshmen, 53% undergrads receive need-based scholarship or grant aid. 57% freshmen, 56% undergrads receive non-need-based scholarship or grant aid. 31% freshmen, 31% undergrads receive need-based self-help aid. 97% undergrads receive any aid. **Criteria for awarding institutional aid:** *Non-need-based:* Academics, art, leadership.

MORAVIAN COLLEGE

1200 Main Street, Bethlehem, PA 18018
Phone: 610-861-1320 **Financial Aid Phone:** 610-861-1320
E-mail: admissions@moravian.edu **CEEB Code:** 2418
Fax: 610-625-7930 **Website:** www.moravian.edu **ACT Code:** 2418

This private school, affiliated with the Moravian Church, was founded in 1742. It has a 60-acre campus.

RATINGS
Admissions Selectivity Rating: 79   **Fire Safety Rating:** 80   **Green Rating:** 75

STUDENTS AND FACULTY

Enrollment: 1,668. **Student Body:** 59% female, 41% male, 39% out-of-state, 1% international (15 countries represented). Asian 2%, African American 2%, Caucasian 89%, Hispanic 4%.
Retention and Graduation: 83% freshmen return for sophomore year. 71% freshmen graduate within 4 years. 17% grads go on to further study within 1 year. 9% grads pursue arts and sciences degrees. 2% grads pursue law degrees. 2% grads pursue business degrees. 3% grads pursue medical degrees. **Faculty:** Student/faculty ratio 11:1. 124 full-time faculty, 88% hold PhDs, 8% are members of minority groups, 51% are women.

ACADEMICS

Degrees: Bachelor's, first professional, master's, post-bachelor's certificate. **Classes:** Most classes have 20–29 students. Most lab/discussion sessions have 10–19 students. **Majors with Highest Enrollment:** Business/commerce; psychology; sociology. **Special Study Options:** Cross-registration, double major, honors program, independent study, internships, student-designed major, study abroad, teacher certification program. **Honors programs:** Students can do honors projects within their selected major. **Combined degree programs:** BA/MEng, occupational therapy (TJU); MBA (Moravian College). Special programs offered to physically disabled students include note-taking services, reader services, tape recorders, tutors. **Career services:** Alumni network, alumni services, career/job search classes, career assessment, internships, regional alumni.

FACILITIES

Housing: Coed dorms, men's dorms, women's dorms, fraternity/sorority housing, apartments for single students, wellness house, theme housing. **Special Academic Facilities/Equipment:** Payne [art] Gallery, Foy [concert] Hall, greenhouse, student art studios, observation room for psychology classes, Leadership Center. **Computers:** 80% of classrooms, 100% of libraries, 100% of dining areas, 100% of student union, 25% of common outdoor areas have wireless network access. Administrative functions (other than registration) can be performed online.

CAMPUS LIFE

Environment: City. **Activities:** Choral groups, concert band, dance, drama/theater, jazz band, literary magazine, marching band, music ensembles, musical theater, radio station, student government, student newspaper, symphony orchestra, yearbook, campus ministries, international student organization. **Organizations:** 80 registered organizations, 16 honor societies, 4 religious organizations. 3 fraternities, 4 sororities. **Athletics (Intercollegiate):** *Men:* Baseball, basketball, cross-country, football, golf, lacrosse, soccer, tennis, track/field (outdoor), track/field (indoor). *Women:* Basketball, cross-country, field hockey, lacrosse, soccer, softball, tennis, track/field (outdoor), track/field (indoor), volleyball. **On-Campus Highlights:** Alternative (on campus club/hang out), Afterwords Cafe (Library Coffee Shop), Priscilla Payne Hurd Academic Complex, Fitness Center, The Quad. **Environmental Initiatives:** Signing of the Talloires Declaration. Moravian College President, Dr. Christopher Thomforde, signed the Talloires Declaration on April 22, 2008. This document, signed by over 290 university presidents in over 40 countries, promotes positive action in environmental sustainability. It also discusses the role of education, research, policy formation and information exchange in managing the human impact on the environment. Sustainability Taskforce: Two main initiatives that were executed by the Taskforce on Sustainability during the 2007–2008 academic year have included a partnership with food services as well as participating in the Focus the Nation project. The partnership with food services has enabled the College to reduce the waste of paper napkins (by using new dispensers), plastic bags (by replacing with reusable bags), and food (by instituting a "no tray" day). Currently the partnership is actively exploring the feasibility of composting on campus. Participation in the National Teach-In "Focus the Nation" in January 2008 has increased awareness of the unsustainable nature of our fossil fuel use and climate change. This theme was introduced by a panel comprised of key members of the College and community and used in class discussions as well. In addition, the taskforce is in the process of completing a greenhouse gas emission inventory and the College's new construction is energy efficient (although not LEED). Partnership with the City of Bethlehem's Committee for Appropriate Transportation Moravian College will introduce a free Bike Loan program. A discount program will be available from local bike shops for purchase of bikes and helmets, etc., for Moravian College students, staff, & faculty. In addition, shared use markings on both sides of Bethlehem's Main Street will be painted by the City of Bethlehem by early summer. There will be a sign saying "Moravian College Bicycle Lane" that will be posted at both ends of Main St. to promote bike usage between the College's north and south campuses.

ADMISSIONS

Freshman Academic Profile: 27% in top 10% of high school class, 57% in top 25% of high school class, 85% in top 50% of high school class. 69% from public high schools. SAT Math middle 50% range 510–610. SAT Critical Reading middle 50% range 500–600. SAT Writing middle 50% range 500–600. ACT middle 50% range 19–23. Minimum paper TOEFL 550. Minimum computer TOEFL 213. **Basis for Candidate Selection:** *Very important factors considered include:* Class rank, academic GPA, rigor of secondary school record, alumni/ae relation, character/personal qualities. *Important factors considered include:* Application essay, recommendation(s), standardized test scores, extracurricular activities, first generation, level of applicant's interest, racial/ethnic status, talent/ability, volunteer work. *Other factors considered include:* Geographical residence, interview, work experience. **Freshman Admission Requirements:** High school diploma is required and GED is accepted. *Academic units required:* 4 English, 3 mathematics, 3 science, (2 science labs), 2 foreign language, 4 social studies. *Academic units recommended:* 4 mathematics, 3 foreign language. **Freshman Admission Statistics:** 2,098 applied, 70% admitted, 26%

enrolled. **Transfer Admission Requirements:** High school transcript, college transcript(s), essay or personal statement, statement of good standing from prior institution(s). Minimum college GPA of 3.0 required. Lowest grade transferable C. **General Admission Information:** Application fee $40. Early decision application deadline 2/1. Regular application deadline 3/1. Regular notification 3/15. Nonfall registration accepted. Admission may be deferred for a maximum of 1 year. Placement offered for CEEB Advanced Placement tests.

COSTS AND FINANCIAL AID

Room and board $8,728. Required fees $515. Average book expense $900. **Required Forms and Deadlines:** FAFSA, CSS/Financial Aid PROFILE, non-custodial PROFILE, business/farm supplement. Copies of parent and student w-2's and 1040's. Financial aid filing deadline 3/15. Priority financial aid filing date 2/14. **Notification of Awards:** Applicants will be notified of awards on or about 4/1. **Types of Aid:** *Need-based scholarships/grants:* Federal Pell, SEOG, state scholarships/grants, the school's own gift aid. *Loans:* FFEL Subsidized Stafford, FFEL Unsubsidized Stafford, FFEL PLUS, Federal Perkins. *Student Employment:* Highest amount earned per year from on-campus jobs $3,000. **Financial Aid Statistics:** 74% freshmen, 73% undergrads receive need-based scholarship or grant aid. 9% freshmen, 7% undergrads receive non-need-based scholarship or grant aid. 66% freshmen, 67% undergrads receive need-based self-help aid. 94% freshmen, 96% undergrads receive any aid. **Criteria for awarding institutional aid:** *Non-need-based:* Academics, alumni affiliation, leadership, minority status, music/drama, religious affiliation.

MOREHEAD STATE UNIVERSITY

Admissions Center, Morehead, KY 40351
Phone: 606-783-2000 **Financial Aid Phone:** 606-783-2011
E-mail: admissions@morehead-st.edu
Fax: 606-783-5038 **Website: ACT Code:** 1530

This public school was founded in 1922. It has a 1016-acre campus.

RATINGS

Admissions Selectivity Rating: 74   **Fire Safety Rating:** 84   **Green Rating:** 72

STUDENTS AND FACULTY

Enrollment: 6,725. **Student Body:** 60% female, 40% male, 14% out-of-state, international (35 countries represented). African American 3%, Caucasian 93%, Hispanic 1%.
Retention and Graduation: 71% freshmen return for sophomore year. **Faculty:** Student/faculty ratio 17:1. 371 full-time faculty, 67% hold PhDs, 11% are are members of minority groups, 48% are women.

ACADEMICS

Degrees: Associate, bachelor's, master's, post-bachelor's certificate, post-master's certificate. **Classes:** Most classes have 20–29 students. Most lab/discussion sessions have 10–19 students. **Majors with Highest Enrollment:** Elementary education and teaching; general studies; nursing/registered nurse (RN, ASN, BSN, MSN). **Special Study Options:** Accelerated program, cooperative education program, cross-registration, distance learning, double major, dual enrollment, exchange student program (domestic), honors program, independent study, internships, student-designed major, study abroad, teacher certification program, weekend college. Special programs offered to physically disabled students include note-taking services, reader services, tutors. **Career services:** Alumni network, alumni services, career/job search classes, career assessment, internships.

FACILITIES

Housing: Coed dorms, special housing for disabled students, special housing for international students, fraternity/sorority housing, apartments for married students, apartments for single students, limited housing available at agriculture complex for agriculture science students. Housing for handicapped students and private rooms available. 90% of campus accessible to physically disabled. **Special Academic Facilities/Equipment:** Ky. Folk Art Center, 320–acre agricultural complex, Space Science Center, Ky. Center for Traditional Music. **Computers:** 100% of classrooms, 20% of dorms, 100% of libraries, 100% of dining areas, 100% of student union, 100% of common outdoor areas have wireless network access. Students can register for classes online. Administrative functions (other than registration) can be performed online.

CAMPUS LIFE

Environment: Village. **Activities:** Choral groups, concert band, dance, drama/theater, jazz band, literary magazine, marching band, music ensembles, musical theater, opera, pep band, radio station, student government, student newspaper, symphony orchestra, television station, yearbook. **Organizations:** 101 registered organizations, 11 honor societies, 7 religious organizations. 10 fraternities, 9 sororities. **Athletics (Intercollegiate):** *Men:* Baseball, basketball, cheerleading, cross-country, football, golf, riflery, tennis, track/field (outdoor). *Women:* Basketball, cheerleading, cross-country, golf, riflery, soccer, softball, tennis, track/field (outdoor), track/field (indoor), volleyball. **On-Campus Highlights:** Adron Doran University Center, Eagle Lake, MSU Wellness Center, Laughlin Health Building. **Environmental Initiatives:** Environmental Education Center: Organizes educational workshops, Earth Day Activities, and community outreach.

ADMISSIONS

Freshman Academic Profile: Average high school GPA 3.31. 21% in top 10% of high school class, 46% in top 25% of high school class, 77% in top 50% of high school class. SAT Math middle 50% range 460–570. SAT Critical Reading middle 50% range 440–560. ACT middle 50% range 19–24. Minimum paper TOEFL 500. Minimum computer TOEFL 173. **Basis for Candidate Selection:** *Very important factors considered include:* Academic GPA, rigor of secondary school record, standardized test scores. *Other factors considered include:* Recommendation(s). **Freshman Admission Requirements:** High school diploma is required and GED is accepted. *Academic units required:* 4 English, 3 mathematics, 3 science, (1 science labs), 2 foreign language, 3 social studies, 1 history, 1 visual/performing arts, 7 academic electives, 1 unit history & appreciation of fine arts required. *Academic units recommended:* 1 computer science. **Freshman Admission Statistics:** 2,772 applied, 80% admitted, 57% enrolled. **Transfer Admission Requirements:** College transcript(s), statement of good standing from prior institution(s). Minimum college GPA of 2.0 required. Lowest grade transferable C. **General Admission Information:** Application fee $30. Nonfall registration accepted. Admission may be deferred for a maximum of one semester. Credit offered for CEEB Advanced Placement tests.

COSTS AND FINANCIAL AID

Required Forms and Deadlines: FAFSA, institution's own financial aid form. Priority financial aid filing date 3/15. **Types of Aid:** *Need-based scholarships/ grants:* Federal Pell, SEOG, state scholarships/grants, private scholarships, the school's own gift aid. *Loans:* Direct Subsidized Stafford, Direct Unsubsidized Stafford, Direct PLUS, FFEL Subsidized Stafford, FFEL Unsubsidized Stafford, FFEL PLUS, Federal Perkins, college/university loans from institutional funds. *Student Employment:* Federal Work-Study Program available. Institutional employment available. **Financial Aid Statistics:** 40% freshmen, 45% undergrads receive need-based scholarship or grant aid. 59% freshmen, 39% undergrads receive non-need-based scholarship or grant aid. 42% freshmen, 47% undergrads receive need-based self-help aid. 6% freshmen, 5% undergrads receive athletic scholarships. 71.5% undergrads borrow to pay for school. Average cumulative indebtedness $20,404. **Criteria for awarding institutional aid:** *Non-need-based:* Academics, alumni affiliation, art, athletics, leadership, minority status, music/drama, state/district residency.

MOREHOUSE COLLEGE

830 Westview Drive, SW, Atlanta, GA 30314
Phone: 404-215-2632
E-mail: janderso@morehouse.edu **CEEB Code:** 5415
Fax: 404-524-5635 **Website:** www.morehouse.edu **ACT Code:** 792

This private school was founded in 1867. It has a 61-acre campus.

RATINGS
Admissions Selectivity Rating: 82 **Fire Safety Rating:** 60* **Green Rating:** 60*

STUDENTS AND FACULTY
Enrollment: 2,891. **Student Body:** 100% male, 70% out-of-state, 3% international African American 94%.
Retention and Graduation: 84% freshmen return for sophomore year. 32% freshmen graduate within 4 years. 25% grads go on to further study within 1 year. 22% grads pursue arts and sciences degrees. 5% grads pursue law degrees. 10% grads pursue business degrees. 14% grads pursue medical degrees. **Faculty:** Student/faculty ratio 15:1. 159 full-time faculty, 81% hold PhDs, 77% are are members of minority groups, 31% are women.

ACADEMICS
Degrees: Bachelor's. **Classes:** Most classes have fewer than 10 students. **Majors with Highest Enrollment:** Biology; business/commerce; computer and information sciences. **Special Study Options:** Cooperative education program, cross-registration, double major, dual enrollment, exchange student program (domestic), honors program, internships, study abroad, dual degree program in engineering and architecture with other institutions. **Combined degree programs:** BA/MEng, degree architecture w/ Michigan U. Special programs offered to physically disabled students include reader services, tape recorders,

tutors. **Career services:** career/job search classes, career assessment, internships

FACILITIES
Housing: Men's dorms, apartments for single students. 100% of campus accessible to physically disabled. **Special Academic Facilities/Equipment:** Three chapels, a meditation room, and an arena that was built by and used for the Olympic games in 1996. **Computers:** Students can register for classes online. Administrative functions (other than registration) can be performed online.

CAMPUS LIFE
Activities: Choral groups, concert band, drama/theater, jazz band, literary magazine, marching band, music ensembles, pep band, student government, student newspaper, yearbook. **Organizations:** 34 registered organizations, 7 honor societies, 4 religious organizations, 6 fraternities. **Athletics (Intercollegiate):** *Men:* Basketball, cross-country, football, track/field (outdoor). **On-Campus Highlights:** Forbes Arena, Graves Hall, Martin Luther King International Chapel, Century Yard, Technology Tower.

ADMISSIONS
Freshman Academic Profile: Average high school GPA 3.24. 20% in top 10% of high school class, 47% in top 25% of high school class, 77% in top 50% of high school class. 80% from public high schools. SAT Math middle 50% range 470–590. SAT Critical Reading middle 50% range 470–580. ACT middle 50% range 19–24. Minimum paper TOEFL 500. **Basis for Candidate Selection:** *Very important factors considered include:* Standardized test scores. *Important factors considered include:* Class rank, application essay, recommendation(s), rigor of secondary school record. *Other factors considered include:* Alumni/ae relation, character/personal qualities, extracurricular activities, geographical residence, interview, racial/ethnic status, talent/ability, volunteer work. **Freshman Admission Requirements:** High school diploma is required and GED is accepted. *Academic units required:* 4 English, 3 mathematics, 2 science, 2 foreign language, 2 social studies. **Freshman Admission Statistics:** 2,277 applied, 67% admitted, 46% enrolled. **Transfer Admission Requirements:** College transcript(s), essay or personal statement, standardized test scores, statement of good standing from prior institution(s). Minimum college GPA of 2.5 required. Lowest grade transferable C. **General Admission Information:** Application fee $45. Early decision application deadline 10/15. Regular application deadline 2/15. Regular notification 4/1. Nonfall registration not accepted. Admission may be deferred for a maximum of 2.

COSTS AND FINANCIAL AID
Annual tuition $14,318. Room and board $8,748. Required fees $1,422. Average book expense $850. **Required Forms and Deadlines:** FAFSA, institution's own financial aid form, CSS/Financial Aid PROFILE. Financial aid filing deadline 4/1. **Notification of Awards:** Applicants will be notified of awards on or about 5/1. **Types of Aid:** *Need-based scholarships/grants:* Federal Pell, SEOG, state scholarships/grants, private scholarships, the school's own gift aid, United Negro College Fund *Loans:* Direct Subsidized Stafford, Direct Unsubsidized Stafford, Direct PLUS, FFEL Subsidized Stafford, FFEL Unsubsidized Stafford, FFEL PLUS, Federal Perkins, state loans, college/university loans from institutional funds. *Student Employment:* Federal Work-Study Program available. Institutional employment available. Highest amount earned per year from on-campus jobs $1,500. Off-campus job opportunities are good. **Financial Aid Statistics:** 38% freshmen, 37% undergrads receive need-based scholarship or grant aid. 73% freshmen, 72% undergrads receive non-need-based scholarship or grant aid. 53% freshmen, 56% undergrads receive need-based self-help aid. 3% freshmen, 4% undergrads receive athletic scholarships. 53% undergrads borrow to pay for school. **Criteria for awarding institutional aid:** *Non-need-based:* Academics, alumni affiliation, art, athletics, leadership, music/drama, state/district residency.

MORGAN STATE UNIVERSITY

1700 East Cold Spring Lane, Baltimore, MD, 21239,
Phone: 800-332-6674
E-mail: tjenness@moac.morgan.edu **CEEB Code:** 5416
Fax: 410-319-3684 **Website:** www.morgan.edu **ACT Code:** 1722

This public school was founded in 1867. It has a 122-acre campus.

RATINGS
Admissions Selectivity Rating: 60* **Fire Safety Rating:** 60* **Green Rating:** 60*

STUDENTS AND FACULTY
Student Body: 40% out-of-state.
Retention and Graduation: 76% freshmen return for sophomore year.

ACADEMICS

Degrees: Bachelor's, master's. **Special Study Options:** Cooperative education program, business, education, engineering, social/behavioral science. **Combined degree programs:** 3-3 pharmacy, 3-4 predental/premed. Special programs offered to physically disabled students include tutors. **Career services:** Career/job search classes, career assessment, internships.

FACILITIES

Housing: Coed dorms, men's dorms, women's dorms, apartments for single students. **Special Academic Facilities/Equipment:** African-American collection, new science complex and school of engineering.

CAMPUS LIFE

Activities: Radio station, student government, student newspaper, television station, yearbook. **Organizations:** 250 registered organizations, 1 religious organizations. 4 fraternities, 4 sororities. **Athletics (Intercollegiate):** *Men:* Basketball, cross-country, football, tennis, track/field (outdoor), volleyball. *Women:* Basketball, cross-country, tennis, track/field (outdoor), volleyball. **On-Campus Highlights:** Fine Arts Center, Hughes Stadium, Mitchell Building, Research Facility, University Museum.

ADMISSIONS

Freshman Academic Profile: 10% in top 10% of high school class, 80% in top 25% of high school class, 96% in top 50% of high school class. 78% from public high schools. Minimum paper TOEFL 570. Minimum computer TOEFL 230. Minimum web-based TOEFL 88. **Basis for Candidate Selection: Freshman Admission Requirements:** High school diploma is required and GED is accepted.High school diploma is required and GED is not accepted. *Academic units recommended:* 4 English, 3 mathematics, 3 science, 2 foreign language, 3 social studies, 2 history. **Freshman Admission Statistics:** Lowest grade transferable C. **General Admission Information:** Early decision application deadline 4/15. Regular application deadline 4/15. Nonfall registration accepted. Credit offered for CEEB Advanced Placement tests.

COSTS AND FINANCIAL AID

Annual in-state tuition $1,853. Annual out-of-state tuition $4,405. Room and board $5,296. Required fees $762. Average book expense $1,500. **Required Forms and Deadlines:** FAFSA, institution's own financial aid form, state aid form **Types of Aid:** *Need-based scholarships/grants:* state scholarships/grants, United Negro College Fund. *Loans:* FFEL Subsidized Stafford, FFEL PLUS. *Student Employment:* Federal Work-Study Program available. Institutional employment available. Off-campus job opportunities are good.

MORNINGSIDE COLLEGE

1501 Morningside Avenue, Sioux City, IA 51106-1751
Phone: 712-274-5511 **Financial Aid Phone:** 712-274-5159
E-mail: mscadm@morningside.edu **CEEB Code:** 6415
Fax: 712-274-5101 **Website:** www.morningside.edu **ACT Code:** 1338

This private school, affiliated with the Methodist Church, was founded in 1894. It has a 68-acre campus.

RATINGS

Admissions Selectivity Rating: 76   **Fire Safety Rating:** 60*   **Green Rating:** 60*

STUDENTS AND FACULTY

Enrollment: 1,180. **Student Body:** 54% female, 46% male, 32% out-of-state, 1% international (4 countries represented). Asian 2%, African American 1%, Caucasian 84%, Hispanic 3%, Native American 1%.
Retention and Graduation: 70% freshmen return for sophomore year. 31% freshmen graduate within 4 years. 11% grads go on to further study within 1 year. 48% grads pursue arts and sciences degrees. 10% grads pursue law degrees. **Faculty:** Student/faculty ratio 17:1. 69 full-time faculty, 77% hold PhDs, 3% are are members of minority groups, 45% are women.

ACADEMICS

Degrees: Bachelor's, master's. **Classes:** Most classes have 10–19 students. Most lab/discussion sessions have 10–19 students. **Majors with Highest Enrollment:** Biology/biological sciences; business administration and management; elementary education and teaching. **Special Study Options:** Distance learning, double major, dual enrollment, English as a Second Language (ESL), honors program, independent study, internships, liberal arts/career combination, student-designed major, study abroad, teacher certification program, health professions. **Combined degree programs:** BA/MA. Special programs offered to physically disabled students include note-taking services, reader services, tape recorders, tutors. **Career services:** Alumni network, alumni services, career/job search classes, career assessment, internships, regional alumni.

FACILITIES

Housing: Coed dorms, fraternity/sorority housing, apartments for married students, apartments for single students. 50% of campus accessible to physically disabled. **Special Academic Facilities/Equipment:** Media-enhanced "smart classroom," high-speed campus Internet connection, art gallery, theatre, totally renovated science facility. **Computers:** 100% of classrooms, 100% of dorms, 100% of libraries, 100% of dining areas, 100% of student union, 100% of common outdoor areas have wireless network access. Students can register for classes online. Administrative functions (other than registration) can be performed online. Undergraduates are required to own a computer.

CAMPUS LIFE

Environment: City. **Activities:** Choral groups, concert band, dance, drama/theater, jazz band, literary magazine, marching band, music ensembles, musical theater, pep band, radio station, student government, student newspaper, television station, yearbook, campus ministries, international student organization. **Organizations:** 40 registered organizations, 15 honor societies, 10 religious organizations. 2 fraternities, 1 sorority. **Athletics (Intercollegiate):** *Men:* Baseball, basketball, cheerleading, cross-country, football, golf, soccer, swimming, tennis, track/field (outdoor), track/field (indoor), wrestling. *Women:* Basketball, cheerleading, cross-country, golf, soccer, softball, swimming, tennis, track/field (outdoor), track/field (indoor), volleyball. **On-Campus Highlights:** New Student Apartments, Health-Fitness Center, Eppley Auditorium, Olsen Student Center, Walker Science Center.

ADMISSIONS

Freshman Academic Profile: Average high school GPA 3.37. 15% in top 10% of high school class, 42% in top 25% of high school class, 78% in top 50% of high school class. 94% from public high schools. ACT middle 50% range 20–25. Minimum paper TOEFL 450. Minimum computer TOEFL 133. **Basis for Candidate Selection:** *Very important factors considered include:* Class rank, academic GPA, recommendation(s), rigor of secondary school record, standardized test scores. *Important factors considered include:* extracurricular activities, interview, talent/ability. *Other factors considered include:* Application essay. **Freshman Admission Requirements:** High school diploma is required and GED is accepted. *Academic units recommended:* 3 English, 2 mathematics, 2 science, 3 social studies. **Freshman Admission Statistics:** 1,349 applied, 74% admitted, 30% enrolled. **Transfer Admission Requirements:** High school transcript, college transcript(s), statement of good standing from prior institution(s). Minimum college GPA of 2.25 required. Lowest grade transferable C–. **General Admission Information:** Application fee $25. Nonfall registration accepted. Admission may be deferred for a maximum of no limit. Credit and/or placement offered for CEEB Advanced Placement tests.

COSTS AND FINANCIAL AID

Annual tuition $21,116. Room and board $6,729. Required fees $1,130. Average book expense $800. **Required Forms and Deadlines:** FAFSA. Priority financial aid filing date 3/1. **Notification of Awards:** Applicants will be notified of awards on a rolling basis beginning 3/31. **Types of Aid:** *Need-based scholarships/grants:* Federal Pell, SEOG, state scholarships/grants, private scholarships, the school's own gift aid. *Loans:* FFEL Subsidized Stafford, FFEL Unsubsidized Stafford, FFEL PLUS, Federal Perkins, state loans, college/university loans from institutional funds. *Student Employment:* Federal Work-Study Program available. Institutional employment available. Highest amount earned per year from on-campus jobs $9,536. Off-campus job opportunities are excellent. **Financial Aid Statistics:** 62% freshmen, 65% undergrads receive need-based scholarship or grant aid. 100% freshmen, 98% undergrads receive non-need-based scholarship or grant aid. 70% freshmen, 75% undergrads receive need-based self-help aid. 56% freshmen, 45% undergrads receive athletic scholarships. 100% freshmen, 100% undergrads receive any aid. 88% undergrads borrow to pay for school. Average cumulative indebtedness $31,208. **Criteria for awarding institutional aid:** *Non-need-based:* Academics, alumni affiliation, art, athletics, job skills, leadership, music/drama, religious affiliation, state/district residency.

MORRIS COLLEGE

100 West College Street, Sumter, SC 29150
Phone: 803-934-3225 **Financial Aid Phone:** 803-934-3238
E-mail: gscriven@morris.edu **CEEB Code:** 5418
Fax: 803-773-8241 **Website:** www.morris.edu **ACT Code:** 3868

This private school, affiliated with the Baptist Church, was founded in 1908. It has a 34-acre campus.

RATINGS

Admissions Selectivity Rating: 61   **Fire Safety Rating:** 64   **Green Rating:** 60*

STUDENTS AND FACULTY

Enrollment: 966. **Student Body:** 58% female, 42% male, 16% out-of-state, African American 100%.

Retention and Graduation: 56% freshmen return for sophomore year. 17% freshmen graduate within 4 years. 12% grads go on to further study within 1 year. 7% grads pursue arts and sciences degrees. 1% grads pursue law degrees. 1% grads pursue business degrees. 1% grads pursue medical degrees. **Faculty:** Student/faculty ratio 18:1. 48 full-time faculty, 71% hold PhDs, 63% are are members of minority groups, 46% are women.

ACADEMICS

Degrees: Bachelor's. **Classes:** Most classes have 10–19 students. Most lab/discussion sessions have fewer than 10 students. **Majors with Highest Enrollment:** Business administration and management; business administration; management and operations, other; community health services/liaison/counseling. **Special Study Options:** Accelerated program, cooperative education program, double major, honors program, internships, liberal arts/career combination, study abroad, teacher certification program, Advanced degree program available for adults aged 25 and older with 60 earned credit hours. **Combined degree programs:** Dual degree, math/engineering with NC A&T State U. **Career services:** Alumni network, alumni services, career/job search classes, career assessment, internships. **Career services highlights include:** The cooperative education internship program allows students to gain invaluable paid work experience closely related to their chosen field of study while earning their undergraduate degrees. The majority of these students are hired full-time by their co-op employers upon graduation from the college.

FACILITIES

Housing: Men's dorms, women's dorms 73% of campus accessible to physically disabled. **Special Academic Facilities/Equipment:** WMMC–640AM Student Radio Station. **Computers:** 100% of classrooms, 100% of dorms, 100% of libraries, 100% of dining areas, 100% of student union, 95% of common outdoor areas have wireless network access. Administrative functions (other than registration) can be performed online.

CAMPUS LIFE

Environment: Town. **Activities:** Choral groups, dance, drama/theater, literary magazine, pep band, radio station, student government, student newspaper, yearbook. **Organizations:** 55 registered organizations, 7 honor societies, 2 religious organizations. 4 fraternities, 4 sororities. **Athletics (Intercollegiate):** *Men:* Baseball, basketball, cheerleading, cross-country, golf, tennis, track/field (outdoor). *Women:* Basketball, cheerleading, cross-country, softball, tennis, track/field (outdoor), volleyball. **On-Campus Highlights:** Student Center, Library, Human Development Center, Outdoor Basketball Court, Auditorium, Computer Labs.

ADMISSIONS

Freshman Academic Profile: Average high school GPA 2.51. 2% in top 10% of high school class, 8% in top 25% of high school class, 30% in top 50% of high school class. 98% from public high schools. Minimum paper TOEFL 500. Minimum computer TOEFL 300. **Basis for Candidate Selection:** *Very important factors considered include:* Academic GPA. *Important factors considered include:* Class rank, rigor of secondary school record, standardized test scores. **Freshman Admission Requirements:** High school diploma is required and GED is accepted. *Academic units required:* 4 English, 4 mathematics, 3 science, 1 foreign language, 2 social studies, 1 history, 7 academic electives, 1–2 government, 1–2 economics. *Academic units recommended:* 2 foreign language. **Freshman Admission Statistics:** 2,350 applied, 91% admitted, 14% enrolled. **Transfer Admission Requirements:** High school transcript, college transcript(s), standardized test scores, statement of good standing from prior institution(s). Minimum college GPA of 2.0 required. Lowest grade transferable C. **General Admission Information:** Application fee $20. Notification on a rolling basis, beginning on or about 11/1; Nonfall registration accepted. Admission may be deferred for a maximum of 1 semester. Credit offered for CEEB Advanced Placement tests.

COSTS AND FINANCIAL AID

Average book expense $1,900. **Required Forms and Deadlines:** FAFSA, institution's own financial aid form. Priority financial aid filing date 3/30. **Notification of Awards:** Applicants will be notified of awards on a rolling basis beginning 6/1. **Types of Aid:** *Need-based scholarships/grants:* Federal Pell, SEOG, state scholarships/grants, private scholarships, the school's own gift aid, United Negro College Fund *Loans:* Direct Subsidized Stafford, Direct Unsubsidized Stafford, Direct PLUS, Federal Perkins. *Student Employment:* Federal Work-Study Program available. Off-campus job opportunities are good. **Financial Aid Statistics:** 96% freshmen, 99% undergrads receive need-based scholarship or grant aid. 11% freshmen, 8% undergrads receive non-need-based scholarship or grant aid. 98% freshmen, 99% undergrads receive need-based self-help aid. 99% freshmen, 99% undergrads receive any aid. 99% undergrads borrow to pay for school. Average cumulative indebtedness $20,000. **Criteria for awarding institutional aid:** *Non-need-based:* Academics, athletics, state/district residency.

MOUNT ALLISON UNIVERSITY

65 York Street, Sackville, NB E4L1E4 Canada
Phone: 506-364-2269 **Financial Aid Phone:** 506-364-2258
E-mail: admissions@mta.ca
Fax: 506-364-2272 **Website:** www.mta.ca

This public school was founded in 1839. It has a 25-acre campus.

RATINGS

Admissions Selectivity Rating: 75 **Fire Safety Rating:** 87 **Green Rating:** 82

STUDENTS AND FACULTY

Enrollment: 2,396. **Student Body:** 60% female, 40% male, 45% out-of-state, (40 countries represented).

Retention and Graduation: 45% freshmen graduate within 4 years. 30% grads go on to further study within 1 year. 10% grads pursue arts and sciences degrees. 3% grads pursue law degrees. 5% grads pursue business degrees. 12% grads pursue medical degrees. **Faculty:** Student/faculty ratio 13:1. 124 full-time faculty, 100% hold PhDs, 31% are women.

ACADEMICS

Degrees: Bachelor's, master's. **Classes:** Most classes have fewer than 10 students. **Majors with Highest Enrollment:** Business/commerce; chemistry; English literature (british and commonwealth); geography; sociology. **Special Study Options:** Distance learning, double major, English as a Second Language (ESL), exchange student program (domestic), honors program, independent study, internships, student-designed major, study abroad. Special programs offered to physically disabled students include reader services, tutors. **Career services:** Career/job search classes.

FACILITIES

Housing: Coed dorms, special housing for disabled students, special housing for international students, women's dorms, cooperative housing, zero environment footprint housing, pet-friendly housing (one residence fosters pets for humane society). 80% of campus accessible to physically disabled. **Special Academic Facilities/Equipment:** Art gallery. **Computers:** 100% of classrooms, 100% of dorms, 100% of libraries, 100% of dining areas, 100% of student union, 85% of common outdoor areas have wireless network access. Students can register for classes online. Administrative functions (other than registration) can be performed online.

CAMPUS LIFE

Environment: Rural. **Activities:** Choral groups, concert band, dance, drama/theater, jazz band, music ensembles, musical theater, radio station, student government, student newspaper, student-run film society, symphony orchestra, yearbook, international student organization. **Organizations:** 106 registered organizations. **Athletics (Intercollegiate):** *Men:* Badminton, basketball, football, rugby, soccer, swimming. *Women:* Badminton, basketball, rugby, soccer, swimming, volleyball. **On-Campus Highlights:** Ownes Art Gallery, Jenings Dinning Hall, library, Student Center **Environmental Initiatives:** Residence Climate Change Challenge expanded this year to include academic and administrative buildings—buildings reduced their consumption of utilities during the month of February from 10 to 25%. New campus Green Plan which studied the waste generated on campus. It identified waste reduction and waste diversion programs to increase our waste diversion from 45% to 70%. Introduced a clean plate program in the dining hall—students scrape their plates just like at home. A 44% reduction in food waste is the result of this "waste in your face" project.

ADMISSIONS

Freshman Academic Profile: 99% from public high schools. Minimum paper TOEFL 550. Minimum computer TOEFL 213. **Basis for Candidate Selection:** *Very important factors considered include:* Academic GPA, rigor of secondary school record, extracurricular activities, interview, talent/ability. *Important factors considered include:* Recommendation(s), character/personal qualities, volunteer work. *Other factors considered include:* Class rank, application essay, standardized test scores, work experience. **Freshman Admission Requirements:** High school diploma is required and GED is accepted. **Freshman Admission Statistics:** 1,997 applied, 46% admitted, 83% enrolled. **Transfer Admission Requirements:** High school transcript, college transcript(s), essay or personal statement, statement of good standing from prior institution(s). Lowest grade transferable C–. **General Admission Information:** Application fee $50. Regular application deadline 5/1. Nonfall registration accepted. Admission may be deferred for a maximum of not avail.

COSTS AND FINANCIAL AID

Annual in-state tuition $6,720. Annual out-of-state tuition $6,720. Room and board $5,130. Required fees $116. Average book expense $1,200. **Required Forms and Deadlines:** FAFSA, institution's own financial aid form **Types of Aid:** *Need-based scholarships/grants:* private scholarships, the school's own gift aid. *Loans:* FFEL Subsidized Stafford, FFEL Unsubsidized Stafford, FFEL PLUS, Canada/Provincial Loan Program. *Student Employment:* Off-campus job opportunities are good. **Financial Aid Statistics:** 25% freshmen, 25% undergrads receive need-based scholarship or grant aid. **Criteria for awarding institutional aid:** *Non-need-based:* Academics, alumni affiliation, art, athletics, job skills, leadership, minority status, music/drama, state/district residency.

MOUNT ALOYSIUS COLLEGE

7373 Admiral Peary Highway, Cresson, PA 16630
Phone: 814-886-6383 **Financial Aid Phone:** 814-886-6463
E-mail: admissions@mtaloy.edu **CEEB Code:** 2420
Fax: 814-886-6441 **Website: ACT Code:** 3635

This private school, affiliated with the Roman Catholic Church, was founded in 1939. It has a 125-acre campus.

RATINGS
Admissions Selectivity Rating: 71   Fire Safety Rating: 60*   Green Rating: 60*

STUDENTS AND FACULTY
Enrollment: 1,482. **Student Body:** 73% female, 27% male, 5% out-of-state, 1% international African American 2%, Caucasian 83%, Hispanic 1%. **Retention and Graduation:** 59% freshmen return for sophomore year. 22% freshmen graduate within 4 years. 22% grads go on to further study within 1 year. **Faculty:** Student/faculty ratio 13.7:1. 62 full-time faculty, 35% hold PhDs, 2% are are members of minority groups, 66% are women.

ACADEMICS
Degrees: Associate, bachelor's, certificate, master's, terminal associate. **Classes:** Most classes have 10–19 students. Most lab/discussion sessions have fewer than 10 students. **Special Study Options:** Accelerated program, distance learning, honors program, independent study, internships, student-designed major, teacher certification program. **Career services:** Alumni services, career/job search classes, career assessment, internships.

FACILITIES
Housing: Coed dorms 90% of campus accessible to physically disabled. **Computers:** 100% of classrooms, 100% of dorms, 100% of libraries, 100% of dining areas, 100% of student union, 100% of common outdoor areas have wireless network access.

CAMPUS LIFE
Environment: Rural. **Activities:** Choral groups, drama/theater, student government, student newspaper. **Organizations:** 16 registered organizations, 2 honor societies, 1 religious organizations. **Athletics (Intercollegiate):** *Men:* Basketball, golf, soccer. *Women:* Basketball, soccer, volleyball.

ADMISSIONS
Freshman Academic Profile: Average high school GPA 3.2. 85% from public high schools. SAT Math middle 50% range 420–510. SAT Critical Reading middle 50% range 420–510. SAT Writing middle 50% range 400–500. ACT middle 50% range 17–21. Minimum paper TOEFL 500. **Basis for Candidate Selection:** *Very important factors considered include:* Academic GPA, rigor of secondary school record, character/personal qualities, extracurricular activities, first generation, interview, talent/ability, volunteer work. *Important factors considered include:* Class rank, recommendation(s), standardized test scores, level of applicant's interest. *Other factors considered include:* Application essay. **Freshman Admission Requirements:** High school diploma is required and GED is accepted. *Academic units required:* 4 English, 3 mathematics, 3 science, 3 social studies, 3 computer science. *Academic units recommended:* 2 foreign language, 3 academic electives. **Freshman Admission Statistics:** 1,219 applied, 80% admitted, 37% enrolled. **Transfer Admission Requirements:** High school transcript, college transcript(s), minimum college GPA of 2.0 required. Lowest grade transferable C. **General Admission Information:** Application fee $30. Notification on a rolling basis, beginning on or about 8/1. Nonfall registration accepted. Admission may be deferred for a maximum of 1 semester. Credit and/or placement offered for CEEB Advanced Placement tests.

COSTS AND FINANCIAL AID
Annual tuition $17,240. Room and board $7,660. Required fees $760. Average book expense $2,000. **Required Forms and Deadlines:** FAFSA. Financial aid filing deadline 5/1. Priority financial aid filing date 4/1. **Notification of Awards:** Applicants will be notified of awards on a rolling basis beginning 3/15. **Types of Aid:** *Need-based scholarships/grants:* Federal Pell, SEOG, state scholarships/grants, private scholarships, the school's own gift aid. *Loans:* FFEL Subsidized Stafford, FFEL Unsubsidized Stafford, FFEL PLUS, Federal Perkins, Federal Nursing, Alternative loans. *Student Employment:* Federal Work-Study Program

available. Institutional employment available. Off-campus job opportunities are poor. **Financial Aid Statistics:** 94% freshmen, 97% undergrads receive need-based scholarship or grant aid. 6% freshmen, 3% undergrads receive non-need-based scholarship or grant aid. 94% freshmen, 97% undergrads receive need-based self-help aid. 30% freshmen, 35% undergrads receive any aid. 80% undergrads borrow to pay for school. Average cumulative indebtedness $29,802. **Criteria for awarding institutional aid:** *Non-need-based:* Academics, art, leadership, music/drama, religious affiliation.

MOUNT HOLYOKE COLLEGE

Newhall Conter, 50 College Stree, South Hadley, MA 01075
Phone: 413-538-2023 **Financial Aid Phone:** 413-538-2291
E-mail: admission@mtholyoke.edu **CEEB Code:** 3529
Fax: 413-538-2409 **Website:** www.mtholyoke.edu **ACT Code:** 1866

This private school was founded in 1837. It has a 800-acre campus.

RATINGS
Admissions Selectivity Rating: 95   Fire Safety Rating: 79   Green Rating: 79

STUDENTS AND FACULTY
Enrollment: 2,182. **Student Body:** 100% female, 74% out-of-state, 17% international (71 countries represented). Asian 12%, African American 5%, Caucasian 49%, Hispanic 5%. **Retention and Graduation:** 92% freshmen return for sophomore year. 79% freshmen graduate within 4 years. 22% grads go on to further study within 1 year. 12% grads pursue arts and sciences degrees. 1% grads pursue law degrees. 2% grads pursue medical degrees. **Faculty:** Student/faculty ratio 10:1. 208 full-time faculty, 94% hold PhDs, 27% are are members of minority groups, 53% are women.

ACADEMICS
Degrees: Bachelor's, certificate, master's, post-bachelor's certificate. **Classes:** Most classes have 10–19 students. Most lab/discussion sessions have 10–19 students. **Majors with Highest Enrollment:** Biology/biological sciences; English language and literature; international relations and affairs. **Special Study Options:** Cooperative education program, cross-registration, double major, exchange student program (domestic), independent study, internships, liberal arts/career combination, student-designed major, study abroad, teacher certification program, Community-based learning courses and First-Year seminars. Special programs offered to physically disabled students include note-taking services, reader services, tape recorders, tutors. **Career services:** Alumni network, alumni services, career/job search classes, career assessment, internships, regional alumni. **Career services highlights include:** www.mtholyoke.edu/cdc/internships.html.

FACILITIES
Housing: Special housing for disabled students, women's dorms, apartments for single students, special housing arrangements are available upon request. 95% of campus accessible to physically disabled. **Special Academic Facilities/Equipment:** Art and historical museums, bronze-casting foundry, child study center, audio-visual center, language learning center, greenhouse, Japanese meditation garden, equestrian center, observatory, linear accelerator, electron microscope, refracting telescope, nuclear magnetic resonance equipment, MCulloch Center for Global Initiatives, Weissman Center for Leadership and the Liberal Arts, Center for the Environment. **Computers:** 20% of classrooms, 100% of dorms, 100% of libraries, 100% of dining areas, 100% of student union, 4% of common outdoor areas have wireless network access. Students can register for classes online. Administrative functions (other than registration) can be performed online.

CAMPUS LIFE
Environment: Town. **Activities:** Choral groups, dance, drama/theater, jazz band, literary magazine, music ensembles, musical theater, radio station, student government, student newspaper, student-run film society, symphony orchestra, yearbook, campus ministries, international student organization, Model UN. **Organizations:** 150 registered organizations, 4 honor societies, 12 religious organizations. **Athletics (Intercollegiate):.** *Women:* Basketball, crew/rowing, cross-country, diving, equestrian sports, field hockey, golf, horseback riding, lacrosse, soccer, squash, swimming, tennis, track/field (outdoor), track/field (indoor), volleyball. **On-Campus Highlights:** Unified Science Center, Kendall Sports and Dance Complex, The Equestrian Center, Blanchard Cam-

pus Center, Williston Memorial Library. The entire campus is an exquisitely maintained botanic garden which includes an arboretum, numerous gardens, and the Talcott Greenhouse. **Environmental Initiatives:** Green Building and Energy: The college has recently received LEED Gold certification for a new residence hall, making it the 5th LEED-certified building on campus. In addition to LEED certification of major construction projects, the college has adopted internal Environmentally Responsible Building Principles and Guidelines to be applied to all construction and renovation projects. Our greenhouse gas inventory indicates that our emissions, primarily associated with building operations, are significantly lower per student than many of our peer institutions. Building lighting retrofits, heat recovery systems, centralized chilled water, cogeneration, and conservation programs have resulted in an 19.5% decrease in GHG emission since 2003. Recycling and Waste Reduction—The college has had an active recycling program since the early 1990's. Over 50% of our routine waste is diverted from disposal through recycling in 2009. Food waste from dining facilities, pre and post comsumer, is composted. Additionally, construction debris is recycled and equestion center waste is composted. Student ECO-Reps and the Environmental Action Coalition routinely conduct waste audits of both residence hall and administrative/academic buildings and organize a variety of information and training activities around recycling and waste reduction as well as other environmental topics. Supporting Local Agriculture—Dining Services has worked diligently to adopt environmentally friendly practices in all aspects of their work, from locating suppliers of local and organic foods to composting waste at local farms. The college procures as much of its food as possible from local growers and purveyors and used produce this year from our own new Student Garden for its Sustainable Agriculture Dinner in September. Our produce company is committed to buying from local farms anytime there is product available. A couple of years ago, Mount Holyoke and the other members of the Five Colleges formalized the buy-local effort as a Five-College initiative. One of the first Five-College efforts was a meeting with local farmers and suppliers of produce, dairy,and meat to discuss the feasibility of buying their products.

ADMISSIONS

Freshman Academic Profile: Average high school GPA 3.65. 62% in top 10% of high school class, 91% in top 25% of high school class, 99% in top 50% of high school class. 59% from public high schools. SAT Math middle 50% range 590–700. SAT Critical Reading middle 50% range 620–720. SAT Writing middle 50% range 625–700. ACT middle 50% range 27–31. Minimum paper TOEFL 600. Minimum computer TOEFL 250. **Basis for Candidate Selection:** *Very important factors considered include:* Class rank, application essay, academic GPA, recommendation(s), rigor of secondary school record. *Important factors considered include:* character/personal qualities, extracurricular activities, first generation, interview, talent/ability, volunteer work, work experience. *Other factors considered include:* Standardized test scores, alumni/ae relation, geographical residence, level of applicant's interest, racial/ethnic status. **Freshman Admission Requirements:** High school diploma is required and GED is accepted. *Academic units recommended:* 4 English, (3 science labs), 3 history, 1 academic electives. **Freshman Admission Statistics:** 3,127 applied, 53% admitted, 32% enrolled. **Transfer Admission Requirements:** High school transcript, college transcript(s), essay or personal statement, statement of good standing from prior institution(s). Minimum college GPA of 3.0 required. Lowest grade transferable C–. **General Admission Information:** Application fee $60. Early decision application deadline 11/15. Regular application deadline 1/15. Regular notification 4/1. Nonfall registration accepted. Credit and/or placement offered for CEEB Advanced Placement tests.

COSTS AND FINANCIAL AID

Annual tuition $38,940. **Required Forms and Deadlines:** FAFSA, CSS/Financial Aid PROFILE, noncustodial PROFILE, business/farm supplement. Financial aid filing deadline 3/1. Priority financial aid filing date 2/15. **Notification of Awards:** Applicants will be notified of awards on or about 4/1. **Types of Aid:** *Need-based scholarships/grants:* Federal Pell, SEOG, state scholarships/grants, private scholarships, the school's own gift aid. *Loans:* Direct Subsidized Stafford, Direct Unsubsidized Stafford, Direct PLUS, Federal Perkins, state loans, college/university loans from institutional funds. *Student Employment:* Federal Work-Study Program available. Institutional employment available. Highest amount earned per year from on-campus jobs $2,100. Off-campus job opportunities are fair. **Financial Aid Statistics:** 59% freshmen, 60% undergrads receive need-based scholarship or grant aid. 58% freshmen, 60% undergrads receive need-based self-help aid. 84% freshmen, 76% undergrads receive any aid. 66% undergrads borrow to pay for school. Average cumulative indebtedness $23,841. **Criteria for awarding institutional aid:** *Non-need-based:* Academics, leadership.

MOUNT IDA COLLEGE

777 Dedham Street, Newton, MA 02459
Phone: 617-928-4553 **Financial Aid Phone:** 617-928-4785
E-mail: admissions@mountida.edu **CEEB Code:** 3530
Fax: 617-928-4507 **Website:** www.mountida.edu **ACT Code:** 1868

This private school was founded in 1899. It has a 72-acre campus.

RATINGS

Admissions Selectivity Rating: 60*   **Fire Safety Rating:** 60*   **Green Rating:** 60*

STUDENTS AND FACULTY

Enrollment: 1,445. **Student Body:** 67% female, 33% male, 40% out-of-state, 5% international (32 countries represented). Asian 2%, African American 10%, Caucasian 56%, Hispanic 6%.
Retention and Graduation: 57% freshmen return for sophomore year. **Faculty:** Student/faculty ratio 13:1. 63 full-time faculty, 57% hold PhDs, 8% are are members of minority groups, 60% are women.

ACADEMICS

Degrees: Associate, bachelor's, certificate, terminal associate, transfer associate. **Classes:** Most classes have 10–19 students. **Special Study Options:** Accelerated program, distance learning, English as a Second Language (ESL), honors program, independent study, internships, student-designed major, study abroad, teacher certification program Special programs offered to physically disabled students include tape recorders, tutors. **Career services:** Alumni network, alumni services, career assessment, internships.

FACILITIES

Housing: Coed dorms, special housing for disabled students, men's dorms, women's dorms. **Special Academic Facilities/Equipment:** Mount Ida College Art Gallery.

CAMPUS LIFE

Environment: Village. **Activities:** Choral groups, dance, drama/theater, literary magazine, radio station, student government, student newspaper, yearbook, international student organization. **Organizations:** 22 registered organizations, 6 honor societies. **Athletics (Intercollegiate):** *Men:* Basketball, football, lacrosse, soccer, volleyball. *Women:* Basketball, cheerleading, cross-country, equestrian sports, soccer, softball, volleyball.

ADMISSIONS

Freshman Academic Profile: SAT Math middle 50% range 380–490. SAT Critical Reading middle 50% range 390–490. SAT Writing middle 50% range 400–500. ACT middle 50% range 15–20. Minimum paper TOEFL 525. Minimum computer TOEFL 197. Minimum web-based TOEFL 70. **Basis for Candidate Selection:** *Very important factors considered include:* Academic GPA. *Important factors considered include:* Recommendation(s), rigor of secondary school record. *Other factors considered include:* Application essay, standardized test scores, character/personal qualities, extracurricular activities, interview, talent/ability, volunteer work, work experience. **Freshman Admission Requirements:** High school diploma is required and GED is accepted. *Academic units recommended:* 4 English, 3 mathematics, 3 science, 2 foreign language, 2 social studies. **Freshman Admission Statistics:** 2,222 applied, 74% admitted, 25% enrolled. **Transfer Admission Requirements:** High school transcript, college transcript(s), essay or personal statement, statement of good standing from prior institution(s). Minimum college GPA of 2.0 required. Lowest grade transferable C. **General Admission Information:** Application fee $45. Nonfall registration accepted. Admission may be deferred for a maximum of 1 year. Credit offered for CEEB Advanced Placement tests.

COSTS AND FINANCIAL AID

Average book expense $1,000. **Required Forms and Deadlines:** FAFSA. Priority financial aid filing date 5/1. **Notification of Awards:** Applicants will be notified of awards on a rolling basis beginning 3/1. **Types of Aid:** *Need-based scholarships/grants:* Federal Pell, SEOG, state scholarships/grants, private scholarships, the school's own gift aid. *Loans:* FFEL Subsidized Stafford, FFEL Unsubsidized Stafford, FFEL PLUS, state loans. *Student Employment:* Federal Work-Study Program available. Institutional employment available. Highest amount earned per year from on-campus jobs $1,500. **Financial Aid Statistics:** 74% freshmen, 75% undergrads receive need-based scholarship or grant aid. 5% freshmen, 4% undergrads receive non-need-based scholarship or grant aid. 72% freshmen, 74% undergrads receive need-based self-help aid. **Criteria for awarding institutional aid:** *Non-need-based:* Academics, art, leadership.

MOUNT MARY COLLEGE

2900 North Menomonee River Parkway, Milwaukee, WI 53222-4597
Phone: 414-256-1219 **Financial Aid Phone:** 414-256-1258
E-mail: admiss@mtmary.edu **CEEB Code:** 1490
Fax: 414-256-0180 **Website:** www.mtmary.edu **ACT Code:** 4620

This private school, affiliated with the Roman Catholic Church, was founded in 1913. It has a 80-acre campus.

RATINGS
Admissions Selectivity Rating: 75   **Fire Safety Rating:** 71   **Green Rating:** 71

STUDENTS AND FACULTY
Enrollment: 1,253. **Student Body:** 98% female, 2% male, 4% out-of-state, 1% international (13 countries represented). Asian 4%, African American 22%, Caucasian 59%, Hispanic 8%, Native American 1%.
Retention and Graduation: 68% freshmen return for sophomore year. 20% freshmen graduate within 4 years. 10% grads go on to further study within 1 year. **Faculty:** Student/faculty ratio 13:1. 66 full-time faculty, 62% hold PhDs, 85% are women.

ACADEMICS
Degrees: Bachelor's, master's, post-bachelor's certificate, post-master's certificate. **Classes:** Most classes have 10–19 students. Most lab/discussion sessions have 10–19 students. **Majors with Highest Enrollment:** fashion/apparel design; nursing/registered nurse (RN, ASN, BSN, MSN). **Special Study Options:** Accelerated program, double major, honors program, independent study, internships, liberal arts/career combination, student-designed major, study abroad, teacher certification program. **Honors programs:** The purpose of the Mount Mary College Honors Program is to reward superior scholarly achievement and to provide special challenges to serious students who wish to achieve maximum benefit from their college education. Students completing the program receive the diploma citation, "Graduation in the Honors Program." Special programs offered to physically disabled students include note-taking services, reader services, tape recorders, tutors. **Career services:** Career/job search classes, career assessment, internships.

FACILITIES
Housing: Women's dorms. 90% of campus accessible to physically disabled. **Special Academic Facilities/Equipment:** Hagerty Library, Marian Art Gallery, Walter and Olive Stiemke Memorial Hall and Conference Center. **Computers:** 100% of dorms, have wireless network access. Students can register for classes online. Administrative functions (other than registration) can be performed online.

CAMPUS LIFE
Environment: Metropolis. **Activities:** Choral groups, dance, literary magazine, music ensembles, student government, student newspaper, campus ministries, international student organization, Model UN. **Organizations:** 42 registered organizations, 14 honor societies, 1 religious organizations. **Athletics (Intercollegiate):** *Women:* Basketball, cross-country, soccer, softball, tennis, volleyball. **On-Campus Highlights:** Cyber Cafe, Gerhardinger Science and Technology Center, Haggerty Library, Notre Dame Hall, Bloechl Recreation Center.

ADMISSIONS
Freshman Academic Profile: Average high school GPA 2.918. 16% in top 10% of high school class, 41% in top 25% of high school class, 70% in top 50% of high school class. 80% from public high schools. ACT middle 50% range 16–22. Minimum paper TOEFL 500. Minimum computer TOEFL 173. Minimum web-based TOEFL 61. **Basis for Candidate Selection:** *Very important factors considered include:* Academic GPA, rigor of secondary school record. *Important factors considered include:* Class rank, standardized test scores, character/personal qualities, talent/ability. *Other factors considered include:* Application essay, recommendation(s), extracurricular activities, interview, volunteer work, work experience. **Freshman Admission Requirements:** High school diploma is required and GED is accepted. *Academic units required:* 4 English, 2 mathematics, 2 science, (2 science labs), 2 social studies, 2 history, 2 academic electives. *Academic units recommended:* 4 English, 3 mathematics, 2 science, (2 science labs), 2 foreign language, 2 social studies, 2 history. **Freshman Admission Statistics:** 808 applied, 50% admitted, 40% enrolled. **Transfer Admission Requirements:** High school transcript, college transcript(s), minimum college GPA of 2.0 required. Lowest grade transferable C. **General Admission Information:** Application fee $25. Notification on a rolling basis, beginning on or about 9/15. Nonfall registration accepted. Admission may be deferred for a maximum of 1 year. Credit and/or placement offered for CEEB Advanced Placement tests.

COSTS AND FINANCIAL AID
Room and board $7,498. Required fees $450. Average book expense $1,260. **Required Forms and Deadlines:** FAFSA. Priority financial aid filing date 3/1. **Notification of Awards:** Applicants will be notified of awards on a rolling basis beginning 3/1. **Types of Aid:** *Need-based scholarships/grants:* Federal Pell, SEOG, state scholarships/grants, private scholarships, the school's own gift aid. *Loans:* FFEL Subsidized Stafford, FFEL Unsubsidized Stafford, FFEL PLUS, Federal Perkins, state loans *Student Employment:* Federal Work-Study Program available. Institutional employment available. Highest amount earned per year from on-campus jobs $1,152. **Financial Aid Statistics:** 92% freshmen, 85% undergrads receive need-based scholarship or grant aid. 3% freshmen, 4% undergrads receive non-need-based scholarship or grant aid. 89% freshmen, 82% undergrads receive need-based self-help aid. 87% freshmen, 86% undergrads receive any aid. 86% undergrads borrow to pay for school. Average cumulative indebtedness $20,729. **Criteria for awarding institutional aid:** *Non-need-based:* Academics, alumni affiliation, art, leadership, music/drama.

MOUNT MERCY COLLEGE

1330 Elmhurst Drive Northeast, Cedar Rapids, IA 52402-4797
Phone: 319-368-6460
E-mail: admission@mtmercy.edu
Fax: 319-363-5270 **Website:** www.mtmercy.edu

This is a private school.

RATINGS
Admissions Selectivity Rating: 74   **Fire Safety Rating:** 60*   **Green Rating:** 60*

STUDENTS AND FACULTY
Enrollment: 1,434. **Student Body:** 70% female, 30% male, 6% out-of-state, international Asian 1%, African American 2%, Caucasian 87%, Hispanic 1%. **Retention and Graduation:** 77% freshmen return for sophomore year. 49% freshmen graduate within 4 years. 9% grads go on to further study within 1 year. 6% grads pursue arts and sciences degrees. 1% grads pursue law degrees. 2% grads pursue business degrees. **Faculty:** Student/faculty ratio 13:1. 72 full-time faculty, 61% hold PhDs, 6% are are members of minority groups, 57% are women.

ACADEMICS
Degrees: Bachelor's. **Classes:** Most classes have 10–19 students. **Majors with Highest Enrollment:** Business/commerce; education; nursing/registered nurse (RN, ASN, BSN, MSN). **Special Study Options:** Accelerated program, cooperative education program, cross-registration, double major, dual enrollment, honors program, independent study, internships, liberal arts/career combination, student-designed major, study abroad, teacher certification program, weekend college. **Combined degree programs:** 2-2 programs with Kirkwood Community College. Special programs offered to physically disabled students include note-taking services, reader services, tape recorders, tutors. **Career services:** Alumni network, alumni services, career/job search classes, career assessment, internships, regional alumni.

FACILITIES
Housing: Coed dorms, apartments for single students. 95% of campus accessible to physically disabled.

CAMPUS LIFE
Activities: Choral groups, drama/theater, literary magazine, pep band, student government, student newspaper. **Organizations:** 35 registered organizations, 16 honor societies, 7 religious organizations. **Athletics (Intercollegiate):** *Men:* Baseball, basketball, cross-country, golf, soccer, track/field (outdoor). *Women:* Basketball, cross-country, golf, soccer, softball, track/field (outdoor), volleyball. **On-Campus Highlights:** Lundy Commons: Game Room, TV Room, Convenience Store, Bookstore, Lounges, Hilltop Grill and Dining Hall, Busse Library, Andrea's House-144 bed, suite style campus residence, Entire campus is connected by underground tunnels.

ADMISSIONS
Freshman Academic Profile: Average high school GPA 3.43. 18% in top 10% of high school class, 44% in top 25% of high school class, 82% in top 50% of high school class. 83% from public high schools. ACT middle 50% range 20–25. Minimum paper TOEFL 550. Minimum computer TOEFL 213. **Basis for Candidate Selection:** *Very important factors considered include:* Class rank, rigor of secondary school record, standardized test scores. *Important factors considered include:* Application essay, recommendation(s), extracurricular activities. *Other factors considered include:* Character/personal qualities, interview, talent/ability, volunteer work. **Freshman Admission Require-**

ments: High school diploma is required and GED is accepted. *Academic units recommended:* 4 English, 4 mathematics, 3 science, 2 foreign language, 2 social studies, 2 history. **Freshman Admission Statistics:** 488 applied, 84% admitted, 48% enrolled. **Transfer Admission Requirements:** College transcript(s), statement of good standing from prior institution(s). Minimum college GPA of 2.5 required. Lowest grade transferable D. **General Admission Information:** Application fee $20. Regular application deadline 8/30. Nonfall registration accepted. Admission may be deferred for a maximum of 1 year. Credit and/or placement offered for CEEB Advanced Placement tests.

COSTS AND FINANCIAL AID
Required Forms and Deadlines: FAFSA. Priority financial aid filing date 3/1. **Notification of Awards:** Applicants will be notified of awards on a rolling basis beginning 3/15. **Types of Aid:** *Need-based scholarships/grants:* Federal Pell, SEOG, state scholarships/grants, the school's own gift aid. *Loans:* Direct Subsidized Stafford, Direct Unsubsidized Stafford, Direct PLUS, Federal Perkins, state loans, college/university loans from institutional funds. *Student Employment:* Federal Work-Study Program available. Institutional employment available. Off-campus job opportunities are excellent. **Financial Aid Statistics:** 87% freshmen, 88% undergrads receive need-based scholarship or grant aid. 12% freshmen, 7% undergrads receive non-need-based scholarship or grant aid. 73% freshmen, 80% undergrads receive need-based self-help aid. 71% undergrads borrow to pay for school. Average cumulative indebtedness $19,656. **Criteria for awarding institutional aid:** *Non-need-based:* Academics, art, leadership, music/drama.

MOUNT OLIVE COLLEGE

634 Henderson Street, Mount Olive, NC 28365
Phone: 919-658-2502
E-mail: admissions@moc.edu **CEEB Code:** 5435
Fax: 919-658-9816 **Website:** www.moc.edu **ACT Code:** 3131

This private school, affiliated with the Baptist Church, was founded in 1951. It has a 138-acre campus.

RATINGS
Admissions Selectivity Rating: 73   **Fire Safety Rating:** 60*   **Green Rating:** 60*

STUDENTS AND FACULTY
Enrollment: 3,390. **Student Body:** 65% female, 35% male, 4% out-of-state, international Asian 1%, African American 34%, Caucasian 55%, Hispanic 3%. **Retention and Graduation:** 20% grads go on to further study within 1 year. **Faculty:** Student/faculty ratio 26:1. 89 full-time faculty, 87% hold PhDs, 16% are are members of minority groups, 33% are women.

ACADEMICS
Degrees: Associate, bachelor's, terminal associate, transfer associate. **Special Study Options:** Accelerated program, cooperative education program, distance learning, double major, dual enrollment, external degree program, honors program, independent study, internships, liberal arts/career combination, teacher certification program. Special programs offered to physically disabled students include tutors. **Career services:** Alumni services, career/job search classes, career assessment, internships.

FACILITIES
Housing: Men's dorms, women's dorms, apartments for single students. 95% of campus accessible to physically disabled.

CAMPUS LIFE
Environment: Rural. **Activities:** Choral groups, concert band, music ensembles, musical theater, student government, campus ministries, international student organization. **Organizations:** 33 registered organizations, 4 honor societies, 6 religious organizations. **Athletics (Intercollegiate):** *Men:* Baseball, basketball, cross-country, golf, soccer, tennis. *Women:* Basketball, cross-country, soccer, softball, tennis, volleyball.

ADMISSIONS
Freshman Academic Profile: 9% in top 10% of high school class, 36% in top 25% of high school class, 67% in top 50% of high school class. Minimum paper TOEFL 500. **Basis for Candidate Selection:** *Very important factors considered include:* Academic GPA, rigor of secondary school record, character/personal qualities. *Important factors considered include:* Class rank, standardized test scores, extracurricular activities, interview, level of applicant's interest, talent/ability. *Other factors considered include:* Recommendation(s), alumni/ae relation, geographical residence. **Freshman Admission Requirements:** High school diploma is required and GED is accepted. *Academic units required:* 4 English, 3 mathematics, 3 science, (1 science labs), 3 social studies, 3 academic

---

electives. **Freshman Admission Statistics:** 1,949 applied, 56% admitted, 35% enrolled. **Transfer Admission Requirements:** High school transcript, college transcript(s), minimum college GPA of 2.0 required. **General Admission Information:** Nonfall registration accepted.

COSTS AND FINANCIAL AID
Annual tuition $13,776. Room and board $5,540. Average book expense $1,400. **Required Forms and Deadlines:** FAFSA, state aid form. **Notification of Awards:** Applicants will be notified of awards on a rolling basis beginning 2/14. **Types of Aid:** *Need-based scholarships/grants:* Federal Pell, SEOG, state scholarships/grants, private scholarships, the school's own gift aid. *Loans:* FFEL Subsidized Stafford, FFEL Unsubsidized Stafford, FFEL PLUS, Federal Perkins, Federal Nursing, state loans. *Student Employment:* Federal Work-Study Program available. Off-campus job opportunities are excellent. **Financial Aid Statistics:** 87% freshmen, 80% undergrads receive need-based scholarship or grant aid. 5% freshmen, 4% undergrads receive non-need-based scholarship or grant aid. 74% freshmen, 74% undergrads receive need-based self-help aid. 3% freshmen, 2% undergrads receive athletic scholarships. 94% undergrads borrow to pay for school. Average cumulative indebtedness $13,854. **Criteria for awarding institutional aid:** *Non-need-based:* Academics, art, athletics, leadership, music/drama, religious affiliation.

MOUNT SAINT MARY COLLEGE

330 Powell Avenue, Newburgh, NY 12550
Phone: 845-569-3248 **Financial Aid Phone:** 845-569-3298
E-mail: admissions@msmc.edu **CEEB Code:** 2423
Fax: 845-562-6762 **Website:** www.msmc.edu **ACT Code:** 2819

This private school was founded in 1959. It has a 70-acre campus.

RATINGS
Admissions Selectivity Rating: 73   **Fire Safety Rating:** 93   **Green Rating:** 72

STUDENTS AND FACULTY
Enrollment: 2,214. **Student Body:** 75% female, 25% male, 13% out-of-state, international (30 countries represented). Asian 2%, African American 7%, Caucasian 78%, Hispanic 10%. **Retention and Graduation:** 72% freshmen return for sophomore year. 39% freshmen graduate within 4 years. 32% grads go on to further study within 1 year. 13% grads pursue arts and sciences degrees. 1% grads pursue business degrees. 3% grads pursue medical degrees. **Faculty:** Student/faculty ratio 17:1. 81 full-time faculty, 85% hold PhDs, 9% are are members of minority groups, 58% are women.

ACADEMICS
Degrees: Bachelor's, certificate, master's, post-master's certificate. **Classes:** Most classes have 20–29 students. Most lab/discussion sessions have fewer than 10 students. **Majors with Highest Enrollment:** nursing/registered nurse (RN, ASN, BSN, MSN); teacher education, multiple levels. **Special Study Options:** Accelerated program, cooperative education program, cross-registration, distance learning, double major, dual enrollment, exchange student program (domestic), honors program, independent study, internships, liberal arts/career combination, student-designed major, study abroad, teacher certification program. **Honors programs:** The Honors Program comprises academic, cultural, and social activities, each of which complements and reinforces the others. **Combined degree programs:** BA/MA. Special programs offered to physically disabled students include tape recorders, tutors. **Career services:** Alumni services, career/job search classes, career assessment **Career services highlights include:** The co-op program helps many students get a jump start on their career choice as well as help clarify their goals.

FACILITIES
Housing: Coed dorms, special housing for disabled students, men's dorms, women's dorms. 95% of campus accessible to physically disabled. **Special Academic Facilities/Equipment:** On-campus elementary school, television studio, and radio station. Multi-media lab. **Computers:** 100% of classrooms, 100% of dorms, 100% of libraries, 100% of dining areas, 100% of student union, 40% of common outdoor areas have wireless network access. Students can register for classes online. Administrative functions (other than registration) can be performed online.

CAMPUS LIFE
Environment: Town. **Activities:** Choral groups, concert band, dance, drama/theater, literary magazine, music ensembles, musical theater, radio station, student government, student newspaper, student-run film society, yearbook, campus ministries. **Organizations:** 30 registered organizations, 12 honor societies, 1 religious organizations. **Athletics (Intercollegiate):** *Men:* Baseball, bas-

ketball, cross-country, lacrosse, soccer, swimming, tennis. *Women:* Basketball, cross-country, lacrosse, soccer, softball, swimming, tennis, volleyball. **On-Campus Highlights:** Athletic Center with indoor pool, cardio/weight room, Knight Court Cyber Cafe, library with wireless Internet access, multi-media production laboratory, theater with student productions/music events. **Environmental Initiatives:** Became a Clean Air Campus with Clean Air New York—distribute information about air quality and invite CANY to campus. Instituted carpool parking spaces on campus. Sponsored a stream clean-up in Spring 09.

ADMISSIONS

Freshman Academic Profile: Average high school GPA 3.2. 9% in top 10% of high school class, 33% in top 25% of high school class, 76% in top 50% of high school class. 50% from public high schools. SAT Math middle 50% range 460–560. SAT Critical Reading middle 50% range 450–540. SAT Writing middle 50% range 450–540. ACT middle 50% range 19–23. Minimum paper TOEFL 550. Minimum computer TOEFL 200. Minimum web-based TOEFL 80. **Basis for Candidate Selection:** *Very important factors considered include:* Academic GPA, rigor of secondary school record. *Important factors considered include:* Class rank, application essay, recommendation(s), standardized test scores, character/personal qualities, interview, talent/ability. *Other factors considered include:* Alumni/ae relation, extracurricular activities, first generation, level of applicant's interest, volunteer work, work experience. **Freshman Admission Requirements:** High school diploma is required and GED is accepted. *Academic units recommended:* 4 English, 3 mathematics, 3 science, 2 foreign language, 3 social studies, 2 history, 1 computer science, 3 academic electives. **Freshman Admission Statistics:** 2,612 applied, 72% admitted, 25% enrolled. **Transfer Admission Requirements:** High school transcript, college transcript(s), standardized test scores, statement of good standing from prior institution(s). Minimum college GPA of 2.0 required. Lowest grade transferable C. **General Admission Information:** Application fee $45. Regular application deadline 8/15. Notification on a rolling basis, beginning on or about 9/15. Nonfall registration accepted. Admission may be deferred for a maximum of 1 year. Credit and/or placement offered for CEEB Advanced Placement tests.

COSTS AND FINANCIAL AID

Annual tuition $22,350. Room and board $11,900. Required fees $950. Average book expense $1,100. **Required Forms and Deadlines:** FAFSA. Financial aid filing deadline 3/1. Priority financial aid filing date 2/15. **Notification of Awards:** Applicants will be notified of awards on a rolling basis beginning 3/15. **Types of Aid:** *Need-based scholarships/grants:* Federal Pell, SEOG, state scholarships/grants, private scholarships, the school's own gift aid, Federal Nursing Scholarships. Academic Competitiveness Grant (ACG) and National Science and Mathematics Access to Retain Talent Grant (National SMART or NSG). *Loans:* FFEL Subsidized Stafford, FFEL Unsubsidized Stafford, FFEL PLUS, Federal Perkins, Federal Nursing *Student Employment:* Federal Work-Study Program available. Institutional employment available. Highest amount earned per year from on-campus jobs $4,204. Off-campus job opportunities are good. **Financial Aid Statistics:** 76% freshmen, 73% undergrads receive need-based scholarship or grant aid. 12% freshmen, 7% undergrads receive non-need-based scholarship or grant aid. 67% freshmen, 71% undergrads receive need-based self-help aid. 96% freshmen, 89% undergrads receive any aid. 94% undergrads borrow to pay for school. Average cumulative indebtedness $32,729. **Criteria for awarding institutional aid:** *Non-need-based:* Academics.

MOUNT ST. MARY'S COLLEGE (CA)

12001 Chalon Road, Los Angeles, CA 90049-1597
Phone: 310-954-4250 **Financial Aid Phone:** 310-954-4190
E-mail: admissions@msmc.la.edu **CEEB Code:** 4493
Fax: 310-954-4259 **Website:** www.msmc.la.edu **ACT Code:** 338

This private school, affiliated with the Roman Catholic Church, was founded in 1925. It has a 53-acre campus.

RATINGS

Admissions Selectivity Rating: 60*   **Fire Safety Rating:** 60*   **Green Rating:** 60*

STUDENTS AND FACULTY

Enrollment: 1,969. **Student Body:** 92% female, 8% male, 2% out-of-state, international (3 countries represented). Asian 20%, African American 9%, Caucasian 12%, Hispanic 48%.
Retention and Graduation: 78% freshmen return for sophomore year. 50% freshmen graduate within 4 years. **Faculty:** Student/faculty ratio 10.5:1. 89 full-time faculty, 61% hold PhDs, 26% are are members of minority groups, 78% are women.

ACADEMICS

Degrees: Associate, bachelor's, certificate, master's, post-bachelor's certificate, post-master's certificate, terminal associate, transfer associate. **Classes:** Most classes have 10–19 students. Most lab/discussion sessions have 10–19 students. **Majors with Highest Enrollment:** Liberal arts and sciences/liberal studies; nursing/registered nurse (RN, ASN, BSN, MSN). **Special Study Options:** Accelerated program, cross-registration, double major, exchange student program (domestic), honors program, independent study, internships, student-designed major, study abroad, teacher certification program, weekend college. **Honors programs:** Honors program is available to qualifying incoming freshmen and college students meeting eligibility requirements. **Combined degree programs:** BA/MA, ADN to MSN. Special programs offered to physically disabled students include note-taking services, reader services, tape recorders, tutors. **Career services:** Alumni services, career/job search classes, career assessment, internships.

FACILITIES

Housing: Men's dorms, women's dorms, limited men's housing. 100% of campus accessible to physically disabled. **Special Academic Facilities/Equipment:** Drudis-Biada Art Gallery. **Computers:** 100% of classrooms, 100% of dorms, 100% of libraries, 100% of dining areas, have wireless network access. Students can register for classes online. Administrative functions (other than registration) can be performed online.

CAMPUS LIFE

Environment: Metropolis. **Activities:** Choral groups, dance, drama/theater, literary magazine, music ensembles, student government, student newspaper, yearbook, campus ministries. **Organizations:** 29 registered organizations, 3 honor societies, 1 religious organizations. 3 sororities. **On-Campus Highlights:** Humanities Building, Chapel, Fitness Center.

ADMISSIONS

Freshman Academic Profile: 51% from public high schools. SAT Math middle 50% range 450–55. SAT Critical Reading middle 50% range 470–56. SAT Writing middle 50% range 470–560. ACT middle 50% range 19–23. Minimum paper TOEFL 550. Minimum computer TOEFL 213. **Basis for Candidate Selection:** *Very important factors considered include:* Application essay, academic GPA, standardized test scores. *Important factors considered include:* Recommendation(s), rigor of secondary school record. *Other factors considered include:* Alumni/ae relation, character/personal qualities, extracurricular activities, first generation, geographical residence, racial/ethnic status, religious affiliation/commitment, state residency, talent/ability, volunteer work, work experience. **Freshman Admission Requirements:** High school diploma is required and GED is accepted. *Academic units required:* 4 English, 3 mathematics, 2 science, (2 science labs), 2 foreign language, 2 social studies, 2 history. *Academic units recommended:* 4 mathematics, 3 science, (3 science labs), 3 foreign language, 3 social studies, 3 history. **Freshman Admission Statistics:** 1,131 applied, 79% admitted, 42% enrolled. **Transfer Admission Requirements:** College transcript(s), essay or personal statement, statement of good standing from prior institution(s). Minimum college GPA of 2.4 required. Lowest grade transferable D. **General Admission Information:** Application fee $40. Notification on a rolling basis, beginning on or about 11/15. Nonfall registration accepted. Admission may be deferred for a maximum of 1 year. Credit and/or placement offered for CEEB Advanced Placement tests.

COSTS AND FINANCIAL AID

Annual tuition $26,280. Room and board $7,832. Required fees $892. Average book expense $1,638. **Required Forms and Deadlines:** FAFSA. Priority financial aid filing date 2/15. **Notification of Awards:** Applicants will be notified of awards on a rolling basis beginning 3/15. **Types of Aid:** *Need-based scholarships/grants:* Federal Pell, SEOG, state scholarships/grants, private scholarships, the school's own gift aid. *Loans:* FFEL Subsidized Stafford, FFEL Unsubsidized Stafford, FFEL PLUS, Federal Nursing, college/university loans from institutional funds. *Student Employment:* Federal Work-Study Program available. Institutional employment available. Off-campus job opportunities are good. **Financial Aid Statistics:** 92% freshmen, 80% undergrads receive need-based scholarship or grant aid. 100% freshmen, 83% undergrads receive non-need-based scholarship or grant aid. 100% freshmen, 83% undergrads receive need-based self-help aid. 90% undergrads borrow to pay for school. Average cumulative indebtedness $33,030. **Criteria for awarding institutional aid:** *Non-need-based:* Academics, alumni affiliation, minority status, religious affiliation, state/district residency.

MOUNT ST. MARY'S UNIVERSITY

16300 Old Emmitsburg Road, Emmitsburg, MD 21727
Phone: 301-447-5214 **Financial Aid Phone:** 301-447-5207
E-mail: admissions@msmary.edu **CEEB Code:** 5421
Fax: 301-447-5860 **Website:** www.msmary.edu **ACT Code:** 1726

This private school, affiliated with the Roman Catholic Church, was founded in 1808. It has a 1400-acre campus.

RATINGS
Admissions Selectivity Rating: 76   **Fire Safety Rating:** 76   **Green Rating:** 78

STUDENTS AND FACULTY
Enrollment: 1,609. **Student Body:** 57% female, 43% male, 44% out-of-state, 1% international (17 countries represented). Asian 3%, African American 8%, Caucasian 80%, Hispanic 6%, Native American 1%.
Retention and Graduation: 78% freshmen return for sophomore year. 70% freshmen graduate within 4 years. 30% grads go on to further study within 1 year. 15% grads pursue arts and sciences degrees. 1% grads pursue law degrees. 6% grads pursue business degrees. 2% grads pursue medical degrees. **Faculty:** Student/faculty ratio 13:1. 112 full-time faculty, 86% hold PhDs, 4% are members of minority groups, 44% are women.

ACADEMICS
Degrees: Bachelor's, master's, post-bachelor's certificate, post-master's certificate. **Classes:** Most classes have 20–29 students. Most lab/discussion sessions have 10–19 students. **Majors with Highest Enrollment:** Business/commerce; communication studies/speech communication and rhetoric; elementary education and teaching. **Special Study Options:** Accelerated program, cross-registration, double major, dual enrollment, honors program, independent study, internships, liberal arts/career combination, student-designed major, study abroad, teacher certification program, weekend college, 3-2 with Johns Hopkins Univ. (BS in Biology; BS in Nursing) 3-3 with Sacred Heart Univ. (BS in Biology; Ph.D in PT) 4-2 with Sacred Heart Univ. (BS in Biology; MS in OT). **Honors programs:** The Honors Program offers talented and motivated students an educational experience that integrates curricular, co-curricular, and extra-curricular learning in both interdisciplinary and major areas of study. **Combined degree programs:** BS Bio, BS nursing; BS bio, Ph.D PT; BS Bio, MS OT. Special programs offered to physically disabled students include note-taking services, reader services, tape recorders, tutors. **Career services:** Alumni network, alumni services, career/job search classes, career assessment, internships. **Career services highlights include:** The Mount's Internship Program provides excellent learning and networking experiences for either credit or non-credit. Internships are tailored to students' majors. 'Mount in Washington' offers full time internships in Washington, DC. The Career Center has also introduced International Internships to London, Dublin and Florence.

FACILITIES
Housing: Coed dorms, special housing for disabled students, apartments for single students, wellness house, theme housing. 85% of campus accessible to physically disabled. **Special Academic Facilities/Equipment:** Historical art collection reflecting Catholic history in America and Marylandia. **Computers:** 100% of classrooms, 100% of dorms, 100% of libraries, 100% of dining areas, 100% of student union, 50% of common outdoor areas have wireless network access. Students can register for classes online. Administrative functions (other than registration) can be performed online.

CAMPUS LIFE
Environment: Rural. **Activities:** Choral groups, concert band, dance, drama/theater, jazz band, literary magazine, music ensembles, musical theater, pep band, radio station, student government, student newspaper, television station, yearbook, campus ministries, international student organization. **Organizations:** 68 registered organizations, 19 honor societies, 8 religious organizations. **Athletics (Intercollegiate):** *Men:* Baseball, basketball, cross-country, golf, lacrosse, soccer, tennis, track/field (outdoor), track/field (indoor). *Women:* Basketball, cross-country, golf, lacrosse, soccer, softball, swimming, tennis, track/field (outdoor), track/field (indoor). **On-Campus Highlights:** McGowan Student Center—Patriot Hall, Knott Athletic Recreation Convocation Complex, Knott Academic Center, Phillips Library, National Shrine Grotto of Lourdes. **Environmental Initiatives:** Our newest dorm is a green building that uses groundwater-source geothermal heating and cooling. Our recycling program is four years old is now an integrated part of campus operations. We are currently eliminating our coal-burning furnace and replacing it with a high-efficiency gas furnace. We are also decentralizing our heating/steam systems to prevent leaks and reduce transmission losses.

ADMISSIONS
Freshman Academic Profile: Average high school GPA 3.11. 21% in top 10% of high school class, 45% in top 25% of high school class, 78% in top 50% of

high school class. 52% from public high schools. SAT Math middle 50% range 460–590. SAT Critical Reading middle 50% range 470–580. SAT Writing middle 50% range 470–580. ACT middle 50% range 20–25. Minimum paper TOEFL 550. Minimum computer TOEFL 213. **Basis for Candidate Selection:** *Important factors considered include:* Academic GPA, rigor of secondary school record, standardized test scores, extracurricular activities, talent/ability, volunteer work. *Other factors considered include:* Application essay, recommendation(s), character/personal qualities, interview, level of applicant's interest, racial/ethnic status, work experience. **Freshman Admission Requirements:** High school diploma is required and GED is accepted. *Academic units required:* 4 English, 3 mathematics, 3 science, (2 science labs), 2 foreign language, 3 social studies, 1 academic electives. **Freshman Admission Statistics:** 2,963 applied, 84% admitted, 19% enrolled. **Transfer Admission Requirements:** College transcript(s), statement of good standing from prior institution(s). Minimum college GPA of 2.0 required. Lowest grade transferable C. **General Admission Information:** Application fee $35. Notification on a rolling basis, beginning on or about 12/1. Nonfall registration accepted. Admission may be deferred for a maximum of 1 year. Credit and/or placement offered for CEEB Advanced Placement tests.

COSTS AND FINANCIAL AID
Average book expense $1,000. **Required Forms and Deadlines:** FAFSA, institution's own financial aid form. Financial aid filing deadline 3/1. Priority financial aid filing date 3/1. **Notification of Awards:** Applicants will be notified of awards on a rolling basis beginning 2/15. **Types of Aid:** *Need-based scholarships/grants:* Federal Pell, SEOG, state scholarships/grants, private scholarships, the school's own gift aid. *Loans:* FFEL Subsidized Stafford, FFEL Unsubsidized Stafford, FFEL PLUS, Federal Perkins. *Student Employment:* Federal Work-Study Program available. Institutional employment available. Off-campus job opportunities are fair. **Financial Aid Statistics:** 74% freshmen, 65% undergrads receive need-based scholarship or grant aid. 15% freshmen, 12% undergrads receive non-need-based scholarship or grant aid. 60% freshmen, 54% undergrads receive need-based self-help aid. 8% freshmen, 10% undergrads receive athletic scholarships. 99% freshmen, 98% undergrads receive any aid. 67% undergrads borrow to pay for school. Average cumulative indebtedness $26,160. **Criteria for awarding institutional aid:** *Non-need-based:* Academics, art, athletics, leadership, minority status, music/drama.

MOUNT UNION COLLEGE

1972 Clark Avenue, Alliance, OH 44601-3993
Phone: 330-823-2590 **Financial Aid Phone:** 877-543-9185
E-mail: admission@muc.edu **CEEB Code:** 1492
Fax: 330-823-5097 **Website:** www.muc.edu

This private school, affiliated with the Methodist Church, was founded in 1846. It has a 115-acre campus.

RATINGS
Admissions Selectivity Rating: 73   **Fire Safety Rating:** 94   **Green Rating:** 84

STUDENTS AND FACULTY
Enrollment: 2,143. **Student Body:** 50% female, 50% male, 11% out-of-state, 3% international (21 countries represented). Asian 1%, African American 5%, Caucasian 84%, Hispanic 2%.
Retention and Graduation: 78% freshmen return for sophomore year. 50% freshmen graduate within 4 years. 29.3% grads go on to further study within 1 year. 8.5% grads pursue arts and sciences degrees. 4.1% grads pursue law degrees. 1.8% grads pursue business degrees. 2.2% grads pursue medical degrees. **Faculty:** Student/faculty ratio 14:1. 124 full-time faculty, 82% hold PhDs, 11% are are members of minority groups, 37% are women.

ACADEMICS
Degrees: Bachelor's, master's. **Classes:** Most classes have 10–19 students. Most lab/discussion sessions have fewer than 10 students. **Majors with Highest Enrollment:** Business administration and management; early childhood education and teaching; sport and fitness administration/management. **Special Study Options:** Cooperative education program, double major, dual enrollment, English as a Second Language (ESL), honors program, independent study, internships, liberal arts/career combination, student-designed major, study abroad, teacher certification program. **Honors programs:** Four honors programs are offered. Honors in Liberal Arts, Honors in the Major, First Year in Honors and Latin Honors. A qualified student may participate in any program and may discontinue honors study without penalty. Students must declare their intent to participate in an honors program no later than the first semester of their junior year Special programs offered to physically disabled students include note-taking services, reader services, tape recorders, tutors. **Career services:** Alumni network, alumni services, career/job search classes, career

assessment, internships, regional alumni. **Career services highlights include:** Employment success results/report.

FACILITIES

Housing: Coed dorms, special housing for disabled students, men's dorms, special housing for international students, women's dorms, fraternity/sorority housing, apartments for single students, theme housing, small, single-sex, college-owned residential homes converted to college housing. 85% of campus accessible to physically disabled. **Special Academic Facilities/Equipment:** Art gallery, ecological center, observatory, educational media center. **Computers:** 100% of classrooms, 90% of dorms, 100% of libraries, 100% of dining areas, 100% of student union, 50% of common outdoor areas have wireless network access. Students can register for classes online. Administrative functions (other than registration) can be performed online.

CAMPUS LIFE

Environment: Village. **Activities:** Choral groups, concert band, dance, drama/theater, jazz band, literary magazine, marching band, music ensembles, musical theater, pep band, radio station, student government, student newspaper, television station, yearbook, campus ministries, international student organization, Model UN. **Organizations:** 80 registered organizations, 16 honor societies, 10 religious organizations. 4 fraternities, 4 sororities. **Athletics (Intercollegiate):** *Men:* Baseball, basketball, cross-country, diving, football, golf, soccer, swimming, tennis, track/field (outdoor), track/field (indoor), wrestling. *Women:* Basketball, cheerleading, cross-country, diving, golf, soccer, softball, swimming, tennis, track/field (outdoor), track/field (indoor), volleyball. **On-Campus Highlights:** Hoover Price Campus Center, Kolenbrander Harter Information Center, McPherson Athletic Building, Dewald Chapel, Bracy Hall Science Building, Welcome Center. **Environmental Initiatives:** Sustainability (Climate Action) Plan; 54 KW Solar Panel; LEED-certified welcome center.

ADMISSIONS

Freshman Academic Profile: Average high school GPA 3.19. 13% in top 10% of high school class, 40% in top 25% of high school class, 74% in top 50% of high school class. SAT Math middle 50% range 440–590. SAT Critical Reading middle 50% range 430–540. ACT middle 50% range 19–25. Minimum paper TOEFL 550. Minimum computer TOEFL 213. **Basis for Candidate Selection:** *Very important factors considered include:* Class rank, academic GPA, rigor of secondary school record, standardized test scores. *Important factors considered include:* Recommendation(s). *Other factors considered include:* Application essay, alumni/ae relation, character/personal qualities, extracurricular activities, racial/ethnic status, talent/ability, volunteer work, work experience. **Freshman Admission Requirements:** High school diploma is required and GED is accepted. *Academic units recommended:* 4 English, 3 mathematics, 3 science, (2 science labs), 2 foreign language, 3 social studies, 1 fine arts. **Freshman Admission Statistics:** 2,320 applied, 75% admitted, 33% enrolled. **Transfer Admission Requirements:** High school transcript, college transcript(s), essay or personal statement, statement of good standing from prior institution(s). Minimum college GPA of 2.0 required. Lowest grade transferable C. **General Admission Information:** Notification on a rolling basis, beginning on or about 10/1. Nonfall registration accepted. Admission may be deferred for a maximum of one semester. Credit and/or placement offered for CEEB Advanced Placement tests.

COSTS AND FINANCIAL AID

Annual tuition $23,630. Room and board $7,420. Required fees $250. **Required Forms and Deadlines:** FAFSA. Priority financial aid filing date 4/1. **Types of Aid:** *Need-based scholarships/grants:* Federal Pell, SEOG, state scholarships/grants, the school's own gift aid. *Loans:* FFEL Subsidized Stafford, FFEL Unsubsidized Stafford, FFEL PLUS, Federal Perkins, college/university loans from institutional funds. *Student Employment:* Federal Work-Study Program available. Institutional employment available. Highest amount earned per year from on-campus jobs $2,600. Off-campus job opportunities are fair. **Financial Aid Statistics:** 83% freshmen, 79% undergrads receive need-based scholarship or grant aid. 4% freshmen, 5% undergrads receive non-need-based scholarship or grant aid. 78% freshmen, 73% undergrads receive need-based self-help aid. 98% freshmen, 98% undergrads receive any aid. 81% undergrads borrow to pay for school. Average cumulative indebtedness $28,158. **Criteria for awarding institutional aid:** *Non-need-based:* Academics, alumni affiliation, art, job skills, minority status, music/drama, state/district residency.

MOUNT VERNON NAZARENE UNIVERSITY

800 Martinsburg Road, Mount Vernon, OH 43050
Phone: 740-392-6868 **Financial Aid Phone:** 866-686-8243
E-mail: admissions@mvnu.edu **CEEB Code:** 1531
Fax: 740-393-0511 **Website:** www.mvnu.edu **ACT Code:** 3372

This private school, affiliated with the Nazarene Church, was founded in 1964. It has a 401-acre campus.

RATINGS
Admissions Selectivity Rating: 76   **Fire Safety Rating:** 62   **Green Rating:** 75

STUDENTS AND FACULTY

Enrollment: 1,939. **Student Body:** 62% female, 38% male, 8% out-of-state, international (7 countries represented). Asian 1%, African American 5%, Caucasian 89%, Hispanic 2%.
Retention and Graduation: 73% freshmen return for sophomore year. 37% freshmen graduate within 4 years. 16% grads go on to further study within 1 year. 3% grads pursue arts and sciences degrees. 7% grads pursue business degrees. 3% grads pursue medical degrees. **Faculty:** Student/faculty ratio 13.9:1. 108 full-time faculty, 64% hold PhDs, 5% are are members of minority groups, 34% are women.

ACADEMICS

Degrees: Associate, bachelor's, master's. **Classes:** Most classes have 10–19 students. **Majors with Highest Enrollment:** Business/commerce; early childhood education and teaching; nursing/registered nurse (RN, ASN, BSN, MSN). **Special Study Options:** Cooperative education program, cross-registration, distance learning, double major, dual enrollment, honors program, independent study, internships, liberal arts/career combination, study abroad, teacher certification program, Cooperative pre-engineering program with Olivet Nazarene University, cooperative pre-occupational therapy/physical therapy/physician's assistant programs with Chatham University, and articulation agreements with Columbus State Community College, Marion Technical College, Zane State College, Central Ohio Technical College, and North Central State College. Several opportunities for students to participate in service learning or mission trips. During the academic year, students may participate in one of the following trips: Germany, Hungary, Venezuela, Costa Rica, Nicaragua, Belize, Benin, Romania, or several out-of-state USA trips. **Honors programs:** Honors Program for outstanding students is designed to provide rewarding challenges for the academically gifted. Specific courses, seminars, and other out-of-the ordinary experiences, both on and off campus, are offered by the Honors Program. A $250 scholarship the first year, increases to $400 in the fourth year. The Honors Program adds depth to your academic development and allows you to have input in designing your own curriculum by proposing study topics for Honors courses and by developing independent projects. You will work closely with a faculty mentor to complete an Honors Project in your major. There are also opportunities for off-campus culural enrichment and entertainment, including travel to musuems, ballet and music performances, or dinner theater. Special programs offered to physically disabled students include note-taking services, reader services, tape recorders, tutors. **Career services:** Alumni services, career/job search classes, career assessment **Career services highlights include:** Missions and ministry opportunities and study aboard.

FACILITIES

Housing: Special housing for disabled students, men's dorms, women's dorms, apartments for single students, wellness house. 95% of campus accessible to physically disabled. **Special Academic Facilities/Equipment:** Art gallery, nature reserve. **Computers:** 95% of classrooms, 5% of dorms, 100% of libraries, 100% of dining areas, 100% of student union, 10% of common outdoor areas have wireless network access. Administrative functions (other than registration) can be performed online.

CAMPUS LIFE

Environment: Rural. **Activities:** Choral groups, concert band, drama/theater, jazz band, literary magazine, music ensembles, musical theater, opera, pep band, radio station, student government, student newspaper, yearbook, campus ministries, international student organization. **Organizations:** 26 registered organizations, 4 honor societies, 16 religious organizations. **Athletics (Intercollegiate):** *Men:* Baseball, basketball, cross-country, golf, soccer. *Women:* Basketball, cross-country, soccer, softball, volleyball. **On-Campus Highlights:** The Prince Student Union, The Chapel, The Cafeteria, The Quad, The Grove. **Environmental Initiatives:** The president has made a public commitment for the university to minimize its "mark" on the environment. Dialogue on how to best develop a university-wide environmental stewardship plan has begun. The university does have an Environmental Stewardship Committee with faculty, staff, and student representation. The university is in the process of finalizing a comprehensive environmental stewardship plan and has recent efforts to increase campus-wide recycling, and conversion of used vegetable oil into biodisel fuel.

ADMISSIONS

Freshman Academic Profile: Average high school GPA 3.27. 21% in top 10% of high school class, 47% in top 25% of high school class, 76% in top 50% of high school class. 77% from public high schools. SAT Math middle 50% range 470–590. SAT Critical Reading middle 50% range 470–570. ACT middle 50% range 19–25. Minimum paper TOEFL 500. Minimum computer TOEFL 173. **Basis for Candidate Selection:** *Very important factors considered include:* Academic GPA, standardized test scores. *Important factors considered include:* Recommendation(s), rigor of secondary school record. *Other factors considered include:* Application essay. **Freshman Admission Requirements:** High school diploma is required and GED is accepted. *Academic units required:* 2 foreign language. *Academic units recommended:* 4 English, 3 mathematics, 3 science, (3 science labs), 3 foreign language, 3 social studies, 1 visual/performing arts, 3 academic electives, 1 health and physical education. **Freshman Admission Statistics:** 875 applied, 72% admitted, 48% enrolled. **Transfer Admission Requirements:** High school transcript, college transcript(s), essay or personal statement, statement of good standing from prior institution(s). Minimum college GPA of 2.0 required. Lowest grade transferable C–. **General Admission Information:** Application fee $25. Regular application deadline 7/15. Notification on a rolling basis, beginning on or about 9/1. Nonfall registration accepted. Admission may be deferred for a maximum of 1 year. Credit offered for CEEB Advanced Placement tests.

COSTS AND FINANCIAL AID

Annual tuition $20,700. Room and board $6,180. Required fees $630. Average book expense $1,200. **Required Forms and Deadlines:** FAFSA, institution's own financial aid form. Priority financial aid filing date 3/15. **Notification of Awards:** Applicants will be notified of awards on a rolling basis beginning 3/15. **Types of Aid:** *Need-based scholarships/grants:* Federal Pell, SEOG, state scholarships/grants, private scholarships, the school's own gift aid. *Loans:* Direct Subsidized Stafford, Direct Unsubsidized Stafford, Direct PLUS. *Student Employment:* Federal Work-Study Program available. Institutional employment available. Highest amount earned per year from on-campus jobs $5,866. Off-campus job opportunities are good. **Financial Aid Statistics:** 89% freshmen, 66% undergrads receive need-based scholarship or grant aid. 15% freshmen, 10% undergrads receive non-need-based scholarship or grant aid. 82% freshmen, 63% undergrads receive need-based self-help aid. 4% freshmen, 3% undergrads receive athletic scholarships. 100% freshmen, 93% undergrads receive any aid. 85% undergrads borrow to pay for school. Average cumulative indebtedness $29,761. **Criteria for awarding institutional aid:** *Non-need-based:* Academics, athletics, minority status, music/drama, religious affiliation, state/district residency.

MOUNTAIN STATE UNIVERSITY

609 South Kanawha Street, Beckley, WV 25801
Phone: 304-929-4636 **Financial Aid Phone:** 304-929-1595
E-mail: gomsu@mountainstate.edu
Fax: 304-253-3463 **Website:** www.mountainstate.edu **ACT Code:** 4510

This private school was founded in 1933. It has a 24-acre campus.

RATINGS

Admissions Selectivity Rating: 63   **Fire Safety Rating:** 99   **Green Rating:** 68

STUDENTS AND FACULTY

Enrollment: 5,137. **Student Body:** 67% female, 33% male, 37.9% out-of-state, 5% international (56 countries represented). Asian 2%, African American 15%, Caucasian 62%, Hispanic 2%, Native American 1%. **Retention and Graduation:** 38% freshmen return for sophomore year. 3% freshmen graduate within 4 years. 15% grads go on to further study within 1 year. 5% grads pursue arts and sciences degrees. 2% grads pursue law degrees. 5% grads pursue business degrees. 2% grads pursue medical degrees. **Faculty:** Student/faculty ratio 14:1. 97 full-time faculty, 29% hold PhDs, 75% are members of minority groups, 71% are women.

ACADEMICS

Degrees: Associate, bachelor's, certificate, doctoral, master's, post-bachelor's certificate, post-master's certificate, terminal associate, transfer associate. **Classes:** Most classes have 10–19 students. Most lab/discussion sessions have fewer than 10 students. **Majors with Highest Enrollment:** Business, management, marketing, and related support services, other; human resources management and services, other; nursing/registered nurse (RN, ASN, BSN, MSN). **Special Study Options:** Accelerated program, cooperative education program,

cross-registration, distance learning, double major, dual enrollment, English as a Second Language (ESL), honors program, independent study, internships, liberal arts/career combination, student-designed major, weekend college. **Honors programs:** President's List and Dean's List Special programs offered to physically disabled students include note-taking services, reader services, tape recorders, tutors. **Career services:** Alumni network, career/job search classes, career assessment, internships. **Career services highlights include:** Internships/Practicum—Qualified bachelor's degree students have an opportunity to work directly in their field of concentration.

FACILITIES

Housing: Coed dorms, Off Campus Housing for Athletes. 80% of campus accessible to physically disabled. **Special Academic Facilities/Equipment:** Robert C. Byrd Learning Resources Center, Botanical Gardens and Greenhouse **Computers:** 90% of classrooms, 100% of libraries, 50% of dining areas, have wireless network access. Students can register for classes online. Administrative functions (other than registration) can be performed online.

CAMPUS LIFE

Environment: Village. **Activities:** Choral groups, drama/theater, literary magazine, music ensembles, pep band, student government, campus ministries, international student organization. **Organizations:** 24 registered organizations, 4 honor societies, 3 religious organizations. 1 fraternity, 1 sorority. **Athletics (Intercollegiate):** *Men:* Basketball, cross-country, soccer, track/field (outdoor). *Women:* cheerleading, cross-country, soccer, softball, track/field (outdoor), volleyball. **On-Campus Highlights:** Cougar Den, Learning Resources Center (LRC), John W. Eye Conference Center (JWE), Culinary Arts building, Hogan Hall, Medicinal Botanical Greenhouse.

ADMISSIONS

Freshman Academic Profile: Average high school GPA 3.02. 2% in top 10% of high school class, 14% in top 25% of high school class, 41% in top 50% of high school class. ACT middle 50% range 17–23. Minimum paper TOEFL 500. Minimum computer TOEFL 173. **Basis for Candidate Selection:** *Very important factors considered include:* Class rank, application essay, academic GPA, recommendation(s), rigor of secondary school record, standardized test scores, alumni/ae relation, character/personal qualities, extracurricular activities, first generation, geographical residence, interview, level of applicant's interest, racial/ethnic status, religious affiliation/commitment, state residency, talent/ability, volunteer work, work experience. **Freshman Admission Requirements:** High school diploma is required and GED is accepted. *Academic units required:* 4 English, 2 mathematics, 2 science, (2 science labs), 3 social studies. *Academic units recommended:* 4 English, 2 mathematics, 2 science, (2 science labs), 3 social studies, 2 history. **Freshman Admission Statistics:** 1,780 applied, 100% admitted, 43% enrolled. **Transfer Admission Requirements:** College transcript(s), Lowest grade transferable C. **General Admission Information:** Application fee $25. Nonfall registration accepted. Admission may be deferred for a maximum of One Semester. Credit offered for CEEB Advanced Placement tests.

COSTS AND FINANCIAL AID

Annual tuition $6,450. Required fees $2,250. Average book expense $1,300. **Required Forms and Deadlines:** FAFSA. Priority financial aid filing date 3/1. **Notification of Awards:** Applicants will be notified of awards on a rolling basis beginning 4/1. **Types of Aid:** *Need-based scholarships/grants:* Federal Pell, SEOG, state scholarships/grants, private scholarships, the school's own gift aid, Federal Nursing Scholarships. *Loans:* FFEL Subsidized Stafford, FFEL Unsubsidized Stafford, FFEL PLUS, Private Educational Loans. *Student Employment:* Federal Work-Study Program available. Institutional employment available. Highest amount earned per year from on-campus jobs $1,600. Off-campus job opportunities are good. **Financial Aid Statistics:** 26% freshmen, 35% undergrads receive need-based scholarship or grant aid. 1% freshmen, 31% freshmen, 46% undergrads receive need-based self-help aid. 2% freshmen, 2% undergrads receive athletic scholarships. 50% freshmen, 54% undergrads receive any aid. 81% undergrads borrow to pay for school. Average cumulative indebtedness $33,218. **Criteria for awarding institutional aid:** *Non-need-based:* Academics, athletics, state/district residency.

See page 1166.

MUHLENBERG COLLEGE

2400 West Chew Street, Allentown, PA 18104-5596
Phone: 484-664-3200 **Financial Aid Phone:** 484-664-3175
E-mail: admission@muhlenberg.edu **CEEB Code:** 2424
Fax: 484-664-3234 **Website:** www.muhlenberg.edu **ACT Code:** 3640

This private school, affiliated with the Lutheran Church, was founded in 1848. It has a 81-acre campus.

RATINGS
Admissions Selectivity Rating: 94   **Fire Safety Rating:** 87   **Green Rating:** 73

STUDENTS AND FACULTY
Enrollment: 2,411. **Student Body:** 58% female, 42% male, 71% out-of-state, international (5 countries represented). Asian 2%, African American 2%, Caucasian 88%, Hispanic 3%.
Retention and Graduation: 92% freshmen return for sophomore year. 79% freshmen graduate within 4 years. 30% grads go on to further study within 1 year. 25% grads pursue arts and sciences degrees. 5% grads pursue law degrees. 1% grads pursue business degrees. 8% grads pursue medical degrees. **Faculty:** Student/faculty ratio 12:1. 166 full-time faculty, 87% hold PhDs, 7% are are members of minority groups, 51% are women.

ACADEMICS
Degrees: Associate, bachelor's, certificate, transfer associate. **Classes:** Most classes have 10–19 students. Most lab/discussion sessions have 10–19 students. **Majors with Highest Enrollment:** Business/commerce; communication studies/speech communication and rhetoric; psychology. **Special Study Options:** Accelerated program, cross-registration, double major, exchange student program (domestic), honors program, independent study, internships, student-designed major, study abroad, teacher certification program. **Honors programs:** Muhlenberg Scholar, Dana Associate, R.J. Fellow (each provides a $4,000 annual stipend, dedicated freshman seminar, and mentored research). **Combined degree programs:** BA/MD, BA/DDS, BA/DDS University of Pennsylvania, BS/MD Drexel Un. Special programs offered to physically disabled students include note-taking services, tutors. **Career services:** Alumni network, alumni services, career/job search classes, career assessment, internships, regional alumni. **Career services highlights include:** The Muhlenberg Shadow Program matches students with alumni in their field of interest to spend a day on the job over winter break. Students are able to learn first-hand about career options of interest to them, and alumni enjoy the feeling of helping a student and remembering why they enjoy their jobs.

FACILITIES
Housing: Coed dorms, special housing for disabled students, special housing for international students, women's dorms, fraternity/sorority housing, apartments for single students, college-owned houses in the neighborhood surrounding the campus. 95% of campus accessible to physically disabled. **Special Academic Facilities/Equipment:** Martin art gallery, biology museum, Graver arboretum, greenhouse, mainstage theatre, recital hall, 20–foot boat for marine studies, 40–acre Raker environmental field station, two electron microscopes, dance studios, experimental theatres, proscenium theatres. **Computers:** 10% of classrooms, 20% of dorms, 100% of libraries, 100% of dining areas, 100% of student union, 10% of common outdoor areas have wireless network access. Students can register for classes online. Administrative functions (other than registration) can be performed online.

CAMPUS LIFE
Environment: City. **Activities:** concert band, dance, drama/theater, jazz band, literary magazine, music ensembles, musical theater, pep band, radio station, student government, student newspaper, student-run film society, symphony orchestra, yearbook. **Organizations:** 100 registered organizations, 12 honor societies, 7 religious organizations. 4 fraternities, 4 sororities. **Athletics (Intercollegiate):** *Men:* Baseball, basketball, cheerleading, cross-country, football, golf, lacrosse, soccer, tennis, track/field (outdoor), track/field (indoor), wrestling. *Women:* Basketball, cheerleading, cross-country, field hockey, golf, lacrosse, soccer, softball, tennis, track/field (outdoor), track/field (indoor), volleyball. **On-Campus Highlights:** Seegers Union by fireplace & Java Joe's, The Life Sports Center-Athletic Facility, Parents Plaza-Outdoor Courtyard, GQ, Seegers Union, Trexler Pavilion for Theatre & Dance. **Environmental Initiatives:** Measurement and evaluation of campus sustainability in progess. New constuction and renovations incorporating sustainable technology including enegy and water conservation and significant materials recycling. Energy conservation and greenhouse gas reduction plan is in progress, building on sub-meter installation and a recent enerty audit.

ADMISSIONS
Freshman Academic Profile: 41% in top 10% of high school class, 43% in top 25% of high school class, 96% in top 50% of high school class. 70% from public high schools. SAT Math middle 50% range 560–660. SAT Critical Reading middle 50% range 560–660. SAT Writing middle 50% range 560–660. ACT middle 50% range 25–31. Minimum paper TOEFL 550. Minimum computer TOEFL 213. **Basis for Candidate Selection:** *Very important factors considered include:* Academic GPA, rigor of secondary school record. *Important factors considered include:* Application essay, recommendation(s), standardized test scores, character/personal qualities, extracurricular activities, interview, talent/ability. *Other factors considered include:* Class rank, alumni/ae relation, first generation, level of applicant's interest, racial/ethnic status, volunteer work, work experience. **Freshman Admission Requirements:** High school diploma is required and GED is accepted. *Academic units required:* 4 English, 3 mathematics, 2 science, 2 foreign language, 2 history. *Academic units recommended:* 4 English, 4 mathematics, 3 science, 4 foreign language, 2 social studies, 3 history. **Freshman Admission Statistics:** 4,410 applied, 44% admitted, 31% enrolled. **Transfer Admission Requirements:** High school transcript, college transcript(s), essay or personal statement, interview, standardized test scores, statement of good standing from prior institution(s). Minimum college GPA of 2.5 required. Lowest grade transferable C. **General Admission Information:** Application fee $50. Early decision application deadline 2/1. Regular application deadline 2/15. Regular notification 4/1. Nonfall registration accepted. Admission may be deferred for a maximum of 1 year. Credit and/or placement offered for CEEB Advanced Placement tests.

COSTS AND FINANCIAL AID
Required Forms and Deadlines: FAFSA, institution's own financial aid form, CSS/Financial Aid PROFILE, noncustodial PROFILE Financial aid filing deadline 2/15. Priority financial aid filing date 2/15. **Notification of Awards:** Applicants will be notified of awards on or about 4/1. **Types of Aid:** *Need-based scholarships/grants:* Federal Pell, SEOG, state scholarships/grants, private scholarships, the school's own gift aid. *Loans:* FFEL Subsidized Stafford, FFEL Unsubsidized Stafford, FFEL PLUS, Federal Perkins, Private. *Student Employment:* Federal Work-Study Program available. Institutional employment available. Highest amount earned per year from on-campus jobs $1,800. Off-campus job opportunities are excellent. **Financial Aid Statistics:** 46% freshmen, 46% undergrads receive need-based scholarship or grant aid. 13% freshmen, 9% undergrads receive non-need-based scholarship or grant aid. 34% freshmen, 37% undergrads receive need-based self-help aid. 80% freshmen, 79.2% undergrads receive any aid. **Criteria for awarding institutional aid:** *Non-need-based:* Academics, art, leadership, music/drama.

MULTNOMAH UNIVERSITY

8435 NE Glisan Street, Portland, OR 97220-5898
Phone: 503-251-6485 **Financial Aid Phone:** 503-251-5335
E-mail: admiss@multnomah.edu
Fax: 503-254-1268 **Website:** www.multnomah.edu

This private school, affiliated with the Christian (Nondenominational) Church, was founded in 1936. It has a 25-acre campus.

RATINGS
Admissions Selectivity Rating: 79   **Fire Safety Rating:** 60*   **Green Rating:** 60*

STUDENTS AND FACULTY
Enrollment: 578. **Student Body:** 42% female, 58% male, 55.4% out-of-state, 1% international (15 countries represented). Asian 3%, African American 1%, Caucasian 72%, Hispanic 2%, Native American 1%.
Retention and Graduation: 27% freshmen graduate within 4 years. **Faculty:** Student/faculty ratio 13:1. 27 full-time faculty, 67% hold PhDs, 22% are women.

ACADEMICS
Degrees: Bachelor's, master's, post-bachelor's certificate. **Classes:** Most classes have fewer than 10 students. Most lab/discussion sessions have 10–19 students. **Majors with Highest Enrollment:** Bible/biblical studies. **Special Study Options:** Cooperative education program, distance learning, double major, internships, liberal arts/career combination, teacher certification program. **Career services:** Career/job search classes, career assessment.

FACILITIES
Housing: Special housing for disabled students, men's dorms, women's dorms, apartments for married students, apartments for single students, houses for

students with spouses or dependents. **Computers:** 100% of classrooms, 100% of dorms, 100% of libraries, 100% of dining areas, 30% of common outdoor areas have wireless network access. Students can register for classes online. Administrative functions (other than registration) can be performed online.

CAMPUS LIFE
Environment: Metropolis. **Activities:** Choral groups, drama/theater, music ensembles, student government, student newspaper. **Athletics (Intercollegiate):** *Men:* Basketball. *Women:* volleyball. **On-Campus Highlights:** Solid Rock Cafe, A-Frame Community Lounge, STUGO Game Room, Cafeteria, Commuter Lounge, The Solid Rock Cafe, STUGO Game Room and cafeteria are all centrally located in our JCA Student Center along with a computer lab, post-office, and health center.

ADMISSIONS
Freshman Academic Profile: Average high school GPA 3.228. 27% in top 10% of high school class, 50% in top 25% of high school class, 85% in top 50% of high school class. SAT Math middle 50% range 450–590. SAT Critical Reading middle 50% range 530–620. SAT Writing middle 50% range 470–610. ACT middle 50% range 19–27. Minimum paper TOEFL 550. Minimum computer TOEFL 213. **Basis for Candidate Selection:** *Very important factors considered include:* Academic GPA, recommendation(s), rigor of secondary school record, standardized test scores, religious affiliation/commitment. *Important factors considered include:* Application essay, character/personal qualities. *Other factors considered include:* Class rank, alumni/ae relation, extracurricular activities, talent/ability, volunteer work, work experience. **Freshman Admission Requirements:** High school diploma is required and GED is accepted. *Academic units recommended:* 4 English, 2 mathematics, 3 science, (1 science labs), 2 foreign language, 3 social studies, 2 history. **Freshman Admission Statistics:** 134 applied, 87% admitted, 53% enrolled. **Transfer Admission Requirements:** College transcript(s), essay or personal statement, statement of good standing from prior institution(s). Minimum college GPA of 2.0 required. Lowest grade transferable C–. **General Admission Information:** Application fee $40. Regular application deadline 7/15. Notification on a rolling basis, beginning on or about 9/1. Nonfall registration accepted. Admission may be deferred for a maximum of one semester. Credit offered for CEEB Advanced Placement tests.

COSTS AND FINANCIAL AID
Annual tuition $14,520. Room and board $6,150. Average book expense $1,000. **Required Forms and Deadlines:** FAFSA, institution's own financial aid form. Financial aid filing deadline 7/1. Priority financial aid filing date 3/1. **Notification of Awards:** Applicants will be notified of awards on a rolling basis beginning 4/1. **Types of Aid:** *Need-based scholarships/grants:* Federal Pell, SEOG, private scholarships, the school's own gift aid. *Loans:* Direct Subsidized Stafford, FFEL Subsidized Stafford, FFEL Unsubsidized Stafford, FFEL PLUS. *Student Employment:* Federal Work-Study Program available. Institutional employment available. Off-campus job opportunities are good. **Financial Aid Statistics:** 75% freshmen, 77% undergrads receive need-based scholarship or grant aid. 4% freshmen, 3% undergrads receive non-need-based scholarship or grant aid. 65% freshmen, 76% undergrads receive need-based self-help aid. 48% freshmen, 89% undergrads receive any aid. **Criteria for awarding institutional aid:** *Non-need-based:* Academics, alumni affiliation, leadership, music/drama.

MURRAY STATE UNIVERSITY

113 Sparks Hall, Murray, KY 42071-0009
Phone: 270-809-3741 **Financial Aid Phone:** 270-809-2546
E-mail: Admissions@murraystate.edu **CEEB Code:** 1494
Fax: 270-809-3780 **Website:** www.murraystate.edu **ACT Code:** 1532

This public school was founded in 1922. It has a 350-acre campus.

RATINGS
Admissions Selectivity Rating: 83   **Fire Safety Rating:** 82   **Green Rating:** 74

STUDENTS AND FACULTY
Enrollment: 7,661. **Student Body:** 58% female, 42% male, 27% out-of-state, 2% international (46 countries represented). Asian 1%, African American 6%, Caucasian 85%, Hispanic 1%.
Retention and Graduation: 72% freshmen return for sophomore year. 33% freshmen graduate within 4 years. **Faculty:** Student/faculty ratio 16:1. 406 full-time faculty, 77% hold PhDs, 13% are are members of minority groups, 41% are women.

ACADEMICS
Degrees: Associate, bachelor's, master's, post-master's certificate. **Classes:** Most classes have fewer than 10 students. Most lab/discussion sessions have

10–19 students. **Majors with Highest Enrollment:** Business/commerce; elementary education and teaching; nursing/registered nurse (RN, ASN, BSN, MSN). **Special Study Options:** Accelerated program, cooperative education program, cross-registration, distance learning, double major, dual enrollment, English as a Second Language (ESL), exchange student program (domestic), external degree program, honors program, independent study, internships, study abroad, teacher certification program, weekend college, agriculture, arts, business/marketing, biological sciences, communications/communication technologies, computer and information sciences, education, engineering/engineering technologies, English, foreign languages, health professions and related sciences, history, home economics, humanities and liberal arts, library sciences, mathematics, natural resources and environmental sciences, natural sciences, parks and recreation, philosophy, physical sciences, protective sciences/public administration, psychology, social/behavioral sciences, technologies, trade and industry, visual and performing arts. **Honors programs:** The Honors Program offers a unique educational experience designed to teach able students how to learn, how to think critically and creatively, and how to communicate effectively. **Combined degree programs:** Engineering program w/ U of L. and U. of Ky. Special programs offered to physically disabled students include note-taking services, tape recorders, tutors. **Career services:** Alumni network, alumni services, career/job search classes, career assessment, internships, regional alumni.

FACILITIES
Housing: Coed dorms, special housing for disabled students, men's dorms, women's dorms, fraternity/sorority housing, apartments for married students, apartments for single students. All housing is operated under a Residential College system. 96% of campus accessible to physically disabled. **Special Academic Facilities/Equipment:** State-of-the-art 73,000 square-foot Student Recreation and Wellness Center nestled in the Residential College housing complex, West Kentucky Museum, 8,500–seat Regional Special Events Center **Computers:** 95% of classrooms, 90% of dorms, 100% of libraries, 100% of dining areas, 100% of student union, have wireless network access. Students can register for classes online. Administrative functions (other than registration) can be performed online.

CAMPUS LIFE
Environment: Village. **Activities:** Choral groups, concert band, dance, drama/theater, jazz band, literary magazine, marching band, music ensembles, musical theater, pep band, radio station, student government, student newspaper, student-run film society, symphony orchestra, television station, yearbook, campus ministries, international student organization. **Organizations:** 175 registered organizations, 30 honor societies, 15 religious organizations. 15 fraternities, 7 sororities. **Athletics (Intercollegiate):** *Men:* Baseball, basketball, bowling, cheerleading, cross-country, equestrian sports, football, golf, horseback riding, riflery, rodeo, tennis. *Women:* Basketball, cheerleading, cross-country, equestrian sports, golf, horseback riding, riflery, rodeo, soccer, softball, tennis, track/field (outdoor), volleyball. **On-Campus Highlights:** New Student Fitness Center, Curris Student Center, Regional Special Events Center, Equine Center, Residential Colleges. **Environmental Initiatives:** Guaranteed Energy performance contracting.6.5 Million Contract Renewable Fuels, BioDiesel, g-35, e-10 Recycling Program Diverting 40% of waste stream from landfill.

ADMISSIONS
Freshman Academic Profile: Average high school GPA 3.53. 27% in top 10% of high school class, 64% in top 25% of high school class, 97% in top 50% of high school class. 80% from public high schools. ACT middle 50% range 21–25. Minimum paper TOEFL 500. Minimum computer TOEFL 173. **Basis for Candidate Selection:** *Very important factors considered include:* Class rank, academic GPA, rigor of secondary school record, standardized test scores. *Important factors considered include:* Alumni/ae relation, talent/ability. *Other factors considered include:* character/personal qualities, extracurricular activities, geographical residence, interview, racial/ethnic status, state residency, volunteer work, work experience. **Freshman Admission Requirements:** High school diploma is required and GED is accepted. *Academic units required:* 4 English, 3 mathematics, 3 science, (1 science labs), 2 foreign language, 3 social studies, 5 academic electives, 2 art appreciation, .5 P.E., .5 health. *Academic units recommended:* 4 mathematics, 4 science. **Freshman Admission Statistics:** 4,233 applied, 73% admitted, 45% enrolled. **Transfer Admission Requirements:** College transcript(s), statement of good standing from prior institution(s). Minimum college GPA of 2.0 required. Lowest grade transferable D. **General Admission Information:** Application fee $30. Regular application deadline 8/3. Nonfall registration accepted. Admission may be deferred for a maximum of 1 year. Credit offered for CEEB Advanced Placement tests.

COSTS AND FINANCIAL AID
Annual in-state tuition $5,130. Annual out-of-state tuition $8,006. Room and board $6,562. Required fees $846. Average book expense $990. **Required Forms and Deadlines:** FAFSA, institution's own financial aid form. Priority financial aid filing date 4/1. **Notification of Awards:** Applicants will be notified of awards on a rolling basis beginning 4/15. **Types of Aid:** *Need-based scholar-*

ships/grants: Federal Pell, SEOG, state scholarships/grants, private scholarships, the school's own gift aid, Federal Nursing Scholarships. A wide variety of private and Foundation scholarships available. Check out the website www.murraystate.edu. *Loans:* Direct Subsidized Stafford, Direct Unsubsidized Stafford, Direct PLUS, FFEL Subsidized Stafford, FFEL Unsubsidized Stafford, FFEL PLUS, Federal Perkins, Federal Nursing, state loans, college/university loans from institutional funds. *Student Employment:* Federal Work-Study Program available. Institutional employment available. Highest amount earned per year from on-campus jobs $3,500. Off-campus job opportunities are good. **Financial Aid Statistics:** 57% freshmen, 38% undergrads receive need-based scholarship or grant aid. 33% freshmen, 28% undergrads receive non-need-based scholarship or grant aid. 32% freshmen, 54% undergrads receive need-based self-help aid. 3% freshmen, 4% undergrads receive athletic scholarships. 83% freshmen, 75% undergrads receive any aid. 51% undergrads borrow to pay for school. Average cumulative indebtedness $18,000. **Criteria for awarding institutional aid:** *Non-need-based:* Academics, alumni affiliation, art, athletics, job skills, leadership, minority status, music/drama, state/district residency.

MUSICIANS INSTITUTE

1655 McCadden Place, Hollywood, CA 90028
Phone: 323-462-1384 **Financial Aid Phone:** 323-462-1121
E-mail: admissions@mi.edu
Fax: 323-462-6978

This private school was founded in 1977.

RATINGS
Admissions Selectivity Rating: 60*   **Fire Safety Rating:** 60*   **Green Rating:** 60*

STUDENTS AND FACULTY
Enrollment: 489. **Student Body:** 14% female, 86% male, 26% out-of-state, international Asian 11%, African American 7%, Caucasian 56%, Hispanic 12%. **Retention and Graduation: Faculty:** 69 full-time faculty, 14% are are members of minority groups, 16% are women.

ACADEMICS
Degrees: Associate, bachelor's, certificate. **Majors with Highest Enrollment:** General studies; multi-/interdisciplinary studies, other. **Career services:** Alumni network, internships.

FACILITIES
Housing: Musicians Institute's Housing Services department assists students and their parents in locating safe, comfortable, affordable, and accessible off-campus housing. MI does not own or operate student housing, but Housing Services manages a vacancy listing service for housing in a variety of locations ad difference price levels.

CAMPUS LIFE
Environment: Metropolis.

ADMISSIONS
Basis for Candidate Selection: *Very important factors considered include:* level of applicant's interest, talent/ability. *Important factors considered include:* Recommendation(s), character/personal qualities, extracurricular activities, interview, work experience. *Other factors considered include:* Class rank, application essay, academic GPA, rigor of secondary school record, standardized test scores, alumni/ae relation, first generation, volunteer work. **Freshman Admission Requirements:** High school diploma is required and GED is accepted. **Freshman Admission Statistics:** 1,057 applied, 98% admitted, 64% enrolled. **Transfer Admission Requirements:** College transcript(s), essay or personal statement, minimum college GPA of 2.0 required. Lowest grade transferable C. **General Admission Information:** Application fee $100. Notification on a rolling basis, beginning on or about 10/1. Nonfall registration accepted. Admission may be deferred for a maximum of 1 year.

COSTS AND FINANCIAL AID
Annual tuition $15,250. Required fees $400. **Required Forms and Deadlines:** FAFSA **Types of Aid:** *Need-based scholarships/grants:* Federal Pell, SEOG, state scholarships/grants, private scholarships *Loans:* FFEL Subsidized Stafford, FFEL Unsubsidized Stafford, FFEL PLUS, alternative loans. *Student Employment:* **Financial Aid Statistics:** 11% freshmen, 21% undergrads receive need-based scholarship or grant aid. 7% freshmen, 17% undergrads receive need-based self-help aid. 25% undergrads borrow to pay for school.

MUSKINGUM COLLEGE

163 Stormont Street, New Concord, OH 43762
Phone: 740-826-8137 **Financial Aid Phone:** 740-826-8137
E-mail: jzellers@muskingum.edu **CEEB Code:** 1496
Fax: 614-826-8100 **ACT Code:** 3305

This private school, affiliated with the Presbyterian Church, was founded in 1837. It has a 245-acre campus.

RATINGS
Admissions Selectivity Rating: 77   **Fire Safety Rating:** 60*   **Green Rating:** 60*

STUDENTS AND FACULTY
Enrollment: 1,655. **Student Body:** 52% female, 48% male, 11% out-of-state, 1% international (11 countries represented). Asian 1%, African American 5%, Caucasian 87%, Hispanic 1%. **Retention and Graduation:** 67% freshmen return for sophomore year. 38% freshmen graduate within 4 years. 20% grads go on to further study within 1 year. 4% grads pursue arts and sciences degrees. 2% grads pursue law degrees. 4% grads pursue business degrees. 2% grads pursue medical degrees. **Faculty:** Student/faculty ratio 16:1. 102 full-time faculty, 93% hold PhDs, 6% are are members of minority groups, 41% are women.

ACADEMICS
Degrees: Bachelor's, master's. **Classes:** Most classes have fewer than 10 students. Most lab/discussion sessions have 20–29 students. **Majors with Highest Enrollment:** Business/commerce; early childhood education and teaching; psychology. **Special Study Options:** Accelerated program, distance learning, double major, dual enrollment, English as a Second Language (ESL), exchange student program (domestic), independent study, internships, liberal arts/career combination, student-designed major, study abroad, teacher certification program, weekend college. **Combined degree programs:** BA/MEng, BA,BS,MAE. Special programs offered to physically disabled students include note-taking services, reader services, tape recorders, tutors. **Career services:** Alumni network, alumni services, career assessment, internships, regional alumni. **Career services highlights include:** Muskingum Leadership Initiative—alumni identify relevant national and regional internships and communicate those opportunities to Muskingum students and faculty.

FACILITIES
Housing: Coed dorms, men's dorms, women's dorms, fraternity/sorority housing, cooperative housing, apartments for single students, theme housing 50% of campus accessible to physically disabled. **Special Academic Facilities/Equipment:** Art gallery, on-campus nursery school, electron microscope, 57-acre biology field station and mobile biology lab. **Computers:** 15% of classrooms, 100% of libraries, 33% of dining areas, 100% of student union, 10% of common outdoor areas have wireless network access. Students can register for classes online. Administrative functions (other than registration) can be performed online.

CAMPUS LIFE
Environment: Rural. **Activities:** Choral groups, concert band, dance, drama/theater, jazz band, literary magazine, marching band, music ensembles, musical theater, pep band, radio station, student government, student newspaper, symphony orchestra, television station, yearbook, campus ministries, international student organization, Model UN. **Organizations:** 95 registered organizations, 16 honor societies, 4 religious organizations. 5 fraternities, 5 sororities. **Athletics (Intercollegiate):** *Men:* Baseball, basketball, cheerleading, cross-country, football, golf, soccer, tennis, track/field (outdoor), track/field (indoor), wrestling. *Women:* Basketball, cheerleading, cross-country, golf, soccer, softball, tennis, track/field (outdoor), track/field (indoor), volleyball. **On-Campus Highlights:** Philip and Betsey Caldwell Hall, Boyd Science Center, Rec Center, Patton Dining Center/ Kelly Coffee House, Walter K. Chess Student Center, New music classroom building opening Fall 2010.

ADMISSIONS
Freshman Academic Profile: Average high school GPA 3.2. 24% in top 10% of high school class, 49% in top 25% of high school class, 76% in top 50% of high school class. 90% from public high schools. SAT Math middle 50% range 480–590. SAT Critical Reading middle 50% range 460–580. SAT Writing middle 50% range 450–590. ACT middle 50% range 19–25. Minimum paper TOEFL 550. Minimum computer TOEFL 213. **Basis for Candidate Selection:** *Very important factors considered include:* Academic GPA, rigor of secondary school record. *Important factors considered include:* Class rank, recommendation(s), standardized test scores. *Other factors considered include:* Application essay, alumni/ae relation, character/personal qualities, extracurricular activities, geographical residence, interview, racial/ethnic status, talent/ability, work experience. **Freshman Admission Requirements:** High school diploma is required and GED is accepted. *Academic units required:* 4 English, 2 mathematics, 2

science, (1 science labs), 2 foreign language, 1 social studies, 2 history. *Academic units recommended:* 4 English, 3 mathematics, 3 science, (2 science labs), 2 foreign language, 1 social studies, 2 history. **Freshman Admission Statistics:** 2,051 applied, 78% admitted, 30% enrolled. **Transfer Admission Requirements:** High school transcript, college transcript(s), minimum college GPA of 2.0 required. Lowest grade transferable C. **General Admission Information:** Regular application deadline 8/1. Notification on a rolling basis, beginning on or about 10/1. Nonfall registration accepted. Admission may be deferred for a maximum of 1 year. Credit and/or placement offered for CEEB Advanced Placement tests.

COSTS AND FINANCIAL AID

Annual tuition $19,190. Room and board $7,740. Required fees $690. Average book expense $1,000. **Required Forms and Deadlines:** FAFSA. Financial aid filing deadline 8/1. Priority financial aid filing date 3/15. **Notification of Awards:** Applicants will be notified of awards on a rolling basis beginning 3/1. **Types of Aid:** *Need-based scholarships/grants:* Federal Pell, SEOG, state scholarships/grants, private scholarships, the school's own gift aid. *Loans:* FFEL Subsidized Stafford, FFEL Unsubsidized Stafford, FFEL PLUS, Federal Perkins, college/university loans from institutional funds. *Student Employment:* Federal Work-Study Program available. Institutional employment available. Highest amount earned per year from on-campus jobs $1,500. Off-campus job opportunities are fair. **Financial Aid Statistics:** 83% freshmen, 78% undergrads receive need-based scholarship or grant aid. 68% freshmen, 68% undergrads receive non-need-based scholarship or grant aid. 70% freshmen, 66% undergrads receive need-based self-help aid. 98% freshmen, 98% undergrads receive any aid. 80% undergrads borrow to pay for school. Average cumulative indebtedness $23,405. **Criteria for awarding institutional aid:** *Non-need-based:* Academics, alumni affiliation, art, leadership, minority status, music/drama, religious affiliation, state/district residency.

NAROPA UNIVERSITY

2130 Araphahoe Avenue, Boulder, CO 80302
Phone: 303-546-3572 **Financial Aid Phone:** 303-546-3534
E-mail: admissions@naropa.edu **CEEB Code:** 908
Fax: 303-546-3583 **Website:** www.naropa.edu **ACT Code:** 4853

This private school was founded in 1974. It has a 12-acre campus.

RATINGS
Admissions Selectivity Rating: 60* **Fire Safety Rating:** 60* **Green Rating:** 96

STUDENTS AND FACULTY
Enrollment: 464. **Student Body:** 61% female, 39% male, 74% out-of-state, 3% international (24 countries represented). Asian 3%, African American 2%, Caucasian 75%, Hispanic 4%, Native American 3%.
Retention and Graduation: 64% freshmen return for sophomore year. 19% freshmen graduate within 4 years. **Faculty:** Student/faculty ratio 9:1. 51 full-time faculty, 51% hold PhDs, 12% are are members of minority groups, 57% are women.

ACADEMICS
Degrees: Bachelor's, certificate, first professional, master's. **Classes:** Most classes have 10–19 students. **Majors with Highest Enrollment:** English language and literature; psychology; visual and performing arts. **Special Study Options:** Double major, independent study, internships, student-designed major, study abroad, Some courses available on-line. Special programs offered to physically disabled students include note-taking services, reader services, tape recorders, tutors.

FACILITIES
Housing: Apartments for married students, apartments for single students, themed housing (living and learning concept). 85% of campus accessible to physically disabled. **Special Academic Facilities/Equipment:** Maitri Rooms, meditation halls, Allen Ginsberg library and a preschool. **Computers:** 100% of classrooms, 100% of dorms, 100% of libraries, 100% of dining areas, 100% of student union, 100% of common outdoor areas have wireless network access. Students can register for classes online. Administrative functions (other than registration) can be performed online.

CAMPUS LIFE
Environment: City. **Activities:** Choral groups, dance, drama/theater, jazz band, literary magazine, music ensembles, student government **Organizations:** 20 registered organizations, 2 religious organizations. **On-Campus Highlights:** Lincoln Building, Nalanda Event Center, Meditation Hall, Naropa Cafe, Visual Arts Studio. **Environmental Initiatives:** We compost all of our paper towels in public restrooms diverting 25% of our landfill waste into compost. The cafe composts which will divert 20–25% of organics into compost from the landfill.

CFL installed in the residential halls, and are converting burned out bulbs to green bulbs throughout the campuses.

ADMISSIONS
Freshman Academic Profile: Average high school GPA 3.026. Minimum paper TOEFL 550. Minimum computer TOEFL 213. **Basis for Candidate Selection:** *Very important factors considered include:* Application essay, academic GPA, recommendation(s), rigor of secondary school record, interview. *Important factors considered include:* Character/personal qualities, extracurricular activities, talent/ability, volunteer work. *Other factors considered include:* Alumni/ae relation, first generation, racial/ethnic status, work experience. **Freshman Admission Requirements:** High school diploma is required and GED is accepted. *Academic units recommended:* 4 English, 3 mathematics, 3 science, (2 science labs), 3 foreign language, 3 social studies, 3 history, 2 academic electives, 2 Art/Dance/Theatre and/or Creative Writing **Freshman Admission Statistics:** 139 applied, 93% admitted, 53% enrolled. **Transfer Admission Requirements:** College transcript(s), essay or personal statement, interview, Lowest grade transferable C. **General Admission Information:** Application fee $50. Nonfall registration accepted. Admission may be deferred for a maximum of 1 year. Credit and/or placement offered for CEEB Advanced Placement tests.

COSTS AND FINANCIAL AID
Annual tuition $23,420. Room and board $8,478. Required fees $100. Average book expense $1,200. **Required Forms and Deadlines:** FAFSA. Priority financial aid filing date 3/1. **Notification of Awards:** Applicants will be notified of awards on a rolling basis beginning 3/1. **Types of Aid:** *Need-based scholarships/grants:* Federal Pell, SEOG, private scholarships, the school's own gift aid. *Loans:* FFEL Subsidized Stafford, FFEL Unsubsidized Stafford, FFEL PLUS, Federal Perkins. *Student Employment:* Federal Work-Study Program available. Off-campus job opportunities are good. **Financial Aid Statistics:** 62% freshmen, 62% undergrads receive need-based scholarship or grant aid. 67% freshmen, 64% undergrads receive need-based self-help aid. 71% freshmen, 71% undergrads receive any aid. 7% undergrads borrow to pay for school. Average cumulative indebtedness $26,582.

See page 1168.

NATIONAL AMERICAN UNVERSITY (NM)

4775 Indian School Rd, NE, Albuquerque, NM 87110
Phone: 505-348-3700
E-mail: NPointer@national.edu
Fax: 505-348-3705

This proprietary school was founded in 1941. It has a 15-acre campus.

RATINGS
Admissions Selectivity Rating: 60* **Fire Safety Rating:** 60* **Green Rating:** 60*

STUDENTS AND FACULTY
Enrollment: 611. **Student Body:** 42% female, 58% male, 1% international (2 countries represented). Asian 2%, African American 5%, Caucasian 42%, Hispanic 38%, Native American 6%.
Retention and Graduation: 5% grads go on to further study within 1 year. 1% grads pursue law degrees. 5% grads pursue business degrees. **Faculty:** Student/faculty ratio 10:1. 6 full-time faculty, 33% hold PhDs, 50% are women.

ACADEMICS
Degrees: Associate, bachelor's, master's. **Classes:** Most classes have fewer than 10 students. **Majors with Highest Enrollment:** accounting; business/commerce; information technology. **Special Study Options:** Accelerated program, cooperative education program, distance learning, double major, dual enrollment, independent study, weekend college. **Career services:** Alumni network, career/job search classes, internships.

FACILITIES
Housing: 100% of campus accessible to physically disabled. **Computers:** Students can register for classes online. Administrative functions (other than registration) can be performed online.

CAMPUS LIFE
Environment: Metropolis. **Activities:** Student government **Organizations:** 1 registered organizations, 1 honor societies.

ADMISSIONS
Freshman Academic Profile: 99% from public high schools. Minimum paper TOEFL 500. Minimum computer TOEFL 173. **Freshman Admission Requirements:** High school diploma is required and GED is accepted. **Fresh-**

man **Admission Statistics: Transfer Admission Requirements:** High school transcript, college transcript(s), Lowest grade transferable C. **General Admission Information:** Application fee $25. Regular application deadline 9/13. Nonfall registration accepted. Admission may be deferred for a maximum of 12.

COSTS AND FINANCIAL AID

Annual tuition $8,100. Required fees $315. **Required Forms and Deadlines: Types of Aid:** *Need-based scholarships/grants:* Federal Pell, SEOG, state scholarships/grants, private scholarships, the school's own gift aid. *Loans:* Direct Subsidized Stafford, Direct Unsubsidized Stafford, Direct PLUS, FFEL Subsidized Stafford, FFEL Unsubsidized Stafford, FFEL PLUS, Federal Perkins, state loans, college/university loans from institutional funds. *Student Employment:* Federal Work-Study Program available. Institutional employment available. Off-campus job opportunities are good.

NATIONAL UNIVERSITY

11255 North Torrey Pinos Road, La Jolla, CA 92037
Phone: 858-642-8180
E-mail: advisor@nu.edu **CEEB Code:** 4557
Fax: 858-642-8710 **Website:** www.nu.edu **ACT Code:** 20015

This private school was founded in 1971.

RATINGS
Admissions Selectivity Rating: 60*   **Fire Safety Rating:** 60*   **Green Rating:** 60*

STUDENTS AND FACULTY
Enrollment: 4,776. **Student Body:** 57% female, 43% male, 1% international Asian 9%, African American 13%, Caucasian 52%, Hispanic 18%, Native American 1%.
Retention and Graduation: 40% freshmen return for sophomore year. **Faculty:** Student/faculty ratio 16:1. 151 full-time faculty, 87% hold PhDs, 19% are are members of minority groups, 42% are women.

ACADEMICS
Degrees: Associate, bachelor's, certificate, diploma, master's, post-bachelor's certificate, terminal associate, transfer associate. **Classes:** Most classes have 10–19 students. **Majors with Highest Enrollment:** criminal justice/law enforcement administration; multi-/interdisciplinary studies, other. **Special Study Options:** Accelerated program, distance learning, double major, dual enrollment, English as a Second Language (ESL), teacher certification program, extensive online offerings are available. Special programs offered to physically disabled students include note-taking services, reader services, tutors. **Career services:** Career assessment, regional alumni.

FACILITIES
Housing: 100% of campus accessible to physically disabled. **Computers:** Students can register for classes online. Administrative functions (other than registration) can be performed online.

CAMPUS LIFE
Activities: Literary magazine.

ADMISSIONS
Freshman Academic Profile: Minimum paper TOEFL 525. Minimum computer TOEFL 197. **Basis for Candidate Selection:** *Important factors considered include:* Interview, work experience. *Other factors considered include:* Application essay, extracurricular activities. **Freshman Admission Requirements:** High school diploma is required and GED is accepted. **Freshman Admission Statistics:** 156 applied, 100% admitted, 36% enrolled. **General Admission Information:** Application fee $60. Nonfall registration accepted. Admission may be deferred for a maximum of 1 year. Neither credit nor placement offered for CEEB Advanced Placement tests.

COSTS AND FINANCIAL AID
Annual tuition $7,965. Required fees $60. **Required Forms and Deadlines:** FAFSA, institution's own financial aid form, state aid form. **Types of Aid:** *Need-based scholarships/grants:* Federal Pell, SEOG, state scholarships/grants, private scholarships, the school's own gift aid. *Loans:* Direct Subsidized Stafford, Direct Unsubsidized Stafford, FFEL Subsidized Stafford, FFEL Unsubsidized Stafford, FFEL PLUS, Federal Perkins. *Student Employment:* Institutional employment available. Off-campus job opportunities are good. **Financial Aid Statistics:** 65% undergrads borrow to pay for school. Average cumulative indebtedness $20,000.

NATIONAL UNIVERSITY OF HEALTH SCIENCES

200 E. Roosevelt Road, Lombard, IL 60148
Phone: 630-889-6566 **Financial Aid Phone:** 630-889-6700
E-mail: admissions@nuhs.edu
Fax: 630-889-6554 **Website:** www.nuhs.edu

This private school was founded in 1906. It has a 32-acre campus.

RATINGS
Admissions Selectivity Rating: 60*   **Fire Safety Rating:** 60*   **Green Rating:** 60*

STUDENTS AND FACULTY
Enrollment: 74. **Student Body:** 16% female, 84% male, 70% out-of-state, 9% international (9 countries represented). Asian 11%, African American 35%, Caucasian 141%, Hispanic 11%.
Retention and Graduation: 90% freshmen return for sophomore year. **Faculty:** Student/faculty ratio 6:1. 46 full-time faculty, 93% hold PhDs, 17% are women.

ACADEMICS
Degrees: Bachelor's, certificate, master's. **Classes:** Most classes have 40–49 students. Most lab/discussion sessions have 20–29 students. **Majors with Highest Enrollment:** Biomedical sciences; massage therapy/therapeutic massage. **Special Study Options:** Internships, accelerated science prerequisite program. **Combined degree programs:** BS/DC.

FACILITIES
Housing: Coed dorms, men's dorms, women's dorms, apartments for married students, apartments for single students, Studio apartments. **Special Academic Facilities/Equipment:** Museum, Fitness Center, Learning Resource Center, Health Care Clinic. **Computers:** 88% of classrooms, 100% of libraries, 100% of common outdoor areas have wireless network access. Students can register for classes online.

CAMPUS LIFE
Environment: Town. **Activities:** student government, student newspaper, yearbook. **Organizations:** 24 registered organizations, 1 religious organizations. 2 fraternities, 1 sorority. **On-Campus Highlights:** Janse Hall, Student Center, Clinic, Learning Resource Center, Dormitories.

ADMISSIONS
Freshman Academic Profile: Minimum paper TOEFL 550. Minimum computer TOEFL 213. Minimum web-based TOEFL 79. **Basis for Candidate Selection: Freshman Admission Requirements:** High school diploma is required and GED is accepted. **Freshman Admission Statistics: Transfer Admission Requirements:** College transcript(s), statement of good standing from prior institution(s). Minimum college GPA of 2.5 required. Lowest grade transferable C. **General Admission Information:** Application fee $55. Nonfall registration accepted. Credit offered for CEEB Advanced Placement tests.

COSTS AND FINANCIAL AID
Types of Aid: *Need-based scholarships/grants:* Federal Pell, SEOG, state scholarships/grants, private scholarships, the school's own gift aid. *Loans:* FFEL Subsidized Stafford, FFEL Unsubsidized Stafford, FFEL PLUS, Federal Perkins. *Student Employment:* Federal Work-Study Program available. Institutional employment available. Off-campus job opportunities are excellent.

NAZARETH COLLEGE

4245 East Avenue, Rochester, NY 14618-3790
Phone: 585-389-2860 **Financial Aid Phone:** 585-389-2310
E-mail: admissions@naz.edu **CEEB Code:** 2511
Fax: 585-389-2826 **Website:** www.naz.edu **ACT Code:** 2826

This private school was founded in 1924. It has a 150-acre campus.

RATINGS
Admissions Selectivity Rating: 84   **Fire Safety Rating:** 60*   **Green Rating:** 60*

STUDENTS AND FACULTY

Enrollment: 2,144. **Student Body:** 76% female, 24% male, 6% out-of-state, 1% international (13 countries represented). Asian 2%, African American 5%, Caucasian 83%, Hispanic 3%.
Retention and Graduation: 81% freshmen return for sophomore year. 60% freshmen graduate within 4 years. **Faculty:** Student/faculty ratio 12:1. 155 full-time faculty, 88% hold PhDs, 14% are are members of minority groups, 61% are women.

ACADEMICS

Degrees: Bachelor's, master's, post-master's certificate. **Classes:** Most classes have 10–19 students. Most lab/discussion sessions have 10–19 students. **Majors with Highest Enrollment:** Business administration, management and operations, other; education; physical therapy/therapist. **Special Study Options:** Cross-registration, distance learning, double major, exchange student program (domestic), honors program, independent study, internships, study abroad, teacher certification program. **Combined degree programs:** BS/DPT Physical Therapy. Special programs offered to physically disabled students include note-taking services, reader services, tape recorders, tutors. **Career services:** Alumni network, alumni services, career/job search classes, career assessment, internships, regional alumni.

FACILITIES

Housing: Coed dorms, special housing for disabled students, apartments for single students, Substance Free Quiet Floors Language House Honors First-year Experience. 80% of campus accessible to physically disabled. **Special Academic Facilities/Equipment:** Arts center, speech/hearing/language clinic, reading clinic, psychology center, center for service learning, Center for Teaching Excellence, and Center for International Education. **Computers:** Students can register for classes online.

CAMPUS LIFE

Environment: Village. **Activities:** Choral groups, concert band, dance, drama/theater, jazz band, literary magazine, music ensembles, musical theater, opera, radio station, student government, student newspaper, symphony orchestra, yearbook, campus ministries, international student organization. **Organizations:** 50 registered organizations, 19 honor societies, 5 religious organizations. **Athletics (Intercollegiate):** *Men:* Basketball, cross-country, diving, equestrian sports, golf, lacrosse, soccer, swimming, tennis, track/field (outdoor), track/field (indoor), volleyball. *Women:* Basketball, cross-country, diving, equestrian sports, field hockey, golf, lacrosse, soccer, softball, swimming, tennis, track/field (outdoor), track/field (indoor), volleyball. **On-Campus Highlights:** Cabaret—informal dining/coffee house, Athletic Facilities, Shults Community Center, Colie's Cafe, library.

ADMISSIONS

Freshman Academic Profile: Average high school GPA 3.3. 30% in top 10% of high school class, 67% in top 25% of high school class, 91% in top 50% of high school class. 90% from public high schools. SAT Math middle 50% range 530–630. SAT Critical Reading middle 50% range 530–630. SAT Writing middle 50% range 510–610. ACT middle 50% range 23–27. Minimum paper TOEFL 550. Minimum computer TOEFL 213. Minimum web-based TOEFL 79. **Basis for Candidate Selection:** *Very important factors considered include:* Class rank, application essay, academic GPA, recommendation(s), rigor of secondary school record. *Important factors considered include:* Character/personal qualities, extracurricular activities, geographical residence, interview, level of applicant's interest, racial/ethnic status, state residency, talent/ability, volunteer work, work experience. *Other factors considered include:* Standardized test scores, alumni/ae relation, first generation. **Freshman Admission Requirements:** High school diploma is required and GED is accepted. *Academic units required:* 4 English, 3 mathematics, 3 science, (2 science labs), 3 foreign language, 3 social studies. *Academic units recommended:* 4 English, 4 mathematics, 4 science, 4 foreign language, 4 social studies. **Freshman Admission Statistics:** 2,181 applied, 74% admitted, 29% enrolled. **Transfer Admission Requirements:** College transcript(s), essay or personal statement, minimum college GPA of 2.5 required. Lowest grade transferable C. **General Admission Information:** Application fee $40. Early decision application deadline 11/15. Regular application deadline 2/15. Regular notification 3/1. Nonfall registration accepted. Admission may be deferred for a maximum of 1 year. Credit and/or placement offered for CEEB Advanced Placement tests.

COSTS AND FINANCIAL AID

Required Forms and Deadlines: FAFSA. Financial aid filing deadline 5/1. Priority financial aid filing date 2/15. **Notification of Awards:** Applicants will be notified of awards on a rolling basis beginning 2/20. **Types of Aid:** *Need-based scholarships/grants:* Federal Pell, SEOG, state scholarships/grants, private scholarships, the school's own gift aid. *Loans:* FFEL Subsidized Stafford, FFEL Unsubsidized Stafford, FFEL PLUS, Federal Perkins. *Student Employment:* Federal Work-Study Program available. Institutional employment available. Off-campus job opportunities are excellent. **Financial Aid Statistics:** 78% freshmen, 79% undergrads receive need-based scholarship or grant aid.

10% freshmen, 9% undergrads receive non-need-based scholarship or grant aid. 66% freshmen, 67% undergrads receive need-based self-help aid. 78% undergrads borrow to pay for school. Average cumulative indebtedness $26,711. **Criteria for awarding institutional aid:** *Non-need-based:* Academics, alumni affiliation, art, minority status, music/drama, state/district residency.

See page 1170.

NEBRASKA CHRISTIAN COLLEGE

1800 Syracuse Avenue, Norfolk, NE 68701
Phone: 402-379-5000
E-mail: admissions@nechristian.edu
Fax: 402-379-5100 **ACT Code:** 2473

This private school was founded in 1945. It has a 40-acre campus.

RATINGS
Admissions Selectivity Rating: 60*   **Fire Safety Rating:** 60*   **Green Rating:** 60*

STUDENTS AND FACULTY
Enrollment: 146. **Student Body:** 45% female, 55% male, 10% out-of-state.

ACADEMICS
Degrees: Associate, bachelor's. **Special Study Options:** Distance learning, internships, study abroad.

FACILITIES
Housing: Private apartments, student plan housing, private rooms.

CAMPUS LIFE
Environment: Rural. **Activities:** Student newspaper. **Athletics (Intercollegiate):** *Men:* Basketball, soccer. *Women:* Basketball, volleyball.

ADMISSIONS
Basis for Candidate Selection: *Very important factors considered include:* Recommendation(s), standardized test scores, character/personal qualities. *Important factors considered include:* Class rank, rigor of secondary school record, extracurricular activities, interview, talent/ability, volunteer work. *Other factors considered include:* Alumni/ae relation, work experience. **Freshman Admission Requirements:** High school diploma is required and GED is accepted. **Freshman Admission Statistics:** 148 applied, 60% admitted, 67% enrolled. **Transfer Admission Requirements:** High school transcript, college transcript(s). **General Admission Information:** Application fee $25. Nonfall registration accepted. Admission may be deferred for a maximum of 1.

COSTS AND FINANCIAL AID
Annual tuition $4,500. Room and board $2,960. Required fees $450. Average book expense $400. **Required Forms and Deadlines:** FAFSA, institution's own financial aid form. **Types of Aid:** *Need-based scholarships/grants:* Federal Pell, SEOG, state scholarships/grants, private scholarships, the school's own gift aid. *Loans:* FFEL Subsidized Stafford, FFEL Unsubsidized Stafford, FFEL PLUS. *Student Employment:* Federal Work-Study Program available. Institutional employment available. Highest amount earned per year from on-campus jobs $1,625. Off-campus job opportunities are excellent. **Financial Aid Statistics:** 93% freshmen, 93% undergrads receive need-based scholarship or grant aid. 59% freshmen, 53% undergrads receive need-based self-help aid. 90% undergrads borrow to pay for school. Average cumulative indebtedness $10,178. **Criteria for awarding institutional aid:** *Non-need-based:* Academics, leadership, music/drama.

NEBRASKA METHODIST COLLEGE

720 North 87th Street, Omaha, NE 68114
Phone: 402-354-7200 **Financial Aid Phone:** 402-354-7225
E-mail: admissions@methodistcollege.edu **CEEB Code:** 6510
Fax: 402-354-7020 **Website: ACT Code:** 2465

This private school, affiliated with the Methodist Church, was founded in 1891. It has a 6-acre campus.

RATINGS
Admissions Selectivity Rating: 77   **Fire Safety Rating:** 60*   **Green Rating:** 60*

STUDENTS AND FACULTY

Enrollment: 504. **Student Body:** 92% female, 8% male, 35% out-of-state, (3 countries represented). Asian 3%, African American 3%, Caucasian 87%, Hispanic 1%, Native American 1%.

Retention and Graduation: 81% freshmen return for sophomore year. 10% grads go on to further study within 1 year. 10% grads pursue arts and sciences degrees. **Faculty:** Student/faculty ratio 10:1. 43 full-time faculty, 28% hold PhDs, 7% are are members of minority groups, 91% are women.

ACADEMICS

Degrees: Associate, bachelor's, certificate, master's, post-master's certificate. **Classes:** Most classes have 10–19 students. Most lab/discussion sessions have 10–19 students. **Majors with Highest Enrollment:** Diagnostic medical sonography/sonographer and ultrasound technician; nursing/registered nurse (RN, ASN, BSN, MSN); radiologic technology/science—radiographer. **Special Study Options:** Accelerated program, distance learning, independent study Special programs offered to physically disabled students include note-taking services, reader services, tape recorders, tutors. **Career services:** Alumni network, alumni services, career/job search classes.

FACILITIES

Housing: Apartments for single students. 90% of campus accessible to physically disabled. **Computers:** 100% of classrooms, 100% of libraries, 100% of dining areas, 100% of student union, have wireless network access. Students can register for classes online. Administrative functions (other than registration) can be performed online.

CAMPUS LIFE

Environment: City. **Activities:** student government **Organizations:** 11 registered organizations, 2 honor societies, **On-Campus Highlights:** Student center, library, human cadaver lab, chapel.

ADMISSIONS

Freshman Academic Profile: Average high school GPA 3.31. 11% in top 10% of high school class, 11% in top 25% of high school class, 50% in top 50% of high school class. 90% from public high schools. ACT middle 50% range 19–23. Minimum paper TOEFL 550. Minimum computer TOEFL 213. Minimum web-based TOEFL 80. **Basis for Candidate Selection:** *Very important factors considered include:* Academic GPA, rigor of secondary school record, standardized test scores. *Important factors considered include:* Class rank, application essay, recommendation(s), character/personal qualities, interview. *Other factors considered include:* Alumni/ae relation, first generation, geographical residence, level of applicant's interest, racial/ethnic status, state residency, volunteer work, work experience. **Freshman Admission Requirements:** High school diploma is required and GED is accepted. *Academic units required:* 4 English, 3 mathematics, 2 science, (2 science labs), 2 social studies. **Freshman Admission Statistics:** 96 applied, 76% admitted, 70% enrolled. **Transfer Admission Requirements:** High school transcript, college transcript(s), essay or personal statement, interview, statement of good standing from prior institution(s). Minimum college GPA of 2.5 required. Lowest grade transferable C. **General Admission Information:** Application fee $25. Regular application deadline 3/1. Notification on a rolling basis, beginning on or about 1/15. Nonfall registration accepted. Admission may be deferred for a maximum of 1 year. Neither credit nor placement offered for CEEB Advanced Placement tests.

COSTS AND FINANCIAL AID

Annual tuition $12,840. Room and board $2,625. Required fees $600. Average book expense $1,300. **Required Forms and Deadlines:** FAFSA, institution's own financial aid form. Priority financial aid filing date 5/1. **Notification of Awards:** Applicants will be notified of awards on a rolling basis beginning 3/1. **Types of Aid:** *Need-based scholarships/grants:* Federal Pell, SEOG, state scholarships/grants, private scholarships, the school's own gift aid. *Loans:* FFEL Subsidized Stafford, FFEL Unsubsidized Stafford, FFEL PLUS, Federal Perkins, Federal Nursing, state loans, college/university loans from institutional funds, alternative loans. *Student Employment:* Federal Work-Study Program available. Institutional employment available. Off-campus job opportunities are good. **Financial Aid Statistics:** 22% freshmen, 38% undergrads receive need-based scholarship or grant aid. 2% freshmen, 3% undergrads receive non-need-based scholarship or grant aid. 20% freshmen, 42% undergrads receive need-based self-help aid. 85% freshmen, 69% undergrads receive any aid. 86% undergrads borrow to pay for school. Average cumulative indebtedness $29,492. **Criteria for awarding institutional aid:** *Non-need-based:* Academics, minority status, religious affiliation.

NEBRASKA WESLEYAN UNIVERSITY

5000 Saint Paul Ave, Lincoln, NE 68504
Phone: 402-465-2218 **Financial Aid Phone:** 402-465-2212
E-mail: admissions@nebrwesleyan.edu **CEEB Code:** 6470
Fax: 402-465-2177 **Website:** www.nebrwesleyan.edu **ACT Code:** 2474

This private school, affiliated with the Methodist Church, was founded in 1887. It has a 50-acre campus.

RATINGS

Admissions Selectivity Rating: 75 **Fire Safety Rating:** 60* **Green Rating:** 74

STUDENTS AND FACULTY

Enrollment: 1,817. **Student Body:** 58% female, 42% male, 11% out-of-state, international (13 countries represented). Asian 2%, African American 2%, Caucasian 89%, Hispanic 1%.

Retention and Graduation: 83% freshmen return for sophomore year. 47% freshmen graduate within 4 years. **Faculty:** Student/faculty ratio 13:1. 105 full-time faculty, 85% hold PhDs, 2% are are members of minority groups, 53% are women.

ACADEMICS

Degrees: Bachelor's, certificate, master's, post-bachelor's certificate, post-master's certificate. **Classes:** Most classes have 20–29 students. Most lab/discussion sessions have 10–19 students. **Majors with Highest Enrollment:** Business administration and management; communication studies/speech communication and rhetoric; psychology. **Special Study Options:** Double major, dual enrollment, independent study, internships, liberal arts/career combination, study abroad, teacher certification program, weekend college, 3-2 Engineering Program with Washington Univ, Columbia Univ, or Univ. of Nebraska-Lincoln; Capitol Hill Internship Program; Chicago Center for Urban Life & Culture. Special programs offered to physically disabled students include note-taking services, reader services, tape recorders, tutors. **Career services:** Alumni network, alumni services, career/job search classes, career assessment, internships, regional alumni. **Career services highlights include:** National and international service learning trips; service learning as part of coursework.

FACILITIES

Housing: Coed dorms, women's dorms, fraternity/sorority housing, apartments for single students, townhouses, residence hall suites. 92% of campus accessible to physically disabled. **Special Academic Facilities/Equipment:** Art galleries, psychology/sleep lab, observatory and planetarium, green house, laboratory theatre, herbarium, nuclear magnetic resonance laboratory. **Computers:** Students can register for classes online. Administrative functions (other than registration) can be performed online.

CAMPUS LIFE

Environment: City. **Activities:** Choral groups, concert band, drama/theater, jazz band, literary magazine, marching band, music ensembles, musical theater, opera, pep band, radio station, student government, student newspaper, symphony orchestra, campus ministries, international student organization. **Organizations:** 80 registered organizations, 18 honor societies, 5 religious organizations. 3 fraternities, 4 sororities. **Athletics (Intercollegiate):** *Men:* Baseball, basketball, cross-country, football, golf, soccer, tennis, track/field (outdoor), track/field (indoor). *Women:* Basketball, cross-country, golf, soccer, softball, tennis, track/field (outdoor), track/field (indoor), volleyball. **On-Campus Highlights:** Weary Center for Health and Fitness, Wesleyan Coffee House, Old Main, Roy G Story Student Center, Great Hall, Smith-Curtis. **Environmental Initiatives:** Completed light inventory; retrofitted 80% of all lights. Recycling including cans, plastic bottles, paper. Updated central heating plant.

ADMISSIONS

Freshman Academic Profile: 26% in top 10% of high school class, 63% in top 25% of high school class, 91% in top 50% of high school class. ACT middle 50% range 23-27. Minimum paper TOEFL 525. Minimum computer TOEFL 195. **Basis for Candidate Selection:** *Very important factors considered include:* Class rank, standardized test scores. *Important factors considered include:* Academic GPA, character/personal qualities, extracurricular activities, talent/ability. *Other factors considered include:* Application essay, recommendation(s), rigor of secondary school record, alumni/ae relation, first generation, geographical residence, interview, racial/ethnic status, volunteer work. **Freshman Admission Requirements:** High school diploma is required and GED is accepted. *Academic units recommended:* 4 English, 3 social studies. **Freshman Admission Statistics:** 1,519 applied, 80% admitted, 32% enrolled. **Transfer Admission Requirements:** College transcript(s), statement of good standing from prior institution(s). Minimum college GPA of 2.0 required. Lowest grade transferable C–. **General Admission Information:** Application fee $20. Regular application deadline 8/15. Regular notification 1/15. Nonfall registration accepted. Admission may be deferred for a maximum of 1 year. Credit offered for CEEB Advanced Placement tests.

COSTS AND FINANCIAL AID

Annual tuition $21,980. Room and board $6,230. Required fees $332. Average book expense $1,200. **Required Forms and Deadlines:** FAFSA. **Types of Aid:** *Need-based scholarships/grants:* Federal Pell, SEOG, state scholarships/grants, private scholarships, the school's own gift aid. *Loans:* FFEL Subsidized Stafford, FFEL Unsubsidized Stafford, FFEL PLUS, Federal Perkins. *Student Employment:* Federal Work-Study Program available. Institutional employment available. Highest amount earned per year from on-campus jobs $7,664. Off-campus job opportunities are good. **Financial Aid Statistics:** 72% freshmen, 66% undergrads receive need-based scholarship or grant aid. 7% freshmen, 7% undergrads receive non-need-based scholarship or grant aid. 60% freshmen, 57% undergrads receive need-based self-help aid. 99% freshmen, 96% undergrads receive any aid. 82% undergrads borrow to pay for school. Average cumulative indebtedness $16,458. **Criteria for awarding institutional aid:** *Non-need-based:* Academics, art, minority status, music/drama.

NEUMANN UNIVERSITY

One Neumann Drive, Aston, PA 19014
Phone: 610-558-5616 **Financial Aid Phone:** 610-558-5532
E-mail: neumann@neumann.edu **CEEB Code:** 2628
Fax: 610-558-5652 **Website:** www.neumann.edu **ACT Code:** 3649

This private school, affiliated with the Roman Catholic Church, was founded in 1965. It has a 55-acre campus.

RATINGS
Admissions Selectivity Rating: 73   **Fire Safety Rating:** 97   **Green Rating:** 60*

STUDENTS AND FACULTY
Enrollment: 2,484. **Student Body:** 66% female, 34% male, 29% out-of-state, 2% international (20 countries represented). Asian 1%, African American 14%, Caucasian 61%, Hispanic 2%.
Retention and Graduation: 70% freshmen return for sophomore year. 34% freshmen graduate within 4 years. 20% grads go on to further study within 1 year. 7% grads pursue arts and sciences degrees. 2% grads pursue law degrees. 10% grads pursue business degrees. 1% grads pursue medical degrees. **Faculty:** Student/faculty ratio 14:1. 88 full-time faculty, 68% hold PhDs, 6% are are members of minority groups, 66% are women.

ACADEMICS
Degrees: Associate, bachelor's, certificate, master's, post-bachelor's certificate, post-master's certificate, terminal associate. **Classes:** Most classes have 20–29 students. Most lab/discussion sessions have 10–19 students. **Majors with Highest Enrollment:** criminal justice/law enforcement administration; elementary education and teaching; nursing/registered nurse (RN, ASN, BSN, MSN). **Special Study Options:** Accelerated program, cooperative education program, distance learning, double major, exchange student program (domestic), honors program, independent study, internships, liberal arts/career combination, student-designed major, study abroad, teacher certification program, weekend college. Special programs offered to physically disabled students include note-taking services, reader services, tape recorders, tutors. **Career services:** Alumni network, alumni services, career/job search classes, career assessment, internships.

FACILITIES
Housing: Coed dorms, special housing for disabled students, off-campus housing. 100% of campus accessible to physically disabled. **Special Academic Facilities/Equipment:** Child development center. **Computers:** 100% of classrooms, 100% of libraries, have wireless network access. Administrative functions (other than registration) can be performed online.

CAMPUS LIFE
Environment: Town. **Activities:** Choral groups, dance, drama/theater, jazz band, literary magazine, music ensembles, musical theater, radio station, student government, student newspaper, yearbook, campus ministries, Model UN. **Organizations:** 14 registered organizations, 4 honor societies, 2 religious organizations. **Athletics (Intercollegiate):** *Men:* Baseball, basketball, cross-country, golf, ice hockey, lacrosse, soccer, tennis. *Women:* Basketball, cross-country, field hockey, ice hockey, lacrosse, soccer, softball, tennis, volleyball. **On-Campus Highlights:** Life Center, training room, on campus chapel, library, computer labs.

ADMISSIONS
Freshman Academic Profile: Average high school GPA 3.25. 30% in top 10% of high school class, 50% in top 25% of high school class, 90% in top 50% of

high school class. 60% from public high schools. SAT Math middle 50% range 400–490. SAT Critical Reading middle 50% range 400–490. Minimum paper TOEFL 550. Minimum computer TOEFL 213. **Basis for Candidate Selection:** *Very important factors considered include:* Recommendation(s), rigor of secondary school record, extracurricular activities, talent/ability. *Important factors considered include:* Class rank, standardized test scores, alumni/ae relation, character/personal qualities, interview, level of applicant's interest. *Other factors considered include:* Application essay, racial/ethnic status, religious affiliation/commitment, volunteer work. **Freshman Admission Requirements:** High school diploma is required and GED is accepted. *Academic units required:* 4 English, 2 mathematics, 2 science, 2 foreign language, 2 social studies, 4 academic electives. *Academic units recommended:* 4 English, 2 mathematics, 3 science, 2 foreign language, 2 social studies, 4 academic electives. **Freshman Admission Statistics:** 2,333 applied, 95% admitted, 24% enrolled. **Transfer Admission Requirements:** College transcript(s), minimum college GPA of 2.0 required. Lowest grade transferable C. **General Admission Information:** Application fee $35. Nonfall registration accepted. Admission may be deferred for a maximum of 1 year. Credit offered for CEEB Advanced Placement tests.

COSTS AND FINANCIAL AID
Annual tuition $19,742. Room and board $9,258. Required fees $660. Average book expense $1,200. **Required Forms and Deadlines:** FAFSA. **Notification of Awards:** Applicants will be notified of awards on a rolling basis beginning 3/1. **Types of Aid:** *Need-based scholarships/grants:* Federal Pell, SEOG, state scholarships/grants, private scholarships, the school's own gift aid, Federal Nursing Scholarships. *Loans:* Direct Subsidized Stafford, Direct Unsubsidized Stafford, Direct PLUS, FFEL Subsidized Stafford, FFEL Unsubsidized Stafford, FFEL PLUS, Federal Nursing *Student Employment:* Federal Work-Study Program available. Highest amount earned per year from on-campus jobs $5,000. Off-campus job opportunities are excellent. **Financial Aid Statistics:** 84% freshmen, 75% undergrads receive need-based scholarship or grant aid. 56% freshmen, 49% undergrads receive non-need-based scholarship or grant aid. 84% freshmen, 75% undergrads receive need-based self-help aid. 98% freshmen, 91% undergrads receive any aid. 80% undergrads borrow to pay for school. Average cumulative indebtedness $25,000. **Criteria for awarding institutional aid:** *Non-need-based:* Academics.

NEUMONT UNIVERSITY

10701 S. River Front Parkway, Suite 300, South Jordan, UT 84095
Phone: 888-638-6668 **Financial Aid Phone:** 801-302-2870
E-mail: admissions@neumont.edu
Fax: 801-302-2880 **Website:** www.neumont.edu

This proprietary school was founded in 2003.

RATINGS
Admissions Selectivity Rating: 60*   **Fire Safety Rating:** 60*   **Green Rating:** 60*

STUDENTS AND FACULTY
Enrollment: 232. **Student Body:** 6% female, 94% male, 73% out-of-state, international (40 countries represented).
Retention and Graduation: 66% freshmen return for sophomore year. **Faculty:** Student/faculty ratio 6:1. 11 full-time faculty.

ACADEMICS
Degrees: Bachelor's, master's. **Special Study Options:** Accelerated program, internships Special programs offered to physically disabled students include note-taking services, reader services, tape recorders, tutors. **Career services:** Career/job search classes, career assessment, internships.

FACILITIES
Housing: Apartments for married students, apartments for single students. **Computers:** 100% of classrooms, 100% of libraries, 100% of dining areas, 100% of student union, have wireless network access. Students can register for classes online. Undergraduates are required to own a computer.

CAMPUS LIFE
Environment: Metropolis. **Activities:** Student government. **Organizations:** 8 registered organizations.

ADMISSIONS
Basis for Candidate Selection: *Very important factors considered include:* Academic GPA, standardized test scores. *Important factors considered include:* Application essay, recommendation(s), interview, level of applicant's interest, work experience. *Other factors considered include:* Class rank, rigor of secondary school record, character/personal qualities, extracurricular activities, talent/ability, volunteer work. **Freshman Admission Requirements:** High

school diploma is required and GED is accepted. **Freshman Admission Statistics: Transfer Admission Requirements:** High school transcript, essay or personal statement, standardized test scores, minimum college GPA of 2.5 required. Lowest grade transferable C. **General Admission Information:** Application fee $35. Nonfall registration accepted. Admission may be deferred for a maximum of 1 year.

COSTS AND FINANCIAL AID

Annual tuition $28,800. Room and board $5,700. Required fees $1,400. **Required Forms and Deadlines:** FAFSA, institution's own financial aid form **Types of Aid:** *Need-based scholarships/grants:* Federal Pell, SEOG, private scholarships, the school's own gift aid. *Loans:* FFEL Subsidized Stafford, FFEL Unsubsidized Stafford, FFEL PLUS, college/university loans from institutional funds. **Criteria for awarding institutional aid:** *Non-need-based:* Academics.

NEW COLLEGE OF CALIFORNIA

741 Valencia street, San Francisco, CA 94110
Phone: 415-437-3460
E-mail: CEEB Code: 4555
Fax: 415-861-0461 **Website:** www.newcollege.edu

This private school was founded in 1971. It has a 1-acre campus.

RATINGS
Admissions Selectivity Rating: 60*   **Fire Safety Rating:** 60*   **Green Rating:** 60*

STUDENTS AND FACULTY
Enrollment: 398. **Student Body:** 70% female, 30% male, % out-of-state, international (6 countries represented). Asian 1%, African American 4%, Caucasian 340%, Hispanic 3%, Native American 3%.
Retention and Graduation: 15% grads go on to further study within 1 year. 5% grads pursue law degrees. **Faculty:** 3% of classes are taught by teaching assistants.

ACADEMICS
Degrees: Associate, bachelor's, certificate, diploma, first professional, master's, terminal associate. **Majors with Highest Enrollment:** music teacher education; music theory and composition; voice and opera. **Special Study Options:** Accelerated program, cooperative education program, distance learning, English as a Second Language (ESL), independent study, internships, liberal arts/career combination, student-designed major, study abroad, teacher certification program, weekend college, summer off-campus field study opportunities. Special programs offered to physically disabled students include tape recorders, tutors. **Career services:** Alumni services.

FACILITIES
Housing: 100% of campus accessible to physically disabled. **Special Academic Facilities/Equipment:** Arts studio, video editing lab, letter press lab.

CAMPUS LIFE
Environment: Metropolis. **Activities:** Choral groups, drama/theater, jazz band, literary magazine, musical theater, radio station, student newspaper.

ADMISSIONS
Basis for Candidate Selection: *Very important factors considered include:* Rigor of secondary school record. *Important factors considered include:* geographical residence, interview, racial/ethnic status, state residency, work experience. *Other factors considered include:* volunteer work. **Freshman Admission Requirements:** High school diploma is required and GED is accepted. **Transfer Admission Requirements:** High school transcript, college transcript(s), essay or personal statement, Lowest grade transferable C. **General Admission Information:** Application fee $50. Early decision application deadline 3/1. Nonfall registration accepted. Admission may be deferred for a maximum of 1 year.

COSTS AND FINANCIAL AID
Required Forms and Deadlines: FAFSA, institution's own financial aid form, state aid form. Financial aid filing deadline 3/2. Priority financial aid filing date 3/2. **Notification of Awards:** Applicants will be notified of awards on a rolling basis beginning 5/15. **Types of Aid:** *Need-based scholarships/grants:* Federal Pell, SEOG, state scholarships/grants, private scholarships, the school's own gift aid. *Loans:* Direct Subsidized Stafford, Direct Unsubsidized Stafford, FFEL PLUS, Federal Perkins. *Student Employment:* Federal Work-Study Program available. Highest amount earned per year from on-campus jobs $3,000. Off-campus job opportunities are good.

NEW COLLEGE OF FLORIDA

5800 Bay Shore Rd, ROB 101, Sarasota, FL 34243-2109
Phone: 941-487-5000 **Financial Aid Phone:** 941-487-5000
E-mail: admissions@ncf.edu **CEEB Code:** 5506
Fax: 941-487-5010 **Website:** www.ncf.edu **ACT Code:** 750

This public school was founded in 1960. It has a 118.6-acre campus.

RATINGS
Admissions Selectivity Rating: 94   **Fire Safety Rating:** 62   **Green Rating:** 80

STUDENTS AND FACULTY
Enrollment: 825. **Student Body:** 62% female, 38% male, 22% out-of-state, international (21 countries represented). Asian 3%, African American 2%, Caucasian 77%, Hispanic 11%, Native American 1%.
Retention and Graduation: 86% freshmen return for sophomore year. 46% freshmen graduate within 4 years. 27% grads go on to further study within 1 year. **Faculty:** Student/faculty ratio 10:1. 71 full-time faculty, 99% hold PhDs, 15% are are members of minority groups, 48% are women.

ACADEMICS
Degrees: Bachelor's. **Classes:** Most classes have 10–19 students. Most lab/discussion sessions have 10–19 students. **Majors with Highest Enrollment:** Biology/biological sciences; political science and government; psychology. **Special Study Options:** Cross-registration, double major, exchange student program (domestic), honors program, independent study, internships, student-designed major, study abroad, academic contract, January interterm (independent study), narrative evaluation/pass-fail, senior thesis, tutorials, undergraduate research. Special or unique academic programs: (1) The New College academic contract whereby each student develops her/his individual academic program of coursework, tutorials, field and lab research, study abroad, and so on, in close consultation with a faculty member. See the General Catalog on the web. www.ncf.edu/resources-for-students. (2) Non-graded, narrative evaluation which encourages exploration and mastery. (3) Intensive "Independent Study Projects" during January which can be highly individual but can also involve group activities, such as an acting workshop or an ecological tour of Florida. (4) Competitive grants programs to support student research. **Honors programs:** New College of Florida is the state's officially-designated "honors college for the liberal arts." Special programs offered to physically disabled students include note-taking services, reader services, tape recorders. **Career services:** Alumni network, alumni services, career/job search classes, career assessment, internships, regional alumni. **Career services highlights include:** The National Student Exchange program.

FACILITIES
Housing: Coed dorms, special housing for disabled students, apartments for single students, specialized housing options may be arranged in response to student interest. 60% of campus accessible to physically disabled. **Special Academic Facilities/Equipment:** Anthropology and psychology labs. Electronic music lab. Individual studio space for senior art students. Marine biology research center with Living Ecosystem Teaching and Research Aquarium, wet lab, and seawater on tap. NMR, scanning electron microscope, inert atmosphere glovebox, transparent fume hoods, greenhouse. **Computers:** 95% of classrooms, 100% of dorms, 100% of libraries, 100% of dining areas, 100% of student union, 20% of common outdoor areas have wireless network access. Students can register for classes online. Administrative functions (other than registration) can be performed online.

CAMPUS LIFE
Environment: Town. **Activities:** Choral groups, dance, drama/theater, literary magazine, music ensembles, musical theater, radio station, student government, student newspaper, student-run film society, campus ministries. **Organizations:** 90 registered organizations, 5 religious organizations. **Athletics (Intercollegiate):** *Men:* Sailing. *Women:* Sailing. **On-Campus Highlights:** The R.V. Heiser Natural Sciences Complex, Pritzker Marine Biology Research Center, The Caples Fine Arts Complex, Four Winds Cafe (Student owned and operated), Jane Bancroft Cook Library, Historic bayfront mansions. **Environmental Initiatives:** Waste Management efforts—recycling of all paper, newsprint, cardboard, phone books, magazines, junk mail, soft-cover books, cotton goods, cans (all types), glass & Plastic, jars & bottles, Auto batteries, used oil & filters, used antifreeze, toner cartridges, chemicals & solvents, white goods, scrap metal, precious metals, wastewater solids, used pallets, yard debris, masonry & concrete, fluorescent tubes, used lumber, etc. Purchasing efforts. All new appliances are EnergyStar. Facility design, construction and renovation efforts. New buildings are typically being made LEED-compliant.

ADMISSIONS

Freshman Academic Profile: Average high school GPA 4.02. 49% in top 10% of high school class, 84% in top 25% of high school class, 96% in top 50% of high school class. 84.4% from public high schools. SAT Math middle 50% range 590–680. SAT Critical Reading middle 50% range 630–730. SAT Writing middle 50% range 600–690. ACT middle 50% range 27–30. Minimum paper TOEFL 560. Minimum computer TOEFL 220. Minimum web-based TOEFL 83. **Basis for Candidate Selection:** *Very important factors considered include:* Application essay, academic GPA, rigor of secondary school record. *Important factors considered include:* Recommendation(s), standardized test scores, character/personal qualities. *Other factors considered include:* Class rank, alumni/ae relation, extracurricular activities, first generation, geographical residence, interview, level of applicant's interest, state residency, talent/ability, volunteer work, work experience. **Freshman Admission Requirements:** High school diploma is required and GED is accepted. *Academic units required:* 4 English, 4 mathematics, 3 science, (2 science labs), 2 foreign language, 3 social studies, 2 academic electives. *Academic units recommended:* 4 English, 4 mathematics, 4 science, (2 science labs), 4 foreign language, 4 social studies, 5 academic electives. **Freshman Admission Statistics:** 1,403 applied, 53% admitted, 29% enrolled. **Transfer Admission Requirements:** College transcript(s), essay or personal statement, minimum college GPA of 2.0 required. Lowest grade transferable C. **General Admission Information:** Application fee $30. Regular application deadline 4/15. Nonfall registration accepted. Admission may be deferred for a maximum of 1 year. Neither credit nor placement offered for CEEB Advanced Placement tests.

COSTS AND FINANCIAL AID

Required Forms and Deadlines: FAFSA. Priority financial aid filing date 2/15. **Notification of Awards:** Applicants will be notified of awards on a rolling basis beginning 10/1. **Types of Aid:** *Need-based scholarships/grants:* Federal Pell, SEOG, state scholarships/grants, private scholarships, the school's own gift aid, Federal Academic Competitiveness Grant. *Loans:* FFEL Subsidized Stafford, FFEL Unsubsidized Stafford, FFEL PLUS, alternative loans. *Student Employment:* Federal Work-Study Program available. Institutional employment available. Highest amount earned per year from on-campus jobs $5,358. Off-campus job opportunities are good. **Financial Aid Statistics:** 50% freshmen, 44% undergrads receive need-based scholarship or grant aid. 12% freshmen, 36% undergrads receive non-need-based scholarship or grant aid. 35% freshmen, 36% undergrads receive need-based self-help aid. 100% freshmen receive any aid. 41% undergrads borrow to pay for school. Average cumulative indebtedness $14,794. **Criteria for awarding institutional aid:** *Non-need-based:* Academics, state/district residency.

NEW ENGLAND COLLEGE

26 Bridge Street, Henniker, NH 03242
Phone: 603-428-2223 **Financial Aid Phone:** 603-428-2226
E-mail: admission@nec.edu **CEEB Code:** 3657
Fax: 603-428-3155 **Website:** www.nec.edu **ACT Code:** 2513

This private school was founded in 1946. It has a 225-acre campus.

RATINGS

Admissions Selectivity Rating: 68 **Fire Safety Rating:** 92 **Green Rating:** 87

STUDENTS AND FACULTY

Enrollment: 997. **Student Body:** 50% female, 50% male, 64% out-of-state, 5% international Asian 1%, African American 6%, Caucasian 86%, Hispanic 3%.
Retention and Graduation: 58% freshmen return for sophomore year. 30% freshmen graduate within 4 years. 21% grads go on to further study within 1 year. 4% grads pursue arts and sciences degrees. 1% grads pursue law degrees. 11% grads pursue business degrees. **Faculty:** Student/faculty ratio 12:1. 65 full-time faculty, 69% hold PhDs, 3% are are members of minority groups, 46% are women.

ACADEMICS

Degrees: Associate, bachelor's, master's. **Classes:** Most classes have 10–19 students. Most lab/discussion sessions have 10–19 students. **Majors with Highest Enrollment:** Business/commerce; elementary education and teaching; sport and fitness administration/management. **Special Study Options:** Accelerated program, cross-registration, distance learning, double major, dual enrollment, English as a Second Language (ESL), exchange student program (domestic), external degree program, honors program, independent study, internships, liberal arts/career combination, student-designed major, study abroad, teacher certification program. **Honors programs:** Honors Program for community college honors transfers **Combined degree programs:** BA/JD, NEC and

New York Law 3+3 Program. Special programs offered to physically disabled students include note-taking services, tape recorders, tutors. **Career services:** Alumni network, career/job search classes, career assessment, internships, regional alumni. **Career services highlights include:** Internships and practical experience throughout the curriculum.

FACILITIES

Housing: Coed dorms, fraternity/sorority housing, theme housingResident freshmen and sophomores are required to live in College housing. Quiet study options, special interest housing is available. 75% of campus accessible to physically disabled. **Special Academic Facilities/Equipment:** New England Art Gallery, Graphic Design and Imaging Lab Center for Educational Innovation (High Tech Building). **Computers:** 100% of classrooms, 100% of dorms, 100% of libraries, 100% of dining areas, 100% of student union, 75% of common outdoor areas have wireless network access. Students can register for classes online. Administrative functions (other than registration) can be performed online.

CAMPUS LIFE

Environment: Rural. **Activities:** Choral groups, dance, drama/theater, literary magazine, radio station, student government, student newspaper, yearbook, international student organization. **Organizations:** 26 registered organizations, 2 honor societies, 1 religious organizations. 2 fraternities, 2 sororities. **Athletics (Intercollegiate):** *Men:* Baseball, basketball, cross-country, ice hockey, lacrosse, soccer. *Women:* Basketball, cheerleading, cross-country, field hockey, ice hockey, lacrosse, soccer, softball. **On-Campus Highlights:** Simon Center (Student Center), Center of Education Innovation, Fitness Center, Gilmore Dining Hall, Coffee House. **Environmental Initiatives:** Addition of sustainability to the mission statement; Environmental Action Committee; capital budgeting to include green projects.

ADMISSIONS

Freshman Academic Profile: Average high school GPA 2.72. 2% in top 10% of high school class, 6% in top 25% of high school class, 37% in top 50% of high school class. 83% from public high schools. SAT Math middle 50% range 390–500. SAT Critical Reading middle 50% range 390–500. SAT Writing middle 50% range 380–480. ACT middle 50% range 17–23. Minimum paper TOEFL 550. Minimum computer TOEFL 213. Minimum web-based TOEFL 13. **Basis for Candidate Selection:** *Very important factors considered include:* Application essay, recommendation(s), rigor of secondary school record, extracurricular activities, interview, level of applicant's interest, talent/ability. *Important factors considered include:* character/personal qualities, volunteer work. *Other factors considered include:* Class rank, academic GPA, standardized test scores, alumni/ae relation, work experience. **Freshman Admission Requirements:** High school diploma is required and GED is accepted. *Academic units required:* 4 English, 2 mathematics, 2 science, (1 science labs). *Academic units recommended:* 4 English, 3 mathematics, 3 science, (2 science labs), 2 foreign language, 3 social studies. **Freshman Admission Statistics:** 1,767 applied, 81% admitted, 18% enrolled. **Transfer Admission Requirements:** High school transcript, college transcript(s), essay or personal statement, statement of good standing from prior institution(s). Lowest grade transferable C–. **General Admission Information:** Application fee $30. Regular application deadline 9/1. Notification on a rolling basis, beginning on or about 11/1. Nonfall registration accepted. Admission may be deferred for a maximum of 1 year. Credit and/or placement offered for CEEB Advanced Placement tests.

COSTS AND FINANCIAL AID

Annual tuition $27,200. Room and board $9,626. Required fees $250. Average book expense $850. **Required Forms and Deadlines:** FAFSA, institution's own financial aid form. Priority financial aid filing date 3/15. **Notification of Awards:** Applicants will be notified of awards on a rolling basis beginning 1/12. **Types of Aid:** *Need-based scholarships/grants:* Federal Pell, SEOG, state scholarships/grants, private scholarships, the school's own gift aid. *Loans:* Direct Subsidized Stafford, Direct Unsubsidized Stafford, Direct PLUS, FFEL Subsidized Stafford, FFEL Unsubsidized Stafford, FFEL PLUS, Federal Perkins, state loans *Student Employment:* Federal Work-Study Program available. Institutional employment available. Highest amount earned per year from on-campus jobs $2,500. Off-campus job opportunities are good. **Financial Aid Statistics:** 80% freshmen, 69% undergrads receive need-based scholarship or grant aid. 5% freshmen, 6% undergrads receive non-need-based scholarship or grant aid. 78% freshmen, 66% undergrads receive need-based self-help aid. 98% freshmen, 90% undergrads receive any aid. 77% undergrads borrow to pay for school. Average cumulative indebtedness $33,466. **Criteria for awarding institutional aid:** *Non-need-based:* Academics, alumni affiliation, art, job skills, leadership, music/drama.

NEW ENGLAND CONSERVATORY OF MUSIC

290 Huntington Avenue, Boston, MA 02115
Phone: 617-585-1101
E-mail: admissions@newenglandconservatory.edu **CEEB Code:** 3659
Fax: 617-585-1115 **Website:** www.newenglandconservatory.edu **ACT Code:** 1872

This private school was founded in 1867.

RATINGS
Admissions Selectivity Rating: 60*   **Fire Safety Rating:** 60*   **Green Rating:** 60*

STUDENTS AND FACULTY
Enrollment: 378. **Student Body:** 45% female, 55% male, 85% out-of-state, 6% international Asian 3%, African American 1%, Caucasian 13%, Hispanic 1%.
Retention and Graduation: 98% freshmen return for sophomore year. 56% freshmen graduate within 4 years. **Faculty:** Student/faculty ratio 4:1. 88 full-time faculty, 26% hold PhDs, 6% are are members of minority groups, 33% are women.

ACADEMICS
Degrees: Bachelor's, diploma, master's. **Classes:** Most classes have 10–19 students. Most lab/discussion sessions have fewer than 10 students. **Majors with Highest Enrollment:** Jazz/jazz studies; violin, viola, guitar and other stringed instruments; voice and opera. **Special Study Options:** Cross-registration, dual enrollment, English as a Second Language (ESL), independent study, internships, study abroad Special programs offered to physically disabled students include note-taking services, tutors. **Career services:** Alumni network, alumni services, career/job search classes, career assessment, internships.

FACILITIES
Housing: Coed dorms 100% of campus accessible to physically disabled.
Special Academic Facilities/Equipment: Rare instrument collection of over 200 pieces, recording and electronic music studios. Over 200 pieces, recording and electronic music studios. Jordan Hall, the Main Concert Hall, is a national Historic Landmark.

CAMPUS LIFE
Activities: Choral groups, concert band, jazz band, music ensembles, musical theater, opera, student government, symphony orchestra. **Organizations:** 7 registered organizations, 1 honor societies, 1 religious organizations. 1 fraternity.

ADMISSIONS
Freshman Academic Profile: Minimum paper TOEFL 500. Minimum computer TOEFL 173. **Basis for Candidate Selection:** *Very important factors considered include:* talent/ability. *Important factors considered include:* Rigor of secondary school record, standardized test scores. *Other factors considered include:* Application essay, academic GPA, recommendation(s), character/personal qualities. **Freshman Admission Requirements:** High school diploma is required and GED is accepted. **Freshman Admission Statistics:** 1,022 applied, 28% admitted, 28% enrolled. **Transfer Admission Requirements:** College transcript(s), essay or personal statement, interview, minimum college GPA of 2.7 required. Lowest grade transferable B. **General Admission Information:** Application fee $100. Notification on a rolling basis, beginning on or about 4/1. Nonfall registration accepted. Admission may be deferred for a maximum of 1 year. Credit offered for CEEB Advanced Placement tests.

COSTS AND FINANCIAL AID
Annual tuition $30,650. Room and board $11,300. Required fees $325. Average book expense $700. **Required Forms and Deadlines:** FAFSA, institution's own financial aid form. Financial aid filing deadline 2/1. Priority financial aid filing date 2/1. **Notification of Awards:** Applicants will be notified of awards on a rolling basis beginning 4/1. **Types of Aid:** *Need-based scholarships/grants:* Federal Pell, SEOG, state scholarships/grants, private scholarships, the school's own gift aid. *Loans:* FFEL Subsidized Stafford, FFEL Unsubsidized Stafford, FFEL PLUS, Federal Perkins, state loans. *Student Employment:* Federal Work-Study Program available. Institutional employment available. Off-campus job opportunities are good. **Financial Aid Statistics:** 63% freshmen, 61% undergrads receive need-based scholarship or grant aid. 28% freshmen, 35% undergrads receive non-need-based scholarship or grant aid. 47% freshmen, 48% undergrads receive need-based self-help aid. 61% undergrads borrow to pay for school. Average cumulative indebtedness $26,628. **Criteria for awarding institutional aid:** *Non-need-based:* Academics, music/drama.

NEW JERSEY CITY UNIVERSITY

2039 Kennedy Boulevard, Jersey City, NJ 07305
Phone: 888-441-6528 **Financial Aid Phone:** 201-200-3378
E-mail: admissions@njcu.edu **CEEB Code:** 2316
Fax: 201-200-2044 **Website:** www.njcu.edu

This public school was founded in 1927. It has a 17-acre campus.

RATINGS
Admissions Selectivity Rating: 79   **Fire Safety Rating:** 96   **Green Rating:** 60*

STUDENTS AND FACULTY
Enrollment: 6,325. **Student Body:** 61% female, 39% male, 1% out-of-state, 1% international (6 countries represented). Asian 7%, African American 20%, Caucasian 26%, Hispanic 35%.
Retention and Graduation: 73% freshmen return for sophomore year. 20% grads go on to further study within 1 year. 13% grads pursue arts and sciences degrees. 1% grads pursue law degrees. 5% grads pursue business degrees. 1% grads pursue medical degrees. **Faculty:** Student/faculty ratio 13:1. 246 full-time faculty, 89% hold PhDs, 25% are are members of minority groups, 50% are women.

ACADEMICS
Degrees: Bachelor's, certificate, master's, post-bachelor's certificate, post-master's certificate. **Classes:** Most classes have 20–29 students. **Majors with Highest Enrollment:** Business administration and management; corrections and criminal justice, other; psychology. **Special Study Options:** Accelerated program, cooperative education program, cross-registration, distance learning, double major, dual enrollment, English as a Second Language (ESL), honors program, independent study, internships, study abroad, teacher certification program, weekend college. **Honors programs:** Honors program in the William Maxwell College of Arts and Sciences. **Combined degree programs:** BA/MA. Special programs offered to physically disabled students include reader services, tape recorders, tutors. **Career services:** Career assessment, internships. **Career services highlights include:** Cooperative education.

FACILITIES
Housing: Coed dorms. 100% of campus accessible to physically disabled.
Special Academic Facilities/Equipment: Art galleries, lab school for special education, criminal justice institute, electron microscope, Raimondo Center for Urban Research and Public Policy. **Computers:** Students can register for classes online. Administrative functions (other than registration) can be performed online.

CAMPUS LIFE
Environment: City. **Activities:** Choral groups, concert band, dance, drama/theater, jazz band, literary magazine, music ensembles, musical theater, opera, radio station, student government, student newspaper, symphony orchestra, yearbook, campus ministries, international student organization. **Organizations:** 50 registered organizations, 2 religious organizations. 7 fraternities, 5 sororities. **Athletics (Intercollegiate):** *Men:* Baseball, basketball, cross-country, soccer, track/field (outdoor), track/field (indoor), volleyball. *Women:* Basketball, bowling, cross-country, soccer, softball, track/field (outdoor), track/field (indoor), volleyball. **On-Campus Highlights:** Student union, physical fitness center, library, cafeteria.

ADMISSIONS
Freshman Academic Profile: Average high school GPA 3.49. 9% in top 10% of high school class, 33% in top 25% of high school class, 73% in top 50% of high school class. 75% from public high schools. SAT Math middle 50% range 430–520. SAT Critical Reading middle 50% range 420–500. SAT Writing middle 50% range 420–500. Minimum paper TOEFL 500. Minimum computer TOEFL 150. **Basis for Candidate Selection:** *Very important factors considered include:* Rigor of secondary school record, standardized test scores, level of applicant's interest, volunteer work. *Important factors considered include:* Application essay, academic GPA, recommendation(s), extracurricular activities. *Other factors considered include:* character/personal qualities, interview, talent/ability. **Freshman Admission Requirements:** High school diploma is required and GED is accepted. *Academic units required:* 4 English, 4 mathematics, 4 science, (2 science labs), 4 social studies. *Academic units recommended:* 4 English, 4 mathematics, 4 science, (3 science labs), 2 foreign language, 4 social studies. **Freshman Admission Statistics:** 4,339 applied, 35% admitted, 50% enrolled. **Transfer Admission Requirements:** College transcript(s), minimum college GPA of 2.0 required. Lowest grade transferable C. **General Admission Information:** Application fee $35. Nonfall registration accepted. Credit and/or placement offered for CEEB Advanced Placement tests.

COSTS AND FINANCIAL AID

Annual in-state tuition $6,542. Annual out-of-state tuition $13,820. Room and board $10,136. Required fees $2,446. Average book expense $1,988. **Required Forms and Deadlines:** FAFSA. Priority financial aid filing date 4/15. **Notification of Awards:** Applicants will be notified of awards on or about 5/15. **Types of Aid:** *Need-based scholarships/grants:* Federal Pell, SEOG, state scholarships/grants, private scholarships, the school's own gift aid, United Negro College Fund *Loans:* FFEL Subsidized Stafford, FFEL Unsubsidized Stafford, FFEL PLUS, Federal Perkins, state loans. *Student Employment:* Federal Work-Study Program available. Institutional employment available. Off-campus job opportunities are good. **Financial Aid Statistics:** 63% freshmen, 54% undergrads receive need-based scholarship or grant aid. 10% freshmen, 6% undergrads receive non-need-based scholarship or grant aid. 31% freshmen, 43% undergrads receive need-based self-help aid. 70% freshmen, 70% undergrads receive any aid. 78% undergrads borrow to pay for school. Average cumulative indebtedness $28,833.

NEW JERSEY INSTITUTE OF TECHNOLOGY

Office of University Admissions, Uni. Heights, Newark, NJ 07102
Phone: 973-596-3300 **Financial Aid Phone:** 973-596-3479
E-mail: admissions@njit.edu **CEEB Code:** 2513
Fax: 973-596-3461 **Website:** www.njit.edu **ACT Code:** 2580

This public school was founded in 1881. It has a 48-acre campus.

RATINGS

Admissions Selectivity Rating: 81　　**Fire Safety Rating:** 88　　**Green Rating:** 83

STUDENTS AND FACULTY

Enrollment: 5,528. **Student Body:** 20% female, 80% male, 4% out-of-state, 4% international (92 countries represented). Asian 21%, African American 10%, Caucasian 36%, Hispanic 20%, Native American 1%.
Retention and Graduation: 84% freshmen return for sophomore year. 17% freshmen graduate within 4 years. 44% grads go on to further study within 1 year. 12% grads pursue arts and sciences degrees. 1% grads pursue law degrees. 25% grads pursue business degrees. 1% grads pursue medical degrees. **Faculty:** Student/faculty ratio 15:1. 403 full-time faculty, 100% hold PhDs, 24% are members of minority groups, 19% are women.

ACADEMICS

Degrees: Bachelor's, doctoral, master's, post-bachelor's certificate. **Classes:** Most classes have 20–29 students. **Majors with Highest Enrollment:** Architecture (BArch, BA/BS, MArch, MA/MS, PhD); civil engineering; mechanical engineering. **Special Study Options:** Accelerated program, cooperative education program, cross-registration, distance learning, double major, English as a Second Language (ESL), honors program, independent study, internships, study abroad **Honors programs:** The Albert Dorman Honors College at the New Jersey Institute of Technology (NJIT) enrolls over 500 exceptional students who excel in the fields of engineering, architecture, computing sciences, management, and the sciences. **Combined degree programs:** BA/MD, BA/MA, BS/MD, BS/DMD, BS/OD, BArch/MS Mang. Special programs offered to physically disabled students include note-taking services, reader services, tape recorders, tutors. **Career services:** Alumni network, alumni services, career/job search classes, career assessment, internships, regional alumni. **Career services highlights include:** Cooperative Education at NJIT is an academically integrated program that gives students the opportunity to gain paid professional work experience before graduation. Although not mandatory, over 400 students choose to participate each year. Most co-op students work fulltime for one or two semesters. The average wage for co-op students exceeds $15.00 per hour Nearly 2,600 different companies have hired NJIT students over the past decade. Employers range from large multinationals to small start-up companies. Students have completed their co-op assignments in New Jersey, ten other states, and four foreign countries.

FACILITIES

Housing: Coed dorms. 100% of campus accessible to physically disabled. **Special Academic Facilities/Equipment:** New Jersey Literary Hall of Fame and more than 50 research centers and sponsored research laboratories, including computer chip manufacturing center, manufacturing systems center, and many others. **Computers:** 100% of classrooms, 100% of dorms, 100% of libraries, 100% of dining areas, 100% of student union, 100% of common outdoor areas have wireless network access. Students can register for classes online. Admin-

istrative functions (other than registration) can be performed online. Undergraduates are required to own a computer.

CAMPUS LIFE

Environment: Metropolis. **Activities:** concert band, dance, drama/theater, literary magazine, marching band, musical theater, radio station, student government, student newspaper, yearbook, international student organization. **Organizations:** 70 registered organizations, 10 honor societies, 5 religious organizations. 15 fraternities, 7 sororities **Athletics (Intercollegiate):** *Men:* Baseball, basketball, cheerleading, cross-country, fencing, soccer, swimming, tennis, track/field (outdoor), track/field (indoor), volleyball. *Women:* Basketball, cheerleading, cross-country, fencing, soccer, swimming, tennis, track/field (outdoor), track/field (indoor), volleyball. **On-Campus Highlights:** Campus Center, Van Houten Library, Zoom Fleisher Athletic Center, East Building—Admissions, Student Mall. **Environmental Initiatives:** Recycling; energy efficiencies on equipment; water conservation devices.

ADMISSIONS

Freshman Academic Profile: 26% in top 10% of high school class, 55% in top 25% of high school class, 83% in top 50% of high school class. 80% from public high schools. SAT Math middle 50% range 550–660. SAT Critical Reading middle 50% range 490–590. SAT Writing middle 50% range 480–580. Minimum paper TOEFL 550. Minimum computer TOEFL 213. Minimum web-based TOEFL 79. **Basis for Candidate Selection:** *Very important factors considered include:* Class rank, rigor of secondary school record, standardized test scores. *Important factors considered include:* Academic GPA. *Other factors considered include:* Application essay, recommendation(s), alumni/ae relation, character/personal qualities, extracurricular activities, geographical residence, interview, level of applicant's interest, racial/ethnic status, religious affiliation/commitment, state residency, talent/ability, volunteer work, work experience. **Freshman Admission Requirements:** High school diploma is required and GED is accepted. *Academic units required:* 4 English, 4 mathematics, 2 science, (2 science labs). *Academic units recommended:* 2 foreign language, 1 social studies, 1 history, 2 academic electives. **Freshman Admission Statistics:** 4,315 applied, 67% admitted, 34% enrolled. **Transfer Admission Requirements:** College transcript(s), minimum college GPA of 2.0 required. Lowest grade transferable C. **General Admission Information:** Application fee $50. Regular application deadline 4/1. Notification on a rolling basis, beginning on or about 11/15. Nonfall registration accepted. Admission may be deferred for a maximum of 1 semester. Credit offered for CEEB Advanced Placement tests.

COSTS AND FINANCIAL AID

Required Forms and Deadlines: FAFSA. Financial aid filing deadline 5/5. Priority financial aid filing date 3/15. **Notification of Awards:** Applicants will be notified of awards on a rolling basis beginning 12/20. **Types of Aid:** *Need-based scholarships/grants:* Federal Pell, SEOG, state scholarships/grants, private scholarships, the school's own gift aid. *Loans:* Direct Subsidized Stafford, Direct Unsubsidized Stafford, Direct PLUS, Federal Perkins, state loans, college/university loans from institutional funds. *Student Employment:* Federal Work-Study Program available. Institutional employment available. Highest amount earned per year from on-campus jobs $5,500. Off-campus job opportunities are good. **Financial Aid Statistics:** 60% freshmen, 38% undergrads receive need-based scholarship or grant aid. 49% freshmen, 31% undergrads receive non-need-based scholarship or grant aid. 64% freshmen, 44% undergrads receive need-based self-help aid. 6% freshmen, 3% undergrads receive athletic scholarships. 70% freshmen, 70% undergrads receive any aid. 40% undergrads borrow to pay for school. Average cumulative indebtedness $20,000. **Criteria for awarding institutional aid:** *Non-need-based:* Academics, athletics, job skills, leadership, state/district residency.

NEW MEXICO INSTITUTE OF MINING AND TECHNOLOGY

Campus Station, 801 Leroy Place, Socorro, NM 87801
Phone: 575-835-5424 **Financial Aid Phone:** 575-835-5333
E-mail: admission@admin.nmt.edu **CEEB Code:** 4533
Fax: 575-835-5989 **Website:** www.nmt.edu **ACT Code:** 2642

This public school was founded in 1889. It has a 320-acre campus.

RATINGS

Admissions Selectivity Rating: 88　　**Fire Safety Rating:** 60*　　**Green Rating:** 60*

STUDENTS AND FACULTY

Enrollment: 1,138. **Student Body:** 27% female, 73% male, 13% out-of-state, 2% international (30 countries represented). Asian 3%, African American 1%, Caucasian 67%, Hispanic 24%, Native American 3%.
Retention and Graduation: 73% freshmen return for sophomore year. 16% freshmen graduate within 4 years. 30% grads go on to further study within 1 year. **Faculty:** Student/faculty ratio 11:1. 119 full-time faculty, 97% hold PhDs, 18% are are members of minority groups, 22% are women.

ACADEMICS

Degrees: Bachelor's, master's, terminal associate. **Classes:** Most classes have fewer than 10 students. Most lab/discussion sessions have 10–19 students. **Majors with Highest Enrollment:** Computer and information sciences; electrical, electronics and communications engineering; mechanical engineering. **Special Study Options:** Accelerated program, cooperative education program, distance learning, double major, dual enrollment, exchange student program (domestic), independent study, internships, student-designed major, teacher certification program. **Combined degree programs:** BS/MS geology, hydrology. Special programs offered to physically disabled students include note-taking services, reader services, tape recorders, tutors. **Career services:** career/job search classes, career assessment, internships.

FACILITIES

Housing: Coed dorms, men's dorms, women's dorms, apartments for married students, apartments for single students. **Special Academic Facilities/Equipment:** Mineral museum, observatory, radio telescope, seismic observatory and library, explosives labs. **Computers:** Students can register for classes online. Administrative functions (other than registration) can be performed online.

CAMPUS LIFE

Environment: Village. **Activities:** Choral groups, concert band, dance, drama/theater, jazz band, music ensembles, musical theater, radio station, student government, student newspaper. **Organizations:** 60 registered organizations, 7 honor societies, 3 religious organizations. **On-Campus Highlights:** Fidel Student Center, Skeen Library, Workman Center.

ADMISSIONS

Freshman Academic Profile: Average high school GPA 3.6. 31% in top 10% of high school class, 63% in top 25% of high school class, 91% in top 50% of high school class. 80% from public high schools. SAT Math middle 50% range 560–680. SAT Critical Reading middle 50% range 530–660. ACT middle 50% range 23–29. Minimum paper TOEFL 540. Minimum computer TOEFL 207. **Basis for Candidate Selection:** *Very important factors considered include:* Academic GPA, rigor of secondary school record, standardized test scores. *Other factors considered include:* Class rank, extracurricular activities, talent/ability. **Freshman Admission Requirements:** High school diploma is required and GED is accepted, *Academic units required:* 4 English, 3 mathematics, 2 science, (2 science labs), 2 social studies, 1 history, 3 academic electives. *Academic units recommended:* 4 English, 4 mathematics, 4 science, (3 science labs), 2 foreign language, 3 social studies, 1 history. **Freshman Admission Statistics:** 763 applied, 55% admitted, 59% enrolled. **Transfer Admission Requirements:** High school transcript, college transcript(s), statement of good standing from prior institution(s). Minimum college GPA of 2.0 required. Lowest grade transferable D. **General Admission Information:** Application fee $15. Regular application deadline 8/1. Notification on a rolling basis, beginning on or about 3/1. Nonfall registration accepted. Admission may be deferred for a maximum of 1 year. Credit and/or placement offered for CEEB Advanced Placement tests.

COSTS AND FINANCIAL AID

Annual in-state tuition $3,980. Annual out-of-state tuition $12,941. Room and board $5,700. Required fees $627. Average book expense $1,000. **Required Forms and Deadlines:** FAFSA, institution's own financial aid form. Financial aid filing deadline 3/1. Priority financial aid filing date 3/1. **Notification of Awards:** Applicants will be notified of awards on a rolling basis beginning 4/1. **Types of Aid:** *Need-based scholarships/grants:* Federal Pell, SEOG, state scholarships/grants, private scholarships, the school's own gift aid. *Loans:* FFEL Subsidized Stafford, FFEL Unsubsidized Stafford, FFEL PLUS, Federal Perkins, state loans. *Student Employment:* Federal Work-Study Program available. Institutional employment available. Highest amount earned per year from on-campus jobs $3,500. Off-campus job opportunities are fair. **Financial Aid Statistics:** 15% freshmen, 27% undergrads receive need-based scholarship or grant aid. 30% freshmen, 29% undergrads receive non-need-based scholarship or grant aid. 17% freshmen, 29% undergrads receive need-based self-help aid. 34% freshmen, 39% undergrads receive any aid. 92% undergrads borrow to pay for school. Average cumulative indebtedness $8,129. **Criteria for awarding institutional aid:** *Non-need-based:* Academics, alumni affiliation, minority status, state/district residency.

NEW MEXICO STATE UNIVERSITY

Box 30001, MSC 3A, Las Cruces, NM 88003-8001
Phone: 575-646-3121
E-mail: admissions@nmsu.edu **CEEB Code:** 4531
Fax: 575-646-6330 **Website:** www.nmsu.edu **ACT Code:** 2638

This public school was founded in 1888. It has a 900-acre campus.

RATINGS

Admissions Selectivity Rating: 71 **Fire Safety Rating:** 60* **Green Rating:** 60*

STUDENTS AND FACULTY

Enrollment: 14,536. **Student Body:** 55% female, 45% male, 18% out-of-state, 5% international (72 countries represented). Asian 1%, African American 3%, Caucasian 35%, Hispanic 44%, Native American 4%.
Retention and Graduation: 23% freshmen graduate within 4 years. **Faculty:** Student/faculty ratio 19.5:1. 699 full-time faculty, 75% hold PhDs, 20% are are members of minority groups, 40% are women.

ACADEMICS

Degrees: Associate, bachelor's, doctoral, master's, post-bachelor's certificate, post-master's certificate. **Classes:** Most classes have 20–29 students. Most lab/discussion sessions have 20–29 students. **Majors with Highest Enrollment:** Business/commerce; curriculum and instruction; electrical, electronics and communications engineering. **Special Study Options:** Accelerated program, cooperative education program, cross-registration, distance learning, double major, dual enrollment, English as a Second Language (ESL), exchange student program (domestic), external degree program, honors program, independent study, internships, student-designed major, study abroad, teacher certification program, weekend college. Special programs offered to physically disabled students include note-taking services, reader services, tape recorders, tutors. **Career services:** Alumni services, career/job search classes, career assessment, internships.

FACILITIES

Housing: Coed dorms, special housing for disabled students, men's dorms, women's dorms, fraternity/sorority housing, apartments for married students, apartments for single students. 95% of campus accessible to physically disabled. **Special Academic Facilities/Equipment:** University and art department museums, theatre, horse farm, sports medicine training clinic, observatory, electron microscope, CRAY supercomputer. **Computers:** Students can register for classes online. Administrative functions (other than registration) can be performed online.

CAMPUS LIFE

Environment: City. **Activities:** Choral groups, concert band, dance, drama/theater, jazz band, literary magazine, marching band, music ensembles, musical theater, opera, pep band, radio station, student government, student newspaper, symphony orchestra, television station, campus ministries. **Organizations:** 263 registered organizations, 24 honor societies, 23 religious organizations. 14 fraternities, 5 sororities. **Athletics (Intercollegiate):** *Men:* Baseball, basketball, cross-country, football, golf, tennis. *Women:* Basketball, cross-country, golf, softball, swimming, tennis, track/field (outdoor), volleyball.

ADMISSIONS

Freshman Academic Profile: Average high school GPA 3.29. 15% in top 10% of high school class, 42% in top 25% of high school class, 75% in top 50% of high school class. SAT Math middle 50% range 430–550. SAT Critical Reading middle 50% range 420–540. SAT Writing middle 50% range 410–533. ACT middle 50% range 18–23. Minimum paper TOEFL 500. **Basis for Candidate Selection:** *Very important factors considered include:* Rigor of secondary school record, standardized test scores. *Other factors considered include:* Academic GPA. **Freshman Admission Requirements:** High school diploma is required and GED is accepted. *Academic units required:* 4 English, 3 mathematics, 2 science, (2 science labs), 1 foreign language. **Freshman Admission Statistics:** 6,650 applied, 96% admitted, 45% enrolled. **Transfer Admission Requirements:** College transcript(s), minimum college GPA of 2.0 required. Lowest grade transferable C. **General Admission Information:** Application fee $20. Nonfall registration accepted. Admission may be deferred for a maximum of 1 year. Credit offered for CEEB Advanced Placement tests.

COSTS AND FINANCIAL AID

Required Forms and Deadlines: FAFSA, institution's own financial aid form. **Notification of Awards:** Applicants will be notified of awards on or about 3/1. **Types of Aid:** *Need-based scholarships/grants:* the school's own gift aid. *Loans:* FFEL Subsidized Stafford, FFEL Unsubsidized Stafford, FFEL PLUS, Federal Perkins, college/university loans from institutional funds. *Student Employment:* Federal Work-Study Program available. Institutional employment available. Off-campus job opportunities are good. **Financial Aid Statistics:**

48% freshmen, 48% undergrads receive need-based scholarship or grant aid. 27% freshmen, 41% undergrads receive need-based self-help aid. 1% freshmen, 1% undergrads receive athletic scholarships. 51.4% undergrads borrow to pay for school. Average cumulative indebtedness $23,262. **Criteria for awarding institutional aid:** *Non-need-based:* Academics, alumni affiliation, athletics, leadership, minority status, state/district residency.

THE NEW SCHOOL FOR JAZZ AND CONTEMPORARY MUSIC

55 W 13th Street, 5th Fl, New York, NY 10011,
Phone: 212-229-5896 x4589 **Financial Aid Phone:** 212 229 8930
E-mail: jazzadm@newschool.edu
Fax: 212-229-8936 **Website:** jazz.newschool.edu

This private school was founded in 1986.

RATINGS
Admissions Selectivity Rating: 73   **Fire Safety Rating:** 73   **Green Rating:** 91

STUDENTS AND FACULTY
Enrollment: 253. **Student Body:** 18% female, 82% male, 77% out-of-state, 26% international (21 countries represented). Asian 2%, African American 6%, Caucasian 43%, Hispanic 6%.
Retention and Graduation: 79% freshmen return for sophomore year. 42% freshmen graduate within 4 years. **Faculty:** Student/faculty ratio 11:1. 2 full-time faculty, 50% are members of minority groups, 50% are women.

ACADEMICS
Degrees: Bachelor's. **Classes:** Most classes have fewer than 10 students. **Majors with Highest Enrollment:** jazz/jazz studies. **Special Study Options:** Accelerated program, cross-registration, dual enrollment, English as a Second Language (ESL), exchange student program (domestic), independent study, internships, study abroad, five year combined BA/BFA. **Combined degree programs:** BA/BFA. Special programs offered to physically disabled students include note-taking services, reader services, tape recorders. **Career services:** Alumni network, alumni services, career/job search classes, career assessment, internships, regional alumni.

FACILITIES
Housing: Coed dorms, special housing for disabled students, apartments for single students 99% of campus accessible to physically disabled. **Computers:** 95% of classrooms, 100% of libraries, 100% of dining areas, 100% of common outdoor areas have wireless network access. Students can register for classes online. Administrative functions (other than registration) can be performed online.

CAMPUS LIFE
Environment: Metropolis. **Activities:** Choral groups, dance, drama/theater, jazz band, literary magazine, music ensembles, opera, radio station, student government, student newspaper, symphony orchestra, international student organization. **Organizations:** 34 registered organizations, **On-Campus Highlights:** Jazz Center, University Welcome Center **Environmental Initiatives:** The New School composts all behind the counter organic wastes and has begun a post-consumer pilot program. Waste Reduction and Recycling: The New School has established a comprehensive waste management and recycling program that includes glass, metal, plastic, paper, cardboard, electronic waste, ink jet cartridges, and compost. These recycling initiatives significantly reduce the amount of trash sent to landfills and/or incinerators by the university. Sustainable Product Procurement The New School currently purchases copy and printer paper composed of is now 100% post-consumer paper across campus. "Energy Star purchasing policy is in place for all computers and appliances; further all computers are EPEAT gold Rated." "Green cleaning products and low-VOC paints are in use across campus." Similarly, all promotional materials are printed on Forest Stewardship Council Certified paper. An Energy Star purchasing policy is in place for all computers and appliances. Green cleaning products are in use across campus, and low-VOC paints are used in high-sensitivity areas. Recent major renovations have featured rapidly renewable or recycled building materials, including linoleum flooring, bamboo flooring, and composite countertops made from post-industrial content. Compostable plates and cutlery are in use in all cafeterias, and locally produced/organic foods are offered in increasing volumes. Energy Management and Carbon Emission Reductions In 2007, The New School signed on to the NYC Mayoral Challenge to Universities to reduce carbon emissions by 30% by 2017. The New School began the challenge with the lowest CO2 footprint of all participating schools, and is already taking steps to further minimize its impact on global climate change. 100% of electricity directly paid for by the university is offset with Renewable Energy Credits from wind power. The New School has conducted a lighting retrofit in its five largest

buildings, and is in the process of conducting an investment grade audit of its mechanical systems

ADMISSIONS
Freshman Academic Profile: Average high school GPA 3.2. Minimum paper TOEFL 550. Minimum computer TOEFL 213. Minimum web-based TOEFL 92. **Basis for Candidate Selection:** *Very important factors considered include:* Level of applicant's interest, talent/ability. *Important factors considered include:* Rigor of secondary school record. *Other factors considered include:* Application essay, academic GPA, recommendation(s), extracurricular activities. **Freshman Admission Requirements:** High school diploma is required and GED is accepted. **Freshman Admission Statistics:** 273 applied, 71% admitted, 25% enrolled. **Transfer Admission Requirements:** College transcript(s), essay or personal statement, Lowest grade transferable C. **General Admission Information:** Application fee $100. Notification on a rolling basis, beginning on or about 4/1. Nonfall registration accepted.

COSTS AND FINANCIAL AID
Required Forms and Deadlines: FAFSA, state aid form. Priority financial aid filing date 3/1. **Notification of Awards:** Applicants will be notified of awards on a rolling basis beginning 3/1. **Types of Aid:** *Need-based scholarships/grants:* Federal Pell, SEOG, state scholarships/grants, private scholarships, the school's own gift aid. *Loans:* FFEL Subsidized Stafford, FFEL Unsubsidized Stafford, FFEL PLUS, Federal Perkins. *Student Employment:* Federal Work-Study Program available. Institutional employment available. Off-campus job opportunities are excellent. **Financial Aid Statistics:** 42% freshmen, 38% undergrads receive need-based scholarship or grant aid. 5% undergrads receive non-need-based scholarship or grant aid. 33% freshmen, 43% undergrads receive need-based self-help aid. 73% freshmen, 78% undergrads receive any aid. 47% undergrads borrow to pay for school. Average cumulative indebtedness $29,809. **Criteria for awarding institutional aid:** *Non-need-based:* Academics, music/drama.

See page 1172.

NEW WORLD SCHOOL OF THE ARTS

300 NE 2nd Avenue, Miami, FL 33132
Phone: 305-237-7007
E-mail: nwsaadm@mdc.edu
Fax: 305-237-3794 **Website:** www.mdc.edu/nwsa

This public school was founded in 1984. It has a 2-acre campus.

RATINGS
Admissions Selectivity Rating: 60*   **Fire Safety Rating:** 60*   **Green Rating:** 60*

STUDENTS AND FACULTY
Enrollment: 359. **Student Body:** 52% female, 48% male, 17% out-of-state, (17 countries represented). Asian 4%, African American 11%, Caucasian 31%, Hispanic 51%.
Retention and Graduation: 50% grads pursue arts and sciences degrees. **Faculty:** Student/faculty ratio 10:1. 20 full-time faculty, 100% hold PhDs, 20% are are members of minority groups, 35% are women.

ACADEMICS
Degrees: Associate, bachelor's. **Majors with Highest Enrollment:** Dance; graphic design. **Special Study Options:** Cooperative education program, distance learning, English as a Second Language (ESL), independent study, liberal arts/career combination.

FACILITIES
Housing: 100% of campus accessible to physically disabled. **Special Academic Facilities/Equipment:** Black box theater, art gallery, dance recital hall. **Computers:** Students can register for classes online. Administrative functions (other than registration) can be performed online.

CAMPUS LIFE
Environment: Metropolis. **Activities:** Dance, drama/theater, music ensembles, musical theater, opera, student government, symphony orchestra.

ADMISSIONS
Freshman Academic Profile: 99% from public high schools. Minimum paper TOEFL 550. Minimum computer TOEFL 213. **Basis for Candidate Selection:** *Very important factors considered include:* Talent/ability. *Other factors considered include:* Application essay, recommendation(s), rigor of secondary school record, character/personal qualities, interview. **Freshman Admission Requirements:** High school diploma is required and GED is accepted. **Transfer Admission Requirements:** High school transcript, college transcript(s),

essay or personal statement, interview, Lowest grade transferable c. **General Admission Information:** Nonfall registration not accepted. Credit and/or placement offered for CEEB Advanced Placement tests.

COSTS AND FINANCIAL AID

Annual in-state tuition $10,000. Annual out-of-state tuition $15,000. Average book expense $600. **Required Forms and Deadlines:** FAFSA. **Types of Aid:** *Need-based scholarships/grants:* Federal Pell, SEOG, state scholarships/grants, private scholarships, the school's own gift aid. *Loans:* Direct Subsidized Stafford, Direct Unsubsidized Stafford, Direct PLUS, FFEL PLUS, Federal Perkins, state loans, college/university loans from institutional funds. *Student Employment:* Federal Work-Study Program available. Off-campus job opportunities are excellent. **Criteria for awarding institutional aid:** *Non-need-based:* Art, music/drama.

NEW YORK INSTITUTE OF TECHNOLOGY

PO Box 8000, Northern Boulevard, Old Westbury, NY 11568
Phone: 516-686-7520
E-mail: admissions@nyit.edu **CEEB Code:** 2561
Fax: 516-686-7613 **Website:** www.nyit.edu **ACT Code:** 2832

This private school was founded in 1955. It has a 525-acre campus.

RATINGS

Admissions Selectivity Rating: 73   **Fire Safety Rating:** 60*   **Green Rating:** 60*

STUDENTS AND FACULTY

Enrollment: 5,141. **Student Body:** 38% female, 62% male, 10% out-of-state, 7% international Asian 10%, African American 11%, Caucasian 33%, Hispanic 10%.
Retention and Graduation: 71% freshmen return for sophomore year. 14% freshmen graduate within 4 years. 29% grads go on to further study within 1 year. 21% grads pursue arts and sciences degrees. 1% grads pursue law degrees. 33% grads pursue business degrees. 2% grads pursue medical degrees. **Faculty:** Student/faculty ratio 16:1. 218 full-time faculty, 89% hold PhDs, 22% are are members of minority groups, 23% are women.

ACADEMICS

Degrees: Associate, bachelor's, certificate, first professional, master's, post-bachelor's certificate, post-master's certificate, terminal associate, transfer associate. **Classes:** Most classes have 10–19 students. Most lab/discussion sessions have 10–19 students. **Majors with Highest Enrollment:** Architecture (BArch, BA/BS, MArch, MA/MS, PhD); business, management, marketing, and related support services, other; communication studies/speech communication and rhetoric. **Special Study Options:** Accelerated program, cooperative education program, cross-registration, distance learning, double major, dual enrollment, English as a Second Language (ESL), honors program, independent study, internships, liberal arts/career combination, study abroad, teacher certification program, weekend college, combined bachelor's/professional degree program in Life Sciences (BS)/Osteopathic Medicine (DO); Architectural Technology (BS)/Energy Managment (MS); Architectural Technology (BS)/MBA; Mechanical Engineering (BS)/Energy Managment (MS); Life Sciences (BS)/Physical Therapy (MS) Life Sciences (BS)/Occupational Therapy (MS); Behavioral Sciences (BS)/Law at Touro Law Center (JD). **Combined degree programs:** BA/JD, BA/MA, BS/MS; BS/MBA. Special programs offered to physically disabled students include tutors. **Career services:** Alumni network, alumni services, career/job search classes, career assessment, internships, regional alumni.

FACILITIES

Housing: Coed dorms, special housing for international students, fraternity/sorority housing, apartments for single students, Housing for graduate, life sciences, first-year experience, student leaders, student government, international, Greek Life organizations and architecture students provided. For the Manhattan Campus, housing is available off-campus. 100% of campus accessible to physically disabled. **Special Academic Facilities/Equipment:** Center for Urban/Suburban Studies; Center for Neighborhood Revitalization; Parkinson's Disease Treatment Center; Center for Energy Policy and Research; Academic Computing Labs; Center for Labor and Industrial Relations; Carleton Group (Advertising) LI News Tonight; Education Enterprise Zone; Center for Teaching and Learning with Technology, Production House, Motion Graphics Laboratory; Academic Health Care Center; Center for Business Information Technologies; de Seversky Culinary Arts Center. **Computers:** Students can register for classes online. Administrative functions (other than registration) can be performed online. Undergraduates are required to own a computer.

CAMPUS LIFE

Environment: Village. **Activities:** Choral groups, dance, drama/theater, literary magazine, musical theater, radio station, student government, student newspaper, student-run film society, television station, yearbook. **Organizations:** 100 registered organizations, 14 honor societies, 4 religious organizations. 5 fraternities, 3 sororities. **Athletics (Intercollegiate):** *Men:* Baseball, basketball, cross-country, lacrosse, soccer, track/field (outdoor). *Women:* Basketball, cross-country, soccer, softball, track/field (outdoor), volleyball. **On-Campus Highlights:** Libraries, computer clusters, radio/television studios, CAD rooms, motion graphics laboratory, engineering labs, allied health facilities, de Seversky Culinary Arts Center.

ADMISSIONS

Freshman Academic Profile: Average high school GPA 3.1. 60% from public high schools. SAT Math middle 50% range 510–630. SAT Critical Reading middle 50% range 470–580. ACT middle 50% range 20–27. Minimum paper TOEFL 550. Minimum computer TOEFL 213. **Basis for Candidate Selection:** *Very important factors considered include:* Rigor of secondary school record. *Important factors considered include:* Application essay, standardized test scores, interview. *Other factors considered include:* Class rank, recommendation(s), character/personal qualities, extracurricular activities, talent/ability, volunteer work, work experience. **Freshman Admission Requirements:** High school diploma is required and GED is accepted. *Academic units required:* 4 English, 2 mathematics, 1 science, (1 science labs), 2 social studies, 7 academic electives. *Academic units recommended:* 4 English, 3 mathematics, 2 science, (1 science labs), 2 social studies, 7 academic electives. **Freshman Admission Statistics:** 3,511 applied, 76% admitted, 33% enrolled. **Transfer Admission Requirements:** College transcript(s), essay or personal statement, minimum college GPA of 2.0 required. Lowest grade transferable C–. **General Admission Information:** Application fee $50. Notification on a rolling basis, beginning on or about 1/1. Nonfall registration accepted. Admission may be deferred for a maximum of 1 year. Credit and/or placement offered for CEEB Advanced Placement tests.

COSTS AND FINANCIAL AID

Annual tuition $16,926. Room and board $7,780. Required fees $300. Average book expense $1,200. **Required Forms and Deadlines:** FAFSA. Priority financial aid filing date 3/1. **Notification of Awards:** Applicants will be notified of awards on a rolling basis beginning 3/15. **Types of Aid:** *Need-based scholarships/grants:* Federal Pell, SEOG, state scholarships/grants, private scholarships, the school's own gift aid. *Loans:* FFEL Subsidized Stafford, FFEL Unsubsidized Stafford, FFEL PLUS, Federal Perkins, Federal Nursing, Alternative loans. *Student Employment:* Federal Work-Study Program available. Institutional employment available. Highest amount earned per year from on-campus jobs $2,200. Off-campus job opportunities are good. **Financial Aid Statistics:** 56% freshmen, 79% undergrads receive need-based scholarship or grant aid. 62% freshmen, 64% undergrads receive non-need-based scholarship or grant aid. 75% freshmen, 84% undergrads receive need-based self-help aid. 5% freshmen, 5% undergrads receive athletic scholarships. 75% undergrads borrow to pay for school. Average cumulative indebtedness $17,125. **Criteria for awarding institutional aid:** *Non-need-based:* Academics, alumni affiliation, athletics.

NEW YORK SCHOOL OF INTERIOR DESIGN

107 East 70th Street, New York, NY 10021
Phone: 212-472-1500 **Financial Aid Phone:** 212-472-1500
E-mail: admissions@nysid.edu **CEEB Code:** 333
Fax: 212-472-1867 **Website:** **ACT Code:** 2829

This private school was founded in 1916.

RATINGS

Admissions Selectivity Rating: 60*   **Fire Safety Rating:** 60*   **Green Rating:** 60*

STUDENTS AND FACULTY

Enrollment: 614. **Student Body:** 93% female, 7% male, 36% out-of-state, 8% international Asian 7%, African American 3%, Caucasian 74%, Hispanic 6%. **Retention and Graduation:** 60% freshmen return for sophomore year. **Faculty:** Student/faculty ratio 10:1. 2 full-time faculty, 50% are women.

ACADEMICS

Degrees: Associate, bachelor's, certificate, first professional, master's, transfer associate. **Classes:** Most classes have 10–19 students. **Majors with Highest Enrollment:** Interior design. **Special Study Options:** Independent study, internships, study abroad. Special programs offered to physically disabled students include tutors. **Career services:** Alumni network, alumni services, internships.

FACILITIES

Housing: 100% of campus accessible to physically disabled. **Special Academic Facilities/Equipment:** Three galleries, lighting laboratory, student atelier.

CAMPUS LIFE

Environment: Metropolis. **Activities: Organizations:** 1 registered organizations.

ADMISSIONS

Freshman Academic Profile: Average high school GPA 3. Minimum paper TOEFL 550. Minimum computer TOEFL 213. **Basis for Candidate Selection:** *Very important factors considered include:* Application essay, rigor of secondary school record, talent/ability. *Important factors considered include:* Academic GPA, recommendation(s), level of applicant's interest. *Other factors considered include:* Class rank, standardized test scores, alumni/ae relation, character/personal qualities, extracurricular activities, interview, work experience. **Freshman Admission Requirements:** High school diploma is required and GED is accepted. *Academic units recommended:* 4 English, 2 mathematics, 2 science, 2 foreign language, 2 social studies, 2 history. **Freshman Admission Statistics:** 38 applied, 76% admitted, 34% enrolled. **Transfer Admission Requirements:** High school transcript, college transcript(s), essay or personal statement, minimum college GPA of 3.0 required. Lowest grade transferable C. **General Admission Information:** Application fee $50. Regular notification 4/1. Nonfall registration accepted. Admission may be deferred for a maximum of 1 year. Credit offered for CEEB Advanced Placement tests.

COSTS AND FINANCIAL AID

Annual tuition $18,600. Required fees $290. **Required Forms and Deadlines:** FAFSA, institution's own financial aid form, state aid form. Priority financial aid filing date 5/1. **Notification of Awards:** Applicants will be notified of awards on a rolling basis beginning 2/1. **Types of Aid:** *Need-based scholarships/grants:* Federal Pell, SEOG, state scholarships/grants, the school's own gift aid. *Loans:* FFEL Subsidized Stafford, FFEL Unsubsidized Stafford, FFEL PLUS. *Student Employment:* Federal Work-Study Program available. Off-campus job opportunities are excellent. **Financial Aid Statistics:** 31% undergrads receive need-based scholarship or grant aid. 19% undergrads receive need-based self-help aid. 15% undergrads receive any aid. 15% undergrads borrow to pay for school. Average cumulative indebtedness $30,000.

See page 1176.

NEW YORK UNIVERSITY

665 Broadway, 11th Floor, New York, NY 10012
Phone: 212-998-4500 **Financial Aid Phone:** 212-998-4444
E-mail: admissions@nyu.edu **CEEB Code:** 2562
Fax: 212-995-4902 **Website:** www.nyu.edu **ACT Code:** 2838

This private school was founded in 1831.

RATINGS

Admissions Selectivity Rating: 96   **Fire Safety Rating:** 82   **Green Rating:** 95

STUDENTS AND FACULTY

Enrollment: 21,227. **Student Body:** 61% female, 39% male, 65% out-of-state, 8% international (133 countries represented). Asian 20%, African American 4%, Caucasian 46%, Hispanic 8%.
Retention and Graduation: 91% freshmen return for sophomore year. 78% freshmen graduate within 4 years. 24% grads go on to further study within 1 year. 5% grads pursue arts and sciences degrees. 7% grads pursue law degrees. 1% grads pursue business degrees. 3% grads pursue medical degrees. **Faculty:** Student/faculty ratio 11:1. 2315 full-time faculty, 92% hold PhDs, 19% are are members of minority groups, 40% are women.

ACADEMICS

Degrees: Associate, bachelor's, certificate, diploma, doctoral, master's, post-bachelor's certificate, post-master's certificate, terminal associate, transfer associate. **Classes:** Most classes have 10–19 students. Most lab/discussion sessions have 10–19 students. **Majors with Highest Enrollment:** Drama and dramatics/theatre arts; finance; liberal arts and sciences/liberal studies. **Special Study Options:** Cross-registration, distance learning, double major, English as a Second Language (ESL), exchange student program (domestic), honors program, independent study, internships, liberal arts/career combination, student-designed major, study abroad, teacher certification program, exchange program with several historically black colleges. **Combined degree programs:** BA/DDS. Special programs offered to physically disabled students include note-taking services, reader services, tape recorders **Career services:** Alumni

network, alumni services, career/job search classes, career assessment, internships, regional alumni. **Career services highlights include:** Students have multiple opportunites to advance their entrepreneurial learning through course work, business planning competitions, workshops, mentoring and coaching.

FACILITIES

Housing: Coed dorms, special housing for disabled students, fraternity/sorority housing, apartments for single students, wellness house, theme housing, Choices substance free communities, FYRE: First Year Residential Experience, Sophomore Year Residential Experience, Explorations Learning Communities, mixed sex housing. 95% of campus accessible to physically disabled. **Special Academic Facilities/Equipment:** Bobst Library and study center; Grey Art Gallery and study center; special academic facilities for arts, business, culture, education, international relations, language, law, media, music, public service, research, and social policy, and Skirball Center for Performing Arts. **Computers:** 70% of classrooms, 100% of libraries, 100% of dining areas, 100% of student union, 50% of common outdoor areas have wireless network access. Students can register for classes online. Administrative functions (other than registration) can be performed online.

CAMPUS LIFE

Environment: Metropolis. **Activities:** Choral groups, concert band, dance, drama/theater, jazz band, literary magazine, music ensembles, musical theater, opera, pep band, radio station, student government, student newspaper, student-run film society, symphony orchestra, television station, yearbook, campus ministries, international student organization, Model UN. **Organizations:** 407 registered organizations, 3 honor societies, 31 religious organizations. 14 fraternities, 10 sororities. **Athletics (Intercollegiate):** *Men:* Basketball, cross-country, diving, fencing, golf, soccer, swimming, tennis, track/field (outdoor), track/field (indoor), volleyball, wrestling. *Women:* Basketball, cross-country, diving, fencing, golf, soccer, swimming, tennis, track/field (outdoor), track/field (indoor), volleyball. **On-Campus Highlights:** Kimmel Center for Student Life, Silver Center for Arts and Science, Coles Athletic Center, Palladium Athletic Facility, Skirball Center for the Performing Arts. **Environmental Initiatives:** 1) Launched a comprehensive sustainability initiative that has learned from earlier schools' efforts, leapfrogging peer schools to achieve new levels of environmental performance—in two years, launched Sustainability Task Force with 60 volunteer members and 8 working groups; Green Grants program and 40 individual grants; Sustainability Advocate Program for more than 100 employees; Student Outreach Initiative reaching 10,000 students in dorms; green purchasing policy that when adopted will affect as much as 100 million dollars of procured goods annually; hired half a dozen full-time-equivalent sustainability staff; executed an annual Environmental Assessment process; released more than 90 recommendations to the university leadership; created a website that has become the networking hub of the green community on campus; etc.! 2) Substantively reduced measured electricity use 5% in one year, with strategies ranging from efficiency upgrades to dorm competitions, and with plans to do it again this next year. 3) Committed to an aggressive 10–year, 30% emissions reduction, and a long-term commitment to climate neutrality—all the more significant because NYU is already extremely efficient because of its location and layout in a dense urban center (NYC), and because it is one of the largest private universities in the world, amounting a substantial portion of NYC's emissions, and NYC 1% of the US.

ADMISSIONS

Freshman Academic Profile: Average high school GPA 3.6. 64% in top 10% of high school class, 92% in top 25% of high school class, 100% in top 50% of high school class. 65% from public high schools. SAT Math middle 50% range 600–720. SAT Critical Reading middle 50% range 610–710. SAT Writing middle 50% range 620–710. ACT middle 50% range 27–31. **Basis for Candidate Selection:** *Very important factors considered include:* Application essay, academic GPA, recommendation(s), rigor of secondary school record, standardized test scores, extracurricular activities, talent/ability. *Important factors considered include:* Class rank, alumni/ae relation, character/personal qualities, first generation, geographical residence. *Other factors considered include:* Racial/ethnic status, volunteer work, work experience. **Freshman Admission Requirements:** High school diploma is required and GED is accepted. *Academic units required:* 4 English, 3 mathematics, 3 science, 2 foreign language, 4 history. *Academic units recommended:* 4 English, 4 mathematics, 4 science, 3 foreign language, 4 history. **Freshman Admission Statistics:** 37,462 applied, 38% admitted, 35% enrolled. **Transfer Admission Requirements:** High school transcript, college transcript(s), essay or personal statement, statement of good standing from prior institution(s). Lowest grade transferable C. **General Admission Information:** Application fee $65. Early decision application deadline 11/1. Regular application deadline 1/1. Regular notification 4/1. Nonfall registration not accepted. Admission may be deferred for a maximum of 1 year. Credit offered for CEEB Advanced Placement tests.

COSTS AND FINANCIAL AID

Required Forms and Deadlines: FAFSA, state aid form, Early Decision applicants may submit an institutional form for an estimated award. Financial aid filing deadline 2/15. **Notification of Awards:** Applicants will be notified of awards on a rolling basis beginning 4/1. **Types of Aid:** *Need-based scholarships/ grants:* Federal Pell, SEOG, state scholarships/grants, private scholarships, the school's own gift aid. *Loans:* FFEL Subsidized Stafford, FFEL Unsubsidized Stafford, FFEL PLUS, Federal Perkins, Federal Nursing *Student Employment:* Federal Work-Study Program available. Institutional employment available. Highest amount earned per year from on-campus jobs $24,026. Off-campus job opportunities are excellent. **Financial Aid Statistics:** 51% freshmen, 49% undergrads receive need-based scholarship or grant aid. 49% freshmen, 47% undergrads receive need-based self-help aid. 58% freshmen, 58% undergrads receive any aid. 59% undergrads borrow to pay for school. Average cumulative indebtedness $33,487. **Criteria for awarding institutional aid:** *Non-need- based:* Academics.

See page 1178.

NEWBERRY COLLEGE

2100 College Street, Newberry, SC 29108
Phone: 803-321-5127
E-mail: admissions@newberry.edu **CEEB Code:** 5493
Fax: 803-321-5138 **Website:** www.newberry.edu **ACT Code:** 3870

This private school, affiliated with the Lutheran Church, was founded in 1856. It has a 60-acre campus.

RATINGS
Admissions Selectivity Rating: 72   **Fire Safety Rating:** 60*   **Green Rating:** 60*

STUDENTS AND FACULTY
Enrollment: 764. **Student Body:** 43% female, 57% male, 25% out-of-state, 2% international (8 countries represented). African American 27%, Caucasian 71%, Hispanic 1%, Native American 1%.
Retention and Graduation: 58% freshmen return for sophomore year. 36% freshmen graduate within 4 years. 15% grads go on to further study within 1 year. **Faculty:** Student/faculty ratio 13:1. 46 full-time faculty, 61% hold PhDs, 9% are are members of minority groups, 37% are women.

ACADEMICS
Degrees: Bachelor's. **Classes:** Most classes have fewer than 10 students. Most lab/discussion sessions have 20–29 students. **Majors with Highest Enrollment:** Business/commerce; communication studies/speech communication and rhetoric; elementary education and teaching. **Special Study Options:** Cooperative education program, double major, dual enrollment, honors program, independent study, internships, liberal arts/career combination, student-designed major, study abroad, teacher certification program **Honors programs:** Summerland Honors Program- Focus is on human identity-honors credit may substitute for cored curriculum. Special programs offered to physically disabled students include tutors. **Career services:** Alumni services, career/job search classes, internships.

FACILITIES
Housing: Coed dorms, men's dorms, women's dorms. 90% of campus accessible to physically disabled. **Special Academic Facilities/Equipment:** TV studio.

CAMPUS LIFE
Environment: Rural. **Activities:** Choral groups, concert band, drama/theater, jazz band, literary magazine, marching band, music ensembles, radio station, student government, student newspaper, television station, yearbook. **Organizations:** 50 registered organizations, 11 honor societies, 4 religious organizations. 5 fraternities, 4 sororities. **Athletics (Intercollegiate):** *Men:* Baseball, basketball, cross-country, football, golf, soccer, tennis. *Women:* Basketball, cheerleading, cross-country, golf, soccer, softball, tennis, volleyball. **On-Campus Highlights:** The Quad—grassy lawn area, Steele Student Center—snack bar, game room, Fitness Center in Physical Education Complex, John F. Clarkson Swimming Pool, Weber Ministries House.

ADMISSIONS
Freshman Academic Profile: Average high school GPA 3.2. 7% in top 10% of high school class, 22% in top 25% of high school class, 61% in top 50% of high school class. 88% from public high schools. SAT Math middle 50% range 460–600. SAT Critical Reading middle 50% range 490–570. ACT middle 50% range 17–22. Minimum paper TOEFL 525. Minimum computer TOEFL 197. **Basis for Candidate Selection:** *Very important factors considered include:* Rigor of secondary school record, standardized test scores. *Important factors considered include:* Class rank. *Other factors considered include:* Application essay, recommendation(s), alumni/ae relation, character/personal qualities,

extracurricular activities, geographical residence, interview, racial/ethnic status, religious affiliation/commitment, state residency, talent/ability, volunteer work, work experience. **Freshman Admission Requirements:** High school diploma is required and GED is accepted. *Academic units required:* 4 English, 3 mathematics, 2 science, (2 science labs), 2 foreign language, 2 social studies, 1 history, 1 academic electives. *Academic units recommended:* 4 English, 3 mathematics, 2 science, (2 science labs), 2 foreign language, 2 social studies, 1 history, 1 academic electives. **Freshman Admission Statistics:** 41% enrolled. **Transfer Admission Requirements:** College transcript(s), minimum college GPA of 2.0 required. Lowest grade transferable C. **General Admission Information:** Application fee $30. Notification on a rolling basis, beginning on or about 9/30. Nonfall registration accepted. Admission may be deferred for a maximum of 2 years. Credit and/or placement offered for CEEB Advanced Placement tests.

COSTS AND FINANCIAL AID
Annual tuition $17,470. Room and board $5,890. Required fees $631. Average book expense $1,195. **Required Forms and Deadlines:** FAFSA, institution's own financial aid form. Priority financial aid filing date 3/15. **Types of Aid:** *Need-based scholarships/grants:* Federal Pell, SEOG, state scholarships/grants, private scholarships, the school's own gift aid. *Loans:* FFEL Subsidized Stafford, FFEL Unsubsidized Stafford, FFEL PLUS, Federal Perkins, state loans *Student Employment:* Federal Work-Study Program available. Institutional employment available. Off-campus job opportunities are poor. **Financial Aid Statistics:** 83% freshmen, 84% undergrads receive need-based scholarship or grant aid. 20% freshmen, 19% undergrads receive non-need-based scholarship or grant aid. 56% freshmen, 59% undergrads receive need-based self-help aid. 16% freshmen, 11% undergrads receive athletic scholarships. 98% undergrads borrow to pay for school. Average cumulative indebtedness $13,477. **Criteria for awarding institutional aid:** *Non-need-based:* Academics, alumni affiliation, athletics, music/drama, religious affiliation, state/district residency.

NEWMAN UNIVERSITY

3100 McCormick Avenue, Wichita, KS 67213-2097
Phone: 316-942-4291
E-mail: admissions@newmanu.edu **CEEB Code:** 6615
Fax: 316-942-4483 **Website:** www.newmanu.edu **ACT Code:** 1452

This private school, affiliated with the Roman Catholic Church, was founded in 1933. It has a 53-acre campus.

RATINGS
Admissions Selectivity Rating: 76   **Fire Safety Rating:** 60*   **Green Rating:** 60*

STUDENTS AND FACULTY
Enrollment: 1,843. **Student Body:** 62% female, 38% male, 11% out-of-state, 6% international (26 countries represented). Asian 3%, African American 5%, Caucasian 77%, Hispanic 7%, Native American 2%.
Retention and Graduation: Faculty: Student/faculty ratio 17:1. 66 full-time faculty.

ACADEMICS
Degrees: Associate, bachelor's, master's, terminal associate, transfer associate. **Classes:** Most classes have 10–19 students. Most lab/discussion sessions have 10–19 students. **Special Study Options:** Cooperative education program, cross-registration, distance learning, double major, dual enrollment, independent study, internships, liberal arts/career combination, student-designed major, study abroad, teacher certification program, weekend college. Special programs offered to physically disabled students include note-taking services, reader services, tape recorders, tutors.

FACILITIES
Housing: Coed dorms, special housing for disabled students, apartments for married students, apartments for single students, Freshmen required to live in college housng first 2 years if not living with parents. 95% of campus accessible to physically disabled. **Special Academic Facilities/Equipment:** Cadaver lab; art gallery.

CAMPUS LIFE
Activities: Choral groups, drama/theater, literary magazine, radio station, student government, student newspaper. **Organizations:** 25 registered organizations, 3 honor societies, 2 religious organizations. **Athletics (Intercollegiate):** *Men:* Baseball, basketball, golf, soccer. *Women:* Basketball, golf, soccer, softball, volleyball.

ADMISSIONS
Freshman Academic Profile: Average high school GPA 3.35. 12% in top 10% of high school class, 26% in top 25% of high school class, 52% in top 50% of high school class. 78% from public high schools. Minimum paper TOEFL 530.

Basis for Candidate Selection: *Very important factors considered include:* Rigor of secondary school record, standardized test scores. *Other factors considered include:* Recommendation(s). **Freshman Admission Requirements:** High school diploma is required and GED is accepted. *Academic units recommended:* 4 English, 3 mathematics, 3 science, 3 social studies. **Transfer Admission Requirements:** College transcript(s), minimum college GPA of 2.0 required. Lowest grade transferable D. **General Admission Information:** Application fee $20. Notification on a rolling basis, beginning on or about 6/1. Nonfall registration accepted. Admission may be deferred for a maximum of 2 years. Credit offered for CEEB Advanced Placement tests.

COSTS AND FINANCIAL AID
Annual tuition $14,650. Room and board $5,060. Required fees $180. Average book expense $800. **Required Forms and Deadlines:** FAFSA, institution's own financial aid form. Priority financial aid filing date 3/1. **Notification of Awards:** Applicants will be notified of awards on a rolling basis beginning 1/2. **Types of Aid:** *Need-based scholarships/grants:* Federal Pell, SEOG, state scholarships/grants, private scholarships, the school's own gift aid. *Loans:* FFEL Subsidized Stafford, FFEL Unsubsidized Stafford, FFEL PLUS, Federal Perkins. *Student Employment:* Highest amount earned per year from on-campus jobs $1,200. **Financial Aid Statistics:** 51% freshmen, 60% undergrads receive need-based scholarship or grant aid. 52% freshmen, 35% undergrads receive non-need-based scholarship or grant aid. 47% freshmen, 60% undergrads receive need-based self-help aid. 36% freshmen, 29% undergrads receive athletic scholarships. 69% undergrads borrow to pay for school. Average cumulative indebtedness $18,808. **Criteria for awarding institutional aid:** *Non-need-based:* Academics, alumni affiliation, athletics, leadership, minority status, music/drama, religious affiliation.

NIAGARA UNIVERSITY

Bailo Hall, PO Box 2011, Niagara University, NY 14109
Phone: 716-286-8700 **Financial Aid Phone:** 716-286-8686
E-mail: admissions@niagara.edu **CEEB Code:** 2558
Fax: 716-286-8710 **Website:** www.niagara.edu **ACT Code:** 2842

This private school, affiliated with the Roman Catholic Church, was founded in 1856. It has a 160-acre campus.

RATINGS
Admissions Selectivity Rating: 76   **Fire Safety Rating:** 60*   **Green Rating:** 81

STUDENTS AND FACULTY
Enrollment: 3,224. **Student Body:** 63% female, 37% male, 7% out-of-state, 16% international (12 countries represented). Asian 1%, African American 4%, Caucasian 68%, Hispanic 2%, Native American 1%.
Retention and Graduation: 76% freshmen return for sophomore year. 54% freshmen graduate within 4 years. 44% grads go on to further study within 1 year. 46% grads pursue arts and sciences degrees. 8% grads pursue law degrees. 33% grads pursue business degrees. 4% grads pursue medical degrees. **Faculty:** Student/faculty ratio 14:1. 149 full-time faculty, 92% hold PhDs, 15% are members of minority groups, 38% are women.

ACADEMICS
Degrees: Associate, bachelor's, certificate, master's, post-bachelor's certificate, post-master's certificate. **Classes:** Most classes have 10–19 students. Most lab/discussion sessions have 10–19 students. **Majors with Highest Enrollment:** Business/commerce; criminal justice/law enforcement administration; teacher education, multiple levels. **Special Study Options:** Accelerated program, cooperative education program, cross-registration, double major, dual enrollment, English as a Second Language (ESL), exchange student program (domestic), honors program, independent study, internships, liberal arts/career combination, study abroad, teacher certification program **Combined degree programs:** BA/MA, BBA/MBA. Special programs offered to physically disabled students include note-taking services, reader services, tape recorders, tutors. **Career services:** Alumni network, career/job search classes, career assessment, internships, regional alumni. **Career services highlights include:** "A cooperative educaton experience enables students to explore the world of work firsthand by providing a unique oportunity for them to earn while they learn. Students majoring in liberal arts, business or hospitality are eligible to particiapte in the co-op program in their junior or senior year, enabling them to gain academic credit as well as paid work experiences in their majors. The cooperative educaton program increases choices for students, and helps employeers to train and hire better qualified personnel." (NU Catalog, p.17)

FACILITIES
Housing: Coed dorms, apartments for single students. **Special Academic**

Facilities/Equipment: Castellani Art Museum. **Computers:** Students can register for classes online.

CAMPUS LIFE
Environment: Town. **Activities:** Choral groups, dance, drama/theater, musical theater, radio station, student government, student newspaper, yearbook, campus ministries, international student organization. **Organizations:** 70 registered organizations, 14 honor societies, 2 religious organizations. 3 fraternities, 2 sororities. **Athletics (Intercollegiate):** *Men:* Baseball, basketball, cross-country, diving, golf, ice hockey, soccer, swimming, tennis. *Women:* Basketball, cross-country, diving, golf, ice hockey, lacrosse, soccer, softball, swimming, tennis, volleyball. **On-Campus Highlights:** Gallagher Center, St.Vincent's Hall, Castellani Art Museum, Clet Hall, Dwyer Arena, Student Apartments. **Environmental Initiatives:** 55,000 sq. ft. academic complex opened in fall 2007 is LEED certifiable. 985 of the university's electricity is hydro-non carbon based.

ADMISSIONS
Freshman Academic Profile: Average high school GPA 3.3. 13% in top 10% of high school class, 41% in top 25% of high school class, 78% in top 50% of high school class. 95% from public high schools. SAT Math middle 50% range 470–570. SAT Critical Reading middle 50% range 490–590. ACT middle 50% range 19–25. Minimum paper TOEFL 500. Minimum computer TOEFL 173. **Basis for Candidate Selection:** *Very important factors considered include:* Rigor of secondary school record. *Important factors considered include:* Recommendation(s), standardized test scores, interview. *Other factors considered include:* Class rank, application essay, alumni/ae relation, character/personal qualities, extracurricular activities, talent/ability, volunteer work. **Freshman Admission Requirements:** High school diploma is required and GED is accepted. *Academic units required:* 4 English, 2 mathematics, 2 science, 2 foreign language, 2 social studies, 4 academic electives. **Freshman Admission Statistics:** 2,942 applied, 80% admitted, 29% enrolled. **Transfer Admission Requirements:** High school transcript, college transcript(s), minimum college GPA of 2.0 required. Lowest grade transferable C. **General Admission Information:** Application fee $30. Regular application deadline 8/1. Nonfall registration accepted. Admission may be deferred for a maximum of 12. Credit offered for CEEB Advanced Placement tests.

COSTS AND FINANCIAL AID
Annual tuition $23,700. Room and board $10,250. Required fees $1,000. Average book expense $1,050. **Required Forms and Deadlines:** FAFSA, state aid form. Priority financial aid filing date 2/15. **Notification of Awards:** Applicants will be notified of awards on a rolling basis beginning 3/1. **Types of Aid:** *Need-based scholarships/grants:* Federal Pell, SEOG, state scholarships/grants, private scholarships, the school's own gift aid. *Loans:* Direct Subsidized Stafford, Direct Unsubsidized Stafford, Direct PLUS, Federal Perkins, Federal Nursing, state loans, college/university loans from institutional funds. *Student Employment:* Federal Work-Study Program available. Highest amount earned per year from on-campus jobs $1,800. Off-campus job opportunities are excellent. **Financial Aid Statistics:** 84% freshmen, 70% undergrads receive need-based scholarship or grant aid. 63% freshmen, 33% undergrads receive non-need-based scholarship or grant aid. 69% freshmen, 57% undergrads receive need-based self-help aid. 4% freshmen, 4% undergrads receive athletic scholarships. 85% freshmen, 82% undergrads receive any aid. 82% undergrads borrow to pay for school. Average cumulative indebtedness $27,215. **Criteria for awarding institutional aid:** *Non-need-based:* Academics, athletics.

See page 1180.

NICHOLLS STATE UNIVERSITY

P.O. Box 2004, Thibodaux, LA 70310
Phone: 985-448-4507 **Financial Aid Phone:** 985-448-4048
E-mail: nicholls@nicholls.edu **CEEB Code:** 6221
Fax: 985-448-4929 **Website:** www.nicholls.edu **ACT Code:** 1580

This public school was founded in 1948. It has a 210-acre campus.

RATINGS
Admissions Selectivity Rating: 73   **Fire Safety Rating:** 71   **Green Rating:** 60*

STUDENTS AND FACULTY
Enrollment: 6,246. **Student Body:** 61% female, 39% male, 4% out-of-state, 2% international (40 countries represented). Asian 1%, African American 18%, Caucasian 73%, Hispanic 1%, Native American 2%.
Retention and Graduation: Faculty: Student/faculty ratio 20:1. 295 full-time faculty, 54% hold PhDs, 11% are are members of minority groups, 51% are women. 1% of classes are taught by teaching assistants.

ACADEMICS

Degrees: Associate, bachelor's, certificate, master's, post-master's certificate. **Classes:** Most classes have 20–29 students. **Majors with Highest Enrollment:** Business administration and management; general studies; nursing/registered nurse (RN, ASN, BSN, MSN). **Special Study Options:** Cooperative education program, cross-registration, distance learning, dual enrollment, honors program, independent study, internships, study abroad, teacher certification program. **Honors programs:** You can learn advanced material in small classes taught by outstanding professors. You can enrich your college experience through intellectually stimulating courses that allow you to reach your potential. The Honors Program invites all academically talented and intellectually curious students to participate. By joining the program you can become a select member of the campus community and associate with students who share similar goals and interests. The Program is designed to meet students' needs and interests. Therefore, students in the program determine their degree of involvement. You may take as many honors courses as you choose or simply successfully complete one-three hour honors course each year. And because honors classes fit degree requirements for all majors, participants graduate on time. **Combined degree programs:** BA/MA. Special programs offered to physically disabled students include note-taking services, reader services, tape recorders, tutors. **Career services:** Alumni network, alumni services, career/job search classes, career assessment, internships.

FACILITIES

Housing: Special housing for disabled students, men's dorms, special housing for international students, women's dorms, apartments for married students, apartments for single students, wellness house. **Special Academic Facilities/Equipment:** Ameen Art Gallery. **Computers:** 100% of classrooms, 100% of dorms, 100% of libraries, 100% of dining areas, 100% of student union, 100% of common outdoor areas have wireless network access. Students can register for classes online. Administrative functions (other than registration) can be performed online.

CAMPUS LIFE

Environment: Village. **Activities:** Choral groups, concert band, dance, drama/theater, jazz band, literary magazine, marching band, music ensembles, musical theater, radio station, student government, student newspaper, student-run film society, television station, yearbook. **Organizations:** 121 registered organizations, 24 honor societies, 6 religious organizations. 10 fraternities, 5 sororities. **Athletics (Intercollegiate):** *Men:* Baseball, basketball, cross-country, football, golf, tennis. *Women:* Basketball, cross-country, golf, soccer, softball, tennis, track/field (outdoor), track/field (indoor), volleyball. **On-Campus Highlights:** Admissions Office, Student Union, Ellender Memorial Library, Guidry Stadium.

ADMISSIONS

Freshman Academic Profile: Average high school GPA 3.17. 18% in top 10% of high school class, 43% in top 25% of high school class, 73% in top 50% of high school class. 68% from public high schools. ACT middle 50% range 24–20. Minimum paper TOEFL 500. Minimum computer TOEFL 173. Minimum web-based TOEFL 61. **Basis for Candidate Selection:** *Very important factors considered include:* Rigor of secondary school record. *Important factors considered include:* standardized test scores. *Other factors considered include:* Class rank, academic GPA, talent/ability. **Freshman Admission Requirements:** High school diploma is required and GED is accepted. *Academic units required:* 4 English, 3 mathematics, 3 science, 2 foreign language, 1 social studies, 2 history, 2 academic electives. **Freshman Admission Statistics:** 2,420 applied, 82% admitted, 63% enrolled. **Transfer Admission Requirements:** College transcript(s), minimum college GPA of 2.0 required. Lowest grade transferable D. **General Admission Information:** Application fee $20. Notification on a rolling basis, beginning on or about 9/1. Nonfall registration accepted. Admission may be deferred for a maximum of 1 semester. Credit and/or placement offered for CEEB Advanced Placement tests.

COSTS AND FINANCIAL AID

Annual in-state tuition $2,231. Annual out-of-state tuition $7,679. Room and board $4,556. Required fees $1,364. Average book expense $1,200. **Required Forms and Deadlines:** FAFSA, institution's own financial aid form, state aid form, noncustodial PROFILE. Financial aid filing deadline 6/30. Priority financial aid filing date 4/15. **Types of Aid:** *Need-based scholarships/grants:* Federal Pell, SEOG, state scholarships/grants, private scholarships, the school's own gift aid. *Loans:* FFEL Subsidized Stafford, FFEL Unsubsidized Stafford, FFEL PLUS, Federal Perkins. *Student Employment:* Federal Work-Study Program available. Institutional employment available. Highest amount earned per year from on-campus jobs $8,112. Off-campus job opportunities are fair. **Financial Aid Statistics:** 44% freshmen, 42% undergrads receive need-based scholarship or grant aid. 32% freshmen, 16% undergrads receive non-need-based scholarship or grant aid. 24% freshmen, 33% undergrads receive need-based self-help aid. 3% freshmen, 3% undergrads receive athletic scholarships. 77% freshmen, 74% undergrads receive any aid. **Criteria for awarding institutional aid:** *Non-need-based:* Academics, athletics, state/district residency.

NICHOLS COLLEGE

PO Box 5000, 124 Center Rd, Dudley, MA 01571-5000
Phone: 508-213-2203 **Financial Aid Phone:** 508-213-2276
E-mail: admissions@nichols.edu **CEEB Code:** 3666
Fax: 508-943-9885 **Website:** www.nichols.edu **ACT Code:** 1878

This private school was founded in 1815. It has a 200-acre campus.

RATINGS

Admissions Selectivity Rating: 70 **Fire Safety Rating:** 60* **Green Rating:** 60*

STUDENTS AND FACULTY

Enrollment: 1,214. **Student Body:** 40% female, 60% male, 35% out-of-state, international (4 countries represented). Asian 1%, African American 4%, Caucasian 78%, Hispanic 3%.
Retention and Graduation: 43% freshmen graduate within 4 years. 7% grads go on to further study within 1 year. 2% grads pursue business degrees. **Faculty:** Student/faculty ratio 20:1. 34 full-time faculty, 56% hold PhDs, 3% are are members of minority groups, 29% are women.

ACADEMICS

Degrees: Associate, bachelor's, master's. **Classes:** Most classes have 20–29 students. Most lab/discussion sessions have 10–19 students. **Majors with Highest Enrollment:** Business/commerce; criminal justice/law enforcement administration; sport and fitness administration/management. **Special Study Options:** Cooperative education program, distance learning, double major, honors program, independent study, internships, liberal arts/career combination, study abroad, teacher certification program. **Combined degree programs:** Five year BSBA/MBA Program. Special programs offered to physically disabled students include tutors. **Career services:** Alumni network, alumni services, career/job search classes, career assessment, internships, regional alumni.

FACILITIES

Housing: Coed dorms, men's dorms, women's dorms, apartments for single students 80% of campus accessible to physically disabled. **Computers:** 10% of classrooms, 100% of libraries, 100% of dining areas, have wireless network access. Students can register for classes online. Administrative functions (other than registration) can be performed online.

CAMPUS LIFE

Environment: Village. **Activities:** drama/theater, literary magazine, musical theater, radio station, student government, student newspaper, yearbook. **Organizations:** 25 registered organizations, 5 honor societies, 1 religious organizations. **Athletics (Intercollegiate):** *Men:* Baseball, basketball, football, golf, ice hockey, lacrosse, soccer, tennis. *Women:* Basketball, field hockey, golf, ice hockey, lacrosse, soccer, softball, tennis **On-Campus Highlights:** Athletic and Recreation Complex, The Currier Center, Snack Bar in Alumni Hall, Davis Cafe, WNRC Radio Station.

ADMISSIONS

Freshman Academic Profile: Average high school GPA 2.61. 82% from public high schools. SAT Math middle 50% range 420–520. SAT Critical Reading middle 50% range 400–490. SAT Writing middle 50% range 418–473. Minimum paper TOEFL 550. Minimum computer TOEFL 213. **Basis for Candidate Selection:** *Very important factors considered include:* Application essay, recommendation(s), rigor of secondary school record. *Important factors considered include:* Academic GPA, standardized test scores, interview. *Other factors considered include:* Class rank, character/personal qualities, extracurricular activities, level of applicant's interest, talent/ability, volunteer work, work experience. **Freshman Admission Requirements:** High school diploma is required and GED is accepted. *Academic units required:* 4 English, 3 mathematics, 2 science, (2 science labs), 2 social studies, 5 academic electives. *Academic units recommended:* 4 mathematics, 3 science, (3 science labs), 2 foreign language. **Freshman Admission Statistics:** 1,894 applied, 77% admitted, 30% enrolled. **Transfer Admission Requirements:** High school transcript, college transcript(s), essay or personal statement, minimum college GPA of 2.0 required. Lowest grade transferable C. **General Admission Information:** Application fee $25. Notification on a rolling basis, beginning on or about 10/1. Nonfall registration accepted. Admission may be deferred for a maximum of 1 year. Neither credit nor placement offered for CEEB Advanced Placement tests.

COSTS AND FINANCIAL AID

Annual tuition $25,400. Room and board $8,960. Required fees $300. Average book expense $1,050. **Required Forms and Deadlines:** FAFSA. Financial aid filing deadline 6/1. Priority financial aid filing date 3/1. **Notification of Awards:** Applicants will be notified of awards on a rolling basis beginning 3/15. **Types of Aid:** *Need-based scholarships/grants:* Federal Pell, SEOG, state scholarships/grants, private scholarships. *Loans:* FFEL Subsidized Stafford, FFEL Unsubsidized Stafford, FFEL PLUS, state loans *Student Employment:* Federal Work-Study Program available. Institutional employment available. Highest amount earned per year from on-campus jobs $3,000. Off-campus job opportunities are fair. **Financial Aid Statistics:** 81% freshmen, 78% undergrads receive need-based scholarship or grant aid. 5% freshmen, 5% undergrads receive non-need-based scholarship or grant aid. 74% freshmen, 73% undergrads receive need-based self-help aid. 70% freshmen, 73% undergrads receive any aid. 84% undergrads borrow to pay for school. Average cumulative indebtedness $17,509. **Criteria for awarding institutional aid:** *Non-need-based:* Academics.

See page 1182.

NORTH CAROLINA A&T STATE UNIVERSITY

1601 East Market Street, Greensboro, NC 27411
Phone: 336-334-7946
E-mail: uadmit@ncat.edu
Fax: 336-334-7478 **Website:** www.ncat.edu

This is a public school.

RATINGS
Admissions Selectivity Rating: 68   **Fire Safety Rating:** 60*   **Green Rating:** 60*

STUDENTS AND FACULTY
Enrollment: 7,245. **Student Body:** 52% female, 48% male, 19% out-of-state, 1% international Asian 1%, African American 92%, Caucasian 5%.
Retention and Graduation: 77% freshmen return for sophomore year. **Faculty:** Student/faculty ratio 16:1. 404 full-time faculty, 90% hold PhDs, 28% are are members of minority groups, 35% are women.

ACADEMICS
Degrees: Bachelor's, master's. **Classes:** Most classes have 20–29 students.
Special Study Options: Cooperative education program, cross-registration, distance learning, double major, external degree program, honors program, independent study, internships, study abroad, teacher certification program.

FACILITIES
Housing: Coed dorms, men's dorms, women's dorms, theme housing, graduate housing.

CAMPUS LIFE
Activities: Choral groups, concert band, dance, drama/theater, jazz band, literary magazine, marching band, music ensembles, musical theater, opera, pep band, radio station, student government, student newspaper, student-run film society, symphony orchestra, television station, yearbook, international student organization, Model UN.

ADMISSIONS
Freshman Academic Profile: Average high school GPA 2.9. 8% in top 10% of high school class, 17% in top 25% of high school class, 49% in top 50% of high school class. 78% from public high schools. SAT Critical Reading middle 50% range 500–390. ACT middle 50% range 12–18. Minimum paper TOEFL 570. Minimum computer TOEFL 230. Minimum web-based TOEFL 88. **Basis for Candidate Selection:** *Very important factors considered include:* Rigor of secondary school record, state residency. *Important factors considered include:* standardized test scores. *Other factors considered include:* Class rank, recommendation(s), alumni/ae relation, character/personal qualities, extracurricular activities, geographical residence, talent/ability, volunteer work, work experience. **Freshman Admission Requirements:** High school diploma is required and GED is accepted. *Academic units required:* 4 English, 3 mathematics, 3 science, 2 social studies, 4 academic electives. **Freshman Admission Statistics:** 5,080 applied, 79% admitted, 44% enrolled. **Transfer Admission Requirements:** High school transcript, minimum college GPA of 2.0 required. Lowest grade transferable C. **General Admission Information:** Application fee $35. Notification on a rolling basis, beginning on or about 9/15. Nonfall registration accepted. Admission may be deferred for a maximum of 1 semester. Credit offered for CEEB Advanced Placement tests.

COSTS AND FINANCIAL AID
Annual in-state tuition $1,172. Annual out-of-state tuition $8,442. Room and board $4,470. Required fees $1,017. Average book expense $750. **Required Forms and Deadlines:** FAFSA. Priority financial aid filing date 3/15. **Notification of Awards:** Applicants will be notified of awards on a rolling basis beginning 4/15. **Types of Aid:** *Need-based scholarships/grants:* Federal Pell, SEOG, state scholarships/grants, private scholarships, the school's own gift aid, United Negro College Fund, Federal Nursing Scholarships. *Loans:* Direct Subsidized Stafford, Direct Unsubsidized Stafford, Direct PLUS, Federal Perkins, alternative loans. *Student Employment:* **Financial Aid Statistics:** 59%

---

freshmen, 49% undergrads receive need-based scholarship or grant aid. 44% freshmen, 34% undergrads receive non-need-based scholarship or grant aid. 59% freshmen, 55% undergrads receive need-based self-help aid. 92% freshmen, 85% undergrads receive athletic scholarships. 73% undergrads borrow to pay for school. Average cumulative indebtedness $15,008. **Criteria for awarding institutional aid:** *Non-need-based:* Academics, alumni affiliation, athletics, minority status, music/drama, state/district residency.

NORTH CAROLINA CENTRAL UNIVERSITY

Fayetteville Street, Durham, NC 27707
Phone: 919-560-6298
E-mail: ebridges@wpo.nccu.edu **CEEB Code:** 5495
Fax: 919-530-7625 **Website:** www.nccu.edu **ACT Code:** 3132

This public school was founded in 1910. It has a 130-acre campus.

RATINGS
Admissions Selectivity Rating: 62   **Fire Safety Rating:** 60*   **Green Rating:** 60*

STUDENTS AND FACULTY
Enrollment: 5,439. **Student Body:** 66% female, 34% male, 10% out-of-state, international (17 countries represented). African American 79%, Caucasian 3%, Hispanic 1%.
Retention and Graduation: 78% freshmen return for sophomore year. **Faculty:** Student/faculty ratio 18:1. 231 full-time faculty, 67% hold PhDs, 77% are are members of minority groups, 47% are women.

ACADEMICS
Degrees: Bachelor's, first professional, master's. **Classes:** Most classes have fewer than 10 students. Most lab/discussion sessions have fewer than 10 students. **Special Study Options:** Cooperative education program, double major, honors program, independent study, internships, study abroad, teacher certification program, weekend college. Special programs offered to physically disabled students include note-taking services, reader services, tape recorders, tutors. **Career services:** Alumni services, career/job search classes, internships.

FACILITIES
Housing: Coed dorms, men's dorms, women's dorms, Coed houses dormitory available. **Special Academic Facilities/Equipment:** Treasury Room—collection of primary resources on black life and culture, art museum with works of Afro-American culture. **Computers:** Administrative functions (other than registration) can be performed online.

CAMPUS LIFE
Activities: Choral groups, concert band, dance, drama/theater, jazz band, literary magazine, marching band, radio station, student government, student newspaper, yearbook. **Organizations:** 4 fraternities, 4 sororities. **Athletics (Intercollegiate):** *Men:* Basketball, cross-country, football, golf, tennis, track/field (outdoor). *Women:* Basketball, cross-country, golf, softball, tennis, track/field (outdoor), volleyball.

ADMISSIONS
Freshman Academic Profile: Average high school GPA 2.6. 4% in top 10% of high school class, 19% in top 25% of high school class, 53% in top 50% of high school class. SAT Math middle 50% range 380–470. SAT Critical Reading middle 50% range 380–470. ACT middle 50% range 14–18. Minimum paper TOEFL 500. Minimum computer TOEFL 173. **Basis for Candidate Selection:** *Very important factors considered include:* Rigor of secondary school record. *Important factors considered include:* Class rank, standardized test scores. *Other factors considered include:* Application essay, recommendation(s), alumni/ae relation, extracurricular activities, interview, racial/ethnic status, state residency, talent/ability. **Freshman Admission Requirements:** High school diploma is required and GED is accepted. *Academic units required:* 4 English, 3 mathematics, 3 science, (1 science labs), 2 social studies, 2 history. *Academic units recommended:* 4 mathematics, 4 science, 2 foreign language, 2 history. **Freshman Admission Statistics:** 2,801 applied, 83% admitted, 50% enrolled. **Transfer Admission Requirements:** High school transcript, college transcript(s), statement of good standing from prior institution(s). Minimum college GPA of 2.0 required. Lowest grade transferable C. **General Admission Information:** Application fee $30. Regular application deadline 7/1. Nonfall registration accepted. Admission may be deferred for a maximum of 4. Credit offered for CEEB Advanced Placement tests.

COSTS AND FINANCIAL AID
Required Forms and Deadlines: FAFSA. Priority financial aid filing date 4/1. **Types of Aid:** *Need-based scholarships/grants:* Federal Pell, SEOG, state scholarships/grants, private scholarships, the school's own gift aid, United

Negro College Fund, Federal Nursing Scholarships. *Loans:* Direct Subsidized Stafford, Direct Unsubsidized Stafford, Direct PLUS, Federal Perkins. *Student Employment:* Federal Work-Study Program available. Off-campus job opportunities are fair. **Financial Aid Statistics:** 58% freshmen, 55% undergrads receive need-based scholarship or grant aid. 69% freshmen, 36% undergrads receive non-need-based scholarship or grant aid. 66% freshmen, 66% undergrads receive need-based self-help aid. 4% freshmen, 2% undergrads receive athletic scholarships. **Criteria for awarding institutional aid:** *Non-need-based:* Academics, alumni affiliation, athletics.

NORTH CAROLINA STATE UNIVERSITY

Box 7103, Raleigh, NC 27695
Phone: 919-515-2434 **Financial Aid Phone:** 919-515-2421
E-mail: undergrad_admissions@ncsu.edu **CEEB Code:** 5496
Fax: 919-515-5039 **Website:** www.ncsu.edu **ACT Code:** 3164

This public school was founded in 1887. It has a 2110-acre campus.

RATINGS
Admissions Selectivity Rating: 91   Fire Safety Rating: 99   Green Rating: 89

STUDENTS AND FACULTY
Enrollment: 23,361. **Student Body:** 43% female, 57% male, 7% out-of-state, 2% international (106 countries represented). Asian 5%, African American 9%, Caucasian 78%, Hispanic 3%, Native American 1%.
Retention and Graduation: 91% freshmen return for sophomore year. 31% grads go on to further study within 1 year. 67% grads pursue arts and sciences degrees. 7% grads pursue law degrees. 19% grads pursue business degrees. 7% grads pursue medical degrees. **Faculty:** Student/faculty ratio 17:1. 1773 full-time faculty, 87% hold PhDs, 20% are are members of minority groups, 31% are women. 9% of classes are taught by teaching assistants.

ACADEMICS
Degrees: Associate, bachelor's, certificate, master's, post-bachelor's certificate. **Classes:** Most classes have 20–29 students. Most lab/discussion sessions have 20–29 students. **Majors with Highest Enrollment:** Biology/biological sciences; business administration and management; mechanical engineering. **Special Study Options:** Accelerated program, cooperative education program, cross-registration, distance learning, double major, dual enrollment, exchange student program (domestic), honors program, independent study, internships, liberal arts/career combination, student-designed major, study abroad. **Honors programs:** The University Honors Program recruits and provides programmatic support for a diverse group of nationally outstanding students, ensuring that they benefit fully from the resources of a major land-grant, research university and the Research Triangle by emphasizing inquiry-, creativity-, and discovery-based learning. The program offers interdisciplinary seminars and a variety of credit-earning opportunites for out-of-classroom experiences. The program emphasizes participation in research by students from all disciplines. Entering students may instead choose to participate in the University Scholars program, which emphasizes enrichment activities and leadership development. There are over 30 honors programs located in the colleges or departments that invite students in their sophomore or junior years. These programs include honors sections of courses, honors seminars, and honors research. Some programs require a senior honor thesis. **Combined degree programs:** BA/BS Humanities/Engineering Humanities/Design. Special programs offered to physically disabled students include note-taking services, reader services, tape recorders **Career services:** Career/job search classes, career assessment, internships, regional alumni.

FACILITIES
Housing: Coed dorms, special housing for disabled students, men's dorms, special housing for international students, women's dorms, fraternity/sorority housing, apartments for married students, apartments for single students, theme housing, living/learning dormitories. 87% of campus accessible to physically disabled. **Special Academic Facilities/Equipment:** Art and arts/crafts galleries, research farms and forest, phytophotron with controlled atmosphere growth chambers. pulp/paper and wood products labs, processing equipment for fiber, fabric, and garment manufacture, electron microscopes, nuclear reactor, stable isotope lab. **Computers:** 94% of classrooms, 100% of libraries, 92% of dining areas, 100% of student union, 52% of common outdoor areas have wireless network access. Students can register for classes online. Administrative functions (other than registration) can be performed online.

CAMPUS LIFE
Environment: Metropolis. **Activities:** Choral groups, concert band, dance, drama/theater, jazz band, literary magazine, marching band, music ensembles, musical theater, pep band, radio station, student government, student newspaper, symphony orchestra, yearbook, campus ministries, international student organization. **Organizations:** 560 registered organizations, 26 honor societies, 25 religious organizations. 33 fraternities, 17 sororities **Athletics (Intercollegiate):** *Men:* Baseball, basketball, cheerleading, cross-country, diving, football, golf, riflery, soccer, swimming, tennis, track/field (outdoor), track/field (indoor), wrestling. *Women:* Basketball, cheerleading, cross-country, diving, golf, gymnastics, riflery, soccer, softball, swimming, tennis, track/field (outdoor), track/field (indoor), volleyball. **On-Campus Highlights:** RBC Center—Sports Arena, Gallery of Art and Design, Carter Finley Stadium, Talley Student Center, University Theatre. **Environmental Initiatives:** Acceptance of a sustainability program that made the Campus Environmental Sustainability Team (CEST) an adminstrative advisory council whose activities and recommendations are approved by the Chancellor. Completion of our first GHG Inventory and in the process of creating a Climate Action Plan. In the process of creating a Sustainability Strategic Plan that will help guide sustainability policies and procedures on campus.

ADMISSIONS
Freshman Academic Profile: Average high school GPA 4.19. 41% in top 10% of high school class, 83% in top 25% of high school class, 99% in top 50% of high school class. 90% from public high schools. SAT Math middle 50% range 560–660. SAT Critical Reading middle 50% range 520–620. SAT Writing middle 50% range 510–610. ACT middle 50% range 23–28. Minimum paper TOEFL 550. Minimum computer TOEFL 213. **Basis for Candidate Selection:** *Very important factors considered include:* Class rank, academic GPA, rigor of secondary school record, standardized test scores. *Other factors considered include:* Application essay, recommendation(s), alumni/ae relation, character/personal qualities, extracurricular activities, first generation, geographical residence, racial/ethnic status, state residency, talent/ability, volunteer work, work experience. **Freshman Admission Requirements:** High school diploma is required and GED is not accepted. *Academic units required:* 4 English, 4 mathematics, 3 science, (1 science labs), 2 foreign language, 1 social studies, 1 history, 1 academic electives. *Academic units recommended:* 4 English, 4 mathematics, 4 science, (2 science labs), 2 foreign language, 1 social studies, 1 history, 4 academic electives. **Freshman Admission Statistics:** 18,782 applied, 55% admitted, 45% enrolled. **Transfer Admission Requirements:** College transcript(s), minimum college GPA of 2.0 required. Lowest grade transferable C–. **General Admission Information:** Application fee $70. Regular application deadline 2/1. Notification on a rolling basis, beginning on or about 10/15. Nonfall registration accepted. Admission may be deferred for a maximum of 1 year. Credit and/or placement offered for CEEB Advanced Placement tests.

COSTS AND FINANCIAL AID
Required Forms and Deadlines: FAFSA, institution's own financial aid form. Priority financial aid filing date 3/1. **Notification of Awards:** Applicants will be notified of awards on a rolling basis beginning 4/1. **Types of Aid:** *Need-based scholarships/grants:* Federal Pell, SEOG, state scholarships/grants, private scholarships, the school's own gift aid, United Negro College Fund *Loans:* FFEL Subsidized Stafford, FFEL Unsubsidized Stafford, FFEL PLUS, Federal Perkins, state loans, college/university loans from institutional funds. *Student Employment:* Federal Work-Study Program available. Institutional employment available. Highest amount earned per year from on-campus jobs $7,300. Off-campus job opportunities are excellent. **Financial Aid Statistics:** 45% freshmen, 42% undergrads receive need-based scholarship or grant aid. 6% freshmen, 4% undergrads receive non-need-based scholarship or grant aid. 32% freshmen, 33% undergrads receive need-based self-help aid. 2% freshmen, 1% undergrads receive athletic scholarships. 70% freshmen, 66% undergrads receive any aid. 48% undergrads borrow to pay for school. Average cumulative indebtedness $19,011. **Criteria for awarding institutional aid:** *Non-need-based:* Academics, alumni affiliation, athletics, leadership, state/district residency.

NORTH CAROLINA WESLEYAN COLLEGE

3400 North Wesleyan Boulevard, Rocky Mount, NC 27804
Phone: 252-985-5200
E-mail: adm@ncwc.edu
Fax: 252-985-5309 **Website:** www.ncwc.edu

This private school, affiliated with the Methodist Church, was founded in 1956.

RATINGS
Admissions Selectivity Rating: 61   Fire Safety Rating: 60*   Green Rating: 60*

STUDENTS AND FACULTY

Enrollment: 1,695. **Student Body:** 59% female, 41% male, 12% out-of-state. Asian 1%, African American 40%, Caucasian 48%, Hispanic 1%, Native American 1%.

Retention and Graduation: 57% freshmen return for sophomore year. 26% freshmen graduate within 4 years. **Faculty:** Student/faculty ratio 15:1. 45 full-time faculty, 62% hold PhDs, 51% are women.

ACADEMICS

Degrees: Bachelor's, certificate. **Classes:** Most classes have 10–19 students. **Majors with Highest Enrollment:** Business/commerce; computer and information science; psychology. **Special Study Options:** Accelerated program, cooperative education program, cross-registration, distance learning, double major, dual enrollment, honors program, independent study, internships, liberal arts/career combination, teacher certification program, weekend college. Special programs offered to physically disabled students include note-taking services, reader services, tape recorders, tutors. **Career services:** Career/job search classes, career assessment, internships. **Career services highlights include:** North Carolina Wesleyan College's Internship and Career Services Center (ICSC) complements the academic program of the college. The ICSC at Wesleyan assists our students' professional development and serves as a resource to students, faculty, and the business community. By emphasizing hands-on learning as an important tool for both full time employment and in developing a career path, the ICSC helps students realize their career goals. The ICSC offers a variety of services that allows students to assess their skills and abilities, make the major declaration, and explore the world of work. Through our resource library and employer files students are able to research possible majors, minors, and careers. To prepare our students for the world of work, the ICSC offers the Career Development Workshop as a required component of the internship for traditional day students. The workshop includes resume and cover letter writing, the value of networking, interviewing skills, appropriate business attire, how to deal with racial discrimination and sexual harassment, and social etiquette. The relevance of practical experience will become evident as students begin to explore their career goals through the Extended Internship (EI) program.

FACILITIES

Housing: Coed dorms, special housing for disabled students, men's dorms, women's dorms. 70% of campus accessible to physically disabled. **Special Academic Facilities/Equipment:** Mims Gallery, Dunn Center for the Performing Arts. **Computers:** Administrative functions (other than registration) can be performed online.

CAMPUS LIFE

Environment: Village. **Activities:** Choral groups, drama/theater, literary magazine, music ensembles, student government, student newspaper, yearbook. **Organizations:** 30 registered organizations, 2 honor societies, 2 religious organizations. 3 fraternities, 3 sororities. **Athletics (Intercollegiate):** *Men:* Baseball, basketball, football, golf, soccer, tennis. *Women:* Basketball, soccer, softball, tennis, volleyball. **On-Campus Highlights:** Dunn Center for the Performing Arts, Mims Gallery, Serpentine Wall, College Fountain, Bellmonte House.

ADMISSIONS

Freshman Academic Profile: Average high school GPA 2.79. 8% in top 10% of high school class, 18% in top 25% of high school class, 59% in top 50% of high school class. 85% from public high schools. SAT Math middle 50% range 5–23. SAT Critical Reading middle 50% range 4–29. Minimum paper TOEFL 500. Minimum computer TOEFL 500. **Basis for Candidate Selection:** *Very important factors considered include:* Recommendation(s), rigor of secondary school record, standardized test scores, talent/ability. *Important factors considered include:* Application essay, alumni/ae relation, character/personal qualities, extracurricular activities, interview, volunteer work, work experience. *Other factors considered include:* Class rank. **Freshman Admission Requirements:** High school diploma is required and GED is accepted. *Academic units recommended:* 4 English, 3 mathematics, (2 science labs), 2 foreign language, 2 social studies. **Freshman Admission Statistics:** 651 applied, 83% admitted, 37% enrolled. **Transfer Admission Requirements:** High school transcript, college transcript(s), standardized test scores, minimum college GPA of 2.0 required. Lowest grade transferable C. **General Admission Information:** Application fee $25. Nonfall registration accepted. Credit and/or placement offered for CEEB Advanced Placement tests.

COSTS AND FINANCIAL AID

Annual tuition $11,225. Room and board $5,555. Required fees $1,218. Average book expense $800. **Required Forms and Deadlines:** FAFSA, state aid form. Priority financial aid filing date 3/15. **Notification of Awards:** Applicants will be notified of awards on a rolling basis beginning 2/1. **Types of Aid:** *Need-based scholarships/grants:* Federal Pell, SEOG, state scholarships/grants, private scholarships, the school's own gift aid. *Loans:* FFEL Subsidized Stafford, FFEL Unsubsidized Stafford, FFEL PLUS, Federal Perkins, alternative loans. *Student Employment:* Federal Work-Study Program available. Highest amount earned per year from on-campus jobs $800. **Financial Aid Statistics:** 100% undergrads borrow to pay for school. **Criteria for awarding institutional aid:** *Non-need-based:* Academics, religious affiliation, state/district residency.

NORTH CENTRAL COLLEGE

Office of Admissions, P.O. Box 3063, Naperville, IL 60566-7063
Phone: 630-637-5800 **Financial Aid Phone:** 630-637-5600
E-mail: admissions@noctrl.edu **CEEB Code:** 1555
Fax: 630-637-5819 **Website:** www.northcentralcollege.edu **ACT Code:** 1096

This private school, affiliated with the Methodist Church, was founded in 1861. It has a 59-acre campus.

RATINGS

Admissions Selectivity Rating: 78   **Fire Safety Rating:** 74   **Green Rating:** 87

STUDENTS AND FACULTY

Enrollment: 2,423. **Student Body:** 57% female, 43% male, 8% out-of-state, 1% international (31 countries represented). Asian 3%, African American 4%, Caucasian 80%, Hispanic 6%.

Retention and Graduation: 77% freshmen return for sophomore year. 53% freshmen graduate within 4 years. **Faculty:** Student/faculty ratio 15.6:1. 118 full-time faculty, 84% hold PhDs, 13% are are members of minority groups, 46% are women.

ACADEMICS

Degrees: Bachelor's, master's, post-bachelor's certificate. **Classes:** Most classes have 20–29 students. Most lab/discussion sessions have 20–29 students. **Majors with Highest Enrollment:** Business administration, management and operations, other; elementary education and teaching; finance. **Special Study Options:** Accelerated program, cross-registration, double major, dual enrollment, English as a Second Language (ESL), exchange student program (domestic), honors program, independent study, internships, student-designed major, study abroad, teacher certification program, 3-2 engineering program with University of Illinois, University of Minnesota; integrated 5 year bachelor's/master's degree programs. **Honors programs:** The College Scholars is a comprehensive four year integrative program culminating in a senior honors thesis. The program is open to students from all academic disciplines. **Combined degree programs:** BA/MA, BA in Acc/MBA; Bachelor's Degree/Masters in Web and Internet Applications. Special programs offered to physically disabled students include note-taking services, reader services, tape recorders, tutors. **Career services:** Alumni network, alumni services, career/job search classes, career assessment, internships, regional alumni. **Career services highlights include:** Because career-related experiences support the mission of the college, the CDC actively assists students in developing Internship opportunities. We have found that real hands on experience within the workforce increases graduates marketability following graduation, be it for seeking employment or pursuing graduate school. Today's' job market is competitive and we offer a strong resource in helping students get involved in these types of opportunities which ultimately helps them reach their goals.

FACILITIES

Housing: Coed dorms, special housing for disabled students, women's dorms, substance-free housing. 85% of campus accessible to physically disabled. **Special Academic Facilities/Equipment:** None **Computers:** 50% of classrooms, 30% of dorms, 100% of libraries, 100% of dining areas, 100% of student union, 100% of common outdoor areas have wireless network access. Students can register for classes online. Administrative functions (other than registration) can be performed online.

CAMPUS LIFE

Environment: City. **Activities:** Choral groups, concert band, dance, drama/theater, jazz band, literary magazine, music ensembles, musical theater, opera, pep band, radio station, student government, student newspaper, campus ministries, international student organization, Model UN. **Organizations:** 54 registered organizations, 14 honor societies, 6 religious organizations. **Athletics (Intercollegiate):** *Men:* Baseball, basketball, cross-country, football, golf, soccer, swimming, tennis, track/field (outdoor), track/field (indoor), wrestling. *Women:* Basketball, cheerleading, cross-country, golf, lacrosse, soccer, softball, swimming, tennis, track/field (outdoor), track/field (indoor), volleyball. **On-Campus Highlights:** Old Main—historic home of North Central College, Benedtti-Wehrli Stadium, Res/Rec Center, Fine Arts Center & Wentz Concert Hall, Oesterle Library, Rolland Boilerhouse Cafe is also a popular on-campus hangout. **Environmental Initiatives:** Development of Sustainabilty Committee; LEED certification for new construction; expansion of recycling program.

ADMISSIONS

Freshman Academic Profile: Average high school GPA 3.5. 88% from public high schools. ACT middle 50% range 22–27. Minimum paper TOEFL 520. Minimum computer TOEFL 190. Minimum web-based TOEFL 68. **Basis for Candidate Selection:** *Very important factors considered include:* Academic GPA, rigor of secondary school record, standardized test scores, character/personal qualities. *Important factors considered include:* Extracurricular activities, talent/ability, volunteer work. *Other factors considered include:* Application essay, recommendation(s), alumni/ae relation, first generation, interview, level of applicant's interest, work experience. **Freshman Admission Requirements:** High school diploma is required and GED is accepted. *Academic units required:* 4 English, 3 mathematics, 3 science, (1 science labs), 2 social studies, 1 history, 3 academic electives. *Academic units recommended:* 4 English, 3 mathematics, 3 science, (3 science labs), 3 foreign language, 2 social studies, 1 history, 3 academic electives. **Freshman Admission Statistics:** 2,762 applied, 67% admitted, 29% enrolled. **Transfer Admission Requirements:** College transcript(s), minimum college GPA of 2.25 required. Lowest grade transferable D. **General Admission Information:** Application fee $25. Notification on a rolling basis, beginning on or about 10/1. Nonfall registration accepted. Admission may be deferred for a maximum of 1 year. Credit and/or placement offered for CEEB Advanced Placement tests.

COSTS AND FINANCIAL AID

Annual tuition $26,676. Room and board $8,379. Required fees $240. Average book expense $1,200. **Required Forms and Deadlines:** FAFSA, institution's own financial aid form, federal income tax returns for both student and parents. **Notification of Awards:** Applicants will be notified of awards on a rolling basis beginning 3/1. **Types of Aid:** *Need-based scholarships/grants:* Federal Pell, SEOG, state scholarships/grants, private scholarships, the school's own gift aid. *Loans:* FFEL Subsidized Stafford, FFEL Unsubsidized Stafford, FFEL PLUS, Federal Perkins, state loans, college/university loans from institutional funds. *Student Employment:* Federal Work-Study Program available. Institutional employment available. Off-campus job opportunities are excellent. **Financial Aid Statistics:** 81% freshmen, 75% undergrads receive need-based scholarship or grant aid. 16% freshmen, 10% undergrads receive non-need-based scholarship or grant aid. 62% freshmen, 62% undergrads receive need-based self-help aid. 99.6% freshmen, 94.6% undergrads receive any aid. 72% undergrads borrow to pay for school. Average cumulative indebtedness $27,285. **Criteria for awarding institutional aid:** *Non-need-based:* Academics, art, leadership, minority status, music/drama, religious affiliation, state/district residency.

NORTH CENTRAL UNIVERSITY

Admissions Office, 910 Elliot Ave, Minneapolis, MN 55404
Phone: 612-343-4460
E-mail: admissions@northcentral.edu
Fax: 612-343-4146 **Website:** www.northcentral.edu

This private school, affiliated with the Pentecostal Church, was founded in 1930. It has a 9-acre campus.

RATINGS
Admissions Selectivity Rating: 65   **Fire Safety Rating:** 60*   **Green Rating:** 60*

STUDENTS AND FACULTY
Enrollment: 1,217. **Student Body:** 57% female, 43% male, 60% out-of-state (11 countries represented).
Retention and Graduation: 75% freshmen return for sophomore year. **Faculty:** Student/faculty ratio 18:1. 40 full-time faculty, 43% hold PhDs, 13% are are members of minority groups, 38% are women.

ACADEMICS
Degrees: Associate, bachelor's, certificate, diploma. **Classes:** Most classes have 10–19 students. **Majors with Highest Enrollment:** Education; music; youth ministry. **Special Study Options:** Distance learning, double major, exchange student program (domestic), independent study, internships. Special programs offered to physically disabled students include note-taking services, reader services, tape recorders, tutors.

FACILITIES
Housing: Men's dorms, women's dorms, apartments for married students, apartments for single students.

CAMPUS LIFE
Environment: Metropolis. **Activities:** Choral groups, concert band, drama/theater, jazz band, music ensembles, radio station, student government, student newspaper, television station. **Organizations:** 30 registered organizations, 15 religious organizations. **Athletics (Intercollegiate):** *Men:* Basketball, cross-country, soccer, track/field (outdoor). *Women:* Basketball, cross-country, soccer, track/field (outdoor), volleyball. **On-Campus Highlights:** Chapel, Library, Cafetria, Philipps Hall, Clay Commons.

ADMISSIONS
Freshman Academic Profile: Average high school GPA 3.1. 2% in top 10% of high school class, 11% in top 25% of high school class, 32% in top 50% of

high school class. SAT Math middle 50% range 440–300. SAT Critical Reading middle 50% range 480–630. ACT middle 50% range 18–24. Minimum paper TOEFL 500. Minimum computer TOEFL 220. **Basis for Candidate Selection:** *Very important factors considered include:* Application essay, academic GPA, recommendation(s), rigor of secondary school record, standardized test scores, character/personal qualities, religious affiliation/commitment. *Important factors considered include:* extracurricular activities, talent/ability, volunteer work. *Other factors considered include:* Class rank, interview. **Freshman Admission Requirements:** High school diploma is required and GED is accepted. *Academic units recommended:* 4 English, 2 mathematics, 2 science, (1 science labs), 1 foreign language, 2 social studies, 2 history, 4 academic electives. **Freshman Admission Statistics:** 422 applied, 98% admitted, 58% enrolled. **Transfer Admission Requirements:** High school transcript, college transcript(s), essay or personal statement, minimum college GPA of 2.0 required. Lowest grade transferable c. **General Admission Information:** Application fee $25. Regular application deadline 6/1. Notification on a rolling basis, beginning on or about 1/1. Nonfall registration accepted. Admission may be deferred for a maximum of 1 year.

COSTS AND FINANCIAL AID
Annual tuition $12,060. Room and board $4,612. Required fees $886. Average book expense $600. **Required Forms and Deadlines:** FAFSA, state aid form. Priority financial aid filing date 4/1. **Notification of Awards:** Applicants will be notified of awards on a rolling basis beginning 3/1. **Types of Aid:** *Need-based scholarships/grants:* Federal Pell, SEOG, state scholarships/grants, private scholarships, the school's own gift aid. *Loans:* FFEL Subsidized Stafford, FFEL Unsubsidized Stafford, FFEL PLUS, Federal Perkins, state loans.

NORTH DAKOTA STATE UNIVERSITY

Box 5454, Fargo, ND 58105
Phone: 701-231-8643 **Financial Aid Phone:** 800-726-3188
E-mail: ndsu.admission@ndsu.edu **CEEB Code:** 6474
Fax: 701-231-8802 **Website:** www.ndsu.edu **ACT Code:** 3202

This public school was founded in 1890. It has a 258-acre campus.

RATINGS
Admissions Selectivity Rating: 77   **Fire Safety Rating:** 60*   **Green Rating:** 60*

STUDENTS AND FACULTY
Enrollment: 10,403. **Student Body:** 45% female, 55% male, 46% out-of-state (58 countries represented).
Retention and Graduation: 82% freshmen return for sophomore year. 17% freshmen graduate within 4 years. **Faculty:** Student/faculty ratio 19:1. 557 full-time faculty, 82% hold PhDs, 20% are are members of minority groups, 30% are women.

ACADEMICS
Degrees: Bachelor's, certificate, first professional, master's, post-master's certificate. **Classes:** Most classes have 20–29 students. Most lab/discussion sessions have 20–29 students. **Majors with Highest Enrollment:** Business, management, marketing, and related support services, other; civil engineering; mechanical engineering. **Special Study Options:** Cooperative education program, cross-registration, distance learning, double major, dual enrollment, English as a Second Language (ESL), honors program, independent study, internships, student-designed major, study abroad, teacher certification program, Tri-College Collaboration and Registration with Minnesota State University and Concordia College. Collaboration with North Dakota University System institutions. **Honors programs:** Scholars Program. Special programs offered to physically disabled students include note-taking services, reader services, tape recorders, tutors. **Career services:** Career/job search classes, internships. **Career services highlights include:** Cooperative Education opportunities are available for most majors. Students are paid for their work experience and earn credit.

FACILITIES
Housing: Coed dorms, men's dorms, women's dorms, apartments for married students, apartments for single students, Designated floors for engineering and architecture students. Learning communities. Wellness community. Freshmen under 19 years of age not living with a parent or guardian must live on campus. Housing is guaranteed for freshmen required to live on campus. Handicapped accessible. 100% of campus accessible to physically disabled. **Special Academic Facilities/Equipment:** Art gallery, language lab, genetics institute, regional studies institute. **Computers:** Students can register for classes online. Administrative functions (other than registration) can be performed online.

CAMPUS LIFE

Environment: City. **Activities:** Choral groups, concert band, drama/theater, jazz band, marching band, music ensembles, musical theater, pep band, radio station, student government, student newspaper. **Organizations:** 218 registered organizations, 22 honor societies, 18 religious organizations. 10 fraternities, 5 sororities. **Athletics (Intercollegiate): Men:** Baseball, basketball, cross-country, football, golf, track/field (outdoor), track/field (indoor), wrestling. *Women:* Basketball, cross-country, golf, soccer, softball, track/field (outdoor), track/field (indoor), volleyball. **On-Campus Highlights:** Wellness Center, Memorial Union, FargoDome, Alumni Center, Industrial Agricultural Communications Center, Residence Halls/Living Learning Center; Newman Outdoor Field; Technology Park.

ADMISSIONS

Freshman Academic Profile: Average high school GPA 3.39. 15.4% in top 10% of high school class, 40% in top 25% of high school class, 73.4% in top 50% of high school class. SAT Math middle 50% range 490–640. SAT Critical Reading middle 50% range 460–600. ACT middle 50% range 20–25. Minimum paper TOEFL 525. Minimum computer TOEFL 193. **Basis for Candidate Selection:** *Very important factors considered include:* Academic GPA, rigor of secondary school record, standardized test scores, *Other factors considered include:* Class rank, recommendation(s). **Freshman Admission Requirements:** High school diploma is required and GED is accepted. *Academic units required:* 4 English, 3 mathematics, 3 science, (3 science labs), 3 social studies. *Academic units recommended:* 2 foreign language. **Freshman Admission Statistics:** 4,382 applied, 85% admitted, 58% enrolled. **Transfer Admission Requirements:** College transcript(s), minimum college GPA of 2.0 required. Lowest grade transferable D. **General Admission Information:** Application fee $35. Regular application deadline 8/15. Notification on a rolling basis, beginning on or about 9/1. Nonfall registration accepted. Admission may be deferred for a maximum of 3 years. Credit and/or placement offered for CEEB Advanced Placement tests.

COSTS AND FINANCIAL AID

Annual in-state tuition $5,013. Annual out-of-state tuition $13,384. Average book expense $700. **Required Forms and Deadlines:** FAFSA. Priority financial aid filing date 3/15. **Notification of Awards:** Applicants will be notified of awards on a rolling basis beginning 3/15. **Types of Aid:** *Need-based scholarships/grants:* Federal Pell, SEOG, state scholarships/grants, private scholarships, the school's own gift aid, Diversity Waivers. *Loans:* FFEL Subsidized Stafford, FFEL Unsubsidized Stafford, FFEL PLUS, Federal Perkins, Federal Nursing, Private loans from various lending institutions. *Student Employment:* Federal Work-Study Program available. Institutional employment available. Off-campus job opportunities are good. **Financial Aid Statistics:** 38% freshmen, 33% undergrads receive need-based scholarship or grant aid. 9% freshmen, 9% undergrads receive non-need-based scholarship or grant aid. 45% freshmen, 46% undergrads receive need-based self-help aid. 3% freshmen, 3% undergrads receive athletic scholarships. 68% undergrads borrow to pay for school. Average cumulative indebtedness $24,001. **Criteria for awarding institutional aid:** *Non-need-based:* Academics, alumni affiliation, art, athletics, leadership, minority status, music/drama, state/district residency.

NORTH GEORGIA COLLEGE
AND STATE UNIVERSITY

Office of Undergraduate Admissions, 82 College Circle, Dahlonega, GA 30597
Phone: 706-864-1800 **Financial Aid Phone:** 706-864-1412
E-mail: admissions@ngcsu.edu **CEEB Code:** 5497
Fax: 706-864-1478 **Website:** www.ngcsu.edu **ACT Code:** 848

This public school was founded in 1873. It has a 120-acre campus.

RATINGS
Admissions Selectivity Rating: 82   **Fire Safety Rating:** 60*   **Green Rating:** 60*

STUDENTS AND FACULTY
Enrollment: 3,983. **Student Body:** 60% female, 40% male, 10% out-of-state, 1% international (34 countries represented). Asian 1%, African American 1%, Caucasian 76%, Hispanic 2%.
Retention and Graduation: 77% freshmen return for sophomore year. 25% freshmen graduate within 4 years. 10% grads go on to further study within 1 year. 1% grads pursue arts and sciences degrees. 1% grads pursue law degrees. 5% grads pursue business degrees. 1% grads pursue medical degrees. **Faculty:** Student/faculty ratio 15:1. 185 full-time faculty, 66% hold PhDs, 6% are members of minority groups, 47% are women.

ACADEMICS

Degrees: Associate, bachelor's, certificate, master's, post-bachelor's certificate, post-master's certificate. **Classes:** Most classes have 20–29 students. Most lab/discussion sessions have fewer than 10 students. **Majors with Highest Enrollment:** Biology/biological sciences; early childhood education and teaching; marketing/marketing management. **Special Study Options:** Cooperative education program, distance learning, double major, dual enrollment, external degree program, honors program, independent study, internships, study abroad, teacher certification program, dual degree in engineering with GA Institute of Technology and Clemson University. Special programs offered to physically disabled students include note-taking services, reader services, tape recorders, tutors.

FACILITIES

Housing: Coed dorms, men's dorms, women's dorms, apartments for single students 90% of campus accessible to physically disabled. **Special Academic Facilities/Equipment:** Planetarium; 2 art galleries; hall of fame; NGCSU museum. **Computers:** Students can register for classes online. Administrative functions (other than registration) can be performed online.

CAMPUS LIFE

Environment: Rural. **Activities:** Choral groups, drama/theater, jazz band, literary magazine, marching band, music ensembles, pep band, student government, student newspaper, symphony orchestra, yearbook. **Organizations:** 60 registered organizations, 8 honor societies, 5 religious organizations. 6 fraternities, 4 sororities. **Athletics (Intercollegiate): Men:** Baseball, basketball, cross-country, football, golf, riflery, soccer, table tennis, tennis, track/field (outdoor), volleyball, water polo. *Women:* Basketball, cheerleading, cross-country, golf, riflery, soccer, softball, table tennis, tennis, track/field (outdoor), volleyball, water polo **On-Campus Highlights:** Canteen, commuter lounge, game room, uniform store, lounge areas.

ADMISSIONS

Freshman Academic Profile: Average high school GPA 3.26. 21% in top 10% of high school class, 53% in top 25% of high school class, 85% in top 50% of high school class. 95% from public high schools. SAT Math middle 50% range 490–580. SAT Critical Reading middle 50% range 500–580. ACT middle 50% range 19–23. Minimum paper TOEFL 550. Minimum computer TOEFL 213. **Basis for Candidate Selection:** *Very important factors considered include:* Rigor of secondary school record, standardized test scores. *Other factors considered include:* Class rank, recommendation(s), alumni/ae relation, character/personal qualities, extracurricular activities, talent/ability, volunteer work, work experience. **Freshman Admission Requirements:** High school diploma is required and GED is accepted. *Academic units required:* 4 English, 4 mathematics, 3 science, (1 science lab), 2 foreign language, 3 social studies. **Freshman Admission Statistics:** 2,103 applied, 60% admitted, 60% enrolled. **Transfer Admission Requirements:** College transcript(s), statement of good standing from prior institution(s). Minimum college GPA of 2.0 required. Lowest grade transferable C. **General Admission Information:** Application fee $25. Regular application deadline 7/1. Nonfall registration accepted. Credit offered for CEEB Advanced Placement tests.

COSTS AND FINANCIAL AID

Annual in-state tuition $2,322. Annual out-of-state tuition $9,290. Room and board $4,424. Required fees $606. Average book expense $750. **Required Forms and Deadlines:** FAFSA, institution's own financial aid form. Priority financial aid filing date 5/1. **Notification of Awards:** Applicants will be notified of awards on a rolling basis beginning 5/15. **Types of Aid:** *Need-based scholarships/grants:* Federal Pell, SEOG, state scholarships/grants, private scholarships, the school's own gift aid. *Loans:* FFEL Subsidized Stafford, FFEL Unsubsidized Stafford, FFEL PLUS, Federal Perkins, state loans, college/university loans from institutional funds. *Student Employment:* **Financial Aid Statistics:** 17% freshmen, 19% undergrads receive need-based scholarship or grant aid. 28% freshmen, 22% undergrads receive non-need-based scholarship or grant aid. 12% freshmen, 10% undergrads receive need-based self-help aid. 2% freshmen, 4% undergrads receive athletic scholarships. **Criteria for awarding institutional aid:** *Non-need-based:* Academics, alumni affiliation, art, athletics, leadership, music/drama, state/district residency.

NORTH GREENVILLE COLLEGE

PO Box 1892, Tigerville, SC 29688-1892
Phone: 864-977-7001
E-mail: admissions@ngc.edu
Fax: 864-977-7177 **Website:** www.ngc.edu

This private school, affiliated with the Southern Baptist Church, was founded in 1892.

RATINGS
Admissions Selectivity Rating: 73   **Fire Safety Rating:** 60*   **Green Rating:** 60*

STUDENTS AND FACULTY
Enrollment: 1,570. **Student Body:** 49% female, 51% male, 19% out-of-state, 2% international (19 countries represented). African American 10%, Caucasian 90%.
Retention and Graduation: Faculty: Student/faculty ratio 17:1. 70 full-time faculty, 37% are women.

ACADEMICS
Degrees: Associate, bachelor's, transfer associate. **Classes:** Most classes have 10–19 students. Most lab/discussion sessions have 10–19 students. **Special Study Options:** Accelerated program, cooperative education program, cross-registration, double major, English as a Second Language (ESL), external degree program, honors program, independent study, internships, student-designed major, study abroad, teacher certification program Special programs offered to physically disabled students include tutors.

FACILITIES
Housing: Men's dorms, women's dorms.

CAMPUS LIFE
Environment: Rural. **Activities:** Choral groups, concert band, drama/theater, jazz band, literary magazine, marching band, music ensembles, radio station, student government, student newspaper, television station, yearbook. **Athletics (Intercollegiate):** *Men:* Baseball, basketball, cross-country, football, golf, soccer, softball, tennis. *Women:* Basketball, cross-country, soccer, softball, tennis, volleyball.

ADMISSIONS
Freshman Academic Profile: Average high school GPA 3.8. 16% in top 10% of high school class, 43% in top 25% of high school class, 70% in top 50% of high school class. SAT Math middle 50% range 460–570. SAT Critical Reading middle 50% range 470–580. ACT middle 50% range 20–24. Minimum paper TOEFL 500. Minimum computer TOEFL 200. **Basis for Candidate Selection:** *Very important factors considered include:* Class rank, rigor of secondary school record, standardized test scores. *Other factors considered include:* Application essay, recommendation(s). **Freshman Admission Requirements:** High school diploma is required and GED is accepted. *Academic units recommended:* 4 English, 2 mathematics, 2 science, (2 science labs), 2 foreign language, 2 social studies, 2 history, 2 academic electives. **Freshman Admission Statistics:** 769 applied, 95% admitted, 56% enrolled. **Transfer Admission Requirements:** College transcript(s), minimum college GPA of 2.0 required. Lowest grade transferable C. **General Admission Information:** Application fee $25. Regular application deadline 8/25. Nonfall registration accepted. Admission may be deferred for a maximum of 1 year.

COSTS AND FINANCIAL AID
Required Forms and Deadlines: FAFSA. Priority financial aid filing date 6/1. **Notification of Awards:** Applicants will be notified of awards on a rolling basis beginning 2/1. **Types of Aid:** *Need-based scholarships/grants:* Federal Pell, SEOG, state scholarships/grants, private scholarships, the school's own gift aid. *Loans:* FFEL Subsidized Stafford, FFEL Unsubsidized Stafford, FFEL PLUS, Federal Perkins, state loans, college/university loans from institutional funds. *Student Employment:* **Financial Aid Statistics:** 71% freshmen, 69% undergrads receive need-based scholarship or grant aid. 18% freshmen, 17% undergrads receive need-based self-help aid. 20% freshmen, 30% undergrads receive athletic scholarships. 50% undergrads borrow to pay for school. Average cumulative indebtedness $3,500. **Criteria for awarding institutional aid:** *Non-need-based:* Academics, art, athletics, music/drama, religious affiliation.

NORTH PARK UNIVERSITY

3225 West Foster Avenue, Chicago, IL 60625-4895
Phone: 773-244-5500 **Financial Aid Phone:** 773-244-5506
E-mail: admission@northpark.edu **CEEB Code:** 1556
Fax: 773-244-5243 **Website:** www.northpark.edu **ACT Code:** 1098

This private school was founded in 1891. It has a 30-acre campus.

RATINGS
Admissions Selectivity Rating: 79   **Fire Safety Rating:** 62   **Green Rating:** 60*

STUDENTS AND FACULTY
Enrollment: 2,188. **Student Body:** 63% female, 37% male, 38% out-of-state, 4% international (31 countries represented). Asian 7%, African American 9%, Caucasian 60%, Hispanic 10%.
Retention and Graduation: 71% freshmen return for sophomore year. 45% freshmen graduate within 4 years. 15% grads go on to further study within 1 year. 15% grads pursue arts and sciences degrees. 2% grads pursue law degrees. 10% grads pursue business degrees. 3% grads pursue medical degrees. **Faculty:** Student/faculty ratio 11:1. 125 full-time faculty, 88% hold PhDs, 17% are members of minority groups, 50% are women.

ACADEMICS
Degrees: Bachelor's, first professional, master's, post-bachelor's certificate. **Classes:** Most classes have 10–19 students. Most lab/discussion sessions have 20–29 students. **Majors with Highest Enrollment:** Business administration and management; education; nursing/registered nurse (RN, ASN, BSN, MSN). **Special Study Options:** Accelerated program, distance learning, double major, English as a Second Language (ESL), honors program, independent study, internships, liberal arts/career combination, student-designed major, study abroad, teacher certification program. **Honors programs:** The North Park University Honors Congress brings together students of high academic ability with faculty in a learning community designed to promote academic excellence, rigorous intellectual development, community involvement, service to others, and vocational direction. As Honors Congress Scholars, students of promise are provided opportunities to excel during their first two years of undergraduate study. Honors courses during the second two years are offered in individual departments. We strive to take the words of Jesus, "To whom much is given, much is required," and give them special consideration in the Honors Congress. Our philosophy is simply this: The Honors Congress gives students of high intellectual ability an array of learning experiences from which to choose, places them sideby-side with faculty mentors who care, and offers them guidance and encouragement along the way. **Combined degree programs:** MDiv/MBA dual degree. Special programs offered to physically disabled students include note-taking services, reader services, tape recorders, tutors. **Career services:** Alumni network, career/job search classes, career assessment, internships. **Career services highlights include:** North Park has hundreds of internship opportunities available throughout the Chicago area. Students can decide between public and private, nonprofit and for profit organizations.

FACILITIES
Housing: Special housing for disabled students, men's dorms, women's dorms, apartments for single students. **Special Academic Facilities/Equipment:** Art gallery, language lab, Swedish Historical Society Archives. **Computers:** 100% of libraries, 25% of dining areas, have wireless network access. Students can register for classes online. Administrative functions (other than registration) can be performed online.

CAMPUS LIFE
Environment: Metropolis. **Activities:** Choral groups, concert band, drama/theater, jazz band, literary magazine, music ensembles, musical theater, opera, pep band, student government, student newspaper, symphony orchestra, yearbook, campus ministries, international student organization. **Organizations:** 4 honor societies, 1 religious organizations. **Athletics (Intercollegiate):** *Men:* Baseball, basketball, cross-country, football, golf, soccer, track/field (outdoor), track/field (indoor). *Women:* Basketball, crew/rowing, cross-country, golf, soccer, softball, track/field (outdoor), track/field (indoor), volleyball. **On-Campus Highlights:** New Student Recreation Center, Brandel Library, new state-of-the-art outdoor athletic facilities, beautiful new campus quadrangle, diverse neighborhood.

ADMISSIONS
Freshman Academic Profile: Average high school GPA 3.1. 11% in top 10% of high school class, 35% in top 25% of high school class, 66% in top 50% of high school class. 80% from public high schools. SAT Math middle 50% range 460–590. SAT Critical Reading middle 50% range 470–580. ACT middle 50% range 19–24. Minimum paper TOEFL 550. Minimum computer TOEFL 213. **Basis for Candidate Selection:** *Very important factors considered include:*

Class rank, application essay, academic GPA, recommendation(s), rigor of secondary school record, standardized test scores, character/personal qualities, talent/ability. *Important factors considered include:* extracurricular activities, first generation, interview, racial/ethnic status, volunteer work. *Other factors considered include:* Alumni/ae relation, geographical residence, level of applicant's interest, work experience. **Freshman Admission Requirements:** High school diploma is required and GED is accepted. *Academic units recommended:* 4 English, 3 mathematics, 3 science, 2 foreign language, 1 social studies, 1 history. **Freshman Admission Statistics:** 1,402 applied, 71% admitted, 42% enrolled. **Transfer Admission Requirements:** College transcript(s), essay or personal statement, statement of good standing from prior institution(s). Minimum college GPA of 2.0 required. Lowest grade transferable D. **General Admission Information:** Application fee $40. Regular application deadline 7/1. Notification on a rolling basis, beginning on or about 9/15. Nonfall registration accepted. Admission may be deferred for a maximum of 1 year. Credit and/or placement offered for CEEB Advanced Placement tests.

COSTS AND FINANCIAL AID

Annual tuition $18,800. Room and board $8,140. Average book expense $950. **Required Forms and Deadlines:** FAFSA. Financial aid filing deadline 8/1. Priority financial aid filing date 5/1. **Notification of Awards:** Applicants will be notified of awards on a rolling basis beginning 3/15. **Types of Aid:** *Need-based scholarships/grants:* Federal Pell, SEOG, state scholarships/grants, private scholarships, the school's own gift aid, Federal Nursing Scholarships. *Loans:* Direct Subsidized Stafford, Direct Unsubsidized Stafford, Direct PLUS, FFEL Subsidized Stafford, FFEL Unsubsidized Stafford, FFEL PLUS, Federal Perkins, Federal Nursing. *Student Employment:* Federal Work-Study Program available. Institutional employment available. Highest amount earned per year from on-campus jobs $1,600. Off-campus job opportunities are excellent. **Financial Aid Statistics:** 50% freshmen receive need-based scholarship or grant aid. 29% freshmen receive non-need-based scholarship or grant aid. 45% freshmen receive need-based self-help aid. 90% freshmen, 90% undergrads receive any aid. 79% undergrads borrow to pay for school. Average cumulative indebtedness $21,140. **Criteria for awarding institutional aid:** *Non-need-based:* Academics, art, music/drama, religious affiliation, state/district residency.

NORTHEASTERN ILLINOIS UNIVERSITY

5500 North St. Louis Avenue, Chicago, IL 60625
Phone: 773-442-4000 **Financial Aid Phone:** 773-442-5000
E-mail: admrec@neiu.edu **CEEB Code:** 1090
Fax: 773-442-4020 **Website:** www.neiu.edu **ACT Code:** 993

This public school was founded in 1961. It has a 63-acre campus.

RATINGS
Admissions Selectivity Rating: 70   **Fire Safety Rating:** 60*   **Green Rating:** 73

STUDENTS AND FACULTY
Enrollment: 9,025. **Student Body:** 58% female, 42% male, 1% out-of-state, 4% international Asian 10%, African American 10%, Caucasian 39%, Hispanic 30%.
Retention and Graduation: 3% freshmen graduate within 4 years. **Faculty:** Student/faculty ratio 17:1. 404 full-time faculty, 73% hold PhDs, 27% are are members of minority groups, 49% are women.

ACADEMICS
Degrees: Bachelor's, master's. **Classes:** Most classes have 20–29 students. **Majors with Highest Enrollment:** Accounting; elementary education and teaching; psychology. **Special Study Options:** Cooperative education program, distance learning, double major, dual enrollment, exchange student program (domestic), honors program, independent study, student-designed major, study abroad, teacher certification program Special programs offered to physically disabled students include note-taking services, reader services, tape recorders, tutors. **Career services:** Career assessment, internships

FACILITIES
Housing: 98% of campus accessible to physically disabled. **Special Academic Facilities/Equipment:** Learning center with audiovisual, TV, multimedia, film, photography, graphic arts, and electronic instructional equipment, listening room. **Computers:** 50% of classrooms, n/a% of dorms, 100% of libraries, 80% of dining areas, 100% of student union, 50% of common outdoor areas have wireless network access. Students can register for classes online. Administrative functions (other than registration) can be performed online.

CAMPUS LIFE
Environment: Metropolis. **Activities:** Choral groups, concert band, dance, drama/theater, jazz band, literary magazine, music ensembles, musical theater,

radio station, student government, student newspaper. **Organizations:** 42 registered organizations, 12 honor societies, 6 religious organizations. 3 fraternities, 3 sororities. **On-Campus Highlights:** International Day, Fine Arst Building/ Art Gallery, Ensemble Dance Company, Health and Wellness Center, Library. **Environmental Initiatives:** Recycling, environmentally friendly chemicals, lighting upgrades.

ADMISSIONS
Freshman Academic Profile: Average high school GPA 2.86. 83% from public high schools. ACT middle 50% range 16–21. Minimum paper TOEFL 500. Minimum computer TOEFL 173. **Basis for Candidate Selection:** *Very important factors considered include:* Class rank, standardized test scores. **Freshman Admission Requirements:** High school diploma is required and GED is accepted. *Academic units required:* 4 English, 3 mathematics, 3 science, 3 social studies, 2 Fine arts, foreign lang. or voc. ed. (only 1 yr voc. ed. allowed). **Freshman Admission Statistics:** 4,035 applied, 74% admitted, 36% enrolled. **Transfer Admission Requirements:** College transcript(s), statement of good standing from prior institution(s). Minimum college GPA of 2.0 required. Lowest grade transferable D. **General Admission Information:** Application fee $25. Regular application deadline 7/1. Regular notification 9/1. Nonfall registration accepted. Admission may be deferred for a maximum of 1 semester. Credit offered for CEEB Advanced Placement tests.

COSTS AND FINANCIAL AID
Required Forms and Deadlines: FAFSA, institution's own financial aid form. Priority financial aid filing date 2/1. **Notification of Awards:** Applicants will be notified of awards on a rolling basis beginning 4/1. **Types of Aid:** *Need-based scholarships/grants:* Federal Pell, SEOG, state scholarships/grants, private scholarships, the school's own gift aid, Federal ACG, SMART. *Loans:* FFEL Subsidized Stafford, FFEL Unsubsidized Stafford, Federal PLUS, Federal Perkins. *Student Employment:* Federal Work-Study Program available. Institutional employment available. Off-campus job opportunities are good. **Financial Aid Statistics:** 52% freshmen, 45% undergrads receive need-based scholarship or grant aid. 5% freshmen, 5% undergrads receive non-need-based scholarship or grant aid. 13% freshmen, 22% undergrads receive need-based self-help aid. 53% freshmen, 61% undergrads receive any aid. 8% undergrads borrow to pay for school. Average cumulative indebtedness $13,418. **Criteria for awarding institutional aid:** *Non-need-based:* Academics, art, leadership, music/drama.

NORTHEASTERN STATE UNIVERSITY

Office of Admissions and Records, 600 N. Grand, Tahlequah, OK 74464-2399
Phone: 918-444-2200 **Financial Aid Phone:** 918-444-6402
E-mail: nsuinfo@nsuok.edu **CEEB Code:** 6485
Fax: 918-458-2342 **Website:** **ACT Code:** 3408

This public school was founded in 1846. It has a 200-acre campus.

RATINGS
Admissions Selectivity Rating: 60*   **Fire Safety Rating:** 60*   **Green Rating:** 60*

STUDENTS AND FACULTY
Enrollment: 8,485. **Student Body:** 61% female, 39% male, 3% out-of-state, 3% international (41 countries represented). Asian 1%, African American 6%, Caucasian 59%, Hispanic 2%, Native American 29%.
Retention and Graduation: 64% freshmen return for sophomore year. 12% freshmen graduate within 4 years. **Faculty:** Student/faculty ratio 23:1. 306 full-time faculty, 70% hold PhDs, 13% are are members of minority groups, 46% are women. 2% of classes are taught by teaching assistants.

ACADEMICS
Degrees: Bachelor's, first professional, master's, post-bachelor's certificate, post-master's certificate. **Classes:** Most classes have 20–29 students. Most lab/discussion sessions have 10–19 students. **Majors with Highest Enrollment:** Accounting; business administration and management; elementary education and teaching. **Special Study Options:** Cooperative education program, distance learning, double major, dual enrollment, honors program, independent study, internships, student-designed major, weekend college. **Honors programs:** NSU Honors Program: The Honors Program at NSU is a challenging educational option for academically talented students who enjoy learning. Honor students work with distinguished faculty members and peers in enhanced courses, pursue independent research, and participate in co-curricular cultural experiences. NSU President's Leadership Class: The President's Leadership Class is a unique scholarship/leadership program designed to identify and cultivate outstanding potential in selected freshmen entering NSU. Membership in the PLC allows students to develop close associations with University administrators, meet scholars and dignitaries who frequently visit

campus, take advantage of some of the most talented faculty members at NSU who teach special sections of selected required courses, and receive scholarship assistance which includes a tuition waiver and a stipend. The PLC Scholarship is renewable for four years if members maintain high academic standards while exercising practical leadership in University activities. Special programs offered to physically disabled students include note-taking services, reader services, tape recorders, tutors. **Career services:** Alumni services, career/job search classes, career assessment.

FACILITIES

Housing: Coed dorms, special housing for disabled students, fraternity/sorority housing, apartments for married students, apartments for single students. **Computers:** Administrative functions (other than registration) can be performed online.

CAMPUS LIFE

Environment: Rural. **Activities:** Choral groups, concert band, dance, drama/theater, jazz band, literary magazine, marching band, music ensembles, musical theater, pep band, student government, student newspaper, symphony orchestra, television station. **Organizations:** 77 registered organizations, 9 honor societies, 5 religious organizations. 7 fraternities, 6 sororities. **Athletics (Intercollegiate):** *Men:* Baseball, basketball, football, golf, soccer. *Women:* Basketball, golf, soccer, softball, tennis. **On-Campus Highlights:** Seminary Hall, University Center, New Science Lab Building, NET Building, Seminary Suites.

ADMISSIONS

Freshman Academic Profile: Average high school GPA 3.24. ACT middle 50% range 18–23. Minimum paper TOEFL 500. Minimum computer TOEFL 173. **Basis for Candidate Selection:** *Very important factors considered include:* Class rank, academic GPA, rigor of secondary school record, standardized test scores. *Other factors considered include:* First generation, geographical residence, state residency. **Freshman Admission Requirements:** High school diploma is required and GED is accepted. *Academic units required:* 4 English, 3 mathematics, 2 science, (2 science labs), 2 history, 4 academic electives. *Academic units recommended:* 2 foreign language, 2 social studies. **Freshman Admission Statistics:** 69% enrolled. **Transfer Admission Requirements:** College transcript(s), minimum college GPA of 2.0 required. Lowest grade transferable 2.0. **General Admission Information:** Regular application deadline 8/1. Nonfall registration accepted. Admission may be deferred for a maximum of one semester. Credit offered for CEEB Advanced Placement tests.

COSTS AND FINANCIAL AID

Average book expense $950. **Required Forms and Deadlines:** FAFSA, institution's own financial aid form. Priority financial aid filing date 4/1. **Notification of Awards:** Applicants will be notified of awards on a rolling basis beginning 2/15. **Types of Aid:** *Need-based scholarships/grants:* Federal Pell, SEOG, state scholarships/grants, private scholarships, the school's own gift aid. *Loans:* FFEL Subsidized Stafford, FFEL Unsubsidized Stafford, FFEL PLUS, Federal Perkins. *Student Employment:* Federal Work-Study Program available. Institutional employment available. **Financial Aid Statistics:** 40% freshmen, 46% undergrads receive need-based scholarship or grant aid. 39% freshmen, 57% undergrads receive non-need-based scholarship or grant aid. 16% freshmen, 41% undergrads receive need-based self-help aid. 4% freshmen, 13% undergrads receive athletic scholarships. 75% freshmen, 75% undergrads receive any aid. 61% undergrads borrow to pay for school. Average cumulative indebtedness $18,981. **Criteria for awarding institutional aid:** *Non-need-based:* Academics, alumni affiliation, art, athletics, job skills, leadership, minority status, music/drama, religious affiliation, state/district residency.

NORTHEASTERN UNIVERSITY

Best 373

360 Huntington Avenue, 150 Richards Hall, Boston, MA 02115
Phone: 617-373-2200 **Financial Aid Phone:** 617-373-3190
E-mail: admissions@neu.edu **CEEB Code:** 3667
Fax: 617-373-8780 **Website:** www.northeastern.edu **ACT Code:** 1880

This private school was founded in 1898. It has a 73-acre campus.

RATINGS

Admissions Selectivity Rating: 93 **Fire Safety Rating:** 81 **Green Rating:** 99

STUDENTS AND FACULTY

Enrollment: 15,699. **Student Body:** 51% female, 49% male, 61% out-of-state, 8% international (113 countries represented). Asian 9%, African American 4%, Caucasian 52%, Hispanic 5%.
Retention and Graduation: 91% freshmen return for sophomore year. 17% grads go on to further study within 1 year. **Faculty:** Student/faculty ratio 15:1. 984 full-time faculty, 88% hold PhDs, 17% are are members of minority groups, 39% are women.

ACADEMICS

Degrees: Bachelor's, master's, post-master's certificate. **Classes:** Most classes have 10–19 students. **Majors with Highest Enrollment:** Business/commerce; engineering; health services/allied health/health sciences. **Special Study Options:** Accelerated program, cooperative education program, cross-registration, distance learning, double major, English as a Second Language (ESL), exchange student program (domestic), honors program, independent study, internships, liberal arts/career combination, student-designed major, study abroad, teacher certification program, ROTC. **Honors programs:** The University Honors Program offers exceptionally motivated students an undergraduate experience charted by meeting academic challenge. The program includes demanding and challenging academic opportunities, connections to an active community of thinkers committed to making a difference, and Living and Learning in the Honors Program thematic communities. The University Honors Program frames opportunities that are intellectually rigorous; promotes global awareness and civic engagement; and empowers students. **Combined degree programs:** BA/MA, BA/MEng Special programs offered to physically disabled students include note-taking services, reader services, tape recorders **Career services:** Alumni network, alumni services, career/job search classes, career assessment, internships, regional alumni. **Career services highlights include:** Northeastern was in Princeton Review's Top 5 in Job Placement Career Services for 2 consecutive years; we host one of the largest Career Fairs in the region each semester—over 500 employers participated in Fall '08 & Spring '09 Career Fairs. We have an "Employer in Residence" program where IBM, Raytheon, and Shawmut Design & Construction make available a company rep one day a week to meet with students to assist in career related topics: resumes, interviews, job openings, and career paths. We also participate in "Call to Serve" (Partnership for Public Service) which educates a new generation about the importance of strong civil service, helps re-establish links between federal agencies and campus, and provides students with information about federal jobs.

FACILITIES

Housing: Coed dorms, special housing for disabled students, special housing for international students, apartments for single students, wellness house, theme housing 95% of campus accessible to physically disabled. **Special Academic Facilities/Equipment:** John D. O'Bryant African American Institute, Egan Science/Engineering Research Center, Behrakis Health Sciences Center, Marine Science Center at Nahant, Center for Subsurfacing Sensing and Imaging Systems (CenSSIS), Center for Complex Network Research, Center for Drug Discovery, Barnett Institute of Chemical and Biological Analysis, Behrakis Health Sciences Center, Center for High Rate Nanomanufacturing, Center for Subsurface Sensing and Imaging Systems (CenSSIS), Egan Science/Engineering Research Center Institute for Information Assurance, Institute on Urban Health Research, Dukakis Center for Urban and Regional Policy, John D. O'Bryant African-American Institute, Institute on Race and Justice, Institute for Global Innovation Management, Marine Science Center, Marino Recreation Center. **Computers:** 100% of classrooms, 20% of dorms, 100% of libraries, 75% of dining areas, 100% of student union, 100% of common outdoor areas have wireless network access. Students can register for classes online. Administrative functions (other than registration) can be performed online.

CAMPUS LIFE

Environment: Metropolis. **Activities:** Choral groups, concert band, dance, drama/theater, jazz band, literary magazine, music ensembles, musical theater, pep band, radio station, student government, student newspaper, symphony orchestra, television station, yearbook, campus ministries, international student organization, Model UN. **Organizations:** 225 registered organizations, 15 honor societies, 20 religious organizations. 9 fraternities, 8 sororities. **Athletics (Intercollegiate):** *Men:* Baseball, basketball, crew/rowing, cross-country, ice hockey, soccer, track/field (outdoor), track/field (indoor). *Women:* Basketball, crew/rowing, cross-country, diving, field hockey, ice hockey, soccer, swimming, track/field (outdoor), track/field (indoor), volleyball. **On-Campus Highlights:** International Village, Curry Student Center, Marino Health and Fitness Center, Levine Marketplace & Stetson West Dining, Cyber Cafe. **Environmental Initiatives:** Presidents' Climate Commitment LEED certification for new buildings and major renovations Aggressive recycling and energy conservation efforts, composting, local produce, fair trade certification, zero transfat, antibiotic free, sustainable seafood, cage free eggs, corporate responsibility partnerships, and active engagement with student groups and individual students.

ADMISSIONS

Freshman Academic Profile: 50% in top 10% of high school class, 81% in top 25% of high school class, 96% in top 50% of high school class. SAT Math middle

50% range 620–700. SAT Critical Reading middle 50% range 580–670. SAT Writing middle 50% range 580–670. ACT middle 50% range 27–31. Minimum paper TOEFL 550. Minimum computer TOEFL 213. Minimum web-based TOEFL 79. **Basis for Candidate Selection:** *Very important factors considered include:* Academic GPA, rigor of secondary school record. *Important factors considered include:* Application essay, recommendation(s), standardized test scores, character/personal qualities, extracurricular activities, first generation, talent/ability, volunteer work. *Other factors considered include:* Class rank, alumni/ae relation, geographical residence, interview, racial/ethnic status, state residency, work experience. **Freshman Admission Requirements:** High school diploma is required and GED is accepted. *Academic units required:* 4 English, 3 mathematics, 3 science, (2 science labs), 2 foreign language, 3 social studies, 2 history. *Academic units recommended:* 4 mathematics, 4 science, (4 science labs), 4 foreign language. **Freshman Admission Statistics:** 34,005 applied, 41% admitted, 20% enrolled. **Transfer Admission Requirements:** College transcript(s), essay or personal statement, statement of good standing from prior institution(s). Minimum college GPA of 2.0 required. Lowest grade transferable C. **General Admission Information:** Application fee $70. Regular application deadline 1/15. Nonfall registration accepted. Admission may be deferred for a maximum of 1 year. Credit and/or placement offered for CEEB Advanced Placement tests.

COSTS AND FINANCIAL AID

Annual tuition $34,950. Room and board $12,350. Required fees $412. Average book expense $1,000. **Required Forms and Deadlines:** FAFSA, CSS/Financial Aid PROFILE Priority financial aid filing date 2/15. **Notification of Awards:** Applicants will be notified of awards on a rolling basis beginning 3/15. **Types of Aid:** *Need-based scholarships/grants:* Federal Pell, SEOG, state scholarships/grants, private scholarships, the school's own gift aid. *Loans:* Direct Subsidized Stafford, Direct Unsubsidized Stafford, Direct PLUS, Federal Perkins, Federal Nursing, state loans *Student Employment:* Federal Work-Study Program available. Institutional employment available. Off-campus job opportunities are excellent. **Criteria for awarding institutional aid:** *Non-need-based:* Academics, athletics, minority status.

See page 1184.

NORTHERN ARIZONA UNIVERSITY

PO Box 4084, Flagstaff, AZ 86011-4084
Phone: 928-523-5511 **Financial Aid Phone:** 928-523-4951
E-mail: undergraduate.admissions@nau.edu **CEEB Code:** 4006
Fax: 928-523-0226 **Website:** www.nau.edu **ACT Code:** 0086

This public school was founded in 1899. It has a 740-acre campus.

RATINGS
Admissions Selectivity Rating: 78   **Fire Safety Rating:** 79   **Green Rating:** 97

STUDENTS AND FACULTY
Enrollment: 18,044. **Student Body:** 59% female, 41% male, 22% out-of-state, 3% international (69 countries represented). Asian 3%, African American 3%, Caucasian 69%, Hispanic 14%, Native American 5%.
Retention and Graduation: 72% freshmen return for sophomore year. 30% freshmen graduate within 4 years. **Faculty:** Student/faculty ratio 19:1. 813 full-time faculty, 10% are are members of minority groups, 48% are women. 5% of classes are taught by teaching assistants.

ACADEMICS
Degrees: Bachelor's, certificate, master's, post-bachelor's certificate. **Classes:** Most classes have 20–29 students. Most lab/discussion sessions have 20–29 students. **Majors with Highest Enrollment:** Biology/biological sciences; elementary education and teaching; hospitality administration/management. **Special Study Options:** Accelerated program, cooperative education program, distance learning, double major, dual enrollment, English as a Second Language (ESL), exchange student program (domestic), honors program, independent study, internships, study abroad, teacher certification program. **Honors programs:** Honors Program Special programs offered to physically disabled students include note-taking services, reader services, tape recorders, tutors. **Career services:** Alumni services, career/job search classes, career assessment, internships.

FACILITIES
Housing: Coed dorms, men's dorms, special housing for international students, women's dorms, fraternity/sorority housing, apartments for married students, apartments for single students. 90% of campus accessible to physically disabled. **Special Academic Facilities/Equipment:** Art gallery, art and music studios, observatory, multidisciplinary research center, 4,000–acre experimental forest. **Computers:** 100% of classrooms, 100% of dorms, 100% of libraries, 100%

of dining areas, 100% of student union, 25% of common outdoor areas have wireless network access. Students can register for classes online. Administrative functions (other than registration) can be performed online.

CAMPUS LIFE
Environment: Town. **Activities:** Choral groups, concert band, dance, drama/theater, jazz band, marching band, music ensembles, musical theater, opera, radio station, student government, student newspaper, symphony orchestra, television station, yearbook, campus ministries, international student organization. **Organizations:** 193 registered organizations, 20 honor societies, 7 religious organizations. 14 fraternities, 9 sororities. **Athletics (Intercollegiate):** *Men:* Basketball, cheerleading, cross-country, football, tennis, track/field (outdoor). *Women:* Basketball, cheerleading, cross-country, diving, golf, soccer, swimming, tennis, track/field (outdoor), volleyball. **On-Campus Highlights:** University Union, NAU Dome, Wall Aquatic Center, Cline Library, Old Main. **Environmental Initiatives:** Green building commitment; 50% of campus landscaping served by reclaimed/non-potable water; ecoPass—free city bus passes offered to all faculty and staff.

ADMISSIONS
Freshman Academic Profile: Average high school GPA 3.4. SAT Math middle 50% range 470–590. SAT Critical Reading middle 50% range 470–580. SAT Writing middle 50% range 450–560. ACT middle 50% range 20–25. Minimum paper TOEFL 525. Minimum computer TOEFL 195. Minimum web-based TOEFL 70. **Basis for Candidate Selection:** *Important factors considered include:* Class rank, academic GPA, rigor of secondary school record, standardized test scores. **Freshman Admission Requirements:** High school diploma is required and GED is accepted. *Academic units required:* 4 English, 4 mathematics, 3 science, (1 science labs), 2 foreign language, 1 social studies, 1 history, 1 fine arts. **Freshman Admission Statistics:** 26,334 applied, 73% admitted, 19% enrolled. Minimum college GPA of 2.0 required. Lowest grade transferable C. **General Admission Information:** Application fee $25. Nonfall registration accepted. Admission may be deferred for a maximum of 2 years. Credit and/or placement offered for CEEB Advanced Placement tests.

COSTS AND FINANCIAL AID
Annual in-state tuition $6,092. Annual out-of-state tuition $17,318. Room and board $7,872. Required fees $540. Average book expense $916. **Required Forms and Deadlines:** FAFSA. Priority financial aid filing date 2/14. **Notification of Awards:** Applicants will be notified of awards on a rolling basis beginning 3/15. **Types of Aid:** *Need-based scholarships/grants:* Federal Pell, SEOG, state scholarships/grants, private scholarships, the school's own gift aid, Federal Nursing Scholarships. *Loans:* Direct Subsidized Stafford, Direct Unsubsidized Stafford, Direct PLUS, Federal Perkins, Federal Nursing, state loans, college/university loans from institutional funds. *Student Employment:* Federal Work-Study Program available. Institutional employment available. Off-campus job opportunities are good. **Financial Aid Statistics:** 29% freshmen, 33% undergrads receive need-based scholarship or grant aid. 25% freshmen, 20% undergrads receive non-need-based scholarship or grant aid. 32% freshmen, 37% undergrads receive need-based self-help aid. 2% freshmen, 2% undergrads receive athletic scholarships. 69% freshmen, 65% undergrads receive any aid. 50.2% undergrads borrow to pay for school. Average cumulative indebtedness $16,703. **Criteria for awarding institutional aid:** *Non-need-based:* Academics, alumni affiliation, art, athletics, leadership, minority status, music/drama, state/district residency.

NORTHERN ILLINOIS UNIVERSITY

Office of Admissions, Williston Hall 101, NIU, DeKalb, IL 60115-2857
Phone: 815-753-0446 **Financial Aid Phone:** 815-753-1395
E-mail: admissions-info@niu.edu **CEEB Code:** 1559
Fax: 815-753-1783 **Website:** www.reg.niu.edu **ACT Code:** 1102

This public school was founded in 1895. It has a 546-acre campus.

RATINGS
Admissions Selectivity Rating: 70   **Fire Safety Rating:** 60*   **Green Rating:** 60*

STUDENTS AND FACULTY
Enrollment: 18,915. **Student Body:** 52% female, 48% male, 4% out-of-state, 1% international Asian 5%, African American 12%, Caucasian 69%, Hispanic 7%.
Retention and Graduation: 78% freshmen return for sophomore year. 26% freshmen graduate within 4 years. 10% grads go on to further study within 1 year. **Faculty:** Student/faculty ratio 17:1. 908 full-time faculty, 82% hold PhDs, 13% are are members of minority groups, 45% are women.

ACADEMICS

Degrees: Bachelor's, first professional, master's. **Classes:** Most classes have 20–29 students. Most lab/discussion sessions have 20–29 students. **Special Study Options:** Cooperative education program, distance learning, double major, dual enrollment, external degree program, honors program, independent study, internships, liberal arts/career combination, student-designed major, study abroad, teacher certification program **Combined degree programs:** BA/JD. Special programs offered to physically disabled students include note-taking services, tape recorders, tutors. **Career services:** Alumni network, alumni services, career/job search classes, internships, regional alumni. **Career services highlights include:** Comprehensive internship and Cooperative ed. program.

FACILITIES

Housing: Coed dorms, special housing for disabled students, special housing for international students, fraternity/sorority housing, apartments for married students, quiet and alcohol-free lifestyle floors, 21 and over/graduates student floors, honors floors. Floors with visitation policies, computer science residential program. 90% of campus accessible to physically disabled. **Special Academic Facilities/Equipment:** Art and anthropology museums, plant molecular biology center. **Computers:** Students can register for classes online.

CAMPUS LIFE

Environment: Rural. **Activities:** Choral groups, concert band, dance, drama/theater, jazz band, marching band, opera, radio station, student government, student newspaper, student-run film society, symphony orchestra, television station **Organizations:** 200 registered organizations, 13 religious organizations. 22 fraternities, 14 sororities. **Athletics (Intercollegiate):** *Men:* Baseball, basketball, diving, football, golf, soccer, swimming, tennis, wrestling. *Women:* Basketball, cross-country, golf, gymnastics, soccer, softball, swimming, tennis, volleyball. **On-Campus Highlights:** Barsema Hall, Convocation Center, Holmes Student Center, Campus Life Building, Recreation Center.

ADMISSIONS

Freshman Academic Profile: 9% in top 10% of high school class, 33% in top 25% of high school class, 75% in top 50% of high school class. ACT middle 50% range 19–24. Minimum paper TOEFL 525. Minimum computer TOEFL 1. **Basis for Candidate Selection:** *Very important factors considered include:* Class rank, rigor of secondary school record, standardized test scores. *Other factors considered include:* Application essay, recommendation(s), extracurricular activities, racial/ethnic status, talent/ability. **Freshman Admission Requirements:** High school diploma is required and GED is accepted. *Academic units required:* 4 English, 2 mathematics, 2 science, (1 science labs), 1 foreign language, 2 social studies, 1 history. *Academic units recommended:* 4 mathematics, 4 science, (2 science labs), 2 foreign language, 3 social studies. **Freshman Admission Statistics:** 16,769 applied, 61% admitted, 29% enrolled. **Transfer Admission Requirements:** College transcript(s), minimum college GPA of 2.0 required. Lowest grade transferable c. **General Admission Information:** Regular application deadline 8/1. Nonfall registration accepted. Credit and/or placement offered for CEEB Advanced Placement tests.

COSTS AND FINANCIAL AID

Annual in-state tuition $4,347. Room and board $5,010. Average book expense $700. **Required Forms and Deadlines:** FAFSA, institution's own financial aid form, noncustodial PROFILE. Priority financial aid filing date 3/1. **Notification of Awards:** Applicants will be notified of awards on a rolling basis beginning 4/15. **Types of Aid:** *Need-based scholarships/grants:* Federal Pell, SEOG, state scholarships/grants, private scholarships, the school's own gift aid, Federal Nursing Scholarships. *Loans:* FFEL Subsidized Stafford, FFEL Unsubsidized Stafford, FFEL PLUS, Federal Perkins. *Student Employment:* Off-campus job opportunities are good. **Financial Aid Statistics:** 41% freshmen, 54% undergrads receive need-based scholarship or grant aid. 20% freshmen, 18% undergrads receive non-need-based scholarship or grant aid. 64% freshmen, 55% undergrads receive need-based self-help aid. 2% freshmen, 2% undergrads receive athletic scholarships. 74% undergrads borrow to pay for school. Average cumulative indebtedness $19,973. **Criteria for awarding institutional aid:** *Non-need-based:* Academics, athletics.

NORTHERN KENTUCKY UNIVERSITY

Administrative Center 401, Nunn Drive, Highland Heights, KY 41099
Phone: 859-572-5220 **Financial Aid Phone:** 859-572-6437
E-mail: admitnku@nku.edu **CEEB Code:** 1574
Fax: 859-572-6665 **Website:** www.nku.edu **ACT Code:** 1566

This public school was founded in 1968. It has a 397-acre campus.

RATINGS

Admissions Selectivity Rating: 60*   **Fire Safety Rating:** 90   **Green Rating:** 74

STUDENTS AND FACULTY

Enrollment: 11,611. **Student Body:** 58% female, 42% male, 39% out-of-state, 2% international (63 countries represented). African American 5%, Caucasian 88%, Hispanic 1%.
Retention and Graduation: 67% freshmen return for sophomore year. **Faculty:** Student/faculty ratio 16:1. 544 full-time faculty, 70% hold PhDs, 10% are are members of minority groups, 49% are women.

ACADEMICS

Degrees: Associate, bachelor's, certificate, first professional, master's, post-bachelor's certificate. **Classes:** Most classes have 20–29 students. Most lab/discussion sessions have 10–19 students. **Majors with Highest Enrollment:** Elementary education and teaching; nursing/registered nurse (RN, ASN, BSN, MSN); psychology. **Special Study Options:** Cooperative education program, cross-registration, distance learning, double major, dual enrollment, exchange student program (domestic), honors program, independent study, internships, liberal arts/career combination, study abroad, teacher certification program, weekend college, web-based programs. **Honors programs:** The NKU Honors Program provides qualified students a 21-hour minor, which includes 15 semester hours of seminars, each having a maximum enrollment of 15 students, PLUS. 6 semester hours for completing the Honors Thesis. At the core of the Honors experience, the seminars emphasize discussion and discovery of ideas. NKU's Honors Program is university-wide. The program showcases open-ended seminars not conforming to the boundaries traditionally dividing fields of experise. Honors learning affords the intellectual challenges of interdisciplinary education. **Combined degree programs:** MBA/JD. Special programs offered to physically disabled students include note-taking services, reader services, tape recorders, tutors. **Career services:** Alumni services, career/job search classes, career assessment, internships. **Career services highlights include:** Cooperative Education—well organized co-op learning program out of the Career Development Center. This program has grown significantly (55%) in the last two years.

FACILITIES

Housing: Coed dorms, special housing for disabled students, men's dorms, women's dorms, cooperative housing, apartments for single studentsOne-Third of all college housing accessible to handicapped. 100% of campus accessible to physically disabled. **Special Academic Facilities/Equipment:** Art gallery, biology, geology, and anthropology museums, research/technical center, two electron microscopes. **Computers:** Students can register for classes online. Administrative functions (other than registration) can be performed online.

CAMPUS LIFE

Environment: Metropolis. **Activities:** Choral groups, concert band, dance, drama/theater, jazz band, literary magazine, music ensembles, musical theater, opera, pep band, radio station, student government, student newspaper, symphony orchestra, television station **Organizations:** 125 registered organizations, 14 honor societies, 9 religious organizations. 8 fraternities, 8 sororities. **Athletics (Intercollegiate):** *Men:* Baseball, basketball, cheerleading, cross-country, golf, soccer, tennis. *Women:* Basketball, cheerleading, cross-country, golf, soccer, softball, tennis, volleyball. **On-Campus Highlights:** Natural Science Center, University Suites (housing), Starbucks Cafe, Albright Health Center, a full service U.S. Bank Branch. **Environmental Initiatives:** Energy savings performance contract that is expected to save $4 million in energy over an 11-year period. Highly successful "U-PASS" partnership with the Transit Authority of Northern Kentucky (TANK) to provide free, unlimited bus rides to students and faculty/staff with a valid university ID. Since August 2007, over 50,000 rides have been taken on TANK buses through the U-PASS program. The campus recycling program was expanded in 2007 to include recycling of #1 and #2 plastic bottles and cans. In addition, NKU is participating in RecycleMania for the first time during 2008. During this 10–week competition, students, faculty/staff and visitors to campus will be encouraged to reduce their waste (trash PLUS recyclables).

ADMISSIONS

Freshman Academic Profile: SAT Math middle 50% range 440–560. SAT Critical Reading middle 50% range 440–540. ACT middle 50% range 18–23. Minimum paper TOEFL 500. Minimum computer TOEFL 173. **Basis for Candidate Selection:** *Very important factors considered include:* Class rank, academic GPA, standardized test scores. **Freshman Admission Requirements:** High school diploma is required and GED is accepted. *Academic units required:* 4 English, 3 mathematics, 3 science, (1 science labs), 2 foreign language, 3 social studies, 6 academic electives, 1 health/physical education. **Freshman Admission Statistics:** 4,317 applied, 75% admitted, 55% enrolled. **Transfer Admission Requirements:** College transcript(s), minimum college GPA of 2.0 required. Lowest grade transferable D. **General Admission Information:** Application fee $30. Regular application deadline 8/1. Notification on a rolling basis, beginning on or about 10/1. Nonfall registration accepted. Credit offered for CEEB Advanced Placement tests.

COSTS AND FINANCIAL AID

Required Forms and Deadlines: FAFSA. Priority financial aid filing date 3/1. **Notification of Awards:** Applicants will be notified of awards on a rolling basis beginning 4/1. **Types of Aid:** *Need-based scholarships/grants:* Federal Pell, SEOG, state scholarships/grants, private scholarships, the school's own gift aid. *Loans:* FFEL Subsidized Stafford, FFEL Unsubsidized Stafford, FFEL PLUS, Federal Perkins, private loans. *Student Employment:* Federal Work-Study Program available. Institutional employment available. Highest amount earned per year from on-campus jobs $5,625. Off-campus job opportunities are good. **Financial Aid Statistics:** 46% freshmen, 36% undergrads receive need-based scholarship or grant aid. 18% freshmen, 13% undergrads receive non-need-based scholarship or grant aid. 36% freshmen, 29% undergrads receive need-based self-help aid. 1% freshmen, 1% undergrads receive athletic scholarships. 90% freshmen, 85% undergrads receive any aid. 3% undergrads borrow to pay for school. Average cumulative indebtedness $21,727. **Criteria for awarding institutional aid:** *Non-need-based:* Academics, alumni affiliation, art, athletics, job skills, leadership, minority status, music/drama, state/district residency.

NORTHERN MICHIGAN UNIVERSITY

1401 Presque Isle Avenue, Marquette, MI 49855
Phone: 906-227-2650 **Financial Aid Phone:** 800-682-9797
E-mail: admiss@nmu.edu **CEEB Code:** 1560
Fax: 906-227-1747 **Website:** www.nmu.edu **ACT Code:** 2038

This public school was founded in 1899. It has a 350-acre campus.

RATINGS
Admissions Selectivity Rating: 72   **Fire Safety Rating:** 83   **Green Rating:** 73

STUDENTS AND FACULTY
Enrollment: 8,386. **Student Body:** 53% female, 47% male, 20.3% out-of-state, 1% international (24 countries represented). Asian 1%, African American 2%, Caucasian 88%, Hispanic 1%, Native American 3%.
Retention and Graduation: 18% freshmen graduate within 4 years. 19% grads go on to further study within 1 year. **Faculty:** Student/faculty ratio 23:1. 317 full-time faculty, 80% hold PhDs, 7% are are members of minority groups, 41% are women. 4% of classes are taught by teaching assistants.

ACADEMICS
Degrees: Associate, bachelor's, certificate, diploma, master's, post-bachelor's certificate, post-master's certificate, terminal associate, transfer associate. **Classes:** Most classes have 20–29 students. **Majors with Highest Enrollment:** art/art studies; criminal justice/safety studies; nursing/registered nurse (RN, ASN, BSN, MSN). **Special Study Options:** Distance learning, double major, dual enrollment, English as a Second Language (ESL), honors program, independent study, internships, liberal arts/career combination, student-designed major, study abroad, teacher certification program, weekend college. **Honors programs:** Honors Program for eligible freshmen and transfer students Special programs offered to physically disabled students include note-taking services, reader services, tape recorders, tutors. **Career services:** Alumni network, career/job search classes, internships. **Career services highlights include:** The offering of internships is specific to each academic department.

FACILITIES
Housing: Coed dorms, special housing for disabled students, apartments for married students, apartments for single students, wellness house, theme housing. 100% of campus accessible to physically disabled. **Special Academic Facilities/Equipment:** Seaborg Science Center, New Science facility, new and remodeled Music and Art and Design instructional rooms, DeVos Art Gallery. **Computers:** 100% of classrooms, 100% of dorms, 100% of libraries, 100% of dining areas, 100% of student union, 100% of common outdoor areas have wireless network access. Students can register for classes online. Administrative functions (other than registration) can be performed online.

CAMPUS LIFE
Environment: Village. **Activities:** Choral groups, concert band, dance, drama/theater, jazz band, literary magazine, marching band, music ensembles, musical theater, opera, pep band, radio station, student government, student newspaper, student-run film society, symphony orchestra, television station, campus ministries, international student organization, Model UN. **Organizations:** 308 registered organizations, 11 honor societies, 19 religious organizations. 3 fraternities, 4 sororities. **Athletics (Intercollegiate):** *Men:* Basketball, cross-country, football, golf, ice hockey, skiing (nordic/cross-country). *Women:* Basketball, cross-country, diving, skiing (nordic/cross-country), soccer, swimming, track/field (outdoor), track/field (indoor), volleyball. **On-Campus Highlights:** Hedgcock Student Service Center, Superior Dome, New Science Facility, Market Place Din-

ing Facility, De Vos Art Galleries, The Starbucks coffee lounge located in the library is a very popular place and doubles as a study lounge. **Environmental Initiatives:** Northern is a member of the Association for the Advancement of Sustainability in Higher Education and USGBC. Reduced energy consumption by providing computer controlled heating and cooling, thermal efficient windows for the dormitories, individual heating controls in dorm rooms, new efficient lighting and controls technology, new energy efficient architectural design components, water efficient fixtures, wells for irrigation and waterless urinals. In 2007 Meyland Hall's renovation received LEED certification, a first for any building in the Upper Peninsula and the first certified residence hall in the states of MI, WI, MN, OH, and IN.

ADMISSIONS
Freshman Academic Profile: Average high school GPA 2.9. ACT middle 50% range 19–24. Minimum paper TOEFL 500. Minimum computer TOEFL 173. Minimum web-based TOEFL 61. **Basis for Candidate Selection:** *Very important factors considered include:* Academic GPA, standardized test scores. **Freshman Admission Requirements:** High school diploma is required and GED is accepted. *Academic units recommended:* 4 English, 4 mathematics, 4 science, 3 foreign language, 4 social studies. **Freshman Admission Statistics:** 5,955 applied, 73% admitted, 41% enrolled. **Transfer Admission Requirements:** College transcript(s), statement of good standing from prior institution(s). Minimum college GPA of 2.0 required. Lowest grade transferable C–. **General Admission Information:** Application fee $30. Notification on a rolling basis, beginning on or about 9/15. Nonfall registration accepted. Admission may be deferred for a maximum of 1 year. Credit and/or placement offered for CEEB Advanced Placement tests.

COSTS AND FINANCIAL AID
Annual in-state tuition $6,840. Annual out-of-state tuition $11,214. Room and board $7,646. Required fees $614. Average book expense $830. **Required Forms and Deadlines:** FAFSA. Priority financial aid filing date 3/1. **Notification of Awards:** Applicants will be notified of awards on a rolling basis beginning 4/1. **Types of Aid:** *Need-based scholarships/grants:* Federal Pell, SEOG, state scholarships/grants, private scholarships, the school's own gift aid, Federal Nursing Scholarships. *Loans:* Direct Subsidized Stafford, Direct Unsubsidized Stafford, Direct PLUS, Federal Perkins, state loans, private loans. *Student Employment:* Federal Work-Study Program available. Institutional employment available. Off-campus job opportunities are fair. **Financial Aid Statistics:** 33% freshmen, 31% undergrads receive need-based scholarship or grant aid. 29% freshmen, 22% undergrads receive non-need-based scholarship or grant aid. 48% freshmen, 48% undergrads receive need-based self-help aid. 86% freshmen, 85% undergrads receive any aid. 67% undergrads borrow to pay for school. Average cumulative indebtedness $24,072. **Criteria for awarding institutional aid:** *Non-need-based:* Academics, art, athletics, leadership, minority status, music/drama, religious affiliation, state/district residency.

NORTHERN STATE UNIVERSITY

1200 South Jay Street, Aberdeen, SD 57401-7198
Phone: 605-626-2544 **Financial Aid Phone:** 605-626-2640
E-mail: admission2@northern.edu **CEEB Code:** 6487
Fax: 605-626-2431 **Website: ACT Code:** 3916

This public school was founded in 1901. It has a 72-acre campus.

RATINGS
Admissions Selectivity Rating: 62   **Fire Safety Rating:** 60*   **Green Rating:** 86

STUDENTS AND FACULTY
Enrollment: 1,667. **Student Body:** 57% female, 43% male, 17% out-of-state, 1% international (12 countries represented). Asian 1%, African American 2%, Caucasian 84%, Hispanic 2%, Native American 3%.
Retention and Graduation: 70% freshmen return for sophomore year. 15% grads go on to further study within 1 year. 7% grads pursue arts and sciences degrees. 1% grads pursue law degrees. 1% grads pursue business degrees. 1% grads pursue medical degrees. **Faculty:** Student/faculty ratio 17:1. 96 full-time faculty, 77% hold PhDs, 11% are are members of minority groups, 36% are women.

ACADEMICS
Degrees: Associate, bachelor's, certificate, master's. **Classes:** Most classes have 10–19 students. **Majors with Highest Enrollment:** Business/commerce; elementary education and teaching; sociology. **Special Study Options:** Accelerated program, cooperative education program, cross-registration, distance learning, double major, dual enrollment, English as a Second Language (ESL), exchange student program (domestic), external degree program, honors program, independent study, internships, liberal arts/career combination,

student-designed major, study abroad, teacher certification program, weekend college, International Business E-Learning Certification. **Honors programs:** Honors Program. **Combined degree programs:** Bachelor's/MBA w/ U of South Dakota. Special programs offered to physically disabled students include note-taking services, reader services, tape recorders, tutors. **Career services:** Alumni network, alumni services, career/job search classes, career assessment, internships, regional alumni. **Career services highlights include:** School of Business Programs School of Education Programs.

FACILITIES

Housing: Coed dorms, men's dorms, women's dorms, apartments for married students, apartments for single students. 90% of campus accessible to physically disabled. **Special Academic Facilities/Equipment:** State-wide E-Learning Center; art galleries. **Computers:** 100% of classrooms, 100% of dorms, 100% of libraries, 100% of dining areas, 100% of student union, have wireless network access. Students can register for classes online. Administrative functions (other than registration) can be performed online.

CAMPUS LIFE

Environment: Rural. **Activities:** Choral groups, concert band, dance, drama/theater, jazz band, marching band, music ensembles, musical theater, pep band, student government, student newspaper, symphony orchestra, television station, yearbook, campus ministries, international student organization. **Organizations:** 100 registered organizations, 5 honor societies, 6 religious organizations. **Athletics (Intercollegiate):** *Men:* Baseball, basketball, cheerleading, cross-country, football, golf, track/field (outdoor), track/field (indoor), wrestling. *Women:* Basketball, cheerleading, cross-country, golf, soccer, softball, swimming, tennis, track/field (outdoor), track/field (indoor), volleyball. **On-Campus Highlights:** NSU Student Center, NSU State-Wide E-Learning Center, NSU Barnett Athletic Center, NSU Johnson Fine Arts Center, NSU International Center of Excellence.

ADMISSIONS

Freshman Academic Profile: 8% in top 10% of high school class, 20% in top 25% of high school class, 36% in top 50% of high school class. ACT middle 50% range 18–24. Minimum paper TOEFL 550. Minimum web-based TOEFL 61. **Basis for Candidate Selection:** *Very important factors considered include:* Class rank, rigor of secondary school record, standardized test scores. *Other factors considered include:* interview, talent/ability. **Freshman Admission Requirements:** High school diploma is required and GED is accepted. *Academic units required:* 4 English, 3 mathematics, 3 science, (3 science labs), 3 social studies. **Freshman Admission Statistics:** 923 applied, 93% admitted, 38% enrolled. **Transfer Admission Requirements:** High school transcript, college transcript(s), statement of good standing from prior institution(s). Minimum college GPA of 2.0 required. Lowest grade transferable C. **General Admission Information:** Application fee $20. Nonfall registration accepted. Credit and/or placement offered for CEEB Advanced Placement tests.

COSTS AND FINANCIAL AID

Annual in-state tuition $2,751. Annual out-of-state tuition $4,124. Room and board $4,875. Required fees $3,312. Average book expense $900. **Required Forms and Deadlines:** FAFSA. Priority financial aid filing date 3/1. **Notification of Awards:** Applicants will be notified of awards on or about 4/15. **Types of Aid:** *Need-based scholarships/grants:* Federal Pell, SEOG, state scholarships/grants, private scholarships, the school's own gift aid. *Loans:* FFEL Subsidized Stafford, FFEL Unsubsidized Stafford, FFEL PLUS, Federal Perkins, college/university loans from institutional funds. *Student Employment:* Federal Work-Study Program available. Institutional employment available. Off-campus job opportunities are excellent. **Criteria for awarding institutional aid:** *Non-need-based:* Academics, art, athletics, leadership, minority status, music/drama, state/district residency.

NORTHLAND COLLEGE

1411 Ellis Avenue, Ashland, WI 54806-3999
Phone: 715-682-1224 **Financial Aid Phone:** 715-682-1255
E-mail: admit@northland.edu **CEEB Code:** 1561
Fax: 715-682-1258 **Website:** www.northland.edu **ACT Code:** 4624

This private school, affiliated with the United Church of Christ Church, was founded in 1892. It has a 130-acre campus.

RATINGS

Admissions Selectivity Rating: 86   **Fire Safety Rating:** 60*   **Green Rating:** 99

STUDENTS AND FACULTY

Enrollment: 624. **Student Body:** 53% female, 47% male, 57% out-of-state, 3% international (5 countries represented). Asian 1%, African American 2%, Caucasian 82%, Hispanic 2%, Native American 3%.

Retention and Graduation: Faculty: Student/faculty ratio 14.6:1. 39 full-time faculty, 82% hold PhDs, 10% are are members of minority groups, 23% are women.

ACADEMICS

Degrees: Bachelor's. **Classes:** Most classes have 10–19 students. Most lab/discussion sessions have 10–19 students. **Majors with Highest Enrollment:** Biology/biological sciences; education; natural resources conservation and research, other. **Special Study Options:** Distance learning, double major, dual enrollment, exchange student program (domestic), honors program, independent study, internships, student-designed major, teacher certification program, 3-2 cooperative programs in Forestry and Engineering with Michigan Technological University and Washington University Eco League consortium with 6 environmental liberal arts colleges around the country (Prescott, Green Mountain, Alaska Pacific University, Antioch College, College of the Atlantic, Northland College) engaging in student semester exchanges. **Combined degree programs:** 3-2 engineering. Special programs offered to physically disabled students include note-taking services, reader services, tape recorders, tutors. **Career services:** Internships.

FACILITIES

Housing: Coed dorms, women's dorms, cooperative housing, apartments for single students, theme housing. **Special Academic Facilities/Equipment:** Native American museum, language lab, field stations in nearby national forest, observatory. **Computers:** 20% of classrooms, 20% of dorms, 100% of libraries, 100% of dining areas, 100% of student union, 75% of common outdoor areas have wireless network access. Students can register for classes online. Administrative functions (other than registration) can be performed online.

CAMPUS LIFE

Environment: Village. **Activities:** Choral groups, concert band, drama/theater, jazz band, music ensembles, radio station, student government, student newspaper, symphony orchestra, yearbook, international student organization. **Organizations:** 30 registered organizations, 1 honor societies, 2 religious organizations. **Athletics (Intercollegiate):** *Men:* Baseball, basketball, cross-country, ice hockey, skiing (nordic/cross-country), soccer. *Women:* Basketball, cross-country, skiing (nordic/cross-country), soccer, softball, volleyball. **On-Campus Highlights:** Campus Center, Science Center, The Fire Ring, The Environmental Living and Learning Center, The Ravine. **Environmental Initiatives:** Signing the ACUPCC; incorporating sustainability into master planning process and throughout the curriculum; student involvement in every major sustainability effort on campus; students promote sustainabile lifestyle through "theme houses": Sunshine House, Ecco House, and Moonbeam Consortium

ADMISSIONS

Freshman Academic Profile: Average high school GPA 3.28. 21% in top 10% of high school class, 39% in top 25% of high school class, 72% in top 50% of high school class. 80% from public high schools. SAT Math middle 50% range 440–600. SAT Critical Reading middle 50% range 530–620. ACT middle 50% range 21–27. Minimum paper TOEFL 525. Minimum computer TOEFL 193. Minimum web-based TOEFL 69. **Basis for Candidate Selection:** *Very important factors considered include:* Rigor of secondary school record. *Important factors considered include:* Class rank, application essay, academic GPA, recommendation(s), standardized test scores. *Other factors considered include:* Alumni/ae relation, character/personal qualities, extracurricular activities, first generation, geographical residence, interview, level of applicant's interest, talent/ability, volunteer work, work experience. **Freshman Admission Requirements:** High school diploma is required and GED is accepted. *Academic units required:* 4 English, 3 mathematics, 3 science, (2 science labs), 3 social studies, 3 academic electives. *Academic units recommended:* 4 English, 3 mathematics, 3 science, (2 science labs), 2 foreign language, 3 social studies, 4 academic electives. **Freshman Admission Statistics:** 634 applied, 74% admitted, 28% enrolled. **Transfer Admission Requirements:** High school transcript, college transcript(s), essay or personal statement, statement of good standing from prior institution(s). Minimum college GPA of 2.0 required. Lowest grade transferable C–. **General Admission Information:** Application fee $25. Notification on a rolling basis, beginning on or about 9/1. Nonfall registration accepted. Admission may be deferred for a maximum of 2 years. Credit and/or placement offered for CEEB Advanced Placement tests.

COSTS AND FINANCIAL AID

Annual tuition $23,380. Room and board $6,765. Required fees $641. Average book expense $800. **Required Forms and Deadlines:** FAFSA. Priority financial aid filing date 3/15. **Notification of Awards:** Applicants will be notified of awards on a rolling basis beginning 3/1. **Types of Aid:** *Need-based scholarships/grants:* Federal Pell, SEOG, state scholarships/grants, private scholarships, the school's own gift aid, Bureau of Indian Affairs Grants. *Loans:* Direct Subsidized Stafford, Direct Unsubsidized Stafford, Direct PLUS, FFEL Subsidized Stafford, FFEL Unsubsidized Stafford, FFEL PLUS, Federal Perkins. *Student Employment:* Federal Work-Study Program available. Institutional employment available. Highest amount earned per year from on-campus jobs $1,600. Off-campus job opportunities are good. **Financial Aid Statistics:** 78% freshmen, 80% undergrads receive need-based scholarship or grant aid. 1% undergrads receive non-need-based scholarship or grant aid. 59% freshmen, 68% undergrads receive need-based self-help aid. 99% freshmen, 95% undergrads receive any aid. 79% undergrads borrow to pay for school. Average cumulative indebtedness $23,630. **Criteria for awarding institutional aid:** *Non-need-based:* Academics, alumni affiliation, art, job skills, leadership, minority status, music/drama, religious affiliation, state/district residency.

NORTHWEST CHRISTIAN COLLEGE

828 East 11th Avenue, Eugene, OR 97401
Phone: 541-684-7201 **Financial Aid Phone:** 541-684-7203
E-mail: admissions@nwcc.edu **CEEB Code:** 4543
Fax: 541-628-7317 **Website: ACT Code:** 10101

This private school was founded in 1895. It has a 8-acre campus.

RATINGS
Admissions Selectivity Rating: 77   **Fire Safety Rating:** 60*   **Green Rating:** 60*

STUDENTS AND FACULTY
Enrollment: 380. **Student Body:** 61% female, 39% male, 10% out-of-state, Asian 2%, African American 1%, Caucasian 64%, Hispanic 4%, Native American 2%.
Retention and Graduation: 66% freshmen return for sophomore year. 23% freshmen graduate within 4 years. **Faculty:** Student/faculty ratio 10:1. 21 full-time faculty, 43% hold PhDs, 52% are women.

ACADEMICS
Degrees: Associate, bachelor's, certificate, master's, post-bachelor's certificate. **Classes:** Most classes have fewer than 10 students. Most lab/discussion sessions have 10–19 students. **Majors with Highest Enrollment:** Business/commerce; teacher education, multiple levels. **Special Study Options:** Accelerated program, distance learning, double major, English as a Second Language (ESL), independent study, internships, liberal arts/career combination, student-designed major, study abroad, teacher certification program Special programs offered to physically disabled students include note-taking services, tape recorders, tutors. **Career services:** Career/job search classes, career assessment, internships. **Career services highlights include:** Internships required of all undergraduate students.

FACILITIES
Housing: Coed dorms, apartments for single students. 80% of campus accessible to physically disabled. **Special Academic Facilities/Equipment:** Morse Event Center with gym, athletic facilities, and weight training room PLUS. Student Life and Athletic Offices. Library Museum and Rare Book Collections. **Computers:** Administrative functions (other than registration) can be performed online.

CAMPUS LIFE
Environment: City. **Activities:** Choral groups, concert band, drama/theater, literary magazine, music ensembles, student government, student newspaper, yearbook. **Organizations:** 10 registered organizations, 1 honor societies, 2 religious organizations. **Athletics (Intercollegiate):** *Men:* Basketball, cross-country, soccer. *Women:* Basketball, cross-country, soccer, softball, volleyball. **On-Campus Highlights:** Morse Event Center, Bookstore/Internet Cafe in Dormitory, Chapel, Library, Pomajevich Faculty Building.

ADMISSIONS
Freshman Academic Profile: Average high school GPA 3.34. 11% in top 10% of high school class, 42% in top 25% of high school class, 74% in top 50% of high school class. 89% from public high schools. SAT Math middle 50% range 470–560. SAT Critical Reading middle 50% range 440–540. SAT Writing middle 50% range 410–510. ACT middle 50% range 21–23. Minimum paper TOEFL 500. Minimum computer TOEFL 173. **Basis for Candidate Selection:** *Very important factors considered include:* Academic GPA. *Important factors considered include:* Class rank, application essay, recommendation(s), standardized test scores. *Other factors considered include:* Rigor of secondary school record, character/personal qualities, work experience. **Freshman Admission Requirements:** High school diploma is required and GED is accepted. *Academic units required:* 4 English, 3 mathematics, 2 science, (1 science labs), 2 foreign language, 2 social studies, 1 history. **Freshman Admission Statistics:** 232 applied, 61% admitted, 46% enrolled. **Transfer Admission Requirements:** College transcript(s), essay or personal statement, statement of good standing from prior institution(s). Minimum college GPA of 2.2 required. Lowest grade transferable C–. **General Admission Information:** Notification on a rolling basis, beginning on or about 10/15. Nonfall registration accepted. Admission

may be deferred for a maximum of 2 years. Credit and/or placement offered for CEEB Advanced Placement tests.

COSTS AND FINANCIAL AID
Average book expense $825. **Required Forms and Deadlines:** FAFSA. Priority financial aid filing date 3/1. **Notification of Awards:** Applicants will be notified of awards on a rolling basis beginning 4/1. **Types of Aid:** *Need-based scholarships/grants:* Federal Pell, SEOG, state scholarships/grants, private scholarships, the school's own gift aid. *Loans:* FFEL Subsidized Stafford, FFEL Unsubsidized Stafford, FFEL PLUS, Federal Perkins. *Student Employment:* Federal Work-Study Program available. Institutional employment available. Off-campus job opportunities are fair. **Financial Aid Statistics:** 85% freshmen, 89% undergrads receive need-based scholarship or grant aid. 11% freshmen, 5% undergrads receive non-need-based scholarship or grant aid. 64% freshmen, 75% undergrads receive need-based self-help aid. 14% freshmen, 5% undergrads receive athletic scholarships. 97% freshmen, 96% undergrads receive any aid. 79% undergrads borrow to pay for school. Average cumulative indebtedness $14,415. **Criteria for awarding institutional aid:** *Non-need-based:* Academics, athletics, leadership, music/drama, religious affiliation.

NORTHWEST COLLEGE

PO Box 579, Kirkland, WA 98083-0579
Phone: 425-889-5231
E-mail: admissions@ncag.edu **CEEB Code:** 4541
Fax: 425-889-5224 **Website:** www.nwcollege.edu **ACT Code:** 4466

This private school, affiliated with the Assemblies of God Church, was founded in 1934. It has a 56-acre campus.

RATINGS
Admissions Selectivity Rating: 60*   **Fire Safety Rating:** 60*   **Green Rating:** 60*

STUDENTS AND FACULTY
Enrollment: 1,054. **Student Body:** 62% female, 38% male, 18% out-of-state, 2% international (9 countries represented). Asian 4%, African American 3%, Caucasian 84%, Hispanic 3%, Native American 1%.
Retention and Graduation: 66% freshmen return for sophomore year. 35% freshmen graduate within 4 years. **Faculty:** Student/faculty ratio 15:1. 50 full-time faculty, 48% hold PhDs, 10% are are members of minority groups, 42% are women.

ACADEMICS
Degrees: Associate, bachelor's, certificate, diploma, master's, post-bachelor's certificate. **Classes:** Most classes have 20–29 students. Most lab/discussion sessions have 10–19 students. **Special Study Options:** Accelerated program, double major, English as a Second Language (ESL), independent study, internships, liberal arts/career combination, study abroad, teacher certification program Special programs offered to physically disabled students include note-taking services, reader services, tape recorders, tutors. **Career services:** Career/job search classes, career assessment, internships.

FACILITIES
Housing: Men's dorms, women's dorms, apartments for married students, apartments for single students, apartments for students with dependent children. 80% of campus accessible to physically disabled. **Computers:** Students can register for classes online.

CAMPUS LIFE
Environment: Village. **Activities:** Choral groups, concert band, drama/theater, jazz band, music ensembles, musical theater, radio station, student government, student newspaper, symphony orchestra, yearbook. **Organizations:** 15 registered organizations, 9 religious organizations. **Athletics (Intercollegiate):** *Men:* Basketball, cross-country, soccer, track/field (outdoor). *Women:* Basketball, cross-country, track/field (outdoor), volleyball.

ADMISSIONS
Freshman Academic Profile: Average high school GPA 3.33. 75% from public high schools. Minimum paper TOEFL 500. Minimum computer TOEFL 173. **Basis for Candidate Selection:** *Very important factors considered include:* Application essay, recommendation(s), rigor of secondary school record, standardized test scores, character/personal qualities. *Important factors considered include:* Class rank, extracurricular activities, religious affiliation/commitment. *Other factors considered include:* Alumni/ae relation, interview, talent/ability, volunteer work. **Freshman Admission Requirements:** High school diploma is required and GED is accepted. *Academic units recommended:* 4 English, 3 mathematics, 2 science, 2 foreign language, 2 social studies, 2 history, 3 academic electives. **Freshman Admission Statistics:** 308 applied, 90% admitted, 60%

enrolled. **Transfer Admission Requirements:** High school transcript, college transcript(s), essay or personal statement, statement of good standing from prior institution(s). Minimum college GPA of 2.3 required. Lowest grade transferable C. **General Admission Information:** Application fee $30. Regular application deadline 8/1. Notification on a rolling basis, beginning on or about 10/1. Nonfall registration accepted. Admission may be deferred for a maximum of 1 year. Credit offered for CEEB Advanced Placement tests.

COSTS AND FINANCIAL AID
Annual tuition $13,200. Room and board $6,124. Required fees $324. Average book expense $850. **Required Forms and Deadlines:** FAFSA, institution's own financial aid form. Priority financial aid filing date 3/1. **Notification of Awards:** Applicants will be notified of awards on a rolling basis beginning 4/15. **Types of Aid:** *Need-based scholarships/grants:* Federal Pell, SEOG, state scholarships/grants, private scholarships, the school's own gift aid. *Loans:* FFEL Subsidized Stafford, FFEL Unsubsidized Stafford, FFEL PLUS, Federal Perkins, state loans, alternative(private) loans. *Student Employment:* Federal Work-Study Program available. Institutional employment available. Highest amount earned per year from on-campus jobs $3,308. Off-campus job opportunities are excellent. **Financial Aid Statistics:** 73% freshmen, 74% undergrads receive need-based scholarship or grant aid. 9% freshmen, 7% undergrads receive non-need-based scholarship or grant aid. 63% freshmen, 68% undergrads receive need-based self-help aid. 4% freshmen, 4% undergrads receive athletic scholarships. 91% undergrads borrow to pay for school. Average cumulative indebtedness $20,015. **Criteria for awarding institutional aid:** *Non-need-based:* Academics, art, athletics, leadership, music/drama, religious affiliation.

NORTHWEST MISSOURI STATE UNIVERSITY

800 University Drive, Maryville, MO 64468
Phone: 800-633-1175
E-mail: admissions@nwmissouri.edu **CEEB Code:** 6488
Fax: 660-562-1121 **Website: ACT Code:** 2338

This public school was founded in 1905. It has a 240-acre campus.

RATINGS
Admissions Selectivity Rating: 77   **Fire Safety Rating:** 60*   **Green Rating:** 60*

STUDENTS AND FACULTY
Enrollment: 4,956. **Student Body:** 55% female, 45% male, 26% out-of-state, 2% international Asian 1%, African American 4%, Caucasian 86%, Hispanic 2%.
Retention and Graduation: 74% freshmen return for sophomore year. **Faculty:** Student/faculty ratio 21:1. 249 full-time faculty, 64% hold PhDs, 6% are are members of minority groups, 45% are women.

ACADEMICS
Degrees: Bachelor's, master's, post-master's certificate. **Classes:** Most classes have 20–29 students. Most lab/discussion sessions have 20–29 students. **Special Study Options:** Accelerated program, distance learning, double major, dual enrollment, English as a Second Language (ESL), honors program, independent study, internships, study abroad, teacher certification program Special programs offered to physically disabled students include note-taking services, reader services, tape recorders, tutors. **Career services:** Alumni services, career/job search classes, career assessment, internships.

FACILITIES
Housing: Coed dorms, special housing for disabled students, fraternity/sorority housing, apartments for single students. **Special Academic Facilities/Equipment:** State history and art collections, earth/science museum, broadcasting museum, on-campus elementary lab school, biomass energy plant. **Computers:** Students can register for classes online.

CAMPUS LIFE
Environment: Rural. **Activities:** Choral groups, concert band, dance, drama/theater, jazz band, literary magazine, marching band, music ensembles, musical theater, pep band, radio station, student government, student newspaper, student-run film society, symphony orchestra, television station, yearbook. **Organizations:** 174 registered organizations, 13 honor societies, 9 religious organizations. 10 fraternities, 6 sororities. **Athletics (Intercollegiate):** *Men:* Baseball, basketball, cheerleading, cross-country, football, rodeo, tennis, track/field (outdoor), track/field (indoor). *Women:* Basketball, cheerleading, cross-country, rodeo, soccer, softball, tennis, track/field (outdoor), track/field (indoor), volleyball.

ADMISSIONS
Freshman Academic Profile: Average high school GPA 3.34. 13% in top 10% of high school class, 41% in top 25% of high school class, 80% in top

50% of high school class. 90% from public high schools. SAT Math middle 50% range 480–610. SAT Critical Reading middle 50% range 450–600. ACT middle 50% range 19–24. Minimum paper TOEFL 500. **Basis for Candidate Selection:** *Very important factors considered include:* Class rank, rigor of secondary school record, standardized test scores. *Important factors considered include:* Academic GPA. *Other factors considered include:* Application essay, recommendation(s), character/personal qualities, extracurricular activities, interview, level of applicant's interest, state residency. **Freshman Admission Requirements:** High school diploma is required and GED is accepted. *Academic units required:* 4 English, 3 mathematics, 2 science, (1 science labs), 3 social studies, 4 academic electives. *Academic units recommended:* 4 mathematics, 3 science, 2 foreign language. **Freshman Admission Statistics:** 3,759 applied, 75% admitted, 45% enrolled. **Transfer Admission Requirements:** College transcript(s), statement of good standing from prior institution(s). Minimum college GPA of 2.0 required. Lowest grade transferable D. **General Admission Information:** Application fee $25. Nonfall registration accepted.

COSTS AND FINANCIAL AID
Annual in-state tuition $5,835. Annual out-of-state tuition $10,080. Room and board $5,854. Required fees $295. Average book expense $500. **Required Forms and Deadlines:** FAFSA. Priority financial aid filing date 4/1. **Notification of Awards:** Applicants will be notified of awards on or about 4/15. **Types of Aid:** *Need-based scholarships/grants:* Federal Pell, SEOG, state scholarships/grants, private scholarships, the school's own gift aid. *Loans:* Direct Subsidized Stafford, Direct Unsubsidized Stafford, Direct PLUS, Federal Perkins, college/university loans from institutional funds. *Student Employment:* Federal Work-Study Program available. Institutional employment available. Off-campus job opportunities are fair. **Financial Aid Statistics:** 28% freshmen, 25% undergrads receive need-based scholarship or grant aid. 39% freshmen, 25% undergrads receive non-need-based scholarship or grant aid. 46% freshmen, 43% undergrads receive need-based self-help aid. 58% undergrads borrow to pay for school. Average cumulative indebtedness $13,799. **Criteria for awarding institutional aid:** *Non-need-based:* Academics, alumni affiliation, art, athletics, leadership, music/drama, state/district residency.

NORTHWEST NAZARENE UNIVERSITY

623 Holly Street, Nampa, ID 83686
Phone: 208-467-8000 **Financial Aid Phone:** 208-467-8774
E-mail: ashlee.jerome@gmail.com **CEEB Code:** 4544
Fax: 208-467-8645 **Website:** 700 E. Fairview sp.8 **ACT Code:** 924

This private school, affiliated with the Nazarene Church, was founded in 1913. It has a 85-acre campus.

RATINGS
Admissions Selectivity Rating: 83   **Fire Safety Rating:** 60*   **Green Rating:** 60*

STUDENTS AND FACULTY
Enrollment: 1,257. **Student Body:** 57% female, 43% male, % out-of-state, 2% international (12 countries represented). Asian 2%, African American 1%, Caucasian 73%, Hispanic 5%, Native American 1%.
Retention and Graduation: Faculty: Student/faculty ratio 13:1. 98 full-time faculty, 86% hold PhDs, 44% are women.

ACADEMICS
Degrees: Bachelor's, master's. **Majors with Highest Enrollment:** Business/commerce; education; nursing/registered nurse (RN, ASN, BSN, MSN). **Special Study Options:** Cooperative education program, cross-registration, distance learning, double major, English as a Second Language (ESL), exchange student program (domestic), honors program, independent study, internships, liberal arts/career combination, student-designed major, study abroad, teacher certification program, Many service and ministry programs and opportunities. **Combined degree programs:** 3-2 engineering program with any co-op institution. Special programs offered to physically disabled students include reader services, tape recorders, tutors. **Career services:** Alumni network, career/job search classes, internships, regional alumni.

FACILITIES
Housing: Coed dorms, men's dorms, women's dorms, apartments for married students, apartments for single students, Off-campus housing owned the by University include rental homes and units. 70% of campus accessible to physically disabled. **Computers:** 100% of classrooms, have wireless network access. Administrative functions (other than registration) can be performed online.

CAMPUS LIFE
Environment: City. **Activities:** Choral groups, concert band, drama/theater, jazz band, literary magazine, music ensembles, musical theater, pep band, stu-

dent government, student newspaper, symphony orchestra, yearbook, campus ministries, international student organization. **Organizations:** 21 registered organizations, 6 honor societies, 8 religious organizations. **Athletics (Intercollegiate):** *Men:* Baseball, basketball, cross-country, golf, soccer, track/field (outdoor), track/field (indoor). *Women:* Basketball, cross-country, soccer, softball, track/field (outdoor), track/field (indoor), volleyball. **On-Campus Highlights:** Helstrom Business Center, The Brandt Center, Ford Hall, Johnson Sports Center, Student Center.

ADMISSIONS

Freshman Academic Profile: 24% in top 10% of high school class, 47% in top 25% of high school class, 76% in top 50% of high school class. 83% from public high schools. Minimum paper TOEFL 500. Minimum computer TOEFL 173. **Basis for Candidate Selection:** *Very important factors considered include:* Class rank, academic GPA, standardized test scores, character/personal qualities. *Other factors considered include:* Recommendation(s), rigor of secondary school record, alumni/ae relation, extracurricular activities, religious affiliation/commitment, talent/ability. **Freshman Admission Requirements:** High school diploma is required and GED is accepted. *Academic units recommended:* 4 English, 3 mathematics, 3 science, 2 foreign language, 3 history. **Freshman Admission Statistics:** 1,999 applied. **Transfer Admission Requirements:** College transcript(s), minimum college GPA of 2.0 required. Lowest grade transferable C–. **General Admission Information:** Application fee $25. Regular application deadline 8/15. Nonfall registration accepted. Credit and/or placement offered for CEEB Advanced Placement tests.

COSTS AND FINANCIAL AID

Annual tuition $21,930. Room and board $5,830. Required fees $320. Average book expense $750. **Required Forms and Deadlines:** FAFSA, institution's own financial aid form. Priority financial aid filing date 3/1. **Notification of Awards:** Applicants will be notified of awards on a rolling basis beginning 4/1. **Types of Aid:** *Need-based scholarships/grants:* Federal Pell, SEOG, state scholarships/grants, private scholarships, the school's own gift aid. *Loans:* FFEL Subsidized Stafford, FFEL Unsubsidized Stafford, FFEL PLUS, Federal Perkins, college/university loans from institutional funds, Bank Loans. *Student Employment:* Federal Work-Study Program available. Institutional employment available. Highest amount earned per year from on-campus jobs $8,739. Off-campus job opportunities are good. **Financial Aid Statistics:** 62% freshmen, 61% undergrads receive need-based scholarship or grant aid. 80% freshmen, 72% undergrads receive non-need-based scholarship or grant aid. 58% freshmen, 55% undergrads receive need-based self-help aid. 17% freshmen, 20% undergrads receive athletic scholarships. 100% freshmen, 99% undergrads receive any aid. 83% undergrads borrow to pay for school. Average cumulative indebtedness $25,626. **Criteria for awarding institutional aid:** *Non-need-based:* Academics, alumni affiliation, art, athletics, leadership, minority status, music/drama, religious affiliation, state/district residency.

NORTHWESTERN COLLEGE (IA)

101 7th St SW, Orange City, IA 51041
Phone: 712-707-7130 **Financial Aid Phone:** 712-707-7131
E-mail: admissions@nwciowa.edu **CEEB Code:** 6490
Fax: 712-707-7164 **Website:** www.nwciowa.edu **ACT Code:** 1346

This private school, affiliated with the Reformed Church Church, was founded in 1882. It has a 100-acre campus.

RATINGS

Admissions Selectivity Rating: 80   **Fire Safety Rating:** 81   **Green Rating:** 67

STUDENTS AND FACULTY

Enrollment: 1,288. **Student Body:** 61% female, 39% male, 45% out-of-state, 3% international (16 countries represented). Asian 1%, African American 1%, Caucasian 95%, Hispanic 1%.
Retention and Graduation: 81% freshmen return for sophomore year. 54% freshmen graduate within 4 years. **Faculty:** Student/faculty ratio 15:1. 77 full-time faculty, 81% hold PhDs, 1% are are members of minority groups, 30% are women.

ACADEMICS

Degrees: Bachelor's, certificate. **Classes:** Most classes have 10–19 students. **Majors with Highest Enrollment:** Biology/biological sciences; business/commerce; education. **Special Study Options:** double major, English as a Second Language (ESL), honors program, independent study, internships, liberal arts/career combination, student-designed major, study abroad, teacher certification program, oOff Campus Study Programs: American Studies Program (Washington, DC), AuSable Inst of Environmental Studies Program (Michigan),

Los Angeles Film Studies Semester, Chicago Metropolitan Studies Program (Chicago), China Studies Program (Xiaman, China), Middle East Studies Program (Cairo, Egypt), Oxford Summer Program (Oxford, England), Romanian Studies Program, Russian Studies Program, Contemporary Music Center (Martha's Vineyard, MA), Latin American Studies Program (Costa Rica), Oxford Honours Programme (England), Trinity Christian College: Semester in Spain, and Creation Care Study Program. **Honors programs:** Honors Program: Affords students an interdisciplinary approach to understanding perennial and contemporary issues, such as technology, war and peace, gender roles, work and calling, and humor. Affords students th eopportunity to delve more deeply into a topic of their choice, workinh with selected faculty members to complete a project that goes beyond the normal upper-division work at the college. Encourages graduate education by sponsoring trips to regional graduate schools and financially supporting graduate school applications. Special programs offered to physically disabled students include note-taking services, reader services, tape recorders, tutors. **Career services:** Alumni services, career/job search classes, career assessment, internships. **Career services highlights include:** Internships.

FACILITIES

Housing: Special housing for disabled students, men's dorms, women's dorms, apartments for single students, theme housing (i.e., Spanish house, etc.). 90% of campus accessible to physically disabled. **Special Academic Facilities/Equipment:** Thea G Korver Visual Arts Center—Art Gallery; DeWitt Theatre Arts Center—proscenium theatre, black box theatre, costume shop. **Computers:** 75% of classrooms, 30% of dorms, 100% of libraries, 100% of dining areas, 100% of student union, 30% of common outdoor areas have wireless network access. Students can register for classes online. Administrative functions (other than registration) can be performed online.

CAMPUS LIFE

Environment: Rural. **Activities:** Choral groups, concert band, dance, drama/theater, jazz band, literary magazine, music ensembles, musical theater, pep band, student government, student newspaper, symphony orchestra, television station, yearbook. **Organizations:** 30 registered organizations, 2 honor societies, 5 religious organizations. **Athletics (Intercollegiate):** *Men:* Baseball, basketball, cheerleading, cross-country, football, golf, soccer, track/field (outdoor), track/field (indoor), wrestling. *Women:* Basketball, cheerleading, cross-country, golf, soccer, softball, track/field (outdoor), track/field (indoor), volleyball. **On-Campus Highlights:** Rowenhorst Student Center, Bultman Center Gym, DeWitt Theatre Arts Center, Korver Visual Arts Center.

ADMISSIONS

Freshman Academic Profile: Average high school GPA 3.5. 28% in top 10% of high school class, 55% in top 25% of high school class, 83% in top 50% of high school class. 87% from public high schools. ACT middle 50% range 21–27. Minimum paper TOEFL 475. Minimum computer TOEFL 150. **Basis for Candidate Selection:** *Very important factors considered include:* Class rank, rigor of secondary school record, standardized test scores. *Important factors considered include:* Application essay, academic GPA, recommendation(s), character/personal qualities, first generation, interview, level of applicant's interest, talent/ability. *Other factors considered include:* extracurricular activities, religious affiliation/commitment. **Freshman Admission Requirements:** High school diploma is required and GED is accepted. *Academic units recommended:* 4 English, 3 mathematics, 3 science, 3 foreign language, 3 social studies. **Freshman Admission Statistics:** 1,277 applied, 85% admitted, 34% enrolled. **Transfer Admission Requirements:** College transcript(s), minimum college GPA of 2.2 required. Lowest grade transferable C. **General Admission Information:** Application fee $25. Notification on a rolling basis, beginning on or about 10/1. Nonfall registration accepted. Admission may be deferred for a maximum of 4 years. Credit and/or placement offered for CEEB Advanced Placement tests.

COSTS AND FINANCIAL AID

Annual tuition $21,648. Room and board $5,792. Average book expense $900. **Required Forms and Deadlines:** FAFSA. Priority financial aid filing date 4/1. **Notification of Awards:** Applicants will be notified of awards on a rolling basis beginning 3/15. **Types of Aid:** *Need-based scholarships/grants:* Federal Pell, SEOG, state scholarships/grants, private scholarships, the school's own gift aid, United Negro College Fund. *Loans:* FFEL Subsidized Stafford, FFEL Unsubsidized Stafford, FFEL PLUS, Federal Perkins, college/university loans from institutional funds. *Student Employment:* Highest amount earned per year from on-campus jobs $2,100. Off-campus job opportunities are fair. **Financial Aid Statistics:** 74% freshmen, 71% undergrads receive need-based scholarship or grant aid. 76% freshmen, 75% undergrads receive non-need-based scholarship or grant aid. 72% freshmen, 72% undergrads receive need-based self-help aid. 37% freshmen, 26% undergrads receive athletic scholarships. 100% freshmen, 99% undergrads receive any aid. 85% undergrads borrow to pay for school. Average cumulative indebtedness $22,286. **Criteria for awarding institutional aid:** *Non-need-based:* Academics, art, athletics, music/drama, religious affiliation.

NORTHWESTERN STATE UNIVERSITY

209 Roy Hall, Natchitoches, LA 71497
Phone: 318-357-4078 **Financial Aid Phone:** 800-823-3008
E-mail: admissions@nsula.edu **CEEB Code:** 6492
Fax: 318-357-4660 **Website:** www.nsula.edu **ACT Code:** 1600

This public school was founded in 1884. It has a 916-acre campus.

RATINGS
Admissions Selectivity Rating: 71   **Fire Safety Rating:** 75   **Green Rating:** 72

STUDENTS AND FACULTY
Enrollment: 7,440. **Student Body:** 68% female, 32% male, 9% out-of-state, 1% international (29 countries represented). Asian 1%, African American 30%, Caucasian 59%, Hispanic 2%, Native American 2%.
Retention and Graduation: 69% freshmen return for sophomore year. 17% freshmen graduate within 4 years. **Faculty:** Student/faculty ratio 16:1. 334 full-time faculty, 59% hold PhDs, 7% are are members of minority groups, 53% are women. 1% of classes are taught by teaching assistants.

ACADEMICS
Degrees: Associate, bachelor's, master's, post-master's certificate. **Classes:** Most classes have 10–19 students. Most lab/discussion sessions have fewer than 10 students. **Majors with Highest Enrollment:** Business administration and management; general studies; nursing/registered nurse (RN, ASN, BSN, MSN). **Special Study Options:** Cooperative education program, distance learning, double major, dual enrollment, honors program, independent study, internships, study abroad, teacher certification program. **Honors programs:** The Louisiana Scholar's College is a special institution at Northwestern that enrolls students in a strong liberal arts program while simultaneously letting them take part in the other great areas of NSU. Special programs offered to physically disabled students include note-taking services, reader services, tape recorders, tutors. **Career services:** Alumni services, career/job search classes, career assessment, internships.

FACILITIES
Housing: Coed dorms, special housing for disabled students, fraternity/sorority housing, apartments for married students, apartments for single students, theme housing. 96% of campus accessible to physically disabled. **Special Academic Facilities/Equipment:** Cammie G. Henry Research Center; Louisiana Creole Heritage Center; Louisiana Folklife Center; Louisiana Regional Folklife Center; The Space Science Group; Williamson Museum. **Computers:** 50% of classrooms, 100% of dorms, 100% of libraries, 50% of dining areas, 100% of student union, 75% of common outdoor areas have wireless network access. Students can register for classes online. Administrative functions (other than registration) can be performed online.

CAMPUS LIFE
Environment: Village. **Activities:** Choral groups, concert band, dance, drama/theater, jazz band, literary magazine, marching band, music ensembles, musical theater, opera, pep band, radio station, student government, student newspaper, symphony orchestra, television station, yearbook, campus ministries, international student organization. **Organizations:** 109 registered organizations, 11 honor societies, 6 religious organizations. 10 fraternities, 7 sororities. **Athletics (Intercollegiate):** *Men:* Baseball, basketball, cheerleading, cross-country, football, soccer, track/field (outdoor), track/field (indoor). *Women:* Basketball, cheerleading, cross-country, soccer, softball, tennis, track/field (outdoor), track/field (indoor), volleyball. **On-Campus Highlights:** Wellness, Recreation, and Activity Center, Student Union, University Place Apartments, University Columns Apartments, BCM/CSO/Wellesley Foundation. **Environmental Initiatives:** Northwestern State University of Louisiana has developed a Request for Proposals for Energy Savings Performance Contracting Services to identify and implement up-grades in the university infrastructure that will result in energy conservation. Northwestern State University of Louisiana has adopted a 'Green' theme for its 22nd Annual Research Day to highlight student and faculty research and projects focused on the environment, energy conservation, and sustainability. Students in the university's orientation course are invited to workshops that address conservation, recycling, and other sustainable practices on campus. Professors of courses in the Arts and the Sciences have adopted green topics for class assignments and projects. Outside the classroom, NSU student groups and organizations participate in recycling, campus beautification, and related green activities.

ADMISSIONS
Freshman Academic Profile: Average high school GPA 3.15. 14% in top 10% of high school class, 38% in top 25% of high school class, 71% in top 50% of high school class. SAT Math middle 50% range 440–550. SAT Critical Reading middle 50% range 420–533. ACT middle 50% range 18–23. Minimum paper TOEFL 500. Minimum computer TOEFL 173. Minimum web-based TOEFL 61. **Basis for Candidate Selection:** *Very important factors considered*

include: Rigor of secondary school record, standardized test scores. *Important factors considered include:* Class rank, academic GPA. *Other factors considered include:* Alumni/ae relation, extracurricular activities, geographical residence, state residency, talent/ability. **Freshman Admission Requirements:** High school diploma is required and GED is accepted. *Academic units required:* 4 English, 3 mathematics, 3 science, (3 science labs), 2 foreign language, 1 social studies, 2 history, 1 visual/performing arts, 1 Other: One additional math or science **Freshman Admission Statistics:** 2,674 applied, 83% admitted, 56% enrolled. **Transfer Admission Requirements:** College transcript(s), statement of good standing from prior institution(s). Minimum college GPA of 2.0 required. Lowest grade transferable D. **General Admission Information:** Application fee $20. Regular application deadline 7/6. Notification on a rolling basis, beginning on or about 1/1. Nonfall registration accepted. Admission may be deferred for a maximum of 3 semesters w/o fee. Credit and/or placement offered for CEEB Advanced Placement tests.

COSTS AND FINANCIAL AID
Required Forms and Deadlines: FAFSA, institution's own financial aid form. Priority financial aid filing date 5/1. **Notification of Awards:** Applicants will be notified of awards on a rolling basis beginning 5/1. **Types of Aid:** *Need-based scholarships/grants:* Federal Pell, SEOG, state scholarships/grants, private scholarships, the school's own gift aid, United Negro College Fund, Federal Nursing Scholarships, Third Party Scholarships. *Loans:* FFEL Subsidized Stafford, FFEL Unsubsidized Stafford, FFEL PLUS, Federal Perkins, alternative loans. *Student Employment:* Federal Work-Study Program available. Institutional employment available. Highest amount earned per year from on-campus jobs $9,218. Off-campus job opportunities are fair. **Financial Aid Statistics:** 38% freshmen, 40% undergrads receive need-based scholarship or grant aid. 42% freshmen, 24% undergrads receive non-need-based scholarship or grant aid. 36% freshmen, 43% undergrads receive need-based self-help aid. 4% freshmen, 4% undergrads receive athletic scholarships. 89.3% freshmen, 77.32% undergrads receive any aid. 72% undergrads borrow to pay for school. Average cumulative indebtedness $22,045. **Criteria for awarding institutional aid:** *Non-need-based:* Academics, alumni affiliation, art, athletics, job skills, leadership, minority status, music/drama, religious affiliation, state/district residency.

NORTHWESTERN UNIVERSITY

PO Box 3060, 1801 Hinman Avenue, Evanston, IL 60204-3060
Phone: 847-491-7271 **Financial Aid Phone:** 847-491-7400
E-mail: ug-admission@northwestern.edu **CEEB Code:** 1565
Fax: 555-555-5555 **Website:** www.northwestern.edu **ACT Code:** 1106

This private school was founded in 1851. It has a 240-acre campus.

RATINGS
Admissions Selectivity Rating: 98   **Fire Safety Rating:** 78   **Green Rating:** 79

STUDENTS AND FACULTY
Enrollment: 8,364. **Student Body:** 52% female, 48% male, 75% out-of-state, 5% international (42 countries represented). Asian 18%, African American 5%, Caucasian 58%, Hispanic 7%.
Retention and Graduation: 97% freshmen return for sophomore year. 86% freshmen graduate within 4 years. 23% grads go on to further study within 1 year. 7% grads pursue arts and sciences degrees. 3% grads pursue law degrees. 1% grads pursue business degrees. 7% grads pursue medical degrees. **Faculty:** Student/faculty ratio 7:1. 1027 full-time faculty, 100% hold PhDs, 17% are are members of minority groups, 29% are women. 2% of classes are taught by teaching assistants.

ACADEMICS
Degrees: Bachelor's, certificate, first professional, master's, post-master's certificate. **Classes:** Most classes have fewer than 10 students. Most lab/discussion sessions have 10–19 students. **Majors with Highest Enrollment:** Economics; engineering; journalism. **Special Study Options:** Accelerated program, cooperative education program, double major, honors program, independent study, internships, liberal arts/career combination, student-designed major, study abroad, teacher certification program. **Honors programs:** Honors Program in Medical Education, Integrated Science Program, MENU, MMSS. **Combined degree programs:** BA/MD, BA/MA, BM/MS, BA/BS, BA/BM, BS/BM, BS/MS. Special programs offered to physically disabled students include note-taking services, reader services, tape recorders, tutors. **Career services:** Alumni

network, alumni services, career/job search classes, career assessment, internships, regional alumni. **Career services highlights include:** At Northwestern, all undergraduates have the opportunity to gain real-world experience through internships, field studies programs, and practicums. These programs place students in corporations, newsrooms, archaeological dig sites, and laboratories throughout Chicago, the United States, and the world.

FACILITIES

Housing: Coed dorms, men's dorms, women's dorms, fraternity/sorority housing, wellness house, theme housing. 100% of campus accessible to physically disabled. **Special Academic Facilities/Equipment:** Art gallery, learning sciences institute, communicative disorders and materials and life sciences buildings, catalysis center, astronomical research center. Ford Motor Compay Engineering Design Center for engineering students. **Computers:** 100% of classrooms, 100% of dorms, 100% of libraries, 100% of dining areas, 100% of student union, 100% of common outdoor areas have wireless network access. Students can register for classes online.

CAMPUS LIFE

Environment: Town. **Activities:** Choral groups, concert band, dance, drama/theater, jazz band, literary magazine, marching band, music ensembles, musical theater, opera, pep band, radio station, student government, student newspaper, student-run film society, symphony orchestra, television station, yearbook, campus ministries, international student organization, Model UN. **Organizations:** 415 registered organizations, 23 honor societies, 29 religious organizations. 17 fraternities, 19 sororities. **Athletics (Intercollegiate):** *Men:* Baseball, basketball, cheerleading, diving, football, golf, soccer, swimming, tennis, wrestling. *Women:* Basketball, cheerleading, cross-country, diving, fencing, field hockey, golf, lacrosse, soccer, softball, swimming, tennis, volleyball. **On-Campus Highlights:** Shakespeare Garden, Dearborn Observatory, Norris Student Center, Henry Crown Sports Pavilion and Acquatic Center, the lakefill on Lake Michigan. **Environmental Initiatives:** Commitment to purchase of renewable energy credits for 20% of the University's usage. 40,000,000 kWh purchased placing NU 2nd in the Big Ten and 9th nationally in green power purchases (US EPA Green Power Partnership). Campus energy audits—Committed to performing investment grade energy audits of all major buildings. Energy saving measures identified as having a 7-year ROI will be implemented. Commitment to LEED certifications awarded (LEED NC Silver and LEED CI Gold) and 4 buildings in process registered for LEED certification with plans for Silver or higher ranking.

ADMISSIONS

Freshman Academic Profile: 85% in top 10% of high school class, 96% in top 25% of high school class, 99% in top 50% of high school class. 65% from public high schools. SAT Math middle 50% range 690–780. SAT Critical Reading middle 50% range 670–750. SAT Writing middle 50% range 670–750. ACT middle 50% range 30–33. Minimum paper TOEFL 600. Minimum computer TOEFL 250. **Basis for Candidate Selection:** *Very important factors considered include:* Class rank, application essay, academic GPA, rigor of secondary school record, standardized test scores. *Important factors considered include:* Recommendation(s), character/personal qualities, extracurricular activities, talent/ability. *Other factors considered include:* Alumni/ae relation, first generation, interview, level of applicant's interest, racial/ethnic status, volunteer work, work experience. **Freshman Admission Requirements:** High school diploma or equivalent is not required. *Academic units recommended:* 4 English, 3 mathematics, 2 science, (2 science labs), 2 foreign language, 2 social studies, 1 academic electives. **Freshman Admission Statistics:** 25,013 applied, 26% admitted, 32% enrolled. **Transfer Admission Requirements:** High school transcript, college transcript(s), essay or personal statement, standardized test scores, statement of good standing from prior institution(s). Minimum college GPA of 3.0 required. Lowest grade transferable C. **General Admission Information:** Application fee $65. Early decision application deadline 11/1. Regular application deadline 1/1. Regular notification 4/15. Nonfall registration accepted. Admission may be deferred for a maximum of 1 year. Credit and/or placement offered for CEEB Advanced Placement tests.

COSTS AND FINANCIAL AID

Annual tuition $38,088. Room and board $11,703. Required fees $373. Average book expense $1,686. **Required Forms and Deadlines:** FAFSA, CSS/Financial Aid PROFILE, noncustodial PROFILE, business/farm supplement. Parent and student federal tax returns. Financial aid filing deadline 2/15. **Notification of Awards:** Applicants will be notified of awards on or about 4/15. **Types of Aid:** *Need-based scholarships/grants:* Federal Pell, SEOG, state scholarships/grants, private scholarships, the school's own gift aid, United Negro College Fund *Loans:* FFEL Subsidized Stafford, FFEL Unsubsidized Stafford, FFEL PLUS, Federal Perkins, college/university loans from institutional funds. *Student Employment:* Federal Work-Study Program available. Institutional employment available. Off-campus job opportunities are excellent. **Financial Aid Statistics:** 38% freshmen, 40% undergrads receive need-based scholarship or grant aid. 34% freshmen, 36% undergrads receive need-based self-help aid. 5% freshmen, 5% undergrads receive athletic scholarships. 60% freshmen, 60%

undergrads receive any aid. 49% undergrads borrow to pay for school. Average cumulative indebtedness $19,908. **Criteria for awarding institutional aid:** *Non-need-based:* Academics, athletics, music/drama.

NORTHWOOD UNIVERSITY

4000 Whiting Drive, Midland, MI 48640
Phone: 989-837-4273 **Financial Aid Phone:** 989-837-4320
E-mail: miadmit@northwood.edu **CEEB Code:** 1568
Fax: 989-837-4490 **Website:** www.northwood.edu **ACT Code:** 2041

This private school was founded in 1959. It has a 434-acre campus.

RATINGS
Admissions Selectivity Rating: 70   **Fire Safety Rating:** 71   **Green Rating:** 60*

STUDENTS AND FACULTY
Enrollment: 1,946. **Student Body:** 37% female, 63% male, 11% out-of-state, 8% international (26 countries represented). Asian 1%, African American 12%, Caucasian 75%, Hispanic 2%.
Retention and Graduation: 74% freshmen return for sophomore year. 31% freshmen graduate within 4 years. **Faculty:** Student/faculty ratio 26:1. 52 full-time faculty, 48% hold PhDs, 4% are are members of minority groups, 37% are women.

ACADEMICS
Degrees: Bachelor's, master's. **Classes:** Most classes have 10–19 students. **Majors with Highest Enrollment:** Business administration and management; sport and fitness administration/management. **Special Study Options:** Accelerated program, distance learning, double major, dual enrollment, external degree program, honors program, independent study, internships, study abroad, weekend college. **Honors programs:** An Honors Program began in Fall Term, 1991. In it, honors sections of six critically important courses are offered. The best instructors and the most demanding material and expectations are used. Additionally, special one credit hour seminars, which include outside speakers, are offered to sophomores and juniors. Special programs offered to physically disabled students include tutors. **Career services:** Alumni network, alumni services, career/job search classes, career assessment, internships.

FACILITIES
Housing: Men's dorms, women's dorms, apartments for single students. **Special Academic Facilities/Equipment:** Hach Student Life Center, Gerstacker Student Union **Computers:** 100% of classrooms, 100% of dorms, 100% of libraries, 100% of dining areas, 100% of student union, have wireless network access. Students can register for classes online. Administrative functions (other than registration) can be performed online.

CAMPUS LIFE
Environment: Town. **Activities:** Choral groups, dance, drama/theater, pep band, student government, student newspaper, yearbook, international student organization. **Organizations:** 42 registered organizations, 2 honor societies, 2 religious organizations. 9 fraternities, 3 sororities. **Athletics (Intercollegiate):** *Men:* Baseball, basketball, cheerleading, cross-country, football, golf, soccer, tennis, track/field (outdoor), track/field (indoor). *Women:* Basketball, cheerleading, cross-country, golf, soccer, softball, tennis, track/field (outdoor), track/field (indoor), volleyball. **On-Campus Highlights:** Hach Student Life Center, Mid—Caf @ Northwood, Bennett Sports Center.

ADMISSIONS
Freshman Academic Profile: Average high school GPA 3.03. 10% in top 10% of high school class, 28% in top 25% of high school class, 56% in top 50% of high school class. 70% from public high schools. SAT Math middle 50% range 440–560. SAT Critical Reading middle 50% range 420–530. ACT middle 50% range 19–23. Minimum paper TOEFL 500. Minimum computer TOEFL 173. **Basis for Candidate Selection:** *Very important factors considered include:* Level of applicant's interest. *Important factors considered include:* Academic GPA, standardized test scores. *Other factors considered include:* Class rank, application essay, recommendation(s), rigor of secondary school record, alumni/ae relation, character/personal qualities, extracurricular activities, interview. **Freshman Admission Requirements:** High school diploma is required and GED is accepted. *Academic units recommended:* 4 English, 3 mathematics, 3 science, 1 foreign language, 3 social studies, 1 computer science. **Freshman Admission Statistics:** 1,720 applied, 75% admitted, 34% enrolled. **Transfer Admission Requirements:** College transcript(s), minimum college GPA of 2.0 required. Lowest grade transferable C. **General Admission Information:** Application fee $25. Notification on a rolling basis, beginning on or about 1/1. Nonfall registration accepted. Admission may be deferred for a maximum of 1 term. Credit and/or placement offered for CEEB Advanced Placement tests.

COSTS AND FINANCIAL AID

Annual tuition $17,451. Room and board $7,923. Required fees $978. Average book expense $1,581. **Required Forms and Deadlines:** FAFSA **Notification of Awards:** Applicants will be notified of awards on a rolling basis beginning 3/1. **Types of Aid:** *Need-based scholarships/grants:* Federal Pell, SEOG, state scholarships/grants, private scholarships, the school's own gift aid. *Loans:* FFEL Subsidized Stafford, FFEL Unsubsidized Stafford, FFEL PLUS, state loans *Student Employment:* Federal Work-Study Program available. Institutional employment available. Off-campus job opportunities are fair. **Financial Aid Statistics:** 61% freshmen, 55% undergrads receive need-based scholarship or grant aid. 32% freshmen, 28% undergrads receive non-need-based scholarship or grant aid. 64% freshmen, 57% undergrads receive need-based self-help aid. 4% freshmen, 5% undergrads receive athletic scholarships. 71% undergrads borrow to pay for school. Average cumulative indebtedness $27,554. **Criteria for awarding institutional aid:** *Non-need-based:* Academics, athletics, leadership, minority status.

NORTHWOOD UNIVERSITY, FLORIDA CAMPUS

2600 North Military Trail, West Palm Beach, FL 33409-2911
Phone: 561-478-5500 **Financial Aid Phone:** 561-478-5590
E-mail: fladmit@northwood.edu **CEEB Code:** 4072
Fax: 561-640-3328 **Website: ACT Code:** 6736

This private school was founded in 1982. It has a 90-acre campus.

RATINGS

Admissions Selectivity Rating: 78   Fire Safety Rating: 73   Green Rating: 60*

STUDENTS AND FACULTY

Enrollment: 619. **Student Body:** 41% female, 59% male, 43% out-of-state, 34% international (40 countries represented). Asian 2%, African American 10%, Caucasian 42%, Hispanic 11%.
Retention and Graduation: 55% freshmen return for sophomore year. 25% freshmen graduate within 4 years. **Faculty:** Student/faculty ratio 23:1. 18 full-time faculty, 33% hold PhDs, 6% are are members of minority groups, 44% are women.

ACADEMICS

Degrees: Bachelor's. **Classes:** Most classes have 10–19 students. **Majors with Highest Enrollment:** Banking and financial support services; marketing/marketing management. **Special Study Options:** Accelerated program, distance learning, double major, dual enrollment, external degree program, honors program, independent study, internships, study abroad, weekend college. **Honors programs:** An Honors Program began in fall term 1991. In it, honors sections of a variety of critically important courses are offered. The best instructors and the most demanding material and expectations are used. Additionally, special one-credit-hour seminars, which include outside speakers, are offered to sophomores and juniors. Honor students having completed 17 credit hours in honors courses may apply for honors admission to Term in Europe, Term in Asia, or Term in Northern Europe and are eligible for a partial scholarship to support these travel abroad programs. This also provides a powerful incentive for students to successfully compete in the Honors Program. Special programs offered to physically disabled students include note-taking services. **Career services:** Alumni network, alumni services, career/job search classes, career assessment, internships.

FACILITIES

Housing: Men's dorms, women's dorms. **Special Academic Facilities/Equipment:** Art gallery. **Computers:** 100% of classrooms, 100% of dorms, 100% of libraries, 100% of dining areas, 100% of student union, have wireless network access. Students can register for classes online. Administrative functions (other than registration) can be performed online.

CAMPUS LIFE

Environment: City. **Activities:** dance, drama/theater, student government, student newspaper, international student organization. **Organizations:** 23 registered organizations, 1 honor societies. **Athletics (Intercollegiate):** *Men:* Baseball, basketball, golf, soccer, tennis. *Women:* Basketball, golf, soccer, softball, tennis, volleyball. **On-Campus Highlights:** Countess de Hoernle Student Life Center **Environmental Initiatives:** We keep use of paper to a minimum (e-mail attachments/files, Blackboard portal). Advertising promotions in small numbers in key locations (as opposed to making up 50 flyers and posting them everywhere!). We are just starting a campus-wide paper recycling program with recycling boxes in key locations and a large bin on campus.

ADMISSIONS

Freshman Academic Profile: Average high school GPA 2.93. 2% in top 10% of high school class, 20% in top 25% of high school class, 55% in top 50% of high school class. 70% from public high schools. SAT Math middle 50% range 410–510. SAT Critical Reading middle 50% range 390–500. SAT Writing middle 50% range 390–470. ACT middle 50% range 17–20. Minimum paper TOEFL 500. Minimum computer TOEFL 173. **Basis for Candidate Selection:** *Very important factors considered include:* Academic GPA, level of applicant's interest. *Important factors considered include:* Class rank, rigor of secondary school record, standardized test scores. *Other factors considered include:* Application essay, recommendation(s), alumni/ae relation, character/personal qualities, extracurricular activities, geographical residence, interview, talent/ability, volunteer work, work experience. **Freshman Admission Requirements:** High school diploma is required and GED is accepted. *Academic units recommended:* 4 English, 3 mathematics, 2 science, (1 science labs), 3 foreign language, 3 social studies. **Freshman Admission Statistics:** 778 applied, 61% admitted, 23% enrolled. **Transfer Admission Requirements:** High school transcript, college transcript(s), minimum college GPA of 2.0 required. Lowest grade transferable C. **General Admission Information:** Application fee $25. Notification on a rolling basis, beginning on or about 10/1. Nonfall registration accepted. Admission may be deferred for a maximum of 1 year. Credit and/or placement offered for CEEB Advanced Placement tests.

COSTS AND FINANCIAL AID

Annual tuition $17,451. Room and board $8,562. Required fees $978. Average book expense $1,581. **Required Forms and Deadlines:** FAFSA, state aid form. **Notification of Awards:** Applicants will be notified of awards on a rolling basis beginning 3/1. **Types of Aid:** *Need-based scholarships/grants:* Federal Pell, SEOG, state scholarships/grants, private scholarships, the school's own gift aid. *Loans:* FFEL Subsidized Stafford, FFEL Unsubsidized Stafford, FFEL PLUS. **Financial Aid Statistics:** 46% freshmen, 33% undergrads receive need-based scholarship or grant aid. 19% freshmen, 14% undergrads receive non-need-based scholarship or grant aid. 46% freshmen, 35% undergrads receive need-based self-help aid. 23% freshmen, 17% undergrads receive athletic scholarships. 61% undergrads borrow to pay for school. Average cumulative indebtedness $22,488. **Criteria for awarding institutional aid:** *Non-need-based:* Academics, alumni affiliation, athletics, leadership, minority status, state/district residency.

NORTHWOOD UNIVERSITY, TEXAS CAMPUS

1114 West FM 1382, Cedar Hill, TX 75104-1204
Phone: 972-293-5400 **Financial Aid Phone:** 972-293-5430
E-mail: txadmit@northwood.edu **CEEB Code:** 6499
Fax: 972-291-3824 **Website: ACT Code:** 4135

This private school was founded in 1966. It has a 360-acre campus.

RATINGS

Admissions Selectivity Rating: 76   Fire Safety Rating: 61   Green Rating: 60*

STUDENTS AND FACULTY

Enrollment: 461. **Student Body:** 46% female, 54% male, 7% out-of-state, 7% international (18 countries represented). Asian 4%, African American 15%, Caucasian 41%, Hispanic 30%, Native American 2%.
Retention and Graduation: 60% freshmen return for sophomore year. 23% freshmen graduate within 4 years. **Faculty:** Student/faculty ratio 15:1. 23 full-time faculty, 22% hold PhDs, 13% are are members of minority groups, 35% are women.

ACADEMICS

Degrees: Bachelor's. **Classes:** Most classes have 10–19 students. **Majors with Highest Enrollment:** Entrepreneurship/entrepreneurial studies; international business/trade/commerce; marketing/marketing management. **Special Study Options:** Accelerated program, distance learning, double major, dual enrollment, external degree program, honors program, independent study, internships, study abroad, weekend college. **Honors programs:** An Honors Program begin in Fall Term, 1991. In it, honors sections of six critically important courses are offered. The best instructors and the most demanding material and expectations are used. Additionally, special one credit hour seminars, which include outside speakers, are offered to sophomores and juniors. Special programs offered to physically disabled students include tutors. **Career services:** Alumni network, alumni services, career assessment, internships.

FACILITIES

Housing: Men's dorms, women's dorms, apartments for single students. **Special Academic Facilities/Equipment:** Butler Gallery, Hopkins Display

Cases, Hach Library **Computers:** 100% of classrooms, 100% of dorms, 100% of libraries, 100% of dining areas, 100% of student union, have wireless network access. Students can register for classes online. Administrative functions (other than registration) can be performed online.

CAMPUS LIFE
Environment: Village. **Activities:** Choral groups, dance, drama/theater, student newspaper, campus ministries, international student organization. **Organizations:** 17 registered organizations, 1 honor societies, 2 religious organizations. 1 fraternity, 1 sorority. **Athletics (Intercollegiate): Men:** Baseball, cross-country, golf, soccer, track/field (outdoor), track/field (indoor). **Women:** cross-country, golf, soccer, softball, track/field (outdoor), track/field (indoor). **Environmental Initiatives:** Paper recycling. We have two large bins in one of the parking lots. The paper is collected twice a week from offices and common areas. During the month of April and for Earth Day, we plan other activities and provide educational flyers about what everyone can do on their own.

ADMISSIONS
Freshman Academic Profile: Average high school GPA 3.2. 12% in top 10% of high school class, 36% in top 25% of high school class, 73% in top 50% of high school class. 90% from public high schools. SAT Math middle 50% range 430–540. SAT Critical Reading middle 50% range 410–540. SAT Writing middle 50% range 400–510. ACT middle 50% range 18–22. Minimum paper TOEFL 500. Minimum computer TOEFL 173. **Basis for Candidate Selection:** *Very important factors considered include:* Class rank, application essay, academic GPA, recommendation(s), rigor of secondary school record, standardized test scores, character/personal qualities, extracurricular activities, interview, level of applicant's interest. *Important factors considered include:* talent/ability, volunteer work, work experience. *Other factors considered include:* Alumni/ae relation, first generation. **Freshman Admission Requirements:** High school diploma is required and GED is accepted. *Academic units recommended:* 4 English, 3 mathematics, 2 science, (1 science labs), 3 foreign language, 3 social studies. **Freshman Admission Statistics:** 503 applied, 55% admitted, 36% enrolled. **Transfer Admission Requirements:** High school transcript, college transcript(s), essay or personal statement, minimum college GPA of 2.0 required. Lowest grade transferable C. **General Admission Information:** Application fee $25. Notification on a rolling basis, beginning on or about 1/1. Nonfall registration accepted. Admission may be deferred for a maximum of 1 year. Credit and/or placement offered for CEEB Advanced Placement tests.

COSTS AND FINANCIAL AID
Annual tuition $17,451. Room and board $7,590. Required fees $978. Average book expense $1,581. **Required Forms and Deadlines:** FAFSA. **Notification of Awards:** Applicants will be notified of awards on a rolling basis beginning 3/1. **Types of Aid:** *Need-based scholarships/grants:* Federal Pell, SEOG, private scholarships, the school's own gift aid. *Loans:* FFEL Subsidized Stafford, FFEL Unsubsidized Stafford, FFEL PLUS. **Financial Aid Statistics:** 66% freshmen, 535% undergrads receive need-based scholarship or grant aid. 21% freshmen, 176% undergrads receive non-need-based scholarship or grant aid. 74% freshmen, 602% undergrads receive need-based self-help aid. 6% freshmen, 100% undergrads receive athletic scholarships. 83% undergrads borrow to pay for school. Average cumulative indebtedness $22,820. **Criteria for awarding institutional aid:** *Non-need-based:* Academics, alumni affiliation, athletics, leadership, minority status, state/district residency.

NORWICH UNIVERSITY

Admissions Office, 27 I.D. White Ave, Northfield, VT 05663
Phone: 802-485-2001
E-mail: nuadm@norwich.edu
Fax: 802-485-2032 **Website:** www.norwich.edu

This private school was founded in 1819. It has a 1125-acre campus.

RATINGS
Admissions Selectivity Rating: 65   **Fire Safety Rating:** 60*   **Green Rating:** 60*

STUDENTS AND FACULTY
Student Body: 77% out-of-state.
Retention and Graduation: 74% freshmen return for sophomore year. 10% grads go on to further study within 1 year. 2% grads pursue arts and sciences degrees. 2% grads pursue law degrees. 2% grads pursue business degrees. 1% grads pursue medical degrees. **Faculty:** Student/faculty ratio 13:1. 104 full-time faculty, 77% hold PhDs, 5% are are members of minority groups, 26% are women.

ACADEMICS
Degrees: Bachelor's, master's, post-bachelor's certificate. **Classes:** Most classes have 10–19 students. **Majors with Highest Enrollment:** Architecture (BArch,

BA/BS, MArch, MA/MS, PhD); criminal justice/law enforcement administration; liberal arts and sciences/liberal studies. **Special Study Options:** Cooperative education program, distance learning, double major, English as a Second Language (ESL), honors program, independent study, internships, study abroad Special programs offered to physically disabled students include tutors. **Career services:** Career/job search classes.

FACILITIES
Housing: Coed dorms. 95% of campus accessible to physically disabled. **Special Academic Facilities/Equipment:** Museum, architecture and art building w/galery, new library.

CAMPUS LIFE
Environment: Rural. **Activities:** Choral groups, concert band, drama/theater, jazz band, literary magazine, marching band, pep band, radio station, student government, student newspaper, yearbook. **Organizations:** 40 registered organizations, 8 honor societies, 4 religious organizations. **Athletics (Intercollegiate): Men:** Baseball, basketball, cross-country, diving, football, ice hockey, lacrosse, riflery, rugby, soccer, swimming, track/field (outdoor), volleyball, wrestling. **Women:** Basketball, cross-country, diving, riflery, rugby, soccer, softball, swimming, track/field (outdoor), volleyball.

ADMISSIONS
Freshman Academic Profile: 90% from public high schools. SAT Math middle 50% range 440–570. SAT Critical Reading middle 50% range 440–560. Minimum paper TOEFL 500. Minimum computer TOEFL 1. **Basis for Candidate Selection:** *Very important factors considered include:* Rigor of secondary school record. *Important factors considered include:* extracurricular activities, talent/ability. *Other factors considered include:* Class rank, application essay, recommendation(s), standardized test scores, alumni/ae relation, character/personal qualities, interview, volunteer work, work experience. **Freshman Admission Requirements:** High school diploma is required and GED is accepted. *Academic units required:* 4 English, 3 mathematics, 2 science, (2 science labs). *Academic units recommended:* 4 English, 4 mathematics, 3 science, (2 science labs), 2 foreign language. **Freshman Admission Statistics:** 1,473 applied, 91% admitted, 37% enrolled. **Transfer Admission Requirements:** High school transcript, college transcript(s), Lowest grade transferable C–. **General Admission Information:** Application fee $35. Early decision application deadline 11/15. Notification on a rolling basis, beginning on or about 10/1. Nonfall registration accepted. Admission may be deferred for a maximum of 1. Credit offered for CEEB Advanced Placement tests.

COSTS AND FINANCIAL AID
Annual tuition $16,710. Room and board $6,372. Required fees $350. Average book expense $500. **Types of Aid:** *Need-based scholarships/grants:* Federal Pell, SEOG *Loans:* Direct Subsidized Stafford, Direct Unsubsidized Stafford, FFEL Subsidized Stafford, FFEL Unsubsidized Stafford, FFEL PLUS, Federal Perkins. *Student Employment:* Federal Work-Study Program available. Institutional employment available. Off-campus job opportunities are fair.

NOTRE DAME COLLEGE

4545 College Road, South Euclid, OH 44121
Phone: 216-381-1680 **Financial Aid Phone:** 216-373-5213
E-mail: admissions@ndc.edu **CEEB Code:** 3085
Fax: 216-373-5278 **Website:** www.notredamecollege.edu **ACT Code:** 3302

This private school, affiliated with the Roman Catholic Church, was founded in 1922. It has a 53-acre campus.

RATINGS
Admissions Selectivity Rating: 74   **Fire Safety Rating:** 60*   **Green Rating:** 60*

STUDENTS AND FACULTY
Enrollment: 835. **Student Body:** 63% female, 37% male, 3% out-of-state, 4% international African American 24%, Caucasian 62%, Hispanic 3%.
Retention and Graduation: 65% freshmen return for sophomore year. 60% grads go on to further study within 1 year. 10% grads pursue arts and sciences degrees. 5% grads pursue law degrees. 10% grads pursue business degrees. 5% grads pursue medical degrees. **Faculty:** Student/faculty ratio 19:1. 36 full-time faculty, 53% hold PhDs, 3% are are members of minority groups, 58% are women.

ACADEMICS
Degrees: Associate, bachelor's, certificate, master's, post-bachelor's certificate. **Classes:** Most classes have 10–19 students. Most lab/discussion sessions have 10–19 students. **Majors with Highest Enrollment:** Business/commerce; psychology; secondary education and teaching. **Special Study Options:** Cooperative education program, cross-registration, distance learning, double major, independent study, internships, student-designed major, study abroad, teacher

certification program, weekend college. Special programs offered to physically disabled students include tutors. **Career services:** Alumni services, career/job search classes, career assessment, internships.

FACILITIES

Housing: Coed dorms, men's dorms, women's dorms 100% of campus accessible to physically disabled. **Special Academic Facilities/Equipment:** Tolerance Resource Center.

CAMPUS LIFE

Environment: Town. **Activities:** Choral groups, dance, drama/theater, literary magazine, pep band, student government, student newspaper, yearbook. **Organizations:** 22 registered organizations, 6 honor societies, 1 religious organizations. **Athletics (Intercollegiate):** *Men:* Baseball, basketball, cross-country, golf, soccer, tennis, track/field (outdoor). *Women:* Basketball, cross-country, golf, lacrosse, soccer, softball, track/field (outdoor), volleyball. **On-Campus Highlights:** Smart classroom, Legacy Walkway, Joseph H. Keller Fitness Center, Tolerance Resource Center, coffee shop.

ADMISSIONS

Freshman Academic Profile: Average high school GPA 2.95. 4% in top 10% of high school class, 22% in top 25% of high school class, 62% in top 50% of high school class. 60% from public high schools. SAT Math middle 50% range 393–520. SAT Critical Reading middle 50% range 440–528. ACT middle 50% range 17–21. Minimum paper TOEFL 550. Minimum computer TOEFL 213. **Basis for Candidate Selection:** *Very important factors considered include:* Academic GPA, rigor of secondary school record, standardized test scores. *Important factors considered include:* Class rank, interview, level of applicant's interest. *Other factors considered include:* Application essay, recommendation(s), alumni/ae relation, character/personal qualities, extracurricular activities, talent/ability, volunteer work, work experience. **Freshman Admission Requirements:** High school diploma is required and GED is accepted. *Academic units recommended:* 4 English, 3 mathematics, 3 science, (3 science labs), 2 foreign language, 3 social studies, 1 fine arts. **Freshman Admission Statistics:** 1,004 applied, 51% admitted, 29% enrolled. **Transfer Admission Requirements:** High school transcript, college transcript(s), interview, minimum college GPA of 2.5 required. Lowest grade transferable C. **General Admission Information:** Application fee $30. Notification on a rolling basis, beginning on or about 9/1. Nonfall registration accepted. Admission may be deferred for a maximum of 1 year. Credit offered for CEEB Advanced Placement tests.

COSTS AND FINANCIAL AID

Annual tuition $18,670. Room and board $6,648. Required fees $550. Average book expense $1,270. **Required Forms and Deadlines:** FAFSA. Priority financial aid filing date 4/1. **Notification of Awards:** Applicants will be notified of awards on a rolling basis beginning 1/1. **Types of Aid:** *Need-based scholarships/grants:* Federal Pell, SEOG, state scholarships/grants, private scholarships, the school's own gift aid. *Loans:* FFEL Subsidized Stafford, FFEL Unsubsidized Stafford, FFEL PLUS, Federal Perkins, state loans, college/university loans from institutional funds. *Student Employment:* Federal Work-Study Program available. Institutional employment available. Off-campus job opportunities are good. **Financial Aid Statistics:** 98% freshmen, 84% undergrads receive need-based scholarship or grant aid. 98% freshmen, 84% undergrads receive non-need-based scholarship or grant aid. 98% freshmen, 84% undergrads receive need-based self-help aid. 6% undergrads receive athletic scholarships. 93% freshmen, 63% undergrads receive any aid. 90% undergrads borrow to pay for school. Average cumulative indebtedness $15,649. **Criteria for awarding institutional aid:** *Non-need-based:* Academics, art, leadership, state/district residency.

See page 1186.

NOTRE DAME DE NAMUR UNIVERSITY

1500 Ralston Avenue, Belmont, CA 94002-1908
Phone: 650-508-3600
E-mail: admiss@ndnu.edu **CEEB Code:** 4063
Fax: 650-508-3426 **Website:** www.ndnu.edu **ACT Code:** 236

This private school, affiliated with the Roman Catholic Church, was founded in 1851. It has a 80-acre campus.

RATINGS

Admissions Selectivity Rating: 71   **Fire Safety Rating:** 60*   **Green Rating:** 60*

STUDENTS AND FACULTY

Enrollment: 855. **Student Body:** 64% female, 36% male, 36% out-of-state, 4% international Asian 17%, African American 5%, Caucasian 44%, Hispanic 20%, Native American 1%.

Retention and Graduation: 70% freshmen return for sophomore year. 40% freshmen graduate within 4 years. 15% grads go on to further study within 1 year. 8% grads pursue arts and sciences degrees. 1% grads pursue law degrees. 5% grads pursue business degrees. 1% grads pursue medical degrees. **Faculty:** Student/faculty ratio 12:1. 56 full-time faculty, 29% are are members of minority groups, 46% are women.

ACADEMICS

Degrees: Bachelor's, master's, post-bachelor's certificate. **Classes:** Most classes have 10–19 students. **Special Study Options:** Accelerated program, double major, English as a Second Language (ESL), exchange student program (domestic), independent study, internships, liberal arts/career combination, student-designed major, study abroad, teacher certification program Special programs offered to physically disabled students include note-taking services, reader services. **Career services:** Career/job search classes, internships.

FACILITIES

Housing: Coed dorms, 2 or 3 person apartments 4-person suites. **Special Academic Facilities/Equipment:** Student art museum, professional art gallery, archives of modern Christian art, theatre, early learning center for Montessori credential training, on-campus elementary school.

CAMPUS LIFE

Environment: Village. **Activities:** Choral groups, dance, literary magazine, music ensembles, musical theater, student government, student newspaper. **Organizations:** 15 registered organizations, 3 honor societies, 1 religious organizations. **Athletics (Intercollegiate):** *Men:* Basketball, cheerleading, soccer, tennis, track/field (outdoor). *Women:* Basketball, cheerleading, cross-country, soccer, softball, tennis, track/field (outdoor), volleyball.

ADMISSIONS

Freshman Academic Profile: Average high school GPA 3.07. 17% in top 10% of high school class, 41% in top 25% of high school class, 74% in top 50% of high school class. 62% from public high schools. SAT Math middle 50% range 450–540. SAT Critical Reading middle 50% range 430–530. SAT Writing middle 50% range 430–540. ACT middle 50% range 18–24. Minimum paper TOEFL 450. **Basis for Candidate Selection:** *Very important factors considered include:* Academic GPA, rigor of secondary school record, character/personal qualities. *Important factors considered include:* Class rank, application essay, recommendation(s), standardized test scores, extracurricular activities, talent/ability, volunteer work. *Other factors considered include:* first generation, interview, work experience. **Freshman Admission Requirements:** High school diploma is required and GED is accepted. *Academic units required:* 4 English, 2 mathematics, 1 science, (1 science labs), 2 foreign language, 2 social studies, 1 history, 3 academic electives. *Academic units recommended:* 3 mathematics, 2 science, (2 science labs), 3 foreign language. **Freshman Admission Statistics:** 706 applied, 97% admitted, 20% enrolled. **Transfer Admission Requirements:** College transcript(s), essay or personal statement, statement of good standing from prior institution(s). Minimum college GPA of 2.0 required. Lowest grade transferable C. **General Admission Information:** Application fee $40. Notification on a rolling basis, beginning on or about 12/1. Nonfall registration accepted. Admission may be deferred for a maximum of 1 year. Credit offered for CEEB Advanced Placement tests.

COSTS AND FINANCIAL AID

Annual tuition $24,450. Room and board $10,580. Required fees $200. Average book expense $1,330. **Required Forms and Deadlines:** FAFSA. Priority financial aid filing date 3/2. **Types of Aid:** *Need-based scholarships/grants:* Federal Pell, SEOG, state scholarships/grants, private scholarships. *Loans:* FFEL Subsidized Stafford, FFEL Unsubsidized Stafford, FFEL PLUS, Federal Perkins. *Student Employment:* Federal Work-Study Program available. Institutional employment available. Highest amount earned per year from on-campus jobs $1,300. Off-campus job opportunities are excellent. **Financial Aid Statistics:** 72% freshmen, 69% undergrads receive need-based scholarship or grant aid. 62% freshmen, 60% undergrads receive need-based self-help aid. 57% undergrads borrow to pay for school. Average cumulative indebtedness $29,687. **Criteria for awarding institutional aid:** *Non-need-based:* Academics, alumni affiliation, art, athletics, leadership, music/drama.

NOVA SCOTIA COLLEGE OF ART AND DESIGN

5163 Duke Street, Halifax, NS B3J 3J6 Canada
Phone: 902-494-8129 **Financial Aid Phone:** 902-494-8130
E-mail: admissions@nscad.ca
Fax: 902-425-2987 **Website:** www.nscad.ca

This public school was founded in 1887. It has a 1-acre campus.

RATINGS
Admissions Selectivity Rating: 60*   **Fire Safety Rating:** 60*   **Green Rating:** 60*

STUDENTS AND FACULTY
Enrollment: 896. **Student Body:** 64% female, 36% male.
Retention and Graduation: Faculty: Student/faculty ratio 11:1. 68 full-time
faculty, 28% are women. 19% of classes are taught by teaching assistants.

ACADEMICS
Degrees: Bachelor's, master's. **Special Study Options:** Cooperative education program, distance learning, double major, exchange student program
(domestic), independent study, internships, study abroad. **Combined degree
programs:** BFA/BD. Special programs offered to physically disabled students
include note-taking services, tape recorders.

FACILITIES
Housing: Men's dorms, women's dorms, apartments for married students. 25%
of campus accessible to physically disabled.

CAMPUS LIFE
Environment: City. **Activities:** Choral groups, concert band, drama/theater,
music ensembles, musical theater, student government, yearbook.

ADMISSIONS
Freshman Academic Profile: Minimum paper TOEFL 575. Minimum
computer TOEFL 233. **Basis for Candidate Selection:** *Very important
factors considered include:* Application essay, rigor of secondary school record,
talent/ability. *Other factors considered include:* Recommendation(s), standardized test scores, character/personal qualities, interview, volunteer work, work
experience. **Freshman Admission Statistics:** 247 applied, 43% admitted.
Transfer Admission Requirements: College transcript(s), essay or personal
statement, statement of good standing from prior institution(s). **General Admission Information:** Application fee $50. Regular application deadline 5/15.
Notification on a rolling basis, beginning on or about 3/15. Nonfall registration
not accepted. Admission may be deferred for a maximum of 1 year. Placement
offered for CEEB Advanced Placement tests.

NOVA SOUTHEASTERN UNIVERSITY

3301 College Avenue, Fort Lauderdale, FL 33314
Phone: 954-262-8000 **Financial Aid Phone:** 954-262-7456
E-mail: ncsinfo@nova.edu **CEEB Code:** 5514
Fax: 954-262-3811 **Website:** www.nova.edu **ACT Code:** 6706

This private school was founded in 1964. It has a 300-acre campus.

RATINGS
Admissions Selectivity Rating: 60*   **Fire Safety Rating:** 60*   **Green Rating:** 60*

STUDENTS AND FACULTY
Enrollment: 5,067. **Student Body:** 73% female, 27% male.
Retention and Graduation: 65% freshmen return for sophomore year. **Faculty:** 712 full-time faculty, 82% hold PhDs, 25% are are members of minority
groups, 46% are women.

ACADEMICS
Degrees: Associate, bachelor's, master's, post-bachelor's certificate, post-
master's certificate. **Classes:** Most classes have 10–19 students. **Majors with
Highest Enrollment:** Biology/biological sciences; business administration and
management; nursing/registered nurse (RN, ASN, BSN, MSN). **Special Study
Options:** distance learning, double major, honors program, independent study,
internships, study abroad, teacher certification program, Dual admission programs with NSU graduate and professional schools. **Honors programs:** http://
undergrad.nova.edu/honors/index.cfm For the academically motivated student,
the NSU Honors program provides a value added experience. Students enjoy
greater interaction with faculty through curricular and co-curricular activities,
special invitations to events, and enhanced engagement in disciplinary inquiry.

Combined degree programs: BA/MD, BA/JD, BA/MA, BA/DDS. Special
programs offered to physically disabled students include note-taking services,
reader services, tape recorders, tutors. **Career services:** Alumni services,
career assessment, internships, regional alumni. **Career services highlights
include:** Our comprehensive career development program encompassing career planning, advisement services, employment and career resources, campus
relations, and employer recruitment program.

FACILITIES
Housing: Coed dorms, special housing for disabled students, special housing
for international students, fraternity/sorority housing, apartments for married
students, apartments for single students, wellness house, theme housing. **Special Academic Facilities/Equipment:** Institute for Early Childhood Studies,
University School for pre-kindergarten to grade 12, Oceanographic Center
and Lab, Biofeedback and Learning Technology Labs, Audiology and Speech
Language Pathology, and Psychology Clinics. **Computers:** 100% of classrooms,
100% of dorms, 100% of libraries, 80% of dining areas, 100% of student union,
70% of common outdoor areas have wireless network access. Students can
register for classes online. Administrative functions (other than registration) can
be performed online.

CAMPUS LIFE
Environment: City. **Activities:** Choral groups, dance, drama/theater, jazz
band, literary magazine, music ensembles, musical theater, pep band, radio
station, student government, student newspaper, international student organization. **Organizations:** 292 registered organizations. **Athletics (Intercollegiate):** *Men:* Baseball, basketball, cross-country, golf, soccer, track/field (outdoor). *Women:* Basketball, cheerleading, crew/rowing, cross-country, golf, soccer, softball, tennis, track/field (outdoor), volleyball. **On-Campus Highlights:**
University Center and Performing Arts W, Alvin Sherman Library, Research &
Inform, Health Professions Division Museum, Miniaci Performing Arts Center,
Law School, University Center includes the sports arena, fitness center, flight
deck, shark mural, and mall-style food court. Performing Arts Wing includes
multiple theaters, costume and scenery shops, performance practice rooms for
music and dance, dressing rooms, and a gallery.

ADMISSIONS
Freshman Academic Profile: 60% from public high schools. **Basis for
Candidate Selection:** *Very important factors considered include:* Academic
GPA, standardized test scores. *Important factors considered include:* Rigor of
secondary school record. *Other factors considered include:* Application essay,
recommendation(s), character/personal qualities, extracurricular activities,
interview, talent/ability, volunteer work. **Freshman Admission Requirements:** High school diploma is required and GED is accepted. *Academic units
recommended:* 4 English, 3 mathematics, 3 science, 3 social studies. **Freshman Admission Statistics: Transfer Admission Requirements:** College
transcript(s), statement of good standing from prior institution(s). Minimum
college GPA of 2.50 required. Lowest grade transferable D. **General Admission Information:** Application fee $50. Regular application deadline 8/1.
Nonfall registration accepted. Admission may be deferred for a maximum of 1
year. Credit and/or placement offered for CEEB Advanced Placement tests.

COSTS AND FINANCIAL AID
Annual tuition $19,800. Room and board $8,360. Required fees $500. Average
book expense $1,500. **Required Forms and Deadlines:** FAFSA, state aid
form. Priority financial aid filing date 4/15. **Notification of Awards:** Applicants
will be notified of awards on a rolling basis beginning 3/15. **Types of Aid:**
Need-based scholarships/grants: Federal Pell, SEOG, state scholarships/grants,
private scholarships, the school's own gift aid. *Loans:* FFEL Subsidized Stafford, FFEL Unsubsidized Stafford, FFEL PLUS, Federal Perkins. *Student
Employment:* Federal Work-Study Program available. Institutional employment
available. Off-campus job opportunities are good. **Criteria for awarding institutional aid:** *Non-need-based:* Academics, athletics, leadership, music/drama.

OAK HILLS CHRISTIAN COLLEGE

1600 Oak Hills Rd SW, Bemidji, MN 56601
Phone: 218-751-8670 **Financial Aid Phone:** 218-751-8670
E-mail: admissions@oakhills.edu
Fax: 218-751-8825 **Website:** www.oakhills.edu **ACT Code:** 2167

This private school was founded in 1946. It has a 180-acre campus.

RATINGS
Admissions Selectivity Rating: 64   **Fire Safety Rating:** 61   **Green Rating:** 60*

STUDENTS AND FACULTY

Enrollment: 149. **Student Body:** 52% female, 48% male, 30% out-of-state, 1% international (1 countries represented). Asian 2%, African American 1%, Caucasian 57%, Hispanic 1%, Native American 1%.
Retention and Graduation: 78% freshmen return for sophomore year. 7% freshmen graduate within 4 years. **Faculty:** Student/faculty ratio 13.7:1. 6 full-time faculty, 67% hold PhDs, 33% are women.

ACADEMICS

Degrees: Associate, bachelor's, certificate, diploma. **Classes:** Most classes have fewer than 10 students. **Majors with Highest Enrollment:** Bible/biblical studies; pastoral studies/counseling; youth ministry. **Special Study Options:** Cooperative education program, double major, independent study, internships Special programs offered to physically disabled students include note-taking services, reader services, tape recorders, tutors. **Career services:** Alumni network, career/job search classes, career assessment, internships.

FACILITIES

Housing: Special housing for disabled students, men's dorms, women's dorms, apartments for married students, apartments for single students. 85% of campus accessible to physically disabled. **Special Academic Facilities/Equipment:** American Indian Resource Center. **Computers:** 50% of classrooms, 100% of dorms, 100% of libraries, 100% of student union, 50% of common outdoor areas have wireless network access. Students can register for classes online. Administrative functions (other than registration) can be performed online.

CAMPUS LIFE

Environment: Village. **Activities:** Choral groups, music ensembles, student government, campus ministries. **Athletics (Intercollegiate):** Men: Basketball. Women: Basketball, volleyball. **On-Campus Highlights:** The Fellowship Center Lounge, Schreiber Activity Center (SAC) Gym, library, chapel, lake front.

ADMISSIONS

Freshman Academic Profile: 17% in top 25% of high school class, 50% in top 50% of high school class. 83% from public high schools. ACT middle 50% range 17–23. Minimum paper TOEFL 500. Minimum computer TOEFL 173. **Basis for Candidate Selection:** *Very important factors considered include:* Class rank, application essay, academic GPA, recommendation(s). *Other factors considered include:* Rigor of secondary school record, interview. **Freshman Admission Requirements:** High school diploma is required and GED is accepted. **Freshman Admission Statistics:** 58 applied, 62% admitted, 106% enrolled. **Transfer Admission Requirements:** High school transcript, college transcript(s), essay or personal statement, minimum college GPA of 2.0 required. Lowest grade transferable C. **General Admission Information:** Application fee $25. Notification on a rolling basis, beginning on or about 9/1. Nonfall registration accepted. Admission may be deferred for a maximum of 2 years. Credit and/or placement offered for CEEB Advanced Placement tests.

COSTS AND FINANCIAL AID

Room and board $4,840. Average book expense $730. **Required Forms and Deadlines:** FAFSA, institution's own financial aid form. **Notification of Awards:** Applicants will be notified of awards on a rolling basis beginning 3/1. **Types of Aid:** *Need-based scholarships/grants:* Federal Pell, SEOG, state scholarships/grants, private scholarships, the school's own gift aid. *Loans:* FFEL Subsidized Stafford, FFEL Unsubsidized Stafford, FFEL PLUS, state loans, Alternative Loan programs. *Student Employment:* Federal Work-Study Program available. Institutional employment available. Highest amount earned per year from on-campus jobs $9. Off-campus job opportunities are excellent. **Financial Aid Statistics:** 95% freshmen, 93% undergrads receive need-based scholarship or grant aid. 71% freshmen, 80% undergrads receive need-based self-help aid. 100% freshmen, 100% undergrads receive any aid. 100% undergrads borrow to pay for school. Average cumulative indebtedness $29,440. **Criteria for awarding institutional aid:** *Non-need-based:* Academics, alumni affiliation.

OAKLAND CITY UNIVERSITY

138 N. Lucretia Street, Oakland City, IN 47660
Phone: 812-749-1221
E-mail: ocuadmit@oak.edu
Fax: 812-749-1433 **Website:** www.oak.edu

This is a private school.

RATINGS
Admissions Selectivity Rating: 72   **Fire Safety Rating:** 60*   **Green Rating:** 60*

STUDENTS AND FACULTY

Enrollment: 1,492. **Student Body:** 53% female, 47% male, 17% out-of-state, 1% international Asian 1%, African American 13%, Caucasian 98%, Native American 1%.
Retention and Graduation: 66% freshmen return for sophomore year. 46% freshmen graduate within 4 years. **Faculty:** Student/faculty ratio 15:1. 58 full-time faculty, 47% are women.

ACADEMICS

Degrees: Associate, bachelor's, certificate, doctoral, master's. **Classes:** Most classes have 10–19 students. Most lab/discussion sessions have fewer than 10 students. **Special Study Options:** distance learning, double major, dual enrollment, independent study, internships, teacher certification program.

FACILITIES

Housing: Men's dorms, women's dorms, apartments for married students, apartments for single students.

CAMPUS LIFE

Activities: Choral groups, drama/theater, pep band, student government, student newspaper, yearbook, campus ministries.

ADMISSIONS

Freshman Academic Profile: Average high school GPA 3.15. 9% in top 10% of high school class, 16% in top 25% of high school class, 41% in top 50% of high school class. SAT Math middle 50% range 420–530. SAT Critical Reading middle 50% range 400–510. SAT Writing middle 50% range 398–500. ACT middle 50% range 17–23. **Basis for Candidate Selection:** *Very important factors considered include:* Academic GPA, rigor of secondary school record, standardized test scores. *Other factors considered include:* Class rank, alumni/ae relation, character/personal qualities, interview, level of applicant's interest. **Freshman Admission Requirements:** High school diploma is required and GED is accepted. *Academic units recommended:* 4 English, 3 mathematics, 3 science, 2 social studies. **Freshman Admission Statistics:** 620 applied, 56% admitted, 100% enrolled. **Transfer Admission Requirements:** High school transcript, college transcript(s), standardized test scores, minimum college GPA of 2.0 required. Lowest grade transferable C. **General Admission Information:** Application fee $35. Regular application deadline 9/5. Nonfall registration accepted.

COSTS AND FINANCIAL AID

Annual tuition $15,200. Room and board $6,000. Required fees $360. Average book expense $1,500. **Required Forms and Deadlines:** FAFSA. Financial aid filing deadline 3/1. **Notification of Awards:** Applicants will be notified of awards on a rolling basis beginning 5/1. **Types of Aid:** *Need-based scholarships/grants:* Federal Pell, SEOG, state scholarships/grants, private scholarships, the school's own gift aid. *Loans:* FFEL Subsidized Stafford, FFEL Unsubsidized Stafford, FFEL PLUS, Federal Perkins. *Student Employment:* **Criteria for awarding institutional aid:** *Non-need-based:* Academics, alumni affiliation, art, athletics, minority status, music/drama, religious affiliation.

OAKLAND UNIVERSITY

Office of Admissions, 101 North Founda, Rochester, MI 48309-4401
Phone: 248-370-3360 **Financial Aid Phone:** 248-370-2550
E-mail: ouinfo@oakland.edu **CEEB Code:** 1497
Fax: 248-370-4462 **Website:** www.oakland.edu **ACT Code:** 2033

This public school was founded in 1957. It has a 1444-acre campus.

RATINGS
Admissions Selectivity Rating: 82   **Fire Safety Rating:** 79   **Green Rating:** 73

STUDENTS AND FACULTY

Enrollment: 14,728. **Student Body:** 61% female, 39% male, 1% out-of-state, 1% international (93 countries represented). Asian 4%, African American 9%, Caucasian 77%, Hispanic 2%.
Retention and Graduation: 74% freshmen return for sophomore year. 12% freshmen graduate within 4 years. **Faculty:** Student/faculty ratio 21:1. 515 full-time faculty, 90% hold PhDs, 21% are members of minority groups, 44% are women. 1% of classes are taught by teaching assistants.

ACADEMICS

Degrees: Bachelor's, doctoral, master's, post-bachelor's certificate, post-master's certificate. **Classes:** Most classes have 20–29 students. Most lab/discussion sessions have 10–19 students. **Majors with Highest Enrollment:** Business/commerce; elementary education and teaching; psychology. **Special Study Options:** Accelerated program, cooperative education program, cross-registration, distance learning, double major, English as a Second Language (ESL), honors program, independent study, internships, student-designed major, study abroad, teacher certification program. **Honors programs:** Honors College. **Combined degree programs:** 5-year MBA program. Special programs offered to physically disabled students include note-taking services, reader services, tape recorders, tutors. **Career services:** Alumni network, alumni services, internships.

FACILITIES

Housing: Coed dorms, special housing for disabled students, special housing for international students, fraternity/sorority housing, apartments for married students, cooperative housing, apartments for single students, wellness house, theme housing, living/learning community. 90% of campus accessible to physically disabled. **Special Academic Facilities/Equipment:** Art gallery, robotics lab, Eye Research institute, Professional theater, Meadowbrook Hall, Meadowbrook Music Festival, two golf courses, Pawley Learning center, Lowry Early Childhood Education Center, Jack's Place for Autism at OU. **Computers:** Students can register for classes online. Administrative functions (other than registration) can be performed online.

CAMPUS LIFE

Environment: Town. **Activities:** Choral groups, concert band, dance, drama/theater, jazz band, literary magazine, music ensembles, musical theater, pep band, radio station, student government, student newspaper, student-run film society, symphony orchestra, television station, campus ministries, international student organization. **Organizations:** 170 registered organizations, 9 honor societies, 12 religious organizations. 6 fraternities, 6 sororities. **Athletics (Intercollegiate): Men:** Baseball, basketball, cross-country, diving, golf, soccer, swimming, track/field (outdoor). **Women:** Basketball, cross-country, diving, golf, soccer, softball, swimming, tennis, track/field (outdoor), volleyball. **On-Campus Highlights:** Recreation Center, Pawley Hall, Oakland Center, Library, Honors College. **Environmental Initiatives:** $8 million facility upgrade from 1998 to save on energy costs. Solar electric power roof installed on the student apartments buildings. Investigating Biomass energy and/ or wind power for campus heating and cooling.

ADMISSIONS

Freshman Academic Profile: Average high school GPA 3.27. 46% in top 25% of high school class, 88% in top 50% of high school class. 90% from public high schools. ACT middle 50% range 19–25. Minimum paper TOEFL 550. Minimum computer TOEFL 213. Minimum web-based TOEFL 79. **Basis for Candidate Selection:** *Very important factors considered include:* Class rank, academic GPA, rigor of secondary school record. *Important factors considered include:* Recommendation(s), character/personal qualities, extracurricular activities, talent/ability, volunteer work. *Other factors considered include:* Application essay, standardized test scores, alumni/ae relation, first generation, interview, level of applicant's interest, work experience. **Freshman Admission Requirements:** High school diploma is required and GED is accepted. *Academic units required:* 4 English, 3 mathematics, 3 science, 3 social studies. *Academic units recommended:* 2 foreign language. **Freshman Admission Statistics:** 10,070 applied, 69% admitted, 36% enrolled. **Transfer Admission Requirements:** College transcript(s), statement of good standing from prior institution(s). Minimum college GPA of 2.50 required. Lowest grade transferable C. **General Admission Information:** Notification on a rolling basis, beginning on or about 9/15. Nonfall registration accepted. Admission may be deferred for a maximum of 1 year. Placement offered for CEEB Advanced Placement tests.

COSTS AND FINANCIAL AID

Annual in-state tuition 9,188. Annual out-of-state tuition $21,236. Room and board $7,350. Average book expense $1,107. **Required Forms and Deadlines:** FAFSA. Priority financial aid filing date 2/15. **Notification of Awards:** Applicants will be notified of awards on a rolling basis beginning 3/15. **Types of Aid:** *Need-based scholarships/grants:* Federal Pell, SEOG, state scholarships/grants, private scholarships, the school's own gift aid. *Loans:* Direct Subsidized Stafford, Direct Unsubsidized Stafford, Direct PLUS, Federal Perkins, Private loans. *Student Employment:* Federal Work-Study Program available. Institutional employment available. Off-campus job opportunities are good. **Financial Aid Statistics:** 37% freshmen, 30% undergrads receive need-based scholarship or grant aid. 20% freshmen, 13% undergrads receive non-need-based scholarship or grant aid. 30% freshmen, 36% undergrads receive need-based self-help aid. 3% freshmen, 2% undergrads receive athletic scholarships. 51% freshmen, 48% undergrads receive any aid. 51% undergrads borrow to pay for school. Average cumulative indebtedness $19,967. **Criteria for awarding institutional aid:** *Non-need-based:* Academics, art, athletics, leadership, music/drama, state/district residency.

OBERLIN COLLEGE

101 North Professor Street, Oberlin College, Oberlin, OH 44074
Phone: 440-775-8411 **Financial Aid Phone:** 440-775-8142
E-mail: college.admissions@oberlin.edu **CEEB Code:** 1587
Fax: 440-775-6905 **Website:** www.oberlin.edu **ACT Code:** 3304

This private school was founded in 1833. It has a 450-acre campus.

RATINGS

Admissions Selectivity Rating: 97   **Fire Safety Rating:** 60*   **Green Rating:** 90

STUDENTS AND FACULTY

Enrollment: 2,839. **Student Body:** 55% female, 45% male, 91% out-of-state, 6% international Asian 7%, African American 6%, Caucasian 75%, Hispanic 5%, Native American 1%.

Retention and Graduation: 94% freshmen return for sophomore year. 69% freshmen graduate within 4 years. 16% grads go on to further study within 1 year. 8% grads pursue arts and sciences degrees. 3% grads pursue law degrees. 2% grads pursue business degrees. 3% grads pursue medical degrees. **Faculty:** Student/faculty ratio 9:1. 285 full-time faculty, 96% hold PhDs, 11% are are members of minority groups, 39% are women.

ACADEMICS

Degrees: Bachelor's, diploma, master's, post-master's certificate. **Classes:** Most classes have 10–19 students. Most lab/discussion sessions have fewer than 10 students. **Majors with Highest Enrollment:** Biology; English language and literature; history. **Special Study Options:** Cross-registration, double major, dual enrollment, English as a Second Language (ESL), exchange student program (domestic), honors program, independent study, internships, student-designed major, study abroad, teacher certification program, 5 year double degree program with Conservatory of Music and College of Arts and Sciences; 3-2 engineering. **Combined degree programs:** BA/B.Music. Special programs offered to physically disabled students include note-taking services, reader services, tape recorders, tutors.

FACILITIES

Housing: Coed dorms, men's dorms, women's dorms, cooperative housing, theme housing. 90% of campus accessible to physically disabled. **Special Academic Facilities/Equipment:** Allen Memorial Art Museum, theaters, music performance halls. **Computers:** Students can register for classes online. Administrative functions (other than registration) can be performed online.

CAMPUS LIFE

Environment: Rural. **Activities:** Choral groups, concert band, dance, drama/theater, jazz band, literary magazine, marching band, music ensembles, musical theater, opera, radio station, student government, student newspaper, student-run film society, symphony orchestra, yearbook, campus ministries, international student organization. **Organizations:** 125 registered organizations, 3 honor societies, 10 religious organizations. **Athletics (Intercollegiate): Men:** Baseball, basketball, cross-country, diving, football, golf, lacrosse, soccer, swimming, tennis, track/field (outdoor), track/field (indoor). **Women:** Basketball, cross-country, diving, field hockey, golf, lacrosse, soccer, softball, swimming, tennis, track/field (outdoor), track/field (indoor), volleyball. **On-Campus Highlights:** Allen Art Museum, Oberlin College Science Center, Adam Joseph Lewis Center for Environmental Studies, Mudd Library, Jesse Philips Recreational Center. **Environmental Initiatives:** Development of Campus Resource Monitoring System http://oberlin.edu/dormenergy. Building of social capital on campus and in the larger community. www.oberlin.edu/sustainability/portfolio/social_capital.html; Adam Joseph Lewis Center for Environmental Studies http://oberlin.edu/ajlc.

ADMISSIONS

Freshman Academic Profile: Average high school GPA 3.6. 69% in top 10% of high school class, 91% in top 25% of high school class, 99% in top 50% of high school class. 60% from public high schools. SAT Math middle 50% range 620–710. SAT Critical Reading middle 50% range 640–740. SAT Writing middle 50% range 640–730. ACT middle 50% range 27–32. Minimum paper TOEFL 600. Minimum computer TOEFL 200. **Basis for Candidate Selection:** *Very important factors considered include:* Class rank, academic GPA, rigor of secondary school record, standardized test scores. *Important factors considered include:* Application essay, recommendation(s), character/personal qualities, extracurricular activities, first generation, talent/ability. *Other factors considered include:* Alumni/ae relation, interview, level of applicant's interest, racial/ethnic status, volunteer work, work experience. **Freshman Admission Require-**

ments: High school diploma is required and GED is accepted. *Academic units required:* 4 English, 4 mathematics, 3 science, 3 foreign language, 3 social studies. **Freshman Admission Statistics:** 7,006 applied, 33% admitted, 34% enrolled. **Transfer Admission Requirements:** High school transcript, college transcript(s), essay or personal statement, standardized test scores, statement of good standing from prior institution(s). Minimum college GPA of 3.0 required. Lowest grade transferable C–. **General Admission Information:** Application fee $35. Early decision application deadline 11/15. Regular application deadline 1/15. Regular notification 4/1. Nonfall registration not accepted. Admission may be deferred for a maximum of 1 year. Credit and/or placement offered for CEEB Advanced Placement tests.

COSTS AND FINANCIAL AID

Annual tuition $38,012. Room and board $9,870. Required fees $268. Average book expense $1,956. **Required Forms and Deadlines:** FAFSA, institution's own financial aid form, CSS/Financial Aid PROFILE, state aid form, noncustodial PROFILE, business/farm supplement. Financial aid filing deadline 2/1. Priority financial aid filing date 1/15. **Notification of Awards:** Applicants will be notified of awards on or about 4/1. **Types of Aid:** *Need-based scholarships/grants:* Federal Pell, SEOG, state scholarships/grants, private scholarships, the school's own gift aid. *Loans:* FFEL Subsidized Stafford, FFEL Unsubsidized Stafford, FFEL PLUS, Federal Perkins, college/university loans from institutional funds. *Student Employment:* Highest amount earned per year from on-campus jobs $1,750. **Financial Aid Statistics:** 52% freshmen, 52% undergrads receive need-based scholarship or grant aid. 29% freshmen, 26% undergrads receive non-need-based scholarship or grant aid. 40% freshmen, 45% undergrads receive need-based self-help aid. 61% freshmen, 60% undergrads receive any aid. **Criteria for awarding institutional aid:** *Non-need-based:* Academics, music/drama.

See page 1188.

OCCIDENTAL COLLEGE

1600 Campus Road, Office of Admission, Los Angeles, CA 90041-3314
Phone: 323-259-2700 **Financial Aid Phone:** 323-259-2548
E-mail: admission@oxy.edu **CEEB Code:** 4581
Fax: 323-341-4875 **Website:** www.oxy.edu **ACT Code:** 350

This private school was founded in 1887. It has a 120-acre campus.

RATINGS

Admissions Selectivity Rating: 94 **Fire Safety Rating:** 64 **Green Rating:** 81

STUDENTS AND FACULTY

Enrollment: 1,959. **Student Body:** 56% female, 44% male, 51% out-of-state, 1% international (23 countries represented). Asian 16%, African American 6%, Caucasian 60%, Hispanic 13%, Native American 1%.
Retention and Graduation: 91% freshmen return for sophomore year. 82% freshmen graduate within 4 years. **Faculty:** Student/faculty ratio 10:1. 163 full-time faculty, 93% hold PhDs, 31% are are members of minority groups, 47% are women.

ACADEMICS

Degrees: Bachelor's, master's. **Classes:** Most classes have 10–19 students. Most lab/discussion sessions have 10–19 students. **Majors with Highest Enrollment:** Economics; English language and literature; international relations and affairs. **Special Study Options:** Cross-registration, double major, exchange student program (domestic), honors program, independent study, internships, student-designed major, study abroad, Richter fellowships for international research; summer undergraduate research program; endowment investment management program (Blyth Fund). **Combined degree programs:** BA/JD, law, Columbia; biotech with Keck Grad Institute. Special programs offered to physically disabled students include note-taking services, tape recorders. **Career services:** Alumni network, alumni services, career/job search classes, internships, regional alumni.

FACILITIES

Housing: Coed dorms, women's dorms, fraternity/sorority housing, theme housing. 75% of campus accessible to physically disabled. **Special Academic Facilities/Equipment:** Keck Theater; Mullin Studio and Art Gallery; Moore Ornithology Collection; Smiley Geological Collection; Morse Collection of Astronomical Instruments; superconducting magnet; vivarium; greenhouses. **Computers:** 100% of classrooms, 100% of dorms, 90% of libraries, 100% of dining areas, 80% of student union, 50% of common outdoor areas have wire-

less network access. Students can register for classes online. Administrative functions (other than registration) can be performed online.

CAMPUS LIFE

Environment: Metropolis. **Activities:** Choral groups, concert band, dance, drama/theater, jazz band, literary magazine, music ensembles, musical theater, radio station, student government, student newspaper, student-run film society, symphony orchestra, yearbook, international student organization. **Organizations:** 8 honor societies, 5 religious organizations. 4 fraternities, 4 sororities. **Athletics (Intercollegiate):** *Men:* Baseball, basketball, cross-country, diving, football, golf, soccer, swimming, tennis, track/field (outdoor), water polo. *Women:* Basketball, cross-country, diving, golf, lacrosse, soccer, softball, swimming, tennis, track/field (outdoor), volleyball, water polo. **On-Campus Highlights:** Johnson Student Center, Student Quad, Samuelson Pavilion, Clapp Library, Alumni Gymnasium. **Environmental Initiatives:** A 20–year campus specific plan that commits the college to Silver LEED standard in new construction and renovation and a host of other sustainabiilty measures; Occidental College Sustainability Group; Student Sustainability Fund.

ADMISSIONS

Freshman Academic Profile: Average high school GPA 3.59. 59% in top 10% of high school class, 90% in top 25% of high school class, 99% in top 50% of high school class. 58% from public high schools. SAT Math middle 50% range 600–680. SAT Critical Reading middle 50% range 600–700. SAT Writing middle 50% range 610–700. ACT middle 50% range 28–32. Minimum paper TOEFL 600. Minimum computer TOEFL 250. **Basis for Candidate Selection:** *Very important factors considered include:* Rigor of secondary school record, extracurricular activities, volunteer work, work experience. *Important factors considered include:* Class rank, application essay, recommendation(s), standardized test scores. *Other factors considered include:* Academic GPA, alumni/ae relation, character/personal qualities, first generation, geographical residence, interview, level of applicant's interest, racial/ethnic status, talent/ability. **Freshman Admission Requirements:** High school diploma is required and GED is accepted. *Academic units recommended:* 4 English, 4 mathematics, 3 science, (2 science labs), 3 foreign language, 2 social studies, 2 history, 2 academic electives. **Freshman Admission Statistics:** 5,924 applied, 44% admitted, 22% enrolled. **Transfer Admission Requirements:** High school transcript, college transcript(s), essay or personal statement, statement of good standing from prior institution(s). Minimum college GPA of 3.0 required. Lowest grade transferable D. **General Admission Information:** Application fee $50. Early decision application deadline 11/15. Regular application deadline 1/10. Regular notification 4/1. Nonfall registration not accepted. Admission may be deferred for a maximum of 1 year. Credit and/or placement offered for CEEB Advanced Placement tests.

COSTS AND FINANCIAL AID

Annual tuition $37,970. Room and board $10,780. Required fees $952. Average book expense $1,054. **Required Forms and Deadlines:** FAFSA, CSS/Financial Aid PROFILE, state aid form, noncustodial PROFILE, business/farm supplement. Financial aid filing deadline 2/1. Priority financial aid filing date 2/1. **Notification of Awards:** Applicants will be notified of awards on a rolling basis beginning 4/1. **Types of Aid:** *Need-based scholarships/grants:* Federal Pell, SEOG, state scholarships/grants, private scholarships, the school's own gift aid. *Loans:* FFEL Subsidized Stafford, FFEL Unsubsidized Stafford, FFEL PLUS, Federal Perkins, college/university loans from institutional funds. *Student Employment:* Federal Work-Study Program available. Institutional employment available. Off-campus job opportunities are good. **Financial Aid Statistics:** 50% freshmen, 52% undergrads receive need-based scholarship or grant aid. 4% freshmen, 3% undergrads receive non-need-based scholarship or grant aid. 48% freshmen, 49% undergrads receive need-based self-help aid. 73% freshmen, 75% undergrads receive any aid. 73% undergrads borrow to pay for school. Average cumulative indebtedness $20,381. **Criteria for awarding institutional aid:** *Non-need-based:* Academics, leadership, music/drama, state/district residency.

OGLETHORPE UNIVERSITY

4484 Peachtree Road N.E, Atlanta, GA 30319
Phone: 404-364-8307 **Financial Aid Phone:** 404-364-8356
E-mail: admission@oglethorpe.edu **CEEB Code:** 5521
Fax: 404-364-8491 **Website:** www.oglethorpe.edu **ACT Code:** 850

This private school was founded in 1835. It has a 102-acre campus.

RATINGS
Admissions Selectivity Rating: 89 **Fire Safety Rating:** 60* **Green Rating:** 72

STUDENTS AND FACULTY
Enrollment: 974. **Student Body:** 60% female, 40% male, 24% out-of-state, 3% international (24 countries represented). Asian 4%, African American 23%, Caucasian 48%, Hispanic 5%.
Retention and Graduation: 75% freshmen return for sophomore year. 43% freshmen graduate within 4 years. 40% grads go on to further study within 1 year. 19% grads pursue arts and sciences degrees. 9% grads pursue law degrees. 10% grads pursue business degrees. 2% grads pursue medical degrees. **Faculty:** Student/faculty ratio 16:1. 46 full-time faculty, 93% hold PhDs, 11% are are members of minority groups, 35% are women.

ACADEMICS
Degrees: Bachelor's, master's. **Classes:** Most classes have 10–19 students. **Majors with Highest Enrollment:** Business/commerce; English language and literature; psychology. **Special Study Options:** Accelerated program, cooperative education program, cross-registration, double major, dual enrollment, exchange student program (domestic), honors program, independent study, internships, liberal arts/career combination, student-designed major, study abroad Special programs offered to physically disabled students include note-taking services, tutors. **Career services:** Alumni services, career/job search classes, career assessment, internships.

FACILITIES
Housing: Coed dorms, fraternity/sorority housing. 60% of campus accessible to physically disabled. **Special Academic Facilities/Equipment:** Art museum, scanning electron microscope. **Computers:** 100% of classrooms, 100% of dorms, 100% of libraries, 100% of student union, 25% of common outdoor areas have wireless network access. Administrative functions (other than registration) can be performed online.

CAMPUS LIFE
Environment: Metropolis. **Activities:** Choral groups, dance, drama/theater, jazz band, literary magazine, music ensembles, musical theater, pep band, radio station, student government, student newspaper, student-run film society, yearbook, campus ministries, international student organization. **Organizations:** 57 registered organizations, 10 honor societies, 5 religious organizations. 4 fraternities, 3 sororities. **Athletics (Intercollegiate):** *Men:* Baseball, basketball, cross-country, golf, lacrosse, soccer, tennis, track/field (outdoor). *Women:* Basketball, cheerleading, cross-country, golf, lacrosse, soccer, tennis, track/field (outdoor), volleyball. **On-Campus Highlights:** Oglethorpe University Museum, Phillip Weltner Library, Conant Performing Arts Center, Hermance Stadium, new residence halls. **Environmental Initiatives:** New buildings are built according to LEED requirements; use of green cleaning chemicals; recycling program on campus—student organized and student run.

ADMISSIONS
Freshman Academic Profile: Average high school GPA 3.55. 24% in top 10% of high school class, 63% in top 25% of high school class, 87% in top 50% of high school class. 79% from public high schools. SAT Math middle 50% range 510–630. SAT Critical Reading middle 50% range 550–650. SAT Writing middle 50% range 510–620. ACT middle 50% range 23–27. Minimum paper TOEFL 550. Minimum computer TOEFL 200. **Basis for Candidate Selection:** *Very important factors considered include:* Academic GPA, rigor of secondary school record, standardized test scores. *Important factors considered include:* Class rank, application essay, recommendation(s), extracurricular activities, interview, level of applicant's interest, volunteer work. *Other factors considered include:* Alumni/ae relation, character/personal qualities, first generation, talent/ability, work experience. **Freshman Admission Requirements:** High school diploma is required and GED is accepted. *Academic units required:* 4 English, 3 mathematics, 2 science, 3 social studies. *Academic units recommended:* 2 foreign language. **Freshman Admission Statistics:** 4,891 applied, 42% admitted, 11% enrolled. **Transfer Admission Requirements:** College transcript(s), statement of good standing from prior institution(s). Minimum college GPA of 2.8 required. Lowest grade transferable C. **General Admission Information:**

Application fee $40. Notification on a rolling basis, beginning on or about 12/1. Nonfall registration accepted. Admission may be deferred for a maximum of 1 year. Credit and/or placement offered for CEEB Advanced Placement tests.

COSTS AND FINANCIAL AID
Annual tuition $26,400. Room and board $9,990. Required fees $250. Average book expense $900. **Required Forms and Deadlines:** FAFSA, institution's own financial aid form **Notification of Awards:** Applicants will be notified of awards on a rolling basis beginning 3/1. **Types of Aid:** *Need-based scholarships/grants:* Federal Pell, SEOG, state scholarships/grants, private scholarships, the school's own gift aid. *Loans:* Direct Subsidized Stafford, Direct Unsubsidized Stafford, Direct PLUS, Federal Perkins. *Student Employment:* Federal Work-Study Program available. Institutional employment available. Off-campus job opportunities are excellent. **Financial Aid Statistics:** 73% freshmen, 57% undergrads receive need-based scholarship or grant aid. 53% freshmen, 41% undergrads receive non-need-based scholarship or grant aid. 66% freshmen, 50% undergrads receive need-based self-help aid. 95% freshmen, 95% undergrads receive any aid. **Criteria for awarding institutional aid:** *Non-need-based:* Academics, music/drama.

OHIO DOMINICAN UNIVERSITY

1216 Sunbury Road, Coumbus, OH 42319-2099
Phone: 614-251-4500 **Financial Aid Phone:** 614-251-4778
E-mail: admissions@ohiodominican.edu **CEEB Code:** 1131
Fax: 614-251-0156 **Website:** www.ohiodominican.edu **ACT Code:** 3256

This private school, affiliated with the Roman Catholic Church, was founded in 1911. It has a 75-acre campus.

RATINGS
Admissions Selectivity Rating: 74 **Fire Safety Rating:** 75 **Green Rating:** 74

STUDENTS AND FACULTY
Enrollment: 1,882. **Student Body:** 60% female, 40% male, 3% out-of-state, 1% international (12 countries represented). Asian 1%, African American 21%, Caucasian 58%, Hispanic 2%.
Retention and Graduation: 61% freshmen return for sophomore year. 30% freshmen graduate within 4 years. **Faculty:** Student/faculty ratio 17:1. 75 full-time faculty, 89% hold PhDs, 5% are are members of minority groups, 51% are women.

ACADEMICS
Degrees: Associate, bachelor's, certificate, master's, transfer associate. **Classes:** Most classes have 10–19 students. **Majors with Highest Enrollment:** Business/commerce; psychology; secondary education and teaching. **Special Study Options:** Accelerated program, cross-registration, distance learning, double major, dual enrollment, exchange student program (domestic), honors program, independent study, internships, study abroad, teacher certification program. **Honors programs:** The Honors Program is designed for high-ability, motivated students. Honors-designed courses will be offered to specifically challenge and engage students in the program. **Career services:** Alumni network, alumni services, career/job search classes, career assessment, internships. **Career services highlights include:** Students gain vital practical experience by participating in internships.

FACILITIES
Housing: Coed dorms. 90% of campus accessible to physically disabled. **Special Academic Facilities/Equipment:** Wehrle Art Gallery. **Computers:** 90% of classrooms, 100% of libraries, 100% of dining areas, 5% of common outdoor areas have wireless network access. Students can register for classes online. Administrative functions (other than registration) can be performed online.

CAMPUS LIFE
Environment: Metropolis. **Activities:** Choral groups, concert band, dance, drama/theater, literary magazine, marching band, music ensembles, musical theater, pep band, radio station, student government, student newspaper, campus ministries, Model UN. **Organizations:** 40 registered organizations, 2 honor societies, 1 religious organizations. **Athletics (Intercollegiate):** *Men:* Baseball, basketball, cross-country, football, golf, soccer, tennis. *Women:* Basketball, cross-country, golf, soccer, softball, tennis, volleyball. **On-Campus Highlights:** Student Center opened Fall 2009, Panther Plaza, Alumni Hall, Wehrle Hall, The Underground in Fitzpatrick Hall. **Environmental Initiatives:** New buildings are to be LEED Silver certified. Recycling program is now in place. Sustainability Council with representation from faculty, staff, and students.

ADMISSIONS
Freshman Academic Profile: Average high school GPA 3.04. 13% in top 10% of high school class, 34% in top 25% of high school class, 62% in top 50% of

high school class. 81% from public high schools. ACT middle 50% range 19–23. Minimum paper TOEFL 550. Minimum computer TOEFL 213. Minimum web-based TOEFL 78. **Basis for Candidate Selection:** *Very important factors considered include:* Academic GPA, rigor of secondary school record. *Important factors considered include:* standardized test scores. *Other factors considered include:* Class rank, application essay, recommendation(s), character/personal qualities, extracurricular activities, interview, talent/ability, volunteer work, work experience. **Freshman Admission Requirements:** High school diploma is required and GED is accepted. *Academic units recommended:* 4 English, 4 mathematics, 3 science, 3 foreign language, 3 social studies. **Freshman Admission Statistics:** 2,367 applied, 59% admitted, 20% enrolled, **Transfer Admission Requirements:** College transcript(s), Lowest grade transferable C. **General Admission Information:** Application fee $25. Notification on a rolling basis, beginning on or about 9/4. Nonfall registration accepted. Admission may be deferred for a maximum of 1 year. Credit and/or placement offered for CEEB Advanced Placement tests.

COSTS AND FINANCIAL AID

Annual tuition $24,116. Room and board $7,900. Required fees $500. Average book expense $1,000. **Required Forms and Deadlines:** FAFSA. Priority financial aid filing date 4/1. **Notification of Awards:** Applicants will be notified of awards on a rolling basis beginning 3/1. *Types of Aid: Need-based scholarships/grants:* Federal Pell, SEOG, state scholarships/grants, private scholarships, the school's own gift aid. *Loans:* FFEL Subsidized Stafford, FFEL Unsubsidized Stafford, FFEL PLUS, Federal Perkins. *Student Employment:* Federal Work-Study Program available. Off-campus job opportunities are good. **Financial Aid Statistics:** 98% freshmen, 88% undergrads receive any aid. 59% undergrads borrow to pay for school. **Criteria for awarding institutional aid:** *Non-need-based:* Academics, athletics, music/drama.

OHIO NORTHERN UNIVERSITY

525 South Main Street, Ada, OH 45810
Phone: 419-772-2260 **Financial Aid Phone:** 419-772-2272
E-mail: admissions-ug@onu.edu **CEEB Code:** 1591
Fax: 419-772-2821 **Website:** www.onu.edu **ACT Code:** 3310

This private school, affiliated with the Methodist Church, was founded in 1871. It has a 300-acre campus.

RATINGS
Admissions Selectivity Rating: 84   **Fire Safety Rating:** 60*   **Green Rating:** 60*

STUDENTS AND FACULTY
Enrollment: 2,591. **Student Body:** 47% female, 53% male, 14% out-of-state, 2% international (18 countries represented). Asian 2%, African American 4%, Caucasian 90%, Hispanic 2%.
Retention and Graduation: 86% freshmen return for sophomore year. 50% freshmen graduate within 4 years. **Faculty:** Student/faculty ratio 13:1. 235 full-time faculty, 79% hold PhDs, 10% are are members of minority groups, 37% are women.

ACADEMICS
Degrees: Bachelor's, post-bachelor's certificate. **Classes:** Most classes have 20–29 students. **Majors with Highest Enrollment:** Biological and biomedical sciences, other; business, management, marketing, and related support services, other; engineering. **Special Study Options:** Cooperative education program, distance learning, double major, dual enrollment, English as a Second Language (ESL), exchange student program (domestic), honors program, independent study, internships, liberal arts/career combination, study abroad, teacher certification program, Washington semester. **Honors programs:** Honors Program consisits of a First-Year Honors Seminar and 3 additional Honors Seminars, 2 "contract" courses and a final Honors project. **Combined degree programs:** BA/JD, Pharm D. Special programs offered to physically disabled students include note-taking services, reader services, tape recorders, tutors. **Career services:** Alumni network, alumni services, career/job search classes, career assessment, internships.

FACILITIES
Housing: Coed dorms, special housing for disabled students, men's dorms, special housing for international students, women's dorms, fraternity/sorority housing, apartments for married students, cooperative housing, apartments for single students, wellness house, theme housing, Honors Residence Halls. 95% of campus accessible to physically disabled. **Special Academic Facilities/Equipment:** Art gallery, performing arts center, language lab, sports center, pharmacy museum. **Computers:** 100% of classrooms, 100% of dorms, 100% of libraries, 100% of dining areas, 100% of student union, have wireless network access. Students can register for classes online. Administrative functions (other than registration) can be performed online.

CAMPUS LIFE
Environment: Village. **Activities:** Choral groups, concert band, dance, drama/theater, jazz band, literary magazine, marching band, music ensembles, musical theater, opera, pep band, radio station, student government, student newspaper, symphony orchestra, television station, yearbook, campus ministries, international student organization, Model UN. **Organizations:** 200 registered organizations, 40 honor societies, 27 religious organizations. 6 fraternities, 4 sororities. **Athletics (Intercollegiate):** *Men:* Baseball, basketball, cross-country, diving, football, golf, soccer, swimming, tennis, track/field (outdoor), track/field (indoor), wrestling. *Women:* Basketball, cross-country, diving, golf, soccer, softball, swimming, tennis, track/field (outdoor), track/field (indoor), volleyball. **On-Campus Highlights:** ONU Sports Center, Northern on Main Coffee Cafe, Performing Arts Center, New Student Apartments, James F. Dicke Hall.

ADMISSIONS
Freshman Academic Profile: Average high school GPA 3.62. 41% in top 10% of high school class, 69% in top 25% of high school class, 89% in top 50% of high school class. SAT Math middle 50% range 530–650. SAT Critical Reading middle 50% range 500–620. SAT Writing middle 50% range 490–620. ACT middle 50% range 23–28. Minimum paper TOEFL 480. Minimum computer TOEFL 157. Minimum web-based TOEFL 54. **Basis for Candidate Selection:** *Very important factors considered include:* Academic GPA, rigor of secondary school record, standardized test scores. *Important factors considered include:* Class rank, extracurricular activities, interview. *Other factors considered include:* Application essay, recommendation(s), alumni/ae relation, character/personal qualities, first generation, level of applicant's interest, talent/ability, volunteer work. **Freshman Admission Requirements:** High school diploma is required and GED is accepted. *Academic units required:* 4 English, 2 mathematics, 2 science, (2 science labs), 2 social studies, 2 history, 4 academic electives. *Academic units recommended:* 4 English, 4 mathematics, 3 science, (2 science labs), 2 foreign language, 3 social studies, 2 history, 1 visual/performing arts, 1 computer science, 4 academic electives. **Freshman Admission Statistics:** 3,032 applied, 88% admitted, 28% enrolled. **Transfer Admission Requirements:** High school transcript, college transcript(s), statement of good standing from prior institution(s). Minimum college GPA of 2.0 required. Lowest grade transferable C. **General Admission Information:** Application fee $30. Regular application deadline 8/15. Notification on a rolling basis, beginning on or about 7/15. Nonfall registration accepted. Admission may be deferred for a maximum of 1 year. Credit and/or placement offered for CEEB Advanced Placement tests.

COSTS AND FINANCIAL AID
Annual tuition $31,626. Room and board $8,280. Required fees $240. Average book expense $1,800. **Required Forms and Deadlines:** FAFSA. Financial aid filing deadline 6/1. Priority financial aid filing date 4/15. **Notification of Awards:** Applicants will be notified of awards on a rolling basis beginning 3/1. **Types of Aid:** *Need-based scholarships/grants:* Federal Pell, SEOG, state scholarships/grants, private scholarships, the school's own gift aid, External Scholarships. *Loans:* FFEL Subsidized Stafford, FFEL Unsubsidized Stafford, FFEL PLUS, Federal Perkins, college/university loans from institutional funds, alternative loans, Federal Health Professions Loan. *Student Employment:* Federal Work-Study Program available. Institutional employment available. Off-campus job opportunities are good. **Financial Aid Statistics:** 79% freshmen, 55% undergrads receive need-based scholarship or grant aid. 43% freshmen, 30% undergrads receive non-need-based scholarship or grant aid. 62% freshmen, 61% undergrads receive need-based self-help aid. 83% undergrads borrow to pay for school. Average cumulative indebtedness $45,753. **Criteria for awarding institutional aid:** *Non-need-based:* Academics, alumni affiliation, art, leadership, minority status, music/drama, state/district residency.

See page 1190.

THE OHIO STATE UNIVERSITY—NEWARK

1179 University Drive, Newark, OH 43055
Phone: 740-366-9333 **Financial Aid Phone:** 614-292-0300
E-mail: donahue.5@osu.edu **CEEB Code:** 752
Fax: 740-364-9645 **Website:** www.newark.ohio-state.edu **ACT Code:** 3312

This public school was founded in 1957. It has a 106-acre campus.

RATINGS
Admissions Selectivity Rating: 61   **Fire Safety Rating:** 78   **Green Rating:** 60*

STUDENTS AND FACULTY
Enrollment: 2,321. **Student Body:** 50% female, 50% male, 5% out-of-state, (1 countries represented). Asian 3%, African American 11%, Caucasian 82%, Hispanic 2%.
Retention and Graduation: 64% freshmen return for sophomore year. 13% freshmen graduate within 4 years. **Faculty:** Student/faculty ratio 19:1. 53 full-time faculty, 98% hold PhDs, 13% are members of minority groups, 40% are women. 1% of classes are taught by teaching assistants.

ACADEMICS
Degrees: Associate, bachelor's, master's. **Classes:** Most classes have 20–29 students. Most lab/discussion sessions have 20–29 students. **Majors with Highest Enrollment:** Elementary education and teaching; nursing/registered nurse (RN, ASN, BSN, MSN); psychology. **Special Study Options:** Accelerated program, cooperative education program, cross-registration, distance learning, double major, dual enrollment, English as a Second Language (ESL), exchange student program (domestic), honors program, independent study, internships, liberal arts/career combination, student-designed major, study abroad, teacher certification program, weekend college. **Honors programs:** The University Honors Program is dedicated to promoting the intellectual and personal development of high-performing students. It strives to promote a more active and enriching relationship between Honors students and the University by connecting them with resources and opportunities that will encourage them to maximize their potential. The University Scholars Program enables talented and motivated students to be part of smaller, selective communnities within the larger university environment. Each of the fourteen programs focuses on a common theme or academic area of interest designed to foster learning and involvement. Scholars live together, attend classes together, and experience diverse opportunities outside the classroom. **Combined degree programs:** BA/MD, BA/DDS, BA/MEng. Special programs offered to physically disabled students include note-taking services, reader services, tape recorders, tutors. **Career services:** career assessment, internships.

FACILITIES
Housing: Coed dorms, apartments for single students, wellness housing 100% of campus accessible to physically disabled. **Computers:** 100% of classrooms, 100% of dorms, 100% of libraries, 100% of dining areas, 100% of student union, have wireless network access. Students can register for classes online. Administrative functions (other than registration) can be performed online.

CAMPUS LIFE
Environment: Village. **Activities:** Choral groups, drama/theater, literary magazine, music ensembles, student government, campus ministries. **Organizations:** 33 registered organizations, 2 honor societies, 2 religious organizations. **Athletics (Intercollegiate):** *Men:* Basketball, golf, soccer. *Women:* Basketball, soccer, softball, volleyball.

ADMISSIONS
Freshman Academic Profile: 4% in top 10% of high school class, 21% in top 25% of high school class, 56% in top 50% of high school class. SAT Math middle 50% range 450–560. SAT Critical Reading middle 50% range 440–540. SAT Writing middle 50% range 440–540. ACT middle 50% range 19–23. Minimum paper TOEFL 527. Minimum computer TOEFL 197. Minimum web-based TOEFL 71. **Basis for Candidate Selection:** *Other factors considered include:* Recommendation(s), rigor of secondary school record. **Freshman Admission Requirements:** High school diploma is required and GED is accepted. *Academic units required:* 4 English, 3 mathematics, 2 science, (2 science labs), 2 foreign language, 2 social studies, 1 academic electives, 1 visual/performing arts. *Academic units recommended:* 4 English, 4 mathematics, 3 science, (3 science labs), 3 foreign language, 3 social studies, 1 academic electives, 1 visual/performing arts. **Freshman Admission Statistics:** 2,282 applied, 99% admitted, 48% enrolled. **Transfer Admission Requirements:** College transcript(s), minimum college GPA of 2.0 required. Lowest grade transferable C–. **General Admission Information:** Application fee $40. Regular application deadline 7/1. Notification on a rolling basis, beginning on or about 12/1. Nonfall registration accepted. Credit and/or placement offered for CEEB Advanced Placement tests.

COSTS AND FINANCIAL AID
Average book expense $1,440. **Required Forms and Deadlines:** FAFSA. Priority financial aid filing date 2/15. **Notification of Awards:** Applicants will be notified of awards on or about 4/5. **Types of Aid:** *Need-based scholarships/grants:* Federal Pell, SEOG, state scholarships/grants, private scholarships, the school's own gift aid. *Loans:* Direct Subsidized Stafford, Direct Unsubsidized Stafford, Direct PLUS, Federal Perkins, Federal Nursing, college/university loans from institutional funds. *Student Employment:* Federal Work-Study Program available. Institutional employment available. Off-campus job opportunities are good. **Financial Aid Statistics:** 40% freshmen, 53% undergrads receive need-based scholarship or grant aid. 1% freshmen, 4% undergrads receive non-need-based scholarship or grant aid. 65% freshmen, 71% undergrads receive need-based self-help aid. 84% freshmen, 82% undergrads receive any aid. **Criteria for awarding institutional aid:** *Non-need-based:* Academics, alumni affiliation, art, athletics, job skills, leadership, minority status, music/drama, state/district residency.

THE OHIO STATE UNIVERSITY AT LIMA

4240 Campus Drive, Lima, OH 45804-3596
Phone: 419-995-8434 **Financial Aid Phone:** 614-688-5712
E-mail: admissions@lima.ohio-state.edu **CEEB Code:** 1541
Fax: 419-995-8483 **Website:** www.lima.ohio-state.edu **ACT Code:** 3312

This public school was founded in 1960. It has a 565-acre campus.

RATINGS
Admissions Selectivity Rating: 62   **Fire Safety Rating:** 60*   **Green Rating:** 60*

STUDENTS AND FACULTY
Enrollment: 1,342. **Student Body:** 53% female, 47% male, 1% out-of-state, Asian 2%, African American 4%, Caucasian 90%, Hispanic 2%, Native American 1%.
Retention and Graduation: 13% freshmen graduate within 4 years. **Faculty:** Student/faculty ratio 17:1. 39 full-time faculty, 97% hold PhDs, 13% are members of minority groups, 36% are women.

ACADEMICS
Degrees: Associate, bachelor's, master's. **Classes:** Most classes have 20–29 students. Most lab/discussion sessions have 20–29 students. **Majors with Highest Enrollment:** Biology/biological sciences; elementary education and teaching; psychology. **Special Study Options:** Accelerated program, cooperative education program, cross-registration, distance learning, double major, dual enrollment, English as a Second Language (ESL), exchange student program (domestic), honors program, independent study, internships, liberal arts/career combination, student-designed major, study abroad, teacher certification program, weekend college. **Honors programs:** The University Honors Program is dedicated to promoting the intellectual and personal development of high-performing students. It strives to promote a more active and enriching relationship between Honors students and the University by connecting them with resources and opportunities that will encourage them to maximize their potential. The University Scholars Program enables talented and motivated students to be part of smaller, selective communnities within the larger university environment. Each of the fourteen programs focuses on a common theme or academic area of interest designed to foster learning and involvement. Scholars live together, attend classes together, and experience diverse opportunities outside the classroom. Special programs offered to physically disabled students include note-taking services, reader services, tape recorders, tutors. **Career services:** Alumni network, alumni services, career/job search classes, career assessment, internships, regional alumni.

FACILITIES
Housing: 100% of campus accessible to physically disabled. **Special Academic Facilities/Equipment:** OhioSeis seismological network; Geological Museum; observatory. **Computers:** 75% of classrooms, 100% of libraries, 100% of dining areas, 100% of student union, 100% of common outdoor areas have wireless network access. Students can register for classes online. Administrative functions (other than registration) can be performed online.

CAMPUS LIFE
Environment: Rural. **Activities:** Choral groups, dance, drama/theater, musical theater, pep band, student government, student-run film society, campus ministries, international student organization. **Organizations:** 32 registered organizations, 1 honor societies, 2 religious organizations.

ADMISSIONS
Freshman Academic Profile: 7% in top 10% of high school class, 22% in top 25% of high school class, 58% in top 50% of high school class. 95% from public high schools. SAT Math middle 50% range 490–637. SAT Critical Reading

middle 50% range 472–572. SAT Writing middle 50% range 432.5–560. ACT middle 50% range 19–24. Minimum paper TOEFL 527. Minimum computer TOEFL 197. Minimum web-based TOEFL 71. **Basis for Candidate Selection:** *Other factors considered include:* Recommendation(s), rigor of secondary school record. **Freshman Admission Requirements:** *Academic units required:* 4 English, 3 mathematics, 2 science, (2 science labs), 2 foreign language, 2 social studies, 1 visual/performing arts, 1 academic electives. *Academic units recommended:* 4 English, 4 mathematics, 3 science, (3 science labs), 3 foreign language, 3 social studies, 1 visual/performing arts, 1 academic electives. **Freshman Admission Statistics:** 996 applied, 98% admitted, 49% enrolled. **Transfer Admission Requirements:** College transcript(s), minimum college GPA of 2.0 required. Lowest grade transferable C–. **General Admission Information:** Application fee $40. Regular application deadline 7/1. Notification on a rolling basis, beginning on or about 12/1. Credit and/or placement offered for CEEB Advanced Placement tests.

COSTS AND FINANCIAL AID

Average book expense $1,440. **Required Forms and Deadlines:** FAFSA. Priority financial aid filing date 2/15. **Notification of Awards:** Applicants will be notified of awards on or about 4/5. **Types of Aid:** *Need-based scholarships/ grants:* Federal Pell, SEOG, state scholarships/grants, private scholarships, the school's own gift aid. *Loans:* Direct Subsidized Stafford, Direct Unsubsidized Stafford, Direct PLUS, Federal Perkins, Federal Nursing, college/university loans from institutional funds. *Student Employment:* Federal Work-Study Program available. Institutional employment available. Off-campus job opportunities are good. **Financial Aid Statistics:** 60% freshmen, 53% undergrads receive need-based scholarship or grant aid. 7% freshmen, 4% undergrads receive non-need-based scholarship or grant aid. 71% freshmen, 71% undergrads receive need-based self-help aid. 95% freshmen, 91% undergrads receive any aid. **Criteria for awarding institutional aid:** *Non-need-based:* Academics, alumni affiliation, art, athletics, job skills, leadership, minority status, music/ drama, state/district residency.

THE OHIO STATE UNIVERSITY AT MANSFIELD

1680 University Drive, Mansfield, OH 44906
Phone: 419-755-4011 **Financial Aid Phone:** 614-292-0300
E-mail: admissions@mansfield.ohio-state.edu **CEEB Code:** 744
Fax: Website: www.mansfield.ohio-stae.edu **ACT Code:** 3312

This public school was founded in 1958. It has a 640-acre campus.

RATINGS
Admissions Selectivity Rating: 62　　**Fire Safety Rating:** 67　　**Green Rating:** 70

STUDENTS AND FACULTY
Enrollment: 1,274. **Student Body:** 54% female, 46% male, 1% out-of-state, international (3 countries represented). Asian 2%, African American 7%, Caucasian 86%, Hispanic 2%, Native American 1%.
Retention and Graduation: 69% freshmen return for sophomore year. 9% freshmen graduate within 4 years. **Faculty:** Student/faculty ratio 18:1. 46 full-time faculty, 98% hold PhDs, 9% are members of minority groups, 46% are women.

ACADEMICS
Degrees: Associate, bachelor's, master's. **Classes:** Most classes have 10–19 students. Most lab/discussion sessions have 40–49 students. **Special Study Options:** Accelerated program, cooperative education program, cross-registration, distance learning, double major, dual enrollment, English as a Second Language (ESL), exchange student program (domestic), honors program, independent study, internships, liberal arts/career combination, student-designed major, study abroad, teacher certification program, weekend college. **Honors programs:** The University Honors Program is dedicated to promoting the intellectual and personal development of high-performing students. It strives to promote a more active and enriching relationship between Honors students and the University by connecting them with resources and opportunities that will encourage them to maximize their potential. The University Scholars Program enables talented and motivated students to be part of smaller, selective communnities within the larger university environment. Each of the fourteen programs focuses on a common theme or academic area of interest designed to foster learning and involvement. Scholars live together, attend classes together, and experience diverse opportunities outside the classroom. **Combined degree programs:** BA/MD, BA/DDS. Special programs offered to physically disabled students include note-taking services, reader services, tape recorders, tutors. **Career services:** Alumni network, alumni services.

FACILITIES
Housing: Special housing for disabled students, apartments for single students, wellness housing. 90% of campus accessible to physically disabled. **Computers:** 100% of classrooms, 100% of dorms, 100% of libraries, 100% of dining areas, 100% of student union, 50% of common outdoor areas have wireless network access. Students can register for classes online. Administrative functions (other than registration) can be performed online.

CAMPUS LIFE
Environment: Town. **Activities:** Choral groups, dance, drama/theater, student newspaper, student-run film society **Organizations:** 16 registered organizations, 2 honor societies, 2 religious organizations. **Athletics (Intercollegiate):** *Men:* Baseball, basketball, soccer. *Women:* Basketball, cheerleading, volleyball. **Environmental Initiatives:** Pursuing HB7 energy savings performance contract; aggressive recycling program; wetlands reclamation, enhancements, and outdoor laboratory.

ADMISSIONS
Freshman Academic Profile: 8% in top 10% of high school class, 29% in top 25% of high school class, 68% in top 50% of high school class. SAT Math middle 50% range 460–580. SAT Critical Reading middle 50% range 450–557. SAT Writing middle 50% range 440–537. ACT middle 50% range 20–24. Minimum paper TOEFL 527. Minimum computer TOEFL 197. Minimum web-based TOEFL 71. **Basis for Candidate Selection:** *Other factors considered include:* Recommendation(s), rigor of secondary school record. **Freshman Admission Requirements:** *Academic units required:* 4 English, 3 mathematics, 2 science, (2 science labs), 2 foreign language, 2 social studies, 1 visual/performing arts, 1 academic electives. *Academic units recommended:* 4 English, 4 mathematics, 3 science, (3 science labs), 3 foreign language, 3 social studies, 1 visual/performing arts, 1 academic electives. **Freshman Admission Statistics:** 1,132 applied, 99% admitted, 44% enrolled. **Transfer Admission Requirements:** College transcript(s), minimum college GPA of 2.0 required. Lowest grade transferable C–. **General Admission Information:** Application fee $40. Regular application deadline 7/1. Notification on a rolling basis, beginning on or about 12/1. Nonfall registration accepted. Credit and/or placement offered for CEEB Advanced Placement tests.

COSTS AND FINANCIAL AID
Room and board $5,205. Average book expense $1,440. **Required Forms and Deadlines:** FAFSA. Priority financial aid filing date 3/1. **Notification of Awards:** Applicants will be notified of awards on or about 4/5. **Types of Aid:** *Need-based scholarships/grants:* Federal Pell, SEOG, state scholarships/grants, private scholarships, the school's own gift aid. *Loans:* Direct Subsidized Stafford, Direct Unsubsidized Stafford, Direct PLUS, Federal Perkins, Federal Nursing, college/university loans from institutional funds. *Student Employment:* Federal Work-Study Program available. Institutional employment available. Off-campus job opportunities are good. **Financial Aid Statistics:** 49% freshmen, 52% undergrads receive need-based scholarship or grant aid. 2% freshmen, 2% undergrads receive non-need-based scholarship or grant aid. 68% freshmen, 71% undergrads receive need-based self-help aid. 91% freshmen, 89% undergrads receive any aid. **Criteria for awarding institutional aid:** *Non-need-based:* Academics, alumni affiliation, art, athletics, job skills, leadership, minority status, music/drama, state/district residency.

THE OHIO STATE UNIVERSITY AT MARION

1465 Mount Vernon Avenue, Marion, OH 43302
Phone: 740-725-6337
E-mail: moreau.1@osu.edu **CEEB Code:** 752
Fax: Website: www.marion.ohio-state.edu **ACT Code:** 3312

This public school was founded in 1957. It has a 188-acre campus.

RATINGS
Admissions Selectivity Rating: 62　　**Fire Safety Rating:** 60*　　**Green Rating:** 60*

STUDENTS AND FACULTY
Enrollment: 1,681. **Student Body:** 54% female, 46% male, internationalAsian 5%, African American 8%, Caucasian 83%, Hispanic 2%, Native American 1%. **Retention and Graduation:** 14% freshmen graduate within 4 years. **Faculty:** Student/faculty ratio 16:1. 38 full-time faculty, 97% hold PhDs, 11% are members of minority groups, 37% are women.

ACADEMICS
Degrees: Associate, bachelor's, master's. **Classes:** Most classes have 20–29 students. Most lab/discussion sessions have 20–29 students. **Special Study Options:** Accelerated program, cooperative education program, cross-registration, distance learning, double major, dual enrollment, English as a Second

Language (ESL), exchange student program (domestic), honors program, independent study, internships, liberal arts/career combination, student-designed major, study abroad, teacher certification program, weekend college. **Honors programs:** The University Honors Program is dedicated to promoting the intellectual and personal development of high-performing students. It strives to promote a more active and enriching relationship between Honors students and the University by connecting them with resources and opportunities that will encourage them to maximize their potential. The University Scholars Program enables talented and motivated students to be part of smaller, selective communities within the larger university environment. Each of the fourteen programs focuses on a common theme or academic area of interest designed to foster learning and involvement. Scholars live together, attend classes together, and experience diverse opportunities outside the classroom. **Combined degree programs:** BA/MD, BA/DDS, BA/MEng. Special programs offered to physically disabled students include note-taking services, reader services, tape recorders, tutors. **Career services:** Alumni network, alumni services, career/job search classes, career assessment, internships, regional alumni.

FACILITIES

Housing: 100% of campus accessible to physically disabled. **Special Academic Facilities/Equipment:** Kuhn Art Gallery **Computers:** 100% of classrooms, 100% of libraries, have wireless network access. Students can register for classes online. Administrative functions (other than registration) can be performed online.

CAMPUS LIFE

Environment: Town. **Activities:** Choral groups, literary magazine, music ensembles, student government, campus ministries. **Organizations:** 33 registered organizations, 1 honor societies, 3 religious organizations. **Athletics (Intercollegiate):** *Men:* Basketball, gymnastics, volleyball. *Women:* Gymnastics.

ADMISSIONS

Freshman Academic Profile: 7% in top 10% of high school class, 28% in top 25% of high school class, 67% in top 50% of high school class. 98% from public high schools. SAT Math middle 50% range 470–590. SAT Critical Reading middle 50% range 440–550. SAT Writing middle 50% range 440–540. ACT middle 50% range 19–24. Minimum paper TOEFL 527. Minimum computer TOEFL 197. Minimum web-based TOEFL 71. **Basis for Candidate Selection:** *Other factors considered include:* Recommendation(s), rigor of secondary school record. **Freshman Admission Requirements:** *Academic units required:* 4 English, 3 mathematics, 2 science, (2 science labs), 2 foreign language, 2 social studies, 1 visual/performing arts, 1 academic electives. *Academic units recommended:* 4 English, 4 mathematics, 3 science, (3 science labs), 3 foreign language, 3 social studies, 1 visual/performing arts, 1 academic electives. **Freshman Admission Statistics:** 980 applied, 98% admitted, 52% enrolled. **Transfer Admission Requirements:** College transcript(s), minimum college GPA of 2.0 required. Lowest grade transferable C–. **General Admission Information:** Application fee $40. Regular application deadline 7/1. Regular notification 12/1. Nonfall registration accepted. Credit and/or placement offered for CEEB Advanced Placement tests.

COSTS AND FINANCIAL AID

Annual in-state tuition $5,661. Annual out-of-state tuition $19,233. Average book expense $1,440. **Required Forms and Deadlines:** FAFSA. Priority financial aid filing date 3/1. **Notification of Awards:** Applicants will be notified of awards on or about 4/5. **Types of Aid:** *Need-based scholarships/grants:* Federal Pell, SEOG, state scholarships/grants, private scholarships, the school's own gift aid. *Loans:* Direct Subsidized Stafford, Direct Unsubsidized Stafford, Direct PLUS, Federal Perkins, Federal Nursing, college/university loans from institutional funds. *Student Employment:* Federal Work-Study Program available. Institutional employment available. Off-campus job opportunities are good. **Financial Aid Statistics:** 49% freshmen, 49% undergrads receive need-based scholarship or grant aid. 2% freshmen, 2% undergrads receive non-need-based scholarship or grant aid. 59% freshmen, 63% undergrads receive need-based self-help aid. 65% freshmen, 67% undergrads receive any aid. **Criteria for awarding institutional aid:** *Non-need-based:* Academics, alumni affiliation, art, athletics, job skills, leadership, minority status, music/drama, state/district residency.

THE OHIO STATE UNIVERSITY—COLUMBUS

Undergraduate Admissions 110 Enarson Hall, 154 W. 12th Avenue, Columbus, OH 43210
Phone: 614-292-3980 **Financial Aid Phone:** 614-292-0300
E-mail: askabuckeye@osu.edu **CEEB Code:** 1592
Fax: 614-292-4818 **Website:** www.osu.edu **ACT Code:** 3312

This public school was founded in 1870. It has a 3469-acre campus.

RATINGS

Admissions Selectivity Rating: 86   **Fire Safety Rating:** 77   **Green Rating:** 96

STUDENTS AND FACULTY

Enrollment: 39,065. **Student Body:** 45% female, 55% male, 11% out-of-state, 4% international (110 countries represented). Asian 6%, African American 7%, Caucasian 81%, Hispanic 3%.
Retention and Graduation: 46% freshmen graduate within 4 years. **Faculty:** Student/faculty ratio 12:1. 3310 full-time faculty, 99% hold PhDs, 20% are members of minority groups, 32% are women. 18% of classes are taught by teaching assistants.

ACADEMICS

Degrees: Associate, bachelor's, certificate, doctoral, master's, post-bachelor's certificate, post-master's certificate. **Classes:** Most classes have 20–29 students. Most lab/discussion sessions have 20–29 students. **Majors with Highest Enrollment:** Biology/biological sciences; finance; political science and government. **Special Study Options:** Accelerated program, cooperative education program, cross-registration, distance learning, double major, dual enrollment, English as a Second Language (ESL), exchange student program (domestic), honors program, independent study, internships, liberal arts/career combination, student-designed major, study abroad, teacher certification program, weekend college. **Honors programs:** The University Honors Program is dedicated to promoting the intellectual and personal development of high-performing students. It strives to promote a more active and enriching relationship between Honors students and the University by connecting them with resources and opportunities that will encourage them to maximize their potential. The University Scholars Program enables talented and motivated students to be part of smaller, selective communities within the larger university environment. Each of the fourteen programs focuses on a common theme or academic area of interest designed to foster learning and involvement. Scholars live together, attend classes together, and experience diverse opportunities outside the classroom. **Combined degree programs:** BA/MD, BA/DDS. Special programs offered to physically disabled students include note-taking services, reader services, tape recorders, tutors. **Career services:** Alumni network, alumni services, career/job search classes, career assessment, internships, regional alumni.

FACILITIES

Housing: Coed dorms, special housing for disabled students, special housing for international students, women's dorms, fraternity/sorority housing, apartments for married students, cooperative housing, apartments for single students, wellness housing, theme housing. 90% of campus accessible to physically disabled. **Special Academic Facilities/Equipment:** Wexner center for the Arts, zoology museum, geology museum, art and photography galleries, nuclear research reactor, electroscience lab, biomedical engineering center, cartoon art museum. **Computers:** 100% of dorms, 90% of libraries, 100% of dining areas, 100% of student union, 4% of common outdoor areas have wireless network access. Students can register for classes online. Administrative functions (other than registration) can be performed online.

CAMPUS LIFE

Environment: Metropolis. **Activities:** Choral groups, dance, drama/theater, jazz band, literary magazine, marching band, music ensembles, musical theater, opera, pep band, radio station, student government, student newspaper, student-run film society, symphony orchestra, television station, yearbook, international student organization. **Organizations:** 950 registered organizations, 39 honor societies, 93 religious organizations. 42 fraternities, 25 sororities. **Athletics (Intercollegiate):** *Men:* Baseball, basketball, cheerleading, cross-country, diving, fencing, football, golf, gymnastics, ice hockey, lacrosse, pistol, riflery, soccer, swimming, tennis, track/field (outdoor), track/field (indoor), volleyball, wrestling. *Women:* Baseball, basketball, cheerleading, crew/rowing, cross-country, diving, fencing, field hockey, golf, gymnastics, ice hockey, lacrosse, pistol, riflery, soccer, softball, swimming, synchronized swimming, tennis, track/field (outdoor), track/field (indoor). **On-Campus Highlights:** Hale Cultural Center, Chadwick Arboretum, Jack Nicklaus Golf Museum, Schottenstein Center and

Value City Arena, Wexner Center for the Arts. **Environmental Initiatives:** Building Energy Auditing Program All-In-One Campus Recycling System Sustainability Education, Research and Outreach

ADMISSIONS

Freshman Academic Profile: 49% in top 10% of high school class, 85% in top 25% of high school class, 99% in top 50% of high school class. 87% from public high schools. SAT Math middle 50% range 580–690. SAT Critical Reading middle 50% range 540–650. SAT Writing middle 50% range 540–640. ACT middle 50% range 25–30. Minimum paper TOEFL 527. Minimum computer TOEFL 197. Minimum web-based TOEFL 71. **Basis for Candidate Selection:** *Very important factors considered include:* Class rank, academic GPA, rigor of secondary school record, standardized test scores. *Important factors considered include:* Application essay, extracurricular activities, first generation, talent/ability, volunteer work, work experience. *Other factors considered include:* Recommendation(s), character/personal qualities, geographical residence, racial/ethnic status, state residency. **Freshman Admission Requirements:** High school diploma is required and GED is accepted. *Academic units required:* 4 English, 3 mathematics, 2 science, (2 science labs), 2 foreign language, 2 social studies, 1 visual/performing arts, 1 academic electives. *Academic units recommended:* 4 English, 4 mathematics, 3 science, (3 science labs), 3 foreign language, 3 social studies, 1 visual/performing arts, 1 academic electives. **Freshman Admission Statistics:** 18,256 applied, 76% admitted, 49% enrolled. **Transfer Admission Requirements:** College transcript(s), minimum college GPA of 2.0 required. Lowest grade transferable C–. **General Admission Information:** Application fee $40. Regular application deadline 2/1. Notification on a rolling basis, beginning on or about 12/1. Nonfall registration accepted. Credit and/or placement offered for CEEB Advanced Placement tests.

COSTS AND FINANCIAL AID

Average book expense $1,440. **Required Forms and Deadlines:** FAFSA. Priority financial aid filing date 2/15. **Notification of Awards:** Applicants will be notified of awards on or about 4/5. **Types of Aid:** *Need-based scholarships/grants:* Federal Pell, SEOG, state scholarships/grants, private scholarships, the school's own gift aid. *Loans:* Direct Subsidized Stafford, Direct Unsubsidized Stafford, Direct PLUS, Federal Perkins, Federal Nursing, college/university loans from institutional funds. *Student Employment:* Federal Work-Study Program available. Institutional employment available. Off-campus job opportunities are good. **Financial Aid Statistics:** 36% freshmen, 33% undergrads receive need-based scholarship or grant aid. 11% freshmen, 6% undergrads receive non-need-based scholarship or grant aid. 52% freshmen, 52% undergrads receive need-based self-help aid. 1% freshmen, 1% undergrads receive athletic scholarships. 93% freshmen, 83% undergrads receive any aid. 54% undergrads borrow to pay for school. Average cumulative indebtedness $18,426. **Criteria for awarding institutional aid:** *Non-need-based:* Academics, alumni affiliation, art, athletics, job skills, leadership, minority status, music/drama, state/district residency.

OHIO UNIVERSITY—ATHENS

120 Chubb Hall, Athens, OH 45701
Phone: 740-593-4100 **Financial Aid Phone:** 740-593-4141
E-mail: admissions@ohio.edu **CEEB Code:** 1593
Fax: 740-593-0560 **Website:** www.ohio.edu **ACT Code:** 3314

This public school was founded in 1804. It has a 1762-acre campus.

RATINGS

Admissions Selectivity Rating: 75   **Fire Safety Rating:** 69   **Green Rating:** 84

STUDENTS AND FACULTY

Enrollment: 18,350. **Student Body:** 52% female, 48% male, 8% out-of-state, 3% international (104 countries represented). Asian 1%, African American 5%, Caucasian 88%, Hispanic 2%.
Retention and Graduation: 82% freshmen return for sophomore year. 48% freshmen graduate within 4 years. 28% grads go on to further study within 1 year. 10% grads pursue arts and sciences degrees. 2% grads pursue law degrees. 2% grads pursue business degrees. 2% grads pursue medical degrees. **Faculty:** Student/faculty ratio 19:1. 907 full-time faculty, 86% hold PhDs, 19% are members of minority groups, 37% are women. 15% of classes are taught by teaching assistants.

ACADEMICS

Degrees: Associate, bachelor's, master's. **Classes:** Most classes have 10–19 students. Most lab/discussion sessions have 10–19 students. **Majors with Highest Enrollment:** Biology/biological sciences; journalism; kinesiology and exercise science. **Special Study Options:** Accelerated program, cooperative education program, cross-registration, distance learning, double major, dual enrollment, English as a Second Language (ESL), external degree program, honors program, independent study, internships, liberal arts/career combination, student-designed major, study abroad, teacher certification program. **Honors programs:** Honors Tutorial College: The most selective of Ohio University's nine undergraduate colleges the Honor's Tutorial College is the oldest, largest, and most academically diverse degree-only degree-granting college in the country. Based on Oxbridge systems of tutorial education developed in England, it offers highly motivated, talented students the opportunity to receive a substantial part of their education through tutorials (one-on-one classes or small seminars). There are generally 220 students in the Honors Tutorial College spread over 26 programs of study. To preserve the tutorial experience, HTC enrolls about 60 new students each year, and admission is highly competitive. Special programs offered to physically disabled students include reader services, tape recorders, tutors. **Career services:** Alumni network, alumni services, career/job search classes, career assessment, regional alumni. **Career services highlights include:** Most internships/co-ops are through college departments as our office focuses on full-time positions.

FACILITIES

Housing: Coed dorms, special housing for disabled students, special housing for international students, women's dorms, apartments for married students. 89% of campus accessible to physically disabled. **Special Academic Facilities/Equipment:** Museum of American Art, Innovation Center, Nuclear Accelerator, Electron Microscope, Biotech Center, Kennedy Museum of Art, Trisolini Gallery, Art Gallery in Multicultural Programs, Voinovich Center, & Academic & Research Center. **Computers:** 100% of classrooms, 100% of dorms, 100% of libraries, 100% of dining areas, 100% of student union, 100% of common outdoor areas have wireless network access. Students can register for classes online. Administrative functions (other than registration) can be performed online.

CAMPUS LIFE

Environment: Village. **Activities:** Choral groups, concert band, dance, drama/theater, jazz band, literary magazine, marching band, music ensembles, musical theater, opera, pep band, radio station, student government, student newspaper, student-run film society, symphony orchestra, television station, yearbook, campus ministries, international student organization. **Organizations:** 323 registered organizations, 16 honor societies, 27 religious organizations. 17 fraternities, 12 sororities. **Athletics (Intercollegiate):** *Men:* Baseball, basketball, cheerleading, cross-country, football, golf, wrestling. *Women:* Basketball, cheerleading, cross-country, diving, field hockey, golf, soccer, softball, swimming, track/field (outdoor), volleyball. **On-Campus Highlights:** Charles J. Ping Recreation Center, Kennedy Museum of Art, Templeton-Blackburn Memorial Auditorium, Convocation Center, Alden Library, 6. Baker University Center. **Environmental Initiatives:** O.U. has the largest invessel composting system at any college or university in the nation. The President's Advisory Council for Sustainability Planning is developing a recommendation for a comprehensive sustainability plan and a climate action plan for the university. The OHIO Ecohouse demonstrates affordable green technology & sustainable living to inform, engage & inspire campus & community members.

ADMISSIONS

Freshman Academic Profile: Average high school GPA 3.36. 16% in top 10% of high school class, 44% in top 25% of high school class, 83% in top 50% of high school class. 85% from public high schools. SAT Math middle 50% range 490–600. SAT Critical Reading middle 50% range 480–600. SAT Writing middle 50% range 470–580. ACT middle 50% range 21–26. **Basis for Candidate Selection:** *Very important factors considered include:* Academic GPA, rigor of secondary school record. *Important factors considered include:* Class rank, standardized test scores. *Other factors considered include:* Application essay, recommendation(s), alumni/ae relation, character/personal qualities, extracurricular activities, talent/ability, volunteer work, work experience. **Freshman Admission Requirements:** High school diploma is required and GED is accepted. *Academic units required:* 4 English, 3 mathematics, 3 science, 2 foreign language, 3 social studies, 1 visual or performing arts. **Freshman Admission Statistics:** 14,204 applied, 82% admitted, 35% enrolled. **Transfer Admission Requirements:** College transcript(s), minimum college GPA of 2.0 required. Lowest grade transferable C–. **General Admission Information:** Application fee $45. Regular application deadline 2/1. Notification on a rolling basis, beginning on or about 9/15. Nonfall registration accepted. Admission may be deferred for a maximum of 1 year. Credit and/or placement offered for CEEB Advanced Placement tests.

COSTS AND FINANCIAL AID

Annual in-state tuition $9,179. Annual out-of-state tuition $18,143. Room and board $9,408. Average book expense $873. **Required Forms and Deadlines:**

FAFSA. Financial aid filing deadline 3/15. Priority financial aid filing date 3/15. **Notification of Awards:** Applicants will be notified of awards on or about 4/1. **Types of Aid:** *Need-based scholarships/grants:* Federal Pell, SEOG, state scholarships/grants, private scholarships, the school's own gift aid. *Loans:* Direct Subsidized Stafford, Direct Unsubsidized Stafford, Direct PLUS, Federal Perkins, Institutional short term loans are repaid in 30–60 days. *Student Employment:* Federal Work-Study Program available. Institutional employment available. Highest amount earned per year from on-campus jobs $1,784. **Financial Aid Statistics:** 57% freshmen, 51% undergrads receive need-based scholarship or grant aid. 32% freshmen, 21% undergrads receive non-need-based scholarship or grant aid. 51% freshmen, 48% undergrads receive need-based self-help aid. 2% freshmen, 2% undergrads receive athletic scholarships. 59% freshmen, 55% undergrads receive any aid. 66% undergrads borrow to pay for school. Average cumulative indebtedness $22,095. **Criteria for awarding institutional aid:** *Non-need-based:* Academics, art, athletics, minority status, music/drama, religious affiliation.

OHIO UNIVERSITY—SOUTHERN

Office of Enrollment Services, 1804 Liberty Avenue, Ironton, OH 45638-2214
Phone: 740-533-4600
E-mail: askousc@mail.southern.ohiou.edu
Fax: 740-533-4632 **Website:** www.southern.ohiou.edu

This public school was founded in 1956. It has a 9-acre campus.

RATINGS
Admissions Selectivity Rating: 60*   **Fire Safety Rating:** 60*   **Green Rating:** 60*

STUDENTS AND FACULTY
Student Body: 11% out-of-state.

ACADEMICS
Degrees: Associate, bachelor's, master's, terminal associate, transfer associate. **Special Study Options:** Distance learning, double major, independent study, student-designed major, teacher certification program, weekend college.

FACILITIES
Computers: Students can register for classes online. Administrative functions (other than registration) can be performed online.

CAMPUS LIFE
Environment: Village. **Activities:** Choral groups, concert band, drama/theater, literary magazine, music ensembles, radio station, student government, television station.

ADMISSIONS
Transfer Admission Requirements: College transcript(s), Lowest grade transferable C. **General Admission Information:** Application fee $20.

COSTS AND FINANCIAL AID
Annual in-state tuition $3,087. Annual out-of-state tuition $3,219. Average book expense $700. **Required Forms and Deadlines:** FAFSA. Priority financial aid filing date 2/15. **Types of Aid:** *Need-based scholarships/grants:* Federal Pell, SEOG, state scholarships/grants, private scholarships, the school's own gift aid. *Loans:* Direct Subsidized Stafford, Direct Unsubsidized Stafford, Direct PLUS, Federal Perkins.

OHIO VALLEY UNIVERSITY

#1 Campus View Drive, Vienna, WV 26105
Phone: 304-865-6200
E-mail: admissions@ovu.edu
Fax: 304-865-6001 **Website: ACT Code:** 4548

This private school was founded in 1960. It has a 267-acre campus.

RATINGS
Admissions Selectivity Rating: 76   **Fire Safety Rating:** 60*   **Green Rating:** 60*

STUDENTS AND FACULTY
Enrollment: 512. **Student Body:** 53% female, 47% male, 6% out-of-state, 7% international (12 countries represented). Asian 1%, African American 4%, Caucasian 86%, Hispanic 1%, Native American 1%.
Retention and Graduation: 72% freshmen return for sophomore year.

Faculty: Student/faculty ratio 14:1. 26 full-time faculty, 38% hold PhDs, 38% are women.

ACADEMICS
Degrees: Associate, bachelor's. **Classes:** Most classes have fewer than 10 students. Most lab/discussion sessions have fewer than 10 students. **Majors with Highest Enrollment:** Business/commerce; elementary education and teaching; psychology. **Special Study Options:** Double major, English as a Second Language (ESL), study abroad, teacher certification program, weekend college, Adult Education: Degree completion program in Business Administration and Saturday college available. Special programs offered to physically disabled students include tutors.

FACILITIES
Housing: Men's dorms, women's dorms, apartments for married students, apartments for single students. 50% of campus accessible to physically disabled.

CAMPUS LIFE
Environment: Village. **Activities:** Choral groups, concert band, drama/theater, jazz band, literary magazine, music ensembles, musical theater, student government, student newspaper, symphony orchestra, yearbook. **Organizations:** 10 registered organizations, 2 honor societies, 3 religious organizations. 4 fraternities, 4 sororities. **Athletics (Intercollegiate): Men:** Baseball, basketball, cross-country, golf, soccer. *Women:* Basketball, cheerleading, cross-country, soccer, softball, volleyball. **On-Campus Highlights:** New men and women's dorm, Memorial Fountain.

ADMISSIONS
Freshman Academic Profile: Average high school GPA 3. 10% in top 10% of high school class, 32% in top 25% of high school class, 57% in top 50% of high school class. 95% from public high schools. SAT Math middle 50% range 540–460. SAT Critical Reading middle 50% range 600–510. ACT middle 50% range 23–17. Minimum paper TOEFL 500. Minimum computer TOEFL 173. **Basis for Candidate Selection:** *Very important factors considered include:* Rigor of secondary school record, standardized test scores, character/personal qualities. *Important factors considered include:* Recommendation(s), alumni/ae relation, talent/ability. *Other factors considered include:* Class rank, application essay, extracurricular activities, interview, religious affiliation/commitment. **Freshman Admission Requirements:** High school diploma is required and GED is accepted. *Academic units recommended:* 3 English, 2 mathematics, 3 science, (1 science labs), 2 social studies, 1 history. **Freshman Admission Statistics:** 326 applied, 59% admitted, 50% enrolled. **Transfer Admission Requirements:** High school transcript, college transcript(s), standardized test scores, minimum college GPA of 2.0 required. Lowest grade transferable D. **General Admission Information:** Application fee $20. Regular application deadline 8/20. Nonfall registration accepted. Admission may be deferred for a maximum of 1 year. Credit and/or placement offered for CEEB Advanced Placement tests.

COSTS AND FINANCIAL AID
Annual tuition $12,750. Room and board $5,850. Required fees $1,512. Average book expense $1,000. **Required Forms and Deadlines:** FAFSA. Priority financial aid filing date 2/15. **Notification of Awards:** Applicants will be notified of awards on a rolling basis beginning 3/15. **Types of Aid:** *Need-based scholarships/grants:* Federal Pell, SEOG, state scholarships/grants, private scholarships, the school's own gift aid. *Loans:* FFEL Subsidized Stafford, FFEL Unsubsidized Stafford, FFEL PLUS, Federal Perkins, Signature student loans. *Student Employment:* Federal Work-Study Program available. Institutional employment available. Highest amount earned per year from on-campus jobs $800. Off-campus job opportunities are good. **Financial Aid Statistics:** 72% freshmen, 63% undergrads receive need-based scholarship or grant aid. 8% freshmen, 9% undergrads receive non-need-based scholarship or grant aid. 64% freshmen, 63% undergrads receive need-based self-help aid. 16% freshmen, 12% undergrads receive athletic scholarships. 81% freshmen, 89% undergrads receive any aid. 80% undergrads borrow to pay for school. **Criteria for awarding institutional aid:** *Non-need-based:* Academics, athletics, job skills, leadership, music/drama, religious affiliation.

OHIO WESLEYAN UNIVERSITY

61 South Sandusky Street, Delaware, OH 43015
Phone: 740-368-3020 **Financial Aid Phone:** 740-368-3050
E-mail: owuadmit@owu.edu **CEEB Code:** 1594
Fax: 740-368-3314 **Website:** www.owu.edu **ACT Code:** 3316

This private school, affiliated with the Methodist Church, was founded in 1842. It has a 200-acre campus.

RATINGS
Admissions Selectivity Rating: 85   **Fire Safety Rating:** 60*   **Green Rating:** 60*

STUDENTS AND FACULTY
Enrollment: 1,960. **Student Body:** 52% female, 48% male, 41% out-of-state, 9% international (41 countries represented). Asian 2%, African American 5%, Caucasian 79%, Hispanic 1%.
Retention and Graduation: 84% freshmen return for sophomore year. 60% freshmen graduate within 4 years. 32% grads go on to further study within 1 year. 14% grads pursue arts and sciences degrees. 3% grads pursue law degrees. 2% grads pursue business degrees. 14% grads pursue medical degrees. **Faculty:** Student/faculty ratio 12:1. 136 full-time faculty, 98% hold PhDs, 7% are are members of minority groups, 35% are women.

ACADEMICS
Degrees: Bachelor's. **Classes:** Most classes have 10–19 students. Most lab/discussion sessions have 10–19 students. **Majors with Highest Enrollment:** Economics; pre-medicine/pre-medical studies; psychology. **Special Study Options:** Double major, dual enrollment, exchange student program (domestic), honors program, independent study, internships, student-designed major, study abroad, teacher certification program **Honors programs:** The Leland F. and Helen Schubert Honors Program recognizes the most talented students among Ohio Wesleyan's community of scholars and challenges them through Honors Tutorials, Honors Seminars, and Honors Scholarships. **Combined degree programs:** Pre-Medical Tech, Pre-Optometry, Pre-Physical Therap. Special programs offered to physically disabled students include note-taking services, tape recorders, tutors. **Career services:** Alumni network, alumni services, career assessment. **Career services highlights include:** Alumni Networking System.

FACILITIES
Housing: Coed dorms, special housing for international students, women's dorms, fraternity/sorority housing, apartments for single students, Small Living Units (SLUs) offer unique living opportunities to groups of 10–15 OWU students. In these theme houses, students create a small community centered on promoting specific interests and concerns. 60% of campus accessible to physically disabled. **Special Academic Facilities/Equipment:** Perkins and Student Observatories Scanning electron microscope Woltemade Center for Economics, Business and Entrepreneurship Nine inch refractor telescope Ross Art Museum Newly renovated fine arts facilities Newly renovated 150,000 square foot science center with state-of-the art classrooms and equipment. Wireless Internet in some areas. Fiber optic network **Computers:** 10% of classrooms, 100% of libraries, 10% of dining areas, 10% of common outdoor areas have wireless network access. Administrative functions (other than registration) can be performed online.

CAMPUS LIFE
Environment: Town. **Activities:** Choral groups, dance, drama/theater, jazz band, literary magazine, music ensembles, musical theater, opera, pep band, radio station, student government, student newspaper, symphony orchestra, yearbook, campus ministries, international student organization, Model UN. **Organizations:** 86 registered organizations, 26 honor societies, 10 religious organizations. 11 fraternity, 7 sororities. **Athletics (Intercollegiate):** *Men:* Baseball, basketball, cross-country, diving, football, golf, lacrosse, sailing, soccer, swimming, tennis, track/field (outdoor), track/field (indoor). *Women:* Basketball, cross-country, diving, field hockey, lacrosse, sailing, soccer, softball, swimming, tennis, track/field (outdoor), track/field (indoor), volleyball. **On-Campus Highlights:** Science Center, Hamilton Williams Campus Center, Selby Stadium, R.W. Corns Building, Sanborn Hall (music), Beeghly Library and Ross Museum are additional popular places on campus.

ADMISSIONS
Freshman Academic Profile: Average high school GPA 3.43. 30% in top 10% of high school class, 59% in top 25% of high school class, 87% in top 50% of high school class. 77% from public high schools. SAT Math middle 50% range 520–650. SAT Critical Reading middle 50% range 520–640. ACT middle 50%

range 22–28. Minimum paper TOEFL 550. Minimum computer TOEFL 213. **Basis for Candidate Selection:** *Very important factors considered include:* Application essay, academic GPA, recommendation(s), rigor of secondary school record, character/personal qualities, interview. *Important factors considered include:* Class rank, standardized test scores, extracurricular activities, talent/ability. *Other factors considered include:* Alumni/ae relation, first generation, geographical residence, level of applicant's interest, racial/ethnic status, volunteer work, work experience. **Freshman Admission Requirements:** High school diploma is required and GED is accepted. *Academic units required:* 4 English, 3 mathematics, 3 science, 2 foreign language, 3 social studies. *Academic units recommended:* 4 mathematics, 4 science, 3 foreign language, 4 social studies. **Freshman Admission Statistics:** 3,814 applied, 66% admitted, 23% enrolled. **Transfer Admission Requirements:** High school transcript, college transcript(s), essay or personal statement, statement of good standing from prior institution(s). Minimum college GPA of 2.5 required. Lowest grade transferable C–. **General Admission Information:** Application fee $35. Early decision application deadline 12/1. Notification on a rolling basis, beginning on or about 10/1. Nonfall registration accepted. Admission may be deferred for a maximum of 2 years. Credit and/or placement offered for CEEB Advanced Placement tests.

COSTS AND FINANCIAL AID
Annual tuition $34,570. Room and board $8,030. Required fees $460. Average book expense $2,402. **Required Forms and Deadlines:** FAFSA, institution's own financial aid form. Financial aid filing deadline 5/1. Priority financial aid filing date 3/1. **Notification of Awards:** Applicants will be notified of awards on a rolling basis beginning 2/15. **Types of Aid:** *Need-based scholarships/grants:* Federal Pell, SEOG, state scholarships/grants, private scholarships, the school's own gift aid. *Loans:* FFEL Subsidized Stafford, FFEL Unsubsidized Stafford, FFEL PLUS, Federal Perkins, college/university loans from institutional funds. *Student Employment:* Federal Work-Study Program available. Institutional employment available. Highest amount earned per year from on-campus jobs $2,400. Off-campus job opportunities are excellent. **Financial Aid Statistics:** 60% freshmen, 56% undergrads receive need-based scholarship or grant aid. 11% freshmen, 9% undergrads receive non-need-based scholarship or grant aid. 50% freshmen, 47% undergrads receive need-based self-help aid. 99% freshmen, 98% undergrads receive any aid. 76% undergrads borrow to pay for school. Average cumulative indebtedness $25,627. **Criteria for awarding institutional aid:** *Non-need-based:* Academics, alumni affiliation, art, leadership, minority status, music/drama, religious affiliation, state/district residency.

See page 1192.

OKLAHOMA BAPTIST UNIVERSITY

500 West University, Shawnee, OK 74804
Phone: 800-654-3285 **Financial Aid Phone:** 405-878-2016
E-mail: admissions@okbu.edu **CEEB Code:** 6541
Fax: 405-878-2046 **Website:** www.okbu.edu **ACT Code:** 3414

This private school, affiliated with the Southern Baptist Church, was founded in 1910. It has a 200-acre campus.

RATINGS
Admissions Selectivity Rating: 93   **Fire Safety Rating:** 70   **Green Rating:** 60*

STUDENTS AND FACULTY
Enrollment: 1,438. **Student Body:** 60% female, 40% male, 42% out-of-state, 4% international (25 countries represented). Asian 1%, African American 3%, Caucasian 83%, Hispanic 2%, Native American 6%.
Retention and Graduation: 71% freshmen return for sophomore year. 48% freshmen graduate within 4 years. 37% grads go on to further study within 1 year. 34% grads pursue arts and sciences degrees. 1% grads pursue law degrees. 1% grads pursue business degrees. 2% grads pursue medical degrees. **Faculty:** Student/faculty ratio 14:1. 112 full-time faculty, 68% hold PhDs, 3% are are members of minority groups, 44% are women.

ACADEMICS
Degrees: Associate, bachelor's, master's. **Classes:** Most classes have fewer than 10 students. Most lab/discussion sessions have fewer than 10 students. **Majors with Highest Enrollment:** Bible/biblical studies; elementary education and teaching; nursing/registered nurse (RN, ASN, BSN, MSN). **Special Study Options:** Cooperative education program, double major, English as a Second Language (ESL), exchange student program (domestic), honors program, independent study, internships, student-designed major, study abroad, teacher certification program, Semester-away programs available. **Honors programs:** The OBU Honors Program is a curricular program designed to enhance the undergraduate study experience for certain exceptionally well-qualified

students. Students completing all of the requirements for gradulation in the Honors Program earn the designation "with Honors" on their OBU diplomas. **Combined degree programs:** BA/MA. Special programs offered to physically disabled students include note-taking services, reader services, tape recorders, tutors. **Career services:** Alumni network, regional alumni.

FACILITIES

Housing: Men's dorms, women's dorms, apartments for married students, apartments for single students. 95% of campus accessible to physically disabled. **Special Academic Facilities/Equipment:** Planetarium, Baptist Historical Society Archives, Avery T. Willis Center for Global Outreach. **Computers:** Students can register for classes online. Administrative functions (other than registration) can be performed online.

CAMPUS LIFE

Environment: Town. **Activities:** Choral groups, concert band, drama/theater, jazz band, literary magazine, music ensembles, musical theater, opera, pep band, student government, student newspaper, symphony orchestra, television station, yearbook, campus ministries. **Organizations:** 80 registered organizations, 15 honor societies, 5 religious organizations. 5 fraternities, 5 sororities. **Athletics (Intercollegiate):** *Men:* Baseball, basketball, cheerleading, cross-country, golf, soccer, tennis, track/field (outdoor), track/field (indoor). *Women:* Basketball, cheerleading, cross-country, golf, soccer, softball, tennis, track/field (outdoor), track/field (indoor), volleyball. **On-Campus Highlights:** Geiger Center (Student Building), Recreation and Wellness Center, Noble Complex (athletics), Mabee Learning Center (Library), Intramural Field.

ADMISSIONS

Freshman Academic Profile: Average high school GPA 3.67. 46% in top 10% of high school class, 73% in top 25% of high school class, 90% in top 50% of high school class. 90% from public high schools. SAT Math middle 50% range 500–630. SAT Critical Reading middle 50% range 510–650. ACT middle 50% range 21–28. Minimum paper TOEFL 500. Minimum computer TOEFL 173. **Basis for Candidate Selection:** *Very important factors considered include:* Academic GPA, rigor of secondary school record. *Important factors considered include:* Class rank, recommendation(s), standardized test scores, character/personal qualities, extracurricular activities. *Other factors considered include:* Application essay, alumni/ae relation, geographical residence, interview, level of applicant's interest, religious affiliation/commitment, state residency, talent/ability, volunteer work, work experience. **Freshman Admission Requirements:** High school diploma is required and GED is accepted. *Academic units recommended:* 4 English, 3 mathematics, 3 science, (2 science labs), 2 foreign language, 1 social studies, 2 history, 2 academic electives, 1 fine arts. **Freshman Admission Statistics: Transfer Admission Requirements:** College transcript(s), minimum college GPA of 2.5 required. Lowest grade transferable D. **General Admission Information:** Application fee $25. Regular application deadline 8/1. Regular notification 9/1. Nonfall registration accepted. Admission may be deferred for a maximum of 1 year. Credit and/or placement offered for CEEB Advanced Placement tests.

COSTS AND FINANCIAL AID

Annual tuition $14,732. Room and board $5,000. Required fees $1,262. Average book expense $1,000. **Required Forms and Deadlines:** FAFSA. Priority financial aid filing date 3/1. **Notification of Awards:** Applicants will be notified of awards on or about 3/1. **Types of Aid:** *Need-based scholarships/grants:* Federal Pell, SEOG, state scholarships/grants, private scholarships, the school's own gift aid, Federal Nursing Scholarships. ACG SMART. *Loans:* FFEL Subsidized Stafford, FFEL Unsubsidized Stafford, FFEL PLUS, Federal Perkins, college/university loans from institutional funds. *Student Employment:* Highest amount earned per year from on-campus jobs $3,200. **Financial Aid Statistics:** 54% freshmen, 55% undergrads receive need-based scholarship or grant aid. 68% freshmen, 64% undergrads receive non-need-based scholarship or grant aid. 17% freshmen, 47% undergrads receive need-based self-help aid. 26% freshmen, 23% undergrads receive athletic scholarships. 87% freshmen, 90% undergrads receive any aid. 58% undergrads borrow to pay for school. Average cumulative indebtedness $17,008. **Criteria for awarding institutional aid:** *Non-need-based:* Academics, alumni affiliation, art, athletics, job skills, leadership, music/drama, religious affiliation.

OKLAHOMA CHRISTIAN UNIVERSITY

P.O. Box 11000, Oklahoma City, OK 73136-1100
Phone: 405-425-5050 **Financial Aid Phone:** 405-425-5190
E-mail: info@oc.edu
Fax: 405-425-5069 **Website:** www.oc.edu **ACT Code:** 3415

This private school, affiliated with the Church of Christ Church, was founded in 1950. It has a 240-acre campus.

RATINGS

Admissions Selectivity Rating: 87   **Fire Safety Rating:** 68   **Green Rating:** 61

STUDENTS AND FACULTY

Enrollment: 1,918. **Student Body:** 48% female, 52% male, 55% out-of-state, 7% international (31 countries represented). Asian 1%, African American 4%, Caucasian 75%, Hispanic 3%, Native American 5%.
Retention and Graduation: 69% freshmen return for sophomore year. 40% freshmen graduate within 4 years. **Faculty:** Student/faculty ratio 14.5:1. 106 full-time faculty, 63% hold PhDs, 30% are women.

ACADEMICS

Degrees: Bachelor's, master's. **Classes:** Most classes have 10–19 students. **Majors with Highest Enrollment:** Biology/biological sciences; elementary education and teaching; nursing/registered nurse (RN, ASN, BSN, MSN). **Special Study Options:** Cross-registration, distance learning, double major, English as a Second Language (ESL), honors program, independent study, internships, student-designed major, study abroad, teacher certification program. **Career services:** Alumni network, alumni services, career/job search classes, career assessment, internships. **Career services highlights include:** They are government sponsored internships with DISA, FBI, CIA, homeland security and more. Also some companies, too many to list.

FACILITIES

Housing: Special housing for disabled students, men's dorms, women's dorms, apartments for married students, apartments for single students. **Special Academic Facilities/Equipment:** Art museum, art gallery. **Computers:** 100% of classrooms, 100% of dorms, 100% of libraries, 100% of dining areas, 100% of student union, 95% of common outdoor areas have wireless network access. Students can register for classes online. Administrative functions (other than registration) can be performed online.

CAMPUS LIFE

Environment: Metropolis. **Activities:** Choral groups, concert band, drama/theater, jazz band, literary magazine, music ensembles, musical theater, opera, pep band, radio station, student government, student newspaper, symphony orchestra, television station, yearbook, campus ministries, international student organization. **Organizations:** 20 registered organizations, 5 honor societies, 2 religious organizations. 6 fraternities, 6 sororities. **Athletics (Intercollegiate):** *Men:* Baseball, basketball, cross-country, golf, soccer, tennis, track/field (outdoor). *Women:* Basketball, cheerleading, cross-country, soccer, softball, tennis, track/field (outdoor) **On-Campus Highlights:** Gaylord University Center, University House Commons, Lawson Commons, Payne Athletic & Fitness Center, Mabee Learning Center.

ADMISSIONS

Freshman Academic Profile: Average high school GPA 3.4. 30% in top 10% of high school class, 54% in top 25% of high school class, 79% in top 50% of high school class. SAT Math middle 50% range 480–610. SAT Critical Reading middle 50% range 470–640. SAT Writing middle 50% range 480–610. ACT middle 50% range 20–27. Minimum paper TOEFL 500. Minimum computer TOEFL 173. Minimum web-based TOEFL 61. **Basis for Candidate Selection:** *Other factors considered include:* Class rank, academic GPA, recommendation(s), rigor of secondary school record, standardized test scores, character/personal qualities, extracurricular activities, interview, talent/ability, volunteer work. **Freshman Admission Requirements:** High school diploma is required and GED is accepted. *Academic units recommended:* 4 English, 4 mathematics, 4 science, (3 science labs), 2 foreign language, 3 social studies. **Freshman Admission Statistics:** 1,718 applied, 56% admitted, 49% enrolled. **Transfer Admission Requirements:** High school transcript, college transcript(s), standardized test scores, statement of good standing from prior institution(s). Lowest grade transferable D. **General Admission Information:** Application fee $25. Notification on a rolling basis, beginning on or about 9/1. Nonfall registration accepted. Admission may be deferred for a maximum of 1 year. Credit offered for CEEB Advanced Placement tests.

COSTS AND FINANCIAL AID

Annual tuition $15,600. Room and board $5,850. Required fees $1,856. Average book expense $1,000. **Required Forms and Deadlines:** FAFSA. Priority financial aid filing date 3/15. **Notification of Awards:** Applicants will be notified of awards on a rolling basis beginning 2/2. **Types of Aid:** *Need-based scholarships/grants:* Federal Pell, SEOG, state scholarships/grants, private scholarships, the school's own gift aid. *Loans:* FFEL Subsidized Stafford, FFEL Unsubsidized Stafford, FFEL PLUS, Federal Perkins. *Student Employment:* Federal Work-Study Program available. Institutional employment available. Highest amount earned per year from on-campus jobs $9,905. Off-campus job opportunities are excellent. **Financial Aid Statistics:** 44% freshmen, 34% undergrads receive need-based scholarship or grant aid. 60% freshmen, 54% undergrads receive non-need-based scholarship or grant aid. 55% freshmen, 51% undergrads receive need-based self-help aid. 10% freshmen, 13% undergrads receive athletic scholarships. 99% freshmen, 98% undergrads receive any aid. 76.6% undergrads borrow to pay for school. Average cumulative indebtedness $24,377. **Criteria for awarding institutional aid:** *Non-need-based:* Academics, alumni affiliation, art, athletics, leadership, music/drama.

OKLAHOMA CITY UNIVERSITY

2501 North Blackwelder, Oklahoma City, OK 73106
Phone: 405-208-5050 **Financial Aid Phone:** 405-208-5211
E-mail: uadmission@okcu.edu **CEEB Code:** 6543
Fax: 405-208-5264 **Website:** www.okcu.edu **ACT Code:** 3416

This private school, affiliated with the Methodist Church, was founded in 1904. It has a 78-acre campus.

RATINGS
Admissions Selectivity Rating: 83   **Fire Safety Rating:** 85   **Green Rating:** 71

STUDENTS AND FACULTY
Enrollment: 2,283. **Student Body:** 60% female, 40% male, 42% out-of-state, 18% international (57 countries represented). Asian 2%, African American 8%, Caucasian 56%, Hispanic 2%, Native American 4%.
Retention and Graduation: 76% freshmen return for sophomore year. 40% freshmen graduate within 4 years. **Faculty:** Student/faculty ratio 11:1. 198 full-time faculty, 80% hold PhDs, 17% are are members of minority groups, 47% are women.

ACADEMICS
Degrees: Bachelor's, master's. **Classes:** Most classes have 10–19 students. Most lab/discussion sessions have fewer than 10 students. **Majors with Highest Enrollment:** Biology/biological sciences; business/commerce; dance. **Special Study Options:** Accelerated program, cooperative education program, distance learning, double major, dual enrollment, English as a Second Language (ESL), exchange student program (domestic), external degree program, honors program, independent study, internships, student-designed major, study abroad, teacher certification program. **Honors programs:** University Honors Program: The mission of the University Honors program is to provide an enhanced learning environment for academically gifted undergraduate students. Each new class of Honors students at OCU will be a spcial community of scholars. Students will have the opportunity to become acquainted with one another and the Honors program in the Honors Colloquium, a course required for all new honors students during their first semester in the program. Honors students will have the opportunities to meet with visiting scholars and participate in special events. As part of a network of honors programs through the National Collegiate Honors Council and the Great Plains Honors Council, students may present research at national and regional honors conferences and participate in exciting summer and semester programs. **Combined degree programs:** BA/JD, MBA/JD. Special programs offered to physically disabled students include reader services, tape recorders, tutors. **Career services:** Alumni network, alumni services, career/job search classes, career assessment, internships, regional alumni. **Career services highlights include:** Career Fairs hosting over 200+ employers on campus.

FACILITIES
Housing: Coed dorms, special housing for disabled students, men's dorms, women's dorms, fraternity/sorority housing, apartments for married students, apartments for single students, Learning Communities. 96% of campus accessible to physically disabled. **Special Academic Facilities/Equipment:** Art museum, audiovisual center, language lab. **Computers:** 100% of classrooms, 100% of dorms, 100% of libraries, 100% of dining areas, 100% of student union, 90% of common outdoor areas have wireless network access. Students can register for classes online. Administrative functions (other than registration) can be performed online.

CAMPUS LIFE
Environment: Metropolis. **Activities:** Choral groups, concert band, dance, drama/theater, jazz band, literary magazine, music ensembles, musical theater,
opera, pep band, student government, student newspaper, symphony orchestra, television station, yearbook, campus ministries, international student organization. **Organizations:** 64 registered organizations, 14 honor societies, 6 religious organizations. 2 fraternities, 4 sororities. **Athletics (Intercollegiate):** *Men:* Baseball, basketball, cheerleading, crew/rowing, golf, soccer, track/field (outdoor), wrestling. *Women:* Basketball, cheerleading, crew/rowing, golf, soccer, softball, track/field (outdoor), volleyball, wrestling. **On-Campus Highlights:** Tom and Brenda McDaniel Univ Center, Henry J Freede Wellness and Activity Center, Meinders' School of Business, Walker Center for Arts and Sciences, Norick Art Center. **Environmental Initiatives:** Computer recycling program, community garden. Purchasing maximum % of wind power allowable by energy supplying and trading company. Install sprinkler system on well system saving city water.

ADMISSIONS
Freshman Academic Profile: Average high school GPA 3.51. 32% in top 10% of high school class, 59% in top 25% of high school class, 86% in top 50% of high school class. 87% from public high schools. SAT Math middle 50% range 480–590. SAT Critical Reading middle 50% range 490–600. Minimum paper TOEFL 550. Minimum computer TOEFL 210. **Basis for Candidate Selection:** *Very important factors considered include:* Class rank, application essay, academic GPA, recommendation(s), standardized test scores. *Important factors considered include:* Rigor of secondary school record, extracurricular activities. *Other factors considered include:* character/personal qualities, talent/ability, volunteer work, work experience. **Freshman Admission Requirements:** High school diploma is required and GED is accepted. *Academic units required:* 4 English, 3 mathematics, 3 science, (1 science labs), 2 foreign language, 3 social studies, 3 history. **Freshman Admission Statistics:** 1,185 applied, 79% admitted, 43% enrolled. **Transfer Admission Requirements:** College transcript(s), essay or personal statement, statement of good standing from prior institution(s). Minimum college GPA of 2.0 required. Lowest grade transferable C–. **General Admission Information:** Application fee $40. Regular application deadline 8/21. Notification on a rolling basis, beginning on or about 10/15. Nonfall registration accepted. Admission may be deferred for a maximum of 1 year. Credit and/or placement offered for CEEB Advanced Placement tests.

COSTS AND FINANCIAL AID
Annual tuition $19,600. Room and board $8,400. Required fees $1,400. Average book expense $1,500. **Required Forms and Deadlines:** FAFSA, institution's own financial aid formTax returns if selected for verification. Financial aid filing deadline 6/30. Priority financial aid filing date 3/1. **Notification of Awards:** Applicants will be notified of awards on a rolling basis beginning 2/20. **Types of Aid:** *Need-based scholarships/grants:* Federal Pell, SEOG, state scholarships/grants, private scholarships, the school's own gift aid, United Negro College Fund, Native American Grants. *Loans:* FFEL Subsidized Stafford, FFEL Unsubsidized Stafford, FFEL PLUS, Federal Perkins. *Student Employment:* Federal Work-Study Program available. Institutional employment available. Highest amount earned per year from on-campus jobs $10,800. Off-campus job opportunities are good. **Financial Aid Statistics:** 59% freshmen, 45% undergrads receive need-based scholarship or grant aid. 17% freshmen, 17% undergrads receive non-need-based scholarship or grant aid. 12% freshmen, 8% undergrads receive need-based self-help aid. 9% freshmen, 7% undergrads receive athletic scholarships. 93% freshmen, 82% undergrads receive any aid. 48% undergrads borrow to pay for school. Average cumulative indebtedness $18,532. **Criteria for awarding institutional aid:** *Non-need-based:* Academics, alumni affiliation, art, athletics, job skills, leadership, music/drama, religious affiliation, state/district residency.

OKLAHOMA STATE UNIVERSITY

219 Student Union, Stillwater, OK 74078
Phone: 405-744-5358 **Financial Aid Phone:** 405-744-6604
E-mail: admissions@okstate.edu **CEEB Code:** 6546
Fax: 405-744-7092 **Website:** http://osu.okstate.edu/welcome/ **ACT Code:** 3424

This public school was founded in 1890. It has a 840-acre campus.

RATINGS
Admissions Selectivity Rating: 79   **Fire Safety Rating:** 60*   **Green Rating:** 75

STUDENTS AND FACULTY
Enrollment: 17,606. **Student Body:** 48% female, 52% male, 17% out-of-state, 2% international (114 countries represented). Asian 2%, African American 4%, Caucasian 80%, Hispanic 3%, Native American 9%.
Retention and Graduation: 31% freshmen graduate within 4 years. **Faculty:** Student/faculty ratio 18:1. 999 full-time faculty, 91% hold PhDs, 10% are are members of minority groups, 32% are women. 13.5% of classes are taught by teaching assistants.

ACADEMICS

Degrees: Bachelor's, master's, post-bachelor's certificate, post-master's certificate. **Classes:** Most classes have 10–19 students. Most lab/discussion sessions have 10–19 students. **Special Study Options:** Accelerated program, cross-registration, distance learning, double major, dual enrollment, English as a Second Language (ESL), exchange student program (domestic), honors program, independent study, internships, student-designed major, study abroad, teacher certification program. **Combined degree programs:** BS/MS Accounting. Special programs offered to physically disabled students include note-taking services, reader services, tape recorders, tutors. **Career services:** Alumni network, alumni services, career/job search classes, career assessment, internships, regional alumni. **Career services highlights include:** Our Entrepreneurship Empowerment in South Africa (EESA) Program involves taking 20 OSU students, pairing them with 20 South African students, and spending six weeks working with a group of historically disadvantaged, township-based entrepreneurs helping them growth their businesses. The students are taught and coached by three of our entrepreneurship faculty members. Over the years we have assisted over 120 entrepreneurs in meaningful ways.

FACILITIES

Housing: Coed dorms, special housing for disabled students, men's dorms, women's dorms, fraternity/sorority housing, apartments for married students, apartments for single students, wellness house, theme housing. 97% of campus accessible to physically disabled. **Special Academic Facilities/Equipment:** Art, history, and natural science museums, wellness center, laser research center. **Computers:** 80% of classrooms, 80% of dorms, 100% of libraries, 80% of student union, have wireless network access. Students can register for classes online. Administrative functions (other than registration) can be performed online.

CAMPUS LIFE

Environment: Town. **Activities:** Choral groups, concert band, dance, drama/theater, jazz band, literary magazine, marching band, music ensembles, musical theater, opera, pep band, radio station, student government, student newspaper, symphony orchestra, television station, campus ministries, international student organization. **Organizations:** 300 registered organizations. **Athletics (Intercollegiate):** *Men:* Baseball, basketball, cross-country, football, golf, tennis, track/field (outdoor), wrestling. *Women:* Basketball, cross-country, equestrian sports, golf, soccer, softball, tennis, track/field (outdoor). **On-Campus Highlights:** Colvin Recreational Center, Gallagher/Iba Arena and Museum, Student Union Building, library, ConocoPhillips Alumni Center. **Environmental Initiatives:** Energy conservation—turning off lights, computers, monitors, speakers, printers, etc when not in use. Reducing thermostat settings during winter and turning it up during summer.

ADMISSIONS

Freshman Academic Profile: Average high school GPA 3.52. 27% in top 10% of high school class, 55% in top 25% of high school class, 86% in top 50% of high school class. SAT Math middle 50% range 500–640. SAT Critical Reading middle 50% range 480–600. ACT middle 50% range 22-27. Minimum paper TOEFL 500. Minimum computer TOEFL 173. Minimum web-based TOEFL 61. **Basis for Candidate Selection:** *Very important factors considered include:* Class rank, academic GPA, standardized test scores. *Other factors considered include:* Application essay, recommendation(s), rigor of secondary school record, character/personal qualities, extracurricular activities, interview, talent/ability. **Freshman Admission Requirements:** High school diploma is required and GED is accepted. *Academic units required:* 4 English, 3 mathematics, 2 science, (2 science labs), 2 social studies, 1 history, 3 academic electives. *Academic units recommended:* 2 foreign language, 1 computer science. **Freshman Admission Statistics:** 7,561 applied, 86% admitted, 48% enrolled. **Transfer Admission Requirements:** College transcript(s), minimum college GPA of 2.25 required. Lowest grade transferable D. **General Admission Information:** Application fee $40. Nonfall registration accepted. Admission may be deferred for a maximum of military. Credit offered for CEEB Advanced Placement tests.

COSTS AND FINANCIAL AID

Annual in-state tuition $3,941. Annual out-of-state tuition $14,295. Room and board $6,402. Required fees $2,261. Average book expense $980. **Required Forms and Deadlines:** FAFSACombined Admissions and Scholarship Application. Priority financial aid filing date 2/1. **Notification of Awards:** Applicants will be notified of awards on a rolling basis beginning 10/1. **Types of Aid:** *Need-based scholarships/grants:* Federal Pell, SEOG, state scholarships/grants, private scholarships, the school's own gift aid, TEACH, ACG, SMART. *Loans:* Direct Subsidized Stafford, Direct Unsubsidized Stafford, Direct PLUS, Federal Perkins. *Student Employment:* Institutional employment available. Off-campus job opportunities are good. **Financial Aid Statistics:** 37% freshmen, 35% undergrads receive need-based scholarship or grant aid. 30% freshmen, 21% undergrads receive non-need-based scholarship or grant aid. 29% freshmen, 33% undergrads receive need-based self-help aid. 1% freshmen, 1% undergrads receive athletic scholarships. 56% undergrads borrow to pay

for school. Average cumulative indebtedness $19,458. **Criteria for awarding institutional aid:** *Non-need-based:* Academics, alumni affiliation, art, athletics, leadership, minority status, music/drama, state/district residency.

OKLAHOMA WESLEYAN UNIVERSITY

2201 Silver Lake Road, Bartlesville, OK 74006
Phone: 918-335-6219
E-mail: admissions@okwu.edu **CEEB Code:** 6135
Fax: 918-335-6229 **Website:** www.okwu.edu **ACT Code:** 3387

This private school was founded in 1972. It has a 127-acre campus.

RATINGS

Admissions Selectivity Rating: 81   **Fire Safety Rating:** 60*   **Green Rating:** 60*

STUDENTS AND FACULTY

Student Body: 43% out-of-state.
Retention and Graduation: 10% grads go on to further study within 1 year. 2% grads pursue arts and sciences degrees. 2% grads pursue law degrees. 5% grads pursue business degrees. 2% grads pursue medical degrees.

ACADEMICS

Degrees: Associate, bachelor's, certificate, master's. **Special Study Options:** Double major, English as a Second Language (ESL), independent study, internships, student-designed major, study abroad. Special programs offered to physically disabled students include tutors.

FACILITIES

Housing: Men's dorms, women's dorms. 70% of campus accessible to physically disabled. **Special Academic Facilities/Equipment:** LaQuinta Mansion. **Computers:** Undergraduates are required to own a computer.

CAMPUS LIFE

Environment: Village. **Activities:** Choral groups, music ensembles, pep band, student government, student newspaper, yearbook. **Organizations:** 10 registered organizations, 2 honor societies, 3 religious organizations. **Athletics (Intercollegiate):** *Men:* Baseball, basketball, cheerleading, golf, soccer. *Women:* Basketball, cheerleading, soccer, softball, volleyball.

ADMISSIONS

Freshman Academic Profile: 90% from public high schools. ACT middle 50% range 19-25. Minimum paper TOEFL 500. **Basis for Candidate Selection:** *Very important factors considered include:* Class rank, recommendation(s), rigor of secondary school record, standardized test scores, character/personal qualities, religious affiliation/commitment, state residency. *Important factors considered include:* Alumni/ae relation, geographical residence, interview, racial/ethnic status. *Other factors considered include:* extracurricular activities, talent/ability. **Freshman Admission Requirements:** High school diploma is required and GED is accepted. *Academic units required:* 4 English, 2 mathematics, 1 science, (1 science labs), 1 social studies, 1 history, 6 academic electives. **Freshman Admission Statistics:** 317 applied, 60% admitted, 62% enrolled. **Transfer Admission Requirements:** High school transcript, college transcript(s), essay or personal statement, statement of good standing from prior institution(s). Minimum college GPA of 2.0 required. Lowest grade transferable D. **General Admission Information:** Application fee $25. Nonfall registration accepted. Admission may be deferred for a maximum of 12. Credit and/or placement offered for CEEB Advanced Placement tests.

COSTS AND FINANCIAL AID

Annual tuition $8,200. Room and board $3,800. Required fees $500. **Required Forms and Deadlines: Types of Aid:** *Need-based scholarships/grants:* Federal Pell, SEOG, state scholarships/grants, private scholarships, the school's own gift aid. *Loans:* Direct Subsidized Stafford, Direct Unsubsidized Stafford, Direct PLUS, Federal Perkins. *Student Employment:* Federal Work-Study Program available. Institutional employment available. Highest amount earned per year from on-campus jobs $1,913. Off-campus job opportunities are excellent.

OLD DOMINION UNIVERSITY

108 Rollins Hall, Hampton Boulevard, Norfolk, VA 23529-0050
Phone: 757-683-3685 **Financial Aid Phone:** 757-683-3683
E-mail: admit@odu.edu **CEEB Code:** 5126
Fax: 757-683-3255 **Website:** www.odu.edu

This public school was founded in 1930. It has a 188-acre campus.

RATINGS

Admissions Selectivity Rating: 78 **Fire Safety Rating:** 73 **Green Rating:** 81

STUDENTS AND FACULTY

Enrollment: 17,819. **Student Body:** 55% female, 45% male, 7% out-of-state, 1% international (130 countries represented). Asian 5%, African American 24%, Caucasian 61%, Hispanic 4%, Native American 1%.
Retention and Graduation: 80% freshmen return for sophomore year. 23% freshmen graduate within 4 years. **Faculty:** Student/faculty ratio 17.9:1. 696 full-time faculty, 79% hold PhDs, 22% are are members of minority groups, 42% are women.

ACADEMICS

Degrees: Bachelor's, doctoral, master's, post-master's certificate. **Classes:** Most classes have 10–19 students. Most lab/discussion sessions have 20–29 students. **Majors with Highest Enrollment:** communication, journalism, and related programs, other; mental and social health services and allied professions, other; multi-/interdisciplinary studies, other. **Special Study Options:** Accelerated program, cooperative education program, cross-registration, distance learning, double major, dual enrollment, English as a Second Language (ESL), exchange student program (domestic), honors program, independent study, internships, liberal arts/career combination, student-designed major, study abroad, teacher certification program, weekend college, experiential learning. **Honors programs:** Honors College. The Honors College was established to further the University's commitment to excellence in education. With an emphasis on teaching, innovation, and small classes, the college offers the experience of a small liberal arts college within the framework of the large university. The four-year experience offers specially designed, low-enrollment courses to honors students and selected juniors and seniors. Several out-of-class and off-campus experiences are often part of these courses— at no extra cost to students. A one credit honors tutorial is required in the junior year, and a senior honors colloquium is taken in the final year of study. All Honors College students are awarded an annual honors stipend. **Combined degree programs:** BA/MD, BA/JD, BA/MA, BA/DDS, BA/MEng, 5-year Master's degree program in education. Special programs offered to physically disabled students include note-taking services, reader services, tutors. **Career services:** Alumni network, alumni services, career/job search classes, career assessment, internships, regional alumni. **Career services highlights include:** The Career Advantage Program is a comprehensive series of programs, services, professional seminars, appointments, and work assignments geared toward helping you determine your future career. The cornerstone of the Career Advantage Program is the Guaranteed Practicum. All undergraduates are guaranteed a practical experience, or classroom experience working in a "real world" setting.

FACILITIES

Housing: Coed dorms, special housing for disabled students, special housing for international students, apartments for single students. 95% of campus accessible to physically disabled. **Special Academic Facilities/Equipment:** Centers for urban research/service, economic education, and child study, planetarium, marine science research vessel, random wave pool. **Computers:** 100% of classrooms, 100% of dorms, 100% of libraries, 100% of dining areas, 100% of student union, 20% of common outdoor areas have wireless network access. Students can register for classes online. Administrative functions (other than registration) can be performed online.

CAMPUS LIFE

Environment: City. **Activities:** Choral groups, concert band, dance, drama/theater, jazz band, marching band, music ensembles, musical theater, pep band, radio station, student government, student newspaper, symphony orchestra, television station, campus ministries, international student organization, Model UN. **Organizations:** 155 registered organizations, 16 honor societies, 25 religious organizations. 14 fraternities, 10 sororities. **Athletics (Intercollegiate):** *Men:* Baseball, basketball, diving, football, golf, sailing, soccer, tennis, wrestling. *Women:* Basketball, crew/rowing, diving, field hockey, golf, lacrosse, sailing, soccer, tennis **On-Campus Highlights:** Webb Student Center, Engineering/Computational Bldg, University Village, Constant Convocation Center, Kaufman Mall. **Environmental Initiatives:** First LEED-certified higher education building in Virginia & Created Environmental Advisory Council Recycling Efforts Incorporate Low-Impact Development Techniques for Storm Water Management.

ADMISSIONS

Freshman Academic Profile: Average high school GPA 3.29. 11% in top 10% of high school class, 39% in top 25% of high school class, 82% in top 50% of high school class. 85% from public high schools. SAT Math middle 50% range 480–580. SAT Critical Reading middle 50% range 480–570. SAT Writing middle 50% range 460–560. ACT middle 50% range 18–23. Minimum paper TOEFL 550. Minimum computer TOEFL 213. Minimum web-based TOEFL 79. **Basis for Candidate Selection:** *Very important factors considered include:* Academic GPA, rigor of secondary school record, standardized test scores, extracurricular activities. *Important factors considered include:* Class rank, application essay, recommendation(s), volunteer work, work experience. *Other factors considered include:* Alumni/ae relation, character/personal qualities, first generation, interview, level of applicant's interest, talent/ability. **Freshman Admission Requirements:** High school diploma is required and GED is accepted. *Academic units required:* 4 English, 3 mathematics, 3 science, 3 foreign language, 3 social studies. **Freshman Admission Statistics:** 9,878 applied, 72% admitted, 39% enrolled. **Transfer Admission Requirements:** College transcript(s), minimum college GPA of 2.2 required. Lowest grade transferable c. **General Admission Information:** Application fee $50. Regular application deadline 2/1. Notification on a rolling basis, beginning on or about 1/15. Nonfall registration accepted. Admission may be deferred for a maximum of 1 year. Credit and/or placement offered for CEEB Advanced Placement tests.

COSTS AND FINANCIAL AID

Annual in-state tuition $7,080. Annual out-of-state tuition $19,530. Room and board $7,868. Required fees $238. Average book expense $1,000. **Required Forms and Deadlines:** FAFSA. Financial aid filing deadline 3/15. Priority financial aid filing date 2/15. **Notification of Awards:** Applicants will be notified of awards on a rolling basis beginning 2/1. **Types of Aid:** *Need-based scholarships/grants:* Federal Pell, SEOG, state scholarships/grants, private scholarships, the school's own gift aid, United Negro College Fund, Federal Nursing Scholarships. *Loans:* Direct Subsidized Stafford, Direct Unsubsidized Stafford, Direct PLUS, Federal Perkins, Federal Nursing, college/university loans from institutional funds. *Student Employment:* Federal Work-Study Program available. Institutional employment available. Highest amount earned per year from on-campus jobs $5,382. Off-campus job opportunities are excellent. **Financial Aid Statistics:** 30% freshmen, 27% undergrads receive need-based scholarship or grant aid. 28% freshmen, 15% undergrads receive non-need-based scholarship or grant aid. 33% freshmen, 33% undergrads receive need-based self-help aid. 3% freshmen, 2% undergrads receive athletic scholarships. 78% freshmen, 74% undergrads receive any aid. 81% undergrads borrow to pay for school. Average cumulative indebtedness $17,250. **Criteria for awarding institutional aid:** *Non-need-based:* Academics, alumni affiliation, art, athletics, leadership, music/drama, state/district residency.

OLIVET COLLEGE

320 S. Main St, Olivet, MI 49076
Phone: 269-749-7635
E-mail: admissions@olivetcollege.edu **CEEB Code:** 1595
Fax: 269-749-6617 **Website:** www.olivetcollege.edu **ACT Code:** 2042

This private school, affiliated with the United Church of Christ Church, was founded in 1844. It has a 45-acre campus.

RATINGS

Admissions Selectivity Rating: 60* **Fire Safety Rating:** 60* **Green Rating:** 60*

STUDENTS AND FACULTY

Enrollment: 1,070. **Student Body:** 42% female, 58% male, 5% out-of-state, 3% international Asian 1%, African American 16%, Caucasian 76%, Hispanic 2%, Native American 1%.
Retention and Graduation: 65% grads go on to further study within 1 year. 72% grads pursue arts and sciences degrees. 20% grads pursue law degrees. 45% grads pursue business degrees. 10% grads pursue medical degrees. **Faculty:** Student/faculty ratio 14:1. 46 full-time faculty, 46% hold PhDs, 26% are are members of minority groups, 37% are women. 1% of classes are taught by teaching assistants.

ACADEMICS

Degrees: Bachelor's, master's. **Special Study Options:** Cooperative education program, dual enrollment, honors program, independent study, internships, liberal arts/career combination, student-designed major, study abroad, teacher certification program, Freshman Year Experience, Portfolio Assessment, Senior Experience, and Service Learning programs. Special programs offered to physically disabled students include reader services, tape recorders, tutors. **Career services:** Career/job search classes, career assessment, internships.

FACILITIES

Housing: Coed dorms, men's dorms, special housing for international students, women's dorms, fraternity/sorority housing, apartments for married students, apartments for single students. 30% of campus accessible to physically disabled. **Computers:** Students can register for classes online. Administrative functions (other than registration) can be performed online.

CAMPUS LIFE

Environment: Rural. **Activities:** Choral groups, concert band, drama/theater, jazz band, music ensembles, musical theater, pep band, radio station, student government, student newspaper, yearbook. **Organizations:** 12 registered organizations, 1 honor societies, 1 religious organizations. 3 fraternities, 3 sororities. **Athletics (Intercollegiate):** *Men:* Baseball, basketball, cross-country, diving, football, golf, soccer, swimming, track/field (outdoor), wrestling. *Women:* Basketball, cheerleading, cross-country, diving, golf, soccer, softball, swimming, tennis, track/field (outdoor), volleyball.

ADMISSIONS

Freshman Academic Profile: Average high school GPA 2.92. 75% from public high schools. Minimum paper TOEFL 550. Minimum computer TOEFL 270. **Basis for Candidate Selection:** *Very important factors considered include:* Rigor of secondary school record, standardized test scores, alumni/ae relation, character/personal qualities, extracurricular activities, volunteer work, work experience. *Important factors considered include:* Recommendation(s), racial/ethnic status. *Other factors considered include:* Class rank, application essay, geographical residence, interview, religious affiliation/commitment, state residency, talent/ability. **Freshman Admission Requirements:** High school diploma is required and GED is accepted. *Academic units recommended:* 4 English, 2 mathematics, 2 science, 3 social studies, 2 academic electives. **Transfer Admission Requirements:** High school transcript, college transcript(s), minimum college GPA of 2.0 required. Lowest grade transferable C–. **General Admission Information:** Application fee $25. Notification on a rolling basis, beginning on or about 8/15. Nonfall registration accepted. Admission may be deferred for a maximum of 1 year. Credit and/or placement offered for CEEB Advanced Placement tests.

COSTS AND FINANCIAL AID

Annual tuition $17,994. Room and board $6,346. Required fees $664. Average book expense $800. **Required Forms and Deadlines:** FAFSA. **Notification of Awards:** Applicants will be notified of awards on a rolling basis beginning 2/1. **Types of Aid:** *Need-based scholarships/grants:* Federal Pell, SEOG, state scholarships/grants, private scholarships, the school's own gift aid. *Loans:* FFEL Subsidized Stafford, FFEL Unsubsidized Stafford, FFEL PLUS, Federal Perkins, state loans. *Student Employment:* Federal Work-Study Program available. Institutional employment available. Highest amount earned per year from on-campus jobs $850. Off-campus job opportunities are fair. **Financial Aid Statistics:** 71% freshmen, 84% undergrads receive need-based scholarship or grant aid. 4% freshmen, 4% undergrads receive non-need-based scholarship or grant aid. 66% freshmen, 78% undergrads receive need-based self-help aid. 80% undergrads borrow to pay for school. Average cumulative indebtedness $6,444. **Criteria for awarding institutional aid:** *Non-need-based:* Academics, art, leadership, music/drama, religious affiliation.

OLIVET NAZARENE UNIVERSITY

One University Avenue, Bourbonnais, IL 60914
Phone: 815-939-5603 **Financial Aid Phone:** 815-939-5249
E-mail: admissions@olivet.edu **CEEB Code:** 32
Fax: 815-935-4998 **Website:** www.olivet.edu **ACT Code:** 1112

This private school, affiliated with the Nazarene Church, was founded in 1907. It has a 225-acre campus.

RATINGS
Admissions Selectivity Rating: 81 **Fire Safety Rating:** 60* **Green Rating:** 60*

STUDENTS AND FACULTY
Enrollment: 2,633. **Student Body:** 60% female, 40% male, 55% out-of-state, 1% international (18 countries represented). Asian 1%, African American 9%, Caucasian 86%, Hispanic 3%.
Retention and Graduation: 79% freshmen return for sophomore year. 39% grads go on to further study within 1 year. 27% grads pursue arts and sciences degrees. 3% grads pursue law degrees. 13% grads pursue business degrees. 9% grads pursue medical degrees. **Faculty:** Student/faculty ratio 20:1. 94 full-time faculty, 68% hold PhDs, 3% are are members of minority groups, 34% are women.

ACADEMICS

Degrees: Associate, bachelor's, master's. **Classes:** Most classes have 20–29 students. **Majors with Highest Enrollment:** Business/commerce; education; health/medical preparatory programs, other. **Special Study Options:** Accelerated program, distance learning, double major, honors program, independent study, internships, student-designed major, study abroad, teacher certification program. **Honors programs:** Phi Delta Lambda Psi Chi (Psychology) Dappa Delta Pi (Education) Kappa Omicron Nu (FACS), Sigma Tau Delta (English), Sigma Theta Tau (Nursing), Kappa Sigma Chapter (Nursing), Phi Alpha Theta (History), Departmental Honors. Special programs offered to physically disabled students include note-taking services, reader services, tape recorders, tutors.

FACILITIES

Housing: Special housing for disabled students, men's dorms, women's dorms, apartments for married students, apartments for single students. 100% of campus accessible to physically disabled. **Special Academic Facilities/Equipment:** Planetarium, "smart" classrooms, radio station. **Computers:** Students can register for classes online. Administrative functions (other than registration) can be performed online.

CAMPUS LIFE

Environment: Town. **Activities:** Choral groups, concert band, dance, drama/theater, jazz band, literary magazine, marching band, music ensembles, musical theater, opera, pep band, radio station, student government, student newspaper, student-run film society, symphony orchestra, television station, yearbook. **Organizations:** 79 registered organizations, 8 honor societies, 23 religious organizations. **Athletics (Intercollegiate):** *Men:* Baseball, basketball, cheerleading, cross-country, football, golf, soccer, tennis, track/field (outdoor), track/field (indoor). *Women:* Basketball, cheerleading, cross-country, soccer, softball, tennis, track/field (outdoor), track/field (indoor), volleyball. **On-Campus Highlights:** Common Grounds (coffee shop), Ludwig Center (student center), McHie Arena, Fitness Center, Red Room (student lounge).

ADMISSIONS

Freshman Academic Profile: Average high school GPA 3.3. 22% in top 10% of high school class, 45% in top 25% of high school class, 75% in top 50% of high school class. 85% from public high schools. SAT Math middle 50% range 480–590. SAT Critical Reading middle 50% range 490–620. ACT middle 50% range 20–26. Minimum paper TOEFL 500. Minimum computer TOEFL 173. **Basis for Candidate Selection:** *Very important factors considered include:* Class rank, recommendation(s), rigor of secondary school record, standardized test scores, character/personal qualities. *Important factors considered include:* Application essay, extracurricular activities, interview, talent/ability. *Other factors considered include:* Religious affiliation/commitment, volunteer work, work experience. **Freshman Admission Requirements:** High school diploma is required and GED is accepted. *Academic units required:* 4 English, 3 mathematics, 3 science, 3 social studies, 2 history. *Academic units recommended:* 4 English, 3 mathematics, 3 science, 2 foreign language, 3 social studies, 2 history. **Freshman Admission Statistics:** 2,747 applied, 64% admitted, 40% enrolled. **Transfer Admission Requirements:** College transcript(s), essay or personal statement, statement of good standing from prior institution(s). Minimum college GPA of 2.0 required. Lowest grade transferable D–. **General Admission Information:** Regular application deadline 5/15. Notification on a rolling basis, beginning on or about 6/1. Nonfall registration accepted. Credit and/or placement offered for CEEB Advanced Placement tests.

COSTS AND FINANCIAL AID

Annual tuition $16,750. Room and board $6,400. Required fees $840. Average book expense $800. **Required Forms and Deadlines:** FAFSA, institution's own financial aid form. Priority financial aid filing date 3/1. **Notification of Awards:** Applicants will be notified of awards on a rolling basis beginning 2/1. **Types of Aid:** *Need-based scholarships/grants:* Federal Pell, SEOG, state scholarships/grants, private scholarships, the school's own gift aid. *Loans:* Direct Subsidized Stafford, Direct Unsubsidized Stafford, Direct PLUS, FFEL Subsidized Stafford, FFEL Unsubsidized Stafford, FFEL PLUS, Federal Perkins. *Student Employment:* Federal Work-Study Program available. **Financial Aid Statistics:** 76% freshmen, 73% undergrads receive need-based scholarship or grant aid. 73% freshmen, 67% undergrads receive non-need-based scholarship or grant aid. 63% freshmen, 64% undergrads receive need-based self-help aid. 15% freshmen, 15% undergrads receive athletic scholarships. 96% undergrads receive any aid. 68% undergrads borrow to pay for school. Average cumulative indebtedness $20,607. **Criteria for awarding institutional aid:** *Non-need-based:* Academics, art, athletics, leadership, music/drama, religious affiliation.

ONONDAGA COMMUNITY COLLEGE

4941, Onondaga Road, Syracuse, NY 13215
Phone: 315-498-2201
E-mail: occinfo@sunyocc.edu
Fax: 315-469-2107 **Website:** www.sunyocc.edu

This public school was founded in 1961. It has a 181-acre campus.

RATINGS
Admissions Selectivity Rating: 60*   **Fire Safety Rating:** 60*   **Green Rating:** 60*

STUDENTS AND FACULTY
Enrollment: 5,097. **Student Body:** 54% female, 46% male.
Retention and Graduation: Faculty: Student/faculty ratio 17:1. 179 full-time faculty, 9% are are members of minority groups, 52% are women.

ACADEMICS
Degrees: associate, certificate. **Classes:** Most classes have 10–19 students. **Special Study Options:** Cooperative education program, double major, dual enrollment, English as a Second Language (ESL), honors program, independent study, internships, liberal arts/career combination, study abroad Special programs offered to physically disabled students include note-taking services, reader services, tape recorders, tutors. **Career services:** Alumni services, career/job search classes.

CAMPUS LIFE
Environment: Village. **Activities:** Choral groups, music ensembles, radio station, student government, student newspaper, television station. **Organizations:** 1 honor societies, **Athletics (Intercollegiate):** *Men:* Baseball, basketball, cross-country, lacrosse, tennis. *Women:* Basketball, cross-country, softball, tennis, volleyball.

ADMISSIONS
Freshman Academic Profile: 95% from public high schools. Minimum paper TOEFL 500. Minimum computer TOEFL 173. **Basis for Candidate Selection:** *Very important factors considered include:* Rigor of secondary school record. *Other factors considered include:* Recommendation(s), character/personal qualities, interview. **Freshman Admission Requirements:** High school diploma is required and GED is accepted. High school diploma or equivalent is not required. *Academic units recommended:* 4 English, 2 mathematics, 3 science, (2 science labs), 2 foreign language, 4 social studies, 4 history. **Freshman Admission Statistics:** 2,899 applied, 79% admitted, 217% enrolled. **Transfer Admission Requirements:** High school transcript, college transcript(s), Lowest grade transferable C. **General Admission Information:** Application fee $30. Nonfall registration accepted. Admission may be deferred for a maximum of 2 semesters.

COSTS AND FINANCIAL AID
Annual in-state tuition $3,180. Annual out-of-state tuition $9,540. Required fees $155. **Required Forms and Deadlines:** FAFSA, state aid form. Priority financial aid filing date 2/15. **Notification of Awards:** Applicants will be notified of awards on or about 4/15. **Types of Aid:** *Need-based scholarships/grants:* Federal Pell, SEOG, state scholarships/grants, Federal work study. *Loans:* FFEL Subsidized Stafford, FFEL Unsubsidized Stafford, FFEL PLUS. *Student Employment:* Federal Work-Study Program available. Off-campus job opportunities are excellent. **Financial Aid Statistics:** 36% freshmen, 41% undergrads receive need-based scholarship or grant aid. 44% freshmen, 49% undergrads receive need-based self-help aid. **Criteria for awarding institutional aid:** *Non-need-based:* Academics, alumni affiliation.

ORAL ROBERTS UNIVERSITY

7777 S. Lewis Avenue, Tulsa, OK 74171
Phone: 918-495-6518
E-mail: admissions@oru.edu **CEEB Code:** 6552
Fax: 918-495-6222 **Website:** www.oru.edu **ACT Code:** 3427

This is a private school. It has a 500-acre campus.

RATINGS
Admissions Selectivity Rating: 80   **Fire Safety Rating:** 60*   **Green Rating:** 60*

STUDENTS AND FACULTY
Enrollment: 2,558. **Student Body:** 58% female, 42% male, 64% out-of-state, international .

Retention and Graduation: 72% freshmen return for sophomore year. 46% freshmen graduate within 4 years. 50% grads go on to further study within 1 year. 25% grads pursue arts and sciences degrees. 1% grads pursue law degrees. 10% grads pursue business degrees. 5% grads pursue medical degrees. **Faculty:** Student/faculty ratio 12:1. 186 full-time faculty, 65% hold PhDs, 12% are are members of minority groups, 41% are women.

ACADEMICS
Degrees: Bachelor's, first professional, master's. **Classes:** Most classes have 10–19 students. Most lab/discussion sessions have 20–29 students. **Majors with Highest Enrollment:** marketing/marketing management; mass communication/media studies; theology/theological studies. **Special Study Options:** Accelerated program, distance learning, double major, dual enrollment, English as a Second Language (ESL), external degree program, honors program, independent study, internships, liberal arts/career combination, student-designed major, study abroad, teacher certification program, weekend college. **Honors programs:** ORU Honors Program includes "Scholars" and "Fellows"—Highly selective; includes Beta Gamma Phi and others. **Combined degree programs:** 3-2 bachelor's/ MBA and bachelor's/MAEd programs. Special programs offered to physically disabled students include note-taking services, reader services, tape recorders, tutors.

FACILITIES
Housing: Men's dorms, women's dorms. 100% of campus accessible to physically disabled. **Special Academic Facilities/Equipment:** Dial Access Information Retrieval System, programmed learning facilities, early learning center, TV production studio.

CAMPUS LIFE
Activities: Choral groups, concert band, dance, drama/theater, jazz band, music ensembles, musical theater, pep band, radio station, student government, student newspaper, television station, yearbook, campus ministries, international student organization, Model UN. **Athletics (Intercollegiate):** *Men:* Baseball, basketball, cheerleading, cross-country, soccer, swimming, tennis, track/field (outdoor). *Women:* Basketball, cheerleading, cross-country, soccer, swimming, tennis, track/field (outdoor), volleyball. **On-Campus Highlights:** Eagle's Nest, Aerobics Center, Prayer Tower, Mabee Center (Multi-purpose Event Complex), Gabrielle Christian Salem Hall.

ADMISSIONS
Freshman Academic Profile: Average high school GPA 3.36. 23% in top 10% of high school class, 45% in top 25% of high school class, 74% in top 50% of high school class. 75% from public high schools. SAT Math middle 50% range 455–570. SAT Critical Reading middle 50% range 465–590. ACT middle 50% range 20–26. Minimum paper TOEFL 500. Minimum computer TOEFL 150. **Basis for Candidate Selection:** *Very important factors considered include:* Application essay, academic GPA, rigor of secondary school record, standardized test scores. *Important factors considered include:* Class rank, recommendation(s). *Other factors considered include:* Alumni/ae relation, character/personal qualities, religious affiliation/commitment. **Freshman Admission Requirements:** High school diploma is required and GED is accepted. *Academic units recommended:* 4 English, 2 mathematics, 1 science, (1 science labs), 2 foreign language, 2 social studies, 4 academic electives. **Freshman Admission Statistics:** 1,127 applied, 73% admitted, 59% enrolled. **Transfer Admission Requirements:** High school transcript, college transcript(s), essay or personal statement, minimum college GPA of 2.0 required. Lowest grade transferable 2. **General Admission Information:** Application fee $35. Nonfall registration accepted. Credit and/or placement offered for CEEB Advanced Placement tests.

COSTS AND FINANCIAL AID
Annual tuition $18,476. Room and board $7,916. Required fees $630. Average book expense $1,500. **Required Forms and Deadlines:** FAFSA. Priority financial aid filing date 3/15. **Types of Aid:** *Need-based scholarships/grants:* Federal Pell, SEOG, state scholarships/grants, private scholarships, the school's own gift aid. *Loans:* FFEL Subsidized Stafford, FFEL Unsubsidized Stafford, FFEL PLUS, Federal Perkins. *Student Employment:* Highest amount earned per year from on-campus jobs $1,800. **Financial Aid Statistics:** 69% freshmen, 67% undergrads receive need-based scholarship or grant aid. 29% freshmen, 25% undergrads receive non-need-based scholarship or grant aid. 63% freshmen, 64% undergrads receive need-based self-help aid. 3% freshmen, 4% undergrads receive athletic scholarships. 67% undergrads borrow to pay for school. Average cumulative indebtedness $34,555. **Criteria for awarding institutional aid:** *Non-need-based:* Academics, alumni affiliation, art, athletics, job skills, leadership, music/drama.

OREGON COLLEGE OF ART AND CRAFT

8245 Southwest Barnes Road, Portland, OR 97225
Phone: 503-297-5544 **Financial Aid Phone:** 503-297-5544
E-mail: dspencer@ocac.edu **CEEB Code:** 4236
Fax: 503-297-9651 **Website:** www.ocac.edu **ACT Code:** 3471

This private school was founded in 1907. It has a 9-acre campus.

RATINGS
Admissions Selectivity Rating: 60*   **Fire Safety Rating:** 61   **Green Rating:** 60*

STUDENTS AND FACULTY
Enrollment: 115. **Student Body:** 71% female, 29% male, 14% out-of-state, (1 countries represented). Asian 3%, Caucasian 79%, Hispanic 2%, Native American 3%.
Retention and Graduation: 76% freshmen return for sophomore year. 15% grads pursue arts and sciences degrees. **Faculty:** Student/faculty ratio 8:1. 9 full-time faculty, 89% hold PhDs, 11% are are members of minority groups, 44% are women.

ACADEMICS
Degrees: Bachelor's, certificate, post-bachelor's certificate. **Classes:** Most classes have fewer than 10 students. **Majors with Highest Enrollment:** drawing; fine arts and art studies, other; metal and jewelry arts. **Special Study Options:** Cross-registration, exchange student program (domestic), independent study, internships, study abroad.

FACILITIES
Housing: cooperative housing, The college offers a small number of on-campus housing for new students straight from high school. In addition, the college has contract with two apartment complexes across the street from the college. 60% of campus accessible to physically disabled. **Special Academic Facilities/Equipment:** Hoffman Gallery, Centrum Gallery, and 7 specialized studios for artmaking.

CAMPUS LIFE
Environment: Metropolis. **Activities:** Student government, student newspaper. **Organizations:** 1 registered organizations, **On-Campus Highlights:** Hands On Cafe, Centrum Art Gallery, Thesis Studios, Library, Computer Lab.

ADMISSIONS
Freshman Academic Profile: 85% from public high schools. ACT middle 50% range 17–24. Minimum paper TOEFL 550. Minimum computer TOEFL 213. **Basis for Candidate Selection:** *Very important factors considered include:* Application essay, academic GPA, level of applicant's interest, talent/ability. *Important factors considered include:* Recommendation(s), rigor of secondary school record, character/personal qualities, interview. *Other factors considered include:* standardized test scores, alumni/ae relation, extracurricular activities, first generation, volunteer work, work experience. **Freshman Admission Requirements:** High school diploma is required and GED is accepted. *Academic units recommended:* 4 English, 3 mathematics, 3 science, 2 foreign language, 1 social studies, 3 history, 2 visual arts **Freshman Admission Statistics:** 27 applied, 93% admitted, 32% enrolled. **Transfer Admission Requirements:** High school transcript, college transcript(s), essay or personal statement, minimum college GPA of 2.0 required. Lowest grade transferable C. **General Admission Information:** Application fee $35. Notification on a rolling basis, beginning on or about 1/1. Nonfall registration accepted. Admission may be deferred for a maximum of 1 year. Credit and/or placement offered for CEEB Advanced Placement tests.

COSTS AND FINANCIAL AID
Required Forms and Deadlines: FAFSA. Priority financial aid filing date 3/1. **Notification of Awards:** Applicants will be notified of awards on a rolling basis beginning 3/15. **Types of Aid:** *Need-based scholarships/grants:* Federal Pell, SEOG, state scholarships/grants, private scholarships, the school's own gift aid. *Loans:* FFEL Subsidized Stafford, FFEL Unsubsidized Stafford, FFEL PLUS, state loans. *Student Employment:* Federal Work-Study Program available. Institutional employment available. **Financial Aid Statistics:** 63% freshmen, 72% undergrads receive need-based scholarship or grant aid. 63% freshmen, 6% undergrads receive non-need-based scholarship or grant aid. 88% freshmen, 72% undergrads receive need-based self-help aid. 65% freshmen, 80% undergrads receive any aid. 100% undergrads borrow to pay for school. Average cumulative indebtedness $31,000. **Criteria for awarding institutional aid:** *Non-need-based:* Academics, art.

OREGON HEALTH & SCIENCE UNIVERSITY

3181 SW Sam Jackson Park Rd, SN-ADM, Portland, OR 97239
Phone: 503-494-2998 **Financial Aid Phone:** 503-494-7800
E-mail: proginfo@ohsu.edu **CEEB Code:** 4900
Fax: 503-494-3400 **Website:** www.ohsu.edu

This public school was founded in 1867. It has a 120-acre campus.

RATINGS
Admissions Selectivity Rating: 60*   **Fire Safety Rating:** 60*   **Green Rating:** 60*

STUDENTS AND FACULTY
Enrollment: 591. **Student Body:** 84% female, 16% male, 10% out-of-state, 1% international Asian 5%, African American 1%, Caucasian 79%, Hispanic 5%, Native American 2%.
Faculty: 1290 full-time faculty.

ACADEMICS
Degrees: Associate, bachelor's, first professional, first professional certificate, master's, post-bachelor's certificate, post-master's certificate. **Majors with Highest Enrollment:** Clinical laboratory science/medical technology/technologist; emergency medical technology/technician (emt paramedic); nursing/registered nurse (RN, ASN, BSN, MSN). **Special Study Options:** Accelerated program, distance learning. **Combined degree programs:** MD/PhD, MD/MPH.

FACILITIES
Computers: Students can register for classes online.

CAMPUS LIFE
Environment: Metropolis. **Activities:** Student government, student newspaper, yearbook. **On-Campus Highlights:** Portland Aerial Tram, Center for Health and Healing Cafe, Marquam Hill Hiking Trails.

ADMISSIONS
Freshman Admission Requirements: High school diploma is required and GED is accepted. **Transfer Admission Requirements:** College transcript(s), essay or personal statement, standardized test scores, statement of good standing from prior institution(s). Lowest grade transferable C. **General Admission Information:** Application fee $120. Regular application deadline 1/15.

COSTS AND FINANCIAL AID
Annual out-of-state tuition $20,176. **Types of Aid:** *Need-based scholarships/grants:* Federal Pell, SEOG, state scholarships/grants, private scholarships, the school's own gift aid, Scholarship for Disadvantaged Student. *Loans:* Direct Subsidized Stafford, Direct Unsubsidized Stafford, Direct PLUS, Federal Perkins, Federal Nursing, college/university loans from institutional funds. *Student Employment:* Federal Work-Study Program available. Institutional employment available. Off-campus job opportunities are poor. **Financial Aid Statistics:** 40% undergrads receive need-based scholarship or grant aid. 80% undergrads receive need-based self-help aid. 70% undergrads receive any aid. **Criteria for awarding institutional aid:** *Non-need-based:* Academics, minority status, state/district residency.

OREGON INSTITUTE OF TECHNOLOGY

3201 Campus Drive, Klamath Falls, OR 97601
Phone: 541-885-1150 **Financial Aid Phone:** 541-885-1280
E-mail: oit@oit.edu **CEEB Code:** 4587
Fax: 541-885-1115 **Website:** **ACT Code:** 3484

This public school was founded in 1947. It has a 173-acre campus.

RATINGS
Admissions Selectivity Rating: 77   **Fire Safety Rating:** 60*   **Green Rating:** 60*

STUDENTS AND FACULTY
Enrollment: 2,663. **Student Body:** 44% female, 56% male, 15% out-of-state, 1% international (11 countries represented). Asian 5%, African American 1%, Caucasian 81%, Hispanic 4%, Native American 2%.
Retention and Graduation: 69% freshmen return for sophomore year. **Faculty:** Student/faculty ratio 16:1. 126 full-time faculty, 33% hold PhDs, 6% are are members of minority groups, 35% are women.

ACADEMICS
Degrees: Associate, bachelor's, certificate, master's. **Classes:** Most classes have 10–19 students. Most lab/discussion sessions have 10–19 students. **Majors with**

Highest Enrollment: Computer engineering technology/technician; computer software technology/technician; mechanical engineering/mechanical technology/technician. **Special Study Options:** Cooperative education program, cross-registration, distance learning, double major, dual enrollment, external degree program, internships, study abroad. Special programs offered to physically disabled students include note-taking services, reader services, tape recorders, tutors.

FACILITIES

Housing: Coed dorms. **Special Academic Facilities/Equipment:** Shaw Historical Library. **Computers:** Students can register for classes online. Administrative functions (other than registration) can be performed online.

CAMPUS LIFE

Environment: Town. **Activities:** Choral groups, pep band, radio station, student government, student newspaper, symphony orchestra, television station. **Organizations:** 30 registered organizations, 5 honor societies, 1 religious organizations. 1 fraternity, 1 sorority. **Athletics (Intercollegiate):** *Men:* Baseball, basketball, cross-country, track/field (outdoor). *Women:* Basketball, cross-country, soccer, softball, track/field (outdoor), volleyball. **On-Campus Highlights:** College Union Bistro, College Union Marketplace, Purvine Coffee Cart, Tech Fit, Fitness Center, Residnece Hall Lounge.

ADMISSIONS

Freshman Academic Profile: Average high school GPA 3.29. 25% in top 10% of high school class, 56% in top 25% of high school class, 92% in top 50% of high school class. SAT Math middle 50% range 480–600. SAT Critical Reading middle 50% range 460–570. ACT middle 50% range 21–26. Minimum paper TOEFL 520. Minimum computer TOEFL 190. **Basis for Candidate Selection:** *Very important factors considered include:* Rigor of secondary school record, standardized test scores. *Other factors considered include:* Class rank, application essay, recommendation(s), character/personal qualities, interview, work experience. **Freshman Admission Requirements:** High school diploma is required and GED is accepted. *Academic units required:* 4 English, 3 mathematics, 2 science, (1 science labs), 2 foreign language, 3 social studies. **Freshman Admission Statistics:** 651 applied, 88% admitted, 46% enrolled. **Transfer Admission Requirements:** College transcript(s), minimum college GPA of 2.0 required. Lowest grade transferable D. **General Admission Information:** Application fee $50. Regular application deadline 10/1. Notification on a rolling basis, beginning on or about 10/15. Nonfall registration accepted. Admission may be deferred for a maximum of 2 years. Credit and/or placement offered for CEEB Advanced Placement tests.

COSTS AND FINANCIAL AID

Annual in-state tuition $4,590. Annual out-of-state tuition $14,760. Room and board $6,480. Required fees $1,329. Average book expense $1,000. **Required Forms and Deadlines:** FAFSA. Priority financial aid filing date 3/1. **Notification of Awards:** Applicants will be notified of awards on a rolling basis beginning 4/1. **Types of Aid:** *Need-based scholarships/grants:* Federal Pell, SEOG, state scholarships/grants, private scholarships, the school's own gift aid. *Loans:* FFEL Subsidized Stafford, FFEL Unsubsidized Stafford, FFEL PLUS, Federal Perkins, college/university loans from institutional funds. *Student Employment:* **Financial Aid Statistics:** 34% freshmen, 43% undergrads receive need-based scholarship or grant aid. 6% freshmen, 5% undergrads receive non-need-based scholarship or grant aid. 55% freshmen, 64% undergrads receive need-based self-help aid. 1% undergrads receive athletic scholarships. 89% freshmen, 86% undergrads receive any aid. 7% undergrads borrow to pay for school. Average cumulative indebtedness $22,351. **Criteria for awarding institutional aid:** *Non-need-based:* Academics, athletics, leadership, minority status.

OREGON STATE UNIVERSITY

104 Kerr Administration Building, Corvallis, OR 97331-2106
Phone: 541-737-4411 **Financial Aid Phone:** 541-737-2241
E-mail: osuadmit@oregonstate.edu **CEEB Code:** 4586
Fax: 541-737-2482 **Website:** oregonstate.edu

This public school was founded in 1858. It has a 421-acre campus.

RATINGS

Admissions Selectivity Rating: 77 **Fire Safety Rating:** 80 **Green Rating:** 98

STUDENTS AND FACULTY

Enrollment: 17,139. **Student Body:** 47% female, 53% male, 15% out-of-state, 2% international Asian 9%, African American 1%, Caucasian 72%, Hispanic 5%, Native American 1%.
Retention and Graduation: 83% freshmen return for sophomore year. 27% freshmen graduate within 4 years. **Faculty:** Student/faculty ratio 20:1. 861 full-time faculty, 75% hold PhDs, 14% are are members of minority groups, 41% are women.

ACADEMICS

Degrees: Bachelor's, certificate, doctoral, master's, post-bachelor's certificate, post-master's certificate. **Classes:** Most classes have 20–29 students. Most lab/discussion sessions have 20–29 students. **Majors with Highest Enrollment:** Business administration and management; health and physical education; human development and family studies. **Special Study Options:** Accelerated program, cooperative education program, cross-registration, distance learning, double major, dual enrollment, English as a Second Language (ESL), exchange student program (domestic), external degree program, honors program, independent study, internships, liberal arts/career combination, student-designed major, study abroad, teacher certification program. **Combined degree programs:** 2-2 food science/technology program w/ U of Alaska. Special programs offered to physically disabled students include note-taking services, reader services, tape recorders, tutors. **Career services:** Alumni network, alumni services, career/job search classes, career assessment, internships, regional alumni.

FACILITIES

Housing: Coed dorms, special housing for disabled students, special housing for international students, fraternity/sorority housing, apartments for married students, cooperative housing, apartments for single students, theme housing. 86% of campus accessible to physically disabled. **Special Academic Facilities/Equipment:** Museums, galleries, collections, exhibits of cultural and scientific materials, language lab. **Computers:** 100% of classrooms, 2% of dorms, 100% of libraries, 50% of dining areas, 100% of student union, 2% of common outdoor areas have wireless network access. Students can register for classes online. Administrative functions (other than registration) can be performed online.

CAMPUS LIFE

Environment: Town. **Activities:** Choral groups, concert band, dance, drama/theater, jazz band, literary magazine, marching band, music ensembles, musical theater, opera, pep band, radio station, student government, student newspaper, student-run film society, symphony orchestra, television station, yearbook, campus ministries, international student organization, Model UN. **Organizations:** 350 registered organizations, 29 honor societies, 23 religious organizations. 24 fraternities, 13 sororities. **Athletics (Intercollegiate):** *Men:* Baseball, basketball, crew/rowing, football, golf, soccer, wrestling. *Women:* Basketball, crew/rowing, cross-country, golf, gymnastics, soccer, softball, swimming, track/field (outdoor), volleyball. **On-Campus Highlights:** Memorial Union, Java II, Weatherford Hall, Dixon Recreation Center, Reser Stadium. **Environmental Initiatives:** Many areas of OSU research have large impacts on sustainability state- and nation-wide. Particularly our climate change research center and our wave and wind research make global impacts. New degrees like ecological engineering offer a greener curriculum. A student fee, combined with donations and administrative money, offsets about 73% of campus electrical use with a green tags purchase. We are in the design phase of installing a large solar hot water system on our rec center. EPA gave OSU a Green Power Leadership Award in 2008. The Student Sustainability Initiative, a student fee funded organization, is a national model for student project and program development. It funds student employees and competitive grants for campus student projects that make campus more sustainable and expose students to sustainable practices.

ADMISSIONS

Freshman Academic Profile: Average high school GPA 3.47. 24% in top 10% of high school class, 52% in top 25% of high school class, 84% in top 50% of high school class. SAT Math middle 50% range 480–610. SAT Critical Reading middle 50% range 460–580. SAT Writing middle 50% range 440–560. ACT middle 50% range 20–26. Minimum paper TOEFL 550. Minimum computer TOEFL 213. **Basis for Candidate Selection:** *Very important factors considered include:* Application essay, academic GPA, rigor of secondary school record. *Important factors considered include:* Class rank, character/personal qualities, level of applicant's interest, talent/ability, volunteer work. *Other factors considered include:* Recommendation(s), standardized test scores, extracurricular activities, first generation, interview, work experience. **Freshman Admission Requirements:** High school diploma is required and GED is accepted. *Academic units required:* 4 English, 3 mathematics, 2 science, (1 science labs), 2 foreign language, 3 social studies. *Academic units recommended:* (2 science labs). **Freshman Admission Statistics:** 10,048 applied, 83% admitted, 41% enrolled. **Transfer Admission Requirements:** College transcript(s), essay or personal statement, statement of good standing from prior institution(s). Minimum college GPA of 2.25 required. Lowest grade transferable D. **General Admission Information:** Application fee $50. Regular application deadline 9/1. Notification on a rolling basis, beginning on or about 10/1. Nonfall registration accepted. Admission may be deferred for a maximum of 1 year. Credit and/or placement offered for CEEB Advanced Placement tests.

COSTS AND FINANCIAL AID

Required Forms and Deadlines: FAFSA. Priority financial aid filing date 2/28. **Notification of Awards:** Applicants will be notified of awards on a rolling basis beginning 4/1. **Types of Aid:** *Need-based scholarships/grants:* Federal Pell, SEOG, state scholarships/grants, private scholarships, the school's own gift aid. *Loans:* Direct Subsidized Stafford, Direct Unsubsidized Stafford, Direct PLUS, Federal Perkins, college/university loans from institutional funds. *Student Employment:* Federal Work-Study Program available. Institutional employment available. Off-campus job opportunities are good. **Financial Aid Statistics:** 41% freshmen, 41% undergrads receive need-based scholarship or grant aid. 2% freshmen, 1% undergrads receive non-need-based scholarship or grant aid. 49% freshmen, 47% undergrads receive need-based self-help aid. 2% freshmen, 3% undergrads receive athletic scholarships. 53% freshmen, 52% undergrads receive any aid. **Criteria for awarding institutional aid:** *Non-need-based:* Academics, alumni affiliation, athletics, job skills, leadership, minority status, state/district residency.

OTIS COLLEGE OF ART AND DESIGN

9045 Lincoln Boulevard, Los Angeles, CA 90045
Phone: 310-665-6820 **Financial Aid Phone:** 310-665-6880
E-mail: admissions@otis.edu **CEEB Code:** 4394
Fax: 310-665-6821 **Website:** www.otis.edu **ACT Code:** 359

This private school was founded in 1918. It has a 5-acre campus.

RATINGS
Admissions Selectivity Rating: 60*   **Fire Safety Rating:** 60*   **Green Rating:** 60*

STUDENTS AND FACULTY
Enrollment: 900. **Student Body:** 63% female, 37% male, % out-of-state, 13% international Asian 32%, African American 3%, Caucasian 36%, Hispanic 14%, Native American 1%.
Retention and Graduation: 75% freshmen return for sophomore year. 36% freshmen graduate within 4 years. 80% grads pursue arts and sciences degrees. **Faculty:** Student/faculty ratio 8:1. 43 full-time faculty, 63% hold PhDs, 5% are are members of minority groups, 56% are women.

ACADEMICS
Degrees: Bachelor's, master's. **Classes:** Most classes have 10–19 students. **Majors with Highest Enrollment:** Animation, interactive technology, video graphics and special effects; fashion/apparel design; graphic design. **Special Study Options:** English as a Second Language (ESL), exchange student program (domestic), honors program, independent study, internships, study abroad **Honors programs:** We have an honors program for qualified enrolled students. Special programs offered to physically disabled students include tape recorders, tutors. **Career services:** Alumni network, alumni services, career/job search classes, career assessment, internships. **Career services highlights include:** Strong and growing network for students to experience real world work.

FACILITIES
Housing: Apartments for single students. 100% of campus accessible to physically disabled. **Special Academic Facilities/Equipment:** Art gallery, student gallery,woodshop, metal shop, photo lab, digital media lab, printmaking lab, letterpress lab. **Computers:** Administrative functions (other than registration) can be performed online.

CAMPUS LIFE
Environment: Metropolis. **Activities:** Literary magazine, student government, student newspaper. **Organizations:** 7 registered organizations,

ADMISSIONS
Freshman Academic Profile: Average high school GPA 3.09. SAT Math middle 50% range 440–580. SAT Critical Reading middle 50% range 420–550. ACT middle 50% range 17–22. Minimum paper TOEFL 550. Minimum computer TOEFL 213. **Basis for Candidate Selection:** *Very important factors considered include:* Rigor of secondary school record, talent/ability. *Important factors considered include:* Application essay, standardized test scores. *Other factors considered include:* Recommendation(s), alumni/ae relation, character/personal qualities, extracurricular activities, interview, volunteer work, work experience. **Freshman Admission Requirements:** High school diploma is required and GED is accepted. *Academic units required:* 4 English, 3 mathematics, 2 science, (1 science labs), 1 social studies, 2 history. *Academic units recommended:* 4 English, 4 mathematics, 4 science, (4 science labs), 2 foreign language, 2 social studies, 3 history. **Freshman Admission Statistics:** 695 applied, 58% admitted, 30% enrolled. **Transfer Admission Requirements:** High school transcript, college transcript(s), essay or personal statement, statement of good standing from prior institution(s). Minimum college GPA of 2.5 required. Lowest grade transferable C. **General Admission Information:** Application fee $50. Nonfall registration accepted. Credit offered for CEEB Advanced Placement tests.

COSTS AND FINANCIAL AID
Annual tuition $25,710. Required fees $600. Average book expense $2,400. **Required Forms and Deadlines:** FAFSA, state aid form. Priority financial aid filing date 2/15. **Notification of Awards:** Applicants will be notified of awards on a rolling basis beginning 3/1. **Types of Aid:** *Need-based scholarships/grants:* Federal Pell, SEOG, state scholarships/grants, private scholarships, the school's own gift aid. *Loans:* FFEL Subsidized Stafford, FFEL Unsubsidized Stafford, FFEL PLUS. *Student Employment:* Federal Work-Study Program available. Institutional employment available. Off-campus job opportunities are excellent. **Financial Aid Statistics:** 87% freshmen, 69% undergrads receive need-based scholarship or grant aid. 72% freshmen, 61% undergrads receive need-based self-help aid. 42% freshmen, 44% undergrads receive any aid. 63% undergrads borrow to pay for school. Average cumulative indebtedness $32,156. **Criteria for awarding institutional aid:** *Non-need-based:* Academics, art.

OTTERBEIN COLLEGE

Office of Admission, One Otterbein College, Westerville, OH 43081
Phone: 614-823-1500 **Financial Aid Phone:** 614-823-1502
E-mail: uotterb@otterbein.edu **CEEB Code:** 1597
Fax: 614-823-1200 **Website:** www.otterbein.edu **ACT Code:** 3318

This private school, affiliated with the Methodist Church, was founded in 1847. It has a 140-acre campus.

RATINGS
Admissions Selectivity Rating: 78   **Fire Safety Rating:** 60*   **Green Rating:** 60*

STUDENTS AND FACULTY
Student Body: 10% out-of-state, international (12 countries represented). **Retention and Graduation:** 92% freshmen return for sophomore year. **Faculty:** Student/faculty ratio 12:1. 161 full-time faculty, 93% hold PhDs, 11% are are members of minority groups, 55% are women.

ACADEMICS
Degrees: Bachelor's, master's. **Majors with Highest Enrollment:** Business/commerce; education; nursing/registered nurse (RN,ASN, BSN, MSN). **Special Study Options:** Accelerated program, cooperative education program, cross-registration, double major, dual enrollment, exchange student program (domestic), honors program, independent study, internships, liberal arts/career combination, student-designed major, study abroad, teacher certification program, weekend college. **Honors programs:** The Honors Program at Otterbein College is designed to provide intellectual stimulation and challenge for students with high academic ability and motivation. The four-year program provides the opportunity to participate in a community of students and faculty who have shared scholarly and creative interests. As part of that community students develop and complete their own Honors research and creative projects. Through the Honors seminars and Honors project, students develop advanced knowledge in their disciplinary fields and acquire the skills for independent work in their own areas of academic and professional interest. The Honors Program at Otterbein College is designed to provide intellectual stimulation and challenge for students with high academic ability and motivation. The four-year program provides the opportunity to participate in a community of students and faculty who have shared scholarly and creative interests. As part of that community students develop and complete their own Honors research and creative projects. Through the Honors seminars and Honors project, students develop advanced knowledge in their disciplinary fields and acquire the skills for independent work in their own areas of academic and professional interest. Special programs offered to physically disabled students include note-taking services, reader services, tape recorders, tutors. **Career services:** Alumni network, alumni services, career/job search classes, career assessment, internships, regional alumni.

FACILITIES
Housing: Coed dorms, men's dorms, women's dorms, fraternity/sorority housing, apartments for single students, theme housing. **Special Academic Facilities/Equipment:** Language lab, horse stable, observatory and planetarium, Celestron 8-inch and 14-inch telescopes, 3 art galleries. **Computers:** Students can register for classes online. Administrative functions (other than registration) can be performed online.

CAMPUS LIFE
Environment: Town. **Activities:** Choral groups, concert band, dance, drama/theater, jazz band, literary magazine, marching band, music ensembles, musical theater, opera, pep band, radio station, student government, student newspaper, symphony orchestra, television station, yearbook, international student organization. **Organizations:** 100 registered organizations, 7 fraternities, 6

sororities. **Athletics (Intercollegiate):** *Men:* Baseball, basketball, cheerleading, cross-country, equestrian sports, football, golf, soccer, tennis, track/field (outdoor), track/field (indoor). *Women:* Basketball, cheerleading, cross-country, equestrian sports, golf, soccer, softball, tennis, track/field (outdoor), track/field (indoor), volleyball. **On-Campus Highlights:** Clements Recreation Center, Cowen Hall—Theatre, Campus Center, Art Galleries/Art Building.

ADMISSIONS

Freshman Academic Profile: Average high school GPA 3.34. 24% in top 10% of high school class, 55% in top 25% of high school class, 85% in top 50% of high school class. SAT Math middle 50% range 480–590. SAT Critical Reading middle 50% range 470–600. SAT Writing middle 50% range 460–600. ACT middle 50% range 20–25. Minimum paper TOEFL 500. Minimum computer TOEFL 193. **Basis for Candidate Selection:** *Important factors considered include:* Class rank, rigor of secondary school record, standardized test scores. *Other factors considered include:* Application essay, recommendation(s), alumni/ae relation, character/personal qualities, extracurricular activities, interview, racial/ethnic status, talent/ability, volunteer work, work experience. **Freshman Admission Requirements:** High school diploma is required and GED is accepted. *Academic units recommended:* 4 English, 3 mathematics, 3 science, 2 foreign language, 3 social studies, 2 performing arts. **Freshman Admission Statistics:** 3,381 applied, 82% admitted, 24% enrolled. **Transfer Admission Requirements:** College transcript(s), minimum college GPA of 2.5 required. Lowest grade transferable C–. **General Admission Information:** Application fee $25. Notification on a rolling basis, beginning on or about 10/15. Nonfall registration accepted. Admission may be deferred for a maximum of 12. Credit and/or placement offered for CEEB Advanced Placement tests.

COSTS AND FINANCIAL AID

Annual tuition $26,319. Room and board $7,461. Average book expense $700. **Required Forms and Deadlines:** FAFSA. Priority financial aid filing date 4/1. **Types of Aid:** *Need-based scholarships/grants:* Federal Pell, SEOG, state scholarships/grants, private scholarships, the school's own gift aid. *Loans:* Direct Subsidized Stafford, Direct Unsubsidized Stafford, Direct PLUS, Federal Perkins. *Student Employment:* Federal Work-Study Program available. Institutional employment available. Highest amount earned per year from on-campus jobs $1,800. Off-campus job opportunities are excellent. **Criteria for awarding institutional aid:** *Non-need-based:* Academics, alumni affiliation, art, leadership, minority status, music/drama, religious affiliation.

See page 1194.

OUACHITA BAPTIST UNIVERSITY

410 Ouachita St, Arkadelphia, AR 71998-0001
Phone: 870-245-5110 **Financial Aid Phone:** 870-245-5587
E-mail: admissions@alpha.obu.edu **CEEB Code:** 6549
Fax: 870-245-5500 **Website: ACT Code:** 134

This private school, affiliated with the Southern Baptist Church, was founded in 1886. It has a 200-acre campus.

RATINGS
Admissions Selectivity Rating: 86   **Fire Safety Rating:** 83   **Green Rating:** 63

STUDENTS AND FACULTY
Enrollment: 1,421. **Student Body:** 53% female, 47% male, 49% out-of-state, 3% international (49 countries represented). Asian 1%, African American 7%, Caucasian 86%, Hispanic 2%, Native American 1%.
Retention and Graduation: 74% freshmen return for sophomore year. 41% freshmen graduate within 4 years. 45% grads go on to further study within 1 year. 16% grads pursue arts and sciences degrees. 8% grads pursue law degrees. 9% grads pursue business degrees. 6% grads pursue medical degrees. **Faculty:** Student/faculty ratio 11:1. 114 full-time faculty, 80% hold PhDs, 2% are are members of minority groups, 33% are women.

ACADEMICS
Degrees: Bachelor's, terminal associate. **Classes:** Most classes have 10–19 students. Most lab/discussion sessions have fewer than 10 students. **Majors with Highest Enrollment:** Biology/biological sciences; business administration and management; mass communication/media studies. **Special Study Options:** Cross-registration, distance learning, double major, English as a Second Language (ESL), honors program, independent study, internships, study abroad, teacher certification program Special programs offered to physically disabled students include note-taking services, reader services, tape recorders, tutors. **Career services:** Alumni network, alumni services, career/job search classes, career assessment, internships. **Career services highlights include:** Tiger Career Connection (online job postings and resources).

FACILITIES
Housing: special housing for disabled students, men's dorms, women's dorms, apartments for married students, apartments for single students 95% of campus accessible to physically disabled. **Special Academic Facilities/Equipment:** Historical archives, Senator John McClellan collection, language lab, TV studio. **Computers:** 100% of classrooms, 100% of dorms, 100% of libraries, 100% of dining areas, 100% of student union, 50% of common outdoor areas have wireless network access. Administrative functions (other than registration) can be performed online.

CAMPUS LIFE
Environment: Village. **Activities:** Choral groups, concert band, dance, drama/theater, jazz band, literary magazine, marching band, music ensembles, musical theater, opera, pep band, student government, student newspaper, television station, yearbook, campus ministries, international student organization, Model UN. **Organizations:** 60 registered organizations, 8 honor societies, 4 religious organizations. 5 fraternities, 5 sororities. **Athletics (Intercollegiate):** *Men:* Baseball, basketball, diving, football, golf, soccer, swimming, tennis, wrestling. *Women:* Basketball, cross-country, diving, golf, soccer, softball, swimming, tennis, volleyball. **On-Campus Highlights:** Starbuck's, Chick-fil-A, Commons (dining), Student Center, Sturgis Recreation Center. **Environmental Initiatives:** Employment of Energy Management Director; faculty and staff initiatives for reduction of utility use; recycling.

ADMISSIONS
Freshman Academic Profile: Average high school GPA 3.52. 32% in top 10% of high school class, 61% in top 25% of high school class, 84% in top 50% of high school class. 85% from public high schools. SAT Math middle 50% range 490–610. SAT Critical Reading middle 50% range 470–590. ACT middle 50% range 21–27. Minimum paper TOEFL 550. Minimum computer TOEFL 213. **Basis for Candidate Selection:** *Very important factors considered include:* Academic GPA, rigor of secondary school record, standardized test scores. *Other factors considered include:* character/personal qualities, talent/ability. **Freshman Admission Requirements:** High school diploma is required and GED is accepted. *Academic units required:* 4 English, 2 mathematics, 2 science, 0 foreign language, 1 social studies, 2 history, 4 academic electives. *Academic units recommended:* 4 English, 3 mathematics, 3 science, 2 foreign language, 1 social studies, 2 history, 4 academic electives. **Freshman Admission Statistics:** 1,592 applied, 67% admitted, 37% enrolled. **Transfer Admission Requirements:** College transcript(s), statement of good standing from prior institution(s). Minimum college GPA of 2.0 required. Lowest grade transferable C. **General Admission Information:** Nonfall registration accepted. Admission may be deferred for a maximum of 1 year. Credit offered for CEEB Advanced Placement tests.

COSTS AND FINANCIAL AID
Annual tuition $19,360. Room and board $5,840. Required fees $460. Average book expense $1,000. **Required Forms and Deadlines:** FAFSA. Financial aid filing deadline 6/1. Priority financial aid filing date 1/15. **Notification of Awards:** Applicants will be notified of awards on a rolling basis beginning 11/1. **Types of Aid:** *Need-based scholarships/grants:* Federal Pell, SEOG, state scholarships/grants, private scholarships, the school's own gift aid. *Loans:* FFEL Subsidized Stafford, FFEL Unsubsidized Stafford, FFEL PLUS, Federal Perkins, state loans, college/university loans from institutional funds, alternative loans. *Student Employment:* Federal Work-Study Program available. Highest amount earned per year from on-campus jobs $1,800. Off-campus job opportunities are fair. **Financial Aid Statistics:** 66% freshmen, 23% undergrads receive need-based scholarship or grant aid. 13% freshmen, 5% undergrads receive non-need-based scholarship or grant aid. 41% freshmen, 16% undergrads receive need-based self-help aid. 6% freshmen, 3% undergrads receive athletic scholarships. 97% freshmen, 96% undergrads receive any aid. 61% undergrads borrow to pay for school. Average cumulative indebtedness $16,230. **Criteria for awarding institutional aid:** *Non-need-based:* Academics, alumni affiliation, art, athletics, leadership, minority status, music/drama, religious affiliation, state/district residency.

OUR LADY OF THE LAKE UNIVERSITY (OLLU)

Admissions Office, 411 South West 24th Street, San Antonio, TX 78207-4689
Phone: 210-434-6711
E-mail: admission@lake.ollusa.edu **CEEB Code:** 6550
Fax: 210-431-4036 **Website:** www.ollusa.edu **ACT Code:** 4140

This private school, affiliated with the Roman Catholic Church, was founded in 1895. It has a 75-acre campus.

RATINGS
Admissions Selectivity Rating: 78   **Fire Safety Rating:** 60*   **Green Rating:** 60*

STUDENTS AND FACULTY

Enrollment: 1,546. **Student Body:** 74% female, 26% male, 1% out-of-state, 1% international Asian 1%, African American 7%, Caucasian 12%, Hispanic 72%.

Retention and Graduation: 53% freshmen return for sophomore year. 15% freshmen graduate within 4 years. 30% grads go on to further study within 1 year. **Faculty:** Student/faculty ratio 12:1. 111 full-time faculty, 74% hold PhDs, 44% are are members of minority groups, 59% are women.

ACADEMICS

Degrees: Bachelor's, master's. **Classes:** Most classes have fewer than 10 students. **Special Study Options:** Cooperative education program, cross-registration, distance learning, double major, dual enrollment, English as a Second Language (ESL), honors program, independent study, internships, liberal arts/career combination, study abroad, teacher certification program, weekend college, service learning. Special programs offered to physically disabled students include note-taking services, reader services, tape recorders, tutors. **Career services:** Alumni services, career assessment.

FACILITIES

Housing: Coed dorms, special housing for disabled students, men's dorms, women's dorms, wellness house. 99% of campus accessible to physically disabled. **Special Academic Facilities/Equipment:** Lab school for children with language and learning disabilities, elementary demonstration school, intercultural institute for training and research, language lab.

CAMPUS LIFE

Activities: Choral groups, dance, drama/theater, jazz band, music ensembles, musical theater, student government, student newspaper, symphony orchestra, television station, campus ministries.

ADMISSIONS

Freshman Academic Profile: Average high school GPA 3.3. 20% in top 10% of high school class, 54% in top 25% of high school class, 82% in top 50% of high school class. SAT Math middle 50% range 430–520. SAT Critical Reading middle 50% range 420–510. ACT middle 50% range 17–21. Minimum paper TOEFL 560. Minimum computer TOEFL 220. Minimum web-based TOEFL 83. **Basis for Candidate Selection:** *Very important factors considered include:* Academic GPA, rigor of secondary school record, standardized test scores. *Important factors considered include:* Class rank. *Other factors considered include:* Application essay, recommendation(s), alumni/ae relation, character/personal qualities, extracurricular activities, first generation, interview, talent/ability, volunteer work, work experience. **Freshman Admission Requirements:** High school diploma is required and GED is accepted. *Academic units required:* 4 English, 2 mathematics, 2 science, (2 science labs), 3 foreign language, 3 social studies, 3 academic electives. *Academic units recommended:* 3 mathematics, 2 academic electives. **Freshman Admission Statistics:** 2,054 applied, 51% admitted, 29% enrolled. **Transfer Admission Requirements:** College transcript(s), minimum college GPA of 2.0 required. Lowest grade transferable D. **General Admission Information:** Application fee $25. Regular application deadline 7/15. Nonfall registration accepted. Admission may be deferred for a maximum of 1 year. Credit offered for CEEB Advanced Placement tests.

COSTS AND FINANCIAL AID

Annual tuition $19,732. Room and board $6,238. Required fees $500. Average book expense $1,200. **Required Forms and Deadlines:** FAFSA. Priority financial aid filing date 2/28. **Notification of Awards:** Applicants will be notified of awards on a rolling basis beginning 4/1. **Types of Aid:** *Need-based scholarships/grants:* Federal Pell, SEOG, state scholarships/grants, private scholarships, the school's own gift aid. *Loans:* FFEL Subsidized Stafford, FFEL Unsubsidized Stafford, FFEL PLUS, Federal Perkins, state loans, private loans. *Student Employment:* Federal Work-Study Program available. Institutional employment available. Highest amount earned per year from on-campus jobs $1,206. Off-campus job opportunities are good. **Criteria for awarding institutional aid:** *Non-need-based:* Academics, alumni affiliation, art, music/drama.

PACE UNIVERSITY

1 Pace Plaza, New York, NY 10038
Phone: 212-346-1323 **Financial Aid Phone:** 914-773-3486
E-mail: infoctr@pace.edu **CEEB Code:** 2635
Fax: 212-346-1040 **Website:** www.pace.edu **ACT Code:** 2852

This private school was founded in 1906. It has a 1-acre campus.

RATINGS

Admissions Selectivity Rating: 75   **Fire Safety Rating:** 84   **Green Rating:** 71

STUDENTS AND FACULTY

Enrollment: 7,206. **Student Body:** 60% female, 40% male, 31% out-of-state, 4% international (92 countries represented). Asian 10%, African American 10%, Caucasian 45%, Hispanic 12%.

Retention and Graduation: 74% freshmen return for sophomore year. 42% freshmen graduate within 4 years. **Faculty:** Student/faculty ratio 15:1. 415 full-time faculty, 89% hold PhDs, 17% are are members of minority groups, 42% are women.

ACADEMICS

Degrees: Associate, bachelor's, certificate, first professional, first professional certificate, master's, post-bachelor's certificate, post-master's certificate. **Classes:** Most classes have 10–19 students. Most lab/discussion sessions have fewer than 10 students. **Majors with Highest Enrollment:** Accounting; finance; nursing/registered nurse (RN, ASN, BSN, MSN). **Special Study Options:** Accelerated program, cooperative education program, cross-registration, distance learning, double major, dual enrollment, English as a Second Language (ESL), honors program, independent study, internships, study abroad, teacher certification program, Evening and freshman studies programs, Pre-freshman summer program, Learning Communities and Service Learning. **Honors programs:** Pforzheimer Honors College for incoming freshmen. **Combined degree programs:** BA/JD, BA/MA, BBA/MBA; BA/MPA. Special programs offered to physically disabled students include note-taking services, reader services, tape recorders. **Career services:** Alumni network, alumni services, career/job search classes, career assessment, internships, regional alumni. **Career services highlights include:** Cooperative Education/Internship Program.

FACILITIES

Housing: Coed dorms, apartments for single students, Apartment style for 3-4 upperclassmen. 100% of campus accessible to physically disabled. **Special Academic Facilities/Equipment:** Laboratory Theatre, Communication Center, Language Center, Center for the Arts, Art Gallery, English Language Institute. **Computers:** 20% of classrooms, 10% of dorms, 100% of libraries, 100% of dining areas, 100% of student union, have wireless network access. Students can register for classes online. Administrative functions (other than registration) can be performed online.

CAMPUS LIFE

Environment: Metropolis. **Activities:** Choral groups, dance, drama/theater, literary magazine, musical theater, radio station, student government, student newspaper, student-run film society, television station, yearbook, international student organization, Model UN. **Organizations:** 79 registered organizations, 25 honor societies, 4 religious organizations. 11 fraternity, 9 sororities. **Athletics (Intercollegiate):** *Men:* Baseball, basketball, cross-country, football, golf, lacrosse, swimming, tennis, track/field (outdoor), track/field (indoor). *Women:* Basketball, cheerleading, cross-country, equestrian sports, soccer, softball, swimming, tennis, track/field (outdoor), track/field (indoor), volleyball. **On-Campus Highlights:** Library, Fitness Center, Theater, Classrooms, Dormitories. **Environmental Initiatives:** Environmental Law Program—Pace Law School Environmental Sciences Program at Dyson College of Arts & Science; New York City Mayoral Challenge; and participation with the Clinton Climate Initiative.

ADMISSIONS

Freshman Academic Profile: Average high school GPA 3.2. 14% in top 10% of high school class, 41% in top 25% of high school class, 75% in top 50% of high school class. 70% from public high schools. SAT Math middle 50% range 490–590. SAT Critical Reading middle 50% range 490–580. ACT middle 50% range 20–26. Minimum paper TOEFL 570. Minimum computer TOEFL 230. **Basis for Candidate Selection:** *Very important factors considered include:* Rigor of secondary school record, standardized test scores. *Important factors considered include:* Class rank, academic GPA. *Other factors considered include:* Application essay, recommendation(s), alumni/ae relation, character/personal qualities, extracurricular activities, talent/ability, volunteer work, work experience. **Freshman Admission Requirements:** High school diploma is required and GED is accepted. *Academic units required:* 4 English, 3 mathematics, 2 science, (2 science labs), 2 foreign language, 1 social studies, 2 history, 2 academic electives. *Academic units recommended:* 4 English, 4 mathematics, 2 science, (2 science labs), 3 foreign language, 2 social studies, 3 history, 2 academic electives. **Freshman Admission Statistics:** 9,123 applied, 75% admitted, 24% enrolled. **Transfer Admission Requirements:** College transcript(s), statement of good standing from prior institution(s). Minimum college GPA of 2.5 required. Lowest grade transferable C. **General Admission Information:** Application fee $45. Regular application deadline 3/1. Notification on a rolling basis, beginning on or about 12/15. Nonfall registration accepted. Admission may be deferred for a maximum of 12 mo. Credit offered for CEEB Advanced Placement tests.

COSTS AND FINANCIAL AID

Annual tuition $30,632. Room and board $11,180. Required fees $743. Average book expense $800. **Required Forms and Deadlines:** FAFSA, state aid form. Priority financial aid filing date 2/15. **Notification of Awards:** Applicants will be notified of awards on a rolling basis beginning 2/25. **Types of Aid:** *Need-based scholarships/grants:* Federal Pell, SEOG, state scholarships/grants, private scholarships, the school's own gift aid, Federal Nursing Scholarships. Endowed and Restricted scholarships and grants. *Loans:* Direct Subsidized Stafford, Direct Unsubsidized Stafford, Direct PLUS, Federal Perkins, Federal Nursing *Student Employment:* Highest amount earned per year from on-campus jobs $1,564. Off-campus job opportunities are good. **Financial Aid Statistics:** 76% freshmen, 70% undergrads receive need-based scholarship or grant aid. 10% freshmen, 8% undergrads receive non-need-based scholarship or grant aid. 66% freshmen, 61% undergrads receive need-based self-help aid. 1% freshmen, 76% freshmen, 70% undergrads receive any aid. 69% undergrads borrow to pay for school. Average cumulative indebtedness $29,622. **Criteria for awarding institutional aid:** *Non-need-based:* Academics, athletics, music/drama.

PACIFIC LUTHERAN UNIVERSITY

Office of Admission, Tacoma, WA 98447
Phone: 253-535-7151 **Financial Aid Phone:** 253-535-7134
E-mail: admission@plu.edu **CEEB Code:** 4597
Fax: 253-536-5136 **Website:** www.plu.edu **ACT Code:** 4597

This private school, affiliated with the Lutheran Church, was founded in 1890. It has a 126-acre campus.

RATINGS
Admissions Selectivity Rating: 86 **Fire Safety Rating:** 82 **Green Rating:** 85

STUDENTS AND FACULTY
Enrollment: 3,265. **Student Body:** 63% female, 37% male, 24% out-of-state, 5% international (21 countries represented). Asian 6%, African American 2%, Caucasian 69%, Hispanic 2%, Native American 1%.
Retention and Graduation: 52% freshmen graduate within 4 years. 11% grads go on to further study within 1 year. **Faculty:** Student/faculty ratio 14:1. 230 full-time faculty, 86% hold PhDs, 9% are are members of minority groups, 48% are women.

ACADEMICS
Degrees: Bachelor's, master's, post-bachelor's certificate, post-master's certificate. **Classes:** Most classes have 20–29 students. Most lab/discussion sessions have 10–19 students. **Majors with Highest Enrollment:** Business administration and management; communication studies/speech communication and rhetoric; nursing/registered nurse (RN, ASN, BSN, MSN). **Special Study Options:** Cooperative education program, cross-registration, double major, dual enrollment, English as a Second Language (ESL), exchange student program (domestic), honors program, independent study, internships, liberal arts/career combination, student-designed major, study abroad, teacher certification program. **Honors programs:** International Honors Program. **Combined degree programs:** BA/MEng Special programs offered to physically disabled students include note-taking services, reader services, tape recorders, tutors. **Career services:** Alumni services, career/job search classes, career assessment.

FACILITIES
Housing: Coed dorms, special housing for disabled students, special housing for international students, women's dorms, apartments for married students, apartments for single students, foreign languages learning housing. 90% of campus accessible to physically disabled. **Special Academic Facilities/Equipment:** Mary Baker Russell Music Center, Wekell Art Gallery, Keck Observatory, Rieke Science Center, Scandinavian Cultural Center, Morken Center for Learning and Technology. **Computers:** 25% of classrooms, 25% of dorms, 100% of libraries, 100% of dining areas, 100% of student union, 25% of common outdoor areas have wireless network access. Students can register for classes online.

CAMPUS LIFE
Environment: City. **Activities:** Choral groups, concert band, dance, drama/theater, jazz band, literary magazine, music ensembles, musical theater, opera, pep band, radio station, student government, student newspaper, student-run film society, symphony orchestra, television station, yearbook, campus ministries, international student organization. **Organizations:** 67 registered organizations, 6 honor societies, 8 religious organizations. **Athletics (Intercollegiate):** *Men:* Baseball, basketball, cheerleading, crew/rowing, cross-country, football, golf, soccer, swimming, tennis, track/field (outdoor), track/field (indoor). *Women:* Basketball, cheerleading, crew/rowing, cross-country, golf, soccer, softball, swimming, tennis, track/field (outdoor), track/field (indoor), volleyball. **On-Campus Highlights:** Keck Observatory, Rieke Science Center, Mary Baker Russell Music Center, Wekell Art Gallery, Names Fitness Center,

Morken Center for Learning and Technology, Scandinavian Cultural Center. **Environmental Initiatives:** Successfully building a community commitment to sustainability that encompasses students, faculty and staff in part through sustainability fellowships. Including environmental goals for waste diversion, reduction of water and electricity consumption, LEED building and carbon neutrality into the campus master plan. PLU is in the leadership circle for the President's Climate Commitment and is planning to meet all goals and deadlines of that commitment.

ADMISSIONS
Freshman Academic Profile: 32% in top 10% of high school class, 66% in top 25% of high school class, 92% in top 50% of high school class. SAT Math middle 50% range 500–620. SAT Critical Reading middle 50% range 490–630. SAT Writing middle 50% range 490–600. ACT middle 50% range 22–28. Minimum paper TOEFL 550. Minimum computer TOEFL 213. Minimum web-based TOEFL 79. **Basis for Candidate Selection:** *Very important factors considered include:* Application essay, rigor of secondary school record. *Important factors considered include:* Class rank, academic GPA, recommendation(s), standardized test scores, character/personal qualities, extracurricular activities, talent/ability, volunteer work. *Other factors considered include:* interview, work experience. **Freshman Admission Requirements:** High school diploma is required and GED is accepted. *Academic units required:* 2 mathematics, 2 foreign language. *Academic units recommended:* 4 English, 3 mathematics, 2 science, (2 science labs), 2 foreign language, 2 social studies, 1 visual/performing arts, 3 academic electives. **Freshman Admission Statistics:** 2,555 applied, 75% admitted, 37% enrolled. **Transfer Admission Requirements:** High school transcript, college transcript(s), essay or personal statement, statement of good standing from prior institution(s). Minimum college GPA of 2.5 required. Lowest grade transferable C–. **General Admission Information:** Application fee $40. Notification on a rolling basis, beginning on or about 10/1. Nonfall registration accepted. Admission may be deferred for a maximum of 2 years. Credit and/or placement offered for CEEB Advanced Placement tests.

COSTS AND FINANCIAL AID
Annual tuition $26,800. Room and board $8,200. Average book expense $924. **Required Forms and Deadlines:** FAFSA. Priority financial aid filing date 1/31. **Notification of Awards:** Applicants will be notified of awards on a rolling basis beginning 3/15. **Types of Aid:** *Need-based scholarships/grants:* Federal Pell, SEOG, state scholarships/grants, private scholarships, the school's own gift aid, Federal Nursing Scholarships. *Loans:* FFEL Subsidized Stafford, FFEL Unsubsidized Stafford, FFEL PLUS, Federal Perkins, Federal Nursing, state loans *Student Employment:* Federal Work-Study Program available. Institutional employment available. Highest amount earned per year from on-campus jobs $13,754. Off-campus job opportunities are good. **Financial Aid Statistics:** 73% freshmen, 66% undergrads receive need-based scholarship or grant aid. 57% freshmen, 50% undergrads receive non-need-based scholarship or grant aid. 63% freshmen, 61% undergrads receive need-based self-help aid. 90.9% freshmen, 86.2% undergrads receive any aid. 71% undergrads borrow to pay for school. Average cumulative indebtedness $22,484. **Criteria for awarding institutional aid:** *Non-need-based:* Academics, alumni affiliation, art, leadership, music/drama, religious affiliation.

PACIFIC NORTHWEST COLLEGE OF ART

1241 NW Johnson Street, Portland, OR 97209
Phone: 503-821-8972
E-mail: admissions@pnca.edu **CEEB Code:** 4504
Fax: 503-821-8978 **Website:** www.pnca.edu **ACT Code:** 3477

This private school was founded in 1909. It has a 1-acre campus.

RATINGS
Admissions Selectivity Rating: 72 **Fire Safety Rating:** 60* **Green Rating:** 60*

STUDENTS AND FACULTY
Enrollment: 288. **Student Body:** 59% female, 41% male, 24% out-of-state, international Asian 3%, African American 1%, Caucasian 92%, Hispanic 3%, Native American 1%.
Retention and Graduation: 66% freshmen return for sophomore year. 18% freshmen graduate within 4 years. **Faculty:** Student/faculty ratio 11:1. 13 full-time faculty, 85% hold PhDs, 38% are women.

ACADEMICS
Degrees: Bachelor's. **Classes:** Most classes have 10–19 students. **Majors with Highest Enrollment:** design and visual communications; painting; photography. **Special Study Options:** Cross-registration, exchange student program (domestic), independent study, internships, student-designed major, study

abroad. **Combined degree programs:** 5-year BA/BFA program with Reed College. **Career services:** Career/job search classes, internships.

FACILITIES

Housing: Apartments for single students, housing/student dorm available through College Housing Northwest in Portland, Oregon. 100% of campus accessible to physically disabled. **Special Academic Facilities/Equipment:** Student galleries, darkrooms, student painting studios, printmaking studio, computer labs. **Computers:** Administrative functions (other than registration) can be performed online.

CAMPUS LIFE

Environment: Metropolis. **Activities:** Student government. **Organizations:** 2 registered organizations. **On-Campus Highlights:** Stevens Studios, Feldman Gallery.

ADMISSIONS

Freshman Academic Profile: Average high school GPA 2.98. 89% from public high schools. SAT Math middle 50% range 370–590. SAT Critical Reading middle 50% range 440–650. ACT middle 50% range 16–26. Minimum paper TOEFL 550. Minimum computer TOEFL 213. **Basis for Candidate Selection:** *Very important factors considered include:* Academic GPA, talent/ability. *Important factors considered include:* Application essay, rigor of secondary school record, extracurricular activities, interview. *Other factors considered include:* Recommendation(s), standardized test scores, character/personal qualities, level of applicant's interest. **Freshman Admission Requirements:** High school diploma is required and GED is accepted. *Academic units recommended:* 4 English, 3 mathematics, 3 science, 3 social studies, 4 art. **Freshman Admission Statistics:** 120 applied, 73% admitted, 31% enrolled. **Transfer Admission Requirements:** College transcript(s), essay or personal statement, minimum college GPA of 2.0 required. Lowest grade transferable C. **General Admission Information:** Application fee $35. Notification on a rolling basis, beginning on or about 1/1. Nonfall registration accepted. Admission may be deferred for a maximum of 2 years. Credit and/or placement offered for CEEB Advanced Placement tests.

COSTS AND FINANCIAL AID

Annual tuition $16,490. Room and board $4,500. Required fees $806. Average book expense $98,500. **Required Forms and Deadlines:** FAFSA. Priority financial aid filing date 3/1. **Notification of Awards:** Applicants will be notified of awards on a rolling basis beginning 4/1. **Types of Aid:** *Need-based scholarships/grants:* Federal Pell, SEOG, state scholarships/grants, private scholarships, the school's own gift aid. *Loans:* FFEL Subsidized Stafford, FFEL Unsubsidized Stafford, FFEL PLUS. *Student Employment:* Highest amount earned per year from on-campus jobs $1,000. **Financial Aid Statistics:** 65% freshmen, 97% undergrads receive need-based scholarship or grant aid. 12% undergrads receive non-need-based scholarship or grant aid. 65% freshmen, 97% undergrads receive need-based self-help aid. 79% undergrads borrow to pay for school. Average cumulative indebtedness $24,974. **Criteria for awarding institutional aid:** *Non-need-based:* Academics, art.

PACIFIC STATES UNIVERSITY

Registrar's Office, 1516 South Western Avenue, Los Angeles, CA 90006
Phone: 323-731-2383
E-mail: admission@psuca.edu
Fax: 323-731-7276 **Website:** www.psuca.edu

This private school was founded in 1928.

RATINGS
Admissions Selectivity Rating: 60*   **Fire Safety Rating:** 60*   **Green Rating:** 60*

STUDENTS AND FACULTY

Enrollment: 56. **Student Body:** 36% female, 64% male, % out-of-state, 77% international Asian 23%.
Retention and Graduation: 75% freshmen return for sophomore year. **Faculty:** Student/faculty ratio 12:1. 10 full-time faculty, 40% hold PhDs, 80% are are members of minority groups, 10% are women.

ACADEMICS

Degrees: Bachelor's, doctoral, master's, post-bachelor's certificate. **Special Study Options:** Distance learning, double major, English as a Second Language (ESL), independent study.

FACILITIES

Housing: Coed dorms.

CAMPUS LIFE

Environment: Metropolis. **Activities:** Television station.

ADMISSIONS

Basis for Candidate Selection: *Important factors considered include:* Standardized test scores. *Other factors considered include:* Application essay, academic GPA, rigor of secondary school record, level of applicant's interest. **Freshman Admission Requirements:** High school diploma is required and GED is accepted. **Freshman Admission Statistics:** 10 applied, 40% admitted, 100% enrolled. **Transfer Admission Requirements:** College transcript(s), minimum college GPA of 2.5 required. Lowest grade transferable C. **General Admission Information:** Nonfall registration not accepted.

COSTS AND FINANCIAL AID

Annual tuition $45,000. Room and board $28,800. Average book expense $400. **Required Forms and Deadlines:** FAFSA. **Types of Aid:** *Need-based scholarships/grants:* Federal Pell. *Loans:* Direct Subsidized Stafford, Direct Unsubsidized Stafford.

PACIFIC UNION COLLEGE

Enrollment Services, One Angwin Avenue, Angwin, CA 94508
Phone: 800-862-7080 **Financial Aid Phone:** 707-965-7200
E-mail: enroll@puc.edu **CEEB Code:** 4600
Fax: 707-965-6432 **Website:** puc.edu **ACT Code:** 362

This private school, affiliated with the Seventh Day Adventist Church, was founded in 1882. It has a 200-acre campus.

RATINGS
Admissions Selectivity Rating: 77   **Fire Safety Rating:** 60*   **Green Rating:** 60*

STUDENTS AND FACULTY

Enrollment: 1,515. **Student Body:** 56% female, 44% male, 16% out-of-state, 5% international (24 countries represented). Asian 21%, African American 3%, Caucasian 30%, Hispanic 13%.
Retention and Graduation: 72% freshmen return for sophomore year. 24% freshmen graduate within 4 years. **Faculty:** Student/faculty ratio 12:1. 94 full-time faculty, 51% hold PhDs, 16% are are members of minority groups, 48% are women.

ACADEMICS

Degrees: Associate, bachelor's, master's. **Classes:** Most classes have fewer than 10 students. Most lab/discussion sessions have fewer than 10 students. **Majors with Highest Enrollment:** Business/commerce; nursing/registered nurse (RN, ASN, BSN, MSN); teacher education, multiple levels. **Special Study Options:** Cooperative education program, double major, external degree program, honors program, independent study, internships, study abroad, teacher certification program. **Honors programs:** The Honors Program offers an alternative general-education program for academically motivated students. There are no other general education requirements. Students fulfilling the Honors Program graduate "With Honors." **Special programs** offered to physically disabled students include note-taking services, reader services, tape recorders, tutors. **Career services:** Career/job search classes, career assessment, internships. **Career services highlights include:** Spring break externship program available to anyone that preregisters.

FACILITIES

Housing: Men's dorms, women's dorms, apartments for married students 80% of campus accessible to physically disabled. **Special Academic Facilities/Equipment:** Art gallery, natural history collection, Pitcairn Island studies center, on-campus elementary and high schools, airport, flight training facility, observatory. **Computers:** Students can register for classes online. Administrative functions (other than registration) can be performed online.

CAMPUS LIFE

Environment: Rural. **Activities:** Choral groups, concert band, drama/theater, jazz band, literary magazine, music ensembles, musical theater, radio station, student government, student newspaper, student-run film society, symphony orchestra, yearbook. **Organizations:** 24 registered organizations, 8 honor societies, **Athletics (Intercollegiate):** *Men:* Basketball, cross-country, volleyball. *Women:* Basketball, cross-country, volleyball. **On-Campus Highlights:** Campus Center, Clark Hall/Museum, Pacific Auditorium (Gym), Paulin Auditorium (Music), 1500 acres of hiking/biking land.

ADMISSIONS

Freshman Academic Profile: Average high school GPA 3.26. SAT Math middle 50% range 430–560. SAT Critical Reading middle 50% range 450–550. SAT Writing middle 50% range 450–550. ACT middle 50% range 16–24. Minimum paper TOEFL 525. Minimum computer TOEFL 195. **Basis for Candidate Selection:** *Very important factors considered include:* Recommendation(s), rigor of secondary school record. *Important factors considered include:* Academic GPA, character/personal qualities, level of applicant's interest. *Other factors considered include:* standardized test scores, extracurricular activities, interview, religious affiliation/commitment. **Freshman Admission Requirements:** High school diploma is required and GED is accepted. *Academic units required:* 4 English, 2 mathematics, 1 science, 1 history. *Academic units recommended:* 3 mathematics, 3 science, 2 foreign language, 2 history, 1 computer literacy **Freshman Admission Statistics:** 1,566 applied, 76% admitted, 21% enrolled. **Transfer Admission Requirements:** High school transcript, college transcript(s), minimum college GPA of 2.0 required. Lowest grade transferable C–. **General Admission Information:** Application fee $30. Notification on a rolling basis, beginning on or about 1/15. Nonfall registration accepted. Admission may be deferred for a maximum of 1 year. Credit offered for CEEB Advanced Placement tests.

COSTS AND FINANCIAL AID
Annual tuition $20,300. Room and board $5,955. Required fees $135. Average book expense $1,385. **Required Forms and Deadlines:** FAFSA, institution's own financial aid form, state aid form, business/farm supplement. Federal tax returns. **Types of Aid:** *Need-based scholarships/grants:* Federal Pell, SEOG, state scholarships/grants, the school's own gift aid. *Loans:* FFEL Subsidized Stafford, FFEL Unsubsidized Stafford, FFEL PLUS, Federal Perkins, college/university loans from institutional funds. *Student Employment:* Federal Work-Study Program available. Institutional employment available. Highest amount earned per year from on-campus jobs $3,000. Off-campus job opportunities are fair. **Financial Aid Statistics:** 61% freshmen, 62% undergrads receive need-based scholarship or grant aid. 58% freshmen, 58% undergrads receive non-need-based scholarship or grant aid. 50% freshmen, 52% undergrads receive need-based self-help aid. 49% undergrads borrow to pay for school. Average cumulative indebtedness $17,500. **Criteria for awarding institutional aid:** *Non-need-based:* Academics, leadership, religious affiliation.

PACIFIC UNIVERSITY

2043 College Way, Forest Grove, OR 97116
Phone: 503-352-2218 **Financial Aid Phone:** 503-352-2222
E-mail: admissions@pacificu.edu **CEEB Code:** 4601
Fax: Website: www.pacificu.edu

This private school was founded in 1849. It has a 60-acre campus.

RATINGS
Admissions Selectivity Rating: 86   **Fire Safety Rating:** 69   **Green Rating:** 76

STUDENTS AND FACULTY
Enrollment: 1,445. **Student Body:** 65% female, 35% male, 47% out-of-state, 2% international (20 countries represented). Asian 23%, African American 1%, Caucasian 59%, Hispanic 5%, Native American 1%.
Retention and Graduation: 76% freshmen return for sophomore year. 52% freshmen graduate within 4 years. 24% grads go on to further study within 1 year. 11% grads pursue arts and sciences degrees. 4% grads pursue law degrees. 2% grads pursue business degrees. 2% grads pursue medical degrees. **Faculty:** Student/faculty ratio 11:1. 205 full-time faculty, 83% hold PhDs, 14% are are members of minority groups, 48% are women.

ACADEMICS
Degrees: Bachelor's, master's. **Classes:** Most classes have 10–19 students. Most lab/discussion sessions have 10–19 students. **Majors with Highest Enrollment:** Biology/biological sciences; business administration and management; kinesiology and exercise science. **Special Study Options:** Cross-registration, double major, English as a Second Language (ESL), independent study, internships, liberal arts/career combination, study abroad, teacher certification program. **Combined degree programs:** 3-2 applied physics program and 4-1 computer scien. Special programs offered to physically disabled students include note-taking services, reader services, tape recorders, tutors. **Career services:** Alumni network, alumni services, career/job search classes, career assessment, internships, regional alumni. **Career services highlights include:** Internships.

FACILITIES
Housing: Coed dorms, special housing for disabled students, apartments for single students, theme housing, 1 wing designated female. **Special Academic Facilities/Equipment:** State history museum, performing arts center, media center, humanitarian center, Holocaust resource center, politics/law forum, Berglund Center for Internet Studies, electron microscopes. **Computers:** 100%

of classrooms, 100% of dorms, 100% of libraries, 100% of dining areas, 100% of student union, 90% of common outdoor areas have wireless network access. Administrative functions (other than registration) can be performed online.

CAMPUS LIFE
Environment: Village. **Activities:** Choral groups, concert band, dance, drama/theater, jazz band, literary magazine, music ensembles, pep band, radio station, student government, student newspaper, student-run film society, campus ministries, international student organization. **Organizations:** 58 registered organizations, 2 honor societies, 4 religious organizations. 3 fraternities, 4 sororities. **Athletics (Intercollegiate):** *Men:* Baseball, basketball, cross-country, golf, soccer, swimming, tennis, track/field (outdoor), wrestling. *Women:* Basketball, cross-country, golf, lacrosse, soccer, softball, swimming, tennis, track/field (outdoor), volleyball, wrestling **On-Campus Highlights:** Pacific Athletic Center, Pacific Library (New Library), Marsh Hall, Old College Hall, New Bookstore/Vera's Cafe. **Environmental Initiatives:** Sustainability Committee; new LEED-certified buldings; B-Street Permaculture Project.

ADMISSIONS
Freshman Academic Profile: Average high school GPA 3.67. 39% in top 10% of high school class, 69% in top 25% of high school class, 95% in top 50% of high school class. 88% from public high schools. SAT Math middle 50% range 510–620. SAT Critical Reading middle 50% range 500–600. ACT middle 50% range 21–27. Minimum paper TOEFL 550. Minimum computer TOEFL 213. **Basis for Candidate Selection:** *Very important factors considered include:* Academic GPA, recommendation(s), rigor of secondary school record, standardized test scores, character/personal qualities, extracurricular activities, level of applicant's interest, volunteer work. *Important factors considered include:* Class rank, application essay, talent/ability. *Other factors considered include:* Alumni/ae relation, first generation, work experience. **Freshman Admission Requirements:** High school diploma is required and GED is accepted. *Academic units recommended:* 4 English, 3 mathematics, 3 science, (1 science labs), 2 foreign language, 3 social studies, 1 history, 4 academic electives. **Freshman Admission Statistics:** 1,627 applied, 78% admitted, 27% enrolled. **Transfer Admission Requirements:** College transcript(s), essay or personal statement, statement of good standing from prior institution(s). Minimum college GPA of 2.70 required. Lowest grade transferable C–. **General Admission Information:** Application fee $40. Regular application deadline 8/15. Notification on a rolling basis, beginning on or about 10/1. Nonfall registration accepted. Admission may be deferred for a maximum of 2 years. Credit and/or placement offered for CEEB Advanced Placement tests.

COSTS AND FINANCIAL AID
Annual tuition $29,290. Room and board $8,118. Required fees $676. Average book expense $950. **Required Forms and Deadlines:** FAFSA. Priority financial aid filing date 3/1. **Notification of Awards:** Applicants will be notified of awards on a rolling basis beginning 3/1. **Types of Aid:** *Need-based scholarships/grants:* Federal Pell, SEOG, state scholarships/grants, private scholarships, the school's own gift aid. *Loans:* FFEL Subsidized Stafford, FFEL Unsubsidized Stafford, FFEL PLUS, Federal Perkins, Private alternative loans. *Student Employment:* Federal Work-Study Program available. Institutional employment available. **Financial Aid Statistics:** 80% freshmen, 74% undergrads receive need-based scholarship or grant aid. 12% freshmen, 7% undergrads receive non-need-based scholarship or grant aid. 71% freshmen, 73% undergrads receive need-based self-help aid. 93% freshmen, 93% undergrads receive any aid. 85% undergrads borrow to pay for school. Average cumulative indebtedness $27,770. **Criteria for awarding institutional aid:** *Non-need-based:* Academics, alumni affiliation, art, music/drama.

PALM BEACH ATLANTIC UNIVERSITY

PO Box 24708, 901 S. Flagler D, West Palm Beach, FL 33416-4708
Phone: 561-803-2100 **Financial Aid Phone:** 561-803-2126
E-mail: admit@pba.edu **CEEB Code:** 5553
Fax: 561-803-2115 **Website:** www.pba.edu **ACT Code:** 739

This private school, affiliated with the Christian (Nondenominational) Church, was founded in 1968. It has a 25-acre campus.

RATINGS
Admissions Selectivity Rating: 77   **Fire Safety Rating:** 60*   **Green Rating:** 60*

STUDENTS AND FACULTY
Enrollment: 2,419. **Student Body:** 64% female, 36% male, 27% out-of-state, 2% international (37 countries represented). Asian 1%, African American 17%, Caucasian 59%, Hispanic 14%.
Retention and Graduation: 69% freshmen return for sophomore year. 41% freshmen graduate within 4 years. **Faculty:** Student/faculty ratio 14:1. 156 full-

time faculty, 77% hold PhDs, 13% are are members of minority groups, 46% are women.

ACADEMICS

Degrees: Associate, bachelor's, master's. **Classes:** Most classes have 10–19 students. Most lab/discussion sessions have 10–19 students. **Majors with Highest Enrollment:** accounting and business/management; education; psychology. **Special Study Options:** Accelerated program, distance learning, double major, dual enrollment, honors program, independent study, internships, student-designed major, study abroad, teacher certification program. **Honors programs:** The Frederick M. Supper Honors Program exists to establish a community of scholars. The program encourages students to develop a thoughtful and insightful Christian worldview through enduring conversation to enable students to live the examined life and to facilitate character formation. **Combined degree programs:** BA/MA. **Career services:** Alumni services, career/job search classes, career assessment, internships. **Career services highlights include:** The Workship program is a distinctive service program at PBA which enables students to offer a Christian response to human needs by serving in nonprofit agencies, churches, and schools outside the university community.

FACILITIES

Housing: Coed dorms, men's dorms, women's dorms, apartments for married students, theme housing. **Special Academic Facilities/Equipment:** DeSantis Family Chapel; Greene Sports Complex (Cafe); Helen K.Persson Recital Hall. **Computers:** Students can register for classes online. Administrative functions (other than registration) can be performed online.

CAMPUS LIFE

Environment: Metropolis. **Activities:** Choral groups, dance, drama/theater, jazz band, literary magazine, music ensembles, musical theater, pep band, radio station, student government, student newspaper, symphony orchestra, television station, yearbook, campus ministries, international student organization. **Organizations:** 56 registered organizations, 29 honor societies, 6 religious organizations. **Athletics (Intercollegiate):** *Men:* Baseball, basketball, cross-country, soccer, tennis. *Women:* Basketball, cross-country, soccer, softball, tennis, volleyball. **On-Campus Highlights:** DeSantis Family Chapel, Greene Complex (athletics, snack shop), Vera Lea Rinker Music Building.

ADMISSIONS

Freshman Academic Profile: Average high school GPA 3.5. SAT Math middle 50% range 450–550. SAT Critical Reading middle 50% range 470–580. SAT Writing middle 50% range 450–570. ACT middle 50% range 20–26. Minimum paper TOEFL 550. Minimum computer TOEFL 213. **Basis for Candidate Selection:** *Very important factors considered include:* Academic GPA, standardized test scores, character/personal qualities. *Important factors considered include:* Application essay, recommendation(s), rigor of secondary school record, interview. *Other factors considered include:* Class rank, alumni/ae relation, extracurricular activities, religious affiliation/commitment, talent/ability, volunteer work. **Freshman Admission Requirements:** High school diploma is required and GED is accepted. *Academic units required:* 4 English, 3 mathematics, 4 science, (2 science labs). **Freshman Admission Statistics:** 1,401 applied, 69% admitted, 44% enrolled. **Transfer Admission Requirements:** College transcript(s), essay or personal statement, minimum college GPA of 2.5 required. Lowest grade transferable C. **General Admission Information:** Notification on a rolling basis, beginning on or about 9/1. Nonfall registration accepted. Admission may be deferred for a maximum of 1 year. Credit offered for CEEB Advanced Placement tests.

COSTS AND FINANCIAL AID

Annual tuition $22,400. Room and board $8,220. Required fees $300. Average book expense $1,200. **Required Forms and Deadlines:** FAFSA. Financial aid filing deadline 8/1. Priority financial aid filing date 2/1. **Notification of Awards:** Applicants will be notified of awards on a rolling basis beginning 2/15. **Types of Aid:** *Need-based scholarships/grants:* Federal Pell, SEOG, state scholarships/grants, private scholarships, the school's own gift aid. *Loans:* FFEL Subsidized Stafford, FFEL Unsubsidized Stafford, FFEL PLUS. *Student Employment:* Federal Work-Study Program available. Institutional employment available. Off-campus job opportunities are good. **Financial Aid Statistics:** 38% freshmen, 43% undergrads receive need-based scholarship or grant aid. 65% freshmen, 64% undergrads receive non-need-based scholarship or grant aid. 58% freshmen, 52% undergrads receive need-based self-help aid. 69% undergrads borrow to pay for school. Average cumulative indebtedness $19,420. **Criteria for awarding institutional aid:** *Non-need-based:* Academics, alumni affiliation, athletics, minority status, music/drama, state/district residency.

PARK UNIVERSITY

8700 River Park Drive, Campus Box 1, Parkville, MO 64152
Phone: 816-584-6214 **Financial Aid Phone:** 816-548-6290
E-mail: admissions@mail.park.edu **CEEB Code:** 6574
Fax: 816-741-4462 **Website: ACT Code:** 2340

This private school was founded in 1875. It has a 700-acre campus.

RATINGS

Admissions Selectivity Rating: 79   **Fire Safety Rating:** 60*   **Green Rating:** 60*

STUDENTS AND FACULTY

Enrollment: 11,135. **Student Body:** 53% female, 47% male, 77% out-of-state, international (93 countries represented).
Retention and Graduation: 71% freshmen return for sophomore year. 18% freshmen graduate within 4 years. 7% grads go on to further study within 1 year. 6% grads pursue arts and sciences degrees. 1% grads pursue business degrees. **Faculty:** Student/faculty ratio 12:1. 119 full-time faculty, 71% hold PhDs, 8% are are members of minority groups, 49% are women.

ACADEMICS

Degrees: Associate, bachelor's, master's, post-bachelor's certificate. **Majors with Highest Enrollment:** Business/commerce; human resources management/personnel administration; management information systems. **Special Study Options:** Accelerated program, cross-registration, distance learning, double major, dual enrollment, English as a Second Language (ESL), honors program, independent study, internships, student-designed major, study abroad, teacher certification program, weekend college. Special programs offered to physically disabled students include note-taking services, reader services, tape recorders, tutors.

FACILITIES

Housing: Coed dorms, apartments for married students. 90% of campus accessible to physically disabled. **Computers:** Students can register for classes online. Administrative functions (other than registration) can be performed online.

CAMPUS LIFE

Environment: Town. **Activities:** Choral groups, drama/theater, literary magazine, radio station, student government, student newspaper, symphony orchestra, yearbook. **Organizations:** 15 registered organizations, 4 honor societies, 13 religious organizations. **Athletics (Intercollegiate):** *Men:* Baseball, basketball, cross-country, soccer, track/field (outdoor), track/field (indoor), volleyball. *Women:* Basketball, cross-country, golf, soccer, softball, track/field (outdoor), track/field (indoor), volleyball. **On-Campus Highlights:** Gym, Cafeteria, Classrooms (Underground), Library, Bookstore.

ADMISSIONS

Freshman Academic Profile: Average high school GPA 3. 24% in top 10% of high school class, 49% in top 25% of high school class, 81% in top 50% of high school class. 80% from public high schools. ACT middle 50% range 18–25. Minimum paper TOEFL 500. Minimum computer TOEFL 173. **Basis for Candidate Selection:** *Very important factors considered include:* Class rank, rigor of secondary school record, standardized test scores. *Other factors considered include:* Application essay, recommendation(s). **Freshman Admission Requirements:** High school diploma is required and GED is accepted. *Academic units recommended:* 3 English, 2 mathematics, 2 science, (1 science labs), 2 foreign language, 3 social studies, 1 history, 6 academic electives. **Freshman Admission Statistics:** 554 applied, 70% admitted, 53% enrolled. **Transfer Admission Requirements:** High school transcript, college transcript(s), minimum college GPA of 2.0 required. Lowest grade transferable C. **General Admission Information:** Application fee $25. Regular application deadline 7/1. Nonfall registration accepted. Admission may be deferred for a maximum of Maximum of 1 year. Credit and/or placement offered for CEEB Advanced Placement tests.

COSTS AND FINANCIAL AID

Average book expense $1,200. **Required Forms and Deadlines:** FAFSA, institution's own financial aid form. Priority financial aid filing date 4/1. **Types of Aid:** *Need-based scholarships/grants:* Federal Pell, SEOG, state scholarships/grants, private scholarships, the school's own gift aid. *Loans:* FFEL Subsidized Stafford, FFEL Unsubsidized Stafford, FFEL PLUS, Federal Perkins, college/university loans from institutional funds. *Student Employment:* Federal Work-Study Program available. **Financial Aid Statistics:** 14% freshmen, 4% undergrads receive need-based scholarship or grant aid. 17% freshmen, 14% undergrads receive non-need-based scholarship or grant aid. 31% freshmen, 38% undergrads receive need-based self-help aid. 11% freshmen, 2% undergrads receive athletic scholarships. 78% freshmen receive any aid. Average cumulative indebtedness $12,800. **Criteria for awarding institutional aid:** *Non-need-based:* Academics, alumni affiliation, art, athletics, job skills, leadership, minority status, music/drama, religious affiliation.

PARSONS THE NEW SCHOOL FOR DESIGN

72 Fifth Avenue, 2nd Floor, New York, NY 10011
Phone: 212-229-8989 **Financial Aid Phone:** 212-229-8930
E-mail: parsadm@newschoo.edu **CEEB Code:** 2638
Fax: 212 229 8975 **Website:** www.parsons.edu **ACT Code:** 2854

This private school was founded in 1896.

RATINGS
Admissions Selectivity Rating: 85   **Fire Safety Rating:** 75   **Green Rating:** 91

STUDENTS AND FACULTY
Enrollment: 4,107. **Student Body:** 78% female, 22% male, 71% out-of-state, 32% international (72 countries represented). Asian 16%, African American 4%, Caucasian 29%, Hispanic 8%.
Retention and Graduation: 84% freshmen return for sophomore year. 54% freshmen graduate within 4 years. **Faculty:** Student/faculty ratio 9:1. 148 full-time faculty, 57% hold PhDs, 14% are are members of minority groups, 48% are women.

ACADEMICS
Degrees: Associate, bachelor's, certificate, master's. **Classes:** Most classes have 10–19 students. Most lab/discussion sessions have 20–29 students. **Majors with Highest Enrollment:** Design and visual communications; fashion/apparel design; illustration. **Special Study Options:** Accelerated program, cross-registration, distance learning, double major, dual enrollment, English as a Second Language (ESL), exchange student program (domestic), independent study, internships, liberal arts/career combination, student-designed major, study abroad, 5-year combined BA/BFA. **Combined degree programs:** BA/BFA, MA/ARC. Special programs offered to physically disabled students include note-taking services, reader services, tape recorders. **Career services:** Alumni network, alumni services, career/job search classes, career assessment, internships, regional alumni.

FACILITIES
Housing: Coed dorms, special housing for disabled students, apartments for single students 99% of campus accessible to physically disabled. **Special Academic Facilities/Equipment:** Fashion Education Center in New York's garment district with labs and studios for fashion design students. **Computers:** 95% of classrooms, 100% of libraries, 100% of dining areas, 100% of common outdoor areas have wireless network access. Students can register for classes online. Administrative functions (other than registration) can be performed online.

CAMPUS LIFE
Environment: Metropolis. **Activities:** Choral groups, dance, drama/theater, jazz band, literary magazine, music ensembles, radio station, student government, student newspaper, symphony orchestra, international student organization. **Organizations:** 34 registered organizations. **On-Campus Highlights:** Sheila Johnson Design Center, Schwartz Fashion Center, University Welcome Center. **Environmental Initiatives:** "The New School composts all behind the counter organic wastes and has begun a post-consumer pilot program. Waste Reduction and Recycling: The New School has established a comprehensive waste management and recycling program that includes glass, metal, plastic, paper, cardboard, electronic waste, ink jet cartridges, and compost. These recycling initiatives significantly reduce the amount of trash sent to landfills and/or incinerators by the university. Sustainable Product Procurement: The New School currently purchases copy and printer paper composed of 100% post-consumer paper across campus. "Energy Star purchasing policy is in place for all computers and appliances; further all computers are EPEAT gold Rated." "Green cleaning products and low-VOC paints are in use across campus." Similarly, all promotional materials are printed on Forest Stewardship Council Certified paper. An Energy Star purchasing policy is in place for all computers and appliances. "Green" cleaning products are in use across campus, and low-VOC paints are used in high-sensitivity areas. Recent major renovations have featured rapidly renewable or recycled building materials, including linoleum flooring, bamboo flooring, and composite countertops made from post-industrial content. Compostable plates and cutlery are in use in all cafeterias, and locally produced/organic foods are offered in increasing volumes. Energy Management and Carbon Emission Reductions In 2007, The New School signed on to the NYC Mayoral Challenge to Universities to reduce carbon emissions by 30% by 2017. The New School began the challenge with the lowest CO_2 footprint of all participating schools, and is already taking steps to further minimize its impact on global climate change. 100% of electricity directly paid for by the university is offset with Renewable Energy Credits from wind power. The New School has conducted a lighting retrofit in its five largest buildings, and is in the process of conducting an investment grade audit of its mechanical systems.

ADMISSIONS
Freshman Academic Profile: Average high school GPA 3.3. 17% in top 10% of high school class, 42% in top 25% of high school class, 77% in top 50% of high school class. SAT Math middle 50% range 490–610. SAT Critical Reading middle 50% range 470–600. SAT Writing middle 50% range 480–600. ACT middle 50% range 21–26. Minimum paper TOEFL 550. Minimum computer TOEFL 213. Minimum web-based TOEFL 92. **Basis for Candidate Selection:** *Very important factors considered include:* Academic GPA, rigor of secondary school record, standardized test scores, level of applicant's interest, talent/ability. *Important factors considered include:* interview. *Other factors considered include:* Class rank, application essay, recommendation(s), extracurricular activities. **Freshman Admission Requirements:** High school diploma is required and GED is accepted. **Freshman Admission Statistics:** 2,719 applied, 62% admitted, 44% enrolled. **Transfer Admission Requirements:** College transcript(s), minimum college GPA of 2.0 required. Lowest grade transferable C. **General Admission Information:** Application fee $50. Notification on a rolling basis, beginning on or about 3/21. Nonfall registration accepted. Admission may be deferred for a maximum of 1 year. Neither credit nor placement offered for CEEB Advanced Placement tests.

COSTS AND FINANCIAL AID
Required Forms and Deadlines: FAFSA, state aid form. Priority financial aid filing date 3/1. **Notification of Awards:** Applicants will be notified of awards on a rolling basis beginning 3/1. **Types of Aid:** *Need-based scholarships/grants:* Federal Pell, SEOG, state scholarships/grants, private scholarships, the school's own gift aid. *Loans:* FFEL Subsidized Stafford, FFEL Unsubsidized Stafford, FFEL PLUS, Federal Perkins. *Student Employment:* Federal Work-Study Program available. Institutional employment available. Off-campus job opportunities are excellent. **Financial Aid Statistics:** 59% freshmen, 44% undergrads receive need-based scholarship or grant aid. 2% freshmen, 1% undergrads receive non-need-based scholarship or grant aid. 44% freshmen, 44% undergrads receive need-based self-help aid. 90% freshmen, 75% undergrads receive any aid. Average cumulative indebtedness $33,576. **Criteria for awarding institutional aid:** *Non-need-based:* Academics, art.

PATRICK HENRY COLLEGE

Ten Patrick Henry Circle, Purcellville, VA 20132
Phone: Financial Aid Phone: 540-441-8142
E-mail: admissions@phc.edu
Fax: 540-441-8119 **Website:** www.phc.edu **ACT Code:** 4383

This private school, affiliated with the Christian (Nondenominational) Church, was founded in 2000. It has a 106-acre campus.

RATINGS
Admissions Selectivity Rating: 60*   **Fire Safety Rating:** 60*   **Green Rating:** 60*

STUDENTS AND FACULTY
Enrollment: 331. **Student Body:** 47% female, 53% male, 88% out-of-state. **Retention and Graduation:** 83% freshmen return for sophomore year. 10% grads go on to further study within 1 year. 23% grads pursue law degrees. **Faculty:** Student/faculty ratio 11:1. 21 full-time faculty, 95% hold PhDs, 10% are women.

ACADEMICS
Degrees: Bachelor's. **Classes:** Most classes have fewer than 10 students. **Majors with Highest Enrollment:** american government and politics (united states); journalism. **Special Study Options:** Distance learning, liberal arts/career combination. Special programs offered to physically disabled students include tutors. **Career services:** Internships.

FACILITIES
Housing: Men's dorms, women's dorms 100% of campus accessible to physically disabled. **Computers:** 100% of classrooms, 100% of dorms, 100% of libraries, 100% of dining areas, 100% of student union, 100% of common outdoor areas have wireless network access. Students can register for classes online. Administrative functions (other than registration) can be performed online. Undergraduates are required to own a computer.

CAMPUS LIFE
Environment: Village. **Activities:** Choral groups, concert band, drama/theater, literary magazine, music ensembles, student government, student newspaper, student-run film society, yearbook, campus ministries, Model UN. **Athletics (Intercollegiate):** *Men:* Basketball, soccer. *Women:* Basketball, soccer. **On-Campus Highlights:** Student coffee lounge, workout facilities, raquetball courts. **Environmental Initiatives:** Water conservation, energy management, recycling.

ADMISSIONS

Freshman Academic Profile: Average high school GPA 3.73. 13% from public high schools. SAT Math middle 50% range 550–650. SAT Critical Reading middle 50% range 620–730. SAT Writing middle 50% range 590–700. ACT middle 50% range 26–31. **Basis for Candidate Selection:** *Very important factors considered include:* Application essay, academic GPA, recommendation(s), rigor of secondary school record, standardized test scores, character/personal qualities, extracurricular activities, interview, religious affiliation/commitment, talent/ability, volunteer work. *Important factors considered include:* level of applicant's interest. *Other factors considered include:* Class rank, alumni/ae relation, first generation, work experience. **Freshman Admission Requirements:** High school diploma is required and GED is accepted. *Academic units required:* 4 English, 3 mathematics, 2 science, 1 foreign language, 3 history, 5 academic electives. *Academic units recommended:* (2 science labs). **Freshman Admission Statistics:** 100% enrolled. **Transfer Admission Requirements:** High school transcript, college transcript(s), essay or personal statement, interview, standardized test scores, statement of good standing from prior institution(s). Lowest grade transferable C. **General Admission Information:** Application fee $40. Regular application deadline 6/15. Notification on a rolling basis, beginning on or about 10/1. Nonfall registration accepted. Admission may be deferred for a maximum of 1 year. Credit and/or placement offered for CEEB Advanced Placement tests.

COSTS AND FINANCIAL AID

Average book expense $500. **Required Forms and Deadlines:** institution's own financial aid form, CSS/Financial Aid PROFILE Financial aid filing deadline 3/15. Priority financial aid filing date 11/1. **Types of Aid:** *Need-based scholarships/grants:* private scholarships, the school's own gift aid. *Loans:* private loans. *Student Employment:* Institutional employment available. Highest amount earned per year from on-campus jobs $2,880. Off-campus job opportunities are good. **Financial Aid Statistics:** 51% freshmen receive need-based scholarship or grant aid. 44% freshmen receive need-based self-help aid. 94% freshmen, 94% undergrads receive any aid. **Criteria for awarding institutional aid:** *Non-need-based:* Academics, leadership, music/drama.

PATTEN UNIVERSITY

2433 Coolidge Avenue, Office of Admissions, Oakland, CA 94601-2699
Phone: 877-472-8836
E-mail: admissions@patten.edu
Fax: 510-534-4344 **Website:** www.patten.edu

This is a private school.

RATINGS
Admissions Selectivity Rating: 60* **Fire Safety Rating:** 60* **Green Rating:** 60*

STUDENTS AND FACULTY
Student Body: 25% out-of-state.
Retention and Graduation: 40% freshmen return for sophomore year.

ACADEMICS
Degrees: Associate, bachelor's, certificate, master's, post-bachelor's certificate, terminal associate, transfer associate.

FACILITIES
Housing: Coed dorms.

CAMPUS LIFE
Organizations: 2 religious organizations.

ADMISSIONS
Freshman Academic Profile: Minimum paper TOEFL 500. **General Admission Information:** Regular application deadline 7/15.

COSTS AND FINANCIAL AID
Annual tuition $11,520. Room and board $6,000. Average book expense $500. **Types of Aid:** *Loans:* FFEL Subsidized Stafford, FFEL PLUS. *Student Employment:* Federal Work-Study Program available. Highest amount earned per year from on-campus jobs $550.

THE PENNSYLVANIA ACADEMY OF THE FINE ARTS

128 North Broad Street, Philadelphia, PA 19102
Phone: 215-972-7625 **Financial Aid Phone:** 215-972-2019
E-mail: admissions@pafa.edu
Fax: 215-569-0153

This private school was founded in 1804.

RATINGS
Admissions Selectivity Rating: 60* **Fire Safety Rating:** 60* **Green Rating:** 60*

STUDENTS AND FACULTY
Student Body: 25% out-of-state (10 countries represented).

ACADEMICS
Degrees: Bachelor's, certificate, master's, post-bachelor's certificate. **Majors with Highest Enrollment:** Painting. **Special Study Options:** Dual enrollment, exchange student program (domestic), independent study, internships. **Combined degree programs:** BFA in conjunction with the University of Pennsylvania.

FACILITIES
Housing: The Pennsylvania Academy has a housing arrangement with International House, Philadelphia. We do not offer our own on-campus housing opportunities.

CAMPUS LIFE
Environment: Metropolis. **Activities:** Student government. **Organizations:** 4 registered organizations. **On-Campus Highlights:** Museum of American Art, World Famous Cast Hall.

ADMISSIONS
Transfer Admission Requirements: College transcript(s), essay or personal statement, minimum college GPA of 3.0 required. Lowest grade transferable C.

COSTS AND FINANCIAL AID
Annual tuition $22,596. Room and board $6,800. Required fees $770. Average book expense $1,314. *Student Employment:* Federal Work-Study Program available. Institutional employment available. Off-campus job opportunities are excellent. **Financial Aid Statistics:** 80% freshmen, 80% undergrads receive any aid.

PENNSYLVANIA COLLEGE OF TECHNOLOGY

One College Avenue, Williamsport, PA 17701
Phone: 570-327-4761 **Financial Aid Phone:** 570-327-4766
E-mail: admissions@pct.edu
Fax: 570-321-5551 **Website:** www.pct.edu/princeton/

This public school was founded in 1989. It has a 984-acre campus.

RATINGS
Admissions Selectivity Rating: 60* **Fire Safety Rating:** 72 **Green Rating:** 60*

STUDENTS AND FACULTY
Enrollment: 6,427. **Student Body:** 36% female, 64% male, 9% out-of-state, international Asian 1%, African American 3%, Caucasian 93%, Hispanic 1%, Native American 1%.
Retention and Graduation: 70% freshmen return for sophomore year. **Faculty:** Student/faculty ratio 18:1. 297 full-time faculty, 3% are are members of minority groups, 29% are women.

ACADEMICS
Degrees: Associate, bachelor's, certificate, transfer associate. **Special Study Options:** Accelerated program, cooperative education program, cross-registration, distance learning, dual enrollment, exchange student program (domestic), honors program, independent study, internships, student-designed major, study abroad, weekend college. Special programs offered to physically disabled students include note-taking services, reader services, tape recorders, tutors. **Career services:** Alumni services. **Career services highlights include:** www.pct.edu/careerservices/.

FACILITIES
Housing: Coed dorms, apartments for single students, wellness house 100% of campus accessible to physically disabled. **Computers:** Students can register

for classes online. Administrative functions (other than registration) can be performed online.

CAMPUS LIFE

Environment: Town. **Activities:** dance, radio station, student government, campus ministries. **Organizations:** 50 registered organizations, 3 honor societies, 4 religious organizations. 3 fraternities, **Athletics (Intercollegiate):** *Men:* archery, baseball, basketball, bowling, cross-country, golf, soccer, tennis, volleyball. *Women:* archery, basketball, bowling, cross-country, golf, soccer, softball, tennis, volleyball. **On-Campus Highlights:** Academic Facilities, Madigan Library, Campus Center, Student & Administrative Services Center, Academic Center.

ADMISSIONS

Freshman Academic Profile: Minimum paper TOEFL 500. Minimum computer TOEFL 173. **Basis for Candidate Selection: Freshman Admission Requirements:** High school diploma is required and GED is accepted. **Freshman Admission Statistics:** 3,002 applied, 95% admitted. **Transfer Admission Requirements:** College transcript(s), Lowest grade transferable C. **General Admission Information:** Application fee $50. Regular application deadline 7/1. Nonfall registration accepted. Admission may be deferred for a maximum of 1 year. Credit and/or placement offered for CEEB Advanced Placement tests.

COSTS AND FINANCIAL AID

Annual in-state tuition $10,020. Annual out-of-state tuition $13,050. Room and board $8,250. Required fees $1,770. Average book expense $1,000. **Required Forms and Deadlines:** FAFSA, institution's own financial aid form. Priority financial aid filing date 4/1. **Notification of Awards:** Applicants will be notified of awards on a rolling basis beginning 6/1. **Types of Aid:** *Need-based scholarships/grants:* Federal Pell, SEOG, state scholarships/grants, private scholarships *Loans:* FFEL Unsubsidized Stafford, FFEL PLUS. *Student Employment:* Federal Work-Study Program available. Institutional employment available. **Criteria for awarding institutional aid:** *Non-need-based:* Academics, alumni affiliation.

See page 1196.

PENNSYLVANIA STATE UNIVERSITY— ABINGTON

106 Sutherland, Abington, PA 19001
Phone: 215-881-7600
E-mail: abingtonadmissions@psu.edu
Fax: 215-881-7655

This public school was founded in 1950. It has a 45-acre campus.

RATINGS

Admissions Selectivity Rating: 70   **Fire Safety Rating:** 60*   **Green Rating:** 60*

STUDENTS AND FACULTY

Enrollment: 2,902. **Student Body:** 49% female, 51% male, 5% out-of-state, 1% international Asian 15%, African American 13%, Caucasian 66%, Hispanic 6%.

Retention and Graduation: Faculty: Student/faculty ratio 21:1. 105 full-time faculty, 59% hold PhDs, 11% are are members of minority groups, 46% are women.

ACADEMICS

Degrees: Bachelor's, terminal associate, transfer associate. **Classes:** Most classes have 20–29 students. Most lab/discussion sessions have 20–29 students. **Special Study Options:** Accelerated program, cooperative education program, distance learning, double major, dual enrollment, English as a Second Language (ESL), exchange student program (domestic), external degree program, honors program, independent study, internships, liberal arts/career combination, student-designed major, study abroad.

CAMPUS LIFE

Environment: Village. **Activities:** Dance, drama/theater, literary magazine, student government, student newspaper, student-run film society, campus ministries. **Athletics (Intercollegiate):** *Men:* Basketball, soccer, softball, tennis. *Women:* Basketball, field hockey, softball, tennis, volleyball.

ADMISSIONS

Freshman Academic Profile: Average high school GPA 3. 9.93% in top 10% of high school class, 28.92% in top 25% of high school class, 64.17% in top 50% of high school class. SAT Math middle 50% range 420–540. SAT Critical

Reading middle 50% range 400–520. Minimum paper TOEFL 550. **Basis for Candidate Selection:** *Very important factors considered include:* Academic GPA, standardized test scores. *Important factors considered include:* Rigor of secondary school record. *Other factors considered include:* Class rank, application essay, recommendation(s), alumni/ae relation, character/personal qualities, extracurricular activities, talent/ability, volunteer work, work experience. **Freshman Admission Requirements:** High school diploma is required and GED is accepted. *Academic units required:* 4 English, 3 mathematics, 3 science, 2 foreign language, 3 social studies. **Freshman Admission Statistics:** 3,604 applied, 80% admitted, 30% enrolled. **Transfer Admission Requirements:** High school transcript, college transcript(s), Lowest grade transferable C. **General Admission Information:** Application fee $50. Notification on a rolling basis, beginning on or about 11/1. Nonfall registration accepted. Admission may be deferred for a maximum of 1 year.

COSTS AND FINANCIAL AID

Annual in-state tuition $10,454. Annual out-of-state tuition $15,954. Room and board $3,360. Required fees $552. Average book expense $1,168. **Required Forms and Deadlines:** FAFSA. Priority financial aid filing date 2/15. **Types of Aid:** *Need-based scholarships/grants:* Federal Pell, SEOG, state scholarships/grants, private scholarships, the school's own gift aid. *Loans:* FFEL Subsidized Stafford, FFEL Unsubsidized Stafford, FFEL PLUS, Federal Perkins, college/university loans from institutional funds, private loans. *Student Employment:* **Financial Aid Statistics:** 52% freshmen, 50% undergrads receive need-based scholarship or grant aid. 33% freshmen, 18% undergrads receive non-need-based scholarship or grant aid. 42% freshmen, 47% undergrads receive need-based self-help aid. 67% undergrads borrow to pay for school. Average cumulative indebtedness $26,300. **Criteria for awarding institutional aid:** *Non-need-based:* Academics, alumni affiliation, athletics, minority status.

PENNSYLVANIA STATE UNIVERSITY—ALTOONA

E108 Raymond Smith Building, Altoona, PA 16601-3760
Phone: 814-949-5466
E-mail: aaadmit@psu.edu
Fax: 814-949-5564

This public school was founded in 1929.

RATINGS

Admissions Selectivity Rating: 73   **Fire Safety Rating:** 60*   **Green Rating:** 60*

STUDENTS AND FACULTY

Enrollment: 3,854. **Student Body:** 49% female, 51% male, 15% out-of-state, 1% international Asian 2%, African American 6%, Caucasian 88%, Hispanic 2%.

Retention and Graduation: Faculty: Student/faculty ratio 19:1. 150 full-time faculty, 72% hold PhDs, 9% are are members of minority groups, 42% are women.

ACADEMICS

Degrees: Bachelor's, terminal associate, transfer associate. **Classes:** Most classes have 20–29 students. Most lab/discussion sessions have 20–29 students. **Special Study Options:** Cooperative education program, cross-registration, distance learning, double major, dual enrollment, English as a Second Language (ESL), exchange student program (domestic), honors program, independent study, internships, liberal arts/career combination, student-designed major, study abroad, teacher certification program .

FACILITIES

Housing: Coed dorms, special housing for disabled students, suites, special interest housing.

CAMPUS LIFE

Environment: Village. **Activities:** Choral groups, dance, drama/theater, jazz band, literary magazine, music ensembles, pep band, student government, student newspaper, student-run film society, yearbook, campus ministries, international student organization. **Athletics (Intercollegiate):** *Men:* Basketball, diving, skiing (downhill/alpine), soccer, swimming, tennis, volleyball. *Women:* Basketball, diving, skiing (downhill/alpine), swimming, tennis, volleyball.

ADMISSIONS

Freshman Academic Profile: Average high school GPA 3.06. 8.37% in top 10% of high school class, 31.79% in top 25% of high school class, 76.91% in top 50% of high school class. SAT Math middle 50% range 460–570. SAT Critical Reading middle 50% range 450–550. **Basis for Candidate Selection:** *Very important factors considered include:* Academic GPA, standardized test scores. *Important factors considered include:* Rigor of secondary school record. *Other* *factors considered include:* Class rank, application essay, recommendation(s), alumni/ae relation, character/personal qualities, extracurricular activities, talent/ability, volunteer work, work experience. **Freshman Admission Requirements:** High school diploma is required and GED is accepted. *Academic units required:* 4 English, 3 mathematics, 3 science, 2 foreign language, 3 social studies. **Freshman Admission Statistics:** 5,930 applied, 70% admitted, 36% enrolled. **Transfer Admission Requirements:** High school transcript, college transcript(s), Lowest grade transferable C. **General Admission Information:** Application fee $50. Notification on a rolling basis, beginning on or about 11/1. Nonfall registration accepted. Admission may be deferred for a maximum of 1 year.

COSTS AND FINANCIAL AID

Annual in-state tuition $10,912. Annual out-of-state tuition $16,694. Room and board $7,180. Required fees $552. Average book expense $1,168. **Required Forms and Deadlines:** FAFSA. Priority financial aid filing date 2/15. **Types of Aid:** *Need-based scholarships/grants:* Federal Pell, SEOG, state scholarships/grants, private scholarships, the school's own gift aid. *Loans:* FFEL Subsidized Stafford, FFEL Unsubsidized Stafford, FFEL PLUS, Federal Perkins, college/university loans from institutional funds, private loans. **Financial Aid Statistics:** 40% freshmen, 48% undergrads receive need-based scholarship or grant aid. 18% freshmen, 21% undergrads receive non-need-based scholarship or grant aid. 52% freshmen, 59% undergrads receive need-based self-help aid. 67% undergrads borrow to pay for school. Average cumulative indebtedness $26,300. **Criteria for awarding institutional aid:** *Non-need-based:* Academics, alumni affiliation, athletics, minority status.

PENNSYLVANIA STATE UNIVERSITY—BERKS

14 Perkins, Student Center, Reading, PA 19610-6009
Phone: 610-396-6060
E-mail: admissionsbk@psu.edu
Fax: 610-396-6077

This public school was founded in 1924. It has a 241-acre campus.

RATINGS
Admissions Selectivity Rating: 70   **Fire Safety Rating:** 60*   **Green Rating:** 60*

STUDENTS AND FACULTY
Enrollment: 2,557. **Student Body:** 42% female, 58% male, 8% out-of-state, 1% international Asian 4%, African American 8%, Caucasian 83%, Hispanic 4%.
Retention and Graduation: Faculty: Student/faculty ratio 19:1. 109 full-time faculty, 68% hold PhDs, 11% are are members of minority groups, 42% are women.

ACADEMICS
Degrees: Bachelor's, certificate, terminal associate, transfer associate. **Classes:** Most classes have 20–29 students. Most lab/discussion sessions have 10–19 students. **Special Study Options:** Accelerated program, cooperative education program, cross-registration, distance learning, dual enrollment, English as a Second Language (ESL), honors program, independent study, internships, study abroad, teacher certification program.

FACILITIES
Housing: Coed dorms, special housing for disabled students, Honor Students, Suites, Special Interest Houses.

CAMPUS LIFE
Environment: Village. **Activities:** Choral groups, dance, drama/theater, pep band, radio station, student government, student newspaper, student-run film society, yearbook, campus ministries, international student organization. **Athletics (Intercollegiate):** *Men:* Baseball, basketball, fencing, soccer, tennis, volleyball. *Women:* Fencing, softball, tennis, volleyball.

ADMISSIONS
Freshman Academic Profile: Average high school GPA 2.85. 5.49% in top 10% of high school class, 23.57% in top 25% of high school class, 60.93% in top 50% of high school class. SAT Math middle 50% range 430–560. SAT Critical Reading middle 50% range 420–540. Minimum paper TOEFL 550. **Basis for Candidate Selection:** *Very important factors considered include:* Academic GPA, standardized test scores. *Important factors considered include:* Rigor of secondary school record. *Other factors considered include:* Class rank, application essay, recommendation(s), alumni/ae relation, character/personal qualities, extracurricular activities, talent/ability, volunteer work, work experience. **Freshman Admission Requirements:** High school diploma is required and GED is accepted. *Academic units required:* 4 English, 3 mathematics, 3 science, 2

foreign language, 3 social studies. **Freshman Admission Statistics:** 3,354 applied, 75% admitted, 37% enrolled. **Transfer Admission Requirements:** High school transcript, college transcript(s), Lowest grade transferable C. **General Admission Information:** Application fee $50. Notification on a rolling basis, beginning on or about 11/1. Nonfall registration accepted. Admission may be deferred for a maximum of 1 year.

COSTS AND FINANCIAL AID

Annual in-state tuition $10,912. Annual out-of-state tuition $16,694. Room and board $7,850. Required fees $552. Average book expense $1,168. **Required Forms and Deadlines:** FAFSA. Priority financial aid filing date 2/15. **Types of Aid:** *Need-based scholarships/grants:* Federal Pell, SEOG, state scholarships/grants, private scholarships, the school's own gift aid. *Loans:* Direct Subsidized Stafford, FFEL Subsidized Stafford, FFEL Unsubsidized Stafford, FFEL PLUS, Federal Perkins, college/university loans from institutional funds, private loans. *Student Employment:* **Financial Aid Statistics:** 36% freshmen, 38% undergrads receive need-based scholarship or grant aid. 14% freshmen, 12% undergrads receive non-need-based scholarship or grant aid. 46% freshmen, 48% undergrads receive need-based self-help aid. 67% undergrads borrow to pay for school. Average cumulative indebtedness $26,300. **Criteria for awarding institutional aid:** *Non-need-based:* Academics, alumni affiliation, athletics, minority status.

PENNSYLVANIA STATE UNIVERSITY—DELAWARE COUNTY

25 Yearsley Mill Road, Media, PA 19063-5596
Phone: 610-892-1200
E-mail: admissions-delco@psu.edu
Fax: 610-892-1320

This public school was founded in 1966. It has a 87-acre campus.

RATINGS
Admissions Selectivity Rating: 68   **Fire Safety Rating:** 60*   **Green Rating:** 60*

STUDENTS AND FACULTY
Enrollment: 1,455. **Student Body:** 43% female, 57% male, 4% out-of-state, international Asian 9%, African American 15%, Caucasian 74%, Hispanic 3%. **Retention and Graduation:** 69% freshmen return for sophomore year. **Faculty:** Student/faculty ratio 19:1. 61 full-time faculty, 57% hold PhDs, 15% are are members of minority groups, 51% are women.

ACADEMICS
Degrees: Bachelor's, certificate, terminal associate, transfer associate. **Classes:** Most classes have 10–19 students. **Special Study Options:** Distance learning, double major, dual enrollment, English as a Second Language (ESL), honors program, independent study, internships, study abroad, teacher certification program.

FACILITIES
Special Academic Facilities/Equipment: Culinary Archives and Museum.

CAMPUS LIFE
Environment: Village. **Activities:** Choral groups, dance, literary magazine, student government, student newspaper, student-run film society. **Athletics (Intercollegiate):** *Men:* Baseball, basketball, ice hockey, riflery, soccer, tennis, volleyball. *Women:* Basketball, ice hockey, riflery, soccer, tennis, volleyball.

ADMISSIONS
Freshman Academic Profile: Average high school GPA 2.88. 5.51% in top 10% of high school class, 22.61% in top 25% of high school class, 58.84% in top 50% of high school class. SAT Math middle 50% range 420–540. SAT Critical Reading middle 50% range 410–520. Minimum paper TOEFL 550. **Basis for Candidate Selection:** *Very important factors considered include:* Academic GPA, standardized test scores. *Important factors considered include:* Rigor of secondary school record. *Other factors considered include:* Class rank, application essay, recommendation(s), alumni/ae relation, character/personal qualities, extracurricular activities, talent/ability, volunteer work, work experience. **Freshman Admission Requirements:** High school diploma is required and GED is accepted. *Academic units required:* 4 English, 3 mathematics, 3 science, 2 foreign language, 3 social studies. **Freshman Admission Statistics:** 1,745 applied, 80% admitted, 31% enrolled. **Transfer Admission Requirements:** High school transcript, college transcript(s), Lowest grade transferable C. **General Admission Information:** Application fee $50. Notification on a rolling basis, beginning on or about 11/1. Nonfall registration accepted. Admission may be deferred for a maximum of 1 year.

COSTS AND FINANCIAL AID

Annual in-state tuition $10,454. Annual out-of-state tuition $15,954. Room and board $3,360. Required fees $552. Average book expense $1,168. **Required Forms and Deadlines:** FAFSA. Priority financial aid filing date 2/15. **Types of Aid:** *Need-based scholarships/grants:* Federal Pell, SEOG, state scholarships/grants, private scholarships, the school's own gift aid. *Loans:* FFEL Subsidized Stafford, FFEL Unsubsidized Stafford, FFEL PLUS, Federal Perkins, college/university loans from institutional funds, private loans. *Student Employment:* **Financial Aid Statistics:** 45% freshmen, 44% undergrads receive need-based scholarship or grant aid. 28% freshmen, 16% undergrads receive non-need-based scholarship or grant aid. 43% freshmen, 45% undergrads receive need-based self-help aid. 67% undergrads borrow to pay for school. Average cumulative indebtedness $26,300. **Criteria for awarding institutional aid:** *Non-need-based:* Academics, alumni affiliation, athletics, minority status.

PENNSYLVANIA STATE UNIVERSITY—DUBOIS

Enrollment Services House, Dubois, PA 15801-3199
Phone: 814-375-4720
E-mail: duboisinfo@psu.edu
Fax: 814-375-4784 **Website:** www.ds.psu.edu

This public school was founded in 1935. It has a 13-acre campus.

RATINGS
Admissions Selectivity Rating: 65   **Fire Safety Rating:** 60*   **Green Rating:** 60*

STUDENTS AND FACULTY
Enrollment: 724. **Student Body:** 51% female, 49% male, 1% out-of-state, African American 1%, Caucasian 99%.
Retention and Graduation: 82% freshmen return for sophomore year. **Faculty:** Student/faculty ratio 13:1. 43 full-time faculty, 65% hold PhDs, 14% are are members of minority groups, 44% are women.

ACADEMICS
Degrees: Bachelor's, certificate, terminal associate, transfer associate. **Classes:** Most classes have 10–19 students. Most lab/discussion sessions have 10–19 students. **Special Study Options:** Accelerated program, cross-registration, distance learning, double major, dual enrollment, honors program, independent study, internships, student-designed major, study abroad.

FACILITIES
Housing: Independtly owned housing nearby.

CAMPUS LIFE
Environment: Village. **Activities:** Choral groups, drama/theater, literary magazine, student government, student newspaper, student-run film society **Athletics (Intercollegiate):** *Men:* Basketball. *Women:* volleyball.

ADMISSIONS
Freshman Academic Profile: Average high school GPA 2.91. 5.39% in top 10% of high school class, 21.08% in top 25% of high school class, 61.27% in top 50% of high school class. SAT Math middle 50% range 415–545. SAT Critical Reading middle 50% range 410–500. Minimum paper TOEFL 550. **Basis for Candidate Selection:** *Very important factors considered include:* Academic GPA, standardized test scores. *Important factors considered include:* Rigor of secondary school record. *Other factors considered include:* Class rank, application essay, recommendation(s), alumni/ae relation, character/personal qualities, extracurricular activities, talent/ability, volunteer work, work experience. **Freshman Admission Requirements:** High school diploma is required and GED is accepted. *Academic units required:* 4 English, 3 mathematics, 3 science, 2 foreign language, 3 social studies. **Freshman Admission Statistics:** 539 applied, 88% admitted, 48% enrolled. **Transfer Admission Requirements:** High school transcript, college transcript(s), Lowest grade transferable C. **General Admission Information:** Application fee $50. Notification on a rolling basis, beginning on or about 11/1. Nonfall registration accepted. Admission may be deferred for a maximum of 1 year.

COSTS AND FINANCIAL AID
Annual in-state tuition $10,454. Annual out-of-state tuition $15,954. Room and board $3,360. Required fees $542. Average book expense $1,168. **Required Forms and Deadlines:** FAFSA. Priority financial aid filing date 2/15. **Notification of Awards:** Applicants will be notified of awards on a rolling basis beginning 3/1. **Types of Aid:** *Need-based scholarships/grants:* Federal Pell, SEOG, state scholarships/grants, private scholarships, the school's own gift aid. *Loans:* FFEL Subsidized Stafford, FFEL Unsubsidized Stafford, FFEL PLUS, Federal Perkins, college/university loans from institutional funds, private loans. *Student Employment:* **Financial Aid Statistics:** 69% freshmen, 74%

---

undergrads receive need-based scholarship or grant aid. 34% freshmen, 28% undergrads receive non-need-based scholarship or grant aid. 68% freshmen, 75% undergrads receive need-based self-help aid. 67% undergrads borrow to pay for school. Average cumulative indebtedness $26,300. **Criteria for awarding institutional aid:** *Non-need-based:* Academics, alumni affiliation, athletics, minority status.

PENNSYLVANIA STATE UNIVERSITY—
ERIE, THE BEHREND COLLEGE

5091 Station Road, Erie, PA 16563-0105
Phone: 814-898-6100
E-mail: behrend.admissions@psu.edu
Fax: 814-898-6044 **Website:** www.pserie.psu.edu **ACT Code:** 3656

This public school was founded in 1948. It has a 732-acre campus.

RATINGS
Admissions Selectivity Rating: 73   **Fire Safety Rating:** 60*   **Green Rating:** 60*

STUDENTS AND FACULTY
Enrollment: 3,843. **Student Body:** 35% female, 65% male, 8% out-of-state, 1% international Asian 2%, African American 3%, Caucasian 91%, Hispanic 2%.
Retention and Graduation: Faculty: Student/faculty ratio 17:1. 208 full-time faculty, 59% hold PhDs, 11% are are members of minority groups, 32% are women.

ACADEMICS
Degrees: Bachelor's, certificate, master's, terminal associate, transfer associate. **Classes:** Most classes have 20–29 students. Most lab/discussion sessions have 10–19 students. **Special Study Options:** Accelerated program, cooperative education program, distance learning, double major, dual enrollment, honors program, independent study, internships, liberal arts/career combination, study abroad, teacher certification program. Special programs offered to physically disabled students include note-taking services, reader services, tape recorders, tutors. **Career services:** Alumni services, career/job search classes, career assessment, internships.

FACILITIES
Housing: Coed dorms, special housing for disabled students, men's dorms, women's dorms, apartments for single students, suites, special interest housing. **Special Academic Facilities/Equipment:** Observatory, plastics lab. **Computers:** Students can register for classes online. Administrative functions (other than registration) can be performed online.

CAMPUS LIFE
Environment: Village. **Activities:** Choral groups, concert band, dance, drama/theater, jazz band, literary magazine, music ensembles, pep band, radio station, student government, student newspaper, student-run film society, campus ministries, international student organization. **Organizations:** 75 registered organizations, 46 honor societies, 26 religious organizations. 6 fraternities, 4 sororities. **Athletics (Intercollegiate):** *Men:* Baseball, basketball, cheerleading, cross-country, golf, soccer, swimming, tennis, track/field (outdoor), water polo, wrestling. *Women:* Basketball, cheerleading, cross-country, golf, soccer, softball, swimming, tennis, track/field (outdoor), volleyball, water polo. **On-Campus Highlights:** Junker Athletic Center, Logan House, Smith Chapel and Carillon, Bruno's Caf Reen Union Building, Historic Behrend Farmhouse.

ADMISSIONS
Freshman Academic Profile: Average high school GPA 3.18. 12.32% in top 10% of high school class, 38.92% in top 25% of high school class, 83.05% in top 50% of high school class. SAT Math middle 50% range 480–590. SAT Critical Reading middle 50% range 460–560. Minimum paper TOEFL 550. **Basis for Candidate Selection:** *Very important factors considered include:* Academic GPA, standardized test scores. *Important factors considered include:* Rigor of secondary school record. *Other factors considered include:* Class rank, application essay, recommendation(s), alumni/ae relation, character/personal qualities, extracurricular activities, talent/ability, volunteer work, work experience. **Freshman Admission Requirements:** High school diploma is required and GED is accepted. *Academic units required:* 4 English, 3 mathematics, 3 science, 2 foreign language, 3 social studies. **Freshman Admission Statistics:** 3,689 applied, 79% admitted, 40% enrolled. **Transfer Admission Requirements:** High school transcript, college transcript(s), Lowest grade transferable C. **General Admission Information:** Application fee $50. Notification on a rolling basis, beginning on or about 11/1. Nonfall registration accepted. Admission may be deferred for a maximum of 1 year. Credit offered for CEEB Advanced Placement tests.

COSTS AND FINANCIAL AID

Annual in-state tuition $10,912. Annual out-of-state tuition $16,694. Room and board $7,180. Required fees $552. Average book expense $1,168. **Required Forms and Deadlines:** FAFSA. Priority financial aid filing date 2/15. **Notification of Awards:** Applicants will be notified of awards on a rolling basis beginning 3/1. **Types of Aid:** *Need-based scholarships/grants:* Federal Pell, SEOG, state scholarships/grants, private scholarships, the school's own gift aid. *Loans:* FFEL Subsidized Stafford, FFEL Unsubsidized Stafford, FFEL PLUS, Federal Perkins, college/university loans from institutional funds, private loans. *Student Employment:* Federal Work-Study Program available. Institutional employment available. Highest amount earned per year from on-campus jobs $656. Off-campus job opportunities are good. **Financial Aid Statistics:** 45% freshmen, 49% undergrads receive need-based scholarship or grant aid. 20% freshmen, 21% undergrads receive non-need-based scholarship or grant aid. 58% freshmen, 61% undergrads receive need-based self-help aid. 67% undergrads borrow to pay for school. Average cumulative indebtedness $26,300. **Criteria for awarding institutional aid:** *Non-need-based:* Academics, alumni affiliation, athletics, minority status.

PENNSYLVANIA STATE UNIVERSITY—FAYETTE, THE EBERLY CAMPUS

PO Box 519, Route 119 North, 108 Williams Building, Uniontown, PA 15401-0519
Phone: 724-430-4130
E-mail: feadm@psu.edu
Fax: 724-430-4175 **Website:** www.fe.psu.edu

This public school was founded in 1934. It has a 193-acre campus.

RATINGS
Admissions Selectivity Rating: 69   **Fire Safety Rating:** 60*   **Green Rating:** 60*

STUDENTS AND FACULTY
Enrollment: 942. **Student Body:** 58% female, 42% male, 1% out-of-state, African American 7%, Caucasian 92%, Hispanic 1%.
Retention and Graduation: Faculty: Student/faculty ratio 14:1. 55 full-time faculty, 51% hold PhDs, 7% are are members of minority groups, 36% are women.

ACADEMICS
Degrees: Bachelor's, terminal associate, transfer associate. **Classes:** Most classes have 20–29 students. Most lab/discussion sessions have fewer than 10 students. **Special Study Options:** Accelerated program, cross-registration, distance learning, double major, dual enrollment, honors program, independent study, internships, student-designed major, study abroad, weekend classes.

FACILITIES
Housing: Privately owned, off-campus housing.

CAMPUS LIFE
Environment: Village. **Activities:** Drama/theater, musical theater, student government.

ADMISSIONS
Freshman Academic Profile: Average high school GPA 2.97. 8.11% in top 10% of high school class, 36.94% in top 25% of high school class, 77.03% in top 50% of high school class. SAT Math middle 50% range 400–520. SAT Critical Reading middle 50% range 400–510. Minimum paper TOEFL 550. **Basis for Candidate Selection:** *Very important factors considered include:* Academic GPA, standardized test scores. *Important factors considered include:* Rigor of secondary school record. *Other factors considered include:* Class rank, application essay, recommendation(s), alumni/ae relation, character/personal qualities, extracurricular activities, talent/ability, volunteer work, work experience. **Freshman Admission Requirements:** High school diploma is required and GED is accepted. *Academic units required:* 4 English, 3 mathematics, 3 science, 2 foreign language, 3 social studies. **Freshman Admission Statistics:** 605 applied, 90% admitted, 45% enrolled. **Transfer Admission Requirements:** High school transcript, college transcript(s), Lowest grade transferable C. **General Admission Information:** Application fee $50. Notification on a rolling basis, beginning on or about 11/1. Nonfall registration accepted. Admission may be deferred for a maximum of 1 year.

COSTS AND FINANCIAL AID
Annual in-state tuition $10,454. Annual out-of-state tuition $15,954. Room and board $3,360. Required fees $542. Average book expense $1,168. **Required Forms and Deadlines:** FAFSA. Priority financial aid filing date 2/15. **Notification of Awards:** Applicants will be notified of awards on a rolling basis

beginning 3/1. **Types of Aid:** *Need-based scholarships/grants:* Federal Pell, SEOG, state scholarships/grants, private scholarships, the school's own gift aid. *Loans:* FFEL Subsidized Stafford, FFEL Unsubsidized Stafford, FFEL PLUS, Federal Perkins, college/university loans from institutional funds, private loans. *Student Employment:* **Financial Aid Statistics:** 68% freshmen, 72% undergrads receive need-based scholarship or grant aid. 28% freshmen, 26% undergrads receive non-need-based scholarship or grant aid. 61% freshmen, 70% undergrads receive need-based self-help aid. 67% undergrads borrow to pay for school. Average cumulative indebtedness $26,300. **Criteria for awarding institutional aid:** *Non-need-based:* Academics, alumni affiliation, athletics, minority status.

PENNSYLVANIA STATE UNIVERSITY— HARRISBURG

Swatara Bldg, 777 W. Harrisburg Pike, Middletown, PA 17057-4898
Phone: 717-948-6250
E-mail: hbgadmit@psu.edu
Fax: 717-948-6325 **Website:** www.hbg.psu.edu

This public school was founded in 1966.

RATINGS
Admissions Selectivity Rating: 74   **Fire Safety Rating:** 60*   **Green Rating:** 60*

STUDENTS AND FACULTY
Enrollment: 2,294. **Student Body:** 46% female, 54% male, 12% out-of-state, 2% international Asian 7%, African American 9%, Caucasian 79%, Hispanic 4%.
Retention and Graduation: Faculty: Student/faculty ratio 12:1. 195 full-time faculty, 85% hold PhDs, 28% are are members of minority groups, 39% are women.

ACADEMICS
Degrees: Bachelor's, certificate, master's, post-bachelor's certificate, terminal associate, transfer associate. **Classes:** Most classes have 20–29 students. Most lab/discussion sessions have fewer than 10 students. **Special Study Options:** Cooperative education program, cross-registration, distance learning, double major, dual enrollment, honors program, independent study, internships, student-designed major, study abroad, teacher certification program.

FACILITIES
Housing: Special housing for disabled students, apartments for single students, special interest housing.

CAMPUS LIFE
Environment: Village. **Activities:** Choral groups, dance, drama/theater, literary magazine, music ensembles, radio station, student government, student newspaper. **Organizations:** 2 honor societies, 1 religious organizations. **Athletics (Intercollegiate):** *Men:* Basketball, skiing (downhill/alpine), soccer, tennis, track/field (outdoor), volleyball. *Women:* Skiing (downhill/alpine), soccer, track/field (outdoor), volleyball.

ADMISSIONS
Freshman Academic Profile: Average high school GPA 3.1. 8.73% in top 10% of high school class, 35.49% in top 25% of high school class, 81.13% in top 50% of high school class. SAT Math middle 50% range 475–580. SAT Critical Reading middle 50% range 460–570. **Basis for Candidate Selection:** *Very important factors considered include:* Academic GPA, standardized test scores. *Important factors considered include:* Rigor of secondary school record. *Other factors considered include:* Class rank, application essay, recommendation(s), alumni/ae relation, character/personal qualities, extracurricular activities, talent/ability, volunteer work, work experience. **Freshman Admission Requirements:** High school diploma is required and GED is accepted. *Academic units required:* 4 English, 3 mathematics, 3 science, 2 foreign language, 3 social studies. **Freshman Admission Statistics:** 2,689 applied, 70% admitted, 22% enrolled. **Transfer Admission Requirements:** High school transcript, college transcript(s), Lowest grade transferable C. **General Admission Information:** Application fee $50. Notification on a rolling basis, beginning on or about 11/1. Nonfall registration accepted. Admission may be deferred for a maximum of 1 year.

COSTS AND FINANCIAL AID
Annual in-state tuition $10,912. Annual out-of-state tuition $16,694. Room and board $8,610. Required fees $542. Average book expense $1,168. **Required Forms and Deadlines:** FAFSA. Priority financial aid filing date 2/15. **Notification of Awards:** Applicants will be notified of awards on a rolling basis

beginning 3/1. **Types of Aid:** *Need-based scholarships/grants:* Federal Pell, SEOG, state scholarships/grants, private scholarships, the school's own gift aid. *Loans:* FFEL Subsidized Stafford, FFEL Unsubsidized Stafford, FFEL PLUS, Federal Perkins, college/university loans from institutional funds, private loans. *Student Employment:* **Financial Aid Statistics:** 43% freshmen, 47% undergrads receive need-based scholarship or grant aid. 22% freshmen, 17% undergrads receive non-need-based scholarship or grant aid. 51% freshmen, 55% undergrads receive need-based self-help aid. 67% undergrads borrow to pay for school. Average cumulative indebtedness $26,300. **Criteria for awarding institutional aid:** *Non-need-based:* Academics, alumni affiliation, athletics, minority status.

PENNSYLVANIA STATE UNIVERSITY—
HAZLETON

110 Admin. Building, 76 University Drive, Hazleton, PA 18202-1291
Phone: 570-450-3142
E-mail: admissions-hn@psu.edu
Fax: 570-450-3182 **Website:** www.hn.psu.edu

This public school was founded in 1934. It has a 73-acre campus.

RATINGS
Admissions Selectivity Rating: 68   **Fire Safety Rating:** 60*   **Green Rating:** 60*

STUDENTS AND FACULTY
Enrollment: 1,192. **Student Body:** 40% female, 60% male, 26% out-of-state, Asian 4%, African American 8%, Caucasian 80%, Hispanic 7%.
Faculty: Student/faculty ratio 19:1. 51 full-time faculty, 65% hold PhDs, 16% are are members of minority groups, 41% are women.

ACADEMICS
Degrees: Bachelor's, terminal associate, transfer associate. **Classes:** Most classes have 20–29 students. **Special Study Options:** Accelerated program, cross-registration, distance learning, double major, dual enrollment, English as a Second Language (ESL), honors program, independent study, internships, student-designed major, study abroad.

FACILITIES
Housing: Coed dorms, townhouses, suites.

CAMPUS LIFE
Environment: Rural. **Activities:** Choral groups, dance, drama/theater, literary magazine, radio station, student government, student newspaper, campus ministries. **Athletics (Intercollegiate):** *Men:* Baseball, basketball, soccer, tennis. *Women:* Softball, tennis, volleyball.

ADMISSIONS
Freshman Academic Profile: Average high school GPA 2.91. 5.94% in top 10% of high school class, 24.36% in top 25% of high school class, 67.33% in top 50% of high school class. SAT Math middle 50% range 420–540. SAT Critical Reading middle 50% range 420–530. Minimum paper TOEFL 550. **Basis for Candidate Selection:** *Very important factors considered include:* Academic GPA, standardized test scores. *Important factors considered include:* Rigor of secondary school record. *Other factors considered include:* Class rank, application essay, recommendation(s), alumni/ae relation, character/personal qualities, extracurricular activities, talent/ability, volunteer work, work experience. **Freshman Admission Requirements:** High school diploma is required and GED is accepted. *Academic units required:* 4 English, 3 mathematics, 3 science, 2 foreign language, 3 social studies. **Freshman Admission Statistics:** 1,613 applied, 89% admitted, 40% enrolled. **Transfer Admission Requirements:** High school transcript, college transcript(s), lowest grade transferable C. **General Admission Information:** Application fee $50. Notification on a rolling basis, beginning on or about 11/1. Nonfall registration accepted. Admission may be deferred for a maximum of 1 year.

COSTS AND FINANCIAL AID
Annual in-state tuition $10,454. Annual out-of-state tuition $15,954. Room and board $7,180. Required fees $552. Average book expense $1,168. **Required Forms and Deadlines:** FAFSA. Priority financial aid filing date 2/15. **Notification of Awards:** Applicants will be notified of awards on a rolling basis beginning 3/1. **Types of Aid:** *Need-based scholarships/grants:* Federal Pell, SEOG, state scholarships/grants, private scholarships, the school's own gift aid. *Loans:* FFEL Subsidized Stafford, FFEL Unsubsidized Stafford, FFEL PLUS, Federal Perkins, college/university loans from institutional funds, private loans. *Student Employment:* **Financial Aid Statistics:** 48% freshmen, 49% undergrads receive need-based scholarship or grant aid. 25% freshmen, 21%

undergrads receive non-need-based scholarship or grant aid. 56% freshmen, 59% undergrads receive need-based self-help aid. 67% undergrads borrow to pay for school. Average cumulative indebtedness $26,300. **Criteria for awarding institutional aid:** *Non-need-based:* Academics, alumni affiliation, athletics, minority status.

PENNSYLVANIA STATE UNIVERSITY—
LEHIGH VALLEY

8380 Mohr Lane, Academic Building, Fogelsville, PA 18051
Phone: 610-285-5035
E-mail: admissions-lv@psu.edu
Fax: 610-285-5220 **Website:** www.lv.psu.edu

This public school was founded in 1912. It has a 42-acre campus.

RATINGS
Admissions Selectivity Rating: 70   **Fire Safety Rating:** 60*   **Green Rating:** 60*

STUDENTS AND FACULTY
Enrollment: 685. **Student Body:** 40% female, 60% male, 5% out-of-state, 1% international Asian 6%, African American 3%, Caucasian 80%, Hispanic 10%.
Retention and Graduation: Faculty: Student/faculty ratio 15:1. 27 full-time faculty, 78% hold PhDs, 15% are are members of minority groups, 52% are women.

ACADEMICS
Degrees: Bachelor's, terminal associate, transfer associate. **Classes:** Most classes have 10–19 students. Most lab/discussion sessions have 10–19 students. **Special Study Options:** Accelerated program, cooperative education program, cross-registration, distance learning, dual enrollment, honors program, independent study, internships, study abroad.

CAMPUS LIFE
Activities: Drama/theater, student government, student newspaper. **Athletics (Intercollegiate):** *Men:* Basketball, cross-country, golf, soccer, tennis, volleyball. *Women:* Basketball, golf, tennis, volleyball.

ADMISSIONS
Freshman Academic Profile: Average high school GPA 2.89. 8.29% in top 10% of high school class, 35.48% in top 25% of high school class, 69.59% in top 50% of high school class. SAT Math middle 50% range 450–570. SAT Critical Reading middle 50% range 420–530. Minimum paper TOEFL 550. **Basis for Candidate Selection:** *Very important factors considered include:* Academic GPA, standardized test scores. *Important factors considered include:* Rigor of secondary school record. *Other factors considered include:* Class rank, application essay, recommendation(s), alumni/ae relation, character/personal qualities, extracurricular activities, talent/ability, volunteer work, work experience. **Freshman Admission Requirements:** High school diploma is required and GED is accepted. *Academic units required:* 4 English, 3 mathematics, 3 science, 2 foreign language, 3 social studies. **Freshman Admission Statistics:** 908 applied, 80% admitted, 34% enrolled. **Transfer Admission Requirements:** High school transcript, college transcript(s), Lowest grade transferable C. **General Admission Information:** Application fee $50. Notification on a rolling basis, beginning on or about 11/1. Nonfall registration accepted. Admission may be deferred for a maximum of 1 year.

COSTS AND FINANCIAL AID
Annual in-state tuition $10,454. Annual out-of-state tuition $15,954. Room and board $3,360. Required fees $552. Average book expense $1,168. **Required Forms and Deadlines:** FAFSA. Priority financial aid filing date 2/15. **Types of Aid:** *Need-based scholarships/grants:* Federal Pell, SEOG, state scholarships/grants, private scholarships, the school's own gift aid. *Loans:* FFEL Subsidized Stafford, FFEL Unsubsidized Stafford, FFEL PLUS, Federal Perkins, college/university loans from institutional funds, private loans. *Student Employment:* **Financial Aid Statistics:** 43% freshmen, 46% undergrads receive need-based scholarship or grant aid. 19% freshmen, 11% undergrads receive non-need-based scholarship or grant aid. 44% freshmen, 50% undergrads receive need-based self-help aid. 67% undergrads borrow to pay for school. Average cumulative indebtedness $26,300. **Criteria for awarding institutional aid:** *Non-need-based:* Academics, alumni affiliation, athletics, minority status.

PENNSYLVANIA STATE UNIVERSITY— MONT ALTO

1 Campus Drive, Mont Alto, PA 17237-9703
Phone: 717-749-6130
E-mail: psuma@psu.edu
Fax: 717-749-6132 **Website:** www.ma.psu.edu

This public school was founded in 1929. It has a 62-acre campus.

RATINGS
Admissions Selectivity Rating: 70   **Fire Safety Rating:** 60*   **Green Rating:** 60*

STUDENTS AND FACULTY
Enrollment: 1,025. **Student Body:** 59% female, 41% male, 17% out-of-state, international Asian 3%, African American 12%, Caucasian 81%, Hispanic 3%. **Retention and Graduation:** 74% freshmen return for sophomore year. 22% grads go on to further study within 1 year. **Faculty:** Student/faculty ratio 14:1. 52 full-time faculty, 50% hold PhDs, 8% are are members of minority groups, 54% are women.

ACADEMICS
Degrees: Bachelor's, terminal associate, transfer associate. **Classes:** Most classes have 10–19 students. Most lab/discussion sessions have 10–19 students. **Special Study Options:** Accelerated program, cross-registration, distance learning, double major, dual enrollment, honors program, independent study, internships, study abroad. **Honors programs:** The Schreyer Honors College is widely recognized as one of the best and most comprehensive undergraduate honors programs in the United States. www.scholars.psu.edu/index.cfm **Combined degree programs:** BA/MD, BA/MEng, Science/MBA Program; JD/MBA. Special programs offered to physically disabled students include note-taking services, reader services, tape recorders, tutors.

FACILITIES
Housing: Coed dorms, special housing for disabled students, suites, special interest housing, townhouses. 99% of campus accessible to physically disabled.

CAMPUS LIFE
Environment: Village. **Activities:** Dance, drama/theater, jazz band, student government, student newspaper, campus ministries. **Athletics (Intercollegiate):** *Men:* Basketball, soccer, tennis. *Women:* Basketball, tennis.

ADMISSIONS
Freshman Academic Profile: Average high school GPA 2.95. 12.75% in top 10% of high school class, 34.31% in top 25% of high school class, 69.61% in top 50% of high school class. SAT Math middle 50% range 430–560. SAT Critical Reading middle 50% range 440–545. **Basis for Candidate Selection:** *Very important factors considered include:* Academic GPA, standardized test scores. *Important factors considered include:* Rigor of secondary school record. *Other factors considered include:* Class rank, application essay, recommendation(s), alumni/ae relation, character/personal qualities, extracurricular activities, talent/ability, volunteer work, work experience. **Freshman Admission Requirements:** High school diploma is required and GED is accepted. *Academic units required:* 4 English, 3 mathematics, 3 science, 2 foreign language, 3 social studies. **Freshman Admission Statistics:** 927 applied, 89% admitted, 44% enrolled. **Transfer Admission Requirements:** High school transcript, college transcript(s), Lowest grade transferable C. **General Admission Information:** Application fee $50. Notification on a rolling basis, beginning on or about 11/1. Nonfall registration accepted. Admission may be deferred for a maximum of 1 year.

COSTS AND FINANCIAL AID
Annual in-state tuition $10,454. Annual out-of-state tuition $15,954. Room and board $7,180. Required fees $552. Average book expense $1,168. **Required Forms and Deadlines:** FAFSA. Priority financial aid filing date 2/15. **Notification of Awards:** Applicants will be notified of awards on a rolling basis beginning 3/1. **Types of Aid:** *Need-based scholarships/grants:* Federal Pell, SEOG, state scholarships/grants, private scholarships, the school's own gift aid. *Loans:* FFEL Subsidized Stafford, FFEL Unsubsidized Stafford, FFEL PLUS, Federal Perkins, college/university loans from institutional funds, private loans. *Student Employment:* **Financial Aid Statistics:** 53% freshmen, 53% undergrads receive need-based scholarship or grant aid. 37% freshmen, 29% undergrads receive non-need-based scholarship or grant aid. 58% freshmen, 60% undergrads receive need-based self-help aid. 67% undergrads borrow to pay for school. Average cumulative indebtedness $26,300. **Criteria for awarding institutional aid:** *Non-need-based:* Academics, alumni affiliation, athletics, minority status.

PENNSYLVANIA STATE UNIVERSITY— NEW KENSINGTON

3550 7th Street Road, Route780, Upper Barrell, PA 15068-1798
Phone: 724-334-5466
E-mail: nkadmissions@psu.edu
Fax: 724-334-6111

This public school was founded in 1958. It has a 71-acre campus.

RATINGS
Admissions Selectivity Rating: 70   **Fire Safety Rating:** 60*   **Green Rating:** 60*

STUDENTS AND FACULTY
Enrollment: 734. **Student Body:** 44% female, 56% male, 2% out-of-state, Asian 1%, African American 3%, Caucasian 95%, Hispanic 1%. **Retention and Graduation: Faculty:** Student/faculty ratio 14:1. 38 full-time faculty, 61% hold PhDs, 16% are are members of minority groups, 45% are women.

ACADEMICS
Degrees: Bachelor's, certificate, terminal associate, transfer associate. **Classes:** Most classes have fewer than 10 students. Most lab/discussion sessions have 10–19 students. **Special Study Options:** Cross-registration, distance learning, double major, dual enrollment, external degree program, honors program, independent study, internships, study abroad.

CAMPUS LIFE
Activities: Choral groups, dance, drama/theater, jazz band, literary magazine, musical theater, student government, student newspaper. **Athletics (Intercollegiate):** *Men:* Baseball, basketball, ice hockey, tennis, volleyball. *Women:* Basketball, ice hockey, tennis, volleyball.

ADMISSIONS
Freshman Academic Profile: Average high school GPA 3.01. 8.7% in top 10% of high school class, 28.8% in top 25% of high school class, 69.02% in top 50% of high school class. SAT Math middle 50% range 440–570. SAT Critical Reading middle 50% range 430–540. Minimum paper TOEFL 550. **Basis for Candidate Selection:** *Very important factors considered include:* Academic GPA, standardized test scores. *Important factors considered include:* Rigor of secondary school record. *Other factors considered include:* Class rank, application essay, recommendation(s), alumni/ae relation, character/personal qualities, extracurricular activities, talent/ability, volunteer work, work experience. **Freshman Admission Requirements:** High school diploma is required and GED is accepted. *Academic units required:* 4 English, 3 mathematics, 3 science, 2 foreign language, 3 social studies. **Freshman Admission Statistics:** 561 applied, 86% admitted, 44% enrolled. **Transfer Admission Requirements:** High school transcript, college transcript(s), Lowest grade transferable C. **General Admission Information:** Application fee $50. Notification on a rolling basis, beginning on or about 11/1. Nonfall registration accepted. Admission may be deferred for a maximum of 1 year.

COSTS AND FINANCIAL AID
Annual in-state tuition $10,454. Annual out-of-state tuition $15,954. Room and board $3,360. Required fees $552. Average book expense $1,168. **Required Forms and Deadlines:** FAFSA. Priority financial aid filing date 2/15. **Types of Aid:** *Need-based scholarships/grants:* Federal Pell, SEOG, state scholarships/grants, private scholarships, the school's own gift aid. *Loans:* FFEL Subsidized Stafford, FFEL Unsubsidized Stafford, FFEL PLUS, Federal Perkins, college/university loans from institutional funds, private loans. *Student Employment:* **Financial Aid Statistics:** 50% freshmen, 54% undergrads receive need-based scholarship or grant aid. 36% freshmen, 22% undergrads receive non-need-based scholarship or grant aid. 51% freshmen, 56% undergrads receive need-based self-help aid. 67% undergrads borrow to pay for school. Average cumulative indebtedness $26,300. **Criteria for awarding institutional aid:** *Non-need-based:* Academics, alumni affiliation, athletics, minority status.

PENNSYLVANIA STATE UNIVERSITY— SCHUYLKILL

200 University Drive, A102 Admin. Bldg, Schuykill Haven, PA 17972-2208
Phone: 570-385-6252
E-mail: sl-admissions@psu.edu
Fax: 570-385-6272 **Website:**

This public school was founded in 1934. It has a 42-acre campus.

RATINGS
Admissions Selectivity Rating: 69   **Fire Safety Rating:** 60*   **Green Rating:** 60*

STUDENTS AND FACULTY
Enrollment: 827. **Student Body:** 54% female, 46% male, 19% out-of-state, international Asian 2%, African American 29%, Caucasian 66%, Hispanic 3%. **Faculty:** Student/faculty ratio 19:1. 38 full-time faculty, 74% hold PhDs, 5% are are members of minority groups, 34% are women.

ACADEMICS
Degrees: Bachelor's, terminal associate, transfer associate. **Classes:** Most classes have 20–29 students. Most lab/discussion sessions have 10–19 students. **Special Study Options:** Accelerated program, cooperative education program, distance learning, double major, dual enrollment, honors program, independent study, internships, student-designed major, study abroad.

FACILITIES
Housing: Special housing for disabled students, apartments for single students.

CAMPUS LIFE
Activities: Choral groups, dance, drama/theater, musical theater, student government, student newspaper, campus ministries. **Athletics (Intercollegiate):** *Men:* Basketball, cross-country, softball, tennis, volleyball. *Women:* Basketball, cross-country, softball, tennis, volleyball.

ADMISSIONS
Freshman Academic Profile: Average high school GPA 2.79. 9.54% in top 10% of high school class, 27.92% in top 25% of high school class, 66.43% in top 50% of high school class. SAT Math middle 50% range 380–520. SAT Critical Reading middle 50% range 380–500. Minimum paper TOEFL 550. **Basis for Candidate Selection:** *Very important factors considered include:* Academic GPA, standardized test scores. *Important factors considered include:* Rigor of secondary school record. *Other factors considered include:* Class rank, application essay, recommendation(s), alumni/ae relation, character/personal qualities, extracurricular activities, talent/ability, volunteer work, work experience. **Freshman Admission Requirements:** High school diploma is required and GED is accepted. *Academic units required:* 4 English, 3 mathematics, 3 science, 2 foreign language, 3 social studies. **Freshman Admission Statistics:** 993 applied, 81% admitted, 42% enrolled. **Transfer Admission Requirements:** High school transcript, college transcript(s), Lowest grade transferable C. **General Admission Information:** Application fee $50. Notification on a rolling basis, beginning on or about 11/1. Nonfall registration accepted. Admission may be deferred for a maximum of 1 year.

COSTS AND FINANCIAL AID
Annual in-state tuition $10,454. Annual out-of-state tuition $15,954. Room and board $8,480. Required fees $542. Average book expense $1,168. **Required Forms and Deadlines:** FAFSA. Priority financial aid filing date 2/15. **Types of Aid:** *Need-based scholarships/grants:* Federal Pell, SEOG, state scholarships/ grants, private scholarships, the school's own gift aid. *Loans:* FFEL Subsidized Stafford, FFEL Unsubsidized Stafford, FFEL PLUS, Federal Perkins, college/ university loans from institutional funds, private loans. *Student Employment:* **Financial Aid Statistics:** 70% freshmen, 71% undergrads receive need-based scholarship or grant aid. 50% freshmen, 32% undergrads receive non-need-based scholarship or grant aid. 70% freshmen, 73% undergrads receive need-based self-help aid. 66% undergrads borrow to pay for school. Average cumulative indebtedness $26,300. **Criteria for awarding institutional aid:** *Non-need-based:* Academics, alumni affiliation, athletics, minority status.

PENNSYLVANIA STATE UNIVERSITY— SHENANGO

147 Shenango Ave, Sharon, PA 16146-1597
Phone: 724-983-2800
E-mail: psushenango@psu.edu
Fax: 724-983-2820

This public school was founded in 1965. It has a 14-acre campus.

RATINGS
Admissions Selectivity Rating: 66   **Fire Safety Rating:** 60*   **Green Rating:** 60*

STUDENTS AND FACULTY
Enrollment: 677. **Student Body:** 65% female, 35% male, 13% out-of-state, Asian 1%, African American 8%, Caucasian 90%, Hispanic 1%. **Retention and Graduation:** 71% freshmen return for sophomore year. **Faculty:** Student/faculty ratio 15:1. 29 full-time faculty, 55% hold PhDs, 10% are are members of minority groups, 45% are women.

ACADEMICS
Degrees: Bachelor's, certificate, terminal associate, transfer associate. **Classes:** Most classes have 10–19 students. Most lab/discussion sessions have 10–19 students. **Special Study Options:** Accelerated program, cross-registration, distance learning, double major, dual enrollment, honors program, independent study, internships, student-designed major, study abroad.

CAMPUS LIFE
Environment: Village. **Activities:** Literary magazine, student government.

ADMISSIONS
Freshman Academic Profile: Average high school GPA 2.91. 2.48% in top 10% of high school class, 19383% in top 25% of high school class, 61.16% in top 50% of high school class. SAT Math middle 50% range 400–520. SAT Critical Reading middle 50% range 400–490. Minimum paper TOEFL 550. **Basis for Candidate Selection:** *Very important factors considered include:* Academic GPA, standardized test scores. *Important factors considered include:* Rigor of secondary school record. *Other factors considered include:* Class rank, application essay, recommendation(s), alumni/ae relation, character/personal qualities, extracurricular activities, talent/ability, volunteer work, work experience. **Freshman Admission Requirements:** High school diploma is required and GED is accepted. *Academic units required:* 4 English, 3 mathematics, 3 science, 2 foreign language, 3 social studies. **Freshman Admission Statistics:** 271 applied, 89% admitted, 61% enrolled. **Transfer Admission Requirements:** High school transcript, college transcript(s), Lowest grade transferable C. **General Admission Information:** Application fee $50. Notification on a rolling basis, beginning on or about 11/1. Nonfall registration accepted. Admission may be deferred for a maximum of 1 year.

COSTS AND FINANCIAL AID
Annual in-state tuition $10,454. Annual out-of-state tuition $15,954. Room and board $3,360. Required fees $552. Average book expense $1,168. **Required Forms and Deadlines:** FAFSA. Priority financial aid filing date 2/15. **Types of Aid:** *Need-based scholarships/grants:* Federal Pell, SEOG, state scholarships/ grants, private scholarships, the school's own gift aid. *Loans:* FFEL Subsidized Stafford, FFEL Unsubsidized Stafford, FFEL PLUS, Federal Perkins, college/ university loans from institutional funds, private loans. *Student Employment:* **Financial Aid Statistics:** 80% freshmen, 80% undergrads receive need-based scholarship or grant aid. 49% freshmen, 34% undergrads receive non-need-based scholarship or grant aid. 78% freshmen, 82% undergrads receive need-based self-help aid. 67% undergrads borrow to pay for school. Average cumulative indebtedness $26,300. **Criteria for awarding institutional aid:** *Non-need-based:* Academics, alumni affiliation, athletics.

PENNSYLVANIA STATE UNIVERSITY— UNIVERSITY PARK

Best 373

201 Shields Building, Box 3000, University Park, PA 16802-3000
Phone: 814-865-5471 **Financial Aid Phone:** 814-865-6301
E-mail: admissions@psu.edu **CEEB Code:** 2660
Fax: 814-863-7590 **Website:** www.psu.edu **ACT Code:** 3656

This public school was founded in 1855. It has a 7264-acre campus.

RATINGS
Admissions Selectivity Rating: 92   **Fire Safety Rating:** 95   **Green Rating:** 89

STUDENTS AND FACULTY
Enrollment: 37,855. **Student Body:** 45% female, 55% male, 25% out-of-state, international (116 countries represented). Asian 5%, African American 4%, Caucasian 78%, Hispanic 4%.
Retention and Graduation: 62% freshmen graduate within 4 years. 22% grads go on to further study within 1 year. **Faculty:** Student/faculty ratio 17:1. 2432 full-time faculty, 78% hold PhDs, 19% are are members of minority groups, 37% are women.

ACADEMICS
Degrees: Associate, bachelor's, certificate, doctoral, master's, post-master's certificate, terminal associate, transfer associate. **Classes:** Most classes have 20–29 students. Most lab/discussion sessions have 20–29 students. **Majors with Highest Enrollment:** Business administration and management; engineering. **Special Study Options:** Accelerated program, cooperative education program, cross-registration, distance learning, double major, dual enrollment, English as a Second Language (ESL), exchange student program (domestic), external degree program, honors program, independent study, internships, liberal arts/career combination, student-designed major, study abroad, teacher certification program, weekend college. **Honors programs:** The Schreyer Honors College is widely recognized as one of the best and most comprehensive undergraduate honors programs in the United States. www.shc.psu.edu/ **Combined degree programs:** BA/MD, BA/MEng, Science/MBA Program; JD/MBA. Special programs offered to physically disabled students include note-taking services, reader services, tape recorders, tutors. **Career services:** Alumni network, alumni services, career/job search classes, career assessment, internships, regional alumni. **Career services highlights include:** All of our e-ship programs are based on problem-based learning for which we have gained both national and international recognition. Course modules are transferable and scalable and have been used by students at other US schools as well as majoe overseas Universities in Germany, Slovakia, Austria, etc.

FACILITIES
Housing: Coed dorms, special housing for disabled students, men's dorms, special housing for international students, women's dorms, fraternity/sorority housing, apartments for married students, apartments for single students, suites, special interest housing. 99% of campus accessible to physically disabled. **Special Academic Facilities/Equipment:** Museums, theatres, language labs, weather station, nuclear reactor. **Computers:** 83% of classrooms, 50% of dorms, 100% of libraries, 100% of dining areas, 100% of student union, 25% of common outdoor areas have wireless network access. Students can register for classes online. Administrative functions (other than registration) can be performed online.

CAMPUS LIFE
Environment: Town. **Activities:** Choral groups, concert band, dance, drama/theater, jazz band, literary magazine, marching band, music ensembles, musical theater, opera, pep band, radio station, student government, student newspaper, student-run film society, symphony orchestra, television station, yearbook, campus ministries, international student organization, Model UN. **Organizations:** 784 registered organizations, 34 honor societies, 49 religious organizations, 58 fraternities, 32 sororities. **Athletics (Intercollegiate):** *Men:* Baseball, basketball, cheerleading, cross-country, diving, fencing, football, golf, gymnastics, lacrosse, soccer, swimming, tennis, track/field (outdoor), track/field (indoor), volleyball, wrestling. *Women:* Basketball, cheerleading, cross-country, diving, fencing, field hockey, golf, gymnastics, lacrosse, soccer, softball, swimming, tennis, track/field (outdoor), track/field (indoor), volleyball. **On-Campus Highlights:** Hetzel Union Building, Pattee Paterno Library, The Creamery, Old Main, The Lion Shrine. **Environmental Initiatives:** To address the issue of climate change, Pennsylvania State University—University Park has

established the goal of reducing greenhouse gas emissions by 17.5%, below 2005/2006 levels, by 2012. In 2009, Pennsylvania State University created its Campus Sustainability Office with three full-time employees. Its mission is to lead and support sustainability initiatives that accomplish Pennsylvania State University business goals and increase long-term value through coordination of energy reduction and conservation strategies, educational programming, and sustainability-performance tracking, reporting and coordination. In FY2008, Pennsylvania State University recycled 53% of its waste stream. Compost (at 44%) and mixed office paper (at 13%) represented the largest proportions of the recycling stream.

ADMISSIONS
Freshman Academic Profile: Average high school GPA 3.55. 49.82% in top 10% of high school class, 85.77% in top 25% of high school class, 97.99% in top 50% of high school class. SAT Math middle 50% range 560–670. SAT Critical Reading middle 50% range 530–630. SAT Writing middle 50% range 540–640. Minimum paper TOEFL 550. Minimum computer TOEFL 213. Minimum web-based TOEFL 80. **Basis for Candidate Selection:** *Very important factors considered include:* Academic GPA, standardized test scores. *Important factors considered include:* Rigor of secondary school record. *Other factors considered include:* Class rank, application essay, recommendation(s), alumni/ae relation, character/personal qualities, extracurricular activities, talent/ability, volunteer work, work experience. **Freshman Admission Requirements:** High school diploma is required and GED is accepted. *Academic units required:* 4 English, 3 mathematics, 3 science, 2 foreign language, 3 social studies. **Freshman Admission Statistics:** 40,714 applied, 52% admitted, 31% enrolled. **Transfer Admission Requirements:** High school transcript, college transcript(s), Lowest grade transferable C. **General Admission Information:** Application fee $50. Notification on a rolling basis, beginning on or about 11/1. Nonfall registration accepted. Admission may be deferred for a maximum of 1 year. Credit and/or placement offered for CEEB Advanced Placement tests.

COSTS AND FINANCIAL AID
Annual in-state tuition $13,604. Annual out-of-state tuition $25,134. Room and board $8,790. Required fees $812. **Required Forms and Deadlines:** FAFSA. Priority financial aid filing date 2/15. **Notification of Awards:** Applicants will be notified of awards on a rolling basis beginning 3/1. **Types of Aid:** *Need-based scholarships/grants:* Federal Pell, SEOG, state scholarships/grants, private scholarships, the school's own gift aid. *Loans:* Direct Subsidized Stafford, Direct Unsubsidized Stafford, Direct PLUS, Federal Perkins, college/university loans from institutional funds, private loans. *Student Employment:* Federal Work-Study Program available. Institutional employment available. Off-campus job opportunities are good. **Financial Aid Statistics:** 21% freshmen, 27% undergrads receive need-based scholarship or grant aid. 20% freshmen, 16% undergrads receive non-need-based scholarship or grant aid. 37% freshmen, 42% undergrads receive need-based self-help aid. 2% freshmen, 1% undergrads receive athletic scholarships. 70% freshmen, 71% undergrads receive any aid. 68% undergrads borrow to pay for school. Average cumulative indebtedness $28,680. **Criteria for awarding institutional aid:** *Non-need-based:* Academics, alumni affiliation, athletics.

PENNSYLVANIA STATE UNIVERSITY— WILKES-BARRE

PO Box PSU, Lehman, PA 18627
Phone: 570-675-9238
E-mail: wbadmissions@psu.edu
Fax: 570-675-9113 **Website:** www.wb.psu.edu

This public school was founded in 1916. It has a 58-acre campus.

RATINGS
Admissions Selectivity Rating: 70   **Fire Safety Rating:** 60*   **Green Rating:** 60*

STUDENTS AND FACULTY
Enrollment: 563. **Student Body:** 29% female, 71% male, 4% out-of-state, international Asian 2%, African American 3%, Caucasian 93%, Hispanic 2%. **Retention and Graduation: Faculty:** Student/faculty ratio 13:1. 37 full-time faculty, 54% hold PhDs, 16% are are members of minority groups, 16% are women.

ACADEMICS
Degrees: Bachelor's, post-bachelor's certificate, terminal associate, transfer associate. **Classes:** Most classes have 10–19 students. **Special Study Options:** Accelerated program, cross-registration, distance learning, double major, dual enrollment, honors program, independent study, internships, student-designed major, study abroad.

CAMPUS LIFE

Environment: Village. **Activities:** Radio station, student government, student newspaper. **Athletics (Intercollegiate): Men:** Baseball, soccer, volleyball. **Women:** Volleyball.

ADMISSIONS

Freshman Academic Profile: Average high school GPA 3.03. 9.26% in top 10% of high school class, 35.19% in top 25% of high school class, 66.67% in top 50% of high school class. SAT Math middle 50% range 440–560. SAT Critical Reading middle 50% range 430–530. Minimum paper TOEFL 550. **Basis for Candidate Selection:** *Very important factors considered include:* Academic GPA, standardized test scores. *Important factors considered include:* Rigor of secondary school record. *Other factors considered include:* Class rank, application essay, recommendation(s), alumni/ae relation, character/personal qualities, extracurricular activities, talent/ability, volunteer work, work experience. **Freshman Admission Requirements:** High school diploma is required and GED is accepted. *Academic units required:* 4 English, 3 mathematics, 3 science, 2 foreign language, 3 social studies. **Freshman Admission Statistics:** 630 applied, 84% admitted, 33% enrolled. **Transfer Admission Requirements:** High school transcript, college transcript(s), Lowest grade transferable C. **General Admission Information:** Application fee $50. Notification on a rolling basis, beginning on or about 11/1. Nonfall registration accepted. Admission may be deferred for a maximum of 1 year.

COSTS AND FINANCIAL AID

Annual in-state tuition $10,454. Annual out-of-state tuition $15,954. Room and board $3,360. Required fees $552. Average book expense $1,168. **Required Forms and Deadlines:** FAFSA. Priority financial aid filing date 2/15. **Types of Aid:** *Need-based scholarships/grants:* Federal Pell, SEOG, state scholarships/grants, private scholarships, the school's own gift aid. *Loans:* FFEL Subsidized Stafford, FFEL Unsubsidized Stafford, FFEL PLUS, Federal Perkins, college/university loans from institutional funds, private loans. *Student Employment:* **Financial Aid Statistics:** 54% freshmen, 53% undergrads receive need-based scholarship or grant aid. 40% freshmen, 27% undergrads receive non-need-based scholarship or grant aid. 58% freshmen, 58% undergrads receive need-based self-help aid. 67% undergrads borrow to pay for school. Average cumulative indebtedness $26,300. **Criteria for awarding institutional aid:** *Non-need-based:* Academics, alumni affiliation, athletics, minority status.

PENNSYLVANIA STATE UNIVERSITY— WORTHINGTON SCRANTON

120 Ridge View Drive, Dunmore, PA 18512-1602
Phone: 570-963-2500
E-mail: wsadmissions@psu.edu
Fax: 570-963-2524 **Website:** www.sn.psu.edu

This public school was founded in 1923. It has a 43-acre campus.

RATINGS

Admissions Selectivity Rating: 65   **Fire Safety Rating:** 60*   **Green Rating:** 60*

STUDENTS AND FACULTY

Enrollment: 1,185. **Student Body:** 50% female, 50% male, 1% out-of-state. Asian 1%, African American 2%, Caucasian 93%, Hispanic 3%. **Retention and Graduation: Faculty:** Student/faculty ratio 16:1. 55 full-time faculty, 62% hold PhDs, 13% are are members of minority groups, 51% are women.

ACADEMICS

Degrees: Bachelor's, terminal associate, transfer associate. **Classes:** Most classes have 20–29 students. Most lab/discussion sessions have 20–29 students. **Special Study Options:** Accelerated program, cooperative education program, cross-registration, distance learning, double major, dual enrollment, honors program, independent study, internships, study abroad.

CAMPUS LIFE

Activities: Choral groups, drama/theater, jazz band, literary magazine, music ensembles, student government, student newspaper. **Athletics (Intercollegiate): Men:** Baseball, basketball, cross-country, soccer. **Women:** volleyball.

ADMISSIONS

Freshman Academic Profile: Average high school GPA 2.84. 4.73% in top 10% of high school class, 18.91% in top 25% of high school class, 63.27% in top 50% of high school class. SAT Math middle 50% range 410–520. SAT Critical Reading middle 50% range 420–530. Minimum paper TOEFL 550. **Basis for Candidate Selection:** *Very important factors considered include:* Academic GPA, standardized test scores. *Important factors considered include:* Rigor of secondary school record. *Other factors considered include:* Class rank, application essay, recommendation(s), alumni/ae relation, character/personal qualities, extracurricular activities, talent/ability, volunteer work, work experience. **Freshman Admission Requirements:** High school diploma is required and GED is accepted. *Academic units required:* 4 English, 3 mathematics, 3 science, 2 foreign language, 3 social studies. **Freshman Admission Statistics:** 903 applied, 86% admitted, 40% enrolled. **Transfer Admission Requirements:** High school transcript, college transcript(s), Lowest grade transferable C. **General Admission Information:** Application fee $50. Notification on a rolling basis, beginning on or about 11/1. Nonfall registration accepted. Admission may be deferred for a maximum of 1 year.

COSTS AND FINANCIAL AID

Annual in-state tuition $10,454. Annual out-of-state tuition $15,954. Room and board $3,360. Required fees $532. Average book expense $1,168. **Required Forms and Deadlines:** FAFSA. Priority financial aid filing date 2/15. **Types of Aid:** *Need-based scholarships/grants:* Federal Pell, SEOG, state scholarships/grants, private scholarships, the school's own gift aid. *Loans:* FFEL Subsidized Stafford, FFEL Unsubsidized Stafford, FFEL PLUS, Federal Perkins, college/university loans from institutional funds, private loans. *Student Employment:* **Financial Aid Statistics:** 55% freshmen, 56% undergrads receive need-based scholarship or grant aid. 17% freshmen, 15% undergrads receive non-need-based scholarship or grant aid. 56% freshmen, 60% undergrads receive need-based self-help aid. 67% undergrads borrow to pay for school. Average cumulative indebtedness $26,300. **Criteria for awarding institutional aid:** *Non-need-based:* Academics, alumni affiliation, athletics, minority status.

PENNSYLVANIA STATE UNIVERSITY—YORK

1031 Edgecomb Avenue, York, PA 17403-3398
Phone: 717-771-4040
E-mail: ykadmission@psu.edu
Fax: 717-771-4005 **Website:** www.yk.psu.edu

This public school was founded in 1926. It has a 52-acre campus.

RATINGS

Admissions Selectivity Rating: 67   **Fire Safety Rating:** 60*   **Green Rating:** 60*

STUDENTS AND FACULTY

Enrollment: 1,070. **Student Body:** 44% female, 56% male, 5% out-of-state, international Asian 6%, African American 5%, Caucasian 83%, Hispanic 5%. **Retention and Graduation:** 71% freshmen return for sophomore year. **Faculty:** Student/faculty ratio 15:1. 59 full-time faculty, 61% hold PhDs, 17% are are members of minority groups, 36% are women.

ACADEMICS

Degrees: Bachelor's, terminal associate, transfer associate. **Classes:** Most classes have 10–19 students. Most lab/discussion sessions have fewer than 10 students. **Special Study Options:** Accelerated program, cross-registration, distance learning, double major, English as a Second Language (ESL), honors program, independent study, internships, student-designed major, study abroad.

FACILITIES

Housing: Nearby rooms, apartments, house rentals in the local community.

CAMPUS LIFE

Environment: Village. **Activities:** Dance, drama/theater, literary magazine, student government, student newspaper, campus ministries, international student organization, Model UN. **Athletics (Intercollegiate): Men:** Basketball, soccer, tennis. **Women:** Tennis, volleyball.

ADMISSIONS

Freshman Academic Profile: Average high school GPA 2.81. 6% in top 10% of high school class, 24% in top 25% of high school class, 55% in top 50% of high school class. SAT Math middle 50% range 440–550. SAT Critical Reading middle 50% range 410–530. Minimum paper TOEFL 550. **Basis for Candidate Selection:** *Very important factors considered include:* Academic GPA, standardized test scores. *Important factors considered include:* Rigor of secondary school record. *Other factors considered include:* Class rank, application essay, recommendation(s), alumni/ae relation, character/personal qualities, extracurricular activities, talent/ability, volunteer work, work experience. **Freshman Admission Requirements:** High school diploma is required and GED is accepted. *Academic units required:* 4 English, 3 mathematics, 3 science, 2 foreign language, 3 social studies. **Freshman Admission Statistics:** 1,328 applied, 84% admitted, 30% enrolled. **Transfer Admission Requirements:** High school transcript, college transcript(s), Lowest grade transferable C. **General Admission Information:** Application fee $50. Notification on a rolling basis, beginning on or about 11/1. Nonfall registration accepted. Admission may be deferred for a maximum of 1 year.

COSTS AND FINANCIAL AID

Annual in-state tuition $10,454. Annual out-of-state tuition $15,954. Room and board $3,360. Required fees $532. Average book expense $1,168. **Required Forms and Deadlines:** FAFSA. Priority financial aid filing date 2/15. **Notification of Awards:** Applicants will be notified of awards on or about 3/1. **Types of Aid:** *Need-based scholarships/grants:* Federal Pell, SEOG, state scholarships/grants, private scholarships, the school's own gift aid. *Loans:* FFEL Subsidized Stafford, FFEL Unsubsidized Stafford, FFEL PLUS, Federal Perkins, college/university loans from institutional funds, private loans. *Student Employment:* **Financial Aid Statistics:** 45% freshmen, 47% undergrads receive need-based scholarship or grant aid. 26% freshmen, 22% undergrads receive non-need-based scholarship or grant aid. 53% freshmen, 50% undergrads receive need-based self-help aid. 67% undergrads borrow to pay for school. Average cumulative indebtedness $26,300. **Criteria for awarding institutional aid:** *Non-need-based:* Academics, alumni affiliation, athletics, minority status.

PEPPERDINE UNIVERSITY

24255 Pacific Coast Highway, Malibu, CA 90263
Phone: 310-506-4392 **Financial Aid Phone:** 310-506-4301
E-mail: admission-seaver@pepperdine.edu **CEEB Code:** 4630
Fax: 310-506-4861 **Website:** www.pepperdine.edu **ACT Code:** 373

This private school, affiliated with the Church of Christ Church, was founded in 1937. It has a 830-acre campus.

RATINGS

Admissions Selectivity Rating: 93　　**Fire Safety Rating:** 70　　**Green Rating:** 81

STUDENTS AND FACULTY

Enrollment: 3,427. **Student Body:** 55% female, 45% male, 43% out-of-state. 6% international (64 countries represented). Asian 10%, African American 7%, Caucasian 58%, Hispanic 12%, Native American 1%.
Retention and Graduation: 90% freshmen return for sophomore year. 73% freshmen graduate within 4 years. **Faculty:** Student/faculty ratio 14.1:1. 365 full-time faculty, 90% hold PhDs, 13% are are members of minority groups, 36% are women.

ACADEMICS

Degrees: Bachelor's, master's. **Classes:** Most classes have 10–19 students. Most lab/discussion sessions have 20–29 students. **Majors with Highest Enrollment:** Business administration and management; communication, journalism, and related programs, other; social sciences, other. **Special Study Options:** double major, honors program, independent study, internships, student-designed major, study abroad, teacher certification program, weekend college, 3-2 programing engineering with University of Southern California, Washington University(MO), Boston University(MA). Special programs offered to physically disabled students include note-taking services, reader services, tape recorders, tutors. **Career services:** Alumni network, alumni services, career/job search classes, career assessment, internships, regional alumni. **Career**

services highlights include: Pepperdine has a very active internship program that reaches into the local LA areas, Washington DC, nationally through our participation in the University Career Action Network, and internationally through an internship emphasis at our international campuses. Students at Pepperdine can receive academic credit for internships. Service-learning is employed as a teaching pedagogy by a variety of faculty members. One example the senior capstone business class "Service Leadership" where class members serve on a consulting team for a nonprofit.

FACILITIES

Housing: Special housing for disabled students, men's dorms, women's dorms, apartments for married students, cooperative housing, apartments for single students, Freshman and sophomores must live on campus or at home with parent or guardian if single and under age 21. **Special Academic Facilities/Equipment:** Weisman Art Museum. **Computers:** 100% of classrooms, 100% of dorms, 100% of libraries, 100% of dining areas, 100% of student union, 100% of common outdoor areas have wireless network access. Students can register for classes online. Administrative functions (other than registration) can be performed online.

CAMPUS LIFE

Environment: City. **Activities:** Choral groups, concert band, dance, drama/theater, jazz band, literary magazine, music ensembles, musical theater, opera, pep band, radio station, student government, student newspaper, student-run film society, symphony orchestra, television station, yearbook, campus ministries, international student organization, Model UN. **Organizations:** 50 registered organizations, 5 honor societies, 8 religious organizations. 5 fraternities, 7 sororities. **Athletics (Intercollegiate):** *Men:* Baseball, basketball, cross-country, golf, tennis, volleyball, water polo. *Women:* Basketball, cheerleading, cross-country, golf, soccer, swimming, tennis, track/field (outdoor), volleyball. **On-Campus Highlights:** Theme Tower, Smother'sTheatre, The Sandbar, Payson Library, Alumni Park. **Environmental Initiatives:** Pepperdine University conserves millions of gallons of drinking water annually dating back to 1972. Pepperdine uses recycled water to irrigate over 90% of the University's managed grounds. The University carefully monitors irrigation practices and uses an automated irrigation program based upon historical trends and current climactic conditions to conserve water and reduce runoff. Pepperdine University recycles all refuse disposed of on campus since 2000. The University has an average diversion rate of 78% meaning that 78% of all refuse gets reused. Pepperdine recycles high-tech equipment. All on-campus tree trimmings and brush clearance debris are either reused for grounds maintenance or turned into compost, which is used in many areas throughout campus. Pepperdine University provides on-campus housing for 52% of our students and 8% of our faculty and staff, resulting in a significant conservation of fossil fuels and improving air quality. The University is currently seeking entitlements for an additional 468 student beds, thereby providing housing for over 75% of our undergraduates with a consequent reduction in student commuters and improvement of air quality. Pepperdine University promotes a Rideshare program that provides incentives and subsidies for participating in carpools, University operated vanpools, mass transit, and walking while offering on-campus shuttles and a fleet of 20 electric vehicles. The University also maintains roughly 500 acres of native vegetation, at no cost to the State, which has a superior carbon balance and thus provides a significant benefit to air quality.

ADMISSIONS

Freshman Academic Profile: Average high school GPA 3.67. 41.6% in top 10% of high school class, 75.7% in top 25% of high school class, 96.1% in top 50% of high school class. SAT Math middle 50% range 560–680. SAT Critical Reading middle 50% range 560–660. SAT Writing middle 50% range 560–660. ACT middle 50% range 24–30. Minimum paper TOEFL 550. Minimum computer TOEFL 220. Minimum web-based TOEFL 80. **Basis for Candidate Selection:** *Very important factors considered include:* Application essay, academic GPA, recommendation(s), rigor of secondary school record, standardized test scores, character/personal qualities, extracurricular activities, talent/ability. *Important factors considered include:* Religious affiliation/commitment, volunteer work. *Other factors considered include:* Alumni/ae relation, first generation, racial/ethnic status, work experience. **Freshman Admission Requirements:** High school diploma is required and GED is accepted. *Academic units recommended:* 4 English, 4 mathematics, 4 science, (3 science labs), 3 foreign language, 3 social studies, 3 history, 3 academic electives, 1 speech. **Freshman Admission Statistics:** 6,426 applied, 41% admitted, 27% enrolled. **Transfer Admission Requirements:** High school transcript, college transcript(s), essay or personal statement, minimum college GPA of 3.00 required. Lowest grade transferable C. **General Admission Information:** Application fee $65. Regular application deadline 1/15. Regular notification 4/1. Nonfall registration accepted. Credit and/or placement offered for CEEB Advanced Placement tests.

COSTS AND FINANCIAL AID

Annual tuition $37,730. Required fees $120. **Required Forms and Deadlines:** FAFSA. Financial aid filing deadline 2/15. Priority financial aid filing date 2/15. **Notification of Awards:** Applicants will be notified of awards on or about 4/15. **Types of Aid:** *Need-based scholarships/grants:* Federal Pell, SEOG, state scholarships/grants, private scholarships, the school's own gift aid, United Negro College Fund, ACG, SMART. *Loans:* FFEL Subsidized Stafford, FFEL Unsubsidized Stafford, FFEL PLUS, Federal Perkins, college/university loans from institutional funds. *Student Employment:* Federal Work-Study Program available. Institutional employment available. Off-campus job opportunities are good. **Financial Aid Statistics:** 54% freshmen, 48% undergrads receive need-based scholarship or grant aid. 26% freshmen, 18% undergrads receive non-need-based scholarship or grant aid. 59% freshmen, 49% undergrads receive need-based self-help aid. 2% freshmen, 3% undergrads receive athletic scholarships. 58% undergrads borrow to pay for school. Average cumulative indebtedness $28,299. **Criteria for awarding institutional aid:** *Non-need-based:* Academics, art, athletics, minority status, music/drama, religious affiliation

PFEIFFER UNIVERSITY

P.O. Box 960, Misenheimer, NC 28109
Phone: 800-338-2060
E-mail: admissions@pfeiffer.edu **CEEB Code:** 5536
Fax: 704-463-1363 **Website:** www.pfeiffer.edu **ACT Code:** 3140

This private school, affiliated with the Methodist Church, was founded in 1885.

RATINGS

Admissions Selectivity Rating: 72   **Fire Safety Rating:** 60*   **Green Rating:** 60*

STUDENTS AND FACULTY

Enrollment: 1,188. **Student Body:** 58% female, 42% male, 19% out-of-state, 5% international (13 countries represented). Asian 1%, African American 16%, Caucasian 59%, Hispanic 1%.
Retention and Graduation: 77% freshmen return for sophomore year. 41% freshmen graduate within 4 years. 23% grads go on to further study within 1 year. 15% grads pursue arts and sciences degrees. 5% grads pursue law degrees. 20% grads pursue business degrees. 2% grads pursue medical degrees. **Faculty:** Student/faculty ratio 13:1. 65 full-time faculty, 66% hold PhDs, 11% are members of minority groups, 37% are women.

ACADEMICS

Degrees: Bachelor's, master's, post-master's certificate. **Classes:** Most classes have fewer than 10 students. **Majors with Highest Enrollment:** Business/commerce; criminal justice/law enforcement administration; elementary education and teaching. **Special Study Options:** Accelerated program, cross-registration, distance learning, double major, dual enrollment, honors program, independent study, internships, study abroad, teacher certification program, Capitol Hill Internship Program. **Honors programs:** Students who have demonstrated strong academic performance are invited to participate in the Honors Program. They enroll in honors-designated courses and are given expanded assignments or complete special projects. They live in honors housing and are invited to join the University Honors Association. Twelve students are chosen each year to serve as marshals at the graduation ceremony and the fall Academic Convocation. In addition, all Pfeiffer students are eligible to graduate cum laude, magna cum laude, and summa cum laude, depending on their grade point average. **Combined degree programs:** BA/MA. Special programs offered to physically disabled students include note-taking services, tutors. **Career services:** Alumni network, alumni services, career/job search classes, career assessment, internships, regional alumni.

FACILITIES

Housing: Coed dorms, men's dorms, women's dorms. **Special Academic Facilities/Equipment:** Beth Haltiwanger Retreat Center, Francis Center for Servant Leadership, new science building. **Computers:** Administrative functions (other than registration) can be performed online.

CAMPUS LIFE

Environment: Rural. **Activities:** Choral groups, concert band, drama/theater, jazz band, literary magazine, music ensembles, musical theater, pep band, student government, student newspaper, yearbook. **Organizations:** 60 registered organizations, 6 honor societies, 1 religious organizations. **Athletics (Intercollegiate):** *Men:* Baseball, basketball, cheerleading, cross-country, golf, lacrosse, soccer, tennis. *Women:* Basketball, cheerleading, cross-country, golf, lacrosse, soccer, softball, swimming, tennis, volleyball. **On-Campus Highlights:** Student Center, Merner Gymnasium, Chapel, Knapp Health and Fitness Center, Beth Haltiwanger Retreat Center, New science building.

ADMISSIONS

Freshman Academic Profile: Average high school GPA 3.1. 11% in top 10% of high school class, 30% in top 25% of high school class, 62% in top 50% of high school class. 90% from public high schools. SAT Math middle 50% range 450–570. SAT Critical Reading middle 50% range 430–540. ACT middle 50% range 18–24. Minimum paper TOEFL 500. Minimum computer TOEFL 173. **Basis for Candidate Selection:** *Very important factors considered include:* Rigor of secondary school record, standardized test scores, character/personal qualities, volunteer work. *Important factors considered include:* Recommendation(s), extracurricular activities, talent/ability. *Other factors considered include:* Class rank, application essay, alumni/ae relation, interview, religious affiliation/commitment, work experience. **Freshman Admission Requirements:** High school diploma is required and GED is accepted. *Academic units required:* 4 English, 3 mathematics, 2 science, (1 science labs), 2 social studies, 2 history. *Academic units recommended:* 2 foreign language. **Freshman Admission Statistics:** 586 applied, 72% admitted, 41% enrolled. **Transfer Admission Requirements:** College transcript(s), statement of good standing from prior institution(s). Minimum college GPA of 2.0 required. Lowest grade transferable D. **General Admission Information:** Application fee $25. Notification on a rolling basis, beginning on or about 9/1. Nonfall registration accepted. Credit offered for CEEB Advanced Placement tests.

COSTS AND FINANCIAL AID

Annual tuition $13,550. Room and board $5,430. Average book expense $500. **Required Forms and Deadlines:** FAFSA **Notification of Awards:** Applicants will be notified of awards on a rolling basis beginning 2/15. **Types of Aid:** *Need-based scholarships/grants:* Federal Pell, SEOG, state scholarships/grants, the school's own gift aid. *Loans:* FFEL Subsidized Stafford, FFEL Unsubsidized Stafford, FFEL PLUS, Federal Perkins. *Student Employment:* Federal Work-Study Program available. Off-campus job opportunities are good. **Financial Aid Statistics:** 77% freshmen, 62% undergrads receive need-based scholarship or grant aid. 25% freshmen, 10% undergrads receive non-need-based scholarship or grant aid. 65% freshmen, 55% undergrads receive need-based self-help aid. 90% freshmen, 90% undergrads receive any aid. **Criteria for awarding institutional aid:** *Non-need-based:* Academics, athletics, religious affiliation, state/district residency.

PHILADELPHIA BIBLICAL UNIVERSITY

200 Manor Avenue, Langhorne, PA 19047
Phone: 215-702-4235 **Financial Aid Phone:** 215-702-4246
E-mail: admissions@pbu.edu
Fax: 215-702-4248 **Website:** www.pbu.edu **ACT Code:** 3658

This private school, affiliated with the Protestant Church, was founded in 1913. It has a 114-acre campus.

RATINGS

Admissions Selectivity Rating: 79   **Fire Safety Rating:** 60*   **Green Rating:** 70

STUDENTS AND FACULTY

Enrollment: 1,044. **Student Body:** 53% female, 47% male, 45% out-of-state, 1% international (25 countries represented). Asian 4%, African American 13%, Caucasian 76%, Hispanic 4%.
Retention and Graduation: 82% freshmen return for sophomore year. 19% freshmen graduate within 4 years. 40% grads go on to further study within 1 year. **Faculty:** Student/faculty ratio 16:1. 52 full-time faculty, 65% hold PhDs, 13% are members of minority groups, 31% are women.

ACADEMICS

Degrees: Bachelor's, certificate, master's. **Classes:** Most classes have 10–19 students. **Majors with Highest Enrollment:** Bible/biblical studies; elementary education and teaching; social work. **Special Study Options:** Accelerated program, double major, honors program, internships, study abroad, teacher certification program. **Combined degree programs:** BS in Bible+MS in Chr Counseling or MS in Education or MS in Org. Leader. Special programs offered to physically disabled students include reader services, tutors. **Career services:** Alumni services, career/job search classes, career assessment.

FACILITIES

Housing: Special housing for disabled students, men's dorms, special housing for international students, women's dorms, apartments for married students, apartments for single students. 99% of campus accessible to physically disabled. **Special Academic Facilities/Equipment:** Biblical Learning Center Museum area. **Computers:** 59% of classrooms, 62% of dorms, 90% of libraries, 100% of dining areas, 100% of student union, 15% of common outdoor areas have wireless network access. Students can register for classes online. Administrative functions (other than registration) can be performed online.

CAMPUS LIFE

Environment: Village. **Activities:** Choral groups, concert band, drama/theater, music ensembles, musical theater, opera, student government, student newspaper, symphony orchestra, yearbook, campus ministries, international student organization. **Organizations:** 25 registered organizations, 4 honor societies, 3 religious organizations. **Athletics (Intercollegiate):** *Men:* Baseball, basketball, cross-country, golf, soccer, volleyball. *Women:* Basketball, cross-country, soccer, softball, tennis, volleyball. **On-Campus Highlights:** Eagle's Nest grill & cafe, Student Lounge, Campus Walkway, Sports Fields, Heritage Hall Lounge. **Environmental Initiatives:** Energy Reduction capital projects including lighting upgrades, occupancy sensors and HVAC controls & equipment.

ADMISSIONS

Freshman Academic Profile: Average high school GPA 3.32. 18% in top 10% of high school class, 35% in top 25% of high school class, 64% in top 50% of high school class. 60% from public high schools. SAT Math middle 50% range 452–570. SAT Critical Reading middle 50% range 480–570. ACT middle 50% range 19.1–26.3. Minimum paper TOEFL 520. Minimum computer TOEFL 190. **Basis for Candidate Selection:** *Very important factors considered include:* Academic GPA, standardized test scores, religious affiliation/commitment. *Important factors considered include:* Application essay, rigor of secondary school record, character/personal qualities, interview. *Other factors considered include:* Class rank, recommendation(s), extracurricular activities, level of applicant's interest. **Freshman Admission Requirements:** High school diploma is required and GED is accepted. *Academic units recommended:* 4 English, 1 mathematics, 2 science, 2 foreign language, 3 social studies. **Freshman Admission Statistics:** 465 applied, 77% admitted, 55% enrolled. **Transfer Admission Requirements:** College transcript(s), essay or personal statement, interview, minimum college GPA of 2.2 required. Lowest grade transferable C. **General Admission Information:** Application fee $25. Notification on a rolling basis, beginning on or about 7/1. Nonfall registration accepted. Admission may be deferred for a maximum of 1 year. Credit and/or placement offered for CEEB Advanced Placement tests.

COSTS AND FINANCIAL AID

Annual tuition $19,797. Room and board $8,050. Required fees $200. Average book expense $1,000. **Required Forms and Deadlines:** FAFSA **Notification of Awards:** Applicants will be notified of awards on a rolling basis beginning 2/15. **Types of Aid:** *Need-based scholarships/grants:* Federal Pell, SEOG, state scholarships/grants, private scholarships, the school's own gift aid. *Loans:* Direct Subsidized Stafford, Direct Unsubsidized Stafford, Direct PLUS, FFEL Subsidized Stafford, FFEL Unsubsidized Stafford, FFEL PLUS, state loans. *Student Employment:* Federal Work-Study Program available. Institutional employment available. Off-campus job opportunities are excellent. **Financial Aid Statistics:** 83% freshmen, 79% undergrads receive need-based scholarship or grant aid. 7% freshmen, 4% undergrads receive non-need-based scholarship or grant aid. 69% freshmen, 74% undergrads receive need-based self-help aid. 85% freshmen, 84% undergrads receive any aid. 97% undergrads borrow to pay for school. Average cumulative indebtedness $28,214. **Criteria for awarding institutional aid:** *Non-need-based:* Academics, leadership, minority status.

PHILADELPHIA UNIVERSITY

School House Lane and Henry Avenue, Philadelphia, PA 19144-5497
Phone: 215-951-2800 **Financial Aid Phone:** 215-951-2940
E-mail: admissions@philau.edu **CEEB Code:** 2666
Fax: 215-951-2907 **Website:** www.PhilaU.edu **ACT Code:** 3668

This private school was founded in 1884. It has a 100-acre campus.

RATINGS

Admissions Selectivity Rating: 79   **Fire Safety Rating:** 60*   **Green Rating:** 60*

STUDENTS AND FACULTY

Enrollment: 2,736. **Student Body:** 70% female, 30% male, 48% out-of-state, 2% international (26 countries represented). Asian 4%, African American 10%, Caucasian 73%, Hispanic 3%.
Retention and Graduation: 73% freshmen return for sophomore year. 36% freshmen graduate within 4 years. 19% grads go on to further study within 1 year. 8% grads pursue arts and sciences degrees. 1% grads pursue law degrees. 10% grads pursue business degrees. 1% grads pursue medical degrees. **Faculty:** Student/faculty ratio 14:1. 108 full-time faculty, 74% hold PhDs, 10% are members of minority groups, 61% are women.

ACADEMICS

Degrees: Associate, bachelor's, certificate, master's, post-bachelor's certificate, post-master's certificate. **Classes:** Most classes have 10–19 students. Most lab/discussion sessions have 10–19 students. **Majors with Highest Enrollment:** Architecture (BArch, BA/BS, MArch, MA/MS, PhD); fashion/apparel design; merchandising and buying operations. **Special Study Options:** distance learning, double major, honors program, independent study, internships, liberal arts/career combination, study abroad. **Honors programs:** University Honors Program. **Combined degree programs:** BS/MS, BS/MBA. Special programs offered to physically disabled students include note-taking services, reader services, tape recorders, tutors. **Career services:** Alumni services, career/job search classes, career assessment, internships.

FACILITIES

Housing: Coed dorms, special housing for disabled students, women's dorms, apartments for single students, townhouses. 63% of campus accessible to physically disabled. **Special Academic Facilities/Equipment:** The Design Center, Industrial Design Studios, Graphic Design Studios, Architecture Design Studios, CAD Labs in fashion design, interior design and architecture. **Computers:** Students can register for classes online. Administrative functions (other than registration) can be performed online.

CAMPUS LIFE

Environment: Metropolis. **Activities:** Choral groups, dance, drama/theater, student government, student newspaper, yearbook. **Organizations:** 32 registered organizations, 3 religious organizations. 1 fraternity, 1 sorority. **Athletics (Intercollegiate):** *Men:* Baseball, basketball, crew/rowing, cross-country, golf, soccer, tennis. *Women:* Basketball, crew/rowing, cross-country, field hockey, lacrosse, soccer, softball, tennis, volleyball. **On-Campus Highlights:** Kanbar Campus Center, Athletic and Recreation Center, Gutman Library, Architecture and Design Building, The Design Center.

ADMISSIONS

Freshman Academic Profile: Average high school GPA 3.41. 11% in top 10% of high school class, 38% in top 25% of high school class, 80% in top 50% of high school class. 80% from public high schools. SAT Math middle 50% range 490–590. SAT Critical Reading middle 50% range 480–560. SAT Writing middle 50% range 470–560. Minimum paper TOEFL 500. Minimum computer TOEFL 170. **Basis for Candidate Selection:** *Very important factors considered include:* Academic GPA, rigor of secondary school record, standardized test scores. *Important factors considered include:* Class rank, recommendation(s), extracurricular activities, interview. *Other factors considered include:* Application essay. **Freshman Admission Requirements:** High school diploma is required and GED is accepted. *Academic units required:* 4 English, 3 mathematics, 3 science, (2 science labs), 2 social studies, 1 history, 2 academic electives. *Academic units recommended:* 4 English, 4 mathematics, 4 science, 2 foreign language, 3 social studies, 2 history. **Freshman Admission Statistics:** 4,307 applied, 61% admitted, 27% enrolled. **Transfer Admission Requirements:** College transcript(s), minimum college GPA of 2.5 required. Lowest grade transferable C. **General Admission Information:** Application fee $35. Notification on a rolling basis, beginning on or about 11/1. Nonfall registration accepted. Admission may be deferred for a maximum of 1 year. Credit and/or placement offered for CEEB Advanced Placement tests.

COSTS AND FINANCIAL AID

Annual tuition $23,748. Average book expense $1,400. **Required Forms and Deadlines:** FAFSA. Financial aid filing deadline 4/15. Priority financial aid filing date 4/15. **Notification of Awards:** Applicants will be notified of awards on a rolling basis beginning 2/10. **Types of Aid:** *Need-based scholarships/grants:* Federal Pell, SEOG, state scholarships/grants, private scholarships, the school's own gift aid, Gift scholarships from outside sources (non-endowed) for which University chooses recipient which may involve a need component. *Loans:* FFEL Subsidized Stafford, FFEL Unsubsidized Stafford, FFEL PLUS, Federal Perkins, Private Loan Programs. *Student Employment:* Federal Work-Study Program available. Institutional employment available. Off-campus job opportunities are good. **Financial Aid Statistics:** 72% freshmen, 68% undergrads receive need-based scholarship or grant aid. 5% freshmen, 4% undergrads receive non-need-based scholarship or grant aid. 67% freshmen, 63% undergrads receive need-based self-help aid. 3% freshmen, 3% undergrads receive athletic scholarships. 99% freshmen, 97% undergrads receive any aid. 74% undergrads borrow to pay for school. Average cumulative indebtedness $27,991. **Criteria for awarding institutional aid:** *Non-need-based:* Academics, athletics.

PIEDMONT COLLEGE

P.O. Box 10, Demorest, GA 30535
Phone: 706-776-0103 **Financial Aid Phone:** 706-778-3000
E-mail: ugrad@piedmont.edu **CEEB Code:** 5537
Fax: 706-776-6635 **Website:** www.piedmont.edu **ACT Code:** 853

This private school, affiliated with the Congregational Church, was founded in 1897. It has a 115-acre campus.

RATINGS

Admissions Selectivity Rating: 78   **Fire Safety Rating:** 60*   **Green Rating:** 60*

STUDENTS AND FACULTY

Enrollment: 939. **Student Body:** 64% female, 36% male, 5% out-of-state, international (23 countries represented). Asian 1%, African American 6%, Caucasian 88%, Hispanic 2%.
Retention and Graduation: 69% freshmen return for sophomore year. 26% freshmen graduate within 4 years. **Faculty:** Student/faculty ratio 13:1. 98 full-time faculty, 77% hold PhDs, 5% are are members of minority groups, 51% are women.

ACADEMICS

Degrees: Bachelor's, master's, post-master's certificate. **Classes:** Most classes have fewer than 10 students. Most lab/discussion sessions have 10–19 students. **Majors with Highest Enrollment:** Business/commerce; elementary education and teaching; sociology. **Special Study Options:** Accelerated program, distance learning, double major, dual enrollment, honors program, independent study, internships, student-designed major, study abroad, teacher certification program. **Combined degree programs:** BA/MAT (Secondary Education). Special programs offered to physically disabled students include note-taking services, reader services, tape recorders, tutors. **Career services:** Alumni network, career/job search classes, career assessment, regional alumni.

FACILITIES

Housing: Coed dorms, special housing for disabled students, men's dorms, women's dorms, apartments for single students. 98% of campus accessible to physically disabled. **Special Academic Facilities/Equipment:** Art gallery; 4 NE Georgia Youth and Tech Center; Botanical Center; Fitness Center. **Computers:** Administrative functions (other than registration) can be performed online.

CAMPUS LIFE

Environment: Rural. **Activities:** Choral groups, concert band, drama/theater, music ensembles, opera, radio station, student government, student newspaper, student-run film society, television station, yearbook. **Organizations:** 20 registered organizations, 7 honor societies, 1 religious organizations. **Athletics (Intercollegiate):** *Men:* Baseball, basketball, cross-country, golf, soccer, tennis. *Women:* Basketball, cross-country, golf, soccer, softball, tennis, volleyball. **On-Campus Highlights:** Johnny Mize Athletic Center, Lane Student Center, Stewart Hall, Center for Music and Worship, Arrendale Library.

ADMISSIONS

Freshman Academic Profile: Average high school GPA 3.4. 19% in top 10% of high school class, 41% in top 25% of high school class, 79% in top 50% of high school class. SAT Math middle 50% range 460–570. SAT Critical Reading middle 50% range 480–570. ACT middle 50% range 18–23. Minimum paper TOEFL 550. Minimum computer TOEFL 213. **Basis for Candidate Selection:** *Very important factors considered include:* Academic GPA, rigor of secondary school record, standardized test scores. *Important factors considered include:* Class rank, application essay, recommendation(s), character/personal qualities, extracurricular activities, first generation, interview, talent/ability. *Other factors considered include:* Alumni/ae relation, geographical residence, level of applicant's interest, state residency, volunteer work, work experience. **Freshman Admission Requirements:** High school diploma is required and GED is accepted. *Academic units recommended:* 4 English, 3 mathematics, 3 science, 2 foreign language, 1 social studies, 2 history. **Freshman Admission Statistics:** 485 applied, 66% admitted, 52% enrolled. **Transfer Admission Requirements:** College transcript(s), statement of good standing from prior institution(s). Minimum college GPA of 2.0 required. Lowest grade transferable C. **General Admission Information:** Regular application deadline 7/11. Regular notification 7/1. Nonfall registration accepted. Admission may be deferred for a maximum of 12. Neither credit nor placement offered for CEEB Advanced Placement tests.

COSTS AND FINANCIAL AID

Annual tuition $15,500. Room and board $5,000. Average book expense $850. **Required Forms and Deadlines:** FAFSA, institution's own financial aid form, state aid form. Priority financial aid filing date 5/5. **Types of Aid:** *Need-based scholarships/grants:* Federal Pell, SEOG, state scholarships/grants, private scholarships, the school's own gift aid. *Loans:* Direct Subsidized Stafford, Direct Unsubsidized Stafford, Direct PLUS. *Student Employment:* Federal Work-Study Program available. Institutional employment available. Highest amount earned per year from on-campus jobs $3,530. Off-campus job opportunities are good. **Financial Aid Statistics:** 45% freshmen, 52% undergrads receive need-based scholarship or grant aid. 64% freshmen, 68% undergrads receive non-need-based scholarship or grant aid. 54% freshmen, 48% undergrads receive need-based self-help aid. 96% freshmen, 87% undergrads receive any aid. 66% undergrads borrow to pay for school. Average cumulative indebtedness $14,408. **Criteria for awarding institutional aid:** *Non-need-based:* Academics, art, leadership, music/drama, religious affiliation, state/district residency.

PIKEVILLE COLLEGE

Admissions Office, 147 Sycamore Street, Pikeville, KY 41501
Phone: 606-218-5251 **Financial Aid Phone:** 606-218-5251
E-mail: wewantyou@pc.edu **CEEB Code:** 1980
Fax: 606-218-5255 **Website:** www.pc.edu **ACT Code:** 1540

This private school, affiliated with the Presbyterian Church, was founded in 1889. It has a 25-acre campus.

RATINGS

Admissions Selectivity Rating: 73   **Fire Safety Rating:** 60*   **Green Rating:** 60*

STUDENTS AND FACULTY

Enrollment: 673. **Student Body:** 51% female, 49% male, 26% out-of-state, international (2 countries represented). Asian 1%, African American 10%, Caucasian 88%, Hispanic 1%.
Retention and Graduation: 53% freshmen return for sophomore year. 18% freshmen graduate within 4 years. 10% grads go on to further study within 1 year. 5% grads pursue arts and sciences degrees. 1% grads pursue law degrees. 2% grads pursue business degrees. 2% grads pursue medical degrees. **Faculty:** Student/faculty ratio 11:1. 53 full-time faculty, 53% hold PhDs, 55% are women.

ACADEMICS

Degrees: Associate, bachelor's, post-bachelor's certificate, terminal associate, transfer associate. **Classes:** Most classes have 10–19 students. **Majors with Highest Enrollment:** Business/commerce; communication studies/speech communication and rhetoric; nursing/registered nurse (RN, ASN, BSN, MSN). **Special Study Options:** Double major, dual enrollment, independent study, internships, liberal arts/career combination, student-designed major, study abroad, teacher certification program. Special programs offered to physically disabled students include tape recorders, tutors.

FACILITIES

Housing: Coed dorms, men's dorms, women's dorms. 90% of campus accessible to physically disabled.

CAMPUS LIFE

Environment: Village. **Activities:** Choral groups, dance, literary magazine, pep band, student government, student newspaper, yearbook, campus ministries. **Organizations:** 40 registered organizations, 6 honor societies, 2 religious organizations. **Athletics (Intercollegiate):** *Men:* Baseball, basketball, bowling, cheerleading, cross-country, football, golf, soccer, tennis. *Women:* Basketball, bowling, cheerleading, cross-country, golf, soccer, softball, tennis, volleyball. **On-Campus Highlights:** Administration Building, Armington Hall, Allara Library, Record Hall, Kinzer Hall.

ADMISSIONS

Freshman Academic Profile: Average high school GPA 3.23. 99% from public high schools. ACT middle 50% range 17–23. **Basis for Candidate Selection: Freshman Admission Requirements:** High school diploma is required and GED is accepted. *Academic units recommended:* 4 English, 3 mathematics, 3 science, 2 social studies, 1 history. **Freshman Admission Statistics:** 770 applied, 100% admitted, 24% enrolled. **Transfer Admission Requirements:** High school transcript, college transcript(s), standardized test scores, statement of good standing from prior institution(s). Lowest grade transferable C. **General Admission Information:** Regular application deadline 8/15. Notification on a rolling basis, beginning on or about 9/15. Nonfall registration accepted. Credit and/or placement offered for CEEB Advanced Placement tests.

COSTS AND FINANCIAL AID

Average book expense $2,000. **Required Forms and Deadlines:** FAFSA, institution's own financial aid form. Priority financial aid filing date 3/15. **Notification of Awards:** Applicants will be notified of awards on a rolling basis beginning 2/1. **Types of Aid:** *Need-based scholarships/grants:* Federal Pell, SEOG, state scholarships/grants, private scholarships, the school's own gift aid. *Loans:* FFEL Subsidized Stafford, FFEL Unsubsidized Stafford, FFEL PLUS, Federal Perkins, college/university loans from institutional funds. *Student Employment:* Federal Work-Study Program available. Off-campus job opportunities are good. **Financial Aid Statistics:** 97% freshmen, 92% undergrads receive need-based scholarship or grant aid. 71% freshmen, 63% undergrads receive need-based self-help aid. 99% freshmen, 93% undergrads receive any aid. 76% undergrads borrow to pay for school. Average cumulative indebtedness $18,103.

PINE MANOR COLLEGE

400 Heath Street, Chestnut Hill, MA 02467-2332
Phone: 617-731-7104 **Financial Aid Phone:** 800-762-1357
E-mail: admission@pmc.edu
Fax: 617-731-7102 **Website:** www.pmc.edu

This is a private school.

RATINGS

Admissions Selectivity Rating: 70   **Fire Safety Rating:** 60*   **Green Rating:** 60*

STUDENTS AND FACULTY

Enrollment: 477. **Student Body:** 100% female, 24% out-of-state, 8% international Asian 4%, African American 32%, Caucasian 25%, Hispanic 21%. **Retention and Graduation:** 58% freshmen return for sophomore year. 31% freshmen graduate within 4 years. 27% grads go on to further study within 1 year. 11% grads pursue arts and sciences degrees. 1% grads pursue law degrees. 11% grads pursue business degrees. 4% grads pursue medical degrees. **Faculty:** Student/faculty ratio 10:1. 30 full-time faculty, 80% hold PhDs, 10% are are members of minority groups, 77% are women.

ACADEMICS

Degrees: Associate, bachelor's, certificate, transfer associate. **Classes:** Most classes have 10–19 students. Most lab/discussion sessions have 10–19 students. **Majors with Highest Enrollment:** Business/commerce; communication and media studies, other; psychology. **Special Study Options:** Cross-registration, double major, English as a Second Language (ESL), honors program, independent study, internships, liberal arts/career combination, student-designed major, study abroad, teacher certification program Special programs offered to physically disabled students include reader services, tape recorders, tutors. **Career services:** Alumni services, career/job search classes, career assessment, internships. **Career services highlights include:** Recognizing a fundamental link between a liberal arts education and the professional world, Pine Manor College integrates the internship experience heavily into the curriculum. Although all students are encouraged to participate in at least one internship

before senior year, each Pine Manor student must complete a senior level internship during fall semester of senior year. The PMC Internship combines student's academic knowledge with practical experience in the workplace, while providing students with the opportunity to explore career options and develop the leadership skills employers seek. Many PMC interns are offered permanent positions at their sites. After working with top professionals at Boston's best corporations, hospitals, museums, laboratories, publications and social service agencies, PMC seniors feel prepared to make informed career choices.

FACILITIES

Housing: Special housing for disabled students, women's dorms. 50% of campus accessible to physically disabled. **Special Academic Facilities/Equipment:** Hess Art Gallery, Annenberg Library and Communications Center, Ann Pappajohn Child Study Center. **Computers:** Administrative functions (other than registration) can be performed online.

CAMPUS LIFE

Activities: Choral groups, dance, drama/theater, literary magazine, radio station, student government, yearbook. **Organizations:** 25 registered organizations, 1 honor societies, 1 religious organizations. **Athletics (Intercollegiate):** *Women:* Basketball, cross-country, lacrosse, soccer, softball, tennis, volleyball.

ADMISSIONS

Freshman Academic Profile: Average high school GPA 2.4. 23% in top 25% of high school class, 49% in top 50% of high school class. 89% from public high schools. SAT Math middle 50% range 340–450. SAT Critical Reading middle 50% range 360–480. ACT middle 50% range 15–19. Minimum paper TOEFL 475. Minimum computer TOEFL 150. **Basis for Candidate Selection:** *Very important factors considered include:* Application essay, recommendation(s), rigor of secondary school record. *Important factors considered include:* standardized test scores, interview. *Other factors considered include:* Class rank, alumni/ae relation, character/personal qualities, extracurricular activities, talent/ability, volunteer work, work experience. **Freshman Admission Requirements:** High school diploma is required and GED is accepted. *Academic units recommended:* 4 English, 3 mathematics, 3 science, 2 foreign language, 2 social studies. **Freshman Admission Statistics:** 478 applied, 75% admitted, 42% enrolled. **Transfer Admission Requirements:** College transcript(s), essay or personal statement, statement of good standing from prior institution(s). Minimum college GPA of 2.0 required. Lowest grade transferable C–. **General Admission Information:** Application fee $25. Nonfall registration accepted. Admission may be deferred for a maximum of 1 year. Credit and/or placement offered for CEEB Advanced Placement tests.

COSTS AND FINANCIAL AID

Annual tuition $3,234. Room and board $5,088. Required fees $826. Average book expense $900. **Required Forms and Deadlines:** FAFSA. Priority financial aid filing date 5/1. **Notification of Awards:** Applicants will be notified of awards on a rolling basis beginning 3/1. **Types of Aid:** *Need-based scholarships/grants:* Federal Pell, SEOG, state scholarships/grants, private scholarships, the school's own gift aid. *Loans:* FFEL Subsidized Stafford, FFEL Unsubsidized Stafford, FFEL PLUS, state loans *Student Employment:* Federal Work-Study Program available. Institutional employment available. Off-campus job opportunities are excellent. **Financial Aid Statistics:** 84% freshmen, 85% undergrads receive any aid. **Criteria for awarding institutional aid:** *Non-need-based:* Academics, alumni affiliation, leadership.

PITTSBURG STATE UNIVERSITY

1701 South Broadway, Pittsburg, KS 66762
Phone: 620-235-4251 **Financial Aid Phone:** 800-854-7488
E-mail: psuadmit@pittstate.edu **CEEB Code:** 6336
Fax: 620-235-6003 **Website:** www.pittstate.edu **ACT Code:** 1449

This public school was founded in 1903. It has a 443-acre campus.

RATINGS

Admissions Selectivity Rating: 73   **Fire Safety Rating:** 75   **Green Rating:** 74

STUDENTS AND FACULTY

Enrollment: 5,793. **Student Body:** 46% female, 54% male, 25% out-of-state, 4% international (39 countries represented). Asian 1%, African American 3%, Caucasian 84%, Hispanic 3%, Native American 2%. **Retention and Graduation:** 75% freshmen return for sophomore year. **Faculty:** Student/faculty ratio 19:1. 308 full-time faculty, 72% hold PhDs, 10% are are members of minority groups, 39% are women.

ACADEMICS

Degrees: Associate, bachelor's, certificate, master's, post-master's certificate. **Classes:** Most classes have 20–29 students. Most lab/discussion sessions have

10–19 students. **Majors with Highest Enrollment:** Biology/biological sciences; elementary education and teaching; nursing/registered nurse (RN, ASN, BSN, MSN). **Special Study Options:** Accelerated program, distance learning, double major, dual enrollment, English as a Second Language (ESL), honors program, independent study, internships, student-designed major, study abroad, teacher certification program **Honors programs:** Honors College Special programs offered to physically disabled students include note-taking services, reader services, tape recorders **Career services:** Alumni network, alumni services, career/job search classes, career assessment, internships.

FACILITIES

Housing: Coed dorms, special housing for disabled students, apartments for married students, substance free and academic excellence floors are available. 90% of campus accessible to physically disabled. **Special Academic Facilities/Equipment:** planetarium, observatory, field biology reserve, nature reach, herbarium, technology center, mammal collection, greenhouse, art gallery, polymer research center, cadaver lab, Veterans Memorial Amphitheater, broadcasting lab, public radio station **Computers:** 100% of classrooms, 100% of dorms, 100% of libraries, 100% of dining areas, 100% of student union, 80% of common outdoor areas have wireless network access. Students can register for classes online. Administrative functions (other than registration) can be performed online.

CAMPUS LIFE

Environment: Village. **Activities:** Choral groups, concert band, dance, drama/theater, jazz band, literary magazine, marching band, music ensembles, pep band, radio station, student government, student newspaper, television station, yearbook, campus ministries, international student organization. **Organizations:** 150 registered organizations, 8 fraternities, 3 sororities. **Athletics (Intercollegiate):** *Men:* Baseball, basketball, cheerleading, cross-country, football, golf, track/field (outdoor), track/field (indoor). *Women:* Basketball, cheerleading, cross-country, softball, track/field (outdoor), track/field (indoor), volleyball. **On-Campus Highlights:** Planetarium, Veterans Memorial Amphitheater, Gorilla Village, Brandenburg Field/Carnie Smith Stadium, Timmons Chapel, Russ Hall, Kansas Technology Center, Nature Reach, Centennial Mural, Centennial Bell Tower, herbarium, art gallery, broadcasting lab, cadaver lab, polymer research lab, mammal collection, ROTC & student fitness center. **Environmental Initiatives:** Establishment of recycling center on campus; installation of energy efficient lighting; installation of water saving fixtures.

ADMISSIONS

Freshman Academic Profile: Average high school GPA 3.3. 18% in top 10% of high school class, 43% in top 25% of high school class, 72% in top 50% of high school class. ACT middle 50% range 19–24. Minimum paper TOEFL 520. Minimum computer TOEFL 190. Minimum web-based TOEFL 68. **Basis for Candidate Selection:** *Very important factors considered include:* Class rank, academic GPA, rigor of secondary school record, standardized test scores. **Freshman Admission Requirements:** High school diploma is required and GED is accepted. *Academic units recommended:* 4 English, 3 mathematics, 3 science, 3 social studies. **Freshman Admission Statistics:** 2,284 applied, 80% admitted, 55% enrolled. **Transfer Admission Requirements:** College transcript(s), minimum college GPA of 2.0 required. Lowest grade transferable D. **General Admission Information:** Application fee $30. Nonfall registration accepted. Credit and/or placement offered for CEEB Advanced Placement tests.

COSTS AND FINANCIAL AID

Annual in-state tuition $3,652. Annual out-of-state tuition $12,176. Room and board $5,744. Required fees $940. Average book expense $1,000. **Required Forms and Deadlines:** FAFSA. Priority financial aid filing date 3/1. **Notification of Awards:** Applicants will be notified of awards on a rolling basis beginning 3/1. **Types of Aid:** *Need-based scholarships/grants:* Federal Pell, SEOG, state scholarships/grants, private scholarships, the school's own gift aid. *Loans:* Direct Subsidized Stafford, Direct Unsubsidized Stafford, Direct PLUS, FFEL Subsidized Stafford, FFEL Unsubsidized Stafford, FFEL PLUS, Federal Perkins, Federal Nursing, college/university loans from institutional funds. *Student Employment:* Federal Work-Study Program available. Institutional employment available. Highest amount earned per year from on-campus jobs $5,100. Off-campus job opportunities are good. **Financial Aid Statistics:** 46% freshmen, 46% undergrads receive need-based scholarship or grant aid. 18% freshmen, 6% undergrads receive non-need-based scholarship or grant aid. 37% freshmen, 48% undergrads receive need-based self-help aid. 2% freshmen, 2% undergrads receive athletic scholarships. 86% freshmen, 83% undergrads receive any aid. 55% undergrads borrow to pay for school. Average cumulative indebtedness $7,746. **Criteria for awarding institutional aid:** *Non-need-based:* Academics, alumni affiliation, art, athletics, leadership, minority status, music/drama.

PITZER COLLEGE

Best 373

1050 North Mills Avenue, Claremont, CA 91711-6101
Phone: 909-621-8129 **Financial Aid Phone:** 909-621-8208
E-mail: admission@pitzer.edu **CEEB Code:** 4619
Fax: 909-621-8770 **Website:** www.pitzer.edu **ACT Code:** 363

This private school was founded in 1963. It has a 35-acre campus.

RATINGS

Admissions Selectivity Rating: 96   **Fire Safety Rating:** 74   **Green Rating:** 98

STUDENTS AND FACULTY

Enrollment: 1,043. **Student Body:** 59% female, 41% male, 46% out-of-state, 3% international (15 countries represented). Asian 8%, African American 6%, Caucasian 40%, Hispanic 15%, Native American 1%.
Retention and Graduation: 90% freshmen return for sophomore year. 70% freshmen graduate within 4 years. 17% grads go on to further study within 1 year. **Faculty:** Student/faculty ratio 11:1. 73 full-time faculty, 100% hold PhDs, 37% are are members of minority groups, 47% are women.

ACADEMICS

Degrees: Bachelor's. **Classes:** Most classes have 10–19 students. **Majors with Highest Enrollment:** film/cinema studies; psychology; sociology. **Special Study Options:** Cooperative education program, cross-registration, double major, English as a Second Language (ESL), exchange student program (domestic), honors program, independent study, internships, liberal arts/career combination, student-designed major, study abroad. **Combined degree programs:** BA/MA, BA/DO (Doctor of Osteopathy); BA/MBA. Special programs offered to physically disabled students include note-taking services, reader services, tape recorders, tutors. **Career services:** Alumni network, career/job search classes, career assessment, internships. **Career services highlights include:** Many of our courses have an internship component which provides students with practical experience as well as classroom learning.

FACILITIES

Housing: Coed dorms, special housing for disabled students, theme housing-Green housing. 95% of campus accessible to physically disabled. **Special Academic Facilities/Equipment:** Theatre arts center, Black, Asian American and Chicano Study centers; film, TV, and videotape studios; arboretum; biological field station; student health services, Gold Student Center **Computers:** 95% of classrooms, 100% of dorms, 95% of libraries, have wireless network access. Students can register for classes online. Administrative functions (other than registration) can be performed online.

CAMPUS LIFE

Environment: Town. **Activities:** Choral groups, dance, drama/theater, literary magazine, music ensembles, radio station, student government, student newspaper, symphony orchestra, campus ministries, international student organization, Model UN. **Organizations:** 120 registered organizations, 1 honor societies. **Athletics (Intercollegiate):** *Men:* Baseball, basketball, cross-country, diving, football, golf, soccer, swimming, tennis, track/field (outdoor), water polo. *Women:* Basketball, cross-country, diving, soccer, softball, swimming, tennis, track/field (outdoor), volleyball, water polo. **On-Campus Highlights:** Grove House, McConnell Center, Gloria and Peter Gold Student Center, Marquis Library, The Mounds. The Claremont Colleges Consortium: Pitzer students may cross-register at any of The Claremont Colleges, and may utilize all Claremont facilities, including Honnold Library, the third-largest academic library in the state, with more than 2 million volumes; Huntley Bookstore; Baxter Medical Center; McAlister Center for Religious Activities and Monsour Counseling Center. Pitzer sponsors the Joint Science Program with Claremont McKenna and Scripps colleges, and the five undergraduate colleges offer a wide range of recreational facilities, student gathering places and dining areas. Pitzer combines with Pomona College for NCAA Division III sports. **Environmental Initiatives:** New green dorms; Campus Climate Challenge through Eco Center; majors in environmental studies and environmental science, class in environmental justice.

ADMISSIONS

Freshman Academic Profile: Average high school GPA 3.84. 47% in top 10% of high school class, 89% in top 25% of high school class, 100% in top 50% of high school class. SAT Math middle 50% range 588–680. SAT Critical Reading middle 50% range 608–693. ACT middle 50% range 56–30. Minimum paper TOEFL 520. Minimum web-based TOEFL 70. **Basis for Candidate Selection:** *Very important factors considered include:* Class rank, application essay, academic GPA, recommendation(s), rigor of secondary school record, character/

personal qualities, extracurricular activities, racial/ethnic status. *Important factors considered include:* first generation, geographical residence, interview, level of applicant's interest, talent/ability, volunteer work. *Other factors considered include:* standardized test scores, alumni/ae relation, work experience. **Freshman Admission Requirements:** High school diploma is required and GED is accepted. *Academic units required:* 4 English, 3 mathematics, 3 science, (3 science labs), 3 foreign language, 3 social studies, 1 history, 1 visual/performing arts. **Freshman Admission Statistics:** 4,081 applied, 20% admitted, 31% enrolled. **Transfer Admission Requirements:** College transcript(s), essay or personal statement, statement of good standing from prior institution(s). Minimum college GPA of 2.0 required. Lowest grade transferable C–. **General Admission Information:** Application fee $60. Early decision application deadline 11/15. Regular application deadline 1/1. Regular notification 4/1. Nonfall registration not accepted. Admission may be deferred for a maximum of 1 year. Placement offered for CEEB Advanced Placement tests.

COSTS AND FINANCIAL AID
Annual tuition $35,840. Room and board $11,440. Required fees $3,490. Average book expense $1,200. **Required Forms and Deadlines:** FAFSA, CSS/Financial Aid PROFILE, state aid form, noncustodial PROFILE, business/farm supplement. Financial aid filing deadline 2/1. **Notification of Awards:** Applicants will be notified of awards on or about 4/1. **Types of Aid:** *Need-based scholarships/grants:* Federal Pell, SEOG, state scholarships/grants, private scholarships, the school's own gift aid, Federal ACG and National SMART. *Loans:* FFEL Subsidized Stafford, FFEL Unsubsidized Stafford, FFEL PLUS, Federal Perkins, college/university loans from institutional funds. *Student Employment:* Federal Work-Study Program available. Institutional employment available. Off-campus job opportunities are good. **Financial Aid Statistics:** 42% freshmen, 37% undergrads receive need-based scholarship or grant aid. 40% freshmen, 39% undergrads receive need-based self-help aid. 45% freshmen, 45% undergrads receive any aid. 45% undergrads borrow to pay for school. Average cumulative indebtedness $20,448. **Criteria for awarding institutional aid:** *Non-need-based:* Academics, leadership.

See page 1198.

PLYMOUTH STATE UNIVERSITY

17 High Street, MSC 52, Plymouth, NH 03264
Phone: 603-535-2237 **Financial Aid Phone:** 877-846-5755
E-mail: plymouthadmit@plymouth.edu **CEEB Code:** 3690
Fax: 603-535-2714 **Website:** www.plymouth.edu **ACT Code:** 2518

This public school was founded in 1871. It has a 170-acre campus.

RATINGS
Admissions Selectivity Rating: 70   **Fire Safety Rating:** 92   **Green Rating:** 91

STUDENTS AND FACULTY
Enrollment: 4,155. **Student Body:** 46% female, 54% male, 39% out-of-state, international (26 countries represented).
Retention and Graduation: 78% freshmen return for sophomore year. 16% grads go on to further study within 1 year. **Faculty:** Student/faculty ratio 17:1. 186 full-time faculty, 7% are are members of minority groups, 41% are women.

ACADEMICS
Degrees: Bachelor's, doctoral, master's, post-bachelor's certificate, post-master's certificate. **Classes:** Most classes have 20–29 students. Most lab/discussion sessions have 10–19 students. **Majors with Highest Enrollment:** Business administration and management; criminal justice/safety studies; elementary education and teaching. **Special Study Options:** Cross-registration, distance learning, double major, dual enrollment, English as a Second Language (ESL), exchange student program (domestic), external degree program, honors program, independent study, internships, student-designed major, study abroad, teacher certification program. **Honors programs:** First and Second Year Honors Program, Business Honors, Psychology Honors Special programs offered to physically disabled students include note-taking services, reader services, tape recorders, tutors. **Career services:** Alumni network, alumni services, career/job search classes, career assessment, internships, regional alumni.

FACILITIES
Housing: Coed dorms, special housing for disabled students, fraternity/sorority housing, apartments for married students, apartments for single students, wellness house, theme housing, non-traditional student apts. Quiet study/academic. 80% of campus accessible to physically disabled. **Special Academic Facilities/Equipment:** Karl Drerup Art gallery, Silver Cultural Arts Center, Sylvestre Planetarium, Child Development and Family Center (NAEYC accredited lab school for children 2–6 years old), meteorology lab, Geographic Information

System lab, psychology lab, graphic design computer lab. **Computers:** 75% of classrooms, 5% of dorms, 100% of libraries, 100% of dining areas, 100% of student union, 10% of common outdoor areas have wireless network access. Students can register for classes online. Administrative functions (other than registration) can be performed online.

CAMPUS LIFE
Environment: Village. **Activities:** Choral groups, concert band, dance, drama/theater, jazz band, literary magazine, music ensembles, musical theater, radio station, student government, student newspaper, student-run film society, yearbook, campus ministries, international student organization, Model UN. **Organizations:** 80 registered organizations, 13 honor societies, 4 religious organizations. 3 sororities. **Athletics (Intercollegiate):** *Men:* Baseball, basketball, football, ice hockey, lacrosse, skiing (downhill/alpine), soccer, wrestling. *Women:* Basketball, cheerleading, diving, field hockey, ice hockey, lacrosse, skiing (downhill/alpine), soccer, softball, swimming, tennis, volleyball. **On-Campus Highlights:** Hartman Union Building, Silver Center for the Arts, PE Center-New-Fall '10 Ice Arena & Welcome Center, Prospect Dining Hall, Lamson Library—Information Commons. **Environmental Initiatives:** New degree program. All new campus construction must achieve LEED Silver standard or the equivalent. Energy conservation projects.

ADMISSIONS
Freshman Academic Profile: Average high school GPA 2.88. 4% in top 10% of high school class, 17% in top 25% of high school class, 53% in top 50% of high school class. 0% from public high schools. SAT Math middle 50% range 440–530. SAT Critical Reading middle 50% range 430–530. ACT middle 50% range 18–23. Minimum paper TOEFL 520. Minimum computer TOEFL 190. **Basis for Candidate Selection:** *Very important factors considered include:* Rigor of secondary school record. *Important factors considered include:* Class rank, application essay, academic GPA, recommendation(s), standardized test scores, character/personal qualities, talent/ability. *Other factors considered include:* Alumni/ae relation, extracurricular activities, racial/ethnic status, volunteer work, work experience. **Freshman Admission Requirements:** High school diploma is required and GED is accepted. *Academic units required:* 4 English, 3 mathematics, 2 science, (1 science labs), 2 social studies, 1 history. *Academic units recommended:* 4 English, 3 mathematics, 3 science, (1 science labs), 2 foreign language, 3 social studies, 2 history. **Freshman Admission Statistics:** 4,239 applied, 70% admitted, 33% enrolled. **Transfer Admission Requirements:** High school transcript, college transcript(s), minimum college GPA of 2.0 required. Lowest grade transferable C. **General Admission Information:** Application fee $45. Regular application deadline 4/1, Notification on a rolling basis, beginning on or about 11/1. Nonfall registration accepted. Admission may be deferred for a maximum of 1 year. Credit offered for CEEB Advanced Placement tests.

COSTS AND FINANCIAL AID
Required Forms and Deadlines: FAFSA. Priority financial aid filing date 3/1. **Notification of Awards:** Applicants will be notified of awards on a rolling basis beginning 3/1. **Types of Aid:** *Need-based scholarships/grants:* Federal Pell, SEOG, state scholarships/grants, private scholarships, the school's own gift aid. *Loans:* Direct Subsidized Stafford, Direct Unsubsidized Stafford, Direct PLUS, Federal Perkins. *Student Employment:* Federal Work-Study Program available. Institutional employment available. Highest amount earned per year from on-campus jobs $3,325. Off-campus job opportunities are good. **Financial Aid Statistics:** 45% freshmen, 42% undergrads receive need-based scholarship or grant aid. 24% freshmen, 20% undergrads receive non-need-based scholarship or grant aid. 61% freshmen, 59% undergrads receive need-based self-help aid. 61% freshmen, 60% undergrads receive any aid. **Criteria for awarding institutional aid:** *Non-need-based:* Academics, music/drama.

POINT LOMA NAZARENE UNIVERSITY

3900 Lomaland Drive, San Diego, CA 92106
Phone: 619-849-2273
E-mail: admissions@pointloma.edu **CEEB Code:** 4605
Fax: 619-849-2601 **Website: ACT Code:** 370

This private school, affiliated with the Nazarene Church, was founded in 1902. It has a 90-acre campus.

RATINGS
Admissions Selectivity Rating: 88   **Fire Safety Rating:** 60*   **Green Rating:** 60*

STUDENTS AND FACULTY
Enrollment: 2,337. **Student Body:** 61% female, 39% male, 21% out-of-state, international (17 countries represented). Asian 6%, African American 2%,

Caucasian 78%, Hispanic 11%, Native American 1%.
Retention and Graduation: 87% freshmen return for sophomore year. 60% freshmen graduate within 4 years. **Faculty:** Student/faculty ratio 16:1. 177 full-time faculty, 73% hold PhDs, 10% are are members of minority groups, 40% are women.

ACADEMICS

Degrees: Bachelor's, master's. **Classes:** Most classes have 20–29 students. **Majors with Highest Enrollment:** Business/commerce; liberal arts and sciences/liberal studies; psychology. **Special Study Options:** Double major, honors program, independent study, internships, study abroad, teacher certification program. **Honors programs:** Honors Scholars Program.

FACILITIES

Housing: Men's dorms, women's dorms, apartments for married students, apartments for single students. 100% of campus accessible to physically disabled. **Special Academic Facilities/Equipment:** Language lab, on-campus preschool, electron microscope. **Computers:** Students can register for classes online. Administrative functions (other than registration) can be performed online.

CAMPUS LIFE

Environment: Metropolis. **Activities:** Choral groups, concert band, drama/theater, jazz band, literary magazine, music ensembles, musical theater, radio station, student government, student newspaper, television station, yearbook, campus ministries, international student organization. **Organizations:** 30 registered organizations, 2 honor societies, 7 religious organizations. 3 fraternities, 3 sororities. **Athletics (Intercollegiate):** *Men:* Baseball, basketball, cross-country, golf, soccer, tennis, track/field (outdoor): *Women:* Basketball, cross-country, softball, tennis, track/field (outdoor), volleyball. **On-Campus Highlights:** Point Break Cafe, Recreation Center, Ryan Library, Greek Ampitheatre, Golden Gymnasium.

ADMISSIONS

Freshman Academic Profile: Average high school GPA 3.72. 45% in top 10% of high school class, 72% in top 25% of high school class, 95% in top 50% of high school class. SAT Math middle 50% range 500–620. SAT Critical Reading middle 50% range 510–620. Minimum paper TOEFL 550. Minimum computer TOEFL 213. **Basis for Candidate Selection:** *Very important factors considered include:* Academic GPA, rigor of secondary school record, standardized test scores, character/personal qualities, religious affiliation/commitment. *Important factors considered include:* Class rank, application essay, recommendation(s), interview. *Other factors considered include:* Alumni/ae relation, extracurricular activities, first generation, level of applicant's interest, talent/ability. **Freshman Admission Requirements:** High school diploma is required and GED is accepted. *Academic units recommended:* 4 English, 3 mathematics, 2 science, (2 science labs), 2 foreign language, 2 social studies, 2 history, 1 academic electives. **Freshman Admission Statistics:** 1,757 applied, 73% admitted, 41% enrolled. **Transfer Admission Requirements:** College transcript(s), essay or personal statement, interview, minimum college GPA of 2.0 required. Lowest grade transferable D. **General Admission Information:** Application fee $50. Regular notification 4/1. Nonfall registration not accepted. Credit and/or placement offered for CEEB Advanced Placement tests.

COSTS AND FINANCIAL AID

Annual tuition $24,580. Room and board $8,170. Required fees $540. Average book expense $1,566. **Required Forms and Deadlines:** FAFSA, institution's own financial aid form. Financial aid filing deadline 3/2. Priority financial aid filing date 3/2. **Notification of Awards:** Applicants will be notified of awards on a rolling basis beginning 3/1. **Types of Aid:** *Need-based scholarships/grants:* Federal Pell, SEOG, state scholarships/grants, private scholarships, the school's own gift aid. *Loans:* FFEL Subsidized Stafford, FFEL Unsubsidized Stafford, FFEL PLUS, Federal Perkins, Federal Nursing. *Student Employment:* **Financial Aid Statistics:** 60% freshmen, 59% undergrads receive need-based scholarship or grant aid. 6% freshmen, 5% undergrads receive non-need-based scholarship or grant aid. 48% freshmen, 52% undergrads receive need-based self-help aid. 3% freshmen, 4% undergrads receive athletic scholarships. 86% undergrads borrow to pay for school. Average cumulative indebtedness $19,525.

POINT PARK UNIVERSITY

201 Wood Street, Pittsburgh, PA 15222
Phone: 412-392-3430 **Financial Aid Phone:** 412-392-3930
E-mail: enroll@pointpark.edu **CEEB Code:** 2676
Fax: 412-391-1980 **Website: ACT Code:** 3530

This private school was founded in 1960.

RATINGS
Admissions Selectivity Rating: 76   **Fire Safety Rating:** 91   **Green Rating:** 73

STUDENTS AND FACULTY

Enrollment: 3,355. **Student Body:** 60% female, 40% male, 17% out-of-state, 1% international (30 countries represented). Asian 1%, African American 19%, Caucasian 76%, Hispanic 2%.
Retention and Graduation: 77% freshmen return for sophomore year. 41% freshmen graduate within 4 years. **Faculty:** Student/faculty ratio 14:1. 122 full-time faculty, 62% hold PhDs, 7% are are members of minority groups, 39% are women.

ACADEMICS

Degrees: Associate, bachelor's, certificate, master's, post-bachelor's certificate. **Classes:** Most classes have 10–19 students. **Majors with Highest Enrollment:** dance; drama and dramatics/theatre arts; teacher education and professional development, specific subject areas, other. **Special Study Options:** Accelerated program, cooperative education program, cross-registration, distance learning, double major, dual enrollment, English as a Second Language (ESL), exchange student program (domestic), honors program, independent study, internships, liberal arts/career combination, student-designed major, study abroad, teacher certification program, weekend college. **Honors programs:** The Point Park Honors Program mission provides the foundation from which honors courses are developed. Honors courses will not be defined by more work but rather by a different kind of learning environment. Students will be introduced to the usual content and objectives of the course, but they will also develop in-depth understandings of topics. Students will be expected to use primary sources when possible and to develop appropriate research skills which should result in major documented papers or projects. Students will be encouraged to become adventurous, independent thinkers. Students should experience a variety of learning activities which may include collaborative learning, field experience, debates, documented projects, interviews, and presentations. Evaluation will be based on performance, creativity, imagination, critical thinking, and risk taking rather than on more assignments and tests. Honors students will be expected to participate in the quest for knowledge by being prepared and willing to contribute to all class activities. Honors students also may join our Honors Student Organization and participate in a variety of community service efforts and projects inside and outside the Point Park community. Students annually are offered the chance to travel for an alternative spring break, and they can present papers and research at national and regional honors conferences. Every effort is made to encourage all of them to assume leadership positions and propose their own activities and endeavors to complement their work in the classroom. Students who complete program requirements will be recognized in the program at graduation and will receive a separate certificate and notation on their transcript. Special programs offered to physically disabled students include note-taking services, reader services, tape recorders, tutors. **Career services:** Alumni network, alumni services, career/job search classes, career assessment, internships, regional alumni.

FACILITIES

Housing: Coed dorms, special housing for disabled students, women's dorms, apartments for single students, theme housing, living & learning communities; suite style. 95% of campus accessible to physically disabled. **Special Academic Facilities/Equipment:** Theater, day care center and elementary school, engineering technology labs, television and radio studios, digital film editing suites, dance studios. **Computers:** 100% of classrooms, 100% of libraries, 100% of dining areas, 100% of student union, 100% of common outdoor areas have wireless network access. Students can register for classes online. Administrative functions (other than registration) can be performed online.

CAMPUS LIFE

Environment: Metropolis. **Activities:** Choral groups, dance, drama/theater, literary magazine, musical theater, radio station, student government, student newspaper, student-run film society, television station, international student organization. **Organizations:** 25 registered organizations, 3 honor societies, 2 religious organizations. **Athletics (Intercollegiate):** *Men:* Baseball, basketball, cross-country, golf, soccer. *Women:* Basketball, cross-country, golf, soccer, softball, volleyball. **On-Campus Highlights:** Point Cafe, Atrium Overlook, Recreation Center, Coffee Kiosk, Outdoor Patio. **Environmental Initiatives:** Recycling, LEED building, creating a greening committee.

ADMISSIONS

Freshman Academic Profile: Average high school GPA 3.24. 16% in top 10% of high school class, 41% in top 25% of high school class, 77% in top 50% of high school class. SAT Math middle 50% range 450–560. SAT Critical Reading middle 50% range 470–570. SAT Writing middle 50% range 460–570. ACT middle 50% range 19–24. Minimum paper TOEFL 500. Minimum computer TOEFL 173. **Basis for Candidate Selection:** *Other factors considered include:* Class rank, academic GPA, rigor of secondary school record, standardized test scores, talent/ability. **Freshman Admission Requirements:** High school diploma is required and GED is accepted. *Academic units recommended:* 4 English, 4 mathematics, 4 science, 2 foreign language, 4 social studies, 4 history, 2 visual/performing arts, 2 academic electives. **Freshman Admission Statistics:** 3,089 applied, 72% admitted, 24% enrolled. **Transfer Admission Requirements:** College transcript(s), minimum college GPA of 2.0 required. Lowest grade transferable C. **General Admission Information:** Application fee $40. Notification on a rolling basis, beginning on or about 10/1. Nonfall registration accepted. Admission may be deferred for a maximum of 1 year. Neither credit nor placement offered for CEEB Advanced Placement tests.

COSTS AND FINANCIAL AID

Annual tuition $20,720. Room and board $9,020. Required fees $614. Average book expense $1,000. **Required Forms and Deadlines:** FAFSA. Priority financial aid filing date 4/15. **Notification of Awards:** Applicants will be notified of awards on a rolling basis beginning 2/15. **Types of Aid:** *Need-based scholarships/grants:* Federal Pell, SEOG, state scholarships/grants, private scholarships, the school's own gift aid. *Loans:* Direct Subsidized Stafford, Direct Unsubsidized Stafford, Direct PLUS, FFEL Subsidized Stafford, FFEL Unsubsidized Stafford, FFEL PLUS, Federal Perkins. *Student Employment:* Federal Work-Study Program available. Institutional employment available. Highest amount earned per year from on-campus jobs $2,500. Off-campus job opportunities are good. **Financial Aid Statistics:** 61% freshmen, 79% undergrads receive need-based scholarship or grant aid. 8% freshmen, 6% undergrads receive non-need-based scholarship or grant aid. 52% freshmen, 74% undergrads receive need-based self-help aid. 3% freshmen, 2% undergrads receive athletic scholarships. 98% freshmen, 90% undergrads receive any aid. 83% undergrads borrow to pay for school. Average cumulative indebtedness $31,656. **Criteria for awarding institutional aid:** *Non-need-based:* Academics, athletics, minority status.

POLYTECHNIC INSTITUTE OF NYU—BROOKLYN

6 Metrotech Center, Brooklyn, NY 11201-2999
Phone: 718-260-3100 **Financial Aid Phone:** 718-260-3300
E-mail: uadmit@poly.edu **CEEB Code:** 2668
Fax: 718-260-3446 **Website:** www.poly.edu **ACT Code:** 2860

This private school was founded in 1854. It has a 3-acre campus.

RATINGS

Admissions Selectivity Rating: 92   **Fire Safety Rating:** 60*   **Green Rating:** 81

STUDENTS AND FACULTY

Enrollment: 1,632. **Student Body:** 20% female, 80% male, 12.7% out-of-state, 12% international (45 countries represented). Asian 28%, African American 10%, Caucasian 25%, Hispanic 11%.

Retention and Graduation: 85% freshmen return for sophomore year. 36% freshmen graduate within 4 years. 27% grads go on to further study within 1 year. **Faculty:** Student/faculty ratio 15:1. 152 full-time faculty, 89% hold PhDs, 24% are are members of minority groups, 18% are women.

ACADEMICS

Degrees: Bachelor's, certificate, doctoral, master's. **Classes:** Most classes have 10–19 students. Most lab/discussion sessions have 10–19 students. **Majors with Highest Enrollment:** Civil engineering; electrical, electronics and communications engineering; mechanical engineering. **Special Study Options:** Accelerated program, cooperative education program, distance learning, double major, dual enrollment, honors program, independent study, internships. **Honors programs:** The Honors College serves as a magnet for attracting academically superior undergraduates to the university. It accepts students of exceptional talent and promise from a variety of backgrounds. It offers outstanding Honors students the opportunity to earn a BS and possibly an MS degree in possibly as few as four years, including summers. Honors College students work one-on-one with faculty mentors, who, among other things, stress interdisciplinary research where appropriate, originality of thought, and active learning. Honors College students form a talented cadre of high-achievers who will become engineers, scientists, managers, and other professionals positioned for leadership roles in our emerging knowledge-based economy. They will also form a highly enthusiastic and supportive part of the university's alumni population

and enhance the overall reputation of the university for delivering excellence in education. **Combined degree programs:** BA/MA, BA/MEng, 2-2 engineering program with CUNY Brooklyn Coll. Special programs offered to physically disabled students include note-taking services, tape recorders, tutors. **Career services:** Alumni network, alumni services, career/job search classes, career assessment, internships.

FACILITIES

Housing: Coed dorms, fraternity/sorority housing. 100% of campus accessible to physically disabled. **Special Academic Facilities/Equipment:** Electron microscope, supersonic wind tunnel. Art Displays in Student Center. **Computers:** 100% of classrooms, 100% of dorms, 100% of libraries, 100% of dining areas, 100% of student union, 100% of common outdoor areas have wireless network access. Students can register for classes online. Administrative functions (other than registration) can be performed online. Undergraduates are required to own a computer.

CAMPUS LIFE

Environment: Metropolis. **Activities:** drama/theater, literary magazine, radio station, student government, student newspaper, student-run film society, yearbook. **Organizations:** 36 registered organizations, 8 honor societies, 4 religious organizations. 3 fraternities, 1 sorority. **Athletics (Intercollegiate):** *Men:* Baseball, basketball, cross-country, soccer, tennis, track/field (outdoor), volleyball. *Women:* Basketball, cross-country, softball, tennis, track/field (outdoor), volleyball. **On-Campus Highlights:** Recreation Center—Wunsch Student Center, Fitness Center—Jacobs Building, Bern Dibner Library for Science and Technology, Jasper H. Kane Dining Hall—Rogers Hall, Gymnasium—Jacobs Building. **Environmental Initiatives:** Enhanced/expanded recycling. Signed Presidents' Climate Committment. Accepted Mayor's Challenge—30% in 10 years.

ADMISSIONS

Freshman Academic Profile: Average high school GPA 3.36. 36% in top 10% of high school class, 69% in top 25% of high school class, 91% in top 50% of high school class. 82% from public high schools. SAT Math middle 50% range 630–720. SAT Critical Reading middle 50% range 560–640. ACT middle 50% range 36–31.5. Minimum paper TOEFL 550. Minimum computer TOEFL 217. **Basis for Candidate Selection:** *Very important factors considered include:* Rigor of secondary school record, standardized test scores. *Important factors considered include:* Class rank. *Other factors considered include:* Application essay, recommendation(s), interview. **Freshman Admission Requirements:** High school diploma is required and GED is accepted. *Academic units required:* 4 English, 4 mathematics, 4 science, 3 social studies, 2 academic electives. *Academic units recommended:* 2 foreign language. **Freshman Admission Statistics:** 3,947 applied, 54% admitted, 17% enrolled. **Transfer Admission Requirements:** College transcript(s), minimum college GPA of 2.5 required. Lowest grade transferable c. **General Admission Information:** Application fee $50. Nonfall registration accepted. Admission may be deferred for a maximum of 1. Credit and/or placement offered for CEEB Advanced Placement tests.

COSTS AND FINANCIAL AID

Annual tuition $32,643. Room and board $9,000. Required fees $1,147. Average book expense $1,000. **Required Forms and Deadlines:** FAFSA, institution's own financial aid form, CSS/Financial Aid PROFILE, state aid form. **Notification of Awards:** Applicants will be notified of awards on a rolling basis beginning 2/15. **Types of Aid:** *Need-based scholarships/grants:* Federal Pell, SEOG, state scholarships/grants, private scholarships, the school's own gift aid, United Negro College Fund *Loans:* FFEL Subsidized Stafford, FFEL Unsubsidized Stafford, FFEL PLUS, Federal Perkins, college/university loans from institutional funds, alternative loans. *Student Employment:* Highest amount earned per year from on-campus jobs $10,500. Off-campus job opportunities are excellent. **Financial Aid Statistics:** 66% freshmen, 60% undergrads receive need-based scholarship or grant aid. 57% freshmen, 51% undergrads receive non-need-based scholarship or grant aid. 61% freshmen, 59% undergrads receive need-based self-help aid. 99% freshmen, 92% undergrads receive any aid. 67% undergrads borrow to pay for school. Average cumulative indebtedness $26,619. **Criteria for awarding institutional aid:** *Non-need-based:* Academics, minority status, state/district residency.

POLYTECHNIC UNIVERSITY OF PUERTO RICO

PO BOX 192017, Hato Rey, PR 00919-2017
Phone: 787.622.8000 **Financial Aid Phone:** 787.622.8000
E-mail:
Fax: 787.764.8712 **Website:** www.pupr.edu

This private school was founded in 1966.

RATINGS
Admissions Selectivity Rating: 60*   **Fire Safety Rating:** 60*   **Green Rating:** 60*

STUDENTS AND FACULTY
Enrollment: 4,844. **Student Body:** 23% female, 77% male, Hispanic 100%. **Retention and Graduation: Faculty:** Student/faculty ratio 20:1. 172 full-time faculty, 23% hold PhDs, 45% are women.

ACADEMICS
Degrees: Bachelor's, master's. **Special Study Options:** Cooperative education program, distance learning, honors program. **Honors programs:** In a continuing effort to provide educational opportunities consistent with the ability of the individual student, the university invites a select group of students to enroll in and benefit from the Honor Program and corresponding Scholarship. This program consists of honors seminars, special courses, and independent study. The special courses enable students who excel to be challenged to their full intellectual capacity. The program is designed both to broaden and deepen the student's intellectual power. At the advanced level, honor students are encouraged to undertake faculty-guided independent research in their areas of special interest or competencies. These courses are conducted as seminars and involve topics at the forefront of current scientific interest. Students who excel in mathematics and physics, regardless of the major preference, are encouraged to enroll in these courses. The program also offers an opportunity for independent study for honor students whose interests lie beyond the topics ordinarily covered by the university program. Special programs offered to physically disabled students include note-taking services, tutors.

FACILITIES
Housing: Computers: 100% of classrooms, 100% of libraries, 100% of dining areas, 100% of student union, 100% of common outdoor areas have wireless network access.

CAMPUS LIFE
Environment: Metropolis. **Activities:** Choral groups, student government. **Organizations:** 20 registered organizations, 1 honor societies, 1 religious organizations. **Athletics (Intercollegiate):** *Men:* Basketball, cross-country, martial arts, table tennis, tennis, track/field (outdoor), volleyball, wrestling. *Women:* cross-country, martial arts, table tennis, tennis, track/field (outdoor), volleyball.

ADMISSIONS
Freshman Academic Profile: 39% from public high schools. **Freshman Admission Requirements:** High school diploma is required and GED is accepted. *Academic units required:* 3 English, 3 mathematics, 3 science, 3 foreign language, 3 social studies. **Freshman Admission Statistics:** 773 applied, 94% admitted, 77% enrolled. **Transfer Admission Requirements:** College transcript(s). **General Admission Information:** Application fee $30. Placement offered for CEEB Advanced Placement tests.

COSTS AND FINANCIAL AID
Annual tuition $5,805. Required fees $525. Average book expense $2,310.
Required Forms and Deadlines: FAFSA.

POMONA COLLEGE

333 N. College Way, Claremont, CA 91711-6312
Phone: 909-621-8134 **Financial Aid Phone:** 909-621-8205
E-mail: admissions@pomona.edu **CEEB Code:** 4607
Fax: 909-621-8952 **Website:** www.pomona.edu **ACT Code:** 372

This private school was founded in 1887. It has a 140-acre campus.

RATINGS
Admissions Selectivity Rating: 99   **Fire Safety Rating:** 84   **Green Rating:** 60*

STUDENTS AND FACULTY
Enrollment: 1,531. **Student Body:** 50% female, 50% male, 67% out-of-state, 4% international (24 countries represented). Asian 14%, African American 9%, Caucasian 46%, Hispanic 11%.
Retention and Graduation: 97% freshmen return for sophomore year. 89% freshmen graduate within 4 years. 33% grads go on to further study within 1 year. 12% grads pursue arts and sciences degrees. 11% grads pursue law degrees. 11% grads pursue medical degrees. **Faculty:** Student/faculty ratio 7:1. 188 full-time faculty, 98% hold PhDs, 27% are are members of minority groups, 43% are women.

ACADEMICS
Degrees: Bachelor's. **Classes:** Most classes have 10–19 students. Most lab/discussion sessions have 10–19 students. **Majors with Highest Enrollment:** Biology/biological sciences; economics; English language and literature. **Special Study Options:** Cross-registration, double major, exchange student program (domestic), independent study, internships, student-designed major, study abroad, The college has a 3-2 combined Bachelors (BA & BS) in Engineering with Washington University in St. Louis and the California Institute of Technology. **Combined degree programs:** BA/MEng Special programs offered to physically disabled students include note-taking services, reader services, tape recorders, tutors. **Career services:** Alumni network, alumni services, career/job search classes, career assessment, internships, regional alumni. **Career services highlights include:** Pomona College Internship Program (PCIP) Students receive school credit for having a part-time internship over the course of a semester, totaling at minimum 60 hours. They can choose from a list of local internship options coordinated through our Career Development Office. Students submit a written evaluation at the end of the semester.

FACILITIES
Housing: Coed dorms, theme housingLanguage Residence Hall. 85% of campus accessible to physically disabled. **Special Academic Facilities/Equipment:** Oldenborg Center for Foreign Languages, Musuem of Art, Brackett Observatory. **Computers:** 75% of classrooms, 50% of dorms, 100% of libraries, 100% of dining areas, 100% of student union, 100% of common outdoor areas have wireless network access. Administrative functions (other than registration) can be performed online.

CAMPUS LIFE
Environment: Town. **Activities:** Choral groups, concert band, dance, drama/theater, jazz band, literary magazine, music ensembles, musical theater, pep band, radio station, student government, student newspaper, student-run film society, symphony orchestra, television station, yearbook, campus ministries, international student organization, Model UN. **Organizations:** 280 registered organizations, 3 honor societies, 5 religious organizations. 3 fraternities, 3 sororities. **Athletics (Intercollegiate):** *Men:* Baseball, basketball, cross-country, diving, football, golf, soccer, swimming, tennis, track/field (outdoor), water polo. *Women:* Basketball, cross-country, diving, golf, lacrosse, soccer, softball, swimming, tennis, track/field (outdoor), volleyball, water polo. **On-Campus Highlights:** Smith Campus Center, Sontag Greek Theater, Rains Center for Sports and Recreation, Brackett Observatory.

ADMISSIONS
Freshman Academic Profile: 64% from public high schools. SAT Math middle 50% range 690–780. SAT Critical Reading middle 50% range 700–780. SAT Writing middle 50% range 680–770. ACT middle 50% range 30–34. Minimum paper TOEFL 600. Minimum computer TOEFL 250. **Basis for Candidate Selection:** *Very important factors considered include:* Class rank, application essay, academic GPA, recommendation(s), rigor of secondary school record, standardized test scores, character/personal qualities, extracurricular activities, talent/ability. *Important factors considered include:* interview. *Other factors considered include:* Alumni/ae relation, first generation, geographical residence, racial/ethnic status, volunteer work, work experience. **Freshman Admission Requirements:** High school diploma or equivalent is not required. *Academic units required:* 4 English, 3 mathematics, 3 science, (2 science labs), 2 foreign language, 2 social studies, 3 history. *Academic units recommended:* 4 mathematics, 4 science, (3 science labs), 3 foreign language, 2 social studies, 3 history. **Freshman Admission Statistics:** 6,149 applied, 16% admitted, 39% enrolled. **Transfer Admission Requirements:** High school transcript, college transcript(s), essay or personal statement, standardized test scores, statement of good standing from prior institution(s). Lowest grade transferable C. **General Admission Information:** Application fee $65. Early decision application deadline 11/1. Regular application deadline 1/2. Nonfall registration not accepted. Admission may be deferred for a maximum of 1 year. Credit and/or placement offered for CEEB Advanced Placement tests.

COSTS AND FINANCIAL AID
Required Forms and Deadlines: FAFSA, CSS/Financial Aid PROFILE, noncustodial PROFILE, business/farm supplement. Tax returns for both the student and parents. Financial aid filing deadline 2/1. Priority financial aid filing date 2/1. **Notification of Awards:** Applicants will be notified of awards

on or about 4/1. **Types of Aid:** *Need-based scholarships/grants:* Federal Pell, SEOG, state scholarships/grants, private scholarships, the school's own gift aid. *Loans:* FFEL Subsidized Stafford, FFEL Unsubsidized Stafford, FFEL PLUS, Federal Perkins, college/university loans from institutional funds. *Student Employment:* Federal Work-Study Program available. Institutional employment available. Off-campus job opportunities are good. **Financial Aid Statistics:** 51% freshmen, 52% undergrads receive need-based scholarship or grant aid. 51% freshmen, 52% undergrads receive need-based self-help aid. 53% freshmen, 50% undergrads receive any aid. 47% undergrads borrow to pay for school. Average cumulative indebtedness $8,776.

PONTIFICAL COLLEGE JOSEPHINUM

7625 North High Street, Columbus, OH 43235-1498
Phone: 614-885-5585 **Financial Aid Phone:** 614-885-5585
E-mail: admissions@pcj.edu
Fax: 614-885-2307

This private school, affiliated with the Roman Catholic Church,, affiliated with the Seminarian Church, was founded in 1888. It has a 100-acre campus.

RATINGS
Admissions Selectivity Rating: 72   **Fire Safety Rating:** 60*   **Green Rating:** 60*

STUDENTS AND FACULTY
Enrollment: 78. **Student Body:** 100% male, 64% out-of-state, 8% international (15 countries represented). Asian 1%, Caucasian 79%, Hispanic 10%, Native American 1%.
Retention and Graduation: 92% freshmen return for sophomore year. 63% freshmen graduate within 4 years. 95% grads go on to further study within 1 year. 5% grads pursue arts and sciences degrees. **Faculty:** Student/faculty ratio 4:1. 17 full-time faculty, 76% hold PhDs, 35% are women.

ACADEMICS
Degrees: Bachelor's, master's. **Classes:** Most classes have 10–19 students. **Special Study Options:** Cross-registration, double major, honors program, independent study.

FACILITIES
Housing: Men's dorms.

CAMPUS LIFE
Environment: Metropolis. **Activities:** Choral groups **Organizations:** 1 religious organizations.

ADMISSIONS
Freshman Academic Profile: 25% in top 10% of high school class, 35% in top 25% of high school class, 60% in top 50% of high school class. SAT Math middle 50% range 360–610. SAT Critical Reading middle 50% range 380–600. SAT Writing middle 50% range 350–610. ACT middle 50% range 17–25. Minimum paper TOEFL 550. Minimum computer TOEFL 173. **Basis for Candidate Selection:** *Very important factors considered include:* Recommendation(s), rigor of secondary school record, standardized test scores, religious affiliation/commitment. *Important factors considered include:* Application essay, academic GPA, interview. *Other factors considered include:* Class rank, character/personal qualities, extracurricular activities, talent/ability, volunteer work. **Freshman Admission Requirements:** High school diploma is required and GED is accepted. *Academic units required:* 4 English, 2 mathematics, 1 science, 1 foreign language, 2 social studies. *Academic units recommended:* 4 mathematics, 4 science, 2 foreign language, 4 social studies. **Freshman Admission Statistics:** 8 applied, 75% admitted, 100% enrolled. **Transfer Admission Requirements:** High school transcript, college transcript(s), essay or personal statement, interview, standardized test scores, Lowest grade transferable C. **General Admission Information:** Application fee $25. Notification on a rolling basis, beginning on or about 1/1. Nonfall registration not accepted.

COSTS AND FINANCIAL AID
Annual tuition $16,701. Room and board $7,908. Required fees $720. Average book expense $1,100. **Required Forms and Deadlines:** FAFSA, institution's own financial aid form. **Types of Aid:** *Need-based scholarships/grants:* Federal Pell, SEOG, state scholarships/grants, private scholarships, the school's own gift aid. *Loans:* FFEL Subsidized Stafford, FFEL Unsubsidized Stafford, FFEL PLUS, Federal Perkins. *Student Employment:* Federal Work-Study Program available. Highest amount earned per year from on-campus jobs $1,200. **Financial Aid Statistics:** 17% undergrads receive need-based scholarship or grant aid. 9% freshmen, 7% undergrads receive need-based self-help aid. 20% undergrads borrow to pay for school. Average cumulative indebtedness $8,575. **Criteria for awarding institutional aid:** *Non-need-based:* Academics.

PORTLAND STATE UNIVERSITY

Office of Admissions and Records, PO Box 751, Portland, OR 97207-0751
Phone: 503-725-3511 **Financial Aid Phone:** 800-547-8887
E-mail: admissions@pdx.edu **CEEB Code:** 4610
Fax: 503-725-5525 **Website:** www.pdx.edu **ACT Code:** 3492

This public school was founded in 1946. It has a 49-acre campus.

RATINGS
Admissions Selectivity Rating: 71   **Fire Safety Rating:** 60*   **Green Rating:** 89

STUDENTS AND FACULTY
Enrollment: 17,930. **Student Body:** 53% female, 47% male, 14% out-of-state, 5% international (97 countries represented). Asian 10%, African American 3%, Caucasian 65%, Hispanic 6%, Native American 1%.
Retention and Graduation: 68% freshmen return for sophomore year. 9% freshmen graduate within 4 years. **Faculty:** Student/faculty ratio 20:1. 800 full-time faculty, 74% hold PhDs, 13% are are members of minority groups, 44% are women. 4% of classes are taught by teaching assistants.

ACADEMICS
Degrees: Bachelor's, certificate, master's, post-bachelor's certificate. **Classes:** Most classes have 20–29 students. Most lab/discussion sessions have 20–29 students. **Majors with Highest Enrollment:** Business/commerce; fine/studio arts; psychology. **Special Study Options:** Accelerated program, cooperative education program, cross-registration, distance learning, double major, English as a Second Language (ESL), exchange student program (domestic), honors program, independent study, internships, study abroad, teacher certification program, Haystack Summer Program in the Arts and Sciences. **Honors programs:** University Honors Program Special programs offered to physically disabled students include note-taking services, reader services, tape recorders, tutors. **Career services:** Alumni network, alumni services, career/job search classes, career assessment, internships. **Career services highlights include:** The Senior Capstone's purpose is to further enhance student learning while cultivating crucial life abilities that are important both academically and professionally; establishing connections within the larger community, developing strategies for analyzing and addressing problems, and working with others trained in fields different from one's own. This 6-credit, community-based learning course is designed to provide students with the opportunity to apply, in a team context, what they have learned in the major and in their other University Studies courses to a real challenge emanating from the metropolitan community.

FACILITIES
Housing: Coed dorms, special housing for disabled students, special housing for international students, fraternity/sorority housing, apartments for married students, apartments for single students, apecial housing for new students. Apartments for students with dependent children. 95% of campus accessible to physically disabled. **Special Academic Facilities/Equipment:** Art galleries, audiovisual resources, classroom multimedia computer systems, learning lab, child development center, Native American Center. **Computers:** 50% of dorms, 100% of libraries, 100% of dining areas, 100% of student union, have wireless network access. Students can register for classes online. Administrative functions (other than registration) can be performed online.

CAMPUS LIFE
Environment: Metropolis. **Activities:** Choral groups, concert band, dance, drama/theater, jazz band, literary magazine, music ensembles, musical theater, opera, pep band, radio station, student government, student newspaper, student-run film society, symphony orchestra, campus ministries, international student organization, Model UN. **Organizations:** 200 registered organizations, 10 honor societies, 14 religious organizations. 4 fraternities, 4 sororities. **Athletics (Intercollegiate):** *Men:* Basketball, cross-country, football, tennis, track/field (outdoor), track/field (indoor). *Women:* Basketball, cross-country, golf, soccer, softball, tennis, track/field (outdoor), track/field (indoor), volleyball. **On-Campus Highlights:** Park Blocks, Student Union Center. **Environmental Initiatives:** Since 2002 PSU has focused on designing new buildings and retrofitting and renovating older campus buildings with sustainability in mind. Several PSU buildings serve as models of these kinds of innovative sustainable design and construction projects. These include the new Engineering Building, Broadway Housing Building, Stephen Epler Hall, and Native American Student and Community Center. In all but the latter, the US Green Building Council's LEED certification program was used as the measuring stick and standard for sustainable design and construction. The Center for Sustainable Processes and Practices collaborates with public and private partners to study eco-roof efficiency. Graduate Sustainability Certificate—This graduate certificate (in process of approval) offers an integrated series of post-baccalaureate courses that comprise a multidisciplinary study of the environmental, social, and economic dimensions of sustainability.

ADMISSIONS

Freshman Academic Profile: Average high school GPA 3.25. SAT Math middle 50% range 460–570. SAT Critical Reading middle 50% range 460–590. SAT Writing middle 50% range 440–560. ACT middle 50% range 18–24. Minimum paper TOEFL 525. Minimum computer TOEFL 197. Minimum web-based TOEFL 71. **Basis for Candidate Selection:** *Very important factors considered include:* Academic GPA, rigor of secondary school record. *Other factors considered include:* Standardized test scores. **Freshman Admission Requirements:** High school diploma is required and GED is accepted. *Academic units required:* 4 English, 3 mathematics, 2 science, 2 foreign language, 2 social studies, 1 history. *Academic units recommended:* (1 science labs). **Freshman Admission Statistics:** 3,757 applied, 90% admitted, 52% enrolled. **Transfer Admission Requirements:** College transcript(s), minimum college GPA of 2.25 required. Lowest grade transferable D-. **General Admission Information:** Application fee $50. Notification on a rolling basis, beginning on or about 1/1. Nonfall registration accepted. Admission may be deferred for a maximum of 1 year. Credit and/or placement offered for CEEB Advanced Placement tests.

COSTS AND FINANCIAL AID

Annual in-state tuition $5,321. Annual out-of-state tuition $19,755. Room and board $9,774. Required fees $1,443. Average book expense $1,911. **Required Forms and Deadlines:** FAFSA. Priority financial aid filing date 2/28. **Types of Aid:** *Need-based scholarships/grants:* Federal Pell, SEOG, state scholarships/grants, private scholarships, the school's own gift aid, United Negro College Fund. *Loans:* Direct Subsidized Stafford, Direct Unsubsidized Stafford, Direct PLUS, FFEL Subsidized Stafford, FFEL Unsubsidized Stafford, FFEL PLUS, Federal Perkins, state loans *Student Employment:* Federal Work-Study Program available. Institutional employment available. Off-campus job opportunities are excellent. **Financial Aid Statistics:** 36% freshmen, 41% undergrads receive need-based scholarship or grant aid. 9% freshmen, 4% undergrads receive non-need-based scholarship or grant aid. 46% freshmen, 50% undergrads receive need-based self-help aid. 4% freshmen, 2% undergrads receive athletic scholarships. 69% freshmen, 61% undergrads receive any aid. 58% undergrads borrow to pay for school. Average cumulative indebtedness $19,512. **Criteria for awarding institutional aid:** *Non-need-based:* Academics, art, athletics, music/drama, state/district residency.

POST UNIVERSITY

PO Box 2540, Waterbury, CT 06723
Phone: 203-596-4520 **Financial Aid Phone:** 204-596-4526
E-mail: admissions@post.edu **CEEB Code:** 3698
Fax: 203-756-5810 **Website:** www.post.edu **ACT Code:** 580

This proprietary school was founded in 1890. It has a 58-acre campus.

RATINGS
Admissions Selectivity Rating: 60*   **Fire Safety Rating:** 60*   **Green Rating:** 69

STUDENTS AND FACULTY
Enrollment: 1,055. **Student Body:** 61% female, 39% male, 13% out-of-state, 1% international (15 countries represented). Asian 1%, African American 15%, Caucasian 33%, Hispanic 7%.
Retention and Graduation: 25% grads go on to further study within 1 year. 20% grads pursue arts and sciences degrees. 5% grads pursue law degrees. 25% grads pursue business degrees.

ACADEMICS
Degrees: Associate, bachelor's, certificate, master's, post-bachelor's certificate, terminal associate, transfer associate. **Majors with Highest Enrollment:** Accounting; business/commerce; criminal justice/law enforcement administration. **Special Study Options:** Accelerated program, cooperative education program, cross-registration, distance learning, double major, honors program, independent study, internships, liberal arts/career combination, study abroad, weekend college. Special programs offered to physically disabled students include tape recorders, tutors. **Career services:** Alumni services, career/job search classes, career assessment, internships.

FACILITIES
Housing: Coed dorms, apartments for single students, Inquire about learning communities. 75% of campus accessible to physically disabled. **Computers:** Students can register for classes online. Administrative functions (other than registration) can be performed online.

CAMPUS LIFE
Environment: City. **Activities:** Choral groups, drama/theater, literary magazine, musical theater, student government, student newspaper. **Organizations:**

---

30 registered organizations, **Athletics (Intercollegiate):** *Men:* Baseball, basketball, cross-country, equestrian sports, golf, soccer, tennis. *Women:* Basketball, cross-country, equestrian sports, soccer, softball, tennis, volleyball. **On-Campus Highlights:** University Hall, Leever Student Center, Drubner Athletic Center.

ADMISSIONS
Freshman Academic Profile: Average high school GPA 2.7. 90% from public high schools. Minimum paper TOEFL 500. Minimum computer TOEFL 170. **Basis for Candidate Selection:** *Very important factors considered include:* Academic GPA, interview, level of applicant's interest. *Important factors considered include:* Standardized test scores, character/personal qualities, extracurricular activities, talent/ability, volunteer work. *Other factors considered include:* Application essay, recommendation(s), alumni/ae relation, first generation. **Freshman Admission Requirements:** High school diploma is required and GED is accepted. *Academic units required:* 4 English, 2 mathematics, 2 science, (1 science labs), 2 foreign language, 1 social studies, 2 history, 2 academic electives. *Academic units recommended:* 4 English, 2 mathematics, 2 science, (1 science labs), 2 foreign language, 1 social studies, 2 history, 2 academic electives. **Freshman Admission Statistics: Transfer Admission Requirements:** College transcript(s), minimum college GPA of 2.0 required. Lowest grade transferable C–. **General Admission Information:** Application fee $40. Nonfall registration accepted. Admission may be deferred for a maximum of 1 year. Credit and/or placement offered for CEEB Advanced Placement tests.

COSTS AND FINANCIAL AID
Annual tuition $22,500. Room and board $9,000. Average book expense $1,000. **Required Forms and Deadlines:** FAFSA, institution's own financial aid form. Priority financial aid filing date 2/15. **Types of Aid:** *Need-based scholarships/grants:* Federal Pell, SEOG, state scholarships/grants, private scholarships, the school's own gift aid. *Loans:* FFEL Subsidized Stafford, FFEL Unsubsidized Stafford, FFEL PLUS, Federal Perkins, state loans, college/university loans from institutional funds. *Student Employment:* Federal Work-Study Program available. Highest amount earned per year from on-campus jobs $2,100. **Financial Aid Statistics:** 80% freshmen, 75% undergrads receive any aid. **Criteria for awarding institutional aid:** *Non-need-based:* Academics, alumni affiliation, athletics, job skills, leadership, minority status, state/district residency.

PRAIRIE VIEW A&M UNIVERSITY

PO Box 519, MS# 1009, Prairie View, TX 77446
Phone: 936-261-3500 **Financial Aid Phone:** 1-877-782-6830
E-mail: admissions@pvamu.edu **CEEB Code:** 6580
Fax: Website: www.pvamu.edu **ACT Code:** 4202

This public school was founded in 1876. It has a 1388-acre campus.

RATINGS
Admissions Selectivity Rating: 75   **Fire Safety Rating:** 60*   **Green Rating:** 60*

STUDENTS AND FACULTY
Enrollment: 6,712. **Student Body:** 58% female, 42% male, 8% out-of-state, 1% international (40 countries represented). Asian 2%, African American 88%, Caucasian 3%, Hispanic 4%.
Retention and Graduation: 8% freshmen graduate within 4 years. **Faculty:** 352 full-time faculty, 78% are are members of minority groups, 40% are women.

ACADEMICS
Degrees: Bachelor's, doctoral, master's. **Majors with Highest Enrollment:** Business administration and management; multi-/interdisciplinary studies, other; nursing/registered nurse (RN, ASN, BSN, MSN). **Special Study Options:** Accelerated program, cooperative education program, distance learning, double major, dual enrollment, English as a Second Language (ESL), honors program, independent study, internships, liberal arts/career combination, study abroad, teacher certification program, weekend college. Special programs offered to physically disabled students include tape recorders, tutors. **Career services:** Alumni network, alumni services, career assessment, internships, regional alumni.

FACILITIES
Housing: Coed dorms, special housing for disabled students, apartments for single students 90% of campus accessible to physically disabled. **Computers:** 100% of classrooms, 100% of dorms, 100% of libraries, 75% of dining areas, 75% of student union, 50% of common outdoor areas have wireless network access. Students can register for classes online.

CAMPUS LIFE
Environment: Rural. **Activities:** Choral groups, concert band, dance, drama/theater, jazz band, marching band, music ensembles, radio station, student gov-

ernment, student newspaper, symphony orchestra, television station, yearbook, campus ministries, international student organization. **Organizations:** 100 registered organizations, 15 honor societies, 6 religious organizations. 9 fraternities, 9 sororities. **Athletics (Intercollegiate):** *Men:* Baseball, basketball, cross-country, football, golf, tennis, track/field (outdoor), track/field (indoor). *Women:* Basketball, cheerleading, cross-country, golf, soccer, softball, tennis, track/field (outdoor), track/field (indoor), volleyball. **On-Campus Highlights:** Purple Zone Student Sports Bar, Memorial Student Center, Baby Dome, J.B. Coleman Library, Jazzman Coffee Cafe, University College and University Village.

ADMISSIONS

Freshman Academic Profile: Average high school GPA 2.91. 6% in top 10% of high school class, 23% in top 25% of high school class, 60% in top 50% of high school class. SAT Math middle 50% range 380–480. SAT Critical Reading middle 50% range 370–460. SAT Writing middle 50% range 360–450. ACT middle 50% range 15–19. Minimum paper TOEFL 500. **Basis for Candidate Selection:** *Very important factors considered include:* Class rank, academic GPA, rigor of secondary school record, standardized test scores. *Other factors considered include:* Character/personal qualities, extracurricular activities, first generation, volunteer work, work experience. **Freshman Admission Requirements:** High school diploma is required and GED is accepted. *Academic units recommended:* 4 English, 3 mathematics, 2 science, 1 visual/performing arts, 1 computer science, 1 academic electives. **Freshman Admission Statistics:** 3,606 applied, 86% admitted, 51% enrolled. **Transfer Admission Requirements:** College transcript(s), statement of good standing from prior institution(s). Minimum college GPA of 2.0 required. Lowest grade transferable C. **General Admission Information:** Application fee $25. Regular application deadline 7/1. Nonfall registration accepted. Admission may be deferred for a maximum of 1. Credit and/or placement offered for CEEB Advanced Placement tests.

COSTS AND FINANCIAL AID

Annual in-state tuition $4,884. Annual out-of-state tuition $13,294. Room and board $6,738. Required fees $1,780. Average book expense $1,000. **Required Forms and Deadlines:** FAFSA, institution's own financial aid form. Financial aid filing deadline 3/1. Priority financial aid filing date 3/1. **Notification of Awards:** Applicants will be notified of awards on or about 6/1. **Types of Aid:** *Need-based scholarships/grants:* Federal Pell, SEOG, state scholarships/grants, the school's own gift aid, United Negro College Fund *Loans:* Direct Subsidized Stafford, Direct Unsubsidized Stafford, Direct PLUS, FFEL Subsidized Stafford, FFEL Unsubsidized Stafford, FFEL PLUS, Federal Perkins, college/university loans from institutional funds. **Criteria for awarding institutional aid:** *Non-need-based:* Academics, athletics.

PRATT INSTITUTE

200 Willoughby Avenue, Brooklyn, NY 11205
Phone: 718-636-3514 **Financial Aid Phone:** 718-636-3599
E-mail: visit@pratt.edu **CEEB Code:** 2669
Fax: 718-636-3670 **Website:** www.pratt.edu **ACT Code:** 2862

This private school was founded in 1887. It has a 25-acre campus.

RATINGS
Admissions Selectivity Rating: 88   **Fire Safety Rating:** 60*   **Green Rating:** 88

STUDENTS AND FACULTY

Enrollment: 2,973. **Student Body:** 62% female, 38% male, 63% out-of-state, 13% international (56 countries represented). Asian 15%, African American 5%, Caucasian 54%, Hispanic 9%.
Retention and Graduation: 83% freshmen return for sophomore year. 40% freshmen graduate within 4 years. **Faculty:** Student/faculty ratio 10.7:1. 120 full-time faculty, 68% hold PhDs, 13% are are members of minority groups, 38% are women.

ACADEMICS

Degrees: Associate, bachelor's, master's, post-master's certificate, terminal associate, transfer associate. **Classes:** Most classes have 10–19 students. **Majors with Highest Enrollment:** Design and visual communications; fashion/apparel design. **Special Study Options:** English as a Second Language (ESL), exchange student program (domestic), independent study, internships, study abroad, teacher certification program. **Combined degree programs:** BA/MA, art history. Special programs offered to physically disabled students include note-taking services, reader services, tutors. **Career services:** Alumni network, alumni services, career/job search classes, career assessment, internships. **Career services highlights include:** As part of the intership program, students can become involved with community matters, contributing their design skills to a community program.

FACILITIES

Housing: Coed dorms, special housing for disabled students, special housing for international students, apartments for single students, wellness houseGlobal Learning (for international and domestic students), Healthy Choice and Quiet Floors are available. **Special Academic Facilities/Equipment:** Five art galleries, fine arts center, printmaking center, computer graphics lab. **Computers:** Undergraduates are required to own a computer.

CAMPUS LIFE

Environment: Metropolis. **Activities:** literary magazine, music ensembles, radio station, student government, student newspaper, student-run film society, television station, yearbook, campus ministries, international student organization. **Organizations:** 50 registered organizations, 4 honor societies, 3 religious organizations. 3 fraternities, 1 sorority. **Athletics (Intercollegiate):** *Men:* Basketball, cross-country, soccer, tennis, track/field (outdoor), track/field (indoor). *Women:* Basketball, cross-country, soccer, tennis, track/field (outdoor), volleyball. **On-Campus Highlights:** Studios, galleries, three cafeterias/coffee shops, athletic center, student union, Pratt is the only East Coast art school with a traditional campus (25 acres). **Environmental Initiatives:** Our new building, breaking ground in April 2008 will be LEED Gold. We received a $475K FIPSE grant "Green by Design" to embed sustainable best practices into every program, create interdisciplinary programs that center around environmental projects and create a "living laboratory" that links greening our facilities with greening our academic programs and providing educational programs to our city. We have a new Center for Sustainable Design and Research that centers faculty and students from various programs around environmental projects and research.

ADMISSIONS

Freshman Academic Profile: Average high school GPA 3.5. 70% from public high schools. SAT Math middle 50% range 520–650. SAT Critical Reading middle 50% range 530–640. SAT Writing middle 50% range 530–630. ACT middle 50% range 22–28. Minimum paper TOEFL 550. Minimum computer TOEFL 213. **Basis for Candidate Selection:** *Very important factors considered include:* Academic GPA, rigor of secondary school record, standardized test scores, talent/ability. *Important factors considered include:* Application essay, recommendation(s), alumni/ae relation, character/personal qualities, level of applicant's interest. *Other factors considered include:* Class rank, extracurricular activities, interview, volunteer work, work experience. **Freshman Admission Requirements:** High school diploma is required and GED is accepted. *Academic units recommended:* 4 English, 1 social studies. **Freshman Admission Statistics:** 5,471 applied, 41% admitted, 28% enrolled. **Transfer Admission Requirements:** High school transcript, college transcript(s), essay or personal statement, statement of good standing from prior institution(s). Lowest grade transferable C. **General Admission Information:** Application fee $50. Regular application deadline 1/5. Regular notification 4/1. Nonfall registration not accepted. Admission may be deferred for a maximum of 1 year. Credit and/or placement offered for CEEB Advanced Placement tests.

COSTS AND FINANCIAL AID

Annual tuition $33,500. Room and board $9,756. Required fees $1,380. Average book expense $3,000. **Required Forms and Deadlines:** FAFSA. Priority financial aid filing date 2/1. *Student Employment:* Federal Work-Study Program available. Institutional employment available. Highest amount earned per year from on-campus jobs $2,500. Off-campus job opportunities are excellent. **Financial Aid Statistics:** 53% freshmen, 60% undergrads receive need-based scholarship or grant aid. 37% freshmen, 51% undergrads receive non-need-based scholarship or grant aid. 49% freshmen, 58% undergrads receive need-based self-help aid. 92.12% freshmen, 82.67% undergrads receive any aid. 65% undergrads borrow to pay for school. Average cumulative indebtedness $27,125.

PRESBYTERIAN COLLEGE

503 South Broad Street, Clinton, SC 29325
Phone: 864-833-8230 **Financial Aid Phone:** 864-833-8287
E-mail: admissions@presby.edu **CEEB Code:** 5540
Fax: 864-833-8195 **Website:** www.presby.edu **ACT Code:** 3874

This private school, affiliated with the Presbyterian Church,, affiliated with the Presbyterian USA Church, was founded in 1880. It has a 240-acre campus.

RATINGS
Admissions Selectivity Rating: 86   **Fire Safety Rating:** 89   **Green Rating:** 74

STUDENTS AND FACULTY

Enrollment: 1,200. **Student Body:** 51% female, 49% male, 36% out-of-state, international (8 countries represented). Asian 1%, African American 8%, Caucasian 87%, Hispanic 1%.

Retention and Graduation: 85% freshmen return for sophomore year. 63% freshmen graduate within 4 years. 31% grads go on to further study within 1 year. Faculty: Student/faculty ratio 11:1. 87 full-time faculty, 92% hold PhDs, 6% are are members of minority groups, 31% are women.

ACADEMICS

Degrees: Bachelor's. Classes: Most classes have 20–29 students. Most lab/discussion sessions have 20–29 students. Majors with Highest Enrollment: Business administration and management; political science and government; psychology. Special Study Options: double major, dual enrollment, exchange student program (domestic), honors program, independent study, internships, study abroad, teacher certification program, program in forestry and environmental science, 3-2 engineering program. Honors programs: A variety of opportunities are available to highly motivated students with above average abilities through the normal programs of the College. These include research, internships, special projects, and directed studies. Presbyterian College also offers a special honors program for students who are chosen on the basis of their demonstrated ability. Students with a 3.20 GPA in all courses and a 3.40 GPA in all courses in the major field may, with the approval of departmental faculty, undertake an honors research program during the junior and/or senior years. Oral and written presentations of the results of the project will be required. Students who successfully complete the departmental honors research program will graduate with honors in the major field. Special programs offered to physically disabled students include tutors. Career services: Alumni network, alumni services, career/job search classes, career assessment, internships, regional alumni. Career services highlights include: Internship Program: Students of all disciplines are coordinated to participate in on-campus seminar sessions at the beginning, middle, and end of the semester to reflect/review, compare/contrast their internship experience as a group.

FACILITIES

Housing: Coed dorms, men's dorms, special housing for international students, women's dorms, fraternity/sorority housing, apartments for single studentsSorority housing is not available. 95% of campus accessible to physically disabled. Special Academic Facilities/Equipment: Art gallery, recital hall, media center, marine/ecological center, scanning and transmission electron microscopes, visible spectrophotometer. Computers: 95% of classrooms, 100% of dorms, 100% of libraries, 100% of dining areas, 100% of student union, 50% of common outdoor areas have wireless network access. Students can register for classes online. Administrative functions (other than registration) can be performed online.

CAMPUS LIFE

Environment: Village. Activities: Choral groups, concert band, dance, drama/theater, jazz band, literary magazine, music ensembles, musical theater, opera, pep band, radio station, student government, student newspaper, symphony orchestra, yearbook, campus ministries. Organizations: 85 registered organizations, 11 honor societies, 6 religious organizations. 6 fraternities, 3 sororities. Athletics (Intercollegiate): Men: Baseball, basketball, cheerleading, cross-country, football, golf, lacrosse, soccer, tennis. Women: Basketball, cheerleading, cross-country, golf, lacrosse, soccer, softball, tennis, volleyball. On-Campus Highlights: Inklings Coffee House, Bailey Stadium, Springs Campus Center, Harrington Peachtree Academic Building, Thompson Library, Inklings—hot spot for open mics and up and coming bands Springs Campus Center—workout facilities, Starbucks, WPCX, ping pong Harrington Peachtree Academic Building—commonly known as H-P it is an ideal study and gathering spot in the late night hours Thompson Library—with the new expansion and renovations to the existing facilities, the library has seen a Renaissance—comfy chairs and cozy corners offer students a relaxing atmosphere for studying and researching. Environmental Initiatives: Energy conservation; use of alternative fuels; Recyling Center.

ADMISSIONS

Freshman Academic Profile: Average high school GPA 3.43. 35% in top 10% of high school class, 69% in top 25% of high school class, 92% in top 50% of high school class. SAT Math middle 50% range 510–630. SAT Critical Reading middle 50% range 490–620. ACT middle 50% range 21–27. Minimum paper TOEFL 550. Minimum computer TOEFL 200. Minimum web-based TOEFL 93. Basis for Candidate Selection: Very important factors considered include: Class rank, application essay, academic GPA, rigor of secondary school record, standardized test scores. Important factors considered include: Recommendation(s), character/personal qualities, extracurricular activities. Other factors considered include: Alumni/ae relation, first generation, interview, level of applicant's interest, talent/ability, volunteer work, work experience. Freshman Admission Requirements: High school diploma is required and GED is accepted. Academic units required: 4 English, 4 mathematics, 2 science, (2 science labs), 2 foreign language, 2 social studies, 2 history, 2 academic electives. Academic units recommended: 4 science, 3 foreign language. Freshman Admission Statistics: 1,455 applied, 70% admitted, 36% enrolled. Transfer Admission Requirements: High school transcript, college transcript(s), essay or personal statement, standardized test scores, statement of good stand-

ing from prior institution(s). Lowest grade transferable C. General Admission Information: Application fee $40. Early decision application deadline 11/1. Regular application deadline 6/30. Regular notification 3/15. Nonfall registration accepted. Admission may be deferred for a maximum of 1 Year. Credit and/or placement offered for CEEB Advanced Placement tests.

COSTS AND FINANCIAL AID

Required Forms and Deadlines: FAFSA. Financial aid filing deadline 6/30. Priority financial aid filing date 3/15. Notification of Awards: Applicants will be notified of awards on a rolling basis beginning 3/1. Types of Aid: Need-based scholarships/grants: Federal Pell, SEOG, state scholarships/grants, private scholarships, the school's own gift aid. Loans: FFEL Subsidized Stafford, FFEL Unsubsidized Stafford, FFEL PLUS, state loans, college/university loans from institutional funds, private loans. Student Employment: Federal Work-Study Program available. Institutional employment available. Highest amount earned per year from on-campus jobs $1,800. Off-campus job opportunities are fair. Financial Aid Statistics: 73% freshmen, 68% undergrads receive need-based scholarship or grant aid. 53% freshmen, 53% undergrads receive non-need-based scholarship or grant aid. 31% freshmen, 32% undergrads receive need-based self-help aid. 11% freshmen, 13% undergrads receive athletic scholarships. 99% freshmen, 98% undergrads receive any aid. 56% undergrads borrow to pay for school. Average cumulative indebtedness $23,391. Criteria for awarding institutional aid: Non-need-based: Academics, alumni affiliation, art, athletics, job skills, leadership, minority status, music/drama, religious affiliation, state/district residency.

PRESCOTT COLLEGE

220 Grove Avenue, Attn: Admissions, Prescott, AZ 86301
Phone: 928-350-2100 **Financial Aid Phone:** 928-350-1112
E-mail: admissions@prescott.edu **CEEB Code:** 9295
Fax: 928-776-5242 **Website:** www.prescott.edu **ACT Code:** 5022

This private school was founded in 1966. It has a 6-acre campus.

RATINGS

Admissions Selectivity Rating: 75   Fire Safety Rating: 65   Green Rating: 95

STUDENTS AND FACULTY

Enrollment: 763. Student Body: 58% female, 42% male, 66% out-of-state, 1% international (6 countries represented). Asian 1%, African American 2%, Caucasian 83%, Hispanic 7%, Native American 2%.
Retention and Graduation: 67% freshmen return for sophomore year. 10% freshmen graduate within 4 years. Faculty: Student/faculty ratio 8:1. 69 full-time faculty, 75% hold PhDs, 9% are are members of minority groups, 49% are women.

ACADEMICS

Degrees: Bachelor's, master's, post-bachelor's certificate, post-master's certificate. Classes: Most classes have 10–19 students. Majors with Highest Enrollment: Education, other; elementary education and teaching; environmental studies. Special Study Options: Cross-registration, double major, exchange student program (domestic), external degree program, independent study, internships, liberal arts/career combination, student-designed major, teacher certification program, Dual Credit. Special programs offered to physically disabled students include note-taking services, tape recorders, tutors. Career services: Alumni network, alumni services, career/job search classes, career assessment, regional alumni. Career services highlights include: One on one career development counseling.

FACILITIES

Housing: Coed dorms. 90% of campus accessible to physically disabled. Special Academic Facilities/Equipment: Wolfberry Farm: An experimental agroecology farm Kino Bay Center, MX: A field station on the Gulf of CA. Sam Hill Warehouse: Our visual arts center GIS Lab (Geographic Information Systems) Several Computer Labs Multi-Media Center Computers: 50% of classrooms, 100% of dorms, 100% of libraries, 100% of dining areas, 75% of common outdoor areas have wireless network access.

CAMPUS LIFE

Environment: Town. Activities: dance, drama/theater, literary magazine, radio station, student government, student newspaper, student-run film society, international student organization. Organizations: 18 registered organizations.

On-Campus Highlights: Crossroads Cafe, Crossroads Library, HUB (Helping Understand Bikes), Sam Hill Visual Arts Building. **Environmental Initiatives:** Curriculum; Environmental awareness is an integral part of our curriculum, with social and environmental literacy as college-wide learning outcomes. Local food initiatives (campus Community Supported Agriculture, college farm and gardens) Progress towards climate neutrality; our non-resident programs have made substantial reductions in their carbon footprint over the last two years: the Adult Degree Program has reduced the carbon footprint for required student travel by approximatley 50%, and the Master of Arts Program has reduced its student travel footprint by about 25%. We are currently undertaking a college-wide energy audit which will result in a five year plan for reducing on-campus greenhouse gas emissions 30–50%.

ADMISSIONS

Freshman Academic Profile: Average high school GPA 3.09. 11% in top 10% of high school class, 32% in top 25% of high school class, 57% in top 50% of high school class. 78% from public high schools. SAT Math middle 50% range 470–580. SAT Critical Reading middle 50% range 530–650. SAT Writing middle 50% range 480–620. ACT middle 50% range 19–26. Minimum paper TOEFL 550. Minimum computer TOEFL 213. Minimum web-based TOEFL 61. **Basis for Candidate Selection:** *Very important factors considered include:* Application essay, recommendation(s), rigor of secondary school record. *Important factors considered include:* Academic GPA, standardized test scores, character/personal qualities, extracurricular activities, interview, level of applicant's interest, talent/ability, volunteer work, work experience. *Other factors considered include:* first generation. **Freshman Admission Requirements:** High school diploma is required and GED is accepted. *Academic units recommended:* 4 English, 3 mathematics, 2 science, 1 foreign language, 3 social studies, 2 history, 1 visual/performing arts. **Freshman Admission Statistics:** 342 applied, 81% admitted, 26% enrolled. **Transfer Admission Requirements:** College transcript(s), essay or personal statement, Lowest grade transferable C. **General Admission Information:** Application fee $25. Early decision application deadline 12/1. Regular application deadline 8/15. Notification on a rolling basis, beginning on or about 1/1. Nonfall registration accepted. Admission may be deferred for a maximum of 2 terms. Credit offered for CEEB Advanced Placement tests.

COSTS AND FINANCIAL AID

Average book expense $624. **Required Forms and Deadlines:** FAFSA. Priority financial aid filing date 3/1. **Notification of Awards:** Applicants will be notified of awards on a rolling basis beginning 3/15. **Types of Aid:** *Need-based scholarships/grants:* Federal Pell, SEOG, state scholarships/grants, private scholarships, the school's own gift aid, ACT & SMART. *Loans:* FFEL Subsidized Stafford, FFEL Unsubsidized Stafford, FFEL PLUS. *Student Employment:* Federal Work-Study Program available. Institutional employment available. Highest amount earned per year from on-campus jobs $2,744. Off-campus job opportunities are good. **Financial Aid Statistics:** 63% freshmen, 57% undergrads receive need-based scholarship or grant aid. 3% freshmen, 2% undergrads receive non-need-based scholarship or grant aid. 62% freshmen, 61% undergrads receive need-based self-help aid. 91% freshmen, 88% undergrads receive any aid. 67% undergrads borrow to pay for school. Average cumulative indebtedness $14,947. **Criteria for awarding institutional aid:** *Non-need-based:* Academics, alumni affiliation, minority status, state/district residency.

PRINCETON UNIVERSITY

PO Box 430, Admission Office, Princeton, NJ 08544-0430
Phone: 609-258-3060 **Financial Aid Phone:** 609-258-3330
E-mail: CEEB Code: 2672
Fax: 609-258-6743 **Website:** www.princeton.edu **ACT Code:** 2588

This private school was founded in 1746. It has a 500-acre campus.

RATINGS
Admissions Selectivity Rating: 99   **Fire Safety Rating:** 99   **Green Rating:** 97

STUDENTS AND FACULTY
Enrollment: 5,029. **Student Body:** 49% female, 51% male, 81% out-of-state, 10% international (115 countries represented). Asian 16%, African American 8%, Caucasian 49%, Hispanic 8%.
Retention and Graduation: 98% freshmen return for sophomore year. 90% freshmen graduate within 4 years. **Faculty:** Student/faculty ratio 6:1. 846 full-

time faculty, 93% hold PhDs, 17% are are members of minority groups, 28% are women.

ACADEMICS
Degrees: Bachelor's, master's. **Classes:** Most classes have 10–19 students. Most lab/discussion sessions have 10–19 students. **Majors with Highest Enrollment:** Economics; history; political science and government. **Special Study Options:** Cross-registration, exchange student program (domestic), independent study, student-designed major, study abroad, teacher certification program Special programs offered to physically disabled students include note-taking services, reader services, tape recorders. **Career services:** Alumni network, alumni services, career/job search classes, career assessment, internships, regional alumni.

FACILITIES
Housing: Coed dorms, special housing for disabled students, apartments for married students, **Special Academic Facilities/Equipment:** Art museum, natural history museum, energy and environmental studies center, plasma physics lab, Center for Jewish Life, Center for Human Values, Woodrow WIlson School of Public and International Affairs, etc. **Computers:** 100% of classrooms, 100% of dorms, 70% of libraries, 100% of dining areas, 100% of student union, 20% of common outdoor areas have wireless network access. Students can register for classes online. Administrative functions (other than registration) can be performed online.

CAMPUS LIFE
Environment: Town. **Activities:** Choral groups, concert band, dance, drama/theater, jazz band, literary magazine, marching band, music ensembles, musical theater, opera, pep band, radio station, student government, student newspaper, student-run film society, symphony orchestra, yearbook, campus ministries, international student organization, Model UN. **Organizations:** 250 registered organizations, 30 honor societies, 28 religious organizations. **Athletics (Intercollegiate):** *Men:* Baseball, basketball, crew/rowing, cross-country, diving, fencing, football, golf, ice hockey, lacrosse, light weight football, soccer, squash, swimming, tennis, track/field (outdoor), track/field (indoor), volleyball, water polo, wrestling. *Women:* Basketball, crew/rowing, cross-country, diving, fencing, field hockey, golf, ice hockey, lacrosse, soccer, softball, squash, swimming, tennis, track/field (outdoor), track/field (indoor), volleyball, water polo. **On-Campus Highlights:** Nassau Hall, Firestone Library, McCarter Theater, Princeton U. Art Museum, University Chapel, Frist Campus Center. **Environmental Initiatives:** Greenhouse Gas reduction goal: 1990 levels by 2020 through local verifiable action, while adding more than 1 million gross square feet of built area, and without the purchase of offsets. Sustainable Building Guidelines: requiring all new buildings and major renovations to be 50% more energy efficient than code requires, 95% demolition and construction debris recycling, and use of sustainable materials. Implementation of transportation demand management program to reduce by 10% the number of cars coming to campus by 2020.

ADMISSIONS
Freshman Academic Profile: Average high school GPA 3.88. 95% in top 10% of high school class, 100% in top 25% of high school class, 100% in top 50% of high school class. 56.2% from public high schools. SAT Math middle 50% range 700–790. SAT Critical Reading middle 50% range 690–790. SAT Writing middle 50% range 700–780. ACT middle 50% range 31–35. Minimum paper TOEFL 600. Minimum computer TOEFL 250. **Basis for Candidate Selection:** *Very important factors considered include:* Class rank, application essay, academic GPA, recommendation(s), rigor of secondary school record, standardized test scores, character/personal qualities, talent/ability. *Important factors considered include:* extracurricular activities. *Other factors considered include:* Alumni/ae relation, first generation, geographical residence, interview, racial/ethnic status, volunteer work, work experience. **Freshman Admission Requirements:** High school diploma or equivalent is not required. *Academic units recommended:* 4 English, 4 mathematics, 4 science, (2 science labs), 4 foreign language, 2 social studies, 2 history, 1 visual/performing arts. **Freshman Admission Statistics:** 21,963 applied, 10% admitted, 60% enrolled. **General Admission Information:** Application fee $65. Regular application deadline 1/1. Regular notification 3/31. Nonfall registration not accepted. Admission may be deferred for a maximum of 1 year. Credit and/or placement offered for CEEB Advanced Placement tests.

COSTS AND FINANCIAL AID
Annual tuition $36,640. Room and board $11,940. Average book expense $1,200. **Required Forms and Deadlines:** FAFSA, institution's own financial aid form. Priority financial aid filing date 2/1. **Notification of Awards:** Applicants will be notified of awards on or about 4/1. **Types of Aid:** *Need-based scholarships/grants:* Federal Pell, SEOG, state scholarships/grants, private scholarships, the school's own gift aid. *Loans:* FFEL Subsidized Stafford, FFEL Unsubsidized Stafford, FFEL PLUS, Federal Perkins, college/university loans from institutional funds. *Student Employment:* Federal Work-Study Program available. Institutional employment available. Highest amount earned per year

from on-campus jobs $3,500. Off-campus job opportunities are good. **Financial Aid Statistics:** 56% freshmen, 56% undergrads receive need-based scholarship or grant aid. 56% freshmen, 56% undergrads receive need-based self-help aid. 59% freshmen, 58% undergrads receive any aid. 21% undergrads borrow to pay for school. Average cumulative indebtedness $4,957.

See page 1200.

PRINCIPIA COLLEGE

1 Maybeck Place, Elsah, IL 62028
Phone: 618-374-5181 **Financial Aid Phone:** 800-277-4648
E-mail: collegeadmissions@prin.edu **CEEB Code:** 1630
Fax: 618-374-4000 **Website:** www.prin.edu **ACT Code:** 1118

This private school, affiliated with the Christian Science Church, was founded in 1898. It has a 2600-acre campus.

RATINGS
Admissions Selectivity Rating: 85   **Fire Safety Rating:** 64   **Green Rating:** 60*

STUDENTS AND FACULTY
Enrollment: 542. **Student Body:** 52% female, 48% male, 88% out-of-state, 13% international (28 countries represented). Asian 1%, African American 1%, Caucasian 81%, Hispanic 1%.
Retention and Graduation: 79% freshmen return for sophomore year. 73% freshmen graduate within 4 years. 27% grads go on to further study within 1 year. 15% grads pursue arts and sciences degrees. 3% grads pursue law degrees. 6% grads pursue business degrees. **Faculty:** Student/faculty ratio 8:1. 55 full-time faculty, 45% hold PhDs, 2% are are members of minority groups, 42% are women.

ACADEMICS
Degrees: Bachelor's. **Classes:** Most classes have 10–19 students. **Majors with Highest Enrollment:** Business/commerce; fine/studio arts; mass communication/media studies. **Special Study Options:** Double major, independent study, internships, liberal arts/career combination, student-designed major, study abroad, teacher certification program, 3-2 Engineering with Washington University (St. Louis, MO), USC (Los Angeles), and Southern Illinois University (SIU) in Edwardsville, IL. **Honors programs:** One honors program of three courses is taught in conjunction with our First Year Experience Program (FYE). **Career services:** Alumni network, career/job search classes, career assessment, internships, regional alumni. **Career services highlights include:** Internship in San Fransisco as part of a school-sponsored program for students interested in practical internships in companies and businesses in the Bay Area.

FACILITIES
Housing: Men's dorms, women's dorms, apartments for married students. Houses with single-sex wings (one side for men and one side for women) and a common living room. This is not really considered "coed" because there are no shared bathrooms or men and women living together on the same floor or on alternate floors. Cottages (for 8 people) are available for non-traditionally aged students, special programs, or theme houses. 75% of campus accessible to physically disabled. **Special Academic Facilities/Equipment:** Science Center with indoor aviary, School of Nations Museum and Classrooms, Voney Art Studio, School of Government, Merrick Wing for Performing Arts.

CAMPUS LIFE
Environment: Rural. **Activities:** Choral groups, dance, drama/theater, jazz band, music ensembles, musical theater, radio station, student government, student newspaper, television station, yearbook. **Organizations:** 29 registered organizations, 1 honor societies, 1 religious organizations. **Athletics (Intercollegiate):** *Men:* Baseball, basketball, cross-country, diving, football, soccer, swimming, tennis, track/field (outdoor), track/field (indoor). *Women:* Basketball, cross-country, diving, soccer, swimming, tennis, track/field (outdoor), track/field (indoor), volleyball. **On-Campus Highlights:** Piasa Pub, Hay Field House, Planetarium, Science Center, Chapel, By January, 2007 a new 68,000 square foot athletic training center will be built. This includes two regulation-size basketball courts and 200 meter indoor track. Also part of the facility will be a 6-lane 25-meter natatorium with four diving boards and am adjacent well-appointed fitness center.

ADMISSIONS
Freshman Academic Profile: Average high school GPA 3.41. 38% in top 10% of high school class, 63% in top 25% of high school class, 79% in top 50% of high school class. 61% from public high schools. SAT Math middle 50% range 500–620. SAT Critical Reading middle 50% range 510–650. ACT middle 50% range 21–30. Minimum paper TOEFL 550. Minimum computer TOEFL 213.

Basis for Candidate Selection: *Very important factors considered include:* Application essay, rigor of secondary school record, character/personal qualities, religious affiliation/commitment. *Important factors considered include:* Class rank, recommendation(s), standardized test scores, extracurricular activities, interview, talent/ability. *Other factors considered include:* Alumni/ae relation, racial/ethnic status, volunteer work, work experience. **Freshman Admission Requirements:** High school diploma is required and GED is accepted. *Academic units required:* 4 English, 4 mathematics, 2 science, (2 science labs), 2 foreign language, 2 social studies, 1 history, 1 academic electives. *Academic units recommended:* 4 English, 4 mathematics, 3 science, (2 science labs), 3 foreign language, 2 social studies, 2 history, 2 academic electives. **Freshman Admission Statistics:** 221 applied, 87% admitted, 61% enrolled. **Transfer Admission Requirements:** High school transcript, college transcript(s), essay or personal statement, minimum college GPA of 2.0 required. Lowest grade transferable C–. **General Admission Information:** Regular application deadline 3/1. Notification on a rolling basis, beginning on or about 11/1. Nonfall registration accepted. Admission may be deferred for a maximum of 1 year. Credit and/or placement offered for CEEB Advanced Placement tests.

COSTS AND FINANCIAL AID
Annual tuition $21,150. Room and board $7,896. Required fees $300. Average book expense $900. **Required Forms and Deadlines:** Institution's own financial aid form, CSS/Financial Aid PROFILE. Financial aid filing deadline 3/1. **Notification of Awards:** Applicants will be notified of awards on a rolling basis beginning 3/15. **Types of Aid:** *Need-based scholarships/grants:* private scholarships, the school's own gift aid. *Loans:* college/university loans from institutional funds. *Student Employment:* Highest amount earned per year from on-campus jobs $1,310. **Financial Aid Statistics:** 55% freshmen, 54% undergrads receive need-based scholarship or grant aid. 26% freshmen, 22% undergrads receive non-need-based scholarship or grant aid. 46% freshmen, 45% undergrads receive need-based self-help aid. 87% freshmen, 79% undergrads receive any aid. 54% undergrads borrow to pay for school. Average cumulative indebtedness $12,740. **Criteria for awarding institutional aid:** *Non-need-based:* Academics, alumni affiliation.

PROVIDENCE COLLEGE

Harkins 222, 1 Cunningham Sq, Providence, RI 02918
Phone: 401-865-2535 **Financial Aid Phone:** 401-865-2286
E-mail: pcadmiss@providence.edu **CEEB Code:** 3693
Fax: 401-865-2826 **Website:** www.providence.edu **ACT Code:** 3806

This private school, affiliated with the Roman Catholic Church, was founded in 1917. It has a 105-acre campus.

RATINGS
Admissions Selectivity Rating: 93   **Fire Safety Rating:** 95   **Green Rating:** 74

STUDENTS AND FACULTY
Enrollment: 3,931. **Student Body:** 56% female, 44% male, 87% out-of-state, 1% international (21 countries represented). Asian 3%, African American 2%, Caucasian 81%, Hispanic 3%.
Retention and Graduation: 92% freshmen return for sophomore year. 84% freshmen graduate within 4 years. 26% grads go on to further study within 1 year. 12% grads pursue arts and sciences degrees. 4% grads pursue law degrees. 4% grads pursue business degrees. 2% grads pursue medical degrees. **Faculty:** Student/faculty ratio 12:1. 295 full-time faculty, 92% hold PhDs, 9% are are members of minority groups, 35% are women.

ACADEMICS
Degrees: Associate, bachelor's, certificate, master's, terminal associate. **Classes:** Most classes have 20–29 students. Most lab/discussion sessions have 10–19 students. **Majors with Highest Enrollment:** Biology/biological sciences; business administration and management; marketing/marketing management. **Special Study Options:** Cross-registration, distance learning, double major, dual enrollment, exchange student program (domestic), honors program, independent study, internships, liberal arts/career combination, student-designed major, study abroad, teacher certification program. **Honors programs:** Liberal Arts Honors Program. **Combined degree programs:** Comb-plan Bio/Opt w/ NE College of Optometry. Special programs offered to physically disabled students include note-taking services, reader services, tape recorders, tutors. **Career services:** Alumni network, alumni services, career/job search classes,

career assessment, internships, regional alumni. **Career services highlights include:** Over 20 departments offer academic internships and field experience courses. We also have the Friar Summer Internship Partner Program in which we pair students with high quality summer internships.

FACILITIES

Housing: Coed dorms, special housing for disabled students, men's dorms, women's dorms, wellness house. 98% of campus accessible to physically disabled. **Special Academic Facilities/Equipment:** Hunt-Cavanagh Art Gallery, Blackfriar Theatre, Science Center Complex, Computer and Language Labs, Smith Center for the Arts. **Computers:** 100% of classrooms, 50% of dorms, 100% of libraries, 100% of dining areas, 100% of student union, 20% of common outdoor areas have wireless network access. Students can register for classes online. Administrative functions (other than registration) can be performed online.

CAMPUS LIFE

Environment: City. **Activities:** Choral groups, concert band, dance, drama/theater, jazz band, literary magazine, music ensembles, musical theater, pep band, radio station, student government, student newspaper, television station, yearbook, campus ministries, international student organization. **Organizations:** 112 registered organizations, 18 honor societies, 2 religious organizations. **Athletics (Intercollegiate):** *Men:* Basketball, cross-country, diving, ice hockey, lacrosse, soccer, swimming, track/field (outdoor), track/field (indoor). *Women:* Basketball, cross-country, diving, field hockey, ice hockey, soccer, softball, swimming, tennis, track/field (outdoor), track/field (indoor), volleyball. **On-Campus Highlights:** McPhails—Student Activity Center, Peterson Center—Athletic Facility, Slavin Center—Student Center, Smith Center for the Arts, St. Dominic Chapel, Harkins Hall—Classrooms, Admin Offices; Blackfriars Theatre; Hunt-Cavanagh Art Gallery.

ADMISSIONS

Freshman Academic Profile: Average high school GPA 3.47. 44% in top 10% of high school class, 80% in top 25% of high school class, 98% in top 50% of high school class. 54% from public high schools. SAT Math middle 50% range 540–640. SAT Critical Reading middle 50% range 530–630. SAT Writing middle 50% range 550–650. ACT middle 50% range 23–28. Minimum paper TOEFL 550. Minimum computer TOEFL 215. Minimum web-based TOEFL 80. **Basis for Candidate Selection:** *Very important factors considered include:* Academic GPA, recommendation(s), rigor of secondary school record. *Important factors considered include:* Application essay, character/personal qualities, extracurricular activities. *Other factors considered include:* Class rank, standardized test scores, alumni/ae relation, first generation, geographical residence, level of applicant's interest, racial/ethnic status, state residency, talent/ability, volunteer work, work experience. **Freshman Admission Requirements:** High school diploma is required and GED is not accepted. *Academic units required:* 4 English, 4 mathematics, 3 science, (2 science labs), 3 foreign language, 2 social studies, 2 history. *Academic units recommended:* 4 English, 4 mathematics, 4 science, (2 science labs), 3 foreign language, 2 social studies, 2 history. **Freshman Admission Statistics:** 8,844 applied, 45% admitted, 25% enrolled. **Transfer Admission Requirements:** High school transcript, college transcript(s), essay or personal statement, statement of good standing from prior institution(s). Minimum college GPA of 3.0 required. Lowest grade transferable c. **General Admission Information:** Application fee $55. Regular application deadline 1/15. Regular notification 4/1. Nonfall registration accepted. Admission may be deferred for a maximum of 1 year. Credit and/or placement offered for CEEB Advanced Placement tests.

COSTS AND FINANCIAL AID

Annual tuition $30,800. Room and board $10,810. Required fees $594. Average book expense $800. **Required Forms and Deadlines:** FAFSA, CSS/Financial Aid PROFILE, business/farm supplement. Financial aid filing deadline 2/1. Priority financial aid filing date 2/1. **Notification of Awards:** Applicants will be notified of awards on or about 4/1. **Types of Aid:** *Need-based scholarships/grants:* Federal Pell, SEOG, state scholarships/grants, private scholarships, the school's own gift aid, Federal Academic Competitive Grant/Smart Grant. *Loans:* Direct Subsidized Stafford, Direct Unsubsidized Stafford, Direct PLUS, FFEL Subsidized Stafford, FFEL Unsubsidized Stafford, FFEL PLUS, Federal Perkins. *Student Employment:* Federal Work-Study Program available. Institutional employment available. Highest amount earned per year from on-campus jobs $6,500. Off-campus job opportunities are good. **Financial Aid Statistics:** 44% freshmen, 52% undergrads receive need-based scholarship or grant aid. 6% freshmen, 6% undergrads receive non-need-based scholarship or grant aid. 45% freshmen, 46% undergrads receive need-based self-help aid. 4% freshmen, 3% undergrads receive athletic scholarships. 75% freshmen, 74% undergrads receive any aid. 64% undergrads borrow to pay for school. Average cumulative indebtedness $33,297. **Criteria for awarding institutional aid:** *Non-need-based:* Academics, athletics, minority status.

PURDUE UNIVERSITY—CALUMET

Office of Admissions, 2200 169th Street, Hammond, IN 46323-2094
Phone: 219-989-2213 **Financial Aid Phone:** 219-989-2301
E-mail: adms@calumet.purdue.edu **CEEB Code:** 1638
Fax: 219-989-2775 **Website:** www.calumet.purdue.edu **ACT Code:** 1233

This public school was founded in 1946. It has a 194-acre campus.

RATINGS
Admissions Selectivity Rating: 70   **Fire Safety Rating:** 88   **Green Rating:** 64

STUDENTS AND FACULTY
Enrollment: 8,403. **Student Body:** 55% female, 45% male, 11% out-of-state, 3% international (39 countries represented). Asian 1%, African American 19%, Caucasian 60%, Hispanic 15%.
Retention and Graduation: 69% freshmen return for sophomore year. 6% freshmen graduate within 4 years. **Faculty:** Student/faculty ratio 21:1. 268 full-time faculty, 69% hold PhDs, 21% are are members of minority groups, 48% are women.

ACADEMICS
Degrees: Associate, bachelor's, certificate, master's, post-bachelor's certificate. **Classes:** Most classes have 20–29 students. Most lab/discussion sessions have 20–29 students. **Majors with Highest Enrollment:** Elementary education and teaching; engineering; marketing/marketing management. **Special Study Options:** Accelerated program, cooperative education program, distance learning, double major, dual enrollment, English as a Second Language (ESL), honors program, independent study, internships, study abroad, teacher certification program, weekend college. **Honors programs:** Purdue Calumet Honors Program **Combined degree programs:** 2-2 nursing program. Special programs offered to physically disabled students include note-taking services, reader services, tape recorders, tutors. **Career services:** Career/job search classes, career assessment, internships.

FACILITIES
Housing: Apartments for single students 100% of campus accessible to physically disabled. **Special Academic Facilities/Equipment:** Audio-visual services, urban development institute. **Computers:** Students can register for classes online. Administrative functions (other than registration) can be performed online.

CAMPUS LIFE
Environment: City. **Activities:** Choral groups, dance, drama/theater, radio station, student government, student newspaper, campus ministries, international student organization. **Organizations:** 56 registered organizations, 25 honor societies, 3 religious organizations, 2 fraternities, 3 sororities. **Athletics (Intercollegiate):** *Men:* Basketball. *Women:* Basketball. **On-Campus Highlights:** Physical Education and Recreation Building, Enrollment Services Center, Challenger Learning Center of Northwest Indiana. **Environmental Initiatives:** Campus-wide recycling; WEP Energy Conservation Measures; alternative transportation including usage of electric vehicles.

ADMISSIONS
Freshman Academic Profile: Average high school GPA 2.58. 10% in top 10% of high school class, 28% in top 25% of high school class, 58% in top 50% of high school class. SAT Math middle 50% range 410–520. SAT Critical Reading middle 50% range 410–510. ACT middle 50% range 17–23. Minimum paper TOEFL 550. Minimum computer TOEFL 213. **Basis for Candidate Selection:** *Important factors considered include:* Class rank, academic GPA, rigor of secondary school record, standardized test scores. **Freshman Admission Requirements:** High school diploma is required and GED is accepted. *Academic units required:* 4 English, 2 mathematics, 1 science, (1 science labs), 2 foreign language, 1 social studies, 1 history. *Academic units recommended:* 4 English, 2 mathematics, 2 science, (2 science labs), 2 foreign language, 2 social studies, 1 history. **Freshman Admission Statistics:** 5,884 applied, 69% admitted, 33% enrolled. **Transfer Admission Requirements:** High school transcript, minimum college GPA of 2.0 required. Lowest grade transferable C. **General Admission Information:** Nonfall registration accepted. Admission may be deferred for a maximum of 1 semester. Credit offered for CEEB Advanced Placement tests.

COSTS AND FINANCIAL AID
Room and board $11. Average book expense $1,125. **Required Forms and Deadlines:** FAFSA. Financial aid filing deadline 6/30. Priority financial aid filing date 3/10. **Notification of Awards:** Applicants will be notified of awards on a rolling basis beginning 4/15. **Types of Aid:** *Need-based scholarships/grants:* Federal Pell, SEOG, state scholarships/grants, the school's own gift aid. *Loans:* Direct Subsidized Stafford, Direct Unsubsidized Stafford, Direct PLUS, Federal Perkins. *Student Employment:* Federal Work-Study Program

available. Off-campus job opportunities are fair. **Financial Aid Statistics:** 36% freshmen, 39% undergrads receive need-based scholarship or grant aid. 15% freshmen, 9% undergrads receive non-need-based scholarship or grant aid. 36% freshmen, 43% undergrads receive need-based self-help aid. 1% freshmen, 62% undergrads borrow to pay for school. Average cumulative indebtedness $19,926. **Criteria for awarding institutional aid:** *Non-need-based:* Academics, athletics, minority status, state/district residency.

PURDUE UNIVERSITY—WEST LAFAYETTE

Best 373

1080 Schleman Hall, West Lafayette, IN 47907-2050
Phone: 765-494-1776 **Financial Aid Phone:** 765-494-0998
E-mail: admissions@purdue.edu **CEEB Code:** 1631
Fax: 765-494-0544 **Website:** www.purdue.edu **ACT Code:** 1230

This public school was founded in 1869. It has a 2552-acre campus.

RATINGS
Admissions Selectivity Rating: 87   **Fire Safety Rating:** 85   **Green Rating:** 81

STUDENTS AND FACULTY
Enrollment: 30,932. **Student Body:** 42% female, 58% male, 36% out-of-state, 9% international (125 countries represented). Asian 5%, African American 3%, Caucasian 79%, Hispanic 3%.
Retention and Graduation: 87% freshmen return for sophomore year. **Faculty:** Student/faculty ratio 13.7:1. 2367 full-time faculty, 82% hold PhDs, 17% are are members of minority groups, 30% are women. 33% of classes are taught by teaching assistants.

ACADEMICS
Degrees: Bachelor's, certificate, doctoral, master's, terminal associate. **Classes:** Most classes have 20–29 students. Most lab/discussion sessions have 20–29 students. **Majors with Highest Enrollment:** Biology/biological sciences; family and consumer sciences/human sciences; mechanical engineering. **Special Study Options:** Accelerated program, cooperative education program, cross-registration, distance learning, double major, dual enrollment, exchange student program (domestic), honors program, independent study, internships, liberal arts/career combination, study abroad, teacher certification program, weekend college. **Honors programs:** University Honors Program. Special programs offered to physically disabled students include note-taking services, reader services, tape recorders, tutors. **Career services:** Alumni network, alumni services, career/job search classes, career assessment, internships, regional alumni. **Career services highlights include:** All of the above.

FACILITIES
Housing: Coed dorms, special housing for disabled students, men's dorms, women's dorms, fraternity/sorority housing, apartments for married students, cooperative housing, apartments for single students, wellness house. 90% of campus accessible to physically disabled. **Special Academic Facilities/Equipment:** Hall of music, child development lab, speech and hearing clinic, small animal veterinary clinic, horticulture park, linear accelerator, tornado simulator, nuclear accelerator. **Computers:** 95% of classrooms, 5% of dorms, 95% of libraries, 90% of dining areas, 95% of student union, 5% of common outdoor areas have wireless network access. Students can register for classes online. Administrative functions (other than registration) can be performed online.

CAMPUS LIFE
Environment: Town. **Activities:** Choral groups, concert band, dance, drama/theater, jazz band, literary magazine, marching band, music ensembles, musical theater, opera, pep band, radio station, student government, student newspaper, student-run film society, symphony orchestra, television station, yearbook, campus ministries, international student organization, Model UN. **Organizations:** 850 registered organizations, 25 honor societies, 66 religious organizations. 48 fraternities, 32 sororities. **Athletics (Intercollegiate): Men:** Baseball, basketball, cross-country, diving, football, golf, swimming, tennis, track/field (outdoor), track/field (indoor), wrestling. *Women:* Basketball, cross-country, diving, golf, soccer, softball, swimming, tennis, track/field (outdoor), track/field (indoor), volleyball. **On-Campus Highlights:** Pudue Memorial Union, Recreational Sports Center, Fountain areas, Libraries, Sporting events. **Environmental Initiatives:** Sustainability Strategic Plan; Enhanced Recycling Program (Desk side recycling); Energy efficiency initiatives.

ADMISSIONS
Freshman Academic Profile: Average high school GPA 3.5. 38% in top 10% of high school class, 72% in top 25% of high school class, 95% in top 50% of high school class. SAT Math middle 50% range 540–670. SAT Critical Reading middle 50% range 500–610. SAT Writing middle 50% range 490–600. ACT middle 50% range 23–29. Minimum paper TOEFL 550. Minimum computer TOEFL 213. Minimum web-based TOEFL 79. **Basis for Candidate Selection:** *Very important factors considered include:* Application essay, rigor of secondary school record, standardized test scores. *Important factors considered include:* Class rank, academic GPA. *Other factors considered include:* Recommendation(s), alumni/ae relation, character/personal qualities, extracurricular activities, first generation, state residency, volunteer work, work experience. **Freshman Admission Requirements:** High school diploma is required and GED is accepted. *Academic units required:* 4 English, 3 mathematics, 3 science, (3 science labs), 2 foreign language, 3 social studies. *Academic units recommended:* 4 mathematics. **Freshman Admission Statistics:** 27,213 applied, 73% admitted, 30% enrolled. **Transfer Admission Requirements:** College transcript(s), essay or personal statement, statement of good standing from prior institution(s). Minimum college GPA of 2.5 required. Lowest grade transferable C. **General Admission Information:** Application fee $50. Regular application deadline 3/1. Notification on a rolling basis, beginning on or about 12/5. Nonfall registration accepted. Admission may be deferred for a maximum of 1 year. Credit and/or placement offered for CEEB Advanced Placement tests.

COSTS AND FINANCIAL AID
Annual in-state tuition $9,070. Annual out-of-state tuition $26,622. **Required Forms and Deadlines:** FAFSA. Priority financial aid filing date 3/1. **Notification of Awards:** Applicants will be notified of awards on or about 4/15. **Types of Aid:** *Need-based scholarships/grants:* Federal Pell, SEOG, state scholarships/grants, private scholarships, the school's own gift aid, Federal Academic Competitiveness Grant (ACG) and National SMART Grant Program. *Loans:* Direct Subsidized Stafford, Direct Unsubsidized Stafford, Direct PLUS, Federal Perkins, college/university loans from institutional funds. *Student Employment:* Federal Work-Study Program available. Institutional employment available. Off-campus job opportunities are good. **Financial Aid Statistics:** 32% freshmen, 30% undergrads receive need-based scholarship or grant aid. 18% freshmen, 11% undergrads receive non-need-based scholarship or grant aid. 41% freshmen, 38% undergrads receive need-based self-help aid. 1% freshmen, 1% undergrads receive athletic scholarships. 52.1% undergrads borrow to pay for school. Average cumulative indebtedness $23,087. **Criteria for awarding institutional aid:** *Non-need-based:* Academics, athletics, leadership, music/drama, state/district residency.

QUEEN'S UNIVERSITY

Admission Services, Gordon Hall, 74 Union St, Kingston, ON K7L3N6 Canada
Phone: 613-533-2218
E-mail: admission@queensu.ca **CEEB Code:** 949
Fax: 613-533-6810 **Website:** www.queensu.ca **ACT Code:** 5236

This public school was founded in 1841. It has a 160-acre campus.

RATINGS
Admissions Selectivity Rating: 60*   **Fire Safety Rating:** 60*   **Green Rating:** 60*

STUDENTS AND FACULTY
Enrollment: 14,130. **Student Body:** 59% female, 41% male, 18% out-of-state, international (129 countries represented).
Retention and Graduation: Faculty: Student/faculty ratio 16:1. 1032 full-time faculty, 94% hold PhDs, 39% are women.

ACADEMICS
Degrees: Bachelor's, master's. **Classes:** Most classes have 20–29 students. Most lab/discussion sessions have 20–29 students. **Majors with Highest Enrollment:** Business/commerce; sport and fitness administration/management. **Special Study Options:** Cooperative education program, distance learning, double major, dual enrollment, English as a Second Language (ESL), exchange student program (domestic), honors program, independent study, internships, study abroad, teacher certification program. The university owns and operates an International Study Centre (ISC) at Herstmonceux,East Sussex, England. Special programs offered to physically disabled students include note-taking services, reader services, tape recorders, tutors. **Career services:** Career/job search classes, career assessment, internships.

FACILITIES
Housing: Coed dorms, men's dorms, special housing for international students, women's dorms, apartments for married students, cooperative housing, apartments for single students. **Special Academic Facilities/Equipment:** Agnes

Etherington Art Centre, Miller Museum of Geology. **Computers:** Students can register for classes online. Administrative functions (other than registration) can be performed online.

CAMPUS LIFE

Environment: City. **Activities:** Choral groups, concert band, dance, drama/theater, jazz band, literary magazine, marching band, music ensembles, musical theater, opera, pep band, radio station, student government, student newspaper, student-run film society, symphony orchestra, television station, yearbook. **Organizations:** 18 religious organizations. **Athletics (Intercollegiate):** *Men:* Baseball, basketball, cheerleading, crew/rowing, cross-country, curling, fencing, football, golf, ice hockey, lacrosse, mountain biking, rodeo, rugby, sailing, skiing (nordic/cross-country), soccer, squash, swimming, tennis, track/field (outdoor), ultimate fr. *Women:* Basketball, cheerleading, crew/rowing, cross-country, curling, fencing, field hockey, ice hockey, lacrosse, mountain biking, rodeo, rugby, sailing, skiing (nordic/cross-country), soccer, squash, swimming, synchronized swimming, tennis, track/field (outdoor). **On-Campus Highlights:** Integrated Learning Centre (ILC), Agnes Etherington Art Centre, Stauffer Library, Biosciences Complex, Chernoff Hall.

ADMISSIONS

Freshman Academic Profile: Minimum paper TOEFL 580. Minimum computer TOEFL 237. **Basis for Candidate Selection:** *Very important factors considered include:* Academic GPA, standardized test scores. *Important factors considered include:* Rigor of secondary school record, extracurricular activities, talent/ability, volunteer work. *Other factors considered include:* Class rank, recommendation(s), work experience. **Freshman Admission Requirements:** High school diploma is required and GED is accepted. **Freshman Admission Statistics:** 25,403 applied, 42% admitted, 31% enrolled. **Transfer Admission Requirements:** High school transcript, college transcript(s). **General Admission Information:** Application fee $135. Regular application deadline 2/16. Notification on a rolling basis, beginning on or about 1/2. Nonfall registration not accepted. Admission may be deferred for a maximum of 1 year.

COSTS AND FINANCIAL AID

Required Forms and Deadlines: institution's own financial aid formP. Financial aid filing deadline 1/31. Priority financial aid filing date 7/1. **Types of Aid:** *Need-based scholarships/grants:* Private scholarships, the school's own gift aid. *Loans:* College/university loans from institutional funds. **Financial Aid Statistics:** 30% undergrads borrow to pay for school. **Criteria for awarding institutional aid:** *Non-need-based:* Academics, leadership, music/drama.

QUEENS UNIVERSITY OF CHARLOTTE

1900 Selwyn Avenue, MSC–1428, Charlotte, NC 28274
Phone: 704-337-2212 **Financial Aid Phone:** 704-337-2225
E-mail: admissions@queens.edu **CEEB Code:** 5560
Fax: 704-337-2403 **Website:** www.queens.edu **ACT Code:** 3148

This private school, affiliated with the Presbyterian Church, was founded in 1857. It has a 30-acre campus.

RATINGS
Admissions Selectivity Rating: 79   **Fire Safety Rating:** 60*   **Green Rating:** 60*

STUDENTS AND FACULTY
Enrollment: 1,718. **Student Body:** 77% female, 23% male, % out-of-state, 5% international Asian 2%, African American 17%, Caucasian 64%, Hispanic 5%. **Retention and Graduation:** 69% freshmen return for sophomore year. **Faculty:** Student/faculty ratio 11:1. 103 full-time faculty, 70% hold PhDs, 12% are are members of minority groups, 67% are women.

ACADEMICS
Degrees: Associate, bachelor's, master's, post-bachelor's certificate, terminal associate. **Classes:** Most classes have 10–19 students. Most lab/discussion sessions have 10–19 students. **Majors with Highest Enrollment:** Business/commerce; communication and media studies, other; nursing/registered nurse (RN, ASN, BSN, MSN). **Special Study Options:** Cross-registration, double major, dual enrollment, honors program, independent study, internships, liberal arts/career combination, student-designed major, study abroad, teacher certification program, weekend college. Special programs offered to physically disabled students include note-taking services, reader services, tape recorders, tutors. **Career services:** Alumni network, career/job search classes, internships. **Career services highlights include:** The internship is a required component of the undergraduate degree here at Queens.

FACILITIES
Housing: Coed dorms, special housing for disabled students, apartment style 2 bedroom suites for traditional-aged undergraduates 1/2 mile from campus.

60% of campus accessible to physically disabled. **Special Academic Facilities/Equipment:** Three art galleries, rare books museum.

CAMPUS LIFE

Environment: Metropolis. **Activities:** Choral groups, dance, drama/theater, literary magazine, music ensembles, musical theater, pep band, student government, student newspaper, yearbook, campus ministries, international student organization, Model UN. **Organizations:** 38 registered organizations, 9 honor societies, 2 religious organizations. 2 fraternities, 4 sororities. **Athletics (Intercollegiate):** *Men:* Basketball, cheerleading, cross-country, golf, lacrosse, soccer, tennis, track/field (outdoor). *Women:* Basketball, cheerleading, cross-country, golf, lacrosse, soccer, softball, tennis, track/field (outdoor), volleyball. **On-Campus Highlights:** Fitness Center, The Lion's Den, Trexler Courtyard, Queens' Off-Campus Athletic Facility.

ADMISSIONS

Freshman Academic Profile: Average high school GPA 3.52. 20% in top 10% of high school class, 47% in top 25% of high school class, 82% in top 50% of high school class. 84% from public high schools. SAT Math middle 50% range 480–580. SAT Critical Reading middle 50% range 470–570. SAT Writing middle 50% range 470–570. ACT middle 50% range 20–24. Minimum paper TOEFL 550. Minimum computer TOEFL 213. Minimum web-based TOEFL 80. **Basis for Candidate Selection:** *Very important factors considered include:* Academic GPA, rigor of secondary school record, standardized test scores, character/personal qualities, extracurricular activities. *Important factors considered include:* Class rank, interview, volunteer work. *Other factors considered include:* Application essay, recommendation(s), alumni/ae relation, first generation, talent/ability, work experience. **Freshman Admission Requirements:** High school diploma is required and GED is accepted. *Academic units required:* 4 English, 3 mathematics, 2 science, (1 science labs), 2 foreign language, 2 social studies. **Freshman Admission Statistics:** 1,538 applied, 77% admitted, 26% enrolled. **Transfer Admission Requirements:** High school transcript, college transcript(s), essay or personal statement, statement of good standing from prior institution(s). Minimum college GPA of 2.0 required. Lowest grade transferable C. **General Admission Information:** Application fee $40. Notification on a rolling basis, beginning on or about 10/1. Nonfall registration accepted. Admission may be deferred for a maximum of 1 year. Credit and/or placement offered for CEEB Advanced Placement tests.

COSTS AND FINANCIAL AID

Required Forms and Deadlines: FAFSA, state aid form. Priority financial aid filing date 3/1. **Notification of Awards:** Applicants will be notified of awards on a rolling basis beginning 3/15. **Types of Aid:** *Need-based scholarships/grants:* Federal Pell, SEOG, state scholarships/grants, private scholarships, the school's own gift aid. *Loans:* FFEL Subsidized Stafford, FFEL Unsubsidized Stafford, FFEL PLUS, Federal Perkins, state loans *Student Employment:* Federal Work-Study Program available. Highest amount earned per year from on-campus jobs $1,500. Off-campus job opportunities are excellent. **Financial Aid Statistics:** 72% freshmen, 65% undergrads receive need-based scholarship or grant aid. 21% freshmen, 12% undergrads receive non-need-based scholarship or grant aid. 53% freshmen, 55% undergrads receive need-based self-help aid. 12% freshmen, 11% undergrads receive athletic scholarships. 85% undergrads borrow to pay for school. Average cumulative indebtedness $22,520. **Criteria for awarding institutional aid:** *Non-need-based:* Academics, art, athletics, minority status, music/drama.

QUINCY UNIVERSITY

1800 College Avenue, Quincy, IL 62301-2699
Phone: 217-228-5210 **Financial Aid Phone:** 217-228-5260
E-mail: admissions@quincy.edu **CEEB Code:** 1645
Fax: 217-228-5479 **Website:** www.quincy.edu **ACT Code:** 1120

This private school, affiliated with the Roman Catholic Church, was founded in 1860. It has a 70-acre campus.

RATINGS
Admissions Selectivity Rating: 71   **Fire Safety Rating:** 60*   **Green Rating:** 74

STUDENTS AND FACULTY
Enrollment: 1,166. **Student Body:** 56% female, 44% male, 27% out-of-state, 1% international (8 countries represented). Asian 1%, African American 10%, Caucasian 75%, Hispanic 4%.
Retention and Graduation: 69% freshmen return for sophomore year. 31% freshmen graduate within 4 years. 32% grads go on to further study within 1 year. 8% grads pursue arts and sciences degrees. 3% grads pursue law degrees. 7% grads pursue business degrees. 3% grads pursue medical degrees. **Faculty:**

Student/faculty ratio 14:1. 53 full-time faculty, 75% hold PhDs, 9% are are members of minority groups, 30% are women.

ACADEMICS

Degrees: Associate, bachelor's, master's. **Classes:** Most classes have 10–19 students. Most lab/discussion sessions have fewer than 10 students. **Majors with Highest Enrollment:** Elementary education and teaching; marketing/marketing management; nursing/registered nurse (RN, ASN, BSN, MSN). **Special Study Options:** Accelerated program, distance learning, double major, dual enrollment, honors program, independent study, internships, student-designed major, study abroad, teacher certification program, 3-2 program in engineering with Washington University; 3-1 program in medical technology with various hospitals. **Honors programs:** The Honors Program provides a challenging course of study which adds an interdisciplinary dimension to a student's major field. The program promotes academic excellence through critical thinking, original research, exceptional writing, and public presentation of scholarship. **Combined degree programs:** Clinical Laboratory Science—BS Special programs offered to physically disabled students include note-taking services, reader services, tape recorders, tutors. **Career services:** Alumni network, alumni services, career/job search classes, career assessment, internships, regional alumni. **Career services highlights include:** The university, in cooperation with the state of Illinois and local businesses and social service agencies, provides early exploratory internships to first and second year students to aid in the career development/decision-making process.

FACILITIES

Housing: Coed dorms, men's dorms, women's dorms, fraternity/sorority housing, apartments for married students, apartments for single students, theme housing, Honors. 90% of campus accessible to physically disabled. **Special Academic Facilities/Equipment:** Reading center for student teachers, multimedia and graphic design labs, TV broadcast studio, temperature-controlled rare books Library archive, art gallery, 200–seat theater, environmental studies institute, hospital simulation lab, aviation facility with flight simulator, College-operated national public radio station. **Computers:** 100% of classrooms, 100% of dorms, 100% of libraries, 100% of dining areas, 100% of student union, 40% of common outdoor areas have wireless network access. Administrative functions (other than registration) can be performed online.

CAMPUS LIFE

Environment: Town. **Activities:** Choral groups, concert band, dance, drama/theater, jazz band, literary magazine, music ensembles, musical theater, opera, pep band, radio station, student government, student newspaper, symphony orchestra, television station, campus ministries. **Organizations:** 40 registered organizations, 8 honor societies, 2 religious organizations. 1 fraternity, 2 sororities. **Athletics (Intercollegiate):** *Men:* Baseball, basketball, cross-country, football, golf, soccer, tennis, volleyball. *Women:* Basketball, cross-country, golf, soccer, softball, tennis, volleyball. **On-Campus Highlights:** Health and Fitness Center, Newly renovated University Center, QU Chapel, Francis Garden, Brenner Library. **Environmental Initiatives:** Residence hall renovation: Centennial Hall east wing renovations included use of recycled furniture and the installation of an energy-efficient VRV hvac system. West-wing renovation slated for this year. The QU Environmental Club planted a rain garden in the form of a native prairie restoration in the center of the circular driveway of North Campus as a part of the Illinois Rain Garden Initiative awarded by the state. See release at www.quincy.edu/newstemplate.php?id=1583 On-going university-wide recycling program for paper, plastic, metal, and ink cartridges.

ADMISSIONS

Freshman Academic Profile: Average high school GPA 3.19. 12% in top 10% of high school class, 35% in top 25% of high school class, 65% in top 50% of high school class. 75% from public high schools. SAT Math middle 50% range 430–540. SAT Critical Reading middle 50% range 420–480. ACT middle 50% range 19–24. Minimum paper TOEFL 500. Minimum computer TOEFL 173. Minimum web-based TOEFL 61. **Basis for Candidate Selection:** *Very important factors considered include:* Academic GPA, rigor of secondary school record. *Important factors considered include:* Class rank, application essay, recommendation(s), standardized test scores, character/personal qualities, extracurricular activities, level of applicant's interest, volunteer work, work experience. *Other factors considered include:* Interview, talent/ability. **Freshman Admission Requirements:** High school diploma is required and GED is accepted. *Academic units recommended:* 4 English, 3 mathematics, 3 science, 2 foreign language, 3 Social Sciences **Freshman Admission Statistics:** 986 applied, 90% admitted, 28% enrolled. **Transfer Admission Requirements:** College transcript(s), statement of good standing from prior institution(s). Minimum college GPA of 2.0 required. Lowest grade transferable D. **General Admission Information:** Application fee $25. Notification on a rolling basis, beginning on or about 9/1. Nonfall registration accepted. Credit offered for CEEB Advanced Placement tests.

COSTS AND FINANCIAL AID

Annual tuition $21,300. Room and board $8,380. Required fees $730. Average book expense $1,250. **Required Forms and Deadlines:** FAFSA. Priority

financial aid filing date 3/1. **Notification of Awards:** Applicants will be notified of awards on a rolling basis beginning 2/15. **Types of Aid:** *Need-based scholarships/grants:* Federal Pell, SEOG, state scholarships/grants, private scholarships, the school's own gift aid. *Loans:* FFEL Subsidized Stafford, FFEL Unsubsidized Stafford, FFEL PLUS, Federal Perkins. *Student Employment:* Federal Work-Study Program available. Institutional employment available. Highest amount earned per year from on-campus jobs $2,000. Off-campus job opportunities are good. **Financial Aid Statistics:** 89% freshmen, 79% undergrads receive need-based scholarship or grant aid. 16% freshmen, 11% undergrads receive non-need-based scholarship or grant aid. 66% freshmen, 62% undergrads receive need-based self-help aid. 9% freshmen, 9% undergrads receive athletic scholarships. 99% freshmen, 93% undergrads receive any aid. 77% undergrads borrow to pay for school. Average cumulative indebtedness $21,785. **Criteria for awarding institutional aid:** *Non-need-based:* Academics, alumni affiliation, art, athletics, music/drama.

QUINNIPIAC UNIVERSITY

275 Mount Carmel Avenue, Hamden, CT 06518
Phone: 203-582-8600 **Financial Aid Phone:** 203-582-8750
E-mail: admissions@quinnipiac.edu **CEEB Code:** 3712
Fax: 203-582-8906 **Website:** www.quinnipiac.edu **ACT Code:** 582

This private school was founded in 1929. It has a 600-acre campus.

RATINGS

Admissions Selectivity Rating: 86   **Fire Safety Rating:** 94   **Green Rating:** 79

STUDENTS AND FACULTY

Enrollment: 5,888. **Student Body:** 62% female, 38% male, 70% out-of-state, 1% international (23 countries represented). Asian 3%, African American 3%, Caucasian 80%, Hispanic 5%.
Retention and Graduation: 86% freshmen return for sophomore year. 69% freshmen graduate within 4 years. 37% grads go on to further study within 1 year. 18% grads pursue arts and sciences degrees. 2% grads pursue law degrees. 9% grads pursue business degrees. 2% grads pursue medical degrees. **Faculty:** Student/faculty ratio 12:1. 304 full-time faculty, 89% hold PhDs, 12% are members of minority groups, 48% are women.

ACADEMICS

Degrees: Bachelor's, doctoral, master's, post-bachelor's certificate, post-master's certificate. **Classes:** Most classes have 10–19 students. Most lab/discussion sessions have 10–19 students. **Majors with Highest Enrollment:** Business/commerce; physical therapy/therapist; psychology. **Special Study Options:** distance learning, double major, exchange student program (domestic), honors program, independent study, internships, liberal arts/career combination, student-designed major, study abroad, teacher certification program, online option for summer course offerings, online degrees offered at the graduate level. **Honors programs:** The University Honors Program, limited to 60–70 freshmen who are selected following their acceptance,provides challenging coursework and opportunities for learning and service. BA/JD, BA/MA. **Career services:** Alumni network, alumni services, career/job search classes, career assessment, internships, regional alumni. **Career services highlights include:** Extensive internship programs in all business and communications fields. Clinical placements in all of the health science fields.

FACILITIES

Housing: Coed dorms, apartments for single students, wellness house, university owned houses provide housing for about 100 seniors/juniors. 100% of campus accessible to physically disabled. **Special Academic Facilities/Equipment:** Quinnipiac Polling Institute, Financial Technology Center, Motion Analysis Lab, Albert Schweitzer Institute, Critical Care Nursing Lab,Fully digital/high definition TV production studio,editing labs, news technology center. Lender family special collection room in Library on the Irish Famine, "An Gorta Mor." **Computers:** 100% of classrooms, 100% of dorms, 100% of libraries, 100% of dining areas, 100% of student union, 100% of common outdoor areas have wireless network access. Students can register for classes online. Administrative functions (other than registration) can be performed online. Undergraduates are required to own a computer.

CAMPUS LIFE

Environment: Town. **Activities:** Choral groups, dance, drama/theater, literary magazine, pep band, radio station, student government, student newspaper, television station, yearbook, campus ministries, international student organization. **Organizations:** 78 registered organizations, 8 honor societies, 3 religious organizations. 2 fraternities, 3 sororities. **Athletics (Intercollegiate):** *Men:* Baseball, basketball, cross-country, ice hockey, lacrosse, soccer, tennis. *Women:* Basketball, cheerleading, cross-country, field hockey, ice hockey, lacrosse, soccer, softball, tennis, track/field (outdoor), track/field (indoor), volleyball. **On-Campus Highlights:** Arnold Bernhard Library, Recreation Center with suspended banked track, An Gorta Mor—Irish famine literature and art, Cafe Q with Zia/Starbucks, Bobcat Den/Coffee Bar, The nearby 250 acre 'York Hill' campus with the TD Bank Sports Center-twin 3500 seat arenas for ice hockey and basketball, includes residence halls with 1800 beds and a student/recreation center. About 5 miles away is the North Haven campus of 104 acres, home to the graduate programs in the School of Health Sciences. Upper division (juniors and seniors) students in Physical Therapy, Occupational Therapy, Nursing, Diagnostic Imaging and Physician Assistant programs also use this outstanding state-of-the-art facility. **Environmental Initiatives:** 100 percent of Quinnipiac electricity requirements on all three of its campuses have been purchased from renewable energy credits. 1,232 photovoltaic solar panels on the roof of the 475,000 square-foot Crescent residence hall, will convert energy from the sun to electricity and generate about 250,000kWH per year. A wind garden composed of 42 vertical-axis wind turbines will generate about 84,000 kilowatt hours per year on the York Hill campus—home to residence halls for 1800 students and the TD Bank Sports Center.

ADMISSIONS

Freshman Academic Profile: Average high school GPA 3.4. 25% in top 10% of high school class, 66% in top 25% of high school class, 95% in top 50% of high school class. 70% from public high schools. SAT Math middle 50% range 560–630. SAT Critical Reading middle 50% range 540–610. ACT middle 50% range 23–27. Minimum paper TOEFL 550. Minimum computer TOEFL 213. Minimum web-based TOEFL 77. **Basis for Candidate Selection:** *Very important factors considered include:* Academic GPA, rigor of secondary school record. *Important factors considered include:* Class rank, application essay, standardized test scores. *Other factors considered include:* Recommendation(s), alumni/ae relation, character/personal qualities, extracurricular activities, interview, level of applicant's interest, racial/ethnic status, talent/ability, volunteer work, work experience. **Freshman Admission Requirements:** High school diploma is required and GED is accepted. *Academic units required:* 4 English, 3 mathematics, 3 science, (2 science labs), 2 foreign language, 2 social studies, 4 years of science and math req. in PT, OT, nursing and, PA. *Academic units recommended:* 4 English, 4 mathematics, 4 science, (3 science labs), 2 foreign language, 3 social studies. **Freshman Admission Statistics:** 13,847 applied, 69% admitted, 17% enrolled. **Transfer Admission Requirements:** College transcript(s), essay or personal statement, minimum college GPA of 2.5 required. Lowest grade transferable C. **General Admission Information:** Application fee $45. Notification on a rolling basis, beginning on or about 12/15. Nonfall registration accepted. Admission may be deferred for a maximum of 1 year. Credit and/or placement offered for CEEB Advanced Placement tests.

COSTS AND FINANCIAL AID

Annual tuition $32,850. Room and board $12,555. Required fees $1,400. Average book expense $800. **Required Forms and Deadlines:** FAFSA, CSS/Financial Aid PROFILE, students applying during 2010–2011 for the spring 2011 or fall 2011 semesters; will need to provide the CSS Profile. Priority financial aid filing date 3/1. **Notification of Awards:** Applicants will be notified of awards on a rolling basis beginning 2/15. **Types of Aid:** *Need-based scholarships/grants:* Federal Pell, SEOG, state scholarships/grants, private scholarships, the school's own gift aid, Federal Nursing Scholarships. *Loans:* Direct Subsidized Stafford, Direct Unsubsidized Stafford, Direct PLUS, FFEL Subsidized Stafford, FFEL Unsubsidized Stafford, FFEL PLUS, Federal Perkins, Federal Nursing, state loans. *Student Employment:* Federal Work-Study Program available. Institutional employment available. Highest amount earned per year from on-campus jobs $2,100. Off-campus job opportunities are excellent. **Financial Aid Statistics:** 60% freshmen, 57% undergrads receive need-based scholarship or grant aid. 27% freshmen, 24% undergrads receive non-need-based scholarship or grant aid. 50% freshmen, 50% undergrads receive need-based self-help aid. 4% freshmen, 5% undergrads receive athletic scholarships. 72% freshmen, 68% undergrads receive any aid. 69% undergrads borrow to pay for school. Average cumulative indebtedness $34,621. **Criteria for awarding institutional aid:** *Non-need-based:* Academics, athletics.

See page 1202.

RADFORD UNIVERSITY

PO Box 6903, RU, Radford, VA 24142
Phone: 540-831-5371 **Financial Aid Phone:** 540-831-5408
E-mail: admissions@radford.edu **CEEB Code:** 5565
Fax: 540-831-5038 **Website:** www.radford.edu **ACT Code:** 4422

This public school was founded in 1910. It has a 191-acre campus.

RATINGS
Admissions Selectivity Rating: 73   **Fire Safety Rating:** 82   **Green Rating:** 87

STUDENTS AND FACULTY
Enrollment: 7,736. **Student Body:** 57% female, 43% male, 7% out-of-state, 1% international (49 countries represented). Asian 2%, African American 6%, Caucasian 86%, Hispanic 3%.
Retention and Graduation: 17% grads go on to further study within 1 year. 9% grads pursue arts and sciences degrees. 3% grads pursue business degrees.
Faculty: Student/faculty ratio 19:1. 387 full-time faculty, 83% hold PhDs, 10% are are members of minority groups, 47% are women. 2% of classes are taught by teaching assistants.

ACADEMICS
Degrees: Bachelor's, doctoral, master's, post-bachelor's certificate, post-master's certificate. **Classes:** Most classes have 20–29 students. Most lab/discussion sessions have 20–29 students. **Majors with Highest Enrollment:** criminal justice/safety studies; multi-/interdisciplinary studies; other; physical education teaching and coaching. **Special Study Options:** Accelerated program, cross-registration, distance learning, double major, dual enrollment, honors program, independent study, internships, student-designed major, study abroad, teacher certification program. **Honors programs:** Student members of Honors Academy work toward graduating as Highlander Scholars. To graduate as a Highlander Scholar, one must complete 27 credit hours of Honors Coursework, present their Honors Capstone Project in a public forum, and have a cumulative GPA of 3.5 at the time of graduation. The 27 hours of honors coursework are completed as follows: 6-12 credits in the Core Curriculum as honors credits (usually earned by taking Honors Classes), 12-15 in one's major as honors credits (usually by contracting the course for honors credit and a 3-6 credit hour honors capstone project in one's major (a piece of scholarship completed under the supervision of a faculty member in one's department). There is also a residential/social component to the Honors Academy. Active members in the Honors Academy enjoy early registration, and their status as a Highlander Scholar Graduate is noted on their diploma and transcript. Students are also supported financially to present the results of their work at professional and undergraduate conferences. **Combined degree programs:** BA/MA. Special programs offered to physically disabled students include note-taking services, reader services, tape recorders, tutors. **Career services:** Alumni network, alumni services, career/job search classes, career assessment, internships, regional alumni. **Career services highlights include:** Radford University has strong job search classes and tools that now include the best software available in the field to assist students in career search training. RU makes available Optimal Resume & Optimal First Impressions software that assists with resume/business letter development; electronic portfolio construction; and virtual interview practice utilizing video and audio tape recording. Our students also have a job board of employer posted openings, a resume posting site, and interview scheduling software powered by CSO and called Hire a Highlander. In addition, each semester the career placement office provides a series of Internship Readiness Seminars and other programs developed to enhance interviewing, business protocol and confidence in the career transition process.

FACILITIES
Housing: Coed dorms, special housing for disabled students, special housing for international students, apartments for single students, wellness house, theme housing. 100% of campus accessible to physically disabled. **Special Academic Facilities/Equipment:** Language Lab, Art Gallery with Sculpture Garden, Planetarium, Selu Conservancy, and on-campus speech/language/hearing clinic. **Computers:** 100% of classrooms, 100% of dorms, 100% of libraries, 100% of dining areas, 100% of student union, 100% of common outdoor areas have wireless network access. Students can register for classes online. Administrative functions (other than registration) can be performed online.

CAMPUS LIFE
Environment: Village. **Activities:** Choral groups, concert band, dance, drama/theater, jazz band, literary magazine, music ensembles, musical theater, pep band, radio station, student government, student newspaper, television station, yearbook, campus ministries, international student organization. **Organizations:** 237 registered organizations, 14 honor societies, 10 religious organizations. 15 fraternities, 10 sororities. **Athletics (Intercollegiate):** *Men:* Baseball, basketball, cheerleading, cross-country, golf, soccer, tennis, track/field

(outdoor), track/field (indoor). *Women:* Basketball, cheerleading, cross-country, diving, field hockey, golf, soccer, softball, swimming, tennis, track/field (outdoor), track/field (indoor), volleyball. **On-Campus Highlights:** Hurlburt Student Center— The Bonnie, Heth Hall—Students Services, Young Hall—High Tech Classrooms, Covington Center for Arts, Muse Hall—New River Grill. **Environmental Initiatives:** Signing the ACUPCC committment. Establishing a high level campus-wide sustainability committee and fourteen subcommittees focused on specific sustainbility targets. Completing a Greenhouse Gas Inventory

ADMISSIONS

Freshman Academic Profile: Average high school GPA 3.19. 90% from public high schools. SAT Math middle 50% range 460–550. SAT Critical Reading middle 50% range 460–550. ACT middle 50% range 19–23. Minimum paper TOEFL 520. Minimum computer TOEFL 190. **Basis for Candidate Selection:** *Very important factors considered include:* Rigor of secondary school record. *Important factors considered include:* Academic GPA. *Other factors considered include:* Class rank, application essay, recommendation(s), standardized test scores, alumni/ae relation, character/personal qualities, extracurricular activities, first generation, geographical residence, level of applicant's interest, racial/ethnic status, state residency, talent/ability, volunteer work, work experience. **Freshman Admission Requirements:** High school diploma is required and GED is accepted. *Academic units recommended:* 4 English, 4 mathematics, 4 science, (3 science labs), 3 foreign language, 2 social studies, 2 history, 5 academic electives. **Freshman Admission Statistics:** 6,166 applied, 71% admitted, 47% enrolled. **Transfer Admission Requirements:** College transcript(s), minimum college GPA of 2.0 required. Lowest grade transferable C. **General Admission Information:** Application fee $50. Regular application deadline 2/1. Regular notification 4/1. Nonfall registration accepted. Admission may be deferred for a maximum of 1 year. Credit and/or placement offered for CEEB Advanced Placement tests.

COSTS AND FINANCIAL AID

Annual in-state tuition $4,396. Annual out-of-state tuition $14,060. Room and board $6,970. Required fees $2,508. Average book expense $1,100. **Required Forms and Deadlines:** FAFSA. Priority financial aid filing date 3/1. **Notification of Awards:** Applicants will be notified of awards on a rolling basis beginning 4/15. **Types of Aid:** *Need-based scholarships/grants:* Federal Pell, SEOG, state scholarships/grants, private scholarships, the school's own gift aid. *Loans:* FFEL Subsidized Stafford, FFEL Unsubsidized Stafford, FFEL PLUS, Federal Perkins, Federal Nursing, state loans, college/university loans from institutional funds. *Student Employment:* Federal Work-Study Program available. Institutional employment available. Highest amount earned per year from on-campus jobs $2,610. Off-campus job opportunities are good. **Financial Aid Statistics:** 21% freshmen, 21% undergrads receive need-based scholarship or grant aid. 5% freshmen, 6% undergrads receive non-need-based scholarship or grant aid. 29% freshmen, 29% undergrads receive need-based self-help aid. 2% freshmen, 2% undergrads receive athletic scholarships. 63% freshmen, 63% undergrads receive any aid. 51% undergrads borrow to pay for school. Average cumulative indebtedness $19,465. **Criteria for awarding institutional aid:** *Non-need-based:* Academics, alumni affiliation, art, athletics, leadership, music/drama, state/district residency.

See page 1204.

RAMAPO COLLEGE OF NEW JERSEY

505 Ramapo Valley Road, Mahwah, NJ 07430-1680
Phone: 201-684-7300 **Financial Aid Phone:** 201-684-7550
E-mail: admissions@ramapo.edu **CEEB Code:** 2884
Fax: 201-684-7964 **Website:** www.ramapo.edu **ACT Code:** 2591

This public school was founded in 1971. It has a 300-acre campus.

RATINGS
Admissions Selectivity Rating: 89   **Fire Safety Rating:** 91   **Green Rating:** 77

STUDENTS AND FACULTY
Enrollment: 5,529. **Student Body:** 58% female, 42% male, 5% out-of-state, 2% international (42 countries represented). Asian 5%, African American 5%, Caucasian 76%, Hispanic 9%. **Retention and Graduation:** 59% freshmen graduate within 4 years. **Faculty:** Student/faculty ratio 18:1. 213 full-time faculty, 94% hold PhDs, 22% are members of minority groups, 45% are women.

ACADEMICS
Degrees: Bachelor's, certificate, master's. **Classes:** Most classes have 20–29 students. Most lab/discussion sessions have 10–19 students. **Majors with High-est Enrollment:** Business administration and management; nursing science (ms, phd); psychology. **Special Study Options:** Accelerated program, cooperative education program, cross-registration, distance learning, double major, dual enrollment, exchange student program (domestic), external degree program, honors program, independent study, internships, liberal arts/career combination, student-designed major, study abroad, teacher certification program, The RCNJ Teacher's Education program is accredited by TEAC. Students with non-Business majors may enroll in courses to earn a Business Essentials Certificate. **Honors programs:** www.ramapo.edu/honors/ The Ramapo College Honors Program is designed for students who desire a scholarly environment and an opportunity to interact with challenging faculty members and like-minded students. The Honors Program provides expanded opportunities for learning and reflection. Other benefits of the College Honors Program include residence hall options, special seminars, and exciting trips. Graduation from the College Honors Program is one indicator of a highly motivated, highly skilled, self-initiating individual. Students may participate in the College Honors Program by completing three H-option courses and receiving an Honors Certificate or by completing three H-option courses and completing a senior project, in which case the student graduates with full college honors. Full college honors is indicated on the diploma. **Combined degree programs:** BA/MD, BA/MA, BA/DDS, BS/DR—PT, Phys.Ast, Chiro, Optom, Osteo. Special programs offered to physically disabled students include note-taking services, reader services, tape recorders, tutors. **Career services:** Alumni network, alumni services, career/job search classes, career assessment, internships. **Career services highlights include:** The college's Cooperative Education Program (created in the 1980–81 academic year) has placed over 8,000 students and received more than $750,000 in grant awards from Federal, State, and private sources as well as nationwide recognition through U.S. Department of Education "national demonstration model" status.

FACILITIES
Housing: Coed dorms, special housing for disabled students, special housing for international students, cooperative housing, apartments for single students, special arrangements are made from time to time. Disabled students live in same residence halls as non-disabled students. 100% of campus accessible to physically disabled. **Special Academic Facilities/Equipment:** Art museum, media center, international telecommunications center, electron microscope, astronomical observatory, Holocaust Studies Center, new sports/fitness complex. A new Center for Science, Education and Technology is underway, as well as a Sustainability Education Center, and a Spirituality Center. **Computers:** 100% of classrooms, 100% of dorms, 100% of libraries, 100% of dining areas, 100% of student union, 60% of common outdoor areas have wireless network access. Students can register for classes online. Administrative functions (other than registration) can be performed online.

CAMPUS LIFE
Environment: Town. **Activities:** Choral groups, dance, drama/theater, literary magazine, music ensembles, musical theater, radio station, student government, student newspaper, television station, yearbook, campus ministries, international student organization, Model UN. **Organizations:** 80 registered organizations, 19 honor societies, 7 religious organizations. 10 fraternities, 11 sorority. **Athletics (Intercollegiate):** *Men:* Baseball, basketball, cross-country, soccer, swimming, tennis, track/field (outdoor), track/field (indoor), volleyball. *Women:* Basketball, cross-country, field hockey, lacrosse, soccer, softball, swimming, tennis, track/field (outdoor), track/field (indoor), volleyball. **On-Campus Highlights:** Berrie Center for Performing and Visual Arts, The Pavilion, The Market Place at the Birch Tree Inn, J Lee's in the Student Center, The Bill Bradley Sports and Fitness center. **Environmental Initiatives:** Curriculum (and a new building for the Sustainability Education Center). Recycling. Energy Conservation.

ADMISSIONS
Freshman Academic Profile: Average high school GPA 3.39. 24% in top 10% of high school class, 62% in top 25% of high school class, 94% in top 50% of high school class. SAT Math middle 50% range 550–630. SAT Critical Reading middle 50% range 520–600. SAT Writing middle 50% range 530–610. Minimum paper TOEFL 550. Minimum computer TOEFL 213. Minimum web-based TOEFL 90. **Basis for Candidate Selection:** *Very important factors considered include:* Class rank, academic GPA, rigor of secondary school record, standardized test scores. *Important factors considered include:* Application essay, recommendation(s), extracurricular activities, talent/ability. *Other factors considered include:* Alumni/ae relation, geographical residence, state residency, volunteer work, work experience. **Freshman Admission Requirements:** High school diploma is required and GED is accepted. *Academic units required:* 4 English, 3 mathematics, 3 science, (2 science labs), 2 foreign language, 3 social studies, 3 academic electives. **Freshman Admission Statistics:** 5,121 applied, 51% admitted, 36% enrolled. **Transfer Admission Requirements:** College transcript(s), essay or personal statement, minimum college GPA of 2.5 required. Lowest grade transferable C. **General Admission Information:** Application fee $60. Regular application deadline 3/1. Nonfall registration

accepted. Admission may be deferred for a maximum of 1 year. Credit and/or placement offered for CEEB Advanced Placement tests.

COSTS AND FINANCIAL AID

Annual in-state tuition $7,683. Annual out-of-state tuition $15,366. Room and board $11,290. Required fees $3,733. Average book expense $1,200. **Required Forms and Deadlines:** FAFSA. Priority financial aid filing date 3/1. **Notification of Awards:** Applicants will be notified of awards on a rolling basis beginning 4/1. **Types of Aid:** *Need-based scholarships/grants:* Federal Pell, SEOG, state scholarships/grants, private scholarships, the school's own gift aid, Federal Nursing Scholarships. Federal TRIO Grant. *Loans:* Direct Subsidized Stafford, Direct Unsubsidized Stafford, Direct PLUS, Federal Perkins, state loans *Student Employment:* Federal Work-Study Program available. Institutional employment available. Highest amount earned per year from on-campus jobs $9,299. Off-campus job opportunities are good. **Financial Aid Statistics:** 23% freshmen, 23% undergrads receive need-based scholarship or grant aid. 18% freshmen, 17% undergrads receive non-need-based scholarship or grant aid. 44% freshmen, 45% undergrads receive need-based self-help aid. 73% freshmen, 71% undergrads receive any aid. 55% undergrads borrow to pay for school. Average cumulative indebtedness $19,789.

RANDOLPH COLLEGE

2500 Rivermont Avenue, Lynchburg, VA 24503-1555
Phone: 434-947-8100 **Financial Aid Phone:** 434-947-8128
E-mail: admissions@randolphcollege.edu **CEEB Code:** 5567
Fax: 434-947-8996 **Website:** www.randolphcollege.edu **ACT Code:** 4388

This private school, affiliated with the Methodist Church, was founded in 1891. It has a 100-acre campus.

RATINGS
Admissions Selectivity Rating: 80   **Fire Safety Rating:** 84   **Green Rating:** 72

STUDENTS AND FACULTY
Enrollment: 549. **Student Body:** 82% female, 18% male, 47% out-of-state, 12% international (33 countries represented). Asian 3%, African American 9%, Caucasian 66%, Hispanic 7%, Native American 1%.
Retention and Graduation: 70% freshmen return for sophomore year. 66% freshmen graduate within 4 years. 31% grads go on to further study within 1 year. 25% grads pursue arts and sciences degrees. 6% grads pursue law degrees. 2% grads pursue business degrees. 5% grads pursue medical degrees. **Faculty:** Student/faculty ratio 7:1. 66 full-time faculty, 92% hold PhDs, 11% are are members of minority groups, 45% are women.

ACADEMICS
Degrees: Bachelor's, master's. **Classes:** Most classes have fewer than 10 students. Most lab/discussion sessions have fewer than 10 students. **Majors with Highest Enrollment:** Biology/biological sciences; political science and government; psychology. **Special Study Options:** Accelerated program, cross-registration, double major, dual enrollment, exchange student program (domestic), honors program, independent study, internships, liberal arts/career combination, student-designed major, study abroad, teacher certification program, 7-college exchange with Washington and Lee University, Hollins University, Hampden-Sydney College, Mary Baldwin College, Sweet Briar College, and Randolph-Macon College. Study abroad is encouraged and facilitated. The College currently offers a program for one or two semesters in Reading,England and affiliated programs in Greece, France, Denmark, Japan, Italy, Spain, N. Ireland, Mexico, and Czech Republic. Qualified students may elect to study abroad on a Randolph College or independent program. Endowed funds provide need-based assistance for study abroad to both American and international students. American Culture Program, a 1-Semester program that includes study on-site at key locations in and near Virginia, open to Randolph College students and students from other colleges who are accepted through a special application process. **Honors programs:** Juniors and seniors who have a cumulative 3.45 in all academic work and a 3.7 in the major are eligible to read for Honors in the Major. The Honors Program encourages students of exceptional ability to engage in independent and intensive study in their fields of interest. **Combined degree programs:** BA/MA, BA/MEng, BA/MS Nursing; BS/BS Engineering. Special programs offered to physically disabled students include note-taking services, reader services, tape recorders, tutors. **Career services:** Alumni network, alumni services, career assessment, internships, regional alumni. **Career**

services highlights include: We are most proud of our Experiential Learning opportunities made available to our students. The Career Development Center continues to provide all aspects of career services and is now within the Experiential Learning Center. The Center serves as a hub for all experiential activities and is responsible for coordination of those activities including service learning, study abroad, volunteerism and internships. The Experiential Learning Center empowers Randolph College students and faculty to creatively combine learning in the classroom with experiential opportunities within our campus and beyond. Through effective communication and collaboration, we help students make meaningful connections between their academic goals and life-long pursuits.

FACILITIES
Housing: Coed dorms, women's dorms, special housing for non-traditional age students. 50% of campus accessible to physically disabled. **Special Academic Facilities/Equipment:** Maier Museum of American Art recognized as one of the most outstanding college collections in the nation, computer-equipped classrooms (including wireless computer networks and smart boards), 100-acre equestrian center, language lab, science and math resource center, learning resources center, writing lab, nursery school, nature preserves, observatory, electron microscope. **Computers:** 100% of classrooms, 100% of dorms, 100% of libraries, 100% of dining areas, 100% of student union, 100% of common outdoor areas have wireless network access. Students can register for classes online. Administrative functions (other than registration) can be performed online.

CAMPUS LIFE
Environment: City. **Activities:** Choral groups, dance, drama/theater, literary magazine, music ensembles, pep band, radio station, student government, student newspaper, student-run film society, yearbook, international student organization, Model UN. **Organizations:** 40 registered organizations, 7 honor societies, 6 religious organizations. **Athletics (Intercollegiate):** *Men:* Basketball, cross-country, equestrian sports, horseback riding, lacrosse, soccer, tennis. *Women:* Basketball, cross-country, equestrian sports, horseback riding, lacrosse, soccer, softball, swimming, tennis, volleyball. **On-Campus Highlights:** The Maier Museum of Art, Macon Bookshop (on Rivermont Avenue), The Whiteside Amphitheater, Botanical Gardens, Main Hall and Main Grounds coffee bar, Randolph College Riding Center Skeller (in Main Hall) Houston Chapel. **Environmental Initiatives:** Instead of a sustainability coordinator, the College has an Environmental Issues Council, composed of faculty, staff and students, who coordinate sustainability initiatives on campus. The College is conducting a comprehensive Greenhouse Gas Inventory and is participating the the STARS pilot program (see above). These will be components of a Green Master Plan that is being developed this year in conjunction with our overall Facilities Master Plan. Environmental Studies faculty and students promote sustainability in the local community by participating in city planning. One member of the faculty chairs the city's Natural Resources Advisory Council, and another serves on the local Planning Commission. One of our honors students is developing an environmental checklist to evaluate the sustainability of development proposals.

ADMISSIONS
Freshman Academic Profile: Average high school GPA 3.3. 20% in top 10% of high school class, 60% in top 25% of high school class, 90% in top 50% of high school class. 78% from public high schools. SAT Math middle 50% range 490–600. SAT Critical Reading middle 50% range 500–630. ACT middle 50% range 23–27. Minimum paper TOEFL 550. Minimum computer TOEFL 213. Minimum web-based TOEFL 79. **Basis for Candidate Selection:** *Very important factors considered include:* Academic GPA, rigor of secondary school record, character/personal qualities. *Important factors considered include:* Class rank, application essay, recommendation(s), standardized test scores, extracurricular activities. *Other factors considered include:* Alumni/ae relation, first generation, interview, level of applicant's interest, talent/ability, volunteer work, work experience. **Freshman Admission Requirements:** High school diploma is required and GED is accepted. *Academic units required:* 4 English, 3 mathematics, 2 science, (2 science labs), 3 foreign language, 2 history, 2 academic electives. **Freshman Admission Statistics:** 1,585 applied, 84% admitted, 11% enrolled. **Transfer Admission Requirements:** High school transcript, college transcript(s), essay or personal statement, Lowest grade transferable C–. **General Admission Information:** Application fee $50. Regular application deadline 4/1. Regular notification 4/15. Nonfall registration accepted. Admission may be deferred for a maximum of 1 year. Credit and/or placement offered for CEEB Advanced Placement tests.

COSTS AND FINANCIAL AID
Annual tuition $25,350. Room and board $9,000. Required fees $510. Average book expense $800. **Required Forms and Deadlines:** FAFSA, state aid form. Priority financial aid filing date 3/1. **Notification of Awards:** Applicants will be notified of awards on a rolling basis beginning 3/1. **Types of Aid:** *Need-based scholarships/grants:* Federal Pell, SEOG, state scholarships/grants, private scholarships, the school's own gift aid. *Loans:* FFEL Subsidized Stafford, FFEL Unsubsidized Stafford, FFEL PLUS, Federal Perkins, college/university loans from institutional funds, private. *Student Employment:* Federal Work-Study

Program available. Institutional employment available. Off-campus job opportunities are good. **Financial Aid Statistics:** 74% freshmen, 66% undergrads receive need-based scholarship or grant aid. 22% freshmen, 18% undergrads receive non-need-based scholarship or grant aid. 66% freshmen, 58% undergrads receive need-based self-help aid. 99% freshmen, 96% undergrads receive any aid. 75% undergrads borrow to pay for school. Average cumulative indebtedness $27,218. **Criteria for awarding institutional aid:** *Non-need-based:* Academics, alumni affiliation, art, leadership, minority status, music/drama, religious affiliation, state/district residency.

RANDOLPH-MACON COLLEGE

P. O. Box 5005, Ashland, VA 23005
Phone: 804-752-7305 **Financial Aid Phone:** 804-752-7259
E-mail: admissions@rmc.edu **CEEB Code:** 5566
Fax: 804-752-4707 **Website:** www.rmc.edu **ACT Code:** 4386

This private school, affiliated with the Methodist Church, was founded in 1830. It has a 120-acre campus.

RATINGS
Admissions Selectivity Rating: 80 **Fire Safety Rating:** 64 **Green Rating:** 68

STUDENTS AND FACULTY
Enrollment: 1,166. **Student Body:** 54% female, 46% male, 30% out-of-state, 2% international (15 countries represented). Asian 2%, African American 9%, Caucasian 85%, Hispanic 2%, Native American 1%.
Retention and Graduation: 72% freshmen return for sophomore year. 45% freshmen graduate within 4 years. 26% grads go on to further study within 1 year. 10% grads pursue arts and sciences degrees. 3% grads pursue law degrees. 3% grads pursue business degrees. 2% grads pursue medical degrees. **Faculty:** Student/faculty ratio 11:1. 91 full-time faculty, 92% hold PhDs, 7% are members of minority groups, 38% are women.

ACADEMICS
Degrees: Bachelor's. **Classes:** Most classes have 10–19 students. **Majors with Highest Enrollment:** Business/managerial economics; psychology; sociology. **Special Study Options:** Accelerated program, cross-registration, double major, dual enrollment, exchange student program (domestic), honors program, independent study, internships, liberal arts/career combination, study abroad, teacher certification program, Member of Seven College Consortium, 3-2 program in engineering with Columbia University University of Virginia, 3-2 forestry with Duke University, 4-1 in accounting with Virginia Commonwealth University. **Honors programs:** The Honors Program offers qualified students the opportunity to take special honors classes, participate in unique programs and events for honors students, and an Honors House for recreation and socializing. **Combined degree programs:** BA/MA, BA/MEng, 3:2 forestry, 4:1 accounting, 4:1 MBA. Special programs offered to physically disabled students include note-taking services, reader services, tape recorders, tutors. **Career services:** Alumni network, alumni services, career/job search classes, career assessment, internships, regional alumni. **Career services highlights include:** Randolph-Macon offers outstanding internship opportunities to students of all class years and majors. Of greatest note is the Bassett Internship Program, open to seniors and juniors.

FACILITIES
Housing: Coed dorms, special housing for disabled students, men's dorms, special housing for international students, women's dorms, fraternity/sorority housing, apartments for single students, Honors House, substance-free housing, special interest housing. 50% of campus accessible to physically disabled. **Special Academic Facilities/Equipment:** Language lab, learning center, media center, greenhouse, observatory with telescope, electron microscopes, nuclear magnetic resonator, art gallery, fine arts center **Computers:** 20% of classrooms, 100% of dorms, 100% of libraries, 100% of dining areas, 100% of student union, 25% of common outdoor areas have wireless network access. Students can register for classes online. Administrative functions (other than registration) can be performed online.

CAMPUS LIFE
Environment: Village. **Activities:** Choral groups, concert band, dance, drama/theater, jazz band, literary magazine, music ensembles, musical theater, pep band, radio station, student government, student newspaper, student-run film society, television station, yearbook, campus ministries, international student organization. **Organizations:** 102 registered organizations, 18 honor societies, 4 religious organizations. 6 fraternities, 4 sororities. **Athletics (Intercollegiate):** *Men:* Baseball, basketball, football, golf, lacrosse, soccer, tennis. *Women:* Basketball, field hockey, lacrosse, soccer, softball, swimming, tennis, volleyball. **On-Campus Highlights:** Randolph-Macon Performing Arts Center, The

Brock Sports and Recreation Center, Frank E. Brown Campus Center, Pace-Armistead Hall and Flippo Gallery, Washington and Franklin Hall, Campus is located on 120 acres in the suburban community of Ashland, Virginia. R-MC has six historic landmarks, including three academic buildings listed on the National Historic Register.

ADMISSIONS
Freshman Academic Profile: Average high school GPA 3.3. 17% in top 10% of high school class, 46% in top 25% of high school class, 77% in top 50% of high school class. 73% from public high schools. SAT Math middle 50% range 500–590. SAT Critical Reading middle 50% range 490–580. SAT Writing middle 50% range 490–580. Minimum paper TOEFL 550. Minimum computer TOEFL 213. **Basis for Candidate Selection:** *Very important factors considered include:* Academic GPA, rigor of secondary school record. *Important factors considered include:* Class rank, application essay, recommendation(s), standardized test scores. *Other factors considered include:* Alumni/ae relation, character/personal qualities, extracurricular activities, first generation, interview, racial/ethnic status, talent/ability, volunteer work, work experience. **Freshman Admission Requirements:** High school diploma is required and GED is accepted. *Academic units required:* 4 English, 3 mathematics, 3 science, (2 science labs), 2 foreign language, 1 social studies, 2 history, 1 academic electives. *Academic units recommended:* 4 English, 4 mathematics, 4 science, (4 science labs), 4 foreign language, 4 social studies, 2 history, 2 academic electives. **Freshman Admission Statistics:** 3,177 applied, 61% admitted, 20% enrolled. **Transfer Admission Requirements:** High school transcript, college transcript(s), essay or personal statement, statement of good standing from prior institution(s). Minimum college GPA of 2.0 required. Lowest grade transferable C–. **General Admission Information:** Application fee $30. Early decision application deadline 11/15. Regular application deadline 3/1. Regular notification 4/1. Nonfall registration accepted. Admission may be deferred for a maximum of 1 year. Credit and/or placement offered for CEEB Advanced Placement tests.

COSTS AND FINANCIAL AID
Annual tuition $26,195. Room and board $8,180. Required fees $635. Average book expense $1,000. **Required Forms and Deadlines:** FAFSA, state aid formR-MC Entitlement Eligibility Form(If applicable) College Prepaid Education Program Form. Financial aid filing deadline 3/1. Priority financial aid filing date 2/1. **Notification of Awards:** Applicants will be notified of awards on or about 3/15. **Types of Aid:** *Need-based scholarships/grants:* Federal Pell, SEOG, state scholarships/grants, private scholarships, the school's own gift aid. *Loans:* FFEL Subsidized Stafford, FFEL Unsubsidized Stafford, FFEL PLUS, Federal Perkins, college/university loans from institutional funds. *Student Employment:* Federal Work-Study Program available. Institutional employment available. Highest amount earned per year from on-campus jobs $1,500. Off-campus job opportunities are excellent. **Financial Aid Statistics:** 62% freshmen, 56% undergrads receive need-based scholarship or grant aid. 8% freshmen, 8% undergrads receive non-need-based scholarship or grant aid. 53% freshmen, 48% undergrads receive need-based self-help aid. 100% freshmen, 95% undergrads receive any aid. **Criteria for awarding institutional aid:** *Non-need-based:* Academics, alumni affiliation, leadership, minority status, religious affiliation, state/district residency.

REED COLLEGE

3203 SE Woodstock Boulevard, Portland, OR 97202-8199
Phone: 503-777-7511 **Financial Aid Phone:** 503-777-7223
E-mail: admission@reed.edu **CEEB Code:** 4654
Fax: 503-777-7553 **Website:** www.reed.edu **ACT Code:** 3494

This private school was founded in 1908. It has a 116-acre campus.

RATINGS
Admissions Selectivity Rating: 97 **Fire Safety Rating:** 60* **Green Rating:** 77

STUDENTS AND FACULTY
Enrollment: 1,408. **Student Body:** 56% female, 44% male, 86% out-of-state, 6% international (41 countries represented). Asian 9%, African American 3%, Caucasian 56%, Hispanic 7%, Native American 1%.
Retention and Graduation: 89% freshmen return for sophomore year. 60% freshmen graduate within 4 years. 65% grads go on to further study within 1 year. 48% grads pursue arts and sciences degrees. 5% grads pursue law degrees. 3% grads pursue business degrees. 4% grads pursue medical degrees. **Faculty:**

Student/faculty ratio 10:1. 128 full-time faculty, 89% hold PhDs, 12% are are members of minority groups, 38% are women.

ACADEMICS

Degrees: Bachelor's, master's. **Classes:** Most classes have 10–19 students. Most lab/discussion sessions have 10–19 students. **Majors with Highest Enrollment:** Biology/biological sciences; English language and literature; psychology. **Special Study Options:** Cross-registration, double major, dual enrollment, exchange student program (domestic), independent study, internships, liberal arts/career combination, study abroad, Computer Science By arrangement with the University of Washington, a student may obtain a bachelor of arts degree from Reed and a bachelor of science degree in computer science from the University of Washington. The program calls for three years at Reed, including completion of the general distribution requirements and major requirements in one department, the passing of the junior qualifying examination, the acquisition of a minimum of 22 Reed units (at least 20 of which, including the distribution requirements, must be earned at Reed), and two years at the University of Washington. The university will admit up to five students per year on the recommendation of Reed College. Recommended students must satisfy the university's GPA requirements for transfer students, which may differ from year to year and which are not necessarily the same for Washington residents and non-residents. Computer science degrees are also available under the engineering programs described later in this section. Course Requirements These vary, depending upon the field of the Reed major -chemistry, mathematics, or physics. Consult the Reed dual degree coordinator for specific information. In special cases, an ad hoc program with the biology or economics department, or with another department, may be approved. Engineering By arrangement with the California Institute of Technology (Caltech), the Columbia University School of Engineering and Applied Sciences, or Rensselaer Polytechnic Institute, a student may obtain a bachelor's degree in engineering (alternatively, computer science or certain earth and planetary sciences) and a bachelor of arts degree from Reed. The program calls for three years at Reed, including the completion of the general college distribution requirements, completion of major requirements in one department (excluding thesis), the passing of the junior qualifying examination, the acquisition of a minimum of 22 Reed units (at least 20 of which, including all but two units of the distribution requirement, must be earned at Reed), and two years at the engineering school. Transfer students entering these programs should expect to spend no fewer than five semesters at Reed to meet this requirement. The two degrees will be awarded concurrently; all requirements for both degrees must be met before either is awarded. Admission to the engineering school is contingent on the college's recommendation and the student's having met certain course requirements of the engineering school while at Reed. Typical course requirements are two years of physics, one or two years of chemistry, and two years of mathematics, including differential equations. Normally, students with a GPA less than 3.0 should not expect to be recommended. Admission to the specific field of engineering preferred by the student is not guaranteed; the student's academic record can be relevant. Admission to Caltech is not automatic upon recommendation, but is subject to review by Caltech and may depend upon factors that cannot be anticipated. Caltech does not guarantee financial aid to otherwise eligible students. While admission to the other programs is also subject to review by the participating school, admission can usually be expected upon recommendation. Course Requirements During the freshman year: Mathematics 111/112 or 211/212; Physics 100. Consult with the Reed dual degree coordinator for information on other required courses. Forestry-Environmental Sciences By arrangement with the Nicholas School of the Environment of Duke University, a student may obtain a bachelor of arts degree at Reed and a professional master's degree from Duke (master of forestry or master of environmental management). Work at Duke emphasizes three aspects of study and research in forest and other renewable natural resources: management, science, and policy. The program calls for three years at Reed, including completion of the general college distribution and major requirements (excluding thesis), passing of the junior qualifying examination, the acquisition of a minimum of 22 Reed units (at least 20 of which, including the distribution requirements, must be earned at Reed), and two years at Duke. Students in all academic majors may qualify for the program. Course Requirements l. Biology 101,102; Mathematics 111 or 112, and Mathematics 141; and Economics 201. 2. Successful completion of the junior qualifying exam before the end of the junior year. Students should plan to take the Graduate Record Examination and make formal application for admission to Duke during the third year at Reed. In the summer following the third year, the student should begin work at Duke. Additional information may be obtained from the faculty adviser for the forestry-environmental sciences program. Pre-Medical and Pre-Veterinary Medical schools value the breadth in educational programs offered by liberal arts colleges. Work in the humanities and social sciences, as well as non-academic factors are all very important. Students should choose a major according to their academic interests and include the following laboratory and other courses to fulfill the admission requirements of most medical schools: 1. General biology: Biology 101 and 102 2. General chemistry: Chemistry 101 and 102 3. Organic chemistry: Chemistry 201 and 202 4. General physics: Physics 100, with lab 5. English or humanities: Humanities 110 6. One year of mathematics, including calculus (Mathematics 111) Course prerequisites for veterinary school usually include the courses above PLUS. additional specific courses, such as biochemistry or upper-level biology. Since there are more than 100 domestic medical schools and 30 veterinary schools, the student may encounter variation in the number and character of admission requirements. Students should be acquainted with the specific requirements and programs of the schools to which they apply. To prepare a competitive application portfolio, students considering medical or veterinary school are strongly encouraged to consult with health professions advisers and the career services office early in their undergraduate careers. In addition to offering advising, the career services office maintains a library of resources essential to the medical school planning process, such as Medical School Admission Requirements, a publication by the American Association of Medical Colleges. The guide Preparation for Medical School at Reed is available online, and includes important timelines, health care internship information, insight into letters of evaluation, and useful web links. It is strongly recommended that students take advantage of additional resources by attending informational seminars, seeking assistance with the application process, and using mock interviews. Graduating students who plan to take time off before applying to medical or veterinary school should discuss their plans with a health-profession adviser before graduation. Visual Arts The college has made arrangements for Reed students to participate in a variety of exchange programs and summer internships at other institutions. They may choose from programs in painting and sculpture, architecture, art history, archaeology, conservation, historic preservation, and museum work. A joint five-year program is also available with the Pacific Northwest College of Art. These programs are described in more detail in the art department section of the catalog. **Combined degree programs:** Computing: Univ. of Washington. Special programs offered to physically disabled students include note-taking services, reader services, tape recorders, tutors. **Career services:** Alumni network, alumni services, career/job search classes, career assessment, internships, regional alumni. **Career services highlights include:** http://web.reed.edu/career/students.html.

FACILITIES

Housing: Coed dorms, special housing for disabled students, women's dorms, cooperative housing, apartments for single students, wellness house, theme housingReed language houses accommodate upper-division students studying Chinese, French, German, Russian, and Spanish. First-year students required to live on campus; exceptions granted for unusual situations. 85% of campus accessible to physically disabled. **Special Academic Facilities/Equipment:** Art gallery, studio art building, language labs, computerized music listening lab, nuclear research reactor, 20 music practice rooms and midi lab, 760 seat auditorium, academic support center (quantitative skills, writing, math support), educational technology center. **Computers:** 100% of classrooms, 100% of dorms, 100% of libraries, 100% of dining areas, 100% of student union, 50% of common outdoor areas have wireless network access. Students can register for classes online. Administrative functions (other than registration) can be performed online.

CAMPUS LIFE

Environment: Metropolis. **Activities:** Choral groups, dance, drama/theater, literary magazine, music ensembles, radio station, student government, student newspaper, student-run film society, symphony orchestra, campus ministries, international student organization, Model UN. **Organizations:** 130 registered organizations, 1 honor societies, 5 religious organizations. **On-Campus Highlights:** Thesis Tower, Nuclear Research Reactor, Crystal Springs Canyon, Cerf Amphitheatre, The Paradox Cafe. **Environmental Initiatives:** LEED construction recycling installation for energy efficiency across campus, i.e., lighting, windows, heating.

ADMISSIONS

Freshman Academic Profile: Average high school GPA 3.9. 65% in top 10% of high school class, 89% in top 25% of high school class, 99% in top 50% of high school class. 59% from public high schools. SAT Math middle 50% range 630–710. SAT Critical Reading middle 50% range 660–760. SAT Writing middle 50% range 650–740. ACT middle 50% range 29–32. Minimum paper TOEFL 600. Minimum computer TOEFL 250. Minimum web-based TOEFL 100. **Basis for Candidate Selection:** *Very important factors considered include:* Application essay, academic GPA, rigor of secondary school record. *Important factors considered include:* Class rank, recommendation(s), standardized test scores, interview, level of applicant's interest. *Other factors considered include:* Alumni/ae relation, character/personal qualities, extracurricular activities, first generation, geographical residence, racial/ethnic status, talent/ability, volunteer work, work experience. **Freshman Admission Requirements:** High school diploma is required and GED is accepted. *Academic units recommended:* 4 English, 4 mathematics, 3 science, 3 foreign language, 1 social studies, 3 history. **Freshman Admission Statistics:** 3,485 applied, 32% admitted, 29% enrolled. **Transfer Admission Requirements:** High school transcript, college transcript(s), essay or personal statement, standardized test scores, statement of good standing from prior institution(s). Lowest grade transferable C–. **General Admission Information:** Application fee $50. Early decision application deadline 11/15. Regular application deadline 1/15. Regular notification 4/1. Nonfall registration not accepted. Admission may be deferred for a maximum of 1 year. Credit and/or placement offered for CEEB Advanced Placement tests.

COSTS AND FINANCIAL AID
Annual tuition $39,440. Room and board $10,250. Required fees $260. Average book expense $950. **Required Forms and Deadlines:** FAFSA, institution's own financial aid form, CSS/Financial Aid PROFILE, noncustodial PROFILE Financial aid filing deadline 1/15. Priority financial aid filing date 1/15. **Notification of Awards:** Applicants will be notified of awards on or about 4/1. **Types of Aid:** *Need-based scholarships/grants:* Federal Pell, SEOG, state scholarships/grants, private scholarships, the school's own gift aid. *Loans:* FFEL Subsidized Stafford, FFEL Unsubsidized Stafford, FFEL PLUS, Federal Perkins. *Student Employment:* Federal Work-Study Program available. Institutional employment available. Highest amount earned per year from on-campus jobs $12,006. **Financial Aid Statistics:** 48% freshmen, 46% undergrads receive need-based scholarship or grant aid. 46% freshmen, 46% undergrads receive need-based self-help aid. 51% freshmen, 49% undergrads receive any aid. 53% undergrads borrow to pay for school. Average cumulative indebtedness $17,296.

See page 1206.

REGENT UNIVERSITY

1000 Regent University Drive, LIB 102, Virginia Beach, VA 23464
Phone: 800-373-5504 **Financial Aid Phone:** 757-352-4125
E-mail: admissions@regent.edu
Fax: 757-352-4381 **Website:** www.regent.edu **ACT Code:** 6738

This private school, affiliated with the Christian (Nondenominational) Church, was founded in 1978. It has a 70-acre campus.

RATINGS
Admissions Selectivity Rating: 78　　**Fire Safety Rating:** 70　　**Green Rating:** 70

STUDENTS AND FACULTY
Enrollment: 1,874. **Student Body:** 66% female, 34% male, 56% out-of-state, 1% international (48 countries represented). Asian 2%, African American 26%, Caucasian 56%, Hispanic 6%, Native American 1%.
Retention and Graduation: 75% freshmen return for sophomore year. **Faculty:** Student/faculty ratio 16:1. 178 full-time faculty, 85% hold PhDs, 19% are are members of minority groups, 32% are women.

ACADEMICS
Degrees: Associate, bachelor's, doctoral, master's, post-master's certificate, terminal associate, transfer associate. **Classes:** Most classes have 20–29 students. **Majors with Highest Enrollment:** Business/commerce; psychology; religion/religious studies. **Special Study Options:** distance learning, double major, dual enrollment, internships, study abroad, teacher certification program Special programs offered to physically disabled students include note-taking services, reader services, tape recorders, tutors. **Career services:** Alumni network, alumni services, career/job search classes, career assessment, internships, regional alumni.

FACILITIES
Housing: Apartments for married students, apartments for single students. 100% of campus accessible to physically disabled. **Special Academic Facilities/Equipment:** The 31,000–square-foot Student Center on Regent's Virginia Beach Campus, opened in 2003, offers a central location for campus and student services. The building houses the University Bookstore, student organizations and meeting rooms, a cafe/coffee shop, computer lab, student lounge and offices for the Registrar, Admissions and Financial Aid. The 135,000–square-foot Communication & Performing Arts Center, opened in 2002, includes film and animation studios, a state-of-the-art main theatre, screening rooms and editing suites in one of the most technologically advanced communication buildings on the east coast. **Computers:** 80% of classrooms, 100% of dorms, 100% of libraries, 100% of student union, 50% of common outdoor areas have wireless network access. Students can register for classes online. Administrative functions (other than registration) can be performed online.

CAMPUS LIFE
Environment: City. **Activities:** Choral groups, concert band, dance, drama/theater, student government, student newspaper, campus ministries, international student organization. **Organizations:** 47 registered organizations, 4 honor societies. **On-Campus Highlights:** The Student Center, Communication & Performing Arts, The Ordinary Cafe and Coffee Shop, Robertson Hall,

University Library, Robertson Hall is equipped with the latest technology in audio/video equipment and cameras for simultaneous broadcasting. The 132,000–square-foot building also boasts a 380–seat moot court/city council chamber. The 135,000–square-foot Communication & Performing Arts Center features a 750–seat theater and a 150–seat experimental theater, cinema-television production studio, film sound stage, screening theaters, technical studios and teaching labs. A back lot area offers space for sets for indoor and outdoor filming. Just opened in 2002, the 31,000–square-foot Student Center houses the University Bookstore, student organization offices, The Ordinary cafe/coffee shop, a computer lab, student lounge and meeting rooms. **Environmental Initiatives:** Our investments in "cool storage" systems since our beginning in 1978 allows us to shave peak demand when the power company desires. This helps reduce the size of the power plant needed to support this area. This results in a major decrease in greenhouse emissions for this area. This fact is recognized by VA Dominion Power—our supplier of electricity. Our campus is one of the most beautiful campuses in Virginia because we have worked diligently to acheive the proper balance between "bricks and mortar" and the natural resources we have been blessed with. Our woods have diverse species of trees and plantings and we strive to enhance the wildlife habitat. For instance den trees are highly valued and preserved. Fruit bearing tree species are highly valued and retained whenever possible. The President and facilities director intensively manages the campus grounds to retain the nature setting. Branches are chipped and composted as are tree leaves and needles. Campus aquatic ecosystems are maintained with similar intensity. We have purposely changed locations for buildings, sidewalks, storm sewer, and other underground utilities in order to preserve natural resources. Additionally we resisted City of Virginia Beach directives to build additional parking lots which would "urbanize" our campus. We hired a lawyer, contested the directive and preserved our green campus. The investments we have made in energy saving devices has been remarkable and worthwhile as evidenced by usage reduction data. ALL building light fixtures have been renovated to T8 fixtures. A state of the art monitoring system is in place. All flat roofs were replaced with white TPO roofs. Most pumps were upgraded with variable frequency drives. All chillers and boilers are high efficiency models. There is much, much more.

ADMISSIONS
Freshman Academic Profile: Average high school GPA 3. SAT Math middle 50% range 420–580. SAT Critical Reading middle 50% range 460–600. SAT Writing middle 50% range 450–570. ACT middle 50% range 16–22. Minimum paper TOEFL 577. Minimum computer TOEFL 233. Minimum web-based TOEFL 90. **Basis for Candidate Selection:** *Very important factors considered include:* Academic GPA, standardized test scores. *Important factors considered include:* Application essay. *Other factors considered include:* Recommendation(s), rigor of secondary school record. **Freshman Admission Requirements:** High school diploma is required and GED is accepted. *Academic units recommended:* 4 English, 3 mathematics, 3 science, 3 foreign language, 3 social studies. **Freshman Admission Statistics:** 223 applied, 64% admitted, 74% enrolled. **Transfer Admission Requirements:** High school transcript, college transcript(s), minimum college GPA of 2.5 required. Lowest grade transferable C. **General Admission Information:** Application fee $50. Regular application deadline 8/1. Nonfall registration accepted. Admission may be deferred for a maximum of 1 year. Credit offered for CEEB Advanced Placement tests.

COSTS AND FINANCIAL AID
Annual tuition $13,800. Room and board $6,250. Required fees $200. Average book expense $598. **Required Forms and Deadlines:** FAFSA, institution's own financial aid form, state aid form. Priority financial aid filing date 3/15. **Notification of Awards:** Applicants will be notified of awards on a rolling basis beginning 3/1. **Types of Aid:** *Need-based scholarships/grants:* Federal Pell, state scholarships/grants, private scholarships, the school's own gift aid. *Loans:* FFEL Subsidized Stafford, FFEL Unsubsidized Stafford, FFEL PLUS. *Student Employment:* Institutional employment available. Highest amount earned per year from on-campus jobs $8,268. Off-campus job opportunities are good. **Financial Aid Statistics:** 48% freshmen, 49% undergrads receive need-based scholarship or grant aid. 76% freshmen, 70% undergrads receive non-need-based scholarship or grant aid. 64% freshmen, 68% undergrads receive need-based self-help aid. 87% freshmen, 88% undergrads receive any aid. 69% undergrads borrow to pay for school. Average cumulative indebtedness $33,451. **Criteria for awarding institutional aid:** *Non-need-based:* Academics, alumni affiliation, leadership.

REGIS COLLEGE

235 Wellesley Street, Weston, MA 02493-1571
Phone: 781-768-7100 **Financial Aid Phone:** 781-768-7180
E-mail: admission@regiscollege.edu **CEEB Code:** 3723
Fax: 781-768-7071 **Website:** www.regiscollege.edu **ACT Code:** 1886

This private school, affiliated with the Roman Catholic Church, was founded in 1927. It has a 131-acre campus.

RATINGS
Admissions Selectivity Rating: 71   **Fire Safety Rating:** 80   **Green Rating:** 77

STUDENTS AND FACULTY
Enrollment: 972. **Student Body:** 82% female, 18% male, 7% out-of-state, 1% international (27 countries represented). Asian 5%, African American 22%, Caucasian 38%, Hispanic 9%, Native American 1%.
Retention and Graduation: 68% freshmen return for sophomore year. 51% freshmen graduate within 4 years. 31% grads go on to further study within 1 year. 19% grads pursue arts and sciences degrees. 1% grads pursue law degrees. 1% grads pursue business degrees. 2% grads pursue medical degrees. **Faculty:** Student/faculty ratio 13:1. 69 full-time faculty. 71% hold PhDs, 4% are are members of minority groups, 77% are women.

ACADEMICS
Degrees: Associate, bachelor's, master's, post-master's certificate, transfer associate. **Classes:** Most classes have 10–19 students. **Majors with Highest Enrollment:** Communication studies/speech communication and rhetoric; nursing/registered nurse (RN, ASN, BSN, MSN); political science and government. **Special Study Options:** Accelerated program, cross-registration, double major, English as a Second Language (ESL), exchange student program (domestic), honors program, independent study, internships, student-designed major, study abroad, teacher certification program. **Honors programs:** The Honors Program at Regis College offers qualified students a stimulating and challenging learning experience, and opportunities for distinguished scholarship. It prepares students to become leaders committed to the betterment of the human condition and our society, a goal that is central to the Regis College mission. **Combined degree programs:** BA/MSCO; BS/MSNU. Special programs offered to physically disabled students include note-taking services, tape recorders, tutors. **Career services:** Alumni network, alumni services, career/job search classes, career assessment, internships. **Career services highlights include:** Internships offer students opportunities to apply classroom learning to the world of work while receiving academic credit.

FACILITIES
Housing: Coed dorms, women's dorms. 85% of campus accessible to physically disabled. **Special Academic Facilities/Equipment:** Fine arts center, philatelic museum. **Computers:** 30% of classrooms, 100% of dorms, 100% of libraries, 100% of dining areas, 100% of student union, 15% of common outdoor areas have wireless network access. Students can register for classes online. Administrative functions (other than registration) can be performed online.

CAMPUS LIFE
Environment: Village. **Activities:** Choral groups, dance, drama/theater, literary magazine, music ensembles, musical theater, radio station, student government, yearbook, campus ministries, Model UN. **Organizations:** 36 registered organizations, 10 honor societies, 2 religious organizations. **Athletics (Intercollegiate):** *Men:* Basketball, diving, soccer, swimming. *Women:* Basketball, diving, field hockey, lacrosse, soccer, softball, swimming, tennis, track/field (outdoor), track/field (indoor), volleyball. **On-Campus Highlights:** College Hall, Student Union, Tower, Athletic Complex, Fine Arts Center. **Environmental Initiatives:** Replacement of steam boilers w/high efficiency designs. Replacement of mercury vapor and incandescent lighting with fluorescent. Elimination of the use of salt for snow/ice control.

ADMISSIONS
Freshman Academic Profile: Average high school GPA 2.84. 10% in top 10% of high school class, 37% in top 25% of high school class, 73% in top 50% of high school class. 70% from public high schools. SAT Math middle 50% range 420–520. SAT Critical Reading middle 50% range 420–520. SAT Writing middle 50% range 420–520. ACT middle 50% range 17–21. Minimum paper TOEFL 550. Minimum computer TOEFL 213. **Basis for Candidate Selection:** *Very important factors considered include:* Application essay, academic GPA, recommendation(s), rigor of secondary school record, character/personal qualities. *Important factors considered include:* Class rank, standardized test scores, extracurricular activities, interview, talent/ability, volunteer work, work experience. *Other factors considered include:* Alumni/ae relation, first generation, level of applicant's interest. **Freshman Admission Requirements:** High school diploma is required and GED is accepted. *Academic units required:* 4

English, 3 mathematics, 2 science, (1 science labs), 2 foreign language, 2 social studies, 3 academic electives. **Freshman Admission Statistics:** 1,735 applied, 73% admitted, 19% enrolled. **Transfer Admission Requirements:** High school transcript, college transcript(s), essay or personal statement, minimum college GPA of 2.0 required. Lowest grade transferable C. **General Admission Information:** Application fee $50. Notification on a rolling basis, beginning on or about 12/1. Nonfall registration accepted. Admission may be deferred for a maximum of 1 year. Credit and/or placement offered for CEEB Advanced Placement tests.

COSTS AND FINANCIAL AID
Annual tuition $28,900. Room and board $12,190. **Required Forms and Deadlines:** FAFSA, institution's own financial aid form. Priority financial aid filing date 2/15. **Notification of Awards:** Applicants will be notified of awards on a rolling basis beginning 3/15. **Types of Aid:** *Need-based scholarships/grants:* Federal Pell, SEOG, state scholarships/grants, private scholarships, the school's own gift aid, Federal Nursing Scholarships. *Loans:* Direct Subsidized Stafford, Direct Unsubsidized Stafford, Direct PLUS, Federal Perkins, Federal Nursing *Student Employment:* Federal Work-Study Program available. Institutional employment available. Highest amount earned per year from on-campus jobs $5,355. Off-campus job opportunities are poor. **Financial Aid Statistics:** 78% freshmen, 76% undergrads receive need-based scholarship or grant aid. 68% freshmen, 57% undergrads receive non-need-based scholarship or grant aid. 83% freshmen, 82% undergrads receive need-based self-help aid. 86% freshmen, 85% undergrads receive any aid. 88% undergrads borrow to pay for school. Average cumulative indebtedness $27,489. **Criteria for awarding institutional aid:** *Non-need-based:* Academics, alumni affiliation, religious affiliation.

REGIS UNIVERSITY

3333 Regis Boulevard, A-12, Denver, CO 80221-1099
Phone: 303-458-4900
E-mail: regisadm@regis.edu/college.asp **CEEB Code:** 4656
Fax: 303-964-5534 **Website:** www.regis.edu **ACT Code:** 526

This private school, affiliated with the Roman Catholic Church, was founded in 1877. It has a 90-acre campus.

RATINGS
Admissions Selectivity Rating: 76   **Fire Safety Rating:** 60*   **Green Rating:** 60*

STUDENTS AND FACULTY
Enrollment: 5,430. **Student Body:** 62% female, 38% male, 24% out-of-state, 1% international (23 countries represented). Asian 3%, African American 5%, Caucasian 64%, Hispanic 8%, Native American 1%.
Retention and Graduation: Faculty: Student/faculty ratio 10:1. 240 full-time faculty, 29% hold PhDs, 9% are are members of minority groups, 55% are women.

ACADEMICS
Degrees: Bachelor's, master's. **Classes:** Most classes have fewer than 10 students. Most lab/discussion sessions have 10–19 students. **Special Study Options:** Accelerated program, cooperative education program, cross-registration, distance learning, double major, dual enrollment, exchange student program (domestic), honors program, independent study, internships, liberal arts/career combination, student-designed major, study abroad, teacher certification program, weekend college. Special programs offered to physically disabled students include tutors. **Career services:** Alumni services, career/job search classes, internships

FACILITIES
Housing: Coed dorms, special housing for disabled students, apartments for single students. 90% of campus accessible to physically disabled. Language lab, wellness center, **Computers:** Administrative functions (other than registration) can be performed online.

CAMPUS LIFE
Environment: Metropolis. **Activities:** Choral groups, drama/theater, literary magazine, music ensembles, musical theater, radio station, student government, student newspaper, yearbook. **Organizations:** 40 registered organizations, 1 honor societies, 1 religious organizations. **Athletics (Intercollegiate):** *Men:* Baseball, basketball, cross-country, golf, soccer. *Women:* Basketball, cross-country, lacrosse, soccer, softball, volleyball.

ADMISSIONS
Freshman Academic Profile: Average high school GPA 3.24. 21% in top 10% of high school class, 47% in top 25% of high school class, 79% in top 50% of

high school class. 65% from public high schools. SAT Math middle 50% range 480–600. SAT Critical Reading middle 50% range 490–590. ACT middle 50% range 21–26. Minimum paper TOEFL 550. Minimum computer TOEFL 1. **Basis for Candidate Selection:** *Very important factors considered include:* Rigor of secondary school record, standardized test scores. *Important factors considered include:* Application essay, recommendation(s). *Other factors considered include:* Class rank, character/personal qualities, extracurricular activities, interview, talent/ability, volunteer work, work experience. **Freshman Admission Requirements:** High school diploma is required and GED is accepted. *Academic units recommended:* 4 English, 2 mathematics, 2 science, 2 foreign language, 2 social studies, 1 history. **Freshman Admission Statistics:** 1,327 applied, 84% admitted, 27% enrolled. **Transfer Admission Requirements:** College transcript(s), essay or personal statement, minimum college GPA of 2.0 required. **General Admission Information:** Application fee $40. Nonfall registration accepted. Admission may be deferred for a maximum of 0. Credit and/or placement offered for CEEB Advanced Placement tests.

COSTS AND FINANCIAL AID

Annual tuition $18,400. Room and board $7,150. Required fees $170. Average book expense $1,187. **Required Forms and Deadlines:** FAFSA. Priority financial aid filing date 3/5. **Notification of Awards:** Applicants will be notified of awards on a rolling basis beginning 3/15. **Types of Aid:** *Need-based scholarships/grants:* Federal Pell, SEOG, state scholarships/grants, private scholarships, the school's own gift aid, Federal Nursing Scholarships. *Loans:* FFEL Subsidized Stafford, FFEL Unsubsidized Stafford, FFEL PLUS, Federal Perkins, Federal Nursing *Student Employment:* Federal Work-Study Program available. Highest amount earned per year from on-campus jobs $1,800. Off-campus job opportunities are good. **Financial Aid Statistics:** 58% freshmen, 41% undergrads receive need-based scholarship or grant aid. 53% freshmen, 23% undergrads receive non-need-based scholarship or grant aid. 51% freshmen, 49% undergrads receive need-based self-help aid. 13% freshmen, 8% undergrads receive athletic scholarships. **Criteria for awarding institutional aid:** *Non-need-based:* Academics, athletics.

REINHARDT COLLEGE

7300 Reinhardt College Circle, Waleska, GA 30183
Phone: 770-720-5526 **Financial Aid Phone:** 770-720- 5667
Fax: 770-720-5899 **Website:** www.reinhardt.edu **ACT Code:** 856

This private school, affiliated with the Methodist Church, was founded in 1883. It has a 600-acre campus.

RATINGS
Admissions Selectivity Rating: 70   **Fire Safety Rating:** 81   **Green Rating:** 72

STUDENTS AND FACULTY

Enrollment: 994. **Student Body:** 60% female, 40% male, 2% out-of-state, international Asian 1%, African American 8%, Caucasian 81%, Hispanic 4%. **Retention and Graduation:** 59% freshmen return for sophomore year. 19% freshmen graduate within 4 years. 35% grads go on to further study within 1 year. 20% grads pursue arts and sciences degrees. 5% grads pursue law degrees. 45% grads pursue business degrees. 5% grads pursue medical degrees. **Faculty:** Student/faculty ratio 13:1. 53 full-time faculty, 72% hold PhDs, 13% are are members of minority groups, 49% are women.

ACADEMICS

Degrees: Associate, bachelor's, master's, transfer associate. **Classes:** Most classes have 10–19 students. **Majors with Highest Enrollment:** Business administration and management; communication and media studies, other; elementary education and teaching. **Special Study Options:** Accelerated program, double major, dual enrollment, external degree program, honors program, independent study, internships, study abroad, teacher certification program. **Honors programs:** The Honors Program is designed for students who are bright, curious and enjoy being challenged. Entering freshman with High School GPA of at least 3.5 or a combined SAT of 1050 or higher, with verbal score of at least 580, will be invited to apply for admission to Reinhardt College's Honors Program Special programs offered to physically disabled students include note-taking services, reader services, tape recorders, tutors. **Career services:** Alumni services, career/job search classes, career assessment, internships, regional alumni. **Career services highlights include:** Internships for the Price School of Education.

FACILITIES

Housing: Coed dorms, special housing for disabled students, men's dorms, women's dorms, honors house. 93% of campus accessible to physically disabled. **Special Academic Facilities/Equipment:** Funk Heritage Center, Falany Per-

forming Arts **Computers:** 100% of classrooms, 100% of dorms, 100% of libraries, 100% of student union, 5% of common outdoor areas have wireless network access. Students can register for classes online. Administrative functions (other than registration) can be performed online.

CAMPUS LIFE

Environment: Rural. **Activities:** Choral groups, concert band, drama/theater, jazz band, music ensembles, student government, student newspaper, student-run film society, television station, yearbook, campus ministries, international student organization. **Organizations:** 40 registered organizations, 6 honor societies, 5 religious organizations. **Athletics (Intercollegiate):** *Men:* Baseball, basketball, cheerleading, cross-country, golf, soccer, tennis. *Women:* Basketball, cheerleading, cross-country, golf, soccer, softball, tennis, volleyball. **On-Campus Highlights:** Falany Performing Arts Center, Funk Heritage Center, Gordy Center, Library, Class room building.

ADMISSIONS

Freshman Academic Profile: Average high school GPA 3.02. 11% in top 10% of high school class, 29% in top 25% of high school class, 57% in top 50% of high school class. 98% from public high schools. SAT Math middle 50% range 430–530. SAT Critical Reading middle 50% range 450–550. ACT middle 50% range 17–21. Minimum paper TOEFL 500. Minimum computer TOEFL 150. **Basis for Candidate Selection:** *Very important factors considered include:* Academic GPA, standardized test scores. *Important factors considered include:* Rigor of secondary school record. *Other factors considered include:* Class rank, recommendation(s), alumni/ae relation, character/personal qualities, extracurricular activities, first generation, geographical residence, level of applicant's interest, racial/ethnic status, religious affiliation/commitment, talent/ability, volunteer work, work experience. **Freshman Admission Requirements:** High school diploma is required and GED is accepted. *Academic units required:* 4 English, 4 mathematics, 3 science, 3 social studies. *Academic units recommended:* 2 foreign language. **Freshman Admission Statistics:** 1,111 applied, 70% admitted, 35% enrolled. **Transfer Admission Requirements:** College transcript(s), statement of good standing from prior institution(s). Minimum college GPA of 2.0 required. Lowest grade transferable C. **General Admission Information:** Application fee $25. Nonfall registration accepted. Credit and/or placement offered for CEEB Advanced Placement tests.

COSTS AND FINANCIAL AID

Annual tuition $15,900. Room and board $6,168. Required fees $170. Average book expense $1,100. **Required Forms and Deadlines:** FAFSA, state aid form. Priority financial aid filing date 5/1. **Notification of Awards:** Applicants will be notified of awards on a rolling basis beginning 3/15. **Types of Aid:** *Need-based scholarships/grants:* Federal Pell, SEOG, state scholarships/grants, private scholarships, the school's own gift aid. *Loans:* FFEL Subsidized Stafford, FFEL Unsubsidized Stafford, FFEL PLUS. *Student Employment:* Federal Work-Study Program available. Highest amount earned per year from on-campus jobs $2,800. Off-campus job opportunities are good. **Financial Aid Statistics:** 62% freshmen, 84% undergrads receive need-based scholarship or grant aid. 12% freshmen, 12% undergrads receive non-need-based scholarship or grant aid. 41% freshmen, 59% undergrads receive need-based self-help aid. 11% freshmen, 7% undergrads receive athletic scholarships. 65% freshmen, 65% undergrads receive any aid. 84.85% undergrads borrow to pay for school. Average cumulative indebtedness $18,329. **Criteria for awarding institutional aid:** *Non-need-based:* Academics, art, athletics, leadership, music/drama, religious affiliation, state/district residency.

RENSSELAER POLYTECHNIC INSTITUTE

110 Eighth Street, Troy, NY 12180-3590
Phone: 518-276-6216 **Financial Aid Phone:** 518-276-6816
E-mail: admissions@rpi.edu **CEEB Code:** 2757
Fax: 518-276-4072 **Website:** www.rpi.edu **ACT Code:** 2866

This private school was founded in 1824. It has a 284-acre campus.

RATINGS
Admissions Selectivity Rating: 95   **Fire Safety Rating:** 72   **Green Rating:** 84

STUDENTS AND FACULTY

Enrollment: 5,539. **Student Body:** 28% female, 72% male, 58% out-of-state, 3% international (60 countries represented). Asian 11%, African American 3%, Caucasian 74%, Hispanic 6%, Native American 1%.

Retention and Graduation: 91% freshmen return for sophomore year. 64% freshmen graduate within 4 years. 24% grads go on to further study within 1 year. 27% grads pursue arts and sciences degrees. 2% grads pursue law degrees. 8% grads pursue business degrees. 3% grads pursue medical degrees. **Faculty:** Student/faculty ratio 16:1. 386 full-time faculty, 99% hold PhDs, 23% are are members of minority groups, 20% are women.

ACADEMICS

Degrees: Bachelor's, certificate, master's. **Classes:** Most classes have 10–19 students. Most lab/discussion sessions have 10–19 students. **Majors with Highest Enrollment:** Business/commerce; computer engineering; electrical, electronics and communications engineering. **Special Study Options:** Accelerated program, cooperative education program, cross-registration, double major, dual enrollment, exchange student program (domestic), honors program, independent study, internships, liberal arts/career combination, student-designed major, study abroad, The accelerated BS-Phd program in the School of Science is possible in all the science departments. Computer Science Physics Applied Physics Biology Biochemistry and Biophysics Geology Hydrogeology. **Honors programs:** The Rensselaer Medal Program, the Presidential Scholars Program. **Combined degree programs:** BA/MEng, BS/MBA, BS/MS, BS/M.Eng, BS/MD, BS/JD, BS/Ph.D. Special programs offered to physically disabled students include note-taking services, reader services, tape recorders, tutors. **Career services:** Alumni network, alumni services, career/job search classes, career assessment, internships, regional alumni. **Career services highlights include:** Rensselaer has actively encouraged the translation of cutting edge academic research into new products and new businesses. Scientific and technological entrepreneurship is a significant part of "The Rensselaer Plan", a comprehensive strategic plan for the Institute. Historically and consistently, faculty, students, and alumni have successfully developed technologies, created innovations, and formed business ventures to bring ideas into practice to create value. Rensselaer's focus on entrepreneurship iscross-campus, interdisciplinary, and presents multiple perspectives. It involves creative thinking, and is not only ideas, but ideas to enterprise. Entrepreneurship at Rensselaer goes beyond curriculum, with a broad spectrum of technology presentations, lecture series, and mentor programs. It has a global focus, and is further focused as technology commercialization and entrepreneurship. The Lally School at Rensselaer has a strong tradition of developing entrepreneurs who create new ventures or bring their entrepreneurial management skills to established organizations. Theory and practice are combined in the classroom, and students interact with experienced entrepreneurs. The Severino Center for Technological Entrepreneurship is the focal point for both entrepreneurship scholarship and learning, and it serves as a bridge to the Rensselaer Incubator and Technology Park. Students participate in lectures and discussions, and events that include both the entire Rensselaer university community as well as professionals from successful start-ups and fast growth companies from the Tech Valley Region.

FACILITIES

Housing: Coed dorms, special housing for disabled students, fraternity/sorority housing, apartments for married students, apartments for single students, theme housing. 75% of campus accessible to physically disabled. **Special Academic Facilities/Equipment:** Shelnutt Art Gallery in the Student Union;The George M. Low Gallery (museum); Center for Terahertz Research; Nanoscale Science and Engineering Centers (NSEC); Center for Biotechnology and Interdisciplinary Studies; Gaerttner Linear Accelerator (LINAC) Laboratory; Hirsch Observatory; RPIdeaLab and Incubator Program (supports student business ventures); Rensselaer Technology Park; Darrin Fresh Water Institute at Lake George; Experimental Media and Performing Arts Center (EMPAC—under construction); Lighting Research Center; Social and Behavioral Research Laboratory; O.T. Swanson Multidisciplinary Laboratory; and other research centers and laboratories as described at www.rpi.edu/research/research_centers. html, Computational Center for Nanotechnology Innovations (CCNI); www.rpi. edu/dept/ess/greening/EECbooks.html. **Computers:** 75% of classrooms, 75% of dorms, 100% of libraries, 75% of dining areas, 100% of student union, 75% of common outdoor areas have wireless network access. Students can register for classes online. Administrative functions (other than registration) can be performed online. Undergraduates are required to own a computer.

CAMPUS LIFE

Environment: City. **Activities:** Choral groups, concert band, dance, drama/theater, jazz band, literary magazine, music ensembles, musical theater, pep band, radio station, student government, student newspaper, student-run film society, symphony orchestra, television station, yearbook, campus ministries, international student organization. **Organizations:** 177 registered organizations, 40 honor societies, 11 religious organizations. 32 fraternities, 5 sororities. **Athletics (Intercollegiate):** *Men:* Baseball, basketball, cross-country, diving, football, golf, ice hockey, lacrosse, soccer, swimming, tennis, track/field (outdoor), track/field (indoor). *Women:* Basketball, cross-country, diving, field hockey, ice hockey, lacrosse, soccer, softball, swimming, tennis, track/field (outdoor), track/field (indoor) **On-Campus Highlights:** Rensselaer Union, Mueller Fitness Center, Experimental Media & Performing Arts Ctr, Houston Field House (hockey arena), ECAV, Quiet and parklike, yet full of all the

conveniences of a self-contained city, Rensselaer's 275-acre campus is a blend of modern style and classic charm. The Institute is in a period of tremendous growth, building new facilities that greatly enhance the lives of our students and faculty. **Environmental Initiatives:** Student Sustainability Task Force; Energy Conservation Program; purchase of wind certificates; sustainability initiatives in new construction.

ADMISSIONS

Freshman Academic Profile: Average high school GPA 3.67. 61% in top 10% of high school class, 80% in top 25% of high school class, 98% in top 50% of high school class. 73% from public high schools. SAT Math middle 50% range 660–750. SAT Critical Reading middle 50% range 610–700. SAT Writing middle 50% range 580–680. ACT middle 50% range 25–30. Minimum paper TOEFL 570. Minimum computer TOEFL 230. Minimum web-based TOEFL 88. **Basis for Candidate Selection:** *Very important factors considered include:* Class rank, academic GPA, rigor of secondary school record, standardized test scores. *Important factors considered include:* Application essay, recommendation(s), character/personal qualities, extracurricular activities, level of applicant's interest. *Other factors considered include:* Alumni/ae relation, geographical residence, interview, racial/ethnic status, talent/ability, volunteer work, work experience. **Freshman Admission Requirements:** High school diploma is required and GED is accepted. *Academic units required:* 4 English, 4 mathematics, 3 science, 2 social studies. *Academic units recommended:* 4 science, 3 social studies. **Freshman Admission Statistics:** 12,350 applied, 43% admitted, 25% enrolled. **Transfer Admission Requirements:** College transcript(s), statement of good standing from prior institution(s). Minimum college GPA of 3.0 required. Lowest grade transferable C. **General Admission Information:** Application fee $70. Early decision application deadline 11/2. Regular application deadline 1/15. Regular notification 3/13. Nonfall registration accepted. Admission may be deferred for a maximum of 1 year. Credit and/or placement offered for CEEB Advanced Placement tests.

COSTS AND FINANCIAL AID

Annual tuition $38,100. Room and board $11,145. Required fees $1,065. Average book expense $1,850. **Required Forms and Deadlines:** FAFSA, CSS/Financial Aid PROFILE Priority financial aid filing date 2/15. **Notification of Awards:** Applicants will be notified of awards on or about 3/25. **Types of Aid:** *Need-based scholarships/grants:* Federal Pell, SEOG, state scholarships/grants, private scholarships, the school's own gift aid, Gates Millennium Scholarship, ACG, Smart Grants. *Loans:* FFEL Subsidized Stafford, FFEL Unsubsidized Stafford, FFEL PLUS, Federal Perkins, state loans, college/university loans from institutional funds. *Student Employment:* Federal Work-Study Program available. Institutional employment available. Highest amount earned per year from on-campus jobs $2,000. Off-campus job opportunities are good. **Financial Aid Statistics:** 66% freshmen, 65% undergrads receive need-based scholarship or grant aid. 17% freshmen, 11% undergrads receive non-need-based scholarship or grant aid. 53% freshmen, 53% undergrads receive need-based self-help aid. 1% freshmen, 1% undergrads receive athletic scholarships. 100% freshmen, 97% undergrads receive any aid. 71% undergrads borrow to pay for school. Average cumulative indebtedness $30,838. **Criteria for awarding institutional aid:** *Non-need-based:* Academics, alumni affiliation, art, athletics, leadership, minority status, music/drama.

RHODE ISLAND SCHOOL OF DESIGN

2 College Street, Providence, RI 02903
Phone: 401-454-6300 **Financial Aid Phone:** 401-454-6661
E-mail: admissions@risd.edu **CEEB Code:** 3726
Fax: 401-454-6309 **Website:** www.risd.edu **ACT Code:** 3812

This private school was founded in 1877. It has a 13-acre campus.

RATINGS

Admissions Selectivity Rating: 90   **Fire Safety Rating:** 60*   **Green Rating:** 60*

STUDENTS AND FACULTY

Enrollment: 1,882. **Student Body:** 66% female, 34% male, % out-of-state, 12% international (44 countries represented). Asian 14%, African American 2%, Caucasian 51%, Hispanic 5%.
Retention and Graduation: Faculty: Student/faculty ratio 11:1. 146 full-time faculty, 12% are are members of minority groups, 45% are women.

ACADEMICS

Degrees: Bachelor's, master's. **Majors with Highest Enrollment:** graphic design; illustration; industrial design. **Special Study Options:** Cross-registration, exchange student program (domestic), independent study, internships, study abroad, Continuing Education program. 6-week precollege summer program for secondary school students. summer workshops for undergraduate credit. 6 week winter session study abroad courses. Special programs offered to physically disabled students include note-taking services, reader services, tape recorders

FACILITIES

Housing: Coed dorms, apartments for single students. **Special Academic Facilities/Equipment:** Art museum with over 45 galleries, extensive facilities for glassblowing, metalsmithing, lithography, sculpture, painting, and other art disciplines, nature lab. **Computers:** Administrative functions (other than registration) can be performed online.

CAMPUS LIFE

Environment: City. **Activities:** Drama/theater, literary magazine, student government, student newspaper, student-run film society, yearbook. **Organizations:** 35 registered organizations, 5 religious organizations. **On-Campus Highlights:** The RISD Museum, The Edna Lawrence Nature Lab, Metcalf 3 dimensional fine art building, 161 S. Main St.—Industrial Design Building, RISD Works.

ADMISSIONS

Freshman Academic Profile: Average high school GPA 3.3. 28% in top 10% of high school class, 54% in top 25% of high school class, 91% in top 50% of high school class. 60% from public high schools. SAT Math middle 50% range 550–670. SAT Critical Reading middle 50% range 530–660. Minimum paper TOEFL 580. Minimum computer TOEFL 237. **Basis for Candidate Selection:** *Very important factors considered include:* Rigor of secondary school record, talent/ability. *Important factors considered include:* Application essay, recommendation(s), standardized test scores, character/personal qualities. *Other factors considered include:* Class rank, alumni/ae relation, extracurricular activities, racial/ethnic status, volunteer work, work experience. **Freshman Admission Requirements:** High school diploma is required and GED is accepted. **Freshman Admission Statistics:** 2,511 applied, 34% admitted, 47% enrolled. **Transfer Admission Requirements:** College transcript(s), essay or personal statement, Lowest grade transferable C. **General Admission Information:** Application fee $50. Regular application deadline 2/15. Regular notification 4/1. Nonfall registration accepted. Admission may be deferred for a maximum of 1 year. Credit and/or placement offered for CEEB Advanced Placement tests.

COSTS AND FINANCIAL AID

Annual tuition $27,510. Room and board $7,709. Required fees $465. Average book expense $2,200. **Required Forms and Deadlines:** FAFSA, CSS/Financial Aid PROFILE. Financial aid filing deadline 2/15. Priority financial aid filing date 2/15. **Notification of Awards:** Applicants will be notified of awards on or about 4/1. **Types of Aid:** *Need-based scholarships/grants:* Federal Pell, SEOG, state scholarships/grants, private scholarships, the school's own gift aid. *Loans:* FFEL Subsidized Stafford, FFEL Unsubsidized Stafford, FFEL PLUS, Federal Perkins. *Student Employment:* Federal Work-Study Program available. Institutional employment available. Highest amount earned per year from on-campus jobs $1,100. Off-campus job opportunities are good. **Financial Aid Statistics:** 27% freshmen, 44% undergrads receive need-based scholarship or grant aid. 1% freshmen, 2% undergrads receive non-need-based scholarship or grant aid. 42% freshmen, 48% undergrads receive need-based self-help aid. 59% undergrads borrow to pay for school. Average cumulative indebtedness $22,500. **Criteria for awarding institutional aid:** *Non-need-based:* Academics, art.

RHODES COLLEGE

Office of Admissions, 2000 North Parkw, Memphis, TN 38112
Phone: 901-843-3700 **Financial Aid Phone:** 901-843-3810
E-mail: adminfo@rhodes.edu **CEEB Code:** 1730
Fax: 901-843-3631 **Website:** www.rhodes.edu **ACT Code:** 4008

This private school, affiliated with the Presbyterian Church, was founded in 1848. It has a 100-acre campus.

RATINGS

Admissions Selectivity Rating: 94   **Fire Safety Rating:** 78   **Green Rating:** 83

STUDENTS AND FACULTY

Enrollment: 1,659. **Student Body:** 57% female, 43% male, 73% out-of-state, 4% international (15 countries represented). Asian 5%, African American 7%, Caucasian 75%, Hispanic 2%, Native American 1%.

Retention and Graduation: 88% freshmen return for sophomore year. 75% freshmen graduate within 4 years. 36% grads go on to further study within 1 year. 16% grads pursue arts and sciences degrees. 5% grads pursue law degrees. 5% grads pursue business degrees. 8% grads pursue medical degrees. **Faculty:** Student/faculty ratio 10:1. 161 full-time faculty, 98% hold PhDs, 11% are are members of minority groups, 45% are women.

ACADEMICS

Degrees: Bachelor's, master's. **Classes:** Most classes have 10–19 students. Most lab/discussion sessions have 10–19 students. **Majors with Highest Enrollment:** Biology/biological sciences; business/commerce; English language and literature. **Special Study Options:** Cooperative education program, cross-registration, double major, dual enrollment, exchange student program (domestic), honors program, independent study, internships, liberal arts/career combination, student-designed major, study abroad, duel degree: Master of Education; Master of Science in Nursing; Master of Science in Biomedical Engineering. **Honors programs:** The Honors program is a culminating experience in the major field, for seniors only. It is the principal means whereby a student may do more independent, intensive, and individual work than can be done in the regular degree programs. The Honors work offers an excellent introduction to graduate study as it employs the full resources of library and laboratory and encourages independent research and study. Honors is available in most majors. **Combined degree programs:** BA/MEd, BA/MSN, BS/MS Biomed Engineering. Special programs offered to physically disabled students include note-taking services, reader services, tape recorders, tutors. **Career services:** Alumni network, alumni services, career/job search classes, career assessment, internships, regional alumni. **Career services highlights include:** The Rhodes St. Jude Summer Plus. program typifies the integrated learning philosophy at Rhodes through which students take classroom skills into the community where they connect knowledge with practice and learn effective leadership through service, internships, international travel and research. The approach also assures that students return to the classroom with the discoveries, problem-solving skills, contextualization, engagement and motivation gained through their experiences. John Sexton '04 describes his experience this way: "I was able to maintain close personal relationships with Rhodes faculty—the kind of relationships a student would be unlikely to have at a larger, research-oriented school—and also access the world-class facilities and experts at St. Jude—the kinds of resources not generally available to students at small liberal arts colleges." Clearly the Summer Plus. program at St. Jude Children's Research Hospital provides the best of both worlds for the Rhodes science major who is ready to commit to two summers and a good deal of the school year working at a research hospital world renowned for its development of treatments for life-threatening diseases of childhood. In this program aspiring physicians and biomedical researchers have a unique opportunity to participate in every phase of the process in which basic research is translated into therapeutic interventions from bench to bedside. The intense and sustained challenge of work in this extraordinary environment fosters both scientific curiosity and humanitarian concern.

FACILITIES

Housing: Coed dorms, men's dorms, women's dorms, apartments for single students, learning communities, substance free, quiet study, restricted visitation, non-smoking, special interest townhouses. 90% of campus accessible to physically disabled. **Special Academic Facilities/Equipment:** 136,000 square foot library; Art gallery; archaeology lab; astronomy observation domes with 14 and 31.5 inch telescopes; machine and woodworking shops; scanning electron microscopes; cell culture lab; nuclear magnetic resonance instrument; gas chromatography systems; UV, X-ray, infrared, and atomic absorption spectrophotometers. **Computers:** 100% of classrooms, 100% of dorms, 100% of libraries, 100% of dining areas, 50% of common outdoor areas have wireless network access. Students can register for classes online. Administrative functions (other than registration) can be performed online.

CAMPUS LIFE

Environment: Metropolis. **Activities:** Choral groups, dance, drama/theater, jazz band, literary magazine, music ensembles, musical theater, pep band, radio station, student government, student newspaper, student-run film society, symphony orchestra, television station, yearbook, campus ministries, international student organization, Model UN. **Organizations:** 115 registered organizations, 14 honor societies, 8 religious organizations. 7 fraternities, 6 sororities. **Athletics (Intercollegiate):** *Men:* Baseball, basketball, cross-country, football, golf, soccer, swimming, tennis, track/field (outdoor). *Women:* Basketball, cross-country, field hockey, golf, soccer, softball, swimming, tennis, track/field (outdoor), volleyball. **On-Campus Highlights:** Barret Library (includes a Starbucks coffee shop), Burrow Center for Student Opportunity, Bryan Campus Life Center (home to the Ly, East Village (apartment-style dorms), McCoy Theater, The Burrow Center for Student Opportunity opened in Spring, 2008. It consolidates most student services under one roof, including a one-stop transaction center, enrolling and financing, student development and academic support, and out of class experiences. It also includes space for student organizations and is open to students 24x7. **Environmental Initiatives:** $500,000 Andrew W. Mellon Foundation grant to expand Environmental Studies initiatives through community partnerships; comprehensive campus-wide recycling program centralized; energy management system and Green Power Switch.

ADMISSIONS

Freshman Academic Profile: Average high school GPA 3.81. 53% in top 10% of high school class, 81% in top 25% of high school class, 96% in top 50% of high school class. 50% from public high schools. SAT Math middle 50% range 580–700. SAT Critical Reading middle 50% range 570–680. SAT Writing middle 50% range 580–680. ACT middle 50% range 26–30. Minimum paper TOEFL 550. Minimum computer TOEFL 213. **Basis for Candidate Selection:** *Very important factors considered include:* Class rank, academic GPA, rigor of secondary school record. *Important factors considered include:* Application essay, recommendation(s), standardized test scores, alumni/ae relation, character/personal qualities, racial/ethnic status. *Other factors considered include:* Extracurricular activities, first generation, geographical residence, interview, level of applicant's interest, state residency, talent/ability, volunteer work, work experience. **Freshman Admission Requirements:** High school diploma is required and GED is accepted. *Academic units required:* 4 English, 3 mathematics, 2 science, (2 science labs), 2 foreign language, 2 social studies, 3 academic electives. **Freshman Admission Statistics:** 5,039 applied, 42% admitted, 20% enrolled. **Transfer Admission Requirements:** High school transcript, college transcript(s), essay or personal statement, standardized test scores, statement of good standing from prior institution(s). Lowest grade transferable C–. **General Admission Information:** Application fee $45. Early decision application deadline 11/1. Regular notification 4/1. Nonfall registration accepted. Admission may be deferred for a maximum of 1 year. Credit and/or placement offered for CEEB Advanced Placement tests.

COSTS AND FINANCIAL AID

Annual tuition $33,400. Room and board $8,314. Required fees $310. Average book expense $1,020. **Required Forms and Deadlines:** FAFSA, CSS/Financial Aid PROFILE, noncustodial PROFILE Financial aid filing deadline 3/1. Priority financial aid filing date 3/1. **Types of Aid:** *Need-based scholarships/grants:* Federal Pell, SEOG, state scholarships/grants, private scholarships, the school's own gift aid. *Loans:* Direct Subsidized Stafford, Direct Unsubsidized Stafford, Direct PLUS, FFEL Subsidized Stafford, FFEL Unsubsidized Stafford, FFEL PLUS, Federal Perkins. *Student Employment:* Federal Work-Study Program available. Institutional employment available. Highest amount earned per year from on-campus jobs $5,140. Off-campus job opportunities are good. **Financial Aid Statistics:** 47% freshmen, 45% undergrads receive need-based scholarship or grant aid. 16% freshmen, 10% undergrads receive non-need-based scholarship or grant aid. 32% freshmen, 32% undergrads receive need-based self-help aid. 85% freshmen, 85% undergrads receive any aid. 47% undergrads borrow to pay for school. Average cumulative indebtedness $26,071. **Criteria for awarding institutional aid:** *Non-need-based:* Academics, art, minority status, music/drama, religious affiliation.

RICE UNIVERSITY

MS 17 PO Box 1892, Houston, TX 77251-1892
Phone: 713-348-7423 **Financial Aid Phone:** 713-348-4958
E-mail: admi@rice.edu **CEEB Code:** 6609
Fax: 713-348-5952 **Website:** www.rice.edu **ACT Code:** 4152

This private school was founded in 1912. It has a 300-acre campus.

RATINGS

Admissions Selectivity Rating: 98   **Fire Safety Rating:** 88   **Green Rating:** 77

STUDENTS AND FACULTY

Enrollment: 3,102. **Student Body:** 48% female, 52% male, 45% out-of-state, 6% international (44 countries represented). Asian 21%, African American 7%, Caucasian 48%, Hispanic 12%.
Retention and Graduation: 97% freshmen return for sophomore year. 82% freshmen graduate within 4 years. 41% grads go on to further study within 1 year. 28% grads pursue arts and sciences degrees. 12% grads pursue law degrees. 1% grads pursue business degrees. 28% grads pursue medical degrees. **Faculty:** Student/faculty ratio 5.2:1. 598 full-time faculty, 97% hold PhDs, 18% are are members of minority groups, 29% are women. 4% of classes are taught by teaching assistants.

ACADEMICS

Degrees: Bachelor's, master's. **Classes:** Most classes have 10–19 students.
Majors with Highest Enrollment: Biology/biological sciences; economics;

psychology. **Special Study Options:** Cross-registration, double major, dual enrollment, English as a Second Language (ESL), honors program, independent study, internships, liberal arts/career combination, student-designed major, study abroad, teacher certification program, 8 year guaranteed medical school program with The Baylor College of Medicine. **Honors programs:** Honors programs through individual departments. **Combined degree programs:** guar.med.school program with Baylor College of Med. Special programs offered to physically disabled students include note-taking services, reader services, tape recorders **Career services:** Alumni network, alumni services, career/job search classes, career assessment, internships, regional alumni. **Career services highlights include:** We are most proud of our relationship with alumni and their support (in terms of professional advice as well as recruitment) of current undergraduate and graduate students.

FACILITIES

Housing: Coed dorms, special housing for disabled students, All undergraduate students are automatically assigned to one of nine (coed) residential colleges and keep affiliation regardless of whether they live on campus or not. 90% of campus accessible to physically disabled. **Special Academic Facilities/Equipment:** Art gallery, museum, media center, language labs, computer labs, civil engineering lab, observatory and NASA equipment for students in space physics courses. **Computers:** 100% of classrooms, 100% of dorms, 1000% of libraries, 100% of dining areas, 100% of student union, 5% of common outdoor areas have wireless network access. Students can register for classes online. Administrative functions (other than registration) can be performed online.

CAMPUS LIFE

Environment: Metropolis. **Activities:** Choral groups, concert band, dance, drama/theater, jazz band, literary magazine, marching band, music ensembles, musical theater, opera, pep band, radio station, student government, student newspaper, student-run film society, symphony orchestra, television station, yearbook, campus ministries, international student organization, Model UN. **Organizations:** 215 registered organizations, 11 honor societies, 14 religious organizations. **Athletics (Intercollegiate):** *Men:* Baseball, basketball, cross-country, football, golf, tennis, track/field (outdoor), track/field (indoor). *Women:* Basketball, cross-country, soccer, swimming, tennis, track/field (outdoor), track/field (indoor), volleyball. **On-Campus Highlights:** Rice Memorial Center, Baker Institute for Public Policy, Brochstein Pavilion (cafe), Shepherd School of Music, Reckling Park—baseball stadium. **Environmental Initiatives:** 1. Green Building. At present, we have roughly 1,000,000 square feet of facilities on campus that are under construction that will receive some level of LEED certification, including the student dormitory Duncan College which is targeted for LEED-Gold. In addition, an off-campus child care center is pursuing LEED certification. Also, an off-campus graduate student apartment complex has been designed to LEED standards although it will not be formally submitted for certification. With this complex, we anticipate savings in energy of about 30% and water savings of 20%. Further, the complex was constructed in an area with excellent pedestrian access, and it includes extensive bicycle storage along with shuttle bus service to campus and to major nearby grocery stores. Our campus standard for on-campus LEED certification for new buildings is LEED-Silver as a minimum. The University has also enjoyed significant successes with construction waste recycling, with many of our largest projects to date logging diversion rates of 85-90% to recycling. 2. Energy Consumption and Prediction Reporting Application. Our campus energy managers have developed an application that provides in near real time a powerful building-level energy consumption and predictive analysis tool that takes into account variations in weather. For a given building, we can accurately model what that building's energy consumption should be based on outdoor temperature, humidity, and past performance of the building. We then plot that versus actual consumption data from the meters. The difference between the two represents energy savings or losses. This tool allows us to see the immediate impact of energy conservation measures. To my knowledge, we are the only university with this capability to create our own weather-normalized predicted baselines. Our energy managers have partnered with Incuity Software to develop this tool into a campus energy management solution. Harvey Mudd College awarded this system with its first annual green engineering award in 2008. See www.incuity.com/HMC%20Award%20News%20Release.pdf 3. Green Cleaning. The custodians of our Facilities Engineering and Planning Department provide the cleaning services for all of our non-residential buildings. Almost all of the cleaning is achieved with hot water, vapor, or a single environmentally-friendly cleaning chemical called H2Orange2 by Envirox. Disposable cleaning rags have been replaced by microfiber cloths, and string mops have been replaced with microfiber flat mops. FE&P custodians can attend optional English language training classes on-campus during work hours, which earns them credit through Houston Community College. They also can enroll in optional computer training, and are offered cross-training opportunities for positions such as plumbers and administrative assistants. Most of our custodians work daytime shifts (which saves building energy and improves customer services, while also being family-friendly and safer), and they receive full employee benefits.

ADMISSIONS

Freshman Academic Profile: 85% in top 10% of high school class, 94% in top 25% of high school class, 99% in top 50% of high school class. SAT Math middle 50% range 670–780. SAT Critical Reading middle 50% range 650–750. SAT Writing middle 50% range 640–750. ACT middle 50% range 30–34. Minimum paper TOEFL 600. Minimum computer TOEFL 250. Minimum web-based TOEFL 100. **Basis for Candidate Selection:** *Very important factors considered include:* Class rank, application essay, academic GPA, recommendation(s), rigor of secondary school record, standardized test scores, character/personal qualities, extracurricular activities, talent/ability. *Other factors considered include:* Alumni/ae relation, first generation, geographical residence, interview, level of applicant's interest, racial/ethnic status, state residency, volunteer work, work experience. **Freshman Admission Requirements:** High school diploma or equivalent is not required. *Academic units required:* 4 English, 3 mathematics, 2 science, (2 science labs), 2 foreign language, 2 social studies, 3 academic electives. *Academic units recommended:* 4 English, 4 mathematics, 4 science, (3 science labs), 4 foreign language, 2 social studies, 2 academic electives. **Freshman Admission Statistics:** 9,813 applied, 23% admitted, 35% enrolled. **Transfer Admission Requirements:** High school transcript, college transcript(s), essay or personal statement, standardized test scores, statement of good standing from prior institution(s). Minimum college GPA of 3.2 required. Lowest grade transferable C–. **General Admission Information:** Application fee $60. Early decision application deadline 11/1. Regular application deadline 1/2. Regular notification 4/1. Nonfall registration not accepted. Admission may be deferred for a maximum of 2 years. Credit and/or placement offered for CEEB Advanced Placement tests.

COSTS AND FINANCIAL AID

Annual tuition $30,782. Room and board $11,230. Required fees $675. Average book expense $800. **Required Forms and Deadlines:** FAFSA, CSS/Financial Aid PROFILE, noncustodial PROFILE, business/farm supplement. Tax returns and W-2s. Priority financial aid filing date 3/1. **Notification of Awards:** Applicants will be notified of awards on a rolling basis beginning 4/1. **Types of Aid:** *Need-based scholarships/grants:* Federal Pell, SEOG, state scholarships/grants, private scholarships, the school's own gift aid. *Loans:* FFEL Subsidized Stafford, FFEL Unsubsidized Stafford, FFEL PLUS, Federal Perkins. *Student Employment:* Federal Work-Study Program available. Institutional employment available. Off-campus job opportunities are excellent. **Financial Aid Statistics:** 35% freshmen, 37% undergrads receive need-based scholarship or grant aid. 5% freshmen, 9% undergrads receive non-need-based scholarship or grant aid. 27% freshmen, 24% undergrads receive need-based self-help aid. 7% freshmen, 9% undergrads receive athletic scholarships. 53% freshmen, 60% undergrads receive any aid. 42% undergrads borrow to pay for school. Average cumulative indebtedness $11,108. **Criteria for awarding institutional aid:** *Non-need-based:* Academics, art, athletics, leadership, minority status, music/drama, state/district residency.

THE RICHARD STOCKTON COLLEGE
OF NEW JERSEY

Jim Leeds Road, PO Box 195, Pomona, NJ 08240-0195
Phone: 609-652-4261 **Financial Aid Phone:** 609-652-4201
E-mail: admissions@stockton.edu **CEEB Code:** 2889
Fax: 609-748-5541 **Website:** www.stockton.edu

This public school was founded in 1969. It has a 1600-acre campus.

RATINGS

Admissions Selectivity Rating: 81   Fire Safety Rating: 88   Green Rating: 76

STUDENTS AND FACULTY

Enrollment: 6,717. **Student Body:** 57% female, 43% male, 1% out-of-state, international (14 countries represented). Asian 5%, African American 8%, Caucasian 76%, Hispanic 6%, Native American 1%.
Retention and Graduation: 39% freshmen graduate within 4 years. 29% grads go on to further study within 1 year. 76% grads pursue arts and sciences degrees. 6% grads pursue business degrees. 6% grads pursue medical degrees. **Faculty:** Student/faculty ratio 18.7:1. 264 full-time faculty, 95% hold PhDs, 22% are members of minority groups, 50% are women.

ACADEMICS

Degrees: Bachelor's, certificate, master's, post-bachelor's certificate, post-master's certificate. **Classes:** Most classes have 30–39 students. Most lab/discussion sessions have 10–19 students. **Majors with Highest Enrollment:** Biology/biological sciences; business administration and management; psychology. **Special Study Options:** Accelerated program, distance learning, double major, English

as a Second Language (ESL), honors program, independent study, internships, liberal arts/career combination, study abroad, teacher certification program, Dual degree bachelor's program in engineering with Rutger's University and New Jersey Institute of Technology, preceptorial advising, opportunities for specialized research, Washington Internship available, and Service-Learning. **Honors programs:** Stockton Honors Program. **Combined degree programs:** BA/MD, BA/MA, BA/DDS, BA/MEng, BA/MA criminal justice, BS/PSM environmental science, BS/ĐPT. Special programs offered to physically disabled students include note-taking services, reader services, tape recorders, tutors. **Career services:** Alumni network, alumni services, career/job search classes, career assessment, internships, regional alumni. **Career services highlights include:** We are proud of all of our programs, but we are proudest of our internship and experiential learning opportunities.

FACILITIES

Housing: Coed dorms, special housing for disabled students, apartments for single students, wellness housing, theme housing, academic units. Living/Learning Communities include themes of Diversity, Global Citizenship, Sustainability, and Wellness. 100% of campus accessible to physically disabled. **Special Academic Facilities/Equipment:** Observatory, Nacote Creek field station, Holocaust Resource Center. **Computers:** 100% of classrooms, 5% of dorms, 100% of libraries, 100% of dining areas, 10% of common outdoor areas have wireless network access. Students can register for classes online. Administrative functions (other than registration) can be performed online.

CAMPUS LIFE

Environment: Town. **Activities:** Choral groups, concert band, dance, drama/theater, literary magazine, music ensembles, musical theater, radio station, student government, student newspaper, television station, yearbook, campus ministries, international student organization. **Organizations:** 130 registered organizations, 6 honor societies, 5 religious organizations. 11 fraternity, 9 sororities. **Athletics (Intercollegiate):** *Men:* Baseball, basketball, cheerleading, cross-country, lacrosse, soccer, track/field (outdoor), track/field (indoor). *Women:* Basketball, cheerleading, crew/rowing, cross-country, field hockey, soccer, softball, tennis, track/field (outdoor), track/field (indoor), volleyball. **On-Campus Highlights:** Performing Arts Center, Library, Housing options, Osprey's Nest, Marine Field Station. **Environmental Initiatives:** Solar generation: 1.2 Megawatts capacity located on campus. This includes rooftop installations and shade canopies over parking lots. The Richad Stockton College Coastal Research Center, located on Nacote Creek in Port Republic,is housed by Richard Stockton College's Nacote Creek Marine and Environmental Science Field Station, which functions in large part as a teaching and training facility for Stockton students. The CRC carries out about 20 research projects a year. The CRC is at the forefront of research groups at Richard Stockton College, and is a leader of coastal geoscience and resource studies in the Mid-Atlantic region. The Geothermal Project provides up to 1,650 tons of cooling capacity and allows portions of the building to be heated and cooled using the same equipment. The Aquifer Thermal Energy Storage system provides additional air conditioning capacity. It is the first project of its kind in the US.

ADMISSIONS

Freshman Academic Profile: 26% in top 10% of high school class, 60% in top 25% of high school class, 96% in top 50% of high school class. 74% from public high schools. SAT Math middle 50% range 510–610. SAT Critical Reading middle 50% range 490–590. SAT Writing middle 50% range 480–580. ACT middle 50% range 19–23. Minimum paper TOEFL 550. Minimum computer TOEFL 217. **Basis for Candidate Selection:** *Very important factors considered include:* Class rank, academic GPA, rigor of secondary school record. *Important factors considered include:* standardized test scores. *Other factors considered include:* Application essay, recommendation(s), alumni/ae relation, character/personal qualities, extracurricular activities, level of applicant's interest, talent/ability, volunteer work, work experience. **Freshman Admission Requirements:** High school diploma is required and GED is accepted. *Academic units required:* 4 English, 3 mathematics, 2 science, (2 science labs), 2 social studies, 5 academic electives. *Academic units recommended:* 4 English, 3 mathematics, 2 science, (2 science labs), 2 foreign language, 2 social studies, 5 academic electives. **Freshman Admission Statistics:** 4,547 applied, 61% admitted, 31% enrolled. Minimum college GPA of 2.5 required. Lowest grade transferable C. **General Admission Information:** Application fee $50. Regular application deadline 5/1. Notification on a rolling basis, beginning on or about 10/1. Nonfall registration accepted. Credit and/or placement offered for CEEB Advanced Placement tests.

COSTS AND FINANCIAL AID

Annual in-state tuition $7,067. Annual out-of-state tuition $12,750. Room and board $10,189. Required fees $3,873. Average book expense $1,500. **Required Forms and Deadlines:** FAFSA. Priority financial aid filing date 3/1. **Notification of Awards:** Applicants will be notified of awards on a rolling basis beginning 4/1. **Types of Aid:** *Need-based scholarships/grants:* Federal Pell, SEOG, state scholarships/grants, the school's own gift aid. *Loans:* Direct Subsidized Stafford, Direct Unsubsidized Stafford, Direct PLUS, Federal Perkins, state loans *Student Employment:* Federal Work-Study Program available. Institutional employment available. Highest amount earned per year from on-campus jobs $1,643. Off-campus job opportunities are excellent. **Financial Aid Statistics:** 35% freshmen, 33% undergrads receive need-based scholarship or grant aid. 30% freshmen, 16% undergrads receive non-need-based scholarship or grant aid. 57% freshmen, 55% undergrads receive need-based self-help aid. 84% freshmen, 77% undergrads receive any aid. 69% undergrads borrow to pay for school. Average cumulative indebtedness $27,847. **Criteria for awarding institutional aid:** *Non-need-based:* Academics, art, leadership, minority status, music/drama, state/district residency.

RICHMOND, THE AMERICAN INTERNATIONAL UNIVERSITY IN LONDON

US Office of Admissions, 343 Congress Street–Suite 3100, Boston, MA 02210
Phone: 617-450-5617 **Financial Aid Phone:** 011-44-20-8332-8244
E-mail: us_admissions@richmond.ac.uk **CEEB Code:** 823
Fax: 617-450-5601 **Website: ACT Code:** 5244

This private school was founded in 1972. It has a 6-acre campus.

RATINGS
Admissions Selectivity Rating: 86   **Fire Safety Rating:** 60*   **Green Rating:** 60*

STUDENTS AND FACULTY
Enrollment: 874. **Student Body:** 55% female, 45% male, % out-of-state. . **Retention and Graduation:** 72% freshmen return for sophomore year. 35% grads go on to further study within 1 year. **Faculty:** Student/faculty ratio 12:1. 41 full-time faculty, 85% hold PhDs, 39% are women.

ACADEMICS
Degrees: Associate, bachelor's, master's, post-bachelor's certificate, terminal associate. **Classes:** Most classes have 10–19 students. **Majors with Highest Enrollment:** Business/commerce; international relations and affairs. **Special Study Options:** English as a Second Language (ESL), independent study, internships, liberal arts/career combination, study abroad, Joint Engineering program with George Washington University.

FACILITIES
Housing: Coed dorms, men's dorms, women's dorms. **Computers:** Administrative functions (other than registration) can be performed online.

CAMPUS LIFE
Environment: Metropolis. **Activities:** Choral groups, dance, drama/theater, literary magazine, music ensembles, musical theater, student government, student newspaper, yearbook. **Organizations:** 1 honor societies, **Athletics (Intercollegiate):** *Men:* rugby, soccer. *Women:* rugby **On-Campus Highlights:** Caffe del Mondo Gourmet Coffee Shop, Wireless Computer Network, Student Common Room, Student Cafeteria.

ADMISSIONS
Freshman Academic Profile: Average high school GPA 3.25. 29% in top 10% of high school class, 40% in top 25% of high school class, 94% in top 50% of high school class. 60% from public high schools. SAT Math middle 50% range 488–610. SAT Critical Reading middle 50% range 495–625. ACT middle 50% range 24–28. Minimum paper TOEFL 550. Minimum computer TOEFL 230. **Basis for Candidate Selection:** *Very important factors considered include:* Application essay, academic GPA, recommendation(s), rigor of secondary school record. *Important factors considered include:* extracurricular activities. *Other factors considered include:* standardized test scores, alumni/ae relation, character/personal qualities, interview, talent/ability. **Freshman Admission Requirements:** High school diploma is required and GED is accepted. *Academic units required:* 4 English, 3 mathematics, 3 science. **Freshman Admission Statistics:** 1,232 applied, 52% admitted, 32% enrolled. **Transfer Admission Requirements:** College transcript(s), essay or personal statement, statement of good standing from prior institution(s). Minimum college GPA of 2.5 required. Lowest grade transferable C. **General Admission Information:** Application fee $50. Regular application deadline 8/1. Notification on a rolling basis, beginning on or about 11/1. Nonfall registration accepted. Admission may be deferred for a maximum of 1 year. Credit and/or placement offered for CEEB Advanced Placement tests.

COSTS AND FINANCIAL AID
Annual tuition $27,000. Room and board $12,900. Average book expense $1,000. **Required Forms and Deadlines:** FAFSA. Priority financial aid filing date 3/15. **Notification of Awards:** Applicants will be notified of awards on or about 3/15. **Types of Aid:** *Need-based scholarships/grants:* private scholarships, the school's own gift aid. *Loans:* FFEL Subsidized Stafford, FFEL Unsubsidized Stafford, FFEL PLUS, college/university loans from institutional funds.

Student Employment: Highest amount earned per year from on-campus jobs $1,500. Off-campus job opportunities are good. **Financial Aid Statistics:** 80% freshmen, 70% undergrads receive any aid. 30% undergrads borrow to pay for school. Average cumulative indebtedness $22,000. **Criteria for awarding institutional aid:** *Non-need-based:* Academics.

RIDER UNIVERSITY

2083 Lawrenceville Road, Lawrenceville, NJ 08648-3099
Phone: 609-896-5042 **Financial Aid Phone:** 609-896-5360
E-mail: admissions@rider.edu **CEEB Code:** 2758
Fax: 609-895-6645 **Website:** www.rider.edu **ACT Code:** 2590

This private school was founded in 1865. It has a 280-acre campus.

RATINGS
Admissions Selectivity Rating: 77   **Fire Safety Rating:** 60*   **Green Rating:** 93

STUDENTS AND FACULTY
Enrollment: 4,712. **Student Body:** 61% female, 39% male, 22% out-of-state, 3% international (50 countries represented). Asian 3%, African American 10%, Caucasian 68%, Hispanic 6%.
Retention and Graduation: 80% freshmen return for sophomore year. 47% freshmen graduate within 4 years. 16% grads go on to further study within 1 year. 2% grads pursue arts and sciences degrees. 1% grads pursue law degrees. 4% grads pursue business degrees. 1% grads pursue medical degrees. **Faculty:** Student/faculty ratio 12.75:1. 243 full-time faculty, 97% hold PhDs, 14% are members of minority groups, 42% are women.

ACADEMICS
Degrees: Associate, bachelor's, master's, post-master's certificate. **Classes:** Most classes have 10–19 students. Most lab/discussion sessions have 10–19 students. **Majors with Highest Enrollment:** Accounting; business/commerce; elementary education and teaching. **Special Study Options:** Cooperative education program, cross-registration, distance learning, double major, honors program, independent study, internships, liberal arts/career combination, study abroad, teacher certification program, weekend college, Learning Communities. **Honors programs:** The Baccalaureate Honors Program is designed to enrich the educational opportunities for Rider students of proven intellectual capability who choose to become Baccalaureate Scholars. Through a series of team-taught seminars, small classes, personal contact with faculty, colloquia and symposia, as well as independent study opportunities, the scholars extend their ability to think critically, coherently, and systematically about the great themes, ideals and movements of their human heritage. Students may apply, or be invited, as entering freshmen, as currently enrolled freshmen or sophomores, or as transfer freshmen or sophomores. To be considered for the program incoming freshmen must be in the top 10 percent of their high school class. **Combined degree programs:** BS/BA. Special programs offered to physically disabled students include reader services, tape recorders, tutors. **Career services:** Alumni network, alumni services, internships.

FACILITIES
Housing: Coed dorms, special housing for disabled students, women's dorms, fraternity/sorority housing, apartments for single students, suites, Special interest areas: wellness, quiet, First Year Experience, science, searning community. 73% of campus accessible to physically disabled. **Special Academic Facilities/ Equipment:** Art gallery, Holocaust/Genocide Resource Center. **Computers:** Students can register for classes online. Administrative functions (other than registration) can be performed online.

CAMPUS LIFE
Environment: Village. **Activities:** Choral groups, concert band, dance, drama/theater, literary magazine, music ensembles, musical theater, opera, pep band, radio station, student government, student newspaper, student-run film society, television station, yearbook, campus ministries, international student organization, Model UN. **Organizations:** 84 registered organizations, 24 honor societies, 6 religious organizations. 4 fraternities, 8 sororities. **Athletics (Intercollegiate):** *Men:* Baseball, basketball, cheerleading, cross-country, diving, golf, soccer, swimming, tennis, track/field (outdoor), wrestling. *Women:* Basketball, cheerleading, cross-country, diving, field hockey, soccer, softball, swimming, tennis, track/field (outdoor), volleyball. **On-Campus Highlights:**

Residence Hall Quad, Alumni Gym, Student Recreation Center, Daly's Dining Hall/Cranberry Cafe, Academic Quad. **Environmental Initiatives:** Signing the American College & University Presidents Climate Commitment and formation of the Energy and Sustainability Steering Committee in 2007 to implement strategic plan establishing sustainability initiatives for the university. Completion of a Greenhouse Gas Inventory for 2007–2008 and 2008–2009 and completion of a Carbon Neutrality Plan in 2010. Development of a student Eco-Rep program and currently employing 10 students. Building Silver LEED-certified new residence hall.

ADMISSIONS

Freshman Academic Profile: Average high school GPA 3.27. 16% in top 10% of high school class, 45% in top 25% of high school class, 79% in top 50% of high school class. 80% from public high schools. SAT Math middle 50% range 470–580. SAT Critical Reading middle 50% range 460–560. SAT Writing middle 50% range 470–580. ACT middle 50% range 19–24. Minimum paper TOEFL 550. Minimum computer TOEFL 213. Minimum web-based TOEFL 80. **Basis for Candidate Selection:** *Very important factors considered include:* Application essay, academic GPA, recommendation(s), rigor of secondary school record, standardized test scores. *Important factors considered include:* level of applicant's interest. *Other factors considered include:* Class rank, alumni/ae relation, character/personal qualities, extracurricular activities, geographical residence, interview, state residency, talent/ability, volunteer work, work experience. **Freshman Admission Requirements:** High school diploma is required and GED is accepted. *Academic units required:* 4 English, 3 mathematics. *Academic units recommended:* 4 mathematics, 4 science, (2 science labs), 2 foreign language, 2 social studies, 2 history. **Freshman Admission Statistics:** 7,372 applied, 75% admitted, 19% enrolled. **Transfer Admission Requirements:** College transcript(s), essay or personal statement, minimum college GPA of 2.5 required. Lowest grade transferable C. **General Admission Information:** Application fee $50. Early decision application deadline 11/15. Notification on a rolling basis, beginning on or about 12/15. Nonfall registration accepted. Admission may be deferred for a maximum of 1 year. Credit and/or placement offered for CEEB Advanced Placement tests.

COSTS AND FINANCIAL AID

Annual tuition $28,470. Room and board $10,720. Required fees $590. Average book expense $1,500. **Required Forms and Deadlines:** FAFSA. Priority financial aid filing date 3/1. **Notification of Awards:** Applicants will be notified of awards on a rolling basis beginning 2/20. **Types of Aid:** *Need-based scholarships/grants:* Federal Pell, SEOG, state scholarships/grants, private scholarships, the school's own gift aid. *Loans:* FFEL Subsidized Stafford, FFEL Unsubsidized Stafford, FFEL PLUS, Federal Perkins, state loans, college/university loans from institutional funds. *Student Employment:* Federal Work-Study Program available. Institutional employment available. Highest amount earned per year from on-campus jobs $6,195. Off-campus job opportunities are good. **Financial Aid Statistics:** 76% freshmen, 68% undergrads receive need-based scholarship or grant aid. 14% freshmen, 11% undergrads receive non-need-based scholarship or grant aid. 57% freshmen, 51% undergrads receive need-based self-help aid. 7% freshmen, 6% undergrads receive athletic scholarships. 77% freshmen, 70% undergrads receive any aid. 72% undergrads borrow to pay for school. Average cumulative indebtedness $35,042. **Criteria for awarding institutional aid:** *Non-need-based:* Academics, alumni affiliation, athletics, leadership, minority status, music/drama, state/district residency.

RINGLING COLLEGE OF ART AND DESIGN

2700 N. Tamiami Trail, Sarasota, FL 34234-5895
Phone: 941-351-5100 **Financial Aid Phone:** 941-359-7534
E-mail: admissions@ringling.edu **CEEB Code:** 5573
Fax: 941-359-7517 **Website:** www.ringling.edu **ACT Code:** 6724

This private school was founded in 1931. It has a 49-acre campus.

RATINGS

Admissions Selectivity Rating: 60* **Fire Safety Rating:** 75 **Green Rating:** 70

STUDENTS AND FACULTY

Enrollment: 1,318. **Student Body:** 57% female, 43% male, 46% out-of-state, 6% international (46 countries represented). Asian 7%, African American 4%, Caucasian 69%, Hispanic 12%, Native American 1%.
Retention and Graduation: 81% freshmen return for sophomore year. 52% freshmen graduate within 4 years. 6% grads go on to further study within 1 year. 6% grads pursue arts and sciences degrees. **Faculty:** Student/faculty ratio 12:1. 83 full-time faculty, 66% hold PhDs, 6% are are members of minority groups, 30% are women.

ACADEMICS

Degrees: Bachelor's, certificate. **Classes:** Most classes have 10–19 students. **Majors with Highest Enrollment:** Animation, interactive technology, video graphics and special effects; graphic design; illustration. **Special Study Options:** Dual enrollment, exchange student program (domestic), independent study, internships, study abroad Special programs offered to physically disabled students include note-taking services, reader services, tape recorders, tutors. **Career services:** Alumni network, alumni services, career/job search classes, career assessment, internships, regional alumni. **Career services highlights include:** Career/job search classes—direct approach to students on areas of interest, review of core approaches and resources; alumni services—helping those who graduated, who, in turn, help us with recruiting, posting jobs, etc.; Regional alumni—help us with conference, workshops, visits to classes; alumni network—same as above; internships—growing opportunities especially in new majors and increasing success as full-time employees by those who interned at the company; career assessment—help students (few) who need to determine best major for their goals.

FACILITIES

Housing: Coed dorms, men's dorms, women's dorms, apartments for married students, apartments for single students, wellness housing. All housing accommodations are ADA compliant. 98% of campus accessible to physically disabled. **Special Academic Facilities/Equipment:** William G. and Marie Selby Gallery, Crossley Gallery, Verman Kimbrough Memorial Library. **Computers:** 60% of classrooms, 100% of dorms, 100% of libraries, 100% of dining areas, 100% of student union, 60% of common outdoor areas have wireless network access. Students can register for classes online. Administrative functions (other than registration) can be performed online.

CAMPUS LIFE

Environment: City. **Activities:** Dance, drama/theater, student government, campus ministries, international student organization. **Organizations:** 22 registered organizations, 2 religious organizations. **On-Campus Highlights:** Student Center, Selby Gallery, Crossley Gallery, Verman Kimbrough Memorial Library, Hammond Commons. **Environmental Initiatives:** In February 2008, the college began construction of two 80,000–square-foot LEED-certified buildings. One building will house 228 students and the other will provide further academic teaching space. In December 2008, the college completed an environmental audit having completed improvements to academic departments and support services. The college employs a Director of Environmental Health and Safety to organize and review the environmental management system.

ADMISSIONS

Freshman Academic Profile: Average high school GPA 3.17. Minimum paper TOEFL 500. Minimum computer TOEFL 173. Minimum web-based TOEFL 61. **Basis for Candidate Selection:** *Very important factors considered include:* Academic GPA, rigor of secondary school record, talent/ability. *Important factors considered include:* Application essay, recommendation(s). *Other factors considered include:* Alumni/ae relation, extracurricular activities, geographical residence, interview, level of applicant's interest, volunteer work, work experience. **Freshman Admission Requirements:** High school diploma is required and GED is accepted. **Freshman Admission Statistics:** 1,147 applied, 73% admitted, 38% enrolled. **Transfer Admission Requirements:** High school transcript, college transcript(s), essay or personal statement, minimum college GPA of 2.0 required. Lowest grade transferable C. **General Admission Information:** Application fee $70. Notification on a rolling basis, beginning on or about 9/1. Nonfall registration not accepted. Admission may be deferred for a maximum of 2 years. Credit and/or placement offered for CEEB Advanced Placement tests.

COSTS AND FINANCIAL AID

Required Forms and Deadlines: FAFSA. Priority financial aid filing date 3/1. **Notification of Awards:** Applicants will be notified of awards on a rolling basis beginning 4/1. **Types of Aid:** *Need-based scholarships/grants:* Federal Pell, SEOG, state scholarships/grants, private scholarships, the school's own gift aid. *Loans:* FFEL Subsidized Stafford, FFEL Unsubsidized Stafford, FFEL PLUS. *Student Employment:* Federal Work-Study Program available. Institutional employment available. Highest amount earned per year from on-campus jobs $5,894. Off-campus job opportunities are good. **Financial Aid Statistics:** 75% freshmen, 75% undergrads receive need-based scholarship or grant aid. 1% freshmen, 1% undergrads receive non-need-based scholarship or grant aid. 70% freshmen, 80% undergrads receive need-based self-help aid. 70% freshmen, 80% undergrads receive any aid. 94% undergrads borrow to pay for school. Average cumulative indebtedness $91,994. **Criteria for awarding institutional aid:** *Non-need-based:* Academics, art.

RIPON COLLEGE

PO Box 248, Ripon, WI 54971
Phone: 920-748-8114 **Financial Aid Phone:** 920-748-8301
E-mail: adminfo@ripon.edu **CEEB Code:** 1664
Fax: 920-748-8335 **Website:** www.ripon.edu **ACT Code:** 4636

This private school was founded in 1851. It has a 250-acre campus.

RATINGS
Admissions Selectivity Rating: 91   **Fire Safety Rating:** 61   **Green Rating:** 73

STUDENTS AND FACULTY
Enrollment: 1,038. **Student Body:** 51% female, 49% male, 27% out-of-state, 3% international (11 countries represented). Asian 1%, African American 1%, Caucasian 85%, Hispanic 3%, Native American 1%.
Retention and Graduation: 83% freshmen return for sophomore year. 60% freshmen graduate within 4 years. 32% grads go on to further study within 1 year. 20% grads pursue arts and sciences degrees. 2% grads pursue law degrees. 3% grads pursue business degrees. 8% grads pursue medical degrees. **Faculty:** Student/faculty ratio 15:1. 60 full-time faculty, 90% hold PhDs, 8% are are members of minority groups, 43% are women.

ACADEMICS
Degrees: Bachelor's. **Classes:** Most classes have 10–19 students. Most lab/discussion sessions have 10–19 students. **Majors with Highest Enrollment:** Business/commerce; history; psychology. **Special Study Options:** Double major, exchange student program (domestic), internships, student-designed major, study abroad, teacher certification program, Argonne Science Semester (Illinois). Newberry Library Program in the Humanities (Illinois). Urban Studies Program (Chicago). Wilderness Field Station Program (Minnesota). Other semester-away programs. Special programs offered to physically disabled students include tutors. **Career services:** Alumni network, career assessment, internships, regional alumni.

FACILITIES
Housing: Coed dorms, men's dorms, women's dorms, fraternity/sorority housing, apartments for single students. **Special Academic Facilities/Equipment:** Art gallery, language labs. **Computers:** 2% of classrooms, 30% of libraries, 100% of dining areas, 60% of student union, have wireless network access.

CAMPUS LIFE
Environment: Village. **Activities:** Choral groups, concert band, dance, drama/theater, jazz band, literary magazine, music ensembles, musical theater, radio station, student government, student newspaper, symphony orchestra, yearbook, campus ministries, international student organization. **Organizations:** 45 registered organizations, 13 honor societies, 2 religious organizations. 5 fraternities, 3 sororities. **Athletics (Intercollegiate):** *Men:* Baseball, basketball, cross-country, cycling, football, golf, soccer, swimming, tennis, track/field (outdoor), track/field (indoor). *Women:* Basketball, cross-country, cycling, golf, soccer, softball, swimming, tennis, track/field (outdoor), track/field (indoor), volleyball. **On-Campus Highlights:** Ceresco Prairie Conservancy, Art Gallery, Storzer Athletic Center, Lane Library.

ADMISSIONS
Freshman Academic Profile: Average high school GPA 3.42. 28% in top 10% of high school class, 61% in top 25% of high school class, 89% in top 50% of high school class. 75% from public high schools. SAT Math middle 50% range 500–640. SAT Critical Reading middle 50% range 490–640. ACT middle 50% range 22–27. Minimum paper TOEFL 550. Minimum computer TOEFL 213. Minimum web-based TOEFL 79. **Basis for Candidate Selection:** *Very important factors considered include:* Rigor of secondary school record, interview. *Important factors considered include:* Class rank, academic GPA, recommendation(s), standardized test scores, character/personal qualities, extracurricular activities. *Other factors considered include:* Application essay, talent/ability, volunteer work. **Freshman Admission Requirements:** High school diploma is required and GED is accepted. *Academic units required:* 4 English, 2 mathematics, 2 science, 2 social studies. *Academic units recommended:* 4 mathematics, 4 science, 2 foreign language, 4 social studies. **Freshman Admission Statistics:** 6,064 applied, 14% admitted, 30% enrolled. **Transfer Admission Requirements:** College transcript(s), essay or personal statement, statement of good standing from prior institution(s). Minimum college GPA of 2.0 required. Lowest grade transferable C. **General Admission Information:** Application fee $30. Notification on a rolling basis, beginning on or about 9/15. Nonfall registration accepted. Admission may be deferred for a maximum of 1 year. Credit and/or placement offered for CEEB Advanced Placement tests.

COSTS AND FINANCIAL AID
Annual tuition $25,170. Room and board $7,270. Required fees $275. Average book expense $1,000. **Required Forms and Deadlines:** FAFSA. Priority financial aid filing date 3/1. **Notification of Awards:** Applicants will be notified of awards on a rolling basis beginning 3/1. **Types of Aid:** *Need-based scholarships/grants:* Federal Pell, SEOG, state scholarships/grants, private scholarships, the school's own gift aid. *Loans:* FFEL Subsidized Stafford, FFEL Unsubsidized Stafford, FFEL PLUS, Federal Perkins. *Student Employment:* Federal Work-Study Program available. Institutional employment available. Highest amount earned per year from on-campus jobs $1,200. Off-campus job opportunities are good. **Financial Aid Statistics:** 81% freshmen, 84% undergrads receive need-based scholarship or grant aid. 10% freshmen, 72% undergrads receive non-need-based scholarship or grant aid. 70% freshmen, 81% undergrads receive need-based self-help aid. 87% freshmen, 89% undergrads receive any aid. 76% undergrads borrow to pay for school. Average cumulative indebtedness $26,073. **Criteria for awarding institutional aid:** *Non-need-based:* Academics, alumni affiliation, art, leadership, minority status, music/drama, religious affiliation, state/district residency.

See page 1208.

RIVIER COLLEGE

420 South Main Street, Nashua, NH 03060
Phone: 603-897-8219 **Financial Aid Phone:** 603-897-8810
E-mail: rivadmit@rivier.edu **CEEB Code:** 3728
Fax: 603-891-1799 **Website:** www.rivier.edu **ACT Code:** 2520

This private school, affiliated with the Roman Catholic Church, was founded in 1933. It has a 68-acre campus.

RATINGS
Admissions Selectivity Rating: 67   **Fire Safety Rating:** 60*   **Green Rating:** 60*

STUDENTS AND FACULTY
Enrollment: 1,406. **Student Body:** 82% female, 18% male, international (12 countries represented). Asian 2%, African American 2%, Caucasian 83%, Hispanic 4%, Native American 1%.
Retention and Graduation: 77% freshmen return for sophomore year. 41% freshmen graduate within 4 years. **Faculty:** Student/faculty ratio 15:1. 71 full-time faculty, 76% hold PhDs, 62% are women.

ACADEMICS
Degrees: Associate, bachelor's, certificate, doctoral, master's, post-bachelor's certificate, post-master's certificate. **Classes:** Most classes have 10–19 students. Most lab/discussion sessions have fewer than 10 students. **Special Study Options:** Cross-registration, double major, honors program, independent study, internships, liberal arts/career combination, student-designed major, teacher certification program **Combined degree programs:** BA/MA. Special programs offered to physically disabled students include note-taking services, reader services, tape recorders, tutors.

FACILITIES
Housing: Coed dorms, coed wellness dorm (substance free). 75% of campus accessible to physically disabled. **Special Academic Facilities/Equipment:** Art gallery, Early Childhood Center/Laboratory School, language lab, TV microscope, video/laser disk system, photospectrometer, high-performance liquid chromatograph, digital imaging lab, several art studios including a photography darkroom. **Computers:** 100% of classrooms, 100% of dorms, 100% of libraries, 100% of dining areas, 100% of student union, 100% of common outdoor areas have wireless network access. Administrative functions (other than registration) can be performed online.

CAMPUS LIFE
Environment: City. **Activities:** Choral groups, dance, drama/theater, music ensembles, student government, student newspaper, television station, yearbook. **Organizations:** 30 registered organizations, 2 honor societies, 2 religious organizations. **Athletics (Intercollegiate):** *Men:* Baseball, basketball, cross-country, soccer, volleyball. *Women:* Basketball, cross-country, soccer, softball, volleyball.

ADMISSIONS
Freshman Academic Profile: Average high school GPA 2.87. SAT Math middle 50% range 420–530. SAT Critical Reading middle 50% range 430–510. SAT Writing middle 50% range 440–530. ACT middle 50% range 17–22. Minimum paper TOEFL 500. Minimum computer TOEFL 173. **Basis for Candidate Selection:** *Very important factors considered include:* Academic GPA, rigor of secondary school record. *Important factors considered include:* Class rank, application essay, standardized test scores, extracurricular activi-

ties, talent/ability, volunteer work, work experience. *Other factors considered include:* Recommendation(s), character/personal qualities, interview. **Freshman Admission Requirements:** High school diploma is required and GED is accepted. *Academic units recommended:* 4 English, 3 mathematics, 1 science, (1 science labs), 2 foreign language, 2 social studies, 1 history, 3 academic electives. **Freshman Admission Statistics:** 878 applied, 81% admitted, 33% enrolled. **Transfer Admission Requirements:** Essay or personal statement, minimum college GPA of 2.0 required. Lowest grade transferable C. **General Admission Information:** Application fee $25. Notification on a rolling basis, beginning on or about 11/1. Nonfall registration not accepted. Admission may be deferred for a maximum of 1 year. Credit and/or placement offered for CEEB Advanced Placement tests.

COSTS AND FINANCIAL AID
Average book expense $1,200. **Required Forms and Deadlines:** FAFSA. Priority financial aid filing date 3/1. **Notification of Awards:** Applicants will be notified of awards on a rolling basis beginning 3/1. **Types of Aid:** *Need-based scholarships/grants:* Federal Pell, SEOG, state scholarships/grants, private scholarships, the school's own gift aid. *Loans:* Direct Subsidized Stafford, Direct Unsubsidized Stafford, Direct PLUS, Federal Perkins, college/university loans from institutional funds. *Student Employment:* Federal Work-Study Program available. Institutional employment available. Highest amount earned per year from on-campus jobs $4,500. Off-campus job opportunities are good. **Financial Aid Statistics:** 84% freshmen, 79% undergrads receive need-based scholarship or grant aid. 3% freshmen, 3% undergrads receive non-need-based scholarship or grant aid. 80% freshmen, 77% undergrads receive need-based self-help aid. 98% freshmen, 97% undergrads receive any aid. 94% undergrads borrow to pay for school. Average cumulative indebtedness $36,389. **Criteria for awarding institutional aid:** *Non-need-based:* Academics, alumni affiliation, leadership.

ROANOKE BIBLE COLLEGE

715 N. Poindexter St, Elizabeth City, NC 27909-4054
Phone: 252-334-2028 **Financial Aid Phone:** 252-334-2020
E-mail: admissions@roanokebible.edu
Fax: 252-334-2064 **ACT Code:** 3153

This private school was founded in 1948. It has a 20-acre campus.

RATINGS
Admissions Selectivity Rating: 72   **Fire Safety Rating:** 60*   **Green Rating:** 72

STUDENTS AND FACULTY
Retention and Graduation: 36% freshmen graduate within 4 years. **Faculty:** Student/faculty ratio 10:1. 9 full-time faculty, 56% hold PhDs, 33% are women.

ACADEMICS
Degrees: Associate, bachelor's, certificate. **Classes:** Most classes have fewer than 10 students. Most lab/discussion sessions have 10–19 students. **Majors with Highest Enrollment:** Bible/biblical studies. **Special Study Options:** Distance learning, double major, dual enrollment, internships, Cross-cultural semester abroad. Special programs offered to physically disabled students include tape recorders, tutors.

FACILITIES
Housing: Special housing for disabled students, men's dorms, women's dorms, apartments for married students, apartments for single students. 90% of campus accessible to physically disabled. **Computers:** 80% of classrooms, 100% of libraries, have wireless network access.

CAMPUS LIFE
Environment: Village. **Activities:** Choral groups, drama/theater, music ensembles, musical theater, student government, yearbook. **Organizations:** 1 honor societies. **Athletics (Intercollegiate):** *Men:* Basketball. *Women:* Basketball, volleyball. **On-Campus Highlights:** On the Pasquotank River, new married housing apartments, new student life center. **Environmental Initiatives:** Geothermal heating & cooling; solar hot water; recycle program.

ADMISSIONS
Freshman Academic Profile: Average high school GPA 2.78. 2% in top 10% of high school class, 14% in top 25% of high school class, 36.6% in top 50% of high school class. 87% from public high schools. SAT Math middle 50% range 420–590. SAT Critical Reading middle 50% range 410–565. Minimum paper TOEFL 500. Minimum computer TOEFL 222. Minimum web-based TOEFL 80. **Basis for Candidate Selection:** *Very important factors considered include:* Class rank, academic GPA, recommendation(s), standardized test scores, character/personal qualities, religious affiliation/commitment. *Important factors considered include:* Application essay, rigor of secondary school record.

Other factors considered include: extracurricular activities, interview, level of applicant's interest, talent/ability, volunteer work, work experience. **Freshman Admission Requirements:** High school diploma is required and GED is accepted. *Academic units required:* 4 English, 3 mathematics, 3 science, (2 science labs), 2 social studies, 2 history, 4 academic electives. *Academic units recommended:* 6 foreign language, 1 computer science. **Freshman Admission Statistics:** 127 applied, 56% admitted, 58% enrolled. **Transfer Admission Requirements:** College transcript(s), essay or personal statement, statement of good standing from prior institution(s). Minimum college GPA of 2.0 required. Lowest grade transferable C. **General Admission Information:** Application fee $50. Notification on a rolling basis, beginning on or about 9/1. Nonfall registration accepted. Admission may be deferred for a maximum of 1 semester. Credit and/or placement offered for CEEB Advanced Placement tests.

COSTS AND FINANCIAL AID
Required Forms and Deadlines: FAFSA, institution's own financial aid form. Priority financial aid filing date 3/1. **Notification of Awards:** Applicants will be notified of awards on a rolling basis beginning 5/1. **Types of Aid:** *Need-based scholarships/grants:* Federal Pell, SEOG, state scholarships/grants, private scholarships, the school's own gift aid. *Loans:* FFEL Subsidized Stafford, FFEL Unsubsidized Stafford, FFEL PLUS, Alternative Loans. *Student Employment:* Federal Work-Study Program available. Institutional employment available. Off-campus job opportunities are good. **Financial Aid Statistics:** 91% freshmen, 86% undergrads receive need-based scholarship or grant aid. 26% freshmen, 20% undergrads receive non-need-based scholarship or grant aid. 62% freshmen, 71% undergrads receive need-based self-help aid. 88% freshmen, 90% undergrads receive any aid. 80% undergrads borrow to pay for school. Average cumulative indebtedness $21,314. **Criteria for awarding institutional aid:** *Non-need-based:* Academics, alumni affiliation, art, athletics, leadership, music/drama, religious affiliation.

ROANOKE COLLEGE

221 College Lane, Salem, VA 24153-3794
Phone: 540-375-2270 **Financial Aid Phone:** 540-375-2235
E-mail: admissions@roanoke.edu **CEEB Code:** 5571
Fax: 540-375-2267 **Website:** www.roanoke.edu **ACT Code:** 4392

This private school, affiliated with the Lutheran Church, was founded in 1842. It has a 68-acre campus.

RATINGS
Admissions Selectivity Rating: 81   **Fire Safety Rating:** 72   **Green Rating:** 60*

STUDENTS AND FACULTY
Enrollment: 1,977. **Student Body:** 56% female, 44% male, 43% out-of-state, 1% international (25 countries represented). Asian 1%, African American 4%, Caucasian 84%, Hispanic 3%, Native American 1%.
Retention and Graduation: 77% freshmen return for sophomore year. 58% freshmen graduate within 4 years. 20% grads go on to further study within 1 year. **Faculty:** Student/faculty ratio 13.4:1. 166 full-time faculty, 82% hold PhDs, 9% are are members of minority groups, 48% are women.

ACADEMICS
Degrees: Bachelor's. **Classes:** Most classes have 10–19 students. Most lab/discussion sessions have 10–19 students. **Majors with Highest Enrollment:** Business/commerce; history; psychology. **Special Study Options:** Accelerated program, cross-registration, double major, dual enrollment, English as a Second Language (ESL), honors program, independent study, internships, liberal arts/career combination, study abroad, teacher certification program. **Honors programs:** The Honors Program is designed for students with excellent academic performance, broad extracurricular interests, and leadership abilities. The Honors Program substitutes a coordinated sequence of interdisciplinary courses for a portion of the core requirements. A Plenary Enrichment Program of supplemental activities, a special scholarship, and a distinct recognition on the diploma and transcript are provided. Special programs offered to physically disabled students include note-taking services, reader services, tape recorders, tutors. **Career services:** Alumni network, alumni services, career/job search classes, career assessment, internships, regional alumni. **Career services highlights include:** Alumni Networking, which is offered to both students and alumni. Roanoke alumni are very open to helping students and fellow graduates in the career development area.

FACILITIES
Housing: Coed dorms, men's dorms, women's dorms, fraternity/sorority housing, apartments for single students, theme housing. 85% of campus accessible to physically disabled. **Special Academic Facilities/Equipment:** Fine arts center, community research center, language lab, church and society center.

Computers: 100% of classrooms, 100% of libraries, 100% of dining areas, 100% of student union, 50% of common outdoor areas have wireless network access. Students can register for classes online. Administrative functions (other than registration) can be performed online.

CAMPUS LIFE

Environment: City. **Activities:** Choral groups, dance, drama/theater, jazz band, literary magazine, music ensembles, musical theater, pep band, radio station, student government, student newspaper, student-run film society, yearbook, campus ministries, international student organization, Model UN. **Organizations:** 85 registered organizations, 30 honor societies, 7 religious organizations. 4 fraternities, 4 sororities. **Athletics (Intercollegiate):** *Men:* Baseball, basketball, cross-country, golf, lacrosse, soccer, tennis, track/field (outdoor), track/field (indoor). *Women:* Basketball, cross-country, field hockey, lacrosse, soccer, softball, tennis, track/field (outdoor), track/field (indoor), volleyball. **On-Campus Highlights:** Colket Student Center, Belk Fitness Center, Fintel Library, Bast Gymnasium & Kerr Stadium, Olin Hall (performing arts).

ADMISSIONS

Freshman Academic Profile: Average high school GPA 3.33. 21% in top 10% of high school class, 47% in top 25% of high school class, 84% in top 50% of high school class. 70% from public high schools. SAT Math middle 50% range 490–590. SAT Critical Reading middle 50% range 500–600. SAT Writing middle 50% range 490–590. Minimum paper TOEFL 520. Minimum computer TOEFL 190. **Basis for Candidate Selection:** *Very important factors considered include:* Class rank, academic GPA, rigor of secondary school record, standardized test scores, character/personal qualities. *Important factors considered include:* Recommendation(s), extracurricular activities, interview. *Other factors considered include:* Application essay, alumni/ae relation, level of applicant's interest, racial/ethnic status, talent/ability, volunteer work, work experience. **Freshman Admission Requirements:** High school diploma is required and GED is accepted. *Academic units required:* 4 English, 3 mathematics, 2 science, (2 science labs), 2 social studies, 5 academic electives. *Academic units recommended:* 4 foreign language. **Freshman Admission Statistics:** 4,169 applied, 68% admitted, 20% enrolled. **Transfer Admission Requirements:** High school transcript, college transcript(s), statement of good standing from prior institution(s). Minimum college GPA of 2.2 required. Lowest grade transferable C–. **General Admission Information:** Application fee $33. Early decision application deadline 12/1. Regular application deadline 3/15. Regular notification 4/1. Nonfall registration accepted. Admission may be deferred for a maximum of 2 years. Credit and/or placement offered for CEEB Advanced Placement tests.

COSTS AND FINANCIAL AID

Annual tuition $28,734. Room and board $9,780. Required fees $850. Average book expense $1,000. **Required Forms and Deadlines:** FAFSA, state aid form. Priority financial aid filing date 3/1. **Notification of Awards:** Applicants will be notified of awards on a rolling basis beginning 11/1. **Types of Aid:** *Need-based scholarships/grants:* Federal Pell, SEOG, state scholarships/grants, private scholarships, the school's own gift aid. *Loans:* FFEL Subsidized Stafford, FFEL Unsubsidized Stafford, FFEL PLUS, Federal Perkins, college/university loans from institutional funds, Alternative loans. *Student Employment:* Federal Work-Study Program available. Institutional employment available. Highest amount earned per year from on-campus jobs $2,000. Off-campus job opportunities are good. **Financial Aid Statistics:** 63% freshmen, 60% undergrads receive need-based scholarship or grant aid. 34% freshmen, 35% undergrads receive non-need-based scholarship or grant aid. 44% freshmen, 45% undergrads receive need-based self-help aid. 94% freshmen, 95% undergrads receive any aid. 74% undergrads borrow to pay for school. Average cumulative indebtedness $21,807. **Criteria for awarding institutional aid:** *Non-need-based:* Academics, minority status, music/drama, religious affiliation.

ROBERT MORRIS COLLEGE (IL)

401 South State Street, Chicago, IL 60605
Phone: 800-762-5960
E-mail: enroll@robertmorris.edu
Fax: 312-935-6819

This is a private school.

RATINGS
Admissions Selectivity Rating: 61   **Fire Safety Rating:** 60*   **Green Rating:** 60*

STUDENTS AND FACULTY
Enrollment: 4,847. **Student Body:** 65% female, 35% male, 1% out-of-state. Asian 2%, African American 37%, Caucasian 34%, Hispanic 24%.

Retention and Graduation: 56% freshmen return for sophomore year. 40% freshmen graduate within 4 years. **Faculty:** Student/faculty ratio 26:1. 134 full-time faculty, 19% hold PhDs, 26% are are members of minority groups, 50% are women.

ACADEMICS
Degrees: Associate, bachelor's, diploma, master's. **Classes:** Most classes have 20–29 students. **Special Study Options:** Accelerated program, cooperative education program, distance learning, dual enrollment, honors program, internships, study abroad.

FACILITIES
Housing: Coed dorms.

CAMPUS LIFE
Activities: Choral groups, dance, drama/theater, literary magazine, student newspaper.

ADMISSIONS
Freshman Academic Profile: Average high school GPA 2.58. 7% in top 10% of high school class, 23% in top 25% of high school class, 50% in top 50% of high school class. **Basis for Candidate Selection:** *Very important factors considered include:* Class rank, rigor of secondary school record, interview. *Other factors considered include:* Application essay, recommendation(s), standardized test scores, character/personal qualities, extracurricular activities, talent/ability, volunteer work, work experience. **Freshman Admission Requirements:** High school diploma is required and GED is accepted. **Freshman Admission Statistics:** 2,714 applied, 80% admitted, 45% enrolled. **Transfer Admission Requirements:** High school transcript, college transcript(s), minimum college GPA of 2.0 required. Lowest grade transferable C. **General Admission Information:** Application fee $30. Nonfall registration accepted. Admission may be deferred for a maximum of unlimited.

COSTS AND FINANCIAL AID
Annual tuition $15,375. Room and board $6,600. **Required Forms and Deadlines:** FAFSA **Notification of Awards: Types of Aid:** *Need-based scholarships/grants:* Federal Pell, SEOG, state scholarships/grants, private scholarships, the school's own gift aid. *Loans:* FFEL Subsidized Stafford, FFEL Unsubsidized Stafford, FFEL PLUS, Federal Perkins. *Student Employment:* **Financial Aid Statistics:** 83% freshmen, 90% undergrads receive need-based scholarship or grant aid. 2% freshmen, 2% undergrads receive non-need-based scholarship or grant aid. 73% freshmen, 77% undergrads receive need-based self-help aid. 1% freshmen, 1% undergrads receive athletic scholarships. 91% undergrads borrow to pay for school. Average cumulative indebtedness $16,666. **Criteria for awarding institutional aid:** *Non-need-based:* Academics, art, athletics, state/district residency.

See page 1210.

ROBERT MORRIS UNIVERSITY

6001 University Boulevard, Moon Township, PA 15108-1189
Phone: 412-397-5200 **Financial Aid Phone:** 412-397-6250
E-mail: admissionsoffice@rmu.edu **CEEB Code:** 2769
Fax: 412-397-2425 **Website:** www.rmu.edu **ACT Code:** 3674

This private school was founded in 1921. It has a 230-acre campus.

RATINGS
Admissions Selectivity Rating: 70   **Fire Safety Rating:** 77   **Green Rating:** 71

STUDENTS AND FACULTY
Enrollment: 3,587. **Student Body:** 44% female, 56% male, 14% out-of-state, 3% international (16 countries represented). Asian 1%, African American 9%, Caucasian 82%, Hispanic 1%.
Retention and Graduation: 79% freshmen return for sophomore year. 34% freshmen graduate within 4 years. 8% grads go on to further study within 1 year. **Faculty:** Student/faculty ratio 15:1. 177 full-time faculty, 81% hold PhDs, 11% are are members of minority groups, 37% are women.

ACADEMICS
Degrees: Bachelor's, certificate, master's, post-bachelor's certificate. **Classes:** Most classes have 20–29 students. **Majors with Highest Enrollment:** Accounting; business administration and management; marketing/marketing management. **Special Study Options:** Cooperative education program, cross-registration, distance learning, double major, honors program, independent study, internships, study abroad, teacher certification program, weekend college, evening, weekend and 5 week/8 week programs. **Honors programs:** International Honors Program **Combined degree programs:** BSBA/MS

BS/MS. Special programs offered to physically disabled students include note-taking services, reader services, tape recorders, tutors. **Career services:** Alumni network, alumni services, career/job search classes, career assessment, internships, regional alumni. **Career services highlights include:** Extensive internship and co-op placement program.

FACILITIES

Housing: Coed dorms, men's dorms, women's dorms, apartments for single students. 75% of campus accessible to physically disabled. **Computers:** 50% of classrooms, 75% of libraries, 100% of dining areas, 100% of student union, 25% of common outdoor areas have wireless network access. Students can register for classes online. Administrative functions (other than registration) can be performed online.

CAMPUS LIFE

Environment: Metropolis. **Activities:** Choral groups, drama/theater, literary magazine, marching band, musical theater, pep band, radio station, student government, student newspaper, television station, campus ministries, international student organization. **Organizations:** 97 registered organizations, 6 honor societies, 5 religious organizations, 4 fraternities, 3 sororities. **Athletics (Intercollegiate):** *Men:* Basketball, football, golf, ice hockey, lacrosse, soccer, tennis, track/field (outdoor), track/field (indoor). *Women:* Basketball, crew/rowing, field hockey, golf, ice hockey, lacrosse, soccer, softball, tennis, track/field (outdoor), track/field (indoor), volleyball. **On-Campus Highlights:** Student Center, RMU Island Sports Center Complex, Computer Labs, Athletic Center, Health Club. **Environmental Initiatives:** Recycling paper, cardboard, plastic, bottles and cans, and florescent bulbs.

ADMISSIONS

Freshman Academic Profile: Average high school GPA 3.26. 9.2% in top 10% of high school class, 32.5% in top 25% of high school class, 68.5% in top 50% of high school class. 87% from public high schools. SAT Math middle 50% range 460–580. SAT Critical Reading middle 50% range 450–540. SAT Writing middle 50% range 440–540. ACT middle 50% range 20–24. Minimum paper TOEFL 500. Minimum computer TOEFL 173. Minimum web-based TOEFL 61. **Basis for Candidate Selection:** *Very important factors considered include:* Academic GPA, standardized test scores. *Important factors considered include:* Class rank, rigor of secondary school record, character/personal qualities, extracurricular activities, interview. *Other factors considered include:* Application essay, recommendation(s), alumni/ae relation, level of applicant's interest, talent/ability, volunteer work, work experience. **Freshman Admission Requirements:** High school diploma is required and GED is accepted. *Academic units required:* 4 English, 3 mathematics, 2 science, 4 social studies, 3 academic electives. *Academic units recommended:* 2 foreign language. **Freshman Admission Statistics:** 3,775 applied, 92% admitted, 21% enrolled. **Transfer Admission Requirements:** College transcript(s), statement of good standing from prior institution(s). Minimum college GPA of 2.0 required. Lowest grade transferable C. **General Admission Information:** Application fee $30. Regular application deadline 7/1. Notification on a rolling basis, beginning on or about 8/1. Nonfall registration accepted. Admission may be deferred for a maximum of 1 year. Credit and/or placement offered for CEEB Advanced Placement tests.

COSTS AND FINANCIAL AID

Required Forms and Deadlines: FAFSA. **Notification of Awards:** Applicants will be notified of awards on a rolling basis beginning 3/15. **Types of Aid:** *Need-based scholarships/grants:* Federal Pell, SEOG, state scholarships/grants, private scholarships, the school's own gift aid. *Loans:* FFEL Subsidized Stafford, FFEL Unsubsidized Stafford, FFEL PLUS, Federal Perkins, Alternative private loans. *Student Employment:* Federal Work-Study Program available. Institutional employment available. Off-campus job opportunities are good. **Financial Aid Statistics:** 79% freshmen, 73% undergrads receive need-based scholarship or grant aid. 9% freshmen, 6% undergrads receive non-need-based scholarship or grant aid. 70% freshmen, 70% undergrads receive need-based self-help aid. 4% freshmen, 3% undergrads receive athletic scholarships. 80% freshmen, 79% undergrads receive any aid. 84% undergrads borrow to pay for school. Average cumulative indebtedness $35,055. **Criteria for awarding institutional aid:** *Non-need-based:* Academics, athletics.

ROBERTS WESLEYAN COLLEGE

2301 Westside Drive, Rochester, NY 14624-1997
Phone: 585-594-6400 **Financial Aid Phone:** 585-594-6150
E-mail: admissions@roberts.edu **CEEB Code:** 2805
Fax: 585-594-6371 **Website:** www.roberts.edu **ACT Code:** 2759

This private school was founded in 1866. It has a 75-acre campus.

RATINGS

Admissions Selectivity Rating: 82   **Fire Safety Rating:** 60*   **Green Rating:** 60*

STUDENTS AND FACULTY

Enrollment: 1,388. **Student Body:** 69% female, 31% male, 8% out-of-state, 1% international (18 countries represented). Asian 1%, African American 10%, Caucasian 78%, Hispanic 4%.
Retention and Graduation: 86% freshmen return for sophomore year. 55% freshmen graduate within 4 years. 29% grads go on to further study within 1 year. **Faculty:** Student/faculty ratio 11:1. 102 full-time faculty, 66% hold PhDs, 9% are are members of minority groups, 47% are women.

ACADEMICS

Degrees: Bachelor's, master's. **Classes:** Most classes have 10–19 students. Most lab/discussion sessions have 10–19 students. **Majors with Highest Enrollment:** Elementary education and teaching; music teacher education; nursing, other. **Special Study Options:** Cross-registration, distance learning, double major, English as a Second Language (ESL), honors program, independent study, internships, study abroad, teacher certification program. **Combined degree programs:** BA/MEng, Pharmacy. Special programs offered to physically disabled students include note-taking services, reader services, tape recorders, tutors. **Career services:** Alumni network, alumni services, career assessment, internships, regional alumni. **Career services highlights include:** Alumni networking and shadowing programs, alumni career panels, alumni career services group on Linkedin.com, mock interviews.

FACILITIES

Housing: Coed dorms, special housing for disabled students, men's dorms, women's dorms, apartments for married students, apartments for single students 71% of campus accessible to physically disabled. **Special Academic Facilities/Equipment:** Davison Art Gallery. **Computers:** 100% of classrooms, 100% of dorms, 100% of libraries, 100% of dining areas, 100% of student union, 70% of common outdoor areas have wireless network access. Students can register for classes online. Administrative functions (other than registration) can be performed online.

CAMPUS LIFE

Environment: City. **Activities:** Choral groups, concert band, dance, drama/theater, jazz band, music ensembles, musical theater, opera, student government, student newspaper, symphony orchestra, yearbook, campus ministries, international student organization, Model UN. **Organizations:** 28 registered organizations, 11 religious organizations. **Athletics (Intercollegiate):** *Men:* Basketball, cross-country, golf, soccer, tennis, track/field (outdoor), track/field (indoor). *Women:* Basketball, cross-country, soccer, tennis, track/field (outdoor), track/field (indoor), volleyball. **On-Campus Highlights:** Voller Athletic Center & Sports Complex, New B. Thomas Golisano Library, Rinker Community Service Center, BT's Cafe, Cultural Life Center.

ADMISSIONS

Freshman Academic Profile: Average high school GPA 3.3. 28% in top 10% of high school class, 56% in top 25% of high school class, 80% in top 50% of high school class. SAT Math middle 50% range 480–610. SAT Critical Reading middle 50% range 470–590. SAT Writing middle 50% range 450–560. ACT middle 50% range 21–27. Minimum paper TOEFL 550. Minimum computer TOEFL 213. Minimum web-based TOEFL 79. **Basis for Candidate Selection:** *Very important factors considered include:* Academic GPA, rigor of secondary school record, standardized test scores, character/personal qualities, interview, religious affiliation/commitment. *Important factors considered include:* Application essay, recommendation(s), extracurricular activities. *Other factors considered include:* Class rank, alumni/ae relation, level of applicant's interest, talent/ability, volunteer work. **Freshman Admission Requirements:** High school diploma is required and GED is accepted. *Academic units required:* 4 English, 3 mathematics, 3 science, (1 science labs), 3 social studies. *Academic units recommended:* 4 mathematics, 4 science, (3 science labs), 3 foreign language. **Freshman Admission Statistics:** 1,358 applied, 65% admitted, 30% enrolled. **Transfer Admission Requirements:** College transcript(s), essay or personal statement, minimum college GPA of 2.70 required. Lowest grade transferable C. **General Admission Information:** Application fee $35. Notification on a rolling basis, beginning on or about 10/1. Nonfall registration accepted. Admission may be deferred for a maximum of 1 year. Credit and/or placement offered for CEEB Advanced Placement tests.

COSTS AND FINANCIAL AID

Annual tuition $22,580. Room and board $8,520. Required fees $866. Average book expense $1,000. **Required Forms and Deadlines:** FAFSA, state aid form. Priority financial aid filing date 3/15. **Notification of Awards:** Applicants will be notified of awards on a rolling basis beginning 3/30. **Types of Aid:** *Need-based scholarships/grants:* Federal Pell, SEOG, state scholarships/grants, private scholarships, the school's own gift aid. *Loans:* Direct Subsidized Stafford, Direct Unsubsidized Stafford, Direct PLUS, Federal Perkins. *Student Employment:* Federal Work-Study Program available. Institutional employment available. Highest amount earned per year from on-campus jobs $3,000. Off-campus job opportunities are fair. **Financial Aid Statistics:** 83% freshmen, 82% undergrads receive need-based scholarship or grant aid. 5% freshmen, 4%

undergrads receive non-need-based scholarship or grant aid. 77% freshmen, 78% undergrads receive need-based self-help aid. 3% freshmen, 2% undergrads receive athletic scholarships. 97% freshmen, 92% undergrads receive any aid. 96% undergrads borrow to pay for school. Average cumulative indebtedness $22,619. **Criteria for awarding institutional aid:** *Non-need-based:* Academics, alumni affiliation, art, athletics, music/drama, religious affiliation.

ROCHESTER COLLEGE

800 West Avon Road, Rochester Hills, MI 48307
Phone: 248-218-2031
E-mail: admissions@rc.edu **CEEB Code:** 1516
Fax: 248-218-2035 **Website:** www.rc.edu **ACT Code:** 2072

This private school, affiliated with the Church of Christ Church, was founded in 1959. It has a 83-acre campus.

RATINGS
Admissions Selectivity Rating: 60*   **Fire Safety Rating:** 60*   **Green Rating:** 60*

STUDENTS AND FACULTY
Student Body: 14% out-of-state. (10 countries represented). **Retention and Graduation:** 69% freshmen return for sophomore year. 8% freshmen graduate within 4 years. **Faculty:** Student/faculty ratio 15:1. 32 full-time faculty, 28% hold PhDs, 34% are women.

ACADEMICS
Degrees: Associate, bachelor's, master's, transfer associate. **Special Study Options:** Accelerated program, cross-registration, double major, dual enrollment, independent study, internships, liberal arts/career combination, study abroad, teacher certification program, weekend college. Special programs offered to physically disabled students include note-taking services, reader services. **Career services:** Alumni services, career/job search classes, career assessment, internships.

FACILITIES
Housing: Special housing for disabled students, men's dorms, women's dorms, apartments for married students.

CAMPUS LIFE
Environment: Village. **Activities:** Choral groups, drama/theater, jazz band, music ensembles, student government, student newspaper, yearbook. **Organizations:** 19 registered organizations, 3 honor societies, 1 religious organizations. **Athletics (Intercollegiate):** *Men:* Baseball, basketball, cross-country, soccer, track/field (outdoor). *Women:* Basketball, cross-country, softball, track/field (outdoor), volleyball.

ADMISSIONS
Freshman Academic Profile: Minimum paper TOEFL 500. Minimum computer TOEFL 173. **Basis for Candidate Selection:** *Important factors considered include:* Rigor of secondary school record, standardized test scores. *Other factors considered include:* interview. **Freshman Admission Requirements:** High school diploma is required and GED is accepted. **Freshman Admission Statistics:** 277 applied, 83% admitted, 65% enrolled. **Transfer Admission Requirements:** High school transcript, college transcript(s), minimum college GPA of 2.0 required. Lowest grade transferable C. **General Admission Information:** Application fee $25. Notification on a rolling basis, beginning on or about 9/1. Nonfall registration accepted. Admission may be deferred for a maximum of 24 months. Credit and/or placement offered for CEEB Advanced Placement tests.

COSTS AND FINANCIAL AID
Annual tuition $9,462. Room and board $5,342. Required fees $600. Average book expense $600. **Required Forms and Deadlines:** FAFSA, institution's own financial aid form. Priority financial aid filing date 8/1. **Notification of Awards:** Applicants will be notified of awards on a rolling basis beginning 6/1. **Types of Aid:** *Need-based scholarships/grants:* Federal Pell, SEOG, state scholarships/grants, private scholarships, the school's own gift aid. *Loans:* Direct Subsidized Stafford, Direct Unsubsidized Stafford, Direct PLUS, Federal Perkins. *Student Employment:* Federal Work-Study Program available. Institutional employment available. Off-campus job opportunities are excellent. **Financial Aid Statistics:** 59% freshmen receive need-based scholarship or grant aid. 53% freshmen receive non-need-based scholarship or grant aid. 56% freshmen receive need-based self-help aid. 29% freshmen receive athletic scholarships. 45% undergrads borrow to pay for school. Average cumulative indebtedness $10,416. **Criteria for awarding institutional aid:** *Non-need-based:* Academics, alumni affiliation, athletics, leadership, music/drama.

ROCHESTER INSTITUTE OF TECHNOLOGY

60 Lomb Memorial Drive, Rochester, NY 14623-5604
Phone: 585-475-5502 **Financial Aid Phone:** 585-475-5502
E-mail: ealfad@rit.edu **CEEB Code:** 2760
Fax: 585-475-7424 **Website:** www.rit.edu **ACT Code:** 2870

This private school was founded in 1829. It has a 1300-acre campus.

RATINGS
Admissions Selectivity Rating: 85   **Fire Safety Rating:** 60*   **Green Rating:** 96

STUDENTS AND FACULTY
Enrollment: 13,056. **Student Body:** 33% female, 67% male, 50% out-of-state, international (95 countries represented). **Retention and Graduation:** 15% grads go on to further study within 1 year. **Faculty:** Student/faculty ratio 14:1. 816 full-time faculty, 70% hold PhDs, 19% are are members of minority groups, 33% are women.

ACADEMICS
Degrees: Associate, bachelor's, certificate, diploma, master's, post-bachelor's certificate, terminal associate, transfer associate. **Classes:** Most classes have 10–19 students. Most lab/discussion sessions have 10–19 students. **Majors with Highest Enrollment:** Business/commerce; information technology; photography. **Special Study Options:** Accelerated program, cooperative education program, cross-registration, distance learning, double major, English as a Second Language (ESL), exchange student program (domestic), honors program, independent study, internships, liberal arts/career combination, student-designed major, study abroad, weekend college. **Honors programs:** The RIT Honors Program provides a variety of curricular and extracurricular options, special Honors housing, and Honors scholarships. **Combined degree programs:** BA/MEng, BS/MS, BS/MBA. Special programs offered to physically disabled students include note-taking services, reader services, tape recorders, tutors. **Career services:** Alumni network, alumni services, career/job search classes, career assessment, internships, regional alumni. **Career services highlights include:** Every academic program at RIT offers some form of experiential education opportunity. Experiential education is designed to enrich the learning experience by providing students the opportunity to apply what they are learning in the lab and classroom to real-world problems, projects, and settings. Experiential education takes many forms including cooperative education, internships, study-abroad, undergraduate research, and industry sponsored project work. Experiential education requirements and opportunities vary among academic programs. Notable among these programs at RIT is cooperative education (co-op). The College of Applied Science and Technology, the E. Philip Saunders College of Business, the B. Thomas Golisano College of Computing and Information Sciences, and the Kate Gleason College of Engineering all require co-op for undergraduate students. It is available on an optional basis in other RIT colleges. Co-op students alternate periods of full-time study with periods of full-time paid work experience in business and industry directly related to their field of study and career interests. Last year more than 3,300 students completed work assignments with nearly 1,500 employers earning collectively in excess of $30 million.

FACILITIES
Housing: Coed dorms, special housing for disabled students, special housing for international students, fraternity/sorority housing, apartments for married students, apartments for single students, Special interest floors for selected majors/ groups. Men's floors Women's floors. 95% of campus accessible to physically disabled. **Special Academic Facilities/Equipment:** Art galleries, microelectronic engineering center, RIT Inn and Conference Center, observatory, student-managed restaurant, packaging testing facility, media resource center, Sunday 2000 printing press, Center for manufacturing studies, two OC3 connections to Internet and Internet2, laser optics laboratory, an observatory, an animal care facility, more than 100 color and black-and-white photography darkrooms, electronic prepress and publishing equipment, ceramic kilns, glass furnaces, a blacksmithing area, and computer graphics and robotic labs. **Computers:** 75% of classrooms, 25% of dorms, 100% of libraries, 100% of dining areas, 100% of student union, 100% of common outdoor areas have wireless network access. Students can register for classes online. Administrative functions (other than registration) can be performed online.

CAMPUS LIFE
Environment: City. **Activities:** Choral groups, concert band, dance, drama/ theater, jazz band, literary magazine, music ensembles, musical theater, pep

---

band, radio station, student government, student newspaper, student-run film society, symphony orchestra, yearbook, campus ministries, international student organization. **Organizations:** 175 registered organizations, 9 honor societies, 5 religious organizations. 19 fraternities, 10 sororities. **Athletics (Intercollegiate):** *Men:* Baseball, basketball, crew/rowing, cross-country, diving, ice hockey, lacrosse, soccer, swimming, tennis, track/field (outdoor), track/field (indoor), wrestling. *Women:* Basketball, cheerleading, crew/rowing, cross-country, diving, ice hockey, lacrosse, soccer, softball, swimming, tennis, track/field (outdoor), track/field (indoor), volleyball. **On-Campus Highlights:** Java Wally's (Wallace Library coffee shop), Student Life Center/Field House/Ice Arena, ESPN Zone @ RIT Student Alumni Union, Ben and Jerry's (RIT Student Alumni Union), The Cafe and Market at Crossroads. **Environmental Initiatives:** 1. President William Destler has just announced that he will sign the American College & University Presidents' Climate Commitment. He noted that, "As part of this commitment, we will need to come up with an institutional strategic plan for reducing energy consumption and greenhouse gas production, and provide institutional structures and support that can move the campus toward the goals set in the plan. This plan will include a green building policy, an energy-star procurement policy, encouragement of public transportation, green power production and purchasing, and waste minimization." In addition, he pledged to make RIT a national center of excellence in the areas of environmental science and sustainability. 2. The institute is processing a $38 million heating and cooling plant replacement project with aim to lower campus emissions and improve the energy efficiency. 3. We have committed to completion of all construction projects according to LEED specification, with a minimum target of LEED Silver. Recently, we achieved our first LEED Gold certification for new construction of the College of Applied Science and Technology (CAST) Building. Additionally, 2 buildings are in process with target for LEED Gold. One building is in the design stage with the target for LEED Platinum.

ADMISSIONS

Freshman Academic Profile: 30.2% in top 10% of high school class, 62% in top 25% of high school class, 91.4% in top 50% of high school class. 85% from public high schools. SAT Math middle 50% range 560–670. SAT Critical Reading middle 50% range 540–630. SAT Writing middle 50% range 520–610. ACT middle 50% range 24–29. Minimum paper TOEFL 550. Minimum computer TOEFL 215. Minimum web-based TOEFL 79. **Basis for Candidate Selection:** *Very important factors considered include:* Academic GPA, rigor of secondary school record. *Important factors considered include:* Class rank, standardized test scores. *Other factors considered include:* Application essay, recommendation(s), alumni/ae relation, character/personal qualities, extracurricular activities, first generation, geographical residence, interview, level of applicant's interest, racial/ethnic status, talent/ability, volunteer work, work experience. **Freshman Admission Requirements:** High school diploma is required and GED is accepted. *Academic units required:* 4 English, 2 mathematics, 2 science, (1 science labs), 4 social studies, 10 academic electives. *Academic units recommended:* 4 English, 3 mathematics, 3 science, (2 science labs), 3 foreign language, 4 social studies, 5 academic electives. **Freshman Admission Statistics:** 12,725 applied, 60% admitted, 34% enrolled. **Transfer Admission Requirements:** College transcript(s), essay or personal statement, minimum college GPA of 2.7 required. Lowest grade transferable C–. **General Admission Information:** Application fee $50. Early decision application deadline 12/1. Regular application deadline 2/1. Notification on a rolling basis, beginning on or about 3/15. Nonfall registration accepted. Admission may be deferred for a maximum of 1 year. Credit and/or placement offered for CEEB Advanced Placement tests.

COSTS AND FINANCIAL AID

Annual tuition $28,886. Room and board $9,642. Required fees $417. Average book expense $900. **Required Forms and Deadlines:** FAFSA, institution's own financial aid form, state aid form. Priority financial aid filing date 3/1. **Notification of Awards:** Applicants will be notified of awards on a rolling basis beginning 3/15. **Types of Aid:** *Need-based scholarships/grants:* Federal Pell, SEOG, state scholarships/grants, private scholarships, the school's own gift aid, NACME. *Loans:* Direct Subsidized Stafford, Direct Unsubsidized Stafford, Direct PLUS, Federal Perkins, RIT Loan program; Alternative loans. *Student Employment:* Federal Work-Study Program available. Institutional employment available. Highest amount earned per year from on-campus jobs $2,500. Off-campus job opportunities are excellent. **Financial Aid Statistics:** 71% freshmen, 65% undergrads receive need-based scholarship or grant aid. 20% freshmen, 20% undergrads receive non-need-based scholarship or grant aid. 66% freshmen, 61% undergrads receive need-based self-help aid. 88% freshmen, 77% undergrads receive any aid. 77% undergrads borrow to pay for school. Average cumulative indebtedness $23,800. **Criteria for awarding institutional aid:** *Non-need-based:* Academics, art, leadership.

See page 1212.

ROCKFORD COLLEGE

Admission, 5050 E. State Street, Rockford, IL 61108-2393
Phone: 815-226-4050 **Financial Aid Phone:** 815-226-4062
E-mail: RCAdmissions@rockford.edu **CEEB Code:** 1665
Fax: 815-226-2822 **Website:** www.rockford.edu **ACT Code:** 1122

This private school was founded in 1847. It has a 130-acre campus.

RATINGS
Admissions Selectivity Rating: 79   **Fire Safety Rating:** 66   **Green Rating:** 60*

STUDENTS AND FACULTY
Enrollment: 857. **Student Body:** 61% female, 39% male, 10% out-of-state, international. Asian 2%, African American 8%, Caucasian 69%, Hispanic 6%. **Retention and Graduation: Faculty:** Student/faculty ratio 9:1. 69 full-time faculty, 68% hold PhDs, 3% are are members of minority groups, 42% are women.

ACADEMICS
Degrees: Bachelor's, master's. **Classes:** Most classes have 10–19 students. Most lab/discussion sessions have fewer than 10 students. **Majors with Highest Enrollment:** Business/commerce; education; nursing/registered nurse (RN, ASN, BSN, MSN). **Special Study Options:** Accelerated program, distance learning, double major, English as a Second Language (ESL), exchange student program (domestic), honors program, independent study, internships, study abroad, teacher certification program, community-based learning, tutorial courses, special studies courses. **Honors programs:** Honors program in Liberal Arts Special programs offered to physically disabled students include note-taking services, reader services, tutors. **Career services:** Career assessment, internships. **Career services highlights include:** Community-Based Learning: Founded at Rockford College in the early 1990s, our community-based learning program is based on the conviction that Rockford College is a citizen of the community and that the community has a stake in Rockford College, as well. The work that the students perform serves the dual function of providing a defined need for the community while also fulfilling a specific learning objective determined by the professor.

FACILITIES
Housing: Coed dorms, special housing for disabled students, theme housing Special housing for first-year students. We offer single rooms, double rooms, and suite style living options. **Special Academic Facilities/Equipment:** Language lab. Art gallery. Sculpture garden. **Computers:** Students can register for classes online. Administrative functions (other than registration) can be performed online.

CAMPUS LIFE
Environment: City. **Activities:** Choral groups, dance, drama/theater, literary magazine, music ensembles, musical theater, opera, pep band, student government, campus ministries, international student organization, Model UN. **Organizations:** 25 registered organizations, 6 honor societies, 1 religious organizations. **Athletics (Intercollegiate):** *Men:* Baseball, basketball, cross-country, football, golf, soccer, tennis, track/field (outdoor), track/field (indoor). *Women:* Basketball, cross-country, golf, soccer, softball, tennis, track/field (outdoor), track/field (indoor), volleyball. **On-Campus Highlights:** Residence Halls, Seaver Gym, Lion's Den-student gathering place, Football/Soccer Stadium, Clark Arts Center, Tour also highlights classroom buildings. **Environmental Initiatives:** Green Week; Trayless Tuesdays in the cafeteria; recycling options readily available.

ADMISSIONS
Freshman Academic Profile: Average high school GPA 3.07. 18% in top 10% of high school class, 33% in top 25% of high school class, 65% in top 50% of high school class. ACT middle 50% range 19–24. Minimum paper TOEFL 550. Minimum computer TOEFL 213. Minimum web-based TOEFL 79. **Basis for Candidate Selection:** *Very important factors considered include:* Academic GPA. *Important factors considered include:* Application essay, rigor of secondary school record, standardized test scores. *Other factors considered include:* Class rank, recommendation(s). **Freshman Admission Requirements:** High school diploma is required and GED is accepted. *Academic units required:* 4 English, 3 mathematics, 3 science, (3 science labs), 3 social studies, 2 academic electives. *Academic units recommended:* 2 foreign language. **Freshman Admission Statistics:** 967 applied, 41% admitted, 23% enrolled. **Transfer Admission Requirements:** College transcript(s), statement of good standing from prior institution(s). Minimum college GPA of 2.3 required. Lowest grade transferable C. **General Admission Information:** Application fee $35. Notification on a rolling basis, beginning on or about 9/15. Nonfall registration accepted. Admission may be deferred for a maximum of 1 year. Credit and/or placement offered for CEEB Advanced Placement tests.

COSTS AND FINANCIAL AID

Annual tuition $24,750. Room and board $6,950. Average book expense $1,200. **Required Forms and Deadlines:** FAFSA. Priority financial aid filing date 3/1. **Notification of Awards:** Applicants will be notified of awards on a rolling basis beginning 3/1. **Types of Aid:** *Need-based scholarships/grants:* Federal Pell, SEOG, state scholarships/grants, private scholarships, the school's own gift aid. *Loans:* FFEL Subsidized Stafford, FFEL Unsubsidized Stafford, FFEL PLUS, Federal Perkins. *Student Employment:* Federal Work-Study Program available. Institutional employment available. Off-campus job opportunities are excellent. **Financial Aid Statistics:** 87% freshmen, 84% undergrads receive need-based scholarship or grant aid. 11% freshmen, 14% undergrads receive non-need-based scholarship or grant aid. 83% freshmen, 87% undergrads receive need-based self-help aid. 99% freshmen, 99% undergrads receive any aid. 92% undergrads borrow to pay for school. Average cumulative indebtedness $29,987. **Criteria for awarding institutional aid:** *Non-need-based:* Academics, alumni affiliation, leadership, minority status, music/drama, state/district residency.

See page 1214.

ROCKHURST UNIVERSITY

1100 Rockhurst Road, Kansas City, MO 64110
Phone: 816-501-4100 **Financial Aid Phone:** 816-501-4100
E-mail: admission@rockhurst.edu **CEEB Code:** 6611
Fax: 816-501-4241 **Website:** www.rockhurst.edu **ACT Code:** 2342

This private school, affiliated with the Roman Catholic Church, was founded in 1910. It has a 55-acre campus.

RATINGS

Admissions Selectivity Rating: 82   **Fire Safety Rating:** 62   **Green Rating:** 60*

STUDENTS AND FACULTY

Enrollment: 1,528. **Student Body:** 59% female, 41% male, 37% out-of-state, 1% international (16 countries represented). Asian 3%, African American 6%, Caucasian 83%, Hispanic 6%, Native American 1%.
Retention and Graduation: 86% freshmen return for sophomore year. 51% freshmen graduate within 4 years. 21% grads go on to further study within 1 year. 4% grads pursue arts and sciences degrees. 4% grads pursue law degrees. 11% grads pursue business degrees. 3% grads pursue medical degrees. **Faculty:** Student/faculty ratio 11:1. 125 full-time faculty, 84% hold PhDs, 5% are are members of minority groups, 45% are women.

ACADEMICS

Degrees: Bachelor's, certificate, master's, post-bachelor's certificate. **Classes:** Most classes have 20–29 students. Most lab/discussion sessions have 10–19 students. **Majors with Highest Enrollment:** Business/commerce; nursing/registered nurse (RN, ASN, BSN, MSN); psychology. **Special Study Options:** Accelerated program, cooperative education program, cross-registration, double major, dual enrollment, exchange student program (domestic), honors program, independent study, internships, study abroad, teacher certification program. **Honors programs:** The Rockhurst University Honors Program is for motivated and talented students, regardless of major, who want to be active participants in designing their education. Students find honors courses to be more innovative, personal, and challenging than other courses. The Benefits Beginning in the first year, honors students have specially designed core courses that are usually small in enrollment and are taught by some of the University's most creative faculty. During the sophomore through senior years, honors students may earn honors credit through "honors options"—individually designed projects that allow students to explore areas of their own interest under the mentorship of a professor. An honors option is typically an offshoot of a regular course, but an option can also be arranged as an independent study course. It is through the honors option that honors students shape their curriculum. **Combined degree programs:** BA/MOT, BA/DPT, BS/CSD, B/MBA. Special programs offered to physically disabled students include note-taking services, reader services, tape recorders, tutors. **Career services:** Alumni network, alumni services, career/job search classes, career assessment, internships, regional alumni. **Career services highlights include:** All three add to the experiential education programs at Rockhurst.

FACILITIES

Housing: Coed dorms, special housing for disabled students, men's dorms, women's dorms, apartments for single students, RU on-campus housing. 90% of campus accessible to physically disabled. **Special Academic Facilities/Equipment:** Greenlease Art Gallery, Richardson Science Center. **Computers:** Students can register for classes online. Administrative functions (other than registration) can be performed online.

CAMPUS LIFE

Environment: Metropolis. **Activities:** Choral groups, drama/theater, literary magazine, musical theater, student government, student newspaper, yearbook. **Organizations:** 44 registered organizations, 4 honor societies, 6 religious organizations. 3 fraternities, 3 sororities. **Athletics (Intercollegiate):** *Men:* Baseball, basketball, golf, soccer, tennis. *Women:* Basketball, golf, soccer, softball, tennis, volleyball. **On-Campus Highlights:** New Bell Tower and Fountains, Richardson Science Center/state-of-art facility, Business School/complete computer lab and classroom renovations, Career and Learning Center, The Old Gym (historic) plus the new.

ADMISSIONS

Freshman Academic Profile: Average high school GPA 3.53. 22% in top 10% of high school class, 55% in top 25% of high school class, 82% in top 50% of high school class. 45% from public high schools. SAT Math middle 50% range 510–610. SAT Critical Reading middle 50% range 480–630. ACT middle 50% range 22–27. Minimum paper TOEFL 550. Minimum computer TOEFL 234. **Basis for Candidate Selection:** *Very important factors considered include:* Academic GPA, standardized test scores. *Important factors considered include:* Class rank, recommendation(s), rigor of secondary school record, character/personal qualities. *Other factors considered include:* Alumni/ae relation, extracurricular activities, interview, level of applicant's interest, religious affiliation/commitment, talent/ability, volunteer work. **Freshman Admission Requirements:** High school diploma is required and GED is accepted. *Academic units recommended:* 4 English, 3 mathematics, 3 science, (1 science labs), 4 academic electives, 3 foreign language/social studies. **Freshman Admission Statistics:** 1,767 applied, 75% admitted, 30% enrolled. **Transfer Admission Requirements:** College transcript(s), minimum college GPA of 2.5 required. Lowest grade transferable C–. **General Admission Information:** Application fee $25. Regular notification 9/15. Nonfall registration accepted. Admission may be deferred for a maximum of 1 year. Credit and/or placement offered for CEEB Advanced Placement tests.

COSTS AND FINANCIAL AID

Annual tuition $22,000. Room and board $6,200. Required fees $840. Average book expense $1,400. **Required Forms and Deadlines:** FAFSA Financial aid filing deadline 6/30. Priority financial aid filing date 3/1. **Notification of Awards:** Applicants will be notified of awards on a rolling basis beginning 1/30. **Types of Aid:** *Need-based scholarships/grants:* Federal Pell, SEOG, state scholarships/grants, private scholarships, the school's own gift aid. *Loans:* FFEL Subsidized Stafford, FFEL Unsubsidized Stafford, FFEL PLUS, Federal Perkins, Alternative Loans. *Student Employment:* Federal Work-Study Program available. Institutional employment available. Highest amount earned per year from on-campus jobs $1,650. Off-campus job opportunities are fair. **Financial Aid Statistics:** 56% freshmen, 50% undergrads receive need-based scholarship or grant aid. 93% freshmen, 78% undergrads receive non-need-based scholarship or grant aid. 48% freshmen, 43% undergrads receive need-based self-help aid. 10% freshmen, 11% undergrads receive athletic scholarships. 89% freshmen, 92% undergrads receive any aid. 67% undergrads borrow to pay for school. Average cumulative indebtedness $17,525. **Criteria for awarding institutional aid:** *Non-need-based:* Academics, alumni affiliation, athletics, leadership, music/drama, state/district residency.

ROCKY MOUNTAIN COLLEGE

1511 Poly Drive, Billings, MT 59102-1796
Phone: 406-657-1026 **Financial Aid Phone:** 406-657-1031
E-mail: admissions@rocky.edu **CEEB Code:** 4660
Fax: 406-657-1189 **Website:** www.rocky.edu **ACT Code:** 2426

This private school was founded in 1878. It has a 60-acre campus.

RATINGS

Admissions Selectivity Rating: 77   **Fire Safety Rating:** 60*   **Green Rating:** 60*

STUDENTS AND FACULTY

Enrollment: 817. **Student Body:** 55% female, 45% male, 38% out-of-state, 5% international (15 countries represented). Asian 1%, African American 1%, Caucasian 84%, Hispanic 2%, Native American 7%.
Retention and Graduation: 67% freshmen return for sophomore year. 28% freshmen graduate within 4 years. 19% grads go on to further study within 1 year. 15% grads pursue arts and sciences degrees. 1% grads pursue law degrees. 3% grads pursue business degrees. 2% grads pursue medical degrees. **Faculty:** Student/faculty ratio 13:1. 48 full-time faculty, 65% hold PhDs, 2% are are members of minority groups, 44% are women.

ACADEMICS

Degrees: Associate, bachelor's, master's, terminal associate, transfer associate. **Classes:** Most classes have 10–19 students. Most lab/discussion sessions have fewer than 10 students. **Majors with Highest Enrollment:** Biology/biological sciences; business/commerce; physician assistant. **Special Study Options:** Accelerated program, distance learning, double major, dual enrollment, English as a Second Language (ESL), honors program, independent study, internships, student-designed major, study abroad, teacher certification program. **Honors programs:** Successful honors students find that participation in this program not only brings them closer to professionals in their chosen fields, but also grants them a substantial credential in their applications to graduate schools or employment opportunities. Special programs offered to physically disabled students include note-taking services, reader services, tape recorders, tutors. **Career services:** Alumni network, alumni services, career/job search classes, career assessment, internships, regional alumni.

FACILITIES

Housing: Coed dorms, apartments for married students, apartments for single students, Suites. 50% of campus accessible to physically disabled. **Special Academic Facilities/Equipment:** Billings Studio Theater, museum, studio, flight simulator/flight school, equestrian facilities, geology collection. **Computers:** Students can register for classes online. Administrative functions (other than registration) can be performed online.

CAMPUS LIFE

Environment: City. **Activities:** Choral groups, concert band, drama/theater, jazz band, literary magazine, music ensembles, musical theater, pep band, student government, student newspaper, yearbook. **Organizations:** 28 registered organizations, 1 honor societies, 4 religious organizations. **Athletics (Intercollegiate):** *Men:* Basketball, cheerleading, football, golf, skiing (downhill/alpine). *Women:* Basketball, cheerleading, golf, skiing (downhill/alpine), soccer, volleyball. **On-Campus Highlights:** Bair Family Student Center, Educational Resource Center, Fortin Center-Gymnasium, Herb Klindt Field-Football Stadium, Losekamp Hall-Music Theatre.

ADMISSIONS

Freshman Academic Profile: Average high school GPA 3.34. 21% in top 10% of high school class, 43% in top 25% of high school class, 78% in top 50% of high school class. SAT Math middle 50% range 450–570. SAT Critical Reading middle 50% range 460–590. ACT middle 50% range 19–24. Minimum paper TOEFL 525. Minimum computer TOEFL 197. **Basis for Candidate Selection:** *Very important factors considered include:* Academic GPA, rigor of secondary school record, standardized test scores. *Important factors considered include:* Class rank. *Other factors considered include:* Application essay, recommendation(s), alumni/ae relation, character/personal qualities, extracurricular activities, interview, level of applicant's interest, talent/ability, volunteer work, work experience. **Freshman Admission Requirements:** High school diploma is required and GED is accepted. *Academic units required:* 4 English, 2 mathematics, 2 science, (1 science labs), 1 foreign language, 2 social studies, 2 history. *Academic units recommended:* 4 English, 3 mathematics, 2 science, (1 science labs), 2 foreign language, 2 social studies, 2 history. **Freshman Admission Statistics:** 596 applied, 72% admitted, 36% enrolled. **Transfer Admission Requirements:** College transcript(s), minimum college GPA of 2.0 required. Lowest grade transferable C–. **General Admission Information:** Application fee $25. Notification on a rolling basis, beginning on or about 9/1. Nonfall registration accepted. Admission may be deferred for a maximum of 1 year. Credit and/or placement offered for CEEB Advanced Placement tests.

COSTS AND FINANCIAL AID

Annual tuition $16,389. Room and board $5,608. Required fees $253. Average book expense $900. **Required Forms and Deadlines:** FAFSA, institution's own financial aid form. Priority financial aid filing date 3/1. **Notification of Awards:** Applicants will be notified of awards on a rolling basis beginning 2/1. **Types of Aid:** *Need-based scholarships/grants:* Federal Pell, SEOG, state scholarships/grants, private scholarships, the school's own gift aid. *Loans:* FFEL Subsidized Stafford, FFEL Unsubsidized Stafford, FFEL PLUS, Federal Perkins. *Student Employment:* Federal Work-Study Program available. Institutional employment available. Highest amount earned per year from on-campus jobs $3,985. Off-campus job opportunities are good. **Financial Aid Statistics:** 67% freshmen, 73% undergrads receive need-based scholarship or grant aid. 28% freshmen, 11% undergrads receive non-need-based scholarship or grant aid. 52% freshmen, 55% undergrads receive need-based self-help aid. 8% freshmen, 4% undergrads receive athletic scholarships. 90% freshmen, 90% undergrads receive any aid. 78% undergrads borrow to pay for school. Average cumulative indebtedness $19,933. **Criteria for awarding institutional aid:** *Non-need-based:* Academics, alumni affiliation, art, athletics, leadership, minority status, music/drama, religious affiliation, state/district residency.

ROCKY MOUNTAIN COLLEGE OF ART & DESIGN

1600 Pierce St, Denver, CO 80214
Phone: 303-753-6046
E-mail: admissions@rmcad.edu
Fax: 303-567-7281 **Website:** www.rmcad.edu **ACT Code:** 5359

This proprietary school was founded in 1963. It has a 23-acre campus.

RATINGS

Admissions Selectivity Rating: 60* **Fire Safety Rating:** 60* **Green Rating:** 60*

STUDENTS AND FACULTY

Student Body: 60% out-of-state.
Faculty: Student/faculty ratio 19:1.

ACADEMICS

Degrees: Bachelor's. **Special Study Options:** Independent study, internships, study abroad. **Career services:** Alumni network, alumni services, career/job search classes, career assessment, internships.

FACILITIES

Special Academic Facilities/Equipment: Philip Steele Gallery, Fine Arts Exhibit Space, Drive Up Gallery.

CAMPUS LIFE

Environment: Metropolis. **Activities:** Dance, music ensembles, student government, student newspaper, campus ministries.

ADMISSIONS

Freshman Academic Profile: Minimum paper TOEFL 500. Minimum computer TOEFL 173. **Basis for Candidate Selection:** *Very important factors considered include:* extracurricular activities. *Important factors considered include:* Academic GPA. **Freshman Admission Requirements:** High school diploma is required and GED is accepted. **Freshman Admission Statistics: Transfer Admission Requirements:** College transcript(s), minimum college GPA of 2.0 required. **General Admission Information:** Nonfall registration accepted. Admission may be deferred for a maximum of one semester.

COSTS AND FINANCIAL AID

Annual tuition $19,752. Average book expense $600. *Student Employment:* Federal Work-Study Program available. Off-campus job opportunities are good.

ROGER WILLIAMS UNIVERSITY

One Old Ferry Road, Bristol, RI 02809-2921
Phone: 401-254-3500 **Financial Aid Phone:** 401-254-3100
E-mail: admit@rwu.edu **CEEB Code:** 3729
Fax: 401-254-3557 **Website:** www.rwu.edu **ACT Code:** 3814

This private school was founded in 1956. It has a 140-acre campus.

RATINGS

Admissions Selectivity Rating: 82 **Fire Safety Rating:** 88 **Green Rating:** 91

STUDENTS AND FACULTY

Enrollment: 4,297. **Student Body:** 48% female, 52% male, 82% out-of-state, 2% international (41 countries represented). Asian 1%, African American 2%, Caucasian 74%, Hispanic 2%.
Retention and Graduation: 82% freshmen return for sophomore year. 40% freshmen graduate within 4 years. 13% grads go on to further study within 1 year. 2% grads pursue law degrees. **Faculty:** Student/faculty ratio 12:1. 210 full-time faculty, 84% hold PhDs, 14% are are members of minority groups, 40% are women.

ACADEMICS

Degrees: Associate, bachelor's, certificate, first professional, master's, post-bachelor's certificate, terminal associate. **Classes:** Most classes have 10–19 students. Most lab/discussion sessions have 10–19 students. **Majors with Highest Enrollment:** Architecture (BArch, BA/BS, MArch, MA/MS, PhD); business/commerce; psychology. **Special Study Options:** Cooperative education program, distance learning, double major, dual enrollment, English as a Second Language (ESL), exchange student program (domestic), external degree program, honors program, independent study, internships, liberal arts/career combination, student-designed major, study abroad, teacher certification program, weekend college. **Honors programs:** 1. Alpha Chi Honors Society-University-wide association for Juniors and Seniors; 2. Four-year Honors Program-For full-time students in any major which includes special sections of general education classes, a unique group service project for juniors and a required senior thesis. The program includes a variety of cultural and co-curricular activities, as well as leadership opportunities; 3. Honors Society Associations-Department-level honors associations within various disciplines **Combined degree programs:** BA/JD, 3-3 law program. Dual Degree Architecture program. Special programs offered to physically disabled students include note-taking services, reader services, tape recorders, tutors.

FACILITIES

Housing: Coed dorms, special housing for disabled students, apartments for single students, wellness housing, theme housing, special interest, academic theme housing, honors, wellness, non-smoking. **Special Academic Facilities/Equipment:** Marine and Natural Sciences Building, School of Law and Law Library, Main Library, Architecture Building and Architecture Library, Performing Arts Center, Thomas J. Paolino Recreation Center, Global Heritage Hall. **Computers:** 100% of classrooms, 100% of dorms, 100% of libraries, 100% of dining areas, 100% of student union, 20% of common outdoor areas have wireless network access. Students can register for classes online. Administrative functions (other than registration) can be performed online.

CAMPUS LIFE

Environment: Village. **Activities:** Choral groups, dance, drama/theater, literary magazine, musical theater, radio station, student government, student newspaper, student-run film society, yearbook, international student organization, Model UN. **Organizations:** 93 registered organizations, 13 honor societies, 4 religious organizations. **Athletics (Intercollegiate):** *Men:* Baseball, basketball, cross-country, diving, equestrian sports, lacrosse, sailing, soccer, swimming, tennis, track/field (outdoor), track/field (indoor), wrestling. *Women:* Basketball, cross-country, diving, equestrian sports, lacrosse, sailing, soccer, softball, swimming, tennis, track/field (outdoor), track/field (indoor), volleyball. **On-Campus Highlights:** Recreation Center, Library, Dining Commons, Marine Science Wet Lab, Bookstore, Students are taken to any specific place they would also like to see. Residence Halls are available for viewing with permission from occupants at certain points in the year. **Environmental Initiatives:** All renovation and new construction on campus meets LEED Silver standards. Committed to reducing power consumption, reuse resources and recycle whenever possible. Incorporating the idea of sustainability in all facets of the university

ADMISSIONS

Freshman Academic Profile: Average high school GPA 3.21. 14% in top 10% of high school class, 38% in top 25% of high school class, 76% in top 50% of high school class. 85% from public high schools. SAT Math middle 50% range 520–600. SAT Critical Reading middle 50% range 500–590. SAT Writing middle 50% range 500–590. ACT middle 50% range 21–25. **Basis for Candidate Selection:** *Very important factors considered include:* Application essay, academic GPA, recommendation(s), rigor of secondary school record, standardized test scores. *Important factors considered include:* Class rank, extracurricular activities. *Other factors considered include:* Alumni/ae relation, first generation, level of applicant's interest, talent/ability, volunteer work, work experience. **Freshman Admission Requirements:** High school diploma is required and GED is accepted. *Academic units required:* 4 English, 3 mathematics, 2 science, (2 science labs), 2 social studies, 2 history, 2 academic electives. *Academic units recommended:* 4 English, 4 mathematics, 4 science, (2 science labs), 2 foreign language, 3 social studies, 3 history, 3 academic electives. **Freshman Admission Statistics:** 8,561 applied, 61% admitted, 18% enrolled. **Transfer Admission Requirements:** College transcript(s), essay or personal statement, minimum college GPA of 2.5 required. Lowest grade transferable C. **General Admission Information:** Application fee $50. Regular application deadline 2/1. Regular notification 3/15. Nonfall registration accepted. Admission may be deferred for a maximum of 1 year. Credit and/or placement offered for CEEB Advanced Placement tests.

COSTS AND FINANCIAL AID

Annual tuition $25,968. Room and board $12,140. Required fees $1,750. Average book expense $900. **Required Forms and Deadlines:** FAFSA, CSS/Financial Aid PROFILE Financial aid filing deadline 2/1. Priority financial aid filing date 1/1. **Notification of Awards:** Applicants will be notified of awards on a rolling basis beginning 3/20. **Types of Aid:** *Need-based scholarships/grants:* Federal Pell, SEOG, state scholarships/grants, private scholarships, the school's own gift aid. *Loans:* FFEL Subsidized Stafford, FFEL Unsubsidized Stafford, FFEL PLUS, Federal Perkins. *Student Employment:* Federal Work-Study Program available. Institutional employment available. Off-campus job opportunities are excellent. **Financial Aid Statistics:** 33% freshmen, 37% undergrads receive need-based scholarship or grant aid. 43% freshmen, 33% undergrads receive non-need-based scholarship or grant aid. 50% freshmen, 53% undergrads receive need-based self-help aid. 89% freshmen, 80% undergrads receive any aid. 79% undergrads borrow to pay for school. Average cumulative indebtedness $30,874. **Criteria for awarding institutional aid:** *Non-need-based:* Academics, leadership.

ROLLINS COLLEGE

1000 Holt Avenue, #1502, Winter Park, FL 32789-4499
Phone: 407-646-2161 **Financial Aid Phone:** 407-646-2395
E-mail: admission@rollins.edu **CEEB Code:** 5572
Fax: 407-646-1502 **Website:** www.rollins.edu **ACT Code:** 748

This private school was founded in 1885. It has a 70-acre campus.

RATINGS
Admissions Selectivity Rating: 91   **Fire Safety Rating:** 84   **Green Rating:** 71

STUDENTS AND FACULTY
Enrollment: 1,773. **Student Body:** 58% female, 42% male, 47% out-of-state, 4% international (52 countries represented). Asian 4%, African American 4%, Caucasian 71%, Hispanic 10%, Native American 1%.
Retention and Graduation: 82% freshmen return for sophomore year. 59% freshmen graduate within 4 years. 41% grads go on to further study within 1 year. 22% grads pursue arts and sciences degrees. 7% grads pursue law degrees. 11% grads pursue business degrees. 2% grads pursue medical degrees. **Faculty:** Student/faculty ratio 10:1. 194 full-time faculty, 94% hold PhDs, 11% are members of minority groups, 39% are women.

ACADEMICS
Degrees: Bachelor's, master's. **Classes:** Most classes have 10–19 students. **Majors with Highest Enrollment:** Economics; international business/trade/commerce; psychology. **Special Study Options:** Accelerated program, cross-registration, double major, dual enrollment, exchange student program (domestic), honors program, independent study, internships, student-designed major, study abroad, teacher certification program **Combined degree programs:** BA/MBA. Special programs offered to physically disabled students include note-taking services, reader services, tape recorders, tutors. **Career services:** Alumni network, alumni services, career/job search classes, career assessment, internships.

FACILITIES
Housing: Coed dorms, special housing for disabled students, fraternity/sorority housing, apartments for single students, theme housing. 60% of campus accessible to physically disabled. **Special Academic Facilities/Equipment:** Art museum, theatres, fine arts center, language lab, skills development building, child development center, psychology center, "state-of-the-art" IT classroom. **Computers:** 100% of classrooms, 100% of dorms, 100% of libraries, 100% of dining areas, 100% of student union, have wireless network access. Students can register for classes online. Administrative functions (other than registration) can be performed online.

CAMPUS LIFE
Environment: Town. **Activities:** Choral groups, concert band, dance, drama/theater, jazz band, literary magazine, music ensembles, musical theater, pep band, radio station, student government, student newspaper, student-run film society, symphony orchestra, television station, yearbook, campus ministries, international student organization. **Organizations:** 125 registered organizations, 5 honor societies, 5 religious organizations. 5 fraternities, 6 sororities. **Athletics (Intercollegiate):** *Men:* Baseball, basketball, crew/rowing, cross-country, golf, lacrosse, sailing, soccer, swimming, tennis, water skiing. *Women:* Basketball, crew/rowing, cross-country, golf, lacrosse, sailing, soccer, swimming, tennis, volleyball, water skiing. **On-Campus Highlights:** Cornell Campus Center, Alfond Sports Center, Art Gallery, Cornell Fine Arts Museum, Olin Library, Rice Family Bookstore. **Environmental Initiatives:** Recycling throughout the campus including in the dorms and dining service areas. Planting of native and drought resistant foliage throughout the campus. An ongoing commitment is in the works for using biodegradable plates and cups in dining service area. Next step is to use them for catering events.

ADMISSIONS
Freshman Academic Profile: Average high school GPA 3.4. 43% in top 10% of high school class, 73% in top 25% of high school class, 91% in top 50% of high school class. 55% from public high schools. SAT Math middle 50% range 555–650. SAT Critical Reading middle 50% range 555–650. ACT middle 50% range 24–29. Minimum paper TOEFL 550. Minimum computer TOEFL 213. Minimum web-based TOEFL 80. **Basis for Candidate Selection:** *Very important factors considered include:* Academic GPA, rigor of secondary school record. *Important factors considered include:* Application essay, recommendation(s), standardized test scores, extracurricular activities, talent/ability. *Other factors considered include:* Class rank, alumni/ae relation, char-

acter/personal qualities, first generation, interview, level of applicant's interest, volunteer work, work experience. **Freshman Admission Requirements:** High school diploma is required and GED is accepted. *Academic units required:* 4 English, 3 mathematics, 2 science, 2 foreign language, 2 social studies, 2 history, 2 academic electives. *Academic units recommended:* 4 English, 4 mathematics, 4 science, 3 foreign language, 3 social studies, 3 history, 3 academic electives. **Freshman Admission Statistics:** 3,485 applied, 53% admitted, 25% enrolled. **Transfer Admission Requirements:** High school transcript, college transcript(s), essay or personal statement, statement of good standing from prior institution(s). Lowest grade transferable C–. **General Admission Information:** Application fee $40. Early decision application deadline 11/15. Regular application deadline 2/15. Regular notification 4/1. Nonfall registration accepted. Admission may be deferred for a maximum of 1 year. Credit and/or placement offered for CEEB Advanced Placement tests.

COSTS AND FINANCIAL AID
Required Forms and Deadlines: FAFSA, institution's own financial aid form Financial aid filing deadline 3/1. Priority financial aid filing date 3/1. **Notification of Awards:** Applicants will be notified of awards on a rolling basis beginning 3/1. **Types of Aid:** *Need-based scholarships/grants:* Federal Pell, SEOG, state scholarships/grants, private scholarships, the school's own gift aid. *Loans:* Direct Subsidized Stafford, Direct Unsubsidized Stafford, Direct PLUS, Federal Perkins, college/university loans from institutional funds. *Student Employment:* Federal Work-Study Program available. Institutional employment available. **Financial Aid Statistics:** 40% freshmen, 41% undergrads receive need-based scholarship or grant aid. 3% freshmen, 4% undergrads receive non-need-based scholarship or grant aid. 31% freshmen, 33% undergrads receive need-based self-help aid. 3% freshmen, 4% undergrads receive athletic scholarships. 78% freshmen, 77% undergrads receive any aid. 48% undergrads borrow to pay for school. Average cumulative indebtedness $21,904. **Criteria for awarding institutional aid:** *Non-need-based:* Academics, art, athletics, leadership, music/drama, state/district residency.

ROOSEVELT UNIVERSITY

430 South Michigan Avenue, Chicago, IL 60605
Phone: 312-341-3515
E-mail: applyRU@roosevelt.edu **CEEB Code:** 1666
Fax: 312-341-3523 **Website:** www.roosevelt.edu **ACT Code:** 1124

This private school was founded in 1945. It has a 34-acre campus.

RATINGS
Admissions Selectivity Rating: 72   **Fire Safety Rating:** 60*   **Green Rating:** 60*

STUDENTS AND FACULTY
Enrollment: 4,113. **Student Body:** 67% female, 33% male, 13.9% out-of-state, 2% international (66 countries represented). Asian 5%, African American 20%, Caucasian 49%, Hispanic 15%.
Retention and Graduation: Faculty: Student/faculty ratio 13:1. 235 full-time faculty, 85% hold PhDs, 20% are are members of minority groups, 43% are women.

ACADEMICS
Degrees: Bachelor's, certificate, master's, post-master's certificate. **Classes:** Most classes have 10–19 students. **Majors with Highest Enrollment:** Biology/biological sciences; elementary education and teaching; psychology. **Special Study Options:** Accelerated program, distance learning, double major, dual enrollment, English as a Second Language (ESL), exchange student program (domestic), honors program, independent study, internships, student-designed major, study abroad, teacher certification program. **Honors programs:** Roosevelt Scholars program offers an enriched academic program combining the students' area of interest with an interdisciplinary approach that includes internships, and research opportunities. Scholars are eligible to receive a special merit scholarship. **Combined degree programs:** BA/JD, MA/JD. Special programs offered to physically disabled students include note-taking services, reader services, tape recorders, tutors.

FACILITIES
Housing: Coed dorms, apartments for single students. 100% of campus accessible to physically disabled. **Special Academic Facilities/Equipment:** The Chicago campus is approx. 1 mile from the Museum of Natural History, Aquarium, Planetarium and Contemporary Art museums; and is 2 blocks from the Art Institute of Chicago. **Computers:** Students can register for classes online. Administrative functions (other than registration) can be performed online.

CAMPUS LIFE
Environment: Metropolis. **Activities:** Dance, literary magazine, radio station, student government, student newspaper, international student organization. **Or-**

---

ganizations: 48 registered organizations, 3 honor societies, 4 religious organizations. 1 fraternities, 2 sororities.

ADMISSIONS
Freshman Academic Profile: Average high school GPA 3.09. 1.8% in top 10% of high school class, 5.5% in top 25% of high school class, 26.2% in top 50% of high school class. 80% from public high schools. SAT Math middle 50% range 470–580. SAT Critical Reading middle 50% range 513–628. ACT middle 50% range 19–25. **Basis for Candidate Selection:** *Very important factors considered include:* Academic GPA, rigor of secondary school record. *Important factors considered include:* standardized test scores. *Other factors considered include:* Class rank, application essay, recommendation(s), alumni/ae relation, character/personal qualities, extracurricular activities, first generation, interview, talent/ability. **Freshman Admission Requirements:** High school diploma is required and GED is accepted. *Academic units required:* 4 English, 3 mathematics, 2 science, (2 science labs), 2 social studies. *Academic units recommended:* 4 English, 4 mathematics, 3 science, (3 science labs), 2 foreign language, 3 social studies, 2 history, 2 academic electives. **Freshman Admission Statistics:** 4,245 applied, 50% admitted, 28% enrolled. **Transfer Admission Requirements:** College transcript(s), statement of good standing from prior institution(s). Minimum college GPA of 2.0 required. Lowest grade transferable D. **General Admission Information:** Application fee $25. Notification on a rolling basis, beginning on or about 10/1. Nonfall registration accepted. Admission may be deferred for a maximum of 1 year. Credit and/or placement offered for CEEB Advanced Placement tests.

COSTS AND FINANCIAL AID
Annual tuition $23,000. Room and board $11,200. Average book expense $1,000. **Required Forms and Deadlines:** FAFSA. Priority financial aid filing date 4/1. **Notification of Awards:** Applicants will be notified of awards on a rolling basis beginning 2/1. **Types of Aid:** *Need-based scholarships/grants:* Federal Pell, SEOG, state scholarships/grants, private scholarships, the school's own gift aid. *Loans:* Direct Subsidized Stafford, Direct Unsubsidized Stafford, Direct PLUS. *Student Employment:* **Financial Aid Statistics:** 61% freshmen, 52% undergrads receive need-based scholarship or grant aid. 74% freshmen, 35% undergrads receive non-need-based scholarship or grant aid. 66% freshmen, 63% undergrads receive need-based self-help aid. **Criteria for awarding institutional aid:** *Non-need-based:* Academics, alumni affiliation, leadership, minority status, music/drama, state/district residency.

ROSE-HULMAN INSTITUTE OF TECHNOLOGY

Best 373

5500 Wabash Avenue-CM 1, Terre Haute, IN 47803-3999
Phone: 812-877-8213 **Financial Aid Phone:** 812-877-8259
E-mail: admissions@rose-hulman.edu **CEEB Code:** 1668
Fax: 812-877-8941 **Website:** www.rose-hulman.edu **ACT Code:** 1232

This private school was founded in 1874. It has a 200-acre campus.

RATINGS
Admissions Selectivity Rating: 91   **Fire Safety Rating:** 93   **Green Rating:** 78

STUDENTS AND FACULTY
Enrollment: 1,842. **Student Body:** 20% female, 80% male, 58.2% out-of-state, 3% international (13 countries represented). Asian 5%, African American 3%, Caucasian 87%, Hispanic 2%.
Retention and Graduation: 69% freshmen graduate within 4 years. 22% grads go on to further study within 1 year. 19% grads pursue arts and sciences degrees. 1% grads pursue law degrees. 1% grads pursue business degrees. 1% grads pursue medical degrees. **Faculty:** Student/faculty ratio 12:1. 160 full-time faculty, 100% hold PhDs, 11% are are members of minority groups, 23% are women.

ACADEMICS
Degrees: Bachelor's, master's. **Classes:** Most classes have 20–29 students. Most lab/discussion sessions have 20–29 students. **Majors with Highest Enrollment:** Chemical engineering; electrical, electronics and communications engineering; mechanical engineering. **Special Study Options:** Accelerated program, cooperative education program, cross-registration, double major, independent study, internships, study abroad **Combined degree programs:** MS/MD in Biomedical Engineering. Special programs offered to physically disabled students include reader services, tutors. **Career services:** Alumni network, alumni services, career/job search classes, career assessment, intern-

ships **Career services highlights include:** For the Rose-Hulman student, experiential learning continually takes place during a student's college career. Whether it is through co-curricular activities, company projects brought to the classroom, or participation in degree related internship/co-op experiences. The Rose-Hulman graduate is fully prepared to enter the workforce running.

FACILITIES

Housing: Coed dorms, men's dorms, fraternity/sorority housing, apartments for single students. 95% of campus accessible to physically-disabled. **Special Academic Facilities/Equipment:** Museums—none officially. Union Bldg—collection of British Watercolors. Moench Hall Section A—Western Sculpture. All Sections—Eclectic Art. Hadley Hall—Hadley Pottery and Salty Seamon Paintings. Other art in various offices. Oakley Observatory. **Computers:** 100% of classrooms, 5% of dorms, 100% of libraries, 100% of dining areas, 100% of student union, 25% of common outdoor areas have wireless network access. Students can register for classes online. Administrative functions (other than registration) can be performed online. Undergraduates are required to own a computer.

CAMPUS LIFE

Environment: Town. **Activities:** Choral groups, concert band, dance, drama/theater, jazz band, literary magazine, music ensembles, musical theater, pep band, radio station, student government, student newspaper, international student organization. **Organizations:** 105 registered organizations, 7 honor societies, 2 religious organizations. 8 fraternities, 3 sororities. **Athletics (Intercollegiate):** *Men:* Baseball, basketball, cross-country, diving, football, golf, riflery, soccer, swimming, tennis, track/field (outdoor), track/field (indoor). *Women:* Basketball, cross-country, diving, golf, riflery, soccer, softball, swimming, tennis, track/field (outdoor), track/field (indoor), volleyball. **On-Campus Highlights:** Sports and Recreation Center, Hatfield Hall, White Chapel, Moench Hall, Chauncey's Place. **Environmental Initiatives:** Signing of the American College & University President's Climate Commitment. Formation of a Sustainability Team responsible for instilling a culture of sustainability integrating sustainability with programs in education, operations, and community service. Serving as a pilot campus for the Sustainability Tracking and Assessment Rating System (STARS) Project through the Association for the Advancement of Sustainability in Higher Education.

ADMISSIONS

Freshman Academic Profile: 60.6% in top 10% of high school class, 88.6% in top 25% of high school class, 99.4% in top 50% of high school class. 79.8% from public high schools. SAT Math middle 50% range 630–720. SAT Critical Reading middle 50% range 560–670. SAT Writing middle 50% range 520–640. ACT middle 50% range 26–32. Minimum paper TOEFL 550. Minimum computer TOEFL 215. Minimum web-based TOEFL 80. **Basis for Candidate Selection:** *Very important factors considered include:* Class rank, rigor of secondary school record. *Important factors considered include:* Academic GPA, recommendation(s), standardized test scores, character/personal qualities. *Other factors considered include:* Application essay, alumni/ae relation, extracurricular activities, interview, talent/ability, volunteer work, work experience. **Freshman Admission Requirements:** High school diploma is required and GED is not accepted. *Academic units required:* 4 English, 4 mathematics, 2 science, (2 science labs), 2 social studies, 4 academic electives. *Academic units recommended:* 5 mathematics, 3 science. **Freshman Admission Statistics:** 3,554 applied, 70% admitted, 19% enrolled. **Transfer Admission Requirements:** College transcript(s), essay or personal statement, statement of good standing from prior institution(s). Minimum college GPA of 3.0 required. Lowest grade transferable C. **General Admission Information:** Application fee $40. Regular application deadline 3/1. Notification on a rolling basis, beginning on or about 10/1. Nonfall registration not accepted. Admission may be deferred for a maximum of 1 year. Credit and/or placement offered for CEEB Advanced Placement tests.

COSTS AND FINANCIAL AID

Annual tuition $33,900. Room and board $9,441. Required fees $660. Average book expense $1,500. **Required Forms and Deadlines:** FAFSA. Priority financial aid filing date 3/1. **Notification of Awards:** Applicants will be notified of awards on or about 3/10. **Types of Aid:** *Need-based scholarships/grants:* Federal Pell, SEOG, state scholarships/grants, the school's own gift aid. *Loans:* Direct Subsidized Stafford, Direct Unsubsidized Stafford, Direct PLUS, FFEL Subsidized Stafford *Student Employment:* Federal Work-Study Program available. Institutional employment available. Highest amount earned per year from on-campus jobs $1,500. **Financial Aid Statistics:** 72% freshmen, 70% undergrads receive need-based scholarship or grant aid. 26% freshmen, 24% undergrads receive non-need-based scholarship or grant aid. 70% freshmen, 68% undergrads receive need-based self-help aid. 100% freshmen, 99% undergrads receive any aid. 73% undergrads borrow to pay for school. Average cumulative indebtedness $35,261. **Criteria for awarding institutional aid:** *Non-need-based:* Academics, minority status.

ROSEMONT COLLEGE

1400 Montgomery Ave, Rosemont, PA 19010
Phone: 610-526-2966 **Financial Aid Phone:** 610 527 0200
E-mail: admissions@rosemont.edu **CEEB Code:** 2763
Fax: 610-520-4399 **Website:** www.rosemont.edu **ACT Code:** 3676

This private school, affiliated with the Roman Catholic Church, was founded in 1921. It has a 56-acre campus.

RATINGS

Admissions Selectivity Rating: 79   **Fire Safety Rating:** 81   **Green Rating:** 76

STUDENTS AND FACULTY

Enrollment: 506. **Student Body:** 95% female, 5% male, 35% out-of-state, 1% international (14 countries represented). Asian 6%, African American 44%, Caucasian 36%, Hispanic 8%.
Retention and Graduation: 76% freshmen return for sophomore year. 78% freshmen graduate within 4 years. 36% grads go on to further study within 1 year. 35% grads pursue arts and sciences degrees. 2% grads pursue law degrees. 5% grads pursue business degrees. 9% grads pursue medical degrees. **Faculty:** Student/faculty ratio 8:1. 26 full-time faculty, 92% hold PhDs, 65% are women.

ACADEMICS

Degrees: Bachelor's, master's, post-bachelor's certificate. **Classes:** Most classes have 10–19 students. **Majors with Highest Enrollment:** Art/art studies; biology/biological sciences; psychology. **Special Study Options:** Accelerated program, cross-registration, distance learning, double major, honors program, independent study, internships, liberal arts/career combination, student-designed major, study abroad, teacher certification program. **Combined degree programs:** BA/MA, BSN in conjunction with Drexel Univ. Special programs offered to physically disabled students include note-taking services, tape recorders, tutors. **Career services:** Alumni services, career/job search classes, career assessment, internships **Career services highlights include:** All students partake of an Internship or a form of Experiential Learning prior to graduation.

FACILITIES

Housing: Women's dorms. Cornelia Connelly Hall located in the center of campus is totally redesigned. It is now a state-of-the-art residence hall. Beginning with fall 2009 Rosemont College welcomes men into the Undergraduate College. 45% of campus accessible to physically disabled. **Special Academic Facilities/Equipment:** McShain Performing Arts Center and Conwell Learning Center **Computers:** 25% of classrooms, 25% of dorms, 50% of libraries, 15% of dining areas, 15% of student union, 10% of common outdoor areas have wireless network access. Students can register for classes online. Administrative functions (other than registration) can be performed online.

CAMPUS LIFE

Environment: Village. **Activities:** Choral groups, concert band, dance, drama/theater, jazz band, literary magazine, marching band, music ensembles, musical theater, opera, pep band, radio station, student government, student newspaper, yearbook, campus ministries. **Organizations:** 23 registered organizations, 6 honor societies, 3 religious organizations. **Athletics (Intercollegiate):** *Men:* Basketball, softball, tennis. *Women:* Basketball, field hockey, lacrosse, softball, tennis, volleyball. **On-Campus Highlights:** Campus Grill, The Grind Coffee Shop, Fitness Center. **Environmental Initiatives:** Energy Star Procurement Policy. Waste Minimization Policy. Indoor Space Temperature Policy.

ADMISSIONS

Freshman Academic Profile: Average high school GPA 3. 25% in top 10% of high school class, 45% in top 25% of high school class, 70% in top 50% of high school class. 61% from public high schools. SAT Math middle 50% range 418–520. SAT Critical Reading middle 50% range 430–573. SAT Writing middle 50% range 435–555. Minimum paper TOEFL 500. Minimum computer TOEFL 173. **Basis for Candidate Selection:** *Very important factors considered include:* Rigor of secondary school record, interview. *Important factors considered include:* Class rank, application essay, academic GPA, recommendation(s), standardized test scores, extracurricular activities, talent/ability, volunteer work. *Other factors considered include:* Alumni/ae relation, character/personal qualities, work experience. **Freshman Admission Requirements:** High school diploma is required and GED is accepted. *Academic units required:* 4 English, 3 mathematics, 3 science, (2 science labs), 1 social studies, 1 history, 7 academic electives. *Academic units recommended:* 4 English, 3 mathematics, 3 science, (2 science labs), 2 foreign language, 2 social studies, 2 history, 4 academic electives. **Freshman Admission Statistics:** 614 applied, 62% admitted, 33% enrolled. **Transfer Admission Requirements:** College transcript(s), minimum college GPA of 2.5 required. Lowest grade transferable C. **General Admission Information:** Application fee $35. Regular application deadline 8/1. Regular notification 3/15. Notification on a rolling basis, beginning on or about 3/1. Nonfall registration accepted. Admission may be deferred for a maximum of 12. Credit and/or placement offered for CEEB Advanced Placement tests.

COSTS AND FINANCIAL AID
Required Forms and Deadlines: FAFSA. Priority financial aid filing date 2/15. **Notification of Awards:** Applicants will be notified of awards on a rolling basis beginning 2/15. **Types of Aid:** *Need-based scholarships/grants:* Federal Pell, SEOG, state scholarships/grants, private scholarships, the school's own gift aid. *Loans:* FFEL Subsidized Stafford, FFEL Unsubsidized Stafford, FFEL PLUS, Federal Perkins, Alternative loans offered, payment plans offered. *Student Employment:* Federal Work-Study Program available. Institutional employment available. Highest amount earned per year from on-campus jobs $2,000. Off-campus job opportunities are good. **Financial Aid Statistics:** 88% freshmen, 84% undergrads receive need-based scholarship or grant aid. 34% freshmen, 9% undergrads receive non-need-based scholarship or grant aid. 75% freshmen, 69% undergrads receive need-based self-help aid. 99% freshmen, 98% undergrads receive any aid. 86% undergrads borrow to pay for school. Average cumulative indebtedness $21,807. **Criteria for awarding institutional aid:** *Non-need-based:* Academics, art, leadership, religious affiliation.

See page 1216.

ROWAN UNIVERSITY

201 Mullica Hill Road, Glassboro, NJ 08028
Phone: 856-256-4200 **Financial Aid Phone:** 856-256-4250
E-mail: admissions@rowan.edu **CEEB Code:** 2515
Fax: 856-256-4430 **Website:** www.rowan.edu **ACT Code:** 2560

This public school was founded in 1923. It has a 800-acre campus.

RATINGS
Admissions Selectivity Rating: 84   **Fire Safety Rating:** 86   **Green Rating:** 90

STUDENTS AND FACULTY
Enrollment: 9,282. **Student Body:** 52% female, 48% male, 2% out-of-state, (17 countries represented). Asian 4%, African American 9%, Caucasian 77%, Hispanic 7%.
Retention and Graduation: 43% freshmen graduate within 4 years. **Faculty:** Student/faculty ratio 15:1. 400 full-time faculty, 84% hold PhDs, 21% are are members of minority groups, 43% are women.

ACADEMICS
Degrees: Bachelor's, master's. **Classes:** Most classes have 20–29 students. **Majors with Highest Enrollment:** Criminal justice/police science; elementary education and teaching; multi-/interdisciplinary studies, other. **Special Study Options:** Cooperative education program, distance learning, double major, English as a Second Language (ESL), exchange student program (domestic), external degree program, honors program, independent study, internships, study abroad, teacher certification program, weekend college. **Honors programs:** The Thomas N. Bantavoglio Honors Concentration offers qualified students access to a variety of academic, enrichment, and service experiences including honors classes, the Honors Student Organization and the 45 activities sponsored by the HSO, as well as travel for cultural and enrichment activities along the eastern seaboard. **Combined degree programs:** BS/MA in mathematics; BS/MS in computer science. Special programs offered to physically disabled students include note-taking service, reader services, tape recorders, tutors. **Career services:** Alumni network, alumni services, career/job search classes, career assessment, internships, regional alumni. **Career services highlights include:** The Rowan University undergraduate Entrepreneurship program has been nationally ranked by The Princeton Review as a Top Program for Entrepreneurship.

FACILITIES
Housing: Coed dorms, special housing for disabled students, apartments for single students, wellness housing, townhouses. 90% of campus accessible to physically disabled. **Special Academic Facilities/Equipment:** Concert hall, glass collection, student recreation center, on-campus early childhood demonstration center, greenhouse for biological studies, observatory, art gallery. **Computers:** 100% of classrooms, 100% of dorms, 100% of libraries, 100% of dining areas, 100% of student union, 100% of common outdoor areas have wireless network access. Students can register for classes online. Administrative functions (other than registration) can be performed online.

CAMPUS LIFE
Environment: Town. **Activities:** Choral groups, concert band, dance, drama/theater, jazz band, literary magazine, music ensembles, musical theater, opera, pep band, radio station, student government, student newspaper, student-run film society, television station, yearbook, campus ministries. **Organizations:** 135 registered organizations, 10 honor societies, 6 religious organizations. 10 fraternities, 10 sororities. **Athletics (Intercollegiate):** *Men:* Baseball, basketball, cross-country, diving, football, soccer, swimming, track/field (outdoor), track/field (indoor). *Women:* Basketball, cross-country, diving, field hockey, lacrosse, soccer, softball, swimming, track/field (outdoor), track/field (indoor), volleyball. **On-Campus Highlights:** Recreation Center, Student Center, Campbell Library, Savitz Hall (Student Services Building), Education Hall. **Environmental Initiatives:** Rowan University purchases 35% of its electricity from wind power sources derived locally and nationally. Rowan University was the first institution of higher education in NJ to sign the American College and University Presidents Climate Commitment (ACUPCC). Rowan was among the first schools in NJ to convert to singe-stream recycling. This innovative program engages students, faculty and staff. The recycling program, coupled with other initiatives, has earned Rowan 9 major awards from federal and state agencies over the last 3 years.

ADMISSIONS
Freshman Academic Profile: Average high school GPA 3.35. 16% in top 10% of high school class, 45% in top 25% of high school class, 86% in top 50% of high school class. SAT Math middle 50% range 490–600. SAT Critical Reading middle 50% range 470–570. SAT Writing middle 50% range 470–570. Minimum paper TOEFL 550. Minimum computer TOEFL 213. Minimum web-based TOEFL 79. **Basis for Candidate Selection:** *Very important factors considered include:* Rigor of secondary school record. *Important factors considered include:* Class rank, academic GPA, standardized test scores. *Other factors considered include:* Recommendation(s), character/personal qualities, extracurricular activities, talent/ability, volunteer work, work experience. **Freshman Admission Requirements:** High school diploma is required and GED is accepted. *Academic units required:* 4 English, 3 mathematics, 2 science, (2 science labs), 2 social studies. *Academic units recommended:* 4 mathematics, 3 science, 2 foreign language. **Freshman Admission Statistics:** 7,696 applied, 66% admitted, 32% enrolled. **Transfer Admission Requirements:** College transcript(s), minimum college GPA of 2.0 required. Lowest grade transferable D. **General Admission Information:** Application fee $50. Regular application deadline 3/1. Regular notification 4/15. Notification on a rolling basis, beginning on or about 10/1. Nonfall registration accepted. Admission may be deferred for a maximum of 1 semester. Credit and/or placement offered for CEEB Advanced Placement tests.

COSTS AND FINANCIAL AID
Annual in-state tuition $8,074. Annual out-of-state tuition $15,148. Room and board $9,958. Required fees $3,160. Average book expense $1,500. **Required Forms and Deadlines:** FAFSA. Priority financial aid filing date 3/15. **Notification of Awards:** Applicants will be notified of awards on a rolling basis beginning 3/15. **Types of Aid:** *Need-based scholarships/grants:* Federal Pell, SEOG, state scholarships/grants, private scholarships, the school's own gift aid. *Loans:* FFEL Subsidized Stafford, FFEL Unsubsidized Stafford, FFEL PLUS. *Student Employment:* Federal Work-Study Program available. Institutional employment available. Highest amount earned per year from on-campus jobs $5,800. Off-campus job opportunities are good. **Financial Aid Statistics:** 19% freshmen, 28% undergrads receive need-based scholarship or grant aid. 11% freshmen, 8% undergrads receive non-need-based scholarship or grant aid. 43% freshmen, 49% undergrads receive need-based self-help aid. 80.74% freshmen, 61.27% undergrads receive any aid. 73% undergrads borrow to pay for school. Average cumulative indebtedness $26,092. **Criteria for awarding institutional aid:** *Non-need-based:* Academics, art, minority status, music/drama.

RUSH UNIVERSITY

600 South Paulina, Suite 440, Chicago, IL 60612-3878
Phone: 312-942-7100 **Financial Aid Phone:** 312-942-6256
E-mail: Rush_Admissions@rush.edu
Fax: 312-942-2219 **Website:** www.rushu.rush.edu **ACT Code:** 1617

This private school was founded in 1972. It has a 35-acre campus.

RATINGS
Admissions Selectivity Rating: 60*   **Fire Safety Rating:** 60*   **Green Rating:** 60*

STUDENTS AND FACULTY
Enrollment: 258. **Student Body:** 87% female, 13% male, 15% out-of-state, 2% international. Asian 18%, African American 7%, Caucasian 69%, Hispanic 3%.
Retention and Graduation: 25% grads go on to further study within 1 year. 5% grads pursue medical degrees. **Faculty:** Student/faculty ratio 8:1. 305 full-time faculty, 65% are women.

ACADEMICS

Degrees: Bachelor's, first professional, master's. **Classes:** Most classes have 10–19 students. **Majors with Highest Enrollment:** Audiology/audiologist and speech-language pathology/pathologist; medicine (MD); nursing/registered nurse (RN, ASN, BSN, MSN). **Special Study Options:** Distance learning. **Combined degree programs:** MD/PhD. Special programs offered to physically disabled students include tape recorders, tutors. **Career services:** Alumni network, alumni services, career/job search classes, career assessment, internships, regional alumni.

FACILITIES

Housing: Apartments for married students, apartments for single students. 85% of campus accessible to physically disabled.

CAMPUS LIFE

Environment: Metropolis. **Activities:** yearbook. **Organizations:** 15 registered organizations, 2 honor societies, 1 religious organizations. **On-Campus Highlights:** Student Lounge, Computer lab (100+ stations), Library, Au Bon Pain. **Environmental Initiatives:** Launched new recycling commitment and awareness campaign on Earth Day 2008.

ADMISSIONS

Freshman Academic Profile: 100% in top 50% of high school class. Minimum paper TOEFL 550. Minimum computer TOEFL 213. **Transfer Admission Requirements:** College transcript(s), essay or personal statement, minimum college GPA of 2.7 required. Lowest grade transferable C. **General Admission Information:** Nonfall registration not accepted. Neither credit nor placement offered for CEEB Advanced Placement tests.

COSTS AND FINANCIAL AID

Annual tuition $5,685. Room and board $4,660. Required fees $490. Average book expense $950. **Required Forms and Deadlines:** FAFSA, institution's own financial aid form, business/farm supplement. **Types of Aid:** *Need-based scholarships/grants:* Federal Pell, SEOG, state scholarships/grants, private scholarships, the school's own gift aid. *Loans:* FFEL Subsidized Stafford, FFEL Unsubsidized Stafford, FFEL PLUS, Federal Perkins, Federal Nursing, college/university loans from institutional funds, credit-based loans. *Student Employment:* Federal Work-Study Program available. Institutional employment available. Off-campus job opportunities are fair. **Financial Aid Statistics:** 54% undergrads receive need-based scholarship or grant aid. 9% undergrads receive non-need-based scholarship or grant aid. 61% undergrads receive need-based self-help aid. 69% undergrads receive any aid. **Criteria for awarding institutional aid:** *Non-need-based:* Academics, leadership, minority status.

RUSSELL SAGE COLLEGE

Office of Admissions, 45 Ferry Street, Troy, NY 12180
Phone: 518-244-2217 **Financial Aid Phone:** 518-244-4525
E-mail: rscadm@sage.edu **CEEB Code:** 2764
Fax: 518-244-6880 **Website:** www.sage.edu/RSC **ACT Code:** 2876

This private school was founded in 1916. It has a 8-acre campus.

RATINGS

Admissions Selectivity Rating: 80   **Fire Safety Rating:** 60*   **Green Rating:** 60*

STUDENTS AND FACULTY

Enrollment: 801. **Student Body:** 100% female, 9% out-of-state, international. Asian 2%, African American 4%, Caucasian 77%, Hispanic 3%.
Retention and Graduation: 79% freshmen return for sophomore year. 46% freshmen graduate within 4 years. 48% grads go on to further study within 1 year. 24% grads pursue arts and sciences degrees. 5% grads pursue business degrees. **Faculty:** Student/faculty ratio 12:1. 61 full-time faculty, 87% hold PhDs, 7% are are members of minority groups, 61% are women.

ACADEMICS

Degrees: Bachelor's. **Classes:** Most classes have 10–19 students. Most lab/discussion sessions have fewer than 10 students. **Majors with Highest Enrollment:** Education; nursing; other; psychology. **Special Study Options:** Accelerated program, cooperative education program, cross-registration, distance learning, double major, honors program, independent study, internships, liberal arts/career combination, student-designed major, study abroad, teacher certification program. **Combined degree programs:** BA/JD, BA/MEng. Special programs offered to physically disabled students include tutors. **Career services:** Alumni services, career/job search classes, career assessment, internships, **Career services highlights include:** Women in the World Curriculum.

FACILITIES

Housing: Women's dorms, Honors Housing, Over 21 Senior Housing, Spanish and French Housing, Returning Adult Housing. 70% of campus accessible to physically disabled. **Special Academic Facilities/Equipment:** Schacht Fine Arts Center (home of NYS Theatre Institute); Robison Athletic and Recreational Center; state-of-the-art lab and research facilities in biology, historic 19th century brownstones. **Computers:** Students can register for classes online. Administrative functions (other than registration) can be performed online.

CAMPUS LIFE

Environment: City. **Activities:** Choral groups, dance, drama/theater, literary magazine, music ensembles, musical theater, student government, student newspaper, yearbook. **Organizations:** 40 registered organizations, 14 honor societies, 4 religious organizations. **Athletics (Intercollegiate):** *Women:* Basketball, soccer, softball, tennis, volleyball. **On-Campus Highlights:** New York State Theatre Institute, Buchman Pavilion, Helen M. Upton Women's Center, Robison Athletic and Recreation Center, James L. Meader Little Theater.

ADMISSIONS

Freshman Academic Profile: Average high school GPA 3.4. 30% in top 10% of high school class, 67% in top 25% of high school class, 95% in top 50% of high school class. SAT Math middle 50% range 480–590. SAT Critical Reading middle 50% range 490–620. ACT middle 50% range 21–25. Minimum paper TOEFL 550. Minimum computer TOEFL 213. **Basis for Candidate Selection:** *Very important factors considered include:* Rigor of secondary school record, standardized test scores. *Important factors considered include:* Class rank, recommendation(s), interview. *Other factors considered include:* Application essay, academic GPA, alumni/ae relation, character/personal qualities, extracurricular activities, talent/ability, volunteer work, work experience. **Freshman Admission Requirements:** High school diploma is required and GED is accepted. *Academic units required:* 4 English, 3 mathematics, 3 science, (3 science labs), 2 foreign language, 4 social studies. *Academic units recommended:* 4 mathematics, 4 science, 4 foreign language. **Freshman Admission Statistics:** 394 applied, 81% admitted, 36% enrolled. **Transfer Admission Requirements:** High school transcript, college transcript(s), statement of good standing from prior institution(s). Minimum college GPA of 2.5 required. Lowest grade transferable C–. **General Admission Information:** Application fee $30. Early decision application deadline 12/1. Notification on a rolling basis, beginning on or about 12/15. Nonfall registration accepted. Admission may be deferred for a maximum of 1 year. Credit and/or placement offered for CEEB Advanced Placement tests.

COSTS AND FINANCIAL AID

Annual tuition $23,800. . Room and board $8,370. Required fees $870. Average book expense $900. **Required Forms and Deadlines:** FAFSA, state aid form. Priority financial aid filing date 3/6. **Notification of Awards:** Applicants will be notified of awards on a rolling basis beginning 3/12. **Types of Aid:** *Need-based scholarships/grants:* Federal Pell, SEOG, state scholarships/grants, private scholarships, the school's own gift aid, Federal Nursing Scholarships. *Loans:* FFEL Subsidized Stafford, FFEL Unsubsidized Stafford, FFEL PLUS, Federal Perkins. *Student Employment:* Highest amount earned per year from on-campus jobs $3,000. Off-campus job opportunities are good. **Financial Aid Statistics:** 60% freshmen, 56% undergrads receive need-based scholarship or grant aid. 59% freshmen, 52% undergrads receive non-need-based scholarship or grant aid. 93% freshmen, 91% undergrads receive need-based self-help aid. 94% freshmen, 89% undergrads receive any aid. 91% undergrads borrow to pay for school. Average cumulative indebtedness $21,500. **Criteria for awarding institutional aid:** *Non-need-based:* Academics, alumni affiliation.

RUST COLLEGE

150 Rust Avenue, Holly Springs, MS 38635
Phone: 662-252-8000
E-mail: jscott2@rustcollege.edu
Fax: 662-252-8895 **Website:** www.rustcollege.edu **ACT Code:** 2240

This private school, affiliated with the Moravian Church, was founded in 1866. It has a 126-acre campus.

RATINGS

Admissions Selectivity Rating: 60*   **Fire Safety Rating:** 60*   **Green Rating:** 60*

STUDENTS AND FACULTY

Enrollment: 1,064. **Student Body:** 63% female, 37% male, (8 countries represented).
Retention and Graduation: 50% freshmen return for sophomore year. 18% freshmen graduate within 4 years. 19% grads go on to further study within 1

year. 12% grads pursue arts and sciences degrees. 7% grads pursue medical degrees. **Faculty:** Student/faculty ratio 20:1. 47 full-time faculty, 87% are are members of minority groups, 43% are women.

ACADEMICS

Degrees: Associate, bachelor's. **Classes:** Most classes have 10–19 students. Most lab/discussion sessions have 10–19 students. **Majors with Highest Enrollment:** Biology/biological sciences; business/commerce; computer and information sciences. **Special Study Options:** Double major, honors program, independent study, internships, liberal arts/career combination, study abroad, teacher certification program, weekend college, 1)Advanced Placement Program. 2)Adult Pathway Program. Dual enrollment includes three Dual Degree Programs with other institutions and one Cooperative Program with another institution. Special programs offered to physically disabled students include tutors.

FACILITIES

Housing: Men's dorms, women's dorms, Honors. 100% of campus accessible to physically disabled. **Special Academic Facilities/Equipment:** Dr. Ron Trojcak collection of African tribal art which includes fabrics, masks and statues used for religious ceremonies, weddings, ritual dance and funerals.

CAMPUS LIFE

Environment: Rural. **Activities:** Choral groups, concert band, dance, drama/theater, marching band, music ensembles, pep band, radio station, student government, student newspaper, television station, yearbook, international student organization. **Organizations:** 35 registered organizations, 7 honor societies, 5 religious organizations. 3 fraternities, 4 sororities. **Athletics (Intercollegiate):** *Men:* Baseball, basketball, cheerleading, cross-country, soccer, tennis, track/field (outdoor). *Women:* Basketball, cheerleading, cross-country, softball, tennis, track/field (outdoor), volleyball. **On-Campus Highlights:** Leontyne Price Library Exhibits, James Elam Chapel, McDonald Science Building, David Beckley Conference Center, McMillan Multi-Purpose Center.

ADMISSIONS

Freshman Academic Profile: Average high school GPA 2.69. 98% from public high schools. ACT middle 50% range 14–18. Minimum paper TOEFL 540. **Basis for Candidate Selection:** *Very important factors considered include:* first generation. *Important factors considered include:* Class rank, application essay, academic GPA, recommendation(s), rigor of secondary school record, standardized test scores, alumni/ae relation, character/personal qualities, level of applicant's interest. *Other factors considered include:* talent/ability, volunteer work. **Freshman Admission Requirements:** High school diploma is required and GED is accepted. *Academic units required:* 4 English, 3 mathematics, 3 science, 3 social studies, 6 academic electives. **Freshman Admission Statistics:** 1,607 applied, 58% admitted, 27% enrolled. **Transfer Admission Requirements:** High school transcript, college transcript(s), statement of good standing from prior institution(s). Minimum college GPA of 2.0 required. Lowest grade transferable C. **General Admission Information:** Application fee $10. Notification on a rolling basis, beginning on or about 7/15. Nonfall registration accepted. Admission may be deferred for a maximum of 1 year. Credit offered for CEEB Advanced Placement tests.

COSTS AND FINANCIAL AID

Annual tuition $7,410. Room and board $2,600. Average book expense $500. **Required Forms and Deadlines:** FAFSA, institution's own financial aid form, state aid form. Priority financial aid filing date 5/9. **Notification of Awards:** Applicants will be notified of awards on a rolling basis beginning 6/9. **Types of Aid:** *Need-based scholarships/grants:* Federal Pell, SEOG, state scholarships/grants, private scholarships, United Negro College Fund. *Loans:* FFEL Subsidized Stafford, FFEL Unsubsidized Stafford, FFEL PLUS, United Methodist. *Student Employment:* Highest amount earned per year from on-campus jobs $1,600. **Financial Aid Statistics:** 91% freshmen, 86% undergrads receive need-based scholarship or grant aid. 5% freshmen, 56% undergrads receive non-need-based scholarship or grant aid. 93% freshmen, 88% undergrads receive need-based self-help aid. 71% undergrads borrow to pay for school. Average cumulative indebtedness $13,055. **Criteria for awarding institutional aid:** *Non-need-based:* Academics, leadership, music/drama, religious affiliation, state/district residency.

RUTGERS, THE STATE UNIVERSITY OF NEW JERSEY—CAMDEN

406 Penn Street, Camden, NJ 08102
Phone: 856-225-6104 **Financial Aid Phone:** 732-932-7305
E-mail: admissions@ugadm.rutgers.edu **CEEB Code:** 2765
Fax: 856-225-6498 **ACT Code:** 2592

This public school was founded in 1927. It has a 25-acre campus.

RATINGS
Admissions Selectivity Rating: 78　　**Fire Safety Rating:** 70　　**Green Rating:** 60*

STUDENTS AND FACULTY
Enrollment: 3,652. **Student Body:** 57% female, 43% male, 2% out-of-state, international (20 countries represented). Asian 8%, African American 15%, Caucasian 67%, Hispanic 6%.
Retention and Graduation: 84% freshmen return for sophomore year. 25% freshmen graduate within 4 years. **Faculty:** Student/faculty ratio 12:1. 252 full-time faculty, 99% hold PhDs, 16% are are members of minority groups, 38% are women. 4% of classes are taught by teaching assistants.

ACADEMICS
Degrees: Bachelor's, master's. **Majors with Highest Enrollment:** Business administration and management; nursing/registered nurse (RN, ASN, BSN, MSN); psychology. **Special Study Options:** Accelerated program, cooperative education program, cross-registration, distance learning, double major, dual enrollment, English as a Second Language (ESL), exchange student program (domestic), honors program, independent study, internships, liberal arts/career combination, student-designed major, study abroad, teacher certification program, weekend college, Cooperative baccalaureate program in engineering with School of Engineering (New Brunswick Campus). Interdisciplinary programs in African-American studies, general science. Cooperative baccalaureate in medical technology with approved hospital. BA/MA in English, history, liberal studies or psychology; BA/MS in biology, chemistry or mathematics (with the Graduate School-Camden). BA in economics or political science/Master of Public Administration (with the Graduate School—Camden). **Combined degree programs:** BA/MD, 2+4 Pharm. D. Special programs offered to physically disabled students include note-taking services, reader services, tape recorders, tutors.

FACILITIES
Housing: Coed dorms, special housing for disabled students, apartments for single students. **Computers:** Students can register for classes online. Administrative functions (other than registration) can be performed online.

CAMPUS LIFE
Environment: City. **Activities:** Drama/theater, literary magazine, radio station, student government, yearbook, international student organization. **Organizations:** 50 registered organizations, 11 honor societies, 4 fraternities, 4 sororities. **Athletics (Intercollegiate):** *Men:* Baseball, basketball, cross-country, golf, soccer, track/field (outdoor). *Women:* Basketball, cross-country, soccer, softball, track/field (outdoor), volleyball.

ADMISSIONS
Freshman Academic Profile: 17% in top 10% of high school class, 23% in top 25% of high school class, 34% in top 50% of high school class. 50% from public high schools. SAT Math middle 50% range 510–600. SAT Critical Reading middle 50% range 490–600. SAT Writing middle 50% range 480–580. Minimum paper TOEFL 500. **Basis for Candidate Selection:** *Very important factors considered include:* Class rank, academic GPA, rigor of secondary school record, standardized test scores. *Other factors considered include:* Application essay, recommendation(s), extracurricular activities, first generation, geographical residence, racial/ethnic status, state residency, volunteer work, work experience. **Freshman Admission Requirements:** High school diploma is required and GED is accepted. *Academic units required:* 4 English, 3 mathematics, 2 science, 2 foreign language, 5 academic electives. *Academic units recommended:* 4 mathematics. **Freshman Admission Statistics:** 5,529 applied, 49% admitted, 13% enrolled. **Transfer Admission Requirements:** High school transcript, college transcript(s), minimum college GPA of NA required. **General Admission Information:** Application fee $65. Regular application deadline 12/1. Nonfall registration accepted. Credit and/or placement offered for CEEB Advanced Placement tests.

COSTS AND FINANCIAL AID
Annual in-state tuition $9,546. Annual out-of-state tuition $20,178. Room and board $9,788. Required fees $2,152. Average book expense $1,431. **Required Forms and Deadlines:** FAFSA. *Student Employment:* Federal Work-Study Program available. Institutional employment available. **Financial Aid Statis-**

tics: 19% freshmen, 38% undergrads receive need-based scholarship or grant aid. 11% freshmen, 15% undergrads receive non-need-based scholarship or grant aid. 22% freshmen, 46% undergrads receive need-based self-help aid. 70% freshmen, 72% undergrads receive any aid. 100% undergrads borrow to pay for school. Average cumulative indebtedness $19,800.

RUTGERS, THE STATE UNIVERSITY OF NEW JERSEY—NEWARK CAMPUS

249 University Avenue, Newark, NJ 07102-1896
Phone: 973-353-5205 **Financial Aid Phone:** 732-932-7305
E-mail: admissions@ugadm.rutgers.edu **CEEB Code:** 2765
Fax: 973-353-1440 **Website: ACT Code:** 2592

This public school was founded in 1930. It has a 36-acre campus.

RATINGS
Admissions Selectivity Rating: 84   **Fire Safety Rating:** 70   **Green Rating:** 60*

STUDENTS AND FACULTY
Enrollment: 6,677. **Student Body:** 54% female, 46% male, 3% out-of-state, 2% international (84 countries represented). Asian 24%, African American 19%, Caucasian 28%, Hispanic 21%.
Retention and Graduation: Faculty: Student/faculty ratio 12:1. 447 full-time faculty, 99% hold PhDs, 21% are are members of minority groups, 38% are women. 9% of classes are taught by teaching assistants.

ACADEMICS
Degrees: Bachelor's, master's. **Majors with Highest Enrollment:** Biology/biological sciences; business administration and management; nursing/registered nurse (RN, ASN, BSN, MSN). **Special Study Options:** Accelerated program, cooperative education program, cross-registration, distance learning, double major, dual enrollment, English as a Second Language (ESL), exchange student program (domestic), honors program, independent study, internships, liberal arts/career combination, student-designed major, study abroad, teacher certification program, weekend college, 5-year baccalaureate-MBA with Rutgers Business School; Baccalaureate/MA in Criminal Justice with the School of Criminal Justice; Baccalaureate/MPA with the School of Public Affairs and Administration; Cooperative baccalaureate program with School of Engineering (New Brunswick campus); Cooperative baccalaureate in medical technology with affiliated hospitals; Interdisciplinary programs in archaeology, international affairs, legal studies, women's studies; continuing professional education; The College of Nursing offers a program on the New Brunswick Campus. Students are admitted in the fall semester only; Baccalaureate in Business Major/Master of Human Resource Management (with School of Management and Labor Relations in New Brunswick); Baccalaureate-master's dual degree programs with the School of Criminal Justice and Rutgers Business School. The Honors College of Rutgers University's Newark College of Arts and Sciences is a four-year program, a college within a college, providing its by-invitation-only students with opportunities for enrichment both in and outside of the classroom. Students invited to join the Honors College benefit from small classes with first-rate faculty, co-curricular internships in major corporations and other institutions, and other special options. Reserved dormitory space, a substantial scholarship program, and research assistantships with faculty members combine to make the RU-Newark Honors College experience unique. For additional information, visit the Honors College web site at http://honorsnewark.rutgers.edu or call (973)353-5860. BA/MD, BA/MA Special programs offered to physically disabled students include note-taking services, reader services, tape recorders, tutors.

FACILITIES
Housing: Coed dorms, fraternity/sorority housing, apartments for single students. **Special Academic Facilities/Equipment:** Institute of Jazz Studies, TV/Radio media center, Institute of Animal Behavior, Center for Crime Prevention Studies, Center for Negotiation and Conflict Resolution, Center for Molecular and Behaviorial Neuroscience, Center for Nursing Research **Computers:** Students can register for classes online. Administrative functions (other than registration) can be performed online.

CAMPUS LIFE
Activities: Choral groups, drama/theater, radio station, student government, student newspaper, yearbook, international student organization. **Organizations:** 80 registered organizations, 16 honor societies, 7 fraternities, 7 sororities. **Athletics (Intercollegiate):** *Men:* Baseball, basketball, soccer, tennis, volleyball. *Women:* Basketball, softball, tennis, volleyball. **On-Campus Highlights:** The Arts at Rutgers Newark, Robeson Campus Center, Athletic Center, Bradley Hall/Bookstore, Dana Library.

ADMISSIONS
Freshman Academic Profile: 29% in top 10% of high school class, 30% in top 25% of high school class, 30% in top 50% of high school class. SAT Math middle 50% range 510–620. SAT Critical Reading middle 50% range 470–570. SAT Writing middle 50% range 480–580. Minimum paper TOEFL 550. Minimum computer TOEFL 123. **Basis for Candidate Selection:** *Very important factors considered include:* Class rank, academic GPA, rigor of secondary school record, standardized test scores. *Other factors considered include:* Application essay, recommendation(s), extracurricular activities, first generation, geographical residence, racial/ethnic status, state residency, volunteer work, work experience. **Freshman Admission Requirements:** High school diploma is required and GED is accepted. *Academic units required:* 4 English, 3 mathematics, 2 science, 2 foreign language, 5 academic electives. *Academic units recommended:* 4 mathematics. **Freshman Admission Statistics:** 12,462 applied, 60% admitted, 12% enrolled. **Transfer Admission Requirements:** High school transcript, college transcript(s), minimum college GPA of na required. **General Admission Information:** Application fee $65. Regular notification 2/28. Nonfall registration accepted. Credit and/or placement offered for CEEB Advanced Placement tests.

COSTS AND FINANCIAL AID
Required Forms and Deadlines: FAFSA. Priority financial aid filing date 3/15. **Notification of Awards:** Applicants will be notified of awards on a rolling basis beginning 2/1. **Types of Aid:** *Need-based scholarships/grants:* Federal Pell, SEOG, state scholarships/grants, private scholarships, the school's own gift aid, Outside Scholarships. *Loans:* Direct Subsidized Stafford, Direct Unsubsidized Stafford, Direct PLUS, Federal Perkins, state loans, college/university loans from institutional funds, Other Educational Loans. **Financial Aid Statistics:** 26% freshmen, 42% undergrads receive need-based scholarship or grant aid. 11% freshmen, 13% undergrads receive non-need-based scholarship or grant aid. 27% freshmen, 41% undergrads receive need-based self-help aid. 80% freshmen, 80% undergrads receive any aid. 85% undergrads borrow to pay for school. Average cumulative indebtedness $17,700. **Criteria for awarding institutional aid:** *Non-need-based:* Academics, alumni affiliation, art, athletics, job skills, minority status, music/drama, religious affiliation, state/district residency.

RUTGERS, THE STATE UNIVERSITY OF NEW JERSEY—NEW BRUNSWICK

65 Davidson Road, Piscataway, NJ 08854-8097
Phone: 732-932-4636 **Financial Aid Phone:** 732-932-7305
E-mail: admissions@ugadm.rutgers.edu **CEEB Code:** 2765
Fax: 732-445-0237 **Website:** www.rutgers.edu **ACT Code:** 2592

This public school was founded in 1766. It has a 2695-acre campus.

RATINGS
Admissions Selectivity Rating: 87   **Fire Safety Rating:** 78   **Green Rating:** 60*

STUDENTS AND FACULTY
Enrollment: 28,817. **Student Body:** 48% female, 52% male, 7% out-of-state, 2% international (117 countries represented). Asian 25%, African American 8%, Caucasian 51%, Hispanic 10%.
Retention and Graduation: Faculty: Student/faculty ratio 14:1. 1678 full-time faculty, 99% hold PhDs, 18% are are members of minority groups, 37% are women. 20% of classes are taught by teaching assistants.

ACADEMICS
Degrees: Bachelor's, master's, post-master's certificate. **Majors with Highest Enrollment:** Biology/biological sciences; engineering. **Special Study Options:** Accelerated program, cooperative education program, cross-registration, distance learning, double major, dual enrollment, English as a Second Language (ESL), exchange student program (domestic), honors program, independent study, internships, liberal arts/career combination, student-designed major, study abroad, teacher certification program, 5-year BA or BS/MBA program in Rutgers Business School; BS in business Discipline/MBA; BA or BS in Science Discipline/MBA; 8-year Bachelor/Medical Dual Degree program with UM-DNJ-Robert Wood Johnson Medical School; 5-year BS/BS in Bioenvironmental Engineering with the School of Engineering; 5-year accelerated baccalaureate-MBA with Rutgers Business School.; Bureau of Engineering Research,

supported by the university, industry, state and federal government, provides research opportunities for students and faculty; Continuing professional education; Exchange program between School of Engineering and the City University of London for qualified students majoring in civil, electrical, or mechanical engineering; 5-year (BA/BS degree) program in liberal arts and engineering; 5-year BA or BS/MEd with the Graduate School of Education; Interdepartmental programs and certificate programs are available; Study Abroad in England, France, Italy, Ireland, Germany, Greece, Mexico, Israel, Australia, India, Japan, Netherlands, Scotland, South Africa, South Korea and Spain; Alumnae externship program; Language and Cultural House Program; 5-year BA/BS in cooperation with Rutgers Business School; BA/Master of communication and information studies (with SCILS); BA/MLER (with School of Management and Labor Relations); Baccalaureate/MCRP, MPH, or MPP with EJB School of Planning and Public Policy; Baccalaureate in Business major/Master of Human Resource Management (with School of Management and Labor Relations {SMLR}). **Combined degree programs:** BA/MD, 5-year BA or BS/MPP, 6-year PharmD, 6-year Bach. Special programs offered to physically disabled students include note-taking services, reader services, tape recorders, tutors. **Career services:** Alumni network, alumni services, career/job search classes, career assessment, internships, regional alumni.

FACILITIES

Housing: Coed dorms, men's dorms, special housing for international students, women's dorms, fraternity/sorority housing, apartments for married students, cooperative housing, apartments for single students, theme housing, special interest housing, language and cultural houses, substance-free house, Math/Science Engineering House for women, first-year residence, transfer center, residence for single mothers and children. **Special Academic Facilities/Equipment:** Geology Museum, Zimmerli Museum, Mason Gross Performing Arts Center; NJ Museum of Agriculture; NJ Film Festival/RU Film Co-op; Rutgers Gardens. **Computers:** Students can register for classes online. Administrative functions (other than registration) can be performed online.

CAMPUS LIFE

Environment: Town. **Activities:** Choral groups, concert band, dance, drama/theater, jazz band, literary magazine, marching band, music ensembles, musical theater, opera, pep band, radio station, student government, student newspaper, student-run film society, symphony orchestra, television station, yearbook, campus ministries, international student organization. **Organizations:** 400 registered organizations, 24 honor societies, 29 fraternities, 15 sororities. **Athletics (Intercollegiate):** *Men:* Baseball, basketball, cheerleading, cross-country, diving, football, golf, lacrosse, soccer, track/field (outdoor), track/field (indoor), wrestling. *Women:* Basketball, cheerleading, crew/rowing, cross-country, diving, field hockey, golf, gymnastics, lacrosse, soccer, softball, swimming, tennis, track/field (outdoor), track/field (indoor), volleyball. **On-Campus Highlights:** Geology Museum, Jane Voorhees Zimmereli Art Museum, Rutgers Display Gardens and Heylar Woods, Hutchenson Memorial Forest.

ADMISSIONS

Freshman Academic Profile: 42% in top 10% of high school class, 38% in top 25% of high school class, 18% in top 50% of high school class. SAT Math middle 50% range 560–680. SAT Critical Reading middle 50% range 530–630. SAT Writing middle 50% range 540–640. Minimum paper TOEFL 550. Minimum computer TOEFL 213. **Basis for Candidate Selection:** *Very important factors considered include:* Class rank, academic GPA, rigor of secondary school record, standardized test scores. *Other factors considered include:* Application essay, recommendation(s), extracurricular activities, first generation, geographical residence, interview, racial/ethnic status, state residency, talent/ability, volunteer work, work experience. **Freshman Admission Requirements:** High school diploma is required and GED is accepted. *Academic units required:* 4 English, 3 mathematics, 2 science, 2 foreign language, 5 academic electives. *Academic units recommended:* 4 mathematics, 2 foreign language. **Freshman Admission Statistics:** 28,624 applied, 61% admitted, 27% enrolled. **Transfer Admission Requirements:** High school transcript, college transcript(s), Lowest grade transferable C. **General Admission Information:** Application fee $65. Regular notification 3/1. Nonfall registration accepted. Credit and/or placement offered for CEEB Advanced Placement tests.

COSTS AND FINANCIAL AID

Annual in-state tuition $9,546. Annual out-of-state tuition $20,178. Room and board $10,676. Required fees $2,340. Average book expense $1,431. **Required Forms and Deadlines:** FAFSA. Priority financial aid filing date 3/15. **Notification of Awards:** Applicants will be notified of awards on a rolling basis beginning 2/1. **Types of Aid:** *Need-based scholarships/grants:* Federal Pell, SEOG, state scholarships/grants, private scholarships, the school's own gift aid, Outside Scholarships. *Loans:* Direct Subsidized Stafford, Direct Unsubsidized Stafford, Direct PLUS, Federal Perkins, state loans, college/university loans from institutional funds, other educational loans. *Student Employment:* Highest amount earned per year from on-campus jobs $1,374. **Financial Aid Statistics:** 27% freshmen, 31% undergrads receive need-based scholarship or grant aid. 27% freshmen, 26% undergrads receive non-need-based scholarship

or grant aid. 38% freshmen, 43% undergrads receive need-based self-help aid. 1% freshmen, 1% undergrads receive athletic scholarships. 67% freshmen, 69% undergrads receive any aid. 74% undergrads borrow to pay for school. Average cumulative indebtedness $16,300. **Criteria for awarding institutional aid:** *Non-need-based:* Academics, alumni affiliation, art, athletics, leadership, minority status, music/drama, religious affiliation.

SACRED HEART UNIVERSITY

5151 Park Avenue, Fairfield, CT 06825
Phone: 203-371-7880 **Financial Aid Phone:** 203-371-7980
E-mail: enroll@sacredheart.edu **CEEB Code:** 3780
Fax: 203-365-7607 **Website:** www.sacredheart.edu **ACT Code:** 589

This private school, affiliated with the Roman Catholic Church, was founded in 1963. It has a 67-acre campus.

RATINGS

Admissions Selectivity Rating: 83   **Fire Safety Rating:** 80   **Green Rating:** 70

STUDENTS AND FACULTY

Enrollment: 4,123. **Student Body:** 61% female, 39% male, 68% out-of-state, 1% international (34 countries represented). Asian 2%, African American 4%, Caucasian 80%, Hispanic 7%.
Retention and Graduation: 82% freshmen return for sophomore year. 56% freshmen graduate within 4 years. 43% grads go on to further study within 1 year. 9% grads pursue arts and sciences degrees. 1% grads pursue law degrees. 2% grads pursue business degrees. 1% grads pursue medical degrees. **Faculty:** Student/faculty ratio 13:1. 204 full-time faculty, 76% hold PhDs, 12% are are members of minority groups, 51% are women.

ACADEMICS

Degrees: Associate, bachelor's, certificate, master's, post-bachelor's certificate, post-master's certificate. **Classes:** Most classes have 20–29 students. **Majors with Highest Enrollment:** Business/commerce; nursing/registered nurse (RN, ASN, BSN, MSN); psychology. **Special Study Options:** Accelerated program, cooperative education program, cross-registration, distance learning, double major, English as a Second Language (ESL), exchange student program (domestic), honors program, independent study, internships, liberal arts/career combination, student-designed major, study abroad, teacher certification program, weekend college, Off-campus study: Summer program in Luxembourg, Summer, Winter Intercession, Spring Break, and Semester in Ireland. Sponsored and approved study abroad programs worldwide. **Combined degree programs:** Combined degree programs in physical therapy (doctoral) and occupational therapy (masters). Accelerated 5th year MBA program. Accelerated MSCIS (Computer Information Systems). **Honors programs:** The Thomas More School of Honors Studies offers a challenging curriculum of Honors-level courses. These studies will provide each student with the quest for the full meaning of our humanity exploring the following three components: (1) the cognitive, (2) the aesthetic and (3) the moral or ethical. The Program also includes advisement, cultural events, dinners with the University President and other events. **Combined degree programs:** BA/MA; BA/S/MBA; BA/S/DPT; BA/S/MSOT; BA/S/MAT; BS/MSCIS; BA/S/MACJ. Special programs offered to physically disabled students include note-taking services, reader services, tape recorders, tutors. **Career services:** Alumni network, alumni services, career/job search classes, career assessment, internships, regional alumni. **Career services highlights include:** The Office of Career Development works diligently to facilitate professional internship opportunities for students in all academic majors and career interests.

FACILITIES

Housing: Coed dorms, special housing for disabled students, apartments for single students, wellness housing, thematic floors; living & learning communities for specific academic programs. 90% of campus accessible to physically disabled. **Special Academic Facilities/Equipment:** WHRT student radio station, WSHU National Public Radio, Edgerton Center for the Performing Arts, Gallery of Contemporary Art. **Computers:** 100% of classrooms, 100% of dorms, 100% of libraries, 100% of dining areas, 100% of student union, 100% of common outdoor areas have wireless network access. Students can register for classes online. Administrative functions (other than registration) can be performed online. Undergraduates are required to own a computer.

CAMPUS LIFE

Environment: Town. **Activities:** Choral groups, concert band, dance, drama/theater, jazz band, literary magazine, marching band, music ensembles, musical theater, pep band, radio station, student government, student newspaper, student-run film society, television station, yearbook, campus ministries, international student organization. **Organizations:** 80 registered organizations, 14 honor societies, 4 religious organizations. 4 fraternities, 6 sororities. **Athletics (Intercollegiate):** *Men:* Baseball, basketball, cross-country, fencing, football, golf, ice hockey, lacrosse, soccer, tennis, track/field (outdoor), track/field (indoor), volleyball, wrestling. *Women:* Basketball, bowling, crew/rowing, cross-country, diving, equestrian sports, fencing, field hockey, golf, ice hockey, lacrosse, soccer, softball, swimming, tennis, track/field (outdoor), track/field (indoor), volleyball. **On-Campus Highlights:** Pitt Health and Recreation Center, Edgerton Center for Performing Arts, Holy Grounds Cafe, Ryan-Matura Library, Hawley Lounge, New University Chapel (Chapel of the Holy Spirit) opened in fall 2009. **Environmental Initiatives:** Lighting renewal for all new construction and renovations, as well as low energy bulbs & motion detection systems. Transfer from 28 chemicals to 6 green chemicals for custodial work. Free shuttle service for students to reduce the number of cars traveling between campuses.

ADMISSIONS

Freshman Academic Profile: Average high school GPA 3.3. 18% in top 10% of high school class, 54% in top 25% of high school class, 83% in top 50% of high school class. 70% from public high schools. SAT Math middle 50% range 490–580. SAT Critical Reading middle 50% range 460–570. Minimum paper TOEFL 550. Minimum computer TOEFL 213. Minimum web-based TOEFL 70. **Basis for Candidate Selection:** *Very important factors considered include:* Academic GPA, rigor of secondary school record. *Important factors considered include:* Class rank, application essay, recommendation(s), character/personal qualities, extracurricular activities, interview, talent/ability, volunteer work, work experience. *Other factors considered include:* standardized test scores, alumni/ae relation, first generation, geographical residence, level of applicant's interest, racial/ethnic status, religious affiliation/commitment, state residency. **Freshman Admission Requirements:** High school diploma is required and GED is accepted. *Academic units required:* 4 English, 3 mathematics, 3 science, (1 science labs), 2 foreign language, 3 social studies, 3 history, 3 academic electives. *Academic units recommended:* 4 English, 4 mathematics, 4 science, (2 science labs), 4 foreign language, 4 social studies, 4 history, 4 academic electives. **Freshman Admission Statistics:** 7,343 applied, 66% admitted, 19% enrolled. **Transfer Admission Requirements:** High school transcript, college transcript(s), essay or personal statement, minimum college GPA of 2.5 required. Lowest grade transferable C–. **General Admission Information:** Application fee $50. Early decision application deadline 12/1. Notification on a rolling basis, beginning on or about 1/1. Nonfall registration accepted. Admission may be deferred for a maximum of 1 year. Credit and/or placement offered for CEEB Advanced Placement tests.

COSTS AND FINANCIAL AID

Annual tuition $30,090. Room and board $11,860. Required fees $208. Average book expense $1,000. **Required Forms and Deadlines:** FAFSA, CSS/Financial Aid PROFILE, noncustodial PROFILE. Priority financial aid filing date 2/15. **Notification of Awards:** Applicants will be notified of awards on a rolling basis beginning 3/1. **Types of Aid:** *Need-based scholarships/grants:* Federal Pell, SEOG, state scholarships/grants, private scholarships, the school's own gift aid. *Loans:* Direct Subsidized Stafford, Direct Unsubsidized Stafford, Direct PLUS, FFEL Subsidized Stafford, FFEL Unsubsidized Stafford, FFEL PLUS, Federal Perkins, state loans, alternative loans. *Student Employment:* Federal Work-Study Program available. Institutional employment available. Off-campus job opportunities are excellent. **Financial Aid Statistics:** 70% freshmen, 68% undergrads receive need-based scholarship or grant aid. 7% freshmen, 5% undergrads receive non-need-based scholarship or grant aid. 59% freshmen, 59% undergrads receive need-based self-help aid. 7% freshmen, 6% undergrads receive athletic scholarships. 70% freshmen, 70% undergrads receive any aid. Average cumulative indebtedness $18,819. **Criteria for awarding institutional aid:** *Non-need-based:* Academics, alumni affiliation, art, athletics, leadership, minority status, music/drama.

SAGINAW VALLEY STATE UNIVERSITY

7400 Bay Road, University Center, MI 48710
Phone: 989-964-4200 **Financial Aid Phone:** 989-964-4103
E-mail: admissions@svsu.edu **CEEB Code:** 1766
Fax: 989-790-0180 **Website: ACT Code:** 2057

This public school was founded in 1963. It has a 782-acre campus.

RATINGS

Admissions Selectivity Rating: 71   **Fire Safety Rating:** 82   **Green Rating:** 62

STUDENTS AND FACULTY

Enrollment: 8,018. **Student Body:** 59% female, 41% male, 1% out-of-state, 3% international (39 countries represented). Asian 1%, African American 7%, Caucasian 82%, Hispanic 2%, Native American 1%.
Retention and Graduation: 9% freshmen graduate within 4 years. 24% grads go on to further study within 1 year. **Faculty:** Student/faculty ratio 20:1. 294 full-time faculty, 75% hold PhDs.

ACADEMICS

Degrees: Bachelor's, master's, post-master's certificate. **Classes:** Most classes have 20–29 students. Most lab/discussion sessions have 10–19 students. **Majors with Highest Enrollment:** Criminal justice/safety studies; elementary education and teaching; nursing/registered nurse (RN, ASN, BSN, MSN). **Special Study Options:** Accelerated program, cooperative education program, distance learning, double major, dual enrollment, English as a Second Language (ESL), honors program, independent study, internships, student-designed major, study abroad, teacher certification program. **Honors programs:** The University Honors Program allows students to pursue their major and minor degree work, while providing enriched academic experiences in Honors courses, seminars, research projects, and social activities. The Honors experience enables students to work more intensively with active teacher/scholars and to participate in interdisciplinary courses. Honors students will have ample opportunity to develop as critical thinkers, active learners, and problem solvers. Special programs offered to physically disabled students include note-taking services, reader services, tutors. **Career services:** Career assessment, internships.

FACILITIES

Housing: Coed dorms, special housing for disabled students, apartments for single students, wellness housing, theme housing. 95% of campus housing accessible to physically disabled. **Special Academic Facilities/Equipment:** Sculpture gallery, fine arts center, center for health and physical education, independent testing lab, center for economic and business research, applied technology research center. **Computers:** Students can register for classes online. Administrative functions (other than registration) can be performed online.

CAMPUS LIFE

Environment: City. **Activities:** Choral groups, concert band, dance, drama/theater, jazz band, literary magazine, marching band, music ensembles, musical theater, pep band, student government, student newspaper, student-run film society, campus ministries, international student organization, Model UN. **Organizations:** 110 registered organizations, 8 honor societies, 9 religious organizations. 4 fraternities, 7 sororities. **Athletics (Intercollegiate):** *Men:* Baseball, basketball, bowling, cheerleading, cross-country, football, golf, soccer, track/field (outdoor), track/field (indoor). *Women:* Basketball, cheerleading, cross-country, soccer, softball, tennis, track/field (outdoor), track/field (indoor), volleyball. **On-Campus Highlights:** Student Center, Student Recreation Center (Ryder), Zahnow Library, Arbury Fine Arts Center, University Village. **Environmental Initiatives:** Building buildings with energy savings in mind for many years. Spending consistently through the years for energy and utility conservation measures. Recycling upgrades, cutting down on areas mowed, etc.

ADMISSIONS

Freshman Academic Profile: Average high school GPA 3.22. 19.1% in top 10% of high school class, 40.1% in top 25% of high school class, 72.8% in top 50% of high school class. ACT middle 50% range 18–24. Minimum paper TOEFL 500. Minimum computer TOEFL 173. Minimum web-based TOEFL 61. **Basis for Candidate Selection:** *Very important factors considered include:* Academic GPA, rigor of secondary school record, standardized test scores. *Other factors considered include:* Recommendation(s). **Freshman Admission Requirements:** High school diploma is required and GED is accepted. *Academic units required:* 4 English, 3 mathematics, 2 science, 3 social studies. *Academic units recommended:* 4 English, 4 mathematics, 4 science, 2 foreign language, 4 social studies, 1 communications. **Freshman Admission Statistics:** 5,467 applied, 88% admitted, 35% enrolled. **Transfer Admission Requirements:** College transcript(s), minimum college GPA of 2.0 required. Lowest grade transferable C–. **General Admission Information:** Application fee $25. Nonfall registration accepted. Admission may be deferred for a maximum of 1. Credit and/or placement offered for CEEB Advanced Placement tests.

COSTS AND FINANCIAL AID

Annual in-state tuition $6,054. Annual out-of-state tuition $14,453. Room and board $6,830. Required fees $438. Average book expense $900. **Required Forms and Deadlines:** FAFSA. Priority financial aid filing date 2/14. **Notification of Awards:** Applicants will be notified of awards on a rolling basis beginning 3/20. **Types of Aid:** *Need-based scholarships/grants:* Federal Pell, SEOG, state scholarships/grants, private scholarships, the school's own gift aid, *Loans:* Direct Subsidized Stafford, Direct Unsubsidized Stafford, Direct PLUS, state loans, CitiAssist Loans, Signature Student Loans. *Student Employment:* Federal Work-Study Program available. Institutional employment available. Off-campus job opportunities are good. **Financial Aid Statistics:** 23% freshmen, 39% undergrads receive need-based scholarship or grant aid. 49% freshmen, 29% undergrads receive non-need-based scholarship or grant aid. 47% freshmen, 50% undergrads receive need-based self-help aid. 5% freshmen, 5% undergrads receive athletic scholarships. 92% freshmen, 83% undergrads receive any aid. 67.6% undergrads borrow to pay for school. Average cumulative indebtedness $23,561. **Criteria for awarding institutional aid:** *Non-need-based:* Academics, art, athletics, leadership, minority status, music/drama.

SAINT ANSELM COLLEGE

Best 373

100 Saint Anselm Drive, Manchester, NH 03102-1310
Phone: 603-641-7500 **Financial Aid Phone:** 603-641-7110
E-mail: admission@anselm.edu **CEEB Code:** 3748
Fax: 603-641-7550 **Website:** www.anselm.edu **ACT Code:** 2522

This private school, affiliated with the Roman Catholic Church, was founded in 1889. It has a 404-acre campus.

RATINGS

Admissions Selectivity Rating: 84   **Fire Safety Rating:** 60*   **Green Rating:** 60*

STUDENTS AND FACULTY

Enrollment: 1,889. **Student Body:** 57% female, 43% male, 79% out-of-state, international (20 countries represented). Asian 1%, African American 1%, Caucasian 87%, Hispanic 2%, Native American 1%.
Retention and Graduation: 85% freshmen return for sophomore year. 71% freshmen graduate within 4 years. 16% grads go on to further study within 1 year. 11% grads pursue arts and sciences degrees. 3% grads pursue law degrees. 1% grads pursue business degrees. 2% grads pursue medical degrees. **Faculty:** Student/faculty ratio 11:1. 144 full-time faculty, 92% hold PhDs, 8% are are members of minority groups, 51% are women.

ACADEMICS

Degrees: Bachelor's, certificate. **Classes:** Most classes have 10–19 students. Most lab/discussion sessions have 10–19 students. **Special Study Options:** Cross-registration, honors program, independent study, internships, liberal arts/career combination, study abroad, teacher certification program **Honors programs:** Honors Program for Presidential Scholars Special programs offered to physically disabled students include note-taking services, reader services, tape recorders, tutors. **Career services:** Alumni network, alumni services, career/job search classes, career assessment, internships, regional alumni.

FACILITIES

Housing: Coed dorms, special housing for disabled students, men's dorms, women's dorms, apartments for single students, theme housing Substance Free Housing. 60% of campus accessible to physically disabled. **Special Academic Facilities/Equipment:** Chapel Art Center, New Hampshire Institute of Politics, Izart Observatory, Koonz Theatre, Comisky Studio (Fine Arts), Poisson Hall. **Computers:** 100% of classrooms, 100% of dorms, 100% of libraries, 100% of dining areas, 100% of student union, have wireless network access. Students can register for classes online. Administrative functions (other than registration) can be performed online.

CAMPUS LIFE

Environment: City. **Activities:** Choral groups, dance, drama/theater, jazz band, literary magazine, musical theater, radio station, student government, student newspaper, television station, yearbook, campus ministries, international student organization, Model UN. **Organizations:** 120 registered organizations, 11 honor societies, 7 religious organizations. **Athletics (Intercollegiate):** *Men:* Baseball, basketball, cross-country, football, golf, ice hockey, lacrosse, skiing (downhill/alpine), soccer, tennis. *Women:* Basketball, cross-country, field hockey,

golf, ice hockey, lacrosse, skiing (downhill/alpine), soccer, softball, tennis, volleyball. **On-Campus Highlights:** Joseph Hall Academic Building, Chapel Arts Center, Davidson Hall Dining Hall, Sullivan Ice Arena & Fitness Center, Abbey Church, Coffee Shop and Pub Cushing Student Center.

ADMISSIONS

Freshman Academic Profile: Average high school GPA 3.13. 65% from public high schools. SAT Math middle 50% range 510–580. SAT Critical Reading middle 50% range 500–590. SAT Writing middle 50% range 490–590. ACT middle 50% range 20–26. Minimum paper TOEFL 550. Minimum computer TOEFL 213. Minimum web-based TOEFL 80. **Basis for Candidate Selection:** *Very important factors considered include:* Application essay, academic GPA, recommendation(s), rigor of secondary school record, standardized test scores. *Other factors considered include:* Class rank, alumni/ae relation, character/personal qualities, extracurricular activities, geographical residence, racial/ethnic status, state residency, talent/ability, volunteer work, work experience. **Freshman Admission Requirements:** High school diploma is required and GED is accepted. *Academic units required:* 4 English, 3 mathematics, 3 science, (2 science labs), 2 foreign language, 2 social studies. *Academic units recommended:* 4 mathematics, 4 science, 4 foreign language. **Freshman Admission Statistics:** 3,664 applied, 77% admitted, 19% enrolled. **Transfer Admission Requirements:** High school transcript, college transcript(s), essay or personal statement, standardized test scores, statement of good standing from prior institution(s). Minimum college GPA of 2.5 required. Lowest grade transferable C. **General Admission Information:** Application fee $55. Early decision application deadline 11/15. Regular application deadline 3/1. Notification on a rolling basis, beginning on or about 1/1. Nonfall registration accepted. Admission may be deferred for a maximum of 1 year. Credit and/or placement offered for CEEB Advanced Placement tests.

COSTS AND FINANCIAL AID

Annual tuition $29,720. Room and board $11,240. Required fees $795. **Required Forms and Deadlines:** FAFSA, CSS/Financial Aid PROFILE, noncustodial PROFILE, business/farm supplement. Financial aid filing deadline 3/15. Priority financial aid filing date 3/15. **Notification of Awards:** Applicants will be notified of awards on a rolling basis beginning 3/1. **Types of Aid:** *Need-based scholarships/grants:* Federal Pell, SEOG, state scholarships/grants, private scholarships, the school's own gift aid. *Loans:* FFEL Subsidized Stafford, FFEL Unsubsidized Stafford, FFEL PLUS, Federal Perkins. *Student Employment:* Federal Work-Study Program available. Institutional employment available. Off-campus job opportunities are excellent. **Financial Aid Statistics:** 74% freshmen, 72% undergrads receive need-based scholarship or grant aid. 7% freshmen, 6% undergrads receive non-need-based scholarship or grant aid. 65% freshmen, 65% undergrads receive need-based self-help aid. 1% freshmen, 1% undergrads receive athletic scholarships. 75% undergrads borrow to pay for school. Average cumulative indebtedness $36,823. **Criteria for awarding institutional aid:** *Non-need-based:* Academics, alumni affiliation, athletics, state/district residency.

See page 1218.

SAINT ANTHONY COLLEGE OF NURSING

5658 East State Street, Rockford, IL 61108-2468
Phone: 815-395-5100 **Financial Aid Phone:** 815-395-5089
E-mail: cheryldelgado@sacn.edu
Fax: 815-395-2275 **Website:** www.sacn.edu

This private school, affiliated with the Roman Catholic Church, was founded in 1915.

RATINGS

Admissions Selectivity Rating: 60*   **Fire Safety Rating:** 60*   **Green Rating:** 60*

STUDENTS AND FACULTY

Enrollment: 86. **Student Body:** 93% female, 7% male, international.
Retention and Graduation: 10% grads go on to further study within 1 year.

ACADEMICS

Degrees: Bachelor's, master's. **Special Study Options:** Distance learning, independent study.

FACILITIES

Housing: Private apartments, student plan housing, private rooms.

CAMPUS LIFE

Environment: City. **Activities:** Student government, student newspaper. **Organizations:** 1 registered organizations.

ADMISSIONS

Freshman Academic Profile: Minimum paper TOEFL 550. Minimum computer TOEFL 213. **Basis for Candidate Selection:** *Important factors considered include:* Application essay, recommendation(s), interview. *Other factors considered include:* Extracurricular activities, volunteer work, work experience. **Freshman Admission Requirements:** High school diploma or equivalent is not required. *Academic units recommended:* 4 English, 3 mathematics, 4 science. **Freshman Admission Statistics: Transfer Admission Requirements:** College transcript(s), essay or personal statement, interview, minimum college GPA of 2.5 required. Lowest grade transferable C. **General Admission Information:** Application fee $50. Regular application deadline 1/15. Credit offered for CEEB Advanced Placement tests.

COSTS AND FINANCIAL AID

Annual tuition $17,220. Required fees $192. **Required Forms and Deadlines: Notification of Awards: Types of Aid:** *Need-based scholarships/grants:* Federal Pell, state scholarships/grants, private scholarships, the school's own gift aid. *Loans:* FFEL Subsidized Stafford, FFEL Unsubsidized Stafford, FFEL PLUS. *Student Employment:* **Financial Aid Statistics:** 93% undergrads receive need-based scholarship or grant aid. 59% undergrads receive non-need-based scholarship or grant aid. 85% undergrads receive need-based self-help aid. 86% undergrads receive any aid. 90% undergrads borrow to pay for school. Average cumulative indebtedness $6,828. **Criteria for awarding institutional aid:** *Non-need-based:* Academics.

SAINT CLOUD STATE UNIVERSITY

720 South 4th Avenue, Saint Cloud, MN 56301-4498
Phone: 320-308-2244 **Financial Aid Phone:** 320-308-2047
E-mail: scsu4u@stcloudstate.edu **CEEB Code:** 6679
Fax: 320-308-2243 **Website: ACT Code:** 2144

This public school was founded in 1869. It has a 920-acre campus.

RATINGS

Admissions Selectivity Rating: 64   **Fire Safety Rating:** 60*   **Green Rating:** 60*

STUDENTS AND FACULTY

Enrollment: 13,120. **Student Body:** 53% female, 47% male, 8% out-of-state, 4% international (85 countries represented). Asian 2%, African American 2%, Caucasian 72%, Hispanic 1%, Native American 1%. **Retention and Graduation:** 71% freshmen return for sophomore year. **Faculty:** Student/faculty ratio 17:1. 650 full-time faculty, 80% hold PhDs, 18% are are members of minority groups, 41% are women.

ACADEMICS

Degrees: Associate, bachelor's, master's, post-bachelor's certificate, post-master's certificate. **Classes:** Most classes have 20–29 students. **Majors with Highest Enrollment:** Elementary education and teaching; marketing/marketing management; mass communication/media studies. **Special Study Options:** Accelerated program, cooperative education program, cross-registration, distance learning, double major, dual enrollment, English as a Second Language (ESL), honors program, independent study, internships, student-designed major, study abroad, teacher certification program Special programs offered to physically disabled students include note-taking services, reader services. **Career services:** Alumni network, alumni services, career/job search classes, career assessment, internships.

FACILITIES

Housing: Coed dorms, special housing for international students. 86% of campus accessible to physically disabled. **Special Academic Facilities/Equipment:** Art and anthropology museums, electron microscope, planetarium, G.I.S. and weather labs. **Computers:** Students can register for classes online. Administrative functions (other than registration) can be performed online.

CAMPUS LIFE

Environment: Town. **Activities:** Choral groups, concert band, dance, drama/theater, music ensembles, musical theater, opera, radio station, student government, student newspaper, symphony orchestra, television station. **Organizations:** 240 registered organizations, 6 honor societies, 12 religious organizations. 5 fraternities, 4 sororities. **Athletics (Intercollegiate):** *Men:* Baseball, basketball, cheerleading, cross-country, diving, football, golf, ice hockey, rugby, swimming, tennis, track/field (outdoor), track/field (indoor), wrestling. *Women:* Basketball, cheerleading, cross-country, diving, golf, ice hockey, rugby, skiing (downhill/alpine), soccer, softball, swimming, tennis, track/field (outdoor), track/field (indoor), volleyball. **On-Campus Highlights:** James W. Miller Learning Resource Center, National Hockey Center.

ADMISSIONS

Freshman Academic Profile: 7% in top 10% of high school class, 29% in top 25% of high school class, 76% in top 50% of high school class. 99% from public high schools. ACT middle 50% range 19–24. Minimum paper TOEFL 500. Minimum computer TOEFL 173. **Basis for Candidate Selection:** *Very important factors considered include:* Class rank, rigor of secondary school record. *Other factors considered include:* Application essay, academic GPA, recommendation(s), standardized test scores, extracurricular activities, talent/ability. **Freshman Admission Requirements:** High school diploma is required and GED is accepted. *Academic units required:* 4 English, 3 mathematics, 3 science, (1 science labs), 2 foreign language, 3 social studies, 1 history, 1 fine arts. **Freshman Admission Statistics:** 5,912 applied, 78% admitted, 47% enrolled. **Transfer Admission Requirements:** College transcript(s), statement of good standing from prior institution(s). Minimum college GPA of 2.0 required. Lowest grade transferable C. **General Admission Information:** Application fee $20. Regular application deadline 6/1. Notification on a rolling basis, beginning on or about 9/15. Nonfall registration accepted. Admission may be deferred for a maximum of 24 months. Credit offered for CEEB Advanced Placement tests.

COSTS AND FINANCIAL AID

Annual in-state tuition $4,760. Annual out-of-state tuition $10,332. Room and board $4,688. Required fees $562. Average book expense $1,000. **Required Forms and Deadlines:** FAFSA, institution's own financial aid form Financial aid filing deadline 6/30. **Notification of Awards:** Applicants will be notified of awards on a rolling basis beginning 6/3. **Types of Aid:** *Need-based scholarships/grants:* Federal Pell, SEOG, state scholarships/grants, private scholarships, the school's own gift aid. *Loans:* FFEL Subsidized Stafford, FFEL Unsubsidized Stafford, FFEL PLUS, Federal Perkins, state loans *Student Employment:* Federal Work-Study Program available. Institutional employment available. **Financial Aid Statistics:** 39% freshmen, 34% undergrads receive need-based scholarship or grant aid. 4% freshmen, 2% undergrads receive non-need-based scholarship or grant aid. 47% freshmen, 44% undergrads receive need-based self-help aid. 2% freshmen, 2% undergrads receive athletic scholarships. 52% undergrads borrow to pay for school. Average cumulative indebtedness $20,431. **Criteria for awarding institutional aid:** *Non-need-based:* Academics, art, athletics, leadership, music/drama.

SAINT FRANCIS MEDICAL CENTER
COLLEGE OF NURSING

511 NE. Greenleaf Street, Peoria, IL 61603
Phone: 309-624-8980
E-mail: janice.e.farquharson@osfhealthcare.org
Fax: 309-624-8973 **Website:** www.sfmccon.edu/

This is a private school.

RATINGS

Admissions Selectivity Rating: 60*   **Fire Safety Rating:** 60*   **Green Rating:** 60*

STUDENTS AND FACULTY

Enrollment: 329. **Student Body:** 90% female, 10% male,. Asian 2%, African American 5%, Caucasian 91%, Hispanic 2%. **Retention and Graduation:** 98% freshmen return for sophomore year. 92% freshmen graduate within 4 years. **Faculty:** Student/faculty ratio 610:1. 32 full-time faculty, 34% hold PhDs, 97% are women.

ACADEMICS

Degrees: Bachelor's, doctoral, master's, post-master's certificate. **Classes:** Most classes have 40–49 students. Most lab/discussion sessions have fewer than 10 students. **Special Study Options:** Accelerated program, distance learning, independent study.

FACILITIES

Housing: Coed dorms.

CAMPUS LIFE

Activities: Student government.

ADMISSIONS

Freshman Admission Requirements: High school diploma is required and GED is accepted. **Transfer Admission Requirements:** High school transcript, college transcript(s), essay or personal statement, statement of good standing from prior institution(s). Minimum college GPA of 2.50 required. Lowest grade transferable C. **General Admission Information:** Application fee $50.

COSTS AND FINANCIAL AID

Annual tuition $14,400. Room and board $2,400. Required fees $260. **Required Forms and Deadlines:** FAFSA, institution's own financial aid form. Priority financial aid filing date 6/1. **Notification of Awards:** Applicants will be notified of awards on a rolling basis beginning 5/15. **Types of Aid:** *Need-based scholarships/grants:* Federal Pell, state scholarships/grants. *Loans:* FFEL Subsidized Stafford, FFEL Unsubsidized Stafford, FFEL PLUS. *Student Employment:* **Financial Aid Statistics:** 72% undergrads receive need-based scholarship or grant aid. 1% undergrads receive non-need-based scholarship or grant aid. 68% undergrads receive need-based self-help aid. **Criteria for awarding institutional aid:** *Non-need-based:* Academics, alumni affiliation.

SAINT FRANCIS UNIVERSITY (PA)

PO Box 600, Loretto, PA 15940
Phone: 814-472-3000 **Financial Aid Phone:** 814-472-3010
E-mail: admissions@francis.edu **CEEB Code:** 2797
Fax: 814-472-3335 **ACT Code:** 3682

This private school, affiliated with the Roman Catholic Church, was founded in 1847. It has a 600-acre campus.

RATINGS

Admissions Selectivity Rating: 72   **Fire Safety Rating:** 62   **Green Rating:** 60*

STUDENTS AND FACULTY

Enrollment: 1,360. **Student Body:** 61% female, 39% male, 31% out-of-state, international (11 countries represented).
Retention and Graduation: 83% freshmen return for sophomore year. 48% freshmen graduate within 4 years. 29% grads go on to further study within 1 year. 5% grads pursue arts and sciences degrees. 3% grads pursue law degrees. 9% grads pursue business degrees. 3% grads pursue medical degrees. **Faculty:** Student/faculty ratio 14:1. 90 full-time faculty.

ACADEMICS

Degrees: Associate, bachelor's, master's, post-bachelor's certificate. **Classes:** Most classes have 10–19 students. Most lab/discussion sessions have 10–19 students. **Majors with Highest Enrollment:** Business/commerce; health professions and related clinical sciences, other; physician assistant. **Special Study Options:** Cooperative education program, distance learning, double major, honors program, independent study, internships, liberal arts/career combination, student-designed major, study abroad, teacher certification program. **Honors programs:** Honors Program. **Combined degree programs:** BA/MD, BA/DDS, BS/MPAS, BS/MOT, BS/DPT, 3-3 BS/PharmD, 2-3 PharmD. Special programs offered to physically disabled students include note-taking services, tape recorders, tutors. **Career services:** Alumni network, career/job search classes, career assessment, internships.

FACILITIES

Housing: Coed dorms, men's dorms, women's dorms, fraternity/sorority housing, apartments for single students, special housing for honors students, special housing for campus ministry. 30% of campus accessible to physically disabled. **Special Academic Facilities/Equipment:** Art museum, elementary-level library for education majors, physician assistant practice facilities, cadaver lab, physical therapy lab, Center of Excellence for Remote and Medically Underserved Areas. **Computers:** Administrative functions (other than registration) can be performed online. Undergraduates are required to own a computer.

CAMPUS LIFE

Environment: Rural. **Activities:** Choral groups, dance, drama/theater, literary magazine, music ensembles, pep band, radio station, student government, student newspaper, student-run film society, television station, yearbook. **Organizations:** 60 registered organizations, 9 honor societies, 10 religious organizations. 3 fraternities, 3 sororities. **Athletics (Intercollegiate):** *Men:* Basketball, cross-country, football, golf, soccer, swimming, tennis, track/field (outdoor), track/field (indoor), volleyball. *Women:* Basketball, cross-country, field hockey, golf, lacrosse, soccer, softball, swimming, tennis, track/field (outdoor), track/field (indoor), volleyball. **On-Campus Highlights:** Christian Hall—residence hall, JFK Student Center, Immaculate Conception Chapel, Stokes Athletics Facility, Mt. Assisi Gardens.

ADMISSIONS

Freshman Academic Profile: Average high school GPA 3.4. 23% in top 10% of high school class, 28% in top 25% of high school class, 78% in top 50% of high school class. 78% from public high schools. SAT Math middle 50% range 480–580. SAT Critical Reading middle 50% range 470–570. ACT middle 50% range 19–26. Minimum paper TOEFL 500. Minimum computer TOEFL 220.

Basis for Candidate Selection: *Very important factors considered include:* Class rank, academic GPA, rigor of secondary school record, standardized test scores, extracurricular activities. *Important factors considered include:* Application essay, recommendation(s), character/personal qualities, interview, level of applicant's interest, talent/ability, volunteer work. *Other factors considered include:* Alumni/ae relation, work experience. **Freshman Admission Requirements:** High school diploma is required and GED is accepted. *Academic units required:* 4 English, 2 mathematics, 1 science, (1 science labs), 2 social studies, 7 academic electives. *Academic units recommended:* 2 science, 1 foreign language. **Freshman Admission Statistics:** 1,246 applied, 91% admitted, 32% enrolled. **Transfer Admission Requirements:** High school transcript, college transcript(s), standardized test scores, statement of good standing from prior institution(s). Minimum college GPA of 2.0 required. Lowest grade transferable C. **General Admission Information:** Application fee $30. Notification on a rolling basis, beginning on or about 10/1. Nonfall registration accepted. Admission may be deferred for a maximum of 12. Credit offered for CEEB Advanced Placement tests.

COSTS AND FINANCIAL AID

Annual tuition $20,360. Room and board $7,568. Required fees $1,050. Average book expense $500. **Required Forms and Deadlines:** FAFSA. Priority financial aid filing date 5/1. **Notification of Awards:** Applicants will be notified of awards on a rolling basis beginning 10/1. **Types of Aid:** *Need-based scholarships/grants:* Federal Pell, SEOG, state scholarships/grants, private scholarships, the school's own gift aid. *Loans:* FFEL Subsidized Stafford, FFEL Unsubsidized Stafford, FFEL PLUS, Federal Perkins. *Student Employment:* Federal Work-Study Program available. Institutional employment available. Highest amount earned per year from on-campus jobs $1,000. Off-campus job opportunities are fair. **Financial Aid Statistics:** 83% freshmen, 84% undergrads receive need-based scholarship or grant aid. 16% freshmen, 12% undergrads receive non-need-based scholarship or grant aid. 64% freshmen, 70% undergrads receive need-based self-help aid. 13% freshmen, 10% undergrads receive athletic scholarships. 94% freshmen receive any aid. 95% undergrads borrow to pay for school. Average cumulative indebtedness $19,690. **Criteria for awarding institutional aid:** *Non-need-based:* Academics, alumni affiliation, athletics, leadership, music/drama, religious affiliation.

SAINT JOSEPH COLLEGE (CT)

1678 Asylum Avenue, West Hartford, CT 06117
Phone: 860-231-5216 **Financial Aid Phone:** 860-231-5223
E-mail: admissions@sjc.edu
Fax: 860-231-5744 **Website:** www.sjc.edu

This private school, affiliated with the Roman Catholic Church, was founded in 1932. It has a 84-acre campus.

RATINGS

Admissions Selectivity Rating: 73   **Fire Safety Rating:** 60*   **Green Rating:** 60*

STUDENTS AND FACULTY

Enrollment: 947. **Student Body:** 99% female, 1% male, 7% out-of-state, international. Asian 2%, African American 11%, Caucasian 65%, Hispanic 10%. **Retention and Graduation:** 75% freshmen return for sophomore year. 31% freshmen graduate within 4 years. **Faculty:** Student/faculty ratio 10:1. 78 full-time faculty, 82% hold PhDs, 13% are are members of minority groups, 72% are women.

ACADEMICS

Degrees: Bachelor's, certificate, master's, post-bachelor's certificate. **Classes:** Most classes have 10–19 students. Most lab/discussion sessions have 10–19 students. **Majors with Highest Enrollment:** nursing/registered nurse (RN, ASN, BSN, MSN); psychology; social work. **Special Study Options:** Accelerated program, cross-registration, distance learning, double major, honors program, independent study, internships, liberal arts/career combination, student-designed major, study abroad, teacher certification program, weekend college. **Combined degree programs:** BA/MA. **Career services:** Alumni services, career/job search classes, career assessment, internships.

FACILITIES

Housing: Special housing for disabled students, women's dorms, Suite living (double rooms with shared common area and kitchen). **Computers:** Students can register for classes online.

CAMPUS LIFE

Environment: Town. **Activities:** Choral groups, dance, drama/theater, music ensembles, student government, student newspaper, yearbook, campus ministries, international student organization. **Organizations:** Athletics (Intercollegiate): *Women:* Basketball, cross-country, diving, lacrosse, soccer, softball, swimming, tennis, volleyball.

ADMISSIONS

Freshman Academic Profile: Average high school GPA 3.2. 19% in top 10% of high school class, 47% in top 25% of high school class, 85% in top 50% of high school class. SAT Math middle 50% range 440–520. SAT Critical Reading middle 50% range 440–520. Minimum paper TOEFL 530. Minimum computer TOEFL 250. **Basis for Candidate Selection:** *Very important factors considered include:* Academic GPA, standardized test scores. *Other factors considered include:* Class rank, application essay, recommendation(s), rigor of secondary school record, alumni/ae relation, character/personal qualities, extracurricular activities, first generation, geographical residence, interview, level of applicant's interest, racial/ethnic status, religious affiliation/commitment, state residency, talent/ability, volunteer work, work experience. **Freshman Admission Requirements:** High school diploma is required and GED is accepted. *Academic units required:* 4 English, 3 mathematics, 3 science, 3 foreign language, 3 social studies. **Freshman Admission Statistics:** 1,150 applied, 84% admitted, 19% enrolled. **Transfer Admission Requirements:** High school transcript, college transcript(s), Lowest grade transferable C. **General Admission Information:** Application fee $50. Notification on a rolling basis, beginning on or about 10/1. Nonfall registration accepted.

COSTS AND FINANCIAL AID

Required Forms and Deadlines: FAFSA. Priority financial aid filing date 2/15. **Notification of Awards:** Applicants will be notified of awards on a rolling basis beginning 3/1. **Types of Aid:** *Need-based scholarships/grants:* Federal Pell, SEOG, state scholarships/grants, private scholarships, the school's own gift aid, Federal Nursing Scholarships. *Loans:* Direct Subsidized Stafford, Direct Unsubsidized Stafford, Direct PLUS, FFEL Subsidized Stafford, FFEL Unsubsidized Stafford, FFEL PLUS, Federal Perkins, state loans *Student Employment:* Off-campus job opportunities are good. **Financial Aid Statistics:** 89% freshmen, 82% undergrads receive need-based scholarship or grant aid. 4% freshmen, 4% undergrads receive non-need-based scholarship or grant aid. 84% freshmen, 77% undergrads receive need-based self-help aid. 82% undergrads borrow to pay for school. Average cumulative indebtedness $39,743. **Criteria for awarding institutional aid:** *Non-need-based:* Academics.

SAINT JOSEPH SEMINARY COLLEGE

75376 River Road, St. Benedict, LA 70457
Phone: 985-867-2248 **Financial Aid Phone:** 985-867-2229
E-mail: georgebinderregistrar@sjasc.edu **CEEB Code:** 6689
Fax: 985-867-2270 **Website: ACT Code:** 1604

This private school, affiliated with the Roman Catholic Church, was founded in 1891. It has a 1200-acre campus.

RATINGS

Admissions Selectivity Rating: 60* **Fire Safety Rating:** 60* **Green Rating:** 60*

STUDENTS AND FACULTY

Student Body: 34% out-of-state.
Retention and Graduation: Faculty: Student/faculty ratio 5:1. 16 full-time faculty, 31% hold PhDs, 44% are women.

ACADEMICS

Degrees: Bachelor's. **Classes:** Most classes have 10–19 students. **Special Study Options:** Distance learning, English as a Second Language (ESL), independent study, study abroad. Special programs offered to physically disabled students include tape recorders, tutors.

FACILITIES

Housing: Men's dorms. 100% of campus accessible to physically disabled.

CAMPUS LIFE

Environment: Rural. **Activities:** Choral groups, drama/theater, literary magazine, student government, student newspaper, yearbook. **Organizations:** 1 religious organizations.

ADMISSIONS

Freshman Academic Profile: Minimum paper TOEFL 520. Minimum computer TOEFL 190. **Basis for Candidate Selection:** *Very important factors considered include:* Rigor of secondary school record, character/personal qualities, religious affiliation/commitment. *Important factors considered include:* Recommendation(s), standardized test scores. *Other factors considered include:* Class rank, extracurricular activities, interview, volunteer work. **Freshman Admission Requirements:** High school diploma is required and GED is ac-

cepted. *Academic units required:* 3 English, 2 mathematics, 2 science, 2 foreign language, 1 history. *Academic units recommended:* 3 English, 2 mathematics, 2 science, 2 foreign language. **Freshman Admission Statistics:** 9 applied, 100% admitted, 100% enrolled. **Transfer Admission Requirements:** High school transcript, college transcript(s), standardized test scores, Lowest grade transferable C. **General Admission Information:** Nonfall registration accepted. Neither credit nor placement offered for CEEB Advanced Placement tests.

COSTS AND FINANCIAL AID

Annual tuition $17,500. Room and board $7,415. Required fees $1,165. Average book expense $1,000. **Required Forms and Deadlines:** FAFSA, institution's own financial aid form, state aid form **Notification of Awards:** Applicants will be notified of awards on a rolling basis beginning 8/3. **Types of Aid:** *Need-based scholarships/grants:* Federal Pell, SEOG, state scholarships/grants, private scholarships, the school's own gift aid. *Loans:* FFEL Subsidized Stafford, FFEL Unsubsidized Stafford, FFEL PLUS, Federal Perkins. *Student Employment:* **Financial Aid Statistics:** 44% freshmen, 43% undergrads receive need-based scholarship or grant aid. 44% freshmen, 9% undergrads receive non-need-based scholarship or grant aid. 44% freshmen, 43% undergrads receive need-based self-help aid. 18% undergrads borrow to pay for school. Average cumulative indebtedness $12,400.

SAINT JOSEPH'S COLLEGE (IN)

P.O. Box 890, Rensselaer, IN 47978
Phone: 219-866-6170 **Financial Aid Phone:** 219-866-6163
E-mail: admissions@saintjoe.edu **CEEB Code:** 1697
Fax: 219-866-6122 **Website:** www.saintjoe.edu **ACT Code:** 1240

This private school, affiliated with the Roman Catholic Church, was founded in 1889. It has a 180-acre campus.

RATINGS

Admissions Selectivity Rating: 74 **Fire Safety Rating:** 76 **Green Rating:** 60*

STUDENTS AND FACULTY

Enrollment: 1,057. **Student Body:** 57% female, 43% male, 27% out-of-state, 1% international (4 countries represented). Asian 1%, African American 9%, Caucasian 84%, Hispanic 4%.
Retention and Graduation: 60% freshmen return for sophomore year. 44% freshmen graduate within 4 years. 22% grads go on to further study within 1 year. 59% grads pursue arts and sciences degrees. 19% grads pursue law degrees. 9% grads pursue business degrees. 3% grads pursue medical degrees. **Faculty:** Student/faculty ratio 15:1. 59 full-time faculty, 86% hold PhDs, 5% are are members of minority groups, 42% are women.

ACADEMICS

Degrees: Associate, bachelor's, certificate, diploma, master's, terminal associate. **Classes:** Most classes have 10–19 students. Most lab/discussion sessions have 10–19 students. **Majors with Highest Enrollment:** Business/commerce; elementary education and teaching; nursing/registered nurse (RN, ASN, BSN, MSN). **Special Study Options:** Accelerated program, cross-registration, double major, dual enrollment, honors program, independent study, internships, liberal arts/career combination, student-designed major, study abroad, teacher certification program. Special programs offered to physically disabled students include note-taking services, reader services, tape recorders, tutors. **Career services:** Alumni network, career assessment, internships.

FACILITIES

Housing: Coed dorms, special housing for disabled students, men's dorms, women's dorms, apartments for single students 74% of campus accessible to physically disabled. **Computers:** 100% of dorms, 100% of libraries, 100% of dining areas, have wireless network access.

CAMPUS LIFE

Environment: Village. **Activities:** Choral groups, concert band, dance, drama/theater, jazz band, literary magazine, marching band, music ensembles, musical theater, pep band, radio station, student government, student newspaper, student-run film society, television station. **Organizations:** 41 registered organizations, 4 honor societies, 7 religious organizations. **Athletics (Intercollegiate):** *Men:* Baseball, basketball, cross-country, football, golf, soccer, tennis, track/field (outdoor), track/field (indoor). *Women:* Basketball, cross-country, golf, soccer, softball, tennis, track/field (outdoor), track/field (indoor), volleyball. **On-Campus Highlights:** Rev. Charles Banet, C.PP.S. Core Education, Saint Joseph's Chapel, Lourdes Grotto, Hanson Recreation Center/Fitness Center, Lake Banet.

ADMISSIONS

Freshman Academic Profile: Average high school GPA 3. 10% in top 10% of high school class, 31% in top 25% of high school class, 62% in top 50% of high school class. 76% from public high schools. SAT Math middle 50% range 420–540. SAT Critical Reading middle 50% range 420–52. ACT middle 50% range 18–24. Minimum paper TOEFL 550. Minimum computer TOEFL 213. **Basis for Candidate Selection:** *Very important factors considered include:* Academic GPA, rigor of secondary school record, standardized test scores. *Important factors considered include:* Class rank, character/personal qualities, extracurricular activities, volunteer work. *Other factors considered include:* Application essay, recommendation(s), alumni/ae relation, interview, talent/ability, work experience. **Freshman Admission Requirements:** High school diploma is required and GED is accepted. *Academic units recommended:* 4 English, 3 mathematics, 3 science, (2 science labs), 2 foreign language, 3 social studies. **Freshman Admission Statistics:** 1,325 applied, 74% admitted, 28% enrolled. **Transfer Admission Requirements:** College transcript(s), minimum college GPA of 2.0 required. Lowest grade transferable C–. **General Admission Information:** Application fee $25. Notification on a rolling basis, beginning on or about 12/1. Nonfall registration accepted. Admission may be deferred for a maximum of 2. Credit offered for CEEB Advanced Placement tests.

COSTS AND FINANCIAL AID

Annual tuition $23,000. Room and board $7,170. Required fees $180. Average book expense $800. **Required Forms and Deadlines:** FAFSA. Priority financial aid filing date 3/1. **Notification of Awards:** Applicants will be notified of awards on a rolling basis beginning 3/1. **Types of Aid:** *Need-based scholarships/grants:* Federal Pell, SEOG, state scholarships/grants, private scholarships, the school's own gift aid. *Loans:* FFEL Subsidized Stafford, FFEL Unsubsidized Stafford, FFEL PLUS, Federal Perkins. *Student Employment:* Federal Work-Study Program available. Institutional employment available. Highest amount earned per year from on-campus jobs $1,500. Off-campus job opportunities are poor. **Financial Aid Statistics:** 79% freshmen, 80% undergrads receive need-based scholarship or grant aid. 23% freshmen, 21% undergrads receive non-need-based scholarship or grant aid. 52% freshmen, 55% undergrads receive need-based self-help aid. 7% freshmen, 8% undergrads receive athletic scholarships. 99% freshmen, 99% undergrads receive any aid. 77% undergrads borrow to pay for school. Average cumulative indebtedness $28,135. **Criteria for awarding institutional aid:** *Non-need-based:* Academics, alumni affiliation, athletics, minority status, music/drama.

SAINT JOSEPH'S COLLEGE OF MAINE

278 Whites Bridge Road, Standish, ME 04084-5263
Phone: 207-893-7746 **Financial Aid Phone:** 207-893-6612
E-mail: admission@sjcme.edu **CEEB Code:** 3755
Fax: 207-893-7862 **Website:** www.sjcme.edu **ACT Code:** 1659

This private school, affiliated with the Roman Catholic Church, was founded in 1912. It has a 350-acre campus.

RATINGS

Admissions Selectivity Rating: 60*   **Fire Safety Rating:** 60*   **Green Rating:** 60*

STUDENTS AND FACULTY

Enrollment: 1,034. **Student Body:** 65% female, 35% male, 44% out-of-state, (1 countries represented). African American 2%, Caucasian 83%, Hispanic 1%. **Retention and Graduation:** 78% freshmen return for sophomore year. 56% freshmen graduate within 4 years. 15% grads go on to further study within 1 year. 1% grads pursue arts and sciences degrees. 3% grads pursue business degrees. 2% grads pursue medical degrees. **Faculty:** Student/faculty ratio 15:1. 68 full-time faculty, 82% hold PhDs, 1% are are members of minority groups, 51% are women.

ACADEMICS

Degrees: Bachelor's. **Classes:** Most classes have 10–19 students. Most lab/discussion sessions have 10–19 students. **Majors with Highest Enrollment:** Business/commerce; elementary education and teaching; nursing/registered nurse (RN, ASN, BSN, MSN). **Special Study Options:** Cross-registration, distance learning, double major, dual enrollment, honors program, independent study, internships, student-designed major, study abroad, teacher certification program. **Honors programs:** 30–40 students per year are admitted for core curriculum Honors Program. Special programs offered to physically disabled students include note-taking services, reader services, tape recorders, tutors.

FACILITIES

Housing: Coed dorms, men's dorms, women's dorms, substance-free housing. 75% of campus accessible to physically disabled. **Special Academic Facilities/**

Equipment: Radio studio, telescope. **Computers:** Administrative functions (other than registration) can be performed online.

CAMPUS LIFE

Environment: Rural. **Activities:** Choral groups, dance, drama/theater, literary magazine, radio station, student government, student newspaper, yearbook. **Organizations:** 25 registered organizations, 2 honor societies, 1 religious organizations. **Athletics (Intercollegiate):** *Men:* Baseball, basketball, cross-country, golf, lacrosse, soccer, swimming. *Women:* Basketball, cross-country, field hockey, lacrosse, soccer, softball, swimming, volleyball. **On-Campus Highlights:** Harold Alford Center, Heffernan Center, Alfond Hall, Java Joe's Cafe, Mercy Hall.

ADMISSIONS

Freshman Academic Profile: 80% from public high schools. SAT Math middle 50% range 440–540. SAT Critical Reading middle 50% range 440–520. Minimum paper TOEFL 500. Minimum computer TOEFL 250. **Basis for Candidate Selection:** *Very important factors considered include:* Application essay, recommendation(s), rigor of secondary school record, character/personal qualities. *Important factors considered include:* Class rank, academic GPA, standardized test scores, talent/ability, volunteer work. *Other factors considered include:* extracurricular activities, interview, level of applicant's interest, work experience. **Freshman Admission Requirements:** High school diploma is required and GED is accepted. *Academic units recommended:* 4 English, 3 mathematics, 2 science, (2 science labs), 2 foreign language, 2 social studies, 2 history. **Freshman Admission Statistics:** 1,094 applied, 82% admitted, 41% enrolled. **Transfer Admission Requirements:** College transcript(s), essay or personal statement, statement of good standing from prior institution(s). Minimum college GPA of 2.0 required. Lowest grade transferable C. **General Admission Information:** Application fee $50. Regular application deadline 8/1. Nonfall registration accepted. Admission may be deferred for a maximum of 1 year. Credit and/or placement offered for CEEB Advanced Placement tests.

COSTS AND FINANCIAL AID

Annual tuition $21,000. Room and board $9,030. Required fees $760. Average book expense $800. **Required Forms and Deadlines:** FAFSA, institution's own financial aid form. Priority financial aid filing date 3/1. **Notification of Awards:** Applicants will be notified of awards on a rolling basis beginning 3/1. **Types of Aid:** *Need-based scholarships/grants:* Federal Pell, SEOG, state scholarships/grants, private scholarships, the school's own gift aid, Federal Nursing Scholarships. *Loans:* FFEL Subsidized Stafford, FFEL Unsubsidized Stafford, FFEL PLUS, Federal Perkins, Federal Nursing, state loans *Student Employment:* Federal Work-Study Program available. Institutional employment available. Highest amount earned per year from on-campus jobs $1,275. Off-campus job opportunities are good. **Financial Aid Statistics:** 84% freshmen, 80% undergrads receive need-based scholarship or grant aid. 10% freshmen, 9% undergrads receive non-need-based scholarship or grant aid. 72% freshmen, 70% undergrads receive need-based self-help aid. 98% freshmen, 95% undergrads receive any aid. 84% undergrads borrow to pay for school. Average cumulative indebtedness $35,518. **Criteria for awarding institutional aid:** *Non-need-based:* Academics, leadership.

SAINT JOSEPH'S UNIVERSITY (PA)

5600 City Avenue, Philadelphia, PA 19131
Phone: 610-660-1300 **Financial Aid Phone:** 610-660-1556
E-mail: admit@sju.edu **CEEB Code:** 2801
Fax: 610-660-1314 **Website:** www.sju.edu **ACT Code:** 3684

This private school, affiliated with the Roman CatholiC–Jesuit Church,, affiliated with the Jesuit Church, was founded in 1851. It has a 103-acre campus.

RATINGS

Admissions Selectivity Rating: 86   **Fire Safety Rating:** 98   **Green Rating:** 78

STUDENTS AND FACULTY

Enrollment: 5,188. **Student Body:** 52% female, 48% male, 52% out-of-state, 1% international (56 countries represented). Asian 2%, African American 7%, Caucasian 82%, Hispanic 4%. **Retention and Graduation:** 86% freshmen return for sophomore year. 71% freshmen graduate within 4 years. 23% grads go on to further study within 1 year. 30% grads pursue arts and sciences degrees. 10% grads pursue law degrees. 11% grads pursue business degrees. 20% grads pursue medical degrees. **Faculty:** Student/faculty ratio 14:1. 284 full-time faculty, 90% hold PhDs, 13% are are members of minority groups, 39% are women.

ACADEMICS

Degrees: Associate, bachelor's, certificate, master's, post-bachelor's certificate, post-master's certificate, transfer associate. **Classes:** Most classes have 20–29 students. Most lab/discussion sessions have 10–19 students. **Majors with Highest Enrollment:** Accounting; finance; marketing/marketing management. **Special Study Options:** Accelerated program, cooperative education program, distance learning, double major, dual enrollment, English as a Second Language (ESL), exchange student program (domestic), honors program, independent study, internships, student-designed major, study abroad, teacher certification program, weekend college, off campus study in Jesuit student exchange. **Honors programs:** There are distinctive benefits attached to belonging to the SJU Honors Program: Team-taught courses allow distinguished faculty members to share their knowledge and expertise with students in a challenging academic environment. Individual honors courses stress a detailed and thorough scholarly exploration of different fields of knowledge. Honors students register ahead of other students in their year. Honors suites in the residence halls allow like-minded students to live together, even as freshmen. Honors students are provided with free tickets and transportation to concerts and performances by world-renowned institutions such as the Arden Theater Company, the Curtis Institute of Music, the Philadelphia Orchestra, the Pennsylvania Ballet, the Academy of Vocal Arts, the Philadelphia Museum of Art, and the Franklin Science Institute. Receptions, concerts and lectures are regularly sponsored by the Honors Program for Honors Students. Students have access to Claver House, a quiet retreat where honors students can study, work with personal computers and attend receptions. Students have opportunities to present research and creative work at national conferences and seminars; they are also kept informed about scholarship and funding opportunities for graduate and professional work. **Combined degree programs:** BS/MS in Education, Psychology; 5th yr MA in Writing Studies. Special programs offered to physically disabled students include note-taking services, reader services, tape recorders, tutors. **Career services:** Alumni network, alumni services, career/job search classes, career assessment, internships, regional alumni. **Career services highlights include:** Saint Joseph's University's Erivan K. Haub School of Business Cooperative Education (Co-op) Program allows students to engage in real-world applications of their academic pursuits. Through two full-time, professionally engaging and paid experiences (creating one year of full-time work experience within the four-year degree), students discover their professional passions and bring real-world experience back to the classroom. In addition, the Co-op Program offers students substantial earning potential. Co-op students earn an average of $8,400 during their four-month work term and $17,000 during their eight-month work term. Employers asked several of these students to continue as part-time employees following their formal Co-op assignment, adding to these earnings. Employers likewise have expressed significant satisfaction with Saint Joseph's Co-op students. Rating Co-op students on dependability, attitude, quality of work and overall performance, the collective rating of all Co-op students (since the Program's inception) is a 4.4 on a scale of 5.0, and 93% of employers would hire their Co-op student(s) full-time, if a full-time job were available.

FACILITIES

Housing: Coed dorms, men's dorms, women's dorms, apartments for single students, theme housing Special accommodations upon need for disabled students. 85% of campus accessible to physically disabled. **Special Academic Facilities/Equipment:** Wall Street Trading Room, Claver House—Honors Program, Mandeville Hall Moot Board Room, University Gallery. **Computers:** 100% of classrooms, 100% of dorms, 100% of libraries, 100% of dining areas, 100% of student union, 10% of common outdoor areas have wireless network access. Students can register for classes online. Administrative functions (other than registration) can be performed online.

CAMPUS LIFE

Environment: Metropolis. **Activities:** Choral groups, concert band, dance, drama/theater, jazz band, literary magazine, music ensembles, musical theater, pep band, radio station, student government, student newspaper, student-run film society, yearbook, campus ministries, international student organization. **Organizations:** 100 registered organizations, 20 honor societies, 4 fraternities, 4 sororities. **Athletics (Intercollegiate):** *Men:* Baseball, basketball, crew/rowing, cross-country, golf, lacrosse, soccer, tennis, track/field (outdoor), track/field (indoor). *Women:* Basketball, crew/rowing, cross-country, field hockey, lacrosse, soccer, softball, tennis, track/field (outdoor), track/field (indoor). **On-Campus Highlights:** Campion Student Center, Hagan Arena and Athletics Center, Chapel of St. Joseph, Mandeville Hall, Maguire Sports Complex, 2008 brought the expansion of the SJU campus through the acquisition of 38 acres of property adjacent to the University as well as the construction of a new parking and retail facility. **Environmental Initiatives:** We have a full-time office of Health, Safety and Environmental compliance. We have a full-time recycling program with full-time staff. We purchase whenever possible Green products and services.

ADMISSIONS

Freshman Academic Profile: Average high school GPA 3.39. 23% in top 10% of high school class, 55% in top 25% of high school class, 86% in top 50% of high school class. 49% from public high schools. SAT Math middle 50% range 510–620. SAT Critical Reading middle 50% range 510–600. SAT Writing middle 50% range 510–610. ACT middle 50% range 21–26. Minimum paper

TOEFL 550. Minimum computer TOEFL 213. Minimum web-based TOEFL 79. **Basis for Candidate Selection:** *Very important factors considered include:* Academic GPA, rigor of secondary school record. *Important factors considered include:* Application essay, recommendation(s), character/personal qualities. *Other factors considered include:* Class rank, standardized test scores, alumni/ae relation, extracurricular activities, first generation, level of applicant's interest, talent/ability, volunteer work, work experience. **Freshman Admission Requirements:** High school diploma is required and GED is not accepted. *Academic units required:* 4 English, 3 mathematics, 2 science, (1 science labs), 2 foreign language, 1 history. *Academic units recommended:* 4 English, 3 mathematics, 2 science, (1 science labs), 2 foreign language, 1 history. **Freshman Admission Statistics:** 6,520 applied, 82% admitted, 22% enrolled. **Transfer Admission Requirements:** High school transcript, college transcript(s), statement of good standing from prior institution(s). Minimum college GPA of 2.5 required. Lowest grade transferable C. **General Admission Information:** Application fee $60. Regular application deadline 2/1. Regular notification 3/15. Nonfall registration accepted. Admission may be deferred for a maximum of 1 year. Credit offered for CEEB Advanced Placement tests.

COSTS AND FINANCIAL AID

Annual tuition $33,940. Room and board $11,575. Required fees $150. Average book expense $1,500. **Required Forms and Deadlines:** FAFSA. Priority financial aid filing date 2/15. **Notification of Awards:** Applicants will be notified of awards on a rolling basis beginning 3/1. **Types of Aid:** *Need-based scholarships/grants:* Federal Pell, SEOG, state scholarships/grants, private scholarships, the school's own gift aid. *Loans:* Direct Subsidized Stafford, Direct Unsubsidized Stafford, Direct PLUS, FFEL Subsidized Stafford, FFEL Unsubsidized Stafford, FFEL PLUS, Federal PerkinsThe Federal Direct Student Loan Program will be in effect beginning with the Fall 2010–11 academic year. *Student Employment:* Federal Work-Study Program available. Institutional employment available. Off-campus job opportunities are excellent. **Financial Aid Statistics:** 54% freshmen, 48% undergrads receive need-based scholarship or grant aid. 51% freshmen, 46% undergrads receive non-need-based scholarship or grant aid. 37% freshmen, 37% undergrads receive need-based self-help aid. 2% freshmen, 3% undergrads receive athletic scholarships. 93% freshmen, 91% undergrads receive any aid. **Criteria for awarding institutional aid:** *Non-need-based:* Academics, alumni affiliation, art, athletics, minority status, music/drama.

SAINT LEO UNIVERSITY

Office of Admission MC2008, PO Box 6665, Saint Leo, FL 33574-6665
Phone: 352)588-8283 **Financial Aid Phone:** 800-240-7658
E-mail: admission@saintleo.edu **CEEB Code:** 5638
Fax: 352)588-8257 **Website:** www.saintleo.edu **ACT Code:** 755

This private school, affiliated with the Roman Catholic Church, was founded in 1889. It has a 186-acre campus.

RATINGS

Admissions Selectivity Rating: 79   **Fire Safety Rating:** 89   **Green Rating:** 60*

STUDENTS AND FACULTY

Enrollment: 1,735. **Student Body:** 51% female, 49% male, 36% out-of-state, 8% international (42 countries represented). Asian 1%, African American 10%, Caucasian 61%, Hispanic 11%.
Retention and Graduation: 24% freshmen graduate within 4 years. **Faculty:** Student/faculty ratio 15:1. 106 full-time faculty, 87% hold PhDs, 11% are are members of minority groups, 36% are women.

ACADEMICS

Degrees: Associate, bachelor's, certificate, master's, post-bachelor's certificate. **Classes:** Most classes have 20–29 students. Most lab/discussion sessions have 10–19 students. **Majors with Highest Enrollment:** Biology/biological sciences; business administration and management; psychology. **Special Study Options:** Distance learning, double major, honors program, independent study, internships, liberal arts/career combination, study abroad, teacher certification program, weekend college. **Honors programs:** The Saint Leo University Honors Program consists of an integrated sequence of six interdisciplinary courses, spread over the first three years of college, and an extensive senior honors project carried out under the supervision of a distinguished faculty mentor. **Combined degree programs:** BA/DDS, BA/DO. Special programs offered to physically disabled students include note-taking services, reader services, tape recorders, tutors. **Career services:** Alumni network, alumni services, career/job search classes, career assessment, internships.

FACILITIES

Housing: Coed dorms, special housing for disabled students, men's dorms, women's dorms, apartments for single students, wellness housing, theme housing Freshmen only housing. 95% of campus accessible to physically disabled. **Computers:** 95% of classrooms, 85% of dorms, 100% of libraries, 100% of dining areas, 100% of student union, 90% of common outdoor areas have wireless network access. Students can register for classes online. Administrative functions (other than registration) can be performed online.

CAMPUS LIFE

Environment: Rural. **Activities:** Choral groups, concert band, dance, drama/theater, literary magazine, music ensembles, musical theater, student government, student newspaper, television station, yearbook, campus ministries, international student organization. **Organizations:** 58 registered organizations, 12 honor societies, 7 religious organizations. 6 fraternities, 4 sororities. **Athletics (Intercollegiate):** *Men:* Baseball, basketball, cross-country, golf, lacrosse, soccer, swimming, tennis. *Women:* Basketball, cross-country, golf, soccer, softball, swimming, tennis, volleyball. **On-Campus Highlights:** Student Community Center, Student Activities Building, Marion Bowman Activities Center, Swimming Pool, Lakefront.

ADMISSIONS

Freshman Academic Profile: Average high school GPA 3.3. 11% in top 10% of high school class, 33% in top 25% of high school class, 64% in top 50% of high school class. 70% from public high schools. SAT Math middle 50% range 450–550. SAT Critical Reading middle 50% range 440–530. SAT Writing middle 50% range 430–520. ACT middle 50% range 20–24. Minimum paper TOEFL 550. Minimum computer TOEFL 213. Minimum web-based TOEFL 80. **Basis for Candidate Selection:** *Very important factors considered include:* Academic GPA, recommendation(s), rigor of secondary school record, standardized test scores, character/personal qualities. *Important factors considered include:* Alumni/ae relation, extracurricular activities, interview, level of applicant's interest, talent/ability, volunteer work. *Other factors considered include:* Class rank, application essay, first generation, racial/ethnic status, work experience. **Freshman Admission Requirements:** High school diploma is required and GED is accepted. *Academic units recommended:* 4 English, 3 mathematics, 2 science, 2 foreign language, 3 social studies, 2 academic electives. **Freshman Admission Statistics:** 2,074 applied, 76% admitted, 31% enrolled. **Transfer Admission Requirements:** College transcript(s), essay or personal statement, statement of good standing from prior institution(s). Minimum college GPA of 2.0 required. Lowest grade transferable D. **General Admission Information:** Application fee $35. Regular application deadline 8/15. Notification on a rolling basis, beginning on or about 10/15. Nonfall registration accepted. Admission may be deferred for a maximum of 1 year. Credit and/or placement offered for CEEB Advanced Placement tests.

COSTS AND FINANCIAL AID

Annual tuition $16,996. Room and board $8,724. Required fees $350. Average book expense $1,200. **Required Forms and Deadlines:** FAFSA. Priority financial aid filing date 3/1. **Notification of Awards:** Applicants will be notified of awards on a rolling basis beginning 1/31. **Types of Aid:** *Need-based scholarships/grants:* Federal Pell, SEOG, state scholarships/grants, private scholarships, the school's own gift aid, United Negro College Fund *Loans:* Direct Subsidized Stafford, Direct Unsubsidized Stafford, Direct PLUS, Federal Perkins, Private Loans Through Lenders. *Student Employment:* Federal Work-Study Program available. Institutional employment available. Highest amount earned per year from on-campus jobs $3,500. Off-campus job opportunities are good. **Financial Aid Statistics:** 78% freshmen, 72% undergrads receive need-based scholarship or grant aid. 8% freshmen, 7% undergrads receive non-need-based scholarship or grant aid. 68% freshmen, 61% undergrads receive need-based self-help aid. 2% freshmen, 4% undergrads receive athletic scholarships. 100% freshmen, 95% undergrads receive any aid. 69% undergrads borrow to pay for school. Average cumulative indebtedness $23,178. **Criteria for awarding institutional aid:** *Non-need-based:* Academics, alumni affiliation, athletics, leadership, minority status, religious affiliation, state/district residency.

SAINT LOUIS UNIVERSITY

221 North Grand Boulevard, DuBourg Hall Room 100, Saint Louis, MO 63103
Phone: 314-977-2500 **Financial Aid Phone:** 314-977-2350
E-mail: admitme@slu.edu **CEEB Code:** 6629
Fax: 314-977-7136 **Website:** www.slu.edu **ACT Code:** 2352

This private school, affiliated with the Roman Catholic Church, was founded in 1818. It has a 235-acre campus.

RATINGS

Admissions Selectivity Rating: 89 **Fire Safety Rating:** 85 **Green Rating:** 75

STUDENTS AND FACULTY

Enrollment: 7,945. **Student Body:** 59% female, 41% male, 58% out-of-state, 7% international (75 countries represented). Asian 6%, African American 8%, Caucasian 65%, Hispanic 3%.
Retention and Graduation: 85% freshmen return for sophomore year. 60% freshmen graduate within 4 years. 35% grads go on to further study within 1 year. 10% grads pursue arts and sciences degrees. 21% grads pursue law degrees. 17% grads pursue business degrees. 21% grads pursue medical degrees. **Faculty:** Student/faculty ratio 13:1. 639 full-time faculty, 90% hold PhDs, 10% are are members of minority groups, 44% are women. 7% of classes are taught by teaching assistants.

ACADEMICS

Degrees: Bachelor's, certificate, doctoral, master's, post-bachelor's certificate, post-master's certificate. **Classes:** Most classes have 10–19 students. Most lab/discussion sessions have 10–19 students. **Majors with Highest Enrollment:** Biology/biological sciences; business administration and management; nursing/registered nurse (RN, ASN, BSN, MSN). **Special Study Options:** Accelerated program, cooperative education program, cross-registration, distance learning, double major, dual enrollment, English as a Second Language (ESL), honors program, independent study, internships, liberal arts/career combination, student-designed major, study abroad, teacher certification program. **Honors programs:** The Honors Program at Saint Louis University offers eligible students the opportunity to develop an individual course of study that complements their undergraduate major, leading to an Honors degree in that discipline. Undergraduates from any of the schools and colleges at Saint Louis University can successfully pursue an honors degree through the University Honors Program. The Saint Louis University Honors Program offers interdisciplinary programs and opportunities with reflective and expressive elements to students in the Honors Program. The Honors Program offers seminar courses with integrated collaborative learning experiences including service learning, internships, and research. The Honors Program offers Honors students study abroad opportunities. The Honors Program offers Honors courses at the Saint Louis University Madrid Campus. The Honors Program offers teaching assistant positions to undergraduate Honors students. The Honors Program offers a residential learning community and several Freshman Interest Groups. The Honors Program provides academic, cultural, and social opportunities. The Honors Program provides peer mentorship programs. **Combined degree programs:** BA/MA, BA/MSW, MD/MBA, MBA/MHA. Special programs offered to physically disabled students include note-taking services, reader services, tape recorders, tutors. **Career services:** Alumni network, alumni services, career/job search classes, career assessment, internships, regional alumni.

FACILITIES

Housing: Coed dorms, special housing for disabled students, men's dorms, women's dorms, fraternity/sorority housing, apartments for married students, apartments for single students, theme housing Foreign Language Housing. 95% of campus accessible to physically disabled. **Special Academic Facilities/Equipment:** Saint Louis University Museum of Art (SLUMA), McNamee Gallery of Samuel Cupples House, Museum of Contemporary Religious Art (MOCRA). **Computers:** 100% of classrooms, 100% of dorms, 100% of libraries, 100% of dining areas, 100% of student union, 100% of common outdoor areas have wireless network access. Students can register for classes online. Administrative functions (other than registration) can be performed online.

CAMPUS LIFE

Environment: Metropolis. **Activities:** Choral groups, dance, drama/theater, jazz band, literary magazine, music ensembles, musical theater, pep band, radio station, student government, student newspaper, student-run film society, television station, yearbook, campus ministries, international student organization, Model UN. **Organizations:** 170 registered organizations, 25 honor societies, 36 religious organizations. 11 fraternities, 6 sororities. **Athletics (Intercollegiate):** *Men:* Baseball, basketball, cross-country, diving, soccer, swimming, tennis, track/field (outdoor), track/field (indoor). *Women:* Basketball, cross-country, diving, field hockey, soccer, softball, swimming, tennis, track/field (outdoor), track/field (indoor), volleyball. **On-Campus Highlights:** St. Francis Xavier Church, Busch Student Center, St. Louis University Museum of Art, Simon Recreation Center, Robert R. Hermann Soccer Stadium, Chaifetz Arena. **Environmental Initiatives:** Recycling Energy efficiencies/reductions Usage of Green Seal certified cleaning products.

ADMISSIONS

Freshman Academic Profile: Average high school GPA 3.71. 39% in top 10% of high school class, 71% in top 25% of high school class, 91% in top 50% of high school class. SAT Math middle 50% range 540–670. SAT Critical Reading middle 50% range 540–650. ACT middle 50% range 24–30. Minimum paper TOEFL 550. Minimum computer TOEFL 213. Minimum web-based TOEFL 80. **Basis for Candidate Selection:** *Very important factors considered include:* Academic GPA, standardized test scores. *Important factors considered include:* Application essay, rigor of secondary school record, character/personal qualities, extracurricular activities, talent/ability. *Other factors considered include:* Recommendation(s), alumni/ae relation, first generation, interview, level of applicant's interest, volunteer work. **Freshman Admission Requirements:** High school diploma is required and GED is accepted. *Academic units required:* 4 English, 4 mathematics, 3 science, 3 foreign language, 3 social studies, 3 academic electives. *Academic units recommended:* 4 English, 4 mathematics, 3 science, 3 foreign language, 3 social studies, 3 academic electives. **Freshman Admission Statistics:** 10,707 applied, 71% admitted, 21% enrolled. **Transfer Admission Requirements:** College transcript(s), minimum college GPA of 2.0 required. Lowest grade transferable C. **General Admission Information:** Application fee $25. Regular application deadline 8/1. Regular notification 8/1. Notification on a rolling basis, beginning on or about 10/1. Nonfall registration accepted. Admission may be deferred for a maximum of 1 Year. Credit and/or placement offered for CEEB Advanced Placement tests.

COSTS AND FINANCIAL AID

Annual tuition $30,940. Room and board $8,900. Required fees $402. Average book expense $1,660. **Required Forms and Deadlines:** FAFSA. Priority financial aid filing date 3/1. **Notification of Awards:** Applicants will be notified of awards on a rolling basis beginning 3/1. **Types of Aid:** *Need-based scholarships/grants:* Federal Pell, SEOG, state scholarships/grants, private scholarships, the school's own gift aid, Federal Nursing Scholarships. *Loans:* FFEL Subsidized Stafford, FFEL Unsubsidized Stafford, FFEL PLUS, Federal Perkins, Federal Nursing, college/university loans from institutional funds. *Student Employment:* Federal Work-Study Program available. Institutional employment available. Highest amount earned per year from on-campus jobs $14,068. Off-campus job opportunities are good. **Financial Aid Statistics:** 63% freshmen, 51% undergrads receive need-based scholarship or grant aid. 8% freshmen, 5% undergrads receive non-need-based scholarship or grant aid. 47% freshmen, 42% undergrads receive need-based self-help aid. 2% freshmen, 2% undergrads receive athletic scholarships. 91% freshmen, 88% undergrads receive any aid. 64% undergrads borrow to pay for school. Average cumulative indebtedness $33,747. **Criteria for awarding institutional aid:** *Non-need-based:* Academics, art, athletics, leadership, music/drama, religious affiliation.

See page 1220.

SAINT MARTIN'S UNIVERSITY

5300 Pacific Avenue SE, Lacey, WA 98503-7500
Phone: 360-438-4596 **Financial Aid Phone:** 360-486-8133
E-mail: admissions@stmartin.edu **CEEB Code:** 4674
Fax: 360-412-6189 **Website:** www.stmartin.edu **ACT Code:** 4474

This private school, affiliated with the Roman Catholic Church, was founded in 1895. It has a 320-acre campus.

RATINGS

Admissions Selectivity Rating: 76   **Fire Safety Rating:** 75   **Green Rating:** 60*

STUDENTS AND FACULTY

Enrollment: 1,298. **Student Body:** 55% female, 45% male, 27% out-of-state, 6% international (17 countries represented). Asian 10%, African American 8%, Caucasian 59%, Hispanic 9%, Native American 2%. **Retention and Graduation:** 71% freshmen return for sophomore year. 35% freshmen graduate within 4 years. 14% grads go on to further study within 1 year. 2% grads pursue arts and sciences degrees. 2% grads pursue law degrees. 8% grads pursue business degrees. 2% grads pursue medical degrees. **Faculty:**

Student/faculty ratio 12.2:1. 78 full-time faculty, 78% hold PhDs, 13% are are members of minority groups, 36% are women.

ACADEMICS

Degrees: Bachelor's, master's, post-bachelor's certificate, post-master's certificate. **Classes:** Most classes have fewer than 10 students. Most lab/discussion sessions have fewer than 10 students. **Majors with Highest Enrollment:** Biology/biological sciences; business administration and management; psychology. **Special Study Options:** Distance learning, double major, English as a Second Language (ESL), exchange student program (domestic), independent study, internships, study abroad, teacher certification program. **Combined degree programs:** BA/MEng. Special programs offered to physically disabled students include note-taking services, reader services, tape recorders, tutors. **Career services:** Alumni network, alumni services, career/job search classes, career assessment, regional alumni. **Career services highlights include:** We invite our local alumni to participate in any and all of our career-related workshops and career advising sessions and we have had a great turnout. The alumni have initiated an online mentor profile so that students may contact an alum with a question or ask advice. Many relationships can be formed by their participation in these two new activities.

FACILITIES

Housing: Coed dorms, special housing for disabled students, apartments for single students. 85% of campus accessible to physically disabled. **Special Academic Facilities/Equipment:** Cap Art Gallery, Waynick Museum. **Computers:** 80% of classrooms, 10% of dorms, 100% of libraries, 100% of dining areas, 100% of student union, have wireless network access. Students can register for classes online. Administrative functions (other than registration) can be performed online.

CAMPUS LIFE

Environment: Town. **Activities:** Choral groups, concert band, dance, drama/theater, jazz band, musical theater, pep band, student government, student newspaper, campus ministries, international student organization, Model UN. **Organizations:** 23 registered organizations, 3 honor societies, 3 religious organizations. **Athletics (Intercollegiate):** *Men:* Baseball, basketball, cross-country, golf, track/field (outdoor), track/field (indoor). *Women:* Basketball, cross-country, golf, softball, track/field (outdoor), track/field (indoor), volleyball. **On-Campus Highlights:** O'Grady Library, Student Union Building, Recreation and Fitness Center, Baran/Burton/Spangler Halls, Abbey Church, Dining Hall renovation completed in December 2009, Spangler Residence Hall opened fall 2005. New residence hall and new academic building opened fall 2008. New Recreation and fitness center opened in January 2010. **Environmental Initiatives:** FoodPlus recycling-for-compost program

ADMISSIONS

Freshman Academic Profile: Average high school GPA 3.27. 19% in top 10% of high school class, 50% in top 25% of high school class, 82% in top 50% of high school class. 95% from public high schools. SAT Math middle 50% range 440–560. SAT Critical Reading middle 50% range 430–550. SAT Writing middle 50% range 410–530. ACT middle 50% range 16–24. Minimum paper TOEFL 525. Minimum computer TOEFL 197. Minimum web-based TOEFL 71. **Basis for Candidate Selection:** *Very important factors considered include:* Academic GPA, rigor of secondary school record. *Important factors considered include:* Application essay, recommendation(s), standardized test scores, character/personal qualities, extracurricular activities, volunteer work. *Other factors considered include:* Class rank, alumni/ae relation, interview, talent/ability, work experience. **Freshman Admission Requirements:** High school diploma is required and GED is accepted. *Academic units recommended:* 4 English, 3 mathematics, 3 science, (1 science labs), 2 foreign language, 2 social studies, 3 academic electives. **Freshman Admission Statistics:** 734 applied, 78% admitted, 31% enrolled. **Transfer Admission Requirements:** College transcript(s), essay or personal statement, minimum college GPA of 2.25 required. Lowest grade transferable C–. **General Admission Information:** Application fee $35. Notification on a rolling basis, beginning on or about 10/1. Nonfall registration accepted. Credit offered for CEEB Advanced Placement tests.

COSTS AND FINANCIAL AID

Annual tuition $26,100. Room and board $8,660. Required fees $302. Average book expense $1,000. **Required Forms and Deadlines:** FAFSA. Priority financial aid filing date 3/1. **Notification of Awards:** Applicants will be notified of awards on a rolling basis beginning 2/15. **Types of Aid:** *Need-based scholarships/grants:* Federal Pell, SEOG, state scholarships/grants, private scholarships, the school's own gift aid. *Loans:* FFEL Subsidized Stafford, FFEL Unsubsidized Stafford, FFEL PLUS, Federal Perkins, state loans, college/university loans from institutional funds, private, alternative educational loans. *Student Employment:* Federal Work-Study Program available. Institutional employment available. Highest amount earned per year from on-campus jobs $2,100. Off-campus job opportunities are good. **Financial Aid Statistics:** 81% freshmen, 79% undergrads receive need-based scholarship or grant aid. 16% freshmen, 10% undergrads receive non-need-based scholarship or grant aid. 65% freshmen, 67% undergrads receive need-based self-help aid. 12%

freshmen, 8% undergrads receive athletic scholarships. 78% freshmen, 86% undergrads receive any aid. 79% undergrads borrow to pay for school. Average cumulative indebtedness $27,807. **Criteria for awarding institutional aid:** *Non-need-based:* Academics, alumni affiliation, art, athletics, leadership, minority status, music/drama, religious affiliation, state/district residency.

SAINT MARY'S COLLEGE (CA)

P.O. Box 4800, Moraga, CA 94575-4800
Phone: 925-631-4224 **Financial Aid Phone:** 925-631-4522
E-mail: smcadmit@stmarys-ca.edu **CEEB Code:** 4675
Fax: 925-376-7193 **Website:** www.stmarys-ca.edu **ACT Code:** 386

This private school, affiliated with the Roman Catholic Church, was founded in 1863. It has a 420-acre campus.

RATINGS
Admissions Selectivity Rating: 74 **Fire Safety Rating:** 83 **Green Rating:** 86

STUDENTS AND FACULTY
Enrollment: 2,379. **Student Body:** 62% female, 38% male, 14% out-of-state, 3% international (29 countries represented). Asian 11%, African American 7%, Caucasian 50%, Hispanic 22%, Native American 1%.
Retention and Graduation: 82% freshmen return for sophomore year. 50% freshmen graduate within 4 years. 24.9% grads go on to further study within 1 year. **Faculty:** Student/faculty ratio 11.7:1. 202 full-time faculty, 92% hold PhDs, 17% are are members of minority groups, 51% are women.

ACADEMICS
Degrees: Associate, bachelor's, doctoral, master's. **Classes:** Most classes have 10–19 students. **Majors with Highest Enrollment:** Business administration, management and operations, other; communication and media studies, other; psychology. **Special Study Options:** Double major, exchange student program (domestic), independent study, student-designed major, study abroad Special programs offered to physically disabled students include note-taking services, reader services, tape recorders, tutors. **Career services:** Alumni network, alumni services, career/job search classes, career assessment, internships. **Career services highlights include:** Career Information Night Series plus our Career and Internship Fair.

FACILITIES
Housing: Coed dorms, special housing for disabled students, theme housing. 90% of campus accessible to physically disabled. **Special Academic Facilities/ Equipment:** Hearst Art Gallery, Brousseau Hall, Science Building Geissberger Observatory. **Computers:** 100% of classrooms, 100% of libraries, 100% of dining areas, 100% of student union, 70% of common outdoor areas have wireless network access. Students can register for classes online. Administrative functions (other than registration) can be performed online.

CAMPUS LIFE
Environment: Village. **Activities:** Choral groups, dance, drama/theater, jazz band, music ensembles, musical theater, pep band, radio station, student government, student newspaper, campus ministries, international student organization. **Organizations:** 56 registered organizations, 3 religious organizations. **Athletics (Intercollegiate):** *Men:* Baseball, basketball, cheerleading, cross-country, golf, soccer, tennis. *Women:* Basketball, cheerleading, crew/rowing, cross-country, lacrosse, soccer, softball, tennis, volleyball. **On-Campus Highlights:** Br. Alfred Brousseau Hall, Cassin Student Union and LeFevre Quad, College Chapel, Hearst Art Gallery, Oliver Dining Hall, Power Plant (exercise facility) McKeon Pavilion, "St. Patty's Cathedral." **Environmental Initiatives:** 2007 summer reading program for incoming students focused on global warming. Energy conservation program (phase 2) reduces consumption by 71KW Student-run organic vegetable garden: http://stmarys-ca.edu/about-smc/sustain-smc/for-students/vegetable-garden.html

ADMISSIONS
Freshman Academic Profile: Average high school GPA 3.4. 52% from public high schools. SAT Math middle 50% range 490–600. SAT Critical Reading middle 50% range 490–590. ACT middle 50% range 20–26. Minimum paper TOEFL 527. Minimum computer TOEFL 197. Minimum web-based TOEFL 71. **Basis for Candidate Selection:** *Very important factors considered include:* Academic GPA, rigor of secondary school record, standardized test scores. *Important factors considered include:* Application essay, recommendation(s),

first generation. *Other factors considered include:* Class rank, alumni/ae relation, character/personal qualities, extracurricular activities, geographical residence, interview, level of applicant's interest, racial/ethnic status, religious affiliation/commitment, talent/ability, volunteer work, work experience. **Freshman Admission Requirements:** High school diploma is required and GED is accepted. *Academic units required:* 4 English, 3 mathematics, 2 science, (1 science labs), 2 foreign language, 1 social studies, 1 history, 2 academic electives. *Academic units recommended:* 4 English, 4 mathematics, 3 science, (1 science labs), 3 foreign language, 1 social studies, 1 history, 2 academic electives. **Freshman Admission Statistics:** 3,241 applied, 79% admitted, 22% enrolled. **Transfer Admission Requirements:** High school transcript, college transcript(s), essay or personal statement, minimum college GPA of 2.3 required. Lowest grade transferable C–. **General Admission Information:** Application fee $55. Regular application deadline 2/1. Regular notification 3/15. Nonfall registration accepted. Admission may be deferred for a maximum of 1 year. Credit and/or placement offered for CEEB Advanced Placement tests.

COSTS AND FINANCIAL AID
Required fees $150. Average book expense $1,512. **Required Forms and Deadlines:** FAFSA, state aid form. Priority financial aid filing date 2/15. **Notification of Awards:** Applicants will be notified of awards on a rolling basis beginning 3/15. **Types of Aid:** *Need-based scholarships/grants:* Federal Pell, SEOG, state scholarships/grants, private scholarships, the school's own gift aid. *Loans:* FFEL Subsidized Stafford, FFEL Unsubsidized Stafford, FFEL PLUS, Federal Perkins. *Student Employment:* Federal Work-Study Program available. Institutional employment available. Highest amount earned per year from on-campus jobs $12,744. Off-campus job opportunities are good. **Financial Aid Statistics:** 71% freshmen, 59% undergrads receive need-based scholarship or grant aid. 29% freshmen, 25% undergrads receive non-need-based scholarship or grant aid. 66% freshmen, 61% undergrads receive need-based self-help aid. 5% freshmen, 4% undergrads receive athletic scholarships. 85% freshmen, 75% undergrads receive any aid. 80% undergrads borrow to pay for school. Average cumulative indebtedness $31,330. **Criteria for awarding institutional aid:** *Non-need-based:* Academics, alumni affiliation, athletics, leadership.

SAINT MARY'S COLLEGE (IN)

Admission office, Notre Dame, IN 46556
Phone: 574-284-4587 **Financial Aid Phone:** 574-284-4557
E-mail: admission@saintmarys.edu **CEEB Code:** 1702
Fax: 574-284-4841 **Website:** www3.saintmarys.edu **ACT Code:** 1244

This private school, affiliated with the Roman Catholic Church, was founded in 1844. It has a 275-acre campus.

RATINGS
Admissions Selectivity Rating: 85 **Fire Safety Rating:** 81 **Green Rating:** 70

STUDENTS AND FACULTY
Enrollment: 1,640. **Student Body:** 100% female, 72% out-of-state, 1% international (6 countries represented). Asian 1%, African American 1%, Caucasian 86%, Hispanic 7%.
Retention and Graduation: 87% freshmen return for sophomore year. 73% freshmen graduate within 4 years. 29% grads go on to further study within 1 year. 14% grads pursue arts and sciences degrees. 0.6% grads pursue law degrees. 1.3% grads pursue business degrees. 2.6% grads pursue medical degrees. **Faculty:** Student/faculty ratio 11:1. 129 full-time faculty, 88% hold PhDs, 9% are are members of minority groups, 65% are women.

ACADEMICS
Degrees: Bachelor's. **Classes:** Most classes have 20–29 students. Most lab/discussion sessions have 10–19 students. **Majors with Highest Enrollment:** Communication studies/speech communication and rhetoric; elementary education and teaching; nursing/registered nurse (RN, ASN, BSN, MSN). **Special Study Options:** Accelerated program, cross-registration, double major, exchange student program (domestic), independent study, internships, liberal arts/career combination, student-designed major, study abroad, teacher certification program Special programs offered to physically disabled students include note-taking services, reader services, tape recorders, tutors. **Career services:** Alumni network, alumni services, career/job search classes, career assessment, internships, regional alumni.

FACILITIES
Housing: Special housing for disabled students, women's dorms, apartments for single students, Intercultural Living Floor. 100% of campus accessible to physically disabled. **Special Academic Facilities/Equipment:** Art gallery, early childhood development center, language lab, electron microscope. **Computers:** 80% of classrooms, 60% of dorms, 100% of libraries, 100% of

dining areas, 100% of student union, have wireless network access. Students can register for classes online. Administrative functions (other than registration) can be performed online.

CAMPUS LIFE

Environment: City. **Activities:** Choral groups, dance, drama/theater, jazz band, literary magazine, marching band, music ensembles, musical theater, opera, pep band, radio station, student government, student newspaper, television station, yearbook, campus ministries, international student organization. **Organizations:** 78 registered organizations, 14 honor societies, 8 religious organizations. **Athletics (Intercollegiate):** *Women:* Basketball, cross-country, diving, golf, soccer, softball, swimming, tennis, volleyball. **On-Campus Highlights:** Student Center/Noble Family Dining hall, Dalloway's Coffee House, Angela Athletic Facility, Spes Unica, Moreau Center for the Arts/O'Laughlin. **Environmental Initiatives:** Campus Recycling Program; environmental considerations in building projects—Spes Unica & Madeleva; hybrid fleet vehicle

ADMISSIONS

Freshman Academic Profile: Average high school GPA 3.71. 38% in top 10% of high school class, 58% in top 25% of high school class, 93% in top 50% of high school class. 54.5% from public high schools. SAT Math middle 50% range 510–600. SAT Critical Reading middle 50% range 510–620. SAT Writing middle 50% range 510–620. ACT middle 50% range 23–28. Minimum paper TOEFL 550. Minimum computer TOEFL 213. **Basis for Candidate Selection:** *Important factors considered include:* Academic GPA, rigor of secondary school record, standardized test scores, level of applicant's interest. *Other factors considered include:* Class rank, application essay, recommendation(s), alumni/ae relation, character/personal qualities, extracurricular activities, first generation, geographical residence, interview, racial/ethnic status, state residency, talent/ability, volunteer work, work experience. **Freshman Admission Requirements:** High school diploma is required and GED is accepted. *Academic units required:* 4 English, 3 mathematics, 2 science, (2 science labs), 2 foreign language, 2 history. *Academic units recommended:* 4 English, 4 mathematics, 4 science, (2 science labs), 4 foreign language, 2 history. **Freshman Admission Statistics:** 1,357 applied, 86% admitted, 37% enrolled. **Transfer Admission Requirements:** High school transcript, college transcript(s), essay or personal statement, standardized test scores, statement of good standing from prior institution(s). Minimum college GPA of 3.0 required. Lowest grade transferable C. **General Admission Information:** Application fee $30. Early decision application deadline 11/15. Notification on a rolling basis, beginning on or about 1/1. Nonfall registration accepted. Credit and/or placement offered for CEEB Advanced Placement tests.

COSTS AND FINANCIAL AID

Annual tuition $28,900. Room and board $9,206. Required fees $636. Average book expense $1,200. **Required Forms and Deadlines:** FAFSA, CSS/Financial Aid PROFILE, noncustodial PROFILE. Priority financial aid filing date 3/1. **Notification of Awards:** Applicants will be notified of awards on a rolling basis beginning 3/15. **Types of Aid:** *Need-based scholarships/grants:* Federal Pell, SEOG, state scholarships/grants, private scholarships, the school's own gift aid. *Loans:* FFEL Subsidized Stafford, FFEL Unsubsidized Stafford, FFEL PLUS, Federal Perkins. *Student Employment:* Federal Work-Study Program available. Institutional employment available. Off-campus job opportunities are good. **Financial Aid Statistics:** 68% freshmen, 64% undergrads receive need-based scholarship or grant aid. 53% freshmen, 50% undergrads receive non-need-based scholarship or grant aid. 56% freshmen, 50% undergrads receive need-based self-help aid. 97% freshmen, 94% undergrads receive any aid. 72% undergrads borrow to pay for school. Average cumulative indebtedness $25,531. **Criteria for awarding institutional aid:** *Non-need-based:* Academics, art.

See page 1222.

SAINT MARY'S UNIVERSITY OF MINNESOTA

700 Terrace Heights #2, Winona, MN 55987-1399
Phone: 507-457-1700 **Financial Aid Phone:** 507-457-1438
E-mail: admission@smumn.edu **CEEB Code:** 6632
Fax: 507-457-1722 **Website:** www.smumn.edu **ACT Code:** 2148

This private school, affiliated with the Roman Catholic Church, was founded in 1912. It has a 400-acre campus.

RATINGS
Admissions Selectivity Rating: 76   **Fire Safety Rating:** 60*   **Green Rating:** 73

STUDENTS AND FACULTY
Enrollment: 2,046. **Student Body:** 52% female, 48% male, 36% out-of-state, 3% international (39 countries represented). Asian 2%, African American 3%, Caucasian 67%, Hispanic 3%.

Retention and Graduation: 75% freshmen return for sophomore year. 46% freshmen graduate within 4 years. **Faculty:** Student/faculty ratio 12:1. 103 full-time faculty, 84% hold PhDs, 3% are are members of minority groups, 38% are women.

ACADEMICS

Degrees: Bachelor's, certificate, diploma, doctoral, master's, post-bachelor's certificate, post-master's certificate. **Classes:** Most classes have 20–29 students. Most lab/discussion sessions have 10–19 students. **Majors with Highest Enrollment:** marketing/marketing management. **Special Study Options:** Cooperative education program, cross-registration, double major, dual enrollment, English as a Second Language (ESL), honors program, independent study, internships, student-designed major, study abroad, teacher certification program. **Honors programs:** The Lasallian Honors Program at Saint Mary's University is a general education program for motivated students who wish to engage in "shared inquiry" in small seminar classes. The hallmarks of the program are study of the Great Books, service learning, and participation in a community of learners who desire to grow intellectually and spiritually, together over four years. Great Books, Shared-Inquiry Seminars The Lasallian Honors Program is an interdisciplinary program of learning in the Great Books and other notable texts of Western and Eastern traditions. All of the courses are shared-inquiry seminars: the students and the professor discuss the works together in lively, interactive, and informed conversations about the most important ideas in human history. Working Smarter Honors courses do not necessarily require more work than other general education courses. What differs is the style of learning, in student-centered seminars. You have the opportunity to participate with other motivated students in small classes taught by professors committed to engaged learning and individualized attention. Streamlined General Education A practical advantage of the Honors program is that it streamlines course requirements. Because of our interdisciplinary 4-credit model, honors students take fewer general education courses. That leaves room for a second major, extracurricular activities, an internship, and/or studying abroad. Future Benefits Participation in the Lasallian Honors Program also has rewards after graduation. When it comes time to compete for a job, internship, or acceptance to graduate school, Honors students have a clear advantage. We have an enviable record (98%) of placing our students in some of the best graduate programs in the country. Personal Growth The most important reason to join the Lasallian Honors Program is the desire to extend yourself intellectually, spiritually, and creatively. We can help you do that in a supportive and challenging academic atmosphere. You will be part of a cohort group that shares your talents and interests – and likely will become your closest college friends. Special programs offered to physically disabled students include note-taking services, reader services, tape recorders, tutors. **Career services:** Alumni network, alumni services, career/job search classes, career assessment, internships.

FACILITIES

Housing: Coed dorms, special housing for disabled students, men's dorms, women's dorms, apartments for single students. 93% of campus accessible to physically disabled. **Special Academic Facilities/Equipment:** Art gallery, performance center, laboratories, observatory. **Computers:** 100% of dorms, 100% of libraries, 100% of dining areas, 100% of student union, have wireless network access. Students can register for classes online. Administrative functions (other than registration) can be performed online.

CAMPUS LIFE

Environment: Town. **Activities:** Choral groups, concert band, dance, drama/theater, jazz band, literary magazine, music ensembles, musical theater, radio station, student government, student newspaper, yearbook, campus ministries, international student organization. **Organizations:** 80 registered organizations, 13 honor societies, 6 religious organizations. **Athletics (Intercollegiate):** *Men:* Baseball, basketball, cross-country, diving, golf, ice hockey, skiing (nordic cross-country), soccer, swimming, tennis, track/field (outdoor), track/field (indoor). *Women:* Basketball, cross-country, diving, golf, ice hockey, skiing (nordic cross-country), soccer, softball, swimming, tennis, track/field (outdoor), track/field (indoor), volleyball. **On-Campus Highlights:** Lillian Hogan Davis Galleries, Gostomski Fieldhouse, Page Theatre, Toner Student Center, Outdoor Track and Field Complex, Saint Mary's also offers an 18 hole disc golf course which runs through the bluffs surrounding the campus. Also, a network of trails run along the bluffs and into wooded valleys allowing for hiking, running, walking, and cross country skiing. **Environmental Initiatives:** ISO 14001 Certified Environmental Management System (EMS); member of the Sustain Winona Collaboration; Green Team—Sustainability Series.

ADMISSIONS

Freshman Academic Profile: Average high school GPA 3.16. 18% in top 10% of high school class, 41% in top 25% of high school class, 71% in top 50% of high school class. 60% from public high schools. SAT Math middle 50% range 463–605. SAT Critical Reading middle 50% range 503–560. ACT middle 50% range 19–26. Minimum paper TOEFL 520. Minimum computer TOEFL 213. Minimum web-based TOEFL 79. **Basis for Candidate Selection:** *Very important factors considered include:* Academic GPA, rigor of secondary school record, standardized test scores. *Important factors considered include:* Class rank, character/personal qualities, interview, talent/ability. *Other factors considered include:* Application essay, recommendation(s), alumni/ae relation, extracurricular activities, level of applicant's interest, volunteer work. **Freshman Admission Requirements:** High school diploma is required and GED is accepted. *Academic units required:* 4 English, 3 mathematics, 3 science, (2 science labs), 2 social studies, 6 academic electives. *Academic units recommended:* 2 foreign language. **Freshman Admission Statistics:** 1,408 applied, 72% admitted, 32% enrolled. **Transfer Admission Requirements:** High school transcript, college transcript(s), statement of good standing from prior institution(s). Minimum college GPA of 2.0 required. Lowest grade transferable C. **General Admission Information:** Application fee $25. Regular application deadline 5/1. Regular notification 5/1. Nonfall registration accepted. Admission may be deferred for a maximum of 1 year. Credit and/or placement offered for CEEB Advanced Placement tests.

COSTS AND FINANCIAL AID
Annual tuition $25,600. Room and board $6,940. Required fees $490. Average book expense $1,300. **Required Forms and Deadlines:** FAFSA. Priority financial aid filing date 3/15. **Notification of Awards:** Applicants will be notified of awards on a rolling basis beginning 2/1. **Types of Aid:** *Need-based scholarships/grants:* Federal Pell, SEOG, state scholarships/grants, the school's own gift aid. *Loans:* FFEL Subsidized Stafford, FFEL Unsubsidized Stafford, FFEL PLUS, Federal Perkins, state loans *Student Employment:* Federal Work-Study Program available. Institutional employment available. Highest amount earned per year from on-campus jobs $3,000. Off-campus job opportunities are good. **Financial Aid Statistics:** 82% freshmen, 73% undergrads receive need-based scholarship or grant aid. 67% freshmen, 59% undergrads receive need-based self-help aid. 81.5% freshmen, 72.5% undergrads receive any aid. 77% undergrads borrow to pay for school. Average cumulative indebtedness $32,166. **Criteria for awarding institutional aid:** *Non-need-based:* Academics, alumni affiliation, art, leadership, minority status, music/drama.

SAINT MARY-OF-THE-WOODS COLLEGE

Office of Admission, Guerin Hall, Saint Mary-of-the-Woods, IN 47876-0068
Phone: 812-535-5106 **Financial Aid Phone:** 812-535-5100
E-mail: smwcadms@smwc.edu **CEEB Code:** 1704
Fax: 812-535-5010 **Website:** www.smwc.edu **ACT Code:** 1242

This private school, affiliated with the Roman Catholic Church, was founded in 1840. It has a 67-acre campus.

RATINGS
Admissions Selectivity Rating: 75   **Fire Safety Rating:** 98   **Green Rating:** 83

STUDENTS AND FACULTY
Enrollment: 1,176. **Student Body:** 97% female, 3% male, 30% out-of-state, international (5 countries represented).
Retention and Graduation: 77% freshmen return for sophomore year. 35% freshmen graduate within 4 years. 18% grads go on to further study within 1 year. 15% grads pursue arts and sciences degrees. 1% grads pursue law degrees. 1% grads pursue business degrees. 1% grads pursue medical degrees. **Faculty:** Student/faculty ratio 8:1. 67 full-time faculty, 54% hold PhDs, 6% are are members of minority groups, 66% are women.

ACADEMICS
Degrees: Associate, bachelor's, certificate, master's, post-bachelor's certificate, post-master's certificate, transfer associate. **Classes:** Most classes have fewer than 10 students. **Majors with Highest Enrollment:** Biology/biological sciences; elementary education and teaching; equestrian/equine studies. **Special Study Options:** Accelerated program, cross-registration, distance learning, double major, external degree program, honors program, independent study, internships, student-designed major, study abroad, teacher certification program Special programs offered to physically disabled students include tutors. **Career services:** Alumni network, alumni services, career/job search classes, career assessment, internships, regional alumni, **Career services highlights include:** Experiential Learning: Externship, Supplemental Learning Experience, and Internship programs.

FACILITIES
Housing: Special housing for disabled students, women's dorms 100% of campus accessible to physically disabled. **Special Academic Facilities/Equipment:** Cecilian Auditorium and Conservatory of Music, SMWC Art Gallery. **Computers:** 100% of classrooms, 100% of dorms, 100% of libraries, 20% of dining areas, 15% of common outdoor areas have wireless network access. Students can register for classes online. Administrative functions (other than registration) can be performed online.

CAMPUS LIFE
Environment: Town. **Activities:** Choral groups, concert band, dance, drama/theater, jazz band, literary magazine, music ensembles, musical theater, student government, student newspaper, yearbook, campus ministries, international student organization. **Organizations:** 30 registered organizations, 6 honor societies, 1 religious organizations. **Athletics (Intercollegiate):** *Women:* Basketball, equestrian sports, golf, soccer, softball, track/field (outdoor) **On-Campus Highlights:** Le Fer Hall (residence hall), Mari Hulman George School of Equine Studies, Softball/Soccer Fields, Cecilian Auditorium, Church of the Immaculate Conception, Saint Mary-of-the-Woods College is a 67-acre wooded campus located five miles northwest of Terre Haute, Indiana. The peaceful and beautiful campus features a fitness trail, lake and stables amid the stately academic buildings. Besides the College, Saint Mary-of-the-Woods is common ground for the Sisters of Providence, Woods Day Care/Pre-School, Providence Center and the White Violet Center for Eco-Justice. **Environmental Initiatives:** recycling food service decreasing waste, composting, use of local/organic foods housekeeping services switched to green chemicals

ADMISSIONS
Freshman Academic Profile: Average high school GPA 3.3. 85% from public high schools. SAT Math middle 50% range 410–520. SAT Critical Reading middle 50% range 430–540. SAT Writing middle 50% range 410–550. ACT middle 50% range 18–25. Minimum paper TOEFL 500. Minimum web-based TOEFL 62. **Basis for Candidate Selection:** *Important factors considered include:* Class rank, application essay, academic GPA, recommendation(s), rigor of secondary school record, standardized test scores. *Other factors considered include:* Character/personal qualities, interview, level of applicant's interest, talent/ability. **Freshman Admission Requirements:** High school diploma is required and GED is accepted. *Academic units required:* 8 English, 6 mathematics, 6 science, (2 science labs), 4 foreign language, 4 social studies, 2 history, 10 academic electives. *Academic units recommended:* 8 English, 8 mathematics, 8 science, (4 science labs), 6 foreign language, 6 social studies, 4 history, 7 academic electives. **Freshman Admission Statistics:** 417 applied, 70% admitted, 44% enrolled. **Transfer Admission Requirements:** College transcript(s), essay or personal statement, minimum college GPA of 2.0 required. Lowest grade transferable C. **General Admission Information:** Application fee $30. Regular application deadline 8/8. Notification on a rolling basis, beginning on or about 10/1. Nonfall registration accepted. Admission may be deferred for a maximum of 1 year. Credit and/or placement offered for CEEB Advanced Placement tests.

COSTS AND FINANCIAL AID
Annual tuition $20,900. . Room and board $7,890. Required fees $650. Average book expense $900. **Required Forms and Deadlines:** FAFSA **Notification of Awards:** Applicants will be notified of awards on a rolling basis beginning 12/1. **Types of Aid:** *Need-based scholarships/grants:* Federal Pell, SEOG, state scholarships/grants, private scholarships, the school's own gift aid. *Loans:* FFEL Subsidized Stafford, FFEL Unsubsidized Stafford, FFEL PLUS, Federal Perkins. *Student Employment:* Federal Work-Study Program available. Institutional employment available. Highest amount earned per year from on-campus jobs $4,665. Off-campus job opportunities are good. **Financial Aid Statistics:** 72% freshmen, 72% undergrads receive need-based scholarship or grant aid. 71% freshmen, 10% undergrads receive non-need-based scholarship or grant aid. 46% freshmen, 64% undergrads receive need-based self-help aid. 10% freshmen, 4% undergrads receive athletic scholarships. 98% freshmen, 96% undergrads receive any aid. 89% undergrads borrow to pay for school. Average cumulative indebtedness $20,310. **Criteria for awarding institutional aid:** *Non-need-based:* Academics, alumni affiliation, art, athletics, leadership, music/drama.

SAINT MICHAEL'S COLLEGE

Best 373

One Winooski Park, Box 7, Colchester, VT 05439
Phone: 802-654-3000 **Financial Aid Phone:** 802-654-3244
E-mail: admission@smcvt.edu **CEEB Code:** 3757
Fax: 802-654-2906 **Website:** www.smcvt.edu **ACT Code:** 4312

This private school, affiliated with the Roman Catholic Church, was founded in 1904. It has a 440-acre campus.

RATINGS
Admissions Selectivity Rating: 84   **Fire Safety Rating:** 74   **Green Rating:** 85

STUDENTS AND FACULTY

Enrollment: 1,915. **Student Body:** 52% female, 48% male, 80.6% out-of-state, 2% international (30 countries represented). Asian 1%, African American 1%, Caucasian 93%, Hispanic 2%.
Retention and Graduation: 71% freshmen graduate within 4 years. 21% grads go on to further study within 1 year. 55% grads pursue arts and sciences degrees. 5% grads pursue law degrees. 15% grads pursue business degrees. 5% grads pursue medical degrees. **Faculty:** Student/faculty ratio 12:1. 154 full-time faculty, 85% hold PhDs, 7% are are members of minority groups, 45% are women.

ACADEMICS

Degrees: Bachelor's, master's, post-bachelor's certificate, post-master's certificate. **Classes:** Most classes have 10–19 students. Most lab/discussion sessions have 20–29 students. **Majors with Highest Enrollment:** Biology/biological sciences; business/commerce; psychology. **Special Study Options:** Cross-registration, distance learning, double major, dual enrollment, English as a Second Language (ESL), honors program, independent study, internships, liberal arts/career combination, student-designed major, study abroad, teacher certification program, Research for Academic Credit: Many majors require students to complete the equivalent of a senior thesis (sometimes called a Senior Seminar) for which they receive academic credit. Students work closely with an academic advisor on these capstone projects. Independent Research with Faculty: Independent research projects with faculty members—which are not-for-credit—often lead to peer-reviewed publications and presentations at major conferences. These projects are an exciting opportunity for students and faculty to work side-by-side, making important discoveries in their fields. For students, these opportunities not only provide excellent resume-building experience, but also the chance to work closely with a mentor. Some students may even qualify for grant-funded research stipends. **Honors programs:** The Honors Program at Saint Michael's provides additional challenges and opportunities to outstanding students through small group discussion, research and extra-curricular activities. Saint Michael's also has chapters of several national honors societies on campus including Phi Beta Kappa, and Delta Epsilon Sigma. **Combined degree programs:** BA/MA, 4+1 MBA w/Clarkson, (BS + DPharm) with Albany College of Pharmacy. Special programs offered to physically disabled students include note-taking services, reader services, tape recorders, tutors. **Career services:** Alumni network, alumni services, career/job search classes, career assessment, internships, regional alumni. **Career services highlights include:** Our Internship Program gives students the opportunity to integrate their academic studies with a supervised work experience. Internships enhance classroom learning by integrating academics with the world of business. This on-the-job experience assists students in their career decision-making process. Internships provide valuable work experiences that increase job opportunities after graduation. Through this process students learn valuable job search and career defining skills.

FACILITIES

Housing: Coed dorms, special housing for disabled students, men's dorms, special housing for international students, women's dorms, apartments for single students, theme housing, honors housing, substance free housing. 75% of campus accessible to physically disabled. **Special Academic Facilities/Equipment:** Holcomb Observatory, McCarthy Arts Center Gallary. **Computers:** 90% of classrooms, 100% of dorms, 100% of libraries, 100% of dining areas, 100% of student union, have wireless network access. Students can register for classes online. Administrative functions (other than registration) can be performed online.

CAMPUS LIFE

Environment: City. **Activities:** Choral groups, concert band, dance, drama/theater, jazz band, literary magazine, music ensembles, musical theater, radio station, student government, student newspaper, yearbook, campus ministries, international student organization. **Organizations:** 50 registered organizations, 11 honor societies, 1 religious organizations. **Athletics (Intercollegiate):** *Men:* Baseball, basketball, cross-country, diving, golf, ice hockey, lacrosse, skiing (downhill/alpine), skiing (nordic cross-country), soccer, swimming, tennis. *Women:* Basketball, cross-country, diving, field hockey, ice hockey, lacrosse, skiing (downhill/alpine), skiing (nordic cross-country), soccer, softball, swimming, tennis, volleyball. **On-Campus Highlights:** Alliot Student Center, McCarthy Arts Center, Chapel of Saint Michael the Archangel, Vincent C. Ross Sports Center, Tarrant Student Recreational Center. **Environmental Initiatives:** Energy Efficiency Programs: "Three Degree Challenge" to further reduce campus wide building temperatures by turning down thermostats to reduce energy consumption (in addition to reducing energy consumption, all new major appliances must be energy star certified); new building aims for LEED certification; all campus buildings on an Energy Management System to ensure efficient use of energy; Creating a culture of sustainability with each First Year class: each first year student receives a green welcome package during their orientation: reusable tote bag, reusable coffee mug, bus map Campus wide Zero-Waste program (recycling is enforced for all Faculty·and staff; every dorm room has a recycling bin and in every Residence Hall there is a recycling room. Dining hall composts

all food scraps as well as residential areas where students volunteer to; all food scraps go to our on-campus compost facility) Finished compost use on campus grounds and college's Organic Garden.

ADMISSIONS

Freshman Academic Profile: Average high school GPA 3.44. 24% in top 10% of high school class, 54% in top 25% of high school class, 81% in top 50% of high school class. 68.6% from public high schools. SAT Math middle 50% range 520–620. SAT Critical Reading middle 50% range 520–630. SAT Writing middle 50% range 510–620. ACT middle 50% range 22–27. Minimum paper TOEFL 550. Minimum computer TOEFL 213. **Basis for Candidate Selection:** *Very important factors considered include:* Class rank, academic GPA, rigor of secondary school record. *Important factors considered include:* Application essay, recommendation(s), standardized test scores, character/personal qualities, extracurricular activities, talent/ability. *Other factors considered include:* Alumni/ae relation, first generation, geographical residence, level of applicant's interest, racial/ethnic status, state residency, volunteer work, work experience. **Freshman Admission Requirements:** High school diploma is required and GED is accepted. *Academic units required:* 4 English, 3 mathematics, 3 science, (2 science labs), 3 foreign language, 3 social studies. *Academic units recommended:* 4 English, 4 mathematics, 4 science, (3 science labs), 4 foreign language, 4 social studies. **Freshman Admission Statistics:** 3,228 applied, 81% admitted, 18% enrolled. **Transfer Admission Requirements:** High school transcript, college transcript(s), essay or personal statement, standardized test scores, minimum college GPA of 2.8 required. Lowest grade transferable C–. **General Admission Information:** Application fee $50. Regular application deadline 2/1. Regular notification 4/1. Nonfall registration accepted. Admission may be deferred for a maximum of 1 year. Credit and/or placement offered for CEEB Advanced Placement tests.

COSTS AND FINANCIAL AID

Required Forms and Deadlines: FAFSA, signed copies of parent's 2009 federal tax return, parent's federal W-2 forms, signed copies of student's 2009 federal tax return, student's federal W-2 forms, Dependent 2009–2010 Verification Worksheet (Please check the Student Financial Services form. Priority financial aid filing date 2/15. **Notification of Awards:** Applicants will be notified of awards on a rolling basis beginning 1/15. **Types of Aid:** *Need-based scholarships/grants:* Federal Pell, SEOG, state scholarships/grants, private scholarships, the school's own gift aid. *Loans:* FFEL Subsidized Stafford, FFEL Unsubsidized Stafford, FFEL PLUS, Federal Perkins. *Student Employment:* Federal Work-Study Program available. Institutional employment available. Highest amount earned per year from on-campus jobs $15,649. Off-campus job opportunities are excellent. **Financial Aid Statistics:** 66% freshmen, 60% undergrads receive need-based scholarship or grant aid. 12% freshmen, 8% undergrads receive non-need-based scholarship or grant aid. 55% freshmen, 52% undergrads receive need-based self-help aid. 1% undergrads receive athletic scholarships. 97.5% freshmen, 93.3% undergrads receive any aid. 76% undergrads borrow to pay for school. Average cumulative indebtedness $30,742. **Criteria for awarding institutional aid:** *Non-need-based:* Academics, alumni affiliation, art, athletics, leadership, minority status, music/drama, state/district residency.

SAINT PAUL'S COLLEGE

115 College Drive, Lawrenceville, VA 23868
Phone: 434-848-1856
E-mail: admissions@saintpauls.edu
Fax: 804-848-6407 **Website:** www.saintpauls.edu **ACT Code:** 4394

This private school, affiliated with the Episcopal Church, was founded in 1888. It has a 185-acre campus.

RATINGS

Admissions Selectivity Rating: 63   **Fire Safety Rating:** 60*   **Green Rating:** 60*

STUDENTS AND FACULTY

Enrollment: 707. **Student Body:** 52% female, 48% male, 31% out-of-state, international (6 countries represented). African American 99%, Caucasian 2%.
Retention and Graduation: 100% freshmen return for sophomore year. 16% freshmen graduate within 4 years. 10% grads go on to further study within 1 year. **Faculty:** Student/faculty ratio 17:1. 30 full-time faculty, 53% hold PhDs, 50% are are members of minority groups, 33% are women.

ACADEMICS

Degrees: Bachelor's. **Classes:** Most classes have fewer than 10 students. Most lab/discussion sessions have fewer than 10 students. **Majors with Highest Enrollment:** Business/commerce; criminal justice/police science; sociology. **Special Study Options:** Accelerated program, cooperative education program, double major, honors program, independent study, internships, liberal arts/career combination, study abroad, teacher certification program, U.S. Army ROTC. **Honors programs:** Alpha Kappa Mu Honor Society Special programs offered to physically disabled students include tape recorders, tutors. **Career services:** Alumni network, alumni services, career/job search classes, career assessment, internships, regional alumni.

FACILITIES

Housing: Men's dorms, women's dorms, apartments for single students. **Special Academic Facilities/Equipment:** The Saul Building (1888) (the first classroom built on SPC campus).

CAMPUS LIFE

Environment: Rural. **Activities:** Choral groups, dance, drama/theater, student government, yearbook. **Organizations:** 30 registered organizations, 2 honor societies, 2 religious organizations. 3 fraternities, 3 sororities. **Athletics (Intercollegiate):** *Men:* Baseball, basketball, cross-country, golf, tennis, track/field (outdoor), track/field (indoor). *Women:* Basketball, cross-country, golf, softball, tennis, track/field (outdoor), track/field (indoor), volleyball. **On-Campus Highlights:** Student Center, Gymnasium, Library, Cafeteria, Dorms.

ADMISSIONS

Freshman Academic Profile: Average high school GPA 2.5. 3% in top 10% of high school class, 8% in top 25% of high school class, 23% in top 50% of high school class. 95% from public high schools. SAT Math middle 50% range 330–410. SAT Critical Reading middle 50% range 330–410. ACT middle 50% range 13–17. **Basis for Candidate Selection:** *Important factors considered include:* Class rank, application essay, recommendation(s), rigor of secondary school record, standardized test scores, character/personal qualities, extracurricular activities, interview, talent/ability. *Other factors considered include:* volunteer work, work experience. **Freshman Admission Requirements:** High school diploma is required and GED is accepted. *Academic units required:* 4 English, 2 mathematics, 2 science. *Academic units recommended:* 4 English, 2 mathematics, 2 science, 2 social studies. **Freshman Admission Statistics:** 641 applied, 71% admitted, 64% enrolled. **Transfer Admission Requirements:** High school transcript, college transcript(s), essay or personal statement, statement of good standing from prior institution(s). Minimum college GPA of 2 required. Lowest grade transferable C. **General Admission Information:** Application fee $20. Nonfall registration accepted. Neither credit nor placement offered for CEEB Advanced Placement tests.

COSTS AND FINANCIAL AID

Annual tuition $10,400. Room and board $5,890. Required fees $681. Average book expense $600. **Required Forms and Deadlines:** FAFSA, state aid form Financial aid filing deadline 6/30. Priority financial aid filing date 3/30. **Notification of Awards:** Applicants will be notified of awards on a rolling basis beginning 1/7. **Types of Aid:** *Need-based scholarships/grants:* Federal Pell, SEOG, state scholarships/grants, private scholarships, the school's own gift aid, United Negro College Fund. *Loans:* Direct Subsidized Stafford, Direct Unsubsidized Stafford, Direct PLUS, Federal Perkins. *Student Employment:* Federal Work-Study Program available. Highest amount earned per year from on-campus jobs $1,300. Off-campus job opportunities are fair. **Financial Aid Statistics:** 80% freshmen, 76% undergrads receive need-based scholarship or grant aid. 84% freshmen, 80% undergrads receive non-need-based scholarship or grant aid. 87% freshmen, 82% undergrads receive need-based self-help aid. 4% freshmen, 11% undergrads receive athletic scholarships. 91% freshmen, 59% undergrads receive any aid. 80% undergrads borrow to pay for school. Average cumulative indebtedness $10,240. **Criteria for awarding institutional aid:** *Non-need-based:* Academics, athletics, state/district residency.

SAINT PETER'S COLLEGE

2641 Kennedy Boulevard, Jersey City, NJ 07306
Phone: 201-761-7100 **Financial Aid Phone:** 201-761-7100
E-mail: admissions@spc.edu **CEEB Code:** 2806
Fax: 201-761-7105 **Website:** www.spc.edu **ACT Code:** 2604

This private school, affiliated with the Roman Catholic Church, was founded in 1872. It has a 10-acre campus.

RATINGS

Admissions Selectivity Rating: 78 **Fire Safety Rating:** 60* **Green Rating:** 60*

STUDENTS AND FACULTY

Enrollment: 2,322. **Student Body:** 57% female, 43% male, 19% out-of-state, 3% international (9 countries represented). Asian 11%, African American 25%, Caucasian 28%, Hispanic 28%.

Retention and Graduation: 76% freshmen return for sophomore year. 27% grads go on to further study within 1 year. 9% grads pursue arts and sciences degrees. 5% grads pursue law degrees. 6% grads pursue business degrees. 7% grads pursue medical degrees. **Faculty:** Student/faculty ratio 15:1. 104 full-time faculty, 10% are are members of minority groups, 41% are women.

ACADEMICS

Degrees: Associate, bachelor's, diploma, master's. **Classes:** Most classes have 10–19 students. **Majors with Highest Enrollment:** Biology/biological sciences; criminal justice/law enforcement administration; education. **Special Study Options:** Accelerated program, cooperative education program, double major, dual enrollment, exchange student program (domestic), honors program, independent study, internships, liberal arts/career combination, student-designed major, study abroad, teacher certification program, weekend college, Joint degree in clinical and laboratory sciences with the University of Medicine and Dentistry of New Jersey (UMDNJ); Joint degree in Pharmacy with Rutgers University. **Honors programs:** While Honors provides academic enrichment for highly motivated students, it is not a formal major or minor. Students enrolled in the program must complete a minimum of 30 credits designated as Honors courses, which include Honors core course seminars, Honors advanced electives, and 6 credits of Honors Thesis: research and independent study. Independent study projects must be approved by the Honors Program and the respective chairs of the student's major department. Independent study projects may carry departmental as well as Honors credit. **Combined degree programs:** BA/MD, BA/JD, Combined-Degree programs at Seton Hall and UMDNJ. Special programs offered to physically disabled students include note-taking services, reader services, tape recorders, tutors.

FACILITIES

Housing: Coed dorms, men's dorms, women's dorms, apartments for single students. **Special Academic Facilities/Equipment:** TV production facilities, center for government affairs.

CAMPUS LIFE

Environment: City. **Activities:** Choral groups, drama/theater, literary magazine, radio station, student government, student newspaper, yearbook. **Organizations:** 45 registered organizations, 11 honor societies. **Athletics (Intercollegiate):** *Men:* Baseball, basketball, cheerleading, cross-country, diving, football, golf, soccer, swimming, tennis, track/field (outdoor). *Women:* Basketball, bowling, cheerleading, cross-country, diving, soccer, softball, swimming, tennis, track/field (outdoor), volleyball.

ADMISSIONS

Freshman Academic Profile: Average high school GPA 3. SAT Math middle 50% range 440–530. SAT Critical Reading middle 50% range 420–520. Minimum paper TOEFL 520. Minimum computer TOEFL 190. **Basis for Candidate Selection:** *Very important factors considered include:* Academic GPA, rigor of secondary school record, standardized test scores. *Important factors considered include:* Class rank, application essay, recommendation(s). *Other factors considered include:* Character/personal qualities, extracurricular activities, interview, talent/ability, volunteer work, work experience. **Freshman Admission Requirements:** High school diploma is required and GED is accepted. *Academic units required:* 4 English, 3 mathematics, 2 science, (1 science labs), 2 foreign language, 2 history, 3 academic electives. *Academic units recommended:* 4 mathematics, 3 science, 3 history. **Freshman Admission Statistics:** 2,863 applied, 69% admitted, 26% enrolled. **Transfer Admission Requirements:** College transcript(s), essay or personal statement, minimum college GPA of 2.0 required. Lowest grade transferable C. **General Admission Information:** Notification on a rolling basis, beginning on or about 11/1. Nonfall registration accepted. Admission may be deferred for a maximum of 24. Credit offered for CEEB Advanced Placement tests.

COSTS AND FINANCIAL AID

Required Forms and Deadlines: FAFSA. Priority financial aid filing date 3/15. **Notification of Awards:** Applicants will be notified of awards on a rolling basis beginning 2/15. **Types of Aid:** *Need-based scholarships/grants:* Federal Pell, SEOG, state scholarships/grants, the school's own gift aid. *Loans:* FFEL Subsidized Stafford, FFEL Unsubsidized Stafford, FFEL PLUS, Federal Perkins, state loans *Student Employment:* Federal Work-Study Program available. Institutional employment available. Highest amount earned per year from on-campus jobs $1,500. Off-campus job opportunities are excellent. **Financial Aid Statistics:** 97% undergrads receive any aid.

See page 1226.

SAINT THOMAS AQUINAS COLLEGE

125 Route 340, Sparkill, NY 10976
Phone: 845-398-4100 **Financial Aid Phone:** 845-398-4098
E-mail: admissions@stac.edu **CEEB Code:** 2807
Fax: 845-398-4114 **Website:** www.stac.edu **ACT Code:** 2897

This private school was founded in 1952. It has a 47-acre campus.

RATINGS
Admissions Selectivity Rating: 70   **Fire Safety Rating:** 85   **Green Rating:** 60*

STUDENTS AND FACULTY
Enrollment: 1,437. **Student Body:** 54% female, 46% male, 27% out-of-state, 1% international. Asian 3%, African American 6%, Caucasian 70%, Hispanic 15%.
Retention and Graduation: 72% freshmen return for sophomore year. 36% grads go on to further study within 1 year. 25% grads pursue arts and sciences degrees. 5% grads pursue law degrees. 5% grads pursue business degrees. 5% grads pursue medical degrees. **Faculty:** Student/faculty ratio 16:1. 64 full-time faculty, 89% hold PhDs, 13% are are members of minority groups, 50% are women.

ACADEMICS
Degrees: Associate, bachelor's, master's, post-master's certificate, terminal associate, transfer associate. **Classes:** Most classes have 20–29 students. **Majors with Highest Enrollment:** Business/commerce; criminal justice/law enforcement administration; elementary education and teaching. **Special Study Options:** Accelerated program, cooperative education program, cross-registration, double major, dual enrollment, exchange student program (domestic), honors program, independent study, internships, liberal arts/career combination, study abroad, teacher certification program, Undergrads may take grad level classes—e.g. cooperative education programs: Combined BS/MSW in social work in partnership with NYU; engineering. **Combined degree programs:** 3-2 engineering programs with George Washington U and Manhattan Coll foreign exchange program(s): study abroad in England. **Honors programs:** Highly selective honors program with maximum 20 student each class. Honor students receive full scholarship. Special programs offered to physically disabled students include note-taking services, tape recorders, tutors. **Career services:** Alumni network, alumni services, career/job search classes, career assessment, internships, regional alumni.

FACILITIES
Housing: Men's dorms, women's dorms, apartments for single students 80% of campus accessible to physically disabled. **Special Academic Facilities/Equipment:** Azarian-McCullough Art Gallery, Sullivan Theatre, Spellman Technology Corridor, Costello Hall Science and Technology Center. **Computers:** Students can register for classes online.

CAMPUS LIFE
Environment: Village. **Activities:** Choral groups, dance, drama/theater, literary magazine, musical theater, opera, radio station, student government, student newspaper, yearbook. **Organizations:** 35 registered organizations, 8 honor societies, 1 religious organizations. **Athletics (Intercollegiate):** *Men:* Baseball, basketball, cross-country, golf, soccer, tennis, track/field (outdoor), track/field (indoor). *Women:* Basketball, cross-country, lacrosse, soccer, softball, tennis, track/field (outdoor). **On-Campus Highlights:** The College Commons, The Fitness Center, The Romano Alumni Center, The Art Gallery, The Techonology Corridor.

ADMISSIONS
Freshman Academic Profile: Average high school GPA 2.6. 5% in top 10% of high school class, 35% in top 25% of high school class, 50% in top 50% of high school class. 70% from public high schools. SAT Math middle 50% range 410–530. SAT Critical Reading middle 50% range 420–510. SAT Writing middle 50% range 420–520. ACT middle 50% range 17–22. Minimum paper TOEFL 530. Minimum computer TOEFL 173. **Basis for Candidate Selection:** *Very important factors considered include:* Rigor of secondary school record. *Important factors considered include:* Application essay, recommendation(s), standardized test scores, extracurricular activities, interview, talent/ability. *Other factors considered include:* Alumni/ae relation, volunteer work, work experience. **Freshman Admission Requirements:** High school diploma is required and GED is accepted. *Academic units required:* 4 English, 3 mathematics, 3 science, (2 science labs), 3 foreign language, 4 social studies. **Freshman Admission Statistics:** 1,331 applied, 80% admitted, 31% enrolled. **Transfer Admission Requirements:** College transcript(s), statement of good standing from prior institution(s). Minimum college GPA of 2.0 required. Lowest grade transferable C. **General Admission Information:** Application fee $30. Early decision application deadline 12/15. Notification on a rolling basis, beginning

on or about 10/1. Nonfall registration accepted. Admission may be deferred for a maximum of 1 year. Credit and/or placement offered for CEEB Advanced Placement tests.

COSTS AND FINANCIAL AID
Annual tuition $19,500. Room and board $9,730. Required fees $500. Average book expense $750. **Required Forms and Deadlines:** FAFSA, state aid form. Priority financial aid filing date 2/15. **Notification of Awards:** Applicants will be notified of awards on a rolling basis beginning 3/1. **Types of Aid:** *Need-based scholarships/grants:* Federal Pell, SEOG, state scholarships/grants, private scholarships, the school's own gift aid. *Loans:* Direct Subsidized Stafford, Direct Unsubsidized Stafford, Direct PLUS, FFEL Subsidized Stafford, FFEL Unsubsidized Stafford, FFEL PLUS, Federal Perkins, Private alternative loans from lending institutions. *Student Employment:* Federal Work-Study Program available. Institutional employment available. Off-campus job opportunities are good. **Financial Aid Statistics:** 63% freshmen, 57% undergrads receive need-based scholarship or grant aid. 8% freshmen, 7% undergrads receive non-need-based scholarship or grant aid. 50% freshmen, 46% undergrads receive need-based self-help aid. 3% freshmen, 3% undergrads receive athletic scholarships. 66% freshmen, 72% undergrads receive any aid. **Criteria for awarding institutional aid:** *Non-need-based:* Academics, athletics.

SAINT VINCENT COLLEGE

Office of Admission and Financial Aid, 300 Fraser Purchase Rd, Latrobe, PA 15650-2690
Phone: 724-537-4540 **Financial Aid Phone:** 800-782-5549
E-mail: admission@stvincent.edu **CEEB Code:** 2808
Fax: 724-532-5069 **Website:** www.stvincent.edu **ACT Code:** 3686

This private school, affiliated with the Roman Catholic Church, was founded in 1846. It has a 200-acre campus.

RATINGS
Admissions Selectivity Rating: 83   **Fire Safety Rating:** 60*   **Green Rating:** 70

STUDENTS AND FACULTY
Enrollment: 1,617. **Student Body:** 50% female, 50% male, 12% out-of-state, 1% international (15 countries represented). Asian 1%, African American 3%, Caucasian 90%, Hispanic 2%.
Retention and Graduation: 60% freshmen graduate within 4 years. 30% grads go on to further study within 1 year. **Faculty:** Student/faculty ratio 13:1. 91 full-time faculty, 84% hold PhDs, 2% are are members of minority groups, 24% are women.

ACADEMICS
Degrees: Bachelor's, certificate, master's, post-bachelor's certificate. **Classes:** Most classes have 20–29 students. Most lab/discussion sessions have 10–19 students. **Majors with Highest Enrollment:** Biology/biological sciences; history; psychology. **Special Study Options:** Accelerated program, cooperative education program, cross-registration, distance learning, double major, dual enrollment, external degree program, honors program, independent study, internships, liberal arts/career combination, study abroad, teacher certification program. **Honors programs:** Honors Classes Professors design Honors classes to challenge and reward students who seek substantial intellectual development in college. The quality, not the quantity of work, distinguishes Honors classes from other courses. Portfolio As part of their coursework in Honors classes, all students are required to submit a short reflective essay and sample of their work at the end of each Honors class. Honors Events Dinner and evening discussions based on a reading, or attendance of a play, a film, an art exhibit, etc, on campus provide a special, congenial setting for intellectual exchange as part of a course or an extracurricular event. Off-Campus Explorations All Honors students and faculty are regularly invited to attend a play, film, art exhibit, etc. Extended trips within the U.S. or abroad may be planned during breaks or the summer. Senior Capstone Projects Honors students in majors with a senior research or capstone project will be strongly encouraged to present their work in a special colloquium at Saint Vincent and at professional meetings in their research areas. **Combined degree programs:** BA/JD, BA/MEng, 3-3 JD, 4-1 MBA w/ Duquesne. Special programs offered to physically disabled students include note-taking services, tutors. **Career services:** Alumni network, alumni services, career assessment, internships, regional alumni. **Career services highlights include:** Students can take internship program for credit, though this is not required. Students are assisted in looking for internships in their field or industry of interest.

FACILITIES
Housing: Coed dorms, apartments for single students. 95% of campus accessible to physically disabled. **Special Academic Facilities/Equipment:** Art

gallery, life sciences research center, spectrophotometer, spectrometer, physiograph work stations, data acquisition work station, planetarium, observatory, radio telescope, instructional technology resource center. **Computers:** 75% of libraries, 100% of student union, 25% of common outdoor areas have wireless network access. Students can register for classes online. Administrative functions (other than registration) can be performed online.

CAMPUS LIFE

Environment: Village. **Activities:** Choral groups, dance, drama/theater, literary magazine, music ensembles, musical theater, pep band, radio station, student government, student newspaper, television station, yearbook, campus ministries, international student organization. **Organizations:** 43 registered organizations, 12 honor societies, 2 religious organizations. **Athletics (Intercollegiate):** *Men:* Baseball, basketball, cross-country, football, golf, lacrosse, soccer, swimming, tennis, track/field (outdoor). *Women:* Basketball, cross-country, field hockey, golf, lacrosse, soccer, softball, swimming, tennis, volleyball. **On-Campus Highlights:** Library, Carey Student Center, St. Benedict Hall, Basilica, Chuck Noll Field. **Environmental Initiatives:** New construction on campus, including a current building project, will be green. Environmental Education Center provides education opportunities to students.

ADMISSIONS

Freshman Academic Profile: Average high school GPA 3.55. 23.8% in top 10% of high school class, 53.9% in top 25% of high school class, 84.3% in top 50% of high school class. 67% from public high schools. SAT Math middle 50% range 490–600. SAT Critical Reading middle 50% range 480–590. SAT Writing middle 50% range 470–570. ACT middle 50% range 20–26. Minimum paper TOEFL 550. Minimum computer TOEFL 213. **Basis for Candidate Selection:** *Very important factors considered include:* Class rank, academic GPA, rigor of secondary school record. *Important factors considered include:* Application essay, standardized test scores, character/personal qualities. *Other factors considered include:* Recommendation(s), extracurricular activities, first generation, interview, talent/ability. **Freshman Admission Requirements:** High school diploma is required and GED is accepted. *Academic units required:* 4 English, 3 mathematics, 1 science, (1 science labs), 3 social studies, 5 academic electives. *Academic units recommended:* 4 English, 3 mathematics, 3 science, (1 science labs), 2 foreign language, 3 social studies, 5 academic electives. **Freshman Admission Statistics:** 1,855 applied, 62% admitted, 37% enrolled. **Transfer Admission Requirements:** High school transcript, college transcript(s), essay or personal statement, statement of good standing from prior institution(s). Minimum college GPA of 2.5 required. Lowest grade transferable C–. **General Admission Information:** Application fee $25. Regular application deadline 5/1. Notification on a rolling basis, beginning on or about 10/1. Nonfall registration accepted. Admission may be deferred for a maximum of 1 year. Credit and/or placement offered for CEEB Advanced Placement tests.

COSTS AND FINANCIAL AID

Annual tuition $22,350. Room and board $7,242. Required fees $650. Average book expense $650. **Required Forms and Deadlines:** FAFSA, state aid form Financial aid filing deadline 5/1. Priority financial aid filing date 3/1. **Notification of Awards:** Applicants will be notified of awards on a rolling basis beginning 3/1. **Types of Aid:** *Need-based scholarships/grants:* Federal Pell, SEOG, state scholarships/grants, private scholarships, the school's own gift aid, United Negro College Fund. *Loans:* FFEL Subsidized Stafford, FFEL Unsubsidized Stafford, FFEL PLUS, Federal Perkins. *Student Employment:* Federal Work-Study Program available. Institutional employment available. Highest amount earned per year from on-campus jobs $2,432. Off-campus job opportunities are good. **Financial Aid Statistics:** 8% freshmen, 74% undergrads receive need-based scholarship or grant aid. 34% freshmen, 62% undergrads receive non-need-based scholarship or grant aid. 59% freshmen, 59% undergrads receive need-based self-help aid. 10% undergrads receive athletic scholarships. 99% freshmen, 96% undergrads receive any aid. **Criteria for awarding institutional aid:** *Non-need-based:* Academics, alumni affiliation, leadership, minority status, music/drama.

See page 1228.

SAINT XAVIER UNIVERSITY

3700 West 103rd Street, Chicago, IL 60655
Phone: 773-298-3050
E-mail: admissions@sxu.edu **CEEB Code:** 1708
Fax: 773-298-3076 **Website: ACT Code:** 1134

This private school, affiliated with the Roman Catholic Church, was founded in 1847. It has a 70-acre campus.

RATINGS
Admissions Selectivity Rating: 86   **Fire Safety Rating:** 60*   **Green Rating:** 60*

STUDENTS AND FACULTY

Enrollment: 3,060. **Student Body:** 70% female, 30% male, 5.7% out-of-state, international. Asian 3%, African American 17%, Caucasian 60%, Hispanic 14%. **Retention and Graduation:** 29% freshmen graduate within 4 years. 10% grads go on to further study within 1 year. **Faculty:** 180 full-time faculty, 100% hold PhDs, 14% are are members of minority groups, 56% are women.

ACADEMICS

Degrees: Bachelor's, certificate, master's, post-bachelor's certificate, post-master's certificate. **Classes:** Most classes have 20–29 students. Most lab/discussion sessions have 10–19 students. **Majors with Highest Enrollment:** Business/commerce; elementary education and teaching; nursing/registered nurse (RN, ASN, BSN, MSN). **Special Study Options:** Accelerated program, cooperative education program, distance learning, double major, dual enrollment, English as a Second Language (ESL), external degree program, honors program, independent study, internships, liberal arts/career combination, student-designed major, study abroad, teacher certification program, weekend college. **Combined degree programs:** BS/RN RN/MS BS/LPN. Special programs offered to physically disabled students include note-taking services, reader services, tape recorders, tutors. **Career services:** Alumni services, career/job search classes, career assessment, internships.

FACILITIES

Housing: Coed dorms, special housing for disabled students, apartments for single students. 98% of campus accessible to physically disabled. **Computers:** Students can register for classes online. Administrative functions (other than registration) can be performed online.

CAMPUS LIFE

Environment: Metropolis. **Activities:** Choral groups, concert band, jazz band, literary magazine, marching band, music ensembles, pep band, radio station, student government, student newspaper, student-run film society, symphony orchestra, yearbook, campus ministries, international student organization. **Organizations:** 41 registered organizations, 2 honor societies, 2 religious organizations. **Athletics (Intercollegiate):** *Men:* Baseball, basketball, football, soccer. *Women:* Basketball, cross-country, soccer, softball, volleyball. **On-Campus Highlights:** Convocation and Athletic Center, McDonough Chapel and Mercy Ministry Center, McCarthy Hall, speech language pathology clinic, art gallery.

ADMISSIONS

Freshman Academic Profile: Average high school GPA 3.2. 17% in top 10% of high school class, 44% in top 25% of high school class, 74% in top 50% of high school class. 55% from public high schools. SAT Math middle 50% range 487–597. SAT Critical Reading middle 50% range 512–580. SAT Writing middle 50% range 455–592. ACT middle 50% range 20–25. Minimum paper TOEFL 550. Minimum computer TOEFL 550. **Basis for Candidate Selection:** *Very important factors considered include:* Application essay, academic GPA, standardized test scores. *Important factors considered include:* Rigor of secondary school record. *Other factors considered include:* Recommendation(s), character/personal qualities, extracurricular activities, interview, level of applicant's interest, talent/ability, volunteer work, work experience. **Freshman Admission Requirements:** High school diploma is required and GED is accepted. *Academic units recommended:* 4 English, 3 mathematics, 2 foreign language, 3 academic electives, 4 science and social science combined **Freshman Admission Statistics:** 12,175 applied, 25% admitted, 14% enrolled. **Transfer Admission Requirements:** College transcript(s), minimum college GPA of 2.5 required. Lowest grade transferable C. **General Admission Information:** Application fee $25. Nonfall registration accepted. Admission may be deferred for a maximum of not avail. Credit offered for CEEB Advanced Placement tests.

COSTS AND FINANCIAL AID

Annual tuition $23,610. Room and board $8,408. Required fees $855. Average book expense $1,200. **Required Forms and Deadlines:** FAFSA. Priority financial aid filing date 3/1. **Notification of Awards:** Applicants will be notified of awards on a rolling basis beginning 2/15. **Types of Aid:** *Need-based scholarships/grants:* Federal Pell, SEOG, state scholarships/grants, private scholarships, the school's own gift aid. *Loans:* FFEL Subsidized Stafford, FFEL Unsubsidized Stafford, FFEL PLUS, Federal Perkins. *Student Employment:* Federal Work-Study Program available. Institutional employment available. Off-campus job opportunities are excellent. **Financial Aid Statistics:** 83% freshmen, 82% undergrads receive need-based scholarship or grant aid. 82% freshmen, 76% undergrads receive non-need-based scholarship or grant aid. 70% freshmen, 72% undergrads receive need-based self-help aid. 12% freshmen, 9% undergrads receive athletic scholarships. 63% undergrads borrow to pay for school. Average cumulative indebtedness $19,374. **Criteria for awarding institutional aid:** *Non-need-based:* Academics, athletics, music/drama.

SALEM COLLEGE

PO Box 10548, Winston-Salem, NC 27108
Phone: 336-721-2621 **Financial Aid Phone:** 336-721-2808
E-mail: admissions@salem.edu **CEEB Code:** 5607
Fax: 336-917-5572 **Website:** www.salem.edu **ACT Code:** 3156

This private school, affiliated with the Moravian Church, was founded in 1772. It has a 57-acre campus.

RATINGS
Admissions Selectivity Rating: 87   **Fire Safety Rating:** 75   **Green Rating:** 61

STUDENTS AND FACULTY
Enrollment: 741. **Student Body:** 98% female, 2% male, 23% out-of-state, 13% international (22 countries represented). Asian 1%, African American 19%, Caucasian 60%, Hispanic 4%.
Retention and Graduation: 78% freshmen return for sophomore year. 50% freshmen graduate within 4 years. 30% grads go on to further study within 1 year. 25% grads pursue arts and sciences degrees. 3% grads pursue law degrees. 5% grads pursue business degrees. **Faculty:** Student/faculty ratio 12:1. 57 full-time faculty, 86% hold PhDs, 9% are are members of minority groups, 61% are women.

ACADEMICS
Degrees: Bachelor's, master's. **Classes:** Most classes have 10–19 students. Most lab/discussion sessions have 10–19 students. **Majors with Highest Enrollment:** Business/commerce; sociology. **Special Study Options:** Cross-registration, double major, dual enrollment, honors program, independent study, internships, liberal arts/career combination, student-designed major, study abroad, teacher certification program. **Career services:** Alumni network, internships.

FACILITIES
Housing: Women's dorms, apartments for single students. 75% of campus accessible to physically disabled. **Special Academic Facilities/Equipment:** Art gallery, fine arts center, Center for Women Writers, videoconferencing center. **Computers:** Administrative functions (other than registration) can be performed online.

CAMPUS LIFE
Environment: City. **Activities:** Choral groups, dance, drama/theater, literary magazine, marching band, music ensembles, musical theater, student government, student newspaper, yearbook. **Organizations:** 26 registered organizations, 14 honor societies, 7 religious organizations. **Athletics (Intercollegiate):** *Women:* Basketball, cross-country, field hockey, swimming, tennis, volleyball. **On-Campus Highlights:** Back porch of Main Hall, Salem Grille/Java City, residence hall basement lounges. **Environmental Initiatives:** Recylcle committment-all residence halls and academic buildings have paper, plastic and aluminum containers. Energy Conservation: 1) systematically changing incandescent lights with CFL; 2)Limited installation of occupancy sensors; 3)removal of lights in vending machines for energy conservation. EPA-self audit and self disclosure program.

ADMISSIONS
Freshman Academic Profile: Average high school GPA 3.7. 39% in top 10% of high school class, 67% in top 25% of high school class, 94% in top 50% of high school class. SAT Math middle 50% range 480–630. SAT Critical Reading middle 50% range 490–650. ACT middle 50% range 20–25. Minimum paper TOEFL 550. Minimum computer TOEFL 213. **Basis for Candidate Selection:** *Very important factors considered include:* Academic GPA, rigor of secondary school record. *Important factors considered include:* Class rank, application essay, recommendation(s), standardized test scores, character/personal qualities, extracurricular activities, talent/ability. *Other factors considered include:* Alumni/ae relation, first generation, interview, level of applicant's interest, volunteer work. **Freshman Admission Requirements:** High school diploma is required and GED is accepted. *Academic units required:* 4 English, 3 mathematics, 3 science, 2 foreign language, 2 history. **Freshman Admission Statistics:** 420 applied, 62% admitted, 46% enrolled. **Transfer Admission Requirements:** High school transcript, college transcript(s), essay or personal statement, statement of good standing from prior institution(s). Minimum college GPA of 2.0 required. Lowest grade transferable C–. **General Admission Information:** Application fee $30. Notification on a rolling basis, beginning on or about 10/1. Nonfall registration accepted. Admission may be deferred for a maximum of 1 year. Credit and/or placement offered for CEEB Advanced Placement tests.

COSTS AND FINANCIAL AID
Annual tuition $18,850. Room and board $10,050. Required fees $340. Average book expense $900. **Required Forms and Deadlines:** FAFSA. Priority financial aid filing date 3/1. **Notification of Awards:** Applicants will be notified of

awards on a rolling basis beginning 3/1. **Types of Aid:** *Need-based scholarships/grants:* Federal Pell, SEOG, state scholarships/grants, private scholarships, the school's own gift aid. *Loans:* FFEL Subsidized Stafford, FFEL Unsubsidized Stafford, FFEL PLUS, Federal Perkins. *Student Employment:* **Financial Aid Statistics:** 45% freshmen, 50% undergrads receive need-based scholarship or grant aid. 54% freshmen, 67% undergrads receive non-need-based scholarship or grant aid. 49% freshmen, 58% undergrads receive need-based self-help aid. 70% undergrads borrow to pay for school. Average cumulative indebtedness $17,125. **Criteria for awarding institutional aid:** *Non-need-based:* Academics, alumni affiliation, leadership, minority status, music/drama, state/district residency.

SALEM INTERNATIONAL UNIVERSITY

223 West Main Street, Salem, WV 26426-0500
Phone: 304-782-5336
E-mail: admissions@salemiu.edu **CEEB Code:** 5608
Fax: 304-782-5592 **Website:** www.salemiu.edu **ACT Code:** 4530

This private school was founded in 1888. It has a 300-acre campus.

RATINGS
Admissions Selectivity Rating: 60*   **Fire Safety Rating:** 60*   **Green Rating:** 60*

STUDENTS AND FACULTY
Enrollment: 439. **Student Body:** 47% female, 53% male, 56% out-of-state, 39% international (20 countries represented). Asian 1%, African American 8%, Caucasian 46%, Hispanic 2%, Native American 1%.
Retention and Graduation: 69% freshmen return for sophomore year. 3% grads go on to further study within 1 year. 2% grads pursue arts and sciences degrees. 1% grads pursue law degrees. 2% grads pursue business degrees. 1% grads pursue medical degrees. **Faculty:** Student/faculty ratio 14:1. 33 full-time faculty, 70% hold PhDs, 24% are are members of minority groups, 39% are women.

ACADEMICS
Degrees: Associate, bachelor's, master's, post-master's certificate. **Classes:** Most classes have fewer than 10 students. **Special Study Options:** Distance learning, double major, English as a Second Language (ESL), independent study, internships, liberal arts/career combination, study abroad, undergrads may take grad level classes foreign exchange program(s): exchange programs abroad in Japan(Teikyo U, Hachioji)and Germany(Teikyo U Berlin). Combined Bachelor's/Graduate degree in molecular biology. Special programs offered to physically disabled students include tutors. **Career services:** Career/job search classes, career assessment, internships.

FACILITIES
Housing: Coed dorms, men's dorms, women's dorms. 90% of campus accessible to physically disabled. **Special Academic Facilities/Equipment:** Living museum of culture and crafts of West Virginia settlers. Fort New Salem. Biotechnology labs, equestrian center.

CAMPUS LIFE
Environment: Rural. **Activities:** Choral groups, dance, student government, student newspaper, television station, yearbook. **Organizations:** 20 registered organizations, 1 honor societies, 2 religious organizations. 4 fraternities, 4 sororities. **Athletics (Intercollegiate):** *Men:* Baseball, basketball, cheerleading, equestrian sports, golf, soccer, swimming, tennis, water polo. *Women:* Basketball, cheerleading, equestrian sports, soccer, softball, swimming, tennis, volleyball, water polo. **On-Campus Highlights:** Barker Center, cafeteria, Tiger's Den, library, computer labs.

ADMISSIONS
Freshman Academic Profile: SAT Math middle 50% range 420–570. SAT Critical Reading middle 50% range 380–550. ACT middle 50% range 16–22. Minimum paper TOEFL 500. Minimum computer TOEFL 173. **Basis for Candidate Selection:** *Very important factors considered include:* Rigor of secondary school record, standardized test scores. *Important factors considered include:* Recommendation(s), extracurricular activities. *Other factors considered include:* Application essay, alumni/ae relation, character/personal qualities, interview, talent/ability. **Freshman Admission Requirements:** High school diploma is required and GED is accepted. *Academic units recommended:* 4 English, 2 mathematics, 2 science, 2 foreign language, 3 social studies. **Freshman Admission Statistics:** 251 applied, 99% admitted, 24% enrolled. **Transfer Admission Requirements:** High school transcript, college transcript(s), statement of good standing from prior institution(s). Minimum college GPA of 2.5 required. Lowest grade transferable C. **General Admission Information:** Application fee $25. Nonfall registration accepted. Admission may be deferred

for a maximum of 1 year. Credit and/or placement offered for CEEB Advanced Placement tests.

COSTS AND FINANCIAL AID
Average book expense $1,000. **Required Forms and Deadlines:** FAFSA, institution's own financial aid form. Priority financial aid filing date 4/15. **Notification of Awards:** Applicants will be notified of awards on a rolling basis beginning 2/15. **Types of Aid:** *Need-based scholarships/grants:* Federal Pell, SEOG, state scholarships/grants, private scholarships, the school's own gift aid. *Loans:* Direct Subsidized Stafford, Direct Unsubsidized Stafford, Direct PLUS, FFEL Subsidized Stafford, FFEL Unsubsidized Stafford, FFEL PLUS, Federal Perkins, college/university loans from institutional funds. *Student Employment:* Federal Work-Study Program available. Institutional employment available. Highest amount earned per year from on-campus jobs $2,000. Off-campus job opportunities are fair. **Financial Aid Statistics:** 43% freshmen, 39% undergrads receive need-based scholarship or grant aid. 6% freshmen, 23% undergrads receive non-need-based scholarship or grant aid. 61% freshmen, 54% undergrads receive need-based self-help aid. 31% freshmen, 6% undergrads receive athletic scholarships. 45% undergrads borrow to pay for school. Average cumulative indebtedness $14,449.

SALEM STATE COLLEGE

352 Lafayette Street, Salem, MA 01970
Phone: 978-542-6210 **Financial Aid Phone:** 978-542-6112
E-mail: admissions@salemstate.edu **CEEB Code:** 3522
Fax: 978-542-6893 **Website:** www.salemstate.edu

This public school was founded in 1854. It has a 108-acre campus.

RATINGS
Admissions Selectivity Rating: 60* **Fire Safety Rating:** 60* **Green Rating:** 60*

STUDENTS AND FACULTY
Enrollment: 7,085. **Student Body:** 62% female, 38% male, 3% out-of-state, 3% international. Asian 3%, African American 9%, Caucasian 75%, Hispanic 7%.
Retention and Graduation: Faculty: Student/faculty ratio 14:1. 331 full-time faculty, 9% are are members of minority groups, 53% are women.

ACADEMICS
Degrees: Bachelor's, master's, post-bachelor's certificate, post-master's certificate. **Classes:** Most classes have 10–19 students. Most lab/discussion sessions have 10–19 students. **Majors with Highest Enrollment:** Business/commerce; criminal justice/law enforcement administration; education. **Special Study Options:** Distance learning, double major, dual enrollment, English as a Second Language (ESL), honors program, independent study, internships, study abroad, teacher certification program. **Combined degree programs:** BS/MS Occupational Therapy. Special programs offered to physically disabled students include reader services, tape recorders.

FACILITIES
Housing: Coed dorms, Faculty in Residence. 100% of campus accessible to physically disabled. **Special Academic Facilities/Equipment:** Aquaculture center, On-campus elementary school, color TV studio, instructional media center. **Computers:**

CAMPUS LIFE
Environment: Village. **Activities:** Choral groups, concert band, dance, drama/theater, jazz band, literary magazine, music ensembles, musical theater, radio station, student government, student newspaper. **Organizations:** 149 registered organizations, 13 honor societies, 3 religious organizations. **Athletics (Intercollegiate):** *Men:* Baseball, basketball, cross-country, diving, golf, ice hockey, lacrosse, soccer, swimming, tennis, track/field (outdoor). *Women:* Basketball, cross-country, diving, field hockey, lacrosse, soccer, softball, swimming, tennis, track/field (outdoor), volleyball.

ADMISSIONS
Freshman Academic Profile: SAT Math middle 50% range 440–540. SAT Critical Reading middle 50% range 440–540. Minimum paper TOEFL 500. Minimum computer TOEFL 173. **Basis for Candidate Selection:** *Very important factors considered include:* Academic GPA, rigor of secondary school record, standardized test scores. *Other factors considered include:* Recommendation(s), character/personal qualities, extracurricular activities, interview, level of applicant's interest, talent/ability, volunteer work, work experience. **Freshman Admission Requirements:** High school diploma is required and GED is accepted. *Academic units required:* 4 English, 3 mathematics, 3 science, (2 science labs), 2 foreign language, 2 social studies, 1 history, 1 visual/performing arts, 1 computer science, 2 academic electives. *Academic*

units recommended: 4 English, 3 mathematics, 3 science, (2 science labs), 2 foreign language, 2 social studies, 3 history, 1 visual/performing arts, 1 computer science, 2 academic electives. **Freshman Admission Statistics:** 5,835 applied, 60% admitted, 28% enrolled. **Transfer Admission Requirements:** College transcript(s), minimum college GPA of 2.0 required. Lowest grade transferable C–. **General Admission Information:** Application fee $30. Notification on a rolling basis, beginning on or about 12/1. Nonfall registration accepted. Admission may be deferred for a maximum of 1 semester. Credit and/or placement offered for CEEB Advanced Placement tests.

COSTS AND FINANCIAL AID
Required Forms and Deadlines: FAFSA. Priority financial aid filing date 4/1. **Notification of Awards:** Applicants will be notified of awards on a rolling basis beginning 6/1. **Financial Aid Statistics:** 73% freshmen, 75% undergrads receive any aid.

SALISBURY UNIVERSITY

Admissions Office, 1101 Camden Avenue, Salisbury, MD 21801
Phone: 410-543-6161 **Financial Aid Phone:** 410-543-6165
E-mail: admissions@salisbury.edu **CEEB Code:** 5403
Fax: 410-546-6016 **Website:** www.salisbury.edu **ACT Code:** 1716

This public school was founded in 1925. It has a 155-acre campus.

RATINGS
Admissions Selectivity Rating: 86 **Fire Safety Rating:** 70 **Green Rating:** 87

STUDENTS AND FACULTY
Enrollment: 7,285. **Student Body:** 55% female, 45% male, 12% out-of-state, 1% international (54 countries represented). Asian 3%, African American 11%, Caucasian 82%, Hispanic 3%, Native American 1%.
Retention and Graduation: 80% freshmen return for sophomore year. 24% grads go on to further study within 1 year. 20.4% grads pursue arts and sciences degrees. 1.1% grads pursue law degrees. 2.2% grads pursue business degrees. 0.3% grads pursue medical degrees. **Faculty:** Student/faculty ratio 17:1. 380 full-time faculty, 85% hold PhDs, 12% are are members of minority groups, 46% are women.

ACADEMICS
Degrees: Bachelor's, certificate, master's, post-bachelor's certificate. **Classes:** Most classes have 20–29 students. Most lab/discussion sessions have 20–29 students. **Majors with Highest Enrollment:** Biology/biological sciences; business administration and management; communication studies/speech communication and rhetoric. **Special Study Options:** Accelerated program, cross-registration, distance learning, double major, dual enrollment, English as a Second Language (ESL), honors program, independent study, internships, liberal arts/career combination, student-designed major, study abroad, teacher certification program **Honors programs:** The Thomas E. Bellavance Honors Program. **Combined degree programs:** BASW/BA, BS/BS biology/envirn, early chidhood educ/elementary educ. Special programs offered to physically disabled students include note-taking services, reader services, tutors. **Career services:** Alumni network, alumni services, career/job search classes, career assessment, internships, regional alumni.

FACILITIES
Housing: Coed dorms, men's dorms, women's dorms, apartments for single students, wellness housing, theme housing Affiliated off-campus apartments, quiet/study housing available. World living/learning option-community of International and American students. 47% of campus accessible to physically disabled. **Special Academic Facilities/Equipment:** Arboretum, University Galleries, Delmarva History and Culture Research Center, Small Business Development Center, Ward Museum of Wildfowl Art. **Computers:** 100% of classrooms, 100% of dorms, 100% of libraries, 100% of dining areas, 100% of student union, have wireless network access. Students can register for classes online. Administrative functions (other than registration) can be performed online.

CAMPUS LIFE
Environment: Town. **Activities:** Choral groups, concert band, dance, drama/theater, jazz band, literary magazine, music ensembles, musical theater, pep band, radio station, student government, student newspaper, student-run film society, symphony orchestra, television station, campus ministries, international student organization. **Organizations:** 126 registered organizations, 23 honor societies, 8 religious organizations. 8 fraternities, 4 sororities. **Athletics (Inter-**

collegiate): *Men:* Baseball, basketball, cross-country, football, lacrosse, soccer, swimming, tennis, track/field (outdoor). *Women:* Basketball, cross-country, field hockey, lacrosse, soccer, softball, swimming, tennis, track/field (outdoor), volleyball. **On-Campus Highlights:** Commons (housing our Dining Hall and Bookstore), Cool Beans Cyber Caf, Scarborough Leadership Center, Honors House, Maggs Physical Activities Center. **Environmental Initiatives:** Energy and water conservation partnership; minimum of LEED Silver for construction; extensive recycling.

ADMISSIONS

Freshman Academic Profile: Average high school GPA 3.59. 23% in top 10% of high school class, 57.5% in top 25% of high school class, 91.1% in top 50% of high school class. SAT Math middle 50% range 520–620. SAT Critical Reading middle 50% range 520–600. SAT Writing middle 50% range 530–600. ACT middle 50% range 21–26. Minimum paper TOEFL 550. Minimum computer TOEFL 213. **Basis for Candidate Selection:** *Very important factors considered include:* Academic GPA, rigor of secondary school record, extracurricular activities, talent/ability. *Important factors considered include:* Class rank, standardized test scores, alumni/ae relation, geographical residence, volunteer work. *Other factors considered include:* Application essay, recommendation(s), character/personal qualities, racial/ethnic status, work experience. **Freshman Admission Requirements:** High school diploma is required and GED is accepted. *Academic units required:* 4 English, 3 mathematics, 3 science, (2 science labs), 2 foreign language, 3 social studies. *Academic units recommended:* 4 English, 4 mathematics, 4 science, (3 science labs), 3 foreign language, 3 social studies, 3 academic electives. **Freshman Admission Statistics:** 7,525 applied, 54% admitted, 32% enrolled. **Transfer Admission Requirements:** College transcript(s), minimum college GPA of 2.0 required. Lowest grade transferable C. **General Admission Information:** Application fee $45. Regular notification 3/15. Nonfall registration accepted. Credit offered for CEEB Advanced Placement tests.

COSTS AND FINANCIAL AID

Annual in-state tuition $4,814. Annual out-of-state tuition $13,310. Room and board $8,070. Required fees $1,804. Average book expense $1,300. **Required Forms and Deadlines:** FAFSA. Financial aid filing deadline 12/31. Priority financial aid filing date 3/1. **Notification of Awards:** Applicants will be notified of awards on a rolling basis beginning 3/15. *Types of Aid: Need-based scholarships/grants:* Federal Pell, SEOG, state scholarships/grants, private scholarships, the school's own gift aid. *Loans:* Direct Subsidized Stafford, Direct Unsubsidized Stafford, Federal Perkins. *Student Employment:* Federal Work-Study Program available. Institutional employment available. Off-campus job opportunities are fair. **Financial Aid Statistics:** 35% freshmen, 31% undergrads receive need-based scholarship or grant aid. 30% freshmen, 33% undergrads receive need-based self-help aid. 79% freshmen, 73% undergrads receive any aid. 55.8% undergrads borrow to pay for school. Average cumulative indebtedness $17,521. **Criteria for awarding institutional aid:** *Non-need-based:* Academics, alumni affiliation, art, leadership, music/drama, state/district residency.

SALVE REGINA UNIVERSITY

100 Ochre Point Avenue, Newport, RI 02840-4192
Phone: 401-341-2908 **Financial Aid Phone:** 401-341-2901
E-mail: sruadmis@salve.edu **CEEB Code:** 3759
Fax: 401-848-2823 **Website:** www.salve.edu **ACT Code:** 3816

This private school, affiliated with the Roman Catholic Church, was founded in 1947. It has a 81-acre campus.

RATINGS
Admissions Selectivity Rating: 85   **Fire Safety Rating:** 86   **Green Rating:** 78

STUDENTS AND FACULTY
Enrollment: 1,976. **Student Body:** 69% female, 31% male, 84% out-of-state, 1% international (17 countries represented). Asian 1%, African American 2%, Caucasian 77%, Hispanic 3%, Native American 1%.
Retention and Graduation: 73% freshmen return for sophomore year. 63% freshmen graduate within 4 years. 20% grads go on to further study within 1 year. 13% grads pursue arts and sciences degrees. 3% grads pursue law degrees. 4% grads pursue business degrees. **Faculty:** Student/faculty ratio 14:1. 117 full-time faculty, 78% hold PhDs, 8% are are members of minority groups, 56% are women.

ACADEMICS
Degrees: Associate, bachelor's, certificate, doctoral, master's, post-bachelor's certificate, post-master's certificate. **Classes:** Most classes have 10–19 students.

Most lab/discussion sessions have 20–29 students. **Majors with Highest Enrollment:** Criminal justice/law enforcement administration; elementary education and teaching; nursing/registered nurse (RN, ASN, BSN, MSN). **Special Study Options:** Accelerated program, distance learning, double major, dual enrollment, English as a Second Language (ESL), honors program, independent study, internships, liberal arts/career combination, study abroad, teacher certification program, Washington Semester. **Honors programs:** The Pell Honors Program is open to students from all majors who receive the Dean's, Trustee's, or Presidential Scholarships, or who are nominated by Salve Regina faculty or the Admissions Office. The goal of the Pell Honors Program is to create a learning community of students from different disciplines. The honors education is an enhancement of the core curriculum with a focus in international relations and public policy emphasizing civic responsibility and action. Students are required to take classes together, participate in either an internship or study abroad experience, and write and publicly defend a senior thesis. **Combined degree programs:** BA/MA, 4-1 MA, 4-1 MS, BA,BS/MBA. Special programs offered to physically disabled students include note-taking services, reader services, tape recorders, tutors. **Career services:** Alumni network, alumni services, career/job search classes, career assessment, internships, regional alumni.

FACILITIES
Housing: Coed dorms, special housing for disabled students, men's dorms, women's dorms, apartments for single students, wellness housing. Both historic style housing and conventional style housing options are available on campus. Off-campus housing is available to upper class students. 85% of campus accessible to physically disabled. **Special Academic Facilities/Equipment:** Art gallery, theater, technology center. **Computers:** 98% of classrooms, 10% of dorms, 100% of libraries, 100% of dining areas, 100% of student union, 25% of common outdoor areas have wireless network access. Students can register for classes online. Administrative functions (other than registration) can be performed online. Undergraduates are required to own a computer.

CAMPUS LIFE
Environment: Town. **Activities:** Choral groups, concert band, dance, drama/theater, jazz band, literary magazine, music ensembles, pep band, radio station, student government, student newspaper, student-run film society, yearbook, campus ministries, international student organization, Model UN. **Organizations:** 42 registered organizations, 14 honor societies, 2 religious organizations. **Athletics (Intercollegiate):** *Men:* Baseball, basketball, cross-country, football, ice hockey, lacrosse, soccer, tennis. *Women:* Basketball, field hockey, ice hockey, lacrosse, soccer, softball, tennis, track/field (outdoor), volleyball. **On-Campus Highlights:** New Residence Hall, Athletic Center, O'Hare Academic & Antone Academic Cntrs, Library and Computer Labs, Historic Mansions on campus. **Environmental Initiatives:** Recycling; energy conservation; water conservation.

ADMISSIONS
Freshman Academic Profile: Average high school GPA 3.34. 21% in top 10% of high school class, 57% in top 25% of high school class, 88% in top 50% of high school class. 65% from public high schools. SAT Math middle 50% range 500–590. SAT Critical Reading middle 50% range 500–585. SAT Writing middle 50% range 500–590. ACT middle 50% range 22–26. Minimum paper TOEFL 500. Minimum computer TOEFL 173. Minimum web-based TOEFL 61. **Basis for Candidate Selection:** *Very important factors considered include:* Class rank, academic GPA, rigor of secondary school record. *Important factors considered include:* Application essay, recommendation(s), standardized test scores. *Other factors considered include:* Alumni/ae relation, character/personal qualities, extracurricular activities, level of applicant's interest, racial/ethnic status, talent/ability, volunteer work, work experience. **Freshman Admission Requirements:** High school diploma is required and GED is accepted. *Academic units required:* 4 English, 3 mathematics, 2 science, (2 science labs), 2 foreign language, 1 social studies, 4 academic electives. **Freshman Admission Statistics:** 5,256 applied, 64% admitted, 15% enrolled. **Transfer Admission Requirements:** High school transcript, college transcript(s), essay or personal statement, statement of good standing from prior institution(s). Minimum college GPA of 2.7 required. Lowest grade transferable C. **General Admission Information:** Application fee $50. Regular notification 4/1. Notification on a rolling basis, beginning on or about 12/15. Nonfall registration accepted. Admission may be deferred for a maximum of 1 year. Credit and/or placement offered for CEEB Advanced Placement tests.

COSTS AND FINANCIAL AID
Average book expense $900. **Required Forms and Deadlines:** FAFSA, CSS/Financial Aid PROFILE, noncustodial PROFILE, business/farm supplement. Financial aid filing deadline 5/15. Priority financial aid filing date 3/1. **Notification of Awards:** Applicants will be notified of awards on or about 4/1. **Types of Aid:** *Need-based scholarships/grants:* Federal Pell, SEOG, state scholarships/grants, private scholarships, the school's own gift aid. *Loans:* FFEL Subsidized Stafford, FFEL Unsubsidized Stafford, FFEL PLUS, Federal Perkins, Federal Nursing, private loans. *Student Employment:* Federal Work-Study Program

available. Institutional employment available. Highest amount earned per year from on-campus jobs $1,200. Off-campus job opportunities are good. **Financial Aid Statistics:** 75% freshmen, 68% undergrads receive need-based scholarship or grant aid. 4% freshmen, 2% undergrads receive non-need-based scholarship or grant aid. 73% freshmen, 68% undergrads receive need-based self-help aid. 68% freshmen, 71% undergrads receive any aid. 80.93% undergrads borrow to pay for school. Average cumulative indebtedness $35,394. **Criteria for awarding institutional aid:** *Non-need-based:* Academics.

SAM HOUSTON STATE UNIVERSITY

Box 2418, SHSU, Huntsville, TX 77341-2418
Phone: 936-294-1828 **Financial Aid Phone:** 936-294-1774
E-mail: admissions@shsu.edu **CEEB Code:** 6643
Fax: 936-294-3758 **Website:** www.shsu.edu **ACT Code:** 4162

This public school was founded in 1879. It has a 272-acre campus.

RATINGS
Admissions Selectivity Rating: 70   **Fire Safety Rating:** 83   **Green Rating:** 66

STUDENTS AND FACULTY
Enrollment: 14,569. **Student Body:** 56% female, 44% male, 0.5% out-of-state, 1% international (48 countries represented). Asian 2%, African American 16%, Caucasian 67%, Hispanic 14%, Native American 1%.
Retention and Graduation: 75% freshmen return for sophomore year. 21% freshmen graduate within 4 years. **Faculty:** Student/faculty ratio 30:1. 532 full-time faculty, 69% hold PhDs, 9% are are members of minority groups, 41% are women.

ACADEMICS
Degrees: Bachelor's, doctoral, master's. **Classes:** Most classes have 20–29 students. Most lab/discussion sessions have 20–29 students. **Majors with Highest Enrollment:** Business/commerce; criminal justice/safety studies; multi-/interdisciplinary studies, other. **Special Study Options:** Distance learning, double major, dual enrollment, English as a Second Language (ESL), honors program, independent study, internships, teacher certification program. **Honors programs:** The Honors student earns Honors credit in a variety of specially designated classes, and works toward the distinction of graduating 'With Honors' or 'With Highest Honors.' To qualify for graduation with honors, a student must have been a participant in the Honors Program and have completed 24 hours of Honors class credit, including participation in two interdisciplinary Honors seminars. To qualify for graduation 'With Highest Honors' a student must, in addition, complete a senior thesis in an approved discipline under the direction of a faculty member of his/her choice. The student will receive 6 credit hours of departmental course credit when completing the senior thesis. Special programs offered to physically disabled students include note-taking services, reader services, tape recorders. **Career services:** Alumni network, alumni services, career/job search classes, career assessment, internships, regional alumni. **Career services highlights include:** We work closely with major public and private accounting firms as well as with a major retailer (Target) to promote their quality internship programs. We publicize, coordinate and host the interviews for these opportunities for our students and recent alumni.

FACILITIES
Housing: Coed dorms, men's dorms, women's dorms, fraternity/sorority housing, apartments for single students. 85% of campus accessible to physically disabled. **Special Academic Facilities/Equipment:** Sam Houston Memorial Museum, on-campus elementary school, communications center for photography, radio, TV, and film, agricultural complex and university farm. **Computers:** Students can register for classes online. Administrative functions (other than registration) can be performed online.

CAMPUS LIFE
Environment: Town. **Activities:** Choral groups, concert band, dance, drama/theater, jazz band, marching band, music ensembles, musical theater, pep band, radio station, student government, student newspaper, symphony orchestra, television station, yearbook, campus ministries, international student organization. **Organizations:** 185 registered organizations, 12 honor societies, 17 religious organizations. 16 fraternities, 10 sororities. **Athletics (Intercollegiate):** *Men:* Baseball, basketball, cheerleading, cross-country, equestrian sports, football, golf, rodeo, soccer, softball, tennis, track/field (outdoor), track/field (indoor). *Women:* Basketball, cheerleading, cross-country, equestrian sports, golf, rodeo, soccer, softball, tennis, track/field (outdoor), track/field (indoor), volleyball. **On-Campus Highlights:** Lowman Student Center, Health and Kinesiology Center, Computer Labs, Mall Area, Old Main Pit. **Environmental Initiatives:** Hired an Energy Manager. Adopted green approach to new building design, but short of LEED certification. Recycling of all brush and organic material picked up on campus.

ADMISSIONS
Freshman Academic Profile: 13.5% in top 10% of high school class, 30.9% in top 25% of high school class, 39% in top 50% of high school class. SAT Math middle 50% range 450–550. SAT Critical Reading middle 50% range 440–540. ACT middle 50% range 18–22. Minimum paper TOEFL 550. Minimum computer TOEFL 213. **Basis for Candidate Selection:** *Very important factors considered include:* Class rank, standardized test scores. *Important factors considered include:* Rigor of secondary school record. *Other factors considered include:* Application essay, academic GPA, recommendation(s), character/personal qualities, extracurricular activities, talent/ability, volunteer work, work experience. **Freshman Admission Requirements:** High school diploma is required and GED is accepted. *Academic units required:* 4 English, 3 mathematics, 2 science, 1 computer science, 1 academic electives. *Academic units recommended:* 4 English, 4 mathematics, 4 science, (1 science labs), 2 foreign language, 1 visual/performing arts, 1 computer science. **Freshman Admission Statistics:** 4,420 applied, 100% admitted, 49% enrolled. **Transfer Admission Requirements:** College transcript(s), statement of good standing from prior institution(s). Minimum college GPA of 2.0 required. Lowest grade transferable D. **General Admission Information:** Application fee $40. Regular application deadline 8/1. Notification on a rolling basis, beginning on or about 9/1. Nonfall registration accepted. Credit and/or placement offered for CEEB Advanced Placement tests.

COSTS AND FINANCIAL AID
Annual in-state tuition $4,650. Annual out-of-state tuition $12,960. Room and board $6,082. Required fees $1,865. Average book expense $1,125. **Required Forms and Deadlines:** FAFSA, institution's own financial aid form **Notification of Awards:** Applicants will be notified of awards on a rolling basis beginning 3/1. **Types of Aid:** *Need-based scholarships/grants:* Federal Pell, SEOG, state scholarships/grants, the school's own gift aid. *Loans:* Direct Subsidized Stafford, Direct Unsubsidized Stafford, Direct PLUS, FFEL Subsidized Stafford, FFEL Unsubsidized Stafford, FFEL PLUS, Federal Perkins, state loans, college/university loans from institutional funds. *Student Employment:* Federal Work-Study Program available. Highest amount earned per year from on-campus jobs $2,500. Off-campus job opportunities are excellent. **Financial Aid Statistics:** 25% freshmen, 19% undergrads receive need-based scholarship or grant aid. 22% freshmen, 7% undergrads receive non-need-based scholarship or grant aid. 21% freshmen, 16% undergrads receive need-based self-help aid. 38% freshmen, 42% undergrads receive any aid. 69.1% undergrads borrow to pay for school. Average cumulative indebtedness $3,259. **Criteria for awarding institutional aid:** *Non-need-based:* Academics, alumni affiliation, art, athletics, job skills, leadership, music/drama, religious affiliation, state/district residency.

SAMFORD UNIVERSITY

Best 373

800 Lakeshore Drive, Birmingham, AL 35229
Phone: 205-726-3673 **Financial Aid Phone:** 205-726-2905
E-mail: admiss@samford.edu **CEEB Code:** 1302
Fax: 205-726-2171 **Website:** www.samford.edu **ACT Code:** 16

This private school, affiliated with the Baptist Church, was founded in 1841. It has a 180-acre campus.

RATINGS
Admissions Selectivity Rating: 82   **Fire Safety Rating:** 86   **Green Rating:** 73

STUDENTS AND FACULTY
Enrollment: 2,824. **Student Body:** 64% female, 36% male, 61% out-of-state, 1% international (19 countries represented). Asian 1%, African American 7%, Caucasian 88%, Hispanic 1%.
Retention and Graduation: 59% freshmen graduate within 4 years. **Faculty:** Student/faculty ratio 11:1. 290 full-time faculty, 83% hold PhDs, 9% are are members of minority groups, 45% are women.

ACADEMICS
Degrees: Associate, bachelor's, certificate, first professional, master's, postmaster's certificate, terminal associate. **Classes:** Most classes have 10–19 students. Most lab/discussion sessions have 10–19 students. **Majors with High-

est **Enrollment:** Biology/biological sciences; nursing/registered nurse (RN, ASN, BSN, MSN); teacher education, multiple levels. **Special Study Options:** Accelerated program, cooperative education program, distance learning, double major, dual enrollment, exchange student program (domestic), honors program, independent study, internships, liberal arts/career combination, study abroad, teacher certification program. **Honors programs:** Samford University Fellows program targets academically gifted high schools students for a highly-competitive program of innovative liberal arts courses, international study and undergraduate research. **Combined degree programs:** The Law School sponsors seven joint-degree programs. Special programs offered to physically disabled students include note-taking services, reader services, tape recorders **Career services:** Career assessment, internships.

FACILITIES

Housing: Special housing for disabled students, men's dorms, women's dorms, fraternity/sorority housing, wellness housing 100% of campus accessible to physically disabled. **Special Academic Facilities/Equipment:** Language lab, reflective telescope, geographic information systems lab, global center, planetarium, conservatory, Pete Hanna Sports Center. **Computers:** 100% of classrooms, 100% of libraries, 100% of dining areas, 100% of student union, have wireless network access. Students can register for classes online. Administrative functions (other than registration) can be performed online.

CAMPUS LIFE

Environment: Town. **Activities:** Choral groups, concert band, dance, drama/theater, jazz band, literary magazine, marching band, music ensembles, musical theater, radio station, student government, student newspaper, symphony orchestra, yearbook, campus ministries, international student organization, Model UN. **Organizations:** 119 registered organizations, 25 honor societies, 16 religious organizations. 6 fraternities, 6 sororities. **Athletics (Intercollegiate):** *Men:* Baseball, basketball, cross-country, football, golf, tennis, track/field (outdoor). *Women:* Basketball, cross-country, golf, soccer, softball, tennis, track/field (outdoor), volleyball. **On-Campus Highlights:** Sciencenter, Pete Hanna Center, University Library, Wright Center Student Center, Beeson University Center, The Quad, Hodges Chapel, Harrison Theatre, and Jane Hollock Brock Recital Hall. **Environmental Initiatives:** Elimination of trays in cafeteria. Decommissioning of old boiler plants and opening of new facility. Implementation of campus recycling program.

ADMISSIONS

Freshman Academic Profile: Average high school GPA 3.58. 36% in top 10% of high school class, 59% in top 25% of high school class, 86% in top 50% of high school class. 53.1% from public high schools. SAT Math middle 50% range 500–610. SAT Critical Reading middle 50% range 510–630. ACT middle 50% range 20–27. Minimum paper TOEFL 550. Minimum computer TOEFL 213. Minimum web-based TOEFL 80. **Basis for Candidate Selection:** *Very important factors considered include:* Application essay, academic GPA, recommendation(s), rigor of secondary school record, standardized test scores, character/personal qualities, religious affiliation/commitment. *Important factors considered include:* Class rank, alumni/ae relation, extracurricular activities, interview. *Other factors considered include:* geographical residence, level of applicant's interest, racial/ethnic status, state residency, talent/ability, volunteer work, work experience. **Freshman Admission Requirements:** High school diploma is required and GED is accepted. *Academic units required:* 4 English, 3 mathematics, 3 science, 2 foreign language, 2 social studies. *Academic units recommended:* (2 science labs). **Freshman Admission Statistics:** 2,153 applied, 89% admitted, 37% enrolled. **Transfer Admission Requirements:** College transcript(s), essay or personal statement, statement of good standing from prior institution(s). Minimum college GPA of 2.5 required. Lowest grade transferable C–. **General Admission Information:** Application fee $35. Notification on a rolling basis, beginning on or about 11/1. Nonfall registration accepted. Admission may be deferred for a maximum of 1 year. Credit and/or placement offered for CEEB Advanced Placement tests.

COSTS AND FINANCIAL AID

Annual tuition $20,200. . Room and board $6,624. Required fees $220. Average book expense $1,200. **Required Forms and Deadlines:** FAFSA, state aid form. Priority financial aid filing date 3/1. **Notification of Awards:** Applicants will be notified of awards on or about 4/1. **Types of Aid:** *Need-based scholarships/grants:* Federal Pell, SEOG, state scholarships/grants, private scholarships, the school's own gift aid. *Loans:* Direct Subsidized Stafford, Direct Unsubsidized Stafford, Direct PLUS, FFEL Subsidized Stafford, FFEL Unsubsidized Stafford, FFEL PLUS, Federal Perkins. *Student Employment:* Federal Work-Study Program available. Institutional employment available. Off-campus job opportunities are excellent. **Financial Aid Statistics:** 37% freshmen, 33% undergrads receive need-based scholarship or grant aid. 29% freshmen, 29% undergrads receive non-need-based scholarship or grant aid. 28% freshmen, 29% undergrads receive need-based self-help aid. 7% freshmen, 8% undergrads receive athletic scholarships. 36% undergrads borrow to pay for school. Average cumulative indebtedness $13,996. **Criteria for awarding institutional aid:** *Non-need-based:* Academics, athletics, leadership, religious affiliation, state/district residency.

SAN DIEGO STATE UNIVERSITY

5500 Campanile Drive, San Diego, CA 92182
Phone: 619-594-6336 **Financial Aid Phone:** 619-594-6323
E-mail: CEEB Code: 4682
Fax: Website: www.sdsu.edu **ACT Code:** 398

This public school was founded in 1897. It has a 300-acre campus.

RATINGS

Admissions Selectivity Rating: 83   **Fire Safety Rating:** 75   **Green Rating:** 93

STUDENTS AND FACULTY

Enrollment: 27,537. **Student Body:** 57% female, 43% male, 6% out-of-state, 3% international (96 countries represented). Asian 15%, African American 4%, Caucasian 41%, Hispanic 26%, Native American 1%.
Retention and Graduation: 81% freshmen return for sophomore year. 29% freshmen graduate within 4 years. **Faculty:** Student/faculty ratio 22:1. 841 full-time faculty, 85% hold PhDs, 25% are are members of minority groups, 43% are women.

ACADEMICS

Degrees: Bachelor's, master's, post-bachelor's certificate. **Classes:** Most classes have 20–29 students. Most lab/discussion sessions have 20–29 students. **Majors with Highest Enrollment:** Business administration and management; kinesiology and exercise science; psychology. **Special Study Options:** Distance learning, double major, English as a Second Language (ESL), exchange student program (domestic), external degree program, honors program, independent study, internships, liberal arts/career combination, study abroad, teacher certification program. **Combined degree programs:** MBA/JD, MSW/MPH, MSW/JD, MPH/MA. Special programs offered to physically disabled students include note-taking services, reader services, tape recorders, tutors. **Career services:** Alumni services, career/job search classes, career assessment, internships.

FACILITIES

Housing: Coed dorms, special housing for international students, fraternity/sorority housing, apartments for single students, extended quiet study hours (more quiet study environment), living/learning center, housing over the break. 99% of campus accessible to physically disabled. **Special Academic Facilities/Equipment:** Art gallery, theatre, recital hall, research bureaus for labor economics, marine studies and social science, audiovisual center, electronic boardroom, multimedia interactive fine arts technology lab, Palomar Observatory (off-campus), field studies stations (off-campus). **Computers:** Students can register for classes online. Administrative functions (other than registration) can be performed online.

CAMPUS LIFE

Environment: City. **Activities:** Choral groups, concert band, dance, drama/theater, jazz band, literary magazine, marching band, music ensembles, musical theater, opera, pep band, radio station, student government, student newspaper, student-run film society, symphony orchestra, television station, campus ministries, international student organization. **Organizations:** 264 registered organizations, 6 honor societies, 14 religious organizations. 21 fraternities, 23 sororities. **Athletics (Intercollegiate):** *Men:* Baseball, basketball, football, golf, soccer, tennis. *Women:* Basketball, crew/rowing, cross-country, diving, golf, soccer, softball, swimming, tennis, track/field (outdoor), track/field (indoor), volleyball, water polo. **Environmental Initiatives:** In 2009 San Diego State launched a Center for Regional Sustainability to support academic engagement, faculty training, reaserch, and programing to further sustainability on campus. The two major building campus projects will have LEED Silver certification in the next three years, a third project a Student Union will be LEED Platinum. A major part of 2008 Student Fee Referendum, which was passed to implement a mandatory student fee and more than doubled student body fees, went to support sustainability on campus.

ADMISSIONS

Freshman Academic Profile: Average high school GPA 3.47. 92% from public high schools. SAT Math middle 50% range 470–600. SAT Critical Reading middle 50% range 460–570. ACT middle 50% range 19–25. Minimum paper TOEFL 550. Minimum computer TOEFL 213. **Basis for Candidate Selection:** *Very important factors considered include:* Academic GPA, rigor of secondary school record, standardized test scores. *Important factors considered include:* geographical residence, state residency. **Freshman Admission Requirements:** High school diploma is required and GED is accepted. *Academic units required:* 4 English, 3 mathematics, 2 science, (2 science labs), 2 foreign language, 1 social studies, 1 history, 1 visual/performing arts, 1 academic electives. *Academic units recommended:* 4 mathematics. **Freshman Admission Statistics:** 41,986 applied, 36% admitted, 28% enrolled. **Transfer Admission Requirements:** College transcript(s), Lowest grade transferable D-. **General**

Admission Information: Application fee $55. Regular application deadline 11/30. Regular notification 3/1. Nonfall registration not accepted. Credit offered for CEEB Advanced Placement tests.

COSTS AND FINANCIAL AID

Required fees $4,902. Average book expense $1,638. **Required Forms and Deadlines:** FAFSA, state aid form. Financial aid filing deadline 3/2. **Notification of Awards:** Applicants will be notified of awards on a rolling basis beginning 2/14. **Types of Aid:** *Need-based scholarships/grants:* Federal Pell, SEOG, state scholarships/grants, private scholarships, the school's own gift aid, Federal Nursing Scholarships. *Loans:* Direct Subsidized Stafford, Direct Unsubsidized Stafford, Direct PLUS, Federal Perkins, college/university loans from institutional funds. *Student Employment:* Federal Work-Study Program available. Institutional employment available. Off-campus job opportunities are good. **Financial Aid Statistics:** 43% freshmen, 39% undergrads receive need-based scholarship or grant aid. 21% freshmen, 11% undergrads receive non-need-based scholarship or grant aid. 61% freshmen, 52% undergrads receive need-based self-help aid. 3% freshmen, 2% undergrads receive athletic scholarships. 67% freshmen, 58% undergrads receive any aid. 44% undergrads borrow to pay for school. Average cumulative indebtedness $14,700. **Criteria for awarding institutional aid:** *Non-need-based:* Academics, alumni affiliation, art, athletics, leadership, music/drama, state/district residency.

SAN FRANCISCO STATE UNIVERSITY

1600 Holloway Avenue, San Francisco, CA 94132
Phone: 415-338-6486 **Financial Aid Phone:** 415-338-7000
E-mail: ugadmit@sfsu.edu **CEEB Code:** 4684
Fax: 415-338-7196 **Website:** www.sfsu.edu

This public school was founded in 1899. It has a 142-acre campus.

RATINGS
Admissions Selectivity Rating: 73   **Fire Safety Rating:** 83   **Green Rating:** 98

STUDENTS AND FACULTY
Enrollment: 25,001. **Student Body:** 59% female, 41% male, 0.8% out-of-state, 7% international (87 countries represented). Asian 28%, African American 5%, Caucasian 30%, Hispanic 18%.
Retention and Graduation: Faculty: 818 full-time faculty, 74% hold PhDs, 39% are are members of minority groups, 48% are women.

ACADEMICS
Degrees: Bachelor's, certificate, master's, post-bachelor's certificate. **Classes:** Most classes have 20–29 students. Most lab/discussion sessions have 10–19 students. **Majors with Highest Enrollment:** Biology/biological sciences; business administration and management; psychology. **Special Study Options:** Cooperative education program, cross-registration, distance learning, double major, dual enrollment, English as a Second Language (ESL), honors program, independent study, internships, liberal arts/career combination, student-designed major, study abroad, teacher certification program. **Combined degree programs:** BA/MA. Special programs offered to physically disabled students include note-taking services, reader services, tape recorders, tutors. **Career services:** Alumni services, career/job search classes, career assessment, internships.

FACILITIES
Housing: Coed dorms, special housing for disabled students, special housing for international students, apartments for married students, apartments for single students, wellness housing, theme housing, women only floors. **Special Academic Facilities/Equipment:** Treganza Anthropology Museum, Moss Landing Marine Laboratories, Romberg Tiburon Center for Environmental Studies, Sierra Nevada Field Campus, Sutro Egyptian Collection. **Computers:** 100% of classrooms, 100% of dorms, 100% of libraries, 100% of dining areas, 100% of student union, 100% of common outdoor areas have wireless network access. Students can register for classes online. Administrative functions (other than registration) can be performed online.

CAMPUS LIFE
Environment: Metropolis. **Activities:** Choral groups, concert band, dance, drama/theater, jazz band, literary magazine, music ensembles, musical theater, opera, pep band, radio station, student government, student newspaper, student-run film society, symphony orchestra, television station, campus ministries, international student organization. **Organizations:** 213 registered organizations, 6 honor societies, 13 religious organizations. 3 fraternities, 4 sororities. **Athletics (Intercollegiate):** *Men:* Baseball, basketball, cross-country, soccer, wrestling. *Women:* Basketball, cross-country, soccer, softball, track/field (outdoor), track/field (indoor), volleyball. **On-Campus Highlights:** Cesar Chavez

Student Center, Cox Stadium, SFSU Fine Arts Gallery, Residential Theme Communities, J. Paul Leonard Library Annex, Malcolm X Plaza, The Village at Centennial Square, and McKenna Theatre. **Environmental Initiatives:** SF State is dedicated to reducing the campus' use of resources and its impact on climate change. Some of the projects that demonstrate that are: the Buy Recycled Campaign, purchasing 15% renewable energy, installing solar panels, implementing a green cleaning program, hiring a Sustainability Coordinator, offering alternative transportation incentives, pursuing LEED certification for two buildings, and diverting over 76% of the waste from the landfill. SF State completed its first Greenhouse Gas Emissions Inventory in May of 2008 and its second one in January 2010. The campus' Sustainability Committee is working on writing a Climate Action Plan which will outline how the campus will reach climate neutrality. SF State is working to institutionalize sustainability into its curriculum. A few of the Departments who have already done so are: Environmental Studies, Geography, Urban Planning, MBA with an emphasis in Sustainability, and the Romburg Tiburon Center for Environmental Studies.

ADMISSIONS
Freshman Academic Profile: Average high school GPA 3.11. 82% from public high schools. SAT Math middle 50% range 450–570. SAT Critical Reading middle 50% range 440–560. SAT Writing middle 50% range 440–560. ACT middle 50% range 19–24. Minimum paper TOEFL 500. Minimum computer TOEFL 173. **Basis for Candidate Selection:** *Very important factors considered include:* Academic GPA, rigor of secondary school record, standardized test scores. *Important factors considered include:* state residency. *Other factors considered include:* Recommendation(s), talent/ability. **Freshman Admission Requirements:** High school diploma is required and GED is accepted. *Academic units required:* 4 English, 3 mathematics, 2 science, (2 science labs), 2 foreign language, 1 social studies, 1 history, 1 visual/performing arts. *Academic units recommended:* 1 academic electives. **Freshman Admission Statistics:** 28,218 applied, 73% admitted, 20% enrolled. **Transfer Admission Requirements:** College transcript(s), statement of good standing from prior institution(s). Minimum college GPA of 2.0 required. Lowest grade transferable D. **General Admission Information:** Application fee $55. Notification on a rolling basis, beginning on or about 10/1. Nonfall registration accepted. Credit offered for CEEB Advanced Placement tests.

COSTS AND FINANCIAL AID
Required Forms and Deadlines: FAFSA. Priority financial aid filing date 3/2. **Notification of Awards:** Applicants will be notified of awards on a rolling basis beginning 2/1. **Types of Aid:** *Need-based scholarships/grants:* Federal Pell, SEOG, state scholarships/grants, private scholarships, the school's own gift aid. *Loans:* Direct Subsidized Stafford, Direct Unsubsidized Stafford, FFEL PLUS, Federal Perkins. *Student Employment:* Federal Work-Study Program available. Institutional employment available. **Financial Aid Statistics:** 37% freshmen, 41% undergrads receive need-based scholarship or grant aid. 8% freshmen, 4% undergrads receive non-need-based scholarship or grant aid. 54% freshmen, 54% undergrads receive need-based self-help aid. 39% undergrads borrow to pay for school. Average cumulative indebtedness $15,636. **Criteria for awarding institutional aid:** *Non-need-based:* Academics, athletics.

SAN JOSE STATE UNIVERSITY

One Washington Square, San Jose, CA 95192-0016
Phone: 408-283-7500 **Financial Aid Phone:** 408-283-7500
E-mail: admissions@sjsu.edu **CEEB Code:** 4687
Fax: 408-924-2050 **Website:** www.sjsu.edu

This public school was founded in 1857. It has a 154-acre campus.

RATINGS
Admissions Selectivity Rating: 74   **Fire Safety Rating:** 60*   **Green Rating:** 60*

STUDENTS AND FACULTY
Enrollment: 25,187. **Student Body:** 52% female, 48% male, 1% out-of-state, 3% international (139 countries represented). Asian 27%, African American 4%, Caucasian 20%, Hispanic 13%.
Retention and Graduation: 80% freshmen return for sophomore year. 6% freshmen graduate within 4 years. **Faculty:** Student/faculty ratio 30:1. 710 full-time faculty, 30% are are members of minority groups, 45% are women. 3.5% of classes are taught by teaching assistants.

ACADEMICS
Degrees: Bachelor's, master's. **Classes:** Most classes have 20–29 students. Most lab/discussion sessions have 20–29 students. **Majors with Highest Enrollment:** Art/art studies; business administration and management; electrical, electronics and communications engineering. **Special Study Options:** Dis-

tance learning, double major, dual enrollment, honors program, independent study, internships, student-designed major, study abroad, teacher certification program Special programs offered to physically disabled students include note-taking services, reader services, tutors. **Career services:** Alumni services, career/job search classes, career assessment, internships. **Career services highlights include:** We are proud of our Neat Ideas Fair program, which was nominated for the 2008 USASBE innovative pedagogy award. The Fair is a venue for students from across the SJSU campus to display and pitch their business ideas and receive feedback from seasoned entrepreneurs, investors, lawyers, professors, and their peers.

FACILITIES

Housing: Coed dorms, special housing for disabled students, men's dorms, special housing for international students, women's dorms, fraternity/sorority housing, cooperative housing, apartments for single students. 100% of campus accessible to physically disabled. **Special Academic Facilities/Equipment:** Martin Luther King, Jr. Library (joint with city); child development lab; Chicano resource center; Beethoven studies center; John Steinbeck research center; art metal foundry; natural history living museum (science education); science resource center, deep-sea research ship, electro-acoustical/recording studios, nuclear science and engineering labs. **Computers:** Students can register for classes online. Administrative functions (other than registration) can be performed online.

CAMPUS LIFE

Environment: Metropolis. **Activities:** Choral groups, dance, drama/theater, literary magazine, marching band, music ensembles, musical theater, radio station, student government, student newspaper, student-run film society, symphony orchestra, campus ministries, international student organization. **Organizations:** 283 registered organizations, 13 honor societies, 20 religious organizations. 20 fraternities, 15 sororities. **Athletics (Intercollegiate):** *Men:* Baseball, basketball, cheerleading, cross-country, diving, football, golf, soccer, softball, swimming, volleyball, water polo. *Women:* Basketball, cheerleading, cross-country, diving, golf, gymnastics, soccer, softball, swimming, tennis, volleyball, water polo. **On-Campus Highlights:** Martin Luther King, Jr. Library, Student Union, Art Quad, Market Cafe/Burger King/Sparro, Gym.

ADMISSIONS

Freshman Academic Profile: Average high school GPA 3.15. 77% from public high schools. SAT Math middle 50% range 450–580. SAT Critical Reading middle 50% range 430–540. SAT Writing middle 50% range 430–530. ACT middle 50% range 18–24. Minimum paper TOEFL 550. Minimum computer TOEFL 213. Minimum web-based TOEFL 80. **Basis for Candidate Selection:** *Very important factors considered include:* Academic GPA, rigor of secondary school record, standardized test scores. *Important factors considered include:* first generation. **Freshman Admission Requirements:** High school diploma is required and GED is accepted. *Academic units required:* 4 English, 3 mathematics, 2 science, (2 science labs), 2 foreign language, 1 social studies, 1 history, 1 visual/performing arts, 1 academic electives. *Academic units recommended:* 4 mathematics, 3 science. **Freshman Admission Statistics:** 24,079 applied, 66% admitted, 23% enrolled. **Transfer Admission Requirements:** College transcript(s), statement of good standing from prior institution(s). Minimum college GPA of 2.0 required. Lowest grade transferable 2. **General Admission Information:** Application fee $55. Regular application deadline 11/30. Notification on a rolling basis, beginning on or about 10/1. Nonfall registration accepted. Credit offered for CEEB Advanced Placement tests.

COSTS AND FINANCIAL AID

Annual out-of-state tuition $10,170. Room and board $8,663. Required fees $3,992. Average book expense $1,656. **Required Forms and Deadlines:** FAFSA. Financial aid filing deadline 6/12. Priority financial aid filing date 3/2. **Notification of Awards:** Applicants will be notified of awards on a rolling basis beginning 4/10. **Types of Aid:** *Need-based scholarships/grants:* Federal Pell, SEOG, state scholarships/grants, private scholarships, the school's own gift aid. *Loans:* FFEL Subsidized Stafford, FFEL Unsubsidized Stafford, FFEL PLUS, Federal Perkins, college/university loans from institutional funds. *Student Employment:* Federal Work-Study Program available. Institutional employment available. Off-campus job opportunities are excellent. **Financial Aid Statistics:** 46% freshmen, 37% undergrads receive need-based scholarship or grant aid. 58% freshmen, 45% undergrads receive need-based self-help aid. 40.45% freshmen, 38.88% undergrads receive any aid. 50% undergrads borrow to pay for school. Average cumulative indebtedness $11,815. **Criteria for awarding institutional aid:** *Non-need-based:* Academics, athletics.

SANTA CLARA UNIVERSITY

500 El Camino Real, Santa Clara, CA 95053
Phone: 408-554-4700 **Financial Aid Phone:** 408-554-4505
E-mail: ugadmissions@scu.edu **CEEB Code:** 4851
Fax: 408-554-5255 **Website:** www.scu.edu

This private school, affiliated with the Roman Catholic Church, was founded in 1851. It has a 106-acre campus.

RATINGS
Admissions Selectivity Rating: 89   **Fire Safety Rating:** 94   **Green Rating:** 90

STUDENTS AND FACULTY

Enrollment: 5,158. **Student Body:** 53% female, 47% male, 36% out-of-state, 3% international (38 countries represented). Asian 17%, African American 4%, Caucasian 42%, Hispanic 15%, Native American 1%.
Retention and Graduation: 78% freshmen graduate within 4 years. 25.7% grads go on to further study within 1 year. 16.3% grads pursue arts and sciences degrees. 5% grads pursue law degrees. 1.5% grads pursue business degrees. 1.5% grads pursue medical degrees. **Faculty:** Student/faculty ratio 12.4:1. 515 full-time faculty, 88% hold PhDs, 20% are are members of minority groups, 43% are women.

ACADEMICS

Degrees: Bachelor's, master's, post-bachelor's certificate, post-master's certificate. **Classes:** Most classes have 20–29 students. Most lab/discussion sessions have 10–19 students. **Majors with Highest Enrollment:** Accounting; communication studies/speech communication and rhetoric; finance. **Special Study Options:** Cooperative education program, double major, honors program, independent study, internships, student-designed major, study abroad, teacher certification program. **Honors programs:** The University Honors Program provides Santa Clara's most able students with intellectual opportunities based in small, seminar-style classes. With 14 to 17 students each, seminars emphasize analytical rigor, effective expression, and interaction among professors and students. The course of study combines broadly based, liberal learning with depth of specialization in a major field. Honors Program classes are designed to fit within the curricula of the humanities, natural and social sciences, business, and engineering. Possible majors include every undergraduate field in the University. **Combined degree programs:** BA/MEng. Special programs offered to physically disabled students include note-taking services, reader services, tape recorders, tutors. **Career services:** Alumni network, alumni services, career/job search classes, career assessment, internships, regional alumni. **Career services highlights include:** The Career Center at Santa Clara University provides students with access to quality internships on a local, national, and international level. Employers from all sectors recruit students for internships that emphasize intentional learning, professional development, real-world experience, skill-building, and networking. Almost 4,000 internships are posted each year that target our students on NACElink. Almost one-third of these are technical internships, reflecting our location in the heart of Silicon Valley. Students also have access to thousands of internships posted on over 100 internship databases through our online resources. In addition, we provide effective and successful co-curricular internship programming through which students effectively connect with employers; educate students, faculty/staff, and parents about all aspects of internships; offer a Freshmen/Sophomore Internship Fair each February; and educate employer organizations about developing substantive internship programs that are committed to intentional learning and provide quality, engaged supervision for the student. We also provide numerous internship-related workshops for students, clubs and organizations, classes, and parents during Parent Weekend.

FACILITIES

Housing: Coed dorms, apartments for single students, theme housing. 95% of campus accessible to physically disabled. **Special Academic Facilities/Equipment:** Art and history museum (de Saisset), mission church, theatre, media lab, retail management institute, computer design center, engineering labs, Markkula Center for Applied Ethics, Center for Science, Technology, and Society, Ignatian Center for Jesuit Education. **Computers:** 100% of classrooms, 100% of dorms, 100% of libraries, 100% of dining areas, 100% of student union, 90% of common outdoor areas have wireless network access. Students can register for classes online. Administrative functions (other than registration) can be performed online.

CAMPUS LIFE

Environment: City. **Activities:** Choral groups, dance, drama/theater, jazz band, literary magazine, music ensembles, musical theater, opera, pep band, radio station, student government, student newspaper, symphony orchestra, yearbook, campus ministries, international student organization, Model UN. **Organizations:** 86 registered organizations, 25 honor societies, 5 religious organizations. **Athletics (Intercollegiate):** *Men:* Baseball, basketball, crew/rowing, cross-country, golf, soccer, tennis, track/field (outdoor), water polo. *Women:* Basketball, crew/rowing, cross-country, golf, soccer, softball, tennis, track/field (outdoor), volleyball, water polo. **On-Campus Highlights:** Historic Mission Church; Mission gardens, Pat Malley Fitness Center, Harrington Learning Commons and Library, Benson Memorial Student Center, Leavey Activities Center, The palm tree dotted campus is gorgeous, with stunning gardens, walkways, Mission style buildings, and lots of greenery. At the heart of Santa Clara University is the historic Mission Santa Clara de Asis. Founded in 1777, it is the eighth oldest of the original 21 California missions. The current Mission Church was dedicated May 13, 1928. From then until now it has served as the University chapel, and is used by the University community for Masses, baptisms, weddings and funerals. The Mission Church is open to the public and welcomes visitors. The de Saisset Museum at Santa Clara University is the South Bay Area's free Museum of art and history. The 19,210 square foot facility was founded adjacent to the Mission Santa Clara de Asis on the Santa Clara University campus in 1955 and is currently one of only two museums in the South Bay accredited by the American Association of Museums. **Environmental Initiatives:** Santa Clara University strives to develop a culture of sustainability. Our Comprehensive Policy on Sustainability (adopted in 2004) targets our efforts toward stewardship, education, and outreach. We are a signatory of the ACUPCC in 2007, committing to transform SCU into a climate-neutral campus. The University's Sustainability Coordinator was hired in 2006. The Office of Sustainability was formally established in 2008 to support campus efforts, coordinate initiatives, serve as the "clearing-house" for campus sustainability data, and to showcase University sustainability programs to the public. The Sustainability Council was also formed at this time to guide the efforts of the Office of Sustainability. EDUCATION: We strive to integrate sustainability across the curriculum to show students that sustainability is ingrained in many disciplines. The Penstemon Project (2007 and 2009), enabled faculty to integrate sustainability into existing courses in multiple disciplines. Nineteen academic departments currently offer a sustainability-related or focused course. Students have created documentaries about sustainability on campus, assessed barriers to greening campus offices, conducted cost/benefit analyses of implementing power strips at residence halls, explored the ethics of GMO crops, and more! Our new core curriculum enables students in all three schools to integrate sustainability into their studies. Students can major in environmental science or environmental studies, and they can participate in international competitions: SCU was one of 20 schools in the 2007 and 2009 Solar Decathlon. Over 100 SCU students designed, built, and operated an energy-efficient, sustainable solar-powered home. SCU earned 3rd place in both competitions! Study abroad opportunities expose students to global dimensions of sustainability. The Sustainable Living Undergraduate Research Project provides undergraduates opportunities to conduct year-long studies of sustainability as it relates to residence life. OUTREACH: SCU undergraduates developed the Sustainability Decathlon–a high school outreach component of the Solar Decathlon. SCU undergraduates mentor local high school students as they explore sustainability and "green" their campuses in 10 categories. Each high school is required to conduct outreach to a local middle or elementary school, further fostering a culture of sustainability. SCU developing half-acre education, demonstration, and community garden. The garden will be used as a living laboratory and training facility for the Bronco Urban Gardens (BUG) Program. BUG helps communities and schools in low-income neighborhoods in San Jose build and utilize new gardens.

ADMISSIONS

Freshman Academic Profile: Average high school GPA 3.53. 40% in top 10% of high school class, 72% in top 25% of high school class, 94% in top 50% of high school class. 47% from public high schools. SAT Math middle 50% range 570–680. SAT Critical Reading middle 50% range 550–650. ACT middle 50% range 25–30. Minimum paper TOEFL 550. Minimum computer TOEFL 213. **Basis for Candidate Selection:** *Very important factors considered include:* Application essay, academic GPA, recommendation(s), rigor of secondary school record. *Important factors considered include:* standardized test scores, character/personal qualities, extracurricular activities, racial/ethnic status, talent/ability, volunteer work. *Other factors considered include:* Class rank, alumni/ae relation, first generation, geographical residence, level of applicant's interest, religious affiliation/commitment, state residency, work experience. **Freshman Admission Requirements:** High school diploma is required and GED is not accepted. *Academic units required:* 4 English, 3 mathematics, 2 science, 2 foreign language, 3 social studies, 1 academic electives. *Academic units recommended:* 4 English, 4 mathematics, 3 science, 3 foreign language, 3 social studies, 1 visual/performing arts, 1 academic electives. **Freshman Admission Statistics:** 10,226 applied, 59% admitted, 18% enrolled. **Transfer Admission**

Requirements: College transcript(s), essay or personal statement, Lowest grade transferable C. **General Admission Information:** Application fee $55. Regular application deadline 1/7. Regular notification 4/1. Nonfall registration not accepted. Admission may be deferred for a maximum of 1 year. Credit and/or placement offered for CEEB Advanced Placement tests.

COSTS AND FINANCIAL AID

Annual tuition $36,000. Room and board $11,400. Average book expense $1,638. **Required Forms and Deadlines:** FAFSA, CSS/Financial Aid PROFILE. Priority financial aid filing date 2/1. **Notification of Awards:** Applicants will be notified of awards on or about 4/1. **Types of Aid:** *Need-based scholarships/grants:* Federal Pell, SEOG, state scholarships/grants, private scholarships, the school's own gift aid. *Loans:* Direct Subsidized Stafford, Direct Unsubsidized Stafford, Direct PLUS, FFEL PLUS, Federal Perkins, Private alternative loans. *Student Employment:* Federal Work-Study Program available. Institutional employment available. Off-campus job opportunities are good. **Financial Aid Statistics:** 32% freshmen, 28% undergrads receive need-based scholarship or grant aid. 20% freshmen, 13% undergrads receive non-need-based scholarship or grant aid. 24% freshmen, 23% undergrads receive need-based self-help aid. 6% freshmen, 5% undergrads receive athletic scholarships. 84.6% freshmen, 76.3% undergrads receive any aid. 43.6% undergrads borrow to pay for school. Average cumulative indebtedness $25,438. **Criteria for awarding institutional aid:** *Non-need-based:* Academics, alumni affiliation, athletics, music/drama.

SARAH LAWRENCE COLLEGE

1 Mead Way, Bronxville, NY 10708-5999
Phone: 914-395-2510 **Financial Aid Phone:** 914-395 2570
E-mail: slcadmit@slc.edu **CEEB Code:** 2810
Fax: 914-395-2515 **Website:** www.sarahlawrence.edu **ACT Code:** 2904

This private school was founded in 1926. It has a 44-acre campus.

RATINGS

Admissions Selectivity Rating: 90   **Fire Safety Rating:** 90   **Green Rating:** 81

STUDENTS AND FACULTY

Enrollment: 1,295. **Student Body:** 73% female, 27% male, 77% out-of-state, 3% international (32 countries represented). Asian 5%, African American 3%, Caucasian 58%, Hispanic 5%.
Retention and Graduation: 82% freshmen return for sophomore year. 64% freshmen graduate within 4 years. **Faculty:** Student/faculty ratio 9:1. 107 full-time faculty, 21% are are members of minority groups, 50% are women.

ACADEMICS

Degrees: Bachelor's, certificate, master's, post-master's certificate. **Classes:** Most classes have 10–19 students. **Special Study Options:** Double major, exchange student program (domestic), independent study, internships, student-designed major, study abroad, teacher certification program, Sarah Lawrence College has no formal majors. However students may concentrate in subject areas. All students design their own educational programs (with faculty advisement), so the equivalent of a "double major" is available. We have a 3-2 program where students can get their BA degree and MSEd in the Art of Teaching or MA in women's history. We also have a 3-2 program in which the student receives a BA in the liberal arts from Sarah Lawrence and a BS in engineering from Columbia. **Combined degree programs:** BA/MA, BA/MEng, BA/MA education, MSW/MA with NYU MA/JD with Pace Law School. Special programs offered to physically disabled students include note-taking services, reader services, tape recorders, tutors. **Career services:** Alumni network, alumni services, career/job search classes, career assessment, internships, **Career services highlights include:** We are proud of both our Internship program as well as our Service Learning and Community Partnership program which offers experiential learning. The Internship Program provides high quality placements in work environments closely related to our students' career, personal, and academic interests. Since Sarah Lawrence College is a 25 minute train ride away from New York City, and NYC is the hub for so many career fields, our office has access to some of the most prestigious organizations available which consistently seek out our students. Our students' stellar performance in the workplace creates future internship opportunities for other students and full-time post-graduation employment.

FACILITIES

Housing: Coed dorms, men's dorms, women's dorms, wellness housing, theme housing. First year students required to live on campus unless living at home. 50% of campus accessible to physically disabled. **Special Academic Facilities/ Equipment:** Performing arts center including a concert hall, dance studios,and theatres; visual arts center including studios, gallery, film theatre, sound stage, visual resources library; music building including music library; science center, early childhood center, greenhouse. **Computers:** 100% of classrooms, 30% of dorms, 100% of libraries, 100% of dining areas, 100% of common outdoor areas have wireless network access. Administrative functions (other than registration) can be performed online.

CAMPUS LIFE

Environment: Metropolis. **Activities:** Choral groups, dance, drama/theater, jazz band, literary magazine, music ensembles, musical theater, radio station, student government, student newspaper, student-run film society, symphony orchestra, yearbook, campus ministries, international student organization, Model UN. **Organizations:** 30 registered organizations, 3 religious organizations. **Athletics (Intercollegiate):** *Men:* Basketball, crew/rowing, cross-country, equestrian sports, soccer, tennis. *Women:* Crew/rowing, cross-country, equestrian sports, softball, swimming, tennis, volleyball. **On-Campus Highlights:** Campbell Sports Center, Communitea House, Siegel Center, Library, Heimbold Visual Arts Center. **Environmental Initiatives:** A new, sustainable dorm opened in 08-09 and a green roof on another dorm. A LEED-certified visual arts building A campus-wide sustainability committee

ADMISSIONS

Freshman Academic Profile: Average high school GPA 3.6. 46% in top 10% of high school class, 79% in top 25% of high school class, 97% in top 50% of high school class. 51% from public high schools. Minimum paper TOEFL 600. Minimum computer TOEFL 250. **Basis for Candidate Selection:** *Very important factors considered include:* Application essay, recommendation(s), rigor of secondary school record. *Important factors considered include:* Academic GPA, extracurricular activities, talent/ability. *Other factors considered include:* Class rank, alumni/ae relation, character/personal qualities, first generation, geographical residence, interview, level of applicant's interest, racial/ethnic status, volunteer work, work experience. **Freshman Admission Requirements:** High school diploma is required and GED is accepted. *Academic units required:* 4 English, 2 mathematics, 2 science, 2 foreign language, 2 history. *Academic units recommended:* 4 mathematics, 4 science, 4 foreign language, 4 social studies, 4 history. **Freshman Admission Statistics:** 2,126 applied, 58% admitted, 29% enrolled. **Transfer Admission Requirements:** High school transcript, college transcript(s), essay or personal statement, statement of good standing from prior institution(s). Lowest grade transferable C. **General Admission Information:** Application fee $60. Early decision application deadline 11/1. Regular application deadline 1/1. Regular notification 4/1. Nonfall registration not accepted. Admission may be deferred for a maximum of 1 year. Credit offered for CEEB Advanced Placement tests.

COSTS AND FINANCIAL AID

Annual tuition $41,040. Room and board $13,820. Required fees $928. Average book expense $600. **Required Forms and Deadlines:** FAFSA, CSS/Financial Aid PROFILE, state aid form, noncustodial PROFILE. Financial aid filing deadline 2/1. **Notification of Awards:** Applicants will be notified of awards on or about 4/1. **Types of Aid:** *Need-based scholarships/grants:* Federal Pell, SEOG, state scholarships/grants, private scholarships, the school's own gift aid. *Loans:* FFEL Subsidized Stafford, FFEL Unsubsidized Stafford, FFEL PLUS, Federal Perkins. *Student Employment:* Federal Work-Study Program available. Institutional employment available. Highest amount earned per year from on-campus jobs $1,500. Off-campus job opportunities are good. **Financial Aid Statistics:** 61% freshmen, 54% undergrads receive need-based scholarship or grant aid. 59% freshmen, 56% undergrads receive need-based self-help aid. 65% freshmen, 58% undergrads receive any aid. 52% undergrads borrow to pay for school. Average cumulative indebtedness $17,246.

SAVANNAH COLLEGE OF ART AND DESIGN

PO Box 3146, Savannah, GA 31402-3146
Phone: 912-525-5100 **Financial Aid Phone:** 912-525-6104
E-mail: admission@scad.edu **CEEB Code:** 5631
Fax: 912-525-5986 **Website:** www.scad.edu **ACT Code:** 0855

This private school was founded in 1978.

RATINGS

Admissions Selectivity Rating: 81   **Fire Safety Rating:** 60*   **Green Rating:** 60*

STUDENTS AND FACULTY

Enrollment: 8,056. **Student Body:** 60% female, 40% male, 78% out-of-state, 9% international (96 countries represented). Asian 1%, African American 4%, Caucasian 26%, Hispanic 3%.
Retention and Graduation: 82% freshmen return for sophomore year. 51% freshmen graduate within 4 years. **Faculty:** Student/faculty ratio 17:1. 491 full-time faculty, 73% hold PhDs, 11% are are members of minority groups, 40% are women.

ACADEMICS

Degrees: Bachelor's, certificate, master's, post-bachelor's certificate. **Classes:** Most classes have 10–19 students. **Majors with Highest Enrollment:** Animation, interactive technology, video graphics and special effects; fashion/apparel design; graphic design. **Special Study Options:** Distance learning, double major, dual enrollment, English as a Second Language (ESL), independent study, internships, study abroad, teacher certification program, Summer quarter programs in New York City and Europe; apprenticeships with artists or designers and internships with museums, agencies, media production companies, architectural firms, and other companies in the United States or abroad. Special programs offered to physically disabled students include note-taking services, tape recorders, tutors. **Career services:** Alumni network, alumni services, career/job search classes, career assessment, internships, regional alumni.

FACILITIES

Housing: Coed dorms, women's dorms, apartments for single students, Learning communities. Accommodations for disabled students are handled on an individual basis. 85% of campus accessible to physically disabled. **Special Academic Facilities/Equipment:** Art galleries; computer, video, photography, and design labs; SCAD Museum of Art. **Computers:** 80% of classrooms, 100% of dorms, 100% of libraries, 100% of dining areas, 100% of student union, 50% of common outdoor areas have wireless network access. Students can register for classes online. Administrative functions (other than registration) can be performed online.

CAMPUS LIFE

Environment: City. **Activities:** Choral groups, dance, drama/theater, music ensembles, musical theater, radio station, student government, student newspaper, television station, international student organization. **Organizations:** 68 registered organizations, 2 honor societies, 3 religious organizations. **Athletics (Intercollegiate):** *Men:* Baseball, basketball, cross-country, equestrian sports, golf, lacrosse, soccer, swimming, tennis. *Women:* Basketball, cross-country, equestrian sports, golf, lacrosse, soccer, softball, swimming, tennis, volleyball. **On-Campus Highlights:** SCAD Museum of Art, Club SCAD, Jen Library, Cafe SCAD, Trustees Theatre.

ADMISSIONS

Freshman Academic Profile: Average high school GPA 3.4. SAT Math middle 50% range 470–590. SAT Critical Reading middle 50% range 490–600. SAT Writing middle 50% range 470–580. ACT middle 50% range 20–26. Minimum paper TOEFL 450. Minimum web-based TOEFL 85. **Basis for Candidate Selection:** *Very important factors considered include:* Academic GPA, standardized test scores. *Important factors considered include:* Rigor of secondary school record, level of applicant's interest. *Other factors considered include:* Class rank, application essay, recommendation(s), character/personal qualities, extracurricular activities, interview, talent/ability, volunteer work, work experience. **Freshman Admission Requirements:** High school diploma is required and GED is accepted. **Freshman Admission Statistics:** 8,108 applied, 68% admitted, 31% enrolled. **Transfer Admission Requirements:** College transcript(s), minimum college GPA of 2.0 required. Lowest grade transferable C. **General Admission Information:** Application fee $50. Regular application deadline 8/1. Nonfall registration accepted. Admission may be deferred for a maximum of 2 consec qtr. Credit and/or placement offered for CEEB Advanced Placement tests.

COSTS AND FINANCIAL AID

Annual tuition $29,070. Room and board $11,750. Average book expense $2,400. **Required Forms and Deadlines:** FAFSA, institution's own financial aid form, state aid form. Priority financial aid filing date 2/15. **Notification of Awards:** Applicants will be notified of awards on a rolling basis beginning 4/1. **Types of Aid:** *Need-based scholarships/grants:* Federal Pell, SEOG, state scholarships/grants, private scholarships, the school's own gift aid. *Loans:* Direct Subsidized Stafford, Direct Unsubsidized Stafford, Direct PLUS, state loans *Student Employment:* Federal Work-Study Program available. Institutional employment available. Off-campus job opportunities are excellent. **Financial Aid Statistics:** 38% freshmen, 28% undergrads receive need-based scholarship or grant aid. 55% freshmen, 45% undergrads receive non-need-based scholarship or grant aid. 60% freshmen, 55% undergrads receive need-based self-help aid. 1% freshmen, 2% undergrads receive athletic scholarships. **Criteria for awarding institutional aid:** *Non-need-based:* Academics, alumni affiliation, art, athletics, music/drama, state/district residency.

See page 1230.

SAVANNAH STATE UNIVERSITY

College Station, PO Box 20209, Savannah, GA 31404
Phone: 912-356-2181
E-mail: SSUAdmissions@savstate.edu **CEEB Code:** 5609
Fax: 912-356-2256 **Website:** www.savstate.edu **ACT Code:** 858

This public school was founded in 1890. It has a 165-acre campus.

RATINGS
Admissions Selectivity Rating: 60*   **Fire Safety Rating:** 60*   **Green Rating:** 60*

STUDENTS AND FACULTY
Student Body: 15% out-of-state, (18 countries represented).
Retention and Graduation: 7% grads go on to further study within 1 year. 7% grads pursue arts and sciences degrees. **Faculty:**

ACADEMICS
Degrees: Bachelor's, master's. **Special Study Options:** internships, study abroad, Undergrads may take grad level classes Off-campus study: summer quarter programs in New York City and Europe; apprenticeships with artists or designers and internships with musuems, agencies, media production companies, architectural firms, and other companies in the United States or abroad. Foreign Exchange Program(s): study abroad in England, France, Germany, Italy, and Spain. **Career services:** Internships.

FACILITIES
Housing: Coed dorms, men's dorms, women's dorms, fraternity/sorority housing.

CAMPUS LIFE
Organizations: 8 honor societies, 3 religious organizations. 5 fraternities, 4 sororities.

ADMISSIONS
Freshman Academic Profile: 94% from public high schools. **Freshman Admission Requirements:** High school diploma is required and GED is accepted.High school diploma is required and GED is not accepted. *Academic units recommended:* 4 English, 3 mathematics, 3 science, 2 foreign language, 3 social studies, 3 academic electives. **Freshman Admission Statistics:** Minimum college GPA of 2.0 required. Lowest grade transferable D. **General Admission Information:** Early decision application deadline 3/1. Regular application deadline 9/1, Nonfall registration accepted. Credit and/or placement offered for CEEB Advanced Placement tests.

COSTS AND FINANCIAL AID
Comprehensive fee $5,100. Room and board $3,495. Average book expense $750. **Required Forms and Deadlines:** FAFSA, institution's own financial aid form. **Types of Aid:** *Need-based scholarships/grants:* State scholarships/grants. *Loans:* FFEL Subsidized Stafford, FFEL PLUS. *Student Employment:* Off-campus job opportunities are good.

SCHOOL OF THE ART INSTITUTE OF CHICAGO

36 South Wabash Avenue, Chicago, IL 60603
Phone: 312-629-6100 **Financial Aid Phone:** 312-629-6600
E-mail: admiss@saic.edu **CEEB Code:** 1713
Fax: 312-629-6101 **Website:** www.saic.edu **ACT Code:** 1136

This private school was founded in 1866.

RATINGS
Admissions Selectivity Rating: 60*   **Fire Safety Rating:** 82   **Green Rating:** 60*

STUDENTS AND FACULTY
Enrollment: 2,359. **Student Body:** 65% female, 35% male, 77% out-of-state, 18% international (34 countries represented). Asian 12%, African-American 3%, Caucasian 56%, Hispanic 9%, Native American 1%.
Retention and Graduation: 74% freshmen return for sophomore year. **Faculty:** Student/faculty ratio 11:1. 134 full-time faculty, 87% hold PhDs, 16% are are members of minority groups, 43% are women.

ACADEMICS
Degrees: Bachelor's, master's, post-bachelor's certificate. **Classes:** Most classes have 10–19 students. **Special Study Options:** Cooperative education program, cross-registration, double major, English as a Second Language (ESL), exchange student program (domestic), independent study, internships, student-

designed major, study abroad, teacher certification program, credit/no credit grading option; multi-disciplinary curriculum; 6 credit off-campus requirement. Special programs offered to physically disabled students include note-taking services, reader services, tape recorders, tutors. **Career services:** Alumni network, alumni services, career/job search classes, career assessment, internships. **Career services highlights include:** SAIC's Cooperative Education Program is the recipient of the National Society for Experiential Education (NSEE) Experiential Education Higher Education Program of the Year Award. The award recognizes an "outstanding educational institution that has demonstrated an exceptional commitment to experiential education in their classrooms or on their campuses."

FACILITIES
Housing: Coed dorms, special housing for disabled students. 99% of campus accessible to physically disabled. **Special Academic Facilities/Equipment:** The School is directly affiliated with the Art Institute of Chicago. Other resources include: The Gene Siskel Film Center; Fashion Resource Center, John M. Flaxman Library and Screening Room Galleries (Betty Rymer, Sullivan Galleries, Student Union Galleries, project space and Gallery X), Joan Flasch Artists' Book Collection,Poetry Center, Roger Brown Resources, Video Data Bank, The Poetry Center, Visiting Artists' Program, Media Center. **Computers:** Students can register for classes online. Administrative functions (other than registration) can be performed online. Undergraduates are required to own a computer.

CAMPUS LIFE
Environment: Metropolis. **Activities:** Dance, drama/theater, literary magazine, radio station, student government, student newspaper, student-run film society, television station, campus ministries, international student organization. **Organizations:** 43 registered organizations, 2 religious organizations. **On-Campus Highlights:** Studio Classrooms, Residence Halls, The Art Institute of Chicago, Gene Siskel Film Center, Galleries.

ADMISSIONS
Freshman Academic Profile: Minimum paper TOEFL 550. Minimum computer TOEFL 213. Minimum web-based TOEFL 80. **Basis for Candidate Selection:** *Very important factors considered include:* Application essay, recommendation(s), rigor of secondary school record, standardized test scores, character/personal qualities, level of applicant's interest, talent/ability. *Important factors considered include:* Class rank, academic GPA, extracurricular activities, first generation, racial/ethnic status, volunteer work. *Other factors considered include:* Alumni/ae relation, geographical residence, interview, state residency, work experience. **Freshman Admission Requirements:** High school diploma is required and GED is accepted. **Freshman Admission Statistics:** 2,075 applied, 81% admitted, 27% enrolled. **Transfer Admission Requirements:** High school transcript, college transcript(s), essay or personal statement, Lowest grade transferable C. **General Admission Information:** Application fee $65. Regular application deadline 6/1. Notification on a rolling basis, beginning on or about 10/1. Nonfall registration accepted. Admission may be deferred for a maximum of 1 year. Credit offered for CEEB Advanced Placement tests.

COSTS AND FINANCIAL AID
Annual tuition $32,550. Room and board $9,200. Required fees $290. Average book expense $2,560. **Required Forms and Deadlines:** FAFSA. Priority financial aid filing date 3/15. **Notification of Awards:** Applicants will be notified of awards on a rolling basis beginning 3/1. **Types of Aid:** *Need-based scholarships/grants:* Federal Pell, SEOG, state scholarships/grants, private scholarships, the school's own gift aid. *Loans:* FFEL Subsidized Stafford, FFEL Unsubsidized Stafford, FFEL PLUS, Federal Perkins, Alternative/private. *Student Employment:* Off-campus job opportunities are fair. **Financial Aid Statistics:** 57% freshmen, 54% undergrads receive need-based scholarship or grant aid. 4% freshmen, 2% undergrads receive non-need-based scholarship or grant aid. 53% freshmen, 53% undergrads receive need-based self-help aid. 63% undergrads borrow to pay for school. Average cumulative indebtedness $33,563. **Criteria for awarding institutional aid:** *Non-need-based:* Academics, art.

SCHOOL OF THE MUSEUM OF FINE ARTS

230 The Fenway, Boston, MA 02115
Phone: 617-369-3626 **Financial Aid Phone:** 617-369-3645
E-mail: admissions@smfa.edu **CEEB Code:** 3794
Fax: 617-369-4264 **Website: ACT Code:** 1895

This private school was founded in 1876. It has a 14-acre campus.

RATINGS
Admissions Selectivity Rating: 60*   **Fire Safety Rating:** 60*   **Green Rating:** 62

STUDENTS AND FACULTY

Enrollment: 564. **Student Body:** 66% female, 34% male, 70% out-of-state, 8% international (39 countries represented). Asian 4%, African American 1%, Caucasian 58%, Hispanic 6%.

Retention and Graduation: 79% freshmen return for sophomore year. 35% freshmen graduate within 4 years. **Faculty:** Student/faculty ratio 10:1. 46 full-time faculty, 70% hold PhDs, 7% are are members of minority groups, 48% are women. 8% of classes are taught by teaching assistants.

ACADEMICS

Degrees: Bachelor's, certificate, diploma, master's, post-bachelor's certificate. **Classes:** Most classes have 10–19 students. **Majors with Highest Enrollment:** Art teacher education; fine arts and art studies; other; fine/studio arts. **Special Study Options:** Cross-registration, double major, English as a Second Language (ESL), exchange student program (domestic), independent study, internships, liberal arts/career combination, student-designed major, study abroad, teacher certification program, Combined Degree opportunity (BFA + BS or BA). All-studio elective program (Diploma). 5th Year study / Certificate for Diploma recipients. Joint BFA with Northeastern University. **Combined degree programs:** BA/BFA, BS/BFA, BFA/Diploma. Special programs offered to physically disabled students include reader services, tape recorders. **Career services:** Alumni network, alumni services, internships. **Career services highlights include:** Our internship program gives students the opportunity to earn studio credit, gain valuable experience, and make contacts in the local art scene. Students in the internship program receive extensive preparation, support and guidance throughout their internship.

FACILITIES

Housing: Coed dorms, Professional off-campus housing assistance. 100% of campus accessible to physically disabled. **Special Academic Facilities/Equipment:** Museum of Fine Arts, Boston; Art galleries; welding equipment; darkrooms; digital equipment; kilns; and more! **Computers:** 100% of classrooms, 100% of dorms, 100% of libraries, 100% of dining areas, 100% of student union, have wireless network access. Students can register for classes online. Administrative functions (other than registration) can be performed online.

CAMPUS LIFE

Environment: Metropolis. **Activities:** Student government, student-run film society. **Organizations:** 10 registered organizations. **On-Campus Highlights:** Classrooms and Studios, Museum of Fine Arts, Boston, Galleries and Exhibition Spaces, Museum and School Libraries, "Art in progress—everywhere you look."

ADMISSIONS

Freshman Academic Profile: SAT Math middle 50% range 450–590. SAT Critical Reading middle 50% range 510–640. SAT Writing middle 50% range 490–628. ACT middle 50% range 21.2–26.2. Minimum paper TOEFL 550. Minimum computer TOEFL 213. Minimum web-based TOEFL 79. **Basis for Candidate Selection:** *Very important factors considered include:* Rigor of secondary school record, talent/ability. *Important factors considered include:* Application essay, academic GPA, interview, level of applicant's interest. *Other factors considered include:* Class rank, recommendation(s), standardized test scores, alumni/ae relation, character/personal qualities, extracurricular activities, first generation, geographical residence, volunteer work, work experience. **Freshman Admission Requirements:** High school diploma is required and GED is accepted. **Freshman Admission Statistics:** 743 applied, 81% admitted, 17% enrolled. **Transfer Admission Requirements:** College transcript(s), essay or personal statement, minimum college GPA of 1.75 required. Lowest grade transferable C–. **General Admission Information:** Application fee $65. Notification on a rolling basis, beginning on or about 3/15. Nonfall registration accepted. Admission may be deferred for a maximum of 1 year. Neither credit nor placement offered for CEEB Advanced Placement tests.

COSTS AND FINANCIAL AID

Annual tuition $29,540. Required fees $2,819. Average book expense $1,500. **Required Forms and Deadlines:** FAFSA, institution's own financial aid form Financial aid filing deadline 3/15. Priority financial aid filing date 3/15. **Notification of Awards:** Applicants will be notified of awards on a rolling basis beginning 4/15. **Types of Aid:** *Need-based scholarships/grants:* Federal Pell, SEOG, state scholarships/grants, private scholarships, the school's own gift aid. *Loans:* FFEL Subsidized Stafford, FFEL Unsubsidized Stafford, FFEL PLUS, state loans *Student Employment:* Federal Work-Study Program available. Institutional employment available. Highest amount earned per year from on-campus jobs $3,500. Off-campus job opportunities are excellent. **Financial Aid Statistics:** 69% freshmen, 75% undergrads receive need-based scholarship or grant aid. 27% freshmen, 4% undergrads receive non-need-based scholarship or grant aid. 65% freshmen, 65% undergrads receive need-based self-help aid. 79% freshmen, 75% undergrads receive any aid. Average cumulative indebtedness $8,179. **Criteria for awarding institutional aid:** *Non-need-based:* Art.

SCHOOL OF VISUAL ARTS

209 East 23rd Street, New York, NY 10010
Phone: 212-592-2100 **Financial Aid Phone:** 212-592-2030
E-mail: admissions@sva.edu **CEEB Code:** 2835
Fax: 212-592-2116 **Website:** www.sva.edu **ACT Code:** 2895

This proprietary school was founded in 1947.

RATINGS

Admissions Selectivity Rating: 78   **Fire Safety Rating:** 96   **Green Rating:** 60*

STUDENTS AND FACULTY

Enrollment: 3,332. **Student Body:** 55% female, 45% male, 57% out-of-state, 15% international (55 countries represented). Asian 13%, African American 3%, Caucasian 49%, Hispanic 10%, Native American 1%.

Retention and Graduation: 86% freshmen return for sophomore year. 60% freshmen graduate within 4 years. **Faculty:** Student/faculty ratio 8.5:1. 163 full-time faculty, 24% hold PhDs, 4% are are members of minority groups, 31% are women.

ACADEMICS

Degrees: Bachelor's, master's. **Classes:** Most classes have 10–19 students. **Majors with Highest Enrollment:** film/video and photographic arts, other; graphic design; photography. **Special Study Options:** English as a Second Language (ESL), exchange student program (domestic), honors program, internships, liberal arts/career combination, study abroad, teacher certification program. **Honors programs:** SVA offers an honors program for incoming freshmen; program involves a two year commitment, with an optional third year. Special programs offered to physically disabled students include note-taking services, reader services, tape recorders, tutors. **Career services:** Alumni network, alumni services, internships.

FACILITIES

Housing: Coed dorms, women's dorms. 100% of campus accessible to physically disabled. **Special Academic Facilities/Equipment:** Visual Art Museum, Milton Glaser Design Study Center and Archives, 8 student galleries. **Computers:** 100% of classrooms, 100% of libraries, 100% of student union, have wireless network access. Students can register for classes online. Administrative functions (other than registration) can be performed online.

CAMPUS LIFE

Environment: Metropolis. **Activities:** Literary magazine, radio station, student government, student-run film society, yearbook. **Organizations:** 23 registered organizations, 3 religious organizations. **On-Campus Highlights:** Visual Arts Gallery, Westside Gallery, Visual Arts Museum, Visual Arts Student Association, Student Lounge. **Environmental Initiatives:** Yes, we do recycle our trash, but we do it off site. Due to space limitations we don't have an area to collect and sort out recyclables from our trash, nor do we have the space to store the recyclables prior to shipment to an appropriate recycler. To accomplish this we rely on an outside contractor to collect our trash and sort it at their facilities. They ensure that anything that can be recycled from our trash finds its way to the recyclers. SVA recycles batteries used in electronic equipment as well as computers, monitors printers and other consumer electronics. We also recycle florescent light bulbs and electronic components. We monitor the waste water that comes from areas like the Photo Labs, Printmaking and the Sculpture Labs. The waste water is tested to make sure that it is in compliance with all city, state and federal regulations. We also do periodic air and water quality checks.

ADMISSIONS

Freshman Academic Profile: Average high school GPA 3.11. 60% from public high schools. SAT Math middle 50% range 460–590. SAT Critical Reading middle 50% range 450–580. SAT Writing middle 50% range 450–580. ACT middle 50% range 20–25. Minimum paper TOEFL 550. Minimum computer TOEFL 213. **Basis for Candidate Selection:** *Very important factors considered include:* Application essay, academic GPA, rigor of secondary school record, interview, level of applicant's interest, talent/ability. *Other factors considered include:* Recommendation(s), standardized test scores, alumni/ae relation, extracurricular activities, volunteer work, work experience. **Freshman Admission Requirements:** High school diploma is required and GED is accepted. *Academic units recommended:* 4 English, 4 social studies, 4 history, 2 visual/performing arts. **Freshman Admission Statistics:** 2,821 applied, 67% admitted, 35% enrolled. **Transfer Admission Requirements:** College transcript(s), essay or personal statement, statement of good standing from prior institution(s). Minimum college GPA of 2.0 required. Lowest grade transferable C. **General Admission Information:** Application fee $50. Notification on a rolling basis, beginning on or about 2/1. Nonfall registration not accepted. Admission may be deferred for a maximum of 1 year. Credit offered for CEEB Advanced Placement tests.

COSTS AND FINANCIAL AID

Annual tuition $26,800. Room and board $12,700. Average book expense $3,150. **Required Forms and Deadlines:** FAFSA, state aid form Financial aid filing deadline 3/1. Priority financial aid filing date 2/1. **Notification of Awards:** Applicants will be notified of awards on a rolling basis beginning 2/15. **Types of Aid:** *Need-based scholarships/grants:* Federal Pell, SEOG, state scholarships/grants, private scholarships, the school's own gift aid, alternate loans. *Loans:* FFEL Subsidized Stafford, FFEL Unsubsidized Stafford, Federal Perkins. *Student Employment:* Federal Work-Study Program available. Off-campus job opportunities are fair. **Financial Aid Statistics:** 39% freshmen, 38% undergrads receive need-based scholarship or grant aid. 11% freshmen, 10% undergrads receive non-need-based scholarship or grant aid. 55% freshmen, 52% undergrads receive need-based self-help aid. 60% freshmen, 55% undergrads receive any aid. 54.9% undergrads borrow to pay for school. Average cumulative indebtedness $34,480. **Criteria for awarding institutional aid:** *Non-need-based:* Art.

SCHREINER UNIVERSITY

2100 Memorial Boulevard, Kerrville, TX 78028-5697
Phone: 830-792-7217 **Financial Aid Phone:** 830-792-7217
E-mail: admissions@schreiner.edu **CEEB Code:** 6647
Fax: 830-896-3232 **Website:** www.schreiner.edu **ACT Code:** 4168

This private school, affiliated with the Presbyterian Church, was founded in 1923. It has a 175-acre campus.

RATINGS

Admissions Selectivity Rating: 78   **Fire Safety Rating:** 60*   **Green Rating:** 60*

STUDENTS AND FACULTY

Enrollment: 1,013. **Student Body:** 56% female, 44% male, international. African American 4%, Caucasian 72%, Hispanic 22%, Native American 2%. **Retention and Graduation:** 68% freshmen return for sophomore year. 26% freshmen graduate within 4 years. **Faculty:** Student/faculty ratio 14:1. 61 full-time faculty, 67% hold PhDs, 8% are are members of minority groups, 48% are women.

ACADEMICS

Degrees: Associate, bachelor's, certificate, master's, post-bachelor's certificate, post-master's certificate. **Classes:** Most classes have 20–29 students. Most lab/discussion sessions have 20–29 students. **Majors with Highest Enrollment:** Biology/biological sciences; design and applied arts, other; psychology. **Special Study Options:** Accelerated program, double major, dual enrollment, honors program, independent study, internships, liberal arts/career combination, student-designed major, study abroad, teacher certification program, weekend college. Special programs offered to physically disabled students include note-taking services, reader services, tape recorders, tutors. **Career services:** Alumni network, alumni services, career/job search classes, career assessment, internships, regional alumni.

FACILITIES

Housing: Coed dorms, special housing for disabled students, apartments for married students, apartments for single students. 95% of campus accessible to physically disabled. **Computers:** 100% of classrooms, 100% of dorms, 100% of libraries, 100% of dining areas, 100% of student union, 30% of common outdoor areas have wireless network access.

CAMPUS LIFE

Environment: Town. **Activities:** Choral groups, dance, drama/theater, literary magazine, music ensembles, musical theater, pep band, student government, student newspaper, symphony orchestra, campus ministries. **Organizations:** 35 registered organizations, 5 honor societies, 7 religious organizations. 2 fraternities, 2 sororities. **Athletics (Intercollegiate):** *Men:* Baseball, basketball, golf, soccer, tennis. *Women:* Basketball, cheerleading, golf, soccer, softball, tennis, volleyball. **On-Campus Highlights:** Caillioux Campus Activity Center, Logan Library, Griffin Welcome Center, Deitert Auditorium, Gus Schreiner Student Center.

ADMISSIONS

Freshman Academic Profile: Average high school GPA 3.54. 16% in top 10% of high school class, 43% in top 25% of high school class, 79% in top 50% of high school class. SAT Math middle 50% range 440–570. SAT Critical Reading middle 50% range 440–550. SAT Writing middle 50% range 420–530. ACT middle 50% range 18–23. Minimum paper TOEFL 550. Minimum computer TOEFL 213. Minimum web-based TOEFL 79. **Basis for Candidate Selection:** *Important factors considered include:* Class rank, application essay, academic GPA, rigor of secondary school record, standardized test scores,

---

character/personal qualities, interview, level of applicant's interest, volunteer work, work experience. *Other factors considered include:* Recommendation(s), extracurricular activities, talent/ability. **Freshman Admission Requirements:** High school diploma is required and GED is accepted. *Academic units recommended:* 4 English, 3 mathematics, 3 science, (2 science labs), 2 foreign language, 2 social studies, 2 history, 1 visual/performing arts, 1 computer science. **Freshman Admission Statistics:** 991 applied, 62% admitted, 47% enrolled. **Transfer Admission Requirements:** College transcript(s), minimum college GPA of 2.0 required. Lowest grade transferable D. **General Admission Information:** Application fee $25. Regular application deadline 8/1. Nonfall registration accepted. Admission may be deferred for a maximum of 1 semester. Credit and/or placement offered for CEEB Advanced Placement tests.

COSTS AND FINANCIAL AID

Annual tuition $18,131. Room and board $8,726. Required fees $600. Average book expense $1,200. **Required Forms and Deadlines:** FAFSA, TAFSA. **Notification of Awards:** Applicants will be notified of awards on a rolling basis beginning 2/15. **Types of Aid:** *Need-based scholarships/grants:* Federal Pell, SEOG, state scholarships/grants, private scholarships, the school's own gift aid. *Loans:* Direct Subsidized Stafford, Direct Unsubsidized Stafford, Direct PLUS, FFEL Subsidized Stafford, FFEL Unsubsidized Stafford, FFEL PLUS, state loans *Student Employment:* Federal Work-Study Program available. Institutional employment available. Off-campus job opportunities are good. **Financial Aid Statistics:** 76% undergrads receive need-based scholarship or grant aid. 9% undergrads receive non-need-based scholarship or grant aid. 64% undergrads receive need-based self-help aid. 100% freshmen, 97% undergrads receive any aid. 97% undergrads borrow to pay for school. Average cumulative indebtedness $27,986. **Criteria for awarding institutional aid:** *Non-need-based:* Academics, art, leadership, music/drama, religious affiliation.

SCRIPPS COLLEGE

1030 Columbia Avenue, Claremont, CA 91711
Phone: 909-621-8149 **Financial Aid Phone:** 909-621-8275
E-mail: admission@scrippscollege.edu **CEEB Code:** 4693
Fax: 909-607-7508 **Website:** www.scrippscollege.edu **ACT Code:** 426

This private school was founded in 1926. It has a 37-acre campus.

RATINGS

Admissions Selectivity Rating: 97   **Fire Safety Rating:** 68   **Green Rating:** 81

STUDENTS AND FACULTY

Enrollment: 898. **Student Body:** 100% female, 58% out-of-state, 2% international (14 countries represented). Asian 13%, African American 4%, Caucasian 46%, Hispanic 9%, Native American 1%. **Retention and Graduation:** 88% freshmen return for sophomore year. 85% freshmen graduate within 4 years. **Faculty:** Student/faculty ratio 10:1. 81 full-time faculty, 100% hold PhDs, 21% are are members of minority groups, 56% are women.

ACADEMICS

Degrees: Bachelor's, post-bachelor's certificate. **Classes:** Most classes have 10–19 students. Most lab/discussion sessions have 10–19 students. **Majors with Highest Enrollment:** English language and literature; international relations and affairs; psychology. **Special Study Options:** Accelerated program, cross-registration, double major, dual enrollment, exchange student program (domestic), independent study, internships, student-designed major, study abroad **Honors programs:** Honors programs in all academic majors available. **Combined degree programs:** BA/MA, BA/MEng, BA/MBA. Special programs offered to physically disabled students include note-taking services, reader services, tape recorders, tutors. **Career services:** Alumni network, alumni services, career/job search classes, career assessment, internships, regional alumni. **Career services highlights include:** Career Planning & Resources offers a variety of internship resources to assist students in their internship search. Scripps is a member of the National Internship Consortium, with 16 schools across the country sharing over 9,000 internship listings. CP&R is pleased to offer a number of internship grants, which allow students to pursue opportunities without having to worry about compensation.

FACILITIES

Housing: special housing for disabled students, women's dorms, apartments for single students, small college-owned houses. 85% of campus accessible to physically disabled. **Special Academic Facilities/Equipment:** Art center, music complex, dance studio, humanities museum and institute, science center, biological field station, field house. **Computers:** 100% of classrooms, 100% of dorms, 100% of libraries, 100% of dining areas, 100% of common outdoor areas have wireless network access. Administrative functions (other than registration) can be performed online.

CAMPUS LIFE

Environment: Town. **Activities:** Choral groups, dance, drama/theater, literary magazine, music ensembles, radio station, student government, student newspaper, symphony orchestra, yearbook, campus ministries, international student organization, Model UN. **Organizations:** 200 registered organizations, 5 honor societies, 7 religious organizations. **Athletics (Intercollegiate):** *Women:* Basketball, cross-country, diving, golf, lacrosse, soccer, softball, swimming, tennis, track/field (outdoor), volleyball, water polo. **On-Campus Highlights:** Williamson Gallery, Rare book room, Denison Library, Margaret Fowler Garden, Malott Commons, Graffitti Wall, Sallie Tiernan Field House. **Environmental Initiatives:** Publication of current practices on the web. Working with students on recycling/composting programs. Requesting information from building contractors on sustainability practices/materials.

ADMISSIONS

Freshman Academic Profile: Average high school GPA 4.05. 69% in top 10% of high school class, 94% in top 25% of high school class, 99% in top 50% of high school class. 55% from public high schools. SAT Math middle 50% range 620–700. SAT Critical Reading middle 50% range 640–730. SAT Writing middle 50% range 640–730. ACT middle 50% range 27–32. Minimum paper TOEFL 600. Minimum computer TOEFL 250. **Basis for Candidate Selection:** *Very important factors considered include:* Class rank, application essay, academic GPA, recommendation(s), rigor of secondary school record, standardized test scores, alumni/ae relation, character/personal qualities, extracurricular activities, first generation, interview, racial/ethnic status, talent/ability, volunteer work, work experience. *Important factors considered include:* geographical residence. **Freshman Admission Requirements:** High school diploma is required and GED is accepted. *Academic units required:* 4 English, 3 mathematics, 3 science, 3 foreign language, 3 social studies. **Freshman Admission Statistics:** 2,061 applied, 33% admitted, 30% enrolled. **Transfer Admission Requirements:** High school transcript, college transcript(s), essay or personal statement, standardized test scores, statement of good standing from prior institution(s). Minimum college GPA of 3.0 required. Lowest grade transferable C. **General Admission Information:** Application fee $60. Early decision application deadline 11/1. Regular application deadline 1/1. Regular notification 4/1. Nonfall registration accepted. Admission may be deferred for a maximum of 1 year. Credit offered for CEEB Advanced Placement tests.

COSTS AND FINANCIAL AID

Annual tuition $38,486. Room and board $11,850. Required fees $214. Average book expense $800. **Required Forms and Deadlines:** FAFSA, CSS/Financial Aid PROFILE, state aid form, noncustodial PROFILE, business/farm supplement. Verification worksheet, signed copies of parent Institution Verification form, parent and student federal tax returns. Financial aid filing deadline 2/1. Priority financial aid filing date 2/1. **Notification of Awards:** Applicants will be notified of awards on or about 4/1. **Types of Aid:** *Need-based scholarships/ grants:* Federal Pell, SEOG, state scholarships/grants, private scholarships, the school's own gift aid. *Loans:* FFEL Subsidized Stafford, FFEL Unsubsidized Stafford, FFEL PLUS, Federal Perkins, college/university loans from institutional funds. *Student Employment:* Federal Work-Study Program available. Institutional employment available. Off-campus job opportunities are good. **Financial Aid Statistics:** 29% freshmen, 42% undergrads receive need-based scholarship or grant aid. 6% freshmen, 12% undergrads receive non-need-based scholarship or grant aid. 25% freshmen, 37% undergrads receive need-based self-help aid. 44% freshmen, 54% undergrads receive any aid. 38% undergrads borrow to pay for school. Average cumulative indebtedness $11,270. **Criteria for awarding institutional aid:** *Non-need-based:* Academics, leadership.

See page 1232.

SEATTLE PACIFIC UNIVERSITY

3307 3rd Avenue West, Seattle, WA 98119-1997
Phone: 206-281-2021 **Financial Aid Phone:** 206-281-2061
E-mail: admissions@spu.edu **CEEB Code:** 4694
Fax: 206-281-2669 **Website:** www.spu.edu **ACT Code:** 4476

This private school, affiliated with the Methodist Church, was founded in 1891. It has a 35-acre campus.

RATINGS

Admissions Selectivity Rating: 87 **Fire Safety Rating:** 74 **Green Rating:** 88

STUDENTS AND FACULTY

Enrollment: 3,001. **Student Body:** 67% female, 33% male, 39% out-of-state, 1% international (43 countries represented). Asian 9%, African American 3%, Caucasian 76%, Hispanic 4%, Native American 1%.
Retention and Graduation: 87% freshmen return for sophomore year. 60% freshmen graduate within 4 years. **Faculty:** Student/faculty ratio 14:1. 191 full-time faculty, 86% hold PhDs, 8% are are members of minority groups, 41% are women.

ACADEMICS

Degrees: Bachelor's, doctoral, master's, post-master's certificate. **Classes:** Most classes have 10–19 students. Most lab/discussion sessions have fewer than 10 students. **Majors with Highest Enrollment:** Biology/biological sciences; business/commerce; nursing/registered nurse (RN, ASN, BSN, MSN). **Special Study Options:** Distance learning, double major, exchange student program (domestic), external degree program, honors program, independent study, internships, liberal arts/career combination, student-designed major, study abroad, teacher certification program. **Honors programs:** University Scholars Special programs offered to physically disabled students include note-taking services, reader services, tape recorders. **Career services:** Alumni network, alumni services, career/job search classes, career assessment, internships **Career services highlights include:** Very strong internship program. Also great 1 & 2 credit classes offered as electives.

FACILITIES

Housing: Coed dorms, apartments for married students, apartments for single students, theme housing. **Special Academic Facilities/Equipment:** Art gallery, theatre facilities **Computers:** 100% of classrooms, 90% of dorms, 100% of libraries, 100% of dining areas, 100% of student union, 50% of common outdoor areas have wireless network access. Students can register for classes online. Administrative functions (other than registration) can be performed online.

CAMPUS LIFE

Environment: Metropolis. **Activities:** Choral groups, drama/theater, jazz band, literary magazine, music ensembles, musical theater, pep band, radio station, student government, student newspaper, symphony orchestra, yearbook, campus ministries. **Organizations:** 63 registered organizations, 1 honor societies, 7 religious organizations. **Athletics (Intercollegiate):** *Men:* Badminton, basketball, bowling, crew/rowing, cross-country, football, soccer, softball, table tennis, tennis, track/field (outdoor), track/field (indoor), volleyball, weight lifting. *Women:* Badminton, basketball, bowling, crew/rowing, cross-country, football, gymnastics, soccer, softball, table tennis, tennis, track/field (outdoor), track/field (indoor), volleyball, weight lifting. **On-Campus Highlights:** Pura Vida Coffee Shop, Royal Brougham Pavilion, Weter Lounge, Student Union Building, The Science Building. **Environmental Initiatives:** 1. Developing relationships between the Facility & Project Management Office and academic departments to support sustainability-related student projects on campus, including an organic garden, solar photovoltaic installation, and building energy audit. 2. Comprehensive waste diversion program, achieving a 52% diversion rate (by weight) in RecycleMania 2009. Year-long programming is supplemented by "donation stations" across campus at the end of each academic year. At these stations, students moving out can donate food, clothing, and household items as well as drop off their recycling. 3. Alternative fleet vehicles: Currently, 5 of our 22 maintenance fleet vehicles are electric. We are in the process of phasing more EVs into our fleet, at a rate of one or two vehicles per year. Because 94% of Seattle's electricity comes from hydro- and wind power, this will allow our fleet to approach carbon neutrality.

ADMISSIONS

Freshman Academic Profile: Average high school GPA 3.56. SAT Math middle 50% range 490–620. SAT Critical Reading middle 50% range 500–630. SAT Writing middle 50% range 500–590. ACT middle 50% range 21–28. Minimum paper TOEFL 550. Minimum computer TOEFL 213. **Basis for Candidate Selection:** *Very important factors considered include:* Application essay, academic GPA, recommendation(s), rigor of secondary school record, standardized test scores. *Important factors considered include:* Character/personal qualities, extracurricular activities, first generation, interview, level of applicant's interest, racial/ethnic status, religious affiliation/commitment, talent/ability, volunteer work, work experience. *Other factors considered include:* Class rank, alumni/ae relation, geographical residence. **Freshman Admission Requirements:** High school diploma is required and GED is accepted. *Academic units recommended:* 4 English, 3 mathematics, 3 science, 3 foreign language, 2 history. **Freshman Admission Statistics:** 1,973 applied, 93% admitted, 37% enrolled. **Transfer Admission Requirements:** College transcript(s), essay or personal statement, minimum college GPA of 2.5 required. Lowest grade transferable C. **General Admission Information:** Application fee $45. Regular application deadline 2/1. Regular notification 3/1. Nonfall registration accepted. Credit offered for CEEB Advanced Placement tests.

COSTS AND FINANCIAL AID

Annual tuition $27,450. . Room and board $8,544. Required fees $360. Average book expense $942. **Required Forms and Deadlines:** FAFSA. Priority financial aid filing date 2/1. **Notification of Awards:** Applicants will be notified of awards on a rolling basis beginning 3/11. **Types of Aid:** *Need-based scholarships/grants:* Federal Pell, SEOG, state scholarships/grants, private scholarships, the school's own gift aid. *Loans:* FFEL Subsidized Stafford, FFEL Unsubsidized Stafford, FFEL PLUS, Federal Perkins, Federal Nursing, college/university loans from institutional funds. *Student Employment:* Federal Work-Study Program available. Institutional employment available. **Financial Aid Statistics:** 74% freshmen, 67% undergrads receive need-based scholarship or grant aid. 68% freshmen, 63% undergrads receive need-based self-help aid. 1% freshmen, 2% undergrads receive athletic scholarships. 70% undergrads borrow to pay for school. Average cumulative indebtedness $25,799. **Criteria for awarding institutional aid:** *Non-need-based:* Academics, alumni affiliation, art, athletics, leadership, minority status, music/drama, religious affiliation.

SEATTLE UNIVERSITY

Admissions Office, 900 Broadway, Seattle, WA 98122-1090
Phone: 206-296-2000 **Financial Aid Phone:** 206-296-2000
E-mail: admissions@seattleu.edu **CEEB Code:** 4695
Fax: 206-296-5656 **Website:** www.seattleu.edu **ACT Code:** 4478

This private school, affiliated with the Roman CatholiC–Jesuit Church, was founded in 1891. It has a 50-acre campus.

RATINGS
Admissions Selectivity Rating: 87   **Fire Safety Rating:** 83   **Green Rating:** 94

STUDENTS AND FACULTY
Enrollment: 4,306. **Student Body:** 60% female, 40% male, 49% out-of-state, 10% international (74 countries represented). Asian 19%, African American 5%, Caucasian 48%, Hispanic 7%, Native American 1%.
Retention and Graduation: 90% freshmen return for sophomore year. 52% freshmen graduate within 4 years. **Faculty:** Student/faculty ratio 13:1. 435 full-time faculty, 79% hold PhDs, 8% are are members of minority groups, 46% are women.

ACADEMICS
Degrees: Bachelor's, master's, post-bachelor's certificate, post-master's certificate. **Classes:** Most classes have 10–19 students. Most lab/discussion sessions have 10–19 students. **Majors with Highest Enrollment:** Finance; marketing/marketing management; nursing/registered nurse (RN, ASN, BSN, MSN). **Special Study Options:** Cooperative education program, cross-registration, double major, English as a Second Language (ESL), honors program, independent study, internships, liberal arts/career combination, student-designed major, study abroad. **Honors programs:** The University Honors program provides students of high ability and motivation the opportunity to join a small, select, two-year-long learning community. The program is taken in the freshman and sophomore years and fulfills most of the university's Core Curriculum requirements. Honors programs are also offered within majors. **Combined degree programs:** BA/MBA. Special programs offered to physically disabled students include note-taking services, reader services, tape recorders, tutors. **Career services:** Alumni network, alumni services, career/job search classes, career assessment, internships

FACILITIES
Housing: Coed dorms, special housing for disabled students, apartments for single students, theme housing. 95% of campus accessible to physically disabled. **Special Academic Facilities/Equipment:** Observatory, electron microscope, St. Ignatius Chapel **Computers:** 100% of classrooms, 20% of dorms, 100% of libraries, 100% of dining areas, 100% of student union, 95% of common outdoor areas have wireless network access. Students can register for classes online. Administrative functions (other than registration) can be performed online.

CAMPUS LIFE
Environment: Metropolis. **Activities:** Choral groups, drama/theater, jazz band, literary magazine, music ensembles, pep band, radio station, student government, student newspaper, campus ministries. **Organizations:** 130 registered organizations. **Athletics (Intercollegiate):** *Men:* Baseball, basketball, cross-country, golf, soccer, swimming, tennis, track/field (outdoor), track/field (indoor). *Women:* Basketball, cross-country, golf, soccer, softball, swimming, tennis, track/field (outdoor), track/field (indoor), volleyball. **On-Campus Highlights:** Chapel of Saint Ignatius, Brand new Student Center, Award Winning

Grounds and Open Space, Sullivan Hall, home of the School of Law. **Environmental Initiatives:** The 48 acres have been maintained pesticide-free since 1986 by using Integrated Pest Management methods. The on-site composting facility annually turns 16 tons of kitchen food waste generated by on-campus restaurants and cafes into compost—which is applied on our landscape. The pre-consumer food waste includes: fruit and veggie trimmings, old bread, expired grains, all the coffee grounds from the cafes and waxed cardboard. There are 14 electric vehicles in the Facilities maintenance staff fleet.

ADMISSIONS
Freshman Academic Profile: Average high school GPA 3.59. 30% in top 10% of high school class, 61% in top 25% of high school class, 93% in top 50% of high school class. 63% from public high schools. SAT Math middle 50% range 520–640. SAT Critical Reading middle 50% range 520–640. SAT Writing middle 50% range 510–620. ACT middle 50% range 23–29. Minimum paper TOEFL 520. Minimum computer TOEFL 190. **Basis for Candidate Selection:** *Very important factors considered include:* Academic GPA, rigor of secondary school record, standardized test scores, character/personal qualities. *Important factors considered include:* Application essay, recommendation(s), extracurricular activities, level of applicant's interest. *Other factors considered include:* Class rank, alumni/ae relation, first generation, geographical residence, interview, racial/ethnic status, religious affiliation/commitment, state residency, talent/ability, volunteer work, work experience. **Freshman Admission Requirements:** High school diploma is required and GED is accepted. *Academic units required:* 4 English, 3 mathematics, 2 science, (2 science labs), 2 foreign language, 2 social studies, 1 history, 2 academic electives. *Academic units recommended:* 4 English, 3 mathematics, 2 science, (2 science labs), 2 foreign language, 2 social studies, 1 history, 2 academic electives. **Freshman Admission Statistics:** 5,578 applied, 66% admitted, 20% enrolled. **Transfer Admission Requirements:** College transcript(s), essay or personal statement, statement of good standing from prior institution(s). Minimum college GPA of 2.25 required. Lowest grade transferable C–. **General Admission Information:** Application fee $50. Notification on a rolling basis, beginning on or about 2/1. Nonfall registration accepted. Admission may be deferred for a maximum of 1 year. Credit and/or placement offered for CEEB Advanced Placement tests.

COSTS AND FINANCIAL AID
Annual tuition $29,340. Room and board $8,805. Average book expense $1,440. **Required Forms and Deadlines:** FAFSA. Priority financial aid filing date 2/1. **Notification of Awards:** Applicants will be notified of awards on a rolling basis beginning 3/21. **Types of Aid:** *Need-based scholarships/grants:* Federal Pell, SEOG, state scholarships/grants, private scholarships, the school's own gift aid, Federal Nursing Scholarships. *Loans:* Direct Subsidized Stafford, Direct Unsubsidized Stafford, Direct PLUS, Federal Perkins, Federal Nursing. **Financial Aid Statistics:** 67% freshmen, 60% undergrads receive need-based scholarship or grant aid. 9% freshmen, 8% undergrads receive non-need-based scholarship or grant aid. 58% freshmen, 52% undergrads receive need-based self-help aid. 1% freshmen, 1% undergrads receive athletic scholarships. 88% freshmen, 76% undergrads receive any aid. 79% undergrads borrow to pay for school. Average cumulative indebtedness $26,665. **Criteria for awarding institutional aid:** *Non-need-based:* Academics, alumni affiliation, athletics, leadership, minority status, music/drama, state/district residency.

See page 1234.

SETON HALL UNIVERSITY

Enrollment Services, 400 South Orange, South Orange, NJ 07079
Phone: 973-761-9332 **Financial Aid Phone:** 973-761-9332
E-mail: thehall@shu.edu **CEEB Code:** 2811
Fax: 973-275-2040 **Website:** www.shu.edu **ACT Code:** 2606

This private school, affiliated with the Roman Catholic Church, was founded in 1856. It has a 58-acre campus.

RATINGS
Admissions Selectivity Rating: 80   **Fire Safety Rating:** 81   **Green Rating:** 60*

STUDENTS AND FACULTY
Enrollment: 4,951. **Student Body:** 55% female, 45% male, 26% out-of-state, 1% international (71 countries represented). Asian 6%, African American 11%, Caucasian 51%, Hispanic 11%.

Retention and Graduation: 83% freshmen return for sophomore year. 41% freshmen graduate within 4 years. 30% grads go on to further study within 1 year. 9% grads pursue arts and sciences degrees. 7% grads pursue law degrees. 5% grads pursue business degrees. 9% grads pursue medical degrees. **Faculty:** Student/faculty ratio 14:1. 441 full-time faculty, 90% hold PhDs, 15% are are members of minority groups, 46% are women. 4% of classes are taught by teaching assistants.

ACADEMICS
Degrees: Bachelor's, first professional, master's, post-master's certificate. **Classes:** Most classes have 10–19 students. Most lab/discussion sessions have 10–19 students. **Majors with Highest Enrollment:** Communication studies/ speech communication and rhetoric; criminal justice/safety studies; nursing/registered nurse (RN, ASN, BSN, MSN). **Special Study Options:** Accelerated program, cooperative education program, cross-registration, distance learning, double major, dual enrollment, English as a Second Language (ESL), honors program, independent study, internships, study abroad, teacher certification program. **Honors programs:** University Honors Program fosters intellectual development through academic challenge. A structured sequence of colloquia and seminars helps to develop critical thinking abilities. Student study the great texts of the past and also have the opportunity to attend operas, theater, museums, concerts and other cultural events. **Combined degree programs:** BA/MA, BA/MEng, BS/MS phys asst or OT or athl trng, BS/D phys ther. Special programs offered to physically disabled students include note-taking services, reader services, tape recorders, tutors. **Career services:** Alumni network, career/job search classes, career assessment, internships, regional alumni. **Career services highlights include:** Internships.

FACILITIES
Housing: Coed dorms, special housing for disabled students, apartments for single students 94% of campus accessible to physically disabled. **Special Academic Facilities/Equipment:** Art, natural history, museums, theatre-in-the-round, archaeological research center, TV studio, radio station. **Computers:** 100% of classrooms, 100% of dorms, 100% of libraries, 100% of dining areas, 100% of student union, 100% of common outdoor areas have wireless network access. Students can register for classes online. Administrative functions (other than registration) can be performed online. Undergraduates are required to own a computer.

CAMPUS LIFE
Environment: Village. **Activities:** Choral groups, drama/theater, pep band, radio station, student government, television station **Organizations:** 100 registered organizations, 13 honor societies, 3 religious organizations. **Athletics (Intercollegiate):** *Men:* Baseball, basketball, cross-country, diving, golf, soccer, swimming, track/field (outdoor). *Women:* Basketball, cross-country, diving, soccer, softball, swimming, tennis, track/field (outdoor). **On-Campus Highlights:** Jubilee Hall, University Center, Walsh Library, Recreation Center, Chapel.

ADMISSIONS
Freshman Academic Profile: Average high school GPA 3.15. 28% in top 10% of high school class, 60% in top 25% of high school class, 88% in top 50% of high school class. 70% from public high schools. SAT Math middle 50% range 500–600. SAT Critical Reading middle 50% range 480–590. Minimum paper TOEFL 550. Minimum computer TOEFL 213. **Basis for Candidate Selection:** *Very important factors considered include:* Application essay, academic GPA, recommendation(s), rigor of secondary school record, standardized test scores. *Important factors considered include:* extracurricular activities, volunteer work, work experience. *Other factors considered include:* Class rank, character/personal qualities, interview, talent/ability. **Freshman Admission Requirements:** High school diploma is required and GED is accepted. *Academic units required:* 4 English, 3 mathematics, 1 science, (1 science labs), 2 foreign language, 2 social studies, 4 academic electives. **Freshman Admission Statistics:** 5,365 applied, 77% admitted, 25% enrolled. Minimum college GPA of 2.5 required. Lowest grade transferable C. **General Admission Information:** Application fee $55. Notification on a rolling basis, beginning on or about 12/1. Nonfall registration accepted. Admission may be deferred for a maximum of 1 year. Credit and/or placement offered for CEEB Advanced Placement tests.

COSTS AND FINANCIAL AID
Annual tuition $22,770. Room and board $10,466. Required fees $1,950. **Required Forms and Deadlines:** FAFSA. Priority financial aid filing date 2/15. **Notification of Awards:** Applicants will be notified of awards on a rolling basis beginning 3/1. **Types of Aid:** *Need-based scholarships/grants:* Federal Pell, SEOG, state scholarships/grants, private scholarships, the school's own gift aid. *Loans:* FFEL Subsidized Stafford, FFEL Unsubsidized Stafford, FFEL PLUS, Federal Perkins, state loans *Student Employment:* Federal Work-Study Program available. Institutional employment available. Highest amount earned per year from on-campus jobs $2,700. Off-campus job opportunities are good. **Financial Aid Statistics:** 54% freshmen, 38% undergrads receive need-based scholarship or grant aid. 47% freshmen, 33% undergrads receive non-need-based scholarship or grant aid. 45% freshmen, 45% undergrads receive need-

based self-help aid. 4% freshmen, 4% undergrads receive athletic scholarships. 91% freshmen, 86% undergrads receive any aid. 6% undergrads borrow to pay for school. Average cumulative indebtedness $16,160. **Criteria for awarding institutional aid:** *Non-need-based:* Academics, alumni affiliation, athletics, minority status, state/district residency.

See page 1236.

SETON HILL UNIVERSITY

1 Seton Hill Drive, Greensburg, PA 15601
Phone: 724-838-4255 **Financial Aid Phone:** 724-838-4293
E-mail: admit@setonhill.edu **CEEB Code:** 2812
Fax: 724-830-1294 **Website:** www.setonhill.edu **ACT Code:** 3688

This private school, affiliated with the Roman Catholic Church, was founded in 1883. It has a 200-acre campus.

RATINGS
Admissions Selectivity Rating: 82   **Fire Safety Rating:** 76   **Green Rating:** 60*

STUDENTS AND FACULTY
Enrollment: 1,483. **Student Body:** 62% female, 38% male, 20% out-of-state, 2% international (23 countries represented). Asian 1%, African American 9%, Caucasian 82%, Hispanic 1%.
Retention and Graduation: 77% freshmen return for sophomore year. 46% freshmen graduate within 4 years. 30% grads go on to further study within 1 year. 21% grads pursue arts and sciences degrees. 1% grads pursue law degrees. 9% grads pursue business degrees. 2% grads pursue medical degrees. **Faculty:** Student/faculty ratio 15:1. 78 full-time faculty, 85% hold PhDs, 6% are are members of minority groups, 54% are women.

ACADEMICS
Degrees: Bachelor's, certificate, master's, post-bachelor's certificate, post-master's certificate. **Classes:** Most classes have 10–19 students. **Majors with Highest Enrollment:** Business/commerce; fine/studio arts; psychology. **Special Study Options:** Accelerated program, cross-registration, distance learning, double major, dual enrollment, English as a Second Language (ESL), exchange student program (domestic), honors program, independent study, internships, liberal arts/career combination, student-designed major, study abroad, teacher certification program, weekend college. **Honors programs:** Honors Program has designated curriculum components. **Combined degree programs:** BA/JD, BS/DO, /DPharm with Lake Erie Coll of Osteopath Med, BA/Law with Duquesne U. Special programs offered to physically disabled students include note-taking services, reader services, tape recorders, tutors. **Career services:** Alumni network, alumni services, career assessment, internships, regional alumni. **Career services highlights include:** Internships encouraged or required in every major.

FACILITIES
Housing: Coed dorms, men's dorms, women's dorms, Special housing for honors students. 95% of campus accessible to physically disabled. **Special Academic Facilities/Equipment:** Art gallery, concert hall, theatre, Child Development Center, NEW—Performing Arts Center, Studio 215, smart classrooms. **Computers:** 100% of classrooms, 100% of dorms, 100% of libraries, 100% of dining areas, 100% of common outdoor areas have wireless network access. Students can register for classes online. Administrative functions (other than registration) can be performed online.

CAMPUS LIFE
Environment: Town. **Activities:** Choral groups, concert band, dance, drama/theater, jazz band, literary magazine, marching band, music ensembles, musical theater, pep band, student government, student newspaper, symphony orchestra, campus ministries, international student organization. **Organizations:** 53 registered organizations, 4 honor societies, 7 religious organizations. **Athletics (Intercollegiate):** *Men:* Baseball, basketball, cross-country, football, lacrosse, soccer, track/field (outdoor), track/field (indoor), wrestling. *Women:* Basketball, cross-country, equestrian sports, field hockey, golf, lacrosse, soccer, softball, tennis, track/field (outdoor), track/field (indoor), volleyball. **On-Campus Highlights:** Griffin's Cove, McKenna Recreation Center, Sullivan Lounge, Residence Halls, Lowe Dining Hall, New additions to Seton Hill include the Center for Performing Arts and Visual Arts Center; both of these venues are located in downtown Greensburg within walking distance of campus. **Environmental Initiatives:** Association of Independent Colleges and Universities of Pennsylvania self/peer assessment program

ADMISSIONS
Freshman Academic Profile: Average high school GPA 3.24. 18% in top 10% of high school class, 44% in top 25% of high school class, 71% in top 50% of

high school class. SAT Math middle 50% range 430–560. SAT Critical Reading middle 50% range 420–540. SAT Writing middle 50% range 420–540. ACT middle 50% range 17–24. Minimum paper TOEFL 600. Minimum computer TOEFL 250. Minimum web-based TOEFL 100. **Basis for Candidate Selection:** *Very important factors considered include:* Academic GPA, rigor of secondary school record, interview. *Important factors considered include:* Class rank, standardized test scores, character/personal qualities, extracurricular activities, talent/ability. *Other factors considered include:* Application essay, recommendation(s), alumni/ae relation, level of applicant's interest, volunteer work, work experience. **Freshman Admission Requirements:** High school diploma is required and GED is accepted. *Academic units required:* 4 English, 2 mathematics, 1 science, (1 science labs), 2 social studies, 4 academic electives. *Academic units recommended:* 4 English, 2 mathematics, 1 science, (1 science labs), 2 foreign language, 2 social studies, 4 academic electives. **Freshman Admission Statistics:** 1,729 applied, 66% admitted, 26% enrolled. **Transfer Admission Requirements:** High school transcript, college transcript(s), statement of good standing from prior institution(s). Minimum college GPA of 2.0 required. Lowest grade transferable C–. **General Admission Information:** Application fee $35. Regular application deadline 8/15. Notification on a rolling basis, beginning on or about 9/1. Nonfall registration accepted. Admission may be deferred for a maximum of 1 year. Credit and/or placement offered for CEEB Advanced Placement tests.

COSTS AND FINANCIAL AID

Required Forms and Deadlines: FAFSA, institution's own financial aid form, state aid form. Priority financial aid filing date 5/1. **Notification of Awards:** Applicants will be notified of awards on a rolling basis beginning 11/15. **Types of Aid:** *Need-based scholarships/grants:* Federal Pell, SEOG, state scholarships/grants, private scholarships, the school's own gift aid. *Loans:* FFEL Subsidized Stafford, FFEL Unsubsidized Stafford, FFEL PLUS, Federal Perkins, college/university loans from institutional funds, Alternative. *Student Employment:* Federal Work-Study Program available. Institutional employment available. Highest amount earned per year from on-campus jobs $1,000. Off-campus job opportunities are good. **Financial Aid Statistics:** 79% freshmen, 78% undergrads receive need-based scholarship or grant aid. 12% freshmen, 10% undergrads receive non-need-based scholarship or grant aid. 65% freshmen, 65% undergrads receive need-based self-help aid. 10% freshmen, 8% undergrads receive athletic scholarships. 98% freshmen, 90% undergrads receive any aid. 91% undergrads borrow to pay for school. Average cumulative indebtedness $25,807. **Criteria for awarding institutional aid:** *Non-need-based:* Academics, alumni affiliation, art, athletics, job skills, music/drama, religious affiliation.

SEWANEE—THE UNIVERSITY OF THE SOUTH

Best 373

735 University Avenue, Sewanee, TN 37383-1000
Phone: 931-598-1238 **Financial Aid Phone:** 800-522-2234
E-mail: admiss@sewanee.edu **CEEB Code:** 1842
Fax: 931-538-3248 **Website:** www.sewanee.edu **ACT Code:** 4924

This private school, affiliated with the Episcopal Church, was founded in 1857. It has a 13000-acre campus.

RATINGS
Admissions Selectivity Rating: 90   **Fire Safety Rating:** 84   **Green Rating:** 92

STUDENTS AND FACULTY
Enrollment: 1,450. **Student Body:** 51% female, 49% male, 77% out-of-state, 2% international (23 countries represented). Asian 3%, African American 5%, Caucasian 87%, Hispanic 3%, Native American 1%.
Retention and Graduation: 90% freshmen return for sophomore year. 75% freshmen graduate within 4 years. 38% grads go on to further study within 1 year. 24% grads pursue arts and sciences degrees. 6% grads pursue law degrees. 4% grads pursue business degrees. 4% grads pursue medical degrees. **Faculty:** Student/faculty ratio 11:1. 134 full-time faculty, 95% hold PhDs, 9% are are members of minority groups, 36% are women.

ACADEMICS
Degrees: Bachelor's, master's, post-bachelor's certificate, post-master's certificate. **Classes:** Most classes have 10–19 students. Most lab/discussion sessions have 20–29 students. **Majors with Highest Enrollment:** Economics; English language and literature; history. **Special Study Options:** Double major, independent study, internships, student-designed major, study abroad

Special programs offered to physically disabled students include note-taking services, reader services, tape recorders. **Career services:** Alumni network, alumni services, career assessment, internships, regional alumni. **Career services highlights include:** Sewanee's Internship Fund Program—Thanks to the help of alumni and the donors of Sewanee's 25 endowed internship funds, 150 students received a total of almost $300,000 in stipends or paid internships in 2007. Sewanee students interned in 20 states and 20 countries in 2007, and these endowed funds enabled the students to do meaningful internships that would otherwise have been unpaid.

FACILITIES
Housing: Coed dorms, special housing for disabled students, men's dorms, special housing for international students, women's dorms, fraternity/sorority housing, apartments for married students, cooperative housing, apartments for single students, wellness housing, theme housing, substance-free housing & Living and Learning Communities. **Special Academic Facilities/Equipment:** Art gallery, observatory, keyboard collection, materials analysis lab with electron microscope. **Computers:** 80% of classrooms, 80% of dorms, 100% of libraries, 100% of dining areas, 100% of student union, 25% of common outdoor areas have wireless network access. Students can register for classes online. Administrative functions (other than registration) can be performed online.

CAMPUS LIFE
Environment: Rural. **Activities:** Choral groups, concert band, dance, drama/theater, jazz band, literary magazine, music ensembles, musical theater, radio station, student government, student newspaper, student-run film society, symphony orchestra, yearbook, campus ministries, international student organization, Model UN. **Organizations:** 110 registered organizations, 9 honor societies, 11 religious organizations. 12 fraternities, 9 sororities. **Athletics (Intercollegiate):** *Men:* Baseball, basketball, cross-country, diving, equestrian sports, football, golf, lacrosse, soccer, swimming, tennis, track/field (outdoor), track/field (indoor). *Women:* Basketball, cheerleading, cross-country, diving, equestrian sports, field hockey, golf, lacrosse, soccer, softball, swimming, tennis, track/field (outdoor), track/field (indoor), volleyball. **On-Campus Highlights:** Outdoor recreation on Sewanee's 10,000 a, All Saints' Chapel, Abbo's Alley Ravine Garden, Memorial Cross and University View, University Golf and Tennis Club. **Environmental Initiatives:** Environmental residents. Current strategic plan initiative for sustainability and environmental programs. Commitment to energy conservation in all building projects including connection to central computer controlled building climate automation system.

ADMISSIONS
Freshman Academic Profile: Average high school GPA 3.6. 43% in top 10% of high school class, 67% in top 25% of high school class, 88% in top 50% of high school class. 50% from public high schools. SAT Math middle 50% range 580–670. SAT Critical Reading middle 50% range 570–690. SAT Writing middle 50% range 560–670. ACT middle 50% range 26–30. Minimum paper TOEFL 550. Minimum computer TOEFL 220. **Basis for Candidate Selection:** *Very important factors considered include:* Academic GPA, recommendation(s), rigor of secondary school record. *Important factors considered include:* Application essay, standardized test scores, character/personal qualities, extracurricular activities, volunteer work, work experience. *Other factors considered include:* Class rank, alumni/ae relation, first generation, geographical residence, interview, level of applicant's interest, racial/ethnic status, talent/ability. **Freshman Admission Requirements:** High school diploma is required and GED is not accepted. *Academic units required:* 4 English, 3 mathematics, 2 science, (2 science labs), 2 foreign language, 1 social studies, 1 history. *Academic units recommended:* 4 English, 4 mathematics, 4 science, (3 science labs), 4 foreign language, 2 social studies, 2 history. **Freshman Admission Statistics:** 2,481 applied, 68% admitted, 24% enrolled. **Transfer Admission Requirements:** High school transcript, college transcript(s), essay or personal statement, standardized test scores, statement of good standing from prior institution(s). Minimum college GPA of 3.00 required. Lowest grade transferable C. **General Admission Information:** Application fee $45. Early decision application deadline 11/15. Regular application deadline 2/1. Regular notification 3/17. Nonfall registration not accepted. Admission may be deferred for a maximum of 1 year. Credit and/or placement offered for CEEB Advanced Placement tests.

COSTS AND FINANCIAL AID
Room and board $9,760. Required fees $272. Average book expense $1,900. **Required Forms and Deadlines:** FAFSA, institution's own financial aid form. Priority financial aid filing date 3/1. **Notification of Awards:** Applicants will be notified of awards on or about 4/1. **Types of Aid:** *Need-based scholarships/grants:* Federal Pell, SEOG, state scholarships/grants, private scholarships, the school's own gift aid. *Loans:* FFEL Subsidized Stafford, FFEL Unsubsidized Stafford, FFEL PLUS, Federal Perkins, state loans, college/university loans from institutional funds, private alternative loans. *Student Employment:* Federal Work-Study Program available. Institutional employment available. Highest amount earned per year from on-campus jobs $1,500. Off-campus job opportunities are fair. **Financial Aid Statistics:** 45% freshmen, 53% undergrads receive need-based scholarship or grant aid. 45% freshmen, 54% undergrads re-

ceive non-need-based scholarship or grant aid. 33% freshmen, 39% undergrads receive need-based self-help aid. 79% freshmen, 70% undergrads receive any aid. 38% undergrads borrow to pay for school. Average cumulative indebtedness $18,717. **Criteria for awarding institutional aid:** *Non-need-based:* Academics, minority status, religious affiliation.

SHASTA BIBLE COLLEGE

2951 Goodwater Ave, Redding, CA 96002
Phone: 530-221-4275
E-mail: admissions@shasta.edu
Fax: 530-221-6929 **Website:** www.shasta.edu **ACT Code:** 427

This private school, affiliated with the Baptist Church, was founded in 1970. It has a 63-acre campus.

RATINGS
Admissions Selectivity Rating: 60*   **Fire Safety Rating:** 60*   **Green Rating:** 60*

STUDENTS AND FACULTY
Enrollment: 89. **Student Body:** 44% female, 56% male, 21% out-of-state, 3% international (5 countries represented). African American 1%, Caucasian 73%, Hispanic 1%.
Retention and Graduation: 40% freshmen return for sophomore year. 100% freshmen graduate within 4 years. 100% grads go on to further study within 1 year. 20% grads pursue arts and sciences degrees. **Faculty:** Student/faculty ratio 12:1. 7 full-time faculty, 71% hold PhDs, 14% are are members of minority groups, 14% are women.

ACADEMICS
Degrees: Associate, bachelor's, certificate, diploma, master's. **Classes:** Most classes have 10–19 students. **Majors with Highest Enrollment:** Electrical, electronic and communications engineering technology/technician. **Special Study Options:** Distance learning, double major, external degree program, independent study, teacher certification program, weekend college, Master's in School Administration. **Combined degree programs:** BA/MA. Special programs offered to physically disabled students include tutors.

FACILITIES
Housing: Coed dorms. 100% of campus accessible to physically disabled.

CAMPUS LIFE
Environment: Rural. **Activities:** Radio station, student government, television station, yearbook.

ADMISSIONS
Freshman Academic Profile: 30% from public high schools. Minimum paper TOEFL 500. Minimum computer TOEFL 173. **Basis for Candidate Selection:** *Very important factors considered include:* Application essay, recommendation(s), character/personal qualities, religious affiliation/commitment, volunteer work. *Important factors considered include:* extracurricular activities, work experience. *Other factors considered include:* Class rank, standardized test scores, alumni/ae relation, interview, talent/ability. **Freshman Admission Requirements:** High school diploma is required and GED is accepted. **Freshman Admission Statistics:** 38 applied, 100% admitted, 100% enrolled. **Transfer Admission Requirements:** High school transcript, college transcript(s), minimum college GPA of 2.0 required. Lowest grade transferable C. **General Admission Information:** Application fee $35. Nonfall registration accepted. Admission may be deferred for a maximum of 1 Semester. Neither credit nor placement offered for CEEB Advanced Placement tests.

COSTS AND FINANCIAL AID
Annual tuition $5,300. Room and board $1,200. Required fees $135. Average book expense $250. **Notification of Awards:** Applicants will be notified of awards on a rolling basis beginning 1/2. **Types of Aid:** *Need-based scholarships/grants:* Federal Pell, state scholarships/grants. *Student Employment:* Federal Work-Study Program available. Highest amount earned per year from on-campus jobs $700. Off-campus job opportunities are excellent.

SHAW UNIVERSITY

118 East South Street, Raleigh, NC 27601
Phone: 919-546-8275 **Financial Aid Phone:** 919-546-8240
E-mail: admissions@shawu.edu **CEEB Code:** 5612
Fax: 919-546-8271 **Website:** www.shawu.edu **ACT Code:** 3158

This private school, affiliated with the Baptist Church, was founded in 1865. It has a 30-acre campus.

RATINGS
Admissions Selectivity Rating: 67   **Fire Safety Rating:** 60*   **Green Rating:** 60*

STUDENTS AND FACULTY
Enrollment: 2,649. **Student Body:** 64% female, 36% male, 36% out-of-state, 2% international (11 countries represented). African American 85%, Caucasian 1%.
Retention and Graduation: 11% freshmen graduate within 4 years. **Faculty:** Student/faculty ratio 15:1. 112 full-time faculty, 63% hold PhDs, 84% are are members of minority groups, 34% are women.

ACADEMICS
Degrees: Associate, bachelor's, first professional, master's. **Classes:** Most classes have fewer than 10 students. **Majors with Highest Enrollment:** Business/commerce; criminal justice/safety studies; psychology. **Special Study Options:** Accelerated program, cross-registration, distance learning, double major, dual enrollment, honors program, independent study, internships, student-designed major, study abroad, teacher certification program, weekend college. Special programs offered to physically disabled students include tape recorders, tutors.

FACILITIES
Housing: Men's dorms, women's dorms. **Special Academic Facilities/Equipment:** TV and film production facilities. Curriculum and Materials Center. **Computers:** Students can register for classes online. Administrative functions (other than registration) can be performed online.

CAMPUS LIFE
Environment: City. **Activities:** Choral groups, concert band, dance, drama/theater, jazz band, marching band, music ensembles, musical theater, pep band, radio station, student government, student newspaper, yearbook. **Organizations:** 4 honor societies, 4 fraternities, 4 sororities. **Athletics (Intercollegiate):** *Men:* Baseball, basketball, cross-country, football, golf, tennis, track/field (outdoor), track/field (indoor). *Women:* Basketball, bowling, cross-country, softball, tennis, track/field (outdoor), track/field (indoor), volleyball.

ADMISSIONS
Freshman Academic Profile: Average high school GPA 2.42. 2% in top 10% of high school class, 9% in top 25% of high school class, 33% in top 50% of high school class. 90% from public high schools. SAT Math middle 50% range 310–420. SAT Critical Reading middle 50% range 320–420. SAT Writing middle 50% range 330–420. ACT middle 50% range 12–17. **Basis for Candidate Selection:** *Very important factors considered include:* Academic GPA, recommendation(s), first generation, geographical residence, level of applicant's interest. *Important factors considered include:* Class rank, application essay, rigor of secondary school record, standardized test scores, character/personal qualities, extracurricular activities, state residency, volunteer work, work experience. *Other factors considered include:* Alumni/ae relation, talent/ability. **Freshman Admission Requirements:** High school diploma is required and GED is accepted. *Academic units required:* 3 English, 2 mathematics, 2 science, 2 social studies, 9 academic electives. **Freshman Admission Statistics:** 5,361 applied, 49% admitted, 28% enrolled. **Transfer Admission Requirements:** College transcript(s), Lowest grade transferable C. **General Admission Information:** Application fee $25. Regular application deadline 7/30. Notification on a rolling basis, beginning on or about 8/1. Nonfall registration accepted. Admission may be deferred for a maximum of indefinite. Credit and/or placement offered for CEEB Advanced Placement tests.

COSTS AND FINANCIAL AID
Required Forms and Deadlines: FAFSA, institution's own financial aid form, state aid form. Financial aid filing deadline 6/1. Priority financial aid filing date 3/1. **Notification of Awards:** Applicants will be notified of awards on a rolling basis beginning 2/1. **Types of Aid:** *Need-based scholarships/grants:* Federal Pell, SEOG, state scholarships/grants, private scholarships, the school's own gift aid, United Negro College Fund *Loans:* FFEL Subsidized Stafford, FFEL Unsubsidized Stafford, FFEL PLUS, Federal Perkins. *Student Employment:* Federal Work-Study Program available. Institutional employment available. Off-campus job opportunities are excellent. **Financial Aid Statistics: Criteria for awarding institutional aid:** *Non-need-based:* Academics, alumni affiliation, art, athletics, music/drama, religious affiliation.

SHAWNEE STATE UNIVERSITY

940 Second Street, Portsmouth, OH 45662
Phone: 740-351-4778 **Financial Aid Phone:** 740-351-4243
E-mail: to_ssu@shawnee.edu **CEEB Code:** 1790
Fax: 740-351-3111 **Website:** www.shawnee.edu **ACT Code:** 3336

This public school was founded in 1986. It has a 50-acre campus.

RATINGS
Admissions Selectivity Rating: 63   **Fire Safety Rating:** 76   **Green Rating:** 70

STUDENTS AND FACULTY
Enrollment: 4,027. **Student Body:** 58% female, 42% male, 9% out-of-state, 1% international (21 countries represented). African American 4%, Caucasian 86%, Native American 1%.
Retention and Graduation: 57% freshmen return for sophomore year. 25% grads go on to further study within 1 year. 2% grads pursue law degrees. 3% grads pursue business degrees. 4% grads pursue medical degrees. **Faculty:** Student/faculty ratio 18:1. 151 full-time faculty, 57% hold PhDs, 9% are are members of minority groups, 44% are women.

ACADEMICS
Degrees: Associate, bachelor's, certificate, master's. **Classes:** Most classes have 10–19 students. Most lab/discussion sessions have 20–29 students. **Majors with Highest Enrollment:** General studies; nursing/registered nurse (RN, ASN, BSN, MSN); psychology. **Special Study Options:** Cross-registration, distance learning, double major, dual enrollment, English as a Second Language (ESL), honors program, independent study, internships, student-designed major, study abroad, teacher certification program Special programs offered to physically disabled students include note-taking services, reader services, tape recorders, tutors. **Career services:** Alumni services, career/job search classes, career assessment, internships..

FACILITIES
Housing: Coed dorms, list of housing in community available. 100% of campus accessible to physically disabled. **Special Academic Facilities/Equipment:** Vern Riffe Center for the Arts. **Computers:** Students can register for classes online.

CAMPUS LIFE
Environment: Town. **Activities:** Choral groups, drama/theater, literary magazine, music ensembles, musical theater, student government, student newspaper, campus ministries. **Organizations:** 36 registered organizations, 2 honor societies, 3 religious organizations. 1 fraternities, 1 sororities. **Athletics (Intercollegiate):** *Men:* Baseball, basketball, cross-country, golf, soccer. *Women:* Basketball, cross-country, soccer, softball, tennis, volleyball. **On-Campus Highlights:** Vern Riffe Center for the Arts, University Center. **Environmental Initiatives:** Geo-thermal chiller plant for new building; single-stream recycle program; pulper for food waste in new kitchen.

ADMISSIONS
Freshman Academic Profile: 12% in top 10% of high school class, 34% in top 25% of high school class, 65% in top 50% of high school class. ACT middle 50% range 17–23. Minimum paper TOEFL 500. Minimum computer TOEFL 170. **Basis for Candidate Selection: Freshman Admission Requirements:** High school diploma is required and GED is accepted. *Academic units recommended:* 4 English, 3 mathematics, 3 science, 2 foreign language, 3 social studies, 1 academic electives. **Freshman Admission Statistics:** 3,785 applied, 84% admitted, 36% enrolled. **Transfer Admission Requirements:** High school transcript, college transcript(s), minimum college GPA of 1.0 required. Lowest grade transferable D. **General Admission Information:** Nonfall registration accepted. Admission may be deferred for a maximum of 1 year. Credit and/or placement offered for CEEB Advanced Placement tests.

COSTS AND FINANCIAL AID
Annual in-state tuition $5,184. Annual out-of-state tuition $9,528. Room and board $8,046. Required fees $948. Average book expense $1,440. **Required Forms and Deadlines:** FAFSA, institution's own financial aid form. Priority financial aid filing date 6/15. **Notification of Awards:** Applicants will be notified of awards on a rolling basis beginning 5/1. **Types of Aid:** *Need-based scholarships/grants:* Federal Pell, SEOG, state scholarships/grants, private scholarships, the school's own gift aid. *Loans:* FFEL Subsidized Stafford, FFEL Unsubsidized Stafford, FFEL PLUS, state loans. *Student Employment:* Off-campus job opportunities are fair. **Financial Aid Statistics:** 58% freshmen, 65% undergrads receive need-based scholarship or grant aid. 30% freshmen, 28% undergrads receive non-need-based scholarship or grant aid. 31% freshmen, 45% undergrads receive need-based self-help aid. 2% freshmen, 1% undergrads receive athletic scholarships. 56% undergrads borrow to pay for school. Average cumulative indebtedness $10,944. **Criteria for awarding**

---

institutional aid: *Non-need-based:* Academics, art, athletics, minority status, music/drama, state/district residency.

SHENANDOAH UNIVERSITY

1460 University Drive, Winchester, VA 22601-5195
Phone: 540-665-4581 **Financial Aid Phone:** 540-665-4538
E-mail: admit@su.edu **CEEB Code:** 5613
Fax: 540-665-4627 **Website:** www.su.edu **ACT Code:** 5613

This private school, affiliated with the Methodist Church, was founded in 1875. It has a 100-acre campus.

RATINGS
Admissions Selectivity Rating: 77   **Fire Safety Rating:** 76   **Green Rating:** 60*

STUDENTS AND FACULTY
Enrollment: 1,562. **Student Body:** 60% female, 40% male, 43% out-of-state, 4% international (46 countries represented). Asian 1%, African American 2%, Caucasian 93%.
Retention and Graduation: 75% freshmen return for sophomore year. 28% freshmen graduate within 4 years. 42% grads go on to further study within 1 year. 34% grads pursue arts and sciences degrees. 1% grads pursue law degrees. 13% grads pursue business degrees. 1% grads pursue medical degrees. **Faculty:** Student/faculty ratio 9:1. 181 full-time faculty, 74% hold PhDs, 7% are are members of minority groups, 46% are women. 1% of classes are taught by teaching assistants.

ACADEMICS
Degrees: Associate, bachelor's, certificate, first professional, master's, post-bachelor's certificate, post-master's certificate, terminal associate. **Classes:** Most classes have 10–19 students. Most lab/discussion sessions have fewer than 10 students. **Majors with Highest Enrollment:** Business/commerce; drama and dramatics/theatre arts; nursing/registered nurse (RN, ASN, BSN, MSN). **Special Study Options:** Accelerated program, cooperative education program, distance learning, double major, English as a Second Language (ESL), independent study, internships, liberal arts/career combination, student-designed major, study abroad, teacher certification program, weekend college. **Combined degree programs:** Pharmacy/MBA; DPT/MBA; DPT/Athletic Training. Special programs offered to physically disabled students include note-taking services, reader services, tape recorders, tutors.

FACILITIES
Housing: Coed dorms, special housing for disabled students, special housing for international students. 91% of campus accessible to physically disabled. **Computers:** 100% of classrooms, 100% of dorms, 100% of libraries, 100% of dining areas, 100% of student union, 25% of common outdoor areas have wireless network access. Students can register for classes online. Administrative functions (other than registration) can be performed online.

CAMPUS LIFE
Environment: Town. **Activities:** Choral groups, concert band, dance, drama/theater, jazz band, music ensembles, musical theater, opera, radio station, student government, student newspaper, symphony orchestra, television station **Organizations:** 65 registered organizations, 2 honor societies, 2 religious organizations. 7 fraternities, 1 sororities. **Athletics (Intercollegiate):** *Men:* Baseball, basketball, cross-country, football, golf, lacrosse, soccer, tennis. *Women:* Basketball, cross-country, field hockey, lacrosse, soccer, softball, tennis, volleyball. **On-Campus Highlights:** Ohrstrom-Bryant Theatre, Aikens Athletic Center, Alson H. Smith, Jr. Library, Health Professions Building, Goodson Chapel/Recital Hall.

ADMISSIONS
Freshman Academic Profile: Average high school GPA 3.21. 15% in top 10% of high school class, 37% in top 25% of high school class, 68% in top 50% of high school class. SAT Math middle 50% range 432–579. SAT Critical Reading middle 50% range 400–639. ACT middle 50% range 20–26. Minimum paper TOEFL 450. Minimum computer TOEFL 133. **Basis for Candidate Selection:** *Very important factors considered include:* Academic GPA, rigor of secondary school record, interview, talent/ability. *Important factors considered include:* Recommendation(s), standardized test scores, extracurricular activities, volunteer work. *Other factors considered include:* Application essay, character/personal qualities, level of applicant's interest, work experience. **Freshman Admission Requirements:** High school diploma is required and GED is accepted. *Academic units required:* 4 English, 3 mathematics, 2 science, (1 science labs), 2 foreign language, 2 social studies, 2 history, 2 academic electives. *Academic units recommended:* 4 mathematics, 4 science, 3 foreign language, 4 academic electives. **Freshman Admission Statistics:** 1,479 applied, 70% admitted, 36% enrolled. **Transfer Admission Requirements:** College

---

transcript(s), statement of good standing from prior institution(s). Minimum college GPA of 2.0 required. Lowest grade transferable C. **General Admission Information:** Application fee $30. Regular notification 8/7. Notification on a rolling basis, beginning on or about 10/6. Nonfall registration accepted. Admission may be deferred for a maximum of 1 year. Credit and/or placement offered for CEEB Advanced Placement tests.

COSTS AND FINANCIAL AID

Annual tuition $19,900. Room and board $7,550. Required fees $150. Average book expense $1,000. **Required Forms and Deadlines:** FAFSA, state aid form. Priority financial aid filing date 2/15. **Notification of Awards:** Applicants will be notified of awards on a rolling basis beginning 3/15. **Types of Aid:** *Need-based scholarships/grants:* Federal Pell, SEOG, state scholarships/grants, private scholarships, the school's own gift aid, Federal Nursing Scholarships. *Loans:* Direct Subsidized Stafford, Direct Unsubsidized Stafford, Direct PLUS, Federal Perkins, Federal Nursing, college/university loans from institutional funds. *Student Employment:* Highest amount earned per year from on-campus jobs $1,500. **Financial Aid Statistics:** 39% freshmen, 55% undergrads receive need-based scholarship or grant aid. 32% freshmen, 34% undergrads receive non-need-based scholarship or grant aid. 48% freshmen, 52% undergrads receive need-based self-help aid. 91% freshmen, 80% undergrads receive any aid. 85% undergrads borrow to pay for school. Average cumulative indebtedness $19,518. **Criteria for awarding institutional aid:** *Non-need-based:* Academics, job skills, music/drama, religious affiliation, state/district residency.

SHEPHERD UNIVERSITY

Office of Admissions, P.O.Box 5000, Shepherdstown, WV 25443-5000
Phone: 304-876-5212 **Financial Aid Phone:** 304-876-5470
E-mail: admissions@shepherd.edu **CEEB Code:** 5615
Fax: 304-876-5165 **Website:** www.shepherd.edu **ACT Code:** 4532

This public school was founded in 1871. It has a 323-acre campus.

RATINGS
Admissions Selectivity Rating: 71   **Fire Safety Rating:** 72   **Green Rating:** 74

STUDENTS AND FACULTY
Enrollment: 3,676. **Student Body:** 58% female, 42% male, 38% out-of-state, international (15 countries represented). Asian 2%, African American 5%, Caucasian 79%, Hispanic 2%.
Retention and Graduation: 66% freshmen return for sophomore year. 21% freshmen graduate within 4 years. 23% grads go on to further study within 1 year. 58% grads pursue arts and sciences degrees. 8% grads pursue law degrees. 23% grads pursue business degrees. 3% grads pursue medical degrees. **Faculty:** Student/faculty ratio 19:1. 124 full-time faculty, 81% hold PhDs, 17% are are members of minority groups, 43% are women.

ACADEMICS
Degrees: Bachelor's, master's. **Classes:** Most classes have 20–29 students. Most lab/discussion sessions have 20–29 students. **Majors with Highest Enrollment:** Business/commerce; nursing/registered nurse (RN, ASN, BSN, MSN); teacher education, multiple levels. **Special Study Options:** Cooperative education program, double major, dual enrollment, honors program, independent study, internships, study abroad, teacher certification program. **Honors programs:** See Honors Program on website www.shepherd.edu. **Combined degree programs:** MedStep with WVU School of Medicine. Special programs offered to physically disabled students include note-taking services, reader services, tape recorders, tutors. **Career services:** Alumni network, alumni services, career/job search classes, career assessment, internships, regional alumni.

FACILITIES
Housing: Coed dorms, special housing for disabled students, apartments for single students, theme housing, suites, first-year housing. 90% of campus accessible to physically disabled. **Special Academic Facilities/Equipment:** Nursery school, elementary education lab, art gallery, theaters, Fazioli Concert Grand Piano, George Tyler Moore Center for the Study of the Civil War, Robert C. Byrd Center for Legislative Studies. **Computers:** 90% of classrooms, 100% of libraries, 100% of dining areas, 100% of student union, 1% of common outdoor areas have wireless network access. Students can register for classes online. Administrative functions (other than registration) can be performed online.

CAMPUS LIFE
Environment: Village. **Activities:** Choral groups, concert band, drama/theater, jazz band, literary magazine, marching band, music ensembles, musical theater, pep band, radio station, student government, student newspaper, symphony orchestra, campus ministries, international student organization. **Organizations:** 85 registered organizations, 9 honor societies, 4 religious organiza-

tions. 4 fraternities, 3 sororities. **Athletics (Intercollegiate):** *Men:* Baseball, basketball, football, golf, soccer, tennis. *Women:* Basketball, lacrosse, soccer, softball, tennis, volleyball. **On-Campus Highlights:** Butcher Athletic Center, Center for Contemporary Arts, Scarborough Library, Wellness Center, Student Center. **Environmental Initiatives:** Recycling; upgrading HVAC equipment; constructing new buildings to LEED standards.

ADMISSIONS
Freshman Academic Profile: Average high school GPA 3.21. 87.4% from public high schools. SAT Math middle 50% range 450–550. SAT Critical Reading middle 50% range 450–560. ACT middle 50% range 20–24. Minimum paper TOEFL 550. Minimum computer TOEFL 213. Minimum web-based TOEFL 79. **Basis for Candidate Selection:** *Very important factors considered include:* Academic GPA, rigor of secondary school record, standardized test scores. *Important factors considered include:* talent/ability. *Other factors considered include:* Class rank, application essay, recommendation(s), alumni/ae relation, character/personal qualities, extracurricular activities, interview, level of applicant's interest. **Freshman Admission Requirements:** High school diploma is required and GED is accepted. *Academic units required:* 4 English, 4 mathematics, 3 science, (3 science labs), 2 foreign language, 2 social studies, 1 history, 1 visual/performing arts, 5 academic electives. **Freshman Admission Statistics:** 1,770 applied, 94% admitted, 48% enrolled. **Transfer Admission Requirements:** College transcript(s), minimum college GPA of 2.0 required. Lowest grade transferable D. **General Admission Information:** Application fee $45. Regular application deadline 8/15. Notification on a rolling basis, beginning on or about 9/15. Nonfall registration accepted. Admission may be deferred for a maximum of 1 year. Credit and/or placement offered for CEEB Advanced Placement tests.

COSTS AND FINANCIAL AID
Annual in-state tuition $5,234. Annual out-of-state tuition $13,574. Room and board $7,228. Average book expense $1,100. **Required Forms and Deadlines:** FAFSA, state aid form. Priority financial aid filing date 3/1. **Notification of Awards:** Applicants will be notified of awards on a rolling basis beginning 3/15. **Types of Aid:** *Need-based scholarships/grants:* Federal Pell, SEOG, state scholarships/grants, private scholarships, the school's own gift aid. *Loans:* Direct Subsidized Stafford, Direct Unsubsidized Stafford, Direct PLUS, Federal Perkins. *Student Employment:* Federal Work-Study Program available. Institutional employment available. Highest amount earned per year from on-campus jobs $12,181. Off-campus job opportunities are good. **Financial Aid Statistics:** 34% freshmen, 33% undergrads receive need-based scholarship or grant aid. 21% freshmen, 14% undergrads receive non-need-based scholarship or grant aid. 40% freshmen, 41% undergrads receive need-based self-help aid. 6% freshmen, 5% undergrads receive athletic scholarships. 74.8% freshmen, 76.9% undergrads receive any aid. 65% undergrads borrow to pay for school. Average cumulative indebtedness $20,053. **Criteria for awarding institutional aid:** *Non-need-based:* Academics, art, athletics, job skills, leadership, minority status, music/drama, state/district residency.

SHIMER COLLEGE

Shimer College, 3424 S. State St, Chicago, IL 60616
Phone: 312-235-3506 **Financial Aid Phone:** 312-235-3507
E-mail: admission@shimer.edu **CEEB Code:** 1717
Fax: 312-235-3501 **Website:** shimer.edu **ACT Code:** 1142

This private school was founded in 1853. It has a 140-acre campus.

RATINGS
Admissions Selectivity Rating: 60*   **Fire Safety Rating:** 60*   **Green Rating:** 60*

STUDENTS AND FACULTY
Enrollment: 91. **Student Body:** 51% female, 49% male, 60% out-of-state, 2% international (4 countries represented). Asian 4%, African American 5%, Caucasian 84%, Hispanic 3%, Native American 1%.
Retention and Graduation: 72% freshmen return for sophomore year. 50% freshmen graduate within 4 years. 50% grads go on to further study within 1 year. 40% grads pursue arts and sciences degrees. 10% grads pursue law degrees. **Faculty:** Student/faculty ratio 8:1. 9 full-time faculty, 122% hold PhDs, 11% are are members of minority groups, 33% are women.

ACADEMICS
Degrees: Bachelor's. **Classes:** Most classes have 10–19 students. **Majors with Highest Enrollment:** humanities/humanistic studies; natural sciences; social sciences. **Special Study Options:** Cross-registration, double major, independent study, internships, liberal arts/career combination, study abroad, weekend college, one-on-one tutorials with faculty member for in depth study in any area

of interest to the student. **Combined degree programs:** BA/JD. **Career services:** Alumni network, alumni services, career/job search classes, internships, regional alumni. **Career services highlights include:** Shimer students may intern off campus during their program. Funded internships are available.

FACILITIES

Housing: Coed dorms, women's dorms, apartments for married students, apartments for single students. 100% of campus accessible to physically disabled. **Special Academic Facilities/Equipment:** The Galvin Library has over one million volumes and 120 digital databases. The MTCC (student center) is an amazing place to eat, play and hang out. **Computers:** 100% of classrooms, 100% of dorms, 100% of libraries, 100% of dining areas, 100% of student union, 100% of common outdoor areas have wireless network access.

CAMPUS LIFE

Environment: Metropolis. **Activities:** Choral groups, concert band, drama/theater, jazz band, literary magazine, music ensembles, radio station, student government, student newspaper, international student organization. **Organizations:** 10 religious organizations. **On-Campus Highlights:** The Shimer College space on the IIT Camp, The Galvin Library/Art Galery, McCormic Tribune Campus Center, Crown Hall, Keating Sports Center, Students are strongly encouraged to visit when classes are in session. The best way to know if Shimer is a good fit for you is if you sit in on a class!

ADMISSIONS

Freshman Academic Profile: Average high school GPA 3.45. 50% from public high schools. Minimum paper TOEFL 625. Minimum computer TOEFL 263. **Basis for Candidate Selection:** *Very important factors considered include:* Application essay, recommendation(s), interview, level of applicant's interest. *Important factors considered include:* Rigor of secondary school record, character/personal qualities, talent/ability, volunteer work. *Other factors considered include:* Class rank, academic GPA, standardized test scores, alumni/ae relation, extracurricular activities, first generation, geographical residence, work experience. **Freshman Admission Requirements:** High school diploma or equivalent is not required. *Academic units recommended:* 4 English, 4 mathematics, 3 science, (1 science labs), 3 foreign language, 1 social studies, 2 history, 1 visual/performing arts, 3 academic electives. **Freshman Admission Statistics:** 59 applied, 90% admitted, 51% enrolled. **Transfer Admission Requirements:** College transcript(s), essay or personal statement, interview, Lowest grade transferable C. **General Admission Information:** Application fee $25. Regular application deadline 8/1. Notification on a rolling basis, beginning on or about 9/15. Nonfall registration accepted. Admission may be deferred for a maximum of 2 years. Neither credit nor placement offered for CEEB Advanced Placement tests.

COSTS AND FINANCIAL AID

Annual tuition $23,750. Room and board $11,200. Required fees $750. Average book expense $1,500. **Required Forms and Deadlines:** FAFSA, institution's own financial aid form. Priority financial aid filing date 3/1. **Notification of Awards:** Applicants will be notified of awards on a rolling basis beginning 2/1. **Types of Aid:** *Need-based scholarships/grants:* Federal Pell, SEOG, state scholarships/grants, private scholarships, the school's own gift aid. *Loans:* FFEL Subsidized Stafford, FFEL Unsubsidized Stafford, FFEL PLUS, Federal Perkins. *Student Employment:* Federal Work-Study Program available. Institutional employment available. Highest amount earned per year from on-campus jobs $1,500. Off-campus job opportunities are excellent. **Financial Aid Statistics:** 58% freshmen, 96% undergrads receive need-based scholarship or grant aid. 4% undergrads receive need-based self-help aid. 85% freshmen, 90% undergrads receive any aid. 100% undergrads borrow to pay for school. Average cumulative indebtedness $35,000. **Criteria for awarding institutional aid:** *Non-need-based:* Academics, alumni affiliation.

SHIPPENSBURG UNIVERSITY
OF PENNSYLVANIA

Old Main 105, 1871 Old Main Drive, Shippensburg, PA 17257-2299
Phone: 717-477-1231 **Financial Aid Phone:** 717-477-1131
E-mail: admiss@ship.edu **CEEB Code:** 2657
Fax: 717-477-4016 **Website:** www.ship.edu **ACT Code:** 3714

This public school was founded in 1871. It has a 200-acre campus.

RATINGS
Admissions Selectivity Rating: 72   **Fire Safety Rating:** 81   **Green Rating:** 80

STUDENTS AND FACULTY
Enrollment: 6,861. **Student Body:** 53% female, 47% male, 5.7% out-of-state, international (16 countries represented). Asian 1%, African American 7%, Caucasian 82%, Hispanic 2%.

Retention and Graduation: 72% freshmen return for sophomore year. 45% freshmen graduate within 4 years. **Faculty:** Student/faculty ratio 20:1. 329 full-time faculty, 93% hold PhDs, 14% are are members of minority groups, 43% are women.

ACADEMICS

Degrees: Bachelor's, certificate, master's, post-bachelor's certificate, post-master's certificate. **Classes:** Most classes have 20–29 students. Most lab/discussion sessions have 10–19 students. **Majors with Highest Enrollment:** Criminal justice/safety studies; elementary education and teaching; psychology. **Special Study Options:** Accelerated program, cooperative education program, distance learning, double major, dual enrollment, honors program, independent study, internships, study abroad, teacher certification program, Raider Plan. **Honors programs:** Program in General Education and Psychology. **Combined degree programs:** 3-2 EngProg/PSU and U of Md; Chem and Bio/Med Tech. Special programs offered to physically disabled students include note-taking services, reader services, tape recorders, tutors. **Career services:** Alumni network, alumni services, career/job search classes, career assessment, internships, regional alumni. **Career services highlights include:** Pennsylvania has been working to transform itself from a manufacturing economy to a diversified service-based economy with strength in technology intensive industries. Pennsylvania's workforce development strategy seeks to align education and training to High Priority Occupations (HPOs), which are fields with identified skill needs and job openings. Internships are a vital link between education and employment. Shippensburg University, and each of the 14 Pennsylvania State System of Higher Education (PASSHE) Universities, received a $30,000 grant to increase internships in the Commonwealth during the 2007–2008 and 2008–2009 academic years. This Economic Development-Internships grant program is designed to help meet the Commonwealth goals to develop and retain employment in the state. The grant project will enhance resources for all stakeholders by increasing university-wide coordination and institutional capacity to manage and increase internships. Student teaching, practicuums, field experiences, and internships are offered by all three colleges at both the undergraduate and graduate levels. Students gain professional experience directly related to their major by working part- or full-time during the fall or spring semesters or during the summer. Students earn credit based upon the number of hours worked; they are supervised by a faculty advisor and are expected to develop a rapport with their employer to fully understand and satisfy the duties and responsibilities of their assignment. Students are expected to complete a variety of academic assignments related to their experience and in a number of programs, also participate in a seminar course associated with their experiential learning placement. Responsibility for assessment rests within the academic departments and is incorporated into departmental five-year program reviews.

FACILITIES

Housing: Coed dorms, wellness housing, theme housing, suites, apartment complex off-campus. 91% of campus accessible to physically disabled. **Special Academic Facilities/Equipment:** Art gallery, vertebrate museum, on-campus elementary school, planetarium, electron microscope, NMR spectrometer, greenhouse, herbarium, Fashion Archives, Women's Center, Closed Circuit TV. **Computers:** 95% of classrooms, 10% of dorms, 100% of libraries, 100% of dining areas, 95% of student union, 75% of common outdoor areas have wireless network access. Students can register for classes online. Administrative functions (other than registration) can be performed online.

CAMPUS LIFE

Environment: Village. **Activities:** Choral groups, concert band, dance, drama/theater, jazz band, literary magazine, marching band, music ensembles, musical theater, radio station, student government, student newspaper, television station, yearbook, campus ministries, international student organization. **Organizations:** 200 registered organizations, 23 honor societies, 8 religious organizations. 12 fraternities, 15 sororities. **Athletics (Intercollegiate):** *Men:* Baseball, basketball, cross-country, football, soccer, swimming, track/field (outdoor), track/field (indoor), wrestling. *Women:* Basketball, cross-country, field hockey, lacrosse, soccer, softball, swimming, tennis, track/field (outdoor), track/field (indoor), volleyball. **On-Campus Highlights:** Ceddia Union Building, Heiges Field House, Student Recreation Center, Ritazza Coffee Shop, Student Fitness Center, Starbucks, Quiznos, Chick-fil-A, Dauphin Humanities Center, Lehman Library, Learning Assistant Center, Reisner Dining Hall. **Environmental Initiatives:** Energy conservation iniatives; Go green carbon footprint analysis; CUB LEED certification/solar panels at Reisner.

ADMISSIONS

Freshman Academic Profile: Average high school GPA 3.23. 9.2% in top 10% of high school class, 31.5% in top 25% of high school class, 68.9% in top 50% of high school class. 88% from public high schools. SAT Math middle 50% range 440–550. SAT Critical Reading middle 50% range 440–530. Minimum paper TOEFL 550. Minimum computer TOEFL 213. Minimum web-based TOEFL 80. **Basis for Candidate Selection:** *Very important factors considered include:* Class rank, academic GPA, rigor of secondary school record, standardized test scores. *Other factors considered include:* Application essay, recommendation(s), character/personal qualities, extracurricular activities, interview, level of applicant's interest, talent/ability, volunteer work, work experience. **Freshman Admission Requirements:** High school diploma is required and GED is accepted. *Academic units recommended:* 4 English, 3 mathematics, 3 science, (3 science labs), 3 foreign language, 3 Social Sciences **Freshman Admission Statistics:** 7,001 applied, 72% admitted, 34% enrolled. **Transfer Admission Requirements:** College transcript(s), statement of good standing from prior institution(s). Minimum college GPA of 2.2 required. Lowest grade transferable C. **General Admission Information:** Application fee $30. Nonfall registration accepted. Admission may be deferred for a maximum of 1 year. Credit and/or placement offered for CEEB Advanced Placement tests.

COSTS AND FINANCIAL AID

Annual in-state tuition $5,554. Annual out-of-state tuition $13,886. Room and board $7,086. Required fees $1,890. Average book expense $1,100. **Required Forms and Deadlines:** FAFSA. Priority financial aid filing date 3/15. **Notification of Awards: Types of Aid:** *Need-based scholarships/grants:* Federal Pell, SEOG, state scholarships/grants, private scholarships, the school's own gift aid, Academic Competitiveness Grant (ACG)and Smart Grant. *Loans:* FFEL Subsidized Stafford, FFEL Unsubsidized Stafford, FFEL PLUS, Federal Perkins, Alternative loans. *Student Employment:* Federal Work-Study Program available. Off-campus job opportunities are good. **Financial Aid Statistics:** 45% freshmen, 39% undergrads receive need-based scholarship or grant aid. 4% freshmen, 3% undergrads receive non-need-based scholarship or grant aid. 54% freshmen, 50% undergrads receive need-based self-help aid. 4% freshmen, 4% undergrads receive athletic scholarships. 85% freshmen, 79% undergrads receive any aid. 74% undergrads borrow to pay for school. Average cumulative indebtedness $21,163. **Criteria for awarding institutional aid:** *Non-need-based:* Academics, athletics.

SHORTER COLLEGE

315 Shorter Avenue, Box 1, Rome, GA 30165
Phone: 706-233-7319 **Financial Aid Phone:** 706-233-7227
E-mail: admissions@shorter.edu **CEEB Code:** 5616
Fax: 706-233-7224 **Website:** www.shorter.edu **ACT Code:** 860

This private school, affiliated with the Southern Baptist Church, was founded in 1873. It has a 150-acre campus.

RATINGS
Admissions Selectivity Rating: 79   **Fire Safety Rating:** 70   **Green Rating:** 68

STUDENTS AND FACULTY
Enrollment: 1,194. **Student Body:** 49% female, 51% male, 9% out-of-state, 5% international (31 countries represented). Asian 1%, African American 14%, Caucasian 75%, Hispanic 2%.
Retention and Graduation: 69% freshmen return for sophomore year. 43% freshmen graduate within 4 years. 30% grads go on to further study within 1 year. **Faculty:** Student/faculty ratio 11:1. 83 full-time faculty, 73% hold PhDs, 12% are are members of minority groups, 48% are women.

ACADEMICS
Degrees: Bachelor's. **Classes:** Most classes have 10–19 students. Most lab/discussion sessions have 10–19 students. **Majors with Highest Enrollment:** Business administration and management; education; visual and performing arts. **Special Study Options:** Cross-registration, double major, dual enrollment, honors program, independent study, internships, student-designed major, study abroad, teacher certification program, weekend college. **Honors programs:** Academy of Aristaeus: A four-year honors program featuring seminar discussions and a research project. Special programs offered to physically disabled students include note-taking services, reader services, tape recorders, tutors. **Career services:** Career/job search classes, career assessment. **Career services highlights include:** Most majors include required internships.

FACILITIES
Housing: Men's dorms, women's dorms, apartments for single students. 70% of campus accessible to physically disabled. **Special Academic Facilities/Equipment:** Shorter History Museum. **Computers:** Students can register for classes online. Administrative functions (other than registration) can be performed online.

CAMPUS LIFE
Environment: Town. **Activities:** Choral groups, concert band, dance, drama/theater, literary magazine, marching band, music ensembles, musical theater, opera, pep band, radio station, student government, student newspaper, student-run film society, yearbook, campus ministries, international student organization, Model UN. **Organizations:** 34 registered organizations, 10 honor

societies, 3 religious organizations. 3 fraternities, 3 sororities. **Athletics (Intercollegiate):** *Men:* Baseball, basketball, cheerleading, cross-country, football, golf, soccer, tennis, track/field (outdoor). *Women:* Basketball, cheerleading, cross-country, golf, lacrosse, soccer, softball, tennis, track/field (outdoor), volleyball. **On-Campus Highlights:** Fitton Student Union, Winthrop-King Activities Center, Brookes Chapel, Ledbetter Baseball Complex.

ADMISSIONS
Freshman Academic Profile: Average high school GPA 3.33. 23% in top 10% of high school class, 50% in top 25% of high school class, 72% in top 50% of high school class. 95% from public high schools. SAT Math middle 50% range 430–550. SAT Critical Reading middle 50% range 430–570. SAT Writing middle 50% range 420–560. ACT middle 50% range 18–23. Minimum paper TOEFL 500. Minimum computer TOEFL 173. **Basis for Candidate Selection:** *Very important factors considered include:* Academic GPA, standardized test scores. *Important factors considered include:* Class rank, application essay, rigor of secondary school record, talent/ability. *Other factors considered include:* Recommendation(s), alumni/ae relation, character/personal qualities, extracurricular activities, first generation, interview, level of applicant's interest, volunteer work, work experience. **Freshman Admission Requirements:** High school diploma is required and GED is accepted. *Academic units required:* 4 English, 4 mathematics, 3 science, 2 foreign language, 3 history. **Freshman Admission Statistics:** 1,672 applied, 65% admitted, 45% enrolled. **Transfer Admission Requirements:** College transcript(s), statement of good standing from prior institution(s). Minimum college GPA of 2.0 required. Lowest grade transferable C. **General Admission Information:** Application fee $25. Notification on a rolling basis, beginning on or about 11/1. Nonfall registration accepted. Admission may be deferred for a maximum of 2 years. Credit and/or placement offered for CEEB Advanced Placement tests.

COSTS AND FINANCIAL AID
Annual tuition $15,950. Room and board $7,800. Required fees $350. Average book expense $1,000. **Required Forms and Deadlines:** FAFSA, institution's own financial aid form, state aid form. Priority financial aid filing date 4/1. **Notification of Awards:** Applicants will be notified of awards on a rolling basis beginning 4/1. **Types of Aid:** *Need-based scholarships/grants:* Federal Pell, SEOG, state scholarships/grants, private scholarships, the school's own gift aid. *Loans:* FFEL Subsidized Stafford, FFEL Unsubsidized Stafford, FFEL PLUS, Federal Perkins, We have moved to using Direct Loans from the US Government. *Student Employment:* Federal Work-Study Program available. Institutional employment available. Highest amount earned per year from on-campus jobs $2,000. Off-campus job opportunities are good. **Financial Aid Statistics:** 78% freshmen, 73% undergrads receive need-based scholarship or grant aid. 15% freshmen, 15% undergrads receive non-need-based scholarship or grant aid. 59% freshmen, 51% undergrads receive need-based self-help aid. 12% freshmen, 15% undergrads receive athletic scholarships. 99% freshmen, 99% undergrads receive any aid. 75% undergrads borrow to pay for school. Average cumulative indebtedness $22,967. **Criteria for awarding institutional aid:** *Non-need-based:* Academics, art, athletics, music/drama, religious affiliation.

SIENA COLLEGE

Best 373

515 Loudon Road, Loudonville, NY 12211
Phone: 518-783-2423 **Financial Aid Phone:** 888-287-4362
E-mail: admit@siena.edu **CEEB Code:** 2814
Fax: 518-783-2436 **Website:** www.siena.edu **ACT Code:** 2878

This private school, affiliated with the Roman Catholic Church, was founded in 1937. It has a 166-acre campus.

RATINGS
Admissions Selectivity Rating: 86   **Fire Safety Rating:** 60*   **Green Rating:** 60*

STUDENTS AND FACULTY
Enrollment: 3,220. **Student Body:** 53% female, 47% male, 16% out-of-state, international (6 countries represented). Asian 3%, African American 2%, Caucasian 81%, Hispanic 4%.
Retention and Graduation: 89% freshmen return for sophomore year. 27% grads go on to further study within 1 year. 7% grads pursue arts and sciences degrees. 4% grads pursue law degrees. 6% grads pursue business degrees. 9% grads pursue medical degrees. **Faculty:** Student/faculty ratio 13:1. 194 full-time faculty, 91% hold PhDs, 12% are are members of minority groups, 36% are women.

ACADEMICS

Degrees: Bachelor's, certificate. **Classes:** Most classes have 20–29 students. Most lab/discussion sessions have 10–19 students. **Majors with Highest Enrollment:** finance; marketing/marketing management; psychology. **Special Study Options:** Accelerated program, cross-registration, double major, English as a Second Language (ESL), honors program, independent study, internships, liberal arts/career combination, study abroad, teacher certification program, Semester in Washington D.C, Gettysburg Semester. **Honors programs:** College-wide Honors program. **Combined degree programs:** BA/MD, BA/JD, BA/MA, BA/DDS, BA/MEng, BBA/MBA. Special programs offered to physically disabled students include note-taking services, reader services, tape recorders, tutors. **Career services:** Alumni network, alumni services, career/job search classes, career assessment, internships, regional alumni. **Career services highlights include:** Students at Siena cultivate internships in almost every field.

FACILITIES

Housing: Coed dorms, special housing for disabled students, special housing for international students, apartments for single students, quiet living area available; on-campus townhouses (men and women). 90% of campus accessible to physically disabled. **Special Academic Facilities/Equipment:** Hickey Financial Center. **Computers:** 20% of classrooms, 40% of dorms, 100% of libraries, 100% of dining areas, 100% of student union, have wireless network access. Students can register for classes online. Administrative functions (other than registration) can be performed online.

CAMPUS LIFE

Environment: Town. **Activities:** Choral groups, dance, drama/theater, literary magazine, musical theater, opera, pep band, radio station, student government, student newspaper, symphony orchestra, television station, yearbook, campus ministries, Model UN. **Organizations:** 70 registered organizations, 15 honor societies, 2 religious organizations. **Athletics (Intercollegiate):** *Men:* Baseball, basketball, cross-country, golf, lacrosse, soccer, tennis. *Women:* Basketball, cross-country, field hockey, golf, lacrosse, soccer, softball, swimming, tennis, volleyball, water polo. **On-Campus Highlights:** Sarazen Student Union, J. Spencer and Patricia Standish Library, MAC/ARC—Athletic Facilities, Siena Hall, Academic Quad, Hickey Financial Technical Center.

ADMISSIONS

Freshman Academic Profile: Average high school GPA 89.8. 27.7% in top 10% of high school class, 61.4% in top 25% of high school class, 92.8% in top 50% of high school class. SAT Math middle 50% range 530–630. SAT Critical Reading middle 50% range 500–600. SAT Writing middle 50% range 500–600. ACT middle 50% range 22–27. Minimum paper TOEFL 550. Minimum computer TOEFL 213. Minimum web-based TOEFL 79. **Basis for Candidate Selection:** *Very important factors considered include:* Academic GPA, rigor of secondary school record. *Important factors considered include:* Recommendation(s), standardized test scores. *Other factors considered include:* Class rank, application essay, alumni/ae relation, character/personal qualities, extracurricular activities, first generation, interview, level of applicant's interest, racial/ethnic status, talent/ability, volunteer work, work experience. **Freshman Admission Requirements:** High school diploma is required and GED is accepted. *Academic units required:* 4 English, 3 mathematics, 3 science, (3 science labs), 1 social studies, 2 history. *Academic units recommended:* 4 English, 4 mathematics, 4 science, (4 science labs), 3 foreign language, 1 social studies, 3 history. **Freshman Admission Statistics:** 7,282 applied, 53% admitted, 20% enrolled. **Transfer Admission Requirements:** College transcript(s), statement of good standing from prior institution(s). Minimum college GPA of 2.5 required. Lowest grade transferable C+. **General Admission Information:** Application fee $50. Early decision application deadline 12/1. Regular application deadline 3/1. Regular notification 3/15. Nonfall registration accepted. Admission may be deferred for a maximum of 1 year. Credit and/or placement offered for CEEB Advanced Placement tests.

COSTS AND FINANCIAL AID

Annual tuition $25,060. Room and board $9,930. Required fees $225. Average book expense $1,080. **Required Forms and Deadlines:** FAFSA, state aid form. Financial aid filing deadline 5/1. Priority financial aid filing date 2/15. **Notification of Awards:** Applicants will be notified of awards on or about 4/1. **Types of Aid:** *Need-based scholarships/grants:* Federal Pell, SEOG, state scholarships/grants, private scholarships, the school's own gift aid. *Loans:* FFEL Subsidized Stafford, FFEL Unsubsidized Stafford, FFEL PLUS, Federal Perkins. *Student Employment:* Highest amount earned per year from on-campus jobs $1,000. **Financial Aid Statistics:** 68% freshmen, 65% undergrads receive need-based scholarship or grant aid. 48% freshmen, 44% undergrads receive non-need-based scholarship or grant aid. 53% freshmen, 53% undergrads receive need-based self-help aid. 9% freshmen, 8% undergrads receive athletic scholarships. 96.1% freshmen, 95.3% undergrads receive any aid. **Criteria for awarding institutional aid:** *Non-need-based:* Academics, athletics, leadership, minority status, state/district residency.

SIERRA NEVADA COLLEGE

999 Tahoe Blvd, Incline Village, NV 89451
Phone: 775-831-1314
E-mail: admissions@sierraneveda.edu
Fax: 702-831-1347 **Website:** www.sierraneveda.edu

This private school was founded in 1969. It has a 25-acre campus.

RATINGS

Admissions Selectivity Rating: 81   **Fire Safety Rating:** 60*   **Green Rating:** 60*

STUDENTS AND FACULTY

Enrollment: 302. **Student Body:** 51% female, 49% male, 70% out-of-state, 3% international. Asian 3%, African American 1%, Caucasian 75%, Hispanic 3%, Native American 1%.
Retention and Graduation: 70% freshmen return for sophomore year. 13% freshmen graduate within 4 years. 33% grads go on to further study within 1 year. **Faculty:** Student/faculty ratio 8:1. 19 full-time faculty, 42% are women.

ACADEMICS

Degrees: Bachelor's, post-bachelor's certificate. **Majors with Highest Enrollment:** Business, management, marketing, and related support services, other; environmental science; humanities/humanistic studies. **Special Study Options:** Double major, honors program, internships, study abroad, teacher certification program. **Combined degree programs:** BA/Dr. Pharmacy. Special programs offered to physically disabled students include note-taking services, tutors. **Career services:** Career/job search classes, career assessment, internships.

FACILITIES

Housing: Coed dorms. 50% of campus accessible to physically disabled. **Special Academic Facilities/Equipment:** McLean Observatory.

CAMPUS LIFE

Environment: Village. **Activities:** Literary magazine, student government, student newspaper. **Organizations:** 10 registered organizations, 1 honor societies, 2 religious organizations. **Athletics (Intercollegiate):** *Men:* Equestrian sports, skiing (downhill/alpine). *Women:* Equestrian sports, skiing (downhill/alpine).

ADMISSIONS

Freshman Academic Profile: Average high school GPA 3.14. 10% in top 10% of high school class, 35% in top 25% of high school class, 70% in top 50% of high school class. 60% from public high schools. SAT Math middle 50% range 480–560. SAT Critical Reading middle 50% range 480–560. ACT middle 50% range 20–26. Minimum paper TOEFL 500. **Basis for Candidate Selection:** *Important factors considered include:* Application essay, recommendation(s), rigor of secondary school record. *Other factors considered include:* Class rank, standardized test scores, alumni/ae relation, character/personal qualities, extracurricular activities, geographical residence, interview, racial/ethnic status, talent/ability, volunteer work, work experience. **Freshman Admission Requirements:** High school diploma is required and GED is accepted. *Academic units recommended:* 4 English, 3 mathematics, 2 science, 2 foreign language, 2 social studies, 2 history. **Freshman Admission Statistics:** 26% enrolled. **Transfer Admission Requirements:** College transcript(s), essay or personal statement, Lowest grade transferable C. **General Admission Information:** Notification on a rolling basis, beginning on or about 12/15. Nonfall registration accepted. Admission may be deferred for a maximum of 1 year. Credit and/or placement offered for CEEB Advanced Placement tests.

COSTS AND FINANCIAL AID

Annual tuition $19,500. Room and board $7,450. Required fees $150. Average book expense $700. **Required Forms and Deadlines:** FAFSA. Priority financial aid filing date 4/1. **Notification of Awards:** Applicants will be notified of awards on a rolling basis beginning 3/1. **Types of Aid:** *Need-based scholarships/grants:* Federal Pell, SEOG, state scholarships/grants, private scholarships, the school's own gift aid. *Loans:* Direct Subsidized Stafford, Direct PLUS. *Student Employment:* Federal Work-Study Program available. Institutional employment available. Off-campus job opportunities are excellent. **Financial Aid Statistics:** 67% freshmen, 67% undergrads receive need-based scholarship or grant aid. 67% freshmen, 67% undergrads receive need-based self-help aid. 70% undergrads borrow to pay for school. Average cumulative indebtedness $13,000. **Criteria for awarding institutional aid:** *Non-need-based:* Academics, art, athletics, state/district residency.

SIMMONS COLLEGE

300 The Fenway, Boston, MA 02115
Phone: 617-521-2051 **Financial Aid Phone:** 617-521-2001
E-mail: ugadm@simmons.edu **CEEB Code:** 3761
Fax: 617-521-3190 **Website:** www.simmons.edu **ACT Code:** 1892

This private school was founded in 1899. It has a 12-acre campus.

RATINGS
Admissions Selectivity Rating: 84   **Fire Safety Rating:** 90   **Green Rating:** 85

STUDENTS AND FACULTY
Enrollment: 1,934. **Student Body:** 100% female, 39% out-of-state, 3% international (46 countries represented). Asian 7%, African American 6%, Caucasian 69%, Hispanic 4%.
Retention and Graduation: 75% freshmen return for sophomore year. 61% freshmen graduate within 4 years. 30% grads go on to further study within 1 year. 20% grads pursue arts and sciences degrees. 1% grads pursue law degrees. 1% grads pursue business degrees. 2% grads pursue medical degrees. **Faculty:** Student/faculty ratio 13:1. 231 full-time faculty, 81% hold PhDs, 24% are are members of minority groups, 69% are women.

ACADEMICS
Degrees: Bachelor's, diploma, doctoral, master's, post-bachelor's certificate, post-master's certificate. **Classes:** Most classes have 10–19 students. **Majors with Highest Enrollment:** nursing/registered nurse (RN, ASN, BSN, MSN); psychology. **Special Study Options:** Accelerated program, cross-registration, double major, dual enrollment, English as a Second Language (ESL), exchange student program (domestic), honors program, independent study, internships, liberal arts/career combination, student-designed major, study abroad, teacher certification program, Exhange program with Mills College (CA), Spellman College (GA), Fisk University (TN), American University (DC), Colleges of the Fenway exchange program, double-degree programs with Massachusetts College of Pharmacy and Health Sciences, and with Hebrew College. **Honors programs:** One Honors Program. **Combined degree programs:** BA/MA, BA/MEng, BA/MAT BS/MS BA/MBA BA/MSW. Special programs offered to physically disabled students include note-taking services, reader services, tape recorders, tutors. **Career services:** Alumni network, alumni services, career/job search classes, career assessment, internships, regional alumni. **Career services highlights include:** Internships that lead to job placement.

FACILITIES
Housing: Special housing for disabled students, women's dorms, wellness housing, theme housing. 99% of campus accessible to physically disabled. **Special Academic Facilities/Equipment:** Art gallery, media center, science center with dream/sleep analysis lab, physical therapy clinic areas, sports center with pool. **Computers:** 100% of classrooms, 5% of dorms, 100% of libraries, 100% of dining areas, 100% of student union, have wireless network access. Students can register for classes online. Administrative functions (other than registration) can be performed online.

CAMPUS LIFE
Environment: City. **Activities:** Choral groups, dance, drama/theater, literary magazine, radio station, student government, student newspaper, student-run film society, symphony orchestra, yearbook. **Organizations:** 91 registered organizations, 4 honor societies, 4 religious organizations. **Athletics (Intercollegiate):** *Women:* Basketball, crew/rowing, diving, field hockey, lacrosse, soccer, softball, swimming, tennis, volleyball. **On-Campus Highlights:** Java City, Beatley Library, Park Science Center, Palace Road Building/Pottruck Technology, School of Management. **Environmental Initiatives:** Recycling and waste management program; mechanical equipment upgrades to improve efficiency and performance; LEED-certified new building.

ADMISSIONS
Freshman Academic Profile: Average high school GPA 3.15. 19% in top 10% of high school class, 55% in top 25% of high school class, 89% in top 50% of high school class. SAT Math middle 50% range 490–600. SAT Critical Reading middle 50% range 500–590. SAT Writing middle 50% range 510–610. ACT middle 50% range 22–26. Minimum paper TOEFL 560. Minimum computer TOEFL 220. Minimum web-based TOEFL 83. **Basis for Candidate Selection:** *Very important factors considered include:* Academic GPA, rigor of secondary school record. *Important factors considered include:* Class rank, application essay, recommendation(s), standardized test scores. *Other factors considered include:* Extracurricular activities, interview, talent/ability, volunteer

work, work experience. **Freshman Admission Requirements:** High school diploma is required and GED is accepted. *Academic units required:* 4 English, 3 mathematics, 3 science, 3 foreign language, 3 social studies, 3 history. *Academic units recommended:* 4 English, 4 mathematics, 3 science, 4 foreign language, 4 social studies, 3 history. **Freshman Admission Statistics:** 3,522 applied, 57% admitted, 18% enrolled. **Transfer Admission Requirements:** High school transcript, college transcript(s), essay or personal statement, statement of good standing from prior institution(s). Minimum college GPA of 2.8 required. Lowest grade transferable C+. **General Admission Information:** Application fee $55. Regular application deadline 2/1. Regular notification 4/15. Nonfall registration accepted. Admission may be deferred for a maximum of 1 year. Credit and/or placement offered for CEEB Advanced Placement tests.

COSTS AND FINANCIAL AID
Annual tuition $30,520. Room and board $12,050. Required fees $930. Average book expense $1,280. **Required Forms and Deadlines:** FAFSA, institution's own financial aid form. Financial aid filing deadline 3/1. Priority financial aid filing date 2/15. **Notification of Awards:** Applicants will be notified of awards on a rolling basis beginning 3/15. **Types of Aid:** *Need-based scholarships/grants:* Federal Pell, SEOG, state scholarships/grants, private scholarships, the school's own gift aid. *Loans:* Direct Subsidized Stafford, Direct Unsubsidized Stafford, Direct PLUS, state loans, college/university loans from institutional funds. *Student Employment:* Federal Work-Study Program available. Institutional employment available. Highest amount earned per year from on-campus jobs $2,000. Off-campus job opportunities are excellent. **Financial Aid Statistics:** 78% freshmen, 70% undergrads receive need-based scholarship or grant aid. 4% freshmen, 3% undergrads receive non-need-based scholarship or grant aid. 73% freshmen, 67% undergrads receive need-based self-help aid. 94% freshmen, 85% undergrads receive any aid. 78% undergrads borrow to pay for school. Average cumulative indebtedness $45,237. **Criteria for awarding institutional aid:** *Non-need-based:* Academics, alumni affiliation, leadership, minority status.

SIMPSON COLLEGE (IA)

701 North C Street, Indianola, IA 50125
Phone: 515-961-1624
E-mail: admiss@simpson.edu **CEEB Code:** 6650
Fax: 515-961-1870 **Website:** www.simpson.edu **ACT Code:** 1354

This private school, affiliated with the Methodist Church, was founded in 1860. It has a 63-acre campus.

RATINGS
Admissions Selectivity Rating: 74   **Fire Safety Rating:** 60*   **Green Rating:** 60*

STUDENTS AND FACULTY
Enrollment: 1,758. **Student Body:** 60% female, 40% male, 10% out-of-state, 2% international (13 countries represented). Asian 1%, African American 1%, Caucasian 93%, Hispanic 1%.
Retention and Graduation: 78% freshmen return for sophomore year. 57% freshmen graduate within 4 years. 11% grads go on to further study within 1 year. 6% grads pursue arts and sciences degrees. 2% grads pursue law degrees. 1% grads pursue business degrees. 2% grads pursue medical degrees. **Faculty:** Student/faculty ratio 14:1. 84 full-time faculty, 87% hold PhDs, 6% are are members of minority groups, 29% are women.

ACADEMICS
Degrees: Bachelor's, post-bachelor's certificate. **Classes:** Most classes have 10–19 students. Most lab/discussion sessions have 10–19 students. **Special Study Options:** Accelerated program, cooperative education program, double major, English as a Second Language (ESL), honors program, independent study, internships, liberal arts/career combination, student-designed major, study abroad, teacher certification program, weekend college, International Program. Special programs offered to physically disabled students include note-taking services, reader services, tape recorders, tutors. **Career services:** Alumni services, career/job search classes, career assessment, internships.

FACILITIES
Housing: Coed dorms, men's dorms, women's dorms, fraternity/sorority housing, apartments for single students, Simpson College owns several homes surrounding campus known as theme houses. Group of students petition for those houses on a yearly basis. **Special Academic Facilities/Equipment:** The biology department hosts a human cadaver lab while Dunn library boasts the Avery O'Craven Room which houses an extensive antebellum collection.

CAMPUS LIFE
Environment: Village. **Activities:** Choral groups, concert band, dance, drama/theater, jazz band, literary magazine, music ensembles, opera, pep band, radio

station, student government, student newspaper, yearbook. **Organizations:** 89 registered organizations, 15 honor societies, 17 religious organizations. 4 fraternities, 4 sororities. **Athletics (Intercollegiate):** *Men:* Baseball, basketball, cheerleading, cross-country, football, golf, soccer, tennis, track/field (outdoor), track/field (indoor), wrestling. *Women:* Basketball, cheerleading, cross-country, golf, soccer, softball, swimming, tennis, track/field (outdoor), track/field (indoor), volleyball. **On-Campus Highlights:** Carse Fitness Center, Blank Performing Arts Center, Carver Science Center and Open Atrium, Pfeiffer Dining Hall, Brenton Student Center.

ADMISSIONS

Freshman Academic Profile: 21% in top 10% of high school class, 57% in top 25% of high school class, 90% in top 50% of high school class. 96% from public high schools. ACT middle 50% range 22–27. Minimum paper TOEFL 550. **Basis for Candidate Selection:** *Very important factors considered include:* Class rank, rigor of secondary school record, standardized test scores. *Important factors considered include:* Recommendation(s), character/personal qualities. *Other factors considered include:* Alumni/ae relation, extracurricular activities, interview, volunteer work. **Freshman Admission Requirements:** High school diploma is required and GED is accepted. *Academic units recommended:* 4 English, 3 mathematics, 3 science, (3 science labs), 3 foreign language, 3 social studies. **Freshman Admission Statistics:** 1,442 applied, 76% admitted, 38% enrolled. **Transfer Admission Requirements:** High school transcript, college transcript(s), standardized test scores, minimum college GPA of 2.5 required. Lowest grade transferable C–. **General Admission Information:** Nonfall registration accepted. Admission may be deferred for a maximum of 24 months. Credit and/or placement offered for CEEB Advanced Placement tests.

COSTS AND FINANCIAL AID

Annual tuition $17,908. Room and board $6,062. Required fees $189. Average book expense $800. **Required Forms and Deadlines:** FAFSA. Priority financial aid filing date 4/1. **Notification of Awards:** Applicants will be notified of awards on a rolling basis beginning 3/15. **Types of Aid:** *Need-based scholarships/grants:* Federal Pell, SEOG, state scholarships/grants, private scholarships, the school's own gift aid. *Loans:* FFEL Subsidized Stafford, FFEL Unsubsidized Stafford, FFEL PLUS, Federal Perkins, state loans, college/university loans from institutional funds, Private Educational Loans. *Student Employment:* Federal Work-Study Program available. Institutional employment available. Highest amount earned per year from on-campus jobs $735. Off-campus job opportunities are fair. **Financial Aid Statistics:** 87% freshmen, 86% undergrads receive need-based scholarship or grant aid. 13% freshmen, 9% undergrads receive non-need-based scholarship or grant aid. 72% freshmen, 75% undergrads receive need-based self-help aid. 91% undergrads borrow to pay for school. Average cumulative indebtedness $20,940. **Criteria for awarding institutional aid:** *Non-need-based:* Academics, alumni affiliation, art, leadership, minority status, music/drama, religious affiliation, state/district residency.

SIMPSON UNIVERSITY

2211 College View Dr, Redding, CA 96003
Phone: 530-226-4606 **Financial Aid Phone:** 530-224-5600
E-mail: admissions@simpsonuniversity.edu
Fax: 530-226-4861 **Website:** www.simpsonuniversity.edu **ACT Code:** 430

This private school, affiliated with the Christian & Missionary Allianc Church, was founded in 1921. It has a 92-acre campus.

RATINGS
Admissions Selectivity Rating: 82   **Fire Safety Rating:** 60*   **Green Rating:** 60*

STUDENTS AND FACULTY
Student Body: international.
Retention and Graduation: 61% freshmen return for sophomore year. **Faculty:** Student/faculty ratio 17:1. 38 full-time faculty, 55% hold PhDs.

ACADEMICS
Degrees: Associate, bachelor's, certificate, master's. **Classes:** Most classes have 10–19 students. Most lab/discussion sessions have 10–19 students. **Majors with Highest Enrollment:** Elementary education and teaching; organizational behavior studies; psychology. **Special Study Options:** Accelerated program, distance learning, double major, honors program, independent study, internships, student-designed major, study abroad, teacher certification program, weekend college. **Honors programs:** Oxford Honours Programme through the CCCU (Coalition of Christian Colleges and Universities). Special programs offered to physically disabled students include note-taking services, reader services, tutors. **Career services:** Career/job search classes, career assessment.

FACILITIES
Housing: Special housing for disabled students, men's dorms, special housing for international students, women's dorms, apartments for married students. 95% of campus accessible to physically disabled. **Computers:** Students can register for classes online. Administrative functions (other than registration) can be performed online.

CAMPUS LIFE
Environment: City. **Activities:** Choral groups, drama/theater, jazz band, music ensembles, pep band, student government, student newspaper, yearbook. **Organizations:** 17 registered organizations, 1 honor societies, 20 religious organizations. **Athletics (Intercollegiate):** *Men:* Baseball, basketball. *Women:* Basketball. **On-Campus Highlights:** Chapel (Heritage Student Life Center), Athletic Events (Heritage Student Life Center), Music Department (Heritage Student Life Center), Bible/Theology Classes (La-Baume Rudat Bldg.), AandB Coffee Shop and Bookstore (Owen Center).

ADMISSIONS
Freshman Academic Profile: Average high school GPA 3.32. 19% in top 10% of high school class, 47% in top 25% of high school class, 79% in top 50% of high school class. 63% from public high schools. SAT Math middle 50% range 430–560. SAT Critical Reading middle 50% range 450–590. ACT middle 50% range 18–23. Minimum paper TOEFL 500. Minimum computer TOEFL 180. **Basis for Candidate Selection:** *Very important factors considered include:* Recommendation(s), rigor of secondary school record, standardized test scores, character/personal qualities, religious affiliation/commitment. *Important factors considered include:* Class rank, volunteer work. *Other factors considered include:* Application essay, extracurricular activities, interview, talent/ability. **Freshman Admission Requirements:** High school diploma is required and GED is accepted. *Academic units recommended:* 4 English, 3 mathematics, 2 science, 2 foreign language, 3 social studies. **Freshman Admission Statistics:** 938 applied, 59% admitted, 34% enrolled. **Transfer Admission Requirements:** High school transcript, college transcript(s), essay or personal statement, statement of good standing from prior institution(s). Minimum college GPA of 2.0 required. Lowest grade transferable C. **General Admission Information:** Application fee $20. Nonfall registration accepted. Admission may be deferred for a maximum of 24 months. Credit and/or placement offered for CEEB Advanced Placement tests.

COSTS AND FINANCIAL AID
Annual tuition $17,000. Room and board $5,900. Average book expense $1,200. **Required Forms and Deadlines:** FAFSA, institution's own financial aid form. Priority financial aid filing date 3/2. **Notification of Awards:** Applicants will be notified of awards on a rolling basis beginning 3/16. **Types of Aid:** *Need-based scholarships/grants:* Federal Pell, SEOG, state scholarships/grants, private scholarships, the school's own gift aid. *Loans:* FFEL Subsidized Stafford, FFEL Unsubsidized Stafford, FFEL PLUS, Federal Perkins, Alternative Loans. *Student Employment:* Federal Work-Study Program available. Institutional employment available. Off-campus job opportunities are good. **Financial Aid Statistics:** 84% freshmen, 91% undergrads receive need-based scholarship or grant aid. 84% freshmen, 91% undergrads receive non-need-based scholarship or grant aid. 82% freshmen, 89% undergrads receive need-based self-help aid. 96% freshmen, 96% undergrads receive any aid. 89% undergrads borrow to pay for school. Average cumulative indebtedness $17,600. **Criteria for awarding institutional aid:** *Non-need-based:* Academics, alumni affiliation, leadership, minority status, music/drama, religious affiliation, state/district residency.

SKIDMORE COLLEGE

815 North Broadway, Saratoga Springs, NY 12866-1632
Phone: 518-580-5570 **Financial Aid Phone:** 518-580-5750
E-mail: admissions@skidmore.edu **CEEB Code:** 2815
Fax: 518-580-5584 **Website:** www.skidmore.edu **ACT Code:** 2906

This private school was founded in 1903. It has a 750-acre campus.

RATINGS
Admissions Selectivity Rating: 94   **Fire Safety Rating:** 60*   **Green Rating:** 60*

STUDENTS AND FACULTY
Enrollment: 2,678. **Student Body:** 60% female, 40% male, 67% out-of-state, 3% international (41 countries represented). Asian 9%, African American 3%, Caucasian 67%, Hispanic 5%, Native American 1%.

Retention and Graduation: 93% freshmen return for sophomore year. 78% freshmen graduate within 4 years. 19% grads go on to further study within 1 year. 7.3% grads pursue arts and sciences degrees. 3.2% grads pursue law degrees. 0.6% grads pursue business degrees. 3.2% grads pursue medical degrees. **Faculty:** Student/faculty ratio 8.4:1. 249 full-time faculty, 80% hold PhDs, 14% are are members of minority groups, 54% are women.

ACADEMICS

Degrees: Bachelor's, master's. **Classes:** Most classes have 10–19 students. Most lab/discussion sessions have 10–19 students. **Majors with Highest Enrollment:** Business/commerce; English language and literature; psychology. **Special Study Options:** Accelerated program, cross-registration, double major, dual enrollment, exchange student program (domestic), honors program, independent study, internships, liberal arts/career combination, student-designed major, study abroad, teacher certification program **Honors programs:** Honors Forum Special programs offered to physically disabled students include note-taking services, reader services, tape recorders, tutors. **Career services:** Alumni network, alumni services, career/job search classes, career assessment, internships, regional alumni. **Career services highlights include:** Alumni Network.

FACILITIES

Housing: Coed dorms, special housing for disabled students, special housing for international students, women's dorms, apartments for single students, gender neutral wing. 75% of campus accessible to physically disabled. **Special Academic Facilities/Equipment:** Tang Teaching Museum and Art Gallery, center for child study, art, music, dance, and theatre facilities, electron microscope, spectrometer. **Computers:** Students can register for classes online. Administrative functions (other than registration) can be performed online.

CAMPUS LIFE

Environment: Town. **Activities:** Choral groups, concert band, dance, drama/theater, jazz band, literary magazine, music ensembles, musical theater, opera, radio station, student government, student newspaper, symphony orchestra, television station, yearbook, campus ministries, international student organization, Model UN. **Organizations:** 80 registered organizations, 10 honor societies, 3 religious organizations. **Athletics (Intercollegiate):** *Men:* Baseball, basketball, crew/rowing, diving, golf, ice hockey, lacrosse, soccer, swimming, tennis. *Women:* Basketball, crew/rowing, diving, equestrian sports, field hockey, lacrosse, soccer, softball, swimming, tennis, volleyball. **On-Campus Highlights:** Tang Teaching Museum, Lucy Scribner Library, Case Student Center, Woodlawn Village Apartments, Murray-Atkins Dining Hall.

ADMISSIONS

Freshman Academic Profile: Average high school GPA 3.403. 37.1% in top 10% of high school class, 79.3% in top 25% of high school class, 96.2% in top 50% of high school class. 61% from public high schools. SAT Math middle 50% range 590–670. SAT Critical Reading middle 50% range 580–680. SAT Writing middle 50% range 590–690. ACT middle 50% range 26–29. Minimum paper TOEFL 590. Minimum computer TOEFL 243. Minimum web-based TOEFL 243. **Basis for Candidate Selection:** *Very important factors considered include:* Rigor of secondary school record. *Important factors considered include:* Class rank, application essay, academic GPA, recommendation(s), character/personal qualities, extracurricular activities, talent/ability, volunteer work, work experience. *Other factors considered include:* Standardized test scores, alumni/ae relation, first generation, geographical residence, interview, level of applicant's interest, racial/ethnic status. **Freshman Admission Requirements:** High school diploma is required and GED is accepted. *Academic units recommended:* 4 English, 4 mathematics, 4 science, (3 science labs), 4 foreign language, 4 social studies. **Freshman Admission Statistics:** 7,316 applied, 30% admitted, 30% enrolled. **Transfer Admission Requirements:** High school transcript, college transcript(s), essay or personal statement, standardized test scores, statement of good standing from prior institution(s). Minimum college GPA of 2.7 required. Lowest grade transferable C. **General Admission Information:** Application fee $60. Early decision application deadline 11/15. Regular application deadline 1/15. Regular notification 4/1. Nonfall registration not accepted. Admission may be deferred for a maximum of 2 years. Credit and/or placement offered for CEEB Advanced Placement tests.

COSTS AND FINANCIAL AID

Annual tuition $39,600. Room and board $10,776. Required fees $820. Average book expense $1,304. **Required Forms and Deadlines:** FAFSA, CSS/Financial Aid PROFILE. Financial aid filing deadline 1/15. **Notification of Awards:** Applicants will be notified of awards on or about 4/1. **Types of Aid:** *Need-based scholarships/grants:* Federal Pell, SEOG, state scholarships/grants, the school's own gift aid. *Loans:* FFEL Subsidized Stafford, FFEL Unsubsidized Stafford, FFEL PLUS, Federal Perkins. *Student Employment:* Federal Work-Study Program available. Institutional employment available. Highest amount earned per year from on-campus jobs $2,300. Off-campus job opportunities are fair. **Financial Aid Statistics:** 41% freshmen, 40% undergrads receive need-based scholarship or grant aid. 17% freshmen, 8% undergrads receive non-need-based

scholarship or grant aid. 41% freshmen, 40% undergrads receive need-based self-help aid. 49% freshmen, 50% undergrads receive any aid. 46.4% undergrads borrow to pay for school. Average cumulative indebtedness $19,163. **Criteria for awarding institutional aid:** *Non-need-based:* Music/drama.

See page 1238.

SLIPPERY ROCK UNIVERSITY OF PENNSYLVANIA

1 Morrow Way, Slippery Rock, PA 16057
Phone: 724-738-2015 **Financial Aid Phone:** 724-738-2044
E-mail: asktherock@sru.edu **CEEB Code:** 2658
Fax: 724-738-2913 **Website:** www.sru.edu **ACT Code:** 3716

This public school was founded in 1889. It has a 600-acre campus.

RATINGS

Admissions Selectivity Rating: 77   **Fire Safety Rating:** 98   **Green Rating:** 78

STUDENTS AND FACULTY

Enrollment: 7,703. **Student Body:** 56% female, 44% male, 9% out-of-state, 1% international (38 countries represented). Asian 1%, African American 5%, Caucasian 85%, Hispanic 1%.
Retention and Graduation: 81% freshmen return for sophomore year. 31% freshmen graduate within 4 years. 22% grads go on to further study within 1 year. 39% grads pursue arts and sciences degrees. 2% grads pursue law degrees. 13% grads pursue business degrees. 1% grads pursue medical degrees. **Faculty:** Student/faculty ratio 20:1. 348 full-time faculty, 89% hold PhDs, 18% are are members of minority groups, 46% are women.

ACADEMICS

Degrees: Bachelor's, certificate, master's, post-bachelor's certificate. **Classes:** Most classes have 20–29 students. Most lab/discussion sessions have fewer than 10 students. **Majors with Highest Enrollment:** Business administration and management; elementary education and teaching; kinesiology and exercise science. **Special Study Options:** Distance learning, double major, dual enrollment, exchange student program (domestic), honors program, independent study, internships, liberal arts/career combination, student-designed major, study abroad, teacher certification program. **Honors programs:** Undergraduate Honors Program **Combined degree programs:** Pre-Osteo 3+4 and Pre-Pharm 3+3 LECOM; Pre-Chiro 3+3 Logan; Pre-PT 3+3 SRU. Special programs offered to physically disabled students include note-taking services, reader services, tape recorders, tutors. **Career services:** Alumni services, career/job search classes, career assessment, internships. **Career services highlights include:** The Office of Career Services offers students and alumni the opportunity to meet individually with career counselors.

FACILITIES

Housing: Coed dorms, special housing for disabled students, apartments for single students, theme housing 80% of campus accessible to physically disabled. **Special Academic Facilities/Equipment:** Special education school for student teachers, physical therapy clinic, microvideo system, planetarium, electron microscope. Residence Halls have academic interest floors with special facilities for specific majors whereby students can interact with faculty and have academically related programs where they live. **Computers:** 80% of classrooms, 100% of dorms, 100% of libraries, 50% of dining areas, 100% of student union, 5% of common outdoor areas have wireless network access. Students can register for classes online. Administrative functions (other than registration) can be performed online.

CAMPUS LIFE

Environment: Rural. **Activities:** Choral groups, concert band, dance, drama/theater, jazz band, literary magazine, marching band, music ensembles, musical theater, radio station, student government, student newspaper, student-run film society, symphony orchestra, television station, campus ministries, international student organization, Model UN. **Organizations:** 145 registered organizations, 37 honor societies, 4 religious organizations. 9 fraternities, 8 sororities. **Athletics (Intercollegiate):** *Men:* Baseball, basketball, cheerleading, cross-country, football, soccer, track/field (outdoor), track/field (indoor). *Women:* Basketball, cheerleading, cross-country, field hockey, lacrosse, soccer, softball, tennis, track/field (outdoor), track/field (indoor), volleyball. **On-Campus Highlights:** Aebersold Recreation Center, New Residential Suite Living Complexes, Bailey Library, Advanced Science and Technology Building, University Union. **Environmental Initiatives:** Recycling; green building designs and renovations; green procurement practices.

ADMISSIONS

Freshman Academic Profile: Average high school GPA 3.39. 12% in top 10% of high school class, 42% in top 25% of high school class, 84% in top 50% of high school class. 80% from public high schools. SAT Math middle 50% range 470–560. SAT Critical Reading middle 50% range 460–550. SAT Writing middle 50% range 450–540. ACT middle 50% range 19–24. Minimum paper TOEFL 500. Minimum computer TOEFL 173. **Basis for Candidate Selection:** *Important factors considered include:* Class rank, academic GPA, rigor of secondary school record, standardized test scores. *Other factors considered include:* Application essay, recommendation(s), talent/ability. **Freshman Admission Requirements:** High school diploma is required and GED is accepted. *Academic units recommended:* 4 English, 3 mathematics, 3 science, (1 science labs), 2 foreign language. **Freshman Admission Statistics:** 5,928 applied, 63% admitted, 42% enrolled. **Transfer Admission Requirements:** College transcript(s), minimum college GPA of 2.0 required. Lowest grade transferable C. **General Admission Information:** Application fee $30. Notification on a rolling basis, beginning on or about 6/15. Nonfall registration accepted. Admission may be deferred for a maximum of 1 year. Credit and/or placement offered for CEEB Advanced Placement tests.

COSTS AND FINANCIAL AID

Annual in-state tuition $5,554. Annual out-of-state tuition $8,331. Room and board $8,454. Required fees $1,681. Average book expense $1,363. **Required Forms and Deadlines:** FAFSA. Priority financial aid filing date 5/1. **Notification of Awards:** Applicants will be notified of awards on a rolling basis beginning 3/15. **Types of Aid:** *Need-based scholarships/grants:* Federal Pell, SEOG, state scholarships/grants, private scholarships, the school's own gift aid. *Loans:* FFEL Subsidized Stafford, FFEL Unsubsidized Stafford, FFEL PLUS, Federal Perkins. *Student Employment:* Federal Work-Study Program available. Institutional employment available. Highest amount earned per year from on-campus jobs $4,000. Off-campus job opportunities are good. **Financial Aid Statistics:** 49% freshmen, 45% undergrads receive need-based scholarship or grant aid. 29% freshmen, 18% undergrads receive non-need-based scholarship or grant aid. 66% freshmen, 61% undergrads receive need-based self-help aid. 4% freshmen, 3% undergrads receive athletic scholarships. 93% freshmen, 85% undergrads receive any aid. 81% undergrads borrow to pay for school. Average cumulative indebtedness $23,879. **Criteria for awarding institutional aid:** *Non-need-based:* Academics, alumni affiliation, art, athletics, job skills, leadership, minority status, music/drama, state/district residency.

SMITH COLLEGE

7 College Lane, Northampton, MA 01063
Phone: 413-585-2500 **Financial Aid Phone:** 413-585-2530
E-mail: admission@smith.edu **CEEB Code:** 3762
Fax: 413-585-2527 **Website:** www.smith.edu **ACT Code:** 1894

This private school was founded in 1871. It has a 147-acre campus.

RATINGS

Admissions Selectivity Rating: 96   **Fire Safety Rating:** 71   **Green Rating:** 96

STUDENTS AND FACULTY

Enrollment: 2,614. **Student Body:** 100% female, 78% out-of-state, 5% international (72 countries represented). Asian 10%, African American 5%, Caucasian 30%, Hispanic 5%, Native American 1%. **Retention and Graduation:** 91% freshmen return for sophomore year. 78% freshmen graduate within 4 years. **Faculty:** Student/faculty ratio 9:1. 281 full-time faculty, 98% hold PhDs, 17% are are members of minority groups, 54% are women.

ACADEMICS

Degrees: Bachelor's, master's, post-bachelor's certificate, post-master's certificate. **Classes:** Most classes have 10–19 students. **Majors with Highest Enrollment:** Economics; political science and government; psychology. **Special Study Options:** Accelerated program, cross-registration, double major, exchange student program (domestic), honors program, independent study, internships, study abroad, teacher certification program Special programs offered to physically disabled students include note-taking services, reader services, tape recorders, tutors. **Career services:** Alumni network, alumni services, career/job search classes, career assessment, internships, regional alumni. **Career services highlights include:** Praxis internship program: guaranteed $2,000 stipend per student for summer internship.

FACILITIES

Housing: Women's dorms, cooperative housing, Apartment complex for limited number of juniors and seniors. Also,one senior house, french speaking house, and Ada Comstock (non-traditional age) house. 85% of campus accessible to physically disabled. **Special Academic Facilities/Equipment:** Art museum, printing, darkroom, and sculpture facilities, dance, electronic music, television, and theatre studios, recital hall, rehearsal rooms, multimedia language lab, early childhood/elementary education campus school, two electronic classrooms, physiology and horticultural labs, animal care facilities, two electron microscopes, greenhouses, observatories. **Computers:** 85% of classrooms, 100% of dorms, 100% of libraries, 100% of dining areas, 100% of student union, 50% of common outdoor areas have wireless network access. Students can register for classes online. Administrative functions (other than registration) can be performed online.

CAMPUS LIFE

Environment: Town. **Activities:** Choral groups, concert band, dance, drama/theater, jazz band, literary magazine, music ensembles, musical theater, radio station, student government, student newspaper, television station, yearbook, campus ministries, international student organization, Model UN. **Organizations:** 133 registered organizations, 3 honor societies, 9 religious organizations. **Athletics (Intercollegiate):** *Women:* Basketball, crew/rowing, cross-country, diving, equestrian sports, field hockey, lacrosse, skiing (downhill/alpine), soccer, softball, squash, swimming, tennis, track/field (outdoor), track/field (indoor), volleyball. **On-Campus Highlights:** Smith Art Museum, The Botanical Gardens, Campus Center, Mendenhall Center for Performing Arts, Lyman Plant House. **Environmental Initiatives:** A new natural gas fired cogeneration facility went online in October 2008. When running it typically generates 90% of campus electricity use and an average of 50% steam for heat. This system will decrease use of #6 fuel oil and greatly reduce greenhouse gas emissions. The addition of steam driven absorption chilling capacity is currently being studied. Hired a full-time Environmental Sustainability Director in August, 2008 who will work closely with shared Energy Manager and Recycling Manager positions (collaboration w/ Five Colleges Inc.). Implemented 18 energy efficiency projects and 7 conservation programs over past 4 years; these have generated substantial financial savings and have reduced greenhouse gas emissions associated with electricity consumption by 18% and steam production by 15%. A recurring fund is being established to fund ongoing efficiency projects.

ADMISSIONS

Freshman Academic Profile: Average high school GPA 3.9. 66% in top 10% of high school class, 94% in top 25% of high school class, 100% in top 50% of high school class. 67% from public high schools. SAT Math middle 50% range 580–690. SAT Critical Reading middle 50% range 610–710. SAT Writing middle 50% range 610–710. ACT middle 50% range 27–30. Minimum paper TOEFL 600. Minimum computer TOEFL 250. Minimum web-based TOEFL 90. **Basis for Candidate Selection:** *Very important factors considered include:* Academic GPA, recommendation(s), rigor of secondary school record, character/personal qualities. *Important factors considered include:* Class rank, application essay, extracurricular activities, interview, talent/ability. *Other factors considered include:* standardized test scores, alumni/ae relation, first generation, racial/ethnic status, volunteer work, work experience. **Freshman Admission Requirements:** High school diploma or equivalent is not required. *Academic units recommended:* 4 English, 3 mathematics, 3 science, (3 science labs), 3 foreign language, 2 history. **Freshman Admission Statistics:** 4,011 applied, 47% admitted, 35% enrolled. **Transfer Admission Requirements:** High school transcript, college transcript(s), essay or personal statement, statement of good standing from prior institution(s). Lowest grade transferable C. **General Admission Information:** Application fee $60. Early decision application deadline 11/15. Regular application deadline 1/15. Regular notification 4/1. Nonfall registration not accepted. Admission may be deferred for a maximum of 1 year. Credit and/or placement offered for CEEB Advanced Placement tests.

COSTS AND FINANCIAL AID

Required Forms and Deadlines: FAFSA, CSS/Financial Aid PROFILE, noncustodial PROFILE, business/farm supplement. Financial aid filing deadline 2/15. **Notification of Awards:** Applicants will be notified of awards on or about 4/1. **Types of Aid:** *Need-based scholarships/grants:* Federal Pell, SEOG, state scholarships/grants, the school's own gift aid. *Loans:* Direct Subsidized Stafford, Direct Unsubsidized Stafford, FFEL PLUS, Federal Perkins, state loans, college/university loans from institutional funds. *Student Employment:* Federal Work-Study Program available. Institutional employment available. Highest amount earned per year from on-campus jobs $2,558. Off-campus job opportunities are excellent. **Financial Aid Statistics:** 57% freshmen, 60% undergrads receive need-based scholarship or grant aid. 1% freshmen, 1% undergrads receive non-need-based scholarship or grant aid. 59% freshmen, 62% undergrads receive need-based self-help aid. 70.2% freshmen, 71.7% undergrads receive any aid. 62% undergrads borrow to pay for school. Average cumulative indebtedness $21,573. **Criteria for awarding institutional aid:** *Non-need-based:* Academics, state/district residency.

SOKA UNIVERSITY OF AMERICA

1 University Drive, Enrollment Services, Aliso Viejo, CA 92656-4105
Phone: 949-480-4150 **Financial Aid Phone:** 949-480-4048
E-mail: admission@soka.edu **CEEB Code:** 4066
Fax: 949-480-4151 **Website:** www.soka.edu **ACT Code:** 467

This private school was founded in 2001. It has a 103-acre campus.

RATINGS
Admissions Selectivity Rating: 93 **Fire Safety Rating:** 79 **Green Rating:** 60*

STUDENTS AND FACULTY
Enrollment: 360. **Student Body:** 62% female, 38% male, 61% out-of-state, 53% international (28 countries represented). Asian 19%, African American 3%, Caucasian 10%, Hispanic 4%.
Retention and Graduation: 91% freshmen return for sophomore year. 40% grads go on to further study within 1 year. 34% grads pursue arts and sciences degrees. 2% grads pursue law degrees. 2% grads pursue business degrees. 2% grads pursue medical degrees. **Faculty:** Student/faculty ratio 8:1. 38 full-time faculty, 95% hold PhDs, 32% are are members of minority groups, 45% are women.

ACADEMICS
Degrees: Bachelor's, master's. **Classes:** Most classes have 10–19 students. Most lab/discussion sessions have 10–19 students. **Special Study Options:** English as a Second Language (ESL), independent study, internships, liberal arts/career combination, study abroad. Special programs offered to physically disabled students include note-taking services, reader services, tape recorders, tutors.

FACILITIES
Housing: Coed dorms, special housing for disabled students. 100% of campus accessible to physically disabled. **Special Academic Facilities/Equipment:** Art Gallery, Athenaeum (Reception Center) **Computers:** Students can register for classes online. Administrative functions (other than registration) can be performed online. Undergraduates are required to own a computer.

CAMPUS LIFE
Environment: Town. **Activities:** Choral groups, concert band, dance, drama/theater, jazz band, literary magazine, music ensembles, student government, student newspaper, student-run film society, symphony orchestra, yearbook. **Organizations:** 38 registered organizations, 1 religious organizations. **Athletics (Intercollegiate):** *Men:* Cross-country, diving, soccer, swimming, track/field (outdoor). *Women:* Cross-country, diving, soccer, swimming, track/field (outdoor) **On-Campus Highlights:** Founders Hall Art Gallery, Student Center Dining Hall, Student Center Bookstore, Recreation Center, Ikeda Library, Hiking trail along canyon rim surrounding campus.

ADMISSIONS
Freshman Academic Profile: Average high school GPA 3.67. 43% in top 10% of high school class, 80% in top 25% of high school class, 94% in top 50% of high school class. 60% from public high schools. SAT Math middle 50% range 570–680. SAT Critical Reading middle 50% range 460–640. SAT Writing middle 50% range 490–630. ACT middle 50% range 23–24. **Basis for Candidate Selection:** *Very important factors considered include:* Class rank, application essay, academic GPA, recommendation(s), rigor of secondary school record, character/personal qualities, extracurricular activities, level of applicant's interest. *Important factors considered include:* Standardized test scores, talent/ability, volunteer work. *Other factors considered include:* geographical residence, interview, racial/ethnic status, work experience. **Freshman Admission Requirements:** High school diploma is required and GED is accepted. *Academic units recommended:* 4 English, 3 mathematics, 2 science, (2 science labs), 2 foreign language, 2 social studies, 2 history. **Freshman Admission Statistics:** 321 applied, 40% admitted, 68% enrolled. **General Admission Information:** Application fee $45. Regular application deadline 1/6. Regular notification 3/15. Nonfall registration not accepted. Admission may be deferred for a maximum of 1 year. Neither credit nor placement offered for CEEB Advanced Placement tests.

COSTS AND FINANCIAL AID
Annual tuition $22,108. Room and board $8,600. Average book expense $1,000. **Required Forms and Deadlines:** FAFSA Financial aid filing deadline 5/1. **Notification of Awards:** Applicants will be notified of awards on a rolling basis beginning 3/15. **Types of Aid:** *Need-based scholarships/grants:* Federal Pell, SEOG, state scholarships/grants, private scholarships, the school's own gift aid, Hispanic Educational Endowment Fund (HEEF). *Loans:* FFEL Subsidized Stafford, FFEL Unsubsidized Stafford, FFEL PLUS, college/university loans from institutional funds. *Student Employment:* Highest amount earned per year from on-campus jobs $5,400. **Financial Aid Statistics:** 35% freshmen,

84% undergrads receive need-based scholarship or grant aid. 35% freshmen, 28% undergrads receive non-need-based scholarship or grant aid. 34% freshmen, 61% undergrads receive need-based self-help aid. 100% freshmen, 100% undergrads receive any aid. 85% undergrads borrow to pay for school. Average cumulative indebtedness $17,125. **Criteria for awarding institutional aid:** *Non-need-based:* Academics.

SONOMA STATE UNIVERSITY

1801 East Cotati Avenue, Rohnert Park, CA 94928
Phone: 707-664-2778 **Financial Aid Phone:** 707-664-2389
E-mail: student.outreach@sonoma.edu **CEEB Code:** 4723
Fax: 707-664-2060 **Website:** www.sonoma.edu **ACT Code:** 431

This public school was founded in 1960. It has a 269-acre campus.

RATINGS
Admissions Selectivity Rating: 72 **Fire Safety Rating:** 60* **Green Rating:** 98

STUDENTS AND FACULTY
Enrollment: 7,483. **Student Body:** 62% female, 38% male, 2% out-of-state, 1% international. Asian 4%, African American 1%, Caucasian 59%, Hispanic 12%, Native American 1%.
Retention and Graduation: 75% freshmen return for sophomore year. 24% grads go on to further study within 1 year. **Faculty:** Student/faculty ratio 23:1. 278 full-time faculty, 91% hold PhDs, 17% are are members of minority groups, 46% are women. 7% of classes are taught by teaching assistants.

ACADEMICS
Degrees: Bachelor's, master's. **Classes:** Most classes have 20–29 students. **Majors with Highest Enrollment:** Business/commerce; liberal arts and sciences studies and humanities, other; psychology. **Special Study Options:** Accelerated program, cooperative education program, cross-registration, distance learning, double major, dual enrollment, English as a Second Language (ESL), exchange student program (domestic), external degree program, honors program, independent study, internships, liberal arts/career combination, student-designed major, study abroad, teacher certification program, **Combined degree programs:** Bachelor's/MBA; bachelor's/MPA. **Combined degree programs:** BA/MA. Special programs offered to physically disabled students include note-taking services, reader services, tape recorders, tutors. **Career services:** Career/job search classes.

FACILITIES
Housing: Coed dorms, men's dorms, special housing for international students, women's dorms, apartments for single students, housing for focused learning communities—freshman seminar dorms, healthy living dorms; women in math/science dorms. 99% of campus accessible to physically disabled. **Special Academic Facilities/Equipment:** Performing arts center, observatory, electron microscope, seismograph, information technology center, environmental technology center, high technology high school, nature preserve. **Computers:** 95% of classrooms, 90% of dorms, 100% of libraries, 85% of dining areas, 100% of student union, 20% of common outdoor areas have wireless network access. Students can register for classes online. Administrative functions (other than registration) can be performed online. Undergraduates are required to own a computer.

CAMPUS LIFE
Environment: Town. **Activities:** Choral groups, dance, drama/theater, jazz band, literary magazine, music ensembles, musical theater, opera, pep band, radio station, student government, student newspaper, symphony orchestra **Organizations:** 109 registered organizations, 2 honor societies, 4 religious organizations. 5 fraternities, 9 sororities. **Athletics (Intercollegiate):** *Men:* Baseball, basketball, soccer, tennis. *Women:* Basketball, cross-country, soccer, softball, tennis, track/field (outdoor), volleyball. **On-Campus Highlights:** Schultz Information Center, Environmental Technology Center, Charlie Brown's (coffee shop), Observatory, University Recreation Center. **Environmental Initiatives:** Energy efficiency; recycling; education.

ADMISSIONS
Freshman Academic Profile: Average high school GPA 3.22. 81% from public high schools. SAT Math middle 50% range 460–570. SAT Critical Reading middle 50% range 450–560. ACT middle 50% range 19–24. Minimum paper TOEFL 500. Minimum computer TOEFL 173. **Basis for Candidate**

Selection: *Very important factors considered include:* Academic GPA, rigor of secondary school record, standardized test scores. *Other factors considered include:* first generation, geographical residence, state residency. **Freshman Admission Requirements:** High school diploma is required and GED is accepted. *Academic units required:* 4 English, 3 mathematics, 2 science, (1 science labs), 2 foreign language, 2 history, 1 visual/performing arts, 1 academic electives, 1 visual/performing arts,US govt. **Freshman Admission Statistics:** 11,244 applied, 77% admitted, 25% enrolled. **Transfer Admission Requirements:** College transcript(s), minimum college GPA of 2.0 required. Lowest grade transferable D. **General Admission Information:** Application fee $55. Regular application deadline 11/30. Regular notification 3/1. Notification on a rolling basis, beginning on or about 11/1. Nonfall registration accepted. Credit and/or placement offered for CEEB Advanced Placement tests.

COSTS AND FINANCIAL AID

Annual out-of-state tuition $10,347. Room and board $10,086. Required fees $5,290. Average book expense $1,732. **Required Forms and Deadlines:** FAFSA. Priority financial aid filing date 1/31. **Notification of Awards:** Applicants will be notified of awards on a rolling basis beginning 3/25. **Types of Aid:** *Need-based scholarships/grants:* Federal Pell, SEOG, state scholarships/grants, private scholarships, ACG, SMART. *Loans:* Direct Subsidized Stafford, Direct Unsubsidized Stafford, Direct PLUS, Federal Perkins. *Student Employment:* Federal Work-Study Program available. Institutional employment available. Highest amount earned per year from on-campus jobs $9,000. Off-campus job opportunities are good. **Financial Aid Statistics:** 12% freshmen, 22% undergrads receive need-based scholarship or grant aid. 4% freshmen, 5% undergrads receive non-need-based scholarship or grant aid. 20% freshmen, 33% undergrads receive need-based self-help aid. 1% freshmen, 1% undergrads receive athletic scholarships. 42% freshmen, 55% undergrads receive any aid. 43% undergrads borrow to pay for school. Average cumulative indebtedness $14,400. **Criteria for awarding institutional aid:** *Non-need-based:* Academics, alumni affiliation, art, athletics, leadership, minority status, music/drama.

SOUTH DAKOTA SCHOOL OF MINES AND TECHNOLOGY

501 East St. Joseph Street, Rapid City, SD 57701-3995
Phone: 605-394-2414 **Financial Aid Phone:** 605-394-2274
E-mail: admissions@sdsmt.edu **CEEB Code:** 003470
Fax: 605-394-1979 **Website:** www.sdsmt.edu **ACT Code:** 3192

This public school was founded in 1885. It has a 118-acre campus.

RATINGS
Admissions Selectivity Rating: 82   **Fire Safety Rating:** 98   **Green Rating:** 86

STUDENTS AND FACULTY
Enrollment: 1,632. **Student Body:** 22% female, 78% male, 41% out-of-state, 3% international (34 countries represented). Asian 1%, Caucasian 85%, Hispanic 1%, Native American 3%.
Retention and Graduation: 9% freshmen graduate within 4 years. 25% grads go on to further study within 1 year. 1% grads pursue law degrees. 1% grads pursue business degrees. 1% grads pursue medical degrees. **Faculty:** Student/faculty ratio 14:1. 121 full-time faculty, 83% hold PhDs, 13% are are members of minority groups, 17% are women.

ACADEMICS
Degrees: Associate, bachelor's, master's, terminal associate. **Classes:** Most classes have 20–29 students. **Majors with Highest Enrollment:** Civil engineering; electrical; electronics and communications engineering; mechanical engineering. **Special Study Options:** Cooperative education program, cross-registration, distance learning, dual enrollment, English as a Second Language (ESL), independent study, internships, liberal arts/career combination, study abroad, Distance Education—SDSMT offfers an MS degree in Technology Management via the Internet. Dual Degrees—We do not offer double majors but students may graduate with more than one degree by completing a minimum of thirty (30) semester hours of credit in residence beyond the credit hours used for the first BS degree. Special programs offered to physically disabled students include note-taking services, reader services, tape recorders, tutors. **Career services:** Alumni network, alumni services, career/job search classes, career assessment, internships, regional alumni. **Career services highlights include:** Both the cooperative/internship programs are very successful and usually lead to permanent employment for the students after graduation.

FACILITIES
Housing: Coed dorms, special housing for disabled students, fraternity/sorority housing, apartments for married students, apartments for single students, well-

ness housing. SDSM&T recently acquired apartments which can be rented by single students or groups of students or married students with families. 80% of campus accessible to physically disabled. **Special Academic Facilities/Equipment:** Museum of geology and paleontology, electron microscope, engineering/mining experiment station, supersonic wind tunnel,3-D visualization lab, polymer processing lab, friction stir welding lab, high-frequency microwave lab, tech development lab, fluid computational dynamics lab, robotics lab, clean manufacturing lab, institute atmospheric science and other research institutes. **Computers:** 100% of classrooms, 100% of dorms, 100% of libraries, 100% of dining areas, 100% of student union, 100% of common outdoor areas have wireless network access. Students can register for classes online. Administrative functions (other than registration) can be performed online.

CAMPUS LIFE
Environment: Town. **Activities:** Choral groups, concert band, dance, drama/theater, jazz band, music ensembles, pep band, radio station, student government, student newspaper, campus ministries, international student organization. **Organizations:** 67 registered organizations, 6 honor societies, 9 religious organizations. 4 fraternities, 2 sororities. **Athletics (Intercollegiate):** *Men:* Basketball, cross-country, football, golf, track/field (outdoor), track/field (indoor). *Women:* Basketball, cross-country, golf, track/field (outdoor), track/field (indoor), volleyball. **On-Campus Highlights:** O'Harra Stadium (football and track), King (Sports) Center—basketball, pool, exercise, Geology and Paleontology Museum, Surbeck Student Center, Apex Gallery. **Environmental Initiatives:** Leed Silver Buildings on all new construction/renovation. Energy Star Appliances Puchasing Policy RecycleMania.

ADMISSIONS
Freshman Academic Profile: Average high school GPA 3.51. 22% in top 10% of high school class, 55% in top 25% of high school class, 86% in top 50% of high school class. SAT Math middle 50% range 550–670. SAT Critical Reading middle 50% range 500–630. ACT middle 50% range 24–28. Minimum paper TOEFL 530. Minimum computer TOEFL 197. Minimum web-based TOEFL 71. **Basis for Candidate Selection:** *Very important factors considered include:* Class rank, academic GPA, rigor of secondary school record, standardized test scores. *Other factors considered include:* Character/personal qualities, extracurricular activities, talent/ability, volunteer work, work experience. **Freshman Admission Requirements:** High school diploma is required and GED is accepted. *Academic units required:* 4 English, 4 mathematics, 4 science, (3 science labs), 2 foreign language, 3 social studies, 1 visual/performing arts. **Freshman Admission Statistics:** 975 applied, 82% admitted, 45% enrolled. **Transfer Admission Requirements:** College transcript(s), statement of good standing from prior institution(s). Minimum college GPA of 2.0 required. Lowest grade transferable D. **General Admission Information:** Application fee $20. Notification on a rolling basis, beginning on or about 11/1. Nonfall registration accepted. Admission may be deferred for a maximum of 1 year. Credit and/or placement offered for CEEB Advanced Placement tests.

COSTS AND FINANCIAL AID
Annual in-state tuition $2,750. Annual out-of-state tuition $4,130. Room and board $5,080. Required fees $4,080. Average book expense $1,950. **Required Forms and Deadlines:** FAFSAFreshman Scholarship Application Form. Priority financial aid filing date 3/15. **Notification of Awards:** Applicants will be notified of awards on a rolling basis beginning 5/1. **Types of Aid:** *Need-based scholarships/grants:* Federal Pell, SEOG, state scholarships/grants, private scholarships, the school's own gift aid, SMART grants, ACG grants. *Loans:* FFEL Subsidized Stafford, FFEL Unsubsidized Stafford, FFEL PLUS, Federal Perkins, Private alternative loans. *Student Employment:* Federal Work-Study Program available. Institutional employment available. Highest amount earned per year from on-campus jobs $2,000. Off-campus job opportunities are good. **Financial Aid Statistics:** 43% freshmen, 35% undergrads receive need-based scholarship or grant aid. 35% freshmen, 19% undergrads receive non-need-based scholarship or grant aid. 47% freshmen, 47% undergrads receive need-based self-help aid. 4% freshmen, 4% undergrads receive athletic scholarships. 57% freshmen, 54% undergrads receive any aid. **Criteria for awarding institutional aid:** *Non-need-based:* Academics, athletics, leadership, minority status.

SOUTH DAKOTA STATE UNIVERSITY

SAD 200, BOX 2201, Brookings, SD 57007-0649
Phone: 605-688-4121 **Financial Aid Phone:** 605-688-4695
E-mail: sdsu.admissions@sdstate.edu **CEEB Code:** 6653
Fax: 605-688-6891 **Website:** www3.sdstate.edu **ACT Code:** 3924

This public school was founded in 1881. It has a 272-acre campus.

RATINGS
Admissions Selectivity Rating: 72 | **Fire Safety Rating:** 77 | **Green Rating:** 63

STUDENTS AND FACULTY
Enrollment: 9,786. **Student Body:** 51% female, 49% male, 30% out-of-state, 1% international (47 countries represented). Asian 1%, African American 1%, Caucasian 87%, Hispanic 1%, Native American 2%.
Retention and Graduation: 78% freshmen return for sophomore year. **Faculty:** 476 full-time faculty, 72% hold PhDs, 14% are are members of minority groups, 44% are women.

ACADEMICS
Degrees: Associate, bachelor's, certificate, master's, post-bachelor's certificate, post-master's certificate, terminal associate. **Classes:** Most classes have 20–29 students. Most lab/discussion sessions have 20–29 students. **Special Study Options:** Accelerated program, cooperative education program, cross-registration, distance learning, double major, dual enrollment, exchange student program (domestic), honors program, independent study, internships, liberal arts/career combination, study abroad, teacher certification program, We offer help and courses in ESL but it is not an official program. **Honors programs:** Have an Honors College. **Combined degree programs:** BS/MS in Economics. Special programs offered to physically disabled students include note-taking services, reader services, tape recorders, tutors. **Career services:** Career/job search classes, career assessment, internships.

FACILITIES
Housing: Coed dorms, special housing for disabled students, special housing for international students, fraternity/sorority housing, apartments for married students, apartments for single students, wellness housing, limited single rooms with optional meal plan for upperclassmen. Students out of high school less than 2 yrs are required to live in campus housing unless living with family. **Special Academic Facilities/Equipment:** SD Art Museum, SD Agricultural Heritage Museum, Northern Plains Bio-stress Laboratory, Animal Disease Research and Diagnostic Lab, McCrory Gardens, new Center for Infectious Disease Research and Vaccinology, EROS-SDSU GISc Center of Excellence. **Computers:** 30% of classrooms, 100% of dorms, 100% of libraries, 100% of dining areas, 100% of student union, 20% of common outdoor areas have wireless network access. Students can register for classes online. Administrative functions (other than registration) can be performed online.

CAMPUS LIFE
Environment: Village. **Activities:** Choral groups, concert band, dance, drama/theater, jazz band, literary magazine, marching band, music ensembles, musical theater, pep band, radio station, student government, student newspaper, symphony orchestra, yearbook. **Organizations:** 200 registered organizations, 32 honor societies, 14 religious organizations. 6 fraternities, 4 sororities. **Athletics (Intercollegiate):** *Men:* Baseball, basketball, cross-country, diving, football, golf, swimming, tennis, track/field (outdoor), track/field (indoor), wrestling. *Women:* Basketball, cross-country, diving, equestrian sports, golf, soccer, softball, swimming, tennis, track/field (outdoor), track/field (indoor), volleyball. **On-Campus Highlights:** Performing Arts Center, Dairy Bar, University Student Union, Frost Arena, South Dakota Art Museum, Northern Plains Bio-Stress Laboratory Enterprise Institute SD Ag Heritage Museum. **Environmental Initiatives:** Asbestos abatement.

ADMISSIONS
Freshman Academic Profile: Average high school GPA 3.34. 15% in top 10% of high school class, 37% in top 25% of high school class, 69% in top 50% of high school class. ACT middle 50% range 20–26. Minimum paper TOEFL 500. Minimum computer TOEFL 173. Minimum web-based TOEFL 61. **Basis for Candidate Selection:** *Very important factors considered include:* Class rank, academic GPA, standardized test scores. *Important factors considered include:* Rigor of secondary school record. *Other factors considered include:* Recommendation(s). **Freshman Admission Requirements:** High school diploma is required and GED is accepted. *Academic units required:* 4 English, 3 mathematics, 3 science, (3 science labs), 3 social studies, 1 Fine arts *Academic units recommended:* 1 computer science. **Freshman Admission Statistics:** 4,191 applied, 93% admitted, 55% enrolled. **Transfer Admission Requirements:** High school transcript, college transcript(s), statement of good standing from prior institution(s). Minimum college GPA of 2.0 required. Lowest grade

transferable D. **General Admission Information:** Application fee $20. Non-fall registration accepted. Admission may be deferred for a maximum of 1 year. Credit and/or placement offered for CEEB Advanced Placement tests.

COSTS AND FINANCIAL AID
Annual in-state tuition $2,646. Annual out-of-state tuition $3,966. Room and board $5,423. Required fees $3,162. Average book expense $1,014. **Required Forms and Deadlines:** FAFSA. Priority financial aid filing date 3/11. **Notification of Awards:** Applicants will be notified of awards on a rolling basis beginning 4/1. **Types of Aid:** *Need-based scholarships/grants:* Federal Pell, SEOG, state scholarships/grants, private scholarships, the school's own gift aid, United Negro College Fund, Federal Nursing Scholarships. Federal SMART grants; Federal Academic Comp Grants, TEACH Grants, TRIO. *Loans:* FFEL Subsidized Stafford, FFEL Unsubsidized Stafford, FFEL PLUS, Federal Perkins, Federal Nursing, college/university loans from institutional funds, Health Profession loans. Private alternative loans. *Student Employment:* Federal Work-Study Program available. Institutional employment available. Highest amount earned per year from on-campus jobs $5,880. Off-campus job opportunities are good. **Financial Aid Statistics:** 36% freshmen, 44% undergrads receive need-based scholarship or grant aid. 53% freshmen, 69% undergrads receive non-need-based scholarship or grant aid. 70% freshmen, 75% undergrads receive need-based self-help aid. 6% freshmen, 4% undergrads receive athletic scholarships. 92% freshmen, 89% undergrads receive any aid. 82% undergrads borrow to pay for school. Average cumulative indebtedness $21,044. **Criteria for awarding institutional aid:** *Non-need-based:* Academics, art, athletics, job skills, leadership, minority status, music/drama, state/district residency.

SOUTHAMPTON COLLEGE OF LONG ISLAND UNIVERSITY

239 Montauk Highway, Southampton, NY 11968
Phone: 631-287-8200
E-mail: admissions@southampton.liunet.edu **CEEB Code:** 2853
Fax: 516-287-8130 **Website:** www.southampton.liu.edu **ACT Code:** 2853

This private school was founded in 1963. It has a 110-acre campus.

RATINGS
Admissions Selectivity Rating: 73 | **Fire Safety Rating:** 60* | **Green Rating:** 60*

STUDENTS AND FACULTY
Enrollment: 1,147. **Student Body:** 67% female, 33% male, 35% out-of-state, 5% international (20 countries represented). Asian 1%, African American 5%, Caucasian 62%, Hispanic 5%, Native American 1%.
Retention and Graduation: 68% freshmen return for sophomore year. **Faculty:** Student/faculty ratio 18:1. 66 full-time faculty.

ACADEMICS
Degrees: Bachelor's, master's, post-bachelor's certificate. **Classes:** Most classes have 10–19 students. Most lab/discussion sessions have 10–19 students. **Majors with Highest Enrollment:** Biopsychology; business/commerce; marine biology. **Special Study Options:** Accelerated program, cooperative education program, distance learning, double major, dual enrollment, English as a Second Language (ESL), exchange student program (domestic), honors program, independent study, internships, liberal arts/career combination, student-designed major, study abroad, teacher certification program, Undergrads may take grad level classes. Co-Op Programs: Arts, Business, Education, Health Professions, Humanities, Natural Science, Social/Behavioral Science, All majors. Off-Campus Study: United Nations, Semester at Sea. Other Special Programs: Travel abroad also available through Friends World Program. **Career services:** Alumni network, alumni services, career/job search classes, career assessment, internships.

FACILITIES
Housing: Coed dorms, women's dormsNon-smoking and substance free; honors; quiet. **Special Academic Facilities/Equipment:** Art galleries, on-campus nursery school, psychobiology lab, marine station and fleet of research vessels, Silicon Graphics Computer Lab. **Computers:** Administrative functions (other than registration) can be performed online.

CAMPUS LIFE
Environment: Village. **Activities:** Choral groups, drama/theater, literary magazine, music ensembles, musical theater, radio station, student government, student newspaper, student-run film society, yearbook. **Organizations:** 40 registered organizations, 4 honor societies, 2 religious organizations. **Athletics (Intercollegiate):** *Men:* Basketball, cross-country, lacrosse, soccer, tennis, volleyball. *Women:* Basketball, cross-country, soccer, softball, tennis, volleyball.

ADMISSIONS

Freshman Academic Profile: Average high school GPA 3.2. 19% in top 10% of high school class, 40% in top 25% of high school class, 77% in top 50% of high school class. 87% from public high schools. Minimum paper TOEFL 525. Minimum computer TOEFL 197. **Basis for Candidate Selection:** *Very important factors considered include:* Rigor of secondary school record, standardized test scores. *Important factors considered include:* Application essay, recommendation(s), character/personal qualities, talent/ability. *Other factors considered include:* Class rank, extracurricular activities, interview, volunteer work, work experience. **Freshman Admission Requirements:** High school diploma is required and GED is accepted. *Academic units required:* 4 English, 2 mathematics, 2 science, (1 science labs), 2 social studies, 2 history. *Academic units recommended:* 4 English, 3 mathematics, 3 science, (1 science labs), 2 foreign language, 2 social studies, 2 history. **Freshman Admission Statistics:** 1,354 applied, 63% admitted, 24% enrolled. Minimum college GPA of 2.0 required. Lowest grade transferable C. **General Admission Information:** Application fee $30. Notification on a rolling basis, beginning on or about 11/15. Nonfall registration accepted. Admission may be deferred for a maximum of 1 year. Credit and/or placement offered for CEEB Advanced Placement tests.

COSTS AND FINANCIAL AID

Annual tuition $15,340. Average book expense $600. **Required Forms and Deadlines:** FAFSA, state aid form. Priority financial aid filing date 2/1. **Notification of Awards:** Applicants will be notified of awards on a rolling basis beginning 3/1. **Types of Aid:** *Need-based scholarships/grants:* Federal Pell, SEOG, state scholarships/grants, private scholarships, the school's own gift aid. *Loans:* Direct Subsidized Stafford, Direct Unsubsidized Stafford, Direct PLUS, Federal Perkins. *Student Employment:* Federal Work-Study Program available. Institutional employment available. Highest amount earned per year from on-campus jobs $1,000. Off-campus job opportunities are good. **Financial Aid Statistics:** 73% freshmen, 74% undergrads receive need-based scholarship or grant aid. 57% freshmen, 44% undergrads receive non-need-based scholarship or grant aid. 80% freshmen, 86% undergrads receive need-based self-help aid. 1% freshmen, 6% undergrads receive athletic scholarships. 81% freshmen, 77% undergrads receive any aid. 89% undergrads borrow to pay for school. Average cumulative indebtedness $19,800. **Criteria for awarding institutional aid:** *Non-need-based:* Academics, alumni affiliation, art, athletics, leadership.

SOUTHEAST MISSOURI STATE UNIVERSITY

One University Plaza, Mail Stop 3550, Cape Girardeau, MO 63701
Phone: 573-651-2590 **Financial Aid Phone:** 573-651-2253
E-mail: admissions@semo.edu **CEEB Code:** 6655
Fax: 573-651-5936 **Website:** www.semo.edu **ACT Code:** 2366

This public school was founded in 1873. It has a 400-acre campus.

RATINGS

Admissions Selectivity Rating: 77   **Fire Safety Rating:** 75   **Green Rating:** 79

STUDENTS AND FACULTY

Enrollment: 8,882. **Student Body:** 58% female, 42% male, 12% out-of-state, 2% international (44 countries represented). Asian 1%, African American 9%, Caucasian 82%, Hispanic 1%.
Retention and Graduation: 74% freshmen return for sophomore year. 24% freshmen graduate within 4 years. **Faculty:** Student/faculty ratio 18:1. 419 full-time faculty, 75% hold PhDs, 13% are are members of minority groups, 46% are women. 4% of classes are taught by teaching assistants.

ACADEMICS

Degrees: Associate, bachelor's, certificate, master's, post-master's certificate. **Classes:** Most classes have 20–29 students. **Majors with Highest Enrollment:** Communication studies/speech communication and rhetoric; elementary education and teaching; general studies. **Special Study Options:** Accelerated program, distance learning, double major, dual enrollment, English as a Second Language (ESL), honors program, independent study, internships, liberal arts/career combination, student-designed major, study abroad, teacher certification program. **Honors programs:** The Honors Program encourages intellectual perspective, addresses special needs of outstanding students and contributes to the general advancement of learning. Special programs offered to physically disabled students include note-taking services, reader services, tape recorders, tutors. **Career services:** Alumni network, alumni services, career/job search classes, career assessment, internships, regional alumni. **Career services highlights include:** Career Linkages assists in locating experiential learning opportunities.

FACILITIES

Housing: Coed dorms, fraternity/sorority housing, wellness housingApartments for students with dependents. 100% of campus accessible to physically disabled.

Special Academic Facilities/Equipment: River Campus at Southeast; Crisp Museum;Bedell Performance Hall; Center for Faulkner Studies; Center for Scholarship in Teaching and Learning; Missouri Statewide Early Literacy Intervention Program (MSELIP); Writing Center; University Demonstration Farm; 4 corporate video studios, 2 radio stations; Southeast Explorer; SHOW (Southeast Health on Wheels); Linda Godwin Center for Science and Math Education. **Computers:** 15% of dorms, 90% of libraries, 90% of dining areas, 90% of student union, 10% of common outdoor areas have wireless network access. Students can register for classes online. Administrative functions (other than registration) can be performed online.

CAMPUS LIFE

Environment: Town. **Activities:** Choral groups, concert band, dance, drama/theater, jazz band, literary magazine, marching band, music ensembles, musical theater, opera, pep band, radio station, student government, student newspaper, symphony orchestra, campus ministries, international student organization, Model UN. **Organizations:** 136 registered organizations, 8 honor societies, 14 religious organizations. 11 fraternities, 7 sororities. **Athletics (Intercollegiate):** *Men:* Baseball, basketball, cheerleading, cross-country, football, track/field (outdoor), track/field (indoor). *Women:* Basketball, cheerleading, cross-country, gymnastics, soccer, softball, tennis, track/field (outdoor), track/field (indoor), volleyball. **On-Campus Highlights:** River Campus at Southeast, Recreation Center & Aquatic Center, Kent Library Information Commons, Otto and Della Seabaugh Polytechnic Bldg, Robert A. Dempster Hall, River Campus: Holland School of Visual adn Performing Arts,Bedell Performance Hall, Crisp Regional Museum, Rust Flexible Theatre, Glenn Convocation Center, Shuck Music Recital Hall. **Environmental Initiatives:** Waste Management Energy management-conduct energy savings workshops and energy audits for area companies. Green certified products

ADMISSIONS

Freshman Academic Profile: Average high school GPA 3.27. 16% in top 10% of high school class, 41% in top 25% of high school class, 71% in top 50% of high school class. SAT Math middle 50% range 460–580. SAT Critical Reading middle 50% range 440–570. ACT middle 50% range 20–25. Minimum paper TOEFL 500. Minimum computer TOEFL 173. Minimum web-based TOEFL 61. **Basis for Candidate Selection:** *Very important factors considered include:* Academic GPA, rigor of secondary school record, standardized test scores. *Other factors considered include:* Class rank. **Freshman Admission Requirements:** High school diploma is required and GED is accepted. *Academic units required:* 4 English, 3 mathematics, 3 science, (1 science labs), 2 social studies, 1 history, 1 visual/performing arts, 3 academic electives. **Freshman Admission Statistics:** 4,164 applied, 92% admitted, 47% enrolled. **Transfer Admission Requirements:** College transcript(s), minimum college GPA of 2.0 required. Lowest grade transferable D. **General Admission Information:** Application fee $25. Regular application deadline 7/1. Notification on a rolling basis, beginning on or about 9/1. Nonfall registration accepted. Credit offered for CEEB Advanced Placement tests.

COSTS AND FINANCIAL AID

Annual in-state tuition $5,544. Annual out-of-state tuition $10,179. Room and board $6,358. Required fees $711. Average book expense $447. **Required Forms and Deadlines:** FAFSA. Priority financial aid filing date 3/1. **Notification of Awards:** Applicants will be notified of awards on a rolling basis beginning 4/1. **Types of Aid:** *Need-based scholarships/grants:* Federal Pell, SEOG, state scholarships/grants, private scholarships, the school's own gift aid. *Loans:* FFEL Subsidized Stafford, FFEL Unsubsidized Stafford, FFEL PLUS, Federal Perkins, state loans. *Student Employment:* Federal Work-Study Program available. Institutional employment available. Off-campus job opportunities are fair. **Financial Aid Statistics:** 52% freshmen, 47% undergrads receive need-based scholarship or grant aid. 8% freshmen, 4% undergrads receive non-need-based scholarship or grant aid. 45% freshmen, 48% undergrads receive need-based self-help aid. 1% freshmen, 2% undergrads receive athletic scholarships. 63% undergrads borrow to pay for school. Average cumulative indebtedness $19,613. **Criteria for awarding institutional aid:** *Non-need-based:* Academics, alumni affiliation, art, athletics, job skills, leadership, minority status, music/drama, state/district residency.

SOUTHEASTERN BIBLE COLLEGE

3001 Highway 280 East, Birmingham, AL 35243
Phone: 205-970-9209
E-mail: admissions@sebc.edu
Fax: 205-970-9207 **Website:** www.sebc.edu **ACT Code:** 38

This private school was founded in 1935. It has a 10-acre campus.

RATINGS
Admissions Selectivity Rating: 60*   **Fire Safety Rating:** 60*   **Green Rating:** 60*

STUDENTS AND FACULTY
Enrollment: 228. **Student Body:** 38% female, 62% male, 30% out-of-state, 1% international (1 countries represented). Asian 1%, African American 18%, Caucasian 79%.
Retention and Graduation: 62% freshmen return for sophomore year. 38% freshmen graduate within 4 years. **Faculty:** Student/faculty ratio 13:1. 11 full-time faculty, 64% hold PhDs, 9% are women.

ACADEMICS
Degrees: Associate, bachelor's, diploma, terminal associate. **Classes:** Most classes have fewer than 10 students. **Majors with Highest Enrollment:** Bible/biblical studies; elementary education and teaching; youth ministry. **Special Study Options:** Independent study, internships Special programs offered to physically disabled students include note-taking services, tape recorders.

FACILITIES
Housing: Men's dorms, women's dorms, apartments for married students. 100% of campus accessible to physically disabled.

CAMPUS LIFE
Environment: Metropolis. **Activities:** Choral groups, music ensembles, student government. **On-Campus Highlights:** Gannett-Estes Library.

ADMISSIONS
Freshman Academic Profile: 60% from public high schools. Minimum paper TOEFL 500. Minimum computer TOEFL 173. **Basis for Candidate Selection:** *Very important factors considered include:* Recommendation(s), rigor of secondary school record, standardized test scores, character/personal qualities, religious affiliation/commitment. *Important factors considered include:* Application essay. *Other factors considered include:* Alumni/ae relation, interview. **Freshman Admission Requirements:** High school diploma is required and GED is accepted. *Academic units required:* 4 English, 4 mathematics, 4 science. **Freshman Admission Statistics:** 279 applied, 52% admitted, 32% enrolled. **Transfer Admission Requirements:** High school transcript, college transcript(s), essay or personal statement, minimum college GPA of 2.0 required. Lowest grade transferable C. **General Admission Information:** Application fee $20. Regular application deadline 8/1. Notification on a rolling basis, beginning on or about 9/1. Nonfall registration accepted. Admission may be deferred for a maximum of 1 year. Credit offered for CEEB Advanced Placement tests.

COSTS AND FINANCIAL AID
Annual tuition $7,500. Room and board $3,450. Required fees $25. Average book expense $500. **Required Forms and Deadlines:** FAFSA, institution's own financial aid form. Priority financial aid filing date 5/1. **Notification of Awards:** Applicants will be notified of awards on or about 6/1. **Types of Aid:** *Need-based scholarships/grants:* Federal Pell, SEOG, state scholarships/grants *Loans:* FFEL Subsidized Stafford, FFEL Unsubsidized Stafford, FFEL PLUS. *Student Employment:* Federal Work-Study Program available. Highest amount earned per year from on-campus jobs $2,000. Off-campus job opportunities are excellent. **Financial Aid Statistics:** 57% freshmen, 56% undergrads receive need-based scholarship or grant aid. 23% freshmen receive non-need-based scholarship or grant aid. 57% freshmen, 66% undergrads receive need-based self-help aid. 18% freshmen, 21% undergrads receive athletic scholarships. 80% freshmen, 85% undergrads receive any aid. 55% undergrads borrow to pay for school. Average cumulative indebtedness $23,000. **Criteria for awarding institutional aid:** *Non-need-based:* Academics, alumni affiliation, state/district residency.

SOUTHEASTERN LOUISIANA UNIVERSITY

SLU 10752, Hammond, LA 70402
Phone: 985-549-2066 **Financial Aid Phone:** 985-549-2244
E-mail: admissions@selu.edu **CEEB Code:** 6656
Fax: 985-549-5632 **Website:** www.selu.edu **ACT Code:** 1608

This public school was founded in 1925. It has a 365-acre campus.

RATINGS
Admissions Selectivity Rating: 68   **Fire Safety Rating:** 93   **Green Rating:** 68

STUDENTS AND FACULTY
Enrollment: 13,086. **Student Body:** 62% female, 38% male, 3% out-of-state, 1% international (63 countries represented). Asian 1%, African American 18%, Caucasian 75%, Hispanic 2%.
Retention and Graduation: 68% freshmen return for sophomore year. 9% freshmen graduate within 4 years. **Faculty:** Student/faculty ratio 22.8:1. 522 full-time faculty, 63% hold PhDs, 13% are are members of minority groups, 44% are women. 1% of classes are taught by teaching assistants.

ACADEMICS
Degrees: Associate, bachelor's, master's. **Classes:** Most classes have 20–29 students. Most lab/discussion sessions have 20–29 students. **Majors with Highest Enrollment:** Business administration and management; general studies; nursing/registered nurse (RN, ASN, BSN, MSN). **Special Study Options:** Accelerated program, cross-registration, distance learning, double major, dual enrollment, English as a Second Language (ESL), honors program, independent study, internships, liberal arts/career combination, study abroad, teacher certification program. **Honors programs:** Reduced size classes, scholarships, honors residence hall, achievement awards, and honor academic credit shown on the transcript. Special programs offered to physically disabled students include note-taking services, tape recorders, tutors. **Career services:** Alumni services, career assessment, internships. **Career services highlights include:** The university offers a wide range of courses and curricula that address emerging regional, national and international priorities. The University embraces active partnerships that benefit students, faculty and the region we serve. Programs enable students to understand themselves and the world around them in a broad intellectual perspective. Such a perspective provides students the opportunity to live full, rich, balanced lives and to assume positions of leadership in the public and private sector. Graduates are prepared to think critically, communicate effectively and become lifelong learners. Emphasis is placed on preparation for careers or graduate study through undergraduate research in collaboration with faculty, "hands-on" internships, field experiences, work-study placements, cooperative education, service-learning, and opportunities to study abroad. Many of these opportunities earn college credit. Southeastern also has honors tracks in place for all degree programs. Undergraduate research programs such as Undergraduate Research and Creative Activities Grants Programs in the College of Arts, Humanities and Social Sciences, PROFIT (Preferred Research Option for Intensive Training) in the College of Business, SOAR (Student Opportunities for Achievement and Research) in the College of Nursing and Health Sciences, SURE (Student Undergraduate Research in Education) in the College of Education and Human Development, and STAR (Science and Technology Awards for Research) in the College of Science and Technology provide opportunities for undergraduate students to conduct research and engage in creative ventures with Southeastern faculty members.

FACILITIES
Housing: Coed dorms, women's dorms, fraternity/sorority housing, apartments for single students. 95% of campus accessible to physically disabled. **Special Academic Facilities/Equipment:** Contemporary Art Gallery, Radio Station, Television Station, Columbia Theatre, Maritime Museum. **Computers:** 5% of classrooms, 100% of dorms, 100% of libraries, 50% of dining areas, 25% of student union, 25% of common outdoor areas have wireless network access. Students can register for classes online. Administrative functions (other than registration) can be performed online.

CAMPUS LIFE
Environment: Village. **Activities:** Choral groups, concert band, dance, drama/theater, jazz band, literary magazine, marching band, music ensembles, musical theater, opera, pep band, radio station, student government, student newspaper, student-run film society, symphony orchestra, television station, yearbook, campus ministries, international student organization. **Organizations:** 105 registered organizations, 11 honor societies, 12 religious organizations. 7 fraternities, 8 sororities. **Athletics (Intercollegiate):** *Men:* Baseball, basketball, cross-country, football, golf, track/field (outdoor), track/field (indoor). *Women:* Basketball, cross-country, soccer, softball, tennis, track/field (outdoor), track/field (indoor), volleyball. **On-Campus Highlights:** Student Union, Student Recreation Center, Library, Bookstore, Campus Dining Complex. **Environ-

mental Initiatives: Computer recycling program campus shuttle Ponchartrain wetland environmental research

ADMISSIONS

Freshman Academic Profile: Average high school GPA 3.12. 11% in top 10% of high school class, 28% in top 25% of high school class, 61% in top 50% of high school class. 74% from public high schools. ACT middle 50% range 19–23. Minimum paper TOEFL 500. Minimum computer TOEFL 173. Minimum web-based TOEFL 61. **Basis for Candidate Selection:** *Very important factors considered include:* Class rank, academic GPA, rigor of secondary school record, standardized test scores. **Freshman Admission Requirements:** High school diploma is required and GED is accepted. *Academic units required:* 4 English, 3 mathematics, 3 science, 2 foreign language, 3 social studies, 1 visual/performing arts, 1 Mathematics or Science **Freshman Admission Statistics:** 3,617 applied, 93% admitted, 82% enrolled. **Transfer Admission Requirements:** College transcript(s), statement of good standing from prior institution(s). Minimum college GPA of 2.0 required. Lowest grade transferable D. **General Admission Information:** Application fee $20. Regular application deadline 8/1. Nonfall registration accepted. Admission may be deferred for a maximum of 1 year. Credit and/or placement offered for CEEB Advanced Placement tests.

COSTS AND FINANCIAL AID

Annual in-state tuition $2,546. Annual out-of-state tuition $9,802. Room and board $6,380. Required fees $1,488. Average book expense $1,200. **Required Forms and Deadlines:** FAFSAInstitutional form for college scholarships only. Priority financial aid filing date 5/1. **Notification of Awards:** Applicants will be notified of awards on a rolling basis beginning 3/1. **Types of Aid:** *Need-based scholarships/grants:* Federal Pell, SEOG, state scholarships/grants, private scholarships, the school's own gift aid, Federal Nursing Scholarships. *Loans:* FFEL Subsidized Stafford, FFEL Unsubsidized Stafford, FFEL PLUS, Federal Perkins, college/university loans from institutional funds. *Student Employment:* Federal Work-Study Program available. Institutional employment available. Highest amount earned per year from on-campus jobs $13,009. Off-campus job opportunities are good. **Financial Aid Statistics:** 29% freshmen, 31% undergrads receive need-based scholarship or grant aid. 28% freshmen, 22% undergrads receive non-need-based scholarship or grant aid. 27% freshmen, 33% undergrads receive need-based self-help aid. 2% freshmen, 1% undergrads receive athletic scholarships. 75.31% freshmen, 74.35% undergrads receive any aid. 60% undergrads borrow to pay for school. Average cumulative indebtedness $18,947. **Criteria for awarding institutional aid:** *Non-need-based:* Academics, athletics, job skills, leadership, music/drama, state/district residency.

SOUTHEASTERN OKLAHOMA STATE UNIVERSITY

1405 North 4th Avenue, PMB 4225, Durant, OK 74701-0609
Phone: 580-745-2060 **Financial Aid Phone:** 580-745-2186
E-mail: admissions@se.edu **CEEB Code:** 6657
Fax: 580-745-4502 **ACT Code:** 3438

This public school was founded in 1909. It has a 268-acre campus.

RATINGS

Admissions Selectivity Rating: 72   **Fire Safety Rating:** 75   **Green Rating:** 60*

STUDENTS AND FACULTY

Enrollment: 3,465. **Student Body:** 55% female, 45% male, 22% out-of-state, 1% international (28 countries represented). Asian 1%, African American 5%, Caucasian 59%, Hispanic 3%, Native American 31%.
Retention and Graduation: 19% freshmen graduate within 4 years. **Faculty:** Student/faculty ratio 18:1. 143 full-time faculty, 74% hold PhDs, 17% are are members of minority groups, 41% are women.

ACADEMICS

Degrees: Bachelor's, master's, post-master's certificate. **Classes:** Most classes have 20–29 students. Most lab/discussion sessions have 20–29 students. **Majors with Highest Enrollment:** Elementary education and teaching; occupational safety and health technology/technician; psychology. **Special Study Options:** Distance learning, double major, honors program, independent study, internships, teacher certification program. **Honors programs:** Our Honors program offers six different scholarships ranging in value from $6,400 to $26,400 over four years Special programs offered to physically disabled students include note-taking services, reader services, tape recorders, tutors. **Career services:** Alumni network, career/job search classes, career assessment, internships.

FACILITIES

Housing: Coed dorms, apartments for single students. 100% of campus accessible to physically disabled. **Special Academic Facilities/Equipment:** Visual and Performing Arts Gallery. **Computers:** 65% of classrooms, 50% of dorms, 100% of libraries, 100% of dining areas, 100% of student union, 50% of common outdoor areas have wireless network access. Students can register for classes online. Administrative functions (other than registration) can be performed online.

CAMPUS LIFE

Environment: Village. **Activities:** Choral groups, concert band, dance, drama/theater, jazz band, literary magazine, marching band, music ensembles, musical theater, opera, pep band, radio station, student government, student newspaper, yearbook, campus ministries, international student organization. **Organizations:** 70 registered organizations, 12 honor societies, 8 religious organizations. 2 fraternities, 2 sororities. **Athletics (Intercollegiate):** *Men:* Baseball, basketball, football, golf, tennis. *Women:* Basketball, cross-country, softball, tennis, volleyball. **On-Campus Highlights:** Shearer Hall and Suites (New Apartments), New Student Union, Newly Renovated Football Stadium, New Basketball Arena, "Campus of a Thousand Magnolias."

ADMISSIONS

Freshman Academic Profile: Average high school GPA 3.29. 16% in top 10% of high school class, 40% in top 25% of high school class, 77% in top 50% of high school class. 99% from public high schools. ACT middle 50% range 18–23. Minimum paper TOEFL 500. Minimum computer TOEFL 173. **Basis for Candidate Selection:** *Very important factors considered include:* Class rank, academic GPA, standardized test scores. *Other factors considered include:* Recommendation(s), rigor of secondary school record, character/personal qualities, interview, level of applicant's interest, state residency, talent/ability. **Freshman Admission Requirements:** High school diploma is required and GED is accepted. *Academic units required:* 4 English, 3 mathematics, 2 science, (2 science labs), 3 history, 2 academic electives. *Academic units recommended:* 1 foreign language, 1 social studies, 1 computer science. **Freshman Admission Statistics:** 916 applied, 82% admitted, 82% enrolled. **Transfer Admission Requirements:** College transcript(s), minimum college GPA of 2.0 required. Lowest grade transferable D. **General Admission Information:** Application fee $20. Nonfall registration accepted. Credit offered for CEEB Advanced Placement tests.

COSTS AND FINANCIAL AID

Annual in-state tuition $3,639. Annual out-of-state tuition $10,010. Room and board $2,005. Required fees $677. Average book expense $800. **Required Forms and Deadlines:** FAFSA, institution's own financial aid form. Priority financial aid filing date 3/1. **Notification of Awards:** Applicants will be notified of awards on a rolling basis beginning 4/15. **Types of Aid:** *Need-based scholarships/grants:* Federal Pell, SEOG, state scholarships/grants, private scholarships, the school's own gift aid. *Loans:* FFEL Subsidized Stafford, FFEL Unsubsidized Stafford, FFEL PLUS, Federal Perkins. *Student Employment:* Federal Work-Study Program available. Institutional employment available. Highest amount earned per year from on-campus jobs $8,259. Off-campus job opportunities are good. **Financial Aid Statistics:** 55% freshmen, 60% undergrads receive need-based scholarship or grant aid. 34% freshmen, 23% undergrads receive non-need-based scholarship or grant aid. 28% freshmen, 43% undergrads receive need-based self-help aid. 10% freshmen, 7% undergrads receive athletic scholarships. 66% freshmen, 65% undergrads receive any aid. 37% undergrads borrow to pay for school. Average cumulative indebtedness $6,852. **Criteria for awarding institutional aid:** *Non-need-based:* Academics, alumni affiliation, art, athletics, leadership, minority status, music/drama, state/district residency.

SOUTHERN ADVENTIST UNIVERSITY

P.O. Box 370, Collegedale, TN 37315
Phone: 423-236-2844 **Financial Aid Phone:** 423-236-2894
E-mail: admissions@southern.edu **CEEB Code:** 3518
Fax: 423-236-1844 **Website: ACT Code:** 4006

This private school, affiliated with the Seventh Day Adventist Church, was founded in 1892. It has a 1000-acre campus.

RATINGS

Admissions Selectivity Rating: 78   **Fire Safety Rating:** 86   **Green Rating:** 64

STUDENTS AND FACULTY

Enrollment: 603. **Student Body:** 54% female, 46% male, 69% out-of-state, 23% international. Asian 18%, African American 41%, Caucasian 255%, Hispanic 51%, Native American 2%.

Retention and Graduation: 69% freshmen return for sophomore year. 21% freshmen graduate within 4 years. 15% grads go on to further study within 1 year. 10% grads pursue arts and sciences degrees. 1% grads pursue business degrees. 3% grads pursue medical degrees. **Faculty:** Student/faculty ratio 15:1. 139 full-time faculty, 64% hold PhDs, 13% are are members of minority groups, 40% are women.

ACADEMICS

Degrees: Associate, bachelor's, certificate, master's, post-master's certificate. **Majors with Highest Enrollment:** Biology/biological sciences; business/commerce; nursing/registered nurse (RN, ASN, BSN, MSN). **Special Study Options:** Double major, dual enrollment, English as a Second Language (ESL), honors program, independent study, internships, study abroad, teacher certification program. **Honors programs:** Southern Scholars program includes special projects, inter-disciplinary studies, and designated honors courses to provide a challenging and intellectually stimulating educational experience. **Combined degree programs:** BA/MA, nursing. Special programs offered to physically disabled students include note-taking services, reader services, tape recorders, tutors.

FACILITIES

Housing: Men's dorms, women's dorms, apartments for married students, apartments for single students. 70% of campus accessible to physically disabled. **Special Academic Facilities/Equipment:** Near-Eastern archaeology teaching collection. **Computers:** 100% of classrooms, 5% of dorms, 100% of libraries, 80% of dining areas, 10% of common outdoor areas have wireless network access. Students can register for classes online. Administrative functions (other than registration) can be performed online.

CAMPUS LIFE

Environment: Rural. **Activities:** Choral groups, concert band, drama/theater, jazz band, music ensembles, radio station, student government, student newspaper, student-run film society, symphony orchestra, television station, yearbook, campus ministries, international student organization. **Organizations:** 30 registered organizations, 8 honor societies, 3 religious organizations. **On-Campus Highlights:** Student Center, Wellness Center, The Village Market, KRs Place, Library. **Environmental Initiatives:** Establishing environmental sustainability committee. Campus-wide chemical cleanout. Using green listed chemicals for cleaning.

ADMISSIONS

Freshman Academic Profile: Average high school GPA 3.4. 18% from public high schools. SAT Math middle 50% range 450–570. ACT middle 50% range 19–26. Minimum computer TOEFL 550. **Basis for Candidate Selection:** *Very important factors considered include:* Academic GPA, rigor of secondary school record, standardized test scores. **Freshman Admission Requirements:** High school diploma is required and GED is accepted. *Academic units required:* 3 English, 2 mathematics, 2 science, 1 social studies, 1 history, 9 academic electives. *Academic units recommended:* 4 English, 3 mathematics, 3 science, 2 foreign language, 1 social studies, 2 history, 9 academic electives, 1 computer competency. **Freshman Admission Statistics:** 1,513 applied, 71% admitted, 56% enrolled. **Transfer Admission Requirements:** College transcript(s), minimum college GPA of 2 required. Lowest grade transferable D. **General Admission Information:** Application fee $25. Regular application deadline 9/8. Nonfall registration accepted. Admission may be deferred for a maximum of 1 year. Credit and/or placement offered for CEEB Advanced Placement tests.

COSTS AND FINANCIAL AID

Annual tuition $16,942. Room and board $5,174. Required fees $770. Average book expense $1,000. **Required Forms and Deadlines:** FAFSA. Priority financial aid filing date 3/31. **Notification of Awards:** Applicants will be notified of awards on a rolling basis beginning 2/15. **Types of Aid:** *Need-based scholarships/grants:* Federal Pell, SEOG, state scholarships/grants, private scholarships, the school's own gift aid. *Loans:* FFEL Subsidized Stafford, FFEL Unsubsidized Stafford, FFEL PLUS, Federal Perkins, Federal Nursing, college/university loans from institutional funds. *Student Employment:* Federal Work-Study Program available. Institutional employment available. Highest amount earned per year from on-campus jobs $2,000. Off-campus job opportunities are good. **Financial Aid Statistics:** 47% freshmen, 45% undergrads receive need-based scholarship or grant aid. 39% freshmen, 26% undergrads receive non-need-based scholarship or grant aid. 39% freshmen, 39% undergrads receive need-based self-help aid. 95% undergrads receive any aid. 58% undergrads borrow to pay for school. Average cumulative indebtedness $22,977. **Criteria for awarding institutional aid:** *Non-need-based:* Academics, alumni affiliation, art, leadership, music/drama.

SOUTHERN ARKANSAS UNIVERSITY

P. O. Box 9382, Magnolia, AR 71754
Phone: 870-235-4040 **Financial Aid Phone:** 870-235-4023
E-mail: muleriders@saumag.edu **CEEB Code:** 142
Fax: 870-235-5072 **Website:** **ACT Code:** 142

This public school was founded in 1909. It has a 1418-acre campus.

RATINGS

Admissions Selectivity Rating: 73 **Fire Safety Rating:** 60* **Green Rating:** 60*

STUDENTS AND FACULTY

Enrollment: 2,671. **Student Body:** 57% female, 43% male, 21% out-of-state, 6% international (29 countries represented). Asian 1%, African American 29%, Caucasian 62%, Hispanic 1%, Native American 1%.
Retention and Graduation: 62% freshmen return for sophomore year. 19% freshmen graduate within 4 years. **Faculty:** Student/faculty ratio 16:1. 148 full-time faculty, 38% are women.

ACADEMICS

Degrees: Associate, bachelor's, master's. **Classes:** Most classes have fewer than 10 students. Most lab/discussion sessions have 20–29 students. **Special Study Options:** Cross-registration, distance learning, double major, dual enrollment, honors program, internships, teacher certification program. Special programs offered to physically disabled students include tape recorders, tutors.

FACILITIES

Housing: Coed dorms, men's dorms, women's dorms, apartments for married students, apartments for single students. 95% of campus accessible to physically disabled. **Computers:** Students can register for classes online. Administrative functions (other than registration) can be performed online.

CAMPUS LIFE

Environment: Rural. **Activities:** Choral groups, concert band, drama/theater, jazz band, marching band, music ensembles, musical theater, pep band, radio station, student government, student newspaper, yearbook. **Organizations:** 80 registered organizations, 10 honor societies, 7 religious organizations. 5 fraternities, 6 sororities. **Athletics (Intercollegiate):** *Men:* Baseball, basketball, cheerleading, cross-country, football, golf, rodeo, track/field (outdoor). *Women:* Basketball, cheerleading, cross-country, rodeo, softball, tennis, track/field (outdoor), volleyball.

ADMISSIONS

Freshman Academic Profile: Average high school GPA 3.23. 38% in top 25% of high school class, 70% in top 50% of high school class. 99% from public high schools. ACT middle 50% range 17–23. Minimum paper TOEFL 500. Minimum computer TOEFL 173. **Basis for Candidate Selection:** *Very important factors considered include:* Class rank, rigor of secondary school record, standardized test scores. *Other factors considered include:* Application essay, recommendation(s). **Freshman Admission Requirements:** High school diploma is required and GED is accepted. *Academic units recommended:* 4 English, 4 mathematics, 3 science, (3 science labs), 2 foreign language, 3 social studies. **Freshman Admission Statistics:** 1,417 applied, 100% admitted, 42% enrolled. **Transfer Admission Requirements:** College transcript(s), statement of good standing from prior institution(s). Lowest grade transferable C. **General Admission Information:** Regular application deadline 8/27. Nonfall registration accepted. Admission may be deferred for a maximum of N/A. Credit offered for CEEB Advanced Placement tests.

COSTS AND FINANCIAL AID

Annual in-state tuition $4,260. Annual out-of-state tuition $6,450. Room and board $3,980. Required fees $630. Average book expense $1,000. **Required Forms and Deadlines:** FAFSA. Priority financial aid filing date 7/2. **Notification of Awards:** Applicants will be notified of awards on a rolling basis beginning 4/15. **Types of Aid:** *Need-based scholarships/grants:* Federal Pell, SEOG, state scholarships/grants, private scholarships, the school's own gift aid. *Loans:* FFEL Subsidized Stafford, FFEL Unsubsidized Stafford, FFEL PLUS, Federal Perkins. *Student Employment:* Highest amount earned per year from on-campus jobs $4,900. **Financial Aid Statistics:** 36% freshmen, 63% undergrads receive need-based scholarship or grant aid. 50% freshmen, 39% undergrads receive non-need-based scholarship or grant aid. 44% freshmen, 56% undergrads receive need-based self-help aid. 85% freshmen, 82% undergrads receive any aid. 61% undergrads borrow to pay for school. Average cumulative indebtedness $14,423. **Criteria for awarding institutional aid:** *Non-need-based:* Academics, alumni affiliation, art, athletics, leadership, minority status, music/drama, state/district residency.

SOUTHERN CALIFORNIA INSTITUTE OF ARCHITECTURE

SCI-Arc Admissions Office, 960 East Third Street, Los Angeles, CA 90013-1822
Phone: 213.356.5320 **Financial Aid Phone:** 213-356-5346
E-mail: admissions@sciarc.edu
Fax: 213-613-2260 **Website:** www.sciarc.edu

This private school was founded in 1972.

RATINGS
Admissions Selectivity Rating: 60*   **Fire Safety Rating:** 60*   **Green Rating:** 60*

STUDENTS AND FACULTY
Enrollment: 245. **Student Body:** 27% female, 73% male, 40% out-of-state, 20% international (45 countries represented). Asian 24%, African American 1%, Caucasian 30%, Hispanic 18%.
Retention and Graduation: 93% freshmen return for sophomore year. **Faculty:** Student/faculty ratio 15:1. 36 full-time faculty, 25% are women.

ACADEMICS
Degrees: Bachelor's, master's. **Special Study Options:** Internships, study abroad. **Career services:** Alumni network, internships.

FACILITIES
Special Academic Facilities/Equipment: SCI-Arc gallery, wood/metal shop, Digital Fabrication shop. **Computers:** Students can register for classes online.

CAMPUS LIFE
Environment: Metropolis. **Activities:** Student government. **On-Campus Highlights:** SCI-Arc Gallery, Kappe Library, wood/metal shop, studios.

ADMISSIONS
Freshman Academic Profile: Minimum paper TOEFL 560. Minimum computer TOEFL 220. Minimum web-based TOEFL 83. **Basis for Candidate Selection:** *Very important factors considered include:* Application essay, academic GPA, recommendation(s), character/personal qualities, level of applicant's interest, talent/ability. *Important factors considered include:* Rigor of secondary school record. *Other factors considered include:* standardized test scores, extracurricular activities, racial/ethnic status, volunteer work, work experience. **Freshman Admission Requirements:** High school diploma is required and GED is accepted. **Freshman Admission Statistics:** 70 applied, 91% admitted, 41% enrolled. **Transfer Admission Requirements:** College transcript(s), essay or personal statement, Lowest grade transferable C. **General Admission Information:** Application fee $75. Regular application deadline 2/1. Regular notification 4/1. Nonfall registration not accepted. Admission may be deferred for a maximum of 1 year.

COSTS AND FINANCIAL AID
Annual tuition $27,500. Required fees $350. **Required Forms and Deadlines:** FAFSA, institution's own financial aid formTax returns or parents' tax returns. Priority financial aid filing date 3/2. **Notification of Awards: Types of Aid:** *Need-based scholarships/grants:* Federal Pell, SEOG, state scholarships/grants, the school's own gift aid. *Loans:* FFEL Subsidized Stafford, FFEL Unsubsidized Stafford, FFEL PLUS. *Student Employment:* Federal Work-Study Program available. **Criteria for awarding institutional aid:** *Non-need-based:* Academics, state/district residency.

SOUTHERN CONNECTICUT STATE UNIVERSITY

SCSU-Admissions House, 131 Farnham Avenue, New Haven, CT 06515-1202
Phone: 203-392-5656
E-mail: adminfo@scsu.ctstateu.edu **CEEB Code:** 3662
Fax: 203-392-5727 **Website:** www.southernct.edu

This public school was founded in 1893. It has a 168-acre campus.

RATINGS
Admissions Selectivity Rating: 68   **Fire Safety Rating:** 60*   **Green Rating:** 60*

STUDENTS AND FACULTY
Enrollment: 8,309. **Student Body:** 62% female, 38% male, 6% out-of-state, 1% international (39 countries represented). Asian 2%, African American 10%, Caucasian 57%, Hispanic 5%.
Retention and Graduation: 75% freshmen return for sophomore year. 12% freshmen graduate within 4 years. 27% grads go on to further study within 1

year. **Faculty:** Student/faculty ratio 17:1. 403 full-time faculty, 90% hold PhDs, 14% are are members of minority groups, 45% are women.

ACADEMICS
Degrees: Bachelor's, master's, post-master's certificate. **Classes:** Most classes have 20–29 students. Most lab/discussion sessions have 10–19 students. **Special Study Options:** Accelerated program, cooperative education program, cross-registration, distance learning, double major, exchange student program (domestic), external degree program, honors program, independent study, internships, liberal arts/career combination, student-designed major, study abroad, teacher certification program, Undergrads may take grad level classes Cooperative Education Programs: Arts, Business, Computer Science, Education, Health Professions, Humanities, Natural Science, Social/Behavioral Science, Technologies. Domestic Exchange Program(s): Exchange programs with other members of state university system. Foreign Exchange Program(s): Study abroad in England, France, and Spain. Evening division. Special programs offered to physically disabled students include note-taking services, reader services, tape recorders, tutors. **Career services:** Career/job search classes, internships.

FACILITIES
Housing: Coed dorms, special housing for disabled students, apartments for single students, freshmen have their own residence halls. Students must be 19 or older to live in upper-classman residence halls. 95% of campus accessible to physically disabled. **Special Academic Facilities/Equipment:** Art gallery, language lab, child development center, communication disorders center, planetarium and observatory, closed-circuit TV center.

CAMPUS LIFE
Environment: Village. **Activities:** Choral groups, concert band, drama/theater, literary magazine, marching band, music ensembles, pep band, radio station, student government, student newspaper, yearbook. **Organizations:** 63 registered organizations, 3 religious organizations. 2 fraternities, 4 sororities. **Athletics (Intercollegiate):** *Men:* Baseball, basketball, cross-country, football, golf, gymnastics, ice hockey, rugby, soccer, softball, swimming, track/field (outdoor), track/field (indoor), volleyball, wrestling. *Women:* Basketball, cheerleading, cross-country, field hockey, golf, gymnastics, rugby, soccer, softball, swimming, track/field (outdoor), track/field (indoor), volleyball.

ADMISSIONS
Freshman Academic Profile: 6% in top 10% of high school class, 22% in top 25% of high school class, 64% in top 50% of high school class. 88% from public high schools. SAT Math middle 50% range 420–520. SAT Critical Reading middle 50% range 430–530. Minimum paper TOEFL 525. Minimum computer TOEFL 1. **Basis for Candidate Selection:** *Very important factors considered include:* Rigor of secondary school record. *Important factors considered include:* Application essay, academic GPA, recommendation(s), standardized test scores. *Other factors considered include:* Class rank, alumni/ae relation, character/personal qualities, extracurricular activities, first generation, racial/ethnic status, talent/ability, volunteer work, work experience. **Freshman Admission Requirements:** High school diploma is required and GED is accepted. *Academic units required:* 4 English, 3 mathematics, 2 science, (1 science labs), 2 foreign language, 2 social studies, 2 history. *Academic units recommended:* 4 mathematics, 3 foreign language. **Freshman Admission Statistics:** 5,037 applied, 54% admitted, 49% enrolled. **Transfer Admission Requirements:** College transcript(s), essay or personal statement, statement of good standing from prior institution(s). Minimum college GPA of 2.0 required. Lowest grade transferable C–. **General Admission Information:** Application fee $50. Regular application deadline 7/1. Notification on a rolling basis, beginning on or about 12/1. Nonfall registration accepted. Admission may be deferred for a maximum of 2 years. Credit offered for CEEB Advanced Placement tests.

COSTS AND FINANCIAL AID
Annual in-state tuition $3,187. Annual out-of-state tuition $10,315. Room and board $8,101. Required fees $3,255. Average book expense $750. **Required Forms and Deadlines:** FAFSA. Financial aid filing deadline 3/10. **Notification of Awards: Types of Aid:** *Need-based scholarships/grants:* Federal Pell, SEOG, state scholarships/grants, the school's own gift aid. *Loans:* FFEL Subsidized Stafford, FFEL Unsubsidized Stafford, FFEL PLUS, Federal Perkins. *Student Employment:* Federal Work-Study Program available. Institutional employment available. Highest amount earned per year from on-campus jobs $1,400. Off-campus job opportunities are good. **Financial Aid Statistics:** 37% freshmen, 37% undergrads receive need-based scholarship or grant aid. 12% freshmen, 7% undergrads receive non-need-based scholarship or grant aid. 37% freshmen, 41% undergrads receive need-based self-help aid. 1% freshmen, 2% undergrads receive athletic scholarships. **Criteria for awarding institutional aid:** *Non-need-based:* Academics, alumni affiliation, athletics.

SOUTHERN ILLINOIS UNIVERSITY CARBONDALE

Southern Illinois University Carbondale MC 4710, Carbondale, IL 62901-4512
Phone: 618-536-4405 **Financial Aid Phone:** 618-453-4334
E-mail: joinsiuc@siu.edu **CEEB Code:** 1726
Fax: 618-453-4609 **Website:** www.siuc.edu **ACT Code:** 1144

This public school was founded in 1869. It has a 1136-acre campus.

RATINGS
Admissions Selectivity Rating: 70   **Fire Safety Rating:** 89   **Green Rating:** 86

STUDENTS AND FACULTY
Enrollment: 15,979. **Student Body:** 43% female, 57% male, 11% out-of-state, 2% international (108 countries represented). Asian 2%, African American 18%, Caucasian 68%, Hispanic 4%.
Retention and Graduation: 58% grads go on to further study within 1 year. **Faculty:** Student/faculty ratio 16.5:1. 931 full-time faculty, 82% hold PhDs, 17% are are members of minority groups, 36% are women. 30% of classes are taught by teaching assistants.

ACADEMICS
Degrees: Associate, bachelor's, first professional, first professional certificate, master's, post-bachelor's certificate. **Classes:** Most classes have 10–19 students. Most lab/discussion sessions have 20–29 students. **Majors with Highest Enrollment:** Business administration and management; elementary education and teaching; health/health care administration/management. **Special Study Options:** Cooperative education program, distance learning, double major, English as a Second Language (ESL), honors program, independent study, internships, student-designed major, study abroad, teacher certification program, ROTC: Army; Air Force. **Honors programs:** University Honors Program—to reward its best undergraduates for their high academic achievement, intended to give the Honors Student a taste of the private-college experience at a state-university price. Classes are small, unique in character, and specially designed for University Honors students by outstanding SIUC faculty. **Combined degree programs:** JD/MD, MA/MBA, MS/MBA, MBA/JD, MBA/MS, MSW/JD. Special programs offered to physically disabled students include note-taking services, reader services, tape recorders, tutors. **Career services:** Alumni services, career/job search classes, career assessment, internships. **Career services highlights include:** Extern Program—a job shodowing program. Business students typically comprise the largest number of participants of this campus-wide program, resulting in a 53+% job/internship offer rate.

FACILITIES
Housing: Coed dorms, special housing for disabled students, men's dorms, women's dorms, fraternity/sorority housing, apartments for married students, apartments for single students, Living Learning Communities, Residential College, General Living Learning, Freshman Interest Groups. 99% of campus accessible to physically disabled. **Special Academic Facilities/Equipment:** Art, natural history, and science museums, outdoor education center, center for crime studies, advertising and public relations agencies, child development lab, community human services center, airport training facility, archaeological research center, fisheries and wildlife research labs, coal research center, electron microscopy center. SIUC's two newest additions: Troutt-Wittmann Academic and Training Center; Student Health Center. **Computers:** 15% of classrooms, 100% of libraries, 95% of dining areas, 100% of student union, 70% of common outdoor areas have wireless network access. Students can register for classes online. Administrative functions (other than registration) can be performed online.

CAMPUS LIFE
Environment: Town. **Activities:** Choral groups, concert band, dance, drama/theater, jazz band, literary magazine, marching band, music ensembles, musical theater, opera, pep band, radio station, student government, student newspaper, student-run film society, symphony orchestra, television station, yearbook, campus ministries, international student organization. **Organizations:** 408 registered organizations, 26 honor societies, 25 religious organizations. 20 fraternities, 8 sororities. **Athletics (Intercollegiate):** *Men:* Baseball, basketball, cheerleading, cross-country, diving, football, golf, swimming, tennis, track/field (outdoor), track/field (indoor). *Women:* Basketball, cheerleading, cross-country, diving, golf, softball, swimming, tennis, track/field (outdoor), track/field (indoor), volleyball. **On-Campus Highlights:** Morris Library, Student Center, Recreation Center, Campus Lake, Faner Museum. **Environmental Initiatives:** $4.0M campus-wide energy efficiency and conservation project to reduce purchased utilities. Vermicomposting facility to compost food waste from campus dining halls and turn it into fertilizer for campus plantings. The facility is heated by a clean-burning oil furnace fired with used motor oil from campus vehicles and is insulated with a soy-based foam product for energy conservation. New Transportation Education Center (currently in design phase) will be Certified under U.S. Green Building Council's LEED-NC 2.2 rating system.

ADMISSIONS
Freshman Academic Profile: 9% in top 10% of high school class, 29% in top 25% of high school class, 62% in top 50% of high school class. SAT Math middle 50% range 440–590. SAT Critical Reading middle 50% range 420–570. SAT Writing middle 50% range 410–520. ACT middle 50% range 19–24. Minimum paper TOEFL 520. Minimum computer TOEFL 190. **Basis for Candidate Selection:** *Very important factors considered include:* Class rank, standardized test scores. *Important factors considered include:* Academic GPA. *Other factors considered include:* Recommendation(s), rigor of secondary school record, extracurricular activities, talent/ability, volunteer work, work experience. **Freshman Admission Requirements:** High school diploma is required and GED is accepted. *Academic units required:* 4 English, 3 mathematics, 3 science, 3 social studies, 2 academic electives. **Freshman Admission Statistics:** 11,785 applied, 69% admitted, 33% enrolled. **Transfer Admission Requirements:** College transcript(s), statement of good standing from prior institution(s). Minimum college GPA of 2.0 required. Lowest grade transferable D. **General Admission Information:** Application fee $30. Notification on a rolling basis, beginning on or about 9/1. Nonfall registration accepted. Credit and/or placement offered for CEEB Advanced Placement tests.

COSTS AND FINANCIAL AID
Annual in-state tuition $6,975. Annual out-of-state tuition $17,438. Room and board $7,673. Required fees $3,121. Average book expense $900. **Required Forms and Deadlines:** FAFSA. Priority financial aid filing date 4/1. **Notification of Awards:** Applicants will be notified of awards on a rolling basis beginning 3/21. **Types of Aid:** *Need-based scholarships/grants:* Federal Pell, SEOG, state scholarships/grants, private scholarships, the school's own gift aid. *Loans:* Direct Subsidized Stafford, Direct Unsubsidized Stafford, Direct PLUS, Federal Perkins, college/university loans from institutional funds. *Student Employment:* Federal Work-Study Program available. Institutional employment available. Highest amount earned per year from on-campus jobs $9,122. Off-campus job opportunities are good. **Financial Aid Statistics:** 48% freshmen, 43% undergrads receive need-based scholarship or grant aid. 35% freshmen, 24% undergrads receive non-need-based scholarship or grant aid. 59% freshmen, 52% undergrads receive need-based self-help aid. 1% freshmen, 1% undergrads receive athletic scholarships. 78% freshmen, 81% undergrads receive any aid. 45% undergrads borrow to pay for school. Average cumulative indebtedness $18,603. **Criteria for awarding institutional aid:** *Non-need-based:* Academics, alumni affiliation, art, athletics, leadership, minority status, music/drama.

SOUTHERN ILLINOIS UNIVERSITY— EDWARDSVILLE

PO Box 1600, Edwardsville, IL 62026-1080
Phone: 618-650-3705 **Financial Aid Phone:** 618-650-3880
E-mail: admissions@siue.edu **CEEB Code:** 1759
Fax: 618-650-5013 **Website:** www.siue.edu **ACT Code:** 1147

This public school was founded in 1957. It has a 2660-acre campus.

RATINGS
Admissions Selectivity Rating: 67   **Fire Safety Rating:** 60*   **Green Rating:** 60*

STUDENTS AND FACULTY
Enrollment: 10,892. **Student Body:** 54% female, 46% male, 1% international (48 countries represented). Asian 2%, African American 10%, Caucasian 80%, Hispanic 2%.
Retention and Graduation: 73% freshmen return for sophomore year. 21% freshmen graduate within 4 years. 31% grads go on to further study within 1 year. 1% grads pursue law degrees. 1% grads pursue medical degrees. **Faculty:** Student/faculty ratio 18:1. 610 full-time faculty, 79% hold PhDs, 15% are are members of minority groups, 47% are women. 3% of classes are taught by teaching assistants.

ACADEMICS
Degrees: Bachelor's, first professional, first professional certificate, master's, post-bachelor's certificate, post-master's certificate. **Classes:** Most classes have 10–19 students. Most lab/discussion sessions have 10–19 students. **Majors with Highest Enrollment:** Business/managerial economics. **Special Study Options:** Accelerated program, cooperative education program, cross-registration, distance learning, double major, English as a Second Language (ESL), honors program, independent study, internships, student-designed major, study abroad, teacher certification program, Independent Study, elementary and secondary teacher certificate programs in art, music, social studies, English, kinesiology, biology, chemistry, foreign languages, history, math, physics, speech communi-

cation. **Combined degree programs:** Econ and finance; chemistry; biological sciences. Special programs offered to physically disabled students include note-taking services, reader services, tape recorders, tutors. **Career services:** Alumni network, alumni services, career/job search classes, career assessment, internships, regional alumni. **Career services highlights include:** Through the SIUE Co-op program, students work in professional assignments for employers throughout the United States and globally.

FACILITIES

Housing: Coed dorms, special housing for disabled students, fraternity/sorority housing, apartments for married students, apartments for single students, Focused Interest Communities. 100% of campus accessible to physically disabled. **Special Academic Facilities/Equipment:** Art gallery, anthropology museum, language lab, center for advanced manufacturing and production, technology commercialization center, electron microscope, psychomotorskills lab, new engineering building and lab. **Computers:** Administrative functions (other than registration) can be performed online.

CAMPUS LIFE

Environment: Village. **Activities:** Choral groups, concert band, dance, drama/theater, jazz band, literary magazine, music ensembles, musical theater, opera, pep band, radio station, student government, student newspaper, symphony orchestra, campus ministries. **Organizations:** 140 registered organizations, 15 honor societies, 9 religious organizations. 10 fraternities, 7 sororities. **Athletics (Intercollegiate):** *Men:* Baseball, basketball, cross-country, golf, soccer, tennis, track/field (outdoor), track/field (indoor), wrestling. *Women:* Basketball, cross-country, golf, soccer, softball, tennis, track/field (outdoor), track/field (indoor), volleyball. **On-Campus Highlights:** Morris University Center, Starbucks Coffee, Auntie Anne's Pretzels, New School of Engineering Building, New School of Pharmacy Building, The SIUE campus sits on 2,660 acres of beautiful woodlands and lakes just 25 minutes from St. Louis, Missouri. Also, SIUE residence halls are among the newest in the state.

ADMISSIONS

Freshman Academic Profile: 17% in top 10% of high school class, 43% in top 25% of high school class, 77% in top 50% of high school class. ACT middle 50% range 20–25. Minimum paper TOEFL 550. Minimum computer TOEFL 213. **Basis for Candidate Selection:** *Very important factors considered include:* Class rank, rigor of secondary school record, standardized test scores. **Freshman Admission Requirements:** High school diploma is required and GED is accepted. *Academic units required:* 4 English, 3 mathematics, 3 science, (3 science labs), 3 social studies, 2 academic electives. *Academic units recommended:* 2 foreign language. **Freshman Admission Statistics:** 5,658 applied, 84% admitted, 39% enrolled. **Transfer Admission Requirements:** College transcript(s), minimum college GPA of 2 required. Lowest grade transferable D. **General Admission Information:** Application fee $30. Regular application deadline 5/1. Notification on a rolling basis, beginning on or about 9/1. Nonfall registration accepted. Admission may be deferred for a maximum of 12. Credit and/or placement offered for CEEB Advanced Placement tests.

COSTS AND FINANCIAL AID

Annual in-state tuition $5,850. Annual out-of-state tuition $14,595. Room and board $8,050. Required fees $1,981. Average book expense $715. **Required Forms and Deadlines:** FAFSA Financial aid filing deadline 6/1. Priority financial aid filing date 3/1. **Notification of Awards:** Applicants will be notified of awards on a rolling basis beginning 3/15. **Types of Aid:** *Need-based scholarships/grants:* Federal Pell, SEOG, state scholarships/grants, private scholarships, the school's own gift aid, Federal Nursing Scholarships. Presidential Scholars Program, Chancellor's Scholars Program, Johnetta Haley Scholarship Program, Provost Scholarship. *Loans:* Direct Subsidized Stafford, Direct Unsubsidized Stafford, Direct PLUS, FFEL Subsidized Stafford, FFEL Unsubsidized Stafford, FFEL PLUS, Federal Perkins, college/university loans from institutional funds, HPL. *Student Employment:* Highest amount earned per year from on-campus jobs $1,348. **Financial Aid Statistics:** 27% freshmen, 30% undergrads receive need-based scholarship or grant aid. 6% freshmen, 6% undergrads receive non-need-based scholarship or grant aid. 45% freshmen, 47% undergrads receive need-based self-help aid. 1% freshmen, 1% undergrads receive athletic scholarships. 40% undergrads borrow to pay for school. Average cumulative indebtedness $16,656. **Criteria for awarding institutional aid:** *Non-need-based:* Academics, art, athletics, leadership, minority status, music/drama.

SOUTHERN METHODIST UNIVERSITY

PO Box 750181, Dallas, TX 75275-0181
Phone: 214-768-3417 **Financial Aid Phone:** 214-768-3417
E-mail: enrol_serv@smu.edu **CEEB Code:** 6660
Fax: 214-768-0202 **Website:** www.smu.edu **ACT Code:** 4171

This private school, affiliated with the Methodist Church, was founded in 1911. It has a 210-acre campus.

RATINGS

Admissions Selectivity Rating: 92 **Fire Safety Rating:** 60* **Green Rating:** 69

STUDENTS AND FACULTY

Enrollment: 6,150. **Student Body:** 53% female, 47% male, 45% out-of-state, 6% international (92 countries represented). Asian 6%, African American 5%, Caucasian 72%, Hispanic 8%, Native American 1%.
Retention and Graduation: 88% freshmen return for sophomore year. 62% freshmen graduate within 4 years. **Faculty:** Student/faculty ratio 12:1. 656 full-time faculty, 84% hold PhDs, 17% are are members of minority groups, 35% are women.

ACADEMICS

Degrees: Bachelor's, certificate, doctoral, master's, post-bachelor's certificate. **Classes:** Most classes have 10–19 students. Most lab/discussion sessions have 20–29 students. **Majors with Highest Enrollment:** Business administration and management; public relations/image management; social sciences. **Special Study Options:** Accelerated program, cooperative education program, distance learning, double major, English as a Second Language (ESL), exchange student program (domestic), honors program, independent study, internships, student-designed major, study abroad, teacher certification program. **Honors programs:** The University Honors Program is designed to prepare Honors students for a new millennium to ensure that they can cope with the challenges of rapid change while taking advantage of the possibilities such a volatile and versatile world presents. The BBA Honors Program, which is separate from the University Honors Program, is composed of special sections of courses in accounting, finance, statistics, operations management, marketing, and management. Advertising Honors Program: A student may apply for the Temerlin Advertising Institute Honors program after completion of his or her first semester as a declared Advertising major. **Combined degree programs:** BS/BA in comp. sci. and music; 3-2 Bachelor's MBA. Special programs offered to physically disabled students include note-taking services, reader services, tape recorders, tutors. **Career services:** Alumni services, career/job search classes, career assessment, internships.

FACILITIES

Housing: Coed dorms, fraternity/sorority housing, apartments for married students, apartments for single students, wellness housing, theme housing. 95% of campus accessible to physically disabled. **Special Academic Facilities/Equipment:** Art, natural history, and paleontology museums, southwest film/video archives, sculpture garden, performing arts theatres, pollen analysis and geothermal labs, electron microbe lab, microscopy lab, seismological observatory, institute of technology services, TV studio. **Computers:** 30% of classrooms, 100% of dorms, 100% of libraries, 100% of dining areas, 100% of student union, 10% of common outdoor areas have wireless network access. Students can register for classes online. Administrative functions (other than registration) can be performed online.

CAMPUS LIFE

Environment: Metropolis. **Activities:** Choral groups, concert band, dance, drama/theater, jazz band, literary magazine, marching band, music ensembles, musical theater, opera, pep band, radio station, student government, student newspaper, student-run film society, symphony orchestra, yearbook, campus ministries, international student organization. **Organizations:** 180 registered organizations, 15 honor societies, 27 religious organizations. 15 fraternities, 13 sororities. **Athletics (Intercollegiate):** *Men:* Basketball, diving, football, golf, soccer, swimming, tennis, volleyball, water polo. *Women:* Basketball, crew/rowing, cross-country, diving, equestrian sports, golf, soccer, swimming, tennis, track/field (outdoor), volleyball, water polo. **On-Campus Highlights:** Gerald J Ford Stadium, Meadows Museum, Hughes Trigg Student Center, Dallas Hall, Fondren Library. **Environmental Initiatives:** Developing a masters certificate program and a masters degree program in sustainability. The Embrey Engineering building is LEED Gold. We purchase 2,100,000 kWh of wind power each year and plan to purchase more with each new LEED building. The student environmental committee host 2-3 events per year.

ADMISSIONS

Freshman Academic Profile: Average high school GPA 3.57. 43% in top 10% of high school class, 73% in top 25% of high school class, 93% in top 50% of high school class. 61% from public high schools. SAT Math middle 50% range 580–680. SAT Critical Reading middle 50% range 560–660. SAT Writing middle 50% range 560–660. ACT middle 50% range 25–30. Minimum paper TOEFL 550. Minimum computer TOEFL 213. **Basis for Candidate Selection:** *Very important factors considered include:* Class rank, application essay, academic GPA, recommendation(s), rigor of secondary school record, standardized test scores. *Important factors considered include:* Character/personal qualities, extracurricular activities, talent/ability, volunteer work, work experience. *Other factors considered include:* Alumni/ae relation, first generation, interview, level of applicant's interest. **Freshman Admission Requirements:** High school diploma is required and GED is not accepted. *Academic units required:* 4 English, 3 mathematics, 3 science, (2 science labs), 2 foreign language, 1 social studies, 2 history. *Academic units recommended:* 4 English, 4 mathematics, 4 science, (3 science labs), 3 foreign language, 2 social studies, 3 history. **Freshman Admission Statistics:** 8,356 applied, 53% admitted, 30% enrolled. **Transfer Admission Requirements:** College transcript(s), essay or personal statement, minimum college GPA of 2.7 required. Lowest grade transferable C–. **General Admission Information:** Application fee $60. Regular application deadline 3/15. Notification on a rolling basis, beginning on or about 12/31. Nonfall registration accepted. Admission may be deferred for a maximum of 1 year. Credit and/or placement offered for CEEB Advanced Placement tests.

COSTS AND FINANCIAL AID

Annual tuition $31,200. Room and board $12,445. Required fees $3,960. Average book expense $800. **Required Forms and Deadlines:** FAFSA, CSS/Financial Aid PROFILE, noncustodial PROFILE, business/farm supplement. Priority financial aid filing date 2/15. **Notification of Awards:** Applicants will be notified of awards on a rolling basis beginning 3/15. **Types of Aid:** *Need-based scholarships/grants:* Federal Pell, SEOG, state scholarships/grants, private scholarships, the school's own gift aid. *Loans:* FFEL Subsidized Stafford, FFEL Unsubsidized Stafford, FFEL PLUS, Federal Perkins, state loans, college/university loans from institutional funds. *Student Employment:* Off-campus job opportunities are good. **Financial Aid Statistics:** 24% freshmen, 27% undergrads receive need-based scholarship or grant aid. 25% freshmen, 20% undergrads receive non-need-based scholarship or grant aid. 28% freshmen, 30% undergrads receive need-based self-help aid. 5% freshmen, 5% undergrads receive athletic scholarships. 82% freshmen, 65% undergrads receive any aid. 38% undergrads borrow to pay for school. Average cumulative indebtedness $20,883. **Criteria for awarding institutional aid:** *Non-need-based:* Academics, art, athletics, leadership, music/drama, religious affiliation, state/district residency.

SOUTHERN NEW HAMPSHIRE UNIVERSITY

2500 North River Road, Manchester, NH 03106-1045
Phone: 603-645-9611 **Financial Aid Phone:** 603-645-9645
E-mail: admission@snhu.edu **CEEB Code:** 3649
Fax: 603-645-9693 **Website:** www.snhu.edu **ACT Code:** 2514

This private school was founded in 1932. It has a 300-acre campus.

RATINGS

Admissions Selectivity Rating: 72 **Fire Safety Rating:** 92 **Green Rating:** 88

STUDENTS AND FACULTY

Enrollment: 1,929. **Student Body:** 52% female, 48% male, 55% out-of-state, 5% international (79 countries represented). Asian 1%, African American 1%, Caucasian 75%, Hispanic 2%.
Retention and Graduation: 49% freshmen graduate within 4 years. 12% grads go on to further study within 1 year. **Faculty:** Student/faculty ratio 16:1. 120 full-time faculty, 76% hold PhDs, 12% are are members of minority groups, 38% are women.

ACADEMICS

Degrees: Associate, bachelor's, certificate, master's, post-bachelor's certificate, post-master's certificate. **Classes:** Most classes have 10–19 students. **Majors with Highest Enrollment:** Business administration and management; culinary arts/chef training; psychology. **Special Study Options:** Accelerated program, cooperative education program, distance learning, double major, dual enrollment, English as a Second Language (ESL), honors program, independent study, internships, student-designed major, study abroad, teacher certification program, weekend college. **Honors programs:** Three-Year Honors Program (BS in Business Administration) and our traditional four-year honors program (available in conjunction with most majors). **Combined degree programs:** Three-Year Bachelor's Degree + 1-Year MBA Special programs offered to

physically disabled students include note-taking services, reader services, tape recorders, tutors. **Career services:** Alumni network, alumni services, career/job search classes, career assessment, internships. **Career services highlights include:** Active internship program at the undergraduate and graduate level.

FACILITIES

Housing: Coed dorms, special housing for disabled students, apartments for single students, wellness housing, theme housing. 85% of campus accessible to physically disabled. **Special Academic Facilities/Equipment:** Art Gallery **Computers:** 100% of classrooms, 40% of dorms, 100% of libraries, 100% of dining areas, 100% of student union, have wireless network access. Students can register for classes online. Undergraduates are required to own a computer.

CAMPUS LIFE

Environment: City. **Activities:** Choral groups, concert band, dance, drama/theater, jazz band, literary magazine, musical theater, radio station, student government, student newspaper, television station, yearbook, campus ministries, international student organization, Model UN. **Organizations:** 58 registered organizations, 7 honor societies, 1 religious organizations. 3 fraternities, 3 sororities. **Athletics (Intercollegiate):** *Men:* Baseball, basketball, cheerleading, cross-country, golf, ice hockey, lacrosse, soccer, tennis. *Women:* Basketball, cheerleading, cross-country, lacrosse, soccer, softball, tennis, volleyball. **On-Campus Highlights:** Center for Financial Studies, Fitness Center/Athletic Complex, Robert Frost Hall (Academic Building), McIninch Art Gallery, Last Chapter Pub, In addition to our five most popular places on campus, we also have a gourmet restaurant on campus run by our culinary and hospitality students, a bakery and coffee shop. **Environmental Initiatives:** Renewable Energy Hedge from 2007–2022 based on 17,500 megawatt hours of wind power output with PPM Energy Inc. By a financial swap, the hedge will flat line SNHU energy budget, and 100% offset energy green house gas use in the voluntary market with RECs, and provide the wind developer a consistent stream of income to facilitate more wind construction. This represents a new sustainable model of utility cost control based on long-term agreements between energy users and renewable developers. The establishment of the SNHU School of Liberal Arts Bachelor of Arts in Environment, Ethics and Public Policy. This new degree program represents the effort by SNHU to provide an interdisciplinary approach to training the next generation of ecological leaders with a wide range of interests, backgrounds and skills, able to respond to the challenges posed by sustainability ion the 21st century. The development of campus sustainability energy plan based on development of initiatives for interconnected campus islands of sustainability. Under development are initiatives including use of sawdust for wood gasification for cogeneration units to supply electricity and heat; the use of geothermal systems based on innovative use of ground water near the Merrimack River for heat pumps; real time price control for optimization of energy use based on 5-minte ISO-NE price signals.

ADMISSIONS

Freshman Academic Profile: Average high school GPA 2.96. 88% from public high schools. SAT Math middle 50% range 440–540. SAT Critical Reading middle 50% range 440–520. SAT Writing middle 50% range 430–520. ACT middle 50% range 18–24. Minimum paper TOEFL 530. Minimum web-based TOEFL 71. **Basis for Candidate Selection:** *Very important factors considered include:* Academic GPA, rigor of secondary school record. *Important factors considered include:* Application essay, recommendation(s), character/personal qualities, extracurricular activities, first generation, level of applicant's interest. *Other factors considered include:* Class rank, standardized test scores, alumni/ae relation, interview, talent/ability, volunteer work, work experience. **Freshman Admission Requirements:** High school diploma is required and GED is accepted. *Academic units required:* 4 English, (2 science labs). **Freshman Admission Statistics:** 3,124 applied, 84% admitted, 18% enrolled. **Transfer Admission Requirements:** High school transcript, college transcript(s), essay or personal statement, minimum college GPA of 2.50 required. Lowest grade transferable C–. **General Admission Information:** Application fee $40. Nonfall registration accepted. Admission may be deferred for a maximum of 1 year. Credit and/or placement offered for CEEB Advanced Placement tests.

COSTS AND FINANCIAL AID

Required Forms and Deadlines: FAFSA. Priority financial aid filing date 3/15. **Notification of Awards:** Applicants will be notified of awards on a rolling basis beginning 3/1. **Types of Aid:** *Need-based scholarships/grants:* Federal Pell, SEOG, state scholarships/grants, private scholarships, the school's own gift aid. *Loans:* Direct Subsidized Stafford, Direct Unsubsidized Stafford, Direct PLUS, FFEL Subsidized Stafford. *Student Employment:* Federal Work-Study Program available. Institutional employment available. Off-campus job opportunities are good. **Financial Aid Statistics:** 94% freshmen, 93% undergrads receive any aid. **Criteria for awarding institutional aid:** *Non-need-based:* Academics, alumni affiliation, athletics, leadership, state/district residency.

SOUTHERN OREGON UNIVERSITY

Office of Admissions, 1250 Siskiyou Blvd, Ashland, OR 97520-5032
Phone: 541-552-6411 **Financial Aid Phone:** 541-552-6600
E-mail: admissions@sou.edu **CEEB Code:** 4702
Fax: 541-552-6614 **Website: ACT Code:** 3496

This public school was founded in 1926. It has a 175-acre campus.

RATINGS
Admissions Selectivity Rating: 60*   **Fire Safety Rating:** 74   **Green Rating:** 60*

STUDENTS AND FACULTY
Enrollment: 4,058. **Student Body:** 58% female, 42% male, 23% out-of-state, 2% international (32 countries represented). Asian 5%, African American 2%, Caucasian 78%, Hispanic 4%, Native American 2%.
Retention and Graduation: Faculty: Student/faculty ratio 21:1. 194 full-time faculty, 79% hold PhDs, 13% are are members of minority groups, 43% are women.

ACADEMICS
Degrees: Bachelor's, master's, post-bachelor's certificate. **Majors with Highest Enrollment:** Business/commerce; criminology; psychology. **Special Study Options:** Accelerated program, cooperative education program, cross-registration, distance learning, double major, dual enrollment, English as a Second Language (ESL), exchange student program (domestic), external degree program, honors program, independent study, internships, liberal arts/career combination, student-designed major, study abroad, teacher certification program, Undergrads may take grad level classes. Nursing programs with Oregon Health Sciences U. Exchange programs with Coll of the Redwoods, Coll of the Siskiyous, and Shasta Coll. Member of National Student Exchange(NSE). Exchange programs abroad in Korea(Dankook U) and Mexico(U of Guanajuato). Study abroad also in Asian, European, and South American countries. Concurrent enrollment with Rogue Community College. Special programs offered to physically disabled students include note-taking services, reader services, tape recorders, tutors. **Career services:** Alumni network, alumni services, career/job search classes, career assessment, internships, regional alumni.

FACILITIES
Housing: Coed dorms, special housing for disabled students, special housing for international students, apartments for married students, apartments for single students, special quiet, substance free, nonsmoking, older students or freshman only residence halls. **Special Academic Facilities/Equipment:** Art and history museums, art galleries, on-campus preschool and kindergarten, National Guard armory, United States Wildlife Forensics Lab. **Computers:** Students can register for classes online. Administrative functions (other than registration) can be performed online.

CAMPUS LIFE
Environment: Village. **Activities:** Choral groups, concert band, dance, drama/theater, jazz band, literary magazine, music ensembles, musical theater, opera, pep band, radio station, student government, student newspaper, student-run film society, symphony orchestra, television station, international student organization. **Organizations:** 52 registered organizations, 13 honor societies, 5 religious organizations. **Athletics (Intercollegiate):** *Men:* Basketball, cross-country, football, track/field (outdoor), wrestling. *Women:* Basketball, cross-country, soccer, softball, tennis, track/field (outdoor), volleyball. **On-Campus Highlights:** Hannon Library, Center for the Visual Arts, Student Union, Theatre Building, Music Building.

ADMISSIONS
Freshman Academic Profile: Average high school GPA 3.2. 90% from public high schools. Minimum paper TOEFL 520. Minimum computer TOEFL 190. **Basis for Candidate Selection:** *Very important factors considered include:* Rigor of secondary school record, standardized test scores. *Other factors considered include:* Application essay, recommendation(s), character/personal qualities, extracurricular activities, talent/ability, volunteer work, work experience. **Freshman Admission Requirements:** High school diploma is required and GED is accepted. *Academic units required:* 4 English, 3 mathematics, 2 science, 2 foreign language, 3 social studies. **Freshman Admission Statistics:** 1,887 applied, 83% admitted, 48% enrolled. **Transfer Admission Requirements:** College transcript(s), minimum college GPA of 2.2 required. Lowest grade transferable D–. **General Admission Information:** Application fee $50. Notification on a rolling basis, beginning on or about 9/1. Nonfall registration accepted. Admission may be deferred for a maximum of 1 year. Credit and/or placement offered for CEEB Advanced Placement tests.

COSTS AND FINANCIAL AID
Required Forms and Deadlines: FAFSA, Institutional scholarship application. Priority financial aid filing date 3/1. **Notification of Awards:** Applicants will be notified of awards on a rolling basis beginning 4/1. **Types of Aid:** *Need-based scholarships/grants:* Federal Pell, SEOG, state scholarships/grants, private scholarships, the school's own gift aid. *Loans:* Direct Subsidized Stafford, Direct Unsubsidized Stafford, Direct PLUS, Federal Perkins, state loans, college/university loans from institutional funds. *Student Employment:* Federal Work-Study Program available. Institutional employment available. Off-campus job opportunities are excellent. **Financial Aid Statistics:** 69% freshmen, 68% undergrads receive need-based scholarship or grant aid. 9% freshmen, 4% undergrads receive non-need-based scholarship or grant aid. 57% freshmen, 70% undergrads receive need-based self-help aid. 1% freshmen, 1% undergrads receive athletic scholarships. 67% freshmen, 67% undergrads receive any aid. 95% undergrads borrow to pay for school. Average cumulative indebtedness $24,416. **Criteria for awarding institutional aid:** *Non-need-based:* Academics, art, athletics, leadership, minority status, music/drama, state/district residency.

SOUTHERN POLYTECHNIC STATE UNIVERSITY

1100 South Marietta Parkway, Marietta, GA 30060-2896
Phone: 678-915-4188 **Financial Aid Phone:** 678-915-7290
E-mail: admiss@spsu.edu **CEEB Code:** 5626
Fax: 678-915-7292 **Website:** www.spsu.edu **ACT Code:** 865

This public school was founded in 1948. It has a 198-acre campus.

RATINGS
Admissions Selectivity Rating: 77   **Fire Safety Rating:** 87   **Green Rating:** 79

STUDENTS AND FACULTY
Enrollment: 4,126. **Student Body:** 18% female, 82% male, 4% out-of-state, 5% international (59 countries represented). Asian 6%, African American 20%, Caucasian 64%, Hispanic 4%.
Retention and Graduation: 6% freshmen graduate within 4 years. **Faculty:** Student/faculty ratio 18:1. 174 full-time faculty, 68% hold PhDs, 27% are are members of minority groups, 29% are women.

ACADEMICS
Degrees: Associate, bachelor's, certificate, master's, post-bachelor's certificate. **Classes:** Most classes have 20–29 students. Most lab/discussion sessions have 10–19 students. **Majors with Highest Enrollment:** Architecture (BArch, BA/BS, MArch, MA/MS, PhD); construction management; mechanical engineering. **Special Study Options:** Cooperative education program, cross-registration, distance learning, double major, dual enrollment, honors program, independent study, internships, study abroad. **Honors programs:** The SPSU Honors Program provides academically talented students the opportunity to develop their talents and skills in an expanded and enriched curriculum. It features seminar-size classes that demand intellectual rigor. The program provides students with a community of peers and ample opportunity for social interaction within the peer group and with Honors faculty. Students work closely with faculty and have opportunities to expand their learning through independent study, special projects, and research. Special programs offered to physically disabled students include note-taking services, reader services, tape recorders, tutors. **Career services:** Alumni services, career/job search classes, career assessment, internships **Career services highlights include:** We are very proud of our co-op and internship programs. Industry actually seek our students and value them greatly.

FACILITIES
Housing: Coed dorms, special housing for disabled students, men's dorms, apartments for single students. 100% of campus accessible to physically disabled. **Computers:** 100% of classrooms, 100% of libraries, 100% of dining areas, 100% of student union, 60% of common outdoor areas have wireless network access. Students can register for classes online. Administrative functions (other than registration) can be performed online.

CAMPUS LIFE
Environment: City. **Activities:** Choral groups, jazz band, pep band, radio station, student government, student newspaper, campus ministries, international student organization. **Organizations:** 87 registered organizations, 3 honor societies, 8 fraternities, 3 sororities. **Athletics (Intercollegiate):** *Men:* Baseball, basketball, cheerleading, soccer. *Women:* Basketball, cheerleading **On-Campus Highlights:** Student Activities Center, Health and Wellness Center, Library, Gym, Administration Building. **Environmental Initiatives:** Recycling Commitment to build all new and renovated buildings to LEED Silver certification. Reducing the university's carbon footprint by using EMS green building materials and voluntary recycling.

ADMISSIONS

Freshman Academic Profile: Average high school GPA 3.24. 95% from public high schools. SAT Math middle 50% range 520–623. SAT Critical Reading middle 50% range 490–580. ACT middle 50% range 21-25. Minimum paper TOEFL 550. Minimum computer TOEFL 213. Minimum web-based TOEFL 79. **Basis for Candidate Selection:** *Very important factors considered include:* Academic GPA, rigor of secondary school record, standardized test scores. **Freshman Admission Requirements:** High school diploma is required and GED is not accepted. *Academic units required:* 4 English, 4 mathematics, 3 science, (2 science labs), 2 foreign language, 3 social studies, 2 academic electives. **Freshman Admission Statistics:** 1,600 applied, 62% admitted, 61% enrolled. **Transfer Admission Requirements:** College transcript(s), minimum college GPA of 2.0 required. Lowest grade transferable C. **General Admission Information:** Application fee $20. Regular application deadline 8/1. Notification on a rolling basis, beginning on or about 9/1. Nonfall registration accepted. Admission may be deferred for a maximum of 1 term. Credit and/or placement offered for CEEB Advanced Placement tests.

COSTS AND FINANCIAL AID

Required Forms and Deadlines: FAFSA. Priority financial aid filing date 4/1. **Notification of Awards:** Applicants will be notified of awards on a rolling basis beginning 6/1. **Types of Aid:** *Need-based scholarships/grants:* Federal Pell, SEOG, state scholarships/grants, private scholarships, the school's own gift aid. *Loans:* FFEL Subsidized Stafford, FFEL Unsubsidized Stafford, FFEL PLUS, state loans *Student Employment:* Federal Work-Study Program available. Institutional employment available. Off-campus job opportunities are good. **Financial Aid Statistics:** 30% freshmen, 26% undergrads receive need-based scholarship or grant aid. 55% freshmen, 15% undergrads receive non-need-based scholarship or grant aid. 37% freshmen, 38% undergrads receive need-based self-help aid. 2% freshmen, 1% undergrads receive athletic scholarships. 86% freshmen receive any aid. 42% undergrads borrow to pay for school. Average cumulative indebtedness $13,244. **Criteria for awarding institutional aid:** *Non-need-based:* Academics, athletics.

SOUTHERN UNIVERSITY AND A&M COLLEGE

P.O. Box 9901, Baton Rouge, LA 70813
Phone: 225-771-2430 **Financial Aid Phone:** 225-771-2790
E-mail: admit@subr.edu **CEEB Code:** 6663
Fax: 225-771-2500 **Website:** subr.edu **ACT Code:** 1610

This public school was founded in 1880. It has a 884-acre campus.

RATINGS

Admissions Selectivity Rating: 71   Fire Safety Rating: 69   Green Rating: 61

STUDENTS AND FACULTY

Enrollment: 6,830. **Student Body:** 61% female, 39% male, 19% out-of-state, 2% international (48 countries represented). African American 96%, Caucasian 3%.
Retention and Graduation: 65% freshmen return for sophomore year. 7% freshmen graduate within 4 years. 16% grads go on to further study within 1 year. 15% grads pursue arts and sciences degrees. 1% grads pursue law degrees. **Faculty:** Student/faculty ratio 16:1. 405 full-time faculty, 66% hold PhDs, 85% are are members of minority groups, 47% are women.

ACADEMICS

Degrees: Associate, bachelor's, master's, post-master's certificate. **Classes:** Most classes have 20–29 students. Most lab/discussion sessions have 10–19 students. **Majors with Highest Enrollment:** Biology/biological sciences; business administration and management; nursing/registered nurse (RN, ASN, BSN, MSN). **Special Study Options:** Cooperative education program, cross-registration, distance learning, double major, dual enrollment, exchange student program (domestic), honors program, independent study, internships, study abroad, teacher certification program, weekend college, undergrads may take grad level classes. Cooperative Education Programs: Engineering **Combined degree programs:** Dual degree programs with Jackson State U and Xavier U. **Honors programs:** The Honors College provides an enhances educational experience for students who have a history of strong academic achievement and who have demonstrated exceptional creativity or talent. The College also provides cultural and intellectual opportunities that are designed to motivae students to perform at the highest level of excellence that they are capable of and through which they may become knowledgeable and effective leaders. Special programs offered to physically disabled students include note-taking services, tape recorders, tutors. **Career services:** Career/job search classes, internships. **Career services highlights include:** The 3.0 credit hour co-op education course.

FACILITIES

Housing: special housing for disabled students, men's dorms, women's dorms 100% of campus accessible to physically disabled. **Special Academic Facilities/Equipment:** Jazz institute Southern Museum of Art. **Computers:** 100% of classrooms, 20% of dorms, 100% of libraries, 50% of dining areas, 90% of student union, 25% of common outdoor areas have wireless network access. Students can register for classes online. Administrative functions (other than registration) can be performed online.

CAMPUS LIFE

Environment: Metropolis. **Activities:** Choral groups, concert band, dance, drama/theater, jazz band, literary magazine, marching band, music ensembles, musical theater, pep band, student government, student newspaper, yearbook. **Organizations:** 88 registered organizations, 11 honor societies, 6 religious organizations. 4 fraternities, 4 sororities. **Athletics (Intercollegiate):** *Men:* Baseball, basketball, cross-country, football, golf, tennis, track/field (outdoor). *Women:* Basketball, cross-country, golf, softball, tennis, track/field (outdoor), volleyball. **On-Campus Highlights:** SUBR Museum of Art, Smith—Brown Student Union, Site of the original Red Stick for Baton, Bluff over the Mississippi River **Environmental Initiatives:** MS4-Stormwater Permit with the Parish of East Baton Rouge; full-time Environmental, Safety and Health Director; Storm Water Plan (Debris Management).

ADMISSIONS

Freshman Academic Profile: Average high school GPA 2.8. 3% in top 10% of high school class, 13% in top 25% of high school class, 40% in top 50% of high school class. 75% from public high schools. SAT Math middle 50% range 380–460. ACT middle 50% range 15–18. Minimum paper TOEFL 500. Minimum computer TOEFL 125. **Basis for Candidate Selection:** *Very important factors considered include:* Class rank, academic GPA, rigor of secondary school record, standardized test scores. *Other factors considered include:* talent/ability. **Freshman Admission Requirements:** High school diploma is required and GED is accepted. *Academic units required:* 4 English, 3 mathematics, 3 science, 2 foreign language, 2 social studies, 1 history, 1 computer science, Arts (1.5 credits). **Freshman Admission Statistics:** 2,179 applied, 56% admitted, 91% enrolled. **Transfer Admission Requirements:** High school transcript, college transcript(s), standardized test scores, statement of good standing from prior institution(s). Minimum college GPA of 2.0 required. Lowest grade transferable C. **General Admission Information:** Application fee $20. Regular application deadline 7/1. Nonfall registration accepted. Admission may be deferred for a maximum of 2 semesters. Credit offered for CEEB Advanced Placement tests.

COSTS AND FINANCIAL AID

Annual in-state tuition $3,666. Annual out-of-state tuition $9,458. Room and board $5,784. Average book expense $1,200. **Required Forms and Deadlines:** FAFSA, institution's own financial aid form. Priority financial aid filing date 5/15. **Notification of Awards:** Applicants will be notified of awards on a rolling basis beginning 6/30. **Types of Aid:** *Need-based scholarships/grants:* Federal Pell, SEOG, state scholarships/grants, private scholarships, the school's own gift aid. *Loans:* Direct Subsidized Stafford, Direct Unsubsidized Stafford, Direct PLUS, FFEL Subsidized Stafford, FFEL Unsubsidized Stafford, FFEL PLUS, college/university loans from institutional funds, TOPS TH Harris LEAP. *Student Employment:* Federal Work-Study Program available. Institutional employment available. Highest amount earned per year from on-campus jobs $1,000. Off-campus job opportunities are fair. **Financial Aid Statistics:** 72% freshmen, 67% undergrads receive need-based scholarship or grant aid. 19% freshmen, 15% undergrads receive non-need-based scholarship or grant aid. 71% freshmen, 76% undergrads receive need-based self-help aid. 5% freshmen, 3% undergrads receive athletic scholarships. 89% freshmen, 85% undergrads receive any aid. 85% undergrads borrow to pay for school. Average cumulative indebtedness $23,000. **Criteria for awarding institutional aid:** *Non-need-based:* Academics, athletics

SOUTHERN UTAH UNIVERSITY

Southern Utah University, Admissions Off, 351 West Univeri, Cedar City, UT 84720
Phone: 435-586-7740
E-mail: adminfo@suu.edu **CEEB Code:** 4092
Fax: 435-865-8223 **Website:** www.suu.edu **ACT Code:** 4271

This public school was founded in 1897. It has a 113-acre campus.

RATINGS

Admissions Selectivity Rating: 79   Fire Safety Rating: 60*   Green Rating: 60*

STUDENTS AND FACULTY

Enrollment: 5,806. **Student Body:** 56% female, 44% male, 12.6% out-of-state, 2% international (7 countries represented). Asian 2%, African American 1%, Caucasian 86%, Hispanic 4%, Native American 2%.
Retention and Graduation: 62% freshmen return for sophomore year. 23% freshmen graduate within 4 years. **Faculty:** Student/faculty ratio 26:1. 216 full-time faculty, 75% hold PhDs, 12% are are members of minority groups, 29% are women.

ACADEMICS

Degrees: Associate, bachelor's, certificate, diploma, master's, terminal associate, transfer associate. **Classes:** Most classes have 20–29 students. Most lab/discussion sessions have 20–29 students. **Special Study Options:** Cooperative education program, distance learning, double major, English as a Second Language (ESL), honors program, independent study, internships, liberal arts/career combination, teacher certification program, weekend college. Special programs offered to physically disabled students include reader services, tape recorders, tutors. **Career services:** Alumni services, career/job search classes, career assessment, internships.

FACILITIES

Housing: Coed dorms, special housing for disabled students, men's dorms, special housing for international students, women's dorms, fraternity/sorority housing, apartments for single students.

CAMPUS LIFE

Environment: Village. **Activities:** Choral groups, concert band, dance, drama/theater, jazz band, literary magazine, marching band, music ensembles, musical theater, opera, pep band, radio station, student government, student newspaper, symphony orchestra, television station, yearbook. **Organizations: Athletics (Intercollegiate):** *Men:* Baseball, basketball, cross-country, football, golf, track/field (outdoor). *Women:* Basketball, cross-country, gymnastics, softball, tennis, track/field (outdoor).

ADMISSIONS

Freshman Academic Profile: Average high school GPA 2.4. 26.3% in top 10% of high school class, 50.8% in top 25% of high school class, 80% in top 50% of high school class. 95% from public high schools. SAT Math middle 50% range 450–570. SAT Critical Reading middle 50% range 450–580. ACT middle 50% range 19–25. Minimum paper TOEFL 500. Minimum computer TOEFL 1.
Basis for Candidate Selection: *Very important factors considered include:* Academic GPA, standardized test scores. *Other factors considered include:* first generation, racial/ethnic status. **Freshman Admission Requirements:** High school diploma is required and GED is accepted. *Academic units recommended:* 4 English, 3 mathematics, 3 science, (1 science labs), 2 foreign language, 3 social studies. **Freshman Admission Statistics:** 3,274 applied, 81% admitted, 49% enrolled. **Transfer Admission Requirements:** College transcript(s), minimum college GPA of 2.25 required. Lowest grade transferable D. **General Admission Information:** Application fee $40. Nonfall registration accepted. Credit and/or placement offered for CEEB Advanced Placement tests.

COSTS AND FINANCIAL AID

Average book expense $1,500. **Required Forms and Deadlines:** FAFSA. Priority financial aid filing date 12/1. **Notification of Awards:** Applicants will be notified of awards on a rolling basis beginning 11/1. **Types of Aid:** *Need-based scholarships/grants:* Federal Pell, SEOG, state scholarships/grants, private scholarships, the school's own gift aid. *Loans:* FFEL Subsidized Stafford, FFEL Unsubsidized Stafford, FFEL PLUS, Federal Perkins. *Student Employment:* Federal Work-Study Program available. Institutional employment available. Highest amount earned per year from on-campus jobs $2,000. Off-campus job opportunities are good. **Financial Aid Statistics:** 51% freshmen, 59% undergrads receive need-based scholarship or grant aid. 34% freshmen, 19% undergrads receive non-need-based scholarship or grant aid. 26% freshmen, 35% undergrads receive need-based self-help aid. 6% freshmen, 6% undergrads receive athletic scholarships. 51% undergrads borrow to pay for school. Average cumulative indebtedness $10,485. **Criteria for awarding institutional aid:** *Non-need-based:* Academics, alumni affiliation, art, athletics, job skills, leadership, minority status, music/drama, state/district residency.

SOUTHERN VERMONT COLLEGE

982 Mansion Drive, Bennington, VT 05201
Phone: 802-447-6304 **Financial Aid Phone:** 800-660-3561
E-mail: admis@svc.edu **CEEB Code:** 3796
Fax: 802-447-4695 **Website:** www.svc.edu **ACT Code:** 4310

This private school was founded in 1974. It has a 371-acre campus.

RATINGS

Admissions Selectivity Rating: 74 **Fire Safety Rating:** 60* **Green Rating:** 60*

STUDENTS AND FACULTY

Enrollment: 464. **Student Body:** 64% female, 36% male, 66% out-of-state.
Retention and Graduation: 61% freshmen return for sophomore year.
Faculty: Student/faculty ratio 11:1. 16 full-time faculty, 25% hold PhDs, 44% are women.

ACADEMICS

Degrees: Associate, bachelor's, terminal associate, transfer associate. **Special Study Options:** Accelerated program, cooperative education program, distance learning, double major, dual enrollment, honors program, independent study, internships, liberal arts/career combination, student-designed major, study abroad. Special programs offered to physically disabled students include note-taking services, tape recorders, tutors. **Career services:** Alumni network, alumni services, career/job search classes, career assessment, internships.

FACILITIES

Housing: Coed dorms, quiet, substance-free and non-smoking, freshmen and upper-classmen residence halls. 60% of campus accessible to physically disabled. **Special Academic Facilities/Equipment:** Mountaineers Field House and Fitness Center, Apartment style Resident Halls and courtyard, Dining Hall and Student Center, Everett Mansion.

CAMPUS LIFE

Environment: Rural. **Activities:** Drama/theater, literary magazine, music ensembles, radio station, student government, student newspaper, yearbook. **Organizations:** 14 registered organizations, 1 honor societies. **Athletics (Intercollegiate):** *Men:* Baseball, basketball, cross-country, rugby, soccer, volleyball. *Women:* Basketball, cross-country, rugby, soccer, softball, volleyball.

ADMISSIONS

Freshman Academic Profile: Average high school GPA 2.63. 5% in top 25% of high school class, 35% in top 50% of high school class. 85% from public high schools. SAT Math middle 50% range 390–490. SAT Critical Reading middle 50% range 420–510. Minimum paper TOEFL 500. Minimum computer TOEFL 173. **Basis for Candidate Selection:** *Very important factors considered include:* Application essay, recommendation(s), rigor of secondary school record, interview. *Important factors considered include:* standardized test scores, character/personal qualities, extracurricular activities, volunteer work. *Other factors considered include:* Class rank, work experience. **Freshman Admission Requirements:** High school diploma is required and GED is accepted. *Academic units required:* 4 English, 2 mathematics. *Academic units recommended:* 4 science, 2 foreign language, 4 social studies, 4 history. **Freshman Admission Statistics:** 373 applied, 71% admitted, 37% enrolled. **Transfer Admission Requirements:** High school transcript, college transcript(s), essay or personal statement, minimum college GPA of 2.0 required. Lowest grade transferable C. **General Admission Information:** Application fee $30. Notification on a rolling basis, beginning on or about 12/1. Nonfall registration accepted. Admission may be deferred for a maximum of 1 year. Credit offered for CEEB Advanced Placement tests.

COSTS AND FINANCIAL AID

Annual tuition $14,374. Room and board $6,948. Average book expense $500. **Required Forms and Deadlines:** FAFSA, institution's own financial aid form. Financial aid filing deadline 5/1. Priority financial aid filing date 3/1. **Notification of Awards:** Applicants will be notified of awards on or about 3/1. **Types of Aid:** *Need-based scholarships/grants:* Federal Pell, SEOG, state scholarships/grants, private scholarships, the school's own gift aid, Southern Vermont College Opportunity Grant Everett Scholarship Leadership Scholarship Vermont Resident Scholarship TRIO Scholarship. *Loans:* Direct Subsidized Stafford, Direct Unsubsidized Stafford, Direct PLUS. *Student Employment:* Federal Work-Study Program available. Off-campus job opportunities are good. **Financial Aid Statistics:** 64% freshmen, 73% undergrads receive need-based scholarship or grant aid. 67% freshmen, 76% undergrads receive need-based self-help aid. 75% freshmen, 75% undergrads receive any aid. **Criteria for awarding institutional aid:** *Non-need-based:* Academics, leadership.

SOUTHERN WESLEYAN UNIVERSITY

Wesleyan Drive, PO Box 1020, Central, SC 29630-1020
Phone: 864-644-5550 **Financial Aid Phone:** 864-644-5500
E-mail: admissions@swu.edu **CEEB Code:** 5896
Fax: 864-644-5972 **Website:** www.swu.edu **ACT Code:** 3837

This private school, affiliated with the Wesleyan Church, was founded in 1906. It has a 330-acre campus.

RATINGS
Admissions Selectivity Rating: 79 **Fire Safety Rating:** 60* **Green Rating:** 61

STUDENTS AND FACULTY
Enrollment: 1,692. **Student Body:** 63% female, 37% male, 17% out-of-state, 1% international (9 countries represented). African American 29%, Caucasian 59%, Hispanic 2%, Native American 1%.
Retention and Graduation: 67% freshmen return for sophomore year. 33% freshmen graduate within 4 years. 31% grads go on to further study within 1 year. **Faculty:** Student/faculty ratio 23:1. 50 full-time faculty, 76% hold PhDs, 14% are are members of minority groups, 30% are women.

ACADEMICS
Degrees: Associate, bachelor's, master's. **Classes:** Most classes have 10–19 students. Most lab/discussion sessions have 20–29 students. **Majors with Highest Enrollment:** Business/commerce; elementary education and teaching; religion/religious studies. **Special Study Options:** Cross-registration, double major, dual enrollment, English as a Second Language (ESL), honors program, independent study, internships, student-designed major, study abroad, teacher certification program **Honors programs:** The honors program consists of specialized coursework, non-credit academic experiences, and service opportunities. Honors students must complete a research-based Honors Major Project in their Junior or Senior years. Special programs offered to physically disabled students include note-taking services, reader services, tape recorders, tutors. **Career services:** Career/job search classes, career assessment, internships **Career services highlights include:** Career assessment.

FACILITIES
Housing: Coed dorms, special housing for disabled students, women's dorms, apartments for single students. 90% of campus accessible to physically disabled. **Special Academic Facilities/Equipment:** Freedom's Hill Historic Site, Clayton Genealogical Research Library, electron microscope lab. **Computers:** 100% of classrooms, 50% of dorms, 100% of libraries, 100% of dining areas, 100% of student union, 25% of common outdoor areas have wireless network access. Students can register for classes online. Administrative functions (other than registration) can be performed online.

CAMPUS LIFE
Environment: Town. **Activities:** Choral groups, concert band, drama/theater, jazz band, literary magazine, music ensembles, musical theater, student government, yearbook, campus ministries. **Organizations:** 12 registered organizations, 2 honor societies, 3 religious organizations. **Athletics (Intercollegiate):** *Men:* Baseball, basketball, cross-country, golf, soccer. *Women:* Basketball, cross-country, soccer, softball, volleyball. **On-Campus Highlights:** Jennings Campus Center, Java City Coffee Shop, Historic Tysinger Gymnasium, Student Apartment Complex. **Environmental Initiatives:** Voluntary recycling of paper and plastic in residence halls and academic buildings. Materials are collected by the city.

ADMISSIONS
Freshman Academic Profile: Average high school GPA 3.6. 13% in top 10% of high school class, 36% in top 25% of high school class, 75% in top 50% of high school class. SAT Math middle 50% range 440–550. SAT Critical Reading middle 50% range 440–540. SAT Writing middle 50% range 410–540. ACT middle 50% range 17–21. Minimum paper TOEFL 500. Minimum computer TOEFL 173. **Basis for Candidate Selection:** *Very important factors considered include:* Academic GPA, standardized test scores. *Other factors considered include:* Class rank, rigor of secondary school record, character/personal qualities, religious affiliation/commitment. **Freshman Admission Requirements:** High school diploma is required and GED is accepted. *Academic units required:* 4 English, 2 mathematics, 2 science, 2 social studies. **Freshman Admission Statistics: Transfer Admission Requirements:** College transcript(s), minimum college GPA of 2.0 required. Lowest grade transferable C. **General Admission Information:** Application fee $25. Regular application deadline 8/1. Nonfall registration accepted. Admission may be deferred for a maximum of 1 semester. Credit and/or placement offered for CEEB Advanced Placement tests.

COSTS AND FINANCIAL AID
Annual tuition $19,000. Room and board $8,150. Required fees $500. Average book expense $950. **Required Forms and Deadlines:** FAFSA, institution's own financial aid form. Financial aid filing deadline 6/30. Priority financial aid filing date 1/31. **Notification of Awards:** Applicants will be notified of awards on a rolling basis beginning 2/1. **Types of Aid:** *Need-based scholarships/grants:* Federal Pell, SEOG, state scholarships/grants, private scholarships, the school's own gift aid. *Loans:* FFEL Subsidized Stafford, FFEL Unsubsidized Stafford, FFEL PLUS, Federal Perkins. *Student Employment:* Federal Work-Study Program available. Institutional employment available. Off-campus job opportunities are good. **Financial Aid Statistics:** 94% freshmen, 43% undergrads receive need-based scholarship or grant aid. 15% freshmen, 4% undergrads receive non-need-based scholarship or grant aid. 69% freshmen, 34% undergrads receive need-based self-help aid. 5% freshmen, 2% undergrads receive athletic scholarships. **Criteria for awarding institutional aid:** *Non-need-based:* Academics, athletics, music/drama, religious affiliation.

SOUTHWEST BAPTIST UNIVERSITY

1600 University Avenue, Bolivar, MO 65613-2597
Phone: 417-328-1810 **Financial Aid Phone:** 417-328-1823
E-mail: admitme@sbuniv.edu **CEEB Code:** 6664
Fax: 417-328-1808 **Website: ACT Code:** 2368

This private school, affiliated with the Southern Baptist Church, was founded in 1878. It has a 180-acre campus.

RATINGS
Admissions Selectivity Rating: 80 **Fire Safety Rating:** 63 **Green Rating:** 60*

STUDENTS AND FACULTY
Enrollment: 2,646. **Student Body:** 66% female, 34% male, 29% out-of-state, 1% international (16 countries represented). Asian 1%, African American 4%, Caucasian 86%, Hispanic 1%, Native American 1%.
Retention and Graduation: 70% freshmen return for sophomore year. 38% freshmen graduate within 4 years. **Faculty:** Student/faculty ratio 13:1. 116 full-time faculty, 59% hold PhDs, 2% are are members of minority groups, 41% are women.

ACADEMICS
Degrees: Associate, bachelor's, certificate, master's, post-master's certificate. **Classes:** Most classes have fewer than 10 students. Most lab/discussion sessions have 10–19 students. **Majors with Highest Enrollment:** Business administration and management; elementary education and teaching; psychology. **Special Study Options:** Cooperative education program, distance learning, double major, dual enrollment, exchange student program (domestic), honors program, independent study, internships, student-designed major, study abroad, teacher certification program. **Honors programs:** Our academic honors program consists of the following components: Academics, servant leadership, intercultural experiences, spiritual growth, and enrichment opportunities. Special programs offered to physically disabled students include note-taking services, reader services, tutors. **Career services:** Career/job search classes, career assessment.

FACILITIES
Housing: Special housing for disabled students, men's dorms, women's dorms, apartments for single students. 95% of campus accessible to physically disabled. **Special Academic Facilities/Equipment:** The Driskell Art Gallery Jester Learning and Performance Center Meyer Wellness and Sports Center **Computers:** 100% of classrooms, 100% of dorms, 100% of libraries, 100% of dining areas, 100% of student union, 40% of common outdoor areas have wireless network access. Administrative functions (other than registration) can be performed online.

CAMPUS LIFE
Environment: Village. **Activities:** Choral groups, concert band, drama/theater, jazz band, music ensembles, musical theater, opera, pep band, student government, student newspaper, symphony orchestra, yearbook, campus ministries. **Organizations:** 34 registered organizations, 8 honor societies, 10 religious organizations. **Athletics (Intercollegiate):** *Men:* Baseball, basketball, cheerleading, cross-country, football, golf, tennis, track/field (outdoor), track/field (indoor). *Women:* Basketball, cheerleading, cross-country, soccer, softball, tennis, track/field (outdoor), track/field (indoor), volleyball. **On-Campus Highlights:** Meyer Wellness and Sports Center, Jester Learning and Performance Center, Felix Goodson Student Union, Harriet K. Hutchens Library, Plaster Stadium.

ADMISSIONS
Freshman Academic Profile: Average high school GPA 3.47. 22% in top 10% of high school class, 41% in top 25% of high school class, 67% in top 50% of high school class. SAT Math middle 50% range 450–600. SAT Critical Reading middle 50% range 410–560. ACT middle 50% range 20–26. Minimum paper TOEFL 550. Minimum computer TOEFL 213. **Basis for Candidate**

Selection: *Very important factors considered include:* Class rank, academic GPA, standardized test scores. *Important factors considered include:* Application essay, recommendation(s), rigor of secondary school record. *Other factors considered include:* Character/personal qualities, interview, talent/ability. **Freshman Admission Requirements:** High school diploma is required and GED is accepted. *Academic units recommended:* 4 English, 3 mathematics, 2 science, 2 social studies, 2 2 additional units from foreign language, computer science, English, mathematics, social studies, or natural sciences recommended. **Freshman Admission Statistics:** 1,617 applied, 92% admitted, 31% enrolled. **Transfer Admission Requirements:** High school transcript, college transcript(s), standardized test scores, minimum college GPA of 2.0 required. Lowest grade transferable D. **General Admission Information:** Application fee $30. Notification on a rolling basis, beginning on or about 9/1. Nonfall registration accepted. Admission may be deferred for a maximum of 1 year. Credit and/or placement offered for CEEB Advanced Placement tests.

COSTS AND FINANCIAL AID

Annual tuition $16,500. . Room and board $5,720. Required fees $780. Average book expense $1,000. **Required Forms and Deadlines:** FAFSA, institution's own financial aid form. Priority financial aid filing date 3/15. **Notification of Awards:** Applicants will be notified of awards on a rolling basis beginning 3/1. **Types of Aid:** *Need-based scholarships/grants:* Federal Pell, SEOG, state scholarships/grants, private scholarships, the school's own gift aid. *Loans:* FFEL Subsidized Stafford, FFEL Unsubsidized Stafford, FFEL PLUS, Federal Perkins, Federal Nursing, Alternative loans. *Student Employment:* Federal Work-Study Program available. Institutional employment available. Off-campus job opportunities are good. **Financial Aid Statistics:** 54% freshmen, 53% undergrads receive need-based scholarship or grant aid. 76% freshmen, 62% undergrads receive non-need-based scholarship or grant aid. 65% freshmen, 65% undergrads receive need-based self-help aid. 16% freshmen, 12% undergrads receive athletic scholarships. 88% freshmen, 71% undergrads receive any aid. 69% undergrads borrow to pay for school. Average cumulative indebtedness $22,913. **Criteria for awarding institutional aid:** *Non-need-based:* Academics, alumni affiliation, art, athletics, job skills, leadership, minority status, music/drama, religious affiliation, state/district residency.

SOUTHWEST MINNESOTA STATE UNIVERSITY

Admission Office, 1501 State Street, Marshall, MN 56258
Phone: 800-642-0684
E-mail: shearerr@southwest.msus.edu **CEEB Code:** 6703
Fax: 507-537-7154 **Website:** www.southwest.msus.edu **ACT Code:** 2151

This public school was founded in 1963. It has a 216-acre campus.

RATINGS
Admissions Selectivity Rating: 60*   **Fire Safety Rating:** 60*   **Green Rating:** 60*

STUDENTS AND FACULTY
Student Body: 17% out-of-state.
Retention and Graduation: 66% freshmen return for sophomore year.

ACADEMICS
Degrees: Associate, bachelor's, master's. **Special Study Options:** Study abroad, exchange program abroad in Japan. Study abroad also in Chile and China. Special programs offered to physically disabled students include note-taking services, reader services, tape recorders, tutors. **Career services:** Alumni services, career/job search classes, career assessment, internships.

FACILITIES
Housing: Apartments for single students. **Special Academic Facilities/Equipment:** Art gallery, natural history museum, science museum, planetarium, greenhouse, wildlife area.

CAMPUS LIFE
Environment: Rural. **Activities:** Literary magazine, radio station, student government, student newspaper, television station, yearbook. **Organizations:** 65 registered organizations, 1 honor societies, 5 religious organizations. **Athletics (Intercollegiate):** *Men:* Cross-country. *Women:* Basketball, cross-country, softball, tennis, volleyball.

ADMISSIONS
Freshman Academic Profile: ACT middle 50% range 19–24. Minimum paper TOEFL 500. **Freshman Admission Requirements:** High school diploma is required and GED is accepted.High school diploma is required and GED is not accepted. *Academic units recommended:* 4 English, 3 mathematics, 3 science, 2 foreign language, 3 social studies, 1 history. **Freshman Admission Statistics:** Minimum college GPA of 2.0 required. Lowest grade transferable C. **General**

Admission Information: Application fee $20. Nonfall registration accepted. Credit offered for CEEB Advanced Placement tests.

COSTS AND FINANCIAL AID
Annual in-state tuition $2,648. Annual out-of-state tuition $5,965. Room and board $3,000. Required fees $484. Average book expense $800. **Required Forms and Deadlines:** FAFSA, institution's own financial aid form. **Notification of Awards: Types of Aid:** *Need-based scholarships/grants:* Federal Pell, SEOG, state scholarships/grants, private scholarships, the school's own gift aid. *Loans:* FFEL Subsidized Stafford, FFEL Unsubsidized Stafford, FFEL PLUS, Federal Perkins, college/university loans from institutional funds. *Student Employment:* Federal Work-Study Program available. Institutional employment available. Highest amount earned per year from on-campus jobs $2,602. Off-campus job opportunities are excellent.

SOUTHWESTERN COLLEGE (AZ)

2625 East Cactus Road, Phoenix, AZ 85032
Phone: 602-386-4100
E-mail: admissions@swcaz.edu
Fax: 602-404-2159 **Website:** www.swcaz.edu

This private school, affiliated with the Baptist Church, was founded in 1960. It has a 17-acre campus.

RATINGS
Admissions Selectivity Rating: 60*   **Fire Safety Rating:** 60*   **Green Rating:** 60*

STUDENTS AND FACULTY
Enrollment: 257. **Student Body:** 43% female, 57% male, 14% out-of-state, 1% international. Asian 2%, African American 4%, Caucasian 84%, Hispanic 5%, Native American 2%.
Retention and Graduation: 67% freshmen return for sophomore year. 70% freshmen graduate within 4 years. **Faculty:** Student/faculty ratio 16:1. 9 full-time faculty, 33% hold PhDs, 33% are women.

ACADEMICS
Degrees: Associate, bachelor's, certificate.

FACILITIES
Housing: Men's dorms, women's dorms, apartments for single students.

CAMPUS LIFE
Environment: Village. **Activities:** Choral groups, drama/theater, music ensembles, student government, student newspaper, yearbook. **Athletics (Intercollegiate):** *Men:* Basketball. *Women:* Basketball, volleyball.

ADMISSIONS
Freshman Academic Profile: 72% from public high schools. ACT middle 50% range 17–23. Minimum paper TOEFL 500. **Basis for Candidate Selection:** *Very important factors considered include:* Application essay, recommendation(s), rigor of secondary school record, standardized test scores, religious affiliation/commitment. *Important factors considered include:* Character/personal qualities. *Other factors considered include:* extracurricular activities, interview. **Freshman Admission Requirements:** High school diploma is required and GED is accepted. **Freshman Admission Statistics:** 95 applied, 86% admitted, 71% enrolled. **Transfer Admission Requirements:** High school transcript, college transcript(s), essay or personal statement, statement of good standing from prior institution(s). Minimum college GPA of 2.0 required. Lowest grade transferable C. **General Admission Information:** Application fee $25. Nonfall registration accepted. Admission may be deferred for a maximum of 1semester.

COSTS AND FINANCIAL AID
Annual tuition $8,600. Room and board $3,400. Required fees $8,600. Average book expense $700. **Required Forms and Deadlines:** FAFSA. Priority financial aid filing date 4/15. **Notification of Awards:** Applicants will be notified of awards on a rolling basis beginning 5/1. **Types of Aid:** *Need-based scholarships/grants:* Federal Pell, SEOG, state scholarships/grants. *Loans:* FFEL Subsidized Stafford, FFEL Unsubsidized Stafford, FFEL PLUS, Federal Perkins. *Student Employment:* Federal Work-Study Program available. Institutional employment available. **Financial Aid Statistics:** 93% freshmen, 79% undergrads receive non-need-based scholarship or grant aid. 93% freshmen, 91% undergrads receive need-based self-help aid. **Criteria for awarding institutional aid:** *Non-need-based:* Academics, alumni affiliation, leadership, music/drama, religious affiliation.

SOUTHWESTERN COLLEGE (KS)

100 College Street, Winfield, KS 67156
Phone: 620-229-6236 **Financial Aid Phone:** 620-229-6215
E-mail: scadmit@sckans.edu **CEEB Code:** 6670
Fax: 620-229-6344 **Website:** www.sckans.edu **ACT Code:** 1464

This private school, affiliated with the Methodist Church, was founded in 1885. It has a 85-acre campus.

RATINGS
Admissions Selectivity Rating: 73   **Fire Safety Rating:** 72   **Green Rating:** 87

STUDENTS AND FACULTY
Enrollment: 1,471. **Student Body:** 48% female, 52% male, 34% out-of-state, 1% international (12 countries represented). Asian 2%, African American 8%, Caucasian 63%, Hispanic 6%, Native American 2%.
Retention and Graduation: 70% freshmen return for sophomore year. 29% freshmen graduate within 4 years. **Faculty:** Student/faculty ratio 12:1. 47 full-time faculty, 60% hold PhDs, 6% are are members of minority groups, 38% are women.

ACADEMICS
Degrees: Bachelor's, master's, post-bachelor's certificate, post-master's certificate. **Classes:** Most classes have fewer than 10 students. Most lab/discussion sessions have fewer than 10 students. **Majors with Highest Enrollment:** Business administration and management; elementary education and teaching; nursing/registered nurse (RN, ASN, BSN, MSN). **Special Study Options:** Accelerated program, distance learning, double major, honors program, independent study, internships, student-designed major, teacher certification program Special programs offered to physically disabled students include reader services, tape recorders, tutors.

FACILITIES
Housing: Coed dorms, men's dorms, women's dorms, apartments for married students, apartments for single students. 90% of campus accessible to physically disabled. **Special Academic Facilities/Equipment:** Ruth Warren Abbott Horticulture Lab; Floyd and Ethel Moore Biological Field Station; Norman E. Hege Education Center. **Computers:** 100% of classrooms, 100% of dorms, 100% of libraries, 100% of dining areas, 100% of student union, 100% of common outdoor areas have wireless network access. Students can register for classes online. Administrative functions (other than registration) can be performed online.

CAMPUS LIFE
Environment: Village. **Activities:** Choral groups, concert band, dance, drama/theater, jazz band, music ensembles, musical theater, pep band, radio station, student government, student newspaper, symphony orchestra, television station, yearbook, campus ministries, international student organization. **Organizations:** 25 registered organizations, 2 honor societies, 7 religious organizations. 2 fraternities. **Athletics (Intercollegiate):** *Men:* Basketball, cheerleading, cross-country, football, golf, soccer, tennis, track/field (outdoor), track/field (indoor). *Women:* Basketball, cheerleading, cross-country, golf, soccer, softball, tennis, track/field (outdoor), track/field (indoor), volleyball. **On-Campus Highlights:** Brand new women's residence hall, Beech Science Center, Historic Stewart Field House, Christy Administration Building, Roy L. Smith Student Center (Newly re-modeled Cafeteria and bookstore). **Environmental Initiatives:** Kansas Envirothon, RecyleMania, encouraging students to recycle old cell phones.

ADMISSIONS
Freshman Academic Profile: Average high school GPA 3.33. 16% in top 10% of high school class, 44% in top 25% of high school class, 73% in top 50% of high school class. 95% from public high schools. SAT Math middle 50% range 430–550. SAT Critical Reading middle 50% range 380–540. SAT Writing middle 50% range 390–560. ACT middle 50% range 19–24. Minimum paper TOEFL 550. Minimum computer TOEFL 213. Minimum web-based TOEFL 80. **Basis for Candidate Selection:** *Very important factors considered include:* Academic GPA, rigor of secondary school record, standardized test scores. *Important factors considered include:* Application essay. *Other factors considered include:* Class rank, recommendation(s), alumni/ae relation, character/personal qualities, extracurricular activities, interview, talent/ability. **Freshman Admission Requirements:** High school diploma is required and GED is accepted. *Academic units required:* 4 English, 3 mathematics, 2 science, (1 science labs), 1 history. **Freshman Admission Statistics:** 293 applied, 90% admitted, 45% enrolled. **Transfer Admission Requirements:** College transcript(s), essay or personal statement, minimum college GPA of 2.25 required. Lowest grade transferable C. **General Admission Information:** Application fee $25. Regular application deadline 8/25. Notification on a rolling basis, beginning on or about 9/15. Nonfall registration accepted. Credit offered for CEEB Advanced Placement tests.

COSTS AND FINANCIAL AID
Annual tuition $19,530. Room and board $5,750. Required fees $150. Average book expense $600. **Required Forms and Deadlines:** FAFSA Financial aid filing deadline 8/15. Priority financial aid filing date 4/1. **Notification of Awards: Types of Aid:** *Need-based scholarships/grants:* Federal Pell, SEOG, state scholarships/grants, the school's own gift aid. *Loans:* Direct Subsidized Stafford, Direct Unsubsidized Stafford, Direct PLUS, FFEL Subsidized Stafford, FFEL Unsubsidized Stafford, FFEL PLUS, Federal Perkins. *Student Employment:* Federal Work-Study Program available. Institutional employment available. Off-campus job opportunities are fair. **Financial Aid Statistics:** 83% freshmen, 78% undergrads receive need-based scholarship or grant aid. 8% freshmen, 5% undergrads receive non-need-based scholarship or grant aid. 68% freshmen, 68% undergrads receive need-based self-help aid. 25% freshmen, 25% undergrads receive athletic scholarships. 100% freshmen, 99% undergrads receive any aid. 86% undergrads borrow to pay for school. Average cumulative indebtedness $27,973. **Criteria for awarding institutional aid:** *Non-need-based:* Academics, athletics, leadership, minority status, music/drama.

SOUTHWESTERN OKLAHOMA STATE UNIVERSITY

100 Campus Drive, Weatherford, OK 73096
Phone: 580-774-3782
E-mail: admissions@swosu.edu **CEEB Code:** 6673
Fax: 580-774-7131 **Website:** www.swosu.edu **ACT Code:** 3340

This public school was founded in 1901. It has a 73-acre campus.

RATINGS
Admissions Selectivity Rating: 72   **Fire Safety Rating:** 60*   **Green Rating:** 60*

STUDENTS AND FACULTY
Enrollment: 4,247. **Student Body:** 58% female, 42% male, 12% out-of-state, 3% international. Asian 1%, African American 5%, Caucasian 79%, Hispanic 4%, Native American 7%.
Retention and Graduation: 65% freshmen return for sophomore year. **Faculty:** Student/faculty ratio 21:1. 211 full-time faculty, 59% hold PhDs, 8% are are members of minority groups, 43% are women. 5% of classes are taught by teaching assistants.

ACADEMICS
Degrees: Associate, bachelor's, first professional, master's. **Classes:** Most classes have 10–19 students. Most lab/discussion sessions have 20–29 students. **Special Study Options:** Accelerated program, distance learning, double major, independent study, internships, student-designed major, teacher certification program, weekend college. **Career services:** Alumni services, career/job search classes, career assessment.

FACILITIES
Housing: Men's dorms, women's dorms, apartments for married students, apartments for single students. **Special Academic Facilities/Equipment:** Writing lab, museum.

CAMPUS LIFE
Environment: Village. **Activities:** Choral groups, concert band, drama/theater, jazz band, literary magazine, marching band, music ensembles, musical theater, pep band, student government, student newspaper, symphony orchestra, television station, yearbook. **Organizations:** 3 religious organizations. 3 fraternities, 3 sororities. **Athletics (Intercollegiate):** *Men:* Baseball, basketball, football, golf, tennis, track/field (outdoor). *Women:* Basketball, tennis.

ADMISSIONS
Freshman Academic Profile: Average high school GPA 3.39. 20% in top 10% of high school class, 43% in top 25% of high school class, 74% in top 50% of high school class. 98% from public high schools. ACT middle 50% range 18–24. Minimum paper TOEFL 500. **Basis for Candidate Selection:** *Very important factors considered include:* Class rank, academic GPA, standardized test scores. **Freshman Admission Requirements:** High school diploma is required and GED is accepted. *Academic units required:* 4 English, 3 mathematics, 2 science, (2 science labs), 1 social studies, 2 history, 3 computer science or foreign language. *Academic units recommended:* 4 English, 3 mathematics, 2 science, (2 science labs), 1 social studies, 2 history, 2 academic electives, 3 computer science or foreign language. **Freshman Admission Statistics:** 1,301 applied, 89% admitted, 74% enrolled. **Transfer Admission Requirements:** College transcript(s), minimum college GPA of 2.0 required. Lowest grade transferable D. **General Admission Information:** Application fee $15. Nonfall registration

accepted. Admission may be deferred for a maximum of 1 year. Credit and/or placement offered for CEEB Advanced Placement tests.

COSTS AND FINANCIAL AID

Annual in-state tuition $2,700. Annual out-of-state tuition $7,200. Room and board $3,550. Required fees $750. Average book expense $1,200. **Required Forms and Deadlines:** FAFSA, institution's own financial aid form Financial aid filing deadline 3/1. Priority financial aid filing date 3/1. **Notification of Awards:** Applicants will be notified of awards on or about 3/20. **Types of Aid:** *Need-based scholarships/grants:* Federal Pell, SEOG, state scholarships/grants, private scholarships, the school's own gift aid. *Loans:* FFEL Subsidized Stafford, FFEL Unsubsidized Stafford, FFEL PLUS, Alternative loans through various institutions. *Student Employment:* Federal Work-Study Program available. Institutional employment available. Off-campus job opportunities are fair. **Financial Aid Statistics:** 39% freshmen, 43% undergrads receive need-based scholarship or grant aid. 45% freshmen, 39% undergrads receive non-need-based scholarship or grant aid. 47% freshmen, 51% undergrads receive need-based self-help aid. 4% freshmen, 4% undergrads receive athletic scholarships. 58% undergrads borrow to pay for school. Average cumulative indebtedness $12,222. **Criteria for awarding institutional aid:** *Non-need-based:* Academics, alumni affiliation, art, athletics, music/drama, state/district residency.

SOUTHWESTERN UNIVERSITY

Admission Office, P.O. Box 770, Georgetown, TX 78627-0770
Phone: 512-863-1200 **Financial Aid Phone:** 512-863-1259
E-mail: admission@southwestern.edu **CEEB Code:** 6674
Fax: 512-863-9601 **Website:** www.southwestern.edu **ACT Code:** 4186

This private school, affiliated with the Methodist Church, was founded in 1840. It has a 703-acre campus.

RATINGS

Admissions Selectivity Rating: 88   **Fire Safety Rating:** 81   **Green Rating:** 72

STUDENTS AND FACULTY

Enrollment: 1,291. **Student Body:** 63% female, 37% male, 7% out-of-state, international (9 countries represented). Asian 4%, African American 3%, Caucasian 76%, Hispanic 15%, Native American 1%.
Retention and Graduation: 84% freshmen return for sophomore year. 64% freshmen graduate within 4 years. 25% grads go on to further study within 1 year. 18% grads pursue arts and sciences degrees. 6% grads pursue law degrees. 1% grads pursue business degrees. 3% grads pursue medical degrees. **Faculty:** Student/faculty ratio 10.4:1. 122 full-time faculty, 100% hold PhDs, 14% are are members of minority groups, 48% are women.

ACADEMICS

Degrees: Bachelor's. **Classes:** Most classes have 10–19 students. Most lab/discussion sessions have 10–19 students. **Majors with Highest Enrollment:** Business/commerce; communication studies/speech communication and rhetoric; political science and government. **Special Study Options:** Double major, honors program, independent study, internships, liberal arts/career combination, student-designed major, study abroad, teacher certification program. Special programs offered to physically disabled students include note-taking services, reader services, tape recorders, tutors. **Career services:** Alumni network, alumni services, career assessment, internships, regional alumni.

FACILITIES

Housing: Coed dorms, special housing for disabled students, men's dorms, special housing for international students, women's dorms, fraternity/sorority housing, apartments for married students, apartments for single students. 100% of campus accessible to physically disabled. **Special Academic Facilities/ Equipment:** Alma Thomas Fine Arts Center; Red and Charline McCombs Campus Center; Corbin J. Robertson Center for Fitness and Wellness; Fountainwood Astronomical Observatory. **Computers:** 100% of classrooms, 100% of dorms, 100% of libraries, 100% of dining areas, 100% of student union, 50% of common outdoor areas have wireless network access. Students can register for classes online. Administrative functions (other than registration) can be performed online.

CAMPUS LIFE

Environment: Town. **Activities:** Choral groups, concert band, dance, drama/theater, jazz band, literary magazine, music ensembles, musical theater, radio station, student government, student newspaper, student-run film society.

Organizations: 99 registered organizations, 14 honor societies, 10 religious organizations. 4 fraternities, 4 sororities. **Athletics (Intercollegiate):** *Men:* Baseball, basketball, cross-country, diving, golf, lacrosse, soccer, swimming, tennis, track/field (outdoor). *Women:* Basketball, cross-country, diving, golf, soccer, softball, swimming, tennis, track/field (outdoor), volleyball. **On-Campus Highlights:** Robertson Center-indoor olympic size pool, McCombs Center-Student Center, Fountainwood Observatory, Korovva Milkbar-student run coffee house, Academic Mall-grassy area in the middle of campus. **Environmental Initiatives:** Signed Talloires Declaration in spring 2007. Gold Certification under the Leadership in Energy and Environmental Design (LEED) Green Building Rating System for new Admission Center in 2009. Second LEED-certfied buliding project slated for opening 2010.

ADMISSIONS

Freshman Academic Profile: 49% in top 10% of high school class, 84% in top 25% of high school class, 98% in top 50% of high school class. 81% from public high schools. SAT Math middle 50% range 570–670. SAT Critical Reading middle 50% range 570–680. ACT middle 50% range 25–30. Minimum paper TOEFL 570. Minimum computer TOEFL 230. **Basis for Candidate Selection:** *Very important factors considered include:* Class rank, application essay, academic GPA, recommendation(s), rigor of secondary school record, standardized test scores. *Important factors considered include:* Alumni/ae relation, character/personal qualities, extracurricular activities, first generation, geographical residence, interview, level of applicant's interest, racial/ethnic status, talent/ability, volunteer work, work experience. **Freshman Admission Requirements:** High school diploma is required and GED is accepted. *Academic units required:* 4 English, 4 mathematics, 3 science, (2 science labs), 2 foreign language, 2 social studies, 1 history, 1 academic electives. *Academic units recommended:* 4 English, 4 mathematics, 4 science, (3 science labs), 3 foreign language, 3 social studies, 2 history. **Freshman Admission Statistics:** 2,490 applied, 63% admitted, 24% enrolled. **Transfer Admission Requirements:** High school transcript, college transcript(s), essay or personal statement, statement of good standing from prior institution(s). Minimum college GPA of 3.0 required. Lowest grade transferable C. **General Admission Information:** Application fee $40. Early decision application deadline 11/1. Regular notification 4/1. Nonfall registration accepted. Admission may be deferred for a maximum of 1 year. Credit offered for CEEB Advanced Placement tests.

COSTS AND FINANCIAL AID

Annual tuition $30,220. Room and board $9,310. Average book expense $1,000. **Required Forms and Deadlines:** FAFSA. Financial aid filing deadline 3/1. Priority financial aid filing date 3/1. **Notification of Awards:** Applicants will be notified of awards on a rolling basis beginning 3/1. **Types of Aid:** *Need-based scholarships/grants:* Federal Pell, SEOG, state scholarships/grants, private scholarships, the school's own gift aid. *Loans:* Direct Subsidized Stafford, Direct Unsubsidized Stafford, Direct PLUS, Federal Perkins, state loans, college/university loans from institutional funds. *Student Employment:* Federal Work-Study Program available. Institutional employment available. Off-campus job opportunities are good. **Financial Aid Statistics:** 59% freshmen, 57% undergrads receive need-based scholarship or grant aid. 54% freshmen, 41% undergrads receive non-need-based scholarship or grant aid. 42% freshmen, 48% undergrads receive need-based self-help aid. 61% undergrads borrow to pay for school. Average cumulative indebtedness $24,036. **Criteria for awarding institutional aid:** *Non-need-based:* Academics, art, minority status, music/drama, religious affiliation.

SPELMAN COLLEGE

350 Spelman Lane, S.W. Box 277, Atlanta, GA 30314-4399
Phone: 404-270-5193 **Financial Aid Phone:** 404-270-5212
E-mail: admiss@spelman.edu **CEEB Code:** 5628
Fax: 404-270-5201 **Website:** www.spelman.edu **ACT Code:** 794

This private school was founded in 1881. It has a 32-acre campus.

RATINGS

Admissions Selectivity Rating: 92   **Fire Safety Rating:** 97   **Green Rating:** 78

STUDENTS AND FACULTY

Enrollment: 2,337. **Student Body:** 100% female, 69% out-of-state, 2% international (18 countries represented). African American 96%.

Retention and Graduation: 88% freshmen return for sophomore year. 67% freshmen graduate within 4 years. **Faculty:** Student/faculty ratio 12:1. 172 full-time faculty, 83% hold PhDs, 67% are women.

ACADEMICS

Degrees: Bachelor's. **Classes:** Most classes have 10–19 students. Most lab/discussion sessions have 20–29 students. **Majors with Highest Enrollment:** Political science and government; psychology. **Special Study Options:** Cross-registration, double major, exchange student program (domestic), honors program, independent study, internships, liberal arts/career combination, student-designed major, study abroad, teacher certification program. **Honors programs:** Ethel Waddell Githii Honors Program Special programs offered to physically disabled students include note-taking services, reader services, tape recorders, tutors. **Career services:** Alumni network, alumni services, career/job search classes, career assessment, internships.

FACILITIES

Housing: Women's dorms, apartments for single students. **Special Academic Facilities/Equipment:** Nursery-elementary school for child development majors, language lab, electron microscope. **Computers:** Students can register for classes online. Administrative functions (other than registration) can be performed online.

CAMPUS LIFE

Environment: Metropolis. **Activities:** Choral groups, dance, drama/theater, jazz band, student government, student newspaper, yearbook, campus ministries, international student organization. **Organizations:** 17 registered organizations, 18 honor societies, 9 religious organizations. 4 sororities. **Athletics (Intercollegiate):** *Women:* Basketball, cross-country, golf, soccer, softball, tennis, volleyball. **On-Campus Highlights:** Sister's Chapel, The Spelman College Art Museum, Camille Olivia Hanks-Cosby Academic Center, Albro, Falconer, Manley Science Center, The Oval and Alumni Arch.

ADMISSIONS

Freshman Academic Profile: Average high school GPA 3.59. 40% in top 10% of high school class, 73% in top 25% of high school class, 95% in top 50% of high school class. 84% from public high schools. SAT Math middle 50% range 490–570. SAT Critical Reading middle 50% range 500–580. ACT middle 50% range 21–25. Minimum paper TOEFL 500. Minimum computer TOEFL 250. **Basis for Candidate Selection:** *Very important factors considered include:* Application essay, academic GPA, rigor of secondary school record, standardized test scores, character/personal qualities. *Important factors considered include:* Recommendation(s), extracurricular activities. *Other factors considered include:* Class rank, alumni/ae relation, first generation, geographical residence, level of applicant's interest, volunteer work, work experience. **Freshman Admission Requirements:** High school diploma is required and GED is accepted. *Academic units required:* 4 English, 3 mathematics, 3 science, (2 science labs), 2 foreign language, 3 social studies, 2 history, 2 academic electives. *Academic units recommended:* 4 English, 4 mathematics, 4 science, (3 science labs), 4 foreign language, 4 social studies, 3 history, 2 academic electives. **Freshman Admission Statistics:** 5,656 applied, 33% admitted, 30% enrolled. **Transfer Admission Requirements:** High school transcript, college transcript(s), minimum college GPA of 2.0 required. Lowest grade transferable C. **General Admission Information:** Application fee $35. Early decision application deadline 11/1. Regular application deadline 2/1. Regular notification 4/1. Nonfall registration not accepted. Admission may be deferred for a maximum of 1 year. Credit offered for CEEB Advanced Placement tests.

COSTS AND FINANCIAL AID

Annual tuition $14,470. Room and board $8,750. Required fees $2,535. Average book expense $1,150. **Required Forms and Deadlines:** institution's own financial aid form, CSS/Financial Aid PROFILE Priority financial aid filing date 3/1. **Notification of Awards: Types of Aid:** *Need-based scholarships/grants:* Federal Pell, SEOG, state scholarships/grants, private scholarships, the school's own gift aid, United Negro College Fund *Loans:* FFEL Subsidized Stafford, FFEL Unsubsidized Stafford, FFEL PLUS. *Student Employment:* Federal Work-Study Program available. Institutional employment available. Off-campus job opportunities are good. **Financial Aid Statistics:** 80% freshmen, 54% undergrads receive need-based scholarship or grant aid. 49% freshmen, 21% undergrads receive non-need-based scholarship or grant aid. 11% freshmen, 72% undergrads receive need-based self-help aid. 82% freshmen, 75% undergrads receive any aid. 75% undergrads borrow to pay for school. **Criteria for awarding institutional aid:** *Non-need-based:* Academics, alumni affiliation, leadership, music/drama, state/district residency.

SPRING ARBOR UNIVERSITY

106 East Main Street, Station #4, Spring Arbor, MI 49283-9799
Phone: 517-750-6458 **Financial Aid Phone:** 800-968-0011
E-mail: admissions@admin.arbor.edu **CEEB Code:** 1732
Fax: 517-750-6620 **Website:** www.arbor.edu **ACT Code:** 2056

This private school was founded in 1873. It has a 100-acre campus.

RATINGS

Admissions Selectivity Rating: 78 **Fire Safety Rating:** 76 **Green Rating:** 60*

STUDENTS AND FACULTY

Enrollment: 2,710. **Student Body:** 69% female, 31% male, 13% out-of-state, international (5 countries represented).
Retention and Graduation: 72% freshmen return for sophomore year. 40% freshmen graduate within 4 years. 29% grads go on to further study within 1 year. 6% grads pursue arts and sciences degrees. 6% grads pursue business degrees. 1% grads pursue medical degrees. **Faculty:** Student/faculty ratio 15:1. 83 full-time faculty, 60% hold PhDs, 6% are are members of minority groups, 31% are women.

ACADEMICS

Degrees: Associate, bachelor's, master's, post-bachelor's certificate. **Classes:** Most classes have 10–19 students. Most lab/discussion sessions have 10–19 students. **Majors with Highest Enrollment:** Business administration, management and operations, other; education; theological and ministerial studies, other. **Special Study Options:** Accelerated program, cross-registration, distance learning, double major, dual enrollment, English as a Second Language (ESL), honors program, independent study, internships, student-designed major, study abroad, teacher certification program, weekend college, Off-Campus Study: Washington Journalism semester, Los Angeles Film Studies program, AuSable Inst of Environmental Studies Program (Michigan). Study abroad programs available: China, Latin America Middle East, Oxford Honors, Russian, Japan, Jerusalem Univ, Russia @ St. Petersburg, People's Republic of China @ Sichuan College. Other programs/destinations are available through petition. **Combined degree programs:** BA/MEng. Special programs offered to physically disabled students include note-taking services, reader services, tape recorders, tutors. **Career services:** Alumni network, alumni services, career/job search classes, career assessment, internships, regional alumni.

FACILITIES

Housing: Special housing for disabled students, men's dorms, special housing for international students, women's dorms, apartments for married students, apartments for single students. 80% of campus accessible to physically disabled. **Special Academic Facilities/Equipment:** State-of-the-art academic building (Poling Center); the Poling Center features the CP Federal Credit Union Trading Center and is equipped with some of the same technology that is used daily on Wall Street including: An electronic wrap-around ticker, large light emitting diode (LED) financial data board, Bloomberg terminal, and continuous financial news feeds. Radio and TV studios, commercial writing/computer graphics lab, science center, art gallery. **Computers:** 90% of classrooms, 100% of dorms, 100% of libraries, 100% of dining areas, 75% of common outdoor areas have wireless network access. Students can register for classes online. Administrative functions (other than registration) can be performed online.

CAMPUS LIFE

Environment: Rural. **Activities:** Choral groups, concert band, drama/theater, jazz band, literary magazine, music ensembles, musical theater, pep band, radio station, student government, student newspaper, student-run film society, symphony orchestra, television station, yearbook, campus ministries, international student organization. **Organizations:** 50 registered organizations, **Athletics (Intercollegiate):** *Men:* Baseball, basketball, cross-country, golf, soccer, tennis, track/field (outdoor), track/field (indoor). *Women:* Basketball, cross-country, soccer, softball, tennis, track/field (outdoor), track/field (indoor), volleyball. **On-Campus Highlights:** Sacred Grounds (Starbucks), Ganton Art Gallery, Poling Center, University Plaza, McKenna Carillon Tower, State-of-the-Art Academic Building (Poling Center) houses a trading center that is equipped with some of the same technology used on Wall Street.

ADMISSIONS

Freshman Academic Profile: Average high school GPA 3.4. 25% in top 10% of high school class, 49% in top 25% of high school class, 78% in top 50% of high school class. SAT Math middle 50% range 470–595. SAT Critical Reading middle 50% range 475–595. SAT Writing middle 50% range 455–570. ACT middle 50% range 20–26. Minimum paper TOEFL 525. Minimum computer TOEFL 197. **Basis for Candidate Selection:** *Very important factors considered include:* Rigor of secondary school record, standardized test scores, character/personal qualities. *Important factors considered include:*

Academic GPA. *Other factors considered include:* Class rank, application essay, recommendation(s), extracurricular activities, interview, religious affiliation/commitment, talent/ability. **Freshman Admission Requirements:** High school diploma is required and GED is accepted. *Academic units required:* 4 English, 3 mathematics, 3 science, (3 science labs), 3 history, 1 Physical Education or Health Related Course *Academic units recommended:* 2 foreign language, 1 computer science. **Freshman Admission Statistics:** 2,022 applied, 78% admitted, 24% enrolled. **Transfer Admission Requirements:** High school transcript, college transcript(s), essay or personal statement, minimum college GPA of 2.0 required. Lowest grade transferable C. **General Admission Information:** Application fee $30. Regular application deadline 8/1. Notification on a rolling basis, beginning on or about 9/1. Nonfall registration accepted. Admission may be deferred for a maximum of No Set Time. Credit offered for CEEB Advanced Placement tests.

COSTS AND FINANCIAL AID
Average book expense $800. **Required Forms and Deadlines:** FAFSA. Priority financial aid filing date 3/1. **Notification of Awards:** Applicants will be notified of awards on a rolling basis beginning 3/1. *Types of Aid: Need-based scholarships/grants:* Federal Pell, SEOG, state scholarships/grants, private scholarships, the school's own gift aid. *Loans:* FFEL Subsidized Stafford, FFEL Unsubsidized Stafford, FFEL PLUS, Federal Perkins, MI-Loan Program and Alternative Loans. *Student Employment:* Federal Work-Study Program available. Institutional employment available. Highest amount earned per year from on-campus jobs $1,550. Off-campus job opportunities are fair. **Financial Aid Statistics:** 87% freshmen, 84% undergrads receive need-based scholarship or grant aid. 7% freshmen, 5% undergrads receive non-need-based scholarship or grant aid. 69% freshmen, 68% undergrads receive need-based self-help aid. 15% freshmen, 14% undergrads receive athletic scholarships. 100% freshmen, 87% undergrads receive any aid. 86% undergrads borrow to pay for school. Average cumulative indebtedness $26,077. **Criteria for awarding institutional aid:** *Non-need-based:* Academics, art, athletics, minority status, music/drama, religious affiliation.

SPRING HILL COLLEGE

4000 Dauphin Street, Mobile, AL 36608
Phone: 251-380-3030 **Financial Aid Phone:** 251-380-3460
E-mail: admit@shc.edu **CEEB Code:** 1733
Fax: 251-460-2186 **Website:** www.shc.edu **ACT Code:** 42

This private school, affiliated with the Roman Catholic Church, was founded in 1830. It has a 450-acre campus.

RATINGS
Admissions Selectivity Rating: 87   **Fire Safety Rating:** 83   **Green Rating:** 62

STUDENTS AND FACULTY
Enrollment: 1,304. **Student Body:** 62% female, 38% male, 52% out-of-state, 1% international (13 countries represented). Asian 1%, African American 18%, Caucasian 68%, Hispanic 7%, Native American 1%.
Retention and Graduation: 77% freshmen return for sophomore year. 50% freshmen graduate within 4 years. 33% grads go on to further study within 1 year. 17% grads pursue arts and sciences degrees. 5% grads pursue law degrees. 3% grads pursue business degrees. 5% grads pursue medical degrees. **Faculty:** Student/faculty ratio 13:1. 82 full-time faculty, 85% hold PhDs, 9% are are members of minority groups, 48% are women.

ACADEMICS
Degrees: Bachelor's, certificate, master's, post-bachelor's certificate, post-master's certificate. **Classes:** Most classes have 10–19 students. Most lab/discussion sessions have 20–29 students. **Majors with Highest Enrollment:** Biology/biological sciences; business administration and management; nursing/registered nurse (RN, ASN, BSN, MSN). **Special Study Options:** Accelerated program, distance learning, double major, dual enrollment, honors program, independent study, internships, student-designed major, study abroad, teacher certification program, 3-2 engineering with Auburn University, University of Alabama Birmingham, Marquette University, University of Florida, and Texas A&M University. Marine biology classes at Dauphin Island Sea Lab in conjunction with the Marine Environmental Sciences Consortium. **Honors programs:** SHC's 4-year Honors Program offers a challenging and rewarding course of study to academically gifted and motivated students. It is comprised of academic courses; seminar experiences; and additional opportunities for service, leadership, cultural exploration, and social interaction both on and off campus. Honors courses cover material in greater depth, use primary materials when possible, stress student participation and responsibility, and encourage high individual achievement. Special programs offered to physically disabled students

include tutors. **Career services:** Alumni network, alumni services, career/job search classes, career assessment, internships, regional alumni.

FACILITIES
Housing: Coed dorms, men's dorms, women's dorms, apartments for single students. 90% of campus accessible to physically disabled. **Special Academic Facilities/Equipment:** Public radio broadcasting station, theater. **Computers:** 50% of classrooms, 15% of dorms, 100% of libraries, 100% of dining areas, 100% of student union, 25% of common outdoor areas have wireless network access. Students can register for classes online. Administrative functions (other than registration) can be performed online.

CAMPUS LIFE
Environment: Metropolis. **Activities:** Choral groups, dance, drama/theater, literary magazine, student government, student newspaper, yearbook, campus ministries. **Organizations:** 66 registered organizations, 16 honor societies, 5 religious organizations. 3 fraternities, 5 sororities. **Athletics (Intercollegiate):** *Men:* Baseball, basketball, cross-country, golf, soccer, tennis. *Women:* Basketball, cross-country, golf, soccer, softball, tennis, volleyball. **On-Campus Highlights:** Arthur Outlaw Recreation Center, Golf Course, Burke Library, Java City Coffee Shop, Dorn Field. **Environmental Initiatives:** Construction of new LEED-certified Student Center Use of a college-wide energy control system Expansion of recycling program

ADMISSIONS
Freshman Academic Profile: Average high school GPA 3.49. 27% in top 10% of high school class, 61% in top 25% of high school class, 86% in top 50% of high school class. 55% from public high schools. SAT Math middle 50% range 480–570. SAT Critical Reading middle 50% range 480–600. SAT Writing middle 50% range 480–590. ACT middle 50% range 21–26. Minimum paper TOEFL 550. Minimum computer TOEFL 213. Minimum web-based TOEFL 80. **Basis for Candidate Selection:** *Very important factors considered include:* Academic GPA, rigor of secondary school record, standardized test scores. *Important factors considered include:* Class rank, recommendation(s), interview. *Other factors considered include:* Application essay, alumni/ae relation, character/personal qualities, extracurricular activities, talent/ability, volunteer work. **Freshman Admission Requirements:** High school diploma is required and GED is accepted. *Academic units recommended:* 4 English, 3 mathematics, 3 science, (1 science labs), 2 foreign language, 2 social studies, 1 history, 1 academic electives. **Freshman Admission Statistics:** 4,234 applied, 55% admitted, 15% enrolled. **Transfer Admission Requirements:** College transcript(s), statement of good standing from prior institution(s). Minimum college GPA of 2.5 required. Lowest grade transferable C–. **General Admission Information:** Application fee $25. Regular application deadline 7/15. Notification on a rolling basis, beginning on or about 11/1. Nonfall registration accepted. Admission may be deferred for a maximum of 1 year. Credit and/or placement offered for CEEB Advanced Placement tests.

COSTS AND FINANCIAL AID
Required Forms and Deadlines: FAFSA, state aid form. Priority financial aid filing date 3/1. **Notification of Awards:** Applicants will be notified of awards on a rolling basis beginning 2/15. *Types of Aid: Need-based scholarships/grants:* Federal Pell, SEOG, state scholarships/grants, private scholarships, the school's own gift aid, ACG, SMART, and TEACH grants. *Loans:* Direct Subsidized Stafford, Direct Unsubsidized Stafford, Direct PLUS, FFEL Subsidized Stafford, FFEL Unsubsidized Stafford, FFEL PLUS, Federal Perkins, Alternative loans (Citiassist, Signature). *Student Employment:* Federal Work-Study Program available. Institutional employment available. Highest amount earned per year from on-campus jobs $1,759. Off-campus job opportunities are good. **Financial Aid Statistics:** 69% freshmen, 66% undergrads receive need-based scholarship or grant aid. 52% freshmen, 51% undergrads receive non-need-based scholarship or grant aid. 51% freshmen, 56% undergrads receive need-based self-help aid. 8% freshmen, 8% undergrads receive athletic scholarships. 100% freshmen, 99% undergrads receive any aid. 72% undergrads borrow to pay for school. Average cumulative indebtedness $13,775. **Criteria for awarding institutional aid:** *Non-need-based:* Academics, alumni affiliation, athletics, job skills, leadership, minority status, state/district residency.

SPRINGFIELD COLLEGE

263 Alden Street, Springfield, MA 01109
Phone: 413-748-3136
E-mail: admissions@spfldcol.edu **CEEB Code:** 3763
Fax: 413-748-3694 **Website:** www.spfldcol.edu

This private school was founded in 1885. It has a 80-acre campus.

RATINGS
Admissions Selectivity Rating: 60*   **Fire Safety Rating:** 60*   **Green Rating:** 60*

STUDENTS AND FACULTY
Student Body: 18 countries represented.
Retention and Graduation: 82% freshmen return for sophomore year. 58% freshmen graduate within 4 years. 20% grads go on to further study within 1 year. **Faculty:** 5% of classes are taught by teaching assistants.

ACADEMICS
Degrees: Bachelor's, master's. **Special Study Options:** Cooperative education program, cross-registration, distance learning, double major, English as a Second Language (ESL), independent study, internships, liberal arts/career combination, study abroad, teacher certification program, weekend college. **Career services:** Alumni services, career/job search classes, career assessment.

FACILITIES
Housing: Coed dorms, special housing for disabled students, men's dorms, special housing for international students, women's dorms, apartments for married students, apartments for single students. **Special Academic Facilities/Equipment:** International center, college-operated summer day camp, hypermedia lab, centers for allied health sciences, emergency medical services management, occupational therapy, and physician assistant.

CAMPUS LIFE
Activities: Choral groups, concert band, dance, drama/theater, jazz band, literary magazine, marching band, music ensembles, musical theater, opera, pep band, radio station, student government, student newspaper, student-run film society, symphony orchestra, yearbook. **Athletics (Intercollegiate):** *Men:* Baseball, basketball, cross-country, diving, football, golf, gymnastics, lacrosse, soccer, swimming, tennis, track/field (outdoor), volleyball, wrestling. *Women:* Basketball, cross-country, diving, field hockey, golf, gymnastics, lacrosse, soccer, softball, swimming, tennis, track/field (outdoor), volleyball. **On-Campus Highlights:** Cheney Hall—dining hall, Caf—dining hall, Wellness Center.

ADMISSIONS
Freshman Academic Profile: 84% from public high schools. SAT Math middle 50% range 450–550. SAT Critical Reading middle 50% range 440–550. Minimum paper TOEFL 525. **Basis for Candidate Selection:** *Other factors considered include:* Class rank, application essay, recommendation(s), rigor of secondary school record, alumni/ae relation, character/personal qualities, extracurricular activities, geographical residence, interview, racial/ethnic status, religious affiliation/commitment, talent/ability, volunteer work, work experience. **Freshman Admission Requirements:** High school diploma is required and GED is accepted. *Academic units recommended:* 4 English, 2 mathematics, 2 science, 2 foreign language, 2 social studies, 4 academic electives. **Freshman Admission Statistics:** 2,249 applied, 59% admitted, 38% enrolled. **Transfer Admission Requirements:** College transcript(s), essay or personal statement, interview, statement of good standing from prior institution(s). Minimum college GPA of 2.5 required. Lowest grade transferable C. **General Admission Information:** Application fee $40. Early decision application deadline 12/1. Regular application deadline 4/11. Nonfall registration accepted. Admission may be deferred for a maximum of 12. Credit and/or placement offered for CEEB Advanced Placement tests.

COSTS AND FINANCIAL AID
Student Employment: Federal Work-Study Program available. Institutional employment available. Highest amount earned per year from on-campus jobs $1,100. Off-campus job opportunities are good.

ST. JOHN FISHER COLLEGE

3690 East Avenue, Rochester, NY 14618-3597
Phone: 585-385-8064 **Financial Aid Phone:** 585-385-8042
E-mail: admissions@sjfc.edu **CEEB Code:** 2798
Fax: 585-385-8386 **Website:** www.sjfc.edu **ACT Code:** 2798

This private school, affiliated with the Roman Catholic Church,, affiliated with the The College is guided by its Catholic heritage. Church, was founded in 1948. It has a 154-acre campus.

RATINGS
Admissions Selectivity Rating: 81   **Fire Safety Rating:** 91   **Green Rating:** 60*

STUDENTS AND FACULTY
Enrollment: 2,810. **Student Body:** 59% female, 41% male, 2% out-of-state, international (9 countries represented). Asian 2%, African American 5%, Caucasian 85%, Hispanic 3%.
Retention and Graduation: 82% freshmen return for sophomore year. 63% freshmen graduate within 4 years. **Faculty:** Student/faculty ratio 13.7:1. 201 full-time faculty, 89% hold PhDs, 13% are are members of minority groups, 49% are women.

ACADEMICS
Degrees: Bachelor's, master's, post-bachelor's certificate, post-master's certificate. **Classes:** Most classes have 20–29 students. Most lab/discussion sessions have 10–19 students. **Majors with Highest Enrollment:** Business administration and management; elementary education and teaching; nursing/registered nurse (RN, ASN, BSN, MSN). **Special Study Options:** Accelerated program, cross-registration, distance learning, double major, exchange student program (domestic), honors program, independent study, internships, liberal arts/career combination, student-designed major, study abroad, teacher certification program, weekend college. **Honors programs:** St John Fisher College Honors Program; Science Scholars Program. Special programs offered to physically disabled students include note-taking services, reader services, tape recorders, tutors. **Career services:** Alumni network, career/job search classes, career assessment, internships, regional alumni.

FACILITIES
Housing: Coed dorms, special housing for disabled students, women's dorms 100% of campus accessible to physically disabled. **Special Academic Facilities/Equipment:** Student Campus Center, state-of-the-art laboratories, 2 electron microscopes, multimedia computer lab, TV studio; Childcare Center (for observation and development), Cyber Cafe, Skalny Welcome Center, art gallery. **Computers:** 25% of classrooms, 100% of libraries, 50% of dining areas, 100% of student union, 10% of common outdoor areas have wireless network access. Students can register for classes online. Administrative functions (other than registration) can be performed online.

CAMPUS LIFE
Environment: City. **Activities:** Choral groups, dance, drama/theater, literary magazine, musical theater, student government, student newspaper, television station, yearbook, campus ministries. **Organizations:** 70 registered organizations, 10 honor societies, 4 religious organizations. **Athletics (Intercollegiate):** *Men:* Baseball, basketball, football, golf, lacrosse, soccer, tennis. *Women:* Basketball, golf, lacrosse, soccer, softball, tennis, volleyball. **On-Campus Highlights:** Campus Center, Cyber Cafe, Golisano Gateway, Growney Stadium, Student Life Center.

ADMISSIONS
Freshman Academic Profile: Average high school GPA 3.49. 25% in top 10% of high school class, 55% in top 25% of high school class, 89% in top 50% of high school class. 93% from public high schools. SAT Math middle 50% range 510–600. SAT Critical Reading middle 50% range 480–570. SAT Writing middle 50% range 460–560. ACT middle 50% range 22–26. Minimum paper TOEFL 550. Minimum computer TOEFL 213. Minimum web-based TOEFL 80. **Basis for Candidate Selection:** *Very important factors considered include:* Academic GPA, recommendation(s), rigor of secondary school record, alumni/ae relation, character/personal qualities. *Important factors considered include:* Class rank, application essay, standardized test scores, extracurricular activities, interview, level of applicant's interest, talent/ability, volunteer work, work experience. *Other factors considered include:* First generation, geographical residence, state residency. **Freshman Admission Requirements:** High school diploma is required and GED is not accepted. *Academic units recommended:* 4 English, 4 mathematics, 4 science, 3 foreign language, 4 social studies. **Freshman Admission Statistics:** 3,440 applied, 65% admitted, 25% enrolled. **Transfer Admission Requirements:** College transcript(s), statement of good standing from prior institution(s). Minimum college GPA of 2.0 required. Lowest grade transferable C. **General Admission Information:** Application fee $30. Early decision application deadline 12/1. Notification on a rolling basis, beginning on or about 12/1. Nonfall registration not accepted. Admission may

be deferred for a maximum of 2 semesters. Credit offered for CEEB Advanced Placement tests.

COSTS AND FINANCIAL AID
Annual tuition $23,850. Room and board $10,090. Required fees $470. Average book expense $900. **Required Forms and Deadlines:** FAFSA, state aid form. Priority financial aid filing date 2/15. **Notification of Awards:** Applicants will be notified of awards on a rolling basis beginning 3/22. **Types of Aid:** *Need-based scholarships/grants:* Federal Pell, SEOG, state scholarships/grants, private scholarships, the school's own gift aid, Federal Nursing Scholarships. *Loans:* Direct Subsidized Stafford, Direct Unsubsidized Stafford, Direct PLUS, Federal Perkins, Bureau of Indian Affairs; Adult Vocational; Federal College Work Study. *Student Employment:* Federal Work-Study Program available. Institutional employment available. Off-campus job opportunities are good. **Financial Aid Statistics:** 80% freshmen, 81% undergrads receive need-based scholarship or grant aid. 53% freshmen, 37% undergrads receive non-need-based scholarship or grant aid. 69% freshmen, 69% undergrads receive need-based self-help aid. 80% freshmen, 81% undergrads receive any aid. 84% undergrads borrow to pay for school. Average cumulative indebtedness $30,281. **Criteria for awarding institutional aid:** *Non-need-based:* Academics, leadership.

ST. AMBROSE UNIVERSITY

518 West Locust Street, Davenport, IA 52803-2898
Phone: 563-333-6300 **Financial Aid Phone:** 563-333-6314
E-mail: admit@sau.edu **CEEB Code:** 6617
Fax: 563-333-6297 **Website:** www.sau.edu **ACT Code:** 1352

This private school, affiliated with the Roman Catholic Church, was founded in 1882. It has a 118-acre campus.

RATINGS
Admissions Selectivity Rating: 74   **Fire Safety Rating:** 73   **Green Rating:** 60*

STUDENTS AND FACULTY
Enrollment: 2,821. **Student Body:** 61% female, 39% male, 56% out-of-state, international (14 countries represented). Asian 1%, African American 3%, Caucasian 83%, Hispanic 4%.
Retention and Graduation: 53% freshmen graduate within 4 years. 18% grads go on to further study within 1 year. **Faculty:** Student/faculty ratio 11:1. 185 full-time faculty, 74% hold PhDs, 8% are are members of minority groups, 46% are women.

ACADEMICS
Degrees: Bachelor's, certificate, master's, post-bachelor's certificate, post-master's certificate. **Classes:** Most classes have 10–19 students. Most lab/discussion sessions have 20–29 students. **Majors with Highest Enrollment:** Business/commerce; nursing/registered nurse (RN, ASN, BSN, MSN); psychology. **Special Study Options:** Accelerated program, cooperative education program, distance learning, double major, independent study, internships, liberal arts/career combination, student-designed major, study abroad, teacher certification program, weekend college, We have overseas academic experiences in England, Ireland, Lithuania, and Ecuador. Our students can, also, take advantage of the overseas experiences thru Central College in Iowa. **Combined degree programs:** BS/D.Phys Therapy, BS/MOT, and BA/MED. Special programs offered to physically disabled students include note-taking services, reader services, tape recorders, tutors. **Career services:** Alumni network, alumni services, career/job search classes, career assessment, internships. **Career services highlights include:** Internships: 70% of our Business majors complete at least one internship.

FACILITIES
Housing: Coed dorms, special housing for disabled students, men's dorms, women's dorms, apartments for single students. The university owns several houses next to campus and will rent them out to graduate or married students. 96% of campus accessible to physically disabled. **Special Academic Facilities/Equipment:** Art gallery, observatory, language lab, and distance learning classrooms (5). **Computers:** 1% of classrooms, 27% of dorms, 100% of libraries, 100% of student union, have wireless network access. Students can register for classes online. Administrative functions (other than registration) can be performed online.

CAMPUS LIFE
Environment: City. **Activities:** Choral groups, concert band, dance, drama/theater, jazz band, literary magazine, music ensembles, musical theater, opera, pep band, radio station, student government, student newspaper, symphony orchestra, television station, campus ministries, international student organization. **Organizations:** 26 registered organizations, 12 honor societies, 3 religious

organizations. **Athletics (Intercollegiate):** *Men:* Baseball, basketball, bowling, cheerleading, cross-country, football, golf, soccer, tennis, track/field (outdoor), track/field (indoor), volleyball. *Women:* Basketball, bowling, cheerleading, cross-country, golf, soccer, softball, tennis, track/field (outdoor), track/field (indoor), volleyball. **On-Campus Highlights:** Rogalski Center (Student Union), Cafeteria, Coffee Shop and Bookstore, Chapel, Galvin Fine Arts Building.
Environmental Initiatives: STORM WATER DETENTION In order to minimize storm water flow into underground storm sewers, the following areas have been developed to detain water during storm events and allow a slower release into the ground.—Townhouse west 2,154 gallons—University Center parking lot islands 9,694 gallons—University Center west grounds 71,808 gallons—Lombard Street at University Center 10,771 gallons—LINK east entry 1,212 gallons—Rohlman north 2,100 gallons—Cosgrove north grounds 8,617 gallons TOTAL: 106,356 gallons of detention STORM WATER RETENTION AREAS In order to minimize underground storm water flows, the following areas have been developed to capture storm water and re use the water for irrigation purposes:—Franklin Hall west retention tanks 12,000 gallons—Chapel east grounds retention tanks 12,000 gallons—New Hall retention tanks 21,000 gallons We have changed cleaning products to use those products that are Green Sealed Certified.—We use mirco fiber rags in glass and mirror cleaning and we use no glass cleaning chemical of any kind.—We use compact fluorescent light bulbs everywhere they can be used for the last 11 years and as we replace old fixtures we replace them with new ones to accomodate the compact fluorescent bulbs.—We no longer use paper or disposable rags or mops.—We no longer use mop oil for our dust mops but instead we use them dry or we use pack vacuums to cut down on the dust.

ADMISSIONS
Freshman Academic Profile: Average high school GPA 3.12. 14% in top 10% of high school class, 34% in top 25% of high school class, 65% in top 50% of high school class. 70% from public high schools. ACT middle 50% range 20–25. Minimum paper TOEFL 500. Minimum computer TOEFL 213. **Basis for Candidate Selection:** *Very important factors considered include:* Class rank, academic GPA, rigor of secondary school record, standardized test scores. *Other factors considered include:* Application essay, recommendation(s), alumni/ae relation, character/personal qualities, extracurricular activities, first generation, geographical residence, interview, racial/ethnic status, talent/ability, volunteer work. **Freshman Admission Requirements:** High school diploma is required and GED is accepted. *Academic units recommended:* 4 English, 3 mathematics, 2 science, (2 science labs), 1 foreign language, 1 social studies, 1 history, 4 academic electives. **Freshman Admission Statistics:** 2,075 applied, 82% admitted, 34% enrolled. **Transfer Admission Requirements:** High school transcript, college transcript(s), standardized test scores, statement of good standing from prior institution(s). Minimum college GPA of 2.0 required. Lowest grade transferable D. **General Admission Information:** Application fee $25. Notification on a rolling basis, beginning on or about 10/1. Nonfall registration accepted. Admission may be deferred for a maximum of 1 semester. Credit and/or placement offered for CEEB Advanced Placement tests.

COSTS AND FINANCIAL AID
Annual tuition $23,680. Room and board $8,585. Required fees $240. Average book expense $1,200. **Required Forms and Deadlines:** FAFSA. Priority financial aid filing date 3/15. **Notification of Awards:** Applicants will be notified of awards on a rolling basis beginning 2/15. **Types of Aid:** *Need-based scholarships/grants:* Federal Pell, SEOG, state scholarships/grants, private scholarships, the school's own gift aid. *Loans:* Direct Subsidized Stafford, Direct Unsubsidized Stafford, Direct PLUS, Federal Perkins. *Student Employment:* Federal Work-Study Program available. Institutional employment available. Highest amount earned per year from on-campus jobs $6,128. Off-campus job opportunities are excellent. **Financial Aid Statistics:** 74% freshmen, 73% undergrads receive need-based scholarship or grant aid. 44% freshmen, 31% undergrads receive non-need-based scholarship or grant aid. 54% freshmen, 58% undergrads receive need-based self-help aid. 9% freshmen, 7% undergrads receive athletic scholarships. 74% freshmen, 74% undergrads receive any aid. 77% undergrads borrow to pay for school. Average cumulative indebtedness $33,216. **Criteria for awarding institutional aid:** *Non-need-based:* Academics, art, athletics, music/drama.

ST. ANDREWS PRESBYTERIAN COLLEGE

1700 Dogwood Mile, Laurinburg, NC 28352
Phone: 910-277-5555 **Financial Aid Phone:** 910-277-5560
E-mail: admissions@sapc.edu **CEEB Code:** 5214
Fax: 910-277-5087 **Website:** sapc.edu **ACT Code:** 3146

This private school, affiliated with the Presbyterian Church, was founded in 1958. It has a 600-acre campus.

RATINGS
Admissions Selectivity Rating: 72   **Fire Safety Rating:** 60*   **Green Rating:** 60*

STUDENTS AND FACULTY
Enrollment: 579. **Student Body:** 57% female, 43% male, 57% out-of-state, 2% international (9 countries represented). Asian 1%, African American 10%, Caucasian 84%, Hispanic 3%, Native American 1%.
Retention and Graduation: 34% freshmen graduate within 4 years. 40% grads go on to further study within 1 year. **Faculty:** Student/faculty ratio 10:1. 34 full-time faculty, 76% hold PhDs, 44% are women.

ACADEMICS
Degrees: Bachelor's, certificate. **Classes:** Most classes have 10–19 students. **Majors with Highest Enrollment:** Business/commerce; elementary education and teaching; English language and literature. **Special Study Options:** Double major, honors program, independent study, internships, student-designed major, study abroad, teacher certification program, weekend college, online classes. Special programs offered to physically disabled students include note-taking services, reader services, tape recorders, tutors. **Career services:** Alumni network, alumni services, career/job search classes, career assessment, internships, regional alumni.

FACILITIES
Housing: Coed dorms, men's dorms, women's dorms. 90% of campus accessible to physically disabled. **Special Academic Facilities/Equipment:** Art gallery, anthropology museum, science lab, electron microscopy center with three electron microscopes, psychology lab, artronics graphics computer, Scottish Heritage Foundation. **Computers:** 100% of libraries, 50% of dining areas, 100% of student union, have wireless network access. Administrative functions (other than registration) can be performed online.

CAMPUS LIFE
Environment: Rural. **Activities:** Choral groups, drama/theater, literary magazine, student government, student newspaper, yearbook, campus ministries. **Organizations:** 30 registered organizations, 3 honor societies, 1 religious organizations. **Athletics (Intercollegiate):** *Men:* Baseball, basketball, cross-country, equestrian sports, golf, horseback riding, lacrosse, soccer, track/field (outdoor), wrestling. *Women:* Basketball, cross-country, equestrian sports, horseback riding, lacrosse, soccer, softball, track/field (outdoor), volleyball, wrestling. **On-Campus Highlights:** Equesterian Center, Morgan Jones Science Labs, Electronic and Fine Arts Center, Athletic Facilities, Art Studios.

ADMISSIONS
Freshman Academic Profile: Average high school GPA 3.039. 4% in top 10% of high school class, 23% in top 25% of high school class, 67% in top 50% of high school class. SAT Math middle 50% range 550–450. SAT Critical Reading middle 50% range 520–450. Minimum paper TOEFL 550. Minimum computer TOEFL 280. **Basis for Candidate Selection:** *Important factors considered include:* Academic GPA, standardized test scores, character/personal qualities, extracurricular activities. *Other factors considered include:* Class rank, application essay, recommendation(s), rigor of secondary school record, first generation, interview, talent/ability, volunteer work, work experience. **Freshman Admission Requirements:** High school diploma is required and GED is accepted. *Academic units required:* 3 English, 3 mathematics, 3 science, 1 foreign language, 3 social studies. **Freshman Admission Statistics:** 743 applied, 76% admitted, 26% enrolled. **Transfer Admission Requirements:** High school transcript, college transcript(s), statement of good standing from prior institution(s). Minimum college GPA of 2.5 required. Lowest grade transferable C–. **General Admission Information:** Application fee $30. Notification on a rolling basis, beginning on or about 9/1. Nonfall registration accepted. Admission may be deferred for a maximum of one term. Credit offered for CEEB Advanced Placement tests.

COSTS AND FINANCIAL AID
Annual tuition $21,190. Average book expense $1,300. **Required Forms and Deadlines:** FAFSA, state aid form **Notification of Awards:** Applicants will be notified of awards on a rolling basis beginning 10/1. **Types of Aid:** *Need-based scholarships/grants:* Federal Pell, SEOG, state scholarships/grants, private scholarships, the school's own gift aid. *Loans:* FFEL Subsidized Stafford, FFEL Unsubsidized Stafford, FFEL PLUS. *Student Employment:* Federal

Work-Study Program available. Institutional employment available. Highest amount earned per year from on-campus jobs $2,000. **Financial Aid Statistics:** 72% freshmen, 73% undergrads receive need-based scholarship or grant aid. 12% freshmen, 11% undergrads receive non-need-based scholarship or grant aid. 59% freshmen, 59% undergrads receive need-based self-help aid. 15% freshmen, 15% undergrads receive athletic scholarships. 99% freshmen, 98% undergrads receive any aid. 57.41% undergrads borrow to pay for school. Average cumulative indebtedness $19,032. **Criteria for awarding institutional aid:** *Non-need-based:* Academics, alumni affiliation, art, athletics, leadership, music/drama.

ST. BONAVENTURE UNIVERSITY

PO Box D, St. Bonaventure, NY 14778
Phone: 716-375-2400 **Financial Aid Phone:** 800-462-5050
E-mail: admissions@sbu.edu **CEEB Code:** 2793
Fax: 716-375-4005 **Website:** www.sbu.edu **ACT Code:** 2882

This private school, affiliated with the Roman Catholic Church, was founded in 1858. It has a 500-acre campus.

RATINGS
Admissions Selectivity Rating: 73   **Fire Safety Rating:** 60*   **Green Rating:** 60*

STUDENTS AND FACULTY
Enrollment: 1,905. **Student Body:** 50% female, 50% male, 24% out-of-state, 2% international (24 countries represented). Asian 2%, African American 4%, Caucasian 18%, Hispanic 2%.
Retention and Graduation: 77% freshmen return for sophomore year. 54% freshmen graduate within 4 years. 33% grads go on to further study within 1 year. 8% grads pursue arts and sciences degrees. 6% grads pursue law degrees. 17% grads pursue business degrees. 2% grads pursue medical degrees. **Faculty:** Student/faculty ratio 14:1. 153 full-time faculty, 79% hold PhDs, 7% are are members of minority groups, 30% are women.

ACADEMICS
Degrees: Bachelor's, master's, post-bachelor's certificate, post-master's certificate. **Classes:** Most classes have 10–19 students. Most lab/discussion sessions have 10–19 students. **Majors with Highest Enrollment:** Business/commerce; elementary education and teaching; journalism. **Special Study Options:** Accelerated program, cross-registration, distance learning, double major, dual enrollment, exchange student program (domestic), honors program, independent study, internships, liberal arts/career combination, student-designed major, study abroad, teacher certification program, weekend college. **Combined degree programs:** BA/MA. Special programs offered to physically disabled students include note-taking services, reader services, tutors. **Career services:** Alumni network, career/job search classes, career assessment, internships, regional alumni.

FACILITIES
Housing: Special housing for disabled students, men's dorms, women's dorms, apartments for single students. 93% of campus accessible to physically disabled. **Special Academic Facilities/Equipment:** Quick Center for the Arts, Digital Conferencing and Media Center, Franciscan Center for Social Concern, Franciscan Institute. **Computers:** 100% of classrooms, have wireless network access. Students can register for classes online.

CAMPUS LIFE
Environment: Village. **Activities:** Choral groups, concert band, dance, drama/theater, jazz band, literary magazine, music ensembles, pep band, radio station, student government, student newspaper, television station, yearbook. **Organizations:** 47 registered organizations, 7 honor societies, 6 religious organizations. **Athletics (Intercollegiate):** *Men:* Baseball, basketball, cross-country, diving, golf, soccer, swimming, tennis. *Women:* Basketball, cross-country, diving, lacrosse, soccer, softball, swimming, tennis. **On-Campus Highlights:** Reilly Center, Richter Center, Quick Arts Center, Allegany River Trail, Golf Course and Clubhouse, Several major construction projects are taking place between 2006 and 2008, including renovation and addition to Hickey Dining Hall, renovation of Shay-Loughlen Residence Hall and addition of rare books wing to Friedsam Library.

ADMISSIONS
Freshman Academic Profile: Average high school GPA 3.13. 12% in top 10% of high school class, 32% in top 25% of high school class, 66% in top 50% of

high school class. 70% from public high schools. SAT Math middle 50% range 480–500. SAT Critical Reading middle 50% range 480–570. ACT middle 50% range 19–23. Minimum paper TOEFL 550. Minimum computer TOEFL 213. **Basis for Candidate Selection:** *Very important factors considered include:* Academic GPA, recommendation(s), rigor of secondary school record, character/personal qualities, interview. *Important factors considered include:* Application essay, standardized test scores, extracurricular activities, level of applicant's interest, talent/ability, volunteer work. *Other factors considered include:* Class rank, alumni/ae relation, first generation, work experience. **Freshman Admission Requirements:** High school diploma is required and GED is accepted. *Academic units required:* 4 English, 3 mathematics, 3 science, 2 foreign language, 4 social studies. *Academic units recommended:* 4 English, 3 mathematics, 3 science, (3 science labs), 2 foreign language, 4 social studies. **Freshman Admission Statistics:** 1,730 applied, 86% admitted, 32% enrolled. **Transfer Admission Requirements:** High school transcript, college transcript(s), statement of good standing from prior institution(s). Minimum college GPA of 2.0 required. Lowest grade transferable C. **General Admission Information:** Application fee $30. Regular application deadline 4/15. Notification on a rolling basis, beginning on or about 10/1. Nonfall registration accepted. Admission may be deferred for a maximum of 1 year. Credit and/or placement offered for CEEB Advanced Placement tests.

COSTS AND FINANCIAL AID

Annual tuition $24,928. Room and board $9,100. Required fees $865. Average book expense $709. **Required Forms and Deadlines:** FAFSA, institution's own financial aid form, state aid form. Priority financial aid filing date 2/1. **Notification of Awards:** Applicants will be notified of awards on a rolling basis beginning 4/1. **Types of Aid:** *Need-based scholarships/grants:* Federal Pell, SEOG, state scholarships/grants, private scholarships, the school's own gift aid. *Loans:* FFEL Subsidized Stafford, FFEL Unsubsidized Stafford, FFEL PLUS, Federal Perkins, college/university loans from institutional funds. *Student Employment:* Highest amount earned per year from on-campus jobs $815. **Financial Aid Statistics:** 73% freshmen, 71% undergrads receive need-based scholarship or grant aid. 13% freshmen, 12% undergrads receive non-need-based scholarship or grant aid. 60% freshmen, 59% undergrads receive need-based self-help aid. 3% freshmen, 4% undergrads receive athletic scholarships. 72% undergrads borrow to pay for school. Average cumulative indebtedness $16,900. **Criteria for awarding institutional aid:** *Non-need-based:* Academics, art, athletics, minority status, music/drama, religious affiliation, state/district residency.

ST. CATHERINE UNIVERSITY

2004 Randolph Avenue, #F-02, Saint Paul, MN 55105
Phone: 651-690-8850 **Financial Aid Phone:** 651-690-6540
E-mail: admissions@stkate.edu **CEEB Code:** 6105
Fax: 651-690-8868 **Website:** www.stkate.edu **ACT Code:** 2096

This private school, affiliated with the Roman Catholic Church, was founded in 1905. It has a 110-acre campus.

RATINGS

Admissions Selectivity Rating: 82   **Fire Safety Rating:** 60*   **Green Rating:** 60*

STUDENTS AND FACULTY

Enrollment: 3,636. **Student Body:** 97% female, 3% male, 8% out-of-state, 1% international (25 countries represented). Asian 8%, African American 11%, Caucasian 72%, Hispanic 3%, Native American 1%.
Retention and Graduation: 76% freshmen return for sophomore year. 38% freshmen graduate within 4 years. 28% grads go on to further study within 1 year. 2% grads pursue arts and sciences degrees. 4% grads pursue law degrees. 10% grads pursue business degrees. 2% grads pursue medical degrees. **Faculty:** Student/faculty ratio 11:1. 271 full-time faculty, 80% are women.

ACADEMICS

Degrees: Associate, bachelor's, certificate, master's, post-bachelor's certificate, post-master's certificate, terminal associate, transfer associate. **Classes:** Most classes have 10–19 students. Most lab/discussion sessions have 10–19 students.
Majors with Highest Enrollment: Elementary education and teaching; nursing/registered nurse (RN, ASN, BSN, MSN); occupational therapy/therapist.
Special Study Options: Cross-registration, double major, dual enrollment, exchange student program (domestic), honors program, independent study, internships, student-designed major, study abroad, weekend college. **Honors programs:** Antonian Scholars are students who exhibit exceptional academic performance in the University and who show promise as learners, researchers, writers, performers, campus or community leaders, and/or creative thinkers. Scholars possess both creativity and love of learning. Scholars are inquisitive

and hard working. They love challenges. Scholars are also students who want to take an active role in "tailoring" their college experiences to their needs, interests and passions. Scholars complete a five-component program that includes interdisciplinary seminars, as well as optional honors sections of TRW and/or GSJ, optional study abroad experiences, and a required Senior Honors Project. Scholars participate in at least two and up to four Honors seminars specifically designed for their learning needs and offered in an interdisciplinary format with two professors. All scholars as seniors are required to enroll in a four-credit independent study course in which they develop a senior project based on an interest, curiosity, or passion. Senior projects are completed with a faculty advisor and an interdisciplinary faculty committee who provide guidance and feedback on the project. Other privileges of membership in the Antonian Scholars Honors Program includes priority registration for courses each semester, special diplomas and commencement recognition, and leadership opportunities in the Honors Program Student Organization. Scholars also have opportunities on a regular basis to socialize, network, and converse with others in the Honors Program. Scholars have access to the Honor's Hub in Coeur de Catherine. The Hub is a quiet place to study when you need one and also a place where Scholars may gather for special activities or conversation. **Combined degree programs:** BA/DPT, BA/MA (Occupational Therapy). Special programs offered to physically disabled students include note-taking services, reader services, tape recorders, tutors. **Career services:** Alumni network, alumni services, career/job search classes, career assessment, internships.

FACILITIES

Housing: Women's dorms, apartments for single students, theme housing Housing for student-parents. 90% of campus accessible to physically disabled. **Special Academic Facilities/Equipment:** Art gallery, theatre, recital hall, experimental psychology lab, language lab, observatory. **Computers:** Students can register for classes online. Administrative functions (other than registration) can be performed online.

CAMPUS LIFE

Environment: Metropolis. **Activities:** Choral groups, drama/theater, literary magazine, music ensembles, musical theater, student government, student newspaper, campus ministries. **Organizations:** 40 registered organizations, 24 honor societies, 4 religious organizations. 1 sororities. **Athletics (Intercollegiate):** *Women:* Basketball, cross-country, diving, ice hockey, soccer, softball, swimming, tennis, track/field (outdoor), track/field (indoor), volleyball. **On-Campus Highlights:** Coeur de Catherine, English garden, Butler Center, Dew Drop Pond, Art Gallery. **Environmental Initiatives:** Retrofitted older building with green roof energy-efficient design in new residence halls sustainable landscaping

ADMISSIONS

Freshman Academic Profile: Average high school GPA 3.6. 33% in top 10% of high school class, 60% in top 25% of high school class, 90% in top 50% of high school class. 86% from public high schools. ACT middle 50% range 22–26. Minimum paper TOEFL 500. Minimum computer TOEFL 173. **Basis for Candidate Selection:** *Very important factors considered include:* Academic GPA, rigor of secondary school record. *Important factors considered include:* Class rank, application essay, recommendation(s), standardized test scores. *Other factors considered include:* interview. **Freshman Admission Requirements:** High school diploma is required and GED is accepted. *Academic units recommended:* 4 English, 3 mathematics, 2 science, 4 foreign language, 2 social studies. **Freshman Admission Statistics:** 1,528 applied, 77% admitted, 31% enrolled. **Transfer Admission Requirements:** High school transcript, college transcript(s), statement of good standing from prior institution(s). Minimum college GPA of 2.0 required. Lowest grade transferable C–. **General Admission Information:** Credit offered for CEEB Advanced Placement tests.

COSTS AND FINANCIAL AID

Annual tuition $26,700. Room and board $6,780. Required fees $378. Average book expense $800. **Required Forms and Deadlines:** FAFSA, institution's own financial aid form. Priority financial aid filing date 4/15. **Notification of Awards:** Applicants will be notified of awards on a rolling basis beginning 3/15. **Types of Aid:** *Need-based scholarships/grants:* Federal Pell, SEOG, state scholarships/grants, private scholarships, the school's own gift aid. *Loans:* Direct Subsidized Stafford, Direct Unsubsidized Stafford, Direct PLUS, Federal Perkins, Federal Nursing, state loans. *Student Employment:* Federal Work-Study Program available. Institutional employment available. Highest amount earned per year from on-campus jobs $2,158. Off-campus job opportunities are excellent. **Financial Aid Statistics:** 77% freshmen, 70% undergrads receive need-based scholarship or grant aid. 70% freshmen, 60% undergrads receive non-need-based scholarship or grant aid. 65% freshmen, 70% undergrads receive need-based self-help aid. 94% freshmen, 90% undergrads receive any aid. 94% undergrads borrow to pay for school. Average cumulative indebtedness $30,886. **Criteria for awarding institutional aid:** *Non-need-based:* Academics, alumni affiliation, leadership, minority status, state/district residency.

ST. CHARLES BORROMENO SEMINARY

100 East Wynnewood Road, Wynnewood, PA 19096
Phone: 610-785-6271 **Financial Aid Phone:** 610-785-6582
E-mail: dandrassy@adphila.org **CEEB Code:** 2794
Fax: 610-617-9267 **Website: ACT Code:** 5923

This private school, affiliated with the Roman Catholic Church, was founded in 1832. It has a 77-acre campus.

RATINGS
Admissions Selectivity Rating: 70   **Fire Safety Rating:** 79   **Green Rating:** 60*

STUDENTS AND FACULTY
Enrollment: 53. **Student Body:** 100% male, 42% out-of-state, 4% international (3 countries represented). Asian 4%, Caucasian 92%.
Retention and Graduation: 75% freshmen return for sophomore year. 33% freshmen graduate within 4 years. 90% grads go on to further study within 1 year. **Faculty:** Student/faculty ratio 7:1. 21 full-time faculty, 67% hold PhDs, 14% are women.

ACADEMICS
Degrees: Bachelor's, first professional, master's. **Classes:** Most classes have 10–19 students. **Special Study Options:** Accelerated program, English as a Second Language (ESL), independent study.

FACILITIES
Housing: Men's dorms, men's and somen's dorms available during Summer sessions. 75% of campus accessible to physically disabled. **Computers:** Students can register for classes online.

CAMPUS LIFE
Environment: Town. **Activities:** Choral groups, drama/theater, music ensembles, student government, student newspaper. **Organizations:** 3 registered organizations, 1 honor societies, 2 religious organizations.

ADMISSIONS
Freshman Academic Profile: 22% in top 10% of high school class, 44% in top 25% of high school class, 67% in top 50% of high school class. 40% from public high schools. SAT Math middle 50% range 470–590. SAT Critical Reading middle 50% range 460–710. Minimum paper TOEFL 450. Minimum computer TOEFL 150. **Basis for Candidate Selection:** *Very important factors considered include:* Application essay, recommendation(s), rigor of secondary school record, character/personal qualities, interview, religious affiliation/commitment. *Important factors considered include:* Class rank, standardized test scores. *Other factors considered include:* Extracurricular activities, talent/ability, work experience. **Freshman Admission Requirements:** High school diploma is required and GED is accepted. *Academic units recommended:* 4 English, 3 mathematics, 3 science, 2 foreign language, 3 social studies. **Freshman Admission Statistics:** 11 applied, 100% admitted, 91% enrolled. **Transfer Admission Requirements:** High school transcript, college transcript(s), essay or personal statement, minimum college GPA of 2.0 required. Lowest grade transferable C. **General Admission Information:** Regular application deadline 7/15. Nonfall registration accepted. Credit and/or placement offered for CEEB Advanced Placement tests.

COSTS AND FINANCIAL AID
Required Forms and Deadlines: FAFSA, institution's own financial aid form. *Student Employment:* Federal Work-Study Program available. Institutional employment available. Off-campus job opportunities are poor. **Financial Aid Statistics:** 100% freshmen, 100% undergrads receive any aid.

ST. EDWARD'S UNIVERSITY

3001 South Congress Avenue, Austin, TX 78704
Phone: 512-448-8500 **Financial Aid Phone:** 512-448-8523
E-mail: seu.admit@stedwards.edu **CEEB Code:** 6619
Fax: 512-464-8877 **Website:** www.gotostedwards.com **ACT Code:** 4156

This private school, affiliated with the Roman Catholic Church, was founded in 1885. It has a 160-acre campus.

RATINGS
Admissions Selectivity Rating: 75   **Fire Safety Rating:** 78   **Green Rating:** 75

STUDENTS AND FACULTY
Enrollment: 4,339. **Student Body:** 59% female, 41% male, 6.7% out-of-state, 3% international (28 countries represented). Asian 3%, African American 5%, Caucasian 54%, Hispanic 30%, Native American 1%.
Retention and Graduation: 44% freshmen graduate within 4 years. **Faculty:** Student/faculty ratio 14.83:1. 184 full-time faculty, 90% hold PhDs, 9% are members of minority groups, 45% are women.

ACADEMICS
Degrees: Bachelor's, master's, post-bachelor's certificate. **Classes:** Most classes have 20–29 students. **Majors with Highest Enrollment:** Biology/biological sciences; communication and media studies, other; psychology, **Special Study Options:** Double major, honors program, internships, study abroad, teacher certification program. **Honors programs:** Honors Program Special programs offered to physically disabled students include note-taking services, reader services, tutors. **Career services:** Alumni network, alumni services, career/job search classes, career assessment, internships, regional alumni. **Career services highlights include:** Service learning initiatives are an integral part of many courses. Faculty receive training on how to integrate service learning into their courses, whereby learning outcomes are achieved while serving the community.

FACILITIES
Housing: Coed dorms, special housing for disabled students, women's dorms, apartments for single students, Community-style living (casas, casitas) and two living-learning communities: Global Understanding and Social Justice. 90% of campus accessible to physically disabled. **Special Academic Facilities/Equipment:** Fine arts facility with digital photography lab; natural sciences center including state-of-the-art labs, classrooms and seminar rooms; interdisciplinary research lab at Wild Basin Wilderness Preserve. **Computers:** 100% of classrooms, 100% of dorms, 100% of libraries, 100% of dining areas, 100% of student union, 100% of common outdoor areas have wireless network access. Students can register for classes online. Administrative functions (other than registration) can be performed online.

CAMPUS LIFE
Environment: Metropolis. **Activities:** Choral groups, dance, drama/theater, literary magazine, music ensembles, musical theater, student government, student newspaper, student-run film society, symphony orchestra, television station, campus ministries, international student organization. **Organizations:** 95 registered organizations, 10 honor societies, 3 religious organizations. **Athletics (Intercollegiate):** *Men:* Baseball, basketball, golf, soccer, tennis. *Women:* Basketball, golf, soccer, softball, tennis, volleyball. **On-Campus Highlights:** Historic Main Building (view of Austin), Meadows Coffee House, new 119,000 sq ft residential villa 2009, John Brooks Williams Natural Sciences Center, Meditation and Prayer Grotto/Sorin Oak, Sorin Oak is the largest oak tree in Austin at 14.6 feet in circumference. **Environmental Initiatives:** High efficiency motors, high efficiency 1,000 ton chiller, cool seal reflective roofs Variable frequency drives. Performance contract to reduce utilities—lighting, retrofit, plumbing fixtures, steam traps, thermal energy storage, replace steam system with hot water boilers.

ADMISSIONS
Freshman Academic Profile: 19% in top 10% of high school class, 54% in top 25% of high school class, 88% in top 50% of high school class. 76% from public high schools. SAT Math middle 50% range 510–610. SAT Critical Reading middle 50% range 520–625. SAT Writing middle 50% range 500–610. ACT middle 50% range 22–27. Minimum paper TOEFL 500. Minimum web-based TOEFL 61. **Basis for Candidate Selection:** *Very important factors considered include:* Application essay, academic GPA, rigor of secondary school record, standardized test scores. *Important factors considered include:* Class rank, recommendation(s), extracurricular activities, volunteer work. *Other factors considered include:* Alumni/ae relation, character/personal qualities, first generation, geographical residence, interview, level of applicant's interest, racial/ethnic status, religious affiliation/commitment, talent/ability, work experience. **Freshman Admission Requirements:** High school diploma is required and GED is accepted. *Academic units required:* 4 English, 3 mathematics, 2 science, (2 science labs), 2 foreign language, 1 social studies, 2 history. *Academic units recommended:* 4 English, 4 mathematics, 3 science, (3 science labs), 3 foreign language, 1 social studies, 3 history, 1 computer science, 1 academic electives. **Freshman Admission Statistics:** 2,981 applied, 66% admitted, 38% enrolled. **Transfer Admission Requirements:** High school transcript, college transcript(s), essay or personal statement, minimum college GPA of 2.50 required. Lowest grade transferable C. **General Admission Information:** Application fee $45. Regular application deadline 5/1. Notification on a rolling basis, beginning on or about 11/1. Nonfall registration accepted. Admission may be deferred for a maximum of 1 year. Credit and/or placement offered for CEEB Advanced Placement tests.

COSTS AND FINANCIAL AID
Annual tuition $26,084. Room and board $9,036. Required fees $400. Average book expense $1,100. **Required Forms and Deadlines:** FAFSA Financial aid filing deadline 4/15. Priority financial aid filing date 3/1. **Notification of Awards:** Applicants will be notified of awards on a rolling basis beginning 1/15. **Types of Aid:** *Need-based scholarships/grants:* Federal Pell, SEOG,

state scholarships/grants, private scholarships, the school's own gift aid, Endowed scholarships. *Loans:* Direct PLUS, FFEL Subsidized Stafford, FFEL Unsubsidized Stafford, FFEL PLUS, Federal Perkins, state loans, Alternative educational loans. *Student Employment:* Federal Work-Study Program available. Institutional employment available. Highest amount earned per year from on-campus jobs $4,800. Off-campus job opportunities are good. **Financial Aid Statistics:** 67% freshmen, 58% undergrads receive need-based scholarship or grant aid. 56% freshmen, 45% undergrads receive non-need-based scholarship or grant aid. 54% freshmen, 47% undergrads receive need-based self-help aid. 4% freshmen, 4% undergrads receive athletic scholarships. 92% freshmen, 87% undergrads receive any aid. 79% undergrads borrow to pay for school. Average cumulative indebtedness $29,810. **Criteria for awarding institutional aid:** *Non-need-based:* Academics, art, athletics, leadership, music/drama, state/district residency.

See page 1240.

ST. FRANCIS COLLEGE (NY)

180 Remsen Street, Brooklyn Heights, NY 11201
Phone: 718-489-5200
E-mail: admissions@stfranciscollege.edu **CEEB Code:** 2796
Fax: 718-522-1274 **Website:** www.stfranciscollege.edu **ACT Code:** 2884

This private school, affiliated with the Roman Catholic Church, was founded in 1884. It has a 1-acre campus.

RATINGS
Admissions Selectivity Rating: 70   **Fire Safety Rating:** 60*   **Green Rating:** 60*

STUDENTS AND FACULTY
Enrollment: 2,294. **Student Body:** 57% female, 43% male, 1% out-of-state, 13% international (52 countries represented). Asian 2%, African American 20%, Caucasian 49%, Hispanic 14%.
Retention and Graduation: 76% freshmen return for sophomore year. 21% freshmen graduate within 4 years. **Faculty:** Student/faculty ratio 18:1. 69 full-time faculty, 77% hold PhDs, 14% are are members of minority groups, 38% are women.

ACADEMICS
Degrees: Associate, bachelor's, master's. **Classes:** Most classes have 10–19 students. Most lab/discussion sessions have 20–29 students. **Special Study Options:** Accelerated program, cooperative education program, cross-registration, double major, dual enrollment, honors program, independent study, internships, study abroad, teacher certification program, Accelerated biomedical science program with New York Colllege of Podiatric Medicine; medical technology program with St. Vincent's Catholic Medical Centers of New York and New York Methodist Hospital; joint program in radiological sciences with St. Vincent's Catholic Medical Centers of New York; 7 year cooperative program with the New York University College of Dentistry; can complete BA at St. Francis and Master of Science in Computer Science from Polytechnic University. **Honors programs:** One college-wide program that is not department specific. **Combined degree programs:** BA/DDS, MS/Computer Science. Special programs offered to physically disabled students include note-taking services, reader services, tape recorders, tutors. **Career services:** Alumni network, alumni services, career/job search classes, career assessment, internships, regional alumni.

FACILITIES
Housing: Students may apply for housing in the recently opened dormitory at Polytechnic University, a few minutes walk from St. Francis College. 100% of campus accessible to physically disabled.

CAMPUS LIFE
Environment: Metropolis. **Activities:** Choral groups, drama/theater, literary magazine, student government, student newspaper, yearbook. **Organizations:** 25 registered organizations, 1 honor societies, 1 religious organizations. 1 fraternities, 1 sororities. **Athletics (Intercollegiate):** *Men:* Basketball, cross-country, diving, golf, soccer, swimming, tennis, track/field (outdoor), track/field (indoor), water polo. *Women:* Basketball, bowling, cross-country, diving, fencing, golf, swimming, tennis, track/field (outdoor), track/field (indoor), volleyball, water polo.

ADMISSIONS
Freshman Academic Profile: Average high school GPA 3.1. 44% from public high schools. SAT Math middle 50% range 400–550. SAT Critical Reading middle 50% range 410–540. Minimum paper TOEFL 500. **Basis for Candidate Selection:** *Very important factors considered include:* Rigor of secondary school record, standardized test scores. *Important factors considered include:* Class rank, application essay, recommendation(s), alumni/ae relation,

character/personal qualities, interview, talent/ability. *Other factors considered include:* extracurricular activities, volunteer work. **Freshman Admission Requirements:** High school diploma is required and GED is accepted. *Academic units required:* 4 English, 3 mathematics, 2 science, (1 science labs), 2 foreign language, 4 social studies, 1 academic electives, 1 music/art. **Freshman Admission Statistics:** 1,304 applied, 88% admitted, 38% enrolled. **Transfer Admission Requirements:** High school transcript, college transcript(s), essay or personal statement, statement of good standing from prior institution(s). Minimum college GPA of 2.0 required. Lowest grade transferable C. **General Admission Information:** Application fee $35. Nonfall registration accepted. Admission may be deferred for a maximum of 1 year. Placement offered for CEEB Advanced Placement tests.

COSTS AND FINANCIAL AID
Annual tuition $13,500. . **Required Forms and Deadlines:** FAFSA, institution's own financial aid form, state aid form. Priority financial aid filing date 2/15. **Notification of Awards: Types of Aid:** *Need-based scholarships/ grants:* Federal Pell, SEOG, state scholarships/grants, private scholarships, the school's own gift aid. *Loans:* FFEL Subsidized Stafford, FFEL Unsubsidized Stafford, FFEL PLUS, Federal Perkins. *Student Employment:* Federal Work-Study Program available. Institutional employment available. Off-campus job opportunities are good. **Financial Aid Statistics:** 50% undergrads receive need-based scholarship or grant aid. 17% undergrads receive non-need-based scholarship or grant aid. 28% undergrads receive need-based self-help aid. 7% undergrads receive athletic scholarships. **Criteria for awarding institutional aid:** *Non-need-based:* Academics, athletics.

ST. JOHN'S COLLEGE (MD)

P.O. Box 2800, Annapolis, MD 21404
Phone: 410-626-2522 **Financial Aid Phone:** 410-295-6932
E-mail: admissions@sjca.edu **CEEB Code:** 5598
Fax: 410-269-7916 **Website:** www.stjohnscollege.edu **ACT Code:** 1732

This private school was founded in 1696. It has a 36-acre campus.

RATINGS
Admissions Selectivity Rating: 85   **Fire Safety Rating:** 84   **Green Rating:** 72

STUDENTS AND FACULTY
Enrollment: 489. **Student Body:** 47% female, 53% male, 85% out-of-state, 2% international (17 countries represented). Asian 2%, African American 1%, Caucasian 87%, Hispanic 5%.
Retention and Graduation: 78% freshmen return for sophomore year. 60% freshmen graduate within 4 years. 10% grads go on to further study within 1 year. 5% grads pursue arts and sciences degrees. 2% grads pursue law degrees. **Faculty:** Student/faculty ratio 8:1. 71 full-time faculty, 79% hold PhDs, 6% are are members of minority groups, 23% are women.

ACADEMICS
Degrees: Bachelor's, master's. **Classes:** Most classes have 10–19 students. **Majors with Highest Enrollment:** liberal arts and sciences studies and humanities, other. **Special Study Options:** internships, Students may spend one or more years at the college's Santa Fe, NM, campus. Special programs offered to physically disabled students include reader services, tape recorders **Career services:** Alumni services, career assessment, internships, regional alumni. **Career services highlights include:** Hodson Internships allowing students to receive a stipend for internships which offer them a substantial opportunity to explore a career and learn related skills.

FACILITIES
Housing: Coed dorms, special housing for disabled students. 80% of campus accessible to physically disabled. **Special Academic Facilities/Equipment:** Art gallery, planetarium, pendulum, Ptolemy stone, Faraday cage, laboratories. **Computers:** 20% of dorms, 30% of common outdoor areas have wireless network access. Administrative functions (other than registration) can be performed online.

CAMPUS LIFE
Environment: Town. **Activities:** Choral groups, dance, drama/theater, literary magazine, music ensembles, student government, student newspaper, student-run film society, yearbook. **Organizations:** 64 registered organizations, 3 religious organizations. **On-Campus Highlights:** Mitchell Art Gallery, Green-filed Library, McDowell Hall, Caroll Barrister House, French Monument. The

entire campus is a registered national landmark. **Environmental Initiatives:** purchasing renewable energy credits for 100% of our electric consumption installing a new central heating plant and disttribution system that will reduce fossil fuel consumption for heating by approximately 25%, as well as smokestack emissions stabilization of 800'+ of waterfront with removal of bulkhead and installation/ restoration of natural wetland

ADMISSIONS

Freshman Academic Profile: 34% in top 10% of high school class, 63% in top 25% of high school class, 89% in top 50% of high school class. 74% from public high schools. SAT Math middle 50% range 590–680. SAT Critical Reading middle 50% range 640–740. Minimum paper TOEFL 600. Minimum computer TOEFL 270. Minimum web-based TOEFL 100. **Basis for Candidate Selection:** *Very important factors considered include:* Application essay. *Important factors considered include:* Recommendation(s), rigor of secondary school record, character/personal qualities. *Other factors considered include:* Class rank, academic GPA, standardized test scores, alumni/ae relation, extracurricular activities, first generation, interview, racial/ethnic status, talent/ability. **Freshman Admission Requirements:** High school diploma is required and GED is accepted. *Academic units required:* 3 mathematics, 2 foreign language. *Academic units recommended:* 4 English, 4 mathematics, 3 science, (3 science labs), 4 foreign language, 2 social studies, 2 history. **Freshman Admission Statistics:** 460 applied, 81% admitted, 42% enrolled. **Transfer Admission Requirements:** High school transcript, college transcript(s), essay or personal statement. **General Admission Information:** Nonfall registration accepted. Admission may be deferred for a maximum of 1 year. Neither credit nor placement offered for CEEB Advanced Placement tests.

COSTS AND FINANCIAL AID

Annual tuition $39,992. Room and board $9,600. Required fees $400. Average book expense $280. **Required Forms and Deadlines:** FAFSA, CSS/Financial Aid PROFILE, state aid form, noncustodial PROFILE, business/farm supplement. Priority financial aid filing date 2/15. **Notification of Awards:** Applicants will be notified of awards on a rolling basis beginning 12/1. **Types of Aid:** *Need-based scholarships/grants:* Federal Pell, SEOG, state scholarships/grants, private scholarships, the school's own gift aid. *Loans:* FFEL Subsidized Stafford, FFEL Unsubsidized Stafford, FFEL PLUS, Federal Perkins, college/university loans from institutional funds. *Student Employment:* Federal Work-Study Program available. Institutional employment available. Highest amount earned per year from on-campus jobs $2,999. Off-campus job opportunities are good. **Financial Aid Statistics:** 56% freshmen, 55% undergrads receive need-based scholarship or grant aid. 1% freshmen, 2% undergrads receive non-need-based scholarship or grant aid. 62% freshmen, 55% undergrads receive need-based self-help aid. 79% freshmen, 73% undergrads receive any aid.

ST. JOHN'S COLLEGE, DEPARTMENT OF NURSING (IL)

421 North Ninth Street, Springfield, IL 62702-5317
Phone: 217-525-5628
E-mail: College@st-johns.org
Fax: 217-757-6870 **Website:** www.st-johns.org/collegeofnursing

This private school, affiliated with the Roman Catholic Church, was founded in 1992.

RATINGS

Admissions Selectivity Rating: 60*   **Fire Safety Rating:** 60*   **Green Rating:** 60*

STUDENTS AND FACULTY

Enrollment: 83. **Student Body:** 93% female, 7% male, 10% out-of-state, 1% international (1 countries represented). African American 1%, Caucasian 98%. **Retention and Graduation:** **Faculty:** Student/faculty ratio 4:1. 12 full-time faculty, 17% hold PhDs, 100% are women.

ACADEMICS

Degrees: Bachelor's. **Classes:** Most classes have 30–39 students. Most lab/discussion sessions have fewer than 10 students. **Majors with Highest Enrollment:** Nursing/registered nurse (RN, ASN, BSN, MSN).

FACILITIES

Housing: Coed dorms, apartments for single students, campus apartments.

CAMPUS LIFE

Activities: Choral groups, drama/theater, literary magazine, student government, student newspaper, campus ministries. **Organizations:** 1 registered organizations.

ADMISSIONS

Freshman Academic Profile: 100% in top 50% of high school class. Minimum paper TOEFL 500. Minimum computer TOEFL 200. **Basis for Candidate Selection:** *Very important factors considered include:* Class rank, application essay, academic GPA, recommendation(s), rigor of secondary school record, standardized test scores, alumni/ae relation, character/personal qualities, extracurricular activities, interview, level of applicant's interest, volunteer work. *Other factors considered include:* Talent/ability, work experience. **Freshman Admission Requirements:** High school diploma is required and GED is accepted. *Academic units required:* 4 English, 3 mathematics, 3 science, (3 science labs, 3 social studies, 2 academic electives. **Freshman Admission Statistics: Transfer Admission Requirements:** High school transcript, college transcript(s), interview, statement of good standing from prior institution(s). Minimum college GPA of 2.5 required. Lowest grade transferable C. **General Admission Information:** Application fee $50. Nonfall registration not accepted. Neither credit nor placement offered for CEEB Advanced Placement tests.

COSTS AND FINANCIAL AID

Annual tuition $11,708. Required fees $444. Average book expense $750.

ST. JOHN'S COLLEGE, SANTA FE

1160 Camino Cruz Blanca, Santa Fe, NM 87505
Phone: 505-984-6060 **Financial Aid Phone:** 505-984-6058
E-mail: admissions@sjcsf.edu **CEEB Code:** 4737
Fax: 505-984-6162 **Website:** www.sjcsf.edu **ACT Code:** 2649

This private school was founded in 1696. It has a 250-acre campus.

RATINGS

Admissions Selectivity Rating: 85   **Fire Safety Rating:** 60*   **Green Rating:** 79

STUDENTS AND FACULTY

Enrollment: 414. **Student Body:** 39% female, 61% male, 93.4% out-of-state, 5% international (17 countries represented). Asian 4%, Caucasian 79%, Hispanic 7%, Native American 1%. **Retention and Graduation:** 74% freshmen return for sophomore year. 54% freshmen graduate within 4 years. 13% grads go on to further study within 1 year. 9% grads pursue arts and sciences degrees. 3% grads pursue law degrees. **Faculty:** Student/faculty ratio 7:1. 68 full-time faculty, 81% hold PhDs, 6% are are members of minority groups, 26% are women.

ACADEMICS

Degrees: Bachelor's, master's. **Classes:** Most classes have 10–19 students. **Special Study Options:** Accelerated program, internships **Career services:** Alumni network, alumni services, career/job search classes, internships, regional alumni. **Career services highlights include:** Ariel Internship Program provides stipends to undergraduates for a limited number of summer internship opportunities regardless of financial need. SJC recognizes that internships have become a significant component of modern academia, whether a student continues on to graduate school or enters the work force.

FACILITIES

Housing: Coed dorms, special housing for disabled students, men's dorms, women's dorms, apartments for married students, apartments for single students, wellness housing, single-sex suites are available. 70% of campus accessible to physically disabled. **Special Academic Facilities/Equipment:** Art gallery. **Computers:** 75% of classrooms, 10% of dorms, 100% of dining areas, 100% of student union, 10% of common outdoor areas have wireless network access. Administrative functions (other than registration) can be performed online.

CAMPUS LIFE

Environment: City. **Activities:** Choral groups, concert band, dance, drama/theater, jazz band, literary magazine, music ensembles, musical theater, student government, student newspaper, student-run film society. **Organizations:** 27 registered organizations. **On-Campus Highlights:** Placita/Fish Pond, Student Activities Center, Great Hall, Coffee Shop, Levan Hall (new building). **Environmental Initiatives:** Paper, glass, plastic, cardboard recycling compost food from cafeteria rainwater collection from roofs.

ADMISSIONS

Freshman Academic Profile: 22% in top 10% of high school class, 50% in top 25% of high school class, 81% in top 50% of high school class. 70% from public high schools. SAT Math middle 50% range 570–690. SAT Critical Reading middle 50% range 610–720. ACT middle 50% range 26–30. Minimum paper TOEFL 550. Minimum computer TOEFL 213. **Basis for Candidate Selection:** *Very important factors considered include:* Application essay. *Important factors considered include:* Recommendation(s), rigor of secondary school record, character/personal qualities, level of applicant's interest. *Other factors considered include:* Class rank, academic GPA, standardized test scores, alumni/ae relation, extracurricular activities, first generation, interview, racial/ethnic status, talent/ability, volunteer work, work experience. **Freshman Admission Requirements:** High school diploma is required and GED is accepted. *Academic units required:* 3 mathematics, 2 foreign language. *Academic units recommended:* 4 English, 1 mathematics, 3 science, (3 science labs), 4 foreign language, 2 history. **Freshman Admission Statistics:** 297 applied, 85% admitted, 49% enrolled. **Transfer Admission Requirements:** High school transcript, college transcript(s), essay or personal statement, **General Admission Information:** Nonfall registration accepted. Admission may be deferred for a maximum of 2 semesters. Neither credit nor placement offered for CEEB Advanced Placement tests.

COSTS AND FINANCIAL AID

Annual tuition $39,992. Room and board $9,600. Required fees $400. Average book expense $275. **Required Forms and Deadlines:** FAFSA, CSS/Financial Aid PROFILE, noncustodial PROFILE, business/farm supplement. Priority financial aid filing date 2/15. **Notification of Awards:** Applicants will be notified of awards on a rolling basis beginning 12/10. **Types of Aid:** *Need-based scholarships/grants:* Federal Pell, SEOG, state scholarships/grants, private scholarships, the school's own gift aid, Academic Competitiveness Grant/SMART Grants. *Loans:* FFEL Subsidized Stafford, FFEL Unsubsidized Stafford, FFEL PLUS, Federal Perkins, college/university loans from institutional funds. *Student Employment:* Federal Work-Study Program available. Institutional employment available. Highest amount earned per year from on-campus jobs $2,800. Off-campus job opportunities are excellent. **Financial Aid Statistics:** 71% freshmen, 61% undergrads receive need-based scholarship or grant aid. 66% freshmen, 56% undergrads receive need-based self-help aid. 79% freshmen, 82% undergrads receive any aid. 65% undergrads borrow to pay for school. Average cumulative indebtedness $27,235.

ST. JOHN'S UNIVERSITY

8000 Utopia Parkway, Queens, NY 11439
Phone: 718-990-2000 **Financial Aid Phone:** 718-990-2000
E-mail: admhelp@stjohns.edu **CEEB Code:** 2799
Fax: 718-990-2096 **Website:** www.stjohns.edu **ACT Code:** 2888

This private school, affiliated with the Roman Catholic Church, was founded in 1870. It has a 122-acre campus.

RATINGS

Admissions Selectivity Rating: 86　　　**Fire Safety Rating:** 86　　　**Green Rating:** 86

STUDENTS AND FACULTY

Enrollment: 12,115. **Student Body:** 54% female, 46% male, 23% out-of-state, 5% international (111 countries represented). Asian 18%, African American 18%, Caucasian 37%, Hispanic 15%.
Retention and Graduation: 78% freshmen return for sophomore year. 38% freshmen graduate within 4 years. 20% grads go on to further study within 1 year. 4% grads pursue arts and sciences degrees. 5% grads pursue law degrees. 4% grads pursue business degrees. 1% grads pursue medical degrees. **Faculty:** Student/faculty ratio 19:1. 669 full-time faculty, 87% hold PhDs, 20% are are members of minority groups, 42% are women.

ACADEMICS

Degrees: Associate, bachelor's, certificate, diploma, doctoral, master's, post-bachelor's certificate, post-master's certificate, terminal associate, transfer associate. **Classes:** Most classes have 20–29 students. Most lab/discussion sessions have 20–29 students. **Majors with Highest Enrollment:** liberal arts and sciences/liberal studies; pharmacy (PharmD [US], PharmD or BS/BPharm [Canada]); psychology. **Special Study Options:** Accelerated program, cross-registration, distance learning, double major, dual enrollment, English as a Second Language (ESL), honors program, independent study, internships, liberal arts/career combination, study abroad, teacher certification program, weekend college. **Honors programs:** The University Honors Program is available to qualified incoming freshmen. The program primarily comprises honors versions of the courses which are part of the core curriculum. Honors students must complete 30 credits of honors-designated courses to complete the program. Additional options for obtaining honors credits are also available. The program also features a range of special activities and events. **Combined degree programs:** BA/JD, BA/MA, BS/MA, BS/MS, BS/MBA, BS/OD, BS/JD, MBA/JD. Special programs offered to physically disabled students include note-taking services, reader services, tape recorders, tutors. **Career services:** Alumni services, career/job search classes, career assessment, internships.

FACILITIES

Housing: Coed dorms, apartments for single students, theme housing Some off-campus apartments are available on a limited basis. 90% of campus accessible to physically disabled. **Special Academic Facilities/Equipment:** University Gallery; Instuctional Media Center; Institute of Asian Studies; Health Education Resource Center; Center for Psychological Services; TV Center; Speech and Hearing Center and Reading and Writing Education Center. **Computers:** 100% of classrooms, 90% of dorms, 100% of libraries, 100% of dining areas, 100% of student union, 100% of common outdoor areas have wireless network access. Students can register for classes online. Administrative functions (other than registration) can be performed online. Undergraduates are required to own a computer.

CAMPUS LIFE

Environment: Metropolis. **Activities:** Choral groups, dance, drama/theater, jazz band, literary magazine, music ensembles, musical theater, pep band, radio station, student government, student newspaper, television station, yearbook, campus ministries. **Organizations:** 180 registered organizations, **Athletics (Intercollegiate):** *Men:* Baseball, basketball, fencing, golf, lacrosse, soccer, softball, table tennis, tennis, volleyball, weight lifting. *Women:* Basketball, cross-country, fencing, soccer, softball, table tennis, tennis, track/field (outdoor), track/field (indoor), volleyball, weight lifting. **On-Campus Highlights:** The Great Lawn, D'Angelo Center, The University Library. **Environmental Initiatives:** Senior management signed the NYC Mayoral Challenge committing to 30% reduction in carbon emissions by the year 2017. Senior management signed a Memorandum of Understanding with the EPA committing to continuous improvement in eight EPA Voluntary Partnership Programs. Establishment of a Sustainability Office within the university's central administration for the purpose of advancing the university efforts for a sustainable future and hiring 17 student workers as Sustainability Coordinators.

ADMISSIONS

Freshman Academic Profile: Average high school GPA 3.3. 24% in top 10% of high school class, 50% in top 25% of high school class, 79% in top 50% of high school class. 65% from public high schools. SAT Math middle 50% range 490–620. SAT Critical Reading middle 50% range 480–590. Minimum paper TOEFL 500. Minimum computer TOEFL 173. Minimum web-based TOEFL 61. **Basis for Candidate Selection:** *Very important factors considered include:* Academic GPA, standardized test scores. *Important factors considered include:* Rigor of secondary school record. *Other factors considered include:* Class rank, application essay, recommendation(s), alumni/ae relation, character/personal qualities, extracurricular activities, geographical residence, interview, level of applicant's interest, volunteer work, work experience. **Freshman Admission Requirements:** High school diploma is required and GED is accepted. *Academic units required:* 4 English. *Academic units recommended:* 3 mathematics, 2 science, (2 science labs), 2 foreign language, 2 history, 1 Social Studies/History units vary **Freshman Admission Statistics:** 52,980 applied, 43% admitted, 14% enrolled. **Transfer Admission Requirements:** College transcript(s), Lowest grade transferable C. **General Admission Information:** Application fee $50. Notification on a rolling basis, beginning on or about 12/1. Nonfall registration accepted. Admission may be deferred for a maximum of 1 year. Credit and/or placement offered for CEEB Advanced Placement tests.

COSTS AND FINANCIAL AID

Annual tuition $29,350. Room and board $13,140. Required fees $690. Average book expense $1,000. **Required Forms and Deadlines:** FAFSA. Priority financial aid filing date 2/1. **Notification of Awards:** Applicants will be notified of awards on a rolling basis beginning 3/15. **Types of Aid:** *Need-based scholarships/grants:* Federal Pell, SEOG, state scholarships/grants, private scholarships, the school's own gift aid. *Loans:* Direct Subsidized Stafford, Direct Unsubsidized Stafford, Direct PLUS, Federal Perkins. *Student Employment:* Federal Work-Study Program available. Institutional employment available. Highest amount earned per year from on-campus jobs $5,000. Off-campus job opportunities are good. **Financial Aid Statistics:** 72% freshmen, 68% undergrads receive need-based scholarship or grant aid. 65% freshmen, 56% undergrads receive non-need-based scholarship or grant aid. 61% freshmen, 63% undergrads receive need-based self-help aid. 1% freshmen, 2% undergrads receive athletic scholarships. 97% freshmen, 97% undergrads receive any aid. 70% undergrads borrow to pay for school. Average cumulative indebtedness $30,692. **Criteria for awarding institutional aid:** *Non-need-based:* Academics, alumni affiliation, art, athletics, leadership, music/drama, religious affiliation.

ST. JOSEPH'S COLLEGE

245 Clinton Avenue, Brooklyn, NY 11205
Phone: 718-636-6868 **Financial Aid Phone:** 631-447-3214
E-mail: www.sjcny.edu
Fax: 718-636-8303 **Website:** www.sjcny.edu

This is a private school.

RATINGS
Admissions Selectivity Rating: 60*　　**Fire Safety Rating:** 60*　　**Green Rating:** 60*

STUDENTS AND FACULTY
Enrollment: 1,037. **Student Body:** 76% female, 24% male, 1.3% out-of-state, international. Asian 7%, African American 36%, Caucasian 38%, Hispanic 14%. **Retention and Graduation:** 81% freshmen return for sophomore year. 70% freshmen graduate within 4 years. 61% grads go on to further study within 1 year. 5% grads pursue arts and sciences degrees. 2% grads pursue law degrees. 3% grads pursue business degrees. 1% grads pursue medical degrees. **Faculty:** Student/faculty ratio 11:1. 50 full-time faculty, 66% hold PhDs, 60% are women.

ACADEMICS
Degrees: Bachelor's, certificate, master's. **Classes:** Most classes have fewer than 10 students. Most lab/discussion sessions have fewer than 10 students. **Special Study Options:** Accelerated program, honors program, independent study, internships, teacher certification program, weekend college, Biomedical Program with New York College of Podiatric medicine. **Honors programs:** Freshman Honors Program provides enriched inter-disciplinary courses. Capstone course includes a travel or global studies component. Honors indicated on transcript. **Combined degree programs:** BS/MBA. Special programs offered to physically disabled students include note-taking services, reader services, tape recorders. **Career services:** Alumni services, career/job search classes, career assessment, internships.

FACILITIES
Housing: 95% of campus accessible to physically disabled. **Special Academic Facilities/Equipment:** Clare Rose Playhouse. **Computers:** Students can register for classes online.

CAMPUS LIFE
Activities: Choral groups, dance, drama/theater, literary magazine, musical theater, student government, student newspaper, yearbook, campus ministries. **Organizations:** 34 registered organizations, 8 honor societies, 2 religious organizations. 2 fraternities, 2 sororities. **On-Campus Highlights:** Athletic Center with pool, Eagles Nest Cafeteria, Student Lounge, Quad Area, Clare Rose Playhouse.

ADMISSIONS
Freshman Academic Profile: 50% from public high schools. SAT Math middle 50% range 430–540. SAT Critical Reading middle 50% range 410–510. SAT Writing middle 50% range 400–500. Minimum paper TOEFL 600. Minimum computer TOEFL 250. Minimum web-based TOEFL 100. **Basis for Candidate Selection:** *Very important factors considered include:* Academic GPA, rigor of secondary school record, standardized test scores. *Important factors considered include:* Class rank, application essay, recommendation(s), extracurricular activities, interview. *Other factors considered include:* Alumni/ae relation, talent/ability, volunteer work, work experience. **Freshman Admission Requirements:** High school diploma is required and GED is accepted. *Academic units required:* 4 English, 3 mathematics, 2 science, 2 foreign language, 4 social studies, 3 academic electives. *Academic units recommended:* 3 foreign language. **Freshman Admission Statistics:** 825 applied, 62% admitted, 25% enrolled. **Transfer Admission Requirements:** College transcript(s), interview, statement of good standing from prior institution(s). Minimum college GPA of 2.0 required. **General Admission Information:** Application fee $25. Credit and/or placement offered for CEEB Advanced Placement tests.

COSTS AND FINANCIAL AID
Annual tuition $15,400. Required fees $563. **Required Forms and Deadlines:** FAFSA, institution's own financial aid form, state aid form. Priority financial aid filing date 2/25. **Notification of Awards:** Applicants will be notified of awards on a rolling basis beginning 3/15. **Types of Aid:** *Need-based scholarships/grants:* Federal Pell, SEOG, state scholarships/grants, private scholarships, the school's own gift aid. *Loans:* FFEL Subsidized Stafford, FFEL

Unsubsidized Stafford, FFEL PLUS, Federal Perkins. *Student Employment:* Federal Work-Study Program available. Institutional employment available. Off-campus job opportunities are good. **Financial Aid Statistics:** 72% freshmen, 68% undergrads receive need-based scholarship or grant aid. 53% freshmen, 46% undergrads receive non-need-based scholarship or grant aid. 65% freshmen, 63% undergrads receive need-based self-help aid. 48% undergrads borrow to pay for school. Average cumulative indebtedness $18,582. **Criteria for awarding institutional aid:** *Non-need-based:* Academics.

See page 1244.

ST. JOSEPH'S COLLEGE, NEW YORK (PATCHOGUE)

155 West Roe Blvd, Patchogue, NY 11772
Phone: 631-447-3219 **Financial Aid Phone:** 631-447-3214
E-mail: longislandas@sjcny.edu **CEEB Code:** 2802
Fax: 631-447-1734 **Website:** www.sjcny.edu **ACT Code:** 2923

This private school was founded in 1916. It has a 30-acre campus.

RATINGS
Admissions Selectivity Rating: 85　　**Fire Safety Rating:** 60*　　**Green Rating:** 60*

STUDENTS AND FACULTY
Enrollment: 3,727. **Student Body:** 72% female, 28% male,. Asian 1%, African American 4%, Caucasian 73%, Hispanic 6%. **Retention and Graduation:** 83% freshmen return for sophomore year. 51% freshmen graduate within 4 years. 61% grads go on to further study within 1 year. 5% grads pursue arts and sciences degrees. 2% grads pursue law degrees. 3% grads pursue business degrees. 1% grads pursue medical degrees. **Faculty:** Student/faculty ratio 16:1. 111 full-time faculty, 68% hold PhDs, 59% are women.

ACADEMICS
Degrees: Bachelor's, certificate, master's. **Classes:** Most classes have 10–19 students. **Majors with Highest Enrollment:** Elementary education and teaching; psychology; secondary education and teaching. **Special Study Options:** Accelerated program, cross-registration, double major, honors program, internships, liberal arts/career combination, study abroad, teacher certification program, weekend college. **Honors programs:** Freshman Honors Program provides enriched inter-disciplinary courses. Capstone course includes a travel or global studies component. Honors indicated on transcript. **Combined degree programs:** BS/MBA. Special programs offered to physically disabled students include note-taking services, reader services, tape recorders **Career services:** Alumni services, career/job search classes, career assessment, internships.

FACILITIES
Housing: 95% of campus accessible to physically disabled. **Special Academic Facilities/Equipment:** Clare Rose Playhouse. **Computers:** Students can register for classes online.

CAMPUS LIFE
Environment: Town. **Activities:** Choral groups, dance, drama/theater, jazz band, literary magazine, music ensembles, musical theater, student government, student newspaper, yearbook, campus ministries. **Organizations:** 34 registered organizations, 8 honor societies, 2 religious organizations. 2 fraternities, 2 sororities. **Athletics (Intercollegiate):** *Men:* Baseball, basketball, cross-country, golf, soccer, tennis, track/field (outdoor). *Women:* Basketball, cross-country, equestrian sports, soccer, softball, swimming, tennis, track/field (outdoor), volleyball. **On-Campus Highlights:** Athletic Center with pool, Eagles Nest Cafeteria, Student Lounge, Quad Area, Clare Rose Playhouse.

ADMISSIONS
Freshman Academic Profile: 88% from public high schools. SAT Math middle 50% range 490–590. SAT Critical Reading middle 50% range 480–560. SAT Writing middle 50% range 460–550. Minimum paper TOEFL 550. Minimum computer TOEFL 213. **Basis for Candidate Selection:** *Very important factors considered include:* Class rank, academic GPA, rigor of secondary school record, standardized test scores. *Important factors considered include:* Application essay, recommendation(s), character/personal qualities, extracurricular activities, interview. *Other factors considered include:* Alumni/ae relation, first generation, level of applicant's interest, talent/ability, volunteer work, work experience. **Freshman Admission Requirements:** High school diploma is required and GED is accepted. *Academic units required:* 4 English, 3 mathematics, 3 science, (3 science labs), 2 foreign language, 4 social studies, 2 academic

electives. **Freshman Admission Statistics:** 1,375 applied, 74% admitted, 50% enrolled. **Transfer Admission Requirements:** College transcript(s), minimum college GPA of 2.0 required. **General Admission Information:** Application fee $25. Notification on a rolling basis, beginning on or about 11/15. Nonfall registration accepted. Admission may be deferred for a maximum of 2 years. Credit offered for CEEB Advanced Placement tests.

COSTS AND FINANCIAL AID
Annual tuition $15,400. Required fees $563. **Required Forms and Deadlines:** FAFSA, institution's own financial aid form, state aid form. Priority financial aid filing date 2/25. **Notification of Awards:** Applicants will be notified of awards on or about 3/15. *Types of Aid: Need-based scholarships/grants:* Federal Pell, SEOG, state scholarships/grants, private scholarships, the school's own gift aid. *Loans:* FFEL Subsidized Stafford, FFEL Unsubsidized Stafford, FFEL PLUS, Federal Perkins. *Student Employment:* Federal Work-Study Program available. Institutional employment available. Off-campus job opportunities are good. **Financial Aid Statistics:** 80% freshmen, 37% undergrads receive need-based scholarship or grant aid. 65% freshmen, 30% undergrads receive non-need-based scholarship or grant aid. 74% freshmen, 38% undergrads receive need-based self-help aid. 69% undergrads borrow to pay for school. Average cumulative indebtedness $14,028. **Criteria for awarding institutional aid:** *Non-need-based:* Academics.

ST. LAWRENCE UNIVERSITY

Payson Hall, Canton, NY 13617
Phone: 315-229-5261 **Financial Aid Phone:** 315-229-5265
E-mail: admissions@stlawu.edu **CEEB Code:** 2805
Fax: 315-229-5818 **Website:** www.stlawu.edu **ACT Code:** 2896

This private school was founded in 1856. It has a 1000-acre campus.

RATINGS
Admissions Selectivity Rating: 93   **Fire Safety Rating:** 67   **Green Rating:** 80

STUDENTS AND FACULTY
Enrollment: 2,271. **Student Body:** 55% female, 45% male, 57% out-of-state, 6% international (44 countries represented). Asian 2%, African American 3%, Caucasian 82%, Hispanic 4%, Native American 1%.
Retention and Graduation: 92% freshmen return for sophomore year. 79% freshmen graduate within 4 years. 20% grads go on to further study within 1 year. 17.9% grads pursue arts and sciences degrees. 3.3% grads pursue law degrees. 1% grads pursue business degrees. 2.3% grads pursue medical degrees. **Faculty:** Student/faculty ratio 11:1. 170 full-time faculty, 98% hold PhDs, 14% are are members of minority groups, 49% are women.

ACADEMICS
Degrees: Bachelor's, master's, post-master's certificate. **Classes:** Most classes have 10–19 students. Most lab/discussion sessions have 10–19 students. **Majors with Highest Enrollment:** Economics; political science and government; psychology. **Special Study Options:** Cross-registration, double major, exchange student program (domestic), independent study, internships, student-designed major, study abroad, teacher certification program, community-based learning. **Honors programs:** The University Fellows program offers a $3500 stipend plus room for summer research on campus. This is a competitive program for students who wish to undertake a serious, independent academic project as their summer employment. **Combined degree programs:** BA/MEng, 4+1 Business Program; 3-2 engineering programs. Special programs offered to physically disabled students include note-taking services, reader services, tape recorders, tutors. **Career services:** Alumni network, alumni services, career/job search classes, career assessment, internships. **Career services highlights include:** Alumni Network.

FACILITIES
Housing: Coed dorms, special housing for disabled students, special housing for international students, women's dorms, fraternity/sorority housing, apartments for single students, theme housing. 60% of campus accessible to physically disabled. **Special Academic Facilities/Equipment:** Art gallery, arts technology center, language lab, center for international education, environmental research facility, 76-acre forest preserve, two electron microscopes, microscopy and sleep labs, neuroscience lab, sustainability lab. **Computers:** 100% of classrooms, 100% of dorms, 100% of libraries, 100% of dining areas,

100% of student union, 100% of common outdoor areas have wireless network access. Students can register for classes online. Administrative functions (other than registration) can be performed online.

CAMPUS LIFE
Environment: Village. **Activities:** Choral groups, concert band, dance, drama/theater, jazz band, literary magazine, music ensembles, radio station, student government, student newspaper, student-run film society, yearbook, campus ministries, international student organization, Model UN. **Organizations:** 117 registered organizations, 22 honor societies, 4 religious organizations. 2 fraternities, 4 sororities. **Athletics (Intercollegiate):** *Men:* Baseball, basketball, crew/rowing, cross-country, equestrian sports, football, golf, ice hockey, lacrosse, skiing (downhill/alpine), skiing (nordic cross-country), soccer, squash, swimming, tennis, track/field (outdoor), track/field (indoor). *Women:* Basketball, crew/rowing, cross-country, equestrian sports, field hockey, golf, ice hockey, lacrosse, skiing (downhill/alpine), skiing (nordic cross-country), soccer, softball, squash, swimming, tennis, track/field (outdoor), track/field (indoor), volleyball. **On-Campus Highlights:** Newell Field House, Brewer Bookstore, Johnson Hall of Science, Owen D. Young Library, Student Center, Student Center opened January 2004, Newell Center for Arts Technology opened 2007, LEED Gold Johnson Hall of Science opened fall 2007. **Environmental Initiatives:** Pledge of climate neutrality. Energy audits of all on and off campus buildings and appropriate retrofits of energy and water efficiency measures. Beginning to re-source our electricity to renewable sources (15% currently) and analyzing a renewable source for our heat.

ADMISSIONS
Freshman Academic Profile: Average high school GPA 3.46. 41.4% in top 10% of high school class, 80.5% in top 25% of high school class, 96.1% in top 50% of high school class. 65% from public high schools. SAT Math middle 50% range 570–650. SAT Critical Reading middle 50% range 570–640. SAT Writing middle 50% range 560–640. ACT middle 50% range 26–29. Minimum paper TOEFL 600. Minimum computer TOEFL 250. **Basis for Candidate Selection:** *Very important factors considered include:* Application essay, academic GPA, recommendation(s), character/personal qualities. *Important factors considered include:* Class rank, rigor of secondary school record, extracurricular activities, interview, racial/ethnic status. *Other factors considered include:* Standardized test scores, alumni/ae relation, first generation, geographical residence, level of applicant's interest, talent/ability, volunteer work, work experience. **Freshman Admission Requirements:** High school diploma is required and GED is accepted. *Academic units recommended:* 4 English, 4 mathematics, 4 science, 4 foreign language, 2 social studies, 2 history. **Freshman Admission Statistics:** 4,715 applied, 39% admitted, 31% enrolled. **Transfer Admission Requirements:** High school transcript, college transcript(s), essay or personal statement, statement of good standing from prior institution(s). Lowest grade transferable C. **General Admission Information:** Application fee $60. Early decision application deadline 11/15. Regular application deadline 2/1. Nonfall registration accepted. Admission may be deferred for a maximum of 1 year. Credit offered for CEEB Advanced Placement tests.

COSTS AND FINANCIAL AID
Average book expense $750. **Required Forms and Deadlines:** FAFSA, noncustodial PROFILE, business/farm supplement. Institution's own financial aid form OR CSS/Financial Aid PROFILE. Financial aid filing deadline 2/1. Priority financial aid filing date 2/1. **Notification of Awards:** Applicants will be notified of awards on or about 3/30. *Types of Aid: Need-based scholarships/grants:* Federal Pell, SEOG, state scholarships/grants, private scholarships, the school's own gift aid. *Loans:* Direct Subsidized Stafford, Direct Unsubsidized Stafford, Direct PLUS, Federal Perkins, college/university loans from institutional funds. *Student Employment:* Federal Work-Study Program available. Institutional employment available. Highest amount earned per year from on-campus jobs $2,000. Off-campus job opportunities are poor. **Financial Aid Statistics:** 66% freshmen, 62% undergrads receive need-based scholarship or grant aid. 11% freshmen, 9% undergrads receive non-need-based scholarship or grant aid. 49% freshmen, 49% undergrads receive need-based self-help aid. 1% freshmen, 2% undergrads receive athletic scholarships. 84.8% freshmen, 82.8% undergrads receive any aid. 74% undergrads borrow to pay for school. Average cumulative indebtedness $31,653. **Criteria for awarding institutional aid:** *Non-need-based:* Academics, alumni affiliation, athletics, leadership, minority status, state/district residency.

See page 1242.

ST. LOUIS COLLEGE OF PHARMACY

4588 Parkview Place, St. Louis, MO 63110
Phone: 314-367-8700
E-mail: pkulage@stlcop.edu **CEEB Code:** 6626
Fax: 314-446-8310 **Website:** www.stlcop.edu **ACT Code:** 2346

This private school was founded in 1864. It has a 7-acre campus.

RATINGS
Admissions Selectivity Rating: 80   **Fire Safety Rating:** 60*   **Green Rating:** 60*

STUDENTS AND FACULTY
Student Body: 21% out-of-state.
Retention and Graduation: Faculty: Student/faculty ratio 13:1. 64 full-time faculty, 91% hold PhDs, 59% are women.

ACADEMICS
Degrees: First professional, master's. **Career services:** Alumni services, internships.

FACILITIES
Housing: Coed dorms, fraternity/sorority housing, apartments for single students.

CAMPUS LIFE
Activities: Choral groups, concert band, drama/theater, literary magazine, musical theater, student government, student newspaper, campus ministries. **Organizations:** 2 honor societies, 6 religious organizations. 5 fraternities. **Athletics (Intercollegiate):** *Men:* Basketball, cheerleading, cross-country. *Women:* Cheerleading, cross-country, volleyball.

ADMISSIONS
Freshman Academic Profile: Average high school GPA 3.4. 20% in top 10% of high school class, 35% in top 25% of high school class, 98% in top 50% of high school class. SAT Math middle 50% range 628–687. SAT Critical Reading middle 50% range 536–562. ACT middle 50% range 25–26. Minimum paper TOEFL 550. **Basis for Candidate Selection:** *Very important factors considered include:* Rigor of secondary school record, standardized test scores. *Important factors considered include:* Class rank. *Other factors considered include:* Application essay, recommendation(s), alumni/ae relation, character/personal qualities, extracurricular activities, volunteer work, work experience. **Freshman Admission Requirements:** High school diploma is required and GED is accepted. *Academic units required:* 4 English, 3 mathematics, 2 science, (2 science labs). *Academic units recommended:* 3 science. **Freshman Admission Statistics:** 356 applied, 80% admitted, 59% enrolled. **Transfer Admission Requirements:** College transcript(s), essay or personal statement, standardized test scores, minimum college GPA of 3.0 required. Lowest grade transferable C. **General Admission Information:** Application fee $35. Regular application deadline 4/2. Notification on a rolling basis, beginning on or about 9/2. Nonfall registration accepted. Credit offered for CEEB Advanced Placement tests.

COSTS AND FINANCIAL AID
Average book expense $1,000. **Required Forms and Deadlines:** FAFSA, institution's own financial aid form. Priority financial aid filing date 3/2. **Notification of Awards:** Applicants will be notified of awards on a rolling basis beginning 2/19. **Types of Aid:** *Need-based scholarships/grants:* Federal Pell, SEOG, state scholarships/grants, private scholarships, the school's own gift aid. *Loans:* FFEL Subsidized Stafford, FFEL Unsubsidized Stafford, FFEL PLUS, Federal Perkins, Health Professions Loan. *Student Employment:* Federal Work-Study Program available. Institutional employment available. Highest amount earned per year from on-campus jobs $800. Off-campus job opportunities are excellent. **Financial Aid Statistics: Criteria for awarding institutional aid:** *Non-need-based:* Job skills, state/district residency.

ST. MARY'S COLLEGE OF MARYLAND

Admissions Office—18952 E. Fisher Rd, St. Marys City, MD 20686-3001
Phone: 240-895-5000 **Financial Aid Phone:** 240-895-3000
E-mail: admissions@smcm.edu **CEEB Code:** 5601
Fax: 240-895-5001 **Website:** www.smcm.edu **ACT Code:** 1736

This public school was founded in 1840. It has a 319-acre campus.

RATINGS
Admissions Selectivity Rating: 91   **Fire Safety Rating:** 77   **Green Rating:** 89

STUDENTS AND FACULTY
Enrollment: 1,978. **Student Body:** 57% female, 43% male, 19% out-of-state, 2% international (38 countries represented). Asian 4%, African American 8%, Caucasian 77%, Hispanic 4%, Native American 1%.
Retention and Graduation: 91% freshmen return for sophomore year. 71% freshmen graduate within 4 years. 34% grads go on to further study within 1 year. 28% grads pursue arts and sciences degrees. 3% grads pursue law degrees. 1% grads pursue business degrees. 2% grads pursue medical degrees. **Faculty:** Student/faculty ratio 11.878:1. 142 full-time faculty, 98% hold PhDs, 15% are are members of minority groups, 46% are women.

ACADEMICS
Degrees: Bachelor's, master's. **Classes:** Most classes have 10–19 students. Most lab/discussion sessions have 10–19 students. **Majors with Highest Enrollment:** Biology/biological sciences; English language and literature; psychology. **Special Study Options:** Double major, dual enrollment, exchange student program (domestic), honors program, independent study, internships, student-designed major, study abroad, teacher certification program. **Honors programs:** Nitze Scholars Program Special programs offered to physically disabled students include note-taking services, reader services, tape recorders, tutors. **Career services:** Alumni network, alumni services, career/job search classes, career assessment, internships, regional alumni. **Career services highlights include:** Our rigorous credit internship program supports students' academic and career goals through the availability of part- to full-time work-learning experiences in the local community and beyond.

FACILITIES
Housing: Coed dorms, special housing for disabled students, men's dorms, women's dorms, apartments for single students, wellness housing, theme housing. There are a variety of different housing options at SMCM. Townhouses for upper-class students as well as suites are offered. There is also special interest housing (ex. SAFE house which is substance and alcohol free housing) and living learning centers (ex. international house, Women in Science House (WiSH), eco-house). 95% of campus accessible to physically disabled. **Special Academic Facilities/Equipment:** Art gallery, archaeological sites, Historic St. Mary's City, historic state house of early Maryland settlers, electron microscope, freshwater and saltwater research facilities, research boat. **Computers:** 100% of classrooms, 20% of dorms, 100% of libraries, 100% of dining areas, 100% of student union, 100% of common outdoor areas have wireless network access. Students can register for classes online. Administrative functions (other than registration) can be performed online.

CAMPUS LIFE
Environment: Rural. **Activities:** Choral groups, dance, drama/theater, jazz band, literary magazine, music ensembles, musical theater, radio station, student government, student newspaper, symphony orchestra, television station, yearbook, campus ministries, international student organization. **Organizations:** 117 registered organizations, 8 honor societies, 4 religious organizations. **Athletics (Intercollegiate):** *Men:* Baseball, basketball, cross-country, lacrosse, sailing, soccer, swimming, tennis. *Women:* Basketball, cross-country, field hockey, lacrosse, sailing, soccer, swimming, tennis, volleyball. **On-Campus Highlights:** Student Center, Library, Athletics and Recreation Center (ARC), Waterfront, Garden of Remembrance. **Environmental Initiatives:** In 2007, students voted overwhelmingly (94%) to increase student fees $25 to purchase renewable energy credits (RECs) to offset 100% of purchased electrical consumption of the school each year, decreasing net emissions by 12,000 metric tons of CO_2, 40% of emissions. In the same year, SGA (Student Government Association) donated $65,000 which went towards a geothermal HVAC system in the new, environmentally designed River Center, preventing the emissions of 33 passenger cars annually. Students continue to be a driving force behind the College's sustainability initiatives. From 2005–2007, the college completed a $2.8 million energy performance contract (EPC) which saved the college 20% of its electric, oil, and water consumption. We are now beginning the process

of another EPC that will again cut consumption by at least 20%. In addition to these large projects, smaller in-house renovations and energy conservation programs have yielded big dividends for the campus and environment. St. Mary's pioneered Maryland's first major public LEED-certified building, Goodpastor Hall, which uses 40% less energy than a conventional building and saves over 300,000 gallons of water each year. All new buildings have been designed and constructed in this vein as this, with all new construction and major renovations being LEED Silver (or comparable) or better.

ADMISSIONS

Freshman Academic Profile: Average high school GPA 3.78. 47% in top 10% of high school class, 78% in top 25% of high school class, 95% in top 50% of high school class. 70% from public high schools. SAT Math middle 50% range 550–650. SAT Critical Reading middle 50% range 580–690. SAT Writing middle 50% range 560–670. ACT middle 50% range 24–29. Minimum paper TOEFL 550. Minimum computer TOEFL 250. Minimum web-based TOEFL 90. **Basis for Candidate Selection:** *Very important factors considered include:* Academic GPA, rigor of secondary school record. *Important factors considered include:* Application essay, recommendation(s), standardized test scores, extracurricular activities, first generation, talent/ability, volunteer work. *Other factors considered include:* Alumni/ae relation, geographical residence, interview, racial/ethnic status, state residency, work experience. **Freshman Admission Requirements:** High school diploma is required and GED is accepted. *Academic units required:* 4 English, 3 mathematics, 3 science, (2 science labs), 2 foreign language, 2 social studies, 1 history, 3 *Academic units recommended:* 4 mathematics, 4 foreign language, 2 history. **Freshman Admission Statistics:** 2,411 applied, 57% admitted, 35% enrolled. **Transfer Admission Requirements:** College transcript(s), essay or personal statement, minimum college GPA of 3.0 required. Lowest grade transferable C–. **General Admission Information:** Application fee $50. Early decision application deadline 11/1. Regular application deadline 1/1. Regular notification 4/1. Nonfall registration accepted. Credit and/or placement offered for CEEB Advanced Placement tests.

COSTS AND FINANCIAL AID

Annual in-state tuition $11,325. Annual out-of-state tuition $22,718. Room and board $10,245. Required fees $2,305. Average book expense $1,000. **Required Forms and Deadlines:** FAFSA Financial aid filing deadline 3/1. Priority financial aid filing date 2/15. **Notification of Awards:** Applicants will be notified of awards on or about 4/1. **Types of Aid:** *Need-based scholarships/grants:* Federal Pell, SEOG, state scholarships/grants, private scholarships, the school's own gift aid. *Loans:* FFEL Subsidized Stafford, FFEL Unsubsidized Stafford, FFEL PLUS, Federal Perkins. *Student Employment:* Federal Work-Study Program available. Institutional employment available. Highest amount earned per year from on-campus jobs $1,100. Off-campus job opportunities are good. **Financial Aid Statistics:** 17% freshmen, 19% undergrads receive need-based scholarship or grant aid. 17% freshmen, 19% undergrads receive non-need-based scholarship or grant aid. 17% freshmen, 19% undergrads receive need-based self-help aid. 59% freshmen, 61% undergrads receive any aid. 70% undergrads borrow to pay for school. Average cumulative indebtedness $17,125. **Criteria for awarding institutional aid:** *Non-need-based:* Academics, alumni affiliation.

See page 1224.

ST. MARY'S UNIVERSITY

One Camino Santa Maria, San Antonio, TX 78228-8503
Phone: 210-436-3126 **Financial Aid Phone:** 210-436-3141
E-mail: uadm@stmarytx.edu **CEEB Code:** 6637
Fax: 210-431-6742 **Website:** www.stmarytx.edu **ACT Code:** 4158

This private school, affiliated with the Roman Catholic Church, was founded in 1852. It has a 135-acre campus.

RATINGS
Admissions Selectivity Rating: 82   **Fire Safety Rating:** 75   **Green Rating:** 65

STUDENTS AND FACULTY
Enrollment: 2,369. **Student Body:** 60% female, 40% male, 4.6% out-of-state, 3% international (19 countries represented). Asian 3%, African American 4%, Caucasian 19%, Hispanic 70%.
Retention and Graduation: 80% freshmen return for sophomore year. 31% freshmen graduate within 4 years. **Faculty:** Student/faculty ratio 13:1. 197 full-time faculty, 92% hold PhDs, 18% are are members of minority groups, 34% are women.

ACADEMICS
Degrees: Bachelor's, master's. **Classes:** Most classes have 20–29 students. Most lab/discussion sessions have 20–29 students. **Majors with Highest**

Enrollment: Biology/biological sciences; political science and government; psychology. **Special Study Options:** Cross-registration, distance learning, double major, dual enrollment, English as a Second Language (ESL), exchange student program (domestic), honors program, independent study, internships, liberal arts/career combination, study abroad, teacher certification program, Evening Studies Program. **Honors programs:** The Honors Program offers an academically challenging and personally enriching course of study designed to cultivate critical analysis, clear oral and written expression, aesthetic awareness and ethical judgment. In and out of the classroom we seek to prepare our future graduates for lives of leadership and service to their communities. **Combined degree programs:** BA/MA, BPhil/MDiv. Special programs offered to physically disabled students include note-taking services, reader services, tape recorders, tutors. **Career services:** Alumni network, alumni services, career/job search classes, career assessment, internships, regional alumni.

FACILITIES
Housing: Coed dorms, Science Learning, Living Community; residence hall for students 22 years old or above/non traditional. 80% of campus accessible to physically disabled. **Computers:** 100% of classrooms, 100% of dorms, 100% of libraries, 100% of dining areas, 100% of student union, 80% of common outdoor areas have wireless network access. Students can register for classes online. Administrative functions (other than registration) can be performed online. Undergraduates are required to own a computer.

CAMPUS LIFE
Environment: Metropolis. **Activities:** Choral groups, concert band, dance, drama/theater, jazz band, literary magazine, music ensembles, musical theater, pep band, student government, student newspaper, campus ministries, international student organization. **Organizations:** 91 registered organizations, 1 religious organizations. 4 fraternities, 4 sororities. **Athletics (Intercollegiate):** *Men:* Baseball, basketball, cheerleading, golf, soccer, tennis. *Women:* Basketball, cheerleading, cross-country, golf, soccer, softball, tennis, volleyball. **On-Campus Highlights:** Alumni Athletics and Convocation Center, University Center, Java City Coffee Shop, The Quad, Barrett Memorial Bell Tower, Pecan Grove and the new 278-bed Founders Hall round out the list of popular campus spots. Founders Hall opened in fall 2009. Designed for freshmen, it provides spacious rooms, welcoming indoor and outdoor common spaces, and a cyber cafe. **Environmental Initiatives:** Energy efficiency electric motors, chillers, lighting. Water conservation pilot program (Recycling).

ADMISSIONS
Freshman Academic Profile: Average high school GPA 3.42. 33.48% in top 10% of high school class, 65.87% in top 25% of high school class, 87.47% in top 50% of high school class. 78.2% from public high schools. SAT Math middle 50% range 470–590. SAT Critical Reading middle 50% range 470–570. SAT Writing middle 50% range 460–560. ACT middle 50% range 20–25. Minimum paper TOEFL 550. Minimum computer TOEFL 213. Minimum web-based TOEFL 80. **Basis for Candidate Selection:** *Very important factors considered include:* Academic GPA, rigor of secondary school record. *Important factors considered include:* Class rank, standardized test scores. *Other factors considered include:* Application essay, recommendation(s), alumni/ae relation, character/personal qualities, extracurricular activities, geographical residence, interview, talent/ability, volunteer work, work experience. **Freshman Admission Requirements:** High school diploma is required and GED is accepted. *Academic units required:* 4 English, 3 mathematics, 3 science, 2 foreign language, 3 social studies, 1 academic electives. *Academic units recommended:* 4 English, 4 mathematics, 4 science, 3 foreign language, 4 social studies. **Freshman Admission Statistics:** 2,448 applied, 76% admitted, 29% enrolled. **Transfer Admission Requirements:** College transcript(s), minimum college GPA of 2.5 required. Lowest grade transferable C–. **General Admission Information:** Application fee $30. Notification on a rolling basis, beginning on or about 10/20. Nonfall registration accepted. Admission may be deferred for a maximum of 1 year. Credit and/or placement offered for CEEB Advanced Placement tests.

COSTS AND FINANCIAL AID
Required Forms and Deadlines: FAFSA. Priority financial aid filing date 3/31. **Notification of Awards:** Applicants will be notified of awards on a rolling basis beginning 3/1. **Types of Aid:** *Need-based scholarships/grants:* Federal Pell, SEOG, state scholarships/grants, private scholarships, the school's own gift aid. *Loans:* Direct Subsidized Stafford, Direct Unsubsidized Stafford, Direct PLUS, Federal Perkins, state loans *Student Employment:* Federal Work-Study Program available. Institutional employment available. Off-campus job opportunities are good. **Financial Aid Statistics:** 78% freshmen, 75% undergrads receive need-based scholarship or grant aid. 67% freshmen, 53% undergrads receive non-need-based scholarship or grant aid. 72% freshmen, 71% undergrads receive need-based self-help aid. 8% freshmen, 7% undergrads receive athletic scholarships. 96% freshmen, 91% undergrads receive any aid. 79% undergrads borrow to pay for school. Average cumulative indebtedness $27,416. **Criteria for awarding institutional aid:** *Non-need-based:* Academics, alumni affiliation, athletics, leadership, minority status, music/drama, state/district residency.

ST. NORBERT COLLEGE

100 Grant Street, De Pere, WI 54115-2099
Phone: 920-403-3005 **Financial Aid Phone:** 920-403-3071
E-mail: admit@snc.edu **CEEB Code:** 1706
Fax: 920-403-4072 **Website:** www.snc.edu **ACT Code:** 4644

This private school, affiliated with the Roman Catholic Church, was founded in 1898. It has a 93-acre campus.

RATINGS
Admissions Selectivity Rating: 78 **Fire Safety Rating:** 70 **Green Rating:** 79

STUDENTS AND FACULTY
Enrollment: 2,060. **Student Body:** 58% female, 42% male, 27% out-of-state, 4% international (31 countries represented). Asian 1%, African American 1%, Caucasian 90%, Hispanic 2%.
Retention and Graduation: 80% freshmen return for sophomore year. 64% freshmen graduate within 4 years. 19% grads go on to further study within 1 year. **Faculty:** Student/faculty ratio 14:1. 134 full-time faculty, 87% hold PhDs, 7% are are members of minority groups, 43% are women.

ACADEMICS
Degrees: Bachelor's, master's. **Classes:** Most classes have 10–19 students. Most lab/discussion sessions have 10–19 students. **Majors with Highest Enrollment:** Business/commerce; communication studies/speech communication and rhetoric; elementary education and teaching. **Special Study Options:** Distance learning, double major, English as a Second Language (ESL), honors program, independent study, internships, student-designed major, study abroad, teacher certification program, Foundation for International Education (London)Internships; Washington Semester. **Honors programs:** The Honors Program at St. Norbert College offers a sophisticated and demanding program of studies and readings to provide the most academically talented students with an enriched academic curriculum that is stimulating and challenging. Special programs offered to physically disabled students include note-taking services, reader services, tape recorders, tutors. **Career services:** Alumni network, alumni services, career assessment, internships, regional alumni. **Career services highlights include:** Students can begin internships on campus or off campus after their freshmen year. Strong emphasis is placed on learning contracts.

FACILITIES
Housing: Coed dorms, special housing for disabled students, special housing for international students, women's dorms, fraternity/sorority housing, apartments for single students, townhouses, off-campus college owned housing. 72% of campus accessible to physically disabled. **Special Academic Facilities/Equipment:** New state-of-the-art Mulva Library, Center for leadership and service, Bush Art Center with three art galleries, scanning electron microscope, visual and performing arts center, center for international education, riverfront campus center with marina, peace and justice center, career services, children's center in cooperation with early childhood education, center of economic education,survey center, Kress Inn, conference services, academic support services, St. Joseph Church, chapels in residence halls, women's center and Journey-Men (men's center). **Computers:** 100% of classrooms, 60% of dorms, 100% of libraries, 100% of dining areas, 100% of student union, have wireless network access. Students can register for classes online. Administrative functions (other than registration) can be performed online.

CAMPUS LIFE
Environment: Village. **Activities:** Choral groups, concert band, drama/theater, jazz band, literary magazine, music ensembles, musical theater, pep band, radio station, student government, student newspaper, student-run film society, television station, campus ministries, international student organization. **Organizations:** 63 registered organizations, 10 honor societies, 3 religious organizations. 3 fraternities, 4 sororities. **Athletics (Intercollegiate):** *Men:* Baseball, basketball, cross-country, football, golf, ice hockey, soccer, tennis, track/field (outdoor), track/field (indoor). *Women:* Basketball, cross-country, golf, ice hockey, soccer, softball, tennis, track/field (outdoor), track/field (indoor), volleyball. **On-Campus Highlights:** The Ray Van Den Heuvel Campus Center, The Bush Fine Arts Center, The F.K. Bemis International Center, Austin E Cofrin Hall, New Mulva Library with Coffee Shop. **Environmental Initiatives:** Designed new Mulva Library with solar water heating system. Converting all campus outdoor lighting to meet "night sky" compliance. Plan and design of future science building will meet Gold standards of LEED certification.

ADMISSIONS
Freshman Academic Profile: Average high school GPA 3.42. 24% in top 10% of high school class, 53% in top 25% of high school class, 86% in top 50% of high school class. 75% from public high schools. ACT middle 50% range 21–26.

Minimum paper TOEFL 550. Minimum web-based TOEFL 80. **Basis for Candidate Selection:** *Very important factors considered include:* Academic GPA, standardized test scores. *Important factors considered include:* Rigor of secondary school record. *Other factors considered include:* Class rank, application essay, recommendation(s), alumni/ae relation, character/personal qualities, extracurricular activities, first generation, geographical residence, interview, level of applicant's interest, racial/ethnic status, religious affiliation/commitment, state residency, talent/ability, volunteer work, work experience. **Freshman Admission Requirements:** High school diploma is required and GED is accepted. *Academic units recommended:* 4 English, 3 mathematics, 3 science, (3 science labs), 2 foreign language, 2 social studies, 2 history. **Freshman Admission Statistics:** 2,024 applied, 83% admitted, 32% enrolled. **Transfer Admission Requirements:** High school transcript, college transcript(s), essay or personal statement, standardized test scores, minimum college GPA of 2.5 required. Lowest grade transferable C. **General Admission Information:** Application fee $25. Notification on a rolling basis, beginning on or about 10/1. Nonfall registration accepted. Admission may be deferred for a maximum of 2 years. Credit and/or placement offered for CEEB Advanced Placement tests.

COSTS AND FINANCIAL AID
Annual tuition $26,522. Room and board $7,052. Required fees $450. Average book expense $900. **Required Forms and Deadlines:** FAFSA. Priority financial aid filing date 3/1. **Notification of Awards:** Applicants will be notified of awards on a rolling basis beginning 3/15. **Types of Aid:** *Need-based scholarships/grants:* Federal Pell, SEOG, state scholarships/grants, private scholarships, the school's own gift aid. *Loans:* Direct Subsidized Stafford, Direct Unsubsidized Stafford, Direct PLUS, Federal Perkins, state loans, college/university loans from institutional funds. *Student Employment:* Federal Work-Study Program available. Institutional employment available. Off-campus job opportunities are good. **Financial Aid Statistics:** 67% freshmen, 63% undergrads receive need-based scholarship or grant aid. 2% freshmen, 2% undergrads receive non-need-based scholarship or grant aid. 56% freshmen, 53% undergrads receive need-based self-help aid. 95% freshmen, 97% undergrads receive any aid. 83% undergrads borrow to pay for school. Average cumulative indebtedness $28,209. **Criteria for awarding institutional aid:** *Non-need-based:* Academics, art, leadership, minority status, music/drama, state/district residency.

ST. OLAF COLLEGE

1520 St. Olaf Avenue, Northfield, MN 55057
Phone: 507-786-3025 **Financial Aid Phone:** 507-786-3019
E-mail: admissions@stolaf.edu **CEEB Code:** 6638
Fax: 507-786-3832 **Website:** www.stolaf.edu **ACT Code:** 2150

This private school, affiliated with the Lutheran Church, was founded in 1874. It has a 300-acre campus.

RATINGS
Admissions Selectivity Rating: 60* **Fire Safety Rating:** 60* **Green Rating:** 60*

STUDENTS AND FACULTY
Enrollment: 3,033. **Student Body:** 55% female, 45% male, 46% out-of-state, 2% international (26 countries represented). Asian 5%, African American 2%, Caucasian 85%, Hispanic 2%.
Retention and Graduation: 93% freshmen return for sophomore year. 82% freshmen graduate within 4 years. 31% grads go on to further study within 1 year. 15% grads pursue arts and sciences degrees. 2% grads pursue law degrees. 6% grads pursue medical degrees. **Faculty:** Student/faculty ratio 12:1. 207 full-time faculty, 90% hold PhDs, 11% are are members of minority groups, 44% are women.

ACADEMICS
Degrees: Bachelor's. **Classes:** Most classes have 10–19 students. Most lab/discussion sessions have 20–29 students. **Majors with Highest Enrollment:** Biology/biological sciences; economics; English language and literature. **Special Study Options:** Cross-registration, double major, dual enrollment, independent study, internships, student-designed major, study abroad, teacher certification program. **Combined degree programs:** Law w/Columbia University. Special programs offered to physically disabled students include note-taking services, reader services, tape recorders, tutors. **Career services:** Alumni network, alumni services, career/job search classes, career assessment, internships, regional alumni, **Career services highlights include:** The Center for Expe-

riential Learning is proud of creating a comprehensive service that is linked to the academic program and offers many types of experiences to complement students' academic programs. The CEL houses four programs: internships, service and civic leadership, entrepreneurial studies, and career services. The CEL has been bery successful in creating programming that meets the needs of students during their four years at St. Olaf. Some programs of which we are proud: entrepreneurial grants to start student-run businesses, service trips, civic engagement initiatives connected to specific courses, career-related seminars preseented in collaboration with academic departments, case study challenges created in conjunction with our corporate partners. Our academic internship program offers students an opportunity to receive credit for experiential learning. Since 2000, there have been over 900 Academic Internships completed by St. Olaf students at over 700 different organizations world wide.

FACILITIES

Housing: Coed dorms, special housing for disabled students, theme housing Honor houses, language houses, quiet halls, first-year only dorms. Disabled students accommodated in dorm of their choice. 80% of campus accessible to physically disabled. **Special Academic Facilities/Equipment:** Finstad Program for Entrepreneurial Studies, Kierkegaard Library, Flaten Art Museum, Norwegian American Historical Association archives. **Computers:** 100% of classrooms, 100% of dorms, 100% of libraries, 100% of dining areas, 100% of student union, 100% of common outdoor areas have wireless network access. Students can register for classes online. Administrative functions (other than registration) can be performed online.

CAMPUS LIFE

Environment: Village. **Activities:** Choral groups, concert band, dance, drama/theater, jazz band, literary magazine, music ensembles, musical theater, opera, pep band, radio station, student government, student newspaper, student-run film society, symphony orchestra, television station, campus ministries, international student organization, Model UN. **Organizations:** 193 registered organizations, 18 honor societies, 16 religious organizations. **Athletics (Intercollegiate): Men:** Baseball, basketball, cross-country, diving, football, golf, ice hockey, skiing (downhill/alpine), skiing (nordic cross-country), soccer, swimming, tennis, track/field (outdoor), track/field (indoor), wrestling. *Women:* Basketball, cross-country, diving, golf, ice hockey, skiing (downhill/alpine), skiing (nordic cross-country), soccer, softball, swimming, tennis, track/field (outdoor), track/field (indoor), volleyball. **On-Campus Highlights:** Regents Hall of Natural Science & Math, Buntrock Commons, Tostrud Recreation Center, The Lion's Pause, Dittman Art Museum, Beautiful 300 acre campus. **Environmental Initiatives:** St. Olaf College's Regents Hall of Natural and Mathematical Sciences has earned platinum certification—the highest rating attainable—from the U.S. Green Building Council's Leadership in Energy and Environmental Design (LEED) rating system. (2009) Self-generating renewable power. A 1.65 wind turbine that feeds the campus distribution directly, with provisions for flowing excess power to the "grid." Infrastructure is in place to add two identical units which would produce kwh equal to all those consumed in 2007. Weekly diversion of 3.5 tons of food waste to on campus composting, and incorporation of compost into grounds and student food producing operations.

ADMISSIONS

Freshman Academic Profile: Average high school GPA 3.63. 53% in top 10% of high school class, 82% in top 25% of high school class, 98% in top 50% of high school class. 82% from public high schools. SAT Math middle 50% range 590–690. SAT Critical Reading middle 50% range 590–710. ACT middle 50% range 26–31. Minimum paper TOEFL 550. Minimum computer TOEFL 213. **Basis for Candidate Selection:** *Very important factors considered include:* Application essay, academic GPA, rigor of secondary school record. *Important factors considered include:* Class rank, recommendation(s), standardized test scores, character/personal qualities, extracurricular activities. *Other factors considered include:* Alumni/ae relation, first generation, geographical residence, interview, level of applicant's interest, racial/ethnic status, religious affiliation/commitment, state residency, talent/ability, volunteer work, work experience. **Freshman Admission Requirements:** High school diploma is required and GED is accepted. *Academic units recommended:* 4 English, 4 mathematics, 4 science, (2 science labs), 4 foreign language, 4 social studies. **Freshman Admission Statistics:** 3,882 applied, 57% admitted, 35% enrolled. **Transfer Admission Requirements:** High school transcript, college transcript(s), essay or personal statement, standardized test scores, statement of good standing from prior institution(s). Minimum college GPA of 2.50 required. Lowest grade transferable C. **General Admission Information:** Application fee $40. Early decision application deadline 11/15. Regular notification 3/20. Nonfall registration not accepted. Admission may be deferred for a maximum of 1 year. Credit and/or placement offered for CEEB Advanced Placement tests.

COSTS AND FINANCIAL AID

Required Forms and Deadlines: FAFSA, CSS/Financial Aid PROFILE, noncustodial PROFILE, business/farm supplement. Financial aid filing deadline 4/15. Priority financial aid filing date 1/15. **Notification of Awards:** Applicants will be notified of awards on a rolling basis beginning 3/1. **Types of**

Aid: *Need-based scholarships/grants:* Federal Pell, SEOG, state scholarships/grants, private scholarships, the school's own gift aid. *Loans:* FFEL Subsidized Stafford, FFEL Unsubsidized Stafford, FFEL PLUS, Federal Perkins, Federal Nursing, state loans, college/university loans from institutional funds. *Student Employment:* Federal Work-Study Program available. Off-campus job opportunities are fair. **Financial Aid Statistics:** 64% freshmen, 65% undergrads receive need-based scholarship or grant aid. 31% freshmen, 30% undergrads receive non-need-based scholarship or grant aid. 64% freshmen, 65% undergrads receive need-based self-help aid. 86% freshmen, 86% undergrads receive any aid. 65% undergrads borrow to pay for school. Average cumulative indebtedness $25,273. **Criteria for awarding institutional aid:** *Non-need-based:* Academics, leadership, music/drama.

ST. THOMAS UNIVERSITY (FL)

16401 Northwest 37th Avenue, Miami Gardens, FL 33054
Phone: 305-628-6546 **Financial Aid Phone:** 305-628-6547
E-mail: signup@stu.edu **CEEB Code:** 5076
Fax: 305-628-6591 **Website:** www.stu.edu **ACT Code:** 719

This private school, affiliated with the Roman Catholic Church, was founded in 1961. It has a 140-acre campus.

RATINGS

Admissions Selectivity Rating: 60+   **Fire Safety Rating:** 90   **Green Rating:** 74

STUDENTS AND FACULTY

Enrollment: 1,176. **Student Body:** 56% female, 44% male, 15% out-of-state, 9% international (57 countries represented). Asian 1%, African American 25%, Caucasian 7%, Hispanic 48%.
Retention and Graduation: 69% freshmen return for sophomore year. 27% freshmen graduate within 4 years. **Faculty:** Student/faculty ratio 13:1. 100 full-time faculty, 83% hold PhDs, 29% are are members of minority groups, 43% are women.

ACADEMICS

Degrees: Bachelor's, certificate, master's, post-bachelor's certificate, post-master's certificate. **Classes:** Most classes have 10–19 students. Most lab/discussion sessions have 10–19 students. **Majors with Highest Enrollment:** Business administration and management; organizational behavior studies; psychology. **Special Study Options:** Distance learning, double major, dual enrollment, honors program, independent study, internships, liberal arts/career combination, teacher certification program. **Honors programs:** The St. Thomas University Honors Program is designed to provide an intensive and stimulating alternative for students who wish to enhance their college academic experience. Qualified students are offered the opportunity to take Honors courses in the subjects of their choice, and, if they desire, to work for an Honors degree. **Combined degree programs:** BA/JD Special programs offered to physically disabled students include note-taking services, reader services, tape recorders, tutors. **Career services:** Career/job search classes, career assessment, internships.

FACILITIES

Housing: Men's dorms, women's dorms 80% of campus accessible to physically disabled. **Special Academic Facilities/Equipment:** Multimedia computer equipment, TV studio, Art Atrium Gallery. **Computers:** 100% of libraries, 100% of dining areas, have wireless network access. Students can register for classes online. Administrative functions (other than registration) can be performed online.

CAMPUS LIFE

Environment: Metropolis. **Activities:** Choral groups, literary magazine, music ensembles, student government, television station, yearbook, campus ministries, international student organization. **Organizations:** 26 registered organizations, 4 honor societies, 2 religious organizations. **Athletics (Intercollegiate):** *Men:* Baseball, basketball, cross-country, golf, soccer, tennis. *Women:* Basketball, cross-country, soccer, softball, tennis, volleyball. **On-Campus Highlights:** Campus Chapel, Library, Fernandez Family Center, Kennedy Hall.

ADMISSIONS

Freshman Academic Profile: SAT Math middle 50% range 382.5–480. SAT Critical Reading middle 50% range 390–480. SAT Writing middle 50% range 380–470. ACT middle 50% range 16–19.25. Minimum paper TOEFL 525. Minimum computer TOEFL 193. **Basis for Candidate Selection:** *Very important factors considered include:* Class rank, academic GPA, standardized test scores. *Important factors considered include:* Application essay, recommendation(s), rigor of secondary school record, alumni/ae relation, level of applicant's interest. *Other factors considered include:* Character/personal qualities, extracurricular activities, talent/ability, volunteer work, work experience. **Freshman Admission Requirements:** High school diploma is required and GED is accepted. *Academic units required:* 4 English, 3 mathematics, 2 science, 3 social studies, 6 academic electives. **Freshman Admission Statistics:** 674 applied, 59% admitted, 60% enrolled. **Transfer Admission Requirements:** College transcript(s), essay or personal statement, statement of good standing from prior institution(s). Minimum college GPA of 2.0 required. Lowest grade transferable C–. **General Admission Information:** Application fee $40. Nonfall registration accepted. Admission may be deferred for a maximum of 1 year. Credit and/or placement offered for CEEB Advanced Placement tests.

COSTS AND FINANCIAL AID

Required Forms and Deadlines: FAFSA, state aid form. Priority financial aid filing date 4/1. **Notification of Awards:** Applicants will be notified of awards on a rolling basis beginning 3/1. **Types of Aid:** *Need-based scholarships/grants:* Federal Pell, SEOG, state scholarships/grants, private scholarships, the school's own gift aid. *Loans:* FFEL Subsidized Stafford, FFEL Unsubsidized Stafford, FFEL PLUS, Federal Perkins. *Student Employment:* Federal Work-Study Program available. Institutional employment available. Off-campus job opportunities are good. **Financial Aid Statistics:** 61% freshmen, 53% undergrads receive need-based scholarship or grant aid. 83% freshmen, 70% undergrads receive non-need-based scholarship or grant aid. 50% freshmen, 51% undergrads receive need-based self-help aid. 14% freshmen, 12% undergrads receive athletic scholarships. **Criteria for awarding institutional aid:** *Non-need-based:* Academics, athletics, leadership.

ST. THOMAS UNIVERSITY (NB)

Admissions Office, St. Thomas University, Fredericton, NB E3B 5G3 Canada
Phone: 506-452-0532
E-mail: admissions@stu.ca
Fax: 506-452-0617 **Website:** www.stu.ca

This private school, affiliated with the Roman Catholic Church, was founded in 1910. It has a 21-acre campus.

RATINGS
Admissions Selectivity Rating: 64   **Fire Safety Rating:** 60*   **Green Rating:** 60*

STUDENTS AND FACULTY
Enrollment: 2,475. **Student Body:** 66% female, 34% male, 27% out-of-state, 5% international (42 countries represented).
Retention and Graduation: 69% freshmen return for sophomore year. 41% freshmen graduate within 4 years. **Faculty:** Student/faculty ratio 19:1. 109 full-time faculty, 95% hold PhDs, 39% are women.

ACADEMICS
Degrees: Bachelor's, certificate, first professional, post-bachelor's certificate. **Classes:** Most classes have 10–19 students. **Majors with Highest Enrollment:** Criminology; English language and literature; psychology. **Special Study Options:** Accelerated program, cross-registration, double major, English as a Second Language (ESL), exchange student program (domestic), honors program, independent study, student-designed major, study abroad, teacher certification program, Aquinas Program: Thematically linked courses from various disciplines. Special programs offered to physically disabled students include note-taking services, reader services, tape recorders, tutors. **Career services:** Career/job search classes, career assessment, internships.

FACILITIES
Housing: Coed dorms, women's dorms. 80% of campus accessible to physically disabled. **Computers:** 100% of dorms, 100% of libraries, 100% of dining areas, have wireless network access. Students can register for classes online. Administrative functions (other than registration) can be performed online.

CAMPUS LIFE
Environment: Town. **Activities:** Choral groups, drama/theater, jazz band, music ensembles, musical theater, radio station, student government, student newspaper, student-run film society, yearbook, campus ministries, international student organization, Model UN. **Organizations:** 5 religious organizations. **Athletics (Intercollegiate):** *Men:* Basketball, cross-country, golf, ice hockey, rugby, soccer, volleyball. *Women:* Basketball, cross-country, golf, ice hockey, rugby, soccer, volleyball. **On-Campus Highlights:** Margaret Norrie McCain Hall, Lower courtyard, J.B. O'Keefe Fitness Centre, Sir James Dunn Hall, The Black Box Theatre. **Environmental Initiatives:** Recycle bins in all areas. Reduction of plastic and styrofoam products in cafeteria. Promotion of reduced energy usage.

ADMISSIONS
Freshman Academic Profile: Average high school GPA 3.3. Minimum paper TOEFL 570. Minimum computer TOEFL 230. Minimum web-based TOEFL 88. **Basis for Candidate Selection:** *Very important factors considered include:* Academic GPA. *Other factors considered include:* Application essay, recommendation(s), standardized test scores. **Freshman Admission Requirements:** High school diploma is required and GED is not accepted. **Freshman Admission Statistics:** 1,345 applied, 81% admitted, 58% enrolled. **Transfer Admission Requirements:** College transcript(s), statement of good standing from prior institution(s). Lowest grade transferable D. **General Admission Information:** Application fee $35. Regular application deadline 8/31. Notification on a rolling basis, beginning on or about 10/15. Nonfall registration accepted. Admission may be deferred for a maximum of 1 year. Credit and/or placement offered for CEEB Advanced Placement tests.

COSTS AND FINANCIAL AID
Average book expense $1,000.

STANFORD UNIVERSITY

Best 373

Undergraduate Admission, Montag Hall, Stanford, CA 94305-6106
Phone: 650-723-2091 **Financial Aid Phone:** 650-723-3058
E-mail: admission@stanford.edu **CEEB Code:** 4704
Fax: 650-725-2846 **Website:** www.stanford.edu **ACT Code:** 434

This private school was founded in 1885. It has a 8180-acre campus.

RATINGS
Admissions Selectivity Rating: 99   **Fire Safety Rating:** 81   **Green Rating:** 97

STUDENTS AND FACULTY
Enrollment: 6,564. **Student Body:** 49% female, 51% male, 54% out-of-state, 7% international (87 countries represented). Asian 23%, African American 10%, Caucasian 36%, Hispanic 13%, Native American 3%.
Retention and Graduation: 98% freshmen return for sophomore year. 79% freshmen graduate within 4 years. 29% grads go on to further study within 1 year. 15% grads pursue arts and sciences degrees. 4% grads pursue law degrees. 1% grads pursue business degrees. 9% grads pursue medical degrees. **Faculty:** Student/faculty ratio 6.1:1. 1008 full-time faculty, 99% hold PhDs, 18% are are members of minority groups, 25% are women. 5% of classes are taught by teaching assistants.

ACADEMICS
Degrees: Bachelor's, master's. **Classes:** Most classes have 10–19 students. Most lab/discussion sessions have 10–19 students. **Majors with Highest Enrollment:** Biology/biological sciences; economics; international relations and affairs. **Special Study Options:** Distance learning, double major, exchange student program (domestic), honors program, independent study, internships, student-designed major, study abroad, Marine research center, Bing Stanford in Washington program, exchange programs with Dartmouth, Howard, Morehouse and Spelman, undergraduate research opportunities, Bing Honors College, overseas study. **Honors programs:** About 100 student annually participate in Bing Honors College. About 25 percent of each graduating class earn departmental honors. **Combined degree programs:** BA/MA, many bachelors/masters coterminal degree. Special programs offered to physically disabled students include note-taking services, reader services, tape recorders, tutors. **Career services:** Alumni network, alumni services, career/job search classes, career assessment, internships, regional alumni. **Career services highlights include:** The Haas Center for Public Service at Stanford connects academic study with public service to strengthen communities and develop effective public leaders.

FACILITIES
Housing: Coed dorms, special housing for disabled students, women's dorms, fraternity/sorority housing, apartments for married students, cooperative housing, apartments for single students, theme housing: Academic, cross-cultural, language theme and ethnic theme houses. 98% of campus accessible to physically disabled. **Special Academic Facilities/Equipment:** Art museum, marine station, observatory, biological preserve, linear accelerator. **Computers:** 100% of classrooms, 100% of dorms, 100% of libraries, 100% of dining areas, 100% of student union, 75% of common outdoor areas have wireless network access.

Students can register for classes online. Administrative functions (other than registration) can be performed online.

CAMPUS LIFE

Environment: City. **Activities:** Choral groups, concert band, dance, drama/theater, jazz band, literary magazine, marching band, music ensembles, musical theater, opera, pep band, radio station, student government, student newspaper, student-run film society, symphony orchestra, television station, yearbook, campus ministries, international student organization, Model UN. **Organizations:** 600 registered organizations, 40 religious organizations. 17 fraternities, 11 sororities. **Athletics (Intercollegiate):** *Men:* Baseball, basketball, crew/rowing, cross-country, diving, fencing, football, golf, gymnastics, sailing, soccer, swimming, tennis, track/field (outdoor), volleyball, water polo, wrestling. *Women:* Basketball, crew/rowing, cross-country, diving, fencing, field hockey, golf, gymnastics, lacrosse, sailing, soccer, softball, squash, swimming, synchronized swimming, tennis, track/field (outdoor), volleyball, water polo. **On-Campus Highlights:** Cantor Center for the Visual Arts, Rodin Sculpture Garden, Memorial Church, Observation Deck at Hoover Tower, athletic facilities. The Stanford campus is among the most beautiful anywhere and is a popular destination for tourists and other visitors. **Environmental Initiatives:** $250 million initiative on Sustainability, Climate and Energy infrastucture and implementation. in addition, Stanford has invested $70 million over the past ten years in energy retrofits, recommissioning and energy efficiency projects. The campus reduced campus energy use by 195 million kWh—enough to run Stanford for a year. Water consumption has been reduced from 2.7 million gallons per day to 2.15 million since 2001. New constructions and major renovations have energy Standards comparable to LEED Gold. 2.Stanford's award-winning Transportation Demand Management program has been recognized by the EPA. It includes a free bus system powered by biodiesel and hybid buses; a commute club, free or pre-tax passes on public transportation; car rental options; commute planning assistance; charter services; and a bike program. A smaller percentage of faculty, staff and student commute by single-occupancy vehicle than the national average (51 versus 77%). 3.Stanford's recycling program, recognized by the EPA, diverts 64% of waste from landfills (including contruction and demolition wmaterails), and the goal is to increase the rate to 75%.

ADMISSIONS

Freshman Academic Profile: 91% in top 10% of high school class, 99% in top 25% of high school class, 100% in top 50% of high school class. 60.2% from public high schools. SAT Math middle 50% range 680–780. SAT Critical Reading middle 50% range 660–760. SAT Writing middle 50% range 670–760. ACT middle 50% range 30–34. **Basis for Candidate Selection:** *Very important factors considered include:* Class rank, application essay, academic GPA, recommendation(s), rigor of secondary school record, standardized test scores, character/personal qualities, extracurricular activities, talent/ability. *Other factors considered include:* Alumni/ae relation, first generation, geographical residence, racial/ethnic status, volunteer work, work experience. **Freshman Admission Requirements:** High school diploma is required and GED is accepted. *Academic units recommended:* 4 English, 4 mathematics, 3 science, (3 science labs), 3 foreign language, 2 social studies, 1 history. **Freshman Admission Statistics:** 15,413 applied, 16% admitted, 70% enrolled. **Transfer Admission Requirements:** High school transcript, college transcript(s), essay or personal statement, standardized test scores, statement of good standing from prior institution(s). Lowest grade transferable C–. **General Admission Information:** Application fee $90. Regular application deadline 1/1. Regular notification 4/1. Nonfall registration not accepted. Admission may be deferred for a maximum of 2 years. Credit and/or placement offered for CEEB Advanced Placement tests.

COSTS AND FINANCIAL AID

Annual tuition $37,380. Room and board $11,463. Required fees $501. Average book expense $1,485. **Required Forms and Deadlines:** FAFSA, CSS/Financial Aid PROFILE Priority financial aid filing date 2/15. **Notification of Awards:** Applicants will be notified of awards on a rolling basis beginning 4/3. **Types of Aid:** *Need-based scholarships/grants:* Federal Pell, SEOG, state scholarships/grants, private scholarships, the school's own gift aid. *Loans:* FFEL Subsidized Stafford, FFEL Unsubsidized Stafford, FFEL PLUS, Federal Perkins. *Student Employment:* Federal Work-Study Program available. Institutional employment available. Off-campus job opportunities are good. **Financial Aid Statistics:** 50% freshmen, 47% undergrads receive need-based scholarship or grant aid. 5% freshmen, 8% undergrads receive non-need-based scholarship or grant aid. 28% freshmen, 30% undergrads receive need-based self-help aid. 11% freshmen, 9% undergrads receive athletic scholarships. 80% undergrads receive any aid. 36% undergrads borrow to pay for school. Average cumulative indebtedness $16,219.

STATE UNIVERSITY OF NEW YORK— ALFRED STATE COLLEGE

Huntington Administration Bldg, Alfred, NY 14802
Phone: 607-587-4215 **Financial Aid Phone:** 607-587-4253
E-mail: admissions@alfredstate.edu **CEEB Code:** 2522
Fax: 607-587-4299 **Website:** www.alfredstate.edu **ACT Code:** 2910

This public school was founded in 1908. It has a 840-acre campus.

RATINGS

Admissions Selectivity Rating: 60*   **Fire Safety Rating:** 60*   **Green Rating:** 61

STUDENTS AND FACULTY

Enrollment: 2,994. **Student Body:** 35% female, 65% male, 11% out-of-state. Asian 3%, African American 7%, Caucasian 94%, Hispanic 3%, Native American 1%.
Retention and Graduation: 38% grads go on to further study within 1 year.
Faculty: Student/faculty ratio 20:1. 148 full-time faculty.

ACADEMICS

Degrees: Associate, bachelor's, certificate, terminal associate, transfer associate. **Classes:** Most classes have 10–19 students. Most lab/discussion sessions have 10–19 students. **Majors with Highest Enrollment:** Architectural technology/technician; automotive engineering technology/technician; engineering technology. **Special Study Options:** Cooperative education program, cross-registration, distance learning, honors program, independent study, internships, student-designed major, study abroad, Internet courses. **Honors programs:** Participants complete a series of seminars, as well as a substantial honors project and 10 hours of volunteer community service. Special programs offered to physically disabled students include note-taking services, reader services, tape recorders, tutors. **Career services:** Alumni network, career/job search classes

FACILITIES

Housing: Coed dorms, special housing for disabled students, Suite, corridor, singles, smoke-free, over 21 yrs, over 24 yrs, wellness living, quiet study, same curriculum housing, baccalaureate, single room options, and computer life style, new upperclassmen apartment suite complex. 100% of campus accessible to physically disabled. **Computers:** 100% of classrooms, 100% of dorms, 100% of libraries, 100% of dining areas, 100% of common outdoor areas have wireless network access. Students can register for classes online. Administrative functions (other than registration) can be performed online.

CAMPUS LIFE

Environment: Rural. **Activities:** Choral groups, concert band, drama/theater, jazz band, literary magazine, music ensembles, musical theater, radio station, student government, student newspaper, symphony orchestra, yearbook. **Organizations:** 60 registered organizations, 4 honor societies, 3 fraternities, 2 sororities. **Athletics (Intercollegiate):** *Men:* Baseball, basketball, cheerleading, cross-country, football, lacrosse, soccer, swimming, track/field (outdoor), wrestling. *Women:* Basketball, cheerleading, cross-country, soccer, softball, swimming, track/field (outdoor), volleyball. **On-Campus Highlights:** Pioneer Center, Orvis (Athletic Center), Peach Pit, Central Dining Hall, Upperclassmen Apartment Suite Complex.

ADMISSIONS

Freshman Academic Profile: Average high school GPA 2.8. SAT Math middle 50% range 440–560. SAT Critical Reading middle 50% range 410–510. ACT middle 50% range 18–24. Minimum paper TOEFL 500. Minimum computer TOEFL 173. **Basis for Candidate Selection:** *Very important factors considered include:* Academic GPA, rigor of secondary school record. *Important factors considered include:* Class rank. *Other factors considered include:* Application essay, recommendation(s), standardized test scores, alumni/ae relation, character/personal qualities, extracurricular activities, interview, talent/ability, volunteer work, work experience. **Freshman Admission Requirements:** High school diploma is required and GED is accepted. *Academic units recommended:* 4 English, 4 mathematics, 4 science, 4 social studies. **Freshman Admission Statistics:** 4,414 applied, 65% admitted, 45% enrolled. **Transfer Admission Requirements:** High school transcript, college transcript(s), statement of good standing from prior institution(s). Minimum college GPA of 2.4 required. Lowest grade transferable C. **General Admission Information:** Application fee $40. Notification on a rolling basis, beginning on or about 11/1. Nonfall registration accepted. Admission may be deferred for a maximum of 1 semester. Credit and/or placement offered for CEEB Advanced Placement tests.

COSTS AND FINANCIAL AID

Annual in-state tuition $4,350. Annual out-of-state tuition $7,210. Room and board $8,430. Required fees $1,109. Average book expense $1,000. **Required Forms and Deadlines:** FAFSA, state aid form. Priority financial aid filing date 1/8. **Notification of Awards:** Applicants will be notified of awards on a rolling basis beginning 3/3. **Types of Aid:** *Need-based scholarships/grants:* Federal Pell, SEOG, state scholarships/grants, private scholarships, the school's own gift aid. *Loans:* FFEL Subsidized Stafford, FFEL Unsubsidized Stafford, FFEL PLUS, Federal Perkins, Federal Nursing *Student Employment:* Federal Work-Study Program available. Institutional employment available. Off-campus job opportunities are fair. **Financial Aid Statistics:** 78% freshmen, 66% undergrads receive need-based scholarship or grant aid. 23% freshmen, 16% undergrads receive non-need-based scholarship or grant aid. 70% freshmen, 61% undergrads receive need-based self-help aid. 21% freshmen, 17% undergrads receive athletic scholarships. 95.84% freshmen, 88.63% undergrads receive any aid. 79.37% undergrads borrow to pay for school. Average cumulative indebtedness $19,999.

STATE UNIVERSITY OF NEW YORK— BINGHAMTON UNIVERSITY

PO Box 6001, Binghamton, NY 13902-6001
Phone: 607-777-2171 **Financial Aid Phone:** 607-777-2428
E-mail: admit@binghamton.edu **CEEB Code:** 2535
Fax: 607-777-4445 **Website:** www.binghamton.edu **ACT Code:** 2956

This public school was founded in 1946. It has a 930-acre campus.

RATINGS
Admissions Selectivity Rating: 94 **Fire Safety Rating:** 76 **Green Rating:** 99

STUDENTS AND FACULTY
Enrollment: 11,661. **Student Body:** 47% female, 53% male, 10% out-of-state, 10% international (98 countries represented). Asian 12%, African American 5%, Caucasian 43%, Hispanic 7%.
Retention and Graduation: 90% freshmen return for sophomore year. 70% freshmen graduate within 4 years. 48% grads go on to further study within 1 year. **Faculty:** Student/faculty ratio 20:1. 596 full-time faculty, 91% hold PhDs, 24% are are members of minority groups, 38% are women. 7% of classes are taught by teaching assistants.

ACADEMICS
Degrees: Bachelor's, master's, post-master's certificate. **Classes:** Most classes have 20–29 students. Most lab/discussion sessions have 20–29 students. **Majors with Highest Enrollment:** Biology/biological sciences; business administration and management; engineering. **Special Study Options:** Accelerated program, cross-registration, distance learning, double major, dual enrollment, English as a Second Language (ESL), exchange student program (domestic), honors program, independent study, internships, liberal arts/career combination, student-designed major, study abroad, teacher certification program, Teacher Certification Program is graduate only. **Honors programs:** Binghamton University Scholars Program—See http://scholars.binghamton.edu Each academic department offers an honors program. Binghamton also has a PricewaterhouseCoopers Scholars program for students in the School of Management. **Combined degree programs:** BA/MA, >40 combined degrees for BA or BS with MBA/MPA/MAT/MA/MS. Special programs offered to physically disabled students include note-taking services, reader services, tape recorders. **Career services:** Alumni network, alumni services, career/job search classes, career assessment, internships, regional alumni. **Career services highlights include:** Binghamton's Career Development Center has received numerous awards for excellence from the SUNY Career Development Organization in regard to programming, operations and recruitment.

FACILITIES
Housing: Coed dorms, special housing for disabled students, apartments for single students, wellness housing, theme housing 90% of campus accessible to physically disabled. **Special Academic Facilities/Equipment:** Art gallery, performing arts center, indoor/outdoor theater, multi-climate and teaching greenhouse, sculpture foundry, 8,000–seat Events Center, Analytical and Diagnostics Laboratory, Electron Microscopy Facility, Public Archaeology Facility, 930–acre Nature Preserve. **Computers:** 95% of classrooms, 100% of dorms, 100% of libraries, 100% of dining areas, 100% of student union, 60% of common outdoor areas have wireless network access. Students can register for classes online. Administrative functions (other than registration) can be performed online.

CAMPUS LIFE
Environment: City. **Activities:** Choral groups, concert band, dance, drama/theater, jazz band, literary magazine, music ensembles, musical theater, opera, pep band, radio station, student government, student newspaper, student-run film society, symphony orchestra, television station, yearbook, campus ministries, international student organization, Model UN. **Organizations:** 23 honor societies, 15 religious organizations. 23 fraternities, 23 sororities. **Athletics (Intercollegiate):** *Men:* Baseball, basketball, cross-country, diving, golf, lacrosse, soccer, swimming, tennis, track/field (outdoor), track/field (indoor), wrestling. *Women:* Basketball, cross-country, diving, lacrosse, soccer, softball, swimming, tennis, track/field (outdoor), track/field (indoor), volleyball. **On-Campus Highlights:** University Union, Fitspace, Nature Preserve, Events Center, Anderson Center for the Arts, Rosefsky Art Gallery, Libraries. **Environmental Initiatives:** Binghamton University's goal is to design, construct, operate and maintain all new buildings following guidelines set forth by the U.S. Green Building Council's LEED rating system. Since 2004, Binghamton has obtained LEED certification on two buildings, as well as LEED Silver certification for a recently constructed building. It is Binghamton's commitment to strive for LEED silver or higher standards for all future buildings. Energy Conservation/Environmental Management Programs: Binghamton University has invested over $1 million dollars in energy conservation projects such as installation of efficient lighting, occupancy sensors, variable speed drives on motors, free-cooling devices to take advantage of cooler outdoor temperature, solar hot water heater and constant improvement to our energy management system. As a result, Binghamton's overall electricity consumption was reduced by 10% from 2007 to 2008 even with additional building spaces and enrollment. Environmental Management Program has also made a tremendous progress in areas such as recycling, waste reduction, composting, and community outreach. Binghamton's waste reduction rate was up from 27% to 42% in 2008. Binghamton University currently provides a student bus system operated jointly by students and the University serving residential student and other needs. Binghamton also has a contract with the county bus system connecting the University with key areas in the community. Binghamton encourages use of public transportation as well as expanded access to public transportation. For the past 5 years there has been an electric vehicle program on campus. Binghamton has also established an HOV carpool program to incur higher occupancy of vehicles coming to campus. Nearly 70% of Binghamton University's 930–acre campus is in its natural state. The core of this undeveloped land is officially designated the Nature Preserve, encompassing 182 acres of land which includes a 20 acre wetland. Binghamton uses this large, valuable resource for teaching and learning, research, ecology, arts, literature and outdoor recreation. Website: http://naturepreserve.binghamton.edu

ADMISSIONS
Freshman Academic Profile: Average high school GPA 3.6. 51% in top 10% of high school class, 84% in top 25% of high school class, 97% in top 50% of high school class. 89% from public high schools. SAT Math middle 50% range 620–710. SAT Critical Reading middle 50% range 580–670. ACT middle 50% range 27–30. Minimum paper TOEFL 550. Minimum computer TOEFL 213. Minimum web-based TOEFL 80. **Basis for Candidate Selection:** *Very important factors considered include:* Academic GPA, rigor of secondary school record, standardized test scores. *Important factors considered include:* Class rank, application essay, recommendation(s), extracurricular activities, first generation. *Other factors considered include:* Alumni/ae relation, character/personal qualities, geographical residence, level of applicant's interest, racial/ethnic status, state residency, talent/ability, volunteer work, work experience. **Freshman Admission Requirements:** High school diploma is required and GED is accepted. *Academic units required:* 4 English, 3 mathematics, 2 science, 3 foreign language, 2 social studies. *Academic units recommended:* 4 mathematics, 4 science, 3 foreign language, 4 social studies, 4 history. **Freshman Admission Statistics:** 29,061 applied, 33% admitted, 22% enrolled. **Transfer Admission Requirements:** College transcript(s), Lowest grade transferable C–. **General Admission Information:** Application fee $40. Regular notification 4/1. Nonfall registration accepted. Admission may be deferred for a maximum of 1 year. Credit offered for CEEB Advanced Placement tests.

COSTS AND FINANCIAL AID
Annual in-state tuition $4,970. Annual out-of-state tuition $12,870. Room and board $10,614. Required fees $1,791. Average book expense $800. **Required Forms and Deadlines:** FAFSA, state aid form. Priority financial aid filing date 2/1. **Notification of Awards:** Applicants will be notified of awards on a rolling basis beginning 4/1. **Types of Aid:** *Need-based scholarships/grants:* Federal Pell, SEOG, state scholarships/grants, private scholarships, the school's own gift aid. *Loans:* Direct Subsidized Stafford, Direct Unsubsidized Stafford, Direct PLUS, Federal Perkins, Federal Nursing, college/university loans from institutional funds. *Student Employment:* Federal Work-Study Program available. Institutional employment available. Highest amount earned per year from on-campus jobs $5,700. Off-campus job opportunities are excellent. **Financial Aid Statistics:** 36% freshmen, 40% undergrads receive need-based scholarship or grant aid. 6% freshmen, 5% undergrads receive non-need-based scholarship

The Princeton Review's Complete Book of Colleges

or grant aid. 44% freshmen, 45% undergrads receive need-based self-help aid. 4% freshmen, 3% undergrads receive athletic scholarships. 77% freshmen, 68% undergrads receive any aid. 49% undergrads borrow to pay for school. Average cumulative indebtedness $14,560. **Criteria for awarding institutional aid:** *Non-need-based:* Academics, art, athletics, leadership, minority status, music/drama, state/district residency.

STATE UNIVERSITY OF NEW YORK— BUFFALO STATE COLLEGE

1300 Elmwood Avenue, Buffalo, NY 14222
Phone: 716-878-4017 **Financial Aid Phone:** 716-878-4902
E-mail: admissions@buffalostate.edu **CEEB Code:** 2533
Fax: 716-878-6100 **Website: ACT Code:** 2930

This public school was founded in 1871. It has a 115-acre campus.

RATINGS
Admissions Selectivity Rating: 74   **Fire Safety Rating:** 60*   **Green Rating:** 74

STUDENTS AND FACULTY
Student Body: 1% out-of-state, (20 countries represented).
Retention and Graduation: 28% grads go on to further study within 1 year. 3% grads pursue arts and sciences degrees. 8% grads pursue law degrees. 5% grads pursue business degrees. **Faculty:** 425 full-time faculty, 84% hold PhDs, 18% are are members of minority groups, 46% are women.

ACADEMICS
Degrees: Bachelor's, master's, post-master's certificate. **Majors with Highest Enrollment:** Business/commerce; elementary education and teaching. **Special Study Options:** Cooperative education program, cross-registration, distance learning, double major, dual enrollment, English as a Second Language (ESL), exchange student program (domestic), honors program, independent study, internships, liberal arts/career combination, study abroad, teacher certification program Special programs offered to physically disabled students include note-taking services, reader services, tape recorders, tutors. **Career services:** Alumni network, alumni services, career/job search classes, career assessment, internships.

FACILITIES
Housing: Coed dorms, special housing for international students, Apartments for students with dependent children. 100% of campus accessible to physically disabled. **Special Academic Facilities/Equipment:** Burchfield Penney Art center, anthropology museum, concert hall with pipe organ, nature preserve. **Computers:** 10% of classrooms, 30% of libraries, 100% of dining areas, 50% of student union, 10% of common outdoor areas have wireless network access. Students can register for classes online. Administrative functions (other than registration) can be performed online.

CAMPUS LIFE
Environment: City. **Activities:** Choral groups, concert band, dance, drama/theater, jazz band, literary magazine, music ensembles, radio station, student government, student newspaper, student-run film society, television station, yearbook, international student organization. **Organizations:** 75 registered organizations, 5 religious organizations. 10 fraternities, 10 sororities. **Athletics (Intercollegiate):** *Men:* Basketball, cross-country, diving, football, ice hockey, soccer, swimming, track/field (outdoor), track/field (indoor). *Women:* Basketball, cheerleading, cross-country, diving, ice hockey, lacrosse, soccer, softball, swimming, tennis, track/field (outdoor), track/field (indoor), volleyball. **On-Campus Highlights:** Burchfield Penny Art Center, Sports Arena, Houston Gymnasium/Fitness Center, Rockwell Hall/Performing Arts Center, Campus House. **Environmental Initiatives:** 1) Creation of a campus wide recycling program for plastic, glass, metal, paper, cardboard, light bulbs, electronics, electronic media (printer cartridges, dvds, cds, VHS, cassettes, etc), batteries, shrink wrap, bubble wrap, and many other misc items! This was applied to every building on campus including the residential halls. 2) "Don't Throw it Out Program"—Move out program for Residential students to bring unwanted furniture, food, clothing, shoes, appliances, etc to centrally located drop off stations. This excess waste, and these items are then donated to nonprofit organizations. 3) Environmental Information Fair- 20—30 organizations ranging from county depts. to coumminty organizations that congritate on campus with the purpose of educating the campus population about environmental events and information that applies to their everyday life. It is a campus event that serves to create awareness among the campus and surrounding community. It is intended to promote and encourage a cleaner Western New York as we inform the community about going green.

ADMISSIONS
Freshman Academic Profile: Average high school GPA 3.1. 7.75% in top 10% of high school class, 30.6% in top 25% of high school class, 69.4% in top 50% of high school class. SAT Math middle 50% range 450–540. SAT Critical Reading middle 50% range 440–530. Minimum paper TOEFL 500. Minimum computer TOEFL 173. **Basis for Candidate Selection:** *Very important factors considered include:* Academic GPA, rigor of secondary school record, standardized test scores. *Important factors considered include:* Class rank. *Other factors considered include:* Application essay, recommendation(s), character/personal qualities, extracurricular activities, first generation, interview, talent/ability, volunteer work, work experience. **Freshman Admission Requirements:** High school diploma is required and GED is accepted. *Academic units required:* 2 mathematics, 2 science. *Academic units recommended:* 4 English, 3 mathematics, 3 science, 3 foreign language, 4 history. **Freshman Admission Statistics:** 9,762 applied, 47% admitted, 30% enrolled. **Transfer Admission Requirements:** College transcript(s), statement of good standing from prior institution(s). Minimum college GPA of 2.0 required. Lowest grade transferable C. **General Admission Information:** Application fee $40. Early decision application deadline 11/15. Notification on a rolling basis, beginning on or about 12/15. Nonfall registration accepted. Admission may be deferred for a maximum of 1 year. Credit offered for CEEB Advanced Placement tests.

COSTS AND FINANCIAL AID
Annual in-state tuition $4,970. Annual out-of-state tuition $12,870. Room and board $9,726. Required fees $1,037. Average book expense $900. **Required Forms and Deadlines:** FAFSA Financial aid filing deadline 5/1. Priority financial aid filing date 3/15. **Notification of Awards:** Applicants will be notified of awards on a rolling basis beginning 5/1. **Types of Aid:** *Need-based scholarships/grants:* Federal Pell, SEOG, state scholarships/grants *Loans:* FFEL Subsidized Stafford, FFEL Unsubsidized Stafford, FFEL PLUS, Federal Perkins. *Student Employment:* **Financial Aid Statistics:** 73% freshmen, 67% undergrads receive need-based scholarship or grant aid. 8% freshmen, 5% undergrads receive non-need-based scholarship or grant aid. 54% freshmen, 54% undergrads receive need-based self-help aid. 71% freshmen, 68% undergrads receive any aid. 69% undergrads borrow to pay for school. Average cumulative indebtedness $17,657. **Criteria for awarding institutional aid:** *Non-need-based:* Academics, minority status.

STATE UNIVERSITY OF NEW YORK—CANTON

French Hall, SUNY Canton, Canton, NY 13617
Phone: 315-386-7123
E-mail: admissions@canton.edu **CEEB Code:** 2523
Fax: 315-386-7929 **Website:** www.canton.edu **ACT Code:** 2912

This public school was founded in 1906. It has a 555-acre campus.

RATINGS
Admissions Selectivity Rating: 60*   **Fire Safety Rating:** 60*   **Green Rating:** 60*

STUDENTS AND FACULTY
Enrollment: 2,119. **Student Body:** 48% female, 52% male, international (5 countries represented). African American 8%, Caucasian 86%, Hispanic 3%, Native American 2%.
Retention and Graduation: 81% freshmen return for sophomore year. 45% grads go on to further study within 1 year. **Faculty:** Student/faculty ratio 23:1. 83 full-time faculty, 20% hold PhDs, 2% are are members of minority groups, 66% are women.

ACADEMICS
Degrees: Associate, bachelor's, certificate, terminal associate, transfer associate. **Classes:** Most classes have 20–29 students. Most lab/discussion sessions have 10–19 students. **Special Study Options:** Cooperative education program, cross-registration, distance learning, dual enrollment, internships, liberal arts/career combination, student-designed major Special programs offered to physically disabled students include note-taking services, reader services, tape recorders, tutors. **Career services:** Career/job search classes, career assessment, internships.

FACILITIES
Housing: Coed dorms, single sex wings, Intensive Quiet Atmosphere, Relaxed Atmosphere, suites, private rooms, computer floors, 21+ floor, Grasse River Community (pet floor), Umoja Ahora Community (multicultural), North Country Experience, alcohol-free, smoke-free. 100% of campus accessible to physically disabled. **Special Academic Facilities/Equipment:** Criminal Investigation Labs, radio station, distance learning classrooms.

CAMPUS LIFE

Environment: Rural. **Activities:** Choral groups, literary magazine, radio station, student government, student newspaper, yearbook. **Organizations:** 50 registered organizations, 2 honor societies, 1 religious organizations. 3 fraternities, 3 sororities. **Athletics (Intercollegiate):** *Men:* Basketball, football, ice hockey, lacrosse, soccer. *Women:* Basketball, soccer, softball, volleyball.

ADMISSIONS

Freshman Academic Profile: Minimum paper TOEFL 550. Minimum computer TOEFL 213. **Basis for Candidate Selection:** *Very important factors considered include:* Rigor of secondary school record. *Other factors considered include:* Class rank, recommendation(s), standardized test scores, character/personal qualities, extracurricular activities, interview, talent/ability, work experience. **Freshman Admission Requirements:** High school diploma is required and GED is accepted. *Academic units recommended:* 4 English, 2 mathematics, 2 science, 4 social studies. **Freshman Admission Statistics:** 1,830 applied, 98% admitted, 45% enrolled. **Transfer Admission Requirements:** High school transcript, college transcript(s), Lowest grade transferable C. **General Admission Information:** Application fee $40. Notification on a rolling basis, beginning on or about 12/1. Nonfall registration accepted. Admission may be deferred for a maximum of 1 year.

COSTS AND FINANCIAL AID

Required Forms and Deadlines: FAFSA, state aid form. Priority financial aid filing date 3/15. **Notification of Awards:** Applicants will be notified of awards on a rolling basis beginning 2/3. **Types of Aid:** *Need-based scholarships/grants:* Federal Pell, SEOG, private scholarships *Loans:* Direct Subsidized Stafford, Direct Unsubsidized Stafford, Direct PLUS, Federal Perkins. *Student Employment:* Federal Work-Study Program available. Institutional employment available. Off-campus job opportunities are fair. **Financial Aid Statistics:** Average cumulative indebtedness $6,000.

STATE UNIVERSITY OF NEW YORK—
COBLESKILL

Office of Admissions, Cobleskill, NY 12043
Phone: 518-255-5525 **Financial Aid Phone:** 518-255-5623
E-mail: admissions@cobleskill.edu **CEEB Code:** 2524
Fax: 518-255-6769 **Website:** www.cobleskill.edu **ACT Code:** 2914

This public school was founded in 1916. It has a 750-acre campus.

RATINGS
Admissions Selectivity Rating: 65   **Fire Safety Rating:** 73   **Green Rating:** 80

STUDENTS AND FACULTY

Enrollment: 2,559. **Student Body:** 47% female, 53% male, 10% out-of-state, 3% international (9 countries represented). Asian 1%, African American 8%, Caucasian 73%, Hispanic 5%. **Retention and Graduation:** 74% freshmen return for sophomore year. 48% freshmen graduate within 4 years. 63% grads go on to further study within 1 year. **Faculty:** Student/faculty ratio 18:1. 110 full-time faculty, 31% hold PhDs, 9% are are members of minority groups, 36% are women.

ACADEMICS

Degrees: Associate, bachelor's, certificate, terminal associate, transfer associate. **Classes:** Most classes have 10–19 students. Most lab/discussion sessions have 10–19 students. **Special Study Options:** Cross-registration, distance learning, English as a Second Language (ESL), honors program, internships, study abroad, weekend college. Special programs offered to physically disabled students include note-taking services, reader services, tape recorders, tutors. **Career services:** Alumni services, career/job search classes, career assessment, internships **Career services highlights include:** A 15 week internship is required for nearly all of the baccalaureate programs. It is the capstone of our 4-year degrees.

FACILITIES

Housing: Coed dorms, special housing for disabled students, men's dorms, women's dorms, LIfestyle floors: Designated quiet study lifestyle, wellness lifestyle, sustainability lifestyle, sophomore experience, upper class experience. **Special Academic Facilities/Equipment:** Art museum, 650 acre agricultural campus, distance learning classrooms, ski area, adult study center. **Computers:** Students can register for classes online. Administrative functions (other than registration) can be performed online.

CAMPUS LIFE

Environment: Rural. **Activities:** Drama/theater, student government, student newspaper, campus ministries, international student organization. **Organiza-**

---

tions: 40 registered organizations, 1 honor societies, 1 religious organizations. **Athletics (Intercollegiate):** *Men:* Baseball, basketball, cross-country, diving, equestrian sports, golf, lacrosse, soccer, swimming, tennis, track/field (outdoor), volleyball. *Women:* Basketball, cross-country, diving, equestrian sports, golf, soccer, softball, swimming, tennis, track/field (outdoor), volleyball. **On-Campus Highlights:** Bouck Hall/Student Union, Brickyard Point, American Heritage, Foundation Equestrian Center, Grosvenor Art Gallery. **Environmental Initiatives:** recycling—paper, plastics, metals, galss and cardboard box waste reduction in dining halls, offices—"Taste Don't Waste" program purchase of green cleaning supplies, recycled building products such as carpet—wear washing chemicals in dining halls.

ADMISSIONS

Freshman Academic Profile: Average high school GPA 80. 3% in top 10% of high school class, 10% in top 25% of high school class, 37% in top 50% of high school class. 98% from public high schools. SAT Math middle 50% range 400–520. SAT Critical Reading middle 50% range 390–500. ACT middle 50% range 17–22. Minimum paper TOEFL 500. **Basis for Candidate Selection:** *Important factors considered include:* Academic GPA, rigor of secondary school record, standardized test scores. *Other factors considered include:* Class rank, application essay, recommendation(s), extracurricular activities, geographical residence, interview, level of applicant's interest, state residency, work experience. **Freshman Admission Requirements:** High school diploma is required and GED is accepted. *Academic units required:* 1 English, 2 mathematics, 1 science, 1 history, 1 academic electives. *Academic units recommended:* (1 science labs), 1 foreign language, 1 social studies, 1 visual/performing arts, 1 computer science. **Freshman Admission Statistics:** 3,045 applied, 81% admitted, 40% enrolled. **Transfer Admission Requirements:** College transcript(s), minimum college GPA of 2.25 required. Lowest grade transferable D. **General Admission Information:** Application fee $40. Notification on a rolling basis, beginning on or about 11/1. Nonfall registration accepted. Admission may be deferred for a maximum of 2 semesters. Credit offered for CEEB Advanced Placement tests.

COSTS AND FINANCIAL AID

Annual in-state tuition $4,350. Annual out-of-state tuition $10,610. Room and board $8,650. Required fees $1,064. Average book expense $1,200. **Required Forms and Deadlines:** FAFSA, state aid form. Priority financial aid filing date 2/15. **Notification of Awards:** Applicants will be notified of awards on a rolling basis beginning 3/20. **Types of Aid:** *Need-based scholarships/grants:* Federal Pell, SEOG, state scholarships/grants, private scholarships, the school's own gift aid. *Loans:* FFEL Subsidized Stafford, FFEL Unsubsidized Stafford, FFEL PLUS, Federal Perkins. *Student Employment:* Federal Work-Study Program available. Institutional employment available. Highest amount earned per year from on-campus jobs $800. Off-campus job opportunities are fair. **Financial Aid Statistics:** 33% freshmen, 66% undergrads receive need-based scholarship or grant aid. 12% freshmen, 8% undergrads receive non-need-based scholarship or grant aid. 31% freshmen, 63% undergrads receive need-based self-help aid. 77% freshmen, 68% undergrads receive any aid. 80% undergrads borrow to pay for school. Average cumulative indebtedness $21,353. **Criteria for awarding institutional aid:** *Non-need-based:* Academics, alumni affiliation, leadership, state/district residency.

STATE UNIVERSITY OF NEW YORK—
THE COLLEGE AT BROCKPORT

350 New Campus Drive, Brockport, NY 14420
Phone: 585-395-2751 **Financial Aid Phone:** 585–395-2501
E-mail: admit@brockport.edu **CEEB Code:** 2537
Fax: 585-395-5452 **Website:** www.brockport.edu **ACT Code:** 2928

This public school was founded in 1835. It has a 464-acre campus.

RATINGS
Admissions Selectivity Rating: 83   **Fire Safety Rating:** 79   **Green Rating:** 83

STUDENTS AND FACULTY

Student Body: 1.1% out-of-state, international (21 countries represented). **Retention and Graduation:** 40% freshmen graduate within 4 years. 23% grads go on to further study within 1 year. 12% grads pursue arts and sciences degrees. 4% grads pursue law degrees. 3% grads pursue business degrees. 1% grads pursue medical degrees. **Faculty:** Student/faculty ratio 18:1. 328 full-time faculty, 87% hold PhDs, 17% are are members of minority groups, 45% are women.

ACADEMICS

Degrees: Bachelor's, master's, post-master's certificate. **Classes:** Most classes have 20–29 students. Most lab/discussion sessions have 10–19 students. **Majors with Highest Enrollment:** Business administration and management; health professions and related clinical sciences, other; physical education teaching and coaching. **Special Study Options:** Accelerated program, cross-registration, distance learning, double major, dual enrollment, honors program, independent study, internships, student-designed major, study abroad, teacher certification program **Honors programs:** 1)College Honors Program, which designs to let students complete general education requirements in small classes; 2) Delta College, which is a time-variable degree program for highly-motivated students. Special programs offered to physically disabled students include note-taking services, reader services, tape recorders, tutors. **Career services:** Alumni network, alumni services, career/job search classes, career assessment, internships, regional alumni. **Career services highlights include:** Brockport has a 91% placement rate for recent graduates.

FACILITIES

Housing: Coed dorms, special housing for international students, apartments for single students, wellness housing, extended housing (open during college breaks-excludes summer). 95% of campus accessible to physically disabled. **Special Academic Facilities/Equipment:** Aquaculture ponds, weather information system, high-resolution germanium detector, research vessel on Lake Ontario, electron microscope, low- temperature physics lab, vacuum deposition lab, computational; physics lab, 2 supercomputers, Doppler Radar system, ultramodern dance facilities including green room, hydrotherapy room, student learning center, academic computing center, and two theaters. **Computers:** 100% of classrooms, 100% of dorms, 100% of libraries, 100% of dining areas, 100% of student union, 80% of common outdoor areas have wireless network access. Students can register for classes online. Administrative functions (other than registration) can be performed online.

CAMPUS LIFE

Environment: Village. **Activities:** Choral groups, dance, drama/theater, literary magazine, music ensembles, musical theater, radio station, student government, student newspaper, television station, campus ministries, international student organization, Model UN. **Organizations:** 71 registered organizations, 20 honor societies, 8 religious organizations. 6 fraternities, 3 sororities. **Athletics (Intercollegiate):** *Men:* Baseball, basketball, cross-country, diving, football, ice hockey, lacrosse, soccer, swimming, track/field (outdoor), track/field (indoor), wrestling. *Women:* Basketball, cross-country, diving, field hockey, gymnastics, lacrosse, soccer, softball, swimming, tennis, track/field (outdoor), track/field (indoor), volleyball. **On-Campus Highlights:** Seymour College Union, Drake Memorial Library, Hartwell Performance Center, Harrison Dining Hall, Tuttle Athletic Complex, Smith Hall Science Center Dailey Hall Computing Center Tower Fine Arts Center. **Environmental Initiatives:** New 208 bed townhomes that are LEED certifiable including: geothermal HVAC, recycled materials, energy efficient systems, etc. Roughly 12 million dollars of investments in a diverse spectrum of energy related facility projects. High recycling rates and alternative energy fuels program including bio-diesels and alternative energy vehicles.

ADMISSIONS

Freshman Academic Profile: Average high school GPA 3.5. 14.7% in top 10% of high school class, 50.1% in top 25% of high school class, 88.3% in top 50% of high school class. SAT Math middle 50% range 500–590. SAT Critical Reading middle 50% range 470–560. SAT Writing middle 50% range 450–560. ACT middle 50% range 21–25. Minimum paper TOEFL 530. Minimum computer TOEFL 197. Minimum web-based TOEFL 71. **Basis for Candidate Selection:** *Very important factors considered include:* Academic GPA, rigor of secondary school record. *Important factors considered include:* Class rank, application essay, recommendation(s), standardized test scores, character/personal qualities, extracurricular activities, talent/ability, volunteer work, work experience. *Other factors considered include:* interview, level of applicant's interest, racial/ethnic status. **Freshman Admission Requirements:** High school diploma is required and GED is accepted. *Academic units required:* 4 English, 3 mathematics, 3 science, (1 science labs), 4 social studies, 3 academic electives. *Academic units recommended:* 3 foreign language. **Freshman Admission Statistics:** 8,671 applied, 45% admitted, 28% enrolled. **Transfer Admission Requirements:** College transcript(s), minimum college GPA of 2.5 required. Lowest grade transferable D–. **General Admission Information:** Application fee $40. Notification on a rolling basis, beginning on or about 11/15. Nonfall registration accepted. Admission may be deferred for a maximum of 1 year. Credit and/or placement offered for CEEB Advanced Placement tests.

COSTS AND FINANCIAL AID

Annual in-state tuition $4,970. Annual out-of-state tuition $12,870. Room and board $9,200. Required fees $1,138. Average book expense $1,000. **Required Forms and Deadlines:** FAFSA, state aid form. Priority financial aid filing date 2/15. **Notification of Awards:** Applicants will be notified of awards on a rolling basis beginning 3/15. **Types of Aid:** *Need-based scholarships/grants:* Federal Pell, SEOG, state scholarships/grants, private scholarships, the school's own gift aid. *Loans:* Direct Subsidized Stafford, Direct Unsubsidized Stafford, Direct PLUS, Federal Perkins, Federal Nursing, Private Alternative loans. *Student Employment:* Federal Work-Study Program available. Institutional employment available. Highest amount earned per year from on-campus jobs $14,059. Off-campus job opportunities are good. **Financial Aid Statistics:** 57% freshmen, 58% undergrads receive need-based scholarship or grant aid. 21% freshmen, 13% undergrads receive non-need-based scholarship or grant aid. 52% freshmen, 57% undergrads receive need-based self-help aid. 91% freshmen, 84% undergrads receive any aid. 81% undergrads borrow to pay for school. Average cumulative indebtedness $26,086. **Criteria for awarding institutional aid:** *Non-need-based:* Academics, alumni affiliation, art, athletics, leadership, minority status, music/drama.

STATE UNIVERSITY OF NEW YORK—COLLEGE OF ENVIRONMENTAL SCIENCE AND FORESTRY

Office of Undergraduate Admissions, SUNY-ESF, Syracuse, NY 13210
Phone: 315-470-6600 **Financial Aid Phone:** 315-470-6706
E-mail: esfinfo@esf.edu **CEEB Code:** 2530
Fax: 315-470-6933 **Website:** www.esf.edu **ACT Code:** 2948

This public school was founded in 1911. It has a 25000-acre campus.

RATINGS

Admissions Selectivity Rating: 83   **Fire Safety Rating:** 92   **Green Rating:** 97

STUDENTS AND FACULTY

Enrollment: 1,541. **Student Body:** 39% female, 61% male, 16% out-of-state, 1% international (30 countries represented). Asian 3%, African American 1%, Caucasian 91%, Hispanic 3%, Native American 1%.
Retention and Graduation: 84% freshmen return for sophomore year. 57% freshmen graduate within 4 years. 20% grads go on to further study within 1 year. **Faculty:** Student/faculty ratio 12:1. 146 full-time faculty, 96% hold PhDs, 11% are are members of minority groups, 24% are women.

ACADEMICS

Degrees: Associate, bachelor's, master's, post-bachelor's certificate. **Classes:** Most classes have 10–19 students. Most lab/discussion sessions have 10–19 students. **Majors with Highest Enrollment:** Environmental biology; environmental science; landscape architecture (BS, BSLA, BLA, MSLA, MLA, PhD). **Special Study Options:** Cooperative education program, cross-registration, distance learning, double major, English as a Second Language (ESL), honors program, independent study, internships, study abroad, teacher certification program, Associate degrees in forest technology & land surveying technology are offered at The Ranger School campus. Graduates of these degrees may then continue their studies at the Syracuse campus to complete bachelor degrees, usually in forest resources management or natural resources management. **Honors programs:** Lower Division Honors Program: freshmen & sophomores, all academic programs, highly selective, associated scholarship, mentoring, honors seminar, honors writing course. Upper Division Thesis Honors Program: juniors and seniors, 16 of 20 academic programs eligible, intensive research or creative projects guided by faculty mentors, thesis exploration seminar, related course work, Honors Thesis/Project course. **Combined degree programs:** BS/ Doctor of Physical Therapy. Special programs offered to physically disabled students include note-taking services, reader services, tape recorders, tutors. **Career services:** Alumni network, alumni services, career/job search classes, career assessment, internships, regional alumni. **Career services highlights include:** Experiential learning is "built in to" all aspects of learning at ESF. Service Learning is an integral part of an ESF education. Required and voluntary undergraduate research, internships and field experiences are components of every degree program. Learn more at www.esf.edu/students/servicelearning/.

FACILITIES

Housing: Coed dorms, special housing for disabled students, special housing for international students, fraternity/sorority housing, apartments for married students, apartments for single students, theme housing. 100% of campus accessible to physically disabled. **Special Academic Facilities/Equipment:** Museums, art galleries, plant growth and animal environmental simulation chambers, wildlife collection, electron microscope, paper making facility, photogrammetric and geodetic facilities, hydrology flumes. **Computers:** 50% of classrooms, 100% of dorms, 100% of libraries, 100% of dining areas, 100% of student union, 10% of common outdoor areas have wireless network access. Students can register for classes online. Administrative functions (other than registration) can be performed online.

CAMPUS LIFE

Environment: City. **Activities:** Choral groups, concert band, dance, drama/theater, jazz band, literary magazine, marching band, music ensembles, musical theater, pep band, radio station, student government, student newspaper, student-run film society, symphony orchestra, television station, yearbook, campus ministries, international student organization. **Organizations:** 300 registered organizations, 1 honor societies, 13 religious organizations. 26 fraternities, 21 sororities. **Athletics (Intercollegiate):** *Men:* Cross-country, golf, soccer. *Women:* Cross-country, golf, soccer **On-Campus Highlights:** Library, green houses, wildlife collection, Labratories & Studios, student lounge, snack bar, student store. SUNY—ESF is on the campus of Syracuse University. The most popular sites on that campus are the Carrier Dome, Crouse College (a historic building), Schine Student Center, Hendricks Chapel. **Environmental Initiatives:** (1)College uses a 250 kilowatt carbonate fuel cell to generate approximately 17% of electrical power. (2)photovoltaic arrays/green roof (3) College owns and manages 25,000 acres of forest (providing carbon offsets). Faculty at SUNY—ESF are conducting nationally recognized and government supported research in the development of ethanol and other renewable products from wood bioimass. We have partnered with the NY State government and private industry to develop the state's first "biorefinery" aimed at producing ethanol and other chemical products from wood sugars. The College has also developed a genetically engineered species of fast growth willow that is being grown as an alternative to corn use in ethanol production. Forty percent of all College vehicles (cars, maintenance vehicles, buses, GEM, etc.) are powered with renewable fuels, electric or hybrid technologies. One fifth of all vehicles are powered with biodeisel, and a significant part of our biodeisel fuel is produced on campus from waste cooking oil.

ADMISSIONS

Freshman Academic Profile: 25% in top 10% of high school class, 65% in top 25% of high school class, 94% in top 50% of high school class. 90% from public high schools. SAT Math middle 50% range 540–630. SAT Critical Reading middle 50% range 510–610. ACT middle 50% range 22–27. Minimum paper TOEFL 550. Minimum computer TOEFL 213. Minimum web-based TOEFL 79. **Basis for Candidate Selection:** *Very important factors considered include:* Application essay, academic GPA, rigor of secondary school record, standardized test scores, level of applicant's interest. *Important factors considered include:* Class rank, recommendation(s), character/personal qualities, extracurricular activities, talent/ability, volunteer work, work experience. *Other factors considered include:* Alumni/ae relation, first generation, geographical residence, interview, racial/ethnic status, state residency. **Freshman Admission Requirements:** High school diploma is required and GED is accepted. *Academic units required:* 4 English, 3 mathematics, 3 science, (3 science labs), 3 social studies. *Academic units recommended:* 4 mathematics, 4 science, (4 science labs), 3 social studies, 1 history. **Freshman Admission Statistics:** 1,544 applied, 49% admitted, 41% enrolled. **Transfer Admission Requirements:** High school transcript, college transcript(s), minimum college GPA of 2.25 required. Lowest grade transferable C. **General Admission Information:** Application fee $40. Notification on a rolling basis, beginning on or about 2/1. Nonfall registration accepted. Admission may be deferred for a maximum of 1 year. Credit offered for CEEB Advanced Placement tests.

COSTS AND FINANCIAL AID

Annual in-state tuition $4,970. Annual out-of-state tuition $12,870. Room and board $12,460. Required fees $849. Average book expense $1,200. **Required Forms and Deadlines:** FAFSA, state aid form. Priority financial aid filing date 3/1. **Notification of Awards:** Applicants will be notified of awards on a rolling basis beginning 3/15. **Types of Aid:** *Need-based scholarships/grants:* Federal Pell, SEOG, state scholarships/grants, private scholarships, the school's own gift aid. Federal SMART Grants, Federal ACG Grants. *Loans:* FFEL Subsidized Stafford, FFEL Unsubsidized Stafford, FFEL PLUS, Federal Perkins. *Student Employment:* Federal Work-Study Program available. Institutional employment available. Highest amount earned per year from on-campus jobs $1,200. Off-campus job opportunities are excellent. **Financial Aid Statistics:** 63% freshmen, 59% undergrads receive need-based scholarship or grant aid. 41% freshmen, 16% undergrads receive non-need-based scholarship or grant aid. 63% freshmen, 59% undergrads receive need-based self-help aid. 80% freshmen, 82% undergrads receive any aid. 80% undergrads borrow to pay for school. Average cumulative indebtedness $23,000. **Criteria for awarding institutional aid:** *Non-need-based:* Academics, alumni affiliation, state/district residency.

See page 1246.

STATE UNIVERSITY OF NEW YORK— THE COLLEGE AT OLD WESTBURY

PO Box 307, Old Westbury, NY 11568-0307
Phone: 516-876-3073 **Financial Aid Phone:** 516-876-3247
E-mail: enroll@oldwestbury.edu **CEEB Code:** 2866
Fax: 516-876-3307 **Website:** www.oldwestbury.edu **ACT Code:** 2939

This public school was founded in 1968. It has a 605-acre campus.

RATINGS
Admissions Selectivity Rating: 76   **Fire Safety Rating:** 85   **Green Rating:** 79

STUDENTS AND FACULTY

Enrollment: 3,696. **Student Body:** 59% female, 41% male, 2% out-of-state, 2% international (34 countries represented). Asian 8%, African American 33%, Caucasian 31%, Hispanic 19%, Native American 1%. **Retention and Graduation:** 75% freshmen return for sophomore year. 18% freshmen graduate within 4 years. 78% grads go on to further study within 1 year. 14% grads pursue arts and sciences degrees. 8% grads pursue law degrees. 31% grads pursue business degrees. 2% grads pursue medical degrees. **Faculty:** Student/faculty ratio 20:1. 131 full-time faculty, 84% hold PhDs, 36% are are members of minority groups, 50% are women.

ACADEMICS

Degrees: Bachelor's, certificate, master's. **Classes:** Most classes have 20–29 students. Most lab/discussion sessions have 20–29 students. **Majors with Highest Enrollment:** Accounting; elementary education and teaching; psychology. **Special Study Options:** Cross-registration, distance learning, double major, English as a Second Language (ESL), exchange student program (domestic), honors program, independent study, internships, liberal arts/career combination, study abroad, teacher certification program, Disabled Student Services; Minority Access to Research Centers; Minority Biomedical Research. **Honors programs:** The Honors College teaches students to integrate learning methods by using in-depth primary source material and complex and intellectually challenging secondary sources. The program emphasizes critical thinking and experiential learning. **Combined degree programs:** BS/DO. Special programs offered to physically disabled students include note-taking services, reader services, tape recorders, tutors. **Career services:** Alumni network, alumni services, career/job search classes, career assessment, internships, regional alumni. **Career services highlights include:** The Community Engagement and Partnership Center founded in 2006, and its First-Year Experience Program, Old Westbury shares its resources to support the programmatic efforts of non-profit organizations and to address issues of shared concern within various communities. The college, as a whole, is using its influential role as a regional employer and developer to contribute directly and tangibly to community revitalization efforts. Critical to this effort is the student community engagement component. Implemented by CEPC and the FYE, the College has initiated a voluntary course-embedded community-based learning and action program in which students engage in community service in areas related to their course of study.

FACILITIES

Housing: Coed dorms, Honors College residence. 90% of campus accessible to physically disabled. **Special Academic Facilities/Equipment:** Art gallery, language lab, TV studio, radio station, recital hall, physical recreation center and Maguire Theatre. **Computers:** 100% of classrooms, 60% of dorms, 100% of libraries, 100% of dining areas, 100% of student union, 30% of common outdoor areas have wireless network access. Students can register for classes online. Administrative functions (other than registration) can be performed online.

CAMPUS LIFE

Environment: Village. **Activities:** Choral groups, dance, drama/theater, radio station, student government, student newspaper, student-run film society, yearbook, campus ministries, international student organization. **Organizations:** 55 registered organizations, 5 honor societies, 2 religious organizations. 6 fraternities, 4 sororities. **Athletics (Intercollegiate):** *Men:* Baseball, basketball, cross-country, golf, soccer, swimming, ultimate frisbee, volleyball. *Women:* Basketball, cross-country, soccer, softball, swimming, ultimate frisbee, volleyball. **On-Campus Highlights:** Student Union, Clark Center (athletic facility), library, theatre, art gallery. **Environmental Initiatives:** SEMPRA Energy Contract, Energy STAR purchases, new building to be constructed and completed by 2010 will be LEED platinum.

ADMISSIONS

Freshman Academic Profile: Average high school GPA 2.8. 88% from public high schools. SAT Math middle 50% range 460–550. SAT Critical Reading middle 50% range 450–530. SAT Writing middle 50% range 430–520. ACT middle 50% range 20–24. Minimum paper TOEFL 513. Minimum computer

TOEFL 183. Minimum web-based TOEFL 65. **Basis for Candidate Selection:** *Very important factors considered include:* Application essay, academic GPA, rigor of secondary school record. *Important factors considered include:* Recommendation(s), standardized test scores. *Other factors considered include:* Character/personal qualities, extracurricular activities, interview, talent/ability, volunteer work, work experience. **Freshman Admission Requirements:** High school diploma is required and GED is accepted. *Academic units required:* 4 English, 3 mathematics, 3 science, (2 science labs), 2 foreign language, 4 social studies, 2 academic electives. *Academic units recommended:* 4 English, 3 mathematics, 3 science, (3 science labs), 3 foreign language, 4 social studies, 1 computer science, 3 academic electives. **Freshman Admission Statistics:** 3,610 applied, 51% admitted, 23% enrolled. **Transfer Admission Requirements:** College transcript(s), essay or personal statement, minimum college GPA of 2.0 required. Lowest grade transferable C. **General Admission Information:** Application fee $40. Notification on a rolling basis, beginning on or about 1/7. Nonfall registration accepted. Admission may be deferred for a maximum of 1 year. Credit and/or placement offered for CEEB Advanced Placement tests.

COSTS AND FINANCIAL AID

Annual in-state tuition $4,970. Annual out-of-state tuition $12,870. Room and board $9,390. Required fees $827. Average book expense $1,000. **Required Forms and Deadlines:** FAFSA, institution's own financial aid form, state aid form. Priority financial aid filing date 4/1. **Notification of Awards:** Applicants will be notified of awards on or about 4/15. **Types of Aid:** *Need-based scholarships/grants:* Federal Pell, SEOG, state scholarships/grants, private scholarships, the school's own gift aid. *Loans:* FFEL Subsidized Stafford, FFEL Unsubsidized Stafford, FFEL PLUS, Federal Perkins, Federal College Work Study Grants Federal Pell Grants Federal Supplemental Education Opportunity Grants State Educational Opportunity Program Grants Supplemental State Tuiti *Student Employment:* Federal Work-Study Program available. Institutional employment available. Off-campus job opportunities are good. **Financial Aid Statistics:** 67% freshmen, 61% undergrads receive need-based scholarship or grant aid. 5% freshmen, 3% undergrads receive non-need-based scholarship or grant aid. 44% freshmen, 42% undergrads receive need-based self-help aid. 70% freshmen, 60% undergrads receive any aid. 50.63% undergrads borrow to pay for school. Average cumulative indebtedness $15,901. **Criteria for awarding institutional aid:** *Non-need-based:* Academics, state/district residency.

STATE UNIVERSITY OF NEW YORK— COLLEGE AT ONEONTA

116 Alumni Hall, State University College, Oneonta, NY 13820
Phone: 607-436-2524 **Financial Aid Phone:** 607-436-2532
E-mail: admissions@oneonta.edu **CEEB Code:** 2542
Fax: 607-436-3074 **Website:** www.oneonta.edu **ACT Code:** 2940

This public school was founded in 1889. It has a 250-acre campus.

RATINGS

Admissions Selectivity Rating: 88   **Fire Safety Rating:** 73   **Green Rating:** 87

STUDENTS AND FACULTY

Enrollment: 5,650. **Student Body:** 57% female, 43% male, 2% out-of-state, 2% international (15 countries represented). Asian 2%, African American 3%, Caucasian 82%, Hispanic 5%.
Retention and Graduation: 83% freshmen return for sophomore year. 48% freshmen graduate within 4 years. 49% grads go on to further study within 1 year. **Faculty:** Student/faculty ratio 17:1. 261 full-time faculty, 80% hold PhDs, 18% are are members of minority groups, 46% are women.

ACADEMICS

Degrees: Bachelor's, master's, post-bachelor's certificate, post-master's certificate. **Classes:** Most classes have 10–19 students. **Majors with Highest Enrollment:** Communication studies/speech communication and rhetoric; elementary education and teaching; visual and performing arts. **Special Study Options:** Cross-registration, distance learning, double major, English as a Second Language (ESL), honors program, independent study, internships, liberal arts/career combination, study abroad, teacher certification program, Variety of 3-1, 3-2, and 2-2 programs with other colleges and universities. **Honors programs:** Oneonta Honors Program. **Combined degree programs:** BA/MA, BA/MEng, acc't, bus. admin, mgmt, fashion, art, med. sci. Special programs offered to physically disabled students include note-taking services, reader services, tape recorders, tutors. **Career services:** Alumni network, alumni services, career/job search classes, career assessment, internships, regional alumni. **Career services highlights include:** Internships available in all academic majors.

FACILITIES

Housing: Coed dorms, Special interest wings in residence halls; apartment-style suites in new hall. 90% of campus accessible to physically disabled. **Special Academic Facilities/Equipment:** Science Discovery Center, Biological Field Station, digital planetarium, observatory, College Camp, children's center **Computers:** 100% of classrooms, 100% of dorms, 100% of libraries, 100% of dining areas, 100% of student union, 100% of common outdoor areas have wireless network access. Students can register for classes online. Administrative functions (other than registration) can be performed online.

CAMPUS LIFE

Environment: Village. **Activities:** Choral groups, concert band, dance, drama/theater, jazz band, literary magazine, music ensembles, musical theater, opera, pep band, radio station, student government, student newspaper, student-run film society, symphony orchestra, television station, yearbook, campus ministries, international student organization, Model UN. **Organizations:** 70 registered organizations, 14 honor societies, 4 religious organizations. 4 fraternities, 6 sororities. **Athletics (Intercollegiate):** *Men:* Baseball, basketball, cross-country, diving, lacrosse, soccer, swimming, tennis, track/field (outdoor), track/field (indoor), wrestling. *Women:* Basketball, cross-country, diving, field hockey, lacrosse, soccer, softball, swimming, tennis, track/field (outdoor), track/field (indoor), volleyball. **On-Campus Highlights:** Alumni Field House, Center for Multicultural Experiences, Hunt College Union, College Camp, Center for Social Responsibility and Community, Newly remodeled Science Building with state-of-the-art Digital Planetarium. **Environmental Initiatives:** Recycling program Green construction standards Campus Sustainability Committee

ADMISSIONS

Freshman Academic Profile: Average high school GPA 3.5. 24% in top 10% of high school class, 66% in top 25% of high school class, 98% in top 50% of high school class. 91% from public high schools. SAT Math middle 50% range 540–620. SAT Critical Reading middle 50% range 520–590. ACT middle 50% range 23–26. Minimum computer TOEFL 173. Minimum paper TOEFL 500. **Basis for Candidate Selection:** *Very important factors considered include:* Rigor of secondary school record. *Important factors considered include:* Application essay, academic GPA, standardized test scores, extracurricular activities, interview, talent/ability, volunteer work. *Other factors considered include:* Recommendation(s), alumni/ae relation, level of applicant's interest, racial/ethnic status, work experience. **Freshman Admission Requirements:** High school diploma is required and GED is accepted. *Academic units required:* 4 English, 2 mathematics, 2 science, (2 science labs), 2 foreign language, 3 social studies. *Academic units recommended:* 3 mathematics, 3 science, 3 foreign language. **Freshman Admission Statistics:** 12,688 applied, 39% admitted, 22% enrolled. **Transfer Admission Requirements:** College transcript(s), minimum college GPA of 2.5 required. Lowest grade transferable C–. **General Admission Information:** Application fee $40. Notification on a rolling basis, beginning on or about 11/15. Nonfall registration accepted. Admission may be deferred for a maximum of 1 year. Credit offered for CEEB Advanced Placement tests.

COSTS AND FINANCIAL AID

Annual in-state tuition $4,970. Annual out-of-state tuition $12,870. Room and board $8,800. Required fees $1,215. Average book expense $900. **Required Forms and Deadlines:** FAFSA, state aid form. Priority financial aid filing date 3/15. **Notification of Awards:** Applicants will be notified of awards on a rolling basis beginning 3/1. **Types of Aid:** *Need-based scholarships/grants:* Federal Pell, SEOG, state scholarships/grants, private scholarships, the school's own gift aid. *Loans:* FFEL Subsidized Stafford, FFEL Unsubsidized Stafford, FFEL PLUS, Federal Perkins. *Student Employment:* Federal Work-Study Program available. Institutional employment available. Highest amount earned per year from on-campus jobs $1,800. Off-campus job opportunities are good. **Financial Aid Statistics:** 45% freshmen, 48% undergrads receive need-based scholarship or grant aid. 47% freshmen, 48% undergrads receive need-based self-help aid. 78% freshmen, 76% undergrads receive any aid. 75% undergrads borrow to pay for school. Average cumulative indebtedness $16,490. **Criteria for awarding institutional aid:** *Non-need-based:* Academics, alumni affiliation, leadership, minority status, music/drama, state/district residency.

STATE UNIVERSITY OF NEW YORK—CORTLAND

PO Box 2000, Cortland, NY 13045-0900
Phone: 607-753-4712 **Financial Aid Phone:** 607-753-4717
E-mail: admissions@cortland.edu **CEEB Code:** 2538
Fax: 607-753-5998 **Website:** www.cortland.edu **ACT Code:** 2932

This public school was founded in 1868. It has a 191-acre campus.

RATINGS
Admissions Selectivity Rating: 83   **Fire Safety Rating:** 60*   **Green Rating:** 60*

STUDENTS AND FACULTY
Enrollment: 6,096. **Student Body:** 57% female, 43% male, 2% out-of-state, 1% international (14 countries represented). Asian 1%, African American 3%, Caucasian 75%, Hispanic 6%, Native American 1%. **Retention and Graduation:** 81% freshmen return for sophomore year. 43% freshmen graduate within 4 years. **Faculty:** Student/faculty ratio 17:1. 306 full-time faculty, 74% hold PhDs, 12% are are members of minority groups, 49% are women.

ACADEMICS
Degrees: Bachelor's, master's, post-master's certificate. **Classes:** Most classes have 20–29 students. Most lab/discussion sessions have 20–29 students. **Special Study Options:** Cooperative education program, cross-registration, distance learning, double major, dual enrollment, exchange student program (domestic), honors program, independent study, internships, liberal arts/career combination, student-designed major, study abroad, teacher certification program Special programs offered to physically disabled students include note-taking services, reader services, tape recorders, tutors.

FACILITIES
Housing: Coed dorms, special housing for disabled students, special housing for international students, cooperative housing, apartments for single students, wellness housingLeadership House, Transfer Floor, Quiet Atmosphere. 75% of campus accessible to physically disabled. **Special Academic Facilities/Equipment:** Natural science museum, greenhouse, center for speech and hearing disorders, classrooms with integrated technologies, specialized labs to support various program offerings. **Computers:** Students can register for classes online. Administrative functions (other than registration) can be performed online.

CAMPUS LIFE
Environment: Village. **Activities:** Choral groups, dance, drama/theater, literary magazine, music ensembles, musical theater, radio station, student government, student newspaper, student-run film society, symphony orchestra, television station, yearbook, campus ministries, international student organization, Model UN. **Organizations:** 100 registered organizations, 16 honor societies, 3 religious organizations. 2 fraternities, 5 sororities. **Athletics (Intercollegiate):** *Men:* Baseball, basketball, cheerleading, cross-country, diving, football, gymnastics, ice hockey, lacrosse, soccer, swimming, track/field (outdoor), track/field (indoor), wrestling. *Women:* Basketball, cheerleading, cross-country, diving, field hockey, golf, gymnastics, ice hockey, lacrosse, soccer, softball, swimming, tennis, track/field (outdoor), track/field (indoor), volleyball. **On-Campus Highlights:** Corey Union, Stadium Complex, Fitness Facilities, Dining Halls, Library.

ADMISSIONS
Freshman Academic Profile: Average high school GPA 3.34. 10% in top 10% of high school class, 45% in top 25% of high school class, 87% in top 50% of high school class. 91% from public high schools. SAT Math middle 50% range 480–560. SAT Critical Reading middle 50% range 510–590. Minimum paper TOEFL 550. **Basis for Candidate Selection:** *Very important factors considered include:* Rigor of secondary school record, standardized test scores. *Important factors considered include:* Application essay, recommendation(s), extracurricular activities, talent/ability. *Other factors considered include:* Class rank, alumni/ae relation, geographical residence, interview, racial/ethnic status, state residency, volunteer work, work experience. **Freshman Admission Requirements:** High school diploma is required and GED is accepted. *Academic units required:* 4 English, 3 mathematics, 3 science, 3 foreign language, 4 social studies. *Academic units recommended:* 4 English, 4 mathematics, 4 science, 4 foreign language, 4 social studies. **Freshman Admission Statistics:** 11,573 applied, 41% admitted, 25% enrolled. **Transfer Admission Requirements:** High school transcript, college transcript(s), minimum college GPA of 2.5 required. Lowest grade transferable C–. **General Admission Information:** Application fee $40. Early decision application deadline 11/15. Notification on a rolling basis, beginning on or about 1/2. Nonfall registration accepted. Admission may be deferred for a maximum of 1 year. Credit offered for CEEB Advanced Placement tests.

COSTS AND FINANCIAL AID
Annual in-state tuition $4,970. Annual out-of-state tuition $12,870. Room and board $9,790. Required fees $1,175. Average book expense $1,000. **Required**

Forms and Deadlines: FAFSA, state aid form. Priority financial aid filing date 3/1. **Notification of Awards:** Applicants will be notified of awards on a rolling basis beginning 3/15. **Types of Aid:** *Need-based scholarships/grants:* Federal Pell, SEOG, state scholarships/grants, private scholarships, the school's own gift aid. *Loans:* FFEL Subsidized Stafford, FFEL Unsubsidized Stafford, FFEL PLUS, Federal Perkins. *Student Employment:* **Financial Aid Statistics:** 47% freshmen, 49% undergrads receive need-based scholarship or grant aid. 1% freshmen, 4% undergrads receive non-need-based scholarship or grant aid. 48% freshmen, 50% undergrads receive need-based self-help aid. **Criteria for awarding institutional aid:** *Non-need-based:* Academics, art, leadership, minority status, music/drama, state/district residency.

STATE UNIVERSITY OF NEW YORK—DELHI

Bush Hall, 2 Main St, Delhi, NY 13753
Phone: 607-746-4550
E-mail: enroll@Delhi.edu
Fax: 607-746-4104 **Website:** www.delhi.edu

This is a public school.

RATINGS
Admissions Selectivity Rating: 60*   **Fire Safety Rating:** 60*   **Green Rating:** 60*

STUDENTS AND FACULTY
Enrollment: 1,791. **Student Body:** 44% female, 56% male, 4% out-of-state, 1% international. Asian 2%, African American 11%, Caucasian 84%, Hispanic 7%. **Retention and Graduation: Faculty:** Student/faculty ratio 15:1.

ACADEMICS
Degrees: Associate, bachelor's, certificate, terminal associate, transfer associate. **Special Study Options:** Distance learning, English as a Second Language (ESL), honors program, internships, student-designed major, weekend college.

FACILITIES
Housing: Coed dorms.

CAMPUS LIFE
Activities: Choral groups, dance, drama/theater, music ensembles, musical theater, radio station, student government, student newspaper, yearbook. **Athletics (Intercollegiate):** *Men:* Basketball, cross-country, diving, golf, lacrosse, soccer, swimming, tennis, track/field (outdoor), track/field (indoor), wrestling. *Women:* Basketball, cross-country, diving, golf, soccer, softball, swimming, tennis, track/field (outdoor), track/field (indoor), volleyball.

ADMISSIONS
Freshman Academic Profile: Basis for Candidate Selection: *Very important factors considered include:* Rigor of secondary school record. *Important factors considered include:* Recommendation(s), character/personal qualities, talent/ability. *Other factors considered include:* Class rank, application essay, standardized test scores, alumni/ae relation, extracurricular activities, geographical residence, interview, state residency, volunteer work, work experience. **Freshman Admission Requirements:** High school diploma is required and GED is accepted. *Academic units required:* 4 English, 1 mathematics, 1 science, 3 social studies, 1 history. *Academic units recommended:* 2 mathematics, 2 science, (1 science labs). **Freshman Admission Statistics: Transfer Admission Requirements:** High school transcript, college transcript(s), Lowest grade transferable C. **General Admission Information:** Application fee $30. Notification on a rolling basis, beginning on or about 11/1. Nonfall registration accepted. Admission may be deferred for a maximum of 12.

COSTS AND FINANCIAL AID
Financial Aid Statistics: 66% undergrads receive need-based scholarship or grant aid. 50% undergrads receive non-need-based scholarship or grant aid. 68% undergrads receive need-based self-help aid. **Criteria for awarding institutional aid:** *Non-need-based:* Academics, leadership, state/district residency.

STATE UNIVERSITY OF NEW YORK— EMPIRE STATE COLLEGE

Two Union Avenue, Saratoga, NY 12866
Phone: 518-587-2100 **Financial Aid Phone:** 518-587-2100
E-mail: admissions@esc.edu **CEEB Code:** 2214
Fax: 518-587-9759 **Website:** esc.edu **ACT Code:** 2737

This public school was founded in 1971.

RATINGS
Admissions Selectivity Rating: 60*   **Fire Safety Rating:** 60*   **Green Rating:** 60*

STUDENTS AND FACULTY
Enrollment: 11,893. **Student Body:** 60% female, 40% male, 6% out-of-state, 5% international. Asian 2%, African American 14%, Caucasian 65%, Hispanic 8%, Native American 1%.
Retention and Graduation: Faculty: Student/faculty ratio 10:1. 169 full-time faculty, 98% hold PhDs, 15% are are members of minority groups, 60% are women.

ACADEMICS
Degrees: Associate, bachelor's, master's. **Majors with Highest Enrollment:** Business/commerce; community organization and advocacy; physical sciences, other. **Special Study Options:** Cross-registration, distance learning, double major, dual enrollment, external degree program, independent study, internships, student-designed major, Student-designed courses of study. **Combined degree programs:** BA/MA, BS/MA; BPS/MA

FACILITIES
Housing: Computers: Students can register for classes online. Administrative functions (other than registration) can be performed online.

CAMPUS LIFE
Environment: Village. **Activities:** Literary magazine.

ADMISSIONS
Freshman Academic Profile: Minimum paper TOEFL 550. Minimum computer TOEFL 213. **Basis for Candidate Selection:** *Very important factors considered include:* Application essay, character/personal qualities. *Other factors considered include:* Recommendation(s), rigor of secondary school record, talent/ability. **Freshman Admission Requirements:** High school diploma is required and GED is accepted. **Freshman Admission Statistics:** 1,023 applied, 78% admitted, 69% enrolled. **Transfer Admission Requirements:** High school transcript, essay or personal statement, Lowest grade transferable C. **General Admission Information:** Nonfall registration accepted. Admission may be deferred for a maximum of 3 years.

COSTS AND FINANCIAL AID
Annual in-state tuition $4,970. Annual out-of-state tuition $12,870. Required fees $225. **Required Forms and Deadlines:** FAFSA, state aid form. Priority financial aid filing date 4/1. **Notification of Awards: Types of Aid:** *Need-based scholarships/grants:* Federal Pell, SEOG, state scholarships/grants, private scholarships, the school's own gift aid. *Loans:* FFEL Subsidized Stafford, FFEL Unsubsidized Stafford, FFEL PLUS, Federal Perkins. *Student Employment:* Federal Work-Study Program available. **Financial Aid Statistics:** 57% undergrads receive any aid.

STATE UNIVERSITY OF NEW YORK— FARMINGDALE STATE UNIVERSITY OF NEW YORK

Admissions Office, 2350 Broadhollow Road, Farmingdale, NY 11735
Phone: 631-420-2200
E-mail: admissions@farmingdale.edu
Fax: 631-420-2633 **Website:** www.farmingdale.edu

This public school was founded in 1912. It has a 380-acre campus.

RATINGS
Admissions Selectivity Rating: 60*   **Fire Safety Rating:** 60*   **Green Rating:** 60*

STUDENTS AND FACULTY
Student Body: 1% out-of-state.
Retention and Graduation: Faculty: Student/faculty ratio 21:1. 187 full-time faculty, 50% hold PhDs, 11% are are members of minority groups, 38% are women.

ACADEMICS
Degrees: Associate, bachelor's, certificate, terminal associate, transfer associate. **Classes:** Most classes have 20–29 students. **Special Study Options:** Distance learning, double major, dual enrollment, internships, study abroad Special programs offered to physically disabled students include reader services, tutors. **Career services:** Alumni services, career/job search classes, career assessment, internships.

FACILITIES
Housing: 90% of campus accessible to physically disabled. **Computers:** Students can register for classes online. Administrative functions (other than registration) can be performed online.

CAMPUS LIFE
Environment: Village. **Activities:** Literary magazine. **Organizations: Athletics (Intercollegiate):** *Men:* Baseball, basketball, cross-country, golf, lacrosse, soccer, track/field (outdoor), track/field (indoor). *Women:* Basketball, cross-country, soccer, softball, track/field (outdoor), track/field (indoor), volleyball.

ADMISSIONS
Freshman Academic Profile: Minimum paper TOEFL 500. Minimum computer TOEFL 173. **Basis for Candidate Selection:** *Very important factors considered include:* Class rank, rigor of secondary school record. *Important factors considered include:* Talent/ability. *Other factors considered include:* Application essay, recommendation(s), standardized test scores, alumni/ae relation, character/personal qualities, extracurricular activities, interview, volunteer work, work experience. **Freshman Admission Requirements:** High school diploma is required and GED is accepted. *Academic units required:* 4 English, 2 mathematics, 1 science, (1 science labs), 4 social studies. *Academic units recommended:* 4 English, 4 mathematics, 3 science, (3 science labs), 4 social studies. **Freshman Admission Statistics:** 2,382 applied, 68% admitted, 56% enrolled. **Transfer Admission Requirements:** High school transcript, college transcript(s), statement of good standing from prior institution(s). Minimum college GPA of 2.0 required. Lowest grade transferable C. **General Admission Information:** Application fee $30. Notification on a rolling basis, beginning on or about 11/1. Nonfall registration accepted. Admission may be deferred for a maximum of 1 year. Credit and/or placement offered for CEEB Advanced Placement tests.

COSTS AND FINANCIAL AID
Required Forms and Deadlines: FAFSA, institution's own financial aid form **Notification of Awards: Types of Aid:** *Need-based scholarships/grants:* Federal Pell, SEOG, state scholarships/grants *Loans:* Direct Subsidized Stafford, Direct Unsubsidized Stafford, Direct PLUS, FFEL Subsidized Stafford, FFEL Unsubsidized Stafford, FFEL PLUS, Federal Perkins, Federal Nursing, state loans *Student Employment:* Federal Work-Study Program available. Institutional employment available. Off-campus job opportunities are good.

STATE UNIVERSITY OF NEW YORK— FASHION INSTITUTE OF TECHNOLOGY

Seventh Avenue at 27th Street, New York, NY 10001
Phone: 212-217-7675
E-mail: fitinfo@fitsuny.edu
Fax: Website: www.fitnyc.suny.edu

This public school was founded in 1944.

RATINGS
Admissions Selectivity Rating: 60*   **Fire Safety Rating:** 60*   **Green Rating:** 60*

STUDENTS AND FACULTY
Student Body: 17% out-of-state.

FACILITIES
Housing: Coed dorms, men's dorms, women's dorms, apartments for single students.

CAMPUS LIFE
Activities: literary magazine, radio station, student government, student newspaper, yearbook. **Organizations:** 70 registered organizations, 7 honor societies, 1 religious organizations.

ADMISSIONS

General Admission Information: Regular application deadline 1/15.

COSTS AND FINANCIAL AID

Annual in-state tuition $2,500. Annual out-of-state tuition $5,950. Room and board $5,600. Required fees $210. Average book expense $1,200. **Required Forms and Deadlines:** FAFSA, institution's own financial aid form, state aid form. **Types of Aid:** *Need-based scholarships/grants: Loans:* FFEL Subsidized Stafford, FFEL PLUS. *Student Employment:* Federal Work-Study Program available. Highest amount earned per year from on-campus jobs $1,400.

STATE UNIVERSITY OF NEW YORK—FREDONIA

178 Central Avenue, Fredonia, NY 14063
Phone: 716-673-3251 **Financial Aid Phone:** 716-673-3253
E-mail: admissions@fredonia.edu **CEEB Code:** 2539
Fax: 716-673-3249 **Website:** www.fredonia.edu **ACT Code:** 2934

This public school was founded in 1826. It has a 249-acre campus.

RATINGS

Admissions Selectivity Rating: 81   **Fire Safety Rating:** 74   **Green Rating:** 60*

STUDENTS AND FACULTY

Enrollment: 5,067. **Student Body:** 56% female, 44% male, 2% out-of-state, 1% international (8 countries represented). Asian 1%, African American 2%, Caucasian 68%, Hispanic 2%.
Retention and Graduation: 85% freshmen return for sophomore year. 49% freshmen graduate within 4 years. 32% grads go on to further study within 1 year. **Faculty:** Student/faculty ratio 16:1. 242 full-time faculty, 79% hold PhDs, 16% are are members of minority groups, 45% are women.

ACADEMICS

Degrees: Bachelor's, master's, post-master's certificate. **Classes:** Most classes have 10–19 students. Most lab/discussion sessions have 20–29 students. **Majors with Highest Enrollment:** Business/commerce; elementary education and teaching; music, other. **Special Study Options:** Accelerated program, distance learning, double major, honors program, independent study, internships, student-designed major, study abroad, teacher certification program **Combined degree programs:** BA/DDS, 3+4 Optometry with SUNY State College of Optometry. Special programs offered to physically disabled students include note-taking services, reader services, tape recorders, tutors. **Career services:** Alumni network, alumni services, career/job search classes, career assessment, internships.

FACILITIES

Housing: Coed dorms, special housing for disabled students, men's dorms, women's dorms, apartments for single students. 85% of campus accessible to physically disabled. **Special Academic Facilities/Equipment:** Art center, education and local history museums, teacher education research center, developmental reading center, Sheldon Communications Lab, SMART class-rooms, greenhouse. **Computers:** 100% of classrooms, 100% of libraries, 100% of dining areas, 100% of student union, 85% of common outdoor areas have wireless network access. Students can register for classes online. Administrative functions (other than registration) can be performed online.

CAMPUS LIFE

Environment: Village. **Activities:** Choral groups, concert band, dance, drama/theater, jazz band, literary magazine, music ensembles, musical theater, opera, pep band, radio station, student government, student newspaper, symphony orchestra, television station, campus ministries, international student organization. **Organizations:** 152 registered organizations, 22 honor societies, 5 religious organizations. 3 fraternities, 3 sororities. **Athletics (Intercollegiate):** *Men:* Baseball, basketball, cross-country, diving, ice hockey, soccer, swimming, track/field (outdoor), track/field (indoor). *Women:* Basketball, cheerleading, cross-country, diving, lacrosse, soccer, softball, swimming, tennis, track/field (outdoor), track/field (indoor), volleyball. **On-Campus Highlights:** University Commons, Michael C. Rockefeller Arts Center, Library, Natatorium-Swimming pool and diving area, Rosch Recital Hall. **Environmental Initiatives:** Campus owned gas well, RecycleMania, Sustainability Committee.

ADMISSIONS

Freshman Academic Profile: Average high school GPA 3.45. 16% in top 10% of high school class, 48% in top 25% of high school class, 90% in top 50% of high school class. 75% from public high schools. SAT Math middle 50% range 510–600. SAT Critical Reading middle 50% range 500–590. ACT middle 50% range 21–26. Minimum paper TOEFL 500. Minimum computer TOEFL 177. Minimum web-based TOEFL 62. **Basis for Candidate Selection:** *Very*

important factors considered include: Academic GPA, rigor of secondary school record. *Important factors considered include:* Class rank, recommendation(s), standardized test scores, extracurricular activities. *Other factors considered include:* Application essay, alumni/ae relation, character/personal qualities, first generation, level of applicant's interest, racial/ethnic status, talent/ability, volunteer work, work experience. **Freshman Admission Requirements:** High school diploma is required and GED is accepted. *Academic units required:* 4 English, 3 mathematics, 3 science, 3 foreign language, 4 social studies. *Academic units recommended:* 4 English, 4 mathematics, 4 science, 3 foreign language, 4 social studies. **Freshman Admission Statistics:** 6,489 applied, 52% admitted, 35% enrolled. **Transfer Admission Requirements:** College transcript(s), minimum college GPA of 2.0 required. Lowest grade transferable D. **General Admission Information:** Application fee $40. Early decision application deadline 11/1. Notification on a rolling basis, beginning on or about 12/1. Nonfall registration accepted. Admission may be deferred for a maximum of 1 year. Credit and/or placement offered for CEEB Advanced Placement tests.

COSTS AND FINANCIAL AID

Annual in-state tuition $4,970. Annual out-of-state tuition $12,870. Room and board $9,140. Required fees $1,238. Average book expense $1,000. **Required Forms and Deadlines:** FAFSA, state aid form. Priority financial aid filing date 2/1. **Notification of Awards:** Applicants will be notified of awards on a rolling basis beginning 3/10. **Types of Aid:** *Need-based scholarships/grants:* Federal Pell, SEOG, state scholarships/grants, private scholarships, the school's own gift aid. *Loans:* FFEL Subsidized Stafford, FFEL Unsubsidized Stafford, FFEL PLUS, Federal Perkins. *Student Employment:* Federal Work-Study Program available. Highest amount earned per year from on-campus jobs $1,000. Off-campus job opportunities are good. **Financial Aid Statistics:** 52% freshmen, 53% undergrads receive need-based scholarship or grant aid. 15% freshmen, 10% undergrads receive non-need-based scholarship or grant aid. 53% freshmen, 54% undergrads receive need-based self-help aid. 81% freshmen, 85% undergrads receive any aid. 88% undergrads borrow to pay for school. Average cumulative indebtedness $19,338. **Criteria for awarding institutional aid:** *Non-need-based:* Academics, alumni affiliation, art, athletics, leadership, minority status, music/drama.

STATE UNIVERSITY OF NEW YORK AT GENESEO

1 College Circle, Geneseo, NY 14454-1401
Phone: 585-245-5571 **Financial Aid Phone:** 585-245-5731
E-mail: admissions@geneseo.edu **CEEB Code:** 2540
Fax: 585-245-5550 **Website:** www.geneseo.edu **ACT Code:** 2936

This public school was founded in 1871. It has a 220-acre campus.

RATINGS

Admissions Selectivity Rating: 94   **Fire Safety Rating:** 87   **Green Rating:** 87

STUDENTS AND FACULTY

Enrollment: 5,488. **Student Body:** 57% female, 43% male, 2% out-of-state, international (24 countries represented). Asian 8%, African American 3%, Caucasian 74%, Hispanic 2%, Native American 1%.
Retention and Graduation: 90% freshmen return for sophomore year. 64% freshmen graduate within 4 years. 41% grads go on to further study within 1 year. 21% grads pursue arts and sciences degrees. 4% grads pursue law degrees. 2% grads pursue business degrees. 4% grads pursue medical degrees. **Faculty:** Student/faculty ratio 19:1. 251 full-time faculty, 84% hold PhDs, 15% are members of minority groups, 41% are women.

ACADEMICS

Degrees: Bachelor's, master's. **Classes:** Most classes have 20–29 students. Most lab/discussion sessions have 10–19 students. **Majors with Highest Enrollment:** Biology/biological sciences; business administration and management; psychology. **Special Study Options:** Cross-registration, double major, dual enrollment, English as a Second Language (ESL), honors program, independent study, internships, study abroad, teacher certification program, Albany semester, Washington semester, 3/2 Engineering, 3-3 Engineering, 4/1 MBA, 3/4 Dentistry, 3/4 Optometry, 3/4 Osteopathic Medicine, 3/2 or 3/1 nursing, 3/3 physical therapy, pre-med and pre-law advisory program. **Combined degree programs:** BA/MA, BA/DDS, BA/DO; BA/OD. Special programs offered to physically disabled students include note-taking services, reader services, tape recorders. **Career services:** Alumni network, alumni services, career/job search classes, career assessment, internships **Career services highlights include:** Career Partners Network.

FACILITIES

Housing: Coed dorms, special housing for disabled students, special housing for international students, town houses and special interest housing is available. Some fraternities and sororities have housing independent of college. 95% of campus accessible to physically disabled. **Special Academic Facilities/Equipment:** Four theatres, electron microscopes. Integrated Science Center **Computers:** 100% of classrooms, 60% of dorms, 100% of libraries, 100% of dining areas, 100% of student union, 10% of common outdoor areas have wireless network access. Students can register for classes online. Administrative functions (other than registration) can be performed online. Undergraduates are required to own a computer.

CAMPUS LIFE

Environment: Village. **Activities:** Choral groups, dance, drama/theater, jazz band, literary magazine, music ensembles, musical theater, pep band, radio station, student government, student newspaper, symphony orchestra, television station, campus ministries, international student organization, Model UN. **Organizations:** 175 registered organizations, 12 honor societies, 7 religious organizations. 8 fraternities, 11 sororities. **Athletics (Intercollegiate):** *Men:* Basketball, cross-country, diving, ice hockey, lacrosse, soccer, swimming, track/field (outdoor), track/field (indoor). *Women:* Basketball, cross-country, diving, equestrian sports, field hockey, lacrosse, soccer, softball, swimming, tennis, track/field (outdoor), track/field (indoor), volleyball. **On-Campus Highlights:** MacVittie College Union, The Gazebo, Milne Library, Alumni Fieldhouse (Workout Center), College Green. **Environmental Initiatives:** Signing of the Presidents Climate Commitment. Currently developing our Climate Action Plan. Establishment of Geneseo's Environmental Impact and Sustainability Task Force. Gold Lecture Series—Live Green Task Force Work/Initiatives.

ADMISSIONS

Freshman Academic Profile: Average high school GPA 3.75. 56% in top 10% of high school class, 88% in top 25% of high school class, 99% in top 50% of high school class. 79% from public high schools. SAT Math middle 50% range 630–690. SAT Critical Reading middle 50% range 610–700. ACT middle 50% range 28–30. Minimum paper TOEFL 525. Minimum computer TOEFL 197. Minimum web-based TOEFL 71. **Basis for Candidate Selection:** *Very important factors considered include:* Rigor of secondary school record, standardized test scores. *Important factors considered include:* Class rank, application essay, academic GPA, recommendation(s), extracurricular activities, racial/ethnic status, talent/ability. *Other factors considered include:* Alumni/ae relation, character/personal qualities, first generation, level of applicant's interest, volunteer work, work experience. **Freshman Admission Requirements:** High school diploma is required and GED is accepted. *Academic units recommended:* 4 English, 4 mathematics, 4 science, 4 foreign language, 4 social studies. **Freshman Admission Statistics:** 10,412 applied, 35% admitted, 26% enrolled. **Transfer Admission Requirements:** High school transcript, college transcript(s), minimum college GPA of 3.0 required. Lowest grade transferable D. **General Admission Information:** Application fee $40. Early decision application deadline 11/15. Regular application deadline 1/1. Regular notification 3/1. Nonfall registration accepted. Admission may be deferred for a maximum of 1 year. Credit offered for CEEB Advanced Placement tests.

COSTS AND FINANCIAL AID

Average book expense $900. **Required Forms and Deadlines:** FAFSA, state aid form. Financial aid filing deadline 2/15. **Notification of Awards:** Applicants will be notified of awards on a rolling basis beginning 3/15. **Types of Aid:** *Need-based scholarships/grants:* Federal Pell, SEOG, state scholarships/grants *Loans:* FFEL Subsidized Stafford, FFEL Unsubsidized Stafford, FFEL PLUS, Federal Perkins. *Student Employment:* Federal Work-Study Program available. Institutional employment available. Highest amount earned per year from on-campus jobs $3,500. Off-campus job opportunities are poor. **Financial Aid Statistics:** 20% freshmen, 44% undergrads receive need-based scholarship or grant aid. 20% freshmen, 15% undergrads receive non-need-based scholarship or grant aid. 21% freshmen, 36% undergrads receive need-based self-help aid. 62% freshmen, 72% undergrads receive any aid. 63% undergrads borrow to pay for school. Average cumulative indebtedness $21,000. **Criteria for awarding institutional aid:** *Non-need-based:* Academics, art, leadership, minority status, music/drama, religious affiliation, state/district residency.

STATE UNIVERSITY OF NEW YORK—INSTITUTE OF TECHNOLOGY AT UTICA/ROME

PO Box 3050, Utica, NY 13504
Phone: 315-792-7500
E-mail: admissions@sunyit.edu **CEEB Code:** 2896
Fax: 315-792-7837 **Website:** www.sunyit.edu **ACT Code:** 2953

This public school was founded in 1966. It has a 850-acre campus.

RATINGS

Admissions Selectivity Rating: 75   **Fire Safety Rating:** 60*   **Green Rating:** 60*

STUDENTS AND FACULTY

Enrollment: 1,993. **Student Body:** 43% female, 57% male, 2% out-of-state, 1% international. Asian 2%, African American 7%, Caucasian 89%, Hispanic 3%, Native American 1%.

Retention and Graduation: Faculty: Student/faculty ratio 19:1. 97 full-time faculty, 78% hold PhDs, 24% are are members of minority groups, 38% are women.

ACADEMICS

Degrees: Bachelor's, master's, post-master's certificate. **Classes:** Most classes have 10–19 students. Most lab/discussion sessions have 10–19 students. **Special Study Options:** Accelerated program, cross-registration, distance learning, double major, dual enrollment, English as a Second Language (ESL), independent study, internships, study abroad. **Combined degree programs:** Computer/Info Science—BS/MS, Nursing—BS/MS. Special programs offered to physically disabled students include note-taking services, reader services, tape recorders, tutors. **Career services:** Alumni services, career/job search classes, career assessment, internships, regional alumni.

FACILITIES

Housing: Coed dorms, special housing for disabled students. 98% of campus accessible to physically disabled. **Special Academic Facilities/Equipment:** Gannett Gallery, New York State Telecommunications Museum. **Computers:** Students can register for classes online. Administrative functions (other than registration) can be performed online.

CAMPUS LIFE

Environment: Village. **Activities:** Drama/theater, jazz band, music ensembles, radio station, student government, student newspaper, television station, yearbook, international student organization. **Organizations:** 30 registered organizations, 4 honor societies, 1 religious organizations. **Athletics (Intercollegiate):** *Men:* Baseball, basketball, golf, lacrosse, soccer. *Women:* Basketball, cross-country, golf, soccer, softball, volleyball.

ADMISSIONS

Freshman Academic Profile: Average high school GPA 88. 10% in top 10% of high school class, 33% in top 25% of high school class, 79% in top 50% of high school class. SAT Math middle 50% range 490–600. SAT Critical Reading middle 50% range 450–560. ACT middle 50% range 22–25. Minimum paper TOEFL 550. Minimum computer TOEFL 213. **Basis for Candidate Selection:** *Very important factors considered include:* Academic GPA, standardized test scores. *Important factors considered include:* Rigor of secondary school record, extracurricular activities. *Other factors considered include:* Application essay, recommendation(s), interview, talent/ability, volunteer work, work experience. **Freshman Admission Requirements:** High school diploma is required and GED is accepted. *Academic units required:* 4 English, 3 mathematics, 3 science, (3 science labs), 2 social studies, 2 history. *Academic units recommended:* 4 mathematics, 4 science, (4 science labs), 3 foreign language, 2 academic electives. **Freshman Admission Statistics:** 1,770 applied, 38% admitted, 30% enrolled. **Transfer Admission Requirements:** College transcript(s), statement of good standing from prior institution(s). Minimum college GPA of 2.5 required. Lowest grade transferable D. **General Admission Information:** Application fee $40. Regular application deadline 8/1. Notification on a rolling basis, beginning on or about 1/15. Nonfall registration accepted. Admission may be deferred for a maximum of 1 year. Neither credit nor placement offered for CEEB Advanced Placement tests.

COSTS AND FINANCIAL AID

Annual in-state tuition $4,970. Annual out-of-state tuition $12,870. Room and board $8,750. Required fees $1,120. Average book expense $1,000. **Required Forms and Deadlines:** FAFSA, state aid form. Priority financial aid filing date 3/15. **Notification of Awards:** Applicants will be notified of awards on a rolling basis beginning 3/17. **Types of Aid:** *Need-based scholarships/grants:* Federal Pell, SEOG, state scholarships/grants, private scholarships *Loans:* Direct Subsidized Stafford, Direct Unsubsidized Stafford, Direct PLUS, Federal Perkins, Federal Nursing *Student Employment:* Federal Work-Study Program available.

Institutional employment available. Off-campus job opportunities are good. **Financial Aid Statistics:** 67% freshmen, 62% undergrads receive need-based scholarship or grant aid. 62% freshmen, 56% undergrads receive need-based self-help aid. **Criteria for awarding institutional aid:** *Non-need-based:* Academics.

STATE UNIVERSITY OF NEW YORK— MARITIME COLLEGE

6 Pennyfield Ave, Throggs Neck, NY 10465
Phone: 718-409-7200 **Financial Aid Phone:** 718-409-7254
E-mail: admissions@sunymaritime.edu
Fax: 718-409-7465 **Website:** www.sunymaritime.edu **ACT Code:** 2954

This public school was founded in 1874. It has a 56-acre campus.

RATINGS
Admissions Selectivity Rating: 78   **Fire Safety Rating:** 77   **Green Rating:** 77

STUDENTS AND FACULTY
Enrollment: 1,562. **Student Body:** 10% female, 90% male, 27% out-of-state, 7% international. Asian 4%, African American 6%, Caucasian 72%, Hispanic 9%.
Retention and Graduation: 76% freshmen return for sophomore year. 5% grads go on to further study within 1 year. 4% grads pursue business degrees. **Faculty:** Student/faculty ratio 17:1. 70 full-time faculty, 49% hold PhDs, 6% are are members of minority groups, 21% are women.

ACADEMICS
Degrees: Associate, bachelor's, master's. **Classes:** Most classes have 20–29 students. Most lab/discussion sessions have 20–29 students. **Majors with Highest Enrollment:** Engineering; transportation/transportation management. **Special Study Options:** Cooperative education program, distance learning, double major, dual enrollment, English as a Second Language (ESL), honors program, independent study, internships, United States Coast Guard-issued deck and engine license program. **Honors programs:** Honors Program **Combined degree programs:** BS/MS. Special programs offered to physically disabled students include note-taking services, reader services, tape recorders, tutors. **Career services:** Alumni network, alumni services, career/job search classes, career assessment, internships, regional alumni. **Career services highlights include:** SUNY Maritime Colleges undergraduate students achieve 99% career placement and earn the top average starting salaries in America. The average starting salary for the Class of 2008 was $61,000. Students who choose to participate in the Regiment of Cadets experience the benefits of a structured learning environment, along with opportunities to develop leadership ability and excel in leadership roles. Each summer, the Regiment of Cadets embarks on a Summer Sea Term onboard the Training Ship Empire State. The training ship is 565 feet long and 17,000 tons. While students reside and operate the Training Ship Empire State, they see the world, stopping in four our more international ports (i.e., Greece, Italy, Ireland, Turkey, etc.).

FACILITIES
Housing: Coed dorms, special housing for disabled studentsMost undergraduates required to live in on-campus housing. 81% of campus accessible to physically disabled. **Special Academic Facilities/Equipment:** Maritime Industry Museum, Fort Schuyler(National Historic Landmark), Bridge Simulator, Liquid Cargo Simulator, 565 ft. Training Ship Empire State VI, Diesel Simulator, 2 Research Ships, State-of-the-Art Electrical Engineering Lab, NY State Strategic Center for Port and Maritime Security (224 ft USS Stalwart), Computerized Weather Station, Maritime College Waterfront Sailboat Fleet:20 Vanguard 420's, 6 Vanguard FJ's, 1 Laser, J-105, J-35, J-24, Colgate 26. **Computers:** 75% of classrooms, 30% of dorms, 100% of libraries, 50% of student union, have wireless network access. Students can register for classes online.

CAMPUS LIFE
Environment: Metropolis. **Activities:** Choral groups, jazz band, marching band, music ensembles, pep band, student government, yearbook, campus ministries, international student organization. **Organizations:** 30 registered organizations, 4 religious organizations. **Athletics (Intercollegiate):** *Men:* Baseball, basketball, cross-country, football, ice hockey, lacrosse, riflery, soccer, swimming. *Women:* Basketball, crew/rowing, cross-country, lacrosse, riflery, soccer, softball, swimming, volleyball. **On-Campus Highlights:** Fort Schuyler, Empire State VI **Environmental Initiatives:** Energy Reduction Programs with NYPA Building a green building with DASNY Partnering with energy management companies

ADMISSIONS
Freshman Academic Profile: Average high school GPA 2.95. 12% in top 10% of high school class, 60% in top 25% of high school class, 92% in top 50% of high school class. SAT Math middle 50% range 510–600. SAT Critical Reading middle 50% range 460–550. ACT middle 50% range 20–24. Minimum paper TOEFL 550. Minimum computer TOEFL 213. Minimum web-based TOEFL 79. **Basis for Candidate Selection:** *Very important factors considered include:* Academic GPA, rigor of secondary school record, standardized test scores. *Important factors considered include:* Recommendation(s), talent/ability, volunteer work, work experience. *Other factors considered include:* Class rank, application essay, alumni/ae relation, extracurricular activities, first generation, interview, level of applicant's interest. **Freshman Admission Requirements:** High school diploma is required and GED is accepted. *Academic units required:* 3 English, 3 mathematics, 3 science, (1 science labs), 1 foreign language, 3 social studies, 3 history. *Academic units recommended:* 4 English, 4 mathematics, 4 science, 3 foreign language. **Freshman Admission Statistics:** 1,386 applied, 63% admitted, 41% enrolled. **Transfer Admission Requirements:** High school transcript, college transcript(s), minimum college GPA of 2.5 required. Lowest grade transferable 2. **General Admission Information:** Application fee $40. Notification on a rolling basis, beginning on or about 9/15. Nonfall registration accepted. Credit offered for CEEB Advanced Placement tests.

COSTS AND FINANCIAL AID
Annual in-state tuition $4,970. Annual out-of-state tuition $12,870. Room and board $9,930. Required fees $1,120. Average book expense $1,260. **Required Forms and Deadlines:** FAFSA, institution's own financial aid form Financial aid filing deadline 7/15. Priority financial aid filing date 3/1. **Notification of Awards:** Applicants will be notified of awards on a rolling basis beginning 3/15. **Types of Aid:** *Need-based scholarships/grants:* Federal Pell, SEOG, state scholarships/grants, private scholarships, the school's own gift aid. *Loans:* FFEL Subsidized Stafford, FFEL Unsubsidized Stafford, FFEL PLUS, Federal Perkins, state loans *Student Employment:* Federal Work-Study Program available. Institutional employment available. Highest amount earned per year from on-campus jobs $9,896. Off-campus job opportunities are fair. **Financial Aid Statistics:** 30% freshmen, 31% undergrads receive need-based scholarship or grant aid. 16% freshmen, 16% undergrads receive non-need-based scholarship or grant aid. 44% freshmen, 40% undergrads receive need-based self-help aid. 73% undergrads borrow to pay for school. Average cumulative indebtedness $30,244. **Criteria for awarding institutional aid:** *Non-need-based:* Academics, leadership, state/district residency.

STATE UNIVERSITY OF NEW YORK—NEW PALTZ

100 Hawk Drive, New Paltz, NY 12561-2499
Phone: 845-257-3200 **Financial Aid Phone:** 845-257-3250
E-mail: admissions@newpaltz.edu **CEEB Code:** 2541
Fax: 845-257-3209 **Website:** www.newpaltz.edu **ACT Code:** 2938

This public school was founded in 1828. It has a 216-acre campus.

RATINGS
Admissions Selectivity Rating: 89   **Fire Safety Rating:** 70   **Green Rating:** 88

STUDENTS AND FACULTY
Enrollment: 6,318. **Student Body:** 66% female, 34% male, 4% out-of-state, 3% international (38 countries represented). Asian 4%, African American 5%, Caucasian 57%, Hispanic 10%, Native American 1%.
Retention and Graduation: 88% freshmen return for sophomore year. 45% freshmen graduate within 4 years. 53% grads go on to further study within 1 year. **Faculty:** Student/faculty ratio 16:1. 325 full-time faculty, 83% hold PhDs, 16% are are members of minority groups, 51% are women. 1.9% of classes are taught by teaching assistants.

ACADEMICS
Degrees: Bachelor's, master's, post-master's certificate. **Classes:** Most classes have 20–29 students. **Majors with Highest Enrollment:** Business administration and management; education; fine/studio arts. **Special Study Options:** Cooperative education program, cross-registration, distance learning, double major, dual enrollment, English as a Second Language (ESL), exchange student program (domestic), honors program, independent study, internships, liberal arts/career combination, student-designed major, study abroad, teacher certification program. **Honors programs:** The Honors Program exists to challenge New Paltz Students beyond what is usually expected of them. It was designed around the philosophy that intense and rigorous courses, taught by outstanding instructors and filled with motivated, focused students would create the optimal learning environment. The Honors Program is small, consisting of around 100 students. Once admitted to the Program, students take special

Honors seminars, which are interdisciplinary and small in size (usually around 10 students). Unlike traditional lecture courses, Honors seminars emphasize dialogue and non-lecture based learning; students are expected to come to class with something to say and to actively participate in debate and discussion. **Combined degree programs:** BS/DO BS/OD BS/MS. Special programs offered to physically disabled students include note-taking services, reader services, tape recorders, tutors. **Career services:** Alumni services, career/job search classes, career assessment, internships. **Career services highlights include:** Internship stipend program provides SUNY New Paltz students with scholarship stipends. These funds allow students to participate in career related experiences regardless of financial constraints.

FACILITIES

Housing: Coed dorms, special housing for disabled students, men's dorms, special housing for international students, women's dorms, The First-Year Initiative, Honors Housing, Art Program Housing. 90% of campus accessible to physically disabled. **Special Academic Facilities/Equipment:** Samuel Dorsky Museum of Art, Resnick Engineering Hall, Coykendall Media Center, Communication Disorders Training Center and Clinic; Music Therapy Training Center and Clinic; Shepherd Recital Hall, Honors Center; Martin Luther King, Jr. Study Center; Fournier Mass Spectrometer;Raymond Kurdt Theatre Collection; more **Computers:** 70% of classrooms, 45% of dorms, 100% of libraries, 90% of dining areas, 90% of student union, 10% of common outdoor areas have wireless network access. Students can register for classes online. Administrative functions (other than registration) can be performed online.

CAMPUS LIFE

Environment: Village. **Activities:** Choral groups, concert band, dance, drama/theater, jazz band, literary magazine, music ensembles, musical theater, radio station, student government, student newspaper, symphony orchestra, television station, campus ministries, international student organization, Model UN. **Organizations:** 196 registered organizations, 12 honor societies, 10 religious organizations. 11 fraternities, 17 sororities. **Athletics (Intercollegiate):** *Men:* Baseball, basketball, cross-country, diving, soccer, swimming, tennis, volleyball. *Women:* Basketball, cross-country, diving, field hockey, lacrosse, soccer, softball, swimming, tennis, volleyball. **On-Campus Highlights:** Samuel Dorsky Museum of Art, Lenape and Esopus Residence Halls, Athletic and Wellness Center, Student Union, Hasbrouck Dining Hall. **Environmental Initiatives:** Investment of large amounts of $ to energy management, for example all new construction of 5,000 sq.or larger ft will be LEED-certified with a target of Silver or higher all renovation will be be have a target of LEED certification using LEED criteria guidelines. Upgrade of recycling efforts including conitnued participation in recylomania, and, increased capture of recylcing materials in construction projects tripling the recycling capture to well over 300 tons, and joining the EPA Waste Wise Program. Participation in the President's climate commitment

ADMISSIONS

Freshman Academic Profile: Average high school GPA 3.5. 24% in top 10% of high school class, 70% in top 25% of high school class, 94% in top 50% of high school class. SAT Math middle 50% range 520–610. SAT Critical Reading middle 50% range 520–610. SAT Writing middle 50% range 520–620. ACT middle 50% range 23–27. Minimum paper TOEFL 550. Minimum computer TOEFL 213. **Basis for Candidate Selection:** *Very important factors considered include:* Academic GPA, rigor of secondary school record, standardized test scores. *Important factors considered include:* Application essay, recommendation(s). *Other factors considered include:* Class rank, extracurricular activities, talent/ability, volunteer work, work experience. **Freshman Admission Requirements:** High school diploma is required and GED is accepted. *Academic units required:* 4 English, 3 mathematics, 3 science, (2 science labs), 2 foreign language, 4 social studies, 1 history. *Academic units recommended:* 4 English, 4 mathematics, 4 science, (4 science labs), 4 foreign language, 4 social studies, 1 history. **Freshman Admission Statistics:** 15,426 applied, 34% admitted, 20% enrolled. **Transfer Admission Requirements:** College transcript(s), statement of good standing from prior institution(s). Minimum college GPA of 2.75 required. Lowest grade transferable C–. **General Admission Information:** Application fee $40. Regular application deadline 4/1. Notification on a rolling basis, beginning on or about 1/1. Nonfall registration not accepted. Credit and/or placement offered for CEEB Advanced Placement tests.

COSTS AND FINANCIAL AID

Annual in-state tuition $4,970. Annual out-of-state tuition $12,870. **Required Forms and Deadlines:** FAFSA, state aid form Financial aid filing deadline 4/1. Priority financial aid filing date 3/15. **Notification of Awards:** Applicants will be notified of awards on a rolling basis beginning 4/1. **Types of Aid:** *Need-based scholarships/grants:* Federal Pell, SEOG, state scholarships/grants, private scholarships, the school's own gift aid. *Loans:* FFEL Subsidized Stafford, FFEL Unsubsidized Stafford, FFEL PLUS, Federal Perkins. *Student Employment:* Federal Work-Study Program available. Institutional employment available. Highest amount earned per year from on-campus jobs $8,569. Off-

campus job opportunities are good. **Financial Aid Statistics:** 27% freshmen, 26% undergrads receive need-based scholarship or grant aid. 6% freshmen, 3% undergrads receive non-need-based scholarship or grant aid. 49% freshmen, 45% undergrads receive need-based self-help aid. 67% freshmen, 62% undergrads receive any aid. 66% undergrads borrow to pay for school. Average cumulative indebtedness $16,823. **Criteria for awarding institutional aid:** *Non-need-based:* Academics, alumni affiliation, art, music/drama.

STATE UNIVERSITY OF NEW YORK—OSWEGO

229 Sheldon Hall, Oswego, NY 13126-3599
Phone: 315-312-2250 **Financial Aid Phone:** 315-312-2248
E-mail: admiss@oswego.edu **CEEB Code:** 2543
Fax: 315-312-3260 **Website:** www.oswego.edu **ACT Code:** 2942

This public school was founded in 1861. It has a 696-acre campus.

RATINGS

Admissions Selectivity Rating: 82   **Fire Safety Rating:** 66   **Green Rating:** 75

STUDENTS AND FACULTY

Enrollment: 7,145. **Student Body:** 52% female, 48% male, 2% out-of-state, 1% international (15 countries represented). Asian 2%, African American 4%, Caucasian 87%, Hispanic 5%.
Retention and Graduation: 81% freshmen return for sophomore year. 40% freshmen graduate within 4 years. 19% grads go on to further study within 1 year. 22% grads pursue arts and sciences degrees. 4% grads pursue law degrees. 6% grads pursue business degrees. 5% grads pursue medical degrees. **Faculty:** Student/faculty ratio 18:1. 312 full-time faculty, 79% hold PhDs, 20% are are members of minority groups, 40% are women.

ACADEMICS

Degrees: Bachelor's, master's, post-master's certificate. **Classes:** Most classes have 10–19 students. Most lab/discussion sessions have 20–29 students. **Majors with Highest Enrollment:** Business/commerce; elementary education and teaching. **Special Study Options:** Accelerated program, cross-registration, distance learning, double major, dual enrollment, English as a Second Language (ESL), exchange student program (domestic), external degree program, honors program, independent study, internships, liberal arts/career combination, study abroad, teacher certification program **Honors programs:** Over 275 students participate in our campus wide Honors Program. Students will take smaller courses based on the program's core multidisciplinary courses in the social sciences, the natural sciences, the humanities, and philosophy, as well as several other courses in math, English, and a foreign language. The courses emphasize the interrelatedness of the disciplines, their historical and intellectual origins, their roles in modern society, and their impact on life in the future. **Combined degree programs:** BA/MA, BS/MBA—5 year accounting BS/MBA program. Special programs offered to physically disabled students include note-taking services, reader services, tape recorders, tutors. **Career services:** Alumni network, alumni services, career/job search classes, career assessment, internships, regional alumni. **Career services highlights include:** We currently have 133 student in Internship Program 43 male student and 90 female students, involving 78 organizations.

FACILITIES

Housing: Coed dorms, wellness housing, theme housing Global living and learning center, suites for upperclassmen, nontraditional student housing, first-year experience residence hall for incoming freshmen only, housing for 21 and over single suites, several rooms equipped with special equipment to meet needs of disabled students available. 85% of campus accessible to physically disabled. **Special Academic Facilities/Equipment:** Tyler Hall Art Galleries, Rice Creek Biological Field Station, curriculum materials center, electron microscopy lab, planetarium. **Computers:** 80% of classrooms, 10% of dorms, 100% of libraries, 100% of dining areas, 100% of student union, have wireless network access. Students can register for classes online. Administrative functions (other than registration) can be performed online.

CAMPUS LIFE

Environment: Village. **Activities:** Choral groups, concert band, dance, drama/theater, jazz band, literary magazine, music ensembles, musical theater, radio station, student government, student newspaper, student-run film society, symphony orchestra, television station, yearbook, international student organization. **Organizations:** 148 registered organizations, 21 honor societies, 6 religious organizations. 13 fraternities, 10 sororities. **Athletics (Intercollegiate):** *Men:* Baseball, basketball, cross-country, diving, golf, ice hockey, lacrosse, soccer, swimming, tennis, track/field (outdoor), track/field (indoor), wrestling. *Women:* Basketball, cross-country, diving, field hockey, ice hockey, lacrosse, soccer, softball, swimming, tennis, track/field (outdoor), track/field (indoor), volleyball. **On-Campus Highlights:** Romney Fieldhouse/ Campus Ctr (Hockey and Conference), Hewitt Union: The Student Union, Rich Hall: The School of Business, Tyler Hall: The Fine Arts Building, Penfield Library and Cafe, Rice Creek Biological field station, The Sweete Shoppe in the Hewitt Union; Laker Hall (Field House), Johnson Hall (1st Year Residence Hall). **Environmental Initiatives:** Commitment to LEED Gold for construction projects President's Climate Commitment (ACUPCC) Actively pursuing on-site generation and geothermal sources.

ADMISSIONS

Freshman Academic Profile: Average high school GPA 3.3. 15% in top 10% of high school class, 54% in top 25% of high school class, 89% in top 50% of high school class. SAT Math middle 50% range 520–600. SAT Critical Reading middle 50% range 530–590. ACT middle 50% range 21–25. Minimum paper TOEFL 550. Minimum computer TOEFL 213. Minimum web-based TOEFL 80. **Basis for Candidate Selection:** *Very important factors considered include:* Academic GPA, rigor of secondary school record. *Important factors considered include:* Class rank, standardized test scores. *Other factors considered include:* Application essay, recommendation(s), character/personal qualities, extracurricular activities, first generation, interview, level of applicant's interest, racial/ethnic status, talent/ability, volunteer work, work experience. **Freshman Admission Requirements:** High school diploma is required and GED is accepted. *Academic units required:* 4 English, 3 mathematics, 3 science, (2 science labs), 2 foreign language, 4 social studies. *Academic units recommended:* 4 English, 4 mathematics, 4 science, (3 science labs), 4 foreign language, 4 social studies. **Freshman Admission Statistics:** 10,464 applied, 47% admitted, 28% enrolled. **Transfer Admission Requirements:** College transcript(s), minimum college GPA of 2.5 required. Lowest grade transferable D. **General Admission Information:** Application fee $40. Early decision application deadline 11/15. Notification on a rolling basis, beginning on or about 1/15. Nonfall registration accepted. Admission may be deferred for a maximum of 1 year. Credit offered for CEEB Advanced Placement tests.

COSTS AND FINANCIAL AID

Annual in-state tuition $4,970. Annual out-of-state tuition $12,870. Room and board $10,870. Required fees $1,286. Average book expense $800. **Required Forms and Deadlines:** FAFSA, state aid form. Priority financial aid filing date 3/1. **Notification of Awards:** Applicants will be notified of awards on a rolling basis beginning 3/1. **Types of Aid:** *Need-based scholarships/grants:* Federal Pell, SEOG, state scholarships/grants, private scholarships, the school's own gift aid. *Loans:* FFEL Subsidized Stafford, FFEL Unsubsidized Stafford, FFEL PLUS, Federal Perkins. *Student Employment:* Federal Work-Study Program available. Institutional employment available. Highest amount earned per year from on-campus jobs $2,000. **Financial Aid Statistics:** 56% freshmen, 56% undergrads receive need-based scholarship or grant aid. 10% freshmen, 5% undergrads receive non-need-based scholarship or grant aid. 56% freshmen, 56% undergrads receive need-based self-help aid. 84% freshmen, 85% undergrads receive any aid. 86% undergrads borrow to pay for school. Average cumulative indebtedness $25,488. **Criteria for awarding institutional aid:** *Non-need-based:* Academics, state/district residency.

STATE UNIVERSITY OF NEW YORK— PLATTSBURGH

1001 Kehoe Bldg, Plattsburgh, NY 12901
Phone: 518-564-2040
E-mail: admissions@plattsburgh.edu **CEEB Code:** 2544
Fax: 518-564-2045 **Website:** www.plattsburgh.edu **ACT Code:** 2944

This public school was founded in 1889. It has a 300-acre campus.

RATINGS

Admissions Selectivity Rating: 73   Fire Safety Rating: 60*   Green Rating: 60*

STUDENTS AND FACULTY

Enrollment: 5,328. **Student Body:** 58% female, 42% male, 4% out-of-state, 7% international (56 countries represented). Asian 2%, African American 5%, Caucasian 76%, Hispanic 3%.
Retention and Graduation: 75% freshmen return for sophomore year. 37% freshmen graduate within 4 years. 34% grads go on to further study within 1 year. 31% grads pursue arts and sciences degrees. 1% grads pursue law degrees. 2% grads pursue business degrees. 1% grads pursue medical degrees. **Faculty:** Student/faculty ratio 18:1. 250 full-time faculty, 90% hold PhDs, 12% are are members of minority groups, 36% are women.

ACADEMICS

Degrees: Bachelor's, master's, post-bachelor's certificate, post-master's certificate. **Classes:** Most classes have 10–19 students. Most lab/discussion sessions have 20–29 students. **Majors with Highest Enrollment:** Business/commerce; early childhood education; special education and teaching. **Special Study Options:** Cooperative education program, cross-registration, distance learning, double major, dual enrollment, English as a Second Language (ESL), exchange student program (domestic), honors program, independent study, internships, liberal arts/career combination, student-designed major, study abroad, teacher certification program. **Honors programs:** The honors program is offered in two levels, General Honors and Advance Honors. Each seminar in General Honors program is limited to about 15 students and is taught by faculty who have a reputation of excellence in teaching. Occasionally distance-learning experiences are available which allow students to work with faculty at other colleges and universities in the US; Advance Honors' work continues the goals and ideals of General Honors, except the work is focused in student's major and requires that students design and carry out a project in research, in performance, in fieldwork, or whatever else would be appropriate to a particular major. **Combined degree programs:** 3-2 French, Spanish; 3-1 Medical Tech. and Cytote. Special programs offered to physically disabled students include note-taking services, reader services, tape recorders, tutors. **Career services:** Alumni network, alumni services, career/job search classes, career assessment, internships.

FACILITIES

Housing: Coed dorms, special housing for disabled students, special housing for international students, Wellness floor, Substance free building and floors, Quiet floors, men's floor, women's floors, Extended lodging. 95% of campus accessible to physically disabled. **Special Academic Facilities/Equipment:** Art galleries, sculpture courtyard, theatre and concert halls, communications/lecture hall, interactive video for telecourses, radio and TV broadcasting facilities, planetarium, on-site research center for biotechnology and environmental science, enzymology lab, electron microscope, remote sensing lab, NMR spectrophotometer, computer-operated infrared spectrophotometer, gas chromatograph, mass spectrometer, computerized liquid scintillation counter, facility for analysis of environmental pollutants in lake water, sediments and biota, lake research/sampling vesel with differential GPS navigation equipment, ubductively coupled plasma/mass spectrometer, ion chromatograph/high performance liquid chromatograph, mercury detector. **Computers:** Students can register for classes online. Administrative functions (other than registration) can be performed online.

CAMPUS LIFE

Environment: Village. **Activities:** Choral groups, concert band, drama/theater, jazz band, literary magazine, music ensembles, radio station, student government, student newspaper, student-run film society, symphony orchestra, television station, yearbook. **Organizations:** 97 registered organizations, 26 honor societies, 3 religious organizations. 6 fraternities, 7 sororities. **Athletics (Intercollegiate):** *Men:* Basketball, cross-country, golf, ice hockey, lacrosse, rugby, soccer, track/field (outdoor), track/field (indoor). *Women:* Basketball, cross-country, golf, ice hockey, rugby, soccer, softball, tennis, track/field (outdoor), track/field (indoor), volleyball. **On-Campus Highlights:** Fitness Center, Art Museums, College Field House, Computer Labs, College Center.

ADMISSIONS

Freshman Academic Profile: Average high school GPA 3. 11% in top 10% of high school class, 33% in top 25% of high school class, 75% in top 50% of high school class. 98% from public high schools. SAT Math middle 50% range 480–560. SAT Critical Reading middle 50% range 480–560. ACT middle 50% range 19–24. Minimum paper TOEFL 450. Minimum computer TOEFL 133. **Basis for Candidate Selection:** *Very important factors considered include:* Rigor of secondary school record, standardized test scores, interview. *Important factors considered include:* Class rank, application essay, recommendation(s), alumni/ae relation, character/personal qualities, extracurricular activities, racial/ethnic status, talent/ability. *Other factors considered include:* Volunteer work, work experience. **Freshman Admission Requirements:** High school diploma is required and GED is accepted. *Academic units required:* 4 English, 3 mathematics, 3 science, 3 foreign language, 3 social studies, 1 history. *Academic units recommended:* 4 English, 4 mathematics, 4 science, 3 foreign language, 3 social studies, 1 history, 2 academic electives. **Freshman Admission Statistics:** 6,798 applied, 62% admitted, 23% enrolled. **Transfer Admission Requirements:** College transcript(s), minimum college GPA of 2.3 required. Lowest grade transferable D. **General Admission Information:** Application fee $40. Early decision application deadline 11/15. Regular application deadline 8/1. Notification on a rolling basis, beginning on or about 1/15. Nonfall registration accepted. Admission may be deferred for a maximum of 1 year. Credit and/or placement offered for CEEB Advanced Placement tests.

COSTS AND FINANCIAL AID

Annual in-state tuition $4,350. Annual out-of-state tuition $10,300. Room and board $6,500. Required fees $850. Average book expense $850. **Required**

Forms and Deadlines: FAFSA, state aid form. Priority financial aid filing date 3/1. **Notification of Awards:** Applicants will be notified of awards on a rolling basis beginning 3/15. **Types of Aid:** *Need-based scholarships/grants:* Federal Pell, SEOG, state scholarships/grants, private scholarships, the school's own gift aid, Scholarships for disavantaged students, State Educational Opportunity Program. *Loans:* Direct Subsidized Stafford, Direct Unsubsidized Stafford, Direct PLUS, Federal Perkins, Federal Nursing, Grace Appleton Loan, privately endowed administered by a Trust Company; Awarded by the College. *Student Employment:* Federal Work-Study Program available. Institutional employment available. Highest amount earned per year from on-campus jobs $1,540. Off-campus job opportunities are good. **Financial Aid Statistics:** 55% freshmen, 55% undergrads receive need-based scholarship or grant aid. 19% freshmen, 18% undergrads receive non-need-based scholarship or grant aid. 52% freshmen, 52% undergrads receive need-based self-help aid. 73% undergrads borrow to pay for school. Average cumulative indebtedness $16,158. **Criteria for awarding institutional aid:** *Non-need-based:* Academics, alumni affiliation, art, leadership, music/drama, state/district residency.

STATE UNIVERSITY OF NEW YORK—POTSDAM

44 Pierrepont Avenue, Potsdam, NY 13676
Phone: 315-267-2180 **Financial Aid Phone:** 315-267-2162
E-mail: admissions@potsdam.edu **CEEB Code:** 2545
Fax: 315-267-2163 **Website:** www.potsdam.edu **ACT Code:** 2946

This public school was founded in 1816. It has a 240-acre campus.

RATINGS
Admissions Selectivity Rating: 75 **Fire Safety Rating:** 74 **Green Rating:** 84

STUDENTS AND FACULTY
Enrollment: 3,691. **Student Body:** 57% female, 43% male, 3% out-of-state, (22 countries represented).
Retention and Graduation: 37% freshmen graduate within 4 years. 42% grads go on to further study within 1 year. 11% grads pursue arts and sciences degrees. 7% grads pursue law degrees. 8% grads pursue business degrees. 6% grads pursue medical degrees. **Faculty:** Student/faculty ratio 14:1. 263 full-time faculty, 78% hold PhDs, 9% are are members of minority groups, 43% are women.

ACADEMICS
Degrees: Bachelor's, master's. **Classes:** Most classes have 10–19 students. Most lab/discussion sessions have 10–19 students. **Majors with Highest Enrollment:** Business administration and management; education, other; music teacher education. **Special Study Options:** Cross-registration, distance learning, double major, dual enrollment, exchange student program (domestic), honors program, independent study, internships, liberal arts/career combination, student-designed major, study abroad, teacher certification program, First-year students may enroll in interdisciplinary program to study art, literature, science, and sociology of the Adirondacks. Extension offers undergraduate and graduate courses with emphasis on teacher education. Combined degree options in engineering with Clarkson University and SUNY Binghamton; accounting, engineering or management with SUNY Institute of Technology. **Honors programs:** The Honors Program is designed to offer special curricular, co-curricular, and extra curricular opportunities for our college's most academically talented students. Benefits include priority registration, honors courses, field trips, mentoring, housing, and select study abroad options. **Combined degree programs:** BA/MA, BA/MST. Special programs offered to physically disabled students include note-taking services, reader services, tape recorders, tutors. **Career services:** Alumni network, alumni services, career/job search classes, career assessment.

FACILITIES
Housing: Coed dorms, special housing for disabled students, special housing for international students, apartments for single students, wellness housing, theme housing, First year experience, Quiet study International House, Transfer student housing, Sustainability. 95% of campus accessible to physically disabled. **Special Academic Facilities/Equipment:** Art gallery, anthropology museum, ecology museum, three performance halls, theatre, synthesizer music studios, planetarium, electron microscope, nuclear magnetic resonator, seismograph. **Computers:** 20% of classrooms, 100% of dorms, 100% of libraries, 100% of dining areas, 100% of student union, 40% of common outdoor areas have wireless network access. Students can register for classes online. Administrative functions (other than registration) can be performed online.

CAMPUS LIFE
Environment: Village. **Activities:** Choral groups, concert band, dance, drama/theater, jazz band, literary magazine, music ensembles, musical theater, opera, radio station, student government, student newspaper, symphony orchestra, yearbook, campus ministries, international student organization. **Organizations:** 100 registered organizations, 17 honor societies, 3 religious organizations. 4 fraternities, 7 sororities. **Athletics (Intercollegiate):** *Men:* Basketball, cross-country, diving, equestrian sports, golf, ice hockey, lacrosse, soccer, swimming. *Women:* Basketball, cross-country, diving, equestrian sports, ice hockey, lacrosse, soccer, softball, swimming, tennis, volleyball. **On-Campus Highlights:** Hosmer Concert Hall, Maxcy Athletic Complex, Townhouses, Gibson Art Gallery, Barrrington Student Union, Becky's Place (new dining facility) Minerva's Cafe. **Environmental Initiatives:** Increase recycle efforts; increase purchase of green products and energy star equipment; increase purchase of renewable energy.

ADMISSIONS
Freshman Academic Profile: Average high school GPA 87.35. 7.2% in top 10% of high school class, 31.4% in top 25% of high school class, 70% in top 50% of high school class. SAT Math middle 50% range 470–570. SAT Critical Reading middle 50% range 470–570. ACT middle 50% range 20–24. Minimum paper TOEFL 550. Minimum computer TOEFL 213. Minimum web-based TOEFL 79. **Basis for Candidate Selection:** *Very important factors considered include:* Academic GPA, rigor of secondary school record. *Important factors considered include:* Class rank, application essay, recommendation(s), character/personal qualities, extracurricular activities, interview, talent/ability. *Other factors considered include:* standardized test scores, alumni/ae relation, level of applicant's interest, volunteer work, work experience. **Freshman Admission Requirements:** High school diploma is required and GED is accepted. *Academic units required:* 4 English, 2 mathematics, 2 science, (1 science labs), 4 social studies, 1 visual/performing arts. *Academic units recommended:* 4 English, 4 mathematics, 4 science, (2 science labs), 4 foreign language, 4 social studies, 1 visual/performing arts. **Freshman Admission Statistics:** 4,525 applied, 66% admitted, 28% enrolled. **Transfer Admission Requirements:** College transcript(s), minimum college GPA of 2.0 required. Lowest grade transferable D. **General Admission Information:** Application fee $40. Notification on a rolling basis, beginning on or about 10/1. Nonfall registration accepted. Admission may be deferred for a maximum of 1 year. Credit and/or placement offered for CEEB Advanced Placement tests.

COSTS AND FINANCIAL AID
Average book expense $1,200. **Required Forms and Deadlines:** FAFSA, state aid form Financial aid filing deadline 5/1. Priority financial aid filing date 3/1. **Notification of Awards:** Applicants will be notified of awards on a rolling basis beginning 2/1. **Types of Aid:** *Need-based scholarships/grants:* Federal Pell, SEOG, state scholarships/grants, private scholarships, the school's own gift aid, VESID, Veteran Benefits, BIA, Native American, Academic Achievement (ACG), SMART (National Math & Science Grant). *Loans:* Direct Subsidized Stafford, Direct Unsubsidized Stafford, Direct PLUS, Federal Perkins, college/university loans from institutional funds, Alternative Loans. *Student Employment:* Federal Work-Study Program available. Institutional employment available. Off-campus job opportunities are good. **Financial Aid Statistics:** 65% freshmen, 60% undergrads receive need-based scholarship or grant aid. 28% freshmen, 22% undergrads receive non-need-based scholarship or grant aid. 62% freshmen, 56% undergrads receive need-based self-help aid. 87% freshmen, 71% undergrads receive any aid. 80% undergrads borrow to pay for school. Average cumulative indebtedness $19,220. **Criteria for awarding institutional aid:** *Non-need-based:* Academics, art, leadership, minority status, music/drama.

STATE UNIVERSITY OF NEW YORK— PURCHASE COLLEGE

Admissions Office, 735 Anderson Hill Road, Purchase, NY 10577
Phone: 914-251-6300
E-mail: admissions@purchase.edu **CEEB Code:** 2878
Fax: 914-251-6314 **Website:** www.purchase.edu **ACT Code:** 2931

This public school was founded in 1967. It has a 550-acre campus.

RATINGS
Admissions Selectivity Rating: 85 **Fire Safety Rating:** 60* **Green Rating:** 85

STUDENTS AND FACULTY

Enrollment: 3,830. **Student Body:** 56% female, 44% male, 19% out-of-state, 2% international (21 countries represented). Asian 3%, African American 7%, Caucasian 55%, Hispanic 12%.

Retention and Graduation: 82% freshmen return for sophomore year. 30% freshmen graduate within 4 years. **Faculty:** Student/faculty ratio 16:1. 150 full-time faculty, 69% hold PhDs, 17% are are members of minority groups, 51% are women. 1% of classes are taught by teaching assistants.

ACADEMICS

Degrees: Bachelor's, master's, post-master's certificate. **Classes:** Most classes have 10–19 students. Most lab/discussion sessions have fewer than 10 students. **Majors with Highest Enrollment:** liberal arts and sciences/liberal studies; visual and performing arts. **Special Study Options:** Cross-registration, distance learning, double major, English as a Second Language (ESL), independent study, internships, liberal arts/career combination, student-designed major, study abroad Special programs offered to physically disabled students include note-taking services, reader services, tape recorders, tutors. **Career services:** Alumni services, career/job search classes, career assessment, internships.

FACILITIES

Housing: Coed dorms, special housing for disabled students, special housing for international students, apartments for married students, apartments for single students, wellness housing, theme housing. 100% of campus accessible to physically disabled. **Special Academic Facilities/Equipment:** Museum, four-theatre performing arts center, visual arts facility, children's center, recording studio, electron microscopes. **Computers:** Students can register for classes online. Administrative functions (other than registration) can be performed online.

CAMPUS LIFE

Environment: Town. **Activities:** Choral groups, dance, drama/theater, jazz band, literary magazine, music ensembles, musical theater, radio station, student government, student newspaper, student-run film society, television station **Organizations:** 30 registered organizations, **Athletics (Intercollegiate):** *Men:* Baseball, basketball, cross-country, golf, soccer, tennis, volleyball. *Women:* Basketball, cross-country, soccer, softball, tennis, volleyball. **On-Campus Highlights:** The Performing Arts Center, The Neuberger Museum, state-of-the-art Athletic Complex, Starbucks, Fort Awesome, new Student Services building. **Environmental Initiatives:** Commited to reduce GHG emissions by 80% by 2050 (Presidents Climate Commitment) Have campus policy that all new buildings constructed be LEED Silver Certified or better Purchase biodegradable and recycled paper products for dining halls and 100% recycled copy paper.

ADMISSIONS

Freshman Academic Profile: Average high school GPA 3.2. 11% in top 10% of high school class, 38% in top 25% of high school class, 81% in top 50% of high school class. SAT Math middle 50% range 490–580. SAT Critical Reading middle 50% range 510–630. SAT Writing middle 50% range 500–620. ACT middle 50% range 21–25. Minimum paper TOEFL 550. Minimum computer TOEFL 213. **Basis for Candidate Selection:** *Very important factors considered include:* Application essay, academic GPA, talent/ability. *Important factors considered include:* standardized test scores. *Other factors considered include:* Class rank, recommendation(s), rigor of secondary school record, character/personal qualities, extracurricular activities, interview. **Freshman Admission Requirements:** High school diploma is required and GED is accepted. **Freshman Admission Statistics:** 8,620 applied, 27% admitted, 30% enrolled. **Transfer Admission Requirements:** College transcript(s), minimum college GPA of 3.0 required. Lowest grade transferable D. **General Admission Information:** Application fee $40. Early decision application deadline 11/1. Regular application deadline 7/15. Regular notification 5/1. Nonfall registration accepted. Admission may be deferred for a maximum of 1 year. Credit and/or placement offered for CEEB Advanced Placement tests.

COSTS AND FINANCIAL AID

Annual in-state tuition $4,970. Annual out-of-state tuition $12,870. Room and board $9,908. Required fees $1,461. Average book expense $1,100. **Required Forms and Deadlines:** FAFSA, state aid form. Priority financial aid filing date 2/1. **Notification of Awards:** Applicants will be notified of awards on a rolling basis beginning 3/1. **Types of Aid:** *Need-based scholarships/grants:* Federal Pell, SEOG, state scholarships/grants, private scholarships, the school's own gift aid. *Loans:* Direct Subsidized Stafford, Direct Unsubsidized Stafford, Direct PLUS, Federal Perkins. *Student Employment:* Federal Work-Study Program available. Institutional employment available. Off-campus job opportunities are excellent. **Financial Aid Statistics:** 42% freshmen, 46% undergrads receive need-based scholarship or grant aid. 1% freshmen, 1% undergrads receive non-need-based scholarship or grant aid. 53% freshmen, 55% undergrads receive need-based self-help aid. 58% undergrads borrow to pay for school. Average cumulative indebtedness $26,275. **Criteria for awarding institutional aid:** *Non-need-based:* Academics, art, minority status, music/drama

See page 1248.

STATE UNIVERSITY OF NEW YORK—
STONY BROOK UNIVERSITY

Office of Admissions, Stony Brook, NY 11794-1901
Phone: 631-632-6868 **Financial Aid Phone:** 631-632-6840
E-mail: enroll@stonybrook.edu **CEEB Code:** 2548
Fax: 631-632-9898 **Website:** www.stonybrook.edu **ACT Code:** 2952

This public school was founded in 1957. It has a 1450-acre campus.

RATINGS
Admissions Selectivity Rating: 91   **Fire Safety Rating:** 60*   **Green Rating:** 92

STUDENTS AND FACULTY

Enrollment: 16,034. **Student Body:** 48% female, 52% male, 7% out-of-state, 7% international (100 countries represented). Asian 23%, African American 7%, Caucasian 37%, Hispanic 9%.

Retention and Graduation: 89% freshmen return for sophomore year. 45% freshmen graduate within 4 years. 34% grads go on to further study within 1 year. **Faculty:** Student/faculty ratio 19:1. 972 full-time faculty, 97% hold PhDs, 19% are are members of minority groups, 34% are women.

ACADEMICS

Degrees: Bachelor's, doctoral, master's, post-bachelor's certificate, post-master's certificate. **Classes:** Most classes have 20–29 students. Most lab/discussion sessions have 20–29 students. **Majors with Highest Enrollment:** Biology/biological sciences; business/commerce; psychology. **Special Study Options:** Cross-registration, distance learning, double major, English as a Second Language (ESL), exchange student program (domestic), honors program, independent study, internships, student-designed major, study abroad, teacher certification program, Albany Semester, Undergrads may take grad level courses BS/MS programs, BE/MS, BS/MA—Living Learning Centers in residence halls, Honors College, undergraduate research and creative activities program where undergraduates work with faculty on research projects, university learning communities and (WISE) Women in Science and Engineering. **Honors programs:** BA/MD **Combined degree programs:** BA/MA, MD/PhD. Special programs offered to physically disabled students include note-taking services, reader services, tape recorders, tutors. **Career services:** Alumni network, alumni services, career/job search classes, career assessment, internships, regional alumni. **Career services highlights include:** Career services internship program modeled after successful corporate internship programs. Includes career counseling, marketing, graphics, human resources, and technology.

FACILITIES

Housing: Coed dorms, special housing for disabled students, apartments for married students, apartments for single students, single sex floors in coed dorms. Living Learning Centers, first year resident members of each college are housed together in the same residential Quadrangle. 75% of campus accessible to physically disabled. **Special Academic Facilities/Equipment:** SAC Gallery, Staller Gallery, Wang Center, Tabler Center for the Arts. **Computers:** 50% of classrooms, 50% of dorms, 50% of libraries, 50% of dining areas, 50% of student union, 50% of common outdoor areas have wireless network access. Students can register for classes online. Administrative functions (other than registration) can be performed online.

CAMPUS LIFE

Environment: Town. **Activities:** Choral groups, concert band, dance, drama/theater, jazz band, literary magazine, marching band, music ensembles, musical theater, opera, pep band, radio station, student government, student newspaper, student-run film society, symphony orchestra, yearbook, campus ministries. **Organizations:** 292 registered organizations, 6 honor societies, 25 religious organizations. 17 fraternities, 16 sororities. **Athletics (Intercollegiate):** *Men:* Baseball, basketball, cross-country, diving, football, lacrosse, soccer, swimming, tennis, track/field (outdoor), track/field (indoor). *Women:* Basketball, cross-country, diving, lacrosse, soccer, softball, swimming, tennis, track/field (outdoor), track/field (indoor), volleyball. **On-Campus Highlights:** Staller Center for the Arts, Sports Complex and Stadium, Student Activities Center, University Hospital, The Charles B. Wang Center, Building and Grounds: Main campus. 1,100 acres. Research and Development Campus, 246 acres adjacent to the main campus. Stony Brook Southampton, 82 acres. Stony Brook Manhattan. New buildings: Humanities Building, undergraduate apartments; Center for Excellence in Wireless and Information Technology under construction. **Environmental Initiatives:** Signing of ACUPCC. Commitment to obtain carbon nuetrality by 2050. Creation of Environmental Stewardship Department which focuses on energy reduction, waste reduction and all areas of sustainability for the campus. Campus 5 Year Plan specifically addresses our commitment to a green campus.

ADMISSIONS

Freshman Academic Profile: Average high school GPA 3.6. 34% in top 10% of high school class, 69% in top 25% of high school class, 93% in top 50% of high school class. 90% from public high schools. SAT Math middle 50% range 580–670. SAT Critical Reading middle 50% range 520–620. SAT Writing middle 50% range 520–620. ACT middle 50% range 24–28. Minimum paper TOEFL 550. Minimum computer TOEFL 213. Minimum web-based TOEFL 80. **Basis for Candidate Selection:** *Very important factors considered include:* Academic GPA, rigor of secondary school record, standardized test scores. *Important factors considered include:* Class rank. *Other factors considered include:* Application essay, recommendation(s), alumni/ae relation, character/personal qualities, extracurricular activities, first generation, interview, level of applicant's interest, state residency, talent/ability, volunteer work, work experience. **Freshman Admission Requirements:** High school diploma is required and GED is accepted. *Academic units required:* 4 English, 3 mathematics, 3 science, 2 foreign language, 4 social studies. *Academic units recommended:* 4 mathematics, 4 science, 3 foreign language. **Freshman Admission Statistics:** 28,497 applied, 40% admitted, 25% enrolled. **Transfer Admission Requirements:** College transcript(s), minimum college GPA of 3.0 required. Lqwest grade transferable C. **General Admission Information:** Application fee $40. Notification on a rolling basis, beginning on or about 2/1. Nonfall registration accepted. Admission may be deferred for a maximum of 2 semesters. Credit and/or placement offered for CEEB Advanced Placement tests.

COSTS AND FINANCIAL AID

Annual in-state tuition $4,970. Annual out-of-state tuition $12,870. Room and board $9,590. Required fees $1,519. Average book expense $900. **Required Forms and Deadlines:** FAFSAProgram Specific Forms. Priority financial aid filing date 3/1. **Notification of Awards:** Applicants will be notified of awards on a rolling basis beginning 3/1. **Types of Aid:** *Need-based scholarships/grants:* Federal Pell, SEOG, state scholarships/grants, the school's own gift aid. *Loans:* Direct Subsidized Stafford, Direct Unsubsidized Stafford, Direct PLUS, Federal Perkins. *Student Employment:* Federal Work-Study Program available. Institutional employment available. Highest amount earned per year from on-campus jobs $12,638. Off-campus job opportunities are excellent. **Financial Aid Statistics:** 48% freshmen, 48% undergrads receive need-based scholarship or grant aid. 2% freshmen, 1% undergrads receive non-need-based scholarship or grant aid. 36% freshmen, 39% undergrads receive need-based self-help aid. 1% freshmen, 1% undergrads receive athletic scholarships. 74% freshmen, 65% undergrads receive any aid. 63% undergrads borrow to pay for school. Average cumulative indebtedness $17,502. **Criteria for awarding institutional aid:** *Non-need-based:* Academics, alumni affiliation, athletics, leadership, music/drama.

STATE UNIVERSITY OF NEW YORK— UPSTATE MEDICAL UNIVERSITY

766 Irving Avenue, Syracuse, NY 13210
Phone: 315-464-4570 **Financial Aid Phone:** 315-464-4329
E-mail: admiss@upstate.edu **CEEB Code:** 2547
Fax: 315-464-8867 **Website:** **ACT Code:** 2981

This public school was founded in 1850. It has a 25-acre campus.

RATINGS

Admissions Selectivity Rating: 60*   **Fire Safety Rating:** 60*   **Green Rating:** 60*

STUDENTS AND FACULTY

Enrollment: 269. **Student Body:** 74% female, 26% male, 4% out-of-state, 2% international. Asian 5%, African American 6%, Caucasian 86%, Native American 1%.
Retention and Graduation: **Faculty:** Student/faculty ratio 12:1. 503 full-time faculty, 91% hold PhDs, 19% are are members of minority groups, 31% are women.

ACADEMICS

Degrees: Bachelor's, first professional, master's, post-master's certificate. **Classes:** Most classes have fewer than 10 students. **Majors with Highest Enrollment:** Medicine (md); Special programs offered to physically disabled students include note-taking services, reader services, tape recorders, tutors. **Career services:** Alumni network, regional alumni.

FACILITIES

Housing: Coed dorms, apartments for married students, apartments for single students. 100% of campus accessible to physically disabled. **Special Academic Facilities/Equipment:** 350 bed Tertiary Care Hospital **Computers:** Administrative functions (other than registration) can be performed online.

CAMPUS LIFE

Environment: City. **Activities:** student government, international student organization. **Organizations:** 51 registered organizations, 3 religious organizations. **On-Campus Highlights:** Weiskotten Hall, Silverman Hall, University Hospital, Institute for Human Performance, Campus Activities Building.

ADMISSIONS

Freshman Academic Profile: 0% from public high schools. Minimum paper TOEFL 550. Minimum computer TOEFL 213. **Basis for Candidate Selection: Freshman Admission Requirements:** High school diploma is required and GED is accepted. *Academic units recommended:* 4 English, 3 mathematics, 3 science, 3 social studies. **Freshman Admission Statistics: Transfer Admission Requirements:** High school transcript, college transcript(s), essay or personal statement, interview, minimum college GPA of 2.0 required. Lowest grade transferable C–. **General Admission Information:** Application fee $40. Nonfall registration not accepted. Admission may be deferred for a maximum of 1 year.

COSTS AND FINANCIAL AID

Annual in-state tuition $4,660. Annual out-of-state tuition $11,740. Room and board $5,768. Required fees $558. Average book expense $975. **Required Forms and Deadlines:** FAFSA. Priority financial aid filing date 3/1. **Notification of Awards:** Applicants will be notified of awards on a rolling basis beginning 6/1. **Types of Aid:** *Need-based scholarships/grants:* Federal Pell, SEOG, state scholarships/grants, the school's own gift aid. *Loans:* FFEL Subsidized Stafford, FFEL Unsubsidized Stafford, FFEL PLUS, Federal Perkins. *Student Employment:* Federal Work-Study Program available. Institutional employment available. Off-campus job opportunities are excellent. **Financial Aid Statistics:** 42% undergrads receive need-based scholarship or grant aid. 52% undergrads receive non-need-based scholarship or grant aid. 67% undergrads receive need-based self-help aid. 76% undergrads borrow to pay for school. Average cumulative indebtedness $17,650.

STATE UNIVERSITY OF NEW YORK— UNIVERSITY AT ALBANY

Office of Undergraduate Admissions, University at Albany-SUNY, 1400 Washington Ave, Albany, NY 12222
Phone: 518-442-5435 **Financial Aid Phone:** 518-442-3202
E-mail: ugadmissions@albany.edu **CEEB Code:** 2532
Fax: 518-442-5383 **Website:** www.albany.edu **ACT Code:** 2926

This public school was founded in 1844. It has a 795-acre campus.

RATINGS

Admissions Selectivity Rating: 86   **Fire Safety Rating:** 80   **Green Rating:** 88

STUDENTS AND FACULTY

Enrollment: 12,797. **Student Body:** 48% female, 52% male, 5% out-of-state, 3% international (84 countries represented). Asian 6%, African American 10%, Caucasian 57%, Hispanic 9%.
Retention and Graduation: 85% freshmen return for sophomore year. 53% freshmen graduate within 4 years. 51% grads go on to further study within 1 year. 13% grads pursue arts and sciences degrees. 6% grads pursue law degrees. 3% grads pursue business degrees. 4% grads pursue medical degrees. **Faculty:** Student/faculty ratio 18.6:1. 637 full-time faculty, 95% hold PhDs, 17% are are members of minority groups, 36% are women. 11% of classes are taught by teaching assistants.

ACADEMICS

Degrees: Bachelor's, master's, post-bachelor's certificate, post-master's certificate. **Classes:** Most classes have 20–29 students. Most lab/discussion sessions have 20–29 students. **Majors with Highest Enrollment:** Business administration and management; English language and literature; psychology. **Special Study Options:** Accelerated program, cross-registration, distance learning, double major, dual enrollment, English as a Second Language (ESL), honors program, independent study, internships, liberal arts/career combination, student-designed major, study abroad, Accelerated 5 year Bachelors/Masters programs in 40 fields; Internships with New York State Legislature; Combined Bachelors/Law degree with Albany Law school; 3+2 Engineering Program with RPI, Clarkson, and others; Biology/Dental Program with Boston University Goldman School of Dental Medicine, Bachelors/Doctor of Optometry with SUNY State College; Early Assurance Program with Albany Medical College and SUNY Upstate Medical College. **Honors programs:** Our Presidential Scholars program combines merit scholarships, honors courses, priority registration, special housing, and faculty mentor opportunities. **Combined degree programs:** BA/JD, BA/MA, BA/MEng, accelerated 5 yr bachelor's/master's in 40 fields. Special programs offered to physically disabled students include note-taking services, reader services, tape recorders, tutors. **Career services:** Alumni network, alumni services, career/job search classes, career assessment, internships, regional alumni. **Career services highlights include:** Internships with New York State Legislature; On-Campus Recruiting for graduates and those seeking internships.

FACILITIES

Housing: Coed dorms, special housing for international students, apartments for married students, apartments for single students, wellness housing, theme housing Disabled Student Services provides individualized services including information on accessible housing. 99% of campus accessible to physically disabled. **Special Academic Facilities/Equipment:** Performing Arts Center, Art Museum, art and dance studios, sculpture foundry, nuclear accelerator and advanced materials facilities, a peptide synthesis facility, recombinatnt DNA sequencing laboratories, and atmospheric science's Whiteface Mountain observational facility. **Computers:** 75% of classrooms, 100% of dorms, 100% of libraries, 75% of dining areas, 100% of student union, 75% of common outdoor areas have wireless network access. Students can register for classes online. Administrative functions (other than registration) can be performed online.

CAMPUS LIFE

Environment: City. **Activities:** Choral groups, concert band, dance, drama/theater, jazz band, literary magazine, music ensembles, musical theater, pep band, radio station, student government, student newspaper, student-run film society, symphony orchestra, television station, yearbook, campus ministries, international student organization. **Organizations:** 200 registered organizations, 20 honor societies, 17 religious organizations. 11 fraternities, 18 sororities. **Athletics (Intercollegiate):** *Men:* Baseball, basketball, cross-country, football, lacrosse, soccer, track/field (outdoor), track/field (indoor). *Women:* Basketball, cross-country, field hockey, golf, lacrosse, soccer, softball, tennis, track/field (outdoor), track/field (indoor), volleyball. **On-Campus Highlights:** Campus Center with bookstore, cafes, and lounges, SEFCU Arena, Science Library /Main Library, Performing Arts Center, University Art Museum, Students often find that a visit to the University at Albany helps them decide whether this is the university for them. Visitors can attend an information session and join a student-led tour during the academic year or the summer. The tour visits classrooms, academic and other facilities, a residence hall and a dining area. Information Sessions begin at 10:00 a.m. and 12:00 p.m. Your visit includes a QandA session and campus tour. Please allow two hours for your visit. **Environmental Initiatives:** Energy conservation waste reduction alternative transport.

ADMISSIONS

Freshman Academic Profile: Average high school GPA 3.4. 21% in top 10% of high school class, 60% in top 25% of high school class, 94% in top 50% of high school class. SAT Math middle 50% range 530–620. SAT Critical Reading middle 50% range 500–590. Minimum paper TOEFL 550. Minimum computer TOEFL 213. Minimum web-based TOEFL 79. **Basis for Candidate Selection:** *Very important factors considered include:* Class rank, academic GPA, recommendation(s), rigor of secondary school record, standardized test scores, character/personal qualities. *Important factors considered include:* Application essay. *Other factors considered include:* Alumni/ae relation, extracurricular activities, first generation, geographical residence, talent/ability, volunteer work, work experience. **Freshman Admission Requirements:** High school diploma is required and GED is accepted. *Academic units required:* 4 English, 2 mathematics, 2 science, (2 science labs), 1 foreign language, 3 social studies, 2 history, 4 academic electives. *Academic units recommended:* 4 mathematics, 3 science, (3 science labs), 3 foreign language. **Freshman Admission Statistics:** 22,188 applied, 47% admitted, 22% enrolled. **Transfer Admission Requirements:** College transcript(s), essay or personal statement, statement of good standing from prior institution(s). Minimum college GPA of 2.5 required. Lowest grade transferable C. **General Admission Information:** Application fee $50. Regular application deadline 3/1. Notification on a rolling basis, beginning on or about 1/1. Nonfall registration accepted. Admission may be deferred for a maximum of 1 year. Credit and/or placement offered for CEEB Advanced Placement tests.

COSTS AND FINANCIAL AID

Annual in-state tuition $4,970. Annual out-of-state tuition $12,870. Room and board $10,238. Required fees $1,778. Average book expense $1,600. **Required**

Forms and Deadlines: FAFSA, NY State residents should apply for TAP on-line at www.tapweb.org. Priority financial aid filing date 3/15. **Notification of Awards:** Applicants will be notified of awards on a rolling basis beginning 3/20. **Types of Aid:** *Need-based scholarships/grants:* Federal Pell, SEOG, state scholarships/grants, private scholarships, the school's own gift aid, NY State residents should apply for TAP on-line at www.tapweb.org. *Loans:* FFEL Subsidized Stafford, FFEL Unsubsidized Stafford, FFEL PLUS, Federal Perkins. *Student Employment:* Federal Work-Study Program available. Institutional employment available. Highest amount earned per year from on-campus jobs $5,532. Off-campus job opportunities are good. **Financial Aid Statistics:** 49% freshmen, 50% undergrads receive need-based scholarship or grant aid. 2% freshmen, 1% undergrads receive non-need-based scholarship or grant aid. 46% freshmen, 46% undergrads receive need-based self-help aid. 2% freshmen, 2% undergrads receive athletic scholarships. 64% freshmen, 62% undergrads receive any aid. Average cumulative indebtedness $22,092. **Criteria for awarding institutional aid:** *Non-need-based:* Academics, athletics, state/district residency.

STATE UNIVERSITY OF NEW YORK—UNIVERSITY AT BUFFALO

12 Capen Hall, Buffalo, NY 14260-1660
Phone: 716-645-6900 **Financial Aid Phone:** 716-645-2450
E-mail: ub-admissions@buffalo.edu **CEEB Code:** 2925
Fax: 716-645-6411 **Website:** www.buffalo.edu **ACT Code:** 2978

This public school was founded in 1846. It has a 1346-acre campus.

RATINGS

Admissions Selectivity Rating: 87 **Fire Safety Rating:** 60* **Green Rating:** 60*

STUDENTS AND FACULTY

Enrollment: 19,149. **Student Body:** 46% female, 54% male, 4% out-of-state, 13% international (108 countries represented). Asian 10%, African American 7%, Caucasian 58%, Hispanic 3%.
Retention and Graduation: 89% freshmen return for sophomore year. 42% freshmen graduate within 4 years. 41% grads go on to further study within 1 year. **Faculty:** Student/faculty ratio 16:1. 1209 full-time faculty, 94% hold PhDs, 24% are are members of minority groups, 35% are women. 11% of classes are taught by teaching assistants.

ACADEMICS

Degrees: Bachelor's, doctoral, master's, post-master's certificate. **Classes:** Most classes have 20–29 students. Most lab/discussion sessions have 20–29 students. **Majors with Highest Enrollment:** Business/commerce; engineering; social sciences. **Special Study Options:** Accelerated program, cooperative education program, cross-registration, distance learning, double major, dual enrollment, English as a Second Language (ESL), exchange student program (domestic), honors program, independent study, internships, liberal arts/career combination, student-designed major, study abroad, teacher certification program, Certificate programs, Combined Degree Programs, Early Assurance Program with School of Medicine & Dentistry, Honors College & Learning Communities. **Honors programs:** There is a University Honors College as well as honors programs within the majors. Undergraduate research is an option in a variety of disciplines and often affords the student an opportunity to participate in cutting-edge research activities. See Website: http://honors.buffalo.edu **Combined degree programs:** BA/MA, BA/MS, BS/MS, BA/MBA, BS/MBA, BA/MA, BA/MSW, BS/DDS, BA/EDM, BA/MFA. Special programs offered to physically disabled students include note-taking services, reader services, tape recorders, tutors. **Career services:** Alumni network, alumni services, career/job search classes, internships.

FACILITIES

Housing: Coed dorms, special housing for disabled students, special housing for international students, apartments for married students, apartments for single students, theme housing Honors Housing, Academic Interest Housing, Freshman Housing. See Website: www.ub-housing.buffalo.edu/special. 90% of campus accessible to physically disabled. **Special Academic Facilities/Equipment:** UB Center for the Arts, Slee Concert Hall, Anthropology Research Museum, Multidisciplinary Center for Earthquake Engineering Research (MCEER), New York State Center of Excellence in Bioinformatics and Life

Sciences, Center for Computational Research (CCR), Poetry and Rare Books Collection, Center of Excellence for Document Analysis and Recognition Center, New York State Center for Engineering Design and Industrial Innovation, Pharmacy Museum, The Virtual Site Museum, Electronic Poetry Center, Archeological Survey Center, Anderson Gallery, Alfiero Center and numerous research centers **Computers:** Students can register for classes online. Administrative functions (other than registration) can be performed online.

CAMPUS LIFE

Environment: City. **Activities:** Choral groups, concert band, dance, drama/theater, jazz band, literary magazine, marching band, music ensembles, musical theater, pep band, radio station, student government, student newspaper, student-run film society, symphony orchestra, television station, campus ministries, international student organization. **Organizations:** 215 registered organizations, 29 honor societies, 35 religious organizations. 22 fraternities, 17 sororities. **Athletics (Intercollegiate):** *Men:* Baseball, basketball, cross-country, football, soccer, swimming, tennis, track/field (outdoor), wrestling. *Women:* Basketball, crew/rowing, cross-country, soccer, softball, swimming, tennis, track/field (outdoor), volleyball. **On-Campus Highlights:** Center for the Arts, Alumni Arena and Athletic Stadium, Center for Computational Research, Apartment style student housing, The Commons (on-campus shopping).

ADMISSIONS

Freshman Academic Profile: Average high school GPA 3.3. 28% in top 10% of high school class, 65% in top 25% of high school class, 95% in top 50% of high school class. SAT Math middle 50% range 550–650. SAT Critical Reading middle 50% range 510–600. ACT middle 50% range 23–28. Minimum paper TOEFL 550. Minimum web-based TOEFL 79. **Basis for Candidate Selection:** *Very important factors considered include:* Academic GPA, rigor of secondary school record, standardized test scores. *Important factors considered include:* Class rank, recommendation(s), interview. *Other factors considered include:* Application essay, character/personal qualities, extracurricular activities, first generation, geographical residence, racial/ethnic status, talent/ability, volunteer work, work experience. **Freshman Admission Requirements:** High school diploma is required and GED is accepted. *Academic units recommended:* 4 English, 3 mathematics, 3 science, 3 foreign language, 4 social studies. **Freshman Admission Statistics:** 21,137 applied, 52% admitted, 29% enrolled. **Transfer Admission Requirements:** High school transcript, college transcript(s), essay or personal statement, minimum college GPA of 2.5 required. Lowest grade transferable D. **General Admission Information:** Application fee $40. Early decision application deadline 11/1. Notification on a rolling basis, beginning on or about 2/1. Nonfall registration accepted. Credit and/or placement offered for CEEB Advanced Placement tests.

COSTS AND FINANCIAL AID

Annual in-state tuition $4,970. Annual out-of-state tuition $12,870. Room and board $9,648. Required fees $2,043. Average book expense $975. **Required Forms and Deadlines:** FAFSA. Priority financial aid filing date 3/1. **Notification of Awards:** Applicants will be notified of awards on a rolling basis beginning 2/1. **Types of Aid:** *Need-based scholarships/grants:* Federal Pell, SEOG, state scholarships/grants, private scholarships, the school's own gift aid, Federal Nursing Scholarships. *Loans:* Direct Subsidized Stafford, Direct Unsubsidized Stafford, Direct PLUS, Federal Perkins, Federal Nursing, college/university loans from institutional funds. *Student Employment:* Federal Work-Study Program available. Institutional employment available. Off-campus job opportunities are good. **Financial Aid Statistics:** 26% freshmen, 13% undergrads receive need-based scholarship or grant aid. 3% freshmen, 4% undergrads receive non-need-based scholarship or grant aid. 12% freshmen, 24% undergrads receive need-based self-help aid. 2% freshmen, 1% undergrads receive athletic scholarships. 50% freshmen, 52% undergrads receive any aid. 44% undergrads borrow to pay for school. Average cumulative indebtedness $15,911. **Criteria for awarding institutional aid:** *Non-need-based:* Academics, athletics, minority status, music/drama, state/district residency.

STEPHEN F. AUSTIN STATE UNIVERSITY

P. O. Box 13051, SFA Station, Nacogdoches, TX 75962
Phone: 936-468-2504 **Financial Aid Phone:** 936-468-2403
E-mail: admissions@sfasu.edu **CEEB Code:** 6682
Fax: 936-468-3849 **Website:** www.sfasu.edu **ACT Code:** 4188

This public school was founded in 1923. It has a 401-acre campus.

RATINGS

Admissions Selectivity Rating: 71   **Fire Safety Rating:** 60*   **Green Rating:** 60*

STUDENTS AND FACULTY

Enrollment: 9,568. **Student Body:** 59% female, 41% male, 2% out-of-state, 1% international (42 countries represented). Asian 1%, African American 16%, Caucasian 74%, Hispanic 7%, Native American 1%. **Retention and Graduation:** 66% freshmen return for sophomore year. 17% freshmen graduate within 4 years. **Faculty:** Student/faculty ratio 18:1. 434 full-time faculty, 76% hold PhDs, 7% are are members of minority groups, 41% are women.

ACADEMICS

Degrees: Bachelor's, master's. **Classes:** Most classes have 20–29 students. Most lab/discussion sessions have 10–19 students. **Majors with Highest Enrollment:** Health and physical education; multi-/interdisciplinary studies, other; nursing/registered nurse (RN, ASN, BSN, MSN). **Special Study Options:** Accelerated program, distance learning, double major, dual enrollment, honors program, independent study, internships, liberal arts/career combination, student-designed major, study abroad, teacher certification program. **Honors programs:** www.sfasu.edu/honors/ **Combined degree programs:** BBA(Accounting)/MPAC(Professional Accountancy). Special programs offered to physically disabled students include note-taking services, reader services, tape recorders, tutors.

FACILITIES

Housing: Coed dorms, special housing for disabled students, men's dorms, women's dorms, fraternity/sorority housing, apartments for married students, apartments for single students, apartments for students with dependent children. 99% of campus accessible to physically disabled. **Special Academic Facilities/Equipment:** Stone Fort Museum, Planetarium, Arboretum, Observatory, GIS Lab, Forest Resources Institute, Soils Analysis Lab, East Texas Historical Assoc, East Texas Research Center, Science Research Center, Research Feed Mill. **Computers:** Students can register for classes online. Administrative functions (other than registration) can be performed online.

CAMPUS LIFE

Environment: Town. **Activities:** Choral groups, concert band, dance, drama/theater, jazz band, literary magazine, marching band, music ensembles, musical theater, opera, pep band, radio station, student government, student newspaper, student-run film society, symphony orchestra, television station, yearbook. **Organizations:** 21 registered organizations, 15 honor societies, 25 religious organizations. 25 fraternities, 14 sororities. **Athletics (Intercollegiate):** *Men:* Basketball, cross-country, football, golf, track/field (outdoor), track/field (indoor). *Women:* Basketball, cross-country, soccer, softball, tennis, track/field (outdoor), track/field (indoor), volleyball. **On-Campus Highlights:** Stone Fort Museum, University Center, Art Galleries—Art Center, Griffith Gallery, Library, Arboretum.

ADMISSIONS

Freshman Academic Profile: 16% in top 10% of high school class, 44% in top 25% of high school class, 83% in top 50% of high school class. 90% from public high schools. SAT Math middle 50% range 450–550. SAT Critical Reading middle 50% range 450–560. ACT middle 50% range 18–23. Minimum paper TOEFL 550. Minimum computer TOEFL 213. **Basis for Candidate Selection:** *Very important factors considered include:* Class rank, rigor of secondary school record, standardized test scores. *Other factors considered include:* Extracurricular activities, geographical residence, talent/ability, volunteer work, work experience. **Freshman Admission Requirements:** High school diploma is required and GED is accepted. *Academic units required:* 4 English, 3 mathematics, 3 science, 2 foreign language. *Academic units recommended:* 1 social studies, 2 history, 3 Fine Arts/Computer/Govt. and Eco. **Freshman Admission Statistics:** 5,873 applied, 75% admitted, 38% enrolled. **Transfer Admission Requirements:** College transcript(s), minimum college GPA of 2.0 required. Lowest grade transferable D. **General Admission Information:** Application fee $25. Notification on a rolling basis, beginning on or about 9/1. Nonfall registration accepted. Credit and/or placement offered for CEEB Advanced Placement tests.

COSTS AND FINANCIAL AID

Annual in-state tuition $3,360. Annual out-of-state tuition $11,100. Room and board $5,012. Required fees $938. Average book expense $905. **Required Forms and Deadlines:** FAFSA. Financial aid filing deadline 4/15. Priority financial aid filing date 4/1. **Notification of Awards:** Applicants will be notified of awards on a rolling basis beginning 5/1. **Types of Aid:** *Need-based scholarships/grants:* Federal Pell, SEOG, state scholarships/grants, private scholarships, the school's own gift aid. *Loans:* FFEL Subsidized Stafford, FFEL Unsubsidized Stafford, FFEL PLUS, Federal Perkins, state loans, college/university loans from institutional funds, Alternative loans. *Student Employment:* Highest amount earned per year from on-campus jobs $4,100. **Financial Aid Statistics:** 39% freshmen, 43% undergrads receive need-based scholarship or grant aid. 27% freshmen, 24% undergrads receive non-need-based scholarship or grant aid. 37% freshmen, 44% undergrads receive need-based self-help aid. 3% freshmen, 3% undergrads receive athletic scholarships. 46% freshmen, 47%

undergrads receive any aid. 62% undergrads borrow to pay for school. Average cumulative indebtedness $16,624. **Criteria for awarding institutional aid:** *Non-need-based:* Academics, alumni affiliation, art, athletics, leadership, music/drama, state/district residency.

STEPHENS COLLEGE

1200 East Broadway, Box 2121, Columbia, MO 65215
Phone: 573-876-7207 **Financial Aid Phone:** 573-876-7106
E-mail: apply@stephens.edu **CEEB Code:** 6683
Fax: 573-876-7237 **Website:** www.stephens.edu **ACT Code:** 2374

This private school was founded in 1833. It has a 86-acre campus.

RATINGS
Admissions Selectivity Rating: 79   Fire Safety Rating: 72   Green Rating: 64

STUDENTS AND FACULTY
Enrollment: 948. **Student Body:** 97% female, 3% male, 46% out-of-state, international (3 countries represented). Asian 1%, African American 13%, Caucasian 76%, Hispanic 3%, Native American 1%.
Retention and Graduation: 65% freshmen return for sophomore year. 43% freshmen graduate within 4 years. 25% grads go on to further study within 1 year. 7% grads pursue arts and sciences degrees. 2% grads pursue law degrees. 7% grads pursue business degrees. 4% grads pursue medical degrees. **Faculty:** Student/faculty ratio 12:1. 60 full-time faculty, 38% hold PhDs, 2% are are members of minority groups, 78% are women.

ACADEMICS
Degrees: Associate, bachelor's, master's, post-bachelor's certificate. **Classes:** Most classes have 10–19 students. Most lab/discussion sessions have 10–19 students. **Majors with Highest Enrollment:** Drama and dramatics/theatre arts; fashion/apparel design; health information/medical records administration/administrator. **Special Study Options:** Cross-registration, distance learning, double major, dual enrollment, external degree program, independent study, internships, liberal arts/career combination, student-designed major, study abroad, teacher certification program. **Combined degree programs:** BA/JD, BA/MA, Occupational Therapy with Washington University. Special programs offered to physically disabled students include note-taking services, tutors. **Career services:** Alumni network, alumni services, career/job search classes, career assessment, internships, regional alumni. **Career services highlights include:** Internships.

FACILITIES
Housing: Special housing for disabled students, women's dorms, fraternity/sorority housing, apartments for single students, Pet Friendly Residence. 80% of campus accessible to physically disabled. **Special Academic Facilities/Equipment:** Art gallery and historical costume collections, on-campus preschool, kindergarten, and elementary school, language lab. **Computers:** 100% of classrooms, 100% of dorms, 100% of libraries, 100% of dining areas, 100% of student union, have wireless network access. Students can register for classes online. Administrative functions (other than registration) can be performed online.

CAMPUS LIFE
Environment: City. **Activities:** Choral groups, dance, drama/theater, literary magazine, music ensembles, musical theater, radio station, student government, student newspaper, student-run film society, television station. **Organizations:** 28 registered organizations, 11 honor societies, 3 religious organizations. 2 sororities. **Athletics (Intercollegiate):** *Women:* Basketball, cross-country, softball, swimming, tennis, volleyball. **On-Campus Highlights:** Equestrian Stables, The Commons, Senior Hall, The Quad, Residence Halls. **Environmental Initiatives:** Recycling, decreased energy usage, meeting LEED criteria on building projects and operations.

ADMISSIONS
Freshman Academic Profile: Average high school GPA 3.31. 11% in top 10% of high school class, 36% in top 25% of high school class, 73% in top 50% of high school class. 78% from public high schools. SAT Math middle 50% range 460–548. SAT Critical Reading middle 50% range 510–600. SAT Writing middle 50% range 500–578. ACT middle 50% range 19–25. Minimum paper TOEFL 550. Minimum computer TOEFL 213. **Basis for Candidate Selection:** *Very important factors considered include:* Application essay, rigor of secondary school record, standardized test scores. *Important factors considered include:* Academic GPA, recommendation(s), extracurricular activities. *Other factors considered include:* Class rank, character/personal qualities, interview, level of applicant's interest, talent/ability, volunteer work, work experience. **Freshman Admission Requirements:** High school diploma is required

and GED is accepted. *Academic units required:* 4 English, 3 mathematics, 2 science, 2 foreign language, 1 social studies. *Academic units recommended:* (2 science labs). **Freshman Admission Statistics:** 675 applied, 72% admitted, 55% enrolled. **Transfer Admission Requirements:** High school transcript, college transcript(s), essay or personal statement, minimum college GPA of 2.0 required. Lowest grade transferable C–. **General Admission Information:** Application fee $25. Notification on a rolling basis, beginning on or about 9/15. Nonfall registration accepted. Admission may be deferred for a maximum of 1 year. Credit offered for CEEB Advanced Placement tests.

COSTS AND FINANCIAL AID
Annual tuition $24,150. Room and board $9,330. Average book expense $1,400. **Required Forms and Deadlines:** FAFSA. Priority financial aid filing date 3/15. **Notification of Awards:** Applicants will be notified of awards on a rolling basis beginning 3/1. **Types of Aid:** *Need-based scholarships/grants:* Federal Pell, SEOG, state scholarships/grants, private scholarships, the school's own gift aid, Federal ACG Federal SMART Grant. *Loans:* FFEL Subsidized Stafford, FFEL Unsubsidized Stafford, FFEL PLUS, Federal Perkins. *Student Employment:* Federal Work-Study Program available. Institutional employment available. Highest amount earned per year from on-campus jobs $1,600. Off-campus job opportunities are good. **Financial Aid Statistics:** 63% freshmen, 77% undergrads receive need-based scholarship or grant aid. 9% freshmen, 11% undergrads receive non-need-based scholarship or grant aid. 50% freshmen, 62% undergrads receive need-based self-help aid. 3% freshmen, 3% undergrads receive athletic scholarships. 99% freshmen, 99% undergrads receive any aid. 78% undergrads borrow to pay for school. Average cumulative indebtedness $22,942. **Criteria for awarding institutional aid:** *Non-need-based:* Academics, alumni affiliation, athletics, leadership, music/drama, state/district residency.

STERLING COLLEGE

125 W. Cooper, Sterling, KS 67579
Phone: 620-278-4275 **Financial Aid Phone:** 620-278-4207
E-mail: admissions@sterling.edu **CEEB Code:** 6684
Fax: 620-278-4416 **Website:** www.sterlingcollege.edu **ACT Code:** 1466

This private school, affiliated with the Presbyterian Church, was founded in 1887. It has a 42-acre campus.

RATINGS
Admissions Selectivity Rating: 75   Fire Safety Rating: 60*   Green Rating: 60*

STUDENTS AND FACULTY
Enrollment: 673. **Student Body:** 48% female, 52% male, 47% out-of-state, 1% international (7 countries represented). Asian 1%, African American 7%, Caucasian 80%, Hispanic 7%, Native American 2%.
Retention and Graduation: 62% freshmen return for sophomore year. 35% freshmen graduate within 4 years. **Faculty:** Student/faculty ratio 14.5:1. 37 full-time faculty, 49% hold PhDs, 8% are are members of minority groups, 27% are women.

ACADEMICS
Degrees: Bachelor's. **Classes:** Most classes have fewer than 10 students. Most lab/discussion sessions have 20–29 students. **Majors with Highest Enrollment:** Business/commerce; elementary education and teaching; health and physical education. **Special Study Options:** Distance learning, double major, dual enrollment, external degree program, honors program, independent study, internships, student-designed major, study abroad, teacher certification program **Honors programs:** The honors program is still being developed. At this point honors level general education classes are offered in interdisciplinary history and literature Special programs offered to physically disabled students include tutors. **Career services:** Alumni network, alumni services, career assessment, internships.

FACILITIES
Housing: Men's dorms, women's dorms. 80% of campus accessible to physically disabled. **Special Academic Facilities/Equipment:** History/cultural museum. **Computers:** Administrative functions (other than registration) can be performed online.

CAMPUS LIFE
Environment: Rural. **Activities:** Choral groups, concert band, drama/theater, jazz band, literary magazine, music ensembles, musical theater, radio station, student government, student newspaper, television station, yearbook, campus ministries. **Organizations:** 16 registered organizations, 4 honor societies, 2 religious organizations. **Athletics (Intercollegiate):** *Men:* Baseball, basketball, cross-country, football, golf, soccer, track/field (outdoor). *Women:* Basketball, cheerleading, cross-country, golf, soccer, softball, track/field (outdoor), vol-

leyball. **On-Campus Highlights:** Gleason Phy. Educ. Center, Student Union, Cooper Hall, Evan's Hall, Campbell Hall.

ADMISSIONS

Freshman Academic Profile: Average high school GPA 3.15. 8% in top 10% of high school class, 25% in top 25% of high school class, 55% in top 50% of high school class. 80% from public high schools. SAT Math middle 50% range 450–540. SAT Critical Reading middle 50% range 410–530. SAT Writing middle 50% range 400–540. ACT middle 50% range 19–24. Minimum paper TOEFL 525. Minimum computer TOEFL 195. Minimum web-based TOEFL 70. **Basis for Candidate Selection:** *Very important factors considered include:* Rigor of secondary school record, standardized test scores, character/personal qualities. *Important factors considered include:* Application essay, academic GPA, recommendation(s), extracurricular activities, interview, level of applicant's interest, religious affiliation/commitment, volunteer work. *Other factors considered include:* Class rank, alumni/ae relation, first generation, talent/ability, work experience. **Freshman Admission Requirements:** High school diploma is required and GED is accepted. *Academic units recommended:* 4 English, 3 mathematics, 3 science, (2 science labs), 2 foreign language, 1 social studies, 2 history, 1 computer science, 1 academic electives, 1 PE. **Freshman Admission Statistics:** 953 applied, 55% admitted, 36% enrolled. **Transfer Admission Requirements:** College transcript(s), essay or personal statement, minimum college GPA of 2.2 required. Lowest grade transferable C–. **General Admission Information:** Application fee $25. Notification on a rolling basis, beginning on or about 9/15. Nonfall registration accepted. Admission may be deferred for a maximum of 1 semester. Credit offered for CEEB Advanced Placement tests.

COSTS AND FINANCIAL AID

Annual tuition $18,000. Room and board $6,430. Average book expense $700. **Required Forms and Deadlines:** FAFSA. Priority financial aid filing date 4/1. **Notification of Awards:** Applicants will be notified of awards on a rolling basis beginning 1/1. **Types of Aid:** *Need-based scholarships/grants:* Federal Pell, SEOG, state scholarships/grants, private scholarships, the school's own gift aid. *Loans:* FFEL Subsidized Stafford, FFEL Unsubsidized Stafford, FFEL PLUS, Federal Perkins. *Student Employment:* Federal Work-Study Program available. Institutional employment available. Highest amount earned per year from on-campus jobs $1,100. Off-campus job opportunities are fair. **Financial Aid Statistics:** 45% freshmen, 45% undergrads receive need-based scholarship or grant aid. 41% freshmen, 42% undergrads receive need-based self-help aid. 7% freshmen, 6% undergrads receive athletic scholarships. 100% freshmen, 96% undergrads receive any aid. 73% undergrads borrow to pay for school. Average cumulative indebtedness $19,187. **Criteria for awarding institutional aid:** *Non-need-based:* Academics, art, athletics, leadership, music/drama.

STERLING COLLEGE (VT)

PO Box 72, Craftsbury Common, VT 05827
Phone: 802-586-7711 **Financial Aid Phone:** 802-586-7711
E-mail: admissions@sterlingcollege.edu **CEEB Code:** 3752
Fax: 802-586-2596 **Website:** www.sterlingcollege.edu **ACT Code:** 6946

This private school was founded in 1958. It has a 430-acre campus.

RATINGS

Admissions Selectivity Rating: 65 **Fire Safety Rating:** 60* **Green Rating:** 60*

STUDENTS AND FACULTY

Enrollment: 98. **Student Body:** 43% female, 57% male, 77% out-of-state, (1 countries represented). Asian 1%, Caucasian 76%, Hispanic 1%.
Retention and Graduation: 47% freshmen return for sophomore year. 27% freshmen graduate within 4 years. 25% grads go on to further study within 1 year. **Faculty:** Student/faculty ratio 5:1. 16 full-time faculty, 25% hold PhDs, 50% are women.

ACADEMICS

Degrees: Bachelor's. **Classes:** Most classes have 10–19 students. **Majors with Highest Enrollment:** Agriculture, agriculture operations, and related sciences, other; natural resources conservation and research, other; parks, recreation and leisure studies. **Special Study Options:** Double major, dual enrollment, exchange student program (domestic), independent study, internships, student-designed major, study abroad, Global Field Studies to Japan, Scandinavia, Belize, Alaska, Sierra Nevada, Newfoundland, Iceland, James Bay, and more. Special programs offered to physically disabled students include tutors. **Career services:** Alumni network, alumni services, career/job search classes, career assessment, internships **Career services highlights include:** The Internship is a ten-week experience (working full time) and two courses prior and post to the experience. It is a total of 8 credits and a requirement of all second year

students. Past Internship sites have included: 58 federal agencies, including National Forests, National Parks, and National Wildlife Refuges, 18 state agencies, 94 educational organizations including environmental, outdoor adventure, classroom, and interpretative centers,112 agricultural producers, 24 environmental advocacy organizations, 21 wildlife rehabilitation, veterinary medicine, and animal shelter organizations, 30 for-profit green businesses, 36 research institutions, and several national organizations including The Sierra Club, National Audubon Society, PETA, Heifer Project International, The Nature Conservancy, Outward Bound, and NOLS.

FACILITIES

Housing: Coed dorms, wellness housing **Special Academic Facilities/Equipment:** Library serves as art gallery. There is a 6–8 week rotation of Vermont artist displays. Campus also includes wind and solar-powered barns that serves as an instructional facility and lab, a greenhouse provides a working lab for plant and soil studies. Other facilities include: A woodshop, logging shop, sugarhouse, root cellar, darkroom, certified organic gardens, and a 32' tall climbing wall provides students with the ability to develop leadership and technical rock-climbing skills. The Center for Northern Studies at Sterling College includes a 300 acre boreal forest. **Computers:** 100% of classrooms, 100% of dorms, 100% of libraries, 100% of dining areas, 100% of student union, 100% of common outdoor areas have wireless network access. Administrative functions (other than registration) can be performed online.

CAMPUS LIFE

Environment: Rural. **Activities:** Choral groups, dance, drama/theater, music ensembles, student government, student-run film society, yearbook. **Organizations: On-Campus Highlights:** Challenge Course and Climbing Wall, Organic Gardens and Livestock Farm, Dining Hall serves local, organic food, 300–acre Boreal Forest, Wind and Solar Powered Barns, Student Lounge, Dancing Goat Cafe, Recreation Room, Lean-toos, XC ski trails, nature trails, Computer labs, common areas in dorms, front porch.

ADMISSIONS

Freshman Academic Profile: Average high school GPA 3. 11% in top 10% of high school class, 21% in top 25% of high school class, 79% in top 50% of high school class. 70% from public high schools. Minimum paper TOEFL 500. Minimum computer TOEFL 173. Minimum web-based TOEFL 61. **Basis for Candidate Selection:** *Very important factors considered include:* Academic GPA, recommendation(s), rigor of secondary school record, level of applicant's interest. *Important factors considered include:* Class rank, application essay, character/personal qualities, extracurricular activities, interview, talent/ability, volunteer work. *Other factors considered include:* Standardized test scores, alumni/ae relation, geographical residence, work experience. **Freshman Admission Requirements:** High school diploma is required and GED is accepted. *Academic units required:* 4 English, 3 mathematics, 2 science, (2 science labs), 0 foreign language, 2 social studies, 2 history. *Academic units recommended:* 4 English, 4 mathematics, 3 science, (3 science labs), 2 foreign language, 2 social studies, 2 history. **Freshman Admission Statistics:** 104 applied, 78% admitted, 33% enrolled. **Transfer Admission Requirements:** High school transcript, college transcript(s), essay or personal statement, minimum college GPA of 2.0 required. Lowest grade transferable C. **General Admission Information:** Application fee $35. Regular application deadline 2/15. Regular notification 4/1. Nonfall registration accepted. Admission may be deferred for a maximum of 1 year. Credit and/or placement offered for CEEB Advanced Placement tests.

COSTS AND FINANCIAL AID

Annual tuition $23,196. Room and board $7,554. Required fees $400. Average book expense $900. **Required Forms and Deadlines:** FAFSA, institution's own financial aid form, state aid form. Priority financial aid filing date 3/1. **Notification of Awards:** Applicants will be notified of awards on a rolling basis beginning 2/1. **Types of Aid:** *Need-based scholarships/grants:* Federal Pell, SEOG, state scholarships/grants, private scholarships, the school's own gift aid. *Loans:* FFEL Subsidized Stafford, FFEL Unsubsidized Stafford, FFEL PLUS. *Student Employment:* Federal Work-Study Program available. Institutional employment available. Highest amount earned per year from on-campus jobs $1,500. Off-campus job opportunities are fair. **Financial Aid Statistics:** 71% freshmen, 74% undergrads receive need-based scholarship or grant aid. 16% undergrads receive non-need-based scholarship or grant aid. 71% freshmen, 74% undergrads receive need-based self-help aid. 71% freshmen, 74% undergrads receive any aid. 40% undergrads borrow to pay for school. Average cumulative indebtedness $15,880. **Criteria for awarding institutional aid:** *Non-need-based:* Academics, leadership, state/district residency.

STETSON UNIVERSITY

421 N. Woodland Blvd, Unit 8378, DeLand, FL 32723
Phone: 386-822-7100 **Financial Aid Phone:** 800-688-7120
E-mail: admissions@stetson.edu **CEEB Code:** 5630
Fax: 386-822-7112 **Website: ACT Code:** 756

This private school was founded in 1883. It has a 175-acre campus.

RATINGS

Admissions Selectivity Rating: 87   **Fire Safety Rating:** 60*   **Green Rating:** 91

STUDENTS AND FACULTY

Enrollment: 2,151. **Student Body:** 57% female, 43% male, 17% out-of-state, 3% international (40 countries represented). Asian 2%, African American 6%, Caucasian 72%, Hispanic 11%.
Retention and Graduation: 77% freshmen return for sophomore year. 50% freshmen graduate within 4 years. 60% grads go on to further study within 1 year. 22% grads pursue arts and sciences degrees. 9% grads pursue law degrees. 16% grads pursue business degrees. 7% grads pursue medical degrees. **Faculty:** Student/faculty ratio 11:1. 229 full-time faculty, 95% hold PhDs, 11% are are members of minority groups, 42% are women.

ACADEMICS

Degrees: Bachelor's, master's. **Classes:** Most classes have 10–19 students. Most lab/discussion sessions have 10–19 students. **Majors with Highest Enrollment:** Business administration and management; elementary education and teaching; psychology. **Special Study Options:** Accelerated program, double major, honors program, independent study, internships, liberal arts/career combination, student-designed major, study abroad, teacher certification program, weekend college. **Combined degree programs:** BA/JD, Cooperative Program in Forestry and Environ. Studies. Special programs offered to physically disabled students include note-taking services, reader services, tape recorders, tutors. **Career services:** Alumni network, alumni services, career/job search classes, career assessment, internships, regional alumni.

FACILITIES

Housing: Coed dorms, men's dorms, women's dorms, fraternity/sorority housing, apartments for single students, wellness housing, theme housing, "Pet" Dorm (pets allowed), Foreign Language House, French House, The Service Station (community service house). **Special Academic Facilities/Equipment:** Language lab, art gallery, greenhouse with growth chambers, mineral museum, electron microscopes. **Computers:** 90% of classrooms, 100% of dorms, 100% of libraries, 95% of dining areas, 100% of student union, 30% of common outdoor areas have wireless network access. Students can register for classes online. Administrative functions (other than registration) can be performed online.

CAMPUS LIFE

Environment: Town. **Activities:** Choral groups, concert band, dance, drama/theater, jazz band, literary magazine, music ensembles, musical theater, opera, pep band, radio station, student government, student newspaper, student-run film society, symphony orchestra, campus ministries, international student organization, Model UN. **Organizations:** 125 registered organizations, 24 honor societies, 8 religious organizations. 6 fraternities, 5 sororities. **Athletics (Intercollegiate):** *Men:* Baseball, basketball, crew/rowing, cross-country, golf, soccer, tennis. *Women:* Basketball, crew/rowing, cross-country, golf, soccer, softball, tennis, volleyball. **On-Campus Highlights:** Lynn Business Center, DuPont-Ball Library, Homer and Dolly Hand Art Center, Hollis Center, Sage Hall. **Environmental Initiatives:** Native Plant Policy, Recycling Program, LEED Certification for buildings.

ADMISSIONS

Freshman Academic Profile: Average high school GPA 3.76. 28% in top 10% of high school class, 63% in top 25% of high school class, 91% in top 50% of high school class. 78% from public high schools. SAT Math middle 50% range 490–600. SAT Critical Reading middle 50% range 500–600. SAT Writing middle 50% range 480–583. ACT middle 50% range 21–26. Minimum paper TOEFL 550. Minimum computer TOEFL 213. **Basis for Candidate Selection:** *Very important factors considered include:* Academic GPA, rigor of secondary school record. *Important factors considered include:* Class rank, application essay, recommendation(s), standardized test scores, character/personal qualities, extracurricular activities, interview, talent/ability, volunteer work, work experience. *Other factors considered include:* Alumni/ae relation, geographical residence, racial/ethnic status, state residency. **Freshman Admission Requirements:** High school diploma is required and GED is accepted. *Academic units required:* 4 English, 3 mathematics, 3 science, 2 foreign language, 2 social studies. **Freshman Admission Statistics:** 4,640 applied, 53% admitted, 20% enrolled. **Transfer Admission Requirements:** High school transcript, college transcript(s), essay or personal statement, standardized test scores, statement of

good standing from prior institution(s). Minimum college GPA of 2.0 required. Lowest grade transferable C. **General Admission Information:** Application fee $40. Early decision application deadline 11/1. Notification on a rolling basis, beginning on or about 12/1. Nonfall registration accepted. Admission may be deferred for a maximum of 1. Credit and/or placement offered for CEEB Advanced Placement tests.

COSTS AND FINANCIAL AID

Required Forms and Deadlines: FAFSA, institution's own financial aid form. Priority financial aid filing date 3/15. **Notification of Awards:** Applicants will be notified of awards on a rolling basis beginning 2/15. **Types of Aid:** *Need-based scholarships/grants:* Federal Pell, SEOG, state scholarships/grants, private scholarships, the school's own gift aid. *Loans:* FFEL Subsidized Stafford, FFEL Unsubsidized Stafford, FFEL PLUS, Federal Perkins. *Student Employment:* Federal Work-Study Program available. Institutional employment available. Highest amount earned per year from on-campus jobs $4,000. Off-campus job opportunities are good. **Financial Aid Statistics:** 71% freshmen, 63% undergrads receive need-based scholarship or grant aid. 11% freshmen, 9% undergrads receive non-need-based scholarship or grant aid. 57% freshmen, 50% undergrads receive need-based self-help aid. 3% freshmen, 4% undergrads receive athletic scholarships. 98.8% freshmen, 96.8% undergrads receive any aid. 83% undergrads borrow to pay for school. Average cumulative indebtedness $30,914. **Criteria for awarding institutional aid:** *Non-need-based:* Academics, alumni affiliation, art, athletics, leadership, minority status, music/drama, religious affiliation, state/district residency.

STEVENS INSTITUTE OF TECHNOLOGY

Castle Point on Hudson, 8th Floor, Hoboken, NJ 07030
Phone: 201-216-5194 **Financial Aid Phone:** 201-216-5555
E-mail: admissions@stevens.edu **CEEB Code:** 2819
Fax: 201-216-8348 **Website:** www.stevens.edu **ACT Code:** 2610

This private school was founded in 1870. It has a 55-acre campus.

RATINGS

Admissions Selectivity Rating: 94   **Fire Safety Rating:** 98   **Green Rating:** 70

STUDENTS AND FACULTY

Enrollment: 2,234. **Student Body:** 26% female, 74% male, 40% out-of-state, 4% international (47 countries represented). Asian 11%, African American 3%, Caucasian 54%, Hispanic 10%.
Retention and Graduation: 90% freshmen return for sophomore year. 20% grads go on to further study within 1 year. 5% grads pursue arts and sciences degrees. 2% grads pursue law degrees. 1% grads pursue business degrees. 2% grads pursue medical degrees. **Faculty:** Student/faculty ratio 7:1. 226 full-time faculty, 25% are are members of minority groups, 20% are women.

ACADEMICS

Degrees: Bachelor's, doctoral, master's, post-bachelor's certificate. **Majors with Highest Enrollment:** Business administration and management; computer/information technology services administration and management, other; mechanical engineering. **Special Study Options:** Accelerated program, cooperative education program, cross-registration, distance learning, double major, dual enrollment, honors program, independent study, internships, study abroad, dual enrollment program with NYU. **Honors programs:** The Scholars Program allows high-achieving students to participate in research over the summer or take up to four tuition-free courses each summer. Scholars students may also complete their Bachelor's in three years or a combined bachelor's and Master's in four years at no extra cost. **Combined degree programs:** BA/MD, BA/JD, BA/DDS, BS/MS; BS/DMD; BS/JD; BS/MD. Special programs offered to physically disabled students include note-taking services, tutors. **Career services:** Alumni network, alumni services, career/job search classes, career assessment, internships, regional alumni. **Career services highlights include:** Our educational philosophy encourages experience with real-world practitioners in business, science and engineering, therefore, 100% of Stevens students participate in coop, research or internships; 40% of students participate in co-op.

FACILITIES

Housing: Coed dorms, women's dorms, fraternity/sorority housing, apartments for married students, apartments for single studentsFreshmen not living at home must live on campus. 100% of campus accessible to physically disabled.

Special Academic Facilities/Equipment: Art museum, electron microscope, ocean engineering lab, HDTV research facility, advanced telecommunications institute, environmental lab, design/manufacturing institute, wind tunnel, robotics lab, product management center, polymer processing institute. DeBaun Theater, a multi-media facility, wireless campus network **Computers:** 95% of classrooms, 100% of dorms, 100% of libraries, 100% of dining areas, 100% of student union, 99% of common outdoor areas have wireless network access. Students can register for classes online. Administrative functions (other than registration) can be performed online. Undergraduates are required to own a computer.

CAMPUS LIFE

Environment: Town. **Activities:** Choral groups, concert band, dance, drama/theater, jazz band, literary magazine, music ensembles, musical theater, pep band, radio station, student government, student newspaper, student-run film society, symphony orchestra, television station, yearbook, campus ministries, international student organization. **Organizations:** 120 registered organizations, 12 honor societies, 6 religious organizations. 10 fraternities, 3 sororities. **Athletics (Intercollegiate):** *Men:* Baseball, basketball, cross-country, fencing, lacrosse, soccer, swimming, tennis, track/field (outdoor), track/field (indoor), volleyball, wrestling. *Women:* Basketball, cross-country, equestrian sports, fencing, field hockey, lacrosse, soccer, swimming, tennis, track/field (outdoor), track/field (indoor), volleyball. **On-Campus Highlights:** Schaefer Athletic Center, DeBaun Auditorium, Castle Point, overlooking Manhattan, Babbio Center, Wesley J. Howe Center. **Environmental Initiatives:** Green minor, Green Book Award.

ADMISSIONS

Freshman Academic Profile: Average high school GPA 3.8. 58% in top 10% of high school class, 85% in top 25% of high school class, 98% in top 50% of high school class. 80% from public high schools. SAT Math middle 50% range 620–710. SAT Critical Reading middle 50% range 550–650. SAT Writing middle 50% range 540–650. ACT middle 50% range 24–29. Minimum paper TOEFL 550. Minimum computer TOEFL 213. Minimum web-based TOEFL 82. **Basis for Candidate Selection:** *Very important factors considered include:* Application essay, academic GPA, recommendation(s), rigor of secondary school record, standardized test scores, character/personal qualities, extracurricular activities, interview, volunteer work, work experience. *Important factors considered include:* Class rank, talent/ability. *Other factors considered include:* Alumni/ae relation. **Freshman Admission Requirements:** High school diploma is required and GED is not accepted. *Academic units required:* 4 English, 4 mathematics, 3 science, (3 science labs). *Academic units recommended:* 4 science, (4 science labs), 2 foreign language, 2 social studies, 2 history, 1 computer science, 4 academic electives. **Freshman Admission Statistics:** 2,972 applied, 51% admitted, 37% enrolled. **Transfer Admission Requirements:** High school transcript, college transcript(s), essay or personal statement, interview, minimum college GPA of 3.0 required. Lowest grade transferable C. **General Admission Information:** Application fee $55. Early decision application deadline 11/15. Regular application deadline 2/1. Regular notification 3/15. Nonfall registration accepted. Admission may be deferred for a maximum of 1 year. Credit and/or placement offered for CEEB Advanced Placement tests.

COSTS AND FINANCIAL AID

Annual tuition $36,600. Room and board $12,150. Required fees $1,380. Average book expense $900. **Required Forms and Deadlines:** FAFSA. Priority financial aid filing date 2/15. **Notification of Awards:** Applicants will be notified of awards on a rolling basis beginning 3/30. **Types of Aid:** *Need-based scholarships/grants:* Federal Pell, SEOG, state scholarships/grants, private scholarships, the school's own gift aid. *Loans:* Direct Subsidized Stafford, Direct Unsubsidized Stafford, Direct PLUS, FFEL Subsidized Stafford, Federal Perkins, state loans, Signature Loans, TERI Loans, NJ CLASS, CitiAssist. *Student Employment:* Federal Work-Study Program available. Institutional employment available. Highest amount earned per year from on-campus jobs $1,300. Off-campus job opportunities are excellent. **Financial Aid Statistics:** 66% freshmen, 54% undergrads receive need-based scholarship or grant aid. 62% freshmen, 55% undergrads receive non-need-based scholarship or grant aid. 65% freshmen, 57% undergrads receive need-based self-help aid. 82.4% freshmen, 75.3% undergrads receive any aid. 65.7% undergrads borrow to pay for school. Average cumulative indebtedness $35,319. **Criteria for awarding institutional aid:** *Non-need-based:* Academics, leadership, minority status, music/drama.

STEVENSON UNIVERSITY

1525 Greenspring Valley Road, Stevenson, MD 21153-0641
Phone: 410-486-7001 **Financial Aid Phone:** 443-334-2559
E-mail: admissions@stevenson.edu
Fax: 443-352-4440 **Website:** www.stevenson.edu

This private school was founded in 1947. It has a 150-acre campus.

RATINGS

Admissions Selectivity Rating: 78   **Fire Safety Rating:** 60*   **Green Rating:** 60*

STUDENTS AND FACULTY

Enrollment: 3,133. **Student Body:** 70% female, 30% male, 8% out-of-state, international (7 countries represented). Asian 3%, African American 17%, Caucasian 70%, Hispanic 2%, Native American 1%.
Retention and Graduation: 46% freshmen graduate within 4 years. 17% grads go on to further study within 1 year. **Faculty:** Student/faculty ratio 15:1. 110 full-time faculty, 65% hold PhDs, 11% are are members of minority groups, 57% are women.

ACADEMICS

Degrees: Bachelor's, master's. **Classes:** Most classes have 10–19 students. **Majors with Highest Enrollment:** Business administration and management; legal assistant/paralegal; nursing/registered nurse (RN, ASN, BSN, MSN). **Special Study Options:** Accelerated program, cooperative education program, cross-registration, distance learning, double major, dual enrollment, honors program, independent study, internships, liberal arts/career combination, student-designed major, study abroad, teacher certification program. **Honors programs:** Consistent with its mission, the Stevenson University Honors Program seeks to admit academically outstanding students who are interested in challenging themselves through a unique and stimulating curriculum that extends beyond traditional academic boundaries. Special programs offered to physically disabled students include note-taking services, reader services, tape recorders, tutors. **Career services:** Alumni network, alumni services, career assessment, internships.

FACILITIES

Housing: Apartments for single students, suite style (2 bedrooms share 1 bath); accommodations made for students with disabilities. 100% of campus accessible to physically disabled. **Special Academic Facilities/Equipment:** Art gallery and theatre. **Computers:** Students can register for classes online. Administrative functions (other than registration) can be performed online.

CAMPUS LIFE

Environment: Village. **Activities:** Choral groups, dance, drama/theater, jazz band, literary magazine, music ensembles, pep band, student government, student newspaper, symphony orchestra, campus ministries, international student organization. **Organizations:** 40 registered organizations, 10 honor societies, 4 religious organizations. 2 sororities. **Athletics (Intercollegiate):** *Men:* Baseball, basketball, cheerleading, cross-country, golf, lacrosse, soccer, tennis, track/field (indoor), volleyball. *Women:* Basketball, cheerleading, cross-country, field hockey, lacrosse, soccer, softball, tennis, track/field (indoor), volleyball. **On-Campus Highlights:** Rockland Center (Dining Hall/Student Ce), Avalon Community Center, The Wellness Center/Caves, Garrison Hall, Theater.

ADMISSIONS

Freshman Academic Profile: Average high school GPA 3.42. 16.08% in top 10% of high school class, 38.69% in top 25% of high school class, 79.4% in top 50% of high school class. 70% from public high schools. SAT Math middle 50% range 450–560. SAT Critical Reading middle 50% range 450–560. SAT Writing middle 50% range 450–560. ACT middle 50% range 18–22. Minimum paper TOEFL 550. Minimum computer TOEFL 213. **Basis for Candidate Selection:** *Very important factors considered include:* Academic GPA, rigor of secondary school record. *Important factors considered include:* Application essay, standardized test scores, extracurricular activities, talent/ability. *Other factors considered include:* Class rank, recommendation(s), alumni/ae relation, character/personal qualities, geographical residence, interview, level of applicant's interest, volunteer work, work experience. **Freshman Admission Requirements:** High school diploma is required and GED is accepted. *Academic units required:* 4 English, 3 mathematics, 3 science, (2 science labs), 2 social studies, 1 history, 4 academic electives. *Academic units recommended:* 4 English, 3 mathematics, 3 science, (2 science labs), 2 foreign language, 2 social studies, 1 history, 4 academic electives. **Freshman Admission Statistics:** 4,107 applied, 57% admitted, 22% enrolled. **Transfer Admission Requirements:** College transcript(s), statement of good standing from prior institution(s). Minimum college GPA of 2.5 required. Lowest grade transferable C. **General Admission Information:** Application fee $40. Notification on a rolling basis, beginning on or about 12/1. Nonfall registration accepted. Admission may be deferred for a maximum of 1 year. Credit and/or placement offered for CEEB Advanced Placement tests.

COSTS AND FINANCIAL AID
Required Forms and Deadlines: FAFSA. Priority financial aid filing date 2/15. **Notification of Awards:** Applicants will be notified of awards on a rolling basis beginning 3/15. **Types of Aid:** *Need-based scholarships/grants:* Federal Pell, SEOG, state scholarships/grants, private scholarships, the school's own gift aid. *Loans:* Direct Subsidized Stafford, Direct Unsubsidized Stafford, Direct PLUS, Federal Perkins. *Student Employment:* Federal Work-Study Program available. Institutional employment available. Off-campus job opportunities are excellent. **Financial Aid Statistics:** 68% freshmen, 61% undergrads receive need-based scholarship or grant aid. 9% freshmen, 7% undergrads receive non-need-based scholarship or grant aid. 48% freshmen, 47% undergrads receive need-based self-help aid. 61.5% undergrads borrow to pay for school. Average cumulative indebtedness $17,896. **Criteria for awarding institutional aid:** *Non-need-based:* Academics, art, leadership, music/drama.

STONEHILL COLLEGE

320 Washington Street, Easton, MA 02357-5610
Phone: 508-565-1373 **Financial Aid Phone:** 508-565-1088
E-mail: admissions@stonehill.edu **CEEB Code:** 3770
Fax: 508-565-1545 **Website:** www.stonehill.edu **ACT Code:** 1918

This private school, affiliated with the Roman Catholic Church, was founded in 1948. It has a 375-acre campus.

RATINGS
Admissions Selectivity Rating: 92   **Fire Safety Rating:** 90   **Green Rating:** 76

STUDENTS AND FACULTY
Enrollment: 2,448. **Student Body:** 60% female, 40% male, 47% out-of-state, international (10 countries represented). Asian 1%, African American 3%, Caucasian 92%, Hispanic 4%.
Retention and Graduation: 89% freshmen return for sophomore year. 80% freshmen graduate within 4 years. 38% grads go on to further study within 1 year. 26% grads pursue arts and sciences degrees. 6% grads pursue law degrees. 4% grads pursue business degrees. **Faculty:** Student/faculty ratio 13.1:1. 151 full-time faculty, 83% hold PhDs, 9% are are members of minority groups, 39% are women.

ACADEMICS
Degrees: Bachelor's. **Classes:** Most classes have 20–29 students. Most lab/discussion sessions have 10–19 students. **Majors with Highest Enrollment:** Biology/biological sciences; English language and literature; psychology. **Special Study Options:** Cross-registration, double major, dual enrollment, honors program, independent study, internships, liberal arts/career combination, student-designed major, study abroad, teacher certification program **Honors programs:** The Honors Program, which requires 5 honors courses and a Senior Honors Experience. Special programs offered to physically disabled students include note-taking services, reader services, tape recorders, tutors. **Career services:** Alumni network, alumni services, career/job search classes, career assessment, internships **Career services highlights include:** We are very proud of the fact that 79% of our senior class has completed some type of internship-related experience.

FACILITIES
Housing: Coed dorms, special housing for disabled students, women's dorms, wellness housing, special interest housing. 80% of campus accessible to physically disabled. **Special Academic Facilities/Equipment:** Institute for law and society, observatory, Stonehill Industrial History Center, shovel museum. **Computers:** 30% of classrooms, 80% of dorms, 100% of libraries, 100% of dining areas, 50% of student union, 20% of common outdoor areas have wireless network access. Students can register for classes online. Administrative functions (other than registration) can be performed online.

CAMPUS LIFE
Environment: Village. **Activities:** Choral groups, dance, drama/theater, literary magazine, music ensembles, musical theater, pep band, radio station, student government, student newspaper, student-run film society, yearbook, campus ministries. **Organizations:** 76 registered organizations, 19 honor societies, 3 religious organizations. **Athletics (Intercollegiate):** *Men:* Baseball, basketball, cross-country, football, ice hockey, soccer, tennis, track/field (outdoor), track/field (indoor). *Women:* Basketball, cross-country, equestrian sports, field hockey, lacrosse, soccer, softball, tennis, track/field (outdoor), track/field (indoor), volleyball. **On-Campus Highlights:** The Hill (entertainment/dining social space), The MacPhaidin Library, The Roche Dining Commons, The Residence Courts (housing/social space), The Sally Blair Ames Sports Complex. **Environmental Initiatives:** OurEnvironmental Stewardship Council (ESC)with membership from all of our administrative divisions and also several students, meets on a regular basis and also prepares meeting minutes to chart progress and issues that are tackled and resolved. Every year for the past five years, we perform several large energy efficiency projects, for example lighting retrofits and HVAC/Controls improvements. We work with our local utilities provider and have always been able to secure rebates (promoting the fact that the work is completed properly and is not just the type of work that is required because it has become "mainstream"). We are now in the process of constructing a new residence hall, and as an ongoing example of our committment to the environment we have made continuous "upgrades" to the original green design to include additional improvements to improve (lower) the energy consumption (e.g., added waterless urinals) and select "green" products requiring less maintenance and upkeep (e.g., substituted linoleum for VCT in the corridors. This level of "efficiency" will be carried over to other capital projects.

ADMISSIONS
Freshman Academic Profile: Average high school GPA 3.49. 50% in top 10% of high school class, 87% in top 25% of high school class, 99% in top 50% of high school class. 64% from public high schools. SAT Math middle 50% range 570–650. SAT Critical Reading middle 50% range 550–630. ACT middle 50% range 24–28. Minimum paper TOEFL 550. Minimum computer TOEFL 213. Minimum web-based TOEFL 79. **Basis for Candidate Selection:** *Very important factors considered include:* Class rank, academic GPA, rigor of secondary school record, character/personal qualities, talent/ability. *Important factors considered include:* Application essay, recommendation(s), extracurricular activities, level of applicant's interest, volunteer work, work experience. *Other factors considered include:* standardized test scores, alumni/ae relation, first generation, geographical residence, interview, racial/ethnic status, religious affiliation/commitment. **Freshman Admission Requirements:** High school diploma is required and GED is accepted. *Academic units required:* 4 English, 3 mathematics, 1 science, (1 science labs), 2 foreign language, 3 history, 3 academic electives. *Academic units recommended:* 4 English, 4 mathematics, 3 science, (2 science labs), 3 foreign language, 3 history, 3 academic electives. **Freshman Admission Statistics:** 5,871 applied, 56% admitted, 21% enrolled. **Transfer Admission Requirements:** High school transcript, college transcript(s), essay or personal statement, statement of good standing from prior institution(s). Minimum college GPA of 2.0 required. Lowest grade transferable C. **General Admission Information:** Application fee $60. Early decision application deadline 11/1. Regular application deadline 1/15. Regular notification 3/15. Nonfall registration accepted. Admission may be deferred for a maximum of 1 year. Credit and/or placement offered for CEEB Advanced Placement tests.

COSTS AND FINANCIAL AID
Required Forms and Deadlines: FAFSA, CSS/Financial Aid PROFILE, noncustodial PROFILE, business/farm supplement. Financial aid filing deadline 2/1. **Notification of Awards:** Applicants will be notified of awards on or about 4/1. **Types of Aid:** *Need-based scholarships/grants:* Federal Pell, SEOG, state scholarships/grants, private scholarships, the school's own gift aid. *Loans:* Direct Subsidized Stafford, Direct Unsubsidized Stafford, Direct PLUS, Federal Perkins, state loans. *Student Employment:* Federal Work-Study Program available. Institutional employment available. Highest amount earned per year from on-campus jobs $2,505. Off-campus job opportunities are good. **Financial Aid Statistics:** 70% freshmen, 64% undergrads receive need-based scholarship or grant aid. 10% freshmen, 8% undergrads receive non-need-based scholarship or grant aid. 60% freshmen, 60% undergrads receive need-based self-help aid. 3% freshmen, 3% undergrads receive athletic scholarships. 98% freshmen, 88% undergrads receive any aid. 73% undergrads borrow to pay for school. Average cumulative indebtedness $29,163. **Criteria for awarding institutional aid:** *Non-need-based:* Academics, athletics, job skills, leadership, minority status, music/drama.

SUFFOLK UNIVERSITY

8 Ashburton Place, Boston, MA 02108
Phone: 617-573-8460 **Financial Aid Phone:** 617-573-8470
E-mail: admission@suffolk.edu **CEEB Code:** 3771
Fax: 617-742-4291 **Website:** www.suffolk.edu **ACT Code:** 1920

This private school was founded in 1906.

RATINGS
Admissions Selectivity Rating: 72   **Fire Safety Rating:** 92   **Green Rating:** 89

STUDENTS AND FACULTY
Enrollment: 5,617. **Student Body:** 56% female, 44% male, 32% out-of-state, 10% international (105 countries represented). Asian 7%, African American 4%, Caucasian 53%, Hispanic 7%.
Retention and Graduation: 72% freshmen return for sophomore year. 36% freshmen graduate within 4 years. 33% grads go on to further study within 1 year. 11% grads pursue arts and sciences degrees. 5% grads pursue law degrees. 12% grads pursue business degrees. 3% grads pursue medical degrees. **Faculty:** Student/faculty ratio 12.7:1. 425 full-time faculty, 91% hold PhDs, 12% are are members of minority groups, 39% are women.

ACADEMICS
Degrees: Associate, bachelor's, certificate, diploma, master's, post-bachelor's certificate, post-master's certificate. **Classes:** Most classes have 10–19 students. Most lab/discussion sessions have 10–19 students. **Majors with Highest Enrollment:** Business/corporate communications; interior design; sociology. **Special Study Options:** Accelerated program, cooperative education program, cross-registration, distance learning, double major, English as a Second Language (ESL), honors program, independent study, internships, liberal arts/career combination, study abroad, weekend college. **Honors programs:** A Community of Scholars Suffolk University honors students work in collaboration with their school's program director and advisory committee to plan events that bring the honors community together on a regular basis outside of the classroom. Lectures by Suffolk University scholars or by noted intellectuals outside of the University, a variety of social events, visits to cultural and historical sites, and public service projects offer intellectual challenge, promote leadership, and develop networking skills with faculty, alumni, community, business, and government leaders. The program provides honors scholars with a broader context for their academic pursuits, while strengthening their sense of community. Special Benefits and Recognition for Honors Scholars: Honors scholars are eligible for a full tuition scholarship. In addition, honors scholars enjoy the following benefits and recognition: Guaranteed housing in University residence halls through the sophomore year; priority course registration; special honors program advisors; application assistance, when applicable, for Fulbright, Marshall, Rhodes, and other post-graduate academic and scholarship programs; Honors Program designation on official academic transcript; and special listing in commencement program. www.suffolk.edu/admission/gchonors.htm. **Combined degree programs:** BA/JD, BA/MA. Special programs offered to physically disabled students include note-taking services, reader services, tape recorders, tutors. **Career services:** Alumni network, alumni services, career/job search classes, career assessment, internships, regional alumni. **Career services highlights include:** The Co-op Program offers both part-time and full-time work options and is available to full-time undergraduate and graduate students. By combining relevant work experience with academic studies, students have the best opportunity for personal, professional and career development. Additionally, students are able to subsidize their education costs while building their resumes in preparation for their professional lives. Students can work either part-time (the most popular option) or full-time. Part-time co-ops usually involve working 15–25 hours per week while continuing to take a full load of courses. Students working full-time must have completed a full load of courses the previous semester and then must return to school for the semester after their co-op placement. Co-ops are available for all majors. Most positions are located in businesses and organizations within easy commuting distance of campus, so that students can balance their work and academic schedules. Some of the employers who have participated in the Suffolk Co-op Program include: 96.9 FM, Biogen, Boston Globe, Cape Cod Potato Chips, Commonwealth of Massachusetts, EF Education, Ernst and Young, LLP Fidelity Investments, Greater Boston Convention and Visitors Bureau, Investors Bank and Trust, Mass General Hospital, Massport, North Suffolk Mental Health Association, PricewaterhouseCoopers. Eligibility for participation in Co-op Program: Undergraduates must have a minimum 2.5 GPA. Undergraduates have completed

their freshman year Transfer students must have completed one semester at Suffolk University Full-time graduate students are eligible upon enrollment in their degree program. Student interested in Co-op must call the office at 617-573-8480 to schedule an appointment with a counselor.

FACILITIES
Housing: Coed dorms, apartments for single students. **Special Academic Facilities/Equipment:** Marine biology field station in Maine, NESAD art gallery, Adams art gallery, C. Walsh Theatre and 10 West Street Theatre **Computers:** 100% of classrooms, 100% of dorms, 100% of libraries, 100% of dining areas, 100% of student union, 20% of common outdoor areas have wireless network access. Students can register for classes online. Administrative functions (other than registration) can be performed online.

CAMPUS LIFE
Environment: Metropolis. **Activities:** Choral groups, dance, drama/theater, literary magazine, music ensembles, musical theater, radio station, student government, student newspaper, television station, yearbook, campus ministries, international student organization. **Organizations:** 75 registered organizations, 11 honor societies, 3 religious organizations. 1 fraternities, 1 sororities. **Athletics (Intercollegiate):** *Men:* Baseball, basketball, cross-country, golf, ice hockey, soccer, tennis. *Women:* Basketball, cross-country, softball, tennis, volleyball. **On-Campus Highlights:** Donahue Student Lounge, Donahue Cafe, Sawyer Library, NESAD Gallery, Alumni Park, Sawyer Computer Lab, Donahue Computer Lab, Sawyer Lounge, 150 Tremont St Dining Room. **Environmental Initiatives:** Energy Management Systems, Green Building Practices, Waste Reduction and Recycling.

ADMISSIONS
Freshman Academic Profile: Average high school GPA 3.02. 12% in top 10% of high school class, 38% in top 25% of high school class, 73% in top 50% of high school class. 70% from public high schools. SAT Math middle 50% range 450–560. SAT Critical Reading middle 50% range 450–560. SAT Writing middle 50% range 450–560. ACT middle 50% range 19–24. Minimum paper TOEFL 525. Minimum computer TOEFL 197. Minimum web-based TOEFL 71. **Basis for Candidate Selection:** *Very important factors considered include:* Rigor of secondary school record. *Important factors considered include:* Class rank, application essay, academic GPA, standardized test scores, character/personal qualities. *Other factors considered include:* Recommendation(s), alumni/ae relation, extracurricular activities, first generation, geographical residence, interview, level of applicant's interest, talent/ability, volunteer work, work experience. **Freshman Admission Requirements:** High school diploma is required and GED is accepted. *Academic units required:* 4 English, 3 mathematics, 2 science, (1 science labs), 2 foreign language, 1 history, 4 academic electives. *Academic units recommended:* 4 English, 4 mathematics, 4 science, (1 science labs), 3 foreign language, 4 history, 4 academic electives. **Freshman Admission Statistics:** 9,036 applied, 85% admitted, 16% enrolled. **Transfer Admission Requirements:** High school transcript, college transcript(s), essay or personal statement, minimum college GPA of 2.5 required. Lowest grade transferable C. **General Admission Information:** Application fee $50. Regular application deadline 3/1. Notification on a rolling basis, beginning on or about 2/5. Nonfall registration accepted. Admission may be deferred for a maximum of 1 year. Credit and/or placement offered for CEEB Advanced Placement tests.

COSTS AND FINANCIAL AID
Annual tuition $27,100. Room and board $14,544. Required fees $108. Average book expense $1,000. **Required Forms and Deadlines:** FAFSA, institution's own financial aid form Financial aid filing deadline 3/1. **Notification of Awards:** Applicants will be notified of awards on a rolling basis beginning 2/5. **Types of Aid:** *Need-based scholarships/grants:* Federal Pell, SEOG, state scholarships/grants, private scholarships, the school's own gift aid. *Loans:* Direct Subsidized Stafford, Direct Unsubsidized Stafford, Direct PLUS, Federal Perkins, state loans, college/university loans from institutional funds. *Student Employment:* Federal Work-Study Program available. Institutional employment available. Highest amount earned per year from on-campus jobs $8,217. Off-campus job opportunities are excellent. **Financial Aid Statistics:** 66% freshmen, 56% undergrads receive need-based scholarship or grant aid. 19% freshmen, 20% undergrads receive non-need-based scholarship or grant aid. 66% freshmen, 57% undergrads receive need-based self-help aid. 82% freshmen, 75% undergrads receive any aid. **Criteria for awarding institutional aid:** *Non-need-based:* Academics, alumni affiliation.

SUSQUEHANNA UNIVERSITY

Best 373

514 University Avenue, Selinsgrove, PA 17870
Phone: 570-372-4260 **Financial Aid Phone:** 570-372-4450
E-mail: suadmiss@susqu.edu **CEEB Code:** 2820
Fax: 570-372-2722 **Website:** www.susqu.edu **ACT Code:** 3720

This private school, affiliated with the Lutheran Church, was founded in 1858. It has a 306-acre campus.

RATINGS
Admissions Selectivity Rating: 80   **Fire Safety Rating:** 87   **Green Rating:** 71

STUDENTS AND FACULTY
Enrollment: 2,066. **Student Body:** 53% female, 47% male, 44.9% out-of-state, 1% international (8 countries represented). Asian 2%, African American 3%, Caucasian 91%, Hispanic 2%.
Retention and Graduation: 80% freshmen graduate within 4 years. 17% grads go on to further study within 1 year. **Faculty:** Student/faculty ratio 13:1. 128 full-time faculty, 92% hold PhDs, 16% are are members of minority groups, 43% are women.

ACADEMICS
Degrees: Bachelor's. **Classes:** Most classes have 10–19 students. Most lab/discussion sessions have 10–19 students. **Majors with Highest Enrollment:** Business administration and management; communication studies/speech communication and rhetoric; creative writing. **Special Study Options:** Accelerated program, cross-registration, distance learning, double major, dual enrollment, exchange student program (domestic), honors program, independent study, internships, student-designed major, study abroad, teacher certification program **Honors programs:** Recognized as a model for similar programs throughout the country, the Honors Program at Susquehanna offers a challenging curriculum to students interested in a more self-directed and interdisciplinary approach at the undergraduate level. The program is well suited to the aggressively curious, active learner who values breadth of study and multiple perspectives. Discussion groups, lectures, off-campus visits and residential programs complement Honors Program courses. **Combined degree programs:** BA/DDS, BA/MEM. or BA/MF with Duke Universit. Special programs offered to physically disabled students include note-taking services, reader services, tape recorders, tutors. **Career services:** Alumni network, alumni services, career/job search classes, career assessment, internships, regional alumni. **Career services highlights include:** Susquehanna University and the Center for Career Services support and encourage student participation in credit internships. Gundaker Enrichment Fund Grants provide qualifying students with supplemental support for internships or volunteer activities. Awards from the funds are intended to provide a range of experiential learning opportunities for students. In addition, Susquehanna University has partnerships with several programs offering students opportunities to combine internships and academic coursework for university credit.

FACILITIES
Housing: Coed dorms, special housing for disabled students, special housing for international students, fraternity/sorority housing, apartments for single students, theme housing. 90% of campus accessible to physically disabled. **Special Academic Facilities/Equipment:** Art gallery, electronic music lab, child development center, foreign language broadcast system, teaching theatre, greenhouse, rare book room, ecological field station, electron microscope, reflecting telescope, fluorescent microscopes, video conference center, and the new Business and Communications Building featuring three multimedia classrooms, three computer laboratories/classrooms, conference and seminar rooms, student team study rooms and alcoves, two video studios, seminar/observation rooms and a room for faculty instructional development. The building facilitates use of laptop computers by offering informational technology dataports for every seat in the classrooms, team study areas and student lounges and faculty offices **Computers:** 90% of classrooms, 10% of dorms, 100% of libraries, 100% of dining areas, 100% of student union, 30% of common outdoor areas have wireless network access. Students can register for classes online. Administrative functions (other than registration) can be performed online.

CAMPUS LIFE
Environment: Town. **Activities:** Choral groups, concert band, dance, drama/theater, jazz band, literary magazine, music ensembles, musical theater, opera, pep band, radio station, student government, student newspaper, student-run film society, symphony orchestra, television station, yearbook, campus ministries, international student organization. **Organizations:** 120 registered organizations, 24 honor societies, 12 religious organizations. 4 fraternities, 5

sororities. **Athletics (Intercollegiate):** *Men:* Baseball, basketball, crew/rowing, cross-country, football, golf, lacrosse, soccer, swimming, tennis, track/field (outdoor), track/field (indoor). *Women:* Basketball, crew/rowing, cross-country, field hockey, golf, lacrosse, soccer, softball, swimming, tennis, track/field (outdoor), track/field (indoor), volleyball. **On-Campus Highlights:** Sports and Fitness Complex, Business and Communications Center, Blough-Weis Library, Trax (campus nightclub), Java City in the Campus Center. **Environmental Initiatives:** New science facility and new student housing will be LEED-certified. This housing and two units built last year utilize geo-thermal energy for heating and cooling. Actively pursuing alternative sources of fuel to replace coal-fired power plant. Cut fuel usage 25% last year by installing highly-efficient insulated steam lines. Susquehanna University is a flagship member of the Graduation Pledge Alliance, a national student organization whose mission is to promote socially and environmentally responsible actions by graduating seniors. Commitments include participation in a recycling cooperative with the borough.

ADMISSIONS
Freshman Academic Profile: Average high school GPA 3.22. 25% in top 10% of high school class, 60% in top 25% of high school class, 87% in top 50% of high school class. 81% from public high schools. SAT Math middle 50% range 520–600. SAT Critical Reading middle 50% range 500–610. SAT Writing middle 50% range 500–610. ACT middle 50% range 21–26. Minimum paper TOEFL 550. Minimum computer TOEFL 213. Minimum web-based TOEFL 81. **Basis for Candidate Selection:** *Very important factors considered include:* Academic GPA, rigor of secondary school record. *Important factors considered include:* Class rank, application essay, recommendation(s), standardized test scores, alumni/ae relation, character/personal qualities, extracurricular activities, interview, level of applicant's interest, racial/ethnic status, talent/ability, volunteer work, work *Other factors considered include:* first generation, geographical residence, religious affiliation/commitment, state residency. **Freshman Admission Requirements:** High school diploma is required and GED is accepted. *Academic units required:* 4 English, 3 mathematics, 3 science, (2 science labs), 2 foreign language, 2 social studies, 2 history, 2 academic electives. *Academic units recommended:* 4 English, 4 mathematics, 4 science, (3 science labs), 4 foreign language, 4 social studies, 2 history, 3 academic electives. **Freshman Admission Statistics:** 2,777 applied, 73% admitted, 31% enrolled. **Transfer Admission Requirements:** High school transcript, college transcript(s), essay or personal statement, statement of good standing from prior institution(s). Minimum college GPA of 2.0 required. Lowest grade transferable C–. **General Admission Information:** Application fee $35. Early decision application deadline 11/15. Regular application deadline 3/1. Notification on a rolling basis, beginning on or about 12/15. Nonfall registration accepted. Admission may be deferred for a maximum of 1 year. Credit and/or placement offered for CEEB Advanced Placement tests.

COSTS AND FINANCIAL AID
Annual tuition $32,050. Room and board $8,800. Required fees $400. Average book expense $850. **Required Forms and Deadlines:** FAFSA, CSS/Financial Aid PROFILE, business/farm supplement. Prior year Federal tax return. Financial aid filing deadline 5/1. Priority financial aid filing date 3/1. **Notification of Awards:** Applicants will be notified of awards on or about 3/1. **Types of Aid:** *Need-based scholarships/grants:* Federal Pell, SEOG, state scholarships/grants, private scholarships, the school's own gift aid. *Loans:* FFEL Subsidized Stafford, FFEL Unsubsidized Stafford, FFEL PLUS, Federal Perkins, college/university loans from institutional funds. *Student Employment:* Federal Work-Study Program available. Institutional employment available. Highest amount earned per year from on-campus jobs $8,337. Off-campus job opportunities are good. **Financial Aid Statistics:** 61% freshmen, 58% undergrads receive need-based scholarship or grant aid. 9% freshmen, 7% undergrads receive non-need-based scholarship or grant aid. 56% freshmen, 54% undergrads receive need-based self-help aid. 96.4% freshmen, 90.6% undergrads receive any aid. **Criteria for awarding institutional aid:** *Non-need-based:* Academics, alumni affiliation, leadership, minority status, music/drama.

SWARTHMORE COLLEGE

500 College Avenue, Swarthmore, PA 19081
Phone: 610-328-8300 **Financial Aid Phone:** 610-328-8358
E-mail: admissions@swarthmore.edu **CEEB Code:** 2821
Fax: 610-328-8580 **Website:** www.swarthmore.edu **ACT Code:** 3722

This private school was founded in 1864. It has a 399-acre campus.

RATINGS
Admissions Selectivity Rating: 99   **Fire Safety Rating:** 87   **Green Rating:** 77

STUDENTS AND FACULTY
Enrollment: 1,505. **Student Body:** 52% female, 48% male, 87% out-of-state, 7% international (57 countries represented). Asian 16%, African American 10%, Caucasian 44%, Hispanic 11%, Native American 1%.
Retention and Graduation: 86% freshmen graduate within 4 years. 23% grads go on to further study within 1 year. 11% grads pursue arts and sciences degrees. 3% grads pursue law degrees. 2% grads pursue medical degrees. **Faculty:** Student/faculty ratio 8:1. 171 full-time faculty, 100% hold PhDs, 15% are are members of minority groups, 40% are women.

ACADEMICS
Degrees: Bachelor's. **Classes:** Most classes have 10–19 students. Most lab/discussion sessions have fewer than 10 students. **Majors with Highest Enrollment:** Biology/biological sciences; economics; political science and government. **Special Study Options:** Accelerated program, cross-registration, double major, exchange student program (domestic), honors program, independent study, internships, student-designed major, study abroad, teacher certification program, Swarthmore offers cooperative exchange programs with Rice and Tufts universities and Harvey Mudd, Pomona, Mills and Middlebury colleges. **Honors programs:** Swarthmore's Honors Program features faculty working with small groups of dedicated and accomplished students; an emphasis on independent learning; students entering into a dialogue with peers, teachers, and examiners; a demanding program of study in major and minor fields; and an examination at the end of two years' study by outside scholars. **Combined degree programs:** BA/BS in engineering and another major. Special programs offered to physically disabled students include note-taking services, reader services, tape recorders, tutors. **Career services:** Alumni network, alumni services, career/job search classes, career assessment, internships, regional alumni. **Career services highlights include:** Swarthmore's externship program matches 200 students annually with over 300 alumni sponsors in diverse career fields and locations nationwide.

FACILITIES
Housing: Coed dorms, men's dorms, women's dorms, Gender Neutral housing (students of any gender may share rooms and/or share bathrooms). 85% of campus accessible to physically disabled. **Special Academic Facilities/Equipment:** The campus is a 399-acre, nationally registered arboretum. The Lang Performing Arts Center's resources include an art gallery, dance studios, cinema, and theater performance space. Highlights of Swarthmore's library facilities include the Friends Historical Library and the Peace Collection. The athletics facilities include a lighted stadium complex, a 400–meter dual durometer track, and synthetic grass playing field, state-of-the-art fitness center and three indoor tennis courts with Rebound Ace surface. The Science Center has been recognized by the U.S. Green Building Council for "leadership in energy and environmental design." The College's two newest residence halls feature loft-style rooms and environmentally friendly green roofs. **Computers:** 100% of classrooms, 100% of dorms, 100% of libraries, 100% of dining areas, 100% of student union, 100% of common outdoor areas have wireless network access. Students can register for classes online. Administrative functions (other than registration) can be performed online.

CAMPUS LIFE
Environment: Village. **Activities:** Choral groups, dance, drama/theater, jazz band, literary magazine, music ensembles, opera, student government, student newspaper, student-run film society, symphony orchestra, yearbook, campus ministries, international student organization. **Organizations:** 138 registered organizations, 3 honor societies, 12 religious organizations. 2 fraternities. **Athletics (Intercollegiate):** Men: Baseball, basketball, cross-country, golf, lacrosse, soccer, swimming, tennis, track/field (outdoor), track/field (indoor). Women: Badminton, basketball, cross-country, field hockey, lacrosse, soccer, softball, swimming, tennis, track/field (outdoor), track/field (indoor), volleyball. **On-Campus Highlights:** Kohlberg & Eldridge Commons Coffee Bars, Parrish Beach (the central campus lawn), Scott Outdoor Amphitheater, Mullan Tennis & Fitness Center, Paces (student-run cafe), Recent years have seen an exciting array of student projects and student spaces develop at Swarthmore. Among them: The acclaimed War News Radio (www.warnewsradio.org), the nation's only student-run national radio program focusing on the wars in Iraq and Afghanistan, now carried by more than 60 stations worldwide; the Genocide Intervention Network (www.genocideintervention.net), a student-founded group that is raising hundreds of thousands of dollars to support peace-keeping in Darfur; two new dormitories, whose student-influenced integrative design features loft-style doubles, wide halls, generous lounge and community kitchens—all aimed at promoting robust hall social life; and the Lang Center for Civic and Social Responsibility (www.swarthmore.edu/langcenter) which prepares students for leadership in civic engagement, public service, advocacy, and social action. **Environmental Initiatives:** 40% of the college's electrical demands are met by renewable wind power The college has approximately 14,300 sq. feet of green roof The College's Sustainability Committee is comprised of faculty, staff, and students and is charged with making recommendations to improve environmental sustainability on campus.

ADMISSIONS
Freshman Academic Profile: 87.4% in top 10% of high school class, 99% in top 25% of high school class, 100% in top 50% of high school class. 59% from public high schools. SAT Math middle 50% range 670–770. SAT Critical Reading middle 50% range 670–760. SAT Writing middle 50% range 670–760. ACT middle 50% range 29.5–33. **Basis for Candidate Selection:** *Very important factors considered include:* Class rank, application essay, academic GPA, recommendation(s), rigor of secondary school record, character/personal qualities. *Important factors considered include:* Standardized test scores, extracurricular activities. *Other factors considered include:* Alumni/ae relation, first generation, geographical residence, interview, level of applicant's interest, racial/ethnic status, talent/ability, volunteer work, work experience. **Freshman Admission Requirements:** High school diploma or equivalent is not required. *Academic units recommended:* 4 English, 3 mathematics, 3 science. **Freshman Admission Statistics:** 5,575 applied, 17% admitted, 41% enrolled. **Transfer Admission Requirements:** High school transcript, college transcript(s), essay or personal statement, standardized test scores, statement of good standing from prior institution(s). Lowest grade transferable C. **General Admission Information:** Application fee $60. Early decision application deadline 11/15. Regular application deadline 1/2. Regular notification 4/1. Nonfall registration not accepted. Admission may be deferred for a maximum of 1 Year. Credit and/or placement offered for CEEB Advanced Placement tests.

COSTS AND FINANCIAL AID
Annual tuition $37,510. Room and board $11,740. Required fees $350. Average book expense $1,150. **Required Forms and Deadlines:** FAFSA, institution's own financial aid form, CSS/Financial Aid PROFILE, state aid form, noncustodial PROFILE, business/farm supplement, federal tax return, W2 statements, year-end paycheck stub. Financial aid filing deadline 2/15. Priority financial aid filing date 2/15. **Notification of Awards:** Applicants will be notified of awards on or about 4/1. **Types of Aid:** *Need-based scholarships/grants:* Federal Pell, SEOG, state scholarships/grants, private scholarships, the school's own gift aid. *Loans:* FFEL Subsidized Stafford, FFEL Unsubsidized Stafford, FFEL PLUS, Federal Perkins, state loans, college/university loans from institutional funds. *Student Employment:* Federal Work-Study Program available. Institutional employment available. Highest amount earned per year from on-campus jobs $1,760. Off-campus job opportunities are good. **Financial Aid Statistics:** 55% freshmen, 49% undergrads receive need-based scholarship or grant aid. 54% freshmen, 48% undergrads receive need-based self-help aid. 55% freshmen, 57% undergrads receive any aid. **Criteria for awarding institutional aid:** *Non-need-based:* Academics, leadership, state/district residency.

See page 1250.

SWEET BRIAR COLLEGE

P. O. Box B, Sweet Briar, VA 24595
Phone: 434-381-6142 **Financial Aid Phone:** 434-381-6156
E-mail: admissions@sbc.edu **CEEB Code:** 5634
Fax: 434-381-6152 **Website:** www.sbc.edu **ACT Code:** 4406

This private school was founded in 1901. It has a 3250-acre campus.

RATINGS
Admissions Selectivity Rating: 82   **Fire Safety Rating:** 99   **Green Rating:** 80

STUDENTS AND FACULTY

Enrollment: 647. **Student Body:** 100% female, 49% out-of-state, 1% international (16 countries represented). Asian 1%, African American 3%, Caucasian 87%, Hispanic 3%, Native American 1%.

Retention and Graduation: 71% freshmen return for sophomore year. 68% freshmen graduate within 4 years. 24% grads go on to further study within 1 year. 6% grads pursue arts and sciences degrees. 1% grads pursue law degrees. 5% grads pursue medical degrees. **Faculty:** Student/faculty ratio 9:1. 65 full-time faculty, 100% hold PhDs, 5% are are members of minority groups, 49% are women.

ACADEMICS

Degrees: Bachelor's, master's. **Classes:** Most classes have 10–19 students. Most lab/discussion sessions have fewer than 10 students. **Majors with Highest Enrollment:** Biology/biological sciences; business/commerce; psychology. **Special Study Options:** Accelerated program, cross-registration, double major, dual enrollment, exchange student program (domestic), honors program, independent study, internships, liberal arts/career combination, student-designed major, study abroad, teacher certification program **Honors programs:** The Honors Program was established and continues to evolve in response to the needs of students who demonstrate exceptional initiative, ability, and creativity. The program consists of challenging courses, Summer Research Fellowships, opportunities for independent work, and a series of extracurricular activities. The program also brings advanced graduate degree candidates to campus, providing role models for students considering graduate studies. **Combined degree programs:** BA/MEng, BA/BS Eng. with Columbia, VaTech, Wash. Univ. Special programs offered to physically disabled students include tutors. **Career services:** Alumni network, alumni services, career/job search classes, career assessment, internships, regional alumni. **Career services highlights include:** The Internship Program has developed into a strong, professionalized program, with resources for providing students with internship and other experiential opportunities for all college majors and fields of interest. The Career Services team has been on the road recently presenting at state and regional conferences on the collaborative relationships forged between college and community. These relationships have greatly augmented the internship program.

FACILITIES

Housing: Women's dorms, Substance-free, Eco Floor, Academic House, International Corridor. 75% of campus accessible to physically disabled. **Special Academic Facilities/Equipment:** Art museum and galleries, college and local history museums, environmental education/nature center, kindergarten/nursery school, riding center, electron microscope, DNA sequencing equipment, 400MHz nuclear magnetic resonance spectrometer. **Computers:** 60% of classrooms, 50% of dorms, 100% of libraries, 100% of dining areas, 100% of student union, 30% of common outdoor areas have wireless network access. Students can register for classes online. Administrative functions (other than registration) can be performed online.

CAMPUS LIFE

Environment: Rural. **Activities:** Choral groups, dance, drama/theater, literary magazine, music ensembles, musical theater, radio station, student government, student newspaper, student-run film society, symphony orchestra, television station, yearbook, campus ministries. **Organizations:** 61 registered organizations, 11 honor societies, 3 religious organizations. **Athletics (Intercollegiate):.** *Women:* field hockey, horseback riding, lacrosse, soccer, softball, swimming, tennis, volleyball. **On-Campus Highlights:** Bistro, Riding Center, Boathouse, Book Shop, Art Barn. **Environmental Initiatives:** Recycling, geothermal, performance contracting.

ADMISSIONS

Freshman Academic Profile: Average high school GPA 3.53. 28% in top 10% of high school class, 53% in top 25% of high school class, 88% in top 50% of high school class. 72% from public high schools. SAT Math middle 50% range 470–600. SAT Critical Reading middle 50% range 510–630. ACT middle 50% range 20–26. Minimum paper TOEFL 550. Minimum computer TOEFL 213. Minimum web-based TOEFL 79. **Basis for Candidate Selection:** *Very important factors considered include:* Academic GPA, rigor of secondary school record. *Important factors considered include:* Application essay, recommendation(s), standardized test scores, interview. *Other factors considered include:* Class rank, alumni/ae relation, character/personal qualities, extracurricular activities, first generation, racial/ethnic status, talent/ability, volunteer work, work experience. **Freshman Admission Requirements:** High school diploma is required and GED is accepted. *Academic units required:* 4 English, 3 mathematics, 3 science, (2 science labs), 2 foreign language, 3 social studies. *Academic units recommended:* 4 English, 4 mathematics, 4 science, (3 science labs), 4 foreign language, 4 social studies. **Freshman Admission Statistics:** 629 applied, 83% admitted, 38% enrolled. **Transfer Admission Requirements:** High school transcript, college transcript(s), essay or personal statement, standardized test scores, statement of good standing from prior institution(s). Minimum college GPA of 2.5 required. Lowest grade transferable C–. **General Admission Information:** Application fee $40. Early decision

application deadline 12/1. Regular application deadline 2/1. Regular notification 3/15. Nonfall registration accepted. Admission may be deferred for a maximum of 1 year. Credit and/or placement offered for CEEB Advanced Placement tests.

COSTS AND FINANCIAL AID

Annual tuition $28,860. Room and board $10,460. Required fees $275. Average book expense $900. **Required Forms and Deadlines:** FAFSA, noncustodial PROFILE Priority financial aid filing date 2/15. **Notification of Awards:** Applicants will be notified of awards on or about 3/1. **Types of Aid:** *Need-based scholarships/grants:* Federal Pell, SEOG, state scholarships/grants, private scholarships, the school's own gift aid. *Loans:* Direct Subsidized Stafford, Direct Unsubsidized Stafford, Direct PLUS, Federal Perkins, college/university loans from institutional funds. *Student Employment:* Federal Work-Study Program available. Institutional employment available. Highest amount earned per year from on-campus jobs $1,000. Off-campus job opportunities are fair. **Financial Aid Statistics:** 62% freshmen, 53% undergrads receive need-based scholarship or grant aid. 33% freshmen, 40% undergrads receive non-need-based scholarship or grant aid. 62% freshmen, 53% undergrads receive need-based self-help aid. 91% freshmen, 93% undergrads receive any aid. 50% undergrads borrow to pay for school. Average cumulative indebtedness $20,118. **Criteria for awarding institutional aid:** *Non-need-based:* Academics, art, leadership, music/drama, state/district residency.

See page 1252.

SYRACUSE UNIVERSITY

100 Crouse-Hinds Hall, 900 S. Crouse Av, Syracuse, NY 13244-2130
Phone: 315-443-3611 **Financial Aid Phone:** 315-443-1513
E-mail: orange@syr.edu **CEEB Code:** 2823
Fax: 315-443-4226 **Website:** www.syr.edu **ACT Code:** 2968

This private school was founded in 1870. It has a 200-acre campus.

RATINGS

Admissions Selectivity Rating: 92   **Fire Safety Rating:** 89   **Green Rating:** 93

STUDENTS AND FACULTY

Enrollment: 13,243. **Student Body:** 56% female, 44% male, 53% out-of-state, 5% international (124 countries represented). Asian 9%, African American 8%, Caucasian 57%, Hispanic 7%, Native American 1%.

Retention and Graduation: 23% grads go on to further study within 1 year. 5% grads pursue arts and sciences degrees. 5% grads pursue law degrees. 1% grads pursue business degrees. 3% grads pursue medical degrees. **Faculty:** Student/faculty ratio 15:1. 962 full-time faculty, 87% hold PhDs, 19% are members of minority groups, 37% are women.

ACADEMICS

Degrees: Associate, bachelor's, certificate, master's, post-bachelor's certificate, post-master's certificate. **Classes:** Most classes have 10–19 students. Most lab/discussion sessions have 20–29 students. **Majors with Highest Enrollment:** Commercial and advertising art; psychology; radio and television. **Special Study Options:** Accelerated program, cooperative education program, distance learning, double major, dual enrollment, English as a Second Language (ESL), honors program, independent study, internships, liberal arts/career combination, student-designed major, study abroad, teacher certification program, SU offers many undergraduate research opportunities, pre-professional programs, and minors. **Honors programs:** The University Honors program combines the benefits of a small intimate community with the advantages of diversity and opportunity found only at larger institutions. Students enjoy provocative coursework in small classes taught by some of the University's most able and experienced faculty, as well as some of the nation's leading research scholars. In the Honors Thesis Project upper class students are closely guided by faculty to pursue intensive research on a topic of their choice. **Combined degree programs:** BA/JD, BA/MEng. Special programs offered to physically disabled students include note-taking services, reader services, tape recorders, tutors. **Career services:** Alumni network, alumni services, career/job search classes, career assessment, internships, regional alumni. **Career services highlights include:** Syracuse University's South Side Entrepreneurial Connect Project (SSECP), launched in June of 2004, works with the challenged inner city neighborhoods on the south side of Syracuse to create sustainable small business ventures. The goal of the SSECP is to foster the development of an entrepreneurial community within the south side through increasing the number of new start ups and developing a supportive infrastructure that ensures the long-term sustainability of existing small businesses within the community. In this comprehensive initiative, students are intimately involved in all facets of SSECP management and implementation, including: Consultation teams with faculty and students from other disciplines that work closely with entrepreneurs in creating and growing ventures; management of a microcredit fund for inner city entrepreneurs; organizing community functions; legal counseling for entrepreneurs from Law School students; youth mentoring and empowerment programs; assistance in coordinating our South Side Entrepreneurs Association; resource mapping and connecting; involvement in the cross-marketing program; and research projects that provide insights that enable the sustainability of the inner city entrepreneurial development model that guides our efforts. Our students intern and work in the SSIC, and it has become the nerve center for a wide range of entrepreneurial initiatives and activities involving the inner city of Syracuse.

FACILITIES

Housing: Coed dorms, special housing for disabled students, special housing for international students, fraternity/sorority housing, apartments for married students, apartments for single students, wellness housing, theme housing International living center, single-sex floors and wings of residence halls, numerous learning communities, and interest housing available. 92% of campus accessible to physically disabled. **Special Academic Facilities/Equipment:** SUArt Galleries; The Warehouse Gallery; digital media convergence center; Syracuse Center of Excellence in Environmental and Energy Systems; Fidelity MOTUS 622i flight simulator for aerospace engineering; Ballentine Investment Institute; community darkrooms; Syracuse Stage professional equity theater; Bernice M. Wright Child Development Laboratory School; Belfer Audio Laboratory and Archive; Gebbie Speech, Language, and Hearing Clinic; Life Sciences Complex; SU Library Special Collections Research Center; UPSTATE: A Center for Design, Research and Real Estate at the SU School of Architecture; Center on Human Policy; Center for Emerging Network Technologies; JPMorgan Chase Technology Center. **Computers:** 75% of classrooms, 100% of dorms, 100% of libraries, 100% of dining areas, 100% of student union, 75% of common outdoor areas have wireless network access. Students can register for classes online. Administrative functions (other than registration) can be performed online.

CAMPUS LIFE

Environment: Metropolis. **Activities:** Choral groups, concert band, dance, drama/theater, jazz band, literary magazine, marching band, music ensembles, musical theater, pep band, radio station, student government, student newspaper, student-run film society, symphony orchestra, television station, yearbook, campus ministries, international student organization. **Organizations:** 347 registered organizations, 43 honor societies, 30 religious organizations. 29 fraternities, 19 sororities. **Athletics (Intercollegiate):** *Men:* Basketball, cheerleading, crew/rowing, cross-country, diving, football, lacrosse, soccer, swimming, track/field (outdoor). *Women:* Basketball, cheerleading, crew/rowing, cross-country, diving, field hockey, ice hockey, lacrosse, soccer, softball, swimming, tennis, track/field (outdoor), volleyball. **On-Campus Highlights:** Schine Student Center, Bird Library Cafe, Hendricks Chapel, Whitman School, Archbold Athletic Complex. **Environmental Initiatives:** 20% renewable energy purchases Created a sustainability department. Making a multi-million dollar investment in temperature controls.

ADMISSIONS

Freshman Academic Profile: Average high school GPA 3.6. 38.5% in top 10% of high school class, 73% in top 25% of high school class, 95.6% in top 50% of high school class. 72% from public high schools. SAT Math middle 50% range 540–650. SAT Critical Reading middle 50% range 510–620. SAT Writing middle 50% range 520–630. ACT middle 50% range 23–28. Minimum paper TOEFL 550. Minimum web-based TOEFL 80. **Basis for Candidate Selection:** *Very important factors considered include:* Class rank, application essay, academic GPA, recommendation(s), rigor of secondary school record, standardized test scores, character/personal qualities, extracurricular activities, interview, level of applicant's interest, talent/ability. *Important factors considered include:* Alumni/ae relation, first generation, geographical residence, state residency, volunteer work, work experience. *Other factors considered include:* Racial/ethnic status. **Freshman Admission Requirements:** High school diploma is required and GED is accepted. *Academic units required:* 4 English, 4 mathematics, 4 science, (4 science labs), 3 foreign language, 4 social studies. **Freshman Admission Statistics:** 20,951 applied, 60% admitted, 26% enrolled. **Transfer Admission Requirements:** College transcript(s), essay or personal statement, statement of good standing from prior institution(s). Lowest grade transferable C. **General Admission Information:** Application fee $70. Early decision application deadline 11/1. Regular application deadline 1/1. Notification on a rolling basis, beginning on or about 3/15. Nonfall registration accepted. Admission may be deferred for a maximum of 1 year. Credit and/or placement offered for CEEB Advanced Placement tests.

COSTS AND FINANCIAL AID

Annual tuition $33,630. Room and board $12,374. Required fees $1,296. Average book expense $1,306. **Required Forms and Deadlines:** FAFSA, CSS/Financial Aid PROFILE, noncustodial PROFILE Financial aid filing deadline 2/2. **Notification of Awards:** Applicants will be notified of awards on or about 3/21. **Types of Aid:** *Need-based scholarships/grants:* Federal Pell, SEOG, state scholarships/grants, private scholarships, the school's own gift aid. *Loans:* Direct Subsidized Stafford, Direct Unsubsidized Stafford, Direct PLUS, Federal Perkins. *Student Employment:* Federal Work-Study Program available. Institutional employment available. Off-campus job opportunities are good. **Financial Aid Statistics:** 57% freshmen, 54% undergrads receive need-based scholarship or grant aid. 3% freshmen, 3% undergrads receive non-need-based scholarship or grant aid. 61% freshmen, 59% undergrads receive need-based self-help aid. 2% freshmen, 3% undergrads receive athletic scholarships. 80% freshmen, 80% undergrads receive any aid. 65% undergrads borrow to pay for school. Average cumulative indebtedness $28,358. **Criteria for awarding institutional aid:** *Non-need-based:* Academics, art, athletics, music/drama, state/district residency.

TALLADEGA COLLEGE

627 West Battle Street, Talladega, AL 35160
Phone: 205-761-6235 **Financial Aid Phone:** 256-761-6341
E-mail: admissions@talladega.edu
Fax: 205-362-0274 **Website:** www.talladega.edu **ACT Code:** 0026

This private school, affiliated with the United Church of Christ Church, was founded in 1867. It has a 50-acre campus.

RATINGS

Admissions Selectivity Rating: 77   **Fire Safety Rating:** 87   **Green Rating:** 60*

STUDENTS AND FACULTY

Enrollment: 601. **Student Body:** 58% female, 42% male, 48% out-of-state,. African American 95%, Hispanic 4%.
Retention and Graduation: 43% freshmen return for sophomore year. 27% freshmen graduate within 4 years. 25% grads go on to further study within 1 year. 25% grads pursue arts and sciences degrees. 25% grads pursue law degrees. 25% grads pursue business degrees. 25% grads pursue medical degrees.
Faculty: Student/faculty ratio 16:1. 29 full-time faculty, 62% hold PhDs, 66% are are members of minority groups, 45% are women.

ACADEMICS

Degrees: Bachelor's. **Classes:** Most classes have fewer than 10 students. Most lab/discussion sessions have fewer than 10 students. **Majors with Highest Enrollment:** Biology/biological sciences; business/commerce; psychology. **Special Study Options:** Double major, dual enrollment, independent study, internships, teacher certification program Special programs offered to physically disabled students include note-taking services, tape recorders, tutors. **Career services:** Alumni network, alumni services, career assessment, internships

FACILITIES

Housing: Men's dorms, women's dorms. 100% of campus accessible to physically disabled. **Special Academic Facilities/Equipment:** Savery Library, Home of the famous Amistad Murals, historic Swayne Hall, which is listed on the National Register; DeForest Chapel, which has the stained glass windows by famous artist, David Driskell; Goodnow Art Building. **Computers:** 100% of libraries, 50% of common outdoor areas have wireless network access. Administrative functions (other than registration) can be performed online.

CAMPUS LIFE

Environment: Rural. **Activities:** Choral groups, concert band, dance, drama/theater, jazz band, student government, student newspaper, yearbook. **Organizations:** 40 registered organizations, 8 honor societies, 1 religious organizations. 4 fraternities, 4 sororities. **Athletics (Intercollegiate):** *Men:* Baseball, basketball, golf. *Women:* Basketball, cheerleading, volleyball. **On-Campus Highlights:** Savery Library, DeForest Chapel, Swayne Hall, Callanan Hall, Fanning Hall.

ADMISSIONS

Freshman Academic Profile: Average high school GPA 2.71. 90% from public high schools. SAT Math middle 50% range 340–410. SAT Critical Reading middle 50% range 320–460. ACT middle 50% range 16–19. Minimum paper TOEFL 500. Minimum computer TOEFL 250. **Basis for Candidate Selection:** *Very important factors considered include:* Application essay, recommendation(s), rigor of secondary school record, standardized test scores, character/personal qualities, extracurricular activities, talent/ability, volunteer work, work experience. *Important factors considered include:* Class rank.

Other factors considered include: interview. **Freshman Admission Requirements:** High school diploma is required and GED is accepted. *Academic units required:* 4 English, 2 mathematics, 2 science, 3 social studies, 2 physical education or health. **Freshman Admission Statistics:** 2,000 applied, 40% admitted, 38% enrolled. **Transfer Admission Requirements:** High school transcript, college transcript(s), essay or personal statement, standardized test scores, statement of good standing from prior institution(s). Minimum college GPA of 2.0 required. Lowest grade transferable C. **General Admission Information:** Application fee $25. Nonfall registration accepted. Admission may be deferred for a maximum of 2 years. Credit and/or placement offered for CEEB Advanced Placement tests.

COSTS AND FINANCIAL AID

Annual tuition $6,720. Room and board $4,290. Required fees $408. Average book expense $1,000. **Required Forms and Deadlines:** FAFSA, institution's own financial aid form, CSS/Financial Aid PROFILE, state aid form Financial aid filing deadline 6/30. Priority financial aid filing date 4/1. **Notification of Awards:** Applicants will be notified of awards on or about 4/1. **Types of Aid:** *Need-based scholarships/grants:* Federal Pell, SEOG, state scholarships/grants, private scholarships, the school's own gift aid, United Negro College Fund. *Loans:* FFEL Subsidized Stafford, FFEL Unsubsidized Stafford, FFEL PLUS, Federal Perkins. *Student Employment:* Highest amount earned per year from on-campus jobs $1,200. Off-campus job opportunities are good. **Financial Aid Statistics:** 42% freshmen, 26% undergrads receive need-based scholarship or grant aid. 42% freshmen, 26% undergrads receive non-need-based scholarship or grant aid. 90% freshmen, 90% undergrads receive any aid. 80% undergrads borrow to pay for school. Average cumulative indebtedness $5,000. **Criteria for awarding institutional aid:** *Non-need-based:* Academics, alumni affiliation, art, athletics, music/drama.

TARLETON STATE UNIVERSITY

PO Box T-0030, Tarleton Station, Stephenville, TX 76402
Phone: 254-968-9125 **Financial Aid Phone:** 254-968-9070
E-mail: uadm@tarleton.edu **CEEB Code:** 6817
Fax: 254-968-9951 **Website:** **ACT Code:** 4204

This public school was founded in 1899. It has a 125-acre campus.

RATINGS
Admissions Selectivity Rating: 70   **Fire Safety Rating:** 85   **Green Rating:** 67

STUDENTS AND FACULTY
Enrollment: 7,781. **Student Body:** 57% female, 43% male, 4% out-of-state, 1% international (33 countries represented). Asian 1%, African American 8%, Caucasian 79%, Hispanic 9%, Native American 1%.
Retention and Graduation: 62% freshmen return for sophomore year. 13% freshmen graduate within 4 years. **Faculty:** Student/faculty ratio 18:1. 318 full-time faculty, 66% hold PhDs, 10% are are members of minority groups, 41% are women. 2% of classes are taught by teaching assistants.

ACADEMICS
Degrees: Associate, bachelor's, master's. **Classes:** Most classes have 20–29 students. Most lab/discussion sessions have 10–19 students. **Majors with Highest Enrollment:** Business/commerce; education. **Special Study Options:** Accelerated program, distance learning, double major, dual enrollment, honors program, internships, study abroad, teacher certification program, Undergrads may take grad level classes. **Honors programs:** Offer honors classes in core curriculum subjects, including English, history, political science, chemistry, biology, geology, and speech. Courses offer intellectually challenging material, innovative approaches to the subject, increased opportunities for honing critical thinking and writing skills, and the opportunity to interact closely with similarly motivated students and with outstanding faculty. Special programs offered to physically disabled students include note-taking services, reader services, tutors. **Career services:** Career/job search classes, career assessment, internships **Career services highlights include:** Education Department and Student Teaching opportunities.

FACILITIES
Housing: Coed dorms, special housing for disabled students, men's dorms, special housing for international students, women's dorms, fraternity/sorority housing, apartments for married students, cooperative housing, apartments for single students. **Special Academic Facilities/Equipment:** Planetarium in Science Bldg. W.K. Gordon Center for Industrial History of Texas. **Computers:** 100% of classrooms, 100% of dorms, 100% of libraries, 100% of student union, have wireless network access. Students can register for classes online. Administrative functions (other than registration) can be performed online.

CAMPUS LIFE
Environment: Village. **Activities:** Choral groups, concert band, dance, drama/theater, jazz band, literary magazine, marching band, music ensembles, musical theater, opera, pep band, radio station, student government, student newspaper, student-run film society, symphony orchestra, television station, yearbook, campus ministries, international student organization. **Organizations:** 117 registered organizations, 13 honor societies, 13 religious organizations. 7 fraternities, 8 sororities. **Athletics (Intercollegiate):** *Men:* Baseball, basketball, cheerleading, cross-country, football, rodeo, track/field (outdoor). *Women:* Basketball, cheerleading, cross-country, golf, rodeo, softball, tennis, track/field (outdoor), volleyball. **On-Campus Highlights:** Barry B. Thompson Student Center, new Recreational Sports Facility, Dick Smith Library, Wisdom Gym, Science Bldg with planetarium. **Environmental Initiatives:** 15% Electric from wind. In compliance with SB12.

ADMISSIONS
Freshman Academic Profile: 8% in top 10% of high school class, 35% in top 25% of high school class, 76% in top 50% of high school class. 99% from public high schools. SAT Math middle 50% range 440–540. SAT Critical Reading middle 50% range 430–530. SAT Writing middle 50% range 420–510. ACT middle 50% range 18–23. Minimum paper TOEFL 520. Minimum computer TOEFL 190. **Basis for Candidate Selection:** *Very important factors considered include:* Class rank, rigor of secondary school record, standardized test scores. *Important factors considered include:* Academic GPA. **Freshman Admission Requirements:** High school diploma is required and GED is accepted. *Academic units required:* 4 English, 3 mathematics, 2 science, (2 science labs), 2 social studies, 1 history, 2 academic electives. *Academic units recommended:* 4 English, 3 mathematics, 3 science, 2 foreign language, 4 academic electives. **Freshman Admission Statistics:** 3,544 applied, 55% admitted, 63% enrolled. **Transfer Admission Requirements:** College transcript(s), minimum college GPA of 2.0 required. Lowest grade transferable D. **General Admission Information:** Application fee $25. Regular application deadline 8/1. Nonfall registration accepted. Credit offered for CEEB Advanced Placement tests.

COSTS AND FINANCIAL AID
Annual in-state tuition $5,166. Annual out-of-state tuition $13,506. Room and board $5,944. Required fees $1,326. Average book expense $1,395. **Required Forms and Deadlines:** FAFSA. Financial aid filing deadline 11/1. Priority financial aid filing date 4/1. **Notification of Awards:** Applicants will be notified of awards on a rolling basis beginning 2/1. **Types of Aid:** *Need-based scholarships/grants:* Federal Pell, SEOG, state scholarships/grants, private scholarships, the school's own gift aid. *Loans:* FFEL Subsidized Stafford, FFEL Unsubsidized Stafford, FFEL PLUS, state loans, college/university loans from institutional funds. *Student Employment:* **Financial Aid Statistics:** 37% freshmen, 46% undergrads receive need-based scholarship or grant aid. 26% freshmen, 20% undergrads receive non-need-based scholarship or grant aid. 42% freshmen, 49% undergrads receive need-based self-help aid. 5% freshmen, 4% undergrads receive athletic scholarships. 57% freshmen, 37% undergrads receive any aid. 55% undergrads borrow to pay for school. Average cumulative indebtedness $16,645. **Criteria for awarding institutional aid:** *Non-need-based:* Academics, alumni affiliation, art, athletics, leadership, music/drama.

TAYLOR UNIVERSITY

236 West Reade Avenue, Upland, IN 46989-1001
Phone: 765-998-5134 **Financial Aid Phone:** 765-998-5358
E-mail: admissions@tayloru.edu **CEEB Code:** 1802
Fax: 765-998-4925 **Website:** www.taylor.edu **ACT Code:** 1248

This private school was founded in 1846. It has a 952-acre campus.

RATINGS
Admissions Selectivity Rating: 87   **Fire Safety Rating:** 89   **Green Rating:** 72

STUDENTS AND FACULTY
Enrollment: 1,938. **Student Body:** 55% female, 45% male, 66% out-of-state, 3% international (29 countries represented). Asian 3%, African American 2%, Caucasian 90%, Hispanic 2%.
Retention and Graduation: 85% freshmen return for sophomore year. 71% freshmen graduate within 4 years. 19% grads go on to further study within 1 year. **Faculty:** Student/faculty ratio 12.7:1. 129 full-time faculty, 80% hold PhDs, 6% are are members of minority groups, 26% are women.

ACADEMICS
Degrees: Associate, bachelor's, certificate, diploma, master's. **Classes:** Most classes have 10–19 students. Most lab/discussion sessions have 10–19 students. **Majors with Highest Enrollment:** Biology/biological sciences; elementary

education and teaching; psychology. **Special Study Options:** Cooperative education program, distance learning, double major, dual enrollment, exchange student program (domestic), honors program, independent study, internships, student-designed major, study abroad, teacher certification program **Honors programs:** Honors Program emphasizes to a greater extent than the general curriculum, integration of faith and learning, ideas and values in content and discussion and student initiative in format. Also offer Freshmen Irish Studies Program in Ireland. **Combined degree programs:** BA/MA, BA and MA in environmental science. Special programs offered to physically disabled students include note-taking services, reader services, tape recorders, tutors. **Career services:** Alumni network, alumni services, career assessment, internships, regional alumni.

FACILITIES

Housing: Men's dorms, women's dorms, apartments for married students, apartments for single students, some off-campus apartments available to upperclassmen with special permission. 85% of campus accessible to physically disabled. **Special Academic Facilities/Equipment:** Compton Art Gallery, Edwin W. Brown Collection/CS Lewis and Friends. **Computers:** 100% of classrooms, 100% of dorms, 100% of libraries, 100% of dining areas, 100% of student union, 50% of common outdoor areas have wireless network access. Students can register for classes online. Administrative functions (other than registration) can be performed online.

CAMPUS LIFE

Environment: Rural. **Activities:** Choral groups, concert band, drama/theater, jazz band, literary magazine, music ensembles, musical theater, opera, pep band, radio station, student government, student newspaper, student-run film society, symphony orchestra, television station, yearbook, campus ministries, international student organization, Model UN. **Organizations:** 87 registered organizations, 7 honor societies, 23 religious organizations. **Athletics (Intercollegiate):** *Men:* Baseball, basketball, cross-country, football, golf, soccer, tennis, track/field (outdoor), track/field (indoor). *Women:* Basketball, cross-country, soccer, softball, tennis, track/field (outdoor), track/field (indoor), volleyball. **On-Campus Highlights:** The Jumping Bean (Student coffee shop), Kesler Student Activities Center, Modelle Metcalf Visual Arts Center, Rediger Chapel and Auditorium, Mitchell Theater. **Environmental Initiatives:** New science facility plan is LEED-certified. Active committee on sustainability. Working on carbon footprint.

ADMISSIONS

Freshman Academic Profile: Average high school GPA 3.61. 41% in top 10% of high school class, 66% in top 25% of high school class, 90% in top 50% of high school class. SAT Math middle 50% range 510–640. SAT Critical Reading middle 50% range 500–650. SAT Writing middle 50% range 490–620. ACT middle 50% range 24–31. Minimum paper TOEFL 550. Minimum computer TOEFL 213. **Basis for Candidate Selection:** *Very important factors considered include:* Application essay, academic GPA, recommendation(s), rigor of secondary school record, standardized test scores, character/personal qualities, religious affiliation/commitment. *Important factors considered include:* Class rank, extracurricular activities, interview, volunteer work. *Other factors considered include:* Alumni/ae relation, first generation, geographical residence, racial/ethnic status, state residency, talent/ability, work experience. **Freshman Admission Requirements:** High school diploma is required and GED is accepted. *Academic units required:* 4 English, 3 mathematics, 3 science, (3 science labs), 2 social studies, 3 academic electives. *Academic units recommended:* 4 mathematics, 4 science, (4 science labs), 2 foreign language, 3 social studies, 1 visual/performing arts, 1 computer science. **Freshman Admission Statistics:** 1,975 applied, 83% admitted, 30% enrolled. **Transfer Admission Requirements:** High school transcript, college transcript(s), essay or personal statement, standardized test scores, statement of good standing from prior institution(s). Minimum college GPA of 2.5 required. Lowest grade transferable C+. **General Admission Information:** Application fee $25. Regular application deadline 8/1. Notification on a rolling basis, beginning on or about 10/1. Nonfall registration accepted. Admission may be deferred for a maximum of 2 years. Credit and/or placement offered for CEEB Advanced Placement tests.

COSTS AND FINANCIAL AID

Average book expense $1,100. **Required Forms and Deadlines:** FAFSA. Financial aid filing deadline 3/10. **Notification of Awards:** Applicants will be notified of awards on a rolling basis beginning 3/1. **Types of Aid:** *Need-based scholarships/grants:* Federal Pell, SEOG, state scholarships/grants, private scholarships, the school's own gift aid. *Loans:* Direct Subsidized Stafford, Direct Unsubsidized Stafford, Direct PLUS, Federal Perkins, college/university loans from institutional funds. *Student Employment:* Federal Work-Study Program available. Institutional employment available. Highest amount earned per year from on-campus jobs $3,500. Off-campus job opportunities are poor. **Financial Aid Statistics:** 63% freshmen, 59% undergrads receive need-based scholarship or grant aid. 8% freshmen, 7% undergrads receive non-need-based scholarship or grant aid. 56% freshmen, 54% undergrads receive need-based self-help aid. 5% freshmen, 4% undergrads receive athletic scholarships. 96% freshmen, 91%

undergrads receive any aid. 53% undergrads borrow to pay for school. Average cumulative indebtedness $22,971. **Criteria for awarding institutional aid:** *Non-need-based:* Academics, alumni affiliation, art, athletics, leadership, minority status, music/drama, religious affiliation, state/district residency.

TAYLOR UNIVERSITY, FORT WAYNE CAMPUS

1025 West Rudisill Boulevard, Fort Wayne, IN 46807
Phone: 260-744-8689
E-mail: admissions_f@tayloru.edu **CEEB Code:** 1227
Fax: 260-744-8660 **Website:** www.tayloru.edu/fw **ACT Code:** 1192

This private school, affiliated with the Protestant Church, was founded in 1846. It has a 32-acre campus.

RATINGS

Admissions Selectivity Rating: 72   **Fire Safety Rating:** 60*   **Green Rating:** 60*

STUDENTS AND FACULTY

Enrollment: 521. **Student Body:** 60% female, 40% male, 25% out-of-state, 1% international (3 countries represented). Asian 1%, African American 6%, Caucasian 86%, Hispanic 2%.
Retention and Graduation: 71% freshmen return for sophomore year. 32% freshmen graduate within 4 years. **Faculty:** Student/faculty ratio 14:1. 26 full-time faculty, 62% hold PhDs, 42% are women.

ACADEMICS

Degrees: Associate, bachelor's, certificate, master's, terminal associate, transfer associate. **Classes:** Most classes have fewer than 10 students. Most lab/discussion sessions have 10–19 students. **Majors with Highest Enrollment:** Elementary education and teaching; nursing/registered nurse (RN, ASN, BSN, MSN); psychology. **Special Study Options:** Accelerated program, cooperative education program, distance learning, double major, exchange student program (domestic), independent study, internships, student-designed major, study abroad, teacher certification program, weekend college. Special programs offered to physically disabled students include reader services, tape recorders, tutors. **Career services:** Alumni services, career/job search classes, career assessment, internships.

FACILITIES

Housing: men's dorms, women's dorms, apartments for single students **Computers:** Students can register for classes online.

CAMPUS LIFE

Environment: City. **Activities:** Choral groups, drama/theater, jazz band, music ensembles, student government, student newspaper, yearbook. **Organizations:** 11 registered organizations, 1 religious organizations. **Athletics (Intercollegiate):** *Men:* Basketball, cheerleading, soccer. *Women:* Basketball, cheerleading, volleyball.

ADMISSIONS

Freshman Academic Profile: Average high school GPA 3.13. 12% in top 10% of high school class, 31% in top 25% of high school class, 65% in top 50% of high school class. 65% from public high schools. SAT Math middle 50% range 418–563. SAT Critical Reading middle 50% range 445–580. ACT middle 50% range 19–26. Minimum paper TOEFL 550. Minimum computer TOEFL 213. **Basis for Candidate Selection:** *Very important factors considered include:* Rigor of secondary school record, religious affiliation/commitment. *Important factors considered include:* Application essay, recommendation(s), standardized test scores, character/personal qualities, interview. *Other factors considered include:* Class rank, extracurricular activities, volunteer work, work experience. **Freshman Admission Requirements:** High school diploma is required and GED is accepted. *Academic units required:* 4 English, 3 mathematics, 3 science, (3 science labs), 2 social studies, 2 history. *Academic units recommended:* 2 foreign language. **Freshman Admission Statistics:** 313 applied, 83% admitted, 46% enrolled. **Transfer Admission Requirements:** High school transcript, college transcript(s), essay or personal statement, statement of good standing from prior institution(s). Minimum college GPA of 2.5 required. Lowest grade transferable C–. **General Admission Information:** Application fee $20. Regular application deadline 8/15. Notification on a rolling basis, beginning on or about 9/1. Nonfall registration accepted. Admission may be deferred for a maximum of 2 years. Neither credit nor placement offered for CEEB Advanced Placement tests.

COSTS AND FINANCIAL AID

Comprehensive fee $20,470. **Required Forms and Deadlines:** FAFSA, institution's own financial aid form. Priority financial aid filing date 3/1. **Notification of Awards:** Applicants will be notified of awards on a rolling basis beginning 3/1. **Types of Aid:** *Need-based scholarships/grants:* Federal Pell,

SEOG, state scholarships/grants, private scholarships, the school's own gift aid, endowed-donor scholarships. *Loans:* FFEL Subsidized Stafford, FFEL Unsubsidized Stafford, FFEL PLUS, Federal Perkins. *Student Employment:* Federal Work-Study Program available. Institutional employment available. Off-campus job opportunities are excellent. **Financial Aid Statistics:** 83% freshmen, 85% undergrads receive need-based scholarship or grant aid. 6% freshmen, 6% undergrads receive non-need-based scholarship or grant aid. 76% freshmen, 79% undergrads receive need-based self-help aid. 1% undergrads receive athletic scholarships. 82% undergrads borrow to pay for school. Average cumulative indebtedness $15,400. **Criteria for awarding institutional aid:** *Non-need-based:* Academics, alumni affiliation, leadership, state/district residency.

TEMPLE UNIVERSITY

1801 North Broad Street (041-09), Philadelphia, PA 19122-6096
Phone: 215-204-7200 **Financial Aid Phone:** 215-204-8760
E-mail: TUADM@TEMPLE.EDU **CEEB Code:** 2906
Fax: 215-204-5694 **Website:** www.temple.edu **ACT Code:** 3724

This public school was founded in 1888. It has a 330-acre campus.

RATINGS
Admissions Selectivity Rating: 84   **Fire Safety Rating:** 94   **Green Rating:** 88

STUDENTS AND FACULTY
Enrollment: 26,244. **Student Body:** 53% female, 47% male, 20% out-of-state, 3% international (117 countries represented). Asian 10%, African American 16%, Caucasian 58%, Hispanic 4%.
Retention and Graduation: 88% freshmen return for sophomore year. 40% freshmen graduate within 4 years. **Faculty:** Student/faculty ratio 16.7:1. 1384 full-time faculty, 76% hold PhDs, 16% are are members of minority groups, 37% are women.

ACADEMICS
Degrees: Associate, bachelor's, certificate, diploma, doctoral, master's, post-bachelor's certificate, post-master's certificate, terminal associate, transfer associate. **Classes:** Most classes have 20–29 students. Most lab/discussion sessions have 20–29 students. **Majors with Highest Enrollment:** Elementary education and teaching; marketing/marketing management; psychology. **Special Study Options:** Cooperative education program, cross-registration, distance learning, double major, dual enrollment, English as a Second Language (ESL), exchange student program (domestic), honors program, independent study, internships, liberal arts/career combination, study abroad, teacher certification program, Programs are offered in a number of foreign countries: Japan, Italy, Costa Rica, France, Germany, Ghana, India, Spain, Turkey, United Kingdom and Brazil. **Honors programs:** 1) Honors Certificate Program 2) Honors Scholars Program **Combined degree programs:** BA/MA, MBA/MA and MBA/MS and BFA with Teaching Certification. Special programs offered to physically disabled students include note-taking services, reader services, tape recorders, tutors. **Career services:** Alumni network, alumni services, career/job search classes, career assessment, internships, regional alumni.

FACILITIES
Housing: Coed dorms, special housing for disabled students, apartments for single students, Living/Learning Centers are available. 100% of campus accessible to physically disabled. **Special Academic Facilities/Equipment:** Blockson Collection, Urban Archieves, observatory **Computers:** 40% of classrooms, 30% of dorms, 80% of libraries, 90% of dining areas, 100% of student union, 40% of common outdoor areas have wireless network access. Students can register for classes online. Administrative functions (other than registration) can be performed online.

CAMPUS LIFE
Environment: Metropolis. **Activities:** Choral groups, concert band, dance, drama/theater, jazz band, literary magazine, marching band, music ensembles, musical theater, opera, pep band, radio station, student government, student newspaper, student-run film society, symphony orchestra, television station, yearbook, campus ministries, international student organization. **Organizations:** 232 registered organizations, 12 honor societies, 24 religious organizations. 11 fraternities, 9 sororities. **Athletics (Intercollegiate):** *Men:* Baseball, basketball, cheerleading, crew/rowing, cross-country, football, golf, gymnastics, soccer, table tennis, tennis, track/field (outdoor), track/field (indoor). *Women:*

Basketball, cheerleading, crew/rowing, cross-country, fencing, field hockey, gymnastics, lacrosse, soccer, softball, table tennis, tennis, track/field (outdoor), track/field (indoor), volleyball. **On-Campus Highlights:** The Tech Center, Howard Gittis Student Center, Liacouras Center (athletic/convocation center), The Shops at Liacouras Walk, Bell Tower, 6. Independence Blue Cross Student Recreation Center 7. Alumni Circle 8. Rock Hall 9. Student Pavilion 10. Campus mall. **Environmental Initiatives:** President Hart signed the American College and University Presidents Climate Commitment in April 2008 The Office of Sustainability was established July 2008. Energy Conservation Policy established December 2008.

ADMISSIONS
Freshman Academic Profile: Average high school GPA 3.41. 21% in top 10% of high school class, 57% in top 25% of high school class, 94% in top 50% of high school class. 71.7% from public high schools. SAT Math middle 50% range 510–610. SAT Critical Reading middle 50% range 490–600. SAT Writing middle 50% range 500–600. ACT middle 50% range 21–26. Minimum paper TOEFL 550. Minimum computer TOEFL 213. Minimum web-based TOEFL 79. **Basis for Candidate Selection:** *Very important factors considered include:* Academic GPA, rigor of secondary school record. *Important factors considered include:* Class rank, standardized test scores. *Other factors considered include:* Application essay, recommendation(s), alumni/ae relation, character/personal qualities, extracurricular activities, talent/ability, volunteer work, work experience. **Freshman Admission Requirements:** High school diploma is required and GED is accepted. *Academic units required:* 4 English, 3 mathematics, 2 science, (1 science labs), 2 foreign language, 2 social studies, 1 history, 1 academic electives. *Academic units recommended:* 4 English, 4 mathematics, 3 science, (2 science labs), 2 foreign language, 2 social studies, 2 history, 3 academic electives. **Freshman Admission Statistics:** 18,574 applied, 61% admitted, 37% enrolled. **Transfer Admission Requirements:** High school transcript, college transcript(s), essay or personal statement, minimum college GPA of 2.50 required. Lowest grade transferable C. **General Admission Information:** Application fee $50. Regular application deadline 3/1. Notification on a rolling basis, beginning on or about 10/15. Nonfall registration accepted. Admission may be deferred for a maximum of 1 year. Credit and/or placement offered for CEEB Advanced Placement tests.

COSTS AND FINANCIAL AID
Annual in-state tuition $11,174. Annual out-of-state tuition $20,454. Room and board $9,198. Required fees $590. Average book expense $1,000. **Required Forms and Deadlines:** FAFSA. Priority financial aid filing date 3/1. **Notification of Awards:** Applicants will be notified of awards on a rolling basis beginning 2/15. **Types of Aid:** *Need-based scholarships/grants:* Federal Pell, SEOG, state scholarships/grants, private scholarships, the school's own gift aid, Federal Nursing Scholarships. *Loans:* FFEL Subsidized Stafford, FFEL Unsubsidized Stafford, FFEL PLUS, Federal Perkins, Federal Nursing, state loans, college/university loans from institutional funds. *Student Employment:* Federal Work-Study Program available. Institutional employment available. Off-campus job opportunities are excellent. **Financial Aid Statistics:** 65% freshmen, 64% undergrads receive need-based scholarship or grant aid. 38% freshmen, 31% undergrads receive non-need-based scholarship or grant aid. 55% freshmen, 56% undergrads receive need-based self-help aid. 1% freshmen, 1% undergrads receive athletic scholarships. 72% freshmen, 63% undergrads receive any aid. 75% undergrads borrow to pay for school. Average cumulative indebtedness $29,886. **Criteria for awarding institutional aid:** *Non-need-based:* Academics, art, athletics, music/drama.

See page 1254.

TENNESSEE STATE UNIVERSITY

3500 John Merritt Boulevard, Nashville, TN, 37209-1561
Phone: 615-963-3101
E-mail: jcade@tnstate.edu
Fax: 615-963-5108 **Website:** www.tnstate.edu

This is a public school.

RATINGS
Admissions Selectivity Rating: 81   **Fire Safety Rating:** 60*   **Green Rating:** 60*

STUDENTS AND FACULTY
Enrollment: 7,000. **Student Body:** 63% female, 37% male, 49% out-of-state, 1% international. Asian 1%, African American 83%, Caucasian 15%, Hispanic 1%.
Retention and Graduation: 77% freshmen return for sophomore year. **Faculty:** Student/faculty ratio 22:1. 383 full-time faculty, 74% hold PhDs, 37% are are members of minority groups, 42% are women.

ACADEMICS

Degrees: Associate, bachelor's, master's. **Classes:** Most classes have fewer than 10 students. Most lab/discussion sessions have 10–19 students. **Special Study Options:** Cooperative education program, cross-registration, double major, exchange student program (domestic), honors program, independent study, internships, liberal arts/career combination, teacher certification program, On-line Degree (courses offered via computer approved by Tennessee Board of Regents).

FACILITIES

Housing: Coed dorms, men's dorms, women's dorms, apartments for single students.

CAMPUS LIFE

Activities: Choral groups, drama/theater, jazz band, marching band, music ensembles, radio station, student government, student newspaper, yearbook.

ADMISSIONS

Freshman Academic Profile: Average high school GPA 2.99. 90% from public high schools. SAT Math middle 50% range 430–510. SAT Critical Reading middle 50% range 430–510. ACT middle 50% range 18–21. Minimum paper TOEFL 500. Minimum computer TOEFL 250. **Basis for Candidate Selection:** *Very important factors considered include:* standardized test scores, state residency. *Important factors considered include:* Class rank, recommendation(s), rigor of secondary school record, geographical residence. *Other factors considered include:* Alumni/ae relation, character/personal qualities, extracurricular activities, talent/ability. **Freshman Admission Requirements:** High school diploma is required and GED is accepted. *Academic units required:* 4 English, 3 mathematics, 2 science, (1 science labs), 2 foreign language, 1 social studies, 1 history, 1 academic electives. **Freshman Admission Statistics:** 6,344 applied, 35% admitted, 59% enrolled. **Transfer Admission Requirements:** College transcript(s), minimum college GPA of 2.9 required. Lowest grade transferable C. **General Admission Information:** Application fee $15. Regular application deadline 8/1. Credit and/or placement offered for CEEB Advanced Placement tests.

COSTS AND FINANCIAL AID

Annual in-state tuition $3,272. Annual out-of-state tuition $10,230. Room and board $3,060. Required fees $150. Average book expense $850. **Required Forms and Deadlines:** FAFSA, CSS/Financial Aid PROFILE, noncustodial PROFILE. **Types of Aid:** *Need-based scholarships/grants:* Federal Pell, SEOG *Loans:* Direct Subsidized Stafford, Direct Unsubsidized Stafford, Direct PLUS, FFEL Subsidized Stafford, FFEL Unsubsidized Stafford, FFEL PLUS, Federal Perkins. *Student Employment:* **Financial Aid Statistics:** 29% freshmen, 11% freshmen, 33% freshmen, 1% freshmen.

TENNESSEE TECHNOLOGICAL UNIVERSITY

PO Box 5006, Cookeville, TN 38505
Phone: 931-372-3888 **Financial Aid Phone:** 931-372-3073
E-mail: admissions@tntech.edu **CEEB Code:** 1804
Fax: 931-372-6250 **Website:** www.tntech.edu **ACT Code:** 4012

This public school was founded in 1915. It has a 235-acre campus.

RATINGS

Admissions Selectivity Rating: 75   **Fire Safety Rating:** 66   **Green Rating:** 60*

STUDENTS AND FACULTY

Enrollment: 8,102. **Student Body:** 47% female, 53% male, 4% out-of-state, 2% international. Asian 1%, African American 3%, Caucasian 82%, Hispanic 1%.
Retention and Graduation: 73% freshmen return for sophomore year. **Faculty:** Student/faculty ratio 19:1. 386 full-time faculty, 72% hold PhDs, 14% are are members of minority groups, 38% are women. 1% of classes are taught by teaching assistants.

ACADEMICS

Degrees: Bachelor's, master's, post-master's certificate. **Classes:** Most classes have 20–29 students. Most lab/discussion sessions have 20–29 students. **Majors with Highest Enrollment:** Business/commerce; elementary education and teaching; mechanical engineering. **Special Study Options:** Cooperative education program, distance learning, double major, dual enrollment, honors program, internships, study abroad, teacher certification program Special programs offered to physically disabled students include note-taking services, reader services, tape recorders, tutors. **Career services:** Alumni network, alumni services, career/job search classes, internships, regional alumni.

FACILITIES

Housing: Coed dorms, special housing for disabled students, men's dorms, special housing for international students, women's dorms, apartments for married students, apartments for single students. 99% of campus accessible to physically disabled. **Special Academic Facilities/Equipment:** 300–acre farm lab, electric power center, water resources center, manufacturing center. **Computers:** Students can register for classes online. Administrative functions (other than registration) can be performed online.

CAMPUS LIFE

Environment: Rural. **Activities:** Choral groups, concert band, dance, drama/theater, jazz band, literary magazine, marching band, music ensembles, musical theater, opera, pep band, radio station, student government, student newspaper, symphony orchestra, television station, yearbook. **Organizations:** 182 registered organizations, 26 honor societies, 16 religious organizations. 12 fraternities, 8 sororities. **Athletics (Intercollegiate):** *Men:* Baseball, basketball, cheerleading, cross-country, football, golf, riflery, tennis. *Women:* Basketball, cheerleading, cross-country, golf, riflery, soccer, softball, tennis, track/field (outdoor), track/field (indoor), volleyball. **On-Campus Highlights:** Recreation/Fitness Center, Barnes and Noble Bookstore, Joan Derryberry Art Gallery, New Residence Halls, Bryan Fine Arts Music Auditorium.

ADMISSIONS

Freshman Academic Profile: Average high school GPA 3.32. 24% in top 10% of high school class, 54% in top 25% of high school class, 84% in top 50% of high school class. 80% from public high schools. SAT Math middle 50% range 510–650. SAT Critical Reading middle 50% range 470–620. ACT middle 50% range 20–26. Minimum paper TOEFL 500. Minimum computer TOEFL 173. **Basis for Candidate Selection:** *Very important factors considered include:* Academic GPA, rigor of secondary school record, standardized test scores. *Other factors considered include:* Application essay, recommendation(s), alumni/ae relation, character/personal qualities, extracurricular activities, interview. **Freshman Admission Requirements:** High school diploma is required and GED is accepted. *Academic units required:* 4 English, 3 mathematics, 2 science, (1 science labs), 2 foreign language, 1 social studies, 1 history, 1 visual/performing art **Freshman Admission Statistics:** 3,499 applied, 91% admitted, 53% enrolled. **Transfer Admission Requirements:** College transcript(s), minimum college GPA of 2.0 required. Lowest grade transferable D. **General Admission Information:** Application fee $15. Regular application deadline 8/1. Nonfall registration accepted. Admission may be deferred for a maximum of 1 semester. Credit and/or placement offered for CEEB Advanced Placement tests.

COSTS AND FINANCIAL AID

Annual in-state tuition $4,582. Annual out-of-state tuition $15,518. Room and board $6,908. Required fees $942. Average book expense $1,200. **Required Forms and Deadlines:** FAFSA. Priority financial aid filing date 3/15. **Notification of Awards:** Applicants will be notified of awards on a rolling basis beginning 3/15. **Types of Aid:** *Need-based scholarships/grants:* Federal Pell, SEOG, state scholarships/grants, private scholarships, the school's own gift aid, United Negro College Fund *Loans:* Direct Subsidized Stafford, Direct Unsubsidized Stafford, FFEL PLUS, Federal Perkins, state loans, college/university loans from institutional funds. *Student Employment:* **Financial Aid Statistics:** 14% freshmen, 26% undergrads receive need-based scholarship or grant aid. 21% freshmen, 21% undergrads receive non-need-based scholarship or grant aid. 13% freshmen, 23% undergrads receive need-based self-help aid. 2% freshmen, 3% undergrads receive athletic scholarships. 91% freshmen, 89% undergrads receive any aid. 40% undergrads borrow to pay for school. Average cumulative indebtedness $13,314. **Criteria for awarding institutional aid:** *Non-need-based:* Academics, alumni affiliation, art, athletics, leadership, minority status, music/drama.

TENNESSEE WESLEYAN COLLEGE

P.O. Box 40, Athens, TN 37371-0040
Phone: 423-745-7504 **Financial Aid Phone:** 423-746-5209
E-mail: twilliams@twcnet.edu
Fax: 423-745-9335 **Website:** www.twcnet.edu **ACT Code:** 4014

This private school was founded in 1857. It has a 40-acre campus.

RATINGS

Admissions Selectivity Rating: 72   **Fire Safety Rating:** 71   **Green Rating:** 60*

STUDENTS AND FACULTY

Enrollment: 847. **Student Body:** 68% female, 32% male, 6% out-of-state, 3% international (13 countries represented). Asian 1%, African American 3%,

Caucasian 75%, Hispanic 2%.
Retention and Graduation: 65% freshmen return for sophomore year. 16% freshmen graduate within 4 years. **Faculty:** Student/faculty ratio 13:1. 46 full-time faculty, 59% hold PhDs, 2% are are members of minority groups, 50% are women.

ACADEMICS

Degrees: Bachelor's. **Classes:** Most classes have 10–19 students. Most lab/discussion sessions have 10–19 students. **Majors with Highest Enrollment:** Business/commerce; education; nursing/registered nurse (RN, ASN, BSN, MSN). **Special Study Options:** Accelerated program, double major, honors program, independent study, internships, student-designed major, study abroad, teacher certification program Special programs offered to physically disabled students include note-taking services, tape recorders, tutors. **Career services:** Alumni services, internships **Career services highlights include:** Cyber and Sounds Cafe.

FACILITIES

Housing: Men's dorms, women's dorms, apartments for single students. Residency Exemption Policy: All students are required to live on campus unless they: Are married; have custody of a child; is a military veteran eligible for benefits under Public Law 358, GI Bill effective 6/66; is a resident in the home of parents or legal guardian who live within the commuting area; is an independent student as defined by financial aid criteria; established residency in the commuting area for 6 months immediately prior to making application to Tennessee Wesleyan College; or enrolled as a senior. 56% of campus accessible to physically disabled. **Special Academic Facilities/Equipment:** Old College—building is on historical register. **Computers:**

CAMPUS LIFE

Environment: Town. **Activities:** Choral groups, drama/theater, literary magazine, musical theater, student government, student newspaper, yearbook. **Organizations:** 19 registered organizations, 5 honor societies, 3 religious organizations. 2 sororities. **Athletics (Intercollegiate):** *Men:* Baseball, basketball, cheerleading, cross-country, golf, soccer, tennis. *Women:* Basketball, cheerleading, cross-country, golf, soccer, softball, tennis, volleyball. **On-Campus Highlights:** Student Activity Center, Student Theatre, Athletic Events (intramural sports), J. Wesley Grill and Starbucks Coffee House, Merner-Pfeiffer Library (book signings, special events, College Quad.

ADMISSIONS

Freshman Academic Profile: Average high school GPA 3.21. 96% from public high schools. ACT middle 50% range 18–24. Minimum paper TOEFL 500. Minimum computer TOEFL 173. **Basis for Candidate Selection:** *Very important factors considered include:* Academic GPA, rigor of secondary school record, standardized test scores. *Important factors considered include:* Application essay, recommendation(s), level of applicant's interest. *Other factors considered include:* Class rank, alumni/ae relation, extracurricular activities, first generation, interview. **Freshman Admission Requirements:** High school diploma is required and GED is accepted. *Academic units recommended:* 4 English, 2 mathematics, 2 science, 1 social studies, 1 history. **Freshman Admission Statistics:** 515 applied, 77% admitted, 42% enrolled. **Transfer Admission Requirements:** College transcript(s), minimum college GPA of 2.0 required. Lowest grade transferable D. **General Admission Information:** Application fee $25. Regular application deadline 8/20. Nonfall registration accepted. Admission may be deferred for a maximum of 1 semester. Credit and/or placement offered for CEEB Advanced Placement tests.

COSTS AND FINANCIAL AID

Annual tuition $14,000. Room and board $5,500. Required fees $550. Average book expense $1,000. **Required Forms and Deadlines:** FAFSA, institution's own financial aid form **Notification of Awards:** Applicants will be notified of awards on a rolling basis beginning 2/1. **Types of Aid:** *Need-based scholarships/grants:* Federal Pell, SEOG, state scholarships/grants, private scholarships, the school's own gift aid. *Loans:* FFEL Subsidized Stafford, FFEL Unsubsidized Stafford, FFEL PLUS, Federal Perkins, United Methodist. *Student Employment:* Highest amount earned per year from on-campus jobs $2,800. **Financial Aid Statistics:** 83% freshmen, 80% undergrads receive need-based scholarship or grant aid. 14% freshmen, 10% undergrads receive non-need-based scholarship or grant aid. 55% freshmen, 61% undergrads receive need-based self-help aid. 20% freshmen, 13% undergrads receive athletic scholarships. 99% freshmen, 99% undergrads receive any aid. 80.9% undergrads borrow to pay for school. Average cumulative indebtedness $15,042. **Criteria for awarding institutional aid:** *Non-need-based:* Academics, alumni affiliation, art, athletics, job skills, leadership, minority status, music/drama, religious affiliation, state/district residency.

TEXAS A&M UNIVERSITY—COLLEGE STATION

P.O. Box 30014, College Station, TX 77843-3014
Phone: 979-845-3741 **Financial Aid Phone:** 979-845-3236
E-mail: admissions@tamu.edu **CEEB Code:** 6003
Fax: 979-847-8737 **Website:** www.tamu.edu **ACT Code:** 4198

This public school was founded in 1876. It has a 5200-acre campus.

RATINGS
Admissions Selectivity Rating: 87   **Fire Safety Rating:** 60*   **Green Rating:** 80

STUDENTS AND FACULTY
Enrollment: 38,729. **Student Body:** 48% female, 52% male, 2% out-of-state, 1% international (125 countries represented). Asian 5%, African American 3%, Caucasian 75%, Hispanic 14%, Native American 1%.
Retention and Graduation: 92% freshmen return for sophomore year. 45% freshmen graduate within 4 years. **Faculty:** Student/faculty ratio 19:1. 2317 full-time faculty, 93% hold PhDs, 23% are are members of minority groups, 30% are women. 25% of classes are taught by teaching assistants.

ACADEMICS
Degrees: Bachelor's, master's, post-bachelor's certificate. **Classes:** Most classes have 20–29 students. Most lab/discussion sessions have 20–29 students. **Majors with Highest Enrollment:** Biological and physical sciences; multi-/interdisciplinary studies, other; operations management and supervision. **Special Study Options:** Accelerated program, cooperative education program, cross-registration, distance learning, double major, dual enrollment, English as a Second Language (ESL), exchange student program (domestic), honors program, independent study, internships, study abroad, teacher certification program Special programs offered to physically disabled students include note-taking services, reader services, tape recorders, tutors. **Career services:** Alumni network, alumni services, career/job search classes, internships.

FACILITIES
Housing: Coed dorms, special housing for disabled students, men's dorms, women's dorms, fraternity/sorority housing, apartments for married students, cooperative housing, apartments for single students, theme housing, Honors Dorm. 65% of campus accessible to physically disabled. **Special Academic Facilities/Equipment:** Bush Library/Museum; Jordan International Collection; Corps of Cadets Center/Museum; Forsyth Center Gallary; MSC Visual Arts Gallary; J.Wayne Stark University Center Gallaries Oran W. Nicks Low Speed Wind Tunnel Astronomical Observatory Ocean Drilling Program Building. **Computers:** 100% of classrooms, 10% of dorms, 100% of libraries, 100% of dining areas, 100% of student union, have wireless network access. Students can register for classes online. Administrative functions (other than registration) can be performed online.

CAMPUS LIFE
Environment: City. **Activities:** Choral groups, concert band, dance, drama/theater, jazz band, literary magazine, marching band, music ensembles, musical theater, radio station, student government, student newspaper, student-run film society, symphony orchestra, television station, yearbook, campus ministries, international student organization. **Organizations:** 725 registered organizations, 34 honor societies, 77 religious organizations. 33 fraternities, 23 sororities. **Athletics (Intercollegiate):** *Men:* Baseball, basketball, cross-country, diving, football, golf, riflery, swimming, tennis, track/field (outdoor), track/field (indoor). *Women:* Basketball, cross-country, diving, equestrian sports, golf, riflery, soccer, softball, swimming, tennis, track/field (outdoor), track/field (indoor), volleyball. **On-Campus Highlights:** Student Recreation Center, Kyle Field, Corps of Cadets, George Bush Presidential Library/Museum, Research Park. **Environmental Initiatives:** LEED Paper Recycling Transportation Fuel

ADMISSIONS
Freshman Academic Profile: 50% in top 10% of high school class, 89% in top 25% of high school class, 99% in top 50% of high school class. SAT Math middle 50% range 570–670. SAT Critical Reading middle 50% range 530–640. SAT Writing middle 50% range 500–620. ACT middle 50% range 24–30. Minimum paper TOEFL 550. **Basis for Candidate Selection:** *Very important factors considered include:* Class rank, academic GPA, rigor of secondary school record, standardized test scores, extracurricular activities, talent/ability. *Important factors considered include:* Application essay, first generation, geographical residence, state residency, volunteer work, work experience. *Other factors considered include:* Recommendation(s), character/personal qualities. **Fresh-**

man Admission Requirements: High school diploma is required and GED is accepted. *Academic units required:* 4 English, 3 mathematics, 3 science, (2 science labs), 2 foreign language, 2 social studies, 1 history. *Academic units recommended:* 4 English, 3 mathematics, 3 science, (2 science labs), 2 foreign language, 2 social studies, 1 history, 1 computer science. **Freshman Admission Statistics:** 22,757 applied, 67% admitted, 53% enrolled. **Transfer Admission Requirements:** High school transcript, college transcript(s), minimum college GPA of 2.5 required. Lowest grade transferable D. **General Admission Information:** Application fee $60. Regular application deadline 1/15. Notification on a rolling basis, beginning on or about 4/1. Nonfall registration accepted. Credit offered for CEEB Advanced Placement tests.

COSTS AND FINANCIAL AID
Annual in-state tuition $5,152. Annual out-of-state tuition $19,585. Room and board $8,039. Required fees $3,024. Average book expense $1,278. **Required Forms and Deadlines:** FAFSA, institution's own financial aid form. Financial Aid Transcripts (for transfer students). Priority financial aid filing date 3/31. **Notification of Awards:** Applicants will be notified of awards on a rolling basis beginning 4/1. **Types of Aid:** *Need-based scholarships/grants:* Federal Pell, SEOG, state scholarships/grants, private scholarships, the school's own gift aid. *Loans:* FFEL Subsidized Stafford, FFEL Unsubsidized Stafford, FFEL PLUS, Federal Perkins, state loans, college/university loans from institutional funds. *Student Employment:* Federal Work-Study Program available. Institutional employment available. Highest amount earned per year from on-campus jobs $2,639. Off-campus job opportunities are excellent. **Financial Aid Statistics:** 37% freshmen, 30% undergrads receive need-based scholarship or grant aid. 7% freshmen, 3% undergrads receive non-need-based scholarship or grant aid. 21% freshmen, 25% undergrads receive need-based self-help aid. 1% freshmen, 1% undergrads receive athletic scholarships. 60.4% freshmen, 50.6% undergrads receive any aid. 51% undergrads borrow to pay for school. Average cumulative indebtedness $21,182. **Criteria for awarding institutional aid:** *Non-need-based:* Academics, alumni affiliation, art, athletics, job skills, leadership, music/drama, state/district residency.

TEXAS A&M UNIVERSITY—COMMERCE

P.O. Box 3011, Commerce, TX 75429
Phone: 903-886-5106
E-mail: admissions@tamu-commerce.edu
Fax: 903-886-5888 **Website: ACT Code:** 6188

This public school was founded in 1889. It has a 140-acre campus.

RATINGS
Admissions Selectivity Rating: 77   **Fire Safety Rating:** 60*   **Green Rating:** 60*

STUDENTS AND FACULTY
Student Body: 4% out-of-state.
Retention and Graduation: Faculty: Student/faculty ratio 16:1. 294 full-time faculty, 64% hold PhDs, 14% are are members of minority groups, 37% are women. 10% of classes are taught by teaching assistants.

ACADEMICS
Degrees: Bachelor's, master's. **Classes:** Most classes have 10–19 students.
Majors with Highest Enrollment: Business/commerce; computer and information science; criminal justice/safety studies. **Special Study Options:** Cooperative education program, distance learning, double major, dual enrollment, honors program, independent study, internships, study abroad, teacher certification program, weekend college, week-end classes for graduate students only. Selected courses available online. **Combined degree programs:** BA/MD Special programs offered to physically disabled students include reader services, tape recorders, tutors. **Career services:** Career/job search classes, internships

FACILITIES
Housing: Coed dorms, special housing for disabled students, men's dorms, special housing for international students, women's dorms, fraternity/sorority housing, apartments for married students, apartments for single students. 35% of campus accessible to physically disabled. **Computers:** Students can register for classes online. Administrative functions (other than registration) can be performed online.

CAMPUS LIFE
Environment: Rural. **Activities:** Choral groups, concert band, dance, drama/theater, jazz band, literary magazine, marching band, music ensembles, musical theater, pep band, radio station, student government, student newspaper, student-run film society, television station, yearbook. **Organizations:** 110 registered organizations, 12 honor societies, 10 religious organizations. 9 fraternities, 9 sororities. **Athletics (Intercollegiate):** *Men:* Basketball, cheerleading, cross-

country, football, golf, track/field (outdoor). *Women:* Basketball, cheerleading, cross-country, golf, soccer, track/field (outdoor), volleyball.

ADMISSIONS
Freshman Academic Profile: Average high school GPA 3.35. 13% in top 10% of high school class, 26% in top 25% of high school class, 33% in top 50% of high school class. 98% from public high schools. SAT Math middle 50% range 460–560. SAT Critical Reading middle 50% range 440–540. ACT middle 50% range 17–23. Minimum paper TOEFL 500. **Basis for Candidate Selection:** *Very important factors considered include:* Class rank, rigor of secondary school record, standardized test scores. *Other factors considered include:* work experience. **Freshman Admission Requirements:** High school diploma is required and GED is accepted. *Academic units required:* 4 English, 3 mathematics, 2 science, 2 History and Social Studies *Academic units recommended:* 2 foreign language. **Freshman Admission Statistics:** 1,899 applied, 51% admitted, 58% enrolled. **Transfer Admission Requirements:** College transcript(s), standardized test scores, statement of good standing from prior institution(s). Minimum college GPA of 2.0 required. Lowest grade transferable D. **General Admission Information:** Application fee $25. Regular application deadline 8/1. Notification on a rolling basis, beginning on or about 10/1. Nonfall registration accepted. Admission may be deferred for a maximum of 1 year. Credit and/or placement offered for CEEB Advanced Placement tests.

COSTS AND FINANCIAL AID
Annual in-state tuition $9,232. Annual out-of-state tuition $25,732. Room and board $6,220. Required fees $1,106. Average book expense $1,010. **Required Forms and Deadlines:** FAFSA. Priority financial aid filing date 5/1. **Notification of Awards:** Applicants will be notified of awards on a rolling basis beginning 6/1. **Types of Aid:** *Need-based scholarships/grants:* Federal Pell, SEOG, state scholarships/grants, private scholarships, the school's own gift aid. *Loans:* Direct Subsidized Stafford, Direct Unsubsidized Stafford, FFEL Subsidized Stafford, FFEL Unsubsidized Stafford, FFEL PLUS, Federal Perkins. *Student Employment:* Federal Work-Study Program available. Institutional employment available. Highest amount earned per year from on-campus jobs $2,500. Off-campus job opportunities are good. **Financial Aid Statistics:** 60% freshmen, 60% undergrads receive need-based scholarship or grant aid. 47% freshmen, 53% undergrads receive need-based self-help aid. 3% freshmen, 2% undergrads receive athletic scholarships. 63% undergrads borrow to pay for school. Average cumulative indebtedness $20,688. **Criteria for awarding institutional aid:** *Non-need-based:* Academics, art, athletics, minority status.

TEXAS A&M UNIVERSITY AT GALVESTON

Admissions Office, PO Box 1675, Galveston, TX 77553
Phone: 409-740-4414 **Financial Aid Phone:** 409-740-4500
E-mail: seaaggie@tamug.edu **CEEB Code:** 6835
Fax: 409-740-4731 **Website:** www.tamug.edu **ACT Code:** 6592

This public school was founded in 1963. It has a 150-acre campus.

RATINGS
Admissions Selectivity Rating: 69   **Fire Safety Rating:** 77   **Green Rating:** 60*

STUDENTS AND FACULTY
Enrollment: 1,566. **Student Body:** 40% female, 60% male, 20% out-of-state, international (13 countries represented). Asian 1%, African American 2%, Caucasian 55%, Hispanic 7%, Native American 1%.
Retention and Graduation: 66% freshmen return for sophomore year. 16% freshmen graduate within 4 years. 60% grads go on to further study within 1 year. 35% grads pursue arts and sciences degrees. 3% grads pursue law degrees. 5% grads pursue business degrees. 2% grads pursue medical degrees. **Faculty:** Student/faculty ratio 14:1. 92 full-time faculty, 65% hold PhDs, 13% are are members of minority groups, 20% are women. 1% of classes are taught by teaching assistants.

ACADEMICS
Degrees: Bachelor's, master's. **Classes:** Most classes have 10–19 students.
Majors with Highest Enrollment: Marine biology and biological oceanography; naval architecture and marine engineering. **Special Study Options:** Accelerated program, cooperative education program, double major, dual enrollment, independent study, internships, study abroad, teacher certification program, Merchant Marine Certification NROTC Naval Sciences. **Combined degree programs:** BS/License Option and BA/License Option. Special programs offered to physically disabled students include note-taking services, reader services, tutors. **Career services:** Alumni network, career assessment, internships, regional alumni. **Career services highlights include:** www.tamug.edu/career/.

FACILITIES

Housing: Coed dorms, special housing for disabled students, women's dorms, Privatized apartment housing available next to campus. 90% of campus accessible to physically disabled. **Special Academic Facilities/Equipment:** USTS Texas Clipper II, Radar School/Ship Bridge Simulator, Engineering Laboratory Building, Sea Camp, Center for Bioacoustics, Center for Marine Training and Safety/TEEX, Laboratory for Oceanographic and Environmental Research, Galveston Bay Information Center, Center for Ports and Waterways, Coastal Zone Laboratory, GulfCet, Marine Mammal Research Program, Naval Science, Texas State Maritime Academy, Texas Institute of Oceanography, Texas Marine Mammal Stranding Network, Sea Turtle/Fisheries Ecology Lab. **Computers:** Students can register for classes online. Administrative functions (other than registration) can be performed online.

CAMPUS LIFE

Environment: Town. **Activities:** Choral groups, dance, drama/theater, literary magazine, student government, student newspaper, television station, yearbook. **Organizations:** 45 registered organizations, 16 honor societies, 4 religious organizations. **Athletics (Intercollegiate):** *Men:* Crew/rowing, sailing. *Women:* Crew/rowing, sailing **On-Campus Highlights:** Mary Moody Northen Student Center, P.E. Facility, Small Boat Basin, Training Ship—Sirius, Jack K. Williams Library.

ADMISSIONS

Freshman Academic Profile: 11% in top 10% of high school class, 40% in top 25% of high school class, 73% in top 50% of high school class. 82% from public high schools. SAT Math middle 50% range 490–600. SAT Critical Reading middle 50% range 460–590. ACT middle 50% range 20–25. Minimum paper TOEFL 550. Minimum computer TOEFL 220. **Basis for Candidate Selection:** *Very important factors considered include:* Class rank, rigor of secondary school record, standardized test scores. *Important factors considered include:* Application essay, academic GPA, recommendation(s), character/personal qualities, extracurricular activities, talent/ability, volunteer work, work experience. *Other factors considered include:* Alumni/ae relation, first generation, interview, level of applicant's interest. **Freshman Admission Requirements:** High school diploma is required and GED is accepted. *Academic units required:* 4 English, 3 mathematics, 3 science, (2 science labs), 3 social studies, 1 computer *Academic units recommended:* 4 English, 4 mathematics, 4 science, 3 foreign language, 3 social studies, 1 computer **Freshman Admission Statistics:** 1,181 applied, 78% admitted, 50% enrolled. **Transfer Admission Requirements:** High school transcript, college transcript(s), essay or personal statement, minimum college GPA of 2.5 required. Lowest grade transferable C. **General Admission Information:** Application fee $45. Nonfall registration accepted. Admission may be deferred for a maximum of 1 Semester. Credit offered for CEEB Advanced Placement tests.

COSTS AND FINANCIAL AID

Annual in-state tuition $4,680. Annual out-of-state tuition $13,020. Room and board $5,203. Required fees $1,375. Average book expense $1,381. **Required Forms and Deadlines:** FAFSA **Notification of Awards:** Applicants will be notified of awards on or about 3/15. **Types of Aid:** *Need-based scholarships/grants:* Federal Pell, SEOG, state scholarships/grants, private scholarships, the school's own gift aid. *Loans:* Direct Subsidized Stafford, Direct Unsubsidized Stafford, Direct PLUS, FFEL Subsidized Stafford, FFEL Unsubsidized Stafford, FFEL PLUS, Federal Perkins, college/university loans from institutional funds. *Student Employment:* Federal Work-Study Program available. Institutional employment available. Highest amount earned per year from on-campus jobs $2,100. Off-campus job opportunities are good. **Financial Aid Statistics:** 25% freshmen, 29% undergrads receive need-based scholarship or grant aid. 2% freshmen, 4% undergrads receive non-need-based scholarship or grant aid. 1% undergrads receive need-based self-help aid. 46% freshmen, 48% undergrads receive any aid. 70% undergrads borrow to pay for school. Average cumulative indebtedness $16,000. **Criteria for awarding institutional aid:** *Non-need-based:* Academics, leadership, state/district residency.

TEXAS A&M UNIVERSITY—KINGSVILLE

MSC 105, Kingsville, TX 78363
Phone: 361-593-2315
E-mail: ksossrx@tamuk.edu
Fax: 361-593-2195 **Website:** www.tamuk.edu

This is a public school.

RATINGS
Admissions Selectivity Rating: 60*   **Fire Safety Rating:** 60*   **Green Rating:** 60*

STUDENTS AND FACULTY

Enrollment: 5,087. **Student Body:** 47% female, 53% male, 2% out-of-state, 1% international. Asian 1%, African American 4%, Caucasian 23%, Hispanic 57%.
Retention and Graduation: 59% freshmen return for sophomore year. **Faculty:** Student/faculty ratio 15:1. 276 full-time faculty, 70% hold PhDs, 24% are are members of minority groups, 35% are women.

ACADEMICS

Degrees: Bachelor's, master's, post-bachelor's certificate, post-master's certificate. **Classes:** Most classes have 10–19 students. Most lab/discussion sessions have 20–29 students. **Special Study Options:** Accelerated program, cooperative education program, distance learning, double major, English as a Second Language (ESL), honors program, internships, study abroad, teacher certification program

FACILITIES

Housing: Coed dorms, men's dorms, women's dorms, apartments for married students.

CAMPUS LIFE

Activities: Choral groups, concert band, dance, drama/theater, jazz band, marching band, music ensembles, musical theater, pep band, radio station, student government, student newspaper, television station.

ADMISSIONS

Freshman Academic Profile: Basis for Candidate Selection: *Important factors considered include:* Class rank, rigor of secondary school record, standardized test scores. **Freshman Admission Requirements:** *Academic units recommended:* 4 English, 3 mathematics, 3 science, 3 foreign language, 4 social studies, 3 history, 3 academic electives. **Freshman Admission Statistics:** 2,105 applied, 99% admitted, 43% enrolled. Minimum college GPA of 2.0 required. **General Admission Information:** Application fee $15. Nonfall registration not accepted. Admission may be deferred for a maximum of varies.

COSTS AND FINANCIAL AID

Annual in-state tuition $1,380. Annual out-of-state tuition $7,590. Room and board $3,966. Required fees $1,602. Average book expense $614. **Required Forms and Deadlines:** FAFSA. Priority financial aid filing date 4/15. **Financial Aid Statistics:** 59% freshmen, 92% undergrads receive need-based scholarship or grant aid. 20% freshmen, 66% undergrads receive non-need-based scholarship or grant aid. 56% freshmen, 76% undergrads receive need-based self-help aid. 46% undergrads borrow to pay for school. Average cumulative indebtedness $2,867.

TEXAS A&M UNIVERSITY—TEXARKANA

P.O. Box 5518, Texarkana, TX 75505
Phone: 903-223-3069
E-mail: admissions@tamut.edu
Fax: 903-223-3140 **Website:**

This public school was founded in 1971. It has a 1-acre campus.

RATINGS
Admissions Selectivity Rating: 60*   **Fire Safety Rating:** 60*   **Green Rating:** 60*

STUDENTS AND FACULTY

Enrollment: 1,030. **Student Body:** 71% female, 29% male, international. Asian 1%, African American 16%, Caucasian 78%, Hispanic 6%, Native American 1%.
Retention and Graduation: Faculty: Student/faculty ratio 13:1. 59 full-time faculty, 15% are are members of minority groups, 41% are women.

ACADEMICS

Degrees: Bachelor's, master's. **Majors with Highest Enrollment:** Accounting; general studies; multi-/interdisciplinary studies, other. **Special Study Options:** Cross-registration, distance learning, independent study, internships, liberal arts/career combination, study abroad, teacher certification program Special programs offered to physically disabled students include note-taking services, tape recorders **Career services:** Career/job search classes.

FACILITIES

Housing: 100% of campus accessible to physically disabled. **Computers:** Students can register for classes online. Administrative functions (other than registration) can be performed online.

CAMPUS LIFE

Environment: Village. **Activities:** Student government, student newspaper. **Organizations:** 20 registered organizations, 5 honor societies, 1 religious organizations.

The Princeton Review's Complete Book of Colleges

ADMISSIONS

Freshman Academic Profile: Minimum paper TOEFL 550. **Transfer Admission Requirements:** College transcript(s), minimum college GPA of 2.0 required. Lowest grade transferable D. **General Admission Information:** Nonfall registration not accepted. Credit offered for CEEB Advanced Placement tests.

COSTS AND FINANCIAL AID

Required Forms and Deadlines: FAFSA, institution's own financial aid form, other documents may be required upon review of student aid reports. **Notification of Awards:** Applicants will be notified of awards on or about 6/1. **Types of Aid:** *Need-based scholarships/grants:* Federal Pell, SEOG, state scholarships/grants, private scholarships, the school's own gift aid. *Loans:* FFEL Subsidized Stafford, FFEL Unsubsidized Stafford, FFEL PLUS, college/university loans from institutional funds. *Student Employment:* Federal Work-Study Program available. Off-campus job opportunities are good. **Financial Aid Statistics: Criteria for awarding institutional aid:** *Non-need-based:* Academics, alumni affiliation, leadership, state/district residency.

TEXAS CHRISTIAN UNIVERSITY

Office of Admissions, TCU Box 297013, Fort Worth, TX 76129
Phone: 817-257-7490 **Financial Aid Phone:** 817-257-7858
E-mail: frogmail@tcu.edu **CEEB Code:** 6820
Fax: 817-257-7268 **Website:** www.tcu.edu **ACT Code:** 4206

This private school, affiliated with the Disciples of Christ Church, was founded in 1873. It has a 300-acre campus.

RATINGS

Admissions Selectivity Rating: 86   **Fire Safety Rating:** 92   **Green Rating:** 83

STUDENTS AND FACULTY

Enrollment: 7,580. **Student Body:** 59% female, 41% male, 21% out-of-state, 5% international (83 countries represented). Asian 3%, African American 5%, Caucasian 73%, Hispanic 10%, Native American 1%.
Retention and Graduation: 85% freshmen return for sophomore year. 55% freshmen graduate within 4 years. 21% grads go on to further study within 1 year. **Faculty:** Student/faculty ratio 13:1. 523 full-time faculty, 84% hold PhDs, 12% are are members of minority groups, 43% are women. 1% of classes are taught by teaching assistants.

ACADEMICS

Degrees: Bachelor's, certificate, first professional, first professional certificate, master's, post-bachelor's certificate. **Classes:** Most classes have 10–19 students. Most lab/discussion sessions have 20–29 students. **Majors with Highest Enrollment:** Business administration and management; nursing/registered nurse (RN, ASN, BSN, MSN); public relations, advertising, and applied communication, other any instructional program in organizational communication, public relations, and advertising. **Special Study Options:** Accelerated program, cross-registration, distance learning, double major, dual enrollment, English as a Second Language (ESL), honors program, independent study, internships, liberal arts/career combination, study abroad, teacher certification program. **Honors programs:** John V. Roach Honors College The Honors College offers programs for students of all majors and complements all areas of study on campus. Entering freshmen who complete the Honors College requirements will graduate with a John V. Roach Honors College Diploma, as well as a specialized degree from the college of their chosen major(s). **Combined degree programs:** BSE/MED. Special programs offered to physically disabled students include note-taking services **Career services:** Alumni network, alumni services, career/job search classes, career assessment, internships, regional alumni. **Career services highlights include:** Career services and entrepreneurship.

FACILITIES

Housing: Coed dorms, men's dorms, women's dorms, fraternity/sorority housing, apartments for married students, apartments for single students, wellness housing, theme housing Designated rooms available for ADA needs. 97% of campus accessible to physically disabled. **Special Academic Facilities/Equipment:** Art exhibition hall, Tandy film library, speech/hearing clinic, TV studios, computer labs, observatory, Moncrief Meteorite, special collections, alumni and visitors center, cable TV, radio station, performance hall, variety of athletic facilities. **Computers:** 100% of classrooms, 100% of dorms, 100% of libraries, 100% of dining areas, 100% of student union, 100% of common outdoor areas

have wireless network access. Students can register for classes online. Administrative functions (other than registration) can be performed online.

CAMPUS LIFE

Environment: Metropolis. **Activities:** Choral groups, concert band, dance, drama/theater, jazz band, literary magazine, marching band, music ensembles, musical theater, opera, pep band, radio station, student government, student newspaper, television station, yearbook, campus ministries, international student organization, Model UN. **Organizations:** 200 registered organizations, 29 honor societies, 17 religious organizations. 15 fraternities, 18 sororities. **Athletics (Intercollegiate):** *Men:* Baseball, basketball, cross-country, diving, football, golf, swimming, tennis, track/field (outdoor), track/field (indoor). *Women:* Basketball, cross-country, diving, equestrian sports, golf, riflery, soccer, swimming, tennis, track/field (outdoor), track/field (indoor), volleyball. **On-Campus Highlights:** Amon Carter Stadium, University Recreation Center, Monnig Meteorite Collection, Brown-Lupton University Union, Campus Commons/Frog Fountain. **Environmental Initiatives:** American Colleges and Universities President's Climate Commitment Climate Commitment Curriculum Committee—planning how to integrate concepts of climate neutrality and sustainability into the curriculum of all TCU students. Academic research initiatives in areas such as green roofs, wind energy, and eco tourism.

ADMISSIONS

Freshman Academic Profile: 30% in top 10% of high school class, 61% in top 25% of high school class, 90% in top 50% of high school class. 72% from public high schools. SAT Math middle 50% range 530–650. SAT Critical Reading middle 50% range 520–630. SAT Writing middle 50% range 520–630. ACT middle 50% range 23–28. Minimum paper TOEFL 550. Minimum computer TOEFL 213. Minimum web-based TOEFL 80. **Basis for Candidate Selection:** *Very important factors considered include:* Class rank, application essay, academic GPA, recommendation(s), rigor of secondary school record, standardized test scores, character/personal qualities. *Important factors considered include:* extracurricular activities, first generation, geographical residence, level of applicant's interest, racial/ethnic status, religious affiliation/commitment, talent/ability, volunteer work, work experience. *Other factors considered include:* Alumni/ae relation, interview. **Freshman Admission Requirements:** High school diploma is required and GED is not accepted. *Academic units required:* 4 English, 3 mathematics, 3 science, 2 foreign language, 3 social studies, 2 academic electives. *Academic units recommended:* 4 English, 4 mathematics, 4 science, 4 foreign language, 4 social studies, 4 academic electives. **Freshman Admission Statistics:** 11,953 applied, 59% admitted, 26% enrolled. **Transfer Admission Requirements:** College transcript(s), essay or personal statement, minimum college GPA of 2.0 required. Lowest grade transferable C. **General Admission Information:** Application fee $40. Regular application deadline 2/15. Regular notification 4/1. Nonfall registration accepted. Admission may be deferred for a maximum of 1 year. Credit offered for CEEB Advanced Placement tests.

COSTS AND FINANCIAL AID

Annual tuition $30,000. Required fees $48. **Required Forms and Deadlines:** FAFSA Financial aid filing deadline 5/1. Priority financial aid filing date 5/1. **Notification of Awards:** Applicants will be notified of awards on a rolling basis beginning 3/15. **Types of Aid:** *Need-based scholarships/grants:* Federal Pell, SEOG, state scholarships/grants, private scholarships, the school's own gift aid. *Loans:* FFEL Subsidized Stafford, FFEL Unsubsidized Stafford, FFEL PLUS, Federal Perkins, Federal Nursing, state loans *Student Employment:* Federal Work-Study Program available. Institutional employment available. Highest amount earned per year from on-campus jobs $12,750. Off-campus job opportunities are excellent. **Financial Aid Statistics:** 39% freshmen, 39% undergrads receive need-based scholarship or grant aid. 27% freshmen, 24% undergrads receive non-need-based scholarship or grant aid. 31% freshmen, 33% undergrads receive need-based self-help aid. 3% freshmen, 3% undergrads receive athletic scholarships. 75% freshmen, 72% undergrads receive any aid. 43% undergrads borrow to pay for school. Average cumulative indebtedness $32,357. **Criteria for awarding institutional aid:** *Non-need-based:* Academics, alumni affiliation, art, minority status, music/drama, religious affiliation, state/district residency.

TEXAS COLLEGE

2404 North Grand Ave, Tyler, TX 75702
Phone: 903-593-8311
E-mail: afrancis@texascollege.edu
Fax: 903-593-0588 **Website:** www.texascollege.edu **ACT Code:** 4210

This private school, affiliated with the Methodist Church, was founded in 1894. It has a 25-acre campus.

RATINGS
Admissions Selectivity Rating: 60*   **Fire Safety Rating:** 60*   **Green Rating:** 60*

STUDENTS AND FACULTY
Enrollment: 1,035. **Student Body:** 49% female, 51% male, 15% out-of-state, (2 countries represented). African American 95%, Caucasian 2%, Hispanic 2%. **Retention and Graduation:** 5% grads go on to further study within 1 year. 5% grads pursue arts and sciences degrees. 2% grads pursue business degrees. 1% grads pursue medical degrees. **Faculty:** Student/faculty ratio 10:1. 28 full-time faculty, 46% hold PhDs, 79% are are members of minority groups, 46% are women.

ACADEMICS
Degrees: Associate, bachelor's. **Classes:** Most classes have 30–39 students. **Majors with Highest Enrollment:** Business/commerce; social work; sociology. **Special Study Options:** Accelerated program, distance learning, dual enrollment, independent study, internships, teacher certification program. **Career services:** Alumni services, career assessment, internships.

FACILITIES
Housing: Men's dorms, women's dorms, apartments for single students. 80% of campus accessible to physically disabled. **Special Academic Facilities/Equipment:** Moody Science-Business Center; D. R. Glass Library; Willie Lee Glass Community Development Services Center.

CAMPUS LIFE
Environment: City. **Activities:** Choral groups, jazz band, marching band, student government, yearbook. **Organizations:** 31 registered organizations, 3 religious organizations. 3 fraternities, 3 sororities. **Athletics (Intercollegiate):** *Men:* Baseball, basketball, cheerleading, football, track/field (outdoor). *Women:* Basketball, cheerleading, softball, track/field (outdoor), volleyball. **On-Campus Highlights:** Gus F. Taylor Gymnasium, Student Union, D. R. Glass Library, Moody Science-Business Center, Mattie Fair Hall (women's residence hall).

ADMISSIONS
Freshman Academic Profile: 98% from public high schools. Minimum paper TOEFL 500. **Basis for Candidate Selection:** *Very important factors considered include:* Rigor of secondary school record. **Freshman Admission Requirements:** High school diploma is required and GED is accepted. *Academic units required:* 4 English, 2 mathematics, 2 science, 2 social studies, 2 history, 4 academic electives. **Freshman Admission Statistics:** 1,066 applied, 98% admitted, 32% enrolled. **Transfer Admission Requirements:** College transcript(s), statement of good standing from prior institution(s). Lowest grade transferable C. **General Admission Information:** Application fee $20. Regular notification 8/15. Notification on a rolling basis, beginning on or about 4/1. Nonfall registration accepted. Admission may be deferred for a maximum of 1 year.

COSTS AND FINANCIAL AID
Annual tuition $6,305. Room and board $4,730. Required fees $20. Average book expense $800. **Required Forms and Deadlines:** FAFSA, institution's own financial aid form. Priority financial aid filing date 4/15. **Notification of Awards:** Applicants will be notified of awards on a rolling basis beginning 4/15. **Types of Aid:** *Need-based scholarships/grants:* Federal Pell, SEOG, state scholarships/grants, private scholarships, the school's own gift aid, United Negro College Fund. *Loans:* state loans. *Student Employment:* Federal Work-Study Program available. Off-campus job opportunities are good. **Financial Aid Statistics:** 100% freshmen, 83% undergrads receive need-based scholarship or grant aid. 100% freshmen, 87% undergrads receive need-based self-help aid. 15% freshmen, 14% undergrads receive athletic scholarships. 100% freshmen, 90% undergrads receive any aid. 90% undergrads borrow to pay for school. Average cumulative indebtedness $2,500. **Criteria for awarding institutional aid:** *Non-need-based:* Academics, athletics.

TEXAS LUTHERAN UNIVERSITY

1000 West Court Street, Seguin, TX 78155
Phone: 830-372-8050 **Financial Aid Phone:** 830-372-8078
E-mail: admissions@tlu.edu
Fax: 830-372-8096 **Website:** www.tlu.edu

This private school, affiliated with the Lutheran Church, was founded in 1891. It has a 184-acre campus.

RATINGS
Admissions Selectivity Rating: 79   **Fire Safety Rating:** 77   **Green Rating:** 71

STUDENTS AND FACULTY
Enrollment: 1,350. **Student Body:** 52% female, 48% male, 4% out-of-state, 1% international (9 countries represented). Asian 1%, African American 10%, Caucasian 61%, Hispanic 23%. **Retention and Graduation:** 31% freshmen graduate within 4 years. **Faculty:** Student/faculty ratio 15:1. 68 full-time faculty, 79% hold PhDs, 13% are are members of minority groups, 41% are women.

ACADEMICS
Degrees: Bachelor's. **Classes:** Most classes have 10–19 students. **Majors with Highest Enrollment:** Accounting; business/commerce; education. **Special Study Options:** Double major, dual enrollment, exchange student program (domestic), honors program, independent study, internships, study abroad, teacher certification program, senior seminars. Special programs offered to physically disabled students include note-taking services, reader services, tutors. **Career services:** Alumni network, alumni services, career/job search classes, internships.

FACILITIES
Housing: Coed dorms, men's dorms, women's dorms, apartments for married students, apartments for single students. 95% of campus accessible to physically disabled. **Special Academic Facilities/Equipment:** Mexican-American studies center, geological museum. **Computers:** 100% of classrooms, 100% of dorms, 100% of libraries, 100% of dining areas, 100% of student union, 100% of common outdoor areas have wireless network access. Students can register for classes online. Administrative functions (other than registration) can be performed online.

CAMPUS LIFE
Environment: Town. **Activities:** Choral groups, concert band, dance, drama/theater, jazz band, literary magazine, music ensembles, musical theater, pep band, student government, student newspaper, symphony orchestra, campus ministries, international student organization. **Organizations:** 53 registered organizations, 10 honor societies, 3 religious organizations. 5 fraternities, 4 sororities. **Athletics (Intercollegiate):** *Men:* Baseball, basketball, football, golf, soccer, tennis. *Women:* Basketball, cross-country, golf, soccer, softball, tennis, track/field (outdoor), track/field (indoor), volleyball. **On-Campus Highlights:** Lucky's Snack Shack, Fitness Center, Alumni Student Center, Residence Halls, Hein Dining Hall. **Environmental Initiatives:** Installation of more efficient HVAC system campus wide. Installation of rainwater collection system creation of a sustainability committee.

ADMISSIONS
Freshman Academic Profile: Average high school GPA 3.52. 22% in top 10% of high school class, 52% in top 25% of high school class, 84% in top 50% of high school class. 94% from public high schools. SAT Math middle 50% range 460–570. SAT Critical Reading middle 50% range 440–550. SAT Writing middle 50% range 420–530. ACT middle 50% range 18–23. Minimum paper TOEFL 550. Minimum computer TOEFL 213. Minimum web-based TOEFL 80. **Basis for Candidate Selection:** *Very important factors considered include:* Class rank, application essay, academic GPA, recommendation(s), rigor of secondary school record, standardized test scores. *Important factors considered include:* Character/personal qualities, interview, talent/ability, volunteer work. *Other factors considered include:* Extracurricular activities, level of applicant's interest, work experience. **Freshman Admission Requirements:** High school diploma is required and GED is accepted. *Academic units required:* 4 English, 3 mathematics, 3 science, (2 science labs), 2 foreign language, 3 social studies. *Academic units recommended:* 4 English, 4 mathematics, 4 science, (2 science labs), 3 foreign language, 4 social studies, 1 computer science, 1 speech. **Freshman Admission Statistics:** 1,070 applied, 66% admitted, 49% enrolled. **Transfer Admission Requirements:** High school transcript, college transcript(s), essay or personal statement, statement of good standing from prior institution(s). Minimum college GPA of 2.25 required. Lowest grade transferable C. **General Admission Information:** Application fee $25. Regular application deadline 8/1. Notification on a rolling basis, beginning on or about 10/1. Nonfall registration accepted. Admission may be deferred for a maximum of 1 year. Credit and/or placement offered for CEEB Advanced Placement tests.

COSTS AND FINANCIAL AID

Required Forms and Deadlines: FAFSA. Priority financial aid filing date 3/1. **Notification of Awards:** Applicants will be notified of awards on a rolling basis beginning 3/1. **Types of Aid:** *Need-based scholarships/grants:* Federal Pell, SEOG, state scholarships/grants, the school's own gift aid. *Loans:* FFEL Subsidized Stafford, FFEL Unsubsidized Stafford, FFEL PLUS, Federal Perkins, state loans *Student Employment:* Federal Work-Study Program available. Institutional employment available. Off-campus job opportunities are good. **Financial Aid Statistics:** 82% freshmen, 72% undergrads receive need-based scholarship or grant aid. 10% freshmen, 7% undergrads receive non-need-based scholarship or grant aid. 66% freshmen, 59% undergrads receive need-based self-help aid. 100% freshmen, 95.6% undergrads receive any aid. 63% undergrads borrow to pay for school. Average cumulative indebtedness $29,200. **Criteria for awarding institutional aid:** *Non-need-based:* Academics, alumni affiliation, leadership, music/drama, religious affiliation.

TEXAS STATE UNIVERSITY—SAN MARCOS

429 North Guadalupe St, San Marcos, TX 78666
Phone: 512-245-2364 **Financial Aid Phone:** 512-245 2315
E-mail: admissions@txstate.edu **CEEB Code:** 6667
Fax: 512-245-8044 **Website:** www.txstate.edu **ACT Code:** 4178

This public school was founded in 1899. It has a 455-acre campus.

RATINGS

Admissions Selectivity Rating: 71   **Fire Safety Rating:** 84   **Green Rating:** 60*

STUDENTS AND FACULTY

Enrollment: 26,002. **Student Body:** 55% female, 45% male, 1% out-of-state, 1% international (69 countries represented). Asian 2%, African American 6%, Caucasian 66%, Hispanic 24%, Native American 1%.
Retention and Graduation: 79% freshmen return for sophomore year. 24% freshmen graduate within 4 years. 21% grads go on to further study within 1 year. 5.1% grads pursue arts and sciences degrees. 1% grads pursue law degrees. 3.7% grads pursue business degrees. 2.2% grads pursue medical degrees. **Faculty:** Student/faculty ratio 19.5:1. 1017 full-time faculty, 72% hold PhDs, 20% are are members of minority groups, 45% are women.

ACADEMICS

Degrees: Bachelor's, doctoral, master's, post-bachelor's certificate. **Classes:** Most classes have 20–29 students. Most lab/discussion sessions have 20–29 students. **Majors with Highest Enrollment:** Business administration and management; multi-/interdisciplinary studies, other; psychology. **Special Study Options:** Accelerated program, distance learning, double major, dual enrollment, English as a Second Language (ESL), exchange student program (domestic), honors program, independent study, internships, study abroad, teacher certification program, weekend college, English as a Second Language is offered to international students or any students for that matter, who wish to improve their command of the English language. But it is not offered as a degree program. **Honors programs:** To graduate in the University Honors Program, a student must complete at least five Honors Classes (which includes the Honors Thesis course) and maintain a minimum GPA of 3.25. Honors courses substitute for certain general education core curriculum and inidividual departmental requirements and thus become integral parts of the degree program. **Combined degree programs:** BA/MD, BA/DDS. See 2008–2010 undgrad catalog page 63 and 64. Special programs offered to physically disabled students include note-taking services, reader services, tape recorders, tutors. **Career services:** Alumni network, alumni services, career/job search classes, career assessment. **Career services highlights include:** Experiential learning through the College of Education. All teacher education majors participate on practice teaching with a supervising teacher mentoring.

FACILITIES

Housing: Coed dorms, special housing for disabled students, men's dorms, women's dorms, fraternity/sorority housing, apartments for married students, apartments for single students, non-smoking, honors, access for the disabled, but not separate housing. 88% of campus accessible to physically disabled. **Special Academic Facilities/Equipment:** Child development center, aquifer research center, two demonstration farms, physical anthropology and archaeology laboratories. Southwestern Writer's Collection. Observatory with a 17 inch telescope. **Computers:** 100% of classrooms, 100% of dorms, 100% of libraries, 100% of dining areas, 100% of student union, 100% of common outdoor areas have wireless network access. Students can register for classes online. Administrative functions (other than registration) can be performed online.

CAMPUS LIFE

Environment: Town. **Activities:** Choral groups, concert band, dance, drama/theater, jazz band, literary magazine, marching band, music ensembles, musical theater, opera, pep band, radio station, student government, student newspaper, student-run film society, symphony orchestra, yearbook, campus ministries, international student organization, Model UN. **Organizations:** 254 registered organizations, 16 honor societies, 27 religious organizations. 18 fraternities, 14 sororities. **Athletics (Intercollegiate):** *Men:* Baseball, basketball, cheerleading, cross-country, football, golf, track/field (outdoor). *Women:* Basketball, cheerleading, cross-country, golf, soccer, softball, tennis, track/field (outdoor), volleyball. **On-Campus Highlights:** LBJ Student Center, Alkek Library, Student Recreation Center, The Quad, Sewell Park, The Quad is a walk way that runs the length of the campus which most academic buildings open on to. Student gather here to socialize between classes. Sewell Park is a general recreational park where students gather to swim, sun bathe, throw frisbees, and play ball. The San Marcos river runs through the park. **Environmental Initiatives:** Established the Texas Rivers Systems Institute. Our programs and projects demonstrate our deep commitment to the careful stewardship of the world's freshwater resources. Through collaborative research, public advocacy, and education on river systems, the Institute affirms the unique role of water in our lives. As one of the earth's most remarkable resources, we are dedicated to preserving and protecting this irreplaceable gift—water. The James and Marilyn Lovell Center for Environmental Geography and Hazards Research located within Texas State University—San Marcos' Department of Geography (one of the largest such departments in the United States), the JMLC provides a focal point around which its scholars can gather to share ideas and mentor students. Faculty Scholars seek to better understand Earth's environment, to analyze and reduce the impacts of natural and technological hazards, and through their work to improve policies directed toward Earth's environment and its hazards. Full-time position of coordinator of recycling and waste management for a campus wide recycling program.

ADMISSIONS

Freshman Academic Profile: 13.9% in top 10% of high school class, 51.9% in top 25% of high school class, 91.9% in top 50% of high school class. 98% from public high schools. SAT Math middle 50% range 490–590. SAT Critical Reading middle 50% range 480–570. SAT Writing middle 50% range 460–550. ACT middle 50% range 21–25. Minimum paper TOEFL 550. Minimum computer TOEFL 213. Minimum web-based TOEFL 78. **Basis for Candidate Selection:** *Very important factors considered include:* Class rank, standardized test scores. *Other factors considered include:* Application essay, rigor of secondary school record, talent/ability. **Freshman Admission Requirements:** High school diploma is required and GED is accepted. *Academic units required:* 4 English, 3 mathematics, 3 science, (2 science labs), 2 foreign language, 1 visual/performing arts, 1 computer science, 3 PE 1.5, Eco.0.5, Health Ed. 0.5, Speech 0.5 *Academic units recommended:* 4 English, 4 mathematics, 4 science, (2 science labs), 3 foreign language, 1 visual/performing arts, 1 computer science, 3 PE 1.5, Eco.0.5, Health Ed. 0.5, Speech 0.5 **Freshman Admission Statistics:** 12,172 applied, 76% admitted, 40% enrolled. **Transfer Admission Requirements:** College transcript(s), statement of good standing from prior institution(s). Minimum college GPA of 2.2 required. Lowest grade transferable D. **General Admission Information:** Application fee $60. Regular application deadline 5/1. Notification on a rolling basis, beginning on or about 9/1. Nonfall registration accepted. Admission may be deferred for a maximum of indefinite, fee req. Credit offered for CEEB Advanced Placement tests.

COSTS AND FINANCIAL AID

Annual in-state tuition $5,460. Annual out-of-state tuition $13,770. Room and board $6,392. Required fees $2,022. Average book expense $1,050. **Required Forms and Deadlines:** FAFSA. Priority financial aid filing date 4/1. **Notification of Awards:** Applicants will be notified of awards on a rolling basis beginning 5/1. **Types of Aid:** *Need-based scholarships/grants:* Federal Pell, SEOG, state scholarships/grants, private scholarships, the school's own gift aid. *Loans:* Direct Subsidized Stafford, Direct Unsubsidized Stafford, Direct PLUS, FFEL Subsidized Stafford, FFEL Unsubsidized Stafford, FFEL PLUS, Federal Perkins, state loans, college/university loans from institutional funds, Alternative Loans, Emergency tuition l. *Student Employment:* Federal Work-Study Program available. Institutional employment available. Highest amount earned per year from on-campus jobs $9,264. Off-campus job opportunities are good. **Financial Aid Statistics:** 38% freshmen, 38% undergrads receive need-based scholarship or grant aid. 19% freshmen, 8% undergrads receive non-need-based scholarship or grant aid. 40% freshmen, 42% undergrads receive need-based self-help aid. 2% freshmen, 1% undergrads receive athletic scholarships. 44% freshmen, 46% undergrads receive any aid. 58.1% undergrads borrow to pay for school. Average cumulative indebtedness $19,691. **Criteria for awarding institutional aid:** *Non-need-based:* Academics, art, athletics, leadership, music/drama, state/district residency.

TEXAS TECH UNIVERSITY

Box 45005, Lubbock, TX 79409-5005
Phone: 806-742-1480 **Financial Aid Phone:** 806-742-3681
E-mail: admissions@ttu.edu **CEEB Code:** 6827
Fax: 806-742-0062 **Website:** www.ttu.edu **ACT Code:** 4220

This public school was founded in 1923. It has a 1839-acre campus.

RATINGS
Admissions Selectivity Rating: 76   **Fire Safety Rating:** 93   **Green Rating:** 60*

STUDENTS AND FACULTY
Enrollment: 23,080. **Student Body:** 44% female, 56% male, 4% out-of-state, 1% international (120 countries represented). Asian 3%, African American 4%, Caucasian 77%, Hispanic 14%, Native American 1%.
Retention and Graduation: 80% freshmen return for sophomore year. 30% freshmen graduate within 4 years. **Faculty:** Student/faculty ratio 18:1. 1099 full-time faculty, 87% hold PhDs, 16% are are members of minority groups, 36% are women. 10.94% of classes are taught by teaching assistants.

ACADEMICS
Degrees: Bachelor's, first professional, master's, post-bachelor's certificate.
Classes: Most classes have 10–19 students. Most lab/discussion sessions have 20–29 students. **Majors with Highest Enrollment:** health and physical education; mechanical engineering; psychology. **Special Study Options:** Accelerated program, cooperative education program, distance learning, double major, dual enrollment, English as a Second Language (ESL), external degree program, honors program, independent study, internships, liberal arts/career combination, student-designed major, study abroad, teacher certification program.
Honors programs: Honors Studies is a special program under our Honors College for highly motivated and academically talented students who want to maximize their college education. It is designed to provide such students with a unique and broadly integrated intellectual experience that is complementary to virtually every major and career path. **Combined degree programs:** BA/MA, MBA/JD; MBA/MD; MPA/JD; MBA/M.Arch; MBA/MS; MS/MS; MBA/MA; JD/MSA; JD/MS; MPA/MA. Special programs offered to physically disabled students include note-taking services, reader services, tape recorders, tutors.
Career services: Alumni services, career/job search classes, internships, regional alumni.

FACILITIES
Housing: Coed dorms, special housing for disabled students, men's dorms, women's dorms, apartments for single students. 100% of campus accessible to physically disabled. **Special Academic Facilities/Equipment:** Museum, child development center, textile research center, agricultural research center, planetarium, ranching heritage center, semi-arid land studies center, ranching heritage center, seismological observatory. **Computers:** Students can register for classes online. Administrative functions (other than registration) can be performed online.

CAMPUS LIFE
Environment: City. **Activities:** Choral groups, concert band, dance, drama/theater, jazz band, marching band, music ensembles, musical theater, pep band, radio station, student government, student newspaper, symphony orchestra, television station, yearbook, campus ministries, international student organization. **Organizations:** 399 registered organizations, 33 honor societies, 35 religious organizations. 25 fraternities, 18 sororities. **Athletics (Intercollegiate):** *Men:* Baseball, basketball, cross-country, football, golf, tennis, track/field (outdoor), track/field (indoor). *Women:* Basketball, cross-country, golf, soccer, softball, tennis, track/field (outdoor), track/field (indoor), volleyball. **On-Campus Highlights:** Student Union Building, Student Recreation Center, Library, Classrooms, United Spirit Arena, Jones AT&T Stadium, Museums, National Ranching and Heritage Center.

ADMISSIONS
Freshman Academic Profile: 21% in top 10% of high school class, 52% in top 25% of high school class, 84% in top 50% of high school class. SAT Math middle 50% range 520–620. SAT Critical Reading middle 50% range 490–590. SAT Writing middle 50% range 460–570. ACT middle 50% range 22-26. Minimum paper TOEFL 550. Minimum computer TOEFL 213. Minimum web-based TOEFL 79. **Basis for Candidate Selection:** *Very important factors considered include:* Class rank, academic GPA, rigor of secondary school record, standardized test scores. *Important factors considered include:* Application essay, alumni/ae relation, character/personal qualities, extracurricular activities, talent/ability, volunteer work, work experience. *Other factors considered include:* Recommendation(s), first generation, level of applicant's interest, racial/ethnic status. **Freshman Admission Requirements:** High school diploma is required and GED is accepted. *Academic units required:* 4 English, 3 mathematics, 2 science, (2 science labs), 2 foreign language. **Freshman**

Admission Statistics: 16,143 applied, 72% admitted, 38% enrolled. **Transfer Admission Requirements:** College transcript(s), statement of good standing from prior institution(s). Minimum college GPA of 2.25 required. Lowest grade transferable D-. **General Admission Information:** Application fee $50. Regular application deadline 5/1. Nonfall registration accepted. Credit offered for CEEB Advanced Placement tests.

COSTS AND FINANCIAL AID
Annual in-state tuition $4,875. Annual out-of-state tuition $13,185. Room and board $7,527. Required fees $2,610. Average book expense $1,000. **Required Forms and Deadlines:** FAFSA. Priority financial aid filing date 4/15. **Notification of Awards: Types of Aid:** *Need-based scholarships/grants:* Federal Pell, SEOG, state scholarships/grants, private scholarships, the school's own gift aid. *Loans:* FFEL Subsidized Stafford, FFEL Unsubsidized Stafford, FFEL PLUS, Federal Perkins, state loans, college/university loans from institutional funds. *Student Employment:* Federal Work-Study Program available. Institutional employment available. Highest amount earned per year from on-campus jobs $5,017. Off-campus job opportunities are excellent. **Financial Aid Statistics:** 26% freshmen, 29% undergrads receive need-based scholarship or grant aid. 18% freshmen, 11% undergrads receive non-need-based scholarship or grant aid. 30% freshmen, 32% undergrads receive need-based self-help aid. 2% freshmen, 2% undergrads receive athletic scholarships. 46% freshmen, 44% undergrads receive any aid. 60% undergrads borrow to pay for school. Average cumulative indebtedness $20,424. **Criteria for awarding institutional aid:** *Non-need-based:* Academics, art, athletics, job skills, leadership, music/drama.

TEXAS WOMAN'S UNIVERSITY

P.O. Box 425589, Denton, TX 76204-5589
Phone: 940-898-3188 **Financial Aid Phone:** 940-898-3050
E-mail: admissions@twu.edu **CEEB Code:** 6826
Fax: 940-898-3081 **Website:** www.twu.edu **ACT Code:** 4224

This public school was founded in 1901. It has a 270-acre campus.

RATINGS
Admissions Selectivity Rating: 74   **Fire Safety Rating:** 98   **Green Rating:** 60*

STUDENTS AND FACULTY
Enrollment: 7,389. **Student Body:** 93% female, 7% male, 1% out-of-state, 2% international (62 countries represented). Asian 8%, African American 21%, Caucasian 51%, Hispanic 18%, Native American 1%.
Retention and Graduation: 71% freshmen return for sophomore year. 22% freshmen graduate within 4 years. 4% grads go on to further study within 1 year. **Faculty:** Student/faculty ratio 17:1. 306 full-time faculty, 17% are are members of minority groups, 71% are women.

ACADEMICS
Degrees: Bachelor's, master's, post-bachelor's certificate, post-master's certificate. **Classes:** Most classes have 10–19 students. **Special Study Options:** Cross-registration, distance learning, double major, dual enrollment, honors program, independent study, internships, study abroad, teacher certification program **Honors programs:** Honors Scholars Program www.twu.edu/honors/index.html **Combined degree programs:** BA/MEng, 3-2 program with UNT. Special programs offered to physically disabled students include note-taking services, reader services, tape recorders, tutors. **Career services:** Internships.

FACILITIES
Housing: Coed dorms, special housing for disabled students, special housing for international students, women's dorms, apartments for married students, apartments for single students, wellness housing, theme housing. 100% of campus accessible to physically disabled. **Special Academic Facilities/Equipment:** Museum, radiation lab, language lab, Texas First Ladies Gown Collection Texas Women's Hall of Fame. **Computers:** Students can register for classes online. Administrative functions (other than registration) can be performed online.

CAMPUS LIFE
Environment: City. **Activities:** Choral groups, dance, drama/theater, jazz band, music ensembles, musical theater, opera, student government, student newspaper, television station, international student organization. **Organizations:** 94 registered organizations, 16 honor societies, 10 religious organizations. 9 sororities. **Athletics (Intercollegiate):** *Women:* Basketball, gymnastics, soccer, softball, volleyball. **On-Campus Highlights:** Student Union, Pioneer Hall, Mega Computer Lab, Guinn/Stark High Rise Resident Halls, Little Chapel-in-the-Woods, TWU has four campuses—two in Dallas, one in Houston and the 270 acre main campus in Denton. The Denton Campus houses the Texas Women's Hall of Fame and the Gowns of Texas First Ladies Collection;

The Houston Campus is located in the Houston Medical Center and recently opened the new facility; The Dallas campuses have begun construction on a new multi-million dollar facility.

ADMISSIONS

Freshman Academic Profile: Average high school GPA 3.2. 18% in top 10% of high school class, 29% in top 25% of high school class, 77% in top 50% of high school class. 93% from public high schools. SAT Math middle 50% range 420–530. SAT Critical Reading middle 50% range 420–520. ACT middle 50% range 18–22. Minimum paper TOEFL 550. Minimum computer TOEFL 213. **Basis for Candidate Selection:** *Very important factors considered include:* Class rank, rigor of secondary school record, standardized test scores. *Important factors considered include:* Academic GPA. **Freshman Admission Requirements:** High school diploma is required and GED is accepted. *Academic units required:* 4 English, 3 mathematics, 2 science, 2 social studies, 3 academic electives. *Academic units recommended:* 4 English, 3 mathematics, 3 science, 3 social studies, 5 academic electives. **Freshman Admission Statistics:** 3,649 applied, 56% admitted, 41% enrolled. **Transfer Admission Requirements:** College transcript(s), minimum college GPA of 2.0 required. Lowest grade transferable D. **General Admission Information:** Application fee $30. Notification on a rolling basis, beginning on or about 10/1. Nonfall registration accepted. Admission may be deferred for a maximum of 2 years. Credit and/or placement offered for CEEB Advanced Placement tests.

COSTS AND FINANCIAL AID

Annual in-state tuition $4,740. Annual out-of-state tuition $13,080. Room and board $6,074. Required fees $1,320. Average book expense $930. **Required Forms and Deadlines:** FAFSA, Financial Aid Certification and Information Form must be completed prior to disbursement of financial aid. Priority financial aid filing date 4/1. **Notification of Awards:** Applicants will be notified of awards on a rolling basis beginning 3/1. **Types of Aid:** *Need-based scholarships/grants:* Federal Pell, SEOG, state scholarships/grants, private scholarships, the school's own gift aid, Federal Nursing Scholarships. Leaveraging Educational Assistance Partnership Grant. *Loans:* FFEL Subsidized Stafford, FFEL Unsubsidized Stafford, FFEL PLUS, Federal Perkins, Federal Nursing, state loans, college/university loans from institutional funds, Alternative non-federal loans. *Student Employment:* Highest amount earned per year from on-campus jobs $5,120. **Financial Aid Statistics:** 39% freshmen, 44% undergrads receive need-based scholarship or grant aid. 40% freshmen, 21% undergrads receive non-need-based scholarship or grant aid. 55% freshmen, 56% undergrads receive need-based self-help aid. 1% undergrads receive athletic scholarships. 77% freshmen, 85% undergrads receive any aid. 58% undergrads borrow to pay for school. Average cumulative indebtedness $19,409. **Criteria for awarding institutional aid:** *Non-need-based:* Academics, art, athletics, music/drama.

THIEL COLLEGE

75 College Avenue, Greenville, PA 16125
Phone: 724-589-2345 **Financial Aid Phone:** 724-589-2178
E-mail: admissions@thiel.edu **CEEB Code:** 2910
Fax: 724-589-2013 **Website:** www.thiel.edu **ACT Code:** 3730

This private school, affiliated with the Lutheran Church, was founded in 1866. It has a 135-acre campus.

RATINGS

Admissions Selectivity Rating: 74   **Fire Safety Rating:** 60*   **Green Rating:** 71

STUDENTS AND FACULTY

Enrollment: 1,091. **Student Body:** 47% female, 53% male, 35% out-of-state, 5% international (14 countries represented). Asian 1%, African American 7%, Caucasian 63%, Hispanic 1%.
Retention and Graduation: 59% freshmen return for sophomore year. 26% freshmen graduate within 4 years. 13% grads go on to further study within 1 year. 86% grads pursue arts and sciences degrees. 1% grads pursue law degrees. 12% grads pursue business degrees. 1% grads pursue medical degrees.
Faculty: Student/faculty ratio 16:1. 64 full-time faculty, 69% hold PhDs, 8% are members of minority groups, 39% are women.

ACADEMICS

Degrees: Associate, bachelor's. **Classes:** Most classes have 10–19 students. Most lab/discussion sessions have 20–29 students. **Majors with Highest Enrollment:** Biology/biological sciences; business/commerce; elementary education and teaching. **Special Study Options:** Cooperative education program, distance learning, double major, dual enrollment, English as a Second Language (ESL), honors program, independent study, internships, liberal arts/career combination, study abroad, teacher certification program. **Honors programs:** Four year Honors Program with special courses for honors students. Special

programs offered to physically disabled students include note-taking services, reader services, tape recorders, tutors. **Career services:** Alumni network, career/job search classes, career assessment, internships.

FACILITIES

Housing: Coed dorms, fraternity/sorority housing, apartments for single students. 90% of campus accessible to physically disabled. **Special Academic Facilities/Equipment:** Art gallery, black box theater, Starbucks Bistro. **Computers:** Students can register for classes online. Undergraduates are required to own a computer.

CAMPUS LIFE

Environment: Rural. **Activities:** Choral groups, concert band, dance, drama/theater, literary magazine, musical theater, pep band, radio station, student government, student newspaper, symphony orchestra, television station, yearbook, campus ministries. **Organizations:** 40 registered organizations, 8 honor societies, 4 religious organizations. 3 fraternities, 4 sororities. **Athletics (Intercollegiate):** *Men:* Baseball, basketball, cheerleading, cross-country, football, golf, soccer, track/field (outdoor), track/field (indoor), wrestling. *Women:* Basketball, cheerleading, cross-country, soccer, softball, track/field (outdoor), track/field (indoor), volleyball. **On-Campus Highlights:** Howard Miller Student Center, Robinson Black Box Theater, new student apartments, Alumni Stadium, Paul Bush Memorial Fitness Center.

ADMISSIONS

Freshman Academic Profile: Average high school GPA 3.02. 19% in top 10% of high school class, 40% in top 25% of high school class, 75% in top 50% of high school class. 88% from public high schools. SAT Math middle 50% range 420–545. SAT Critical Reading middle 50% range 400–510. ACT middle 50% range 17–24. Minimum paper TOEFL 450. Minimum computer TOEFL 140. **Basis for Candidate Selection:** *Very important factors considered include:* Application essay, academic GPA, recommendation(s), rigor of secondary school record, standardized test scores, interview, level of applicant's interest. *Important factors considered include:* Class rank, character/personal qualities. *Other factors considered include:* Extracurricular activities, talent/ability, volunteer work, work experience. **Freshman Admission Requirements:** High school diploma is required and GED is accepted. *Academic units recommended:* 4 English, 2 mathematics, 2 science, (2 science labs), 2 foreign language, 3 social studies, 1 academic electives. **Freshman Admission Statistics:** 1,439 applied, 71% admitted, 31% enrolled. **Transfer Admission Requirements:** High school transcript, college transcript(s), essay or personal statement, interview, standardized test scores, statement of good standing from prior institution(s). Minimum college GPA of 2.0 required. Lowest grade transferable C. **General Admission Information:** Application fee $35. Regular application deadline 6/30. Notification on a rolling basis, beginning on or about 9/15. Nonfall registration accepted. Admission may be deferred for a maximum of 1 year. Credit and/or placement offered for CEEB Advanced Placement tests.

COSTS AND FINANCIAL AID

Required Forms and Deadlines: FAFSA, state aid form. Priority financial aid filing date 3/15. **Notification of Awards:** Applicants will be notified of awards on a rolling basis beginning 2/15. **Types of Aid:** *Need-based scholarships/grants:* Federal Pell, SEOG, state scholarships/grants, private scholarships, the school's own gift aid. *Loans:* FFEL Subsidized Stafford, FFEL Unsubsidized Stafford, FFEL PLUS, Federal Perkins, college/university loans from institutional funds. *Student Employment:* Federal Work-Study Program available. Institutional employment available. Off-campus job opportunities are fair. **Financial Aid Statistics:** 84% freshmen, 78% undergrads receive need-based scholarship or grant aid. 5% freshmen, 5% undergrads receive non-need-based scholarship or grant aid. 76% freshmen, 70% undergrads receive need-based self-help aid. 84% undergrads borrow to pay for school. Average cumulative indebtedness $21,712. **Criteria for awarding institutional aid:** *Non-need-based:* Academics, alumni affiliation, leadership, religious affiliation, state/district residency.

THOMAS AQUINAS COLLEGE

10000 North Ojai Road, Santa Paula, CA 93060
Phone: 805-525-4417 **Financial Aid Phone:** 800-634-9797
E-mail: admissions@thomasaquinas.edu **CEEB Code:** 4828
Fax: 805-421-5905 **Website:** www.thomasaquinas.edu **ACT Code:** 425

This private school, affiliated with the Roman Catholic Church, was founded in 1971. It has a 131-acre campus.

RATINGS
Admissions Selectivity Rating: 91   **Fire Safety Rating:** 87   **Green Rating:** 60*

STUDENTS AND FACULTY
Enrollment: 345. **Student Body:** 54% female, 46% male, 63% out-of-state, 6% international (8 countries represented). Asian 2%, Caucasian 75%, Hispanic 8%, Native American 1%.
Retention and Graduation: 79% freshmen return for sophomore year. 71% freshmen graduate within 4 years. 28% grads go on to further study within 1 year. 11% grads pursue arts and sciences degrees. 1% grads pursue law degrees. 1% grads pursue medical degrees. **Faculty:** Student/faculty ratio 11:1. 28 full-time faculty, 64% hold PhDs, 7% are women.

ACADEMICS
Degrees: Bachelor's. **Classes:** Most classes have 10–19 students. **Special Study Options:** The sole academic program offered: a "cross-disciplinary" curriculum of liberal education through reading and analyzing the "Great Books," with special emphasis on philosophy, theology, mathematics, science, and literature. **Career services:** Alumni network, alumni services, career/job search classes, career assessment, internships, regional alumni. **Career services highlights include:** Career Assessment: We work directly with our students, one on one, in order to help them determine their strengths. We then talk with them about their various interests, and advise them on possible options, given their strengths and interests. We encourage them to talk to people within those fields, including networking with our alumni. We also have guest speakers and discernment classes that help as well.

FACILITIES
Housing: Men's dorms, women's dorms, students living with their families may live off campus. 100% of campus accessible to physically disabled. **Special Academic Facilities/Equipment:** St. Bernardine Library.

CAMPUS LIFE
Environment: Rural. **Activities:** Choral groups, dance, drama/theater, music ensembles, musical theater **Organizations:** 2 registered organizations, 4 religious organizations. **On-Campus Highlights:** St. Joseph Commons, The Dumb Ox Coffee Shop, Dorm Commons, St. Bernardine Library, Student Lounge. **Environmental Initiatives:** The college recycles recyclable material.

ADMISSIONS
Freshman Academic Profile: Average high school GPA 3.74. 50% in top 10% of high school class, 80% in top 25% of high school class, 100% in top 50% of high school class. 14% from public high schools. SAT Math middle 50% range 550–640. SAT Critical Reading middle 50% range 610–730. SAT Writing middle 50% range 590–690. ACT middle 50% range 25–30. Minimum paper TOEFL 570. Minimum computer TOEFL 230. **Basis for Candidate Selection:** *Very important factors considered include:* Application essay, recommendation(s), rigor of secondary school record, standardized test scores, character/personal qualities, level of applicant's interest. *Important factors considered include:* Academic GPA. *Other factors considered include:* Class rank, extracurricular activities, interview, religious affiliation/commitment, talent/ability, volunteer work, work experience. **Freshman Admission Requirements:** High school diploma is required and GED is accepted. *Academic units required:* 4 English, 3 mathematics, 2 science, 2 foreign language, 2 history. *Academic units recommended:* 4 English, 4 mathematics, 3 science, (2 science labs), 2 history, 3 academic electives. **Freshman Admission Statistics:** 184 applied, 78% admitted, 71% enrolled. **General Admission Information:** Notification on a rolling basis, beginning on or about 10/1. Nonfall registration not accepted. Admission may be deferred for a maximum of 1 year. Neither credit nor placement offered for CEEB Advanced Placement tests.

COSTS AND FINANCIAL AID
Annual tuition $22,400. Room and board $7,400. Average book expense $450. **Required Forms and Deadlines:** FAFSA, institution's own financial aid form, state aid form, business/farm supplement. Tax return, Noncustodial Parent

Statement. Financial aid filing deadline 3/2. **Notification of Awards:** Applicants will be notified of awards on a rolling basis beginning 1/1. **Types of Aid:** *Need-based scholarships/grants:* Federal Pell, state scholarships/grants, private scholarships, the school's own gift aid. *Loans:* FFEL Subsidized Stafford, FFEL Unsubsidized Stafford, FFEL PLUS, college/university loans from institutional funds, Canadian student Loans. *Student Employment:* Off-campus job opportunities are fair. **Financial Aid Statistics:** 78% freshmen, 68% undergrads receive need-based scholarship or grant aid. 85% freshmen, 75% undergrads receive need-based self-help aid. 88% freshmen, 80% undergrads receive any aid. 71% undergrads borrow to pay for school. Average cumulative indebtedness $15,000.

THOMAS COLLEGE

180 West River Road, Waterville, ME 04901
Phone: 207-859-1101 **Financial Aid Phone:** 207-859-1105
E-mail: admiss@thomas.edu **CEEB Code:** 2052
Fax: 207-859-1114 **Website:** www.thomas.edu **ACT Code:** 1663

This private school was founded in 1894. It has a 120-acre campus.

RATINGS
Admissions Selectivity Rating: 70   **Fire Safety Rating:** 98   **Green Rating:** 60*

STUDENTS AND FACULTY
Enrollment: 739. **Student Body:** 49% female, 51% male, 20% out-of-state. Asian 1%, African American 2%, Caucasian 88%, Hispanic 1%.
Retention and Graduation: 7% grads go on to further study within 1 year. 7% grads pursue business degrees. **Faculty:** Student/faculty ratio 18:1. 21 full-time faculty, 48% hold PhDs, 38% are women.

ACADEMICS
Degrees: Associate, bachelor's, master's, terminal associate, transfer associate. **Classes:** Most classes have 20–29 students. **Majors with Highest Enrollment:** Accounting; accounting and business/management; sport and fitness administration/management. **Special Study Options:** Cross-registration, distance learning, double major, internships, study abroad, teacher certification program **Combined degree programs:** BS/MBA. **Career services:** Career assessment, internships.

FACILITIES
Housing: Coed dorms, residence halls are designated coed—male or female by floor or suite, not by building. 71% of campus accessible to physically disabled. **Computers:** Students can register for classes online. Administrative functions (other than registration) can be performed online.

CAMPUS LIFE
Environment: Rural. **Activities:** Choral groups, dance, drama/theater, student government, student newspaper, yearbook. **Organizations:** 26 registered organizations, 3 honor societies, 1 fraternities, 1 sororities. **Athletics (Intercollegiate):** *Men:* Baseball, basketball, golf, lacrosse, soccer, tennis. *Women:* Basketball, field hockey, lacrosse, soccer, softball, volleyball.

ADMISSIONS
Freshman Academic Profile: Average high school GPA 2.7. 7% in top 10% of high school class, 19% in top 25% of high school class, 54% in top 50% of high school class. SAT Math middle 50% range 390–510. SAT Critical Reading middle 50% range 400–500. SAT Writing middle 50% range 380–500. ACT middle 50% range 13–22. Minimum paper TOEFL 530. Minimum computer TOEFL 197. **Basis for Candidate Selection:** *Very important factors considered include:* Class rank, application essay, academic GPA, recommendation(s), rigor of secondary school record, standardized test scores. *Important factors considered include:* Character/personal qualities, extracurricular activities, interview. *Other factors considered include:* Alumni/ae relation, first generation, level of applicant's interest, talent/ability, volunteer work, work experience. **Freshman Admission Requirements:** High school diploma is required and GED is accepted. *Academic units recommended:* 4 English, 3 mathematics, 3 science, 2 foreign language, 2 social studies, 2 history. **Freshman Admission Statistics:** 668 applied, 81% admitted, 45% enrolled. **Transfer Admission Requirements:** High school transcript, college transcript(s), essay or personal statement, minimum college GPA of 2.0 required. Lowest grade transferable C. **General Admission Information:** Application fee $50. Notification on a rolling basis, beginning on or about 12/1. Nonfall registration accepted. Admission may be deferred for a maximum of 2 years. Credit and/or placement offered for CEEB Advanced Placement tests.

COSTS AND FINANCIAL AID
Annual tuition $17,280. Room and board $7,430. Required fees $450. Average book expense $800. **Required Forms and Deadlines:** FAFSA. Priority

financial aid filing date 2/15. **Notification of Awards:** Applicants will be notified of awards on a rolling basis beginning 3/15. **Types of Aid:** *Need-based scholarships/grants:* Federal Pell, SEOG, state scholarships/grants, private scholarships, the school's own gift aid. *Loans:* Direct Subsidized Stafford, Direct Unsubsidized Stafford, Direct PLUS, Federal Perkins. *Student Employment:* Federal Work-Study Program available. Institutional employment available. Off-campus job opportunities are excellent. **Financial Aid Statistics:** 96% freshmen, 90% undergrads receive need-based scholarship or grant aid. 30% freshmen, 17% undergrads receive non-need-based scholarship or grant aid. 86% freshmen, 82% undergrads receive need-based self-help aid. 95% freshmen, 90% undergrads receive any aid. 75% undergrads borrow to pay for school. Average cumulative indebtedness $38,734. **Criteria for awarding institutional aid:** *Non-need-based:* Academics.

THOMAS EDISON STATE COLLEGE

101 West State Street, Trenton, NJ 08608-1176
Phone: 888-442-8372 **Financial Aid Phone:** 609-633-9658
E-mail: admissions@tesc.edu **CEEB Code:** 2612
Fax: 609-984-8447 **Website:** www.tesc.edu **ACT Code:** 274872

This public school was founded in 1972. It has a 2-acre campus.

RATINGS
Admissions Selectivity Rating: 60*   **Fire Safety Rating:** 60*   **Green Rating:** 60*

STUDENTS AND FACULTY
Enrollment: 16,797. **Student Body:** 37% female, 63% male, 68% out-of-state, 2% international (74 countries represented). Asian 3%, African American 16%, Caucasian 60%, Hispanic 8%, Native American 1%.
Retention and Graduation: Faculty:

ACADEMICS
Degrees: Associate, bachelor's, certificate, master's, post-bachelor's certificate, post-master's certificate. **Majors with Highest Enrollment:** Business administration and management; liberal arts and sciences/liberal studies; nuclear engineering technology/technician. **Special Study Options:** Distance learning, dual enrollment, external degree program, independent study, Joint degree program with the University of Medicine and Dentistry of New Jersey for Bachelor of Science in Health Sciences. Graduates of associate degree and diploma programs of nursing may enroll for a BSN degree only (RN-BSN program), or both a BSN and a MSN degree (RN-BSN/MSN program) with preparation as a Nurse Educator at the Master's level. **Combined degree programs:** BSN/MSN. **Career services:** Alumni network.

FACILITIES
Housing: Thomas Edison State College serves adult students at a distance. The College doesn't own/operate any housing units and/or dorms. 97% of campus accessible to physically disabled. **Computers:** Students can register for classes online. Administrative functions (other than registration) can be performed online.

CAMPUS LIFE
Environment: City. **Activities: Organizations:** 3 honor societies, **On-Campus Highlights:** Prudence Townsend Kelsey Memorial Roo **Environmental Initiatives:** Only recycled paper to be used. Purchased hybrid vehicle for Vice Presidents to use. Adopted recycling programs.

ADMISSIONS
Freshman Academic Profile: Minimum paper TOEFL 500. Minimum computer TOEFL 173. **Freshman Admission Requirements:** High school diploma is required and GED is accepted. **Transfer Admission Requirements:** College transcript(s), Lowest grade transferable D. **General Admission Information:** Application fee $75. Credit offered for CEEB Advanced Placement tests.

COSTS AND FINANCIAL AID
Required Forms and Deadlines: FAFSA, institution's own financial aid form. **Types of Aid:** *Need-based scholarships/grants:* Federal Pell, state scholarships/grants, private scholarships *Loans:* FFEL Subsidized Stafford, FFEL Unsubsidized Stafford, FFEL PLUS, state loans, Private Educational Loans. **Financial Aid Statistics:** 11% undergrads receive any aid.

THOMAS JEFFERSON UNIVERSITY

130 South 9th Street, Suite 100, Philadelphia, PA 19107
Phone: 215-503-8890 **Financial Aid Phone:** 215 9552867
E-mail: jchp@jefferson.edu **CEEB Code:** 2903
Fax: 215-503-7241 **Website:** www.jefferson.edu/jchp

This private school was founded in 1967.

RATINGS
Admissions Selectivity Rating: 60*   **Fire Safety Rating:** 60*   **Green Rating:** 60*

STUDENTS AND FACULTY
Enrollment: 827. **Student Body:** 83% female, 17% male, 27% out-of-state, 1% international. Asian 8%, African American 9%, Caucasian 71%, Hispanic 3%.
Retention and Graduation: Faculty: Student/faculty ratio 14:1. 82 full-time faculty, 43% hold PhDs, 12% are members of minority groups, 85% are women.

ACADEMICS
Degrees: Associate, bachelor's, master's, post-bachelor's certificate, post-master's certificate, transfer associate. **Majors with Highest Enrollment:** Clinical laboratory science/medical technology/technologist; health services/allied health/health sciences; nursing/registered nurse (RN, ASN, BSN, MSN). **Special Study Options:** Accelerated program, distance learning, double major, independent study, internships, study abroad Special programs offered to physically disabled students include note-taking services, reader services, tutors. **Career services:** Alumni network, alumni services, career/job search classes, career assessment, regional alumni.

FACILITIES
Housing: Coed dorms, special housing for disabled students, apartments for married students, apartments for single students. 80% of campus accessible to physically disabled. **Special Academic Facilities/Equipment:** Copy of the famous Gross Clinic, new building with simulation labs. Located in the heart of Center City close to all historical sights as well as cultural events and museums. **Computers:** 100% of classrooms, 100% of dorms, 100% of libraries, have wireless network access. Students can register for classes online. Administrative functions (other than registration) can be performed online.

CAMPUS LIFE
Environment: Metropolis. **Activities:** Choral groups, student government, yearbook, international student organization. **On-Campus Highlights:** New Education and Research Building, famous painting called the Gross Clinic, close to historic sites, close to famous museums, many fine restaurants and theaters. Jefferson is located in Center City Philadelphia, near the Convention Center with many fine restaurants, shops, and other cultural sights.

ADMISSIONS
Freshman Academic Profile: Freshman Admission Requirements: High school diploma is required and GED is accepted. **Transfer Admission Requirements:** College transcript(s), essay or personal statement, statement of good standing from prior institution(s). Minimum college GPA of 2.5 required. Lowest grade transferable C. **General Admission Information:** Application fee $50. Notification on a rolling basis, beginning on or about 11/1. Nonfall registration accepted.

COSTS AND FINANCIAL AID
Annual tuition $23,685. Room and board $8,280. Required fees $400. Average book expense $1,495. **Required Forms and Deadlines:** FAFSA, institution's own financial aid form Financial aid filing deadline 5/1. **Types of Aid:** *Need-based scholarships/grants:* Federal Pell, SEOG, state scholarships/grants, private scholarships, the school's own gift aid, Federal Nursing Scholarships. *Loans:* Direct Subsidized Stafford, Direct Unsubsidized Stafford, FFEL Subsidized Stafford, FFEL Unsubsidized Stafford, FFEL PLUS, Federal Perkins, Federal Nursing, state loans, college/university loans from institutional funds. *Student Employment:* Federal Work-Study Program available. Institutional employment available. Off-campus job opportunities are excellent. **Financial Aid Statistics: Criteria for awarding institutional aid:** *Non-need-based:* Academics, leadership, state/district residency.

THOMAS MORE COLLEGE

333 Thomas More Pkwy, Crestview Hill, KY 41017-3495
Phone: 859-344-3332 **Financial Aid Phone:** 859-344-3319
E-mail: admissions@thomasmore.edu **CEEB Code:** 3892
Fax: 859-344-3444 **Website:** www.thomasmore.edu **ACT Code:** 1560

This private school, affiliated with the Roman Catholic Church, was founded in 1921. It has a 100-acre campus.

RATINGS
Admissions Selectivity Rating: 60*   **Fire Safety Rating:** 60*   **Green Rating:** 60*

STUDENTS AND FACULTY
Enrollment: 1,371. **Student Body:** 51% female, 49% male, 66% out-of-state, 1% international. Asian 1%, African American 5%, Caucasian 79%.
Retention and Graduation: 62% freshmen return for sophomore year. 39% freshmen graduate within 4 years. 25% grads go on to further study within 1 year. 44% grads pursue arts and sciences degrees. 6% grads pursue law degrees. 5% grads pursue business degrees. 5% grads pursue medical degrees. **Faculty:** Student/faculty ratio 15:1. 71 full-time faculty, 66% hold PhDs, 7% are members of minority groups, 39% are women.

ACADEMICS
Degrees: Associate, bachelor's, certificate, master's, terminal associate. **Classes:** Most classes have 10–19 students. Most lab/discussion sessions have 10–19 students. **Majors with Highest Enrollment:** Business/commerce; teacher education and professional development, specific subject areas, other. **Special Study Options:** Accelerated program, cooperative education program, cross-registration, double major, dual enrollment, English as a Second Language (ESL), honors program, independent study, internships, liberal arts/career combination, student-designed major, study abroad, teacher certification program, weekend college. **Honors programs:** Thomas More Honors Program. Special programs offered to physically disabled students include note-taking services, reader services, tape recorders, tutors.

FACILITIES
Housing: Coed dorms, men's dorms, women's dorms. 99% of campus accessible to physically disabled. **Computers:** Students can register for classes online. Administrative functions (other than registration) can be performed online.

CAMPUS LIFE
Environment: Village. **Activities:** Choral groups, drama/theater, literary magazine, student government, yearbook. **Organizations:** 29 registered organizations, 5 honor societies, 1 religious organizations. 1 fraternities, **Athletics (Intercollegiate):** *Men:* Baseball, basketball, cross-country, football, golf, soccer, tennis. *Women:* Basketball, cross-country, golf, soccer, softball, tennis, volleyball. **On-Campus Highlights:** Steigerwald Student Center, Connor Convocation Center (Athletic Center), Bank of KY Observatory at Thomas More College, Biology Field Station on the Ohio River, Murphy Hall.

ADMISSIONS
Freshman Academic Profile: Average high school GPA 2.88. 7% in top 10% of high school class, 31% in top 25% of high school class, 85% in top 50% of high school class. 69% from public high schools. SAT Math middle 50% range 460–600. SAT Critical Reading middle 50% range 460–580. ACT middle 50% range 19–24. Minimum paper TOEFL 515. Minimum computer TOEFL 187. **Basis for Candidate Selection:** *Very important factors considered include:* Rigor of secondary school record, standardized test scores. *Important factors considered include:* Class rank. *Other factors considered include:* Application essay, recommendation(s), character/personal qualities, extracurricular activities, interview, talent/ability, volunteer work. **Freshman Admission Requirements:** High school diploma is required and GED is accepted. *Academic units required:* 4 English, 3 mathematics, 3 science, (1 science labs), 2 foreign language, 3 social studies. *Academic units recommended:* 2 Arts AppreciationandComputer Literacy **Freshman Admission Statistics:** 1,363 applied, 61% admitted, 31% enrolled. **Transfer Admission Requirements:** College transcript(s), statement of good standing from prior institution(s). Minimum college GPA of 2.0 required. Lowest grade transferable C. **General Admission Information:** Application fee $25. Notification on a rolling basis, beginning on or about 3/15. Nonfall registration accepted. Admission may be deferred for a maximum of 1 year. Credit and/or placement offered for CEEB Advanced Placement tests.

COSTS AND FINANCIAL AID
Annual tuition $19,500. Room and board $5,400. Required fees $450. Average book expense $800. **Required Forms and Deadlines:** FAFSA, institution's own financial aid form. Priority financial aid filing date 3/15. **Notification of Awards:** Applicants will be notified of awards on a rolling basis beginning 3/1. **Types of Aid:** *Need-based scholarships/grants:* Federal Pell, SEOG, private scholarships, the school's own gift aid, United Negro College Fund *Loans:* FFEL Subsidized Stafford, FFEL Unsubsidized Stafford, FFEL PLUS, Federal Perkins, Federal Nursing, college/university loans from institutional funds. *Student Employment:* Highest amount earned per year from on-campus jobs $1,400. **Financial Aid Statistics:** 94% freshmen, 89% undergrads receive need-based scholarship or grant aid. 99% freshmen, 99% undergrads receive non-need-based scholarship or grant aid. 65% freshmen, 61% undergrads receive need-based self-help aid. 90% freshmen, 74% undergrads receive any aid. 62% undergrads borrow to pay for school. Average cumulative indebtedness $21,980. **Criteria for awarding institutional aid:** *Non-need-based:* Academics, alumni affiliation, art, job skills, leadership, minority status, music/drama, religious affiliation.

See page 1256.

THOMAS MORE COLLEGE OF LIBERAL ARTS

6 Manchester Street, Merrimack, NH 03054-4818
Phone: 603-880-8308
E-mail: admissions@thomasmorecollege.edu
Fax: 603-880-9280 **Website:** www.thomasmorecollege.edu **ACT Code:** 3892

This private school, affiliated with the Roman Catholic Church, was founded in 1978. It has a 13-acre campus.

RATINGS
Admissions Selectivity Rating: 75   **Fire Safety Rating:** 60*   **Green Rating:** 60*

STUDENTS AND FACULTY
Enrollment: 92. **Student Body:** 48% female, 52% male, 84% out-of-state, 4% international. Caucasian 52%, Hispanic 1%.
Retention and Graduation: 60% freshmen return for sophomore year. 52% grads go on to further study within 1 year. 48% grads pursue arts and sciences degrees. 8% grads pursue law degrees. 2% grads pursue business degrees. 2% grads pursue medical degrees. **Faculty:** Student/faculty ratio 12:1. 5 full-time faculty, 100% hold PhDs, 20% are women.

ACADEMICS
Degrees: Bachelor's. **Classes:** Most classes have 10–19 students. **Majors with Highest Enrollment:** Biology; business/commerce; computer and information sciences. **Special Study Options:** internships, study abroad, Spring semester in Rome for all sophomores.

FACILITIES
Housing: Men's dorms, women's dorms 70% of campus accessible to physically disabled.

CAMPUS LIFE
Environment: Village. **Activities:** Choral groups, drama/theater.

ADMISSIONS
Freshman Academic Profile: 12% from public high schools. **Basis for Candidate Selection:** *Very important factors considered include:* Application essay, recommendation(s), character/personal qualities, interview. *Important factors considered include:* talent/ability. *Other factors considered include:* Class rank, academic GPA, rigor of secondary school record, standardized test scores, extracurricular activities, level of applicant's interest, religious affiliation/commitment. **Freshman Admission Requirements:** High school diploma is required and GED is accepted. *Academic units required:* 4 English, 3 mathematics, 2 science, (2 science labs), 2 foreign language, 2 social studies, 2 history. *Academic units recommended:* 2 music, art. **Freshman Admission Statistics:** 75 applied, 55% admitted, 63% enrolled. **Transfer Admission Requirements:** College transcript(s), essay or personal statement, Lowest grade transferable C. **General Admission Information:** Notification on a rolling basis, beginning on or about 1/6. Nonfall registration accepted. Admission may be deferred for a maximum of n/a. Neither credit nor placement offered for CEEB Advanced Placement tests.

COSTS AND FINANCIAL AID
Annual tuition $11,100. Room and board $8,000. Average book expense $525. **Required Forms and Deadlines:** FAFSA. Priority financial aid filing date 4/15. **Notification of Awards:** Applicants will be notified of awards on a rolling basis beginning 3/15. **Types of Aid:** *Need-based scholarships/grants:* Federal Pell, SEOG, state scholarships/grants, private scholarships, the school's own gift aid. *Loans:* FFEL Subsidized Stafford, FFEL Unsubsidized Stafford, FFEL PLUS. *Student Employment:* Off-campus job opportunities are good. **Financial Aid Statistics:** 74% freshmen, 69% undergrads receive need-based scholarship or grant aid. 97% freshmen, 74% undergrads receive non-need-based scholarship or grant aid. 52% freshmen, 42% undergrads receive need-based self-help

aid. 79% undergrads borrow to pay for school. Average cumulative indebtedness $22,555. **Criteria for awarding institutional aid:** *Non-need-based:* Academics.

THOMPSON RIVERS UNIVERISTY

TRU Admissions, P.O. Box 3010, Kamloops, BC V2C 5N3 Canada
Phone: 250-828-5071
E-mail: admissions@tru.ca
Fax: 250-371-5513 **Website:** www.tru.ca

This public school was founded in 1970. It has a 200-acre campus.

RATINGS
Admissions Selectivity Rating: 60*   Fire Safety Rating: 60*   Green Rating: 60*

STUDENTS AND FACULTY
Enrollment: 4,497. **Student Body:** 61% female, 39% male, 15% out-of-state (43 countries represented).
Retention and Graduation: Faculty: Student/faculty ratio 20:1. 375 full-time faculty, 28% hold PhDs.

ACADEMICS
Degrees: Associate, bachelor's, certificate, diploma, master's, post-bachelor's certificate, terminal associate, transfer associate. **Classes:** Most classes have 20–29 students. Most lab/discussion sessions have 10–19 students. **Special Study Options:** Accelerated program, cooperative education program, distance learning, double major, English as a Second Language (ESL), external degree program, honors program, independent study, internships, liberal arts/career combination, study abroad, teacher certification program Special programs offered to physically disabled students include note-taking services, reader services, tape recorders, tutors. **Career services:** Alumni network, career/job search classes, career assessment

FACILITIES
Housing: 95% of campus accessible to physically disabled. **Computers:** Students can register for classes online. Administrative functions (other than registration) can be performed online.

CAMPUS LIFE
Activities: literary magazine, student government **Organizations:** 5 religious organizations. **Athletics (Intercollegiate):** *Men:* Baseball, basketball, soccer, volleyball. *Women:* Basketball, soccer, volleyball.

ADMISSIONS
Freshman Academic Profile: 95% from public high schools. **Basis for Candidate Selection:** *Very important factors considered include:* Rigor of secondary school record. *Important factors considered include:* Standardized test scores. *Other factors considered include:* Recommendation(s), character/personal qualities, interview, racial/ethnic status, talent/ability, volunteer work, work experience. **Transfer Admission Requirements:** High school transcript, college transcript(s), **General Admission Information:** Application fee $60. Regular application deadline 3/1. Notification on a rolling basis, beginning on or about 10/1. Nonfall registration accepted. Admission may be deferred for a maximum of 1 Year. Neither credit nor placement offered for CEEB Advanced Placement tests.

COSTS AND FINANCIAL AID
Room and board $2,100. Required fees $200. Average book expense $1,000. *Student Employment:* Off-campus job opportunities are good.

THOPMSON RIVERS UNIVERSITY— OPEN LEARNING

Student Services, Box 82080, Burnaby, BC V5C 6J8 Canada
Phone: 604-431-3300
E-mail: admissions@tru.ca
Fax: 604-431-3444 **Website:** www.bcou.ca

This is a public school.

RATINGS
Admissions Selectivity Rating: 60*   Fire Safety Rating: 60*   Green Rating: 60*

ACADEMICS
Degrees: Associate, bachelor's, certificate. **Majors with Highest Enrollment:** Business, management, marketing, and related support services, other; communication, journalism, and related programs, other; computer and information sciences and support services, other.

TIFFIN UNIVERSITY

155 Miami Street, Tiffin, OH 44883
Phone: 419-448-3423 **Financial Aid Phone:** 419-448-3415
E-mail: admiss@tiffin.edu **CEEB Code:** 1817
Fax: Website: www.tiffin.edu **ACT Code:** 3334

This private school was founded in 1888. It has a 110-acre campus.

RATINGS
Admissions Selectivity Rating: 75   Fire Safety Rating: 67   Green Rating: 68

STUDENTS AND FACULTY
Enrollment: 2,277. **Student Body:** 55% female, 45% male, 29% out-of-state, 3% international (19 countries represented). Asian 1%, African American 19%, Caucasian 57%, Hispanic 3%.
Retention and Graduation: 62% freshmen return for sophomore year. 37% freshmen graduate within 4 years. 25% grads go on to further study within 1 year. **Faculty:** Student/faculty ratio 18.5:1. 66 full-time faculty, 67% hold PhDs, 12% are members of minority groups, 48% are women.

ACADEMICS
Degrees: Associate, bachelor's, certificate, master's, post-bachelor's certificate. **Classes:** Most classes have fewer than 10 students. Most lab/discussion sessions have fewer than 10 students. **Majors with Highest Enrollment:** Business administration and management; forensic science and technology; marketing/marketing management. **Special Study Options:** Accelerated program, cross-registration, distance learning, double major, dual enrollment, English as a Second Language (ESL), honors program, independent study, internships, study abroad, teacher certification program. **Honors programs:** We offer a Freshman Honors Program. **Career services:** Alumni network, alumni services, career/job search classes, career assessment, internships, regional alumni.

FACILITIES
Housing: Coed dorms, special housing for disabled students, men's dorms, special housing for international students, women's dorms, fraternity/sorority housing, apartments for married students, theme housing. 85% of campus accessible to physically disabled. **Special Academic Facilities/Equipment:** University Art Gallery, multimedia lab. **Computers:** 100% of classrooms, 25% of dorms, 100% of libraries, 100% of dining areas, 100% of student union, have wireless network access. Students can register for classes online. Administrative functions (other than registration) can be performed online.

CAMPUS LIFE
Environment: Village. **Activities:** Choral groups, concert band, dance, drama/theater, jazz band, literary magazine, marching band, music ensembles, musical theater, pep band, student government, student newspaper, campus ministries, international student organization. **Organizations:** 32 registered organizations, 1 honor societies, 2 religious organizations. 3 fraternities, 3 sororities. **Athletics (Intercollegiate):** *Men:* Baseball, basketball, cheerleading, cross-country, equestrian sports, football, golf, soccer, tennis, track/field (outdoor), track/field (indoor). *Women:* Basketball, cheerleading, cross-country, equestrian sports, golf, lacrosse, soccer, softball, tennis, track/field (outdoor), track/field (indoor), volleyball. **On-Campus Highlights:** Gillmor Student Center, Hayes Center for the Arts, Hertzer Technology Center, Main Classroom Building, Franks Hall. **Environmental Initiatives:** Establishment of a Green Committee. All future buildings will be considered for LEED certification (silver level). Paper recycling program has been implemented at the University along with a trayless program in the dining hall.

ADMISSIONS
Freshman Academic Profile: Average high school GPA 3.05. 75% from public high schools. SAT Math middle 50% range 433–528. SAT Critical Reading middle 50% range 430–528. ACT middle 50% range 18–23. Minimum paper TOEFL 500. Minimum web-based TOEFL 61. **Basis for Candidate Selection:** *Very important factors considered include:* Academic GPA, rigor of secondary school record, standardized test scores. *Important factors considered include:* Class rank, application essay, recommendation(s), extracurricular activities, geographical residence, state residency. *Other factors considered include:* Alumni/ae relation, character/personal qualities, first generation, interview, level of applicant's interest, racial/ethnic status, talent/ability, volunteer work. **Fresh-**

man Admission Requirements: High school diploma is required and GED is accepted. *Academic units required:* 4 English, 3 mathematics, 3 science, 3 social studies. *Academic units recommended:* 2 foreign language. **Freshman Admission Statistics:** 3,526 applied, 60% admitted, 32% enrolled. **Transfer Admission Requirements:** High school transcript, college transcript(s), minimum college GPA of 2.0 required. Lowest grade transferable C. **General Admission Information:** Application fee $20. Notification on a rolling basis, beginning on or about 9/15. Nonfall registration accepted. Credit offered for CEEB Advanced Placement tests.

COSTS AND FINANCIAL AID
Annual tuition $18,390. Room and board $8,340. Average book expense $1,500. **Required Forms and Deadlines:** FAFSA **Notification of Awards:** Applicants will be notified of awards on a rolling basis beginning 1/15. **Types of Aid:** *Need-based scholarships/grants:* Federal Pell, SEOG, state scholarships/grants, private scholarships, the school's own gift aid. *Loans:* Direct Subsidized Stafford, Direct Unsubsidized Stafford, Direct PLUS, FFEL Subsidized Stafford, FFEL Unsubsidized Stafford, FFEL PLUS, Federal Perkins, college/university loans from institutional funds. *Student Employment:* Federal Work-Study Program available. Institutional employment available. Highest amount earned per year from on-campus jobs $1,600. Off-campus job opportunities are good. **Financial Aid Statistics:** 70% freshmen, 63% undergrads receive need-based scholarship or grant aid. 66% freshmen, 53% undergrads receive non-need-based scholarship or grant aid. 90% freshmen, 80% undergrads receive need-based self-help aid. 2% freshmen, 2% undergrads receive athletic scholarships. 98% freshmen, 86% undergrads receive any aid. 82% undergrads borrow to pay for school. Average cumulative indebtedness $26,345. **Criteria for awarding institutional aid:** *Non-need-based:* Academics, alumni affiliation, athletics, music/drama, state/district residency.

TOCCOA FALLS COLLEGE

Toccoa Falls College, Office of Admissions, Toccoa Falls, GA 30598
Phone: 888-785-5624 **Financial Aid Phone:** 706-886-6831
E-mail: admissions@tfc.edu
Fax: 706-282-6012 **Website:** www.tfc.edu **ACT Code:** 0868

This private school, affiliated with the Christian & Missionary Allianc Church, was founded in 1907. It has a 1100-acre campus.

RATINGS
Admissions Selectivity Rating: 81   **Fire Safety Rating:** 61   **Green Rating:** 60*

STUDENTS AND FACULTY
Enrollment: 858. **Student Body:** 54% female, 46% male, 46% out-of-state, 1% international. Asian 8%, African American 3%, Caucasian 86%, Hispanic 2%.
Retention and Graduation: 60% freshmen return for sophomore year. 46% freshmen graduate within 4 years. **Faculty:** Student/faculty ratio 17:1. 47 full-time faculty, 57% hold PhDs, 4% are members of minority groups, 21% are women.

ACADEMICS
Degrees: Associate, bachelor's, certificate. **Classes:** Most classes have fewer than 10 students. **Majors with Highest Enrollment:** Counseling psychology; elementary education and teaching; missions/missionary studies and missiology. **Special Study Options:** Distance learning, double major, dual enrollment, independent study, internships, teacher certification program Special programs offered to physically disabled students include note-taking services, reader services, tutors. **Career services:** Career assessment

FACILITIES
Housing: Men's dorms, special housing for international students, women's dorms, apartments for married students, mobile home court living available for married students. 70% of campus accessible to physically disabled. **Computers:** 40% of classrooms, 50% of dorms, 100% of libraries, 100% of dining areas, 50% of student union, 1% of common outdoor areas have wireless network access. Students can register for classes online. Administrative functions (other than registration) can be performed online.

CAMPUS LIFE
Environment: Rural. **Activities:** Choral groups, concert band, drama/theater, jazz band, music ensembles, radio station, student government, student newspaper, yearbook, campus ministries. **Athletics (Intercollegiate):** *Men:* Baseball, basketball, cross-country, golf, soccer, tennis. *Women:* Basketball, cheerleading, cross-country, golf, soccer, tennis, volleyball. **On-Campus Highlights:** The Waterfall, Student Center, Gymnatorium, Eagle's Nest, Grace Chapel & Performing Arts Center.

ADMISSIONS
Freshman Academic Profile: Average high school GPA 3.4. 12% in top 10% of high school class, 38% in top 25% of high school class, 70% in top 50% of high school class. 57% from public high schools. SAT Math middle 50% range 430–550. SAT Critical Reading middle 50% range 460–570. ACT middle 50% range 18–25. Minimum paper TOEFL 500. Minimum computer TOEFL 173. **Basis for Candidate Selection:** *Very important factors considered include:* Application essay, academic GPA, recommendation(s), rigor of secondary school record, standardized test scores, character/personal qualities, religious affiliation/commitment, *Other factors considered include:* Extracurricular activities, interview, level of applicant's interest, talent/ability, volunteer work, work experience. **Freshman Admission Requirements:** High school diploma is required and GED is accepted. *Academic units recommended:* 4 English, 3 mathematics, 3 science, (2 science labs), 3 social studies, 6 academic electives. **Freshman Admission Statistics:** 1,188 applied, 45% admitted, 31% enrolled. **Transfer Admission Requirements:** College transcript(s), essay or personal statement, minimum college GPA of 2.0 required. Lowest grade transferable C–. **General Admission Information:** Application fee $20. Regular application deadline 8/1. Regular notification 3/1. Nonfall registration accepted. Admission may be deferred for a maximum of 2 years. Credit and/or placement offered for CEEB Advanced Placement tests.

COSTS AND FINANCIAL AID
Annual tuition $15,450. Room and board $5,650. Required fees $125. Average book expense $1,000. **Required Forms and Deadlines:** FAFSA, institution's own financial aid form, state aid form. Priority financial aid filing date 5/1. **Notification of Awards:** Applicants will be notified of awards on a rolling basis beginning 3/1. **Types of Aid:** *Need-based scholarships/grants:* Federal Pell, SEOG, state scholarships/grants, private scholarships, the school's own gift aid. *Loans:* FFEL Subsidized Stafford, FFEL Unsubsidized Stafford, FFEL PLUS, Federal Perkins, state loans, college/university loans from institutional funds. *Student Employment:* Highest amount earned per year from on-campus jobs $6,000. **Financial Aid Statistics:** 35% freshmen, 43% undergrads receive need-based scholarship or grant aid. 76% freshmen, 83% undergrads receive non-need-based scholarship or grant aid. 16% freshmen, 13% undergrads receive need-based self-help aid. 100% freshmen, 98% undergrads receive any aid. 78% undergrads borrow to pay for school. Average cumulative indebtedness $6,284. **Criteria for awarding institutional aid:** *Non-need-based:* Academics, alumni affiliation, leadership, music/drama, religious affiliation, state/district residency.

TOUGALOO COLLEGE

500 West Country Line Road, Tougaloo, MS 39174
Phone: 888-424-2566 **Financial Aid Phone:** 601-977-7769
E-mail: jjacobs@mail.tougaloo.edu
Fax: 601-977-6185 **Website:** tougaloo.edu

This private school, affiliated with the Church of Christ Church, was founded in 1869. It has a 500-acre campus.

RATINGS
Admissions Selectivity Rating: 60*   **Fire Safety Rating:** 84   **Green Rating:** 60*

STUDENTS AND FACULTY
Enrollment: 967. **Student Body:** 72% female, 28% male, 18% out-of-state, (3 countries represented). African American 99%.
Retention and Graduation: 70% freshmen return for sophomore year. 63% freshmen graduate within 4 years. 69% grads go on to further study within 1 year. 50% grads pursue arts and sciences degrees. 20% grads pursue law degrees. 10% grads pursue business degrees. 20% grads pursue medical degrees. **Faculty:** Student/faculty ratio 15:1. 78 full-time faculty, 60% hold PhDs, 55% are members of minority groups, 51% are women.

ACADEMICS
Degrees: Associate, bachelor's, certificate, terminal associate, transfer associate. **Classes:** Most classes have 20–29 students. Most lab/discussion sessions have 10–19 students. **Special Study Options:** Cooperative education program, cross-registration, double major, dual enrollment, exchange student program (domestic), honors program, independent study, internships, liberal arts/career combination, study abroad, teacher certification program. **Honors programs:** There is a general Honors Program **Combined degree programs:** Nursing with Univ. of MS Medical School. Special programs offered to physically disabled students include tape recorders, tutors. **Career services:** Alumni network, alumni services, career/job search classes, career assessment, internships.

FACILITIES

Housing: Men's dorms, women's dorms. 70% of campus accessible to physically disabled. **Special Academic Facilities/Equipment:** Tougaloo Art Collections, Bailey-Ward Black Collection **Computers:** Students can register for classes online. Administrative functions (other than registration) can be performed online.

CAMPUS LIFE

Environment: City. **Activities:** Choral groups, dance, drama/theater, jazz band, literary magazine, music ensembles, student government, student newspaper, television station, yearbook. **Organizations:** 50 registered organizations, 2 honor societies, 7 religious organizations. 4 fraternities, 4 sororities. **Athletics (Intercollegiate):** Men: Baseball, basketball, cross-country, golf, tennis, track/field (outdoor). Women: Basketball, cross-country, golf, softball, tennis, track/field (outdoor). **On-Campus Highlights:** Woodworth Chapel, L. Zenobia Coleman Library and Archives, Warren Hall Student Center, Owens Health and Wellness Center, Blackmon Administration Center.

ADMISSIONS

Freshman Academic Profile: Average high school GPA 3.2. 95% from public high schools. ACT middle 50% range 16–21. Minimum paper TOEFL 500. Minimum computer TOEFL 200. **Basis for Candidate Selection:** Important factors considered include: Recommendation(s), rigor of secondary school record, standardized test scores, character/personal qualities, talent/ability. Other factors considered include: Class rank, application essay, alumni/ae relation, extracurricular activities, interview. **Freshman Admission Requirements:** High school diploma is required and GED is accepted. Academic units required: 3 English, 2 mathematics, 2 science, 1 social studies, 1 history, 7 academic electives. Academic units recommended: 4 English, 3 mathematics, 3 science, 2 foreign language, 2 social studies, 2 history, 7 academic electives. **Transfer Admission Requirements:** College transcript(s), standardized test scores, statement of good standing from prior institution(s). Minimum college GPA of 2.0 required. Lowest grade transferable C. **General Admission Information:** Application fee $25. Notification on a rolling basis, beginning on or about 10/15. Nonfall registration accepted. Admission may be deferred for a maximum of 1 semester. Credit and/or placement offered for CEEB Advanced Placement tests.

COSTS AND FINANCIAL AID

Annual tuition $9,240. Room and board $6,330. Required fees $470. Average book expense $1,200. **Required Forms and Deadlines:** FAFSA, institution's own financial aid form, CSS/Financial Aid PROFILE. **Notification of Awards:** Applicants will be notified of awards on a rolling basis beginning 10/15. **Types of Aid:** Need-based scholarships/grants: Federal Pell, SEOG, state scholarships/grants, private scholarships, the school's own gift aid, United Negro College Fund. Loans: Direct Subsidized Stafford, Direct PLUS, FFEL Unsubsidized Stafford, Federal Perkins, Federal Nursing. Student Employment: Federal Work-Study Program available. Highest amount earned per year from on-campus jobs $2,800. Off-campus job opportunities are excellent. **Financial Aid Statistics:** 96% freshmen, 88% undergrads receive need-based scholarship or grant aid. 15% undergrads receive non-need-based scholarship or grant aid. 20% undergrads receive need-based self-help aid. 1% undergrads receive athletic scholarships. 95% freshmen, 95% undergrads receive any aid. 85% undergrads borrow to pay for school. Average cumulative indebtedness $8,000. **Criteria for awarding institutional aid:** Non-need-based: Academics, art, athletics, leadership, music/drama.

TOWSON UNIVERSITY

8000 York Road, Towson, MD 21252-0001
Phone: 410-704-2113 **Financial Aid Phone:** 410-704-4236
E-mail: admissions@towson.edu **CEEB Code:** 5404
Fax: 410-704-3030 **Website:** www.towson.edu **ACT Code:** 1718

This public school was founded in 1866. It has a 328-acre campus.

RATINGS

Admissions Selectivity Rating: 80   **Fire Safety Rating:** 95   **Green Rating:** 84

STUDENTS AND FACULTY

Enrollment: 16,598. **Student Body:** 60% female, 40% male, 17.8% out-of-state, 3% international (94 countries represented). Asian 4%, African American 12%, Caucasian 68%, Hispanic 3%.
Retention and Graduation: 46% freshmen graduate within 4 years. **Faculty:** Student/faculty ratio 17:1. 822 full-time faculty, 74% hold PhDs, 14% are members of minority groups, 53% are women.

ACADEMICS

Degrees: Bachelor's, master's, post-bachelor's certificate, post-master's certificate. **Classes:** Most classes have 20–29 students. Most lab/discussion sessions

have 10–19 students. **Majors with Highest Enrollment:** Business administration, management and operations, other; elementary education and teaching; social sciences. **Special Study Options:** Cooperative education program, cross-registration, distance learning, double major, dual enrollment, English as a Second Language (ESL), exchange student program (domestic), honors program, independent study, internships, liberal arts/career combination, student-designed major, study abroad, teacher certification program. **Honors programs:** Honors College Special programs offered to physically disabled students include note-taking services, reader services. **Career services:** Alumni network, alumni services, career/job search classes, career assessment, internships, regional alumni. **Career services highlights include:** Internships.

FACILITIES

Housing: Coed dorms, special housing for disabled students, special housing for international students, apartments for single students. 80% of campus accessible to physically disabled. **Special Academic Facilities/Equipment:** Art galleries, animal museum, Asian art collection, elementary school, media center, speech/language clinic, planetarium/observatory, herbarium, electron microscope, argon laser. **Computers:** 100% of classrooms, 100% of dorms, 100% of libraries, 100% of dining areas, 100% of student union, 100% of common outdoor areas have wireless network access. Students can register for classes online. Administrative functions (other than registration) can be performed online.

CAMPUS LIFE

Environment: Metropolis. **Activities:** Choral groups, concert band, dance, drama/theater, jazz band, literary magazine, marching band, music ensembles, musical theater, pep band, radio station, student government, student newspaper, symphony orchestra, television station, yearbook, campus ministries, international student organization. **Organizations:** 198 registered organizations, 15 honor societies, 12 religious organizations. 12 fraternities, 10 sororities. **Athletics (Intercollegiate):** Men: Baseball, basketball, cheerleading, cross-country, diving, football, golf, lacrosse, soccer, swimming, tennis. Women: Basketball, cheerleading, cross-country, diving, field hockey, gymnastics, lacrosse, soccer, softball, swimming, tennis, track/field (outdoor), volleyball. **On-Campus Highlights:** Johnny Unitas Stadium, University Union, Burdick Hall—athletic facilities, The Den, Towson Center—events. **Environmental Initiatives:** RecycleMania; Stream Clean-Up; Earth Week Plus.

ADMISSIONS

Freshman Academic Profile: Average high school GPA 3.55. 9.2% in top 10% of high school class, 22.6% in top 25% of high school class, 40.3% in top 50% of high school class. SAT Math middle 50% range 490–590. SAT Critical Reading middle 50% range 490–580. SAT Writing middle 50% range 500–580. ACT middle 50% range 21–24. Minimum paper TOEFL 500. Minimum computer TOEFL 173. Minimum web-based TOEFL 61. **Basis for Candidate Selection:** Very important factors considered include: Academic GPA. Important factors considered include: Rigor of secondary school record, standardized test scores. Other factors considered include: Class rank, application essay, recommendation(s), first generation, talent/ability. **Freshman Admission Requirements:** High school diploma is required and GED is accepted. Academic units required: 4 English, 3 mathematics, 3 science, (2 science labs), 2 foreign language, 3 social studies, 6 academic electives. **Freshman Admission Statistics:** 15,423 applied, 63% admitted, 25% enrolled. **Transfer Admission Requirements:** College transcript(s), minimum college GPA of 2.0 required. Lowest grade transferable D. **General Admission Information:** Application fee $45. Regular application deadline 2/15. Notification on a rolling basis, beginning on or about 10/15. Nonfall registration accepted. Admission may be deferred for a maximum of Up to 1 year. Credit and/or placement offered for CEEB Advanced Placement tests.

COSTS AND FINANCIAL AID

Annual in-state tuition $5,180. Annual out-of-state tuition $15,994. Room and board $8,670. Required fees $2,238. Average book expense $984. **Required Forms and Deadlines:** FAFSA. Priority financial aid filing date 2/10. **Notification of Awards:** Applicants will be notified of awards on a rolling basis beginning 3/21. **Types of Aid:** Need-based scholarships/grants: Federal Pell, SEOG, state scholarships/grants, private scholarships, the school's own gift aid. Loans: Direct Subsidized Stafford, Direct Unsubsidized Stafford, Direct PLUS, Federal Perkins. Student Employment: Federal Work-Study Program available. Institutional employment available. Off-campus job opportunities are excellent. **Financial Aid Statistics:** 32% freshmen, 31% undergrads receive need-based scholarship or grant aid. 22% freshmen, 13% undergrads receive non-need-based scholarship or grant aid. 38% freshmen, 34% undergrads receive need-based self-help aid. 1% undergrads receive athletic scholarships. 76% freshmen, 68% undergrads receive any aid. 23% undergrads borrow to pay for school. Average cumulative indebtedness $13,245. **Criteria for awarding institutional aid:** Non-need-based: Academics, art, athletics, music/drama.

TRANSYLVANIA UNIVERSITY

Best 373

300 North Broadway, Lexington, KY 40508-1797
Phone: 859-233-8242 **Financial Aid Phone:** 859-233-8239
E-mail: admissions@transy.edu **CEEB Code:** 1808
Fax: 859-281-3649 **Website:** www.transy.edu **ACT Code:** 1550

This private school, affiliated with the Christian (Nondenominational) Church, was founded in 1780. It has a 36-acre campus.

RATINGS
Admissions Selectivity Rating: 86   **Fire Safety Rating:** 83   **Green Rating:** 72

STUDENTS AND FACULTY
Enrollment: 1,154. **Student Body:** 60% female, 40% male, 18% out-of-state, international (3 countries represented). Asian 2%, African American 3%, Caucasian 83%, Hispanic 1%.
Retention and Graduation: 84% freshmen return for sophomore year. 63% freshmen graduate within 4 years. 41% grads go on to further study within 1 year. 11% grads pursue arts and sciences degrees. 6% grads pursue law degrees. 2% grads pursue business degrees. 4% grads pursue medical degrees. **Faculty:** Student/faculty ratio 12.6:1. 85 full-time faculty, 92% hold PhDs, 7% are members of minority groups, 39% are women.

ACADEMICS
Degrees: Bachelor's. **Classes:** Most classes have 10–19 students. Most lab/discussion sessions have 10–19 students. **Majors with Highest Enrollment:** Biology/biological sciences; business/commerce; psychology. **Special Study Options:** Double major, independent study, internships, liberal arts/career combination, student-designed major, study abroad, teacher certification program Special programs offered to physically disabled students include note-taking services, reader services, tape recorders, tutors. **Career services:** Alumni network, alumni services, career/job search classes, career assessment, internships, regional alumni. **Career services highlights include:** Internship Programs.

FACILITIES
Housing: Coed dorms, special housing for disabled students, men's dorms, women's dorms, apartments for single students, theme housing, efficiency apartment option for upperclassmen. Units with facilities for disabled students. 90% of campus accessible to physically disabled. **Special Academic Facilities/Equipment:** Art gallery, museum of early scientific apparatus, medical museum, language lab, transmission electron microscope. **Computers:** 20% of classrooms, 20% of dorms, 75% of libraries, 20% of dining areas, 100% of student union, 10% of common outdoor areas have wireless network access. Administrative functions (other than registration) can be performed online.

CAMPUS LIFE
Environment: City. **Activities:** Choral groups, concert band, dance, drama/theater, jazz band, literary magazine, music ensembles, musical theater, opera, pep band, radio station, student government, student newspaper, yearbook. **Organizations:** 55 registered organizations, 10 honor societies, 7 religious organizations. 4 fraternities, 4 sororities. **Athletics (Intercollegiate):** *Men:* Baseball, basketball, cheerleading, cross-country, diving, golf, soccer, swimming, tennis, track/field (outdoor). *Women:* Basketball, cheerleading, cross-country, diving, field hockey, golf, soccer, softball, swimming, tennis, track/field (outdoor), volleyball. **On-Campus Highlights:** Beck Athletic and Recreation Center, William T. Young Campus Center, Mitchell Fine Arts Center, Little Theater, 1780 Cafe. **Environmental Initiatives:** All campus education initiatives including RecycleMania. Developing climate action plan. Developed all-campus Energy Star purchase requirement for equipment.

ADMISSIONS
Freshman Academic Profile: Average high school GPA 3.66. 40% in top 10% of high school class, 66% in top 25% of high school class, 91% in top 50% of high school class. 79% from public high schools. SAT Math middle 50% range 530–640. SAT Critical Reading middle 50% range 530–640. ACT middle 50% range 24–29. Minimum paper TOEFL 550. Minimum computer TOEFL 213. **Basis for Candidate Selection:** *Very important factors considered include:* Academic GPA, rigor of secondary school record, standardized test scores. *Important factors considered include:* Application essay, recommendation(s), extracurricular activities. *Other factors considered include:* Class rank, alumni/ae relation, character/personal qualities, first generation, geographical residence, interview, talent/ability, volunteer work, work experience. **Freshman Admission Requirements:** High school diploma is required and GED is accepted. *Academic units required:* 4 English, 3 mathematics, 3 science, 2 social studies.

Academic units recommended: 4 English, 4 mathematics, 4 science, (2 science labs), 2 foreign language, 2 social studies, 1 history, 1 academic electives. **Freshman Admission Statistics:** 1,334 applied, 80% admitted, 30% enrolled. **Transfer Admission Requirements:** High school transcript, college transcript(s), essay or personal statement, minimum college GPA of 2.75 required. Lowest grade transferable C–. **General Admission Information:** Application fee $30. Regular application deadline 2/1. Regular notification 3/1. Nonfall registration accepted. Admission may be deferred for a maximum of 1 year. Credit and/or placement offered for CEEB Advanced Placement tests.

COSTS AND FINANCIAL AID
Annual tuition $24,250. Room and board $7,770. Required fees $1,030. Average book expense $1,000. **Required Forms and Deadlines:** FAFSA. Priority financial aid filing date 3/1. **Notification of Awards:** Applicants will be notified of awards on a rolling basis beginning 3/15. **Types of Aid:** *Need-based scholarships/grants:* Federal Pell, SEOG, state scholarships/grants, private scholarships, the school's own gift aid. *Loans:* FFEL Subsidized Stafford, FFEL Unsubsidized Stafford, FFEL PLUS, Federal Perkins, college/university loans from institutional funds. *Student Employment:* Federal Work-Study Program available. Institutional employment available. Off-campus job opportunities are excellent. **Financial Aid Statistics:** 69% freshmen, 64% undergrads receive need-based scholarship or grant aid. 12% freshmen, 9% undergrads receive non-need-based scholarship or grant aid. 51% freshmen, 51% undergrads receive need-based self-help aid. 99% freshmen, 98% undergrads receive any aid. 63.6% undergrads borrow to pay for school. Average cumulative indebtedness $17,885. **Criteria for awarding institutional aid:** *Non-need-based:* Academics, art, leadership, minority status, music/drama, religious affiliation, state/district residency.

See page 1258.

TRENT UNIVERSITY

Registrar's Office, 1600 West Bank Dr, Trent University, Peterborough, ON K9J 7B8 Canada
Phone: 705-748-1011 x 7410
E-mail: jclee@trentu.ca
Fax: 705-748-1629 **Website:** www.trentu.ca

This is a public school.

RATINGS
Admissions Selectivity Rating: 60*   **Fire Safety Rating:** 60*   **Green Rating:** 60*

ACADEMICS
Degrees: Bachelor's, diploma, doctoral, master's, transfer associate. **Classes:** **Special Study Options:** Accelerated program, double major, English as a Second Language (ESL), exchange student program (domestic), honors program, liberal arts/career combination, student-designed major, study abroad, teacher certification program.

FACILITIES
Housing: Coed dorms, special housing for disabled students, women's dorms, apartments for married students, apartments for single students, theme housing.

CAMPUS LIFE
Activities: Choral groups, dance, drama/theater, jazz band, literary magazine, radio station, student government, student newspaper, student-run film society, yearbook, international student organization, Model UN. **Organizations:**

ADMISSIONS
Transfer Admission Requirements: High school transcript, college transcript(s), minimum college GPA of 2.65 required. Lowest grade transferable C.

COSTS AND FINANCIAL AID
Annual in-state tuition $5,000. Average book expense $1,000. **Required Forms and Deadlines:** institution's own financial aid form, OSAP. Financial aid filing deadline 3/1. Priority financial aid filing date 3/1. **Types of Aid:** *Need-based scholarships/grants:* State scholarships/grants, private scholarships, the school's own gift aid. *Loans:* college/university loans from institutional funds. **Criteria for awarding institutional aid:** *Non-need-based:* Academics.

TREVECCA NAZARENE UNIVERSITY

333 Murfreesboro Road, Nashville, TN 37210
Phone: 615-248-1320 **Financial Aid Phone:** 615-248-1242
E-mail: admissions_und@trevecca.edu
Fax: 615-248-7406 **Website: ACT Code:** 4016

This private school, affiliated with the Nazarene Church, was founded in 1901. It has a 65-acre campus.

RATINGS
Admissions Selectivity Rating: 79   **Fire Safety Rating:** 60*   **Green Rating:** 60*

STUDENTS AND FACULTY
Enrollment: 1,234. **Student Body:** 55% female, 45% male, 37% out-of-state, 1% international (12 countries represented). Asian 1%, African American 7%, Caucasian 83%, Hispanic 3%.
Retention and Graduation: 71% freshmen return for sophomore year. 37% freshmen graduate within 4 years. **Faculty:** Student/faculty ratio 12:1. 87 full-time faculty, 83% hold PhDs, 8% are members of minority groups, 31% are women.

ACADEMICS
Degrees: Associate, bachelor's, master's. **Classes:** Most classes have 10–19 students. **Majors with Highest Enrollment:** Business administration and management; elementary education and teaching; religion/religious studies. **Special Study Options:** Double major, internships, study abroad, teacher certification program, four adult degree-completion programs offer non-traditional class schedules (night/on-line). Special programs offered to physically disabled students include note-taking services, reader services, tutors. **Career services:** Career/job search classes, internships.

FACILITIES
Housing: Men's dorms, women's dorms, apartments for married students, apartments for single students. **Computers:** 100% of classrooms, 100% of dorms, 100% of libraries, 100% of dining areas, 100% of student union, 100% of common outdoor areas have wireless network access. Administrative functions (other than registration) can be performed online.

CAMPUS LIFE
Environment: Metropolis. **Activities:** Choral groups, concert band, drama/theater, jazz band, literary magazine, marching band, music ensembles, musical theater, pep band, radio station, student government, student newspaper, symphony orchestra, television station, yearbook, campus ministries, international student organization. **Athletics (Intercollegiate):** *Men:* Baseball, basketball, golf, soccer. *Women:* Basketball, golf, soccer, softball, volleyball. **On-Campus Highlights:** Library, Student Center.

ADMISSIONS
Freshman Academic Profile: Average high school GPA 3.17. 17% in top 10% of high school class, 39% in top 25% of high school class, 68% in top 50% of high school class. SAT Math middle 50% range 420–570. SAT Critical Reading middle 50% range 440–570. ACT middle 50% range 19–25. Minimum paper TOEFL 500. Minimum computer TOEFL 173. **Basis for Candidate Selection:** *Very important factors considered include:* Academic GPA, standardized test scores, character/personal qualities. *Important factors considered include:* level of applicant's interest. *Other factors considered include:* Class rank, application essay, recommendation(s), extracurricular activities, interview, talent/ability. **Freshman Admission Requirements:** High school diploma is required and GED is accepted. *Academic units recommended:* 4 English, 2 mathematics, 1 science, 2 foreign language, 1 social studies, 1 history, 4 academic electives. **Freshman Admission Statistics:** 899 applied, 69% admitted, 39% enrolled. **Transfer Admission Requirements:** College transcript(s), lowest grade transferable D. **General Admission Information:** Application fee $25. Regular application deadline 8/1. Nonfall registration accepted. Credit offered for CEEB Advanced Placement tests.

COSTS AND FINANCIAL AID
Average book expense $1,100. **Required Forms and Deadlines:** FAFSA. Financial aid filing deadline 7/30. Priority financial aid filing date 2/25. **Notification of Awards:** Applicants will be notified of awards on a rolling basis beginning 3/1. **Types of Aid:** *Need-based scholarships/grants:* Federal Pell, SEOG, state scholarships/grants, private scholarships, the school's own gift aid. *Loans:* FFEL Subsidized Stafford, FFEL Unsubsidized Stafford, FFEL PLUS, Federal Perkins. *Student Employment:* Federal Work-Study Program available. Institutional employment available. Off-campus job opportunities are good. **Financial Aid Statistics:** 94% undergrads receive any aid. **Criteria for awarding institutional aid:** *Non-need-based:* Academics, alumni affiliation, art, athletics, leadership, minority status, music/drama, religious affiliation.

TRINE UNIVERSITY

1 University Avenue, Angola, IN 46703
Phone: 260-665-4100 **Financial Aid Phone:** 260-664-4158
E-mail: admit@trine.edu **CEEB Code:** 1811
Fax: 260-665-4578 **Website:** www.trine.edu **ACT Code:** 1250

This private school was founded in 1884. It has a 400-acre campus.

RATINGS
Admissions Selectivity Rating: 83   **Fire Safety Rating:** 85   **Green Rating:** 78

STUDENTS AND FACULTY
Enrollment: 1,384. **Student Body:** 31% female, 69% male, 43% out-of-state, 2% international (10 countries represented). Asian 1%, African American 3%, Caucasian 69%, Hispanic 1%.
Retention and Graduation: 25% grads go on to further study within 1 year. 10% grads pursue arts and sciences degrees. 5% grads pursue law degrees. 10% grads pursue business degrees. **Faculty:** Student/faculty ratio 17:1. 69 full-time faculty, 65% hold PhDs, 4% are members of minority groups, 25% are women.

ACADEMICS
Degrees: Associate, bachelor's, master's. **Classes:** Most classes have 20–29 students. Most lab/discussion sessions have 10–19 students. **Majors with Highest Enrollment:** Civil engineering; criminal justice/safety studies; mechanical engineering. **Special Study Options:** Cooperative education program, distance learning, double major, dual enrollment, English as a Second Language (ESL), honors program, internships, liberal arts/career combination, study abroad, teacher certification program. **Honors programs:** Honors program began with fall 2006 entering class of freshmen. **Combined degree programs:** BA/MEng Special programs offered to physically disabled students include tutors. **Career services:** Alumni network, alumni services, career/job search classes, career assessment, internships, regional alumni. **Career services highlights include:** Students may elect to incorporate cooperative education (Co-op) as a part of their academic curriculum. Co-op students alternate semesters of employment with semesters of full-time study, that provides both academic knowledge, relevant work experience, and a salary or stipend. A Co-op background is highly regarded by prospective employers; seniors seeking full-time employment with the cooperative education credential are consistently selected over candidates without this major-related experience.

FACILITIES
Housing: Coed dorms, men's dorms, women's dorms, apartments for single students, Honors housing. 95% of campus accessible to physically disabled. **Special Academic Facilities/Equipment:** Lewis Hershey Museum; Wells Gallery of Engravings; Zollner Golf Course. **Computers:** 100% of classrooms, 100% of dorms, 100% of libraries, 100% of dining areas, 100% of student union, have wireless network access. Students can register for classes online. Administrative functions (other than registration) can be performed online.

CAMPUS LIFE
Environment: Village. **Activities:** Choral groups, dance, drama/theater, music ensembles, pep band, radio station, student government, student newspaper, yearbook. **Organizations:** 35 registered organizations, 13 honor societies, 3 religious organizations. 8 fraternities, 6 sororities. **Athletics (Intercollegiate):** *Men:* Baseball, basketball, cross-country, football, golf, lacrosse, soccer, tennis, track/field (outdoor), track/field (indoor), wrestling. *Women:* Basketball, cross-country, golf, lacrosse, soccer, softball, tennis, track/field (outdoor), track/field (indoor), volleyball. **On-Campus Highlights:** University Center/Ctr for online Technol, Fawick Hall of Engineering, Taylor Hall of Humanities, Zollner Golf Course (on campus), Hershey Hall (Recreational Facilities). **Environmental Initiatives:** IDEM—MS4 Storm Water Program— Erosion control best management practices, public outreach, World Wide Water Sampling Day, Water retention projects, water gardens, storm water inlet identification. Audubon Certification—green chemicals on golf course, campus, and athletic fields, water-based paints. Green Cleaning chemicals and floor scrubbing equipment that reduces water consumption.

ADMISSIONS
Freshman Academic Profile: Average high school GPA 3.38. 22% in top 10% of high school class, 48% in top 25% of high school class, 85% in top 50% of high school class. 80% from public high schools. SAT Math middle 50% range 490–600. SAT Critical Reading middle 50% range 440–570. ACT middle 50% range 20–25. Minimum paper TOEFL 550. Minimum computer TOEFL 217. Minimum web-based TOEFL 80. **Basis for Candidate Selection:** *Very important factors considered include:* Class rank, academic GPA, rigor of secondary school record, standardized test scores. *Important factors considered include:* Application essay, recommendation(s), extracurricular activities, interview. *Other factors considered include:* Alumni/ae relation, character/personal qualities, talent/ability, volunteer work, work experience. **Freshman Admission Requirements:** High school diploma is required and GED is accepted.

Academic units required: 4 English, 3 mathematics, 3 science, (2 science labs), 3 social studies, 2 history, 3 academic electives. **Freshman Admission Statistics:** 2,277 applied, 53% admitted, 36% enrolled. **Transfer Admission Requirements:** High school transcript, college transcript(s), statement of good standing from prior institution(s). Minimum college GPA of 2.0 required. Lowest grade transferable C. **General Admission Information:** Regular application deadline 8/1. Nonfall registration accepted. Admission may be deferred for a maximum of 1 year. Credit and/or placement offered for CEEB Advanced Placement tests.

COSTS AND FINANCIAL AID
Annual tuition $24,100. Room and board $8,300. Required fees $100. Average book expense $1,500. **Required Forms and Deadlines:** FAFSA. Financial aid filing deadline 3/10. Priority financial aid filing date 3/10. **Notification of Awards:** Applicants will be notified of awards on a rolling basis beginning 2/15. **Types of Aid:** *Need-based scholarships/grants:* Federal Pell, SEOG, state scholarships/grants, private scholarships, the school's own gift aid. *Loans:* FFEL Subsidized Stafford, FFEL Unsubsidized Stafford, FFEL PLUS. *Student Employment:* Federal Work-Study Program available. Highest amount earned per year from on-campus jobs $2,420. Off-campus job opportunities are good. **Financial Aid Statistics:** 44% freshmen, 37% undergrads receive need-based scholarship or grant aid. 68% freshmen, 68% undergrads receive non-need-based scholarship or grant aid. 68% freshmen, 68% undergrads receive need-based self-help aid. 99% freshmen, 98% undergrads receive any aid. 79% undergrads borrow to pay for school. Average cumulative indebtedness $17,380. **Criteria for awarding institutional aid:** *Non-need-based:* Academics, music/drama.

See page 1260.

TRINITY (WASHINGTON) UNIVERSITY

125 Michigan Avenue, NE, Washington, DC 20017
Phone: 202-884-9400 **Financial Aid Phone:** 202-884-9530
E-mail: admissions@trinitydc.edu **CEEB Code:** 5796
Fax: 202-884-9403 **Website:** www.trinitydc.edu **ACT Code:** 696

This private school was founded in 1897. It has a 26-acre campus.

RATINGS
Admissions Selectivity Rating: 65　　**Fire Safety Rating:** 60*　　**Green Rating:** 60*

STUDENTS AND FACULTY
Enrollment: 962. **Student Body:** 98% female, 2% male, 48% out-of-state, 1% international (42 countries represented). Asian 2%, African American 68%, Caucasian 7%, Hispanic 11%, Native American 1%.
Retention and Graduation: 66% freshmen return for sophomore year. 29% freshmen graduate within 4 years. **Faculty:** Student/faculty ratio 11:1. 61 full-time faculty, 100% hold PhDs, 30% are members of minority groups, 72% are women.

ACADEMICS
Degrees: Bachelor's, master's, post-bachelor's certificate. **Classes:** Most classes have 10–19 students. **Majors with Highest Enrollment:** Business administration and management; communication studies/speech communication and rhetoric; social psychology. **Special Study Options:** Accelerated program, cross-registration, distance learning, double major, dual enrollment, honors program, independent study, internships, student-designed major, study abroad, teacher certification program, weekend college. **Honors programs:** The Honors Program at Trinity encourages students to take advantage of small, seminar-style classes with the rich cultural benefits of our location in the nation's capital. It provides academically motivated students with the intellectual stimulation that comes not only from courses designed specifically for them by faculty members but also from intensive debate and discussion with their peers. **Combined degree programs:** BA/BS—with GWU or Univ. Maryland. Special programs offered to physically disabled students include note-taking services, reader services, tape recorders, tutors. **Career services:** Alumni network, alumni services, career/job search classes, career assessment, internships, regional alumni. **Career services highlights include:** Service learning component of required first year seminar.

FACILITIES
Housing: Women's dorms. **Special Academic Facilities/Equipment:** Art Gallery, Media Technology Center, Writing Center, Marilley Computer Classroom. **Computers:** Students can register for classes online.

CAMPUS LIFE
Activities: Choral groups, dance, drama/theater, literary magazine, student government, student newspaper, student-run film society, yearbook. **Organiza-**

tions: 34 registered organizations, 5 honor societies, 2 religious organizations. **Athletics (Intercollegiate):** *Women:* Basketball, field hockey, lacrosse, soccer, softball, swimming, tennis, volleyball. **On-Campus Highlights:** Trinity Center for Women and Girls in Sports, University Chapel, Main Hall.

ADMISSIONS
Freshman Academic Profile: Average high school GPA 2.8. SAT Math middle 50% range 330–480. SAT Critical Reading middle 50% range 360–482. ACT middle 50% range 13–18. Minimum paper TOEFL 550. Minimum computer TOEFL 213. **Basis for Candidate Selection:** *Very important factors considered include:* Rigor of secondary school record, character/personal qualities. *Important factors considered include:* Application essay, recommendation(s), alumni/ae relation, extracurricular activities, talent/ability, volunteer work. *Other factors considered include:* Class rank, standardized test scores, geographical residence, interview, work experience. **Freshman Admission Requirements:** High school diploma is required and GED is accepted. *Academic units required:* 4 English, 3 mathematics, 2 science, (1 science labs), 2 foreign language, 3 social studies, 2 history. **Freshman Admission Statistics:** 441 applied, 86% admitted, 39% enrolled. **Transfer Admission Requirements:** College transcript(s), essay or personal statement, minimum college GPA of 2.5 required. Lowest grade transferable C. **General Admission Information:** Application fee $40. Nonfall registration accepted. Admission may be deferred for a maximum of 1 year. Credit and/or placement offered for CEEB Advanced Placement tests.

COSTS AND FINANCIAL AID
Annual tuition $17,200. Room and board $7,574. Required fees $160. Average book expense $1,000. **Required Forms and Deadlines:** FAFSA. Priority financial aid filing date 3/1. **Notification of Awards:** Applicants will be notified of awards on a rolling basis beginning 2/1. **Types of Aid:** *Need-based scholarships/grants:* Federal Pell, SEOG, state scholarships/grants, private scholarships, the school's own gift aid. *Loans:* FFEL Subsidized Stafford, FFEL Unsubsidized Stafford, FFEL PLUS, Federal Perkins. *Student Employment:* Federal Work-Study Program available. Institutional employment available. Highest amount earned per year from on-campus jobs $2,000. Off-campus job opportunities are excellent. **Financial Aid Statistics:** 93% freshmen, 86% undergrads receive need-based scholarship or grant aid. 8% freshmen, 3% undergrads receive non-need-based scholarship or grant aid. 75% freshmen, 74% undergrads receive need-based self-help aid. 97% freshmen, 94% undergrads receive any aid. 78% undergrads borrow to pay for school. Average cumulative indebtedness $29,875. **Criteria for awarding institutional aid:** *Non-need-based:* Academics, alumni affiliation, leadership.

TRINITY BIBLE COLLEGE

50 South 6th Avenue, Ellendale, ND 58436-7150
Phone: 701-349-5403
E-mail: admissions@trinitybiblecollege.edu
Fax: 701-349-5443 **Website:** www.trinitybiblecollege.edu

This is a private school.

RATINGS
Admissions Selectivity Rating: 60*　　**Fire Safety Rating:** 60*　　**Green Rating:** 60*

STUDENTS AND FACULTY
Enrollment: 305. **Student Body:** 54% female, 46% male, 60% out-of-state,. Asian 1%, African American 3%, Caucasian 91%, Hispanic 2%, Native American 4%.
Retention and Graduation: 77% freshmen return for sophomore year.

ACADEMICS
Degrees: Associate, bachelor's, certificate. **Special Study Options:** Distance learning, double major, dual enrollment, independent study, teacher certification program.

FACILITIES
Housing: Apartments for married students, apartments for single students.

CAMPUS LIFE
Activities: Student government.

ADMISSIONS
Basis for Candidate Selection: *Very important factors considered include:* Recommendation(s), standardized test scores, character/personal qualities. *Important factors considered include:* Application essay. *Other factors considered include:* Rigor of secondary school record, religious affiliation/commitment. **Freshman Admission Requirements:** High school diploma is required and GED is accepted. **Transfer Admission Requirements:** High

school transcript, college transcript(s), essay or personal statement, statement of good standing from prior institution(s). Lowest grade transferable C. **General Admission Information:** Application fee $25. Notification on a rolling basis, beginning on or about 9/2. Nonfall registration accepted. Admission may be deferred for a maximum of indefinitely.

COSTS AND FINANCIAL AID
Annual tuition $9,680. Room and board $4,370. Required fees $1,478. Average book expense $700. **Required Forms and Deadlines:** FAFSA, information provided on student application for admission. Priority financial aid filing date 3/1. **Notification of Awards:** Applicants will be notified of awards on a rolling basis beginning 3/1. **Types of Aid:** *Need-based scholarships/grants:* Federal Pell, SEOG, state scholarships/grants, private scholarships, the school's own gift aid. *Loans:* FFEL Subsidized Stafford, FFEL Unsubsidized Stafford, FFEL PLUS, Federal Perkins. **Financial Aid Statistics:** 94% freshmen, 95% undergrads receive need-based scholarship or grant aid. 93% freshmen, 93% undergrads receive need-based self-help aid. **Criteria for awarding institutional aid:** *Non-need-based:* Academics, alumni affiliation, art, leadership, music/drama, religious affiliation.

TRINITY CHRISTIAN COLLEGE

6601 West College Drive, Palos Heights, IL 60463
Phone: 708-239-4708 **Financial Aid Phone:** 708-239-4706
E-mail: admissions@trnty.edu **CEEB Code:** 1820
Fax: 708-239-4826 **Website:** www.trnty.edu **ACT Code:** 1165

This private school was founded in 1959. It has a 60-acre campus.

RATINGS
Admissions Selectivity Rating: 74   **Fire Safety Rating:** 72   **Green Rating:** 60*

STUDENTS AND FACULTY
Enrollment: 1,345. **Student Body:** 69% female, 31% male, 28% out-of-state, 2% international (12 countries represented). Asian 2%, African American 8%, Caucasian 75%, Hispanic 7%.
Retention and Graduation: 73% freshmen return for sophomore year. 54% freshmen graduate within 4 years. 12% grads go on to further study within 1 year. 4% grads pursue arts and sciences degrees. 1% grads pursue law degrees. 1% grads pursue business degrees. 2% grads pursue medical degrees. **Faculty:** Student/faculty ratio 12:1. 79 full-time faculty, 67% hold PhDs, 11% are members of minority groups, 41% are women.

ACADEMICS
Degrees: Bachelor's. **Classes:** Most classes have 10–19 students. Most lab/discussion sessions have 10–19 students. **Majors with Highest Enrollment:** Business/commerce; elementary education and teaching; nursing/registered nurse (RN, ASN, BSN, MSN). **Special Study Options:** Cooperative education program, double major, English as a Second Language (ESL), honors program, independent study, internships, liberal arts/career combination, study abroad, teacher certification program. **Honors programs:** The Trinity Honors Program challenges and academically supports gifted students through seminars, unique opportunities within the major program, and participation in co-curricular activities. Special programs offered to physically disabled students include reader services, tape recorders, tutors. **Career services:** Alumni network, alumni services, career assessment, internships, regional alumni. **Career services highlights include:** Chicago Semester Internships.

FACILITIES
Housing: Coed dorms, apartments for married students, apartments for single students. 98% of campus accessible to physically disabled. **Special Academic Facilities/Equipment:** Dutch Heritage Center. **Computers:** 100% of classrooms, 100% of dorms, 100% of libraries, 100% of dining areas, 100% of student union, 15% of common outdoor areas have wireless network access. Students can register for classes online. Administrative functions (other than registration) can be performed online.

CAMPUS LIFE
Environment: Metropolis. **Activities:** Choral groups, concert band, dance, drama/theater, jazz band, music ensembles, musical theater, student government, student newspaper, yearbook, campus ministries. **Organizations:** 15 registered organizations, 2 honor societies, 1 religious organizations. **Athletics (Intercollegiate):** *Men:* Baseball, basketball, cross-country, soccer, track/field (outdoor), track/field (indoor). *Women:* Basketball, cross-country, soccer, softball, track/field (outdoor), track/field (indoor), volleyball. **On-Campus Highlights:** Bootsma Bookstore/Cafe, West Hall Rec, Chapel, South Hall Lobby **Environmental Initiatives:** Recycling of paper, aluminum, and glass Maintenance of a nature trail on campus

ADMISSIONS
Freshman Academic Profile: Average high school GPA 3.37. 17% in top 10% of high school class, 40% in top 25% of high school class, 67% in top 50% of high school class. 54% from public high schools. SAT Math middle 50% range 430–674. SAT Critical Reading middle 50% range 443–642. ACT middle 50% range 17–29. Minimum paper TOEFL 550. Minimum computer TOEFL 213. **Basis for Candidate Selection:** *Very important factors considered include:* Academic GPA, rigor of secondary school record, standardized test scores. *Important factors considered include:* Class rank, application essay, recommendation(s), character/personal qualities, extracurricular activities, interview, level of applicant's interest, religious affiliation/commitment, talent/ability. *Other factors considered include:* Alumni/ae relation, first generation, geographical residence, racial/ethnic status, state residency, volunteer work, work experience. **Freshman Admission Requirements:** High school diploma is required and GED is accepted. *Academic units required:* 3 English, 3 mathematics, 2 science, 2 social studies. *Academic units recommended:* 4 English, 3 mathematics, 2 foreign language, 3 social studies, 2 history. **Freshman Admission Statistics:** 625 applied, 86% admitted, 38% enrolled. **Transfer Admission Requirements:** College transcript(s), essay or personal statement, interview, statement of good standing from prior institution(s). Minimum college GPA of 2.0 required. Lowest grade transferable C. **General Admission Information:** Application fee $20. Notification on a rolling basis, beginning on or about 9/1. Nonfall registration accepted. Admission may be deferred for a maximum of 2 semesters. Credit and/or placement offered for CEEB Advanced Placement tests.

COSTS AND FINANCIAL AID
Annual tuition $17,920. Room and board $7,010. Average book expense $925. **Required Forms and Deadlines:** FAFSA, institution's own financial aid form. Financial aid filing deadline 4/15. Priority financial aid filing date 2/15. **Notification of Awards:** Applicants will be notified of awards on or about 3/15. **Types of Aid:** *Need-based scholarships/grants:* Federal Pell, SEOG, state scholarships/grants, private scholarships, the school's own gift aid. *Loans:* FFEL Subsidized Stafford, FFEL Unsubsidized Stafford, FFEL PLUS, Federal Perkins, Federal Nursing *Student Employment:* Federal Work-Study Program available. Institutional employment available. Highest amount earned per year from on-campus jobs $10,905. Off-campus job opportunities are good. **Financial Aid Statistics:** 74% freshmen, 65% undergrads receive need-based scholarship or grant aid. 75% freshmen, 67% undergrads receive non-need-based scholarship or grant aid. 74% freshmen, 69% undergrads receive need-based self-help aid. 36% freshmen, 15% undergrads receive athletic scholarships. 98% freshmen, 94% undergrads receive any aid. 82% undergrads borrow to pay for school. Average cumulative indebtedness $29,943. **Criteria for awarding institutional aid:** *Non-need-based:* Academics, alumni affiliation, art, athletics, leadership, minority status, music/drama, religious affiliation, state/district residency.

TRINITY COLLEGE (CT)

300 Summit Street, Hartford, CT 06016
Phone: 860-297-2180 **Financial Aid Phone:** 860-297-2047
E-mail: admissions.office@trincoll.edu **CEEB Code:** 3899
Fax: 860-297-2287 **Website:** www.trincoll.edu **ACT Code:** 598

This private school was founded in 1823. It has a 100-acre campus.

RATINGS
Admissions Selectivity Rating: 95   **Fire Safety Rating:** 86   **Green Rating:** 60*

STUDENTS AND FACULTY
Enrollment: 2,234. **Student Body:** 49% female, 51% male, 82% out-of-state, 5% international (48 countries represented). Asian 6%, African American 6%, Caucasian 65%, Hispanic 6%.
Retention and Graduation: 91% freshmen return for sophomore year. 76% freshmen graduate within 4 years. 19% grads go on to further study within 1 year. 10% grads pursue arts and sciences degrees. 4% grads pursue law degrees. 1% grads pursue business degrees. 1% grads pursue medical degrees. **Faculty:** Student/faculty ratio 9:1. 193 full-time faculty, 92% hold PhDs, 21% are members of minority groups, 39% are women.

ACADEMICS
Degrees: Bachelor's, master's. **Classes:** Most classes have 10–19 students. Most lab/discussion sessions have 10–19 students. **Majors with Highest

Enrollment: Economics; English language and literature; political science and government. **Special Study Options:** Accelerated program, cross-registration, double major, exchange student program (domestic), honors program, independent study, internships, liberal arts/career combination, student-designed major, study abroad, teacher certification program, 5-year BS/MS in Electrical Engineering or Mechanical Engineering with Rensselaer Polytechnic Institute, Community Learning Initiative. **Combined degree programs:** BA/MEng, BA/MS in Elect, Engg,or Mech Engg. with RPI. Special programs offered to physically disabled students include note-taking services, reader services, tape recorders, tutors. **Career services:** Alumni network, alumni services, career/job search classes, career assessment, internships, regional alumni. **Career services highlights include:** Our academic internships provide real-life experiences within the framework of an academic analysis. They range from internships in for-profit governmental to non-profit organizations. Over half of our students take courses with a community-based experiential component also linking community engagement with an academic course.

FACILITIES

Housing: Coed dorms, special housing for disabled students, fraternity/sorority housing, community service dorm, quiet dorm, wellness and substance-free, 21+ only, cooking. All dorms are non-smoking. 60% of campus accessible to physically disabled. **Special Academic Facilities/Equipment:** Watkinson Library; Austin Arts Center. **Computers:** 95% of classrooms, 85% of dorms, 100% of libraries, 100% of dining areas, 100% of student union, 90% of common outdoor areas have wireless network access. Students can register for classes online. Administrative functions (other than registration) can be performed online.

CAMPUS LIFE

Environment: Metropolis. **Activities:** Choral groups, dance, drama/theater, jazz band, literary magazine, music ensembles, musical theater, radio station, student government, student newspaper, student-run film society, yearbook, campus ministries, international student organization, Model UN. **Organizations:** 105 registered organizations, 5 honor societies, 5 religious organizations. 7 fraternities, 3 sororities. **Athletics (Intercollegiate):** *Men:* Baseball, basketball, crew/rowing, cross-country, diving, football, golf, ice hockey, lacrosse, soccer, squash, swimming, tennis, track/field (outdoor), track/field (indoor), wrestling. *Women:* Basketball, crew/rowing, cross-country, diving, field hockey, ice hockey, lacrosse, soccer, softball, squash, swimming, tennis, track/field (outdoor), track/field (indoor), volleyball. **On-Campus Highlights:** The Learning Corridor, library, the Science/Engineering Labs, Summit Suites (newest residence hall), the Chapel. **Environmental Initiatives:** Energy conservation measures to help reduce and eliminate greenhouse gas emissions in accordance with the Presidents' Climate Commitment. Development of The Treehouse (Trinity Recreational and Environmental Education House) as a social house where students can come together and share their common interests of nature appreciation and conservation. Participation in RecycleMania.

ADMISSIONS

Freshman Academic Profile: 68% in top 10% of high school class, 93% in top 25% of high school class, 99% in top 50% of high school class. 44% from public high schools. SAT Math middle 50% range 610–690. SAT Critical Reading middle 50% range 590–680. SAT Writing middle 50% range 610–710. ACT middle 50% range 26–30. **Basis for Candidate Selection:** *Very important factors considered include:* Rigor of secondary school record. *Important factors considered include:* Class rank, application essay, academic GPA, recommendation(s), standardized test scores, character/personal qualities, extracurricular activities, interview, racial/ethnic status, talent/ability. *Other factors considered include:* Alumni/ae relation, first generation, geographical residence, level of applicant's interest, volunteer work, work experience. **Freshman Admission Requirements:** High school diploma is required and GED is accepted. *Academic units required:* 4 English, 3 mathematics, 2 science, (2 science labs), 3 foreign language, 2 history. **Freshman Admission Statistics:** 4,532 applied, 41% admitted, 31% enrolled. **Transfer Admission Requirements:** High school transcript, college transcript(s), essay or personal statement, standardized test scores, statement of good standing from prior institution(s). Minimum college GPA of 3.0 required. Lowest grade transferable C–. **General Admission Information:** Application fee $60. Early decision application deadline 11/15. Regular application deadline 1/1. Regular notification 4/1. Nonfall registration not accepted. Admission may be deferred for a maximum of 1 year. Credit and/or placement offered for CEEB Advanced Placement tests.

COSTS AND FINANCIAL AID

Annual tuition $38,900. Room and board $10,560. Required fees $1,940. Average book expense $1,000. **Required Forms and Deadlines:** FAFSA, CSS/Financial Aid PROFILE, noncustodial PROFILE, business/farm supplement, federal income tax returns. Financial aid filing deadline 3/1. Priority financial aid filing date 2/1. **Notification of Awards:** Applicants will be notified of awards on or about 4/1. **Types of Aid:** *Need-based scholarships/grants:* Federal Pell, SEOG, state scholarships/grants, private scholarships, the school's own gift aid. *Loans:* Direct Subsidized Stafford, Direct Unsubsidized Stafford, Direct PLUS, FFEL Subsidized Stafford, FFEL Unsubsidized Stafford, FFEL PLUS, Federal Perkins, college/university loans from institutional funds. *Student*

Employment: Federal Work-Study Program available. Institutional employment available. Highest amount earned per year from on-campus jobs $6,000. Off-campus job opportunities are good. **Financial Aid Statistics:** 41% freshmen, 39% undergrads receive need-based scholarship or grant aid. 10% freshmen, 8% undergrads receive non-need-based scholarship or grant aid. 35% freshmen, 32% undergrads receive need-based self-help aid. 53% freshmen, 52% undergrads receive any aid. 42% undergrads borrow to pay for school. Average cumulative indebtedness $20,174. **Criteria for awarding institutional aid:** *Non-need-based:* Academics, leadership.

See page 1262.

TRINITY COLLEGE OF FLORIDA

2430 Welbilt Boulevard, Trinity, FL 34655
Phone: 727-569-1411 **Financial Aid Phone:** 727-569-1413
E-mail: admissions@trinitycollege.edu
Fax: 727-569-1410 **Website:** www.trinitycollege.edu **ACT Code:** 4876

This private school was founded in 1932. It has a 40-acre campus.

RATINGS
Admissions Selectivity Rating: 70   **Fire Safety Rating:** 71   **Green Rating:** 62

STUDENTS AND FACULTY
Enrollment: 210. **Student Body:** 39% female, 61% male, 28% out-of-state, 1% international (2 countries represented). African American 18%, Caucasian 64%, Hispanic 16%.
Retention and Graduation: 67% freshmen return for sophomore year. 30% freshmen graduate within 4 years. 14% grads go on to further study within 1 year. **Faculty:** Student/faculty ratio 13.9:1. 6 full-time faculty, 83% hold PhDs, 17% are women.

ACADEMICS
Degrees: Associate, bachelor's, certificate, terminal associate. **Classes:** Most classes have fewer than 10 students. **Majors with Highest Enrollment:** pastoral studies/counseling; pre-theology/pre-ministerial studies; youth ministry. **Special Study Options:** Accelerated program, double major, dual enrollment, honors program, independent study, internships, weekend college. **Honors programs:** Our honors program consists of 4 Great Books Seminars Special programs offered to physically disabled students include tutors. **Career services:** Career assessment, internships.

FACILITIES
Housing: Special housing for disabled students, men's dorms, women's dorms, apartments available for double occupancy or more. 100% of campus accessible to physically disabled. **Computers:** 100% of classrooms, 100% of dorms, 100% of libraries, 100% of dining areas, 100% of student union, have wireless network access.

CAMPUS LIFE
Environment: City. **Activities:** Choral groups, drama/theater, student government, yearbook, campus ministries. **Organizations:** 4 religious organizations. **Athletics (Intercollegiate):** *Men:* Basketball. *Women:* Volleyball. **On-Campus Highlights:** Epiphanies Coffee Shop, library, lounge areas, outdoor gazebo, horseshoe pits.

ADMISSIONS
Freshman Academic Profile: Average high school GPA 2.8. SAT Math middle 50% range 370–480. SAT Critical Reading middle 50% range 460–550. ACT middle 50% range 19–23. Minimum paper TOEFL 500. Minimum computer TOEFL 173. **Basis for Candidate Selection:** *Very important factors considered include:* Application essay, academic GPA, recommendation(s), standardized test scores, religious affiliation/commitment. *Important factors considered include:* Character/personal qualities. *Other factors considered include:* Extracurricular activities. **Freshman Admission Requirements:** High school diploma is required and GED is accepted. *Academic units required:* 4 English, 4 mathematics, 4 science, 2 foreign language, 2 social studies, 2 history. **Freshman Admission Statistics:** 79 applied, 85% admitted, 49% enrolled. **Transfer Admission Requirements:** High school transcript, college transcript(s), essay or personal statement, minimum college GPA of 2.0 required. Lowest grade transferable C. **General Admission Information:** Application fee $25. Regular application deadline 8/2. Nonfall registration accepted. Admission may be deferred for a maximum of 1 year. Credit and/or placement offered for CEEB Advanced Placement tests.

COSTS AND FINANCIAL AID
Annual tuition $11,024. Room and board $6,656. Required fees $800. Average book expense $1,185. **Required Forms and Deadlines:** FAFSA, institution's

own financial aid form. Priority financial aid filing date 3/15. **Types of Aid:** *Need-based scholarships/grants:* Federal Pell, SEOG, state scholarships/grants, private scholarships, the school's own gift aid. *Loans:* FFEL Subsidized Stafford, FFEL Unsubsidized Stafford, FFEL PLUS, Private Loans. *Student Employment:* Federal Work-Study Program available. Institutional employment available. Highest amount earned per year from on-campus jobs $4,350. Off-campus job opportunities are excellent. **Financial Aid Statistics:** 77% freshmen, 78% undergrads receive need-based scholarship or grant aid. 77% freshmen, 66% undergrads receive non-need-based scholarship or grant aid. 58% freshmen, 71% undergrads receive need-based self-help aid. 99% freshmen, 99% undergrads receive any aid. 80% undergrads borrow to pay for school. Average cumulative indebtedness $20,523. **Criteria for awarding institutional aid:** *Non-need-based:* Academics, music/drama.

TRINITY INTERNATIONAL UNIVERSITY

2065 Half Day Road, Deerfield, IL 60015
Phone: 847-317-7000 **Financial Aid Phone:** 847-317-7033
E-mail: tcadmissions@tiu.edu **CEEB Code:** 1810
Fax: 847-317-8097 **Website:** www.tiu.edu **ACT Code:** 1150

This private school was founded in 1897. It has a 111-acre campus.

RATINGS
Admissions Selectivity Rating: 82   **Fire Safety Rating:** 70   **Green Rating:** 60*

STUDENTS AND FACULTY
Enrollment: 950. **Student Body:** 57% female, 43% male, 41% out-of-state, 1% international (38 countries represented). Asian 5%, African American 17%, Caucasian 63%, Hispanic 4%.
Retention and Graduation: 66% freshmen return for sophomore year. 40% freshmen graduate within 4 years. 32% grads go on to further study within 1 year. **Faculty:** Student/faculty ratio 12:1. 43 full-time faculty, 84% hold PhDs, 14% are members of minority groups, 42% are women.

ACADEMICS
Degrees: Bachelor's, certificate, first professional, master's, post-bachelor's certificate. **Classes:** Most classes have 20–29 students. Most lab/discussion sessions have 10–19 students. **Majors with Highest Enrollment:** Business/commerce; elementary education and teaching; theology and religious vocations, other. **Special Study Options:** Cross-registration, double major, dual enrollment, honors program, independent study, internships, study abroad, teacher certification program, REACH (for nontraditional students with previous college credit), graduate courses. **Honors programs:** Trinity has adopted a model for an Honors Program that is intended to enhance the breadth and depth of your liberal-arts learning, but without the burden of many additional requirements. Hence, you will do honors work in the areas of your disciplinary major, general education, and special interdisciplinary classes, but virtually all of your honors work will also fulfill regular Trinity requirements. **Combined degree programs:** BA/MA. Special programs offered to physically disabled students include note-taking services, reader services, tape recorders, tutors. **Career services:** Alumni services, career/job search classes, career assessment, internships. **Career services highlights include:** Students in Trinity International University's Athletic Training Education Program have benefited through Trinity's partnership with Condell Health Network in Libertyville, Illinois. Condell's internship opportunities provide our students with necessary clinical experience while they work under the supervision of certified athletic trainers.

FACILITIES
Housing: Special housing for disabled students, men's dorms, women's dorms, apartments for married students, apartments for single students. 75% of campus accessible to physically disabled. **Special Academic Facilities/Equipment:** None **Computers:** 100% of classrooms, 50% of dorms, 100% of libraries, 100% of student union, have wireless network access. Students can register for classes online. Administrative functions (other than registration) can be performed online.

CAMPUS LIFE
Environment: Village. **Activities:** Choral groups, concert band, drama/theater, jazz band, music ensembles, musical theater, pep band, student government, student newspaper, symphony orchestra, yearbook, campus ministries. **Organizations:** 33 registered organizations, 2 honor societies. **Athletics (Intercollegiate):** *Men:* Baseball, basketball, football, soccer. *Women:* Basketball, soccer, softball, volleyball. **On-Campus Highlights:** Lew Student Center, Trinity Hall, McLennan Academic Building, Rodine Global Ministry Building, Melton Dining Hall.

ADMISSIONS
Freshman Academic Profile: Average high school GPA 3.26. 37% in top 10% of high school class, 43% in top 25% of high school class, 68% in top 50% of high school class. 69% from public high schools. SAT Math middle 50% range 440–600. SAT Critical Reading middle 50% range 445–610. ACT middle 50% range 19–26. Minimum paper TOEFL 530. Minimum computer TOEFL 197. **Basis for Candidate Selection:** *Very important factors considered include:* Class rank, application essay, academic GPA, recommendation(s), standardized test scores, character/personal qualities, religious affiliation/commitment, *Other factors considered include:* Rigor of secondary school record, extracurricular activities, first generation, talent/ability. **Freshman Admission Requirements:** High school diploma is required and GED is accepted. *Academic units required:* 4 English, 2 mathematics, 2 science, (1 science labs), 2 foreign language, 2 social studies, 2 history, 2 visual/performing arts. **Freshman Admission Statistics:** 548 applied, 63% admitted, 39% enrolled. **Transfer Admission Requirements:** High school transcript, college transcript(s), essay or personal statement, statement of good standing from prior institution(s). Minimum college GPA of 2.0 required. Lowest grade transferable C–. **General Admission Information:** Application fee $25. Notification on a rolling basis, beginning on or about 9/1. Nonfall registration accepted. Admission may be deferred for a maximum of 1 year. Credit and/or placement offered for CEEB Advanced Placement tests.

COSTS AND FINANCIAL AID
Annual tuition $21,980. Room and board $7,430. Required fees $390. **Required Forms and Deadlines:** FAFSA. Priority financial aid filing date 4/1. **Notification of Awards:** Applicants will be notified of awards on a rolling basis beginning 2/15. **Types of Aid:** *Need-based scholarships/grants:* Federal Pell, SEOG, state scholarships/grants, private scholarships, the school's own gift aid. *Loans:* FFEL Subsidized Stafford, FFEL Unsubsidized Stafford, FFEL PLUS, Federal Perkins. *Student Employment:* Federal Work-Study Program available. Institutional employment available. Off-campus job opportunities are excellent. **Financial Aid Statistics:** 77% freshmen, 75% undergrads receive need-based scholarship or grant aid. 77% freshmen, 74% undergrads receive non-need-based scholarship or grant aid. 66% freshmen, 61% undergrads receive need-based self-help aid. 90% freshmen, 86% undergrads receive any aid. 79% undergrads borrow to pay for school. Average cumulative indebtedness $22,155. **Criteria for awarding institutional aid:** *Non-need-based:* Academics, alumni affiliation, athletics, minority status, music/drama, religious affiliation.

TRINITY LUTHERAN COLLEGE

4221 228th Avenue SE, Issaquah, WA 98029
Phone: 425-961-5510 **Financial Aid Phone:** 425-961-5514
E-mail: admission@tlc.edu
Fax: 425-392-0404 **Website:** www.tlc.edu

This private school, affiliated with the Lutheran Church, was founded in 1944.

RATINGS
Admissions Selectivity Rating: 60*   **Fire Safety Rating:** 60*   **Green Rating:** 60*

STUDENTS AND FACULTY
Enrollment: 91. **Student Body:** 53% female, 47% male, 35% out-of-state,. Asian 4%, African American 1%, Caucasian 112%, Hispanic 4%, Native American 1%.
Retention and Graduation: 78% freshmen return for sophomore year. **Faculty:** 13 full-time faculty.

ACADEMICS
Degrees: Associate, bachelor's, diploma, post-bachelor's certificate, terminal associate, transfer associate. **Majors with Highest Enrollment:** Bible/biblical studies; music, other; youth ministry. **Special Study Options:** Double major, independent study, internships, liberal arts/career combination, student-designed major, study abroad, teacher certification program Special programs offered to physically disabled students include note-taking services, reader services, tape recorders, tutors. **Career services:** Alumni network, alumni services, career assessment, internships, regional alumni. **Career services highlights include:** 10–week internships are a graduation requirement for all students.

FACILITIES
Housing: Coed dorms, special housing for disabled students, men's dorms, women's dorms, apartments for married students, apartments for single students, special housing for married students and non-traditional age students.
Computers: Administrative functions (other than registration) can be performed online.

CAMPUS LIFE

Environment: Village. **Activities:** Choral groups, drama/theater, music ensembles, musical theater, student government, student newspaper, yearbook. **Athletics (Intercollegiate):** *Men:* Basketball, softball. *Women:* Softball. **On-Campus Highlights:** Student Center, The Running Cup, Chapel, YMCA, bookstore.

ADMISSIONS

Freshman Academic Profile: 33% in top 25% of high school class, 60% in top 50% of high school class. Minimum paper TOEFL 525. Minimum computer TOEFL 197. **Basis for Candidate Selection:** *Very important factors considered include:* Recommendation(s), character/personal qualities. *Important factors considered include:* Academic GPA, rigor of secondary school record, standardized test scores, religious affiliation/commitment, volunteer work. *Other factors considered include:* Alumni/ae relation, extracurricular activities, first generation, level of applicant's interest, talent/ability, work experience. **Freshman Admission Requirements:** High school diploma is required and GED is accepted. **Transfer Admission Requirements:** College transcript(s), minimum college GPA of 2.0 required. Lowest grade transferable C–. **General Admission Information:** Application fee $30. Regular application deadline 8/15. Nonfall registration accepted. Admission may be deferred for a maximum of 2 years. Credit and/or placement offered for CEEB Advanced Placement tests.

COSTS AND FINANCIAL AID

Annual tuition $13,714. Room and board $6,078. Required fees $450. Average book expense $500. **Required Forms and Deadlines:** FAFSA, institution's own financial aid form. **Notification of Awards:** Applicants will be notified of awards on a rolling basis beginning 1/1. **Types of Aid:** *Need-based scholarships/grants:* Federal Pell, SEOG, private scholarships, the school's own gift aid. *Loans:* Direct Subsidized Stafford, Direct Unsubsidized Stafford, Direct PLUS, FFEL Subsidized Stafford, FFEL PLUS. *Student Employment:* Federal Work-Study Program available. Institutional employment available. Off-campus job opportunities are excellent. **Financial Aid Statistics: Criteria for awarding institutional aid:** *Non-need-based:* Academics, alumni affiliation, art, leadership, music/drama, religious affiliation.

TRINITY UNIVERSITY

One Trinity Place, San Antonio, TX 78212-7200
Phone: 210-999-7207
E-mail: admissions@trinity.edu **CEEB Code:** 6831
Fax: 210-999-8164 **Website:** www.trinity.edu **ACT Code:** 4226

This private school was founded in 1869. It has a 117-acre campus.

RATINGS

Admissions Selectivity Rating: 93 **Fire Safety Rating:** 97 **Green Rating:** 76

STUDENTS AND FACULTY

Enrollment: 2,458. **Student Body:** 54% female, 46% male, 29% out-of-state, 7% international (66 countries represented). Asian 7%, African American 4%, Caucasian 62%, Hispanic 11%, Native American 1%.
Retention and Graduation: 89% freshmen return for sophomore year. 68% freshmen graduate within 4 years. 34% grads go on to further study within 1 year. **Faculty:** Student/faculty ratio 9:1. 243 full-time faculty, 100% hold PhDs, 12% are members of minority groups, 38% are women.

ACADEMICS

Degrees: Bachelor's, master's. **Classes:** Most classes have 10–19 students. Most lab/discussion sessions have 10–19 students. **Majors with Highest Enrollment:** Business administration, management and operations, other; English language and literature. **Special Study Options:** Accelerated program, double major, honors program, independent study, internships, liberal arts/career combination, student-designed major, study abroad, teacher certification program. **Honors programs:** Honors Program **Combined degree programs:** BA/MA, BA/MA-education; BS/MS-accounting. Special programs offered to physically disabled students include note-taking services, reader services, tutors. **Career services:** Alumni network, career assessment, internships. **Career services highlights include:** The Alumni Network is an amazing program, with over 500 alumni in our Career Network making themselves available for networking with students and fellow graduates.

FACILITIES

Housing: Coed dorms, wellness housing, theme housing. **Special Academic Facilities/Equipment:** Steiren Theatre, Richardson Communication Center, Ruth Taylor Arts Complex including art gallery, Laurie Auditorium. **Computers:** 100% of classrooms, 100% of dorms, 100% of libraries, 100% of dining areas, 100% of student union, 100% of common outdoor areas have wireless network access. Students can register for classes online. Administrative functions (other than registration) can be performed online.

CAMPUS LIFE

Environment: Metropolis. **Activities:** Choral groups, concert band, dance, drama/theater, jazz band, literary magazine, music ensembles, musical theater, opera, pep band, radio station, student government, student newspaper, student-run film society, symphony orchestra, television station, yearbook, campus ministries, international student organization, Model UN. **Organizations:** 130 registered organizations, 24 honor societies, 4 religious organizations, 7 fraternities, 6 sororities. **Athletics (Intercollegiate):** *Men:* Baseball, basketball, cross-country, diving, football, golf, soccer, swimming, tennis, track/field (outdoor). *Women:* Basketball, cross-country, diving, golf, soccer, softball, swimming, tennis, track/field (outdoor), volleyball. **On-Campus Highlights:** Stieren Theatre, Laurie Auditorium, Coates Library, Bell Athletic Center, Coates University Center, Northrup Hall.

ADMISSIONS

Freshman Academic Profile: Average high school GPA 3.56. 55% in top 10% of high school class, 86% in top 25% of high school class, 98% in top 50% of high school class. 62% from public high schools. SAT Math middle 50% range 610–690. SAT Critical Reading middle 50% range 590–700. ACT middle 50% range 27–31. Minimum paper TOEFL 600. Minimum computer TOEFL 250. **Basis for Candidate Selection:** *Very important factors considered include:* Class rank, academic GPA, rigor of secondary school record. *Important factors considered include:* Application essay, recommendation(s), standardized test scores, character/personal qualities, extracurricular activities, interview, talent/ability. *Other factors considered include:* Alumni/ae relation, first generation, geographical residence, level of applicant's interest, racial/ethnic status, volunteer work, work experience. **Freshman Admission Requirements:** High school diploma is required and GED is accepted. *Academic units required:* 4 English, 3 mathematics, 3 science, (2 science labs), 2 foreign language, 3 social studies. *Academic units recommended:* 4 English, 3 mathematics, 3 science, (3 science labs), 3 foreign language, 3 social studies, 3 academic electives. **Freshman Admission Statistics:** 4,209 applied, 59% admitted, 26% enrolled. **Transfer Admission Requirements:** High school transcript, college transcript(s), essay or personal statement, statement of good standing from prior institution(s). Minimum college GPA of 3.0 required. Lowest grade transferable C–. **General Admission Information:** Application fee $50. Early decision application deadline 11/1. Regular application deadline 2/1. Regular notification 4/1. Nonfall registration not accepted. Admission may be deferred for a maximum of 1 year. Credit and/or placement offered for CEEB Advanced Placement tests.

COSTS AND FINANCIAL AID

Required Forms and Deadlines: FAFSA. Financial aid filing deadline 4/1. Priority financial aid filing date 2/15. **Notification of Awards:** Applicants will be notified of awards on or about 4/1. **Types of Aid:** *Need-based scholarships/grants:* Federal Pell, SEOG, state scholarships/grants, private scholarships, the school's own gift aid. *Loans:* FFEL Subsidized Stafford, FFEL Unsubsidized Stafford, FFEL PLUS, Federal Perkins, state loans, college/university loans from institutional funds. *Student Employment:* Federal Work-Study Program available. Institutional employment available. Off-campus job opportunities are good. **Financial Aid Statistics:** 44% freshmen, 38% undergrads receive need-based scholarship or grant aid. 13% freshmen, 8% undergrads receive non-need-based scholarship or grant aid. 34% freshmen, 33% undergrads receive need-based self-help aid. 91% freshmen, 83% undergrads receive any aid. **Criteria for awarding institutional aid:** *Non-need-based:* Academics, leadership, music/drama.

TRINITY WESTERN UNIVERSITY

P.O Box 1409, Blaine, WA 98231
Phone: 604-513-2019
E-mail: admissions@twu.ca **CEEB Code:** 876
Fax: 604-513-2064 **Website:** www.twu.ca **ACT Code:** 5242

This private school was founded in 1962. It has a 100-acre campus.

RATINGS

Admissions Selectivity Rating: 60* **Fire Safety Rating:** 60* **Green Rating:** 60*

STUDENTS AND FACULTY

Enrollment: 1,968. **Student Body:** 57% female, 43% male, 3% out-of-state. **Retention and Graduation:** 80% freshmen return for sophomore year. 15% grads go on to further study within 1 year. 3% grads pursue law degrees. 3% grads pursue medical degrees. **Faculty:** Student/faculty ratio 18:1. 77 full-time faculty, 90% hold PhDs, 4% are members of minority groups, 18% are women.

ACADEMICS

Degrees: Bachelor's, certificate, diploma, first professional, master's. **Majors with Highest Enrollment:** Electrical, electronic and communications engineering technology/technician. **Special Study Options:** Cooperative education program, double major, English as a Second Language (ESL), honors program, internships, study abroad. **Career services:** Alumni services, career/job search classes, career assessment, internships.

FACILITIES

Housing: 95% of campus accessible to physically disabled. **Special Academic Facilities/Equipment:** Museum of Biblical History. **Computers:** Administrative functions (other than registration) can be performed online.

CAMPUS LIFE

Environment: Town. **Activities:** Drama/theater, literary magazine, student government, student newspaper, student-run film society **Organizations:** 33 registered organizations, **Athletics (Intercollegiate):** *Men:* Basketball, cross-country, ice hockey, rugby, soccer, track/field (outdoor), volleyball. *Women:* Basketball, cross-country, rugby, soccer, track/field (outdoor), volleyball.

ADMISSIONS

Freshman Academic Profile: 80% from public high schools. Minimum paper TOEFL 570. **Basis for Candidate Selection:** *Very important factors considered include:* Recommendation(s), rigor of secondary school record, standardized test scores. *Important factors considered include:* Application essay. *Other factors considered include:* Class rank, character/personal qualities, extracurricular activities, religious affiliation/commitment, talent/ability. **Freshman Admission Requirements:** High school diploma is required and GED is accepted. *Academic units required:* 4 English, 3 mathematics, 2 science, (1 science labs), 2 social studies, 2 academic electives. **Freshman Admission Statistics:** 1,371 applied, 78% admitted, 39% enrolled. **Transfer Admission Requirements:** High school transcript, college transcript(s), essay or personal statement, minimum college GPA of 2.0 required. Lowest grade transferable D. **General Admission Information:** Application fee $35. Regular application deadline 6/15. Notification on a rolling basis, beginning on or about 10/15. Nonfall registration accepted. Admission may be deferred for a maximum of 3 semesters. Credit and/or placement offered for CEEB Advanced Placement tests.

COSTS AND FINANCIAL AID

Annual tuition $10,350. Room and board $5,990. Required fees $120. Average book expense $800. **Required Forms and Deadlines:** institution's own financial aid form Financial aid filing deadline 3/15. **Notification of Awards:** Applicants will be notified of awards on a rolling basis beginning 4/1. **Types of Aid:** *Need-based scholarships/grants:* State scholarships/grants, private scholarships, the school's own gift aid. *Loans:* Direct Subsidized Stafford, Direct Unsubsidized Stafford, Direct PLUS. *Student Employment:* Institutional employment available. Highest amount earned per year from on-campus jobs $1,000. Off-campus job opportunities are good. **Financial Aid Statistics:** 1% freshmen, 10% undergrads receive need-based scholarship or grant aid. 1% freshmen, 2% undergrads receive non-need-based scholarship or grant aid. 19% freshmen, 20% undergrads receive need-based self-help aid. 65% undergrads borrow to pay for school. Average cumulative indebtedness $17,000. **Criteria for awarding institutional aid:** *Non-need-based:* Academics, athletics, leadership, music/drama.

TROY UNIVERSITY DOTHAN

P.O. Box 8368, Dothan, AL 36304-0368
Phone: 334-983-6556
E-mail: ariversjr@troyst.edu
Fax: 334-983-6322 **Website:** www.tsud.edu **ACT Code:** 15

This public school was founded in 1864. It has a 265-acre campus.

RATINGS

Admissions Selectivity Rating: 74   **Fire Safety Rating:** 60*   **Green Rating:** 60*

STUDENTS AND FACULTY

Enrollment: 1,470. **Student Body:** 68% female, 32% male, 7% out-of-state. Asian 1%, African American 22%, Caucasian 71%, Hispanic 2%, Native American 1%.

Retention and Graduation: 62% freshmen return for sophomore year. 20% freshmen graduate within 4 years. **Faculty:** Student/faculty ratio 15:1. 57 full-time faculty, 72% hold PhDs, 9% are members of minority groups, 32% are women.

ACADEMICS

Degrees: Associate, bachelor's, master's, post-master's certificate, terminal associate, transfer associate. **Classes:** Most classes have 10–19 students. Most lab/discussion sessions have 10–19 students. **Majors with Highest Enrollment:** accounting; computer and information sciences; elementary education and teaching. **Special Study Options:** Distance learning, external degree program, independent study, internships, teacher certification program, weekend college Special programs offered to physically disabled students include note-taking services, reader services, tape recorders, tutors. **Career services:** Alumni services, career/job search classes, career assessment, internships.

FACILITIES

Housing: 100% of campus accessible to physically disabled. **Computers:** Students can register for classes online. Administrative functions (other than registration) can be performed online.

CAMPUS LIFE

Activities: Literary magazine, student government. **Organizations:** 18 registered organizations, 6 honor societies, 1 religious organizations.

ADMISSIONS

Freshman Academic Profile: Average high school GPA 3.19. 98% from public high schools. ACT middle 50% range 20–24. Minimum paper TOEFL 550. Minimum computer TOEFL 213. **Basis for Candidate Selection:** *Very important factors considered include:* Rigor of secondary school record, standardized test scores. *Important factors considered include:* geographical residence, state residency. *Other factors considered include:* character/personal qualities. **Freshman Admission Requirements:** High school diploma is required and GED is accepted. *Academic units required:* 4 English, 4 mathematics, 4 science, 4 social studies, 6 academic electives. **Freshman Admission Statistics:** 176 applied, 66% admitted, 70% enrolled. **Transfer Admission Requirements:** College transcript(s), statement of good standing from prior institution(s). Minimum college GPA of 2.0 required. Lowest grade transferable D. **General Admission Information:** Application fee $20. Nonfall registration accepted. Admission may be deferred for a maximum of 1 year.

COSTS AND FINANCIAL AID

Annual in-state tuition $3,850. Annual out-of-state tuition $7,700. Required fees $312. **Required Forms and Deadlines:** FAFSA, institution's own financial aid form. Priority financial aid filing date 3/1. **Notification of Awards:** Applicants will be notified of awards on a rolling basis beginning 2/1. **Types of Aid:** *Need-based scholarships/grants:* Federal Pell, SEOG, state scholarships/grants, private scholarships, the school's own gift aid. *Loans:* FFEL Subsidized Stafford, FFEL Unsubsidized Stafford, FFEL PLUS. *Student Employment:* Federal Work-Study Program available. Off-campus job opportunities are fair. **Financial Aid Statistics:** 34% freshmen, 41% undergrads receive need-based scholarship or grant aid. 28% freshmen, 9% undergrads receive non-need-based scholarship or grant aid. 56% freshmen, 63% undergrads receive need-based self-help aid. **Criteria for awarding institutional aid:** *Non-need-based:* Academics.

TROY UNIVERSITY MONTGOMERY

P.O. Drawer 4419, Montgomery, AL 36103-4419
Phone: 334-241-9506
E-mail: admit@tsum.edu
Fax: 334-241-5448 **Website:** www.tsum.edu

This public school was founded in 1965. It has a 6-acre campus.

RATINGS

Admissions Selectivity Rating: 60*   **Fire Safety Rating:** 60*   **Green Rating:** 60*

STUDENTS AND FACULTY

Enrollment: 2,893. **Student Body:** 67% female, 33% male. Asian 1%, African American 52%, Caucasian 43%, Hispanic 1%.
Retention and Graduation: **Faculty:** Student/faculty ratio 47:1. 36 full-time faculty, 78% hold PhDs, 22% are members of minority groups, 31% are women.

ACADEMICS

Degrees: Associate, bachelor's, master's, post-master's certificate, terminal associate. **Classes:** Most classes have 10–19 students. **Majors with Highest Enrollment:** Business/commerce; human resources management/personnel administration; liberal arts and sciences/liberal studies. **Special Study

Options: Accelerated program, cross-registration, distance learning, double major, dual enrollment, exchange student program (domestic), external degree program, honors program, independent study, internships, teacher certification program, weekend college. Echange student program equates to our transient program. Internships and Tercher Certification Program are graduate programs only. Special programs offered to physically disabled students include note-taking services, reader services, tape recorders, tutors. **Career services:** Alumni services, career/job search classes, career assessment.

FACILITIES

Housing: No on-campus housing available. 98% of campus accessible to physically disabled. **Special Academic Facilities/Equipment:** W. A Gayle Planetarium, Davis Theater, Rosa L. Parks Library and Museum **Computers:** Students can register for classes online.

CAMPUS LIFE

Organizations: 7 registered organizations, 2 honor societies,

ADMISSIONS

Freshman Academic Profile: Basis for Candidate Selection: *Very important factors considered include:* Rigor of secondary school record, *Other factors considered include:* Standardized test scores. **Freshman Admission Requirements:** High school diploma is required and GED is accepted. *Academic units required:* 3 English. *Academic units recommended:* 4 English. **Transfer Admission Requirements:** College transcript(s), statement of good standing from prior institution(s). Lowest grade transferable D. **General Admission Information:** Application fee $20. Nonfall registration accepted. Admission may be deferred for a maximum of 2 semesters.

COSTS AND FINANCIAL AID

Required Forms and Deadlines: FAFSA, institution's own financial aid form. Financial aid filing deadline 5/1. **Types of Aid:** *Need-based scholarships/grants:* Federal Pell, SEOG, state scholarships/grants, private scholarships. *Loans:* FFEL Subsidized Stafford, FFEL Unsubsidized Stafford, FFEL PLUS. *Student Employment:* Federal Work-Study Program available. Off-campus job opportunities are good. **Financial Aid Statistics:** 44% freshmen, 42% undergrads receive need-based scholarship or grant aid. 38% freshmen, 44% undergrads receive need-based self-help aid. **Criteria for awarding institutional aid:** *Non-need-based:* Academics.

TROY UNIVERSITY—TROY (FORMERLY TROY STATE UNIVERSITY)

111 Adams Administration, Troy, AL 36082
Phone: 334-670-3179 **Financial Aid Phone:** 334-670-3186
E-mail: admit@troy.edu **CEEB Code:** 1738
Fax: 334-670-3733 **Website:** www.troy.edu **ACT Code:** 48

This public school was founded in 1887. It has a 512-acre campus.

RATINGS

Admissions Selectivity Rating: 81   **Fire Safety Rating:** 82   **Green Rating:** 72

STUDENTS AND FACULTY

Enrollment: 22,029. **Student Body:** 60% female, 40% male, 44% out-of-state, 2% international. Asian 1%, African American 42%, Caucasian 47%, Hispanic 3%, Native American 2%.
Retention and Graduation: 69% freshmen return for sophomore year. **Faculty:** Student/faculty ratio 21:1. 516 full-time faculty, 67% hold PhDs, 16% are members of minority groups, 42% are women. 1% of classes are taught by teaching assistants.

ACADEMICS

Degrees: Associate, bachelor's, doctoral, master's, post-master's certificate. **Classes:** Most classes have 10–19 students. Most lab/discussion sessions have 20–29 students. **Majors with Highest Enrollment:** Business administration and management; criminal justice/safety studies; liberal arts and sciences studies and humanities, other. **Special Study Options:** Accelerated program, cross-registration, distance learning, double major, dual enrollment, English as a Second Language (ESL), external degree program, honors program, independent study, internships, study abroad, teacher certification program, weekend college. **Honors programs:** The University Honors Program, open to students in all undergraduate divisions of the university, is administered by the Honors Council and the director of university honors. The purpose of the University Honors Program is to offer the academically superior student a specially designed program, within a supportive community, that fosters critical thinking, intellectual development and social responsibility. This enhanced program is de-

signed to provide a balance of common experience and flexibility addressed to individual achievement as well as a comprehensive framework on which to build disciplinary studies. The Honors Program also has an honors house on campus which houses both male and female students. Students should consult with the director of the University Honors Program and the director of University Housing for availabilities and stipulations. The house serves as a residence and a focal point for meetings and activities with the Honors Alliance, faculty and staff in the Honors Program. The official student voice within the program is the University Honors Alliance. Membership to the University Honors Alliance is offered to any student with a 3.3 grade point average or higher. There is an annual membership fee of $5. Special programs offered to physically disabled students include note-taking services, reader services, tape recorders, tutors.

FACILITIES

Housing: Coed dorms, men's dorms, special housing for international students, women's dorms, fraternity/sorority housing, apartments for married students, apartments for single students, Substance Free Housing, Honor Student Housing. 95% of campus accessible to physically disabled. **Special Academic Facilities/Equipment:** Art museum, recording studio. **Computers:** Students can register for classes online.

CAMPUS LIFE

Environment: Town. **Activities:** Choral groups, concert band, dance, drama/theater, jazz band, marching band, music ensembles, musical theater, opera, pep band, radio station, student government, student newspaper, symphony orchestra, television station, yearbook. **Organizations:** 125 registered organizations, 22 honor societies, 7 religious organizations. 12 fraternities, 9 sororities. **Athletics (Intercollegiate):** *Men:* Baseball, basketball, cheerleading, cross-country, football, golf, rodeo, tennis, track/field (outdoor). *Women:* Basketball, cheerleading, cross-country, golf, rodeo, soccer, softball, tennis, track/field (outdoor), volleyball. **On-Campus Highlights:** Movie Gallery Veterans Stadium, Malone Art Gallery, Hall of Honor/National Band Hall of Fame, Trojan Center, Rosa Parks Museum—Montgomery Campus. **Environmental Initiatives:** Recycling; alternative fuel sources; landscaping.

ADMISSIONS

Freshman Academic Profile: Average high school GPA 3.46. 4% in top 10% of high school class, 78% in top 25% of high school class, 80% in top 50% of high school class. ACT middle 50% range 17.8–23.2. Minimum paper TOEFL 500. Minimum computer TOEFL 173. **Basis for Candidate Selection:** *Very important factors considered include:* Academic GPA, rigor of secondary school record, standardized test scores, *Other factors considered include:* Application essay, recommendation(s), alumni/ae relation, character/personal qualities, extracurricular activities, interview, talent/ability. **Freshman Admission Requirements:** High school diploma is required and GED is accepted. *Academic units required:* 4 English, 4 mathematics, 4 science, 4 social studies. *Academic units recommended:* 2 foreign language. **Freshman Admission Statistics:** 6,413 applied, 66% admitted, 78% enrolled. **Transfer Admission Requirements:** College transcript(s), minimum college GPA of 2.0 required. Lowest grade transferable D. **General Admission Information:** Application fee $30. Nonfall registration accepted. Admission may be deferred for a maximum of 2 years. Credit and/or placement offered for CEEB Advanced Placement tests.

COSTS AND FINANCIAL AID

Annual in-state tuition $4,200. Annual out-of-state tuition $12,600. Required fees $1,110. Average book expense $1,100. **Required Forms and Deadlines:** FAFSA, institution's own financial aid form. Priority financial aid filing date 5/1. **Notification of Awards:** Applicants will be notified of awards on a rolling basis beginning 5/1. **Types of Aid:** *Need-based scholarships/grants:* Federal Pell, SEOG, state scholarships/grants, private scholarships, the school's own gift aid. *Loans:* FFEL Subsidized Stafford, FFEL Unsubsidized Stafford, FFEL PLUS, Federal Perkins. **Financial Aid Statistics:** 52% freshmen, 50% undergrads receive need-based scholarship or grant aid. 28% freshmen, 16% undergrads receive non-need-based scholarship or grant aid. 77% freshmen, 71% undergrads receive need-based self-help aid. 1% freshmen, 1% undergrads receive athletic scholarships. **Criteria for awarding institutional aid:** *Non-need-based:* Academics, athletics, leadership, music/drama.

TRUMAN STATE UNIVERSITY

100 E. Normal, Kirksville, MO 63501
Phone: 660-785-4114 **Financial Aid Phone:** 660-785-4310
E-mail: admissions@truman.edu **CEEB Code:** 6483
Fax: 660-785-7456 **Website:** www.truman.edu **ACT Code:** 2336

This public school was founded in 1867. It has a 140-acre campus.

RATINGS
Admissions Selectivity Rating: 91   **Fire Safety Rating:** 85   **Green Rating:** 73

STUDENTS AND FACULTY
Enrollment: 5,381. **Student Body:** 58% female, 42% male, 23% out-of-state, 5% international (43 countries represented). Asian 2%, African American 4%, Caucasian 75%, Hispanic 2%, Native American 1%.
Retention and Graduation: 84% freshmen return for sophomore year. 47% freshmen graduate within 4 years. 50% grads go on to further study within 1 year. **Faculty:** Student/faculty ratio 16:1. 345 full-time faculty, 82% hold PhDs, 11% are members of minority groups, 38% are women. 1% of classes are taught by teaching assistants.

ACADEMICS
Degrees: Bachelor's, master's. **Classes:** Most classes have 20–29 students. Most lab/discussion sessions have 20–29 students. **Majors with Highest Enrollment:** Biology/biological sciences; business administration and management; English language and literature. **Special Study Options:** Double major, dual enrollment, honors program, independent study, internships, student-designed major, study abroad, teacher certification program. **Honors programs:** General Honors Program: Students must complete five upper-level courses in math, social science, science and humanities with a 3.5 GPA in these 5 courses. Departmental honors are also available in some disciplines. Special programs offered to physically disabled students include note-taking services, reader services, tape recorders, tutors. **Career services:** Alumni network, alumni services, career assessment, internships, regional alumni. **Career services highlights include:** Truman offers a wide variety of experiential internships through the "Truman in Washington" program in Washington, DC Included are work-experience opportunities in such areas as foreign affairs/diplomacy, government affairs, criminal justice, international relations, health and human services, and communications as well as other areas.

FACILITIES
Housing: Coed dorms, special housing for disabled students, special housing for international students, apartments for married students, apartments for single students, theme housing, sorority housing, French language housing, and Spanish language housing. 98% of campus accessible to physically disabled.
Special Academic Facilities/Equipment: Art gallery, local history and artifacts museum, human performance lab, greenhouse, observatory, IR and NMR instrumentation, and convergent media center (TV studio, newspaper, and radio station). **Computers:** 100% of classrooms, 100% of dorms, 100% of libraries, 75% of dining areas, 100% of student union, 90% of common outdoor areas have wireless network access. Students can register for classes online. Administrative functions (other than registration) can be performed online.

CAMPUS LIFE
Environment: Village. **Activities:** Choral groups, concert band, dance, drama/theater, jazz band, literary magazine, marching band, music ensembles, musical theater, opera, pep band, radio station, student government, student newspaper, student-run film society, symphony orchestra, television station, campus ministries, international student organization, Model UN. **Organizations:** 282 registered organizations, 18 honor societies, 16 religious organizations, 16 fraternities, 11 sororities. **Athletics (Intercollegiate):** *Men:* Baseball, basketball, cross-country, football, golf, soccer, swimming, tennis, track/field (outdoor), track/field (indoor), wrestling. *Women:* Basketball, cross-country, golf, soccer, softball, swimming, tennis, track/field (outdoor), track/field (indoor), volleyball. **On-Campus Highlights:** Student Recreation Center, Pickler Memorial Library, Student Union Building, The Quadrangle, Jazzman's Coffee Shop. **Environmental Initiatives:** Recycling program; Bulldog Biodiesel (convert waste vegetable oil from cafeterias and area restaurants to biodiesel fuel); compost recycling.

ADMISSIONS
Freshman Academic Profile: Average high school GPA 3.74. 46% in top 10% of high school class, 95% in top 25% of high school class, 98% in top 50% of high school class. 78% from public high schools. SAT Math middle 50% range 560–660. SAT Critical Reading middle 50% range 540–660. ACT middle 50% range 25–30. Minimum paper TOEFL 550. Minimum computer TOEFL 173. Minimum web-based TOEFL 79. **Basis for Candidate Selection:** *Very important factors considered include:* Class rank, academic GPA, rigor of secondary school record, standardized test scores. *Important factors considered include:* Application essay. *Other factors considered include:* Recommendation(s), alumni/ae relation, character/personal qualities, extracurricular activities, first generation, geographical residence, racial/ethnic status, state residency, talent/ability, volunteer work, work experience. **Freshman Admission Requirements:** High school diploma is required and GED is accepted. *Academic units required:* 4 English, 3 mathematics, 3 science, (1 science labs), 2 foreign language, 2 social studies, 1 history, 1 visual/performing arts. *Academic units recommended:* 4 mathematics, (2 science labs). **Freshman Admission Statistics:** 4,608 applied, 72% admitted, 40% enrolled. **Transfer Admission Requirements:** College transcript(s), essay or personal statement. **General Admission Information:** Nonfall registration accepted. Admission may be deferred for a maximum of 1 year. Credit and/or placement offered for CEEB Advanced Placement tests.

COSTS AND FINANCIAL AID
Average book expense $1,000. **Required Forms and Deadlines:** FAFSA, institution's own financial aid form. Priority financial aid filing date 4/1. **Notification of Awards:** Applicants will be notified of awards on a rolling basis beginning 3/1. **Types of Aid:** *Need-based scholarships/grants:* Federal Pell, SEOG, state scholarships/grants, private scholarships, the school's own gift aid, Federal ACG, SMART and TEACH Grants. *Loans:* FFEL Subsidized Stafford, FFEL Unsubsidized Stafford, FFEL PLUS, Federal Perkins, Federal Nursing, college/university loans from institutional funds, alternative loans. *Student Employment:* Federal Work-Study Program available. Institutional employment available. Highest amount earned per year from on-campus jobs $4,208. Off-campus job opportunities are good. **Financial Aid Statistics:** 35% freshmen, 30% undergrads receive need-based scholarship or grant aid. 44% freshmen, 31% undergrads receive non-need-based scholarship or grant aid. 28% freshmen, 32% undergrads receive need-based self-help aid. 6% freshmen, 6% undergrads receive athletic scholarships. 98% freshmen, 95% undergrads receive any aid. 53% undergrads borrow to pay for school. Average cumulative indebtedness $21,858. **Criteria for awarding institutional aid:** *Non-need-based:* Academics, alumni affiliation, art, athletics, leadership, minority status, music/drama, state/district residency.

See page 1264.

TUFTS UNIVERSITY

Bendetson Hall, Medford, MA 02155
Phone: 617-627-3170 **Financial Aid Phone:** 617-627-2000
E-mail: admissions.inquiry@ase.tufts.edu **CEEB Code:** 3901
Fax: 617-627-3860 **Website:** www.tufts.edu **ACT Code:** 1922

This private school was founded in 1852. It has a 150-acre campus.

RATINGS
Admissions Selectivity Rating: 98   **Fire Safety Rating:** 96   **Green Rating:** 86

STUDENTS AND FACULTY
Enrollment: 5,146. **Student Body:** 51% female, 49% male, 75.5% out-of-state, 6% international (93 countries represented). Asian 13%, African American 5%, Caucasian 58%, Hispanic 6%.
Retention and Graduation: 85% freshmen graduate within 4 years. **Faculty:** Student/faculty ratio 8.8:1. 675 full-time faculty, 95% hold PhDs, 21% are members of minority groups, 40% are women. 1% of classes are taught by teaching assistants.

ACADEMICS
Degrees: Bachelor's, master's, post-bachelor's certificate, post-master's certificate. **Classes:** Most classes have 10–19 students. Most lab/discussion sessions have 10–19 students. **Majors with Highest Enrollment:** Economics; English language and literature; international relations and affairs. **Special Study Options:** Cross-registration, double major, exchange student program (domestic), honors program, independent study, internships, liberal arts/career combination, student-designed major, study abroad, teacher certification program. **Combined degree programs:** BA/MD, BA/MA, BA/DDS, 5-yr BA/BFA with museum school of Fine Arts. Special programs offered to physically disabled students include note-taking services, reader services, tape recorders, tutors.

Career services: Alumni network, alumni services, career/job search classes, career assessment, internships, regional alumni. **Career services highlights include:** Thanks to our proximity to Boston, most of our students are able to pursue an internship during their 4 years, many for academic credit. Tufts also has a program geared at providing a stipend to students who pursue an internship with non-profit or public sector organizations.

FACILITIES

Housing: Coed dorms, special housing for disabled students, women's dorms, fraternity/sorority housing, cooperative housing, special interest housing. **Special Academic Facilities/Equipment:** Language lab, nutrition institute, research lab for physical electronics, bioelectrical and biochemical labs, computer-aided design (CAD) facility, electro-optics technology and environmental management centers. **Computers:** 50% of classrooms, 20% of dorms, 100% of libraries, 75% of dining areas, 100% of student union, 75% of common outdoor areas have wireless network access. Students can register for classes online. Administrative functions (other than registration) can be performed online.

CAMPUS LIFE

Environment: Town. **Activities:** Choral groups, concert band, dance, drama/theater, jazz band, literary magazine, marching band, music ensembles, musical theater, opera, pep band, radio station, student government, student newspaper, student-run film society, symphony orchestra, television station, yearbook, campus ministries, international student organization, Model UN. **Organizations:** 160 registered organizations, 4 honor societies, 6 religious organizations. 11 fraternities, 3 sororities. **Athletics (Intercollegiate):** *Men:* Baseball, basketball, crew/rowing, cross-country, diving, football, golf, ice hockey, lacrosse, sailing, soccer, squash, swimming, tennis, track/field (outdoor), track/field (indoor). *Women:* Basketball, cheerleading, crew/rowing, cross-country, diving, fencing, field hockey, golf, lacrosse, sailing, soccer, softball, squash, swimming, tennis, track/field (outdoor), track/field (indoor), volleyball. **On-Campus Highlights:** The Aidekman Arts Center, Tisch Library, Edwin Ginn Library, Cousens Gymnasium, Ellis Oval, Meyer Campus Center. **Environmental Initiatives:** Reduced green house gas emissions to below 1998 levels LEED Gold building and comprehensive energy efficiency efforts Comprehensive recycling and green purchasing and green dining initiatives

ADMISSIONS

Freshman Academic Profile: 85% in top 10% of high school class, 98% in top 25% of high school class, 100% in top 50% of high school class. 59% from public high schools. SAT Math middle 50% range 680–750. SAT Critical Reading middle 50% range 680–750. SAT Writing middle 50% range 680–760. ACT middle 50% range 30–33. Minimum paper TOEFL 600. Minimum computer TOEFL 100. **Basis for Candidate Selection:** *Very important factors considered include:* Application essay, academic GPA, rigor of secondary school record, character/personal qualities. *Important factors considered include:* Class rank, recommendation(s), standardized test scores, extracurricular activities, talent/ability, volunteer work, work experience. *Other factors considered include:* Alumni/ae relation, first generation, geographical residence, interview, racial/ethnic status. **Freshman Admission Requirements:** High school diploma is required and GED is accepted. *Academic units recommended:* 4 English, 4 mathematics, 4 science, 4 foreign language, 4 social studies, 4 history. **Freshman Admission Statistics:** 15,042 applied, 27% admitted, 33% enrolled. **Transfer Admission Requirements:** High school transcript, college transcript(s), essay or personal statement, standardized test scores, statement of good standing from prior institution(s). Lowest grade transferable C. **General Admission Information:** Application fee $70. Early decision application deadline 11/1. Regular application deadline 1/1. Regular notification 4/1. Nonfall registration not accepted. Admission may be deferred for a maximum of 1 year. Credit and/or placement offered for CEEB Advanced Placement tests.

COSTS AND FINANCIAL AID

Required Forms and Deadlines: FAFSA, CSS/Financial Aid PROFILE, noncustodial PROFILE, parent and student federal income tax returns. Financial aid filing deadline 2/15. Priority financial aid filing date 2/15. **Notification of Awards:** Applicants will be notified of awards on or about 4/1. **Types of Aid:** *Need-based scholarships/grants:* Federal Pell, SEOG, state scholarships/grants, the school's own gift aid. *Loans:* Direct Subsidized Stafford, Direct Unsubsidized Stafford, Federal Perkins, college/university loans from institutional funds. *Student Employment:* Federal Work-Study Program available. Institutional employment available. Off-campus job opportunities are good. **Financial Aid Statistics:** 37% freshmen, 36% undergrads receive need-based scholarship or grant aid. 2% freshmen, 1% undergrads receive non-need-based scholarship or grant aid. 36% freshmen, 37% undergrads receive need-based self-help aid. 52% freshmen, 52% undergrads receive any aid. 41% undergrads borrow to pay for school. Average cumulative indebtedness $23,731. **Criteria for awarding institutional aid:** *Non-need-based:* Academics.

TULANE UNIVERSITY

6823 St. Charles Avenue, New Orleans, LA 70118
Phone: 504-865-5260 **Financial Aid Phone:** 504-865-5723
E-mail: undergrad.admission@tulane.edu **CEEB Code:** 6832
Fax: 504-862-8715 **Website:** www.tulane.edu **ACT Code:** 1614

This private school was founded in 1834. It has a 110-acre campus.

RATINGS
Admissions Selectivity Rating: 96 **Fire Safety Rating:** 97 **Green Rating:** 87

STUDENTS AND FACULTY
Enrollment: 7,160. **Student Body:** 55% female, 45% male, 65% out-of-state, 3% international (45 countries represented). Asian 4%, African American 10%, Caucasian 69%, Hispanic 4%, Native American 2%.
Retention and Graduation: 91% freshmen return for sophomore year. 60% freshmen graduate within 4 years. **Faculty:** Student/faculty ratio 8:1. 572 full-time faculty, 94% hold PhDs, 18% are members of minority groups, 35% are women.

ACADEMICS
Degrees: Associate, bachelor's, certificate, doctoral, master's, post-bachelor's certificate. **Classes:** Most classes have 10–19 students. **Majors with Highest Enrollment:** Business/commerce; health services/allied health/health sciences; psychology. **Special Study Options:** Accelerated program, cross-registration, distance learning, double major, English as a Second Language (ESL), exchange student program (domestic), honors program, independent study, internships, liberal arts/career combination, student-designed major, study abroad, teacher certification program. **Honors programs:** Tulane Honors Program **Combined degree programs:** BA/MD, BA/JD, BA/MA, Integrated Graduate Studies 4+1 programs. Special programs offered to physically disabled students include note-taking services, reader services, tape recorders, tutors. **Career services:** Alumni network, alumni services, career/job search classes, career assessment, internships, regional alumni.

FACILITIES
Housing: Coed dorms, special housing for disabled students, special housing for international students, women's dorms, apartments for married students, apartments for single students, wellness housing. 60% of campus accessible to physically disabled. **Special Academic Facilities/Equipment:** Newcomb Art Gallery, Amistad Research Center, Latin American Library, Maxwell Music Library, Hogan Jazz Archives, Louisiana Special Collection, Manuscripts Department, Koch Herbarium, Tulane Museum of Natural History, Government Documents. **Computers:** 100% of classrooms, 100% of dorms, 100% of libraries, 100% of dining areas, 100% of student union, 100% of common outdoor areas have wireless network access. Students can register for classes online. Administrative functions (other than registration) can be performed online.

CAMPUS LIFE
Environment: City. **Activities:** Choral groups, concert band, dance, drama/theater, jazz band, literary magazine, marching band, music ensembles, musical theater, pep band, radio station, student government, student newspaper, student-run film society, television station, yearbook. **Organizations:** 250 registered organizations, 43 honor societies, 16 religious organizations. 15 fraternities, 11 sororities. **Athletics (Intercollegiate):** *Men:* Baseball, basketball, cross-country, football, tennis, track/field (outdoor). *Women:* Basketball, cross-country, diving, golf, swimming, tennis, track/field (outdoor), track/field (indoor), volleyball. **On-Campus Highlights:** Amistad Research Center, Newcomb Art Gallery, Reily Recreation Center, Howard Tilton Memorial Library, PJ's Coffee Shop. **Environmental Initiatives:** Almost every school within the university offers undergraduates or graduates an environmental major or focus. These include a top-ranked Environmental Law program, Environmental Health Sciences degrees at the graduate and undergraduate levels, an Environmental Science degree, an interdisciplinary Environmental Studies degree and studios that focus on sustainable design in the School of Architecture. In addition, the Ecology and Evolutionary Biology and Earth and Environmental Sciences departments have strong programs that address coastal sustainability and global environmental change. Tulane's Center for Public Service and the public service requirement ensures that academic inquiry is integrated with active civic engagement, largely within the context of helping New Orleans rebuild as a more sustainable community. Tulane has a number of green building projects on campus, and since Hurricane Katrina many Tulane students, staff and faculty have been engaged in sustainable building, design, and neighborhood planning projects in the larger community. Most recently on campus, the renovation of

the Lavin-Bernick Center for University Life included the installation of natural ventilation and daylighting features, including solar chimneys, extensive fans, exterior sunshades, and lighting systems that adjust to daylight. Off-campus, projects such as a Tulane-facilitated energy efficient neighborhood plan and green, affordable homes designed and constructed by Tulane architecture students have advanced sustainable rebuilding efforts in New Orleans. Tulane is currently implementing numerous energy efficiency and water conservation measures that will reduce annual uptown campus greenhouse gas emissions by a projected 10%. In addition to heating, cooling, lighting and water conversation improvements, the university has student-led energy savings education programs, such the country's first Energy Star Showcase Dorm Room. To further this effort to reduce energy use and carbon emissions, Tulane has joined the Presidents Climate Commitment.

ADMISSIONS

Freshman Academic Profile: Average high school GPA 3.49. 60.02% in top 10% of high school class, 87.73% in top 25% of high school class, 97.32% in top 50% of high school class. SAT Math middle 50% range 620–700. SAT Critical Reading middle 50% range 630–700. SAT Writing middle 50% range 630–710. ACT middle 50% range 29–32. Minimum paper TOEFL 550. Minimum computer TOEFL 213. **Basis for Candidate Selection:** *Very important factors considered include:* Class rank, academic GPA, rigor of secondary school record, standardized test scores. *Important factors considered include:* Application essay, recommendation(s), character/personal qualities. *Other factors considered include:* Alumni/ae relation, extracurricular activities, first generation, interview, talent/ability, volunteer work, work experience. **Freshman Admission Requirements:** High school diploma is required and GED is accepted. *Academic units recommended:* 4 English, 4 mathematics, 4 science, (4 science labs), 3 foreign language, 3 social studies, 3 academic electives. **Freshman Admission Statistics:** 39,887 applied, 26% admitted, 14% enrolled. **Transfer Admission Requirements:** High school transcript, college transcript(s), essay or personal statement, minimum college GPA of 2.5 required. Lowest grade transferable C. **General Admission Information:** Regular application deadline 1/15. Regular notification 4/1. Nonfall registration accepted. Admission may be deferred for a maximum of 1 year. Credit and/or placement offered for CEEB Advanced Placement tests.

COSTS AND FINANCIAL AID

Annual tuition $37,200. Room and board $9,606. Required fees $3,384. Average book expense $1,200. **Required Forms and Deadlines:** FAFSA, CSS/Financial Aid PROFILE, noncustodial PROFILE, business/farm supplement. Financial aid filing deadline 2/15. Priority financial aid filing date 2/15. **Notification of Awards:** Applicants will be notified of awards on a rolling basis beginning 3/15. **Types of Aid:** *Need-based scholarships/grants:* Federal Pell, SEOG, state scholarships/grants, private scholarships, the school's own gift aid, Academic Competitiveness Grant, SMART Grant. *Loans:* FFEL Subsidized Stafford, FFEL Unsubsidized Stafford, FFEL PLUS, Federal Perkins. *Student Employment:* Federal Work-Study Program available. Institutional employment available. Highest amount earned per year from on-campus jobs $2,500. Off-campus job opportunities are good. **Financial Aid Statistics:** 39% freshmen, 36% undergrads receive need-based scholarship or grant aid. 18% freshmen, 11% undergrads receive non-need-based scholarship or grant aid. 21% freshmen, 24% undergrads receive need-based self-help aid. 2% freshmen, 2% undergrads receive athletic scholarships. 48% undergrads borrow to pay for school. Average cumulative indebtedness $25,284. **Criteria for awarding institutional aid:** *Non-need-based:* Academics, athletics, leadership, music/drama, state/district residency.

TUSCULUM COLLEGE

PO Box 5051, Greenville, TN 37743
Phone: 423-636-7300 **Financial Aid Phone:** 800-729-0256
E-mail: admissions@tusculum.edu **CEEB Code:** 1812
Fax: 423-638-7166 **Website: ACT Code:** 4018

This private school, affiliated with the Presbyterian Church, was founded in 1794. It has a 142-acre campus.

RATINGS

Admissions Selectivity Rating: 71 **Fire Safety Rating:** 60* **Green Rating:** 60*

STUDENTS AND FACULTY

Enrollment: 2,600. **Student Body:** 60% female, 40% male, 18% out-of-state, 2% international (8 countries represented). African American 11%, Caucasian 83%, Hispanic 2%.
Retention and Graduation: 62% freshmen return for sophomore year. 26% freshmen graduate within 4 years. 10% grads go on to further study within 1

year. 12% grads pursue arts and sciences degrees. 1% grads pursue law degrees. 5% grads pursue business degrees. 2% grads pursue medical degrees. **Faculty:** Student/faculty ratio 16:1. 75 full-time faculty, 63% hold PhDs, 3% are members of minority groups, 44% are women.

ACADEMICS

Degrees: Bachelor's, master's. **Classes:** Most classes have 10–19 students. **Majors with Highest Enrollment:** Biology/biological sciences; business administration and management; elementary education and teaching. **Special Study Options:** Double major, honors program, independent study, internships, student-designed major, study abroad, teacher certification program, 16 month accelerated evening program for non-traditional students. **Honors programs:** Honors program for those students meeting gpa and act standards—available after the first semester Special programs offered to physically disabled students include tutors. **Career services:** Alumni network, alumni services, career assessment, internships, regional alumni. **Career services highlights include:** Service-Learning.

FACILITIES

Housing: Coed dorms, men's dorms, women's dorms, apartments for single students. 80% of campus accessible to physically disabled. **Special Academic Facilities/Equipment:** The Andrew Johnson Presidential Museum and Library. The College Archives. The Charles Coffin Collection. **Computers:** Administrative functions (other than registration) can be performed online.

CAMPUS LIFE

Environment: Village. **Activities:** dance, drama/theater, radio station, student government, student newspaper, yearbook. **Organizations:** 12 registered organizations, 1 honor societies, 2 religious organizations. 1 fraternities, 1 sororities. **Athletics (Intercollegiate):** *Men:* Baseball, basketball, cheerleading, cross-country, football, golf, soccer, tennis. *Women:* Basketball, cheerleading, cross-country, golf, soccer, softball, tennis, volleyball. **On-Campus Highlights:** Niswonger Commons Center, Perk Coffee House, Indoor Athletic Facility

ADMISSIONS

Freshman Academic Profile: Average high school GPA 2.85. 16% in top 10% of high school class, 42% in top 25% of high school class, 78% in top 50% of high school class. SAT Math middle 50% range 410–540. SAT Critical Reading middle 50% range 410–540. ACT middle 50% range 18–23. Minimum paper TOEFL 550. Minimum computer TOEFL 250. **Basis for Candidate Selection:** *Very important factors considered include:* Rigor of secondary school record, standardized test scores. *Important factors considered include:* Application essay. *Other factors considered include:* Class rank, recommendation(s), character/personal qualities, extracurricular activities, interview, talent/ability, volunteer work. **Freshman Admission Requirements:** High school diploma is required and GED is accepted. *Academic units required:* 4 English, 3 mathematics, 2 science, 3 social studies. **Freshman Admission Statistics:** 1,456 applied, 81% admitted, 24% enrolled. **Transfer Admission Requirements:** College transcript(s), statement of good standing from prior institution(s). Minimum college GPA of 2.0 required. Lowest grade transferable D. **General Admission Information:** Notification on a rolling basis, beginning on or about 1/3. Nonfall registration accepted. Admission may be deferred for a maximum of 1 year. Credit offered for CEEB Advanced Placement tests.

COSTS AND FINANCIAL AID

Required Forms and Deadlines: FAFSA. Financial aid filing deadline 2/15. Priority financial aid filing date 2/15. **Notification of Awards:** Applicants will be notified of awards on a rolling basis beginning 3/15. **Types of Aid:** *Need-based scholarships/grants:* Federal Pell, SEOG, state scholarships/grants, private scholarships, the school's own gift aid. *Loans:* FFEL Subsidized Stafford, FFEL Unsubsidized Stafford, FFEL PLUS, Federal Perkins. *Student Employment:* Federal Work-Study Program available. Institutional employment available. Off-campus job opportunities are good. **Financial Aid Statistics:** 60% freshmen, 40% undergrads receive need-based scholarship or grant aid. 73% freshmen, 37% undergrads receive non-need-based scholarship or grant aid. 62% freshmen, 51% undergrads receive need-based self-help aid. 15% freshmen, 14% undergrads receive athletic scholarships. 90% freshmen, 85% undergrads receive any aid. Average cumulative indebtedness $14,633. **Criteria for awarding institutional aid:** *Non-need-based:* Academics, athletics, leadership, music/drama, state/district residency.

TUSKEGEE UNIVERSITY

Best 373

Old Administration Building, Suite 101, Tuskegee, AL 36088
Phone: 334-727-8500 **Financial Aid Phone:** 334-727-8500
E-mail: admi@tuskegee.edu **CEEB Code:** 1813
Fax: 334-727-5750 **Website:** www.tuskegee.edu **ACT Code:** 50

This private school was founded in 1881. It has a 5200-acre campus.

RATINGS
Admissions Selectivity Rating: 80   **Fire Safety Rating:** 60*   **Green Rating:** 60*

STUDENTS AND FACULTY
Enrollment: 2,475. **Student Body:** 57% female, 43% male, 72% out-of-state, 1% international (90 countries represented). African American 88%. **Retention and Graduation:** 65% freshmen return for sophomore year. 16% freshmen graduate within 4 years. 23% grads go on to further study within 1 year. 11% grads pursue arts and sciences degrees. 2% grads pursue law degrees. 4% grads pursue business degrees. 3% grads pursue medical degrees. **Faculty:** Student/faculty ratio 11:1. 267 full-time faculty, 82% hold PhDs, 75% are members of minority groups, 34% are women.

ACADEMICS
Degrees: Bachelor's, doctoral, master's. **Classes:** Most classes have 10–19 students. **Majors with Highest Enrollment:** Electrical, electronics and communications engineering; veterinary medicine (dvm). **Special Study Options:** Cooperative education program, double major, dual enrollment, honors program, independent study, internships, teacher certification program **Career services:** Alumni network, career/job search classes, career assessment, internships, regional alumni.

FACILITIES
Housing: Coed dorms, men's dorms, women's dorms, apartments for married students, apartments for single students. **Special Academic Facilities/Equipment:** Agricultural and natural history museum, electron microscopes, two nursery schools. **Computers:** 100% of classrooms, 100% of dorms, 100% of libraries, 100% of dining areas, 100% of student union, 100% of common outdoor areas have wireless network access. Students can register for classes online.

CAMPUS LIFE
Environment: Rural. **Activities:** Choral groups, drama/theater, marching band, student government, student newspaper, yearbook, campus ministries, international student organization. **Organizations:** 36 registered organizations, 22 honor societies, 6 religious organizations. 5 fraternities, 6 sororities. **Athletics (Intercollegiate):** *Men:* Baseball, basketball, cheerleading, cross-country, diving, fencing, football, golf, gymnastics, riflery, soccer, swimming, tennis, track/field (outdoor), track/field (indoor), volleyball. *Women:* Basketball, cheerleading, cross-country, diving, fencing, golf, gymnastics, riflery, soccer, swimming, tennis, track/field (outdoor), track/field (indoor), volleyball. **On-Campus Highlights:** George Washington Carver Museum, Kellogg Conference Center, Tuskegee Chapel, The Tuskegee Cemetery, General Daniel.

ADMISSIONS
Freshman Academic Profile: Average high school GPA 3.07. 20% in top 10% of high school class, 59% in top 25% of high school class, 100% in top 50% of high school class. SAT Math middle 50% range 390–480. SAT Critical Reading middle 50% range 390–490. ACT middle 50% range 17–21. Minimum paper TOEFL 500. Minimum computer TOEFL 62. **Basis for Candidate Selection:** *Very important factors considered include:* Class rank, academic GPA, recommendation(s), rigor of secondary school record, standardized test scores, talent/ability. *Important factors considered include:* Alumni/ae relation, character/personal qualities. *Other factors considered include:* Application essay, extracurricular activities, first generation, geographical residence, interview, state residency, volunteer work, work experience. **Freshman Admission Requirements:** High school diploma is required and GED is accepted. *Academic units required:* 4 English, 3 mathematics, 2 science, 3 social studies, 4 academic electives. **Freshman Admission Statistics:** 2,692 applied, 58% admitted, 44% enrolled. **Transfer Admission Requirements:** College transcript(s), minimum college GPA of 2.0 required. Lowest grade transferable C. **General Admission Information:** Application fee $25. Regular application deadline 7/15. Regular notification 3/15. Notification on a rolling basis, beginning on or about 3/1. Nonfall registration accepted. Credit and/or placement offered for CEEB Advanced Placement tests.

COSTS AND FINANCIAL AID
Annual tuition $16,100. Room and board $7,570. Required fees $650. Average book expense $1,109. **Required Forms and Deadlines:** FAFSA, institution's own financial aid form, CSS/Financial Aid PROFILE Priority financial aid filing date 3/31. **Types of Aid:** *Need-based scholarships/grants:* Federal Pell, SEOG, state scholarships/grants, private scholarships, the school's own gift aid, United Negro College Fund, Federal Nursing Scholarships. *Loans:* Direct Subsidized Stafford, Direct Unsubsidized Stafford, Direct PLUS, FFEL Subsidized Stafford, FFEL Unsubsidized Stafford, FFEL PLUS, Federal Perkins, Federal Nursing, state loans, college/university loans from institutional funds. *Student Employment:* Federal Work-Study Program available. Institutional employment available. Highest amount earned per year from on-campus jobs $1,540. Off-campus job opportunities are good. **Financial Aid Statistics:** 66% freshmen, 77% undergrads receive need-based scholarship or grant aid. 44% freshmen, 26% undergrads receive non-need-based scholarship or grant aid. 51% freshmen, 58% undergrads receive need-based self-help aid. 8% freshmen, 5% undergrads receive athletic scholarships. 80% freshmen, 92% undergrads receive any aid. 91% undergrads borrow to pay for school. Average cumulative indebtedness $28,000. **Criteria for awarding institutional aid:** *Non-need-based:* Academics, athletics, state/district residency.

UNION COLLEGE

310 College Street, Barbourville, KY 40906
Phone: 606-546-1229 **Financial Aid Phone:** 606-546-1224
E-mail: enrollme@unionky.edu
Fax: 606-546-1667 **Website:** www.unionky.edu **ACT Code:** 015520

This private school, affiliated with the Methodist Church, was founded in 1879.

RATINGS
Admissions Selectivity Rating: 80   **Fire Safety Rating:** 60*   **Green Rating:** 60*

STUDENTS AND FACULTY
Enrollment: 811. **Student Body:** 46% female, 54% male, 24.61% out-of-state, 3% international (9 countries represented). African American 12%, Caucasian 79%, Hispanic 1%. **Retention and Graduation:** 14% freshmen graduate within 4 years. **Faculty:** Student/faculty ratio 16:1. 61 full-time faculty, 72% hold PhDs, 10% are members of minority groups, 44% are women.

ACADEMICS
Degrees: Bachelor's, master's, post-bachelor's certificate, post-master's certificate. **Classes:** Most classes have 10–19 students. Most lab/discussion sessions have 10–19 students. **Majors with Highest Enrollment:** Business administration and management; psychology; special education and teaching. **Special Study Options:** Distance learning, double major, honors program, independent study, internships, liberal arts/career combination, student-designed major, study abroad, teacher certification program Special programs offered to physically disabled students include reader services, tape recorders, tutors. **Career services:** Alumni network, career/job search classes, career assessment, internships, regional alumni.

FACILITIES
Housing: Men's dorms, women's dorms, apartments for married students, apartments for single students. 50% of campus accessible to physically disabled. **Computers:** 100% of classrooms, 100% of dorms, 100% of libraries, 100% of dining areas, 100% of student union, 50% of common outdoor areas have wireless network access. Students can register for classes online. Administrative functions (other than registration) can be performed online.

CAMPUS LIFE
Environment: Rural. **Activities:** Choral groups, drama/theater, literary magazine, pep band, student government, television station, yearbook. **Organizations:** 23 registered organizations, 2 honor societies, 2 religious organizations. **Athletics (Intercollegiate):** *Men:* Baseball, basketball, bowling, cheerleading, cross-country, cycling, football, golf, soccer, swimming, tennis, track/field (outdoor). *Women:* Basketball, bowling, cheerleading, cross-country, cycling, golf, soccer, softball, swimming, tennis, track/field (outdoor), volleyball. **On-Campus Highlights:** Student Center, Sharp Center Coffee Shop, Fitness Center.

ADMISSIONS
Freshman Academic Profile: Average high school GPA 2.91. SAT Math middle 50% range 438–508. SAT Critical Reading middle 50% range 415–455. ACT middle 50% range 17–21. Minimum paper TOEFL 550. **Basis for Candidate Selection:** *Important factors considered include:* Class rank,

academic GPA, rigor of secondary school record, standardized test scores, level of applicant's interest. *Other factors considered include:* Recommendation(s), alumni/ae relation, character/personal qualities, extracurricular activities, first generation, geographical residence, talent/ability, volunteer work. **Freshman Admission Requirements:** High school diploma is required and GED is accepted. *Academic units recommended:* 4 English, 3 mathematics, 2 science, (2 science labs), 1 foreign language, 2 social studies. **Freshman Admission Statistics:** 1,226 applied, 28% admitted, 55% enrolled. **Transfer Admission Requirements:** College transcript(s), minimum college GPA of 2.0 required. Lowest grade transferable 2. **General Admission Information:** Application fee $10. Nonfall registration accepted.

COSTS AND FINANCIAL AID

Annual tuition $18,244. Room and board $5,950. Required fees $605. Average book expense $1,400. **Required Forms and Deadlines:** FAFSA. Priority financial aid filing date 3/15. **Notification of Awards:** Applicants will be notified of awards on a rolling basis beginning 3/1. **Types of Aid:** *Need-based scholarships/grants:* Federal Pell, SEOG, state scholarships/grants, private scholarships, the school's own gift aid. *Loans:* FFEL Subsidized Stafford, FFEL Unsubsidized Stafford, FFEL PLUS, college/university loans from institutional funds. *Student Employment:* Federal Work-Study Program available. Institutional employment available. Off-campus job opportunities are fair. **Financial Aid Statistics:** 84% freshmen, 85% undergrads receive need-based scholarship or grant aid. 9% freshmen, 10% undergrads receive non-need-based scholarship or grant aid. 78% freshmen, 77% undergrads receive need-based self-help aid. 73% undergrads borrow to pay for school. Average cumulative indebtedness $22,388. **Criteria for awarding institutional aid:** *Non-need-based:* Academics, athletics, job skills, religious affiliation, state/district residency.

UNION COLLEGE

Grant Hall, Union College, Schenectady, NY 12308
Phone: 518-388-6112 **Financial Aid Phone:** 518-388-6123
E-mail: admissions@union.edu **CEEB Code:** 2920
Fax: 518-388-6986 **Website:** www.union.edu **ACT Code:** 2970

This private school was founded in 1795. It has a 100-acre campus.

RATINGS
Admissions Selectivity Rating: 60*   **Fire Safety Rating:** 60*   **Green Rating:** 60*

STUDENTS AND FACULTY
Enrollment: 2,141. **Student Body:** 49% female, 51% male, 59% out-of-state, 3% international (32 countries represented). Asian 7%, African American 5%, Caucasian 79%, Hispanic 5%.
Retention and Graduation: 91% freshmen return for sophomore year. 80% freshmen graduate within 4 years. 35% grads go on to further study within 1 year. 11% grads pursue arts and sciences degrees. 5% grads pursue law degrees. 7% grads pursue business degrees. 6% grads pursue medical degrees. **Faculty:** Student/faculty ratio 10:1. 199 full-time faculty, 96% hold PhDs, 13% are members of minority groups, 43% are women.

ACADEMICS
Degrees: Bachelor's. **Classes:** Most classes have 10–19 students. Most lab/discussion sessions have 10–19 students. **Majors with Highest Enrollment:** Economics; English language and literature; political science and government. **Special Study Options:** Accelerated program, cross-registration, double major, dual enrollment, honors program, independent study, internships, liberal arts/career combination, student-designed major, study abroad, teacher certification program. **Honors programs:** The Union Scholars program offers selected students the opportunity to take full advantage of the diverse intellectual experiences at Union. Specific features of the program are an enriched two-term version of First-Year Preceptorial; a sophomore independent study project with a professor of the student's choosing; the option to participate as a junior in a program in which students take a leadership role in the College's intellectual and social life; and a Scholars Colloquium run by students for presenting faculty and student research, in the senior year. Union Scholars use their extra courses to create an enriched program that meets their specific needs and interests. **Combined degree programs:** BA/JD, BS/MS or MBA/MD; BS/MS;BA or BS/MBA(joint pgms). Special programs offered to physically disabled students include note-taking services, reader services, tape recorders **Career services:** Alumni network, alumni services, career/job search classes, career assess-

ment, internships, regional alumni. **Career services highlights include:** Faculty, alumni, and athletics involvement in student career planning.

FACILITIES
Housing: Coed dorms, fraternity/sorority housing, apartments for single students, theme housing, Minerva Houses. Up to 45 students live in each. All students and faculty members have (Minerva) house affiliations. Each house contributes intellectual, cultural, and social events to the campus. **Special Academic Facilities/Equipment:** The Nott Memorial and its Mandeville Gallery; Yulman Theater; Burns Arts Atrium; Taylor Music Center and its Emerson Auditorium; Special Collections at Schaffer Library; Memorial Chapel; Jackson's Garden, an eight-acre formal garden and woodland. Academic facilities include the F.W. Olin Center, with high technology classrooms and laboratories, a multi-media auditorium, collaborative computer classrooms, and a 20-inch remote-controlled telescope. Science and engineering facilities include superconducting nuclear magnetic resonance spectrometer, two electron microscopes, tandem pelletron positive ion accelerator, a fully accessible machine lab, and Aerogel fabrication and analysis lab. **Computers:** 100% of classrooms, 75% of dorms, 100% of libraries, 100% of dining areas, 100% of student union, 100% of common outdoor areas have wireless network access. Students can register for classes online. Administrative functions (other than registration) can be performed online.

CAMPUS LIFE
Environment: Town. **Activities:** Choral groups, concert band, dance, drama/theater, jazz band, literary magazine, music ensembles, radio station, student government, student newspaper, student-run film society, symphony orchestra, television station, yearbook, campus ministries, international student organization, Model UN. **Organizations:** 100 registered organizations, 13 honor societies, 7 religious organizations. 12 fraternities, 5 sororities. **Athletics (Intercollegiate):** *Men:* Baseball, basketball, crew/rowing, cross-country, diving, football, ice hockey, lacrosse, soccer, swimming, tennis, track/field (outdoor), track/field (indoor). *Women:* Basketball, crew/rowing, cross-country, diving, field hockey, ice hockey, lacrosse, soccer, softball, swimming, tennis, track/field (outdoor), track/field (indoor), volleyball. **On-Campus Highlights:** The Nott Memorial, Schaffer Library, Reamer Campus Center, Jackson's Garden, Memorial Chapel. **Environmental Initiatives:** President green grants. U Sustain website. Conversion to electric vehicles.

ADMISSIONS
Freshman Academic Profile: Average high school GPA 3.56. 58% in top 10% of high school class, 84% in top 25% of high school class, 99% in top 50% of high school class. 74% from public high schools. SAT Math middle 50% range 620–700. SAT Critical Reading middle 50% range 590–670. SAT Writing middle 50% range 580–670. ACT middle 50% range 27–30. Minimum paper TOEFL 600. Minimum computer TOEFL 250. Minimum web-based TOEFL 90. **Basis for Candidate Selection:** *Very important factors considered include:* Class rank, academic GPA, rigor of secondary school record. *Important factors considered include:* Recommendation(s), standardized test scores, character/personal qualities, extracurricular activities, talent/ability. *Other factors considered include:* Application essay, alumni/ae relation, first generation, geographical residence, interview, level of applicant's interest, racial/ethnic status, state residency, volunteer work, work experience. **Freshman Admission Requirements:** High school diploma is required and GED is not accepted. *Academic units required:* 4 English, 3 mathematics, 2 science, (2 science labs), 2 foreign language, 1 social studies, 1 history. *Academic units recommended:* 4 English, 4 mathematics, 4 science, (4 science labs), 4 foreign language, 2 social studies, 2 history. **Freshman Admission Statistics:** 4,829 applied, 41% admitted, 26% enrolled. **Transfer Admission Requirements:** High school transcript, college transcript(s), essay or personal statement, statement of good standing from prior institution(s). Minimum college GPA of 3.0 required. Lowest grade transferable C. **General Admission Information:** Application fee $50. Early decision application deadline 11/15. Regular application deadline 1/15. Regular notification 4/1. Nonfall registration not accepted. Admission may be deferred for a maximum of 1 year. Credit and/or placement offered for CEEB Advanced Placement tests.

COSTS AND FINANCIAL AID
Comprehensive fee $50,439. **Required Forms and Deadlines:** FAFSA, CSS/Financial Aid PROFILE, state aid form, noncustodial PROFILE, business/farm supplement. Financial aid filing deadline 2/1. Priority financial aid filing date 2/1. **Types of Aid:** *Need-based scholarships/grants:* Federal Pell, SEOG, state scholarships/grants, private scholarships, the school's own gift aid. *Loans:* Direct Subsidized Stafford, Direct Unsubsidized Stafford, Direct PLUS, Federal Perkins, college/university loans from institutional funds. *Student Employment:* Federal Work-Study Program available. Institutional employment available. Highest amount earned per year from on-campus jobs $3,800. Off-campus job opportunities are good. **Financial Aid Statistics:** 51% freshmen, 46% undergrads receive need-based scholarship or grant aid. 2% freshmen, 2% undergrads receive non-need-based scholarship or grant aid. 51% freshmen, 45% undergrads receive need-based self-help aid. 69% freshmen, 68% undergrads receive any aid. 61% undergrads borrow to pay for school. Average cumulative

indebtedness $24,739. **Criteria for awarding institutional aid:** *Non-need-based:* Academics.

See page 1266.

UNION COLLEGE (NE)

3800 South 48th Street, Lincoln, NE 68506-4300
Phone: 402-486-2504 **Financial Aid Phone:** 402-426-2505
E-mail: ucenroll@ucollege.edu
Fax: 402-486-2566 **Website:** www.ucollege.edu **ACT Code:** 2480

This private school, affiliated with the Seventh Day Adventist Church, was founded in 1891.

RATINGS
Admissions Selectivity Rating: 74   **Fire Safety Rating:** 60*   **Green Rating:** 60*

STUDENTS AND FACULTY
Enrollment: 845. **Student Body:** 56% female, 44% male, 79% out-of-state, 11% international (34 countries represented). Asian 2%, African American 2%, Caucasian 75%, Hispanic 6%, Native American 1%.
Retention and Graduation: 69% freshmen return for sophomore year. 21% grads go on to further study within 1 year. 8% grads pursue arts and sciences degrees. 2% grads pursue law degrees. 5% grads pursue business degrees. 6% grads pursue medical degrees. **Faculty:** Student/faculty ratio 13:1. 54 full-time faculty, 54% hold PhDs, 13% are members of minority groups, 35% are women.

ACADEMICS
Degrees: Associate, bachelor's, master's. **Classes:** Most classes have fewer than 10 students. **Majors with Highest Enrollment:** Business/commerce; nursing/registered nurse (RN, ASN, BSN, MSN); physician assistant. **Special Study Options:** Cross-registration, distance learning, double major, dual enrollment, English as a Second Language (ESL), honors program, independent study, internships, student-designed major, study abroad, teacher certification program. **Honors programs:** The honors program is available for students who have demonstrated superior scholastic ability. Special programs offered to physically disabled students include note-taking services, reader services, tape recorders, tutors. **Career services:** Career assessment, internships.

FACILITIES
Housing: Men's dorms, women's dorms, apartments for married students, apartments for single students 75% of campus accessible to physically disabled. **Computers:** Administrative functions (other than registration) can be performed online.

CAMPUS LIFE
Environment: Village. **Activities:** Choral groups, concert band, drama/theater, literary magazine, music ensembles, student government, student newspaper, yearbook. **Organizations:** 1 honor societies, 3 religious organizations. **Athletics (Intercollegiate):** *Men:* Basketball, volleyball. *Women:* Basketball, volleyball. **On-Campus Highlights:** Cafeteria, The Ortner Center, The Arboretum, Dick Administration Bldg, Larson Life Style Center.

ADMISSIONS
Freshman Academic Profile: 17% in top 10% of high school class, 14% in top 25% of high school class, 57% in top 50% of high school class. 10% from public high schools. ACT middle 50% range 19–25. Minimum paper TOEFL 550. Minimum computer TOEFL 213. **Basis for Candidate Selection:** *Very important factors considered include:* Recommendation(s), rigor of secondary school record, standardized test scores, character/personal qualities. *Important factors considered include:* Class rank, extracurricular activities, interview, religious affiliation/commitment. *Other factors considered include:* Application essay, alumni/ae relation, geographical residence, state residency, talent/ability. **Freshman Admission Requirements:** High school diploma is required and GED is accepted. *Academic units required:* 3 English, 2 mathematics, 2 science, (1 science labs), 1 social studies, 1 history, 3 academic electives. *Academic units recommended:* 4 English, 3 mathematics, 3 science, 1 foreign language. **Freshman Admission Statistics:** 635 applied, 43% admitted, 66% enrolled. **Transfer Admission Requirements:** High school transcript, college transcript(s), minimum college GPA of 2.0 required. Lowest grade transferable C–. **General Admission Information:** Nonfall registration accepted. Credit and/or placement offered for CEEB Advanced Placement tests.

COSTS AND FINANCIAL AID
Annual tuition $13,990. Room and board $4,720. Required fees $420. Average book expense $950. **Required Forms and Deadlines:** FAFSA. Priority financial aid filing date 3/15. **Notification of Awards:** Applicants will be notified of awards on a rolling basis beginning 5/1. **Types of Aid:** *Need-based scholarships/*

grants: Federal Pell, SEOG, state scholarships/grants, private scholarships, the school's own gift aid. *Loans:* FFEL Subsidized Stafford, FFEL Unsubsidized Stafford, FFEL PLUS, Federal Perkins, Federal Nursing, college/university loans from institutional funds. *Student Employment:* Highest amount earned per year from on-campus jobs $1,300. **Financial Aid Statistics:** 86% freshmen, 87% undergrads receive need-based scholarship or grant aid. 12% freshmen, 9% undergrads receive non-need-based scholarship or grant aid. 73% freshmen, 77% undergrads receive need-based self-help aid. 100% freshmen, 58% undergrads receive any aid. **Criteria for awarding institutional aid:** *Non-need-based:* Academics, leadership, religious affiliation.

UNION INSTITUTE & UNIVERSITY

440 East McMillan Street, Cincinnati, OH 45206
Phone: 513-861-6400 **Financial Aid Phone:** 800-486-3116
E-mail: admissions@myunion.edu
Fax: 513-861-3238 **Website:** www.myunion.edu

This private school was founded in 1964.

RATINGS
Admissions Selectivity Rating: 60*   **Fire Safety Rating:** 60*   **Green Rating:** 68

STUDENTS AND FACULTY
Enrollment: 963. **Student Body:** 60% female, 40% male, 17% out-of-state, (24 countries represented). Asian 2%, African American 30%, Caucasian 44%, Hispanic 13%, Native American 1%.
Retention and Graduation: 79% freshmen return for sophomore year. 21% freshmen graduate within 4 years. **Faculty:** 35 full-time faculty, 291% hold PhDs, 11% are members of minority groups, 46% are women.

ACADEMICS
Degrees: Bachelor's, doctoral, master's, post-bachelor's certificate, post-master's certificate. **Majors with Highest Enrollment:** child development; criminal justice/law enforcement administration; liberal arts and sciences studies and humanities, other. **Special Study Options:** Cross-registration, distance learning, external degree program, independent study, internships, teacher certification program **Career services:** Alumni services, career assessment.

FACILITIES
Housing: Housing (not university-owned) available for learners participating in brief on-campus residencies at Montpelier, Vermont, center (applicable to BA and MEd programs only). 100% of campus accessible to physically disabled. **Computers:** Students can register for classes online. Administrative functions (other than registration) can be performed online.

CAMPUS LIFE
Environment: Metropolis.

ADMISSIONS
Basis for Candidate Selection: *Very important factors considered include:* Application essay, recommendation(s), interview. *Important factors considered include:* level of applicant's interest. *Other factors considered include:* character/personal qualities, extracurricular activities, talent/ability, volunteer work, work experience. **Freshman Admission Requirements:** High school diploma is required and GED is accepted. **Transfer Admission Requirements:** College transcript(s), essay or personal statement, interview, Lowest grade transferable D. **General Admission Information:** Application fee $35. Nonfall registration accepted. Admission may be deferred for a maximum of 1 year. Credit offered for CEEB Advanced Placement tests.

COSTS AND FINANCIAL AID
Annual tuition $10,896. Required fees $174. **Required Forms and Deadlines:** FAFSA, institution's own financial aid form. Financial aid filing deadline 8/1. **Notification of Awards:** Applicants will be notified of awards on a rolling basis beginning 5/1. **Types of Aid:** *Need-based scholarships/grants:* Federal Pell, SEOG, state scholarships/grants, private scholarships, the school's own gift aid. *Loans:* FFEL Subsidized Stafford, FFEL Unsubsidized Stafford, FFEL PLUS, Federal Perkins. *Student Employment:* Federal Work-Study Program available. Off-campus job opportunities are good. **Criteria for awarding institutional aid:** *Non-need-based:* Academics, state/district residency.

UNION UNIVERSITY

1050 Union University Drive, Jackson, TN 38305-3697
Phone: 731-661-5000 **Financial Aid Phone:** 731-661-5015
E-mail: rgrimm@uu.edu **CEEB Code:** 1826
Fax: 731-661-5017 **Website: ACT Code:** 4020

This private school, affiliated with the Southern Baptist Church, was founded in 1823. It has a 360-acre campus.

RATINGS
Admissions Selectivity Rating: 86   **Fire Safety Rating:** 73   **Green Rating:** 75

STUDENTS AND FACULTY
Enrollment: 2,439. **Student Body:** 61% female, 39% male, % out-of-state, 2% international (36 countries represented). Asian 1%, African American 11%, Caucasian 82%, Hispanic 1%.
Retention and Graduation: 92% freshmen return for sophomore year. 40% grads go on to further study within 1 year. **Faculty:** Student/faculty ratio 12:1.

ACADEMICS
Degrees: Associate, bachelor's, diploma, doctoral, master's, post-master's certificate, transfer associate. **Classes:** Most classes have 10–19 students. Most lab/discussion sessions have 10–19 students. **Majors with Highest Enrollment:** christian studies; elementary education and teaching; nursing/registered nurse (RN, ASN, BSN, MSN). **Special Study Options:** Accelerated program, cross-registration, distance learning, double major, dual enrollment, English as a Second Language (ESL), exchange student program (domestic), honors program, independent study, internships, study abroad, teacher certification program Special programs offered to physically disabled students include note-taking services, reader services, tape recorders, tutors. **Career services:** Alumni network, alumni services, career/job search classes, career assessment, internships, regional alumni. **Career services highlights include:** Our department is proudest of the career development and recruitment opportunities that are discipline-specific (What Can I Do With a Major In…? workshops) and recruitment-specific (College to Career, professional development and prep; Career "U"niversity, internship opportunities; the Job Market, career recruitment, and Teacher Expo, education recruitment).

FACILITIES
Housing: Special housing for disabled students, men's dorms, women's dorms, apartments for married students. 98% of campus accessible to physically disabled. **Special Academic Facilities/Equipment:** Elementary education lab, 21st-century classroom, TV communications truck, nursing/health assessment labs, health and wellness center, art gallery. **Computers:** 75% of classrooms, 100% of dorms, 100% of libraries, 50% of dining areas, 100% of student union, have wireless network access. Administrative functions (other than registration) can be performed online.

CAMPUS LIFE
Environment: City. **Activities:** Choral groups, concert band, drama/theater, jazz band, literary magazine, music ensembles, pep band, student government, student newspaper, student-run film society, yearbook, campus ministries, international student organization. **Organizations:** 67 registered organizations, 12 honor societies, 4 religious organizations. 3 fraternities, 3 sororities **Athletics (Intercollegiate):** *Men:* Baseball, basketball, cheerleading, cross-country, golf, soccer. *Women:* Basketball, cheerleading, cross-country, soccer, softball, volleyball. **On-Campus Highlights:** Bowld Commons, New Residence Life Complexes, Pharmacy Building, White Hall, Jennings Hall, Athletic Facility, Penick Academic Complex, Barefoot's Joe Coffee Shop. **Environmental Initiatives:** Campus wide recycling campaign for cans, plastics (#1 and #2), and paper. This includes pick up from all student residential areas as well as all buildings/offices. Participation in RecycleMania; organizing new student sustainability organization. Working towards energy efficiency in all new buildings/appliances.

ADMISSIONS
Freshman Academic Profile: Average high school GPA 3.616. 35% in top 10% of high school class, 63% in top 25% of high school class, 89% in top 50% of high school class. 60% from public high schools. SAT Math middle 50% range 510–630. SAT Critical Reading middle 50% range 510–660. ACT middle 50% range 23–30. Minimum paper TOEFL 550. Minimum web-based TOEFL 80. **Basis for Candidate Selection:** *Very important factors considered include:* Academic GPA, rigor of secondary school record, character/personal qualities, level of applicant's interest. *Important factors considered include:* Class rank, standardized test scores, extracurricular activities, interview, religious affiliation/commitment, talent/ability. *Other factors considered include:* Application essay, recommendation(s), alumni/ae relation, first generation, volunteer work, work experience. **Freshman Admission Requirements:** High school diploma is required and GED is accepted. *Academic units required:* 4 English,

3 mathematics, 3 science, (2 science labs), 1 foreign language, 2 social studies, 1 history, 1 academic electives. *Academic units recommended:* 4 English, 4 mathematics, 4 science, (2 science labs), 2 foreign language, 2 social studies, 2 history, 1 visual/performing arts, 1 computer science, 4 academic electives. **Freshman Admission Statistics:** 1,526 applied, 84% admitted, 42% enrolled. **Transfer Admission Requirements:** College transcript(s), statement of good standing from prior institution(s). Minimum college GPA of 2.3 required. Lowest grade transferable C. **General Admission Information:** Application fee $35. Regular application deadline 8/1. Notification on a rolling basis, beginning on or about 10/1. Nonfall registration accepted. Admission may be deferred for a maximum of 1 year. Credit offered for CEEB Advanced Placement tests.

COSTS AND FINANCIAL AID
Annual tuition $17,990. Room and board $6,200. Required fees $630. Average book expense $1,000. **Required Forms and Deadlines:** FAFSA, institution's own financial aid form. Priority financial aid filing date 2/15. **Notification of Awards:** Applicants will be notified of awards on a rolling basis beginning 12/1. **Types of Aid:** *Need-based scholarships/grants:* Federal Pell, SEOG, state scholarships/grants, private scholarships, the school's own gift aid. *Loans:* Direct Subsidized Stafford, Direct Unsubsidized Stafford, Direct PLUS, Federal Perkins, Alternative Loans. *Student Employment:* Federal Work-Study Program available. Institutional employment available. Highest amount earned per year from on-campus jobs $1,500. Off-campus job opportunities are excellent. **Financial Aid Statistics:** 55% freshmen, 51% undergrads receive need-based scholarship or grant aid. 72% freshmen, 68% undergrads receive non-need-based scholarship or grant aid. 42% freshmen, 45% undergrads receive need-based self-help aid. 9% freshmen, 10% undergrads receive athletic scholarships. 92% freshmen, 85% undergrads receive any aid. 58% undergrads borrow to pay for school. Average cumulative indebtedness $24,253. **Criteria for awarding institutional aid:** *Non-need-based:* Academics, alumni affiliation, art, athletics, leadership, minority status, music/drama, religious affiliation.

UNITED STATES AIR FORCE ACADEMY

HQ USAFA/ RRS, 2304 Cadet Drive, Suite 2300, USAF Academy, CO 80840-5025
Phone: 719-333-2520
E-mail: rr_webmail@usafa.edu
Fax: 719-333-3012 **Website:** www.academyadmissions.com **ACT Code:** 530

This public school was founded in 1954. It has a 18000-acre campus.

RATINGS
Admissions Selectivity Rating: 96   **Fire Safety Rating:** 60*   **Green Rating:** 80

STUDENTS AND FACULTY
Enrollment: 4,620. **Student Body:** 20% female, 80% male, 93% out-of-state, 1% international (36 countries represented). Asian 8%, African American 5%, Caucasian 73%, Hispanic 8%, Native American 1%.
Retention and Graduation: 91% freshmen return for sophomore year. 77% freshmen graduate within 4 years. 8.6% grads go on to further study within 1 year. 2.2% grads pursue arts and sciences degrees. 1% grads pursue business degrees. 1.9% grads pursue medical degrees. **Faculty:** Student/faculty ratio 9:1. 506 full-time faculty, 51% hold PhDs, 8% are members of minority groups, 23% are women.

ACADEMICS
Degrees: Bachelor's. **Classes:** Most classes have 10–19 students. Most lab/discussion sessions have 10–19 students. **Majors with Highest Enrollment:** Aerospace, aeronautical and astronautical engineering; business/commerce; social sciences. **Special Study Options:** Double major, English as a Second Language (ESL), exchange student program (domestic), honors program, independent study, internships, student-designed major, study abroad, Academically At-Risk Program Hospital Instruction Program Extra Instruction Program Summer Programs.

FACILITIES
Housing: Coed dormsAll students are required to live on campus all four years. **Special Academic Facilities/Equipment:** Language learning center, laser and optics research center, USAFA observatory, Dept. of Engineering Mechanics Lab, US Air Force Academy visitor's center, consolidated educational training facility, Air Force Academy cadet chapel, American Legion Memorial Tower, Clune area athletic and speaking events (seats 6,000), air garden, Falcon

Stadium, Aeronautics Lab, Meterology Lab, Arnold Hall Broadway Theater, ballroom and conference rooms, and historical displays. **Computers:** 100% of classrooms, 100% of libraries, 100% of student union, have wireless network access. Students can register for classes online. Administrative functions (other than registration) can be performed online. Undergraduates are required to own a computer.

CAMPUS LIFE
Environment: Metropolis. **Activities:** Choral groups, dance, drama/theater, marching band, musical theater, pep band, radio station, yearbook, campus ministries, Model UN. **Organizations:** 77 registered organizations, 2 honor societies, 14 religious organizations. **Athletics (Intercollegiate):** *Men:* Baseball, basketball, boxing, cheerleading, cross-country, diving, fencing, football, golf, gymnastics, ice hockey, lacrosse, riflery, soccer, swimming, tennis, track/field (outdoor), track/field (indoor), water polo, wrestling. *Women:* Basketball, cheerleading, cross-country, diving, fencing, gymnastics, riflery, soccer, swimming, tennis, track/field (outdoor), track/field (indoor), volleyball. **On-Campus Highlights:** USAF Academy Chapel, Thunderbird Lookout and Air Field, Falcon Stadium, Cadet Sports Complex, Visitor Center. **Environmental Initiatives:** Solar Hydro Geo Thermal

ADMISSIONS
Freshman Academic Profile: Average high school GPA 3.86. 52% in top 10% of high school class, 81% in top 25% of high school class, 97% in top 50% of high school class. 90% from public high schools. SAT Math middle 50% range 630–700. SAT Critical Reading middle 50% range 600–680. SAT Writing middle 50% range 570–650. ACT middle 50% range 28–32. **Basis for Candidate Selection:** *Very important factors considered include:* Class rank, application essay, academic GPA, recommendation(s), rigor of secondary school record, standardized test scores, character/personal qualities, interview. *Important factors considered include:* Extracurricular activities, talent/ability, volunteer work, work experience. *Other factors considered include:* Alumni/ae relation, first generation, geographical residence, racial/ethnic status, state residency. **Freshman Admission Requirements:** High school diploma is required and GED is accepted. *Academic units recommended:* 4 English, 4 mathematics, 4 science, (4 science labs), 2 foreign language, 3 social studies, 3 history, 1 computer science. **Freshman Admission Statistics:** 9,897 applied, 17% admitted, 82% enrolled. **Transfer Admission Requirements:** High school transcript, college transcript(s), essay or personal statement, interview, standardized test scores, minimum college GPA of 2.0 required. **General Admission Information:** Regular application deadline 2/15. Notification on a rolling basis, beginning on or about 11/15. Nonfall registration not accepted. Credit and/or placement offered for CEEB Advanced Placement tests.

See page 1268.

UNITED STATES COAST GUARD ACADEMY

31 Mohegan Avenue, New London, CT 06320-8103
Phone: 860-444-8503
E-mail: CEEB Code: 5807
Fax: 860-701-6700 **Website:** www.uscga.edu **ACT Code:** 0600

This public school was founded in 1876. It has a 120-acre campus.

RATINGS
Admissions Selectivity Rating: 95   **Fire Safety Rating:** 72   **Green Rating:** 82

STUDENTS AND FACULTY
Enrollment: 973. **Student Body:** 27% female, 73% male, 94% out-of-state, 2% international (10 countries represented). Asian 4%, African American 3%, Caucasian 82%, Hispanic 7%, Native American 1%.
Retention and Graduation: 89% freshmen return for sophomore year. 73% freshmen graduate within 4 years. **Faculty:** Student/faculty ratio 7:1. 139 full-time faculty, 48% hold PhDs, 7% are members of minority groups, 26% are women.

ACADEMICS
Degrees: Bachelor's. **Classes:** Most classes have 10–19 students. Most lab/discussion sessions have fewer than 10 students. **Majors with Highest Enrollment:** Business administration and management; civil engineering; political science and government. **Special Study Options:** Double major, exchange student program (domestic), honors program, independent study, internships.

Career services: Alumni network, career assessment, regional alumni. **Career services highlights include:** All graduates are "employed" and assigned to operational field units upon graduation.

FACILITIES
Housing: Coed dorms 95% of campus accessible to physically disabled. **Special Academic Facilities/Equipment:** CG Museum; Library; Visitors Center; Alumni Center **Computers:** 100% of classrooms, 65% of dorms, 100% of libraries, 50% of dining areas, 100% of student union, 50% of common outdoor areas have wireless network access. Students can register for classes online. Administrative functions (other than registration) can be performed online. Undergraduates are required to own a computer.

CAMPUS LIFE
Environment: City. **Activities:** Choral groups, concert band, dance, drama/theater, jazz band, marching band, pep band, yearbook, campus ministries. **Organizations:** 2 honor societies, 7 religious organizations. **Athletics (Intercollegiate):** *Men:* Baseball, basketball, crew/rowing, cross-country, diving, football, pistol, riflery, sailing, soccer, swimming, tennis, track/field (outdoor), track/field (indoor), wrestling. *Women:* Basketball, cheerleading, crew/rowing, cross-country, diving, pistol, riflery, sailing, soccer, softball, swimming, track/field (outdoor), track/field (indoor), volleyball. **On-Campus Highlights:** Coast Guard Barque EAGLE, Coast Guard Museum, Sailing Center and Waterfront, Souvenier Shop (Military Exchange), Coast Guard Academy Chapel and Crown Park. **Environmental Initiatives:** Federal Electronic Recycling Challenge Participant and winner 2008 and 2009. RecycleMania www.campusdish.com/en-US/csne/uscga/Sustainability. Federal electronics challenge facility partner 2009 and 2010.

ADMISSIONS
Freshman Academic Profile: Average high school GPA 3.7. 49% in top 10% of high school class, 83% in top 25% of high school class, 99% in top 50% of high school class. 81% from public high schools. SAT Math middle 50% range 600–680. SAT Critical Reading middle 50% range 560–660. ACT middle 50% range 24–30. Minimum paper TOEFL 560. Minimum computer TOEFL 220. **Basis for Candidate Selection:** *Very important factors considered include:* Class rank, academic GPA, rigor of secondary school record, standardized test scores, character/personal qualities, extracurricular activities. *Important factors considered include:* Application essay, recommendation(s), talent/ability. *Other factors considered include:* Alumni/ae relation, interview, level of applicant's interest, volunteer work, work experience. **Freshman Admission Requirements:** High school diploma is required and GED is accepted. *Academic units required:* 4 English, 4 mathematics, 3 science, (3 science labs). **Freshman Admission Statistics:** 1,672 applied, 25% admitted, 70% enrolled. **Transfer Admission Requirements:** High school transcript, essay or personal statement, standardized test scores, statement of good standing from prior institution(s). **General Admission Information:** Regular application deadline 2/1. Notification on a rolling basis, beginning on or about 12/15. Nonfall registration not accepted. Placement offered for CEEB Advanced Placement tests.

UNITED STATES MERCHANT MARINE ACADEMY

Office of Admissions, Kings Point, NY 11024-1699
Phone: 516-773-5391 **Financial Aid Phone:** 516-773-5295
E-mail: admissions@usmma.edu **CEEB Code:** 2923
Fax: 516-773-5390 **Website:** www.usmma.edu **ACT Code:** 2974

This public school was founded in 1943. It has a 82-acre campus.

RATINGS
Admissions Selectivity Rating: 93   **Fire Safety Rating:** 60*   **Green Rating:** 60*

STUDENTS AND FACULTY
Enrollment: 985. **Student Body:** 12% female, 88% male, 86% out-of-state, 3% international (5 countries represented). Asian 5%, African American 3%, Caucasian 84%, Hispanic 5%, Native American 1%.
Retention and Graduation: 92% freshmen return for sophomore year. 2% grads go on to further study within 1 year. 1% grads pursue arts and sciences degrees. **Faculty:** Student/faculty ratio 11:1. 95 full-time faculty, 100% hold PhDs, 15% are women.

ACADEMICS

Degrees: Bachelor's, master's. **Classes:** Most classes have 10–19 students. Most lab/discussion sessions have 10–19 students. **Majors with Highest Enrollment:** Engineering; naval architecture and marine engineering; transportation and materials moving, other. **Special Study Options:** honors program, independent study, internships. **Career services:** Alumni network, alumni services, career/job search classes, career assessment, internships.

FACILITIES

Housing: Coed dorms, all students required to live on campus in dormitories provided. **Special Academic Facilities/Equipment:** American Merchant Marine Museum. **Computers:** Students can register for classes online. Administrative functions (other than registration) can be performed online. Undergraduates are required to own a computer.

CAMPUS LIFE

Environment: Village. **Activities:** Choral groups, concert band, drama/theater, marching band, student government, student newspaper, yearbook, campus ministries. **Organizations:** 3 religious organizations. **Athletics (Intercollegiate):** *Men:* Baseball, basketball, crew/rowing, cross-country, diving, football, golf, lacrosse, riflery, sailing, soccer, swimming, tennis, track/field (outdoor), volleyball, water polo, wrestling. *Women:* Basketball, crew/rowing, cross-country, diving, golf, riflery, sailing, softball, swimming, tennis, track/field (outdoor), volleyball.

ADMISSIONS

Freshman Academic Profile: Average high school GPA 3.6. 18% in top 10% of high school class, 23% in top 25% of high school class, 85% in top 50% of high school class. 71% from public high schools. SAT Math middle 50% range 600–660. SAT Critical Reading middle 50% range 540–640. ACT middle 50% range 25–29. Minimum paper TOEFL 533. Minimum computer TOEFL 200. Minimum web-based TOEFL 73. **Basis for Candidate Selection:** *Very important factors considered include:* Rigor of secondary school record, standardized test scores, character/personal qualities. *Important factors considered include:* Class rank, application essay, academic GPA, recommendation(s), extracurricular activities, level of applicant's interest, talent/ability. *Other factors considered include:* geographical residence, interview, racial/ethnic status, state residency, volunteer work, work experience. **Freshman Admission Requirements:** High school diploma is required and GED is accepted. *Academic units required:* 4 English, 3 mathematics, 3 science, (1 science labs), 8 academic electives. *Academic units recommended:* 4 English, 4 mathematics, 4 science, (2 science labs), 2 foreign language, 4 social studies. **Freshman Admission Statistics:** 1,734 applied, 18% admitted, 100% enrolled. **Transfer Admission Requirements:** High school transcript, college transcript(s), essay or personal statement, standardized test scores, statement of good standing from prior institution(s). Minimum college GPA of 2.5 required. **General Admission Information:** Regular application deadline 3/1. Notification on a rolling basis, beginning on or about 11/1. Nonfall registration not accepted. Credit offered for CEEB Advanced Placement tests.

COSTS AND FINANCIAL AID

Required fees $2,843. **Required Forms and Deadlines:** FAFSA, institution's own financial aid form Financial aid filing deadline 5/1. **Notification of Awards:** Applicants will be notified of awards on a rolling basis beginning 1/31. **Types of Aid:** *Need-based scholarships/grants:* Federal Pell, private scholarships, Federal SMART Grants & Federal Academic Competitiveness Grants. *Loans:* Direct PLUS, FFEL Subsidized Stafford, FFEL Unsubsidized Stafford, FFEL PLUS. *Student Employment:* Off-campus job opportunities are poor.

UNITED STATES MILITARY ACADEMY

646 Swift Road, West Point, NY 10996-1905
Phone: 845-938-4041
E-mail: admissions@usma.edu **CEEB Code:** 2924
Fax: 845-938-3021 **Website:** www.westpoint.edu **ACT Code:** 2976

This public school was founded in 1802. It has a 16080-acre campus.

RATINGS

Admissions Selectivity Rating: 96   **Fire Safety Rating:** 83   **Green Rating:** 60*

STUDENTS AND FACULTY

Enrollment: 4,553. **Student Body:** 15% female, 85% male, 93% out-of-state, 1% international (35 countries represented). Asian 7%, African American 6%, Caucasian 75%, Hispanic 8%, Native American 1%.

College Directory

Retention and Graduation: 91% freshmen return for sophomore year. 77% freshmen graduate within 4 years. 100% grads go on to further study within 1 year. 2% grads pursue medical degrees. **Faculty:** Student/faculty ratio 7:1. 637 full-time faculty, 43% hold PhDs, 12% are members of minority groups, 19% are women.

ACADEMICS

Degrees: Bachelor's. **Classes:** Most classes have 10–19 students. Most lab/discussion sessions have 10–19 students. **Majors with Highest Enrollment:** Business administration and management; economics; engineering/industrial management. **Special Study Options:** Double major, exchange student program (domestic), honors program, independent study, internships, study abroad, Opportunities to attend Army Schools (Airborne, Air Assault, etc.) to learn special skills.

FACILITIES

Housing: Coed dorms, coed dorms are called barracks. **Special Academic Facilities/Equipment:** West Point Museum (oldest of U.S. army museums. The athletic facilities rate as highly as the academic plant. Arvin gymnasium, featuring swimming pools, wrestling, squash, racquetball, handball, and volleyball. courts has undergone a major renovation to modernize and improve its contribution to the physical development of the corps of cadets. Michie Stadium, home of the Army football team, is considered one of America's most picturesque stadiums to watch a college football game. Holleder Center houses Tate Rink for the Army hockey team and Christl Arena is the home of the Army men and women's basketball teams. Additionally, the Shea Stadium outdoor track facility and Gillis Field House indoor practice facility are newly renovated to include an all-weather track, an astroturf football field and new lighting. There is also a redesigned 18-hole golf course and a new indoor tennis facility. Eisenhower Hall, the modern "student union," contains a 4,500– seat auditorium, a 1,000–seat snack bar and cafeteria, a large ballroom, and other social and recreational rooms. About 60 major productions, to include Broadway shows, musicals, popular rock, jazz, country/western, and alternative music concerts are staged annually in the theater. The new cadet library, Jefferson Hall opened this year. **Computers:** 100% of classrooms, 100% of libraries, 100% of student union, have wireless network access. Students can register for classes online. Administrative functions (other than registration) can be performed online. Undergraduates are required to own a computer.

CAMPUS LIFE

Environment: Village. **Activities:** Choral groups, drama/theater, jazz band, music ensembles, pep band, radio station, student government, student newspaper, television station, yearbook, campus ministries, international student organization, Model UN. **Organizations:** 105 registered organizations, 7 honor societies, 13 religious organizations. **Athletics (Intercollegiate):** *Men:* Baseball, basketball, cross-country, football, golf, gymnastics, ice hockey, lacrosse, riflery, soccer, swimming, tennis, track/field (outdoor), track/field (indoor), wrestling. *Women:* Basketball, cross-country, riflery, soccer, softball, swimming, tennis, track/field (outdoor), track/field (indoor), volleyball. **On-Campus Highlights:** Cadet Chapel, West Point Museum, Eisenhower Hall, Michie Stadium, Trophy Point, Fort Putnam, West Point Cemetery.

ADMISSIONS

Freshman Academic Profile: Average high school GPA 3.75. 43% in top 10% of high school class, 75% in top 25% of high school class, 96% in top 50% of high school class. 86% from public high schools. SAT Math middle 50% range 600–690. SAT Critical Reading middle 50% range 570–670. ACT middle 50% range 21–36. **Basis for Candidate Selection:** *Very important factors considered include:* Class rank, application essay, academic GPA, recommendation(s), rigor of secondary school record, standardized test scores, character/personal qualities, extracurricular activities, talent/ability. *Important factors considered include:* geographical residence, interview, level of applicant's interest, racial/ethnic status, volunteer work. *Other factors considered include:* Alumni/ae relation, state residency, work experience. **Freshman Admission Requirements:** High school diploma is required and GED is accepted. *Academic units recommended:* 4 English, 4 mathematics, 4 science, (2 science labs), 2 foreign language, 3 social studies, 1 history, 3 academic electives. **Freshman Admission Statistics:** 10,778 applied, 14% admitted, 77% enrolled. **General Admission Information:** Regular application deadline 2/28. Notification on a rolling basis, beginning on or about 11/15. Nonfall registration not accepted. Placement offered for CEEB Advanced Placement tests.

COSTS AND FINANCIAL AID

Types of Aid: *Need-based scholarships/grants:* All students receive an annual salary of approximately $10,148. Room and board, medical and dental care is provided by the institution. A one-time deposit of $2,900 is required upon admission to pay for the initial issue of uniforms, books, supplies, equipment and fees. If needed, loans for the deposit are available for $100 to $2,400. *Loans:* All students receive an annual salary of approximately $10,148. Room and board, medical and dental care is provided by the institution. A one-time deposit of $2,900 is required upon admission to pay for the initial issue of uniforms, books, supplies, etc.

See page 1272.

UNITED STATES NAVAL ACADEMY

117 Decatur Road, Annapolis, MD 21402
Phone: 410-293-1914
E-mail: stroop@usna.edu **CEEB Code:** 5809
Fax: 410-293-4348 **Website:** www.usna.edu **ACT Code:** 1742

This public school was founded in 1845. It has a 330-acre campus.

RATINGS
Admissions Selectivity Rating: 96   **Fire Safety Rating:** 60*   **Green Rating:** 60*

STUDENTS AND FACULTY
Enrollment: 4,552. **Student Body:** 20% female, 80% male, 96% out-of-state, 1% international (28 countries represented). Asian 4%, African American 5%, Caucasian 71%, Hispanic 12%.
Retention and Graduation: 96% freshmen return for sophomore year. 84% freshmen graduate within 4 years. 2% grads go on to further study within 1 year. 1% grads pursue medical degrees. **Faculty:** Student/faculty ratio 8.7:1. 522 full-time faculty, 64% hold PhDs, 9% are members of minority groups, 23% are women.

ACADEMICS
Degrees: Bachelor's. **Classes:** Most classes have 10–19 students. **Majors with Highest Enrollment:** Economics; political science and government; systems engineering. **Special Study Options:** Double major, exchange student program (domestic), honors program, independent study, Voluntary Graduate Education Program. **Honors programs:** Voluntary Graduate Education Program—second semester seniors may enroll in graduate school at a nearby college or university **Career services highlights include:** The United States Navy and the United States Marine Corps hire all our graduates.

FACILITIES
Housing: Coed dorms. All midshipmen live in same dormitory. **Special Academic Facilities/Equipment:** Naval history museum, Naval Institute Proceedings, propulsion lab, wind tunnels, flight simulator, ship tow tanks, satellite dish, coastal chamber facilities, fleet of small training craft (power and sail), oceanographic research vessel. **Computers:** Students can register for classes online. Administrative functions (other than registration) can be performed online. Undergraduates are required to own a computer.

CAMPUS LIFE
Environment: Town. **Activities:** Choral groups, concert band, drama/theater, jazz band, literary magazine, marching band, musical theater, pep band, radio station, student government, yearbook, campus ministries, international student organization. **Organizations:** 70 registered organizations, 10 honor societies; 8 religious organizations. **Athletics (Intercollegiate):** *Men:* Baseball, basketball, crew/rowing, cross-country, diving, football, golf, gymnastics, lacrosse, light weight football, riflery, sailing, soccer, squash, swimming, tennis, track/field (outdoor), track/field (indoor), water polo, wrestling. *Women:* Basketball, crew/rowing, cross-country, diving, lacrosse, riflery, sailing, soccer, swimming, tennis, track/field (outdoor), track/field (indoor), volleyball. **On-Campus Highlights:** Bancroft Hall, U.S. Naval Academy Museum, Armel-Leftwich Visitor Center, U.S. Naval Academy Chapel, Lejeune Hall.

ADMISSIONS
Freshman Academic Profile: 56% in top 10% of high school class, 81% in top 25% of high school class, 96% in top 50% of high school class. 60% from public high schools. SAT Math middle 50% range 600–700. SAT Critical Reading middle 50% range 560–700. **Basis for Candidate Selection:** *Very important factors considered include:* Class rank, application essay, academic GPA, recommendation(s), rigor of secondary school record, character/personal qualities, extracurricular activities, interview, level of applicant's interest. *Important factors considered include:* Standardized test scores, talent/ability. *Other factors considered include:* Alumni/ae relation, first generation, geographical residence, racial/ethnic status, state residency, volunteer work, work experience. **Freshman Admission Requirements:** High school diploma or equivalent is not required. *Academic units recommended:* 4 English, 4 mathematics, 2 science, (1 science labs), 2 foreign language, 2 history, 1 Introductory computer courses **Freshman Admission Statistics:** 15,342 applied, 10% admitted, 85% enrolled. **General Admission Information:** Regular application deadline 1/31. Regular notification 4/15. Notification on a rolling basis, beginning on or about 9/1. Nonfall registration not accepted. Credit and/or placement offered for CEEB Advanced Placement tests.

UNIVERSITÉ LAVAL—FACULTÉ DES SCIENCES DE L'ADMINISTRATION

2345 Allée des bibliothèques, local 2440, Université Laval, Québec, QC G1V 0A6 Canada
Phone: 418 656-3080 **Financial Aid Phone:** 418 656-3332
E-mail: reg@reg.ulaval.ca
Fax: 1 418 656-5216 **Website:** www.fsa.ulaval.ca

This public school was founded in 1924.

RATINGS
Admissions Selectivity Rating: 60*   **Fire Safety Rating:** 60*   **Green Rating:** 60*

STUDENTS AND FACULTY
Enrollment: 2,009. **Student Body:** 43% female, 57% male, % out-of-state, 3% international.
Retention and Graduation: 75% freshmen return for sophomore year. 65% freshmen graduate within 4 years. **Faculty:**

ACADEMICS
Degrees: Bachelor's, certificate, diploma, master's, post-bachelor's certificate. **Classes: Special Study Options:** Cooperative education program, exchange student program (domestic), internships, student-designed major, study abroad Special programs offered to physically disabled students include note-taking services, reader services, tape recorders **Career services:** Alumni network, alumni services, career/job search classes, internships

FACILITIES
Housing: Coed dorms, men's dorms, women's dorms 100% of campus accessible to physically disabled. **Computers:** 100% of classrooms, 100% of dorms, 100% of libraries, 100% of dining areas, 100% of student union, 100% of common outdoor areas have wireless network access. Students can register for classes online. Administrative functions (other than registration) can be performed online. Undergraduates are required to own a computer.

CAMPUS LIFE
Environment: Metropolis. **Activities:** Choral groups, concert band, dance, drama/theater, jazz band, literary magazine, music ensembles, radio station, student government, student newspaper, international student organization, Model UN. **Organizations:** 200 registered organizations, **Athletics (Intercollegiate):** *Men:* Badminton, basketball, diving, golf, rugby, skiing (downhill/alpine), skiing (nordic/cross-country), soccer, swimming, track/field (outdoor), track/field (indoor), volleyball. *Women:* Badminton, basketball, diving, golf, rugby, skiing (downhill/alpine), skiing (nordic/cross-country), soccer, swimming, track/field (outdoor), track/field (indoor), volleyball. **Environmental Initiatives:** Table de concertation sur le développement durabla See www.developpementdurable.ulaval.ca/agir/la_table_de_concertation_sur_le_developpement_durable/ Fonds de développement durable/Sustainable Developement: 2M$ in 5 years to support on-campus sustainable development projects. All other initiatives: www.developpementdurable.ulaval.ca/agir/

ADMISSIONS
Freshman Academic Profile: Basis for Candidate Selection: *Very important factors considered include:* Academic GPA, rigor of secondary school record. *Other factors considered include:* Standardized test scores, extracurricular activities, work experience. **Freshman Admission Requirements:** High school diploma is required and GED is not accepted. **Freshman Admission Statistics:** 1,377 applied, 71% admitted, 57% enrolled. **General Admission Information:** Application fee $30. Nonfall registration accepted.

COSTS AND FINANCIAL AID
Annual in-state tuition $2,500. Annual out-of-state tuition $5,956. Room and board $2,232. Average book expense $2,000. *Student Employment:* Off-campus job opportunities are good.

UNIVERSITY OF ADVANCING TECHNOLOGY (UAT)

2625 W. Baseline Rd, Tempe, AZ 85283-1056
Phone: 602-383-8228 **Financial Aid Phone:** 602-383-8228
E-mail: admissions@uat.edu
Fax: 602-383-8222 **Website:** www.uat.edu

This proprietary school was founded in 1983.

RATINGS
Admissions Selectivity Rating: 60*   **Fire Safety Rating:** 60*   **Green Rating:** 60*

STUDENTS AND FACULTY
Enrollment: 1,090. **Student Body:** 10% female, 90% male, 8% out-of-state, international. Asian 4%, African American 7%, Caucasian 61%, Hispanic 6%, Native American 1%.
Retention and Graduation: Faculty: Student/faculty ratio 15:1. 35 full-time faculty, 17% hold PhDs, 34% are women.

ACADEMICS
Degrees: Associate, bachelor's, diploma, master's. **Classes:** Most classes have 20–29 students. **Special Study Options:** Accelerated program, cooperative education program, distance learning, double major, independent study, internships, student-designed major **Career services:** Alumni network, alumni services, career/job search classes, career assessment, internships, regional alumni. **Career services highlights include:** UAT expends its resources on seeking out internship opportunities for all of our majors. For example, many of our game design students are currently interns at Rainbow Studios, Buena Vista Games and many other prominent game development companies. Internships are also a graduation requirements for all UAT students.

FACILITIES
Housing: 100% of campus accessible to physically disabled. **Computers:** Administrative functions (other than registration) can be performed online.

CAMPUS LIFE
Environment: Metropolis. **Activities:** Student government **Organizations:** 1 religious organizations. **On-Campus Highlights:** Cuban Pete's Cafe, UAT Library, Computer Commons, Campus Game Stations.

ADMISSIONS
Freshman Academic Profile: Minimum paper TOEFL 550. Minimum computer TOEFL 213. **Basis for Candidate Selection:** *Very important factors considered include:* Character/personal qualities, interview, level of applicant's interest, talent/ability. *Important factors considered include:* Rigor of secondary school record. *Other factors considered include:* Academic GPA, standardized test scores, volunteer work. **Freshman Admission Requirements:** High school diploma is required and GED is accepted. **Transfer Admission Requirements:** High school transcript, college transcript(s), minimum college GPA of 2.0 required. Lowest grade transferable C. **General Admission Information:** Nonfall registration accepted. Admission may be deferred for a maximum of 1 year.

COSTS AND FINANCIAL AID
Annual tuition $18,800. Average book expense $1,000. **Required Forms and Deadlines:** FAFSA. Priority financial aid filing date 4/10. **Types of Aid:** *Need-based scholarships/grants:* Federal Pell, SEOG, private scholarships, the school's own gift aid. *Loans:* FFEL Subsidized Stafford, FFEL Unsubsidized Stafford, FFEL PLUS. **Financial Aid Statistics:** 72% undergrads borrow to pay for school.

THE UNIVERSITY OF AKRON

The University of Akron, Akron, OH 44325-2001
Phone: 330-972-7100 **Financial Aid Phone:** 800-621-3847
E-mail: admissions@uakron.edu **CEEB Code:** 1829
Fax: 330-972-7022 **Website:** www.uakron.edu **ACT Code:** 3338

This public school was founded in 1870. It has a 223-acre campus.

RATINGS
Admissions Selectivity Rating: 70   **Fire Safety Rating:** 84   **Green Rating:** 60*

STUDENTS AND FACULTY
Enrollment: 21,378. **Student Body:** 49% female, 51% male, 3% out-of-state, 1% international (76 countries represented). Asian 2%, African American 14%, Caucasian 77%, Hispanic 1%.
Retention and Graduation: Faculty: Student/faculty ratio 20.5:1. 798 full-time faculty, 82% hold PhDs, 16% are members of minority groups, 42% are women. 4% of classes are taught by teaching assistants.

ACADEMICS
Degrees: Associate, bachelor's, certificate, doctoral, master's, post-bachelor's certificate, post-master's certificate. **Classes:** Most classes have 20–29 students. Most lab/discussion sessions have 10–19 students. **Majors with Highest Enrollment:** Biology/biological sciences; mechanical engineering; nursing/registered nurse (RN, ASN, BSN, MSN). **Special Study Options:** Accelerated program, cooperative education program, distance learning, double major, English as a Second Language (ESL), external degree program, honors program, independent study, internships, student-designed major, study abroad, teacher certification program, weekend college, Undergraduates may take graduate level courses. Co-Op Programs: Arts, Business, Computer Science, Engineering, Family and Consumer Sciences, Humanities, Natural Science, Technologies. Dual Enrollment offered for select graduate level programs. **Honors programs:** Honors Delegates, Engineering Program, Emerging Leaders Program **Combined degree programs:** BA/MD, RN/MSN in Nursing, BS/MS in Accounting and Math. Special programs offered to physically disabled students include note-taking services, reader services, tape recorders, tutors. **Career services:** alumni services, career/job search classes, career assessment, internships. **Career services highlights include:** One of two finalists for the "Most innovative Pedagogy for Entrepreneurship Education Award" at the United States Assocatiation for Small Business and Entrepreneurship (USASBE) annual conference, 2009.

FACILITIES
Housing: Coed dorms, special housing for disabled students, men's dorms, special housing for international students, women's dorms, fraternity/sorority housing, Honors student dormitory. 90% of campus accessible to physically disabled. Performing arts hall, nursery center, language lab, speech and hearing center, nursing learning resource labs, institute of polymer science and engineering, chemical lab, institute for health and social policy, Bliss Institute of Applied Politics. **Computers:** 100% of classrooms, 100% of dorms, 100% of libraries, 100% of dining areas, 100% of student union, 100% of common outdoor areas have wireless network access. Students can register for classes online. Administrative functions (other than registration) can be performed online.

CAMPUS LIFE
Environment: City. **Activities:** Choral groups, concert band, dance, drama/theater, jazz band, marching band, music ensembles, musical theater, pep band, radio station, student government, student newspaper, symphony orchestra, television station, yearbook, campus ministries, international student organization. **Organizations:** 216 registered organizations, 30 honor societies, 12 religious organizations. 15 fraternities, 8 sororities **Athletics (Intercollegiate):** *Men:* Baseball, basketball, cheerleading, cross-country, football, golf, riflery, soccer, track/field (outdoor), track/field (indoor). *Women:* Basketball, cheerleading, cross-country, diving, riflery, soccer, softball, swimming, tennis, track/field (outdoor), track/field (indoor), volleyball. **On-Campus Highlights:** Recreation Center, Student Union (includes food court, Starbucks), E.J. Thomas Performing Arts Hall, James A. Rhodes Arena, Robertson Cafe, Student Recreation and Wellness Center, which features a 56-foot rock-climbing wall, recreation pool, "lazy river," spa, ball courts and fitness facilities; Student Union with a movie theatre, bowling and billiards, a food court and a Starbucks Cafe.

ADMISSIONS
Freshman Academic Profile: Average high school GPA 2.95. 11% in top 10% of high school class, 28% in top 25% of high school class, 56% in top 50% of high school class. SAT Math middle 50% range 430–590. SAT Critical Reading middle 50% range 430–560. ACT middle 50% range 18–24. Minimum paper TOEFL 500. Minimum computer TOEFL 173. Minimum web-based TOEFL 61. **Basis for Candidate Selection:** *Very important factors considered include:* Class rank, academic GPA, rigor of secondary school record, standardized test scores. **Freshman Admission Requirements:** High school diploma is required and GED is accepted. *Academic units recommended:* 4 English, 3 mathematics, 3 science, 2 foreign language, 3 social studies. **Freshman Admission Statistics:** 13,902 applied, 76% admitted, 43% enrolled. **Transfer Admission Requirements:** College transcript(s), statement of good standing from prior institution(s). Lowest grade transferable D–. **General Admission Information:** Application fee $30. Regular application deadline 8/10. Notification on a rolling basis, beginning on or about 9/15. Nonfall registration accepted. Admission may be deferred for a maximum of 2 semesters. Credit offered for CEEB Advanced Placement tests.

COSTS AND FINANCIAL AID
Annual in-state tuition $7,345. Annual out-of-state tuition $16,593. Room and board $8,697. Required fees $1,407. Average book expense $900. **Required**

Forms and Deadlines: FAFSA, institution's own financial aid form. Priority financial aid filing date 2/1. **Notification of Awards:** Applicants will be notified of awards on a rolling basis beginning 4/1. **Types of Aid:** *Need-based scholarships/grants:* Federal Pell, SEOG *Loans:* FFEL Subsidized Stafford, FFEL Unsubsidized Stafford, FFEL PLUS, Federal Perkins, Federal Nursing *Student Employment:* Federal Work-Study Program available. Institutional employment available. Highest amount earned per year from on-campus jobs $5,800. Off-campus job opportunities are excellent. **Financial Aid Statistics:** 35% freshmen, 33% undergrads receive need-based scholarship or grant aid. 37% freshmen, 29% undergrads receive non-need-based scholarship or grant aid. 53% freshmen, 53% undergrads receive need-based self-help aid. 1% freshmen, 1% undergrads receive athletic scholarships. 72% freshmen, 72% undergrads receive any aid. 65% undergrads borrow to pay for school. Average cumulative indebtedness $19,000. **Criteria for awarding institutional aid:** *Non-need-based:* Academics, art, athletics, leadership, music/drama, state/district residency.

THE UNIVERSITY OF ALABAMA AT BIRMINGHAM

Office of Undergraduate Admissions, HUC 260, 1530 3r, Birmingham, AL 35294-1150
Phone: 205-934-8221 **Financial Aid Phone:** 205-934-8223
E-mail: undergradadmit@uab.edu **CEEB Code:** 1856
Fax: 205-975-7114 **Website:** www.uab.edu/home **ACT Code:** 56

This public school was founded in 1969. It has a 183-acre campus.

RATINGS
Admissions Selectivity Rating: 78   **Fire Safety Rating:** 92   **Green Rating:** 60*

STUDENTS AND FACULTY
Enrollment: 10,265. **Student Body:** 58% female, 42% male, 6% out-of-state, 2% international (82 countries represented). Asian 4%, African American 26%, Caucasian 61%, Hispanic 2%.
Retention and Graduation: Faculty: Student/faculty ratio 16:1. 845 full-time faculty, 86% hold PhDs, 20% are members of minority groups, 43% are women.

ACADEMICS
Degrees: Bachelor's, certificate, doctoral, master's, post-bachelor's certificate, post-master's certificate. **Classes:** Most classes have 10–19 students. Most lab/discussion sessions have 20–29 students. **Majors with Highest Enrollment:** Accounting; biology/biological sciences; psychology. **Special Study Options:** Accelerated program, cooperative education program, cross-registration, distance learning, double major, dual enrollment, English as a Second Language (ESL), honors program, independent study, internships, student-designed major, study abroad, teacher certification program. **Honors programs:** The University Honors Program is designed for students who want to satisfy their intellectual curiosity both inside and outside the classroom. The program is limited in size to 200 students who represent a wide variety of disciplines, backgrounds and interests. Without delaying progress toward a degree, the Honors Program provides students an opportunity to participate in a community of committed scholars, to form close relationships with faculty, to explore new ideas, and to share their ideas, interests, and lives on a daily basis in the Honors House. Students have opportunities to work on independent projects, to travel, and to participate in special extracurricular activities. Those who complete the program are recognized with the designation "With University Honors" on their transcripts and in the graduation program. **Combined degree programs:** BA/MD, BA/MA, Fifth Year BS/MS in Biology Program; EMSAP. Special programs offered to physically disabled students include note-taking services, reader services, tape recorders **Career services:** alumni services, career/job search classes, career assessment, regional alumni.

FACILITIES
Housing: Coed dorms, special housing for disabled students, special housing for international students, apartments for married students, apartments for single students, theme housing. 100% of campus accessible to physically disabled. **Special Academic Facilities/Equipment:** Museum of health sciences. **Computers:** Students can register for classes online. Administrative functions (other than registration) can be performed online.

CAMPUS LIFE
Environment: Metropolis. **Activities:** Choral groups, concert band, dance, drama/theater, jazz band, literary magazine, marching band, music ensembles,

musical theater, opera, pep band, radio station, student government, student newspaper, campus ministries, international student organization. **Organizations:** 150 registered organizations, 45 honor societies, 9 religious organizations. 9 fraternities, 8 sororities. **Athletics (Intercollegiate):** *Men:* Baseball, basketball, football, golf, soccer, tennis. *Women:* Basketball, cross-country, golf, riflery, soccer, softball, synchronized swimming, tennis, track/field (outdoor), track/field (indoor), volleyball. **On-Campus Highlights:** Student Rec Center, Commons Dining Hall, Hill University Center, Blazer Hall, Heritage Hall. **Environmental Initiatives:** Electric cars; PV charging station for electric cars; recycling.

ADMISSIONS
Freshman Academic Profile: Average high school GPA 3.5. 27% in top 10% of high school class, 55% in top 25% of high school class, 77% in top 50% of high school class. ACT middle 50% range 21–27. Minimum paper TOEFL 500. Minimum computer TOEFL 173. Minimum web-based TOEFL 61. **Basis for Candidate Selection:** *Very important factors considered include:* Academic GPA, rigor of secondary school record, standardized test scores. **Freshman Admission Requirements:** High school diploma is required and GED is accepted. *Academic units required:* 4 English, 3 mathematics, 3 science, (2 science labs), 1 foreign language, 3 social studies, 3 academic electives. **Freshman Admission Statistics:** 4,418 applied, 84% admitted, 41% enrolled. **Transfer Admission Requirements:** College transcript(s), minimum college GPA of 2.0 required. **General Admission Information:** Application fee $35. Regular application deadline 3/1. Nonfall registration accepted. Admission may be deferred for a maximum of 1 year. Credit offered for CEEB Advanced Placement tests.

COSTS AND FINANCIAL AID
Annual in-state tuition $4,224. Annual out-of-state tuition $10,560. Room and board $8,142. Required fees $872. Average book expense $1,000. **Required Forms and Deadlines:** FAFSA. Priority financial aid filing date 4/1. **Notification of Awards:** Applicants will be notified of awards on a rolling basis beginning 4/1. **Types of Aid:** *Need-based scholarships/grants:* Federal Pell, SEOG, state scholarships/grants, private scholarships, the school's own gift aid, United Negro College Fund. *Loans:* Direct Subsidized Stafford, Direct Unsubsidized Stafford, Direct PLUS, Federal Perkins, state loans, college/university loans from institutional funds. *Student Employment:* Federal Work-Study Program available. Institutional employment available. Off-campus job opportunities are excellent. **Financial Aid Statistics:** 25% freshmen, 28% undergrads receive need-based scholarship or grant aid. 24% freshmen, 13% undergrads receive non-need-based scholarship or grant aid. 32% freshmen, 39% undergrads receive need-based self-help aid. 4% freshmen, 4% undergrads receive athletic scholarships. **Criteria for awarding institutional aid:** *Non-need-based:* Academics, alumni affiliation, art, athletics, leadership, minority status, music/drama.

See page 1270.

THE UNIVERSITY OF ALABAMA IN HUNTSVILLE

UAH Office of Admissions, 301 Sparkman Dr., Huntsville, AL 35899
Phone: 256-824-6070 **Financial Aid Phone:** 256-824-2761
E-mail: admitme@uah.edu **CEEB Code:** 1854
Fax: 256-824-6073 **Website:** www.uah.edu **ACT Code:** 53

This public school was founded in 1950. It has a 400-acre campus.

RATINGS
Admissions Selectivity Rating: 84   **Fire Safety Rating:** 87   **Green Rating:** 81

STUDENTS AND FACULTY
Enrollment: 5,956. **Student Body:** 47% female, 53% male, 10% out-of-state, 3% international (84 countries represented). Asian 3%, African American 15%, Caucasian 73%, Hispanic 2%, Native American 2%.
Retention and Graduation: 76% freshmen return for sophomore year. 17% freshmen graduate within 4 years. **Faculty:** Student/faculty ratio 17:1. 303 full-time faculty, 90% hold PhDs, 22% are members of minority groups, 38% are women. 7% of classes are taught by teaching assistants.

ACADEMICS
Degrees: Bachelor's, doctoral, master's, post-bachelor's certificate, post-master's certificate. **Classes:** Most classes have 20–29 students. Most lab/discussion sessions have fewer than 10 students. **Majors with Highest Enrollment:** Biology/biological sciences; mechanical engineering; nursing/registered nurse (RN, ASN, BSN, MSN). **Special Study Options:** Cooperative education program, cross-registration, distance learning, double major, dual enrollment, English as a Second Language (ESL), honors program, independent study, internships, study abroad, teacher certification program, Intensive English Program. **Honors programs:** The Honors Program at UAH provides academically talented

undergraduate students with opportunities to develop their special talents and skills within an expanded and enriched version of the curriculum leading to an Honors Diploma. Honors coursework parallels regular offerings in all majors and programs. The courses include special interdisciplinary seminars, and opportunities for independent study and research/creative work, including the opportunity to work closely with faculty on special student projects. Students may participate in an Honors internship that offers active involvement in a business enterprise, professional organization, or government agency that has particular interest and relevance to the student's course of study. Participating students also benefit from the interaction the Honors Program affords with other talented and highly motivated students. See honors.uah.edu for more information. **Combined degree programs:** BA/MA, biological sciences, physics, computer science. Special programs offered to physically disabled students include note-taking services, reader services, tape recorders, tutors. **Career services:** Alumni services, career/job search classes, career assessment, internships. **Career services highlights include:** Coop program is one of the largest in the state of Alabama and is accredited by the Accreditation Council for Cooperative Education.

FACILITIES

Housing: Coed dorms, special housing for disabled students, fraternity/sorority housing, apartments for married students, cooperative housing, apartments for single students, theme housing, Athletic Teammates. 98% of campus accessible to physically disabled. **Special Academic Facilities/Equipment:** Art museum and galleries, observatory with a Solar Magnetometer, optics building, centers for applied optics, micro-gravity research, robotics, solar research, space plasma, and aeronomic research. **Computers:** 25% of classrooms, 30% of dorms, 100% of libraries, 100% of dining areas, 100% of student union, 90% of common outdoor areas have wireless network access. Students can register for classes online. Administrative functions (other than registration) can be performed online.

CAMPUS LIFE

Environment: City. **Activities:** Choral groups, concert band, dance, drama/theater, jazz band, literary magazine, music ensembles, pep band, student government, student newspaper, campus ministries, international student organization. **Organizations:** 52 registered organizations, 24 honor societies, 5 religious organizations. 7 fraternities, 4 sororities. **Athletics (Intercollegiate):** *Men:* Baseball, basketball, cheerleading, cross-country, ice hockey, soccer, tennis, track/field (outdoor), track/field (indoor). *Women:* Basketball, cheerleading, cross-country, soccer, softball, tennis, track/field (outdoor), track/field (indoor), volleyball. **On-Campus Highlights:** University Fitness Center, Shelby Center, Salmon Library, University Center, Central Campus Residence Hall. **Environmental Initiatives:** Improved Control and Proper disposal of lab chemicals An Energy Conservation program that has been in place for over 20 years and is ever expanding. A recycling program that has been in place for over 20 years.

ADMISSIONS

Freshman Academic Profile: Average high school GPA 3.56. 34% in top 10% of high school class, 63% in top 25% of high school class, 85% in top 50% of high school class. 87% from public high schools. SAT Math middle 50% range 520–640. SAT Critical Reading middle 50% range 500–630. ACT middle 50% range 22–28. Minimum paper TOEFL 500. Minimum computer TOEFL 173. Minimum web-based TOEFL 62. **Basis for Candidate Selection:** *Very important factors considered include:* Academic GPA, rigor of secondary school record, standardized test scores, *Other factors considered include:* Class rank, application essay, recommendation(s), level of applicant's interest. **Freshman Admission Requirements:** High school diploma is required and GED is accepted. *Academic units required:* 4 English, 3 mathematics, 3 science, 4 social studies, 6 academic electives. *Academic units recommended:* 4 English, 4 mathematics, 4 science, (2 science labs), 2 foreign language, 4 social studies, 6 academic electives. **Freshman Admission Statistics:** 1,924 applied, 72% admitted, 58% enrolled. **Transfer Admission Requirements:** College transcript(s), statement of good standing from prior institution(s). Minimum college GPA of 2.0 required. Lowest grade transferable D. **General Admission Information:** Application fee $30. Regular application deadline 8/19. Nonfall registration accepted. Admission may be deferred for a maximum of 1 year. Credit and/or placement offered for CEEB Advanced Placement tests.

COSTS AND FINANCIAL AID

Annual in-state tuition $6,510. Annual out-of-state tuition $15,628. Room and board $7,208. Required fees $651. Average book expense $1,542. **Required Forms and Deadlines:** FAFSA. Financial aid filing deadline 7/31. Priority financial aid filing date 4/1. **Notification of Awards:** Applicants will be notified of awards on a rolling basis beginning 4/1. **Types of Aid:** *Need-based scholarships/grants:* Federal Pell, SEOG, state scholarships/grants, private scholarships, the school's own gift aid, Federal Nursing Scholarships. *Loans:* Direct Subsidized Stafford, Direct Unsubsidized Stafford, Direct PLUS. *Student Employment:* Federal Work-Study Program available. Institutional employment available. Off-campus job opportunities are fair. **Financial Aid Statistics:** 42% freshmen, 37% undergrads receive need-based scholarship or grant aid. 6% freshmen, 2% undergrads receive non-need-based scholarship or grant aid. 37%

freshmen, 44% undergrads receive need-based self-help aid. 5% freshmen, 4% undergrads receive athletic scholarships. 87% freshmen, 76% undergrads receive any aid. 26% undergrads borrow to pay for school. Average cumulative indebtedness $24,938. **Criteria for awarding institutional aid:** *Non-need-based:* Academics, art, athletics, leadership, minority status, music/drama.

UNIVERSITY OF ALABAMA—TUSCALOOSA

Box 870132, Tuscaloosa, AL 35487-0132
Phone: 205-348-5666 **Financial Aid Phone:** 205-348-6756
E-mail: admissions@ua.edu **CEEB Code:** 1830
Fax: 205-348-9046 **Website:** www.ua.edu **ACT Code:** 52

This public school was founded in 1831. It has a 1000-acre campus.

RATINGS

Admissions Selectivity Rating: 87   **Fire Safety Rating:** 75   **Green Rating:** 87

STUDENTS AND FACULTY

Enrollment: 23,296. **Student Body:** 52% female, 48% male, 28.5% out-of-state, 1% international (70 countries represented). Asian 1%, African American 12%, Caucasian 83%, Hispanic 2%, Native American 1%.
Retention and Graduation: 38% freshmen graduate within 4 years. 24% grads go on to further study within 1 year. 2% grads pursue law degrees. 2% grads pursue medical degrees. **Faculty:** Student/faculty ratio 20:1. 1068 full-time faculty, 88% hold PhDs, 16% are members of minority groups, 41% are women. 11% of classes are taught by teaching assistants.

ACADEMICS

Degrees: Bachelor's, doctoral, master's, post-master's certificate. **Classes:** Most classes have 10–19 students. Most lab/discussion sessions have 20–29 students. **Majors with Highest Enrollment:** Elementary education and teaching; finance; nursing/registered nurse (RN, ASN, BSN, MSN). **Special Study Options:** Accelerated program, cooperative education program, cross-registration, distance learning, double major, dual enrollment, English as a Second Language (ESL), exchange student program (domestic), external degree program, honors program, independent study, internships, liberal arts/career combination, student-designed major, study abroad, teacher certification program, weekend college. **Honors programs:** University Honors College is composed of the University Honors Program, Computer-Based Honors Program and the International Honors Program. There is also a program called the University Fellows Experience. **Combined degree programs:** BS/MBA. Special programs offered to physically disabled students include note-taking services, reader services, tape recorders, tutors. **Career services:** Alumni network, alumni services, career/job search classes, career assessment, internships, regional alumni. **Career services highlights include:** Cooperative Education is a special academic program at The University of Alabama. In order to promote, encourage, and improve the education of students and to provide maximum service to industry, business, and government agencies, The University of Alabama offers qualified students and approved employers the opportunity to participate in Cooperative Education (Co-op) where students alternate periods of full-time study with periods of full-time employment.

FACILITIES

Housing: Coed dorms, special housing for disabled students, men's dorms, special housing for international students, women's dorms, fraternity/sorority housing, apartments for married students, apartments for single students, theme housing, apartments for visiting scholars. 98% of campus accessible to physically disabled. **Special Academic Facilities/Equipment:** Art gallery, natural history museum, concert hall, archaeologic site and museum, arboretum, observatory, simulated coal mine, robotics lab, wind tunnel, artificial intelligence lab, jet propulsion engine mini-lab, special collections building. **Computers:** 55% of classrooms, 100% of dorms, 100% of libraries, 75% of dining areas, 100% of student union, 22% of common outdoor areas have wireless network access. Students can register for classes online. Administrative functions (other than registration) can be performed online.

CAMPUS LIFE

Environment: City. **Activities:** Choral groups, concert band, dance, drama/theater, jazz band, literary magazine, marching band, music ensembles, musical theater, opera, pep band, radio station, student government, student newspaper, student-run film society, symphony orchestra, television station, yearbook, campus ministries, international student organization, Model UN. **Organizations:** 294 registered organizations, 66 honor societies, 30 religious organizations. 31

fraternities, 23 sororities. **Athletics (Intercollegiate):** *Men:* Baseball, basketball, cross-country, diving, football, golf, swimming, tennis, track/field (outdoor), track/field (indoor). *Women:* Basketball, crew/rowing, cross-country, diving, golf, gymnastics, soccer, softball, swimming, tennis, track/field (outdoor), track/field (indoor), volleyball. **On-Campus Highlights:** University of Alabama Museum of Natural History, Amelia Gayle Gorgas Library, Bryant-Denny Stadium, The Gorgas House Museum (built in 1829), Paul W. Bryant Museum, Located right on campus is a wonderful blend of cultures and ethnic foods. Interesting shops, a new shopping center, great coffee shops, local and visiting musical talent—all located on University Blvd. **Environmental Initiatives:** Recycling has increased by 86% over fiscal year 2008. Currently we are recycling over 885 tons of recyclable material. Game day recycling at UA home football games. Working on a community organic garden on campus.

ADMISSIONS

Freshman Academic Profile: Average high school GPA 3.47. 43.3% in top 10% of high school class, 56.1% in top 25% of high school class, 78.5% in top 50% of high school class. SAT Math middle 50% range 500–620. SAT Critical Reading middle 50% range 500–600. ACT middle 50% range 21–28. Minimum paper TOEFL 500. Minimum computer TOEFL 173. Minimum web-based TOEFL 61. **Basis for Candidate Selection:** *Very important factors considered include:* Academic GPA, rigor of secondary school record, standardized test scores. *Important factors considered include:* Class rank. *Other factors considered include:* Application essay, recommendation(s), alumni/ae relation, character/personal qualities, extracurricular activities, first generation, interview, talent/ability, volunteer work, work experience. **Freshman Admission Requirements:** High school diploma is required and GED is accepted. *Academic units required:* 4 English, 3 mathematics, 3 science, (2 science labs), 1 foreign language, 4 social studies, 1 history, 5 academic electives. *Academic units recommended:* 4 English, 3 mathematics, 3 science, (2 science labs), 1 foreign language, 4 social studies, 1 history, 5 academic electives. **Freshman Admission Statistics:** 19,518 applied, 57% admitted, 46% enrolled. **Transfer Admission Requirements:** College transcript(s), minimum college GPA of 2.0 required. Lowest grade transferable D. **General Admission Information:** Application fee $40. Notification on a rolling basis, beginning on or about 8/1. Nonfall registration accepted. Credit and/or placement offered for CEEB Advanced Placement tests.

COSTS AND FINANCIAL AID

Annual in-state tuition $7,000. Annual out-of-state tuition $19,200. Room and board $7,796. Average book expense $1,100. **Required Forms and Deadlines:** FAFSA. Priority financial aid filing date 3/1. **Notification of Awards:** Applicants will be notified of awards on a rolling basis beginning 4/1. **Types of Aid:** *Need-based scholarships/grants:* Federal Pell, SEOG, state scholarships/grants, private scholarships, the school's own gift aid, Federal Nursing Scholarships. *Loans:* Direct Subsidized Stafford, Direct Unsubsidized Stafford, Direct PLUS, Federal Perkins, college/university loans from institutional funds. *Student Employment:* Federal Work-Study Program available. Institutional employment available. Highest amount earned per year from on-campus jobs $2,466. Off-campus job opportunities are good. **Financial Aid Statistics:** 25% freshmen, 26% undergrads receive need-based scholarship or grant aid. 26% freshmen, 21% undergrads receive non-need-based scholarship or grant aid. 26% freshmen, 32% undergrads receive need-based self-help aid. 2% freshmen, 2% undergrads receive athletic scholarships. 68% freshmen, 63% undergrads receive any aid. 51.7% undergrads borrow to pay for school. Average cumulative indebtedness $23,964. **Criteria for awarding institutional aid:** *Non-need-based:* Academics, alumni affiliation, art, athletics, leadership, minority status, music/drama, state/district residency.

UNIVERSITY OF ALASKA—ANCHORAGE

3211 Providence Drive, Anchorage, AK 99508-8046
Phone: 907-786-1480
E-mail: enroll@uaa.alaska.edu **CEEB Code:** 4896
Fax: 907-786-4888 **Website:** www.uaa.alaska.edu **ACT Code:** 137

This public school was founded in 1954. It has a 384-acre campus.

RATINGS
Admissions Selectivity Rating: 73   **Fire Safety Rating:** 60*   **Green Rating:** 60*

STUDENTS AND FACULTY
Enrollment: 11,878. **Student Body:** 59% female, 41% male, 9% out-of-state, 1% international (35 countries represented). Asian 8%, African American 3%, Caucasian 61%, Hispanic 5%, Native American 10%.
Retention and Graduation: Faculty: 617 full-time faculty, 52% hold PhDs, 12% are members of minority groups, 52% are women.

ACADEMICS
Degrees: Associate, bachelor's, certificate, master's, post-bachelor's certificate, post-master's certificate. **Classes:** Most classes have fewer than 10 students. Most lab/discussion sessions have 10–19 students. **Special Study Options:** Cooperative education program, cross-registration, distance learning, double major, dual enrollment, English as a Second Language (ESL), exchange student program (domestic), honors program, independent study, internships, liberal arts/career combination, student-designed major, study abroad, teacher certification program. **Honors programs:** University Honors Program Special programs offered to physically disabled students include note-taking services, reader services, tape recorders **Career services:** Alumni services, career/job search classes, career assessment, internships.

FACILITIES
Housing: Coed dorms, special housing for disabled students, special housing for international students, apartments for single students, wellness housing-Separate floors for: Alaska natives studying engineering, nursing students, honor students, language and cultures, first-year students under age 20, healthy lifestyle, quiet lifestyle, WWAMI program, Far East exchange program. 95% of campus accessible to physically disabled. **Special Academic Facilities/Equipment:** Kimura and student Center Galleries. **Computers:** Students can register for classes online. Administrative functions (other than registration) can be performed online.

CAMPUS LIFE
Environment: City. **Activities:** Choral groups, dance, drama/theater, jazz band, literary magazine, music ensembles, musical theater, opera, radio station, student government, student newspaper, student-run film society, campus ministries, international student organization, Model UN. **Organizations:** 70 registered organizations, 5 honor societies, 5 religious organizations. 1 fraternities, 2 sororities. **Athletics (Intercollegiate):** *Men:* Basketball, cross-country, ice hockey, skiing (downhill/alpine), skiing (nordic/cross-country). *Women:* Basketball, cross-country, gymnastics, skiing (downhill/alpine), skiing (nordic/cross-country), volleyball. **On-Campus Highlights:** Campus Center, Wells Fargo Sports Center, Creakside Eatery, Cuddy Center, Student Health Center, The University of Alaska Anchorage campus has covered walkways across much of the campus as well as bike trails that connect the camus to the town's bike trail system. Student Housing is adjacent to the campus with shuttle buses running every 15 minutes throughout the main campus and University Center area of campus.

ADMISSIONS
Freshman Academic Profile: 9% in top 10% of high school class, 26% in top 25% of high school class, 57% in top 50% of high school class. 95% from public high schools. SAT Math middle 50% range 420–560. SAT Critical Reading middle 50% range 430–450. ACT middle 50% range 17–24. Minimum paper TOEFL 450. **Basis for Candidate Selection:** *Very important factors considered include:* Rigor of secondary school record, *Other factors considered include:* Class rank, standardized test scores, talent/ability. **Freshman Admission Requirements:** High school diploma is required and GED is accepted. **Transfer Admission Requirements:** College transcript(s), statement of good standing from prior institution(s). Minimum college GPA of 2.0 required. Lowest grade transferable C. **General Admission Information:** Application fee $50. Regular application deadline 7/1. Nonfall registration accepted. Admission may be deferred for a maximum of 1 years. Credit offered for CEEB Advanced Placement tests.

COSTS AND FINANCIAL AID
Annual in-state tuition $4,230. Annual out-of-state tuition $14,130. Room and board $8,605. Required fees $576. Average book expense $990. **Required Forms and Deadlines:** FAFSA, institution's own financial aid form Financial aid filing deadline 8/1. Priority financial aid filing date 4/1. **Notification of Awards:** Applicants will be notified of awards on a rolling basis beginning 3/15. **Types of Aid:** *Need-based scholarships/grants:* Federal Pell, SEOG, state scholarships/grants, private scholarships, the school's own gift aid, Federal Work Study. *Loans:* FFEL Subsidized Stafford, FFEL Unsubsidized Stafford, FFEL PLUS, state loans *Student Employment:* Federal Work-Study Program available. Institutional employment available. Off-campus job opportunities are good. **Financial Aid Statistics: Criteria for awarding institutional aid:** *Non-need-based:* Academics, athletics.

UNIVERSITY OF ALASKA—FAIRBANKS

PO Box 757480, Fairbanks, AK 99775-7480
Phone: 907-474-7500 **Financial Aid Phone:** 888-474-7256
E-mail: admissions@uaf.edu **CEEB Code:** 4866
Fax: 907-474-5379 **Website:** www.uaf.edu **ACT Code:** 64

This public school was founded in 1917. It has a 2250-acre campus.

RATINGS
Admissions Selectivity Rating: 74 **Fire Safety Rating:** 85 **Green Rating:** 60*

STUDENTS AND FACULTY
Enrollment: 5,273. **Student Body:** 57% female, 43% male, 13% out-of-state, 2% international (42 countries represented). Asian 3%, African American 3%, Caucasian 61%, Hispanic 4%, Native American 19%.
Retention and Graduation: 80% freshmen return for sophomore year. 11% freshmen graduate within 4 years. **Faculty:** 341 full-time faculty, 55% hold PhDs, 43% are women.

ACADEMICS
Degrees: Associate, bachelor's, certificate, master's, post-bachelor's certificate, terminal associate, transfer associate. **Majors with Highest Enrollment:** Biology/biological sciences; business administration and management; elementary education and teaching. **Special Study Options:** Accelerated program, cooperative education program, distance learning, double major, dual enrollment, exchange student program (domestic), external degree program, honors program, independent study, internships, student-designed major, study abroad, teacher certification program, Legislative Aide Intern Program; Undergraduate Research Opportunities. **Honors programs:** The Honors Program at UAF provides superior undergraduate students with intellectual opportunities greater than those generally found in university lecture halls. Honors students experience small classes, direct contact with top faculty members, a flexible curriculum and great encouragement to pursue their own intellectual interests. **Combined degree programs:** BS/MS Computer Science, BS/MS Mechanical Engineering. Special programs offered to physically disabled students include note-taking services, reader services, tape recorders, tutors. **Career services:** Alumni network, alumni services, career/job search classes, career assessment, internships.

FACILITIES
Housing: Coed dorms, special housing for disabled students, apartments for married students, apartments for single students, wellness housing, Alaska Native cultural housing. 90% of campus accessible to physically disabled.
Special Academic Facilities/Equipment: Museum of natural/cultural history of Alaska and the North, Cray Super Computer, extensive telecommunication network, Geophysical Institute, NASA earth station, Poker Flat Research Range, electron microscope, microprobe, International Arctic Research Center, Institute of Arctic Biology, Institute of Northern Engineering, Arctic Region Supercomputing Center, Institute of Marine Biology, Agriculture and Forestry Experiment Station, Office of Electronic Miniaturization, Alaska Native Language Center, Georgeson Botanical Gardens, Cold Climate Housing Research Center, Large Animal Research Station. **Computers:** 100% of classrooms, 100% of dorms, 100% of libraries, 100% of dining areas, 100% of student union, 50% of common outdoor areas have wireless network access. Students can register for classes online. Administrative functions (other than registration) can be performed online.

CAMPUS LIFE
Environment: City. **Activities:** Choral groups, concert band, dance, drama/theater, jazz band, literary magazine, music ensembles, pep band, radio station, student government, student newspaper, symphony orchestra, television station, campus ministries, international student organization, Model UN. **Organizations:** 122 registered organizations, 11 honor societies, 10 religious organizations. 1 fraternities, 1 sororities. **Athletics (Intercollegiate):** *Men:* Basketball, cross-country, ice hockey, riflery, skiing (nordic/cross-country). *Women:* Basketball, cross-country, riflery, skiing (nordic/cross-country), volleyball. **On-Campus Highlights:** Wood Center (includes food court), Student Recreation Center (SRC), Rasmuson Library, Groomed cross-country ski trails on campus, Hess Recreation Center, Wood Center (includes food court, coffee shop, bowling alley and pool tables, Outdoor Adventures, the Pub and various spaces for groups to gather or hold meetings) The 2,250 acre Fairbanks campus includes two lakes and 17 miles of ski and hiking trails as well as a major student recreation complex. We often refer to UAF as having a 360–million-acre campus because research and field work might take you anywhere in Alaska.

ADMISSIONS
Freshman Academic Profile: Average high school GPA 3.19. 15% in top 10% of high school class, 34% in top 25% of high school class, 65% in top 50% of high school class. SAT Math middle 50% range 430–590. SAT Critical Reading middle 50% range 450–600. SAT Writing middle 50% range 420–550. ACT middle 50% range 18–25. Minimum paper TOEFL 550. Minimum computer TOEFL 213. Minimum web-based TOEFL 80. **Basis for Candidate Selection:** *Very important factors considered include:* Academic GPA, standardized test scores. **Freshman Admission Requirements:** High school diploma is required and GED is not accepted. *Academic units required:* 4 English, 3 mathematics, 3 science, (1 science labs), 3 social studies. *Academic units recommended:* 2 foreign language. **Freshman Admission Statistics:** 2,030 applied, 74% admitted, 67% enrolled. **Transfer Admission Requirements:** College transcript(s), minimum college GPA of 2.0 required. Lowest grade transferable C. **General Admission Information:** Application fee $50. Regular application deadline 7/1. Regular notification 9/1. Notification on a rolling basis, beginning on or about 1/1. Nonfall registration accepted. Admission may be deferred for a maximum of 1 calendar year. Credit and/or placement offered for CEEB Advanced Placement tests.

COSTS AND FINANCIAL AID
Annual in-state tuition $4,755. Annual out-of-state tuition $15,345. Room and board $6,800. Required fees $913. Average book expense $1,300. **Required Forms and Deadlines:** FAFSA. Financial aid filing deadline 7/1. Priority financial aid filing date 2/15. **Notification of Awards:** Applicants will be notified of awards on a rolling basis beginning 3/1. **Types of Aid:** *Need-based scholarships/grants:* Federal Pell, SEOG, state scholarships/grants, private scholarships, the school's own gift aid. *Loans:* FFEL Subsidized Stafford, FFEL Unsubsidized Stafford, FFEL PLUS, state loans *Student Employment:* Federal Work-Study Program available. Institutional employment available. Highest amount earned per year from on-campus jobs $5,320. Off-campus job opportunities are good. **Financial Aid Statistics:** 31% freshmen, 31% undergrads receive need-based scholarship or grant aid. 4% freshmen, 3% undergrads receive non-need-based scholarship or grant aid. 28% freshmen, 32% undergrads receive need-based self-help aid. 2% freshmen, 3% undergrads receive athletic scholarships. 73% freshmen, 60% undergrads receive any aid. 54% undergrads borrow to pay for school. Average cumulative indebtedness $29,485. **Criteria for awarding institutional aid:** *Non-need-based:* Academics, art, athletics, leadership, minority status, music/drama, state/district residency.

UNIVERSITY OF ARIZONA

PO Box 210040, Tucson, AZ 85721-0040
Phone: 520-621-3237 **Financial Aid Phone:** 520-621-5200
E-mail: appinfo@arizona.edu **CEEB Code:** 4832
Fax: 520-621-9799 **Website:** www.arizona.edu **ACT Code:** 96

This public school was founded in 1885. It has a 378-acre campus.

RATINGS
Admissions Selectivity Rating: 83 **Fire Safety Rating:** 92 **Green Rating:** 60*

STUDENTS AND FACULTY
Enrollment: 30,333. **Student Body:** 52% female, 48% male, 30.3% out-of-state, 3% international (123 countries represented). Asian 7%, African American 4%, Caucasian 63%, Hispanic 18%, Native American 3%.
Retention and Graduation: 78% freshmen return for sophomore year. 32% freshmen graduate within 4 years. 42% grads go on to further study within 1 year. **Faculty:** Student/faculty ratio 19.7:1. 1546 full-time faculty, 91% hold PhDs, 17% are members of minority groups, 36% are women. 22% of classes are taught by teaching assistants.

ACADEMICS
Degrees: Bachelor's, master's, post-bachelor's certificate, post-master's certificate. **Classes:** Most classes have 20–29 students. Most lab/discussion sessions have 20–29 students. **Majors with Highest Enrollment:** cell/cellular and molecular biology; political science and government; psychology. **Special Study Options:** Accelerated program, cooperative education program, cross-registration, distance learning, double major, dual enrollment, English as a Second Language (ESL), exchange student program (domestic), external degree program, independent study, internships, liberal arts/career combination, study abroad, teacher certification program, weekend college. **Honors programs:** For information on our Honors College, visit: www.honors.arizona.edu. Special programs offered to physically disabled students include note-taking services, reader services, tape recorders, tutors. **Career services:** Alumni services, career/job search classes, career assessment, internships.

FACILITIES

Housing: Coed dorms, special housing for disabled students, special housing for international students, women's dorms, fraternity/sorority housing, apartments for single students. 85% of campus accessible to physically disabled. **Special Academic Facilities/Equipment:** Art, photography, and natural history museums, tree-ring lab, planetarium, optical sciences center, nuclear reactor. **Computers:** 100% of classrooms, 100% of dorms, 100% of libraries, 100% of dining areas, 100% of student union, 75% of common outdoor areas have wireless network access. Students can register for classes online. Administrative functions (other than registration) can be performed online.

CAMPUS LIFE

Environment: Metropolis. **Activities:** Choral groups, concert band, dance, drama/theater, jazz band, literary magazine, marching band, music ensembles, musical theater, opera, pep band, radio station, student government, student newspaper, symphony orchestra, television station, yearbook, campus ministries, international student organization, Model UN. **Organizations:** 504 registered organizations, 13 honor societies, 13 religious organizations. 25 fraternities, 20 sororities. **Athletics (Intercollegiate):** *Men:* Baseball, basketball, cross-country, diving, football, golf, swimming, tennis, track/field (outdoor). *Women:* Basketball, cross-country, diving, golf, gymnastics, soccer, softball, swimming, tennis, track/field (outdoor), track/field (indoor), volleyball. **On-Campus Highlights:** Flandrau Science Center, Center for Creative Photography, UA Museum of Art, Athletics Events, Arizona State Museum.

ADMISSIONS

Freshman Academic Profile: Average high school GPA 3.37. 34% in top 10% of high school class, 62% in top 25% of high school class, 88% in top 50% of high school class. 90% from public high schools. SAT Math middle 50% range 490–620. SAT Critical Reading middle 50% range 460–600. ACT middle 50% range 21–27. **Basis for Candidate Selection:** *Very important factors considered include:* Academic GPA, rigor of secondary school record, *Other factors considered include:* Class rank, application essay, recommendation(s), standardized test scores, character/personal qualities, extracurricular activities, first generation, geographical residence, interview, racial/ethnic status, state residency, talent/ability, volunteer work, work experience. **Freshman Admission Requirements:** High school diploma is required and GED is accepted. *Academic units required:* 4 English, 3 mathematics, 3 science, (3 science labs), 2 foreign language, 1 social studies, 1 history, 1 Fine Art *Academic units recommended:* 4 English, 3 mathematics, 3 science, (3 science labs), 2 foreign language, 2 social studies, 1 history, 1 Fine Art **Freshman Admission Statistics:** 24,625 applied, 78% admitted, 36% enrolled. **Transfer Admission Requirements:** College transcript(s), Lowest grade transferable C. **General Admission Information:** Application fee $50. Regular application deadline 5/1. Notification on a rolling basis, beginning on or about 11/1. Nonfall registration accepted. Credit offered for CEEB Advanced Placement tests.

COSTS AND FINANCIAL AID

Annual in-state tuition $6,540. Annual out-of-state tuition $21,949. Room and board $8,614. Required fees $315. Average book expense $1,000. **Required Forms and Deadlines:** FAFSA. **Types of Aid:** *Need-based scholarships/grants:* Federal Pell, SEOG, state scholarships/grants, private scholarships, the school's own gift aid, Federal Nursing Scholarships. *Loans:* FFEL Subsidized Stafford, FFEL Unsubsidized Stafford, FFEL PLUS, Federal Perkins, Federal Nursing, college/university loans from institutional funds. *Student Employment:* Federal Work-Study Program available. Institutional employment available. Off-campus job opportunities are good. **Financial Aid Statistics:** 36% freshmen, 36% undergrads receive need-based scholarship or grant aid. 5% freshmen, 3% undergrads receive non-need-based scholarship or grant aid. 20% freshmen, 26% undergrads receive need-based self-help aid. 1% freshmen, 1% undergrads receive athletic scholarships. 65.3% freshmen, 63.9% undergrads receive any aid. 43% undergrads borrow to pay for school. Average cumulative indebtedness $18,712. **Criteria for awarding institutional aid:** *Non-need-based:* Academics, art, music/drama.

UNIVERSITY OF ARKANSAS—FAYETTEVILLE

232 Silas Hunt Hall, Fayetteville, AR 72701
Phone: 479-575-5346 **Financial Aid Phone:** 479-575-3806
E-mail: uofa@uark.edu **CEEB Code:** 6866
Fax: 479-575-7515 **Website:** www.uark.edu **ACT Code:** 144

This public school was founded in 1871. It has a 410-acre campus.

RATINGS

Admissions Selectivity Rating: 88   **Fire Safety Rating:** 60*   **Green Rating:** 93

STUDENTS AND FACULTY

Enrollment: 15,347. **Student Body:** 48% female, 52% male, 26.5% out-of-state, 3% international (106 countries represented). Asian 3%, African American 5%, Caucasian 82%, Hispanic 4%, Native American 2%.
Retention and Graduation: 83% freshmen return for sophomore year. 34% freshmen graduate within 4 years. **Faculty:** Student/faculty ratio 17:1. 899 full-time faculty, 89% hold PhDs, 12% are members of minority groups, 34% are women. 24.5% of classes are taught by teaching assistants.

ACADEMICS

Degrees: Bachelor's, master's, post-bachelor's certificate, post-master's certificate. **Classes:** Most classes have 20–29 students. Most lab/discussion sessions have 20–29 students. **Majors with Highest Enrollment:** finance; journalism; marketing/marketing management. **Special Study Options:** Accelerated program, cooperative education program, distance learning, double major, dual enrollment, English as a Second Language (ESL), honors program, independent study, internships, liberal arts/career combination, student-designed major, study abroad, teacher certification program. **Honors programs:** The Honors College provides exceptional opportunities for outstanding undergraduates. The College incorporates 4 areas of responsiblity: recruitment, administration of honors fellowships, coordination of honors program and curricula, and coordination of related services. **Combined degree programs:** BA/MD, BA/JD, BA/DDS, MBA/JD. Special programs offered to physically disabled students include note-taking services, reader services, tape recorders, tutors. **Career services:** Alumni network, alumni services, career assessment, internships

FACILITIES

Housing: Coed dorms, women's dorms, fraternity/sorority housing, apartments for single students, Suites with private bedrooms. Special interest floors. Enhanced learning centers. First year experience program area. Adaptable housing for disabled students. Several residences remain open over holiday and winter breaks. Honors housing. Sophmore and beyond program area. 100% of campus accessible to physically disabled. **Special Academic Facilities/Equipment:** Public Radio-KUAF, High Density Electronics Center, Reynolds Center for Enterprise Development, Center for Excellence in Poultry Science, Genesis Small Business Incubation Center, Chemical Hazards Research Center (NEW) Honors College. **Computers:** Students can register for classes online. Administrative functions (other than registration) can be performed online.

CAMPUS LIFE

Environment: Town. **Activities:** Choral groups, concert band, dance, drama/theater, jazz band, literary magazine, marching band, music ensembles, musical theater, opera, pep band, radio station, student government, student newspaper, student-run film society, symphony orchestra, television station, yearbook, campus ministries, international student organization. **Organizations:** 340 registered organizations, 39 honor societies, 32 religious organizations. 16 fraternities, 11 sororities. **Athletics (Intercollegiate):** *Men:* Baseball, basketball, cross-country, football, golf, tennis, track/field (outdoor), track/field (indoor). *Women:* Basketball, cross-country, diving, golf, gymnastics, soccer, softball, swimming, tennis, track/field (outdoor), track/field (indoor), volleyball. **On-Campus Highlights:** Bud Walton Arena, Old Main, Reynolds Razorback Stadium, Greek AmphiTheater, Senior Walk (every graduate's name engraved). **Environmental Initiatives:** ACUPCC Signatory, GHG inventory, climate action plan, $40 million investment in conservation on campus Razorback Recycling

ADMISSIONS

Freshman Academic Profile: Average high school GPA 3.55. 30.3% in top 10% of high school class, 60.1% in top 25% of high school class, 88.6% in top 50% of high school class. 84% from public high schools. SAT Math middle 50% range 520–640. SAT Critical Reading middle 50% range 500–620. ACT middle 50% range 23–29. Minimum paper TOEFL 550. Minimum computer TOEFL 213. Minimum web-based TOEFL 80. **Basis for Candidate Selection:** *Very important factors considered include:* Class rank, academic GPA, rigor of secondary school record, standardized test scores, *Other factors considered include:* Application essay, recommendation(s), alumni/ae relation, character/personal qualities, extracurricular activities, first generation, geographical residence, racial/ethnic status, state residency, talent/ability, volunteer work, work experience. **Freshman Admission Requirements:** High school diploma is required and GED is accepted. *Academic units required:* 4 English, 4 mathematics, 3 science, (2 science labs), 3 social studies, 2 academic electives. *Academic units recommended:* 2 foreign language. **Freshman Admission Statistics:** 12,035 applied, 56% admitted, 43% enrolled. **Transfer Admission Requirements:** College transcript(s), minimum college GPA of 2.0 required. Lowest grade transferable C–. **General Admission Information:** Application fee $40. Regular application deadline 8/1. Notification on a rolling basis, beginning on or about 9/15. Nonfall registration accepted. Credit and/or placement offered for CEEB Advanced Placement tests.

COSTS AND FINANCIAL AID

Annual in-state tuition $5,010. Annual out-of-state tuition $13,888. Room and board $7,422. Required fees $1,390. Average book expense $1,008. **Required Forms and Deadlines:** FAFSA. Priority financial aid filing date 3/15. **Notification of Awards:** Applicants will be notified of awards on a rolling basis beginning 4/1. **Types of Aid:** *Need-based scholarships/grants:* Federal Pell, SEOG, state scholarships/grants, private scholarships, the school's own gift aid. *Loans:* FFEL Subsidized Stafford, FFEL Unsubsidized Stafford, FFEL PLUS, Federal Perkins, state loans, college/university loans from institutional funds, Alternative Loans. *Student Employment:* Federal Work-Study Program available. Institutional employment available. Highest amount earned per year from on-campus jobs $3,000. **Financial Aid Statistics:** 30% freshmen, 27% undergrads receive need-based scholarship or grant aid. 6% freshmen, 3% undergrads receive non-need-based scholarship or grant aid. 24% freshmen, 28% undergrads receive need-based self-help aid. 3% freshmen, 3% undergrads receive athletic scholarships. 71.7% freshmen, 65.1% undergrads receive any aid. 43.8% undergrads borrow to pay for school. Average cumulative indebtedness $19,248. **Criteria for awarding institutional aid:** *Non-need-based:* Academics, alumni affiliation, art, athletics, leadership, minority status, music/drama, state/district residency.

See page 1274.

UNIVERSITY OF ARKANSAS—LITTLE ROCK

2801 South University Avenue, Little Rock, AR 72204
Phone: 501-569-3127
E-mail: admissions@ualr.edu
Fax: 501-569-8915 **Website:** www.ualr.edu

This is a public school.

RATINGS
Admissions Selectivity Rating: 60* **Fire Safety Rating:** 60* **Green Rating:** 60*

STUDENTS AND FACULTY
Student Body: 2% out-of-state.
Retention and Graduation: 59% freshmen return for sophomore year.

ACADEMICS
Degrees: Associate, bachelor's, certificate, master's, post-bachelor's certificate.

FACILITIES
Housing: Coed dorms, men's dorms, women's dorms, fraternity/sorority housing.

CAMPUS LIFE
Activities: Radio station, student government, student newspaper, television station, yearbook.

ADMISSIONS
Freshman Academic Profile: Average high school GPA 2.5. 93% from public high schools. Minimum paper TOEFL 500. Minimum computer TOEFL 173. **Freshman Admission Requirements:** High school diploma is required and GED is accepted. *Academic units recommended:* 4 English, 3 mathematics, 2 science, (2 science labs), 2 foreign language, 1 social studies, 2 history. **Transfer Admission Requirements:** College transcript(s), minimum college GPA of 2.0 required. Lowest grade transferable C. **General Admission Information:** Nonfall registration accepted. Credit offered for CEEB Advanced Placement tests.

COSTS AND FINANCIAL AID
Annual in-state tuition $1,131. Annual out-of-state tuition $2,916. Room and board $2,435. Required fees $138. Average book expense $1,000. **Required**

Forms and Deadlines: FAFSA, state aid form **Types of Aid:** *Need-based scholarships/grants:* State scholarships/grants. *Loans:* FFEL Subsidized Stafford, FFEL PLUS.

UNIVERSITY OF ARKANSAS AT PINE BLUFF

1200 N. University Drive, Mail Slot 4983, Pine Bluff, AR 71601
Phone: 870-575-8492
E-mail: fultone@uapb.edu
Fax: 870-575-4608 **Website:** www.uapb.edu

This is a public school.

RATINGS
Admissions Selectivity Rating: 60* **Fire Safety Rating:** 60* **Green Rating:** 60*

STUDENTS AND FACULTY
Enrollment: 3,048. **Student Body:** 58% female, 42% male, 33% out-of-state, international. African American 96%, Caucasian 3%.
Retention and Graduation: 57% freshmen return for sophomore year. 14% freshmen graduate within 4 years. **Faculty:** Student/faculty ratio 18:1. 164 full-time faculty, 46% are members of minority groups, 54% are women.

ACADEMICS
Degrees: Associate, bachelor's, certificate, master's. **Classes:** Most classes have fewer than 10 students. **Special Study Options:** Cooperative education program, distance learning, double major, dual enrollment, honors program, internships, study abroad, teacher certification program.

FACILITIES
Housing: Men's dorms, women's dorms.

CAMPUS LIFE
Activities: Choral groups, concert band, drama/theater, jazz band, marching band, radio station, student government, student newspaper, television station, yearbook.

ADMISSIONS
Freshman Academic Profile: 93% from public high schools. SAT Math middle 50% range 350–450. SAT Critical Reading middle 50% range 350–440. ACT middle 50% range 14–18. Minimum paper TOEFL 500. Minimum computer TOEFL 173. **Basis for Candidate Selection:** *Very important factors considered include:* Rigor of secondary school record, standardized test scores. *Important factors considered include:* Academic GPA. **Freshman Admission Requirements:** High school diploma is required and GED is accepted. *Academic units required:* 4 English, 3 mathematics, 3 science, (2 science labs), 2 foreign language, 1 social studies, 2 history, 4 academic electives. **Freshman Admission Statistics:** 2,169 applied, 64% admitted, 59% enrolled. **Transfer Admission Requirements:** High school transcript, college transcript(s), **General Admission Information:** Nonfall registration accepted. Credit offered for CEEB Advanced Placement tests.

COSTS AND FINANCIAL AID
Annual in-state tuition $3,300. Annual out-of-state tuition $7,710. Room and board $6,070. Required fees $1,199. Average book expense $1,000. **Required Forms and Deadlines:** FAFSA. **Types of Aid:** *Need-based scholarships/grants:* Federal Pell, SEOG, state scholarships/grants, private scholarships, the school's own gift aid. *Loans:* FFEL Subsidized Stafford, FFEL Unsubsidized Stafford, Federal Perkins.

UNIVERSITY OF THE ARTS

320 South Broad Street, Philadelphia, PA 19102
Phone: 215-717-6049
E-mail: admissions@uarts.edu **CEEB Code:** 2664
Fax: 215-717-6045 **Website:** www.uarts.edu **ACT Code:** 3664

This private school was founded in 1876. It has a 18-acre campus.

RATINGS
Admissions Selectivity Rating: 79 **Fire Safety Rating:** 60* **Green Rating:** 60*

STUDENTS AND FACULTY
Enrollment: 2,100. **Student Body:** 54% female, 46% male, 62% out-of-state, 3% international (40 countries represented). Asian 3%, African American 11%,

Caucasian 65%, Hispanic 4%.
Retention and Graduation: 76% freshmen return for sophomore year. 55% freshmen graduate within 4 years. 68% grads go on to further study within 1 year. **Faculty:** Student/faculty ratio 9:1. 114 full-time faculty, 49% hold PhDs, 8% are members of minority groups, 38% are women.

ACADEMICS
Degrees: Bachelor's, certificate, diploma, master's, post-bachelor's certificate. **Classes:** Most classes have 10–19 students. **Majors with Highest Enrollment:** drama and dramatics/theatre arts; graphic design; photography. **Special Study Options:** Accelerated program, cross-registration, double major, dual enrollment, English as a Second Language (ESL), exchange student program. (domestic), independent study, internships, study abroad, teacher certification program **Combined degree programs:** BFA/MAT Teaching Visual Arts, BM/MAT Music Ed. Special programs offered to physically disabled students include note-taking services, reader services, tape recorders, tutors. **Career services:** Alumni services, career/job search classes, career assessment, internships.

FACILITIES
Housing: Coed dorms, apartments for single students 85% of campus accessible to physically disabled. **Special Academic Facilities/Equipment:** Rosenwald-Wolf Gallery, Merriam Theater, Arts Bank, Borowsky Center for Publication arts, Gershman Y.

CAMPUS LIFE
Environment: Metropolis. **Activities:** Choral groups, concert band, dance, drama/theater, jazz band, music ensembles, musical theater, radio station, student government. **Organizations:** 5 registered organizations, 1 religious organizations.

ADMISSIONS
Freshman Academic Profile: Average high school GPA 2.88. 10% in top 10% of high school class, 32% in top 25% of high school class, 66% in top 50% of high school class. 85% from public high schools. SAT Math middle 50% range 450–570. SAT Critical Reading middle 50% range 470–580. SAT Writing middle 50% range 460–580. ACT middle 50% range 19–26. Minimum paper TOEFL 500. Minimum computer TOEFL 173. **Basis for Candidate Selection:** *Very important factors considered include:* Rigor of secondary school record, interview, talent/ability. *Important factors considered include:* Class rank, application essay, standardized test scores, character/personal qualities, extracurricular activities. *Other factors considered include:* Recommendation(s), alumni/ae relation, racial/ethnic status, volunteer work, work experience. **Freshman Admission Requirements:** High school diploma is required and GED is accepted. *Academic units required:* 4 English. *Academic units recommended:* 3 mathematics, 2 science, 2 foreign language, 2 social studies, 2 history, 2 Study in visual art, music, dance, drama, or creative writing. **Freshman Admission Statistics:** 2,349 applied, 49% admitted, 49% enrolled. **Transfer Admission Requirements:** High school transcript, college transcript(s), essay or personal statement, standardized test scores, minimum college GPA of 2.0 required. Lowest grade transferable C. **General Admission Information:** Application fee $60. Notification on a rolling basis, beginning on or about 11/1. Nonfall registration accepted. Admission may be deferred for a maximum of 1 year. Credit and/or placement offered for CEEB Advanced Placement tests.

COSTS AND FINANCIAL AID
Annual tuition $23,380. Room and board $7,800. Required fees $950. Average book expense $2,000. **Required Forms and Deadlines:** FAFSA. Financial aid filing deadline 3/1. Priority financial aid filing date 3/1. **Notification of Awards:** Applicants will be notified of awards on a rolling basis beginning 3/15. **Types of Aid:** *Need-based scholarships/grants:* Federal Pell, SEOG, state scholarships/grants, private scholarships, the school's own gift aid, merit scholarships. *Loans:* FFEL Subsidized Stafford, FFEL Unsubsidized Stafford, FFEL PLUS, Federal Perkinsalternative loans. *Student Employment:* Federal Work-Study Program available. Institutional employment available. Highest amount earned per year from on-campus jobs $1,200. Off-campus job opportunities are excellent. **Financial Aid Statistics:** 43% freshmen, 40% undergrads receive need-based scholarship or grant aid. 65% freshmen, 90% undergrads receive non-need-based scholarship or grant aid. 65% freshmen, 90% undergrads receive need-based self-help aid. 87% freshmen, 90% undergrads receive any aid. 85% undergrads borrow to pay for school. Average cumulative indebtedness $17,500. **Criteria for awarding institutional aid:** *Non-need-based:* Academics, art, music/drama.

UNIVERSITY OF BALTIMORE

1420 North Charles Street, Baltimore, MD 21201
Phone: 410-837-4777 **Financial Aid Phone:** 410-837-4763
E-mail: admissions@ubmall.ubalt.edu **CEEB Code:** 5810
Fax: 410-837-4793 **Website:** www.ubalt.edu/admissionsad/01FF09.cfm?ad_source=princetonreview

This public school was founded in 1925. It has a 47-acre campus.

RATINGS
Admissions Selectivity Rating: 60*   **Fire Safety Rating:** 60*   **Green Rating:** 83

STUDENTS AND FACULTY
Enrollment: 2,967. **Student Body:** 58% female, 42% male, 1% out-of-state, 1% international. Asian 4%, African American 38%, Caucasian 34%, Hispanic 2%, Native American 1%.
Retention and Graduation: 18% grads go on to further study within 1 year. 10% grads pursue arts and sciences degrees. 2% grads pursue law degrees. 9% grads pursue business degrees. **Faculty:** Student/faculty ratio 20:1. 178 full-time faculty, 84% hold PhDs, 23% are members of minority groups, 43% are women.

ACADEMICS
Degrees: Bachelor's, master's, post-bachelor's certificate. **Classes:** Most classes have 20–29 students. **Majors with Highest Enrollment:** Business/commerce; criminal justice/police science; health/health care administration/management. **Special Study Options:** Accelerated program, cooperative education program, distance learning, honors program, independent study, internships, student-designed major, study abroad. **Combined degree programs:** BA/JD, BA/MA, MBA/JD. Special programs offered to physically disabled students include note-taking services, reader services, tape recorders, tutors. **Career services:** Alumni network, alumni services, career/job search classes, career assessment, internships, regional alumni. **Career services highlights include:** The internship program serves students who do not have experimental learning built into their academic units.

FACILITIES
Housing: The university works with several apartment complexes in the area to provide direct leases to students. 100% of campus accessible to physically disabled. **Computers:** Students can register for classes online. Administrative functions (other than registration) can be performed online.

CAMPUS LIFE
Environment: Metropolis. **Activities:** drama/theater, literary magazine, student government, student newspaper, international student organization. **Organizations:** 26 registered organizations, 11 honor societies, 2 religious organizations. **On-Campus Highlights:** Student Union **Environmental Initiatives:** 30% energy reduction contract with Energy Systems Group, Single. steam recycling Certificate of Sustainabilty (MBA Program). Creation of human ecology and sustainabilty minor in 2010 and major in 2011.

ADMISSIONS
Freshman Academic Profile: Minimum paper TOEFL 550. Minimum computer TOEFL 275. **Basis for Candidate Selection:** *Important factors considered include:* Class rank, academic GPA, rigor of secondary school record, standardized test scores. *Other factors considered include:* Application essay, recommendation(s), alumni/ae relation, character/personal qualities, extracurricular activities, first generation, talent/ability, volunteer work, work experience. **Freshman Admission Requirements:** High school diploma is required and GED is accepted. *Academic units required:* 4 English, 3 mathematics, 3 science, (2 science labs), 3 social studies, 4 academic electives. **Transfer Admission Requirements:** College transcript(s), minimum college GPA of 2.0 required. Lowest grade transferable D. **General Admission Information:** Application fee $30. Regular notification 4/1. Nonfall registration accepted. Admission may be deferred for a maximum of 1 year. Credit and/or placement offered for CEEB Advanced Placement tests.

COSTS AND FINANCIAL AID
Annual in-state tuition $5,325. Annual out-of-state tuition $18,832. Required fees $1,846. **Required Forms and Deadlines:** FAFSA. Priority financial aid filing date 3/1. **Types of Aid:** *Need-based scholarships/grants:* Federal Pell, SEOG, state scholarships/grants, private scholarships, the school's own gift aid. *Loans:* Direct Subsidized Stafford, Direct Unsubsidized Stafford, Direct PLUS. *Student Employment:* Federal Work-Study Program available. Institutional employment available. **Financial Aid Statistics:** 75% freshmen, 57% undergrads receive need-based scholarship or grant aid. 52% freshmen, 48% undergrads receive need-based self-help aid. 100% freshmen, 70% undergrads receive any aid. 51% undergrads borrow to pay for school. **Criteria for awarding institutional aid:** *Non-need-based:* Academics, state/district residency.

UNIVERSITY OF BRIDGEPORT

126 Park Avenue, Bridgeport, CT 06604
Phone: 203-576-4552 **Financial Aid Phone:** 203-576-4568
E-mail: admit@.bridgeport.edu **CEEB Code:** 3914
Fax: 203-576-4941 **Website: ACT Code:** 602

This private school was founded in 1927. It has a 86-acre campus.

RATINGS
Admissions Selectivity Rating: 73   **Fire Safety Rating:** 60*   **Green Rating:** 60*

STUDENTS AND FACULTY
Enrollment: 2,248. **Student Body:** 68% female, 32% male, 35% out-of-state, 11% international (80 countries represented). Asian 3%, African American 37%, Caucasian 27%, Hispanic 15%.
Retention and Graduation: 52% freshmen return for sophomore year. 15% grads go on to further study within 1 year. 10% grads pursue arts and sciences degrees. 10% grads pursue law degrees. 10% grads pursue business degrees. 5% grads pursue medical degrees. **Faculty:** Student/faculty ratio 12:1. 125 full-time faculty, 82% hold PhDs, 19% are members of minority groups, 37% are women.

ACADEMICS
Degrees: Associate, bachelor's, certificate, master's, post-master's certificate. **Classes:** Most classes have 10–19 students. **Majors with Highest Enrollment:** Business/commerce; dental hygiene/hygienist; psychology. **Special Study Options:** Accelerated program, cooperative education program, cross-registration, distance learning, double major, English as a Second Language (ESL), honors program, independent study, internships, liberal arts/career combination, student-designed major, study abroad, teacher certification program, weekend college **Combined degree programs:** BS/DC, BS/MBA. Special programs offered to physically disabled students include note-taking services, reader services, tape recorders, tutors. **Career services:** Alumni network, alumni services, career/job search classes, career assessment, internships, regional alumni.

FACILITIES
Housing: Coed dorms, men's, women's floors. 80% of campus accessible to physically disabled. **Computers:** 80% of classrooms, 100% of dorms, 100% of libraries, 30% of dining areas, 50% of student union, have wireless network access. Students can register for classes online. Administrative functions (other than registration) can be performed online.

CAMPUS LIFE
Environment: City. **Activities:** Choral groups, dance, literary magazine, music ensembles, student government, student newspaper, yearbook, international student organization. **Organizations:** 30 registered organizations, 11 honor societies, 6 religious organizations. 2 fraternities, 4 sororities. **Athletics (Intercollegiate):** *Men:* Baseball, basketball, cross-country, soccer, swimming. *Women:* Basketball, cross-country, gymnastics, lacrosse, soccer, softball, swimming, volleyball. **On-Campus Highlights:** Arnold Bernhard Center, Wheeler Recreation Center, John J. Cox Student Center, The University Gallery, Hubbell Gymnasium.

ADMISSIONS
Freshman Academic Profile: Average high school GPA 2.84. 7% in top 10% of high school class, 29% in top 25% of high school class, 64% in top 50% of high school class. 89% from public high schools. SAT Math middle 50% range 410–500. SAT Critical Reading middle 50% range 400–490. SAT Writing middle 50% range 400–480. ACT middle 50% range 15–20. Minimum paper TOEFL 500. Minimum computer TOEFL 173. Minimum web-based TOEFL 61. **Basis for Candidate Selection:** *Very important factors considered include:* Rigor of secondary school record, standardized test scores. *Important factors considered include:* Class rank, application essay, academic GPA, recommendation(s), talent/ability. *Other factors considered include:* Alumni/ae relation, character/personal qualities, extracurricular activities, interview, level of applicant's interest, volunteer work, work experience. **Freshman Admission Requirements:** High school diploma is required and GED is accepted. *Academic units required:* 4 English, 3 mathematics, 2 science, (2 science labs), 2 social studies, 5 academic electives. *Academic units recommended:* 4 English, 3 mathematics, 2 science, (2 science labs), 2 social studies, 5 academic electives. **Freshman Admission Statistics:** 8,165 applied, 55% admitted, 10% enrolled. **Transfer Admission Requirements:** College transcript(s), essay or personal statement, minimum college GPA of 2.0 required. Lowest grade transferable C–. **General Admission Information:** Application fee $25. Notification on a rolling basis, beginning on or about 10/1. Nonfall registration accepted. Admission may be deferred for a maximum of 1 year. Credit and/or placement offered for CEEB Advanced Placement tests.

COSTS AND FINANCIAL AID
Annual tuition $23,400. Room and board $11,080. Required fees $2,065. Average book expense $1,500. **Required Forms and Deadlines:** FAFSA, institution's own financial aid form. Priority financial aid filing date 4/1. **Notification of Awards:** Applicants will be notified of awards on a rolling basis beginning 3/1. **Types of Aid:** *Need-based scholarships/grants:* Federal Pell, SEOG, state scholarships/grants, private scholarships, the school's own gift aid. *Loans:* Direct Subsidized Stafford, Direct Unsubsidized Stafford, Direct PLUS, FFEL Subsidized Stafford, FFEL Unsubsidized Stafford, FFEL PLUS, Federal Perkins. *Student Employment:* Federal Work-Study Program available. Institutional employment available. Highest amount earned per year from on-campus jobs $2,000. Off-campus job opportunities are good. **Financial Aid Statistics:** 74% freshmen, 73% undergrads receive need-based scholarship or grant aid. 75% freshmen, 67% undergrads receive non-need-based scholarship or grant aid. 77% freshmen, 74% undergrads receive need-based self-help aid. 3% freshmen, 5% undergrads receive athletic scholarships. 98% freshmen, 95% undergrads receive any aid. **Criteria for awarding institutional aid:** *Non-need-based:* Academics, athletics, leadership, music/drama, state/district residency.

THE UNIVERSITY OF BRITISH COLUMBIA

Room 2016, 1874 East Mall, Vancouver, BC V6T 1Z1 Canada
Phone: 1-604-822-3014 **Financial Aid Phone:** 604-822-5111
E-mail: askme@interchange.ubc.ca
Fax: 604-822-3599 **Website:** https://you.ubc.ca

This public school was founded in 1908. It has a 1000-acre campus.

RATINGS
Admissions Selectivity Rating: 60*   **Fire Safety Rating:** 60*   **Green Rating:** 92

STUDENTS AND FACULTY
Enrollment: 31,517. **Student Body:** 54% female, 46% male, % out-of-state, 11% international (142 countries represented).
Retention and Graduation: 30% freshmen graduate within 4 years. 50% grads go on to further study within 1 year. **Faculty:** Student/faculty ratio 15:1.

ACADEMICS
Degrees: Bachelor's, certificate, diploma, doctoral, master's. **Classes:** Most classes have 50–59 students. Most lab/discussion sessions have 20–29 students. **Majors with Highest Enrollment:** Biological and physical sciences; computer and information sciences; psychology. **Special Study Options:** Cooperative education program, distance learning, double major, dual enrollment, English as a Second Language (ESL), exchange student program (domestic), honors program, internships, liberal arts/career combination, student-designed major, study abroad, teacher certification program, cross-disciplinary first year options. **Honors programs:** UBC offers many honours programs for academically strong undergraduates. **Combined degree programs:** BA/BSc. Special programs offered to physically disabled students include note-taking services, reader services, tape recorders, tutors. **Career services:** Alumni network, alumni services, career/job search classes, career assessment, internships, regional alumni. **Career services highlights include:** Outstanding Coop (Work Learn) programs in six major Faculties.

FACILITIES
Housing: Coed dorms, special housing for disabled students, men's dorms, special housing for international students, women's dorms, fraternity/sorority housing, apartments for married students, apartments for single students, theme housing. National theme housing in association with partner universities in Japan, Mexico, Korea, and Hong Kong SAR. 90% of campus accessible to physically disabled. **Special Academic Facilities/Equipment:** Museum of Anthropology, Barber Learning Centre Beaty Biodiversity Museum, Geological Museum, TRIUMF, sub-atomic particle research, Botanical Gardens, Nitobe Garden, Belkin Art Gallery, Chan Centre for Performing Arts, Liu International Studies Centre, St.John's College (Graduate College), Pulp and Paper Centre Centre for Intergrated Systems Research, Wall Centre for Interdisciplinary Studies. **Computers:** 100% of classrooms, 100% of dorms, 100% of libraries, 100% of dining areas, 100% of student union, 100% of common outdoor areas have wireless network access. Students can register for classes online. Administrative functions (other than registration) can be performed online.

CAMPUS LIFE
Environment: Metropolis. **Activities:** Choral groups, concert band, dance, drama/theater, literary magazine, music ensembles, musical theater, opera, radio station, student government, student newspaper, student-run film society, symphony orchestra, international student organization. **Organizations:** 250 registered organizations, 1 honor societies, 7 religious organizations. 9 fraterni-

ties, 8 sororities. **Athletics (Intercollegiate):** *Men:* Baseball, basketball, crew/rowing, cross-country, field hockey, football, golf, ice hockey, rugby, soccer, swimming, track/field (outdoor), volleyball. *Women:* Basketball, crew/rowing, cross-country, field hockey, golf, ice hockey, rugby, soccer, swimming, track/field (outdoor), volleyball. **On-Campus Highlights:** Koerner Library, Museum of Anthropology, Chan Centre, Student Union Building, Barber Learning Centre. **Environmental Initiatives:** UBC is a signatory to the Talloires Declaration. It has integrated sustainability into its vision statement and strategic plan and formed a President's Advisory Council on Sustainability. The UBC Sustainability Office opened in 1998—the first of its kind in a Canadian university. UBC has created an advisory committee of faculty, staff, students and alumni on socially responsible investing. The committee advises the Board of Governors on issues of transparency, proxy votes, and socially responsible investment practices. UBC met 2012 Kyoto Protocol targets in 2006, having reduced over the past 16 years greenhouse gas emissions by 25 per cent. UBC currently reduces carbon emissions by 14,000 tonnes annually. UBC recently finished a capital upgrade campaign that rebuilt or retrofitted nearly 300 buildings on campus to increase energy and water efficiency and reduce emissions. In addition to the numerous green building on campus, all new construction is required to achieve LEED Gold certification and all new residential constructions follows equivalent residential construction guidelines set forth in UBC's Residential Environmental Assessment Program. Numerous other initiatives: Initiatives such as the Student Ambassadors Initiative, Sustainability Pledge Program and Student Environment Centre fully engage students in sustainable living. UBC's dining services exclusively serves local eggs, poultry and milk. UBC currently offers more than 300 sustainability-related courses. UBC Okanagan heating energy is projected to come from fully sustainable resources (ground source) within the next two to three years. For other commitments see: www.sustain.ubc.ca.

ADMISSIONS

Freshman Academic Profile: Basis for Candidate Selection: *Very important factors considered include:* Academic GPA, rigor of secondary school record. *Other factors considered include:* Application essay, recommendation(s), standardized test scores, character/personal qualities, extracurricular activities, level of applicant's interest, talent/ability, volunteer work, work experience. **Freshman Admission Requirements:** High school diploma is required and GED is not accepted. *Academic units required:* 4 English, 3 mathematics, 12 academic electives. **Transfer Admission Requirements:** College transcript(s), statement of good standing from prior institution(s). **General Admission Information:** Application fee $100. Regular application deadline 2/28. Notification on a rolling basis, beginning on or about 2/15. Nonfall registration accepted. Admission may be deferred for a maximum of up to one year. Credit and/or placement offered for CEEB Advanced Placement tests.

COSTS AND FINANCIAL AID

Average book expense $1,500. **Required Forms and Deadlines:** institution's own financial aid form Financial aid filing deadline 2/15. Priority financial aid filing date 2/15. **Types of Aid:** *Need-based scholarships/grants:* Provincial scholarships and grants are available for Canadian citizens permanent residents of Canada. International students are eligible for modest merit awards. No application is necessary for merit-based awards. International students of outstanding academic merit and personal accomplishment who would otherwise not have the means to attend university may be nominated for awards, of which a limited number are awarded annually of between $15,000 -$35,000, depending on means. These awards are by nomination only (deadline for nominations February 1). Athletic scholarships are available for outstanding athletes, at head coach discretion in accordance with CIS rules. *Loans:* Direct Subsidized Stafford, Direct Unsubsidized Stafford, Direct PLUS, FFEL Subsidized Stafford, FFEL Unsubsidized Stafford, FFEL PLUS. *Student Employment:* Institutional employment available. Off-campus job opportunities are good. **Financial Aid Statistics: Criteria for awarding institutional aid:** *Non-need-based:* Academics, athletics, leadership.

UNIVERSITY OF CALIFORNIA—BERKELEY

110 Sproul Hall, #5800, Berkeley, CA 94720-5800
CEEB Code: 4833
Fax: 510-642-7333 **Website:** www.berkeley.edu **ACT Code:** 444

This public school was founded in 1868. It has a 1232-acre campus.

RATINGS
Admissions Selectivity Rating: 97   **Fire Safety Rating:** 76   **Green Rating:** 99

STUDENTS AND FACULTY
Student Body: 7% out-of-state.

ACADEMICS
Degrees: Bachelor's, master's, post-bachelor's certificate. **Majors with Highest Enrollment:** Computer engineering; English language and literature; political science and government. **Special Study Options:** Accelerated program, cross-registration, double major, dual enrollment, English as a Second Language (ESL), exchange student program (domestic), honors program, independent study, internships, student-designed major, study abroad, teacher certification program **Combined degree programs:** 10 Engineering double majors BS degree. Special programs offered to physically disabled students include note-taking services, reader services, tape recorders, tutors. **Career services:** Alumni services, career/job search classes, career assessment, internships.

FACILITIES
Housing: Coed dorms, special housing for disabled students, men's dorms, special housing for international students, women's dorms, fraternity/sorority housing, apartments for married students, cooperative housing, apartments for single students, theme housing. 95% of campus accessible to physically disabled. **Special Academic Facilities/Equipment:** Lawrence Berkeley National Lab; Pacific Film Archive; Earthquake Data Center; Museums of art, anthropology, natural history, paleontology; Botanical Garden. **Computers:** Students can register for classes online. Administrative functions (other than registration) can be performed online.

CAMPUS LIFE
Activities: Choral groups, concert band, dance, drama/theater, jazz band, literary magazine, marching band, music ensembles, musical theater, pep band, radio station, student government, student newspaper, student-run film society, symphony orchestra, television station, yearbook, international student organization, Model UN. **Organizations:** 300 registered organizations, 6 honor societies, 28 religious organizations. 38 fraternities, 19 sororities. **Athletics (Intercollegiate):** *Men:* Baseball, basketball, crew/rowing, cross-country, diving, football, golf, gymnastics, rugby, sailing, soccer, swimming, tennis, track/field (outdoor), water polo. *Women:* Basketball, crew/rowing, cross-country, diving, field hockey, golf, gymnastics, lacrosse, sailing, soccer, softball, swimming, tennis, track/field (outdoor), volleyball, water polo. **On-Campus Highlights:** Botanical Gardens, Lawrence Hall of Science, Museum of Anthropology, Museum of Art. **Environmental Initiatives:** Planning and Reporting: Completion of 2008 Campus Sustainability Assessment, 2009 Campus Sustainability Report, 2009 Campus Sustainability Plan; Establishment of campus Sustainability Metrics; Completion of 2009 Climate Action Plan; System-wide sustainability metrics included in UCOP Accountability Framework Implementation: We aggressively pursue measures to reduce greenhouse gas emissions on campus in order to achieve our goal of achieving 1990 levels by 2014. Our strategies for achieving this ambitious target include increasing the efficiency of our energy usage (especially in existing buildings), greening our electricity supply, and promoting sustainable transportation. We will be commissioning all large buildings in the next 3-4 years, having recently completed around 20 energy efficiency projects that will reduce emissions by 3,500 tons each year. We have completed a pilot of computer energy management software, and completed water and energy efficiency upgrades and changes at our recreational facility. The first two rounds of The Green Initiative Fund projects have been awarded, allocating around $450,000 of student fees to worthy student projects. Our new Green Department and Event certifications have been successful — at least 7,500 faculty, staff, students, and guests have been participants in a certified event or department. Communication and Coordination: In the past year, we have greatly expanded our outreach to and coordination with students, faculty, and staff. In addtition to our newsletter, we have updated our websites, guest lectured at numerous classes, launched a Facebook page, and supported a campus-wide energy and water conservation campaign (www.facilities.berkeley.edu/green-buildings/CACS_campaign/campaign.html). We also host Student Sustainability Forums four times a year, intended to be a space for members of the campus community to become more informed about how various campus entities are working towards sustainability and to provide networking opportunities.

ADMISSIONS
Freshman Academic Profile: 98% in top 10% of high school class, 100% in top 25% of high school class, 100% in top 50% of high school class. 85% from public high schools. SAT Math middle 50% range 640–760. SAT Critical Reading middle 50% range 590–710. SAT Writing middle 50% range 610–720. Minimum paper TOEFL 550. Minimum computer TOEFL 213. **Basis for Candidate Selection:** *Very important factors considered include:* Application essay, academic GPA, rigor of secondary school record, state residency. *Important factors considered include:* Standardized test scores, character/personal qualities, extracurricular activities, talent/ability, volunteer work, work experience. *Other factors considered include:* First generation, geographical residence. **Freshman Admission Requirements:** High school diploma is required and GED is accepted. *Academic units required:* 4 English, 3 mathematics, 2 science, (2 science labs), 2 foreign language, 2 history, 1 visual/performing arts, 1 academic electives. *Academic units recommended:* 4 English, 4 mathematics, 3 science, (3

science labs), 3 foreign language, 2 history, 1 visual/performing arts, 1 academic electives. **Freshman Admission Statistics:** 48,465 applied. **Transfer Admission Requirements:** essay or personal statement, minimum college GPA of 2.4 required. Lowest grade transferable D. **General Admission Information:** Application fee $60. Regular application deadline 11/30. Nonfall registration accepted. Neither credit nor placement offered for CEEB Advanced Placement tests.

COSTS AND FINANCIAL AID

Required Forms and Deadlines: FAFSA, state aid form. Financial aid filing deadline 3/2. Priority financial aid filing date 3/2. **Notification of Awards:** Applicants will be notified of awards on or about 4/15. **Types of Aid:** *Need-based scholarships/grants:* Federal Pell, SEOG, state scholarships/grants, private scholarships, the school's own gift aid. *Loans:* Direct Subsidized Stafford, Direct Unsubsidized Stafford, Direct PLUS, Federal Perkins. *Student Employment:* Federal Work-Study Program available. Institutional employment available. Off-campus job opportunities are excellent. **Financial Aid Statistics: Criteria for awarding institutional aid:** *Non-need-based:* Academics.

UNIVERSITY OF CALIFORNIA—DAVIS

178 Mrak Hall, One Shields Ave, Davis, CA 95616
Phone: 530-752-2971 **Financial Aid Phone:** 530-752-2396
E-mail: undergraduateadmissions@ucdavis.edu **CEEB Code:** 4834
Fax: 530-752-1280 **Website:** www.ucdavis.edu **ACT Code:** 454

This public school was founded in 1908. It has a 5200-acre campus.

RATINGS
Admissions Selectivity Rating: 96   **Fire Safety Rating:** 76   **Green Rating:** 94

STUDENTS AND FACULTY
Enrollment: 24,453. **Student Body:** 56% female, 44% male, 2% out-of-state, 2% international (121 countries represented). Asian 40%, African American 3%, Caucasian 35%, Hispanic 14%, Native American 1%.
Retention and Graduation: 92% freshmen return for sophomore year. 48% freshmen graduate within 4 years. 40% grads go on to further study within 1 year. 23% grads pursue arts and sciences degrees. 4% grads pursue law degrees. 1% grads pursue business degrees. 12% grads pursue medical degrees. **Faculty:** Student/faculty ratio 19:1. 1586 full-time faculty, 98% hold PhDs, 19% are members of minority groups, 33% are women.

ACADEMICS
Degrees: Bachelor's, doctoral, master's, post-bachelor's certificate, post-master's certificate. **Classes:** Most classes have 20–29 students. Most lab/discussion sessions have 20–29 students. **Majors with Highest Enrollment:** Biology/biological sciences; economics; psychology. **Special Study Options:** Accelerated program, cross-registration, double major, dual enrollment, English as a Second Language (ESL), honors program, independent study, internships, student-designed major, study abroad, teacher certification program, Washington, DC, Center. **Honors programs:** The Davis Honors Challenge (DHC) is an innovative, open-application, campuswide honors program for highly motivated students. In addition to a mentor program and a residential living-learning option for first-year students, DHC offers students the opportunity to participate in an honors program for four years. Integrated Studies Honors Program (ISHP), the oldest continuous residential learning community in the UC system, is an invitational, residential honors program for first-year students. ISHP provides an academic residential community similar to those of the best small colleges and helps students integrate knowledge from the arts and humanities, natural sciences and engineering, and social sciences. Special programs offered to physically disabled students include note-taking services, reader services, tape recorders, tutors.

FACILITIES
Housing: Coed dorms, special housing for disabled students, women's dorms, apartments for married students, cooperative housing, apartments for single students, wellness housing, theme housing. Special Interest Communities: Davis Honors Challenge, Hammar-skold, International Relations, Integrated Studies, Multiethnic Program, Music, Arts & Performance, Quiet Program, Rainbow House, Women's Community. **Special Academic Facilities/Equipment:** Art galleries, 150–acre university arboretum, equestrian center, craft center, student experimental farm, nuclear lab, human performance lab, natural reserves, early

childhood lab, raptor center, primate research center. **Computers:** Students can register for classes online. Administrative functions (other than registration) can be performed online.

CAMPUS LIFE
Environment: Town. **Activities:** Choral groups, concert band, dance, drama/theater, jazz band, literary magazine, marching band, music ensembles, musical theater, pep band, radio station, student government, student newspaper, student-run film society, symphony orchestra, television station, yearbook, campus ministries, international student organization, Model UN. **Organizations:** 364 registered organizations, 1 honor societies, 50 religious organizations. 28 fraternities, 21 sororities. **Athletics (Intercollegiate):** *Men:* Baseball, basketball, cross-country, diving, football, golf, soccer, swimming, tennis, track/field (outdoor), track/field (indoor), water polo, wrestling. *Women:* Basketball, crew/rowing, cross-country, diving, field hockey, golf, gymnastics, lacrosse, soccer, softball, swimming, tennis, track/field (outdoor), track/field (indoor), volleyball, water polo. **On-Campus Highlights:** Mondavi Center for the Performing Arts, Memorial Union/Coffee House, Activities and Recreation Center (The ARC), Sciences Laboratory Building, The UC Davis Arboretum, http://daviswiki.org/. **Environmental Initiatives:** Davis, known as the bicycle capital of the United States, is the first community to achieve the Platinum level from the League of American Bicyclists. On any given day, up to 20,000 bikes are on campus. The Bike Barn helps on-campus cyclists with over 10,000 repairs per year. Unitrans, the community bus system (www.unitrans.ucdavis.edu), is operated by UC Davis students, has a fleet of clean busses that runs on compressed natural gas, and provides more than 3,000,000 rides per year. UC Davis students make remarkable use of busses with more than 85 percent of local trips on these environmentally friendly alternative transportation systems. UC Davis recently conducted a Bikeway and Transit Network Study, which outlines plans for additional bicycling infrastructure. UC Davis is a leader in green building design. For example, the Tahoe Environmental Research Center is one of the first laboratory buildings in the world to be awarded LEED Platinum, the highest rating given by the US Green Building Council. All new buildings are at least 20% more efficient than required by California's strict energy code and typically are designed to meet LEED Silver or Gold standards. Gladys Valley Hall, a classroom building, won the 2005 Best Practice Award in Overall Sustainable Design from the Higher Education Energy Efficiency Partnership Program and is expected to be awarded LEED Silver. The new Graduate School of Management employs an innovative radiant heating and cooling system coupled with a ground source heat pump and is expected to be awarded LEED Gold. The Brewery, Winery and Food Processing facility under construction will have innovative waste management and stormwater capture systems and is expected to be awarded LEED Platinum. To ensure that students, staff and faculty can walk and bike to campus and participate in all aspects of campus life, UC Davis broke ground in 2009 on West Village, a mixed use housing community adjacent to the central campus. The community aims to be zero net energy from the electrical grid, and has won federal and state grants to assist with the design and implementation of community-scaled renewable energy sources. When complete, the 200–acre neighborhood will include housing for 3,000 students, 500 faculty and staff family homes, recreation fields, and a community college and commercial space on a village square. Residents will walk, bike, and use transit for access to the heart of campus, leaving cars at home. Employing sustainable strategies for transportation, solar access, and storm water drainage with a compact, mixed use layout will create an equitable, environmentally effective, and economically viable neighborhood. The first students housing is expected to open in fall 2011.

ADMISSIONS
Freshman Academic Profile: Average high school GPA 3.85. 96% in top 10% of high school class, 100% in top 25% of high school class, 100% in top 50% of high school class. 84% from public high schools. SAT Math middle 50% range 560–680. SAT Critical Reading middle 50% range 510–640. SAT Writing middle 50% range 520–640. ACT middle 50% range 23–29. Minimum paper TOEFL 550. Minimum computer TOEFL 213. Minimum web-based TOEFL 60. **Basis for Candidate Selection:** *Very important factors considered include:* Academic GPA, rigor of secondary school record, standardized test scores. *Important factors considered include:* Application essay, character/personal qualities, extracurricular activities, first generation, talent/ability. *Other factors considered include:* State residency, volunteer work, work experience. **Freshman Admission Requirements:** High school diploma is required and GED is accepted. *Academic units required:* 4 English, 3 mathematics, 2 science, (2 science labs), 2 foreign language, 2 social studies, 1 visual/performing arts, 1 academic electives. *Academic units recommended:* 4 English, 4 mathematics, 3 science, (3 science labs), 3 foreign language, 2 social studies, 1 visual/performing arts, 1 academic electives. **Freshman Admission Statistics:** 42,382 applied, 47% admitted, 22% enrolled. **Transfer Admission Requirements:** High school transcript, college transcript(s), essay or personal statement, statement of good standing from prior institution(s). Lowest grade transferable D-. **General Admission Information:** Application fee $60. Regular application deadline 11/30. Regular notification 3/15. Nonfall registration not accepted. Credit and/or placement offered for CEEB Advanced Placement tests.

COSTS AND FINANCIAL AID

Annual out-of-state tuition $22,021. Room and board $12,361. Required fees $9,364. Average book expense $1,590. **Required Forms and Deadlines:** FAFSA. Priority financial aid filing date 3/2. **Notification of Awards:** Applicants will be notified of awards on a rolling basis beginning 3/12. **Types of Aid:** *Need-based scholarships/grants:* Federal Pell, SEOG, state scholarships/grants, private scholarships, the school's own gift aid, specify):Academic Competitiveness Grant (ACG) and National Science and Mathematics Access to Retain Talent Grant (SMART). *Loans:* Direct Subsidized Stafford, Direct Unsubsidized Stafford, Direct PLUS, Federal Perkins, college/university loans from institutional funds. *Student Employment:* Highest amount earned per year from on-campus jobs $7,280. **Financial Aid Statistics:** 53% freshmen, 51% undergrads receive need-based scholarship or grant aid. 1% freshmen, 41% freshmen, 38% undergrads receive need-based self-help aid. 1% freshmen, 1% undergrads receive athletic scholarships. 46% freshmen, 59% undergrads receive any aid. 47% undergrads borrow to pay for school. Average cumulative indebtedness $15,155. **Criteria for awarding institutional aid:** *Non-need-based:* Academics, athletics.

UNIVERSITY OF CALIFORNIA—IRVINE

Office of Admissions and Relations with Schools, 204 Administration Bldg, Irvine, CA 92697-1075
Phone: 949-824-6703 **Financial Aid Phone:** 949-824-8262
E-mail: admissions@uci.edu **CEEB Code:** 4859
Fax: 949-824-2711 **Website:**

This public school was founded in 1965. It has a 1500-acre campus.

RATINGS
Admissions Selectivity Rating: 96   **Fire Safety Rating:** 60*   **Green Rating:** 97

STUDENTS AND FACULTY
Enrollment: 22,226. **Student Body:** 53% female, 47% male, 2% out-of-state, 3% international (105 countries represented). Asian 53%, African American 2%, Caucasian 22%, Hispanic 14%.
Retention and Graduation: 58% freshmen graduate within 4 years. **Faculty:** Student/faculty ratio 19:1. 1464 full-time faculty, 98% hold PhDs, 28% are members of minority groups, 35% are women.

ACADEMICS
Degrees: Bachelor's, master's, post-bachelor's certificate. **Classes:** Most classes have 20–29 students. Most lab/discussion sessions have fewer than 10 students. **Majors with Highest Enrollment:** Biology/biological sciences; psychology; social psychology. **Special Study Options:** Accelerated program, distance learning, double major, dual enrollment, English as a Second Language (ESL), honors program, independent study, internships, liberal arts/career combination, study abroad, teacher certification program. **Honors programs:** Campuswide Honors Program (CHP). **Combined degree programs:** 3-2 MBA. Special programs offered to physically disabled students include note-taking services, reader services, tape recorders. **Career services:** Alumni network, alumni services, career/job search classes, career assessment, internships.

FACILITIES
Housing: Coed dorms, special housing for disabled students, men's dorms, special housing for international students, women's dorms, fraternity/sorority housing, apartments for married students, cooperative housing, apartments for single students, theme housing. 95% of campus accessible to physically disabled. **Special Academic Facilities/Equipment:** Museum of systemic biology, freshwater marsh reserve, electron microscope, nuclear reactor, laser institute, research facilities. **Computers:** 90% of classrooms, 100% of libraries, 100% of dining areas, 100% of student union, have wireless network access. Students can register for classes online. Administrative functions (other than registration) can be performed online.

CAMPUS LIFE
Environment: City. **Activities:** Choral groups, concert band, dance, drama/theater, jazz band, literary magazine, music ensembles, musical theater, opera, pep band, radio station, student government, student newspaper, student-run film society, symphony orchestra, yearbook, international student organization, Model UN. **Organizations:** 484 registered organizations, 18 honor societies, 51 religious organizations. 21 fraternities, 23 sororities. **Athletics (Intercollegiate):** *Men:* Baseball, basketball, cross-country, golf, sailing, soccer, tennis, track/field (outdoor), volleyball, water polo. *Women:* Basketball, cross-country, golf, sailing, soccer, tennis, track/field (outdoor), volleyball, water polo.
On-Campus Highlights: Anteater Recreation Center, Bren Events Center, Cross-Cultural Center, Beall Center for Art and Technology, Arts Plaza. **Envi-**

ronmental Initiatives: Conversion of campus shuttle fleet to B100 biodiesel. Primary source of fuel is rercovreed waste cooking oil. See www.abs.uci.edu/b100retrofitprocess.pdf. First campus-wide LEED submittal in U.S. See www.sustainability.uci.edu/UCIUSGBCsmartsustainablecampus.pdf. 1.2 megawatt DC solar power system being installed on campus.

ADMISSIONS
Freshman Academic Profile: Average high school GPA 3.85. 96% in top 10% of high school class, 100% in top 25% of high school class, 100% in top 50% of high school class. 85% from public high schools. SAT Math middle 50% range 570–680. SAT Critical Reading middle 50% range 520–640. SAT Writing middle 50% range 530–640. Minimum paper TOEFL 550. Minimum computer TOEFL 213. **Basis for Candidate Selection:** *Very important factors considered include:* Application essay, academic GPA, rigor of secondary school record, standardized test scores, extracurricular activities, level of applicant's interest, talent/ability, volunteer work, work experience. *Important factors considered include:* Character/personal qualities. *Other factors considered include:* first generation, state residency. **Freshman Admission Requirements:** High school diploma is required and GED is accepted. *Academic units required:* 4 English, 3 mathematics, 2 science, (2 science labs), 2 foreign language, 2 history, 1 visual/performing arts, 1 academic electives. *Academic units recommended:* 4 English, 4 mathematics, 3 science, (3 science labs), 3 foreign language, 2 history, 1 visual/performing arts, 1 academic electives. **Freshman Admission Statistics:** 44,123 applied, 44% admitted, 21% enrolled. **Transfer Admission Requirements:** High school transcript, college transcript(s), essay or personal statement, minimum college GPA of 2.0 required. Lowest grade transferable C. **General Admission Information:** Application fee $60. Regular application deadline 11/30. Regular notification 3/31. Nonfall registration not accepted. Credit offered for CEEB Advanced Placement tests.

COSTS AND FINANCIAL AID
Annual in-state tuition $9,402. Annual out-of-state tuition $32,281. Room and board $10,655. Required fees $2,511. Average book expense $1,645. **Required Forms and Deadlines:** FAFSA, state aid form, GPA verification form to state agency. Financial aid filing deadline 5/2. Priority financial aid filing date 3/2. **Notification of Awards:** Applicants will be notified of awards on a rolling basis beginning 4/1. **Types of Aid:** *Need-based scholarships/grants:* Federal Pell, SEOG, state scholarships/grants, private scholarships, the school's own gift aid. *Loans:* Direct Subsidized Stafford, Direct Unsubsidized Stafford, Direct PLUS, FFEL Subsidized Stafford, FFEL Unsubsidized Stafford, FFEL PLUS, Federal Perkins, college/university loans from institutional funds, Private Loans. *Student Employment:* Federal Work-Study Program available. Institutional employment available. **Financial Aid Statistics:** 46% freshmen, 45% undergrads receive need-based scholarship or grant aid. 1% freshmen, 1% undergrads receive non-need-based scholarship or grant aid. 36% freshmen, 33% undergrads receive need-based self-help aid. 1% freshmen, 1% undergrads receive athletic scholarships. 46% undergrads borrow to pay for school. Average cumulative indebtedness $14,323. **Criteria for awarding institutional aid:** *Non-need-based:* Academics, art, athletics, job skills, leadership, music/drama, state/district residency.

UNIVERSITY OF CALIFORNIA—LOS ANGELES

Best 373

1147 Murphy Hall, Box 951436, Los Angeles, CA 90095-1436
Phone: 310-825-3101 **Financial Aid Phone:** 310-206-0400
E-mail: ugadm@saonet.ucla.edu **CEEB Code:** 4837
Fax: 310-206-1206 **Website:** www.ucla.edu **ACT Code:** 448

This public school was founded in 1919. It has a 419-acre campus.

RATINGS
Admissions Selectivity Rating: 98   **Fire Safety Rating:** 84   **Green Rating:** 87

STUDENTS AND FACULTY
Enrollment: 26,536. **Student Body:** 55% female, 45% male, 6% out-of-state, 4% international (104 countries represented). Asian 38%, African American 4%, Caucasian 34%, Hispanic 15%.
Retention and Graduation: 97% freshmen return for sophomore year. 65% freshmen graduate within 4 years. **Faculty:** Student/faculty ratio 16:1. 1948 full-time faculty, 98% hold PhDs, 23% are members of minority groups, 31% are women.

ACADEMICS

Degrees: Bachelor's, first professional, master's. **Classes:** Most classes have 10–19 students. Most lab/discussion sessions have 20–29 students. **Majors with Highest Enrollment:** Business/managerial economics; political science and government; psychology. **Special Study Options:** Accelerated program, double major, English as a Second Language (ESL), honors program, independent study, internships, liberal arts/career combination, student-designed major, study abroad. **Honors programs:** The College Honors Program Special programs offered to physically disabled students include note-taking services, reader services, tape recorders, tutors. **Career services:** Alumni network, alumni services, career/job search classes, career assessment, internships, regional alumni. **Career services highlights include:** Based at the UC Washington Center, CAPPP students carry out a research project on a topic of their own choosing, and complete a challenging, substantive internship at one of DC's hundreds of government agencies, think tanks, NGOs, non-profits, media outlets, advocacy, trade, and business organizations. Program participants earn up to 16 upper division units while remaining full-time UCLA students.

FACILITIES

Housing: Coed dorms, special housing for disabled students, fraternity/sorority housing, apartments for married students, apartments for single students, wellness housing, theme housing. 100% of campus accessible to physically disabled. **Special Academic Facilities/Equipment:** Art gallery, cultural history museum, sculpture garden, graphic arts center, numerous study centers, research institutes, UCLA Armand Hammer Museum of Art and Cultural Center, Murphy Sculpture Garden, Fowler Museum of Cultural History. **Computers:** Students can register for classes online. Administrative functions (other than registration) can be performed online.

CAMPUS LIFE

Environment: Metropolis. **Activities:** Choral groups, concert band, dance, drama/theater, jazz band, literary magazine, marching band, music ensembles, musical theater, opera, pep band, radio station, student government, student newspaper, student-run film society, symphony orchestra, television station, yearbook, campus ministries, international student organization, Model UN. **Organizations:** 870 registered organizations, 21 honor societies, 38 religious organizations. 36 fraternities, 28 sororities. **Athletics (Intercollegiate):** *Men:* Baseball, basketball, cross-country, football, golf, soccer, tennis, track/field (outdoor), track/field (indoor), volleyball, water polo. *Women:* Basketball, crew/rowing, cross-country, diving, golf, gymnastics, soccer, softball, swimming, tennis, track/field (outdoor), track/field (indoor), volleyball, water polo. **On-Campus Highlights:** The UCLA Library, UCLA Fowler Museum of Cultural History, UCLA Book Store, DeNeve Plaza, Kerckhoff Coffee House. **Environmental Initiatives:** The university is engaged in several efforts to integrate green procurement initiatives into strategic procurement programs, including development of restructured purchasing contracts that will include sustainability principles in various strategic sourcing areas such as paper, janitorial, and equipment products. In addition, a UC–wide committee on strategic food service sourcing has been tasked with responsibility to develop an RFP for organically grown and sustainable food products for the university and its campuses. At the campus level, green products already do make up a portion of the total procurement (for example, approximately 26 percent of all office, dining and janitorial paper products purchased by UCLA in 2002–03 included recycled content). The UC Sustainable Food Systems Campaign (SFS) is a student organization that collaborates with campus administrators, faculty, staff, local farmers, and other student groups in efforts to adopt more sustainable food practices at the university level. Through education and outreach with programs such as the UCLA Community Organic Garden and an official university-accredited experiential course, the campaign communicates a sound future of food for UCLA. In the past six months, the SFS campaign has gathered over 6,000 signatures from students statewide in support of local, organic, and socially responsible food, as well as green dining facility standards. Past efforts and events also include the passing of a statewide referendum for a better future in food, a college-night organic dinner that was in collaboration with the local farmers market, and organic taste-tests on campus. The recently adopted UC Green Building and Clean Energy Policy ("Policy") recognizes that resource sustainability is critically important. The Policy promotes "...the principles of energy efficiency and sustainability in the planning, financing, design, construction, renewal, maintenance, operation, space management, facilities utilization, and commissioning of facilities and infrastructure to the fullest extent possible, consistent with budgetary constraints and regulatory and programmatic requirements," and provides detailed guidelines for implementing practices in support of Green Building Design and Clean Energy Standards. In that context, the University is establishing a UC–equivalent certification process (equivalent to the USGBC/LEED certification process) to be applied to all major new construction/renovation projects approved as of July 2004.

ADMISSIONS

Freshman Academic Profile: Average high school GPA 4.22. 97% in top 10% of high school class, 100% in top 25% of high school class, 100% in top 50% of high school class. 81% from public high schools. SAT Math middle 50% range 600–730. SAT Critical Reading middle 50% range 570–680. SAT Writing middle 50% range 580–700. ACT middle 50% range 25–31. Minimum paper TOEFL 550. Minimum computer TOEFL 220. Minimum web-based TOEFL 83. **Basis for Candidate Selection:** *Very important factors considered include:* Application essay, academic GPA, rigor of secondary school record, standardized test scores. *Important factors considered include:* Character/personal qualities, extracurricular activities, talent/ability, volunteer work, work experience. *Other factors considered include:* First generation, geographical residence. **Freshman Admission Requirements:** High school diploma is required and GED is accepted. *Academic units required:* 4 English, 3 mathematics, 2 science, (2 science labs), 2 foreign language, 2 history, 1 academic electives, 1 visual and performing arts. *Academic units recommended:* 4 English, 4 mathematics, 3 science, (3 science labs), 3 foreign language, 2 history, 1 academic electives, 1 visual and performing arts. **Freshman Admission Statistics:** 55,437 applied, 23% admitted, 37% enrolled. **Transfer Admission Requirements:** College transcript(s), essay or personal statement, statement of good standing from prior institution(s). Minimum college GPA of 2.4 required. Lowest grade transferable D. **General Admission Information:** Application fee $60. Regular application deadline 11/30. Notification on a rolling basis, beginning on or about 3/31. Nonfall registration not accepted. Credit and/or placement offered for CEEB Advanced Placement tests.

COSTS AND FINANCIAL AID

Annual out-of-state tuition $22,021. Room and board $13,314. Required fees $9,151. Average book expense $1,599. **Required Forms and Deadlines:** FAFSA. **Notification of Awards:** Applicants will be notified of awards on a rolling basis beginning 3/15. **Types of Aid:** *Need-based scholarships/grants:* Federal Pell, SEOG, state scholarships/grants, private scholarships, the school's own gift aid, United Negro College Fund, Federal Nursing Scholarships. *Loans:* FFEL Subsidized Stafford, FFEL Unsubsidized Stafford, FFEL PLUS, Federal Perkins, Federal Nursing, state loans, college/university loans from institutional funds. *Student Employment:* Federal Work-Study Program available. Institutional employment available. Off-campus job opportunities are good. **Financial Aid Statistics:** 47% freshmen, 47% undergrads receive need-based scholarship or grant aid. 1% freshmen, 1% undergrads receive non-need-based scholarship or grant aid. 31% freshmen, 34% undergrads receive need-based self-help aid. 2% freshmen, 2% undergrads receive athletic scholarships. 46% freshmen, 50% undergrads receive any aid. 43% undergrads borrow to pay for school. Average cumulative indebtedness $16,733. **Criteria for awarding institutional aid:** *Non-need-based:* Academics, alumni affiliation, athletics.

See page 1276.

UNIVERSITY OF CALIFORNIA—RIVERSIDE

3106 Student Services Building, Riverside, CA 92521
Phone: 951-827-3411 **Financial Aid Phone:** 951-827-3878
E-mail: admin@ucr.edu **CEEB Code:** 4839
Fax: 951-827-6344 **Website:** www.ucr.edu

This public school was founded in 1954. It has a 1200-acre campus.

RATINGS

Admissions Selectivity Rating: 92   **Fire Safety Rating:** 85   **Green Rating:** 93

STUDENTS AND FACULTY

Enrollment: 16,996. **Student Body:** 52% female, 48% male, 1% out-of-state, 2% international (66 countries represented). Asian 40%, African American 8%, Caucasian 17%, Hispanic 29%.
Retention and Graduation: 39% freshmen graduate within 4 years. **Faculty:** Student/faculty ratio 18.5:1. 765 full-time faculty, 98% hold PhDs, 32% are members of minority groups, 33% are women.

ACADEMICS

Degrees: Bachelor's, master's, post-bachelor's certificate. **Classes:** Most classes have 20–29 students. Most lab/discussion sessions have 20–29 students. **Majors with Highest Enrollment:** Biology/biological sciences; business administration and management; psychology. **Special Study Options:** Accelerated program, cross-registration, double major, English as a Second Language (ESL), honors program, independent study, internships, student-designed major, study abroad, teacher certification program. Special programs offered to physically disabled students include note-taking services, reader services, tape recorders, tutors. **Career services:** Alumni network, alumni services, career/job search classes, career assessment, internships. **Career services highlights include:** Today's students do not always have the time to come to the brinks and mortar home of the traditional Career Center. The UCR Career Center has responded by developing state-of-the-art best practices to deliver services whether this is job search, internships, or career counseling. These new alternatives and virtual services range from a highly interactive website using podcast and YouTube features to providing workshops either in the classroom or in a virtual environment.

FACILITIES

Housing: Coed dorms, special housing for disabled students, special housing for international students, apartments for married students, apartments for single students, theme housing. **Special Academic Facilities/Equipment:** Art gallery, photography museum, botanical gardens, audio-visual resource center/studios, media resource center, statistical consulting center, citrus research center and agricultural experiment station, air pollution research center, center for environmental research and technology, water resources center, geophysics and planetary physics institute, center for bibliographical studies, center for family studies, center for crime and justice studies, natural reserve system, water resources center, salinity lab. **Computers:** 100% of classrooms, 15% of dorms, 100% of libraries, 100% of dining areas, 100% of student union, 100% of common outdoor areas have wireless network access. Students can register for classes online. Administrative functions (other than registration) can be performed online.

CAMPUS LIFE

Environment: City. **Activities:** Choral groups, concert band, dance, drama/theater, jazz band, literary magazine, music ensembles, musical theater, pep band, radio station, student government, student newspaper, student-run film society, international student organization. **Organizations:** 264 registered organizations, 9 honor societies, 27 religious organizations. 20 fraternities, 20 sororities. **Athletics (Intercollegiate):** *Men:* Baseball, basketball, cross-country, golf, soccer, tennis, track/field (outdoor), track/field (indoor). *Women:* Basketball, cross-country, golf, soccer, softball, tennis, track/field (outdoor), track/field (indoor), volleyball. **On-Campus Highlights:** Basketball games, Student Recreation Center and intramural sports, The Barn (music and comedy acts), Coffee Bean and Tea Leaf, The Highlander Union Building (HUB). **Environmental Initiatives:** Developing a climate neutrality plan. Planning a LEED Platinum new building for Environmental Health & Safety—not yet approved. Developing a sustainable, native landscape plan for UCR-Palm Desert Campus.

ADMISSIONS

Freshman Academic Profile: Average high school GPA 3.49. 94% in top 10% of high school class, 100% in top 25% of high school class, 100% in top 50% of high school class. 89% from public high schools. SAT Math middle 50% range 480–620. SAT Critical Reading middle 50% range 450–570. SAT Writing middle 50% range 460–570. ACT middle 50% range 19–25. Minimum paper TOEFL 550. Minimum computer TOEFL 213. **Basis for Candidate Selection:** *Very important factors considered include:* Academic GPA, rigor of secondary school record, standardized test scores, state residency. *Important factors considered include:* Application essay. *Other factors considered include:* first generation. **Freshman Admission Requirements:** High school diploma is required and GED is accepted. *Academic units required:* 4 English, 3 mathematics, 2 science, (2 science labs), 2 foreign language, 2 history, 1 visual/performing arts, 1 academic electives. *Academic units recommended:* 4 mathematics, 3 science, (3 science labs), 3 foreign language. **Freshman Admission Statistics:** 24,969 applied, 80% admitted, 22% enrolled. **Transfer Admission Requirements:** College transcript(s), essay or personal statement, statement of good standing from prior institution(s). Minimum college GPA of 2.4 required. Lowest grade transferable D-. **General Admission Information:** Application fee $60. Regular application deadline 11/30. Notification on a rolling basis, beginning on or about 2/1. Nonfall registration not accepted. Credit and/or placement offered for CEEB Advanced Placement tests.

COSTS AND FINANCIAL AID

Annual in-state tuition $6,888. Annual out-of-state tuition $29,556. Room and board $10,900. Required fees $1,619. Average book expense $1,750. **Required Forms and Deadlines:** FAFSA, state aid form. Financial aid filing deadline 3/2. Priority financial aid filing date 3/2. **Notification of Awards:** Applicants will be notified of awards on a rolling basis beginning 3/1. **Types of Aid:** *Need-based scholarships/grants:* Federal Pell, SEOG, state scholarships/grants, private scholarships, the school's own gift aid. *Loans:* Direct Subsidized Stafford, Direct Unsubsidized Stafford, Direct PLUS, Federal Perkins, college/university loans from institutional funds. *Student Employment:* Federal Work-Study Program available. Institutional employment available. Off-campus job opportunities are excellent. **Financial Aid Statistics:** 66% freshmen, 64% undergrads receive need-based scholarship or grant aid. 1% freshmen, 1% undergrads receive non-need-based scholarship or grant aid. 58% freshmen, 53% undergrads receive need-based self-help aid. 1% freshmen, 1% undergrads receive athletic scholarships. 83% freshmen, 77% undergrads receive any aid. 62% undergrads

borrow to pay for school. Average cumulative indebtedness $16,398. **Criteria for awarding institutional aid:** *Non-need-based:* Academics, art, athletics, job skills, leadership, music/drama, state/district residency.

UNIVERSITY OF CALIFORNIA—SAN DIEGO

9500 Gilman Drive, 0021, La Jolla, CA 92093-0021
Phone: 858-534-4831 **Financial Aid Phone:** 858-534-4480
E-mail: admissionsinfo@ucsd.edu **CEEB Code:** 4836
Fax: 858-534-5723 **Website:** www.ucsd.edu

This public school was founded in 1960. It has a 1976-acre campus.

RATINGS

Admissions Selectivity Rating: 97   **Fire Safety Rating:** 82   **Green Rating:** 96

STUDENTS AND FACULTY

Enrollment: 23,143. **Student Body:** 52% female, 48% male, 3% out-of-state, 7% international (70 countries represented). Asian 44%, African American 2%, Caucasian 25%, Hispanic 13%.
Retention and Graduation: 94% freshmen return for sophomore year. 56% freshmen graduate within 4 years. 35% grads go on to further study within 1 year. 34% grads pursue arts and sciences degrees. 15% grads pursue law degrees. 8% grads pursue business degrees. 16% grads pursue medical degrees.
Faculty: Student/faculty ratio 19:1. 943 full-time faculty, 98% hold PhDs, 24% are members of minority groups, 25% are women.

ACADEMICS

Degrees: Bachelor's, master's. **Classes:** Most classes have 10–19 students. Most lab/discussion sessions have 20–29 students. **Majors with Highest Enrollment:** Biology/biological sciences; economics; psychology. **Special Study Options:** Accelerated program, cooperative education program, cross-registration, double major, English as a Second Language (ESL), exchange student program (domestic), honors program, independent study, internships, liberal arts/career combination, student-designed major, study abroad, teacher certification program, Summer sessions for credit; special services for students with learning disabilities; Research programs, freshman honors program, in-depth academic assignments working in small groups or one-to-one with faculty. **Honors programs:** Each of UCSD's six colleges offers an honors program. Honors programs differ from college to college and year to year.

FACILITIES

Housing: Coed dorms, special housing for disabled students, men's dorms, special housing for international students, women's dorms, fraternity/sorority housing, apartments for married students, cooperative housing, apartments for single students, International House for international students and others interested in international living. 100% of campus accessible to physically disabled. **Special Academic Facilities/Equipment:** Art galleries, center for U.S.-Mexican studies, music recording studio, audiovisual center, center for music experimentation, aquarium, structural lab, San Diego supercomputer center, electron microscopes lab, the UC San Diego Medical Center, Scripps Institution of Oceanography, California Institute for Telecommunications and Information Technology (Calit2), Institute on Global Conflict and Cooperation, Institute of the Americas. **Computers:** 100% of classrooms, 100% of dorms, 100% of libraries, 100% of dining areas, 100% of student union, 30% of common outdoor areas have wireless network access. Students can register for classes online. Administrative functions (other than registration) can be performed online.

CAMPUS LIFE

Environment: Metropolis. **Activities:** Choral groups, concert band, dance, drama/theater, jazz band, literary magazine, marching band, music ensembles, musical theater, opera, pep band, radio station, student government, student newspaper, student-run film society, symphony orchestra, television station, yearbook, campus ministries, international student organization, Model UN. **Organizations:** 406 registered organizations, 5 honor societies, 46 religious organizations. 19 fraternities, 14 sororities. **Athletics (Intercollegiate):** *Men:* Baseball, basketball, crew/rowing, cross-country, diving, fencing, golf, soccer, swimming, tennis, track/field (outdoor), volleyball, water polo. *Women:* Basketball, crew/rowing, cross-country, diving, fencing, soccer, softball, swimming, tennis, track/field (outdoor), volleyball, water polo. **On-Campus Highlights:** Geisel Library, Stuart Art (sculpture) Gallery, Sun God Statue, Ocean Cliffs,

Stephen Birch Aquarium and Museum, Price Center Expansion. **Environmental Initiatives:** The Sustainability Resource Center (SRC), completed November 20, 2009 was constructed to provide a centralized, collaborative space in which to realize the common goals of maximizing campus environmental, social, and economic stewardship and sustainability reducing the campus impact on the environment, programs, maximizing campus and local outreach and participation, and establishing a model for contributing to local, national, and global sustainability.

ADMISSIONS

Freshman Academic Profile: Average high school GPA 3.96. 100% in top 10% of high school class, 100% in top 25% of high school class, 100% in top 50% of high school class. SAT Math middle 50% range 610–720. SAT Critical Reading middle 50% range 540–660. SAT Writing middle 50% range 560–680. ACT middle 50% range 24–30. Minimum paper TOEFL 550. **Basis for Candidate Selection:** *Very important factors considered include:* Application essay, academic GPA, rigor of secondary school record, standardized test scores, character/personal qualities, state residency, talent/ability. *Important factors considered include:* Extracurricular activities, volunteer work. *Other factors considered include:* first generation, work experience. **Freshman Admission Requirements:** High school diploma is required and GED is accepted. *Academic units required:* 4 English, 3 mathematics, 2 science, (2 science labs), 2 foreign language, 2 history, 1 visual/performing arts, 1 academic electives. *Academic units recommended:* 4 English, 4 mathematics, 3 science, (3 science labs), 3 foreign language, 2 history, 1 academic electives. **Freshman Admission Statistics:** 47,046 applied, 38% admitted, 21% enrolled. **Transfer Admission Requirements:** College transcript(s), essay or personal statement, statement of good standing from prior institution(s). Minimum college GPA of 2.4 required. Lowest grade transferable D. **General Admission Information:** Application fee $60. Regular application deadline 11/30. Regular notification 3/31. Notification on a rolling basis, beginning on or about 3/15. Nonfall registration accepted. Credit and/or placement offered for CEEB Advanced Placement tests.

COSTS AND FINANCIAL AID

Annual in-state tuition $8,798. Annual out-of-state tuition $22,669. Room and board $11,057. Required fees $900. Average book expense $1,560. **Required Forms and Deadlines:** FAFSA, state aid form Financial aid filing deadline 6/1. Priority financial aid filing date 3/2. **Notification of Awards:** Applicants will be notified of awards on a rolling basis beginning 3/15. **Types of Aid:** *Need-based scholarships/grants:* Federal Pell, SEOG, state scholarships/grants, private scholarships, the school's own gift aid, Federal Academic Competitive Grant Federal National SMART Grant. *Loans:* FFEL Subsidized Stafford, FFEL Unsubsidized Stafford, FFEL PLUS, Federal Perkins, college/university loans from institutional funds, Alternative Loans. *Student Employment:* Federal Work-Study Program available. Institutional employment available. Highest amount earned per year from on-campus jobs $15,840. Off-campus job opportunities are good. **Financial Aid Statistics:** 53% freshmen, 51% undergrads receive need-based scholarship or grant aid. 1% freshmen, 47% freshmen, 45% undergrads receive need-based self-help aid. 3% freshmen, 2% undergrads receive athletic scholarships. 77% freshmen, 63% undergrads receive any aid. 50% undergrads borrow to pay for school. Average cumulative indebtedness $16,317. **Criteria for awarding institutional aid:** *Non-need-based:* Academics, art, athletics, leadership, minority status, music/drama.

UNIVERSITY OF CALIFORNIA— SANTA BARBARA

Office of Admissions, 1210 Cheadle Hall, Santa Barbara, CA 93106-2014
Phone: 805-893-2881 **Financial Aid Phone:** 805-893-2118
E-mail: admissions@sa.ucsb.edu **CEEB Code:** 4835
Fax: 805-893-2676 **Website:** www.ucsb.edu

This public school was founded in 1909. It has a 989-acre campus.

RATINGS
Admissions Selectivity Rating: 95 **Fire Safety Rating:** 88 **Green Rating:** 99

STUDENTS AND FACULTY
Enrollment: 19,793. **Student Body:** 54% female, 46% male, 4% out-of-state, 1% international (72 countries represented). Asian 13%, African American 2%, Caucasian 39%, Hispanic 16%, Native American 1%.
Retention and Graduation: 91% freshmen return for sophomore year. 63%

freshmen graduate within 4 years. **Faculty:** Student/faculty ratio 17:1. 919 full-time faculty, 100% hold PhDs, 17% are members of minority groups, 33% are women.

ACADEMICS
Degrees: Bachelor's, master's, post-bachelor's certificate, post-master's certificate. **Classes:** Most classes have fewer than 10 students. Most lab/discussion sessions have 20–29 students. **Majors with Highest Enrollment:** Biology/biological sciences; economics; psychology. **Special Study Options:** Accelerated program, cross-registration, double major, dual enrollment, English as a Second Language (ESL), exchange student program (domestic), honors program, independent study, internships, student-designed major, study abroad, teacher certification program, Undergrads may take grad level classes. Off-Campus Study: Washington, DC. Freshman Seminars, pre-professional programs and advising, academic minors, and undergraduate research. **Honors programs:** The College Honors Program is designed to give students in the College of Letters and Science the opportunity to pursue their interests as part of a small community of scholars. The program connects such students to the resources of a large university, while providing an intimate collegiate atmosphere where students work closely with peers and professors in small classes, research laboratories, and special program and activities. **Combined degree programs:** BA/MA, BS/MS. Special programs offered to physically disabled students include note-taking services, reader services, tape recorders, tutors. **Career services:** Career/job search classes, career assessment, internships.

FACILITIES
Housing: Coed dorms, fraternity/sorority housing, apartments for married students, cooperative housing, apartments for single students, wellness housing, theme housing. **Special Academic Facilities/Equipment:** Art museum, centers for black studies, Chicano studies, and study of developing nations, institutes for applied behavioral sciences, community/organizational research, marine science, and theoretical physics, Channel Islands field station. **Computers:** 100% of dorms, 100% of dining areas, 100% of student union, have wireless network access. Students can register for classes online. Administrative functions (other than registration) can be performed online.

CAMPUS LIFE
Environment: City. **Activities:** Choral groups, concert band, dance, drama/theater, jazz band, literary magazine, music ensembles, musical theater, opera, pep band, radio station, student government, student newspaper, student-run film society, symphony orchestra, television station, yearbook, campus ministries, international student organization, Model UN. **Organizations:** 508 registered organizations, 5 honor societies, 19 religious organizations. 17 fraternities, 18 sororities. **Athletics (Intercollegiate):** *Men:* Baseball, basketball, cross-country, diving, golf, gymnastics, soccer, swimming, tennis, track/field (outdoor), volleyball, water polo. *Women:* Basketball, cross-country, diving, gymnastics, soccer, softball, swimming, tennis, track/field (outdoor), volleyball, water polo. **On-Campus Highlights:** Storke Tower Plaza/University Center, University Art Museum, UCSB Davidson Library, Recreation Center, Career and Counseling Services Center. **Environmental Initiatives:** 1) Green buildings: minimum silver and strive for gold LEED certification – six buildings are currently certified, including San Clemente Villages Graduate Housing – one of the largest Gold certified housing projects in the US – and Bren Hall – the first building in the US to receive two Platinum ratings for new construction and existing buildings. Plus, 24 additional existing buildings scheduled to be certified in the next couple years through the USGBC Portfolio Program. UCSB has the most LEED EB buildings in the UC System. We created Low Environmental Impact Cleaning Policy for the campus custodial services. All cleaning products and soaps used by the custodial staff are Green Seal certified. Plus toilet tissue, seat covers, and brown paper towels have 100% recycled content. Housing & Residential Services, supports solar water heating providing hot water for dorms, recycling used cooking oil from dining commons for biofuel, extensive recycling program including composting of food waste, purchasing local and/or organic foods for dining commons, using Green Seal cleaning products for custodial duties. 2) Energy: through HVAC and lighting retrofits, delamping (removing unnecessary lights), Flex Your Power campaigns, etc, the campus has decreased its per-square-footage electrical consumption by 31% and its natural gas consumption by 23% since 1998. We are part of a Strategic Energy Partnership—$1.5 million in energy retrofits taking place in 2009 with $14.5 million in additional retrofits occurring over the next two years 3) Creation of a high-level Chancellor's Sustainability Committee that includes administration, deans, Nobel laureates, senior faculty, staff and students in charge of making recommendations for sustainability projects to the Chancellor.

ADMISSIONS
Freshman Academic Profile: Average high school GPA 3.85. 87% from public high schools. SAT Math middle 50% range 550–670. SAT Critical Reading middle 50% range 540–660. SAT Writing middle 50% range 540–660. ACT middle 50% range 24–30. Minimum paper TOEFL 550. Minimum computer TOEFL 213. Minimum web-based TOEFL 79. **Basis for Candidate Selection:** *Very important factors considered include:* Application essay, academic GPA, rigor of secondary school record, standardized test scores, *Other factors considered include:* Class rank, character/personal qualities, extracurricular

activities, first generation, state residency, talent/ability, volunteer work, work experience. **Freshman Admission Requirements:** High school diploma is required and GED is accepted. *Academic units required:* 4 English, 3 mathematics, (2 science labs), 2 foreign language, 2 history, 1 visual/performing arts, 1 academic electives. *Academic units recommended:* 4 mathematics, (3 science labs), 3 foreign language. **Freshman Admission Statistics:** 44,707 applied, 48% admitted, 21% enrolled. **Transfer Admission Requirements:** High school transcript, college transcript(s), essay or personal statement, minimum college GPA of 2.4 required. Lowest grade transferable D. **General Admission Information:** Application fee $60. Regular application deadline 11/30. Regular notification 3/1. Nonfall registration not accepted. Credit and/or placement offered for CEEB Advanced Placement tests.

COSTS AND FINANCIAL AID
Required Forms and Deadlines: FAFSA. Financial aid filing deadline 5/31. Priority financial aid filing date 3/2. **Notification of Awards:** Applicants will be notified of awards on a rolling basis beginning 3/15. **Types of Aid:** *Need-based scholarships/grants:* Federal Pell, SEOG, state scholarships/grants, private scholarships, the school's own gift aid, Work Study is also available as need-based aid. *Loans:* Direct Subsidized Stafford, Direct Unsubsidized Stafford, Direct PLUS, Federal Perkins. *Student Employment:* Federal Work-Study Program available. Institutional employment available. Off-campus job opportunities are good. **Financial Aid Statistics:** 47% freshmen, 41% undergrads receive need-based scholarship or grant aid. 1% freshmen, 38% freshmen, 34% undergrads receive need-based self-help aid. 1% freshmen, 1% undergrads receive athletic scholarships. 47% undergrads borrow to pay for school. Average cumulative indebtedness $17,107. **Criteria for awarding institutional aid:** *Non-need-based:* Academics, athletics.

UNIVERSITY OF CALIFORNIA—SANTA CRUZ

Office of Admissions; Cook House, 1156 High Street, Santa Cruz, CA 95064
Phone: 831-459-4008 **Financial Aid Phone:** 831-459-2963
E-mail: admissions@ucsc.edu **CEEB Code:** 4860
Fax: 831-459-4452 **Website:** www.ucsc.edu

This public school was founded in 1965. It has a 2000-acre campus.

RATINGS
Admissions Selectivity Rating: 94 **Fire Safety Rating:** 78 **Green Rating:** 99

STUDENTS AND FACULTY
Enrollment: 15,206. **Student Body:** 53% female, 47% male, 3% out-of-state, international (72 countries represented). Asian 22%, African American 3%, Caucasian 49%, Hispanic 18%, Native American 1%.
Retention and Graduation: 49% freshmen graduate within 4 years. **Faculty:** Student/faculty ratio 19.24:1. 586 full-time faculty, 98% hold PhDs, 24% are members of minority groups, 37% are women.

ACADEMICS
Degrees: Bachelor's, doctoral, master's, post-bachelor's certificate. **Classes:** Most classes have 10–19 students. Most lab/discussion sessions have 10–19 students. **Majors with Highest Enrollment:** art/art studies; business/commerce; psychology. **Special Study Options:** Cooperative education program, cross-registration, double major, exchange student program (domestic), independent study, internships, student-designed major, study abroad, teacher certification program **Combined degree programs:** BA/MA, economics/applied economics, business management economics, global economic. Special programs offered to physically disabled students include note-taking services, reader services, tape recorders, tutors. **Career services:** Alumni network, alumni services, career/job search classes, career assessment, internships. **Career services highlights include:** Chancellor's Undergraduate Internship Program (CUIP)- CUIP provides professional level on-campus internships in administrative departments throughout campus. Interns work with a mentor to develop personal and professional skills and take a lead role in producing a product or result in thir one-year internship. Interns receive a scholarship equivalent to their registration fees for a year in exchange for 450 hours of work. Students attend a 2-unit leadership seminar led by the Dean of Undergraduate Education during both Fall and Spring quarters. This program places an average of 35 students per year. Professions Training Program and Bonner Leaders (PTP/BL)- The PTP/BL service-learning program provides internships in local non-profit organizations along with an academic component focused on leader-

ship development. Students receive a $1000 scholarship for 300 hours of work. This program is a partnership with the Bonner Foundation and AmeriCorps and places 15-20 students each year.

FACILITIES
Housing: Coed dorms, men's dorms, special housing for international students, women's dorms, apartments for married students, apartments for single students, theme housing, university-sponsored off-campus housing, RV park, -University Inn and Conference Center. **Special Academic Facilities/Equipment:** Eloise Pickard Smith Gallery Mary Porter Sesnon Gallery Center for Agroecology Wellness Center Long Marine Laboratory. **Computers:** 100% of classrooms, 100% of dorms, 100% of libraries, 100% of dining areas, 100% of student union, have wireless network access. Students can register for classes online. Administrative functions (other than registration) can be performed online.

CAMPUS LIFE
Environment: City. **Activities:** Choral groups, dance, drama/theater, jazz band, literary magazine, music ensembles, musical theater, opera, radio station, student government, student newspaper, student-run film society, symphony orchestra, television station, campus ministries, international student organization, Model UN. **Organizations:** 138 registered organizations, 3 honor societies, 19 religious organizations. 9 fraternities, 11 sororities. **Athletics (Intercollegiate):** *Men:* Basketball, diving, soccer, swimming, tennis, volleyball. *Women:* Basketball, cross-country, diving, golf, soccer, swimming, tennis, volleyball. **On-Campus Highlights:** Arboretum, Farm and Garden, East Field House, Bay Tree Bookstore/Grad Student Commons, Pogonip Open Area Reserve. **Environmental Initiatives:** Formation of the Chancellor's Committee on Climate Change to create a Climate Action Plan to achieve carbon neutrality and create demonstration and city/county/campus collaborative projects (2008). Completion of UCSC's first Campus Sustainability Assessment (2007). LEED certification projects underway (one LEED-EB, several LEED-CI, and a potential LEED-NC).

ADMISSIONS
Freshman Academic Profile: Average high school GPA 3.61. 96% in top 10% of high school class, 100% in top 25% of high school class, 100% in top 50% of high school class. 87% from public high schools. SAT Math middle 50% range 520–640. SAT Critical Reading middle 50% range 510–630. SAT Writing middle 50% range 520–630. ACT middle 50% range 22–28. Minimum paper TOEFL 550. Minimum computer TOEFL 220. Minimum web-based TOEFL 83. **Basis for Candidate Selection:** *Very important factors considered include:* Application essay, academic GPA, rigor of secondary school record, standardized test scores, state residency. *Important factors considered include:* Class rank, character/personal qualities, extracurricular activities, first generation, geographical residence, talent/ability. *Other factors considered include:* volunteer work, work experience. **Freshman Admission Requirements:** High school diploma is required and GED is accepted. *Academic units required:* 4 English, 3 mathematics, 2 science, (2 science labs), 2 foreign language, 1 social studies, 1 history, 1 visual/performing arts, 1 academic electives. 1 *Academic units recommended:* 4 English, 4 mathematics, 3 science, (3 science labs), 3 foreign language. **Freshman Admission Statistics:** 27,237 applied, 64% admitted, 18% enrolled. **Transfer Admission Requirements:** College transcript(s), essay or personal statement, statement of good standing from prior institution(s). Minimum college GPA of 2.4 required. Lowest grade transferable D. **General Admission Information:** Application fee $60. Regular application deadline 11/30. Regular notification 3/31. Notification on a rolling basis, beginning on or about 3/15. Nonfall registration accepted. Neither credit nor placement offered for CEEB Advanced Placement tests.

COSTS AND FINANCIAL AID
Annual out-of-state tuition $22,668. Room and board $13,641. Required fees $10,095. Average book expense $1,392. **Required Forms and Deadlines:** FAFSA, state aid formCA Student Adi Commission GPA verification form for CA residents. Financial aid filing deadline 3/2. **Notification of Awards:** Applicants will be notified of awards on a rolling basis beginning 4/1. **Types of Aid:** *Need-based scholarships/grants:* Federal Pell, SEOG, state scholarships/grants, private scholarships, the school's own gift aid. *Loans:* Direct Subsidized Stafford, Direct Unsubsidized Stafford, Direct PLUS, Federal Perkins. *Student Employment:* Federal Work-Study Program available. Institutional employment available. Off-campus job opportunities are excellent. **Financial Aid Statistics:** 44% freshmen, 44% undergrads receive need-based scholarship or grant aid. 45% freshmen, 43% undergrads receive need-based self-help aid. 54.6% freshmen, 58.6% undergrads receive any aid. 53% undergrads borrow to pay for school. Average cumulative indebtedness $15,918. **Criteria for awarding institutional aid:** *Non-need-based:* Academics, alumni affiliation, art, leadership, music/drama.

UNIVERSITY OF CENTRAL ARKANSAS

201 Donaghey Avenue, Bernard Hall 101, Conway, AR 72035
Phone: 501-450-3128 **Financial Aid Phone:** 501-450-3140
E-mail: admissions@uca.edu **CEEB Code:** 6012
Fax: 501-450-5228 **Website:** www.uca.edu/ **ACT Code:** 118

This public school was founded in 1907. It has a 262-acre campus.

RATINGS
Admissions Selectivity Rating: 84 **Fire Safety Rating:** 60* **Green Rating:** 60*

STUDENTS AND FACULTY
Enrollment: 9,921. **Student Body:** 58% female, 42% male, 6% out-of-state,
4% international (61 countries represented). Asian 1%, African American 16%,
Caucasian 71%, Hispanic 2%, Native American 1%.
Retention and Graduation: 23% freshmen graduate within 4 years. **Faculty:**
Student/faculty ratio 18:1. 510 full-time faculty, 69% hold PhDs, 11% are mem-
bers of minority groups, 47% are women.

ACADEMICS
Degrees: Associate, bachelor's, certificate, master's, post-bachelor's certificate,
post-master's certificate. **Classes:** Most classes have 20–29 students. **Special
Study Options:** Accelerated program, cooperative education program, distance
learning, double major, dual enrollment, English as a Second Language (ESL),
honors program, independent study, internships, liberal arts/career combination, study abroad, teacher certification program, 5 year professional program
in Physical and Occupational Therapy. Special programs offered to physically
disabled students include note-taking services, reader services, tape recorders.
Career services: Internships.

FACILITIES
Housing: Coed dorms, special housing for disabled students, men's dorms, special housing for international students, women's dorms, fraternity/sorority housing, apartments for married students, apartments for single students, residential
colleges are offered, as well as Honors housing. **Special Academic Facilities/
Equipment:** Greenhouse, Baum Gellery, HPER Center, Planetarium, Technology Plaza, Smartboards, H.L. Minton Center for Geospatial Analysis and
Research. **Computers:** 100% of classrooms, 100% of dorms, 100% of libraries,
100% of dining areas, 100% of student union, 100% of common outdoor areas
have wireless network access. Students can register for classes online. Administrative functions (other than registration) can be performed online.

CAMPUS LIFE
Environment: Town. **Activities:** Choral groups, concert band, dance, drama/
theater, jazz band, literary magazine, marching band, music ensembles, pep
band, radio station, student government, student newspaper, student-run film
society, symphony orchestra, television station, yearbook, campus ministries,
international student organization, Model UN. **Organizations:** 158 registered
organizations, 11 honor societies, 16 religious organizations. 12 fraternities, 8
sororities. **Athletics (Intercollegiate):** *Men:* Baseball, basketball, cheerleading, cross-country, football, golf, soccer, tennis, track/field (outdoor), track/field
(indoor). *Women:* Basketball, cheerleading, cross-country, golf, soccer, softball,
tennis, track/field (outdoor), track/field (indoor), volleyball. **On-Campus Highlights:** Student Center, HPER Center, Baum Gallery, Estes Stadium, Farris
Center.

ADMISSIONS
Freshman Academic Profile: Average high school GPA 3.3. ACT middle
50% range 20–27. Minimum paper TOEFL 500. Minimum computer TOEFL
173. Minimum web-based TOEFL 61. **Basis for Candidate Selection:** *Very
important factors considered include:* Academic GPA, standardized test scores.
Important factors considered include: Class rank. **Freshman Admission Requirements:** High school diploma is required and GED is accepted. *Academic
units recommended:* 4 English, 4 mathematics, 3 science, 1 social studies, 2
history, 10 academic electives. **Freshman Admission Statistics:** 5,780 applied,
49% admitted, 64% enrolled. **Transfer Admission Requirements:** College
transcript(s), statement of good standing from prior institution(s). Minimum
college GPA of 2.0 required. Lowest grade transferable C. **General Admission
Information:** Notification on a rolling basis, beginning on or about 10/1. Nonfall registration accepted. Credit and/or placement offered for CEEB Advanced
Placement tests.

COSTS AND FINANCIAL AID
Required Forms and Deadlines: FAFSA. Financial aid filing deadline 7/1.
Priority financial aid filing date 4/15. **Notification of Awards:** Applicants will
be notified of awards on a rolling basis beginning 5/4. **Types of Aid:** *Need-
based scholarships/grants:* Federal Pell, SEOG, state scholarships/grants,
private scholarships, the school's own gift aid, Federal Nursing Scholarships.
Loans: FFEL Subsidized Stafford, FFEL Unsubsidized Stafford, FFEL

PLUS, Federal Perkins, Federal Nursing, state loans, external loans. *Student
Employment:* Federal Work-Study Program available. Institutional employment available. **Financial Aid Statistics:** 6% freshmen, 6% undergrads receive
need-based scholarship or grant aid. 9% freshmen, 7% undergrads receive
non-need-based scholarship or grant aid. 16% freshmen, 17% undergrads
receive need-based self-help aid. 1% freshmen, 1% undergrads receive athletic
scholarships. 83.46% freshmen, 80.17% undergrads receive any aid. **Criteria
for awarding institutional aid:** *Non-need-based:* Academics, art, athletics,
leadership, minority status, music/drama, state/district residency.

UNIVERSITY OF CENTRAL FLORIDA

P.O. Box 160111, Orlando, FL 32816-0111
Phone: 407-823-3000 **Financial Aid Phone:** 407-823-2827
E-mail: admission@mail.ucf.edu **CEEB Code:** 5233
Fax: 407-823-5625 **Website:** www.ucf.edu **ACT Code:** 735

This public school was founded in 1963. It has a 1415-acre campus.

RATINGS
Admissions Selectivity Rating: 90 **Fire Safety Rating:** 81 **Green Rating:** 83

STUDENTS AND FACULTY
Enrollment: 45,048. **Student Body:** 55% female, 45% male, 5% out-of-state,
1% international (141 countries represented). Asian 6%, African American 9%,
Caucasian 66%, Hispanic 15%.
Retention and Graduation: 87% freshmen return for sophomore year. 34%
freshmen graduate within 4 years. **Faculty:** Student/faculty ratio 30.9:1. 1240
full-time faculty, 78% hold PhDs, 23% are members of minority groups, 39%
are women. 5% of classes are taught by teaching assistants.

ACADEMICS
Degrees: Associate, bachelor's, certificate, master's, post-bachelor's certificate. **Classes:** Most classes have 20–29 students. Most lab/discussion sessions
have 30–39 students. **Majors with Highest Enrollment:** health services/al-
lied health/health sciences; marketing/marketing management; psychology.
Special Study Options: Cooperative education program, distance learning,
double major, dual enrollment, English as a Second Language (ESL), honors
program, internships, study abroad, teacher certification program. **Honors
programs:** The Burnett Honors College combines the intimacy of a small
liberal arts college with the benefits of a large, metropolitan research university.
The college fosters an atmosphere of intellectual excitement and a passion
for learning; offers cutting-edge courses and innovative teaching methods;
provides academic and professional advisement, mentoring, select co-curricular
activities to Honors students; and develops sound values of social responsibility, inclusiveness, and good citizenship. The Burnett Honors College offers
two main tracks, University Honors and Honors in the Major, and a special
accelerated Medical School program in partnership with University of South
Florida. University Honors targets primarily incoming freshmen and comprises
a special freshman symposium, General Education Program (GEP) courses, and
upper-division seminars and disciplinary core courses. Honors GEP courses are
taught across the curriculum and are limited to enrollments of 20 students for
all courses except English Composition, which is limited to 15 students. Honors
English Composition also differs from regular Composition offerings that follow
a standardized curriculum in that each Honors section is "themed." Upper
division University Honors students take 9–15 hours of special interdisciplinary,
team-taught seminars or, in the case of the professional colleges, a combination of core courses in their fields and interdisciplinary seminars. In addition,
students participating in University Honors enroll in a well-respected and
established first-year experience course, the Honors Symposium. Honors in the
Major is a senior thesis Honors program. Honors in the Major students engage
in a two-semester course of study consisting of preparing a research proposal,
conducting original research, and writing a thesis. The student selects a three-
member faculty committee to oversee the thesis process that culminates in the
thesis defense. UCF/USF Early Acceptance/Accelerated Medical Program:
This unique program offers qualified UCF Honors students the opportunity
to complete the baccalaureate and Doctor in Medicine degrees in seven years.
Through a special partnership with the College of Medicine at the University
of South Florida, UCF Honors students are guaranteed admission to the USF
medical school once they have successfully completed the program requirements. **Combined degree programs:** BA/MD, BA/MA, BA/MEng, BS/MS.
Special programs offered to physically disabled students include note-taking

services, reader services, tape recorders, tutors. **Career services:** Career/job search classes, career assessment.

FACILITIES

Housing: Coed dorms, men's dorms, women's dorms, fraternity/sorority housing, apartments for single students, wellness housing, theme housing, affiliated student residences available across street from campus with university resident assistants. On-campus: Honors Center; Living Learning Communities, Lead Scholars Center. 97% of campus accessible to physically disabled. **Special Academic Facilities/Equipment:** Center for research and education in optics and lasers, arboretum, observatory, new student union, student recreation center. **Computers:** 100% of classrooms, 100% of dorms, 100% of libraries, 90% of dining areas, 100% of student union, 90% of common outdoor areas have wireless network access. Students can register for classes online. Administrative functions (other than registration) can be performed online.

CAMPUS LIFE

Environment: City. **Activities:** Choral groups, concert band, drama/theater, jazz band, literary magazine, marching band, music ensembles, musical theater, pep band, radio station, student government, student newspaper, student-run film society, symphony orchestra, campus ministries, international student organization, Model UN. **Organizations:** 361 registered organizations, 36 honor societies, 29 religious organizations. 21 fraternities, 18 sororities. **Athletics (Intercollegiate):** *Men:* Baseball, basketball, cheerleading, cross-country, football, golf, soccer, tennis. *Women:* Basketball, cheerleading, crew/rowing, cross-country, golf, soccer, softball, tennis, track/field (outdoor), track/field (indoor), volleyball. **On-Campus Highlights:** Student Union, Recreation and Wellness Center, bookstore (Barnes and Noble cafe), Reflecting Pond, new Arena and Football Stadium. **Environmental Initiatives:** In-House Building Commissioning Team; full-time Sustainability Marketing and Outreach; retrofitting water conservation devices on campus.

ADMISSIONS

Freshman Academic Profile: Average high school GPA 3.71. 35% in top 10% of high school class, 77% in top 25% of high school class, 95% in top 50% of high school class. SAT Math middle 50% range 560–650. SAT Critical Reading middle 50% range 530–620. SAT Writing middle 50% range 510–600. ACT middle 50% range 23–28. Minimum paper TOEFL 550. Minimum computer TOEFL 213. **Basis for Candidate Selection:** *Very important factors considered include:* Academic GPA, rigor of secondary school record, standardized test scores. *Important factors considered include:* Application essay, recommendation(s). *Other factors considered include:* Class rank, alumni/ae relation, character/personal qualities, extracurricular activities, first generation, geographical residence, interview, level of applicant's interest, state residency, talent/ability, volunteer work, work experience. **Freshman Admission Requirements:** High school diploma is required and GED is accepted. *Academic units required:* 4 English, 4 mathematics, 3 science, (2 science labs), 2 foreign language, 3 social studies, 2 academic electives. **Freshman Admission Statistics:** 32,335 applied, 47% admitted, 42% enrolled. **Transfer Admission Requirements:** College transcript(s), minimum college GPA of 2.0 required. Lowest grade transferable D. **General Admission Information:** Application fee $30. Regular application deadline 5/1. Notification on a rolling basis, beginning on or about 10/1. Nonfall registration accepted. Credit offered for CEEB Advanced Placement tests.

COSTS AND FINANCIAL AID

Annual in-state tuition $4,526. Annual out-of-state tuition $20,005. Room and board $8,540. Average book expense $924. **Required Forms and Deadlines:** FAFSA. Financial aid filing deadline 6/30. Priority financial aid filing date 3/1. **Notification of Awards:** Applicants will be notified of awards on a rolling basis beginning 3/15. **Types of Aid:** *Need-based scholarships/grants:* Federal Pell, SEOG, state scholarships/grants, private scholarships, the school's own gift aid, University scholarships and grants. *Loans:* FFEL Subsidized Stafford, FFEL Unsubsidized Stafford, FFEL PLUS, Federal Perkins. *Student Employment:* Federal Work-Study Program available. Institutional employment available. **Financial Aid Statistics:** 24% freshmen, 28% undergrads receive need-based scholarship or grant aid. 39% freshmen, 27% undergrads receive non-need-based scholarship or grant aid. 16% freshmen, 24% undergrads receive need-based self-help aid. 1% freshmen, 1% undergrads receive athletic scholarships. 90% freshmen, 74% undergrads receive any aid. 41.2% undergrads borrow to pay for school. Average cumulative indebtedness $17,044. **Criteria for awarding institutional aid:** *Non-need-based:* Academics, alumni affiliation, athletics, leadership, state/district residency.

See page 1278.

UNIVERSITY OF CENTRAL MISSOURI

Office of Admissions, WDE 1400, Warrensburg, MO 64093
Phone: 660-543-4290 **Financial Aid Phone:** 660-543-4040
E-mail: admit@ucmovmb.edu **CEEB Code:** 6090
Fax: 660-543-8517 **Website:** www.cmsu.edu **ACT Code:** 2272

This public school was founded in 1871. It has a 1561-acre campus.

RATINGS
Admissions Selectivity Rating: 71   **Fire Safety Rating:** 67   **Green Rating:** 60*

STUDENTS AND FACULTY

Enrollment: 8,441. **Student Body:** 56% female, 44% male, 7% out-of-state, 2% international (53 countries represented). Asian 1%, African American 5%, Caucasian 76%, Hispanic 2%.
Retention and Graduation: 68% freshmen return for sophomore year. 23% freshmen graduate within 4 years. **Faculty:** Student/faculty ratio 19:1. 449 full-time faculty, 73% hold PhDs, 7% are members of minority groups, 40% are women. 4% of classes are taught by teaching assistants.

ACADEMICS

Degrees: Associate, bachelor's, master's, post-bachelor's certificate, post-master's certificate. **Classes:** Most classes have 20–29 students. **Majors with Highest Enrollment:** Criminal justice/law enforcement administration; education; marketing/marketing management. **Special Study Options:** Accelerated program, cooperative education program, cross-registration, distance learning, double major, dual enrollment, English as a Second Language (ESL), honors program, internships, student-designed major, study abroad, teacher certification program, weekend college Special programs offered to physically disabled students include note-taking services, reader services, tape recorders, tutors.

FACILITIES

Housing: Coed dorms, special housing for disabled students, special housing for international students, women's dorms, fraternity/sorority housing, apartments for married students, apartments for single students, Economy Suites and Townhouses. 95% of campus accessible to physically disabled. **Special Academic Facilities/Equipment:** Art gallery, Nance Museum and Library of Antiquities, natural history museum, English language center, child development lab, speech and hearing lab, 260–acre farm, Missouri Safety center, National Police Institute, driving/safety range, center for technology and business research, airport for aviation program. Extended campus, Lee's Summit, MO. KCMW-FM, KMOS-TV, Public Broadcasting Stations. **Computers:** Students can register for classes online. Administrative functions (other than registration) can be performed online.

CAMPUS LIFE

Environment: Rural. **Activities:** Choral groups, concert band, dance, drama/theater, jazz band, literary magazine, marching band, music ensembles, musical theater, opera, pep band, radio station, student government, student newspaper, student-run film society, symphony orchestra, television station, yearbook. **Organizations:** 150 registered organizations, 24 honor societies, 14 religious organizations. 9 fraternities, 10 sororities. **Athletics (Intercollegiate):** *Men:* Baseball, basketball, bowling, cross-country, football, golf, soccer, track/field (outdoor), wrestling. *Women:* Basketball, bowling, cross-country, soccer, softball, track/field (outdoor), volleyball. **On-Campus Highlights:** Union Commons, Library, Pertle Springs, multi-purpose building.

ADMISSIONS

Freshman Academic Profile: Average high school GPA 3.29. 12% in top 10% of high school class, 36% in top 25% of high school class, 71% in top 50% of high school class. 90% from public high schools. ACT middle 50% range 20–24. Minimum paper TOEFL 500. Minimum computer TOEFL 173. **Basis for Candidate Selection:** *Very important factors considered include:* Class rank, rigor of secondary school record, standardized test scores, *Other factors considered include:* Recommendation(s), alumni/ae relation, character/personal qualities, extracurricular activities, talent/ability. **Freshman Admission Requirements:** High school diploma is required and GED is accepted. *Academic units required:* 4 English, 3 mathematics, 2 science, (1 science labs), 3 social studies, 3 academic electives, 1 arts. *Academic units recommended:* 2 foreign language. **Freshman Admission Statistics:** 3,631 applied, 84% admitted, 52% enrolled. **Transfer Admission Requirements:** College transcript(s), minimum college GPA of 2.0 required. Lowest grade transferable C. **General Admission Information:** Application fee $30. Regular application deadline 8/18. Notification on a rolling basis, beginning on or about 9/3. Nonfall registration accepted. Admission may be deferred for a maximum of 3 semesters. Credit offered for CEEB Advanced Placement tests.

COSTS AND FINANCIAL AID

Required Forms and Deadlines: FAFSA. Priority financial aid filing date 3/1. **Notification of Awards:** Applicants will be notified of awards on or about

3/1. **Types of Aid:** *Need-based scholarships/grants:* Federal Pell, SEOG, state scholarships/grants, private scholarships, the school's own gift aid. *Loans:* Direct Subsidized Stafford, Direct Unsubsidized Stafford, Direct PLUS, Federal Perkins, state loans *Student Employment:* Highest amount earned per year from on-campus jobs $2,000. **Financial Aid Statistics:** 27% freshmen, 36% undergrads receive need-based scholarship or grant aid. 36% freshmen, 32% undergrads receive non-need-based scholarship or grant aid. 43% freshmen, 55% undergrads receive need-based self-help aid. 5% freshmen, 5% undergrads receive athletic scholarships. 51% freshmen, 61% undergrads receive any aid. 68% undergrads borrow to pay for school. Average cumulative indebtedness $13,184. **Criteria for awarding institutional aid:** *Non-need-based:* Academics, alumni affiliation, art, athletics, leadership, minority status, music/drama, state/district residency.

UNIVERSITY OF CENTRAL OKLAHOMA

100 North University Drive, Edmond, OK 73034
Phone: 405-974-2338 **Financial Aid Phone:** 405-974-3334
E-mail: admituco@uco.edu **CEEB Code:** 6091
Fax: 405-341-4964 **ACT Code:** 3390

This public school was founded in 1890. It has a 200-acre campus.

RATINGS
Admissions Selectivity Rating: 73   **Fire Safety Rating:** 78   **Green Rating:** 77

STUDENTS AND FACULTY
Enrollment: 14,019. **Student Body:** 58% female, 42% male, 3% out-of-state, 6% international (75 countries represented). Asian 3%, African American 9%, Caucasian 60%, Hispanic 4%, Native American 5%.
Retention and Graduation: 61% freshmen return for sophomore year. **Faculty:** Student/faculty ratio 21:1. 441 full-time faculty, 68% hold PhDs, 13% are members of minority groups, 48% are women.

ACADEMICS
Degrees: Bachelor's, certificate, master's. **Classes:** Most classes have 20–29 students. Most lab/discussion sessions have 10–19 students. **Majors with Highest Enrollment:** Business administration and management; elementary education and teaching; nursing/registered nurse (RN, ASN, BSN, MSN). **Special Study Options:** Accelerated program, distance learning, double major, dual enrollment, English as a Second Language (ESL), honors program, independent study, internships, teacher certification program Special programs offered to physically disabled students include note-taking services, reader services, tape recorders, tutors. **Career services:** Alumni services, career/job search classes, career assessment, internships.

FACILITIES
Housing: Coed dorms, men's dorms, women's dorms, fraternity/sorority housing, apartments for married students, apartments for single students. 95% of campus accessible to physically disabled. **Special Academic Facilities/Equipment:** Art and history museums, archives. **Computers:** 100% of classrooms, 100% of dorms, 100% of libraries, 100% of dining areas, 100% of student union, 50% of common outdoor areas have wireless network access. Students can register for classes online. Administrative functions (other than registration) can be performed online.

CAMPUS LIFE
Environment: Metropolis. **Activities:** Choral groups, concert band, dance, drama/theater, jazz band, marching band, music ensembles, musical theater, pep band, radio station, student government, student newspaper, symphony orchestra, television station, yearbook. **Organizations:** 150 registered organizations, 27 honor societies, 16 religious organizations. 9 fraternities, 10 sororities. **Athletics (Intercollegiate):** *Men:* Baseball, basketball, football, golf, wrestling. *Women:* Basketball, cross-country, golf, soccer, softball, tennis, volleyball. **On-Campus Highlights:** Starbucks, Wellness Center, University Center. **Environmental Initiatives:** Use 100% wind power; waterless urinals; motion sensor lighting.

ADMISSIONS
Freshman Academic Profile: Average high school GPA 3.28. 12% in top 10% of high school class, 35% in top 25% of high school class, 72% in top 50% of high school class. ACT middle 50% range 19–23. Minimum paper TOEFL 560. Minimum computer TOEFL 220. Minimum web-based TOEFL 83. **Basis for Candidate Selection:** *Very important factors considered include:* Class rank, academic GPA, rigor of secondary school record, standardized test scores, *Other factors considered include:* Extracurricular activities, talent/ability. **Freshman Admission Requirements:** High school diploma is required and GED is accepted. *Academic units required:* 4 English, 3 mathematics, 2 science, (2 sci-

ence labs), 1 social studies, 2 history. *Academic units recommended:* 4 English, 4 mathematics, 3 science, (2 science labs), 2 foreign language, 1 social studies, 2 history. **Freshman Admission Statistics:** 4,614 applied, 69% admitted, 67% enrolled. **Transfer Admission Requirements:** College transcript(s), statement of good standing from prior institution(s). Minimum college GPA of 2.0 required. Lowest grade transferable D. **General Admission Information:** Application fee $25. Notification on a rolling basis, beginning on or about 4/1. Nonfall registration accepted. Admission may be deferred for a maximum of 1 semester. Credit and/or placement offered for CEEB Advanced Placement tests.

COSTS AND FINANCIAL AID
Annual in-state tuition $3,681. Annual out-of-state tuition $10,110. Room and board $7,468. Required fees $542. Average book expense $1,000. **Required Forms and Deadlines:** FAFSA, institution's own financial aid form. Financial aid filing deadline 5/31. Priority financial aid filing date 5/31. **Notification of Awards:** Applicants will be notified of awards on a rolling basis beginning 5/1. **Types of Aid:** *Need-based scholarships/grants:* Federal Pell, SEOG, state scholarships/grants, private scholarships, the school's own gift aid. *Loans:* FFEL Subsidized Stafford, FFEL Unsubsidized Stafford, FFEL PLUS, Federal Perkins. *Student Employment:* Federal Work-Study Program available. Institutional employment available. Highest amount earned per year from on-campus jobs $7,200. Off-campus job opportunities are excellent. **Financial Aid Statistics:** 37% freshmen, 42% undergrads receive need-based scholarship or grant aid. 1% freshmen, 2% undergrads receive non-need-based scholarship or grant aid. 38% freshmen, 44% undergrads receive need-based self-help aid. 2% freshmen, 2% undergrads receive athletic scholarships. 66% freshmen, 75% undergrads receive any aid. 48% undergrads borrow to pay for school. Average cumulative indebtedness $17,385. **Criteria for awarding institutional aid:** *Non-need-based:* Academics, alumni affiliation, art, athletics, leadership, minority status, music/drama, state/district residency.

UNIVERSITY OF CHARLESTON

2300 MacCorkle Ave SE, Charleston, WV 25304
Phone: 304-357-4750 **Financial Aid Phone:** 304-357-4759
E-mail: admissions@ucwv.edu **CEEB Code:** 5419
Fax: 304-357-4781 **Website:** www.ucwv.edu **ACT Code:** 4528

This private school was founded in 1888. It has a 24-acre campus.

RATINGS
Admissions Selectivity Rating: 76   **Fire Safety Rating:** 60*   **Green Rating:** 69

STUDENTS AND FACULTY
Enrollment: 1,006. **Student Body:** 59% female, 41% male, 40% out-of-state, 10% international (19 countries represented). Asian 1%, African American 8%, Caucasian 57%, Hispanic 1%.
Retention and Graduation: 57% freshmen return for sophomore year. 38% freshmen graduate within 4 years. **Faculty:** Student/faculty ratio 14:1. 86 full-time faculty, 59% hold PhDs, 10% are members of minority groups, 62% are women.

ACADEMICS
Degrees: Associate, bachelor's, master's. **Classes:** Most classes have 10–19 students. Most lab/discussion sessions have fewer than 10 students. **Majors with Highest Enrollment:** Biology/biological sciences; business administration and management; health services/allied health/health sciences. **Special Study Options:** Double major, English as a Second Language (ESL), independent study, internships, liberal arts/career combination, study abroad Special programs offered to physically disabled students include note-taking services, reader services, tape recorders, tutors.

FACILITIES
Housing: Coed dorms, special housing for disabled students, apartments for single students. **Special Academic Facilities/Equipment:** Erma Byrd Art Gallery. **Computers:** 75% of classrooms, 100% of dorms, 100% of libraries, 100% of dining areas, 100% of student union, 50% of common outdoor areas have wireless network access. Students can register for classes online. Administrative functions (other than registration) can be performed online.

CAMPUS LIFE
Environment: City. **Activities:** Choral groups, dance, drama/theater, music ensembles, pep band, student government, student newspaper, yearbook,

campus ministries, international student organization, Model UN. **Organizations:** 39 registered organizations, 7 honor societies, 2 religious organizations. 2 fraternities, 3 sororities. **Athletics (Intercollegiate):** *Men:* Baseball, basketball, football, golf, soccer, tennis. *Women:* Basketball, crew/rowing, cross-country, golf, soccer, softball, tennis, track/field (outdoor), volleyball. **On-Campus Highlights:** New Fitness Center, School of Pharmacy, Coffee Tavern, University of Charleston Stadium, Graduate School of Business. **Environmental Initiatives:** Recycling on campus; planting trees; energy conservation, specifically electricity.

ADMISSIONS

Freshman Academic Profile: Average high school GPA 3.33. 20% in top 10% of high school class, 44% in top 25% of high school class, 74% in top 50% of high school class. SAT Math middle 50% range 430–520. SAT Critical Reading middle 50% range 440–530. ACT middle 50% range 19–24. Minimum paper TOEFL 550. Minimum computer TOEFL 213. Minimum web-based TOEFL 79. **Basis for Candidate Selection:** *Very important factors considered include:* Academic GPA, standardized test scores. *Important factors considered include:* Class rank, rigor of secondary school record, alumni/ae relation, extracurricular activities. *Other factors considered include:* Application essay, recommendation(s), character/personal qualities, first generation, interview, level of applicant's interest, talent/ability, volunteer work, work experience. **Freshman Admission Requirements:** High school diploma is required and GED is accepted. *Academic units required:* 1 Algebra for BS Nursing *Academic units recommended:* 4 English, 3 mathematics, 3 science, 1 foreign language, 3 social studies, 2 history. **Freshman Admission Statistics:** 1,225 applied, 79% admitted, 28% enrolled. **Transfer Admission Requirements:** College transcript(s), minimum college GPA of 2.25 required. Lowest grade transferable C. **General Admission Information:** Application fee $25. Notification on a rolling basis, beginning on or about 10/1. Nonfall registration accepted. Credit and/or placement offered for CEEB Advanced Placement tests.

COSTS AND FINANCIAL AID

Annual tuition $24,000. Room and board $8,700. Average book expense $1,500. **Required Forms and Deadlines:** FAFSA. Priority financial aid filing date 3/1. **Notification of Awards:** Applicants will be notified of awards on a rolling basis beginning 3/1. **Types of Aid:** *Need-based scholarships/grants:* Federal Pell, SEOG, state scholarships/grants, private scholarships, the school's own gift aid, TEACH/Academic Competitiveness/SMART. *Loans:* FFEL Subsidized Stafford, FFEL Unsubsidized Stafford, FFEL PLUS, Federal Perkins, Federal Nursing *Student Employment:* Federal Work-Study Program available. Off-campus job opportunities are good. **Financial Aid Statistics:** 80% freshmen, 59% undergrads receive need-based scholarship or grant aid. 80% freshmen, 73% undergrads receive non-need-based scholarship or grant aid. 82% freshmen, 81% undergrads receive need-based self-help aid. 1% freshmen, 2% undergrads receive athletic scholarships. 98% freshmen, 97% undergrads receive any aid. 91% undergrads borrow to pay for school. Average cumulative indebtedness $23,250. **Criteria for awarding institutional aid:** *Non-need-based:* Academics, alumni affiliation, athletics, leadership, music/drama.

UNIVERSITY OF CHICAGO

1101 E 58th Street, Rosenwald Hall Suite 105, Chicago, IL 60637
Phone: 773-702-8650 **Financial Aid Phone:** 773-702-8655
E-mail: collegeadmissions@uchicago.edu **CEEB Code:** 1832
Fax: 773-702-4199 **Website:** www.uchicago.edu **ACT Code:** 1152

This private school was founded in 1890. It has a 211-acre campus.

RATINGS

Admissions Selectivity Rating: 98   **Fire Safety Rating:** 60*   **Green Rating:** 85

STUDENTS AND FACULTY

Enrollment: 5,063. **Student Body:** 49% female, 51% male, 77% out-of-state, 9% international (71 countries represented). Asian 15%, African American 6%, Caucasian 43%, Hispanic 9%.
Retention and Graduation: 98% freshmen return for sophomore year. 86% freshmen graduate within 4 years. **Faculty:** Student/faculty ratio 6:1. 1082 full-time faculty, 100% hold PhDs, 19% are members of minority groups, 29% are women.

ACADEMICS

Degrees: Bachelor's, doctoral, master's. **Classes:** Most classes have fewer than 10 students. Most lab/discussion sessions have 10–19 students. **Majors with Highest Enrollment:** Biology/biological sciences; economics; political science and government. **Special Study Options:** Accelerated program, cross-registration, double major, dual enrollment, English as a Second Language (ESL), exchange student program (domestic), honors program, independent study, internships, student-designed major, study abroad, teacher certification program. **Combined degree programs:** BA/MA. **Career services:** Alumni network, alumni services, career/job search classes, career assessment, internships, regional alumni. **Career services highlights include:** Internship program: Jeff Metcalf Fellows Program provides outstanding opportunities for both students and hosting organizations. It has grown dramatically since its creation in 1997, and this year placed 210 students in internships across the US. We are particularly proud of the relationships this program has built with alumni.

FACILITIES

Housing: Coed dorms, special housing for disabled students, special housing for international students, fraternity/sorority housing, apartments for married students, cooperative housing. **Special Academic Facilities/Equipment:** Smart Museum, Renaissance Society, Oriental Institute, Business and Economics Resource Center, D'Angelo Law Library, Echhart Library, John Crerar Library, Joseph Regenstein Library, Special Collections Research Center, Social Services Administration Library, Yerkes Obseavtory Library, On Campus Lab School(PreK-12), Argonne National Laboratory, Enrico Fermi Institute, Court Theater, Observatory, Two Telescopes, Fermi National Accelerator Laboratory. **Computers:** 100% of classrooms, 100% of dorms, 100% of libraries, 100% of dining areas, 100% of student union, 100% of common outdoor areas have wireless network access. Students can register for classes online.

CAMPUS LIFE

Environment: Metropolis. **Activities:** Choral groups, concert band, dance, drama/theater, jazz band, literary magazine, music ensembles, musical theater, pep band, radio station, student government, student newspaper, student-run film society, symphony orchestra, yearbook, campus ministries, international student organization, Model UN. **Organizations:** 400 registered organizations, 5 honor societies, 36 religious organizations. 10 fraternities, 3 sororities. **Athletics (Intercollegiate):** *Men:* Baseball, basketball, cross-country, diving, football, soccer, swimming, tennis, track/field (outdoor), track/field (indoor), volleyball, wrestling. *Women:* Basketball, cross-country, diving, soccer, softball, swimming, tennis, track/field (outdoor), track/field (indoor), volleyball. **On-Campus Highlights:** Gerald Ratner Athletics Center, Joseph Regenstein Library, Robie House, Court Theatre, Rockefeller Memorial Chapel, Food on Campus UChicago boasts over a dozen on-campus coffee shops and three residential dining halls, as well as a host of delis and snack shops. Of note, Bartlett Dining Commons, once an athletic field house, is a large dining hall that offers excellent a la carte options and a kosher deli and Hallowed Grounds, a student-run lounge that offers international food from neighborhood restaurants, two pool tables, and popular open-mic nights. Books on Campus Seminary Co-op Bookstore (58th Street and University Avenue) One of the best academic bookstores in the world, the Co-Op also has a veritable maze of fiction, poetry, drama, and everything in-between. It also carries the textbooks for most social sciences and humanities courses. University of Chicago Bookstore (Barnes and Noble) (58th Street and Ellis Ave) University t-shirts, pennants, and math and science textbooks. Also contains a Starbucks. O'Gara and Wilson, Chicago's 'oldest' bookstore, specializing in rare and used books. Arts and Music on campus Professional companies and artists in residence include Court Theatre, one of the top reparatory theater companies in the city; the critically acclaimed (and Grammy award winning) Pacifica Quartet; the Newberry Consort, famed for their performances of medieval and Renaissance music on period instruments; the Saint Paul Chamber Orchestra; and the modern ensemble 'eighth blackbird.' The University of Chicago Presents series brings musicians from all over the world to Mandel Hall in the Reynolds Club (the main student center). **Environmental Initiatives:** Formation of the Program on the Global Environment Facilities Services has increased University attention in this area by leading the construction of energy efficient central utilities plants to provide steam and chilled water, aggressive program promoting alternative transportation, green roof initiatives, and Silver LEED certification pursuit on renovation project. Support of the Sustainability Council to engage students, faculty and staff in sustainability issues and hiring of a full-time sustainability officer.

ADMISSIONS

Freshman Academic Profile: 87% in top 10% of high school class, 97% in top 25% of high school class, 100% in top 50% of high school class. 64% from public high schools. SAT Math middle 50% range 680–780. SAT Critical Reading middle 50% range 690–780. SAT Writing middle 50% range 670–760. ACT middle 50% range 28–32. Minimum paper TOEFL 600. Minimum computer TOEFL 250. Minimum web-based TOEFL 104. **Basis for Candidate Selection:** *Very important factors considered include:* Application essay, recommendation(s), rigor of secondary school record, character/personal qualities, talent/ability. *Important factors considered include:* Class rank, academic GPA, extracurricular activities, volunteer work. *Other factors considered include:* Standardized test scores, alumni/ae relation, first generation, interview, level of applicant's interest, racial/ethnic status, work experience. **Freshman Admission Requirements:** High school diploma or equivalent is not required. *Academic units recommended:* 4 English, 4 mathematics, 4 science, 3 foreign language, 2 social studies, 2 history. **Freshman Admission Statistics:** 13,564 applied, 27% admitted, 36% enrolled. **Transfer Admission Requirements:** High school transcript, college transcript(s), essay or personal statement, standardized test scores, statement of good standing from prior institution(s). Minimum college GPA of 3.0 required. Lowest grade transferable 2. **General Admission Information:** Application fee $65. Regular application deadline 1/2. Regular notification 4/1. Nonfall registration not accepted. Admission may be deferred for a maximum of 1 year. Credit and/or placement offered for CEEB Advanced Placement tests.

COSTS AND FINANCIAL AID
Required Forms and Deadlines: FAFSA, institution's own financial aid form, CSS/Financial Aid PROFILE, noncustodial PROFILE Financial aid filing deadline 2/1. **Notification of Awards:** Applicants will be notified of awards on or about 4/15. **Types of Aid:** *Need-based scholarships/grants:* Federal Pell, SEOG, state scholarships/grants, private scholarships, the school's own gift aid. *Loans:* FFEL Subsidized Stafford, FFEL Unsubsidized Stafford, FFEL PLUS, Federal Perkins. **Financial Aid Statistics:** 51% freshmen, 39% undergrads receive need-based scholarship or grant aid. 40% freshmen, 39% undergrads receive need-based self-help aid. 48% freshmen, 46% undergrads receive any aid. 48% undergrads borrow to pay for school. Average cumulative indebtedness $24,238. **Criteria for awarding institutional aid:** *Non-need-based:* Academics, leadership.

See page 1280.

UNIVERSITY OF CINCINNATI

P.O. Box 210091, Cincinnati, OH 45221-0091
Phone: 513-556-1100 **Financial Aid Phone:** 513-556-6982
E-mail: admissions@uc.edu **CEEB Code:** 1833
Fax: 513-556-1105 **Website:** www.uc.edu **ACT Code:** 3340

This public school was founded in 1819. It has a 392-acre campus.

RATINGS
Admissions Selectivity Rating: 81   **Fire Safety Rating:** 90   **Green Rating:** 86

STUDENTS AND FACULTY
Enrollment: 20,183. **Student Body:** 51% female, 49% male, 10% out-of-state, 1% international (115 countries represented). Asian 3%, African American 11%, Caucasian 78%, Hispanic 2%.
Retention and Graduation: 83% freshmen return for sophomore year. 19% freshmen graduate within 4 years. **Faculty:** Student/faculty ratio 15:1. 1208 full-time faculty, 59% hold PhDs, 18% are members of minority groups, 41% are women.

ACADEMICS
Degrees: Associate, bachelor's, certificate, first professional, master's, post-bachelor's certificate, terminal associate, transfer associate. **Classes:** Most classes have 20–29 students. **Majors with Highest Enrollment:** communication studies/speech communication and rhetoric; marketing/marketing management; psychology. **Special Study Options:** Accelerated program, cooperative education program, distance learning, double major, English as a Second Language (ESL), honors program, independent study, internships, liberal arts/career combination, study abroad, teacher certification program, weekend college. **Honors programs:** www.uc.edu/honors. Special programs offered to physically disabled students include note-taking services, reader services, tape recorders, tutors. **Career services:** Alumni network, alumni services, career/job search classes, career assessment, internships, regional alumni. **Career services highlights include:** Cooperative Learning: UC Professional Practice Program—over 100 years of service.

FACILITIES
Housing: Coed dorms, men's dorms, women's dorms, fraternity/sorority housing, apartments for married students, apartments for single students. **Special Academic Facilities/Equipment:** Art museum, language lab, observatory. **Computers:** 50% of classrooms, 75% of libraries, 75% of dining areas, 55% of

student union, 75% of common outdoor areas have wireless network access. Students can register for classes online. Administrative functions (other than registration) can be performed online.

CAMPUS LIFE
Environment: Metropolis. **Activities:** Choral groups, concert band, dance, drama/theater, jazz band, marching band, music ensembles, musical theater, opera, pep band, radio station, student government, student newspaper, student-run film society, symphony orchestra, yearbook. **Organizations:** 250 registered organizations, 16 honor societies, 23 religious organizations. 23 fraternities, 10 sororities. **Athletics (Intercollegiate):** *Men:* Baseball, basketball, cheerleading, cross-country, diving, football, golf, soccer, swimming, track/field (outdoor). *Women:* Basketball, cheerleading, cross-country, diving, golf, lacrosse, soccer, swimming, tennis, track/field (outdoor), track/field (indoor), volleyball. **Environmental Initiatives:** OH HB 251—Requirement to reduce energy emissions by 25%. ACUPPC—working on carbon footprint; working on implementation plan. All new buildings are required to be LEED Silver; 3 buildings on campus are rated Silver.

ADMISSIONS
Freshman Academic Profile: Average high school GPA 3.4. 22% in top 10% of high school class, 49% in top 25% of high school class, 81% in top 50% of high school class. SAT Math middle 50% range 520–640. SAT Critical Reading middle 50% range 500–610. SAT Writing middle 50% range 490–600. ACT middle 50% range 22–27. Minimum paper TOEFL 515. **Basis for Candidate Selection:** *Very important factors considered include:* Class rank, academic GPA, rigor of secondary school record, standardized test scores, *Other factors considered include:* Application essay, extracurricular activities. **Freshman Admission Requirements:** High school diploma is required and GED is accepted. *Academic units required:* 4 English, 3 mathematics, 2 science, 2 foreign language, 2 social studies, 2 academic electives, 1 *Academic units recommended:* 4 mathematics, 3 science, 1 history. **Freshman Admission Statistics:** 14,333 applied, 61% admitted, 36% enrolled. **General Admission Information:** Application fee $40. Regular application deadline 9/1. Nonfall registration accepted. Admission may be deferred for a maximum of 1 year. Credit and/or placement offered for CEEB Advanced Placement tests.

COSTS AND FINANCIAL AID
Annual in-state tuition $7,896. Annual out-of-state tuition $22,419. Room and board $9,702. Required fees $1,503. Average book expense $1,275. **Required Forms and Deadlines:** FAFSA. **Notification of Awards:** Applicants will be notified of awards on a rolling basis beginning 3/10. **Types of Aid:** *Need-based scholarships/grants:* Federal Pell, SEOG, state scholarships/grants, private scholarships, the school's own gift aid, United Negro College Fund, Federal Nursing Scholarships. ACG, SMART, TEACH. *Loans:* FFEL Subsidized Stafford, FFEL Unsubsidized Stafford, FFEL PLUS, Federal Perkins, Federal Nursing, state loans, college/university loans from institutional funds. *Student Employment:* Federal Work-Study Program available. Institutional employment available. Off-campus job opportunities are excellent. **Financial Aid Statistics:** 25% freshmen, 23% undergrads receive need-based scholarship or grant aid. 27% freshmen, 22% undergrads receive non-need-based scholarship or grant aid. 21% freshmen, 18% undergrads receive need-based self-help aid. 1% freshmen, 1% undergrads receive athletic scholarships. 78% freshmen, 75% undergrads receive any aid. 65% undergrads borrow to pay for school. Average cumulative indebtedness $24,431. **Criteria for awarding institutional aid:** *Non-need-based:* Academics, alumni affiliation, art, athletics, leadership, minority status, music/drama, state/district residency.

UNIVERSITY OF COLORADO AT COLORADO SPRINGS

Admissions Office, PO Box 7150, Colorado Springs, CO 80933-7150
Phone: 719-262-3383 **Financial Aid Phone:** 719-262-3460
E-mail: admrec@uccs.edu **CEEB Code:** 4874
Fax: 719-262-3116 **Website:** www.uccs.edu **ACT Code:** 535

This public school was founded in 1965. It has a 504-acre campus.

RATINGS
Admissions Selectivity Rating: 78   **Fire Safety Rating:** 60*   **Green Rating:** 60*

STUDENTS AND FACULTY
Enrollment: 6,098. **Student Body:** 60% female, 40% male, 7% out-of-state, international (35 countries represented). Asian 5%, African American 4%, Caucasian 76%, Hispanic 9%, Native American 1%.

Retention and Graduation: 64% freshmen return for sophomore year. 19% freshmen graduate within 4 years. **Faculty:** Student/faculty ratio 18:1. 200 full-time faculty, 100% hold PhDs, 14% are members of minority groups, 36% are women. 1% of classes are taught by teaching assistants.

ACADEMICS

Degrees: Bachelor's, certificate, master's, post-bachelor's certificate, post-master's certificate. **Classes:** Most classes have 10–19 students. Most lab/discussion sessions have 20–29 students. **Special Study Options:** Accelerated program, cooperative education program, cross-registration, distance learning, double major, dual enrollment, English as a Second Language (ESL), exchange student program (domestic), independent study, internships, liberal arts/career combination, student-designed major, study abroad, teacher certification program Special programs offered to physically disabled students include note-taking services, reader services, tape recorders, tutors.

FACILITIES

Housing: Coed dorms, special housing for disabled students, men's dorms, women's dorms, apartments for single students. 100% of campus accessible to physically disabled. **Special Academic Facilities/Equipment:** Gallery of contemporary art. **Computers:** Students can register for classes online.

CAMPUS LIFE

Environment: Metropolis. **Activities:** Choral groups, dance, drama/theater, jazz band, literary magazine, music ensembles, musical theater, radio station, student government, student newspaper, student-run film society. **Organizations:** 55 registered organizations, 7 religious organizations. 1 sororities. **Athletics (Intercollegiate):** *Men:* Basketball, cross-country, golf, soccer, tennis, track/field (outdoor). *Women:* Basketball, cross-country, softball, tennis, track/field (outdoor), volleyball. **On-Campus Highlights:** El Pomar Center (Kramer family Library), University Center, The Lodge, Gallery of Contemporary Art.

ADMISSIONS

Freshman Academic Profile: Average high school GPA 3.36. 16% in top 10% of high school class, 42% in top 25% of high school class, 78% in top 50% of high school class. SAT Math middle 50% range 470–610. SAT Critical Reading middle 50% range 470–590. SAT Writing middle 50% range 450–560. ACT middle 50% range 20–25. Minimum paper TOEFL 550. Minimum computer TOEFL 213. **Basis for Candidate Selection:** *Very important factors considered include:* Class rank, academic GPA, rigor of secondary school record, standardized test scores. *Important factors considered include:* Recommendation(s), level of applicant's interest. *Other factors considered include:* Application essay, alumni/ae relation, character/personal qualities, extracurricular activities, geographical residence, state residency, talent/ability, volunteer work. **Freshman Admission Requirements:** High school diploma is required and GED is accepted. *Academic units required:* 4 English, 3 mathematics, 3 science, (2 science labs), 2 foreign language, 2 social studies, 1 academic electives. *Academic units recommended:* 4 English, 4 mathematics, 3 science, (2 science labs), 2 foreign language, 2 social studies, 1 academic electives. **Freshman Admission Statistics:** 3,243 applied, 63% admitted, 37% enrolled. **Transfer Admission Requirements:** High school transcript, college transcript(s), minimum college GPA of 2.0 required. Lowest grade transferable C. **General Admission Information:** Application fee $50. Regular application deadline 7/1. Notification on a rolling basis, beginning on or about 10/1. Nonfall registration accepted. Admission may be deferred for a maximum of 1 year. Neither credit nor placement offered for CEEB Advanced Placement tests.

COSTS AND FINANCIAL AID

Annual in-state tuition $5,490. Annual out-of-state tuition $22,950. Room and board $7,662. Required fees $1,047. Average book expense $1,296. **Required Forms and Deadlines:** FAFSA. Priority financial aid filing date 4/1. **Notification of Awards:** Applicants will be notified of awards on a rolling basis beginning 4/15. **Types of Aid:** *Need-based scholarships/grants:* Federal Pell, SEOG, state scholarships/grants, private scholarships, the school's own gift aid, Federal Nursing Scholarships. *Loans:* FFEL Subsidized Stafford, FFEL Unsubsidized Stafford, FFEL PLUS, Federal Perkins, college/university loans from institutional funds. **Financial Aid Statistics:** 34% freshmen, 36% undergrads receive need-based scholarship or grant aid. 31% freshmen, 42% undergrads receive need-based self-help aid. 2% freshmen, 1% undergrads receive athletic scholarships. 45% undergrads borrow to pay for school. Average cumulative indebtedness $12,694. **Criteria for awarding institutional aid:** *Non-need-based:* Academics, athletics, leadership, state/district residency.

UNIVERSITY OF COLORADO AT DENVER

P.O. Box 173364, Campus Box 167, Denver, CO 80217
Phone: 303-556-2704 **Financial Aid Phone:** 303-556-2886
E-mail: admissions@cudenver.edu **CEEB Code:** 4875
Fax: 303-556-4838 **Website:** www.cudenver.edu **ACT Code:** 533

This public school was founded in 1912. It has a 127-acre campus.

RATINGS
Admissions Selectivity Rating: 76   **Fire Safety Rating:** 60*   **Green Rating:** 60*

STUDENTS AND FACULTY
Enrollment: 8,327. **Student Body:** 55% female, 45% male, 4% out-of-state, 1% international (57 countries represented). Asian 10%, African American 5%, Caucasian 63%, Hispanic 12%, Native American 1%.
Retention and Graduation: 71% freshmen return for sophomore year. 7% grads go on to further study within 1 year. 19% grads pursue arts and sciences degrees. 8% grads pursue business degrees. **Faculty:** Student/faculty ratio 15:1. 2186 full-time faculty, 81% hold PhDs, 11% are members of minority groups, 47% are women.

ACADEMICS
Degrees: Bachelor's, first professional, master's, post-master's certificate. **Classes:** Most classes have 20–29 students. Most lab/discussion sessions have 20–29 students. **Majors with Highest Enrollment:** Biology/biological sciences; business/commerce; psychology. **Special Study Options:** Accelerated program, cooperative education program, cross-registration, distance learning, double major, English as a Second Language (ESL), honors program, independent study, internships, student-designed major, study abroad, teacher certification program, weekend college. **Combined degree programs:** BS/MBA. Special programs offered to physically disabled students include note-taking services, reader services, tape recorders, tutors. **Career services:** Alumni services, career assessment, internships.

FACILITIES
Housing: Coed dorms. 100% of campus accessible to physically disabled. **Special Academic Facilities/Equipment:** Emmanual Gallery **Computers:** Students can register for classes online. Administrative functions (other than registration) can be performed online.

CAMPUS LIFE
Environment: Metropolis. **Activities:** Choral groups, dance, drama/theater, jazz band, music ensembles, musical theater, student government, student newspaper. **Organizations:** 77 registered organizations, 5 honor societies, 4 religious organizations. **On-Campus Highlights:** PE/Events Center and Emmanuel Gallery, The Auraria Library, Tivoli Student Union, St. Elizabeth's Church, King Academic and Performing Arts Center.

ADMISSIONS
Freshman Academic Profile: Average high school GPA 3.3. 17% in top 10% of high school class, 43% in top 25% of high school class, 78% in top 50% of high school class. SAT Math middle 50% range 490–590. SAT Critical Reading middle 50% range 490–600. ACT middle 50% range 19–25. Minimum paper TOEFL 525. Minimum computer TOEFL 197. Minimum web-based TOEFL 71. **Basis for Candidate Selection:** *Very important factors considered include:* Class rank, academic GPA, rigor of secondary school record, standardized test scores. *Important factors considered include:* Application essay, recommendation(s), level of applicant's interest. *Other factors considered include:* Character/personal qualities, extracurricular activities, talent/ability. **Freshman Admission Requirements:** High school diploma is required and GED is accepted. *Academic units required:* 4 English, 3 mathematics, 3 science, 2 foreign language, 2 social studies, 1 academic electives. *Academic units recommended:* 4 English, 3 mathematics, 3 science, (2 science labs), 2 foreign language, 2 social studies, 1 history, 1 academic electives. **Freshman Admission Statistics:** 3,521 applied, 68% admitted, 45% enrolled. **Transfer Admission Requirements:** College transcript(s), statement of good standing from prior institution(s). Minimum college GPA of 2.4 required. Lowest grade transferable C–. **General Admission Information:** Application fee $50. Nonfall registration accepted. Admission may be deferred for a maximum of 12 mos. Credit and/or placement offered for CEEB Advanced Placement tests.

COSTS AND FINANCIAL AID
Annual in-state tuition $5,054. Annual out-of-state tuition $17,010. Room and board $9,990. Required fees $878. Average book expense $1,700. **Required Forms and Deadlines:** FAFSA, institution's own financial aid form. Priority financial aid filing date 4/1. **Notification of Awards:** Applicants will be notified of awards on a rolling basis beginning 5/1. **Types of Aid:** *Need-based scholarships/grants:* Federal Pell, SEOG, state scholarships/grants, private scholarships, the school's own gift aid, Federal Nursing Scholarships. *Loans:*

The Princeton Review's Complete Book of Colleges

Direct Subsidized Stafford, Direct Unsubsidized Stafford, Direct PLUS, FFEL Subsidized Stafford, FFEL Unsubsidized Stafford, FFEL PLUS, Federal Perkins, Federal Nursing. *Student Employment:* Federal Work-Study Program available. Off-campus job opportunities are good. **Financial Aid Statistics:** 42% freshmen, 54% undergrads receive need-based scholarship or grant aid. 5% freshmen, 3% undergrads receive non-need-based scholarship or grant aid. 31% freshmen, 53% undergrads receive need-based self-help aid. 44% undergrads borrow to pay for school. Average cumulative indebtedness $16,321. **Criteria for awarding institutional aid:** *Non-need-based:* Academics, art, leadership, music/drama.

UNIVERSITY OF COLORADO AT DENVER AND HEALTH SCIENCES CENTER

4200 E. 9th Ave, A-054, Denver, CO 80262
Phone: 303-315-7676 **Financial Aid Phone:** 303-315-8364
E-mail: student.services@uchsc.edu
Fax: 303-315-3358 **Website:** www.uchsc.edu

This public school was founded in 1883.

RATINGS
Admissions Selectivity Rating: 60*   **Fire Safety Rating:** 60*   **Green Rating:** 60*

STUDENTS AND FACULTY
Enrollment: 359. **Student Body:** 90% female, 10% male, 1% international. Asian 5%, African American 2%, Caucasian 79%, Hispanic 6%, Native American 1%.
Retention and Graduation: Faculty: Student/faculty ratio 2:1. 1342 full-time faculty, 97% hold PhDs.

ACADEMICS
Degrees: Bachelor's, first professional, master's, post-master's certificate. **Special Study Options:** Cross-registration, distance learning, independent study, internships.

FACILITIES
Housing: 90% of campus accessible to physically disabled. **Computers:** Students can register for classes online. Administrative functions (other than registration) can be performed online.

CAMPUS LIFE
Environment: Metropolis. **Activities:** Dance, drama/theater, musical theater, student government, student newspaper, yearbook.

ADMISSIONS
Freshman Academic Profile: Minimum paper TOEFL 550. Minimum computer TOEFL 213. **Transfer Admission Requirements:** College transcript(s), essay or personal statement, minimum college GPA of 2.0 required. Lowest grade transferable C. **General Admission Information:** Nonfall registration not accepted.

COSTS AND FINANCIAL AID
Required Forms and Deadlines: Financial aid filing deadline 3/15. **Types of Aid:** *Need-based scholarships/grants:* Federal Pell, SEOG, state scholarships/grants, private scholarships, the school's own gift aid. *Loans:* Direct Subsidized Stafford, Direct Unsubsidized Stafford, Direct PLUS, Federal Perkins, Federal Nursing, college/university loans from institutional funds. **Financial Aid Statistics:** 19% undergrads receive need-based scholarship or grant aid. 12% undergrads receive non-need-based scholarship or grant aid. 71% undergrads receive need-based self-help aid. 93% undergrads borrow to pay for school. Average cumulative indebtedness $21,592.

UNIVERSITY OF COLORADO—BOULDER

552 UCB, Boulder, CO 80309-0552
Phone: 303-492-6301 **Financial Aid Phone:** 303-492-5091
E-mail: CEEB Code: 4841
Fax: 303-492-7115 **Website:** www.colorado.edu **ACT Code:** 532

This public school was founded in 1876. It has a 600-acre campus.

RATINGS
Admissions Selectivity Rating: 82   **Fire Safety Rating:** 83   **Green Rating:** 87

STUDENTS AND FACULTY
Enrollment: 26,405. **Student Body:** 47% female, 53% male, 33% out-of-state, 2% international (113 countries represented). Asian 6%, African American 2%, Caucasian 78%, Hispanic 6%, Native American 1%.
Retention and Graduation: 83% freshmen return for sophomore year. 41% freshmen graduate within 4 years. 21% grads go on to further study within 1 year. 12% grads pursue arts and sciences degrees. 2% grads pursue law degrees. 2% grads pursue business degrees. 3% grads pursue medical degrees. **Faculty:** Student/faculty ratio 18.4:1. 1392 full-time faculty, 90% hold PhDs, 16% are members of minority groups, 37% are women. 9% of classes are taught by teaching assistants.

ACADEMICS
Degrees: Bachelor's, master's, post-master's certificate. **Classes:** Most classes have 10–19 students. Most lab/discussion sessions have 20–29 students. **Majors with Highest Enrollment:** International/global studies; physiology; psychology. **Special Study Options:** Accelerated program, cooperative education program, cross-registration, distance learning, double major, dual enrollment, English as a Second Language (ESL), exchange student program (domestic), honors program, independent study, internships, liberal arts/career combination, student-designed major, study abroad, teacher certification program, *Research and combined BA/MA include Undergraduate Research Opportunities and Concurrent Bachelor's/Master's Programs. **Small Group Academic Programs include Residence Hall Academic Programs, FallFEST, and Presidents Leadership Class. **Honors programs:** The CU Honors Program provides special educational opportunities for academically prepared, highly motivated undergraduate students. The Honors Program offers a wide-ranging curriculum supported by thoughtful advising and close contact with faculty. The program aspires to provide the best education possible for the leaders of the future. The Honors Residential Academic Program (HRAP) is a residential academic program within the general Honors Program. Qualified first-year students who are invited to participate in the Honors Program may elect to live in an honors part of the Kittredge residence hall complex. In this living and learning environment, students experience all of the advantages of a small liberal arts college while also enjoying the diverse resources of a major university. We offer incoming students the opportunity to associate with other bright, highly motivated students and to become part of a special community of peers and faculty. The Norlin Scholars Program is a community of students with a broad, synthetic view of education that embraces active learning, creativity, and interdisciplinary scholarship. Norlin Scholars participate in small, specialized courses and other small-group experiences emphasizing critical thinking, collaboration, and written and oral communications skills. They also engage in research or creative work with faculty mentors. The Presidents Leadership Class (PLC) offers a unique opportunity to those students who want to make a difference for themselves and their community. The core of PLC is an academic program focusing on leadership, service, ethics, American communities, and global challenges. PLC scholars receive a four-year scholarship. **Combined degree programs:** BA/MA, BS/MS. Special programs offered to physically disabled students include note-taking services, reader services, tape recorders, tutors. **Career services:** Alumni network, alumni services, career/job search classes, career assessment, internships, regional alumni. **Career services highlights include:** International and National Voluntary Service Training (INVST) Based on service learning principles, INVST is a two-year leadership-training program in community service. It offers a unique educational experience to all majors in the College of Arts and Sciences. Aspects of the program include small innovative classes, a community-building experience in the mountains, two summer programs of service in the US and abroad, and supervised community service positions during the fall and spring semesters. Issues of global development, nonviolent social change, interpersonal conflict and conflict resolution, community development, and solving community problems are all addressed, with focus on poverty, racism, and other manifestations of social inequality and injustice.

FACILITIES

Housing: Coed dorms, special housing for disabled students, fraternity/sorority housing, apartments for married students, apartments for single students, wellness housing, theme housing, residential academic programs within specific dorms. 80% of campus accessible to physically disabled. **Special Academic Facilities/Equipment:** Art galleries, natural history museum, heritage center, observatory, planetarium and science center, electron microscopes, outdoor theater, video interactive foreign language laboratory, mountain research station, centrifuge, hands-on teaching and learning laboratory for engineering, multipurpose cultural/athletics/educational events and conference center, a premier concert hall, and an innovative multi-disciplinary Information Technology center. **Computers:** 100% of classrooms, 65% of dorms, 100% of libraries, 100% of dining areas, 100% of student union, 50% of common outdoor areas have wireless network access. Students can register for classes online. Administrative functions (other than registration) can be performed online.

CAMPUS LIFE

Environment: City. **Activities:** Choral groups, concert band, dance, drama/theater, jazz band, literary magazine, marching band, music ensembles, musical theater, opera, pep band, radio station, student government, student newspaper, student-run film society, symphony orchestra, television station, campus ministries, international student organization, Model UN. **Organizations:** 300 registered organizations, 26 honor societies, 35 religious organizations. 20 fraternities, 19 sororities. **Athletics (Intercollegiate):** *Men:* Basketball, cross-country, football, golf, skiing (downhill/alpine), skiing (nordic/cross-country), track/field (outdoor), track/field (indoor). *Women:* Basketball, cross-country, golf, skiing (downhill/alpine), skiing (nordic/cross-country), soccer, tennis, track/field (outdoor), track/field (indoor), volleyball. **On-Campus Highlights:** University Memorial Center (UMC), Student Recreation Center, Norlin Library, ATLAS Building, Farrand Field, CU-Boulder's Outdoor Program, at the Recreation Center, offers many opportunities to explore the wonderful backcountry regions of Colorado and other unique locations. The program provides recreational experiences emphasizing adventure, skill acquisition, environmental awareness, safety, challenge, a sense of community, and fun. **Environmental Initiatives:** EDUCATION AND RESEARCH: Campus commitment to environmental education and research has helped CU—Boulder become one of the nation's top environmental research universities. According to the National Science Foundation (NSF), CU—Boulder's $90.8 million in funded environmental research ranks third among the nation's universities. When oceanography research is excluded from the total (reflecting CU—Boulder's landlocked geography), however, the University is ranked first in the aggregate of remaining environmental research categories (according to 2004 NSF data, the latest year available for categorical NSF data). CU—Boulder's reputation and performance as a national leader in environmental issues and sustainability helps recruit and retain faculty with the recognized expertise to win leading-edge research awards, to contribute to the global sustainability knowledge base, and to enhance an already respected environmental studies department—one with integrated environmental content across the campus. STUDENT ENGAGEMENT: CU-Boulder students have a decades-long legacy of leadership in environmental action. On Earth Day 1970, students founded the Environmental Center, now the nation's oldest, largest, and most accomplished student-led center of its kind. In 1974, CU—Boulder students founded the nation's first campus recycling program; in 1991, students voted to raise student fees to purchase pre-paid bus passes for all students; in 2000, students on our campus became the nation's first to raise student fees to buy wind energy credits for student buildings; and in 2007, the student government became the nation's first to sign the ACUPCC commitment for student buildings. CAMPUS GREENING: An aggressive campus operational greening campaign has produced consistently reduced energy and potable water consumption trends since 2001 in spite of ongoing growth in student population and in research funding that leads to increased lab activity. Overall, electricity usage has fallen from 14.57 kWh/ft2 to 13.02 kWh/ft2. Chilled water use is down from 2.98 ton-hr/ft2 to 2.86 ton-hr/ft2. Steam use decreased from 75.19 lbs/ft2 to 65.40 lbs/ ft2. Potable water consumption has declined from 61.69 Gal/ft2 to 30.63 Gal/ft2 for over 9.5 million square feet of campus buildings. These reductions are direct results of a large number of energy conservation projects such as: HVAC recommissioning, weather-stripping, IR scanning of buildings to add insulation, lighting and lighting controls upgrade, energy audits of campus buildings, computer/desktop energy management, building scheduling improvements, water conservation in research labs, ditch water for irrigation, etc. Also, the campus has engaged in numerous educational and behavioral initiatives including Buff Energy Star competition, campus pledge card, stickers/posters, and ongoing outreach/public events.

ADMISSIONS

Freshman Academic Profile: Average high school GPA 3.55. 25% in top 10% of high school class, 58% in top 25% of high school class, 92% in top 50% of high school class. SAT Math middle 50% range 550–650. SAT Critical Reading middle 50% range 530–630. ACT middle 50% range 24–29. Minimum paper TOEFL 500. Minimum computer TOEFL 173. Minimum web-based TOEFL 61. **Basis for Candidate Selection:** *Very important factors considered include:*

Class rank, application essay, academic GPA, recommendation(s), rigor of secondary school record. *Important factors considered include:* Standardized test scores, character/personal. qualities, first generation, state residency. *Other factors considered include:* Alumni/ae relation, extracurricular activities, geographical residence, level of applicant's interest, talent/ability, volunteer work, work experience. **Freshman Admission Requirements:** High school diploma is required and GED is accepted. *Academic units required:* 4 English, 4 mathematics, 3 science, (2 science labs), 3 foreign language, 3 social studies, 1 history, 1 geography **Freshman Admission Statistics:** 19,694 applied, 84% admitted, 34% enrolled. **Transfer Admission Requirements:** High school transcript, college transcript(s), essay or personal statement, Lowest grade transferable C–. **General Admission Information:** Application fee $50. Regular application deadline 1/15. Regular notification 4/1. Nonfall registration accepted. Admission may be deferred for a maximum of 1 year. Credit and/or placement offered for CEEB Advanced Placement tests.

COSTS AND FINANCIAL AID

Annual in-state tuition $6,446. Annual out-of-state tuition $25,400. Room and board $10,378. Required fees $1,486. Average book expense $1,749. **Required Forms and Deadlines:** FAFSATax return required. Priority financial aid filing date 4/1. **Notification of Awards:** Applicants will be notified of awards on a rolling basis beginning 3/1. **Types of Aid:** *Need-based scholarships/grants:* Federal Pell, SEOG, state scholarships/grants, private scholarships, the school's own gift aid. *Loans:* Direct Subsidized Stafford, Direct Unsubsidized Stafford, Direct PLUS, Federal Perkins, college/university loans from institutional funds, private lenders. *Student Employment:* Federal Work-Study Program available. Institutional employment available. Highest amount earned per year from on-campus jobs $12,050. Off-campus job opportunities are excellent. **Financial Aid Statistics:** 35% freshmen, 29% undergrads receive need-based scholarship or grant aid. 1% freshmen, 1% undergrads receive non-need-based scholarship or grant aid. 36% freshmen, 32% undergrads receive need-based self-help aid. 1% freshmen, 1% undergrads receive athletic scholarships. 86% freshmen, 63% undergrads receive any aid. 42% undergrads borrow to pay for school. Average cumulative indebtedness $19,211. **Criteria for awarding institutional aid:** *Non-need-based:* Academics, alumni affiliation, art, athletics, leadership, music/drama, state/district residency.

UNIVERSITY OF CONNECTICUT

2131 Hillside Road, Unit 3088, Storrs, CT 06268-3088
Phone: 860-486-3137 **Financial Aid Phone:** 860-486-2819
E-mail: beahusky@uconn.edu **CEEB Code:** 3915
Fax: 860-486-1476 **Website:** www.uconn.edu **ACT Code:** 604

This public school was founded in 1881. It has a 4104-acre campus.

RATINGS

Admissions Selectivity Rating: 89   **Fire Safety Rating:** 86   **Green Rating:** 95

STUDENTS AND FACULTY

Enrollment: 16,691. **Student Body:** 50% female, 50% male, 23% out-of-state, 1% international (109 countries represented). Asian 8%, African American 5%, Caucasian 64%, Hispanic 5%.
Retention and Graduation: 92% freshmen return for sophomore year. 61% freshmen graduate within 4 years. 30% grads go on to further study within 1 year. 19% grads pursue arts and sciences degrees. 2% grads pursue law degrees. 3% grads pursue business degrees. 1% grads pursue medical degrees. **Faculty:** Student/faculty ratio 18:1. 1030 full-time faculty, 93% hold PhDs, 19% are members of minority groups, 35% are women. 24% of classes are taught by teaching assistants.

ACADEMICS

Degrees: Associate, bachelor's, doctoral, master's, post-bachelor's certificate, post-master's certificate, terminal associate, transfer associate. **Classes:** Most classes have 10–19 students. Most lab/discussion sessions have 10–19 students. **Majors with Highest Enrollment:** Business/commerce; political science and government; psychology. **Special Study Options:** Accelerated program, cooperative education program, distance learning, double major, dual enrollment, English as a Second Language (ESL), exchange student program (domestic), honors program, independent study, internships, liberal arts/career combination, student-designed major, study abroad, teacher certification program, Winter inter-session, summer session, and urban semester. **Honors pro-**

grams: Honors Scholar Program for all undergraduates. **Combined degree programs:** BA/MD, BA/MA, BA/DDS, PharmD. Special programs offered to physically disabled students include note-taking services, reader services, tape recorders, tutors.

FACILITIES

Housing: Coed dorms, special housing for disabled students, men's dorms, special housing for international students, women's dorms, fraternity/sorority housing, apartments for married students, apartments for single students, wellness housing, theme housing, special interests, Honors, Foreign Languages, Older-Student Housing, Freshman Year Experience Housing, "Global House," Women in Math, Science, and Engineering, other learning communities. 90% of campus accessible to physically disabled. **Special Academic Facilities/ Equipment:** Art and natural history museums, child development labs, national undersea research center, arboretum, institute for social inquiry, institute of materials science, electron microscope labs. **Computers:** 90% of libraries, 5% of dining areas, 25% of student union, have wireless network access. Students can register for classes online. Administrative functions (other than registration) can be performed online.

CAMPUS LIFE

Environment: Town. **Activities:** Choral groups, concert band, dance, drama/ theater, jazz band, literary magazine, marching band, music ensembles, musical theater, opera, pep band, radio station, student government, student newspaper, student-run film society, symphony orchestra, television station, yearbook, campus ministries, international student organization, Model UN. **Organizations:** 303 registered organizations, 29 honor societies, 17 religious organizations. 14 fraternities, 12 sororities. **Athletics (Intercollegiate):** *Men:* Baseball, basketball, cross-country, diving, football, golf, ice hockey, soccer, swimming, tennis, track/field (outdoor), track/field (indoor). *Women:* Basketball, crew/rowing, cross-country, diving, field hockey, ice hockey, lacrosse, soccer, softball, swimming, tennis, track/field (outdoor), track/field (indoor), volleyball. **On-Campus Highlights:** William Benton Museum of Art, Dairy Product Salesroom, Puppetry Museum, Green Houses, Jorgensen Auditorium and Connecticut Repertory Theater. **Environmental Initiatives:** Signed ACUPCC and began developing Climate Action Plan Adopted Sustainable Design & Construction Policy (March 2007) setting LEED Silver rating as minimum performance standard for all new construction and major renovation projects—especially significant because UConn has 10 years and $1.3 billion remaining on a 20-year, $2.3 billion, state bond-funded capital improvement program Developed Academic Plan for 2008–2013 which includes the environment as one of three "areas of excellence"—has already resulted in corresponding investment in academic programs and research infrastructure focused on environmental sustainability, e.g., start-up of EcoHouse (Environmental Living and Learning Community) in Fall 2009, hiring of numerous faculty with expertise in sustainable energy, climate and atmosphere, and consideration of ways to improve environmental literacy at UConn, such as new majors and certification programs

ADMISSIONS

Freshman Academic Profile: 44% in top 10% of high school class, 83% in top 25% of high school class, 99% in top 50% of high school class. 95% from public high schools. SAT Math middle 50% range 570–670. SAT Critical Reading middle 50% range 550–640. SAT Writing middle 50% range 550–650. ACT middle 50% range 24–29. Minimum paper TOEFL 550. Minimum computer TOEFL 213. Minimum web-based TOEFL 79. **Basis for Candidate Selection:** *Very important factors considered include:* Class rank, academic GPA, rigor of secondary school record, standardized test scores. *Important factors considered include:* Application essay, recommendation(s), character/personal qualities, extracurricular activities, first generation, racial/ethnic status, talent/ ability, volunteer work. *Other factors considered include:* Alumni/ae relation, geographical residence, level of applicant's interest, state residency, work experience. **Freshman Admission Requirements:** High school diploma is required and GED is accepted. *Academic units required:* 4 English, 3 mathematics, 2 science, (2 science labs), 2 foreign language, 2 social studies, 3 academic electives. *Academic units recommended:* 3 foreign language. **Freshman Admission Statistics:** 21,999 applied, 50% admitted, 29% enrolled. **Transfer Admission Requirements:** High school transcript, college transcript(s), essay or personal statement, minimum college GPA of 2.7 required. Lowest grade transferable C. **General Admission Information:** Application fee $70. Regular application deadline 2/1. Notification on a rolling basis, beginning on or about 1/1. Nonfall registration accepted. Admission may be deferred for a maximum of 1 year. Credit and/or placement offered for CEEB Advanced Placement tests.

COSTS AND FINANCIAL AID

Annual in-state tuition $7,632. Annual out-of-state tuition $23,232. Room and board $10,120. Required fees $2,254. Average book expense $800. **Required Forms and Deadlines:** FAFSA. Priority financial aid filing date 3/1. **Notification of Awards:** Applicants will be notified of awards on a rolling basis beginning 3/1. **Types of Aid:** *Need-based scholarships/grants:* Federal Pell, SEOG, state scholarships/grants, private scholarships, the school's own gift aid. *Loans:* FFEL Subsidized Stafford, FFEL Unsubsidized Stafford, FFEL PLUS,

Federal Perkins. *Student Employment:* Federal Work-Study Program available. Institutional employment available. Highest amount earned per year from on-campus jobs $3,500. Off-campus job opportunities are good. **Financial Aid Statistics:** 37% freshmen, 34% undergrads receive need-based scholarship or grant aid. 37% freshmen, 24% undergrads receive non-need-based scholarship or grant aid. 36% freshmen, 38% undergrads receive need-based self-help aid. 2% freshmen, 2% undergrads receive athletic scholarships. 49% freshmen, 48% undergrads receive any aid. 61% undergrads borrow to pay for school. Average cumulative indebtedness $21,521. **Criteria for awarding institutional aid:** *Non-need-based:* Academics, art, athletics, leadership, minority status, music/drama.

UNIVERSITY OF THE CUMBERLANDS

6178 College Station Drive, Williamsburg, KY 40769
Phone: 606-539-4241 **Financial Aid Phone:** 606-539-4220
E-mail: admiss@ucumberlands.edu **CEEB Code:** 1145
Fax: 606-539-4303 **Website: ACT Code:** 1510

This private school was founded in 1888. It has a 50-acre campus.

RATINGS

Admissions Selectivity Rating: 75   **Fire Safety Rating:** 87   **Green Rating:** 60*

STUDENTS AND FACULTY

Enrollment: 1,389. **Student Body:** 53% female, 47% male, 38% out-of-state, 2% international (22 countries represented). Asian 1%, African American 5%, Caucasian 65%, Hispanic 1%.
Retention and Graduation: 62% freshmen return for sophomore year. 22% freshmen graduate within 4 years. 7% grads go on to further study within 1 year. 3% grads pursue arts and sciences degrees. 1% grads pursue law degrees. 2% grads pursue business degrees. 3% grads pursue medical degrees. **Faculty:** Student/faculty ratio 14:1. 85 full-time faculty, 74% hold PhDs, 6% are members of minority groups, 36% are women.

ACADEMICS

Degrees: Bachelor's, master's. **Classes:** Most classes have 10–19 students. Most lab/discussion sessions have fewer than 10 students. **Majors with Highest Enrollment:** Biology/biological sciences; business/commerce; elementary education and teaching. **Special Study Options:** Accelerated program, cooperative education program, distance learning, double major, dual enrollment, English as a Second Language (ESL), honors program, independent study, internships, liberal arts/career combination, student-designed major, study abroad, teacher certification program Special programs offered to physically disabled students include tutors. **Career services:** Alumni network, alumni services, career/job search classes, career assessment, internships, regional alumni. **Career services highlights include:** Internships with Rollins Corporation.

FACILITIES

Housing: Men's dorms, women's dorms. 55% of campus accessible to physically disabled. **Special Academic Facilities/Equipment:** Natural Science History, distance learning lab, and student art museums. **Computers:** Students can register for classes online. Administrative functions (other than registration) can be performed online.

CAMPUS LIFE

Environment: Rural. **Activities:** Choral groups, concert band, dance, drama/ theater, jazz band, marching band, music ensembles, musical theater, pep band, radio station, student government, student newspaper, television station **Organizations:** 45 registered organizations, 11 honor societies, 18 religious organizations. **Athletics (Intercollegiate):** *Men:* Baseball, basketball, cheerleading, cross-country, football, golf, soccer, swimming, tennis, track/field (outdoor), wrestling. *Women:* Basketball, cheerleading, cross-country, golf, soccer, softball, swimming, tennis, track/field (outdoor), volleyball, wrestling **On-Campus Highlights:** Cumberland Inn and Museum, O. Wayne Rollins Center, Rollins Fine Arts Center, Taylor Stadium, Boswell Campus Center.

ADMISSIONS

Freshman Academic Profile: Average high school GPA 3.4. 20% in top 10% of high school class, 44% in top 25% of high school class, 79% in top 50% of high school class. 90% from public high schools. SAT Math middle 50% range 410–570. SAT Critical Reading middle 50% range 410–560. ACT middle 50% range 19–24. Minimum paper TOEFL 550. Minimum computer TOEFL 215. **Basis for Candidate Selection:** *Very important factors considered include:* Rigor of secondary school record, *Other factors considered include:* Class rank, application essay, academic GPA, recommendation(s), standardized test scores, character/personal qualities, extracurricular activities, first generation, interview, level of applicant's interest, talent/ability, volunteer work. **Freshman Admis-**

sion Requirements: High school diploma is required and GED is accepted. *Academic units required:* 4 English, 3 mathematics, 2 science, 1 social studies. *Academic units recommended:* 4 English, 3 mathematics, 3 science, 1 foreign language, 2 social studies. **Freshman Admission Statistics:** 849 applied, 83% admitted, 50% enrolled. **Transfer Admission Requirements:** College transcript(s), essay or personal statement, statement of good standing from prior institution(s). Minimum college GPA of 2.0 required. Lowest grade transferable C. **General Admission Information:** Application fee $30. Regular notification 8/15. Notification on a rolling basis, beginning on or about 9/1. Nonfall registration accepted. Admission may be deferred for a maximum of 1 semester. Credit offered for CEEB Advanced Placement tests.

COSTS AND FINANCIAL AID
Annual tuition $13,298. Room and board $6,626. Required fees $360. Average book expense $1,000. **Required Forms and Deadlines:** FAFSA. Priority financial aid filing date 3/1. **Notification of Awards:** Applicants will be notified of awards on a rolling basis beginning 2/1. **Types of Aid:** *Need-based scholarships/grants:* Federal Pell, SEOG, state scholarships/grants, private scholarships, the school's own gift aid. *Loans:* FFEL Subsidized Stafford, FFEL Unsubsidized Stafford, FFEL PLUS, Federal Perkins, college/university loans from institutional funds. *Student Employment:* Federal Work-Study Program available. Institutional employment available. Highest amount earned per year from on-campus jobs $2,400. Off-campus job opportunities are fair. **Financial Aid Statistics:** 87% freshmen, 85% undergrads receive need-based scholarship or grant aid. 87% freshmen, 85% undergrads receive non-need-based scholarship or grant aid. 67% freshmen, 59% undergrads receive need-based self-help aid. 4% freshmen, 3% undergrads receive athletic scholarships. 94% freshmen, 92% undergrads receive any aid. 72% undergrads borrow to pay for school. Average cumulative indebtedness $19,118. **Criteria for awarding institutional aid:** *Non-need-based:* Academics, alumni affiliation, art, athletics, leadership, music/drama, religious affiliation, state/district residency.

See page 1282.

UNIVERSITY OF DALLAS

1845 East Northgate Drive, Irving, TX 75062
Phone: 972-721-5266 **Financial Aid Phone:** 972-721-5266
E-mail: ugadmis@udallas.edu **CEEB Code:** 6868
Fax: 972-721-5017 **Website:** www.udallas.edu **ACT Code:** 4234

This private school, affiliated with the Roman Catholic Church, was founded in 1956. It has a 450-acre campus.

RATINGS
Admissions Selectivity Rating: 85   **Fire Safety Rating:** 93   **Green Rating:** 68

STUDENTS AND FACULTY
Enrollment: 1,297. **Student Body:** 51% female, 49% male, 54% out-of-state, 3% international (20 countries represented). Asian 5%, African American 1%, Caucasian 65%, Hispanic 15%.
Retention and Graduation: 82% freshmen return for sophomore year. 62% freshmen graduate within 4 years. 40% grads go on to further study within 1 year. 14% grads pursue arts and sciences degrees. 3% grads pursue law degrees. 4% grads pursue business degrees. 3% grads pursue medical degrees. **Faculty:** Student/faculty ratio 13:1. 125 full-time faculty, 94% hold PhDs, 6% are members of minority groups, 30% are women.

ACADEMICS
Degrees: Bachelor's, master's, post-bachelor's certificate, post-master's certificate. **Classes:** Most classes have 20–29 students. Most lab/discussion sessions have 10–19 students. **Majors with Highest Enrollment:** Biology/biological sciences; business administration and management; English language and literature. **Special Study Options:** Double major, dual enrollment, independent study, internships, liberal arts/career combination, student-designed major, study abroad, teacher certification program. **Combined degree programs:** BA/MA, BA/MBA BA/M-Psy BA/MA philosophy. Special programs offered to physically disabled students include note-taking services, reader services, tape recorders, tutors. **Career services:** Alumni network, alumni services, career/ job search classes, career assessment, internships. **Career services highlights include:** Recruiting program for graduating students.

FACILITIES
Housing: Coed dorms, men's dorms, women's dorms, apartments for single students. 50% of campus accessible to physically disabled. **Special Academic Facilities/Equipment:** Art gallery, theater, language science, and computer labs, observatory. **Computers:** 50% of classrooms, 100% of dorms, 100% of libraries, 20% of dining areas, 100% of student union, 50% of common outdoor areas have wireless network access. Students can register for classes online. Administrative functions (other than registration) can be performed online.

CAMPUS LIFE
Environment: City. **Activities:** Choral groups, dance, drama/theater, literary magazine, music ensembles, musical theater, radio station, student government, student newspaper, student-run film society, yearbook, campus ministries, international student organization. **Organizations:** 35 registered organizations, 4 honor societies, 5 religious organizations. **Athletics (Intercollegiate):** *Men:* Baseball, basketball, cross-country, golf, lacrosse, soccer, track/field (outdoor). *Women:* Basketball, cross-country, lacrosse, soccer, softball, track/field (outdoor), volleyball. **On-Campus Highlights:** Church of the Incarnation, Capp Bar, The Mall, The Rathskeller, Art Village. **Environmental Initiatives:** Student Government recycling committee and Environmental Alliance Club. SG provides recycling receptacles for cans and papers. Replacing all water faucets with reduction flow fixtures (low flow). Energy survey of all buildings to determine current efficiency and needed improvements. Upgraded HVAC systems in many buildings.

ADMISSIONS
Freshman Academic Profile: Average high school GPA 3.7. 36% in top 10% of high school class, 58% in top 25% of high school class, 87% in top 50% of high school class. 43% from public high schools. SAT Math middle 50% range 530–650. SAT Critical Reading middle 50% range 560–700. SAT Writing middle 50% range 540–670. ACT middle 50% range 20–30. Minimum paper TOEFL 550. Minimum computer TOEFL 213. Minimum web-based TOEFL 79. **Basis for Candidate Selection:** *Very important factors considered include:* Application essay, academic GPA, recommendation(s), rigor of secondary school record, standardized test scores, character/personal qualities. *Important factors considered include:* Class rank, talent/ability. *Other factors considered include:* Alumni/ae relation, extracurricular activities, first generation, interview, level of applicant's interest, volunteer work, work experience. **Freshman Admission Requirements:** High school diploma is required and GED is accepted. *Academic units required:* 4 English, 3 mathematics, 3 science, 2 foreign language, 3 social studies, 3 history, 2 visual/performing arts, 4 academic electives. *Academic units recommended:* 4 English, 4 mathematics, 3 science, (3 science labs), 3 foreign language, 4 social studies, 4 history, 2 visual/performing arts, 4 academic electives. **Freshman Admission Statistics:** 1,056 applied, 92% admitted, 33% enrolled. **Transfer Admission Requirements:** College transcript(s), essay or personal statement, statement of good standing from prior institution(s). Minimum college GPA of 2.5 required. Lowest grade transferable C–. **General Admission Information:** Application fee $40. Regular application deadline 8/1. Notification on a rolling basis, beginning on or about 3/1. Nonfall registration accepted. Admission may be deferred for a maximum of 1 year. Credit and/or placement offered for CEEB Advanced Placement tests.

COSTS AND FINANCIAL AID
Annual tuition $26,100. Room and board $8,650. Required fees $1,715. Average book expense $1,700. **Required Forms and Deadlines:** FAFSA. Priority financial aid filing date 3/1. **Notification of Awards:** Applicants will be notified of awards on a rolling basis beginning 3/30. **Types of Aid:** *Need-based scholarships/grants:* Federal Pell, SEOG, state scholarships/grants, the school's own gift aid. *Loans:* FFEL Subsidized Stafford, FFEL Unsubsidized Stafford, FFEL PLUS, state loans. *Student Employment:* Federal Work-Study Program available. Institutional employment available. Highest amount earned per year from on-campus jobs $1,500. Off-campus job opportunities are fair. **Financial Aid Statistics:** 61% freshmen, 60% undergrads receive need-based scholarship or grant aid. 7% freshmen, 5% undergrads receive non-need-based scholarship or grant aid. 53% freshmen, 53% undergrads receive need-based self-help aid. 96% freshmen, 93% undergrads receive any aid. 57% undergrads borrow to pay for school. Average cumulative indebtedness $24,650. **Criteria for awarding institutional aid:** *Non-need-based:* Academics, art, leadership, music/drama.

UNIVERSITY OF DAYTON

Best 373

300 College Park, Dayton, OH 45469-1300
Phone: 937-229-4411 **Financial Aid Phone:** 800-427-5029
E-mail: admission@udayton.edu **CEEB Code:** 1834
Fax: 937-229-4729 **Website:** www.udayton.edu **ACT Code:** 3342

This private school, affiliated with the Roman Catholic Church, was founded in 1850. It has a 259-acre campus.

RATINGS
Admissions Selectivity Rating: 84   **Fire Safety Rating:** 60*   **Green Rating:** 80

STUDENTS AND FACULTY
Enrollment: 7,183. **Student Body:** 49% female, 51% male, 39% out-of-state, 2% international (50 countries represented). Asian 1%, African American 3%, Caucasian 86%, Hispanic 2%.
Retention and Graduation: 87% freshmen return for sophomore year. 58% freshmen graduate within 4 years. **Faculty:** Student/faculty ratio 15:1. 475 full-time faculty, 91% hold PhDs, 14% are members of minority groups, 36% are women. 7% of classes are taught by teaching assistants.

ACADEMICS
Degrees: Bachelor's, master's, post-master's certificate. **Classes:** Most classes have 20–29 students. Most lab/discussion sessions have 10–19 students. **Majors with Highest Enrollment:** Business, management, marketing, and related support services, other; mechanical engineering; psychology. **Special Study Options:** Accelerated program, cooperative education program, cross-registration, distance learning, double major, dual enrollment, English as a Second Language (ESL), exchange student program (domestic), honors program, independent study, internships, liberal arts/career combination, student-designed major, study abroad, teacher certification program, distance learning courses are offered, but not programs; domestic exchange only among other Marianist institutions; student-designed major is general studies. **Honors programs:** The University Honors Program offers courses, programming, fellowship advising, funding, guidance and benefits to undergraduates who have superior academic records, culminating in an Honors-designated diploma. Through the Honors Program, students can develop their academic talents, explore the world, undertake extensive, self-directed research, and apply their knowledge for the benefit of others. **Combined degree programs:** BA/MA, ACC/MBA. Special programs offered to physically disabled students include note-taking services, reader services, tape recorders, tutors. **Career services:** Alumni network, alumni services, career/job search classes, career assessment, internships, regional alumni.

FACILITIES
Housing: Coed dorms, special housing for disabled students, men's dorms, special housing for international students, women's dorms, fraternity/sorority housing, apartments for single students, wellness housing, theme housingUniversity-owned houses. 95% of campus accessible to physically disabled. **Special Academic Facilities/Equipment:** UD Research Institute, Bombeck Family Learning Center, Learning Teaching Center, Davis Center for Portfolio Management, Marian Library, ArtStreet living-learning complex, RecPlex. **Computers:** 100% of classrooms, 100% of dorms, 100% of libraries, 100% of dining areas, 100% of student union, 100% of common outdoor areas have wireless network access. Students can register for classes online. Administrative functions (other than registration) can be performed online. Undergraduates are required to own a computer.

CAMPUS LIFE
Environment: City. **Activities:** Choral groups, concert band, dance, drama/theater, jazz band, literary magazine, marching band, music ensembles, musical theater, opera, pep band, radio station, student government, student newspaper, symphony orchestra, television station, yearbook, campus ministries, international student organization, Model UN. **Organizations:** 200 registered organizations, 14 honor societies, 30 religious organizations. 13 fraternities, 9 sororities. **Athletics (Intercollegiate):** *Men:* Baseball, basketball, cheerleading, cross-country, football, golf, soccer, tennis. *Women:* Basketball, cheerleading, crew/rowing, cross-country, golf, soccer, softball, tennis, track/field (outdoor), track/field (indoor), volleyball. **On-Campus Highlights:** John F. Kennedy Memorial Union, Ryan C. Harris Learning-Teaching Center, University of Dayton Arena, University of Dayton Science Center, Kettering Laboratories; UDRI, ArtStreet, an innovative living-learning complex, combines student residential quarters with performance and visual arts spaces, a recording studio, radio

station and cafe. Marianst Hall, a multifunctional facility consisting of student housing, a book store, post office, credit union, food emporium, worship space and learning center, was completed in fall 2004. A $22 million addition to and renovation of Sherman and Wohlleben Halls, home to UD science programs, connects them and provides close to 55,000 square feet for new laboratories, classrooms, offices and gathering spaces. A fitness and recreation complex, or RecPlex, opened in January 2006. It consists of three levels and totals 129,540 square feet. **Environmental Initiatives:** Composting program that has eliminated ~90% of waste from all campus dining halls complete with a total conversion to compostable disposable products for takeout and washable service ware for dine-in customers. A commingle single-stream recycling program for plastic, steel and aluminum cans, cardboard and paper, with additional recycling of ink and toner, electronics, scrap metal, batteries, and construction and renovation debris. Coupled with a program to divert usable items to charity during student move out, we have reduced waste leaving campus by 40% in 5 years. To reduce energy use, the following measures have been taken: efficient equipment including tankless hot water heaters and 92% efficient furnaces are standard when upgrading the houses in the student neighborhood; campus buildings have been set to 74 in summer and 68 in winter; building HVAC equipment has been optimized and control systems installed to reduce over-conditioning; boiler controls have increased efficiency of the central boiler plant by 15%; a demand reduction program implemented this past summer resulted in 10%+ savings each month and has been continued permanently; a student behavior change campaign culminated with a dorm energy competition in which the winning dorm reduced energy use by over 20% compared to the same period last year.

ADMISSIONS
Freshman Academic Profile: Average high school GPA 3.6. 27% in top 10% of high school class, 58% in top 25% of high school class, 87% in top 50% of high school class. 52% from public high schools. SAT Math middle 50% range 520–640. SAT Critical Reading middle 50% range 510–610. ACT middle 50% range 23–28. Minimum paper TOEFL 523. Minimum computer TOEFL 193. Minimum web-based TOEFL 70. **Basis for Candidate Selection:** *Very important factors considered include:* Academic GPA. *Important factors considered include:* Class rank, rigor of secondary school record, standardized test scores, talent/ability. *Other factors considered include:* Application essay, recommendation(s), alumni/ae relation, character/personal qualities, extracurricular activities, first generation, interview, racial/ethnic status, volunteer work, work experience. **Freshman Admission Requirements:** High school diploma is required and GED is accepted. *Academic units required:* 2 units of foreign language are required for admission to the College of Arts and Sciences. *Academic units recommended:* 4 English, 3 mathematics, 2 science, (1 science labs), 3 social studies, 4 academic electives. **Freshman Admission Statistics:** 12,212 applied, 73% admitted, 19% enrolled. **Transfer Admission Requirements:** High school transcript, college transcript(s), essay or personal statement, minimum college GPA of 2.0 required. Lowest grade transferable C–. **General Admission Information:** Regular application deadline 3/1. Nonfall registration accepted. Admission may be deferred for a maximum of 2 years. Credit and/or placement offered for CEEB Advanced Placement tests.

COSTS AND FINANCIAL AID
Required Forms and Deadlines: FAFSA. Priority financial aid filing date 3/31. **Notification of Awards:** Applicants will be notified of awards on a rolling basis beginning 3/15. **Types of Aid:** *Need-based scholarships/grants:* Federal Pell, SEOG, state scholarships/grants, private scholarships, the school's own gift aid, ACG, SMART. *Loans:* FFEL Subsidized Stafford, FFEL Unsubsidized Stafford, FFEL PLUS, Federal Perkins. *Student Employment:* Federal Work-Study Program available. Institutional employment available. Off-campus job opportunities are good. **Financial Aid Statistics:** 39% freshmen, 48% undergrads receive need-based scholarship or grant aid. 53% freshmen, 51% undergrads receive non-need-based scholarship or grant aid. 48% freshmen, 48% undergrads receive need-based self-help aid. 1% freshmen, 1% undergrads receive athletic scholarships. 95% freshmen, 95% undergrads receive any aid. 87% undergrads borrow to pay for school. Average cumulative indebtedness $32,862. **Criteria for awarding institutional aid:** *Non-need-based:* Academics, alumni affiliation, art, athletics, leadership, music/drama, state/district residency.

UNIVERSITY OF DELAWARE

Best 373

210 South College Ave, Newark, DE 19716-6210
Phone: 302-831-8123 **Financial Aid Phone:** 302-831-8761
E-mail: admissions@udel.edu **CEEB Code:** 5811
Fax: 302-831-6905 **Website:** www.udel.edu **ACT Code:** 634

This public school was founded in 1743. It has a 1000-acre campus.

RATINGS
Admissions Selectivity Rating: 93   **Fire Safety Rating:** 96   **Green Rating:** 88

STUDENTS AND FACULTY
Enrollment: 15,757. **Student Body:** 58% female, 42% male, 64% out-of-state, 2% international (91 countries represented). Asian 5%, African American 5%, Caucasian 4%, Hispanic 6%.
Retention and Graduation: 61% freshmen graduate within 4 years. 15% grads go on to further study within 1 year. 21% grads pursue arts and sciences degrees. 14% grads pursue law degrees. 4% grads pursue business degrees. 17% grads pursue medical degrees. **Faculty:** Student/faculty ratio 12:1. 1159 full-time faculty, 85% hold PhDs, 17% are members of minority groups, 39% are women. 5% of classes are taught by teaching assistants.

ACADEMICS
Degrees: Associate, bachelor's, master's. **Classes:** Most classes have 20–29 students. Most lab/discussion sessions have 10–19 students. **Majors with Highest Enrollment:** Biology/biological sciences; nursing/registered nurse (RN, ASN, BSN, MSN); psychology. **Special Study Options:** Accelerated program, cooperative education program, distance learning, double major, dual enrollment, English as a Second Language (ESL), honors program, independent study, internships, liberal arts/career combination, student-designed major, study abroad, teacher certification program. **Honors programs:** University Honors Program, http://honors.udel.edu/ **Combined degree programs:** 4+1 BS Hotel Restaurant and Inst. Mgmt./MBA. Special programs offered to physically disabled students include note-taking services, reader services, tape recorders, tutors. **Career services:** Alumni network, alumni services, career/job search classes, career assessment, internships. **Career services highlights include:** Extensive web-based career workshop series. Strong relationships with academic departments and colleges to deliver services to students. Discovery Learning: internships, study abroad, undergraduate research, and service learning.

FACILITIES
Housing: Coed dorms, special housing for disabled students, women's dorms, fraternity/sorority housing, apartments for married students, apartments for single students, theme housing, special interest housing. 95% of campus accessible to physically disabled. **Special Academic Facilities/Equipment:** $20 million Lammont du Pont Laboratory, $11 million Biotechnology Center, $1,8 million Fischer Greenhouse Laboratory, 23,000–seat Delaware Football Stadium, 350–acre Agricultural Teaching and Research Complex, 35-acre Woodlot harboring numerous wild species of animals and birds, 28 micro-computing sites, 6-acre Morris Library containing pver 2.8 million books and over 270 networked databases, 2 student/University centers, art coservation laboratories at Winterthur Museum and Gardens, Bob Carpenter Sports/Convocation Center, livestock arena and working farm, composites manufacturing science laboratory, Delaware Field House, Fred P. Rullo Stadium, Gerald Culley foreign language media center, historic costume and textile collection, laboratory for the analysis of cultural materials, medical technology laboratory, the mineralogical museum, nursing practice practice laboratories, orthopedic and biomechanical engineering center, Rust and Gold ice skating arenas, textiles, botanical gardens, the University gallery, University honors center, University laboratory preschool, Vita Nova, 40+ research centers and institutes, Center for the Arts. **Computers:** 100% of classrooms, 100% of dorms, 100% of libraries, 100% of dining areas, 100% of student union, 50% of common outdoor areas have wireless network access. Students can register for classes online. Administrative functions (other than registration) can be performed online.

CAMPUS LIFE
Environment: Town. **Activities:** Choral groups, concert band, dance, drama/theater, jazz band, literary magazine, marching band, music ensembles, musical theater, opera, pep band, radio station, student government, student newspaper, student-run film society, symphony orchestra, television station, campus ministries, international student organization, Model UN. **Organizations:** 250 registered organizations, 23 honor societies, 24 religious organizations. 22 fraternities, 15 sororities. **Athletics (Intercollegiate):** *Men:* Baseball, basketball, cross-country, diving, football, golf, lacrosse, soccer, swimming, tennis,

track/field (outdoor). *Women:* Basketball, crew/rowing, cross-country, diving, field hockey, lacrosse, soccer, softball, swimming, tennis, track/field (outdoor), track/field (indoor), volleyball. **On-Campus Highlights:** Trabant University Center, Gore Hall, Memorial Hall, Morris Library, Delaware Stadium/Bob Carpenter Center. **Environmental Initiatives:** Carbon Footprint Initiative In April of last year the University of Delaware launched the Carbon Footprint Initiative, a comprehensive effort to produce a greenhouse gas inventory and a climate action plan. This effort has been led by Dr. John Byrne, Distinguished Professor of Public Policy and member of the International Panel on Climate Change. The Carbon Footprint Initiative included a comprehensive inventory of all emissions as well as energy audits of 21 representative buildings across campus. A University Climate Action Plan was produced detailing specific implementation steps and produced a goal of reducing University emissions by 20% by 2020. Expanding Renewable Energy Use Over the last six months, the University has initiated two separate projects to expand the amount of renewable energy used by the University. In October, the University signed an agreement to install a 2MW wind turbine on its Lewes Campus in 2010. See: www.udel.edu/udaily/2010/oct/gamesa101909.html In addition to pursuing the use of wind power, the University also issued a request for proposals for up to six megawatts of solar power to be installed at its Newark campus. The University is currently in the process of evaluating proposals. Implementation of Green Liasions Program and Single Stream Recycling In the fall of 2009, the University launched a Green Liaison Program (GLP)with the goal of raising environemental awareness and encouraging environmental action in the University community. Members of the campus community are encouraged to identify and implement environmentally-friendly initiatives. The program is open to all students, staff and faculty. See: www.udel.edu/udaily/2010/sep/green091609. html See: www.udel.edu/sustainability/green/ In the fall of 2009, the University redesigned its campus recycling program. Every campus building, including all dorm rooms and offices, now have a single stream recycling container next to all trash receptacles. The expansion of the University recycling program raised the University's diversion rate to it's highest point in history: 31% in the month of October. See: www.udel.edu/udaily/2010/nov/recycle113009.html See: www. udel.edu/udaily/2010/aug/recycle082709.html

ADMISSIONS
Freshman Academic Profile: Average high school GPA 3.5. 37% in top 10% of high school class, 74% in top 25% of high school class, 96% in top 50% of high school class. 80% from public high schools. SAT Math middle 50% range 540–650. SAT Critical Reading middle 50% range 520–630. SAT Writing middle 50% range 520–640. ACT middle 50% range 24–28. Minimum paper TOEFL 550. Minimum computer TOEFL 213. Minimum web-based TOEFL 80. **Basis for Candidate Selection:** *Very important factors considered include:* Academic GPA, rigor of secondary school record, state residency. *Important factors considered include:* Application essay, recommendation(s), standardized test scores, character/personal qualities, extracurricular activities, talent/ability, volunteer work, work experience. *Other factors considered include:* Class rank, alumni/ae relation, first generation, geographical residence, interview, level of applicant's interest, racial/ethnic status. **Freshman Admission Requirements:** High school diploma is required and GED is accepted. *Academic units required:* 4 English, 3 mathematics, 3 science, (2 science labs), 2 foreign language, 2 social studies, 2 history, 2 academic electives. *Academic units recommended:* 4 English, 4 mathematics, 4 science, (3 science labs), 4 foreign language, 2 social studies, 2 history. **Freshman Admission Statistics:** 24,744 applied, 57% admitted, 30% enrolled. **Transfer Admission Requirements:** High school transcript, college transcript(s), essay or personal statement, statement of good standing from prior institution(s). Minimum college GPA of 2.5 required. Lowest grade transferable C. **General Admission Information:** Application fee $75. Regular application deadline 1/15. Regular notification 3/15. Nonfall registration accepted. Admission may be deferred for a maximum of 1 year. Credit offered for CEEB Advanced Placement tests.

COSTS AND FINANCIAL AID
Annual in-state tuition $8,540. Annual out-of-state tuition $22,240. Room and board $9,066. Required fees $946. Average book expense $800. **Required Forms and Deadlines:** FAFSA. Financial aid filing deadline 3/15. Priority financial aid filing date 2/1. **Notification of Awards:** Applicants will be notified of awards on a rolling basis beginning 3/15. **Types of Aid:** *Need-based scholarships/grants:* Federal Pell, SEOG, state scholarships/grants, private scholarships, the school's own gift aid. *Loans:* Direct Subsidized Stafford, Direct Unsubsidized Stafford, Direct PLUS, Federal Perkins, Federal Nursing, college/university loans from institutional funds. *Student Employment:* Federal Work-Study Program available. Institutional employment available. Highest amount earned per year from on-campus jobs $2,000. Off-campus job opportunities are excellent. **Financial Aid Statistics:** 36% freshmen, 39% undergrads receive need-based scholarship or grant aid. 22% freshmen, 16% undergrads receive non-need-based scholarship or grant aid. 39% freshmen, 48% undergrads receive need-based self-help aid. 4% freshmen, 4% undergrads receive athletic scholarships. 57% freshmen, 55% undergrads receive any aid. 44% undergrads borrow to pay for school. Average cumulative indebtedness $17,200.

Criteria for awarding institutional aid: *Non-need-based:* Academics, alumni affiliation, art, athletics, leadership, minority status, music/drama, state/district residency.

See page 1284.

UNIVERSITY OF DENVER

Office of Admission, 2197 S. University Blvd, Denver, CO 80208
Phone: 303-871-2036 **Financial Aid Phone:** 303.871.2880
E-mail: admission@du.edu **CEEB Code:** 4842
Fax: 303-871-3301 **Website:** www.du.edu **ACT Code:** 534

This private school was founded in 1864. It has a 125-acre campus.

RATINGS
Admissions Selectivity Rating: 89   **Fire Safety Rating:** 82   **Green Rating:** 90

STUDENTS AND FACULTY
Enrollment: 5,314. **Student Body:** 56% female, 44% male, 55% out-of-state, 6% international (91 countries represented). Asian 5%, African American 4%, Caucasian 71%, Hispanic 8%, Native American 1%.
Retention and Graduation: 86% freshmen return for sophomore year. 58% freshmen graduate within 4 years. **Faculty:** Student/faculty ratio 8:1. 612 full-time faculty, 90% hold PhDs, 15% are members of minority groups, 50% are women. 0.5% of classes are taught by teaching assistants.

ACADEMICS
Degrees: Bachelor's, certificate, doctoral, master's, post-bachelor's certificate, post-master's certificate. **Classes:** Most classes have 10–19 students. Most lab/discussion sessions have 20–29 students. **Majors with Highest Enrollment:** Biology/biological sciences; business, management, marketing, and related support services, other; business/commerce. **Special Study Options:** Accelerated program, cooperative education program, distance learning, double major, dual enrollment, English as a Second Language (ESL), honors program, independent study, internships, student-designed major, study abroad, teacher certification program, weekend college, Learning disabilities services. **Honors programs:** The University of Denver offers a challenging Honors Program for talented students who seek an advanced liberal education, lively dialogue with their peers and faculty on important issues, study abroad in first-rate universities, and inspiring in-depth work in their majors. The aim of the program is to challenge students to cultivate strong habits of critical thinking, creativity, and scholarship and to offer close support for advanced work. Students in the Honors Program have the best of both worlds: the small classes and close community of a liberal arts college and the opportunities and resources of a research university. **Combined degree programs:** BA/MA, BA/MPP, BSBA/MBA, BA or BS and MSW, BS/MS in engineering, others. Special programs offered to physically disabled students include note-taking services, reader services, tape recorders, tutors. **Career services:** Alumni network, alumni services, career/job search classes, career assessment, internships, regional alumni. **Career services highlights include:** The Backpacks to Briefcases program guides and supports students from their first year at Daniels through their transition to the working world. To symbolize this important time of growth, Daniels students receive a complimentary backpack when they enroll and briefcases embossed with the Daniels logo when they graduate. The mission of Backpacks to Briefcases is two-fold: —Help students get the most of out of their college experience. —Prepare students to realize their full potential when transitioning to the business world. This mission is accomplished through fun and informative workshops, professional development programs, networking opportunities and other memorable experiences. Past events have included a "Fashion your Future" fashion show and seminar of business attire and etiquette, a Career Conference on "Negotiating your Career Path in a Difficult Economy" with specialized breakout sessions for everyone from first-year students to graduating seniors, and a workshop on "The Art of Small Talk" to help you make a great first impression at networking receptions, job fairs and other events.

FACILITIES
Housing: Coed dorms, fraternity/sorority housing, apartments for married students, apartments for single students, wellness housing, theme housing. 85% of campus accessible to physically disabled. **Special Academic Facilities/Equipment:** Art gallery, performing arts center, centers for Judaic and Latin American studies, Anthropology Museum, center for child study, center for gifted and talented children, regional conservation center, high altitude research

lab, law enforcement technology center, observatory. **Computers:** 75% of classrooms, 10% of dorms, 100% of libraries, 100% of dining areas, 100% of student union, 50% of common outdoor areas have wireless network access. Students can register for classes online. Administrative functions (other than registration) can be performed online. Undergraduates are required to own a computer.

CAMPUS LIFE
Environment: Metropolis. **Activities:** Choral groups, concert band, dance, drama/theater, jazz band, literary magazine, music ensembles, musical theater, opera, pep band, radio station, student government, student newspaper, student-run film society, symphony orchestra, campus ministries, international student organization, Model UN. **Organizations:** 160 registered organizations, 19 honor societies, 14 religious organizations. 9 fraternities, 6 sororities. **Athletics (Intercollegiate):** *Men:* Basketball, diving, golf, ice hockey, lacrosse, skiing (downhill/alpine), skiing (nordic/cross-country), soccer, swimming, tennis. *Women:* Basketball, diving, golf, gymnastics, lacrosse, skiing (downhill/alpine), skiing (nordic/cross-country), soccer, swimming, tennis, volleyball. **On-Campus Highlights:** Campus Green (Driscoll Lawn), Ritchie Center (athletic facility), Newman Center (performing arts), Daniels College of Business building, Jazzman's Cafe (located inside Driscoll Center). **Environmental Initiatives:** On Sept. 24, 2009 the University of Denver launched a free bicycle library with high-tech bikes available on request for all-day use. The DU Undergraduate Student Government—in partnership with local businesses, the city of Denver and DU academic departments—launched the bike lending program. The new program allows students, faculty or staff members to check out one of 20 new bikes from Nelson or Centennial residence halls with just a Pioneer card. The bikes can be used all day until 7 p.m. and come with a lock and helmet. The program will be free through the winter and early spring, eventually folding into a citywide Denver bike-sharing network that will station some 600 bikes at self-service, solar powered kiosks all over the city. DU is expected to have at least two kiosks on campus. The new Katherine A. Ruffatto Hall (scheduled to open Summer 2010) will house the Morgridge College of Education (MCE), the Learning Effectiveness Program (LEP) and the Disability Services Program (DSP) at the University of Denver. When finished, Ruffatto Hall will be one of three recent DU structures to be built "green." The building incorporates the U.S. Green Building Council's LEED standards for environmental construction. Nagel Hall and the Ricketson Law building have received LEED Gold ratings. Ruffatto Hall also will also be submitted for a gold rating, continuing DU's commitment to sustainable building. The University of Denver is committed to the "greening" of Residence Life. There is an effort toward mindful consumption, recycling, green procurement and composting. As part of a reorganization plan, part of a staff position was allocated for a sustainability coordinator for Residence Life. The coordinator organized a residence hall enenergy and water conservation contest. Nelson Hall is the residence hall that won the contest by reducing electricity consumption by 28.9% and natural gas consumption by 8.0% compared to the previous fall quarter.

ADMISSIONS
Freshman Academic Profile: Average high school GPA 3.68. 45% in top 10% of high school class, 75% in top 25% of high school class, 96% in top 50% of high school class. SAT Math middle 50% range 550–650. SAT Critical Reading middle 50% range 540–640. SAT Writing middle 50% range 520–620. ACT middle 50% range 24–29. Minimum paper TOEFL 525. Minimum computer TOEFL 193. **Basis for Candidate Selection:** *Very important factors considered include:* Academic GPA, rigor of secondary school record, standardized test scores, character/personal qualities. *Important factors considered include:* Application essay, recommendation(s), extracurricular activities, interview, level of applicant's interest, talent/ability, volunteer work, work experience. **Freshman Admission Requirements:** High school diploma is required and GED is accepted. *Academic units recommended:* 4 English, 4 mathematics, 4 science, (2 science labs), 4 foreign language, 2 social studies, 2 history. **Freshman Admission Statistics:** 8,411 applied, 70% admitted, 20% enrolled. **Transfer Admission Requirements:** College transcript(s), essay or personal statement, statement of good standing from prior institution(s). Lowest grade transferable C. **General Admission Information:** Application fee $50. Regular application deadline 1/15. Regular notification 3/15. Nonfall registration accepted. Admission may be deferred for a maximum of 1 year. Credit and/or placement offered for CEEB Advanced Placement tests.

COSTS AND FINANCIAL AID
Annual tuition $34,596. Average book expense $1,749. **Required Forms and Deadlines:** FAFSA, CSS/Financial Aid PROFILE, noncustodial PROFILE Priority financial aid filing date 3/1. **Notification of Awards:** Applicants will be notified of awards on or about 4/1. **Types of Aid:** *Need-based scholarships/grants:* Federal Pell, SEOG, state scholarships/grants, private scholarships, the school's own gift aid. *Loans:* Direct Subsidized Stafford, Direct Unsubsidized Stafford, Direct PLUS, FFEL Subsidized Stafford, FFEL Unsubsidized Stafford, FFEL PLUS, Federal Perkins, college/university loans from institutional funds. *Student Employment:* Off-campus job opportunities are excellent.
Financial Aid Statistics: 43% freshmen, 43% undergrads receive need-based

scholarship or grant aid. 5% freshmen, 4% undergrads receive non-need-based scholarship or grant aid. 30% freshmen, 31% undergrads receive need-based self-help aid. 4% freshmen, 5% undergrads receive athletic scholarships. 34% undergrads borrow to pay for school. Average cumulative indebtedness $23,950. **Criteria for awarding institutional aid:** *Non-need-based:* Academics, art, athletics, leadership, music/drama, state/district residency.

UNIVERSITY OF DETROIT MERCY

P.O. Box 19900, Detroit, MI 48219
Phone: 313-993-1245
E-mail: admissions@udmercy.edu **CEEB Code:** 1835
Fax: 313-993-3326 **Website:** www.udmercy.edu **ACT Code:** 2060

This private school, affiliated with the Roman Catholic-Jesuit Church, was founded in 1877. It has a 70-acre campus.

RATINGS
Admissions Selectivity Rating: 75   **Fire Safety Rating:** 60*   **Green Rating:** 60*

STUDENTS AND FACULTY
Enrollment: 2,986. **Student Body:** 68% female, 32% male, 4% out-of-state, 3% international. Asian 2%, African American 32%, Caucasian 52%, Hispanic 2%, Native American 1%.
Retention and Graduation: 76% freshmen return for sophomore year. 33% freshmen graduate within 4 years. 20% grads go on to further study within 1 year. 5% grads pursue arts and sciences degrees. 4% grads pursue law degrees. 8% grads pursue business degrees. 3% grads pursue medical degrees. **Faculty:** Student/faculty ratio 15:1. 270 full-time faculty, 85% hold PhDs, 14% are members of minority groups, 44% are women.

ACADEMICS
Degrees: Associate, bachelor's, certificate, first professional, first professional certificate, master's, post-bachelor's certificate, post-master's certificate, terminal associate, transfer associate. **Classes: Special Study Options:** Accelerated program, cooperative education program, double major, dual enrollment, English as a Second Language (ESL), honors program, independent study, internships, liberal arts/career combination, study abroad, teacher certification program, weekend college. **Combined degree programs:** BA/DDS Special programs offered to physically disabled students include note-taking services **Career services:** alumni services, career/job search classes, career assessment, internships

FACILITIES
Housing: Coed dorms, fraternity/sorority housing, apartments for married students, Peace and Justice Floor Honors Floors WISE (Women in Science and Engineering) floor.

CAMPUS LIFE
Activities: Dance, drama/theater, literary magazine, pep band, radio station, student government, student newspaper. **Organizations:** 55 registered organizations, 1 honor societies, 7 fraternities, 3 sororities. **Athletics (Intercollegiate):** *Men:* Baseball, basketball, cheerleading, cross-country, fencing, golf, soccer, track/field (outdoor), track/field (indoor). *Women:* Basketball, cheerleading, cross-country, fencing, soccer, softball, tennis, track/field (outdoor), track/field (indoor).

ADMISSIONS
Freshman Academic Profile: Average high school GPA 3.33. 22% in top 10% of high school class, 50% in top 25% of high school class, 83% in top 50% of high school class. ACT middle 50% range 19–25. **Basis for Candidate Selection:** *Very important factors considered include:* Rigor of secondary school record, standardized test scores, *Other factors considered include:* Class rank, application essay, recommendation(s), alumni/ae relation, extracurricular activities, interview, volunteer work. **Freshman Admission Requirements:** High school diploma is required and GED is accepted. *Academic units required:* 4 English, 3 mathematics, 2 science, (1 science labs), 1 social studies, 1 history. *Academic units recommended:* 2 foreign language, 2 academic electives. **Freshman Admission Statistics:** 2,181 applied, 81% admitted, 27% enrolled. **Transfer Admission Requirements:** College transcript(s), minimum college GPA of 2.0 required. Lowest grade transferable C. **General Admission Information:** Application fee $25. Regular application deadline 7/1. Notification on a rolling basis, beginning on or about 9/1. Nonfall registration accepted. Admission may be deferred for a maximum of 12. Credit and/or placement offered for CEEB Advanced Placement tests.

COSTS AND FINANCIAL AID
Annual tuition $20,400. Room and board $7,040. Required fees $570. Average book expense $1,300. **Required Forms and Deadlines:** FAFSA. Priority financial aid filing date 3/1. **Notification of Awards:** Applicants will be noti-

fied of awards on or about 3/1. **Types of Aid:** *Need-based scholarships/grants:* Federal Pell, SEOG, state scholarships/grants, private scholarships, the school's own gift aid, Federal Nursing Scholarships. *Loans:* FFEL Subsidized Stafford, FFEL Unsubsidized Stafford, FFEL PLUS, Federal Perkins, Federal Nursing, college/university loans from institutional funds. *Student Employment:* Federal Work-Study Program available. Institutional employment available. Off-campus job opportunities are good. **Financial Aid Statistics:** 66% freshmen, 71% undergrads receive need-based scholarship or grant aid. 99% freshmen, 63% undergrads receive non-need-based scholarship or grant aid. 59% freshmen, 68% undergrads receive need-based self-help aid. 2% freshmen, 1% undergrads receive athletic scholarships. **Criteria for awarding institutional aid:** *Non-need-based:* Academics, athletics, leadership, minority status, music/drama, religious affiliation.

UNIVERSITY OF THE DISTRICT OF COLUMBIA

4200 Connecticut Avenue Northwest, Washington, DC 20008
Phone: 202-274-6110
E-mail: lflannagan@udc.edu **CEEB Code:** 5929
Fax: 202-274-5552 **Website:** www.udc.edu **ACT Code:** 695

This public school was founded in 1976. It has a 23-acre campus.

RATINGS
Admissions Selectivity Rating: 60*   **Fire Safety Rating:** 60*   **Green Rating:** 60*

STUDENTS AND FACULTY
Enrollment: 5,300. **Student Body:** 60% female, 40% male, 27% out-of-state,. Asian 2%, African American 73%, Caucasian 6%, Hispanic 5%.
Retention and Graduation: 6% grads go on to further study within 1 year. 1% grads pursue arts and sciences degrees. 1% grads pursue law degrees. 3% grads pursue business degrees. 1% grads pursue medical degrees. **Faculty:** Student/faculty ratio 13:1. 215 full-time faculty, 66% hold PhDs, 60% are members of minority groups, 47% are women.

ACADEMICS
Degrees: Associate, bachelor's, master's. **Classes:** Most classes have 30–39 students. Most lab/discussion sessions have 20–29 students. **Special Study Options:** Cooperative education program, English as a Second Language (ESL), honors program, independent study, teacher certification program, weekend college, Business, Computer Science, Home Economics, Technologies. Special programs offered to physically disabled students include reader services, tape recorders, tutors.

FACILITIES
Housing: The University of the District of Columbia is a Commuter School with an open-admission policy. 100% of campus accessible to physically disabled. **Special Academic Facilities/Equipment:** Theatre, greenhouse.

CAMPUS LIFE
Activities: Choral groups, concert band, dance, drama/theater, jazz band, literary magazine, music ensembles, opera, pep band, student government, student newspaper, symphony orchestra, television station, yearbook. **Organizations:** 28 registered organizations, 8 honor societies, 3 fraternities, 3 sororities. **Athletics (Intercollegiate):** *Men:* Basketball, cross-country, soccer, tennis. *Women:* Basketball, tennis, track/field (outdoor), volleyball. **On-Campus Highlights:** Library, Recruitment Office, Office of Admission, gym.

ADMISSIONS
Freshman Academic Profile: 90% from public high schools. Minimum paper TOEFL 550. **Basis for Candidate Selection:** *Very important factors considered include:* Rigor of secondary school record, *Other factors considered include:* Recommendation(s), character/personal qualities, extracurricular activities, state residency, talent/ability. **Freshman Admission Requirements:** High school diploma is required and GED is accepted. *Academic units required:* 4 English, 2 mathematics, 2 science, (2 science labs), 2 foreign language, 2 social studies, 2 history. *Academic units recommended:* 4 English, 2 mathematics, 2 science, (2 science labs), 2 foreign language, 2 social studies, 2 history. **Transfer Admission Requirements:** College transcript(s), minimum college GPA of 2.0 required. Lowest grade transferable C. **General Admission Information:** Application fee $20. Regular application deadline 6/14. Nonfall registration accepted. Admission may be deferred for a maximum of 1 semester. Placement offered for CEEB Advanced Placement tests.

COSTS AND FINANCIAL AID
Annual in-state tuition $2,160. Annual out-of-state tuition $4,800. Required fees $510. Average book expense $900. **Required Forms and Deadlines:** FAFSA, institution's own financial aid form. Priority financial aid filing date 5/5.

Notification of Awards: Applicants will be notified of awards on a rolling basis beginning 5/5. **Types of Aid:** *Need-based scholarships/grants:* Federal Pell, SEOG, state scholarships/grants, private scholarships, the school's own gift aid. *Loans:* FFEL Subsidized Stafford, FFEL Unsubsidized Stafford, FFEL PLUS, Federal Perkins. *Student Employment:* Federal Work-Study Program available. Institutional employment available. Highest amount earned per year from on-campus jobs $1,950. Off-campus job opportunities are good. **Financial Aid Statistics:** 55% freshmen, 57% undergrads receive need-based scholarship or grant aid. 21% freshmen, 1% undergrads receive non-need-based scholarship or grant aid. 10% freshmen, 10% undergrads receive need-based self-help aid. 5% freshmen, 5% undergrads receive athletic scholarships. 63% undergrads borrow to pay for school. Average cumulative indebtedness $18,800. **Criteria for awarding institutional aid:** *Non-need-based:* Academics, alumni affiliation, athletics.

UNIVERSITY OF DUBUQUE

2000 University Avenue, Dubuque, IA 52001-5050
Phone: 319-589-3200 **Financial Aid Phone:** 563-589-3396
E-mail: admssns@dbq.edu **CEEB Code:** 6869
Fax: 319-589-3690 **Website:** www.dbq.edu **ACT Code:** 1358

This private school, affiliated with the Presbyterian Church, was founded in 1852. It has a 56-acre campus.

RATINGS

Admissions Selectivity Rating: 71   **Fire Safety Rating:** 93   **Green Rating:** 84

STUDENTS AND FACULTY

Enrollment: 1,431. **Student Body:** 45% female, 55% male, 53% out-of-state, 1% international. Asian 2%, African American 12%, Caucasian 72%, Hispanic 4%, Native American 1%.
Retention and Graduation: 71% freshmen return for sophomore year. 21% freshmen graduate within 4 years. 20% grads go on to further study within 1 year. 10% grads pursue arts and sciences degrees. 2% grads pursue law degrees. 3% grads pursue business degrees. 2% grads pursue medical degrees. **Faculty:** Student/faculty ratio 14:1. 83 full-time faculty, 49% hold PhDs, 7% are members of minority groups, 36% are women.

ACADEMICS

Degrees: Associate, bachelor's, master's. **Classes:** Most classes have 10–19 students. Most lab/discussion sessions have fewer than 10 students. **Majors with Highest Enrollment:** airline/commercial/professional pilot and flight crew; animation, interactive technology, video graphics and special effects; business/commerce. **Special Study Options:** Cooperative education program, cross-registration, distance learning, double major, dual enrollment, independent study, internships, liberal arts/career combination, student-designed major, study abroad, teacher certification program, Undergrads may take grad level classes. Off-Campus Study: Semester-away programs. **Combined degree programs:** BA/MA, 3-3. M.Div. program, BBA/MBA (4+1). Special programs offered to physically disabled students include note-taking services, reader services, tape recorders, tutors. **Career services:** Alumni network, alumni services, career/job search classes, career assessment, internships, regional alumni.

FACILITIES

Housing: Coed dorms, special housing for disabled students, apartments for married students, apartments for single students, Houses and Townhouses and Suites. 50% of campus accessible to physically disabled. **Special Academic Facilities/Equipment:** Art gallery, language labs, electron microscope, gas chromatograph/mass spectrometer, floating science lab on the Mississippi River, computer graphics/interactive media stduios, multimedia project production studio in the new Charles C. Myers Library **Computers:** 20% of classrooms, 100% of libraries, 100% of student union, have wireless network access. Students can register for classes online. Administrative functions (other than registration) can be performed online.

CAMPUS LIFE

Environment: Town. **Activities:** Choral groups, dance, drama/theater, jazz band, literary magazine, music ensembles, musical theater, pep band, student government, student newspaper, student-run film society, yearbook, campus ministries, international student organization. **Organizations:** 50 registered organizations, 2 honor societies, 3 religious organizations. 7 fraternities, 4 sororities. **Athletics (Intercollegiate):** *Men:* Baseball, basketball, cross-country, football, golf, soccer, tennis, track/field (outdoor), track/field (indoor), wrestling. *Women:* Basketball, cross-country, golf, soccer, softball, tennis, track/field (outdoor), track/field (indoor), volleyball. **On-Campus Highlights:** Coffee Shop, Stoltz Sports Center, Library, Student Union, Chlapaty Recreation & Wellness Center. **Environmental Initiatives:** Campus-wide recycling; heating, cooling, recycling, etc. standards

ADMISSIONS

Freshman Academic Profile: Average high school GPA 2.94. 8% in top 10% of high school class, 22% in top 25% of high school class, 55% in top 50% of high school class. 85% from public high schools. SAT Math middle 50% range 440–540. SAT Critical Reading middle 50% range 440–530. ACT middle 50% range 18–23. Minimum paper TOEFL 500. Minimum computer TOEFL 275. **Basis for Candidate Selection:** *Very important factors considered include:* Class rank, application essay, recommendation(s), rigor of secondary school record, standardized test scores, character/personal qualities, *Other factors considered include:* Alumni/ae relation, extracurricular activities, interview, talent/ability, volunteer work, work experience. **Freshman Admission Requirements:** High school diploma is required and GED is accepted. *Academic units required:* 4 English, 3 mathematics, 3 science, 3 social studies, 3 academic electives. *Academic units recommended:* 4 English, 3 mathematics, 3 science, 3 social studies, 3 academic electives. **Freshman Admission Statistics:** 1,181 applied, 75% admitted, 40% enrolled. **Transfer Admission Requirements:** College transcript(s), minimum college GPA of 2.0 required. Lowest grade transferable C. **General Admission Information:** Application fee $25. Notification on a rolling basis, beginning on or about 9/1. Nonfall registration accepted. Admission may be deferred for a maximum of 1 year. Credit offered for CEEB Advanced Placement tests.

COSTS AND FINANCIAL AID

Annual tuition $20,200. Room and board $6,790. Required fees $570. Average book expense $950. **Required Forms and Deadlines:** FAFSA. Priority financial aid filing date 4/1. **Notification of Awards:** Applicants will be notified of awards on a rolling basis beginning 3/1. **Types of Aid:** *Need-based scholarships/ grants:* Federal Pell, SEOG, state scholarships/grants, private scholarships, the school's own gift aid. *Loans:* Direct Subsidized Stafford, Direct Unsubsidized Stafford, Direct PLUS, FFEL Subsidized Stafford, FFEL Unsubsidized Stafford, FFEL PLUS, Federal Perkins, state loans, college/university loans from institutional funds. *Student Employment:* Federal Work-Study Program available. Institutional employment available. Highest amount earned per year from on-campus jobs $1,500. Off-campus job opportunities are excellent. **Financial Aid Statistics:** 91% freshmen, 89% undergrads receive need-based scholarship or grant aid. 15% freshmen, 11% undergrads receive non-need-based scholarship or grant aid. 74% freshmen, 74% undergrads receive need-based self-help aid. 85% freshmen, 85% undergrads receive any aid. 96.81% undergrads borrow to pay for school. Average cumulative indebtedness $37,936. **Criteria for awarding institutional aid:** *Non-need-based:* Academics, alumni affiliation, leadership, music/drama, state/district residency.

UNIVERSITY OF EVANSVILLE

1800 Lincoln Avenue, Evansville, IN 47722
Phone: 812-488-2468 **Financial Aid Phone:** 812-488-2364
E-mail: admission@evansville.edu **CEEB Code:** 1208
Fax: 812-488-4076 **Website:** www.evansville.edu **ACT Code:** 1188

This private school, affiliated with the Methodist Church, was founded in 1854. It has a 75-acre campus.

RATINGS

Admissions Selectivity Rating: 85   **Fire Safety Rating:** 74   **Green Rating:** 73

STUDENTS AND FACULTY

Enrollment: 2,549. **Student Body:** 59% female, 41% male, 39% out-of-state, 6% international (50 countries represented). Asian 1%, African American 2%, Caucasian 72%, Hispanic 2%.
Retention and Graduation: 52% freshmen graduate within 4 years. 23% grads go on to further study within 1 year. **Faculty:** Student/faculty ratio 14:1. 172 full-time faculty, 87% hold PhDs, 8% are members of minority groups, 35% are women.

ACADEMICS

Degrees: Associate, bachelor's, master's. **Classes:** Most classes have 10–19 students. Most lab/discussion sessions have 20–29 students. **Majors with Highest Enrollment:** Drama and dramatics/theatre arts; kinesiology and exercise science; nursing/registered nurse (RN, ASN, BSN, MSN). **Special Study Options:** Accelerated program, cooperative education program, double major, dual enrollment, English as a Second Language (ESL), external degree program, honors program, independent study, internships, student-designed major, study abroad, teacher certification program. **Honors programs:** The Honors Program incorporates unique courses with distinct learning environments to provide enhanced educational learning experiences for exceptional students. Students openly discuss different viewpoints in small, seminar-style classes offered in various academic disciplines. Intellectually curious students who desire academic challenges will enjoy the collaborative learning atmosphere of the Honors Program, as well as the opportunity to engage in advanced independent study, a senior project, and special social programs. **Combined degree programs:** BS/MS in health services administration. Special programs offered to physically disabled students include note-taking services, tutors. **Career services:** Alumni network, alumni services, career/job search classes, career assessment, internships, regional alumni.

FACILITIES

Housing: Coed dorms, men's dorms, women's dorms, fraternity/sorority housing, apartments for single students, theme housing. 87% of campus accessible to physically disabled. **Computers:** 100% of classrooms, 100% of dorms, 100% of libraries, 100% of dining areas, 100% of student union, 100% of common outdoor areas have wireless network access. Students can register for classes online. Administrative functions (other than registration) can be performed online.

CAMPUS LIFE

Environment: City. **Activities:** Choral groups, concert band, dance, drama/theater, jazz band, literary magazine, music ensembles, musical theater, opera, pep band, radio station, student government, student newspaper, student-run film society, symphony orchestra, yearbook, campus ministries, international student organization, Model UN. **Organizations:** 154 registered organizations, 11 honor societies, 10 religious organizations. 6 fraternities, 5 sororities. **Athletics (Intercollegiate):** *Men:* Baseball, basketball, cross-country, diving, golf, soccer, swimming. *Women:* Basketball, cross-country, diving, golf, soccer, softball, swimming, tennis, volleyball. **On-Campus Highlights:** Koch Center, Fitness Center, School of Business Administration, Ridgway Student Center, Jazzman's Cafe, The library and Memorial Plaza are also popular places on campus. **Environmental Initiatives:** Recycling of paper, plastic, aluminum, cardboard, newspaper, magazines, books, electronic equipment, batteries and ink cartridges. LEED certification of new buildings. Ecology focused classes.

ADMISSIONS

Freshman Academic Profile: Average high school GPA 3.67. 38% in top 10% of high school class, 70% in top 25% of high school class, 96% in top 50% of high school class. SAT Math middle 50% range 510–628. SAT Critical Reading middle 50% range 510–610. SAT Writing middle 50% range 490–600. ACT middle 50% range 22–28. Minimum paper TOEFL 500. Minimum computer TOEFL 173. Minimum web-based TOEFL 61. **Basis for Candidate Selection:** *Very important factors considered include:* Academic GPA, rigor of secondary school record. *Important factors considered include:* Standardized test scores, extracurricular activities. *Other factors considered include:* Class rank, recommendation(s), alumni/ae relation, character/personal qualities, level of applicant's interest, racial/ethnic status, talent/ability, volunteer work, work experience. **Freshman Admission Requirements:** High school diploma is required and GED is accepted. *Academic units required:* 4 English, 3 mathematics, 2 science, (2 science labs), 1 social studies, 1 history. *Academic units recommended:* 4 mathematics, 3 science, 2 foreign language. **Freshman Admission Statistics:** 3,012 applied, 86% admitted, 27% enrolled. **Transfer Admission Requirements:** High school transcript, college transcript(s), statement of good standing from prior institution(s). Minimum college GPA of 2.0 required. Lowest grade transferable C. **General Admission Information:** Application fee $35. Regular application deadline 2/1. Regular notification 2/15. Nonfall registration accepted. Admission may be deferred for a maximum of 1 year. Credit and/or placement offered for CEEB Advanced Placement tests.

COSTS AND FINANCIAL AID

Annual tuition $26,010. Room and board $8,670. Required fees $746. Average book expense $1,000. **Required Forms and Deadlines:** FAFSA. Priority financial aid filing date 3/10. **Notification of Awards:** Applicants will be notified of awards on a rolling basis beginning 3/25. **Types of Aid:** *Need-based scholarships/grants:* Federal Pell, SEOG, state scholarships/grants, the school's own gift aid. *Loans:* Direct Subsidized Stafford, Direct Unsubsidized Stafford, Direct PLUS, Federal Perkins, Federal Nursing, college/university loans from institutional funds. *Student Employment:* Federal Work-Study Program available. Institutional employment available. Highest amount earned per year from on-campus jobs $1,300. Off-campus job opportunities are good. **Financial Aid Statistics:** 78% freshmen, 71% undergrads receive need-based scholarship or grant aid. 74% freshmen, 62% undergrads receive non-need-based scholarship or grant aid. 48% freshmen, 49% undergrads receive need-based self-help aid. 2% freshmen, 4% undergrads receive athletic scholarships. 99% freshmen, 95% undergrads receive any aid. 72% undergrads borrow to pay for school. Average cumulative indebtedness $25,598. **Criteria for awarding institutional aid:** *Non-need-based:* Academics, alumni affiliation, art, athletics, leadership, minority status, music/drama, religious affiliation, state/district residency.

THE UNIVERSITY OF FINDLAY

1000 North Main Street, Findlay, OH 45840
Phone: 419-434-4732
E-mail: admissions@findlay.edu **CEEB Code:** 1223
Fax: 419-434-4898 **ACT Code:** 3272

This private school was founded in 1882. It has a 175-acre campus.

RATINGS

Admissions Selectivity Rating: 80   **Fire Safety Rating:** 60*   **Green Rating:** 60*

STUDENTS AND FACULTY

Enrollment: 3,381. **Student Body:** 57% female, 43% male, 20% out-of-state, 1% international. Asian 4%, African American 4%, Caucasian 72%, Hispanic 2%.
Retention and Graduation: 72% freshmen return for sophomore year. 32% freshmen graduate within 4 years. 18% grads go on to further study within 1 year. 3% grads pursue arts and sciences degrees. 4% grads pursue law degrees. 3% grads pursue business degrees. 1% grads pursue medical degrees. **Faculty:** Student/faculty ratio 16:1. 160 full-time faculty, 51% hold PhDs, 41% are members of minority groups, 40% are women.

ACADEMICS

Degrees: Associate, bachelor's, master's. **Classes:** Most classes have 10–19 students. **Special Study Options:** Accelerated program, cooperative education program, distance learning, double major, dual enrollment, English as a Second Language (ESL), external degree program, honors program, independent study, internships, liberal arts/career combination, student-designed major, study abroad, teacher certification program, weekend college, BS in nursing with Mount Carmel College of Nursing, 3-1 arrangement with Art Institute Consortium. **Combined degree programs:** 3-1 medical technology and nuclear medicine tech. Special programs offered to physically disabled students include note-taking services, tutors. **Career services:** Alumni services, career/job search classes, career assessment, internships.

FACILITIES

Housing: Special housing for disabled students, men's dorms, special housing for international students, women's dorms, fraternity/sorority housing, apartments for single students, Honors house, Special Interest houses. 90% of campus accessible to physically disabled. **Special Academic Facilities/ Equipment:** Fine arts pavilion, planetarium. Mazza Gallery (Children's Book Illustrations.).

CAMPUS LIFE

Environment: Village. **Activities:** Choral groups, concert band, drama/theater, jazz band, literary magazine, marching band, music ensembles, musical theater, pep band, radio station, student government, student newspaper, student-run film society, television station, yearbook. **Organizations:** 40 registered organizations, 1 honor societies, 1 religious organizations. 3 fraternities, 2 sororities. **Athletics (Intercollegiate):** *Men:* Baseball, basketball, cross-country, diving, equestrian sports, football, golf, ice hockey, soccer, swimming, tennis, track/field (outdoor), track/field (indoor), volleyball, wrestling. *Women:* Basketball, cross-country, diving, equestrian sports, golf, ice hockey, soccer, softball, swimming, tennis, track/field (outdoor), track/field (indoor), volleyball.

ADMISSIONS

Freshman Academic Profile: Average high school GPA 3.38. 26% in top 10% of high school class, 54% in top 25% of high school class, 80% in top 50% of high school class. 92% from public high schools. SAT Math middle 50% range 470–580. SAT Critical Reading middle 50% range 470–580. SAT Writing middle 50% range 460–590. ACT middle 50% range 20–25. Minimum paper TOEFL 500. **Basis for Candidate Selection:** *Very important factors considered include:* Application essay, academic GPA, recommendation(s), rigor of secondary school record, standardized test scores. *Important factors considered include:* Interview. *Other factors considered include:* Class rank, alumni/ae relation, character/personal qualities, extracurricular activities, religious affiliation/commitment, talent/ability, volunteer work. **Freshman Admission Requirements:** High school diploma is required and GED is accepted. *Academic units recommended:* 4 English, 3 mathematics, 3 science, 2 foreign language, 2 social studies, 1 history, 1 academic electives. **Freshman Admission Statistics:** 2,708 applied, 72% admitted, 37% enrolled. **Transfer Admission Requirements:** College transcript(s), minimum college GPA of 2.0 required. Lowest grade transferable C. **General Admission Information:** Regular application deadline 7/1. Notification on a rolling basis, beginning on or about 9/1. Nonfall registration accepted. Admission may be deferred for a maximum of 1 year. Credit and/or placement offered for CEEB Advanced Placement tests.

COSTS AND FINANCIAL AID

Required Forms and Deadlines: FAFSA. Financial aid filing deadline 8/1. Priority financial aid filing date 3/1. **Notification of Awards:** Applicants will be notified of awards on a rolling basis beginning 3/1. **Types of Aid:** *Need-based scholarships/grants:* Federal Pell, SEOG, state scholarships/grants, private scholarships, the school's own gift aid. *Loans:* Direct Subsidized Stafford, Direct Unsubsidized Stafford, Direct PLUS, Federal Perkins, college/university loans from institutional funds. *Student Employment:* Federal Work-Study Program available. Institutional employment available. Highest amount earned per year from on-campus jobs $600. Off-campus job opportunities are excellent. **Financial Aid Statistics:** 78% freshmen, 64% undergrads receive need-based scholarship or grant aid. 19% freshmen, 17% undergrads receive non-need-based scholarship or grant aid. 80% freshmen, 64% undergrads receive need-based self-help aid. 15% freshmen, 10% undergrads receive athletic scholarships. 85% undergrads borrow to pay for school. Average cumulative indebtedness $17,000. **Criteria for awarding institutional aid:** *Non-need-based:* Academics, alumni affiliation, athletics, music/drama, religious affiliation, state/district residency.

See page 1286.

UNIVERSITY OF FLORIDA

201 Criser Hall, Box 114000, Gainesville, FL 32611-4000
Phone: 352-392-1365 **Financial Aid Phone:** 352-392-1271
E-mail: CEEB Code: 5812
Fax: 904-392-3987 **Website:** www.ufl.edu

This public school was founded in 1853. It has a 2000-acre campus.

RATINGS
Admissions Selectivity Rating: 95   **Fire Safety Rating:** 72   **Green Rating:** 96

STUDENTS AND FACULTY
Enrollment: 34,094. **Student Body:** 54% female, 46% male, 3.6% out-of-state, 1% international (134 countries represented). Asian 8%, African American 10%, Caucasian 63%, Hispanic 15%. **Retention and Graduation:** 95% freshmen return for sophomore year. **Faculty:** Student/faculty ratio 20.3:1. 1937 full-time faculty, 85% hold PhDs, 20% are members of minority groups, 31% are women. 27% of classes are taught by teaching assistants.

ACADEMICS
Degrees: Bachelor's, first professional, master's. **Classes:** Most classes have 10–19 students. Most lab/discussion sessions have 10–19 students. **Majors with Highest Enrollment:** Finance; political science and government; psychology. **Special Study Options:** Accelerated program, cooperative education program, cross-registration, distance learning, double major, dual enrollment, English as a Second Language (ESL), exchange student program (domestic), external degree program, honors program, independent study, internships, liberal arts/career combination, student-designed major, study abroad, teacher certification program, weekend college, Adult/Continuing Education, TV-delivered credit-bearing courses, Honors Program, and distance learning courses. **Honors programs:** The University of Florida Honors Program blends the vast resources of a research university with the individualized attention often available only at small liberal arts colleges. With small classes taught by the top faculty at the university, the program offers students the opportunity to make the most of their education al experience. Close interaction with faculty often leads to undergraduate research projects, and students are encouraged to pursue such activities. Students in the Honors Program have the opportunity to live in the Honors Residential College at Hume Hall, the university's newest and most modern dormitory, where they will be surrounded by like-minded individuals and engage in a unique living-learning community. **Combined degree programs:** www.registrar.ufl.edu/catalog/programs/combined.html. Special programs offered to physically disabled students include note-taking services, reader services, tape recorders. **Career services:** Alumni services, career/job search classes, career assessment, internships. **Career services highlights include:** Major Career Showcase conducted each semester—one of the largest fairs of its type nationally. Number one Career Center in United States for 2010.

FACILITIES
Housing: Coed dorms, special housing for disabled students, special housing for international students, fraternity/sorority housing, apartments for married students, apartments for single students, Honors Residential College at Hume Hall, International House at Weaver Hall, Career Exploration Community at Graham Hall, Wellness Communities at Springs and Beaty Towers, Faculty-In-Residence Program, First-Year Experience Program, No-Visitation by Opposite

Sex Floor available by request, East Hall Engineering Community, Community Service Floor in Fletcher, Fine Arts Living Learning Community in Reid hall, Global Learning Community in Yulee. 98% of campus accessible to physically disabled. **Special Academic Facilities/Equipment:** Natural history museum, art museum, art gallery, center for the performing arts, Aeolian Skinner organ, cast-bell carillon, citrus research center, coastal engineering wave tank, 100–kilowatt training and research reactor, academic computing center, microkelvin lab, self-contained intensive care hyperbaric chamber. **Computers:** 80% of classrooms, 100% of dorms, 100% of libraries, 100% of dining areas, 100% of student union, 100% of common outdoor areas have wireless network access. Students can register for classes online. Administrative functions (other than registration) can be performed online.

CAMPUS LIFE
Environment: City. **Activities:** Choral groups, concert band, dance, drama/theater, jazz band, literary magazine, marching band, music ensembles, musical theater, pep band, radio station, student government, student newspaper, student-run film society, symphony orchestra, television station, yearbook. **Organizations:** 853 registered organizations. **Athletics (Intercollegiate):** *Men:* Baseball, basketball, cross-country, diving, football, golf, swimming, tennis, track/field (outdoor), track/field (indoor). *Women:* Basketball, cross-country, diving, golf, gymnastics, lacrosse, soccer, softball, swimming, tennis, track/field (outdoor), track/field (indoor), volleyball. **On-Campus Highlights:** Center for Performing Arts, Florida Museum of Natural History, Cancer & Genetic Research Complex, Brain Institute, Lake Alice Wildlife Reserve. **Environmental Initiatives:** Zero Waste by 2015: As a result of Dr. Machen's goal for Zero Waste by 2015, UF now recycles over 6,500 tons of material annually, nearly 40% of the waste stream. Additionally, UF strives to recycle at least 75% of its deconstruction debris and has instituted an Electronics Reuse/Recycling Policy and accompanying step-by-step guide for disposal and recycling. Indoor collection of paper, cans & bottles is institution-wide. UF initiated a Tail-gator recycling program for home game days in 2006. This volunteer-based program collected over 17,000 lbs of recyclables from 6 home games in the first year and over 26,000 lbs during the 2007 season. With expansion into the stadium in 2009, the program diverted more than 55,000 lbs of recyclables. UF researchers recycle Helium on campus and the Veterinary Medical Center repurposes animal waste through a composting partnership with the Forestry Service. Carbon Neutrality by 2025: UF completed its first greenhouse gas inventory and assessment in 2004. In October 2006, UF President J. Bernard Machen, was the first to sign the American College and University Presidents Climate Commitment, which committed UF to creating an action plan for becoming carbon neutral and to adding the impacts of air travel and commuting to its original greenhouse gas inventory. In 2009, UF completed a carbon inventory and developed a carbon action plan in accordance with the ACUPCC. UF hosted the first-ever carbon neutral college football game against FSU in 2007. The game inspired a Gator alumnus and his family to start a non-profit that generated all of the carbon offsets required for a fully carbon neutral 2008 home football season—the first of its kind in the NCAA, and in 2009, this partnership continued to work on carbon emissions in athletics, taking the entire athletic program carbon neutral. LEED Gold certification for all new construction: In 2001, UF adopted the Leadership in Energy and Environmental Design (LEED) standards for all major new construction and renovation projects. In 2006, this commitment was re-confirmed and strengthened by requiring LEED-Silver criteria for design and construction of all major new construction and renovation projects to deliver high performance and sustainable building design. To date, the campus boasts one Platinum certified building, four Gold certified buildings, 2 Silver certified buildings, and 10 certified buildings. The first Platinum and Gold certified buildings in the state were on the UF campus. The Facilities, Planning, and Construction Department, which administers this program, has undertaken a LEED portfolio program for existing buildings; UF was selected by the US Green Building Council as one of 12 entities to pursue this portfolio approach. The Campus Historic District is listed on the National Register of Historic Places; the university is committed to preservation of the campus in a manner that meets its goals for energy efficiency. UF built its first green roof atop the Charles R. Perry Construction Yard building this year. The roof, which contains soil and live plants, helps reduce storm water runoff and insulates the building against heat and sound. In support of the indoor health of the built environment, Green Seal-certified cleaning products are used by custodial staff whenever possible.

ADMISSIONS
Freshman Academic Profile: Average high school GPA 4.1. 76% in top 10% of high school class, 92% in top 25% of high school class, 98% in top 50% of high school class. 81% from public high schools. SAT Math middle 50% range 590–700. SAT Critical Reading middle 50% range 570—680. ACT middle 50% range 25—30. **Basis for Candidate Selection:** *Very important factors considered include:* Academic GPA, rigor of secondary school record. *Important factors considered include:* Application essay, character/personal qualities, extracurricular activities, first generation, talent/ability. *Other factors considered include:* Class rank, standardized test scores, alumni/ae relation, geographical

residence, level of applicant's interest, state residency, volunteer work, work experience. **Freshman Admission Requirements:** High school diploma is required and GED is accepted. *Academic units required:* 4 English, 3 mathematics, 3 science, (2 science labs), 2 foreign language, 3 social studies, 3 academic electives. **Freshman Admission Statistics:** 27,612 applied, 39% admitted, 59% enrolled. **Transfer Admission Requirements:** High school transcript, college transcript(s), standardized test scores, minimum college GPA of 2.0 required. **General Admission Information:** Application fee $30. Regular application deadline 11/1. Nonfall registration accepted. Credit and/or placement offered for CEEB Advanced Placement tests.

COSTS AND FINANCIAL AID

Annual in-state tuition $4,373. Annual out-of-state tuition $23,744. Room and board $7,500. Average book expense $990. **Required Forms and Deadlines:** FAFSA. Priority financial aid filing date 3/15. **Notification of Awards:** Applicants will be notified of awards on a rolling basis beginning 4/1. **Types of Aid:** *Need-based scholarships/grants:* Federal Pell, SEOG, state scholarships/grants, private scholarships, the school's own gift aid. State, Academic, Creative arts/performance, Special achievements/activities, Special characteristics, Athletic and ROTC. *Loans:* Direct Subsidized Stafford, Direct Unsubsidized Stafford, Direct PLUS, Federal Perkins, college/university loans from institutional funds. *Student Employment:* Federal Work-Study Program available. Institutional employment available. Highest amount earned per year from on-campus jobs $19,744. Off-campus job opportunities are fair. **Financial Aid Statistics:** 26% freshmen, 23% undergrads receive need-based scholarship or grant aid. 39% freshmen, 29% undergrads receive non-need-based scholarship or grant aid. 15% freshmen, 19% undergrads receive need-based self-help aid. 1% freshmen, 1% undergrads receive athletic scholarships. 97% freshmen, 85% undergrads receive any aid. 41% undergrads borrow to pay for school. Average cumulative indebtedness $15,318. **Criteria for awarding institutional aid:** *Non-need-based:* Academics, art, athletics, leadership, minority status, music/drama, state/district residency.

UNIVERSITY OF GEORGIA

Terrell Hall, Athens, GA 30602
Phone: 706-542-8776 **Financial Aid Phone:** 706-542-6147
E-mail: undergrad@admissions.uga.edu **CEEB Code:** 5813
Fax: 706-542-1466 **Website:** www.uga.edu **ACT Code:** 872

This public school was founded in 1785. It has a 324-acre campus.

RATINGS
Admissions Selectivity Rating: 60*   **Fire Safety Rating:** 60*   **Green Rating:** 60*

STUDENTS AND FACULTY
Enrollment: 25,882. **Student Body:** 57% female, 43% male, 10% out-of-state, 1% international (133 countries represented). Asian 7%, African American 7%, Caucasian 80%, Hispanic 3%.
Retention and Graduation: 51% freshmen graduate within 4 years. 23% grads go on to further study within 1 year. **Faculty:** Student/faculty ratio 18:1. 1775 full-time faculty, 89% hold PhDs, 17% are members of minority groups, 35% are women. 19% of classes are taught by teaching assistants.

ACADEMICS
Degrees: Bachelor's, certificate, doctoral, master's, post-bachelor's certificate, post-master's certificate. **Classes:** Most classes have 20–29 students. **Majors with Highest Enrollment:** Biology/biological sciences; English language and literature; psychology. **Special Study Options:** Accelerated program, cooperative education program, cross-registration, distance learning, double major, dual enrollment, exchange student program (domestic), external degree program, honors program, independent study, internships, liberal arts/career combination, student-designed major, study abroad, teacher certification program. **Honors programs:** General Honors Program (university-wide), Foundation Fellows, Center for Undergraduate Research Summer Research Fellows, CURO Apprentice Program Special programs offered to physically disabled students include note-taking services, reader services, tape recorders, tutors. **Career services:** Alumni network, alumni services, career/job search classes, career assessment, internships, regional alumni. **Career services highlights include:** Career Academy: Approximately 200 students participated. This event is scheduled the day "before" classes start at UGA and is dedicated to help students begin their job search. The University of Georgia Career Academy

is a one-day, intensive career conference that jump starts the career skills of participating students so that they can immediately launch a successful job search campaign. During the event, students heard from employers representing McKesson, Eli Lilly, Altria, Target, FBI, Sherwin Williams, Liberty Mutual, State Department, Unum, E & J Gallo, and PWC.

FACILITIES
Housing: Coed dorms, special housing for disabled students, special housing for international students, women's dorms, fraternity/sorority housing, apartments for married students, apartments for single students, theme housing, Honors and Language focused dorms are available. 90% of campus accessible to physically disabled. **Special Academic Facilities/Equipment:** Miller Learning Center, Georgia Museum of Art, Georgia Museum of Natural History, Ramsey Student Center for Physical Activities, Performing Arts Center, Tate Student Center. **Computers:** 90% of classrooms, 15% of dorms, 100% of libraries, 100% of dining areas, 100% of student union, 100% of common outdoor areas have wireless network access. Students can register for classes online. Administrative functions (other than registration) can be performed online.

CAMPUS LIFE
Environment: City. **Activities:** Choral groups, concert band, dance, drama/theater, jazz band, literary magazine, marching band, music ensembles, musical theater, opera, pep band, radio station, student government, student newspaper, student-run film society, symphony orchestra, television station, yearbook, campus ministries, international student organization, Model UN. **Organizations:** 597 registered organizations, 22 honor societies, 35 religious organizations. 34 fraternities, 25 sororities. **Athletics (Intercollegiate):** *Men:* Baseball, basketball, cross-country, diving, football, golf, swimming, tennis, track/field (outdoor), track/field (indoor). *Women:* Basketball, cross-country, diving, equestrian sports, golf, gymnastics, soccer, softball, swimming, tennis, track/field (outdoor), track/field (indoor), volleyball. **On-Campus Highlights:** Zell B. Miller Learning Center, Sanford Stadium, Ramsey Student Center for Physical Activ, Performing and Visual Arts Complex, Tate Student Center. **Environmental Initiatives:** Sustainability is a primary directive in the University's Strategic Plan for 2010–2020. Administratively in 2010, UGA established an Office of Sustainability to communicate and advance sustainability efforts on campus. In 2007, UGA created the Eugene Odom School of Ecology the world's first stand-alone school devoted to teaching, research and public service in the areas of ecology and environmental studies. Also, more than 100 UGA faculty members from a broad spectrum of academic disciplines have joined together to create the Academy of the Environment. The academy provides a venue for cross-disciplinary collaboration in research, graduate and undergraduate training and public education and outreach. In development of the physical campus, UGA has created over 46 acres of new green space since the adoption of the University master plan in 1998 and recently opened its first LEED Certified building, Tate Student Center Expansion, at the Gold Level. Four other campus buildings are currently tracking LEED certification at the gold or silver level. In total, UGA will have over 500,000 s.f. of LEED certified building space. In response to the recent historic drought, UGA has taken aggressive steps to conserve water such as installing rain gardens, planting native species, installing low-flow toilets and shower heads, reducing water use and recycling water in research labs and including cisterns in new construction. UGA currently has over 50 rain gardens and 14 cisterns installed or under construction totaling over 530,000 gallons storage capacity for continuous reuse. The result is a 30 percent reduction in water use from 2008.

ADMISSIONS
Freshman Academic Profile: Average high school GPA 3.83. 54% in top 10% of high school class, 89% in top 25% of high school class, 98% in top 50% of high school class. 77% from public high schools. SAT Math middle 50% range 570–670. SAT Critical Reading middle 50% range 560–660. SAT Writing middle 50% range 570–660. ACT middle 50% range 25–29. Minimum paper TOEFL 550. Minimum computer TOEFL 213. **Basis for Candidate Selection:** *Very important factors considered include:* Academic GPA, rigor of secondary school record. *Important factors considered include:* Standardized test scores. *Other factors considered include:* Application essay, recommendation(s), character/personal qualities, extracurricular activities, first generation, talent/ability, volunteer work, work experience. **Freshman Admission Requirements:** High school diploma is required and GED is accepted. *Academic units required:* 4 English, 4 mathematics, 3 science, (2 science labs), 2 foreign language, 3 social studies. *Academic units recommended:* 4 English, 4 mathematics, 3 science, (2 science labs), 3 foreign language, 1 social studies, 2 history, 1 academic electives. **Freshman Admission Statistics:** 17,776 applied, 54% admitted, 49% enrolled. **Transfer Admission Requirements:** College transcript(s), Lowest grade transferable D. **General Admission Information:** Application fee $60. Regular application deadline 1/15. Nonfall registration accepted. Admission may be deferred for a maximum of 1 year. Credit and/or placement offered for CEEB Advanced Placement tests.

COSTS AND FINANCIAL AID
Required Forms and Deadlines: FAFSA. Priority financial aid filing date 3/1. **Notification of Awards:** Applicants will be notified of awards on a rolling basis

beginning 5/15. **Types of Aid:** *Need-based scholarships/grants:* Federal Pell, SEOG, state scholarships/grants, private scholarships, the school's own gift aid. *Loans:* Direct Subsidized Stafford, Direct Unsubsidized Stafford, Direct PLUS, Federal Perkins, state loans, college/university loans from institutional funds. **Financial Aid Statistics:** 34% freshmen, 29% undergrads receive need-based scholarship or grant aid. 10% freshmen, 5% undergrads receive non-need-based scholarship or grant aid. 17% freshmen, 21% undergrads receive need-based self-help aid. 2% freshmen, 2% undergrads receive athletic scholarships. 41% freshmen, 38% undergrads receive any aid. 44% undergrads borrow to pay for school. Average cumulative indebtedness $14,766. **Criteria for awarding institutional aid:** *Non-need-based:* Academics, athletics, state/district residency.

UNIVERSITY OF GREAT FALLS

1301 20th Street South, Great Falls, MT 59405
Phone: 406-791-5200 **Financial Aid Phone:** 406-791-5235
E-mail: enroll@ugf.edu **CEEB Code:** 4058
Fax: 406-791-5209 **Website:** www.ugf.edu **ACT Code:** 2410

This private school, affiliated with the Roman Catholic Church, was founded in 1932. It has a 44-acre campus.

RATINGS
Admissions Selectivity Rating: 77   **Fire Safety Rating:** 60*   **Green Rating:** 60*

STUDENTS AND FACULTY
Enrollment: 612. **Student Body:** 63% female, 37% male, 20% out-of-state, international.
Retention and Graduation: 59% freshmen return for sophomore year. 20% grads pursue arts and sciences degrees. 100% grads pursue medical degrees. **Faculty:** Student/faculty ratio 12:1. 33 full-time faculty, 61% hold PhDs, 6% are members of minority groups, 33% are women.

ACADEMICS
Degrees: Associate, bachelor's, master's, terminal associate, transfer associate. **Classes:** Most classes have fewer than 10 students. **Majors with Highest Enrollment:** Criminal justice/safety studies; elementary education and teaching; psychology. **Special Study Options:** Cooperative education program, distance learning, double major, independent study, internships, liberal arts/career combination, teacher certification program. Special programs offered to physically disabled students include note-taking services, reader services, tape recorders, tutors. **Career services:** Alumni network, alumni services, career/job search classes, internships.

FACILITIES
Housing: Coed dorms, apartments for married students, apartments for single students. 85% of campus accessible to physically disabled. **Special Academic Facilities/Equipment:** Art museum; Dr. Hong Herbarium. **Computers:** 70% of classrooms, 100% of dorms, 100% of libraries, 100% of student union, have wireless network access. Students can register for classes online.

CAMPUS LIFE
Environment: Town. **Activities:** Choral groups, concert band, dance, drama/theater, jazz band, music ensembles, musical theater, pep band, radio station, student government, student newspaper, symphony orchestra, campus ministries. **Organizations:** 10 registered organizations, 2 honor societies, 1 religious organizations. **Athletics (Intercollegiate): Men:** Basketball, cheerleading, cross-country, golf, track/field (outdoor), wrestling. *Women:* Basketball, cheerleading, cross-country, golf, soccer, softball, track/field (outdoor), volleyball. **On-Campus Highlights:** Student Center, Wellness Center, Athletic Facility, Art Gallery.

ADMISSIONS
Freshman Academic Profile: Average high school GPA 3.37. 87% from public high schools. SAT Math middle 50% range 360–490. SAT Critical Reading middle 50% range 330–430. ACT middle 50% range 18–24. Minimum paper TOEFL 500. Minimum computer TOEFL 173. **Basis for Candidate Selection:** *Important factors considered include:* Application essay, academic GPA, rigor of secondary school record, standardized test scores, character/personal qualities, interview, level of applicant's interest, religious affiliation/commitment. *Other factors considered include:* Class rank, recommendation(s), extracurricular activities, first generation, racial/ethnic status, talent/ability, volunteer work, work experience. **Freshman Admission Requirements:** High school diploma is required and GED is accepted. *Academic units required:* 4 English, 3 mathematics, 3 science, (1 science labs), 1 social studies, 3 history, 5 academic electives. *Academic units recommended:* 4 English, 3 mathematics, 3 science, (1 science labs), 2 foreign language, 2 social studies, 3 history, 3 academic electives. **Freshman Admission Statistics:** 351 applied, 57% admit-

ted, 74% enrolled. **Transfer Admission Requirements:** College transcript(s), essay or personal statement, minimum college GPA of 2.0 required. Lowest grade transferable C. **General Admission Information:** Application fee $35. Regular application deadline 8/30. Notification on a rolling basis, beginning on or about 10/1. Nonfall registration accepted. Admission may be deferred for a maximum of 2 Semesters. Credit and/or placement offered for CEEB Advanced Placement tests.

COSTS AND FINANCIAL AID
Annual tuition $15,500. Room and board $6,490. Required fees $900. Average book expense $500. **Required Forms and Deadlines:** FAFSA. Priority financial aid filing date 4/1. **Notification of Awards:** Applicants will be notified of awards on a rolling basis beginning 3/1. **Types of Aid:** *Need-based scholarships/grants:* Federal Pell, SEOG, state scholarships/grants, private scholarships, the school's own gift aid. *Loans:* FFEL Subsidized Stafford, FFEL Unsubsidized Stafford, FFEL PLUS, Federal Perkins. *Student Employment:* Federal Work-Study Program available. Institutional employment available. Highest amount earned per year from on-campus jobs $2,000. Off-campus job opportunities are fair. **Financial Aid Statistics:** 47% freshmen, 54% undergrads receive need-based scholarship or grant aid. 63% freshmen, 68% undergrads receive non-need-based scholarship or grant aid. 62% freshmen, 69% undergrads receive need-based self-help aid. 47% freshmen, 38% undergrads receive athletic scholarships. 46% freshmen, 50% undergrads receive any aid. 83% undergrads borrow to pay for school. **Criteria for awarding institutional aid:** *Non-need-based:* Academics, alumni affiliation, art, athletics, job skills, leadership, minority status, music/drama, religious affiliation, state/district residency.

UNIVERSITY OF HARTFORD

200 Bloomfield Avenue, West Hartford, CT 06117
Phone: 860-768-4296 **Financial Aid Phone:** 800-947-4303
E-mail: admissions@mail.hartford.edu **CEEB Code:** 3436
Fax: 860-768-4961 **Website:** www.hartford.edu **ACT Code:** 606

This private school was founded in 1877. It has a 320-acre campus.

RATINGS
Admissions Selectivity Rating: 60*   **Fire Safety Rating:** 60*   **Green Rating:** 60*

STUDENTS AND FACULTY
Enrollment: 5,318. **Student Body:** 51% female, 49% male, 61% out-of-state, 3% international (65 countries represented). Asian 3%, African American 10%, Caucasian 67%, Hispanic 5%.
Retention and Graduation: 78% freshmen return for sophomore year. 45% freshmen graduate within 4 years. 22% grads go on to further study within 1 year. 39% grads pursue arts and sciences degrees. 2% grads pursue law degrees. 14% grads pursue business degrees. 2% grads pursue medical degrees. **Faculty:** Student/faculty ratio 13:1. 325 full-time faculty, 72% hold PhDs, 11% are members of minority groups, 36% are women.

ACADEMICS
Degrees: Associate, bachelor's, certificate, diploma, master's, post-bachelor's certificate, post-master's certificate. **Classes:** Most classes have 10–19 students. Most lab/discussion sessions have fewer than 10 students. **Majors with Highest Enrollment:** Architectural engineering technology/technician; communication studies/speech communication and rhetoric; psychology. **Special Study Options:** Cooperative education program, cross-registration, distance learning, double major, dual enrollment, English as a Second Language (ESL), exchange student program (domestic), honors program, independent study, internships, liberal arts/career combination, student-designed major, study abroad, teacher certification program **Combined degree programs:** BS health science/MS physical therapy. Special programs offered to physically disabled students include note-taking services, reader services, tutors.

FACILITIES
Housing: Coed dorms, special housing for disabled students, women's dorms, apartments for single students, Honors Housing. **Special Academic Facilities/Equipment:** Museum of presidential memorabilia, Art Gallery, off-campus child care center for student teaching, learning skills and language lab, audiovisual aids center, 8,000-acre environmental center. **Computers:** Students can register for classes online. Administrative functions (other than registration) can be performed online.

CAMPUS LIFE
Environment: Metropolis. **Activities:** Choral groups, concert band, dance, drama/theater, jazz band, literary magazine, music ensembles, musical theater, opera, pep band, radio station, student government, student newspaper, symphony orchestra, television station, yearbook. **Organizations:** 93 registered

organizations, 22 honor societies, 7 religious organizations. 16 fraternities, 14 sororities. **Athletics (Intercollegiate): Men:** Baseball, basketball, cross-country, golf, lacrosse, soccer, tennis, track/field (outdoor), track/field (indoor). *Women:* Basketball, cross-country, golf, soccer, softball, tennis, track/field (outdoor), track/field (indoor), volleyball. **On-Campus Highlights:** Museum of American Political Life, Art Gallery, Sports Center, Java City Coffee House, Hawk's Nest.

ADMISSIONS

Freshman Academic Profile: 76% from public high schools. SAT Math middle 50% range 490–590. SAT Critical Reading middle 50% range 480–580. ACT middle 50% range 21–25. Minimum paper TOEFL 550. Minimum computer TOEFL 213. **Basis for Candidate Selection:** *Very important factors considered include:* Rigor of secondary school record. *Important factors considered include:* Class rank, standardized test scores. *Other factors considered include:* Application essay, recommendation(s), character/personal qualities, extracurricular activities, interview, talent/ability. **Freshman Admission Requirements:** High school diploma is required and GED is accepted. *Academic units required:* 4 English, 2 mathematics, 2 science, 2 social studies, 2 history, 4 academic electives. *Academic units recommended:* 3 mathematics, 3 science, 2 foreign language, 3 social studies. **Freshman Admission Statistics:** 12,065 applied, 66% admitted, 19% enrolled. **Transfer Admission Requirements:** College transcript(s), minimum college GPA of 2.2 required. Lowest grade transferable C–. **General Admission Information:** Application fee $35. Notification on a rolling basis, beginning on or about 10/1. Nonfall registration accepted. Admission may be deferred for a maximum of 1 year. Credit and/or placement offered for CEEB Advanced Placement tests.

COSTS AND FINANCIAL AID

Annual tuition $24,576. Room and board $9,922. Required fees $1,190. Average book expense $860. **Required Forms and Deadlines:** FAFSA, institution's own financial aid form. Priority financial aid filing date 2/1. **Notification of Awards:** Applicants will be notified of awards on a rolling basis beginning 3/1. **Types of Aid:** *Need-based scholarships/grants:* Federal Pell, SEOG, state scholarships/grants, private scholarships, the school's own gift aid. *Loans:* FFEL Subsidized Stafford, FFEL Unsubsidized Stafford, FFEL PLUS, Federal Perkins. **Financial Aid Statistics:** 64% freshmen, 61% undergrads receive need-based scholarship or grant aid. 63% freshmen, 60% undergrads receive non-need-based scholarship or grant aid. 59% freshmen, 59% undergrads receive need-based self-help aid. 2% freshmen, 3% undergrads receive athletic scholarships. 97% freshmen, 95% undergrads receive any aid. 66% undergrads borrow to pay for school. Average cumulative indebtedness $25,553. **Criteria for awarding institutional aid:** *Non-need-based:* Academics, art, athletics, music/drama.

See page 1288.

UNIVERSITY OF HAWAII AT HILO

200 West Kawili Street, Hilo, HI 96720-4091
Phone: 808-974-7414 **Financial Aid Phone:** 808-974-7323
E-mail: uhhadm@hawaii.edu
Fax: 808-933-0861 **Website: ACT Code:** 904

This public school was founded in 1970. It has a 225-acre campus.

RATINGS
Admissions Selectivity Rating: 83   **Fire Safety Rating:** 60*   **Green Rating:** 60*

STUDENTS AND FACULTY
Enrollment: 3,148. **Student Body:** 60% female, 40% male, 35% out-of-state, 9% international. Asian 40%, African American 1%, Caucasian 36%, Hispanic 2%, Native American 1%.
Retention and Graduation: 66% freshmen return for sophomore year. 11% freshmen graduate within 4 years. **Faculty:** Student/faculty ratio 11:1. 238 full-time faculty, 63% hold PhDs, 34% are members of minority groups, 45% are women.

ACADEMICS
Degrees: Bachelor's, certificate, first professional, master's, post-bachelor's certificate. **Classes:** Most classes have 10–19 students. **Majors with Highest Enrollment:** Business, management, marketing, and related support services, other; psychology. **Special Study Options:** Cross-registration, distance learning, double major, dual enrollment, English as a Second Language (ESL), exchange student program (domestic), honors program, independent study, internships, student-designed major, study abroad, teacher certification program. Special programs offered to physically disabled students include note-taking services, reader services, tape recorders, tutors. **Career services:** Alumni

network, alumni services, career assessment, internships. **Career services highlights include:** Service Learning opportunities.

FACILITIES
Housing: Coed dorms, special housing for disabled students, apartments for married students, apartments for single students. 90% of campus accessible to physically disabled. **Computers:** Students can register for classes online. Administrative functions (other than registration) can be performed online.

CAMPUS LIFE
Environment: Town. **Activities:** Choral groups, dance, drama/theater, jazz band, literary magazine, music ensembles, radio station, student government, student newspaper. **Organizations:** 43 registered organizations, 4 religious organizations. **Athletics (Intercollegiate): Men:** Baseball, basketball, cross-country, golf, tennis. *Women:* cross-country, softball, tennis, volleyball. **On-Campus Highlights:** University Classroom Building (opened fall '02), University Campus Center Plaza (opening sp '04), University Lava Landing (Student Cyber Lounge), University Mo'okini Library, University Theatre, Student Life Center Facilities (Opening spr 08).

ADMISSIONS
Freshman Academic Profile: Average high school GPA 3.3. 22% in top 10% of high school class, 46% in top 25% of high school class, 82% in top 50% of high school class. SAT Math middle 50% range 440–600. SAT Critical Reading middle 50% range 440–560. ACT middle 50% range 17–24. Minimum paper TOEFL 500. Minimum computer TOEFL 173. **Basis for Candidate Selection:** *Very important factors considered include:* Rigor of secondary school record. *Important factors considered include:* Class rank, standardized test scores. *Other factors considered include:* Application essay, recommendation(s), extracurricular activities, talent/ability. **Freshman Admission Requirements:** High school diploma is required and GED is accepted. *Academic units required:* 4 English, 3 mathematics, 3 science, (3 science labs), 7 academic electives. *Academic units recommended:* 4 English, 4 mathematics, 4 science, (3 science labs), 2 foreign language, 2 social studies, 2 history. **Freshman Admission Statistics:** 1,612 applied, 51% admitted, 57% enrolled. **Transfer Admission Requirements:** College transcript(s), minimum college GPA of 2.0 required. Lowest grade transferable C. **General Admission Information:** Application fee $50. Regular application deadline 7/1. Notification on a rolling basis, beginning on or about 10/1. Nonfall registration accepted. Admission may be deferred for a maximum of 1 semester. Credit offered for CEEB Advanced Placement tests.

COSTS AND FINANCIAL AID
Annual in-state tuition $3,000. Annual out-of-state tuition $9,550. Room and board $6,292. Required fees $148. Average book expense $1,017. **Required Forms and Deadlines:** FAFSA. Priority financial aid filing date 3/1. **Notification of Awards:** Applicants will be notified of awards on a rolling basis beginning 4/12. **Types of Aid:** *Need-based scholarships/grants:* Federal Pell, SEOG, state scholarships/grants, private scholarships, the school's own gift aid. *Loans:* FFEL Subsidized Stafford, FFEL Unsubsidized Stafford, FFEL PLUS, Federal Perkins, state loans *Student Employment:* Federal Work-Study Program available. Institutional employment available. Highest amount earned per year from on-campus jobs $1,832. **Financial Aid Statistics:** 35% freshmen, 23% undergrads receive need-based scholarship or grant aid. 10% freshmen, 3% undergrads receive non-need-based scholarship or grant aid. 30% freshmen, 20% undergrads receive need-based self-help aid. 22% freshmen, 37% undergrads borrow to pay for school. Average cumulative indebtedness $11,806. **Criteria for awarding institutional aid:** *Non-need-based:* Academics, art, athletics, leadership, minority status, music/drama.

UNIVERSITY OF HAWAII AT MANOA

2600 Campus Road, QLCSS Room 001, Honolulu, HI 96822
Phone: 808-956-8975 **Financial Aid Phone:** 808-956-7251
E-mail: uhmanoa.admissions@hawaii.edu **CEEB Code:** 4867
Fax: 808-956-4148 **Website:** http://manoa.hawaii.edu **ACT Code:** 902

This public school was founded in 1907. It has a 320-acre campus.

RATINGS
Admissions Selectivity Rating: 84   **Fire Safety Rating:** 60*   **Green Rating:** 94

STUDENTS AND FACULTY
Enrollment: 13,583. **Student Body:** 54% female, 46% male, 23.3% out-of-state, 4% international (98 countries represented). Asian 67%, African American 1%, Caucasian 24%, Hispanic 3%, Native American 1%.
Retention and Graduation: Faculty: Student/faculty ratio 14.6:1. 1200 full-time faculty, 87% hold PhDs, 34% are members of minority groups, 41% are women.

ACADEMICS

Degrees: Bachelor's, master's, post-bachelor's certificate. **Classes:** Most classes have 10–19 students. Most lab/discussion sessions have 20–29 students. **Majors with Highest Enrollment:** art/art studies; biology/biological sciences; hospitality administration/management, other. **Special Study Options:** Cooperative education program, distance learning, double major, English as a Second Language (ESL), exchange student program (domestic), honors program, independent study, internships, student-designed major, study abroad, teacher certification program. **Honors programs:** Selected Studies Program. **Combined degree programs:** Architecture. Special programs offered to physically disabled students include note-taking services, reader services, tape recorders. **Career services:** alumni services, career/job search classes, career assessment, internships. **Career services highlights include:** Research has shown that out of classroom experiences are positively linked to academic persistence and educational attainment. Work-based experiences can contribute to students finding meaning in their academic pursuits, and vice versa. As a result, a partnership with the Colleges of Arts and Sciences was implemented. The Arts & Sciences Internship Program (ASIP) supports the mission of the Center for Career Development and Student Employment (CCDSE) at UH, to empower students to engage in career life planning through awareness, exploration, experience, and reflection.

FACILITIES

Housing: Coed dorms, special housing for disabled students, apartments for married students, apartments for single students. 40% of campus accessible to physically disabled. **Special Academic Facilities/Equipment:** UH Art and Commons Galleries, John Young Museum, John F. Kennedy Theatre, Lyon Arboretum, Waikiki Aquarium, Sunset (travel industry) Library, Chuck Gee Technology Learning Center, Advanced Computing Research Laboratory, Environmental Engineering Lab, Hawaii Center for Advanced Communications, Coral Reef Science Laboratory, traditionally designed Korean Studies Building, Coconut Island marine biology labs, Wong Audio-Visual Center, language lab, speech and hearing and dental hygiene clinics, law library, Hawaiian lo'i(garden), electron microscope and laser laboratories, ship and submersible research fleet, and Maui Super Computer, Jakuan Tea House. **Computers:** Students can register for classes online. Administrative functions (other than registration) can be performed online.

CAMPUS LIFE

Environment: Metropolis. **Activities:** Choral groups, concert band, dance, drama/theater, jazz band, literary magazine, marching band, music ensembles, musical theater, pep band, radio station, student government, student newspaper, student-run film society, symphony orchestra, campus ministries, international student organization. **Organizations:** 161 registered organizations, 7 honor societies, 24 religious organizations. 3 fraternities, 2 sororities. **Athletics (Intercollegiate):** *Men:* Baseball, basketball, cheerleading, diving, football, golf, sailing, swimming, tennis, volleyball. *Women:* Basketball, cheerleading, cross-country, diving, golf, sailing, soccer, softball, swimming, tennis, track/field (outdoor), track/field (indoor), volleyball, water polo. **On-Campus Highlights:** Campus Center, Queen Lili'uokalani Ctr for Student Svcs, Quad Courtyard, Sinclair Library, Hamilton Library. **Environmental Initiatives:** Creation & convening of Manoa Sustainability Corps. Manoa Green Days—our energy reduction program to consolidate building uses & completely shut down buildings. Sustainable UH—a student run sustainability organization.

ADMISSIONS

Freshman Academic Profile: Average high school GPA 3.435. 27.9% in top 10% of high school class, 60.3% in top 25% of high school class, 66.4% from public high schools. SAT Math middle 50% range 510–620. SAT Critical Reading middle 50% range 480–580. SAT Writing middle 50% range 480–570. ACT middle 50% range 21–25. Minimum paper TOEFL 500. Minimum computer TOEFL 173. Minimum web-based TOEFL 61. **Basis for Candidate Selection:** *Very important factors considered include:* Academic GPA, rigor of secondary school record, standardized test scores. *Important factors considered include:* Class rank, state residency. *Other factors considered include:* Application essay, recommendation(s), extracurricular activities, geographical residence, interview, talent/ability. **Freshman Admission Requirements:** High school diploma is required and GED is accepted. *Academic units required:* 4 English, 3 mathematics, 3 science, 3 social studies, 5 academic electives, 4 College Prep Courses **Freshman Admission Statistics:** 7,196 applied, 67% admitted, 40% enrolled. **Transfer Admission Requirements:** College transcript(s), minimum college GPA of 2.5 required. Lowest grade transferable D. **General Admission Information:** Application fee $50. Regular application deadline 5/1. Notification on a rolling basis, beginning on or about 12/1. Nonfall registration accepted. Credit and/or placement offered for CEEB Advanced Placement tests.

COSTS AND FINANCIAL AID

Annual in-state tuition $7,584. Annual out-of-state tuition $21,024. Room and board $8,493. Required fees $399. Average book expense $1,123. **Required Forms and Deadlines:** FAFSA. Priority financial aid filing date 3/1. **Noti-**

fication of Awards: Applicants will be notified of awards on a rolling basis beginning 4/1. **Types of Aid:** *Need-based scholarships/grants:* Federal Pell, SEOG, state scholarships/grants, private scholarships, the school's own gift aid. *Loans:* FFEL Subsidized Stafford, FFEL Unsubsidized Stafford, FFEL PLUS, Federal Perkins, Federal Nursing, state loans *Student Employment:* Federal Work-Study Program available. Institutional employment available. Highest amount earned per year from on-campus jobs $5,897. Off-campus job opportunities are good. **Financial Aid Statistics:** 27% freshmen, 26% undergrads receive need-based scholarship or grant aid. 8% freshmen, 6% undergrads receive non-need-based scholarship or grant aid. 20% freshmen, 22% undergrads receive need-based self-help aid. 2% freshmen, 2% undergrads receive athletic scholarships. 61.9% freshmen, 58.8% undergrads receive any aid. 34.5% undergrads borrow to pay for school. Average cumulative indebtedness $14,835. **Criteria for awarding institutional aid:** *Non-need-based:* Academics, alumni affiliation, art, athletics, leadership, music/drama.

UNIVERSITY OF HAWAII—WEST O`AHU

96-129 Ala Ike, Pearl City, HI 96782
Phone: 808-454-4700 **Financial Aid Phone:** 808-454-4700
E-mail: admissions@uhwo.hawaii.edu
Fax: 808-453-6075 **Website:** www.uhwo.hawaii.edu

This public school was founded in 1976.

RATINGS

Admissions Selectivity Rating: 60*   **Fire Safety Rating:** 60*   **Green Rating:** 60*

STUDENTS AND FACULTY

Enrollment: 1,253. **Student Body:** 71% female, 29% male, 1.8% out-of-state, 3% international (16 countries represented). Asian 64%, African American 2%, Caucasian 17%, Hispanic 2%.
Retention and Graduation: 60% freshmen return for sophomore year. 20% freshmen graduate within 4 years. **Faculty:** Student/faculty ratio 13:1. 46 full-time faculty, 96% hold PhDs, 50% are members of minority groups, 46% are women.

ACADEMICS

Degrees: Bachelor's, certificate. **Classes:** Most classes have 10–19 students. Most lab/discussion sessions have 20–29 students. **Majors with Highest Enrollment:** Business/commerce; psychology; public administration. **Special Study Options:** Distance learning, double major, teacher certification program. Special programs offered to physically disabled students include note-taking services, reader services.

FACILITIES

Housing: 100% of campus accessible to physically disabled. **Computers:** 10% of classrooms, 30% of common outdoor areas have wireless network access. Students can register for classes online.

CAMPUS LIFE

Environment: Town. **Activities:** Student government. **Organizations:** 12 registered organizations, 1 honor societies.

ADMISSIONS

Freshman Academic Profile: Average high school GPA 3.167. Minimum paper TOEFL 550. Minimum computer TOEFL 213. **Basis for Candidate Selection:** *Very important factors considered include:* Academic GPA. *Important factors considered include:* Rigor of secondary school record. *Other factors considered include:* Application essay, recommendation(s), standardized test scores, extracurricular activities, first generation, geographical residence, state residency. **Freshman Admission Requirements:** High school diploma is required and GED is accepted. *Academic units required:* 4 English, 3 mathematics, 3 science, 3 social studies, 5 academic electives, 4 college prepatory courses. **Freshman Admission Statistics:** 241 applied, 81% admitted, 39% enrolled. Minimum college GPA of 2.0 required. Lowest grade transferable D. **General Admission Information:** Application fee $50. Regular application deadline 8/1. Notification on a rolling basis, beginning on or about 2/1. Nonfall registration accepted. Admission may be deferred for a maximum of 1 semester. Credit and/or placement offered for CEEB Advanced Placement tests.

COSTS AND FINANCIAL AID

Annual in-state tuition $4,656. Annual out-of-state tuition $14,352. Required fees $10. Average book expense $1,123. **Required Forms and Deadlines:** FAFSA. Priority financial aid filing date 4/1. **Notification of Awards:** Applicants will be notified of awards on a rolling basis beginning 4/1. **Types of Aid:** *Need-based scholarships/grants:* Federal Pell, SEOG, state scholarships/grants, private scholarships, the school's own gift aid. *Loans:* FFEL Subsidized

Stafford, FFEL Unsubsidized Stafford, FFEL PLUS. *Student Employment:* Federal Work-Study Program available. Institutional employment available. Highest amount earned per year from on-campus jobs $8,000. Off-campus job opportunities are good. **Financial Aid Statistics:** 60% freshmen, 39% undergrads receive need-based scholarship or grant aid. 20% freshmen, 30% undergrads receive need-based self-help aid. 70% freshmen, 57% undergrads receive any aid.

UNIVERSITY OF HOUSTON

Office of Admissions, 4400 University Drive, Houston, TX 77204-2023
Phone: 713-743-1010 **Financial Aid Phone:** 713-743-1010
E-mail: admissions@uh.edu **CEEB Code:** 6870
Fax: 713-743-9633 **Website:** www.uh.edu **ACT Code:** 4236

This public school was founded in 1927. It has a 667-acre campus.

RATINGS
Admissions Selectivity Rating: 79   **Fire Safety Rating:** 89   **Green Rating:** 82

STUDENTS AND FACULTY
Enrollment: 28,056. **Student Body:** 51% female, 49% male, 1% out-of-state, 4% international (125 countries represented). Asian 22%, African American 15%, Caucasian 32%, Hispanic 24%.
Retention and Graduation: 79% freshmen return for sophomore year. 15% freshmen graduate within 4 years. **Faculty:** Student/faculty ratio 22:1. 1,256 full-time faculty, 88% hold PhDs, 23% are members of minority groups, 36% are women. 4% of classes are taught by teaching assistants.

ACADEMICS
Degrees: Bachelor's, first professional, master's. **Classes:** Most classes have 20–29 students. Most lab/discussion sessions have 20–29 students. **Majors with Highest Enrollment:** Business administration and management; psychology; Biological/Life Sciences. **Special Study Options:** Accelerated program, cooperative education program, cross-registration, distance learning, double major, dual enrollment, English as a Second Language (ESL), exchange student program (domestic), honors program, independent study, internships, study abroad, teacher certification program, weekend college, Academic Enrichment programs, certification programs, affiliated studies, and continuing education. **Honors programs:** The Honors College at the University of Houston is a nationally recognized, intellectually stimulating learning community. As a vibrant, leading presence within the university, the Honors College attracts highly talented and motivated students and educators to a collegial environment where tradition is honored and possibilities are both realized and created. **Combined degree programs:** Pharmacy, Engineering, Accounting. Special programs offered to physically disabled students include note-taking services, reader services, tape recorders, tutors. **Career services:** Alumni network, alumni services, career/job search classes, career assessment, internships. **Career services highlights include:** The Campus Recruitment program is the one we are most proud of.

FACILITIES
Housing: Coed dorms, special housing for disabled students, fraternity/sorority housing, apartments for married students, apartments for single students, special housing for honors students, upper level and graduate students. Calhoun Loft, Cambridge Oaks and Cullen Apartment. 98% of campus accessible to physically disabled. **Special Academic Facilities/Equipment:** Art gallery, language lab, human development lab school, University Hilton (staffed in part by students in Coll. of Hotel and Restaurant Management), opera studio. **Computers:** 100% of classrooms, 25% of dorms, 100% of libraries, 25% of dining areas, 100% of student union, 25% of common outdoor areas have wireless network access. Students can register for classes online. Administrative functions (other than registration) can be performed online.

CAMPUS LIFE
Environment: Metropolis. **Activities:** Choral groups, concert band, dance, drama/theater, jazz band, literary magazine, marching band, music ensembles, musical theater, opera, pep band, radio station, student government, student newspaper, student-run film society, symphony orchestra, television station, yearbook, campus ministries, international student organization. **Organizations:** 518 registered organizations, 25 honor societies, 39 religious organizations. 23 social fraternities, 20 social sororities. **Athletics (Intercollegiate):** *Men:* Baseball, basketball, cross-country, football, golf, track/field (outdoor), track/field (indoor). *Women:* Basketball, cross-country, diving, soccer, softball, swimming, tennis, track/field (outdoor), track/field (indoor), volleyball. **On-Campus Highlights:** University Center, Campus Recreation and Wellness Center, University Center Sattelite, Blaffer Gallery, Campus Activities. **Environmental Initiatives:** Recycling/waste minimization; commute modal split; energy conservation/retro commissioning of existing buildings.

ADMISSIONS
Freshman Academic Profile: Average high school GPA 3.6. 24% in top 10% of high school class, 60% in top 25% of high school class, 88% in top 50% of high school class. SAT Math middle 50% range 500–620. SAT Critical Reading middle 50% range 470–570. ACT middle 50% range 20–25. Minimum paper TOEFL 550. Minimum web-based TOEFL 79. **Basis for Candidate Selection:** *Very important factors considered include:* Class rank, rigor of secondary school record. *Important factors considered include:* Academic GPA, standardized test scores. *Other factors considered include:* Recommendation(s), character/personal qualities, extracurricular activities, first generation, talent/ability, volunteer work, work experience. **Freshman Admission Requirements:** High school diploma is required and GED is accepted. *Academic units recommended:* 4 English, 3 mathematics, 2 science, 2 foreign language, 3 social studies. **Freshman Admission Statistics:** 11,393 applied, 70% admitted, 41% enrolled. **Transfer Admission Requirements:** College transcript(s), minimum college GPA of 2.0 required. Lowest grade transferable C–. **General Admission Information:** Application fee $50. Regular application deadline 4/1. Nonfall registration accepted. Credit and/or placement offered for CEEB Advanced Placement tests.

COSTS AND FINANCIAL AID
Annual in-state tuition $5,542. Annual out-of-state tuition $13,852. Room and board $7,164. Required fees $2,954. Average book expense $1,100. **Required Forms and Deadlines:** FAFSA. Priority financial aid filing date 4/1. **Notification of Awards:** Applicants will be notified of awards on a rolling basis beginning 5/1. **Types of Aid:** *Need-based scholarships/grants:* Federal Pell, SEOG, state scholarships/grants, private scholarships, the school's own gift aid. *Loans:* FFEL Subsidized Stafford, FFEL Unsubsidized Stafford, FFEL PLUS, Federal Perkins, state loans *Student Employment:* Federal Work-Study Program available. Institutional employment available. Off-campus job opportunities are good. **Financial Aid Statistics:** 55.4% freshmen, 46.2% undergrads receive need-based scholarship or grant aid. 10% freshmen, 4% undergrads receive non-need-based scholarship or grant aid. 43% freshmen, 45% undergrads receive need-based self-help aid. 84% freshmen, 66% undergrads receive any aid. **Criteria for awarding institutional aid:** *Non-need-based:* Academics, alumni affiliation, art, athletics, job skills, leadership, music/drama, state/district residency.

UNIVERSITY OF HOUSTON—CLEAR LAKE

2700 Bay Area Boulevard, Houston, TX 77058-1098
Phone: 281-283-2521 **Financial Aid Phone:** 281-283-2480
E-mail: admissions@uhcl.edu **CEEB Code:** 6916
Fax: 281-283-2530

This public school was founded in 1974. It has a 524-acre campus.

RATINGS
Admissions Selectivity Rating: 60*   **Fire Safety Rating:** 60*   **Green Rating:** 60*

STUDENTS AND FACULTY
Enrollment: 4,104. **Student Body:** 69% female, 31% male, 1% out-of-state, 2% international (84 countries represented). Asian 6%, African American 8%, Caucasian 57%, Hispanic 26%, Native American 1%.
Retention and Graduation: Faculty: Student/faculty ratio 10.24:1. 220 full-time faculty, 86% hold PhDs, 23% are members of minority groups, 43% are women.

ACADEMICS
Degrees: Bachelor's, certificate, doctoral, master's, post-bachelor's certificate, post-master's certificate. **Classes:** Most classes have 10–19 students. **Majors with Highest Enrollment:** Accounting; education; psychology. **Special Study Options:** Cooperative education program, distance learning, double major, dual enrollment, independent study, internships, student-designed major, study abroad, teacher certification program, weekend college. **Combined degree programs:** BS/MS, BS/MHBA. Special programs offered to physically disabled students include note-taking services, reader services, tape recorders, tutors. **Career services:** Alumni network, alumni services, career/job search classes, career assessment, internships.

FACILITIES
Housing: Privatized housing apartments. 100% of campus accessible to physically disabled. **Special Academic Facilities/Equipment:** Student Art Gallery Fitness Center/Fitness Zone. **Computers:** 100% of classrooms, 100% of libraries, 100% of dining areas, 100% of student union, 100% of common outdoor areas have wireless network access. Students can register for classes online. Administrative functions (other than registration) can be performed online.

CAMPUS LIFE

Environment: Metropolis. **Activities:** Literary magazine, student government, student newspaper, student-run film society, international student organization. **Organizations:** 70 registered organizations, 16 honor societies, 5 religious organizations. **On-Campus Highlights:** Student Service Building, Bayou Building, library, Delta Building, computer labs.

ADMISSIONS

Freshman Academic Profile: Minimum paper TOEFL 550. Minimum computer TOEFL 213. **Freshman Admission Requirements: Transfer Admission Requirements:** College transcript(s), standardized test scores, statement of good standing from prior institution(s). Minimum college GPA of 2.0 required. Lowest grade transferable D–. **General Admission Information:** Application fee $35. Regular application deadline 8/1. Nonfall registration accepted. Admission may be deferred for a maximum of 1 year.

COSTS AND FINANCIAL AID

Annual in-state tuition $4,560. Annual out-of-state tuition $13,770. Room and board $7,896. Required fees $1,148. **Required Forms and Deadlines: Types of Aid:** *Need-based scholarships/grants:* Federal Pell, SEOG, state scholarships/grants, private scholarships, the school's own gift aid. *Loans:* Direct Subsidized Stafford, Direct Unsubsidized Stafford, Direct PLUS, Federal Perkins, state loans. *Student Employment:* Federal Work-Study Program available. Institutional employment available. Off-campus job opportunities are good. **Financial Aid Statistics:** 37% undergrads receive need-based scholarship or grant aid. 19% undergrads receive non-need-based scholarship or grant aid. 38% undergrads receive need-based self-help aid. 61% undergrads receive any aid. Average cumulative indebtedness $18,286.

UNIVERSITY OF HOUSTON—DOWNTOWN

Admissions Office, One Main Street, Houston, TX 77002-1001
Phone: 713-221-8522 **Financial Aid Phone:** 713-221-8041
E-mail: uhdadmit@dt.uh.edu
Fax: 713-221-5220

This public school was founded in 1974.

RATINGS

Admissions Selectivity Rating: 60*   **Fire Safety Rating:** 60*   **Green Rating:** 60*

STUDENTS AND FACULTY

Enrollment: 11,344. **Student Body:** 59% female, 41% male, 1% out-of-state, 3% international (73 countries represented). Asian 10%, African American 26%, Caucasian 23%, Hispanic 38%.
Retention and Graduation: 52% freshmen return for sophomore year. 2% freshmen graduate within 4 years. **Faculty:** Student/faculty ratio 20:1. 292 full-time faculty, 80% hold PhDs, 31% are members of minority groups, 46% are women.

ACADEMICS

Degrees: Bachelor's, master's. **Classes:** Most classes have 20–29 students. Most lab/discussion sessions have 20–29 students. **Majors with Highest Enrollment:** Accounting; criminal justice/safety studies; finance. **Special Study Options:** Cooperative education program, distance learning, double major, dual enrollment, English as a Second Language (ESL), honors program, independent study, internships, study abroad, teacher certification program, weekend college.

FACILITIES

Computers: Students can register for classes online. Administrative functions (other than registration) can be performed online.

CAMPUS LIFE

Environment: Metropolis. **Activities:** drama/theater, jazz band, literary magazine, student government, student newspaper. **Organizations:** 52 registered organizations, 3 honor societies, 2 religious organizations. 4 fraternities, 4 sororities. **Athletics (Intercollegiate):** *Men:* Badminton, basketball, bowling, football, soccer, softball, tennis, volleyball, weight lifting. *Women:* Badminton, basketball, bowling, soccer, softball, tennis, volleyball, weight lifting. **On-Campus Highlights:** Special Events Center, O' Kane Gallery, Food court and adjoining Coffee House, Jesse H. Jones Student Life Center, O' Kane Theatre.

ADMISSIONS

Freshman Academic Profile: Minimum paper TOEFL 550. Minimum computer TOEFL 213. **Freshman Admission Requirements:** High school diploma is required and GED is accepted. *Academic units recommended:* 4 English, 3 mathematics, 3 science, 3 foreign language, 3 social studies, 1 academic electives, 7 economics, fine arts, health education, physical educa-

tion, speech, and technology. **Freshman Admission Statistics:** 1,957 applied, 99% admitted, 50% enrolled. **Transfer Admission Requirements:** College transcript(s), Lowest grade transferable C. **General Admission Information:** Application fee $35. Regular application deadline 7/1. Nonfall registration accepted. Admission may be deferred for a maximum of text. Credit offered for CEEB Advanced Placement tests.

COSTS AND FINANCIAL AID

Annual in-state tuition $2,898. Annual out-of-state tuition $9,498. Required fees $758. Average book expense $1,020. **Required Forms and Deadlines:** FAFSA. Financial aid filing deadline 4/1. **Notification of Awards:** Applicants will be notified of awards on a rolling basis beginning 4/1. **Types of Aid:** *Need-based scholarships/grants:* Federal Pell, SEOG, state scholarships/grants, private scholarships, the school's own gift aid. *Loans:* FFEL Subsidized Stafford, FFEL Unsubsidized Stafford, FFEL PLUS, state loans **Financial Aid Statistics:** 62% freshmen, 70% undergrads receive need-based scholarship or grant aid. 23% freshmen, 47% undergrads receive need-based self-help aid. 35% freshmen, 77% undergrads receive any aid. 72.1% undergrads borrow to pay for school. Average cumulative indebtedness $13,371. **Criteria for awarding institutional aid:** *Non-need-based:* Academics, leadership, state/district residency.

UNIVERSITY OF HOUSTON—VICTORIA

Admissions and Records, UW #104, 3007 N, Victoria, TX 77901-4450
Phone: 361-570-4110 **Financial Aid Phone:** 316-570-4131
E-mail: admissions@uhv.edu
Fax: 361-570-4114

This public school was founded in 1973.

RATINGS

Admissions Selectivity Rating: 60*   **Fire Safety Rating:** 60*   **Green Rating:** 60*

STUDENTS AND FACULTY

Enrollment: 1,779. **Student Body:** 70% female, 30% male, 1% out-of-state, 2% international (20 countries represented). Asian 7%, African American 12%, Caucasian 57%, Hispanic 21%, Native American 1%.
Retention and Graduation: Faculty: Student/faculty ratio 15:1. 106 full-time faculty, 92% hold PhDs, 38% are members of minority groups, 45% are women.

ACADEMICS

Degrees: Bachelor's, master's, post-bachelor's certificate, post-master's certificate. **Classes:** Most classes have 20–29 students. **Majors with Highest Enrollment:** Business/commerce; education; multi-/interdisciplinary studies, other. **Special Study Options:** Distance learning, double major, honors program, independent study, internships, study abroad, teacher certification program. Special programs offered to physically disabled students include note-taking services, tutors. **Career services:** Alumni services, career/job search classes, career assessment, internships.

FACILITIES

Housing: Coed dorms. Dorm will open in fall 2011. 100% of campus accessible to physically disabled. **Special Academic Facilities/Equipment:** Museum of Coastal Bend. **Computers:** Students can register for classes online. Administrative functions (other than registration) can be performed online.

CAMPUS LIFE

Environment: City. **Activities:** Student government, international student organization. **Athletics (Intercollegiate):** *Men:* Baseball. *Women:* Softball.

ADMISSIONS

Freshman Academic Profile: Minimum paper TOEFL 550. Minimum computer TOEFL 213. **Freshman Admission Requirements:** High school diploma is required and GED is accepted. **Transfer Admission Requirements:** College transcript(s), standardized test scores, minimum college GPA of 2.0 required. Lowest grade transferable C. **General Admission Information:** Nonfall registration accepted.

COSTS AND FINANCIAL AID

Annual in-state tuition $4,200. Annual out-of-state tuition $12,600. Required fees $1,110. Average book expense $1,100. **Required Forms and Deadlines:** FAFSA. Priority financial aid filing date 4/15. **Notification of Awards:** Applicants will be notified of awards on a rolling basis beginning 5/1. **Types of Aid:** *Need-based scholarships/grants:* Federal Pell, SEOG, state scholarships/grants, private scholarships, the school's own gift aid. *Loans:* FFEL Subsidized Stafford, FFEL Unsubsidized Stafford, FFEL PLUS, Federal Nursing, state loans. *Student Employment:* Federal Work-Study Program available. Institutional employment available. Off-campus job opportunities are good. **Financial**

UNIVERSITY OF IDAHO

UI Admissions Office, PO Box 444264, Moscow, ID 83844-4264
Phone: 208-885-6326 **Financial Aid Phone:** 208-885-6312
E-mail: admissions@uidaho.edu **CEEB Code:** 4843
Fax: 208-885-9119 **Website:** www.uihome.uidaho.edu/uihome/ **ACT Code:** 928

This public school was founded in 1889. It has a 12500-acre campus.

RATINGS
Admissions Selectivity Rating: 77   **Fire Safety Rating:** 60*   **Green Rating:** 98

STUDENTS AND FACULTY
Enrollment: 8,757. **Student Body:** 47% female, 53% male, 32% out-of-state, 2% international (74 countries represented). Asian 2%, African American 1%, Caucasian 81%, Hispanic 6%, Native American 1%.
Retention and Graduation: 25% freshmen graduate within 4 years. **Faculty:** Student/faculty ratio 17:1. 545 full-time faculty, 77% hold PhDs, 8% are members of minority groups, 30% are women. 15% of classes are taught by teaching assistants.

ACADEMICS
Degrees: Bachelor's, certificate, master's, post-bachelor's certificate, post-master's certificate. **Classes:** Most classes have 20–29 students. Most lab/discussion sessions have 10–19 students. **Majors with Highest Enrollment:** Elementary education and teaching; mechanical engineering; psychology. **Special Study Options:** Accelerated program, cooperative education program, cross-registration, distance learning, double major, dual enrollment, English as a Second Language (ESL), exchange student program (domestic), honors program, independent study, internships, student-designed major, study abroad, teacher certification program. **Honors programs:** Established in 1983, the University Honors Program offers a stimulating course of study and the advantages of an enriched learning community for over 500 students from all colleges and majors. The UHP's diverse curriculum, including special topic courses and innovative seminars, serves a variety of needs and interests. Beyond the classroom, the program's extracurricular opportunities include concerts, plays, films, lectures and other off-campus excursions that foster cultural enrichment, friendship, and learning. Honors classes offer opportunities to explore subjects and methods in significant depth—students find that their education and their academic performance are enhanced by strong mentoring relationships with faculty devoted to enabling each student to fulfill his or her potential, and by the lively, participation-based modes of learning in small classes. Lower-division honors core courses enable students to learn with their peers in small classes taught by honors faculty. Moreover, each year the program offers innovative upper-division seminars, with each class limited to fifteen students. Honors students are frequently interested in and encouraged to apply for exchanges to other American universities or to universities abroad. As part of a dynamic, broad-based education, members are also encouraged to participate in domestic or international exchange programs, and to take advantage of opportunities to engage in laboratory or field-based research programs as well as internships and other forms of cooperative education. Special programs offered to physically disabled students include note-taking services, reader services, tape recorders, tutors. **Career services:** Alumni network, alumni services, career/job search classes, career assessment, internships, regional alumni. **Career services highlights include:** Internships.

FACILITIES
Housing: Coed dorms, special housing for disabled students, men's dorms, special housing for international students, women's dorms, fraternity/sorority housing, apartments for married students, apartments for single students. 85% of campus accessible to physically disabled. **Special Academic Facilities/Equipment:** On-campus preschool, experimental forest, electron microscope. **Computers:** 100% of classrooms, 100% of dorms, 100% of libraries, 100% of dining areas, 100% of student union, have wireless network access. Students can register for classes online. Administrative functions (other than registration) can be performed online.

CAMPUS LIFE
Environment: Town. **Activities:** Choral groups, concert band, dance, drama/theater, jazz band, marching band, music ensembles, musical theater, opera, pep band, radio station, student government, student newspaper, student-run film society, symphony orchestra, television station, campus ministries, international student organization. **Organizations:** 190 registered organizations, 13 honor societies, 20 religious organizations. 18 fraternities, 9 sororities. **Athletics (Intercollegiate):** *Men:* Basketball, cross-country, football, golf, track/field (outdoor), track/field (indoor). *Women:* Basketball, cross-country, golf, soccer, swimming, track/field (outdoor), track/field (indoor), volleyball. **On-Campus Highlights:** Idaho Commons—food and meeting rooms, 18 hole golf course, Kibbie Dome—athletics, Student Recreation Center, Borah Theater, 6. Rec Center/Outdoors Program 7. Frisbee Golf Course 8. Religious Centers. See our campus live with web cams at www.uidaho.edu/webcams. **Environmental Initiatives:** $35 mil ESCO for energy conservation projects currently underway. Built institutional infrastructure: hired a Sustainability Coordinator, launched a Sustainability Center, formed committees, task forces, etc. to assess and develop long-term plans for sustainability issues. Converted steam plant to a biomass boiler.

ADMISSIONS
Freshman Academic Profile: Average high school GPA 3.38. 19% in top 10% of high school class, 46% in top 25% of high school class, 79% in top 50% of high school class. 90% from public high schools. SAT Math middle 50% range 400–610. SAT Critical Reading middle 50% range 490–600. SAT Writing middle 50% range 460–570. ACT middle 50% range 20–26. Minimum paper TOEFL 525. Minimum computer TOEFL 193. Minimum web-based TOEFL 70. **Basis for Candidate Selection:** *Very important factors considered include:* Academic GPA, standardized test scores, *Other factors considered include:* Recommendation(s). **Freshman Admission Requirements:** High school diploma is required and GED is accepted. *Academic units required:* 4 English, 3 mathematics, 3 science, (1 science labs), 1 foreign language. **Freshman Admission Statistics:** 5,110 applied, 80% admitted, 44% enrolled. **Transfer Admission Requirements:** College transcript(s), minimum college GPA of 2.0 required. Lowest grade transferable D. **General Admission Information:** Application fee $40. Regular application deadline 8/1. Nonfall registration accepted. Credit and/or placement offered for CEEB Advanced Placement tests.

COSTS AND FINANCIAL AID
Annual out-of-state tuition $10,080. Room and board $7,242. Required fees $4,932. Average book expense $1,474. **Required Forms and Deadlines:** FAFSA. Priority financial aid filing date 2/15. **Notification of Awards:** Applicants will be notified of awards on a rolling basis beginning 3/30. **Types of Aid:** *Need-based scholarships/grants:* Federal Pell, SEOG, state scholarships/grants, private scholarships, the school's own gift aid. *Loans:* Direct Subsidized Stafford, Direct Unsubsidized Stafford, Direct PLUS, Federal Perkins, college/university loans from institutional funds. *Student Employment:* Federal Work-Study Program available. Institutional employment available. Off-campus job opportunities are good. **Financial Aid Statistics:** 34% freshmen, 37% undergrads receive need-based scholarship or grant aid. 49% freshmen, 47% undergrads receive non-need-based scholarship or grant aid. 41% freshmen, 48% undergrads receive need-based self-help aid. 3% freshmen, 3% undergrads receive athletic scholarships. 56.3% freshmen, 57.6% undergrads receive any aid. 66% undergrads borrow to pay for school. Average cumulative indebtedness $21,702. **Criteria for awarding institutional aid:** *Non-need-based:* Academics, alumni affiliation, art, athletics, leadership, minority status, music/drama, state/district residency.

UNIVERSITY OF ILLINOIS AT CHICAGO

Office of Admissions & Records, Box 5220 m/c 018, Chicago, IL 60680-5220
Phone: 312-996-4350 **Financial Aid Phone:** 312-996-3126
E-mail: www.uic.edu/depts/oar/contact/htm **CEEB Code:** 1851
Fax: 312-996-2953 **Website:** www.uic.edu **ACT Code:** 1155

This public school was founded in 1965. It has a 218-acre campus.

RATINGS
Admissions Selectivity Rating: 79   **Fire Safety Rating:** 60*   **Green Rating:** 85

STUDENTS AND FACULTY
Enrollment: 15,986. **Student Body:** 52% female, 48% male, 1.7% out-of-state, 1% international (88 countries represented). Asian 22%, African American 8%, Caucasian 44%, Hispanic 18%.
Retention and Graduation: 23% grads go on to further study within 1 year. **Faculty:** Student/faculty ratio 17.8:1. 1160 full-time faculty, 24% are members of minority groups, 45% are women.

ACADEMICS

Degrees: Bachelor's, doctoral, master's, post-bachelor's certificate, post-master's certificate. **Classes:** Most classes have 20–29 students. Most lab/discussion sessions have 20–29 students. **Majors with Highest Enrollment:** Biology/biological sciences; business administration and management; psychology. **Special Study Options:** Accelerated program, cooperative education program, distance learning, double major, dual enrollment, exchange student program (domestic), honors program, independent study, internships, student-designed major, study abroad, teacher certification program. **Combined degree programs:** BA/MD, BA/DDS. Special programs offered to physically disabled students include note-taking services, reader services, tape recorders, tutors. **Career services:** Alumni network, alumni services, career/job search classes, career assessment, internships, regional alumni. **Career services highlights include:** The Entrepreneurship Consulting Program provides an opportunity for teams of students to work with a professional consultant to solve real business problems for entrepreneurial firms. Also, we are equally proud because this year we received a National Award for Excellence from the National (Global) Consortium of Entrepreneurship Centers, held at Syracuse University. It was for founding (1997) and growing the national Collegiate Entrepreneurs' Organization (CEO), one of our UIC programs. We have student entrepreneurship clubs on more than 140 university campuses and the Annual CEO Conference attracted 1300 students (and faculty)

FACILITIES

Housing: Coed dorms, special housing for disabled students, apartments for single students, honors floor, Presidential Awards House. 80% of campus accessible to physically disabled. **Computers:** 95% of classrooms, 100% of dorms, 100% of libraries, 100% of dining areas, 100% of student union, have wireless network access. Students can register for classes online. Administrative functions (other than registration) can be performed online.

CAMPUS LIFE

Environment: Metropolis. **Activities:** Choral groups, concert band, drama/theater, jazz band, literary magazine, music ensembles, pep band, radio station, student government, student newspaper, international student organization. **Organizations:** 370 registered organizations, 10 honor societies, 33 religious organizations. 13 fraternities, 15 sororities. **Athletics (Intercollegiate):** *Men:* Baseball, basketball, cross-country, diving, gymnastics, soccer, swimming, tennis, track/field (outdoor). *Women:* Basketball, cross-country, diving, gymnastics, softball, swimming, tennis, track/field (outdoor), volleyball. **On-Campus Highlights:** Student Center East, Student Center West, UIC Pavilion, Student Services Building, Student Recreation Facility. **Environmental Initiatives:** establishment of Office of Sustainability and appointment of associate chancellor for sustainability and signing the Illinois sustainability University Compact Preparation of a climate action plan. Jane Addams Hull House, Urban farm, and Rethinking soup. A grass roots effort at local, sustainable food systems in an urban environment.

ADMISSIONS

Freshman Academic Profile: 28% in top 10% of high school class, 62% in top 25% of high school class, 93% in top 50% of high school class. SAT Math middle 50% range 510–660. SAT Critical Reading middle 50% range 460–630. SAT Writing middle 50% range 490–630. ACT middle 50% range 21–26. Minimum paper TOEFL 520. Minimum computer TOEFL 190. **Basis for Candidate Selection:** *Very important factors considered include:* Class rank, application essay, academic GPA, rigor of secondary school record, standardized test scores, *Other factors considered include:* Recommendation(s), character/personal qualities, extracurricular activities. **Freshman Admission Requirements:** High school diploma is required and GED is accepted. *Academic units required:* 4 English, 3 mathematics, 3 science, 2 foreign language, 3 social studies. *Academic units recommended:* 4 mathematics. **Freshman Admission Statistics:** 14,661 applied, 63% admitted, 34% enrolled. **Transfer Admission Requirements:** College transcript(s), minimum college GPA of 2.5 required. **General Admission Information:** Application fee $40. Regular application deadline 1/15. Notification on a rolling basis, beginning on or about 11/30. Nonfall registration not accepted. Credit and/or placement offered for CEEB Advanced Placement tests.

COSTS AND FINANCIAL AID

Average book expense $1,200. **Required Forms and Deadlines:** FAFSA. Priority financial aid filing date 3/1. **Notification of Awards:** Applicants will be notified of awards on a rolling basis beginning 3/15. **Types of Aid:** *Need-based scholarships/grants:* Federal Pell, SEOG, state scholarships/grants, private scholarships, the school's own gift aid. *Loans:* Direct Subsidized Stafford, Direct Unsubsidized Stafford, Direct PLUS, Federal Perkins, Federal Nursing, state loans, college/university loans from institutional funds, Alternative loans. *Student Employment:* Federal Work-Study Program available. Institutional employment available. Off-campus job opportunities are good. **Financial Aid Statistics:** 52% freshmen, 49% undergrads receive need-based scholarship or grant aid. 4% freshmen, 2% undergrads receive non-need-based scholarship or grant aid. 48% freshmen, 48% undergrads receive need-based self-help aid.

1% freshmen, 1% undergrads receive athletic scholarships. 77% freshmen, 80% undergrads receive any aid. 57% undergrads borrow to pay for school. Average cumulative indebtedness $17,276. **Criteria for awarding institutional aid:** *Non-need-based:* Academics, art, music/drama.

UNIVERSITY OF ILLINOIS AT SPRINGFIELD

One University Plaza, MS UHB 1080, Springfield, IL 62703-5407
Phone: 217-206-4847 **Financial Aid Phone:** 217-206-6724
E-mail: admissions@uis.edu **CEEB Code:** 834
Fax: 217-206-6620 **Website: ACT Code:** 1137

This public school was founded in 1969. It has a 746-acre campus.

RATINGS

Admissions Selectivity Rating: 78   **Fire Safety Rating:** 60*   **Green Rating:** 76

STUDENTS AND FACULTY

Enrollment: 2,920. **Student Body:** 55% female, 45% male, 8.6% out-of-state, 1% international (23 countries represented). Asian 3%, African American 13%, Caucasian 71%, Hispanic 3%, Native American 1%.
Retention and Graduation: 47% freshmen graduate within 4 years. **Faculty:** Student/faculty ratio 12.7:1. 211 full-time faculty, 90% hold PhDs, 17% are members of minority groups, 42% are women.

ACADEMICS

Degrees: Bachelor's, master's, post-bachelor's certificate, post-master's certificate. **Classes:** Most classes have 20–29 students. Most lab/discussion sessions have 10–19 students. **Majors with Highest Enrollment:** Business administration and management; computer science; psychology. **Special Study Options:** Distance learning, double major, English as a Second Language (ESL), honors program, independent study, internships, study abroad, teacher certification program. **Honors programs:** Interdisciplinary four-year baccalaureate experience for highly qualified freshman. **Combined degree programs:** BA/MA. Special programs offered to physically disabled students include note-taking services, reader services, tape recorders **Career services:** Alumni network, alumni services, career/job search classes, career assessment, internships, regional alumni.

FACILITIES

Housing: Coed dorms, special housing for disabled students, special housing for international students, apartments for married students, apartments for single students, wellness housing, theme housing, Family Housing. 99% of campus accessible to physically disabled. **Special Academic Facilities/Equipment:** Norris L. Brookens Library, Sangamon Auditorium, Observatory. **Computers:** 100% of classrooms, 100% of dorms, 100% of libraries, 100% of dining areas, 100% of student union, 100% of common outdoor areas have wireless network access. Students can register for classes online. Administrative functions (other than registration) can be performed online.

CAMPUS LIFE

Environment: City. **Activities:** Choral groups, concert band, dance, drama/theater, jazz band, music ensembles, pep band, student government, student newspaper, student-run film society, campus ministries, international student organization, Model UN. **Organizations:** 76 registered organizations, **Athletics (Intercollegiate):** *Men:* Basketball, golf, soccer, tennis. *Women:* Basketball, cheerleading, golf, soccer, softball, tennis, volleyball. **On-Campus Highlights:** University Hall, Public Affairs Center **Environmental Initiatives:** Construction of a residence hall with a green roof. With the support of a grant from the State of Illinois, the university has expanded the recycling program from only academic buildings to include housing. The university has committed 1.95 million dollars to retrofit old single glazed windows in one campus building with double-glazed windows for energy conservation.

ADMISSIONS

Freshman Academic Profile: Average high school GPA 3.24. 17.5% in top 10% of high school class, 43.4% in top 25% of high school class, 77.7% in top 50% of high school class. 88.7% from public high schools. ACT middle 50% range 20–26. Minimum paper TOEFL 500. Minimum computer TOEFL 173. **Basis for Candidate Selection:** *Very important factors considered include:* Application essay, academic GPA, rigor of secondary school record. *Important factors considered include:* Standardized test scores. *Other factors considered include:* Class rank, recommendation(s), extracurricular activities, first generation, level of applicant's interest, work experience. **Freshman Admission Requirements:** High school diploma is required and GED is accepted. *Academic units required:* 4 English, 3 mathematics, 3 science, (2 science labs), 2 foreign language, 2 social studies, 2 history, 2 visual/performing arts. **Freshman**

Admission Statistics: 1,349 applied, 58% admitted, 37% enrolled. **Transfer Admission Requirements:** College transcript(s), minimum college GPA of 2.0 required. Lowest grade transferable D. **General Admission Information:** Application fee $40. Nonfall registration not accepted. Admission may be deferred for a maximum of 1 year. Credit and/or placement offered for CEEB Advanced Placement tests.

COSTS AND FINANCIAL AID

Average book expense $1,200. **Required Forms and Deadlines:** FAFSA. Financial aid filing deadline 11/15. Priority financial aid filing date 4/1. **Notification of Awards:** Applicants will be notified of awards on a rolling basis beginning 1/1. **Types of Aid:** *Need-based scholarships/grants:* Federal Pell, SEOG, state scholarships/grants, private scholarships, the school's own gift aid. *Loans:* Direct Subsidized Stafford, Direct Unsubsidized Stafford, Direct PLUS, Federal Perkins, college/university loans from institutional funds. **Financial Aid Statistics:** 68% freshmen, 50% undergrads receive need-based scholarship or grant aid. 18% freshmen, 8% undergrads receive non-need-based scholarship or grant aid. 61% freshmen, 52% undergrads receive need-based self-help aid. 4% freshmen, 2% undergrads receive athletic scholarships. 64% undergrads borrow to pay for school. Average cumulative indebtedness $14,717. **Criteria for awarding institutional aid:** *Non-need-based:* Academics, alumni affiliation, art, athletics, job skills, leadership, minority status, music/drama, state/district residency.

UNIVERSITY OF ILLINOIS AT URBANA-CHAMPAIGN

Best 373

901 West Illinois Street, Urbana, IL 61801
Phone: 217-333-0302 **Financial Aid Phone:** 217-333-0100
E-mail: ugradadmissions@uiuc.edu **CEEB Code:** 4607
Fax: 217-244-0903 **Website:** www.illinois.edu **ACT Code:** 1154

This public school was founded in 1867. It has a 4724-acre campus.

RATINGS

Admissions Selectivity Rating: 88 **Fire Safety Rating:** 62 **Green Rating:** 95

STUDENTS AND FACULTY

Enrollment: 30,395. **Student Body:** 47% female, 53% male, 7% out-of-state, 5% international (123 countries represented). Asian 13%, African American 7%, Caucasian 66%, Hispanic 7%.
Retention and Graduation: 93% freshmen return for sophomore year. 63% freshmen graduate within 4 years. 26% grads go on to further study within 1 year. 18% grads pursue arts and sciences degrees. 3% grads pursue law degrees. 2% grads pursue business degrees. 3% grads pursue medical degrees. **Faculty:** Student/faculty ratio 17:1. 1974 full-time faculty, 92% hold PhDs, 23% are members of minority groups, 30% are women. 26% of classes are taught by teaching assistants.

ACADEMICS

Degrees: Bachelor's, certificate, first professional, master's, post-bachelor's certificate, post-master's certificate. **Classes:** Most classes have 20–29 students. Most lab/discussion sessions have 20–29 students. **Majors with Highest Enrollment:** Cell/cellular and molecular biology; political science and government; psychology. **Special Study Options:** Accelerated program, cooperative education program, cross-registration, distance learning, double major, dual enrollment, English as a Second Language (ESL), exchange student program (domestic), honors program, independent study, internships, liberal arts/career combination, student-designed major, study abroad, teacher certification program, Jonathan Baldwin Turner Honors program, Campus Honors, Illinois Leadership & Entrepreneurial Programs. **Honors programs:** Campus Honors Program, James Scholars Program. **Combined degree programs:** BA/MEng, MD/Ph.D. Special programs offered to physically disabled students include note-taking services, reader services, tape recorders, tutors. **Career services:** Alumni network, alumni services, career/job search classes, career assessment, internships, regional alumni. **Career services highlights include:** Illinois'"elementhouse," placed ninth overall (out of 20 entries) in the U.S. Department of Energy's Solar Decathlon competition. The 8-day event culminated with an awards ceremony on Friday, October 19 on the National Mall in Washington, DC. "We were very pleased to win the Market Viability contest, which reflects the practical aspects of our design. Winning the Comfort Zone

---

contest really demonstrated that all of the individual comfort-related principles we chose for our system were considered the best." "The Solar Decathlon was a great experience for our students," Newell added. Approximately 40 students went to Washington, DC over the three-week period for the competition. They did a wonderful job and were great representatives of our state and university. "We left some of Illinois in Washington, DC, too," he added. "The new Native American Smithsonian Museum is planting several of the prairie plants around the museum that our landscape architecture students brought to Washington."

FACILITIES

Housing: Coed dorms, special housing for disabled students, men's dorms, special housing for international students, women's dorms, fraternity/sorority housing, apartments for married students, cooperative housing, apartments for single students, Living and Learning Communities housed within the residence halls; Private Certified Housing. 100% of campus accessible to physically disabled. **Special Academic Facilities/Equipment:** Art, cultural and natural history museums, performing arts center, National Center for Supercomputing Applications, Beckman Institute, Siebel Computer Science Center, University Library (37 separate libraries and centers on campus), Japan House and Gardens, Assembly Hall for large concerts, Allerton Park and Conference Center, Arboretum, and the Illini Student Union. **Computers:** 85% of classrooms, 100% of dorms, 100% of libraries, 100% of dining areas, 100% of student union, 1% of common outdoor areas have wireless network access. Students can register for classes online. Administrative functions (other than registration) can be performed online.

CAMPUS LIFE

Environment: City. **Activities:** Choral groups, concert band, dance, drama/theater, jazz band, literary magazine, marching band, music ensembles, musical theater, opera, pep band, radio station, student government, student newspaper, student-run film society, symphony orchestra, television station, yearbook, campus ministries, international student organization, Model UN. **Organizations:** 1000 registered organizations, 30 honor societies, 95 religious organizations. 60 fraternities, 36 sororities. **Athletics (Intercollegiate):** *Men:* Baseball, basketball, cheerleading, cross-country, football, golf, gymnastics, tennis, track/field (outdoor), wrestling. *Women:* Basketball, cheerleading, cross-country, diving, golf, gymnastics, soccer, softball, swimming, tennis, track/field (outdoor), volleyball. **On-Campus Highlights:** Campus Town restaurants and shops, Krannert Center for Performing Arts, Assembly Hall, Multiple Campus Recreation Centers, Illini Student Union, on-campus Arboretum; The Japan House; extensive athletic facilities; historic round barns; Siebel Computer Science Center; spacious green space at the Central and Bardeen Quads; Papa Dels Pizza and Za's Italian Cafe. **Environmental Initiatives:** The state-of-the-art Business Instructional Facility at the University of Illinois has earned the world's highest honor for sustainable, environmentally friendly construction and design. The year-old building is the first business facility at a public university anywhere in the world to earn platinum certification. Illinois has recently completed a Sustainability Vision process and is now implementing steps that will infuse sustainability into education, research, outreach and operations. The University's retrocommissioning team has completed nearly 2 million square feet of upgrades to campus buildings, resulting in ~10% energy reduction in 2 years.

ADMISSIONS

Freshman Academic Profile: 55% in top 10% of high school class, 89% in top 25% of high school class, 99% in top 50% of high school class. 75% from public high schools. SAT Math middle 50% range 630–740. SAT Critical Reading middle 50% range 540–670. ACT middle 50% range 26–31. Minimum paper TOEFL 550. Minimum computer TOEFL 213. Minimum web-based TOEFL 79. **Basis for Candidate Selection:** *Very important factors considered include:* Class rank, application essay, academic GPA, rigor of secondary school record, standardized test scores. *Important factors considered include:* Character/personal qualities, extracurricular activities, first generation, talent/ability, volunteer work, work experience. *Other factors considered include:* geographical residence, racial/ethnic status, state residency. **Freshman Admission Requirements:** High school diploma is required and GED is accepted. *Academic units required:* 4 English, 3 mathematics, 2 science, (2 science labs), 2 foreign language, 2 social studies, 2 academic electives, 3.5 years of mathematics including trigonometry are required in the following programs: Agricultural. **Freshman Admission Statistics:** 21,645 applied, 71% admitted, 45% enrolled. **Transfer Admission Requirements:** College transcript(s), essay or personal statement, Lowest grade transferable D. **General Admission Information:** Application fee $40. Regular application deadline 1/2. Regular notification 12/14. Nonfall registration not accepted. Admission may be deferred for a maximum of 1 year. Credit and/or placement offered for CEEB Advanced Placement tests.

COSTS AND FINANCIAL AID

Annual in-state tuition $8,502. Annual out-of-state tuition $21,895. Room and board $8,196. Required fees $2,001. Average book expense $1,200. **Required Forms and Deadlines:** FAFSA. Priority financial aid filing date 3/15. **Types of Aid:** *Need-based scholarships/grants:* Federal Pell, SEOG, state scholarships/grants, private scholarships, the school's own gift aid, United Negro College Fund. *Loans:* Direct Subsidized Stafford, Direct Unsubsidized Stafford, Direct PLUS, Federal Perkins, college/university loans from institutional funds. *Student Employment:* Federal Work-Study Program available. Institutional employment available. Highest amount earned per year from on-campus jobs $13,377. Off-campus job opportunities are excellent. **Financial Aid Statistics:** 36% freshmen, 39% undergrads receive need-based scholarship or grant aid. 13% freshmen, 12% undergrads receive non-need-based scholarship or grant aid. 34% freshmen, 36% undergrads receive need-based self-help aid. 1% freshmen, 1% undergrads receive athletic scholarships. 69% freshmen, 72% undergrads receive any aid. 51% undergrads borrow to pay for school. Average cumulative indebtedness $17,057. **Criteria for awarding institutional aid:** *Non-need-based:* Academics, alumni affiliation, art, athletics, leadership, music/drama, state/district residency.

UNIVERSITY OF THE INCARNATE WORD

4301 Broadway, Box 285, San Antonio, TX 78209-6397
Phone: 210-829-6005 **Financial Aid Phone:** 210-829-6008
E-mail: admis@uiwtx.edu **CEEB Code:** 006303
Fax: 210-829-3921 **Website:** www.uiw.edu **ACT Code:** 4106

This private school, affiliated with the Roman Catholic Church, was founded in 1881. It has a 154-acre campus.

RATINGS
Admissions Selectivity Rating: 77   **Fire Safety Rating:** 60*   **Green Rating:** 60*

STUDENTS AND FACULTY
Enrollment: 5,071. **Student Body:** 66% female, 34% male, 5% out-of-state, 2% international (48 countries represented). Asian 2%, African American 7%, Caucasian 24%, Hispanic 58%.
Retention and Graduation: 63% freshmen return for sophomore year. **Faculty:** Student/faculty ratio 13:1. 200 full-time faculty, 63% hold PhDs, 28% are members of minority groups, 54% are women.

ACADEMICS
Degrees: Associate, bachelor's, first professional, master's, post-bachelor's certificate. **Classes:** Most classes have 20–29 students. Most lab/discussion sessions have 10–19 students. **Majors with Highest Enrollment:** Business administration and management; elementary education and teaching; nursing/registered nurse (RN, ASN, BSN, MSN). **Special Study Options:** Accelerated program, cross-registration, distance learning, double major, dual enrollment, English as a Second Language (ESL), honors program, independent study, internships, student-designed major, study abroad, teacher certification program, weekend college. **Honors programs:** UIW Honors Program. **Combined degree programs:** BBA/MS—Accounting. Special programs offered to physically disabled students include note-taking services, reader services, tape recorders, tutors. **Career services:** Alumni services, career/job search classes, career assessment, internships.

FACILITIES
Housing: Coed dorms, special housing for disabled students, men's dorms, women's dorms, apartments for single students. 95% of campus accessible to physically disabled. **Computers:** 100% of classrooms, 100% of dorms, 100% of libraries, 100% of dining areas, 100% of student union, 100% of common outdoor areas have wireless network access. Students can register for classes online. Administrative functions (other than registration) can be performed online. Undergraduates are required to own a computer.

CAMPUS LIFE
Environment: Metropolis. **Activities:** Choral groups, dance, drama/theater, jazz band, literary magazine, music ensembles, musical theater, radio station, student government, student newspaper, symphony orchestra, campus ministries, international student organization. **Organizations:** 58 registered organizations, 8 honor societies, 2 religious organizations. 2 fraternities, 4 sororities. **Athletics (Intercollegiate):** *Men:* Baseball, basketball, cross-country, football, golf, soccer, swimming, tennis, track/field (outdoor). *Women:* Basketball, cross-country, golf, soccer, softball, swimming, synchronized swimming, tennis, track/field (outdoor), volleyball. **On-Campus Highlights:** Student Center, Chick-Fil-A, Library, Wellness Center, Dubuis Lawn.

ADMISSIONS
Freshman Academic Profile: Average high school GPA 3.46. 19.97% in top 10% of high school class, 48.25% in top 25% of high school class, 80.03% in top 50% of high school class. SAT Math middle 50% range 430–540. SAT Critical Reading middle 50% range 420–530. SAT Writing middle 50% range 420–520. ACT middle 50% range 17–22. Minimum paper TOEFL 560. Minimum computer TOEFL 220. Minimum web-based TOEFL 83. **Basis for Candidate**

Selection: *Very important factors considered include:* Academic GPA, rigor of secondary school record. *Important factors considered include:* Class rank, standardized test scores. *Other factors considered include:* Application essay, recommendation(s), alumni/ae relation, character/personal qualities, extracurricular activities, geographical residence, interview, level of applicant's interest, talent/ability, volunteer work, work experience. **Freshman Admission Requirements:** High school diploma is required and GED is accepted. *Academic units required:* 4 English, 3 mathematics, 3 science, 2 foreign language, 3 social studies, 1 visual/performing arts. *Academic units recommended:* 4 English, 4 mathematics, 3 science, 2 foreign language, 4 social studies, 1 visual/performing arts. **Freshman Admission Statistics:** 3,390 applied, 67% admitted, 39% enrolled. **Transfer Admission Requirements:** College transcript(s), minimum college GPA of 2.50 required. Lowest grade transferable C. **General Admission Information:** Application fee $20. Nonfall registration accepted. Admission may be deferred for a maximum of 1 term. Credit offered for CEEB Advanced Placement tests.

COSTS AND FINANCIAL AID
Annual tuition $20,400. Room and board $8,780. Required fees $890. Average book expense $1,200. **Required Forms and Deadlines:** FAFSA. Priority financial aid filing date 4/1. **Notification of Awards:** Applicants will be notified of awards on a rolling basis beginning 2/15. **Types of Aid:** *Need-based scholarships/grants:* Federal Pell, SEOG, state scholarships/grants, private scholarships, the school's own gift aid, United Negro College Fund, Federal Nursing Scholarships. *Loans:* FFEL Subsidized Stafford, FFEL Unsubsidized Stafford, FFEL PLUS, Federal Perkins, Federal Nursing, state loans. *Student Employment:* Federal Work-Study Program available. Institutional employment available. Off-campus job opportunities are good. **Financial Aid Statistics:** 61% freshmen, 61% undergrads receive need-based scholarship or grant aid. 76% freshmen, 53% undergrads receive non-need-based scholarship or grant aid. 47% freshmen, 56% undergrads receive need-based self-help aid. 4% freshmen, 4% undergrads receive athletic scholarships. 90% freshmen, 70% undergrads receive any aid. 86% undergrads borrow to pay for school. Average cumulative indebtedness $39,985. **Criteria for awarding institutional aid:** *Non-need-based:* Academics, alumni affiliation, art, athletics, leadership, music/drama, religious affiliation, state/district residency.

UNIVERSITY OF INDIANAPOLIS

1400 East Hanna Avenue, Indianapolis, IN 46227-3697
Phone: 317-788-3216 **Financial Aid Phone:** 317-788-3217
E-mail: admissions@uindy.edu **CEEB Code:** 1321
Fax: 317-788-3300 **Website:** www.uindy.edu **ACT Code:** 1204

This private school, affiliated with the Methodist Church, was founded in 1902. It has a 65-acre campus.

RATINGS
Admissions Selectivity Rating: 78   **Fire Safety Rating:** 60*   **Green Rating:** 60*

STUDENTS AND FACULTY
Enrollment: 3,734. **Student Body:** 67% female, 33% male, 11% out-of-state, 5% international (47 countries represented). Asian 1%, African American 11%, Caucasian 74%, Hispanic 2%.
Retention and Graduation: 73% freshmen return for sophomore year. 38% freshmen graduate within 4 years. **Faculty:** Student/faculty ratio 13:1. 205 full-time faculty.

ACADEMICS
Degrees: Associate, bachelor's, master's. **Classes:** Most classes have 10–19 students. Most lab/discussion sessions have 20–29 students. **Majors with Highest Enrollment:** Business/commerce; education; nursing/registered nurse (RN, ASN, BSN, MSN). **Special Study Options:** Accelerated program, cross-registration, double major, dual enrollment, English as a Second Language (ESL), honors program, independent study, internships, liberal arts/career combination, student-designed major, study abroad, teacher certification program, Spring Term Session (4-4-1). Special programs offered to physically disabled students include note-taking services, reader services, tape recorders, tutors.

FACILITIES
Housing: Coed dorms, women's dorms, apartments for married students, apartments for single students. 90% of campus accessible to physically disabled. **Special Academic Facilities/Equipment:** Developmental preschool, art gallery, observatory. **Computers:** 100% of classrooms, 100% of dorms, 100% of libraries, 100% of dining areas, 100% of student union, 100% of common outdoor areas have wireless network access.

CAMPUS LIFE

Environment: Metropolis. **Activities:** Choral groups, concert band, dance, drama/theater, jazz band, literary magazine, music ensembles, musical theater, opera, pep band, radio station, student government, student newspaper, television station, yearbook, campus ministries, international student organization. **Organizations:** 53 registered organizations, 14 honor societies, 4 religious organizations. **Athletics (Intercollegiate): Men:** Baseball, basketball, cross-country, diving, football, golf, soccer, swimming, tennis, track/field (outdoor), wrestling. **Women:** Basketball, cross-country, diving, golf, soccer, softball, swimming, tennis, track/field (outdoor), volleyball. **On-Campus Highlights:** Ruth Lilly Fitness Center, Schwitzer Center, Krannert Memorial Library, Christel Dehaan Fine Arts Center, Martin Hall.

ADMISSIONS

Freshman Academic Profile: Average high school GPA 3.36. 26% in top 10% of high school class, 59% in top 25% of high school class, 89% in top 50% of high school class. SAT Math middle 50% range 460–570. SAT Critical Reading middle 50% range 450–560. SAT Writing middle 50% range 440–550. ACT middle 50% range 19–25. Minimum paper TOEFL 500. Minimum computer TOEFL 173. **Basis for Candidate Selection:** *Very important factors considered include:* Academic GPA, rigor of secondary school record. *Important factors considered include:* Class rank, standardized test scores. *Other factors considered include:* Recommendation(s), extracurricular activities, interview. **Freshman Admission Requirements:** High school diploma is required and GED is accepted. *Academic units required:* 4 English, 3 mathematics, 3 science, (2 science labs), 2 foreign language, 1 social studies, 1 history, 1 academic electives. *Academic units recommended:* 4 English, 4 mathematics, 4 science, (3 science labs), 2 foreign language, 2 social studies, 1 history, 3 academic electives. **Freshman Admission Statistics:** 3,944 applied, 80% admitted, 24% enrolled. **Transfer Admission Requirements:** High school transcript, college transcript(s), standardized test scores, statement of good standing from prior institution(s). Minimum college GPA of 2.0 required. Lowest grade transferable C–. **General Admission Information:** Application fee $25. Notification on a rolling basis, beginning on or about 9/1. Nonfall registration accepted. Admission may be deferred for a maximum of N/A. Credit offered for CEEB Advanced Placement tests.

COSTS AND FINANCIAL AID

Required Forms and Deadlines: FAFSA, institution's own financial aid form. Priority financial aid filing date 3/10. **Notification of Awards:** Applicants will be notified of awards on a rolling basis beginning 3/1. **Types of Aid:** *Need-based scholarships/grants:* Federal Pell, SEOG, state scholarships/grants, private scholarships, the school's own gift aid. *Loans:* FFEL Subsidized Stafford, FFEL Unsubsidized Stafford, FFEL PLUS, Federal Perkins. *Student Employment:* Federal Work-Study Program available. Institutional employment available. Off-campus job opportunities are good. **Financial Aid Statistics: Criteria for awarding institutional aid:** *Non-need-based:* Academics, alumni affiliation, art, athletics, job skills, leadership, music/drama, religious affiliation, state/district residency.

UNIVERSITY OF IOWA

107 Calvin Hall, Iowa City, IA 52242
Phone: 319-335-3847 **Financial Aid Phone:** 319-335-1450
E-mail: admissions@uiowa.edu **CEEB Code:** 6681
Fax: 319-333-1535 **Website:** www.uiowa.edu **ACT Code:** 1356

This public school was founded in 1847. It has a 1900-acre campus.

RATINGS

Admissions Selectivity Rating: 81   **Fire Safety Rating:** 79   **Green Rating:** 89

STUDENTS AND FACULTY

Enrollment: 19,899. **Student Body:** 51% female, 49% male, 38% out-of-state, 4% international (116 countries represented). Asian 4%, African American 2%, Caucasian 82%, Hispanic 3%, Native American 1%.
Retention and Graduation: 83% freshmen return for sophomore year. 42% freshmen graduate within 4 years. **Faculty:** Student/faculty ratio 15:1. 1586 full-time faculty, 97% hold PhDs, 16% are members of minority groups, 31% are women.

ACADEMICS

Degrees: Bachelor's, certificate, master's, post-master's certificate. **Classes:** Most classes have 10–19 students. Most lab/discussion sessions have 20–29 students. **Majors with Highest Enrollment:** Business/commerce; engineering; psychology. **Special Study Options:** Accelerated program, cooperative education program, distance learning, double major, dual enrollment, English as a Second Language (ESL), exchange student program (domestic), external degree program, honors program, independent study, internships, liberal arts/career combination, student-designed major, study abroad, teacher certification program. **Honors programs:** The University of Iowa Honors Program is dedicated to the academic and personal enrichment of its students. This enrichment is accomplished through special academic opportunities and programs that are sponsored by the Honors Program and open to all Honors students. **Combined degree programs:** BA/MA, BA/DDS, BA/MEng, BBA/BA,BS BSE/BA, BS BSN/BA,BS. Special programs offered to physically disabled students include note-taking services, reader services, tape recorders, tutors. **Career services:** Alumni network, alumni services, career/job search classes, career assessment, internships, regional alumni. **Career services highlights include:** The University of Iowa Pomerantz Career Center is a world-class facility with a national reputation for excellence. The Center directly serves more than 20,000 students from the Henry B. Tippie College of Business, the College of Engineering, and the College of Liberal Arts and Sciences.

FACILITIES

Housing: Coed dorms, special housing for disabled students, fraternity/sorority housing, apartments for married students, apartments for single students, wellness housing, theme housing, Quiet Houses available. Living-Learning Communities for the following interests: Honors; Iowa Writers; Health Sciences; Business and Entrepreneurship, Women in Science and Engineering; Men in Engineering; performing arts; international interests; citizenship and service; Law Study and Legal Careers, Sustainability, Career Leadership Academy, Healthy Living Network, Hispanic Culture and Language. 98% of campus accessible to physically disabled. **Special Academic Facilities/Equipment:** National Advanced Driving Simulator, electron microscope, laser facility, Oakdale Research park, UI Hygienic Lab, UI Center for Biocatalysis & Bioprocessing, UI Research Foundation, survey research facilities natural history museum, Medical Museum, Old Capitol Museum, Main Library and 10 departmental libraries, information arcade, newspaper. production lab, TV lab, UI Technology Innovation Center, and Project Art. **Computers:** 100% of classrooms, 25% of dorms, 100% of libraries, 25% of dining areas, 90% of student union, 15% of common outdoor areas have wireless network access. Students can register for classes online. Administrative functions (other than registration) can be performed online.

CAMPUS LIFE

Environment: City. **Activities:** Choral groups, concert band, dance, drama/theater, jazz band, literary magazine, marching band, music ensembles, musical theater, opera, pep band, radio station, student government, student newspaper, student-run film society, symphony orchestra, television station, campus ministries, international student organization. **Organizations:** 488 registered organizations, 21 honor societies, 24 religious organizations. 18 fraternities, 18 sororities. **Athletics (Intercollegiate): Men:** Baseball, basketball, cheerleading, cross-country, diving, football, golf, gymnastics, swimming, tennis, track/field (outdoor), track/field (indoor), wrestling. **Women:** Basketball, cheerleading, crew/rowing, cross-country, diving, field hockey, golf, gymnastics, soccer, softball, swimming, tennis, track/field (outdoor), track/field (indoor), volleyball. **On-Campus Highlights:** Kinnick Stadium/Carver Hawkeye Arena, The University of Iowa Museum of Natural History, UI Recreational Services, Hawkeye Hall of Fame, UIHC Project Art. **Environmental Initiatives:** The University of Iowa's Energy Conservation and Management Plan sets aggressive targets for performance: 10% energy reduction and 15% energy from renewable sources by 2013. Investigations into renewable energies are ongoing and the UI is currently developing a 100% renewable energy power system for its research campus. The University of Iowa was one of the first institutions of higher education to sign the Chicago Climate Exchange. Under this legally-binding agreement, the UI will be required to achieve a 6% reduction in greenhouse gas emissions by 2010, based on a 1998–2001 baseline. Currently, the UI is ahead of its pace toward this goal. Any exceeding reductions will earn carbon credits, which the UI will retire permanently or sell to fund additional conservation measures. The University of Iowa is committed to integrating sustainability into its academic mission through the creation of ten new interdisciplinary faculty positions and the development of a sustainability studies certificate, available this academic year. A new sustainable living/learning community will be available to students fall 2010.

ADMISSIONS

Freshman Academic Profile: Average high school GPA 3.57. 23% in top 10% of high school class, 55% in top 25% of high school class, 91% in top 50% of high school class. 90% from public high schools. SAT Math middle 50% range 560–690. SAT Critical Reading middle 50% range 500–640. ACT middle 50%

range 23–28. Minimum paper TOEFL 530. Minimum computer TOEFL 197. Minimum web-based TOEFL 71. **Basis for Candidate Selection:** *Very important factors considered include:* Class rank, academic GPA, rigor of secondary school record, standardized test scores. *Other factors considered include:* Recommendation(s), character/personal qualities, state residency, talent/ability. **Freshman Admission Requirements:** High school diploma is required and GED is accepted. *Academic units required:* 4 English, 3 mathematics, 3 science, 2 foreign language, 3 social studies. *Academic units recommended:* 4 mathematics, 4 foreign language. **Freshman Admission Statistics:** 15,060 applied, 83% admitted, 32% enrolled. **Transfer Admission Requirements:** High school transcript, college transcript(s), minimum college GPA of 2.5 required. Lowest grade transferable D. **General Admission Information:** Application fee $40. Regular application deadline 4/1. Notification on a rolling basis, beginning on or about 9/15. Nonfall registration accepted. Admission may be deferred for a maximum of 12. Credit and/or placement offered for CEEB Advanced Placement tests.

COSTS AND FINANCIAL AID

Annual in-state tuition $5,782. Annual out-of-state tuition $21,156. Room and board $8,004. Required fees $1,042. Average book expense $1,090. **Required Forms and Deadlines:** FAFSA, institution's own financial aid form **Notification of Awards:** Applicants will be notified of awards on a rolling basis beginning 3/15. **Types of Aid:** *Need-based scholarships/grants:* Federal Pell, SEOG, state scholarships/grants, private scholarships, the school's own gift aid. *Loans:* Direct Subsidized Stafford, Direct Unsubsidized Stafford, Direct PLUS, Federal Perkins, Federal Nursing, college/university loans from institutional funds, short term. *Student Employment:* Federal Work-Study Program available. Institutional employment available. Highest amount earned per year from on-campus jobs $7,200. Off-campus job opportunities are good. **Financial Aid Statistics:** 32% freshmen, 30% undergrads receive need-based scholarship or grant aid. 26% freshmen, 17% undergrads receive non-need-based scholarship or grant aid. 39% freshmen, 42% undergrads receive need-based self-help aid. 2% freshmen, 2% undergrads receive athletic scholarships. 80% freshmen, 82% undergrads receive any aid. 61% undergrads borrow to pay for school. Average cumulative indebtedness $22,856. **Criteria for awarding institutional aid:** *Non-need-based:* Academics, alumni affiliation, art, athletics, leadership, minority status, music/drama.

UNIVERSITY OF KANSAS

Best 373

Office of Admissions and Scholarships, 1502 Iowa Street, Lawrence, KS 66045-7576
Phone: 785-864-3911 **Financial Aid Phone:** 785-864-4700
E-mail: adm@ku.edu **CEEB Code:** 6871
Fax: 785-864-5017 **Website:** www.ku.edu **ACT Code:** 1470

This public school was founded in 1866. It has a 1100-acre campus.

RATINGS
Admissions Selectivity Rating: 82   **Fire Safety Rating:** 81   **Green Rating:** 81

STUDENTS AND FACULTY
Enrollment: 20,755. **Student Body:** 50% female, 50% male, 22% out-of-state, 4% international (108 countries represented). Asian 4%, African American 4%, Caucasian 80%, Hispanic 4%, Native American 1%.
Retention and Graduation: 78% freshmen return for sophomore year. 38% grads go on to further study within 1 year. **Faculty:** Student/faculty ratio 19:1. 1246 full-time faculty, 97% hold PhDs, 17% are members of minority groups, 37% are women. 18% of classes are taught by teaching assistants.

ACADEMICS
Degrees: Bachelor's, master's, post-master's certificate. **Classes:** Most classes have 20–29 students. Most lab/discussion sessions have 10–19 students. **Majors with Highest Enrollment:** Biology/biological sciences; business/commerce; psychology. **Special Study Options:** Accelerated program, cooperative education program, distance learning, double major, dual enrollment, English as a Second Language (ESL), honors program, independent study, internships, liberal arts/career combination, study abroad, teacher certification program, Off Campus Study: Washington DC semester; Study abroad in over 60 countries. **Honors programs:** The University Honors Program gives outstanding and creative students opportunities for intellectual growth and achievement through its small, challenging classes. web site at www.honors.ku.edu Special programs offered to physically disabled students include note-taking services, reader services, tape recorders, tutors. **Career services:** Career/job search classes, career

assessment, internships. **Career services highlights include:** Alternative Breaks, In the Streets Week, Center for Community Outreach.

FACILITIES
Housing: Coed dorms, women's dorms, fraternity/sorority housing, apartments for married students, cooperative housing, apartments for single students 95% of campus accessible to physically disabled. **Special Academic Facilities/Equipment:** 12 libraries (including art and architecture, engineering, law, medical, music and dance, rare research materials, special collections, and science), performing arts center, organ recital hall, museums (art, anthropology, classical, entomology, invertebrate paleontology, and natural history), film studio, student operated radio and television stations, public radio station, herbarium, space technology center, observatory, Robert J. Dole Institute for Politics, Hall Center for the Humanities, Center for International Business Education and Research, ecological reserves, Biological Survey, Geological Survey, Information and Telecommunication Technology Center, energy research center, flight research lab, Transportation Research Center, 400+ bed hospital for clinical learning, Hoglund Brain Imaging Center, Center on Aging.

CAMPUS LIFE
Environment: City. **Activities:** Choral groups, concert band, dance, drama/theater, jazz band, literary magazine, marching band, music ensembles, musical theater, opera, pep band, radio station, student government, student newspaper, symphony orchestra, television station, international student organization. **Organizations:** 476 registered organizations, 14 honor societies, 39 religious organizations. 27 fraternities, 16 sororities. **Athletics (Intercollegiate):** *Men:* Baseball, basketball, cross-country, football, golf, track/field (outdoor), track/field (indoor). *Women:* Basketball, crew/rowing, cross-country, diving, golf, soccer, softball, swimming, tennis, track/field (outdoor), track/field (indoor), volleyball. **On-Campus Highlights:** Spencer Museum of Art, Kansas Union and Bookstore, Natural History Museum, Athletic Hall of Fame, Robert J. Dole Institute of Politics, Beautiful campus to walk around. **Environmental Initiatives:** In 2008, a Renewable Energy and Sustainability student fee was established. The first projects were funded in 2009 and include:—ReRev Regeneration devices for energy generation on KU Rec Center elliptical exercise machines, including a display unit showing amounts of energy produced and raising student awareness—Wind Credit purchase to offset the electricity usage of Anschutz Library for 1 year—Helping to fund an earth day speaker on sustainable energy—Insulation for steam delivery system Students from Environmental Studies, Architecture, and Engineering worked University staff and professionals to design and construct a 5,200 sq. ft. raingarden to absorb rainwater runoff from the Student Recreation Center; this pilot project should help promote more sustainable landscaping and storm water management practices. (www.sustainability.ku.edu/raingarden/) KU faculty and researchers conduct research that addresses transportation (www.kutri.ku.edu), the use and development of alternative fuels (www2.ku.edu/~features/biodiesel, www.cebc.ku.edu), measuring ice sheets (www.cresis.ku.edu) and other environmental issues.

ADMISSIONS
Freshman Academic Profile: Average high school GPA 3.4. 27% in top 10% of high school class, 57% in top 25% of high school class, 88% in top 50% of high school class. ACT middle 50% range 22–27. **Basis for Candidate Selection:** *Very important factors considered include:* Class rank, academic GPA, standardized test scores. **Freshman Admission Requirements:** High school diploma is required and GED is accepted. *Academic units required:* 4 English, 3 mathematics, 3 science, 3 social studies. *Academic units recommended:* 4 English, 4 mathematics, 3 science, 2 foreign language, 3 social studies. **Freshman Admission Statistics:** 10,653 applied, 91% admitted, 40% enrolled. **Transfer Admission Requirements:** College transcript(s), minimum college GPA of 2.5 required. Lowest grade transferable C. **General Admission Information:** Application fee $30. Regular application deadline 4/1. Notification on a rolling basis, beginning on or about 9/1. Nonfall registration accepted. Credit and/or placement offered for CEEB Advanced Placement tests.

COSTS AND FINANCIAL AID
Annual in-state tuition $6,567. Annual out-of-state tuition $17,250. Room and board $6,802. Required fees $847. Average book expense $800. **Required Forms and Deadlines:** FAFSA. Priority financial aid filing date 3/1. **Notification of Awards:** Applicants will be notified of awards on a rolling basis beginning 4/1. **Types of Aid:** *Need-based scholarships/grants:* Federal Pell, SEOG, state scholarships/grants, private scholarships, the school's own gift aid. *Loans:* Direct Subsidized Stafford, Direct Unsubsidized Stafford, Direct PLUS, FFEL Subsidized Stafford, FFEL Unsubsidized Stafford, FFEL PLUS, Federal Perkins, college/university loans from institutional funds. *Student Employment:* Federal Work-Study Program available. Institutional employment available. Highest amount earned per year from on-campus jobs $4,800. Off-campus job opportunities are excellent. **Financial Aid Statistics:** 25% freshmen, 25% undergrads receive need-based scholarship or grant aid. 17% freshmen, 12% undergrads receive non-need-based scholarship or grant aid. 30% freshmen, 32% undergrads receive need-based self-help aid. 2% freshmen, 2% undergrads

receive athletic scholarships. 60% freshmen, 51% undergrads receive any aid. 45% undergrads borrow to pay for school. Average cumulative indebtedness $22,478. **Criteria for awarding institutional aid:** *Non-need-based:* Academics, alumni affiliation, art, athletics, leadership, minority status, music/drama, state/district residency.

UNIVERSITY OF KENTUCKY

100 Funkhouser Building, Lexington, KY 40506
Phone: 859-257-2000 **Financial Aid Phone:** 859-257-3172
E-mail: admissions@uky.edu **CEEB Code:** 1837
Fax: 859-257-3823 **Website:** www.uky.edu **ACT Code:** 1554

This public school was founded in 1865. It has a 687-acre campus.

RATINGS
Admissions Selectivity Rating: 81   **Fire Safety Rating:** 82   **Green Rating:** 60*

STUDENTS AND FACULTY
Enrollment: 18,591. **Student Body:** 50% female, 50% male, 21% out-of-state, 1% international (117 countries represented). Asian 2%, African American 7%, Caucasian 87%, Hispanic 1%.
Retention and Graduation: 81% freshmen return for sophomore year. 29% freshmen graduate within 4 years. **Faculty:** Student/faculty ratio 18:1. 1265 full-time faculty, 92% hold PhDs, 17% are members of minority groups, 33% are women. 20% of classes are taught by teaching assistants.

ACADEMICS
Degrees: Bachelor's, certificate, first professional, master's. **Classes:** Most classes have 20–29 students. Most lab/discussion sessions have 20–29 students. **Special Study Options:** Accelerated program, cooperative education program, distance learning, double major, English as a Second Language (ESL), exchange student program (domestic), honors program, independent study, internships, study abroad, teacher certification program, weekend college **Combined degree programs:** BA/MA, JD/MBA. Special programs offered to physically disabled students include note-taking services, reader services

FACILITIES
Housing: Coed dorms, special housing for disabled students, men's dorms, special housing for international students, women's dorms, fraternity/sorority housing, apartments for married students, apartments for single students. 95% of campus accessible to physically disabled. **Special Academic Facilities/Equipment:** Anthropology and art museums, center for the humanities, centers for equine research, cancer research, and robotics, pharmacy manufacturing lab. **Computers:** 30% of classrooms, 10% of dorms, 100% of libraries, 80% of dining areas, 70% of student union, 50% of common outdoor areas have wireless network access. Students can register for classes online. Administrative functions (other than registration) can be performed online.

CAMPUS LIFE
Environment: City. **Activities:** Choral groups, concert band, dance, drama/theater, jazz band, literary magazine, marching band, music ensembles, musical theater, opera, pep band, radio station, student government, student newspaper, symphony orchestra, yearbook, international student organization. **Organizations:** 348 registered organizations, 28 honor societies, 20 religious organizations, 19 fraternities, 16 sororities. **Athletics (Intercollegiate):** *Men:* Baseball, basketball, cheerleading, cross-country, diving, football, golf, riflery, soccer, swimming, tennis, track/field (outdoor), track/field (indoor). *Women:* Basketball, cheerleading, cross-country, diving, golf, gymnastics, riflery, soccer, softball, swimming, tennis, track/field (outdoor), track/field (indoor), volleyball. **On-Campus Highlights:** W.T. Young Library, Johnson Fitness Center, Memorial Coliseum, Arboretum, Memorial Hall.

ADMISSIONS
Freshman Academic Profile: Average high school GPA 3.4. 26% in top 10% of high school class, 54% in top 25% of high school class, 82% in top 50% of high school class. SAT Math middle 50% range 500–630. SAT Critical Reading middle 50% range 490–610. SAT Writing middle 50% range 480–600. ACT middle 50% range 22–27. Minimum paper TOEFL 527. Minimum computer TOEFL 197. **Basis for Candidate Selection:** *Very important factors considered include:* Academic GPA, rigor of secondary school record, standardized test scores, *Other factors considered include:* Class rank, application essay, recommendation(s), alumni/ae relation, character/personal qualities, extracurricular activities, first generation, geographical residence, interview, racial/

ethnic status, talent/ability, volunteer work. **Freshman Admission Requirements:** High school diploma is required and GED is accepted. *Academic units required:* 4 English, 3 mathematics, 3 science, 2 foreign language, 3 social studies, 5 academic electives, 2 fine or performing arts (1), health (.5), and physical ed. (.5). *Academic units recommended:* 4 English, 4 mathematics, 4 science, 2 foreign language, 3 social studies, 3 academic electives, 2 fine or performing arts (1), health (.5), and physical ed. (.5). **Freshman Admission Statistics:** 11,120 applied, 79% admitted, 47% enrolled. **Transfer Admission Requirements:** College transcript(s), minimum college GPA of 2.0 required. Lowest grade transferable D. **General Admission Information:** Application fee $50. Regular application deadline 2/15. Notification on a rolling basis, beginning on or about 10/1. Nonfall registration accepted. Admission may be deferred for a maximum of 1 year. Credit and/or placement offered for CEEB Advanced Placement tests.

COSTS AND FINANCIAL AID
Annual in-state tuition $7,214. Annual out-of-state tuition $15,769. Room and board $9,125. Required fees $909. Average book expense $800. **Required Forms and Deadlines:** FAFSA. Financial aid filing deadline 2/15. Priority financial aid filing date 2/15. **Notification of Awards:** Applicants will be notified of awards on a rolling basis beginning 4/1. **Types of Aid:** *Need-based scholarships/grants:* Federal Pell, SEOG, state scholarships/grants, private scholarships, the school's own gift aid. *Loans:* Direct Subsidized Stafford, Direct Unsubsidized Stafford, Direct PLUS, FFEL Subsidized Stafford, FFEL Unsubsidized Stafford, FFEL PLUS, Federal Perkins, state loans, college/university loans from institutional funds. *Student Employment:* Federal Work-Study Program available. **Financial Aid Statistics:** 18% freshmen, 18% undergrads receive need-based scholarship or grant aid. 41% freshmen, 27% undergrads receive non-need-based scholarship or grant aid. 28% freshmen, 28% undergrads receive need-based self-help aid. 3% freshmen, 3% undergrads receive athletic scholarships. 40% freshmen, 38% undergrads receive any aid. 33% undergrads borrow to pay for school. Average cumulative indebtedness $15,891. **Criteria for awarding institutional aid:** *Non-need-based:* Academics, alumni affiliation, art, athletics, job skills, leadership, minority status, music/drama, state/district residency.

UNIVERSITY OF KING'S COLLEGE

Registrars Office, Halifax, NS B3H 2A1 Canada
Phone: 902-422-1271
E-mail: admissions@ukings.ns.ca
Fax: 902-423-3357 **Website:** www.ukings.ca

This public school was founded in 1789. It has a 3-acre campus.

RATINGS
Admissions Selectivity Rating: 60*   **Fire Safety Rating:** 60*   **Green Rating:** 60*

STUDENTS AND FACULTY
Enrollment: 1,137. **Student Body:** 57% female, 43% male, 53% out-of-state, international (6 countries represented).
Retention and Graduation: Faculty: Student/faculty ratio 25:1. 51 full-time faculty, 71% hold PhDs, 31% are women.

ACADEMICS
Degrees: Bachelor's. **Majors with Highest Enrollment:** English language and literature; psychology; sociology. **Special Study Options:** Cooperative education program, double major, honors program, internships, study abroad. **Career services:** Career/job search classes, career assessment.

FACILITIES
Housing: Coed dorms, men's dorms, women's dorms. **Computers:** Students can register for classes online. Administrative functions (other than registration) can be performed online.

CAMPUS LIFE
Environment: Metropolis. **Activities:** Choral groups, dance, drama/theater, literary magazine, radio station, student government, student newspaper, student-run film society, yearbook. **Athletics (Intercollegiate):** *Men:* Badminton, basketball, soccer, volleyball. *Women:* Badminton, basketball, soccer, volleyball. **On-Campus Highlights:** The Pit, The Wardroom, The Manning Room, The Library, The Quad.

ADMISSIONS
Freshman Academic Profile: Minimum paper TOEFL 580. Minimum computer TOEFL 237. **Basis for Candidate Selection:** *Very important factors considered include:* Rigor of secondary school record, standardized test scores. **Freshman Admission Requirements:** High school diploma is required

and GED is not accepted. **Freshman Admission Statistics:** 1,043 applied, 41% admitted, 83% enrolled. **Transfer Admission Requirements:** College transcript(s), lowest grade transferable C. **General Admission Information:** Application fee $45. Regular application deadline 6/1. Notification on a rolling basis, beginning on or about 3/1. Nonfall registration not accepted. Admission may be deferred for a maximum of 1 year.

COSTS AND FINANCIAL AID
Average book expense $1,000. *Student Employment:* Off-campus job opportunities are good.

UNIVERSITY OF LA VERNE

1950 Third Street, La Verne, CA 91750
Phone: 909-392-2800 **Financial Aid Phone:** 1-800-649-0160
E-mail: admissions@ulv.edu **CEEB Code:** 4381
Fax: 909-392-2714 **Website:** www.laverne.edu **ACT Code:** 295

This private school was founded in 1891. It has a 38-acre campus.

RATINGS
Admissions Selectivity Rating: 85   **Fire Safety Rating:** 66   **Green Rating:** 90

STUDENTS AND FACULTY
Enrollment: 1,507. **Student Body:** 59% female, 41% male, 1% out-of-state, 1% international (12 countries represented). Asian 4%, African American 7%, Caucasian 26%, Hispanic 39%, Native American 1%. **Retention and Graduation:** 78% freshmen return for sophomore year. 43% freshmen graduate within 4 years. **Faculty:** Student/faculty ratio 12:1. 190 full-time faculty, 86% hold PhDs, 19% are members of minority groups, 47% are women.

ACADEMICS
Degrees: Associate, bachelor's, certificate, master's, post-bachelor's certificate. **Classes:** Most classes have 10–19 students. Most lab/discussion sessions have fewer than 10 students. **Majors with Highest Enrollment:** Business/commerce; liberal arts and sciences/liberal studies; psychology. **Special Study Options:** Distance learning, double major, English as a Second Language (ESL), exchange student program (domestic), honors program, independent study, internships, liberal arts/career combination, student-designed major, study abroad, teacher certification program, weekend college. **Honors programs:** For students who have demonstrated exceptional academic achievement and motivation, the ULV Honors Program offers increased opportunities for intellectual and personal growth. Participants in the Honors Program can enrich their undergraduate experience through a special Honors curriculum that emphasizes critical thinking skills and the integration of knowledge from various disciplines, through individualized attention from faculty mentors, and through community outreach activities and cultural programs. All eligible undergraduate students, regardless of major, are invited to apply, but participation in the program is completely voluntary. Students who complete the entire program receive the designation "Honors Program Graduate" on their diplomas and transcripts. Students who complete a minimum of two Interdisciplinary Seminars and a total of at least 10 units in Honors receive the designation "Honors Program Participant" on their transcripts. Besides these benefits, students in the program also receive specialized academic advising, greater opportunities for original research and study, and additional enrichment activities, including guest lectures. They may also be eligible for Honors Scholarships. The Honors Center, available to Honors Program students, offers a study lounge, computer laboratory, and a seminar room. **Combined degree programs:** JD/MBA. Special programs offered to physically disabled students include note-taking services, reader services, tape recorders, tutors. **Career services:** career/job search classes, career assessment, internships. **Career services highlights include:** Career Services has numerous internship listings in all career fields.

FACILITIES
Housing: Coed dorms, special housing for disabled students, women's dorms. 95% of campus accessible to physically disabled. **Special Academic Facilities/Equipment:** Greenhouse and Animal Care Facility; Montana Field Station—Magpie Ranch; Jeagar science specimen Museum; Photography and Art galleries. **Computers:** 100% of classrooms, 100% of dorms, 100% of libraries, 100% of dining areas, 100% of student union, 100% of common outdoor areas have wireless network access. Students can register for classes online. Administrative functions (other than registration) can be performed online.

CAMPUS LIFE
Environment: Town. **Activities:** Choral groups, dance, drama/theater, literary magazine, music ensembles, musical theater, radio station, student government, student newspaper, student-run film society, television station, campus minis-

tries, international student organization, Model UN. **Organizations:** 40 registered organizations, 2 honor societies, 1 religious organizations. 3 fraternities, 6 sororities. **Athletics (Intercollegiate):** *Men:* Baseball, basketball, cross-country, diving, football, golf, soccer, swimming, tennis, track/field (outdoor), water polo. *Women:* Basketball, cross-country, diving, soccer, softball, swimming, tennis, track/field (outdoor), volleyball, water polo. **On-Campus Highlights:** Campus Center, Sneaky Park (outdoor events), Davenport Dining Hall, Dailey Theater (Fine Arts Performances), University Quad. **Environmental Initiatives:** Recycling Program; Energy Management: central cooler, lighting fixtures; Water Conservation: plumbing fixtures, irrigation, xeriscaping.

ADMISSIONS
Freshman Academic Profile: Average high school GPA 3.32. 24.3% in top 10% of high school class, 54.8% in top 25% of high school class, 84.8% in top 50% of high school class. SAT Math middle 50% range 440–560. SAT Critical Reading middle 50% range 440–550. SAT Writing middle 50% range 430–540. ACT middle 50% range 17–23. Minimum paper TOEFL 500. Minimum computer TOEFL 173. **Basis for Candidate Selection:** *Very important factors considered include:* Application essay, academic GPA, recommendation(s), rigor of secondary school record, standardized test scores, character/personal qualities. *Important factors considered include:* Class rank, extracurricular activities. *Other factors considered include:* Alumni/ae relation, first generation, interview, level of applicant's interest, racial/ethnic status, talent/ability, volunteer work, work experience. **Freshman Admission Requirements:** High school diploma is required and GED is accepted. *Academic units required:* 4 English, 3 mathematics, 2 science, (1 science labs), 2 social studies, 3 history. *Academic units recommended:* 4 English, 4 mathematics, 2 science, (2 science labs), 2 foreign language, 2 social studies, 3 history, 2 academic electives. **Freshman Admission Statistics:** 1,452 applied, 68% admitted, 34% enrolled. **Transfer Admission Requirements:** College transcript(s), essay or personal statement, minimum college GPA of 2.7 required. Lowest grade transferable C–. **General Admission Information:** Application fee $50. Notification on a rolling basis, beginning on or about 12/1. Nonfall registration accepted. Admission may be deferred for a maximum of 1 year. Credit and/or placement offered for CEEB Advanced Placement tests.

COSTS AND FINANCIAL AID
Annual tuition $29,800. Room and board $10,440. Average book expense $1,638. **Required Forms and Deadlines:** FAFSA, state aid form. Priority financial aid filing date 3/2. **Notification of Awards:** Applicants will be notified of awards on a rolling basis beginning 3/17. **Types of Aid:** *Need-based scholarships/grants:* Federal Pell, SEOG, state scholarships/grants, private scholarships, the school's own gift aid. *Loans:* FFEL Subsidized Stafford, FFEL Unsubsidized Stafford, FFEL PLUS, Federal Perkins, college/university loans from institutional funds, Private Alternative Loans. *Student Employment:* Federal Work-Study Program available. **Financial Aid Statistics:** 57% freshmen, 71% undergrads receive need-based scholarship or grant aid. 83% freshmen, 72% undergrads receive non-need-based scholarship or grant aid. 74% freshmen, 78% undergrads receive need-based self-help aid. 83% freshmen, 83% undergrads receive any aid. 83% undergrads borrow to pay for school. Average cumulative indebtedness $25,491. **Criteria for awarding institutional aid:** *Non-need-based:* Academics, alumni affiliation, art, leadership, minority status, music/drama, religious affiliation.

THE UNIVERSITY OF LETHBRIDGE

4401 University Drive, Lethbridge, AB T1K 3M4 Canada
Phone: 403-320-5700 **Financial Aid Phone:** 403-3292585
E-mail: inquiries@uleth.ca
Fax: 403-329-5159 **Website:** www.uleth.ca **ACT Code:** 5202

This public school was founded in 1967. It has a 568-acre campus.

RATINGS
Admissions Selectivity Rating: 60*   **Fire Safety Rating:** 60*   **Green Rating:** 60*

STUDENTS AND FACULTY
Student Body: 12% out-of-state.
Retention and Graduation: Faculty: Student/faculty ratio 15:1.

ACADEMICS
Degrees: Bachelor's, certificate, diploma, doctoral, master's, post-bachelor's certificate. **Classes:** Most classes have 10–19 students. Most lab/discussion sessions have 10–19 students. **Majors with Highest Enrollment:** Accounting; business administration and management; kinesiology and exercise science. **Special Study Options:** Accelerated program, cooperative education program, double major, English as a Second Language (ESL), exchange student program (domestic), honors program, independent study, internships, student-designed

major, study abroad, teacher certification program, Applied Studies. **Combined degree programs:** BA or BSc/BEd, BA or BSc/BMgt, BMgt/Bed. Special programs offered to physically disabled students include note-taking services, reader services, tape recorders, tutors. **Career services:** Alumni services, career/job search classes, career assessment, internships.

FACILITIES
Housing: Coed dorms, special housing for disabled students, apartments for married students, apartments for single students, townhouses for single and married students and students with families. 100% of campus accessible to physically disabled. **Special Academic Facilities/Equipment:** Art Gallery, Theatres. **Computers:** 100% of classrooms, 100% of libraries, 100% of dining areas, 100% of student union, have wireless network access. Students can register for classes online. Administrative functions (other than registration) can be performed online.

CAMPUS LIFE
Environment: City. **Activities:** Choral groups, dance, drama/theater, jazz band, literary magazine, music ensembles, musical theater, radio station, student government, student newspaper, student-run film society, symphony orchestra, international student organization. **Organizations:** 1 fraternities, 1 sororities. **Athletics (Intercollegiate):** *Men:* Basketball, ice hockey, soccer, swimming, track/field (outdoor). *Women:* Basketball, ice hockey, rugby, soccer, swimming, track/field (outdoor).

ADMISSIONS
Freshman Academic Profile: Minimum paper TOEFL 550. Minimum computer TOEFL 213. Minimum web-based TOEFL 80. **Basis for Candidate Selection:** *Very important factors considered include:* Rigor of secondary school record. *Other factors considered include:* Class rank, standardized test scores. **Freshman Admission Requirements:** High school diploma is required and GED is not accepted. **Freshman Admission Statistics:** 2,228 applied, 58% admitted, 80% enrolled. **Transfer Admission Requirements:** College transcript(s). **General Admission Information:** Application fee $75. Regular application deadline 6/1. Nonfall registration accepted. Admission may be deferred for a maximum of 1 semester.

COSTS AND FINANCIAL AID
Annual in-state tuition $4,910. Room and board $6,652. Required fees $649. *Student Employment:* Institutional employment available. Off-campus job opportunities are good. **Financial Aid Statistics:** 35% freshmen receive any aid.

UNIVERSITY OF LOUISIANA AT LAFAYETTE

Best 373

P.O. Drawer 41210, Lafayette, LA 70504
Phone: 337-482-6553 **Financial Aid Phone:** 337-482-6506
E-mail: enroll@louisiana.edu **CEEB Code:** 6672
Fax: 337-482-1112 **Website:** www.louisiana.edu **ACT Code:** 1612

This public school was founded in 1898. It has a 1375-acre campus.

RATINGS
Admissions Selectivity Rating: 74   **Fire Safety Rating:** 87   **Green Rating:** 60*

STUDENTS AND FACULTY
Enrollment: 14,240. **Student Body:** 58% female, 42% male, 4% out-of-state, 2% international (97 countries represented). Asian 2%, African American 19%, Caucasian 74%, Hispanic 2%.
Retention and Graduation: 74% freshmen return for sophomore year. 12% freshmen graduate within 4 years. **Faculty:** Student/faculty ratio 23:1. 591 full-time faculty, 74% hold PhDs, 15% are members of minority groups, 42% are women.

ACADEMICS
Degrees: Bachelor's, doctoral, master's, post-master's certificate. **Classes:** Most classes have 20–29 students. **Majors with Highest Enrollment:** Biology/biological sciences; business administration and management; nursing/registered nurse (RN, ASN, BSN, MSN). **Special Study Options:** Accelerated program, cooperative education program, cross-registration, distance learning, double major, dual enrollment, exchange student program (domestic), honors program, independent study, internships, student-designed major, study abroad, teacher certification program. **Honors programs:** Honors Baccalaureate degree is available. Special programs offered to physically disabled students include

note-taking services, reader services, tape recorders, tutors. **Career services:** Career/job search classes, career assessment.

FACILITIES
Housing: Men's dorms, women's dorms, fraternity/sorority housing, apartments for married students, apartments for single students. 85% of campus accessible to physically disabled. **Special Academic Facilities/Equipment:** Art museum, experimental farm, primate center, CAD/CAM laboratory, marine research facility, on campus restaurant and hotel with instructional facilities, 2 nuclear accelerators, 2 electron microscopes, radio station and television production studio, nursery school laboratory, Louisiana Emersive Technologies Enterprise. **Computers:** Students can register for classes online. Administrative functions (other than registration) can be performed online.

CAMPUS LIFE
Environment: City. **Activities:** Choral groups, concert band, dance, drama/theater, jazz band, literary magazine, marching band, music ensembles, musical theater, opera, radio station, student government, student newspaper, symphony orchestra, yearbook, campus ministries, international student organization. **Organizations:** 155 registered organizations, 14 honor societies, 8 religious organizations. 11 fraternities, 9 sororities. **Athletics (Intercollegiate):** *Men:* Baseball, basketball, cheerleading, cross-country, football, golf, tennis, track/field (outdoor), track/field (indoor). *Women:* Basketball, cheerleading, cross-country, soccer, softball, tennis, track/field (outdoor), track/field (indoor), volleyball. **On-Campus Highlights:** University Museum, Student Center, Cajun Field, Cajundome, Dupre Library.

ADMISSIONS
Freshman Academic Profile: Average high school GPA 3.23. 15% in top 10% of high school class, 39% in top 25% of high school class, 73% in top 50% of high school class. ACT middle 50% range 20–24. Minimum paper TOEFL 525. Minimum computer TOEFL 195. **Basis for Candidate Selection:** *Very important factors considered include:* Class rank, academic GPA, rigor of secondary school record, standardized test scores, *Other factors considered include:* State residency. **Freshman Admission Requirements:** High school diploma is required and GED is accepted. *Academic units required:* 4 English, 4 mathematics, 3 science, 2 foreign language, 1 social studies, 2 history, 1 visual/performing arts, 1 computer science/literacy. **Freshman Admission Statistics:** 7,634 applied, 68% admitted, 50% enrolled. **Transfer Admission Requirements:** College transcript(s), Lowest grade transferable D. **General Admission Information:** Application fee $25. Nonfall registration accepted. Admission may be deferred for a maximum of 1 semester. Credit and/or placement offered for CEEB Advanced Placement tests.

COSTS AND FINANCIAL AID
Annual in-state tuition $3,574. Annual out-of-state tuition $9,754. Room and board $4,200. Average book expense $1,200. **Required Forms and Deadlines:** FAFSA. Priority financial aid filing date 5/1. **Notification of Awards:** Applicants will be notified of awards on a rolling basis beginning 4/1. **Types of Aid:** *Need-based scholarships/grants:* Federal Pell, SEOG, state scholarships/grants, private scholarships, the school's own gift aid, Federal Nursing Scholarships. *Loans:* FFEL Subsidized Stafford, FFEL Unsubsidized Stafford, FFEL PLUS, Federal Perkins, Federal Nursing *Student Employment:* Federal Work-Study Program available. Institutional employment available. Off-campus job opportunities are good. **Financial Aid Statistics:** 46% freshmen, 41% undergrads receive need-based scholarship or grant aid. 9% freshmen, 4% undergrads receive non-need-based scholarship or grant aid. 22% freshmen, 30% undergrads receive need-based self-help aid. 2% freshmen, 3% undergrads receive athletic scholarships. 87% freshmen, 72% undergrads receive any aid.

THE UNIVERSITY OF LOUISIANA AT MONROE

700 University Avenue, Monroe, LA 71209
Phone: 318-342-5252
E-mail: hood@ulm.edu **CEEB Code:** 6482
Fax: 318-342-5274 **Website:** www.ulm.edu **ACT Code:** 1598

This public school was founded in 1931. It has a 238-acre campus.

RATINGS
Admissions Selectivity Rating: 60*   **Fire Safety Rating:** 60*   **Green Rating:** 60*

STUDENTS AND FACULTY
Enrollment: 8,542. **Student Body:** 61% female, 39% male, 7% out-of-state, 1% international (47 countries represented). Asian 3%, African American 27%, Caucasian 95%, Hispanic 1%.
Retention and Graduation: 8% freshmen graduate within 4 years. **Faculty:** Student/faculty ratio 17:1.

ACADEMICS

Degrees: Associate, bachelor's, certificate, master's, post-master's certificate.
Classes: Special Study Options: Accelerated program, cooperative education program, distance learning, English as a Second Language (ESL), honors program, internships, teacher certification program. Special programs offered to physically disabled students include note-taking services, reader services, tape recorders. **Career services:** Career/job search classes.

FACILITIES

Housing: Coed dorms, men's dorms, women's dorms, fraternity/sorority housing. 95% of campus accessible to physically disabled. **Special Academic Facilities/Equipment:** Agricultural farm lab, soil/plant analysis lab, climatic research center, herbarium, pre-school child lab, educational media center, cancer research center.

CAMPUS LIFE

Environment: Village. **Activities:** Choral groups, concert band, dance, drama/theater, jazz band, literary magazine, marching band, music ensembles, musical theater, pep band, radio station, student government, student newspaper, television station, yearbook. **Organizations:** 128 registered organizations, 22 honor societies, 11 religious organizations. 8 fraternities, 8 sororities. **Athletics (Intercollegiate):** *Men:* Baseball, basketball, cross-country, soccer, tennis. *Women:* Basketball, cross-country, soccer, softball, tennis, volleyball.

ADMISSIONS

Freshman Academic Profile: ACT middle 50% range 16–22. **Freshman Admission Requirements: Freshman Admission Statistics:** 2,657 applied, 92% admitted, 74% enrolled. **Transfer Admission Requirements:** High school transcript, college transcript(s), **General Admission Information:** Application fee $15. Notification on a rolling basis, beginning on or about 4/1. Nonfall registration accepted.

COSTS AND FINANCIAL AID

Annual in-state tuition $1,644. Annual out-of-state tuition $2,400. Room and board $3,380. Required fees $282. Average book expense $668. **Required Forms and Deadlines:** FAFSA. **Types of Aid:** *Need-based scholarships/grants:* Federal Pell, private scholarships, the school's own gift aid. *Student Employment:* Federal Work-Study Program available. Highest amount earned per year from on-campus jobs $1,000. Off-campus job opportunities are good.

UNIVERSITY OF LOUISVILLE

Admissions Office, University of Louisville, Louisville, KY 40292
Phone: 502-852-6531 **Financial Aid Phone:** 502-852-5511
E-mail: admitme@louisville.edu
Fax: 502-852-4776 **Website:** www.louisville.edu **ACT Code:** 1556

This public school was founded in 1798. It has a 274-acre campus.

RATINGS

Admissions Selectivity Rating: 80   **Fire Safety Rating:** 60*   **Green Rating:** 60*

STUDENTS AND FACULTY

Enrollment: 14,591. **Student Body:** 51% female, 49% male, 16% out-of-state, 1% international. Asian 3%, African American 13%, Caucasian 79%, Hispanic 2%.
Retention and Graduation: 78% freshmen return for sophomore year. **Faculty:** Student/faculty ratio 17:1. 802 full-time faculty, 89% hold PhDs, 18% are members of minority groups, 37% are women.

ACADEMICS

Degrees: Associate, bachelor's, certificate, diploma, doctoral, master's, post-bachelor's certificate, post-master's certificate, terminal associate, transfer associate. **Classes:** Most classes have 20–29 students. **Special Study Options:** Accelerated program, cooperative education program, cross-registration, distance learning, double major, dual enrollment, English as a Second Language (ESL), honors program, independent study, internships, student-designed major, study abroad, teacher certification program. **Combined degree programs:** BS-BA/MBA. Special programs offered to physically disabled students include note-taking services, reader services, tape recorders, tutors.

FACILITIES

Housing: Coed dorms, special housing for disabled students, fraternity/sorority housing, apartments for married students, cooperative housing, apartments for single students, theme housing. 100% of campus accessible to physically disabled. **Special Academic Facilities/Equipment:** Natural history and art museums, planetarium, numerous institutes and centers. **Computers:** Administrative functions (other than registration) can be performed online.

CAMPUS LIFE

Environment: Metropolis. **Activities:** Choral groups, concert band, dance, drama/theater, jazz band, literary magazine, marching band, music ensembles, musical theater, opera, pep band, radio station, student government, student newspaper, symphony orchestra, campus ministries, international student organization. **Organizations:** 237 registered organizations, 7 honor societies, 18 religious organizations. 13 fraternities, 10 sororities. **Athletics (Intercollegiate):** *Men:* Baseball, basketball, cheerleading, cross-country, diving, football, golf, soccer, swimming, tennis, track/field (outdoor). *Women:* Basketball, cheerleading, crew/rowing, cross-country, diving, field hockey, golf, lacrosse, soccer, softball, swimming, tennis, track/field (outdoor), volleyball. **On-Campus Highlights:** Student Activity Center, J.B. Speed Art Museum.

ADMISSIONS

Freshman Academic Profile: Average high school GPA 3.46. 25% in top 10% of high school class, 53% in top 25% of high school class, 84% in top 50% of high school class. SAT Math middle 50% range 510–640. SAT Critical Reading middle 50% range 500–628. ACT middle 50% range 21–28. Minimum paper TOEFL 550. Minimum computer TOEFL 213. **Basis for Candidate Selection:** *Very important factors considered include:* Academic GPA, rigor of secondary school record, standardized test scores. *Other factors considered include:* Class rank, recommendation(s), extracurricular activities, racial/ethnic status, state residency, talent/ability, volunteer work, work experience. **Freshman Admission Requirements:** High school diploma is required and GED is accepted. *Academic units required:* 4 English, 3 mathematics, 3 science, (1 science labs), 2 foreign language, 3 social studies, 1 visual/performing arts, 5 academic electives, 5 electives must be rigorous; history is included in social studies. *Academic units recommended:* 4 mathematics, 4 science, 3 foreign language. **Freshman Admission Statistics:** 7,755 applied, 73% admitted, 44% enrolled. **Transfer Admission Requirements:** College transcript(s), minimum college GPA of 2.0 required. Lowest grade transferable D. **General Admission Information:** Application fee $40. Regular application deadline 8/25. Nonfall registration accepted. Credit and/or placement offered for CEEB Advanced Placement tests.

COSTS AND FINANCIAL AID

Annual in-state tuition $7,944. Annual out-of-state tuition $19,272. Room and board $5,437. Average book expense $1,000.

UNIVERSITY OF MAINE

5713 Chadbourne Hall, Orono, ME 04469-5713
Phone: 207-581-1561 **Financial Aid Phone:** 207-581-1324
E-mail: um-admit@maine.edu **CEEB Code:** 3916
Fax: 207-581-1213 **Website:** www.umaine.edu **ACT Code:** 1664

This public school was founded in 1865. It has a 660-acre campus.

RATINGS

Admissions Selectivity Rating: 76   **Fire Safety Rating:** 86   **Green Rating:** 99

STUDENTS AND FACULTY

Enrollment: 8,759. **Student Body:** 48% female, 52% male, 15% out-of-state, 2% international (67 countries represented). Asian 1%, African American 1%, Caucasian 81%, Hispanic 1%, Native American 2%.
Retention and Graduation: 79% freshmen return for sophomore year. 34% freshmen graduate within 4 years. 25% grads go on to further study within 1 year. **Faculty:** Student/faculty ratio 15:1. 567 full-time faculty, 76% hold PhDs, 6% are members of minority groups, 34% are women. 17% of classes are taught by teaching assistants.

ACADEMICS

Degrees: Bachelor's, doctoral, master's, post-master's certificate. **Classes:** Most classes have 10–19 students. Most lab/discussion sessions have 10–19 students. **Majors with Highest Enrollment:** Business/commerce; education; engineering. **Special Study Options:** Accelerated program, cooperative education program, distance learning, double major, dual enrollment, English as a Second Language (ESL), honors program, independent study, internships, liberal arts/career combination, study abroad, teacher certification program. **Honors programs:** The Honors College at the University of Maine provides a unique opportunity for a community of five hundred motivated students to investigate diverse academic areas of the university, to be challenged in a supportive intellectual environment, and to critically engage fellow students and enthusiastic, distinguished faculty in thoughtful, provocative discussion. The benefits and rewards are substantial, and the program is flexible enough to be tailored precisely to the individual student's needs and interests. **Combined degree programs:** BA/MD, BA/MA, BA/DO. Special programs offered to physically disabled students include note-taking services, reader services, tape recorders, tutors. **Career services:** Alumni network, alumni services, career/job search classes, career assessment, internships, regional alumni. **Career services highlights include:** Visit us at www.umaine.edu/career/coop.html for information about these programs.

FACILITIES

Housing: Coed dorms, special housing for disabled students, special housing for international students, fraternity/sorority housing, apartments for married students, apartments for single students, wellness housing, theme **Housing:** Honor's College Housing; graduate student housing; smoke free; chem free; clusters for engineering and science majors. First Year Residential Experience (FYRE). 90% of campus accessible to physically disabled. **Special Academic Facilities/Equipment:** Laboratory for Advanced Surface Science and Technology (LASST), Advanced Manufacturing Center, Anthropology museum, Digital Media Lab, folklore and oral history museum, art museum, Canadian-American center, social sciences research institute, exceptional child research lab, preschool, experimental farms, land/water resources center, center for marine studies, planetarium/observatory, electron microscopes, farm museum, papermaking machine, aquaculture production facility, woodland preserve, botanical garden, arts center, Franco-American Center. **Computers:** 100% of classrooms, 10% of dorms, 100% of libraries, 100% of dining areas, 100% of student union, 50% of common outdoor areas have wireless network access. Students can register for classes online. Administrative functions (other than registration) can be performed online.

CAMPUS LIFE

Environment: Village. **Activities:** Choral groups, concert band, dance, drama/theater, jazz band, literary magazine, marching band, music ensembles, musical theater, opera, pep band, radio station, student government, student newspaper, student-run film society, symphony orchestra, television station, yearbook, campus ministries, international student organization. **Organizations:** 224 registered organizations, 42 honor societies, 7 religious organizations. 13 fraternities, 6 sororities. **Athletics (Intercollegiate):** *Men:* Baseball, basketball, cross-country, diving, football, ice hockey, soccer, swimming, track/field (outdoor), track/field (indoor). *Women:* Basketball, cross-country, diving, field hockey, ice hockey, soccer, softball, swimming, track/field (outdoor), track/field (indoor), volleyball. **On-Campus Highlights:** Collins Center for the Arts, Alfond Arena, Market Place—Memorial Union, Student Recreation Center, The Mall. **Environmental Initiatives:** UMaine is developing a master plan centered on sustainablility, restoring habitat, avoiding sprawl, maximizing solar orientation, and reducing carbon emissions. Installation of a back-pressure turbine, with plans to install a cogeneration facility at the university's steam plant An institutional commitment (including a $300,000 Green Loan Fund supported by the University of Maine Foundation)to research and practical solutions related to sustainable energy, including cellulosic ethanol, wind power and tidal power

ADMISSIONS

Freshman Academic Profile: Average high school GPA 3.18. 20% in top 10% of high school class, 49% in top 25% of high school class, 85% in top 50% of high school class. SAT Math middle 50% range 480–590. SAT Critical Reading middle 50% range 470–580. SAT Writing middle 50% range 460–560. ACT middle 50% range 20–26. Minimum paper TOEFL 530. Minimum computer TOEFL 197. Minimum web-based TOEFL 71. **Basis for Candidate Selection:** *Very important factors considered include:* Class rank, academic GPA, rigor of secondary school record, standardized test scores. *Important factors considered include:* Application essay, recommendation(s). *Other factors considered include:* Character/personal qualities, extracurricular activities, geographical residence, interview, talent/ability, volunteer work, work experience. **Freshman Admission Requirements:** High school diploma is required and GED is accepted. *Academic units required:* 4 English, 3 mathematics, 2 science, (2 science labs), 2 foreign language, 2 social studies, 4 academic electives, 1 physical education for education majors. *Academic units recommended:* 4 English, 4 mathematics, 4 science, (3 science labs), 2 foreign language, 3 social studies, 1 history, 4 academic electives, 1 physical education for education majors. **Freshman Admission Statistics:** 6,786 applied, 80% admitted, 32% enrolled. **Transfer Admission Requirements:** High school transcript, college transcript(s), essay or personal statement, minimum college GPA of 2.0 required. Lowest grade transferable C–. **General Admission Information:** Application fee $40. Notification on a rolling basis, beginning on or about 2/1. Nonfall registration accepted. Admission may be deferred for a maximum of 2 semesters. Credit offered for CEEB Advanced Placement tests.

COSTS AND FINANCIAL AID

Required Forms and Deadlines: FAFSA. Priority financial aid filing date 3/1. **Notification of Awards:** Applicants will be notified of awards on a rolling

basis beginning 3/15. **Types of Aid:** *Need-based scholarships/grants:* Federal Pell, SEOG, state scholarships/grants, private scholarships, the school's own gift aid. *Loans:* FFEL Subsidized Stafford, FFEL Unsubsidized Stafford, FFEL PLUS, Federal Perkins, state loans *Student Employment:* Federal Work-Study Program available. Institutional employment available. Highest amount earned per year from on-campus jobs $4,000. Off-campus job opportunities are good. **Financial Aid Statistics:** 53% freshmen, 46% undergrads receive need-based scholarship or grant aid. 4% freshmen, 3% undergrads receive non-need-based scholarship or grant aid. 52% freshmen, 52% undergrads receive need-based self-help aid. 76% freshmen, 93% undergrads receive any aid. 76% undergrads borrow to pay for school. Average cumulative indebtedness $22,630. **Criteria for awarding institutional aid:** *Non-need-based:* Academics, alumni affiliation, art, athletics, job skills, leadership, minority status, music/drama, religious affiliation, state/district residency.

See page 1292.

UNIVERSITY OF MAINE—AUGUSTA

46 University Drive, Augusta, ME 04330
Phone: 207-621-3185 **Financial Aid Phone:** 207-621-3455
E-mail: umaadm@maine.edu **CEEB Code:** 3929
Fax: 207-621-3333 **Website:** www.uma.edu **ACT Code:** 1641

This public school was founded in 1965. It has a 159-acre campus.

RATINGS
Admissions Selectivity Rating: 60* **Fire Safety Rating:** 60* **Green Rating:** 82

STUDENTS AND FACULTY
Enrollment: 4,370. **Student Body:** 74% female, 26% male, 2% out-of-state, international (8 countries represented). Asian 1%, African American 1%, Caucasian 77%, Hispanic 1%, Native American 3%.
Retention and Graduation: 55% freshmen return for sophomore year. 40% grads go on to further study within 1 year. **Faculty:** Student/faculty ratio 18:1. 104 full-time faculty, 54% hold PhDs, 57% are women.

ACADEMICS
Degrees: Associate, bachelor's, certificate, post-bachelor's certificate, terminal associate, transfer associate. **Classes:** Most classes have 10–19 students. Most lab/discussion sessions have 10–19 students. **Majors with Highest Enrollment:** Business/commerce; health services/allied health/health sciences; social sciences. **Special Study Options:** Cross-registration, distance learning, double major, dual enrollment, honors program, independent study, internships, liberal arts/career combination, student-designed major, study abroad. **Honors programs:** UMA Honors Program—augments a student's academic and co-curricular experience Special programs offered to physically disabled students include note-taking services **Career services:** Career/job search classes, career assessment.

FACILITIES
Housing: 99% of campus accessible to physically disabled. **Special Academic Facilities/Equipment:** Jewett Gallery, Katz Library, Student Center. **Computers:** 100% of classrooms, 100% of libraries, 100% of dining areas, 100% of student union, 100% of common outdoor areas have wireless network access. Students can register for classes online. Administrative functions (other than registration) can be performed online.

CAMPUS LIFE
Environment: Village. **Activities:** Drama/theater, jazz band, music ensembles, pep band, student government, student newspaper, international student organization. **Organizations:** 23 registered organizations, 1 honor societies, 1 religious organizations. **Athletics (Intercollegiate):** *Men:* Basketball, golf. *Women:* Basketball, golf, soccer. **On-Campus Highlights:** Katz Library, Student Center, Campus Center at UCB, Huskins Lounge at UCB. **Environmental Initiatives:** Reduce—Reuse—Recycle program in place since 1990. Energy policy states UMA will purchase at least 15% of its electicity from renewable sources. All new facilities over 5,000 square feet and major capital renovations over 50% of building replacement value will seek LEED Silver rating or equivalent.

ADMISSIONS
Freshman Academic Profile: Minimum paper TOEFL 500. Minimum computer TOEFL 173. **Basis for Candidate Selection:** *Important factors considered include:* Class rank, academic GPA, rigor of secondary school record. *Other factors considered include:* Application essay, recommendation(s), standardized test scores, character/personal qualities, interview, level of applicant's interest, talent/ability, volunteer work, work experience. **Freshman Admission**

Requirements: High school diploma is required and GED is accepted. *Academic units recommended:* 4 English, 2 mathematics, 2 science, (2 science labs), 2 social studies, 2 history. **Freshman Admission Statistics:** 1,053 applied, 96% admitted, 58% enrolled. **Transfer Admission Requirements:** College transcript(s), minimum college GPA of 2.0 required. Lowest grade transferable C. **General Admission Information:** Application fee $40. Regular application deadline 8/30. Nonfall registration accepted. Admission may be deferred for a maximum of 1 year. Credit offered for CEEB Advanced Placement tests.

COSTS AND FINANCIAL AID

Required Forms and Deadlines: FAFSA. Priority financial aid filing date 3/1. **Notification of Awards:** Applicants will be notified of awards on a rolling basis beginning 3/15. **Types of Aid:** *Need-based scholarships/grants:* Federal Pell, SEOG, state scholarships/grants, private scholarships, the school's own gift aid. *Loans:* Direct Subsidized Stafford, Direct Unsubsidized Stafford, FFEL Subsidized Stafford, FFEL Unsubsidized Stafford, FFEL PLUS, Federal Perkins, Federal Nursing, state loans *Student Employment:* Federal Work-Study Program available. Institutional employment available. Highest amount earned per year from on-campus jobs $3,800. Off-campus job opportunities are fair. **Financial Aid Statistics:** 73% freshmen, 84% undergrads receive need-based scholarship or grant aid. 2% freshmen, 1% undergrads receive non-need-based scholarship or grant aid. 55% freshmen, 75% undergrads receive need-based self-help aid. 1% undergrads receive athletic scholarships. 63% freshmen, 70% undergrads receive any aid. 66% undergrads borrow to pay for school. Average cumulative indebtedness $14,473. **Criteria for awarding institutional aid:** *Non-need-based:* Academics, athletics, leadership, music/drama, state/district residency.

UNIVERSITY OF MAINE AT FARMINGTON

246 Main Street, Farmington, ME 04938
Phone: 207-778-7050 **Financial Aid Phone:** 207-778-7100
E-mail: umfadmit@maine.edu **CEEB Code:** 3506
Fax: 207-778-8182 **Website:** www.farmington.edu **ACT Code:** 1640

This public school was founded in 1863. It has a 55-acre campus.

RATINGS

Admissions Selectivity Rating: 74   **Fire Safety Rating:** 96   **Green Rating:** 91

STUDENTS AND FACULTY

Enrollment: 2,046. **Student Body:** 65% female, 35% male, 12.9% out-of-state, international (12 countries represented). Asian 1%, African American 1%, Caucasian 82%, Hispanic 1%, Native American 1%.
Retention and Graduation: 70% freshmen return for sophomore year. 46% freshmen graduate within 4 years. 20% grads go on to further study within 1 year. 15% grads pursue arts and sciences degrees. 1% grads pursue law degrees. 3% grads pursue business degrees. 1% grads pursue medical degrees. **Faculty:** Student/faculty ratio 14:1. 120 full-time faculty, 91% hold PhDs, 4% are members of minority groups, 53% are women.

ACADEMICS

Degrees: Bachelor's, master's. **Classes:** Most classes have 10–19 students. Most lab/discussion sessions have 10–19 students. **Majors with Highest Enrollment:** Elementary education and teaching; multi-/interdisciplinary studies, other; psychology. **Special Study Options:** Cooperative education program, cross-registration, double major, dual enrollment, exchange student program (domestic), honors program, independent study, internships, liberal arts/career combination, student-designed major, study abroad, teacher certification program, SALT, Documentary Field Study in Portland, ME, National Student Exchange, Service Learning. **Honors programs:** UMF Honors Program Special programs offered to physically disabled students include note-taking services, reader services **Career services:** Career assessment. **Career services highlights include:** Student Teaching programs.

FACILITIES

Housing: Coed dorms, special housing for international students, women's dorms, wellness housing, theme housing: Housing for students maintaining a certain GPA, medical rooms, quiet floors, wellness community, international community, independent living environment housing available. 75% of campus accessible to physically disabled. **Special Academic Facilities/Equipment:** Art gallery, health and fitness center, computer center, Mantor Library, Alumni theater, Nordica Auditorium, observatory. **Computers:** 100% of classrooms, 100% of dorms, 100% of libraries, 100% of dining areas, 100% of student union, 100% of common outdoor areas have wireless network access. Students can register for classes online. Administrative functions (other than registration) can be performed online.

CAMPUS LIFE

Environment: Village. **Activities:** Choral groups, concert band, dance, drama/theater, literary magazine, music ensembles, musical theater, radio station, student government, student newspaper, yearbook, international student organization. **Organizations:** 52 registered organizations, 3 honor societies, 3 religious organizations. **Athletics (Intercollegiate):** *Men:* Baseball, basketball, cross-country, golf, soccer. *Women:* Basketball, cross-country, field hockey, soccer, softball, volleyball. **On-Campus Highlights:** Recreation and Fitness Center, Landing, Computer Center, Education Center, Student Center. **Environmental Initiatives:** Completion of two LEED-certified buildings and commitment to new construction and major renovations at the LEED Silver level. ACUPCC signatory with completion of GHG inventory and Climate Action Plan as of January 2010. Energy conservation resulting in an energy footprint 20% below national average for comparable colleges.

ADMISSIONS

Freshman Academic Profile: Average high school GPA 3.17. 13% in top 10% of high school class, 39% in top 25% of high school class, 77% in top 50% of high school class. 88% from public high schools. SAT Math middle 50% range 440–550. SAT Critical Reading middle 50% range 450–560. Minimum paper TOEFL 550. Minimum computer TOEFL 213. **Basis for Candidate Selection:** *Very important factors considered include:* Class rank, rigor of secondary school record, extracurricular activities. *Important factors considered include:* Application essay, academic GPA, recommendation(s), character/personal qualities, interview, talent/ability, volunteer work, work experience. *Other factors considered include:* Alumni/ae relation, first generation, geographical residence, level of applicant's interest, racial/ethnic status, state residency. **Freshman Admission Requirements:** High school diploma is required and GED is accepted. *Academic units required:* 4 English, 3 mathematics, 2 science, (2 science labs), 2 foreign language, 2 social studies. *Academic units recommended:* 4 English, 4 mathematics, 3 science, (3 science labs), 3 foreign language, 3 social studies, 2 history, 3 academic electives, 3 academic electives **Freshman Admission Statistics:** 1,817 applied, 71% admitted, 38% enrolled. **Transfer Admission Requirements:** High school transcript, college transcript(s), essay or personal statement, minimum college GPA of 2.5 required. Lowest grade transferable C. **General Admission Information:** Application fee $40. Notification on a rolling basis, beginning on or about 12/15. Nonfall registration accepted. Admission may be deferred for a maximum of 1 year. Credit and/or placement offered for CEEB Advanced Placement tests.

COSTS AND FINANCIAL AID

Annual in-state tuition $7,744. Annual out-of-state tuition $16,128. Room and board $7,552. Required fees $966. Average book expense $720. **Required Forms and Deadlines:** FAFSA. Financial aid filing deadline 3/1. Priority financial aid filing date 3/1. **Notification of Awards:** Applicants will be notified of awards on a rolling basis beginning 3/15. **Types of Aid:** *Need-based scholarships/grants:* Federal Pell, SEOG, state scholarships/grants, private scholarships, the school's own gift aid, Native American scholarships and waivers. *Loans:* Direct Subsidized Stafford, Direct Unsubsidized Stafford, Direct PLUS, FFEL Subsidized Stafford, FFEL Unsubsidized Stafford, FFEL PLUS, Federal Perkins, state loans, college/university loans from institutional funds, Teachers for Maine Loans. *Student Employment:* Federal Work-Study Program available. Institutional employment available. Highest amount earned per year from on-campus jobs $5,530. Off-campus job opportunities are fair. **Financial Aid Statistics:** 63% freshmen, 57% undergrads receive need-based scholarship or grant aid. 50% freshmen, 26% undergrads receive non-need-based scholarship or grant aid. 66% freshmen, 62% undergrads receive need-based self-help aid. 96% freshmen, 94% undergrads receive any aid. 81% undergrads borrow to pay for school. Average cumulative indebtedness $19,490. **Criteria for awarding institutional aid:** *Non-need-based:* Academics, leadership, minority status, state/district residency.

UNIVERSITY OF MAINE—FORT KENT

23 University Drive, Fort Kent, ME 04774
Phone: 888-879-8635 **Financial Aid Phone:** 207-834-7605
E-mail: umfkadm@maine.maine.edu **CEEB Code:** 3393
Fax: 207-834-7609 **Website:** www.umfk.maine.edu **ACT Code:** 1642

This public school was founded in 1878. It has a 52-acre campus.

RATINGS

Admissions Selectivity Rating: 64   **Fire Safety Rating:** 95   **Green Rating:** 78

STUDENTS AND FACULTY

Enrollment: 1,063. **Student Body:** 66% female, 34% male, 4% out-of-state, 12% international. African American 2%, Caucasian 52%, Native American 1%.

Retention and Graduation: 63% freshmen return for sophomore year. 25% freshmen graduate within 4 years. 5% grads go on to further study within 1 year. 3% grads pursue arts and sciences degrees. **Faculty:** Student/faculty ratio 17:1. 39 full-time faculty, 82% hold PhDs, 3% are members of minority groups, 41% are women.

ACADEMICS

Degrees: Associate, bachelor's. **Classes:** Most classes have 10–19 students. Most lab/discussion sessions have fewer than 10 students. **Majors with Highest Enrollment:** Business/commerce; elementary education and teaching; nursing/registered nurse (RN, ASN, BSN, MSN). **Special Study Options:** Cross-registration, distance learning, double major, English as a Second Language (ESL), honors program, independent study, internships, liberal arts/career combination, student-designed major, teacher certification program, distance learning within entire UMaine system. Special programs offered to physically disabled students include note-taking services, reader services, tape recorders, tutors. **Career services:** Alumni services, career/job search classes, career assessment, internships.

FACILITIES

Housing: Coed dorms, special housing for disabled students, men's dorms, women's dorms. 80% of campus accessible to physically disabled. **Computers:** 100% of classrooms, 100% of dorms, 100% of libraries, 100% of dining areas, 100% of student union, 100% of common outdoor areas have wireless network access. Students can register for classes online. Administrative functions (other than registration) can be performed online.

CAMPUS LIFE

Environment: Rural. **Activities:** Choral groups, drama/theater, student government **Organizations:** 25 registered organizations, 1 honor societies, 1 religious organizations. 1 sororities. **Athletics (Intercollegiate):** Men: Basketball, cross-country, golf, skiing (downhill/alpine), skiing (nordic/cross-country), soccer. Women: Basketball, cross-country, golf, skiing (downhill/alpine), skiing (nordic/cross-country), soccer, volleyball. **On-Campus Highlights:** Bengal's Lair, The Lodge (res hall), library.

ADMISSIONS

Freshman Academic Profile: Average high school GPA 2.64. 2% in top 10% of high school class, 19% in top 25% of high school class, 62% in top 50% of high school class. 96% from public high schools. SAT Math middle 50% range 350–465. SAT Critical Reading middle 50% range 350–482. SAT Writing middle 50% range 324–471. ACT middle 50% range 18–22. Minimum paper TOEFL 500. Minimum computer TOEFL 175. **Basis for Candidate Selection:** *Very important factors considered include:* level of applicant's interest. *Important factors considered include:* Class rank, application essay, academic GPA, recommendation(s), rigor of secondary school record, character/personal qualities, first generation, geographical residence, state residency, talent/ability, volunteer work. *Other factors considered include:* Standardized test scores, alumni/ae relation, extracurricular activities, interview, work experience. **Freshman Admission Requirements:** High school diploma is required and GED is accepted. *Academic units required:* 4 English, 2 mathematics, 2 science, (2 science labs). *Academic units recommended:* 2 foreign language. **Freshman Admission Statistics:** 280 applied, 78% admitted, 58% enrolled. **Transfer Admission Requirements:** High school transcript, college transcript(s), essay or personal statement, Lowest grade transferable C–. **General Admission Information:** Application fee $40. Notification on a rolling basis, beginning on or about 12/1. Nonfall registration accepted. Credit and/or placement offered for CEEB Advanced Placement tests.

COSTS AND FINANCIAL AID

Annual in-state tuition $6,030. Annual out-of-state tuition $15,180. Room and board $7,080. Required fees $773. Average book expense $1,100. **Required Forms and Deadlines:** FAFSA, institution's own financial aid form, CSS/Financial Aid PROFILE, state aid form. **Types of Aid:** *Need-based scholarships/grants:* Federal Pell, SEOG, state scholarships/grants, private scholarships, the school's own gift aid, Federal Nursing Scholarships. *Loans:* Direct Subsidized Stafford, Direct Unsubsidized Stafford, Direct PLUS, FFEL Subsidized Stafford, FFEL Unsubsidized Stafford, FFEL PLUS, Federal Perkins, Federal Nursing, state loans, college/university loans from institutional funds. *Student Employment:* Federal Work-Study Program available. Institutional employment available. Highest amount earned per year from on-campus jobs $1,500. Off-campus job opportunities are good. **Financial Aid Statistics:** 47% freshmen, 35% undergrads receive need-based scholarship or grant aid. 81% freshmen, 56% undergrads receive non-need-based scholarship or grant aid. 62% freshmen, 46% undergrads receive need-based self-help aid. 86% freshmen, 80% undergrads receive any aid. **Criteria for awarding institutional aid:** *Non-need-based:* Academics, alumni affiliation, job skills, leadership, state/district residency.

See page 1290.

UNIVERSITY OF MAINE AT MACHIAS

Office of Admissions, 9 O Brien Avenue, Machias, ME 04654
Phone: 207-255-1318 **Financial Aid Phone:** 207-255-1203
E-mail: ummadmissions@maine.edu **CEEB Code:** 3956
Fax: 207-255-1363 **Website:** www.umm.maine.edu **ACT Code:** 1666

This public school was founded in 1909. It has a 42-acre campus.

RATINGS
Admissions Selectivity Rating: 71   **Fire Safety Rating:** 60*   **Green Rating:** 60*

STUDENTS AND FACULTY

Enrollment: 554. **Student Body:** 65% female, 35% male, 24% out-of-state, 4% international (18 countries represented). Asian 1%, African American 1%, Caucasian 88%, Hispanic 2%, Native American 4%.
Retention and Graduation: 12% freshmen graduate within 4 years. **Faculty:** Student/faculty ratio 15:1. 30 full-time faculty, 73% hold PhDs, 3% are members of minority groups, 33% are women.

ACADEMICS

Degrees: Bachelor's. **Classes:** Most classes have 10–19 students. Most lab/discussion sessions have 10–19 students. **Majors with Highest Enrollment:** Elementary education and teaching; marine biology and biological oceanography; parks, recreation and leisure facilities management. **Special Study Options:** Cooperative education program, distance learning, double major, dual enrollment, honors program, independent study, internships, student-designed major, study abroad, teacher certification program. Special programs offered to physically disabled students include reader services, tape recorders, tutors. **Career services:** Career assessment, internships.

FACILITIES

Housing: Coed dorms. 85% of campus accessible to physically disabled. **Special Academic Facilities/Equipment:** Art Gallery, Book Arts Print Shop, Geographic Information Systems Laboratory and Service Center **Computers:** 100% of classrooms, 100% of dorms, 100% of libraries, 100% of dining areas, 100% of student union, 100% of common outdoor areas have wireless network access. Students can register for classes online. Administrative functions (other than registration) can be performed online.

CAMPUS LIFE

Environment: Rural. **Activities:** Choral groups, dance, drama/theater, literary magazine, music ensembles, musical theater, pep band, radio station, student government, campus ministries. **Organizations:** 38 registered organizations, 2 religious organizations. 5 fraternities, 4 sororities. **Athletics (Intercollegiate):** Men: Basketball, soccer. Women: Basketball, soccer, volleyball. **On-Campus Highlights:** Aquatics/Fitness Center/Gymnasium, Residence Halls, Wireless Computer Lab/Classroom, Performing Arts Center, Early Care and Education Center, The Portal—multi-media center, Marine Biology lab facilities, Campus Radio Station, Art Studios and Gallery, Bookstore, Book Arts Print Shop, Kilburn Commons, The Galley. **Environmental Initiatives:** Green Council; RecycleMania.

ADMISSIONS

Freshman Academic Profile: 12.8% in top 10% of high school class, 24.4% in top 25% of high school class, 62.8% in top 50% of high school class. SAT Math middle 50% range 400–530. SAT Critical Reading middle 50% range 440–530. ACT middle 50% range 15–25. Minimum paper TOEFL 500. Minimum computer TOEFL 173. **Basis for Candidate Selection:** *Very important factors considered include:* Application essay, recommendation(s), rigor of secondary school record, interview. *Important factors considered include:* Class rank, standardized test scores, extracurricular activities. *Other factors considered include:* character/personal qualities, talent/ability, volunteer work, work experience. **Freshman Admission Requirements:** High school diploma is required and GED is accepted. *Academic units required:* 4 English, 3 mathematics, 2 science, (2 science labs), 2 social studies. *Academic units recommended:* 2 foreign language, 3 academic electives. **Freshman Admission Statistics:** 381 applied, 92% admitted, 32% enrolled. **Transfer Admission Requirements:** High school transcript, college transcript(s), statement of good standing from prior institution(s). Minimum college GPA of 2.0 required. Lowest grade transferable C–. **General Admission Information:** Application fee $40. Regular application deadline 8/15. Nonfall registration accepted. Admission may be deferred for a maximum of 1 year. Credit offered for CEEB Advanced Placement tests.

COSTS AND FINANCIAL AID

Annual in-state tuition $6,410. Annual out-of-state tuition $16,550. Room and board $6,574. Average book expense $650. **Required Forms and Deadlines:** FAFSA. Priority financial aid filing date 3/1. **Notification of Awards:** Applicants will be notified of awards on a rolling basis beginning 3/1. **Types of Aid:** *Need-based scholarships/grants:* Federal Pell, SEOG, state scholarships/

grants, private scholarships, the school's own gift aid. *Loans:* FFEL Subsidized Stafford, FFEL Unsubsidized Stafford, FFEL PLUS, Federal Perkins. *Student Employment:* Federal Work-Study Program available. Institutional employment available. Highest amount earned per year from on-campus jobs $1,200. Off-campus job opportunities are good. **Financial Aid Statistics:** 79% freshmen, 70% undergrads receive need-based scholarship or grant aid. 7% freshmen, 4% undergrads receive non-need-based scholarship or grant aid. 66% freshmen, 64% undergrads receive need-based self-help aid. 82% freshmen, 74% undergrads receive any aid. 69% undergrads borrow to pay for school. Average cumulative indebtedness $16,127. **Criteria for awarding institutional aid:** *Non-need-based:* Academics, alumni affiliation, art, leadership, minority status, music/drama, state/district residency.

UNIVERSITY OF MAINE—PRESQUE ISLE

Office of Admissions, 181 Main Street, Presque Isle, ME 04769
Phone: 207-768-9532 **Financial Aid Phone:** 207-768-9510
E-mail: adventure@umpi.maine.edu **CEEB Code:** 3008
Fax: 207-768-9777 **Website:** www.umpi.edu

This public school was founded in 1903. It has a 150-acre campus.

RATINGS
Admissions Selectivity Rating: 67   **Fire Safety Rating:** 72   **Green Rating:** 60*

STUDENTS AND FACULTY
Enrollment: 1,266. **Student Body:** 64% female, 36% male, 2% out-of-state, 9% international (5 countries represented). Asian 1%, African American 1%, Caucasian 71%, Hispanic 1%, Native American 4%.
Retention and Graduation: 55% freshmen return for sophomore year.
Faculty: Student/faculty ratio 16:1. 54 full-time faculty, 81% hold PhDs, 4% are members of minority groups, 44% are women.

ACADEMICS
Degrees: Associate, bachelor's, certificate. **Classes:** Most classes have 10–19 students. Most lab/discussion sessions have 10–19 students. **Majors with Highest Enrollment:** Elementary education and teaching; liberal arts and sciences/liberal studies; social work. **Special Study Options:** Accelerated program, cooperative education program, cross-registration, distance learning, double major, exchange student program (domestic), honors program, independent study, internships, student-designed major, study abroad, teacher certification program. **Honors programs:** HON 300 Honors Seminar HON/HTY 401 Oral History HON 421 Honors Senior Year Project. Special programs offered to physically disabled students include note-taking services, reader services, tape recorders, tutors. **Career services:** Alumni services, career/job search classes, career assessment, internships.

FACILITIES
Housing: Coed dorms, apartments for married students. 100% of campus accessible to physically disabled. **Special Academic Facilities/Equipment:** Museum and art gallery, Gentile Hall. **Computers:** Students can register for classes online. Administrative functions (other than registration) can be performed online.

CAMPUS LIFE
Environment: Village. **Activities:** drama/theater, radio station, student government, student newspaper. **Organizations:** 27 registered organizations, 1 honor societies, 1 religious organizations. 1 fraternities, 1 sororities. **Athletics (Intercollegiate):** *Men:* Baseball, basketball, cross-country, golf, skiing (nordic/cross-country), soccer. *Women:* Basketball, cross-country, skiing (nordic/cross-country), soccer, softball, volleyball. **On-Campus Highlights:** Caroline D. Gentile Hall, Campus Center, Library, Fitness Center, Owl's Nest, Caroline D. Gentile Hall, the newest building at the University of Maine at Presque Isle, will officially open to the public on January 21, 2006. Named in honor of the university's longest serving faculty member, Gentile Hall features a large multipurpose court, fitness center, pool, elevated track, and climbing wall. The facility will support the university's academic programs and student body, but the community will also be welcomed and encouraged to use its resources.

ADMISSIONS
Freshman Academic Profile: Average high school GPA 3.04. 8% in top 10% of high school class, 23% in top 25% of high school class, 51% in top 50% of high school class. SAT Math middle 50% range 390–500. SAT Critical Reading middle 50% range 390–530. Minimum paper TOEFL 550. Minimum computer TOEFL 230. **Basis for Candidate Selection:** *Very important factors considered include:* Class rank, application essay, academic GPA, recommendation(s), rigor of secondary school record. *Important factors considered include:* Interview. *Other factors considered include:* Standardized test

scores, alumni/ae relation, character/personal qualities, extracurricular activities, racial/ethnic status, state residency, talent/ability, volunteer work, work experience. **Freshman Admission Requirements:** High school diploma is required and GED is accepted. *Academic units recommended:* 4 English, 3 mathematics, 2 science, (2 science labs), 2 foreign language, 3 social studies, 2 academic electives. **Freshman Admission Statistics:** 483 applied, 86% admitted, 51% enrolled. **Transfer Admission Requirements:** High school transcript, college transcript(s), essay or personal statement, statement of good standing from prior institution(s). Minimum college GPA of 2.0 required. Lowest grade transferable C–. **General Admission Information:** Application fee $40. Nonfall registration accepted. Admission may be deferred for a maximum of up to one year. Credit offered for CEEB Advanced Placement tests.

COSTS AND FINANCIAL AID
Annual in-state tuition $4,290. Annual out-of-state tuition $10,680. Room and board $5,246. Required fees $530. Average book expense $800. **Required Forms and Deadlines:** FAFSA. Priority financial aid filing date 4/1. **Notification of Awards:** Applicants will be notified of awards on a rolling basis beginning 3/1. **Types of Aid:** *Need-based scholarships/grants:* Federal Pell, SEOG, state scholarships/grants, private scholarships, the school's own gift aid. *Loans:* Direct Subsidized Stafford, Direct Unsubsidized Stafford, Direct PLUS, Federal Perkins, state loans, college/university loans from institutional funds. **Financial Aid Statistics:** 66% freshmen, 52% undergrads receive need-based scholarship or grant aid. 5% freshmen, 3% undergrads receive non-need-based scholarship or grant aid. 50% freshmen, 43% undergrads receive need-based self-help aid. 89% freshmen, 89% undergrads receive any aid. 33% undergrads borrow to pay for school. Average cumulative indebtedness $11,181. **Criteria for awarding institutional aid:** *Non-need-based:* Academics, alumni affiliation, art, job skills, leadership, minority status, music/drama, state/district residency.

UNIVERSITY OF MARY

7500 University Drive, Bismarck, ND 58504
Phone: 701-255-7500
E-mail: suerood@umary.edu **CEEB Code:** 6428
Fax: 701-255-7687 **Website:** www.umary.edu **ACT Code:** 3201

This private school, affiliated with the Roman Catholic Church, was founded in 1959. It has a 107-acre campus.

RATINGS
Admissions Selectivity Rating: 70   **Fire Safety Rating:** 60*   **Green Rating:** 60*

STUDENTS AND FACULTY
Enrollment: 1,722. **Student Body:** 62% female, 38% male.
Retention and Graduation: 70% freshmen return for sophomore year. 1% grads pursue arts and sciences degrees. 2% grads pursue law degrees. 4% grads pursue business degrees. **Faculty:** Student/faculty ratio 17:1.

ACADEMICS
Degrees: Associate, bachelor's, master's. **Majors with Highest Enrollment:** Business/commerce; health services/allied health/health sciences; nursing/registered nurse (RN, ASN, BSN, MSN). **Special Study Options:** Accelerated program, cooperative education program, distance learning, double major, dual enrollment, external degree program, honors program, independent study, internships, study abroad, teacher certification program. **Combined degree programs:** BA/MA Special programs offered to physically disabled students include tape recorders, tutors. **Career services:** Alumni services, career/job search classes, career assessment, internships.

FACILITIES
Housing: Men's dorms, women's dorms, apartments for single students 75% of campus accessible to physically disabled. **Special Academic Facilities/Equipment:** Art gallery.

CAMPUS LIFE
Environment: Village. **Activities:** Choral groups, concert band, drama/theater, jazz band, literary magazine, music ensembles, musical theater, pep band, radio station, student government, student newspaper, television station, yearbook. **Organizations:** 50 registered organizations, 5 honor societies, 6 religious organizations. **Athletics (Intercollegiate):** *Men:* Baseball, basketball, cross-country, football, golf, soccer, tennis, track/field (outdoor), track/field (indoor), wrestling. *Women:* Basketball, cheerleading, cross-country, golf, soccer, softball, tennis, track/field (outdoor), track/field (indoor), volleyball.

ADMISSIONS
Freshman Academic Profile: ACT middle 50% range 19–24. Minimum paper TOEFL 500. **Basis for Candidate Selection:** *Very important factors consid-*

ered *include:* Standardized test scores. *Important factors considered include:* Class rank, recommendation(s), rigor of secondary school record. *Other factors considered include:* Application essay, character/personal qualities, interview. **Freshman Admission Requirements:** High school diploma is required and GED is accepted. *Academic units recommended:* 4 English, 2 mathematics, 2 science, 3 social studies. **Freshman Admission Statistics:** 943 applied, 95% admitted, 48% enrolled. **Transfer Admission Requirements:** College transcript(s), minimum college GPA of 2.0 required. Lowest grade transferable D. **General Admission Information:** Application fee $15. Regular application deadline 8/23. Notification on a rolling basis, beginning on or about 9/2. Nonfall registration accepted. Admission may be deferred for a maximum of 12. Credit and/or placement offered for CEEB Advanced Placement tests.

COSTS AND FINANCIAL AID

Annual tuition $9,200. Room and board $3,540. Required fees $300. Average book expense $610. **Required Forms and Deadlines:** FAFSA. Priority financial aid filing date 5/1. *Types of Aid: Need-based scholarships/grants:* Federal Pell, SEOG, state scholarships/grants, private scholarships, the school's own gift aid. *Loans:* FFEL Subsidized Stafford, FFEL Unsubsidized Stafford, FFEL PLUS, Federal Perkins, Federal Nursing *Student Employment:* Federal Work-Study Program available. Institutional employment available. Highest amount earned per year from on-campus jobs $1,000. Off-campus job opportunities are good. **Financial Aid Statistics:** 79% freshmen, 52% undergrads receive need-based scholarship or grant aid. 79% freshmen, 32% undergrads receive non-need-based scholarship or grant aid. 79% freshmen, 52% undergrads receive need-based self-help aid. 77% undergrads borrow to pay for school. Average cumulative indebtedness $18,000.

UNIVERSITY OF MARY HARDIN-BAYLOR

UMHB Box 8004, 900 College Street, Belton, TX 76513
Phone: 254-295-4520 **Financial Aid Phone:** 254-295-4517
E-mail: admissions@umhb.edu
Fax: 254-295-5049 **Website:** www.umhb.edu

This private school, affiliated with the Baptist Church, was founded in 1845. It has a 170-acre campus.

RATINGS
Admissions Selectivity Rating: 73   **Fire Safety Rating:** 66   **Green Rating:** 60*

STUDENTS AND FACULTY
Enrollment: 2,547. **Student Body:** 61% female, 39% male, 2% out-of-state, 1% international (11 countries represented). Asian 2%, African American 13%, Caucasian 68%, Hispanic 14%.
Retention and Graduation: 65% freshmen return for sophomore year. 29% freshmen graduate within 4 years. **Faculty:** Student/faculty ratio 14:1. 143 full-time faculty, 63% hold PhDs, 11% are members of minority groups, 55% are women.

ACADEMICS
Degrees: Bachelor's, doctoral, master's. **Classes:** Most classes have 10–19 students. Most lab/discussion sessions have 10–19 students. **Majors with Highest Enrollment:** Elementary education and teaching; nursing/registered nurse (RN, ASN, BSN, MSN); psychology. **Special Study Options:** Accelerated program, double major, dual enrollment, English as a Second Language (ESL), honors program, independent study, internships, student-designed major, study abroad, teacher certification program, tuition exchange program with other participating universities. Undergrads may take grad level classes. Military degree completion programs. Servicemember Opportunity Colleges (SOCS) programs. **Honors programs:** Lower Level Honors Program—approximately the top 10% of UMHB's entering freshman class. Freshman year offerings include English and religion, and sophomore year offerings are interdisciplinary courses in the humanities and social sciences. Upper Level Honors Program—Minimum requirements for completion of this program is the completion of three upper level courses designated as honors level and the completion of HNRS 3110 "Great Books and Ideas" and HNRS 3120 "Living Issues." Successful completion of these requirements will allow the student to graduate with the cum laude designation. To receive the higher designations of magna cum laude or summa cum laude, the student must also successfully complete an Honors Research Project. This project must include original research and both written and oral presentations of that research to the Honors Committee. **Combined degree programs:** BBA/MBA; 3-1 Clinical Lab Science with local hospital. Special programs offered to physically disabled students include note-taking services, reader services, tape recorders, tutors. **Career services:** Alumni network, alumni services, career/job search classes, career assessment, internships, regional alumni. **Career services highlights include:** The UMHB Career

Development Center offers an array of self assessments, exploration, document preparation, and career planning opportunities. The most used and results-generated career program is the one on one Resume Clinic which involves an interactive session with our students drafting a successful career document. Many times this is their first resume, and the new confidence that is reflective by the student after completing this document is most exciting. Additional popular programs and workshops include, Show Me the Money: Salary negotiations; Facebook, My Space and My Future Employer; and the President's Senior Etiquette Dinner Program.

FACILITIES
Housing: Special housing for disabled students, men's dorms, women's dorms, apartments for single students. 85% of campus accessible to physically disabled. **Special Academic Facilities/Equipment:** Language lab. **Computers:** 100% of classrooms, 100% of dorms, 100% of libraries, 100% of dining areas, 100% of student union, 80% of common outdoor areas have wireless network access. Students can register for classes online. Administrative functions (other than registration) can be performed online.

CAMPUS LIFE
Environment: City. **Activities:** Choral groups, concert band, drama/theater, jazz band, literary magazine, marching band, music ensembles, musical theater, opera, pep band, student government, student newspaper, symphony orchestra, yearbook, campus ministries, international student organization. **Organizations:** 51 registered organizations, 5 honor societies, 7 religious organizations. **Athletics (Intercollegiate):** *Men:* Baseball, basketball, football, golf, soccer, tennis. *Women:* Basketball, golf, soccer, softball, tennis, volleyball. **On-Campus Highlights:** SUB (Student Union Building), Sportsplex or ANY sporting event, Millennium Oaks Park (gazebo, pond), Mayborn Center exercise/fitness facilities, Quad area.

ADMISSIONS
Freshman Academic Profile: SAT Math middle 50% range 480–590. SAT Critical Reading middle 50% range 470–590. SAT Writing middle 50% range 450–570. ACT middle 50% range 20–26. **Basis for Candidate Selection:** *Very important factors considered include:* Class rank, standardized test scores. *Important factors considered include:* Academic GPA, level of applicant's interest. *Other factors considered include:* Application essay, recommendation(s), rigor of secondary school record, alumni/ae relation, character/personal qualities, extracurricular activities, first generation, geographical residence, interview, racial/ethnic status, religious affiliation/commitment, state residency, talent/ability, volunteer work, work experience. **Freshman Admission Requirements:** High school diploma is required and GED is accepted. *Academic units required:* 4 English, 3 mathematics, 3 science, 2 foreign language, 3 social studies. **Transfer Admission Requirements:** College transcript(s), minimum college GPA of 2.0 required. Lowest grade transferable C. **General Admission Information:** Application fee $35. Nonfall registration accepted. Admission may be deferred for a maximum of no set limit. Credit offered for CEEB Advanced Placement tests.

COSTS AND FINANCIAL AID
Annual tuition $18,300. Room and board $5,350. Required fees $2,350. Average book expense $1,200. **Required Forms and Deadlines:** FAFSA, institution's own financial aid form. Priority financial aid filing date 3/1. **Notification of Awards:** Applicants will be notified of awards on a rolling basis beginning 2/1. *Types of Aid: Need-based scholarships/grants:* Federal Pell, SEOG, state scholarships/grants, private scholarships, the school's own gift aid, Federal Nursing Scholarships. federal work study, Texas state work study, UMHB work duty. *Loans:* Direct Subsidized Stafford, Direct Unsubsidized Stafford, FFEL Subsidized Stafford, FFEL Unsubsidized Stafford, FFEL PLUS, Federal Perkins, state loans, college/university loans from institutional funds. *Student Employment:* Federal Work-Study Program available. Institutional employment available. Highest amount earned per year from on-campus jobs $3,500. Off-campus job opportunities are good. **Financial Aid Statistics:** 87% freshmen, 90% undergrads receive need-based scholarship or grant aid. 32% freshmen, 16% undergrads receive non-need-based scholarship or grant aid. 62% freshmen, 69% undergrads receive need-based self-help aid. 98% freshmen, 89% undergrads receive any aid. 86% undergrads borrow to pay for school. **Criteria for awarding institutional aid:** *Non-need-based:* Academics, art, leadership, music/drama, religious affiliation.

UNIVERSITY OF MARY WASHINGTON

1301 College Avenue, Fredericksburg, VA 22401
Phone: 540-654-2000 **Financial Aid Phone:** 540-654-2468
E-mail: admit@umw.edu **CEEB Code:** 5398
Fax: 540-654-1857 **Website:** www.umw.edu **ACT Code:** 4414

This public school was founded in 1908. It has a 176-acre campus.

RATINGS

Admissions Selectivity Rating: 87   **Fire Safety Rating:** 80   **Green Rating:** 77

STUDENTS AND FACULTY

Enrollment: 4,258. **Student Body:** 65% female, 35% male, 20% out-of-state, international (11 countries represented). Asian 5%, African American 28%, Caucasian 60%, Hispanic 4%.
Retention and Graduation: 83% freshmen return for sophomore year. 65% freshmen graduate within 4 years. 24% grads go on to further study within 1 year. 60% grads pursue arts and sciences degrees. 5% grads pursue law degrees. 1% grads pursue business degrees. 1% grads pursue medical degrees. **Faculty:** Student/faculty ratio 16:1. 242 full-time faculty, 90% hold PhDs, 13% are members of minority groups, 48% are women.

ACADEMICS

Degrees: Bachelor's, certificate, master's, post-bachelor's certificate. **Classes:** Most classes have 20–29 students. Most lab/discussion sessions have 20–29 students. **Majors with Highest Enrollment:** Business administration and management; English language and literature; psychology. **Special Study Options:** Accelerated program, distance learning, double major, independent study, internships, student-designed major, study abroad, teacher certification program. **Combined degree programs:** BA/BS & MS elementary education, BS computer science & MSMIS, MBA/MSMIS. Special programs offered to physically disabled students include note-taking services, reader services, tape recorders. **Career services:** Alumni network, alumni services, career/job search classes, career assessment, internships, regional alumni. **Career services highlights include:** Our academic credit internship program allows students to take up to 12 experiential credits toward graduation. Most experiences are graded and in many cases count toward the major.

FACILITIES

Housing: Coed dorms, special housing for disabled students, men's dorms, special housing for international students, women's dorms, apartments for single students, wellness housing, theme housing, substance-free. 63% of campus accessible to physically disabled. **Special Academic Facilities/Equipment:** Two art galleries, Center for Historic Preservation, language labs, Leidecker Center for Asian Studies, cartography lab, greenhouse. **Computers:** 100% of classrooms, 100% of dorms, 100% of libraries, 100% of dining areas, 100% of student union, 5% of common outdoor areas have wireless network access. Students can register for classes online. Administrative functions (other than registration) can be performed online.

CAMPUS LIFE

Environment: City. **Activities:** Choral groups, concert band, dance, drama/theater, jazz band, literary magazine, music ensembles, musical theater, opera, radio station, student government, student newspaper, student-run film society, symphony orchestra, yearbook, campus ministries, international student organization, Model UN. **Organizations:** 120 registered organizations, 23 honor societies, 10 religious organizations. **Athletics (Intercollegiate):** *Men:* Baseball, basketball, crew/rowing, cross-country, equestrian sports, lacrosse, soccer, swimming, tennis, track/field (outdoor), track/field (indoor). *Women:* Basketball, crew/rowing, cross-country, equestrian sports, field hockey, lacrosse, soccer, softball, swimming, tennis, track/field (outdoor), track/field (indoor), volleyball. **On-Campus Highlights:** Woodard Campus Center, Battleground Athletic facilities/Fitness Center, Palmieri Plaza Fountain, Ball Circle, Lee Hall. **Environmental Initiatives:** UMW has seen a significant reduction in costs and use of resources since the university entered this program. For more information, see www.umw.edu/news/?a=615. In 2009, the President's Council on Sustainability was formed as an advisory committee to the University's President and Cabinet on how the university can best act and articulate the institutions commitment to sustainability and environmental stewardship as outlined in the Strategic Plan. The committee is directly responsible to the Executive Vice President for Administration and Finance and the Provost. UMW has a significant university-wide recycling program in place for aluminum, paper, newspaper, cardboard, plastic, motor oil, oil filters, printer cartridges, antifreeze, tires, auto parts, refrigerators, freon, latex paint, computer monitors, CPUs without hard drives, printers and fluorescent tubes. Waste reduction includes composting of yard waste and re-use of wood chips from tree removal. Second annual RecycleMania www.umw.edu/recycle.

ADMISSIONS

Freshman Academic Profile: Average high school GPA 3.58. 78% from public high schools. SAT Math middle 50% range 520–620. SAT Critical Reading middle 50% range 540–650. SAT Writing middle 50% range 530–630. ACT middle 50% range 24–28. Minimum paper TOEFL 570. Minimum computer TOEFL 230. Minimum web-based TOEFL 88. **Basis for Candidate Selection:** *Very important factors considered include:* Academic GPA, rigor of secondary school record. *Important factors considered include:* Class rank, application essay, recommendation(s), standardized test scores, extracurricular activities. *Other factors considered include:* Alumni/ae relation, character/personal qualities, first generation, geographical residence, racial/ethnic status, state residency, talent/ability, volunteer work, work experience. **Freshman Admission Requirements:** High school diploma is required and GED is accepted. *Academic units required:* 4 English, 3 mathematics, 3 science, (3 science labs), 2 foreign language, 2 social studies, 1 history. *Academic units recommended:* 4 English, 4 mathematics, 4 science, (4 science labs), 4 foreign language, 2 social studies, 2 history. **Freshman Admission Statistics:** 4,761 applied, 74% admitted, 27% enrolled. **Transfer Admission Requirements:** High school transcript, college transcript(s), essay or personal statement, statement of good standing from prior institution(s). Minimum college GPA of 2.0 required. Lowest grade transferable C. **General Admission Information:** Application fee $50. Regular application deadline 2/1. Regular notification 4/1. Nonfall registration accepted. Admission may be deferred for a maximum of 2 semesters. Credit offered for CEEB Advanced Placement tests.

COSTS AND FINANCIAL AID

Annual in-state tuition $3,900. Annual out-of-state tuition $16,810. Room and board $8,200. Required fees $3,900. Average book expense $1,000. **Required Forms and Deadlines:** FAFSA, institution's own financial aid form Financial aid filing deadline 5/31. Priority financial aid filing date 3/1. **Notification of Awards:** Applicants will be notified of awards on or about 4/15. **Types of Aid:** *Need-based scholarships/grants:* Federal Pell, SEOG, state scholarships/grants, private scholarships, the school's own gift aid, Unendowed gifts. *Loans:* FFEL Subsidized Stafford, FFEL Unsubsidized Stafford, FFEL PLUS, Federal Perkins. *Student Employment:* Federal Work-Study Program available. Institutional employment available. Highest amount earned per year from on-campus jobs $5,200. Off-campus job opportunities are good. **Financial Aid Statistics:** 13% freshmen, 13% undergrads receive need-based scholarship or grant aid. 13% freshmen, 7% undergrads receive non-need-based scholarship or grant aid. 22% freshmen, 17% undergrads receive need-based self-help aid. 56% freshmen, 58% undergrads receive any aid. 44% undergrads borrow to pay for school. Average cumulative indebtedness $15,630. **Criteria for awarding institutional aid:** *Non-need-based:* Academics, alumni affiliation, art, leadership, music/drama, state/district residency.

UNIVERSITY OF MARYLAND
UNIVERSITY COLLEGE

3501 University Blvd. East, Adelphi, MD 20783
Phone: 301-985-7000
E-mail: umucinfo@nova.umuc.edu
Fax: 301-985-7364 **Website:** www.umuc.edu **ACT Code:** 20097

This public school was founded in 1947.

RATINGS

Admissions Selectivity Rating: 60*   **Fire Safety Rating:** 60*   **Green Rating:** 60*

STUDENTS AND FACULTY

Enrollment: 17,527. **Student Body:** 58% female, 42% male, 31% out-of-state. **Faculty:** Student/faculty ratio 24:1. 119 full-time faculty, 66% hold PhDs, 38% are women.

ACADEMICS

Degrees: Associate, bachelor's, certificate, master's, post-bachelor's certificate. **Classes:** Most classes have 20–29 students. **Majors with Highest Enrollment:** Business/commerce; information science/studies; multi-/interdisciplinary studies, other. **Special Study Options:** Accelerated program, cooperative education program, cross-registration, distance learning, double major, dual enrollment, external degree program, teacher certification program, weekend college Special programs offered to physically disabled students include note-taking services, reader services, tape recorders, tutors. **Career services:** Alumni services, career/job search classes, career assessment.

FACILITIES

Housing: 85% of campus accessible to physically disabled. **Computers:** Students can register for classes online. Administrative functions (other than registration) can be performed online.

CAMPUS LIFE

Environment: Village.

ADMISSIONS

Freshman Academic Profile: Minimum paper TOEFL 550. Minimum computer TOEFL 213. **Freshman Admission Requirements:** High school diploma is required and GED is accepted. **Freshman Admission Statistics:** 994 applied, 100% admitted, 53% enrolled. **Transfer Admission Requirements:** High school transcript, college transcript(s), minimum college GPA of 2.0 required. Lowest grade transferable D. **General Admission Information:** Application fee $30. Nonfall registration accepted. Admission may be deferred for a maximum of 24 months. Credit and/or placement offered for CEEB Advanced Placement tests.

COSTS AND FINANCIAL AID

Annual in-state tuition $5,208. Annual out-of-state tuition $9,576. Required fees $120. Average book expense $1,362. **Required Forms and Deadlines:** FAFSA, institution's own financial aid form. Priority financial aid filing date 6/1. **Notification of Awards:** Applicants will be notified of awards on a rolling basis beginning 5/1. **Types of Aid:** *Need-based scholarships/grants:* Federal Pell, SEOG, state scholarships/grants, private scholarships, the school's own gift aid. *Loans:* Direct Subsidized Stafford, Direct Unsubsidized Stafford, Direct PLUS, Federal Perkins. *Student Employment:* Off-campus job opportunities are good. **Financial Aid Statistics:** 30% freshmen, 34% undergrads receive need-based scholarship or grant aid. 2% undergrads receive non-need-based scholarship or grant aid. 37% freshmen, 46% undergrads receive need-based self-help aid. **Criteria for awarding institutional aid:** *Non-need-based:* Academics, leadership.

UNIVERSITY OF MARYLAND, BALTIMORE COUNTY

Best 373

1000 Hilltop Circle, Baltimore, MD 21250
Phone: 410-455-2291 **Financial Aid Phone:** 410-455-2387
E-mail: admissions@umbc.edu **CEEB Code:** 5835
Fax: 410-455-1094 **Website:** www.umbc.edu **ACT Code:** 1751

This public school was founded in 1966. It has a 530-acre campus.

RATINGS

Admissions Selectivity Rating: 83   **Fire Safety Rating:** 85   **Green Rating:** 91

STUDENTS AND FACULTY

Enrollment: 9,815. **Student Body:** 46% female, 54% male, 6.7% out-of-state, 4% international (92 countries represented). Asian 21%, African American 17%, Caucasian 52%, Hispanic 4%, Native American 1%.
Retention and Graduation: 43% grads go on to further study within 1 year. 30% grads pursue arts and sciences degrees. 1.4% grads pursue law degrees. 2.3% grads pursue business degrees. 4.7% grads pursue medical degrees. **Faculty:** Student/faculty ratio 19:1. 480 full-time faculty, 87% hold PhDs, 18% are members of minority groups, 43% are women. 1.8% of classes are taught by teaching assistants.

ACADEMICS

Degrees: Bachelor's, master's, post-bachelor's certificate. **Classes:** Most classes have 20–29 students. Most lab/discussion sessions have 10–19 students. **Majors with Highest Enrollment:** Biology/biological sciences; computer and information sciences; psychology. **Special Study Options:** Accelerated program, cooperative education program, cross-registration, double major, dual enrollment, English as a Second Language (ESL), exchange student program (domestic), honors program, independent study, internships, student-designed major, study abroad, teacher certification program. **Honors programs:** UMBC Honors College, Merehoff (Science, Technology, Engineering, and Mathematics), Scholars Program, Sherman Teacher Education Scholars Program, Sondheim Scholars Programs, Center for Women and Information Technology (CWIT) Scholars Program, Humanities Scholars Program, Lineman Scholars Program. **Combined degree programs:** BA/MA, BA/MEng, biochemistry, chemistry, economics, info. systems. Special programs offered to physically disabled students

include note-taking services, reader services, tape recorders, tutors. **Career services:** Alumni network, alumni services, career/job search classes, career assessment, internships, regional alumni. **Career services highlights include:** UMBC Career Services is proud of many of the programs and stellar customer service that it delivers to multiple constituents. Collaboration is high with internal and external partners and a primary example of this type of collaboration is demonstrated by the development of Career Path, a website that is intended to help students understand what they can do with their major within a variety of industries, access current jobs and hear the stories of UMBC alumni. We are also extremely proud of consistent and continual employer recruitment activities and presence on campus despite a downturn in the economy. Our graduates continue to report very good job offers.

FACILITIES

Housing: Coed dorms, special housing for disabled students, apartments for single students, theme housingSame sex floors, honors floors, quiet lifestyle, Substance-free, and living-learning communities: Center for Women and Information Technology, Emergency Health Services, Exploratory Majors, Honors College, Humanities Floor, Intercultural Living Exchange, Shriver Living Learning Center, Visual and Performing Arts Floor, and Women Involved in Learning and Leadership, gender neutral. 95% of campus accessible to physically disabled. **Special Academic Facilities/Equipment:** Albin O. Kuhn Library and Gallery, Center for Art and Visual Culture, Women's Center, Center for Environmental Science, Center for Photonics Technology, Center for Women and Information Technology, Center on Research and Teaching in Social Work, Howard Hughes Medical Institute at UMBC, Imaging Research Center, Institute for Global Electronic Commerce, Joint Center for Earth Systems Technology, Laboratory for Healthcare Informatics, Maryland Center for Telecommunications Research, Maryland Institute for Policy Analysis and Research, bwtech@umbc Research and Technology Park and Incubator and Accelerator, Shriver Center, UMBC Technology Center, Goddard Earth Science and Technology Center. **Computers:** 100% of classrooms, 80% of dorms, 100% of libraries, 100% of dining areas, 100% of student union, 40% of common outdoor areas have wireless network access. Students can register for classes online. Administrative functions (other than registration) can be performed online.

CAMPUS LIFE

Environment: Metropolis. **Activities:** Choral groups, dance, drama/theater, jazz band, literary magazine, music ensembles, musical theater, pep band, radio station, student government, student newspaper, student-run film society, symphony orchestra, campus ministries, international student organization, Model UN. **Organizations:** 230 registered organizations, 8 honor societies, 20 religious organizations. 11 fraternities, 12 sororities. **Athletics (Intercollegiate):** *Men:* Baseball, basketball, cheerleading, cross-country, diving, lacrosse, soccer, swimming, tennis, track/field (outdoor), track/field (indoor). *Women:* Basketball, cheerleading, cross-country, diving, lacrosse, soccer, softball, swimming, tennis, track/field (outdoor), track/field (indoor), volleyball. **On-Campus Highlights:** Albin O. Kuhn Library and Gallery, The Commons (Student Center), Center for Art Design and Visual Cultu, Howard Hughes Medical Institute Lab, Retriever Activities Center, Students attend, and take part in, a world of excellent theatre, music and dance performances on campus. They go to art openings and lectures, start clubs and exchange ideas through the campus paper and literary magazines. **Environmental Initiatives:** Climate Commitment Task Force (students, faculty, staff) will commence implementation of its Climate Action Plan and reduce our carbon footprint. Implement energy performance contract. Pursuing LEED Silver certification for new Performing Arts and Humanities Facility, which is expected to start contruction in June 2010 and begin design on LEED certified residence hall.

ADMISSIONS

Freshman Academic Profile: Average high school GPA 3.61. 24.2% in top 10% of high school class, 52% in top 25% of high school class, 83.6% in top 50% of high school class. SAT Math middle 50% range 550–660. SAT Critical Reading middle 50% range 530–630. SAT Writing middle 50% range 530–630. ACT middle 50% range 22–29. Minimum paper TOEFL 460. Minimum computer TOEFL 140. Minimum web-based TOEFL 48. **Basis for Candidate Selection:** *Very important factors considered include:* Academic GPA, rigor of secondary school record, standardized test scores. *Important factors considered include:* Class rank, application essay, recommendation(s), talent/ability. *Other factors considered include:* Character/personal qualities, extracurricular activities. **Freshman Admission Requirements:** High school diploma is required and GED is accepted. *Academic units required:* 4 English, 3 mathematics, 3 science, 2 foreign language, 3 social studies, 3 Social Studies & History *Academic units recommended:* 4 mathematics. **Freshman Admission Statistics:** 6,047 applied, 69% admitted, 37% enrolled. **Transfer Admission Requirements:** College transcript(s), statement of good standing from prior institution(s). Minimum college GPA of 2.5 required. Lowest grade transferable D. **General Admission Information:** Application fee $50. Regular application deadline 2/1. Notification on a rolling basis, beginning on or about 12/15. Nonfall registration accepted. Admission may be deferred for a maximum of 1 year. Credit and/or placement offered for CEEB Advanced Placement tests.

COSTS AND FINANCIAL AID

Annual in-state tuition $8,872. Annual out-of-state tuition $18,213. Room and board $9,050. Average book expense $1,200. **Required Forms and Deadlines:** FAFSA. Priority financial aid filing date 2/14. **Notification of Awards:** Applicants will be notified of awards on a rolling basis beginning 3/15. **Types of Aid:** *Need-based scholarships/grants:* Federal Pell, SEOG, state scholarships/grants, private scholarships, the school's own gift aid. *Loans:* Direct Subsidized Stafford, Direct Unsubsidized Stafford, Direct PLUS, Federal Perkins. *Student Employment:* Federal Work-Study Program available. Institutional employment available. Off-campus job opportunities are excellent. **Financial Aid Statistics:** 38% freshmen, 39% undergrads receive need-based scholarship or grant aid. 7% freshmen, 4% undergrads receive non-need-based scholarship or grant aid. 38% freshmen, 43% undergrads receive need-based self-help aid. 5% freshmen, 4% undergrads receive athletic scholarships. 70% freshmen, 61% undergrads receive any aid. 51% undergrads borrow to pay for school. Average cumulative indebtedness $19,353. **Criteria for awarding institutional aid:** *Non-need-based:* Academics, alumni affiliation, art, athletics, music/drama.

See page 1294.

UNIVERSITY OF MARYLAND, COLLEGE PARK

Mitchell Building, College Park, MD 20742-5235
Phone: 301-314-8385 **Financial Aid Phone:** 301-314-9000
E-mail: um-admit@uga.umd.edu **CEEB Code:** 5814
Fax: 301-314-9693 **Website:** www.maryland.edu **ACT Code:** 1746

This public school was founded in 1856. It has a 1382-acre campus.

RATINGS

Admissions Selectivity Rating: 95   Fire Safety Rating: 76   Green Rating: 99

STUDENTS AND FACULTY

Enrollment: 25,898. **Student Body:** 47% female, 53% male, 24% out-of-state, 2% international (135 countries represented). Asian 15%, African American 12%, Caucasian 58%, Hispanic 6%.
Retention and Graduation: 93% freshmen return for sophomore year. 63% freshmen graduate within 4 years. **Faculty:** Student/faculty ratio 18.19996:1. 1644 full-time faculty, 92% hold PhDs, 19% are members of minority groups, 34% are women. 15% of classes are taught by teaching assistants.

ACADEMICS

Degrees: Bachelor's, certificate, master's, post-bachelor's certificate, post-master's certificate. **Classes:** Most classes have 20–29 students. Most lab/discussion sessions have 20–29 students. **Majors with Highest Enrollment:** criminology; economics; political science and government. **Special Study Options:** Accelerated program, cooperative education program, cross-registration, distance learning, double major, dual enrollment, English as a Second Language (ESL), exchange student program (domestic), external degree program, honors program, independent study, internships, liberal arts/career combination, student-designed major, study abroad, teacher certification program, Living-Learning programs including Gemstone Program, Honors, First-Year Focus, Jiminez-Porter Writers House, Civicus, College Park Scholars, and others. **Honors programs:** Gemstones, Honors, Honors Humanities. **Combined degree programs:** BA/JD, BA/MA, BA/MBA. Special programs offered to physically disabled students include note-taking services, reader services, tape recorders, tutors. **Career services:** Internships.

FACILITIES

Housing: Coed dorms, special housing for disabled students, special housing for international students, women's dorms, fraternity/sorority housing, cooperative housing, apartments for single students, wellness housing, theme housing, Living/Learning program housing includes Gemstone program, College Park Scholars, Language House, Beyond the Classroom, Civicus, Hinman CEOs, Global Communities, Jimenz-Porter Writer's House, Honors, International House, Honors Humanities, smoke-free/alcohol-free. **Special Academic Facilities/Equipment:** Aerospace buoyancy lab, art gallery, international piano archives, center for architectural design and research, model nuclear reactor, wind tunnel. **Computers:** 100% of classrooms, 100% of dorms, 100% of libraries, 100% of dining areas, 100% of student union, 100% of common outdoor areas have wireless network access. Students can register for classes online. Administrative functions (other than registration) can be performed online.

CAMPUS LIFE

Environment: Metropolis. **Activities:** Choral groups, concert band, dance, drama/theater, jazz band, literary magazine, marching band, music ensembles, musical theater, opera, pep band, radio station, student government, student newspaper, student-run film society, symphony orchestra, television station, yearbook, campus ministries, international student organization, Model UN. **Organizations:** 574 registered organizations, 53 honor societies, 55 religious organizations. 36 fraternities, 27 sororities. **Athletics (Intercollegiate):** *Men:* Baseball, basketball, cross-country, football, golf, lacrosse, soccer, swimming, tennis, track/field (outdoor), track/field (indoor), wrestling. *Women:* Basketball, cheerleading, cross-country, field hockey, golf, gymnastics, lacrosse, soccer, softball, swimming, tennis, track/field (outdoor), track/field (indoor), volleyball, water polo. **On-Campus Highlights:** Clarice Smith Performing Arts Center, Adele H. Stamp Student Union, Eppley Recreation Center, Chevy Chase Bank Field at Byrd Stadium, Comcast Center, 6. Memorial Chapel 7. Riggs Alumni Center. **Environmental Initiatives:** Developing a Climate Action Plan consistent with the American College and University Presidents Climate Commitment. Working to integrate sustainability across the University curriculum and develop a sustainability ethic in campus culture through multiple programs. Designing and construction all new buildings and major renovations to at least LEED-Silver standards and developing storm water management controls to improve the quality of local streams and the Chesapeake Bay.

ADMISSIONS

Freshman Academic Profile: Average high school GPA 3.93. 71% in top 10% of high school class, 91% in top 25% of high school class, 99% in top 50% of high school class. SAT Math middle 50% range 620–710. SAT Critical Reading middle 50% range 580–680. Minimum paper TOEFL 575. **Basis for Candidate Selection:** *Very important factors considered include:* Academic GPA, rigor of secondary school record, standardized test scores. *Important factors considered include:* Class rank, application essay, recommendation(s), first generation, state residency, talent/ability. *Other factors considered include:* Alumni/ae relation, character/personal qualities, extracurricular activities, geographical residence, racial/ethnic status, volunteer work, work experience. **Freshman Admission Requirements:** High school diploma is required and GED is accepted. *Academic units required:* 4 English, 3 mathematics, 3 science, (2 science labs), 2 foreign language, 3 social studies. *Academic units recommended:* 4 mathematics. **Freshman Admission Statistics:** 28,331 applied, 42% admitted, 35% enrolled. **Transfer Admission Requirements:** College transcript(s), essay or personal statement, statement of good standing from prior institution(s). Lowest grade transferable C. **General Admission Information:** Application fee $55. Regular application deadline 1/20. Nonfall registration accepted. Admission may be deferred for a maximum of 1 year. Credit and/or placement offered for CEEB Advanced Placement tests.

COSTS AND FINANCIAL AID

Annual in-state tuition $6,556. Annual out-of-state tuition $22,503. Room and board $9,377. Required fees $1,487. Average book expense $1,025. **Required Forms and Deadlines:** FAFSA. Priority financial aid filing date 2/15. **Notification of Awards:** Applicants will be notified of awards on a rolling basis beginning 4/1. **Types of Aid:** *Need-based scholarships/grants:* Federal Pell, SEOG, state scholarships/grants, private scholarships, the school's own gift aid. *Loans:* FFEL Subsidized Stafford, FFEL Unsubsidized Stafford, FFEL PLUS, Federal Perkins. *Student Employment:* Federal Work-Study Program available. Institutional employment available. Off-campus job opportunities are good. **Financial Aid Statistics:** 25% freshmen, 26% undergrads receive need-based scholarship or grant aid. 21% freshmen, 14% undergrads receive non-need-based scholarship or grant aid. 23% freshmen, 26% undergrads receive need-based self-help aid. 1% freshmen, 1% undergrads receive athletic scholarships. 67.8% freshmen, 59.5% undergrads receive any aid. 44% undergrads borrow to pay for school. Average cumulative indebtedness $20,091. **Criteria for awarding institutional aid:** *Non-need-based:* Academics, art, athletics.

UNIVERSITY OF MASSACHUSETTS—AMHERST

Best 373

University Admissions Center, 37 Mather Dr, Amherst, MA 01003-9291
Phone: 413-545-0222 **Financial Aid Phone:** 413-545-0801
E-mail: mail@admissions.umass.edu **CEEB Code:** 3917
Fax: 413-545-4312 **Website:** www.umass.edu **ACT Code:** 1924

This public school was founded in 1863. It has a 1463-acre campus.

RATINGS
Admissions Selectivity Rating: 86   **Fire Safety Rating:** 80   **Green Rating:** 89

STUDENTS AND FACULTY
Enrollment: 20,287. **Student Body:** 50% female, 50% male, 17% out-of-state, 1% international (44 countries represented). Asian 8%, African American 5%, Caucasian 70%, Hispanic 4%.
Retention and Graduation: 49% freshmen graduate within 4 years. 22.1% grads go on to further study within 1 year. 8.2% grads pursue law degrees. 19.1% grads pursue business degrees. 5.6% grads pursue medical degrees.
Faculty: Student/faculty ratio 18:1. 1170 full-time faculty, 93% hold PhDs, 19% are members of minority groups, 38% are women.

ACADEMICS
Degrees: Associate, bachelor's, certificate, doctoral, master's, post-bachelor's certificate, post-master's certificate. **Classes:** Most classes have 20–29 students. Most lab/discussion sessions have 20–29 students. **Majors with Highest Enrollment:** Biology/biological sciences; business administration and management; psychology. **Special Study Options:** Cooperative education program, cross-registration, distance learning, double major, dual enrollment, English as a Second Language (ESL), exchange student program (domestic), honors program, independent study, internships, liberal arts/career combination, student-designed major, study abroad, teacher certification program. **Honors programs:** Commonwealth Honors College offers the advantages of a small honors college, but also the wide-ranging opportunities of a nationally recognized research university. There are approximately 2,800 academically talented students in the Commonwealth College, all experiencing the challenges of a dynamic curriculum that includes interdisciplinary seminars, enriched honors courses, colloquia, independent study, service learning, a "culminating experience" and an honors thesis or project, as well as the option of special living-learning accommodations. Special programs offered to physically disabled students include note-taking services, reader services, tape recorders, tutors. **Career services:** Alumni network, alumni services, career/job search classes, career assessment, internships, regional alumni. **Career services highlights include:** We are very proud of the comprehensive career planning services we provide to the students at the university. There is no program that we feel is better than the others.

FACILITIES
Housing: Coed dorms, special housing for disabled students, men's dorms, special housing for international students, women's dorms, fraternity/sorority housing, apartments for married students, apartments for single students, wellness housing, theme housing, first year housing. **Special Academic Facilities/Equipment:** Computer Science Complex, Polymer Research Institute, Herter (Art) Gallery, University Art Gallery, Natural History Museum, Fine Arts Center, Mullins Center (sports and entertainment arena, Learning Commons. **Computers:** 97% of classrooms, 10% of dorms, 100% of libraries, 100% of dining areas, 100% of student union, 20% of common outdoor areas have wireless network access. Students can register for classes online. Administrative functions (other than registration) can be performed online.

CAMPUS LIFE
Environment: Town. **Activities:** Choral groups, concert band, dance, drama/theater, jazz band, literary magazine, marching band, music ensembles, musical theater, opera, pep band, radio station, student government, student newspaper, student-run film society, symphony orchestra, television station, campus ministries, international student organization, Model UN. **Organizations:** 291 registered organizations, 30 honor societies, 14 religious organizations. 21 fraternities, 15 sororities. **Athletics (Intercollegiate):** *Men:* Baseball, basketball, cross-country, diving, football, ice hockey, lacrosse, soccer, swimming, track/field (outdoor), track/field (indoor). *Women:* Basketball, crew/rowing, cross-country, diving, field hockey, lacrosse, soccer, softball, swimming, tennis, track/field (outdoor), track/field (indoor). **On-Campus Highlights:** The Campus Center / Student Union, The Learning Commons, Recreation Center, The Mullins Center, The Fine Arts Center, www.umass.edu/umhome/visit_campus.html. **Environmental Initiatives:** Central Heating Plant: Our new Central Heating

Plant now allows us to produce roughly 70% of our campus' energy through co-generation. The Central Heating Plant is fueled by mostly natural gas with some oil in the winter time. Climate Action Plan: The development of our campus' Climate Action Plan is our most recent success that will help UMass Amherst move toward a more sustainable future. Our Climate Action Plan not only lists what UMass Amherst has done, but how we plan to recude our greenhouse gas emissions and other negative environmental impacts in important areas such as energy conservation, green building, transportation, etc. Student Involvement: UMass Amherst is dedicated to not only reducing our greenhouse gas emissions and other environmental impacts through infrastructural changes, but also through actively involving student sin all parts of its sustainability initiative. The UMass Amherst Eco-Rep Program is one of the largest in the country with upwards of 70 Eco-Reps working to educate their peers about environmental issues that they can have a positive impact on as college students. Also, UMass Amherst has just hired its first seven Sustainability Interns to aid the Sustainability Coordinator and our Environmental Performance Advisory Committee in carrying out the Climate Action Plan.

ADMISSIONS
Freshman Academic Profile: Average high school GPA 3.6. 27% in top 10% of high school class, 67% in top 25% of high school class, 97% in top 50% of high school class. SAT Math middle 50% range 540–650. SAT Critical Reading middle 50% range 520–630. ACT middle 50% range 23–28. Minimum paper TOEFL 550. Minimum computer TOEFL 213. **Basis for Candidate Selection:** *Very important factors considered include:* Academic GPA, rigor of secondary school record. *Important factors considered include:* Class rank, standardized test scores. *Other factors considered include:* Application essay, recommendation(s), character/personal qualities, extracurricular activities, first generation, geographical residence, level of applicant's interest, racial/ethnic status, state residency, talent/ability, volunteer work, work experience. **Freshman Admission Requirements:** High school diploma is required and GED is accepted. *Academic units required:* 4 English, 3 mathematics, 3 science, (2 science labs), 2 foreign language, 2 social studies, 2 academic electives. **Freshman Admission Statistics:** 29,452 applied, 67% admitted, 21% enrolled. **Transfer Admission Requirements:** College transcript(s), essay or personal statement, minimum college GPA of 2.5 required. Lowest grade transferable C–. **General Admission Information:** Regular application deadline 1/15. Nonfall registration accepted. Admission may be deferred for a maximum of 1 year. Credit and/or placement offered for CEEB Advanced Placement tests.

COSTS AND FINANCIAL AID
Required Forms and Deadlines: FAFSA. Priority financial aid filing date 2/14. **Notification of Awards:** Applicants will be notified of awards on a rolling basis beginning 3/1. **Types of Aid:** *Need-based scholarships/grants:* Federal Pell, SEOG, state scholarships/grants, private scholarships, the school's own gift aid. *Loans:* Direct Subsidized Stafford, Direct Unsubsidized Stafford, Direct PLUS, Federal Perkins, state loans *Student Employment:* Federal Work-Study Program available. Institutional employment available. Off-campus job opportunities are good. **Financial Aid Statistics:** 43% freshmen, 41% undergrads receive need-based scholarship or grant aid. 3% freshmen, 3% undergrads receive non-need-based scholarship or grant aid. 45% freshmen, 46% undergrads receive need-based self-help aid. 1% freshmen, 1% undergrads receive athletic scholarships. 84% freshmen, 89% undergrads receive any aid. 67% undergrads borrow to pay for school. Average cumulative indebtedness $23,614. **Criteria for awarding institutional aid:** *Non-need-based:* Academics, art, athletics, music/drama, state/district residency.

UNIVERSITY OF MASSACHUSETTS—BOSTON

100 Morrissey Boulevard, Boston, MA 02125-3393
Phone: 617-287-6000 **Financial Aid Phone:** 617-287-6300
E-mail: enrollment.info@umb.edu **CEEB Code:** 3924
Fax: 617-287-5999 **Website:** www.umb.edu

This public school was founded in 1964. It has a 177-acre campus.

RATINGS
Admissions Selectivity Rating: 76   **Fire Safety Rating:** 60*   **Green Rating:** 96

STUDENTS AND FACULTY
Enrollment: 10,130. **Student Body:** 58% female, 42% male, 5% out-of-state, 4% international (138 countries represented). Asian 3%, African American 16%, Caucasian 48%, Hispanic 9%.
Retention and Graduation: 77% freshmen return for sophomore year. 119% freshmen graduate within 4 years. **Faculty:** Student/faculty ratio 16:1. 499 full-time faculty, 93% hold PhDs, 21% are members of minority groups, 48% are women.

ACADEMICS

Degrees: Bachelor's, certificate, master's, post-bachelor's certificate, post-master's certificate. **Classes:** Most classes have 20–29 students. Most lab/discussion sessions have fewer than 10 students. **Majors with Highest Enrollment:** Management science; nursing/registered nurse (RN, ASN, BSN, MSN); psychology. **Special Study Options:** Cooperative education program, cross-registration, distance learning, double major, dual enrollment, English as a Second Language (ESL), exchange student program (domestic), honors program, independent study, internships, liberal arts/career combination, student-designed major, study abroad, teacher certification program. **Honors programs:** The University Honors Program seeks to meet the needs of students who thrive on intellectual challenge by offering special interdisciplinary academic opportunities outside the major. **Combined degree programs:** BA/MA, BA/MBA BA/MA applied science, BA/MA sociology. Special programs offered to physically disabled students include note-taking services, reader services, tape recorders, tutors. **Career services:** Alumni network, alumni services, career/job search classes, career assessment, internships, regional alumni.

FACILITIES

Housing: University housing referral service. 100% of campus accessible to physically disabled. **Special Academic Facilities/Equipment:** Art gallery, tropical greenhouse, observatory, adaptive computer lab. **Computers:** 100% of classrooms, 100% of libraries, 100% of dining areas, 100% of student union, have wireless network access. Students can register for classes online. Administrative functions (other than registration) can be performed online.

CAMPUS LIFE

Environment: Metropolis. **Activities:** Choral groups, concert band, dance, drama/theater, jazz band, literary magazine, music ensembles, radio station, student government, student newspaper, student-run film society, symphony orchestra, yearbook, campus ministries, international student organization, Model UN. **Organizations:** 75 registered organizations, 1 honor societies. **Athletics (Intercollegiate):** *Men:* Baseball, basketball, cross-country, ice hockey, lacrosse, soccer, tennis, track/field (outdoor), track/field (indoor). *Women:* Basketball, cross-country, ice hockey, soccer, softball, tennis, track/field (outdoor), track/field (indoor), volleyball. **On-Campus Highlights:** New Campus Center, Clark Athletic Center, Waterfront area and weekly boat tours, Greenhouse, Healey Library. **Environmental Initiatives:** 1. Comprehensive sustainability program, toxics use reduction program, energy conservation and management efforts, master planning. UMB awarded MA Sustainable Campus of the Year in 2004. 2. Sigining Tailories and ACUPCC commitments—only public university in Boston to do so. 3. Academic program with environmental focus in both graduate and undergraduate levels—in many colleges within the university.

ADMISSIONS

Freshman Academic Profile: Average high school GPA 3. SAT Math middle 50% range 480–580. SAT Critical Reading middle 50% range 460–570. Minimum paper TOEFL 550. Minimum computer TOEFL 213. Minimum web-based TOEFL 79. **Basis for Candidate Selection:** *Very important factors considered include:* Academic GPA, rigor of secondary school record, standardized test scores, character/personal qualities. *Important factors considered include:* Application essay, recommendation(s). *Other factors considered include:* Extracurricular activities, first generation, interview, level of applicant's interest, talent/ability, volunteer work, work experience. **Freshman Admission Requirements:** High school diploma is required and GED is accepted. *Academic units required:* 4 English, 3 mathematics, 3 science, (2 science labs), 2 foreign language, 1 social studies, 1 history, 2 academic electives. **Freshman Admission Statistics:** 6,050 applied, 61% admitted, 27% enrolled. **Transfer Admission Requirements:** College transcript(s), essay or personal statement, statement of good standing from prior institution(s). Minimum college GPA of 2.5 required. Lowest grade transferable C–. **General Admission Information:** Application fee $40. Regular application deadline 6/1. Nonfall registration accepted. Admission may be deferred for a maximum of 1 year. Credit offered for CEEB Advanced Placement tests.

COSTS AND FINANCIAL AID

Annual in-state tuition $1,714. Annual out-of-state tuition $9,758. Required fees $8,897. **Required Forms and Deadlines:** FAFSA. Priority financial aid filing date 3/1. **Notification of Awards:** Applicants will be notified of awards on a rolling basis beginning 3/21. **Types of Aid:** *Need-based scholarships/grants:* Federal Pell, SEOG, state scholarships/grants, private scholarships, the school's own gift aid, Federal Nursing Scholarships. *Loans:* Direct Subsidized Stafford, Direct Unsubsidized Stafford, Direct PLUS, Federal Perkins. *Student Employment:* Off-campus job opportunities are excellent. **Financial Aid Statistics:** 58% freshmen, 52% undergrads receive need-based scholarship or grant aid. 3% freshmen, 2% undergrads receive non-need-based scholarship or grant aid. 57% freshmen, 58% undergrads receive need-based self-help aid. 67% undergrads borrow to pay for school. Average cumulative indebtedness $19,327. **Criteria for awarding institutional aid:** *Non-need-based:* Academics, leadership, state/district residency.

See page 1296.

UNIVERSITY OF MASSACHUSETTS— DARTMOUTH

285 Old Westport Road, N Dartmouth, MA 02747-2300
Phone: 508-999-8605 **Financial Aid Phone:** 508-999-8857
E-mail: admissions@umassd.edu **CEEB Code:** 3786
Fax: 508-999-8755 **Website:** www.umassd.edu **ACT Code:** 1906

This public school was founded in 1895. It has a 710-acre campus.

RATINGS

Admissions Selectivity Rating: 74   **Fire Safety Rating:** 60*   **Green Rating:** 72

STUDENTS AND FACULTY

Enrollment: 7,775. **Student Body:** 48% female, 52% male, 4% out-of-state, international (41 countries represented). Asian 3%, African American 8%, Caucasian 79%, Hispanic 3%, Native American 1%.
Retention and Graduation: 73% freshmen return for sophomore year. 32% freshmen graduate within 4 years. **Faculty:** Student/faculty ratio 18:1. 369 full-time faculty, 86% hold PhDs, 23% are members of minority groups, 40% are women. 3% of classes are taught by teaching assistants.

ACADEMICS

Degrees: Bachelor's, doctoral, master's, post-bachelor's certificate, post-master's certificate. **Classes:** Most classes have 20–29 students. Most lab/discussion sessions have 20–29 students. **Majors with Highest Enrollment:** Business administration and management; nursing; other; psychology. **Special Study Options:** Cooperative education program, cross-registration, distance learning, double major, dual enrollment, exchange student program (domestic), honors program, independent study, internships, student-designed major, study abroad, teacher certification program. **Honors programs:** Honors Program **Combined degree programs:** BA/JD, BA/MA, BS/MS chemistry, biology,engineering, and nursing; BS/MAT and BA/MAT. Special programs offered to physically disabled students include note-taking services, reader services, tape recorders, tutors. **Career services:** Alumni network, career/job search classes, internships

FACILITIES

Housing: Coed dorms, special housing for disabled students, apartments for single students, apartments for upperclassmen and graduate students. Program dedicated suites. 97% of campus accessible to physically disabled. **Special Academic Facilities/Equipment:** Art gallery, language center, center for Jewish culture, Robert F. Kennedy assassination archives, electron microscope, observatory, marine research vessels, Advanced Manufacturing and Technology Center, School of Marine Science and Technology. **Computers:** 100% of classrooms, 100% of dorms, 100% of libraries, 100% of dining areas, 100% of student union, 100% of common outdoor areas have wireless network access. Students can register for classes online. Administrative functions (other than registration) can be performed online.

CAMPUS LIFE

Environment: Town. **Activities:** Choral groups, concert band, dance, drama/theater, jazz band, literary magazine, music ensembles, musical theater, pep band, radio station, student government, student newspaper, symphony orchestra, yearbook, international student organization. **Organizations:** 103 registered organizations, 5 honor societies, 6 religious organizations. 5 fraternities, 3 sororities. **Athletics (Intercollegiate):** *Men:* Baseball, basketball, cross-country, diving, football, golf, ice hockey, lacrosse, soccer, swimming, tennis, track/field (outdoor), track/field (indoor). *Women:* Basketball, cheerleading, cross-country, diving, equestrian sports, field hockey, golf, lacrosse, soccer, softball, swimming, tennis, track/field (outdoor), track/field (indoor), volleyball. **On-Campus Highlights:** Underground Cafe, Tripp Athletic Center, Woodlawn Commons, MacLean Campus Center, Observatory.

ADMISSIONS

Freshman Academic Profile: Average high school GPA 3.06. 14% in top 10% of high school class, 36% in top 25% of high school class, 75% in top 50% of high school class. 89% from public high schools. SAT Math middle 50% range 490–590. SAT Critical Reading middle 50% range 470–560. ACT middle 50% range 20–25. Minimum paper TOEFL 520. Minimum computer TOEFL 190. Minimum web-based TOEFL 68. **Basis for Candidate Selection:** *Very important factors considered include:* Academic GPA, rigor of secondary school record, standardized test scores, *Other factors considered include:* Class rank, application essay, recommendation(s), alumni/ae relation, character/personal qualities, extracurricular activities, first generation, talent/ability, volunteer work, work experience. **Freshman Admission Requirements:** High school diploma is required and GED is accepted. *Academic units required:* 4 English, 3 mathematics, 3 science, (2 science labs), 2 foreign language, 1 social studies, 1 history, 2 academic electives. *Academic units recommended:* 1 additional math and science for some majors. **Freshman Admission Statistics:** 7,149 applied, 68% admitted, 31% enrolled. **Transfer Admission Requirements:** College transcript(s), essay or personal statement, minimum college GPA of 2.5 required. Lowest grade transferable C–. **General Admission Information:** Application fee $40. Early decision application deadline 11/15. Notification on a rolling basis, beginning on or about 12/15. Nonfall registration accepted. Admission may be deferred for a maximum of 2 semesters. Credit and/or placement offered for CEEB Advanced Placement tests.

COSTS AND FINANCIAL AID

Annual in-state tuition $1,417. Annual out-of-state tuition $8,099. Average book expense $1,200. **Required Forms and Deadlines:** FAFSA. Priority financial aid filing date 3/1. **Notification of Awards:** Applicants will be notified of awards on a rolling basis beginning 3/25. **Types of Aid:** *Need-based scholarships/grants:* Federal Pell, SEOG, state scholarships/grants, private scholarships, the school's own gift aid. *Loans:* Direct Subsidized Stafford, Direct Unsubsidized Stafford, Direct PLUS, Federal Perkins, Federal Nursing, state loans. *Student Employment:* Federal Work-Study Program available. Institutional employment available. Off-campus job opportunities are excellent. **Financial Aid Statistics:** 51% freshmen, 45% undergrads receive need-based scholarship or grant aid. 2% freshmen, 2% undergrads receive non-need-based scholarship or grant aid. 58% freshmen, 55% undergrads receive need-based self-help aid. 62% freshmen, 58% undergrads receive any aid. 73% undergrads borrow to pay for school. Average cumulative indebtedness $21,905. **Criteria for awarding institutional aid:** *Non-need-based:* Academics, minority status, state/district residency.

UNIVERSITY OF MASSACHUSETTS—LOWELL

Office of Undergrad Admissions, 883 Broadway Street Suite 110, Lowell, MA 01854-5104

Phone: 978-934-3931 **Financial Aid Phone:** 978-934-4237
E-mail: admissions@uml.edu **CEEB Code:** 3911
Fax: 978-934-3086 **Website:** www.uml.edu **ACT Code:** 1854

This public school was founded in 1894. It has a 150-acre campus.

RATINGS
Admissions Selectivity Rating: 77 **Fire Safety Rating:** 88 **Green Rating:** 84

STUDENTS AND FACULTY
Enrollment: 9,615. **Student Body:** 40% female, 60% male, 8.4% out-of-state, 1% international (73 countries represented). Asian 9%, African American 6%, Caucasian 74%, Hispanic 7%.
Retention and Graduation: 28% freshmen graduate within 4 years. **Faculty:** Student/faculty ratio 15:1. 402 full-time faculty, 76% hold PhDs, 17% are members of minority groups, 35% are women.

ACADEMICS
Degrees: Associate, bachelor's, master's, post-master's certificate. **Classes:** Most classes have 20–29 students. Most lab/discussion sessions have 10–19 students. **Majors with Highest Enrollment:** Business/commerce; electrical, electronics and communications engineering; nursing, other. **Special Study Options:** Accelerated program, cooperative education program, cross-registration, distance learning, double major, dual enrollment, honors program, internships, liberal arts/career combination, study abroad, teacher certification program, Teacher Certification program for Education is Graduate only. **Honors programs:** The Honors Program at UMass Lowell offers high-achieving students individualized instruction in small groups, often in seminar format; opportunities for undergraduate research; special "Commonwealth Honors Program Scholar" designation on transcripts and diplomas—upon completion of program requirements; opportunity to live on one of the Honors floors in the residence halls; and Honors Program social events. LEARN PROGRAM—All first year students participate in the LEARN Program. LEARN, which stands for Living Education and Resource Networking, links academic, residential and personal development experiences by clustering offices, labs and classrooms among residence hall rooms, and offering a year-long schedule of programs that address a range of pertinent social and personal issues. **Combined degree programs:** BA/MA, BA/MEng. Special programs offered to physically disabled students include note-taking services, reader services, tape recorders, tutors. **Career services:** Alumni network, alumni services, career/job search classes, career assessment, internships, regional alumni.

FACILITIES
Housing: Coed dorms, special housing for disabled students, apartments for married students, cooperative housing, apartments for single students 80% of campus accessible to physically disabled. **Special Academic Facilities/Equipment:** Language lab, media center, audio-visual department, Centers for Learning, Center for field studies, Center for Performing and Visual Arts, Center for

Health Promotion, Research Nuclear Reactor. New $19.5 million recreation center which includes multi court gymnasium, 1/8 mile indoor elevated track, aerobics room, game rooms, locker rooms, and a sauna. Also included are meeting rooms and an indoor/outdoor food court. **Computers:** 50% of classrooms, 90% of dorms, 100% of libraries, 100% of dining areas, 100% of student union, 75% of common outdoor areas have wireless network access. Students can register for classes online. Administrative functions (other than registration) can be performed online.

CAMPUS LIFE
Environment: City. **Activities:** Choral groups, concert band, dance, drama/theater, jazz band, literary magazine, marching band, music ensembles, pep band, radio station, student government, student newspaper, student-run film society, symphony orchestra, yearbook, international student organization. **Organizations:** 100 registered organizations, 16 honor societies, 4 religious organizations. **Athletics (Intercollegiate):** *Men:* Baseball, basketball, crew/rowing, cross-country, golf, ice hockey, soccer, track/field (outdoor), track/field (indoor). *Women:* Basketball, crew/rowing, cross-country, field hockey, soccer, softball, track/field (outdoor), track/field (indoor), volleyball. **On-Campus Highlights:** Campus Recreation Center, South Campus Quad, McGauvran Student Center, Fox Multi-purpose Room, Southwick Lounge, New updated state of the art dining facility in the Southwick Lounge. **Environmental Initiatives:** Zero sort university wide recycling program, energy conservation & submetering utilities, pursuing renewable energy programs—PV Solar.

ADMISSIONS
Freshman Academic Profile: Average high school GPA 3.25. 14.85% in top 10% of high school class, 42.89% in top 25% of high school class, 78.29% in top 50% of high school class. 87% from public high schools. SAT Math middle 50% range 500–610. SAT Critical Reading middle 50% range 480–570. Minimum paper TOEFL 550. Minimum computer TOEFL 213. **Basis for Candidate Selection:** *Very important factors considered include:* Application essay, academic GPA, rigor of secondary school record, standardized test scores. *Important factors considered include:* Recommendation(s), first generation, level of applicant's interest. *Other factors considered include:* Class rank, character/personal qualities, extracurricular activities, interview, talent/ability, volunteer work, work experience. **Freshman Admission Requirements:** High school diploma is required and GED is accepted. *Academic units required:* 4 English, 3 mathematics, 3 science, (2 science labs), 2 foreign language, 2 social studies, 2 academic electives. *Academic units recommended:* 4 mathematics, 4 science. **Freshman Admission Statistics:** 5,913 applied, 73% admitted, 36% enrolled. **Transfer Admission Requirements:** College transcript(s), minimum college GPA of 2.0 required. Lowest grade transferable C–. **General Admission Information:** Application fee $60. Notification on a rolling basis, beginning on or about 12/1. Nonfall registration accepted. Admission may be deferred for a maximum of 1 year. Credit offered for CEEB Advanced Placement tests.

COSTS AND FINANCIAL AID
Annual in-state tuition $1,454. Annual out-of-state tuition $8,567. Room and board $8,635. Required fees $9,227. Average book expense $800. **Required Forms and Deadlines:** FAFSA. Priority financial aid filing date 3/1. **Notification of Awards:** Applicants will be notified of awards on a rolling basis beginning 3/25. **Types of Aid:** *Need-based scholarships/grants:* Federal Pell, SEOG, state scholarships/grants, private scholarships *Loans:* Direct Subsidized Stafford, Direct Unsubsidized Stafford, Direct PLUS, Federal Perkins. *Student Employment:* Federal Work-Study Program available. Institutional employment available. Highest amount earned per year from on-campus jobs $4,000. Off-campus job opportunities are good. **Financial Aid Statistics:** 61% freshmen, 56% undergrads receive need-based scholarship or grant aid. 4% freshmen, 3% undergrads receive non-need-based scholarship or grant aid. 56% freshmen, 53% undergrads receive need-based self-help aid. 1% freshmen, 2% undergrads receive athletic scholarships. 94% freshmen, 94% undergrads receive any aid. 73% undergrads borrow to pay for school. Average cumulative indebtedness $21,542. **Criteria for awarding institutional aid:** *Non-need-based:* Academics, alumni affiliation, art, athletics, job skills, leadership, minority status, music/drama, religious affiliation, state/district residency.

See page 1298.

THE UNIVERSITY OF MEMPHIS

101 Wilder Tower, Memphis, TN 38152
Phone: 901-678-2111 **Financial Aid Phone:** 901-678-4825
E-mail: recruitment@memphis.edu **CEEB Code:** 1459
Fax: 901-678-3053 **Website:** www.memphis.edu **ACT Code:** 3992

This public school was founded in 1912. It has a 1160-acre campus.

RATINGS
Admissions Selectivity Rating: 75   **Fire Safety Rating:** 86   **Green Rating:** 98

STUDENTS AND FACULTY
Enrollment: 16,011. **Student Body:** 61% female, 39% male, 9.1% out-of-state, 1% international (78 countries represented). Asian 3%, African American 40%, Caucasian 51%, Hispanic 2%.
Retention and Graduation: 76% freshmen return for sophomore year. 14% freshmen graduate within 4 years. **Faculty:** Student/faculty ratio 15:1. 840 full-time faculty, 78% hold PhDs, 21% are members of minority groups, 41% are women.

ACADEMICS
Degrees: Bachelor's, master's, post-bachelor's certificate, post-master's certificate. **Classes:** Most classes have 20–29 students. Most lab/discussion sessions have 10–19 students. **Majors with Highest Enrollment:** liberal arts and sciences/liberal studies; multi-/interdisciplinary studies, other; teacher education, multiple levels. **Special Study Options:** Accelerated program, cooperative education program, cross-registration, distance learning, double major, dual enrollment, English as a Second Language (ESL), exchange student program (domestic), external degree program, honors program, independent study, internships, liberal arts/career combination, student-designed major, study abroad, teacher certification program. **Honors programs:** The Honors Program offers students the opportunity to take small classes and interdisciplinary seminars with the university's most outstanding faculty. The program also includes many wonderful opportunities beyond the classroom such as study abroad, independent research, and co-curricular activities. Honors students also have the chance to participate in nationally recognized undergraduate research conferences and extend their learning through internships and public service. Special programs offered to physically disabled students include note-taking services, reader services, tape recorders. **Career services:** Alumni network, alumni services, career/job search classes, career assessment, internships, regional alumni. **Career services highlights include:** Fresh Connections are learning communities that use clusters of courses to connect different disciplines to a common theme. Students in the Learning Communitites take these courses together to develop a deeper understanding of the material.

FACILITIES
Housing: Coed dorms, special housing for disabled students, men's dorms, women's dorms, fraternity/sorority housing, apartments for married students, apartments for single students, Living-Learning communities. 95% of campus accessible to physically disabled. **Special Academic Facilities/Equipment:** Center for Earthquake Research & Information, Institute of Egyptian Art & Archaeology, Bureau of Business and Economic Research. **Computers:** 100% of classrooms, 55% of dorms, 100% of libraries, 100% of dining areas, 100% of student union, 10% of common outdoor areas have wireless network access. Students can register for classes online. Administrative functions (other than registration) can be performed online.

CAMPUS LIFE
Environment: Metropolis. **Activities:** Choral groups, concert band, dance, drama/theater, jazz band, literary magazine, marching band, music ensembles, musical theater, opera, pep band, radio station, student government, student newspaper, symphony orchestra, campus ministries, international student organization. **Organizations:** 140 registered organizations, 20 honor societies, 12 religious organizations. 14 fraternities, 11 sororities. **Athletics (Intercollegiate):** *Men:* Baseball, basketball, cross-country, football, golf, riflery, soccer, tennis, track/field (outdoor). *Women:* Basketball, cross-country, golf, riflery, soccer, softball, tennis, track/field (outdoor), volleyball. **On-Campus Highlights:** Rose Theater Lecture Hall, FedEx Institute of Technology, Finch Recreation Facility, Harris Concert Hall, Institute of Egyptian Art & Archaeology. **Environmental Initiatives:** Energy conservation, recycling, University of Memphis Campus Sustainability Strategic Plan.

ADMISSIONS
Freshman Academic Profile: Average high school GPA 3.23. 15.1% in top 10% of high school class, 42.2% in top 25% of high school class, 77.9% in top 50% of high school class. ACT middle 50% range 19–24. Minimum paper TOEFL 500. Minimum computer TOEFL 173. Minimum web-based TOEFL 61. **Basis for Candidate Selection:** *Very important factors considered include:* Academic GPA, rigor of secondary school record, standardized test scores, *Other factors considered include:* Application essay, recommendation(s),

character/personal qualities, talent/ability, work experience. **Freshman Admission Requirements:** High school diploma is required and GED is accepted. *Academic units required:* 4 English, 3 mathematics, 2 science, (1 science labs), 2 foreign language, 2 social studies, 1 history, 1 visual/performing arts. **Freshman Admission Statistics:** 6,156 applied, 67% admitted, 55% enrolled. **Transfer Admission Requirements:** College transcript(s), standardized test scores, Lowest grade transferable C. **General Admission Information:** Application fee $25. Regular application deadline 7/1. Nonfall registration accepted. Credit and/or placement offered for CEEB Advanced Placement tests.

COSTS AND FINANCIAL AID
Required Forms and Deadlines: FAFSA. Financial aid filing deadline 6/1. Priority financial aid filing date 3/1. **Notification of Awards:** Applicants will be notified of awards on a rolling basis beginning 3/1. **Types of Aid:** *Need-based scholarships/grants:* Federal Pell, SEOG, state scholarships/grants, private scholarships, the school's own gift aid. *Loans:* Direct Subsidized Stafford, Direct Unsubsidized Stafford, Direct PLUS, Federal Perkins, state loans, college/university loans from institutional funds. *Student Employment:* Federal Work-Study Program available. Institutional employment available. Off-campus job opportunities are excellent. **Financial Aid Statistics:** 58% freshmen, 50% undergrads receive need-based scholarship or grant aid. 30% freshmen, 38% undergrads receive non-need-based scholarship or grant aid. 54% freshmen, 57% undergrads receive need-based self-help aid. 2% freshmen, 2% undergrads receive athletic scholarships. 95% freshmen, 91% undergrads receive any aid. 32% undergrads borrow to pay for school. Average cumulative indebtedness $22,600. **Criteria for awarding institutional aid:** *Non-need-based:* Academics, alumni affiliation, art, athletics, leadership, minority status, music/drama, state/district residency.

UNIVERSITY OF MIAMI

Office of Admission, PO Box 248025, Coral Gables, FL 33124-4616
Phone: 305-284-4323 **Financial Aid Phone:** 305-284-2270
E-mail: admissions@miami.edu **CEEB Code:** 5815
Fax: 305-284-2507 **Website:** www.miami.edu **ACT Code:** 760

This private school was founded in 1925. It has a 260-acre campus.

RATINGS
Admissions Selectivity Rating: 95   **Fire Safety Rating:** 81   **Green Rating:** 89

STUDENTS AND FACULTY
Enrollment: 9,855. **Student Body:** 52% female, 48% male, 49% out-of-state, 9% international. Asian 5%, African American 8%, Caucasian 45%, Hispanic 24%.
Retention and Graduation: 90% freshmen return for sophomore year. 66% freshmen graduate within 4 years. **Faculty:** Student/faculty ratio 11:1. 961 full-time faculty, 87% hold PhDs, 28% are members of minority groups, 36% are women.

ACADEMICS
Degrees: Bachelor's, certificate, master's, post-bachelor's certificate, post-master's certificate. **Classes:** Most classes have 10–19 students. Most lab/discussion sessions have 10–19 students. **Special Study Options:** Accelerated program, distance learning, double major, dual enrollment, English as a Second Language (ESL), honors program, independent study, internships, liberal arts/career combination, student-designed major, study abroad, teacher certification program, weekend college. **Honors programs:** Honors Program in Medicine (HPM) BA/MD, BA/JD, BA/MEng **Combined degree programs:** Special programs offered to physically disabled students include note-taking services, reader services, tutors. **Career services:** Alumni network, alumni services, career/job search classes, career assessment, internships, regional alumni.

FACILITIES
Housing: Coed dorms, special housing for disabled students, fraternity/sorority housing, apartments for single students, theme housing. **Special Academic Facilities/Equipment:** Lowe Art Museum, Gusman Concert Hall, Jerry Herman Ring Theatre, Bill Cosford Cinema, Convocation Center, Wellness Center. **Computers:** 100% of classrooms, 100% of dorms, 100% of libraries, 100% of dining areas, 100% of student union, 100% of common outdoor areas have wireless network access. Students can register for classes online. Administrative functions (other than registration) can be performed online.

CAMPUS LIFE

Environment: Town. **Activities:** Choral groups, concert band, dance, drama/theater, jazz band, literary magazine, marching band, music ensembles, musical theater, opera, pep band, radio station, student government, student newspaper, student-run film society, symphony orchestra, television station, yearbook, campus ministries, international student organization, Model UN. **Athletics (Intercollegiate):** *Men:* Baseball, basketball, cheerleading, cross-country, football, tennis, track/field (outdoor), track/field (indoor). *Women:* Basketball, cheerleading, crew/rowing, cross-country, diving, golf, soccer, swimming, tennis, track/field (outdoor), track/field (indoor), volleyball. **On-Campus Highlights:** Lowe Art Museum, Jerry Herman Ring Theater, Bank United Center, Mark Light Stadium (Baseball), Gusman Concert Hall & Recording Studio, University Center Breezeway/Student Union, The Rock (free speech area). **Environmental Initiatives:** The President signing the ACUPCC and the Talloires Declaration. The university has implemented new building standards for new construction and major renovations to attempt to meet USGBC LEED Silver certification. The University has signed the Panama Pact: a collaboration on a world-class education and research facility addressing present and 22nd century challenges focusing on technologies that are sustainable.

ADMISSIONS

Freshman Academic Profile: Average high school GPA 4.2. 63% in top 10% of high school class, 87% in top 25% of high school class, 97% in top 50% of high school class. SAT Math middle 50% range 600–700. SAT Critical Reading middle 50% range 570–680. SAT Writing middle 50% range 570–670. ACT middle 50% range 27–31. Minimum paper TOEFL 550. Minimum computer TOEFL 213. Minimum web-based TOEFL 80. **Basis for Candidate Selection:** *Very important factors considered include:* Class rank, application essay, academic GPA, recommendation(s), rigor of secondary school record, standardized test scores, extracurricular activities. *Important factors considered include:* volunteer work. *Other factors considered include:* Alumni/ae relation, character/personal qualities, first generation, geographical residence, racial/ethnic status, talent/ability, work experience. **Freshman Admission Requirements:** High school diploma is required and GED is accepted. *Academic units recommended:* 4 English, 4 mathematics, 3 science, (2 science labs), 2 foreign language, 3 social studies, 2 history, 1 visual/performing arts, 1 computer science. **Freshman Admission Statistics:** 21,844 applied, 44% admitted, 21% enrolled. **Transfer Admission Requirements:** College transcript(s), statement of good standing from prior institution(s). Lowest grade transferable C. **General Admission Information:** Application fee $65. Early decision application deadline 11/1. Regular application deadline 1/15. Regular notification 4/15. Nonfall registration accepted. Admission may be deferred for a maximum of 1 year. Credit and/or placement offered for CEEB Advanced Placement tests.

COSTS AND FINANCIAL AID

Annual tuition $35,540. Room and board $10,800. Required fees $648. **Required Forms and Deadlines:** FAFSA. Priority financial aid filing date 2/1. **Notification of Awards:** Applicants will be notified of awards on a rolling basis beginning 3/1. **Types of Aid:** *Need-based scholarships/grants:* Federal Pell, SEOG, state scholarships/grants, private scholarships, the school's own gift aid, Federal Nursing Scholarships. Federal Academic Competitiveness Grant Federal SMART Grant. *Loans:* FFEL Subsidized Stafford, FFEL Unsubsidized Stafford, FFEL PLUS, Federal Perkins, Federal Nursing, college/university loans from institutional funds, Private Alternative Education Loans. *Student Employment:* Federal Work-Study Program available. Institutional employment available. Highest amount earned per year from on-campus jobs $3,000. Off-campus job opportunities are excellent. **Financial Aid Statistics:** 47% freshmen, 47% undergrads receive need-based scholarship or grant aid. 16% freshmen, 15% undergrads receive non-need-based scholarship or grant aid. 40% freshmen, 42% undergrads receive need-based self-help aid. 3% freshmen, 2% undergrads receive athletic scholarships. 55% undergrads borrow to pay for school. Average cumulative indebtedness $24,396. **Criteria for awarding institutional aid:** *Non-need-based:* Academics, athletics, music/drama.

UNIVERSITY OF MICHIGAN—ANN ARBOR

1220 Student Activities Building, Ann Arbor, MI 48109-1316
Phone: 734-764-7433 **Financial Aid Phone:** 734-763-6600
E-mail: CEEB Code: 1839
Fax: 734-936-0740 **Website:** www.umich.edu **ACT Code:** 2062

This public school was founded in 1817. It has a 3177-acre campus.

RATINGS

Admissions Selectivity Rating: 96   **Fire Safety Rating:** 88   **Green Rating:** 84

STUDENTS AND FACULTY

Enrollment: 26,127. **Student Body:** 49% female, 51% male, 31% out-of-state, 5% international (120 countries represented). Asian 9%, African American 5%, Caucasian 49%, Hispanic 3%, Native American 1%.
Retention and Graduation: 96% freshmen return for sophomore year. 36.6% grads go on to further study within 1 year. 12.1% grads pursue arts and sciences degrees. 19.7% grads pursue law degrees. 1.8% grads pursue business degrees. 20.5% grads pursue medical degrees. **Faculty:** Student/faculty ratio 15:1. 2479 full-time faculty, 91% hold PhDs, 23% are members of minority groups, 37% are women. 39% of classes are taught by teaching assistants.

ACADEMICS

Degrees: Bachelor's, doctoral, master's, post-bachelor's certificate, post-master's certificate. **Classes:** Most classes have 10–19 students. Most lab/discussion sessions have 20–29 students. **Majors with Highest Enrollment:** Business administration and management; mechanical engineering; psychology. **Special Study Options:** Accelerated program, cooperative education program, cross-registration, distance learning, double major, dual enrollment, English as a Second Language (ESL), exchange student program (domestic), external degree program, honors program, independent study, internships, liberal arts/career combination, student-designed major, study abroad, teacher certification program, weekend college. **Honors programs:** LSA Honors Program; departmental honors programs **Combined degree programs:** BA/MA, BA/MEng, BA/MArch; BS/M.SBE; BA Ling/MA Info; BS/MPH. Special programs offered to physically disabled students include note-taking services, reader services, tape recorders, tutors. **Career services:** Alumni network, alumni services, career/job search classes, career assessment, internships. **Career services highlights include:** The University of Michigan is equally proud of all its cooperative, experiential, and internship learning opportunities.

FACILITIES

Housing: Coed dorms, special housing for disabled students, women's dorms, fraternity/sorority housing, apartments for married students, cooperative housing, apartments for single students, wellness housing, theme housing, Living/learning communities, substance free dorms. 97% of campus accessible to physically disabled. **Special Academic Facilities/Equipment:** Anthropology, archaeology, art, natural science, paleontology, and zoology museums; audiovisual center, planetarium, electron microscope, biology station, geology camp, athletic campus, medical center, nuclear lab, botanical garden, herbarium, arboretum. **Computers:** 85% of classrooms, 40% of dorms, 80% of libraries, 95% of dining areas, 80% of student union, 10% of common outdoor areas have wireless network access. Students can register for classes online. Administrative functions (other than registration) can be performed online.

CAMPUS LIFE

Environment: City. **Activities:** Choral groups, concert band, dance, drama/theater, jazz band, literary magazine, marching band, music ensembles, musical theater, opera, pep band, radio station, student government, student newspaper, student-run film society, symphony orchestra, television station, yearbook, campus ministries, international student organization, Model UN. **Organizations:** 1000 registered organizations, 13 honor societies, 67 religious organizations. 39 fraternities, 27 sororities. **Athletics (Intercollegiate):** *Men:* Baseball, basketball, cheerleading, cross-country, diving, football, golf, gymnastics, ice hockey, swimming, tennis, track/field (outdoor), track/field (indoor), wrestling. *Women:* Basketball, cheerleading, crew/rowing, cross-country, diving, field hockey, golf, gymnastics, soccer, softball, swimming, tennis, track/field (outdoor), track/field (indoor), volleyball, water polo. **On-Campus Highlights:** Michigan Stadium, Museum of Natural History, Museum of Art, Margaret Dow Towsley Sports Museum. **Environmental Initiatives:** Planet Blue—Recycling & Waste Reduction; Climate Savers Computing Initiative; Green Lights Initiative.

ADMISSIONS

Freshman Academic Profile: Average high school GPA 3.75. 92% in top 10% of high school class, 99% in top 25% of high school class, 100% in top 50% of

The Princeton Review's Complete Book of Colleges

high school class. SAT Math middle 50% range 640–740. SAT Critical Reading middle 50% range 590–690. SAT Writing middle 50% range 600–700. ACT middle 50% range 27–31. Minimum paper TOEFL 570. Minimum computer TOEFL 230. Minimum web-based TOEFL 88. **Basis for Candidate Selection:** *Very important factors considered include:* Rigor of secondary school record. *Important factors considered include:* Application essay, academic GPA, recommendation(s), standardized test scores, character/personal qualities, first generation. *Other factors considered include:* Class rank, alumni/ae relation, extracurricular activities, geographical residence, level of applicant's interest, state residency, talent/ability, volunteer work, work experience. **Freshman Admission Requirements:** High school diploma is required and GED is accepted. *Academic units required:* 4 English, (1 science labs), 3 social studies, 3 history, 1 academic electives. *Academic units recommended:* 4 English, 4 mathematics, 4 science, (1 science labs), 4 foreign language, 3 social studies, 3 history, 2 visual/performing arts, 1 computer science, 1 academic electives. **Freshman Admission Statistics:** 29,965 applied, 50% admitted, 41% enrolled. **Transfer Admission Requirements:** High school transcript, college transcript(s), essay or personal statement, statement of good standing from prior institution(s). Minimum college GPA of 3.0 required. Lowest grade transferable C. **General Admission Information:** Application fee $40. Regular application deadline 2/1. Notification on a rolling basis, beginning on or about 11/1. Nonfall registration accepted. Admission may be deferred for a maximum of 1 year. Credit and/or placement offered for CEEB Advanced Placement tests.

COSTS AND FINANCIAL AID

Annual in-state tuition $12,211. Annual out-of-state tuition $35,974. Room and board $8,924. Required fees $189. Average book expense $1,048. **Required Forms and Deadlines:** FAFSA, CSS/Financial Aid PROFILE Financial aid filing deadline 5/30. Priority financial aid filing date 4/29. **Notification of Awards:** Applicants will be notified of awards on a rolling basis beginning 3/14. **Types of Aid:** *Need-based scholarships/grants:* Federal Pell, SEOG, state scholarships/grants, private scholarships, the school's own gift aid, Academic Competitive Grant (ACG); National SMART; DC Tag Program; Byrd; Teach Grant. *Loans:* Direct Subsidized Stafford, Direct Unsubsidized Stafford, Direct PLUS, Federal Perkins, Federal Nursing, college/university loans from institutional funds, Direct Loan Grad Plus; Health Professional Student Loans. *Student Employment:* Federal Work-Study Program available. Institutional employment available. Off-campus job opportunities are excellent. **Financial Aid Statistics:** 24% freshmen, 25% undergrads receive need-based scholarship or grant aid. 40% freshmen, 30% undergrads receive non-need-based scholarship or grant aid. 46% freshmen, 46% undergrads receive need-based self-help aid. 2% freshmen, 2% undergrads receive athletic scholarships. 46% undergrads borrow to pay for school. Average cumulative indebtedness $26,819. **Criteria for awarding institutional aid:** *Non-need-based:* Academics, alumni affiliation, art, athletics, leadership, music/drama, religious affiliation, state/district residency.

UNIVERSITY OF MICHIGAN—DEARBORN

4901 Evergreen Road, Dearborn, MI 48128-1491
Phone: 313-593-5100 **Financial Aid Phone:** 734-763-6600
E-mail: admissions@umd.umich.edu
Fax: 313-436-9167 **Website:** www.umd.umich.edu

This is a public school.

RATINGS
Admissions Selectivity Rating: 60*   **Fire Safety Rating:** 60*   **Green Rating:** 60*

STUDENTS AND FACULTY
Enrollment: 5,895. **Student Body:** 53% female, 47% male, 2% out-of-state, 1% international. Asian 6%, African American 7%, Caucasian 75%, Hispanic 2%, Native American 1%.
Retention and Graduation: 79% freshmen return for sophomore year. **Faculty:** Student/faculty ratio 15:1. 259 full-time faculty, 89% hold PhDs, 23% are members of minority groups, 31% are women.

ACADEMICS
Degrees: Bachelor's, master's, post-bachelor's certificate. **Classes:** Most classes have 20–29 students. Most lab/discussion sessions have 10–19 students. **Special Study Options:** Accelerated program, cooperative education program, cross-registration, distance learning, double major, dual enrollment, honors program, independent study, internships, liberal arts/career combination, student-designed major, study abroad, teacher certification program.

FACILITIES
Housing: Fraternity/sorority housing.

CAMPUS LIFE
Activities: Drama/theater, literary magazine, radio station, student government, student newspaper, student-run film society, television station.

ADMISSIONS
Freshman Academic Profile: Average high school GPA 3.4. 25% in top 10% of high school class, 60% in top 25% of high school class, 94% in top 50% of high school class. 84% from public high schools. ACT middle 50% range 21–26. Minimum paper TOEFL 550. Minimum computer TOEFL 213. **Basis for Candidate Selection:** *Very important factors considered include:* Rigor of secondary school record, standardized test scores, *Other factors considered include:* Class rank, application essay, recommendation(s), interview. **Freshman Admission Requirements:** High school diploma is required and GED is accepted. *Academic units recommended:* 4 English, 4 mathematics, 3 science, (1 science labs), 3 foreign language, 3 social studies. **Freshman Admission Statistics:** 2,334 applied, 65% admitted, 47% enrolled. **Transfer Admission Requirements:** High school transcript, college transcript(s), Lowest grade transferable C. **General Admission Information:** Application fee $30. Nonfall registration accepted. Admission may be deferred for a maximum of no limit. Credit and/or placement offered for CEEB Advanced Placement tests.

COSTS AND FINANCIAL AID
Annual in-state tuition $12,211. Annual out-of-state tuition $35,974. Room and board $8,924. Required fees $189. Average book expense $1,048. **Required Forms and Deadlines:** FAFSA. Priority financial aid filing date 4/1. **Notification of Awards:** Applicants will be notified of awards on a rolling basis beginning 5/1. **Types of Aid:** *Need-based scholarships/grants:* Federal Pell, SEOG, state scholarships/grants, private scholarships, the school's own gift aid. *Loans:* Direct Subsidized Stafford, Direct Unsubsidized Stafford, Direct PLUS, Federal Perkins, state loans, college/university loans from institutional funds. *Student Employment:* Federal Work-Study Program available. Institutional employment available. Off-campus job opportunities are excellent. **Financial Aid Statistics:** 22% freshmen, 24% undergrads receive need-based scholarship or grant aid. 21% freshmen, 8% undergrads receive non-need-based scholarship or grant aid. 8% freshmen, 22% undergrads receive need-based self-help aid. 2% freshmen, 1% undergrads receive athletic scholarships. 27% undergrads borrow to pay for school. Average cumulative indebtedness $14,673. **Criteria for awarding institutional aid:** *Non-need-based:* Academics, alumni affiliation, art, athletics, job skills, leadership, minority status, music/drama, state/district residency.

UNIVERSITY OF MICHIGAN—FLINT

303 E. Kearsley St, 245 UPAV, Flint, MI 48502
Phone: 810-762-3300 **Financial Aid Phone:** 810-762-3444
E-mail: admissions@umflint.edu **CEEB Code:** 1853
Fax: 810-762-3272 **Website:** www.umflint.edu **ACT Code:** 2063

This public school was founded in 1956. It has a 72-acre campus.

RATINGS
Admissions Selectivity Rating: 73   **Fire Safety Rating:** 60*   **Green Rating:** 70

STUDENTS AND FACULTY
Enrollment: 6,280. **Student Body:** 61% female, 39% male, 1.46% out-of-state, 1% international (30 countries represented). Asian 2%, African American 14%, Caucasian 70%, Hispanic 3%, Native American 1%.
Retention and Graduation: 13% freshmen graduate within 4 years. **Faculty:** Student/faculty ratio 17:1. 257 full-time faculty, 70% hold PhDs, 17% are members of minority groups, 52% are women.

ACADEMICS
Degrees: Bachelor's, master's. **Classes:** Most classes have 20–29 students. Most lab/discussion sessions have 20–29 students. **Majors with Highest Enrollment:** Business administration and management; elementary education and teaching; nursing/registered nurse (RN, ASN, BSN, MSN). **Special Study Options:** Cooperative education program, distance learning, double major, dual enrollment, English as a Second Language (ESL), honors program, independent study, internships, student-designed major, study abroad, teacher certification program. **Honors programs:** 4-yr University Honors Scholar Program 2-yr Junior/Senior University Honors Scholar Program. **Combined degree programs:** BBA/MBA. Special programs offered to physically disabled students include note-taking services, reader services, tape recorders, tutors. **Career services:** Career/job search classes, career assessment, internships.

FACILITIES
Housing: Coed dorms. 97% of campus accessible to physically disabled. **Special Academic Facilities/Equipment:** Frances Willson Thompson Library.

Computers: 100% of classrooms, 100% of dorms, 100% of libraries, 100% of dining areas, 100% of student union, have wireless network access. Students can register for classes online. Administrative functions (other than registration) can be performed online.

CAMPUS LIFE

Environment: City. **Activities:** Choral groups, concert band, dance, drama/theater, jazz band, literary magazine, music ensembles, musical theater, student government, student newspaper, television station, international student organization. **Organizations:** 99 registered organizations, 7 honor societies, 6 religious organizations. 4 fraternities, 5 sororities. **On-Campus Highlights:** Recreation Center, University Center/Student Union, University Pavilion/Food Court/Bookstore, Resident's Hall, Frances Willson Thompson Library. **Environmental Initiatives:** Recycling and waste minimization; energy conservation; and use of biodegradable paper dinning products; protecton of campus' natural resources.

ADMISSIONS

Freshman Academic Profile: Average high school GPA 3.19. 18.85% in top 10% of high school class, 43.3% in top 25% of high school class, 76.29% in top 50% of high school class. 87.6% from public high schools. SAT Math middle 50% range 425–547.5. SAT Critical Reading middle 50% range 385–567.5. SAT Writing middle 50% range 400–535. ACT middle 50% range 18–24. Minimum paper TOEFL 550. Minimum computer TOEFL 173. **Basis for Candidate Selection:** *Very important factors considered include:* Academic GPA, rigor of secondary school record, standardized test scores. *Important factors considered include:* Extracurricular activities. *Other factors considered include:* Class rank, application essay, recommendation(s), interview, talent/ability. **Freshman Admission Requirements:** High school diploma is required and GED is accepted. *Academic units required:* 4 English, 3 mathematics, 2 science, 3 social studies. *Academic units recommended:* 4 English, 4 mathematics, 4 science, (2 science labs), 2 foreign language, 3 social studies, 3 history. **Freshman Admission Statistics:** 2,693 applied, 82% admitted, 35% enrolled. **Transfer Admission Requirements:** High school transcript, college transcript(s), minimum college GPA of 2.0 required. Lowest grade transferable 2. **General Admission Information:** Application fee $30. Notification on a rolling basis, beginning on or about 12/1. Nonfall registration accepted. Admission may be deferred for a maximum of 1 Year. Credit and/or placement offered for CEEB Advanced Placement tests.

COSTS AND FINANCIAL AID

Annual in-state tuition $7,899. Annual out-of-state tuition $15,413. Room and board $6,874. Required fees $380. Average book expense $1,000. **Required Forms and Deadlines:** FAFSA, institution's own financial aid formInstitution's own financial aid form used in Spring/Summer Sessions only. Priority financial aid filing date 3/1. **Notification of Awards:** Applicants will be notified of awards on a rolling basis beginning 3/15. **Types of Aid:** *Need-based scholarships/grants:* Federal Pell, SEOG, state scholarships/grants, private scholarships, the school's own gift aid. *Loans:* Direct Subsidized Stafford, Direct Unsubsidized Stafford, Direct PLUS, Federal Perkins, state loans *Student Employment:* Federal Work-Study Program available. Institutional employment available. Off-campus job opportunities are poor. **Financial Aid Statistics:** 47% freshmen, 42% undergrads receive need-based scholarship or grant aid. 59% freshmen, 56% undergrads receive non-need-based scholarship or grant aid. 55% freshmen, 54% undergrads receive need-based self-help aid. 77.9% freshmen, 78% undergrads borrow to pay for school. Average cumulative indebtedness $23,120. **Criteria for awarding institutional aid:** *Non-need-based:* Academics, art, leadership, minority status, music/drama.

UNIVERSITY OF MINNESOTA, CROOKSTON

University of Minnesota, Crookston, 2900 University Avenue, Crookston, MN 56716-5001
Phone: 218-281-8569 **Financial Aid Phone:** 218-281-8563
E-mail: UMCinfo@umn.edu
Fax: 218-281-8575 **Website:** www.crk.umn.edu **ACT Code:** 2129

This public school was founded in 1966. It has a 237-acre campus.

RATINGS

Admissions Selectivity Rating: 77   **Fire Safety Rating:** 99   **Green Rating:** 69

STUDENTS AND FACULTY

Enrollment: 1,207. **Student Body:** 41% female, 59% male, 32% out-of-state, 8% international (23 countries represented). Asian 1%, African American 4%, Caucasian 78%, Hispanic 1%, Native American 1%. **Retention and Graduation:** 68% freshmen return for sophomore year. 21% freshmen graduate within 4 years. 3% grads go on to further study within 1

year. 2% grads pursue business degrees. **Faculty:** Student/faculty ratio 16:1. 53 full-time faculty, 47% hold PhDs, 11% are members of minority groups, 34% are women.

ACADEMICS

Degrees: Bachelor's, certificate. **Classes:** Most classes have 10–19 students. Most lab/discussion sessions have 10–19 students. **Majors with Highest Enrollment:** Business administration and management; equestrian/equine studies; natural resources/conservation. **Special Study Options:** Cross-registration, distance learning, double major, dual enrollment, English as a Second Language (ESL), honors program, independent study, internships, student-designed major, study abroad, teacher certification program. **Honors programs:** The University of Minnesota, Crookston Honor's Program was developed to inspire and transform the students' writing, discussion and critical thinking skills that reflect high expectations for academically successful students. Students will be nurtured and challenged to explore ideas, assess values and develop leadership skills. Honors coursework will address the diverse and global atmosphere in which we live. In addition, students in the Honors Program will have the opportunity for various social outings outside of the normal campus experience. ° Designed for academically highly-motivated students who want more than a degree. ° Small class sizes ensure one-on-one time with faculty, who invest in your success. ° Flexible curriculum helps you meet career goals while meeting discipline and honors specific requirements. ° Innovative program structure involves honor courses, student led discussion groups and individual studies in discipline specific courses. ° You will develop and conduct an original scholarly project as a senior to satisfy final program requirements. ° Exposure to culturally-rich experiences will enable you to develop a global perspective and leadership skills. Special programs offered to physically disabled students include note-taking services, reader services, tape recorders, tutors. **Career services:** Alumni services, career/job search classes, career assessment, internships. **Career services highlights include:** Internships that provide experiential learning and on-the-job training for all students.

FACILITIES

Housing: Coed dorms, special housing for disabled students, apartments for single students, theme housing. 90% of campus accessible to physically disabled. **Special Academic Facilities/Equipment:** Red River Valley Natural History Area; Northwest Research and Outreach Center; UMC Horse Riding Arena; Valley Technology Park. **Computers:** 20% of classrooms, 100% of dorms, 100% of libraries, 75% of dining areas, 100% of student union, 25% of common outdoor areas have wireless network access. Students can register for classes online. Administrative functions (other than registration) can be performed online.

CAMPUS LIFE

Environment: Village. **Activities:** Choral groups, drama/theater, pep band, radio station, student government, campus ministries, international student organization. **Organizations:** 38 registered organizations, 1 honor societies, 2 religious organizations. 1 fraternities, 1 sororities. **Athletics (Intercollegiate):** *Men:* Baseball, basketball, football, golf, ice hockey. *Women:* Basketball, equestrian sports, golf, soccer, softball, tennis, volleyball. **On-Campus Highlights:** Sargeant Student Center, University Teaching and Outreach Center, Sports Center, Bergland Laboratory, Centennial Hall Student Apartments, Campus Mall Dairy Barns Kiehle Auditorium. **Environmental Initiatives:** The 2007–2008 Crookston Student Association has recommitted its efforts to increase recycling on campus. January 11, 2008, President Robert Bruininks letter sent to all campuses entitled: "The University of Minnesota's Ongoing Committment to Sustainability." Our campus Mission-Vision-Core Values state: "The University of Minnesota, Crookston serving as a regional hub for innovation, entrepreneurism, and regional sustainability."

ADMISSIONS

Freshman Academic Profile: Average high school GPA 3.12. 10% in top 10% of high school class, 33% in top 25% of high school class, 64% in top 50% of high school class. SAT Math middle 50% range 430–530. SAT Critical Reading middle 50% range 420–520. SAT Writing middle 50% range 480–560. ACT middle 50% range 19–24. Minimum paper TOEFL 520. Minimum computer TOEFL 190. Minimum web-based TOEFL 68. **Basis for Candidate Selection:** *Very important factors considered include:* Class rank, academic GPA, rigor of secondary school record, standardized test scores, *Other factors considered include:* Application essay, recommendation(s). **Freshman Admission Requirements:** High school diploma is required and GED is accepted. *Academic units required:* 4 English, 3 mathematics, 3 science, (2 science labs), 3 social studies. *Academic units recommended:* 2 foreign language. **Freshman Admission Statistics:** 776 applied, 454% admitted, 8% enrolled. **Transfer Admission Requirements:** College transcript(s), minimum college GPA of 2.0 required. Lowest grade transferable D. **General Admission Information:** Application fee $30. Notification on a rolling basis, beginning on or about 9/1. Nonfall registration accepted. Admission may be deferred for a maximum of 1 year. Credit and/or placement offered for CEEB Advanced Placement tests.

COSTS AND FINANCIAL AID

Annual in-state tuition $7,388. Annual out-of-state tuition $7,388. Room and board $6,254. Required fees $2,600. Average book expense $800. **Required Forms and Deadlines:** FAFSA. Priority financial aid filing date 3/1. **Notification of Awards:** Applicants will be notified of awards on a rolling basis beginning 3/1. **Types of Aid:** *Need-based scholarships/grants:* Federal Pell, SEOG, state scholarships/grants, private scholarships, the school's own gift aid, Federal Academic Competitiveness Grant and SMART Grant. *Loans:* Direct Subsidized Stafford, Direct Unsubsidized Stafford, Direct PLUS, Federal Perkins, state loans, private loans. *Student Employment:* Federal Work-Study Program available. Institutional employment available. Highest amount earned per year from on-campus jobs $2,000. Off-campus job opportunities are fair. **Financial Aid Statistics:** 64% freshmen, 60% undergrads receive need-based scholarship or grant aid. 21% freshmen, 13% undergrads receive non-need-based scholarship or grant aid. 55% freshmen, 57% undergrads receive need-based self-help aid. 66% freshmen, 64% undergrads receive any aid. 84% undergrads borrow to pay for school. Average cumulative indebtedness $26,565. **Criteria for awarding institutional aid:** *Non-need-based:* Academics, alumni affiliation, athletics, leadership, minority status, music/drama, state/district residency.

UNIVERSITY OF MINNESOTA, DULUTH

25 Solon Campus Center, 1117 University, Duluth, MN 55812-3000
Phone: 218-726-7171 **Financial Aid Phone:** 218-726-8000
E-mail: umdadmis@d.umn.edu **CEEB Code:** 6873
Fax: 218-726-7040 **Website:** www.d.umn.edu **ACT Code:** 2157

This public school was founded in 1947. It has a 247-acre campus.

RATINGS

Admissions Selectivity Rating: 71　　　**Fire Safety Rating:** 88　　　**Green Rating:** 89

STUDENTS AND FACULTY

Enrollment: 9,422. **Student Body:** 47% female, 53% male, 11.36% out-of-state, 1% international (42 countries represented). Asian 3%, African American 1%, Caucasian 90%, Hispanic 1%, Native American 1%.
Retention and Graduation: 81% freshmen return for sophomore year. 16% grads go on to further study within 1 year. **Faculty:** Student/faculty ratio 21:1. 463 full-time faculty, 75% hold PhDs, 19% are members of minority groups, 43% are women.

ACADEMICS

Degrees: Bachelor's, master's, post-bachelor's certificate. **Classes:** Most classes have 20–29 students. Most lab/discussion sessions have 10–19 students. **Majors with Highest Enrollment:** Biology/biological sciences; business administration and management; elementary education and teaching. **Special Study Options:** Accelerated program, cross-registration, distance learning, double major, dual enrollment, exchange student program (domestic), honors program, independent study, internships, liberal arts/career combination, study abroad, teacher certification program, weekend college. **Honors programs:** The Honors Program offers motivated students who are serious about their intellectual and personal growth a variety of special classes enhanced by cultural events and activities, as well as leadership and research opportunities. Special programs offered to physically disabled students include note-taking services, reader services, tape recorders, tutors. **Career services:** Alumni services, career/job search classes, career assessment, internships.

FACILITIES

Housing: Coed dorms, special housing for disabled students, men's dorms, women's dorms. 100% of campus accessible to physically disabled. **Special Academic Facilities/Equipment:** Art museum, planetarium, music performance hall, theatre. **Computers:** 100% of classrooms, 100% of libraries, 100% of dining areas, 100% of student union, have wireless network access. Students can register for classes online. Administrative functions (other than registration) can be performed online.

CAMPUS LIFE

Environment: Village. **Activities:** Choral groups, concert band, dance, drama/theater, jazz band, literary magazine, marching band, music ensembles, musical theater, opera, pep band, radio station, student government, student newspaper, student-run film society, symphony orchestra, campus ministries, international student organization, Model UN. **Organizations:** 150 registered organizations, 10 honor societies, 7 religious organizations. 2 fraternities, 2 sororities. **Athletics (Intercollegiate):** *Men:* Baseball, basketball, cross-country, football, ice hockey, track/field (outdoor), track/field (indoor). *Women:* Basketball, cross-country, ice hockey, soccer, softball, tennis, track/field (outdoor), track/field (indoor), volleyball. **On-Campus Highlights:** Solon Campus Center, library,

residence halls, Kirby Student Center Food Court, Sports and Health Center. **Environmental Initiatives:** LEED, Stormwater Management Plan, Energy Conservation Projects.

ADMISSIONS

Freshman Academic Profile: 16.49% in top 10% of high school class, 41.75% in top 25% of high school class, 85.14% in top 50% of high school class. 94% from public high schools. SAT Math middle 50% range 480–620. SAT Critical Reading middle 50% range 480–590. SAT Writing middle 50% range 460–580. ACT middle 50% range 20–26. Minimum paper TOEFL 550. Minimum computer TOEFL 213. Minimum web-based TOEFL 80. **Basis for Candidate Selection:** *Very important factors considered include:* Class rank, standardized test scores. *Important factors considered include:* Rigor of secondary school record. *Other factors considered include:* Application essay, academic GPA, recommendation(s), alumni/ae relation, extracurricular activities, first generation, geographical residence, racial/ethnic status, state residency, talent/ability. **Freshman Admission Requirements:** High school diploma is required and GED is accepted. *Academic units required:* 4 English, 3 mathematics, 3 science, 2 foreign language, 2 social studies, 1 history. *Academic units recommended:* 1 visual/performing arts, 1 computer science. **Freshman Admission Statistics:** 7,936 applied, 71% admitted, 37% enrolled. **Transfer Admission Requirements:** High school transcript, college transcript(s), minimum college GPA of 2.0 required. Lowest grade transferable D. **General Admission Information:** Application fee $35. Regular application deadline 8/1. Notification on a rolling basis, beginning on or about 9/17. Nonfall registration accepted. Admission may be deferred for a maximum of 3 semesters. Credit and/or placement offered for CEEB Advanced Placement tests.

COSTS AND FINANCIAL AID

Annual in-state tuition $8,230. Annual out-of-state tuition $10,230. Room and board $6,078. Required fees $2,030. Average book expense $1,248. **Required Forms and Deadlines:** FAFSA. Priority financial aid filing date 3/31. **Notification of Awards:** Applicants will be notified of awards on or about 3/1. **Types of Aid:** *Need-based scholarships/grants:* Federal Pell, SEOG, state scholarships/grants, private scholarships, the school's own gift aid. *Loans:* Direct Subsidized Stafford, Direct Unsubsidized Stafford, Direct PLUS, Federal Perkins, state loans, college/university loans from institutional funds. *Student Employment:* Federal Work-Study Program available. Institutional employment available. Off-campus job opportunities are excellent. **Financial Aid Statistics:** 58% freshmen, 56% undergrads receive need-based scholarship or grant aid. 15% freshmen, 15% undergrads receive non-need-based scholarship or grant aid. 49% freshmen, 50% undergrads receive need-based self-help aid. 85% freshmen, 81% undergrads receive any aid. 72% undergrads borrow to pay for school. Average cumulative indebtedness $27,921. **Criteria for awarding institutional aid:** *Non-need-based:* Academics, alumni affiliation, art, athletics, leadership, minority status, music/drama, state/district residency.

UNIVERSITY OF MINNESOTA, MORRIS

600 E 4th St, Morris, MN 56267
Phone: 320-589-6035 **Financial Aid Phone:** 800-992-8863
E-mail: admissions@morris.umn.edu **CEEB Code:** 6890
Fax: 320-589-1673 **Website:** www.morris.umn.edu **ACT Code:** 2155

This public school was founded in 1959. It has a 130-acre campus.

RATINGS

Admissions Selectivity Rating: 75　　　**Fire Safety Rating:** 60*　　　**Green Rating:** 60*

STUDENTS AND FACULTY

Enrollment: 1,667. **Student Body:** 61% female, 39% male, 13% out-of-state, 1% international (15 countries represented). Asian 3%, African American 2%, Caucasian 74%, Hispanic 1%, Native American 9%.
Retention and Graduation: 86% freshmen return for sophomore year. 40% freshmen graduate within 4 years. 48% grads go on to further study within 1 year. 30% grads pursue arts and sciences degrees. 11% grads pursue law degrees. 3% grads pursue business degrees. 4% grads pursue medical degrees. **Faculty:** Student/faculty ratio 13:1. 121 full-time faculty, 93% hold PhDs, 16% are members of minority groups, 43% are women.

ACADEMICS

Degrees: Bachelor's, certificate. **Classes:** Most classes have 10–19 students. Most lab/discussion sessions have 10–19 students. **Majors with Highest Enrollment:** Biology; elementary education and teaching; psychology. **Special Study Options:** Accelerated program, cooperative education program, distance learning, double major, exchange student program (domestic), honors program, independent study, internships, student-designed major, study abroad, teacher certification program. **Honors programs:** The purpose of the Honors Program is to provide a distinctive, academically challenging, intellectual experience that amplifies and complements the liberal arts mission of UMM for motivated and high-achieving students. It does this by relying upon an interdisciplinary curriculum that is team-taught by UMM's finest faculty. The program consists of a core course, "Traditions in Human Thought." This course explores significant works from history, literature, philosophy, and science from an interdisciplinary perspective. Following the core course, students choose from a variety of interdisciplinary honors courses, participate in service learning and volunteer programs, and complete a senior honors project. Special programs offered to physically disabled students include note-taking services, reader services, tape recorders, tutors. **Career services:** Alumni services, career/job search classes, career assessment, internships. **Career services highlights include:** The Undergraduate Research Opportunities Program (UROP) is a competitive, merit-based program that provides student stipends and expense allowances for students to partner with a faculty member on research, scholarly, or creative projects in laboratories, studios, libraries, and field sites. Students develop detailed knowledge of research methods and may choose to work with faculty members from UMM or from other University of Minnesota campuses, thus giving students access to the university's wide range of faculty and research facilities.

FACILITIES

Housing: Coed dorms, special housing for disabled students, men's dorms, women's dorms, apartments for single students. 70% of campus accessible to physically disabled. **Special Academic Facilities/Equipment:** HFA Art Gallery, conservatory, observatory. **Computers:** Students can register for classes online. Administrative functions (other than registration) can be performed online.

CAMPUS LIFE

Environment: Rural. **Activities:** Choral groups, concert band, dance, drama/theater, jazz band, literary magazine, music ensembles, musical theater, radio station, student government, student newspaper, symphony orchestra, television station **Organizations:** 90 registered organizations, 5 honor societies, 12 religious organizations. **Athletics (Intercollegiate):** *Men:* Baseball, basketball, football, golf, tennis, track/field (outdoor), track/field (indoor). *Women:* Basketball, cross-country, diving, golf, soccer, softball, swimming, tennis, track/field (outdoor), track/field (indoor), volleyball. **On-Campus Highlights:** Student Center—KUMM, cafe, Louis' Lower Level, Regional Fitness Center—Outdoor Center, pools, Science Center—completed '02, Humanities Fine Arts Center—gallery, recitals, The Mall—outdoor recreation area.

ADMISSIONS

Freshman Academic Profile: 32% in top 10% of high school class, 60% in top 25% of high school class, 88% in top 50% of high school class. 92% from public high schools. SAT Math middle 50% range 510–650. SAT Critical Reading middle 50% range 520–640. ACT middle 50% range 23–28. Minimum paper TOEFL 550. Minimum computer TOEFL 213. **Basis for Candidate Selection:** *Very important factors considered include:* Class rank, rigor of secondary school record, standardized test scores. *Important factors considered include:* Application essay, recommendation(s), character/personal qualities, extracurricular activities, talent/ability, volunteer work, work experience. *Other factors considered include:* Alumni/ae relation, interview, racial/ethnic status. **Freshman Admission Requirements:** High school diploma is required and GED is accepted. *Academic units required:* 4 English, 3 mathematics, 3 science, (2 science labs), 2 foreign language, 4 social studies, 4 history. *Academic units recommended:* 4 mathematics, 4 science, 3 foreign language. **Freshman Admission Statistics:** 1,067 applied, 84% admitted, 43% enrolled. **Transfer Admission Requirements:** College transcript(s), essay or personal statement, statement of good standing from prior institution(s). Minimum college GPA of 2.5 required. Lowest grade transferable D. **General Admission Information:** Application fee $35. Regular application deadline 3/15. Regular notification 4/1. Notification on a rolling basis, beginning on or about 9/1. Nonfall registration accepted. Admission may be deferred for a maximum of 1 year. Credit and/or placement offered for CEEB Advanced Placement tests.

COSTS AND FINANCIAL AID

Annual in-state tuition $8,720. Annual out-of-state tuition $8,720. Room and board $6,150. Required fees $1,592. Average book expense $900. **Required Forms and Deadlines:** FAFSA. Priority financial aid filing date 3/1. **Notification of Awards:** Applicants will be notified of awards on a rolling basis beginning 3/15. **Types of Aid:** *Need-based scholarships/grants:* Federal Pell, SEOG, state scholarships/grants, private scholarships, the school's own gift aid. *Loans:* Direct Subsidized Stafford, Direct Unsubsidized Stafford, Direct PLUS, Federal Perkins, state loans. **Student Employment:** Federal Work-Study Program available. Institutional employment available. Highest amount earned per year from on-campus jobs $2,343. Off-campus job opportunities are good. **Financial Aid Statistics:** 59% freshmen, 58% undergrads receive need-based scholarship or grant aid. 23% freshmen, 22% undergrads receive non-need-based scholarship or grant aid. 58% freshmen, 61% undergrads receive need-based self-help aid. 90% freshmen, 87% undergrads receive any aid. 74% undergrads borrow to pay for school. Average cumulative indebtedness $20,942. **Criteria for**

awarding institutional aid: *Non-need-based:* Academics, alumni affiliation, leadership, minority status, music/drama, state/district residency.

UNIVERSITY OF MINNESOTA, TWIN CITIES

Best 373

240 Williamson Hall, 231 Pillsbury Drive SE, Minneapolis, MN 55455-0213
Phone: 612-625-2008 **Financial Aid Phone:** 612-624-1111
E-mail: CEEB Code: 6874
Fax: 612-626-1693 **Website:** www.umn.edu **ACT Code:** 2156

This public school was founded in 1851. It has a 2000-acre campus.

RATINGS
Admissions Selectivity Rating: 89   **Fire Safety Rating:** 60*   **Green Rating:** 94

STUDENTS AND FACULTY
Enrollment: 29,921. **Student Body:** 52% female, 48% male, 25% out-of-state, 5% international. Asian 10%, African American 5%, Caucasian 75%, Hispanic 2%, Native American 1%.
Retention and Graduation: 90% freshmen return for sophomore year. **Faculty:** Student/faculty ratio 19:1. 1834 full-time faculty, 81% hold PhDs, 15% are members of minority groups, 39% are women.

ACADEMICS
Degrees: Bachelor's, certificate, diploma, master's, post-bachelor's certificate, post-master's certificate. **Classes:** Most classes have 20–29 students. Most lab/discussion sessions have 10–19 students. **Majors with Highest Enrollment:** Biology/biological sciences; journalism; psychology. **Special Study Options:** Accelerated program, cooperative education program, cross-registration, distance learning, double major, dual enrollment, English as a Second Language (ESL), exchange student program (domestic), external degree program, honors program, independent study, internships, liberal arts/career combination, student-designed major, study abroad, teacher certification program, Minors offered in most majors. Students may register in the College of Continuing Education and take courses in any division for BA or BS degrees. Programs in Foreign Service and pre-social work. Phi Beta Kappa. Pass/fail grading option. Internships. Qualified undergraduates may take graduate level classes. Preprofessional programs in law, medicine, veterinary science, pharmacy, dentistry, architecture, biology, education, journalism, landscape architecture, management, medical technology, mortuary science, nursing, and occupational/physical therapy. **Honors programs:** Honors, Undergraduate Research Opportunities Program. Special programs offered to physically disabled students include note-taking services, reader services, tape recorders, tutors. **Career services:** Alumni network, alumni services, career/job search classes, career assessment, internships, regional alumni. **Career services highlights include:** Very unique experiential classes described below. Intern program described below. New business hatchery in which 17 undergraduate students receive pro bono legal support, advice from entrepreneurs-in-residence and access to seed funding.

FACILITIES
Housing: Coed dorms, special housing for disabled students, special housing for international students, fraternity/sorority housing, apartments for married students, cooperative housing, apartments for single students, Honors housing, residential college (academic programs in residence). Eight conventional residence halls, plus three new apartment style residence halls. Housing application, $25 non-refundable residence hall application fee, and $100 residence hall advance payment (refundable), required by May 1 for guaranteed freshman housing. Off-campus housing office provides off-campus housing listings. **Special Academic Facilities/Equipment:** Frederick R. Weisman Art Museum, Bell Museum of Natural History, Ted Mann Concert Hall, Recreational Sports Center, Civil Engineering Building, Basic Sciences/Biomedical Engineering Building, Coffman Memorial Union, West Bank Arts Quarter, Goldstein Gallery, Arboretum. **Computers:** Students can register for classes online. Administrative functions (other than registration) can be performed online.

CAMPUS LIFE
Environment: Metropolis. **Activities:** Choral groups, concert band, dance, drama/theater, jazz band, literary magazine, marching band, music ensembles, musical theater, opera, pep band, radio station, student government, student newspaper, student-run film society, symphony orchestra, television station, international student organization. **Organizations:** 600 registered organi-

zations, 10 religious organizations. 22 fraternities, 12 sororities. **Athletics (Intercollegiate):** *Men:* Baseball, basketball, cross-country, diving, football, golf, gymnastics, ice hockey, swimming, tennis, track/field (outdoor), track/field (indoor), wrestling. *Women:* Basketball, cheerleading, cross-country, diving, golf, gymnastics, ice hockey, soccer, softball, swimming, tennis, track/field (outdoor), track/field (indoor), volleyball. **On-Campus Highlights:** Weisman Art Museum, McNamara Alumni Center, TCF Bank Stadium, Goldstein Gallery, Northrup Memorial Auditorium, Coffman Memorial Union, Mariucci Arena, University Theater, Rarig Center. **Environmental Initiatives:** Long established programs integrate sustainability throughout operations: Examples include our 25 year old recycling program, Parking & Transportations efforts to reduce emissions and fuel consumption while increasing use of alternative transportation; use of biomass on campus..An early participant in the Chicago Climate Exchange. U of MN implemented significant energy efficiency improvements and worked with State of MN to establish and adopt progressive sustainable building guidelines (B3) for new construction and renovations. Pioneering Interdisciplinary Research and Curricula: Formed the Institute on the Environment (and Initiative for Renewable Energy and the Environment) to support research that addresses today's grand environmental challenges with interdisciplinary approaches and partnerships. Established one of the first Sustainability Minor programs in the country (open to all majors) and more recently formed the Center for Sustainable Enterprise Development. http://environment.umn.edu/index.html www.csed.umn.edu/aboutus.html Our commitment to be a sustainable public research land grant institution: Formed a university system -wide Committee consisting of staff, students and faculty to set sustainability goals and performance measures in leadership, operations, energy efficiency, research, education and outreach according to our Regents Sustainability and Energy Efficiency policy adopted in 2004.

ADMISSIONS

Freshman Academic Profile: 43% in top 10% of high school class, 83% in top 25% of high school class, 99% in top 50% of high school class. SAT Math middle 50% range 600–710. SAT Critical Reading middle 50% range 520–670. SAT Writing middle 50% range 530–650. ACT middle 50% range 24–29. Minimum paper TOEFL 550. Minimum computer TOEFL 213. **Basis for Candidate Selection:** *Very important factors considered include:* Class rank, academic GPA, rigor of secondary school record, standardized test scores, *Other factors considered include:* Alumni/ae relation, character/personal qualities, extracurricular activities, first generation, geographical residence, racial/ethnic status, talent/ability, volunteer work, work experience. **Freshman Admission Requirements:** High school diploma is required and GED is accepted. *Academic units required:* 4 English, 3 mathematics, 3 science, 2 foreign language, 3 social studies, 1 history. **Freshman Admission Statistics:** 33,910 applied, 50% admitted, 32% enrolled. **Transfer Admission Requirements:** College transcript(s), minimum college GPA of 2.0 required. Lowest grade transferable D. **General Admission Information:** Application fee $45. Nonfall registration accepted. Admission may be deferred for a maximum of 1 year. Neither credit nor placement offered for CEEB Advanced Placement tests.

COSTS AND FINANCIAL AID

Required Forms and Deadlines: FAFSA, institution's own financial aid form. Priority financial aid filing date 3/1. **Notification of Awards:** Applicants will be notified of awards on a rolling basis beginning 2/15. **Types of Aid:** *Need-based scholarships/grants:* Federal Pell, SEOG, state scholarships/grants, private scholarships, the school's own gift aid, Federal Nursing Scholarships. *Loans:* Direct Subsidized Stafford, Direct Unsubsidized Stafford, Direct PLUS, Federal Perkins, Federal Nursing, state loans, college/university loans from institutional funds. *Student Employment:* Federal Work-Study Program available. Institutional employment available. **Financial Aid Statistics:** 51% freshmen, 50% undergrads receive need-based scholarship or grant aid. 12% freshmen, 11% undergrads receive non-need-based scholarship or grant aid. 44% freshmen, 46% undergrads receive need-based self-help aid. 63% undergrads borrow to pay for school. Average cumulative indebtedness $26,516. **Criteria for awarding institutional aid:** *Non-need-based:* Academics, art, athletics, job skills, leadership, minority status, music/drama, state/district residency.

UNIVERSITY OF MISSISSIPPI

145 Martindale, University, MS 38677
Phone: 662-915-7226 **Financial Aid Phone:** 800-891-4596
E-mail: admissions@olemiss.edu **CEEB Code:** 1840
Fax: 662-915-5869 **Website:** www.olemiss.edu **ACT Code:** 2250

This public school was founded in 1844. It has a 2500-acre campus.

RATINGS
Admissions Selectivity Rating: 72   **Fire Safety Rating:** 84   **Green Rating:** 84

STUDENTS AND FACULTY
Enrollment: 13,024. **Student Body:** 53% female, 47% male, 32% out-of-state, 1% international (65 countries represented). Asian 2%, African American 15%, Caucasian 80%, Hispanic 1%.
Retention and Graduation: Faculty: Student/faculty ratio 17:1. 729 full-time faculty, 84% hold PhDs, 19% are members of minority groups, 39% are women.

ACADEMICS
Degrees: Bachelor's, certificate, master's. **Classes:** Most classes have 10–19 students. Most lab/discussion sessions have 20–29 students. **Majors with Highest Enrollment:** Accounting; elementary education and teaching; marketing/marketing management. **Special Study Options:** Accelerated program, cooperative education program, distance learning, double major, dual enrollment, English as a Second Language (ESL), honors program, independent study, internships, study abroad, teacher certification program. **Honors programs:** Sally McDonnell-Barksdale Honors College. Special programs offered to physically disabled students include note-taking services, reader services, tape recorders.

FACILITIES
Housing: Men's dorms, special housing for international students, women's dorms, fraternity/sorority housing, apartments for married students, apartments for single students, Graduate/Older Students, intensive study floors, special interest, substance free, environmental interest housing available. **Special Academic Facilities/Equipment:** Sally McDonnell-Barksdale Honors College, Croft Institute for International Studies, National Food Service Management Institute, Mississippi Center for Supercomputing Research,Art and archaeology museums, women's studies center, Center for Study of Southern Culture,William Faulkner home, Marine Minerals Research Institute, National Center for Physical Acoustics, National Center for Natural Products Research, Biological Field Station, Barksdale Reading Institute, Ford Center for the Performing Arts, William Winter Institutue for Racial Reconciliation, Paris-Yates Chapel, Trent Lott Leadership Institute, Living Blues Archive, Student Media Center. **Computers:** 30% of classrooms, 100% of dorms, 100% of libraries, 80% of dining areas, 100% of student union, 30% of common outdoor areas have wireless network access. Students can register for classes online. Administrative functions (other than registration) can be performed online.

CAMPUS LIFE
Environment: Village. **Activities:** Choral groups, concert band, dance, drama/theater, jazz band, marching band, music ensembles, musical theater, opera, pep band, radio station, student government, student newspaper, symphony orchestra, television station, yearbook, campus ministries, international student organization. **Organizations:** 250 registered organizations, 25 honor societies, 21 religious organizations. 18 fraternities, 13 sororities. **Athletics (Intercollegiate):** *Men:* Baseball, basketball, cheerleading, cross-country, football, golf, tennis, track/field (outdoor), track/field (indoor). *Women:* Basketball, cheerleading, cross-country, golf, riflery, soccer, softball, tennis, track/field (outdoor), track/field (indoor), volleyball. **On-Campus Highlights:** Lyceum, Gertrude C. Ford Center for the Performing Arts, Intramural Sports Practice Facility, Student Union, Business School, INFORMATION SESSIONS at 9 am, 11 am, 1pm, 2 pm; TOURS-10 am, and 3 pm (Please register by phone, email, or online); RED/BLUE PREVIEWS-select Saturdays 8:30–1:00 pm (Register online); Fall and Spring Visit Days-8 am to noon (No advanced registration required). **Environmental Initiatives:** Energy management, green buildings, alternative transportation.

ADMISSIONS
Freshman Academic Profile: 70% from public high schools. Minimum paper TOEFL 550. Minimum computer TOEFL 213. **Basis for Candidate Selection:** *Very important factors considered include:* Academic GPA, rigor of secondary school record. *Important factors considered include:* Class rank, standardized test scores. *Other factors considered include:* Alumni/ae relation, state residency, talent/ability. **Freshman Admission Requirements:** High school

diploma is required and GED is accepted. *Academic units required:* 4 English, 3 mathematics, 3 science, (2 science labs), 1 foreign language, 1 social studies, 2 history, 1 academic electives. *Academic units recommended:* 4 mathematics, 4 science, 2 foreign language, 2 social studies. **Transfer Admission Requirements:** College transcript(s), minimum college GPA of 2.0 required. Lowest grade transferable D. **General Admission Information:** Application fee $25. Regular application deadline 7/20. Notification on a rolling basis, beginning on or about 10/1. Nonfall registration accepted. Credit offered for CEEB Advanced Placement tests.

COSTS AND FINANCIAL AID

Required Forms and Deadlines: FAFSA. Priority financial aid filing date 3/15. **Notification of Awards:** Applicants will be notified of awards on a rolling basis beginning 4/1. **Types of Aid:** *Need-based scholarships/grants:* Federal Pell, SEOG, state scholarships/grants, private scholarships, the school's own gift aid. *Loans:* FFEL Subsidized Stafford, FFEL Unsubsidized Stafford, FFEL PLUS, Federal Perkins, college/university loans from institutional funds. *Student Employment:* Federal Work-Study Program available. Institutional employment available. Off-campus job opportunities are fair. **Financial Aid Statistics:** 37% freshmen, 38% undergrads receive need-based scholarship or grant aid. 6% freshmen, 4% undergrads receive non-need-based scholarship or grant aid. 28% freshmen, 33% undergrads receive need-based self-help aid. 3% freshmen, 3% undergrads receive athletic scholarships. 68% freshmen, 71% undergrads receive any aid. 39% undergrads borrow to pay for school. Average cumulative indebtedness $22,866. **Criteria for awarding institutional aid:** *Non-need-based:* Academics, alumni affiliation, art, athletics, leadership, minority status, music/drama, state/district residency.

UNIVERSITY OF MISSOURI

230 Jesse Hall, Columbia, MO 65211
Phone: 573-882-7786 **Financial Aid Phone:** 573-882-7506
E-mail: MU4U@missouri.edu
Fax: 573-882-7887 **Website:** www.missouri.edu **ACT Code:** 2382

This public school was founded in 1839. It has a 1372-acre campus.

RATINGS

Admissions Selectivity Rating: 77   **Fire Safety Rating:** 73   **Green Rating:** 88

STUDENTS AND FACULTY

Enrollment: 23,529. **Student Body:** 52% female, 48% male, 22% out-of-state, 2% international (121 countries represented). Asian 2%, African American 7%, Caucasian 83%, Hispanic 2%, Native American 1%.
Retention and Graduation: 85% freshmen return for sophomore year. 43% freshmen graduate within 4 years. **Faculty:** Student/faculty ratio 19:1. 1266 full-time faculty, 91% hold PhDs, 18% are members of minority groups, 35% are women.

ACADEMICS

Degrees: Bachelor's, doctoral, master's, post-master's certificate. **Classes:** Most classes have 10–19 students. Most lab/discussion sessions have 20–29 students. **Majors with Highest Enrollment:** Biological and biomedical sciences, other; business/commerce. **Special Study Options:** Accelerated program, cooperative education program, cross-registration, distance learning, double major, dual enrollment, English as a Second Language (ESL), exchange student program (domestic), external degree program, honors program, independent study, internships, student-designed major, study abroad, teacher certification program, Evening College, MU Direct. **Honors programs:** Honors College **Combined degree programs:** BA/MA, Accounting. Special programs offered to physically disabled students include note-taking services, reader services, tape recorders, tutors. **Career services:** Alumni network, alumni services, career/job search classes, career assessment, internships, regional alumni. **Career services highlights include:** Our new recruitment website: www.HireMizzouGrads.com.

FACILITIES

Housing: Coed dorms, men's dorms, women's dorms, fraternity/sorority housing, apartments for married students, Freshmen Interest Groups and unique learning communities allow students to live in coed residence halls and share in exploring the same academic area of interest. 100% of campus accessible to physically disabled. **Special Academic Facilities/Equipment:** Life Sciences Center for Research TigerPlace—licensed care facility; Department of Nursing; James B Nutter Family Information Commons; Ellis Library; Museum of

Anthropology Museum of Art and Archeology; world's most powerful university research reactor for Nuclear Medicine one of 15 European Union Centers on college campuses. **Computers:** 100% of classrooms, 10% of dorms, 100% of libraries, 100% of dining areas, 100% of student union, 10% of common outdoor areas have wireless network access. Students can register for classes online. Administrative functions (other than registration) can be performed online.

CAMPUS LIFE

Environment: City. **Activities:** Choral groups, concert band, dance, drama/theater, jazz band, literary magazine, marching band, music ensembles, musical theater, opera, pep band, radio station, student government, student newspaper, student-run film society, symphony orchestra, television station, yearbook, campus ministries, international student organization, Model UN. **Organizations:** 598 registered organizations, 25 honor societies, 47 religious organizations. 32 fraternities, 19 sororities. **Athletics (Intercollegiate):** *Men:* Baseball, basketball, cross-country, diving, football, golf, swimming, track/field (outdoor), track/field (indoor), wrestling. *Women:* Basketball, cheerleading, cross-country, diving, golf, gymnastics, soccer, softball, swimming, tennis, track/field (outdoor), track/field (indoor), volleyball. **On-Campus Highlights:** Student Recreation Center—amazing recr, Mizzou Arena—home of Tiger Basketball, Memorial Stadium—home of Tiger Football, Jesse Hall—home to administ and various concerts, Life Sciences Center—home of research, Renovation and construction on campus—Life Sciences Center, Mizzou Arena, James B Nutter Family Infomration Center in Ellis Library, Virginia Avenue Housing and Dining Expansion. **Environmental Initiatives:** Signatory to ACUPCC climate change commitment. Recent purchase of 100% biomass boiler that will reduce greenhouse gas emissions by up to 25%. Major commitment to energy conservation for the past 20 years, currently saves MU 20 % of its energy cost. We have an ongoing goal to save an additional 1% cost each year.

ADMISSIONS

Freshman Academic Profile: 25% in top 10% of high school class, 55% in top 25% of high school class, 86% in top 50% of high school class. SAT Math middle 50% range 530–650. SAT Critical Reading middle 50% range 530–650. ACT middle 50% range 23–28. Minimum paper TOEFL 500. Minimum web-based TOEFL 61. **Basis for Candidate Selection:** *Very important factors considered include:* Class rank, academic GPA, standardized test scores. *Important factors considered include:* Rigor of secondary school record. *Other factors considered include:* Application essay, recommendation(s), first generation, level of applicant's interest, racial/ethnic status, talent/ability, volunteer work, work experience. **Freshman Admission Requirements:** High school diploma is required and GED is accepted. *Academic units required:* 4 English, 4 mathematics, 3 science, (1 science labs), 2 foreign language, 3 social studies, 1 fine arts. **Freshman Admission Statistics:** 16,436 applied, 83% admitted, 41% enrolled. **Transfer Admission Requirements:** College transcript(s), minimum college GPA of 2.5 required. **General Admission Information:** Application fee $45. Notification on a rolling basis, beginning on or about 1/15. Nonfall registration accepted. Admission may be deferred for a maximum of 1 year. Credit and/or placement offered for CEEB Advanced Placement tests.

COSTS AND FINANCIAL AID

Annual in-state tuition $7,077. Annual out-of-state tuition $17,733. Room and board $7,002. Required fees $1,629. **Required Forms and Deadlines:** FAFSA. Priority financial aid filing date 3/1. **Notification of Awards:** Applicants will be notified of awards on a rolling basis beginning 4/1. **Types of Aid:** *Need-based scholarships/grants:* Federal Pell, SEOG, state scholarships/grants, private scholarships, the school's own gift aid, outside. *Loans:* Direct Subsidized Stafford, Direct Unsubsidized Stafford, Direct PLUS, FFEL PLUS, Federal Perkins, Federal Nursing, state loans, college/university loans from institutional funds, outside or 3rd party. *Student Employment:* Federal Work-Study Program available. Institutional employment available. Off-campus job opportunities are excellent. **Financial Aid Statistics:** 42% freshmen, 37% undergrads receive need-based scholarship or grant aid. 3% freshmen, 2% undergrads receive non-need-based scholarship or grant aid. 34% freshmen, 34% undergrads receive need-based self-help aid. 4% freshmen, 4% undergrads receive athletic scholarships. 61% undergrads borrow to pay for school. Average cumulative indebtedness $20,814. **Criteria for awarding institutional aid:** *Non-need-based:* Academics, alumni affiliation, art, athletics, leadership, minority status, music/drama, state/district residency.

UNIVERSITY OF MISSOURI—KANSAS CITY

5100 Rockhill Road, 101 AC, Kansas City, mo 64114
Phone: 816-235-1111 **Financial Aid Phone:** 816-235-1154
E-mail: admit@umkc.edu **CEEB Code:** 6872
Fax: 816-235-5544 **Website:** www.umkc.edu **ACT Code:** 2380

This private school was founded in 1929. It has a 191-acre campus.

RATINGS

Admissions Selectivity Rating: 85   **Fire Safety Rating:** 60*   **Green Rating:** 71

STUDENTS AND FACULTY

Enrollment: 7,721. **Student Body:** 58% female, 42% male, 26% out-of-state, 3% international (66 countries represented). Asian 6%, African American 15%, Caucasian 59%, Hispanic 5%, Native American 1%.
Retention and Graduation: 74% freshmen return for sophomore year. 19% freshmen graduate within 4 years. **Faculty:** Student/faculty ratio 13:1. 721 full-time faculty, 75% hold PhDs, 22% are members of minority groups, 44% are women.

ACADEMICS

Degrees: Bachelor's, master's, post-master's certificate. **Classes:** Most classes have 10–19 students. Most lab/discussion sessions have 10–19 students. **Special Study Options:** Accelerated program, distance learning, double major, dual enrollment, English as a Second Language (ESL), honors program, independent study, internships, liberal arts/career combination, student-designed major, study abroad, teacher certification program. **Honors programs:** UMKC Honors Program **Combined degree programs:** BA/MD, BA/JD, BA/DDS, BLA/MD, BA/MPA, BBA/MBA. Special programs offered to physically disabled students include note-taking services, reader services, tape recorders, tutors. **Career services:** Alumni network, alumni services, career/job search classes, career assessment, internships. **Career services highlights include:** Cooperative Learning Programs.

FACILITIES

Housing: Coed dorms, special housing for disabled students, fraternity/sorority housing, apartments for married students, apartments for single students, University owned houses. 98% of campus accessible to physically disabled. **Special Academic Facilities/Equipment:** Art gallery, professional theater, geosciences museums, language lab, observatory. **Computers:** 90% of classrooms, 100% of dorms, 100% of libraries, 100% of dining areas, 100% of student union, have wireless network access. Students can register for classes online. Administrative functions (other than registration) can be performed online.

CAMPUS LIFE

Environment: Metropolis. **Activities:** Choral groups, concert band, dance, drama/theater, jazz band, literary magazine, music ensembles, musical theater, opera, pep band, student government, student newspaper, symphony orchestra, campus ministries, international student organization, Model UN. **Organizations:** 200 registered organizations, 32 honor societies, 13 religious organizations. 6 fraternities, 7 sororities. **Athletics (Intercollegiate):** *Men:* Basketball, cheerleading, cross-country, golf, riflery, soccer, tennis, track/field (outdoor). *Women:* Basketball, cheerleading, cross-country, golf, riflery, softball, tennis, track/field (outdoor), volleyball. **On-Campus Highlights:** Muddy's Coffee Shop, Nelson Atkins Museum, Sweeney Recreation Center, Minsky's restaurant, Planet Sub restaurant. **Environmental Initiatives:** Recycling, energy management, building design.

ADMISSIONS

Freshman Academic Profile: Average high school GPA 3.31. 31% in top 10% of high school class, 58% in top 25% of high school class, 89% in top 50% of high school class. SAT Math middle 50% range 550–690. SAT Critical Reading middle 50% range 520–650. ACT middle 50% range 21–28. Minimum paper TOEFL 500. Minimum computer TOEFL 213. Minimum web-based TOEFL 79. **Basis for Candidate Selection:** *Very important factors considered include:* Class rank, academic GPA, rigor of secondary school record, standardized test scores. *Other factors considered include:* Application essay, recommendation(s), character/personal qualities, extracurricular activities, first generation, interview, talent/ability, volunteer work, work experience. **Freshman Admission Requirements:** High school diploma is required and GED is accepted. *Academic units required:* 4 English, 4 mathematics, 3 science, (1 science labs), 2 foreign language, 3 social studies, 1 Fine Arts **Freshman Admission Statistics:** 4,117 applied, 62% admitted, 39% enrolled. **Transfer Admission Requirements:** College transcript(s), minimum college GPA of 2.0 required. Lowest grade transferable D. **General Admission Information:** Application fee $45. Nonfall registration accepted. Admission may be deferred for a maximum of 2 semesters. Credit offered for CEEB Advanced Placement tests.

COSTS AND FINANCIAL AID

Annual tuition $7,368. Room and board $10,467. Required fees $905. **Required Forms and Deadlines:** FAFSA. Priority financial aid filing date 3/1. **Notification of Awards:** Applicants will be notified of awards on a rolling basis beginning 4/15. **Types of Aid:** *Need-based scholarships/grants:* Federal Pell, SEOG, state scholarships/grants, private scholarships, the school's own gift aid, United Negro College Fund, Federal Nursing Scholarships. *Loans:* Direct Subsidized Stafford, Direct Unsubsidized Stafford, Direct PLUS, Federal Perkins, Federal Nursing, state loans, college/university loans from institutional funds. *Student Employment:* Federal Work-Study Program available. Institutional employment available. Highest amount earned per year from on-campus jobs $5,700. Off-campus job opportunities are excellent. **Financial Aid Statistics:** 63% freshmen, 53% undergrads receive need-based scholarship or grant aid. 3% freshmen, 1% undergrads receive non-need-based scholarship or grant aid. 46% freshmen, 54% undergrads receive need-based self-help aid. 3% freshmen, 2% undergrads receive athletic scholarships. 62.6% freshmen, 62% undergrads receive any aid. 65% undergrads borrow to pay for school. Average cumulative indebtedness $20,512. **Criteria for awarding institutional aid:** *Non-need-based:* Academics, alumni affiliation, art, athletics, leadership, minority status, music/drama, state/district residency.

UNIVERSITY OF MISSOURI—SAINT LOUIS

351 Millenium Student Center, 1 University Boulevard, Saint Louis, MO 63121-4400
Phone: 314-516-5451 **Financial Aid Phone:** 314-516-5526
E-mail: admissions@umsl.edu **CEEB Code:** 6889
Fax: 314-516-5310 **Website:** www.umsl.edu **ACT Code:** 2383

This public school was founded in 1963. It has a 475-acre campus.

RATINGS

Admissions Selectivity Rating: 77   **Fire Safety Rating:** 88   **Green Rating:** 72

STUDENTS AND FACULTY

Enrollment: 8,933. **Student Body:** 58% female, 42% male, 10% out-of-state, 3% international (53 countries represented). Asian 3%, African American 21%, Caucasian 61%, Hispanic 2%.
Retention and Graduation: 69% freshmen return for sophomore year. 21% freshmen graduate within 4 years. 16% grads go on to further study within 1 year. 41% grads pursue arts and sciences degrees. 1% grads pursue law degrees. 20% grads pursue business degrees. **Faculty:** Student/faculty ratio 17:1. 480 full-time faculty, 76% hold PhDs, 18% are members of minority groups, 48% are women. 8% of classes are taught by teaching assistants.

ACADEMICS

Degrees: Bachelor's, doctoral, master's, post-bachelor's certificate, post-master's certificate. **Classes:** Most classes have 10–19 students. Most lab/discussion sessions have 10–19 students. **Majors with Highest Enrollment:** accounting; business/commerce; psychology. **Special Study Options:** Accelerated program, cooperative education program, cross-registration, distance learning, double major, dual enrollment, English as a Second Language (ESL), exchange student program (domestic), honors program, independent study, internships, student-designed major, study abroad, teacher certification program, Engineering UMSL/WU, 2+3 BS/MA Program in Economics, 2+3 BA/BS-Ed and MA Program in History, 2+3 BA/MA Program in Philosophy, 2+3 BA/MA Program in Political Science, 2+3 BA in Psychology and MS in Gerontology Program, 2+3 BA/MA Program in Sociology, Art and Art History 3+4 Program for School of Architecture at Washington University, Biology 3+4 Program for UMSL College of Optometry, Physics and Astronomy 3+4 Program for UMSL College of Optometry, Biology 3+3 Program for Logan Chiropractic College. **Honors programs:** Pierre Laclede Honors College offers a four-year (for freshmen) and a two-year (for internal and external transfers) honors program through which students can meet their General Education and some other graduation requirements (e.g., advanced composition, global awareness, cultural diversity). Most instruction is in small seminars (average enrollment is 13). There is a six-hour independent study requirement, and a writing program engages all students. **Combined degree programs:** BA/MA, BA/DOPT; BS/DOPT. Special programs offered to physically disabled students include note-taking services, reader services, tape recorders **Career services:** alumni services, career assessment, internships. **Career services highlights include:** Experiential learning as it includes our Internship and Cooperative Education programs.

FACILITIES

Housing: Coed dorms, special housing for disabled students, special housing for international students, fraternity/sorority housing, apartments for married students, apartments for single students, theme housingHousing for graduate students and students over 21 in apartments; other themed communities. 100%

of campus accessible to physically disabled. **Special Academic Facilities/Equipment:** Art galleries, language, writing labs, math labs Mercantile Library, and observatory, radio station. **Computers:** 68% of classrooms, 90% of dorms, 90% of libraries, 100% of dining areas, 90% of student union, 60% of common outdoor areas have wireless network access. Students can register for classes online. Administrative functions (other than registration) can be performed online.

CAMPUS LIFE

Environment: Metropolis. **Activities:** Choral groups, dance, drama/theater, jazz band, literary magazine, music ensembles, musical theater, opera, pep band, radio station, student government, student newspaper, student-run film society, campus ministries, international student organization, Model UN. **Organizations:** 125 registered organizations, 24 honor societies, 9 religious organizations. 3 fraternities, 3 sororities. **Athletics (Intercollegiate):** *Men:* Baseball, basketball, golf, soccer, tennis. *Women:* Basketball, golf, soccer, softball, tennis, volleyball. **On-Campus Highlights:** Millennium Student Center, Touhill Performing Arts Center, Mark Twain Athletic Complex, Gallery 210, Pilot House. **Environmental Initiatives:** Energy conservation; waste management and recycling; pollution prevention.

ADMISSIONS

Freshman Academic Profile: 22% in top 10% of high school class, 48% in top 25% of high school class, 81% in top 50% of high school class. 91% from public high schools. SAT Math middle 50% range 470–670. ACT middle 50% range 20–26. Minimum paper TOEFL 500. Minimum computer TOEFL 173. **Basis for Candidate Selection:** *Very important factors considered include:* Class rank, academic GPA, rigor of secondary school record, standardized test scores, *Other factors considered include:* Application essay, recommendation(s). **Freshman Admission Requirements:** High school diploma is required and GED is accepted: *Academic units required:* 4 English, 4 mathematics, 3 science, (1 science labs), 2 foreign language, 3 social studies, 1 fine arts **Freshman Admission Statistics:** 1,619 applied, 79% admitted, 41% enrolled. **Transfer Admission Requirements:** College transcript(s), minimum college GPA of 2.0 required. Lowest grade transferable D. **General Admission Information:** Application fee $35. Regular application deadline 8/23. Notification on a rolling basis, beginning on or about 10/1. Nonfall registration accepted. Credit and/or placement offered for CEEB Advanced Placement tests.

COSTS AND FINANCIAL AID

Average book expense $950. **Required Forms and Deadlines:** FAFSA. Priority financial aid filing date 4/1. **Notification of Awards:** Applicants will be notified of awards on a rolling basis beginning 4/1. **Types of Aid:** *Need-based scholarships/grants:* Federal Pell, SEOG, state scholarships/grants, private scholarships, the school's own gift aid, Federal Nursing Scholarships. Federal ACG and SMART grants. *Loans:* FFEL Subsidized Stafford, FFEL Unsubsidized Stafford, FFEL PLUS, Federal Perkins, Federal Nursing, Federal Teach Grants. *Student Employment:* Federal Work-Study Program available. Institutional employment available. Highest amount earned per year from on-campus jobs $8,000. Off-campus job opportunities are good. **Financial Aid Statistics:** 67% freshmen, 54% undergrads receive need-based scholarship or grant aid. 5% freshmen, 1% undergrads receive non-need-based scholarship or grant aid. 51% freshmen, 56% undergrads receive need-based self-help aid. 2% freshmen, 1% undergrads receive athletic scholarships. 84% freshmen, 74% undergrads receive any aid. 65% undergrads borrow to pay for school. Average cumulative indebtedness $25,776. **Criteria for awarding institutional aid:** *Non-need-based:* Academics, alumni affiliation, art, athletics, music/drama, state/district residency.

UNIVERSITY OF MOBILE

5735 College Parkway, Mobile, AL 36613-2842
Phone: 251-442-2273 **Financial Aid Phone:** 251-442-2239
E-mail: adminfo@mail.umobile.edu **CEEB Code:** 1515
Fax: 251-442-2498 **Website:** www.umobile.edu **ACT Code:** 29

This private school, affiliated with the Southern Baptist Church, was founded in 1961. It has a 830-acre campus.

RATINGS

Admissions Selectivity Rating: 78   **Fire Safety Rating:** 60*   **Green Rating:** 66

STUDENTS AND FACULTY

Enrollment: 1,417. **Student Body:** 66% female, 34% male, 18.4% out-of-state, 2% international (25 countries represented). African American 22%, Caucasian 65%, Hispanic 1%, Native American 2%.
Retention and Graduation: 77% freshmen return for sophomore year. 28% freshmen graduate within 4 years. **Faculty:** Student/faculty ratio 12:1. 84 full-time faculty, 61% hold PhDs, 5% are members of minority groups, 45% are women.

ACADEMICS

Degrees: Associate, bachelor's, master's. **Classes:** Most classes have 10–19 students. Most lab/discussion sessions have 10–19 students. **Majors with Highest Enrollment:** Business administration and management; elementary education and teaching; nursing/registered nurse (RN, ASN, BSN, MSN). **Special Study Options:** Accelerated program, double major, honors program, independent study, internships, teacher certification program. **Honors programs:** Exploring the great books and the enduring questions; join a community of enthusiastic students like yourself; take courses designed not to make you do more work, but do the kind of work that will help you become a thinking leader; earn the "Honors Scholar" designation and seal on your diploma and transcript; participate in special events, such as an annual honor dinner hosted by President Foley; have frequent access to honors faculty; benefit from honors roundtable designed to help students prepare for and apply to graduate school, seek grants and scholarships, and pursue post-graduate career opportunities. **Combined degree programs:** BS/MBA. Special programs offered to physically disabled students include tutors. **Career services:** Alumni services, career/job search classes, career assessment, internships.

FACILITIES

Housing: Men's dorms, women's dorms 100% of campus accessible to physically disabled. **Special Academic Facilities/Equipment:** Art gallery, forest learning center. **Computers:** 10% of classrooms, 100% of dorms, 100% of libraries, 50% of dining areas, 100% of student union, 20% of common outdoor areas have wireless network access. Students can register for classes online. Administrative functions (other than registration) can be performed online.

CAMPUS LIFE

Environment: City. **Activities:** Choral groups, concert band, jazz band, music ensembles, musical theater, opera, pep band, student government, campus ministries. **Organizations:** 52 registered organizations, 12 honor societies, 3 religious organizations. **Athletics (Intercollegiate):** *Men:* Baseball, basketball, cross-country, golf, soccer, tennis. *Women:* Basketball, cheerleading, cross-country, golf, soccer, softball, tennis, volleyball. **On-Campus Highlights:** Ram Hall—state-of-the-art Auditorium, Newly renovated dining hall, Martin Hall—Donald Art Gallery, New Dorms—Faulkner and Samford Halls, Baseball Field/Swimming Pool. **Environmental Initiatives:** Recycling, wildlife conservation, green energy, sanitary underground injection system.

ADMISSIONS

Freshman Academic Profile: Average high school GPA 3.33. 27% in top 10% of high school class, 55% in top 25% of high school class, 79% in top 50% of high school class. SAT Math middle 50% range 430–540. SAT Critical Reading middle 50% range 470–590. ACT middle 50% range 19–25. Minimum paper TOEFL 500. Minimum computer TOEFL 173. Minimum web-based TOEFL 61. **Basis for Candidate Selection:** *Very important factors considered include:* Academic GPA, standardized test scores, *Other factors considered include:* Class rank, recommendation(s), rigor of secondary school record, character/personal qualities, extracurricular activities, level of applicant's interest, talent/ability. **Freshman Admission Requirements:** High school diploma is required and GED is accepted. *Academic units recommended:* 4 English, 3 mathematics, 2 foreign language, 3 social studies. **Freshman Admission Statistics:** 796 applied, 78% admitted, 37% enrolled. **Transfer Admission Requirements:** College transcript(s), minimum college GPA of 2.75 required. Lowest grade transferable C. **General Admission Information:** Application fee $50. Regular application deadline 8/1. Nonfall registration accepted. Admission may be deferred for a maximum of 1 year. Credit offered for CEEB Advanced Placement tests.

COSTS AND FINANCIAL AID

Required Forms and Deadlines: FAFSA, state aid form **Types of Aid:** *Need-based scholarships/grants:* Federal Pell, SEOG, state scholarships/grants, private scholarships, the school's own gift aid, Federal Nursing Scholarships. *Loans:* FFEL Subsidized Stafford, FFEL Unsubsidized Stafford, FFEL PLUS, Federal Perkins. *Student Employment:* Federal Work-Study Program available. Institutional employment available. Highest amount earned per year from on-campus jobs $1,855. Off-campus job opportunities are fair. **Financial Aid Statistics:** 86% freshmen, 71% undergrads receive need-based scholarship or grant aid. 10% freshmen, 11% undergrads receive non-need-based scholarship or grant aid. 54% freshmen, 60% undergrads receive need-based self-help aid. 3% freshmen, 2% undergrads receive athletic scholarships. 96% freshmen, 96% undergrads receive any aid. 25% undergrads borrow to pay for school. Average cumulative indebtedness $18,840. **Criteria for awarding institutional aid:** *Non-need-based:* Academics, alumni affiliation, athletics, music/drama, religious affiliation.

THE UNIVERSITY OF MONTANA

Best 373

Lommasson Center 103, Missoula, MT 59812
Phone: 406-243-6266 **Financial Aid Phone:** 406-243-5373
E-mail: admiss@umontana.edu **CEEB Code:** 4489
Fax: 406-243-5711 **Website:** www.umontana.edu **ACT Code:** 2422

This public school was founded in 1893. It has a 220-acre campus.

RATINGS
Admissions Selectivity Rating: 72   **Fire Safety Rating:** 77   **Green Rating:** 94

STUDENTS AND FACULTY
Enrollment: 12,038. **Student Body:** 53% female, 47% male, 25% out-of-state, 2% international (65 countries represented). Asian 2%, African American 1%, Caucasian 83%, Hispanic 2%, Native American 4%.
Retention and Graduation: 72% freshmen return for sophomore year. 19% freshmen graduate within 4 years. 33% grads go on to further study within 1 year. **Faculty:** Student/faculty ratio 19:1. 564 full-time faculty, 82% hold PhDs, 12% are members of minority groups, 37% are women. 9% of classes are taught by teaching assistants.

ACADEMICS
Degrees: Associate, bachelor's, certificate, first professional, master's, post-master's certificate, terminal associate. **Classes:** Most classes have 10–19 students. Most lab/discussion sessions have 20–29 students. **Majors with Highest Enrollment:** Business administration and management; education; psychology. **Special Study Options:** Cooperative education program, cross-registration, distance learning, double major, English as a Second Language (ESL), exchange student program (domestic), external degree program, honors program, independent study, internships, study abroad, teacher certification program, Bachelor of Nursing in Missoula in cooperation with Montana State University—Bozeman. **Honors programs:** The Davidson Honors College offers talented and motivated students an academic and social community as an important part of their undergraduate experience at The University of Montana, regardless of their major disciplines. Honors courses are taught by many of the best scholars on campus and are generally limited to twenty students. The Honors College encourages its students to participate in community service activities, international educational experiences and undergraduate research. **Combined degree programs:** JD/MBA, MBA/PharmD, JD/MPA. Special programs offered to physically disabled students include note-taking services, reader services, tape recorders, tutors. **Career services:** Alumni network, alumni services, career/job search classes, career assessment, internships, regional alumni.

FACILITIES
Housing: Coed dorms, special housing for disabled students, men's dorms, special housing for international students, women's dorms, fraternity/sorority housing, apartments for married students, apartments for single students, theme housing, apartments for students and families, Honors floors, International floors, and quiet floors in dorms, activity dorms, personal development housing. **Special Academic Facilities/Equipment:** On main campus: clinical psychology center; environmental studies lab; geology field camp; several biological, biomedical, kinesiology, physiology, forestry-related, and other research labs or centers; art galleries; broadcast media center (public radio and television) and performing arts-radio-television building; practical ethics center; extensive presentation technology equipment and services, and others. Other locations: biological station, experimental forest, two-year college of technology (two locations), Fort Missoula field research center, and others. **Computers:** 20% of classrooms, 100% of libraries, 60% of dining areas, 100% of student union, 5% of common outdoor areas have wireless network access. Students can register for classes online. Administrative functions (other than registration) can be performed online.

CAMPUS LIFE
Environment: City. **Activities:** Choral groups, concert band, dance, drama/theater, jazz band, literary magazine, marching band, music ensembles, musical theater, opera, pep band, radio station, student government, student newspaper, symphony orchestra, television station **Organizations:** 150 registered organizations, 5 fraternities, 4 sororities. **Athletics (Intercollegiate):** *Men:* Basketball, cheerleading, cross-country, football, tennis, track/field (outdoor), track/field (indoor). *Women:* Basketball, cheerleading, cross-country, golf, soccer, tennis, track/field (outdoor), track/field (indoor), volleyball. **On-Campus Highlights:** Adams Event Center (basketball, shows, etc.), Washington-Grizzly Stadium (football, other), Campus Recreation Center (student recreation), University Center (student center, movie theater), Performing Arts-RadioTV Center (public radio-TV), 2. Washington-Grizzly Stadium also used for MAJOR events, like Pearl Jam concert a few years ago (kicking off their annual tour), the Rolling Stones concert Oct 2006, and Elton John concerts (2007 and 2008). **Environmental Initiatives:** Full-time Sustainability Coordinator and professional Recycling Coordinator in Facilities Services. These and others at UM completed a Greenhouse Gas Inventory and have embarked on a Carbon Neutrality Action Plan. Campus committee on sustainability, Farm to College Program.

ADMISSIONS
Freshman Academic Profile: Average high school GPA 3.22. 17% in top 10% of high school class, 39% in top 25% of high school class, 71% in top 50% of high school class. 44% from public high schools. SAT Math middle 50% range 480–590. SAT Critical Reading middle 50% range 480–580. SAT Writing middle 50% range 450–580. ACT middle 50% range 20–26. Minimum paper TOEFL 500. Minimum computer TOEFL 173. **Basis for Candidate Selection:** *Very important factors considered include:* Class rank, academic GPA, rigor of secondary school record, standardized test scores. *Important factors considered include:* Extracurricular activities, talent/ability. *Other factors considered include:* Application essay, recommendation(s). **Freshman Admission Requirements:** High school diploma is required and GED is accepted. *Academic units required:* 4 English, 3 mathematics, 2 science, (2 science labs), 3 social studies, 2 history. *Academic units recommended:* 2 foreign language, 2 visual/performing arts, 2 computer science, 2 Foreign language or vocational education **Freshman Admission Statistics:** 5,342 applied, 96% admitted, 47% enrolled. **Transfer Admission Requirements:** College transcript(s), minimum college GPA of 2.0 required. Lowest grade transferable D. **General Admission Information:** Application fee $30. Notification on a rolling basis, beginning on or about 9/15. Nonfall registration accepted. Admission may be deferred for a maximum of 1 year. Credit and/or placement offered for CEEB Advanced Placement tests.

COSTS AND FINANCIAL AID
Annual in-state tuition $4,054. Annual out-of-state tuition $16,894. Room and board $6,611. Required fees $1,479. Average book expense $900. **Required Forms and Deadlines:** FAFSAUM Supplemental Information Sheet. Priority financial aid filing date 2/15. **Notification of Awards:** Applicants will be notified of awards on a rolling basis beginning 4/1. **Types of Aid:** *Need-based scholarships/grants:* Federal Pell, SEOG, state scholarships/grants, private scholarships, the school's own gift aid. *Loans:* FFEL Subsidized Stafford, FFEL Unsubsidized Stafford, FFEL PLUS, Federal Perkins. *Student Employment:* Federal Work-Study Program available. Institutional employment available. Off-campus job opportunities are good. **Financial Aid Statistics:** 35% freshmen, 36% undergrads receive need-based scholarship or grant aid. 2% freshmen, 1% undergrads receive non-need-based scholarship or grant aid. 46% freshmen, 46% undergrads receive need-based self-help aid. 2% freshmen, 3% undergrads receive athletic scholarships. 78% freshmen, 73% undergrads receive any aid. 67% undergrads borrow to pay for school. Average cumulative indebtedness $17,527. **Criteria for awarding institutional aid:** *Non-need-based:* Academics, alumni affiliation, athletics, leadership, music/drama, state/district residency.

THE UNIVERSITY OF MONTANA—WESTERN

710 South Atlantic, Dillon, MT 59725
Phone: 406-683-7331
E-mail: admissions@umwestern.edu **CEEB Code:** 4945
Fax: 406-683-7493 **Website:** www.umwestern.edu **ACT Code:** 2428

This public school was founded in 1893. It has a 34-acre campus.

RATINGS
Admissions Selectivity Rating: 63   **Fire Safety Rating:** 60*   **Green Rating:** 60*

STUDENTS AND FACULTY
Enrollment: 1,159. **Student Body:** 59% female, 41% male, 15% out-of-state, (5 countries represented).
Retention and Graduation: 62% freshmen return for sophomore year. 8% freshmen graduate within 4 years. 50% grads go on to further study within 1 year. **Faculty:** Student/faculty ratio 16:1. 50 full-time faculty, 74% hold PhDs, 8% are members of minority groups, 44% are women.

ACADEMICS
Degrees: Associate, bachelor's. **Classes:** Most classes have 10–19 students. **Majors with Highest Enrollment:** Business/commerce; elementary education and teaching; environmental studies. **Special Study Options:** Cooperative education program, distance learning, double major, dual enrollment, honors

program, independent study, internships, teacher certification program Special programs offered to physically disabled students include note-taking services, reader services, tape recorders, tutors. **Career services:** Alumni services, career/job search classes, career assessment, internships.

FACILITIES

Housing: Coed dorms, special housing for disabled students, men's dorms, women's dorms, apartments for married students, apartments for single students, students with fewer than 30 credits not living w/ family required to live in dorm. Transfer students under 21 w/ less than 30 credits not living with parents must live in dorm. 90% of campus accessible to physically disabled. **Special Academic Facilities/Equipment:** Art gallery, outdoor education center, learning center. **Computers:** Students can register for classes online. Administrative functions (other than registration) can be performed online.

CAMPUS LIFE

Environment: Rural. **Activities:** Choral groups, concert band, drama/theater, jazz band, literary magazine, music ensembles, radio station, student government, student newspaper, yearbook. **Organizations:** 25 registered organizations, 2 honor societies, 2 religious organizations. **Athletics (Intercollegiate):** *Men:* Basketball, cheerleading, football, golf, rodeo. *Women:* Basketball, cheerleading, golf, rodeo, volleyball. **On-Campus Highlights:** SUB (Student Union Building), Straugh Arena, The Cup, STC Tech Building, Bark'n Bite.

ADMISSIONS

Freshman Academic Profile: Average high school GPA 2.99. 5% in top 10% of high school class, 18% in top 25% of high school class, 49% in top 50% of high school class. 96% from public high schools. SAT Math middle 50% range 430–520. SAT Critical Reading middle 50% range 410–510. ACT middle 50% range 16–22. Minimum paper TOEFL 500. Minimum computer TOEFL 173. **Basis for Candidate Selection:** *Very important factors considered include:* Class rank, rigor of secondary school record, standardized test scores, *Other factors considered include:* Alumni/ae relation, extracurricular activities, racial/ethnic status, state residency, talent/ability. **Freshman Admission Requirements:** High school diploma is required and GED is accepted. *Academic units required:* 4 English, 3 mathematics, 2 science, (2 science labs), 3 social studies, 4 academic electives. **Freshman Admission Statistics:** 428 applied, 99% admitted, 57% enrolled. **Transfer Admission Requirements:** College transcript(s), minimum college GPA of 2.0 required. Lowest grade transferable c. **General Admission Information:** Application fee $30. Regular application deadline 7/1. Notification on a rolling basis, beginning on or about 9/1. Nonfall registration accepted. Admission may be deferred for a maximum of 18. Credit and/or placement offered for CEEB Advanced Placement tests.

COSTS AND FINANCIAL AID

Annual in-state tuition $3,538. Room and board $4,920. Required fees $815. Average book expense $850. **Required Forms and Deadlines:** FAFSA. Priority financial aid filing date 3/1. **Notification of Awards:** Applicants will be notified of awards on a rolling basis beginning 3/1. **Types of Aid:** *Need-based scholarships/grants:* Federal Pell, SEOG, state scholarships/grants, the school's own gift aid. *Loans:* FFEL Subsidized Stafford, FFEL Unsubsidized Stafford, FFEL PLUS, Federal Perkins. *Student Employment:* Federal Work-Study Program available. Institutional employment available. Highest amount earned per year from on-campus jobs $1,350. Off-campus job opportunities are good. **Financial Aid Statistics:** 65% freshmen, 73% undergrads receive need-based scholarship or grant aid. 3% freshmen, 3% undergrads receive non-need-based scholarship or grant aid. 65% freshmen, 74% undergrads receive need-based self-help aid. 10% freshmen, 17% undergrads receive athletic scholarships. 84% undergrads borrow to pay for school. Average cumulative indebtedness $20,703. **Criteria for awarding institutional aid:** *Non-need-based:* Academics, alumni affiliation, art, athletics, job skills, leadership, minority status, music/drama, religious affiliation, state/district residency.

UNIVERSITY OF MONTEVALLO

Station 6030, Montevallo, AL 35115
Phone: 205-665-6030 **Financial Aid Phone:** 205-665-6050
E-mail: admissions@montevallo.edu **CEEB Code:** 1004
Fax: 205-665-6032 **Website:** www.montevallo.edu/ **ACT Code:** 4

This public school was founded in 1896. It has a 160-acre campus.

RATINGS
Admissions Selectivity Rating: 60*   **Fire Safety Rating:** 65   **Green Rating:** 78

STUDENTS AND FACULTY
Enrollment: 2,547. **Student Body:** 67% female, 33% male, 4% out-of-state, 2% international (20 countries represented). Asian 5%, African American 10%, Caucasian 75%, Hispanic 2%, Native American 1%.
Retention and Graduation: 78% freshmen return for sophomore year. **Faculty:** Student/faculty ratio 16:1. 137 full-time faculty, 94% hold PhDs, 12% are members of minority groups, 51% are women.

ACADEMICS
Degrees: Bachelor's, master's, post-master's certificate. **Classes:** Most classes have 10–19 students. Most lab/discussion sessions have 20–29 students. **Majors with Highest Enrollment:** Business administration and management; elementary education and teaching; health and physical education. **Special Study Options:** Accelerated program, cross-registration, double major, dual enrollment, exchange student program (domestic), honors program, independent study, internships, study abroad, teacher certification program, Advanced Placement credit; academic remediation; and Learning disabilities services. **Honors programs:** Honors History; Honors Composition; Honors Literature; Honors Thesis. **Combined degree programs:** 3-2 engineering program with U of Alabama at Birmingham. Special programs offered to physically disabled students include note-taking services, reader services, tape recorders, tutors. **Career services:** Alumni services, career assessment. **Career services highlights include:** The Career Center assists students through all aspects of the career-planning process. Career counseling, including career assessments is available to all enrolled students. Other services include employability skills training, job postings, internship information, on-campus interviewing, career events and seminars and graduate school information.

FACILITIES
Housing: Coed dorms, men's dorms, women's dorms, fraternity/sorority housing, apartments for married students. **Special Academic Facilities/Equipment:** Art gallery, child development, speech and hearing, traffic safety, and undergraduate liberal studies centers, mass communications center with cable TV broadcasting capabilities. **Computers:** 98% of classrooms, 85% of dorms, 100% of libraries, 100% of dining areas, 100% of student union, 75% of common outdoor areas have wireless network access. Students can register for classes online. Administrative functions (other than registration) can be performed online.

CAMPUS LIFE
Environment: Rural. **Activities:** Choral groups, concert band, dance, drama/theater, jazz band, literary magazine, music ensembles, musical theater, student government, student newspaper, television station, yearbook. **Organizations:** 93 registered organizations, 26 honor societies, 8 religious organizations. 7 fraternities, 8 sororities. **Athletics (Intercollegiate):** *Men:* Baseball, basketball, golf, soccer. *Women:* Basketball, cross-country, golf, soccer, tennis, volleyball. **On-Campus Highlights:** Cafeteria, Student Activity Center, Main Quad, University of Montevallo Student Lake, Intramural Fields. **Environmental Initiatives:** Campus lighting retrofit to energy saving bulbs. Campus-wide retrofit of all toilets, showers and faucets to low use fixtures. An aggressive energy management program.

ADMISSIONS
Freshman Academic Profile: 90% from public high schools. ACT middle 50% range 20–26. Minimum paper TOEFL 525. Minimum computer TOEFL 193. Minimum web-based TOEFL 71. **Basis for Candidate Selection:** *Very important factors considered include:* Rigor of secondary school record, standardized test scores, *Other factors considered include:* Class rank, recommendation(s), alumni/ae relation, character/personal qualities, extracurricular activities, interview, talent/ability, work experience. **Freshman Admission Requirements:** High school diploma is required and GED is accepted. *Academic units required:* 4 English, 2 mathematics, 2 science, 2 social studies, 2 history, 4 academic electives. *Academic units recommended:* 3 mathematics, 3 science, 2 foreign language. **Freshman Admission Statistics:** 1,350 applied, 72% admitted, 44% enrolled. **Transfer Admission Requirements:** College transcript(s), minimum college GPA of 2.0 required. Lowest grade transferable D. **General Admission Information:** Application fee $25. Regular application deadline 8/1. Notification on a rolling basis, beginning on or about 9/1. Nonfall registration accepted. Admission may be deferred for a maximum of 2 years.

COSTS AND FINANCIAL AID
Required Forms and Deadlines: FAFSA. Priority financial aid filing date 4/1. **Notification of Awards:** Applicants will be notified of awards on a rolling basis beginning 4/20. **Types of Aid:** *Need-based scholarships/grants:* Federal Pell, SEOG, state scholarships/grants, private scholarships, the school's own gift aid. *Loans:* FFEL Subsidized Stafford, FFEL Unsubsidized Stafford, FFEL PLUS, Federal Perkins. *Student Employment:* Federal Work-Study Program available. Institutional employment available. Highest amount earned per year from on-campus jobs $3,100. Off-campus job opportunities are good. **Financial Aid Statistics:** 44% freshmen, 38% undergrads receive need-based scholarship or grant aid. 11% freshmen, 6% undergrads receive non-need-based scholarship or grant aid. 39% freshmen, 41% undergrads receive need-based self-help aid. 1% freshmen, 3% undergrads receive athletic scholarships. 78% freshmen, 74% undergrads receive any aid. 54% undergrads borrow to pay for school. Aver-

age cumulative indebtedness $16,581. **Criteria for awarding institutional aid:** *Non-need-based:* Academics, art, athletics, leadership, minority status, music/drama.

UNIVERSITY OF NEBRASKA AT KEARNEY

905 West 25th, Kearney, NE 68849
Phone: 800-532-7639
E-mail: admissionsug@unk.edu **CEEB Code:** 6467
Fax: 308-865-8987 **Website:** www.unk.edu **ACT Code:** 2468

This public school was founded in 1903. It has a 235-acre campus.

RATINGS
Admissions Selectivity Rating: 60*   **Fire Safety Rating:** 60*   **Green Rating:** 60*

STUDENTS AND FACULTY
Enrollment: 5,886. **Student Body:** 56% female, 44% male, 6% out-of-state, 3% international. Asian 1%, African American 1%, Caucasian 88%, Hispanic 2%.

ACADEMICS
Degrees: Bachelor's, master's. **Classes: Special Study Options:** Distance learning, double major, English as a Second Language (ESL), exchange student program (domestic), external degree program, honors program, internships, study abroad, teacher certification program. **Combined degree programs:** 3-1 medical technology program. Special programs offered to physically disabled students include note-taking services, reader services, tape recorders, tutors. **Career services:** Career assessment, internships.

FACILITIES
Housing: Coed dorms, men's dorms, women's dorms, fraternity/sorority housing, apartments for married students, apartments for single students. **Special Academic Facilities/Equipment:** Art gallery, language lab, museum of Nebraska art.

CAMPUS LIFE
Environment: Village. **Activities:** Choral groups, concert band, dance, drama/theater, jazz band, literary magazine, marching band, music ensembles, musical theater, opera, pep band, radio station, student government, student newspaper, symphony orchestra, television station. **Organizations:** 1 religious organizations. 10 fraternities, 6 sororities. **Athletics (Intercollegiate):** *Men:* Baseball, basketball, cross-country, diving, football, golf, soccer, softball, swimming, tennis, volleyball. *Women:* Basketball, cross-country, diving, football, golf, soccer, softball, swimming, tennis, volleyball.

ADMISSIONS
Freshman Academic Profile: 90% from public high schools. Minimum paper TOEFL 520. **Basis for Candidate Selection:** *Very important factors considered include:* Class rank, rigor of secondary school record, standardized test scores. *Other factors considered include:* Religious affiliation/commitment, talent/ability. **Freshman Admission Requirements:** High school diploma is required and GED is accepted. *Academic units required:* 4 English, 3 mathematics, 3 science, (1 science labs), 2 foreign language, 1 social studies, 2 history, 1 academic electives. **Freshman Admission Statistics:** 2,672 applied, **Transfer Admission Requirements:** High school transcript, college transcript(s), minimum college GPA of 2.0 required. Lowest grade transferable C. **General Admission Information:** Application fee $25. Regular application deadline 8/1. Notification on a rolling basis, beginning on or about 10/1. Nonfall registration accepted. Credit and/or placement offered for CEEB Advanced Placement tests.

COSTS AND FINANCIAL AID
Annual in-state tuition $2,715. Annual out-of-state tuition $5,550. Room and board $4,156. Required fees $498. Average book expense $700. **Required Forms and Deadlines:** FAFSA, institution's own financial aid form C. Priority financial aid filing date 3/1. **Notification of Awards:** Applicants will be notified of awards on or about 5/1. **Types of Aid:** *Need-based scholarships/grants:* Federal Pell, SEOG, state scholarships/grants, private scholarships, the school's own gift aid. *Loans:* FFEL Subsidized Stafford, FFEL Unsubsidized Stafford, FFEL PLUS, Federal Perkins. *Student Employment:* Federal Work-Study Program available. Institutional employment available. Off-campus job opportunities are excellent. **Financial Aid Statistics:** 43% undergrads borrow to pay for school. Average cumulative indebtedness $13,400. **Criteria for awarding institutional aid:** *Non-need-based:* Academics, art, athletics, leadership, music/drama.

UNIVERSITY OF NEBRASKA AT OMAHA

Office of Admissions, 6001 Dodge Street, EAB Room 103, Omaha, NE 68182
Phone: 402-554-2393 **Financial Aid Phone:** 402-554-2327
E-mail: unoadm@mail.unomaha.edu **CEEB Code:** 6420
Fax: 402-554-3472 **Website:** www.unomaha.edu **ACT Code:** 2464

This public school was founded in 1908. It has a 472-acre campus.

RATINGS
Admissions Selectivity Rating: 73   **Fire Safety Rating:** 96   **Green Rating:** 74

STUDENTS AND FACULTY
Enrollment: 11,323. **Student Body:** 52% female, 48% male, 9% out-of-state, 2% international (72 countries represented). Asian 3%, African American 6%, Caucasian 80%, Hispanic 4%, Native American 1%.
Retention and Graduation: 74% freshmen return for sophomore year. 13% freshmen graduate within 4 years. 18% grads go on to further study within 1 year. **Faculty:** Student/faculty ratio 18:1. 479 full-time faculty, 81% hold PhDs, 18% are members of minority groups, 43% are women. 4% of classes are taught by teaching assistants.

ACADEMICS
Degrees: Bachelor's, master's, post-bachelor's certificate, post-master's certificate. **Classes:** Most classes have 20–29 students. Most lab/discussion sessions have 20–29 students. **Majors with Highest Enrollment:** Biology/biological sciences; elementary education and teaching; psychology. **Special Study Options:** Cooperative education program, cross-registration, distance learning, double major, dual enrollment, English as a Second Language (ESL), exchange student program (domestic), honors program, independent study, internships, student-designed major, study abroad, teacher certification program, Business, Engineering. **Honors programs:** UNO Honors Program includes many opportunities such as Early Registration, Honors-only courses, Honors-priority Housing, Honors domestic and international semesters, Honors internships, and a Washington Center affiliation. **Combined degree programs:** MPA/MSW in Public Administration and Social Work. Special programs offered to physically disabled students include note-taking services, reader services, tape recorders, tutors. **Career services:** Career/job search classes, career assessment, internships. **Career services highlights include:** The internships are a UNO strength.

FACILITIES
Housing: Coed dorms, leased apartment dwellings. 99% of campus accessible to physically disabled. **Special Academic Facilities/Equipment:** Center for Afghanistan studies, physical education facility, Strauss Performing Arts Center, Speech Center, Writing Center, Math/Science Center, Peter Kiewit Information Technology Building, and Career Center. **Computers:** 100% of classrooms, 100% of dorms, 100% of libraries, 100% of dining areas, 100% of student union, 85% of common outdoor areas have wireless network access. Students can register for classes online. Administrative functions (other than registration) can be performed online.

CAMPUS LIFE
Environment: Metropolis. **Activities:** Choral groups, concert band, dance, drama/theater, jazz band, literary magazine, marching band, music ensembles, musical theater, opera, pep band, radio station, student government, student newspaper, student-run film society, symphony orchestra, television station, campus ministries, international student organization, Model UN. **Organizations:** 127 registered organizations, 23 honor societies, 14 religious organizations. 6 fraternities, 8 sororities. **Athletics (Intercollegiate):** *Men:* Baseball, basketball, football, ice-hockey, wrestling. *Women:* Basketball, cross-country, diving, golf, soccer, softball, swimming, tennis, track/field (outdoor), track/field (indoor), volleyball. **On-Campus Highlights:** University Library, Strauss Performing Arts Center, Milo Bail Student Center, Durham Science Center, Peter Kiewit Institute. **Environmental Initiatives:** Examination of our Sustainable Operations (with commitment from our VC for B & F and our FMP Director). Engaging our campus students & community in such efforts Focus on energy reduction

ADMISSIONS
Freshman Academic Profile: Average high school GPA 3.3. 11.3% in top 10% of high school class, 34.6% in top 25% of high school class, 70.9% in top 50% of high school class. 90% from public high schools. ACT middle 50% range 20–26. Minimum paper TOEFL 500. Minimum web-based TOEFL 61. **Basis for Candidate Selection:** *Very important factors considered include:* Class rank, rigor of secondary school record, standardized test scores. *Other factors considered include:* character/personal qualities. **Freshman Admission Requirements:** High school diploma is required and GED is accepted. *Academic units required:* 4 English, 3 mathematics, 3 science, (1 science labs),

2 foreign language, 1 social studies, 2 history, 1 academic electives. **Freshman Admission Statistics:** 4,845 applied, 80% admitted, 68% enrolled. **Transfer Admission Requirements:** College transcript(s), statement of good standing from prior institution(s). Minimum college GPA of 2.0 required. Lowest grade transferable C–. **General Admission Information:** Application fee $45. Regular application deadline 8/1. Nonfall registration accepted.

COSTS AND FINANCIAL AID

Annual in-state tuition $5,115. Annual out-of-state tuition $15,075. Room and board $7,230. Required fees $1,114. Average book expense $900. **Required Forms and Deadlines:** FAFSA. Priority financial aid filing date 3/1. **Notification of Awards:** Applicants will be notified of awards on a rolling basis beginning 4/15. **Types of Aid:** *Need-based scholarships/grants:* Federal Pell, SEOG, state scholarships/grants, private scholarships, the school's own gift aid. *Loans:* FFEL Subsidized Stafford, FFEL Unsubsidized Stafford, FFEL PLUS, Federal Perkins, college/university loans from institutional funds. *Student Employment:* Federal Work-Study Program available. Institutional employment available. Highest amount earned per year from on-campus jobs $15,600. Off-campus job opportunities are excellent. **Financial Aid Statistics:** 30% freshmen, 30% undergrads receive need-based scholarship or grant aid. 33% freshmen, 21% undergrads receive non-need-based scholarship or grant aid. 27% freshmen, 34% undergrads receive need-based self-help aid. 1% freshmen, 80% freshmen, 81% undergrads receive any aid. 48% undergrads borrow to pay for school. Average cumulative indebtedness $19,000. **Criteria for awarding institutional aid:** *Non-need-based:* Academics, alumni affiliation, art, athletics, leadership, minority status, music/drama, state/district residency.

UNIVERSITY OF NEBRASKA MEDICAL CENTER

984230 Nebr Med Ctr, Omaha, NE 68198-4230
Phone: 402-559-6864 **Financial Aid Phone:** 402-559-4109
E-mail: ttonjes@unmc.edu
Fax: 402-559-6796 **Website:** www.unmc.edu

This public school was founded in 1902.

RATINGS
Admissions Selectivity Rating: 60*   **Fire Safety Rating:** 60*   **Green Rating:** 60*

STUDENTS AND FACULTY
Enrollment: 812. **Student Body:** 88% female, 12% male, 12% out-of-state, 1% international. Asian 1%, African American 1%, Caucasian 93%, Hispanic 3%, Native American 1%.
Retention and Graduation: Faculty: 768 full-time faculty, 90% hold PhDs, 14% are members of minority groups, 39% are women.

ACADEMICS
Degrees: Bachelor's, first professional, master's, post-bachelor's certificate, post-master's certificate. **Majors with Highest Enrollment:** medicine (MD); nursing/registered nurse (RN, ASN, BSN, MSN); pharmacy (PharmD [US], PharmD or BS/BPharm [Canada]). **Special Study Options:** Accelerated program, distance learning, honors program, independent study. Special programs offered to physically disabled students include note-taking services, tutors.

CAMPUS LIFE
Environment: Metropolis. **Activities:** Student government, student newspaper.

ADMISSIONS
Freshman Academic Profile: Minimum paper TOEFL 551. Minimum computer TOEFL 235. **Transfer Admission Requirements:** College transcript(s), Lowest grade transferable c. **General Admission Information:** Nonfall registration not accepted.

COSTS AND FINANCIAL AID
Annual in-state tuition $6,450. Annual out-of-state tuition $18,900. Required fees $310. Average book expense $950. **Required Forms and Deadlines:** FAFSA, institution's own financial aid form. Financial aid filing deadline 3/15. Priority financial aid filing date 3/15. **Notification of Awards:** Applicants will be notified of awards on or about 4/1. **Types of Aid:** *Need-based scholarships/grants:* Federal Pell, SEOG, state scholarships/grants, private scholarships, the school's own gift aid. *Loans:* FFEL Subsidized Stafford, FFEL Unsubsidized Stafford, FFEL PLUS, Federal Perkins, Federal Nursing, state loans. *Student Employment:* Federal Work-Study Program available. Institutional employment available. Off-campus job opportunities are fair. **Financial Aid Statistics:** 56% undergrads receive need-based scholarship or grant aid. 3% undergrads receive non-need-based scholarship or grant aid. 63% undergrads receive self-help aid. **Criteria for awarding institutional aid:** *Non-need-based:* Academics, leadership, minority status.

UNIVERSITY OF NEBRASKA—LINCOLN

1410 Q Street, Lincoln, NE 68588-0256
Phone: 402-472-2023 **Financial Aid Phone:** 402-472-2030
E-mail: admissions@unl.edu **CEEB Code:** 6877
Fax: 402-472-0670 **Website:** www.unl.edu **ACT Code:** 2482

This public school was founded in 1869. It has a 617-acre campus.

RATINGS
Admissions Selectivity Rating: 78   **Fire Safety Rating:** 68   **Green Rating:** 70

STUDENTS AND FACULTY
Enrollment: 18,053. **Student Body:** 46% female, 54% male, 17% out-of-state, 3% international (117 countries represented). Asian 3%, African American 2%, Caucasian 83%, Hispanic 3%, Native American 1%.
Retention and Graduation: 83% freshmen return for sophomore year. 23% freshmen graduate within 4 years. **Faculty:** Student/faculty ratio 19:1. 1068 full-time faculty, 97% hold PhDs, 16% are members of minority groups, 28% are women. 18% of classes are taught by teaching assistants.

ACADEMICS
Degrees: Associate, bachelor's, first professional, master's, post-bachelor's certificate, post-master's certificate, terminal associate. **Classes:** Most classes have 20–29 students. Most lab/discussion sessions have 20–29 students. **Majors with Highest Enrollment:** Business administration and management; finance; psychology. **Special Study Options:** Accelerated program, cooperative education program, cross-registration, distance learning, double major, dual enrollment, English as a Second Language (ESL), exchange student program (domestic), honors program, independent study, internships, liberal arts/career combination, student-designed major, study abroad, teacher certification program. **Honors programs:** University Honors Program: Acceptance into the program is based on a comprehensive evaluation of student's potential by the Honors Program Faculty Committee. A special notation is made on the transcript and diploma upon graduation. J.D. Edwards Honors Program: Purpose is to produce top quality graduates who combine business knowledge and computing fundamentals for enterprise information and software systems. Special programs offered to physically disabled students include note-taking services, reader services, tape recorders, tutors. **Career services:** Alumni services, career/job search classes, career assessment.

FACILITIES
Housing: Coed dorms, special housing for disabled students, men's dorms, special housing for international students, women's dorms, fraternity/sorority housing, apartments for married students, cooperative housing, apartments for single students. 85% of campus accessible to physically disabled. **Special Academic Facilities/Equipment:** Art gallery, performing arts center, food industries complex, planetarium, center for mass spectrometry, natural science museum, animal science complex, veterinary animal research/diagnosis center.

CAMPUS LIFE
Environment: City. **Activities:** Choral groups, concert band, dance, drama/theater, jazz band, literary magazine, marching band, music ensembles, musical theater, opera, pep band, radio station, student government, student newspaper, student-run film society, symphony orchestra, television station, yearbook, campus ministries, international student organization, Model UN. **Organizations:** 335 registered organizations, 57 honor societies, 25 religious organizations. 27 fraternities, 18 sororities. **Athletics (Intercollegiate):** *Men:* Baseball, basketball, cross-country, football, golf, gymnastics, rodeo, tennis, track/field (outdoor), track/field (indoor), wrestling. *Women:* Basketball, bowling, cross-country, diving, golf, gymnastics, riflery, rodeo, soccer, softball, swimming, tennis, track/field (outdoor), track/field (indoor), volleyball. **On-Campus Highlights:** Student Union, Student Recreation, Library, Memorial Stadium and Hewitt Center, Residence Halls. **Environmental Initiatives:** Recycling of paper, plastic, and aluminum; green' new construction; use of ethynol in university fleet.

ADMISSIONS
Freshman Academic Profile: 27% in top 10% of high school class, 53% in top 25% of high school class, 83% in top 50% of high school class. SAT Math middle 50% range 530–670. SAT Critical Reading middle 50% range 500–650. ACT middle 50% range 22–28. Minimum paper TOEFL 525. Minimum computer TOEFL 193. **Basis for Candidate Selection:** *Very important factors considered include:* Class rank, standardized test scores. *Important factors considered*

include: Rigor of secondary school record. *Other factors considered include:* Academic GPA, recommendation(s), first generation, talent/ability. **Freshman Admission Requirements:** High school diploma is required and GED is accepted. *Academic units required:* 4 English, 4 mathematics, 3 science, (1 science labs), 2 foreign language, 3 social studies. *Academic units recommended:* 1 history. **Freshman Admission Statistics:** 9,598 applied, 62% admitted, 71% enrolled. **Transfer Admission Requirements:** High school transcript, college transcript(s), minimum college GPA of 2.0 required. Lowest grade transferable D. **General Admission Information:** Application fee $45. Regular application deadline 5/1. Notification on a rolling basis, beginning on or about 9/1. Nonfall registration accepted. Neither credit nor placement offered for CEEB Advanced Placement tests.

COSTS AND FINANCIAL AID

Annual in-state tuition $6,315. Annual out-of-state tuition $17,028. Average book expense $950. **Required Forms and Deadlines:** FAFSA **Notification of Awards:** Applicants will be notified of awards on a rolling basis beginning 4/1. **Types of Aid:** *Need-based scholarships/grants:* Federal Pell, SEOG, state scholarships/grants, private scholarships, the school's own gift aid. *Loans:* Direct Subsidized Stafford, Direct Unsubsidized Stafford, Direct PLUS, FFEL Subsidized Stafford, FFEL Unsubsidized Stafford, FFEL PLUS, Federal Perkins, college/university loans from institutional funds. *Student Employment:* Federal Work-Study Program available. Institutional employment available. Off-campus job opportunities are excellent. **Financial Aid Statistics:** 36% freshmen, 33% undergrads receive need-based scholarship or grant aid. 5% freshmen, 3% undergrads receive non-need-based scholarship or grant aid. 30% freshmen, 34% undergrads receive need-based self-help aid. 2% freshmen, 3% undergrads receive athletic scholarships. 41% freshmen, 36% undergrads receive any aid. 61% undergrads borrow to pay for school. Average cumulative indebtedness $19,075. **Criteria for awarding institutional aid:** *Non-need-based:* Academics, alumni affiliation, art, athletics, leadership, minority status, music/drama, state/district residency.

UNIVERSITY OF NEVADA, LAS VEGAS

4505 Maryland Parkway, Box 451021, Las Vegas, NV 89154-1021
Phone: 702-774-8658
E-mail: Undergraduate.Recruitment@ccmail.nevada.edu **CEEB Code:** 4861
Fax: 702-774-8008 **Website:** www.unlv.edu **ACT Code:** 2496

This public school was founded in 1957. It has a 337-acre campus.

RATINGS
Admissions Selectivity Rating: 74   **Fire Safety Rating:** 60*   **Green Rating:** 60*

STUDENTS AND FACULTY
Enrollment: 20,607. **Student Body:** 56% female, 44% male, 22% out-of-state, 4% international (84 countries represented). Asian 14%, African American 8%, Caucasian 53%, Hispanic 11%, Native American 1%.
Retention and Graduation: 73% freshmen return for sophomore year. 12% freshmen graduate within 4 years. **Faculty:** Student/faculty ratio 20:1. 776 full-time faculty, 90% hold PhDs, 18% are members of minority groups, 33% are women. 11% of classes are taught by teaching assistants.

ACADEMICS
Degrees: Bachelor's, certificate, first professional, master's, post-bachelor's certificate, post-master's certificate. **Classes:** Most classes have 20–29 students. Most lab/discussion sessions have 20–29 students. **Majors with Highest Enrollment:** Elementary education and teaching; hospitality administration/management; psychology. **Special Study Options:** Accelerated program, cooperative education program, cross-registration, distance learning, double major, dual enrollment, English as a Second Language (ESL), exchange student program (domestic), honors program, independent study, internships, student-designed major, study abroad, teacher certification program **Combined degree programs:** Interdisciplinary program in environmental science. Special programs offered to physically disabled students include note-taking services, reader services, tape recorders, tutors. **Career services:** Alumni network, alumni services, career/job search classes, career assessment, internships, regional alumni.

FACILITIES
Housing: Coed dorms. **Special Academic Facilities/Equipment:** Art galleries, national supercomputing center for energy and environment, natural history museum, arboretum, 3 theaters, concert hall, law school, dental school, international gaming institute, professional practice school for teachers. **Computers:** Students can register for classes online. Administrative functions (other than registration) can be performed online.

CAMPUS LIFE
Environment: Metropolis. **Activities:** Choral groups, concert band, dance, drama/theater, jazz band, literary magazine, marching band, music ensembles, musical theater, opera, pep band, radio station, student government, student newspaper, student-run film society, symphony orchestra, television station. **Organizations:** 24 honor societies, 14 religious organizations. 8 fraternities, 6 sororities. **Athletics (Intercollegiate):** *Men:* Baseball, basketball, football, golf, soccer, swimming, tennis. *Women:* Basketball, cross-country, equestrian sports, golf, soccer, softball, swimming, tennis, track/field (outdoor), volleyball. **On-Campus Highlights:** Lied Library, Artemus W. Ham Concert Hall, Moyer Student Union, Judy Bailey Theatre, Student Services Complex, Thomas and Mack and Cox Pavilion Event Centers, Lied Athletic Complex, Tonopah Residence Complex.

ADMISSIONS
Freshman Academic Profile: Average high school GPA 3.34. 18% in top 10% of high school class, 47% in top 25% of high school class, 82% in top 50% of high school class. SAT Math middle 50% range 450–580. SAT Critical Reading middle 50% range 440–560. ACT middle 50% range 18–24. Minimum paper TOEFL 500. **Basis for Candidate Selection:** *Very important factors considered include:* Rigor of secondary school record, standardized test scores, *Other factors considered include:* Recommendation(s). **Freshman Admission Requirements:** High school diploma is required and GED is accepted. *Academic units required:* 4 English, 3 mathematics, 3 science, (2 science labs), 3 social studies. *Academic units recommended:* 4 English, 3 mathematics, 3 science, (2 science labs), 3 social studies. **Freshman Admission Statistics:** 7,042 applied, 81% admitted, 58% enrolled. **Transfer Admission Requirements:** College transcript(s), minimum college GPA of 2.0 required. Lowest grade transferable D–. **General Admission Information:** Application fee $60. Regular application deadline 4/1. Notification on a rolling basis, beginning on or about 11/1. Nonfall registration accepted. Admission may be deferred for a maximum of 1 year. Credit and/or placement offered for CEEB Advanced Placement tests.

COSTS AND FINANCIAL AID
Required Forms and Deadlines: FAFSA, institution's own financial aid form. Priority financial aid filing date 2/1. **Notification of Awards:** Applicants will be notified of awards on a rolling basis beginning 4/1. **Types of Aid:** *Need-based scholarships/grants:* Federal Pell, SEOG, state scholarships/grants, private scholarships, the school's own gift aid. *Loans:* Direct Subsidized Stafford, Direct Unsubsidized Stafford, Direct PLUS, Federal Perkins, state loans, college/university loans from institutional funds. *Student Employment:* Federal Work-Study Program available. Institutional employment available. Highest amount earned per year from on-campus jobs $3,680. Off-campus job opportunities are excellent. **Financial Aid Statistics:** 20% freshmen, 24% undergrads receive need-based scholarship or grant aid. 27% freshmen, 14% undergrads receive non-need-based scholarship or grant aid. 15% freshmen, 20% undergrads receive need-based self-help aid. 4% freshmen, 3% undergrads receive athletic scholarships. 39% undergrads borrow to pay for school. Average cumulative indebtedness $12,818. **Criteria for awarding institutional aid:** *Non-need-based:* Academics, alumni affiliation, art, athletics, job skills, leadership, minority status, music/drama, state/district residency.

UNIVERSITY OF NEVADA, RENO

Mail Stop 120, Reno, NV 89557
Phone: 775-784-4700
E-mail: asknevada@unr.edu **CEEB Code:** 4844
Fax: 775-784-4283 **Website:** www.unr.edu **ACT Code:** 2497

This public school was founded in 1864. It has a 200-acre campus.

RATINGS
Admissions Selectivity Rating: 72   **Fire Safety Rating:** 60*   **Green Rating:** 60*

STUDENTS AND FACULTY
Enrollment: 11,605. **Student Body:** 55% female, 45% male, 18% out-of-state, 3% international (56 countries represented). Asian 7%, African American 2%, Caucasian 73%, Hispanic 7%, Native American 1%.
Retention and Graduation: 76% freshmen return for sophomore year. 15% freshmen graduate within 4 years. **Faculty:** Student/faculty ratio 15:1. 682 full-time faculty, 88% hold PhDs, 14% are members of minority groups, 35% are women.

ACADEMICS
Degrees: Bachelor's, first professional, first professional certificate, master's, post-bachelor's certificate, post-master's certificate. **Classes:** Most classes have

20–29 students. Most lab/discussion sessions have 20–29 students. **Special Study Options:** Distance learning, double major, dual enrollment, English as a Second Language (ESL), exchange student program (domestic), honors program, independent study, internships, study abroad, teacher certification program Special programs offered to physically disabled students include note-taking services, reader services, tutors. **Career services:** Alumni services, career/job search classes, career assessment, internships.

FACILITIES

Housing: Coed dorms, special housing for disabled students, men's dorms, women's dorms, apartments for married students, apartments for single students.

CAMPUS LIFE

Activities: Choral groups, concert band, dance, drama/theater, jazz band, literary magazine, marching band, music ensembles, musical theater, opera, pep band, radio station, student government, student newspaper, yearbook. **Athletics (Intercollegiate):** *Men:* Basketball, cross-country, diving, softball, swimming, tennis, track/field (outdoor), volleyball. *Women:* Basketball, cross-country, diving, soccer, softball, swimming, tennis, track/field (outdoor), volleyball.

ADMISSIONS

Freshman Academic Profile: Average high school GPA 3.36. SAT Math middle 50% range 480–600. SAT Critical Reading middle 50% range 470–590. ACT middle 50% range 20–25. **Basis for Candidate Selection:** *Very important factors considered include:* Rigor of secondary school record, *Other factors considered include:* Standardized test scores. **Freshman Admission Requirements:** High school diploma is required and GED is not accepted. *Academic units required:* 4 English, 3 mathematics, 3 science, (2 science labs), 3 social studies. **Freshman Admission Statistics:** 4,024 applied, 88% admitted, 59% enrolled. **Transfer Admission Requirements:** College transcript(s), minimum college GPA of 2.0 required. Lowest grade transferable D–. **General Admission Information:** Application fee $60. Nonfall registration accepted. Admission may be deferred for a maximum of 1 year. Credit and/or placement offered for CEEB Advanced Placement tests.

COSTS AND FINANCIAL AID

Required Forms and Deadlines: FAFSA. Priority financial aid filing date 2/1. **Notification of Awards:** Applicants will be notified of awards on a rolling basis beginning 4/1. **Types of Aid:** *Need-based scholarships/grants:* Federal Pell, SEOG, private scholarships, the school's own gift aid. *Loans:* FFEL Subsidized Stafford, FFEL Unsubsidized Stafford, FFEL PLUS, Federal Perkins, college/university loans from institutional funds. *Student Employment:* Federal Work-Study Program available. Institutional employment available. Highest amount earned per year from on-campus jobs $3,000. Off-campus job opportunities are excellent. **Financial Aid Statistics:** 14% freshmen, 17% undergrads receive need-based scholarship or grant aid. 28% freshmen, 19% undergrads receive non-need-based scholarship or grant aid. 14% freshmen, 20% undergrads receive need-based self-help aid. 3% freshmen, 4% undergrads receive athletic scholarships. 44% undergrads borrow to pay for school. Average cumulative indebtedness $15,548.

UNIVERSITY OF NEW ENGLAND

11 Hills Beach Road, Biddeford, ME 04005-9599
Phone: 207-602-2297 **Financial Aid Phone:** 207-602-2342
E-mail: admissions@une.edu **CEEB Code:** 3751
Fax: 207-602-5900 **Website:** www.une.edu **ACT Code:** 3751

This private school was founded in 1831. It has a 550-acre campus.

RATINGS
Admissions Selectivity Rating: 76   **Fire Safety Rating:** 60*   **Green Rating:** 60*

STUDENTS AND FACULTY

Enrollment: 1,698. **Student Body:** 77% female, 23% male, 59% out-of-state, international (11 countries represented). Asian 1%, African American 1%, Caucasian 91%, Hispanic 1%.
Retention and Graduation: 75% freshmen return for sophomore year. 49% freshmen graduate within 4 years. **Faculty:** Student/faculty ratio 11:1. 137 full-time faculty, 85% hold PhDs, 4% are members of minority groups, 49% are women.

ACADEMICS

Degrees: Associate, bachelor's, certificate, diploma, first professional, master's, post-bachelor's certificate, post-master's certificate, terminal associate. **Classes:** Most classes have 20–29 students. Most lab/discussion sessions have 10–19 students. **Majors with Highest Enrollment:** athletic training/trainer;

biomedical sciences; marine biology and biological oceanography. **Special Study Options:** Cross-registration, distance learning, double major, English as a Second Language (ESL), honors program, independent study, internships, student-designed major, study abroad, teacher certification program, Advanced standing options are available for qualified undergraduates to both our Physician Assistant and Doctor of Osteopathic Medicine graduate programs. **Honors programs:** The College of Arts and Sciences offers and honors program to qualified applicants. **Combined degree programs:** DO/MPH and DO/PhD. Special programs offered to physically disabled students include note-taking services, reader services, tutors. **Career services:** Alumni network, career/job search classes, career assessment, internships.

FACILITIES

Housing: Coed dorms, women's dorms. 85% of campus accessible to physically disabled. **Special Academic Facilities/Equipment:** Payson Art Gallery; Maine Women Writers Collection; Marine Science Education and Research Center; Marine Animal Rehabilitation Center (MARC); Performance Enhancement and Evaluation Center for health sciences (PEEC); Center for Health Ethics, Law and Policy; Center for Transcultural Health; and New England Institute of Cognitive Science and Evolutionary Psychology. **Computers:** Students can register for classes online.

CAMPUS LIFE

Environment: Village. **Activities:** Choral groups, dance, literary magazine, music ensembles, student government, student newspaper, yearbook. **Organizations:** 36 registered organizations, 3 honor societies, 1 religious organizations. **Athletics (Intercollegiate):** *Men:* Basketball, cross-country, golf, lacrosse, soccer. *Women:* Basketball, cross-country, field hockey, golf, lacrosse, soccer, softball, swimming, volleyball. **On-Campus Highlights:** Marine Science and Research Center, Alfond Health Science Center, UNE Beach (on Atlantic Ocean and Saco River), The Point Picnic Area, Campus Center.

ADMISSIONS

Freshman Academic Profile: Average high school GPA 3.2. 17% in top 10% of high school class, 49% in top 25% of high school class, 86% in top 50% of high school class. SAT Math middle 50% range 470–580. SAT Critical Reading middle 50% range 540–570. Minimum paper TOEFL 550. Minimum computer TOEFL 213. **Basis for Candidate Selection:** *Very important factors considered include:* Academic GPA, rigor of secondary school record. *Important factors considered include:* Class rank, interview. *Other factors considered include:* Application essay, recommendation(s), standardized test scores, alumni/ae relation, character/personal qualities, extracurricular activities, geographical residence, level of applicant's interest, talent/ability, volunteer work, work experience. **Freshman Admission Requirements:** High school diploma is required and GED is accepted. *Academic units required:* 4 English, 3 mathematics, 3 science, (2 science labs), 2 social studies, 2 history. *Academic units recommended:* 4 mathematics, 4 science, (3 science labs), 2 foreign language, 4 social studies, 4 history, 4 academic electives. **Freshman Admission Statistics:** 2,055 applied, 92% admitted, 25% enrolled. **Transfer Admission Requirements:** College transcript(s), minimum college GPA of 2.0 required. Lowest grade transferable C–. **General Admission Information:** Application fee $40. Notification on a rolling basis, beginning on or about 12/15. Nonfall registration accepted. Admission may be deferred for a maximum of 12. Credit and/or placement offered for CEEB Advanced Placement tests.

COSTS AND FINANCIAL AID

Annual tuition $22,940. Room and board $9,255. Required fees $850. Average book expense $1,000. **Required Forms and Deadlines:** FAFSA, tax returns, verification worksheet. Financial aid filing deadline 5/1. Priority financial aid filing date 3/1. **Notification of Awards:** Applicants will be notified of awards on a rolling basis beginning 3/15. **Types of Aid:** *Need-based scholarships/grants:* Federal Pell, SEOG, state scholarships/grants, private scholarships, the school's own gift aid. *Loans:* FFEL Subsidized Stafford, FFEL Unsubsidized Stafford, FFEL PLUS, Federal Perkins, Federal Nursing *Student Employment:* Federal Work-Study Program available. Institutional employment available. Highest amount earned per year from on-campus jobs $2,000. Off-campus job opportunities are good. **Financial Aid Statistics:** 83% freshmen, 83% undergrads receive need-based scholarship or grant aid. 9% freshmen, 5% undergrads receive non-need-based scholarship or grant aid. 72% freshmen, 76% undergrads receive need-based self-help aid. 93% freshmen, 94% undergrads receive any aid. 88% undergrads borrow to pay for school. Average cumulative indebtedness $37,507. **Criteria for awarding institutional aid:** *Non-need-based:* Academics, alumni affiliation, leadership.

See page 1300.

UNIVERSITY OF NEW HAMPSHIRE

UNH Office of Admissions, 4 Garrison Ave, Durham, NH 03824
Phone: 603-862-1360 **Financial Aid Phone:** 603-862-3600
E-mail: admissions@unh.edu **CEEB Code:** 3918
Fax: 603-862-0077 **Website:** www.unh.edu **ACT Code:** 2524

This public school was founded in 1866. It has a 2600-acre campus.

RATINGS
Admissions Selectivity Rating: 80   **Fire Safety Rating:** 96   **Green Rating:** 97

STUDENTS AND FACULTY
Enrollment: 12,226. **Student Body:** 56% female, 44% male, 42% out-of-state, 1% international (52 countries represented). Asian 2%, African American 2%, Caucasian 77%, Hispanic 2%.
Retention and Graduation: 35% grads go on to further study within 1 year. 15% grads pursue arts and sciences degrees. 1% grads pursue law degrees. 3% grads pursue business degrees. 1% grads pursue medical degrees. **Faculty:** Student/faculty ratio 19:1. 618 full-time faculty, 84% hold PhDs, 9% are members of minority groups, 36% are women. 1% of classes are taught by teaching assistants.

ACADEMICS
Degrees: Associate, bachelor's, doctoral, master's, post-bachelor's certificate, post-master's certificate, terminal associate. **Classes:** Most classes have 20–29 students. Most lab/discussion sessions have 20–29 students. **Majors with Highest Enrollment:** Business administration and management; English language and literature; psychology. **Special Study Options:** Accelerated program, cooperative education program, cross-registration, distance learning, double major, English as a Second Language (ESL), exchange student program (domestic), honors program, independent study, internships, student-designed major, study abroad, teacher certification program, weekend college, Research/Creative Projects, Learning Communities, Experiential Learning, Senior Capstone, Service Learning, Work Study, Honors. **Honors programs:** The UNH honors program offers small and dynamic classes, opportunities for research and study overseas, individualized advising and a close and supportive community. **Combined degree programs:** BA/MA, BS/MS OT, BA/BS and MBA, BS/MS Account, BA/BS and MEduc, BS/MS in biochem. Special programs offered to physically disabled students include note-taking services, reader services, tape recorders, tutors. **Career services:** Alumni network, alumni services, career/job search classes, career assessment, internships, regional alumni. **Career services highlights include:** UNH's Washington Internship Program through the Washington Internship Program allows UNH students to earn academic credit while working and living in Washington, DC. Recent internships for UNH students have included the US Senate, State Department, US Attorney Generals Office, Environmental Protection Agency, Smithsonian Museum, public interest law firms, lobbyists, and non-profit organizations.

FACILITIES
Housing: Coed dorms, special housing for international students, fraternity/sorority housing, apartments for married students, apartments for single students, theme housingThere are 11 theme dorms for only freshman and 11 others for all students. Four "small halls" of 45 to 50 people in mostly single rooms are also available. 85% of campus accessible to physically disabled. **Special Academic Facilities/Equipment:** Journalism laboratory, Milne Special Collections Archives and Museum, optical observatory, marine research laboratory, experiential learning center, child development center, language lab, art gallery, agricultural and equine facilities, electron microscope, sawmill, nature preserves and trails, survey center, radio station. **Computers:** 5% of classrooms, 100% of dorms, 100% of libraries, 100% of student union, 2% of common outdoor areas have wireless network access. Students can register for classes online. Administrative functions (other than registration) can be performed online.

CAMPUS LIFE
Environment: Village. **Activities:** Choral groups, concert band, dance, drama/theater, jazz band, literary magazine, marching band, music ensembles, musical theater, pep band, radio station, student government, student newspaper, student-run film society, symphony orchestra, television station, yearbook, campus ministries, international student organization, Model UN. **Organizations:** 187 registered organizations, 18 honor societies, 10 religious organizations. 10 fraternities, 7 sororities. **Athletics (Intercollegiate):** *Men:* Basketball, cross-country, football, ice hockey, skiing (downhill/alpine), skiing (nordic/cross-country), soccer, track/field (outdoor), track/field (indoor). *Women:* Basketball,
cross-country, diving, field hockey, gymnastics, ice hockey, lacrosse, skiing (downhill/alpine), skiing (nordic/cross-country), soccer, swimming, track/field (outdoor), track/field (indoor), volleyball. **On-Campus Highlights:** Dimond Library, Whittemore Center, Hamel Recreation Center, Student Union/Holloway Commons, College Woods, Other spots include Dairy Bar/Train Station, Art Gallery, Thompson Hall, Morse Hall. **Environmental Initiatives:** 1. The UNH University Office of Sustainability (UOS) is the oldest endowed sustainability program in higher education in the U.S. and has worked with the larger campus community over 10 years to develop UNH's unique sustainable learning community model and to foster sustainability locally, statewide, and regionally www.sustainableunh.unh.edu. Under our comprehensive Climate Education Initiative and as a key component of its climate action plan, WildCAP and signature to the American College and University Presidents Climate Commitment, UNH has committed to cut its greenhouse gas emission 50% by 2020 and 80% by 2050 on the road to carbon neutrality by 2100. We also use processed landfill gas from the EcoLine project, a landfill gas-to-energy project that uses methane gas from a nearby landfill, as the primary fuel for our on-campus cogeneration plant. By selling the renewable energy credits associate with EcoLine we are able to help finance this project and invest in more energy efficiency on campus via a new revolving energy efficiency fund. More info at www.sustainableunh. unh.edu/climate_ed/cogen_landfillgas.html, unh.edu/etf/wildcap.html and www. sustainableunh.unh.edu/climate_ed/recs.html Responding to a need by farmers for scientific research to support organic dairy efforts, UNH is the first land grant university to have an organic dairy farm and education/research center. The organic dairy is a research center for organic production and management and an education center for organic dairy farmers, farmers considering the transition to organic, and students of sustainable agriculture. The organic dairy research farm is part of UNH's broader Food & Society Initiative (FAS) through which UNH meets its commitment to being a sustainable food community. Other efforts include a Dual Major in EcoGastronomy for undergraduate students and a Local Harvest Initiative in the dining halls. More info at www. sustainableunh.unh.edu/fas/index.html.

ADMISSIONS
Freshman Academic Profile: 25% in top 10% of high school class, 71% in top 25% of high school class, 97% in top 50% of high school class. 81% from public high schools. SAT Math middle 50% range 520–630. SAT Critical Reading middle 50% range 510–610. Minimum paper TOEFL 550. Minimum computer TOEFL 213. Minimum web-based TOEFL 80. **Basis for Candidate Selection:** *Very important factors considered include:* Class rank, rigor of secondary school record. *Important factors considered include:* Academic GPA, recommendation(s). *Other factors considered include:* Application essay, standardized test scores, alumni/ae relation, character/personal qualities, extracurricular activities, first generation, geographical residence, racial/ethnic status, state residency, talent/ability, volunteer work, work experience. **Freshman Admission Requirements:** High school diploma is required and GED is accepted. *Academic units required:* 4 English, 3 mathematics, 3 science, (2 science labs), 2 foreign language, 3 social studies. *Academic units recommended:* 4 English, 4 mathematics, 4 science, (3 science labs), 3 foreign language, 3 social studies, 1 academic electives. **Freshman Admission Statistics:** 16,132 applied, 72% admitted, 25% enrolled. **Transfer Admission Requirements:** High school transcript, college transcript(s), essay or personal statement, interview, standardized test scores, minimum college GPA of 2.8 required. Lowest grade transferable C. **General Admission Information:** Application fee $50. Regular application deadline 2/1. Notification on a rolling basis, beginning on or about 2/1. Nonfall registration accepted. Admission may be deferred for a maximum of 1 year. Credit and/or placement offered for CEEB Advanced Placement tests.

COSTS AND FINANCIAL AID
Annual in-state tuition $10,080. Annual out-of-state tuition $24,050. Room and board $8,874. Required fees $2,663. Average book expense $1,200. **Required Forms and Deadlines:** FAFSA. Financial aid filing deadline 3/1. **Notification of Awards:** Applicants will be notified of awards on a rolling basis beginning 3/1. **Types of Aid:** *Need-based scholarships/grants:* Federal Pell, SEOG, state scholarships/grants, private scholarships, the school's own gift aid, Veterans Educational Benefits. *Loans:* FFEL Subsidized Stafford, FFEL Unsubsidized Stafford, FFEL PLUS, Federal Perkins, college/university loans from institutional funds. *Student Employment:* Federal Work-Study Program available. Institutional employment available. Highest amount earned per year from on-campus jobs $25,487. Off-campus job opportunities are excellent. **Financial Aid Statistics:** 39% freshmen, 37% undergrads receive need-based scholarship or grant aid. 6% freshmen, 4% undergrads receive non-need-based scholarship or grant aid. 58% freshmen, 57% undergrads receive need-based self-help aid. 2% freshmen, 2% undergrads receive athletic scholarships. 84% freshmen, 79% undergrads receive any aid. 74% undergrads borrow to pay for school. Average cumulative indebtedness $30,760. **Criteria for awarding institutional aid:** *Non-need-based:* Academics, art, athletics, leadership, music/drama, religious affiliation.

UNIVERSITY OF NEW HAMPSHIRE AT MANCHESTER

400 Commercial Street, Manchester, NH 03101
Phone: 603-641-4150
E-mail: unhm.admissions@unh.edu **CEEB Code:** 2094
Fax: 603-641-4125 **Website:** www.unh.edu/unhm/

This public school was founded in 1985.

RATINGS
Admissions Selectivity Rating: 63 **Fire Safety Rating:** 60* **Green Rating:** 60*

STUDENTS AND FACULTY
Enrollment: 704. **Student Body:** 64% female, 36% male, 1% out-of-state, 1% international (5 countries represented). Asian 1%, African American 2%, Caucasian 94%, Hispanic 1%.
Retention and Graduation: Faculty: Student/faculty ratio 18:1. 23 full-time faculty, 78% hold PhDs, 52% are women. 3% of classes are taught by teaching assistants.

ACADEMICS
Degrees: Associate, bachelor's. **Classes:** Most classes have 10–19 students. **Special Study Options:** Cross-registration, double major, English as a Second Language (ESL), exchange student program (domestic), independent study, internships, study abroad, teacher certification program Special programs offered to physically disabled students include note-taking services, reader services, tape recorders, tutors. **Career services:** Alumni services, career/job search classes, career assessment, internships.

FACILITIES
Housing: 85% of campus accessible to physically disabled.

CAMPUS LIFE
Activities: Student government.

ADMISSIONS
Freshman Academic Profile: SAT Math middle 50% range 440–550. SAT Critical Reading middle 50% range 460–550. Minimum paper TOEFL 550. Minimum computer TOEFL 213. Minimum web-based TOEFL 75. **Basis for Candidate Selection:** *Very important factors considered include:* Rigor of secondary school record. *Important factors considered include:* Class rank, application essay, recommendation(s), standardized test scores. *Other factors considered include:* Alumni/ae relation, character/personal qualities, extracurricular activities, interview, racial/ethnic status, state residency, talent/ability, volunteer work, work experience. **Freshman Admission Requirements:** High school diploma is required and GED is accepted. *Academic units required:* 4 English, 3 mathematics, (3 science labs), 2 foreign language, 2 social studies. *Academic units recommended:* 4 mathematics, (4 science labs), 3 foreign language. **Freshman Admission Statistics:** 218 applied, 74% admitted, 66% enrolled. **Transfer Admission Requirements:** High school transcript, college transcript(s), essay or personal statement, statement of good standing from prior institution(s). Minimum college GPA of 2.5 required. Lowest grade transferable C. **General Admission Information:** Application fee $50. Regular application deadline 6/15. Notification on a rolling basis, beginning on or about 1/31. Nonfall registration accepted. Admission may be deferred for a maximum of 2 Semesters. Credit offered for CEEB Advanced Placement tests.

COSTS AND FINANCIAL AID
Annual in-state tuition $4,630. Annual out-of-state tuition $12,190. Required fees $54. Average book expense $700. **Required Forms and Deadlines:** FAFSA, noncustodial PROFILE, business/farm supplement. Priority financial aid filing date 5/1. **Notification of Awards:** Applicants will be notified of awards on a rolling basis beginning 4/1. **Types of Aid:** *Need-based scholarships/grants:* Federal Pell, SEOG, state scholarships/grants, private scholarships, the school's own gift aid. *Loans:* FFEL Subsidized Stafford, FFEL Unsubsidized Stafford, FFEL PLUS, Federal Perkins, Outside Loans. *Student Employment:* Federal Work-Study Program available. Institutional employment available. Off-campus job opportunities are excellent. **Criteria for awarding institutional aid:** *Non-need-based:* Academics, minority status.

UNIVERSITY OF NEW HAVEN

300 Orange Avenue, West Haven, CT 06516
Phone: 203-932-7319
E-mail: adminfo@newhaven.edu **CEEB Code:** 3663
Fax: 203-931-6093 **Website:** www.newhaven.edu **ACT Code:** 576

This private school was founded in 1920. It has a 78-acre campus.

RATINGS
Admissions Selectivity Rating: 76 **Fire Safety Rating:** 60* **Green Rating:** 60*

STUDENTS AND FACULTY
Enrollment: 2,627. **Student Body:** 45% female, 55% male, 38% out-of-state, 4% international. Asian 1%, African American 9%, Caucasian 50%, Hispanic 4%.
Retention and Graduation: 78% freshmen return for sophomore year. **Faculty:** Student/faculty ratio 10:1. 178 full-time faculty, 90% hold PhDs, 10% are members of minority groups, 19% are women.

ACADEMICS
Degrees: Associate, bachelor's, certificate, master's, post-bachelor's certificate. **Classes:** Most classes have 10–19 students. Most lab/discussion sessions have 10–19 students. **Majors with Highest Enrollment:** Business/commerce; criminal justice/law enforcement administration; engineering. **Special Study Options:** Accelerated program, cooperative education program, cross-registration, double major, dual enrollment, English as a Second Language (ESL), honors program, independent study, internships, student-designed major, study abroad **Combined degree programs:** BS/MS in environmental science. Special programs offered to physically disabled students include note-taking services, reader services, tape recorders, tutors. **Career services:** Alumni network, alumni services, career/job search classes, career assessment, internships.

FACILITIES
Housing: Coed dorms, apartments for single students. 82% of campus accessible to physically disabled. **Special Academic Facilities/Equipment:** Art gallery, forensic science lab, radio station, tv station, theater Orchestra New England, music and sound recording studio.

CAMPUS LIFE
Environment: Village. **Activities:** Choral groups, dance, drama/theater, music ensembles, musical theater, pep band, radio station, student government, student newspaper, television station, yearbook. **Organizations:** 50 registered organizations, 5 honor societies, 1 religious organizations. 2 fraternities, 3 sororities. **Athletics (Intercollegiate):** *Men:* Baseball, basketball, cross-country, golf, lacrosse, soccer, track/field (outdoor), track/field (indoor), volleyball. *Women:* Basketball, cheerleading, cross-country, lacrosse, soccer, softball, tennis, volleyball. **On-Campus Highlights:** Bartel's Student Union, Student Run Dance Hall, Coffe Shop.

ADMISSIONS
Freshman Academic Profile: Average high school GPA 3. 14% in top 10% of high school class, 35% in top 25% of high school class, 67% in top 50% of high school class. 85% from public high schools. SAT Math middle 50% range 450–570. SAT Critical Reading middle 50% range 460–560. Minimum paper TOEFL 520. Minimum computer TOEFL 190. **Basis for Candidate Selection:** *Very important factors considered include:* Rigor of secondary school record, standardized test scores. *Important factors considered include:* Class rank, application essay, recommendation(s). *Other factors considered include:* Alumni/ae relation, character/personal qualities, extracurricular activities, interview, talent/ability, volunteer work, work experience. **Freshman Admission Requirements:** High school diploma is required and GED is accepted. *Academic units required:* 4 English, 3 mathematics, 2 science, 2 history, 3 academic electives. *Academic units recommended:* 2 foreign language, 2 social studies. **Freshman Admission Statistics:** 3,025 applied, 67% admitted, 31% enrolled. **Transfer Admission Requirements:** High school transcript, college transcript(s), minimum college GPA of 2.5 required. Lowest grade transferable C. **General Admission Information:** Application fee $50. Notification on a rolling basis, beginning on or about 9/15. Nonfall registration accepted. Admission may be deferred for a maximum of 1 year. Credit and/or placement offered for CEEB Advanced Placement tests.

COSTS AND FINANCIAL AID
Annual tuition $20,130. Room and board $8,040. Required fees $482. Average book expense $750. **Required Forms and Deadlines:** FAFSA, institution's own financial aid form, tax returns. Priority financial aid filing date 3/2. **Notification of Awards:** Applicants will be notified of awards on a rolling basis beginning 3/15. **Types of Aid:** *Need-based scholarships/grants:* Federal Pell, SEOG, state scholarships/grants, private scholarships, the school's own gift aid. *Loans:* FFEL Subsidized Stafford, FFEL Unsubsidized Stafford, FFEL PLUS,

Federal Perkins. *Student Employment:* Federal Work-Study Program available. Institutional employment available. Highest amount earned per year from on-campus jobs $900. Off-campus job opportunities are excellent. **Financial Aid Statistics:** 71% freshmen, 68% undergrads receive need-based scholarship or grant aid. 5% freshmen, 5% undergrads receive non-need-based scholarship or grant aid. 68% freshmen, 67% undergrads receive need-based self-help aid. 2% freshmen, 3% undergrads receive athletic scholarships. 73% undergrads borrow to pay for school. Average cumulative indebtedness $16,300. **Criteria for awarding institutional aid:** *Non-need-based:* Academics, athletics.

See page 1302.

UNIVERSITY OF NEW MEXICO

Office of Admissions, PO Box 4895, Albuquerque, NM 87196-4895
Phone: 505-277-2446 **Financial Aid Phone:** 505-277-8900
E-mail: apply@unm.edu **CEEB Code:** 4845
Fax: 505-277-6686 **Website:** www.unm.edu **ACT Code:** 2650

This public school was founded in 1889. It has a 769-acre campus.

RATINGS
Admissions Selectivity Rating: 77   **Fire Safety Rating:** 70   **Green Rating:** 91

STUDENTS AND FACULTY
Enrollment: 18,330. **Student Body:** 58% female, 42% male, 21% out-of-state, 1% international (92 countries represented). Asian 4%, African American 3%, Caucasian 46%, Hispanic 35%, Native American 6%.
Retention and Graduation: Faculty: Student/faculty ratio 20:1. 885 full-time faculty, 86% hold PhDs, 22% are members of minority groups, 59% are women.

ACADEMICS
Degrees: Associate, bachelor's, certificate, first professional, master's, post-master's certificate. **Classes:** Most classes have 20–29 students. Most lab/discussion sessions have 10–19 students. **Majors with Highest Enrollment:** Biology/biological sciences; business administration and management; psychology. **Special Study Options:** Accelerated program, cooperative education program, distance learning, double major, dual enrollment, English as a Second Language (ESL), exchange student program (domestic), honors program, independent study, internships, student-designed major, study abroad, teacher certification program, weekend college. **Honors programs:** The University Honors Program offers the chance to explore major contemporary ideas and values in small interdisciplinary seminars with the additional benefits of personal interaction with outstanding UNM faculty, opportunities for upper-division independent research, social and cultural events, lecture series, and opportunities to participate in regional and national honors conferences. UHP students do not major in University Honors. They graduate with a degree from one of UNM's degree-granting colleges or schools. **Combined degree programs:** BA/MD, 3-2 Latin American Studies/MBA. Special programs offered to physically disabled students include note-taking services, reader services, tape recorders, tutors. **Career services:** Alumni network, alumni services, career/job search classes, career assessment, internships, regional alumni.

FACILITIES
Housing: Coed dorms, fraternity/sorority housing, apartments for married students, apartments for single students, Special living options include graduate and senior housing, academic floors, scholars wing, and outdoor/wellness units. Computer Science and Engineering unit also available. 100% of campus accessible to physically disabled. **Special Academic Facilities/Equipment:** Museums of art, anthropology, geology, and Southwestern biology, lithography institute, meteoritics institute, electron and electron scanning microscopes, nuclear reactor, robotics lab, observatory, planetarium, Science and Technology Park. **Computers:** 100% of classrooms, 100% of dorms, 100% of libraries, 100% of dining areas, 100% of student union, 85% of common outdoor areas have wireless network access. Students can register for classes online. Administrative functions (other than registration) can be performed online.

CAMPUS LIFE
Environment: Metropolis. **Activities:** Choral groups, concert band, dance, drama/theater, jazz band, literary magazine, marching band, music ensembles, musical theater, opera, pep band, radio station, student government, student newspaper, student-run film society, symphony orchestra, television station. **Organizations:** 375 registered organizations, 20 honor societies, 23 religious

organizations. 9 fraternities, 10 sororities. **Athletics (Intercollegiate):** *Men:* Baseball, basketball, cross-country, football, golf, skiing (downhill/alpine), skiing (nordic/cross-country), soccer, tennis, track/field (outdoor), track/field (indoor). *Women:* Basketball, cross-country, diving, golf, skiing (downhill/alpine), skiing (nordic/cross-country), soccer, softball, swimming, tennis, track/field (outdoor), track/field (indoor), volleyball. **On-Campus Highlights:** SUB (Student Union Building), Duck Pond, Zimmerman Library, Popejoy Hall—Performing Arts Center, Residency Halls, Maxwell Museum, Trolly Tour of Campus for new and prospective students.

ADMISSIONS
Freshman Academic Profile: Average high school GPA 3.33. 21% in top 10% of high school class, 45% in top 25% of high school class, 79% in top 50% of high school class. SAT Math middle 50% range 470–590. SAT Critical Reading middle 50% range 470–600. ACT middle 50% range 19–25. Minimum paper TOEFL 520. Minimum computer TOEFL 190. Minimum web-based TOEFL 68. **Basis for Candidate Selection:** *Very important factors considered include:* Academic GPA, rigor of secondary school record. *Important factors considered include:* Class rank, standardized test scores. *Other factors considered include:* Application essay, recommendation(s), character/personal qualities, extracurricular activities, first generation, volunteer work, work experience. **Freshman Admission Requirements:** High school diploma is required and GED is accepted. *Academic units required:* 4 English, 3 mathematics, 2 science, (1 science labs), 2 foreign language, 1 social studies, 1 history. **Freshman Admission Statistics:** 7,134 applied, 74% admitted, 59% enrolled. **Transfer Admission Requirements:** College transcript(s), minimum college GPA of 2.0 required. Lowest grade transferable C. **General Admission Information:** Application fee $20. Regular application deadline 6/15. Nonfall registration accepted. Admission may be deferred for a maximum of 1 year. Credit and/or placement offered for CEEB Advanced Placement tests.

COSTS AND FINANCIAL AID
Annual in-state tuition $6,094. Annual out-of-state tuition $19,923. **Required Forms and Deadlines:** FAFSA. Priority financial aid filing date 3/1. **Notification of Awards:** Applicants will be notified of awards on a rolling basis beginning 4/15. **Types of Aid:** *Need-based scholarships/grants:* Federal Pell, SEOG, state scholarships/grants, private scholarships, the school's own gift aid, United Negro College Fund, Federal Nursing Scholarships. *Loans:* Direct Subsidized Stafford, Direct Unsubsidized Stafford, Direct PLUS, Federal Perkins, Federal Nursing, state loans, college/university loans from institutional funds. *Student Employment:* Federal Work-Study Program available. **Financial Aid Statistics: Criteria for awarding institutional aid:** *Non-need-based:* Academics, alumni affiliation, art, athletics, job skills, leadership, minority status, music/drama, religious affiliation, state/district residency.

UNIVERSITY OF NEW ORLEANS

University of New Orleans Admissions, 10 Admin Bldg, New Orleans, LA 70148
Phone: 504-280-6595 **Financial Aid Phone:** 504-280-6603
E-mail: admissions@uno.edu **CEEB Code:** 6379
Fax: 504-280-5522 **Website:** www.uno.edu **ACT Code:** 1591

This public school was founded in 1956. It has a 195-acre campus.

RATINGS
Admissions Selectivity Rating: 77   **Fire Safety Rating:** 60*   **Green Rating:** 60*

STUDENTS AND FACULTY
Enrollment: 8,515. **Student Body:** 51% female, 49% male, 5% out-of-state, 4% international (85 countries represented). Asian 6%, African American 18%, Caucasian 57%, Hispanic 7%, Native American 1%.
Retention and Graduation: 69% freshmen return for sophomore year.
Faculty: Student/faculty ratio 18:1. 442 full-time faculty, 69% hold PhDs, 15% are members of minority groups, 41% are women. 5% of classes are taught by teaching assistants.

ACADEMICS
Degrees: Bachelor's, master's, post-bachelor's certificate. **Classes:** Most classes have 20–29 students. **Majors with Highest Enrollment:** Business administration and management; general studies; psychology. **Special Study Options:** Cooperative education program, cross-registration, distance learning, double major, dual enrollment, English as a Second Language (ESL), exchange student

program (domestic), honors program, independent study, internships, student-designed major, study abroad, teacher certification program, weekend college Special programs offered to physically disabled students include note-taking services, reader services, tape recorders, tutors. **Career services:** Alumni services, career assessment, internships.

FACILITIES
Housing: Coed dorms, special housing for disabled students, apartments for married students, apartments for single students. 100% of campus accessible to physically disabled. **Special Academic Facilities/Equipment:** Performing arts center, audiovisual center, TV studio, Eisenhower leadership studies center, child care center, Louisiana collection. **Computers:** 100% of libraries, 100% of student union, have wireless network access. Students can register for classes online. Administrative functions (other than registration) can be performed online.

CAMPUS LIFE
Environment: Metropolis. **Activities:** Choral groups, concert band, dance, drama/theater, jazz band, literary magazine, music ensembles, musical theater, opera, pep band, radio station, student government, student newspaper, student-run film society, campus ministries, international student organization. **Organizations:** 120 registered organizations, 7 religious organizations. 9 fraternities, 8 sororities. **Athletics (Intercollegiate):** *Men:* Baseball, basketball, diving, golf, swimming, tennis. *Women:* Basketball, diving, swimming, tennis, volleyball. **On-Campus Highlights:** Recreation and Fitness Center, The University Center, The Homer L. Hitt Alumni and Visitors Ce, Earl K. Long Library.

ADMISSIONS
Freshman Academic Profile: Average high school GPA 3.08. 13% in top 10% of high school class, 33% in top 25% of high school class, 64% in top 50% of high school class. 62% from public high schools. SAT Math middle 50% range 480–625. SAT Critical Reading middle 50% range 470–600. SAT Writing middle 50% range 460–570. ACT middle 50% range 20–24. Minimum paper TOEFL 525. Minimum computer TOEFL 195. Minimum web-based TOEFL 71. **Basis for Candidate Selection:** *Very important factors considered include:* Class rank, academic GPA, rigor of secondary school record, standardized test scores, *Other factors considered include:* Recommendation(s), geographical residence, state residency. **Freshman Admission Requirements:** High school diploma is required and GED is accepted. *Academic units required:* 4 English, 3 mathematics, 3 science, 2 foreign language, 1 social studies, 2 history, 1 visual/performing arts. **Freshman Admission Statistics:** 3,764 applied, 57% admitted, 59% enrolled. **Transfer Admission Requirements:** College transcript(s), minimum college GPA of 2.25 required. Lowest grade transferable D. **General Admission Information:** Application fee $40. Regular application deadline 8/20. Notification on a rolling basis, beginning on or about 10/1. Nonfall registration accepted. Admission may be deferred for a maximum of 1 year. Credit and/or placement offered for CEEB Advanced Placement tests.

COSTS AND FINANCIAL AID
Annual in-state tuition $3,704. Annual out-of-state tuition $11,860. Room and board $6,700. Required fees $628. Average book expense $1,200. **Required Forms and Deadlines:** FAFSA. Priority financial aid filing date 5/15. **Notification of Awards:** Applicants will be notified of awards on a rolling basis beginning 4/20. **Types of Aid:** *Need-based scholarships/grants:* Federal Pell, SEOG, state scholarships/grants, private scholarships, the school's own gift aid. *Loans:* Direct Subsidized Stafford, Direct Unsubsidized Stafford, Direct PLUS, FFEL Subsidized Stafford, FFEL Unsubsidized Stafford, FFEL PLUS, Federal Perkins, college/university loans from institutional funds. **Student Employment:** Federal Work-Study Program available. Institutional employment available. Highest amount earned per year from on-campus jobs $23,920. **Financial Aid Statistics:** 43% freshmen, 42% undergrads receive need-based scholarship or grant aid. 40% freshmen, 23% undergrads receive non-need-based scholarship or grant aid. 23% freshmen, 31% undergrads receive need-based self-help aid. 2% freshmen, 2% undergrads receive athletic scholarships. 75% freshmen, 66% undergrads borrow to pay for school. 16% undergrads borrow to pay for school. Average cumulative indebtedness $13,623. **Criteria for awarding institutional aid:** *Non-need-based:* Academics, athletics.

UNIVERSITY OF NORTH ALABAMA

UNA Box 5011, Florence, AL 35632-0001
Phone: 256-765-4318 **Financial Aid Phone:** 256-765-4278
E-mail: admissions@una.edu
Fax: 256-765-4329 **Website:** www.una.edu **ACT Code:** 14

This public school was founded in 1830. It has a 130-acre campus.

RATINGS
Admissions Selectivity Rating: 77   **Fire Safety Rating:** 60*   **Green Rating:** 60*

STUDENTS AND FACULTY
Enrollment: 5,235. **Student Body:** 57% female, 43% male, 19% out-of-state, 9% international (67 countries represented). Asian 1%, African American 10%, Caucasian 70%, Hispanic 1%, Native American 1%.
Retention and Graduation: 68% freshmen return for sophomore year. **Faculty:** Student/faculty ratio 21:1. 247 full-time faculty, 63% hold PhDs, 14% are members of minority groups, 47% are women.

ACADEMICS
Degrees: Bachelor's, master's, post-master's certificate. **Classes:** Most classes have fewer than 10 students. Most lab/discussion sessions have 20–29 students. **Majors with Highest Enrollment:** Business/commerce; nursing/registered nurse (RN, ASN, BSN, MSN); secondary education and teaching. **Special Study Options:** Accelerated program, cooperative education program, distance learning, double major, dual enrollment, English as a Second Language (ESL), honors program, independent study, internships, student-designed major, teacher certification program, weekend college Special programs offered to physically disabled students include tutors.

FACILITIES
Housing: Coed dorms, men's dorms, special housing for international students, women's dorms, fraternity/sorority housing, apartments for married students, apartments for single students. 99% of campus accessible to physically disabled. **Special Academic Facilities/Equipment:** On-campus lab school (N-6), planetarium, observatory, art gallery. **Computers:** Students can register for classes online.

CAMPUS LIFE
Environment: Town. **Activities:** Choral groups, concert band, drama/theater, jazz band, literary magazine, marching band, music ensembles, musical theater, pep band, radio station, student government, student newspaper, yearbook. **Organizations:** 98 registered organizations. **Athletics (Intercollegiate):** *Men:* Baseball, basketball, cross-country, football, golf, tennis. *Women:* Basketball, cross-country, soccer, softball, tennis, volleyball. **On-Campus Highlights:** Guillot University Center, Academic Resource Center, Entertainment Industry Center, Recreation Center, Flowers Hall.

ADMISSIONS
Freshman Academic Profile: Average high school GPA 2.97. 44% in top 25% of high school class, 76% in top 50% of high school class. 99% from public high schools. ACT middle 50% range 18–24. Minimum paper TOEFL 500. Minimum computer TOEFL 173. **Basis for Candidate Selection:** *Very important factors considered include:* Class rank, academic GPA, standardized test scores. *Important factors considered include:* Rigor of secondary school record, character/personal qualities. **Freshman Admission Requirements:** High school diploma is required and GED is accepted. *Academic units required:* 4 English, 2 mathematics, 2 science, 2 foreign language, 3 social studies. **Freshman Admission Statistics:** 2,227 applied, 84% admitted, 54% enrolled. **Transfer Admission Requirements:** College transcript(s), minimum college GPA of 2.0 required. Lowest grade transferable C. **General Admission Information:** Application fee $25. Notification on a rolling basis, beginning on or about 6/15. Nonfall registration accepted. Admission may be deferred for a maximum of 1 semester. Credit offered for CEEB Advanced Placement tests.

COSTS AND FINANCIAL AID
Annual in-state tuition $3,768. Annual out-of-state tuition $7,536. Room and board $4,372. Required fees $883. Average book expense $830. **Required Forms and Deadlines:** FAFSA. Priority financial aid filing date 4/1. **Notification of Awards:** Applicants will be notified of awards on a rolling basis beginning 5/31. **Types of Aid:** *Need-based scholarships/grants:* Federal Pell, SEOG, state scholarships/grants, private scholarships, the school's own gift aid. *Loans:* FFEL Subsidized Stafford, FFEL Unsubsidized Stafford, FFEL PLUS, Federal Perkins. **Financial Aid Statistics:** 28% freshmen, 29% undergrads receive need-based scholarship or grant aid. 35% freshmen, 26% undergrads receive non-need-based scholarship or grant aid. 26% freshmen, 34% undergrads receive need-based self-help aid. 5% freshmen, 5% undergrads receive athletic scholarships. 47.2% undergrads borrow to pay for school. Average cumulative indebtedness $18,245. **Criteria for awarding institutional aid:** *Non-need-*

based: Academics, art, athletics, leadership, minority status, music/drama, state/district residency.

THE UNIVERSITY OF NORTH CAROLINA AT ASHEVILLE

CPO #1320, One University Heights, Asheville, NC 28804-8502
Phone: 828-251-6481 **Financial Aid Phone:** 828-251-6535
E-mail: admissions@unca.edu **CEEB Code:** 5013
Fax: 828-251-6482 **Website:** www.unca.edu **ACT Code:** 3064

This public school was founded in 1927. It has a 265-acre campus.

RATINGS
Admissions Selectivity Rating: 84   **Fire Safety Rating:** 82   **Green Rating:** 77

STUDENTS AND FACULTY
Enrollment: 3,320. **Student Body:** 57% female, 43% male, 87% out-of-state, 1% international (19 countries represented). Asian 1%, African American 2%, Caucasian 88%, Hispanic 3%.
Retention and Graduation: 82% freshmen return for sophomore year. 29% freshmen graduate within 4 years. 21% grads go on to further study within 1 year. 18% grads pursue arts and sciences degrees. 1% grads pursue law degrees. 1% grads pursue business degrees. 1% grads pursue medical degrees. **Faculty:** Student/faculty ratio 14:1. 208 full-time faculty, 85% hold PhDs, 11% are members of minority groups, 44% are women.

ACADEMICS
Degrees: Bachelor's, master's, post-bachelor's certificate. **Classes:** Most classes have 10–19 students. Most lab/discussion sessions have 20–29 students. **Majors with Highest Enrollment:** English language and literature; psychology; sociology. **Special Study Options:** Cross-registration, distance learning, double major, dual enrollment, exchange student program (domestic), honors program, independent study, internships, liberal arts/career combination, student-designed major, study abroad, teacher certification program. **Honors programs:** University Honors Program—Designed for talented and motivated students, the Honors curriculum complements the General Education and major curricula. Successful completion of the Honors Program enables the student to graduate with Distinction as a University Scholar. (See www.unca.edu/honors/ for further information.) Undergraduate Research Program—The Undergraduate Research Program at UNCA seeks to encourage the establishment of faculty/student research pairs who work together on a project of mutual interest. Research may be performed in any discipline on campus. Students who have made oral presentations at symposia and have had their work reviewed and published can receive recognition as University Research Scholars. (See www.unca.edu/urp/ for more information.) Special programs offered to physically disabled students include note-taking services, reader services, tape recorders, tutors. **Career services:** Alumni network, alumni services, career/job search classes, career assessment, internships, regional alumni.

FACILITIES
Housing: Coed dorms, special housing for disabled students, men's dorms, women's dorms, substance-free dorms, 24 hour quiet dorms. 95% of campus accessible to physically disabled. **Special Academic Facilities/Equipment:** Undergraduate Research Center, Steelcase Teleconference Center, Music Recording Center, Asheville Botanical Gardens, NC Arboretum, Center for Creative Retirement. **Computers:** 1% of classrooms, 100% of libraries, 100% of dining areas, 90% of student union, have wireless network access. Students can register for classes online. Administrative functions (other than registration) can be performed online.

CAMPUS LIFE
Environment: Town. **Activities:** Choral groups, concert band, dance, drama/theater, jazz band, literary magazine, music ensembles, musical theater, pep band, radio station, student government, student newspaper, campus ministries, international student organization. **Organizations:** 82 registered organizations, 14 honor societies, 10 religious organizations. 1 fraternities, 2 sororities. **Athletics (Intercollegiate):** *Men:* Baseball, basketball, cheerleading, cross-country, soccer, tennis, track/field (outdoor). *Women:* Basketball, cheerleading, cross-country, soccer, tennis, track/field (outdoor), volleyball. **On-Campus Highlights:** Health and Fitness Center, Main Campus Quadrangle, High-

smith University Union, Asheville Botanical Gardens, Cafe Ramsey in Ramsey Library. **Environmental Initiatives:** New and Planned Campus Construction that incorporates sustainable features. UNC Asheville's four newest buildings and a fifth project, now in the design phase, all incorporate sustainable features. Examples: The New Hall classroom building, which opened in January 2006, has an innovative vegetative roof that minimizes rainwater runoff, and geothermal heat pumps for heating and cooling. New Hall geothermal heating and cooling resulted in a savings of 87.4% of combined energy consumption compared to the campus average during 2007. Sam Millar Facilities Management Complex, which opened in September 2007, is a 27,660–square-foot complex made up of three buildings that are home to some 115 employees working in 18 trade fields, including grounds, housekeeping, plumbing and mail services. Sustainable features include solar panels, a 10,000–gallon underground grey water cistern, geothermal heating and cooling, recycled cotton batt insulation, pervious pavements in the parking areas and roadways, and bioretention ponds to clean up water runoff prior to entering area streams. UNC Asheville is pursuing LEED Silver Certification for the complex. The Steve and Frosene Zeis Science & Multimedia Building, a four-story, 88,500–square-foot building now under construction, will house the biology, chemistry and multimedia arts and sciences departments. The design includes advanced storm water management, low-emitting interior materials, water efficient landscaping, and significant use of natural light throughout the structure. Pisgah House, now under construction, is a new, multi-purpose facility that will serve as the residence for current and future UNC Asheville Chancellors, as well as a location for University-hosted meetings, receptions, dinners, programs and performances. It is being built using sustainable construction practices, materials and equipment and will comply with the principles currently being developed for the residential application of the LEED Green Building Rating System. The Craft Campus, now in the design phase, will provide a much-need facility for UNC Asheville students pursuing studio crafts and is expected to serve as a national model for green building and add to Western North Carolina's $144-million craft economy. The Craft Campus will be located off campus, adjacent to Buncombe County's former landfill. The University is leasing the 153-acre site from Buncombe County for $1 per year for 99 years. The Craft Campus will be a "green" facility, including its energy sources, building materials and studio operations. Methane from Buncombe County's former landfill will provide the primary energy source for studios, kilns, glass furnaces and a visitors' center. In 2004, the University was awarded a $100,000 grant from the Kresge Foundation to aid with planning costs for the Craft Campus green building design. It is the maximum amount the foundation awards through its Green Building Initiative. Establishment of the Student Environmental Center The Student Environmental Center (SEC) is funded by a student-initiated "green fee" that will fund new technology, educational displays concerning UNC Asheville's green campus buildings, and campaigns to increase students' engagement in environmentally responsible behaviors such as recycling, use of alternative transportation, and energy and resource conservation. The SEC reports directly to the Student Affairs Division as a student-run entity. Current SEC projects include working with faculty to integrate sustainability issues into freshman colloquia courses, developing signage to improve recycling on our campus and working with the Alumni & Development division to pursue outside funding for renewable energy projects. Student interns worked with the student group Active Students for a Healthy Environment (ASHE) to plan a regional discussion on climate change that took place in January and featured a number of distinguished campus and community leaders engaging in a dialogue about mitigating climate change. An example of a recent use of student sustainability fees for technology upgrade was the purchase of GEM electric vehicle for use by Campus Parking Enforcement. Commitment to a reduction in energy use and promotion of transportation alternatives. Among the examples we can offer are these: UNC Asheville's commitment to the reduction of energy use was recognized with two top awards from the North Carolina State Energy Office in 2006. The first was an award for the lowest per-square-foot energy consumption of all public universities in the western half of the state, and noted a number of energy savings initiatives, including upgraded mechanical systems, improved maintenance techniques for heating-and-cooling systems, and the replacement of windows in older building with new energy-efficient models. The second award was for the implementation of a number of energy-reduction efforts that emphasized teamwork and individual employee responsibility. UNC Asheville is actively pursuing transportation alternatives for students, faculty and staff. UNC Asheville's Great Bus About was recently recognized by the Association of Commuter Transportation with a first-place award for creative excellence. The Great Bus About, a partnership between UNC Asheville and the City of Asheville, was launched in 2006 as a marketing tool to promote the Passport program, which provides unlimited free bus service to UNC Asheville students, staff and faculty. The Passport program led to a 146% increase in UNC Asheville bus boarding between November 2006 and May 2007. The 2006 Great Bus About led to a one-day 2000% increase in bus ridership. UNC Asheville's Chancellor, Anne Ponder, is the only chancellor in the 16-campus UNC system to request a hybrid vehicle as her official, state-supplied transportation. She drives a Ford Escape hybrid. Alternative fuel vehicles are used by the staff of Facilities Management.

ADMISSIONS

Freshman Academic Profile: Average high school GPA 3.9. 22% in top 10% of high school class, 60% in top 25% of high school class, 95% in top 50% of high school class. 87% from public high schools. SAT Math middle 50% range 530–630. SAT Critical Reading middle 50% range 540–640. SAT Writing middle 50% range 510–625. ACT middle 50% range 23–27. Minimum paper TOEFL 550. Minimum computer TOEFL 213. Minimum web-based TOEFL 79. **Basis for Candidate Selection:** *Very important factors considered include:* Class rank, academic GPA, rigor of secondary school record. *Important factors considered include:* Application essay, recommendation(s), standardized test scores. *Other factors considered include:* Alumni/ae relation, extracurricular activities, first generation, geographical residence, interview, level of applicant's interest, racial/ethnic status, state residency, talent/ability, volunteer work, work experience. **Freshman Admission Requirements:** High school diploma is required and GED is not accepted. *Academic units required:* 4 English, 4 mathematics, 3 science, (1 science labs), 2 foreign language, 1 social studies, 1 history. *Academic units recommended:* 4 academic electives. **Freshman Admission Statistics:** 2,510 applied, 77% admitted, 33% enrolled. **Transfer Admission Requirements:** College transcript(s), minimum college GPA of 2.50 required. Lowest grade transferable C. **General Admission Information:** Application fee $50. Regular application deadline 2/15. Regular notification 4/1. Nonfall registration accepted. Admission may be deferred for a maximum of 1 year. Credit and/or placement offered for CEEB Advanced Placement tests.

COSTS AND FINANCIAL AID

Annual in-state tuition $2,389. Annual out-of-state tuition $14,106. Room and board $6,890. Required fees $2,022. Average book expense $850. **Required Forms and Deadlines:** FAFSA. Priority financial aid filing date 3/1. **Notification of Awards:** Applicants will be notified of awards on a rolling basis beginning 3/15. **Types of Aid:** *Need-based scholarships/grants:* Federal Pell, SEOG, state scholarships/grants, private scholarships, the school's own gift aid. *Loans:* Direct Subsidized Stafford, Direct Unsubsidized Stafford, Direct PLUS, Federal Perkins, state loans, college/university loans from institutional funds. *Student Employment:* Federal Work-Study Program available. Institutional employment available. Off-campus job opportunities are good. **Financial Aid Statistics:** 44% freshmen, 42% undergrads receive need-based scholarship or grant aid. 8% freshmen, 6% undergrads receive non-need-based scholarship or grant aid. 30% freshmen, 32% undergrads receive need-based self-help aid. 3% freshmen, 3% undergrads receive athletic scholarships. 70% freshmen, 65% undergrads receive any aid. 50% undergrads borrow to pay for school. Average cumulative indebtedness $14,596. **Criteria for awarding institutional aid:** *Non-need-based:* Academics, alumni affiliation, art, athletics, job skills, leadership, minority status, music/drama, state/district residency.

THE UNIVERSITY OF NORTH CAROLINA AT CHAPEL HILL

Office of Undergraduate Admissions, Jackson Hall, Chapel Hill, NC 27599-2200
Phone: 919-966-3621 **Financial Aid Phone:** 919-962-8396
E-mail: unchelp@admissions.unc.edu **CEEB Code:** 5816
Fax: 919-962-3045 **Website:** www.unc.edu **ACT Code:** 3162

This public school was founded in 1789. It has a 729-acre campus.

RATINGS

Admissions Selectivity Rating: 97 **Fire Safety Rating:** 87 **Green Rating:** 95

STUDENTS AND FACULTY

Enrollment: 17,565. **Student Body:** 59% female, 41% male, 16% out-of-state, 2% international (133 countries represented). Asian 7%, African American 11%, Caucasian 69%, Hispanic 5%, Native American 1%.
Retention and Graduation: 74% freshmen graduate within 4 years. 28.4% grads go on to further study within 1 year. 12.9% grads pursue arts and sciences degrees. 6.2% grads pursue law degrees. 4.9% grads pursue business degrees. 2.6% grads pursue medical degrees. **Faculty:** Student/faculty ratio 14:1. 1628 full-time faculty, 91% hold PhDs, 22% are members of minority groups, 41% are women. 25% of classes are taught by teaching assistants.

ACADEMICS

Degrees: Bachelor's, certificate, doctoral, master's, post-bachelor's certificate, post-master's certificate. **Classes:** Most classes have 10–19 students. Most lab/discussion sessions have 10–19 students. **Majors with Highest Enrollment:** Biology/biological sciences; business administration and management; psychology. **Special Study Options:** Cross-registration, distance learning, double major, dual enrollment, honors program, independent study, internships, student-designed major, study abroad, teacher certification program. **Honors programs:** See www.honors.unc.edu/ Special programs offered to physically disabled students include note-taking services, reader services, tape recorders **Career services:** Alumni network, alumni services, career/job search classes, career assessment, internships, regional alumni. **Career services highlights include:** The eight networking nights we do each year. For each night we bring in 20–30 professionals deep in one career area that is very difficult to break into for internships and full-time jobs. This gives students multiple opportunities to make contacts that they can follow up with to gain a "foot in the door" in fields/industries where it is hard to find an internship/job.

FACILITIES

Housing: Coed dorms, special housing for disabled students, men's dorms, special housing for international students, women's dorms, fraternity/sorority housing, apartments for married students, apartments for single students, wellness housing, theme housingSpecial Options in Housing—Learning Communities such as RELIC—Religion as Explorative Learning Integrated in our Community, Language Houses, The Carolina Experience, Men@Carolina, W.E.L.L.—Women's Experiences: Learning and Leadership, Connected Learning Program, Service and Leadership, Substance Free Environments, Sustainability, UNITAS. 98% of campus accessible to physically disabled. **Special Academic Facilities/Equipment:** Art museum, Folklore council, Institute of Folk Music, communications center, Basketball Museum, Institute of Latin American Studies, Institute of fisheries research, Sitterson Hall Computer Museum, Institute of Natural Science, Research Laboratory of Anthropology, Hayden Planetarium, Paul Green Theatre, Playmakers Theater, Memorial Hall. **Computers:** 75% of classrooms, 15% of dorms, 100% of libraries, 100% of dining areas, 100% of student union, 50% of common outdoor areas have wireless network access. Students can register for classes online. Administrative functions (other than registration) can be performed online. Undergraduates are required to own a computer.

CAMPUS LIFE

Environment: Town. **Activities:** Choral groups, concert band, dance, drama/theater, jazz band, literary magazine, marching band, music ensembles, musical theater, opera, pep band, radio station, student government, student newspaper, student-run film society, symphony orchestra, television station, yearbook, campus ministries, international student organization, Model UN. **Organizations:** 635 registered organizations, 19 honor societies, 42 religious organizations. 35 fraternities, 23 sororities. **Athletics (Intercollegiate):** *Men:* Baseball, basketball, cross-country, diving, fencing, football, golf, lacrosse, soccer, swimming, tennis, track/field (outdoor), track/field (indoor), wrestling. *Women:* Basketball, crew/rowing, cross-country, diving, fencing, field hockey, golf, gymnastics, lacrosse, soccer, softball, swimming, tennis, track/field (outdoor), track/field (indoor), volleyball. **On-Campus Highlights:** The Pit, McCorkle Place, Polk Place, Dean Smith Center, Student Union, Old Well, Coker Arboretum, Morehead Planetarium, Ackland Art Museum, Kenan Stadium. **Environmental Initiatives:** Partnered with Orange (County) Water and Sewer Authority (OWASA) to install a water reclamation and reuse system that replaces more than 210 million gallons of potable water annually. This system reduces total daily water demand in the OWASA service territory by 10%. Started in summer 2009, the system provides makeup water in cooling towers and irrigates landscapes. Reclaimed water will be used to flush toilets in new buildings once code approval has been granted. 32 MW.Cogeneration Facility, district heating and cooling, and 5 million gallon thermal storage facility Fare Free Transit and Commuter Alternatives Program. More than 6 million free bus rides provided annually. UNC contributes more than $6 million annually to fund Chapel Hill Transit.

ADMISSIONS

Freshman Academic Profile: Average high school GPA 4.47. 80% in top 10% of high school class, 96% in top 25% of high school class, 99% in top 50% of high school class. 80% from public high schools. SAT Math middle 50% range 620–710. SAT Critical Reading middle 50% range 590–700. SAT Writing middle 50% range 580–680. ACT middle 50% range 26–31. Minimum paper TOEFL 600. Minimum computer TOEFL 250. Minimum web-based TOEFL 100. **Basis for Candidate Selection:** *Very important factors considered include:* Class rank, application essay, academic GPA, recommendation(s), rigor of secondary school record, standardized test scores, character/personal qualities, extracurricular activities, state residency, talent/ability. *Important factors considered include:* Alumni/ae relation, first generation, racial/ethnic status, volunteer work, work experience. **Freshman Admission Requirements:** High school diploma is required and GED is not accepted. *Academic units required:* 4 English, 4 mathematics, 3 science, (1 science labs), 2 foreign language, 1 social studies, 1 history. **Freshman Admission Statistics:** 23,224 applied, 32% admitted, 54% enrolled. **Transfer Admission Requirements:** High school transcript, college transcript(s), essay or personal statement, statement of good standing from prior institution(s). Minimum college GPA of 2.0 required. Lowest grade transferable C. **General Admission Information:** Application fee $70. Regular application deadline 1/15. Nonfall registration not accepted. Admission may be deferred for a maximum of 1 year. Credit and/or placement offered for CEEB Advanced Placement tests.

COSTS AND FINANCIAL AID

Annual in-state tuition $3,865. Annual out-of-state tuition $21,753. Room and board $8,670. Required fees $1,761. Average book expense $1,000. **Required Forms and Deadlines:** FAFSA, CSS/Financial Aid PROFILE. Priority financial aid filing date 3/1. **Notification of Awards:** Applicants will be notified of awards on a rolling basis beginning 3/15. **Types of Aid:** *Need-based scholarships/grants:* Federal Pell, SEOG, state scholarships/grants, private scholarships, the school's own gift aid, State Grants. *Loans:* FFEL Subsidized Stafford, FFEL Unsubsidized Stafford, FFEL PLUS, Federal Perkins, state loans, college/university loans from institutional funds, Alternative Loans. *Student Employment:* Federal Work-Study Program available. Institutional employment available. Off-campus job opportunities are good. **Financial Aid Statistics:** 31% freshmen, 32% undergrads receive need-based scholarship or grant aid. 16% freshmen, 10% undergrads receive non-need-based scholarship or grant aid. 12% freshmen, 17% undergrads receive need-based self-help aid. 2% freshmen, 2% undergrads receive athletic scholarships. 63% freshmen, 58% undergrads receive any aid. **Criteria for awarding institutional aid:** *Non-need-based:* Academics, alumni affiliation, art, athletics, leadership, music/drama, religious affiliation, state/district residency.

THE UNIVERSITY OF NORTH CAROLINA AT CHARLOTTE

9201 University City Boulevard, Charlotte, NC 28223-0001
Phone: 704-687-2213 **Financial Aid Phone:** 704-687-2461
E-mail: unccadm@uncc.edu **CEEB Code:** 5105
Fax: 704-687-6483 **Website:** www.uncc.edu **ACT Code:** 3163

This public school was founded in 1946. It has a 1000-acre campus.

RATINGS

Admissions Selectivity Rating: 77   **Fire Safety Rating:** 60*   **Green Rating:** 76

STUDENTS AND FACULTY

Enrollment: 17,531. **Student Body:** 52% female, 48% male, 9% out-of-state, 2% international (92 countries represented). Asian 5%, African American 14%, Caucasian 75%, Hispanic 4%.
Retention and Graduation: 75% freshmen return for sophomore year. 13% grads go on to further study within 1 year. **Faculty:** Student/faculty ratio 15:1. 945 full-time faculty, 85% hold PhDs, 21% are members of minority groups, 41% are women. 7% of classes are taught by teaching assistants.

ACADEMICS

Degrees: Bachelor's, master's, post-master's certificate. **Classes:** Most classes have 20–29 students. Most lab/discussion sessions have 10–19 students. **Majors with Highest Enrollment:** Finance; psychology. **Special Study Options:** Accelerated program, cooperative education program, cross-registration, distance learning, double major, dual enrollment, English as a Second Language (ESL), honors program, independent study, internships, study abroad, teacher certification program, weekend college, Wilderness Exploration Program. Special programs offered to physically disabled students include note-taking services, reader services, tape recorders, tutors. **Career services:** Career/job search classes, career assessment, internships.

FACILITIES

Housing: Coed dorms, special housing for disabled students, special housing for international students, women's dorms, fraternity/sorority housing, apartments for single students, rooms for students with disabilities limited, apply early. Graduate and older non-traditional student housing and substance free housing available upon request. 95% of campus accessible to physically disabled. **Special Academic Facilities/Equipment:** Urban studies and community service institute, mock court room, applied research center, language lab, 63-acre ecological reserve, botanical and horticultural complex, tropical rainforest conservatory. **Computers:** 10% of classrooms, 10% of dorms, 30% of libraries, 70% of dining areas, 30% of student union, 10% of common outdoor areas have wireless network access. Students can register for classes online. Administrative functions (other than registration) can be performed online.

CAMPUS LIFE

Environment: Metropolis. **Activities:** Choral groups, concert band, dance, drama/theater, jazz band, literary magazine, music ensembles, musical theater, opera, pep band, student government, student newspaper, television station, yearbook, campus ministries. **Organizations:** 222 registered organizations, 25 honor societies, 22 religious organizations. 14 fraternities, 10 sororities. **Athletics (Intercollegiate):** *Men:* Baseball, basketball, cross-country, golf, soccer, tennis, track/field (outdoor). *Women:* Basketball, cross-country, soccer, softball, tennis, track/field (outdoor), volleyball. **On-Campus Highlights:** Bonnie E. Cone University Center, James H. Barnhardt Student Activity Center, J. Murrey Atkins Library, UNCC Botanical Gardens and Greenhouse, Ritazza Coffee Shop, After Hours at the Rathskeller, Robinson Hall Theatre. **Environmental Initiatives:** Recycling, alternative fuel vehicles, Student Green Energy initiative (just starting).

ADMISSIONS

Freshman Academic Profile: Average high school GPA 3.55. 14.66% in top 10% of high school class, 46.91% in top 25% of high school class, 88.71% in top 50% of high school class. SAT Math middle 50% range 480–590. SAT Critical Reading middle 50% range 470–560. SAT Writing middle 50% range 460–550. ACT middle 50% range 19–24. Minimum paper TOEFL 507. Minimum computer TOEFL 180. **Basis for Candidate Selection:** *Very important factors considered include:* Academic GPA, rigor of secondary school record, standardized test scores, *Other factors considered include:* character/personal qualities, extracurricular activities, geographical residence, level of applicant's interest, state residency, talent/ability. **Freshman Admission Requirements:** High school diploma is required and GED is accepted. *Academic units required:* 4 English, 4 mathematics, 3 science, (1 science labs), 2 foreign language, 2 social studies. *Academic units recommended:* 1 foreign language, 1 history. **Freshman Admission Statistics:** 9,911 applied, 75% admitted, 40% enrolled. **Transfer Admission Requirements:** High school transcript, college transcript(s), statement of good standing from prior institution(s). Minimum college GPA of 2.0 required. Lowest grade transferable C. **General Admission Information:** Application fee $50. Regular application deadline 7/1. Notification on a rolling basis, beginning on or about 11/1. Nonfall registration accepted. Credit and/or placement offered for CEEB Advanced Placement tests.

COSTS AND FINANCIAL AID

Annual in-state tuition $2,461. Annual out-of-state tuition $12,873. Room and board $6,034. Required fees $1,692. Average book expense $1,200. **Required Forms and Deadlines:** FAFSA. Priority financial aid filing date 4/1. **Notification of Awards:** Applicants will be notified of awards on a rolling basis beginning 3/15. **Types of Aid:** *Need-based scholarships/grants:* Federal Pell, SEOG, state scholarships/grants, private scholarships, the school's own gift aid. *Loans:* FFEL Subsidized Stafford, FFEL Unsubsidized Stafford, FFEL PLUS, Federal Perkins, college/university loans from institutional funds. *Student Employment:* Highest amount earned per year from on-campus jobs $2,000. Off-campus job opportunities are good. **Financial Aid Statistics:** 37% freshmen, 37% undergrads receive need-based scholarship or grant aid. 9% freshmen, 5% undergrads receive non-need-based scholarship or grant aid. 35% freshmen, 38% undergrads receive need-based self-help aid. 1% freshmen, 1% undergrads receive athletic scholarships. 59% freshmen, 62% undergrads receive any aid. 56% undergrads borrow to pay for school. Average cumulative indebtedness $18,402. **Criteria for awarding institutional aid:** *Non-need-based:* Academics, athletics, leadership, music/drama.

THE UNIVERSITY OF NORTH CAROLINA AT GREENSBORO

1400 Spring Garden Street, Greensboro, NC 27402-6170
Phone: 336-334-5243 **Financial Aid Phone:** 336-334-5702
E-mail: admissions@uncg.edu **CEEB Code:** 5913
Fax: 336-334-4180 **Website:** www.uncg.edu **ACT Code:** 3166

This public school was founded in 1891. It has a 357-acre campus.

RATINGS

Admissions Selectivity Rating: 82   **Fire Safety Rating:** 67   **Green Rating:** 60*

STUDENTS AND FACULTY

Enrollment: 14,275. **Student Body:** 67% female, 33% male, 5.5% out-of-state, 1% international (12 countries represented). Asian 4%, African American 23%, Caucasian 65%, Hispanic 2%.

Retention and Graduation: 77% freshmen return for sophomore year. 28% freshmen graduate within 4 years. **Faculty:** Student/faculty ratio 16.5:1. 788 full-time faculty, 80% hold PhDs, 34% are members of minority groups, 50% are women.

ACADEMICS

Degrees: Bachelor's, master's, post-bachelor's certificate, post-master's certificate. **Classes:** Most classes have 20–29 students. Most lab/discussion sessions have 20–29 students. **Majors with Highest Enrollment:** Biology/biological sciences; business administration and management; nursing/registered nurse (RN, ASN, BSN, MSN). **Special Study Options:** Accelerated program, cross-registration, distance learning, double major, dual enrollment, honors program, independent study, internships, study abroad, teacher certification program, Evening University. **Combined degree programs:** BA/MA, accounting, mathematics, chem, various BA and MBA. Special programs offered to physically disabled students include note-taking services, reader services, tape recorders, tutors. **Career services:** Alumni services, career/job search classes, career assessment, internships.

FACILITIES

Housing: Coed dorms, special housing for international students, women's dorms, apartments for single students. **Special Academic Facilities/Equipment:** 42-acre recreational site, art gallery, 45,000-square-foot Student Center, New Music Building, New Science Building. **Computers:** 90% of dorms, 35% of libraries, have wireless network access. Students can register for classes online. Administrative functions (other than registration) can be performed online.

CAMPUS LIFE

Environment: City. **Activities:** Choral groups, concert band, dance, drama/theater, jazz band, literary magazine, music ensembles, musical theater, opera, pep band, radio station, student government, student newspaper, student-run film society, symphony orchestra, international student organization. **Organizations:** 200 registered organizations, 23 honor societies, 13 religious organizations. 11 fraternities, 11 sororities. **Athletics (Intercollegiate):** *Men:* Baseball, basketball, cross-country, golf, soccer, tennis, wrestling. *Women:* Basketball, cross-country, golf, soccer, softball, tennis, volleyball. **On-Campus Highlights:** Elliott University Center, Student Rec Center, Weatherspoon Art Museum, Peabody Park, UNCG Theatre.

ADMISSIONS

Freshman Academic Profile: Average high school GPA 3.58. 13.74% in top 10% of high school class, 43.09% in top 25% of high school class, 85.7% in top 50% of high school class. 95% from public high schools. SAT Math middle 50% range 460–570. SAT Critical Reading middle 50% range 460–560. SAT Writing middle 50% range 450–540. Minimum paper TOEFL 550. Minimum computer TOEFL 213. Minimum web-based TOEFL 79. **Basis for Candidate Selection:** *Very important factors considered include:* Academic GPA, rigor of secondary school record. *Important factors considered include:* Standardized test scores. *Other factors considered include:* Recommendation(s). **Freshman Admission Requirements:** High school diploma is required and GED is not accepted. *Academic units required:* 4 English, 4 mathematics, 3 science, (1 science labs), 2 foreign language, 2 social studies. **Freshman Admission Statistics:** 9,104 applied, 73% admitted, 38% enrolled. **Transfer Admission Requirements:** High school transcript, college transcript(s), standardized test scores, statement of good standing from prior institution(s). Minimum college GPA of 2.0 required. Lowest grade transferable 2. **General Admission Information:** Application fee $45. Regular application deadline 3/1. Notification on a rolling basis, beginning on or about 12/15. Nonfall registration accepted. Admission may be deferred for a maximum of 1 semester. Credit and/or placement offered for CEEB Advanced Placement tests.

COSTS AND FINANCIAL AID

Annual in-state tuition $2,590. Annual out-of-state tuition $14,351. Room and board $6,506. Required fees $1,644. Average book expense $1,282. **Required Forms and Deadlines:** FAFSA. Priority financial aid filing date 3/1. **Notification of Awards:** Applicants will be notified of awards on a rolling basis beginning 3/15. **Types of Aid:** *Need-based scholarships/grants:* Federal Pell, SEOG, state scholarships/grants, private scholarships, the school's own gift aid. *Loans:* Direct Subsidized Stafford, Direct Unsubsidized Stafford, Direct PLUS, FFEL Subsidized Stafford, FFEL Unsubsidized Stafford, FFEL PLUS, Federal Perkins, college/university loans from institutional funds. *Student Employment:* Federal Work-Study Program available. Institutional employment available. Off-campus job opportunities are good. **Financial Aid Statistics:** 40% freshmen, 40% undergrads receive need-based scholarship or grant aid. 56% freshmen, 52% undergrads receive non-need-based scholarship or grant aid. 37% freshmen, 44% undergrads receive need-based self-help aid. 1% freshmen, 1% undergrads receive athletic scholarships. 77% freshmen, 71% undergrads receive any aid. 67% undergrads borrow to pay for school. Average cumulative indebtedness $18,604. **Criteria for awarding institutional aid:** *Non-need-based:* Academics, alumni affiliation, art, athletics, music/drama, state/district residency.

THE UNIVERSITY OF NORTH CAROLINA AT PEMBROKE

One University Drive, P.O. Box 1510, Pembroke, NC 28372
Phone: 910-521-6262 **Financial Aid Phone:** 910-521-6366
E-mail: admissions@uncp.edu **CEEB Code:** 5534
Fax: 910-521-6497 **Website:** www.uncp.edu **ACT Code:** 3138

This public school was founded in 1887. It has a 161-acre campus.

RATINGS

Admissions Selectivity Rating: 70   **Fire Safety Rating:** 60*   **Green Rating:** 72

STUDENTS AND FACULTY

Enrollment: 5,631. **Student Body:** 61% female, 39% male, 6% out-of-state, 1% international (19 countries represented). Asian 1%, African American 25%, Caucasian 33%, Hispanic 4%, Native American 12%.
Retention and Graduation: 23% freshmen graduate within 4 years. **Faculty:** Student/faculty ratio 15:1. 323 full-time faculty, 67% hold PhDs, 24% are members of minority groups, 46% are women.

ACADEMICS

Degrees: Bachelor's, certificate, master's. **Classes:** Most classes have 20–29 students. Most lab/discussion sessions have fewer than 10 students. **Majors with Highest Enrollment:** Biology/biological sciences; business administration and management; elementary education and teaching. **Special Study Options:** Accelerated program, cooperative education program, cross-registration, distance learning, double major, dual enrollment, English as a Second Language (ESL), exchange student program (domestic), external degree program, honors program, independent study, internships, study abroad, teacher certification program. **Honors programs:** The Esther G. Maynor Honors College began in 2001 to attract top scholars to UNCP, and provide an environment that stimulates academic and personal growth. **Combined degree programs:** BA/MA Special programs offered to physically disabled students include note-taking services, reader services, tape recorders, tutors. **Career services:** Alumni network, alumni services, career/job search classes, career assessment, internships. **Career services highlights include:** We are very proud of the opportunities for experiential learning/internships that we offer. This is something we believe is very important and we encourage students to seek out these opportunities.

FACILITIES

Housing: Coed dorms, special housing for disabled students, men's dorms, women's dorms, apartments for single students. 99% of campus accessible to physically disabled. **Special Academic Facilities/Equipment:** Native American Resources Center and Museum. **Computers:** 100% of classrooms, 50% of dorms, 100% of libraries, 100% of dining areas, 100% of student union, 30% of common outdoor areas have wireless network access. Students can register for classes online. Administrative functions (other than registration) can be performed online. Undergraduates are required to own a computer.

CAMPUS LIFE

Environment: Rural. **Activities:** Choral groups, concert band, dance, drama/theater, jazz band, literary magazine, marching band, music ensembles, musical theater, pep band, student government, student newspaper, student-run film society, television station, yearbook, campus ministries, international student organization, Model UN. **Organizations:** 70 registered organizations, 11 honor societies, 5 religious organizations. 10 fraternities, 11 sororities. **Athletics (Intercollegiate):** *Men:* Baseball, basketball, cheerleading, cross-country, football, golf, soccer, track/field (outdoor), wrestling. *Women:* Basketball, cheerleading, cross-country, golf, soccer, softball, tennis, track/field (outdoor), volleyball. **On-Campus Highlights:** Newly renovated athletic facility, Native American Resource Center/Museum, Givens Performing Arts Center, Newly renovated Bookstore, Higher Ground Ropes Course. **Environmental Initiatives:** Planning & Construction Dept. mandates all new facilities to be LEED certified. Campus wide single-stream recycling program. Housekeeping staff utilize green cleaning products.

ADMISSIONS

Freshman Academic Profile: Average high school GPA 3.1. 9% in top 10% of high school class, 31% in top 25% of high school class, 64% in top 50% of high school class. 99% from public high schools. SAT Math middle 50% range 420–510. SAT Critical Reading middle 50% range 410–490. SAT Writing middle 50% range 390–480. ACT middle 50% range 16–19. Minimum paper TOEFL 500. Minimum computer TOEFL 173. Minimum web-based TOEFL 61. **Basis for Candidate Selection:** *Very important factors considered include:* Class rank, academic GPA, rigor of secondary school record, standardized test scores. *Other factors considered include:* Application essay, recommendation(s), character/personal qualities, interview, talent/ability. **Freshman Admission Requirements:** High school diploma is required and GED is accepted. *Academic* *units required:* 4 English, 4 mathematics, 3 science, (1 science labs), 2 foreign language, 1 social studies, 1 history. **Freshman Admission Statistics:** 3,031 applied, 79% admitted, 51% enrolled. **Transfer Admission Requirements:** High school transcript, college transcript(s), statement of good standing from prior institution(s). Minimum college GPA of 2.0 required. Lowest grade transferable C. **General Admission Information:** Application fee $40. Regular application deadline 7/31. Notification on a rolling basis, beginning on or about 9/15. Nonfall registration accepted. Admission may be deferred for a maximum of 1 year. Credit offered for CEEB Advanced Placement tests.

COSTS AND FINANCIAL AID

Annual in-state tuition $2,060. Annual out-of-state tuition $11,267. Room and board $6,430. Required fees $1,676. Average book expense $1,184. **Required Forms and Deadlines:** FAFSA. Priority financial aid filing date 3/15. **Notification of Awards:** Applicants will be notified of awards on a rolling basis beginning 4/15. **Types of Aid:** *Need-based scholarships/grants:* Federal Pell, SEOG, state scholarships/grants, private scholarships, the school's own gift aid. *Loans:* FFEL Subsidized Stafford, FFEL Unsubsidized Stafford, FFEL PLUS, Federal Perkins, college/university loans from institutional funds. *Student Employment:* Federal Work-Study Program available. Off-campus job opportunities are fair. **Financial Aid Statistics:** 64% freshmen, 65% undergrads receive need-based scholarship or grant aid. 9% freshmen, 5% undergrads receive non-need-based scholarship or grant aid. 44% freshmen, 55% undergrads receive need-based self-help aid. 75% freshmen, 73% undergrads receive any aid. **Criteria for awarding institutional aid:** *Non-need-based:* Academics, alumni affiliation, art, athletics, music/drama, state/district residency.

THE UNIVERSITY OF NORTH CAROLINA AT WILMINGTON

601 South College Rd, Wilmington, NC 28403-5904
Phone: 910-962-3243 **Financial Aid Phone:** 910-962-3177
E-mail: admissions@uncw.edu **CEEB Code:** 5907
Fax: 910-962-3038 **Website:** www.uncw.edu **ACT Code:** 3174

This public school was founded in 1947. It has a 656-acre campus.

RATINGS

Admissions Selectivity Rating: 87   **Fire Safety Rating:** 89   **Green Rating:** 79

STUDENTS AND FACULTY

Enrollment: 10,761. **Student Body:** 58% female, 42% male, 14% out-of-state, international (44 countries represented). Asian 2%, African American 4%, Caucasian 84%, Hispanic 4%, Native American 1%.
Retention and Graduation: 44% freshmen graduate within 4 years. **Faculty:** Student/faculty ratio 17:1. 587 full-time faculty, 86% hold PhDs, 13% are members of minority groups, 43% are women.

ACADEMICS

Degrees: Bachelor's, certificate, master's, post-bachelor's certificate, post-master's certificate. **Classes:** Most classes have 20–29 students. Most lab/discussion sessions have 20–29 students. **Majors with Highest Enrollment:** Business/managerial economics; elementary education and teaching; psychology. **Special Study Options:** Accelerated program, cooperative education program, cross-registration, distance learning, double major, dual enrollment, English as a Second Language (ESL), exchange student program (domestic), honors program, independent study, internships, study abroad, teacher certification program, 2+2 Pre-Engineering Program. **Honors programs:** The HONORS SCHOLARS PROGRAM at UNCW is designed to offer academically talented students challenging and exciting experiences both in and out of the classroom. A student may begin with general honors in the first two years, and then go on to departmental honors in their major. In their freshman and sophomore years, students take special interdisciplinary honors seminars and honors sections of basic studies courses. Honors classes are small—generally not over 20 students—to encourage discussion and faculty-student interaction. In any given semester, an honors scholar will enroll in both honors and other university classes, enhancing his or her experiences in many academic areas with a wide variety of students. In their junior and senior years, honors students will propose and carry out an honors "capstone" experience—a scholarly project in the student's major. This involves independent work and close interaction with a faculty sponsor. Many of these have led to publication and presentations at professional conferences. Overall, the program encourages curiosity, critical thinking, and independent work skills by offering exciting academic and cultural activities as well as the opportunity for close working and social relationships with the faculty. Special programs offered to physically disabled students include note-taking services, reader services, tape recorders, tutors. **Career services:** Alumni network,

alumni services, career assessment, internships, regional alumni. **Career services highlights include:** The UNCW Virtual Career Center is nationally recognized for its comprehensive web site.

FACILITIES

Housing: Coed dorms, special housing for international students, women's dorms, apartments for single students, wellness housing, theme housing 95% of campus accessible to physically disabled. **Special Academic Facilities/Equipment:** Upperman African American Cultural Arts Center, N.C. Teachers Legacy Hall, Ev-Henwood Nature Preserve, Center for Marine Science at Myrtle Grove, Almkuist-Nixon Sports Medicine Building, Museum of World Cultures, Claude Howell Gallery, UNCW Library Archives and Special Collections. **Computers:** 100% of classrooms, 100% of dorms, 100% of libraries, 100% of dining areas, 100% of student union, 50% of common outdoor areas have wireless network access. Students can register for classes online. Administrative functions (other than registration) can be performed online.

CAMPUS LIFE

Environment: City. **Activities:** Choral groups, concert band, dance, drama/theater, jazz band, literary magazine, music ensembles, pep band, radio station, student government, student newspaper, student-run film society, symphony orchestra, television station, campus ministries, international student organization, Model UN. **Organizations:** 173 registered organizations, 8 honor societies, 14 religious organizations. 11 fraternities, 11 sororities. **Athletics (Intercollegiate):** *Men:* Baseball, basketball, cheerleading, cross-country, diving, golf, soccer, swimming, tennis, track/field (outdoor). *Women:* Basketball, cheerleading, cross-country, diving, golf, soccer, softball, swimming, tennis, track/field (outdoor), volleyball. **On-Campus Highlights:** Fisher Student Center, William Randall Library, UNCW Student Recreation Center, Trask Coliseum, Cultural Arts Building. **Environmental Initiatives:** Bio diesel fuel program LEED certification for new housing and parking development. Current residence halls going green with students turning in regular lightbulbs for energy efficient ones and conserving water. Dining services—using biopak containers, going trayless, offering free trade coffee, using reusable clean cloths.

ADMISSIONS

Freshman Academic Profile: Average high school GPA 3.78. 24% in top 10% of high school class, 62% in top 25% of high school class, 99% in top 50% of high school class. SAT Math middle 50% range 550–630. SAT Critical Reading middle 50% range 530–620. SAT Writing middle 50% range 520–610. ACT middle 50% range 22–27. Minimum paper TOEFL 525. Minimum computer TOEFL 197. Minimum web-based TOEFL 71. **Basis for Candidate Selection:** *Very important factors considered include:* Application essay, academic GPA, recommendation(s), rigor of secondary school record, standardized test scores. *Important factors considered include:* Class rank. *Other factors considered include:* Alumni/ae relation, character/personal qualities, extracurricular activities, first generation, geographical residence, level of applicant's interest, racial/ethnic status, state residency, talent/ability, volunteer work, work experience. **Freshman Admission Requirements:** High school diploma is required and GED is accepted. *Academic units required:* 4 English, 4 mathematics, 3 science, (1 science labs), 2 foreign language, 2 social studies, 1 history. **Freshman Admission Statistics:** 9,283 applied, 58% admitted, 36% enrolled. **Transfer Admission Requirements:** High school transcript, college transcript(s), essay or personal statement, minimum college GPA of 2.5 required. Lowest grade transferable C. **General Admission Information:** Application fee $60. Regular application deadline 2/1. Regular notification 4/1. Nonfall registration accepted. Admission may be deferred for a maximum of 1 year. Credit and/or placement offered for CEEB Advanced Placement tests.

COSTS AND FINANCIAL AID

Annual in-state tuition $2,565. Annual out-of-state tuition $13,447. Room and board $7,798. Required fees $2,308. Average book expense $934. **Required Forms and Deadlines:** FAFSA. Priority financial aid filing date 4/1. **Notification of Awards:** Applicants will be notified of awards on a rolling basis beginning 4/1. **Types of Aid:** *Need-based scholarships/grants:* Federal Pell, SEOG, state scholarships/grants, private scholarships, the school's own gift aid. *Loans:* Direct Subsidized Stafford, Direct Unsubsidized Stafford, Direct PLUS, FFEL Subsidized Stafford, FFEL Unsubsidized Stafford, FFEL PLUS, Federal Perkins, state loans, college/university loans from institutional funds. *Student Employment:* Federal Work-Study Program available. Institutional employment available. Off-campus job opportunities are good. **Financial Aid Statistics:** 38% freshmen, 39% undergrads receive need-based scholarship or grant aid. 19% freshmen, 16% undergrads receive non-need-based scholarship or grant aid. 26% freshmen, 31% undergrads receive need-based self-help aid. 2% freshmen, 2% undergrads receive athletic scholarships. 43% freshmen, 43% undergrads receive any aid. 54% undergrads borrow to pay for school. Average cumulative indebtedness $16,115. **Criteria for awarding institutional aid:** *Non-need-based:* Academics, alumni affiliation, art, athletics, leadership, music/drama, state/district residency.

UNIVERSITY OF NORTH DAKOTA

205 Twamley Hall 264 Centennial Drive St, Grand Forks, ND 58202-8357
Phone: 800-225-5863 **Financial Aid Phone:** 701-777-3121
E-mail: enrollmentservices@mail.und.edu **CEEB Code:** 6878
Fax: 701-777-3367 **Website:** www.und.edu **ACT Code:** 3218

This public school was founded in 1883. It has a 549-acre campus.

RATINGS
Admissions Selectivity Rating: 77   **Fire Safety Rating:** 78   **Green Rating:** 85

STUDENTS AND FACULTY
Enrollment: 10,440. **Student Body:** 45% female, 55% male, 49% out-of-state, 5% international (76 countries represented). Asian 1%, African American 1%, Caucasian 85%, Hispanic 1%, Native American 3%.
Retention and Graduation: 77% freshmen return for sophomore year. 21% grads go on to further study within 1 year. 12% grads pursue arts and sciences degrees. 1% grads pursue law degrees. 1% grads pursue business degrees. 2% grads pursue medical degrees. **Faculty:** Student/faculty ratio 18:1. 594 full-time faculty, 80% hold PhDs, 12% are members of minority groups, 39% are women.

ACADEMICS
Degrees: Bachelor's, certificate, diploma, master's, post-bachelor's certificate. **Classes:** Most classes have 20–29 students. Most lab/discussion sessions have fewer than 10 students. **Majors with Highest Enrollment:** airline/commercial/professional pilot and flight crew; nursing/registered nurse (RN, ASN, BSN, MSN); psychology. **Special Study Options:** Accelerated program, cooperative education program, cross-registration, distance learning, double major, dual enrollment, English as a Second Language (ESL), exchange student program (domestic), external degree program, honors program, independent study, internships, liberal arts/career combination, student-designed major, study abroad, teacher certification program, weekend college. **Honors programs:** Students may participate in the Honors Program throughout their undergraduate career. Students in any college of the University may enroll in the Honors Program. Most students graduate from the Program as "Scholars in the Honors Program" while also fulfilling a major in the Colleges, but the Honors Program also offers the option of creating an individually designed program of study through Honors. This option may result in either a BA or a BS degree earned through the College of Arts and Sciences. **Combined degree programs:** www.und.edu/dept/registrar/catalogs/catalog. Special programs offered to physically disabled students include note-taking services, reader services, tape recorders. **Career services:** Alumni network, alumni services, career/job search classes, career assessment, internships. **Career services highlights include:** Cooperative Learning. Internships. Students work closely with entrepreneur practitioners.

FACILITIES
Housing: Coed dorms, special housing for disabled students, men's dorms, women's dorms, fraternity/sorority housing, apartments for married students, apartments for single students, wellness housing, theme housing 99% of campus accessible to physically disabled. **Special Academic Facilities/Equipment:** Hughes Fine Arts Center, Burtness Theatre, North Dakota Museum of Art, Chester Fritz Auditorium, mining/mineral resources research institute/energy research center, remote sensing institute, aviation facilities, meteorology data center, Ralph Engelstad Arena. **Computers:** 70% of classrooms, 100% of dorms, 100% of libraries, 50% of dining areas, 100% of student union, have wireless network access. Students can register for classes online. Administrative functions (other than registration) can be performed online.

CAMPUS LIFE
Environment: Town. **Activities:** Choral groups, concert band, dance, drama/theater, jazz band, literary magazine, marching band, music ensembles, musical theater, opera, pep band, radio station, student government, student newspaper, student-run film society, symphony orchestra, television station, campus ministries, international student organization. **Organizations:** 230 registered organizations, 42 honor societies, 3 religious organizations. 13 fraternities, 7 sororities. **Athletics (Intercollegiate):** *Men:* Baseball, basketball, cross-country, diving, football, golf, ice hockey, swimming, track/field (outdoor), track/field (indoor). *Women:* Basketball, cross-country, diving, golf, ice hockey, soccer, softball, swimming, tennis, track/field (outdoor), track/field (indoor), volleyball. **On-Campus Highlights:** Engelstad Arena, Memorial Union, Archives Coffee shop, International Centre, North Dakota Museum of Art. **Environmental Initiatives:** Energy conservation programs, Presidential Climate Committment, recycling.

ADMISSIONS
Freshman Academic Profile: Average high school GPA 3.38. 17% in top 10% of high school class, 40% in top 25% of high school class, 74% in top 50% of high school class. 92% from public high schools. ACT middle 50% range 20–25. Minimum paper TOEFL 525. Minimum computer TOEFL 195. **Basis for Candidate Selection:** *Very important factors considered include:* Academic GPA, standardized test scores, *Other factors considered include:* Class rank, rigor of secondary school record. **Freshman Admission Requirements:** High school diploma is required and GED is accepted. *Academic units required:* 4 English, 3 mathematics, 3 science, (3 science labs), 3 social studies. *Academic units recommended:* 1 foreign language. **Freshman Admission Statistics:** 4,111 applied, 73% admitted, 66% enrolled. **Transfer Admission Requirements:** College transcript(s), minimum college GPA of 2.0 required. **General Admission Information:** Application fee $35. Notification on a rolling basis, beginning on or about 9/1. Nonfall registration accepted. Admission may be deferred for a maximum of 1 Semester. Credit and/or placement offered for CEEB Advanced Placement tests.

COSTS AND FINANCIAL AID
Required Forms and Deadlines: FAFSA. Priority financial aid filing date 3/15. **Notification of Awards:** Applicants will be notified of awards on a rolling basis beginning 5/15. **Types of Aid:** *Need-based scholarships/grants:* Federal Pell, SEOG, state scholarships/grants, private scholarships, the school's own gift aid, Federal Nursing Scholarships. *Loans:* FFEL Subsidized Stafford, FFEL Unsubsidized Stafford, FFEL PLUS, Federal Perkins, Federal Nursing, Alternative Commercial Loans. *Student Employment:* Federal Work-Study Program available. Institutional employment available. Highest amount earned per year from on-campus jobs $2,071. Off-campus job opportunities are excellent. **Financial Aid Statistics:** 38% freshmen, 34% undergrads receive need-based scholarship or grant aid. 1% freshmen, 45% freshmen, 46% undergrads receive need-based self-help aid. 4% freshmen, 4% undergrads receive athletic scholarships. 69% freshmen, 77% undergrads receive any aid. 85% undergrads borrow to pay for school. Average cumulative indebtedness $38,804. **Criteria for awarding institutional aid:** *Non-need-based:* Academics, alumni affiliation, art, athletics, job skills, leadership, music/drama, religious affiliation.

UNIVERSITY OF NORTH FLORIDA

1 UNF Drive, Jacksonville, FL 32224-7699
Phone: 904-620-5555 **Financial Aid Phone:** 904-620-2698
E-mail: admissions@unf.edu **CEEB Code:** 9841
Fax: 904-620-2414 **Website:** www.unf.edu **ACT Code:** 5490

This public school was founded in 1965. It has a 1300-acre campus.

RATINGS
Admissions Selectivity Rating: 79   **Fire Safety Rating:** 60*   **Green Rating:** 85

STUDENTS AND FACULTY
Enrollment: 14,216. **Student Body:** 56% female, 44% male, 2.6% out-of-state, 1% international (114 countries represented). Asian 6%, African American 11%, Caucasian 74%, Hispanic 7%.
Retention and Graduation: **Faculty:** Student/faculty ratio 23:1. 495 full-time faculty, 79% hold PhDs, 14% are members of minority groups, 47% are women.

ACADEMICS
Degrees: Associate, bachelor's, master's, post-bachelor's certificate, post-master's certificate, terminal associate, transfer associate. **Classes:** Most classes have 20–29 students. Most lab/discussion sessions have 20–29 students. **Majors with Highest Enrollment:** Business administration and management; mass communication/media studies; psychology. **Special Study Options:** Accelerated program, cooperative education program, distance learning, double major, dual enrollment, English as a Second Language (ESL), exchange student program (domestic), honors program, independent study, internships, student-designed major, study abroad, teacher certification program, weekend college, Learning Communities. **Honors programs:** The Honors Program at the University of North Florida offers talented and ambitious students a unique approach to higher education. Honors Classes are limited to 20 students, combining active and experiential learning in an interdisciplinary setting. The goal is to build a community of learners who have the ability to take their learning outside the classroom and into the real world helping to bridge the gap between education and experience. The honors program is a limited access program and spaces are filled on a first-come-first-serve basis. Special programs offered to physically disabled students include note-taking services, reader services, tape recorders. **Career services:** Alumni services, career/job search classes, internships.

FACILITIES

Housing: Coed dorms, special housing for disabled students, apartments for single students, suite style housing. **Special Academic Facilities/Equipment:** Art gallery, bird sanctuary, Fine Arts Center. **Computers:** 100% of classrooms, 50% of dorms, 100% of libraries, 50% of dining areas, 100% of student union, 100% of common outdoor areas have wireless network access. Students can register for classes online. Administrative functions (other than registration) can be performed online.

CAMPUS LIFE

Environment: Metropolis. **Activities:** Choral groups, concert band, dance, drama/theater, jazz band, literary magazine, music ensembles, pep band, radio station, student government, student newspaper, television station, campus ministries, international student organization. **Organizations:** 140 registered organizations, 8 honor societies, 29 religious organizations. 14 fraternities, 10 sororities. **Athletics (Intercollegiate):** *Men:* Baseball, basketball, cheerleading, cross-country, golf, soccer, tennis, track/field (outdoor), track/field (indoor). *Women:* Basketball, cheerleading, cross-country, diving, soccer, softball, swimming, tennis, track/field (outdoor), track/field (indoor), volleyball. **On-Campus Highlights:** Student Union, Bookstore, Art Gallery, Nature Trails, Campus skate park, Greek Affairs, Earth Music Festival, Athletics NCAA I, Free movies on Campus, Jazz Program (nationally recognized), Division I sports.

ADMISSIONS

Freshman Academic Profile: Average high school GPA 3.49. 22% in top 10% of high school class, 53% in top 25% of high school class, 86% in top 50% of high school class. SAT Math middle 50% range 510–600. SAT Critical Reading middle 50% range 510–610. ACT middle 50% range 21–24. Minimum paper TOEFL 500. Minimum computer TOEFL 173. Minimum web-based TOEFL 61. **Basis for Candidate Selection:** *Very important factors considered include:* Academic GPA, rigor of secondary school record, standardized test scores, *Other factors considered include:* Class rank, application essay, recommendation(s), extracurricular activities, level of applicant's interest, talent/ability, volunteer work, work experience. **Freshman Admission Requirements:** High school diploma is required and GED is accepted. *Academic units required:* 4 English, 3 mathematics, 3 science, (1 science labs), 2 foreign language, 3 social studies, 4 academic electives. **Freshman Admission Statistics:** 10,159 applied, 64% admitted, 34% enrolled. **Transfer Admission Requirements:** College transcript(s), minimum college GPA of 2.0 required. Lowest grade transferable D. **General Admission Information:** Application fee $30. Regular application deadline 6/11. Regular notification 12/11. Notification on a rolling basis, beginning on or about 11/13. Nonfall registration accepted. Admission may be deferred for a maximum of 2 Semesters. Credit offered for CEEB Advanced Placement tests.

COSTS AND FINANCIAL AID

Required Forms and Deadlines: FAFSA, financial aid transcript for transfer students. Priority financial aid filing date 4/1. **Notification of Awards:** Applicants will be notified of awards on a rolling basis beginning 3/15. **Types of Aid:** *Need-based scholarships/grants:* Federal Pell, SEOG, state scholarships/grants, private scholarships, the school's own gift aid, 2-2 Scholarships jointly sponsored with Florida Community College at Jacksonville. *Loans:* FFEL Subsidized Stafford, FFEL Unsubsidized Stafford, FFEL PLUS, Federal Perkins. *Student Employment:* Federal Work-Study Program available. Institutional employment available. Highest amount earned per year from on-campus jobs $3,750. Off-campus job opportunities are good. **Financial Aid Statistics:** 33% freshmen, 29% undergrads receive need-based scholarship or grant aid. 41% freshmen, 24% undergrads receive non-need-based scholarship or grant aid. 20% freshmen, 26% undergrads receive need-based self-help aid. 2% freshmen, 2% undergrads receive athletic scholarships. 89.7% freshmen, 71.9% undergrads receive any aid. 40.87% undergrads borrow to pay for school. Average cumulative indebtedness $15,619. **Criteria for awarding institutional aid:** *Non-need-based:* Academics, athletics, leadership, minority status, music/drama, state/district residency.

UNIVERSITY OF NORTH TEXAS

1155 Union Circle #311277, Denton, TX 76203
Phone: 940-565-2681 **Financial Aid Phone:** 940-565-3901
E-mail: undergrad@unt.edu **CEEB Code:** 6481
Fax: 940-565-2408 **Website:** www.unt.edu **ACT Code:** 4136

This public school was founded in 1890. It has a 850-acre campus.

RATINGS

Admissions Selectivity Rating: 74   **Fire Safety Rating:** 86   **Green Rating:** 95

STUDENTS AND FACULTY

Enrollment: 28,474. **Student Body:** 54% female, 46% male, 4% out-of-state, 2% international (122 countries represented). Asian 6%, African American 14%, Caucasian 62%, Hispanic 14%, Native American 1%.
Retention and Graduation: 76% freshmen return for sophomore year. 19% freshmen graduate within 4 years. **Faculty:** Student/faculty ratio 24:1. 1035 full-time faculty, 89% hold PhDs, 21% are members of minority groups, 38% are women.

ACADEMICS

Degrees: Bachelor's, master's, post-bachelor's certificate. **Classes:** Most classes have 20–29 students. Most lab/discussion sessions have 20–29 students. **Majors with Highest Enrollment:** criminal justice/safety studies; education; sociology. **Special Study Options:** Accelerated program, cooperative education program, cross-registration, distance learning, double major, dual enrollment, English as a Second Language (ESL), honors program, independent study, internships, study abroad, teacher certification program, weekend college. **Honors programs:** University of North Texas Honors College. **Combined degree programs:** BA/MD, BA/JD, BA/MA, BA/DDS, BA/MEng. Special programs offered to physically disabled students include note-taking services, reader services, tape recorders, tutors. **Career services:** Alumni network, alumni services, career/job search classes, career assessment, internships, regional alumni. **Career services highlights include:** We offer our Alumni Services to our alumni at no cost (very important in these times especially), and have developed some very strong programs for the alumni to help them in their tranisition.

FACILITIES

Housing: Coed dorms, special housing for disabled students, women's dorms, fraternity/sorority housing, apartments for married students, cooperative housing, apartments for single students, theme housing. 90% of campus accessible to physically disabled. **Special Academic Facilities/Equipment:** Laser, observatory, accelerators, recreational facility, music facilities, environmental sciences, planetarium, art galleries **Computers:** 75% of classrooms, 30% of dorms, 100% of libraries, 100% of dining areas, 100% of student union, 10% of common outdoor areas have wireless network access. Students can register for classes online. Administrative functions (other than registration) can be performed online.

CAMPUS LIFE

Environment: City. **Activities:** Choral groups, concert band, dance, drama/theater, jazz band, literary magazine, marching band, music ensembles, musical theater, opera, pep band, radio station, student government, student newspaper, student-run film society, symphony orchestra, television station, campus ministries, international student organization. **Organizations:** 330 registered organizations, 40 honor societies, 34 religious organizations. 23 fraternities, 16 sororities. **Athletics (Intercollegiate):** *Men:* Basketball, cross-country, football, golf, softball, track/field (indoor). *Women:* Basketball, cross-country, diving, golf, soccer, softball, swimming, tennis, track/field (indoor), volleyball. **On-Campus Highlights:** University Union, Student Recreation Center, Library Mall and pavilion, Murchison Performing Arts Center, Eagle Student Services Center, Chestnut Hall. **Environmental Initiatives:** Recycling waste materials (over 600 tons recycled last year). Tree advisory committee. Large green spaces on campus. Monitoring conservation of electrical consumption and water usage. Developing Climate Action Plan

ADMISSIONS

Freshman Academic Profile: 21% in top 10% of high school class, 51% in top 25% of high school class, 89% in top 50% of high school class. 95% from public high schools. SAT Math middle 50% range 490–600. SAT Critical Reading middle 50% range 480–590. SAT Writing middle 50% range 460–570. ACT middle 50% range 20–25. Minimum paper TOEFL 550. Minimum computer TOEFL 213. Minimum web-based TOEFL 79. **Basis for Candidate Selection:** *Very important factors considered include:* Class rank, academic GPA, standardized test scores. *Important factors considered include:* Application essay, recommendation(s), rigor of secondary school record. *Other factors considered include:* character/personal qualities, extracurricular activities, first generation, geographical residence, level of applicant's interest, talent/ability, volunteer work, work experience. **Freshman Admission Requirements:** High school diploma is required and GED is accepted. *Academic units required:* 4 English, 3 mathematics, 3 science, (3 science labs), 2 foreign language, 2 social studies, 2 history, 3 academic electives. **Freshman Admission Statistics:** 12,883 applied, 64% admitted, 40% enrolled. **Transfer Admission Requirements:** College transcript(s), statement of good standing from prior institution(s). Minimum college GPA of 2.5 required. Lowest grade transferable D. **General Admission Information:** Application fee $40. Regular application deadline 8/1. Notification on a rolling basis, beginning on or about 10/15. Nonfall registration accepted. Credit and/or placement offered for CEEB Advanced Placement tests.

COSTS AND FINANCIAL AID

Annual in-state tuition $5,360. Annual out-of-state tuition $13,670. Room and board $6,534. Required fees $1,941. Average book expense $1,250. **Required Forms and Deadlines:** FAFSA. Priority financial aid filing date 4/15. **No-**

tification of Awards: Applicants will be notified of awards on a rolling basis beginning 4/1. **Types of Aid:** *Need-based scholarships/grants:* Federal Pell, SEOG, state scholarships/grants, private scholarships, the school's own gift aid. *Loans:* Direct Subsidized Stafford, Direct Unsubsidized Stafford, Direct PLUS, Federal Perkins, state loans *Student Employment:* Federal Work-Study Program available. Institutional employment available. Highest amount earned per year from on-campus jobs $8,726. Off-campus job opportunities are excellent. **Financial Aid Statistics:** 46% freshmen, 39% undergrads receive need-based scholarship or grant aid. 22% freshmen, 11% undergrads receive non-need-based scholarship or grant aid. 43% freshmen, 43% undergrads receive need-based self-help aid. 1% freshmen, 1% undergrads receive athletic scholarships. 81% freshmen, 66% undergrads receive any aid. **Criteria for awarding institutional aid:** *Non-need-based:* Academics.

UNIVERSITY OF NORTHERN COLORADO

UNC Admissions Office, Campus Box 10, Greeley, CO 80639
Phone: 970-351-2881 **Financial Aid Phone:** 970-351-2502
E-mail: admissions.help@unco.edu **CEEB Code:** 4074
Fax: 970-351-2984 **Website:** www.unco.edu **ACT Code:** 0502

This public school was founded in 1890. It has a 243-acre campus.

RATINGS
Admissions Selectivity Rating: 71   **Fire Safety Rating:** 90   **Green Rating:** 73

STUDENTS AND FACULTY
Enrollment: 9,690. **Student Body:** 61% female, 39% male, 12% out-of-state, 1% international (49 countries represented). Asian 3%, African American 3%, Caucasian 78%, Hispanic 9%, Native American 1%.
Retention and Graduation: 3% grads go on to further study within 1 year. 3.1% grads pursue arts and sciences degrees. 1.3% grads pursue business degrees. **Faculty:** Student/faculty ratio 23:1. 371 full-time faculty, 9% are members of minority groups, 49% are women. 14% of classes are taught by teaching assistants.

ACADEMICS
Degrees: Bachelor's, master's, post-master's certificate. **Classes:** Most classes have 20–29 students. Most lab/discussion sessions have 20–29 students. **Majors with Highest Enrollment:** Business administration and management; kinesiology and exercise science; multi-/interdisciplinary studies, other. **Special Study Options:** Cooperative education program, cross-registration, distance learning, double major, English as a Second Language (ESL), exchange student program (domestic), external degree program, honors program, independent study, internships, student-designed major, study abroad, teacher certification program. **Honors programs:** The University Honors Program is designed to offer exceptional students both the resources of a comprehensive university and the individual attention traditionally associated with a small college. It asks that they be alive to the life of the mind and pushes them to raise the expectations they have for themselves and their education. It seeks to involve them in learning, heighten their critical awareness, and encourage their independent thinking and research. Special programs offered to physically disabled students include note-taking services, reader services, tape recorders, tutors. **Career services:** Alumni services, career/job search classes, career assessment, internships.

FACILITIES
Housing: Coed dorms, special housing for disabled students, women's dorms, fraternity/sorority housing, apartments for married students, apartments for single students. 100% of campus accessible to physically disabled. **Special Academic Facilities/Equipment:** Art Museum, Music Library, James A. Michener Collection. **Computers:** 100% of classrooms, 100% of dorms, 100% of libraries, 100% of dining areas, 100% of student union, 5% of common outdoor areas have wireless network access. Students can register for classes online. Administrative functions (other than registration) can be performed online.

CAMPUS LIFE
Environment: City. **Activities:** Choral groups, concert band, dance, drama/theater, jazz band, literary magazine, marching band, music ensembles, musical theater, opera, pep band, radio station, student government, student newspaper, student-run film society, symphony orchestra, television station, campus ministries, international student organization. **Organizations:** 137 registered organizations, 9 honor societies, 18 religious organizations. 9 fraternities, 8 sororities. **Athletics (Intercollegiate):** *Men:* Baseball, basketball, football, golf, tennis, track/field (outdoor), wrestling. *Women:* Basketball, cross-country, diving, golf, soccer, softball, swimming, tennis, track/field (outdoor), volleyball. **On-Campus Highlights:** University Center, James Michener Library, Recreation Center, Cultural Centers. **Environmental Initiatives:** Performance contracting, recycling, non-potable water usage for irrigation.

ADMISSIONS
Freshman Academic Profile: Average high school GPA 3.19. 12% in top 10% of high school class, 33% in top 25% of high school class, 67% in top 50% of high school class. 92% from public high schools. SAT Math middle 50% range 470–590. SAT Critical Reading middle 50% range 460–580. SAT Writing middle 50% range 460–560. ACT middle 50% range 20–25. Minimum paper TOEFL 520. Minimum computer TOEFL 190. **Basis for Candidate Selection:** *Very important factors considered include:* Class rank, academic GPA, standardized test scores. *Important factors considered include:* Recommendation(s). *Other factors considered include:* Rigor of secondary school record, character/personal qualities, extracurricular activities, interview, racial/ethnic status, state residency, talent/ability, work experience. **Freshman Admission Requirements:** High school diploma is required and GED is accepted. *Academic units required:* 4 English, 3 mathematics, 3 science, (2 science labs), 3 social studies, 2 academic electives. **Freshman Admission Statistics:** 5,609 applied, 93% admitted, 40% enrolled. **Transfer Admission Requirements:** College transcript(s), statement of good standing from prior institution(s). Minimum college GPA of 2.4 required. Lowest grade transferable C. **General Admission Information:** Application fee $45. Nonfall registration accepted. Admission may be deferred for a maximum of 3 semesters. Credit offered for CEEB Advanced Placement tests.

COSTS AND FINANCIAL AID
Annual in-state tuition $3,942. Annual out-of-state tuition $13,344. Room and board $7,784. Required fees $738. Average book expense $1,200. **Required Forms and Deadlines:** FAFSA. Priority financial aid filing date 3/1. **Notification of Awards:** Applicants will be notified of awards on a rolling basis beginning 4/15. **Types of Aid:** *Need-based scholarships/grants:* Federal Pell, SEOG, state scholarships/grants, private scholarships, the school's own gift aid. *Loans:* FFEL Subsidized Stafford, FFEL Unsubsidized Stafford, FFEL PLUS, Federal Perkins, college/university loans from institutional funds. *Student Employment:* Federal Work-Study Program available. Institutional employment available. Highest amount earned per year from on-campus jobs $4,726. Off-campus job opportunities are fair. **Financial Aid Statistics:** 35% freshmen, 34% undergrads receive need-based scholarship or grant aid. 23% freshmen, 15% undergrads receive non-need-based scholarship or grant aid. 32% freshmen, 34% undergrads receive need-based self-help aid. 1% undergrads receive athletic scholarships. 81% freshmen, 73.5% undergrads receive any aid. **Criteria for awarding institutional aid:** *Non-need-based:* Academics, athletics, music/drama.

UNIVERSITY OF NORTHERN IOWA

1227 West 27th Street, Cedar Falls, IA 50614-0018
Phone: 319-273-2281 **Financial Aid Phone:** 319-273-2701
E-mail: admissions@uni.edu **CEEB Code:** 6307
Fax: 319-273-2885 **Website:** www.uni.edu **ACT Code:** 1322

This public school was founded in 1876. It has a 910-acre campus.

RATINGS
Admissions Selectivity Rating: 75   **Fire Safety Rating:** 70   **Green Rating:** 92

STUDENTS AND FACULTY
Enrollment: 11,061. **Student Body:** 56% female, 44% male, 4.9% out-of-state, 2% international (68 countries represented). Asian 1%, African American 3%, Caucasian 90%, Hispanic 2%.
Retention and Graduation: 35% freshmen graduate within 4 years. 15% grads go on to further study within 1 year. 9% grads pursue arts and sciences degrees. 1% grads pursue law degrees. 1% grads pursue business degrees. 1% grads pursue medical degrees. **Faculty:** Student/faculty ratio 17:1. 632 full-time faculty, 72% hold PhDs, 13% are members of minority groups, 45% are women. 2% of classes are taught by teaching assistants.

ACADEMICS
Degrees: Bachelor's, doctoral, master's. **Classes:** Most classes have 20–29 students. Most lab/discussion sessions have 10–19 students. **Majors with Highest Enrollment:** Business administration and management; elementary education and teaching; marketing/marketing management. **Special Study Options:** Accelerated program, cooperative education program, distance learning, double major, dual enrollment, English as a Second Language (ESL), exchange student program (domestic), external degree program, honors program, independent study, internships, liberal arts/career combination, student-designed major, study abroad, teacher certification program, weekend college, combined bachelor's/master's degree programs (BA/MA, BS/MS, BA/MS); undergraduate Dual Degree Majors; 2+2 Programs; undergraduate and graduate certificates. **Honors programs:** University Honors Program—includes all 5 colleges and is open

to all majors www.uni.edu/honors. **Combined degree programs:** BA/MA, BA/MS, BA/MAcc, biology, chemistry, technology. Special programs offered to physically disabled students include note-taking services, reader services, tape recorders, tutors. **Career services:** Alumni services, career/job search classes, career assessment, internships. **Career services highlights include:** UNI has had over 10,000 students conduct internships for credit over the past 30 years, with thousands more participating in an internship for no credit.

FACILITIES

Housing: Coed dorms, men's dorms, women's dorms, fraternity/sorority housing, apartments for married students, apartments for single students, Facilities accessible by persons with disabilities. 90% of campus accessible to physically disabled. **Special Academic Facilities/Equipment:** Natural history museum, art gallery, greenhouse and biological preserves, Lakeside biology lab and field lab for conservation problems, Tallgrass Prairie Center, Educational Technology Center, curriculum lab, on-campus school for student teachers, NASA Regional Teacher Resource Center, speech and hearing clinic, Small Business Development Center, Iowa Waste Reduction Center, Center for Applied Research in Metal Casting. Iowa Communications Network provides two-way audio/video link between classrooms across the state. Satellite video production truck with three cameras. Performing Arts Center. **Computers:** 80% of classrooms, 75% of libraries, 100% of dining areas, 100% of student union, have wireless network access. Students can register for classes online. Administrative functions (other than registration) can be performed online.

CAMPUS LIFE

Environment: Town. **Activities:** Choral groups, concert band, dance, drama/theater, jazz band, literary magazine, marching band, music ensembles, musical theater, opera, pep band, radio station, student government, student newspaper, symphony orchestra, yearbook, campus ministries, international student organization, Model UN. **Organizations:** 278 registered organizations, 18 honor societies, 21 religious organizations. 5 fraternities, 4 sororities. **Athletics (Intercollegiate):** *Men:* Basketball, cross-country, football, golf, track/field (outdoor), track/field (indoor), wrestling. *Women:* Basketball, cross-country, diving, golf, soccer, softball, swimming, tennis, track/field (outdoor), track/field (indoor), volleyball. **On-Campus Highlights:** Wellness Recreation Center, Gallagher-Bluedorn Performing Arts Center, Piazza and Rialto Dining Centers, Maucker University Union, UNI-DOME and McLeod Center. **Environmental Initiatives:** Currently in the process of hiring a sustainability officer/energy conservation coordinator. Energy Conservation/Sustainability Committee with representatives from faculty, staff, students, and the community. Recycling and Reuse Technology Transfer Center. CEEE funding

ADMISSIONS

Freshman Academic Profile: Average high school GPA 3.41. 18.9% in top 10% of high school class, 48.7% in top 25% of high school class, 85% in top 50% of high school class. ACT middle 50% range 21.04–25.89. Minimum paper TOEFL 550. Minimum web-based TOEFL 79. **Basis for Candidate Selection:** *Very important factors considered include:* Class rank, academic GPA, rigor of secondary school record, standardized test scores, *Other factors considered include:* Application essay, recommendation(s), first generation, interview, talent/ability. **Freshman Admission Requirements:** High school diploma is required and GED is accepted. *Academic units required:* 4 English, 3 mathematics, 3 science, 3 social studies, 2 academic electives. *Academic units recommended:* (1 science labs), 2 foreign language. **Freshman Admission Statistics:** 4,133 applied, 85% admitted, 56% enrolled. **Transfer Admission Requirements:** College transcript(s), Lowest grade transferable D. **General Admission Information:** Application fee $40. Regular application deadline 8/15. Notification on a rolling basis, beginning on or about 9/1. Nonfall registration accepted. Admission may be deferred for a maximum of indefinitely. Credit and/or placement offered for CEEB Advanced Placement tests.

COSTS AND FINANCIAL AID

Annual in-state tuition $5,756. Annual out-of-state tuition $14,020. Room and board $6,960. Required fees $880. Average book expense $1,035. **Required Forms and Deadlines:** FAFSA. **Notification of Awards:** Applicants will be notified of awards on a rolling basis beginning 3/1. **Types of Aid:** *Need-based scholarships/grants:* Federal Pell, SEOG, state scholarships/grants, private scholarships, the school's own gift aid. *Loans:* Direct Subsidized Stafford, Direct Unsubsidized Stafford, Direct PLUS, Federal Perkins, Private, Alternative Loans. *Student Employment:* Federal Work-Study Program available. Institutional employment available. Highest amount earned per year from on-campus jobs $5,872. Off-campus job opportunities are good. **Financial Aid Statistics:** 29% freshmen, 32% undergrads receive need-based scholarship or grant aid. 40% freshmen, 23% undergrads receive non-need-based scholarship or grant aid. 44% freshmen, 48% undergrads receive need-based self-help aid. 3% freshmen, 3% undergrads receive athletic scholarships. 92% freshmen, 87% undergrads receive any aid. 80% undergrads borrow to pay for school. Average cumulative indebtedness $24,123. **Criteria for awarding institutional aid:** *Non-need-based:* Academics, alumni affiliation, art, athletics, leadership, minority status, music/drama, state/district residency.

UNIVERSITY OF NOTRE DAME

220 Main Building, Notre Dame, IN 46556
Phone: 574-631-7505 **Financial Aid Phone:** 574-631-6436
E-mail: admissions@nd.edu **CEEB Code:** 1841
Fax: 574-631-8865 **Website:** www.nd.edu **ACT Code:** 1252

This private school, affiliated with the Roman Catholic Church, was founded in 1842. It has a 1250-acre campus.

RATINGS
Admissions Selectivity Rating: 98   **Fire Safety Rating:** 89   **Green Rating:** 88

STUDENTS AND FACULTY
Enrollment: 8,354. **Student Body:** 47% female, 53% male, 92% out-of-state, 3% international (89 countries represented). Asian 7%, African American 4%, Caucasian 77%, Hispanic 9%, Native American 1%.
Retention and Graduation: 97% freshmen return for sophomore year. 32% grads go on to further study within 1 year. 13% grads pursue arts and sciences degrees. 7% grads pursue law degrees. 3% grads pursue business degrees. 9% grads pursue medical degrees. **Faculty:** Student/faculty ratio 12:1. 907 full-time faculty, 93% hold PhDs, 14% are members of minority groups, 27% are women. 7% of classes are taught by teaching assistants.

ACADEMICS
Degrees: Bachelor's, first professional, master's. **Classes:** Most classes have 10–19 students. Most lab/discussion sessions have 10–19 students. **Majors with Highest Enrollment:** finance; political science and government; psychology. **Special Study Options:** Accelerated program, cross-registration, double major, dual enrollment, exchange student program (domestic), honors program, independent study, internships, liberal arts/career combination, student-designed major, study abroad, teacher certification program, Teacher Certification only available through Cross Registration with St. Mary's College. **Combined degree programs:** BS Engr./MBA. Special programs offered to physically disabled students include note-taking services, reader services, tape recorders **Career services:** Alumni network, alumni services, career/job search classes, career assessment, internships. **Career services highlights include:** Employer Development and Alumni Networking: To continue forming and growing relationships with employers during difficult economic times, The Career Center has increased it efforts and outreach to employers to identify career opportunities for students. The importance of networking continues to grow given the current state of the economy. Also recognizing that building and maintaining professional networking relationships will be critical to the hiring process this year. The Career Center has several programs planned for the spring semester that will help students network. ° The Career Center sent emails to 24,000 alumni in select industries to identify opportunities for Notre Dame students. As a result, employers including IBM, Skanska USA, Switch-Fast, Radio Flyer, Fidelity, Bristol Myers Squibb, Lockheed Martin, Draftfcb, and Societe Generale registered for the Winter Career Fair and/or posted job opportunities for our students. ° Career Counselors have received additional training on searching for jobs within the federal government and public service, a key sector of employment opportunities. ° The Career Center has successfully developed recruiting relationships with small, mid-sized, and family-owned companies to post jobs and internships. ° The Career Center will host a special program in NYC with ND alumni working in private equity and banking, to expand placement opportunities and internships on Wall Street. Also arranging two-week unpaid externships on Wall Street to help students gain experience in a very tough job market. ° The Career Center has added DirectEmployers Association to its Employer Advisory Board and gained instant access to 420 Fortune 500 employers ° The Career Center is working with Alumni Clubs to help seniors find jobs in or near their hometowns ° The Career Center is networking with GradStaff.com, CityStaff.com, Adecco and other professional organizations to help students connect to short-term, paid, professional jobs to gain experience with Fortune 500 companies. ° The Career Center has also implemented distance interviewing with Skype, and Polycam technology as an additional service for employers who cannot travel to campus to interview. ° A Notre Dame Alumni Group has been established on LinkedIn and currently has over 8,200 members. ° The Career Center launched a Job Shadow Program in Fall 2008 with over 1,200 alumni volunteering to host students at their companies for a one day networking visit ° The Career Center also has an agreement with the ND Alumni Association to grant seniors access to Irish Online, the online community of the Notre Dame Alumni Association. Senior students can create an account on this website before graduation and find alumni contacts. Additionally, networking workshops are being offered, providing students with access to

Irish Online that will enable them to find key contacts for career development. Additional programs and information: ° Confirmed 1,475 internships for ND students documented in the Intern Survey for the Summer of 2008 ° Raised funding to reimburse students $200 for travel to the Big East Career Fair in March 2008 and March 2009.

FACILITIES

Housing: Men's dorms, women's dorms 95% of campus accessible to physically disabled. **Special Academic Facilities/Equipment:** Art museum, theater, germ-free research facility, radiation laboratory. **Computers:** Students can register for classes online. Administrative functions (other than registration) can be performed online.

CAMPUS LIFE

Environment: City. **Activities:** Choral groups, concert band, dance, drama/theater, jazz band, literary magazine, marching band, music ensembles, musical theater, opera, pep band, radio station, student government, student newspaper, student-run film society, symphony orchestra, yearbook, campus ministries, international student organization, Model UN. **Organizations:** 299 registered organizations, 10 honor societies, 11 religious organizations. **Athletics (Intercollegiate):** *Men:* Baseball, basketball, cross-country, diving, fencing, football, golf, ice hockey, lacrosse, soccer, swimming, tennis, track/field (outdoor). *Women:* Basketball, crew/rowing, cross-country, diving, fencing, golf, lacrosse, soccer, softball, swimming, tennis, track/field (outdoor), volleyball. **On-Campus Highlights:** Grotto, The Dome (Main Building), Basilica of the Sacred Heart, Notre Dame Stadium, Eck Center. **Environmental Initiatives:** Expansion of Office of Sustainability to include 3 full time staff and 7 interns; development of metrics and quantitative goals in 7 key sustainability areas. Investment of $4 million this year to improve lighting and/or HVAC efficiency in 24 campus buildings. Continuous utilization of $2 million Green Loan Fund to support capital projects that save energy and natural resources

ADMISSIONS

Freshman Academic Profile: 86% in top 10% of high school class, 95% in top 25% of high school class, 100% in top 50% of high school class. 50% from public high schools. SAT Math middle 50% range 670–760. SAT Critical Reading middle 50% range 650–740. SAT Writing middle 50% range 640–730. ACT middle 50% range 31–34. Minimum paper TOEFL 560. Minimum computer TOEFL 250. Minimum web-based TOEFL 100. **Basis for Candidate Selection:** *Very important factors considered include:* Rigor of secondary school record. *Important factors considered include:* Class rank, application essay, academic GPA, recommendation(s), standardized test scores, alumni/ae relation, character/personal qualities, extracurricular activities, talent/ability, volunteer work. *Other factors considered include:* First generation, level of applicant's interest, racial/ethnic status, religious affiliation/commitment, work experience. **Freshman Admission Requirements:** High school diploma is required and GED is not accepted. *Academic units required:* 4 English, 3 mathematics, 2 science, (2 science labs), 2 foreign language, 2 history, 3 academic electives. *Academic units recommended:* 4 English, 4 mathematics, 4 science, (2 science labs), 4 foreign language, 4 history. **Freshman Admission Statistics:** 13,945 applied, 27% admitted, 54% enrolled. **Transfer Admission Requirements:** High school transcript, college transcript(s), essay or personal statement, standardized test scores, statement of good standing from prior institution(s). Minimum college GPA of 3.0 required. Lowest grade transferable C. **General Admission Information:** Application fee $65. Regular application deadline 12/31. Regular notification 4/10. Nonfall registration accepted. Admission may be deferred for a maximum of 1 year.

COSTS AND FINANCIAL AID

Annual tuition $37,970. Room and board $10,368. Required fees $507. Average book expense $950. **Required Forms and Deadlines:** FAFSA, CSS/Financial Aid PROFILE, business/farm supplement. Financial aid filing deadline 2/15. Priority financial aid filing date 2/15. **Notification of Awards:** Applicants will be notified of awards on or about 4/1. **Types of Aid:** *Need-based scholarships/grants:* Federal Pell, SEOG, state scholarships/grants, private scholarships, the school's own gift aid, Federal ACG and SMART Grants. *Loans:* FFEL Subsidized Stafford, FFEL Unsubsidized Stafford, FFEL PLUS, Federal Perkins, Private Student Loans. *Student Employment:* Highest amount earned per year from on-campus jobs $6,300. Off-campus job opportunities are fair. **Financial Aid Statistics:** 45% freshmen, 44% undergrads receive need-based scholarship or grant aid. 30% freshmen, 28% undergrads receive non-need-based scholarship or grant aid. 35% freshmen, 39% undergrads receive need-based self-help aid. 5% freshmen, 5% undergrads receive athletic scholarships. 57% undergrads borrow to pay for school. Average cumulative indebtedness $29,835. **Criteria for awarding institutional aid:** *Non-need-based:* Athletics.

UNIVERSITY OF OKLAHOMA

1000 Asp Aveune, Norman, OK 73019-4076
Phone: 405-325-2252 **Financial Aid Phone:** 405-325-5505
E-mail: admrec@ou.edu **CEEB Code:** 6879
Fax: 405-325-7124 **Website:** www.ou.edu **ACT Code:** 6879

This public school was founded in 1890. It has a 3914-acre campus.

RATINGS
Admissions Selectivity Rating: 83   **Fire Safety Rating:** 97   **Green Rating:** 89

STUDENTS AND FACULTY
Enrollment: 20,685. **Student Body:** 53% female, 47% male, 28% out-of-state, 2% international (85 countries represented). Asian 6%, African American 6%, Caucasian 74%, Hispanic 5%, Native American 7%.
Retention and Graduation: 29% freshmen graduate within 4 years. **Faculty:** Student/faculty ratio 17.9:1. 1442 full-time faculty, 82% hold PhDs, 18% are members of minority groups, 41% are women. 19% of classes are taught by teaching assistants.

ACADEMICS
Degrees: Bachelor's, certificate, master's, post-bachelor's certificate, post-master's certificate. **Classes:** Most classes have 10–19 students. Most lab/discussion sessions have 20–29 students. **Majors with Highest Enrollment:** journalism; management science; psychology. **Special Study Options:** Accelerated program, cooperative education program, distance learning, double major, dual enrollment, English as a Second Language (ESL), external degree program, honors program, independent study, internships, liberal arts/career combination, student-designed major, study abroad, teacher certification program, weekend college. **Honors programs:** Honors at Oxford: This summer program enables students to study at Oxford (while living at Brasenose College). While there, students work in private tutorials with distinguished Oxford dons. Students can earn up to 6 hours of honors credit in one of our four classes that are offered. Honors in Italy: Honors in Italy is built around a three-hours course called "Imagining Italy" which is taught in the Tuscan town of Arezzo and includes side trips to Florence, Venice, and Rome where students are led on walking tours of the art and history of Italy. The focus is on how Italian culture has influenced writers, filmmakers, and artists from John Adams to Henry James and from Mark Twain to Martin Scorsese. Honors in Germany (new for summer 2010): Honors students and other OU students travel to Leipzig, Germany in June, live at the University of Leipzig, study German, and take a course on German-American literary relations (American writers who wrote in Germany about German culture.) Additionally, students focus on experiencing and exploring major sites for the history and memory of WWII in Germany by taking day trips from Leipzig to major WWII-related sites in Germany. The course will be for six hours credit and will be offered each summer. Honors Undergraduate Research Assistant Program: Honors Undergraduate Research Assistant Program provides undergraduates the opportunity to work with professors as research assistants on specific projects. Student assistants are expected to work 10 hours a week for 10 weeks for $6 an hour. Honors College students with at least 15 hours of college credit and a 3.4+ GPA are eligible to apply. Medical Humanities Scholars Program: The Honors College and the University of Oklahoma College of Medicine have created a special pathway (through a bachelor of arts degree leading to a medical doctorate) for up to five high school students each year who wish to study the humanistic aspects of medicine as undergraduates. Through a special admissions process, the Medical Humanities Scholars are accepted at the medical school as part of their application to OU's undergraduate honors program. The Honors College has also created a Medical Humanities Minor open to all honors students wishing to study medicine from the perspectives of history, sociology, anthropology, bioethics, literature, and economics. Honors Undergraduate Writing Assistant Program: The Honors Undergraduate Writing Assistant Program includes assistants who receive a stipend to work as writing assistants for the required freshman American Perspectives courses. Students who wish to be writing assistants apply to the program and, if they are selected, participate in a required upper-division preparatory course that focuses on composition pedagogy, research and writing skills, and strategies for commenting and conferencing on students writing. Honors Undergraduate Research Opportunities Program: The Undergraduate Research Opportunities Program is open to all undergraduates at OU. Each semester the Honors College awards more than $12,500 to undergraduate students and their faculty mentors for research and creative activity. Undergraduate Research Day: Each spring the college hosts an Undergraduate Research Day, in which

scholars, Honors students or not, share their research with the peers. The Honors College, Phi Beta Kappa and Phi Kappa Phi give cash awards to the best presentations in various categories. Conversations with the Dean: Each week the Dean of the Honors College has in a distinguished professor, author, diplomat, politician, or some other important community or intellectual figure to discuss world events. With the Dean as moderator, students are encouraged to participate in vibrant discussion with the week's important guest. Honors College Reading Groups: The Dean and Honors College faculty assign a book of their individual choosing to students who voluntarily join an Honors College Reading Group. Limited to 15 students per group, the books are provided free of charge to participants who then meet as a group, one hour a week, to discuss the assigned pages with the professor. There is no charge for this activity, there are no grades, and students may come and go as they please. The aim is to encourage students to read, think, and discuss with other Honors College students important topics of mutual interest, whether fiction or non-fiction. The Honors Undergraduate Research Journal: The Honors Undergraduate Research Journal is a forum in which Honors students of all majors have the opportunity to have their work published. A panel of Honors College professors who annually appoint an editorial board of about eight Honors students advises THURJ. The board accepts research papers, poetry, and short stories of which the top submissions are published every spring. Freshman Summer Reading Series: Each summer all incoming freshmen receive a free, theme-based book chosen by the faculty. The students are encouraged to actively engage the material (the book arrives at the student's home in late June), which provides the incoming class with a common intellectual experience that the faculty and students can build on during their first semester in order to develop and nurture a collective intellectual community. **Combined degree programs:** BA/MA, BA/MEng, BAC/MAC. Special programs offered to physically disabled students include note-taking services, reader services, tutors. **Career services:** Alumni network, alumni services, career/job search classes, career assessment, internships. **Career services highlights include:** Alumni Network—Alumni provide career mentoring to currently enrolled students.

FACILITIES

Housing: Coed dorms, special housing for disabled students, men's dorms, special housing for international students, women's dorms, fraternity/sorority housing, apartments for married students, apartments for single students, Honors House, Cultural Housing, National Merit, and Scholastics floors. 92% of campus accessible to physically disabled. **Special Academic Facilities/Equipment:** Fred Jones Museum of Art, Sam Noble Museum of Natural History, National Weather Center, National Severe Storms Library, OU Biological Station, History of Science Collection, Western History Collection, Oklahoma Geological Survey. **Computers:** 60% of classrooms, 80% of dorms, 100% of libraries, 75% of dining areas, 100% of student union, 80% of common outdoor areas have wireless network access. Students can register for classes online. Administrative functions (other than registration) can be performed online.

CAMPUS LIFE

Environment: City. **Activities:** Choral groups, concert band, dance, drama/theater, jazz band, literary magazine, marching band, music ensembles, musical theater, opera, pep band, radio station, student government, student newspaper, student-run film society, symphony orchestra, television station, yearbook, campus ministries, international student organization, Model UN. **Organizations:** 388 registered organizations, 17 honor societies, 39 religious organizations. 30 fraternities, 20 sororities. **Athletics (Intercollegiate):** *Men:* Baseball, basketball, cross-country, football, golf, gymnastics, tennis, track/field (outdoor), track/field (indoor), wrestling. *Women:* Basketball, crew/rowing, cross-country, golf, gymnastics, soccer, softball, tennis, track/field (outdoor), track/field (indoor), volleyball. **On-Campus Highlights:** Fred Jones Jr. Museum of Art, The Gaylord Family Oklahoma Memorial Sta, Sam Noble Ok. Museum of Natural History, Oklahoma Memorial Union, Lloyd Noble Center. **Environmental Initiatives:** Membership in the Chicago Climate Exchange. Joining with the University Presidents' Campus Climate Challenge. Operation of the Academic Department for Interdisciplinary Perspectives on the Environment

ADMISSIONS

Freshman Academic Profile: Average high school GPA 3.59. 34% in top 10% of high school class, 68% in top 25% of high school class, 93% in top 50% of high school class. SAT Math middle 50% range 530–660. SAT Critical Reading middle 50% range 510–640. ACT middle 50% range 23–29. Minimum paper TOEFL 550. Minimum computer TOEFL 213. Minimum web-based TOEFL 79. **Basis for Candidate Selection:** *Very important factors considered include:* Class rank, academic GPA, rigor of secondary school record, standardized test scores, *Other factors considered include:* Application essay, recommendation(s), state residency. **Freshman Admission Requirements:** High school diploma is required and GED is accepted. *Academic units required:* 4 English, 3 mathematics, 3 science, (3 science labs), 2 social studies, 1 history, 2 academic electives. *Academic units recommended:* 2 foreign language, 1 computer science. **Freshman Admission Statistics:** 8,960 applied, 93% admitted, 45% enrolled. **Transfer Admission Requirements:** College transcript(s), Lowest

grade transferable D. **General Admission Information:** Application fee $40. Regular application deadline 4/1. Nonfall registration accepted. Credit and/or placement offered for CEEB Advanced Placement tests.

COSTS AND FINANCIAL AID

Annual in-state tuition $2,830. Annual out-of-state tuition $10,814. Room and board $7,598. Required fees $2,415. Average book expense $1,016. **Required Forms and Deadlines:** FAFSA. Priority financial aid filing date 3/1. **Notification of Awards:** Applicants will be notified of awards on a rolling basis beginning 3/15. **Types of Aid:** *Need-based scholarships/grants:* Federal Pell, SEOG, state scholarships/grants, private scholarships, the school's own gift aid, United Negro College Fund. *Loans:* FFEL Subsidized Stafford, FFEL Unsubsidized Stafford, FFEL PLUS, Federal Perkins, Federal Nursing, college/university loans from institutional funds. *Student Employment:* Federal Work-Study Program available. Institutional employment available. Highest amount earned per year from on-campus jobs $3,108. Off-campus job opportunities are excellent. **Financial Aid Statistics:** 5% freshmen, 14% undergrads receive need-based scholarship or grant aid. 52% freshmen, 32% undergrads receive non-need-based scholarship or grant aid. 39% freshmen, 39% undergrads receive need-based self-help aid. 1% freshmen, 1% undergrads receive athletic scholarships. 82% freshmen, 76% undergrads receive any aid. 45% undergrads borrow to pay for school. Average cumulative indebtedness $15,659. **Criteria for awarding institutional aid:** *Non-need-based:* Academics, alumni affiliation, art, athletics, leadership, music/drama, religious affiliation.

UNIVERSITY OF OREGON

1217 University of Oregon, Eugene, OR 97403-1217
Phone: 541-346-3201 **Financial Aid Phone:** 800-760-6953
E-mail: uoadmit@uoregon.edu **CEEB Code:** 4846
Fax: 541-346-5815 **Website:** www.uoregon.edu

This public school was founded in 1876. It has a 295-acre campus.

RATINGS

Admissions Selectivity Rating: 83   **Fire Safety Rating:** 70   **Green Rating:** 96

STUDENTS AND FACULTY

Enrollment: 18,213. **Student Body:** 51% female, 49% male, 32% out-of-state, 6% international (85 countries represented). Asian 6%, African American 2%, Caucasian 74%, Hispanic 4%, Native American 1%.
Retention and Graduation: 83% freshmen return for sophomore year. 46% freshmen graduate within 4 years. 28% grads go on to further study within 1 year. **Faculty:** Student/faculty ratio 20:1. 892 full-time faculty, 96% hold PhDs, 16% are members of minority groups, 41% are women. 13% of classes are taught by teaching assistants.

ACADEMICS

Degrees: Bachelor's, master's, post-bachelor's certificate. **Classes:** Most classes have 20–29 students. Most lab/discussion sessions have 20–29 students. **Majors with Highest Enrollment:** Business/commerce; journalism; psychology. **Special Study Options:** Cross-registration, distance learning, double major, English as a Second Language (ESL), exchange student program (domestic), honors program, independent study, internships, liberal arts/career combination, student-designed major, study abroad, teacher certification program, Semester at Sea program; Professional distinctions program, a certificate program in which students gain direct professional preparation through internships, special courses, a professional mentor program, and the development of an electronic resume and portfolio. There is also a dual enrollment program that allows you to enroll in both UO and Lane Community College or UO and Southwestern Oregon Community College (differs from CDS definition in that it is not a high school dual enrollment program). **Honors programs:** Robert D. Clark Honors College, College of Arts and Sciences Society of College Scholars, Professional Distinctions program, Dean's List, Junior Scholars. Special programs offered to physically disabled students include note-taking services, reader services, tape recorders, tutors. **Career services:** Alumni network, alumni services, career/job search classes, career assessment, internships, regional alumni. **Career services highlights include:** Career Assessment Program: This is a free opportunity available to all students that assists them in assessing values, interests, preferences and strengths. Through this process students gain confidence and self direction which helps them gain insight in major selection and career direction.

FACILITIES

Housing: Coed dorms, fraternity/sorority housing, apartments for married students, cooperative housing, apartments for single students, wellness housing, theme housing, graduate student housing. Most residence halls have separate men's and women's floors. 95% of campus accessible to physically disabled. **Special Academic Facilities/Equipment:** Jordan Schnitzer Museum of Art; Museum of Natural and Cultural History; James Warsaw Sports Marketing Center; Lundquist Center for Entrepreneurship; University of Oregon Many Nations Longhouse; Green Chemistry Laboratory and Alice C. Tyler Instrumentation Center; Future Music Oregon, a computer music center in the School of Music; Pine Mountain Observatory (Bend, Oregon); Oregon Institute of Marine Biology (Oregon Coast); Central Oregon programs affiliated with the Oregon University System Cascades Campus (Bend, Oregon); Urban Architecture program and BetterBricks Daylighting Laboratory at the University of Oregon Portland Center (Portland, Oregon). **Computers:** 95% of classrooms, 35% of dorms, 100% of libraries, 100% of dining areas, 100% of student union, 30% of common outdoor areas have wireless network access. Students can register for classes online. Administrative functions (other than registration) can be performed online.

CAMPUS LIFE

Environment: City. **Activities:** Choral groups, concert band, dance, drama/theater, jazz band, literary magazine, marching band, music ensembles, musical theater, opera, pep band, radio station, student government, student newspaper, student-run film society, symphony orchestra, campus ministries, international student organization. **Organizations:** 250 registered organizations, 22 honor societies, 20 religious organizations. 12 fraternities, 10 sororities. **Athletics (Intercollegiate):** *Men:* Baseball, basketball, cross-country, football, golf, tennis, track/field (outdoor). *Women:* Basketball, cross-country, golf, gymnastics, lacrosse, soccer, softball, tennis, track/field (outdoor), volleyball. **On-Campus Highlights:** University of Oregon Duckstore, Knight Library, Erb Memorial Union, Laverne Krauss Gallery in Lawrence Hall, watch sports at Autzen, Hayward, or Mac Court. The University of Oregon's 295-acre, park-like campus is home to more than 500 varieties of trees, various private spots to study or simply stare at the sky, and tons of quick stops where you can grab a bite between classes. With a wealth of campus resources to make your life as a student easier, the UO campus feeds the mind, body, and spirit. On average, each course you take at the UO will have a person from another country, six people from different states, and several people with religious, cultural, and ethnic heritage different from your own. You'll thrive because this diversity pushes you to see the world differently. You'll listen to new ideas, and maybe even change the world because you changed your mind. **Environmental Initiatives:** Signed ACUPCC and completed climate action plan. Massive energy efficiency upgrades; lighting retrofits, building upgrades Major education and research inititatives in green chemistry, product design, sustainable materials, sustainable cities, green leadership.

ADMISSIONS

Freshman Academic Profile: Average high school GPA 3.54. 28% in top 10% of high school class, 62% in top 25% of high school class, 93% in top 50% of high school class. SAT Math middle 50% range 498–614. SAT Critical Reading middle 50% range 492–611. Minimum paper TOEFL 500. Minimum web-based TOEFL 61. **Basis for Candidate Selection:** *Very important factors considered include:* Academic GPA, rigor of secondary school record, *Other factors considered include:* Class rank, application essay, recommendation(s), standardized test scores, extracurricular activities, first generation, geographical residence, racial/ethnic status, state residency, talent/ability, volunteer work, work experience. **Freshman Admission Requirements:** High school diploma is required and GED is accepted. *Academic units required:* 4 English, 3 mathematics, 2 science, 2 foreign language, 3 social studies. *Academic units recommended:* (1 science labs), 2 2 additional units in required college preparatory areas recommended. **Freshman Admission Statistics:** 16,780 applied, 80% admitted, 29% enrolled. **Transfer Admission Requirements:** College transcript(s), minimum college GPA of 2.25 required. Lowest grade transferable D-. **General Admission Information:** Application fee $50. Regular application deadline 1/15. Notification on a rolling basis, beginning on or about 12/15. Nonfall registration accepted. Credit and/or placement offered for CEEB Advanced Placement tests.

COSTS AND FINANCIAL AID

Annual in-state tuition $6,180. Annual out-of-state tuition $22,470. Room and board $8,939. Required fees $1,250. Average book expense $1,050. **Required Forms and Deadlines:** FAFSA. Priority financial aid filing date 3/1. **Notification of Awards:** Applicants will be notified of awards on a rolling basis beginning 4/15. **Types of Aid:** *Need-based scholarships/grants:* Federal Pell, SEOG, state scholarships/grants, private scholarships, the school's own gift aid. *Loans:* Direct Subsidized Stafford, Direct Unsubsidized Stafford, Direct PLUS, Federal Perkins, college/university loans from institutional funds. *Student Employment:* Federal Work-Study Program available. Institutional employment available. Off-campus job opportunities are good. **Financial Aid Statistics:**

21% freshmen, 23% undergrads receive need-based scholarship or grant aid. 22% freshmen, 13% undergrads receive non-need-based scholarship or grant aid. 33% freshmen, 35% undergrads receive need-based self-help aid. 2% undergrads receive athletic scholarships. 64.8% freshmen, 62.9% undergrads receive any aid. 55% undergrads borrow to pay for school. Average cumulative indebtedness $19,336. **Criteria for awarding institutional aid:** *Non-need-based:* Academics, art, athletics, leadership, minority status, music/drama, state/district residency.

See page 1304.

UNIVERSITY OF THE OZARKS

415 N College Avenue, Clarksville, AR 72830
Phone: 479-979-1227 **Financial Aid Phone:** 479-979-1221
E-mail: admiss@ozarks.edu **CEEB Code:** 6111
Fax: 479-979-1417 **Website:** www.ozarks.edu **ACT Code:** 120

This private school, affiliated with the Presbyterian Church, was founded in 1834. It has a 56-acre campus.

RATINGS

Admissions Selectivity Rating: 77   **Fire Safety Rating:** 81   **Green Rating:** 60*

STUDENTS AND FACULTY

Enrollment: 595. **Student Body:** 51% female, 49% male, 29% out-of-state, 18% international (21 countries represented). Asian 1%, African American 5%, Caucasian 68%, Hispanic 4%, Native American 3%.
Retention and Graduation: 69% freshmen return for sophomore year. 31% freshmen graduate within 4 years. **Faculty:** Student/faculty ratio 10:1. 47 full-time faculty, 79% hold PhDs, 9% are members of minority groups, 30% are women.

ACADEMICS

Degrees: Bachelor's. **Classes:** Most classes have 10–19 students. **Majors with Highest Enrollment:** Biology/biological sciences; business administration and management; marketing/marketing management. **Special Study Options:** Cooperative education program, double major, dual enrollment, independent study, internships, liberal arts/career combination, study abroad, teacher certification program. Special programs offered to physically disabled students include note-taking services, reader services, tape recorders, tutors. **Career services:** Alumni network, alumni services, career assessment, internships, regional alumni.

FACILITIES

Housing: Coed dorms, men's dorms, women's dorms, apartments for married students, apartments for single students, university owned housing. 100% of campus accessible to physically disabled. **Special Academic Facilities/Equipment:** Walton Fine Arts Center; Stephens Gallery; Smith-Broyles Science Center; Walker Hall Teacher Education and Communications Center. **Computers:** 100% of libraries, have wireless network access.

CAMPUS LIFE

Environment: Village. **Activities:** Choral groups, drama/theater, literary magazine, music ensembles, radio station, student government, student-run film society, television station, yearbook, campus ministries, international student organization. **Organizations:** 40 registered organizations, 5 honor societies, 6 religious organizations. **Athletics (Intercollegiate):** *Men:* Baseball, basketball, cheerleading, cross-country, soccer, tennis. *Women:* Basketball, cheerleading, cross-country, soccer, softball, tennis **On-Campus Highlights:** Seay Student Center, Walton Fine Arts Center, Walker Education and Communications Buil, Robson Library, Gilbert's Park.

ADMISSIONS

Freshman Academic Profile: Average high school GPA 3.35. 14% in top 10% of high school class, 41% in top 25% of high school class, 75% in top 50% of high school class. 92% from public high schools. SAT Math middle 50% range 460–560. SAT Critical Reading middle 50% range 430–530. ACT middle 50% range 19–24.5. Minimum paper TOEFL 500. Minimum computer TOEFL 173. **Basis for Candidate Selection:** *Important factors considered include:* Standardized test scores. *Other factors considered include:* Application essay, academic GPA, recommendation(s), rigor of secondary school record, alumni/ae relation, character/personal qualities, extracurricular activities, interview, level of applicant's interest, talent/ability, volunteer work, work experience. **Freshman Admission Requirements:** High school diploma is required and GED is accepted. *Academic units recommended:* 4 English, 4 mathematics, 3 science, (2 science labs), 2 foreign language, 1 social studies, 2 history. **Freshman Admission Statistics:** 596 applied, 89% admitted, **Transfer Admission Require-**

ments: College transcript(s), minimum college GPA of 2.0 required. Lowest grade transferable C. **General Admission Information:** Application fee $30. Nonfall registration accepted. Credit and/or placement offered for CEEB Advanced Placement tests.

COSTS AND FINANCIAL AID
Annual tuition $18,300. Room and board $6,050. Required fees $600. Average book expense $800. **Required Forms and Deadlines:** FAFSA. Priority financial aid filing date 2/15. **Notification of Awards:** Applicants will be notified of awards on a rolling basis beginning 3/1. **Types of Aid:** *Need-based scholarships/grants:* Federal Pell, SEOG, state scholarships/grants, private scholarships, the school's own gift aid, United Negro College Fund, Federal Nursing Scholarships. *Loans:* FFEL Subsidized Stafford, FFEL Unsubsidized Stafford, FFEL PLUS, Federal Perkins, college/university loans from institutional funds. *Student Employment:* Federal Work-Study Program available. Institutional employment available. Highest amount earned per year from on-campus jobs $5,726. Off-campus job opportunities are fair. **Financial Aid Statistics:** 73% freshmen, 58% undergrads receive need-based scholarship or grant aid. 57% freshmen, 49% undergrads receive need-based self-help aid. 95% freshmen, 94% undergrads receive any aid. 44% undergrads borrow to pay for school. Average cumulative indebtedness $16,852. **Criteria for awarding institutional aid:** *Non-need-based:* Academics, alumni affiliation, art, leadership, minority status, music/drama, religious affiliation, state/district residency.

UNIVERSITY OF THE PACIFIC

3601 Pacific Avenue, Stockton, CA 95211
Phone: 209-946-2211 **Financial Aid Phone:** 209-946-2421
E-mail: admissions@pacific.edu **CEEB Code:** 4065
Fax: 209-946-2413 **Website:** web.pacific.edu **ACT Code:** 240

This private school was founded in 1851. It has a 175-acre campus.

RATINGS
Admissions Selectivity Rating: 91   **Fire Safety Rating:** 88   **Green Rating:** 82

STUDENTS AND FACULTY
Enrollment: 3,489. **Student Body:** 55% female, 45% male, 12.5% out-of-state (66 countries represented). **Retention and Graduation:** 41% freshmen graduate within 4 years. **Faculty:** Student/faculty ratio 13:1. 434 full-time faculty, 88% hold PhDs, 20% are members of minority groups, 40% are women.

ACADEMICS
Degrees: Bachelor's, master's. **Classes:** Most classes have fewer than 10 students. Most lab/discussion sessions have 10–19 students. **Majors with Highest Enrollment:** Biology/biological sciences; business/commerce; engineering. **Special Study Options:** Accelerated program, double major, dual enrollment, English as a Second Language (ESL), exchange student program (domestic), honors program, independent study, internships, liberal arts/career combination, student-designed major, study abroad, teacher certification program, minors, practicum, thematic minors, undergraduate research, ethnic studies, envirnomental science, gender studies, service learning. **Combined degree programs:** BA/DDS, BA or BS/MBA, BA or BS/DDS, BS/PharmD. Special programs offered to physically disabled students include note-taking services, reader services, tape recorders, tutors. **Career services:** Alumni network, alumni services, career/job search classes, career assessment, internships

FACILITIES
Housing: Coed dorms, fraternity/sorority housing, apartments for single students. 90% of campus accessible to physically disabled. **Special Academic Facilities/Equipment:** John Muir Collection, Dave and Iola Brubeck Collection, Brubeck Istitute for Jazz Studies, Reynolds Art Gallery. **Computers:** 100% of classrooms, 90% of dorms, 100% of libraries, 100% of dining areas, 100% of student union, 30% of common outdoor areas have wireless network access. Students can register for classes online. Administrative functions (other than registration) can be performed online.

CAMPUS LIFE
Environment: City. **Activities:** Choral groups, concert band, dance, drama/theater, jazz band, literary magazine, music ensembles, musical theater, opera, pep band, radio station, student government, student newspaper, student-run film society, symphony orchestra, yearbook, campus ministries, international

student organization, Model UN. **Organizations:** 100 registered organizations, 14 honor societies, 10 religious organizations. 8 fraternities, 7 sororities. **Athletics (Intercollegiate):** *Men:* Baseball, basketball, golf, swimming, tennis, volleyball, water polo. *Women:* Basketball, cross-country, field hockey, soccer, softball, swimming, tennis, volleyball, water polo. **On-Campus Highlights:** Brubeck Istitute for Jazz Studies, John Muir Collection and Center, Alex Spanos Center, Reynolds Art Gallery, Pharmacy and Health Sciences Bldg. **Environmental Initiatives:** Natural Resource Institute, Calaveras River Restoration Project, LEED certification of New Student Center.

ADMISSIONS
Freshman Academic Profile: Average high school GPA 3.49. 41.6% in top 10% of high school class, 75.6% in top 25% of high school class, 95.2% in top 50% of high school class. 82% from public high schools. SAT Math middle 50% range 540–680. SAT Critical Reading middle 50% range 510–640. SAT Writing middle 50% range 500–640. ACT middle 50% range 23–30. Minimum paper TOEFL 475. Minimum computer TOEFL 150. Minimum web-based TOEFL 52. **Basis for Candidate Selection:** *Very important factors considered include:* Rigor of secondary school record. *Important factors considered include:* Application essay, academic GPA, recommendation(s), standardized test scores, extracurricular activities, first generation. *Other factors considered include:* Class rank, alumni/ae relation, character/personal qualities, geographical residence, level of applicant's interest, talent/ability, volunteer work, work experience. **Freshman Admission Requirements:** High school diploma is required and GED is accepted. *Academic units recommended:* 4 English, 2 foreign language, 2 social studies, 1 history, 1 visual/performing arts, 1 academic electives. **Freshman Admission Statistics:** 14,970 applied, 42% admitted, 14% enrolled. **Transfer Admission Requirements:** College transcript(s), statement of good standing from prior institution(s). Minimum college GPA of 3.0 required. Lowest grade transferable C. **General Admission Information:** Application fee $60. Regular application deadline 1/15. Notification on a rolling basis, beginning on or about 3/15. Nonfall registration accepted. Admission may be deferred for a maximum of 1 year. Credit and/or placement offered for CEEB Advanced Placement tests.

COSTS AND FINANCIAL AID
Annual tuition $31,730. Room and board $10,616. Required fees $500. Average book expense $1,638. **Required Forms and Deadlines:** FAFSA. Priority financial aid filing date 2/15. **Notification of Awards:** Applicants will be notified of awards on a rolling basis beginning 3/15. **Types of Aid:** *Need-based scholarships/grants:* Federal Pell, SEOG, state scholarships/grants, private scholarships, the school's own gift aid, ACG, SMART. *Loans:* Direct Subsidized Stafford, Direct Unsubsidized Stafford, Direct PLUS, FFEL Subsidized Stafford, FFEL Unsubsidized Stafford, FFEL PLUS, Federal Perkins, Direct Graduate/Professional PLUS. Loans. **Financial Aid Statistics:** 72% freshmen, 66% undergrads receive need-based scholarship or grant aid. 69% freshmen, 65% undergrads receive need-based self-help aid. 3% freshmen, 3% undergrads receive athletic scholarships. 91% freshmen, 83% undergrads receive any aid. **Criteria for awarding institutional aid:** *Non-need-based:* Academics, athletics, leadership, music/drama, religious affiliation.

UNIVERSITY OF PENNSYLVANIA

1 College Hall, Philadelphia, PA 19104
Phone: 215-898-7507 **Financial Aid Phone:** 215-898-1988
E-mail: info@admissions.ugao.upenn.edu **CEEB Code:** 2926
Fax: 215-898-9670 **Website:** www.upenn.edu **ACT Code:** 3732

This private school was founded in 1740. It has a 279-acre campus.

RATINGS
Admissions Selectivity Rating: 99   **Fire Safety Rating:** 70   **Green Rating:** 90

STUDENTS AND FACULTY
Enrollment: 9,756. **Student Body:** 50% female, 50% male, 83% out-of-state, 10% international (103 countries represented). Asian 18%, African American 8%, Caucasian 43%, Hispanic 6%. **Retention and Graduation:** 98% freshmen return for sophomore year. 88% freshmen graduate within 4 years. 18% grads go on to further study within 1 year. 4% grads pursue arts and sciences degrees. 5% grads pursue law degrees. 1% grads pursue business degrees. 6% grads pursue medical degrees. **Faculty:** Student/faculty ratio 5.81:1. 1413 full-time faculty, 100% hold PhDs, 18% are

members of minority groups, 35% are women. 5% of classes are taught by teaching assistants.

ACADEMICS

Degrees: Associate, bachelor's, certificate, first professional, first professional certificate, master's, post-bachelor's certificate, post-master's certificate, terminal associate. **Classes:** Most classes have 10–19 students. **Majors with Highest Enrollment:** Business administration and management; finance; nursing/registered nurse (RN, ASN, BSN, MSN). **Special Study Options:** Accelerated program, cross-registration, double major, dual enrollment, English as a Second Language (ESL), exchange student program (domestic), honors program, independent study, internships, liberal arts/career combination, student-designed major, study abroad, teacher certification program, Joint degree programs among schools. Accelerated degree programs. Opportunities for preprofessional programs in predentistry, prelaw, premedicine, and preveterinary studies (not actual majors). Washington semester. **Honors programs:** Penn's general honors program is called the Benjamin Franklin Scholars program, although the honors program for students in business is called Joseph Wharton Scholars. There are specialized honors programs including Fisher Program in Management and Technology, the Huntsman Program in International Studies and Business, the Vagelos Scholars Program in Molecular Life Sciences, and the Civic Scholars Program which offers opportunities to integrate community service and academics. The University Scholars Program is open to already matriculated students who are interested in engaging in high-level research. **Combined degree programs:** BA/JD, BA/MA, BA/DDS, BA/MEng, 4-yr. BSE/BS, BSE/MBA, BA/MS Ed, BAS/MS Ed. Special programs offered to physically disabled students include note-taking services, reader services, tape recorders, tutors. **Career services:** Alumni network, alumni services, career assessment, internships, regional alumni. **Career services highlights include:** In addition to a full on-campus recruiting program (over 13,000 interviews conducted annually), Career Services sponsors the following career days for undergraduates: CareerLink (business fair), Engineering Career Day, Government and Public Policy Career Day, International Opportunities Fair, Nursing Career Day, and a Spring Career Fair for non-profits and just in time opportunities as well as internships.

FACILITIES

Housing: Coed dorms, special housing for disabled students, fraternity/sorority housing, apartments for married students, apartments for single students, wellness housing private off-campus. 92% of campus accessible to physically disabled. **Special Academic Facilities/Equipment:** Art gallery, anthropology museum, institute for contemporary art, language lab, large animal research center, primate research center, arboretum, observatory, wind tunnel, electron microscope. **Computers:** 85% of classrooms, 100% of dorms, 100% of libraries, 85% of dining areas, 100% of student union, 25% of common outdoor areas have wireless network access. Students can register for classes online. Administrative functions (other than registration) can be performed online.

CAMPUS LIFE

Environment: Metropolis. **Activities:** Choral groups, concert band, dance, drama/theater, jazz band, literary magazine, marching band, music ensembles, musical theater, opera, pep band, radio station, student government, student newspaper, student-run film society, symphony orchestra, television station, yearbook, campus ministries, international student organization, Model UN. **Organizations:** 350 registered organizations, 9 honor societies, 29 religious organizations. 35 fraternities, 13 sororities. **Athletics (Intercollegiate):** *Men:* Baseball, basketball, crew/rowing, cross-country, diving, fencing, football, golf, lacrosse, light weight football, soccer, squash, swimming, tennis, track/field (outdoor), track/field (indoor), wrestling. *Women:* Basketball, crew/rowing, cross-country, diving, fencing, field hockey, golf, gymnastics, lacrosse, soccer, softball, squash, swimming, tennis, track/field (outdoor), track/field (indoor), volleyball. **On-Campus Highlights:** University of Pennsylvania Museum, Institute of Contemporary Art, Walnut Street shops and restuarants, Annenberg Center, Franklin Field. **Environmental Initiatives:** 1) Continued purchase of Renewable Energy Credits in the form of wind-generated electricity. Penn is the nation's leader in wind-energy purchase, with over 45% of our electricity (192,727 MWH) being offset by Renewable Energy Credits. 2) Building optimization implementation, a program to optimize building systems in high-energy-use buildings to reduce their utility use and carbon footprint. 3) Signing on the Presidents Climate Commitment, with ongoing planning for publication of a Climate Action Plan.

ADMISSIONS

Freshman Academic Profile: Average high school GPA 3.83. 99% in top 10% of high school class, 100% in top 25% of high school class, 100% in top 50% of high school class. 55% from public high schools. SAT Math middle 50% range 680–780. SAT Critical Reading middle 50% range 650–740. SAT Writing middle 50% range 670–760. ACT middle 50% range 30–33. Minimum paper TOEFL 600. Minimum computer TOEFL 220. Minimum web-based TOEFL 100. **Basis for Candidate Selection:** *Very important factors considered include:* Recommendation(s), rigor of secondary school record, character/personal

qualities. *Important factors considered include:* Class rank, application essay, academic GPA, standardized test scores, extracurricular activities, work experience. *Other factors considered include:* Alumni/ae relation, first generation, geographical residence, interview, racial/ethnic status, talent/ability, volunteer work. **Freshman Admission Requirements:** High school diploma or equivalent is not required. *Academic units required:* 4 English, 4 mathematics, 3 science, (3 science labs), 4 foreign language, 3 history. **Freshman Admission Statistics:** 22,935 applied, 17% admitted, 63% enrolled. **Transfer Admission Requirements:** High school transcript, college transcript(s), essay or personal statement, standardized test scores, statement of good standing from prior institution(s). Lowest grade transferable C. **General Admission Information:** Application fee $75. Early decision application deadline 11/1. Regular application deadline 1/1. Regular notification 4/1. Nonfall registration not accepted. Admission may be deferred for a maximum of 1 year. Credit and/or placement offered for CEEB Advanced Placement tests.

COSTS AND FINANCIAL AID

Annual tuition $34,868. Room and board $11,016. Required fees $4,102. Average book expense $1,094. **Required Forms and Deadlines:** FAFSA, institution's own financial aid form, CSS/Financial Aid PROFILE, noncustodial PROFILE, business/farm supplement. Parents' and student's most recently completed income tax. Priority financial aid filing date 2/15. **Notification of Awards:** Applicants will be notified of awards on or about 4/1. **Types of Aid:** *Need-based scholarships/grants:* Federal Pell, SEOG, state scholarships/grants, private scholarships, the school's own gift aid. *Loans:* FFEL Subsidized Stafford, FFEL Unsubsidized Stafford, FFEL PLUS, Federal Perkins, Federal Nursing, college/university loans from institutional funds, Supplemental 3rd Party Loans guaranteed by institution. *Student Employment:* Federal Work-Study Program available. Institutional employment available. Off-campus job opportunities are excellent. **Financial Aid Statistics:** 37% freshmen, 39% undergrads receive need-based scholarship or grant aid. 38% freshmen, 41% undergrads receive need-based self-help aid. 60% freshmen, 55% undergrads receive any aid. 41% undergrads borrow to pay for school. Average cumulative indebtedness $19,085.

UNIVERSITY OF PHOENIX

4035 S. Riverpoint Parkway, Phoenix, AZ 85040
Phone: 480-446-4600 **Financial Aid Phone:** 1-800-921-1904
Website: www.phoenix.edu

This proprietary school was founded in 1976.

RATINGS

Admissions Selectivity Rating: 60*   **Fire Safety Rating:** 60*   **Green Rating:** 60*

STUDENTS AND FACULTY

Enrollment: 310,170. **Student Body:** 68% female, 32% male, % out-of-state, 3% international. Asian 2%, African American 18%, Caucasian 39%, Hispanic 9%, Native American 1%.
Retention and Graduation: 1% freshmen graduate within 4 years. **Faculty:** Student/faculty ratio 43:1. 1410 full-time faculty, 23% hold PhDs, 19% are members of minority groups, 46% are women.

ACADEMICS

Degrees: Associate, bachelor's, certificate, master's, post-bachelor's certificate, post-master's certificate, transfer associate. **Majors with Highest Enrollment:** accounting; business administration and management; health/health care administration/management. **Special Study Options:** Accelerated program, distance learning, independent study, Evening courses meeting 4 hours per night, one night per week for 5 weeks at the bachelor level and 6 weeks at the master level. Special programs offered to physically disabled students include tape recorders **Career services:** Alumni network.

FACILITIES

Housing: 100% of campus accessible to physically disabled. **Computers:** Students can register for classes online. Administrative functions (other than registration) can be performed online.

CAMPUS LIFE

Environment: Metropolis. **Organizations:** 2 honor societies.

ADMISSIONS

Freshman Academic Profile: Minimum paper TOEFL 550. Minimum computer TOEFL 213. **Basis for Candidate Selection:** *Very important factors considered include:* Work experience. *Other factors considered include:* Recommendation(s). **Freshman Admission Requirements:** High school diploma is required and GED is accepted. **Transfer Admission Requirements:**

College transcript(s), **General Admission Information:** Nonfall registration accepted. Neither credit nor placement offered for CEEB Advanced Placement tests.

UNIVERSITY OF PITTSBURGH AT BRADFORD

Office of Admissions - Hanley Library, 300 Campus Drive, Bradford, PA 16701
Phone: 814-362-7555 **Financial Aid Phone:** 814-362-7550
E-mail: Admissions@upb.pitt.edu **CEEB Code:** 2935
Fax: 814-362-5150 **Website:** www.upb.pitt.edu **ACT Code:** 3731

This public school was founded in 1963. It has a 317-acre campus.

RATINGS
Admissions Selectivity Rating: 71   **Fire Safety Rating:** 81   **Green Rating:** 75

STUDENTS AND FACULTY
Enrollment: 1,600. **Student Body:** 55% female, 45% male, 15% out-of-state, international (7 countries represented). Asian 2%, African American 6%, Caucasian 85%, Hispanic 1%, Native American 1%.
Retention and Graduation: 72% freshmen return for sophomore year. 28% freshmen graduate within 4 years. 22% grads go on to further study within 1 year. 14% grads pursue arts and sciences degrees. 2% grads pursue law degrees. 3% grads pursue business degrees. 3% grads pursue medical degrees. **Faculty:** Student/faculty ratio 18:1. 72 full-time faculty, 63% hold PhDs, 15% are members of minority groups, 32% are women.

ACADEMICS
Degrees: Associate, bachelor's, terminal associate, transfer associate. **Classes:** Most classes have 20–29 students. Most lab/discussion sessions have 10–19 students. **Majors with Highest Enrollment:** Business/commerce; elementary education and teaching; nursing/registered nurse (RN, ASN, BSN, MSN). **Special Study Options:** Cross-registration, distance learning, double major, dual enrollment, external degree program, honors program, independent study, internships, study abroad, teacher certification program. **Honors programs:** The University of Pittsburgh at Bradford offers the Scholars Program which is designed to create a learning community for outstanding students at Pitt-Bradford. Special programs offered to physically disabled students include note-taking services, reader services, tape recorders, tutors. **Career services:** Alumni network, alumni services, career assessment, internships, regional alumni. **Career services highlights include:** Career Messenger is a monthly newsletter that will be distributed via e-mail. To receive this newsletter you must subscribe.

FACILITIES
Housing: Coed dorms, special housing for disabled students, apartments for single students. 99% of campus accessible to physically disabled. **Special Academic Facilities/Equipment:** Ceramics Studio, Biodiesal Lab, Television and Radio Broadcast Labs. **Computers:** 100% of classrooms, 100% of dorms, 90% of libraries, 90% of dining areas, 100% of student union, 50% of common outdoor areas have wireless network access. Students can register for classes online. Administrative functions (other than registration) can be performed online.

CAMPUS LIFE
Environment: Village. **Activities:** Choral groups, dance, drama/theater, literary magazine, radio station, student government, student newspaper, campus ministries. **Organizations:** 54 registered organizations, 8 honor societies, 1 religious organizations. 3 fraternities, 3 sororities. **Athletics (Intercollegiate):** *Men:* Baseball, basketball, cross-country, golf, soccer, swimming, tennis. *Women:* Basketball, cross-country, golf, soccer, softball, swimming, tennis, volleyball. **On-Campus Highlights:** Sport and Fitness Center, The Commons, student apartments, Blaisdell Hall (Fine Arts Building), smart classrooms. **Environmental Initiatives:** Development of an Alternative Energy Institute. Partnership in a consortium that includes the University of Pittsburgh, Penn State, and others for development of an alternative energy university consortium.

ADMISSIONS
Freshman Academic Profile: Average high school GPA 3.11. 0.29% in top 10% of high school class, 6.47% in top 25% of high school class, 42.06% in top 50% of high school class. 95% from public high schools. SAT Math middle 50% range 450–550. SAT Critical Reading middle 50% range 440–520. SAT Writing middle 50% range 430–530. ACT middle 50% range 19–22. Minimum paper TOEFL 550. Minimum computer TOEFL 213. **Basis for Candidate Selection:** *Very important factors considered include:* level of applicant's interest. *Important factors considered include:* Academic GPA, rigor of secondary school record, standardized test scores, interview. *Other factors considered include:* Class rank, application essay, recommendation(s), character/personal qualities, extracurricular activities, talent/ability, volunteer work, work experience. **Freshman Admission Requirements:** High school diploma is required

and GED is accepted. *Academic units required:* 4 English, 2 mathematics, 1 science, (1 science labs), 2 foreign language, 1 history, 5 academic electives. *Academic units recommended:* 4 English, 2 science, (2 science labs), 2 foreign language, 1 history, 5 academic electives. **Freshman Admission Statistics:** 987 applied, 83% admitted, 51% enrolled. **Transfer Admission Requirements:** College transcript(s), statement of good standing from prior institution(s). Minimum college GPA of 2.0 required. Lowest grade transferable C–. **General Admission Information:** Application fee $45. Notification on a rolling basis, beginning on or about 11/1. Nonfall registration accepted. Admission may be deferred for a maximum of 1 year. Credit and/or placement offered for CEEB Advanced Placement tests.

COSTS AND FINANCIAL AID
Annual in-state tuition $11,012. Annual out-of-state tuition $20,572. Room and board $7,480. Required fees $710. Average book expense $1,050. **Required Forms and Deadlines:** FAFSA. Priority financial aid filing date 3/1. **Notification of Awards:** Applicants will be notified of awards on a rolling basis beginning 4/1. **Types of Aid:** *Need-based scholarships/grants:* Federal Pell, SEOG, state scholarships/grants, private scholarships, the school's own gift aid. *Loans:* FFEL Subsidized Stafford, FFEL Unsubsidized Stafford, FFEL PLUS, Federal Perkins. *Student Employment:* Federal Work-Study Program available. Institutional employment available. Off-campus job opportunities are fair. **Financial Aid Statistics:** 56% freshmen, 36% undergrads receive need-based scholarship or grant aid. 61% freshmen, 31% undergrads receive non-need-based scholarship or grant aid. 86% freshmen, 57% undergrads receive need-based self-help aid. 86.27% freshmen, 84% undergrads receive any aid. 81.7% undergrads borrow to pay for school. Average cumulative indebtedness $21,683. **Criteria for awarding institutional aid:** *Non-need-based:* Academics, alumni affiliation, state/district residency.

UNIVERSITY OF PITTSBURGH AT JOHNSTOWN

157 Blackington Hall, 450 Schoolhouse Road, Johnstown, PA 15904
Phone: 814-269-7050 **Financial Aid Phone:** 814-269-7045
E-mail: upjadmit@pitt.edu **CEEB Code:** 2934
Fax: 814-269-7044 **Website:** www.upj.pitt.edu

This public school was founded in 1927. It has a 650-acre campus.

RATINGS
Admissions Selectivity Rating: 71   **Fire Safety Rating:** 60*   **Green Rating:** 60*

STUDENTS AND FACULTY
Enrollment: 3,043. **Student Body:** 46% female, 54% male, 2% out-of-state, 1% international (20 countries represented). Asian 2%, African American 2%, Caucasian 92%, Hispanic 1%.
Retention and Graduation: 73% freshmen return for sophomore year. 42% freshmen graduate within 4 years. 8% grads pursue arts and sciences degrees. 1% grads pursue law degrees. 1% grads pursue business degrees. 2% grads pursue medical degrees. **Faculty:** Student/faculty ratio 18:1. 143 full-time faculty, 71% hold PhDs, 7% are members of minority groups, 39% are women.

ACADEMICS
Degrees: Associate, bachelor's, certificate. **Classes:** Most classes have 20–29 students. Most lab/discussion sessions have 10–19 students. **Special Study Options:** Accelerated program, cooperative education program, cross-registration, distance learning, double major, dual enrollment, independent study, internships, liberal arts/career combination, student-designed major, study abroad, teacher certification program. **Honors programs:** President's Scholars Program Special programs offered to physically disabled students include tutors. **Career services:** Alumni network, alumni services, internships

FACILITIES
Housing: Coed dorms, special housing for disabled students, fraternity/sorority housing, apartments for single students, theme housing, townhouses, lodges, single-sex residence upon request. 100% of campus accessible to physically disabled. **Special Academic Facilities/Equipment:** Art museum, performing arts center, language lab. **Computers:** 75% of classrooms, 100% of libraries, 50% of dining areas, 100% of student union, 50% of common outdoor areas have wireless network access. Administrative functions (other than registration) can be performed online.

CAMPUS LIFE
Environment: City. **Activities:** Choral groups, concert band, dance, drama/theater, literary magazine, music ensembles, musical theater, pep band, radio station, student government, student newspaper, television station, yearbook, campus ministries, Model UN. **Organizations:** 70 registered organizations, 11 honor societies, 3 religious organizations. 5 fraternities, 3 sororities. **Athletics (Intercollegiate):** *Men:* Baseball, basketball, golf, soccer, wrestling. *Women:*

Basketball, cheerleading, cross-country, golf, soccer, track/field (outdoor), volleyball. **On-Campus Highlights:** Student Union Building, Sports Center, Cafeteria, Living/Learning Center, Performing Arts Center.

ADMISSIONS

Freshman Academic Profile: Average high school GPA 3.36. 10% in top 10% of high school class, 35% in top 25% of high school class, 73% in top 50% of high school class. SAT Math middle 50% range 460–570. SAT Critical Reading middle 50% range 450–540. SAT Writing middle 50% range 440–540. ACT middle 50% range 18–23. Minimum paper TOEFL 550. Minimum computer TOEFL 213. Minimum web-based TOEFL 80. **Basis for Candidate Selection:** *Very important factors considered include:* Class rank, academic GPA, rigor of secondary school record. *Important factors considered include:* Application essay, recommendation(s), standardized test scores, extracurricular activities, interview, level of applicant's interest, talent/ability, volunteer work, work experience. *Other factors considered include:* character/personal qualities, racial/ethnic status. **Freshman Admission Requirements:** High school diploma is required and GED is accepted. *Academic units required:* 4 English, 2 mathematics, 2 science, (1 science labs), 2 foreign language, 4 social studies. *Academic units recommended:* 3 mathematics. **Freshman Admission Statistics:** 1,652 applied, 89% admitted, 56% enrolled. **Transfer Admission Requirements:** High school transcript, college transcript(s), minimum college GPA of 2.0 required. Lowest grade transferable C. **General Admission Information:** Application fee $45. Notification on a rolling basis, beginning on or about 9/1. Nonfall registration accepted. Admission may be deferred for a maximum of 1 year. Credit and/or placement offered for CEEB Advanced Placement tests.

COSTS AND FINANCIAL AID

Annual in-state tuition $11,012. Annual out-of-state tuition $20,572. Room and board $7,530. Required fees $836. Average book expense $1,030. **Required Forms and Deadlines:** FAFSA, state aid form. Priority financial aid filing date 4/1. **Notification of Awards:** Applicants will be notified of awards on a rolling basis beginning 3/15. **Types of Aid:** *Need-based scholarships/grants:* Federal Pell, SEOG, state scholarships/grants, private scholarships, the school's own gift aid. *Loans:* FFEL Subsidized Stafford, FFEL Unsubsidized Stafford, FFEL PLUS, Federal Perkins. *Student Employment:* Federal Work-Study Program available. Institutional employment available. Off-campus job opportunities are good. **Financial Aid Statistics:** 55% freshmen, 51% undergrads receive need-based scholarship or grant aid. 22% freshmen, 19% undergrads receive non-need-based scholarship or grant aid. 69% freshmen, 64% undergrads receive need-based self-help aid. 5% freshmen, 4% undergrads receive athletic scholarships. 80% freshmen, 80% undergrads receive any aid. 85% undergrads borrow to pay for school. Average cumulative indebtedness $23,243. **Criteria for awarding institutional aid:** *Non-need-based:* Academics, athletics, leadership, minority status, state/district residency.

UNIVERSITY OF PITTSBURGH— PITTSBURGH CAMPUS

4227 Fifth Avenue, First Floor Alumni Hall, Pittsburgh, PA 15260
Phone: 412-624-7488 **Financial Aid Phone:** 412-624-7488
E-mail: oafa@pitt.edu **CEEB Code:** 2927
Fax: 412-648-8815 **Website:** www.pitt.edu **ACT Code:** 3734

This public school was founded in 1787. It has a 132-acre campus.

RATINGS

Admissions Selectivity Rating: 92　　　**Fire Safety Rating:** 82　　　**Green Rating:** 80

STUDENTS AND FACULTY

Enrollment: 17,682. **Student Body:** 51% female, 49% male, 19% out-of-state, 1% international (48 countries represented). Asian 5%, African American 8%, Caucasian, 79%, Hispanic 1%.
Retention and Graduation: 93% freshmen return for sophomore year. 57% freshmen graduate within 4 years. 38.8% grads go on to further study within 1 year. 5.8% grads pursue arts and sciences degrees. 5.2% grads pursue law degrees. 3.1% grads pursue business degrees. 4.2% grads pursue medical degrees.

ACADEMICS

Degrees: Bachelor's, certificate, doctoral, master's, post-bachelor's certificate, post-master's certificate. **Classes:** Most classes have 10–19 students. Most lab/

discussion sessions have 20–29 students. **Majors with Highest Enrollment:** marketing/marketing management; psychology; speech and rhetorical studies. **Special Study Options:** Accelerated program, cooperative education program, cross-registration, distance learning, double major, dual enrollment, English as a Second Language (ESL), exchange student program (domestic), external degree program, honors program, independent study, internships, liberal arts/career combination, student-designed major, study abroad, teacher certification program, weekend college. **Honors programs:** University Honors College. **Combined degree programs:** BA/MD, BA/DMD. Special programs offered to physically disabled students include note-taking services, reader services, tape recorders. **Career services:** Alumni network, alumni services, career/job search classes, career assessment, internships, regional alumni. **Career services highlights include:** The Pitt Career Network is an extremely valuable tool to which Pitt students have access. This is a database of over 6,000 alumni volunteers worldwide searchable by students. They also provide job shadowing opportunities nationwide. The Office of Student Employment and Placement Assistance (SEPA) hosted its first Career Kickoff event this past fall. The theme for this event was "On the Road With SEPA," since this was an event that would be held in multiple locations and the tag line was "Amp Up Your Career" to tie into the road/concert theme. Career Kickoff was created as a weeklong event held in various locations throughout campus making it convenient for students to stop by in between classes. The goal of this event was to provide students with valuable information before the career fair. We gave seniors and juniors a CD filled with valuabe information such as resume templates, sample cover letters, and acceptance letters. We also gave students a long-sleeved American Eagle t-shirt that listed every career-related event and date on the back of the shirt (similar to a concert t-shirt to tie into the "On the Road" theme.), magnets with the dates of the career-related events, networking tips, career fair tips, and an opportunity to win a pair of donated Cirque du Soleil tickets. Several components made this event unique. While most schools host a career week prior to their career fairs in their offices, we were in a different location each day making it convenient for students to attend. We also invited various regional employers to participate reviewing student resumes, discussing career opportunities in their companies, and providing students tips on networking with employers. Students had the opportunity to hear first hand from an employer tips on improving their resume. Students also had the opportunity to discuss possible positions with employers prior to the career fair, giving them a competitive edge in their job search. This event was extremely successful attacting over 2,300 students, making this the largest non-career fair event in our office.

FACILITIES

Housing: Coed dorms, special housing for disabled students, women's dorms, fraternity/sorority housing, apartments for single students, wellness housing, theme housing. 90% of campus accessible to physically disabled. **Special Academic Facilities/Equipment:** Stephen Foster Memorial, observatory. **Computers:** 100% of classrooms, 25% of dorms, 100% of libraries, 100% of dining areas, 100% of student union, 50% of common outdoor areas have wireless network access. Students can register for classes online. Administrative functions (other than registration) can be performed online.

CAMPUS LIFE

Environment: Metropolis. **Activities:** Choral groups, concert band, dance, drama/theater, jazz band, literary magazine, marching band, music ensembles, pep band, radio station, student government, student newspaper, student-run film society, television station, yearbook, campus ministries, international student organization, Model UN. **Organizations:** 395 registered organizations, 17 honor societies, 20 fraternities, 16 sororities. **Athletics (Intercollegiate):** *Men:* Baseball, basketball, cross-country, diving, football, soccer, swimming, track/field (outdoor), wrestling. *Women:* Basketball, cross-country, diving, gymnastics, soccer, softball, swimming, tennis, track/field (outdoor), volleyball. **On-Campus Highlights:** Cathedral of Learning, William Pitt Union, Heinz Chapel, Peterson Event Center, Sennott Square. **Environmental Initiatives:** The University recently constructed and began operation of a new steam plant which houses six 100,000 pound per hour national gas fired boilers. The Carillo Street Steam Plant provides partial steam service for both the University and the University of Pittsburgh Medical Center. Transfer of Pitt's steam production from the current steam provider to the new facility is projected to ultimately reduce steam-related greenhouse gas emissions by approximately 47%. The new plant is equipped with state of the art emission control technology and ultra-low NOx burners whcih emit less than 9 parts per million (ppm) NOx. The University of Pittsburgh is the only University in the country to own a plant permitted at 9 ppm NOx. The university has invested in a comprehensive building automation/energy management system and has converted many of its buildings from pneumatic to direct digital control (DDC). The system provides automatic control of building temperatures and operating schedules, allowing for setbacks during unoccupied periods. In conjunction with the energy management system, significant investments have been made in energy conservation measures, including lighting upgrades, installation of occupancy sensors, and the expansion of the university's central steam and chilled water infrastructure to eliminate stand-alone chillers and boilers. Pitt has also converted selected buildings from constant volume to variable volume air systems and has installed heat recovery systems in recent mechanical system upgrades. Over the past 13 years, an estimated cost avoidance of over $28 million has been achieved via energy management and conservation projects. The University pursues LEED certification for many large projects, selected on a case-by-case basis. The McGowan Institute for Regenerative Medicine was the first laboratory building in Pennsylvania to achieve LEED Gold certification. Four current projects are pursuing LEED certification (either Gold or Silver). The university has incorporated many sustainable design standards into its Professional Design Manual. This manual is distributed to all design professionals, who apply the standards to all renovation and construction projects. Examples of these standards include the requirement for occupancy sensors in all new construction and renovation projects, direct digital controls for all mechanical system installations or upgrades, energy efficient control schemes, energy efficient standard lighting, carpet with a minimum of 25% recycled content, carpet adhesives containing no bolatile organic compounds (VOC's), low VOC paints, premium efficiency motors, and VAV controls, among others. To highlight these standards, sustainable items are marked in the design manual with a green leaf symbol.

ADMISSIONS

Freshman Academic Profile: Average high school GPA 3.87. 49% in top 10% of high school class, 86% in top 25% of high school class, 99% in top 50% of high school class. SAT Math middle 50% range 590–680. SAT Critical Reading middle 50% range 570–680. SAT Writing middle 50% range 560–660. ACT middle 50% range 25–30. Minimum paper TOEFL 550. Minimum computer TOEFL 213. Minimum web-based TOEFL 80. **Basis for Candidate Selection:** *Very important factors considered include:* Academic GPA, rigor of secondary school record. *Important factors considered include:* Standardized test scores. *Other factors considered include:* Class rank, application essay, recommendation(s), character/personal qualities, extracurricular activities, first generation, geographical residence, interview, level of applicant's interest, racial/ethnic status, talent/ability, volunteer work, work experience. **Freshman Admission Requirements:** High school diploma is required and GED is not accepted. *Academic units required:* 4 English, 3 mathematics, 3 science, (3 science labs), 2 foreign language, 2 social studies, 3 academic electives. *Academic units recommended:* 4 English, 4 mathematics, 4 science, (4 science labs), 3 foreign language, 3 social studies, 5 academic electives. **Freshman Admission Statistics:** 21,737 applied, 59% admitted, 29% enrolled. **Transfer Admission Requirements:** High school transcript, college transcript(s), essay or personal statement, Lowest grade transferable C. **General Admission Information:** Application fee $45. Notification on a rolling basis, beginning on or about 10/1. Nonfall registration accepted. Credit offered for CEEB Advanced Placement tests.

COSTS AND FINANCIAL AID

Annual in-state tuition $13,344. Annual out-of-state tuition $23,042. Room and board $8,900. Required fees $810. Average book expense $1,050. **Required Forms and Deadlines:** FAFSA. Priority financial aid filing date 3/1. **Notification of Awards:** Applicants will be notified of awards on a rolling basis beginning 3/15. **Types of Aid:** *Need-based scholarships/grants:* Federal Pell, SEOG, state scholarships/grants, private scholarships, the school's own gift aid, Federal Nursing Scholarships. *Loans:* FFEL Subsidized Stafford, FFEL Unsubsidized Stafford, FFEL PLUS, Federal Perkins, Federal Nursing, college/university loans from institutional funds. *Student Employment:* Federal Work-Study Program available. Institutional employment available. Off-campus job opportunities are excellent. **Financial Aid Statistics:** 41% freshmen, 38% undergrads receive need-based scholarship or grant aid. 22% freshmen, 16% undergrads receive non-need-based scholarship or grant aid. 43% freshmen, 45% undergrads receive need-based self-help aid. 1% freshmen, 1% undergrads receive athletic scholarships. 63.8% freshmen, 62.8% undergrads receive any aid. **Criteria for awarding institutional aid:** *Non-need-based:* Academics, athletics.

UNIVERSITY OF PITTSBURGH—GREENSBURG

150 Finoli Drive, Greensburg, PA 15601
Phone: 724-836-9880 **Financial Aid Phone:** 724-836-9881
E-mail: upgadmit@pitt.edu **CEEB Code:** 2936
Fax: 724-836-7471 **Website:** www.upg.pitt.edu **ACT Code:** 3733

This public school was founded in 1963. It has a 217-acre campus.

RATINGS
Admissions Selectivity Rating: 74   **Fire Safety Rating:** 60*   **Green Rating:** 60*

STUDENTS AND FACULTY
Enrollment: 1,785. **Student Body:** 49% female, 51% male, 1% out-of-state, international. Asian 2%, African American 5%, Caucasian 80%, Hispanic 2%.

Retention and Graduation: 79% freshmen return for sophomore year. 32% freshmen graduate within 4 years. 21% grads go on to further study within 1 year. 15% grads pursue arts and sciences degrees. 1% grads pursue law degrees. 4% grads pursue business degrees. 1% grads pursue medical degrees. **Faculty:** Student/faculty ratio 18:1. 74 full-time faculty, 84% hold PhDs, 15% are members of minority groups, 51% are women.

ACADEMICS

Degrees: Bachelor's, certificate. **Classes:** Most classes have 30–39 students. Most lab/discussion sessions have 20–29 students. **Majors with Highest Enrollment:** Biology/biological sciences; management information systems; psychology. **Special Study Options:** Cross-registration, double major, dual enrollment, exchange student program (domestic), independent study, internships, liberal arts/career combination, student-designed major, study abroad Special programs offered to physically disabled students include note-taking services, reader services, tape recorders, tutors. **Career services:** Alumni network, alumni services, career/job search classes, career assessment, internships, regional alumni.

FACILITIES

Housing: Coed dorms, theme housing. 95% of campus accessible to physically disabled. **Computers:** 100% of libraries, 100% of dining areas, 100% of student union, have wireless network access. Students can register for classes online. Administrative functions (other than registration) can be performed online.

CAMPUS LIFE

Environment: Village. **Activities:** Choral groups, dance, drama/theater, literary magazine, musical theater, radio station, student government, student newspaper, campus ministries, international student organization. **Organizations:** 25 registered organizations, 8 honor societies, 3 religious organizations. **Athletics (Intercollegiate):** *Men:* Baseball, basketball, cross-country, golf, soccer, tennis. *Women:* Basketball, cross-country, golf, soccer, softball, volleyball. **On-Campus Highlights:** Academic Villages, Exchange—Coffee House, Fireside Lounge, Wagner Dining Hall, Ferguson Theater.

ADMISSIONS

Freshman Academic Profile: Average high school GPA 3.37. 10% in top 10% of high school class, 38% in top 25% of high school class, 80% in top 50% of high school class. 95% from public high schools. SAT Math middle 50% range 470–570. SAT Critical Reading middle 50% range 460–550. SAT Writing middle 50% range 450–540. ACT middle 50% range 19–23. Minimum paper TOEFL 550. Minimum computer TOEFL 213. **Basis for Candidate Selection:** *Very important factors considered include:* Class rank, academic GPA, rigor of secondary school record, standardized test scores, *Other factors considered include:* Application essay, recommendation(s), character/personal qualities, extracurricular activities, interview, level of applicant's interest, talent/ability, volunteer work. **Freshman Admission Requirements:** High school diploma is required and GED is accepted. *Academic units required:* 4 English, 2 mathematics, 1 science, (1 science labs), 3 foreign language, 2 social studies, 2 history, 1 academic electives. *Academic units recommended:* 4 English, 4 mathematics, 2 science, 3 foreign language, 2 social studies, 2 history, 1 computer science, 3 academic electives. **Freshman Admission Statistics:** 1,276 applied, 74% admitted, 87% enrolled. **Transfer Admission Requirements:** High school transcript, college transcript(s), statement of good standing from prior institution(s). Minimum college GPA of 2.0 required. Lowest grade transferable C. **General Admission Information:** Application fee $45. Notification on a rolling basis, beginning on or about 9/15. Nonfall registration accepted. Admission may be deferred for a maximum of 1 year. Credit and/or placement offered for CEEB Advanced Placement tests.

COSTS AND FINANCIAL AID

Required Forms and Deadlines: FAFSA, state aid form. Priority financial aid filing date 2/15. **Notification of Awards:** Applicants will be notified of awards on a rolling basis beginning 3/15. **Types of Aid:** *Need-based scholarships/grants:* Federal Pell, SEOG, state scholarships/grants, private scholarships, the school's own gift aid, United Negro College Fund *Loans:* FFEL Subsidized Stafford, FFEL Unsubsidized Stafford, FFEL PLUS, Federal Perkins, college/university loans from institutional funds. *Student Employment:* Federal Work-Study Program available. Institutional employment available. Off-campus job opportunities are good. **Financial Aid Statistics:** 31% freshmen, 32% undergrads receive need-based scholarship or grant aid. 19% freshmen, 9% undergrads receive non-need-based scholarship or grant aid. 65% freshmen, 63% undergrads receive need-based self-help aid. 82% undergrads borrow to pay for school. Average cumulative indebtedness $24,707. **Criteria for awarding institutional aid:** *Non-need-based:* Academics, leadership, minority status.

UNIVERSITY OF PORTLAND

5000 North Willamette Blvd, Portland, OR 97203-7147
Phone: 503-943-7147 **Financial Aid Phone:** 503-943-7311
E-mail: admissions@up.edu **CEEB Code:** 4847
Fax: 503-943-7315 **Website:** www.up.edu **ACT Code:** 3500

This private school, affiliated with the Roman Catholic Church, was founded in 1901. It has a 130-acre campus.

RATINGS
Admissions Selectivity Rating: 91   **Fire Safety Rating:** 60*   **Green Rating:** 93

STUDENTS AND FACULTY
Enrollment: 3,077. **Student Body:** 61% female, 39% male, 59% out-of-state, 2% international (32 countries represented). Asian 12%, African American 1%, Caucasian 67%, Hispanic 5%, Native American 1%.
Retention and Graduation: 86% freshmen return for sophomore year. 68% freshmen graduate within 4 years. 25% grads go on to further study within 1 year. **Faculty:** Student/faculty ratio 13:1. 207 full-time faculty, 90% hold PhDs, 4% are members of minority groups, 44% are women.

ACADEMICS
Degrees: Bachelor's, master's, post-master's certificate. **Classes:** Most classes have 20–29 students. Most lab/discussion sessions have 10–19 students. **Majors with Highest Enrollment:** Biology/biological sciences; finance; nursing/registered nurse (RN, ASN, BSN, MSN). **Special Study Options:** Cross-registration, double major, honors program, independent study, internships, liberal arts/career combination, study abroad, teacher certification program. **Honors programs:** The honors program provides an exciting intellectual challenge for highly motivated students whit above average high school records. The program is designed to facilitate learning through special small classes which permit a high level of student-faculty interaction. Honors students may be enrolled in any major. Special programs offered to physically disabled students include note-taking services, reader services, tutors. **Career services:** Alumni network, alumni services, career/job search classes, career assessment, internships, regional alumni.

FACILITIES
Housing: Coed dorms, men's dorms, women's dorms, theme housingRental housing. 80% of campus accessible to physically disabled. **Special Academic Facilities/Equipment:** Art gallery, observatory. **Computers:** 100% of classrooms, 100% of dorms, 100% of libraries, 100% of dining areas, 100% of student union, 100% of common outdoor areas have wireless network access. Students can register for classes online. Administrative functions (other than registration) can be performed online.

CAMPUS LIFE
Environment: Metropolis. **Activities:** Choral groups, concert band, dance, drama/theater, jazz band, literary magazine, music ensembles, musical theater, pep band, radio station, student government, student newspaper, student-run film society, symphony orchestra, yearbook, campus ministries, international student organization. **Organizations:** 40 registered organizations, 15 honor societies, 9 religious organizations. **Athletics (Intercollegiate):** *Men:* Baseball, basketball, cross-country, golf, soccer, tennis, track/field (outdoor). *Women:* Basketball, cross-country, golf, soccer, tennis, track/field (outdoor), volleyball. **On-Campus Highlights:** The Cove, St. Mary's Lounge, Howard Recreation Hall. **Environmental Initiatives:** Portland host and active participant of Focus the Nation. Promotion and availability of alternative transportation sources for students. New building construction meet LEED standards.

ADMISSIONS
Freshman Academic Profile: Average high school GPA 3.63. 43% in top 10% of high school class, 76% in top 25% of high school class, 94% in top 50% of high school class. 60% from public high schools. SAT Math middle 50% range 550–650. SAT Critical Reading middle 50% range 530–640. Minimum paper TOEFL 550. Minimum computer TOEFL 197. **Basis for Candidate Selection:** *Very important factors considered include:* Academic GPA, rigor of secondary school record, standardized test scores. *Important factors considered include:* Class rank, application essay, recommendation(s), extracurricular activities, talent/ability, volunteer work. *Other factors considered include:* Alumni/ae relation, character/personal qualities, first generation, geographical residence, interview, level of applicant's interest, racial/ethnic status, religious affiliation/commitment, work experience. **Freshman Admission Requirements:** High school diploma is required and GED is accepted. *Academic units required:* 3 English, 2 mathematics, 2 science, 2 social studies, 2 history, 7 academic electives. *Academic units recommended:* 4 English, 3 mathematics, 2 science, 2 social studies, 2 history, 7 academic electives. **Freshman Admission Statistics:** 9,381 applied, 56% admitted, 16% enrolled. **Transfer Admission Require-**

ments: College transcript(s), essay or personal statement, minimum college GPA of 2.5 required. Lowest grade transferable C. **General Admission Information:** Application fee $50. Regular application deadline 6/1. Notification on a rolling basis, beginning on or about 10/1. Nonfall registration accepted. Credit and/or placement offered for CEEB Advanced Placement tests.

COSTS AND FINANCIAL AID
Annual tuition $30,800. Room and board $9,135. Required fees $1,196. Average book expense $1,000. **Required Forms and Deadlines:** FAFSA. Priority financial aid filing date 3/1. **Notification of Awards:** Applicants will be notified of awards on a rolling basis beginning 3/15. **Types of Aid:** *Need-based scholarships/grants:* Federal Pell, SEOG, state scholarships/grants, private scholarships, the school's own gift aid. *Loans:* FFEL Subsidized Stafford, FFEL Unsubsidized Stafford, FFEL PLUS, Federal Perkins, Federal Nursing, college/university loans from institutional funds. *Student Employment:* Federal Work-Study Program available. Highest amount earned per year from on-campus jobs $1,377. Off-campus job opportunities are good. **Financial Aid Statistics:** 50% freshmen, 48% undergrads receive need-based scholarship or grant aid. 67% freshmen, 62% undergrads receive non-need-based scholarship or grant aid. 52% freshmen, 51% undergrads receive need-based self-help aid. 4% freshmen, 5% undergrads receive athletic scholarships. 96% freshmen, 93% undergrads receive any aid. 62% undergrads borrow to pay for school. Average cumulative indebtedness $23,955. **Criteria for awarding institutional aid:** *Non-need-based:* Academics, alumni affiliation, athletics, music/drama, religious affiliation.

UNIVERSITY OF PRINCE EDWARD ISLAND

Office of the Registrar, Charlottetown, PE C1A 4P3 Canada
Phone: 902-566-0439 **Financial Aid Phone:** 902-566-0358
E-mail: registrar@upei.ca
Fax: 902-566-0795 **Website:** www.upei.ca

This public school was founded in 1969. It has a 130-acre campus.

RATINGS
Admissions Selectivity Rating: 60*   **Fire Safety Rating:** 60*   **Green Rating:** 60*

STUDENTS AND FACULTY
Student Body: 15% out-of-state (50 countries represented).
Retention and Graduation: Faculty: Student/faculty ratio 12:1. 244 full-time faculty.

ACADEMICS
Degrees: Bachelor's, certificate, diploma, first professional, master's. **Classes:** Most classes have 20–29 students. Most lab/discussion sessions have fewer than 10 students. **Special Study Options:** Accelerated program, cooperative education program, distance learning, double major, English as a Second Language (ESL), exchange student program (domestic), honors program, internships, study abroad, teacher certification program. Special programs offered to physically disabled students include tutors.

FACILITIES
Housing: Coed dorms, special housing for disabled students, men's dorms, women's dorms, apartments for single students. **Computers:** Students can register for classes online. Administrative functions (other than registration) can be performed online.

CAMPUS LIFE
Environment: Town. **Activities:** Choral groups, concert band, drama/theater, music ensembles, radio station, student government, student newspaper, yearbook. **Organizations:** 25 registered organizations, 3 religious organizations. **Athletics (Intercollegiate):** *Men:* Basketball, ice hockey, soccer. *Women:* Basketball, field hockey, ice hockey, rugby, soccer, volleyball. **On-Campus Highlights:** Chi-Wan Young Sports Centre, W.A. Murphy Student Centre, MacLauchlan Arena and Aquatic Centre, Atlantic Veterinary College, Robertson Library.

ADMISSIONS
Freshman Academic Profile: 90% from public high schools. Minimum paper TOEFL 550. Minimum computer TOEFL 213. **Basis for Candidate Selection:** *Very important factors considered include:* Academic GPA, rigor of secondary school record. *Important factors considered include:* Class rank, recommendation(s). *Other factors considered include:* Standardized test scores. **Freshman Admission Statistics:** 1,044 applied, 61% admitted, 91% enrolled. **Transfer Admission Requirements:** College transcript(s), statement of good standing from prior institution(s). **General Admission Information:** Application fee $50. Regular application deadline 8/1. Regular notification 8/31. Nonfall

registration accepted. Admission may be deferred for a maximum of 1 semester. Neither credit nor placement offered for CEEB Advanced Placement tests.

COSTS AND FINANCIAL AID
Average book expense $500.

UNIVERSITY OF PUGET SOUND

1500 North Warner Street, Tacoma, WA 98416-1062
Phone: 253-879-3211 **Financial Aid Phone:** 253-879-3214
E-mail: admission@ups.edu **CEEB Code:** 4067
Fax: 253-879-3993 **Website:** www.ups.edu **ACT Code:** 4450

This private school was founded in 1888. It has a 97-acre campus.

RATINGS
Admissions Selectivity Rating: 89   **Fire Safety Rating:** 72   **Green Rating:** 60*

STUDENTS AND FACULTY
Enrollment: 2,531. **Student Body:** 58% female, 42% male, 71% out-of-state, international (14 countries represented). Asian 9%, African American 3%, Caucasian 75%, Hispanic 3%, Native American 1%.
Retention and Graduation: 83% freshmen return for sophomore year. 68% freshmen graduate within 4 years. 34% grads go on to further study within 1 year. 11% grads pursue arts and sciences degrees. 3% grads pursue law degrees. 1% grads pursue business degrees. 3% grads pursue medical degrees. **Faculty:** Student/faculty ratio 11:1. 223 full-time faculty, 88% hold PhDs, 9% are members of minority groups, 45% are women.

ACADEMICS
Degrees: Bachelor's, first professional, master's, post-master's certificate.
Classes: Most classes have 10–19 students. Most lab/discussion sessions have 10–19 students. **Majors with Highest Enrollment:** Business/commerce; English language and literature; psychology. **Special Study Options:** Cooperative education program, double major, honors program, independent study, internships, student-designed major, study abroad, teacher certification program, 1 year of study in Asia, 3-2 engineering program, Business Leadership Program.
Honors programs: Business Leadership Program; Honors Program Special programs offered to physically disabled students include note-taking services, reader services, tape recorders, tutors. **Career services:** Alumni network, alumni services, career/job search classes, career assessment, internships, regional alumni. **Career services highlights include:** Internship Seminar 497/8, 1.0 Unit. In this seminar students examine issues related to work and its meaning in individual and collective life. Among the requirements are the completion of 120 hours of field experience at a site prearranged in consultation with the internship coordinator. The seminar provides the context to reflect on concrete experiences at the site and link them to political, psychological, social, economic and intellectual forces that shape our views on work and its meaning.

FACILITIES
Housing: Coed dorms, special housing for disabled students, women's dorms, fraternity/sorority housing, Small residential houses, theme floors in halls. 85% of campus accessible to physically disabled. **Special Academic Facilities/Equipment:** Art gallery, natural history museum, concert hall, transmission and scanning electron microscopes, spectrometers, exercise science lab, observatory, paleomagnetic and X-ray lab, physiology labs, and DNA Sequencer. **Computers:** 30% of classrooms, 30% of dorms, 95% of libraries, 95% of dining areas, 85% of student union, 10% of common outdoor areas have wireless network access. Students can register for classes online. Administrative functions (other than registration) can be performed online.

CAMPUS LIFE
Environment: City. **Activities:** Choral groups, concert band, dance, drama/theater, jazz band, literary magazine, music ensembles, musical theater, opera, radio station, student government, student newspaper, student-run film society, symphony orchestra, yearbook. **Organizations:** 77 registered organizations, 2 honor societies, 12 religious organizations. 4 fraternities, 4 sororities. **Athletics (Intercollegiate):** *Men:* Baseball, basketball, crew/rowing, cross-country, football, golf, soccer, swimming, tennis, track/field (outdoor), track/field (indoor). *Women:* Basketball, crew/rowing, cross-country, golf, lacrosse, soccer, softball, swimming, tennis, track/field (outdoor), track/field (indoor), volleyball.
On-Campus Highlights: 3-story Dale Chihuly glass sculpture in Wyatt Hall, Harned Hall, new state-of-the-art science facility, Diversions Caf, 97 acres

---

of rolling lawns, native fir groves, and Tudor Gothic architecture. Music and theater productions directed by faculty and students on campus.

ADMISSIONS
Freshman Academic Profile: Average high school GPA 3.54. 40% in top 10% of high school class, 69% in top 25% of high school class, 95% in top 50% of high school class. 76% from public high schools. SAT Math middle 50% range 550–660. SAT Critical Reading middle 50% range 570–690. SAT Writing middle 50% range 560–660. ACT middle 50% range 25–30. Minimum paper TOEFL 550. Minimum computer TOEFL 213. **Basis for Candidate Selection:** *Very important factors considered include:* Academic GPA, rigor of secondary school record, standardized test scores. *Important factors considered include:* Application essay, recommendation(s), alumni/ae relation, character/personal qualities, extracurricular activities, racial/ethnic status, talent/ability. *Other factors considered include:* Class rank, first generation, interview, level of applicant's interest, volunteer work, work experience. **Freshman Admission Requirements:** High school diploma is required and GED is accepted. *Academic units recommended:* 4 English, 4 mathematics, 4 science, (4 science labs), 3 foreign language, 3 social studies, 3 history, 1 fine/visual/performing arts **Freshman Admission Statistics:** 5,231 applied, 65% admitted, 20% enrolled. **Transfer Admission Requirements:** College transcript(s), essay or personal statement, statement of good standing from prior institution(s). Minimum college GPA of 2.0 required. Lowest grade transferable D. **General Admission Information:** Application fee $40. Early decision application deadline 11/15. Regular application deadline 2/15. Regular notification 4/1. Nonfall registration accepted. Admission may be deferred for a maximum of 1 year. Credit and/or placement offered for CEEB Advanced Placement tests.

COSTS AND FINANCIAL AID
Average book expense $1,000. **Required Forms and Deadlines:** FAFSA. Priority financial aid filing date 2/1. **Notification of Awards:** Applicants will be notified of awards on a rolling basis beginning 3/15. **Types of Aid:** *Need-based scholarships/grants:* Federal Pell, SEOG, state scholarships/grants, private scholarships, the school's own gift aid. *Loans:* FFEL Subsidized Stafford, FFEL Unsubsidized Stafford, FFEL PLUS, Federal Perkins. *Student Employment:* Federal Work-Study Program available. Institutional employment available. Highest amount earned per year from on-campus jobs $2,650. Off-campus job opportunities are excellent. **Financial Aid Statistics:** 56% freshmen, 58% undergrads receive need-based scholarship or grant aid. 29% freshmen, 29% undergrads receive non-need-based scholarship or grant aid. 44% freshmen, 48% undergrads receive need-based self-help aid. 88% freshmen, 90% undergrads receive any aid. 88% undergrads borrow to pay for school. Average cumulative indebtedness $27,648. **Criteria for awarding institutional aid:** *Non-need-based:* Academics, alumni affiliation, art, leadership, music/drama, religious affiliation.

UNIVERSITY OF REDLANDS

1200 E. Colton Avenue, Redlands, CA 92373
Phone: 909-335-4074 **Financial Aid Phone:** 909-748-8047
E-mail: admissions@redlands.edu **CEEB Code:** 4848
Fax: 909-335-4089 **Website:** www.redlands.edu **ACT Code:** 464

This private school was founded in 1907. It has a 160-acre campus.

RATINGS
Admissions Selectivity Rating: 86   **Fire Safety Rating:** 74   **Green Rating:** 81

STUDENTS AND FACULTY
Enrollment: 2,819. **Student Body:** 56% female, 44% male, 33% out-of-state, 2% international (17 countries represented). Asian 5%, African American 4%, Caucasian 57%, Hispanic 13%, Native American 1%.
Retention and Graduation: 62% freshmen graduate within 4 years. 25% grads go on to further study within 1 year. 6% grads pursue law degrees. 6% grads pursue business degrees. 5% grads pursue medical degrees. **Faculty:** Student/faculty ratio 13:1. 224 full-time faculty, 87% hold PhDs, 46% are women.

ACADEMICS
Degrees: Associate, bachelor's, certificate, master's, post-bachelor's certificate, post-master's certificate. **Classes:** Most classes have 10–19 students. **Majors with Highest Enrollment:** Business/commerce; liberal arts and sciences/liberal studies; psychology. **Special Study Options:** Cross-registration, double major, dual enrollment, exchange student program (domestic), honors program,

independent study, internships, liberal arts/career combination, student-designed major, study abroad, teacher certification program. **Honors programs:** The Johnston Center for Integrative Studies allows students to design their own majors in consultation with faculty advisors. Students write contracts for their courses and receive narrative evaluations in lieu of traditional grades. The center has received national acclaim for its innovative approaches to education. Special programs offered to physically disabled students include note-taking services, reader services, tutors. **Career services:** Alumni services, career/job search classes, regional alumni.

FACILITIES

Housing: Coed dorms, special housing for disabled students, men's dorms, women's dorms, fraternity/sorority housing, apartments for single students, abroad programming, apartments for students with dependent children. 75% of campus accessible to physically disabled. **Special Academic Facilities/Equipment:** Art gallery, Far East art collection, Southwest collection, center for communicative disorders, language lab, Helen and Vernon Farquar Anthropology Lab, Physics Laser Photonics Lab, Irvine Map Library, Geographic Information System lab. **Computers:** 100% of classrooms, 100% of dorms, 100% of libraries, 100% of dining areas, 100% of student union, 100% of common outdoor areas have wireless network access. Students can register for classes online. Administrative functions (other than registration) can be performed online.

CAMPUS LIFE

Environment: Town. **Activities:** Choral groups, concert band, dance, drama/theater, jazz band, literary magazine, music ensembles, musical theater, opera, radio station, student government, student newspaper, student-run film society, symphony orchestra, yearbook. **Organizations:** 105 registered organizations, 8 honor societies, 8 religious organizations. 5 fraternities, 5 sororities. **Athletics (Intercollegiate):** *Men:* Baseball, basketball, cross-country, diving, football, golf, soccer, swimming, tennis, track/field (outdoor), water polo. *Women:* Basketball, cross-country, diving, golf, lacrosse, soccer, softball, swimming, tennis, track/field (outdoor), volleyball, water polo. **On-Campus Highlights:** Armacost Library, Peppers Art Center, Currier Gymnasium/Fitness Center, Chapel, Post Office, Other popular places on campus: Math and Physics Building, Aquatic Center, Football Stadium, Jasper's Corner, and Plaza Cafe. **Environmental Initiatives:** Co-Generation facility to provide power to much of the campus Lewis Hall—a high performance earth-sheltered green building that houses the department of Environmental Studies, the GIS program, and the Resdlands Institute A planned Art & Theater Center LEED (green) building—about to begin construction.

ADMISSIONS

Freshman Academic Profile: Average high school GPA 3.58. 31% in top 10% of high school class, 69% in top 25% of high school class, 92% in top 50% of high school class. SAT Math middle 50% range 540–620. SAT Critical Reading middle 50% range 520–620. ACT middle 50% range 21–27. Minimum paper TOEFL 550. Minimum computer TOEFL 213. **Basis for Candidate Selection:** *Very important factors considered include:* Academic GPA, recommendation(s), rigor of secondary school record, character/personal qualities, talent/ability. *Important factors considered include:* Application essay, standardized test scores. *Other factors considered include:* Alumni/ae relation, extracurricular activities, first generation, geographical residence, interview, racial/ethnic status, volunteer work, work experience. **Freshman Admission Requirements:** High school diploma is required and GED is accepted. *Academic units required:* 4 English, 3 mathematics, 2 science, (1 science labs), 2 foreign language, 2 social studies. *Academic units recommended:* 4 English, 4 mathematics, 3 science, (1 science labs), 3 foreign language, 2 social studies, 1 history. **Freshman Admission Statistics:** 3,443 applied, 68% admitted, 25% enrolled. **Transfer Admission Requirements:** High school transcript, college transcript(s), essay or personal statement, minimum college GPA of 2.5 required. Lowest grade transferable C. **General Admission Information:** Application fee $30. Regular application deadline 6/1. Notification on a rolling basis, beginning on or about 11/1. Nonfall registration accepted. Admission may be deferred for a maximum of 1 year. Credit and/or placement offered for CEEB Advanced Placement tests.

COSTS AND FINANCIAL AID

Annual tuition $31,994. Room and board $10,122. Required fees $300. Average book expense $1,566. **Required Forms and Deadlines:** FAFSA, state aid form, GPA Verification form for California Residents. Priority financial aid filing date 2/15. **Notification of Awards:** Applicants will be notified of awards on a rolling basis beginning 2/28. **Types of Aid:** *Need-based scholarships/grants:* Federal Pell, SEOG, state scholarships/grants, private scholarships, the school's own gift aid. *Loans:* FFEL Subsidized Stafford, FFEL Unsubsidized Stafford, FFEL PLUS, Federal Perkins, college/university loans from institutional funds. *Student Employment:* Federal Work-Study Program available. Highest amount earned per year from on-campus jobs $2,000. Off-campus job opportunities are fair. **Financial Aid Statistics:** 60% freshmen, 63% undergrads receive need-based scholarship or grant aid. 8% freshmen, 7% undergrads receive non-need-based scholarship or grant aid. 45% freshmen, 52% undergrads receive

need-based self-help aid. 82% freshmen, 81% undergrads receive any aid. 69.9% undergrads borrow to pay for school. Average cumulative indebtedness $17,290. **Criteria for awarding institutional aid:** *Non-need-based:* Academics, art, music/drama.

UNIVERSITY OF RHODE ISLAND

Newman Hall, 14 Upper College Road, Kingston, RI 02881
Phone: 401-874-7100 **Financial Aid Phone:** 401-874-7530
E-mail: admission@uri.edu **CEEB Code:** 3919
Fax: 401-874-5523 **Website:** www.uri.edu **ACT Code:** 3818

This public school was founded in 1892. It has a 1300-acre campus.

RATINGS
Admissions Selectivity Rating: 76   **Fire Safety Rating:** 80   **Green Rating:** 93

STUDENTS AND FACULTY
Enrollment: 12,520. **Student Body:** 56% female, 44% male, 39% out-of-state, international (64 countries represented). Asian 3%, African American 5%, Caucasian 73%, Hispanic 5%.
Retention and Graduation: 80% freshmen return for sophomore year. 40% freshmen graduate within 4 years. **Faculty:** Student/faculty ratio 16.5:1. 683 full-time faculty, 89% hold PhDs, 14% are members of minority groups, 42% are women. 2.8% of classes are taught by teaching assistants.

ACADEMICS
Degrees: Bachelor's, first professional, master's, post-bachelor's certificate. **Classes:** Most classes have 20–29 students. Most lab/discussion sessions have 10–19 students. **Majors with Highest Enrollment:** communication studies/speech communication and rhetoric; nursing/registered nurse (RN, ASN, BSN, MSN); psychology. **Special Study Options:** Distance learning, double major, dual enrollment, exchange student program (domestic), honors program, independent study, internships, study abroad, teacher certification program, weekend college. **Honors programs:** The Honors Program at URI features small classes, a nationally renowned Honors Colloquium, National Scholarship for upper class students, advising and honors housing for upper class students. **Combined degree programs:** MCP/JD, MPA/MDS, PhD/MMA, MS/JD, MA/MLIS, MMA/JD, PharmD/MBA, MPA/MLIS, MP. Special programs offered to physically disabled students include note-taking services, tape recorders. **Career services:** Alumni network, alumni services, career assessment, internships, regional alumni. **Career services highlights include:** Career assessments and job search assistance.

FACILITIES
Housing: Coed dorms, special housing for disabled students, fraternity/sorority housing, apartments for married students, cooperative housing, apartments for single students, wellness housing, theme housingLearning communities for undecided majors, honor program, health sciences, engineering, college environment and health sciences majors, and nursing. 100% of campus accessible to physically disabled. **Special Academic Facilities/Equipment:** Center for robotic research, animal science farm, planetarium, Watson House Museum, Narragansett Bay Campus for Marine Sciences, American historic textiles museum, aquaculture center, fisheries and marine technology laboratory, center for biotechnology and life sciences, human performance laboratory. **Computers:** 50% of classrooms, 100% of dorms, 100% of libraries, 75% of dining areas, 100% of student union, 25% of common outdoor areas have wireless network access. Students can register for classes online. Administrative functions (other than registration) can be performed online.

CAMPUS LIFE
Environment: Village. **Activities:** Choral groups, concert band, dance, drama/theater, jazz band, literary magazine, marching band, music ensembles, musical theater, pep band, radio station, student government, student newspaper, student-run film society, television station, yearbook, campus ministries, international student organization. **Organizations:** 100 registered organizations, 40 honor societies, 5 religious organizations. 11 fraternities, 9 sororities. **Athletics (Intercollegiate):** *Men:* Baseball, basketball, cheerleading, cross-country, football, golf, soccer, track/field (outdoor), track/field (indoor). *Women:* Basketball, cheerleading, crew/rowing, cross-country, diving, soccer, softball, swimming, tennis, track/field (outdoor), track/field (indoor), volleyball. **On-Campus Highlights:** Ryan Center and Boss Ice Arena, Ballentine Hall (Business building), Memorial Student Union, Multi-Cultural Center in heart of campus, Hope Dining Commons, Center for Biotechnology and Life Sciences—LEED certi-

fied and the focal point of a statewide effort to build a new, knowledge-based economy for Rhode Island. Green Hall—historic building houses Registrar, Financial Aid and Bursar, as well as Administrative Offices. **Environmental Initiatives:** Reduce Greenhouse Gas Emissions, LEED certification for new buildings, public transportation access.

ADMISSIONS

Freshman Academic Profile: Average high school GPA 3.09. 16% in top 10% of high school class, SAT Math middle 50% range 500–590. SAT Critical Reading middle 50% range 480–570. Minimum paper TOEFL 550. Minimum computer TOEFL 213. Minimum web-based TOEFL 79. **Basis for Candidate Selection:** *Very important factors considered include:* Rigor of secondary school record. *Important factors considered include:* Class rank, application essay, academic GPA, standardized test scores. *Other factors considered include:* Recommendation(s), alumni/ae relation, character/personal qualities, extracurricular activities, first generation, geographical residence, level of applicant's interest, racial/ethnic status, state residency, talent/ability, volunteer work, work experience. **Freshman Admission Requirements:** High school diploma is required and GED is accepted. *Academic units required:* 4 English, 3 mathematics, 2 science, (1 science labs), 2 foreign language, 2 social studies, 5 academic electives. **Freshman Admission Statistics:** 15,887 applied, 80% admitted, 25% enrolled. **Transfer Admission Requirements:** College transcript(s), essay or personal statement, statement of good standing from prior institution(s). Minimum college GPA of 2.5 required. Lowest grade transferable C. **General Admission Information:** Application fee $65. Regular application deadline 2/1. Regular notification 3/31. Notification on a rolling basis, beginning on or about 12/1. Nonfall registration accepted. Credit and/or placement offered for CEEB Advanced Placement tests.

COSTS AND FINANCIAL AID

Annual in-state tuition $8,238. Annual out-of-state tuition $24,736. Room and board $9,892. Required fees $1,290. Average book expense $1,200. **Required Forms and Deadlines:** FAFSA. Priority financial aid filing date 3/1. **Notification of Awards:** Applicants will be notified of awards on a rolling basis beginning 3/31. **Types of Aid:** *Need-based scholarships/grants:* Federal Pell, SEOG, state scholarships/grants, private scholarships, the school's own gift aid. *Loans:* Direct Subsidized Stafford, Direct Unsubsidized Stafford, Direct PLUS, Federal Perkins, Federal Nursing, state loans, college/university loans from institutional funds. *Student Employment:* Federal Work-Study Program available. Institutional employment available. Highest amount earned per year from on-campus jobs $2,000. Off-campus job opportunities are good. **Financial Aid Statistics:** 53% freshmen, 55% undergrads receive need-based scholarship or grant aid. 5% freshmen, 5% undergrads receive non-need-based scholarship or grant aid. 50% freshmen, 52% undergrads receive need-based self-help aid. 57% freshmen, 57% undergrads receive any aid. 71% undergrads borrow to pay for school. Average cumulative indebtedness $22,500. **Criteria for awarding institutional aid:** *Non-need-based:* Academics, alumni affiliation, art, athletics, music/drama.

UNIVERSITY OF RICHMOND

28 Westhampton Way, University of Richmond, VA 23173
Phone: 804-289-8640
E-mail: www.richmond.edu/admission/index. **CEEB Code:** 5569
Fax: 804-287-6003 **Website:** www.richmond.edu **ACT Code:** 4410

This private school was founded in 1830. It has a 350-acre campus.

RATINGS
Admissions Selectivity Rating: 94　　**Fire Safety Rating:** 77　　**Green Rating:** 95

STUDENTS AND FACULTY
Enrollment: 2,826. **Student Body:** 53% female, 47% male, 80% out-of-state, 5% international (68 countries represented). Asian 5%, African American 8%, Caucasian 64%, Hispanic 4%.
Retention and Graduation: 92% freshmen return for sophomore year. 82% freshmen graduate within 4 years. 39% grads go on to further study within 1 year. 15% grads pursue arts and sciences degrees. 5% grads pursue law degrees. 5% grads pursue medical degrees. **Faculty:** Student/faculty ratio 8:1. 321 full-time faculty, 80% hold PhDs, 11% are members of minority groups, 40% are women.

ACADEMICS
Degrees: Associate, bachelor's, certificate, diploma, master's, post-bachelor's certificate. **Classes:** Most classes have 10–19 students. Most lab/discussion sessions have 10–19 students. **Majors with Highest Enrollment:** Business administration and management; English language and literature; political science and government. **Special Study Options:** Accelerated program, cross-registration, distance learning, double major, English as a Second Language (ESL), exchange student program (domestic), honors program, independent study, internships, student-designed major, study abroad, teacher certification program, Notes on above: Summer English Language Institute is for accepted International Students only. Distance Learning offered through School of Continuing Studies. **Career services:** Alumni network, alumni services, career/job search classes, career assessment, internships. **Career services highlights include:** Spider Road Trips. Trips include Spiders on Wall Street to visit Wall Street firms; Spiders in Media and Communications to New York City; Spiders for the Common Good to public service organizations in Washington D.C. and day trips to selected organizations in the Richmond area. Accompanied by staff, groups of approximately 25 students are given the opportunity to see the operations and hear speakers in different organizations.

FACILITIES
Housing: Coed dorms, special housing for disabled students, men's dorms, women's dorms, apartments for single students, theme housing*Global House, Outdoor House, and Civic Engagement represent co-ed housing. Other housing options include: Spinning your Web (for first-year males) and Ready for Moore (for first-year females). 90% of campus accessible to physically disabled. **Special Academic Facilities/Equipment:** Art gallery, mineral museum, Virginia Baptist archives, language lab, Neuroscience lab, Speech Center, Music Technology lab, Jepson School of Leadership, Center for Civic Engagement. **Computers:** 100% of classrooms, 100% of dorms, 100% of libraries, 100% of dining areas, 100% of student union, 100% of common outdoor areas have wireless network access. Students can register for classes online. Administrative functions (other than registration) can be performed online.

CAMPUS LIFE
Environment: Metropolis. **Activities:** Choral groups, concert band, dance, drama/theater, jazz band, literary magazine, music ensembles, musical theater, pep band, radio station, student government, student newspaper, student-run film society, symphony orchestra, campus ministries, international student organization, Model UN. **Organizations:** 208 registered organizations, 28 honor societies, 17 religious organizations. 6 fraternities, 8 sororities. **Athletics (Intercollegiate):** *Men:* Baseball, basketball, cross-country, football, golf, soccer, tennis, track/field (outdoor), track/field (indoor). *Women:* Basketball, cross-country, diving, field hockey, golf, lacrosse, soccer, swimming, tennis, track/field (outdoor), track/field (indoor). **On-Campus Highlights:** Tyler Haynes Commons, Robins Center (Athletic Center), Boatwright Memorial Library and Coffee Shop, Stern Plaza (Weinstein Hall, Jepson Hall, etc.), Westhampton Green (Modlin Center for the Arts). **Environmental Initiatives:** Signing the ACUPCC and subsequent creation of the Climate Action Plan (in process); waste diversion initiatives; energy conservation and efficiency projects.

ADMISSIONS
Freshman Academic Profile: 58% in top 10% of high school class, 87% in top 25% of high school class, 98% in top 50% of high school class. 59% from public high schools. SAT Math middle 50% range 590–680. SAT Critical Reading middle 50% range 580–670. SAT Writing middle 50% range 580–690. ACT middle 50% range 26–30. Minimum paper TOEFL 550. Minimum computer TOEFL 213. Minimum web-based TOEFL 80. **Basis for Candidate Selection:** *Very important factors considered include:* Academic GPA, rigor of secondary school record. *Important factors considered include:* Class rank, application essay, standardized test scores, character/personal qualities, first generation, talent/ability. *Other factors considered include:* Recommendation(s), alumni/ae relation, extracurricular activities, geographical residence, interview, racial/ethnic status, state residency, volunteer work, work experience. **Freshman Admission Requirements:** High school diploma is required and GED is accepted. *Academic units required:* 4 English, 3 mathematics, 2 science, (2 science labs), 2 foreign language, 2 history. *Academic units recommended:* 4 English, 4 mathematics, 4 science, (4 science labs), 4 foreign language, 4 history. **Freshman Admission Statistics:** 7,880 applied, 39% admitted, 30% enrolled. **Transfer Admission Requirements:** High school transcript, college transcript(s), essay or personal statement, statement of good standing from prior institution(s). Minimum college GPA of 2.0 required. Lowest grade transferable C. **General Admission Information:** Application fee $50. Early decision application deadline 11/15. Regular application deadline 1/15. Regular notification 4/1. Nonfall registration not accepted. Admission may be deferred for a maximum of 1 year. Credit and/or placement offered for CEEB Advanced Placement tests.

COSTS AND FINANCIAL AID
Annual tuition $41,610. Room and board $8,810. Average book expense $1,050. **Required Forms and Deadlines:** FAFSA, institution's own financial aid form Financial aid filing deadline 2/15. **Notification of Awards:** Applicants will be

notified of awards on or about 4/1. **Types of Aid:** *Need-based scholarships/ grants:* Federal Pell, SEOG, state scholarships/grants, private scholarships, the school's own gift aid. *Loans:* Direct Subsidized Stafford, Direct Unsubsidized Stafford, Direct PLUS, Federal Perkins. *Student Employment:* Federal Work-Study Program available. Institutional employment available. Off-campus job opportunities are excellent. **Financial Aid Statistics:** 52% freshmen, 46% undergrads receive need-based scholarship or grant aid. 5% freshmen, 5% undergrads receive non-need-based scholarship or grant aid. 46% freshmen, 39% undergrads receive need-based self-help aid. 6% freshmen, 6% undergrads receive athletic scholarships. 68% freshmen, 70% undergrads receive any aid. 42% undergrads borrow to pay for school. Average cumulative indebtedness $21,555. **Criteria for awarding institutional aid:** *Non-need-based:* Academics, art, athletics, leadership, minority status, music/drama.

UNIVERSITY OF RIO GRANDE

218 North College Avenue, Admissions, Rio Grande, OH 45774
Phone: 740-245-7206 **Financial Aid Phone:** 740-245-7219
E-mail: admissions@rio.edu **CEEB Code:** 1663
Fax: 740-245-7260 **Website:** rio.edu **ACT Code:** 3324

This private school was founded in 1876. It has a 68-acre campus.

RATINGS
Admissions Selectivity Rating: 77   **Fire Safety Rating:** 98   **Green Rating:** 68

STUDENTS AND FACULTY
Enrollment: 1,534. **Student Body:** 61% female, 39% male, 2% out-of-state, 1% international. African American 4%, Caucasian 74%, Hispanic 1%.
Retention and Graduation: 56% freshmen return for sophomore year.
Faculty: Student/faculty ratio 16:1. 95 full-time faculty, 41% hold PhDs, 7% are members of minority groups, 61% are women.

ACADEMICS
Degrees: Associate, bachelor's, certificate, master's. **Classes:** Most classes have fewer than 10 students. Most lab/discussion sessions have 20–29 students. **Majors with Highest Enrollment:** Business/office automation/technology/ data entry; elementary education and teaching; nursing/registered nurse (RN, ASN, BSN, MSN). **Special Study Options:** Accelerated program, cooperative education program, distance learning, double major, dual enrollment, English as a Second Language (ESL), honors program, independent study, internships, liberal arts/career combination, student-designed major, study abroad, teacher certification program. **Combined degree programs:** 2-2 programs: nursing, business, industrial tech. Special programs offered to physically disabled students include note-taking services, reader services, tape recorders, tutors. **Career services:** Alumni services, career assessment, internships.

FACILITIES
Housing: Coed dorms, special housing for disabled students, men's dorms, women's dorms, wellness housing, private housing owned and operated by university available to responsible students. 75% of campus accessible to physically disabled. **Special Academic Facilities/Equipment:** Archives of local and college history, art museum, fine woodworking, theater, art annex. **Computers:** 75% of classrooms, 100% of dorms, 100% of libraries, 100% of dining areas, 100% of student union, 25% of common outdoor areas have wireless network access. Students can register for classes online. Administrative functions (other than registration) can be performed online.

CAMPUS LIFE
Environment: Rural. **Activities:** Choral groups, concert band, dance, drama/ theater, jazz band, literary magazine, music ensembles, musical theater, pep band, radio station, student government, student newspaper, television station. **Organizations:** 34 registered organizations, 4 honor societies, 3 religious organizations. 4 fraternities, 5 sororities. **Athletics (Intercollegiate):** *Men:* Baseball, basketball, cross-country, soccer, track/field (outdoor), track/field (indoor). *Women:* Basketball, cheerleading, cross-country, soccer, softball, track/ field (outdoor), track/field (indoor), volleyball. **On-Campus Highlights:** Food Court, Red Zone, Basketball Court **Environmental Initiatives:** Recycling program, some solar powered equipment, energy usage reduction program, trayless Tuesdays in the cafeteria.

ADMISSIONS
Freshman Academic Profile: Average high school GPA 2.8. 6% in top 10% of high school class, 16% in top 25% of high school class, 52% in top 50% of high school class. 95% from public high schools. Minimum paper TOEFL 400. Minimum computer TOEFL 97. **Basis for Candidate Selection:** *Other factors considered include:* Class rank, academic GPA, standardized test scores.
Freshman Admission Requirements: High school diploma is required

and GED is accepted. *Academic units required:* 4 English, 3 mathematics, 3 science, (1 science labs), 3 social studies, 7 academic electives. *Academic units recommended:* (2 science labs), 2 foreign language, 2 history, 9 academic electives. **Freshman Admission Statistics:** 2,733 applied, 80% admitted, 23% enrolled. **Transfer Admission Requirements:** High school transcript, college transcript(s), statement of good standing from prior institution(s). Minimum college GPA of 0 required. Lowest grade transferable D. **General Admission Information:** Application fee $25. Nonfall registration accepted. Credit and/or placement offered for CEEB Advanced Placement tests.

COSTS AND FINANCIAL AID
Annual tuition $18,260. Room and board $7,600. Required fees $96. Average book expense $1,000. **Required Forms and Deadlines:** FAFSA, institution's own financial aid form. Priority financial aid filing date 3/15. **Notification of Awards:** Applicants will be notified of awards on a rolling basis beginning 1/15. **Types of Aid:** *Need-based scholarships/grants:* Federal Pell, SEOG, state scholarships/grants, private scholarships, the school's own gift aid. *Loans:* Direct Subsidized Stafford, Direct Unsubsidized Stafford, Direct PLUS, FFEL Subsidized Stafford, FFEL PLUS, Federal Perkins, Federal Nursing, college/university loans from institutional funds. *Student Employment:* Off-campus job opportunities are fair. **Financial Aid Statistics:** 73% freshmen, 53% undergrads receive need-based scholarship or grant aid. 76% freshmen, 52% undergrads receive non-need-based scholarship or grant aid. 58% freshmen, 47% undergrads receive need-based self-help aid. 3% freshmen, 10% undergrads receive athletic scholarships. 75% undergrads borrow to pay for school. Average cumulative indebtedness $17,862. **Criteria for awarding institutional aid:** *Non-need-based:* Academics, alumni affiliation, athletics, leadership, music/drama, state/district residency.

UNIVERSITY OF ROCHESTER

300 Wilson Blvd, PO Box 270251, Rochester, NY 14627
Phone: 585-275-3221 **Financial Aid Phone:** 585-275-3226
E-mail: admit@admissions.rochester.edu **CEEB Code:** 2928
Fax: 585-461-4595 **Website:** www.rochester.edu **ACT Code:** 2980

This private school was founded in 1850. It has a 655-acre campus.

RATINGS
Admissions Selectivity Rating: 96   **Fire Safety Rating:** 70   **Green Rating:** 88

STUDENTS AND FACULTY
Enrollment: 5,291. **Student Body:** 51% female, 49% male, 50% out-of-state, 8% international (92 countries represented). Asian 10%, African American 4%, Caucasian 54%, Hispanic 4%.
Retention and Graduation: 96% freshmen return for sophomore year. 74% freshmen graduate within 4 years. 51% grads go on to further study within 1 year. 33% grads pursue arts and sciences degrees. 19% grads pursue law degrees. 6% grads pursue business degrees. 20% grads pursue medical degrees. **Faculty:** Student/faculty ratio 9:1. 524 full-time faculty, 90% hold PhDs, 14% are members of minority groups, 27% are women.

ACADEMICS
Degrees: Bachelor's, master's, post-bachelor's certificate, post-master's certificate. **Classes:** Most classes have 10–19 students. **Majors with Highest Enrollment:** Biology/biological sciences; economics; psychology. **Special Study Options:** Accelerated program, cooperative education program, cross-registration, double major, dual enrollment, English as a Second Language (ESL), honors program, independent study, internships, liberal arts/career combination, student-designed major, study abroad, teacher certification program, "Take 5" a fifth year tuition free to supplement regular requirements; Washington Semester Program; Rochester Curriculum (clusters); Quest Courses. **Combined degree programs:** BA/MD, BA/MA, medicine, business, education, engineering. Special programs offered to physically disabled students include note-taking services, reader services, tape recorders, tutors. **Career services:** Alumni network, alumni services, career assessment, internships. **Career services highlights include:** Rochester students pursue internship, externship, research and volunteer experiences at a high rate. Many are involved in programs directed by other organizations, including 67 study abroad programs in which the University is a partner. The campus career center guides individualized plans for student career development and enjoys extraordinary success. A partial listing of the programs the University has created and manages on its own: internships at

the Parliament in London, Parlement in France or the European Parliament in Brussels; "Art New York," a semester spent living in New York City working at galleries or museums; REU programs at Rochester in Chemistry, Engineering, and Medicine; similar programs at Fermilab in Chicago, at NIH and NASA in the DC area; the Urban Scholars summer program in Rochester, now extended as a fifth Rochester Youth Year; a fifth Kaufmann Entrepreneurial Year in which students as individuals or in groups create and manage a new enterprise; the Malawi Immersion Seminar, a summer program centering on a 10–day homestay in a rural African village; a guided summer investigation of Italian architecture, archaeology and engineering, which is now the capstone experience in a new major; intensive in-country immersion language programs for several foreign languages; earth sciences research expeditions in the Arctic and South Africa each year; numerous developmental programs in music and in clinical medical research; the Mt. Hope Family Clinic in developmental and social psychology; engineering industry practicum opportunities with Google, Apple, Microsoft, Kodak, Xerox, IBM, etc.; cognitive research with the use of an academic MRI facility on the undergraduate campus; undergraduate study and research programs at Rochester's Laboratory for Laser Energetics, home of the Omega EP laser system, one of the world's most powerful.

FACILITIES

Housing: Coed dorms, special housing for disabled students, men's dorms, special housing for international students, women's dorms, fraternity/sorority housing, apartments for married students, apartments for single students, wellness housing, theme housingFreshman housing; special interest housing; suite style living. 90% of campus accessible to physically disabled. **Special Academic Facilities/Equipment:** Art center and gallery, African and African-American studies institute, center for women's studies, visual science and space science centers, institute of optics, observatory, laser energetics and nuclear structure research labs, electron microscopes. Judaic studies center, political economy institute, sign language research center, biomedical ultrasound center, Polish and central European studies center, electronic imaging systems center, center for future health. **Computers:** 100% of classrooms, 30% of dorms, 100% of libraries, 100% of dining areas, 100% of student union, have wireless network access. Students can register for classes online. Administrative functions (other than registration) can be performed online.

CAMPUS LIFE

Environment: Metropolis. **Activities:** Choral groups, concert band, dance, drama/theater, jazz band, literary magazine, music ensembles, musical theater, opera, pep band, radio station, student government, student newspaper, student-run film society, symphony orchestra, television station, international student organization, Model UN. **Organizations:** 224 registered organizations, 6 honor societies, 14 religious organizations. 17 fraternities, 13 sororities. **Athletics (Intercollegiate):** *Men:* Baseball, basketball, cross-country, diving, football, golf, soccer, squash, swimming, tennis, track/field (outdoor), track/field (indoor). *Women:* Basketball, crew/rowing, cross-country, diving, field hockey, golf, lacrosse, soccer, softball, swimming, tennis, track/field (outdoor), track/field (indoor), volleyball. **On-Campus Highlights:** Eastman Theater, Memorial Art Gallery, Rush Rhees Library, Interfaith Chapel, Robert B. Goergen Athletic Center, Recent New Buildings on Campus: ° Robert B. Goergen Hall for Biomedical Engineering and Optics—A five-story facility that pairs biomedical engineering and optics in an environment of teaching laboratories, high-tech demonstration areas, and gathering spaces for collaboration. ° The Gleason Library—A collaborative study space, designed with student input, which features an open floor plan and lightweight furniture that students are encouraged to reconfigure. ° Riverview Student Apartments—A five-building, 120–unit dormitory complex. The waterfront building features fully furnished apartments and offers amenities not found in other on-campus housing, including air conditioning, kitchens and separate living rooms. Each of the three- and four-story buildings is equipped with laundry and vending facilities. ° University Health Services Building -The new facility brings together UHS medical care services, physical therapy, health promotion, administrative offices, and the University Counseling Center. The UHS building is the primary health-care stop for Arts, Sciences & Engineering students, as well as faculty, staff, and other members of the University community. **Environmental Initiatives:** This year, university leadership supported two major long term student initiatives: EcoReps program and Biodiesel bus program: a)EcoReps educate the students in their halls on environmental issues like waste reduction and energy conservation by helping to plan dorm activities and events, and by serving as a resource for every day sustainability issues. EcoReps are enthusiastic incoming freshman with a desire to promote change. There are 20–22 EcoReps each year—one on each floor of the freshman dorms. The EcoReps are guided by two upperclassmen student leads who are experienced in on-campus environmental efforts. EcoReps educate the students in their halls on environmental issues like waste reduction and energy conservation by helping to plan dorm activities and events. www.rochester.edu/sustainability/ecoreps/ b)UR Biodiesel bus made its maiden voyage on May 14, 2009; it now runs 5 days per week as a campus shuttle. The program was developed by students with financial support by the facilities department. Over 20% of the fuel is collected from dining services. A video describing the fuel processing and bus operations is found at: www.youtube.com/watch?v=m-TZyAFgyQk

An article describing the launch is available at: www.rochester.edu/news/show.php?id=3353 Under the direction of the president and University Council on Sustainability the university developed 25 sustainability initiatives; they include programs in Energy, Maintenance and Construction, Purchasing and Business Practices, Dining Services, Transportation and Parking, and Communication. Eight (8) initiatives are complete: distribution of compact fluorescent light bulbs, adherence to smart growth principles, hiring a recycling coordinator, adherence to green printing practices, recycling 100% of the glass, plastic and metal containers in all dining facilities, composting pre-consumer dining services waste, implementation of a fry oil biodiesel fuel shuttle bus program, and pursuing the use of existing remote parking facilities and minimize the paving of campus areas. Significant progress has been made in the areas of improving communication of sustainability initiatives, maximizing cogeneration load, retrofitting lighting and occupancy sensors, participation in the EPA's Energy Star program, and incentives for using mass transit. On Monday, October 19, 2009, Richard Pifer, Associate Vice President for University Facilities and Services updated the University Council on Sustainability the status of the 25 Task Force Initiatives. An article describing the status of the initiatives may be found at: http://blogs.rochester.edu/greennotes/?p=119 On January 15, 2010, the University of Rochester announced it is getting more than $1 million to build a better light bulb. The U of R was awarded $1,239,071 from the U.S. Department of Energy to build OLED's. It stands for Organic Light-Emitting Diodes, a technologically advanced light bulb that uses white phosphorus. The goal of the project is to produce efficient OLED bulbs that operate for more than 10,000 hours. www.energy.gov/news2009/documents2009/SSL_Selections_011510.pdf

ADMISSIONS

Freshman Academic Profile: Average high school GPA 3.8. 76% in top 10% of high school class, 91% in top 25% of high school class, 99% in top 50% of high school class. 75% from public high schools. SAT Math middle 50% range 640–720. SAT Critical Reading middle 50% range 590–690. SAT Writing middle 50% range 590–690. ACT middle 50% range 28–33. Minimum paper TOEFL 600. Minimum computer TOEFL 250. Minimum web-based TOEFL 100. **Basis for Candidate Selection:** *Very important factors considered include:* Recommendation(s), rigor of secondary school record, character/personal qualities. *Important factors considered include:* Application essay, academic GPA, standardized test scores, extracurricular activities, interview, talent/ability. *Other factors considered include:* Class rank, alumni/ae relation, first generation, geographical residence, level of applicant's interest, racial/ethnic status, volunteer work, work experience. **Freshman Admission Requirements:** High school diploma is required and GED is accepted. **Freshman Admission Statistics:** 12,111 applied, 39% admitted, 23% enrolled. **Transfer Admission Requirements:** College transcript(s), essay or personal statement, Lowest grade transferable C. **General Admission Information:** Application fee $60. Early decision application deadline 11/1. Regular application deadline 1/1. Regular notification 4/1. Nonfall registration accepted. Admission may be deferred for a maximum of 1. Credit and/or placement offered for CEEB Advanced Placement tests.

COSTS AND FINANCIAL AID

Annual tuition $37,870. Room and board $11,200. Required fees $820. Average book expense $1,250. **Required Forms and Deadlines:** FAFSA, CSS/Financial Aid PROFILE, state aid form, noncustodial PROFILE, business/farm supplement. Financial aid filing deadline 2/1. Priority financial aid filing date 2/1. **Notification of Awards:** Applicants will be notified of awards on or about 4/1. **Types of Aid:** *Need-based scholarships/grants:* Federal Pell, SEOG, state scholarships/grants, the school's own gift aid. *Loans:* Direct Subsidized Stafford, Direct Unsubsidized Stafford, Direct PLUS, Federal Perkins, Federal Nursing, college/university loans from institutional funds. *Student Employment:* Federal Work-Study Program available. Institutional employment available. Off-campus job opportunities are excellent. **Financial Aid Statistics:** 61% freshmen, 57% undergrads receive need-based scholarship or grant aid. 7% freshmen, 5% undergrads receive non-need-based scholarship or grant aid. 53% freshmen, 51% undergrads receive need-based self-help aid. 88% freshmen, 88% undergrads receive any aid. 55% undergrads borrow to pay for school. Average cumulative indebtedness $27,121. **Criteria for awarding institutional aid:** *Non-need-based:* Academics, alumni affiliation, leadership, music/drama.

UNIVERSITY OF SAINT MARY (KS)

4100 South Fourth Street Trafficway, Leavenworth, KS 66048
Phone: 913-758-6118
E-mail: admis@hub.smcks.edu **CEEB Code:** 6630
Fax: 913-758-6140 **Website:** www.stmary.edu **ACT Code:** 1455

This private school, affiliated with the Roman Catholic Church, was founded in 1923. It has a 240-acre campus.

RATINGS
Admissions Selectivity Rating: 75   **Fire Safety Rating:** 60*   **Green Rating:** 60*

STUDENTS AND FACULTY
Enrollment: 575. **Student Body:** 61% female, 39% male, 41% out-of-state, international. Asian 1%, African American 12%, Caucasian 71%, Hispanic 8%, Native American 1%.
Retention and Graduation: 71% freshmen return for sophomore year. 35% freshmen graduate within 4 years. **Faculty:** Student/faculty ratio 12:1. 42 full-time faculty, 52% hold PhDs, 2% are members of minority groups, 55% are women.

ACADEMICS
Degrees: Associate, bachelor's, master's, transfer associate. **Classes:** Most classes have fewer than 10 students. **Majors with Highest Enrollment:** Business/commerce; elementary education and teaching; psychology. **Special Study Options:** Accelerated program, distance learning, double major, dual enrollment, honors program, independent study, internships, student-designed major, study abroad, teacher certification program, semester-away programs available. Special programs offered to physically disabled students include note-taking services, tutors.

FACILITIES
Housing: Coed dorms. **Special Academic Facilities/Equipment:** Lincoln Library Collection, art gallery, Bible Collection. **Computers:** Students can register for classes online. Administrative functions (other than registration) can be performed online.

CAMPUS LIFE
Environment: Town. **Activities:** Choral groups, concert band, drama/theater, literary magazine, music ensembles, musical theater, pep band, student government, campus ministries. **Organizations:** 22 registered organizations, 2 honor societies, 2 religious organizations. **Athletics (Intercollegiate):** *Men:* Baseball, basketball, football, soccer. *Women:* Basketball, soccer, softball, volleyball.

ADMISSIONS
Freshman Academic Profile: Average high school GPA 3.24. 13% in top 10% of high school class, 42% in top 25% of high school class, 68% in top 50% of high school class. 80% from public high schools. SAT Math middle 50% range 420–510. SAT Critical Reading middle 50% range 420–500. ACT middle 50% range 18–22. Minimum paper TOEFL 500. **Basis for Candidate Selection:** *Very important factors considered include:* Academic GPA, rigor of secondary school record, character/personal qualities. *Important factors considered include:* Standardized test scores, extracurricular activities, interview, talent/ability, volunteer work. *Other factors considered include:* Class rank, application essay, recommendation(s), alumni/ae relation, work experience. **Freshman Admission Requirements:** High school diploma is required and GED is accepted. *Academic units required:* 4 English, 2 mathematics, 2 science, 2 history. *Academic units recommended:* 4 English, 4 mathematics, 4 science, (2 science labs), 2 foreign language, 2 social studies, 4 history, 2 academic electives, 2 computer programming. **Freshman Admission Statistics:** 535 applied, 69% admitted, 31% enrolled. **Transfer Admission Requirements:** College transcript(s), minimum college GPA of 2.0 required. Lowest grade transferable C. **General Admission Information:** Application fee $25. Nonfall registration accepted. Admission may be deferred for a maximum of 1 semester. Credit and/or placement offered for CEEB Advanced Placement tests.

COSTS AND FINANCIAL AID
Annual tuition $18,500. Room and board $5,900. Required fees $390. Average book expense $700. **Required Forms and Deadlines:** FAFSA. Priority financial aid filing date 4/1. **Notification of Awards:** Applicants will be notified of awards on a rolling basis beginning 2/1. **Types of Aid:** *Need-based scholarships/grants:* Federal Pell, SEOG, state scholarships/grants, private scholarships, the school's own gift aid. *Loans:* FFEL Subsidized Stafford, FFEL Unsubsidized Stafford, FFEL PLUS, Federal Perkins. *Student Employment:* Highest amount earned per year from on-campus jobs $1,500. **Financial Aid Statistics:** 72% freshmen, 76% undergrads receive need-based scholarship or grant aid. 5% freshmen, 5% undergrads receive non-need-based scholarship or grant aid. 67% freshmen, 74% undergrads receive need-based self-help aid. 31% freshmen, 30% undergrads receive athletic scholarships. **Criteria for awarding institutional aid:** *Non-need-based:* Academics, art, athletics, leadership, music/drama.

UNIVERSITY OF SAINT THOMAS (MN)

2115 Summit Avenue, Mail #32F, St. Paul, MN 55105-1096
Phone: 651-962-6150 **Financial Aid Phone:** 651-962-6550
E-mail: admissions@stthomas.edu **CEEB Code:** 6110
Fax: 651-962-6160 **Website:** www.stthomas.edu **ACT Code:** 2102

This private school, affiliated with the Roman Catholic Church, was founded in 1885. It has a 78-acre campus.

RATINGS
Admissions Selectivity Rating: 78   **Fire Safety Rating:** 98   **Green Rating:** 83

STUDENTS AND FACULTY
Enrollment: 5,992. **Student Body:** 45% female, 55% male, 17% out-of-state, 1% international. Asian 5%, African American 3%, Caucasian 81%, Hispanic 4%.
Retention and Graduation: 86% freshmen return for sophomore year. 56% freshmen graduate within 4 years. **Faculty:** Student/faculty ratio 15:1. 420 full-time faculty, 11% are members of minority groups, 40% are women.

ACADEMICS
Degrees: Bachelor's, certificate, master's, post-bachelor's certificate, post-master's certificate. **Classes:** Most classes have 20–29 students. Most lab/discussion sessions have 10–19 students. **Special Study Options:** Cross-registration, double major, English as a Second Language (ESL), exchange student program (domestic), honors program, independent study, internships, student-designed major, study abroad, teacher certification program. **Honors programs:** The Aquinas Scholars Program is the undergraduate honors program. Its purpose is to provide opportunities for motivated and curious students to deepen and enrich their undergraduate education. **Combined degree programs:** BA/MEng. Special programs offered to physically disabled students include note-taking services, reader services, tape recorders, tutors. **Career services:** Alumni network, alumni services, career assessment, internships, regional alumni.

FACILITIES
Housing: Men's dorms, special housing for international students, women's dorms, apartments for single students, chemical-free lifestyle, women in science house, first year experience houses, Catholic women's and Catholic men's communities. **Special Academic Facilities/Equipment:** Seminary. **Computers:** 100% of classrooms, 100% of dorms, 100% of libraries, 100% of dining areas, 100% of student union, 100% of common outdoor areas have wireless network access. Students can register for classes online. Administrative functions (other than registration) can be performed online.

CAMPUS LIFE
Environment: Metropolis. **Activities:** Choral groups, concert band, dance, drama/theater, jazz band, literary magazine, music ensembles, pep band, radio station, student government, student newspaper, television station, yearbook, campus ministries, international student organization, Model UN. **Organizations:** 114 registered organizations, 7 religious organizations. 1 fraternities. **Athletics (Intercollegiate):** *Men:* Baseball, basketball, cross-country, diving, football, golf, ice hockey, soccer, swimming, tennis, track/field (outdoor), track/field (indoor). *Women:* Basketball, cross-country, diving, golf, ice hockey, soccer, softball, swimming, tennis, track/field (outdoor), track/field (indoor), volleyball. **On-Campus Highlights:** O'Shaughnessy—Frey Library, Scooters non-alcoholic pub and restaurant, Koch Commons (workout facility residence hall area), Frey Science and Engineering Center, Chapel of St. Thomas Aquinas. **Environmental Initiatives:** New Anderson Student Union to be LEED Silver certified. Completion date, summer of 2012. Center Solar Panels are currently being installed on roof of Brady Hall residence. Two HourCars, hybrids in the local car sharing program, are purchased and placed on campus for student and neighbor use. www.hourcar.org

ADMISSIONS
Freshman Academic Profile: Average high school GPA 3.52. 21% in top 10% of high school class, 50% in top 25% of high school class, 87% in top 50% of high school class. 72% from public high schools. SAT Math middle 50% range 540–650. SAT Critical Reading middle 50% range 520–630. ACT middle 50% range 23–28. Minimum paper TOEFL 550. Minimum computer TOEFL 213. Minimum web-based TOEFL 80. **Basis for Candidate Selection:** *Very important factors considered include:* Academic GPA, rigor of secondary school record, standardized test scores. *Important factors considered include:* Class rank, application essay. *Other factors considered include:* Recommendation(s), alumni/ae relation, character/personal qualities, extracurricular activities, geographical residence, racial/ethnic status, talent/ability, volunteer work. **Freshman Admission Requirements:** High school diploma is required and GED is accepted. *Academic units required:* 3 mathematics, 2 science. *Academic units recommended:* 4 English, 4 mathematics, 4 foreign language, 2 social

studies. **Freshman Admission Statistics:** 5,065 applied, 87% admitted, 31% enrolled. **Transfer Admission Requirements:** High school transcript, college transcript(s), essay or personal statement, statement of good standing from prior institution(s). Minimum college GPA of 2.3 required. Lowest grade transferable C–. **General Admission Information:** Notification on a rolling basis, beginning on or about 10/1. Nonfall registration accepted. Credit and/or placement offered for CEEB Advanced Placement tests.

COSTS AND FINANCIAL AID

Required Forms and Deadlines: FAFSA. Priority financial aid filing date 4/1. **Notification of Awards:** Applicants will be notified of awards on a rolling basis beginning 3/1. **Types of Aid:** *Need-based scholarships/grants:* Federal Pell, SEOG, state scholarships/grants, private scholarships, the school's own gift aid. *Loans:* Direct Subsidized Stafford, Direct Unsubsidized Stafford, Direct PLUS, Federal Perkins, state loans, private loans. *Student Employment:* Federal Work-Study Program available. Institutional employment available. Off-campus job opportunities are fair. **Financial Aid Statistics:** 62% freshmen, 57% undergrads receive need-based scholarship or grant aid. 10% freshmen, 6% undergrads receive non-need-based scholarship or grant aid. 48% freshmen, 49% undergrads receive need-based self-help aid. 97% freshmen, 91% undergrads receive any aid. 67% undergrads borrow to pay for school. Average cumulative indebtedness $32,132. **Criteria for awarding institutional aid:** *Non-need-based:* Academics, music/drama.

UNIVERSITY OF SAN DIEGO

5998 Alcala Park, San Diego, CA 92110-2492
Phone: 619-260-4506 **Financial Aid Phone:** 619-260-4514
E-mail: admissions@sandiego.edu **CEEB Code:** 4849
Fax: 619-260-6836 **Website:** www.sandiego.edu **ACT Code:** 394

This private school, affiliated with the Roman Catholic Church, was founded in 1949. It has a 180-acre campus.

RATINGS
Admissions Selectivity Rating: 94   **Fire Safety Rating:** 77   **Green Rating:** 82

STUDENTS AND FACULTY
Enrollment: 5,066. **Student Body:** 57% female, 43% male, 37% out-of-state, 4% international (61 countries represented). Asian 11%, African American 3%, Caucasian 60%, Hispanic 15%, Native American 2%.
Retention and Graduation: 85% freshmen return for sophomore year. 66% freshmen graduate within 4 years. 20% grads go on to further study within 1 year. 5% grads pursue arts and sciences degrees. 3% grads pursue law degrees. 4% grads pursue business degrees. 4% grads pursue medical degrees. **Faculty:** Student/faculty ratio 15:1. 381 full-time faculty, 94% hold PhDs, 18% are members of minority groups, 45% are women.

ACADEMICS
Degrees: Bachelor's, master's, post-bachelor's certificate, post-master's certificate. **Classes:** Most classes have 30–39 students. Most lab/discussion sessions have 10–19 students. **Majors with Highest Enrollment:** Business administration and management; communication studies/speech communication and rhetoric; finance. **Special Study Options:** Double major, English as a Second Language (ESL), honors program, independent study, internships, liberal arts/career combination, study abroad, teacher certification program. **Honors programs:** Phi Beta Kappa, Honors Program. **Combined degree programs:** BS/MSN, MBA/JD. **Career services:** Alumni network, alumni services, career/job search classes, career assessment, internships, regional alumni.

FACILITIES
Housing: Coed dorms, special housing for disabled students, men's dorms, women's dorms, apartments for married students, apartments for single students, wellness housing, theme housing. 85% of campus accessible to physically disabled. **Special Academic Facilities/Equipment:** Art gallery, peace and justice institute, child development center, language labs. **Computers:** 100% of classrooms, 100% of dorms, 100% of libraries, 100% of dining areas, 100% of student union, 100% of common outdoor areas have wireless network access. Students can register for classes online. Administrative functions (other than registration) can be performed online.

CAMPUS LIFE
Environment: Metropolis. **Activities:** Choral groups, dance, drama/theater, jazz band, literary magazine, music ensembles, musical theater, pep band, radio

station, student government, student newspaper, symphony orchestra, television station, yearbook, campus ministries, international student organization, Model UN. **Organizations:** 129 registered organizations, 20 honor societies, 2 religious organizations. 5 fraternities, 6 sororities. **Athletics (Intercollegiate):** *Men:* Baseball, basketball, crew/rowing, cross-country, football, golf, soccer, tennis. *Women:* Basketball, cheerleading, crew/rowing, cross-country, diving, soccer, softball, swimming, tennis, track/field (outdoor), volleyball. **On-Campus Highlights:** Aromas Coffee House, Donald P. Shiley Center for Science and Technology, Jenny Craig Pavilion (Sporting/concert venue), Joan B. Kroc Institute for Peace and Justice, Student Life Pavilion. **Environmental Initiatives:** University has committed to building a 1.23 MW solar system, and is currently investigating other clean energy sources. University has invested over $8 million in energy conservation projects over the next 3 years. Last year the university saved 8 million gallons of water through scaling back landscaping and irrigation. Another reduction of an additional 30 million gallons of water is slated for this year. (Total consumption is approximately 120 million gallons)

ADMISSIONS
Freshman Academic Profile: Average high school GPA 3.84. 45% in top 10% of high school class, 80% in top 25% of high school class, 98% in top 50% of high school class. 60% from public high schools. SAT Math middle 50% range 565–660. SAT Critical Reading middle 50% range 550–640. SAT Writing middle 50% range 550–650. ACT middle 50% range 25–29. Minimum paper TOEFL 550. Minimum computer TOEFL 213. Minimum web-based TOEFL 80. **Basis for Candidate Selection:** *Very important factors considered include:* Academic GPA, rigor of secondary school record, standardized test scores, religious affiliation/commitment. *Important factors considered include:* Class rank, application essay, recommendation(s), character/personal qualities, extracurricular activities, talent/ability, volunteer work. *Other factors considered include:* Alumni/ae relation, first generation, geographical residence, level of applicant's interest, racial/ethnic status, work experience. **Freshman Admission Requirements:** High school diploma is required and GED is accepted. *Academic units required:* 4 English, 3 mathematics, 3 science, (2 science labs), 2 foreign language, 3 social studies. *Academic units recommended:* 4 English, 4 mathematics, 4 science, (3 science labs), 3 foreign language, 4 social studies. **Freshman Admission Statistics:** 11,000 applied, 30% admitted, 33% enrolled. **Transfer Admission Requirements:** High school transcript, college transcript(s), essay or personal statement, minimum college GPA of 3.0 required. Lowest grade transferable C. **General Admission Information:** Application fee $55. Regular application deadline 3/1. Regular notification 4/15. Nonfall registration accepted. Admission may be deferred for a maximum of 1 year. Credit and/or placement offered for CEEB Advanced Placement tests.

COSTS AND FINANCIAL AID
Required Forms and Deadlines: FAFSA. Financial aid filing deadline 3/2. **Notification of Awards:** Applicants will be notified of awards on a rolling basis beginning 3/1. **Types of Aid:** *Need-based scholarships/grants:* Federal Pell, SEOG, state scholarships/grants, private scholarships, the school's own gift aid, Federal Nursing Scholarships. *Loans:* FFEL Subsidized Stafford, FFEL Unsubsidized Stafford, FFEL PLUS, Federal Perkins, college/university loans from institutional funds. *Student Employment:* Federal Work-Study Program available. Institutional employment available. Off-campus job opportunities are good. **Financial Aid Statistics:** 46% freshmen, 42% undergrads receive need-based scholarship or grant aid. 26% freshmen, 19% undergrads receive non-need-based scholarship or grant aid. 34% freshmen, 36% undergrads receive need-based self-help aid. 2% freshmen, 3% undergrads receive athletic scholarships. 71% freshmen, 66% undergrads receive any aid. 57% undergrads borrow to pay for school. Average cumulative indebtedness $27,999. **Criteria for awarding institutional aid:** *Non-need-based:* Academics, athletics, leadership, music/drama, religious affiliation.

UNIVERSITY OF SAN FRANCISCO

2130 Fulton Street, San Francisco, CA 94117
Phone: 415-422-6563
E-mail: admission@usfca.edu **CEEB Code:** 4850
Fax: 415-422-2217 **Website:** www.usfca.edu

This private school, affiliated with the Roman Catholic Church,, affiliated with the Jesuit Church, was founded in 1855. It has a 55-acre campus.

RATINGS
Admissions Selectivity Rating: 85   **Fire Safety Rating:** 60*   **Green Rating:** 81

STUDENTS AND FACULTY

Enrollment: 4,934. **Student Body:** 64% female, 36% male, 27.4% out-of-state, 9% international (78 countries represented). Asian 22%, African American 5%, Caucasian 39%, Hispanic 14%, Native American 1%.
Retention and Graduation: 51% freshmen graduate within 4 years. 1% grads pursue medical degrees. **Faculty:** Student/faculty ratio 13:1. 380 full-time faculty, 92% hold PhDs, 21% are members of minority groups, 46% are women.

ACADEMICS

Degrees: Bachelor's, certificate, first professional, master's, post-master's certificate. **Classes:** Most classes have 10–19 students. Most lab/discussion sessions have 10–19 students. **Majors with Highest Enrollment:** Business/commerce; nursing/registered nurse (RN, ASN, BSN, MSN); psychology. **Special Study Options:** Accelerated program, cross-registration, distance learning, double major, English as a Second Language (ESL), exchange student program (domestic), external degree program, honors program, independent study, internships, liberal arts/career combination, student-designed major, study abroad, teacher certification program. **Combined degree programs:** BA/JD, BA/MA, BA/MEng. Special programs offered to physically disabled students include note-taking services, reader services, tape recorders, tutors. **Career services:** Career/job search classes, career assessment, internships.

FACILITIES

Housing: Coed dorms, women's dorms, apartments for single students, Several off campus buildings with flats have been purchased and converted into multiple student housing units. 100% of campus accessible to physically disabled. **Special Academic Facilities/Equipment:** Rare Book Room, Ricci Institute for Chinese-Western Cultural History. **Computers:** 25% of classrooms, 25% of dorms, 25% of dining areas, 75% of student union, 25% of common outdoor areas have wireless network access. Students can register for classes online. Administrative functions (other than registration) can be performed online.

CAMPUS LIFE

Environment: Metropolis. **Activities:** Choral groups, dance, drama/theater, literary magazine, music ensembles, musical theater, pep band, radio station, student government, student newspaper, television station, yearbook. **Organizations:** 90 registered organizations, 14 honor societies, 4 fraternities, 4 sororities. **Athletics (Intercollegiate):** *Men:* Baseball, basketball, cross-country, golf, riflery, soccer, tennis, track/field (outdoor). *Women:* Basketball, cross-country, golf, riflery, soccer, tennis, track/field (outdoor), volleyball. **On-Campus Highlights:** Koret Health and Recreation Center, War Memorial Gym, St. Ignatius Church, Geschke Learning Resourse Center, Loan Mountain Campus. **Environmental Initiatives:** Sustainability. Placed 5th in National competition in RecycleMania. Currently, USF's co-generation plant produces about half of lower campus' peak energy needs. Located in the basement of Gleeson Library, the plant converts natural gas into electricity. Although the conversion of natural gas to energy does produce some emissions, natural gas is considered the cleanest of the fossil fuels. The plant gets its co-generation designation because it also captures heat lost during the conversion process and uses that to provide some of the heat lower campus uses. The plant provides about 38 percent of lower campus' heating needs. Additionally, the university uses thermal panels on top of Phelan, Gillson, and Hayes-Healy halls. The panels differ from solar panels in that they heat water directly rather than producing electricity, providing some of the hot water needed in those halls. LEED Goals on new projects Incorporation of "green" building practices in construction, including the renovation of Kalmanovitz Hall (formerly Campion Hall). London said USF will try to achieve LEED certification for the new Integrated Science Center, currently being designed. Awarded by the U.S. Green Building Council, LEED provides a suite of standards for environmentally sustainable construction. If the Integrated Science Center receives the certification, it would be the first such building on campus. Installation of Photo voltaic panels. As part of that process, USF is installing new solar panels on top of the Koret Health and Recreation Center, University Center, Cowell Hall, and Kalmanovitz Hall. Together with the solar panels already on Gleeson Library, the panels will produce about 16 percent of lower campus' peak electricity needs.

ADMISSIONS

Freshman Academic Profile: Average high school GPA 3.503. 25.8% in top 10% of high school class, 61.2% in top 25% of high school class, 91.4% in top 50% of high school class. 52% from public high schools. SAT Math middle 50% range 520–620. SAT Critical Reading middle 50% range 510–620. SAT Writing middle 50% range 510–620. ACT middle 50% range 22–27. Minimum paper TOEFL 550. Minimum computer TOEFL 213. Minimum web-based TOEFL 79. **Basis for Candidate Selection:** *Very important factors considered include:* Academic GPA, recommendation(s), rigor of secondary school record, standardized test scores. *Important factors considered include:* Class rank, application essay. *Other factors considered include:* Alumni/ae relation, character/personal qualities, extracurricular activities, interview, talent/ability, volunteer work. **Freshman Admission Requirements:** High school diploma is required and GED is accepted. *Academic units recommended:* 4 English, 3 mathematics, 2 science, (2 science labs), 2 foreign language, 3 social studies, 6 academic

electives, 2 One chemistry and 1 biology or physics is required of nursing and science applicants **Freshman Admission Statistics:** 8,485 applied, 64% admitted, 19% enrolled. **Transfer Admission Requirements:** College transcript(s), essay or personal statement, minimum college GPA of 2.5 required. Lowest grade transferable C. **General Admission Information:** Application fee $55. Regular notification 4/1. Nonfall registration accepted. Admission may be deferred for a maximum of 1 semester. Credit offered for CEEB Advanced Placement tests.

COSTS AND FINANCIAL AID

Annual tuition $34,430. Room and board $11,540. Required fees $340. Average book expense $1,000. **Required Forms and Deadlines:** FAFSA. Priority financial aid filing date 2/1. **Notification of Awards:** Applicants will be notified of awards on a rolling basis beginning 4/1. **Types of Aid:** *Need-based scholarships/grants:* Federal Pell, SEOG, state scholarships/grants, private scholarships, the school's own gift aid, Federal Nursing Scholarships. *Loans:* Direct Subsidized Stafford, Direct Unsubsidized Stafford, Direct PLUS, FFEL Subsidized Stafford, FFEL Unsubsidized Stafford, FFEL PLUS, Federal Perkins, Federal Nursing, college/university loans from institutional funds, Note: FFEL Loans are for Graduate. *Student Employment:* Federal Work-Study Program available. Institutional employment available. Highest amount earned per year from on-campus jobs $2,000. Off-campus job opportunities are excellent. **Financial Aid Statistics:** 54% freshmen, 51% undergrads receive need-based scholarship or grant aid. 50% freshmen, 49% undergrads receive need-based self-help aid. 5% freshmen, 3% undergrads receive athletic scholarships. 65% undergrads borrow to pay for school. Average cumulative indebtedness $27,260. **Criteria for awarding institutional aid:** *Non-need-based:* Academics, athletics.

See page 1306.

UNIVERSITY OF SCIENCE & ARTS OF OKLAHOMA

1727 West Alabama, Chickasha, OK 73018
Phone: 405-574-1357 **Financial Aid Phone:** 405-574-1240
E-mail: usao-admissions@usao.edu **CEEB Code:** 6544
Fax: 405-574-1220 **Website:** www.usao.edu **ACT Code:** 3418

This public school was founded in 1908. It has a 75-acre campus.

RATINGS
Admissions Selectivity Rating: 78   **Fire Safety Rating:** 82   **Green Rating:** 60*

STUDENTS AND FACULTY

Enrollment: 1,013. **Student Body:** 64% female, 36% male, 7.74% out-of-state, 6% international (19 countries represented). Asian 1%, African American 5%, Caucasian 73%, Hispanic 9%, Native American 11%.
Retention and Graduation: 72% freshmen return for sophomore year. 20% freshmen graduate within 4 years. 35% grads go on to further study within 1 year. 15% grads pursue arts and sciences degrees. 3% grads pursue law degrees. 8% grads pursue business degrees. 3% grads pursue medical degrees. **Faculty:** Student/faculty ratio 15:1. 55 full-time faculty, 89% hold PhDs, 11% are members of minority groups, 49% are women.

ACADEMICS

Degrees: Bachelor's. **Classes:** Most classes have 10–19 students. Most lab/discussion sessions have 10–19 students. **Majors with Highest Enrollment:** Business administration and management; elementary education and teaching; psychology. **Special Study Options:** Accelerated program, double major, dual enrollment, honors program, independent study, internships, student-designed major, study abroad, teacher certification program. Special programs offered to physically disabled students include note-taking services, tutors. **Career services:** Career/job search classes, career assessment, internships.

FACILITIES

Housing: Coed dorms, apartments for single students. 95% of campus accessible to physically disabled. **Special Academic Facilities/Equipment:** Language labs, speech and hearing clinic, multiple computer labs, herbarium **Computers:** 100% of classrooms, 85% of dorms, 100% of libraries, 100% of dining areas, 100% of student union, 100%·of common outdoor areas have wireless network access.

CAMPUS LIFE

Environment: Village. **Activities:** Choral groups, concert band, drama/theater, jazz band, literary magazine, music ensembles, musical theater, pep band, student government, student newspaper, television station, campus ministries. **Organizations:** 24 registered organizations, 7 honor societies, 4 religious organizations. 1 fraternities, 1 sororities. **Athletics (Intercollegiate):** *Men:* Baseball, basketball, cheerleading, soccer. *Women:* Basketball, cheerleading, soccer, softball **On-Campus Highlights:** Lawson Court, Nash Library, Student Center, Bill Smith Ballpark, Scooter's Grill.

ADMISSIONS

Freshman Academic Profile: Average high school GPA 3.42. 21.2% in top 10% of high school class, 51.9% in top 25% of high school class, 80.8% in top 50% of high school class. 75% from public high schools. SAT Math middle 50% range 480–570. SAT Critical Reading middle 50% range 380–480. ACT middle 50% range 19–26. Minimum paper TOEFL 500. Minimum computer TOEFL 173. **Basis for Candidate Selection:** *Very important factors considered include:* Class rank, academic GPA, rigor of secondary school record, standardized test scores. *Important factors considered include:* talent/ability. *Other factors considered include:* Recommendation(s), character/personal qualities. **Freshman Admission Requirements:** High school diploma is required and GED is accepted. *Academic units required:* 4 English, 3 mathematics, 3 science, (3 science labs), 2 social studies, 1 history, 2 academic electives. *Academic units recommended:* 4 mathematics, 2 foreign language, 2 visual/performing arts, 1 computer science. **Freshman Admission Statistics:** 395 applied, 74% admitted, 64% enrolled. **Transfer Admission Requirements:** College transcript(s), minimum college GPA of 2.0 required. Lowest grade transferable D. **General Admission Information:** Application fee $25. Regular application deadline 9/1. Notification on a rolling basis, beginning on or about 2/10. Nonfall registration accepted. Credit offered for CEEB Advanced Placement tests.

COSTS AND FINANCIAL AID

Required Forms and Deadlines: FAFSA, institution's own financial aid form. Priority financial aid filing date 3/15. **Notification of Awards:** Applicants will be notified of awards on a rolling basis beginning 3/15. **Types of Aid:** *Need-based scholarships/grants:* Federal Pell, SEOG, state scholarships/grants, private scholarships, the school's own gift aid. *Loans:* FFEL Subsidized Stafford, FFEL Unsubsidized Stafford, FFEL PLUS, Federal Perkins, college/university loans from institutional funds. *Student Employment:* Federal Work-Study Program available. Institutional employment available. Highest amount earned per year from on-campus jobs $8,600. Off-campus job opportunities are good. **Financial Aid Statistics:** 71% freshmen, 58% undergrads receive need-based scholarship or grant aid. 8% freshmen, 5% undergrads receive non-need-based scholarship or grant aid. 42% freshmen, 39% undergrads receive need-based self-help aid. 7% freshmen, 9% undergrads receive athletic scholarships. 73% freshmen, 61% undergrads receive any aid. 58% undergrads borrow to pay for school. Average cumulative indebtedness $15,598. **Criteria for awarding institutional aid:** *Non-need-based:* Academics, art, athletics, leadership, music/drama, state/district residency.

UNIVERSITY OF THE SCIENCES
IN PHILADELPHIA

600 South 43rd Street, Admission Office, Philadelphia, PA 19104-4495
Phone: 215-596-8810 **Financial Aid Phone:** 215-596-8894
E-mail: admit@usip.edu **CEEB Code:** 2663
Fax: 215-596-8821 **ACT Code:** 3671

This private school was founded in 1821. It has a 35-acre campus.

RATINGS
Admissions Selectivity Rating: 89 **Fire Safety Rating:** 81 **Green Rating:** 72

STUDENTS AND FACULTY
Enrollment: 2,602. **Student Body:** 60% female, 40% male, 50% out-of-state, 1% international (14 countries represented). Asian 38%, African American 4%, Caucasian 48%, Hispanic 2%.
Retention and Graduation: 85% freshmen return for sophomore year. 51% freshmen graduate within 4 years. **Faculty:** Student/faculty ratio 14:1. 166 full-time faculty, 73% hold PhDs, 17% are members of minority groups, 48% are women.

ACADEMICS
Degrees: Bachelor's, master's, post-bachelor's certificate, post-master's certificate. **Classes:** Most classes have 20–29 students. Most lab/discussion sessions have 20–29 students. **Majors with Highest Enrollment:** Biology/biological sciences; pharmacy (pharmd [usa], pharmd or bs/bpharm [canada]); physical therapy/therapist. **Special Study Options:** Distance learning, double major, English as a Second Language (ESL), honors program, internships, liberal

arts/career combination, teacher certification program, academic remediation, advanced placement credit, learning disabilities services, off-campus study. **Honors programs:** The Honors Program at University of the Sciences offers exceptional students the opportunity for specialized, intensive learning experiences both inside and outside the classroom. As an honors student, you will take part in special honors classes and recitations. The workload for these classes is not harder than others at University of the Sciences, but different. For example you may do smaller, more advanced experiments in a lab course. You may tour historic sites for a history class, or meet with a visiting author in your writing class. You will work in smaller classes and have more independent and group projects. **Combined degree programs:** PharmD/MBA; BSHS/MOT; BSHS/MPT; BSHS/DPT. Special programs offered to physically disabled students include note-taking services, reader services, tape recorders, tutors. **Career services:** alumni services, career/job search classes, career assessment, internships. **Career services highlights include:** USP Alumni Career Panels.

FACILITIES
Housing: Coed dorms, fraternity/sorority housing, apartments for single students, wellness housing honor halls in certain dormitories, upper level floor for upper level students. 90% of campus accessible to physically disabled. **Special Academic Facilities/Equipment:** Pharmacy museum, electron microscope. **Computers:** 80% of classrooms, 100% of dorms, 100% of libraries, 100% of dining areas, 40% of common outdoor areas have wireless network access. Students can register for classes online. Administrative functions (other than registration) can be performed online.

CAMPUS LIFE
Environment: Metropolis. **Activities:** Choral groups, concert band, dance, drama/theater, literary magazine, musical theater, student government, student newspaper, yearbook. **Organizations:** 66 registered organizations, 6 honor societies, 6 religious organizations. 2 fraternities, 2 sororities. **Athletics (Intercollegiate):** *Men:* Baseball, basketball, cross-country, golf, riflery, tennis. *Women:* Basketball, cross-country, golf, riflery, softball, tennis, volleyball. **On-Campus Highlights:** McNeil Science and Technology Center, Athletic Recreation Center, Wilson Hall, Marvin Sampson Museum, Griffith Hall, More than 80 state-of-the-art laboratories, including the Center for Advanced Pharmacy Studies (CAPS), the first laboratory of its kind at any college of pharmacy nationwide. In September 2003, USP opened a new 78,000–square-foot athletic/recreation center that provides exercise and practice space for varsity and intramural sports as well as general recreational facilities. The new building, part of a $30 million campus expansion and beautification project, contains a 3,500–square-foot, three-lane swimming pool; additional classrooms and faculty offices; and space for student organizations to meet and for students to gather informally. In August 2006, USP opened the McNeil Science and Technology Center, a three-story, 77,000–square-foot leading edge facility that reflects the University's commitment to its innovative curriculum. The Center's research laboratories and state-of-the-art-equipped support spaces will accommodate more undergraduate, graduate, post-doctoral, and faculty researchers in biology, microbiology, physics, and other scientific fields. The Center features a 400–seat auditorium, classrooms, computer workrooms and other flexible space that supports innovative teaching and learning through multi-media technology. The Center's two-story, light-filled commons provides a comfortable space for students to relax and study. **Environmental Initiatives:** All "On the Go" containers are fully recyclable. Five meal periods a week are trayless to conserve water and reduce chemical use. We have an Eco-Clam Shell program where a guest can purchase a re-usable fully recyclable clam shell and trade it in for a clean one at each meal period.

ADMISSIONS
Freshman Academic Profile: Average high school GPA 3.6. 47% in top 10% of high school class, 78% in top 25% of high school class, 98% in top 50% of high school class. SAT Math middle 50% range 560–650. SAT Critical Reading middle 50% range 520–600. ACT middle 50% range 23–27. Minimum paper TOEFL 550. Minimum computer TOEFL 213. **Basis for Candidate Selection:** *Very important factors considered include:* Class rank, academic GPA, rigor of secondary school record, standardized test scores. *Important factors considered include:* Character/personal qualities, level of applicant's interest. *Other factors considered include:* Application essay, recommendation(s), alumni/ae relation, extracurricular activities, interview, talent/ability, volunteer work, work experience. **Freshman Admission Requirements:** High school diploma is required and GED is accepted. *Academic units required:* 4 English, 3 mathematics, 3 science, (3 science labs), 1 foreign language, 1 social studies, 1 history, 4 academic electives. *Academic units recommended:* 4 mathematics, 4 science. **Freshman Admission Statistics:** 4,178 applied, 62% admitted, 20% enrolled. **Transfer Admission Requirements:** College transcript(s), standardized test scores, minimum college GPA of 3.0 required. Lowest grade transferable C. **General Admission Information:** Application fee $45. Notification on a rolling basis, beginning on or about 10/1. Nonfall registration not accepted. Admission may be deferred for a maximum of 1 year. Credit offered for CEEB Advanced Placement tests.

COSTS AND FINANCIAL AID

Average book expense $1,050. **Required Forms and Deadlines:** FAFSA. Financial aid filing deadline 3/15. Priority financial aid filing date 3/15. **Notification of Awards:** Applicants will be notified of awards on a rolling basis beginning 1/15. **Types of Aid:** *Need-based scholarships/grants:* Federal Pell, SEOG, state scholarships/grants, private scholarships, the school's own gift aid. *Loans:* FFEL Subsidized Stafford, FFEL Unsubsidized Stafford, FFEL PLUS, Federal Perkins, college/university loans from institutional funds. *Student Employment:* Federal Work-Study Program available. Institutional employment available. Highest amount earned per year from on-campus jobs $4,899. **Financial Aid Statistics:** 54% freshmen, 40% undergrads receive need-based scholarship or grant aid. 82% freshmen, 82% undergrads receive non-need-based scholarship or grant aid. 73% freshmen, 70% undergrads receive need-based self-help aid. 1% undergrads receive athletic scholarships. 100% freshmen, 89% undergrads receive any aid. 90% undergrads borrow to pay for school. Average cumulative indebtedness $87,096. **Criteria for awarding institutional aid:** *Non-need-based:* Academics, athletics.

UNIVERSITY OF SCRANTON

800 Linden Street, Scranton, PA 18510-4699
Phone: 570-941-7540 **Financial Aid Phone:** 570-941-7700
E-mail: admissions@scranton.edu **CEEB Code:** 2929
Fax: 570-941-5928 **Website:** www.scranton.edu **ACT Code:** 3736

This private school, affiliated with the Roman CatholiC–Jesuit Church, was founded in 1888. It has a 50-acre campus.

RATINGS
Admissions Selectivity Rating: 85 **Fire Safety Rating:** 80 **Green Rating:** 71

STUDENTS AND FACULTY
Enrollment: 4,010. **Student Body:** 57% female, 43% male, 51% out-of-state, 1% international (23 countries represented). Asian 2%, African American 1%, Caucasian 80%, Hispanic 4%.
Retention and Graduation: 91% freshmen return for sophomore year. 73% freshmen graduate within 4 years. 39% grads go on to further study within 1 year. 14% grads pursue arts and sciences degrees. 3% grads pursue law degrees. 2% grads pursue business degrees. 5% grads pursue medical degrees. **Faculty:** Student/faculty ratio 11.3:1. 20 full-time faculty, 1095% hold PhDs, 135% are members of minority groups, 520% are women.

ACADEMICS
Degrees: Associate, bachelor's, certificate, master's, post-bachelor's certificate, post-master's certificate. **Classes:** Most classes have 10–19 students. Most lab/discussion sessions have 10–19 students. **Majors with Highest Enrollment:** Biology/biological sciences; elementary education and teaching; marketing/marketing management. **Special Study Options:** Accelerated program, cross-registration, distance learning, double major, dual enrollment, English as a Second Language (ESL), exchange student program (domestic), honors program, independent study, internships, study abroad, teacher certification program, Baccalaureate/masters degree program. **Combined degree programs:** BA/MA, BS/MA, MS/MHA, BS/MS, BS/MBA. Special programs offered to physically disabled students include note-taking services, reader services, tape recorders, tutors.

FACILITIES
Housing: Coed dorms, men's dorms, women's dorms, apartments for single students, theme housing. 100% of campus accessible to physically disabled. **Special Academic Facilities/Equipment:** Art gallery, fine arts facility, theatre, center for music groups, language lab, microbiology institute, electron microscope, greenhouse. **Computers:** 40% of classrooms, 100% of dorms, 100% of libraries, 100% of dining areas, 100% of student union, 90% of common outdoor areas have wireless network access. Students can register for classes online. Administrative functions (other than registration) can be performed online.

CAMPUS LIFE
Environment: City. **Activities:** Choral groups, concert band, dance, drama/theater, jazz band, literary magazine, music ensembles, radio station, student government, student newspaper, television station, yearbook, campus ministries, international student organization. **Organizations:** 50 registered organizations, 32 honor societies, 14 religious organizations. **Athletics (Intercollegiate):**

Men: Baseball, basketball, cross-country, golf, ice hockey, lacrosse, soccer, swimming, tennis, wrestling. *Women:* Basketball, cross-country, field hockey, lacrosse, soccer, softball, swimming, tennis, volleyball. **On-Campus Highlights:** Brennan Hall (Home of the Kania School of Management), DeNaples Campus Center, The Harry and Jeanette Weiberg Memorial Library, The Murray Room (workout facility) **Environmental Initiatives:** The ongoing infusion of sustainability across the curriculum: http://matrix.scranton.edu/sustainability/done-academics.shtml. In addition we have a long standing and internationally known program/commitment to green(sustainable) chemistry: http://academic.scranton.edu/faculty/CANNM1/greenchemistry.html. Physical Plant: http://matrix.scranton.edu/sustainability/done-plant.shtml. Community Awareness: http://matrix.scranton.edu/sustainability/done-community.shtml. Events on Campus include: local organic foods dinner; Sustainability Fair: climate change lectures/movies.

ADMISSIONS
Freshman Academic Profile: Average high school GPA 3.36. 30% in top 10% of high school class, 64% in top 25% of high school class, 91.4% in top 50% of high school class. SAT Math middle 50% range 520–610. SAT Critical Reading middle 50% range 510–600. Minimum paper TOEFL 500. Minimum computer TOEFL 173. **Basis for Candidate Selection:** *Very important factors considered include:* Class rank, academic GPA, rigor of secondary school record, standardized test scores. *Important factors considered include:* Extracurricular activities. *Other factors considered include:* Application essay, recommendation(s), alumni/ae relation, character/personal qualities, interview, level of applicant's interest, talent/ability, volunteer work, work experience. **Freshman Admission Requirements:** High school diploma is required and GED is accepted. *Academic units required:* 4 English, 3 mathematics, 3 science, (1 science labs), 2 foreign language, 2 social studies, 2 history, 4 academic electives. *Academic units recommended:* 4 English, 4 mathematics, 3 science, (1 science labs), 2 foreign language, 3 social studies, 3 history, 4 academic electives. **Freshman Admission Statistics:** 7,890 applied, 66% admitted, 19% enrolled. **Transfer Admission Requirements:** High school transcript, college transcript(s), minimum college GPA of 2.75 required. Lowest grade transferable C. **General Admission Information:** Regular application deadline 3/1. Notification on a rolling basis, beginning on or about 12/15. Nonfall registration accepted. Admission may be deferred for a maximum of 1 year. Credit and/or placement offered for CEEB Advanced Placement tests.

COSTS AND FINANCIAL AID
Annual tuition $31,502. Room and board $11,440. Required fees $300. Average book expense $1,150. **Required Forms and Deadlines:** FAFSA. Priority financial aid filing date 2/15. **Notification of Awards:** Applicants will be notified of awards on a rolling basis beginning 3/15. **Types of Aid:** *Need-based scholarships/grants:* Federal Pell, SEOG, state scholarships/grants, private scholarships, the school's own gift aid. *Loans:* Direct Subsidized Stafford, Direct Unsubsidized Stafford, Direct PLUS, Federal Perkins, Federal Nursing. *Student Employment:* Federal Work-Study Program available. Institutional employment available. Off-campus job opportunities are good. **Financial Aid Statistics:** 68% freshmen, 63% undergrads receive need-based scholarship or grant aid. 7% freshmen, 5% undergrads receive non-need-based scholarship or grant aid. 59% freshmen, 56% undergrads receive need-based self-help aid. 85% freshmen, 82% undergrads receive any aid. 77% undergrads borrow to pay for school. Average cumulative indebtedness $28,251. **Criteria for awarding institutional aid:** *Non-need-based:* Academics.

See page 1308.

UNIVERSITY OF SOUTH ALABAMA

Meisler Hall, Room 2500, Mobile, AL 36688-0002
Phone: 251-460-6141 **Financial Aid Phone:** 251-460-6231
E-mail: admiss@usouthal.edu **CEEB Code:** 1880
Fax: 251-460-7023 **ACT Code:** 59

This public school was founded in 1963. It has a 1215-acre campus.

RATINGS
Admissions Selectivity Rating: 60* **Fire Safety Rating:** 60* **Green Rating:** 60*

STUDENTS AND FACULTY
Enrollment: 11,250. **Student Body:** 57% female, 43% male, 19% out-of-state, 4% international (101 countries represented). Asian 3%, African American 19%, Caucasian 66%, Hispanic 2%, Native American 1%.
Retention and Graduation: 67% freshmen return for sophomore year. 13% freshmen graduate within 4 years. **Faculty:** Student/faculty ratio 14:1. 740 full-time faculty, 80% hold PhDs, 39% are women.

ACADEMICS

Degrees: Bachelor's, certificate, master's, post-bachelor's certificate, post-master's certificate. **Classes: Special Study Options:** Accelerated program, cooperative education program, distance learning, double major, dual enrollment, English as a Second Language (ESL), honors program, independent study, internships, student-designed major, study abroad, teacher certification program, weekend college. **Honors programs:** Honor Program Special programs offered to physically disabled students include note-taking services, reader services, tape recorders, tutors.

FACILITIES

Housing: Coed dorms, special housing for disabled students, men's dorms, women's dorms, fraternity/sorority housing, apartments for married students, apartments for single students. **Special Academic Facilities/Equipment:** Museum/gallery complex, three hospitals, center for clinical education in health programs, engineering labs. **Computers:** Students can register for classes online. Administrative functions (other than registration) can be performed online. Undergraduates are required to own a computer.

CAMPUS LIFE

Environment: City. **Activities:** Choral groups, concert band, dance, drama/theater, jazz band, literary magazine, marching band, music ensembles, musical theater, opera, student government, student newspaper, student-run film society, symphony orchestra, television station, campus ministries. **Organizations:** 185 registered organizations, 2 honor societies, 1 religious organizations. 8 fraternities, 8 sororities. **Athletics (Intercollegiate):** *Men:* Baseball, basketball, cross-country, football, golf, tennis, track/field (outdoor). *Women:* Basketball, cross-country, golf, soccer, softball, tennis, track/field (outdoor), volleyball. **On-Campus Highlights:** Mitchell Center (arena), Stanky Field, John W. Laidlaw Performing Arts Center, Intramural Field Complex.

ADMISSIONS

Freshman Academic Profile: 92% from public high schools. SAT Math middle 50% range 430–550. SAT Critical Reading middle 50% range 440–560. ACT middle 50% range 18–24. Minimum paper TOEFL 500. **Basis for Candidate Selection:** *Very important factors considered include:* Rigor of secondary school record, standardized test scores. **Freshman Admission Requirements:** High school diploma is required and GED is accepted. *Academic units recommended:* 4 English, 3 mathematics, 2 science, 2 social studies, 2 history, 2 academic electives, 3 **Freshman Admission Statistics:** 4,050 applied, 90% admitted, 51% enrolled. **Transfer Admission Requirements:** College transcript(s), minimum college GPA of 2.0 required. Lowest grade transferable D. **General Admission Information:** Application fee $35. Regular application deadline 9/10. Nonfall registration accepted. Admission may be deferred for a maximum of N/A. Credit and/or placement offered for CEEB Advanced Placement tests.

COSTS AND FINANCIAL AID

Annual in-state tuition $4,860. Annual out-of-state tuition $9,720. Room and board $5,344. Required fees $1,102. Average book expense $1,200. **Required Forms and Deadlines:** FAFSA, institution's own financial aid form, state aid form **Notification of Awards:** Applicants will be notified of awards on a rolling basis beginning 5/15. **Types of Aid:** *Need-based scholarships/grants:* Federal Pell, SEOG, state scholarships/grants, private scholarships, the school's own gift aid. *Loans:* FFEL Subsidized Stafford, FFEL Unsubsidized Stafford, FFEL PLUS, Federal Perkins, college/university loans from institutional funds. *Student Employment:* Federal Work-Study Program available. **Financial Aid Statistics:** 31% freshmen, 27% undergrads receive need-based scholarship or grant aid. 38% freshmen, 37% undergrads receive non-need-based scholarship or grant aid. 32% freshmen, 34% undergrads receive need-based self-help aid. 4% freshmen, 3% undergrads receive athletic scholarships. **Criteria for awarding institutional aid:** *Non-need-based:* Academics, alumni affiliation, art, athletics, minority status, music/drama.

UNIVERSITY OF SOUTH CAROLINA—AIKEN

471 University Parkway, Aiken, SC 29801
Phone: 803-641-3366 **Financial Aid Phone:** 803-641-3476
E-mail: admit@usca.edu **CEEB Code:** 5840
Fax: 803-641-3727 **Website:** web.usca.edu **ACT Code:** 3879

This public school was founded in 1961. It has a 453-acre campus.

RATINGS

Admissions Selectivity Rating: 83   **Fire Safety Rating:** 99   **Green Rating:** 60*

STUDENTS AND FACULTY

Enrollment: 2,919. **Student Body:** 66% female, 34% male, 9% out-of-state, 1% international (24 countries represented). Asian 1%, African American 28%, Caucasian 61%, Hispanic 3%.
Retention and Graduation: 69% freshmen return for sophomore year. 17% freshmen graduate within 4 years. **Faculty:** Student/faculty ratio 15:1. 150 full-time faculty, 73% hold PhDs, 8% are members of minority groups, 47% are women.

ACADEMICS

Degrees: Bachelor's, master's. **Classes:** Most classes have 20–29 students. Most lab/discussion sessions have 20–29 students. **Majors with Highest Enrollment:** Business/commerce; education; nursing/registered nurse (RN, ASN, BSN, MSN). **Special Study Options:** Cooperative education program, distance learning, double major, dual enrollment, English as a Second Language (ESL), honors program, independent study, internships, student-designed major, study abroad, teacher certification program. **Honors programs:** The USCA Honors Program is designed to increase the educational opportunities for the academically well qualified and highly motivated student. Designed in accordance with the principles of the National Collegiate Honors Council, the USC Aiken Honors Program provides an enriched academic experience, both in and out of the classroom, for outstanding students committed to reaching their highest potential as scholars and creative thinkers. For details on our Honors Program or the other high quality academic opportunities awaiting you at USC Aiken, please call on our Office of Admissions toll free at 888.WOW.USCA or locally at 803.641.3366. The Honors Director may be reached at 803.641.3226. Special programs offered to physically disabled students include note-taking services, reader services, tape recorders. **Career services:** Alumni network, alumni services, career/job search classes, career assessment, internships, regional alumni.

FACILITIES

Housing: Coed dorms, special housing for disabled students, apartments for single students, wellness housing, theme housing. 100% of campus accessible to physically disabled. **Special Academic Facilities/Equipment:** Ruth Patrick Science Education Center, Etherredge Center (fine arts center), Wellness Center, planetarium. **Computers:** 100% of classrooms, 100% of dorms, 100% of libraries, 100% of dining areas, 100% of student union, 100% of common outdoor areas have wireless network access. Students can register for classes online. Administrative functions (other than registration) can be performed online.

CAMPUS LIFE

Environment: Town. **Activities:** Concert band, dance, drama/theater, music ensembles, musical theater, pep band, student government, student newspaper, symphony orchestra, yearbook, campus ministries, international student organization. **Organizations:** 89 registered organizations, 12 honor societies, 7 religious organizations. 5 fraternities, 7 sororities. **Athletics (Intercollegiate):** *Men:* Baseball, basketball, cheerleading, golf, soccer, tennis. *Women:* Basketball, cheerleading, cross-country, soccer, softball, tennis, volleyball. **On-Campus Highlights:** DuPont Planetarium in the Ruth Patrick Science Education Center, The Etherredge Center for Visual and Performing Arts, The Wellness Center and Natatorium, The Alan B. Miller Nursing Building, Pacer Commons Student Housing, Roberto Hernandez Baseball Stadium, USC Aiken Convocation Center.

ADMISSIONS

Freshman Academic Profile: Average high school GPA 3.58. 15% in top 10% of high school class, 43% in top 25% of high school class, 78% in top 50% of high school class. SAT Math middle 50% range 450–550. SAT Critical Reading middle 50% range 430–540. SAT Writing middle 50% range 410–520. ACT middle 50% range 18–23. Minimum paper TOEFL 550. Minimum computer TOEFL 213. Minimum web-based TOEFL 80. **Basis for Candidate Selection:** *Very important factors considered include:* Class rank, academic GPA, rigor of secondary school record, standardized test scores. **Freshman Admission Requirements:** High school diploma is required and GED is accepted. *Academic units required:* 4 English, 4 mathematics, 3 science, (3 science labs), 2 foreign language, 2 social studies, 1 history, 4 academic electives, 1 1 elective must be PE or ROTC. *Academic units recommended:* 1 visual/performing arts, 1 computer science. **Freshman Admission Statistics:** 2,712 applied, 38% admitted, 68% enrolled. **Transfer Admission Requirements:** College transcript(s), statement of good standing from prior institution(s). Minimum college GPA of 2.0 required. Lowest grade transferable C. **General Admission Information:** Application fee $45. Regular application deadline 8/1. Notification on a rolling basis, beginning on or about 9/1. Nonfall registration accepted. Credit and/or placement offered for CEEB Advanced Placement tests.

COSTS AND FINANCIAL AID

Annual in-state tuition $7,700. Annual out-of-state tuition $15,432. Room and board $6,400. Required fees $250. Average book expense $1,080. **Required Forms and Deadlines:** FAFSA. Priority financial aid filing date 3/15. **Notification of Awards:** Applicants will be notified of awards on a rolling basis beginning 4/20. **Types of Aid:** *Need-based scholarships/grants:* Federal Pell, SEOG, state scholarships/grants, private scholarships, the school's own gift aid. *Loans:* Direct Subsidized Stafford, Direct Unsubsidized Stafford, Direct PLUS, FFEL Subsidized Stafford, FFEL Unsubsidized Stafford, FFEL PLUS, Federal Perkins, state loans *Student Employment:* Federal Work-Study Program available. Institutional employment available. Off-campus job opportunities are fair. **Financial Aid Statistics:** 60% freshmen, 48% undergrads receive need-based scholarship or grant aid. 7% freshmen, 7% undergrads receive non-need-based scholarship or grant aid. 46% freshmen, 46% undergrads receive need-based self-help aid. 3% freshmen, 5% undergrads receive athletic scholarships. 47% undergrads borrow to pay for school. Average cumulative indebtedness $24,668. **Criteria for awarding institutional aid:** *Non-need-based:* Academics, alumni affiliation, art, athletics, leadership, minority status, music/drama, state/district residency.

UNIVERSITY OF SOUTH CAROLINA—BEAUFORT

1 University Boulevard, Bluffton, SC 29909
Phone: 843-208-8000 **Financial Aid Phone:** 843-521-3104
E-mail: admissions@uscb.edu **CEEB Code:** 5845
Fax: 843-208-8290 **Website:** www.uscb.edu **ACT Code:** 3835

This public school was founded in 1959. It has a 213-acre campus.

RATINGS
Admissions Selectivity Rating: 60*   **Fire Safety Rating:** 60*   **Green Rating:** 60*

STUDENTS AND FACULTY
Enrollment: 1,319. **Student Body:** 63% female, 37% male, 23.1% out-of-state, 1% international (14 countries represented). Asian 1%, African American 16%, Caucasian 70%, Hispanic 6%, Native American 1%.
Retention and Graduation: Faculty: 62 full-time faculty, 76% hold PhDs, 11% are members of minority groups, 39% are women.

ACADEMICS
Degrees: Associate, bachelor's, post-bachelor's certificate, transfer associate. **Classes:** Most classes have 10–19 students. **Majors with Highest Enrollment:** Business administration and management; psychology; social sciences. **Special Study Options:** Cooperative education program, cross-registration, distance learning, dual enrollment, independent study, internships, study abroad, teacher certification program, weekend college Special programs offered to physically disabled students include note-taking services, reader services, tape recorders, tutors. **Career services:** Career/job search classes, internships.

FACILITIES
Housing: Coed dorms, special housing for disabled students, apartments for single students. **Computers:** Students can register for classes online. Administrative functions (other than registration) can be performed online.

CAMPUS LIFE
Environment: Village. **Activities:** Choral groups, drama/theater, literary magazine, musical theater, student government, student newspaper. **Organizations:** 11 registered organizations. **Athletics (Intercollegiate):** *Men:* Baseball, cross-country, golf, track/field (outdoor) **On-Campus Highlights:** Sandbar Cafe, Campus Center Gym, library.

ADMISSIONS
Freshman Academic Profile: Minimum paper TOEFL 550. Minimum computer TOEFL 213. **Basis for Candidate Selection:** *Very important factors considered include:* Academic GPA, standardized test scores. *Important factors considered include:* Class rank, rigor of secondary school record. **Freshman Admission Requirements:** High school diploma is required and GED is accepted. *Academic units required:* 4 English, 3 mathematics, 3 science, (3 science labs), 2 foreign language, 2 social studies, 1 history, 4 academic electives, 1 physical education. **Transfer Admission Requirements:** College transcript(s), minimum college GPA of 2.0 required. Lowest grade transferable C–. **General Admission Information:** Application fee $40. Notification on a rolling basis, beginning on or about 2/1. Nonfall registration accepted. Credit offered for CEEB Advanced Placement tests.

COSTS AND FINANCIAL AID
Required Forms and Deadlines: FAFSA. Priority financial aid filing date 4/15. **Notification of Awards:** Applicants will be notified of awards on a rolling basis beginning 5/31. **Types of Aid:** *Need-based scholarships/grants:* Federal Pell, SEOG, state scholarships/grants, private scholarships, the school's own gift aid. *Loans:* FFEL Subsidized Stafford, FFEL Unsubsidized Stafford, FFEL PLUS, state loans **Financial Aid Statistics:** 35% freshmen, 65% undergrads

receive any aid. **Criteria for awarding institutional aid:** *Non-need-based:* Academics, state/district residency.

UNIVERSITY OF SOUTH CAROLINA—COLUMBIA

Office of Undergraduate Admissions, University of South Carolina, Columbia, SC 29208
Phone: 803-777-7700 **Financial Aid Phone:** 803-777-8134
E-mail: admissions@sc.edu **CEEB Code:** 5818
Fax: 803-777-0101 **Website:** www.sc.edu **ACT Code:** 3880

This public school was founded in 1801. It has a 384-acre campus.

RATINGS
Admissions Selectivity Rating: 87   **Fire Safety Rating:** 89   **Green Rating:** 94

STUDENTS AND FACULTY
Enrollment: 20,135. **Student Body:** 54% female, 46% male, 26% out-of-state, 1% international (120 countries represented). African American 11%, Caucasian 78%, Hispanic 3%.
Retention and Graduation: 46% freshmen graduate within 4 years. **Faculty:** Student/faculty ratio 18:1. 1142 full-time faculty, 84% hold PhDs, 11% are members of minority groups, 40% are women. 11% of classes are taught by teaching assistants.

ACADEMICS
Degrees: Associate, bachelor's, doctoral, master's, post-bachelor's certificate, post-master's certificate. **Classes:** Most classes have 20–29 students. Most lab/discussion sessions have 20–29 students. **Majors with Highest Enrollment:** Experimental psychology; nursing/registered nurse (RN, ASN, BSN, MSN); sport and fitness administration/management. **Special Study Options:** Accelerated program, cooperative education program, cross-registration, distance learning, double major, dual enrollment, English as a Second Language (ESL), exchange student program (domestic), external degree program, honors program, independent study, internships, student-designed major, study abroad, teacher certification program, weekend college, Alternative Spring Break, Dobson Internship Program, Volunteer Service Program, International Program for Students, Undergraduate Research. **Honors programs:** The Honors College is a small college of about 1,000 students, all of whom excel in academics. What makes the Honors College different is its ability to weave engaging, exciting course offerings into any undergraduate major. You choose your major and set up your course schedule just like any other student at the University. But your choices include classes especially for Honors College students over 100 courses each semester. **Combined degree programs:** BA/MEng. Special programs offered to physically disabled students include note-taking services, reader services, tape recorders. **Career services:** Alumni services, career/job search classes, career assessment, internships. **Career services highlights include:** Experiential learning through consulting with and assisting with startup of new businesses.

FACILITIES
Housing: Coed dorms, special housing for disabled students, men's dorms, special housing for international students, women's dorms, fraternity/sorority housing, apartments for married students, apartments for single students, wellness housing, Honors housing (first year freshman and upperclass), Preston Residential College, Pre-Medical (first year and upperclass), Pre-Law, Engineering and Computing Community, Athletic, Greek, Teaching Fellows, Global, Green, Magellan Explorers, Capstone Scholars, Bridge Community, Journalism, Music, French House, Spanish Language, other special interest. 95% of campus accessible to physically disabled. **Special Academic Facilities/Equipment:** Art gallery, movie theater, McKissick Museum, South Caroliniana Library, Melton Observatory, Gibbes Planetarium, Melton Observatory, Filtration Research Engineering Demonstration Unit, Belser Arboretum, A.C. Moore Gardens. **Computers:** Students can register for classes online. Administrative functions (other than registration) can be performed online.

CAMPUS LIFE
Environment: City. **Activities:** Choral groups, concert band, dance, drama/theater, jazz band, literary magazine, marching band, music ensembles, musical theater, opera, pep band, radio station, student government, student newspaper, symphony orchestra. **Organizations:** 300 registered organizations, 25 honor societies, 32 religious organizations. 20 fraternities, 14 sororities. **Athletics (Intercollegiate):** *Men:* Baseball, basketball, diving, football, golf, racquetball,

soccer, softball, swimming, tennis, track/field (outdoor). *Women:* Basketball, cross-country, diving, equestrian sports, golf, racquetball, soccer, softball, swimming, tennis, track/field (outdoor), volleyball. **On-Campus Highlights:** Strom Thurmond Wellness & Fitness Center, Russell House, Greek Village, Williams Brice Stadium, Historic Horseshoe. **Environmental Initiatives:** Operation of biomass plant producing 76% of campus heat & hot water and 1.2% of campus electricity from renewable sources, in addition the Performance Contract has reduced energy and water consmption in over 2/3rds of the campus buildings. The campus energy consumption has been reduced by 33% and water consumption by 44% since 2004. Campus has committed to converting 100% of its fleet to alternative fuel vehicles by 2015, which will eliminate 2,000 tons of CO2 emissions/year. Green Learning Center utilizes 25 graduate and undergraduate interns and assistants to develop and provide co-curricular education to the campus and community.

ADMISSIONS

Freshman Academic Profile: Average high school GPA 3.9. 27% in top 10% of high school class, 60% in top 25% of high school class, 91% in top 50% of high school class. SAT Math middle 50% range 560–650. SAT Critical Reading middle 50% range 530–640. ACT middle 50% range 24–29. Minimum paper TOEFL 550. Minimum computer TOEFL 210. Minimum web-based TOEFL 77. **Basis for Candidate Selection:** *Very important factors considered include:* Academic GPA, rigor of secondary school record, standardized test scores. *Important factors considered include:* Class rank. *Other factors considered include:* Application essay, recommendation(s), alumni/ae relation, character/personal qualities, extracurricular activities, first generation, racial/ethnic status, state residency, talent/ability, volunteer work, work experience. **Freshman Admission Requirements:** High school diploma is required and GED is accepted. *Academic units required:* 4 English, 4 mathematics, 3 science, (3 science labs), 2 foreign language, 2 social studies, 1 history, 1 academic electives, 2 PE or ROTC and fine arts. **Freshman Admission Statistics:** 17,694 applied, 64% admitted, 35% enrolled. **Transfer Admission Requirements:** College transcript(s), minimum college GPA of 2.25 required. Lowest grade transferable C−. **General Admission Information:** Application fee $50. Regular application deadline 12/1. Notification on a rolling basis, beginning on or about 3/15. Nonfall registration accepted. Credit and/or placement offered for CEEB Advanced Placement tests.

COSTS AND FINANCIAL AID

Annual in-state tuition $8,756. Annual out-of-state tuition $23,332. Room and board $7,328. Required fees $400. Average book expense $936. **Required Forms and Deadlines:** FAFSA. Priority financial aid filing date 1/4. **Notification of Awards:** Applicants will be notified of awards on a rolling basis beginning 1/4. **Types of Aid:** *Need-based scholarships/grants:* Federal Pell, SEOG, state scholarships/grants, private scholarships, the school's own gift aid, United Negro College Fund, Federal Nursing Scholarships. USC Opportunity Grant—Institutional Gamecock Guarantee. *Loans:* FFEL Subsidized Stafford, FFEL Unsubsidized Stafford, FFEL PLUS, Federal Perkins, Federal Nursing *Student Employment:* Federal Work-Study Program available. Institutional employment available. Off-campus job opportunities are good. **Financial Aid Statistics:** 17% freshmen, 22% undergrads receive need-based scholarship or grant aid. 37% freshmen, 28% undergrads receive non-need-based scholarship or grant aid. 28% freshmen, 35% undergrads receive need-based self-help aid. 3% freshmen, 3% undergrads receive athletic scholarships. 93% freshmen, 90% undergrads receive any aid. 46% undergrads borrow to pay for school. Average cumulative indebtedness $21,755. **Criteria for awarding institutional aid:** *Non-need-based:* Academics, alumni affiliation, art, athletics, job skills, leadership, minority status, music/drama, religious affiliation, state/district residency.

THE UNIVERSITY OF SOUTH DAKOTA

414 East Clark, Vermillion, SD 57069
Phone: 605-677-5434 **Financial Aid Phone:** 605-677-5446
E-mail: admissions@usd.edu **CEEB Code:** 6881
Fax: 605-677-6323 **Website:** www.usd.edu **ACT Code:** 3928

This public school was founded in 1862. It has a 273-acre campus.

RATINGS

Admissions Selectivity Rating: 73   **Fire Safety Rating:** 89   **Green Rating:** 86

STUDENTS AND FACULTY

Enrollment: 6,043. **Student Body:** 62% female, 38% male, 25% out-of-state, (30 countries represented). Asian 1%, African American 2%, Caucasian 83%, Hispanic 1%, Native American 2%.
Retention and Graduation: 72% freshmen return for sophomore year. 22% freshmen graduate within 4 years. 48% grads go on to further study within 1 year. 20% grads pursue arts and sciences degrees. 8% grads pursue law degrees. 25% grads pursue business degrees. 8% grads pursue medical degrees. **Faculty:** Student/faculty ratio 15:1. 395 full-time faculty, 74% hold PhDs, 16% are members of minority groups, 48% are women. 5% of classes are taught by teaching assistants.

ACADEMICS

Degrees: Associate, bachelor's, certificate, doctoral, master's, post-bachelor's certificate, post-master's certificate, terminal associate. **Classes:** Most classes have 10–19 students. Most lab/discussion sessions have 20–29 students. **Majors with Highest Enrollment:** Business/commerce; education; psychology. **Special Study Options:** Accelerated program, cross-registration, distance learning, double major, dual enrollment, English as a Second Language (ESL), exchange student program (domestic), external degree program, honors program, independent study, internships, liberal arts/career combination, student-designed major, study abroad, teacher certification program. **Honors programs:** University Honors Program. The program has its own core curriculum that replaces the University's general education requirements. Thesis Scholars Program, Alumni Student Scholars Program, Law Honors Scholars Program. **Combined degree programs:** BA/MA. Special programs offered to physically disabled students include note-taking services, reader services, tape recorders, tutors. **Career services:** Alumni network, alumni services, career/job search classes, career assessment, internships. **Career services highlights include:** USD, as the flagship liberal arts institution in the state, provides the framework for an extraordinary education and includes the Interdisciplinary Education & Action or "IdEA" Program. The U. has purposefully designed a contemporary liberal arts education that includes a solid foundation of knowledge, exposure to many different academic disciplines, immersion in interdisciplinary and diverse ways of thinkingt, and understanding of service and citizenship. All students at the U. follow a flexible course of study that first exposes them to great ideas, but ultimately challenges them to integrate their knowledge in ways that serve their own careers and other citizens (http://catalog.usd.edu/content.php?catoid=3&navoid=34). The integration component of this education is found in the IdEA Program, which invites USD students to explore interdisciplinary approaches to questions that matter in a global, contemporary society. It occurs when juniors and seniors are experiencing the conclusion of their academic careers at USD and at a time when individuals are moving beyond their immediate and personal identities and defining their roles and responsibilities in a wider social, political, economic and physical environments. It provides key liberal learning outcomes such as critical thinking, integrative approaches and active citizenship.

FACILITIES

Housing: Coed dorms, special housing for disabled students, fraternity/sorority housing, apartments for married students, apartments for single students, apartments for students with dependent children. Brand new state of the art apartment style housing currently under construction with a new wellness center being constructed due to open in 2010. 98% of campus accessible to physically disabled. **Special Academic Facilities/Equipment:** W.H. Over Museum, The National Music Museum, Oscar Howe Art Gallery, Center for Instructional Design and Delivery, Institute of American Indian Studies, Native American Cultural Center, Disaster Mental Health Institute, Neuharth Center for Excellence in Journalism, Missouri Rive Institute. **Computers:** 60% of classrooms, 100% of libraries, 100% of dining areas, 100% of student union, have wireless network access. Students can register for classes online. Administrative functions (other than registration) can be performed online.

CAMPUS LIFE

Environment: Village. **Activities:** Choral groups, concert band, dance, drama/theater, jazz band, literary magazine, marching band, music ensembles, musical theater, opera, pep band, radio station, student government, student newspaper, symphony orchestra, television station, campus ministries, international student organization. **Organizations:** 120 registered organizations, 6 honor societies, 6 religious organizations. 8 fraternities, 3 sororities. **Athletics (Intercollegiate):** *Men:* Basketball, cross-country, diving, football, golf, swimming, track/field (outdoor), track/field (indoor). *Women:* Basketball, cross-country, diving, golf, soccer, softball, swimming, tennis, track/field (outdoor), track/field (indoor), volleyball. **On-Campus Highlights:** Al Neuharth Media Center, The National Music Museum, The Dakota Dome, Belbus Student Service Center, Coyote Student Center. **Environmental Initiatives:** Recycling, signed Climate Commitment, formation of the Sustainability Task Force.

ADMISSIONS

Freshman Academic Profile: Average high school GPA 3.31. 13% in top 10% of high school class, 38% in top 25% of high school class, 71% in top 50% of

high school class. SAT Math middle 50% range 440–610. SAT Critical Reading middle 50% range 430–630. ACT middle 50% range 20–26. Minimum paper TOEFL 550. Minimum computer TOEFL 213. Minimum web-based TOEFL 79. **Basis for Candidate Selection:** *Very important factors considered include:* Class rank, academic GPA, rigor of secondary school record, standardized test scores. *Important factors considered include:* Alumni/ae relation. *Other factors considered include:* Application essay, recommendation(s), character/personal qualities, extracurricular activities, geographical residence, racial/ethnic status, state residency, talent/ability, volunteer work, work experience. **Freshman Admission Requirements:** High school diploma is required and GED is accepted. *Academic units required:* 4 English, 3 mathematics, 3 science, (3 science labs), 3 social studies, 1 Fine Arts *Academic units recommended:* 4 English, 4 mathematics, 4 science, (3 science labs), 2 foreign language, 3 social studies, 1 fine arts. **Freshman Admission Statistics:** 3,129 applied, 87% admitted, 41% enrolled. **Transfer Admission Requirements:** High school transcript, college transcript(s), minimum college GPA of 2.0 required. Lowest grade transferable D. **General Admission Information:** Application fee $20. Notification on a rolling basis, beginning on or about 9/10. Nonfall registration accepted. Admission may be deferred for a maximum of One Semester. Credit and/or placement offered for CEEB Advanced Placement tests.

COSTS AND FINANCIAL AID

Annual in-state tuition $2,751. Annual out-of-state tuition $4,124. Room and board $5,787. Required fees $3,717. Average book expense $900. **Required Forms and Deadlines:** FAFSA. Priority financial aid filing date 3/15. **Notification of Awards:** Applicants will be notified of awards on a rolling basis beginning 3/1. **Types of Aid:** *Need-based scholarships/grants:* Federal Pell, SEOG, private scholarships, the school's own gift aid, Federal Nursing Scholarships. *Loans:* FFEL Subsidized Stafford, FFEL Unsubsidized Stafford, FFEL PLUS, Federal Perkins, Federal Nursing, college/university loans from institutional funds. *Student Employment:* Federal Work-Study Program available. Institutional employment available. Highest amount earned per year from on-campus jobs $3,300. Off-campus job opportunities are good. **Financial Aid Statistics:** 26% freshmen, 28% undergrads receive need-based scholarship or grant aid. 71% freshmen, 48% undergrads receive non-need-based scholarship or grant aid. 32% freshmen, 36% undergrads receive need-based self-help aid. 6% freshmen, 5% undergrads receive athletic scholarships. 92% freshmen, 88% undergrads receive any aid. **Criteria for awarding institutional aid:** *Non-need-based:* Academics, art, athletics, leadership, minority status, music/drama.

UNIVERSITY OF SOUTH FLORIDA

4202 East Fowler Avenue, SVC–1036, Tampa, FL 33620-9951
Phone: 813-974-3350 **Financial Aid Phone:** 813-974-4700
E-mail: admissions@admin.usf.edu **CEEB Code:** 5828
Fax: 813-974-9689 **Website:** www.usf.edu **ACT Code:** 761

This public school was founded in 1956. It has a 1797-acre campus.

RATINGS
Admissions Selectivity Rating: 87   **Fire Safety Rating:** 60*   **Green Rating:** 92

STUDENTS AND FACULTY
Enrollment: 35,750. **Student Body:** 57% female, 43% male, 3% out-of-state, 1% international (136 countries represented). Asian 6%, African American 12%, Caucasian 64%, Hispanic 14%.
Retention and Graduation: 86% freshmen return for sophomore year. 20% grads go on to further study within 1 year. **Faculty:** Student/faculty ratio 27:1. 1292 full-time faculty, 79% hold PhDs, 24% are members of minority groups, 42% are women. 17% of classes are taught by teaching assistants.

ACADEMICS
Degrees: Associate, bachelor's, master's. **Classes:** Most classes have 20–29 students. Most lab/discussion sessions have 20–29 students. **Majors with Highest Enrollment:** Biomedical sciences; business/commerce; psychology. **Special Study Options:** Accelerated program, cooperative education program, cross-registration, distance learning, double major, dual enrollment, exchange student program (domestic), honors program, internships, study abroad, teacher certification program, weekend college, Honors undergraduate research majors. **Honors programs:** Honors College: http://honors.usf.edu/. **Combined degree programs:** BA/MD, BA/MA, BA/MEng. Special programs offered to physically disabled students include note-taking services, reader services, tutors.

Career services: Alumni services, career/job search classes, career assessment, internships.

FACILITIES
Housing: Coed dorms, special housing for disabled students, men's dorms, special housing for international students, women's dorms, fraternity/sorority housing, apartments for married students, cooperative housing, apartments for single students, grad students only, medical students only. 100% of campus accessible to physically disabled. **Special Academic Facilities/Equipment:** Art museum and galleries, contemporary art museum, graphic studio, anthropology museum, fitness center, par course. **Computers:** 80% of classrooms, 35% of dorms, 100% of library, 50% of dining areas, 100% of student union, 50% of common outdoor areas have wireless network access. Students can register for classes online. Administrative functions (other than registration) can be performed online.

CAMPUS LIFE
Environment: Metropolis. **Activities:** Choral groups, concert band, dance, drama/theater, jazz band, literary magazine, marching band, music ensembles, musical theater, opera, pep band, radio station, student government, student newspaper, student-run film society, symphony orchestra, television station **Organizations:** 507 registered organizations, 33 honor societies, 42 religious organizations. 16 fraternities, 22 sororities. **Athletics (Intercollegiate):** *Men:* Baseball, basketball, cheerleading, cross-country, football, golf, sailing, soccer, tennis, track/field (outdoor), track/field (indoor). *Women:* Basketball, cheerleading, cross-country, golf, sailing, soccer, softball, tennis, track/field (outdoor), track/field (indoor), volleyball. **On-Campus Highlights:** Marshall Center, The Tampa Campus Library, Contemporary Art Museum, Botanical Gardens, Sun Dome. **Environmental Initiatives:** USF's 2008 Going Green Tampa Bay sustainability EXPO which drew over 3,000 visitors. Our USF Sustainability Initiative and 14 subcommittees. Our rapidly expanding recycling program, our campus transportation program. We have incorporated sustainability into our USF Strategic Plan.

ADMISSIONS
Freshman Academic Profile: 26.35% in top 10% of high school class, 58.7% in top 25% of high school class, 81.62% in top 50% of high school class. 95% from public high schools. SAT Math middle 50% range 520–630. SAT Critical Reading middle 50% range 510–620. SAT Writing middle 50% range 500–600. ACT middle 50% range 22–28. Minimum paper TOEFL 550. Minimum computer TOEFL 213. **Basis for Candidate Selection:** *Very important factors considered include:* Academic GPA, rigor of secondary school record. *Important factors considered include:* Standardized test scores, first generation. *Other factors considered include:* Class rank, application essay, recommendation(s), character/personal qualities, extracurricular activities, geographical residence, state residency, talent/ability, volunteer work, work experience. **Freshman Admission Requirements:** High school diploma is required and GED is accepted. *Academic units required:* 4 English, 4 mathematics, 3 science, (2 science labs), 2 foreign language, 3 social studies, 3 academic electives. *Academic units recommended:* 4 science, (3 science labs), 4 foreign language. **Freshman Admission Statistics:** 29,631 applied, 43% admitted, 34% enrolled. **Transfer Admission Requirements:** College transcript(s), statement of good standing from prior institution(s). Minimum college GPA of 2.3 required. Lowest grade transferable D. **General Admission Information:** Application fee $30. Regular application deadline 4/15. Regular notification 4/15. Notification on a rolling basis, beginning on or about 10/1. Nonfall registration accepted. Credit and/or placement offered for CEEB Advanced Placement tests.

COSTS AND FINANCIAL AID
Annual in-state tuition $4,503. Annual out-of-state tuition $15,312. Room and board $8,750. Required fees $74. Average book expense $1,500. **Required Forms and Deadlines:** FAFSA. Priority financial aid filing date 3/1. **Notification of Awards:** Applicants will be notified of awards on a rolling basis beginning 3/15. **Types of Aid:** *Need-based scholarships/grants:* Federal Pell, SEOG, state scholarships/grants, private scholarships, the school's own gift aid. *Loans:* FFEL Subsidized Stafford, FFEL Unsubsidized Stafford, FFEL PLUS, Federal Perkins, college/university loans from institutional funds. *Student Employment:* Federal Work-Study Program available. Institutional employment available. Off-campus job opportunities are good. **Financial Aid Statistics:** 29% freshmen, 8% undergrads receive need-based scholarship or grant aid. 52% freshmen, 3% undergrads receive non-need-based scholarship or grant aid. 25% freshmen, 35% undergrads receive need-based self-help aid. 2% freshmen, 1% undergrads receive athletic scholarships. 98% freshmen, 76% undergrads receive any aid. 52% undergrads borrow to pay for school. Average cumulative indebtedness $19,963. **Criteria for awarding institutional aid:** *Non-need-based:* Academics, alumni affiliation, art, athletics, job skills, leadership, minority status, music/drama, religious affiliation, state/district residency.

UNIVERSITY OF SOUTHERN CALIFORNIA

Office of Admission/ John Hubbard Hall, 700 Childs Way, Los Angeles, CA 90089-0911
Phone: 213-740-1111 **Financial Aid Phone:** 213-740-1111
E-mail: admitusc@usc.edu **CEEB Code:** 4852
Fax: 213-821-0200 **Website:** www.usc.edu **ACT Code:** 470

This private school was founded in 1880. It has a 155-acre campus.

RATINGS
Admissions Selectivity Rating: 98   **Fire Safety Rating:** 96   **Green Rating:** 89

STUDENTS AND FACULTY
Enrollment: 16,445. **Student Body:** 50% female, 50% male, 34.8% out-of-state, 10% international (150 countries represented). Asian 24%, African American 6%, Caucasian 45%, Hispanic 13%, Native American 1%. **Retention and Graduation:** 96% freshmen return for sophomore year. 72% freshmen graduate within 4 years. 23.9% grads go on to further study within 1 year. 5% grads pursue law degrees. 2.3% grads pursue medical degrees. **Faculty:** Student/faculty ratio 9:1. 1638 full-time faculty, 89% hold PhDs, 26% are members of minority groups, 34% are women.

ACADEMICS
Degrees: Bachelor's, doctoral, master's, post-bachelor's certificate, post-master's certificate. **Classes:** Most classes have 10–19 students. Most lab/discussion sessions have 20–29 students. **Majors with Highest Enrollment:** Business administration and management; communication studies/speech communication and rhetoric; psychology. **Special Study Options:** Cooperative education program, distance learning, double major, English as a Second Language (ESL), exchange student program (domestic), honors program, independent study, internships, liberal arts/career combination, student-designed major, study abroad, learning communities, Thematic Option, undergraduate research, and Freshman Seminars. **Honors programs:** Thematic Option Program; Multimedia Scholarship. **Combined degree programs:** BA/MD, BA/MA, BA/MEng, BS/MA, BS/MS. Special programs offered to physically disabled students include note-taking services, reader services, tape recorders, tutors. **Career services:** Alumni network, alumni services, career assessment, internships, regional alumni. **Career services highlights include:** Joint Educational Project, a service learning program that provides an interface between USC and the local community.

FACILITIES
Housing: Coed dorms, special housing for disabled students, special housing for international students, fraternity/sorority housing, apartments for married students, apartments for single students, wellness housing, theme housingSpecial interest floors. 97% of campus accessible to physically disabled. **Special Academic Facilities/Equipment:** USC Fisher Museum of Art; Hancock Memorial Museum; specialized architecture and fine arts galleries, studios and labs; media labs; cinema scoring sound stage; recording studios; theatres and recital halls; exercise physiology lab; specialized engineering laboratories; biomedical imaging labs; Center for Electron Microscopy and Microanalysis; genomic research facilities; GIS research lab; USC Shoah Foundation Institute visual history archive; Archival Research Center; High-Performance Computing Center; public computing centers and labs; extensive wireless access to the USC network; classrooms outfitted with multiple webcams and microphones. **Computers:** 15% of classrooms, 10% of dorms, 100% of libraries, 100% of dining areas, 100% of student union, 90% of common outdoor areas have wireless network access. Students can register for classes online. Administrative functions (other than registration) can be performed online.

CAMPUS LIFE
Environment: Metropolis. **Activities:** Choral groups, concert band, dance, drama/theater, jazz band, literary magazine, marching band, music ensembles, musical theater, opera, pep band, radio station, student government, student newspaper, student-run film society, symphony orchestra, television station, yearbook, campus ministries, international student organization, Model UN. **Organizations:** 676 registered organizations, 49 honor societies, 74 religious organizations. 41 fraternities, 23 sororities. **Athletics (Intercollegiate):** *Men:* Baseball, basketball, diving, football, golf, swimming, tennis, track/field (outdoor), volleyball, water polo. *Women:* Basketball, crew/rowing, cross-country, diving, golf, soccer, swimming, tennis, track/field (outdoor), volleyball, water polo. **On-Campus Highlights:** USC Fisher Museum of Art, Galen Center (event & training pavilion), Leavey Library (open 24 hours), Heritage Hall (athletic awards), Tutor Campus Center (opens fall 2010), USC's University

Park campus—located three miles south of downtown Los Angeles, adjacent to the museums and recreational facilities of historic Exposition Park—is an urban oasis, offering a park-like atmosphere and rich architectural history. **Environmental Initiatives:** Energy Efficiency & Innovation: USC employs a full time Director of Energy Services to manage energy programs including lighting retrofits, equipment upgrades, and a recent retrofit of chillers, cooling towers, and pumps throughout the university, including a three million gallon centralized thermal energy storage tank installed below ground. The 3 million-gallon thermal energy water storage (TES) system was built 40 feet below ground. It is estimated that the new system conserves about 4,500 megawatt-hours of electricity a year by circulating chilled water to air conditioning systems throughout the University Park Campus, significantly expanding the capacity of the campus' existing chilled-water system while reducing utility use. The warmer water coming back through pipes has a chance to chill overnight before it is recirculated which allows USC to shift much of the kilowatt-hour usage to off-peak hours when electricity is more available. The entire system was conceived in 2001 and completed in 2005. Transportation Initiatives: USC counts on the services of a full time Rideshare Coordinator to ensure that transportation programs are available to all members of the university community. In 2006 USC achieved an Average Vehicle Ridership (AVR) of 1.69, exceeding the target of 1.50 established by the South Coast Air Quality Management District (SCAQMD). Seventeen strategies are used to achieve this AVR, most notably: a carpool/vanpool program; transit and parking charge subsidies; telecommuting; various incentives and raffles; availability of compressed work weeks; bicycle accessibility; and various support strategies like providing transit information and ridesharing assistance. There are five primary ride sharing options available to the USC community. Students, Staff, and Faculty are encouraged to ride the MTA Bus Lines, DASH Bus Lines, Metrolink Trains, or participate in carpools and vanpools. Eligible full time employees of USC who participate in the programs receive a subsidy of $30 as a benefit for not purchasing a parking pass. The subsidies provided to employees may be applied to the purchase of monthly passes for Metro (light rail or bus), LADOT, Metrolink, or other services not sold through the Transportation Office. In order to facilitate participation in the carpool program, employees are encouraged to participate in L.A. County's "ridematch" program to find potential carpool partners. The online database matches potential rideshare partners from the five county regions of Los Angeles, San Bernardino, Orange, Ventura, and Riverside. In addition, USC's Rideshare Office conducts an annual rideshare survey to generate a customized "rideguide" to match potential carpoolers in a given area. Trojan Transportation has three alternative fuel trams that run on biodiesel which provide service to off-campus housing, between campuses, and to Union Train Station. Recently purchased electriC–powered, three-wheeled vehicles and bicycles are now used daily to patrol the campus by the Department of Public Safety. Eight of the three wheeled carts are used daily and offer a green alternative to gasoline powered patrol cars. In addition, the Facilities Management Services organization counts on a fleet of electric and hybrid vehicles for campus use. Also of note, USC has partnered with Flexcar, a unique car-sharing service that offers members affordable hourly access to vehicles, thus reducing the need for vehicles on campus. The service is available to everyone in the USC community. Sustainability Steering Committee: The Sustainability Steering Committee's core intent is to help USC maintain its current needs without compromising the ability of future generations to do the same. Specific responsibilities of this oversight committee include: a. Benchmarking trends in institutional sustainability and identifying the best economic, social, environmental opportunities on which USC can act; b. Identifying USC's strengths and opportunities relative to advancing sustainability in the areas of campus operations, and community outreach; c. Communicating USC's sustainability initiatives and their benefits to the university community; and d. Making recommendations to the Senior Vice President of Administration detailing specific actions and resources required to best allow USC administrative functions to operationalize sustainable practices. The Sustainability Steering Committee consists of at least 12 voting members appointed by the Senior Vice President, Administration and General Counsel. Members are drawn from a group of senior level administrators, staff, students, and faculty representatives who are knowledgeable of and/or play a potentially large role in the area of sustainability. Sub-committees (such as the Operations Sustainability Steering Committee, which is overseen by the Sustainability Steering Committee) are used as needed to carry out individual initiatives. Committee created the sustainability program manager position to launch new program and has guided the recent establishment of the Sustainability Office.

ADMISSIONS
Freshman Academic Profile: Average high school GPA 3.7. 86% in top 10% of high school class, 97% in top 25% of high school class, 100% in top 50% of high school class. 57% from public high schools. SAT Math middle 50% range 650–740. SAT Critical Reading middle 50% range 620–710. SAT Writing middle 50% range 640–730. ACT middle 50% range 29–32. **Basis for Candidate Selection:** *Very important factors considered include:* Application essay, academic GPA, recommendation(s), rigor of secondary school record, standardized test scores. *Important factors considered include:* Extracurricular activities, talent/ability. *Other factors considered include:* Class rank, alumni/ae

relation, character/personal qualities, first generation, interview, racial/ethnic status, volunteer work, work experience. **Freshman Admission Requirements:** High school diploma is required and GED is not accepted. *Academic units required:* 4 English, 3 mathematics, 2 science, (2 science labs), 2 foreign language, 2 social studies, 3 academic electives. *Academic units recommended:* 4 English, 4 mathematics, 3 science, (3 science labs), 3 foreign language, 3 social studies, 3 academic electives. **Freshman Admission Statistics:** 35,753 applied, 24% admitted, 33% enrolled. **Transfer Admission Requirements:** High school transcript, college transcript(s), essay or personal statement, Lowest grade transferable C–. **General Admission Information:** Application fee $65. Regular application deadline 1/10. Regular notification 4/1. Nonfall registration accepted. Credit and/or placement offered for CEEB Advanced Placement tests.

COSTS AND FINANCIAL AID

Required Forms and Deadlines: FAFSA, CSS/Financial Aid PROFILE, parent and student federal income tax form with all schedules and W2s. USC Non-filing Forms for those not required to file. Priority financial aid filing date 2/2. **Notification of Awards:** Applicants will be notified of awards on a rolling basis beginning 3/15. **Types of Aid:** *Need-based scholarships/grants:* Federal Pell, SEOG, state scholarships/grants, private scholarships, the school's own gift aid. *Loans:* FFEL Subsidized Stafford, FFEL Unsubsidized Stafford, FFEL PLUS, Federal Perkins, "Credit Ready" and Credit Based loans. *Student Employment:* Federal Work-Study Program available. Institutional employment available. Off-campus job opportunities are excellent. **Financial Aid Statistics:** 37% freshmen, 37% undergrads receive need-based scholarship or grant aid. 25% freshmen, 18% undergrads receive non-need-based scholarship or grant aid. 42% freshmen, 41% undergrads receive need-based self-help aid. 4% freshmen, 2% undergrads receive athletic scholarships. 68% freshmen, 62% undergrads receive any aid. 45% undergrads borrow to pay for school. Average cumulative indebtedness $30,097. **Criteria for awarding institutional aid:** *Non-need-based:* Academics, alumni affiliation, art, athletics, leadership, music/drama.

UNIVERSITY OF SOUTHERN INDIANA

8600 University Boulevard, Evansville, IN 47712
Phone: 812-464-1765 **Financial Aid Phone:** 812-464-1767
E-mail: enroll@usi.edu **CEEB Code:** 1335
Fax: 812-465-7154 **Website:** www.usi.edu **ACT Code:** 1207

This public school was founded in 1965. It has a 330-acre campus.

RATINGS
Admissions Selectivity Rating: 70   **Fire Safety Rating:** 71   **Green Rating:** 74

STUDENTS AND FACULTY
Enrollment: 9,442. **Student Body:** 58% female, 42% male, 10% out-of-state, 2% international (40 countries represented). Asian 1%, African American 5%, Caucasian 89%, Hispanic 1%.
Retention and Graduation: 68% freshmen return for sophomore year. 17% freshmen graduate within 4 years. 16% grads go on to further study within 1 year. **Faculty:** Student/faculty ratio 18:1. 338 full-time faculty, 64% hold PhDs, 6% are members of minority groups, 54% are women.

ACADEMICS
Degrees: Associate, bachelor's, certificate, master's, post-bachelor's certificate, terminal associate, transfer associate. **Classes:** Most classes have 20–29 students. Most lab/discussion sessions have 20–29 students. **Majors with Highest Enrollment:** Business administration and management; elementary education and teaching; health/health care administration/management. **Special Study Options:** Cooperative education program, distance learning, double major, dual enrollment, English as a Second Language (ESL), honors program, independent study, internships, study abroad, teacher certification program. **Combined degree programs:** RN/MSN. Special programs offered to physically disabled students include note-taking services, reader services, tape recorders, tutors. **Career services:** Alumni network, alumni services, career/job search classes, career assessment, internships.

FACILITIES
Housing: Coed dorms, special housing for disabled students, fraternity/sorority housing, apartments for married students, apartments for single students, wellness housing, theme housing. 95% of campus accessible to physically disabled. **Computers:** 100% of classrooms, 100% of dorms, 100% of libraries, 100% of dining areas, 100% of student union, 100% of common outdoor areas have wireless network access. Students can register for classes online. Administrative functions (other than registration) can be performed online.

CAMPUS LIFE
Environment: City. **Activities:** Choral groups, dance, drama/theater, jazz band, literary magazine, pep band, radio station, student government, student newspaper, campus ministries, international student organization, Model UN. **Organizations:** 102 registered organizations, 6 honor societies, 7 religious organizations. 7 fraternities, 4 sororities. **Athletics (Intercollegiate):** *Men:* Baseball, basketball, cross-country, golf, soccer, tennis, track/field (outdoor), track/field (indoor). *Women:* Basketball, cross-country, golf, soccer, softball, tennis, track/field (outdoor), track/field (indoor), volleyball. **On-Campus Highlights:** Eagle's Nest, The Loft, Recreation and Fitness Center, Rice Library. **Environmental Initiatives:** Established environmental stewardship committee. Being more conscious of sustainable materials such as CFL lighting and reducing energy consumption. Highlight starter program to recycle materials from new construction and renovation projects.

ADMISSIONS
Freshman Academic Profile: Average high school GPA 3.02. 12% in top 10% of high school class, 31% in top 25% of high school class, 64% in top 50% of high school class. SAT Math middle 50% range 430–540. SAT Critical Reading middle 50% range 420–530. SAT Writing middle 50% range 405–510. ACT middle 50% range 18–23. Minimum paper TOEFL 525. Minimum computer TOEFL 197. Minimum web-based TOEFL 71. **Basis for Candidate Selection:** *Important factors considered include:* Class rank, academic GPA, standardized test scores. *Other factors considered include:* Application essay, recommendation(s), rigor of secondary school record, alumni/ae relation, character/personal qualities, extracurricular activities, interview, talent/ability, work experience. **Freshman Admission Requirements:** High school diploma is required and GED is accepted. *Academic units recommended:* 4 English, 4 mathematics, 2 science, 2 foreign language, 2 social studies, 2 history, 2 academic electives. **Freshman Admission Statistics:** 5,324 applied, 88% admitted, 45% enrolled. **Transfer Admission Requirements:** High school transcript, college transcript(s), minimum college GPA of 2.0 required. Lowest grade transferable C–. **General Admission Information:** Application fee $25. Regular application deadline 8/15. Notification on a rolling basis, beginning on or about 7/1. Nonfall registration accepted. Credit and/or placement offered for CEEB Advanced Placement tests.

COSTS AND FINANCIAL AID
Annual in-state tuition $5,274. Annual out-of-state tuition $12,555. Room and board $6,700. Required fees $200. Average book expense $1,100. **Required Forms and Deadlines:** FAFSA, institution's own financial aid form. Priority financial aid filing date 3/1. **Notification of Awards:** Applicants will be notified of awards on a rolling basis beginning 4/1. **Types of Aid:** *Need-based scholarships/grants:* Federal Pell, SEOG, state scholarships/grants, private scholarships, the school's own gift aid, Federal Nursing Scholarships. *Loans:* Direct Subsidized Stafford, Direct Unsubsidized Stafford, Direct PLUS. *Student Employment:* Federal Work-Study Program available. Institutional employment available. Off-campus job opportunities are good. **Financial Aid Statistics:** 48% freshmen, 43% undergrads receive need-based scholarship or grant aid. 6% freshmen, 4% undergrads receive non-need-based scholarship or grant aid. 58% freshmen, 55% undergrads receive need-based self-help aid. 1% freshmen, 1% undergrads receive athletic scholarships. 70% freshmen, 71% undergrads receive any aid. **Criteria for awarding institutional aid:** *Non-need-based:* Academics, art, athletics, leadership, music/drama, state/district residency.

UNIVERSITY OF SOUTHERN MAINE

37 College Avenue, Gorham, ME 04038
Phone: 207-780-5670 **Financial Aid Phone:** 207-780-5250
E-mail: usmadm@usm.maine.edu **CEEB Code:** 3691
Fax: 207-780-5640 **Website:** www.usm.maine.edu **ACT Code:** 1644

This public school was founded in 1878. It has a 144-acre campus.

RATINGS
Admissions Selectivity Rating: 71   **Fire Safety Rating:** 60*   **Green Rating:** 60*

STUDENTS AND FACULTY
Enrollment: 6,548. **Student Body:** 57% female, 43% male, % out-of-state, 2% international (40 countries represented). Asian 2%, African American 2%, Caucasian 92%, Hispanic 1%, Native American 2%.
Retention and Graduation: **Faculty:** 335 full-time faculty.

ACADEMICS
Degrees: Bachelor's, certificate, master's, post-master's certificate. **Majors with Highest Enrollment:** Perioperative/operating room and surgical nurse/nursing; psychology. **Special Study Options:** Accelerated program, coopera-

tive education program, cross-registration, distance learning, double major, English as a Second Language (ESL), exchange student program (domestic), honors program, independent study, internships, liberal arts/career combination, student-designed major, study abroad, teacher certification program, weekend college, Preengineering program with University of Maine at Orono, living/learning scholars program, Greater Portland Alliance—cross registration with University of New England, St. Joseph's (Maine), Southern Maine Technical College, and Maine College of Art. **Honors programs:** Russell Scholars—living/learning community, USM honors program Special programs offered to physically disabled students include note-taking services, tape recorders, tutors. **Career services:** Career/job search classes, internships.

FACILITIES

Housing: Coed dorms, special housing for disabled students, fraternity/sorority housing, apartments for married students, apartments for single students, Fine Arts House, Russell Scholars (living/learning), Chemical Free Floor 24 Hour Quiet Floor, Community Living program. 100% of campus accessible to physically disabled. **Special Academic Facilities/Equipment:** Southworth Planetarium, Osher Map Collection and Smith Center for Cartographic Education, WMPG (radio station), GTV (cable TV station), Free Press (campus newspaper), various art galleries on all three campuses. **Computers:** Students can register for classes online. Administrative functions (other than registration) can be performed online.

CAMPUS LIFE

Environment: Town. **Activities:** Choral groups, concert band, dance, drama/theater, jazz band, literary magazine, music ensembles, musical theater, opera, radio station, student government, student newspaper, symphony orchestra, television station, yearbook, international student organization. **Organizations:** 100 registered organizations, 2 honor societies, 3 religious organizations. 4 fraternities, 4 sororities. **Athletics (Intercollegiate):** *Men:* Baseball, basketball, cheerleading, cross-country, golf, ice hockey, lacrosse, soccer, tennis, track/field (outdoor), track/field (indoor), wrestling. *Women:* Basketball, cheerleading, cross-country, field hockey, golf, ice hockey, lacrosse, soccer, softball, tennis, track/field (outdoor), track/field (indoor), volleyball. **On-Campus Highlights:** Art gallery, Costello Sports Complex, Russell Theater and Concert Hall, Southworth Planetarium, TV/radio station.

ADMISSIONS

Freshman Academic Profile: Average high school GPA 3.04. 8% in top 10% of high school class, 29% in top 25% of high school class, 66% in top 50% of high school class. SAT Math middle 50% range 450–560. SAT Critical Reading middle 50% range 450–560. SAT Writing middle 50% range 440–550. ACT middle 50% range 18–23. Minimum paper TOEFL 550. Minimum computer TOEFL 213. **Basis for Candidate Selection:** *Very important factors considered include:* Class rank, rigor of secondary school record, standardized test scores. *Important factors considered include:* Application essay, recommendation(s). *Other factors considered include:* Academic GPA, alumni/ae relation, character/personal qualities, extracurricular activities, geographical residence, interview, level of applicant's interest, racial/ethnic status, state residency, talent/ability, volunteer work, work experience. **Freshman Admission Requirements:** High school diploma is required and GED is accepted. *Academic units required:* 4 English, 3 mathematics, 2 science, (2 science labs), 2 foreign language, 2 social studies, 2 history. *Academic units recommended:* 4 mathematics, 3 science, (3 science labs), 3 foreign language, 3 social studies, 3 history. **Freshman Admission Statistics:** 4,141 applied, 84% admitted, 27% enrolled. **Transfer Admission Requirements:** High school transcript, college transcript(s), essay or personal statement, minimum college GPA of 2.0 required. Lowest grade transferable C–. **General Admission Information:** Application fee $40. Notification on a rolling basis, beginning on or about 1/1. Nonfall registration accepted. Admission may be deferred for a maximum of 1 year. Credit and/or placement offered for CEEB Advanced Placement tests.

COSTS AND FINANCIAL AID

Annual in-state tuition $6,930. Annual out-of-state tuition $19,140. Room and board $8,762. Required fees $884. Average book expense $1,000. **Required Forms and Deadlines:** FAFSA. Priority financial aid filing date 2/15. **Notification of Awards:** Applicants will be notified of awards on a rolling basis beginning 3/15. **Types of Aid:** *Need-based scholarships/grants:* Federal Pell, SEOG, state scholarships/grants, private scholarships, the school's own gift aid. *Loans:* FFEL Subsidized Stafford, FFEL Unsubsidized Stafford, FFEL PLUS, Federal Perkins, Federal Nursing, state loans *Student Employment:* Federal Work-Study Program available. Off-campus job opportunities are excellent. **Financial Aid Statistics:** 70% freshmen, 79% undergrads receive any aid. **Criteria for awarding institutional aid:** *Non-need-based:* Academics, music/drama, state/district residency.

UNIVERSITY OF SOUTHERN MISSISSIPPI

118 College Drive #5166, Hattiesburg, MS 39406
Phone: 601-266-5000 **Financial Aid Phone:** 601-266-4774
E-mail: admissions@usm.edu **CEEB Code:** 1479
Fax: 601-266-5148 **Website:** www.usm.edu **ACT Code:** 2218

This public school was founded in 1910. It has a 1090-acre campus.

RATINGS
Admissions Selectivity Rating: 76 **Fire Safety Rating:** 81 **Green Rating:** 83

STUDENTS AND FACULTY
Enrollment: 12,383. **Student Body:** 61% female, 39% male, 12% out-of-state, 1% international. Asian 1%, African American 30%, Caucasian 61%, Hispanic 2%.

Retention and Graduation: 74% freshmen return for sophomore year. 21% freshmen graduate within 4 years. **Faculty:** Student/faculty ratio 16:1. 758 full-time faculty, 75% hold PhDs, 15% are members of minority groups, 47% are women.

ACADEMICS
Degrees: Bachelor's, certificate, doctoral, master's, post-master's certificate. **Classes:** Most classes have 10–19 students. Most lab/discussion sessions have 10–19 students. **Majors with Highest Enrollment:** Elementary education and teaching; nursing/registered nurse (RN, ASN, BSN, MSN); psychology. **Special Study Options:** Distance learning, double major, dual enrollment, honors program, independent study, internships, study abroad, teacher certification program Special programs offered to physically disabled students include note-taking services, reader services, tape recorders, tutors. **Career services:** Alumni services, career/job search classes, career assessment, internships. **Career services highlights include:** Career Assesment Individualized counselors and 24/7 online career center.

FACILITIES
Housing: Special housing for disabled students, men's dorms, women's dorms, fraternity/sorority housing, apartments for married students, theme housing. **Special Academic Facilities/Equipment:** Museum of Art. **Computers:** 100% of classrooms, 100% of dorms, 100% of libraries, 100% of dining areas, 100% of student union, 30% of common outdoor areas have wireless network access. Students can register for classes online. Administrative functions (other than registration) can be performed online.

CAMPUS LIFE
Environment: City. **Activities:** Choral groups, concert band, dance, drama/theater, jazz band, literary magazine, marching band, music ensembles, musical theater, opera, pep band, radio station, student government, student newspaper, student-run film society, symphony orchestra, yearbook, campus ministries, international student organization. **Organizations:** 8 honor societies, 20 religious organizations. 15 fraternities, 11 sororities. **Athletics (Intercollegiate):** *Men:* Baseball, basketball, football, golf, tennis, track/field (outdoor), track/field (indoor). *Women:* Basketball, cross-country, golf, soccer, softball, tennis, track/field (outdoor), track/field (indoor), volleyball. **On-Campus Highlights:** Starbucks, Thad Cochran Center, Barnes & Nobles Bookstore. **Environmental Initiatives:** Recycling (12+ years), energy conservation, LEED certification on new buildings. Pursuing use of Green Seal cleaning products and organic grounds maintenance.

ADMISSIONS
Freshman Academic Profile: Average high school GPA 3.06. 15% in top 10% of high school class, 41% in top 25% of high school class, 74% in top 50% of high school class. 88% from public high schools. SAT Math middle 50% range 450–565. SAT Critical Reading middle 50% range 460–560. ACT middle 50% range 18–24. Minimum paper TOEFL 525. Minimum computer TOEFL 197. Minimum web-based TOEFL 71. **Basis for Candidate Selection:** *Very important factors considered include:* Academic GPA, standardized test scores. *Other factors considered include:* Class rank. **Freshman Admission Requirements:** High school diploma is required and GED is accepted. *Academic units required:* 4 English, 3 mathematics, 3 science, 3 social studies, 2 academic electives. **Freshman Admission Statistics:** 5,081 applied, 56% admitted, 56% enrolled. **Transfer Admission Requirements:** College transcript(s), statement of good standing from prior institution(s). Minimum college GPA of 2.0 required. Lowest grade transferable D. **General Admission Information:** Application fee $35. Notification on a rolling basis, beginning on or about 9/1. Nonfall registration accepted. Credit and/or placement offered for CEEB Advanced Placement tests.

COSTS AND FINANCIAL AID
Annual in-state tuition $5,096. Annual out-of-state tuition $12,746. Room and board $6,200. Required fees $402. Average book expense $1,400. **Required**

Forms and Deadlines: FAFSA, institution's own financial aid form. Priority financial aid filing date 3/15. **Notification of Awards:** Applicants will be notified of awards on a rolling basis beginning 4/1. **Types of Aid:** *Need-based scholarships/grants:* Federal Pell, SEOG, state scholarships/grants, private scholarships, the school's own gift aid. *Loans:* Direct Subsidized Stafford, Direct Unsubsidized Stafford, Direct PLUS, FFEL Subsidized Stafford. *Student Employment:* Federal Work-Study Program available. Institutional employment available. Highest amount earned per year from on-campus jobs $3,668. Off-campus job opportunities are good. **Financial Aid Statistics:** 43% freshmen, 42% undergrads receive need-based scholarship or grant aid. 39% freshmen, 29% undergrads receive non-need-based scholarship or grant aid. 51% freshmen, 52% undergrads receive need-based self-help aid. 4% freshmen, 4% undergrads receive athletic scholarships. 62% freshmen, 63% undergrads receive any aid. 63% undergrads borrow to pay for school. Average cumulative indebtedness $19,915.

UNIVERSITY OF THE SOUTHWEST

6610 Lovington Highway, Hobbs, NM 88240
Phone: 505-392-6563 **Financial Aid Phone:** 505-392-6561
E-mail: admissions@csw.edu **CEEB Code:** 4116
Fax: 505-392-6006 **Website:** www.csw.edu **ACT Code:** 2633

This private school was founded in 1962. It has a 162-acre campus.

RATINGS
Admissions Selectivity Rating: 79   **Fire Safety Rating:** 75   **Green Rating:** 60*

STUDENTS AND FACULTY
Enrollment: 430. **Student Body:** 64% female, 36% male, 39% out-of-state, 1% international (12 countries represented). Asian 1%, African American 4%, Caucasian 52%, Hispanic 39%, Native American 2%.
Retention and Graduation: 32% freshmen return for sophomore year. 10% freshmen graduate within 4 years. 30% grads go on to further study within 1 year. 30% grads pursue arts and sciences degrees. **Faculty:** Student/faculty ratio 11:1. 20 full-time faculty, 60% hold PhDs, 10% are members of minority groups, 45% are women.

ACADEMICS
Degrees: Bachelor's, master's. **Classes:** Most classes have fewer than 10 students. Most lab/discussion sessions have fewer than 10 students. **Majors with Highest Enrollment:** Business/commerce; criminal justice/police science; elementary education and teaching. **Special Study Options:** Distance learning, double major, internships, teacher certification program Special programs offered to physically disabled students include tutors.

FACILITIES
Housing: Men's dorms, women's dorms. 90% of campus accessible to physically disabled.

CAMPUS LIFE
Environment: Town. **Activities:** Choral groups, drama/theater, literary magazine, student government, student newspaper. **Organizations:** 3 honor societies, 1 religious organizations. **Athletics (Intercollegiate):** *Men:* Baseball, cross-country, golf, rodeo, soccer, track/field (outdoor). *Women:* cross-country, golf, rodeo, soccer, softball, track/field (outdoor), volleyball. **On-Campus Highlights:** Residential Halls-East and West, Scarborough Memorial Library, Mabee Southwest Heritage Center, Jack Williams Baseball Field, Joan M. Tucker Center for Business Leadership, 6. The Mabee Teaching and Learning Center 7. Fadke Arts and Science Building 8. Bill Danies Campus Center.

ADMISSIONS
Freshman Academic Profile: Average high school GPA 3.11. 1% in top 10% of high school class, 16% in top 25% of high school class, 69% in top 50% of high school class. SAT Math middle 50% range 340–500. SAT Critical Reading middle 50% range 340–470. SAT Writing middle 50% range 330–460. ACT middle 50% range 14–20. Minimum paper TOEFL 550. Minimum computer TOEFL 218. **Basis for Candidate Selection:** *Very important factors considered include:* Class rank, academic GPA, standardized test scores. **Freshman Admission Requirements:** High school diploma is required and GED is accepted. **Freshman Admission Statistics:** 2,207 applied, 23% admitted, 10% enrolled. **Transfer Admission Requirements:** College transcript(s), minimum college GPA of 2.0 required. Lowest grade transferable D. **General Admission Information:** Application fee $25. Notification on a rolling basis, beginning on or about 10/5. Nonfall registration accepted. Credit offered for CEEB Advanced Placement tests.

COSTS AND FINANCIAL AID
Annual tuition $11,700. Room and board $5,400. Average book expense $800. **Required Forms and Deadlines:** FAFSA, institution's own financial aid form Financial aid filing deadline 6/2. Priority financial aid filing date 4/2. **Notification of Awards:** Applicants will be notified of awards on or about 4/2. **Types of Aid:** *Need-based scholarships/grants:* Federal Pell, SEOG, state scholarships/grants, private scholarships, the school's own gift aid. *Loans:* FFEL Subsidized Stafford, FFEL Unsubsidized Stafford, FFEL PLUS. *Student Employment:* Highest amount earned per year from on-campus jobs $3,000. **Financial Aid Statistics:** 61% freshmen, 60% undergrads receive need-based scholarship or grant aid. 8% freshmen, 58% undergrads receive non-need-based scholarship or grant aid. 8% freshmen, 14% undergrads receive need-based self-help aid. 12% freshmen, 26% undergrads receive athletic scholarships. 75% freshmen, 77% undergrads receive any aid. 85% undergrads borrow to pay for school. Average cumulative indebtedness $12,420. **Criteria for awarding institutional aid:** *Non-need-based:* Academics, athletics, job skills, leadership, music/drama, religious affiliation, state/district residency.

UNIVERSITY OF ST. FRANCIS

500 Wilcox Street, Joliet, IL 60435
Phone: 815-740-5037 **Financial Aid Phone:** 866-890-8331
E-mail: admissions@stfrancis.edu **CEEB Code:** 1130
Fax: 815-740-5032 **Website:** www.stfrancis.edu **ACT Code:** 1000

This private school, affiliated with the Roman Catholic Church, was founded in 1920. It has a 22-acre campus.

RATINGS
Admissions Selectivity Rating: 83   **Fire Safety Rating:** 90   **Green Rating:** 81

STUDENTS AND FACULTY
Enrollment: 1,247. **Student Body:** 68% female, 32% male, 5% out-of-state, 1% international. Asian 4%, African American 7%, Caucasian 74%, Hispanic 12%.
Retention and Graduation: 76% freshmen return for sophomore year. 33% freshmen graduate within 4 years. **Faculty:** Student/faculty ratio 12:1. 88 full-time faculty, 68% hold PhDs, 9% are members of minority groups, 58% are women.

ACADEMICS
Degrees: Bachelor's, master's, post-master's certificate. **Classes:** Most classes have 10–19 students. Most lab/discussion sessions have 10–19 students. **Majors with Highest Enrollment:** Business administration and management; elementary education and teaching; nursing/registered nurse (RN, ASN, BSN, MSN). **Special Study Options:** Cross-registration, distance learning, double major, honors program, independent study, internships, student-designed major, study abroad, teacher certification program. **Honors programs:** Duns Scotus Fellow/Scholars Program is designed to create a learning community of motivated students who are challenged to excel academically. **Combined degree programs:** BBA/MBA. Special programs offered to physically disabled students include note-taking services, reader services, tape recorders, tutors. **Career services:** Alumni network, alumni services, career/job search classes, career assessment, internships, regional alumni.

FACILITIES
Housing: Coed dorms, apartments for single students, wellness housing. 100% of campus accessible to physically disabled. **Special Academic Facilities/Equipment:** Rialto City Center Campus, new home of the Art & Design Department; Student Center/Bistro in the Motherhouse; Abbey in Marian Residence Hall; Moser Performing Arts Center. **Computers:** 100% of classrooms, 100% of dorms, 100% of libraries, 100% of dining areas, 100% of student union, 100% of common outdoor areas have wireless network access. Students can register for classes online. Administrative functions (other than registration) can be performed online.

CAMPUS LIFE
Environment: City. **Activities:** Choral groups, dance, drama/theater, literary magazine, music ensembles, musical theater, opera, radio station, student government, student newspaper, symphony orchestra, television station, campus ministries, international student organization. **Organizations:** 29 registered organizations, 13 honor societies, 1 religious organizations. **Athletics (Intercollegiate):** *Men:* Baseball, basketball, cross-country, football, golf, soccer, tennis, track/field (outdoor), track/field (indoor). *Women:* Basketball, cheerleading, cross-country, golf, soccer, softball, tennis, track/field (outdoor), track/field (indoor), volleyball. **On-Campus Highlights:** Rialto City Center Campus, Student Center/Bistro in Motherhouse, Abbey (in Marian Residence Hall), Moser

Performing Arts Center. **Environmental Initiatives:** Campus-wide recycling, energy efficient lighting, water conservation project (P3) in progress.

ADMISSIONS
Freshman Academic Profile: Average high school GPA 3.3. 20% in top 10% of high school class, 50% in top 25% of high school class, 90% in top 50% of high school class. 83% from public high schools. ACT middle 50% range 21–26. Minimum paper TOEFL 550. Minimum computer TOEFL 213. **Basis for Candidate Selection:** *Very important factors considered include:* Class rank, academic GPA, rigor of secondary school record, standardized test scores, *Other factors considered include:* Application essay, recommendation(s), interview. **Freshman Admission Requirements:** High school diploma is required and GED is accepted. *Academic units required:* 4 English, 3 mathematics, 2 science, (1 science labs), 2 social studies, 3 academic electives, 3 3 units from 2 areas: language, computer science, music or art. **Freshman Admission Statistics:** 1,274 applied, 50% admitted, 35% enrolled. **Transfer Admission Requirements:** College transcript(s), statement of good standing from prior institution(s). Minimum college GPA of 2.5 required. **General Admission Information:** Application fee $30. Regular application deadline 8/1. Notification on a rolling basis, beginning on or about 9/15. Nonfall registration accepted. Admission may be deferred for a maximum of 1 year. Credit and/or placement offered for CEEB Advanced Placement tests.

COSTS AND FINANCIAL AID
Required Forms and Deadlines: FAFSA, institution's own financial aid form. Priority financial aid filing date 3/15. **Notification of Awards:** Applicants will be notified of awards on a rolling basis beginning 2/15. **Types of Aid:** *Need-based scholarships/grants:* Federal Pell, SEOG, state scholarships/grants, private scholarships, the school's own gift aid, Federal Nursing Scholarships. Federal ACG and SMART funds. *Loans:* Direct Subsidized Stafford, Direct Unsubsidized Stafford, Direct PLUS, Federal Perkins. *Student Employment:* Federal Work-Study Program available. Institutional employment available. Highest amount earned per year from on-campus jobs $9,350. Off-campus job opportunities are good. **Financial Aid Statistics:** 48% freshmen, 56% undergrads receive need-based scholarship or grant aid. 47% freshmen, 75% undergrads receive non-need-based scholarship or grant aid. 50% freshmen, 62% undergrads receive need-based self-help aid. 10% freshmen, 7% undergrads receive athletic scholarships. 100% freshmen, 99% undergrads receive any aid. 96% undergrads borrow to pay for school. Average cumulative indebtedness $21,594. **Criteria for awarding institutional aid:** *Non-need-based:* Academics, alumni affiliation, art, athletics, leadership, music/drama, religious affiliation, state/district residency.

UNIVERSITY OF ST. THOMAS

3800 Montrose Boulevard, Houston, TX 77006-4696
Phone: 713-525-3500 **Financial Aid Phone:** 713-525-2151
E-mail: admissions@stthom.edu **CEEB Code:** 6880
Fax: 713-525-3558 **Website:** www.stthom.edu **ACT Code:** 4238

This private school, affiliated with the Roman Catholic Church, was founded in 1947. It has a 20-acre campus.

RATINGS
Admissions Selectivity Rating: 80   **Fire Safety Rating:** 83   **Green Rating:** 67

STUDENTS AND FACULTY
Enrollment: 1,668. **Student Body:** 59% female, 41% male, 3% out-of-state, 4% international (58 countries represented). Asian 12%, African American 5%, Caucasian 34%, Hispanic 34%, Native American 1%.
Retention and Graduation: 70% freshmen return for sophomore year. 30% freshmen graduate within 4 years. **Faculty:** Student/faculty ratio 12:1. 125 full-time faculty, 92% hold PhDs, 14% are members of minority groups, 33% are women.

ACADEMICS
Degrees: Bachelor's, diploma, master's. **Classes:** Most classes have 10–19 students. Most lab/discussion sessions have 10–19 students. **Majors with Highest Enrollment:** Accounting; biology/biological sciences; psychology. **Special Study Options:** Accelerated program, distance learning, double major, dual enrollment, honors program, independent study, internships, liberal arts/career combination, student-designed major, study abroad, teacher certification program, weekend college. **Honors programs:** The Honors Program at the University of St. Thomas is a four-year interdisciplinary program for students of exceptional intellectual ability, motivation, and curiosity. It is designed not simply to provoke students to master specific disciplines such as philosophy, history, mathematics, and natural science but to offer an experience which

integrates, on the deepest and most profound level, the intellectual, cultural and spiritual foundations of a liberal arts education. **Combined degree programs:** BBA/MBA. Special programs offered to physically disabled students include note-taking services, reader services, tape recorders, tutors. **Career services:** Career/job search classes, career assessment, internships.

FACILITIES
Housing: Coed dorms, apartments for single students. **Special Academic Facilities/Equipment:** Learning and Writing Center, Chapel of St. Basil, Doherty Library. **Computers:** 100% of classrooms, 100% of libraries, 100% of dining areas, 100% of common outdoor areas have wireless network access. Students can register for classes online. Administrative functions (other than registration) can be performed online.

CAMPUS LIFE
Environment: Metropolis. **Activities:** Choral groups, dance, drama/theater, jazz band, literary magazine, music ensembles, musical theater, student government, student newspaper, campus ministries, international student organization. **Organizations:** 69 registered organizations, 22 honor societies, 5 religious organizations. **Athletics (Intercollegiate):** *Men:* Basketball, soccer. *Women:* volleyball. **On-Campus Highlights:** Jerabeck Activity and Athletic Center, Crooker Student Center, Chapel of St. Basil, The Lounge, Academic Mall.

ADMISSIONS
Freshman Academic Profile: Average high school GPA 3.44. 28.25% in top 10% of high school class, 58.3% in top 25% of high school class, 82.51% in top 50% of high school class. 67% from public high schools. SAT Math middle 50% range 510–630. SAT Critical Reading middle 50% range 510–620. SAT Writing middle 50% range 500–600. ACT middle 50% range 23–27. Minimum paper TOEFL 550. Minimum computer TOEFL 213. Minimum web-based TOEFL 79. **Basis for Candidate Selection:** *Very important factors considered include:* Class rank, application essay, academic GPA, rigor of secondary school record, standardized test scores, *Other factors considered include:* Recommendation(s), character/personal qualities, extracurricular activities, interview, level of applicant's interest, talent/ability, volunteer work, work experience. **Freshman Admission Requirements:** High school diploma is required and GED is accepted. *Academic units required:* 4 English, 3 mathematics, 3 science, (2 science labs), 2 foreign language, 2 social studies, 1 history, 3 Electives in college preparatory classes. *Academic units recommended:* 4 English, 3 mathematics, 3 science, (2 science labs), 2 foreign language, 2 social studies, 1 history, 3 electives in college preparatory classes. **Freshman Admission Statistics:** 866 applied, 80% admitted, 41% enrolled. **Transfer Admission Requirements:** College transcript(s), minimum college GPA of 2.50 required. Lowest grade transferable C. **General Admission Information:** Application fee $25. Regular application deadline 5/1. Notification on a rolling basis, beginning on or about 11/15. Nonfall registration accepted. Admission may be deferred for a maximum of 1 year. Credit and/or placement offered for CEEB Advanced Placement tests.

COSTS AND FINANCIAL AID
Required Forms and Deadlines: FAFSA. Priority financial aid filing date 4/15. **Notification of Awards:** Applicants will be notified of awards on a rolling basis beginning 3/22. **Types of Aid:** *Need-based scholarships/grants:* Federal Pell, SEOG, state scholarships/grants, private scholarships, the school's own gift aid, ACG Grant, SMART grant. *Loans:* FFEL Subsidized Stafford, FFEL Unsubsidized Stafford, FFEL PLUS, Federal Perkins, state loans *Student Employment:* Federal Work-Study Program available. Off-campus job opportunities are excellent. **Financial Aid Statistics:** 64% freshmen, 57% undergrads receive need-based scholarship or grant aid. 7% freshmen, 4% undergrads receive non-need-based scholarship or grant aid. 41% freshmen, 42% undergrads receive need-based self-help aid. 2% freshmen, 1% undergrads receive athletic scholarships. 90% freshmen, 67% undergrads receive any aid. 71% undergrads borrow to pay for school. Average cumulative indebtedness $22,857. **Criteria for awarding institutional aid:** *Non-need-based:* Academics, athletics.

UNIVERSITY OF TAMPA

401 West Kennedy Boulevard, Tampa, FL 33606-1490
Phone: 813-253-6211 **Financial Aid Phone:** 813-253-6219
E-mail: admissions@ut.edu **CEEB Code:** 5819
Fax: 813-258-7398 **Website: ACT Code:** 762

This private school was founded in 1931. It has a 100-acre campus.

RATINGS
Admissions Selectivity Rating: 84   **Fire Safety Rating:** 85   **Green Rating:** 60*

STUDENTS AND FACULTY

Enrollment: 5,518. **Student Body:** 57% female, 43% male, 56.7% out-of-state, 9% international (100 countries represented). Asian 2%, African American 5%, Caucasian 63%, Hispanic 10%.

Retention and Graduation: 44% freshmen graduate within 4 years. 24% grads go on to further study within 1 year. 8% grads pursue arts and sciences degrees. 7% grads pursue law degrees. 14% grads pursue business degrees. 4% grads pursue medical degrees. **Faculty:** Student/faculty ratio 17:1. 238 full-time faculty, 91% hold PhDs, 9% are members of minority groups, 42% are women.

ACADEMICS

Degrees: Associate, bachelor's, certificate, master's, post-master's certificate. **Classes:** Most classes have 20–29 students. Most lab/discussion sessions have 10–19 students. **Majors with Highest Enrollment:** Business administration and management; communication studies/speech communication and rhetoric; psychology. **Special Study Options:** Double major, dual enrollment, exchange student program (domestic), honors program, independent study, internships, liberal arts/career combination, study abroad, teacher certification program, Certificate in International Studies program. **Honors programs:** UT's Honors Program offers special classes that are developed to enhance creative thinking processes while meeting general distribution requirements. **Combined degree programs:** MSN-MBA; BS Chemistry-MBA; RN-MSN. Special programs offered to physically disabled students include note-taking services, reader services, tutors. **Career services:** Alumni network, alumni services, career/job search classes, career assessment, internships. **Career services highlights include:** From their first day on campus, students are supported and involved. They are rewarded with an unlimited array of opportunities that take them to the edge of their imaginations and beyond. All students have opportunities to balance "learning by thinking" with "learning by doing." Both in-class hands on projects and out-of-classroom learning activities help students integrate classroom theory with real world practices. Interactive learning activities such as case studies, behavioral and computer simulations, internships, performances, exhibitions, research, service learning, study abroad, etc, are offered across the curriculum.

FACILITIES

Housing: Coed dorms, special housing for disabled students, apartments for single students, theme housing. 100% of campus accessible to physically disabled. **Special Academic Facilities/Equipment:** Victorian art and furniture museum, theatres, studios, music center, language lab, fully equipped research vessel for marine science, H.B. Plant Museum, marine science research center on Tampa Bay. **Computers:** 50% of classrooms, 25% of dorms, 100% of libraries, 80% of dining areas, 100% of student union, 80% of common outdoor areas have wireless network access. Students can register for classes online. Administrative functions (other than registration) can be performed online.

CAMPUS LIFE

Environment: Metropolis. **Activities:** Choral groups, concert band, dance, drama/theater, jazz band, literary magazine, music ensembles, musical theater, pep band, radio station, student government, student newspaper, student-run film society, symphony orchestra, television station, yearbook, campus ministries, international student organization, Model UN. **Organizations:** 145 registered organizations, 13 honor societies, 8 religious organizations. 9 fraternities, 10 sororities. **Athletics (Intercollegiate):** *Men:* Baseball, basketball, cross-country, golf, soccer, swimming. *Women:* Basketball, crew/rowing, cross-country, soccer, softball, swimming, tennis, volleyball. **On-Campus Highlights:** Vaughn Student Center, Plant Hall, Stadium Center, Vaughn Center Courtyard, Martinez Sports Center.

ADMISSIONS

Freshman Academic Profile: Average high school GPA 3.24. 15% in top 10% of high school class, 43% in top 25% of high school class, 83% in top 50% of high school class. 75% from public high schools. SAT Math middle 50% range 490–580. SAT Critical Reading middle 50% range 480–570. SAT Writing middle 50% range 480–570. ACT middle 50% range 21–25. Minimum paper TOEFL 550. Minimum computer TOEFL 213. **Basis for Candidate Selection:** *Very important factors considered include:* Academic GPA, rigor of secondary school record, standardized test scores. *Important factors considered include:* Application essay, recommendation(s), talent/ability. *Other factors considered include:* Class rank, alumni/ae relation, character/personal qualities, extracurricular activities, first generation, interview, level of applicant's interest, volunteer work, work experience. **Freshman Admission Requirements:** High school diploma is required and GED is accepted. *Academic units required:* 4 English, 3 mathematics, 3 science, (2 science labs), 2 foreign language, 3 social studies, 3 academic electives. **Freshman Admission Statistics:** 9,929 applied, 62% admitted, 23% enrolled. **Transfer Admission Requirements:** College transcript(s), minimum college GPA of 2.2 required. Lowest grade transferable C. **General Admission Information:** Application fee $40. Notification on a rolling basis, beginning on or about 10/1. Nonfall registration accepted. Admission may be deferred for a maximum of 1 term. Credit and/or placement offered for CEEB Advanced Placement tests.

COSTS AND FINANCIAL AID

Required Forms and Deadlines: FAFSA, state aid form. **Notification of Awards:** Applicants will be notified of awards on a rolling basis beginning 2/1. **Types of Aid:** *Need-based scholarships/grants:* Federal Pell, SEOG, state scholarships/grants, private scholarships, the school's own gift aid. *Loans:* FFEL Subsidized Stafford, FFEL Unsubsidized Stafford, FFEL PLUS, Federal Perkins, college/university loans from institutional funds. *Student Employment:* Federal Work-Study Program available. Institutional employment available. Off-campus job opportunities are fair. **Financial Aid Statistics:** 58% freshmen, 52% undergrads receive need-based scholarship or grant aid. 55% freshmen, 43% undergrads receive non-need-based scholarship or grant aid. 49% freshmen, 45% undergrads receive need-based self-help aid. 90% freshmen, 89% undergrads receive any aid. 62% undergrads borrow to pay for school. Average cumulative indebtedness $24,812. **Criteria for awarding institutional aid:** *Non-need-based:* Academics, alumni affiliation, art, athletics, leadership, music/drama, state/district residency.

See page 1310.

UNIVERSITY OF TENNESSEE AT MARTIN

200 Hall-Moody, Administrative Building, Martin, TN 38238
Phone: 731-881-7020 **Financial Aid Phone:** 731-881-7040
E-mail: admitme@utm.edu
Fax: 731-881-7029 **Website:** www.utm.edu **ACT Code:** 4032

This public school was founded in 1900. It has a 930-acre campus.

RATINGS

Admissions Selectivity Rating: 77   **Fire Safety Rating:** 65   **Green Rating:** 84

STUDENTS AND FACULTY

Enrollment: 6,476. **Student Body:** 57% female, 43% male, 4% out-of-state, 2% international (28 countries represented). Asian 1%, African American 16%, Caucasian 80%, Hispanic 1%.

Retention and Graduation: 72% freshmen return for sophomore year. 24% freshmen graduate within 4 years. 20% grads go on to further study within 1 year. **Faculty:** Student/faculty ratio 19:1. 270 full-time faculty, 75% hold PhDs, 8% are members of minority groups, 43% are women.

ACADEMICS

Degrees: Bachelor's, master's. **Classes:** Most classes have 10–19 students. Most lab/discussion sessions have 10–19 students. **Majors with Highest Enrollment:** Biology/biological sciences; multi-/interdisciplinary studies, other; nursing/registered nurse (RN, ASN, BSN, MSN). **Special Study Options:** Accelerated program, cooperative education program, cross-registration, distance learning, double major, dual enrollment, English as a Second Language (ESL), exchange student program (domestic), honors program, independent study, internships, student-designed major, study abroad, teacher certification program, 3-1 programs in pharmacy, veterinary medicine, dentistry, medicine, optometry, podiatry and chiropractory. **Honors programs:** University Scholars Honors Seminar Special programs offered to physically disabled students include note-taking services, reader services, tape recorders, tutors. **Career services:** Alumni network, alumni services, career/job search classes, internships, regional alumni. **Career services highlights include:** erecruiting.com allows our students faster and more significant information on employers and job openings from their computers.

FACILITIES

Housing: Coed dorms, special housing for disabled students, men's dorms, special housing for international students, women's dorms, fraternity/sorority housing, apartments for married students, apartments for single students, theme housing. 100% of campus accessible to physically disabled. **Special Academic Facilities/Equipment:** Paul Meek Library contains Houston Gordon University. Museum **Computers:** 100% of classrooms, 50% of dorms, 100% of libraries, 100% of dining areas, 100% of student union, 100% of common outdoor areas have wireless network access. Students can register for classes online. Administrative functions (other than registration) can be performed online.

CAMPUS LIFE

Environment: Rural. **Activities:** Choral groups, concert band, dance, drama/theater, jazz band, literary magazine, marching band, music ensembles, opera, pep band, radio station, student government, student newspaper, television station, yearbook, campus ministries, international student organization. **Organizations:** 100 registered organizations, 27 honor societies, 11 religious organizations. 12 fraternities, 8 sororities. **Athletics (Intercollegiate):** *Men:* Baseball, basketball, cross-country, football, golf, riflery, rodeo. *Women:* Basketball, cheerleading, cross-country, equestrian sports, riflery, rodeo, soccer, softball, tennis, volleyball. **On-Campus Highlights:** Boling University Center, Paul Meek Library, Fitness Center, Elam Center and Intramural facilities, Quad, Captain's Coffee in Paul Meek Library Student Life Center. **Environmental Initiatives:** Establishing a Recycling Facility to collect camups and community recyclables. The campus recycles its paper, cardboard, cans and plastic bottles. Purchasing green products such as carpet made from recycled materials and re-cycled paper products. Retrofit lighting with new, more energy-efficient lamps and ballasts, updating HVAC controls, and installing low flush toilets and urinals and occupancy lighting sensors.

ADMISSIONS

Freshman Academic Profile: Average high school GPA 3.39. 20% in top 10% of high school class, 50% in top 25% of high school class, 88% in top 50% of high school class. 90% from public high schools. ACT middle 50% range 20–25. Minimum paper TOEFL 500. Minimum computer TOEFL 173. Minimum web-based TOEFL 61. **Basis for Candidate Selection:** *Very important factors considered include:* Academic GPA, rigor of secondary school record, standardized test scores. **Freshman Admission Requirements:** High school diploma is required and GED is accepted. *Academic units required:* 4 English, 3 mathematics, 2 science, (1 science labs), 2 foreign language, 0 social studies, 2 history, 1 visual/performing arts. **Freshman Admission Statistics:** 3,333 applied, 76% admitted, 55% enrolled. **Transfer Admission Requirements:** High school transcript, college transcript(s), minimum college GPA of 2.0 required. Lowest grade transferable D. **General Admission Information:** Application fee $30. Regular application deadline 8/1. Notification on a rolling basis, beginning on or about 9/1. Nonfall registration accepted. Admission may be deferred for a maximum of rolling. Credit and/or placement offered for CEEB Advanced Placement tests.

COSTS AND FINANCIAL AID

Required Forms and Deadlines: FAFSA. Priority financial aid filing date 3/1. **Notification of Awards:** Applicants will be notified of awards on a rolling basis beginning 4/1. **Types of Aid:** *Need-based scholarships/grants:* Federal Pell, SEOG, state scholarships/grants, private scholarships, the school's own gift aid. *Loans:* FFEL Subsidized Stafford, FFEL Unsubsidized Stafford, FFEL PLUS, Federal Perkins. *Student Employment:* Federal Work-Study Program available. Institutional employment available. Highest amount earned per year from on-campus jobs $9,668. Off-campus job opportunities are fair. **Financial Aid Statistics:** 47% freshmen, 46% undergrads receive need-based scholarship or grant aid. 63% freshmen, 40% undergrads receive non-need-based scholarship or grant aid. 34% freshmen, 43% undergrads receive need-based self-help aid. 2% freshmen, 2% undergrads receive athletic scholarships. 96% freshmen, 88% undergrads receive any aid. 44% undergrads borrow to pay for school. Average cumulative indebtedness $24,480. **Criteria for awarding institutional aid:** *Non-need-based:* Academics, art, athletics, leadership, music/drama, state/district residency.

UNIVERSITY OF TENNESSEE, KNOXVILLE

320 Student Service Building, Circle Park Drive, Knoxville, TN 37996-0230
Phone: 865-974-2184 **Financial Aid Phone:** 865-974-3131
E-mail: admissions@utk.edu **CEEB Code:** 1843
Fax: Website: www.utk.edu **ACT Code:** 4026

This public school was founded in 1794. It has a 520-acre campus.

RATINGS
Admissions Selectivity Rating: 88   **Fire Safety Rating:** 85   **Green Rating:** 87

STUDENTS AND FACULTY
Enrollment: 20,849. **Student Body:** 49% female, 51% male, 13% out-of-state, 1% international (115 countries represented). Asian 3%, African American 8%, Caucasian 84%, Hispanic 2%, Native American 1%.
Retention and Graduation: 84% freshmen return for sophomore year. 31% freshmen graduate within 4 years. **Faculty:** Student/faculty ratio 16:1. 1536 full-time faculty, 82% hold PhDs, 16% are members of minority groups, 39% are women. 9% of classes are taught by teaching assistants.

ACADEMICS
Degrees: Bachelor's, doctoral, master's, post-master's certificate. **Classes:** Most classes have 20–29 students. Most lab/discussion sessions have 20–29 students.
Majors with Highest Enrollment: Business administration and manage-

ment; journalism; psychology. **Special Study Options:** Accelerated program, cooperative education program, cross-registration, distance learning, double major, dual enrollment, English as a Second Language (ESL), exchange student program (domestic), external degree program, honors program, independent study, internships, liberal arts/career combination, student-designed major, study abroad, teacher certification program. **Honors programs:** 1. Chancellor's Honors Program 2. Haslam Scholars Program 3. College Scholars Program 4. Global Leadership Scholars Program 5. College of Engineering Honors Program 6. College of Agricultural and Natural Resources Honors Program 7. College of Social Work Honors Program 8. Howard H. Baker Jr. Center for Public Policy's Baker Scholars Program 9. The Math Honors Program 10. Additional departmental honors programs. **Combined degree programs:** JD/MBA, JD/MPA. Special programs offered to physically disabled students include note-taking services, reader services, tape recorders, tutors. **Career services:** Alumni network, alumni services, career/job search classes, career assessment, internships. **Career services highlights include:** Office of Professional Practice in Engineering's Cooperative Education Program. This program matches students with employers to ensure a real world work experience that significantly enhances the students chances for quality work opportunities at graduation. Approximately 250 students participate in this program annually.

FACILITIES
Housing: Coed dorms, special housing for disabled students, men's dorms, special housing for international students, women's dorms, fraternity/sorority housing, apartments for married students, apartments for single students, theme housing, transfer student floors. 95% of campus accessible to physically disabled. **Special Academic Facilities/Equipment:** Comprehensive museum of anthropology, archaeology, art, geology, natural history, and medicine, theatre-in-the-round,livestock farms, robotics research center, electron microscope, McClung Museum. **Computers:** 100% of classrooms, 100% of dorms, 100% of libraries, 100% of dining areas, 100% of student union, 25% of common outdoor areas have wireless network access. Students can register for classes online.

CAMPUS LIFE
Environment: City. **Activities:** Choral groups, concert band, dance, drama/theater, jazz band, literary magazine, marching band, music ensembles, musical theater, opera, pep band, radio station, student government, student newspaper, student-run film society, symphony orchestra, television station, yearbook, campus ministries, international student organization, Model UN. **Organizations:** 450 registered organizations, 90 honor societies, 30 religious organizations. 23 fraternities, 18 sororities. **Athletics (Intercollegiate):** *Men:* Baseball, basketball, cheerleading, cross-country, diving, football, golf, swimming, tennis, track/field (outdoor), track/field (indoor). *Women:* Basketball, cheerleading, crew/rowing, cross-country, diving, golf, soccer, softball, swimming, tennis, track/field (outdoor), track/field (indoor), volleyball. **On-Campus Highlights:** Ayres Hall and the Hill, Neyland Stadium, Hodges Library, Rec Sports Center, Howard Baker, Jr. Ctr. for Public Policy, McClung Museum, Alumni Memorial Building and Cox Auditorium, Thompson-Boling Arena. **Environmental Initiatives:** Climate Action Plan, Switch Your Thinking energy conservation campaign, game day recycling program.

ADMISSIONS
Freshman Academic Profile: Average high school GPA 3.78. 39% in top 10% of high school class, 70% in top 25% of high school class, 92% in top 50% of high school class. SAT Math middle 50% range 530–650. SAT Critical Reading middle 50% range 510–640. ACT middle 50% range 24–29. Minimum paper TOEFL 523. Minimum computer TOEFL 193. Minimum web-based TOEFL 70. **Basis for Candidate Selection:** *Very important factors considered include:* Academic GPA, rigor of secondary school record, standardized test scores, *Other factors considered include:* Class rank, application essay, recommendation(s), alumni/ae relation, character/personal qualities, extracurricular activities, first generation, geographical residence, level of applicant's interest, racial/ethnic status, state residency, talent/ability, volunteer work, work experience. **Freshman Admission Requirements:** High school diploma is required and GED is accepted. *Academic units required:* 4 English, 3 mathematics, 2 science, (1 science labs), 2 foreign language, 1 social studies, 1 history, 1 visual/performing arts. **Freshman Admission Statistics:** 12,234 applied, 73% admitted, 42% enrolled. **Transfer Admission Requirements:** High school transcript, college transcript(s), statement of good standing from prior institution(s). Minimum college GPA of 2.0 required. Lowest grade transferable C. **General Admission Information:** Application fee $30. Regular application deadline 12/1. Regular notification 3/15. Nonfall registration accepted. Credit offered for CEEB Advanced Placement tests.

COSTS AND FINANCIAL AID
Annual in-state tuition $5,918. Annual out-of-state tuition $19,714. Room and board $6,652. Required fees $932. Average book expense $1,366. **Required Forms and Deadlines:** FAFSA. **Notification of Awards:** Applicants will be notified of awards on a rolling basis beginning 3/15. **Types of Aid:** *Need-based scholarships/grants:* Federal Pell, SEOG, state scholarships/grants, private

scholarships, the school's own gift aid, Federal Nursing Scholarships. *Loans:* FFEL Subsidized Stafford, FFEL Unsubsidized Stafford, FFEL PLUS, Federal Perkins, college/university loans from institutional funds. *Student Employment:* Federal Work-Study Program available. Off-campus job opportunities are fair. **Financial Aid Statistics:** 45% freshmen, 38% undergrads receive need-based scholarship or grant aid. 22% freshmen, 28% undergrads receive need-based self-help aid. 2% freshmen, 2% undergrads receive athletic scholarships. 51% undergrads borrow to pay for school. Average cumulative indebtedness $24,690. **Criteria for awarding institutional aid:** *Non-need-based:* Academics, art, athletics, leadership, minority status, music/drama, state/district residency.

UNIVERSITY OF TENNESSEE—CHATTANOOGA

615 McCallie Avenue, Dept 5105, Chattanooga, TN 37403
Phone: 423-425-4662 **Financial Aid Phone:** 423-425-4677
E-mail: Yancy-Freeman@utc.edu **CEEB Code:** 1831
Fax: 423-425-4157 **Website:** www.utc.edu **ACT Code:** 4022

This public school was founded in 1886. It has a 120-acre campus.

RATINGS
Admissions Selectivity Rating: 78   **Fire Safety Rating:** 60*   **Green Rating:** 75

STUDENTS AND FACULTY
Enrollment: 8,855. **Student Body:** 56% female, 44% male, 6% out-of-state, 1% international (45 countries represented). Asian 2%, African American 16%, Caucasian 78%, Hispanic 2%, Native American 1%.
Retention and Graduation: 67% freshmen return for sophomore year. 16% freshmen graduate within 4 years. 24% grads go on to further study within 1 year. **Faculty:** Student/faculty ratio 18:1. 411 full-time faculty, 73% hold PhDs, 12% are members of minority groups, 45% are women. 5% of classes are taught by teaching assistants.

ACADEMICS
Degrees: Bachelor's, certificate, master's, post-bachelor's certificate, post-master's certificate. **Classes:** Most classes have 20–29 students. Most lab/discussion sessions have 20–29 students. **Majors with Highest Enrollment:** Business administration and management; kinesiology and exercise science; psychology. **Special Study Options:** Cooperative education program, cross-registration, distance learning, double major, dual enrollment, English as a Second Language (ESL), honors program, independent study, internships, study abroad, teacher certification program. **Honors programs:** The University Honors curriculum is a 37-hour sequence of specially designed and enhanced seminar courses in the humanities, the fine arts, cultural perspectives, the history of science, and the social sciences, culminating in a senior-year departmental honors project. These seminars fulfill all of the student's general education course requirements except mathematics and laboratory science. www.utc.edu/Academic/UniversityHonors/ Special programs offered to physically disabled students include note-taking services, reader services, tape recorders, tutors. **Career services:** Alumni network, alumni services, internships.

FACILITIES
Housing: Coed dorms, fraternity/sorority housing, apartments for married students, apartments for single students. 95% of campus accessible to physically disabled. **Special Academic Facilities/Equipment:** Walker Teaching Resource Center; Jones Observatory; Institute of Archaeology; Odor Research Center; SIM Center; Challenger Center; Center for Applied Social Research; The Ochs Center for Metropolitan Studies. **Computers:** 90% of classrooms, 100% of libraries, 100% of dining areas, 100% of student union, 60% of common outdoor areas have wireless network access. Students can register for classes online. Administrative functions (other than registration) can be performed online.

CAMPUS LIFE
Environment: City. **Activities:** Choral groups, concert band, dance, drama/theater, jazz band, literary magazine, marching band, music ensembles, opera, pep band, radio station, student government, student newspaper, student-run film society, symphony orchestra, television station, campus ministries, international student organization, Model UN. **Organizations:** 130 registered organizations, 34 honor societies, 8 religious organizations. 7 fraternities, 7 sororities. **Athletics (Intercollegiate):** *Men:* Basketball, cross-country, football, golf, tennis, track/field (outdoor), wrestling. *Women:* Basketball, cross-country, golf, soccer, softball, tennis, track/field (outdoor), volleyball. **On-Campus Highlights:** Challenger Center, University Center, The Aquatic and Recreation Center (ARC), The Crossroads **Environmental Initiatives:** Recycling Energy conservation LEED Certified Building Design (new UTC Library)

ADMISSIONS
Freshman Academic Profile: Average high school GPA 3.26. 75% from public high schools. ACT middle 50% range 20–25. Minimum paper TOEFL 500. Minimum computer TOEFL 173. Minimum web-based TOEFL 61. **Basis for Candidate Selection:** *Very important factors considered include:* Academic GPA, rigor of secondary school record, standardized test scores. *Important factors considered include:* Character/personal qualities. *Other factors considered include:* Application essay, recommendation(s), extracurricular activities, talent/ability, volunteer work, work experience. **Freshman Admission Requirements:** High school diploma is required and GED is accepted. *Academic units required:* 4 English, 3 mathematics, 2 science, (2 science labs), 2 foreign language, 1 social studies, 1 history, 1 visual/performing arts. **Freshman Admission Statistics:** 6,700 applied, 79% admitted, 42% enrolled. **Transfer Admission Requirements:** College transcript(s), minimum college GPA of 2.0 required. Lowest grade transferable D. **General Admission Information:** Application fee $30. Regular application deadline 8/1. Nonfall registration accepted. Admission may be deferred for a maximum of 1 semester. Credit and/or placement offered for CEEB Advanced Placement tests.

COSTS AND FINANCIAL AID
Annual in-state tuition $4,506. Annual out-of-state tuition $15,804. Room and board $8,056. Required fees $1,150. Average book expense $1,000. **Required Forms and Deadlines:** FAFSA, institution's own financial aid form. Priority financial aid filing date 4/1. **Notification of Awards:** Applicants will be notified of awards on a rolling basis beginning 3/1. **Types of Aid:** *Need-based scholarships/grants:* Federal Pell, SEOG, state scholarships/grants, private scholarships, the school's own gift aid, United Negro College Fund. *Loans:* FFEL Subsidized Stafford, FFEL Unsubsidized Stafford, FFEL PLUS, Federal Perkins, college/university loans from institutional funds. *Student Employment:* Federal Work-Study Program available. Institutional employment available. Highest amount earned per year from on-campus jobs $19,500. Off-campus job opportunities are good. **Financial Aid Statistics:** 57% freshmen, 52% undergrads receive need-based scholarship or grant aid. 45% freshmen, 40% undergrads receive non-need-based scholarship or grant aid. 58% freshmen, 59% undergrads receive need-based self-help aid. 2% freshmen, 3% undergrads receive athletic scholarships. 57% freshmen, 51% undergrads receive any aid. 65% undergrads borrow to pay for school. Average cumulative indebtedness $19,456. **Criteria for awarding institutional aid:** *Non-need-based:* Academics, alumni affiliation, art, athletics, job skills, leadership, minority status, music/drama, religious affiliation, state/district residency.

THE UNIVERSITY OF TEXAS AT ARLINGTON

Office of Admissions, PO Box 19111, Arlington, TX 76019-0111
Phone: 817-272-6287 **Financial Aid Phone:** 817-272-3561
E-mail: admissions@uta.edu **CEEB Code:** 6013
Fax: 817-272-3435 **Website:** www.uta.edu **ACT Code:** 4200

This public school was founded in 1895. It has a 394-acre campus.

RATINGS
Admissions Selectivity Rating: 75   **Fire Safety Rating:** 89   **Green Rating:** 74

STUDENTS AND FACULTY
Enrollment: 18,762. **Student Body:** 52% female, 48% male, 2% out-of-state (147 countries represented).
Retention and Graduation: 15% freshmen graduate within 4 years. **Faculty:** Student/faculty ratio 19:1. 794 full-time faculty, 24% are members of minority groups, 37% are women. 8% of classes are taught by teaching assistants.

ACADEMICS
Degrees: Bachelor's, master's, post-bachelor's certificate, post-master's certificate. **Classes:** Most classes have 20–29 students. **Majors with Highest Enrollment:** Biology/biological sciences; business administration and management; nursing/registered nurse (RN, ASN, BSN, MSN). **Special Study Options:** Cross-registration, distance learning, double major, dual enrollment, English as a Second Language (ESL), honors program, independent study, internships, student-designed major, study abroad, teacher certification program. **Honors programs:** We have the only Honors College in N. Texas. Freshmen interest groups, honors study abroad. **Combined degree programs:** BA/MD, BS/MBA. Special programs offered to physically disabled students include note-taking services, reader services, tape recorders, tutors. **Career services:** Alumni services, career/job search classes, career assessment, internships.

FACILITIES
Housing: Coed dorms, men's dorms, women's dorms, fraternity/sorority housing, apartments for married students, apartments for single students, Family

housing (priority given to students with dependent children). 95% of campus accessible to physically disabled. **Special Academic Facilities/Equipment:** Cartographic history library, maps collection, minority cultures collection, library of Texana and Mexican war. Continuing Education Work Force Development Center. material, planetarium, Automation and Robotics Research institute, Wave Scattering Research Center **Computers:** Students can register for classes online. Administrative functions (other than registration) can be performed online.

CAMPUS LIFE

Environment: Metropolis. **Activities:** Choral groups, concert band, dance, drama/theater, jazz band, literary magazine, marching band, music ensembles, opera, radio station, student government, student newspaper, student-run film society, symphony orchestra, campus ministries, international student organization. **Organizations:** 459 registered organizations, 30 honor societies, 27 religious organizations. 12 fraternities, 13 sororities. **Athletics (Intercollegiate):** *Men:* Baseball, basketball, cross-country, golf, tennis, track/field (outdoor). *Women:* Basketball, cross-country, softball, tennis, track/field (outdoor), volleyball. **On-Campus Highlights:** Click Cafe in Library, E. H. Herford University Center, Activities Bldg, Library Mall/Free speech area, Architectue courtyard. **Environmental Initiatives:** Sustainability is prominent component of master plan (www.uta.edu/masterplan/ut_arlington_master_plan. pdf); sustainable design guidelines (e.g., LEED Silver Engineering Research Building now being designed); energy conservation (via energy performance contracts) is prominent component of Capital Improvement Plan ($30+ million invested in energy conservation since 1973, much of it since 2005) Formation of President's Sustainability Committee, 2007, comprising 40+ administrative staff, faculty, grad students, undergrad students, and community/NGO representatives (http://blog.uta.edu/sustainability), leading to: launch of sustainability web page (www.uta.edu/sustainability); formation of 10 working groups focusing on every aspect of campus life (http://blog.uta.edu/sustainability/contacts/work-groups-related-resources/); active generation and deliberation of extensive set of sustainability recommendations (http://mavspace.uta.edu/xythoswfs/webui/_xy-575263_4) Partnering with City of Arlington on sustainability grants (e.g., for $125,000 composting unit) and sustainability initiatives such as carbon footprint analysis undertaken in 2008 (http://blog.uta.edu/sustainability/2008/01/18/ut-arlington-carbon-footprint-analysis/).

ADMISSIONS

Freshman Academic Profile: 22% in top 10% of high school class, 63% in top 25% of high school class, 89% in top 50% of high school class. SAT Math middle 50% range 480–590. SAT Critical Reading middle 50% range 450–560. ACT middle 50% range 19–23. Minimum paper TOEFL 550. Minimum computer TOEFL 213. **Basis for Candidate Selection:** *Very important factors considered include:* Class rank, academic GPA, standardized test scores. *Important factors considered include:* Rigor of secondary school record. *Other factors considered include:* Application essay, recommendation(s), character/personal qualities, extracurricular activities, first generation, level of applicant's interest, talent/ability, volunteer work, work experience. **Freshman Admission Requirements:** High school diploma is required and GED is not accepted. *Academic units required:* 4 English, 3 mathematics, 3 science, 2 foreign language, 3 social studies, 5 academic electives, 5 physical education 1.5; health 0.5; computer proficiency 1; fine arts; 1 music. *Academic units recommended:* 4 English, 4 mathematics, 3 science, 3 foreign language, 4 social studies, 5 academic electives. **Freshman Admission Statistics:** 5,811 applied, 77% admitted, 49% enrolled. **Transfer Admission Requirements:** High school transcript, college transcript(s), minimum college GPA of 2.25 required. Lowest grade transferable C. **General Admission Information:** Application fee $35. Nonfall registration accepted. Admission may be deferred for a maximum of 1 year. Credit offered for CEEB Advanced Placement tests.

COSTS AND FINANCIAL AID

Annual in-state tuition $8,186. Annual out-of-state tuition $16,496. Room and board $6,658. Average book expense $908. **Required Forms and Deadlines:** FAFSA. Priority financial aid filing date 5/15. **Notification of Awards:** Applicants will be notified of awards on a rolling basis beginning 4/1. **Types of Aid:** *Need-based scholarships/grants:* Federal Pell, SEOG, state scholarships/grants, private scholarships, the school's own gift aid, United Negro College Fund *Loans:* FFEL Subsidized Stafford, FFEL Unsubsidized Stafford, FFEL PLUS, Federal Perkins, college/university loans from institutional funds. *Student Employment:* Federal Work-Study Program available. Institutional employment available. Off-campus job opportunities are excellent. **Financial Aid Statistics:** 39% freshmen, 58% undergrads receive need-based scholarship or grant aid. 26% freshmen, 16% undergrads receive non-need-based scholarship or grant aid. 50% freshmen, 51% undergrads receive need-based self-help aid. 58% freshmen, 51% undergrads receive any aid.

P.O. Box 8058, Austin, TX 78713-8058
Phone: 512-475-7440 **Financial Aid Phone:** 512-475-6282
E-mail: CEEB Code: 6882
Fax: 512-475-7475 **Website:** www.utexas.edu **ACT Code:** 4240

This public school was founded in 1883. It has a 350-acre campus.

RATINGS

Admissions Selectivity Rating: 94   **Fire Safety Rating:** 60*   **Green Rating:** 60*

STUDENTS AND FACULTY

Enrollment: 36,711. **Student Body:** 52% female, 48% male, 4.2% out-of-state, 4% international (125 countries represented). Asian 18%, African American 5%, Caucasian 54%, Hispanic 18%.

Retention and Graduation: 48% freshmen graduate within 4 years. **Faculty:** Student/faculty ratio 17.34:1. 2687 full-time faculty, 88% hold PhDs, 19% are members of minority groups, 37% are women.

ACADEMICS

Degrees: Bachelor's, first professional, master's. **Classes:** Most classes have 10–19 students. Most lab/discussion sessions have 10–19 students. **Majors with Highest Enrollment:** Biology/biological sciences; business/commerce; liberal arts and sciences/liberal studies. **Special Study Options:** Accelerated program, cooperative education program, distance learning, double major, dual enrollment, English as a Second Language (ESL), honors program, independent study, internships, liberal arts/career combination, student-designed major, study abroad, teacher certification program Special programs offered to physically disabled students include note-taking services, reader services. **Career services:** Alumni network, career/job search classes, career assessment, internships, regional alumni. **Career services highlights include:** Internships- All BBA students must complete at least one internship in order to graduate. Our internship programs allow our BBAs to compete on a national level.

FACILITIES

Housing: Coed dorms, men's dorms, women's dorms, apartments for married students, apartments for single students, Honors Residence, Living Learning Centers (First-time Freshmen). 98% of campus accessible to physically disabled. **Special Academic Facilities/Equipment:** Blanton Museum of Art, Lyndon Baines Johnson Presidential Library/Museum, Performing Arts Center, Texas Memorial Museum, Harry Ransom Humanities Research Center. **Computers:** Students can register for classes online. Administrative functions (other than registration) can be performed online.

CAMPUS LIFE

Environment: Metropolis. **Activities:** Choral groups, concert band, dance, drama/theater, jazz band, literary magazine, marching band, music ensembles, musical theater, opera, pep band, radio station, student government, student newspaper, student-run film society, symphony orchestra, television station, yearbook, campus ministries, international student organization. **Organizations:** 900 registered organizations, 15 honor societies, 95 religious organizations. 26 fraternities, 22 sororities. **Athletics (Intercollegiate):** *Men:* Baseball, basketball, cross-country, diving, football, golf, swimming, tennis, track/field (outdoor). *Women:* Basketball, crew/rowing, cross-country, diving, golf, soccer, softball, swimming, tennis, track/field (outdoor), volleyball. **On-Campus Highlights:** Texas Union, Frank Erwin Special Events Center, Performing Arts Center, Harry Ransom Humanities Research Center, Blanton Museum of Art.

ADMISSIONS

Freshman Academic Profile: 75.2% in top 10% of high school class, 94.7% in top 25% of high school class, 99.2% in top 50% of high school class. SAT Math middle 50% range 570–690. SAT Critical Reading middle 50% range 540–660. SAT Writing middle 50% range 540–670. ACT middle 50% range 24–30. Minimum paper TOEFL 550. Minimum computer TOEFL 213. Minimum web-based TOEFL 79. **Basis for Candidate Selection:** *Very important factors considered include:* Class rank, rigor of secondary school record. *Important factors considered include:* Application essay, standardized test scores, extracurricular activities, talent/ability, volunteer work, work experience. *Other factors considered include:* Recommendation(s), character/personal qualities, first generation, level of applicant's interest, racial/ethnic status, state residency. **Freshman Admission Requirements:** High school diploma is required and GED is accepted. *Academic units required:* 4 English, 3 mathematics, 2 science, (2 science labs), 2 foreign language, 3 social studies. *Academic units recommended:*

4 English, 4 mathematics, 4 science, (3 science labs), 3 foreign language, 3 social studies. **Freshman Admission Statistics:** 29,501 applied, 44% admitted, 52% enrolled. **Transfer Admission Requirements:** College transcript(s), essay or personal statement, minimum college GPA of 3.0 required. Lowest grade transferable C. **General Admission Information:** Application fee $60. Regular application deadline 12/15. Nonfall registration accepted. Credit and/or placement offered for CEEB Advanced Placement tests.

COSTS AND FINANCIAL AID
Annual in-state tuition $8,930. Annual out-of-state tuition $30,006. Room and board $9,602. Average book expense $860. **Required Forms and Deadlines:** FAFSA. Priority financial aid filing date 4/1. **Notification of Awards:** Applicants will be notified of awards on a rolling basis beginning 3/15. **Types of Aid:** *Need-based scholarships/grants:* Federal Pell, SEOG, state scholarships/grants, private scholarships, the school's own gift aid. *Loans:* FFEL Subsidized Stafford, FFEL Unsubsidized Stafford, FFEL PLUS, Federal Perkins, state loans *Student Employment:* Federal Work-Study Program available. Off-campus job opportunities are fair. **Financial Aid Statistics:** 57% freshmen, 44% undergrads receive need-based scholarship or grant aid. 60% freshmen, 51% undergrads receive need-based self-help aid. 60% freshmen, 54% undergrads receive any aid. 42% undergrads borrow to pay for school. Average cumulative indebtedness $17,000. **Criteria for awarding institutional aid:** *Non-need-based:* Academics, art, athletics, leadership, music/drama, state/district residency.

THE UNIVERSITY OF TEXAS AT BROWNSVILLE

80 Fort Brown, Brownsville, TX 78520
Phone: 956-882-8295 **Financial Aid Phone:** 956-882-8814
E-mail: admissions@utb.edu **CEEB Code:** 6825
Fax: 956-882-7810 **Website:** www.utb.edu

This public school was founded in 1926.

RATINGS
Admissions Selectivity Rating: 61   **Fire Safety Rating:** 60*   **Green Rating:** 60*

STUDENTS AND FACULTY
Enrollment: 10,145. **Student Body:** 60% female, 40% male, 4% out-of-state, 4% international (21 countries represented). Caucasian 5%, Hispanic 90%. **Retention and Graduation:** **Faculty:** 366 full-time faculty, 59% hold PhDs, 46% are members of minority groups, 43% are women.

ACADEMICS
Degrees: Associate, bachelor's, certificate, master's, terminal associate, transfer associate. **Majors with Highest Enrollment:** Business/commerce; multi-/interdisciplinary studies, other; psychology. **Special Study Options:** Cooperative education program, distance learning, double major, dual enrollment, English as a Second Language (ESL), independent study, internships, teacher certification program Special programs offered to physically disabled students include note-taking services, reader services, tape recorders, tutors.

FACILITIES
Housing: Coed dorms, special housing for disabled students, men's dorms, women's dorms, apartments for single students. **Computers:** Students can register for classes online. Administrative functions (other than registration) can be performed online.

CAMPUS LIFE
Environment: City. **Activities:** Choral groups, concert band, dance, drama/theater, jazz band, music ensembles, opera, radio station, student government, student newspaper. **Organizations:** 56 registered organizations, 6 honor societies, **Athletics (Intercollegiate):** *Men:* Baseball, golf. *Women:* Golf, volleyball.

ADMISSIONS
Freshman Academic Profile: Average high school GPA 2.61. 10% in top 10% of high school class, 27% in top 25% of high school class, 57% in top 50% of high school class. 95% from public high schools. **Freshman Admission Requirements:** High school diploma or equivalent is not required. *Academic units required:* 4 English, 2 mathematics, 2 science, (2 science labs), 2 foreign language, 4 social studies, 2 history, 1 academic electives. *Academic units recommended:* 4 English, 4 mathematics, 3 science, (3 science labs), 3 foreign language, 4 social studies, 2 history, 4 academic electives. **Freshman Admission Statistics:** 3,174 applied, 100% admitted, 57% enrolled. **Transfer Admission Requirements:** High school transcript, college transcript(s), minimum college GPA of 2.0 required. Lowest grade transferable C. **General Admission Information:** Regular application deadline 7/1. Nonfall registration accepted. Admission may be deferred for a maximum of 1 year. Credit offered for CEEB Advanced Placement tests.

COSTS AND FINANCIAL AID
Average book expense $615. **Required Forms and Deadlines:** FAFSA. Financial aid filing deadline 6/1. Priority financial aid filing date 4/1. **Notification of Awards:** Applicants will be notified of awards on or about 5/1. **Types of Aid:**

Need-based scholarships/grants: Federal Pell, SEOG, state scholarships/grants, private scholarships, the school's own gift aid. *Loans:* FFEL Subsidized Stafford, FFEL Unsubsidized Stafford, FFEL PLUS, college/university loans from institutional funds. **Financial Aid Statistics: Criteria for awarding institutional aid:** *Non-need-based:* Academics, art, athletics, leadership, music/drama.

THE UNIVERSITY OF TEXAS AT DALLAS

800 West Campbell Road, HH 10, Richardson, TX 75080
Phone: 972-883-2270 **Financial Aid Phone:** 972-883-2941
E-mail: interest@utdallas.edu **CEEB Code:** 6897
Fax: 972-883-2599 **Website:** www.utdallas.edu **ACT Code:** 4243

This public school was founded in 1969. It has a 500-acre campus.

RATINGS
Admissions Selectivity Rating: 89   **Fire Safety Rating:** 60*   **Green Rating:** 69

STUDENTS AND FACULTY
Enrollment: 9,634. **Student Body:** 45% female, 55% male, 3% out-of-state, 4% international (108 countries represented). Asian 22%, African American 7%, Caucasian 53%, Hispanic 12%, Native American 1%. **Retention and Graduation:** 84% freshmen return for sophomore year. 43% freshmen graduate within 4 years. **Faculty:** Student/faculty ratio 20:1. 533 full-time faculty, 92% hold PhDs, 26% are members of minority groups, 27% are women. 3% of classes are taught by teaching assistants.

ACADEMICS
Degrees: Bachelor's, master's, post-bachelor's certificate. **Classes:** Most classes have 10–19 students. Most lab/discussion sessions have 20–29 students. **Majors with Highest Enrollment:** Biology/biological sciences; business/commerce; electrical, electronics and communications engineering. **Special Study Options:** Accelerated program, cooperative education program, cross-registration, distance learning, double major, dual enrollment, English as a Second Language (ESL), honors program, independent study, internships, liberal arts/career combination, student-designed major, study abroad, teacher certification program, 3-2 Engineering programs, 2-2 Transfer programs. **Honors programs:** Collegium V offers small classes, innovative instruction, world class faculty, bright and inquisitive colleagues, and an array of extracurricular events to provide special opportunities for professional and personal growth. **Combined degree programs:** BA/MA, BS/MS, BA/MPA, BS/MPA, MS/PhD. Special programs offered to physically disabled students include note-taking services, reader services, tape recorders, tutors. **Career services:** Career/job search classes, career assessment, internships.

FACILITIES
Housing: Coed dorms, apartments for married students, apartments for single students, living learning communities for freshmen. 100% of campus accessible to physically disabled. **Special Academic Facilities/Equipment:** McDermott Library Special Collections which includes History of Aviation Collection, Wineburgh Philatelic Research Library and Louise B. Belsterling Botanical Library. **Computers:** 80% of classrooms, 100% of dorms, 100% of libraries, 100% of student union, 5% of common outdoor areas have wireless network access. Students can register for classes online.

CAMPUS LIFE
Environment: Metropolis. **Activities:** Choral groups, concert band, dance, drama/theater, jazz band, literary magazine, music ensembles, musical theater, pep band, radio station, student government, student newspaper, student-run film society, symphony orchestra, television station, international student organization. **Organizations:** 142 registered organizations, 8 honor societies, 9 religious organizations. 9 fraternities, 6 sororities. **Athletics (Intercollegiate):** *Men:* Baseball, basketball, cross-country, golf, soccer, tennis. *Women:* Basketball, cross-country, golf, soccer, softball, tennis, volleyball. **On-Campus Highlights:** The Pub (coffeehouse), Comet Cafe, Student Union, Activity Center, University Village clubhouses. **Environmental Initiatives:** Campus recycling program; DART shuttle program; free DART passes for students, faculty, staff.

ADMISSIONS
Freshman Academic Profile: Average high school GPA 3.58. 36% in top 10% of high school class, 70% in top 25% of high school class, 92% in top 50% of high school class. 92% from public high schools. SAT Math middle 50% range 560–690. SAT Critical Reading middle 50% range 520–660. SAT Writing middle 50% range 500–620. ACT middle 50% range 24–30. Minimum paper TOEFL 550. Minimum computer TOEFL 215. Minimum web-based TOEFL 80. **Basis for Candidate Selection:** *Very important factors considered include:* Class rank, academic GPA, rigor of secondary school record, standardized test scores. *Important factors considered include:* Application essay, extracurricular activities. *Other factors considered include:* Recommendation(s), character/personal qualities, first generation, geographical residence, level of applicant's interest, state residency, talent/ability, volunteer work, work experience. **Freshman Admission Requirements:** High school diploma is required and GED is

accepted. *Academic units required:* 4 English, 4 mathematics, 3 science, (3 science labs), 2 foreign language, 3 social studies. *Academic units recommended:* 4 English, 4 mathematics, 3 science, (3 science labs), 3 foreign language, 4 social studies, 1 visual/performing arts, 1 computer science, 2 health, PE. **Freshman Admission Statistics:** 5,554 applied, 52% admitted, 47% enrolled. **Transfer Admission Requirements:** College transcript(s), minimum college GPA of 2.5 required. Lowest grade transferable C. **General Admission Information:** Application fee $50. Regular application deadline 7/1. Nonfall registration accepted. Admission may be deferred for a maximum of 1 year. Credit and/or placement offered for CEEB Advanced Placement tests.

COSTS AND FINANCIAL AID

Annual in-state tuition $8,950. Annual out-of-state tuition $19,250. Room and board $7,733. Average book expense $1,200. **Required Forms and Deadlines:** FAFSA. Priority financial aid filing date 3/31. **Notification of Awards:** Applicants will be notified of awards on a rolling basis beginning 3/1. **Types of Aid:** *Need-based scholarships/grants:* Federal Pell, SEOG, state scholarships/grants, private scholarships, the school's own gift aid. *Loans:* FFEL Subsidized Stafford, FFEL Unsubsidized Stafford, FFEL PLUS, Federal Perkins, state loans, college/university loans from institutional funds. *Student Employment:* Federal Work-Study Program available. Institutional employment available. Highest amount earned per year from on-campus jobs $15,318. Off-campus job opportunities are excellent. **Financial Aid Statistics:** 41% freshmen, 42% undergrads receive need-based scholarship or grant aid. 8% freshmen, 3% undergrads receive non-need-based scholarship or grant aid. 20% freshmen, 33% undergrads receive need-based self-help aid. 73% freshmen, 62% undergrads receive any aid. 42% undergrads borrow to pay for school. Average cumulative indebtedness $7,343. **Criteria for awarding institutional aid:** *Non-need-based:* Academics.

THE UNIVERSITY OF TEXAS AT EL PASO

500 W. University Ave, El Paso, TX 79968-0510
Phone: 915-747-5890
E-mail: futureminer@utep.edu **CEEB Code:** 6829
Fax: 915-747-8893 **Website:** www.utep.edu **ACT Code:** 4223

This public school was founded in 1913. It has a 330-acre campus.

RATINGS
Admissions Selectivity Rating: 68   **Fire Safety Rating:** 60*   **Green Rating:** 60*

STUDENTS AND FACULTY
Enrollment: 16,658. **Student Body:** 55% female, 45% male, 3% out-of-state, 10% international (69 countries represented). Asian 1%, African American 3%, Caucasian 9%, Hispanic 77%.
Retention and Graduation: 68% freshmen return for sophomore year. **Faculty:** Student/faculty ratio 20:1. 662 full-time faculty, 19% are members of minority groups, 38% are women. 2% of classes are taught by teaching assistants.

ACADEMICS
Degrees: Bachelor's, master's. **Classes:** Most classes have 20–29 students. Most lab/discussion sessions have 10–19 students. **Majors with Highest Enrollment:** Criminal justice/safety studies; multi-/interdisciplinary studies, other; psychology. **Special Study Options:** Accelerated program, cooperative education program, cross-registration, distance learning, double major, dual enrollment, English as a Second Language (ESL), exchange student program (domestic), honors program, independent study, internships, study abroad, teacher certification program, weekend college **Combined degree programs:** BA/MA. Special programs offered to physically disabled students include note-taking services, reader services, tape recorders. **Career services:** Alumni services, career assessment, internships.

FACILITIES
Housing: Special housing for disabled students, apartments for single students. 90% of campus accessible to physically disabled. **Special Academic Facilities/Equipment:** Cross-cultural ethnic study center, natural history and cultural museum, solar pond and solar house, electron microscope, atmospheric and acoustic research lab, seismic observatory. **Computers:** Students can register for classes online. Administrative functions (other than registration) can be performed online.

CAMPUS LIFE
Environment: Metropolis. **Activities:** Choral groups, concert band, dance, drama/theater, jazz band, literary magazine, marching band, music ensembles, musical theater, opera, pep band, radio station, student government, student newspaper, student-run film society, symphony orchestra. **Organizations:** 1 honor societies, 1 religious organizations. 6 fraternities, 4 sororities. **Athletics (Intercollegiate):** *Men:* Basketball, cross-country, football, golf, track/field (outdoor), track/field (indoor). *Women:* Basketball, cross-country, golf, riflery, soccer, softball, tennis, track/field (outdoor), track/field (indoor), volleyball.

ADMISSIONS
Freshman Academic Profile: Average high school GPA 3.15. 18% in top 10% of high school class, 43% in top 25% of high school class, 74% in top 50% of high school class. 94% from public high schools. SAT Math middle 50% range 410–530. ACT middle 50% range 16–21. **Basis for Candidate Selection:** *Very important factors considered include:* Class rank, rigor of secondary school record. *Important factors considered include:* Standardized test scores, state residency. *Other factors considered include:* Recommendation(s), alumni/ae relation, character/personal qualities, extracurricular activities, geographical residence, interview, talent/ability, volunteer work, work experience. **Freshman Admission Requirements:** High school diploma is required and GED is accepted. *Academic units recommended:* 4 English, 4 mathematics, 3 science, 2 foreign language, 2 social studies, 2 history. **Freshman Admission Statistics:** 5,147 applied, 99% admitted, 45% enrolled. **Transfer Admission Requirements:** College transcript(s), minimum college GPA of 2.0 required. Lowest grade transferable D. **General Admission Information:** Regular application deadline 7/31. Nonfall registration accepted. Admission may be deferred for a maximum of 1 semester.

COSTS AND FINANCIAL AID
Annual in-state tuition $4,311. Room and board $4,185. Required fees $1,299. Average book expense $900. **Required Forms and Deadlines:** institution's own financial aid form. Priority financial aid filing date 3/15. **Notification of Awards:** Applicants will be notified of awards on or about 6/30. **Types of Aid:** *Need-based scholarships/grants:* Federal Pell, SEOG, state scholarships/grants, private scholarships, the school's own gift aid, United Negro College Fund, Federal Nursing Scholarships. *Loans:* FFEL Subsidized Stafford, FFEL Unsubsidized Stafford, FFEL PLUS, Federal Perkins, state loans, college/university loans from institutional funds. *Student Employment:* Federal Work-Study Program available. Institutional employment available. Off-campus job opportunities are good. **Financial Aid Statistics:** 52% freshmen, 47% undergrads receive need-based scholarship or grant aid. 6% freshmen, 5% undergrads receive non-need-based scholarship or grant aid. 54% freshmen, 51% undergrads receive need-based self-help aid. 1% freshmen, 1% undergrads receive athletic scholarships. 77% freshmen, 65% undergrads receive any aid. 50.6% undergrads borrow to pay for school. Average cumulative indebtedness $7,230. **Criteria for awarding institutional aid:** *Non-need-based:* Academics, alumni affiliation, art, athletics, job skills, leadership, minority status, music/drama, religious affiliation, state/district residency.

THE UNIVERSITY OF TEXAS AT SAN ANTONIO

One UTSA Circle, San Antonio, TX 78249-0617
Phone: 210-458-8000 **Financial Aid Phone:** 210-458-8000
E-mail: prospects@utsa.edu **CEEB Code:** 6919
Fax: 210-458-2001 **Website:** www.utsa.edu **ACT Code:** 4239

This public school was founded in 1969. It has a 600-acre campus.

RATINGS
Admissions Selectivity Rating: 64   **Fire Safety Rating:** 60*   **Green Rating:** 60*

STUDENTS AND FACULTY
Enrollment: 24,883. **Student Body:** 50% female, 50% male, 2% out-of-state, 2% international (66 countries represented). Asian 7%, African American 9%, Caucasian 37%, Hispanic 44%.
Retention and Graduation: 56% freshmen return for sophomore year. 8% freshmen graduate within 4 years. **Faculty:** Student/faculty ratio 23:1. 966 full-time faculty, 72% hold PhDs, 37% are members of minority groups, 43% are women.

ACADEMICS
Degrees: Bachelor's, doctoral, master's, post-bachelor's certificate. **Classes:** Most classes have 20–29 students. Most lab/discussion sessions have 10–19 students. **Majors with Highest Enrollment:** Biology/biological sciences; multi-/interdisciplinary studies, other; psychology. **Special Study Options:** Accelerated program, cooperative education program, distance learning, double major, dual enrollment, English as a Second Language (ESL), exchange student program (domestic), honors program, independent study, internships, study abroad, teacher certification program. **Honors programs:** The mission of the Honors College is to provide enhanced educational opportunities for selected, motivated, enthusiastic, diverse, and inquisitive students and to foster the pursuit of excellence in undergraduate, higher education. The underlying philosophy of the program is that well-educated individuals should understand broad, interdisciplinary perspectives while demonstrating expertise in their chosen field. The Honors College is open to students from all academic disciplines. Members of the Honors College pursue a rigorous academic program which satisfies all requirements of their academic departments and Colleges and goes beyond those requirements to provide the basis for outstanding achievement and appropriate recognition for that achievement. The Honors College offers small classes with greater opportunities for student participation, increased student-faculty contact, greater individual attention, lively discussions of important

issues, special interdisciplinary seminars, community service opportunities, and supervised research experiences, all designed to challenge talented students. Special programs offered to physically disabled students include note-taking services, reader services, tape recorders.

FACILITIES

Housing: Coed dorms, special housing for disabled students, apartments for married students, apartments for single students. 100% of campus accessible to physically disabled. **Special Academic Facilities/Equipment:** Art gallery, audiovisual center, Institute of Texan Cultures Museum. **Computers:** Students can register for classes online. Administrative functions (other than registration) can be performed online.

CAMPUS LIFE

Environment: Metropolis. **Activities:** Choral groups, concert band, dance, drama/theater, jazz band, literary magazine, music ensembles, opera, pep band, student government, student newspaper, symphony orchestra, yearbook, campus ministries, international student organization. **Organizations:** 140 registered organizations, 40 honor societies, 9 religious organizations. 10 fraternities, 9 sororities. **Athletics (Intercollegiate):** *Men:* Baseball, basketball, cross-country, golf, tennis, track/field (outdoor), track/field (indoor). *Women:* Basketball, cross-country, soccer, softball, tennis, track/field (outdoor), track/field (indoor), volleyball.

ADMISSIONS

Freshman Academic Profile: 10.25% in top 10% of high school class, 38.14% in top 25% of high school class, 74.46% in top 50% of high school class. 94% from public high schools. SAT Math middle 50% range 470–580. SAT Critical Reading middle 50% range 450–560. SAT Writing middle 50% range 430–540. ACT middle 50% range 19–24. Minimum paper TOEFL 500. Minimum computer TOEFL 173. **Basis for Candidate Selection:** *Very important factors considered include:* Class rank, academic GPA, standardized test scores, *Other factors considered include:* Recommendation(s). **Freshman Admission Requirements:** High school diploma is required and GED is accepted. *Academic units recommended:* 4 English, 3 mathematics, 3 science, 2 foreign language, 1 visual/performing arts. **Freshman Admission Statistics:** 11,993 applied, 87% admitted, 47% enrolled. **Transfer Admission Requirements:** College transcript(s), minimum college GPA of 2.0 required. Lowest grade transferable D. **General Admission Information:** Application fee $40. Regular application deadline 7/1. Regular notification 9/1. Nonfall registration accepted. Credit and/or placement offered for CEEB Advanced Placement tests.

COSTS AND FINANCIAL AID

Annual in-state tuition $5,126. Annual out-of-state tuition $13,436. Room and board $8,937. Required fees $2,401. Average book expense $1,000. **Required Forms and Deadlines:** FAFSA, institution's own financial aid form. Priority financial aid filing date 3/31. **Notification of Awards:** Applicants will be notified of awards on a rolling basis beginning 4/1. **Types of Aid:** *Need-based scholarships/grants:* Federal Pell, SEOG, state scholarships/grants, private scholarships, the school's own gift aid. *Loans:* Direct Subsidized Stafford, Direct Unsubsidized Stafford, Direct PLUS, FFEL Subsidized Stafford, FFEL Unsubsidized Stafford, FFEL PLUS, Federal Perkins, state loans, college/university loans from institutional funds. **Financial Aid Statistics:** 42% freshmen, 45% undergrads receive need-based scholarship or grant aid. 16% freshmen, 10% undergrads receive non-need-based scholarship or grant aid. 38% freshmen, 45% undergrads receive need-based self-help aid. 2% freshmen, 1% undergrads receive athletic scholarships. 65% freshmen, 67% undergrads receive any aid. 65% undergrads borrow to pay for school. Average cumulative indebtedness $22,118. **Criteria for awarding institutional aid:** *Non-need-based:* Academics, alumni affiliation, art, athletics, job skills, leadership, music/drama, state/district residency.

THE UNIVERSITY OF TEXAS AT TYLER

3900 University Blvd, Tyler, TX 75799
Phone: 903-566-7202 **Financial Aid Phone:** 903-566-7180
E-mail: admissions@mail.uttyl.edu
Fax: 903-566-7068 **Website:** www.uttyler.edu

This public school was founded in 1971. It has a 204-acre campus.

RATINGS

Admissions Selectivity Rating: 60*   **Fire Safety Rating:** 95   **Green Rating:** 60*

STUDENTS AND FACULTY

Enrollment: 4,700. **Student Body:** 60% female, 40% male, 2% out-of-state, 1% international (45 countries represented). Asian 2%, African American 10%, Caucasian 79%, Hispanic 6%, Native American 1%.

Retention and Graduation: 59% freshmen return for sophomore year. 14% grads go on to further study within 1 year. **Faculty:** Student/faculty ratio 21:1. 234 full-time faculty, 70% hold PhDs, 12% are members of minority groups, 49% are women.

ACADEMICS

Degrees: Bachelor's, master's. **Classes:** Most classes have 20–29 students. **Majors with Highest Enrollment:** Business/managerial economics; multi-/interdisciplinary studies, other; nursing/registered nurse (RN, ASN, BSN, MSN). **Special Study Options:** Cooperative education program, distance learning, double major, English as a Second Language (ESL), exchange student program (domestic), independent study, internships, student-designed major, study abroad, teacher certification program, weekend college Special programs offered to physically disabled students include note-taking services, reader services **Career services:** Career/job search classes, career assessment.

FACILITIES

Housing: Coed dorms, apartments for married students, apartments for single students, Univ Pines Apts—384 beds, Patriot Village Apts—200 bed residence hall, www.uttyler.edu/housing. **Computers:** Students can register for classes online. Administrative functions (other than registration) can be performed online.

CAMPUS LIFE

Environment: City. **Activities:** Choral groups, concert band, drama/theater, jazz band, literary magazine, music ensembles, musical theater, opera, pep band, student government, student newspaper, student-run film society. **Organizations:** 73 registered organizations, 6 honor societies, 4 fraternities, 4 sororities. **Athletics (Intercollegiate):** *Men:* Baseball, basketball, cheerleading, cross-country, golf, soccer, tennis. *Women:* Basketball, cheerleading, cross-country, golf, soccer, tennis, volleyball. **On-Campus Highlights:** Herrington Patriot Center, Riter Tower and Plaza, Cowan Fine and Performing Art Center, Bill Ratliff Engineering and Science Complex, University Center.

ADMISSIONS

Freshman Academic Profile: SAT Math middle 50% range 480–580. SAT Critical Reading middle 50% range 470–570. ACT middle 50% range 20–25. Minimum paper TOEFL 550. Minimum computer TOEFL 213. **Basis for Candidate Selection:** *Very important factors considered include:* Class rank, academic GPA, standardized test scores. *Important factors considered include:* Rigor of secondary school record, extracurricular activities, first generation, volunteer work, work experience. **Freshman Admission Requirements:** High school diploma is required and GED is accepted. *Academic units required:* 4 English, 3 mathematics, 3 science, (1 science labs), 2 foreign language, 3 social studies. *Academic units recommended:* 4 mathematics, (3 science labs). **Freshman Admission Statistics:** 1,823 applied, 76% admitted, 46% enrolled. **Transfer Admission Requirements:** College transcript(s), minimum college GPA of 2.0 required. Lowest grade transferable C. **General Admission Information:** Application fee $25. Notification on a rolling basis, beginning on or about 9/1. Nonfall registration accepted. Admission may be deferred for a maximum of 1 year.

COSTS AND FINANCIAL AID

Required Forms and Deadlines: FAFSA, institution's own financial aid form. Priority financial aid filing date 4/1. **Notification of Awards:** Applicants will be notified of awards on a rolling basis beginning 4/15. **Types of Aid:** *Need-based scholarships/grants:* Federal Pell, SEOG, state scholarships/grants, private scholarships, the school's own gift aid, Texas Grant Program, Teach for Texas Conditional Program. *Loans:* FFEL Subsidized Stafford, FFEL Unsubsidized Stafford, FFEL PLUS, Federal Perkins, state loans. **Financial Aid Statistics:** 35% freshmen, 42% undergrads receive need-based scholarship or grant aid. 6% freshmen, 3% undergrads receive non-need-based scholarship or grant aid. 35% freshmen, 47% undergrads receive need-based self-help aid. 44% undergrads borrow to pay for school. Average cumulative indebtedness $11,286. **Criteria for awarding institutional aid:** *Non-need-based:* Academics, art, music/drama.

THE UNIVERSITY OF TEXAS HEALTH SCIENCE CENTER AT HOUSTON

PO Box 20036, Houston, TX 77225
Phone: 713-500-3361
E-mail: admissions@uth.tmc.edu
Fax: 713-500-3356 **Website:** www.uth.tmc.edu

This public school was founded in 1972.

RATINGS

Admissions Selectivity Rating: 60*   **Fire Safety Rating:** 60*   **Green Rating:** 60*

STUDENTS AND FACULTY

Enrollment: 381. **Student Body:** 88% female, 12% male, % out-of-state, 2% international. Asian 17%, African American 7%, Caucasian 58%, Hispanic 15%, Native American 1%.
Faculty: 985 full-time faculty, 41% are women.

ACADEMICS

Degrees: Bachelor's, certificate, first professional, master's, post-master's certificate.

FACILITIES

Housing: University owns an apartment complex which is located approximately 1 1/2 miles from campus. It is competitively priced with other apartment complexes in the area and does not cater exclusively to students. 100% of campus accessible to physically disabled. **Special Academic Facilities/Equipment:** The student's learning experience takes place in the heart of the Texas Medical Center. Among state of the art hospitals and research facilites.
Computers: Students can register for classes online. Administrative functions (other than registration) can be performed online. Undergraduates are required to own a computer.

CAMPUS LIFE

Activities: Student government.

ADMISSIONS

Freshman Academic Profile: Minimum paper TOEFL 565. **Transfer Admission Requirements:** College transcript(s), interview, standardized test scores, statement of good standing from prior institution(s). Minimum college GPA of 2.8 required. Lowest grade transferable C. **General Admission Information:** Application fee $30. Regular application deadline 1/1. Nonfall registration not accepted.

COSTS AND FINANCIAL AID

Required Forms and Deadlines: FAFSA, institution's own financial aid form. Priority financial aid filing date 3/1. **Types of Aid:** *Need-based scholarships/grants:* Federal Pell, SEOG, state scholarships/grants, the school's own gift aid, Federal Nursing Scholarships. outside Scholarships. *Loans:* FFEL Subsidized Stafford, FFEL Unsubsidized Stafford, FFEL PLUS, Federal Perkins, Federal Nursing, college/university loans from institutional funds, Outside Loans. *Student Employment:* Off-campus job opportunities are excellent. **Financial Aid Statistics:** 69% undergrads receive need-based scholarship or grant aid. 75% undergrads receive need-based self-help aid. 90% undergrads borrow to pay for school. Average cumulative indebtedness $14,361.

THE UNIVERSITY OF TEXAS MEDICAL BRANCH

301 University Boulevard, Galveston, TX 77555-1305
Phone: 409-772-1215 **Financial Aid Phone:** 409-772-1215
E-mail: enrollment.services@utmb.edu **CEEB Code:** 6887
Fax: 409-772-4466 **Website:** www.utmb.edu

This public school was founded in 1891. It has a 85-acre campus.

RATINGS

Admissions Selectivity Rating: 60*   **Fire Safety Rating:** 60*   **Green Rating:** 60*

STUDENTS AND FACULTY

Enrollment: 492. **Student Body:** 80% female, 20% male, 1% out-of-state, 2% international (34 countries represented). Asian 18%, African, American 18%, Caucasian 42%, Hispanic 14%, Native American 1%.

ACADEMICS

Degrees: Bachelor's, master's, post-master's certificate. **Majors with Highest Enrollment:** Clinical laboratory science/medical technology/technologist; nursing/registered nurse (RN, ASN, BSN, MSN); respiratory care therapy/therapist. **Special Study Options:** Distance learning, independent study, internships. **Combined degree programs:** MD/PhD. Special programs offered to physically disabled students include note-taking services, reader services, tape recorders, tutors. **Career services:** Alumni network, alumni services, internships.

FACILITIES

Housing: Coed dorms, fraternity/sorority housing, apartments for married students, apartments for single students. 100% of campus accessible to physically disabled. **Special Academic Facilities/Equipment:** Moody Medical Library. **Computers:** Students can register for classes online. Administrative functions (other than registration) can be performed online.

CAMPUS LIFE

Environment: Town. **Activities:** Student government, student newspaper, yearbook. **Organizations:** 94 registered organizations, 4 honor societies, 7 reli-

gious organizations. 5 fraternities. **On-Campus Highlights:** Joe Jamail Student Center, Rosenberg House, Ashbel Smith Building, Alumni Field House, Moody Medical Library.

ADMISSIONS

Freshman Academic Profile: Minimum paper TOEFL 550. Minimum computer TOEFL 213. **Transfer Admission Requirements:** College transcript(s), minimum college GPA of 2.0 required. Lowest grade transferable C. **General Admission Information:** Neither credit nor placement offered for CEEB Advanced Placement tests.

COSTS AND FINANCIAL AID

Required Forms and Deadlines: FAFSA. **Types of Aid:** *Need-based scholarships/grants:* Federal Pell, SEOG, state scholarships/grants, private scholarships, the school's own gift aid. *Loans:* Direct Subsidized Stafford, Direct Unsubsidized Stafford, Direct PLUS, Federal Perkins, Federal Nursing, college/university loans from institutional funds. *Student Employment:* Federal Work-Study Program available. Institutional employment available. Off-campus job opportunities are good. **Criteria for awarding institutional aid:** *Non-need-based:* Academics, minority status, state/district residency.

THE UNIVERSITY OF TEXAS—PAN AMERICAN

Admissions and New Student Services, 1201 West Univer, Edinburg, TX 78541
Phone: 956-381-2999 **Financial Aid Phone:** 956-381-2501
E-mail: admissions@utpa.edu **CEEB Code:** 006570
Fax: Website: www.utpa.edu **ACT Code:** 4142

This public school was founded in 1927. It has a 330-acre campus.

RATINGS

Admissions Selectivity Rating: 65   **Fire Safety Rating:** 60*   **Green Rating:** 63

STUDENTS AND FACULTY

Enrollment: 15,064. **Student Body:** 58% female, 42% male, 0.4% out-of-state, 5% international (51 countries represented). Asian 1%, African American 1%, Caucasian 5%, Hispanic 88%.
Retention and Graduation: 13% freshmen graduate within 4 years. **Faculty:** Student/faculty ratio 19:1. 668 full-time faculty, 40% are members of minority groups, 38% are women.

ACADEMICS

Degrees: Bachelor's, master's, post-bachelor's certificate. **Classes:** Most classes have 30–39 students. Most lab/discussion sessions have 20–29 students. **Majors with Highest Enrollment:** Business administration and management; multi-/interdisciplinary studies, other; speech and rhetorical studies. **Special Study Options:** Accelerated program, cooperative education program, distance learning, double major, dual enrollment, English as a Second Language (ESL), exchange student program (domestic), honors program, independent study, internships, study abroad, teacher certification program, weekend college. **Honors programs:** PRE-MEDICAL HONORS COLLEGE with Baylor College of Medicine. Special programs offered to physically disabled students include note-taking services, reader services, tape recorders, tutors. **Career services:** Alumni services, career assessment, internships.

FACILITIES

Housing: Coed dorms, men's dorms, women's dorms, apartments for married students, apartments for single students. 100% of campus accessible to physically disabled. **Computers:** Students can register for classes online. Administrative functions (other than registration) can be performed online.

CAMPUS LIFE

Environment: Town. **Activities:** Choral groups, concert band, dance, drama/theater, jazz band, music ensembles, musical theater, pep band, student government, student newspaper, symphony orchestra, campus ministries, international student organization. **Organizations:** 80 registered organizations, 9 honor societies, 7 religious organizations. 4 fraternities, 1 sororities. **Athletics (Intercollegiate):** *Men:* Baseball, basketball, cross-country, golf, tennis, track/field (outdoor). *Women:* Basketball, cross-country, golf, tennis, track/field (outdoor), volleyball. **On-Campus Highlights:** Visitors Center, Science Courtyard, Residence Halls, Student Union. **Environmental Initiatives:** The direction of disposal of hazardous waste streams toward recycling or reuse. The use of environmentally friendly (low water) landscaping materials. The upgrade of lighting fixtures, energy management system components, and chiller systems for energy reduction and emissions friendlier to the environment.

ADMISSIONS

Freshman Academic Profile: 19% in top 10% of high school class, 49% in top 25% of high school class, 80% in top 50% of high school class. 99% from public high schools. SAT Math middle 50% range 420–530. SAT Critical Reading middle 50% range 410–510. ACT middle 50% range 17–21. Minimum paper TOEFL 500. Minimum computer TOEFL 173. Minimum web-based TOEFL 61. **Basis for Candidate Selection:** *Very important factors considered include:* Standardized test scores. *Important factors considered include:* Class rank, academic GPA, rigor of secondary school record. **Freshman Admission Requirements:** High school diploma is required and GED is accepted. *Academic units required:* 4 English, 3 mathematics, 3 science, 2 foreign language. **Freshman Admission Statistics:** 5,235 applied, 85% admitted, 60% enrolled. **Transfer Admission Requirements:** College transcript(s), minimum college GPA of 2.0 required. Lowest grade transferable D. **General Admission Information:** Regular application deadline 8/11. Nonfall registration accepted. Credit and/or placement offered for CEEB Advanced Placement tests.

COSTS AND FINANCIAL AID
Annual in-state tuition $3,305. Annual out-of-state tuition $10,049. Room and board $6,038. Required fees $999. Average book expense $1,000. **Required Forms and Deadlines:** FAFSA. Priority financial aid filing date 3/1. **Notification of Awards:** Applicants will be notified of awards on or about 3/15. **Types of Aid:** *Need-based scholarships/grants:* Federal Pell, SEOG, state scholarships/grants, private scholarships, the school's own gift aid. *Loans:* FFEL Subsidized Stafford, FFEL Unsubsidized Stafford, FFEL PLUS, Federal Perkins, state loans. *Student Employment:* Federal Work-Study Program available. Institutional employment available. Off-campus job opportunities are good. **Financial Aid Statistics:** 76% freshmen, 71% undergrads receive need-based scholarship or grant aid. 2% freshmen, 2% undergrads receive non-need-based scholarship or grant aid. 21% freshmen, 39% undergrads receive need-based self-help aid. 1% freshmen, 1% undergrads receive athletic scholarships. 67.7% freshmen, 84.5% undergrads receive any aid. 64% undergrads borrow to pay for school. Average cumulative indebtedness $12,302. **Criteria for awarding institutional aid:** *Non-need-based:* Academics, alumni affiliation, art, athletics, leadership, music/drama.

UNIVERSITY OF TOLEDO

2801 West Bancroft, Toledo, OH 43606
Phone: 419-530-8700 **Financial Aid Phone:** 419-530-8700
E-mail: enroll@utnet.utoledo.edu **CEEB Code:** 1845
Fax: 419-530-5713 **Website:** www.utoledo.edu **ACT Code:** 3344

This public school was founded in 1872. It has a 400-acre campus.

RATINGS
Admissions Selectivity Rating: 72   **Fire Safety Rating:** 60*   **Green Rating:** 60*

STUDENTS AND FACULTY
Enrollment: 15,288. **Student Body:** 49% female, 51% male, 8% out-of-state, 1% international (108 countries represented). Asian 2%, African American 13%, Caucasian 76%, Hispanic 3%.
Retention and Graduation: 69% freshmen return for sophomore year. 17% freshmen graduate within 4 years. **Faculty:** Student/faculty ratio 18:1. 813 full-time faculty, 73% hold PhDs, 17% are members of minority groups, 35% are women.

ACADEMICS
Degrees: Associate, bachelor's, certificate, first professional, master's, post-bachelor's certificate, post-master's certificate. **Majors with Highest Enrollment:** Education; engineering; marketing/marketing management. **Special Study Options:** Accelerated program, cooperative education program, cross-registration, distance learning, double major, dual enrollment, exchange student program (domestic), honors program, independent study, internships, liberal arts/career combination, student-designed major, study abroad, teacher certification program, weekend college. Special programs offered to physically disabled students include note-taking services, reader services, tutors.

FACILITIES
Housing: Coed dorms, special housing for disabled students, men's dorms, special housing for international students, women's dorms, fraternity/sorority housing. 95% of campus accessible to physically disabled. **Special Academic Facilities/Equipment:** Language lab, arboretum, planetariums, two observatories, electron microscope. **Computers:** Students can register for classes online.

CAMPUS LIFE
Environment: City. **Activities:** Choral groups, concert band, dance, drama/theater, jazz band, literary magazine, marching band, music ensembles, musical theater, opera, pep band, radio station, student government, student newspaper, student-run film society, symphony orchestra, television station. **Organizations:** 200 registered organizations, 14 fraternities, 13 sororities. **Athletics**

(Intercollegiate): *Men:* Baseball, basketball, cheerleading, cross-country, diving, football, golf, lacrosse, softball, swimming, tennis, track/field (outdoor), track/field (indoor), volleyball. *Women:* Basketball, cheerleading, cross-country, diving, golf, lacrosse, softball, swimming, tennis, track/field (outdoor), track/field (indoor), volleyball.

ADMISSIONS
Freshman Academic Profile: Average high school GPA 3.08. 16% in top 10% of high school class, 37% in top 25% of high school class, 64% in top 50% of high school class. SAT Math middle 50% range 460–600. SAT Critical Reading middle 50% range 450–570. ACT middle 50% range 19–25. Minimum paper TOEFL 500. Minimum computer TOEFL 173. **Basis for Candidate Selection:** *Very important factors considered include:* Rigor of secondary school record, standardized test scores, state residency. **Freshman Admission Requirements:** High school diploma is required and GED is accepted. *Academic units required:* 4 English, 3 mathematics, 3 science, 3 social studies. *Academic units recommended:* 4 English, 3 mathematics, 3 science, (1 science labs), 2 foreign language, 3 social studies, 1 history. **Freshman Admission Statistics:** 8,126 applied, 80% admitted, 49% enrolled. **Transfer Admission Requirements:** College transcript(s), statement of good standing from prior institution(s). Minimum college GPA of 2.0 required. Lowest grade transferable C. **General Admission Information:** Application fee $40. Notification on a rolling basis, beginning on or about 10/1. Nonfall registration accepted. Admission may be deferred for a maximum of 1 year. Credit and/or placement offered for CEEB Advanced Placement tests.

COSTS AND FINANCIAL AID
Annual in-state tuition $6,430. Annual out-of-state tuition $15,242. Room and board $8,213. Required fees $1,091. Average book expense $690. **Required Forms and Deadlines:** FAFSA. Priority financial aid filing date 4/1. **Notification of Awards:** Applicants will be notified of awards on a rolling basis beginning 4/1. **Types of Aid:** *Need-based scholarships/grants:* Federal Pell, SEOG, state scholarships/grants, private scholarships, the school's own gift aid. *Loans:* Direct Subsidized Stafford, Direct Unsubsidized Stafford, Direct PLUS, Federal Perkins, state loans. *Student Employment:* Federal Work-Study Program available. **Financial Aid Statistics:** 55% undergrads receive any aid. 65% undergrads borrow to pay for school. Average cumulative indebtedness $20,859. **Criteria for awarding institutional aid:** *Non-need-based:* Academics, art, athletics, minority status, music/drama, state/district residency.

UNIVERSITY OF TORONTO

Best 373

315 Bloor Street West, Toronto, ON M5S1A3 Canada
Phone: 416-978-2190
E-mail: admissions.help@utoronto.ca **CEEB Code:** 982
Fax: 416-978-7022 **Website:** www.utoronto.ca

This public school was founded in 1827. It has a 1767-acre campus.

RATINGS
Admissions Selectivity Rating: 60*   **Fire Safety Rating:** 60*   **Green Rating:** 83

STUDENTS AND FACULTY
Enrollment: 61,156. **Student Body:** 55% female, 45% male, 8% out-of-state, 11% international (166 countries represented).
Retention and Graduation: **Faculty:** Student/faculty ratio 21:1. 2757 full-time faculty, 36% are women.

ACADEMICS
Degrees: Bachelor's, certificate, diploma, master's. **Classes: Special Study Options:** Cooperative education program, double major, English as a Second Language (ESL), exchange student program (domestic), honors program, internships, study abroad, teacher certification program. **Combined degree programs:** JD/MBA, JD/MA, JD/PhD/, JD/MISt, JD/MSW. Special programs offered to physically disabled students include note-taking services, reader services, tape recorders, tutors. **Career services:** Career/job search classes.

FACILITIES
Housing: Coed dorms, men's dorms, women's dorms, apartments for married students, cooperative housing. **Computers:** Students can register for classes online. Administrative functions (other than registration) can be performed online.

CAMPUS LIFE

Environment: Metropolis. **Activities:** Choral groups, concert band, dance, drama/theater, jazz band, literary magazine, music ensembles, opera, radio station, student government, student newspaper, student-run film society, symphony orchestra. **Organizations:** 200 registered organizations, 49 religious organizations. **Athletics (Intercollegiate):** *Men:* Badminton, baseball, basketball, crew/rowing, cross-country, curling, fencing, football, golf, ice hockey, lacrosse, mountain biking, rugby, skiing (nordic/cross-country), soccer, squash, swimming, tennis, track/field (outdoor), track/field (indoor), volleyball. *Women:* Badminton, basketball, crew/rowing, cross-country, curling, fencing, field hockey, ice hockey, lacrosse, mountain biking, rugby, skiing (nordic/cross-country), soccer, squash, swimming, tennis, track/field (outdoor), track/field (indoor), volleyball, water polo. **On-Campus Highlights:** Hart House, The Athletic Centre, Justine Barnike Gallery, Thomas Fisher Rare Book Library, Convocation Hall.

ADMISSIONS

Freshman Academic Profile: Minimum paper TOEFL 600. Minimum computer TOEFL 250. **Basis for Candidate Selection:** *Very important factors considered include:* Academic GPA, standardized test scores. **Freshman Admission Requirements:** High school diploma is required and GED is accepted. **Freshman Admission Statistics:** 63,955 applied, 71% admitted, 30% enrolled. **Transfer Admission Requirements:** High school transcript, college transcript(s), standardized test scores. **General Admission Information:** Application fee $80. Regular application deadline 3/1. Notification on a rolling basis, beginning on or about 3/15. Nonfall registration not accepted.

COSTS AND FINANCIAL AID

Required Forms and Deadlines: OSAP.

THE UNIVERSITY OF TULSA

800 South Tucker Drive, Tulsa, OK 74104
Phone: 918-631-2307 **Financial Aid Phone:** 918-631-2526
E-mail: admission@utulsa.edu **CEEB Code:** 6883
Fax: 918-631-5003 **Website:** www.utulsa.edu **ACT Code:** 3444

This private school, affiliated with the Presbyterian Church, was founded in 1894. It has a 209-acre campus.

RATINGS

Admissions Selectivity Rating: 95 **Fire Safety Rating:** 88 **Green Rating:** 83

STUDENTS AND FACULTY

Enrollment: 3,027. **Student Body:** 47% female, 53% male, 41% out-of-state, 14% international (62 countries represented). Asian 3%, African American 6%, Caucasian 62%, Hispanic 4%, Native American 4%.
Retention and Graduation: 88% freshmen return for sophomore year. 44% freshmen graduate within 4 years. 41% grads go on to further study within 1 year. 17% grads pursue arts and sciences degrees. 2% grads pursue law degrees. 7% grads pursue business degrees. 5% grads pursue medical degrees. **Faculty:** Student/faculty ratio 11:1. 311 full-time faculty, 96% hold PhDs, 16% are members of minority groups, 32% are women. 4% of classes are taught by teaching assistants.

ACADEMICS

Degrees: Bachelor's, master's, post-bachelor's certificate. **Classes:** Most classes have 10–19 students. Most lab/discussion sessions have 10–19 students. **Majors with Highest Enrollment:** Marketing/marketing management; petroleum engineering; psychology. **Special Study Options:** Accelerated program, double major, English as a Second Language (ESL), honors program, independent study, internships, liberal arts/career combination, student-designed major, study abroad, teacher certification program. **Honors programs:** The Honors Program is a four-year course of study consisting of 21 hours of academic credit. In small classes and individual tutorials, students pursue a critical examination of the moral and political commitments, scientific achievments, and artistic sensibilities that have shaped the modern world. The program culminates in the senior year with students designing and executing individual research projects. The Tulsa Undergraduate Research Challenge (TURC) is an innovative program that enables undergraduates to take challenging courses and conduct advanced research with the guidance of top professors. Its aim is to create leaders in scholarship, research, and public life. The centerpiece of the program

---

is research; the goal of such research may be to deliver papers at academic conferences, to produce publishable articles, or to initiate meaningful community projects. **Combined degree programs:** BA/JD, Bachelor's and MBA. Special programs offered to physically disabled students include note-taking services, reader services, tape recorders, tutors. **Career services:** Alumni network, alumni services, career/job search classes, career assessment, internships, regional alumni. **Career services highlights include:** Internships provide students with the opportunity to supplement classroom training with real-world experience in a position related to their major or career goals. Students may be paid or may receive academic credit or a combination of pay and credit.

FACILITIES

Housing: Coed dorms, special housing for disabled students, men's dorms, women's dorms, fraternity/sorority housing, apartments for married students, apartments for single students, Honors House. 80% of campus accessible to physically disabled. **Special Academic Facilities/Equipment:** Alexandre Hogue Art Gallery, Biotechnology Institute, Center for Communicative Disorders, Charge-Coupled Camera Microscope, Donald W. Reynolds Center (site of a state-of-the-art athletic training program), Education Technology Lab, Electron Microscopes, Kendall Theatre, McFarlin Library Special Collections (focus on American, British, and Irish Literature of the late 19th and early 20th centuries, and on Native American History and Law), Multimedia "boardroom" style classrooms (3), ONEOK Multimedia Auditorium, Sadie Adwan Communication Lab, Sidney Born Technical Library (contains an outstanding collection concerning energy, most notably petroleum), Sun Computer Work Stations, World's largest research flow-loop in Petroleum Engr. **Computers:** 100% of classrooms, 100% of dorms, 100% of libraries, 100% of dining areas, 100% of student union, 100% of common outdoor areas have wireless network access. Students can register for classes online. Administrative functions (other than registration) can be performed online.

CAMPUS LIFE

Environment: Metropolis. **Activities:** Choral groups, concert band, dance, drama/theater, jazz band, literary magazine, marching band, music ensembles, musical theater, opera, pep band, radio station, student government, student newspaper, symphony orchestra, television station, yearbook, campus ministries, international student organization, Model UN. **Organizations:** 245 registered organizations, 40 honor societies, 21 religious organizations. 7 fraternities, 9 sororities. **Athletics (Intercollegiate):** *Men:* Basketball, cheerleading, cross-country, football, golf, soccer, tennis, track/field (outdoor), track/field (indoor). *Women:* Basketball, cheerleading, crew/rowing, cross-country, golf, soccer, softball, tennis, track/field (outdoor), track/field (indoor), volleyball. **On-Campus Highlights:** Collins Fitness Center, Reynolds Center, McFarlin Library, Allen Chapman Activity Center, Fraternity/Sorority Row, Collins College of Business, The College of Engineering and Natural Sciences, Chapman Hall—The College of Arts and Sciences, Phillips Hall—School of Art, Kendall Hall Theatre, Collins Hall—Visitors Center and Office of Admission, H.A. Chapman Stadium. **Environmental Initiatives:** All campus shuttles run on compressed natural gas Recycling program includes events and all buildings, and covers plastics, aluminum, paper, and glass in targeted areas. Earth Day Week—trayless meals in dining halls, and distribution of recycling bags and totes to students and campus organizations.

ADMISSIONS

Freshman Academic Profile: Average high school GPA 3.8. 71% in top 10% of high school class, 89% in top 25% of high school class, 97% in top 50% of high school class. 75% from public high schools. SAT Math middle 50% range 560–690. SAT Critical Reading middle 50% range 570–700. ACT middle 50% range 25–32. Minimum paper TOEFL 500. Minimum computer TOEFL 173. Minimum web-based TOEFL 61. **Basis for Candidate Selection:** *Very important factors considered include:* Class rank, academic GPA, rigor of secondary school record, standardized test scores, interview, level of applicant's interest. *Important factors considered include:* Application essay, recommendation(s), character/personal qualities, extracurricular activities, talent/ability. *Other factors considered include:* Alumni/ae relation, first generation, racial/ethnic status, volunteer work, work experience. **Freshman Admission Requirements:** High school diploma is required and GED is accepted. *Academic units recommended:* 4 English, 3 mathematics, 3 science, (2 science labs), 2 foreign language, 1 social studies, 2 history, 1 academic electives. **Freshman Admission Statistics:** 4,698 applied, 50% admitted, 30% enrolled. **Transfer Admission Requirements:** College transcript(s), essay or personal statement, statement of good standing from prior institution(s). Minimum college GPA of 2.5 required. Lowest grade transferable C. **General Admission Information:** Application fee $35. Notification on a rolling basis, beginning on or about 10/1. Nonfall registration accepted. Admission may be deferred for a maximum of 1 year. Credit and/or placement offered for CEEB Advanced Placement tests.

COSTS AND FINANCIAL AID

Annual tuition $28,060. Room and board $9,018. Required fees $100. Average book expense $1,200. **Required Forms and Deadlines:** FAFSA, institution's own financial aid form. Priority financial aid filing date 4/1. **Notification of Awards:** Applicants will be notified of awards on a rolling basis beginning 3/1. **Types of Aid:** *Need-based scholarships/grants:* Federal Pell, SEOG, state scholarships/grants, private scholarships, the school's own gift aid. *Loans:* FFEL Subsidized Stafford, FFEL Unsubsidized Stafford, FFEL PLUS, Federal Perkins. *Student Employment:* Federal Work-Study Program available. Institutional employment available. Highest amount earned per year from on-campus jobs $4,700. Off-campus job opportunities are good. **Financial Aid Statistics:** 20% freshmen, 18% undergrads receive need-based scholarship or grant aid. 50% freshmen, 39% undergrads receive non-need-based scholarship or grant aid. 40% freshmen, 34% undergrads receive need-based self-help aid. 13% freshmen, 12% undergrads receive athletic scholarships. 91% freshmen, 88% undergrads receive any aid. 36% undergrads borrow to pay for school. Average cumulative indebtedness $28,364. **Criteria for awarding institutional aid:** *Non-need-based:* Academics, alumni affiliation, art, athletics, leadership, minority status, music/drama, religious affiliation.

UNIVERSITY OF UTAH

Best 373

201 South 1460 East, Room 250 S, Salt Lake City, UT 84112
Phone: 801-581-7281 **Financial Aid Phone:** 801-581-6211
E-mail: admissions@sa.utah.edu **CEEB Code:** 4853
Fax: 801-585-7864 **Website:** www.utah.edu **ACT Code:** 42740

This public school was founded in 1850. It has a 1535-acre campus.

RATINGS
Admissions Selectivity Rating: 79   **Fire Safety Rating:** 87   **Green Rating:** 90

STUDENTS AND FACULTY
Enrollment: 20,983. **Student Body:** 45% female, 55% male, 21% out-of-state, 3% international (130 countries represented). Asian 6%, African American 1%, Caucasian 78%, Hispanic 5%, Native American 1%. **Retention and Graduation:** 22% freshmen graduate within 4 years. **Faculty:** Student/faculty ratio 15:1. 1269 full-time faculty, 82% hold PhDs, 11% are members of minority groups, 39% are women. 17% of classes are taught by teaching assistants.

ACADEMICS
Degrees: Bachelor's, doctoral, master's, post-bachelor's certificate, post-master's certificate. **Classes:** Most classes have 20–29 students. Most lab/discussion sessions have 10–19 students. **Majors with Highest Enrollment:** Biology/biological sciences; business/commerce; economics. **Special Study Options:** Accelerated program, cooperative education program, cross-registration, distance learning, double major, dual enrollment, English as a Second Language (ESL), exchange student program (domestic), honors program, independent study, internships, liberal arts/career combination, student-designed major, study abroad, teacher certification program. **Honors programs:** The Honors Program promotes an enriched academic environment for talented and highly motivated students. We foster values of social responsibility, inclusiveness and academic quality—in short a community of excellence. The Honors Program provides talented students with an enhanced undergraduate experience through a number of opportunities. Honors students typically enroll in one or two Honors classes each semester during their first two years. This will put students in contact with other students who set high goals for themselves, like to be challenged and are highly motivated. Rather than the large auditorium classes so many freshmen or sophomore students take, honors classes will be small and students will get to know their professors well. Students will have personal, intense advising at key moments in the next four years that will help them plan for graduation with the Honors degree at each step along the way. **Combined degree programs:** BA/MEng, Neuroscience MD/Phd. Special programs offered to physically disabled students include note-taking services, reader services, tape recorders, tutors. **Career services:** Alumni network, alumni services, career/job search classes, career assessment, internships.

FACILITIES
Housing: Coed dorms, special housing for disabled students, special housing for international students, fraternity/sorority housing, apartments for married students, theme housing, Limited Visitation, 24-hour Quiet, First Year Students only. 100% of campus accessible to physically disabled. **Special Academic Facilities/Equipment:** Museums of natural history and fine arts, government institute, environmental biological research facilities, human genetics lab.

Computers: 100% of classrooms, 100% of dorms, 100% of libraries, 100% of dining areas, 100% of student union, 60% of common outdoor areas have wireless network access. Students can register for classes online. Administrative functions (other than registration) can be performed online.

CAMPUS LIFE
Environment: Metropolis. **Activities:** Choral groups, concert band, dance, drama/theater, jazz band, literary magazine, marching band, music ensembles, musical theater, opera, pep band, radio station, student government, student newspaper, student-run film society, symphony orchestra, television station, campus ministries, international student organization, Model UN. **Organizations:** 238 registered organizations, 41 honor societies, 9 religious organizations. 7 fraternities, 6 sororities. **Athletics (Intercollegiate):** *Men:* Baseball, basketball, cheerleading, diving, football, golf, skiing (downhill/alpine), skiing (nordic/cross-country), swimming, tennis. *Women:* Basketball, cheerleading, cross-country, diving, gymnastics, skiing (downhill/alpine), skiing (nordic/cross-country), soccer, softball, swimming, tennis, track/field (outdoor), track/field (indoor), volleyball. **On-Campus Highlights:** Rice Eccles Stadium, Jon M. Huntsman Center, Huntsman Cancer Institute, Utah Museum of Fine Arts, Utah Museum of Natural History, Marriott Library Red Butte Gardens Olympic Cauldron Park Fort Douglas Museum and Cemetery Kingsbury Hall/Gardner Hall. **Environmental Initiatives:** 1. Transportation: Free public transportation (Ed-Pass) for all students, staff and faculty; gas-electric hybrid, biodiesel, and natural gas-powered campus vehicles. 2. Energy Initiatives: Offset more than 10% of our electricity consumption with windpower purchases; new co-generation plant under construction will cut outside energy purchases by another 10%, ongoing building retrofits for lighting, HVAC, and other efficiency gains. 3. Student Involvement: campus as a sustainability learning lab for courses; numerous on-campus "green" groups; environmental service opportunities with Bennion Community Service Center, student internships available through the Office of Sustainability, and also the greater community through Environmental Studies and Master's in Science and Technology programs.

ADMISSIONS
Freshman Academic Profile: Average high school GPA 3.52. 23% in top 10% of high school class, 48% in top 25% of high school class, 82% in top 50% of high school class. 96% from public high schools. SAT Math middle 50% range 500–630. SAT Critical Reading middle 50% range 490–630. SAT Writing middle 50% range 480–600. ACT middle 50% range 21–27. Minimum paper TOEFL 500. Minimum web-based TOEFL 61. **Basis for Candidate Selection:** *Very important factors considered include:* Academic GPA, rigor of secondary school record, standardized test scores. *Important factors considered include:* talent/ability. *Other factors considered include:* Class rank; recommendation(s), extracurricular activities, interview, racial/ethnic status. **Freshman Admission Requirements:** High school diploma is required and GED is accepted. *Academic units required:* 4 English, 2 mathematics, 3 science, (1 science labs), 2 foreign language, 1 history, 4 academic electives. **Freshman Admission Statistics:** 7,890 applied, 80% admitted, 43% enrolled. **Transfer Admission Requirements:** College transcript(s), statement of good standing from prior institution(s). Minimum college GPA of 2.6 required. Lowest grade transferable D-. **General Admission Information:** Application fee $45. Regular application deadline 4/1. Nonfall registration accepted. Credit and/or placement offered for CEEB Advanced Placement tests.

COSTS AND FINANCIAL AID
Average book expense $1,080. **Required Forms and Deadlines:** FAFSA, institution's own financial aid form. Priority financial aid filing date 4/1. **Notification of Awards:** Applicants will be notified of awards on a rolling basis beginning 4/15. **Types of Aid:** *Need-based scholarships/grants:* Federal Pell, SEOG, state scholarships/grants, private scholarships, the school's own gift aid, Federal Nursing Scholarships. ACG, National SMART Grant, and TEACH Grant. *Loans:* FFEL Subsidized Stafford, FFEL Unsubsidized Stafford, FFEL PLUS, Federal Perkins, Federal Nursing, college/university loans from institutional funds, Private Alternative Loans. *Student Employment:* Federal Work-Study Program available. Institutional employment available. Highest amount earned per year from on-campus jobs $8,800. Off-campus job opportunities are excellent. **Financial Aid Statistics:** 31% freshmen, 32% undergrads receive need-based scholarship or grant aid. 3% freshmen, 1% undergrads receive non-need-based scholarship or grant aid. 23% freshmen, 30% undergrads receive need-based self-help aid. 1% undergrads receive athletic scholarships. 40% freshmen, 40% undergrads receive any aid. 40% undergrads borrow to pay for school. Average cumulative indebtedness $15,201. **Criteria for awarding institutional aid:** *Non-need-based:* Academics, alumni affiliation, art, athletics, leadership, minority status, music/drama, state/district residency.

UNIVERSITY OF VERMONT

Admissions Office, 194 South Prospect Street, Burlington, VT 05401-3596
Phone: 802-656-3370 **Financial Aid Phone:** 802-656-5700
E-mail: admissions@uvm.edu **CEEB Code:** 3920
Fax: 802-656-8611 **Website:** www.uvm.edu **ACT Code:** 4322

This public school was founded in 1791. It has a 460-acre campus.

RATINGS
Admissions Selectivity Rating: 83   **Fire Safety Rating:** 89   **Green Rating:** 93

STUDENTS AND FACULTY
Enrollment: 10,371. **Student Body:** 56% female, 44% male, 65% out-of-state, 1% international (54 countries represented). Asian 2%, African American 1%, Caucasian 91%, Hispanic 2%.
Retention and Graduation: 85% freshmen return for sophomore year. 57% freshmen graduate within 4 years. 25% grads go on to further study within 1 year. 7% grads pursue arts and sciences degrees. 2% grads pursue law degrees. 1% grads pursue business degrees. 3% grads pursue medical degrees. **Faculty:** Student/faculty ratio 17:1. 597 full-time faculty, 86% hold PhDs, 15% are members of minority groups, 41% are women. 2% of classes are taught by teaching assistants.

ACADEMICS
Degrees: Bachelor's, master's, post-bachelor's certificate, post-master's certificate. **Classes:** Most classes have fewer than 10 students. Most lab/discussion sessions have 20–29 students. **Majors with Highest Enrollment:** Biology/biological sciences; business administration and management; psychology. **Special Study Options:** Cooperative education program, distance learning, double major, dual enrollment, exchange student program (domestic), honors program, independent study, internships, liberal arts/career combination, student-designed major, study abroad, teacher certification program, Evening University option in several programs. **Honors programs:** University wide Honors College, a residential learning community where students live together and take classes in one of UVM's newest residence halls. Honors College students are simultaneously enrolled in one of seven other UVM undergraduate colleges or schools. Honors College courses comprise approximately 20% of a students overall coursework and include a year-long common first year seminar, a choice of a variety of sophomore seminars, a junior year thesis prep course, and a senior year thesis, creative project or practicum. Upon graduation program completers are designated as Honors College Scholars. **Combined degree programs:** BA/JD, BS/DVM with Tufts University, BA/BS-DPT. Special programs offered to physically disabled students include note-taking services, reader services, tape recorders, tutors. **Career services:** alumni services, career assessment, internships. **Career services highlights include:** Dollar Enterprise, an award winning service learning activity in which students are provided with $1 of working capital and develop and run a campus based entrepreneurial activity for one week. The activity is done for one week. All profits are donated to a charity of the group's choice.

FACILITIES
Housing: Coed dorms, fraternity/sorority housing, apartments for married students, apartments for single students, wellness housing, theme housing. 90% of campus accessible to physically disabled. **Special Academic Facilities/Equipment:** Art/ethnography museum, chemistry/physics library, medical library, on-campus preschool, government research and world affairs centers, agricultural experiment station, horse farm, multinuclear magnetic resonance spectrometers, mass spectrometer. **Computers:** 10% of classrooms, 15% of dorms, 100% of libraries, 100% of dining areas, 100% of student union, 5% of common outdoor areas have wireless network access. Students can register for classes online. Administrative functions (other than registration) can be performed online.

CAMPUS LIFE
Environment: Town. **Activities:** Choral groups, concert band, dance, drama/theater, jazz band, literary magazine, music ensembles, musical theater, pep band, radio station, student government, student newspaper, student-run film society, symphony orchestra, television station, campus ministries, international student organization. **Organizations:** 140 registered organizations, 30 honor societies, 10 religious organizations. 9 fraternities, 6 sororities. **Athletics (Intercollegiate):** *Men:* Basketball, cross-country, ice hockey, lacrosse, skiing (downhill/alpine), skiing (nordic/cross-country), soccer, track/field (outdoor), track/field (indoor). *Women:* Basketball, cross-country, diving, field hockey, ice hockey, lacrosse, skiing (downhill/alpine), skiing (nordic/cross-country), soccer, swimming, track/field (outdoor), track/field (indoor). **On-Campus Highlights:** Davis Student Center, Fleming Museum, Campus Green, Athletic Complex/Fitness Center, Spear Street Research Farm and Equine Center. **Environmental Initiatives:** Office of Sustainability supports infusion of sustainability into operations, student life, curriculum, and communications. Eco-Reps Program provides peer education in residence halls, supports campus-wide events, develops student leaders, and connects them with key administrative, faculty, and community leaders. LEED Silver minimum has changed thinking on cmapus; energy efficiency investments have yielded millions of dollars in avoided costs; Clean Energy Fund is teaching us about renewables

ADMISSIONS
Freshman Academic Profile: 29% in top 10% of high school class, 66% in top 25% of high school class, 96% in top 50% of high school class. 70% from public high schools. SAT Math middle 50% range 550–640. SAT Critical Reading middle 50% range 540–640. SAT Writing middle 50% range 540–640. ACT middle 50% range 24–28. Minimum paper TOEFL 550. Minimum computer TOEFL 213. **Basis for Candidate Selection:** *Very important factors considered include:* Rigor of secondary school record. *Important factors considered include:* Class rank, application essay, academic GPA, standardized test scores, character/personal qualities, state residency. *Other factors considered include:* Recommendation(s), alumni/ae relation, extracurricular activities, first generation, geographical residence, interview, level of applicant's interest, racial/ethnic status, talent/ability, volunteer work, work experience. **Freshman Admission Requirements:** High school diploma is required and GED is accepted. *Academic units required:* 4 English, 3 mathematics, 2 science, (1 science labs), 2 foreign language, 3 social studies. **Freshman Admission Statistics:** 22,365 applied, 71% admitted, 17% enrolled. **Transfer Admission Requirements:** High school transcript, college transcript(s), essay or personal statement, minimum college GPA of 2.5 required. Lowest grade transferable C. **General Admission Information:** Application fee $45. Regular application deadline 1/15. Regular notification 3/31. Nonfall registration accepted. Admission may be deferred for a maximum of 1 year. Credit and/or placement offered for CEEB Advanced Placement tests.

COSTS AND FINANCIAL AID
Annual in-state tuition $11,712. Annual out-of-state tuition $29,568. Room and board $8,996. Required fees $1,842. Average book expense $1,050. **Required Forms and Deadlines:** FAFSA. Priority financial aid filing date 2/10. **Notification of Awards:** Applicants will be notified of awards on a rolling basis beginning 3/15. **Types of Aid:** *Need-based scholarships/grants:* Federal Pell, SEOG, state scholarships/grants, private scholarships, the school's own gift aid, Federal Nursing Scholarships. *Loans:* FFEL Subsidized Stafford, FFEL Unsubsidized Stafford, FFEL PLUS, Federal Perkins, Federal Nursing, college/university loans from institutional funds. *Student Employment:* Federal Work-Study Program available. Institutional employment available. Off-campus job opportunities are good. **Financial Aid Statistics:** 55% freshmen, 50% undergrads receive need-based scholarship or grant aid. 4% freshmen, 3% undergrads receive non-need-based scholarship or grant aid. 48% freshmen, 47% undergrads receive need-based self-help aid. 2% freshmen, 2% undergrads receive athletic scholarships. 90% freshmen, 84% undergrads receive any aid. 63% undergrads borrow to pay for school. Average cumulative indebtedness $27,682. **Criteria for awarding institutional aid:** *Non-need-based:* Academics, art, athletics.

UNIVERSITY OF THE VIRGIN ISLANDS

2 John Brewers Bay, St. Thomas, VI 00802-9990
Phone: 340-693-1150
E-mail: admissions@uvi.edu **CEEB Code:** 879
Fax: 340-693-1220 **Website:** www.uvi.edu

This public school was founded in 1962.

RATINGS
Admissions Selectivity Rating: 60*   **Fire Safety Rating:** 60*   **Green Rating:** 60*

STUDENTS AND FACULTY
Enrollment: 1,972. **Student Body:** 80% female, 20% male, 36% out-of-state, 7% international. Asian 1%, African American 71%, Caucasian 2%, Hispanic 3%.
Retention and Graduation: Faculty: Student/faculty ratio 14:1. 99 full-time faculty, 68% hold PhDs, 53% are members of minority groups, 44% are women.

ACADEMICS
Degrees: Associate, master's. **Classes: Special Study Options:** Cooperative education program, distance learning, dual enrollment, exchange student program (domestic), independent study, internships, teacher certification program.

FACILITIES

Housing: Men's dorms, women's dorms. **Computers:** Administrative functions (other than registration) can be performed online.

CAMPUS LIFE

Environment: Village. **Activities:** Choral groups, concert band, dance, drama/theater, jazz band, music ensembles, student government, student newspaper, yearbook. **Organizations:** 27 registered organizations, 2 honor societies, 2 religious organizations. 1 fraternities, 3 sororities. **Athletics (Intercollegiate):** *Men:* Basketball, soccer, swimming, tennis, volleyball. *Women:* Basketball, swimming, tennis, volleyball.

ADMISSIONS

Freshman Academic Profile: SAT Math middle 50% range 330–450. SAT Critical Reading middle 50% range 360–470. **Basis for Candidate Selection:** *Very important factors considered include:* Rigor of secondary school record. *Other factors considered include:* Standardized test scores, state residency. **Freshman Admission Requirements:** High school diploma is required and GED is accepted. *Academic units recommended:* 4 English, 2 mathematics, 2 science, 1 foreign language, 2 social studies. **Freshman Admission Statistics:** 854 applied, 73% admitted, 45% enrolled. **Transfer Admission Requirements:** High school transcript, college transcript(s), statement of good standing from prior institution(s). Minimum college GPA of 2.0 required. Lowest grade transferable C. **General Admission Information:** Application fee $20. Regular application deadline 4/30. Nonfall registration accepted. Admission may be deferred for a maximum of not specific.

COSTS AND FINANCIAL AID

Annual in-state tuition $1,500. Annual out-of-state tuition $4,500. Room and board $2,715. Required fees $133. Average book expense $400. **Types of Aid:** *Need-based scholarships/grants:* Federal Pell.

UNIVERSITY OF VIRGINIA

Office of Admission, PO Box 400160, Charlottesville, VA 22906
Phone: 434-982-3200 **Financial Aid Phone:** 434-982-6000
E-mail: undergradadmission@virginia.edu **CEEB Code:** 5820
Fax: 434-924-3587 **Website:** www.virginia.edu **ACT Code:** 4412

This public school was founded in 1819. It has a 1167-acre campus.

RATINGS

Admissions Selectivity Rating: 98   **Fire Safety Rating:** 69   **Green Rating:** 92

STUDENTS AND FACULTY

Enrollment: 14,225. **Student Body:** 56% female, 44% male, 28% out-of-state, 5% international (130 countries represented). Asian 12%, African American 8%, Caucasian 60%, Hispanic 4%.
Retention and Graduation: 97% freshmen return for sophomore year. **Faculty:** Student/faculty ratio 15.9:1. 1220 full-time faculty, 92% hold PhDs, 12% are members of minority groups, 33% are women. 19% of classes are taught by teaching assistants.

ACADEMICS

Degrees: Bachelor's, master's, post-master's certificate. **Classes:** Most classes have 10–19 students. Most lab/discussion sessions have 20–29 students. **Majors with Highest Enrollment:** Business/commerce; economics; history. **Special Study Options:** Accelerated program, cooperative education program, double major, English as a Second Language (ESL), exchange student program (domestic), honors program, independent study, internships, liberal arts/career combination, student-designed major, study abroad, teacher certification program, Special January term (during Winter Break) where students can take one course. Semester at Sea option of spending an academic semester on board a ship travelling to multiple countries. **Honors programs:** Jefferson Scholars: Full scholarship given to approximately 30 students per year. Special lectures and discussions with distinguished University faculty; all first year Jefferson Scholars take part in an outdoor leadership experience; all rising-second year Jefferson Scholars, prior to the beginning of school, participate in a two-week Institute for Leadership and Citizenship designed to foster a deeper understanding of the art of leadership and the importance of citizenship. Additionally, all Jefferson Scholars are granted an opportunity to travel and study abroad between their second and third year. Scholars may elect to spend three weeks of study at either Regent's College in England or the Erasmus Institute in Tuscany,

Italy. Following the structured tutorial, each Scholar designs and completes two weeks of travel and independent inquiry. Echols Scholars-School of Arts and Sciences. Separate dormitory, with Rodman Scholars, for first-year students. Flexible degree requirements; exemption from some requirements; preference for courses. Rodman Scholars-School of Engineering and Applied Sciences. Separate dormitory, with Echols Scholars, for first-year students. Special courses designed only for Rodman Scholars in first two years. **Combined degree programs:** 5-year B.A./M.Teaching. Special programs offered to physically disabled students include note-taking services, reader services, tape recorders, tutors. **Career services:** Alumni network, alumni services, career/job search classes, career assessment, internships, regional alumni. **Career services highlights include:** (a tie) (1) on-grounds interviewing because, for our size school, we not only have an exceedingly robust program (7,000 to 10,000 individual student interviews per year; and most of the top tier organizations you'd find listed in the Fortune 100), but also because student interviews here are very often evenly distributed among the College, Commerce, and SEAS (Engineering School); and, (2) the dramatic growth and popularity of our internship programs among our students—not only corporate internships, but also non-profit/public policy/community service internships, an initiative you rarely find on a large public university campus.

FACILITIES

Housing: Coed dorms, special housing for international students, fraternity/sorority housing, apartments for married students, apartments for single students, theme housing, French, German, Spanish and Russian houses, a multi-lingual house, and three residential colleges. 100% of campus accessible to physically disabled. **Special Academic Facilities/Equipment:** 15 libraries, art museum, experimental farm, biological station, observatory/planetarium, nuclear information center, media center (multimedia editing). **Computers:** 100% of classrooms, 100% of dorms, 100% of libraries, 100% of dining areas, 100% of student union, 26–50% of common outdoor areas have wireless network access. Students can register for classes online. Administrative functions (other than registration) can be performed online.

CAMPUS LIFE

Environment: City. **Activities:** Choral groups, concert band, dance, drama/theater, jazz band, literary magazine, marching band, music ensembles, musical theater, opera, pep band, radio station, student government, student newspaper, student-run film society, symphony orchestra, television station, campus ministries, international student organization, Model UN. **Organizations:** 7 honor societies, 44 religious organizations. 28 fraternities, 15 sororities. **Athletics (Intercollegiate):** *Men:* Baseball, basketball, cross-country, diving, football, golf, lacrosse, soccer, swimming, tennis, track/field (outdoor), track/field (indoor), wrestling. *Women:* Basketball, crew/rowing, cross-country, diving, field hockey, golf, lacrosse, soccer, softball, swimming, tennis, track/field (outdoor), track/field (indoor), volleyball. **On-Campus Highlights:** Rotunda/Academical Village (orig campus), Alderman and Clemons Libraries, John Paul Jones Arena, Football and Soccer Stadiums, Aquatic and Fitness Center, Location of the future "arts precinct"; new library housing original rare and early American manuscripts; Birdwood Golf Course; Observatory; Old Cabell Hall (music performances); Culbreth Theatre (drama); Newcomb Hall (student services building); University of Virginia Bookstore. **Environmental Initiatives:** Academics: The University of Virginia offers 70+ courses in 8 different schools with significant focus on sustainability, including a global sustainability course, a new course model cross listed and taught jointly by faculty from Engineering, Architecture, and Commerce. Sustainable Design and Construction: The University's policy to achieve LEED certification on all new buildings and major renovations has led to 30 projects registered with the U.S. Green Building Council, with 2 of these complete and certified (1 Gold, 1 Silver). Ongoing efficiency and conservation efforts, including: award winning recycling and stormwater management program, extensive building retro-commissioning team, Environmental Management System implementation across multiple departments, and Green Dining that include composting, reusable to-go containers, and local farm relationships.

ADMISSIONS

Freshman Academic Profile: Average high school GPA 4.11. 89% in top 10% of high school class, 97% in top 25% of high school class, 99% in top 50% of high school class. 76% from public high schools. SAT Math middle 50% range 630–730. SAT Critical Reading middle 50% range 600–710. SAT Writing middle 50% range 610–710. ACT middle 50% range 27–32. **Basis for Candidate Selection:** *Very important factors considered include:* Class rank, academic GPA, recommendation(s), rigor of secondary school record, alumni/ae relation, first generation, racial/ethnic status, state residency. *Important factors considered include:* Application essay, standardized test scores, character/personal qualities, extracurricular activities, talent/ability. *Other factors considered include:* geographical residence, volunteer work, work experience. **Freshman Admission Requirements:** High school diploma is required and GED is accepted. *Academic units required:* 4 English, 4 mathematics, 2 science, 2 foreign language, 1 social studies. *Academic units recommended:* 5 mathematics, 4 science, 5 foreign language, 4 social studies. **Freshman Admission Statistics:** 21,108 applied, 32% admitted, 48% enrolled. **Transfer Admission Requirements:** High school transcript, college transcript(s), essay or personal statement, standardized test scores, statement of good standing from prior institution(s). Minimum college GPA of 2.0 required. Lowest grade transferable C. **General Admission Information:** Application fee $60. Regular application deadline 1/1. Regular notification 4/1. Nonfall registration not accepted. Admission may be deferred for a maximum of 1 year. Credit and/or placement offered for CEEB Advanced Placement tests.

COSTS AND FINANCIAL AID

Required Forms and Deadlines: FAFSA, institution's own financial aid form. Priority financial aid filing date 3/1. **Notification of Awards:** Applicants will be notified of awards on or about 4/5. **Types of Aid:** *Need-based scholarships/ grants:* Federal Pell, SEOG, state scholarships/grants, private scholarships, the school's own gift aid, Federal Nursing Scholarships. *Loans:* FFEL Subsidized Stafford, FFEL Unsubsidized Stafford, FFEL PLUS, Federal Perkins, Federal Nursing, college/university loans from institutional funds, Alternative/Private Loans. *Student Employment:* Federal Work-Study Program available. Institutional employment available. **Financial Aid Statistics:** 28% freshmen, 25% undergrads receive need-based scholarship or grant aid. 4% freshmen, 3% undergrads receive non-need-based scholarship or grant aid. 19% freshmen, 18% undergrads receive need-based self-help aid. 3% freshmen, 3% undergrads receive athletic scholarships. 58% freshmen, 51% undergrads receive any aid. 33.9% undergrads borrow to pay for school. Average cumulative indebtedness $19,939. **Criteria for awarding institutional aid:** *Non-need-based:* Academics, athletics, leadership, minority status, music/drama, state/district residency.

UNIVERSITY OF VIRGINIA'S COLLEGE AT WISE

1 College Avenue, Wise, VA 24293
Phone: 276-328-0102
E-mail: admissions@uvawise.edu **CEEB Code:** 5124
Fax: 276-328-0251 **Website:** www.uvawise.edu **ACT Code:** 4343

This public school was founded in 1954. It has a 367-acre campus.

RATINGS
Admissions Selectivity Rating: 77 **Fire Safety Rating:** 60* **Green Rating:** 60*

STUDENTS AND FACULTY
Enrollment: 1,629. **Student Body:** 52% female, 48% male, 5% out-of-state, international. Asian 1%, African American 7%, Caucasian 90%, Hispanic 2%. **Retention and Graduation:** 73% freshmen return for sophomore year. 25% freshmen graduate within 4 years. 14% grads go on to further study within 1 year. 7% grads pursue arts and sciences degrees. 6% grads pursue law degrees. 4% grads pursue business degrees. 1% grads pursue medical degrees. **Faculty:** Student/faculty ratio 16:1. 91 full-time faculty, 29% hold PhDs, 13% are members of minority groups, 41% are women.

ACADEMICS
Degrees: Bachelor's. **Classes:** Most classes have 10–19 students. Most lab/discussion sessions have 10–19 students. **Special Study Options:** Accelerated program, cooperative education program, distance learning, double major, dual enrollment, honors program, independent study, internships, student-designed major, study abroad, teacher certification program. Special programs offered to physically disabled students include note-taking services, reader services, tape recorders, tutors. **Career services:** Alumni services, career/job search classes, career assessment, internships.

FACILITIES
Housing: Coed dorms, special housing for disabled students, men's dorms, women's dorms, apartments for single students. 95% of campus accessible to physically disabled. **Computers:** Administrative functions (other than registration) can be performed online.

CAMPUS LIFE
Environment: Rural. **Activities:** Choral groups, concert band, dance, drama/theater, literary magazine, music ensembles, musical theater, pep band, radio station, student government, student newspaper, television station, yearbook. **Organizations:** 40 registered organizations, 3 honor societies, 3 religious organizations. 3 fraternities, 2 sororities. **Athletics (Intercollegiate):** *Men:* Baseball, basketball, cross-country, football, golf, tennis, track/field (outdoor). *Women:* Basketball, cross-country, softball, tennis, track/field (outdoor), volleyball.

ADMISSIONS
Freshman Academic Profile: Average high school GPA 3.3. 18% in top 10% of high school class, 40% in top 25% of high school class, 78% in top

50% of high school class. 99% from public high schools. SAT Math middle 50% range 430–530. SAT Critical Reading middle 50% range 420–530. SAT Writing middle 50% range 16–21. ACT middle 50% range 16–21. Minimum paper TOEFL 550. **Basis for Candidate Selection:** *Very important factors considered include:* Class rank, rigor of secondary school record. *Important factors considered include:* Standardized test scores, talent/ability. *Other factors considered include:* Application essay, recommendation(s), character/personal qualities, extracurricular activities, interview, racial/ethnic status, volunteer work, work experience. **Freshman Admission Requirements:** High school diploma is required and GED is accepted. *Academic units required:* 4 English, 3 mathematics, 2 science, (2 science labs), 2 foreign language, 1 social studies, 1 history, 5 academic electives. **Freshman Admission Statistics:** 1,084 applied, 81% admitted, 45% enrolled. **Transfer Admission Requirements:** College transcript(s), minimum college GPA of 2.3 required. Lowest grade transferable C–. **General Admission Information:** Application fee $25. Regular application deadline 8/1. Notification on a rolling basis, beginning on or about 9/15. Nonfall registration accepted. Admission may be deferred for a maximum of 1 year. Credit and/or placement offered for CEEB Advanced Placement tests.

COSTS AND FINANCIAL AID
Required Forms and Deadlines: FAFSA. Priority financial aid filing date 4/1. **Notification of Awards:** Applicants will be notified of awards on a rolling basis beginning 4/1. **Types of Aid:** *Need-based scholarships/grants:* Federal Pell, SEOG, state scholarships/grants, private scholarships, the school's own gift aid. *Loans:* FFEL Subsidized Stafford, FFEL Unsubsidized Stafford, FFEL PLUS, Federal Perkins, state loans, college/university loans from institutional funds. *Student Employment:* Federal Work-Study Program available. Institutional employment available. Highest amount earned per year from on-campus jobs $900. Off-campus job opportunities are fair. **Financial Aid Statistics: Criteria for awarding institutional aid:** *Non-need-based:* Academics, alumni affiliation, art, athletics, job skills, leadership, music/drama, state/district residency.

UNIVERSITY OF WASHINGTON

1410 NE Campus Parkway, UW Box 355852, Seattle, WA 98195-5852
Phone: 206-543-9686 **Financial Aid Phone:** 206-543-6101
E-mail: CEEB Code: 4854
Fax: 206-685-3655 **Website:** www.washington.edu **ACT Code:** 4484

This public school was founded in 1861. It has a 700-acre campus.

RATINGS
Admissions Selectivity Rating: 94 **Fire Safety Rating:** 94 **Green Rating:** 96

STUDENTS AND FACULTY
Enrollment: 27,365. **Student Body:** 52% female, 48% male, 12% out-of-state, 5% international (107 countries represented). Asian 28%, African American 3%, Caucasian 52%, Hispanic 6%, Native American 1%. **Retention and Graduation:** 93% freshmen return for sophomore year. 51% freshmen graduate within 4 years. **Faculty:** Student/faculty ratio 11:1. 3019 full-time faculty, 89% hold PhDs, 20% are members of minority groups, 37% are women.

ACADEMICS
Degrees: Bachelor's, first professional, first professional certificate, master's, post-master's certificate. **Classes:** Most classes have 20–29 students. Most lab/discussion sessions have 20–29 students. **Majors with Highest Enrollment:** Economics; political science and government; psychology. **Special Study Options:** Cooperative education program, distance learning, double major, English as a Second Language (ESL), exchange student program (domestic), honors program, independent study, internships, student-designed major, study abroad, teacher certification program, Friday Harbor Labs. **Honors programs:** We have a University Honors Program, as well as departmental honors options. Special programs offered to physically disabled students include note-taking services, reader services, tape recorders, tutors. **Career services:** Alumni network, alumni services, career/job search classes, career assessment, internships, regional alumni.

FACILITIES
Housing: Coed dorms, special housing for disabled students, special housing for international students, fraternity/sorority housing, apartments for married students, apartments for single students, theme housing. 100% of campus

accessible to physically disabled. **Special Academic Facilities/Equipment:** Multiple art galleries, an anthropology and natural history museum, arboretum, closed-circuit TV studio. **Computers:** 100% of dorms, 100% of libraries, 100% of student union, have wireless network access. Students can register for classes online. Administrative functions (other than registration) can be performed online.

CAMPUS LIFE

Environment: Metropolis. **Activities:** Choral groups, concert band, dance, drama/theater, jazz band, literary magazine, marching band, music ensembles, musical theater, opera, pep band, radio station, student government, student newspaper, student-run film society, symphony orchestra, television station, campus ministries, international student organization, Model UN. **Organizations:** 711 registered organizations, 13 honor societies, 52 religious organizations. 31 fraternities, 16 sororities. **Athletics (Intercollegiate):** *Men:* Baseball, basketball, crew/rowing, cross-country, football, golf, soccer, tennis, track/field (outdoor). *Women:* Basketball, crew/rowing, cross-country, golf, gymnastics, soccer, softball, tennis, track/field (outdoor), volleyball. **On-Campus Highlights:** Henry Art Gallery, Burke Museum, Meany Hall for Performing Arts, football games at Husky Stadium, Waterfront Activities Center (WAC). **Environmental Initiatives:** College of the Environment http://coenv.washington.edu/ Environmental Stewardship and Sustainability Office; Strategy Management Finance and Facilities http://green.washington.edu. This office supports the Environmental Stewardship Advisory Committee (ESAC) http://green.washington.edu/esac. Charter signatory of the American College & University Presidents Climate Commitment (ACUPCC); development and submission of a Climate Action Plan http://green.washington.edu/cap.

ADMISSIONS

Freshman Academic Profile: Average high school GPA 3.72. 87% in top 10% of high school class, 13% in top 25% of high school class, 100% in top 50% of high school class. SAT Math middle 50% range 570–680. SAT Critical Reading middle 50% range 530–650. SAT Writing middle 50% range 530–640. ACT middle 50% range 24–29. Minimum paper TOEFL 537. Minimum computer TOEFL 207. Minimum web-based TOEFL 76. **Basis for Candidate Selection:** *Very important factors considered include:* Application essay, academic GPA, rigor of secondary school record. *Important factors considered include:* Standardized test scores, character/personal qualities, extracurricular activities, first generation, talent/ability, volunteer work, work experience. *Other factors considered include:* State residency. **Freshman Admission Requirements:** High school diploma or equivalent is not required. *Academic units required:* 4 English, 3 mathematics, 2 science, (1 science labs), 2 foreign language, 3 social studies. *Academic units recommended:* 4 English, 4 mathematics, 3 science, (3 science labs), 3 foreign language, 4 social studies, 1 history, 1 visual/performing arts, 1 computer science. **Freshman Admission Statistics:** 20,224 applied, 61% admitted, 45% enrolled. **Transfer Admission Requirements:** High school transcript, college transcript(s), essay or personal statement, minimum college GPA of 2.5 required. Lowest grade transferable .7. **General Admission Information:** Application fee $50. Regular application deadline 1/15. Regular notification 4/15. Notification on a rolling basis, beginning on or about 11/1. Nonfall registration accepted. Credit and/or placement offered for CEEB Advanced Placement tests.

COSTS AND FINANCIAL AID

Annual in-state tuition $7,692. Annual out-of-state tuition $24,367. **Required Forms and Deadlines:** FAFSA. Priority financial aid filing date 2/28. **Notification of Awards:** Applicants will be notified of awards on or about 3/31. **Types of Aid:** *Need-based scholarships/grants:* Federal Pell, SEOG, state scholarships/grants, private scholarships, the school's own gift aid. *Loans:* Direct Subsidized Stafford, Direct Unsubsidized Stafford, Direct PLUS, Federal Perkins, Federal Nursing, college/university loans from institutional funds. *Student Employment:* Federal Work-Study Program available. Institutional employment available. Off-campus job opportunities are excellent. **Financial Aid Statistics:** 29% freshmen, 29% undergrads receive need-based scholarship or grant aid. 7% freshmen, 4% undergrads receive non-need-based scholarship or grant aid. 21% freshmen, 24% undergrads receive need-based self-help aid. 1% freshmen, 1% undergrads receive athletic scholarships. 50% freshmen, 50% undergrads receive any aid. 50% undergrads borrow to pay for school. Average cumulative indebtedness $16,800. **Criteria for awarding institutional aid:** *Non-need-based:* Academics, alumni affiliation, art, athletics, leadership, music/drama.

UNIVERSITY OF WEST ALABAMA

Station 4, Livingston, AL 35470
Phone: 888-636-8800
E-mail: admissions@uwa.edu **CEEB Code:** 1737
Fax: 205-652-3522 **Website:** www.uwa.edu **ACT Code:** 24

This public school was founded in 1835. It has a 600-acre campus.

RATINGS
Admissions Selectivity Rating: 60*   **Fire Safety Rating:** 60*   **Green Rating:** 60*

STUDENTS AND FACULTY
Enrollment: 1,945. **Student Body:** 61% female, 39% male, 19% out-of-state, international. African American 47%, Caucasian 36%, Hispanic 1%. **Retention and Graduation:** 15% grads go on to further study within 1 year. 12% grads pursue arts and sciences degrees. 1% grads pursue law degrees. 1% grads pursue business degrees. 1% grads pursue medical degrees. **Faculty:** Student/faculty ratio 19:1. 116 full-time faculty, 79% hold PhDs, 16% are members of minority groups, 47% are women.

ACADEMICS
Degrees: Associate, bachelor's, master's. **Classes:** Most classes have fewer than 10 students. Most lab/discussion sessions have 10–19 students. **Special Study Options:** Accelerated program, cooperative education program, distance learning, double major, dual enrollment, exchange student program (domestic), honors program, independent study, internships, teacher certification program. **Combined degree programs:** BA/MEng, 2-yr transfer program in fisheries and wildlife ma. Special programs offered to physically disabled students include tutors. **Career services:** Alumni services, career assessment.

FACILITIES
Housing: Coed dorms, men's dorms, women's dorms, apartments for married students, apartments for single students. 100% of campus accessible to physically disabled. **Computers:** Administrative functions (other than registration) can be performed online.

CAMPUS LIFE
Environment: Rural. **Activities:** Choral groups, concert band, dance, drama/theater, marching band, student government, student newspaper, television station, yearbook, campus ministries, international student organization. **Organizations:** 30 registered organizations, 8 honor societies, 5 religious organizations. 7 fraternities, 6 sororities. **Athletics (Intercollegiate):** *Men:* Baseball, basketball, cheerleading, cross-country, football, rodeo. *Women:* Basketball, cheerleading, cross-country, rodeo, softball, volleyball.

ADMISSIONS
Freshman Academic Profile: 88% from public high schools. ACT middle 50% range 18–34. Minimum paper TOEFL 500. **Basis for Candidate Selection:** *Very important factors considered include:* Rigor of secondary school record, standardized test scores. **Freshman Admission Requirements:** High school diploma is required and GED is accepted. *Academic units required:* 3 English, 3 mathematics, 3 science, 3 social studies, 3 academic electives. **Freshman Admission Statistics:** 690 applied, 61% admitted, 73% enrolled. **Transfer Admission Requirements:** College transcript(s), statement of good standing from prior institution(s). Minimum college GPA of 2.0 required. Lowest grade transferable C. **General Admission Information:** Application fee $50. Nonfall registration accepted. Admission may be deferred for a maximum of 1 year. Credit and/or placement offered for CEEB Advanced Placement tests.

COSTS AND FINANCIAL AID
Annual in-state tuition $5,060. Annual out-of-state tuition $10,120. Room and board $3,748. Required fees $360. Average book expense $900. **Required Forms and Deadlines:** FAFSA. Priority financial aid filing date 4/1. **Notification of Awards:** Applicants will be notified of awards on a rolling basis beginning 6/1. **Types of Aid:** *Need-based scholarships/grants:* Federal Pell, SEOG, state scholarships/grants, the school's own gift aid. *Loans:* FFEL Subsidized Stafford, FFEL Unsubsidized Stafford, FFEL PLUS, Federal Perkins, Stafford Federal Loan Teacher Loan Forgiveness. *Student Employment:* Federal Work-Study Program available. Highest amount earned per year from on-campus jobs $1,317. Off-campus job opportunities are good. **Financial Aid Statistics:** 47% freshmen, 48% undergrads receive need-based scholarship or grant aid. 39% freshmen, 37% undergrads receive non-need-based scholarship or grant aid. 40% freshmen, 22% undergrads receive need-based self-help aid. 8% freshmen, 7% undergrads receive athletic scholarships. 54% undergrads borrow to pay for school. Average cumulative indebtedness $3,846. **Criteria for awarding institutional aid:** *Non-need-based:* Academics, alumni affiliation, athletics, leadership, music/drama, state/district residency.

UNIVERSITY OF WEST FLORIDA

11000 University Parkway, Pensacola, FL 32514-5750
Phone: 850-474-2230 **Financial Aid Phone:** 850-474-2400
E-mail: admissions@uwf.edu **CEEB Code:** 5833
Fax: 850-474-3360 **Website:** http://uwf.edu **ACT Code:** 771

This public school was founded in 1963. It has a 1600-acre campus.

RATINGS
Admissions Selectivity Rating: 87   **Fire Safety Rating:** 82   **Green Rating:** 84

STUDENTS AND FACULTY
Enrollment: 8,718. **Student Body:** 59% female, 41% male, 9% out-of-state, 1% international (80 countries represented). Asian 5%, African American 10%, Caucasian 76%, Hispanic 6%, Native American 1%.
Retention and Graduation: 21% freshmen graduate within 4 years. **Faculty:** Student/faculty ratio 22:1. 312 full-time faculty, 81% hold PhDs, 17% are members of minority groups, 41% are women.

ACADEMICS
Degrees: Associate, bachelor's, doctoral, master's, post-master's certificate. **Classes:** Most classes have 20–29 students. Most lab/discussion sessions have 20–29 students. **Majors with Highest Enrollment:** Elementary education and teaching; mass communication/media studies; psychology. **Special Study Options:** Cooperative education program, distance learning, dual enrollment, exchange student program (domestic), honors program, independent study, internships, study abroad, teacher certification program, learning disability services. **Combined degree programs:** BS/MS Biology,Chemistry—called Fast Track. Special programs offered to physically disabled students include note-taking services, reader services, tape recorders, tutors. **Career services:** career assessment. **Career services highlights include:** UWF is an accredited cooperative education school. We offer the Myers Briggs Type Indicator and Strong Interest Inventory as career assessments.

FACILITIES
Housing: Coed dorms, fraternity/sorority housing, apartments for married students, apartments for single students, Special dorm rooms for disabled students. 80% of campus accessible to physically disabled. **Special Academic Facilities/Equipment:** Archeology museum,instructional media center, biology, chemistry, physics, and psychology labs, property on the Gulf of Mexico for marine and ecology research. **Computers:** 100% of classrooms, 100% of libraries, 100% of dining areas, 100% of student union, 100% of common outdoor areas have wireless network access. Students can register for classes online. Administrative functions (other than registration) can be performed online.

CAMPUS LIFE
Environment: City. **Activities:** Choral groups, concert band, dance, drama/theater, jazz band, music ensembles, musical theater, radio station, student government, student newspaper, symphony orchestra, television station. **Organizations:** 157 registered organizations, 15 honor societies, 17 religious organizations. 10 fraternities, 7 sororities. **Athletics (Intercollegiate):** *Men:* Baseball, basketball, cross-country, golf, soccer, tennis. *Women:* Basketball, cross-country, golf, soccer, softball, tennis, volleyball. **On-Campus Highlights:** The Commons (has cafeteria and bookstore), Fitness Facilities, Center for Fine and Performing Arts, Nature Trails, Library, Archeology Institute Artifact Display. **Environmental Initiatives:** All new buildings must be at least LEED Silver certified; energy consumption program; environmentally friendly/green purchasing initiative.

ADMISSIONS
Freshman Academic Profile: Average high school GPA 3.46. 18% in top 10% of high school class, 43% in top 25% of high school class, 79% in top 50% of high school class. 92% from public high schools. SAT Math middle 50% range 470–570. SAT Critical Reading middle 50% range 490–590. ACT middle 50% range 21–25. Minimum paper TOEFL 525. Minimum computer TOEFL 213. **Basis for Candidate Selection:** *Very important factors considered include:* Academic GPA, rigor of secondary school record, standardized test scores, state residency. *Other factors considered include:* Class rank, application essay, recommendation(s), alumni/ae relation, character/personal qualities, extracurricular activities, first generation, geographical residence, level of applicant's interest, talent/ability, volunteer work, work experience. **Freshman Admission Requirements:** High school diploma is required and GED is accepted. *Academic units required:* 4 English, 3 mathematics, 3 science, (2 science labs), 2 foreign language, 3 social studies, 4 academic electives. **Freshman Admission Statistics:** 4,513 applied, 70% admitted, 35% enrolled. **Transfer Admission Requirements:** College transcript(s); minimum college GPA of 2.0 required. Lowest grade transferable D. **General Admission Information:** Application fee $30. Regular application deadline 6/30. Notification on a rolling basis,

beginning on or about 10/1. Nonfall registration accepted. Admission may be deferred for a maximum of 1 year. Credit offered for CEEB Advanced Placement tests.

COSTS AND FINANCIAL AID
Average book expense $1,200. **Required Forms and Deadlines:** FAFSA, institution's own financial aid form. **Notification of Awards:** Applicants will be notified of awards on a rolling basis beginning 2/1. **Types of Aid:** *Need-based scholarships/grants:* Federal Pell, SEOG, state scholarships/grants, private scholarships, the school's own gift aid. *Loans:* Direct Subsidized Stafford, Direct Unsubsidized Stafford, Direct PLUS, Federal Perkins, college/university loans from institutional funds. *Student Employment:* Federal Work-Study Program available. Institutional employment available. Off-campus job opportunities are good. **Financial Aid Statistics:** 68% freshmen, 65% undergrads receive any aid. **Criteria for awarding institutional aid:** *Non-need-based:* Academics, alumni affiliation, art, athletics, minority status, music/drama.

UNIVERSITY OF WEST GEORGIA

1601 Maple Street, Carrollton, GA 30118
Phone: 678-839-4000 **Financial Aid Phone:** 678-839-6421
E-mail: admiss@westga.edu **CEEB Code:** 5900
Fax: 678-839-4747 **Website:** www.westga.edu **ACT Code:** 878

This public school was founded in 1906. It has a 645-acre campus.

RATINGS
Admissions Selectivity Rating: 75   **Fire Safety Rating:** 79   **Green Rating:** 60*

STUDENTS AND FACULTY
Enrollment: 9,622. **Student Body:** 60% female, 40% male, 3% out-of-state, 1% international (76 countries represented). Asian 1%, African American 27%, Caucasian 64%, Hispanic 2%.
Retention and Graduation: 12% freshmen graduate within 4 years. **Faculty:** Student/faculty ratio 17:1. 431 full-time faculty, 78% hold PhDs, 16% are members of minority groups, 50% are women.

ACADEMICS
Degrees: Bachelor's, certificate, doctoral, master's, post-bachelor's certificate, post-master's certificate. **Classes:** Most classes have 20–29 students. Most lab/discussion sessions have 20–29 students. **Majors with Highest Enrollment:** Biology/biological sciences; elementary education and teaching; nursing/registered nurse (RN, ASN, BSN, MSN). **Special Study Options:** Accelerated program, cooperative education program, distance learning, double major, dual enrollment, external degree program, honors program, independent study, internships, study abroad, teacher certification program. Special programs offered to physically disabled students include note-taking services, reader services, tape recorders, tutors. **Career services:** alumni services, internships

FACILITIES
Housing: Coed dorms, special housing for disabled students, women's dorms, fraternity/sorority housing. 85% of campus accessible to physically disabled. **Special Academic Facilities/Equipment:** Archalolgical laboratory, art gallery, electron microscope, observatory, preschool, performing arts center, TV studio. **Computers:** 20% of classrooms, 10% of dorms, 100% of libraries, 100% of dining areas, 100% of student union, 80% of common outdoor areas have wireless network access. Students can register for classes online. Administrative functions (other than registration) can be performed online.

CAMPUS LIFE
Environment: City. **Activities:** Choral groups, concert band, dance, drama/theater, jazz band, literary magazine, marching band, music ensembles, musical theater, opera, pep band, radio station, student government, student newspaper, television station, campus ministries, international student organization. **Organizations:** 131 registered organizations, 32 honor societies, 17 religious organizations. 14 fraternities, 8 sororities. **Athletics (Intercollegiate):** *Men:* Baseball, basketball, cheerleading, cross-country, football, golf. *Women:* Basketball, cheerleading, cross-country, golf, soccer, softball, volleyball. **On-Campus Highlights:** Technology Learning Center (TLC), Bookstore, Ingram Library, Football Stadium, Campus Recreation Center, University Community Center, Coliseum, and Campus Visitor's Center.

ADMISSIONS
Freshman Academic Profile: Average high school GPA 2.93. 91% from public high schools. SAT Math middle 50% range 450–530. SAT Critical Reading middle 50% range 450–540. SAT Writing middle 50% range 440–520. ACT middle 50% range 18–22. Minimum paper TOEFL 523. Minimum computer TOEFL 193. **Basis for Candidate Selection:** *Very important factors consid-*

ered include: Academic GPA, rigor of secondary school record, standardized test scores. **Freshman Admission Requirements:** High school diploma is required and GED is not accepted. *Academic units required:* 4 English, 4 mathematics, 3 science, (2 science labs), 2 foreign language, 1 social studies, 2 history. *Academic units recommended:* 4 science. **Freshman Admission Statistics:** 5,981 applied, 58% admitted, 59% enrolled. **Transfer Admission Requirements:** College transcript(s), minimum college GPA of 2.0 required. Lowest grade transferable D. **General Admission Information:** Application fee $30. Regular application deadline 6/1. Notification on a rolling basis, beginning on or about 8/1. Nonfall registration accepted. Credit and/or placement offered for CEEB Advanced Placement tests.

COSTS AND FINANCIAL AID

Annual in-state tuition $7,722. Annual out-of-state tuition $25,269. Room and board $7,546. Required fees $891. Average book expense $792. **Required Forms and Deadlines:** FAFSA. **Notification of Awards:** Applicants will be notified of awards on a rolling basis beginning 6/1. **Types of Aid:** *Need-based scholarships/grants:* Federal Pell, SEOG, state scholarships/grants, private scholarships, the school's own gift aid, United Negro College Fund, Federal Nursing Scholarships. *Loans:* Direct Subsidized Stafford, Direct Unsubsidized Stafford, Direct PLUS, Federal Perkins, state loans, college/university loans from institutional funds. *Student Employment:* Federal Work-Study Program available. Institutional employment available. Highest amount earned per year from on-campus jobs $5,220. **Financial Aid Statistics:** 57% freshmen, 50% undergrads receive need-based scholarship or grant aid. 17% freshmen, 11% undergrads receive non-need-based scholarship or grant aid. 46% freshmen, 46% undergrads receive need-based self-help aid. 2% freshmen, 2% undergrads receive athletic scholarships. 65% freshmen, 60% undergrads receive any aid. **Criteria for awarding institutional aid:** *Non-need-based:* Academics, alumni affiliation, art, athletics, leadership, minority status, music/drama, religious affiliation, state/district residency.

THE UNIVERSITY OF WESTERN ONTARIO

Western Student Services Bldg, RM 3140, London, ON N6A 3K7 Canada
Phone: 519-661-2100 **Financial Aid Phone:** 519-661-2100
E-mail: reg-admissions@uwo.ca
Fax: 519-661-3710 **Website:** www.uwo.ca

This public school was founded in 1878. It has a 1178-acre campus.

RATINGS
Admissions Selectivity Rating: 60*   **Fire Safety Rating:** 60*   **Green Rating:** 84

STUDENTS AND FACULTY
Enrollment: 26,507. **Student Body:** 58% female, 42% male, 6% out-of-state (85 countries represented).
Retention and Graduation: 92% freshmen return for sophomore year. 65% freshmen graduate within 4 years. **Faculty:** Student/faculty ratio 20:1. 1374 full-time faculty, 30% are women.

ACADEMICS
Degrees: Bachelor's, certificate, diploma, doctoral, master's. **Majors with Highest Enrollment:** Biology/biological sciences; health services/allied health/health sciences; social sciences, other. **Special Study Options:** Accelerated program, cooperative education program, cross-registration, distance learning, double major, dual enrollment, English as a Second Language (ESL), exchange student program (domestic), honors program, independent study, internships, liberal arts/career combination, student-designed major, study abroad, teacher certification program. **Honors programs:** Scholar's Electives **Combined degree programs:** BESc/MD, BESc/LLB, LLB/MBA, BSc/LLB, HBA/BMSc. Special programs offered to physically disabled students include note-taking services, reader services, tape recorders. **Career services:** Alumni network, alumni services, career/job search classes, career assessment, internships, regional alumni. **Career services highlights include:** Western's Internship Program www.career.uwo.ca/wip, Backpack2briefcase www.alumni.uwo.ca/b2b/, Interview Stream—online mock interview tool! Career Week/Job Fairs.

FACILITIES
Housing: Coed dorms, special housing for disabled students, men's dorms, special housing for international students, women's dorms, apartments for married students, apartments for single students. 92% of campus accessible to physically disabled. **Special Academic Facilities/Equipment:** McIntosh Gallery Hume Cronyn Memorial Observatory Student Recreation Centre **Computers:** 100% of libraries, 100% of student union, have wireless network access. Students can register for classes online. Administrative functions (other than registration) can be performed online.

CAMPUS LIFE
Environment: City. **Activities:** Choral groups, concert band, dance, drama/theater, jazz band, marching band, music ensembles, musical theater, opera, pep band, radio station, student government, student newspaper, student-run film society, symphony orchestra, television station, campus ministries, international student organization, Model UN. **Organizations:** 189 registered organizations, 14 fraternities, 5 sororities. **Athletics (Intercollegiate):** *Men:* Badminton, baseball, basketball, crew/rowing, cross-country, curling, fencing, football, golf, ice hockey, rugby, soccer, squash, swimming, tennis, track/field (outdoor), track/field (indoor), volleyball, water polo, wrestling. *Women:* Badminton, basketball, crew/rowing, cross-country, curling, fencing, field hockey, golf, ice hockey, lacrosse, rugby, soccer, squash, swimming, tennis, track/field (outdoor), track/field (indoor), volleyball, wrestling. **On-Campus Highlights:** University Community Centre, Student Recreation Centre, TD Waterhouse Stadium, Von Kuster Hall, McIntosh Gallery, McIntosh Gallery—oldest university art gallery in Canada. **Environmental Initiatives:** Signatories of Ontario University; committed to a Greener World; undergraduate/Masters programs in Environment and Sustainability; LEED Building Development—all new construction and renovation will be LEED Silver Certified or better.

ADMISSIONS
Freshman Academic Profile: Average high school GPA 85.1. Minimum paper TOEFL 550. Minimum web-based TOEFL 83. **Basis for Candidate Selection:** *Very important factors considered include:* Academic GPA, rigor of secondary school record, standardized test scores, *Other factors considered include:* Class rank, recommendation(s), extracurricular activities, first generation, talent/ability, volunteer work. **Freshman Admission Requirements: Freshman Admission Statistics:** 31,128 applied, 53% admitted, 27% enrolled. **Transfer Admission Requirements:** College transcript(s), **General Admission Information:** Application fee $120. Regular application deadline 6/1. Notification on a rolling basis, beginning on or about 2/1. Nonfall registration not accepted. Admission may be deferred for a maximum of 1 year. Credit offered for CEEB Advanced Placement tests.

COSTS AND FINANCIAL AID
Required fees $887. **Required Forms and Deadlines:** FAFSA, institution's own financial aid form, state aid form. **Types of Aid:** *Need-based scholarships/grants:* State scholarships/grants, private scholarships, the school's own gift aid, Federal Bursaries and Grants. *Loans:* Federal and provincial loan programs administered by governments. *Student Employment:* Off-campus job opportunities are good. **Financial Aid Statistics: Criteria for awarding institutional aid:** *Non-need-based:* Academics, alumni affiliation, art, athletics, leadership, minority status, music/drama, state/district residency.

UNIVERSITY OF WINDSOR

Office of the Registrar, 401 Sunset Ave, Windsor, ON N9B3P4 Canada
Phone: 519-253-3000 **Financial Aid Phone:** 519-253-3000
E-mail: registrar@uwindsor.ca
Fax: 519-971-3653 **Website:** www.uwindsor.ca

This public school was founded in 1857. It has a 125-acre campus.

RATINGS
Admissions Selectivity Rating: 60*   **Fire Safety Rating:** 60*   **Green Rating:** 75

STUDENTS AND FACULTY
Enrollment: 13,835. **Student Body:** 54% female, 46% male, % out-of-state, international (89 countries represented).
Retention and Graduation: Faculty: Student/faculty ratio 18:1. 592 full-time faculty, 81% hold PhDs, 40% are women.

ACADEMICS
Degrees: Bachelor's, certificate, master's. **Majors with Highest Enrollment:** Business/commerce; engineering; social sciences, other. **Special Study Options:** Cooperative education program, distance learning, double major, English as a Second Language (ESL), exchange student program (domestic), honors program, independent study, internships, study abroad, teacher certification program, MBA for Managers and Professionals, which is offered on weekends (Centre for Executive Education). **Honors programs:** As a comprehensive university we have distinguished ourselves at many levels. **Combined degree programs:** BA (French)/BEd, BA/BEd/ECE, BScBEd, BMath/BEd, BCS/BEd, JD/LLB. Special programs offered to physically disabled students include note-taking services, reader services, tape recorders, tutors. **Career services:** Career/job search classes, career assessment, internships. **Career services highlights include:** The Centre for Career Education contributes to the holistic education of students and complements academic programs of study by supporting a wide range of career-related programs and resources with an

emphasis on excellence in learning from experience. We guide students through the career development process including the exploration of personal workplace preferences and strengths, the development of career competencies, and the construction of a career plan.

FACILITIES

Housing: Coed dorms, special housing for disabled students, special housing for international students, fraternity/sorority housing, apartments for married students, cooperative housing, apartments for single students, off campus housing lists for tenants and landlords. 100% of campus accessible to physically disabled. **Special Academic Facilities/Equipment:** Centre for Engineering Innovation (completion date 2011); C.A.R.E. (Centre for Automotive Research and Education); GLIER (Great Lakes Institute for Environemntal Research); Jackman Dramatic Art Centre (theatrical space); Bio-Learning Centre (BLC); Biotechnology Laboratory. **Computers:** 100% of classrooms, 100% of dorms, 100% of libraries, 100% of dining areas, 100% of student union, 100% of common outdoor areas have wireless network access. Students can register for classes online. Administrative functions (other than registration) can be performed online.

CAMPUS LIFE

Environment: City. **Activities:** Choral groups, dance, drama/theater, jazz band, literary magazine, music ensembles, musical theater, radio station, student government, student newspaper, student-run film society, campus ministries, international student organization. **Organizations:** 116 registered organizations, 1 honor societies, 13 religious organizations. 3 fraternities, 3 sororities. **Athletics (Intercollegiate):** *Men:* Basketball, cross-country, football, ice hockey, soccer, track/field (outdoor), track/field (indoor), volleyball. *Women:* Basketball, cross-country, ice hockey, soccer, track/field (outdoor), track/field (indoor), volleyball. **On-Campus Highlights:** CAW Student Centre, Forge Fitness facility, The Basement Pub, St. Denis Athletic Centre/University Sta, Leddy Library, Odette Sculpture Garden which includes a scenic 5km waterfront trail. Many students will exercise or study/relax by the water. **Environmental Initiatives:** LEEDS Certified Buildings—Medical School will qualify after completion of the third floor. LEEDS Certified Bldg. $113 Million Centre for Engineering Innovation forthcoming. Consistent internationally recognized research from The Great Lakes Institute for Environmental Research,and many other areas on campus.

ADMISSIONS

Freshman Academic Profile: Basis for Candidate Selection: *Very important factors considered include:* Academic GPA, rigor of secondary school record. *Other factors considered include:* Recommendation(s), standardized test scores, extracurricular activities, geographical residence, interview. **Freshman Admission Requirements:** High school diploma is required and GED is not accepted. **Freshman Admission Statistics:** 12,082 applied, 68% admitted, 35% enrolled. **Transfer Admission Requirements:** College transcript(s). **General Admission Information:** Application fee $75. Notification on a rolling basis, beginning on or about 1/1. Nonfall registration accepted.

COSTS AND FINANCIAL AID

Required Forms and Deadlines: institution's own financial aid form, Ontario Student Assistance Program (OSAP). Financial aid filing deadline 1/31. Priority financial aid filing date 6/30. **Notification of Awards:** Applicants will be notified of awards on a rolling basis beginning 6/1. **Types of Aid:** *Need-based scholarships/grants:* the school's own gift aid. *Loans:* Ontario Student Assistance Program (OSAP). *Student Employment:* Off-campus job opportunities are good. **Financial Aid Statistics: Criteria for awarding institutional aid:** *Non-need-based:* Academics, art, athletics, leadership, minority status, music/drama, state/district residency.

UNIVERSITY OF WISCONSIN—EAU CLAIRE

105 Garfield Avenue, Schofield 112, Eau Claire, WI 54701
Phone: 715-836-5415 **Financial Aid Phone:** 715-836-3373
E-mail: admissions@uwec.edu **CEEB Code:** 1913
Fax: 715-836-2409 **Website:** www.uwec.edu **ACT Code:** 4670

This public school was founded in 1916. It has a 333-acre campus.

RATINGS

Admissions Selectivity Rating: 79   **Fire Safety Rating:** 71   **Green Rating:** 86

STUDENTS AND FACULTY

Enrollment: 10,384. **Student Body:** 59% female, 41% male, 22% out-of-state, 1% international (39 countries represented). Asian 3%, African American 1%, Caucasian 91%, Hispanic 1%, Native American 1%.
Retention and Graduation: 84% freshmen return for sophomore year. 25% freshmen graduate within 4 years. 10% grads go on to further study within 1

year. **Faculty:** Student/faculty ratio 21:1. 410 full-time faculty, 81% hold PhDs, 11% are members of minority groups, 46% are women.

ACADEMICS

Degrees: Associate, bachelor's, certificate, master's, post-bachelor's certificate, post-master's certificate, terminal associate, transfer associate. **Classes:** Most classes have 20–29 students. Most lab/discussion sessions have 20–29 students. **Majors with Highest Enrollment:** Biology/biological sciences; elementary education and teaching; nursing/registered nurse (RN, ASN, BSN, MSN). **Special Study Options:** Accelerated program, cooperative education program, cross-registration, distance learning, double major, dual enrollment, English as a Second Language (ESL), exchange student program (domestic), external degree program, honors program, independent study, internships, student-designed major, study abroad, teacher certification program, collaborative programs in Early Childhood Education. Special programs offered to physically disabled students include note-taking services, reader services, tutors. **Career services:** Alumni network, alumni services, career/job search classes, career assessment, internships, regional alumni.

FACILITIES

Housing: Coed dorms, men's dorms, women's dorms, apartments for single students. 80% of campus accessible to physically disabled. **Special Academic Facilities/Equipment:** Art gallery, human development center, bird museum, field station, planetarium. **Computers:** 50% of classrooms, 10% of dorms, 100% of libraries, 100% of dining areas, 100% of student union, 100% of common outdoor areas have wireless network access. Students can register for classes online. Administrative functions (other than registration) can be performed online.

CAMPUS LIFE

Environment: Town. **Activities:** Choral groups, concert band, dance, drama/theater, jazz band, literary magazine, marching band, music ensembles, musical theater, opera, pep band, radio station, student government, student newspaper, student-run film society, symphony orchestra, television station, campus ministries, international student organization, Model UN. **Organizations:** 240 registered organizations, 30 honor societies, 16 religious organizations. 2 fraternities, 3 sororities. **Athletics (Intercollegiate):** *Men:* Basketball, cross-country, diving, football, golf, ice hockey, swimming, tennis, track/field (outdoor), track/field (indoor), wrestling. *Women:* Basketball, cross-country, diving, golf, gymnastics, ice hockey, soccer, softball, swimming, tennis, track/field (outdoor), track/field (indoor), volleyball. **On-Campus Highlights:** Chippewa River Footbridge, Davies Center (Student Center/Union), McPhee Center (Athletic Facility), Hass Fine Arts Center, Higher Ground (Recreational Facility). **Environmental Initiatives:** In 2009, beginning the development of our Climate Action Plan, which will reflect the efforts of faculty, staff, and students. In 2010 (early) the finalization of our climate Action Plan. The faculty/staff/student Clean Commute Initiative, which is reaching out to work with the City of Eau Claire on key biking/pedestrian/busing issues. The continued support for the Chancellor's Sustainability Fellow to serve as intra-campus liaison and campus-community liaison, and to represent our campus at regional and statewide gathering of sustainability workers.

ADMISSIONS

Freshman Academic Profile: 29% in top 10% of high school class, 61% in top 25% of high school class, 98% in top 50% of high school class. 93% from public high schools. SAT Math middle 50% range 520–670. SAT Critical Reading middle 50% range 520–640. SAT Writing middle 50% range 490–620. ACT middle 50% range 23–26. Minimum paper TOEFL 550. Minimum computer TOEFL 213. Minimum web-based TOEFL 79. **Basis for Candidate Selection:** *Very important factors considered include:* Class rank, rigor of secondary school record. *Important factors considered include:* Standardized test scores. *Other factors considered include:* Application essay, academic GPA, recommendation(s), character/personal qualities, extracurricular activities, first generation, interview, level of applicant's interest, racial/ethnic status, talent/ability, volunteer work, work experience. **Freshman Admission Requirements:** High school diploma is required and GED is accepted. *Academic units required:* 4 English, 3 mathematics, 3 science, 2 foreign language, 3 social studies, 2 academic electives. **Freshman Admission Statistics:** 7,414 applied, 67% admitted, 40% enrolled. **Transfer Admission Requirements:** High school transcript, college transcript(s), statement of good standing from prior institution(s). Minimum college GPA of 2.0 required. Lowest grade transferable D–. **General Admission Information:** Application fee $44. Notification on a rolling basis, beginning on or about 9/15. Nonfall registration accepted. Credit and/or placement offered for CEEB Advanced Placement tests.

COSTS AND FINANCIAL AID

Annual in-state tuition $5,527. Annual out-of-state tuition $13,100. Room and board $5,730. Required fees $1,106. Average book expense $460. **Required Forms and Deadlines:** FAFSA. Priority financial aid filing date 4/15. **Notification of Awards:** Applicants will be notified of awards on a rolling basis beginning 4/15. **Types of Aid** *Need-based scholarships/grants:* Federal Pell,

SEOG, state scholarships/grants, private scholarships, the school's own gift aid, Federal Nursing Scholarships. Academic Competetiveness Grant, SMART Grant, BIA Excellence in Math/Comp. Science, EMAC, Student Support Services Grant. *Loans:* Direct Subsidized Stafford, Direct Unsubsidized Stafford, Direct PLUS, Federal Perkins, state loans, college/university loans from institutional funds, Private. *Student Employment:* Federal Work-Study Program available. Institutional employment available. Highest amount earned per year from on-campus jobs $10,023. Off-campus job opportunities are fair. **Financial Aid Statistics:** 26% freshmen, 26% undergrads receive need-based scholarship or grant aid. 23% freshmen, 41% undergrads receive need-based self-help aid. 72% freshmen, 69% undergrads receive any aid. 68% undergrads borrow to pay for school. Average cumulative indebtedness $19,687. **Criteria for awarding institutional aid:** *Non-need-based:* Academics, art, leadership, minority status, music/drama, state/district residency.

UNIVERSITY OF WISCONSIN—GREEN BAY

2420 Nicolet Drive, Green Bay, WI 53411-7001
Phone: 920-465-2111 **Financial Aid Phone:** 920-465-2075
E-mail: uwgb@uwgb.edu **CEEB Code:** 1859
Fax: 920-465-5754 **Website:** www.uwgb.edu **ACT Code:** 4688

This public school was founded in 1965. It has a 700-acre campus.

RATINGS
Admissions Selectivity Rating: 74   **Fire Safety Rating:** 60*   **Green Rating:** 79

STUDENTS AND FACULTY
Enrollment: 6,068. **Student Body:** 64% female, 36% male, 5% out-of-state, 1% international (41 countries represented). Asian 3%, African American 1%, Caucasian 90%, Hispanic 1%, Native American 2%.
Retention and Graduation: 75% freshmen return for sophomore year. 25% freshmen graduate within 4 years. 15% grads go on to further study within 1 year. 10% grads pursue arts and sciences degrees. 1% grads pursue law degrees. 3% grads pursue business degrees. 1% grads pursue medical degrees. **Faculty:** Student/faculty ratio 25:1. 189 full-time faculty, 80% hold PhDs, 15% are members of minority groups, 46% are women.

ACADEMICS
Degrees: Associate, bachelor's, master's, post-bachelor's certificate. **Classes:** Most classes have 20–29 students. Most lab/discussion sessions have 20–29 students. **Majors with Highest Enrollment:** Biological and biomedical sciences, other; business/commerce; psychology. **Special Study Options:** Cross-registration, distance learning, double major, exchange student program (domestic), external degree program, independent study, internships, liberal arts/career combination, student-designed major, study abroad, teacher certification program. **Combined degree programs:** BS/MS Environmental Science/Env Science & Policy. Special programs offered to physically disabled students include note-taking services, reader services, tape recorders. **Career services:** Alumni network, alumni services, career/job search classes, internships.

FACILITIES
Housing: Coed dorms, apartments for single students, Suites w/ private bedrooms. 99% of campus accessible to physically disabled. **Special Academic Facilities/Equipment:** 290–acre arboretum, Herbarium, regional Performing Arts Center. **Computers:** 75% of classrooms, 100% of dorms, 100% of libraries, 100% of dining areas, 100% of student union, 10% of common outdoor areas have wireless network access. Students can register for classes online. Administrative functions (other than registration) can be performed online.

CAMPUS LIFE
Environment: City. **Activities:** Choral groups, concert band, dance, drama/theater, jazz band, literary magazine, music ensembles, musical theater, pep band, radio station, student government, student newspaper, student-run film society, television station, campus ministries, international student organization. **Organizations:** 100 registered organizations, 7 honor societies, 5 religious organizations. 2 fraternities, 2 sororities. **Athletics (Intercollegiate):** *Men:* Basketball, cheerleading, cross-country, diving, golf, skiing (nordic/cross-country), soccer, swimming, tennis. *Women:* Basketball, cheerleading, cross-country, diving, golf, skiing (nordic/cross-country), soccer, softball, swimming, tennis, volleyball. **On-Campus Highlights:** Mary Ann Cofrin Hall—State-of-the-art academic bldg, Kress Event Center -recently remodeled, Weidner Center for Performing Arts, Lambeau Cottage on the shores of Green B, Student Union-recently remodeled. **Environmental Initiatives:** Building integrated photovoltaics in Mary Ann Cofrin Hall (www.buildingsolar.com/index.html). Historically strong academic programs in environmental science and environmental policy and planning at both bachelor's and master's level. Campus design connects buildings with energy efficient underground tunnels.

ADMISSIONS
Freshman Academic Profile: Average high school GPA 3.25. 95% from public high schools. ACT middle 50% range 20–24. Minimum paper TOEFL 500. Minimum computer TOEFL 173. Minimum web-based TOEFL 61. **Basis for Candidate Selection:** *Very important factors considered include:* Academic GPA, rigor of secondary school record, standardized test scores, extracurricular activities. *Important factors considered include:* Application essay, level of applicant's interest, volunteer work, work experience. *Other factors considered include:* Recommendation(s), character/personal qualities, geographical residence, interview, racial/ethnic status, state residency, talent/ability. **Freshman Admission Requirements:** High school diploma is required and GED is accepted. *Academic units required:* 4 English, 3 mathematics, 3 science, (1 science labs), 3 social studies, 4 academic electives. *Academic units recommended:* 4 English, 3 mathematics, 3 science, (1 science labs), 2 foreign language, 3 social studies, 4 academic electives. **Freshman Admission Statistics:** 3,563 applied, 70% admitted, 42% enrolled. **Transfer Admission Requirements:** College transcript(s), minimum college GPA of 2.0 required. Lowest grade transferable D. **General Admission Information:** Application fee $44. Notification on a rolling basis, beginning on or about 9/15. Nonfall registration accepted. Admission may be deferred for a maximum of 1 year. Credit and/or placement offered for CEEB Advanced Placement tests.

COSTS AND FINANCIAL AID
Average book expense $800. **Required Forms and Deadlines:** FAFSA. Priority financial aid filing date 4/1. **Notification of Awards:** Applicants will be notified of awards on a rolling basis beginning 1/1. **Types of Aid:** *Need-based scholarships/grants:* Federal Pell, SEOG, state scholarships/grants, private scholarships, the school's own gift aid. *Loans:* FFEL Subsidized Stafford, FFEL Unsubsidized Stafford, FFEL PLUS, Federal Perkins. *Student Employment:* Federal Work-Study Program available. Institutional employment available. Off-campus job opportunities are good. **Financial Aid Statistics:** 39% freshmen, 35% undergrads receive need-based scholarship or grant aid. 24% freshmen, 23% undergrads receive non-need-based scholarship or grant aid. 47% freshmen, 48% undergrads receive need-based self-help aid. 3% freshmen, 2% undergrads receive athletic scholarships. 62% freshmen, 61% undergrads receive any aid. 71% undergrads borrow to pay for school. Average cumulative indebtedness $19,636. **Criteria for awarding institutional aid:** *Non-need-based:* Academics, art, athletics, leadership, minority status, music/drama.

UNIVERSITY OF WISCONSIN—LA CROSSE

1725 State Street, Cleary Center, La Crosse, WI 54601-3742
Phone: 608-785-8939 **Financial Aid Phone:** 608-785-8604
E-mail: admissions@uwlax.edu **CEEB Code:** 1914
Fax: 608-785-8940 **Website:** www.uwlax.edu **ACT Code:** 4672

This public school was founded in 1909. It has a 120-acre campus.

RATINGS
Admissions Selectivity Rating: 87   **Fire Safety Rating:** 60*   **Green Rating:** 60*

STUDENTS AND FACULTY
Enrollment: 8,493. **Student Body:** 58% female, 42% male, 16% out-of-state, 2% international (41 countries represented). Asian 3%, African American 1%, Caucasian 89%, Hispanic 2%.
Retention and Graduation: 86% freshmen return for sophomore year. 34% freshmen graduate within 4 years. 21% grads go on to further study within 1 year. **Faculty:** Student/faculty ratio 21:1. 376 full-time faculty, 75% hold PhDs, 15% are members of minority groups, 43% are women.

ACADEMICS
Degrees: Associate, bachelor's, certificate, master's, post-bachelor's certificate. **Classes:** Most classes have 20–29 students. Most lab/discussion sessions have 20–29 students. **Majors with Highest Enrollment:** Elementary education and teaching; kinesiology and exercise science; marketing/marketing management. **Special Study Options:** Cooperative education program, cross-registration, distance learning, double major, dual enrollment, English as a Second Language (ESL), honors program, independent study, internships, liberal arts/career combination, study abroad, teacher certification program, Weekend college: grad only. **Honors programs:** University Honors Program lt;www.uwlax. edu/honors/gt. **Combined degree programs:** BS/MSPT; BS/MSOT. Special programs offered to physically disabled students include note-taking services, reader services, tape recorders, tutors.

FACILITIES
Housing: Coed dorms, special housing for international students, wellness housing, First Year Experience. 98% of campus accessible to physically dis-

abled. **Special Academic Facilities/Equipment:** Greenhouse, planetarium, Health Science Center,Mississippi Valley Archaeology Center, River Studies center, Business Development Center, La Crosse Exercise and Health Program. **Computers:** Students can register for classes online. Administrative functions (other than registration) can be performed online.

CAMPUS LIFE

Environment: City. **Activities:** Choral groups, concert band, drama/theater, jazz band, marching band, music ensembles, pep band, radio station, student government, student newspaper, symphony orchestra, international student organization. **Organizations:** 180 registered organizations, 13 honor societies, 10 religious organizations. 4 fraternities, 2 sororities. **Athletics (Intercollegiate):** *Men:* Baseball, basketball, cross-country, diving, football, swimming, tennis, track/field (outdoor), track/field (indoor), wrestling. *Women:* Basketball, cross-country, diving, gymnastics, soccer, softball, swimming, tennis, track/field (outdoor), track/field (indoor), volleyball. **On-Campus Highlights:** Recreation Eagle Center, Cyber Cafe, Archaeology Museum, Murphy Library, Wing Technology Computer Lab, The 119 acre campus has 32 buildings, including 19 used for instruction, academic support and administrative purposes; 10 residence halls and three student centers.

ADMISSIONS

Freshman Academic Profile: Average high school GPA 3.57. 30% in top 10% of high school class, 79% in top 25% of high school class, 98% in top 50% of high school class. ACT middle 50% range 23–27. Minimum paper TOEFL 550. Minimum computer TOEFL 213. **Basis for Candidate Selection:** *Very important factors considered include:* Class rank, academic GPA, rigor of secondary school record, standardized test scores. *Important factors considered include:* Application essay, extracurricular activities, level of applicant's interest, volunteer work. *Other factors considered include:* Recommendation(s), alumni/ae relation, character/personal qualities, first generation, geographical residence, interview, racial/ethnic status, state residency, talent/ability, work experience. **Freshman Admission Requirements:** High school diploma is required and GED is accepted. *Academic units required:* 4 English, 3 mathematics, 3 science, (2 science labs), 3 social studies, 4 academic electives. *Academic units recommended:* 4 English, 4 mathematics, 4 science, (3 science labs), 3 foreign language, 4 social studies, 4 academic electives. **Freshman Admission Statistics:** 6,504 applied, 69% admitted, 40% enrolled. **Transfer Admission Requirements:** College transcript(s), statement of good standing from prior institution(s). Minimum college GPA of 3.0 required. Lowest grade transferable D-. **General Admission Information:** Application fee $44. Notification on a rolling basis, beginning on or about 9/15. Nonfall registration accepted. Credit and/or placement offered for CEEB Advanced Placement tests.

COSTS AND FINANCIAL AID

Annual in-state tuition $6,425. Annual out-of-state tuition $13,998. Room and board $5,630. Required fees $1,084. Average book expense $300. **Required Forms and Deadlines:** FAFSA. Priority financial aid filing date 3/15. **Notification of Awards:** Applicants will be notified of awards on a rolling basis beginning 4/1. **Types of Aid:** *Need-based scholarships/grants:* Federal Pell, SEOG, state scholarships/grants, private scholarships, the school's own gift aid. *Loans:* FFEL Subsidized Stafford, FFEL Unsubsidized Stafford, FFEL PLUS, Federal Perkins. *Student Employment:* Highest amount earned per year from on-campus jobs $7,020. **Financial Aid Statistics:** 16% freshmen, 18% undergrads receive need-based scholarship or grant aid. 5% freshmen, 4% undergrads receive non-need-based scholarship or grant aid. 38% freshmen, 37% undergrads receive need-based self-help aid. 65% freshmen, 72% undergrads receive any aid. 65% undergrads borrow to pay for school. Average cumulative indebtedness $21,998. **Criteria for awarding institutional aid:** *Non-need-based:* Academics, art, athletics, leadership, music/drama.

UNIVERSITY OF WISCONSIN—MADISON

Best 373

Armory and Gymnasium, 716 Langdon Street, Madison, WI 53706-1481
Phone: 608-262-3961 **Financial Aid Phone:** 608-262-3060
E-mail: onwisconsin@admissions.wisc.edu **CEEB Code:** 1846
Fax: 608-262-7706 **Website:** www.wisc.edu **ACT Code:** 4656

This public school was founded in 1848. It has a 933-acre campus.

RATINGS

Admissions Selectivity Rating: 94   **Fire Safety Rating:** 60*   **Green Rating:** 60*

STUDENTS AND FACULTY

Enrollment: 28,690. **Student Body:** 52% female, 48% male, 32% out-of-state, 5% international (132 countries represented). Asian 6%, African American 3%, Caucasian 78%, Hispanic 4%, Native American 1%.
Retention and Graduation: 94% freshmen return for sophomore year. 50% freshmen graduate within 4 years. **Faculty:** Student/faculty ratio 17:1. 2397 full-time faculty, 91% hold PhDs, 16% are members of minority groups, 36% are women. 22% of classes are taught by teaching assistants.

ACADEMICS

Degrees: Bachelor's, doctoral, master's, post-master's certificate. **Classes:** Most classes have 10–19 students. Most lab/discussion sessions have 20–29 students. **Majors with Highest Enrollment:** Biology/biological sciences; economics; political science and government. **Special Study Options:** Accelerated program, cooperative education program, distance learning, double major, dual enrollment, English as a Second Language (ESL), exchange student program (domestic), honors program, independent study, internships, liberal arts/career combination, student-designed major, study abroad, teacher certification program Special programs offered to physically disabled students include note-taking services, reader services, tape recorders, tutors. **Career services:** Alumni network, career/job search classes, career assessment, internships. **Career services highlights include:** We have multiple career placement centers for different schools and colleges. Futhermore, we have all of the services above, but they are not all offered through a career placement center. For example, internships are generally organized through academic departments and alumni services are provided through our alumni association.

FACILITIES

Housing: Coed dorms, men's dorms, special housing for international students, women's dorms, fraternity/sorority housing, apartments for married students, cooperative housing, apartments for single students, theme housing, Residential Learning Communities. 80% of campus accessible to physically disabled. **Special Academic Facilities/Equipment:** Art, physics, and geology museums, nuclear reactor, arboretum, botanical gardens, observatory, campus dairy store (campus-made ice cream and cheese), American Indian burial mounds. **Computers:** 100% of classrooms, 25% of dorms, 100% of libraries, 100% of dining areas, 100% of student union, 100% of common outdoor areas have wireless network access. Students can register for classes online. Administrative functions (other than registration) can be performed online.

CAMPUS LIFE

Environment: City. **Activities:** Choral groups, concert band, dance, drama/theater, jazz band, literary magazine, marching band, music ensembles, musical theater, opera, pep band, radio station, student government, student newspaper, student-run film society, symphony orchestra, television station, yearbook, international student organization. **Organizations:** 685 registered organizations, 27 honor societies, 26 fraternities, 11 sororities. **Athletics (Intercollegiate):** *Men:* Basketball, cheerleading, crew/rowing, cross-country, football, golf, ice hockey, soccer, swimming, tennis, track/field (outdoor), wrestling. *Women:* Basketball, cheerleading, crew/rowing, cross-country, golf, ice hockey, soccer, softball, swimming, tennis, track/field (outdoor), volleyball. **On-Campus Highlights:** Allen Centennial Gardens, Kohl Center, Memorial Union Terrace, Chazen Museum of Art, Babcock Hall Dairy Plant and Store, www.visit.wisc.edu/todo.html.

ADMISSIONS

Freshman Academic Profile: Average high school GPA 3.69. 56.5% in top 10% of high school class, 91.3% in top 25% of high school class, 99.1% in top 50% of high school class. SAT Math middle 50% range 620–720. SAT Critical Reading middle 50% range 500–670. SAT Writing middle 50% range 570–670. ACT middle 50% range 26–30. Minimum paper TOEFL 550. Minimum computer TOEFL 213. **Basis for Candidate Selection:** *Very important factors considered include:* Class rank, academic GPA, rigor of secondary school record. *Important factors considered include:* Application essay, standardized test scores, state residency. *Other factors considered include:* Recommendation(s), alumni/ae relation, character/personal qualities, extracurricular activities, first generation, level of applicant's interest, racial/ethnic status, talent/ability, volunteer work, work experience. **Freshman Admission Requirements:** High school diploma is required and GED is accepted. *Academic units required:* 4 English, 3 mathematics, 3 science, 2 foreign language, 3 social studies, 2 academic electives. *Academic units recommended:* 4 English, 4 mathematics, 4 science, 4 foreign language, 4 social studies, 2 academic electives. **Freshman Admission Statistics:** 24,855 applied, 57% admitted, 40% enrolled. **Transfer Admission Requirements:** High school transcript, college transcript(s), essay or personal statement, Lowest grade transferable D. **General Admission Information:** Application fee $44. Regular application deadline 2/1. Notification on a rolling basis, beginning on or about 10/1. Nonfall registration accepted. Admission may be deferred for a maximum of 1 year. Credit and/or placement offered for CEEB Advanced Placement tests.

COSTS AND FINANCIAL AID

Required Forms and Deadlines: FAFSA, institution's own financial aid form. **Notification of Awards:** Applicants will be notified of awards on a rolling basis beginning 4/1. **Types of Aid:** *Need-based scholarships/grants:* Federal Pell, SEOG, state scholarships/grants, private scholarships, the school's own gift aid. *Loans:* FFEL Subsidized Stafford, FFEL Unsubsidized Stafford, FFEL PLUS, Federal Perkins, Federal Nursing, state loansWe are transitioning to direct lending within the next year. *Student Employment:* Federal Work-Study Program available. Institutional employment available. Off-campus job opportunities are excellent. **Financial Aid Statistics:** 23% freshmen, 23% undergrads receive need-based scholarship or grant aid. 18% freshmen, 12% undergrads receive non-need-based scholarship or grant aid. 26% freshmen, 28% undergrads receive need-based self-help aid. 2% freshmen, 2% undergrads receive athletic scholarships. 48.7% undergrads borrow to pay for school. Average cumulative indebtedness $21,552. **Criteria for awarding institutional aid:** *Non-need-based:* Academics, alumni affiliation, art, athletics, job skills, leadership, minority status, music/drama, religious affiliation, state/district residency.

UNIVERSITY OF WISCONSIN—MILWAUKEE

PO Box 749, Milwaukee, WI 53201
Phone: 414-229-2222
E-mail: uwmlook@uwm.edu **CEEB Code:** 1473
Fax: 414-229-6940 **Website:** www4.uwm.edu **ACT Code:** 4658

This public school was founded in 1956. It has a 93-acre campus.

RATINGS
Admissions Selectivity Rating: 71   **Fire Safety Rating:** 60*   **Green Rating:** 82

STUDENTS AND FACULTY
Enrollment: 23,553. **Student Body:** 50% female, 50% male, 1.7% out-of-state, 1% international. Asian 5%, African American 7%, Caucasian 78%, Hispanic 5%, Native American 1%.
Retention and Graduation: 73% freshmen return for sophomore year.
Faculty: Student/faculty ratio 21:1. 1050 full-time faculty, 24% are members of minority groups, 45% are women.

ACADEMICS
Degrees: Bachelor's, certificate, master's, post-bachelor's certificate, post-master's certificate. **Classes:** Most classes have 20–29 students. Most lab/discussion sessions have 20–29 students. **Special Study Options:** Accelerated program, cooperative education program, cross-registration, distance learning, double major, dual enrollment, English as a Second Language (ESL), external degree program, honors program, independent study, internships, liberal arts/career combination, student-designed major, study abroad, teacher certification program. Special programs offered to physically disabled students include note-taking services, reader services, tape recorders, tutors. **Career services:** career assessment, internships. **Career services highlights include:** LaMacchia Enterprises Entrepreneur Internship.

FACILITIES
Housing: Coed dorms, special housing for disabled students, apartments for single students. **Special Academic Facilities/Equipment:** Art and geology museums, childhood education center, foreign language resource center, Great Lakes research facility and environmental studies field station, planetarium.

CAMPUS LIFE
Activities: Choral groups, concert band, dance, drama/theater, jazz band, literary magazine, marching band, music ensembles, musical theater, pep band, radio station, student government, student newspaper, student-run film society, symphony orchestra, campus ministries, international student organization, Model UN. **Organizations:** 250 registered organizations, 1 honor societies, 4 religious organizations. 8 fraternities, 4 sororities. **Athletics (Intercollegiate):** *Men:* Baseball, basketball, cross-country, diving, soccer, swimming, track/field (outdoor). *Women:* Basketball, cross-country, soccer, swimming, tennis, track/field (outdoor), volleyball. **Environmental Initiatives:** Renewed Recycling Commitment, including increased recycling, E-Waste project, and a Construction & Demolition Debris recycling program. Stormwater Management and green roofs projects. Use of green cleaning supplies.

ADMISSIONS
Freshman Academic Profile: Average high school GPA 3.05. 8% in top 10% of high school class, 26% in top 25% of high school class, 63% in top 50% of high school class. SAT Math middle 50% range 490–620. SAT Critical Reading middle 50% range 470–600. SAT Writing middle 50% range 450–590. ACT middle 50% range 19–24. Minimum paper TOEFL 500. **Basis for Candidate Selection:** *Very important factors considered include:* Academic GPA, rigor of secondary school record. *Important factors considered include:* Class rank, standardized test scores, talent/ability. *Other factors considered include:* Application essay, recommendation(s), character/personal qualities, extracurricular

activities, first generation, geographical residence, interview, level of applicant's interest, racial/ethnic status, state residency, volunteer work, work experience. **Freshman Admission Requirements:** High school diploma is required and GED is accepted. *Academic units required:* 4 English, 3 mathematics, 3 science, (1 science labs), 3 social studies, 2 academic electives; 2 from the above areas, computer science, fine arts, or other appropriate courses. *Academic units recommended:* 4 English, 4 mathematics, 3 science, (1 science labs), 2 foreign language, 3 social studies, 2 academic electives; 2 from the above areas, computer science, fine arts, or other appropriate courses. **Freshman Admission Statistics:** 11,469 applied, 77% admitted, 46% enrolled. **Transfer Admission Requirements:** High school transcript, college transcript(s), minimum college GPA of 2.0 required. Lowest grade transferable D–. **General Admission Information:** Application fee $44. Regular application deadline 7/1. Notification on a rolling basis, beginning on or about 9/15. Nonfall registration accepted. Admission may be deferred for a maximum of 1 semester. Credit offered for CEEB Advanced Placement tests.

COSTS AND FINANCIAL AID
Required Forms and Deadlines: FAFSA. Priority financial aid filing date 3/1. **Notification of Awards:** Applicants will be notified of awards on a rolling basis beginning 3/10. **Types of Aid:** *Need-based scholarships/grants:* Federal Pell, SEOG, state scholarships/grants, private scholarships, the school's own gift aid, Federal Nursing Scholarships. *Loans:* FFEL Subsidized Stafford, FFEL Unsubsidized Stafford, FFEL PLUS, Federal Perkins, Federal Nursing, state loans, Alternative Loans. *Student Employment:* Federal Work-Study Program available. Institutional employment available. Off-campus job opportunities are good. **Financial Aid Statistics:** 28% freshmen, 29% undergrads receive need-based scholarship or grant aid. 11% freshmen, 6% undergrads receive non-need-based scholarship or grant aid. 51% freshmen, 50% undergrads receive need-based self-help aid. 67% undergrads borrow to pay for school. Average cumulative indebtedness $19,830. **Criteria for awarding institutional aid:** *Non-need-based:* Academics, art, athletics, music/drama.

UNIVERSITY OF WISCONSIN—OSHKOSH

Dempsey Hall 135, 800 Algoma Boulevard, Oshkosh, WI 54901
Phone: 920-424-0202 **Financial Aid Phone:** 920-424-4025
E-mail: oshadmuw@uwosh.edu **CEEB Code:** 1916
Fax: 920-424-1098 **Website:** www.uwosh.edu/home **ACT Code:** 4674

This public school was founded in 1871. It has a 192-acre campus.

RATINGS
Admissions Selectivity Rating: 71   **Fire Safety Rating:** 60*   **Green Rating:** 82

STUDENTS AND FACULTY
Enrollment: 10,078. **Student Body:** 58% female, 42% male, 2% out-of-state, 1% international (32 countries represented). Asian 3%, African American 1%, Caucasian 91%, Hispanic 2%, Native American 1%.
Retention and Graduation: 76% freshmen return for sophomore year. **Faculty:** Student/faculty ratio 20:1. 386 full-time faculty, 81% hold PhDs, 10% are members of minority groups, 45% are women.

ACADEMICS
Degrees: Associate, bachelor's, certificate, master's. **Classes:** Most classes have 20–29 students. Most lab/discussion sessions have 20–29 students. **Majors with Highest Enrollment:** Business/commerce; elementary education and teaching; nursing/registered nurse (RN, ASN, BSN, MSN). **Special Study Options:** Accelerated program, cooperative education program, cross-registration, distance learning, double major, dual enrollment, English as a Second Language (ESL), exchange student program (domestic), honors program, independent study, internships, liberal arts/career combination, student-designed major, study abroad, teacher certification program, weekend college Special programs offered to physically disabled students include note-taking services, reader services, tape recorders, tutors.

FACILITIES
Housing: Coed dorms, special housing for disabled students, men's dorms, women's dorms, fraternity/sorority housing. **Special Academic Facilities/Equipment:** Art gallery, ceramics lab, electron microscope. **Computers:** Students can register for classes online.

CAMPUS LIFE
Environment: Village. **Activities:** Choral groups, concert band, dance, drama/theater, jazz band, literary magazine, music ensembles, pep band, radio station, student government, student newspaper, student-run film society, television station, campus ministries, international student organization, Model UN. **Organizations:** 175 registered organizations, 15 honor societies, 6 religious

organizations. 8 fraternities, 5 sororities. **Athletics (Intercollegiate):** *Men:* Baseball, basketball, cross-country, diving, football, soccer, swimming, tennis, track/field (outdoor), track/field (indoor), wrestling. *Women:* Basketball, cross-country, diving, golf, gymnastics, soccer, softball, swimming, tennis, track/field (outdoor), track/field (indoor), volleyball. **Environmental Initiatives:** The recent development of a comprehensive campus sustainability plan that covers the four areas of operations, teaching, research and outreach. The leadership of the campus in the purchase of alternative energy. The campus was the first major educational institution in the State of Wisconsin to purchase alternative energy, and continues to be a leader in this area. This May the campus will conduct a faculty college on intergrating sustainability across the urriculum based on the AASHE model. We hope it will be an annual event.

ADMISSIONS

Freshman Academic Profile: Average high school GPA 3.25. 10% in top 10% of high school class, 37% in top 25% of high school class, 87% in top 50% of high school class. ACT middle 50% range 20–24. Minimum paper TOEFL 525. Minimum computer TOEFL 197. Minimum web-based TOEFL 70. **Basis for Candidate Selection:** *Very important factors considered include:* Rigor of secondary school record. *Important factors considered include:* Class rank, academic GPA, standardized test scores. *Other factors considered include:* Application essay, recommendation(s), alumni/ae relation, character/personal qualities, extracurricular activities, first generation, racial/ethnic status, talent/ability, volunteer work, work experience. **Freshman Admission Requirements:** High school diploma is required and GED is accepted. *Academic units required:* 4 English, 3 mathematics, 3 science, (3 science labs), 3 social studies, 4 academic electives. *Academic units recommended:* 4 mathematics, 4 science, (4 science labs). **Freshman Admission Statistics:** 5,329 applied, 81% admitted, 43% enrolled. **Transfer Admission Requirements:** College transcript(s), minimum college GPA of 2.50 required. Lowest grade transferable D. **General Admission Information:** Application fee $44. Regular application deadline 8/1. Notification on a rolling basis, beginning on or about 9/15. Nonfall registration accepted. Admission may be deferred for a maximum of 12. Credit offered for CEEB Advanced Placement tests.

COSTS AND FINANCIAL AID

Annual in-state tuition $6,038. Annual out-of-state tuition $13,610. Room and board $5,898. Average book expense $800. **Required Forms and Deadlines:** FAFSA. Priority financial aid filing date 3/15. **Notification of Awards:** Applicants will be notified of awards on or about 4/15. **Types of Aid:** *Need-based scholarships/grants:* Federal Pell, SEOG, state scholarships/grants, private scholarships, the school's own gift aid, Federal Nursing Scholarships. *Loans:* FFEL Subsidized Stafford, FFEL Unsubsidized Stafford, FFEL PLUS, Federal Perkins, Federal Nursing, state loans, college/university loans from institutional funds. *Student Employment:* Federal Work-Study Program available. Institutional employment available. **Financial Aid Statistics:** 19% freshmen, 32% undergrads receive need-based scholarship or grant aid. 19% freshmen, 22% undergrads receive non-need-based scholarship or grant aid. 19% freshmen, 22% undergrads receive need-based self-help aid. 44% freshmen, 36% undergrads receive any aid. 68% undergrads borrow to pay for school. Average cumulative indebtedness $19,000. **Criteria for awarding institutional aid:** *Non-need-based:* Academics, art, job skills, leadership, minority status, music/drama, state/district residency.

UNIVERSITY OF WISCONSIN—PARKSIDE

Box 2000, Kenosha, WI 53141-2000
Phone: 262-595-2355 **Financial Aid Phone:** 262-595-2574
E-mail: matthew.jensen@uwp.edu **CEEB Code:** 1860
Fax: 262-595-2008 **Website:** www.uwp.edu **ACT Code:** 4690

This public school was founded in 1968. It has a 700-acre campus.

RATINGS

Admissions Selectivity Rating: 61   **Fire Safety Rating:** 60*   **Green Rating:** 60*

STUDENTS AND FACULTY

Enrollment: 4,590. **Student Body:** 57% female, 43% male, 7% out-of-state, 1% international (28 countries represented). Asian 3%, African American 8%, Caucasian 69%, Hispanic 6%, Native American 1%.
Retention and Graduation: 65% freshmen return for sophomore year. 9% freshmen graduate within 4 years. **Faculty:** Student/faculty ratio 18:1. 181 full-time faculty, 74% hold PhDs, 22% are members of minority groups, 45% are women.

ACADEMICS

Degrees: Bachelor's, certificate, master's. **Classes:** Most classes have fewer than 10 students. Most lab/discussion sessions have 20–29 students. **Majors**

with Highest Enrollment: Business/commerce; criminal justice/law enforcement administration; sociology. **Special Study Options:** Accelerated program, distance learning, double major, dual enrollment, exchange student program (domestic), honors program, independent study, internships, liberal arts/career combination, study abroad, teacher certification program, weekend college, Cooperative nursing program with University of Wisconsin: Milwaukee. Special programs offered to physically disabled students include note-taking services, reader services, tape recorders. **Career services:** Alumni services, career/job search classes, career assessment, internships.

FACILITIES

Housing: Coed dorms, special housing for disabled students, special housing for international students, apartments for single students. 99% of campus accessible to physically disabled. **Special Academic Facilities/Equipment:** Language lab, electron microscope. **Computers:** Students can register for classes online. Administrative functions (other than registration) can be performed online.

CAMPUS LIFE

Environment: City. **Activities:** Choral groups, concert band, dance, drama/theater, jazz band, literary magazine, music ensembles, musical theater, pep band, radio station, student government, student newspaper, symphony orchestra **Organizations:** 48 registered organizations, 5 honor societies, 1 religious organizations. 3 fraternities, 3 sororities. **Athletics (Intercollegiate):** *Men:* Baseball, basketball, cross-country, golf, soccer, track/field (outdoor), track/field (indoor), wrestling. *Women:* Basketball, cross-country, soccer, softball, track/field (outdoor), track/field (indoor), volleyball. **On-Campus Highlights:** Wyllie Library/Main Place, Communication Arts Building, Student Union, Student Activities Center, Molinaro Hall.

ADMISSIONS

Freshman Academic Profile: 5% in top 10% of high school class, 23% in top 25% of high school class, 56% in top 50% of high school class. 92% from public high schools. ACT middle 50% range 18–22. Minimum paper TOEFL 525. Minimum computer TOEFL 197. **Basis for Candidate Selection:** *Very important factors considered include:* Class rank, academic GPA, rigor of secondary school record, standardized test scores. *Other factors considered include:* Application essay, recommendation(s), alumni/ae relation, character/personal qualities, extracurricular activities, first generation, interview, level of applicant's interest, racial/ethnic status, talent/ability, volunteer work, work experience. **Freshman Admission Requirements:** High school diploma is required and GED is accepted. *Academic units required:* 4 English, 3 mathematics, 3 science, 3 social studies, 4 academic electives. *Academic units recommended:* 4 English, 4 mathematics, 4 science, (2 science labs), 2 foreign language, 3 social studies, 1 history, 4 academic electives. **Freshman Admission Statistics:** 1,868 applied, 92% admitted, 51% enrolled. **Transfer Admission Requirements:** High school transcript, college transcript(s), statement of good standing from prior institution(s). Minimum college GPA of 2.0 required. Lowest grade transferable D-. **General Admission Information:** Application fee $35. Regular application deadline 8/1. Notification on a rolling basis, beginning on or about 9/15. Nonfall registration accepted. Admission may be deferred for a maximum of 1 year. Credit and/or placement offered for CEEB Advanced Placement tests.

COSTS AND FINANCIAL AID

Annual in-state tuition $4,277. Annual out-of-state tuition $14,323. Room and board $5,550. Required fees $720. Average book expense $784. **Required Forms and Deadlines:** FAFSA. Priority financial aid filing date 3/15. **Notification of Awards:** Applicants will be notified of awards on a rolling basis beginning 4/1. **Types of Aid:** *Need-based scholarships/grants:* Federal Pell, SEOG, state scholarships/grants, private scholarships, the school's own gift aid, Federal Nursing Scholarships. *Loans:* FFEL Subsidized Stafford, FFEL Unsubsidized Stafford, FFEL PLUS, Federal Perkins, state loans *Student Employment:* Federal Work-Study Program available. Institutional employment available. Off-campus job opportunities are excellent. **Financial Aid Statistics:** 46% freshmen, 47% undergrads receive need-based scholarship or grant aid. 19% freshmen, 9% undergrads receive non-need-based scholarship or grant aid. 44% freshmen, 37% undergrads receive need-based self-help aid. 56% undergrads borrow to pay for school. Average cumulative indebtedness $17,158. **Criteria for awarding institutional aid:** *Non-need-based:* Academics, art, athletics, minority status, music/drama, state/district residency.

UNIVERSITY OF WISCONSIN—PLATTEVILLE

1 University Plaza, Platteville, WI 53818
Phone: 608)342-1125 **Financial Aid Phone:** 608-342-1836
E-mail: admit@uwplatt.edu **CEEB Code:** 1917
Fax: 608)342-1122 **Website:** www.uwplatt.edu **ACT Code:** 4676

This public school was founded in 1866. It has a 820-acre campus.

RATINGS
Admissions Selectivity Rating: 65   **Fire Safety Rating:** 63   **Green Rating:** 60*

STUDENTS AND FACULTY
Enrollment: 5,631. **Student Body:** 38% female, 62% male, 10% out-of-state, international (20 countries represented). Asian 1%, African American 1%, Caucasian 95%, Hispanic 1%.
Retention and Graduation: 76% freshmen return for sophomore year. **Faculty:** Student/faculty ratio 20:1. 249 full-time faculty, 83% hold PhDs, 16% are members of minority groups, 31% are women.

ACADEMICS
Degrees: Associate, bachelor's, certificate, diploma, master's, transfer associate. **Classes:** Most classes have fewer than 10 students. Most lab/discussion sessions have 20–29 students. **Majors with Highest Enrollment:** Business administration and management; criminal justice/safety studies; mechanical engineering. **Special Study Options:** Cooperative education program, distance learning, double major, dual enrollment, English as a Second Language (ESL), exchange student program (domestic), external degree program, honors program, independent study, internships, liberal arts/career combination, student-designed major, study abroad, teacher certification program. **Honors programs:** UW—Platteville has a University Honors Program that provides exceptional students with opportunities to study the problems, ideas, and methods of the liberal arts with an intensity, depth, and perspective that cannot usually be achieved in regular courses. Special programs offered to physically disabled students include note-taking services, reader services, tape recorders, tutors.

FACILITIES
Housing: Coed dorms, men's dorms, women's dorms, fraternity/sorority housing 100% of campus accessible to physically disabled. **Special Academic Facilities/Equipment:** Electron microscope, Nohr Art Gallery, The Wisconsin Room. **Computers:** Students can register for classes online. Administrative functions (other than registration) can be performed online.

CAMPUS LIFE
Environment: Village. **Activities:** Choral groups, concert band, drama/theater, jazz band, literary magazine, marching band, music ensembles, musical theater, pep band, radio station, student government, student newspaper, symphony orchestra, television station **Organizations:** 180 registered organizations, 15 honor societies, 9 religious organizations. 9 fraternities, 5 sororities. **Athletics (Intercollegiate): Men:** Baseball, basketball, cross-country, football, soccer, track/field (outdoor), track/field (indoor), wrestling. *Women:* Basketball, cross-country, golf, soccer, softball, track/field (outdoor), track/field (indoor), volleyball. **On-Campus Highlights:** Pioneer Student Center, Resident Halls, Field House, Ullrich Hall, New Athletic Fields, Check out our virtual tour at www.uwplatt.edu/university/vtour/.

ADMISSIONS
Freshman Academic Profile: 12% in top 10% of high school class, 35% in top 25% of high school class, 77% in top 50% of high school class. 94% from public high schools. ACT middle 50% range 20–25. Minimum paper TOEFL 550. **Basis for Candidate Selection:** *Very important factors considered include:* Class rank, rigor of secondary school record, standardized test scores. *Important factors considered include:* Geographical residence, state residency. *Other factors considered include:* Academic GPA, recommendation(s), extracurricular activities, interview, talent/ability. **Freshman Admission Requirements:** High school diploma is required and GED is accepted. *Academic units required:* 4 English, 3 mathematics, 3 science, (2 science labs), 3 social studies, 4 academic electives. *Academic units recommended:* 3 mathematics. **Freshman Admission Statistics:** 3,075 applied, 85% admitted, 46% enrolled. **Transfer Admission Requirements:** College transcript(s), statement of good standing from prior institution(s). Minimum college GPA of 2.0 required. Lowest grade transferable D. **General Admission Information:** Application fee $35. Notification on a rolling basis, beginning on or about 9/15. Nonfall registration accepted. Admission may be deferred for a maximum of 1 semester. Credit offered for CEEB Advanced Placement tests.

COSTS AND FINANCIAL AID
Annual in-state tuition $4,277. Annual out-of-state tuition $14,323. Room and board $4,654. Required fees $848. Average book expense $320. **Required Forms and Deadlines:** FAFSA. Priority financial aid filing date 1/3. **Notifica-**

tion of Awards: Applicants will be notified of awards on a rolling basis beginning 4/15. **Types of Aid:** *Need-based scholarships/grants:* State scholarships/grants. *Loans:* FFEL Subsidized Stafford, FFEL Unsubsidized Stafford, FFEL PLUS, Federal Perkins. **Financial Aid Statistics:** 60% undergrads borrow to pay for school. Average cumulative indebtedness $10,030. **Criteria for awarding institutional aid:** *Non-need-based:* Academics, leadership.

UNIVERSITY OF WISCONSIN—RIVER FALLS

410 South Third Street, 112 South Hall, River Falls, WI 54022
Phone: 715-425-3500 **Financial Aid Phone:** 715-425-3141
E-mail: admit@uwrf.edu **CEEB Code:** 1918
Fax: 715-425-0676 **Website:** www.uwrf.edu **ACT Code:** 4678

This public school was founded in 1874. It has a 225-acre campus.

RATINGS
Admissions Selectivity Rating: 60*   **Fire Safety Rating:** 60*   **Green Rating:** 60*

STUDENTS AND FACULTY
Enrollment: 5,880. **Student Body:** 58% female, 42% male, 42% out-of-state (18 countries represented).
Retention and Graduation: 26% freshmen graduate within 4 years. 17% grads go on to further study within 1 year. **Faculty:** Student/faculty ratio 22:1. 241 full-time faculty, 9% are members of minority groups, 42% are women.

ACADEMICS
Degrees: Bachelor's, master's, post-bachelor's certificate, post-master's certificate. **Classes:** Most classes have 20–29 students. Most lab/discussion sessions have 10–19 students. **Majors with Highest Enrollment:** Animal sciences; biological and physical sciences; business/commerce. **Special Study Options:** Accelerated program, cooperative education program, distance learning, double major, dual enrollment, exchange student program (domestic), honors program, independent study, internships, student-designed major, study abroad, teacher certification program. **Honors programs:** The UW—River Falls Honors Program is designed to meet the educational needs of students who have an outstanding record of academic achievement and a true sense of intellectual adventure. It allows students to experience a variety of course types and educationally related experiences while gaining academic credit. Students enrolled in the program may choose Honors sections of many general education classes, take introductory and advanced Honors seminars, participate in Honors colloquia, complete an Honors thesis/project, enroll in a service-learning experience for credit and receive credits for participation in the intellectual and creative life of the UW—RF community and elsewhere. All of these experiences are gained while still keeping within the major and minor requirements of an Honors student's academic program. Special programs offered to physically disabled students include note-taking services, reader services, tape recorders, tutors. **Career services:** Alumni network, alumni services, career/job search classes, career assessment, internships, regional alumni. **Career services highlights include:** Professional staff are available for one hour appointments to help you with placement, resume writing, portfolio help, licensing, etc.

FACILITIES
Housing: Coed dorms, women's dorms, fraternity/sorority housing, apartments for single students. 95% of campus accessible to physically disabled. **Special Academic Facilities/Equipment:** Local history museum, 20–inch reflecting telescope, observatory, electron microscope, greenhouse, lab farms, educational technology center. **Computers:** Students can register for classes online. Administrative functions (other than registration) can be performed online.

CAMPUS LIFE
Environment: Village. **Activities:** Choral groups, concert band, dance, drama/theater, jazz band, literary magazine, music ensembles, musical theater, pep band, radio station, student government, student newspaper, symphony orchestra, television station. **Organizations:** 120 registered organizations, 9 honor societies, 12 religious organizations. 5 fraternities, 4 sororities. **Athletics (Intercollegiate): Men:** Basketball, cross-country, football, ice hockey, swimming, track/field (outdoor), track/field (indoor). *Women:* Basketball, cross-country, golf, ice hockey, soccer, softball, swimming, tennis, track/field (outdoor), track/field (indoor), volleyball. **On-Campus Highlights:** University Student Center, Leadership Center, Knowles/Hunt Recreation Complex, Chalmer Davee Library, Educational Technology Center, Swenson Sundial (world's largest), Carillon, Fine Arts performing complex, Two campus laboratory farms, and Kansas City Chiefs summer camp.

ADMISSIONS
Freshman Academic Profile: 95% from public high schools. ACT middle 50% range 18–24. Minimum paper TOEFL 500. Minimum computer TOEFL

180. Basis for Candidate Selection: *Very important factors considered include:* Class rank, rigor of secondary school record, standardized test scores, *Other factors considered include:* Academic GPA, recommendation(s). **Freshman Admission Requirements:** High school diploma is required and GED is accepted. *Academic units required:* 4 English, 3 mathematics, 3 science, 3 social studies, 4 academic electives. *Academic units recommended:* 2 foreign language. **Freshman Admission Statistics:** 2,886 applied, 91% admitted, 49% enrolled. **Transfer Admission Requirements:** College transcript(s), statement of good standing from prior institution(s). Minimum college GPA of 2.6 required. Lowest grade transferable D. **General Admission Information:** Application fee $44. Notification on a rolling basis, beginning on or about 9/15. Nonfall registration accepted. Admission may be deferred for a maximum of 1 year. Credit and/or placement offered for CEEB Advanced Placement tests.

COSTS AND FINANCIAL AID

Annual in-state tuition $6,220. Annual out-of-state tuition $13,793. Room and board $5,106. Average book expense $300. **Required Forms and Deadlines:** FAFSA, institution's own financial aid form. Priority financial aid filing date 3/15. **Notification of Awards:** Applicants will be notified of awards on a rolling basis beginning 4/1. **Types of Aid:** *Need-based scholarships/grants:* Federal Pell, SEOG, state scholarships/grants, private scholarships, the school's own gift aid. *Loans:* FFEL Subsidized Stafford, FFEL Unsubsidized Stafford, FFEL PLUS, Federal Perkins. *Student Employment:* Federal Work-Study Program available. Institutional employment available. Off-campus job opportunities are good. **Financial Aid Statistics:** 30% freshmen, 38% undergrads receive need-based scholarship or grant aid. 5% freshmen, 5% undergrads receive non-need-based scholarship or grant aid. 37% freshmen, 49% undergrads receive need-based self-help aid.

UNIVERSITY OF WISCONSIN—STEVENS POINT

102 Student Services Center, Stevens Point, WI 54481
Phone: 715-346-2441 **Financial Aid Phone:** 715-346-4771
E-mail: admiss@uwsp.edu **CEEB Code:** 1919
Fax: 715-346-3296 **Website:** www.uwsp.edu **ACT Code:** 4680

This public school was founded in 1894. It has a 335-acre campus.

RATINGS
Admissions Selectivity Rating: 79   **Fire Safety Rating:** 65   **Green Rating:** 97

STUDENTS AND FACULTY
Enrollment: 8,610. **Student Body:** 52% female, 48% male, 8% out-of-state, 2% international (31 countries represented). Asian 3%, African American 1%, Caucasian 90%, Hispanic 1%, Native American 1%.
Retention and Graduation: 78% freshmen return for sophomore year. 20% freshmen graduate within 4 years. 10% grads go on to further study within 1 year. **Faculty:** Student/faculty ratio 20:1. 398 full-time faculty, 78% hold PhDs, 8% are members of minority groups, 41% are women.

ACADEMICS
Degrees: Associate, bachelor's, master's, terminal associate. **Classes:** Most classes have 20–29 students. Most lab/discussion sessions have 20–29 students. **Majors with Highest Enrollment:** Biological and physical sciences; business/commerce; elementary education and teaching. **Special Study Options:** Accelerated program, distance learning, double major, dual enrollment, English as a Second Language (ESL), independent study, internships, student-designed major, study abroad, teacher certification program. Special programs offered to physically disabled students include note-taking services, reader services, tape recorders, tutors. **Career services:** Alumni network, career/job search classes, career assessment, internships.

FACILITIES
Housing: Coed dorms, men's dorms, women's dorms, wellness housing, theme housing, Freshman Interest Groups. 100% of campus accessible to physically disabled. **Special Academic Facilities/Equipment:** Art galleries, costume and goblet collections, museum of natural history, early childhood study institute, communicative disorders center, map center, observatory, planetarium, Foucault pendulum, nature preserve, environmental station, groundwater center, herbarium, aviary, wellness institute. **Computers:** 100% of classrooms, 10% of dorms, 100% of libraries, 100% of dining areas, 100% of student union, have wireless network access. Students can register for classes online. Administrative functions (other than registration) can be performed online.

CAMPUS LIFE
Environment: Town. **Activities:** Choral groups, concert band, dance, drama/theater, jazz band, literary magazine, music ensembles, musical theater, opera, pep band, radio station, student government, student newspaper, student-run film society, symphony orchestra, television station, campus ministries, international student organization, Model UN. **Organizations:** 185 registered organizations, 12 honor societies, 9 religious organizations, 4 fraternities, 3 sororities. **Athletics (Intercollegiate):** *Men:* Baseball, basketball, cross-country, diving, football, ice hockey, swimming, track/field (outdoor), wrestling. *Women:* Basketball, cross-country, diving, golf, ice hockey, soccer, softball, swimming, tennis, track/field (outdoor), volleyball. **On-Campus Highlights:** University Center/Brewhouse, Schmeeckle Reserve/Wisconsin Conservation Hall of, Health Enhancement Center, Allen Recreation Center, Fine Arts Building, The University Center houses the Information Center, Student Activities and Involvement Center, the university bookstore, meeting rooms, study lounges, Multicultural Center, and several dining options. The Schmeeckle Reserve is a 265-acre reserve available for educational and recreational use by students and community alike. The reserve includes a 24-acre lake and a 2 1/2 mile trail system used for recreational purposes. The Health Enhancement Center houses athletics, facilities for physical education programs, an OlympiC–sized swimming pool, 7,500 square foot weight room, state-of-the-art training room, 8-lane indoor track with an infield for 6 tennis courts or 4 full-sized basketball courts, a fieldhouse and the Berg Gym. Allen Recreation Center provides a cardio-fitness facility, massage rooms, and a recreation center with rental equipment available for students. The Fine Arts Center houses the departments of Art and Design, Music, and Theatre and Dance. Concerts and drama productions are scheduled throughout the year in its two theatres. The Carlsten Art Gallery is also located here. Other highlights on campus include a huge mosaic on the outer, south wall of the College of Natural Resources building; a plenetarium located in the Science Building; the Learning Resources Center which contains Instructional Media Services, the library, and the Museum of Natural History; and the Communication Arts Center which houses the student radio station, student newspaper. and several television studios. **Environmental Initiatives:** UWSP has a long-standing commitment to the environment. We established the first the nation's first "conservation education" major in 1946 and subsequently, in 1970, a College of Natural Resources that is the largest and premier undergraduate institution for natural resources and environmental management in the nation. A new Operations and Waste Management Facility currently is in design and is slated for construction in the 2009–11 biennium. The project will result in the first waste management facility of its kind built at a university in Wisconsin and will feature a pilot wastewater treatment plant, a composting lab, a microbiology lab, and an adjoined recycling center offering co-training opportunities in materials recycling. UWSP's award-winning recycling and composting program originated in 1989. The Greenest Room in Knutzen Hall is an ongoing demonstration of how students and the public can live an affordable and comfortable environmentally friendly lifestyle by utilizing products and practices that are sustainable and earth friendly. One of the residence halls, Knutson Hall, has been UWSP's "Eco-Hall" for 10 years.

ADMISSIONS
Freshman Academic Profile: Average high school GPA 3.4. 15% in top 10% of high school class, 46% in top 25% of high school class, 93% in top 50% of high school class. SAT Math middle 50% range 490–652. SAT Critical Reading middle 50% range 515–655. SAT Writing middle 50% range 490–667. ACT middle 50% range 21–25. Minimum paper TOEFL 523. Minimum computer TOEFL 193. Minimum web-based TOEFL 70. **Basis for Candidate Selection:** *Very important factors considered include:* Class rank, academic GPA, rigor of secondary school record, standardized test scores. *Important factors considered include:* Application essay, recommendation(s). *Other factors considered include:* character/personal qualities, extracurricular activities, first generation, level of applicant's interest, racial/ethnic status, talent/ability, volunteer work, work experience. **Freshman Admission Requirements:** High school diploma is required and GED is accepted. *Academic units required:* 4 English, 3 mathematics, 3 science, 3 social studies, 4 academic electives, 4 Additional 2 units from English, mathematics, social sciences, sciences, or foreign language and 2 units from above areas or other academic areas. *Academic units recommended:* 4 mathematics, 4 science, 4 social studies, 4 Additional 2 units from English, mathematics, social sciences, sciences, or foreign language and 2 units from above areas or other academic areas. **Freshman Admission Statistics:** 5,178 applied, 73% admitted, 44% enrolled. **Transfer Admission Requirements:** High school transcript, college transcript(s), statement of good standing from prior institution(s). Minimum college GPA of 2.25 required. Lowest grade transferable D. **General Admission Information:** Application fee $44. Nonfall registration accepted. Admission may be deferred for a maximum of semester. Credit and/or placement offered for CEEB Advanced Placement tests.

COSTS AND FINANCIAL AID
Annual in-state tuition $6,530. Annual out-of-state tuition $14,104. Room and board $5,612. Required fees $1,168. Average book expense $500. **Required Forms and Deadlines:** FAFSA. Financial aid filing deadline 6/15. Priority financial aid filing date 5/15. **Notification of Awards:** Applicants will be notified of awards on a rolling basis beginning 5/1. **Types of Aid:** *Need-based scholarships/grants:* Federal Pell, SEOG, state scholarships/grants, private scholarships, the school's own gift aid. *Loans:* FFEL Subsidized Stafford, FFEL

Unsubsidized Stafford, FFEL PLUS, Federal Perkins. *Student Employment:* Federal Work-Study Program available. Institutional employment available. Off-campus job opportunities are good. **Financial Aid Statistics:** 23% freshmen, 26% undergrads receive need-based scholarship or grant aid. 5% freshmen, 6% undergrads receive non-need-based scholarship or grant aid. 42% freshmen, 45% undergrads receive need-based self-help aid. 73% freshmen, 72% undergrads receive any aid. 73% undergrads borrow to pay for school. Average cumulative indebtedness $19,738. **Criteria for awarding institutional aid:** *Non-need-based:* Academics, alumni affiliation, art, music/drama.

UNIVERSITY OF WISCONSIN—STOUT

Admissions UW-Stout, Menomonie, WI 54751
Phone: 715-232-1411 **Financial Aid Phone:** 715-232-1363
E-mail: admissions@uwstout.edu **CEEB Code:** 1740
Fax: 715-232-1667 **Website:** www.uwstout.edu **ACT Code:** 4652

This public school was founded in 1891. It has a 110-acre campus.

RATINGS
Admissions Selectivity Rating: 71 **Fire Safety Rating:** 60* **Green Rating:** 60*

STUDENTS AND FACULTY
Enrollment: 7,893. **Student Body:** 48% female, 52% male, 30% out-of-state, 1% international (28 countries represented). Asian 3%, African American 1%, Caucasian 89%, Hispanic 1%, Native American 1%.
Retention and Graduation: 19% freshmen graduate within 4 years. 9% grads go on to further study within 1 year. **Faculty:** Student/faculty ratio 20:1. 346 full-time faculty, 79% hold PhDs, 13% are members of minority groups, 41% are women.

ACADEMICS
Degrees: Bachelor's, certificate, master's, post-bachelor's certificate, post-master's certificate. **Classes:** Most classes have 20–29 students. Most lab/discussion sessions have 20–29 students. **Majors with Highest Enrollment:** Business/commerce; design and applied arts, other; hospitality administration/management. **Special Study Options:** Accelerated program, cooperative education program, cross-registration, distance learning, double major, dual enrollment, exchange student program (domestic), external degree program, honors program, independent study, internships, study abroad, teacher certification program. **Honors programs:** The University Honors Program (UHP) is designed to enhance the education of students challenging them to think in more depth and detail and to provide the opportunity to meet other students while doing so. Special programs offered to physically disabled students include note-taking services, reader services, tutors. **Career services:** Alumni services, career/job search classes, internships. **Career services highlights include:** Our Co-op Program now exceeds 676 co-op students per year.

FACILITIES
Housing: Coed dorms, special housing for disabled students, apartments for single students, freshmen housing, smoke-free housing, upperclass/graduate housing, alcohol-free housing. 100% of campus accessible to physically disabled. **Special Academic Facilities/Equipment:** Specialized labs support degree programs throughout the campus. Furlong Art Gallery in Micheal's Hall. **Computers:** Students can register for classes online. Administrative functions (other than registration) can be performed online. Undergraduates are required to own a computer.

CAMPUS LIFE
Environment: Village. **Activities:** Choral groups, concert band, dance, drama/theater, jazz band, literary magazine, marching band, music ensembles, musical theater, pep band, radio station, student government, student newspaper, student-run film society, campus ministries, international student organization, Model UN. **Organizations:** 120 registered organizations, 1 honor societies, 12 religious organizations. 5 fraternities, 3 sororities. **Athletics (Intercollegiate):** *Men:* Baseball, basketball, cross-country, football, ice hockey, track/field (outdoor). *Women:* Basketball, cross-country, gymnastics, soccer, softball, tennis, track/field (outdoor), volleyball. **On-Campus Highlights:** Millenium Hall, Athletic Complex, Ropes Course, Climbing Wall, In-line Skating, Student Center, Micheels Hall.

ADMISSIONS
Freshman Academic Profile: 7.3% in top 10% of high school class, 25.5% in top 25% of high school class, 72.7% in top 50% of high school class. ACT middle 50% range 19–23. Minimum paper TOEFL 500. Minimum computer TOEFL 173. **Basis for Candidate Selection:** *Very important factors considered include:* Class rank, standardized test scores. *Important factors considered include:* Application essay, rigor of secondary school record. *Other factors*

considered include: Academic GPA, recommendation(s), alumni/ae relation, character/personal qualities, extracurricular activities, first generation, interview, level of applicant's interest, racial/ethnic status, talent/ability, volunteer work, work experience. **Freshman Admission Requirements:** High school diploma is required and GED is accepted. *Academic units required:* 4 English, 3 mathematics, 3 science, 3 social studies, 4 academic electives. *Academic units recommended:* 2 foreign language. **Transfer Admission Requirements:** College transcript(s), statement of good standing from prior institution(s). Minimum college GPA of 2.5 required. Lowest grade transferable D–. **General Admission Information:** Application fee $44. Notification on a rolling basis, beginning on or about 9/15. Nonfall registration accepted. Credit offered for CEEB Advanced Placement tests.

COSTS AND FINANCIAL AID
Annual in-state tuition $5,974. Annual out-of-state tuition $13,719. Room and board $5,336. Required fees $1,847. Average book expense $356. **Required Forms and Deadlines:** FAFSA. Priority financial aid filing date 3/15. **Notification of Awards:** Applicants will be notified of awards on a rolling basis beginning 4/1. **Types of Aid:** *Need-based scholarships/grants:* Federal Pell, SEOG, state scholarships/grants, private scholarships, the school's own gift aid. *Loans:* FFEL Subsidized Stafford, FFEL Unsubsidized Stafford, FFEL PLUS, Federal Perkins, Alternative Educational Loans. *Student Employment:* Federal Work-Study Program available. Institutional employment available. Highest amount earned per year from on-campus jobs $948. Off-campus job opportunities are good. **Financial Aid Statistics:** 28% freshmen, 31% undergrads receive need-based scholarship or grant aid. 11% freshmen, 7% undergrads receive non-need-based scholarship or grant aid. 52% freshmen, 53% undergrads receive need-based self-help aid. 71% freshmen, 74% undergrads receive any aid. 78% undergrads borrow to pay for school. Average cumulative indebtedness $25,134. **Criteria for awarding institutional aid:** *Non-need-based:* Academics.

UNIVERSITY OF WISCONSIN—SUPERIOR

Belknap and Catlin, P.O. Box 2000, Superior, WI 54880-4500
Phone: 715-394-8230 **Financial Aid Phone:** 715-394-8200
E-mail: admissions@uwsuper.edu **CEEB Code:** 1920
Fax: 715-394-8407 **Website:** www.uwsuper.edu **ACT Code:** 4682

This public school was founded in 1893. It has a 230-acre campus.

RATINGS
Admissions Selectivity Rating: 70 **Fire Safety Rating:** 61 **Green Rating:** 61

STUDENTS AND FACULTY
Enrollment: 2,515. **Student Body:** 57% female, 43% male, 44% out-of-state, 6% international (30 countries represented). Asian 1%, African American 2%, Caucasian 85%, Hispanic 1%, Native American 3%.
Retention and Graduation: 72% freshmen return for sophomore year. 20% freshmen graduate within 4 years. 13% grads go on to further study within 1 year. 2% grads pursue arts and sciences degrees. 1% grads pursue law degrees. 2% grads pursue business degrees. 1% grads pursue medical degrees. **Faculty:** Student/faculty ratio 18:1. 112 full-time faculty, 73% hold PhDs, 10% are members of minority groups, 46% are women.

ACADEMICS
Degrees: Associate, bachelor's, certificate, master's, post-master's certificate. **Classes:** Most classes have 10–19 students. Most lab/discussion sessions have 10–19 students. **Majors with Highest Enrollment:** Biology/biological sciences; business administration and management; elementary education and teaching. **Special Study Options:** Cooperative education program, cross-registration, distance learning, double major, dual enrollment, English as a Second Language (ESL), exchange student program (domestic), external degree program, independent study, internships, liberal arts/career combination, student-designed major, study abroad, teacher certification program. **Combined degree programs:** 3-2 Forestry program w/ Michigan Tech U. Special programs offered to physically disabled students include note-taking services, tape recorders, tutors. **Career services:** Alumni network, career/job search classes, career assessment, internships.

FACILITIES
Housing: Coed dorms, special housing for disabled students, women's dorms, apartments for married students, apartments for single students, 90% of campus accessible to physically disabled. **Special Academic Facilities/Equipment:** TV, radio, and film facilities,observatory, greenhouse,two art galleries, recital hall, four theaters, modern health and wellness center. Major Library renovations to be completed and major student center renovation in works.

Computers: 40% of classrooms, 100% of libraries, 100% of dining areas, 100% of student union, 20% of common outdoor areas have wireless network access. Students can register for classes online. Administrative functions (other than registration) can be performed online.

CAMPUS LIFE

Environment: City. **Activities:** Choral groups, concert band, dance, drama/theater, jazz band, literary magazine, music ensembles, musical theater, pep band, radio station, student government, student newspaper, student-run film society, symphony orchestra, television station, campus ministries, international student organization. **Organizations:** 70 registered organizations, 1 honor societies, 5 religious organizations. 1 sororities. **Athletics (Intercollegiate):** *Men:* Baseball, basketball, cross-country, ice hockey, soccer, track/field (outdoor), track/field (indoor). *Women:* Basketball, cross-country, golf, ice hockey, soccer, softball, track/field (outdoor), track/field (indoor), volleyball. **On-Campus Highlights:** New Health and Wellness Center, Coffee Nook, Snack Bar, Rothwell Student Center Student Lounge, Multicultural Center, Health and Wellness Center is a new $17 million facility complete with running track, climbing wall, raquetball courts and much more. Library renovations underway, new student center renovations starting soon. **Environmental Initiatives:** LEED certification for new buildings that are now in the planning/construction process; establishing a Sustainability Council that will guide the implementation of our environmental commitment; A new student group—SWARM.

ADMISSIONS

Freshman Academic Profile: 11% in top 10% of high school class, 33% in top 25% of high school class, 75% in top 50% of high school class. 90% from public high schools. ACT middle 50% range 19–24. Minimum paper TOEFL 525. Minimum computer TOEFL 195. **Basis for Candidate Selection:** *Very important factors considered include:* Rigor of secondary school record. *Important factors considered include:* Class rank, standardized test scores. *Other factors considered include:* Application essay, recommendation(s), character/personal qualities, extracurricular activities, first generation, interview, level of applicant's interest, racial/ethnic status, talent/ability, volunteer work, work experience. **Freshman Admission Requirements:** High school diploma is required and GED is accepted. *Academic units required:* 4 English, 3 mathematics, 3 science, 3 social studies, 4 academic electives. *Academic units recommended:* 2 foreign language. **Freshman Admission Statistics:** 965 applied, 68% admitted, 56% enrolled. **Transfer Admission Requirements:** College transcript(s), minimum college GPA of 2.0 required. Lowest grade transferable D. **General Admission Information:** Application fee $44. Notification on a rolling basis, beginning on or about 10/1. Nonfall registration accepted. Admission may be deferred for a maximum of 1 year. Credit offered for CEEB Advanced Placement tests.

COSTS AND FINANCIAL AID

Annual in-state tuition $5,571. Annual out-of-state tuition $13,143. Room and board $5,600. Required fees $1,165. Average book expense $750. **Required Forms and Deadlines:** FAFSA. Priority financial aid filing date 4/15. **Notification of Awards:** Applicants will be notified of awards on a rolling basis beginning 3/15. **Types of Aid:** *Need-based scholarships/grants:* Federal Pell, SEOG, state scholarships/grants, private scholarships, the school's own gift aid. *Loans:* Direct Subsidized Stafford, Direct Unsubsidized Stafford, Direct PLUS, Federal Perkins, state loans, college/university loans from institutional funds. *Student Employment:* Federal Work-Study Program available. Institutional employment available. Highest amount earned per year from on-campus jobs $11,000. Off-campus job opportunities are good. **Financial Aid Statistics:** 33% freshmen, 37% undergrads receive need-based scholarship or grant aid. 23% freshmen, 13% undergrads receive non-need-based scholarship or grant aid. 48% freshmen, 53% undergrads receive need-based self-help aid. 72% freshmen, 73% undergrads receive any aid. 75% undergrads borrow to pay for school. Average cumulative indebtedness $22,516. **Criteria for awarding institutional aid:** *Non-need-based:* Academics, alumni affiliation, art, leadership, minority status, music/drama, state/district residency.

UNIVERSITY OF WISCONSIN—WHITEWATER

800 West Main Street, Whitewater, WI 53190-1791
Phone: 262-472-1440 **Financial Aid Phone:** 262-472-1130
E-mail: uwwadmit@uww.edu **CEEB Code:** 1921
Fax: 262-472-1515 **Website:** www.uww.edu **ACT Code:** 4684

This public school was founded in 1868. It has a 385-acre campus.

RATINGS
Admissions Selectivity Rating: 66   **Fire Safety Rating:** 71   **Green Rating:** 60*

STUDENTS AND FACULTY

Enrollment: 8,999. **Student Body:** 50% female, 50% male, 4% out-of-state, international (69 countries represented). Asian 2%, African American 4%, Caucasian 90%, Hispanic 2%.
Retention and Graduation: 74% freshmen return for sophomore year. 21% freshmen graduate within 4 years. **Faculty:** Student/faculty ratio 22:1. 392 full-time faculty, 85% hold PhDs, 18% are members of minority groups, 44% are women.

ACADEMICS

Degrees: Associate, bachelor's, master's. **Classes:** Most classes have 30–39 students. **Majors with Highest Enrollment:** Elementary education and teaching; journalism; physical education teaching and coaching. **Special Study Options:** Accelerated program, cooperative education program, cross-registration, distance learning, double major, dual enrollment, English as a Second Language (ESL), exchange student program (domestic), external degree program, honors program, independent study, internships, liberal arts/career combination, student-designed major, study abroad, teacher certification program, weekend college. **Honors programs:** General academic honors program Special programs offered to physically disabled students include note-taking services, reader services, tape recorders, tutors. **Career services:** Career/job search classes, career assessment, internships. **Career services highlights include:** Internships.

FACILITIES

Housing: Coed dorms, special housing for disabled students, special housing for international students, women's dorms. 100% of campus accessible to physically disabled. **Special Academic Facilities/Equipment:** Two electron microscopes, state-of-the-art Theater/Auditorium. **Computers:** Students can register for classes online. Administrative functions (other than registration) can be performed online.

CAMPUS LIFE

Environment: Village. **Activities:** Choral groups, concert band, dance, drama/theater, jazz band, literary magazine, marching band, music ensembles, musical theater, opera, radio station, student government, student newspaper, symphony orchestra, television station. **Organizations:** 130 registered organizations, 4 honor societies, 8 religious organizations. 9 fraternities, 8 sororities. **Athletics (Intercollegiate):** *Men:* Baseball, basketball, cross-country, diving, football, soccer, swimming, tennis, track/field (outdoor), track/field (indoor), wrestling. *Women:* Basketball, bowling, cross-country, diving, golf, gymnastics, soccer, softball, swimming, tennis, track/field (outdoor), track/field (indoor), volleyball. **On-Campus Highlights:** New Kachel Field House, University Center, Underground Dance Club, Ritazza Coffee Shop, Warhawk Room.

ADMISSIONS

Freshman Academic Profile: 9% in top 10% of high school class, 32% in top 25% of high school class, 77% in top 50% of high school class. 90% from public high schools. SAT Math middle 50% range 480–600. SAT Writing middle 50% range 470–610. ACT middle 50% range 20–24. Minimum paper TOEFL 500. Minimum computer TOEFL 214. **Basis for Candidate Selection:** *Very important factors considered include:* Class rank, rigor of secondary school record, standardized test scores. *Other factors considered include:* Application essay, academic GPA, recommendation(s), character/personal qualities, extracurricular activities, first generation, geographical residence, interview, level of applicant's interest, racial/ethnic status, state residency, talent/ability, volunteer work, work experience. **Freshman Admission Requirements:** High school diploma is required and GED is accepted. *Academic units required:* 4 English, 3 mathematics, 3 science, (1 science labs), 3 social studies, 4 academic electives. *Academic units recommended:* 4 mathematics, 4 science, 2 foreign language, 4 social studies. **Transfer Admission Requirements:** High school transcript, college transcript(s), minimum college GPA of 2.0 required. Lowest grade transferable D–. **General Admission Information:** Application fee $35. Notification on a rolling basis, beginning on or about 9/15. Nonfall registration accepted. Admission may be deferred for a maximum of 3 terms or 1. Credit offered for CEEB Advanced Placement tests.

COSTS AND FINANCIAL AID

Annual in-state tuition $5,568. Annual out-of-state tuition $13,042. Room and board $4,322. Required fees $710. Average book expense $170. **Required Forms and Deadlines:** FAFSA. Priority financial aid filing date 3/15. **Notification of Awards:** Applicants will be notified of awards on a rolling basis beginning 4/1. **Types of Aid:** *Need-based scholarships/grants:* Federal Pell, SEOG, state scholarships/grants, private scholarships, the school's own gift aid. *Loans:* Direct Subsidized Stafford, Direct Unsubsidized Stafford, Direct PLUS, Federal Perkins, college/university loans from institutional funds, Alternative Loans. *Student Employment:* Highest amount earned per year from on-campus jobs $3,000. **Financial Aid Statistics:** 20% freshmen, 21% undergrads receive need-based scholarship or grant aid. 14% freshmen, 6% undergrads receive non-need-based scholarship or grant aid. 45% freshmen, 39% undergrads receive need-based self-help aid. 52% freshmen, 42% undergrads receive any aid. 64.7% undergrads borrow to pay for school. Average cumulative indebtedness

$15,602. **Criteria for awarding institutional aid:** *Non-need-based:* Academics, alumni affiliation, art, leadership, minority status, music/drama, state/district residency.

UNIVERSITY OF WYOMING

Best 373

Dept 3435, 1000 E University Ave, Laramie, WY 82071
Phone: 307-766-5160 **Financial Aid Phone:** 307-766-2116
E-mail: Why-Wyo@uwyo.edu **CEEB Code:** 4855
Fax: 307-766-4042 **Website:** www.uwyo.edu **ACT Code:** 5006

This public school was founded in 1886. It has a 785-acre campus.

RATINGS
Admissions Selectivity Rating: 88   **Fire Safety Rating:** 60*   **Green Rating:** 85

STUDENTS AND FACULTY
Enrollment: 9,587. **Student Body:** 53% female, 47% male, 289% out-of-state, 3% international (86 countries represented). Asian 1%, African American 1%, Caucasian 81%, Hispanic 4%, Native American 1%.
Retention and Graduation: Faculty: Student/faculty ratio 14:1. 730 full-time faculty, 85% hold PhDs, 9% are members of minority groups, 36% are women. 10% of classes are taught by teaching assistants.

ACADEMICS
Degrees: Bachelor's, certificate, doctoral, master's, post-bachelor's certificate, post-master's certificate. **Classes:** Most classes have 20–29 students. Most lab/discussion sessions have 20–29 students. **Majors with Highest Enrollment:** Elementary education and teaching; nursing/registered nurse (RN, ASN, BSN, MSN); psychology. **Special Study Options:** Accelerated program, distance learning, double major, English as a Second Language (ESL), exchange student program (domestic), external degree program, honors program, independent study, internships, student-designed major, study abroad. **Honors programs:** The University Honors Program provides highly motivated students a series of curricular and extracurricular opportunities. Most students are selected for the program prior to their freshman year, although the program welcomes UW and transfer students up to the beginning of the junior year. Each year the Honors Program awards scholarships to qualifying students who are beginning their undergraduate education or who are entering the University as transfer students. The honors students organize extracurricular activities, have a student lounge and computers for their use, and have the option of living on one of the honors floors in the residence halls or in the Honors House. Courses offered in the honors program are restricted to honors program students; exceptions must be approved by the Honors program office. Special programs offered to physically disabled students include note-taking services, reader services, tape recorders, tutors. **Career services:** Alumni network, alumni services, career/job search classes, career assessment, internships, regional alumni.

FACILITIES
Housing: Coed dorms, special housing for disabled students, fraternity/sorority housing, apartments for married students, apartments for single students, Floor specific living plans in the residence halls; Health Sciences Living house. 95% of campus accessible to physically disabled. **Special Academic Facilities/Equipment:** Art gallery, Geology museum, American Heritage Center, Rocky Mountain Herbarium, Solheim Mycology Herbarium, art museum, planetarium, environmental biology lab, anthropology museum, on-site elementary school, state veterinary lab, infrared telescope observatory, lysimeter lab, insect museum and gallery room, Wyoming Geographic Information Science Center, Writing Center, Wyoming Cooperative Fishery and Wildlife Research Unit. **Computers:** 75% of classrooms, 20% of dorms, 100% of libraries, 5% of dining areas, 100% of student union, 10% of common outdoor areas have wireless network access. Students can register for classes online. Administrative functions (other than registration) can be performed online.

CAMPUS LIFE
Environment: Town. **Activities:** Choral groups, concert band, dance, drama/theater, jazz band, literary magazine, marching band, music ensembles, musical theater, opera, pep band, radio station, student government, student newspaper, symphony orchestra, television station, campus ministries, international student organization, Model UN. **Organizations:** 223 registered organizations, 41 honor societies, 17 religious organizations. 8 fraternities, 6 sororities. **Athletics (Intercollegiate):** *Men:* Basketball, cheerleading, cross-country, diving, football, golf, swimming, track/field (outdoor), track/field (indoor), wrestling.

Women: Basketball, cheerleading, cross-country, diving, golf, soccer, swimming, tennis, track/field (outdoor), track/field (indoor), volleyball. **On-Campus Highlights:** Student Union, American Heritage Center and Art Museum, Geology Museum, Fine Arts Center, Half-Acre Gym. **Environmental Initiatives:** Campus Sustainability Committee; College of Business Sustainable Business Program; Presidents' Climate Commitment.

ADMISSIONS
Freshman Academic Profile: Average high school GPA 3.43. 21.7% in top 10% of high school class, 49.4% in top 25% of high school class, 80.6% in top 50% of high school class. SAT Math middle 50% range 490–620. SAT Critical Reading middle 50% range 480–600. ACT middle 50% range 21–27. Minimum paper TOEFL 525. Minimum computer TOEFL 197. Minimum web-based TOEFL 71. **Basis for Candidate Selection:** *Very important factors considered include:* Academic GPA, rigor of secondary school record, standardized test scores. *Important factors considered include:* level of applicant's interest. *Other factors considered include:* Application essay, recommendation(s), character/personal qualities, extracurricular activities, interview, state residency, talent/ability. **Freshman Admission Requirements:** High school diploma is required and GED is accepted. *Academic units required:* 4 English, 3 mathematics, 3 science, (3 science labs), 3 Cultural Context Electives. *Academic units recommended:* 3 behavioral or social sciences, 3 visual or performing arts, 3 humanities or earth/space sciences. **Freshman Admission Statistics:** 3,709 applied, 96% admitted, 45% enrolled. **Transfer Admission Requirements:** College transcript(s), minimum college GPA of 2.0 required. Lowest grade transferable D. **General Admission Information:** Application fee $40. Regular application deadline 8/10. Nonfall registration accepted. Admission may be deferred for a maximum of 1 year. Credit and/or placement offered for CEEB Advanced Placement tests.

COSTS AND FINANCIAL AID
Annual in-state tuition $2,820. Annual out-of-state tuition $10,740. Room and board $8,006. Required fees $906. Average book expense $1,200. **Required Forms and Deadlines:** FAFSA. Priority financial aid filing date 2/1. **Notification of Awards:** Applicants will be notified of awards on a rolling basis beginning 3/15. **Types of Aid:** *Need-based scholarships/grants:* Federal Pell, SEOG, state scholarships/grants, private scholarships, the school's own gift aid. *Loans:* FFEL Subsidized Stafford, FFEL Unsubsidized Stafford, FFEL PLUS, Federal Perkins. *Student Employment:* Federal Work-Study Program available. Institutional employment available. Off-campus job opportunities are good. **Financial Aid Statistics:** 21% freshmen, 23% undergrads receive need-based scholarship or grant aid. 39% freshmen, 29% undergrads receive non-need-based scholarship or grant aid. 22% freshmen, 27% undergrads receive need-based self-help aid. 5% freshmen, 5% undergrads receive athletic scholarships. 89.63% freshmen, 63.45% undergrads receive any aid. 53% undergrads borrow to pay for school. Average cumulative indebtedness $18,760. **Criteria for awarding institutional aid:** *Non-need-based:* Academics, alumni affiliation, art, athletics, leadership, minority status, music/drama, religious affiliation, state/district residency.

See page 1312.

UPPER IOWA UNIVERSITY

Parker Fox Hall Box 1859, Fayette, IA 52142-1859
Phone: 800-553-4150 **Financial Aid Phone:** 563-425-5274
E-mail: admission@uiu.edu
Fax: 319-425-5277 **Website: ACT Code:** 1360

This private school was founded in 1857. It has a 80-acre campus.

RATINGS
Admissions Selectivity Rating: 64   **Fire Safety Rating:** 61   **Green Rating:** 60*

STUDENTS AND FACULTY
Enrollment: 5,811. **Student Body:** 61% female, 39% male (19 countries represented).
Retention and Graduation: 70% freshmen return for sophomore year. 21% freshmen graduate within 4 years. 8% grads go on to further study within 1 year. 4% grads pursue arts and sciences degrees. 1% grads pursue law degrees. 2% grads pursue business degrees. 1% grads pursue medical degrees. **Faculty:** Student/faculty ratio 23.5:1. 60 full-time faculty, 82% hold PhDs, 7% are members of minority groups, 43% are women.

ACADEMICS
Degrees: Associate, bachelor's, certificate, master's, terminal associate, transfer associate. **Classes:** Most classes have 10–19 students. Most lab/discussion sessions have 10–19 students. **Majors with Highest Enrollment:** Elementary education and teaching; marketing/marketing management; natural resources/

conservation. **Special Study Options:** Accelerated program, distance learning, double major, dual enrollment, English as a Second Language (ESL), external degree program, independent study, internships, liberal arts/career combination, student-designed major, study abroad, teacher certification program Special programs offered to physically disabled students include reader services, tape recorders, tutors. **Career services:** Alumni services, career/job search classes, career assessment, internships.

FACILITIES

Housing: Coed dorms, men's dorms, women's dorms, Apartment-style housing. 70% of campus accessible to physically disabled. **Computers:** 100% of classrooms, 100% of dorms, 100% of libraries, 100% of dining areas, 100% of student union, 33% of common outdoor areas have wireless network access. Students can register for classes online. Administrative functions (other than registration) can be performed online.

CAMPUS LIFE

Environment: Rural. **Activities:** Choral groups, pep band, student government, student newspaper, campus ministries, international student organization. **Organizations:** 40 registered organizations, 1 honor societies, 1 religious organizations. 4 fraternities, 5 sororities. **Athletics (Intercollegiate):** *Men:* Baseball, basketball, cross-country, football, golf, soccer, wrestling. *Women:* Basketball, cross-country, golf, soccer, softball, tennis, volleyball. **On-Campus Highlights:** Rec Center, Grill 151, Dorman Gym, Andres Center for Business and Education, Cafeteria, We have 3 new buildings that will be opening in 2010. A new student center, liberal arts building and new housing unit.

ADMISSIONS

Freshman Academic Profile: Average high school GPA 2.94. Minimum paper TOEFL 500. Minimum computer TOEFL 173. Minimum web-based TOEFL 61. **Basis for Candidate Selection:** *Very important factors considered include:* Standardized test scores. *Important factors considered include:* Academic GPA. *Other factors considered include:* Class rank, recommendation(s), rigor of secondary school record, alumni/ae relation, first generation. **Freshman Admission Requirements:** High school diploma is required and GED is accepted. **Freshman Admission Statistics:** 1,293 applied, 42% admitted, 32% enrolled. **Transfer Admission Requirements:** High school transcript, college transcript(s), Lowest grade transferable D-. **General Admission Information:** Application fee $15. Regular application deadline 8/23. Nonfall registration accepted. Admission may be deferred for a maximum of one term. Credit and/or placement offered for CEEB Advanced Placement tests.

COSTS AND FINANCIAL AID

Annual tuition $22,350. Room and board $6,870. Average book expense $1,400. **Required Forms and Deadlines:** FAFSA. Priority financial aid filing date 3/1. **Types of Aid:** *Need-based scholarships/grants:* Federal Pell, SEOG, state scholarships/grants, private scholarships, the school's own gift aid. *Loans:* FFEL Subsidized Stafford, FFEL Unsubsidized Stafford, FFEL PLUS, Federal Perkins, Alternative Loans. *Student Employment:* Federal Work-Study Program available. Highest amount earned per year from on-campus jobs $1,860. Off-campus job opportunities are fair. **Financial Aid Statistics:** 52% freshmen, 61% undergrads receive need-based scholarship or grant aid. 15% freshmen, 11% undergrads receive non-need-based scholarship or grant aid. 34% freshmen, 58% undergrads receive need-based self-help aid. 4% freshmen, 2% undergrads receive athletic scholarships. 100% freshmen, 100% undergrads receive any aid. **Criteria for awarding institutional aid:** *Non-need-based:* Academics, alumni affiliation, athletics.

URSINUS COLLEGE

Ursinus College, Admissions Offic, Collegeville, PA 19426
Phone: 610-409-3200 **Financial Aid Phone:** 610-409-3600
E-mail: admissions@ursinus.edu **CEEB Code:** 2931
Fax: 610-409-3662 **Website:** www.ursinus.edu **ACT Code:** 3738

This private school was founded in 1869. It has a 170-acre campus.

RATINGS

Admissions Selectivity Rating: 92   **Fire Safety Rating:** 87   **Green Rating:** 85

STUDENTS AND FACULTY

Enrollment: 1,655. **Student Body:** 55% female, 45% male, 42% out-of-state, 1% international (13 countries represented). Asian 4%, African American 6%, Caucasian 73%, Hispanic 3%.

Retention and Graduation: 88% freshmen return for sophomore year. 72% freshmen graduate within 4 years. 34% grads go on to further study within 1 year. 19% grads pursue arts and sciences degrees. 3% grads pursue law degrees. 2% grads pursue business degrees. 10% grads pursue medical degrees. **Faculty:** Student/faculty ratio 12:1. 123 full-time faculty, 91% hold PhDs, 14% are members of minority groups, 46% are women.

ACADEMICS

Degrees: Bachelor's. **Classes:** Most classes have fewer than 10 students. Most lab/discussion sessions have 10–19 students. **Majors with Highest Enrollment:** Biology/biological sciences; economics; psychology. **Special Study Options:** Double major, dual enrollment, English as a Second Language (ESL), honors program, independent study, internships, student-designed major, study abroad, teacher certification program, Howard University Semester. **Honors programs:** The Ursinus Summer Fellows program provides stipends to rising juniors and seniors to live on campus and do faculty-mentored research over the summer months. Fellows' projects often lead to senior honors projects. **Combined degree programs:** BA/MD, BA/MEng, Early Assurance-Drexel Univ. College of Medicine. Special programs offered to physically disabled students include note-taking services, reader services, tape recorders, tutors. **Career services:** Alumni network, alumni services, career/job search classes, career assessment, internships, regional alumni. **Career services highlights include:** Our internship opportunities are exceptional and numerous and have taken our students on all sorts of adventures: to nearby pharmaceutical labs, to U.S. embassies overseas, to the summer stock stages of the Berkshires, and to a marine mammal rescue station at the Jersey Shore. Internships are available to students in every major, and even to those studying abroad. With a full range of staffing and Internet resources to find, match and place students in internships that are right for them, Ursinus has a high percentage of students who participate in these experiences.

FACILITIES

Housing: Coed dorms, men's dorms, special housing for international students, women's dorms, Ursinus features the Residential Village, a cluster of 25 restored Victorian-era houses. Theme houses include: Musser International, Unity, Wellness, Language, Biology, Service, Zwingli Literary House and Wicks Honors House. 40% of Ursinus students reside in these houses. 95% of campus accessible to physically disabled. **Special Academic Facilities/Equipment:** The Kaleidoscope (performing arts center); new field house; new 143-bed dormitory; Berman Museum of Art; 6 new telescopes; scanning electron microscopelt; Bruker 300 MHz NMR; Perkin Elmer Spectrum 1000 FTIR; LKB Isothermal Calorimeter; an assortment of spectrometers and an HPLC; recently-renovated Pfahler Hall of Science. **Computers:** 100% of classrooms, 100% of libraries, 100% of dining areas, 100% of student union, 50% of common outdoor areas have wireless network access. Students can register for classes online. Administrative functions (other than registration) can be performed online. Undergraduates are required to own a computer.

CAMPUS LIFE

Environment: City. **Activities:** Choral groups, concert band, dance, drama/theater, jazz band, literary magazine, music ensembles, musical theater, pep band, radio station, student government, student newspaper, student-run film society, television station, yearbook. **Organizations:** 88 registered organizations, 27 honor societies, 4 religious organizations. 7 fraternities, 7 sororities. **Athletics (Intercollegiate):** *Men:* Baseball, basketball, cross-country, football, golf, lacrosse, soccer, swimming, tennis, track/field (outdoor), track/field (indoor), wrestling. *Women:* Basketball, cross-country, field hockey, golf, gymnastics, lacrosse, soccer, softball, swimming, tennis, track/field (outdoor), track/field (indoor), volleyball. **On-Campus Highlights:** The Kaleidoscope Performing Arts Centerl, Berman Museum of Art, Pfahler Hall of Science, Richter-North Hall (new dormitory) Bakes Center (field house and fitnes, Wismer Center houses campus bookstore and dining facilities. Victorian dormitories along Main Street and traditional campus buildings give Ursinus a classic college ambience. **Environmental Initiatives:** Establishment of an Environmental Studies Program that requires public service of its students, who in turn develop problem solving skills in sustainability and conservation through course and extracurricular work. Active participation in Focus the Nation, including four days of programming in 2008. See http://academic.ursinus.edu/ftn. Energy efficiency study and implementation: Ursinus College has established an independent, annual budget to fund energy efficiency initiatives.

ADMISSIONS

Freshman Academic Profile: Average high school GPA 3.67. 48% in top 10% of high school class, 78% in top 25% of high school class, 96% in top 50% of high school class. 61% from public high schools. SAT Math middle 50% range 570–670. SAT Critical Reading middle 50% range 570–680. SAT Writing middle 50% range 560–660. ACT middle 50% range 25–29. Minimum paper TOEFL 500. Minimum computer TOEFL 173. **Basis for Candidate Selection:** *Very important factors considered include:* Class rank, rigor of secondary school record, extracurricular activities. *Important factors considered include:* Application essay, academic GPA, recommendation(s), standardized test scores, alumni/

ae relation, racial/ethnic status, talent/ability, volunteer work, work experience. *Other factors considered include:* character/personal qualities, first generation, geographical residence, interview, level of applicant's interest. **Freshman Admission Requirements:** High school diploma is required and GED is accepted. *Academic units required:* 4 English, 3 mathematics, 1 science, (1 science labs), 2 foreign language, 1 social studies. *Academic units recommended:* 4 English, 4 mathematics, 4 science, (2 science labs), 4 foreign language, 4 social studies. **Freshman Admission Statistics:** 6,192 applied, 55% admitted, 32% enrolled. **Transfer Admission Requirements:** High school transcript, college transcript(s), essay or personal statement, standardized test scores, minimum college GPA of 3.0 required. Lowest grade transferable C. **General Admission Information:** Application fee $50. Early decision application deadline 1/15. Regular application deadline 2/15. Regular notification 4/1. Nonfall registration accepted. Admission may be deferred for a maximum of 1 year. Credit and/or placement offered for CEEB Advanced Placement tests.

COSTS AND FINANCIAL AID

Average book expense $1,000. **Required Forms and Deadlines:** FAFSA, institution's own financial aid form, CSS/Financial Aid PROFILE Financial aid filing deadline 2/15. **Notification of Awards:** Applicants will be notified of awards on or about 4/1. **Types of Aid:** *Need-based scholarships/grants:* Federal Pell, SEOG, state scholarships/grants, private scholarships, the school's own gift aid. *Loans:* FFEL Subsidized Stafford, FFEL Unsubsidized Stafford, FFEL PLUS, Federal Perkins. *Student Employment:* Federal Work-Study Program available. Institutional employment available. Highest amount earned per year from on-campus jobs $1,200. Off-campus job opportunities are excellent. **Financial Aid Statistics:** 64% freshmen, 66% undergrads receive need-based scholarship or grant aid. 17% freshmen, 16% undergrads receive non-need-based scholarship or grant aid. 50% freshmen, 55% undergrads receive need-based self-help aid. 92% freshmen, 91% undergrads receive any aid. 75% undergrads borrow to pay for school. Average cumulative indebtedness $21,171. **Criteria for awarding institutional aid:** *Non-need-based:* Academics, alumni affiliation, art, music/drama.

URSULINE COLLEGE

2550 Lander Road, Pepper Pike, OH 44124-4398
Phone: 440-449-4203 **Financial Aid Phone:** 440-646-8309
E-mail: admission@ursuline.edu **CEEB Code:** 1848
Fax: 440-684-6138 **Website:** www.ursuline.edu

This private school, affiliated with the Roman Catholic Church, was founded in 1871. It has a 110-acre campus.

RATINGS

Admissions Selectivity Rating: 73   **Fire Safety Rating:** 81   **Green Rating:** 62

STUDENTS AND FACULTY

Enrollment: 1,062. **Student Body:** 91% female, 9% male, 2% out-of-state, international (6 countries represented). Asian 1%, African American 26%, Caucasian 69%, Hispanic 2%.
Retention and Graduation: 68% freshmen return for sophomore year. 30% freshmen graduate within 4 years. **Faculty:** Student/faculty ratio 9:1. 70 full-time faculty, 64% hold PhDs, 6% are members of minority groups, 86% are women.

ACADEMICS

Degrees: Bachelor's, certificate, master's, post-bachelor's certificate, post-master's certificate. **Classes:** Most classes have 10–19 students. Most lab/discussion sessions have 10–19 students. **Majors with Highest Enrollment:** Early childhood education and teaching; nursing/registered nurse (RN, ASN, BSN, MSN); psychology. **Special Study Options:** Accelerated program, cooperative education program, cross-registration, double major, independent study, internships, teacher certification program. Special programs offered to physically disabled students include note-taking services, reader services, tape recorders, tutors. **Career services:** Career assessment, internships. **Career services highlights include:** Our e-recruiting program that assists students in their search.

FACILITIES

Housing: Coed dorms, women's dorms 98% of campus accessible to physically disabled. **Special Academic Facilities/Equipment:** Fritsche Gallery (Art), Fitness Center Swimming Pool. **Computers:** 100% of classrooms, 100% of libraries, 100% of dining areas, have wireless network access.

CAMPUS LIFE

Environment: City. **Activities:** Choral groups, drama/theater, literary magazine, student government, campus ministries. **Organizations:** 21 registered organizations, 4 honor societies, **Athletics (Intercollegiate):** *Women:*

Basketball, bowling, cross-country, golf, soccer, softball, swimming, tennis, track/field (outdoor), volleyball. **On-Campus Highlights:** Bishop Anthony M. Pilla Student Learning Center, Florence O'Donnell Wasmer Gallery, Matthew J. O'Brien Campus Center, Joseph J. Mullen Academic Center, Ralph M. Besse Library. **Environmental Initiatives:** Increased recycling; energy conservation; renewable energy .

ADMISSIONS

Freshman Academic Profile: Average high school GPA 3.085. 5% in top 10% of high school class, 34% in top 25% of high school class, 78% in top 50% of high school class. 73% from public high schools. SAT Math middle 50% range 400–530. SAT Critical Reading middle 50% range 410–510. SAT Writing middle 50% range 400–500. ACT middle 50% range 19–23. Minimum paper TOEFL 500. Minimum computer TOEFL 173. Minimum web-based TOEFL 60. **Basis for Candidate Selection:** *Very important factors considered include:* Academic GPA, standardized test scores. *Important factors considered include:* Application essay, recommendation(s). *Other factors considered include:* Class rank, rigor of secondary school record, alumni/ae relation, interview. **Freshman Admission Requirements:** High school diploma is required and GED is accepted. *Academic units recommended:* 4 English, 3 mathematics, 3 science, (2 science labs), 2 foreign language, 3 social studies, 1 visual/performing arts, 1 PE/health. **Freshman Admission Statistics:** 248 applied, 90% admitted, 43% enrolled. **Transfer Admission Requirements:** College transcript(s), essay or personal statement, minimum college GPA of 2.5 required. Lowest grade transferable c. **General Admission Information:** Application fee $25. Nonfall registration accepted. Admission may be deferred for a maximum of 1 year. Credit and/or placement offered for CEEB Advanced Placement tests.

COSTS AND FINANCIAL AID

Average book expense $1,100. **Required Forms and Deadlines:** FAFSA. Priority financial aid filing date 3/1. **Notification of Awards:** Applicants will be notified of awards on a rolling basis beginning 2/20. **Types of Aid:** *Need-based scholarships/grants:* Federal Pell, SEOG, state scholarships/grants, private scholarships, the school's own gift aid, Federal Nursing Scholarships. *Loans:* FFEL Subsidized Stafford, FFEL Unsubsidized Stafford, FFEL PLUS, Federal Perkins, state loans, college/university loans from institutional funds. *Student Employment:* Federal Work-Study Program available. Off-campus job opportunities are good. **Financial Aid Statistics:** 95% freshmen, 84% undergrads receive need-based scholarship or grant aid. 6% freshmen, 5% undergrads receive non-need-based scholarship or grant aid. 85% freshmen, 80% undergrads receive need-based self-help aid. 3% freshmen, 3% undergrads receive athletic scholarships. 95% freshmen, 86% undergrads receive any aid. 83.6% undergrads borrow to pay for school. Average cumulative indebtedness $22,723. **Criteria for awarding institutional aid:** *Non-need-based:* Academics, alumni affiliation, art, athletics, leadership, religious affiliation.

USC UPSTATE

800 University Way, Spartanburg, SC 29303
Phone: 864-503-5246
E-mail: dstewart@uscs.edu **CEEB Code:** 5850
Fax: 864-503-5727 **Website:** www.uscs.edu **ACT Code:** 3889

This public school was founded in 1967. It has a 298-acre campus.

RATINGS

Admissions Selectivity Rating: 79   **Fire Safety Rating:** 60*   **Green Rating:** 60*

STUDENTS AND FACULTY

Enrollment: 4,237. **Student Body:** 65% female, 35% male, 7% out-of-state, 2% international (30 countries represented). Asian 3%, African American 26%, Caucasian 64%, Hispanic 1%.
Retention and Graduation: 67% freshmen return for sophomore year. 17% freshmen graduate within 4 years. 20% grads go on to further study within 1 year. **Faculty:** Student/faculty ratio 17:1. 179 full-time faculty, 79% hold PhDs, 54% are women.

ACADEMICS

Degrees: Associate, bachelor's, master's, terminal associate. **Classes:** Most classes have 20–29 students. Most lab/discussion sessions have 20–29 students. **Majors with Highest Enrollment:** Business/commerce; education; nursing/registered nurse (RN, ASN, BSN, MSN). **Special Study Options:** Accelerated program, cross-registration, distance learning, double major, exchange student program (domestic), honors program, independent study, internships, student-designed major, study abroad, teacher certification program. Special programs offered to physically disabled students include note-taking services, reader services, tape recorders, tutors. **Career services:** Alumni services, career/job search classes, career assessment, internships.

FACILITIES

Housing: Coed dorms, apartments for single students 100% of campus accessible to physically disabled. **Special Academic Facilities/Equipment:** Campus Life Center; performing arts building, including 450 seat theater; arts studies film theater; recital hall; language laboratory; Quality Institute. **Computers:** Students can register for classes online. Administrative functions (other than registration) can be performed online.

CAMPUS LIFE

Activities: Choral groups, dance, drama/theater, jazz band, literary magazine, music ensembles, musical theater, student government, student newspaper. **Organizations:** 61 registered organizations, 5 religious organizations. 2 fraternities, 3 sororities. **Athletics (Intercollegiate):** Men: Baseball, basketball, cross-country, soccer, tennis. Women: Basketball, cross-country, soccer, softball, tennis, volleyball. **On-Campus Highlights:** Campus Life Center, Aboretum.

ADMISSIONS

Freshman Academic Profile: Average high school GPA 3.4. 11% in top 10% of high school class, 37% in top 25% of high school class, 68% in top 50% of high school class. SAT Math middle 50% range 450–540. SAT Critical Reading middle 50% range 440–530. ACT middle 50% range 18–21. Minimum paper TOEFL 500. Minimum computer TOEFL 173. **Basis for Candidate Selection:** *Very important factors considered include:* Rigor of secondary school record, standardized test scores. **Freshman Admission Requirements:** High school diploma is required and GED is accepted. *Academic units required:* 4 English, 3 mathematics, 3 science, (2 science labs), 2 foreign language, 2 social studies, 1 history, 4 academic electives, 1 physical education or ROTC. **Freshman Admission Statistics:** 1,904 applied, 49% admitted, 75% enrolled. **Transfer Admission Requirements:** College transcript(s), statement of good standing from prior institution(s). Minimum college GPA of 2.0 required. Lowest grade transferable C. **General Admission Information:** Application fee $35. Notification on a rolling basis, beginning on or about 9/15. Nonfall registration accepted. Admission may be deferred for a maximum of 1 year. Credit offered for CEEB Advanced Placement tests.

COSTS AND FINANCIAL AID

Annual in-state tuition $5,310. Annual out-of-state tuition $10,936. Room and board $4,940. Required fees $226. Average book expense $700. **Required Forms and Deadlines:** FAFSAScholarship Application. Financial aid filing deadline 7/15. Priority financial aid filing date 3/1. **Types of Aid:** *Need-based scholarships/grants:* Federal Pell, SEOG, state scholarships/grants, private scholarships, the school's own gift aid, Non-need-based (college-administered): Academic merit Athletic State scholarships/grants ROTC scholarships. *Loans:* FFEL Subsidized Stafford, FFEL Unsubsidized Stafford, FFEL PLUS, Federal Perkins, Federal Nursing, state loans *Student Employment:* Federal Work-Study Program available. Institutional employment available. Off-campus job opportunities are excellent. **Financial Aid Statistics:** 33% freshmen, 37% undergrads receive need-based scholarship or grant aid. 37% freshmen, 14% undergrads receive non-need-based scholarship or grant aid. 31% freshmen, 45% undergrads receive need-based self-help aid. 3% freshmen, 3% undergrads receive athletic scholarships. 64% undergrads borrow to pay for school. Average cumulative indebtedness $15,779. **Criteria for awarding institutional aid:** *Non-need-based:* Academics, athletics, minority status, state/district residency.

UTAH STATE UNIVERSITY

0160 Old Main Hill, Logan, UT 84322-0160
Phone: 435-797-1079 **Financial Aid Phone:** 435-797-0173
E-mail: admit@usu.edu
Fax: 435-797-3708 **Website:** www.usu.edu **ACT Code:** 4276

This public school was founded in 1888. It has a 400-acre campus.

RATINGS

Admissions Selectivity Rating: 75   **Fire Safety Rating:** 60*   **Green Rating:** 88

STUDENTS AND FACULTY

Enrollment: 13,652. **Student Body:** 49% female, 51% male, 23% out-of-state, 4% international (78 countries represented). Asian 2%, African American 1%, Caucasian 85%, Hispanic 3%, Native American 1%.
Retention and Graduation: 23% grads go on to further study within 1 year. 1% grads pursue medical degrees. **Faculty:** Student/faculty ratio 17.8:1. 708 full-time faculty, 86% hold PhDs, 6% are members of minority groups, 32% are women. 7% of classes are taught by teaching assistants.

ACADEMICS

Degrees: Associate, bachelor's, certificate, master's, post-bachelor's certificate, post-master's certificate, terminal associate, transfer associate. **Classes:** Most classes have 20–29 students. Most lab/discussion sessions have 10–19 students.

Majors with Highest Enrollment: accounting; information science/studies; marketing/marketing management. **Special Study Options:** Accelerated program, cooperative education program, cross-registration, distance learning, double major, dual enrollment, English as a Second Language (ESL), exchange student program (domestic), honors program, independent study, internships, liberal arts/career combination, student-designed major, study abroad, teacher certification program, weekend college. **Honors programs:** The Honors Program is a community of scholars whose curiosity, creativity, and enthusiasm for learning foster educational achievement and personal growth. Our students are going places—graduate school, professional school, terrific jobs. Honors offers undergraduate students intensive seminars, experimental and interdisciplinary courses, writing projects, leadership opportunities, artistic and social activities. Our classes are smaller, allowing students to get to know professors and encouraging classroom interaction and discussion. We allow students to define their own interests and pursue them through "contracts" with professors, fostering close contact with professors. Other advantages include priority registration, an Honors-only computer lab, the Honors lounge and study areas. Starting in Fall 2005, Honors expects to offer housing. Special programs offered to physically disabled students include reader services, tape recorders. **Career services:** Alumni network, career/job search classes, career assessment, internships.

FACILITIES

Housing: Coed dorms, special housing for disabled students, men's dorms, special housing for international students, women's dorms, fraternity/sorority housing, apartments for married students, apartments for single students, theme housing, mobile home park. 96% of campus accessible to physically disabled. **Special Academic Facilities/Equipment:** Art gallery, agricultural and engineering experiment station, water research lab, wildlife and fishery research unit, on-campus school, intermountain herbarium, electron microscope, space dynamics lab. **Computers:** 99% of classrooms, 95% of dorms, 99% of libraries, 99% of dining areas, 99% of student union, 50% of common outdoor areas have wireless network access. Students can register for classes online. Administrative functions (other than registration) can be performed online.

CAMPUS LIFE

Environment: Town. **Activities:** Choral groups, concert band, dance, drama/theater, jazz band, marching band, music ensembles, musical theater, opera, pep band, radio station, student government, student newspaper, student-run film society, symphony orchestra, television station, campus ministries, international student organization. **Organizations:** 194 registered organizations, 32 honor societies, 8 religious organizations. 5 fraternities, 3 sororities. **Athletics (Intercollegiate):** Men: Basketball, cross-country, football, golf, tennis, track/field (outdoor), track/field (indoor). Women: Basketball, cross-country, gymnastics, soccer, softball, tennis, track/field (outdoor), track/field (indoor), volleyball. **On-Campus Highlights:** Outdoor Recreation Center, Nora Eccles Jones Art Museum, Fieldhouse athletic facility, Taggart Student Center, The quad. **Environmental Initiatives:** Increased energy efficiency in buildings, recycling, Aggie Blue Bikes.

ADMISSIONS

Freshman Academic Profile: Average high school GPA 3.54. 23.7% in top 10% of high school class, 49.4% in top 25% of high school class, 82.2% in top 50% of high school class. SAT Math middle 50% range 460–630. SAT Critical Reading middle 50% range 470–630. ACT middle 50% range 21–27. Minimum paper TOEFL 500. Minimum computer TOEFL 173. **Basis for Candidate Selection:** *Very important factors considered include:* Academic GPA, standardized test scores. *Important factors considered include:* Rigor of secondary school record. *Other factors considered include:* Class rank, recommendation(s). **Freshman Admission Requirements:** High school diploma is required and GED is accepted. *Academic units required:* 4 English, 3 mathematics, 3 science, (1 science labs), 1 history, 4 academic electives. *Academic units recommended:* 2 foreign language. **Freshman Admission Statistics:** 6,438 applied, 98% admitted, 45% enrolled. **Transfer Admission Requirements:** College transcript(s), minimum college GPA of 2.2 required. Lowest grade transferable D. **General Admission Information:** Application fee $40. Nonfall registration accepted. Admission may be deferred for a maximum of 2 years+ one semester. Credit and/or placement offered for CEEB Advanced Placement tests.

COSTS AND FINANCIAL AID

Annual in-state tuition $4,043. Annual out-of-state tuition $13,017. Room and board $4,900. Required fees $785. Average book expense $1,150. **Required Forms and Deadlines:** FAFSA **Notification of Awards:** Applicants will be notified of awards on a rolling basis beginning 4/1. **Types of Aid:** *Need-based scholarships/grants:* Federal Pell, SEOG, state scholarships/grants, private scholarships, the school's own gift aid. *Loans:* FFEL Subsidized Stafford, FFEL Unsubsidized Stafford, FFEL PLUS, Federal Perkins, college/university loans from institutional funds. *Student Employment:* Federal Work-Study Program available. Institutional employment available. Highest amount earned per year from on-campus jobs $10,200. Off-campus job opportunities are excellent. **Financial Aid Statistics:** 17% freshmen, 30% undergrads receive need-based scholarship or grant aid. 18% freshmen, 19% undergrads receive non-need-based scholarship or grant aid. 22% freshmen, 31% undergrads receive need-based self-help aid. 2% freshmen, 2% undergrads receive athletic scholarships. 61% freshmen, 63% undergrads receive any aid. **Criteria for awarding institutional aid:** *Non-need-based:* Academics, alumni affiliation, art, athletics, leadership, minority status, music/drama, religious affiliation, state/district residency.

UTICA COLLEGE

1600 Burrstone Road, Utica, NY 13502-4892
Phone: 315-792-3006 **Financial Aid Phone:** 315-792-3179
E-mail: admiss@utica.edu **CEEB Code:** 2932
Fax: 315-792-3003 **Website:** www.utica.edu **ACT Code:** 2932

This private school was founded in 1946. It has a 128-acre campus.

RATINGS
Admissions Selectivity Rating: 70   **Fire Safety Rating:** 77   **Green Rating:** 79

STUDENTS AND FACULTY
Enrollment: 2,478. **Student Body:** 57% female, 43% male, 19% out-of-state, 2% international (25 countries represented). Asian 2%, African American 11%, Caucasian 59%, Hispanic 4%, Native American 1%.
Retention and Graduation: 64% freshmen return for sophomore year. 38% freshmen graduate within 4 years. 46% grads go on to further study within 1 year. 1% grads pursue medical degrees. **Faculty:** Student/faculty ratio 11:1. 131 full-time faculty, 86% hold PhDs, 5% are members of minority groups, 50% are women.

ACADEMICS
Degrees: Bachelor's, certificate, master's, post-bachelor's certificate. **Classes:** Most classes have 10–19 students. Most lab/discussion sessions have 10–19 students. **Majors with Highest Enrollment:** Business/commerce; corrections and criminal justice, other; health services/allied health/health sciences. **Special Study Options:** Accelerated program, cooperative education program, cross-registration, distance learning, double major, dual enrollment, exchange student program (domestic), honors program, independent study, internships, liberal arts/career combination, study abroad, teacher certification program, weekend college, BS Health Studies/ MS OT weekend program; ECI online program for undergraduate transfer students. **Honors programs:** www.utica.edu/academic/opportunities/honors.cfm **Combined degree programs:** BS(Health Studies)/MS OT; BS(Health Stud. Special programs offered to physically disabled students include note-taking services, reader services, tape recorders, tutors. **Career services:** Alumni network, alumni services, career/job search classes, career assessment, internships.

FACILITIES
Housing: Coed dorms, special housing for disabled students, apartments for single students, women's floors, men's floors. 85% of campus accessible to physically disabled. **Special Academic Facilities/Equipment:** Edith Langley Barrett Art Gallery **Computers:** 95% of classrooms, 10% of dorms, 100% of libraries, 100% of dining areas, 100% of student union, have wireless network access. Students can register for classes online. Administrative functions (other than registration) can be performed online.

CAMPUS LIFE
Environment: City. **Activities:** Choral groups, concert band, dance, drama/theater, literary magazine, radio station, student government, student newspaper, student-run film society, yearbook. **Organizations:** 80 registered organizations, 8 honor societies, 4 religious organizations. 5 fraternities, 4 sororities. **Athletics (Intercollegiate):** *Men:* Baseball, basketball, cross-country, diving, football, golf, ice hockey, lacrosse, soccer, swimming, tennis, track/field (outdoor). *Women:* Basketball, cross-country, diving, field hockey, ice hockey, lacrosse, soccer, softball, swimming, tennis, track/field (outdoor), volleyball, water polo. **On-Campus Highlights:** Strebel Student Center and Lounge, Pioneer Cafe, Clark Athletic Center, Romano Hall Lounge, Library Cafe. **Environmental Initiatives:** Committee on sustainability formed in 2007. Extensive recycling program. Partnership in co-generation electrical generation plant.

ADMISSIONS
Freshman Academic Profile: Average high school GPA 2.91. 8% in top 10% of high school class, 30% in top 25% of high school class, 63% in top 50% of high school class. SAT Math middle 50% range 420–520. SAT Critical Reading middle 50% range 410–510. SAT Writing middle 50% range 390–490. ACT middle 50% range 18–23. Minimum paper TOEFL 525. Minimum computer TOEFL 195. **Basis for Candidate Selection:** *Very important factors considered include:* Academic GPA, rigor of secondary school record. *Important factors considered include:* Application essay, recommendation(s), character/

personal qualities, extracurricular activities, interview, talent/ability, volunteer work, work experience. *Other factors considered include:* Class rank, standardized test scores, alumni/ae relation, first generation, level of applicant's interest. **Freshman Admission Requirements:** High school diploma is required and GED is accepted. *Academic units required:* 4 English, 3 mathematics, 3 science, 2 foreign language, 3 social studies, 1 academic electives. **Freshman Admission Statistics:** 2,930 applied, 78% admitted, 25% enrolled. **Transfer Admission Requirements:** College transcript(s), essay or personal statement, minimum college GPA of 2.50 required. Lowest grade transferable C. **General Admission Information:** Application fee $40. Notification on a rolling basis, beginning on or about 9/1. Nonfall registration accepted. Admission may be deferred for a maximum of 1 year. Credit and/or placement offered for CEEB Advanced Placement tests.

COSTS AND FINANCIAL AID
Average book expense $984. **Required Forms and Deadlines:** FAFSA. Priority financial aid filing date 2/15. **Notification of Awards:** Applicants will be notified of awards on a rolling basis beginning 2/1. **Types of Aid:** *Need-based scholarships/grants:* Federal Pell, SEOG, state scholarships/grants, private scholarships, the school's own gift aid, Federal Nursing Scholarships. *Loans:* Direct Subsidized Stafford, Direct Unsubsidized Stafford, Direct PLUS, Federal Perkins, Alternative loans. *Student Employment:* Federal Work-Study Program available. Institutional employment available. Off-campus job opportunities are good. **Financial Aid Statistics:** 93% freshmen, 90% undergrads receive need-based scholarship or grant aid. 5% freshmen, 6% undergrads receive non-need-based scholarship or grant aid. 87% freshmen, 83% undergrads receive need-based self-help aid. 86% freshmen, 86% undergrads receive any aid. 86% undergrads borrow to pay for school. Average cumulative indebtedness $35,534. **Criteria for awarding institutional aid:** *Non-need-based:* Academics.

VALDOSTA STATE UNIVERSITY

1500 North Patterson Street, Valdosta, GA 31698
Phone: 229-333-5791 **Financial Aid Phone:** 229-333-5935
E-mail: admissions@valdosta.edu **CEEB Code:** 5855
Fax: 229-333-5482 **Website:** www.valdosta.edu **ACT Code:** 874

This public school was founded in 1906. It has a 178-acre campus.

RATINGS
Admissions Selectivity Rating: 74   **Fire Safety Rating:** 78   **Green Rating:** 60*

STUDENTS AND FACULTY
Enrollment: 9,401. **Student Body:** 59% female, 41% male, 6% out-of-state, 2% international. Asian 1%, African American 23%, Caucasian 71%, Hispanic 2%.
Retention and Graduation: 74% freshmen return for sophomore year. 18% freshmen graduate within 4 years. **Faculty:** Student/faculty ratio 20:1. 438 full-time faculty, 10% are members of minority groups, 44% are women.

ACADEMICS
Degrees: Associate, bachelor's, master's, post-master's certificate. **Classes:** Most classes have 20–29 students. Most lab/discussion sessions have 20–29 students. **Majors with Highest Enrollment:** Biology/biological sciences; early childhood education and teaching; nursing/registered nurse (RN, ASN, BSN, MSN). **Special Study Options:** Cooperative education program, distance learning, double major, dual enrollment, English as a Second Language (ESL), external degree program, honors program, independent study, internships, study abroad, teacher certification program, weekend college. **Honors programs:** Honors Program Special programs offered to physically disabled students include note-taking services, reader services, tape recorders, tutors. **Career services:** Alumni services, career/job search classes, career assessment, internships.

FACILITIES
Housing: Coed dorms, special housing for disabled students, men's dorms, special housing for international students, women's dorms, apartments for married students, apartments for single students, wellness floors, and honors floors. 100% of campus accessible to physically disabled. **Special Academic Facilities/Equipment:** Planetarium; Herbarium; Art Gallery; VSU Archives. **Computers:** Students can register for classes online. Administrative functions (other than registration) can be performed online.

CAMPUS LIFE
Environment: City. **Activities:** Choral groups, concert band, dance, drama/theater, jazz band, literary magazine, marching band, music ensembles, pep band, radio station, student government, student newspaper, symphony orchestra, television station **Organizations:** 140 registered organizations, 22 honor

societies, 11 religious organizations. 12 fraternities, 10 sororities. **Athletics (Intercollegiate):** *Men:* Baseball, basketball, cross-country, football, golf, tennis. *Women:* Basketball, cheerleading, cross-country, softball, tennis, volleyball. **On-Campus Highlights:** Student Recreation Center, Game Room, Internet Cafe, The Loop, Palms Dining Center and quad.

ADMISSIONS

Freshman Academic Profile: Average high school GPA 3.03. SAT Math middle 50% range 470–560. SAT Critical Reading middle 50% range 480–560. ACT middle 50% range 20–23. Minimum paper TOEFL 523. Minimum computer TOEFL 193. **Basis for Candidate Selection:** *Very important factors considered include:* Standardized test scores. *Important factors considered include:* Class rank, academic GPA, rigor of secondary school record. **Freshman Admission Requirements:** High school diploma is required and GED is not accepted. *Academic units required:* 4 English, 4 mathematics, 3 science, (2 science labs), 2 foreign language, 3 social studies. **Freshman Admission Statistics:** 6,281 applied, 61% admitted, 52% enrolled. **Transfer Admission Requirements:** College transcript(s), minimum college GPA of 2.0 required. Lowest grade transferable D. **General Admission Information:** Application fee $40. Regular application deadline 7/1. Notification on a rolling basis, beginning on or about 8/1. Nonfall registration accepted. Admission may be deferred for a maximum of 2 years. Credit and/or placement offered for CEEB Advanced Placement tests.

COSTS AND FINANCIAL AID

Annual in-state tuition $2,536. Annual out-of-state tuition $10,144. Room and board $5,680. Required fees $930. Average book expense $1,000. **Required Forms and Deadlines:** FAFSA. Priority financial aid filing date 5/1. **Notification of Awards:** Applicants will be notified of awards on a rolling basis beginning 5/15. **Types of Aid:** *Need-based scholarships/grants:* Federal Pell, SEOG, state scholarships/grants, private scholarships, the school's own gift aid, LEAP, ACG SMART Grant. *Loans:* Direct Subsidized Stafford, Direct Unsubsidized Stafford, Direct PLUS, FFEL Subsidized Stafford, FFEL Unsubsidized Stafford, FFEL PLUS. *Student Employment:* Federal Work-Study Program available. Institutional employment available. Highest amount earned per year from on-campus jobs $4,000. Off-campus job opportunities are good. **Financial Aid Statistics:** 47% freshmen, 47% undergrads receive need-based scholarship or grant aid. 7% freshmen, 4% undergrads receive non-need-based scholarship or grant aid. 45% freshmen, 53% undergrads receive need-based self-help aid. 2% freshmen, 3% undergrads receive athletic scholarships. 99% freshmen, 90% undergrads receive any aid. 65% undergrads borrow to pay for school. Average cumulative indebtedness $17,000. **Criteria for awarding institutional aid:** *Non-need-based:* Academics, art, athletics, leadership, music/drama, state/district residency.

VALLEY CITY STATE UNIVERSITY

101 College St. SW, Valley City, ND 58072
Phone: 701-845-7101 **Financial Aid Phone:** 701-845-7412
E-mail: enrollment.services@vcsu.edu
Fax: 701-845-7299 **Website:** www.vcsu.edu **ACT Code:** 3216

This public school was founded in 1890. It has a 55-acre campus.

RATINGS

Admissions Selectivity Rating: 70 **Fire Safety Rating:** 60* **Green Rating:** 60*

STUDENTS AND FACULTY

Enrollment: 1,013. **Student Body:** 53% female, 47% male, 28% out-of-state, 5% international (7 countries represented). African American 2%, Caucasian 89%, Hispanic 1%, Native American 2%.
Retention and Graduation: 64% freshmen return for sophomore year.
Faculty: Student/faculty ratio 18:1. 55 full-time faculty, 36% hold PhDs, 51% are women.

ACADEMICS

Degrees: Bachelor's, master's. **Majors with Highest Enrollment:** computer and information sciences and support services, other; elementary education and teaching. **Special Study Options:** Accelerated program, cooperative education program, distance learning, double major, dual enrollment, internships, liberal arts/career combination, student-designed major, teacher certification program Special programs offered to physically disabled students include note-taking services, reader services, tape recorders, tutors. **Career services:** Career/job search classes, career assessment, internships.

FACILITIES

Housing: Coed dorms, special housing for disabled students, men's dorms, women's dorms, fraternity/sorority housing, apartments for married students,

Apts. for students with dependant children. 85% of campus accessible to physically disabled. **Special Academic Facilities/Equipment:** Planetarium. **Computers:** Students can register for classes online. Administrative functions (other than registration) can be performed online.

CAMPUS LIFE

Environment: Rural. **Activities:** Choral groups, concert band, drama/theater, jazz band, music ensembles, musical theater, pep band, student government, student newspaper, yearbook. **Organizations:** 16 registered organizations, 5 honor societies, 3 religious organizations. 1 fraternities, 1 sororities. **Athletics (Intercollegiate):** *Men:* Baseball, basketball, football. *Women:* Basketball, cheerleading, softball, volleyball. **On-Campus Highlights:** Planetarium, Medicine Wheel, Fieldhouse, Vangstad Auditorium, Student Center.

ADMISSIONS

Freshman Academic Profile: Average high school GPA 3. 6% in top 10% of high school class, 22% in top 25% of high school class, 54% in top 50% of high school class. 98% from public high schools. SAT Math middle 50% range 450–570. SAT Critical Reading middle 50% range 450–580. ACT middle 50% range 18–23. Minimum paper TOEFL 525. Minimum computer TOEFL 195. **Basis for Candidate Selection:** *Very important factors considered include:* Rigor of secondary school record, *Other factors considered include:* Class rank, standardized test scores. **Freshman Admission Requirements:** High school diploma is required and GED is accepted. *Academic units required:* 4 English, 3 mathematics, 3 science, (3 science labs), 3 social studies. *Academic units recommended:* 2 foreign language. **Freshman Admission Statistics:** 256 applied, 94% admitted, 73% enrolled. **Transfer Admission Requirements:** College transcript(s), statement of good standing from prior institution(s). Minimum college GPA of 2.0 required. Lowest grade transferable D. **General Admission Information:** Application fee $35. Nonfall registration accepted. Admission may be deferred for a maximum of indefinete. Neither credit nor placement offered for CEEB Advanced Placement tests.

COSTS AND FINANCIAL AID

Annual in-state tuition $3,536. Annual out-of-state tuition $9,761. Room and board $4,694. Required fees $1,504. Average book expense $700. **Required Forms and Deadlines:** FAFSA. Priority financial aid filing date 3/15. **Notification of Awards:** Applicants will be notified of awards on a rolling basis beginning 1/15. **Types of Aid:** *Need-based scholarships/grants:* Federal Pell, SEOG, state scholarships/grants *Loans:* FFEL Subsidized Stafford, FFEL Unsubsidized Stafford, FFEL PLUS, Federal Perkins. **Financial Aid Statistics:** 36% freshmen, 33% undergrads receive need-based scholarship or grant aid. 52% freshmen, 33% undergrads receive non-need-based scholarship or grant aid. 62% freshmen, 54% undergrads receive need-based self-help aid. 6% freshmen, 5% undergrads receive athletic scholarships. 93% freshmen, 86% undergrads receive any aid. 36% undergrads borrow to pay for school. Average cumulative indebtedness $18,209. **Criteria for awarding institutional aid:** *Non-need-based:* Academics, alumni affiliation, athletics, leadership, minority status, music/drama.

VALPARAISO UNIVERSITY

Office of Admission, Kretzmann Hall, 1700 Chapel Dr, Valparaiso, IN 46383
Phone: 219-464-5011 **Financial Aid Phone:** 219-464-5015
E-mail: undergrad.admissions@valpo.edu **CEEB Code:** 1874
Fax: 219-464-6898 **Website:** www.valpo.edu **ACT Code:** 1256

This private school, affiliated with the Lutheran Church, was founded in 1859. It has a 320-acre campus.

RATINGS

Admissions Selectivity Rating: 85 **Fire Safety Rating:** 62 **Green Rating:** 79

STUDENTS AND FACULTY

Enrollment: 2,823. **Student Body:** 52% female, 48% male, 60% out-of-state, 3% international (46 countries represented). Asian 2%, African American 6%, Caucasian 82%, Hispanic 5%, Native American 1%.
Retention and Graduation: 63% freshmen graduate within 4 years. 24% grads go on to further study within 1 year. 16% grads pursue arts and sciences degrees. 3% grads pursue law degrees. 2% grads pursue business degrees. 1% grads pursue medical degrees. **Faculty:** Student/faculty ratio 14:1. 242 full-time faculty, 92% hold PhDs, 7% are members of minority groups, 35% are women.

ACADEMICS

Degrees: Associate, bachelor's, certificate, master's, post-bachelor's certificate, post-master's certificate, terminal associate. **Classes:** Most classes have 10–19 students. Most lab/discussion sessions have 10–19 students. **Majors with Highest Enrollment:** nursing/registered nurse (RN, ASN, BSN, MSN); political science and government; psychology. **Special Study Options:** Accelerated program, cooperative education program, cross-registration, distance learning, double major, English as a Second Language (ESL), exchange student program (domestic), honors program, independent study, internships, liberal arts/career combination, student-designed major, study abroad, teacher certification program. **Honors programs:** Christ College, VU's honors college, provides an honors-level liberal arts curriculum dedicated to the study and practice of the basic arts of inquiry and committed to educational processes that enable students to achieve a measure of intellectual independence. **Combined degree programs:** BA/JD, BA/MA, JD/MA, JD/MBA, JD/MALS, JD/MS, BSN/MSN, BA/EdS. Special programs offered to physically disabled students include note-taking services, reader services, tape recorders, tutors. **Career services:** Alumni network, alumni services, career/job search classes, career assessment, internships, regional alumni.

FACILITIES

Housing: Coed dorms, women's dorms, fraternity/sorority housing, apartments for single students, theme housing, Residence hall for German language students. 86% of campus accessible to physically disabled. **Special Academic Facilities/Equipment:** Art museum, galleries, language lab, planetarium, electron microscope, observatory, TV Studio, weather station, Virtual Nursing Learning Center, VisBox, non-linear video editing, Christopher Center for Learning and Information Resources, Doppler Radar faciltiy. **Computers:** 60% of classrooms, 100% of dorms, 100% of libraries, 100% of dining areas, 100% of student union, 15% of common outdoor areas have wireless network access. Students can register for classes online. Administrative functions (other than registration) can be performed online.

CAMPUS LIFE

Environment: Town. **Activities:** Choral groups, concert band, dance, drama/theater, jazz band, literary magazine, music ensembles, musical theater, pep band, radio station, student government, student newspaper, symphony orchestra, yearbook, campus ministries, international student organization. **Organizations:** 94 registered organizations, 33 honor societies, 7 religious organizations. 9 fraternities, 7 sororities. **Athletics (Intercollegiate):** *Men:* Baseball, basketball, cross-country, diving, football, golf, soccer, swimming, tennis, track/field (outdoor), track/field (indoor). *Women:* Basketball, bowling, cross-country, diving, golf, soccer, softball, swimming, tennis, track/field (outdoor), track/field (indoor), volleyball. **On-Campus Highlights:** Harre Union, Christopher Center for Library & Infor, VU Center for the Arts, Brauer Art Museum, Athletics-Recreation Center, Kallay-Christopher Hall Kade Duesenberg German House Grinder's Cafe. **Environmental Initiatives:** Development of environmental sustainability intranet and Internet web sites Increased the number of waterless urinals Continued to increase the number of hand dryers Used fry oil routed to recycler who converts it to biodiesel and lube oil for roller mills Recycled all used furniture resulting from move into the new Union Pilot for lighting occupancy sensors Pilot for unplugging water coolers Development of draft environmental sustainability statement "Green Tips" column in staff newsletter New construction and renovation projects in compliance with Leadership in Energy and Environmental Design (LEED) standards. All new buildings and major renovations are required to be LEED Silver or comparable. In addition, a project has been targeted to be compliant at the LEED Gold level. An Environmental Sustainability Committee has been established. The University has received a second grant for a rain garden and has a seat on the City of Valparaiso's water conservation taskforce. Ground tires in asphalt mix Ground tires in new artificial turf eliminating lawn mowing and chemicals Mulch from chipped yard waste Storm water detention on campus, now adding bioswales Smaller service vehicles Fewer service vehicles Electric service vehicles

ADMISSIONS

Freshman Academic Profile: Average high school GPA 3.48. 26% in top 10% of high school class, 58% in top 25% of high school class, 86% in top 50% of high school class. SAT Math middle 50% range 500–620. SAT Critical Reading middle 50% range 480–630. SAT Writing middle 50% range 480–610. ACT middle 50% range 22–29. Minimum paper TOEFL 550. Minimum computer TOEFL 213. Minimum web-based TOEFL 80. **Basis for Candidate Selection:** *Very important factors considered include:* Academic GPA, rigor of secondary school record. *Important factors considered include:* Class rank, standardized test scores, alumni/ae relation, character/personal qualities, extracurricular activities, talent/ability. *Other factors considered include:* Application essay, recommendation(s), first generation, interview, level of applicant's interest, racial/ethnic status, religious affiliation/commitment, volunteer work. **Freshman Admission Requirements:** High school diploma is required and GED is accepted. *Academic units required:* 4 English, 3 mathematics, 2 science, (2 science labs), 2 foreign language, 2 history, 3 academic electives. *Academic units recommended:* 4 English, 4 mathematics, 3 science, (3 science labs), 2 foreign language, 1 social studies, 2 history, 3 academic electives. **Freshman Admission Statistics:** 2,932 applied, 91% admitted, 25% enrolled. **Transfer Admission Requirements:** College transcript(s), essay or personal statement, statement of good standing from prior institution(s). Minimum college GPA of 2.0 required. Lowest grade transferable C–. **General Admission Information:** Application fee $30. Regular application deadline 8/15. Notification on a rolling basis, beginning on or about 10/1. Nonfall registration accepted. Admission may be deferred for a maximum of 1 year. Credit and/or placement offered for CEEB Advanced Placement tests.

COSTS AND FINANCIAL AID

Annual tuition $27,360. Room and board $7,960. Required fees $960. Average book expense $1,200. **Required Forms and Deadlines:** Priority financial aid filing date 3/1. **Notification of Awards:** Applicants will be notified of awards on a rolling basis beginning 3/1. **Types of Aid:** *Need-based scholarships/grants:* Federal Pell, SEOG, state scholarships/grants, private scholarships, the school's own gift aid. *Loans:* Direct Subsidized Stafford, Direct Unsubsidized Stafford, Direct PLUS, Federal Perkins, college/university loans from institutional funds, Private/alternative education loans if credit standards are met. *Student Employment:* Federal Work-Study Program available. Institutional employment available. Highest amount earned per year from on-campus jobs $5,481. Off-campus job opportunities are good. **Financial Aid Statistics:** 75% freshmen, 71% undergrads receive need-based scholarship or grant aid. 9% freshmen, 9% undergrads receive non-need-based scholarship or grant aid. 59% freshmen, 57% undergrads receive need-based self-help aid. 3% freshmen, 3% undergrads receive athletic scholarships. 94% freshmen, 94% undergrads receive any aid. 73% undergrads borrow to pay for school. Average cumulative indebtedness $31,783. **Criteria for awarding institutional aid:** *Non-need-based:* Academics, alumni affiliation, art, athletics, leadership, music/drama, religious affiliation, state/district residency.

VANDERBILT UNIVERSITY

2305 West End Avenue, Nashville, TN 37203
Phone: 615-322-2561 **Financial Aid Phone:** 800-288-0204
E-mail: admissions@vanderbilt.edu **CEEB Code:** 1871
Fax: 615-343-7765 **Website:** www.vanderbilt.edu **ACT Code:** 4036

This private school was founded in 1873. It has a 323-acre campus.

RATINGS

Admissions Selectivity Rating: 99   **Fire Safety Rating:** 93   **Green Rating:** 81

STUDENTS AND FACULTY

Enrollment: 6,764. **Student Body:** 52% female, 48% male, 84% out-of-state, 4% international (55 countries represented). Asian 8%, African American 9%, Caucasian 56%, Hispanic 6%, Native American 1%.
Retention and Graduation: 96% freshmen return for sophomore year. 84% freshmen graduate within 4 years. 38% grads go on to further study within 1 year. **Faculty:** Student/faculty ratio 8:1. 866 full-time faculty, 97% hold PhDs, 15% are members of minority groups, 34% are women.

ACADEMICS

Degrees: Bachelor's, doctoral, master's. **Classes:** Most classes have 10–19 students. Most lab/discussion sessions have 10–19 students. **Majors with Highest Enrollment:** Engineering science; psychology; sociology. **Special Study Options:** Accelerated program, cooperative education program, cross-registration, distance learning, double major, dual enrollment, English as a Second Language (ESL), honors program, independent study, internships, liberal arts/career combination, student-designed major, study abroad, teacher certification program. **Honors programs:** Psychology, Child Development, Cognitive Studies, and Child Studies, Biomedical Engineering, Biological Sciences. **Combined degree programs:** BA/MBA, MBA/JD, MBA/MD, JD/MDIV, JD/MTS. Special programs offered to physically disabled students include note-taking services, reader services, tape recorders, tutors. **Career services:** Alumni network, alumni services, career/job search classes, career assessment, internships, regional alumni.

FACILITIES

Housing: Coed dorms, special housing for disabled students, men's dorms, special housing for international students, women's dorms, apartments for married students, apartments for single students, theme housing. The Commons is a community of first-year students, residential faculty, and professional staff. 95% of campus accessible to physically disabled. **Special Academic Facilities/Equipment:** Art galleries, center for research on education and human development, multimedia classrooms, teaching center, observatories, free-electron laser, electron microscope. **Computers:** 100% of classrooms, 100% of dorms, 100% of libraries, 100% of dining areas, 100% of student union, 100% of common outdoor areas have wireless network access. Students can register for classes online. Administrative functions (other than registration) can be performed online.

CAMPUS LIFE

Environment: Metropolis. **Activities:** Choral groups, concert band, dance, drama/theater, jazz band, literary magazine, marching band, music ensembles, musical theater, opera, pep band, radio station, student government, student newspaper, student-run film society, symphony orchestra, television station, yearbook, campus ministries, international student organization, Model UN. **Organizations:** 329 registered organizations, 20 honor societies, 18 religious organizations. 19 fraternities, 12 sororities. **Athletics (Intercollegiate):** *Men:* Baseball, basketball, cross-country, football, golf, tennis. *Women:* Basketball, cross-country, golf, lacrosse, soccer, tennis, track/field (outdoor). **On-Campus Highlights:** The Commons, Jean and Alexander Heard Library, Student Recreation Center, Student Life Center, Sarratt Student Center. **Environmental Initiatives:** LEED certification—Vanderbilt was the first university in TN to have any LEED certified buildings. Currently, we have three LEED-Silver certified residence halls, a LEED-Gold Commons Center, the largest concentration in TN and one of the largest in the Southeast. Commuter Choice programs—Vanderbilt employs around 22,000 people and is the largest private employer in middle TN. We have implemented robust commuter choice programs and was designated as the 2006 TN Governor's Environmental Stewardship Program winner for pollution prevention. We are also a designated "Best Workplaces for Commuters" by the EPA and DOT. We fully cover the cost of bus fare for any employee that wants to use mass transit to commute to work, we subsidize the cost of train transportation for those that are eligible. In 2008, we implemented a Vandy-specific carpool/vanpool matching service and a ZipCar hourly rental car program. Vanderbilt has 1 full-time recycling coordinator and recently hired 1 part-time recycling coordinator to direct the activities of 2 recycling technicians and a number of part-time students. VU has a central Recycling Center and additional outdoor recycling facilities. In 2008, Vanderbilt recycled 898 tons of cardboard paper, plastic and aluminum, and 46 tons of electronic waste. Additionally, recycling was implemented at large scale events for the first time, such as Commencement and football games.

ADMISSIONS

Freshman Academic Profile: Average high school GPA 3.7. 86% in top 10% of high school class, 97% in top 25% of high school class, 100% in top 50% of high school class. 57% from public high schools. SAT Math middle 50% range 690—770. SAT Critical Reading middle 50% range 660—750. SAT Writing middle 50% range 660—750. ACT middle 50% range 30—34. Minimum paper TOEFL 570. **Basis for Candidate Selection:** *Very important factors considered include:* Class rank, application essay, academic GPA, rigor of secondary school record, standardized test scores, character/personal qualities, extracurricular activities. *Important factors considered include:* Recommendation(s), talent/ability. *Other factors considered include:* Alumni/ae relation, first generation, geographical residence, interview, racial/ethnic status, state residency, volunteer work, work experience. **Freshman Admission Requirements:** High school diploma is required and GED is accepted. *Academic units required:* 4 English, 3 mathematics, 3 science, (2 science labs), 2 foreign language, 2 social studies, 1 history, 3 academic electives. *Academic units recommended:* 4 English, 4 mathematics, 4 science, (3 science labs), 2 foreign language, 3 social studies, 1 history, 3 academic electives. **Freshman Admission Statistics:** 19,353 applied, 20% admitted, 41% enrolled. **Transfer Admission Requirements:** College transcript(s), essay or personal statement, statement of good standing from prior institution(s). Lowest grade transferable C. **General Admission Information:** Application fee $50. Early decision application deadline 11/1. Regular application deadline 1/3. Regular notification 4/1. Nonfall registration not accepted. Admission may be deferred for a maximum of 1 year. Credit and/or placement offered for CEEB Advanced Placement tests.

COSTS AND FINANCIAL AID

Annual tuition $37,632. Room and board $12,650. Required fees $946. Average book expense $1,208. **Required Forms and Deadlines:** FAFSA, CSS/Financial Aid PROFILE Priority financial aid filing date 2/1. **Notification of Awards:** Applicants will be notified of awards on or about 4/1. **Types of Aid:** *Need-based scholarships/grants:* Federal Pell, SEOG, state scholarships/grants, private scholarships, the school's own gift aid. *Loans:* FFEL Subsidized Stafford, FFEL Unsubsidized Stafford, FFEL PLUS, Federal Perkins, Federal Nursing, college/university loans from institutional funds, Undergrad Education Loan. *Student Employment:* Federal Work-Study Program available. Institutional employment available. Highest amount earned per year from on-campus jobs $2,000. Off-campus job opportunities are excellent. **Financial Aid Statistics:** 42% freshmen, 41% undergrads receive need-based scholarship or grant aid. 26% freshmen, 20% undergrads receive non-need-based scholarship or grant aid. 25% freshmen, 26% undergrads receive need-based self-help aid. 4% freshmen, 4% undergrads receive athletic scholarships. 62% freshmen, 62% undergrads receive any aid. 40% undergrads borrow to pay for school. Average cumulative indebtedness $19,563. **Criteria for awarding institutional aid:** *Non-need-based:* Academics, athletics, leadership, minority status, music/drama, state/district residency.

See page 1314.

VANDERCOOK COLLEGE OF MUSIC

3140 South Federal Street, Chicago, IL 60616-3886
Phone: 312-225-6288
E-mail: admissions@vandercook.edu **CEEB Code:** 1872
Fax: 312-225-5211 **Website:** www.vandercook.edu **ACT Code:** 1156

This private school was founded in 1909. It has a 1-acre campus.

RATINGS
Admissions Selectivity Rating: 74   **Fire Safety Rating:** 60*   **Green Rating:** 60*

STUDENTS AND FACULTY
Enrollment: 93. **Student Body:** 48% female, 52% male, 34% out-of-state, 2% international (2 countries represented). Asian 2%, African American 15%, Caucasian 71%, Hispanic 9%.
Retention and Graduation: 39% freshmen graduate within 4 years.

ACADEMICS
Degrees: Bachelor's, master's. **Special Study Options:** Independent study, teacher certification program.

FACILITIES
Housing: Coed dorms, men's dorms, women's dorms, fraternity/sorority housing.

CAMPUS LIFE
Environment: Metropolis. **Activities:** Choral groups, concert band, jazz band, music ensembles, musical theater, student newspaper. **Organizations:** 5 registered organizations, 1 fraternities.

ADMISSIONS
Freshman Academic Profile: SAT Math middle 50% range 350–590. SAT Critical Reading middle 50% range 440–670. ACT middle 50% range 16–22. Minimum paper TOEFL 500. Minimum computer TOEFL 173. **Basis for Candidate Selection:** *Very important factors considered include:* Interview, talent/ability. *Important factors considered include:* Application essay, rigor of secondary school record, extracurricular activities. *Other factors considered include:* Class rank, recommendation(s), standardized test scores, alumni/ae relation, character/personal qualities, volunteer work, work experience. **Freshman Admission Requirements:** High school diploma is required and GED is accepted. *Academic units required:* 3 English, 2 mathematics, 2 science, 2 foreign language, 3 social studies, 3 academic electives. **Freshman Admission Statistics:** 43 applied, 91% admitted, 72% enrolled. **Transfer Admission Requirements:** High school transcript, college transcript(s), essay or personal statement, interview, standardized test scores, minimum college GPA of 2.5 required. Lowest grade transferable C. **General Admission Information:** Application fee $35. Regular application deadline 5/1. Nonfall registration accepted. Admission may be deferred for a maximum of case by case. Credit offered for CEEB Advanced Placement tests.

COSTS AND FINANCIAL AID
Annual tuition $15,130. Room and board $6,900. Required fees $630. Average book expense $1,200. **Required Forms and Deadlines:** FAFSA **Types of Aid:** *Need-based scholarships/grants:* State scholarships/grants. *Loans:* FFEL Subsidized Stafford, FFEL PLUS.

VANGUARD UNIVERSITY OF SOUTHERN CALIFORNIA

55 Fair Drive, Costa Mesa, CA 92626
Phone: 714-556-3610 **Financial Aid Phone:** 714-556-3610
E-mail: admissions@vanguard.edu **CEEB Code:** 4701
Fax: 714-966-5471 **Website:** www.vanguard.edu **ACT Code:** 432

This private school, affiliated with the Assemblies of God Church, was founded in 1920. It has a 38-acre campus.

RATINGS
Admissions Selectivity Rating: 75   **Fire Safety Rating:** 78   **Green Rating:** 60*

STUDENTS AND FACULTY
Enrollment: 1,847. **Student Body:** 63% female, 37% male, 14% out-of-state, 1% international (17 countries represented). Asian 4%, African American 3%, Caucasian 66%, Hispanic 17%, Native American 1%.
Retention and Graduation: 76% freshmen return for sophomore year. 37% freshmen graduate within 4 years. **Faculty:** Student/faculty ratio 16:1. 66 full-time faculty, 77% hold PhDs, 14% are members of minority groups, 39% are women.

ACADEMICS
Degrees: Bachelor's, master's. **Classes:** Most classes have 10–19 students. Most lab/discussion sessions have fewer than 10 students. **Majors with Highest Enrollment:** Business/commerce; education; psychology. **Special Study Options:** Accelerated program, cooperative education program, cross-registration, double major, dual enrollment, external degree program, independent study, internships, study abroad, teacher certification program. Special programs offered to physically disabled students include note-taking services, tutors.

FACILITIES
Housing: Special housing for disabled students, men's dorms, women's dorms, apartments for married students, apartments for single students, One dorm is coed (Floors 1, 2, 4 for males; floor 3 for females). 95% of campus accessible to physically disabled. **Special Academic Facilities/Equipment:** Lyceum Theater; Computer Lab; Communications Lab. **Computers:** Students can register for classes online. Administrative functions (other than registration) can be performed online.

CAMPUS LIFE
Environment: City. **Activities:** Choral groups, concert band, dance, drama/theater, jazz band, music ensembles, musical theater, opera, pep band, student government, student newspaper, symphony orchestra, yearbook. **Organizations:** 50 registered organizations, 5 honor societies, 25 religious organizations. **Athletics (Intercollegiate):** *Men:* Baseball, basketball, cross-country, soccer, tennis, track/field (outdoor), track/field (indoor). *Women:* Basketball, cross-country, soccer, softball, tennis, track/field (outdoor), track/field (indoor), volleyball. **On-Campus Highlights:** Cove-Student Union, The Library, The Pit-our gymnasium, Heath Academic Center, The Dining Commons.

ADMISSIONS
Freshman Academic Profile: Average high school GPA 3.35. 22% in top 10% of high school class, 49% in top 25% of high school class, 78% in top 50% of high school class. 73% from public high schools. SAT Math middle 50% range 430–560. SAT Critical Reading middle 50% range 450–570. ACT middle 50% range 19–24. Minimum paper TOEFL 550. Minimum computer TOEFL 213. **Basis for Candidate Selection:** *Very important factors considered include:* Application essay, academic GPA, recommendation(s), rigor of secondary school record, character/personal qualities. *Important factors considered include:* Standardized test scores, religious affiliation/commitment. *Other factors considered include:* Extracurricular activities, interview, level of applicant's interest, talent/ability, volunteer work, work experience. **Freshman Admission Requirements:** High school diploma is required and GED is accepted. *Academic units recommended:* 4 English, 2 mathematics, 2 science, 3 social studies. **Freshman Admission Statistics:** 899 applied, 83% admitted, 53% enrolled. **Transfer Admission Requirements:** College transcript(s), essay or personal statement, minimum college GPA of 2.0 required. Lowest grade transferable C–. **General Admission Information:** Application fee $45. Notification on a rolling basis, beginning on or about 1/15. Nonfall registration accepted. Credit offered for CEEB Advanced Placement tests.

COSTS AND FINANCIAL AID
Annual tuition $22,466. Room and board $7,270. Required fees $520. Average book expense $1,314. **Required Forms and Deadlines:** FAFSA, state aid form Financial aid filing deadline 3/2. Priority financial aid filing date 3/2. **Notification of Awards:** Applicants will be notified of awards on a rolling basis

beginning 4/1. **Types of Aid:** *Need-based scholarships/grants:* Federal Pell, SEOG, state scholarships/grants, private scholarships, the school's own gift aid. *Loans:* FFEL Subsidized Stafford, FFEL Unsubsidized Stafford, FFEL PLUS, Federal Perkins. *Student Employment:* Federal Work-Study Program available. Institutional employment available. Highest amount earned per year from on-campus jobs $6,000. Off-campus job opportunities are excellent. **Financial Aid Statistics:** 54% freshmen, 58% undergrads receive need-based scholarship or grant aid. 61% freshmen, 74% undergrads receive non-need-based scholarship or grant aid. 54% freshmen, 79% undergrads receive need-based self-help aid. 2% freshmen, 2% undergrads receive athletic scholarships. 94% freshmen, 99% undergrads receive any aid. 76% undergrads borrow to pay for school. Average cumulative indebtedness $16,979. **Criteria for awarding institutional aid:** *Non-need-based:* Academics, athletics, music/drama.

VASSAR COLLEGE

124 Raymond Avenue, Poughkeepsie, NY 12604
Phone: 845-437-7300 **Financial Aid Phone:** 845-437-5320
E-mail: admissions@vassar.edu **CEEB Code:** 2956
Fax: 845-437-7063 **Website:** www.vassar.edu **ACT Code:** 2982

This private school was founded in 1861. It has a 1000-acre campus.

RATINGS
Admissions Selectivity Rating: 98   **Fire Safety Rating:** 81   **Green Rating:** 90

STUDENTS AND FACULTY
Enrollment: 2,394. **Student Body:** 59% female, 41% male, 73% out-of-state, 6% international (43 countries represented). Asian 11%, African American 5%, Caucasian 70%, Hispanic 7%.
Retention and Graduation: 96% freshmen return for sophomore year. 88% freshmen graduate within 4 years. 23% grads go on to further study within 1 year. 11% grads pursue arts and sciences degrees. 3% grads pursue law degrees. 3% grads pursue medical degrees. **Faculty:** Student/faculty ratio 8:1. 296 full-time faculty, 89% hold PhDs, 25% are members of minority groups, 48% are women.

ACADEMICS
Degrees: Bachelor's, master's. **Classes:** Most classes have 10–19 students. Most lab/discussion sessions have 10–19 students. **Majors with Highest Enrollment:** English language and literature; political science and government; psychology. **Special Study Options:** Cooperative education program, cross-registration, double major, exchange student program (domestic), independent study, internships, liberal arts/career combination, student-designed major, study abroad, teacher certification program. **Combined degree programs:** BA/MA Special programs offered to physically disabled students include note-taking services, reader services, tape recorders **Career services:** Alumni network, alumni services, career/job search classes, career assessment, internships, regional alumni.

FACILITIES
Housing: Coed dorms, special housing for disabled students, special housing for international students, women's dorms, apartments for married students, cooperative housing, apartments for single students, wellness housing, quiet housing. 69% of campus accessible to physically disabled. **Special Academic Facilities/Equipment:** Art center, theatres, nursery school, environmental field station, geology museum, electron microscope, observatory, Skinner Music Hall, Fitness Center. **Computers:** 100% of classrooms, 100% of dorms, 100% of libraries, 100% of dining areas, 100% of student union, 80% of common outdoor areas have wireless network access. Students can register for classes online. Administrative functions (other than registration) can be performed online.

CAMPUS LIFE
Environment: Town. **Activities:** Choral groups, concert band, dance, drama/theater, jazz band, literary magazine, marching band, music ensembles, musical theater, opera, radio station, student government, student newspaper, student-run film society, symphony orchestra, television station, yearbook, campus ministries, international student organization, Model UN. **Organizations:** 105 registered organizations, 2 honor societies, 11 religious organizations. **Athletics (Intercollegiate):** *Men:* Baseball, basketball, crew/rowing, cross-country, diving, fencing, lacrosse, soccer, squash, swimming, tennis, track/field (outdoor), volleyball. *Women:* Basketball, crew/rowing, cross-country, diving, fencing, field

hockey, golf, lacrosse, soccer, squash, swimming, tennis, track/field (outdoor), volleyball. **On-Campus Highlights:** Library, Shakespeare Garden, Class of 1951 Observatory, Frances Lehman Loeb Art Center, Center for Drama and Film. **Environmental Initiatives:** composting nearly. 100% of food waste on site purchasing local food. 30% locally grown or purchased shared bicycle program

ADMISSIONS

Freshman Academic Profile: Average high school GPA 3.77. 67% in top 10% of high school class, 95% in top 25% of high school class, 99% in top 50% of high school class. 61% from public high schools. SAT Math middle 50% range 640–720. SAT Critical Reading middle 50% range 660–750. SAT Writing middle 50% range 660–750. ACT middle 50% range 29–32. Minimum paper TOEFL 600. Minimum computer TOEFL 250. Minimum web-based TOEFL 100. **Basis for Candidate Selection:** *Very important factors considered include:* Rigor of secondary school record. *Important factors considered include:* Class rank, application essay, academic GPA, recommendation(s), standardized test scores, extracurricular activities, talent/ability. *Other factors considered include:* Alumni/ae relation, character/personal qualities, first generation, geographical residence, interview, level of applicant's interest, racial/ethnic status, volunteer work, work experience. **Freshman Admission Requirements:** High school diploma is required and GED is accepted. *Academic units required:* 4 English, 4 mathematics, 4 science, (3 science labs), 3 foreign language, 2 social studies, 2 history, 4 academic electives. *Academic units recommended:* 4 English, 4 mathematics, 4 science, (3 science labs), 4 foreign language, 4 social studies, 2 history. **Freshman Admission Statistics:** 7,577 applied, 25% admitted, 35% enrolled. **Transfer Admission Requirements:** High school transcript, college transcript(s), essay or personal statement, standardized test scores, statement of good standing from prior institution(s). Minimum college GPA of 3.0 required. Lowest grade transferable C. **General Admission Information:** Application fee $60. Early decision application deadline 11/15. Regular application deadline 1/1. Regular notification 4/1. Nonfall registration not accepted. Admission may be deferred for a maximum of 1 year. Credit and/or placement offered for CEEB Advanced Placement tests.

COSTS AND FINANCIAL AID

Annual tuition $41,335. Room and board $9,370. Required fees $595. Average book expense $860. **Required Forms and Deadlines:** FAFSA, CSS/Financial Aid PROFILE, noncustodial PROFILE, business/farm supplement. Financial aid filing deadline 2/1. **Notification of Awards:** Applicants will be notified of awards on or about 3/30. **Types of Aid:** *Need-based scholarships/grants:* Federal Pell, SEOG, state scholarships/grants, private scholarships, the school's own gift aid. *Loans:* Direct Subsidized Stafford, Direct Unsubsidized Stafford, Direct PLUS, Federal Perkins, Loans for Non-citizens with need. *Student Employment:* Federal Work-Study Program available. Institutional employment available. Highest amount earned per year from on-campus jobs $4,350. Off-campus job opportunities are fair. **Financial Aid Statistics:** 60% freshmen, 56% undergrads receive need-based scholarship or grant aid. 60% freshmen, 56% undergrads receive need-based self-help aid. 60.5% freshmen, 55.7% undergrads receive any aid. 49% undergrads borrow to pay for school. Average cumulative indebtedness $18,876.

VAUGHN COLLEGE OF AERONAUTICS AND TECHNOLOGY

86-01 23rd Avenue, 86-01 23rd Avenue, Flushing, NY 11369
Phone: 718-429-6600 **Financial Aid Phone:** 718-429-6600
E-mail: admitme@vaughn.edu **CEEB Code:** 2001
Fax: 718-779-2231 **Website:** www.vaughn.edu

This private school was founded in 1932. It has a 6-acre campus.

RATINGS
Admissions Selectivity Rating: 60*　　**Fire Safety Rating:** 94　　**Green Rating:** 60*

STUDENTS AND FACULTY
Enrollment: 1,283. **Student Body:** 11% female, 89% male, 8% out-of-state, 2% international. Asian 12%, African American 21%, Caucasian 14%, Hispanic 38%, Native American 1%.
Retention and Graduation: 88% freshmen return for sophomore year. 31% freshmen graduate within 4 years. **Faculty:** Student/faculty ratio 15:1. 39 full-time faculty, 36% hold PhDs, 28% are members of minority groups, 10% are women.

ACADEMICS
Degrees: Associate, bachelor's, certificate, master's. **Classes:** Most classes have 20–29 students. Most lab/discussion sessions have 20–29 students. **Majors with Highest Enrollment:** airframe mechanics and aircraft maintenance technol-

ogy/technician; business/commerce; transportation/transportation management. **Special Study Options:** Accelerated program, distance learning, double major, independent study, internships, liberal arts/career combination. **Career services:** Alumni network, alumni services, career/job search classes, career assessment, internships. **Career services highlights include:** Internship program.

FACILITIES
Housing: Coed dorms. **Computers:** 100% of classrooms, 100% of dorms, 100% of libraries, 100% of dining areas, 100% of common outdoor areas have wireless network access. Administrative functions (other than registration) can be performed online.

CAMPUS LIFE
Environment: City. **Activities:** Dance, drama/theater, student government, yearbook, international student organization. **Organizations:** 21 registered organizations, 1 honor societies. **Athletics (Intercollegiate):** *Men:* Basketball, soccer. *Women:* Tennis. **On-Campus Highlights:** Complex of six flight simulators, Laboratories, Observation Tower, Cafeteria, Library.

ADMISSIONS
Freshman Academic Profile: SAT Math middle 50% range 471–552. SAT Critical Reading middle 50% range 440–536. Minimum paper TOEFL 600. Minimum computer TOEFL 218. **Basis for Candidate Selection:** *Very important factors considered include:* Rigor of secondary school record. *Important factors considered include:* Academic GPA, standardized test scores, level of applicant's interest. *Other factors considered include:* Application essay, recommendation(s), character/personal qualities, extracurricular activities, first generation, interview, talent/ability, volunteer work, work experience. **Freshman Admission Requirements:** High school diploma is required and GED is accepted. *Academic units required:* 4 English, 3 mathematics, 2 science, (2 science labs), 1 social studies. *Academic units recommended:* 4 English, 4 mathematics, 3 science, (3 science labs), 4 social studies. **Freshman Admission Statistics:** 492 applied, 92% admitted, 58% enrolled. **Transfer Admission Requirements:** College transcript(s), minimum college GPA of 2.0 required. Lowest grade transferable C. **General Admission Information:** Application fee $40. Notification on a rolling basis, beginning on or about 10/1. Nonfall registration accepted. Admission may be deferred for a maximum of 1 year. Credit and/or placement offered for CEEB Advanced Placement tests.

COSTS AND FINANCIAL AID
Annual tuition $17,115. Room and board $11,025. Required fees $400. Average book expense $1,500. **Required Forms and Deadlines:** FAFSA, state aid form. Priority financial aid filing date 3/1. **Notification of Awards:** Applicants will be notified of awards on a rolling basis beginning 4/15. **Types of Aid:** *Need-based scholarships/grants:* Federal Pell, SEOG, state scholarships/grants, private scholarships, the school's own gift aid. *Loans:* FFEL Subsidized Stafford, FFEL Unsubsidized Stafford, FFEL PLUS. *Student Employment:* Federal Work-Study Program available. Institutional employment available. Off-campus job opportunities are excellent. **Financial Aid Statistics:** 96% freshmen, 70% undergrads receive need-based scholarship or grant aid. 15% freshmen, 17% undergrads receive non-need-based scholarship or grant aid. 98% freshmen, 89% undergrads receive need-based self-help aid. 99% freshmen, 89% undergrads receive any aid. 93% undergrads borrow to pay for school. Average cumulative indebtedness $3,491. **Criteria for awarding institutional aid:** *Non-need-based:* Academics, alumni affiliation, job skills, leadership.

See page 1316.

VERMONT TECHNICAL COLLEGE

PO Box 500, Randolph Center, VT 05061
Phone: 802-728-1242
E-mail: Admissions@vtc.edu
Fax: 802-728-1321 **Website:** www.vtc.edu

This is a public school.

RATINGS
Admissions Selectivity Rating: 70　　**Fire Safety Rating:** 60*　　**Green Rating:** 60*

STUDENTS AND FACULTY
Enrollment: 1,378. **Student Body:** 40% female, 60% male, 21% out-of-state, international.
Retention and Graduation: 65% freshmen return for sophomore year. **Faculty:** Student/faculty ratio 12:1. 79 full-time faculty, 80% hold PhDs, 47% are women.

ACADEMICS

Degrees: Associate, bachelor's, certificate, diploma. **Classes:** Most classes have 10–19 students. Most lab/discussion sessions have 10–19 students. **Special Study Options:** Distance learning, double major, dual enrollment, internships

FACILITIES

Housing: Coed dorms.

CAMPUS LIFE

Activities: Radio station, student government, television station, yearbook.

ADMISSIONS

Freshman Academic Profile: 8% in top 10% of high school class, 27% in top 25% of high school class, 60% in top 50% of high school class. SAT Math middle 50% range 450–560. SAT Critical Reading middle 50% range 410–520. SAT Writing middle 50% range 410–520. **Basis for Candidate Selection:** *Very important factors considered include:* Academic GPA, rigor of secondary school record. *Important factors considered include:* Recommendation(s), standardized test scores, interview. *Other factors considered include:* Application essay, alumni/ae relation, character/personal qualities, extracurricular activities, first generation, volunteer work, work experience. **Freshman Admission Requirements:** High school diploma is required and GED is accepted. *Academic units required:* 4 English, 3 mathematics, 2 science, (1 science labs), 2 social studies, 2 history. *Academic units recommended:* 4 mathematics, 3 science, (2 science labs), 2 foreign language. **Freshman Admission Statistics:** 920 applied, 58% admitted, 54% enrolled. **Transfer Admission Requirements:** College transcript(s), statement of good standing from prior institution(s). Lowest grade transferable C–. **General Admission Information:** Application fee $36. Notification on a rolling basis, beginning on or about 10/1. Nonfall registration accepted.

COSTS AND FINANCIAL AID

Financial Aid Statistics: 55% freshmen, 52% undergrads receive need-based scholarship or grant aid. 2% freshmen, 3% undergrads receive non-need-based scholarship or grant aid. 58% freshmen, 58% undergrads receive need-based self-help aid.

VILLA MARIA COLLEGE OF BUFFALO

240 Pine Ridge Road, Buffalo, NY 14225
Phone: 716-961-1805 **Financial Aid Phone:** 716-961-1850
E-mail: admissions@villa.edu
Fax: 716-896-0705 **Website: ACT Code:** 2983

This private school, affiliated with the Roman Catholic Church, was founded in 1960. It has a 9-acre campus.

RATINGS

Admissions Selectivity Rating: 65   **Fire Safety Rating:** 60*   **Green Rating:** 60*

STUDENTS AND FACULTY

Enrollment: 497. **Student Body:** 65% female, 35% male, 1% out-of-state, (2 countries represented). Asian 1%, African American 22%, Caucasian 71%, Hispanic 3%, Native American 1%.
Retention and Graduation: 69% freshmen return for sophomore year.
Faculty: Student/faculty ratio 10:1. 31 full-time faculty, 39% hold PhDs, 6% are members of minority groups, 55% are women.

ACADEMICS

Degrees: Associate, bachelor's. **Classes:** Most classes have 10–19 students. Most lab/discussion sessions have 10–19 students. **Majors with Highest Enrollment:** Interior design; music management and merchandising; visual and performing arts. **Special Study Options:** Cooperative education program, cross-registration, dual enrollment, internships, liberal arts/career combination, study abroad, Selected courses are offered in evening modules primarily with non-traditional students in mind. These offerings are limited. Special programs offered to physically disabled students include tutors. **Career services:** Alumni services, career/job search classes, career assessment, internships.

FACILITIES

Housing: Apartments for married students, apartments for single students Housing is available at Collegiate Village (college affiliated) which is a mile off-campus; however van service to campus is available. There is no on-campus housing. 100% of campus accessible to physically disabled. **Special Academic Facilities/Equipment:** Art Gallery, Music Building, Recording Studio, Student Center, Athletic Center, Art Shop. **Computers:** 100% of libraries, 100% of dining areas, have wireless network access. Students can register for classes online. Administrative functions (other than registration) can be performed online.

CAMPUS LIFE

Environment: City. **Activities:** Choral groups, jazz band, literary magazine, music ensembles, student government, student newspaper, campus ministries. **Organizations:** 1 honor societies. **On-Campus Highlights:** Athletic/Student Center, Recording Studio.

ADMISSIONS

Freshman Academic Profile: Average high school GPA 2.6. 1% in top 10% of high school class, 11% in top 25% of high school class, 48% in top 50% of high school class. 94% from public high schools. SAT Math middle 50% range 400–500. SAT Critical Reading middle 50% range 380–510. ACT middle 50% range 18–22. Minimum paper TOEFL 450. Minimum computer TOEFL 133. **Basis for Candidate Selection:** *Very important factors considered include:* Application essay, academic GPA, interview, talent/ability. *Important factors considered include:* Level of applicant's interest. *Other factors considered include:* Recommendation(s), rigor of secondary school record, standardized test scores, volunteer work, work experience. **Freshman Admission Requirements:** High school diploma is required and GED is accepted. *Academic units recommended:* 4 English, 3 mathematics, 3 science, 4 social studies, 4 history. **Freshman Admission Statistics:** 572 applied, 71% admitted, 37% enrolled. **Transfer Admission Requirements:** College transcript(s), interview, Lowest grade transferable C. **General Admission Information:** Nonfall registration accepted. Admission may be deferred for a maximum of 2 semesters. Credit and/or placement offered for CEEB Advanced Placement tests.

COSTS AND FINANCIAL AID

Required Forms and Deadlines: FAFSA. **Notification of Awards:** Applicants will be notified of awards on a rolling basis beginning 2/15. **Types of Aid:** *Need-based scholarships/grants:* Federal Pell, SEOG, state scholarships/grants, private scholarships, the school's own gift aid. *Loans:* FFEL Subsidized Stafford, FFEL Unsubsidized Stafford, FFEL PLUS. *Student Employment:* Federal Work-Study Program available. Off-campus job opportunities are fair. **Financial Aid Statistics:** 76% freshmen, 77% undergrads receive need-based scholarship or grant aid. 31% freshmen, 13% undergrads receive non-need-based scholarship or grant aid. 81% freshmen, 73% undergrads receive need-based self-help aid. 83% freshmen, 86% undergrads receive any aid. 100% undergrads borrow to pay for school. **Criteria for awarding institutional aid:** *Non-need-based:* Academics, alumni affiliation, art, leadership, minority status, music/drama.

VILLANOVA UNIVERSITY

Best 373

800 Lancaster Avenue, Villanova, PA 19085-1672
Phone: 610-519-4000 **Financial Aid Phone:** 610-519-4010
E-mail: gotovu@villanova.edu **CEEB Code:** 2959
Fax: 610-519-6450 **Website:** www.villanova.edu **ACT Code:** 3744

This private school, affiliated with the Roman Catholic Church, was founded in 1842. It has a 254-acre campus.

RATINGS

Admissions Selectivity Rating: 95   **Fire Safety Rating:** 85   **Green Rating:** 86

STUDENTS AND FACULTY

Enrollment: 6,897. **Student Body:** 51% female, 49% male, 70% out-of-state, 3% international (53 countries represented). Asian 7%, African American 5%, Caucasian 76%, Hispanic 7%.
Retention and Graduation: 94% freshmen return for sophomore year. 82% freshmen graduate within 4 years. 22% grads go on to further study within 1 year. 7% grads pursue arts and sciences degrees. 6% grads pursue law degrees. 2% grads pursue business degrees. 4% grads pursue medical degrees. **Faculty:** Student/faculty ratio 11:1. 570 full-time faculty, 89% hold PhDs, 14% are members of minority groups, 37% are women.

ACADEMICS

Degrees: Associate, bachelor's, master's, post-bachelor's certificate, post-master's certificate. **Classes:** Most classes have 10–19 students. Most lab/discussion sessions have 10–19 students. **Majors with Highest Enrollment:** communication studies/speech communication and rhetoric; finance; nursing/registered nurse (RN, ASN, BSN, MSN). **Special Study Options:** Accelerated program, cooperative education program, cross-registration, distance learning, double major, dual enrollment, English as a Second Language (ESL), exchange student program (domestic), honors program, independent study, internships, liberal arts/career combination, study abroad, teacher certification program. **Honors programs:** Honors at Villanova is a comprehensive four-year program that offers challenging seminars, research opportunities, service projects, and cultural and social events designed to bring together superior students and dedicated faculty. Honors courses and co-curricular activities enrich and complement the academic experience inherent in a Villanova education. The Honors Program also works closely with the University's Center for Undergraduate Grants and Awards, which administers the Presidential Scholarship program for incoming students; Connelly-Delouvrier International Scholarships for study abroad; and Villanova's support for students pursuing prestigious national fellowships. The Villanova University Honors Program is an active member of both the National Collegiate Honors Council and the Northeast Region of the National Collegiate Honors Council. **Combined degree programs:** BS/MD, BS/OD, BS/MS, BS/DDM. Special programs offered to physically disabled students include note-taking services, reader services, tape recorders, tutors. **Career services:** Alumni network, alumni services, career/job search classes, career assessment, internships, regional alumni. **Career services highlights include:** Hundreds of companies recruit Villanova students for internships—either on campus or via job boards—each year. Many internships ultimately lead to full-time job offers.

FACILITIES

Housing: Coed dorms, men's dorms, women's dorms, apartments for single students, wellness housing, theme housing, Learning Communities. 100% of campus accessible to physically disabled. **Special Academic Facilities/Equipment:** Driscoll Hall, home of the Villanova College of Nursing; the Villanova School of Business Applied Finance Lab; the Structural Engineering Teaching and Research Laboratory; the Augustinian Historical Museum, and the Villanova Observatory. **Computers:** 90% of classrooms, 90% of dorms, 100% of libraries, 100% of dining areas, 100% of student union, 10% of common outdoor areas have wireless network access. Students can register for classes online. Administrative functions (other than registration) can be performed online. Undergraduates are required to own a computer.

CAMPUS LIFE

Environment: Village. **Activities:** Choral groups, concert band, dance, drama/theater, jazz band, literary magazine, marching band, music ensembles, musical theater, pep band, radio station, student government, student newspaper, student-run film society, symphony orchestra, television station, yearbook, campus ministries, international student organization, Model UN. **Organizations:** 250 registered organizations, 34 honor societies, 15 religious organizations. 9 fraternities, 9 sororities. **Athletics (Intercollegiate):** *Men:* Baseball, basketball, cheerleading, cross-country, diving, football, golf, lacrosse, soccer, swimming, tennis, track/field (outdoor), track/field (indoor). *Women:* Basketball, cheerleading, crew/rowing, cross-country, diving, field hockey, lacrosse, soccer, softball, swimming, tennis, track/field (outdoor), track/field (indoor), volleyball, water polo. **On-Campus Highlights:** St. Thomas of Villanova Church, Davis Center for Athletics and Fitness, Villanova University Shop, Connelly Center and Cinema, Bartley Hall Exchange. **Environmental Initiatives:** Academic programs: the master's degree in sustainable engineering; the first-year environmental leadership learning community; bachelor's degrees in environmental science and environmental studies; an undergraduate concentration in environmental studies; a new minor in sustainability studies; a biology master's degree, graduate certificate, and advanced graduate certificate with a concentration in ecology, evolution, and organismal biology; a master's degree in water resources and environmental engineering, and a graduate certificate in urban water resources design. Non-academic programs: In addition to the contributions of academic departments, several groups of students, faculty, and staff are working together to strengthen Villanova's commitment to the environment. These groups include the President's Environmental Sustainability Committee, the Villanova Environmental Group, and the Villanova Ecological Society. Villanova has a green dorm, as well as an ongoing dorm energy conservation competition. The Sustainable Endowments Institute gives Villanova an "A" in several categories of its annual Green Report Card, including Food & Recycling. The Institute also considers Villanova to be an "Endowment Sustainability Leader," a title given to only 12 colleges that earned an average grade of A- or better on three endowment management categories: transparency, investment priorities, and shareholder engagement. Lastly, the university implements green building practices, with features that include green roofs, extensive natural lighting and other energy-conserving building features, efficient plumbing, and a 90% construction waste diversion rate. Dining Services: Villanova has implemented a comprehensive composting initiative, and has transitioned one of its locations into a green facility, reducing its trash volume by two thirds. Villanova partners with the Monterey Bay Aquarium, following the Seafood Watch program (exclusively purchasing and serving seafood which is abundant, and caught or farmed in environmentally-friendly ways.) 100% of the resident dining halls are trayless and have complete vegetarian options available. In addition, Villanova Dining Services purchases 32% of its food from local and organic sources.

ADMISSIONS

Freshman Academic Profile: Average high school GPA 3.76. 58% in top 10% of high school class, 88% in top 25% of high school class, 98% in top 50% of high school class. 56% from public high schools. SAT Math middle 50% range 620–710. SAT Critical Reading middle 50% range 580–680. ACT middle 50% range 28–31. Minimum paper TOEFL 550. Minimum computer TOEFL 213. **Basis for Candidate Selection:** *Very important factors considered include:* Class rank, academic GPA, rigor of secondary school record, standardized test scores. *Important factors considered include:* Application essay, recommendation(s), character/personal qualities, extracurricular activities, talent/ability, volunteer work, work experience. *Other factors considered include:* Alumni/ae relation, first generation, geographical residence, level of applicant's interest, racial/ethnic status, state residency. **Freshman Admission Requirements:** High school diploma is required and GED is accepted. *Academic units required:* 4 English, 4 mathematics, 4 science, (2 science labs), 2 foreign language, 2 academic electives. *Academic units recommended:* 4 English, 4 mathematics, 4 science, (3 science labs), 4 foreign language, 2 academic electives. **Freshman Admission Statistics:** 13,098 applied, 46% admitted, 27% enrolled. **Transfer Admission Requirements:** High school transcript, college transcript(s), essay or personal statement, standardized test scores, statement of good standing from prior institution(s). Lowest grade transferable C. **General Admission Information:** Application fee $75. Regular application deadline 1/7. Regular notification 4/1. Nonfall registration not accepted. Admission may be deferred for a maximum of 1 year. Credit and/or placement offered for CEEB Advanced Placement tests.

COSTS AND FINANCIAL AID

Annual tuition $37,210. Room and board $10,320. Required fees $580. Average book expense $950. **Required Forms and Deadlines:** FAFSA, institution's own financial aid form. Financial aid filing deadline 2/7. **Notification of Awards:** Applicants will be notified of awards on or about 4/1. **Types of Aid:** *Need-based scholarships/grants:* Federal Pell, SEOG, state scholarships/grants, private scholarships, the school's own gift aid. *Loans:* FFEL Subsidized Stafford, FFEL Unsubsidized Stafford, FFEL PLUS, Federal Perkins, Federal Nursing *Student Employment:* Federal Work-Study Program available. Institutional employment available. Off-campus job opportunities are excellent. **Financial Aid Statistics:** 49% freshmen, 42% undergrads receive need-based scholarship or grant aid. 16% freshmen, 13% undergrads receive non-need-based scholarship or grant aid. 50% freshmen, 45% undergrads receive need-based self-help aid. 2% freshmen, 2% undergrads receive athletic scholarships. 53% freshmen, 48% undergrads receive any aid. 55% undergrads borrow to pay for school. Average cumulative indebtedness $31,048. **Criteria for awarding institutional aid:** *Non-need-based:* Academics, alumni affiliation, athletics, leadership, minority status, religious affiliation.

VIRGINIA COMMONWEALTH UNIVERSITY

821 West Franklin Street, PO Box 842526, Richmond, VA 23284
Phone: 804-828-1222 **Financial Aid Phone:** 804-828-6669
E-mail: upgrad@vcu.edu **CEEB Code:** 5570
Fax: 804-828-1899 **Website:** www.vcu.edu

This public school was founded in 1838. It has a 143-acre campus.

RATINGS

Admissions Selectivity Rating: 80   **Fire Safety Rating:** 80   **Green Rating:** 97

STUDENTS AND FACULTY

Enrollment: 21,500. **Student Body:** 57% female, 43% male, 7% out-of-state, 3% international (110 countries represented). Asian 12%, African American 20%, Caucasian 52%, Hispanic 4%, Native American 1%.
Retention and Graduation: 84% freshmen return for sophomore year. 25% freshmen graduate within 4 years. **Faculty:** Student/faculty ratio 18:1. 1919 full-time faculty, 19% are members of minority groups, 42% are women.

ACADEMICS

Degrees: Bachelor's, certificate, master's, post-bachelor's certificate, post-master's certificate. **Classes:** Most classes have 10–19 students. Most lab/discussion sessions have 20–29 students. **Special Study Options:** Accelerated program, cooperative education program, distance learning, double major, dual enrollment, English as a Second Language (ESL), honors program, independent study, internships, liberal arts/career combination, student-designed major, study abroad, teacher certification program. **Honors programs:** Mentorship Programs—All first year students are invited to participate in this program. In this program upper classmen volunteer to serve as mentors offering support and assistance to new honors students during their first semester. **Combined degree programs:** BA/MD, BA/DDS, Pharmacy (PharmD) as a part of Honors Program. Special programs offered to physically disabled students include note-taking services, reader services, tape recorders, tutors. **Career services:** Alumni network, alumni services, career/job search classes, career assessment, internships.

FACILITIES

Housing: Coed dorms, special housing for disabled students, apartments for single students. 90% of campus accessible to physically disabled. **Special Academic Facilities/Equipment:** Anderson Gallery, Student Art Gallery, Larrick Student Center, Shafer Ct. Dining Facilities, Student Commons, Siegel Center, Cabell Library, Biotech Research Bldgs, Tompkins McCaw Library and VCU Bookstores. **Computers:** 75% of classrooms, 100% of dorms, 100% of libraries, 100% of dining areas, 100% of student union, 25% of common outdoor areas have wireless network access. Students can register for classes online. Administrative functions (other than registration) can be performed online. Undergraduates are required to own a computer.

CAMPUS LIFE

Environment: Metropolis. **Activities:** Choral groups, concert band, dance, drama/theater, jazz band, literary magazine, musical theater, pep band, radio station, student government, student newspaper, television station, yearbook, campus ministries, international student organization. **Organizations:** 377 registered organizations, 30 religious organizations. 22 fraternities, 13 sororities. **Athletics (Intercollegiate): Men:** Baseball, basketball, cross-country, golf, soccer, tennis, track/field (outdoor). *Women:* Basketball, cross-country, field hockey, soccer, tennis, track/field (outdoor), volleyball. **On-Campus Highlights:** Student Commons, Cabell Library, Siegel Center, Anderson Gallery, Shafer Court Dining Facility, Cary Street Recreation Complex. **Environmental Initiatives:** GHG Emissions Inventory and Climate Action Plan Securing of stimulus funds for $3M of solar (renewable) energy projects Development of a capital project for a bio-mass steam plant.

ADMISSIONS

Freshman Academic Profile: Average high school GPA 3.43. 16% in top 10% of high school class, 47% in top 25% of high school class, 87% in top 50% of high school class. SAT Math middle 50% range 490–590. SAT Critical Reading middle 50% range 490–600. SAT Writing middle 50% range 480–580. ACT middle 50% range 20–25. Minimum paper TOEFL 550. Minimum web-based TOEFL 80. **Basis for Candidate Selection:** *Very important factors considered include:* Academic GPA, rigor of secondary school record. *Important factors considered include:* Standardized test scores, talent/ability. *Other factors considered include:* Class rank, application essay, recommendation(s), extracurricular activities, first generation, volunteer work, work experience. **Freshman Admission Requirements:** High school diploma is required and GED is accepted. *Academic units required:* 4 English, 3 mathematics, 3 science, (1 science labs), 2 foreign language, 1 social studies, 2 history. *Academic units recommended:* 4 English, 4 mathematics, 4 science, (1 science labs), 3 foreign language, 1 social studies, 3 history, 1 visual/performing arts. **Freshman Admission Statistics:** 16,915 applied, 59% admitted, 36% enrolled. **Transfer Admission Requirements:** College transcript(s), minimum college GPA of 2.25 required. Lowest grade transferable C. **General Admission Information:** Application fee $40. Notification on a rolling basis, beginning on or about 12/1. Nonfall registration accepted. Admission may be deferred for a maximum of 1 semester. Credit offered for CEEB Advanced Placement tests.

COSTS AND FINANCIAL AID

Required Forms and Deadlines: FAFSA. Priority financial aid filing date 3/1. **Notification of Awards:** Applicants will be notified of awards on a rolling basis beginning 4/1. **Types of Aid:** *Need-based scholarships/grants:* Federal Pell, SEOG, state scholarships/grants, private scholarships, the school's own gift aid. *Loans:* Direct Subsidized Stafford, Direct Unsubsidized Stafford, Direct PLUS, Federal Perkins, Federal Nursing. *Student Employment:* Federal Work-Study Program available. Institutional employment available. Off-campus job opportunities are good. **Financial Aid Statistics:** 31% freshmen, 34% undergrads receive need-based scholarship or grant aid. 23% freshmen, 14% undergrads receive non-need-based scholarship or grant aid. 36% freshmen, 40% undergrads receive need-based self-help aid. 1% freshmen, 1% undergrads receive athletic scholarships. 70% freshmen, 61% undergrads receive any aid. 61% undergrads borrow to pay for school. Average cumulative indebtedness $22,864. **Criteria for awarding institutional aid:** *Non-need-based:* Academics, alumni affiliation, art, athletics, leadership, music/drama.

VIRGINIA INTERMONT COLLEGE

1013 Moore Street, Bristol, VA 24201-4298
Phone: 276-466-7856 **Financial Aid Phone:** 276-466-7872
E-mail: viadmit@vic.edu **CEEB Code:** 5857
Fax: 276-466-7855 **Website: ACT Code:** 4416

This private school, affiliated with the Baptist Church, was founded in 1884. It has a 27-acre campus.

RATINGS

Admissions Selectivity Rating: 75   **Fire Safety Rating:** 77   **Green Rating:** 60*

STUDENTS AND FACULTY

Enrollment: 885. **Student Body:** 69% female, 31% male, 68% out-of-state, 8% international. Asian 1%, African American 7%, Caucasian 78%, Hispanic 2%, Native American 1%.
Retention and Graduation: 74% freshmen return for sophomore year. 10% grads go on to further study within 1 year. 3% grads pursue arts and sciences degrees. 1% grads pursue law degrees. 2% grads pursue business degrees. 1% grads pursue medical degrees. **Faculty:** Student/faculty ratio 12:1. 44 full-time faculty, 61% hold PhDs, 5% are members of minority groups, 41% are women.

ACADEMICS

Degrees: Associate, bachelor's. **Classes:** Most classes have fewer than 10 students. Most lab/discussion sessions have fewer than 10 students. **Majors with Highest Enrollment:** Business/commerce; equestrian/equine studies; photography. **Special Study Options:** Accelerated program, cross-registration, distance learning, double major, English as a Second Language (ESL), honors program, independent study, internships, study abroad, teacher certification program. **Honors programs:** Honors program available for students who meet the necessary academic requirements. Special programs offered to physically disabled students include note-taking services, reader services, tape recorders, tutors. **Career services:** Alumni services, career/job search classes, internships.

FACILITIES

Housing: Coed dorms, special housing for disabled students, men's dorms, women's dorms, apartments for married students, apartments for single students. 25% of campus accessible to physically disabled. **Special Academic Facilities/Equipment:** Museum/gallery, 129-acre riding center for equestrian program. Newly constructed Fine Arts Center. **Computers:** Students can register for classes online. Administrative functions (other than registration) can be performed online.

CAMPUS LIFE

Environment: Town. **Activities:** Choral groups, dance, drama/theater, musical theater, student government, yearbook. **Organizations:** 26 registered organizations, 4 honor societies, 2 religious organizations. **Athletics (Intercollegiate):** *Men:* Baseball, basketball, cross-country, equestrian sports, golf, soccer, tennis, track/field (outdoor), track/field (indoor). *Women:* Basketball, cheerleading, cross-country, equestrian sports, soccer, softball, tennis, track/field (outdoor), track/field (indoor), volleyball. **On-Campus Highlights:** Fine Arts Gallery, Van Dyke Davis Alumni House, President's Home, Equestrian Center, Bell Tower.

ADMISSIONS

Freshman Academic Profile: Average high school GPA 3.2. 8% in top 10% of high school class, 20% in top 25% of high school class, 58% in top 50% of high school class. 85% from public high schools. SAT Math middle 50% range 410–540. SAT Critical Reading middle 50% range 410–530. ACT middle 50% range 17–25. Minimum paper TOEFL 500. Minimum computer TOEFL 173. **Basis for Candidate Selection:** *Very important factors considered include:* Academic GPA, rigor of secondary school record, standardized test scores, *Other factors considered include:* Class rank, application essay, recommendation(s), alumni/ae relation, character/personal qualities, extracurricular activities, first generation, interview, level of applicant's interest, talent/ability, work experience. **Freshman Admission Requirements:** High school diploma is required and GED is accepted. *Academic units required:* 4 English, 2 mathematics, 1 science, (1 science labs), 2 social studies, 6 academic electives. **Freshman Admission Statistics:** 624 applied, 55% admitted, 44% enrolled. **Transfer Admission Requirements:** College transcript(s), essay or personal statement, statement of good standing from prior institution(s). Minimum college GPA of 2.0 required. Lowest grade transferable C. **General Admission Information:** Application fee $25. Nonfall registration accepted. Admission may be deferred for a maximum of 2 terms. Credit and/or placement offered for CEEB Advanced Placement tests.

COSTS AND FINANCIAL AID

Annual tuition $16,895. Room and board $6,095. Required fees $950. Average book expense $900. **Required Forms and Deadlines:** FAFSA, state aid form. Priority financial aid filing date 3/1. **Notification of Awards:** Applicants will be notified of awards on a rolling basis beginning 2/15. **Types of Aid:** *Need-based scholarships/grants:* Federal Pell, SEOG, state scholarships/grants, private scholarships, the school's own gift aid. *Loans:* FFEL Subsidized Stafford, FFEL Unsubsidized Stafford, FFEL PLUS, Federal Perkins. *Student Employment:* Federal Work-Study Program available. Highest amount earned per year from on-campus jobs $1,500. Off-campus job opportunities are good. **Financial Aid Statistics:** 65% freshmen, 73% undergrads receive need-based scholarship or grant aid. 5% freshmen, 4% undergrads receive non-need-based scholarship or grant aid. 50% freshmen, 67% undergrads receive need-based self-help aid. 14% freshmen, 10% undergrads receive athletic scholarships. 65% freshmen, 73% undergrads receive any aid. 79% undergrads borrow to pay for school. Average cumulative indebtedness $20,051. **Criteria for awarding institutional aid:** *Non-need-based:* Academics, alumni affiliation, art, athletics, minority status, music/drama, religious affiliation, state/district residency.

VIRGINIA MILITARY INSTITUTE

VMI Office of Admissions, Lexington, VA 24450-0304
Phone: 540-464-7211 **Financial Aid Phone:** 540-464-7208
E-mail: admissions@vmi.edu **CEEB Code:** 5858
Fax: 540-464-7746 **Website:** www.vmi.edu **ACT Code:** 4418

This public school was founded in 1839. It has a 140-acre campus.

RATINGS
Admissions Selectivity Rating: 82　　**Fire Safety Rating:** 60*　　**Green Rating:** 60*

STUDENTS AND FACULTY
Enrollment: 1,428. **Student Body:** 8% female, 92% male, 40.7% out-of-state, 2% international (9 countries represented). Asian 4%, African American 6%, Caucasian 84%, Hispanic 4%.
Retention and Graduation: 8% grads go on to further study within 1 year. 3% grads pursue arts and sciences degrees. 2% grads pursue law degrees. 1% grads pursue business degrees. 1% grads pursue medical degrees. **Faculty:** Student/faculty ratio 10.4:1. 120 full-time faculty, 98% hold PhDs, 7% are members of minority groups, 19% are women.

ACADEMICS
Degrees: Bachelor's. **Classes:** Most classes have 10–19 students. **Majors with Highest Enrollment:** Business/managerial economics; history; mechanical engineering. **Special Study Options:** Accelerated program, double major, exchange student program (domestic), honors program, independent study, internships, study abroad, teacher certification program, Summer Transition Program: Optional for incoming freshman. **Honors programs:** Institute Honors Program, departmental honors programs. **Career services:** Alumni network, career/job search classes, career assessment, internships.

FACILITIES
Housing: Barracks (3–5 students/room). 50% of campus accessible to physically disabled. **Special Academic Facilities/Equipment:** VMI Museum George C. Marshall Museum. **Computers:** Students can register for classes online. Administrative functions (other than registration) can be performed online.

CAMPUS LIFE
Environment: Village. **Activities:** Choral groups, concert band, drama/theater, jazz band, literary magazine, marching band, music ensembles, musical theater, pep band, student government, student newspaper, yearbook. **Organizations:** 50 registered organizations, 11 honor societies, 3 religious organizations. **Athletics (Intercollegiate):** *Men:* Baseball, basketball, cross-country, football, golf, lacrosse, riflery, soccer, swimming, track/field (outdoor), track/field (indoor), wrestling. *Women:* cross-country, riflery, soccer, swimming, track/field (outdoor), track/field (indoor). **On-Campus Highlights:** VMI Museum, George C. Marshall Museum.

ADMISSIONS
Freshman Academic Profile: Average high school GPA 3.351. 9.9% in top 10% of high school class, 39.9% in top 25% of high school class, 81.5% in top 50% of high school class. 84% from public high schools. SAT Math middle 50% range 530–620. SAT Critical Reading middle 50% range 510–620. SAT Writing middle 50% range 480–590. ACT middle 50% range 21–26. Minimum paper TOEFL 500. Minimum computer TOEFL 173. **Basis for Candidate Selection:** *Very important factors considered include:* Class rank, rigor of secondary school record, standardized test scores, character/personal qualities. *Important factors considered include:* Extracurricular activities, interview, racial/ethnic status, state residency, volunteer work. *Other factors considered include:* Recommendation(s), alumni/ae relation, geographical residence, talent/ability. **Freshman Admission Requirements:** High school diploma is required and GED is not accepted. *Academic units required:* 4 English, 3 mathematics,

3 science, (3 science labs), 3 foreign language. *Academic units recommended:* 4 mathematics, 4 foreign language. **Freshman Admission Statistics:** 1,600 applied, 54% admitted, 48% enrolled. **Transfer Admission Requirements:** High school transcript, college transcript(s), standardized test scores, minimum college GPA of 2.0 required. Lowest grade transferable C. **General Admission Information:** Application fee $35. Early decision application deadline 11/15. Regular application deadline 2/15. Notification on a rolling basis, beginning on or about 1/1. Nonfall registration not accepted. Credit and/or placement offered for CEEB Advanced Placement tests.

COSTS AND FINANCIAL AID
Required Forms and Deadlines: FAFSA, institution's own financial aid form. Priority financial aid filing date 3/1. **Notification of Awards:** Applicants will be notified of awards on a rolling basis beginning 3/15. **Types of Aid:** *Need-based scholarships/grants:* Federal Pell, SEOG, state scholarships/grants, private scholarships, the school's own gift aid. *Loans:* Direct Subsidized Stafford, Direct Unsubsidized Stafford, Direct PLUS, Federal Perkins. *Student Employment:* Highest amount earned per year from on-campus jobs $850. **Financial Aid Statistics:** 35% freshmen, 32% undergrads receive need-based scholarship or grant aid. 13% freshmen, 12% undergrads receive non-need-based scholarship or grant aid. 20% freshmen, 20% undergrads receive need-based self-help aid. 11% freshmen, 7% undergrads receive athletic scholarships. 85% freshmen, 82% undergrads receive any aid. 52% undergrads borrow to pay for school. Average cumulative indebtedness $19,114. **Criteria for awarding institutional aid:** *Non-need-based:* Academics, alumni affiliation, athletics, leadership, music/drama.

VIRGINIA STATE UNIVERSITY

One Hayden Drive, PO Box 9018, Petersburg, VA 23806
Phone: 804-524-5902 **Financial Aid Phone:** 804-524-5990
E-mail: admiss@vsu.edu **CEEB Code:** 5860
Fax: 804-524-5055 **Website:** www.vsu.edu **ACT Code:** 4424

This public school was founded in 1882. It has a 246-acre campus.

RATINGS
Admissions Selectivity Rating: 71　　**Fire Safety Rating:** 60*　　**Green Rating:** 60*

STUDENTS AND FACULTY
Enrollment: 4,420. **Student Body:** 61% female, 39% male, 34% out-of-state, international (29 countries represented). African American 94%, Caucasian 2%.
Retention and Graduation: 68% freshmen return for sophomore year. 21% freshmen graduate within 4 years. **Faculty:** Student/faculty ratio 16:1. 254 full-time faculty, 75% are members of minority groups, 42% are women.

ACADEMICS
Degrees: Associate, bachelor's, certificate, master's, post-master's certificate. **Majors with Highest Enrollment:** Liberal arts and sciences/liberal studies; physical education teaching and coaching; sociology. **Special Study Options:** Cooperative education program, double major, dual enrollment, exchange student program (domestic), honors program, independent study, internships, teacher certification program Special programs offered to physically disabled students include note-taking services, reader services, tutors. **Career services:** Alumni network, internships.

FACILITIES
Housing: Coed dorms, men's dorms, women's dorms, apartments for single students. Note: Coed dorm—students required to have a 3.0 GPA and a record of leadership and service. (Honors Co-educational Residence Facility). 90% of campus accessible to physically disabled. **Computers:** Administrative functions (other than registration) can be performed online.

CAMPUS LIFE
Environment: Town. **Activities:** Choral groups, concert band, dance, drama/theater, jazz band, literary magazine, marching band, music ensembles, pep band, radio station, student government, student newspaper, television station, yearbook, campus ministries. **Organizations:** 70 registered organizations, 6 honor societies, 4 religious organizations. 5 fraternities, 4 sororities. **Athletics (Intercollegiate):** *Men:* Baseball, basketball, cheerleading, cross-country, football, golf, tennis, track/field (outdoor), track/field (indoor). *Women:* Basketball, bowling, cheerleading, cross-country, golf, softball, tennis, track/field (outdoor), track/field (indoor), volleyball.

ADMISSIONS
Freshman Academic Profile: Average high school GPA 2.8. 5% in top 10% of high school class, 23% in top 25% of high school class, 60% in top 50% of high school class. SAT Math middle 50% range 380–460. SAT Critical Reading

middle 50% range 380–460. Minimum paper TOEFL 500. Minimum computer TOEFL 173. **Basis for Candidate Selection:** *Very important factors considered include:* Application essay, recommendation(s), rigor of secondary school record, standardized test scores. *Important factors considered include:* Academic GPA. *Other factors considered include:* Class rank, alumni/ae relation, character/personal qualities, extracurricular activities, geographical residence, state residency, talent/ability, volunteer work, work experience. **Freshman Admission Requirements:** High school diploma is required and GED is accepted. *Academic units required:* 4 English, 3 mathematics, 2 science, (1 science labs), 2 social studies. *Academic units recommended:* 2 foreign language. **Transfer Admission Requirements:** College transcript(s), essay or personal statement, statement of good standing from prior institution(s). Minimum college GPA of 2.0 required. Lowest grade transferable C. **General Admission Information:** Application fee $25. Regular application deadline 5/1. Notification on a rolling basis, beginning on or about 11/1. Nonfall registration accepted. Credit offered for CEEB Advanced Placement tests.

COSTS AND FINANCIAL AID

Annual in-state tuition $3,584. Annual out-of-state tuition $11,646. Room and board $8,050. Required fees $2,590. Average book expense $900. **Required Forms and Deadlines:** FAFSA, institution's own financial aid form Financial aid filing deadline 5/1. Priority financial aid filing date 3/31. **Notification of Awards:** Applicants will be notified of awards on a rolling basis beginning 5/1. **Types of Aid:** *Need-based scholarships/grants:* Federal Pell, SEOG, state scholarships/grants, private scholarships, the school's own gift aid. *Loans:* Direct Subsidized Stafford, Direct Unsubsidized Stafford, Direct PLUS, FFEL PLUS, Federal Perkins, college/university loans from institutional funds. *Student Employment:* Federal Work-Study Program available. Institutional employment available. **Financial Aid Statistics:** 89% undergrads borrow to pay for school. **Criteria for awarding institutional aid:** *Non-need-based:* Academics, alumni affiliation, art, job skills, leadership, music/drama, religious affiliation.

VIRGINIA TECH

Undergraduate Admissions, 201 Burruss Hall, Blacksburg, VA 24061
Phone: 540-231-6267 **Financial Aid Phone:** 540-231-5179
E-mail: vtadmiss@vt.edu **CEEB Code:** 5859
Fax: 540-231-3242 **Website:** www.vt.edu **ACT Code:** 4420

This public school was founded in 1872. It has a 2600-acre campus.

RATINGS
Admissions Selectivity Rating: 90 **Fire Safety Rating:** 78 **Green Rating:** 98

STUDENTS AND FACULTY
Enrollment: 23,461. **Student Body:** 43% female, 57% male, 24% out-of-state, 2% international (112 countries represented). Asian 8%, African American 4%, Caucasian 74%, Hispanic 3%.
Retention and Graduation: 26% grads go on to further study within 1 year.
Faculty: Student/faculty ratio 16:1. 1364 full-time faculty, 90% hold PhDs, 17% are members of minority groups, 32% are women.

ACADEMICS
Degrees: Associate, bachelor's, master's, post-master's certificate. **Classes:** Most classes have 20–29 students. Most lab/discussion sessions have 20–29 students. **Majors with Highest Enrollment:** Biology/biological sciences; engineering. **Special Study Options:** Accelerated program, cooperative education program, distance learning, double major, dual enrollment, English as a Second Language (ESL), honors program, independent study, internships, study abroad, teacher certification program **Combined degree programs:** BA/MA Special programs offered to physically disabled students include note-taking services, reader services, tape recorders, tutors. **Career services:** Alumni network, alumni services, career/job search classes, career assessment, internships

FACILITIES
Housing: Coed dorms, special housing for disabled students, men's dorms, special housing for international students, women's dorms, fraternity/sorority housing, wellness housing, theme housingHousing for Corps of Cadets and athletes. The World—a cross cultural environment. The W.E.L.L—a personal health/development community. Foreign language hall and academic success hall available. The Wing—a transitional/orientation community for freshmen. Residential Leadership Community Biological and Life Sciences Learning Community Virginia Tech Design Collaborative. 60% of campus accessible to physically disabled. **Special Academic Facilities/Equipment:** Art gallery, digital music facilities, multimedia labs, Black Cultural Center, television studio, anaerobic lab, CAD-CAM labs, observatory, wind tunnel, farms, Math Emporium, the CAVE (virtual reality learning facility). Virtual Reality Cave. **Computers:** Students can register for classes online. Administrative functions (other than registration) can be performed online. Undergraduates are required to own a computer.

CAMPUS LIFE
Environment: Town. **Activities:** Choral groups, concert band, dance, drama/theater, jazz band, literary magazine, marching band, music ensembles, musical theater, pep band, radio station, student government, student newspaper, yearbook. **Organizations:** 600 registered organizations, 32 honor societies, 53 religious organizations. 31 fraternities, 12 sororities. **Athletics (Intercollegiate):** *Men:* Baseball, basketball, cheerleading, cross-country, diving, football, golf, soccer, swimming, tennis, track/field (outdoor), track/field (indoor), ultimate frisbee, water polo. *Women:* Basketball, cheerleading, cross-country, diving, lacrosse, soccer, softball, swimming, tennis, track/field (outdoor), track/field (indoor), ultimate frisbee, volleyball, water polo. **Environmental Initiatives:** "The Virginia Tech Climate Action Commitment Resolution" and Sustainability Plan On April 25, 2008 Virginia Tech President Charles W. Steger charged the Energy and Sustainability Committee to develop a climate commitment and sustainability plan specific to the university, to utilize the university governance system to review the documentation, and to have the University Council act on the climate commitment by the end of the 2009 Spring Semester. The Energy and Sustainability Committee successfully met that challenge. On April 22, 2009 (Earth Day) the University Council recommended approval of "The Virginia Tech Climate Action Commitment (VTCAC) Resolution" and accepted the accompanying Sustainability Plan. On June 1, 2009 the Board of Visitors unanimously approved the "VTCAC Resolution." The documents may be viewed on the newly established Office of Sustainability website at: www.facilities.vt.edu/sustainability. Under this new university policy, the Office of Sustainability was officially established to plan and coordinate sustainability programs. The Office of Sustainability is currently overseeing more than 80 sustainability initiatives, and it is developing a strategic plan of how to implement the VTCAC effectively through keeping communication lines open with the university community and general public. Energy Reduction, Efficiency, and Conservation Measures: 1. Significant energy reduction has been achieved through the implementation of temperature settings in accordance with the Campus Energy and Water Policy 5505: 68 degrees Fahrenheit for the heating season and 74 degrees Fahrenheit for the cooling season. These measures have resulted in substantial energy saving, cost savings, and reductions in greenhouse gas emissions. 2. Significant energy reduction has been achieved through the select shutdown of building air handlers during periods of reduced occupancy using the Building Automation System. Substantial energy savings, cost savings, and reductions in greenhouse gas emissions have been realized. 3. Implementation of the use of the "free cooling" during the winter months for campus chilled water systems. 4. Nearing the completion of a $28 million capital project that will significantly enhance the Central Steam Plant efficiency and campus-wide steam distribution infrastructure. 5. Energy Service Company (ESCO) has completed an energy conservation "Technical Audit" for six major buildings: Central Steam Plant, Cassell Coliseum, Dietrick Dining Hall, Pritchard Residence Hall, McBryde Hall (Academic), and Hahn Hall (Research). Specific energy conservation recommendations are under review. 6. The Virginia Tech Climate Action Commitment Resolution, item #6 states the university "will pursue LEED Silver Certification or better for all new buildings and major renovations." Twelve new construction and major renovation capital projects totally over 1 million gross square feet are registered in the Leadership in Energy and Environmental Design (LEED) program with the U.S. Green Building Council. 7. The Energy and Sustainability Committee is revising Campus Policy 5505 to incorporate new energy use, water use, waste reduction, and transportation/travel requirements in the Commonwealth of Virginia's Governor's Executive Order 82 (2009) "Greening of State Government." 8. Virginia Tech finished in third place in the Governor's "Green Commonwealth Challenge." Campus Life and Student Involvement: 1. All of the initiatives that were listed last year are still running effectively. The following list is one to supplement the list from last year. 2. The Student Government Association has partnered with Residence Life and the Office of Sustainability to host the first ever energy and waste reduction competition. The Virginia Tech Eco-Olympics will run the entire month of April and will include: a kickoff event that ties into the International Earth Hour initiative; a point system to encourage students to attend sustainability related events; a weekly tracking system for energy consumption, water consumption, waste production, and recycling rate; and a "greened" Relay for Life event. 3. Students from five different student organizations developed a "Sustainable Living Guide" that will be distributed to all of the students that live on campus. This guide was "developed by students for students." This collaborative group of students then partnered with the Office of Sustainability and Student Programs to be able to provide a reusable bag with the guide to create a small scale "sustainability kit." 4. The second annual "Green Effect" football game was held this

fall. Over 200 students volunteered to engage tailgaters about the importance of recycling and handed out recycling bags. Due to the success of this program, the amount of material recycled was over one ton more than an average football game. Stadium recycling of plastic bottles is standard clean-up procedures at football games. The SGA is also planning a "Green Effect" basketball game for this season. 5. The Office of Sustainability met with all of the Transfer and Freshman Orientation leaders to talk about the sustainability efforts being made on campus. Orientation Leaders were then given all of the information needed to facilitate small group discussions with their new students about the important aspects of sustainability and what sustainability means to the Hokies. 6. The Office of Sustainability is in the process of establishing a steering committee to develop a comprehensive campus-wide recycling system. There is currently recycling available almost everywhere on campus, but the system needs to be looked at in its entirety, not just the pieces. This comprehensive plan will lay out a coordinated and streamlined system that will bring continuity to the campus-wide infrastructure. 7. Dining Services is now successfully composting in two large dining facilities and planning on bringing a third one on line shortly. On average, 12,960 lbs of food waste per week is being diverted from the landfill to the compost site. 8. Team ECCO, a sustainability committee within the Division of Student Affairs, is developing a "Green Events Guide" through collaborating with over 10 different departments. This guide provides step by step guidance on how to make an event more sustainable, and provides a rating system to measure the effort made to reduce its impact. 9. The Coalition for Campus Sustainability, a coalition of 24 different environmental and non-environmental student organizations, has partnered with the Student Government Association to run a massive campaign to establish an optional "green fee" that students can opt out of. 10. The Virginia Tech GREEN Team (the Office of Sustainability's sustainability education team) partnered with Hokie F-6 two years in a row to hold a "Sustainable Picnic" for all incoming freshman. See also www.recycle.vt.edu/greenteam 11. Virginia Tech is participating in the RecycleMania national competition for the fifth consecutive year. This year, several student environmental organizations and the Student Government Association are partnering with the Office of Sustainability to run the biggest campaign yet.

ADMISSIONS

Freshman Academic Profile: Average high school GPA 3.91. 44% in top 10% of high school class, 85% in top 25% of high school class, 99% in top 50% of high school class. 95% from public high schools. SAT Math middle 50% range 570–670. SAT Critical Reading middle 50% range 540–640. SAT Writing middle 50% range 540–630. Minimum paper TOEFL 550. Minimum computer TOEFL 207. **Basis for Candidate Selection:** *Very important factors considered include:* Academic GPA, rigor of secondary school record, standardized test scores, *Other factors considered include:* Recommendation(s), alumni/ae relation, character/personal qualities, extracurricular activities, first generation, geographical residence, racial/ethnic status, state residency, talent/ability, volunteer work, work experience. **Freshman Admission Requirements:** High school diploma is required and GED is accepted. *Academic units required:* 4 English, 3 mathematics, 2 science, (2 science labs), 1 social studies, 1 history, 4 academic electives. *Academic units recommended:* 4 mathematics, 3 science, 3 foreign language. **Freshman Admission Statistics:** 21,053 applied, 67% admitted, 36% enrolled. **Transfer Admission Requirements:** High school transcript, college transcript(s), minimum college GPA of 3.0 required. Lowest grade transferable C. **General Admission Information:** Application fee $50. Early decision application deadline 11/1. Regular application deadline 1/15. Regular notification 4/1. Nonfall registration accepted. Admission may be deferred for a maximum of 1 year. Credit and/or placement offered for CEEB Advanced Placement tests.

COSTS AND FINANCIAL AID

Annual in-state tuition $6,639. Annual out-of-state tuition $19,522. Room and board $5,824. Required fees $1,966. Average book expense $1,080. **Required Forms and Deadlines:** FAFSA General Scholarship Application. Priority financial aid filing date 3/1. **Notification of Awards:** Applicants will be notified of awards on a rolling basis beginning 3/30. **Types of Aid:** *Need-based scholarships/grants:* Federal Pell, SEOG, state scholarships/grants, private scholarships, the school's own gift aid, cadet scholarships/grants. *Loans:* Direct Subsidized Stafford, Direct Unsubsidized Stafford, Direct PLUS, Federal Perkins, college/university loans from institutional funds. *Student Employment:* Federal Work-Study Program available. Off-campus job opportunities are excellent. **Financial Aid Statistics:** 26% freshmen, 27% undergrads receive need-based scholarship or grant aid. 8% freshmen, 6% undergrads receive non-need-based scholarship or grant aid. 29% freshmen, 29% undergrads receive need-based self-help aid. 2% freshmen, 2% undergrads receive athletic scholarships. 36% freshmen, 36% undergrads receive any aid. 52.3% undergrads borrow to pay for school. Average cumulative indebtedness $22,870. **Criteria for awarding institutional aid:** *Non-need-based:* Academics, art, athletics, leadership, minority status, music/drama, state/district residency.

VIRGINIA WESLEYAN COLLEGE

1584 Wesleyan Drive, Norfolk/Virginia Beach, VA 23502-5599
Phone: 757-455-3208 **Financial Aid Phone:** 757-455-3345
E-mail: admissions@vwc.edu **CEEB Code:** 5867
Fax: 757-461-5238 **Website:** www.vwc.edu **ACT Code:** 4429

This private school, affiliated with the Methodist Church, was founded in 1961. It has a 300-acre campus.

RATINGS

Admissions Selectivity Rating: 72   **Fire Safety Rating:** 60*   **Green Rating:** 85

STUDENTS AND FACULTY

Enrollment: 1,300. **Student Body:** 62% female, 38% male, 21% out-of-state, 1% international (7 countries represented). Asian 2%, African American 21%, Caucasian 67%, Hispanic 4%.
Retention and Graduation: 35% freshmen graduate within 4 years. **Faculty:** Student/faculty ratio 11.3:1. 84 full-time faculty, 89% hold PhDs, 10% are members of minority groups, 40% are women.

ACADEMICS

Degrees: Bachelor's. **Classes:** Most classes have 10–19 students. **Majors with Highest Enrollment:** Business administration and management; communication studies/speech communication and rhetoric; criminal justice/safety studies. **Special Study Options:** Double major, honors program, independent study, internships, liberal arts/career combination, student-designed major, study abroad, teacher certification program, Externships; PORTfolio, a 4-year competitive program designed to integrate liberal arts and experiential learning. **Honors programs:** Wesleyan Scholars is an honors program which is designed for applicants with superior high school achievement records. The Honors and Scholars program, including Wesleyan Scholars, offers academically challenging honors courses and stimulating co-curricular experiences. Program enhancement is also offered through PORTfolio, a selective program designed to integrate the liberal arts with experiential learning opportunities available in Hampton Roads. **Combined degree programs:** 2-2 program in business/accounting with Tidewater. Special programs offered to physically disabled students include note-taking services, reader services, tape recorders, tutors. **Career services:** Alumni network, career/job search classes, internships, regional alumni.

FACILITIES

Housing: Coed dorms, special housing for disabled students, special housing for international students, women's dorms, fraternity/sorority housing, apartments for single students, wellness housing, townhouses, Honors and Scholars Hall, Wellness Hall—a substance free hall which provides special programs focusing on social, physical, spiritual, emotional, and intellectual wellness. 90% of campus accessible to physically disabled. **Special Academic Facilities/Equipment:** Greenhouse, language lab, teleconferencing facility, social science teach. and learn. lab, radio station, TV studio, Barclay Sheaks Art Gallery, computerized classrooms, Internet access all classrooms, 24-hr. computer lab, Lambuth M. Clarke Hall with state-of-the-art teaching technologies, three academic villages combining residences and campus offices and services. **Computers:** 20% of classrooms, 100% of libraries, 100% of student union, have wireless network access. Students can register for classes online. Administrative functions (other than registration) can be performed online.

CAMPUS LIFE

Environment: Metropolis. **Activities:** Choral groups, dance, drama/theater, literary magazine, music ensembles, musical theater, radio station, student government, student newspaper, yearbook, campus ministries, international student organization, Model UN. **Organizations:** 60 registered organizations, 19 honor societies, 4 religious organizations. 3 fraternities, 4 sororities. **Athletics (Intercollegiate):** *Men:* Baseball, basketball, cross-country, golf, lacrosse, soccer, tennis, track/field (outdoor), track/field (indoor). *Women:* Basketball, cheerleading, cross-country, field hockey, lacrosse, soccer, softball, tennis, track/field (outdoor), track/field (indoor), volleyball. **On-Campus Highlights:** The Marlin Restaurant, Jane P. Batten Student Center, Village III, Trinder Athletic Center **Environmental Initiatives:** Green Roof Recycling Sustainable Purchasing

ADMISSIONS

Freshman Academic Profile: Average high school GPA 3.1. 10.4% in top 10% of high school class, 34.3% in top 25% of high school class, 70.2% in top 50% of high school class. 86% from public high schools. SAT Math middle 50% range 440–540. SAT Critical Reading middle 50% range 440–530. SAT Writing middle 50% range 430–520. ACT middle 50% range 18–23. Minimum paper TOEFL 550. Minimum computer TOEFL 213. **Basis for Candidate Selection:** *Very important factors considered include:* Academic GPA, rigor of secondary school record, level of applicant's interest. *Important factors considered include:* Application essay, recommendation(s), standardized test scores, extracurricular activities. *Other factors considered include:* Alumni/ae relation, character/personal qualities, first generation, interview, talent/ability, volunteer work, work experience. **Freshman Admission Requirements:** High school diploma is required and GED is accepted. *Academic units required:* 4 English, 3 mathematics, 2 science, (2 science labs); 2 foreign language, 1 history, 1 computer science. *Academic units recommended:* 4 English, 3 mathematics, 2 science, (2 science labs), 2 foreign language, 1 history, 1 computer science, 4 academic electives. **Freshman Admission Statistics:** 1,372 applied, 75% admitted, 31% enrolled. **Transfer Admission Requirements:** High school transcript, college transcript(s), essay or personal statement, statement of good standing from prior institution(s). Minimum college GPA of 2.5 required. Lowest grade transferable C. **General Admission Information:** Application fee $40. Notification on a rolling basis, beginning on or about 9/15. Nonfall registration accepted. Credit and/or placement offered for CEEB Advanced Placement tests.

COSTS AND FINANCIAL AID

Annual tuition $26,976. Room and board $7,384. Required fees $500. Average book expense $1,000. **Required Forms and Deadlines:** FAFSA, state aid form. Priority financial aid filing date 3/1. **Notification of Awards:** Applicants will be notified of awards on a rolling basis beginning 2/1. **Types of Aid:** *Need-based scholarships/grants:* Federal Pell, SEOG, state scholarships/grants, private scholarships, the school's own gift aid, Virginia Coalition for Independent Colleges; United Methodist Greater Higher Education Board. *Loans:* FFEL Subsidized Stafford, FFEL Unsubsidized Stafford, FFEL PLUS, Federal Perkins, state loans, Private Alternative Loan Program. *Student Employment:* Federal Work-Study Program available. Institutional employment available. Highest amount earned per year from on-campus jobs $1,200. Off-campus job opportunities are good. **Financial Aid Statistics:** 76% freshmen, 73% undergrads receive need-based scholarship or grant aid. 18% freshmen, 15% undergrads receive non-need-based scholarship or grant aid. 62% freshmen, 61% undergrads receive need-based self-help aid. 96% freshmen, 91.1% undergrads receive any aid. 79.55% undergrads borrow to pay for school. Average cumulative indebtedness $27,658. **Criteria for awarding institutional aid:** *Non-need-based:* Academics, alumni affiliation, leadership, religious affiliation, state/district residency.

VITERBO UNIVERSITY

900 Viterbo Drive, La Crosse, WI 54601
Phone: 608-796-3010 **Financial Aid Phone:** 608-496-3900
E-mail: admission@viterbo.edu **CEEB Code:** 1878
Fax: 608-796-3020 **Website: ACT Code:** 4662

This private school, affiliated with the Roman Catholic Church, was founded in 1890. It has a 25-acre campus.

RATINGS
Admissions Selectivity Rating: 72   **Fire Safety Rating:** 61   **Green Rating:** 60*

STUDENTS AND FACULTY
Enrollment: 1,922. **Student Body:** 71% female, 29% male, 19% out-of-state, 1% international (15 countries represented). Asian 1%, African American 1%, Caucasian 93%, Hispanic 1%, Native American 1%.
Retention and Graduation: 74% freshmen return for sophomore year. 30% freshmen graduate within 4 years. 7% grads go on to further study within 1 year. 4% grads pursue arts and sciences degrees. 1% grads pursue law degrees. 2% grads pursue medical degrees. **Faculty:** Student/faculty ratio 13:1. 110 full-time faculty, 56% hold PhDs, 4% are members of minority groups, 56% are women.

ACADEMICS
Degrees: Associate, bachelor's, master's, post-bachelor's certificate, terminal associate, transfer associate. **Classes:** Most classes have 10–19 students. Most lab/discussion sessions have 10–19 students. **Majors with Highest Enrollment:** Business administration and management; elementary education and teaching; nursing/registered nurse (RN, ASN, BSN, MSN). **Special Study Options:** Accelerated program, cross-registration, distance learning, double major, dual enrollment, honors program, independent study, internships, liberal arts/career combination, student-designed major, study abroad, teacher certification program, weekend college, Weekend college is basically for our Master's level programs. **Honors programs:** The mission of the Viterbo University Honors Program is to provide a supportive, enriched learning environment responsive to the educational needs of highly able and exceptionally motivated undergraduate students who are committed to achieving academic excellence. The program provides honors sections of regular, general education courses, honors credit within regular sections, interdisciplinary Honors Capstone courses, oversight of senior honors projects, and increased opportunity for undergraduate research and creative activity. The program complements and enhances the Liberal Arts mission of the university. Together, honors students and faculty constitute a community of scholars. **Combined degree programs:** chiropractic. Special programs offered to physically disabled students include note-taking services, reader services, tape recorders, tutors. **Career services:** Alumni network, alumni services, career/job search classes, career assessment, internships, regional alumni. **Career services highlights include:** We have been very successful placing our students in internships that have not only assisted the student but the larger La Crosse community.

FACILITIES
Housing: Coed dorms, apartments for single students, theme floors in dorms and university owned theme houses. 90% of campus accessible to physically disabled. **Special Academic Facilities/Equipment:** Fine Arts Center; Center for Ethics, Science and Technology with distance education labs and video conferencing; Nursing center with labs and simulated equipment; new recreation and education center co-sponsored by Viterbo University and the Boys and Girls Club. **Computers:** Students can register for classes online. Administrative functions (other than registration) can be performed online.

CAMPUS LIFE
Environment: Town. **Activities:** Choral groups, dance, drama/theater, literary magazine, music ensembles, musical theater, opera, pep band, student government, student newspaper. **Organizations:** 22 registered organizations, 2 honor societies, 2 religious organizations. **Athletics (Intercollegiate):** *Men:* Baseball, basketball, golf, soccer. *Women:* Basketball, golf, soccer, softball, volleyball. **On-Campus Highlights:** Reinhart Center for Ethics, Science and Technology, Fine Arts Center, Amie Mathy Center for Recreation and Education, Student Activity Center, Dancing Francis. Center for Ethics, Science and Technology opened the Fall of 2003. Center for Recreation and Wellness opened fall 2005, co-sponsored by Viterbo and the Boys/Girls club. Dancing Francis is a bronze sculpture of Francis of Assisi by Paul Granland. Fine Arts Center is home of performing arts in the region. Student Activity Center is home to the V-Hawks as well as fitness center for all students.

ADMISSIONS
Freshman Academic Profile: Average high school GPA 3.3. 12.6% in top 10% of high school class, 38.8% in top 25% of high school class, 72.9% in top 50% of high school class. 97% from public high schools. ACT middle 50% range 20–24. Minimum paper TOEFL 550. Minimum computer TOEFL 213. **Basis for Candidate Selection:** *Very important factors considered include:* Academic GPA, rigor of secondary school record, standardized test scores, character/personal qualities, level of applicant's interest. *Important factors considered include:* Class rank, interview, talent/ability. *Other factors considered include:* Application essay, recommendation(s), alumni/ae relation, extracurricular activities, first generation, volunteer work. **Freshman Admission Requirements:** High school diploma is required and GED is accepted. *Academic units required:* 3 English, 2 mathematics, 2 science, 2 social studies, 5 academic electives. *Academic units recommended:* 4 English, 2 mathematics, 2 science, (2 science labs), 2 foreign language, 2 social studies, 5 academic electives. **Freshman Admission Statistics:** 1,148 applied, 88% admitted, 36% enrolled. **Transfer Admission Requirements:** High school transcript, college transcript(s), statement of good standing from prior institution(s). Minimum college GPA of 2.0 required. Lowest grade transferable C–. **General Admission Information:** Application fee $25. Nonfall registration accepted. Admission may be deferred for a maximum of Two years. Credit offered for CEEB Advanced Placement tests.

COSTS AND FINANCIAL AID
Annual tuition $18,170. Room and board $6,140. Required fees $420. Average book expense $800. **Required Forms and Deadlines:** FAFSA, institution's own financial aid form. Priority financial aid filing date 3/15. **Notification of Awards:** Applicants will be notified of awards on a rolling basis beginning 4/1. **Types of Aid:** *Need-based scholarships/grants:* Federal Pell, SEOG, state scholarships/grants, private scholarships, the school's own gift aid. *Loans:* FFEL Subsidized Stafford, FFEL Unsubsidized Stafford, FFEL PLUS, Federal Perkins, Federal Nursing, state loans *Student Employment:* Federal Work-Study Program available. Institutional employment available. Highest amount earned per year from on-campus jobs $2,500. Off-campus job opportunities are good. **Financial Aid Statistics:** 95% freshmen, 79% undergrads receive need-based scholarship or grant aid. 6% freshmen, 5% undergrads receive non-need-based scholarship or grant aid. 91% freshmen, 76% undergrads receive need-based self-help aid. 1% undergrads receive athletic scholarships. 98% freshmen, 89% undergrads receive any aid. 86% undergrads borrow to pay for school. Average cumulative indebtedness $15,703. **Criteria for awarding institutional aid:** *Non-need-based:* Academics, alumni affiliation, art, athletics, leadership, minority status, music/drama.

VOORHEES COLLEGE

P.O. BOX 678, Denmark, SC 29042
Phone: 803-703-7111
E-mail: white@voorhees.edu **CEEB Code:** 5863
Fax: 803-793-1117 **Website:** www.voorhees.edu **ACT Code:** 3882

This private school, affiliated with the Episcopal Church, was founded in 1897. It has a 350-acre campus.

RATINGS
Admissions Selectivity Rating: 71   **Fire Safety Rating:** 60*   **Green Rating:** 60*

STUDENTS AND FACULTY
Enrollment: 738. **Student Body:** 64% female, 36% male, 30% out-of-state, 1% international. African American 98%, Caucasian 1%.
Retention and Graduation: 70% freshmen return for sophomore year. 100% freshmen graduate within 4 years. 25% grads go on to further study within 1 year. 17% grads pursue arts and sciences degrees. 2% grads pursue law degrees. 5% grads pursue business degrees. 4% grads pursue medical degrees. **Faculty:** Student/faculty ratio 20:1. 43 full-time faculty, 44% hold PhDs, 91% are members of minority groups, 37% are women.

ACADEMICS
Degrees: Bachelor's, terminal associate. **Classes: Special Study Options:** Cooperative education program, honors program, internships, weekend college Special programs offered to physically disabled students include tape recorders, tutors. **Career services:** Alumni network, career/job search classes, internships.

FACILITIES
Housing: Men's dorms, women's dorms, fraternity/sorority housing, Faculty + Staff Apartments, Housing for Single Mothers. **Computers:** Administrative functions (other than registration) can be performed online.

CAMPUS LIFE
Environment: Rural. **Activities:** Choral groups, drama/theater, literary magazine, pep band, radio station, student government, student newspaper, yearbook. **Organizations:** 33 registered organizations, 2 honor societies, 3 religious organizations. 4 fraternities, 4 sororities. **Athletics (Intercollegiate):** *Men:* Baseball, basketball, cheerleading, cross-country. *Women:* Basketball, cheerleading, cross-country, softball, volleyball.

ADMISSIONS
Freshman Academic Profile: Average high school GPA 2. 1% in top 10% of high school class, 44% in top 25% of high school class, 50% in top 50% of high school class. 95% from public high schools. SAT Math middle 50% range 390–410. SAT Critical Reading middle 50% range 300–400. ACT middle 50% range 11–18. Minimum paper TOEFL 500. **Basis for Candidate Selection:** *Very important factors considered include:* Class rank, rigor of secondary school record, standardized test scores. *Important factors considered include:* Recommendation(s), alumni/ae relation, character/personal qualities, talent/ability. *Other factors considered include:* Extracurricular activities. **Freshman Admission Requirements:** High school diploma is required and GED is accepted. *Academic units required:* 4 English, 3 mathematics, 2 science, 2 foreign language, 1 social studies, 1 history, 7 academic electives. *Academic units recommended:* 4 English, 3 mathematics, 3 science, 2 foreign language, 1 social studies, 1 history, 7 academic electives. **Freshman Admission Statistics:** 3,511 applied, 37% admitted, 19% enrolled. **Transfer Admission Requirements:** College transcript(s), statement of good standing from prior institution(s). Minimum college GPA of 2.0 required. Lowest grade transferable c. **General Admission Information:** Application fee $25. Notification on a rolling basis, beginning on or about 1/1. Nonfall registration accepted. Admission may be deferred for a maximum of 2 years. Credit offered for CEEB Advanced Placement tests.

COSTS AND FINANCIAL AID
Annual tuition $6,460. Room and board $3,516. Required fees $170. Average book expense $2,500. **Required Forms and Deadlines:** FAFSA, institution's own financial aid form. Priority financial aid filing date 4/15. **Notification of Awards:** Applicants will be notified of awards on a rolling basis beginning 5/1. **Types of Aid:** *Need-based scholarships/grants:* Federal Pell, SEOG, state scholarships/grants, private scholarships, the school's own gift aid, United Negro College Fund. *Loans:* FFEL Subsidized Stafford, FFEL Unsubsidized Stafford, FFEL PLUS, Federal Perkins. *Student Employment:* Federal Work-Study Program available. Institutional employment available. Off-campus job opportunities are poor. **Financial Aid Statistics:** 88% freshmen, 85% undergrads receive need-based scholarship or grant aid. 1% freshmen, 1% undergrads receive non-need-based scholarship or grant aid. 85% freshmen, 88% undergrads receive need-based self-help aid. 70% undergrads borrow to pay for school. Average

cumulative indebtedness $8,939. **Criteria for awarding institutional aid:** *Non-need-based:* Academics, art, athletics, leadership.

WABASH COLLEGE

PO Box 352, 301 W. Wabash Av, Crawfordsville, IN 47933
Phone: 765-361-6225 **Financial Aid Phone:** 765-361-6370
E-mail: admissions@wabash.edu **CEEB Code:** 1895
Fax: 765-361-6437 **Website:** www.wabash.edu **ACT Code:** 1260

This private school was founded in 1832. It has a 60-acre campus.

RATINGS
Admissions Selectivity Rating: 88   **Fire Safety Rating:** 79   **Green Rating:** 74

STUDENTS AND FACULTY
Enrollment: 874. **Student Body:** 100% male, 22% out-of-state, 7% international (21 countries represented). Asian 2%, African American 6%, Caucasian 77%, Hispanic 5%, Native American 1%.
Retention and Graduation: 85% freshmen return for sophomore year. 62% freshmen graduate within 4 years. 27% grads go on to further study within 1 year. 10% grads pursue arts and sciences degrees. 7% grads pursue law degrees. 8% grads pursue medical degrees. **Faculty:** Student/faculty ratio 9.7:1. 90 full-time faculty, 99% hold PhDs, 8% are members of minority groups, 36% are women.

ACADEMICS
Degrees: Bachelor's. **Classes:** Most classes have 10–19 students. Most lab/discussion sessions have fewer than 10 students. **Majors with Highest Enrollment:** history; psychology; religion/religious studies. **Special Study Options:** Double major, independent study, internships, liberal arts/career combination, study abroad, teacher certification program, Student designed majors, minors, or areas of concentration. Immersion Learning courses are offered, which involve travel domestically and abroad. **Combined degree programs:** BA/JD, BA/MEng, Columbia University School of Law. Special programs offered to physically disabled students include note-taking services, reader services, tape recorders, tutors. **Career services:** Alumni network, alumni services, career/job search classes, career assessment, internships, regional alumni. **Career services highlights include:** Our brand new (beginning Fall 09)Wabash Business Leaders Program: Co-curricular program, designed to provide a comprehensive background in business, regardless of major. Couples our Business Sequence with experiential learning through internships, immersion programs, case studies, and speaker events.

FACILITIES
Housing: Special housing for disabled students, men's dorms, fraternity/sorority housing, college-owned houses and apartments. 80% of campus accessible to physically disabled. **Special Academic Facilities/Equipment:** Malcolm X Institute of Black Studies, two art galleries, language lab, electron microscope, atomic absorption, nuclear and infrared spectrometers, Beowulf Supercomputer, Center of Inquiry in the Liberal Arts, Wabash Center for Teaching and Learning in Theology and Religion, Ramsey Archival Center **Computers:** 100% of classrooms, 100% of dorms, 100% of libraries, 100% of dining areas, 100% of student union, 100% of common outdoor areas have wireless network access. Administrative functions (other than registration) can be performed online.

CAMPUS LIFE
Environment: Village. **Activities:** Choral groups, concert band, drama/theater, jazz band, literary magazine, music ensembles, pep band, radio station, student government, student newspaper, student-run film society, symphony orchestra, yearbook, campus ministries, international student organization, Model UN. **Organizations:** 65 registered organizations, 7 honor societies, 5 religious organizations. 9 fraternities. **Athletics (Intercollegiate):** *Men:* Baseball, basketball, cross-country, diving, football, golf, soccer, swimming, tennis, track/field (outdoor), track/field (indoor), wrestling. **On-Campus Highlights:** Allen Athletics and Recreation Center, Wabash Chapel, New Science Building, Hays Hall, Trippet Hall, Lilly Library, Malcolm X Institute of Black Studies. **Environmental Initiatives:** Campus-wide recycling Environmental Concerns Committee driving LEED Certification New, state-of-the-art, energy efficient boilers Green Bikes

ADMISSIONS

Freshman Academic Profile: Average high school GPA 3.52. 31% in top 10% of high school class, 70% in top 25% of high school class, 91% in top 50% of high school class. 91% from public high schools. SAT Math middle 50% range 530–660. SAT Critical Reading middle 50% range 500–600. SAT Writing middle 50% range 470–600. ACT middle 50% range 21–27. Minimum paper TOEFL 550. Minimum computer TOEFL 213. **Basis for Candidate Selection:** *Very important factors considered include:* Class rank, academic GPA, rigor of secondary school record. *Important factors considered include:* Recommendation(s), standardized test scores, extracurricular activities, interview, level of applicant's interest, talent/ability. *Other factors considered include:* Application essay, alumni/ae relation, character/personal qualities, first generation, geographical residence, racial/ethnic status, volunteer work, work experience. **Freshman Admission Requirements:** High school diploma is required and GED is accepted. *Academic units recommended:* 4 English, 4 mathematics, 2 science, (2 science labs), 2 foreign language, 2 social studies, 2 history, 3 academic electives. **Freshman Admission Statistics:** 1,588 applied, 49% admitted, 32% enrolled. **Transfer Admission Requirements:** High school transcript, college transcript(s), essay or personal statement, standardized test scores, statement of good standing from prior institution(s). Lowest grade transferable C. **General Admission Information:** Application fee $40. Early decision application deadline 11/15. Notification on a rolling basis, beginning on or about 11/15. Nonfall registration accepted. Admission may be deferred for a maximum of 1 year. Credit and/or placement offered for CEEB Advanced Placement tests.

COSTS AND FINANCIAL AID

Annual tuition $29,100. Room and board $7,600. Required fees $650. Average book expense $800. **Required Forms and Deadlines:** FAFSA, CSS/Financial Aid PROFILE, noncustodial PROFILE, Federal tax returns and W-2 statements. Financial aid filing deadline 3/1. Priority financial aid filing date 2/15. **Notification of Awards:** Applicants will be notified of awards on or about 3/31. **Types of Aid:** *Need-based scholarships/grants:* Federal Pell, state scholarships/grants, private scholarships, the school's own gift aid. *Loans:* Direct Subsidized Stafford, Direct Unsubsidized Stafford, Direct PLUS, college/university loans from institutional funds. *Student Employment:* Institutional employment available. Highest amount earned per year from on-campus jobs $3,000. Off-campus job opportunities are good. **Financial Aid Statistics:** 82% freshmen, 79% undergrads receive need-based scholarship or grant aid. 24% freshmen, 30% undergrads receive non-need-based scholarship or grant aid. 76% freshmen, 69% undergrads receive need-based self-help aid. 92% freshmen, 88% undergrads receive any aid. 70% undergrads borrow to pay for school. Average cumulative indebtedness $28,383. **Criteria for awarding institutional aid:** *Non-need-based:* Academics, art, job skills, music/drama.

WAGNER COLLEGE

Best 373

One Campus Road, Staten Island, NY 10301-4495
Phone: 718-390-3411 **Financial Aid Phone:** 718-390-3183
E-mail: adm@wagner.edu **CEEB Code:** 2966
Fax: 718-390-3105 **Website:** www.wagner.edu **ACT Code:** 2984

This private school was founded in 1883. It has a 110-acre campus.

RATINGS

Admissions Selectivity Rating: 88   **Fire Safety Rating:** 96   **Green Rating:** 74

STUDENTS AND FACULTY

Enrollment: 1,911. **Student Body:** 62% female, 38% male, 52% out-of-state, 1% international (19 countries represented). Asian 2%, African American 5%, Caucasian 83%, Hispanic 6%.
Retention and Graduation: 77% freshmen return for sophomore year. 62% freshmen graduate within 4 years. 43% grads go on to further study within 1 year. 17% grads pursue arts and sciences degrees. 7% grads pursue law degrees. 19% grads pursue business degrees. 7% grads pursue medical degrees. **Faculty:** Student/faculty ratio 14:1. 101 full-time faculty, 92% hold PhDs, 10% are members of minority groups, 49% are women.

ACADEMICS

Degrees: Bachelor's, master's, post-bachelor's certificate. **Classes:** Most classes have 10–19 students. Most lab/discussion sessions have 10–19 students. **Majors with Highest Enrollment:** Biology/biological sciences; business/commerce;

psychology. **Special Study Options:** Double major, exchange student program (domestic), honors program, independent study, internships, study abroad, teacher certification program, Learning Communities. **Combined degree programs:** BA/DDS, 7-year dental program with New York University. Special programs offered to physically disabled students include note-taking services, reader services, tape recorders, tutors. **Career services:** Alumni network, alumni services, internships. **Career services highlights include:** The Wagner Plan for the Practical Liberal Arts involves both of the above.

FACILITIES

Housing: Coed dorms, fraternity/sorority housing, apartments for single students, theme housing. **Special Academic Facilities/Equipment:** Art gallery, early childhood center, nursing resource center, planetarium, two electron microscopes, solar energy project. **Computers:** 90% of classrooms, 100% of dorms, 100% of libraries, 100% of dining areas, 100% of student union, 50% of common outdoor areas have wireless network access. Students can register for classes online. Administrative functions (other than registration) can be performed online.

CAMPUS LIFE

Environment: Metropolis. **Activities:** Choral groups, dance, drama/theater, jazz band, literary magazine, music ensembles, musical theater, pep band, radio station, student government, student newspaper, yearbook, campus ministries, international student organization, Model UN. **Organizations:** 66 registered organizations, 11 honor societies, 4 religious organizations. 5 fraternities, 4 sororities. **Athletics (Intercollegiate):** *Men:* Baseball, basketball, cross-country, football, golf, lacrosse, tennis, track/field (outdoor), track/field (indoor). *Women:* Basketball, cross-country, golf, lacrosse, soccer, softball, swimming, tennis, track/field (outdoor), track/field (indoor), water polo. **On-Campus Highlights:** Coffee House, Spiro Sports Center, Wagner Student Union, Main Hall Theatre, Foundation Hall, Hawk's Nest. **Environmental Initiatives:** Competing in Recylemania, spring 2009 going trayless in all dining venues.

ADMISSIONS

Freshman Academic Profile: Average high school GPA 89. 17% in top 10% of high school class, 70% in top 25% of high school class, 92% in top 50% of high school class. SAT Math middle 50% range 530–650. SAT Critical Reading middle 50% range 530–640. SAT Writing middle 50% range 520–650. ACT middle 50% range 23–28. Minimum paper TOEFL 550. Minimum computer TOEFL 217. Minimum web-based TOEFL 17. **Basis for Candidate Selection:** *Very important factors considered include:* Class rank, academic GPA, rigor of secondary school record. *Important factors considered include:* Application essay, recommendation(s), standardized test scores, extracurricular activities, interview. *Other factors considered include:* character/personal qualities, geographical residence, level of applicant's interest, talent/ability, volunteer work, work experience. **Freshman Admission Requirements:** High school diploma is required and GED is accepted. *Academic units required:* 4 English, 3 mathematics, 2 science, (1 science labs), 2 foreign language, 1 social studies, 3 history, 6 academic electives. **Freshman Admission Statistics:** 3,012 applied, 61% admitted, 26% enrolled. **Transfer Admission Requirements:** College transcript(s), essay or personal statement, statement of good standing from prior institution(s). Minimum college GPA of 3.0 required. Lowest grade transferable C. **General Admission Information:** Application fee $50. Early decision application deadline 1/1. Regular application deadline 2/15. Regular notification 3/1. Nonfall registration accepted. Admission may be deferred for a maximum of 1 year. Credit offered for CEEB Advanced Placement tests.

COSTS AND FINANCIAL AID

Annual tuition $32,430. Room and board $9,700. Required fees $150. Average book expense $745. **Required Forms and Deadlines:** FAFSA, institution's own financial aid form, state aid form. Priority financial aid filing date 2/15. **Notification of Awards:** Applicants will be notified of awards on a rolling basis beginning 3/1. **Types of Aid:** *Need-based scholarships/grants:* Federal Pell, SEOG, state scholarships/grants, private scholarships. *Loans:* FFEL Subsidized Stafford, FFEL Unsubsidized Stafford, FFEL PLUS, Federal Perkins, Federal Nursing, Alternative Loans. *Student Employment:* Federal Work-Study Program available. Institutional employment available. Highest amount earned per year from on-campus jobs $1,000. Off-campus job opportunities are good. **Financial Aid Statistics:** 63% freshmen, 55% undergrads receive need-based scholarship or grant aid. 48% freshmen, 44% undergrads receive need-based self-help aid. 6% freshmen, 6% undergrads receive athletic scholarships. 92% freshmen, 90% undergrads receive any aid. 56% undergrads borrow to pay for school. Average cumulative indebtedness $34,326. **Criteria for awarding institutional aid:** *Non-need-based:* Academics, athletics, music/drama.

WAKE FOREST UNIVERSITY

Best 373

P.O. Box 7305, Reynolda Station, Winston Salem, NC 27109
Phone: 336-758-5201 **Financial Aid Phone:** 336-758-5154
E-mail: admissions@wfu.edu **CEEB Code:** 5885
Fax: 336-758-4324 **Website:** www.wfu.edu **ACT Code:** 3168

This private school was founded in 1834. It has a 340-acre campus.

RATINGS

Admissions Selectivity Rating: 95   **Fire Safety Rating:** 88   **Green Rating:** 81

STUDENTS AND FACULTY

Enrollment: 4,466. **Student Body:** 51% female, 49% male, 75% out-of-state, 1% international. Asian 5%, African American 7%, Caucasian 82%, Hispanic 3%, Native American 1%.
Retention and Graduation: 93% freshmen return for sophomore year. 83% freshmen graduate within 4 years. 36% grads go on to further study within 1 year. 22% grads pursue arts and sciences degrees. 6% grads pursue law degrees. 1% grads pursue business degrees. 4% grads pursue medical degrees. **Faculty:** Student/faculty ratio 10:1. 71 full-time faculty, 604% hold PhDs, 94% are members of minority groups, 249% are women.

ACADEMICS

Degrees: first professional, master's, post-bachelor's certificate. **Classes:** Most classes have 10–19 students. Most lab/discussion sessions have 10–19 students. **Majors with Highest Enrollment:** Business/commerce; political science and government; psychology. **Special Study Options:** Cross-registration, double major, dual enrollment, honors program, independent study, internships, study abroad, teacher certification program. **Honors programs:** For highly qualified students, a series of interdisciplinary honors courses are offered. Additionally, for students especially talented in individual areas of study, most departments in the College offer special studies leading to graduation with honors in a particular discipline. **Combined degree programs:** BS/MS in accountancy. Special programs offered to physically disabled students include note-taking services, reader services, tape recorders, tutors. **Career services:** Alumni network, alumni services, career/job search classes, career assessment, internships, regional alumni.

FACILITIES

Housing: Coed dorms, fraternity/sorority housing, apartments for single students, wellness housing, theme housing, Wellness = Substance Free. **Special Academic Facilities/Equipment:** Museum of Anthropology; Charlotte and Philip Hanes Art Gallery; Scales Fine Arts Center; Reynolda House, Museum of American Art; Laser and Electron Microscope Labs. **Computers:** 100% of classrooms, 100% of dorms, 100% of libraries, 100% of dining areas, 100% of student union, 5% of common outdoor areas have wireless network access. Students can register for classes online. Administrative functions (other than registration) can be performed online. Undergraduates are required to own a computer.

CAMPUS LIFE

Environment: City. **Activities:** Choral groups, concert band, dance, drama/theater, jazz band, literary magazine, marching band, music ensembles, pep band, radio station, student government, student newspaper, student-run film society, symphony orchestra, television station, yearbook, campus ministries, international student organization, Model UN. **Organizations:** 168 registered organizations, 16 honor societies, 16 religious organizations. 14 fraternities, 9 sororities. **Athletics (Intercollegiate):** *Men:* Baseball, basketball, cheerleading, cross-country, football, golf, soccer, tennis, track/field (outdoor), track/field (indoor). *Women:* Basketball, cheerleading, cross-country, field hockey, golf, soccer, tennis, track/field (outdoor), track/field (indoor), volleyball. **On-Campus Highlights:** Charlotte and Philip Hanes Art Gallery, Museum of Anthropology, The Z. Smith Reynolds Library, Wait Chapel, Benson University Center. **Environmental Initiatives:** Campus Master Plan: Wake Forest has completed a new campus master plan that will guide development over the next 50 years. Heavily integrated into that plan are tenets for sustainable design (e.g., LEED) as well as stormwater management and biohabitat protection. This new master plan will guide the campus in integrating sustainability within the built and natural environments for the years ahead. Energy management: the university has a robust Energy Management software system to conserve energy during normal operating periods and to cycle down energy use to minimal levels during low- or no-occupancy periods. Also, energy reduction projects are underway in FY09—lighting retrofits, motor replacements, central plant upgrades,

etc. Also, new capital projects are designed to achieve energy savings in excess of 30% greater than ASHRAE requirements. Recycling: Approximately 30 percent of the WFU waste stream is diverted from the landfill as either recycled or reused. A renewed emphasis on recycling—to include deskside capture and more functional campus collection containers—is seeing significant success.

ADMISSIONS

Freshman Academic Profile: 64.3% in top 10% of high school class, 90.8% in top 25% of high school class, 98% in top 50% of high school class. 65% from public high schools. SAT Math middle 50% range 630–710. SAT Critical Reading middle 50% range 610–690. ACT middle 50% range 27–31. Minimum paper TOEFL 600. Minimum computer TOEFL 250. **Basis for Candidate Selection:** *Very important factors considered include:* Class rank, application essay, academic GPA, rigor of secondary school record, character/personal qualities. *Important factors considered include:* Recommendation(s), extracurricular activities, interview, talent/ability. *Other factors considered include:* Standardized test scores, alumni/ae relation, first generation, geographical residence, level of applicant's interest, racial/ethnic status, religious affiliation/commitment, state residency, volunteer work. **Freshman Admission Requirements:** High school diploma is required and GED is accepted. *Academic units required:* 4 English, 3 mathematics, 1 science, 2 foreign language, 2 social studies. *Academic units recommended:* 4 English, 4 mathematics, 4 science, 4 foreign language, 4 social studies. **Freshman Admission Statistics:** 9,050 applied, 38% admitted, 35% enrolled. **Transfer Admission Requirements:** High school transcript, college transcript(s), essay or personal statement, statement of good standing from prior institution(s). Minimum college GPA of 2.0 required. Lowest grade transferable C. **General Admission Information:** Application fee $50. Early decision application deadline 11/15. Regular application deadline 1/15. Regular notification 4/1. Nonfall registration not accepted. Admission may be deferred for a maximum of 1 year. Credit and/or placement offered for CEEB Advanced Placement tests.

COSTS AND FINANCIAL AID

Annual tuition $38,206. Room and board $10,410. Required fees $416. Average book expense $900. **Required Forms and Deadlines:** FAFSA, CSS/Financial Aid PROFILE, state aid form, noncustodial PROFILE Financial aid filing deadline 3/1. Priority financial aid filing date 2/1. **Notification of Awards:** Applicants will be notified of awards on a rolling basis beginning 4/1. **Types of Aid:** *Need-based scholarships/grants:* Federal Pell, SEOG, state scholarships/grants, private scholarships, the school's own gift aid. *Loans:* FFEL Subsidized Stafford, FFEL Unsubsidized Stafford, FFEL PLUS, Federal Perkins, state loans, college/university loans from institutional funds. *Student Employment:* Federal Work-Study Program available. Institutional employment available. Highest amount earned per year from on-campus jobs $2,495. Off-campus job opportunities are excellent. **Financial Aid Statistics:** 27% freshmen, 33% undergrads receive need-based scholarship or grant aid. 19% freshmen, 22% undergrads receive non-need-based scholarship or grant aid. 23% freshmen, 29% undergrads receive need-based self-help aid. 6% freshmen, 4% undergrads receive athletic scholarships. 39% freshmen, 34% undergrads receive any aid. 38% undergrads borrow to pay for school. Average cumulative indebtedness $24,827. **Criteria for awarding institutional aid:** *Non-need-based:* Academics, alumni affiliation, art, athletics, leadership, music/drama, religious affiliation, state/district residency.

WALDORF COLLEGE

106 South 6th St, Forest City, IA 50436
Phone: 641-585-8112
E-mail: admissions@waldorf.edu
Fax: 641-585-8125 **Website:** www.waldorf.edu **ACT Code:** 1895

This private school, affiliated with the Lutheran Church, was founded in 1903. It has a 40-acre campus.

RATINGS

Admissions Selectivity Rating: 60*   **Fire Safety Rating:** 60*   **Green Rating:** 60*

STUDENTS AND FACULTY

Enrollment: 573. **Student Body:** 53% female, 47% male, 17% out-of-state, 6% international. Asian 1%, African American 4%, Caucasian 99%, Hispanic 1%.
Retention and Graduation: **Faculty:** Student/faculty ratio 15:1. 64 full-time faculty, 25% hold PhDs.

ACADEMICS

Degrees: Associate, bachelor's. **Classes:** Most classes have 10–19 students. Most lab/discussion sessions have fewer than 10 students. **Majors with Highest **Enrollment:** Business, management, marketing, and related support services, other; communication, journalism, and related programs, other; computer and information sciences and support services, other. **Special Study Options:** Accelerated program, cooperative education program, double major, English as a Second Language (ESL), honors program, internships, student-designed major, study abroad, teacher certification program **Combined degree programs:** BA/MD Special programs offered to physically disabled students include note-taking services, reader services, tutors. **Career services:** Alumni network, alumni services, career/job search classes, career assessment, internships. **Career services highlights include:** Internships.

FACILITIES
Housing: Coed dorms, special housing for disabled students, suites, special interest housing, townhouses. **Computers:** Administrative functions (other than registration) can be performed online.

CAMPUS LIFE
Environment: Rural. **Activities:** dance, drama/theater, jazz band, student government, student newspaper, campus ministries. **Athletics (Intercollegiate):** *Men:* Baseball, basketball, football, golf, soccer, wrestling. *Women:* Basketball, cheerleading, golf, soccer, softball, volleyball. **On-Campus Highlights:** Walucks (coffee/snacks), Wellness Center, Video-Production Studio, Library (new), Breen Hall.

ADMISSIONS
Freshman Academic Profile: Average high school GPA 3.01. 95% from public high schools. Minimum paper TOEFL 500. Minimum computer TOEFL 173. **Basis for Candidate Selection:** *Very important factors considered include:* Recommendation(s), rigor of secondary school record, standardized test scores. *Important factors considered include:* Extracurricular activities, talent/ability. *Other factors considered include:* Class rank, alumni/ae relation, character/personal qualities, interview, racial/ethnic status, religious affiliation/commitment. **Freshman Admission Requirements:** High school diploma is required and GED is accepted. *Academic units recommended:* 4 English, 3 mathematics, 3 science, 2 foreign language, 4 history. **Freshman Admission Statistics:** 584 applied, 67% admitted, 50% enrolled. **Transfer Admission Requirements:** High school transcript, college transcript(s), standardized test scores, statement of good standing from prior institution(s). Minimum college GPA of 2.0 required. Lowest grade transferable C–. **General Admission Information:** Notification on a rolling basis, beginning on or about 10/4. Nonfall registration not accepted. Admission may be deferred for a maximum of 1 year.

WALLA WALLA UNIVERSITY

Office of Admissions, 204 South Colleg, College Place, WA 99324-1198
Phone: 509-527-2327 **Financial Aid Phone:** 509-527-2815
E-mail: info@wallawalla.edu **CEEB Code:** 4940
Fax: 509-527-2397 **Website:** www.wallawalla.edu **ACT Code:** 4486

This private school, affiliated with the Seventh Day Adventist Church, was founded in 1892. It has a 77-acre campus.

RATINGS
Admissions Selectivity Rating: 73   **Fire Safety Rating:** 60*   **Green Rating:** 60*

STUDENTS AND FACULTY
Enrollment: 1,555. **Student Body:** 48% female, 52% male, 60% out-of-state, 1% international (30 countries represented). Asian 6%, African American 3%, Caucasian 78%, Hispanic 10%, Native American 1%. **Retention and Graduation:** 69% freshmen return for sophomore year. 19% freshmen graduate within 4 years. **Faculty:** Student/faculty ratio 13:1. 117 full-time faculty, 71% hold PhDs, 5% are members of minority groups, 36% are women.

ACADEMICS
Degrees: Associate, bachelor's, master's. **Classes:** Most classes have fewer than 10 students. Most lab/discussion sessions have fewer than 10 students. **Majors with Highest Enrollment:** Business/commerce; engineering; social work. **Special Study Options:** Cooperative education program, distance learning, double major, honors program, independent study, internships, liberal arts/career combination, study abroad, teacher certification program Special programs offered to physically disabled students include note-taking services, reader services, tape recorders, tutors. **Career services:** Alumni network, career/job search classes, career assessment, internships. **Career services highlights include:** All of our accounting and management students participate in internships.

FACILITIES
Housing: Special housing for disabled students, men's dorms, women's dorms, apartments for married students, apartments for single students, wellness housing, 75% of campus accessible to physically disabled. **Special Academic Facilities/Equipment:** Marine station on the Rosario Strait of the Puget Sound in Washington state. **Computers:** Students can register for classes online.

CAMPUS LIFE
Environment: Town. **Activities:** Choral groups, concert band, drama/theater, literary magazine, music ensembles, radio station, student government, student newspaper, symphony orchestra, television station, yearbook, campus ministries, international student organization. **Organizations:** 33 registered organizations, 7 honor societies, 6 religious organizations. **Athletics (Intercollegiate):** *Men:* Basketball, golf, soccer, volleyball. *Women:* Basketball, softball, volleyball. **On-Campus Highlights:** The Dairy Express, Peterson Memorial Library, The Student Association Center, Winter Educational Complex: gym/climbing wall/pool, The College Store, Clyde and Mary Harris Gallery.

ADMISSIONS
Freshman Academic Profile: Average high school GPA 3.41. 9% from public high schools. Minimum paper TOEFL 550. Minimum computer TOEFL 213. **Basis for Candidate Selection:** *Very important factors considered include:* Academic GPA, recommendation(s), rigor of secondary school record. *Important factors considered include:* Character/personal qualities, level of applicant's interest. *Other factors considered include:* Class rank, standardized test scores, extracurricular activities, talent/ability. **Freshman Admission Requirements:** High school diploma is required and GED is accepted. *Academic units required:* 4 English, 3 mathematics, 2 science, (2 science labs), 2 history. *Academic units recommended:* 4 English, 4 mathematics, 3 science, (2 science labs), 2 foreign language, 1 social studies, 2 history. **Freshman Admission Statistics:** 505 applied, 98% admitted, 64% enrolled. **Transfer Admission Requirements:** College transcript(s), minimum college GPA of 2.0 required. Lowest grade transferable D–. **General Admission Information:** Application fee $40. Notification on a rolling basis, beginning on or about 9/25. Nonfall registration accepted. Admission may be deferred for a maximum of 1 year. Credit and/or placement offered for CEEB Advanced Placement tests.

COSTS AND FINANCIAL AID
Annual tuition $21,726. Room and board $4,320. Required fees $210. Average book expense $1,014. **Required Forms and Deadlines:** FAFSA, institution's own financial aid form. Priority financial aid filing date 4/30. **Notification of Awards:** Applicants will be notified of awards on a rolling basis beginning 3/15. **Types of Aid:** *Need-based scholarships/grants:* Federal Pell, SEOG, state scholarships/grants, private scholarships, the school's own gift aid, Federal Nursing Scholarships. *Loans:* FFEL Subsidized Stafford, FFEL Unsubsidized Stafford, FFEL PLUS, Federal Perkins, Federal Nursing, college/university loans from institutional funds. *Student Employment:* Federal Work-Study Program available. Institutional employment available. Off-campus job opportunities are good. **Financial Aid Statistics:** 58% freshmen, 53% undergrads receive need-based scholarship or grant aid. 68% freshmen, 52% undergrads receive non-need-based scholarship or grant aid. 65% freshmen, 65% undergrads receive need-based self-help aid. 84% freshmen, 83% undergrads receive any aid. 79% undergrads borrow to pay for school. Average cumulative indebtedness $28,287. **Criteria for awarding institutional aid:** *Non-need-based:* Academics, leadership, music/drama.

WALSH COLLEGE OF ACCOUNTANCY AND BUSINESS ADMINISTRATION

3838 Livernois Road, PO Box 7006, Troy, MI 48007-7006
Phone: 248-689-8282 **Financial Aid Phone:** 248-823-1285
E-mail: admissions@walshcollege.edu
Fax: 248-689-0938

This private school was founded in 1922. It has a 20-acre campus.

RATINGS
Admissions Selectivity Rating: 60*   **Fire Safety Rating:** 60*   **Green Rating:** 64

STUDENTS AND FACULTY
Enrollment: 984. **Student Body:** 55% female, 45% male, 0.5% out-of-state, 4% international (46 countries represented). Asian 3%, African American 5%, Caucasian 65%, Hispanic 1%. **Retention and Graduation: Faculty:** Student/faculty ratio 17.44:1. 18 full-time faculty, 72% hold PhDs, 6% are members of minority groups, 44% are women.

ACADEMICS

Degrees: Bachelor's, master's, post-bachelor's certificate, post-master's certificate. **Classes:** Most classes have 20–29 students. **Majors with Highest Enrollment:** Liberal arts and sciences/liberal studies; pharmacy (pharmd [usa], pharmd or bs/bpharm [canada]); psychology. **Special Study Options:** Distance learning, double major, dual enrollment, independent study, internships Special programs offered to physically disabled students include note-taking services, reader services, tape recorders, tutors. **Career services:** Alumni network, alumni services, career/job search classes, career assessment, internships

FACILITIES

Housing: 100% of campus accessible to physically disabled. **Computers:** 100% of classrooms, 100% of libraries, 100% of dining areas, have wireless network access. Students can register for classes online. Administrative functions (other than registration) can be performed online.

CAMPUS LIFE

Environment: City. **Activities:** Student government, student newspaper, student-run film society **Organizations:** 6 registered organizations, 1 honor societies. **On-Campus Highlights:** Barry Center.

ADMISSIONS

Freshman Academic Profile: Minimum paper TOEFL 550. Minimum computer TOEFL 213. Minimum web-based TOEFL 79. **Freshman Admission Requirements: Transfer Admission Requirements:** College transcript(s), minimum college GPA of 2.0 required. Lowest grade transferable C. **General Admission Information:** Application fee $25.

COSTS AND FINANCIAL AID

Required Forms and Deadlines: FAFSA. Priority financial aid filing date 3/23. **Types of Aid:** *Need-based scholarships/grants:* Federal Pell, SEOG, state scholarships/grants, the school's own gift aid. *Loans:* FFEL Subsidized Stafford, FFEL Unsubsidized Stafford, state loans *Student Employment:* Federal Work-Study Program available. Off-campus job opportunities are fair. **Financial Aid Statistics:** 28% undergrads receive need-based scholarship or grant aid. 8% undergrads receive non-need-based scholarship or grant aid. 44% undergrads receive need-based self-help aid. 61% undergrads borrow to pay for school. Average cumulative indebtedness $12,367. **Criteria for awarding institutional aid:** *Non-need-based:* Academics.

WALSH UNIVERSITY

Walsh University, 2020 E Maple St, North Canton, OH 44720-3396
Phone: 800-362-9846 **Financial Aid Phone:** 330-490-7146
E-mail: admissions@walsh.edu **CEEB Code:** 1926
Fax: 330-490-7165 **Website:** www.walsh.edu **ACT Code:** 3349

This private school, affiliated with the Roman Catholic Church, was founded in 1958. It has a 140-acre campus.

RATINGS

Admissions Selectivity Rating: 73   **Fire Safety Rating:** 95   **Green Rating:** 70

STUDENTS AND FACULTY

Enrollment: 2,278. **Student Body:** 63% female, 37% male, 2% out-of-state, 1% international (22 countries represented). Asian 1%, African American 4%, Caucasian 79%, Hispanic 1%.
Retention and Graduation: 71% freshmen return for sophomore year. 25% grads go on to further study within 1 year. 6% grads pursue arts and sciences degrees. 1% grads pursue law degrees. 6% grads pursue business degrees. 2% grads pursue medical degrees. **Faculty:** Student/faculty ratio 14:1. 108 full-time faculty, 75% hold PhDs, 8% are members of minority groups, 53% are women.

ACADEMICS

Degrees: Associate, bachelor's, master's. **Classes:** Most classes have 10–19 students. Most lab/discussion sessions have fewer than 10 students. **Majors with Highest Enrollment:** Biological and physical sciences; business/commerce; nursing/registered nurse (RN, ASN, BSN, MSN). **Special Study Options:** Accelerated program, double major, dual enrollment, English as a Second Language (ESL), exchange student program (domestic), external degree program, honors program, independent study, internships, liberal arts/career combination, study abroad, teacher certification program, Combined bachelor's/master's degree programs CCSA College Consortium for Study Abroad Rome Experience. **Honors programs:** Honors Program students may pursue any major and have opportunity annually to attend the national honors conference, where Walsh students frequently present their research. **Combined degree programs:** BA/MA, 3-1 med-tech, 3-4 dentistry. Special programs offered to physically disabled students include reader services, tape recorders, tutors.

Career services: Alumni network, alumni services, career assessment, internships, regional alumni.

FACILITIES

Housing: Coed dorms, special housing for disabled students, special housing for international students, apartments for single students, wellness housin Apartment-style residence hall with kitchens. 100% of campus accessible to physically disabled. **Special Academic Facilities/Equipment:** bioinformatics lab, Hoover Museum, human cadaver lab (prosection for undergrad), Gathering Garden for Education activities with schoolchildren, Religious Education Center. **Computers:** 10% of classrooms, 12% of dorms, 100% of libraries, 100% of dining areas, 100% of student union, 5% of common outdoor areas have wireless network access. Students can register for classes online. Administrative functions (other than registration) can be performed online.

CAMPUS LIFE

Environment: City. **Activities:** Choral groups, dance, drama/theater, literary magazine, music ensembles, pep band, radio station, student government, student newspaper, campus ministries, international student organization. **Organizations:** 30 registered organizations, 10 honor societies, 3 religious organizations. **Athletics (Intercollegiate):** *Men:* Baseball, basketball, cheerleading, cross-country, football, golf, soccer, tennis, track/field (outdoor), track/field (indoor). *Women:* Basketball, cheerleading, cross-country, golf, soccer, softball, tennis, track/field (outdoor), track/field (indoor), volleyball. **On-Campus Highlights:** David Campus Center, Alumni Arena, University Apartments, Barrette Business and Community Center, Wellness Center. **Environmental Initiatives:** HVAC & electrical managament system recycling program for paper, plastic, and aluminum ink cartridge recycle system

ADMISSIONS

Freshman Academic Profile: Average high school GPA 3.31. 16% in top 10% of high school class, 41% in top 25% of high school class, 75% in top 50% of high school class. 76.5% from public high schools. SAT Math middle 50% range 460–550. SAT Critical Reading middle 50% range 440–530. ACT middle 50% range 19–24. Minimum paper TOEFL 500. Minimum computer TOEFL 173. Minimum web-based TOEFL 61. **Basis for Candidate Selection:** *Very important factors considered include:* Academic GPA, rigor of secondary school record, standardized test scores. *Important factors considered include:* Recommendation(s), character/personal qualities. *Other factors considered include:* Class rank, application essay, interview, volunteer work. **Freshman Admission Requirements:** High school diploma is required and GED is accepted. *Academic units recommended:* 4 English, 3 mathematics, 3 science, 2 foreign language, 3 social studies, 1 academic electives. **Freshman Admission Statistics:** 1,466 applied, 81% admitted, 41% enrolled. **Transfer Admission Requirements:** High school transcript, college transcript(s), minimum college GPA of 2.0 required. Lowest grade transferable C. **General Admission Information:** Application fee $25. Regular application deadline 8/15. Notification on a rolling basis, beginning on or about 10/1. Nonfall registration accepted. Admission may be deferred for a maximum of 1 year. Credit offered for CEEB Advanced Placement tests.

COSTS AND FINANCIAL AID

Annual tuition $21,380. Room and board $8,360. Required fees $900. Average book expense $1,062. **Required Forms and Deadlines:** FAFSA, institution's own financial aid form. Priority financial aid filing date 2/14. **Notification of Awards:** Applicants will be notified of awards on a rolling basis beginning 2/15. **Types of Aid:** *Need-based scholarships/grants:* Federal Pell, SEOG, state scholarships/grants, private scholarships, the school's own gift aid. *Loans:* Direct Subsidized Stafford, Direct Unsubsidized Stafford, Direct PLUS, Federal Perkins, state loans. *Student Employment:* Federal Work-Study Program available. Institutional employment available. Highest amount earned per year from on-campus jobs $3,000. **Financial Aid Statistics:** 74% freshmen, 65% undergrads receive need-based scholarship or grant aid. 83% freshmen, 56% undergrads receive non-need-based scholarship or grant aid. 66% freshmen, 56% undergrads receive need-based self-help aid. 25% freshmen, 20% undergrads receive athletic scholarships. 92% freshmen, 92% undergrads receive any aid. 92% undergrads borrow to pay for school. Average cumulative indebtedness $23,446. **Criteria for awarding institutional aid:** *Non-need-based:* Academics, alumni affiliation, athletics, music/drama, religious affiliation, state/district residency.

WARNER PACIFIC COLLEGE

Office of Admissions, 2219 SE 68th Ave, Portland, OR 97215
Phone: 503-517-1020 **Financial Aid Phone:** 503-517-1091
E-mail: admissions@warnerpacific.edu **CEEB Code:** 4595
Fax: 503-517-1540 **Website:** www.warnerpacific.edu

This private school, affiliated with the Church of God Church, was founded in 1937. It has a 15-acre campus.

RATINGS
Admissions Selectivity Rating: 60* **Fire Safety Rating:** 60* **Green Rating:** 60*

STUDENTS AND FACULTY
Enrollment: 1,181. **Student Body:** 62% female, 38% male, % out-of-state, international (12 countries represented). Asian 3%, African American 4%, Caucasian 57%, Hispanic 4%.
Retention and Graduation: 36% freshmen graduate within 4 years. **Faculty:** Student/faculty ratio 11:1. 24 full-time faculty, 58% hold PhDs, 8% are members of minority groups, 29% are women.

ACADEMICS
Degrees: Associate, bachelor's, certificate, master's. **Classes:** Most classes have 10–19 students. **Special Study Options:** Cooperative education program, double major, independent study, internships, student-designed major, study abroad, teacher certification program, weekend college, Adult Degree Program. Special programs offered to physically disabled students include note-taking services, reader services, tape recorders, tutors. **Career services:** Career assessment, internships.

FACILITIES
Housing: Men's dorms, women's dorms, apartments for married students, apartments for single students. 50% of campus accessible to physically disabled. **Special Academic Facilities/Equipment:** Early learning center, electron microscopes. **Computers:** 100% of classrooms, 10% of dorms, 100% of libraries, 100% of dining areas, 100% of student union, 50% of common outdoor areas have wireless network access.

CAMPUS LIFE
Environment: Metropolis. **Activities:** Choral groups, concert band, dance, drama/theater, jazz band, literary magazine, music ensembles, musical theater, student government, student newspaper, yearbook, campus ministries, international student organization. **Organizations:** 20 registered organizations, 2 religious organizations. **Athletics (Intercollegiate):** *Men:* Basketball, cross-country, golf, soccer, track/field (outdoor), track/field (indoor). *Women:* Basketball, cross-country, golf, soccer, track/field (outdoor), track/field (indoor), volleyball. **On-Campus Highlights:** Tabor Grind Coffee Shop, Dining Hall, Student Union Building, Otto F. Linn Library, A.F. Gray lawn.

ADMISSIONS
Freshman Academic Profile: SAT Math middle 50% range 430–570. SAT Critical Reading middle 50% range 440–580. SAT Writing middle 50% range 440–560. ACT middle 50% range 17–25. Minimum paper TOEFL 525. Minimum computer TOEFL 195. Minimum web-based TOEFL 71. **Basis for Candidate Selection:** *Important factors considered include:* Application essay, academic GPA, standardized test scores. *Other factors considered include:* Class rank, recommendation(s), rigor of secondary school record. **Freshman Admission Requirements:** High school diploma is required and GED is accepted. *Academic units recommended:* 4 English, 2 mathematics, 2 science, (2 science labs), 3 social studies. **Transfer Admission Requirements:** College transcript(s), essay or personal statement, minimum college GPA of 2.5 required. Lowest grade transferable d. **General Admission Information:** Application fee $50. Early decision application deadline 6/1. Nonfall registration accepted. Admission may be deferred for a maximum of 1 year. Credit offered for CEEB Advanced Placement tests.

COSTS AND FINANCIAL AID
Average book expense $1,100. **Required Forms and Deadlines:** FAFSA. Priority financial aid filing date 3/1. **Notification of Awards:** Applicants will be notified of awards on a rolling basis beginning 3/1. **Types of Aid:** *Need-based scholarships/grants:* Federal Pell, SEOG, state scholarships/grants, private scholarships, the school's own gift aid. *Loans:* Direct Subsidized Stafford, Direct Unsubsidized Stafford, Direct PLUS, FFEL Subsidized Stafford, FFEL Unsubsidized Stafford, FFEL PLUS, Federal Perkins. *Student Employment:* Federal Work-Study Program available. Institutional employment available. Highest amount earned per year from on-campus jobs $4,000. **Financial Aid Statistics:** 77% freshmen, 79% undergrads receive need-based scholarship or grant aid. 84% freshmen, 85% undergrads receive non-need-based scholarship or grant aid. 80% freshmen, 82% undergrads receive need-based self-help aid. 2% freshmen, 3% undergrads receive athletic scholarships. 96% freshmen, 97%

undergrads receive any aid. 93% undergrads borrow to pay for school. Average cumulative indebtedness $22,433. **Criteria for awarding institutional aid:** *Non-need-based:* Academics, alumni affiliation, athletics, leadership, music/drama, religious affiliation.

WARNER SOUTHERN COLLEGE

13985 Hwy. 27, Lake Wales, FL 33859
Phone: 863-638-7212 **Financial Aid Phone:** 863-638-7203
E-mail: admissions@warner.edu **CEEB Code:** 5883
Fax: 863-638-7290 **Website:** **ACT Code:** 777

This private school, affiliated with the Church of God Church, was founded in 1968. It has a 320-acre campus.

RATINGS
Admissions Selectivity Rating: 72 **Fire Safety Rating:** 60* **Green Rating:** 60*

STUDENTS AND FACULTY
Enrollment: 937. **Student Body:** 58% female, 42% male, % out-of-state, 1% international (17 countries represented). Asian 1%, African American 17%, Caucasian 56%, Hispanic 8%.
Retention and Graduation: 26% freshmen graduate within 4 years. **Faculty:** Student/faculty ratio 13:1. 34 full-time faculty, 59% hold PhDs, 12% are members of minority groups, 38% are women.

ACADEMICS
Degrees: Associate, bachelor's, certificate, master's, terminal associate. **Classes:** Most classes have 10–19 students. **Majors with Highest Enrollment:** Business/commerce; education; pastoral studies/counseling. **Special Study Options:** Accelerated program, distance learning, double major, dual enrollment, English as a Second Language (ESL), independent study, internships, study abroad, teacher certification program.

FACILITIES
Housing: Men's dorms, women's dorms. 80% of campus accessible to physically disabled.

CAMPUS LIFE
Environment: Rural. **Activities:** Choral groups, music ensembles, student government, student newspaper. **Organizations:** 2 registered organizations, 6 honor societies, 1 religious organizations. 2 fraternities, 2 sororities. **Athletics (Intercollegiate):** *Men:* Baseball, basketball, cheerleading, cross-country, golf, soccer, tennis, track/field (outdoor), track/field (indoor). *Women:* Basketball, cheerleading, cross-country, golf, soccer, softball, tennis, track/field (outdoor), track/field (indoor), volleyball. **On-Campus Highlights:** Lion's Den, Turner Athletic Center, Pontious Learning Resource Center, Caffe Cristiano

ADMISSIONS
Freshman Academic Profile: Average high school GPA 3. 11% in top 10% of high school class, 23% in top 25% of high school class, 66% in top 50% of high school class. 90% from public high schools. SAT Math middle 50% range 351–613. SAT Critical Reading middle 50% range 342–580. ACT middle 50% range 15–24. Minimum paper TOEFL 500. Minimum computer TOEFL 173. **Basis for Candidate Selection:** *Important factors considered include:* Class rank, academic GPA, recommendation(s), standardized test scores, level of applicant's interest. *Other factors considered include:* Application essay, rigor of secondary school record, alumni/ae relation, character/personal qualities, extracurricular activities, interview, talent/ability, volunteer work. **Freshman Admission Requirements:** High school diploma is required and GED is accepted. *Academic units recommended:* 4 English, 3 mathematics, 2 science, 1 social studies, 1 history, 2 academic electives. **Freshman Admission Statistics:** 363 applied, 66% admitted, 47% enrolled. **Transfer Admission Requirements:** College transcript(s), essay or personal statement, statement of good standing from prior institution(s). Minimum college GPA of 2.0 required. Lowest grade transferable D. **General Admission Information:** Application fee $20. Notification on a rolling basis, beginning on or about 9/1. Nonfall registration accepted. Admission may be deferred for a maximum of No time set. Neither credit nor placement offered for CEEB Advanced Placement tests.

COSTS AND FINANCIAL AID
Annual tuition $13,600. Room and board $5,730. Required fees $150. Average book expense $1,000. **Required Forms and Deadlines:** FAFSA, state aid form, Verification Form. Priority financial aid filing date 5/1. **Notification of Awards:** Applicants will be notified of awards on a rolling basis beginning 1/15. **Types of Aid:** *Need-based scholarships/grants:* Federal Pell, SEOG, state scholarships/grants, private scholarships, the school's own gift aid. *Loans:* FFEL Subsidized Stafford, FFEL Unsubsidized Stafford, FFEL PLUS, Federal

PerkinsAlternative Loans. *Student Employment:* Federal Work-Study Program available. Institutional employment available. Highest amount earned per year from on-campus jobs $1,200. Off-campus job opportunities are good. **Financial Aid Statistics:** 56% freshmen, 45% undergrads receive need-based scholarship or grant aid. 71% freshmen, 67% undergrads receive non-need-based scholarship or grant aid. 58% freshmen, 61% undergrads receive need-based self-help aid. 66% freshmen, 34% undergrads receive athletic scholarships. 100% freshmen, 93% undergrads receive any aid. **Criteria for awarding institutional aid:** *Non-need-based:* Academics, alumni affiliation, athletics, leadership, minority status, music/drama, religious affiliation, state/district residency.

WARREN WILSON COLLEGE

PO Box 9000, Asheville, NC 28815-9000
Phone: 800-934-3536 **Financial Aid Phone:** 828-771-2082
E-mail: admit@warren-wilson.edu **CEEB Code:** 5886
Fax: 828-298-1440 **Website:** www.warren-wilson.edu **ACT Code:** 3170

This private school, affiliated with the Presbyterian Church, was founded in 1894. It has a 1100-acre campus.

RATINGS

Admissions Selectivity Rating: 84 **Fire Safety Rating:** 60* **Green Rating:** 99

STUDENTS AND FACULTY

Enrollment: 923. **Student Body:** 60% female, 40% male, 84% out-of-state, 3% international (12 countries represented). Asian 1%, African American 1%, Caucasian 91%, Hispanic 2%.
Retention and Graduation: 69% freshmen return for sophomore year. 33% freshmen graduate within 4 years. 30% grads go on to further study within 1 year. 30% grads pursue arts and sciences degrees. 1% grads pursue business degrees. **Faculty:** Student/faculty ratio 13:1. 65 full-time faculty, 92% hold PhDs, 11% are members of minority groups, 40% are women.

ACADEMICS

Degrees: Bachelor's, master's. **Classes:** Most classes have 10–19 students. Most lab/discussion sessions have 10–19 students. **Majors with Highest Enrollment:** parks, recreation, leisure, and fitness studies, other; psychology. **Special Study Options:** Cross-registration, double major, dual enrollment, English as a Second Language (ESL), exchange student program (domestic), honors program, independent study, internships, liberal arts/career combination, student-designed major, study abroad. Special programs offered to physically disabled students include tape recorders. **Career services:** Career assessment, internships, regional alumni.

FACILITIES

Housing: Coed dorms, men's dorms, women's dorms, apartments for married students, cooperative housing, apartments for single students. 100% of campus accessible to physically disabled. **Special Academic Facilities/Equipment:** 300–acre farm, 700–acre forest, community gardens, archaeological dig on campus, organically managed garden, GIS lab, photomicroscopy lab. **Computers:**

CAMPUS LIFE

Environment: Village. **Activities:** Choral groups, dance, drama/theater, jazz band, literary magazine, music ensembles, musical theater, student government, student newspaper, yearbook. **Organizations:** 25 registered organizations, 5 religious organizations. **Athletics (Intercollegiate):** *Men:* Basketball, cross-country, diving, kayaking, mountain biking, soccer, swimming, ultimate frisbee. *Women:* Basketball, cross-country, diving, kayaking, mountain biking, soccer, swimming, ultimate frisbee. **On-Campus Highlights:** Sage Caf, Pond, Witherspoon/Morse Science Center, Dogwood-a short hike to this great view, Cow Pie Caf. **Environmental Initiatives:** Climate Action Plan to achieve 80% reduction in emissions campus wide by 2020 includes our formal climate change partnership with city of Asheville; quarterly emissions reports to support changes; solar array KW's sold to NC Green Power for sustainability outreach to community to influence reduction in GHGs Curriculum: Environmental studies largest major on campus (since '70s) with 6 concentrations; new inter-disciplinary sustainability curriculum; formal campus commitment to environmental responsibility; Environmental Leadership Center to support work. Built Environment: More than 30% of core campus buildings are either LEED Gold(3), LEED EB platinum(1) or green. 2 more LEED applications in process. Student energy crew conducts energy audits of old buildings to plan efficiency retrofits; energy usage measured monthly for all buildings.

ADMISSIONS

Freshman Academic Profile: Average high school GPA 3.2. 17% in top 10% of high school class, 46% in top 25% of high school class, 76% in top 50% of high school class. 71% from public high schools. SAT Math middle 50% range 500–610. SAT Critical Reading middle 50% range 540–660. SAT Writing middle 50% range 520–630. ACT middle 50% range 23–28. Minimum paper TOEFL 550. **Basis for Candidate Selection:** *Very important factors considered include:* Application essay, rigor of secondary school record, standardized test scores, character/personal qualities, interview, volunteer work, work experience. *Important factors considered include:* Class rank, recommendation(s). *Other factors considered include:* Alumni/ae relation, extracurricular activities, state residency, talent/ability. **Freshman Admission Requirements:** High school diploma is required and GED is accepted. *Academic units required:* 4 English, 3 mathematics, 2 science, (2 science labs), 3 history. *Academic units recommended:* 2 foreign language. **Freshman Admission Statistics:** 919 applied, 76% admitted, 35% enrolled. **Transfer Admission Requirements:** High school transcript, college transcript(s), standardized test scores, minimum college GPA of 3.0 required. Lowest grade transferable C. **General Admission Information:** Early decision application deadline 11/15. Regular application deadline 2/15. Nonfall registration accepted. Admission may be deferred for a maximum of 1. Credit and/or placement offered for CEEB Advanced Placement tests.

COSTS AND FINANCIAL AID

Annual tuition $24,195. Room and board $7,730. Required fees $300. Average book expense $870. **Required Forms and Deadlines:** FAFSA, institution's own financial aid form, state aid form. Priority financial aid filing date 4/1. **Notification of Awards:** Applicants will be notified of awards on a rolling basis beginning 3/2. **Types of Aid:** *Need-based scholarships/grants:* Federal Pell, SEOG, state scholarships/grants, the school's own gift aid. *Loans:* FFEL Subsidized Stafford, FFEL Unsubsidized Stafford, FFEL PLUS, Federal Perkins, college/university loans from institutional funds. *Student Employment:* Highest amount earned per year from on-campus jobs $3,144. Off-campus job opportunities are good. **Financial Aid Statistics:** 52% freshmen, 54% undergrads receive need-based scholarship or grant aid. 14% freshmen, 10% undergrads receive non-need-based scholarship or grant aid. 57% freshmen, 60% undergrads receive need-based self-help aid. 44% undergrads borrow to pay for school. Average cumulative indebtedness $17,533. **Criteria for awarding institutional aid:** *Non-need-based:* Academics, art, leadership, state/district residency.

WARTBURG COLLEGE

100 Wartburg Blvd, PO Box 1003, Waverly, IA 50677-0903
Phone: 319-352-8264 **Financial Aid Phone:** 319-352-8262
E-mail: admissions@wartburg.edu **CEEB Code:** 6926
Fax: 319-352-8579 **Website:** www.wartburg.edu **ACT Code:** 1364

This private school, affiliated with the Lutheran Church, was founded in 1852. It has a 118-acre campus.

RATINGS

Admissions Selectivity Rating: 81 **Fire Safety Rating:** 85 **Green Rating:** 74

STUDENTS AND FACULTY

Enrollment: 1,755. **Student Body:** 52% female, 48% male, 25% out-of-state, 5% international (38 countries represented). Asian 2%, African American 5%, Caucasian 82%, Hispanic 1%.
Retention and Graduation: 82% freshmen return for sophomore year. 61% freshmen graduate within 4 years. 23.4% grads go on to further study within 1 year. 10.8% grads pursue arts and sciences degrees. 0.5% grads pursue law degrees. 1.6% grads pursue business degrees. 6% grads pursue medical degrees. **Faculty:** Student/faculty ratio 12:1. 109 full-time faculty, 84% hold PhDs, 5% are members of minority groups, 48% are women.

ACADEMICS

Degrees: Bachelor's. **Classes:** Most classes have 20–29 students. Most lab/discussion sessions have 20–29 students. **Majors with Highest Enrollment:** Biology/biological sciences; business, management, marketing, and related support services, other; communication studies/speech communication and rhetoric. **Special Study Options:** Accelerated program, double major, dual enrollment, honors program, independent study, internships, student-designed major, study abroad, teacher certification program. **Honors programs:** Scholars Program—features small seminar classes, distinguished speaker series, sophomore-year program of lectures, concerts, and performances, student involvement in designing courses and activities, variety of social and travel opportunities, student-designed senior project **Combined degree programs:** 2-2 nursing, 3-1 occup. therapy, 3-2 phys therapy. Special programs offered to physically disabled students include note-taking services, reader services, tutors. **Career services:** Alumni network

FACILITIES

Housing: Coed dorms, men's dorms, women's dorms, apartments for single students, theme housing, suite-style living. 85% of campus accessible to physically disabled. **Special Academic Facilities/Equipment:** Art gallery, fine arts center, institute for leadership education, planetarium, prairie preserve, state-of-the-art library, center for community engagement, wellness center. **Computers:** 30% of classrooms, 10% of dorms, 100% of libraries, 100% of dining areas, 100% of student union, 10% of common outdoor areas have wireless network access. Students can register for classes online. Administrative functions (other than registration) can be performed online.

CAMPUS LIFE

Environment: Village. **Activities:** Choral groups, concert band, dance, drama/theater, jazz band, literary magazine, music ensembles, musical theater, opera, pep band, radio station, student government, student newspaper, student-run film society, symphony orchestra, television station, yearbook, campus ministries, international student organization. **Organizations:** 90 registered organizations, 12 honor societies, 9 religious organizations. **Athletics (Intercollegiate):** *Men:* Baseball, basketball, cross-country, football, golf, soccer, tennis, track/field (outdoor), track/field (indoor), wrestling. *Women:* Basketball, cross-country, golf, soccer, softball, tennis, track/field (outdoor), track/field (indoor), volleyball. **On-Campus Highlights:** Konditorei Coffee Shop/Vogel Library, Sports and Wellness Center (new 2007), Saemann Student Center (renovated 2004), Walston-Hoover Stadium (new 2001), Old Main (on National Historic Registry), $31 million Sports and Wellness Center. **Environmental Initiatives:** LEED requirements for new Sports and Wellness Center. Partnership with Waverly Light and Power on wind generation to offset-carbon-based energy in new Sports and Wellness Center. Trayless dining; use of front load washers to reduce water and energy use.

ADMISSIONS

Freshman Academic Profile: Average high school GPA 3.48. 28% in top 10% of high school class, 56% in top 25% of high school class, 84% in top 50% of high school class. SAT Math middle 50% range 470–610. SAT Critical Reading middle 50% range 420–600. SAT Writing middle 50% range 410–570. ACT middle 50% range 21–27. Minimum paper TOEFL 480. Minimum computer TOEFL 157. Minimum web-based TOEFL 55. **Basis for Candidate Selection:** *Very important factors considered include:* Class rank, academic GPA, recommendation(s), rigor of secondary school record, standardized test scores. *Important factors considered include:* Character/personal qualities, interview. *Other factors considered include:* Application essay, extracurricular activities, level of applicant's interest, racial/ethnic status, talent/ability, volunteer work, work experience. **Freshman Admission Requirements:** High school diploma is required and GED is accepted. *Academic units recommended:* 4 English, 3 mathematics, 3 science, 2 foreign language, 2 social studies, 1 computer science. **Freshman Admission Statistics:** 2,278 applied, 73% admitted, 29% enrolled. **Transfer Admission Requirements:** High school transcript, college transcript(s), standardized test scores, statement of good standing from prior institution(s). Minimum college GPA of 2.0 required. Lowest grade transferable C–. **General Admission Information:** Notification on a rolling basis, beginning on or about 7/1. Nonfall registration accepted. Admission may be deferred for a maximum of 1 year. Credit and/or placement offered for CEEB Advanced Placement tests.

COSTS AND FINANCIAL AID

Required Forms and Deadlines: FAFSA. Priority financial aid filing date 3/1. **Notification of Awards:** Applicants will be notified of awards on a rolling basis beginning 3/21. **Types of Aid:** *Need-based scholarships/grants:* Federal Pell, SEOG, state scholarships/grants, private scholarships, the school's own gift aid. *Loans:* FFEL Subsidized Stafford, FFEL Unsubsidized Stafford, FFEL PLUS, Federal Perkins, Alternative. *Student Employment:* Federal Work-Study Program available. Institutional employment available. Highest amount earned per year from on-campus jobs $8,435. Off-campus job opportunities are good. **Financial Aid Statistics:** 77% freshmen, 77% undergrads receive need-based scholarship or grant aid. 15% freshmen, 11% undergrads receive non-need-based scholarship or grant aid. 61% freshmen, 64% undergrads receive need-based self-help aid. 99% freshmen, 98% undergrads receive any aid. 81% undergrads borrow to pay for school. Average cumulative indebtedness $27,225. **Criteria for awarding institutional aid:** *Non-need-based:* Academics, alumni affiliation, leadership, music/drama, religious affiliation.

WASHBURN UNIVERSITY

1700 SW College Ave, MO 114, Topeka, KS 66621
Phone: 785-670-1030
E-mail: admissions@washburn.edu
Fax: 785-670-1113 **Website:** www.washburn.edu

This is a public school.

RATINGS
Admissions Selectivity Rating: 69   **Fire Safety Rating:** 60*   **Green Rating:** 60*

STUDENTS AND FACULTY
Enrollment: 5,396. **Student Body:** 61% female, 39% male, 7% out-of-state. **Retention and Graduation:** 63% freshmen return for sophomore year. **Faculty:** Student/faculty ratio 15:1. 265 full-time faculty, 83% hold PhDs, 11% are members of minority groups, 50% are women.

ACADEMICS
Degrees: Associate, bachelor's, certificate, first professional, first professional certificate, master's, post-bachelor's certificate. **Classes:** Most classes have 20–29 students. Most lab/discussion sessions have 10–19 students. **Special Study Options:** Cooperative education program, cross-registration, distance learning, double major, dual enrollment, English as a Second Language (ESL), honors program, independent study, internships, liberal arts/career combination, student-designed major, study abroad, teacher certification program, Transformational Experience.

FACILITIES
Housing: Coed dorms, fraternity/sorority housing, apartments for single students, wellness housing, pecial interest housing.

CAMPUS LIFE
Activities: Choral groups, concert band, dance, drama/theater, jazz band, literary magazine, marching band, music ensembles, musical theater, pep band, student government, student newspaper, student-run film society, symphony orchestra, television station, yearbook, campus ministries, international student organization, Model UN.

ADMISSIONS
Freshman Academic Profile: Average high school GPA 3.16. 12% in top 10% of high school class, 32% in top 25% of high school class, 62% in top 50% of high school class. 96% from public high schools. ACT middle 50% range 19–25. Minimum paper TOEFL 450. Minimum computer TOEFL 133. **Basis for Candidate Selection:** *Very important factors considered include:* Academic GPA, rigor of secondary school record, standardized test scores. **Freshman Admission Requirements:** High school diploma is required and GED is accepted. *Academic units recommended:* 4 English, 3 mathematics, 3 science, 2 foreign language, 3 social studies, 1 history, 1 computer science. **Freshman Admission Statistics:** 1,573 applied, 100% admitted, 53% enrolled. **Transfer Admission Requirements:** College transcript(s), statement of good standing from prior institution(s). Minimum college GPA of 2.0 required. Lowest grade transferable 1. **General Admission Information:** Application fee $20. Regular application deadline 8/1. Notification on a rolling basis, beginning on or about 9/1. Nonfall registration accepted. Credit and/or placement offered for CEEB Advanced Placement tests.

COSTS AND FINANCIAL AID
Annual in-state tuition $5,910. Annual out-of-state tuition $13,410. Room and board $5,602. Required fees $86. Average book expense $1,400. **Required Forms and Deadlines:** FAFSA, Admission/Scholarship Application. Priority financial aid filing date 2/15. **Notification of Awards:** Applicants will be notified of awards on a rolling basis beginning 3/15. **Types of Aid:** *Need-based scholarships/grants:* Federal Pell, SEOG, state scholarships/grants, private scholarships, the school's own gift aid. *Loans:* Direct Subsidized Stafford, Direct Unsubsidized Stafford, Direct PLUS, Federal Perkins, college/university loans from institutional funds, Alternative Loans. **Financial Aid Statistics:** 31% freshmen, 32% undergrads receive need-based scholarship or grant aid. 29% freshmen, 26% undergrads receive non-need-based scholarship or grant aid. 53% freshmen, 55% undergrads receive need-based self-help aid. 4% freshmen, 4% undergrads receive athletic scholarships. 59% undergrads borrow to pay for school. Average cumulative indebtedness $20,562. **Criteria for awarding institutional aid:** *Non-need-based:* Academics, alumni affiliation, art, athletics, job skills, leadership, minority status, music/drama, religious affiliation, state/district residency.

WASHINGTON & JEFFERSON COLLEGE

60 South Lincoln Street, Washington, PA 15301
Phone: 724-223-6025 **Financial Aid Phone:** 724-223-6019
E-mail: admission@washjeff.edu **CEEB Code:** 2967
Fax: 724-223-6534 **Website:** www.washjeff.edu **ACT Code:** 3746

This private school was founded in 1781. It has a 60-acre campus.

RATINGS
Admissions Selectivity Rating: 92   **Fire Safety Rating:** 85   **Green Rating:** 82

STUDENTS AND FACULTY
Enrollment: 1,479. **Student Body:** 47% female, 53% male, 24% out-of-state, (11 countries represented). Asian 1%, African American 3%, Caucasian 84%, Hispanic 1%.
Retention and Graduation: 86% freshmen return for sophomore year. 69% freshmen graduate within 4 years. 37% grads go on to further study within 1 year. 15% grads pursue arts and sciences degrees. 12% grads pursue law degrees. 1% grads pursue business degrees. 11% grads pursue medical degrees. **Faculty:** Student/faculty ratio 12:1. 116 full-time faculty, 91% hold PhDs, 13% are members of minority groups, 41% are women.

ACADEMICS
Degrees: Bachelor's. **Classes:** Most classes have 10–19 students. Most lab/discussion sessions have 10–19 students. **Majors with Highest Enrollment:** accounting; business/commerce; psychology. **Special Study Options:** Accelerated program, double major, dual enrollment, honors program, independent study, internships, student-designed major, study abroad, teacher certification program, Advanced placement credit. **Combined degree programs:** BA/MD, BA/JD, BA/MEng, 3/3 law, 3/4 podiatry, 3/4 optometry. Special programs offered to physically disabled students include tutors. **Career services:** Alumni network, alumni services, career/job search classes, career assessment, internships, regional alumni. **Career services highlights include:** While we are proud of many programs, we especially appreciate the support of the alumni of the college, particularly with hosting interns. Many of these experiences result in full time employment.

FACILITIES
Housing: Coed dorms, special housing for disabled students, men's dorms, women's dorms, fraternity/sorority housing, apartments for single students, wellness housing, theme housing, on-campus suites. 48% of campus accessible to physically disabled. **Special Academic Facilities/Equipment:** Microplate Reader, Cell Culture Labs, Isolator Lab, X-Ray Diffraction Unit, Neuropsychology Lab, Atomic Absorption Unit, Nuclear Magnetic Resonance (NMR) Lab, Refrigerated Centrifuge, Global Learning Unit, Language Lab, Spectrometers, Laser Scanning Confocal Microscope Facility, Abernathy Field Station. **Computers:** 100% of classrooms, 100% of dorms, 100% of libraries, 100% of dining areas, 100% of student union, 95% of common outdoor areas have wireless network access. Students can register for classes online. Administrative functions (other than registration) can be performed online.

CAMPUS LIFE
Environment: Village. **Activities:** Choral groups, concert band, dance, drama/theater, jazz band, literary magazine, music ensembles, musical theater, pep band, radio station, student government, student newspaper, student-run film society, symphony orchestra, yearbook, campus ministries, international student organization, Model UN. **Organizations:** 94 registered organizations, 21 honor societies, 4 religious organizations. 6 fraternities, 4 sororities. **Athletics (Intercollegiate):** *Men:* Baseball, basketball, cheerleading, cross-country, diving, football, golf, lacrosse, soccer, swimming, tennis, track/field (outdoor), track/field (indoor), water polo, wrestling. *Women:* Basketball, cheerleading, cross-country, diving, field hockey, golf, lacrosse, soccer, softball, swimming, tennis, track/field (outdoor), track/field (indoor), volleyball, water polo. **On-Campus Highlights:** The Hub (Student Center), Swanson Wellness Center, Monticellos Coffee House, Burnett (for meetings/studying), Ski Lodge/Barista in the Commons. **Environmental Initiatives:** President's Climate Commitment Silver LEED Certification for new Science building Food service sustainability initiatives. Food service at W&J purchases 20% of their products locally, recycles fryer grease into bio-diesel fuel and uses it in their delivery trucks, is in the process of becoming trayless, recycles all of their cardboard, and uses bio-degradable "to go" packaging, recycled paper, napkins made from recycled materials, and paper cups.

ADMISSIONS
Freshman Academic Profile: Average high school GPA 3.34. 38% in top 10% of high school class, 71% in top 25% of high school class, 94% in top 50% of high school class. 82% from public high schools. SAT Math middle 50% range 520–620. SAT Critical Reading middle 50% range 510–610. ACT middle 50% range 22–28. Minimum paper TOEFL 567. Minimum computer TOEFL 227. Minimum web-based TOEFL 86. **Basis for Candidate Selection:** *Very important factors considered include:* Class rank, application essay, academic GPA, recommendation(s), rigor of secondary school record, character/personal qualities, interview. *Important factors considered include:* Standardized test scores, extracurricular activities. *Other factors considered include:* Alumni/ae relation, geographical residence, level of applicant's interest, racial/ethnic status, state residency, talent/ability, volunteer work, work experience. **Freshman Admission Requirements:** High school diploma is required and GED is accepted. *Academic units required:* 3 English, 3 mathematics, 2 foreign language, 1 history, 6 Six or more academic courses from English, Mathematics, Foreign Language, History (Social or Natural **Freshman Admission Statistics:** 6,658 applied, 42% admitted, 14% enrolled. **Transfer Admission Requirements:** High school transcript, college transcript(s), essay or personal statement, standardized test scores, statement of good standing from prior institution(s). Minimum college GPA of 2.50 required. Lowest grade transferable C. **General Admission Information:** Application fee $25. Early decision application deadline 12/1. Regular application deadline 3/1. Notification on a rolling basis, beginning on or about 10/1. Nonfall registration accepted. Admission may be deferred for a maximum of 1 Year. Credit and/or placement offered for CEEB Advanced Placement tests.

COSTS AND FINANCIAL AID
Average book expense $800. **Required Forms and Deadlines:** FAFSA. Priority financial aid filing date 2/15. **Notification of Awards:** Applicants will be notified of awards on a rolling basis beginning 3/1. **Types of Aid:** *Need-based scholarships/grants:* Federal Pell, SEOG, state scholarships/grants, private scholarships, the school's own gift aid, ACG and SMART Grants. *Loans:* FFEL Subsidized Stafford, FFEL Unsubsidized Stafford, FFEL PLUS, Federal Perkins, college/university loans from institutional funds. *Student Employment:* Federal Work-Study Program available. Institutional employment available. Highest amount earned per year from on-campus jobs $3,440. Off-campus job opportunities are good. **Financial Aid Statistics:** 65% freshmen, 65% undergrads receive need-based scholarship or grant aid. 71% freshmen, 65% undergrads receive non-need-based scholarship or grant aid. 69% freshmen, 68% undergrads receive need-based self-help aid. 100% freshmen, 98% undergrads receive any aid. 75% undergrads borrow to pay for school. Average cumulative indebtedness $23. **Criteria for awarding institutional aid:** *Non-need-based:* Academics, alumni affiliation.

WASHINGTON AND LEE UNIVERSITY

Letcher Avenue, Lexington, VA 24450-0303
Phone: 540-458-8710
E-mail: admissions@wlu.edu **CEEB Code:** 5887
Fax: 540-458-8062 **Website:** www2.wlu.edu **ACT Code:** 4430

This private school was founded in 1749. It has a 322-acre campus.

RATINGS
Admissions Selectivity Rating: 97   **Fire Safety Rating:** 60*   **Green Rating:** 60*

STUDENTS AND FACULTY
Enrollment: 1,747. **Student Body:** 49% female, 51% male, 85% out-of-state, 4% international (47 countries represented). Asian 3%, African American 4%, Caucasian 86%, Hispanic 1%.
Retention and Graduation: 94% freshmen return for sophomore year. 84% freshmen graduate within 4 years. 24% grads go on to further study within 1 year. 6% grads pursue arts and sciences degrees. 9% grads pursue law degrees. 1% grads pursue business degrees. 5% grads pursue medical degrees. **Faculty:** Student/faculty ratio 10:1. 215 full-time faculty, 94% hold PhDs, 7% are members of minority groups, 30% are women.

ACADEMICS
Degrees: Bachelor's, first professional, master's. **Classes:** Most classes have 10–19 students. Most lab/discussion sessions have fewer than 10 students. **Majors with Highest Enrollment:** Business/commerce; economics; history. **Special Study Options:** Double major, exchange student program (domestic), honors program, independent study, internships, liberal arts/career combination, student-designed major, study abroad, teacher certification program. **Honors programs:** University Scholars, Bonner Scholars. **Combined degree programs:** BA/JD, 3-3 JD with Washington and Lee School of Law. **Career**

services: Alumni network, career/job search classes, career assessment, internships, regional alumni.

FACILITIES

Housing: Coed dorms, special housing for international students, fraternity/sorority housing, apartments for single students, Outing Club House, Spanish House, Chavis House. 80% of campus accessible to physically disabled. **Special Academic Facilities/Equipment:** History and porcelain museums performing arts center communications labs nuclear science lab scanning electron microscope **Computers:** Students can register for classes online. Administrative functions (other than registration) can be performed online.

CAMPUS LIFE

Environment: Village. **Activities:** Choral groups, dance, drama/theater, jazz band, literary magazine, music ensembles, radio station, student government, student newspaper, student-run film society, symphony orchestra, television station, yearbook. **Organizations:** 90 registered organizations, 5 honor societies, 11 religious organizations. 14 fraternities, 5 sororities. **Athletics (Intercollegiate): Men:** Baseball, basketball, cross-country, equestrian sports, football, golf, lacrosse, soccer, swimming, tennis, track/field (outdoor), track/field (indoor), wrestling. **Women:** Basketball, cheerleading, cross-country, equestrian sports, field hockey, lacrosse, soccer, swimming, tennis, track/field (outdoor), track/field (indoor), volleyball. **On-Campus Highlights:** Lee Chapel, Elrod University Commons, Lenfest Center for the Arts, Doremus Fitness Center, Reeves Center and Watson Pavillion.

ADMISSIONS

Freshman Academic Profile: 81% in top 10% of high school class, 98% in top 25% of high school class, 100% in top 50% of high school class. SAT Math middle 50% range 650–730. SAT Critical Reading middle 50% range 660–730. ACT middle 50% range 28–31. **Basis for Candidate Selection:** *Very important factors considered include:* Class rank, rigor of secondary school record, standardized test scores, character/personal qualities, extracurricular activities. *Important factors considered include:* Recommendation(s), interview. *Other factors considered include:* Application essay, alumni/ae relation, geographical residence, racial/ethnic status, state residency, talent/ability, volunteer work, work experience. **Freshman Admission Requirements:** High school diploma or equivalent is not required. *Academic units required:* 4 English, 3 mathematics, 1 science, (1 science labs), 3 foreign language, 1 social studies, 1 history, 4 academic electives. *Academic units recommended:* 4 mathematics, 3 science, 4 foreign language, 2 history. **Freshman Admission Statistics:** 4,215 applied, 27% admitted, 39% enrolled. **Transfer Admission Requirements:** High school transcript, college transcript(s), essay or personal statement, standardized test scores, statement of good standing from prior institution(s). Minimum college GPA of 2.0 required. Lowest grade transferable C. **General Admission Information:** Application fee $50. Early decision application deadline 11/15. Regular application deadline 1/15. Regular notification 4/1. Nonfall registration not accepted. Admission may be deferred for a maximum of 1 year. Credit and/or placement offered for CEEB Advanced Placement tests.

COSTS AND FINANCIAL AID

Annual tuition $27,960. Room and board $7,225. Required fees $675. Average book expense $1,500. **Required Forms and Deadlines:** FAFSA, CSS/Financial Aid PROFILE, noncustodial PROFILE, business/farm supplement. Financial aid filing deadline 2/9. **Notification of Awards:** Applicants will be notified of awards on or about 4/6. **Types of Aid:** *Need-based scholarships/grants:* Federal Pell, SEOG, state scholarships/grants, private scholarships, the school's own gift aid. *Loans:* FFEL Subsidized Stafford, FFEL Unsubsidized Stafford, FFEL PLUS, Federal Perkins, college/university loans from institutional funds. *Student Employment:* Federal Work-Study Program available. Institutional employment available. Off-campus job opportunities are fair. **Financial Aid Statistics:** 31% freshmen, 27% undergrads receive need-based scholarship or grant aid. 10% freshmen, 10% undergrads receive non-need-based scholarship or grant aid. 13% freshmen, 14% undergrads receive need-based self-help aid. 25% undergrads borrow to pay for school. Average cumulative indebtedness $17,105. **Criteria for awarding institutional aid:** *Non-need-based:* Academics.

WASHINGTON BIBLE COLLEGE

6511 Princess Garden Parkway, Lanham, MD 20706-3599
Phone: 301-552-1400
E-mail: admissions@bible.edu
Fax: 301-552-2775 **Website:** www.bible.edu **ACT Code:** 1462

This private school was founded in 1938. It has a 63-acre campus.

RATINGS

Admissions Selectivity Rating: 60*   **Fire Safety Rating:** 60*   **Green Rating:** 60*

STUDENTS AND FACULTY

Enrollment: 352. **Student Body:** 42% female, 58% male.
Retention and Graduation: 10% freshmen graduate within 4 years. **Faculty:** 70% of classes are taught by teaching assistants.

ACADEMICS

Degrees: Associate, bachelor's, certificate. **Classes: Special Study Options:** English as a Second Language (ESL), independent study, internships. **Career services:** Aumni services.

FACILITIES

Housing: Men's dorms, women's dorms, apartments for married students 60% of campus accessible to physically disabled.

CAMPUS LIFE

Environment: Village. **Activities:** Choral groups, music ensembles, student government, yearbook. **Organizations:** 1 honor societies. **Athletics (Intercollegiate): Men:** Basketball, soccer. **Women:** Basketball, cheerleading, volleyball.

ADMISSIONS

Freshman Academic Profile: Minimum paper TOEFL 550. **Basis for Candidate Selection:** *Very important factors considered include:* Application essay, recommendation(s), religious affiliation/commitment. *Important factors considered include:* Class rank, rigor of secondary school record, standardized test scores, character/personal qualities. *Other factors considered include:* Alumni/ae relation, extracurricular activities, interview, talent/ability, volunteer work. **Freshman Admission Requirements:** High school diploma is required and GED is accepted. *Academic units recommended:* 4 English, 2 mathematics, 2 science, 2 social studies, 5 academic electives. **Freshman Admission Statistics:** 56 applied, 29% admitted, 263% enrolled. **Transfer Admission Requirements:** College transcript(s), essay or personal statement, statement of good standing from prior institution(s). Minimum college GPA of 2.0 required. Lowest grade transferable C. **General Admission Information:** Application fee $25. Regular application deadline 8/4. Nonfall registration accepted. Admission may be deferred for a maximum of 36.

COSTS AND FINANCIAL AID

Annual tuition $10,140. Room and board $4,180. Required fees $100. Average book expense $300. **Required Forms and Deadlines:** FAFSA, institution's own financial aid formV. Priority financial aid filing date 6/1. **Notification of Awards:** Applicants will be notified of awards on a rolling basis beginning 1/30. **Types of Aid:** *Need-based scholarships/grants:* Federal Pell, SEOG, state scholarships/grants, private scholarships, the school's own gift aid. *Loans:* FFEL Subsidized Stafford, FFEL Unsubsidized Stafford, FFEL PLUS. *Student Employment:* Federal Work-Study Program available. Institutional employment available. Highest amount earned per year from on-campus jobs $3,000. Off-campus job opportunities are excellent. **Financial Aid Statistics:** 20% freshmen, 13% undergrads receive need-based scholarship or grant aid. 8% freshmen, 4% undergrads receive non-need-based scholarship or grant aid. 32% freshmen, 66% undergrads receive need-based self-help aid. 20% undergrads borrow to pay for school. Average cumulative indebtedness $13,000. **Criteria for awarding institutional aid:** *Non-need-based:* Academics, leadership, minority status, music/drama.

WASHINGTON COLLEGE

300 Washington Avenue, Chestertown, MD 21620
Phone: 410-778-7700 **Financial Aid Phone:** 410-778-7214
E-mail: adm.off@washcoll.edu **CEEB Code:** 5888
Fax: 410-778-7287 **Website:** www.washcoll.edu **ACT Code:** 1754

This private school was founded in 1782. It has a 144-acre campus.

RATINGS

Admissions Selectivity Rating: 86   **Fire Safety Rating:** 95   **Green Rating:** 60*

STUDENTS AND FACULTY

Enrollment: 1,268. **Student Body:** 59% female, 41% male, 48% out-of-state, 2% international (25 countries represented). Asian 2%, African American 5%, Caucasian 86%, Hispanic 1%.
Retention and Graduation: 84% freshmen return for sophomore year. 76% freshmen graduate within 4 years. 50% grads go on to further study within 1 year. 12% grads pursue arts and sciences degrees. 4% grads pursue law degrees.

8% grads pursue business degrees. 3% grads pursue medical degrees. **Faculty:** Student/faculty ratio 11.9:1. 87 full-time faculty, 93% hold PhDs, 13% are members of minority groups, 37% are women.

ACADEMICS

Degrees: Bachelor's, master's. **Classes:** Most classes have 10–19 students. Most lab/discussion sessions have fewer than 10 students. **Majors with Highest Enrollment:** Business administration and management; English language and literature; psychology. **Special Study Options:** Cross-registration, double major, dual enrollment, exchange student program (domestic), honors program, independent study, internships, liberal arts/career combination, student-designed major, study abroad, teacher certification program. **Honors programs:** The Douglass Cater Society of Junior Fellows is the College's flagship academic enrichment program—one that rewards creativity, initiative and intellectual curiosity with competitive grants to support self-directed undergraduate research and scholarship anywhere in the world. The intent is to bring together the best and brightest in what founder Douglass Cater called "a companionship of learning." **Combined degree programs:** 3+2 nursing. **Career services:** Alumni network, alumni services, career assessment, internships, regional alumni. **Career services highlights include:** The Washington Center has over 35,000 alumni, many of whom are leaders in numerous professions and nations around the world. Based in the nation's capitol it offers exceptional experiential learning opportunities in various government and public service sectors.

FACILITIES

Housing: Coed dorms, special housing for disabled students, men's dorms, special housing for international students, women's dorms, fraternity/sorority housing, wellness housing, theme housing. 90% of campus accessible to physically disabled. **Special Academic Facilities/Equipment:** Language lab, computer classroom, C.V. Starr Center for the Study of the American Experience, The Center for the Environment and Society, O'Neil Literary House. **Computers:** Administrative functions (other than registration) can be performed online.

CAMPUS LIFE

Environment: Rural. **Activities:** Choral groups, concert band, dance, drama/theater, jazz band, literary magazine, music ensembles, radio station, student government, student newspaper, yearbook, campus ministries, international student organization, Model UN. **Organizations:** 50 registered organizations, 13 honor societies, 4 religious organizations. 4 fraternities, 3 sororities. **Athletics (Intercollegiate):** *Men:* Baseball, basketball, crew/rowing, lacrosse, sailing, soccer, swimming, tennis. *Women:* Basketball, crew/rowing, field hockey, lacrosse, sailing, soccer, softball, swimming, tennis, volleyball. **On-Campus Highlights:** Miller Library, Johnson Lifetime Fitness Center, Gibson Center for the Arts, O'Neill Literary House, Hodson Commons Student Center, Hynson Pavillion and Washington College Boathouse providing water access and kayaks, sail boats, pantoons, canoes, motor boats, wakeboarding boats, etc. **Environmental Initiatives:** George Goes Green (G3) is Washington College's initiative for stewardship and sustainability. Situated on Maryland's Eastern Shore, the College is surrounded by the coastal and inland waters of the Chesapeake Bay, which informs our sense of history, our sense of self, and our sense of place. Our benefactor George Washington promoted sustainable economic cycles by advocating compost as a method to amend damaged soils. Today, Washington College is nationally renowned for promoting sustainability. Green at a Glance: Chesapeake Semester composting recycling environmentally-friendly products local foods native plant landscaping green facilities Recycling is now available in every building on campus. On campus, we recycle plastic and glass bottles, aluminum and tin cans, cardboard, and most types of paper. In the academic buildings, bottles and cans can be recycled in the blue bins, while paper can be recycled in the tall green bins or the locked blue paper bins where they are available. Student Environmental Alliance: The Washington College Student Environmental Alliance (SEA) is a student-run organization on campus. It promotes sustainability on campus and within the community, and works with various outside organizations to help promote sustainable practices. SEA welcomes all majors and disciplines to join at weekly meetings and events. SEA primarily focuses on: Promoting awareness of local, national, and international environmental issues and concerns Environmental education Keeping a record of accomplishments to provide for future SEA generations Providing a group that fosters personal environmental well-being Positively impacting the Washington College, Chestertown, and outside communities through its environmental initiatives

ADMISSIONS

Freshman Academic Profile: Average high school GPA 3.44. 30% in top 10% of high school class, 71% in top 25% of high school class, 92% in top 50% of high school class. 67% from public high schools. SAT Math middle 50% range 510–610. SAT Critical Reading middle 50% range 520–620. SAT Writing middle 50% range 520–620. ACT middle 50% range 22–29. **Basis for Candidate Selection:** *Very important factors considered include:* Academic GPA, rigor of secondary school record, interview. *Important factors considered include:* Class rank, standardized test scores, level of applicant's interest, work experience. *Other factors considered include:* Application essay, recommendation(s),

alumni/ae relation, character/personal qualities, extracurricular activities, first generation, geographical residence, racial/ethnic status, state residency, talent/ability, volunteer work. **Freshman Admission Requirements:** High school diploma is required and GED is accepted. *Academic units required:* 4 English, 3 mathematics, 3 science, (2 science labs), 2 foreign language, 2 social studies, 2 history. *Academic units recommended:* 4 English, 4 mathematics, 4 science, (3 science labs), 4 foreign language, 4 social studies. **Freshman Admission Statistics:** 4,498 applied, 72% admitted, 12% enrolled. **Transfer Admission Requirements:** High school transcript, college transcript(s), essay or personal statement, statement of good standing from prior institution(s). **General Admission Information:** Application fee $55. Early decision application deadline 11/1. Regular application deadline 3/1. Notification on a rolling basis, beginning on or about 10/15. Nonfall registration accepted. Admission may be deferred for a maximum of 0ne year. Credit and/or placement offered for CEEB Advanced Placement tests.

COSTS AND FINANCIAL AID

Annual tuition $34,690. Room and board $7,460. Required fees $660. Average book expense $1,250. **Required Forms and Deadlines:** FAFSA, institution's own financial aid form. Priority financial aid filing date 2/15. **Notification of Awards:** Applicants will be notified of awards on a rolling basis beginning 2/15. **Types of Aid:** *Need-based scholarships/grants:* Federal Pell, SEOG, state scholarships/grants, private scholarships, the school's own gift aid. *Loans:* FFEL Subsidized Stafford, FFEL Unsubsidized Stafford, FFEL PLUS, Federal Perkins. *Student Employment:* Federal Work-Study Program available. Institutional employment available. Highest amount earned per year from on-campus jobs $2,000. Off-campus job opportunities are good. **Financial Aid Statistics:** 57% freshmen, 53% undergrads receive need-based scholarship or grant aid. 7% freshmen, 7% undergrads receive non-need-based scholarship or grant aid. 50% freshmen, 47% undergrads receive need-based self-help aid. 88% freshmen, 82% undergrads receive any aid. 58% undergrads borrow to pay for school. Average cumulative indebtedness $28,727. **Criteria for awarding institutional aid:** *Non-need-based:* Academics

See page 1318.

WASHINGTON STATE UNIVERSITY

PO Box 641067, Pullman, WA 99164-1067
Phone: 509-335-5586 **Financial Aid Phone:** 509-335-9711
E-mail: admiss2@wsu.edu **CEEB Code:** 4705
Fax: 509-335-4902 **Website:** www.wsu.edu **ACT Code:** 4482

This public school was founded in 1890. It has a 1745-acre campus.

RATINGS

Admissions Selectivity Rating: 83   **Fire Safety Rating:** 76   **Green Rating:** 88

STUDENTS AND FACULTY

Enrollment: 21,312. **Student Body:** 52% female, 48% male, 8% out-of-state, 3% international (92 countries represented). Asian 5%, African American 2%, Caucasian 73%, Hispanic 7%, Native American 1%.
Retention and Graduation: 84% freshmen return for sophomore year. 40% freshmen graduate within 4 years. 23% grads go on to further study within 1 year. **Faculty:** Student/faculty ratio 15:1. 1151 full-time faculty, 90% hold PhDs, 14% are members of minority groups, 39% are women. 8.1% of classes are taught by teaching assistants.

ACADEMICS

Degrees: Bachelor's, certificate, master's, post-bachelor's certificate, post-master's certificate. **Classes:** Most classes have 20–29 students. **Majors with Highest Enrollment:** Business administration and management; communication, journalism, and related programs, other; social sciences. **Special Study Options:** Accelerated program, cooperative education program, cross-registration, distance learning, double major, dual enrollment, English as a Second Language (ESL), exchange student program (domestic), external degree program, honors program, independent study, internships, liberal arts/career combination, student-designed major, study abroad, teacher certification program. **Honors programs:** Now in its fiftieth year, the Honors College is one of the oldest and most highly regarded public university honors colleges in the country. It attracts top students in all majors from throughout the United States and around the world. The Honors College curriculum emphasizes global awareness and international impact. It immerses students in the study of international issues, builds their proficiency in a second language, and encourages them to study abroad. Instead of lecturing, professors teach courses interactively, inspiring discussions among students. Honors students conduct research as undergraduates, exploring an academic question of importance to them, documenting their analysis and conclusions, and orally presenting their work to faculty. The Honors College deepens students' intellectual curiosity and builds a lifelong love of learning, as well as skills in critical thinking, writing, public presentation, and information literacy. Graduates emerge with the tools required to become leaders in their fields. Special programs offered to physically disabled students include note-taking services, reader services, tape recorders, tutors. **Career services:** Alumni network, alumni services, career/job search classes, career assessment, internships. **Career services highlights include:** Experiential Learning opportunities and Internships. The Internship Program at The Center for Advising and Career Development provides comprehensive career counseling and services to help students integrate educational experiences with internships in the government, business, industry and non-profit sectors. The program is free for participants. The program is also a resource to WSU faculty, staff and employers. It provides faculty/staff assistance regarding internship concerns and issues. The program assists employers with creating internship programs, recruiting for interns, and connecting with faculty/staff and students. On average, 1600 students participate in internships per academic year.

FACILITIES

Housing: Coed dorms, special housing for disabled students, men's dorms, special housing for international students, women's dorms, fraternity/sorority housing, apartments for married students, apartments for single students, wellness housing, theme housingfreshman focus-living/learning communities. 90% of campus accessible to physically disabled. **Special Academic Facilities/Equipment:** Anthropology museum; arboretum; art museum; audio labs; bear research center; beef center; behavioral lab; cadaver anatomy laboratory; child development laboratory; composite materials and engineering center; creamery; culinary lab and teaching kitchen; dairy center; ecological reserve; electronic piano/music computer lab; electronic trading room; engineering and teaching research laboratory; feed preparation laboratory; food sensory evaluation laboratory; geological collections; greenhouses; historic textiles and costume collection; horticultural orchard and organic farm; entomological collection; natural history museum; observatory; oil and gas processing laboratory; planetarium; herbarium and mycological herbarium; soil monolith collection; veterinary anatomy teaching museum; laboratory for atmospheric research; laboratory for biotechnology and bioanalysis; electron microscopy center; environmental research center; geoanalytical laboratory; music listening library; music recording studio; nuclear radiation center; planetarium; public and student-run television stations; student-run radio stations; social and economic sciences research center; state of Washington water research center; center for spectroscopy; speech and hearing clinic; center for teaching, learning and technology; TV production studios and editing suites; vet teaching hospital; vertebrate zoology museum **Computers:** 100% of classrooms, 100% of dorms, 100% of libraries, 100% of dining areas, 100% of student union, 25% of common outdoor areas have wireless network access. Students can register for classes online. Administrative functions (other than registration) can be performed online.

CAMPUS LIFE

Environment: Town. **Activities:** Choral groups, concert band, dance, drama/theater, jazz band, literary magazine, marching band, music ensembles, musical theater, opera, pep band, radio station, student government, student newspaper, student-run film society, symphony orchestra, television station, yearbook, campus ministries, international student organization, Model UN. **Organizations:** 300 registered organizations, 36 honor societies, 19 religious organizations. 26 fraternities, 13 sororities. **Athletics (Intercollegiate):** *Men:* Baseball, basketball, cross-country, football, golf, track/field (outdoor). *Women:* Basketball, crew/rowing, cross-country, golf, soccer, swimming, tennis, track/field (outdoor), volleyball. **On-Campus Highlights:** Compton Union Building (CUB), Terrell Friendship Mall, Student Recreation Center, Beasley Performing Arts Coliseum, Martin Stadium, The newly renovated CUB stands at the heart of student leadership, engagement, and culture on campus. It is home to offices for student government and many student services. The building houses a selection of food vendors, the campus bookstore, banks, and a post office. Both wired and wireless Internet services serve students and faculty. Ballrooms, meeting rooms, and a surround-sound auditorium host a variety of events. A passage through the CUB gives students 24-hour access to the library. The whole student body comes together on Glenn Terrell Friendship Mall. Located at the heart of campus, the Mall is where culture, ideas, and lively dialogue are exchanged daily. It is the site of many outdoor events, including frequent live performances by student musicians. Students gather here as they walk to and from the library, the Compton Union Building (student union), and academic buildings, often staking out favorite spots to talk, relax, study, or catch a bite to eat. The 160,000–square-foot Student Recreation Center features the largest student weight and cardio center in the country, basketball and volleyball courts, indoor soccer, a four-lane indoor track, racquetball and squash courts, roller hockey, badminton, and much more. Swimmers enjoy the five-lane lap pool, leisure pool, and 53-person spa. Big crowds pack Beasley Performing Arts Coliseum for PaC–10 Cougar men's and women's basketball games and for big name entertainment for Dad's and Mom's Weekends. WSU students turn out for entertainment ranging from pop music concerts to ballet to wresting. Located in the center of campus, Martin Stadium is home to the PaC–10 Cougars. 2008 stadium rénovations include a north-side concourse, additional concession and restroom areas, and a state-of-the-art scoreboard. Still to come are the addition of more seats and premium seating, slated for completion by fall of 2012. **Environmental Initiatives:** Sustainability & Environment Committee, established by the President of WSU. Meets monthly and has campus-wide representation. Greenhouse Gas Inventory for the Pullman campus Ongoing Environmental Management System Implementation

ADMISSIONS

Freshman Academic Profile: Average high school GPA 3.42. 30% in top 10% of high school class, 55% in top 25% of high school class, 86% in top 50% of high school class. 99% from public high schools. SAT Math middle 50% range 490–610. SAT Critical Reading middle 50% range 480–590. SAT Writing middle 50% range 460–570. ACT middle 50% range 21-26. Minimum paper TOEFL 520. Minimum web-based TOEFL 68. **Basis for Candidate Selection:** *Very important factors considered include:* Academic GPA, standardized test scores. *Important factors considered include:* Class rank, application essay, rigor of secondary school record. *Other factors considered include:* Recommendation(s), character/personal qualities, extracurricular activities, talent/ability, volunteer work, work experience. **Freshman Admission Requirements:** High school diploma is required and GED is accepted. *Academic units required:* 4 English, 3 mathematics, 2 science, (3 science labs), 1 One unit of fine, visual, or performing arts, or one additional unit of academic elective. *Academic units recommended:* 4 English, 4 mathematics, 2 science, (3 science labs), 1 One unit of fine, visual, or performing arts, or one additional unit of academic elective. **Freshman Admission Statistics:** 12,478 applied, 76% admitted, 39% enrolled. **Transfer Admission Requirements:** College transcript(s), minimum college GPA of 2.5 required. Lowest grade transferable D. **General Admission Information:** Application fee $50. Notification on a rolling basis, beginning on or about 11/1. Nonfall registration accepted. Credit offered for CEEB Advanced Placement tests.

COSTS AND FINANCIAL AID

Required Forms and Deadlines: FAFSA. Priority financial aid filing date 2/15. **Notification of Awards:** Applicants will be notified of awards on a rolling basis beginning 4/15. **Types of Aid:** *Need-based scholarships/grants:* Federal Pell, SEOG, state scholarships/grants, private scholarships, the school's own gift aid, United Negro College Fund, Federal Nursing Scholarships. *Loans:* FFEL Subsidized Stafford, FFEL Unsubsidized Stafford, FFEL PLUS, Federal Perkins, Federal Nursing. *Student Employment:* Federal Work-Study Program available. Institutional employment available. Highest amount earned per year from on-campus jobs $8,517. Off-campus job opportunities are good. **Financial Aid Statistics:** 27% freshmen, 34% undergrads receive need-based scholarship or grant aid. 32% freshmen, 19% undergrads receive non-need-based scholarship or grant aid. 35% freshmen, 43% undergrads receive need-based self-help aid. 3% freshmen, 2% undergrads receive athletic scholarships. 82% freshmen, 74% undergrads receive any aid. **Criteria for awarding institutional aid:** *Non-need-based:* Academics, alumni affiliation, art, athletics, job skills, leadership, minority status, music/drama, religious affiliation, state/district residency.

WASHINGTON UNIVERSITY IN ST. LOUIS

Campus Box 1089, One Brookings Drive, St. Louis, MO 63130-4899
Phone: 314-935-6000 **Financial Aid Phone:** 888-547-6670
E-mail: admissions@wustl.edu **CEEB Code:** 6929
Fax: 314-935-4290 **Website:** wustl.edu **ACT Code:** 2386

This private school was founded in 1853. It has a 169-acre campus.

RATINGS
Admissions Selectivity Rating: 99   **Fire Safety Rating:** 85   **Green Rating:** 60*

STUDENTS AND FACULTY
Enrollment: 6,436. **Student Body:** 50% female, 50% male, 91% out-of-state, 6% international (90 countries represented). Asian 14%, African American 9%, Caucasian 59%, Hispanic 3%.
Retention and Graduation: 97% freshmen return for sophomore year. 33%

grads go on to further study within 1 year. **Faculty:** Student/faculty ratio 7:1. 916 full-time faculty, 98% hold PhDs, 35% are women.

ACADEMICS

Degrees: Bachelor's, certificate, doctoral, master's, post-bachelor's certificate, post-master's certificate. **Classes:** Most classes have fewer than 10 students. Most lab/discussion sessions have 10–19 students. **Majors with Highest Enrollment:** Biology/biological sciences; finance; psychology. **Special Study Options:** Accelerated program, cooperative education program, cross-registration, double major, dual enrollment, English as a Second Language (ESL), exchange student program (domestic), independent study, internships, liberal arts/career combination, student-designed major, study abroad, teacher certification program. The University Scholars Program at Washington University gives selected students the opportunity to be admitted to undergraduate study and a graduate program at the same time. **Combined degree programs:** BA/MA, BA/MEng, 5 year BA/BFA 3/2 AB/MSOT. Special programs offered to physically disabled students include note-taking services, reader services, tape recorders, tutors. **Career services:** Alumni network, alumni services, career/job search classes, career assessment, internships, regional alumni. **Career services highlights include:** Opportunities are provided for cooperative education programs in Engineering. Internships are available in most areas including business, communications, social service, and many others. Internships and study abroad are available in numerous foreign countries.

FACILITIES

Housing: Coed dorms, fraternity/sorority housing, apartments for married students, cooperative housing, apartments for single students, wellness housing, special interest suites, upper-class housing, single sex floors in coed buildings, on-campus transfer-specific housing, and small-group housing for students who share common interests and goals. 95% of campus accessible to physically disabled. **Special Academic Facilities/Equipment:** Art gallery, business/economics experimental lab, botanical garden, NASA planetary imaging facility, TAP reactor system, triple monochromator, Computer Automated Radioactive Particle Tracking and gamma ray Computed Tomography, Observatory, EADS learning center, Student Enterprise Zone, Edison Theatre, lab science building, outdoor Tyson Research Center. **Computers:** Students can register for classes online. Administrative functions (other than registration) can be performed online.

CAMPUS LIFE

Environment: City. **Activities:** Choral groups, concert band, dance, drama/theater, jazz band, literary magazine, music ensembles, musical theater, opera, pep band, radio station, student government, student newspaper, student-run film society, symphony orchestra, television station, campus ministries, international student organization, Model UN. **Organizations:** 200 registered organizations, 18 honor societies, 19 religious organizations. 12 fraternities, 6 sororities. **Athletics (Intercollegiate):** *Men:* Baseball, basketball, cross-country, diving, football, soccer, swimming, tennis, track/field (outdoor), track/field (indoor). *Women:* Basketball, cross-country, diving, golf, soccer, softball, swimming, tennis, track/field (outdoor), track/field (indoor), volleyball. **On-Campus Highlights:** Gallery of Art, Edison Theatre, Ursa's Cafe, Francis Gymnasium and Francis Field, Residence Halls.

ADMISSIONS

Freshman Academic Profile: 96% in top 10% of high school class, 100% in top 25% of high school class, 100% in top 50% of high school class. 63% from public high schools. SAT Math middle 50% range 710–780. SAT Critical Reading middle 50% range 680–750. ACT middle 50% range 32–34. Minimum paper TOEFL 550. Minimum computer TOEFL 213. Minimum web-based TOEFL 79. **Basis for Candidate Selection:** *Very important factors considered include:* Class rank, application essay, academic GPA, recommendation(s), rigor of secondary school record, standardized test scores, character/personal qualities, extracurricular activities, talent/ability, volunteer work, work experience. *Other factors considered include:* Alumni/ae relation, first generation, interview, level of applicant's interest, racial/ethnic status. **Freshman Admission Requirements:** High school diploma is required and GED is accepted. *Academic units recommended:* 4 English, 4 mathematics, 4 science, (4 science labs), 2 foreign language, 4 social studies, 4 history. **Freshman Admission Statistics:** 23,105 applied, 22% admitted, 29% enrolled. **Transfer Admission Requirements:** College transcript(s), essay or personal statement, statement of good standing from prior institution(s). Lowest grade transferable C. **General Admission Information:** Application fee $55. Early decision application deadline 11/15. Regular application deadline 1/15. Regular notification 4/1. Nonfall registration not accepted. Admission may be deferred for a maximum of 24 months. Credit and/or placement offered for CEEB Advanced Placement tests.

COSTS AND FINANCIAL AID

Annual tuition $39,400. Room and board $12,941. Required fees $974. Average book expense $1,300. **Required Forms and Deadlines:** FAFSA, CSS/Financial Aid PROFILE, noncustodial PROFILE, student and parent 1040 tax return or signed waiver if there is no tax return. Financial aid filing deadline

2/15. **Notification of Awards:** Applicants will be notified of awards on or about 4/1. **Types of Aid:** *Need-based scholarships/grants:* Federal Pell, SEOG, state scholarships/grants, private scholarships, the school's own gift aid, United Negro College Fund, Federal Academic Competitive Grant, Federal SMART Grant. *Loans:* Direct Subsidized Stafford, Direct Unsubsidized Stafford, Direct PLUS, FFEL Subsidized Stafford, FFEL Unsubsidized Stafford, FFEL PLUS, Federal Perkins, state loans, college/university loans from institutional funds. *Student Employment:* Federal Work-Study Program available. Institutional employment available. Highest amount earned per year from on-campus jobs $2,000. Off-campus job opportunities are excellent. **Financial Aid Statistics:** 36% freshmen, 41% undergrads receive need-based scholarship or grant aid. 4% freshmen, 3% undergrads receive non-need-based scholarship or grant aid. 28% freshmen, 29% undergrads receive need-based self-help aid. 37% freshmen, 42% undergrads receive any aid. 39% undergrads borrow to pay for school. **Criteria for awarding institutional aid:** *Non-need-based:* Academics.

WATKINS COLLEGE OF ART, DESIGN & FILM

2298 Rosa L Parks Blvd, Nashville, TN 37228
Phone: 615-277-7418 **Financial Aid Phone:** 615-277-7421
E-mail: admissions@watkins.edu
Fax: 615-383-4849 **Website:** www.watkins.edu **ACT Code:** 4027

This private school was founded in 1895. It has a 13-acre campus.

RATINGS

Admissions Selectivity Rating: 60*   **Fire Safety Rating:** 94   **Green Rating:** 60*

STUDENTS AND FACULTY

Enrollment: 367. **Student Body:** 53% female, 47% male, 25% out-of-state, (4 countries represented).
Retention and Graduation: 10% freshmen graduate within 4 years. 10% grads go on to further study within 1 year. 10% grads pursue arts and sciences degrees. **Faculty:** Student/faculty ratio 8:1. 20 full-time faculty, 70% hold PhDs, 50% are women.

ACADEMICS

Degrees: Bachelor's, post-bachelor's certificate. **Classes:** Most classes have 10–19 students. **Majors with Highest Enrollment:** Film/cinema studies; fine/studio arts; graphic design. **Special Study Options:** Dual enrollment, independent study, internships, study abroad. Special programs offered to physically disabled students include note-taking services, reader services, tape recorders, tutors. **Career services:** Alumni network, alumni services, career/job search classes, career assessment, internships. **Career services highlights include:** Internships available in all majors.

FACILITIES

Housing: Coed dorms, special housing for disabled students, women's dorms, apartments for single students. 100% of campus accessible to physically disabled. **Special Academic Facilities/Equipment:** Brownlee O. Currey Gallery **Computers:** 100% of classrooms, 100% of dorms, 100% of libraries, 100% of dining areas, 100% of student union, 50% of common outdoor areas have wireless network access. Administrative functions (other than registration) can be performed online.

CAMPUS LIFE

Environment: Metropolis. **Activities:** Student newspaper, student-run film society **Organizations: Environmental Initiatives:** Recycling Program. Filtered Water Bottle filling stations. Sustainability classes in certain majors.

ADMISSIONS

Freshman Academic Profile: 60% from public high schools. Minimum paper TOEFL 340. Minimum computer TOEFL 150. Minimum web-based TOEFL 60. **Basis for Candidate Selection:** *Very important factors considered include:* Application essay, level of applicant's interest, talent/ability. *Important factors considered include:* Academic GPA, recommendation(s), standardized test scores, character/personal qualities. *Other factors considered include:* Class rank, rigor of secondary school record, extracurricular activities, interview, volunteer work. **Freshman Admission Requirements:** High school diploma is required and GED is accepted. *Academic units recommended:* 3 English, 2 mathematics, 2 science, 1 foreign language, 3 social studies, 3 history, 4 visual/performing arts, 3 computer science. **Freshman Admission Statistics:** 112 applied, 75% admitted, 67% enrolled. **Transfer Admission Requirements:** College transcript(s), essay or personal statement, statement of good standing from prior institution(s). Minimum college GPA of 2.6 required. Lowest grade transferable c. **General Admission Information:** Application fee $50. Regular application deadline 7/15. Notification on a rolling basis, beginning on or about 1/1. Nonfall registration accepted. Admission may be deferred for a maximum of 1 semester. Credit offered for CEEB Advanced Placement tests.

COSTS AND FINANCIAL AID

Required Forms and Deadlines: FAFSA, institution's own financial aid form. Financial aid filing deadline 10/1. Priority financial aid filing date 4/1. **Notification of Awards:** Applicants will be notified of awards on a rolling basis beginning 5/1. **Types of Aid:** *Need-based scholarships/grants:* Federal Pell, SEOG, state scholarships/grants, private scholarships, the school's own gift aid. *Loans:* FFEL Subsidized Stafford, FFEL Unsubsidized Stafford, FFEL PLUS. *Student Employment:* Federal Work-Study Program available. Institutional employment available. Off-campus job opportunities are good. **Financial Aid Statistics:** 56% freshmen, 80% undergrads receive need-based scholarship or grant aid. 30% freshmen, 10% undergrads receive non-need-based scholarship or grant aid. 82% freshmen, 80% undergrads receive need-based self-help aid. 50% freshmen, 40% undergrads receive any aid. 50% undergrads borrow to pay for school. Average cumulative indebtedness $20,000. **Criteria for awarding institutional aid:** *Non-need-based:* Academics, art.

WAYLAND BAPTIST UNIVERSITY

1900 West 7th Street, CMB 712, Plainview, TX 79072
Phone: 806-291-3500 **Financial Aid Phone:** 806-291-3520
E-mail: admityou@wbu.edu
Fax: 806-291-1963 **ACT Code:** 4246

This private school, affiliated with the Southern Baptist Church, was founded in 1908. It has a 80-acre campus.

RATINGS
Admissions Selectivity Rating: 72   **Fire Safety Rating:** 81   **Green Rating:** 60*

STUDENTS AND FACULTY

Enrollment: 862. **Student Body:** 53% female, 47% male, 15% out-of-state, 3% international (18 countries represented). Asian 1%, African American 6%, Caucasian 59%, Hispanic 23%, Native American 1%.
Retention and Graduation: 66% freshmen return for sophomore year. 20% freshmen graduate within 4 years. **Faculty:** Student/faculty ratio 8:1. 92 full-time faculty, 71% hold PhDs, 4% are members of minority groups, 29% are women.

ACADEMICS

Degrees: Associate, bachelor's, master's, transfer associate. **Classes:** Most classes have 10–19 students. **Majors with Highest Enrollment:** Business/commerce; christian studies; elementary education and teaching. **Special Study Options:** Accelerated program, distance learning, double major, dual enrollment, external degree program, honors program, internships, study abroad, teacher certification program. **Honors programs:** The Honors Program offered by Wayland is designed to challenge the academically superior student to develop initiative and abilities beyond what is expected in a normal course of study. Electing an Honors program offers breadth and depth of content through independent study and research, aiding the student in preparation for entering a career upon graduation or attending graduate school in a field of choice. Honors work represents the highest level of academic work available at Wayland on the undergraduate level. Special programs offered to physically disabled students include note-taking services, reader services, tutors. **Career services:** Career assessment.

FACILITIES

Housing: Men's dorms, women's dorms, apartments for married students 100% of campus accessible to physically disabled. **Special Academic Facilities/Equipment:** Llano Estacado Museum. **Computers:** 80% of classrooms, 80% of dorms, 100% of libraries, 100% of dining areas, have wireless network access. Students can register for classes online. Administrative functions (other than registration) can be performed online.

CAMPUS LIFE

Environment: Town. **Activities:** Choral groups, concert band, drama/theater, marching band, music ensembles, musical theater, pep band, radio station, student government, student newspaper, television station, yearbook, campus ministries. **Organizations:** 34 registered organizations, 4 honor societies, 7 religious organizations. **Athletics (Intercollegiate):** *Men:* Baseball, basketball, cheerleading, cross-country, golf, soccer, track/field (outdoor), track/field (indoor). *Women:* Basketball, cheerleading, cross-country, golf, soccer, track/field (outdoor), track/field (indoor), volleyball. **On-Campus Highlights:** McClung University Center, Mabee Learning Resource Center, Gates Hall, Hutcherson Gymnasium, Harral Auditorium, Pete and Nelda Laney Activities Center. **Environmental Initiatives:** Installed energy efficient lighting in major buildings across campus.

ADMISSIONS

Freshman Academic Profile: Average high school GPA 3.55. 18% in top 10% of high school class, 41% in top 25% of high school class, 72% in top 50% of high school class. SAT Math middle 50% range 430–570. SAT Critical Reading middle 50% range 410–540. SAT Writing middle 50% range 420–545. ACT middle 50% range 18–23. Minimum paper TOEFL 500. Minimum computer TOEFL 173. Minimum web-based TOEFL 61. **Basis for Candidate Selection:** *Very important factors considered include:* Class rank, standardized test scores. *Important factors considered include:* Rigor of secondary school record. **Freshman Admission Requirements:** High school diploma is required and GED is accepted. *Academic units required:* 3 English, 2 mathematics, 2 science, 2 history. *Academic units recommended:* 3 mathematics, 3 science. **Freshman Admission Statistics:** 307 applied, 93% admitted, 77% enrolled. **Transfer Admission Requirements:** College transcript(s), statement of good standing from prior institution(s). Minimum college GPA of 2.0 required. Lowest grade transferable D. **General Admission Information:** Application fee $35. Notification on a rolling basis, beginning on or about 3/1. Nonfall registration accepted. Credit offered for CEEB Advanced Placement tests.

COSTS AND FINANCIAL AID

Annual tuition $11,850. Room and board $3,986. Required fees $890. Average book expense $1,248. **Required Forms and Deadlines:** FAFSA, institution's own financial aid form, Tax returns/Verification worksheet. Priority financial aid filing date 6/1. **Notification of Awards:** Applicants will be notified of awards on a rolling basis beginning 2/15. **Types of Aid:** *Need-based scholarships/grants:* Federal Pell, SEOG, state scholarships/grants, private scholarships, the school's own gift aid. *Loans:* FFEL Subsidized Stafford, FFEL Unsubsidized Stafford, FFEL PLUS, Federal Perkins, state loans *Student Employment:* Federal Work-Study Program available. Institutional employment available. Off-campus job opportunities are fair. **Financial Aid Statistics:** 71% freshmen, 70% undergrads receive need-based scholarship or grant aid. 13% freshmen, 8% undergrads receive non-need-based scholarship or grant aid. 43% freshmen, 52% undergrads receive need-based self-help aid. 74% freshmen, 69% undergrads receive any aid. 78% undergrads borrow to pay for school. Average cumulative indebtedness $25,387. **Criteria for awarding institutional aid:** *Non-need-based:* Academics, alumni affiliation, art, athletics, music/drama, religious affiliation.

WAYNE STATE COLLEGE

1111 Main Street, Wayne, NE 68787
Phone: 402-375-7234 **Financial Aid Phone:** 402-375-7230
E-mail: admit1@wsc.edu **CEEB Code:** 6469
Fax: 402-375-7204 **Website:** www.wsc.edu **ACT Code:** 2472

This public school was founded in 1909. It has a 128-acre campus.

RATINGS
Admissions Selectivity Rating: 67   **Fire Safety Rating:** 60*   **Green Rating:** 60*

STUDENTS AND FACULTY

Enrollment: 2,924. **Student Body:** 54% female, 46% male, 14% out-of-state, 1% international (23 countries represented). Asian 1%, African American 3%, Caucasian 84%, Hispanic 2%, Native American 1%.
Retention and Graduation: 67% freshmen return for sophomore year. **Faculty:** Student/faculty ratio 20:1. 122 full-time faculty, 76% hold PhDs, 6% are members of minority groups, 48% are women. 2% of classes are taught by teaching assistants.

ACADEMICS

Degrees: Bachelor's, master's, post-master's certificate. **Classes:** Most classes have 20–29 students. Most lab/discussion sessions have 30–39 students. **Majors with Highest Enrollment:** Business administration and management; criminal justice/safety studies; elementary education and teaching. **Special Study Options:** Cooperative education program, distance learning, double major, dual enrollment, honors program, independent study, internships, student-designed major, study abroad, teacher certification program, Learning Communities; First-Year Experience; Service Learning. Special programs offered to physically disabled students include note-taking services, reader services, tape recorders, tutors. **Career services:** Alumni network, alumni services, career/job search classes, career assessment, internships

FACILITIES

Housing: Coed dorms. **Special Academic Facilities/Equipment:** Art gallery, fine arts center, planetarium, recreation center, telecommunications network. **Computers:** 100% of classrooms, 100% of dorms, 100% of libraries, 100% of dining areas, 100% of student union, 40% of common outdoor areas have wireless network access. Students can register for classes online. Administrative functions (other than registration) can be performed online.

CAMPUS LIFE

Environment: Rural. **Activities:** Choral groups, concert band, dance, drama/theater, jazz band, literary magazine, marching band, music ensembles, musical theater, pep band, radio station, student government, student newspaper, television station, campus ministries, international student organization. **Organizations:** 96 registered organizations, 18 honor societies, 7 religious organizations. 2 fraternities, 3 sororities. **Athletics (Intercollegiate):** *Men:* Baseball, basketball, cross-country, football, golf, track/field (outdoor), track/field (indoor). *Women:* Basketball, cross-country, golf, soccer, softball, track/field (outdoor), track/field (indoor), volleyball. **Environmental Initiatives:** Recycling Program, Gray Water Project.

ADMISSIONS

Freshman Academic Profile: Average high school GPA 3.21. 11% in top 10% of high school class, 30% in top 25% of high school class, 61% in top 50% of high school class. ACT middle 50% range 18–24. Minimum paper TOEFL 550. Minimum computer TOEFL 213. **Freshman Admission Requirements:** High school diploma is required and GED is accepted. *Academic units recommended:* 4 English, 3 mathematics, 2 science, 2 foreign language, 3 social studies, 2 visual/performing arts, 2 computer science. **Freshman Admission Statistics:** 2,055 applied, 100% admitted, 32% enrolled. **Transfer Admission Requirements:** College transcript(s), minimum college GPA of 2.0 required. Lowest grade transferable C–. **General Admission Information:** Application fee $30. Regular application deadline 8/24. Notification on a rolling basis, beginning on or about 9/15. Nonfall registration accepted. Admission may be deferred for a maximum of 1 semester. Credit and/or placement offered for CEEB Advanced Placement tests.

COSTS AND FINANCIAL AID

Required Forms and Deadlines: FAFSA. Priority financial aid filing date 4/1. **Notification of Awards:** Applicants will be notified of awards on a rolling basis beginning 3/1. **Types of Aid:** *Need-based scholarships/grants:* Federal Pell, SEOG, state scholarships/grants, private scholarships, the school's own gift aid. *Loans:* FFEL Subsidized Stafford, FFEL Unsubsidized Stafford, FFEL PLUS, Federal Perkins. *Student Employment:* Federal Work-Study Program available. Institutional employment available. Off-campus job opportunities are fair. **Financial Aid Statistics:** 54% freshmen, 49% undergrads receive need-based scholarship or grant aid. 27% freshmen, 23% undergrads receive non-need-based scholarship or grant aid. 54% freshmen, 53% undergrads receive need-based self-help aid. 3% freshmen, 4% undergrads receive athletic scholarships. **Criteria for awarding institutional aid:** *Non-need-based:* Academics, art, athletics, leadership, minority status, music/drama, religious affiliation, state/district residency.

WAYNE STATE UNIVERSITY

42 West Warren, "The Welcome Center", Detroit, MI 48202
Phone: 313-577-3577 **Financial Aid Phone:** 313-577-3378
E-mail: Admissions@wayne.edu **CEEB Code:** 1898
Fax: 313-577-7536 **Website:** www.wayne.edu **ACT Code:** 2064

This public school was founded in 1868. It has a 219-acre campus.

RATINGS

Admissions Selectivity Rating: 60*   **Fire Safety Rating:** 60*   **Green Rating:** 60*

STUDENTS AND FACULTY

Enrollment: 19,113. **Student Body:** 59% female, 41% male, 1% out-of-state, 4% international (90 countries represented). Asian 5%, African American 32%, Caucasian 47%, Hispanic 3%.
Retention and Graduation: 76% freshmen return for sophomore year. **Faculty:** Student/faculty ratio 17:1. 1001 full-time faculty, 61% hold PhDs, 24% are members of minority groups, 38% are women.

ACADEMICS

Degrees: Bachelor's, first professional, master's, post-bachelor's certificate, post-master's certificate. **Majors with Highest Enrollment:** Elementary education and teaching; nursing/registered nurse (RN, ASN, BSN, MSN); psychology. **Special Study Options:** Accelerated program, cooperative education program, cross-registration, distance learning, double major, dual enrollment, English as a Second Language (ESL), external degree program, honors program, independent study, internships, liberal arts/career combination, study abroad, teacher certification program, weekend college Special programs offered to physically disabled students include note-taking services, reader services, tape recorders, tutors. **Career services:** Career/job search classes, career assessment, internships.

FACILITIES

Housing: Coed dorms, special housing for disabled students, fraternity/sorority housing, apartments for married students, apartments for single students. 100% of campus accessible to physically disabled. **Special Academic Facilities/Equipment:** Detroit Institute of Arts; Detroit Historical Museum; Detroit Science Museum; Charles H Wright Museum of African American History. **Computers:** Students can register for classes online. Administrative functions (other than registration) can be performed online.

CAMPUS LIFE

Environment: Metropolis. **Activities:** Choral groups, concert band, dance, drama/theater, jazz band, literary magazine, music ensembles, musical theater, opera, pep band, student government, student newspaper, student-run film society, symphony orchestra, yearbook. **Organizations:** 166 registered organizations, 4 honor societies, 12 religious organizations. 7 fraternities, 8 sororities. **Athletics (Intercollegiate):** *Men:* Baseball, basketball, cross-country, diving, fencing, football, golf, ice hockey, swimming, tennis. *Women:* Basketball, cross-country, diving, fencing, ice hockey, softball, swimming, tennis, volleyball. **On-Campus Highlights:** Recreation and Fitness Center, Student Center Building, Subway, Starbucks, Residence Halls.

ADMISSIONS

Freshman Academic Profile: ACT middle 50% range 16–24. Minimum paper TOEFL 550. Minimum computer TOEFL 213. **Basis for Candidate Selection:** *Very important factors considered include:* Rigor of secondary school record, standardized test scores, *Other factors considered include:* Class rank, extracurricular activities. **Freshman Admission Requirements:** High school diploma is required and GED is accepted. *Academic units recommended:* 4 English, 4 mathematics, 3 science, 2 foreign language, 3 social studies, 2 academic electives. **Freshman Admission Statistics:** 9,680 applied, 63% admitted, 51% enrolled. **Transfer Admission Requirements:** College transcript(s), minimum college GPA of 2.0 required. Lowest grade transferable C. **General Admission Information:** Application fee $30. Regular application deadline 8/1. Nonfall registration accepted. Admission may be deferred for a maximum of 1 year. Credit and/or placement offered for CEEB Advanced Placement tests.

COSTS AND FINANCIAL AID

Annual in-state tuition $4,773. Annual out-of-state tuition $10,941. Room and board $6,700. Required fees $626. **Required Forms and Deadlines:** FAFSA. Priority financial aid filing date 3/1. **Notification of Awards:** Applicants will be notified of awards on a rolling basis beginning 4/1. **Types of Aid:** *Need-based scholarships/grants:* Federal Pell, SEOG, state scholarships/grants, private scholarships, the school's own gift aid. *Loans:* FFEL Subsidized Stafford, FFEL Unsubsidized Stafford, FFEL PLUS, Federal Perkins, Federal Nursing, state loans, college/university loans from institutional funds. *Student Employment:* Institutional employment available. Off-campus job opportunities are fair. **Financial Aid Statistics:** 43% freshmen, 40% undergrads receive need-based scholarship or grant aid. 37% freshmen, 20% undergrads receive non-need-based scholarship or grant aid. 31% freshmen, 41% undergrads receive need-based self-help aid. 3% freshmen, 3% undergrads receive athletic scholarships. 45% undergrads borrow to pay for school. Average cumulative indebtedness $19,563. **Criteria for awarding institutional aid:** *Non-need-based:* Academics, art, athletics, leadership, music/drama.

WAYNESBURG UNIVERSITY

51 West College Street, Waynesburg, PA 15370
Phone: 724-852-3248 **Financial Aid Phone:** 724-852-3208
E-mail: admissions@waynesburg.edu **CEEB Code:** 2969
Fax: 724-627-8124 **ACT Code:** 3748

This private school, affiliated with the Presbyterian Church, was founded in 1849. It has a 30-acre campus.

RATINGS

Admissions Selectivity Rating: 76   **Fire Safety Rating:** 91   **Green Rating:** 60*

STUDENTS AND FACULTY

Enrollment: 1,533. **Student Body:** 59% female, 41% male, 14% out-of-state, (6 countries represented). African American 3%, Caucasian 95%, Hispanic 1%.
Retention and Graduation: 76% freshmen return for sophomore year. 48% freshmen graduate within 4 years. 16% grads go on to further study within 1 year. 1% grads pursue law degrees. 3% grads pursue business degrees. 1% grads pursue medical degrees. **Faculty:** Student/faculty ratio 15:1. 72 full-time faculty, 68% hold PhDs, 8% are members of minority groups, 51% are women.

ACADEMICS

Degrees: Associate, bachelor's, master's. **Classes:** Most classes have 10–19 students. Most lab/discussion sessions have 10–19 students. **Majors with Highest Enrollment:** Business, management, marketing, and related support services, other; communication studies/speech communication and rhetoric; nursing/registered nurse (RN, ASN, BSN, MSN). **Special Study Options:** Accelerated program, distance learning, double major, dual enrollment, English as a Second Language (ESL), honors program, independent study, internships, liberal arts/career combination, study abroad, teacher certification program, 3-2 program in engineering with Penn State University in State College, PA and Washington University in Saint Louis, MO, 3-1 program in marine bioloy with Florida Institute of Technology; 3-3 law program with Duquesne University. **Combined degree programs:** BA/JD, 3/2 Pre-Law -Waynesburg and Duquense. Special programs offered to physically disabled students include tutors. **Career services:** Alumni network, alumni services, career/job search classes, career assessment, internships, regional alumni. **Career services highlights include:** Professional Development course for second semester juniors and seniors.

FACILITIES

Housing: Coed dorms, men's dorms, women's dorms. 90% of campus accessible to physically disabled. **Special Academic Facilities/Equipment:** Geology, biology, archaeology, and ceramics museum, arboretum, 174-acre farm, Center for Research and Economic Development . **Computers:** 95% of classrooms, 95% of libraries, 100% of dining areas, 100% of student union, 20% of common outdoor areas have wireless network access. Students can register for classes online. Administrative functions (other than registration) can be performed online.

CAMPUS LIFE

Environment: Village. **Activities:** Choral groups, concert band, dance, drama/theater, literary magazine, marching band, music ensembles, musical theater, pep band, radio station, student government, student newspaper, television station, yearbook. **Organizations:** 40 registered organizations, 16 honor societies, 7 religious organizations. **Athletics (Intercollegiate):** *Men:* Baseball, basketball, cross-country, football, golf, soccer, tennis, track/field (outdoor), wrestling. *Women:* Basketball, cross-country, golf, lacrosse, soccer, softball, tennis, track/field (outdoor), volleyball. **On-Campus Highlights:** Communication Department, Stover Campus Center, Museum, Alumni Hall/Chapel, New Residence Halls.

ADMISSIONS

Freshman Academic Profile: Average high school GPA 3.43. 15% in top 10% of high school class, 43% in top 25% of high school class, 77% in top 50% of high school class. SAT Math middle 50% range 450–560. SAT Critical Reading middle 50% range 450–540. Minimum paper TOEFL 550. Minimum computer TOEFL 213. **Basis for Candidate Selection:** *Very important factors considered include:* Class rank, academic GPA, rigor of secondary school record, standardized test scores, interview. *Important factors considered include:* Extracurricular activities. *Other factors considered include:* Application essay, recommendation(s), alumni/ae relation, character/personal qualities, level of applicant's interest, volunteer work, work experience. **Freshman Admission Requirements:** High school diploma is required and GED is accepted. *Academic units required:* 4 English, 3 mathematics, 2 science, 2 social studies, 5 academic electives. *Academic units recommended:* 3 science, 2 foreign language. **Freshman Admission Statistics:** 1,875 applied, 71% admitted, 29% enrolled. **Transfer Admission Requirements:** High school transcript, college transcript(s), statement of good standing from prior institution(s). Minimum college GPA of 2.5 required. Lowest grade transferable C. **General Admission Information:** Application fee $20. Nonfall registration accepted. Credit offered for CEEB Advanced Placement tests.

COSTS AND FINANCIAL AID

Annual tuition $17,400. Room and board $7,370. Required fees $360. Average book expense $1,300. **Required Forms and Deadlines:** FAFSA. Priority financial aid filing date 3/15. **Notification of Awards:** Applicants will be notified of awards on a rolling basis beginning 2/15. **Types of Aid:** *Need-based scholarships/grants:* Federal Pell, SEOG, state scholarships/grants, private scholarships, the school's own gift aid. *Loans:* FFEL Subsidized Stafford, FFEL Unsubsidized Stafford, FFEL PLUS, Federal Perkins, Federal Nursing, Private Alternative Loans. *Student Employment:* Federal Work-Study Program available. Institutional employment available. Highest amount earned per year from on-campus jobs $3,000. Off-campus job opportunities are good. **Financial Aid Statistics:** 39% freshmen, 58% undergrads receive need-based scholarship or grant aid. 5% freshmen, 4% undergrads receive non-need-based scholarship or grant aid. 31% freshmen, 54% undergrads receive need-based self-help aid. 85% freshmen, 84% undergrads receive any aid. 88% undergrads borrow to pay for school. Average cumulative indebtedness $22,000. **Criteria for awarding institutional aid:** *Non-need-based:* Academics, alumni affiliation, art, job skills, leadership, minority status, music/drama, religious affiliation, state/district residency.

WEBB INSTITUTE

298 Crescent Beach Road, Glen Cove, NY 11542
Phone: 516-674-9838 **Financial Aid Phone:** 516-671-2213
E-mail: admissions@webb-institute.edu **CEEB Code:** 2970
Fax: 516-674-9838 **Website:** www.webb-institute.edu **ACT Code:** 2987

This private school was founded in 1889. It has a 26-acre campus.

RATINGS
Admissions Selectivity Rating: 97 **Fire Safety Rating:** 63 **Green Rating:** 60*

STUDENTS AND FACULTY
Enrollment: 90. **Student Body:** 18% female, 82% male, 78% out-of-state, Asian 4%, Caucasian 91%, Hispanic 2%.
Retention and Graduation: 88% freshmen return for sophomore year. 56% freshmen graduate within 4 years. 25% grads go on to further study within 1 year. **Faculty:** 11 full-time faculty, 55% hold PhDs, 9% are women.

ACADEMICS
Degrees: Bachelor's. **Classes:** Most classes have 20–29 students. **Special Study Options:** Double major, independent study, internships. **Career services:** Alumni network, career/job search classes, internships, regional alumni. **Career services highlights include:** Winter Work program. All students are required to work in the industry for 2 months of each academic year. Freshmen work in shipyards; Sophomore work onboard ships; Juniors and Seniors work in engineering design offices.

FACILITIES
Housing: Coed dorms, men's dorms, women's dorms. 70% of campus accessible to physically disabled. **Special Academic Facilities/Equipment:** Towing tank for model testing, marine engineering lab. **Computers:** 100% of classrooms, 100% of dorms, 100% of libraries, 100% of dining areas, 100% of student union, 100% of common outdoor areas have wireless network access.

CAMPUS LIFE
Environment: Village. **Activities:** Choral groups, drama/theater, music ensembles, student government, yearbook. **Organizations:** 2 registered organizations. **Athletics (Intercollegiate):** *Men:* Basketball, cross-country, sailing, soccer, tennis, volleyball. *Women:* Basketball, cross-country, sailing, soccer, tennis, volleyball. **On-Campus Highlights:** Stevenson Taylor Hall, Brockett Pub, Waterfront Facility.

ADMISSIONS
Freshman Academic Profile: Average high school GPA 3.9. 71% in top 10% of high school class, 93% in top 25% of high school class, 100% in top 50% of high school class. 76% from public high schools. SAT Math middle 50% range 670–740. SAT Critical Reading middle 50% range 610–670. SAT Writing middle 50% range 610–680. **Basis for Candidate Selection:** *Very important factors considered include:* Class rank, academic GPA, rigor of secondary school record, standardized test scores, character/personal qualities, interview, level of applicant's interest. *Important factors considered include:* Recommendation(s), extracurricular activities. *Other factors considered include:* talent/ability, volunteer work, work experience. **Freshman Admission Requirements:** High school diploma is required and GED is not accepted. *Academic units required:* 4 English, 4 mathematics, 2 science, (2 science labs), 2 social studies, 4 academic electives. **Freshman Admission Statistics:** 73 applied, 41% admitted, 73% enrolled. **Transfer Admission Requirements:** High school transcript, college transcript(s), interview, standardized test scores, minimum college GPA of 3.5 required. **General Admission Information:** Application fee $25. Early decision application deadline 10/15. Regular application deadline 2/15. Notification on a rolling basis, beginning on or about 4/15. Nonfall registration not accepted. Neither credit nor placement offered for CEEB Advanced Placement tests.

COSTS AND FINANCIAL AID
Room and board $10,200. Average book expense $750. **Required Forms and Deadlines:** FAFSA. Financial aid filing deadline 7/1. Priority financial aid filing date 7/1. **Notification of Awards:** Applicants will be notified of awards on or about 8/1. **Types of Aid:** *Need-based scholarships/grants:* Federal Pell, state scholarships/grants, private scholarships, the school's own gift aid. *Loans:* FFEL Subsidized Stafford, FFEL Unsubsidized Stafford, FFEL PLUS. *Student Employment:* Off-campus job opportunities are fair. **Financial Aid Statistics:** 8% freshmen, 14% undergrads receive need-based scholarship or grant aid. 4% freshmen, 10% undergrads receive non-need-based scholarship or grant aid. 21% freshmen, 11% undergrads receive need-based self-help aid. 25%

---

freshmen, 20% undergrads receive any aid. 20% undergrads borrow to pay for school. Average cumulative indebtedness $7,303. **Criteria for awarding institutional aid:** *Non-need-based:* Academics.

WEBBER INTERNATIONAL UNIVERSITY

PO Box 96, Babson Park, FL 33827
Phone: 863-638-2910 **Financial Aid Phone:** 863-638-2930
E-mail: admissions@webber.edu **CEEB Code:** 5893
Fax: 863-638-1591 **Website:** www.webber.edu **ACT Code:** 773

This private school was founded in 1927. It has a 110-acre campus.

RATINGS
Admissions Selectivity Rating: 70   **Fire Safety Rating:** 82   **Green Rating:** 60*

STUDENTS AND FACULTY
Enrollment: 603. **Student Body:** 35% female, 65% male, 4% out-of-state, 13% international (36 countries represented). African American 20%, Caucasian 47%, Hispanic 8%.
Retention and Graduation: 49% freshmen return for sophomore year. 24% freshmen graduate within 4 years. 7% grads go on to further study within 1 year. 2% grads pursue law degrees. 5% grads pursue business degrees. **Faculty:** Student/faculty ratio 18:1. 20 full-time faculty, 70% hold PhDs, 10% are members of minority groups, 45% are women.

ACADEMICS
Degrees: Associate, bachelor's, master's. **Classes:** Most classes have 20–29 students. **Majors with Highest Enrollment:** Business administration and management; business/commerce; parks, recreation and leisure facilities management. **Special Study Options:** Cooperative education program, cross-registration, distance learning, double major, dual enrollment, English as a Second Language (ESL), exchange student program (domestic), external degree program, independent study, internships, study abroad, weekend college. **Career services:** Career/job search classes, career assessment, internships. **Career services highlights include:** As a Career Counselor I am most proud of the experiential learning in the classroom in classes like Career Development where we engage the learner at a more personal level by addressing the needs of the individual. In career development each student is treated as an individual and the learning process is individual not necessarily as a group. Students are given individual personality assessments and must demonstrate goal setting abilities while observing different occupations, in hands on setting and finally presenting the occupation they have chosen as a career. I am also very proud of our internship program which gives students a valuable learning tooland hands-on opportunity in the field they are most intersted in.

FACILITIES
Housing: Men's dorms, women's dorms. 70% of campus accessible to physically disabled. **Computers:** Administrative functions (other than registration) can be performed online.

CAMPUS LIFE
Environment: Rural. **Activities:** marching band, pep band, student government, student newspaper, international student organization. **Organizations:** 6 registered organizations. **Athletics (Intercollegiate):** *Men:* Baseball, basketball, bowling, cheerleading, cross-country, football, golf, soccer, tennis, track/field (outdoor). *Women:* Basketball, bowling, cheerleading, cross-country, golf, soccer, softball, tennis, track/field (outdoor), volleyball. **On-Campus Highlights:** Student Union, Fitness Center, Computer Lab, Career Center

ADMISSIONS
Freshman Academic Profile: Average high school GPA 3.14. 8% in top 10% of high school class, 27% in top 25% of high school class, 57% in top 50% of high school class. 76% from public high schools. SAT Math middle 50% range 430–530. SAT Critical Reading middle 50% range 420–510. ACT middle 50% range 18–21. Minimum paper TOEFL 500. Minimum computer TOEFL 173. **Basis for Candidate Selection:** *Very important factors considered include:* Academic GPA, standardized test scores. *Important factors considered include:* Rigor of secondary school record. *Other factors considered include:* Class rank, application essay, recommendation(s), alumni/ae relation, character/personal qualities, interview. **Freshman Admission Requirements:** High school diploma is required and GED is accepted. *Academic units required:* 4 English, 2 mathematics, 1 science, 2 social studies, 2 *Academic units recommended:* 3 mathematics, 3 science, 1 foreign language, 2 history, 4 academic electives. **Freshman Admission Statistics:** 411 applied, 74% admitted, 57% enrolled. **Transfer Admission Requirements:** College transcript(s), statement of good standing from prior institution(s). Minimum college GPA of 2.0 required. Lowest grade transferable C. **General Admission Information:** Application fee

$35. Regular application deadline 8/1. Notification on a rolling basis, beginning on or about 12/1. Nonfall registration accepted. Admission may be deferred for a maximum of 1 semester. Credit offered for CEEB Advanced Placement tests.

COSTS AND FINANCIAL AID
Annual tuition $17,850. Room and board $6,822. Average book expense $800. **Required Forms and Deadlines:** FAFSA, state aid form. Financial aid filing deadline 8/1. Priority financial aid filing date 5/1. **Notification of Awards:** Applicants will be notified of awards on a rolling basis beginning 4/1. **Types of Aid:** *Need-based scholarships/grants:* Federal Pell, SEOG, state scholarships/grants, private scholarships, the school's own gift aid. *Loans:* FFEL Subsidized Stafford, FFEL Unsubsidized Stafford, FFEL PLUS, Federal Perkins. *Student Employment:* Federal Work-Study Program available. Institutional employment available. Highest amount earned per year from on-campus jobs $1,950. Off-campus job opportunities are good. **Financial Aid Statistics:** 60% freshmen, 58% undergrads receive need-based scholarship or grant aid. 60% freshmen, 43% undergrads receive non-need-based scholarship or grant aid. 54% freshmen, 52% undergrads receive need-based self-help aid. 29% freshmen, 31% undergrads receive athletic scholarships. 100% freshmen, 99% undergrads receive any aid. Average cumulative indebtedness $23,902. **Criteria for awarding institutional aid:** *Non-need-based:* Academics, alumni affiliation, athletics, leadership, state/district residency.

See page 1320.

WEBER STATE UNIVERSITY

1137 University Circle, Ogden, UT 84408-1137
Phone: 801-626-6744 **Financial Aid Phone:** 801-626-6586
E-mail: admissions@weber.edu **CEEB Code:** 4941
Fax: 801-626-6747 **Website:** weber.edu **ACT Code:** 4282

This public school was founded in 1889. It has a 526-acre campus.

RATINGS
Admissions Selectivity Rating: 71   **Fire Safety Rating:** 60*   **Green Rating:** 74

STUDENTS AND FACULTY
Enrollment: 16,831. **Student Body:** 51% female, 49% male, 7% out-of-state, 1% international (35 countries represented). Asian 3%, African American 1%, Caucasian 65%, Hispanic 5%, Native American 1%.
Retention and Graduation: 70% freshmen return for sophomore year. 28% freshmen graduate within 4 years. **Faculty:** Student/faculty ratio 22:1. 460 full-time faculty, 85% hold PhDs, 10% are members of minority groups, 41% are women.

ACADEMICS
Degrees: Associate, bachelor's, certificate, master's, post-bachelor's certificate, terminal associate, transfer associate. **Classes:** Most classes have 10–19 students. Most lab/discussion sessions have 10–19 students. **Majors with Highest Enrollment:** Business administration and management; elementary education and teaching; nursing/registered nurse (RN, ASN, BSN, MSN). **Special Study Options:** Accelerated program, cooperative education program, distance learning, double major, dual enrollment, English as a Second Language (ESL), exchange student program (domestic), external degree program, honors program, independent study, internships, student-designed major, study abroad, teacher certification program, First Year Experience. Special programs offered to physically disabled students include note-taking services, reader services, tape recorders, tutors. **Career services:** Alumni network, alumni services, career/job search classes, career assessment, internships, regional alumni.

FACILITIES
Housing: Special housing for disabled students, men's dorms, women's dorms, apartments for married students, apartments for single students. 99% of campus accessible to physically disabled. **Special Academic Facilities/Equipment:** Art gallery, language lab, TV studio, communication arts/technologies facilities, natural science museum, herbarium, planetarium, aerospace technology equipment for developing satellite projects, dental hygiene clinic. **Computers:** 50% of classrooms, 50% of dorms, 100% of libraries, 100% of dining areas, 100% of student union, 100% of common outdoor areas have wireless network access. Students can register for classes online. Administrative functions (other than registration) can be performed online.

CAMPUS LIFE
Environment: Town. **Activities:** Choral groups, concert band, dance, drama/theater, jazz band, literary magazine, marching band, music ensembles, musical theater, opera, pep band, radio station, student government, student newspaper, student-run film society, symphony orchestra, television station. **Organiza-

tions: 100 registered organizations, 1 honor societies, 4 religious organizations. 2 fraternities, 3 sororities. **Athletics (Intercollegiate):** *Men:* Basketball, cheerleading, cross-country, football, golf, tennis, track/field (outdoor), track/field (indoor). *Women:* Basketball, cheerleading, cross-country, golf, soccer, tennis, track/field (outdoor), track/field (indoor), volleyball. **On-Campus Highlights:** Health and Physical Education Center, Bowling Alley and Arcade, Student Union Building, Kimball Visual Arts Building, Val A. Browning Center, Student Union Building is under renovation, West side is completed, the East side as completed summer 2008. Pool tables and games have been moved to Promontory Tower for the time being. Bowling has been contracted out to a local alley. **Environmental Initiatives:** Total lighting upgrades in two of our major campus buildings and re-commissioning of two more. Construction of a new Central Chilled Water Plant. We are seeing about a 30% increase in plant efficiency. Most importantly, we have contracted with an Energy Services Corporation for implementation of approximately $7,000,000 of energy conservation initiatives.

ADMISSIONS

Freshman Academic Profile: Average high school GPA 3.3. 100% in top 50% of high school class. 99% from public high schools. ACT middle 50% range 18–24. **Basis for Candidate Selection:** *Important factors considered include:* Rigor of secondary school record, standardized test scores. *Other factors considered include:* Character/personal qualities, extracurricular activities, interview. **Freshman Admission Requirements:** High school diploma is required and GED is accepted. *Academic units recommended:* 4 English, 2 mathematics, 2 science, 2 foreign language, 1 history, 4 academic electives. **Freshman Admission Statistics:** 4,297 applied, 100% admitted, 57% enrolled. **Transfer Admission Requirements:** College transcript(s), minimum college GPA of 2.0 required. Lowest grade transferable C. **General Admission Information:** Application fee $45. Regular application deadline 8/22. Nonfall registration accepted. Admission may be deferred for a maximum of 1 year. Placement offered for CEEB Advanced Placement tests.

COSTS AND FINANCIAL AID

Annual in-state tuition $3,153. Annual out-of-state tuition $10,460. Room and board $3,118. Required fees $702. Average book expense $1,200. **Required Forms and Deadlines:** FAFSA, institution's own financial aid form. Priority financial aid filing date 3/1. **Notification of Awards:** Applicants will be notified of awards on a rolling basis beginning 3/15. **Types of Aid:** *Need-based scholarships/grants:* Federal Pell, SEOG, state scholarships/grants, private scholarships, the school's own gift aid. *Loans:* FFEL Subsidized Stafford, FFEL Unsubsidized Stafford, FFEL PLUS, Federal Perkins, Short-term Tuition Loan. *Student Employment:* Federal Work-Study Program available. Institutional employment available. Off-campus job opportunities are good. **Financial Aid Statistics:** 20% freshmen, 30% undergrads receive need-based scholarship or grant aid. 41% freshmen, 30% undergrads receive non-need-based scholarship or grant aid. 15% freshmen, 27% undergrads receive need-based self-help aid. 6% freshmen, 3% undergrads receive athletic scholarships. 42% freshmen, 53% undergrads receive any aid. **Criteria for awarding institutional aid:** *Non-need-based:* Academics, alumni affiliation, art, athletics, job skills, leadership, minority status, music/drama, state/district residency.

WEBSTER UNIVERSITY

470 East Lockwood Avenue, Saint Louis, MO 63119-3194
Phone: 314-968-6991 **Financial Aid Phone:** 314-968-6992
E-mail: admit@webster.edu **CEEB Code:** 6933
Fax: 314-968-7115 **Website:** www.webster.edu **ACT Code:** 2388

This private school was founded in 1915. It has a 47-acre campus.

RATINGS

Admissions Selectivity Rating: 85 **Fire Safety Rating:** 86 **Green Rating:** 60*

STUDENTS AND FACULTY

Enrollment: 3,411. **Student Body:** 58% female, 42% male, 21% out-of-state, 1% international (64 countries represented). Asian 2%, African American 12%, Caucasian 71%, Hispanic 3%, Native American 1%.
Retention and Graduation: 47% freshmen graduate within 4 years. 20% grads go on to further study within 1 year. **Faculty:** Student/faculty ratio 11.8:1. 187 full-time faculty, 73% hold PhDs, 9% are members of minority groups, 46% are women.

ACADEMICS

Degrees: Bachelor's, certificate, master's, post-bachelor's certificate, post-master's certificate. **Classes:** Most classes have 10–19 students. **Majors with Highest Enrollment:** Business/commerce; computer science; education. **Special Study Options:** Accelerated program, cooperative education program, cross-registration, distance learning, double major, dual enrollment, English as a Second Language (ESL), exchange student program (domestic), independent study, internships, liberal arts/career combination, student-designed major, study abroad, teacher certification program, Certificate Programs, Combination bachelor's/master's degree in many subject areas, Independent study, Student Leadership Development Program. In addition to the programs offered at its four St. Louis area campuses, Webster University offers undergraduate degree completion programs at the following extended campus locations in the United States: Charleston, SC—Website: http://explore.webster.edu/admissions/undergraduate/worldwide/charleston.asp Columbia, SC—Website: http://explore.webster.edu/admissions/undergraduate/worldwide/columbia.asp Greenville, SC—Website: http://explore.webster.edu/admissions/undergraduate/worldwide/greenville.asp Kansas City, MO Website: www.webster.edu/kc/ Orlando, FL Website: http://explore.webster.edu/admissions/undergraduate/worldwide/orlando.asp Irvine, CA—Website: http://explore.webster.edu/admissions/undergraduate/worldwide/irvine.asp San Diego, CA Website: http://explore.webster.edu/admissions/undergraduate/worldwide/sandiego.asp Undergraduate students may also study at Webster's international campuses, where they may complete their entire degree at the following locations: Geneva, Switzerland Website: www.webster.ch Leiden, The Netherlands Website: www.webster.nl London, UK, at Webster at Regent's College Website: www.bacl.ac.uk Vienna, Austria Website: www.webster.ac.at Cha-am, Thailand Website: www.webster.ac.th. **Combined degree programs:** BA/MA, 3/4 BA-BFA/MS w/ Washington Univ. in Architecture. Special programs offered to physically disabled students include note-taking services, reader services, tape recorders, tutors. **Career services:** Alumni network, alumni services, career assessment, internships

FACILITIES

Housing: Coed dorms, special housing for international students, women's dorms, apartments for married students, apartments for single students. 85% of campus accessible to physically disabled. **Special Academic Facilities/Equipment:** Loretto-Hilton Center for Performing Arts (Houses St. Louis Repertory company, Opera Theatre of St. Louis, and Webster Symphony); Community Music School of Webster University. **Computers:** 10% of classrooms, 12% of dorms, 50% of libraries, 100% of dining areas, 100% of student union, 60% of common outdoor areas have wireless network access. Students can register for classes online. Administrative functions (other than registration) can be performed online.

CAMPUS LIFE

Environment: Metropolis. **Activities:** Choral groups, dance, drama/theater, jazz band, literary magazine, music ensembles, musical theater, opera, radio station, student government, student newspaper, student-run film society, symphony orchestra, television station, yearbook, campus ministries. **Organizations:** 62 registered organizations, 1 honor societies, 1 religious organizations. 1 fraternities, **Athletics (Intercollegiate):** *Men:* Baseball, basketball, cross-country, golf, soccer, tennis, track/field (outdoor). *Women:* Basketball, cross-country, soccer, softball, tennis, track/field (outdoor), volleyball. **On-Campus Highlights:** University Center, The Quadrangle, Emerson Library, Fitness Center, Marletto's Marketplace (dining hall). **Environmental Initiatives:** Recycling program.

ADMISSIONS

Freshman Academic Profile: Average high school GPA 3.45. 24% in top 10% of high school class, 55% in top 25% of high school class, 83% in top 50% of high school class. 79% from public high schools. SAT Math middle 50% range 460–630. SAT Critical Reading middle 50% range 520–650. ACT middle 50% range 21–28. Minimum paper TOEFL 550. Minimum computer TOEFL 210. **Basis for Candidate Selection:** *Very important factors considered include:* Academic GPA, standardized test scores, talent/ability. *Important factors considered include:* Class rank, application essay, recommendation(s), rigor of secondary school record, level of applicant's interest. *Other factors considered include:* Extracurricular activities, geographical residence, interview, racial/ethnic status, volunteer work. **Freshman Admission Requirements:** High school diploma is required and GED is accepted. *Academic units recommended:* 4 English, 3 mathematics, 3 science, (2 science labs), 2 foreign language, 3 social studies, 4 academic electives, 1 fine art. **Freshman Admission Statistics:** 1,584 applied, 52% admitted, 60% enrolled. **Transfer Admission Requirements:** College transcript(s), essay or personal statement, minimum college GPA of 2.5 required. Lowest grade transferable C. **General Admission Information:** Application fee $35. Regular application deadline 6/1. Notification on a rolling basis, beginning on or about 9/1. Nonfall registration accepted. Admission may be deferred for a maximum of 1 year. Credit offered for CEEB Advanced Placement tests.

COSTS AND FINANCIAL AID

Annual tuition $21,056. Room and board $9,070. Average book expense $800. **Required Forms and Deadlines:** FAFSA, institution's own financial aid form. Priority financial aid filing date 4/1. **Notification of Awards:** Applicants will be notified of awards on a rolling basis beginning 2/1. **Types of Aid:** *Need-based scholarships/grants:* Federal Pell, SEOG, state scholarships/grants, private scholarships, the school's own gift aid. *Loans:* FFEL Subsidized Stafford, FFEL Unsubsidized Stafford, FFEL PLUS, Federal Perkins. *Student Employment:* Federal Work-Study Program available. Institutional employment available. Off-campus job opportunities are good. **Financial Aid Statistics:** 58% freshmen, 57% undergrads receive need-based scholarship or grant aid. 52% freshmen, 42% undergrads receive non-need-based scholarship or grant aid. 65% freshmen, 63% undergrads receive need-based self-help aid. 96% freshmen, 70% undergrads receive any aid. 54% undergrads borrow to pay for school. Average cumulative indebtedness $24,224. **Criteria for awarding institutional aid:** *Non-need-based:* Academics, art, music/drama, state/district residency.

WELLESLEY COLLEGE

Board of Admission, 106 Central Street, Wellesley, MA 02481-8203
Phone: 781-283-2270 **Financial Aid Phone:** 781-283-2360
E-mail: admission@wellesley.edu **CEEB Code:** 3957
Fax: 781-283-3678 **Website:** www.wellesley.edu **ACT Code:** 1926

This private school was founded in 1870. It has a 500-acre campus.

RATINGS
Admissions Selectivity Rating: 97   Fire Safety Rating: 83   Green Rating: 88

STUDENTS AND FACULTY
Enrollment: 2,193. **Student Body:** 100% female, 84% out-of-state, 10% international (70 countries represented). Asian 26%, African American 7%, Caucasian 43%, Hispanic 8%, Native American 1%.
Retention and Graduation: 94% freshmen return for sophomore year. 84% freshmen graduate within 4 years. 25% grads go on to further study within 1 year. 26% grads pursue arts and sciences degrees. 11% grads pursue law degrees. 1% grads pursue business degrees. 9% grads pursue medical degrees. **Faculty:** Student/faculty ratio 8:1. 259 full-time faculty, 96% hold PhDs, 24% are members of minority groups, 56% are women.

ACADEMICS
Degrees: Bachelor's. **Classes:** Most classes have 10–19 students. Most lab/discussion sessions have 10–19 students. **Majors with Highest Enrollment:** Economics; political science and government; psychology. **Special Study Options:** Cross-registration, double major, dual enrollment, exchange student program (domestic), honors program, independent study, internships, student-designed major, study abroad, teacher certification program **Combined degree programs:** BA/MA, Brandeis MA ief (International Economics and Finance). Special programs offered to physically disabled students include note-taking services, reader services, tape recorders, tutors. **Career services:** Alumni network, alumni services, career/job search classes, career assessment, internships, regional alumni. **Career services highlights include:** Wellesley College funded at least one internship for more than half the class of 2009. This included grants of up $3,500 for what otherwise would have been unpaid internships over the summer.

FACILITIES
Housing: Women's dorms, cooperative housing, apartments for single students, wellness housing, theme housing. 85% of campus accessible to physically disabled. **Special Academic Facilities/Equipment:** Clapp Library Davis Museum and Cultural Center Harambee House Houghton Memorial Chapel Hunnewell Arboretum, Alexandra Botanic Gardens, and Ferguson Greenhouses Jewett Art Museum Keohane Sports Center Knapp Media and Technology Center Knapp Social Science Center Lake Waban Pforzheimer Learning and Teaching Center Ruth Nagel Jones Theatre Science Center, including NMR Spectrometers Slater International Center Wang Campus Center Wellesley Centers for Women Whitin Observatory, including 3 telescopes. **Computers:** 100% of classrooms, 100% of dorms, 100% of libraries, 100% of dining areas, 100% of student union, 5% of common outdoor areas have wireless network access. Students can register for classes online. Administrative functions (other than registration) can be performed online.

CAMPUS LIFE
Environment: Town. **Activities:** Choral groups, dance, drama/theater, jazz band, literary magazine, music ensembles, radio station, student government, student newspaper, student-run film society, symphony orchestra, yearbook, campus ministries, international student organization. **Organizations:** 160 registered organizations, 7 honor societies, 30 religious organizations. **Athletics**

(Intercollegiate):. *Women:* Basketball, crew/rowing, cross-country, diving, fencing, field hockey, golf, lacrosse, soccer, softball, squash, swimming, tennis, track/field (outdoor), track/field (indoor), volleyball. **On-Campus Highlights:** Wang Campus Center, Davis Museum and Cultural Center, Clapp Library and Knapp Media Center, Science Center, Lake Waban. **Environmental Initiatives:** 1. The College has made a large difference in improving the landscape by turning two significant brown field sites into green space. This effort reduced paved surfaces by 5.7 acres, greatly improved storm water management and quality, and reduced potable water consumption. This initiative also resulted in the planting of thousands of trees and shrubs. 2. We have greatly increased the recycling program over the past several years. We are recycling more than 10% of all solid waste. Wellesley College has a strong focus on reduction in consumption of materials while maintaining a strong recycling program. 3. Wellesley has been a leader in the efficient utilization of energy in many areas of the campus for nearly 30 years. Since 2003, we have reduced electrical consumption by 12% even though a new, highly programmed, 50,000 square foot building was brought on line during that period. In this effort, we are implementing additional practices and equipment to further reduce electrical use.

ADMISSIONS
Freshman Academic Profile: 78% in top 10% of high school class, 96% in top 25% of high school class, 100% in top 50% of high school class. 63% from public high schools. SAT Math middle 50% range 640–730. SAT Critical Reading middle 50% range 640–740. SAT Writing middle 50% range 650–740. ACT middle 50% range 29–32. **Basis for Candidate Selection:** *Very important factors considered include:* Application essay, academic GPA, recommendation(s), rigor of secondary school record, standardized test scores, character/personal qualities. *Important factors considered include:* Class rank, extracurricular activities. *Other factors considered include:* Alumni/ae relation, first generation, geographical residence, interview, level of applicant's interest, racial/ethnic status, state residency, talent/ability, volunteer work, work experience. **Freshman Admission Requirements:** High school diploma or equivalent is not required. High school diploma is required and GED is not accepted. *Academic units recommended:* 4 English, 4 mathematics, 3 science, (2 science labs), 4 foreign language, 4 social studies, 4 history. **Freshman Admission Statistics:** 4,156 applied, 35% admitted, 40% enrolled. **Transfer Admission Requirements:** High school transcript, college transcript(s), essay or personal statement, interview, standardized test scores, statement of good standing from prior institution(s). Lowest grade transferable C. **General Admission Information:** Application fee $50. Early decision application deadline 11/1. Regular application deadline 1/15. Regular notification 4/1. Nonfall registration not accepted. Admission may be deferred for a maximum of 1 year. Credit and/or placement offered for CEEB Advanced Placement tests.

COSTS AND FINANCIAL AID
Required Forms and Deadlines: FAFSA, CSS/Financial Aid PROFILE, noncustodial PROFILE, business/farm supplement. Business taxes, if applicable. Priority financial aid filing date 1/15. **Notification of Awards:** Applicants will be notified of awards on or about 4/1. **Types of Aid:** *Need-based scholarships/grants:* Federal Pell, SEOG, state scholarships/grants, private scholarships, the school's own gift aid, ACG Grant and SMART Grant. *Loans:* Direct Subsidized Stafford, Direct Unsubsidized Stafford, Direct PLUS, Federal Perkins, state loans, college/university loans from institutional funds. *Student Employment:* Federal Work-Study Program available. Institutional employment available. Off-campus job opportunities are excellent. **Financial Aid Statistics:** 57% freshmen, 60% undergrads receive need-based scholarship or grant aid. 51% freshmen, 56% undergrads receive need-based self-help aid. 58% freshmen, 62% undergrads receive any aid. 56% undergrads borrow to pay for school. Average cumulative indebtedness $13,324.

WELLS COLLEGE

Route 90, Aurora, NY 13026
Phone: 315-364-3264 **Financial Aid Phone:** 315-364-3289
E-mail: admissions@wells.edu **CEEB Code:** 2971
Fax: 315-364-3227 **Website:** www.wells.edu **ACT Code:** 2971

This private school was founded in 1868. It has a 365-acre campus.

RATINGS
Admissions Selectivity Rating: 85   Fire Safety Rating: 81   Green Rating: 75

STUDENTS AND FACULTY

Enrollment: 552. **Student Body:** 71% female, 29% male, 32% out-of-state, 2% international (13 countries represented). Asian 2%, African American 6%, Caucasian 67%, Hispanic 4%, Native American 1%.
Retention and Graduation: 53% freshmen graduate within 4 years. 25% grads go on to further study within 1 year. 18% grads pursue arts and sciences degrees. 4% grads pursue law degrees. 1% grads pursue business degrees. 2% grads pursue medical degrees. **Faculty:** Student/faculty ratio 9.7:1. 39 full-time faculty, 95% hold PhDs, 18% are members of minority groups, 54% are women.

ACADEMICS

Degrees: Bachelor's. **Classes:** Most classes have 10–19 students. **Majors with Highest Enrollment:** English language and literature; molecular biology; psychology. **Special Study Options:** Accelerated program, cross-registration, double major, English as a Second Language (ESL), independent study, internships, student-designed major, study abroad, teacher certification program, Cross registration with Cornell University, Ithaca College, and Cayuga Community College. **Combined degree programs:** BA/MBA, BA/MPH, BA/DVM, BA/M.Ed. Special programs offered to physically disabled students include tutors. **Career services:** Alumni network, alumni services, career assessment, internships, regional alumni. **Career services highlights include:** Wells College's ability to connect our students to the real world, through the use of internships, study abroad and experiential learning makes us unlike any other.

FACILITIES

Housing: Coed dorms, women's dorms, off campus college affiliated housing as well as an Environmental Science theme house. 58% of campus accessible to physically disabled. **Special Academic Facilities/Equipment:** Two greenhouses, environmentally regulated animal room, the college theatre (Phillips Auditorium), recital hall, electronic music studio, 15 pianos, a Dowd harpsichord, an early instrument collection, a sculpture and ceramics studio, dark rooms, painting and drawing studio, a Book Arts Center, lithography presses, an extensive art library, art gallery, general and specialized clusters for the social sciences, foreign languages, and natural and mathematical sciences. **Computers:** 10% of classrooms, 90% of dorms, 100% of libraries, 100% of student union, have wireless network access. Students can register for classes online. Administrative functions (other than registration) can be performed online.

CAMPUS LIFE

Environment: Rural. **Activities:** Choral groups, dance, drama/theater, literary magazine, music ensembles, student government, student newspaper, yearbook, Model UN. **Organizations:** 35 registered organizations, 2 honor societies, 2 religious organizations. **Athletics (Intercollegiate):** *Men:* Basketball, cross-country, golf, lacrosse, soccer, swimming. *Women:* Basketball, cross-country, field hockey, golf, lacrosse, soccer, softball, swimming, tennis **On-Campus Highlights:** Sommer Center, Boat House, Schwartz Student Union, Macmillan Hall, Main Building.

ADMISSIONS

Freshman Academic Profile: Average high school GPA 3.5. 31% in top 10% of high school class, 65% in top 25% of high school class, 91% in top 50% of high school class. 88% from public high schools. SAT Math middle 50% range 480–600. SAT Critical Reading middle 50% range 500–630. SAT Writing middle 50% range 480–590. ACT middle 50% range 22–27. Minimum paper TOEFL 550. Minimum computer TOEFL 213. **Basis for Candidate Selection:** *Very important factors considered include:* Academic GPA, recommendation(s), rigor of secondary school record, standardized test scores, extracurricular activities. *Important factors considered include:* Application essay, interview. *Other factors considered include:* Class rank, alumni/ae relation, character/personal qualities, level of applicant's interest, talent/ability, volunteer work, work experience. **Freshman Admission Requirements:** High school diploma is required and GED is accepted. *Academic units required:* 4 English, 3 mathematics, 2 science, (2 science labs), 1 social studies, 3 history, 2 academic electives. *Academic units recommended:* 4 mathematics, 3 science, (3 science labs), 2 foreign language, 2 social studies, 2 history, 3 academic electives, 2 music, art, computer science. **Freshman Admission Statistics:** 1,673 applied, 71% admitted, 12% enrolled. **Transfer Admission Requirements:** High school transcript, college transcript(s), essay or personal statement, standardized test scores, statement of good standing from prior institution(s). Minimum college GPA of 2.0 required. Lowest grade transferable C–. **General Admission Information:** Application fee $40. Early decision application deadline 12/15. Regular application deadline 3/1. Regular notification 4/1. Nonfall registration accepted. Admission may be deferred for a maximum of 1 year. Credit and/or placement offered for CEEB Advanced Placement tests.

COSTS AND FINANCIAL AID

Annual tuition $28,180. Room and board $9,000. Required fees $1,500. Average book expense $800. **Required Forms and Deadlines:** FAFSA, CSS/Financial Aid Profile for Early Decision Applicants only. Priority financial aid filing date 2/15. **Notification of Awards:** Applicants will be notified of awards on a rolling basis beginning 3/1. **Types of Aid:** *Need-based scholarships/grants:* Federal

Pell, SEOG, state scholarships/grants, private scholarships, the school's own gift aid. *Loans:* FFEL Subsidized Stafford, FFEL Unsubsidized Stafford, FFEL PLUS, Federal Perkins. *Student Employment:* Federal Work-Study Program available. Institutional employment available. Highest amount earned per year from on-campus jobs $1,600. Off-campus job opportunities are poor. **Financial Aid Statistics:** 86% freshmen, 83% undergrads receive need-based scholarship or grant aid. 57% freshmen, 49% undergrads receive non-need-based scholarship or grant aid. 78% freshmen, 80% undergrads receive need-based self-help aid. 96% freshmen, 95% undergrads receive any aid. 82% undergrads borrow to pay for school. Average cumulative indebtedness $24,182. **Criteria for awarding institutional aid:** *Non-need-based:* Academics, alumni affiliation, leadership.

See page 1322.

WENTWORTH INSTITUTE OF TECHNOLOGY

550 Huntington Avenue, Admissions Office, Boston, MA 02115-5998
Phone: 617-989-4000 **Financial Aid Phone:** 617-989-4174
E-mail: admissions@wit.edu **CEEB Code:** 3958
Fax: 617-989-4010 **Website:** www.wit.edu

This private school was founded in 1904. It has a 35-acre campus.

RATINGS

Admissions Selectivity Rating: 77   **Fire Safety Rating:** 84   **Green Rating:** 87

STUDENTS AND FACULTY

Enrollment: 3,781. **Student Body:** 19% female, 81% male, 42% out-of-state, 3% international (46 countries represented). Asian 5%, African American 4%, Caucasian 70%, Hispanic 4%.
Retention and Graduation: 79% freshmen return for sophomore year. 2% grads go on to further study within 1 year. **Faculty:** Student/faculty ratio 15:1. 139 full-time faculty, 56% hold PhDs, 11% are members of minority groups, 23% are women.

ACADEMICS

Degrees: Associate, bachelor's, master's, terminal associate. **Classes:** Most classes have 20–29 students. Most lab/discussion sessions have 10–19 students. **Majors with Highest Enrollment:** architecture (barch, ba/bs, march, ma/ms, phd); construction management; mechanical engineering/mechanical technology/technician. **Special Study Options:** Cooperative education program, cross-registration, distance learning, study abroad, Cross registration available through the Colleges of the Fenway Consortium with member colleges: Simmons College, Emmanuel College, Wheelock College, Massachusetts College of Pharmacy and Health Sciences, Massachusetts College of Art, and Wentworth Institute of Technology. Special programs offered to physically disabled students include note-taking services, reader services, tape recorders, tutors. **Career services:** Alumni network, career/job search classes, internships. **Career services highlights include:** Active for over 30 years, WIT's co-op program is one of the largest and most comprehensive cooperative education programs of its kind in the nation. Co-op is a requirement for all majors. 100% of WIT's co-op placements are directly related to the student's field of study.

FACILITIES

Housing: Coed dorms. 75% of campus accessible to physically disabled. **Computers:** 100% of classrooms, 100% of dorms, 100% of libraries, 100% of dining areas, have wireless network access. Students can register for classes online. Administrative functions (other than registration) can be performed online.

CAMPUS LIFE

Environment: Metropolis. **Activities:** Choral groups, dance, drama/theater, music ensembles, musical theater, radio station, student government, student newspaper, student-run film society, yearbook, international student organization. **Organizations:** 50 registered organizations, 3 honor societies, 1 religious organizations. **Athletics (Intercollegiate):** *Men:* Baseball, basketball, golf, ice hockey, lacrosse, riflery, soccer, tennis, volleyball. *Women:* Basketball, golf, riflery, soccer, softball, tennis, volleyball. **On-Campus Highlights:** 550 Huntington Ave (newest residence hall), Beatty Hall (cafe, library, student activities), Computer Info Systems Networking Lab (, Tansey Gymnasium, Annex (architecture and design studios), Daily tours and info sessions, fall Open Houses, spring Special Events, see website www.wit.edu (under Prospective Students) for details. **Environmental Initiatives:** Cogeneration System, High Efficient Boilers, Lighting Upgrade.

ADMISSIONS

Freshman Academic Profile: Average high school GPA 3. 65% from public high schools. SAT Math middle 50% range 500–610. SAT Critical Reading middle 50% range 460–560. SAT Writing middle 50% range 450–550. ACT middle 50% range 20–25. Minimum paper TOEFL 525. Minimum computer TOEFL 197. **Basis for Candidate Selection:** *Important factors considered include:* Application essay, recommendation(s), rigor of secondary school record, standardized test scores. *Other factors considered include:* Academic GPA, alumni/ae relation, character/personal qualities, extracurricular activities, first generation, geographical residence, level of applicant's interest, talent/ability, volunteer work, work experience. **Freshman Admission Requirements:** High school diploma is required and GED is accepted. *Academic units required:* 4 English, 3 mathematics, 2 science, (1 science labs), 1 social studies, 3 college-preparatory math, 1 physics recommended for many programs. *Academic units recommended:* 4 mathematics, 3 college-preparatory math, 1 physics recommended for many programs. **Freshman Admission Statistics:** 4,845 applied, 67% admitted, 26% enrolled. **Transfer Admission Requirements:** High school transcript, college transcript(s), essay or personal statement, Lowest grade transferable C. **General Admission Information:** Application fee $50. Notification on a rolling basis, beginning on or about 10/30. Nonfall registration accepted. Admission may be deferred for a maximum of 1 year. Credit offered for CEEB Advanced Placement tests.

COSTS AND FINANCIAL AID

Annual tuition $21,800. Room and board $10,500. Average book expense $1,500. **Required Forms and Deadlines:** FAFSA. Priority financial aid filing date 3/1. **Notification of Awards:** Applicants will be notified of awards on a rolling basis beginning 3/15. **Types of Aid:** *Need-based scholarships/grants:* Federal Pell, SEOG, state scholarships/grants, private scholarships, the school's own gift aid. *Loans:* FFEL Subsidized Stafford, FFEL Unsubsidized Stafford, FFEL PLUS, Federal Perkins, state loans *Student Employment:* Federal Work-Study Program available. Institutional employment available. Highest amount earned per year from on-campus jobs $875. Off-campus job opportunities are good. **Financial Aid Statistics:** 23% freshmen, 23% undergrads receive need-based scholarship or grant aid. 70% freshmen, 57% undergrads receive non-need-based scholarship or grant aid. 68% freshmen, 63% undergrads receive need-based self-help aid. 67% freshmen, 75% undergrads receive any aid. 83% undergrads borrow to pay for school. Average cumulative indebtedness $22,000. **Criteria for awarding institutional aid:** *Non-need-based:* Academics, leadership, state/district residency.

WESLEY COLLEGE (DE)

120 North State Street, Dover, DE 19901-3875
Phone: 302-736-2400
E-mail: admissions@wesley.edu **CEEB Code:** 1433
Fax: 302-736-2382 **Website:** www.wesley.eud **ACT Code:** 636

This private school, affiliated with the Methodist Church, was founded in 1873. It has a 40-acre campus.

RATINGS

Admissions Selectivity Rating: 78   **Fire Safety Rating:** 60*   **Green Rating:** 60*

STUDENTS AND FACULTY

Enrollment: 1,605. **Student Body:** 52% female, 48% male, 63% out-of-state, 1% international. Asian 2%, African American 22%, Caucasian 72%, Hispanic 3%, Native American 1%.
Retention and Graduation: 82% freshmen return for sophomore year. 34% freshmen graduate within 4 years. 30% grads go on to further study within 1 year. 2% grads pursue arts and sciences degrees. 1% grads pursue law degrees. 10% grads pursue business degrees. **Faculty:** Student/faculty ratio 19:1. 66 full-time faculty, 79% hold PhDs, 11% are members of minority groups, 50% are women.

ACADEMICS

Degrees: Associate, bachelor's, certificate, master's, post-bachelor's certificate. **Classes:** Most classes have 20–29 students. Most lab/discussion sessions have fewer than 10 students. **Majors with Highest Enrollment:** Business/commerce; elementary education and teaching; psychology. **Special Study Options:** Double major, honors program, independent study, internships, liberal arts/career combination, teacher certification program. Special programs offered to physically disabled students include tape recorders, tutors. **Career services:** Internships.

FACILITIES

Housing: Coed dorms, men's dorms, women's dorms, apartments for single students. 80% of campus accessible to physically disabled. **Special Academic Facilities/Equipment:** 1 **Computers:** Students can register for classes online. Administrative functions (other than registration) can be performed online.

CAMPUS LIFE

Environment: Town. **Activities:** Choral groups, drama/theater, literary magazine, music ensembles, radio station, student government, student newspaper, yearbook. **Organizations:** 30 registered organizations, 2 honor societies, 2 religious organizations. 3 fraternities, 3 sororities. **Athletics (Intercollegiate):** *Men:* Baseball, basketball, cheerleading, cross-country, football, golf, lacrosse, soccer, tennis. *Women:* Baseball, basketball, cheerleading, cross-country, field hockey, golf, lacrosse, soccer, softball, tennis.

ADMISSIONS

Freshman Academic Profile: Average high school GPA 2.98. 24% in top 10% of high school class, 56% in top 25% of high school class, 78% in top 50% of high school class. 80% from public high schools. SAT Math middle 50% range 400–500. SAT Critical Reading middle 50% range 499–490. SAT Writing middle 50% range 390–490. Minimum paper TOEFL 550. Minimum computer TOEFL 250. **Basis for Candidate Selection:** *Very important factors considered include:* Academic GPA. *Important factors considered include:* Class rank, rigor of secondary school record, standardized test scores. *Other factors considered include:* Application essay, recommendation(s), alumni/ae relation, character/personal qualities, extracurricular activities, interview, level of applicant's interest, talent/ability, volunteer work, work experience. **Freshman Admission Requirements:** High school diploma is required and GED is accepted. *Academic units recommended:* 4 English, 4 mathematics, 4 science, (2 science labs), 2 foreign language, 2 social studies, 2 academic electives. **Freshman Admission Statistics:** 2,633 applied, 76% admitted, 25% enrolled. **Transfer Admission Requirements:** High school transcript, college transcript(s), minimum college GPA of 2.0 required. Lowest grade transferable C. **General Admission Information:** Application fee $25. Nonfall registration accepted. Admission may be deferred for a maximum of 2 sems (1 yr). Credit and/or placement offered for CEEB Advanced Placement tests.

COSTS AND FINANCIAL AID

Annual tuition $16,750. Room and board $7,800. Required fees $829. Average book expense $1,000. **Required Forms and Deadlines:** FAFSA, institution's own financial aid form. Priority financial aid filing date 4/15. **Notification of Awards:** Applicants will be notified of awards on a rolling basis beginning 1/1. **Types of Aid:** *Need-based scholarships/grants:* Federal Pell, SEOG, state scholarships/grants, private scholarships *Loans:* Direct PLUS, FFEL Subsidized Stafford, FFEL Unsubsidized Stafford, FFEL PLUS, Federal Perkins. *Student Employment:* Highest amount earned per year from on-campus jobs $2,550. **Financial Aid Statistics:** 60% freshmen, 75% undergrads receive need-based scholarship or grant aid. 35% freshmen, 43% undergrads receive non-need-based scholarship or grant aid. 77% freshmen, 86% undergrads receive need-based self-help aid. 95% freshmen, 95% undergrads receive any aid. 93% undergrads borrow to pay for school. **Criteria for awarding institutional aid:** *Non-need-based:* Academics, alumni affiliation, religious affiliation.

WESLEYAN COLLEGE

Best 373

4760 Forsyth Road, Macon, GA 31210-4462
Phone: 478-477-1110 **Financial Aid Phone:** 478-757-5205
E-mail: admissions@wesleyancollege.edu **CEEB Code:** 5895
Fax: 478-757-4030 **Website:** www.wesleyancollege.edu **ACT Code:** 876

This private school, affiliated with the Methodist Church, was founded in 1836. It has a 200-acre campus.

RATINGS

Admissions Selectivity Rating: 88   **Fire Safety Rating:** 60*   **Green Rating:** 78

STUDENTS AND FACULTY

Enrollment: 610. **Student Body:** 100% female, 85% out-of-state, 14% international (21 countries represented). Asian 2%, African American 16%, Caucasian 29%, Hispanic 1%.
Retention and Graduation: 76% freshmen return for sophomore year. 26% grads go on to further study within 1 year. 6% grads pursue arts and sciences degrees. 2% grads pursue law degrees. 5% grads pursue business degrees. 3% grads pursue medical degrees. **Faculty:** Student/faculty ratio 12:1. 47 full-time faculty, 100% hold PhDs, 9% are members of minority groups, 55% are women.

ACADEMICS

Degrees: Bachelor's, master's. **Classes:** Most classes have 10–19 students. **Majors with Highest Enrollment:** Business administration, management and operations, other; international business/trade/commerce; psychology. **Special Study Options:** Accelerated program, cross-registration, double major, dual enrollment, exchange student program (domestic), honors program, independent study, internships, liberal arts/career combination, student-designed major, study abroad, teacher certification program, weekend college, Dual degree engineering(3/2) with Georgia Tech, Auburn University and Mercer University. **Honors programs:** Honors Program **Combined degree programs:** 3-2 eng. prg. w/ Auburn U, Georgia Tech, Mercer. Special programs offered to physically disabled students include note-taking services, tutors. **Career services:** Alumni network, career/job search classes, career assessment, internships. **Career services highlights include:** Internships are required for all graduating seniors.

FACILITIES

Housing: Special housing for disabled students, women's dorms, apartments for single studentsStudents required to live on campus unless married or living with family in the local area. 70% of campus accessible to physically disabled. **Special Academic Facilities/Equipment:** Art and history museums, special collection of Georgiana and Americana, on-campus equestrian center. **Computers:** 80% of classrooms, 100% of libraries, 100% of dining areas, 100% of student union, 50% of common outdoor areas have wireless network access. Students can register for classes online. Administrative functions (other than registration) can be performed online.

CAMPUS LIFE

Environment: City. **Activities:** Choral groups, dance, drama/theater, literary magazine, music ensembles, student government, student newspaper, yearbook, campus ministries, international student organization, Model UN. **Organizations:** 40 registered organizations, 10 honor societies, 5 religious organizations. **Athletics (Intercollegiate):.** *Women:* Basketball, cross-country, equestrian sports, soccer, softball, tennis, volleyball. **On-Campus Highlights:** Historic quad of buildings Georgian brick design, Equestrian and Fitness Centers, Lake, Residence Halls, Art Galleries. **Environmental Initiatives:** We are currently renovating one of our main teaching buildings to achieve LEED Silver Certification. We have established an Energy Star purchasing policy in accordance with the President's Climate Commitment. We have begun a campus-wide recycling program.

ADMISSIONS

Freshman Academic Profile: 81% from public high schools. SAT Math middle 50% range 440–590. SAT Critical Reading middle 50% range 470–600. SAT Writing middle 50% range 460–590. ACT middle 50% range 20–28. Minimum paper TOEFL 550. Minimum computer TOEFL 213. **Basis for Candidate Selection:** *Very important factors considered include:* Rigor of secondary school record. *Important factors considered include:* Class rank, academic GPA, recommendation(s), standardized test scores, extracurricular activities, interview, talent/ability. *Other factors considered include:* Application essay, alumni/ae relation, level of applicant's interest, volunteer work, work experience. **Freshman Admission Requirements:** High school diploma is required and GED is accepted. *Academic units required:* 4 English, 3 mathematics, 3 science, (2 science labs), 2 foreign language, 3 social studies. *Academic units recommended:* 4 English, 4 mathematics, 4 science, (3 science labs), 4 foreign language, 4 social studies, 2 academic electives. **Freshman Admission Statistics:** 507 applied, 51% admitted, 38% enrolled. **Transfer Admission Requirements:** College transcript(s), essay or personal statement, statement of good standing from prior institution(s). Minimum college GPA of 2.5 required. Lowest grade transferable C. **General Admission Information:** Application fee $30. Early decision application deadline 11/15. Regular application deadline 6/1. Notification on a rolling basis, beginning on or about 10/1. Nonfall registration accepted. Admission may be deferred for a maximum of 1 year. Credit and/or placement offered for CEEB Advanced Placement tests.

COSTS AND FINANCIAL AID

Annual tuition $17,500. Room and board $8,000. Average book expense $1,000. **Required Forms and Deadlines:** FAFSA, institution's own financial aid form, state aid form Financial aid filing deadline 6/3. Priority financial aid filing date 2/15. **Notification of Awards:** Applicants will be notified of awards on a rolling basis beginning 3/1. **Types of Aid:** *Need-based scholarships/grants:* Federal Pell, SEOG, state scholarships/grants, private scholarships, the school's own gift aid. *Loans:* FFEL Subsidized Stafford, FFEL Unsubsidized Stafford, FFEL PLUS, Federal Perkins, state loans, college/university loans from institutional funds, CitiAssist, Wells FARGO,Collegiate Loans, Key Alternative Loans. *Student Employment:* Federal Work-Study Program available. Highest amount earned per year from on-campus jobs $1,500. Off-campus job opportunities are good. **Financial Aid Statistics:** 70% freshmen, 61% undergrads receive need-based scholarship or grant aid. 22% freshmen, 15% undergrads receive non-need-based scholarship or grant aid. 48% freshmen, 46% undergrads receive need-based self-help aid. 96% freshmen, 91% undergrads receive any aid. 62% undergrads borrow to pay for school. Average cumulative indebtedness $20,896. **Criteria for awarding institutional aid:** *Non-need-based:* Academics, alumni affiliation, art, job skills, leadership, minority status, music/drama, religious affiliation, state/district residency.

WESLEYAN UNIVERSITY

70 Wyllys Avenue, Middletown, CT 06459-0265
Phone: 860-685-3000 **Financial Aid Phone:** 860-685-2800
E-mail: admissions@wesleyan.edu **CEEB Code:** 3959
Fax: 860-685-3001 **Website:** www.wesleyan.edu **ACT Code:** 614

This private school was founded in 1831. It has a 240-acre campus.

RATINGS
Admissions Selectivity Rating: 98   **Fire Safety Rating:** 86   **Green Rating:** 86

STUDENTS AND FACULTY
Enrollment: 2,766. **Student Body:** 50% female, 50% male, 92% out-of-state, 7% international (53 countries represented). Asian 10%, African American 7%, Caucasian 58%, Hispanic 9%, Native American 1%.
Retention and Graduation: 95% freshmen return for sophomore year. 88% freshmen graduate within 4 years. **Faculty:** Student/faculty ratio 9:1. 330 full-time faculty, 94% hold PhDs, 18% are members of minority groups, 42% are women.

ACADEMICS
Degrees: Bachelor's, master's, post-master's certificate. **Classes:** Most classes have 10–19 students. Most lab/discussion sessions have 20–29 students. **Majors with Highest Enrollment:** English language and literature; political science and government; psychology. **Special Study Options:** Cross-registration, double major, dual enrollment, exchange student program (domestic), honors program, independent study, student-designed major, study abroad **Combined degree programs:** BA/MA Special programs offered to physically disabled students include note-taking services, reader services, tape recorders, tutors.

FACILITIES
Housing: Coed dorms, special housing for disabled students, fraternity/sorority housing, apartments for married students, apartments for single students, wellness housing, theme housing14 Residence halls, 32 program houses, 139 woodframe houses. **Special Academic Facilities/Equipment:** Art center, art galleries, Center for Afro-American studies, East Asian Studies Center, Cinema Archives, concert hall, public affairs center, language lab, electron microscope, observatory, nuclear magnetic resonance spectrometers. **Computers:** 90% of classrooms, 100% of dorms, 90% of libraries, 90% of dining areas, 100% of student union, 90% of common outdoor areas have wireless network access. Students can register for classes online. Administrative functions (other than registration) can be performed online.

CAMPUS LIFE
Environment: Town. **Activities:** Choral groups, concert band, dance, drama/theater, jazz band, literary magazine, music ensembles, musical theater, pep band, radio station, student government, student newspaper, student-run film society, symphony orchestra, yearbook, campus ministries. **Organizations:** 220 registered organizations, 2 honor societies, 10 religious organizations. 9 fraternities, 4 sororities. **Athletics (Intercollegiate):** *Men:* Baseball, basketball, crew/rowing, cross-country, diving, football, golf, ice hockey, lacrosse, soccer, squash, swimming, tennis, track/field (outdoor), track/field (indoor), wrestling. *Women:* Basketball, crew/rowing, cross-country, diving, field hockey, ice hockey, lacrosse, soccer, softball, squash, swimming, tennis, track/field (outdoor), track/field (indoor), volleyball. **On-Campus Highlights:** Center for the Arts, Freeman Athletic Center, Center for Film Studies, Olin Memorial Library, Van Vleck Observatory, Freeman East Asian Studies Center. **Environmental Initiatives:** Education of campus community on Wesleyan's Carbon footprint and the steps required to meet the 2010, 2020 and 2050 goals towards carbon neutrality. Reduction of GHG to 1990 levels by 2010 Campus community commitment to climate change and education of personal impact on global climate change starting with your home and office.

ADMISSIONS
Freshman Academic Profile: Average high school GPA 3.82. 70% in top 10% of high school class, 90% in top 25% of high school class, 100% in top 50% of high school class. 57% from public high schools. SAT Math middle 50% range 650–750. SAT Critical Reading middle 50% range 640–750. SAT Writing middle 50% range 640–740. ACT middle 50% range 29–33. Minimum paper TOEFL 600. Minimum computer TOEFL 250. Minimum web-based TOEFL 100. **Basis for Candidate Selection:** *Very important factors considered include:* Rigor of secondary school record. *Important factors considered include:* Class rank, application essay, academic GPA, recommendation(s), standardized test scores,

character/personal qualities, first generation, racial/ethnic status, talent/ability. *Other factors considered include:* Alumni/ae relation, extracurricular activities, geographical residence, interview, volunteer work, work experience. **Freshman Admission Requirements:** High school diploma is required and GED is accepted. *Academic units recommended:* 4 English, 4 mathematics, 4 science, (3 science labs), 4 foreign language, 4 social studies, 4 history. **Freshman Admission Statistics:** 10,068 applied, 22% admitted, 34% enrolled. **Transfer Admission Requirements:** High school transcript, college transcript(s), essay or personal statement, standardized test scores, statement of good standing from prior institution(s). Lowest grade transferable C–. **General Admission Information:** Application fee $55. Early decision application deadline 11/15. Regular application deadline 1/1. Regular notification 4/1. Nonfall registration not accepted. Admission may be deferred for a maximum of 1 year. Credit and/or placement offered for CEEB Advanced Placement tests.

COSTS AND FINANCIAL AID

Required Forms and Deadlines: FAFSA, CSS/Financial Aid PROFILE, state aid form, noncustodial PROFILE. Financial aid filing deadline 2/15. **Notification of Awards:** Applicants will be notified of awards on or about 4/1. *Types of Aid: Need-based scholarships/grants:* Federal Pell, SEOG, state scholarships/grants, private scholarships, the school's own gift aid. *Loans:* Direct Subsidized Stafford, Direct Unsubsidized Stafford, Direct PLUS, Federal Perkins, college/university loans from institutional funds. *Student Employment:* Federal Work-Study Program available. Institutional employment available. Off-campus job opportunities are good. **Financial Aid Statistics:** 43% freshmen, 42% undergrads receive need-based scholarship or grant aid. 47% freshmen, 47% undergrads receive need-based self-help aid. 43% freshmen, 44% undergrads receive any aid. 44% undergrads borrow to pay for school. Average cumulative indebtedness $29,174. **Criteria for awarding institutional aid:** *Non-need-based:* Academics.

WEST CHESTER UNIVERSITY OF PENNSYLVANIA

Messikomer Hall, 100 W. Rosedale Avenue, West Chester, PA 19383
Phone: 610-436-3411 **Financial Aid Phone:** 610-436-2627
E-mail: ugadmiss@wcupa.edu **CEEB Code:** 3328
Fax: 610-436-2907 **Website:** www.wcupa.edu

This public school was founded in 1871. It has a 403.4-acre campus.

RATINGS

Admissions Selectivity Rating: 85   **Fire Safety Rating:** 93   **Green Rating:** 80

STUDENTS AND FACULTY

Enrollment: 11,561. **Student Body:** 60% female, 40% male, 11.62% out-of-state, international (57 countries represented). Asian 2%, African American 9%, Caucasian 85%, Hispanic 3%.
Retention and Graduation: 40% freshmen graduate within 4 years. **Faculty:** Student/faculty ratio 17.3:1. 560 full-time faculty, 51% are women.

ACADEMICS

Degrees: Bachelor's, master's, post-bachelor's certificate, post-master's certificate. **Classes:** Most classes have 20–29 students. **Majors with Highest Enrollment:** Elementary education and teaching; history; psychology. **Special Study Options:** Cooperative education program, cross-registration, distance learning, double major, dual enrollment, English as a Second Language (ESL), exchange student program (domestic), honors program, independent study, internships, liberal arts/career combination, student-designed major, study abroad, teacher certification program. **Honors programs:** See the Honors College section of the WCU Website: www.wcupa.edu/honors/. Special programs offered to physically disabled students include note-taking services, reader services, tape recorders, tutors. **Career services:** Alumni network, alumni services, career/job search classes, career assessment, internships, regional alumni. **Career services highlights include:** Student Teaching.

FACILITIES

Housing: Coed dorms, special housing for disabled students, men's dorms, special housing for international students, women's dorms, fraternity/sorority housing, apartments for single students, wellness housing. 95% of campus accessible to physically disabled. **Special Academic Facilities/Equipment:** McKinney Gallery, Long Gallery, Emile K. Asplundh Concert Hall, Swope Auditorium, EO Bull Main Stage, Sykes Theater, Frances Harvey Green Library, Presser Music Library, Darlington Herbarium, Geology Museum, Speech and Hearing Clinic, Philips Autograph Library, Farrell Stadium, Hollinger Fieldhouse, Schmucker Science Center, The Center for Advanced Scientific Imaging and

the Materials Research Center, WCU Planetarium, WCU Observatory, Robert B. Gordon Natural Area for Environmental Studies, The Children's Center, Southeastern PA Autism Resource Center, Geography and Planning Geographic Informatino Systems Lab, Philips Auditorium, Main Hall Auditorium, Schmucker Auditorium, Boucher Lecture Hall, Center for Government and Community Affairs, The Poetry Center. **Computers:** 100% of classrooms, 20% of dorms, 100% of libraries, 100% of dining areas, 100% of student union, 100% of common outdoor areas have wireless network access. Students can register for classes online. Administrative functions (other than registration) can be performed online.

CAMPUS LIFE

Environment: Village. **Activities:** Choral groups, concert band, dance, drama/theater, jazz band, literary magazine, marching band, music ensembles, musical theater, opera, pep band, radio station, student government, student newspaper, symphony orchestra, television station, yearbook, campus ministries, international student organization. **Organizations:** 233 registered organizations, 26 honor societies, 12 religious organizations. 12 fraternities, 13 sororities. **Athletics (Intercollegiate):** *Men:* Baseball, basketball, cross-country, diving, football, golf, soccer, swimming, tennis, track/field (outdoor). *Women:* Basketball, cheerleading, cross-country, diving, field hockey, golf, gymnastics, lacrosse, rugby, soccer, softball, swimming, tennis, track/field (outdoor), volleyball. **On-Campus Highlights:** Emilie K. Asplundh Concert Hall, E.O. Bull Main Stage, Farrell Stadium, Sykes Student Union Building, Educational Center for Earth Observation Systems, Please see our website for a campus events calendar: www.wcupa.edu/_INFORMATION/events/. **Environmental Initiatives:** Construction of new buildings and the renovation of existing buildings are done so that they could meet LEED Silver if the necessary paper work was filed and fees paid. Geothermal heating and cooling used for new residence halls, renovations, and buildings. Also, all buildings undergoing lifecycle renovations and some old existing buildings are having their HVAC systems changed out to geothermal systems. University vehicle fleet includes some that use compressed natural gas.

ADMISSIONS

Freshman Academic Profile: Average high school GPA 3.32. 9.42% in top 10% of high school class, 33.1% in top 25% of high school class, 76.31% in top 50% of high school class. SAT Math middle 50% range 490–580. SAT Critical Reading middle 50% range 480–560. SAT Writing middle 50% range 480–570. Minimum paper TOEFL 550. Minimum computer TOEFL 213. Minimum web-based TOEFL 80. **Basis for Candidate Selection:** *Very important factors considered include:* Class rank, academic GPA, rigor of secondary school record. *Important factors considered include:* Standardized test scores. *Other factors considered include:* Application essay, character/personal qualities, extracurricular activities, racial/ethnic status, talent/ability, volunteer work, work experience. **Freshman Admission Requirements:** High school diploma is required and GED is accepted. *Academic units required:* 4 English, 3 mathematics, 2 science, (1 science labs), 2 social studies, 2 history, 1 academic electives. *Academic units recommended:* 4 English, 4 mathematics, 3 science, (2 science labs), 2 foreign language, 1 visual/performing arts, 1 computer science, 2 academic electives. **Freshman Admission Statistics:** 13,619 applied, 49% admitted, 34% enrolled. **Transfer Admission Requirements:** College transcript(s), essay or personal statement, minimum college GPA of 2.0 required. Lowest grade transferable C. **General Admission Information:** Application fee $35. Notification on a rolling basis, beginning on or about 10/1. Nonfall registration accepted. Admission may be deferred for a maximum of Varies. Credit and/or placement offered for CEEB Advanced Placement tests.

COSTS AND FINANCIAL AID

Annual in-state tuition $5,554. Annual out-of-state tuition $13,886. Room and board $7,214. Required fees $1,657. Average book expense $1,320. **Required Forms and Deadlines:** FAFSA. Priority financial aid filing date 3/1. **Notification of Awards:** Applicants will be notified of awards on or about 4/1. **Types of Aid:** *Need-based scholarships/grants:* Federal Pell, SEOG, state scholarships/grants, the school's own gift aid. *Loans:* FFEL Subsidized Stafford, FFEL Unsubsidized Stafford, FFEL PLUS, Federal Perkins, Federal Nursing. *Student Employment:* Federal Work-Study Program available. Institutional employment available. Off-campus job opportunities are good. **Financial Aid Statistics:** 41% freshmen, 34% undergrads receive need-based scholarship or grant aid. 8% freshmen, 5% undergrads receive non-need-based scholarship or grant aid. 66% freshmen, 61% undergrads receive need-based self-help aid. 1% freshmen, 1% undergrads receive athletic scholarships. 54.9% freshmen, 60% undergrads receive any aid. 72% undergrads borrow to pay for school. Average cumulative indebtedness $19,820.

WEST LIBERTY STATE COLLEGE

PO Box 295, West Liberty, WV 26074
Phone: 304-336-8076 **Financial Aid Phone:** 304-336-8016
E-mail: wladmsn1@wlsc.edu **CEEB Code:** 5901
Fax: 304-336-8403 **Website:** www.wlsc.edu **ACT Code:** 4534

This public school was founded in 1837. It has a 290-acre campus.

RATINGS
Admissions Selectivity Rating: 66   **Fire Safety Rating:** 60*   **Green Rating:** 60*

STUDENTS AND FACULTY
Enrollment: 2,305. **Student Body:** 55% female, 45% male, 28% out-of-state, 1% international. African American 3%, Caucasian 95%, Hispanic 1%.
Retention and Graduation: 43% grads go on to further study within 1 year. 6% grads pursue arts and sciences degrees. 1% grads pursue law degrees. 1% grads pursue business degrees. 1% grads pursue medical degrees. **Faculty:** Student/faculty ratio 18:1. 98 full-time faculty, 45% hold PhDs, 5% are members of minority groups, 40% are women.

ACADEMICS
Degrees: Associate, bachelor's. **Classes:** Most classes have 10–19 students. Most lab/discussion sessions have 10–19 students. **Majors with Highest Enrollment:** Business/commerce; criminal justice/safety studies; elementary education and teaching. **Special Study Options:** Accelerated program, double major, external degree program, honors program, independent study, internships, student-designed major, teacher certification program. **Honors programs:** The goal of the Honors Program is to foster excellence through personal endeavors. These are original challenging studies, experiemnts, or other creative accomplishments which students wish to pursue in order to enhance their intellectual development. Special programs offered to physically disabled students include note-taking services, reader services, tape recorders, tutors.

FACILITIES
Housing: Coed dorms, men's dorms, women's dorms, apartments for married students, Honors Dorm. 90% of campus accessible to physically disabled. **Special Academic Facilities/Equipment:** Book museums, language lab, clinical lab sciences and dental hygiene labs. clinical lab sciences and dental hygiene labs.

CAMPUS LIFE
Environment: Rural. **Activities:** Choral groups, concert band, drama/theater, jazz band, literary magazine, marching band, music ensembles, musical theater, pep band, radio station, student government, student newspaper, television station **Organizations:** 50 registered organizations, 10 honor societies, 4 religious organizations, 5 fraternities, 4 sororities. **Athletics (Intercollegiate):** *Men:* Baseball, basketball, cheerleading, cross-country, football, golf, swimming, tennis, track/field (outdoor), wrestling. *Women:* Basketball, cheerleading, cross-country, golf, softball, swimming, tennis, track/field (outdoor), volleyball.

ADMISSIONS
Freshman Academic Profile: Average high school GPA 3.05. 5% in top 10% of high school class, 32% in top 25% of high school class, 58% in top 50% of high school class. 88% from public high schools. SAT Math middle 50% range 390–490. SAT Critical Reading middle 50% range 400–500. ACT middle 50% range 17–22. Minimum paper TOEFL 500. Minimum computer TOEFL 173. **Basis for Candidate Selection:** *Very important factors considered include:* Rigor of secondary school record, standardized test scores. **Freshman Admission Requirements:** High school diploma is required and GED is accepted. *Academic units required:* 4 English, 2 mathematics, 2 science, (2 science labs), 2 social studies, 1 history. *Academic units recommended:* 2 foreign language. **Freshman Admission Statistics:** 1,202 applied, 98% admitted, 38% enrolled. **Transfer Admission Requirements:** College transcript(s), minimum college GPA of 2.0 required. Lowest grade transferable D. **General Admission Information:** Notification on a rolling basis, beginning on or about 10/1. Nonfall registration accepted. Credit offered for CEEB Advanced Placement tests.

COSTS AND FINANCIAL AID
Annual in-state tuition $3,138. Annual out-of-state tuition $7,790. Room and board $4,730. Average book expense $800. **Required Forms and Deadlines:** FAFSA. Priority financial aid filing date 3/1. **Notification of Awards:** Applicants will be notified of awards on a rolling basis beginning 2/15. **Types of Aid:** *Need-based scholarships/grants:* Federal Pell, SEOG, state scholarships/grants, private scholarships, the school's own gift aid. *Loans:* Direct Subsidized Stafford, Direct Unsubsidized Stafford, Direct PLUS, Federal Perkins, Federal Nursing. *Student Employment:* Off-campus job opportunities are good. **Financial Aid Statistics:** 46% freshmen, 44% undergrads receive need-based scholarship or grant aid. 44% freshmen, 21% undergrads receive non-need-based scholarship or grant aid. 40% freshmen, 58% undergrads receive need-based self-help aid. 64% undergrads borrow to pay for school. Average cumulative

indebtedness $13,800. **Criteria for awarding institutional aid:** *Non-need-based:* State/district residency.

WEST SUBURBAN COLLEGE OF NURSING

3 Erie Court, Oak Park, IL 60302
Phone: 708-763-6530 **Financial Aid Phone:** 708-763-1426
E-mail: admission@wscn.edu
Fax: 708-763-1531 **Website:** www.wscn.edu

This private school, affiliated with the Roman Catholic Church, was founded in 1914.

RATINGS
Admissions Selectivity Rating: 60*   **Fire Safety Rating:** 60*   **Green Rating:** 60*

STUDENTS AND FACULTY
Enrollment: 236. **Student Body:** 86% female, 14% male, % out-of-state,. Asian 24%, African American 10%, Caucasian 40%, Hispanic 13%. **Faculty:** Student/faculty ratio 10.1:1. 23 full-time faculty, 17% hold PhDs, 17% are members of minority groups, 100% are women.

ACADEMICS
Degrees: Bachelor's, master's. **Classes:** Most classes have 10–19 students. Most lab/discussion sessions have fewer than 10 students. **Special Study Options:** Accelerated program, WSCN offers an Evening & Weekend program. There is also a Master of Science in Nursing program, which offers four separate majors. **Career services:** alumni services, career assessment.

FACILITIES
Computers: 100% of classrooms, 100% of libraries, 100% of dining areas, have wireless network access. Students can register for classes online. Administrative functions (other than registration) can be performed online. Undergraduates are required to own a computer.

CAMPUS LIFE
Environment: Metropolis. **Activities:** Student government **Organizations:** 2 registered organizations.

ADMISSIONS
Freshman Admission Requirements: High school diploma is required and GED is accepted. **Transfer Admission Requirements:** College transcript(s), essay or personal statement, standardized test scores, minimum college GPA of 2.75 required. Lowest grade transferable C. **General Admission Information:** Application fee $30. Regular application deadline 4/1. Admission may be deferred for a maximum of .1 semester.

COSTS AND FINANCIAL AID
Types of Aid: *Need-based scholarships/grants:* Federal Pell, SEOG, state scholarships/grants, private scholarships, the school's own gift aid, Federal Nursing Scholarships. *Loans:* FFEL Subsidized Stafford, FFEL Unsubsidized Stafford, FFEL PLUS, college/university loans from institutional funds. *Student Employment:* Federal Work-Study Program available. Institutional employment available. Highest amount earned per year from on-campus jobs $5,353. Off-campus job opportunities are good. **Financial Aid Statistics:** 91% undergrads receive need-based scholarship or grant aid. 16% undergrads receive non-need-based scholarship or grant aid. 72% undergrads receive need-based self-help aid. 86% undergrads receive any aid. 86% undergrads borrow to pay for school. **Criteria for awarding institutional aid:** *Non-need-based:* Academics.

WEST TEXAS A&M UNIVERSITY

PO Box 60907, Canyon, TX 79016-0001
Phone: 806-651-2020 **Financial Aid Phone:** 806-651-2055
E-mail: admissions@mail.wtamu.edu **CEEB Code:** 3665
Fax: 806-651-5268 **Website:** www.wtamu.edu **ACT Code:** 4250

This public school was founded in 1910. It has a 135-acre campus.

RATINGS
Admissions Selectivity Rating: 71   **Fire Safety Rating:** 60*   **Green Rating:** 60*

STUDENTS AND FACULTY
Enrollment: 6,051. **Student Body:** 55% female, 45% male, 8% out-of-state, 1% international (37 countries represented). Asian 2%, African American 5%, Caucasian 72%, Hispanic 19%, Native American 1%.

Retention and Graduation: 64% freshmen return for sophomore year. 17% freshmen graduate within 4 years. **Faculty:** Student/faculty ratio 18:1. 252 full-time faculty, 68% hold PhDs, 6% are members of minority groups, 44% are women. 4% of classes are taught by teaching assistants.

ACADEMICS

Degrees: Bachelor's, diploma, master's. **Classes:** Most classes have 20–29 students. Most lab/discussion sessions have 20–29 students. **Majors with Highest Enrollment:** Business/commerce; multi-/interdisciplinary studies, other; nursing/registered nurse (RN, ASN, BSN, MSN). **Special Study Options:** Cooperative education program, distance learning, double major, English as a Second Language (ESL), honors program, independent study, internships, liberal arts/career combination, study abroad, teacher certification program. **Honors programs:** The Honors Program at West Texas AandM University is committed to providing exceptional students with challenging academic studies, innovative approaches to instruction; increased opportunities for improving skills in critical thinking, research, developing creative works and writing; expanded cultural knowledge; and the opportunity to interact closely with faculty and similarly motivated students. **Combined degree programs:** BBA/MPA. Special programs offered to physically disabled students include note-taking services, reader services, tape recorders, tutors. **Career services:** Alumni network, alumni services, career/job search classes, career assessment, internships, regional alumni.

FACILITIES

Housing: Coed dorms, special housing for disabled students, men's dorms, women's dorms, fraternity/sorority housing, Honors Program. 100% of campus accessible to physically disabled. **Special Academic Facilities/Equipment:** Regional History Museum, Research Center, Panhandle Plains Historical Museum, Killgore Research Center. **Computers:** Students can register for classes online. Administrative functions (other than registration) can be performed online.

CAMPUS LIFE

Environment: Village. **Activities:** Choral groups, concert band, dance, drama/theater, jazz band, literary magazine, marching band, music ensembles, musical theater, opera, radio station, student government, student newspaper, symphony orchestra, campus ministries, international student organization. **Organizations:** 110 registered organizations, 15 honor societies, 13 religious organizations. 5 fraternities, 5 sororities. **Athletics (Intercollegiate):** *Men:* Baseball, basketball, cross-country, football, golf, soccer. *Women:* Basketball, cheerleading, cross-country, equestrian sports, golf, soccer, softball, volleyball. **On-Campus Highlights:** Panhandle-Plains Historical Museum, Jack B. Kelley Student Center, Virgil Henson Activities Center, Old Main (first building built on campus), WTAMU Horse Center, Panhandle-Plains Historical Museum is the largest historical museum in the State of Texas.

ADMISSIONS

Freshman Academic Profile: 18% in top 10% of high school class, 47% in top 25% of high school class, 84% in top 50% of high school class. 99% from public high schools. SAT Math middle 50% range 420–520. SAT Critical Reading middle 50% range 460–600. SAT Writing middle 50% range 440–530. ACT middle 50% range 18–23. Minimum paper TOEFL 520. Minimum computer TOEFL 190. **Basis for Candidate Selection:** *Very important factors considered include:* Class rank, academic GPA, standardized test scores. *Important factors considered include:* Rigor of secondary school record. *Other factors considered include:* Recommendation(s). **Freshman Admission Requirements:** High school diploma is required and GED is accepted. *Academic units required:* 4 English, 3 mathematics, 3 science. *Academic units recommended:* 2 foreign language, 4 social studies. **Freshman Admission Statistics:** 2,340 applied, 71% admitted, 58% enrolled. **Transfer Admission Requirements:** College transcript(s), minimum college GPA of 2.0 required. Lowest grade transferable C. **General Admission Information:** Application fee $25. Notification on a rolling basis, beginning on or about 9/1. Nonfall registration accepted. Admission may be deferred for a maximum of 1 term. Credit offered for CEEB Advanced Placement tests.

COSTS AND FINANCIAL AID

Average book expense $900. **Required Forms and Deadlines:** FAFSA. **Notification of Awards:** Applicants will be notified of awards on a rolling basis beginning 2/1. **Types of Aid:** *Need-based scholarships/grants:* Federal Pell, SEOG, state scholarships/grants, private scholarships, the school's own gift aid. *Loans:* FFEL Subsidized Stafford, FFEL Unsubsidized Stafford, FFEL PLUS, Federal Perkins, state loans. *Student Employment:* Highest amount earned per year from on-campus jobs $5,850. **Financial Aid Statistics:** 32% freshmen, 42% undergrads receive need-based scholarship or grant aid. 49% freshmen, 17% undergrads receive non-need-based scholarship or grant aid. 35% freshmen, 41% undergrads receive need-based self-help aid. 6% freshmen, 5% undergrads receive athletic scholarships. 52% freshmen, 53% undergrads receive any aid. **Criteria for awarding institutional aid:** *Non-need-based:* Academics, art, athletics, leadership, music/drama, state/district residency.

WEST VIRGINIA STATE UNIVERSITY

106 Ferrell Hall, Institute, WV 25112
Phone: 304-766-3033 **Financial Aid Phone:** 304-766-3131
E-mail: admissions@wvstateu.edu **CEEB Code:** 5903
Fax: 304-766-5182 **Website:** www.wvstateu.edu **ACT Code:** 4538

This public school was founded in 1891. It has a 95-acre campus.

RATINGS

Admissions Selectivity Rating: 60*   **Fire Safety Rating:** 60*   **Green Rating:** 60*

STUDENTS AND FACULTY

Enrollment: 3,455. **Student Body:** 59% female, 41% male, 8% out-of-state, (8 countries represented). Asian 1%, African American 15%, Caucasian 81%, Hispanic 1%.
Retention and Graduation: 6% grads go on to further study within 1 year. 3% grads pursue arts and sciences degrees. 1% grads pursue law degrees. 1% grads pursue business degrees. 1% grads pursue medical degrees.

ACADEMICS

Degrees: Bachelor's, master's. **Majors with Highest Enrollment:** Business administration and management; elementary education and teaching; general studies. **Special Study Options:** Cooperative education program, off-campus study: Washington, DC. Special programs offered to physically disabled students include tutors.

FACILITIES

Housing: Coed dorms, men's dorms, women's dorms, apartments for married students. **Special Academic Facilities/Equipment:** On-campus day-care center, art gallery, ROTC Hall of Fame, Sports Hall of Fame.

CAMPUS LIFE

Environment: Village. **Activities:** Choral groups, concert band, jazz band, literary magazine, marching band, music ensembles, radio station, student government, student newspaper, television station, yearbook. **Organizations:** 4 honor societies, 2 religious organizations. 6 fraternities, 3 sororities. **Athletics (Intercollegiate):** *Men:* Baseball, basketball, cross-country, football, softball, tennis, track/field (outdoor), volleyball. *Women:* Basketball, cross-country, softball, tennis, track/field (outdoor), volleyball.

ADMISSIONS

Freshman Academic Profile: 99% from public high schools. **Freshman Admission Requirements:** High school diploma is required and GED is accepted.High school diploma is required and GED is not accepted. *Academic units required:* 4 English, 2 mathematics, 2 science, 2 foreign language, 3 social studies, 1 history. **Transfer Admission Requirements:** College transcript(s), minimum college GPA of 2.0 required. Lowest grade transferable D. **General Admission Information:** Regular application deadline 8/22. Nonfall registration accepted. Credit and/or placement offered for CEEB Advanced Placement tests.

COSTS AND FINANCIAL AID

Annual in-state tuition $2,116. Annual out-of-state tuition $5,150. Room and board $3,550. Required fees $125. Average book expense $500. **Required Forms and Deadlines:** FAFSA, institution's own financial aid form. **Types of Aid:** *Need-based scholarships/grants: Loans:* FFEL Subsidized Stafford, FFEL PLUS. *Student Employment:* Highest amount earned per year from on-campus jobs $1,300.

WEST VIRGINIA UNIVERSITY

Admissions Office, PO Box 6009, Morgantown, WV 26506-6009
Phone: 304-293-2121 **Financial Aid Phone:** 304-293-5242
E-mail: go2wvu@mail.wvu.edu **CEEB Code:** 5904
Fax: 304-293-3080 **Website:** www.wvu.edu **ACT Code:** 4540

This public school was founded in 1867.

RATINGS

Admissions Selectivity Rating: 76   **Fire Safety Rating:** 96   **Green Rating:** 99

STUDENTS AND FACULTY

Enrollment: 21,720. **Student Body:** 45% female, 55% male, 45.4% out-of-state, international (67 countries represented).

Retention and Graduation: Faculty: Student/faculty ratio 23:1. 935 full-time faculty, 80% hold PhDs, 13% are members of minority groups, 39% are women.

ACADEMICS

Degrees: Bachelor's, master's. **Classes:** Most classes have 20–29 students. Most lab/discussion sessions have 20–29 students. **Majors with Highest Enrollment:** Business/commerce; engineering; health professions and related clinical sciences, other. **Special Study Options:** Accelerated program, cooperative education program, distance learning, double major, English as a Second Language (ESL), exchange student program (domestic), external degree program, honors program, independent study, internships, student-designed major, study abroad, teacher certification program, weekend college. **Honors programs:** Honors Leadership Academy **Combined degree programs:** BA/MA, BA/MA in Ed,BSBAd/BA Lang,BA/MOT,BA/MPT,MPA/BSW. Special programs offered to physically disabled students include note-taking services, reader services, tape recorders, tutors. **Career services:** Alumni network, alumni services, career/job search classes, career assessment, internships

FACILITIES

Housing: Coed dorms, special housing for disabled students, men's dorms, special housing for international students, women's dorms, fraternity/sorority housing, apartments for married students, cooperative housing, apartments for single students, Special interest "floors" available, Operation Jump Start places faculty residence hall leaders adjacent to residence halls allowing frequent opportunities for faculty-student interaction outside classroom. This program mandatory for freshmen. 90% of campus accessible to physically disabled. **Special Academic Facilities/Equipment:** Art galleries, creative arts center, arboretum, herbarium, planetarium, concurrent engineering research center, discovery lab (for inventors), Appalachian hardwood center, small business development center, pharmacy museum, coal and energy museum, center for economic research, fluidization center, center for software development. **Computers:** 80% of classrooms, 75% of dorms, 100% of libraries, 40% of dining areas, 100% of student union, 10% of common outdoor areas have wireless network access. Students can register for classes online. Administrative functions (other than registration) can be performed online.

CAMPUS LIFE

Environment: Town. **Activities:** Choral groups, concert band, dance, drama/theater, jazz band, literary magazine, marching band, music ensembles, musical theater, pep band, radio station, student government, student newspaper, symphony orchestra, television station, yearbook, campus ministries, international student organization. **Organizations:** 370 registered organizations, 31 honor societies, 28 religious organizations. 14 fraternities, 9 sororities. **Athletics (Intercollegiate):** *Men:* Baseball, basketball, diving, football, riflery, soccer, swimming, wrestling. *Women:* Basketball, crew/rowing, cross-country, diving, gymnastics, riflery, soccer, swimming, tennis, track/field (outdoor), track/field (indoor), volleyball. **On-Campus Highlights:** New state-of-the-art Student Recreation Center, Mountainlair (Student Union), Personal Rapid Transit (PRT), Mountaineer Field, Historic Woodburn Circle, Core Arboretum. **Environmental Initiatives:** 1. Energy (Performance Contracting): Performance-based contract between WVU and Siemens Building Systems 2. Trayless Dining: A trayless dining beta study was conducted at Arnold's Diner (residence hall) and Hatfields restaurant to demonstrate that savings in energy and food waste can be achieved. This study was successful and revealed a 42% reduction of waste per customer served when compared to residence hall of similar size and usage. The next phase is to evaluate the feasibility and implement trayless dining at other residence halls and cafeteria's. 3. Academics/Curriculum Development: Energy efficiency coursework, Sustainable Design & Development coursework, and the establishment of WVU Sustainable Design Studio.

ADMISSIONS

Freshman Academic Profile: Average high school GPA 3.3. 19.3% in top 10% of high school class, 45.4% in top 25% of high school class, 76.8% in top 50% of high school class. SAT Math middle 50% range 480–580. SAT Critical Reading middle 50% range 460–560. ACT middle 50% range 21–26. Minimum paper TOEFL 550. Minimum computer TOEFL 173. **Basis for Candidate Selection:** *Very important factors considered include:* Academic GPA, standardized test scores. *Important factors considered include:* Rigor of secondary school record, level of applicant's interest, state residency. *Other factors considered include:* Recommendation(s), extracurricular activities, talent/ability, volunteer work. **Freshman Admission Requirements:** High school diploma is required and GED is accepted. *Academic units required:* 4 English, 4 mathematics, 3 science, (3 science labs), 2 foreign language, 3 social studies, 1 visual/performing arts. **Freshman Admission Statistics:** 14,053 applied, 88% admitted, 37% enrolled. **Transfer Admission Requirements:** College transcript(s), minimum college GPA of 2.0 required. Lowest grade transferable D. **General Admission Information:** Application fee $25. Regular application deadline 8/1. Notification on a rolling basis, beginning on or about 10/1. Nonfall registration

accepted. Admission may be deferred for a maximum of 1 year. Credit and/or placement offered for CEEB Advanced Placement tests.

COSTS AND FINANCIAL AID

Annual in-state tuition $5,304. Annual out-of-state tuition $16,402. Room and board $7,770. Average book expense $1,178. **Required Forms and Deadlines:** FAFSA, state aid form Financial aid filing deadline 3/1. **Notification of Awards:** Applicants will be notified of awards on a rolling basis beginning 3/15. **Types of Aid:** *Need-based scholarships/grants:* Federal Pell, SEOG, state scholarships/grants, private scholarships, the school's own gift aid. *Loans:* Direct Subsidized Stafford, Direct Unsubsidized Stafford, Direct PLUS, Federal Perkins, college/university loans from institutional funds. *Student Employment:* Federal Work-Study Program available. Institutional employment available. Highest amount earned per year from on-campus jobs $2,500. Off-campus job opportunities are good. **Financial Aid Statistics:** 33% freshmen, 34% undergrads receive need-based scholarship or grant aid. 33% freshmen, 36% undergrads receive non-need-based scholarship or grant aid. 35% freshmen, 41% undergrads receive need-based self-help aid. 1% freshmen, 1% undergrads receive athletic scholarships. 72% freshmen, 75% undergrads receive any aid. Average cumulative indebtedness $17,321. **Criteria for awarding institutional aid:** *Non-need-based:* Academics, alumni affiliation, art, athletics, job skills, leadership, minority status, music/drama, state/district residency.

WEST VIRGINIA UNIVERSITY INSTITUTE OF TECHNOLOGY

Box 10 Old Main, Montgomery, WV 25136
Phone: 304-442-3167
E-mail: admissions@wvutech.edu
Fax: 304-442-3097 **Website:** www.wvutech.edu

This is a public school.

RATINGS

Admissions Selectivity Rating: 60*   **Fire Safety Rating:** 60*   **Green Rating:** 60*

STUDENTS AND FACULTY

Enrollment: 2,001. **Student Body:** 39% female, 61% male, 6% out-of-state, 4% international. Asian 1%, African American 8%, Caucasian 87%, Hispanic 1%.

Retention and Graduation: 62% freshmen return for sophomore year. **Faculty:** Student/faculty ratio 16:1. 119 full-time faculty, 47% hold PhDs, 18% are members of minority groups, 28% are women.

ACADEMICS

Degrees: Associate, bachelor's, certificate, master's. **Classes:** Most classes have 10–19 students. Most lab/discussion sessions have 20–29 students. **Special Study Options:** Cooperative education program, distance learning, double major, dual enrollment, internships, student-designed major

FACILITIES

Housing: Coed dorms, men's dorms, women's dorms, fraternity/sorority housing.

CAMPUS LIFE

Activities: Choral groups, concert band, drama/theater, jazz band, marching band, music ensembles, pep band, student government, student newspaper. **Organizations:**

ADMISSIONS

Freshman Academic Profile: Average high school GPA 3.16. 20% in top 10% of high school class, 21% in top 25% of high school class, 43% in top 50% of high school class. 88% from public high schools. SAT Math middle 50% range 400–580. SAT Critical Reading middle 50% range 380–530. ACT middle 50% range 17–23. Minimum paper TOEFL 500. Minimum computer TOEFL 173. **Basis for Candidate Selection:** *Very important factors considered include:* Rigor of secondary school record, standardized test scores, *Other factors considered include:* Class rank, recommendation(s), alumni/ae relation, character/personal qualities, extracurricular activities, interview, state residency, talent/ability, volunteer work. **Freshman Admission Requirements:** High school diploma is required and GED is accepted. *Academic units required:* 4 English, 2 mathematics, 2 science, (2 science labs), 3 social studies. *Academic units recommended:* 4 English, 3 mathematics, 2 science, (2 science labs), 2 foreign language, 3 social studies. **Freshman Admission Statistics:** 1,191 applied, 74% admitted, 47% enrolled. **Transfer Admission Requirements:** College transcript(s), minimum college GPA of 1.7 required. Lowest grade transferable D. **General Admission Information:** Notification on a rolling basis, beginning on or about 9/30. Nonfall registration accepted. Admission may be deferred for a maximum of 1 semester. Credit offered for CEEB Advanced Placement tests.

COSTS AND FINANCIAL AID

Annual in-state tuition $3,200. Annual out-of-state tuition $8,400. Room and board $4,896. Average book expense $800. **Required Forms and Deadlines:** FAFSA, institution's own financial aid form Financial aid filing deadline 4/3. Priority financial aid filing date 2/3. **Notification of Awards:** Applicants will be notified of awards on a rolling basis beginning 3/3. **Types of Aid:** *Need-based scholarships/grants:* Federal Pell, SEOG, state scholarships/grants, private scholarships, the school's own gift aid. *Loans:* Direct Subsidized Stafford, Direct Unsubsidized Stafford, Direct PLUS, FFEL Subsidized Stafford, FFEL Unsubsidized Stafford, FFEL PLUS, Federal Perkins. **Financial Aid Statistics:** 47% freshmen, 43% undergrads receive need-based scholarship or grant aid. 42% freshmen, 26% undergrads receive non-need-based scholarship or grant aid. 35% freshmen, 38% undergrads receive need-based self-help aid. 2% freshmen, 6% undergrads receive athletic scholarships. 47% undergrads borrow to pay for school. **Criteria for awarding institutional aid:** *Non-need-based:* Academics, alumni affiliation, art, athletics, music/drama.

WEST VIRGINIA WESLEYAN COLLEGE

59 College Avenue, Buckhannon, WV 26201
Phone: 304-473-8510 **Financial Aid Phone:** 304-473-8080
E-mail: admission@wvwc.edu **CEEB Code:** 5905
Fax: 304-473-8108 **Website:** www.wvwc.edu **ACT Code:** 4544

This private school, affiliated with the Methodist Church, was founded in 1890. It has a 120-acre campus.

RATINGS
Admissions Selectivity Rating: 79   **Fire Safety Rating:** 60*   **Green Rating:** 72

STUDENTS AND FACULTY

Enrollment: 1,353. **Student Body:** 54% female, 46% male, 39% out-of-state, 4% international (12 countries represented). Asian 1%, African American 8%, Caucasian 81%, Hispanic 3%, Native American 1%.
Retention and Graduation: 75% freshmen return for sophomore year. 43% freshmen graduate within 4 years. 35% grads go on to further study within 1 year. 57% grads pursue arts and sciences degrees. 11% grads pursue law degrees. 16% grads pursue business degrees. 6% grads pursue medical degrees. **Faculty:** Student/faculty ratio 13:1. 75 full-time faculty, 76% hold PhDs, 1% are members of minority groups, 44% are women.

ACADEMICS

Degrees: Bachelor's, master's. **Classes:** Most classes have 10–19 students. Most lab/discussion sessions have 10–19 students. **Majors with Highest Enrollment:** Biology/biological sciences; business administration and management; elementary education and teaching. **Special Study Options:** Double major, English as a Second Language (ESL), exchange student program (domestic), honors program, independent study, internships, liberal arts/career combination, student-designed major, study abroad, teacher certification program. **Honors programs:** The Honors Program is offered to recognize and challenge the College's most academically talented students. Participation is voluntary for all qualified students. **Combined degree programs:** BA/MA. Special programs offered to physically disabled students include note-taking services, reader services, tape recorders, tutors. **Career services:** Alumni network, alumni services, career/job search classes, internships.

FACILITIES

Housing: Coed dorms, special housing for disabled students, men's dorms, women's dorms, fraternity/sorority housing. **Computers:** Students can register for classes online. Undergraduates are required to own a computer.

CAMPUS LIFE

Environment: Village. **Activities:** Choral groups, dance, drama/theater, jazz band, literary magazine, music ensembles, musical theater, opera, radio station, student government, student newspaper, yearbook, campus ministries, international student organization. **Organizations:** 75 registered organizations, 31 honor societies, 6 religious organizations. 6 fraternities, 5 sororities. **Athletics (Intercollegiate):** *Men:* Baseball, basketball, cross-country, football, golf, soccer, softball, swimming, tennis, track/field (outdoor), track/field (indoor). *Women:* Basketball, cross-country, golf, lacrosse, soccer, swimming, tennis, track/field (outdoor), track/field (indoor), volleyball. **On-Campus Highlights:** Cat's Claw (alternate dining facility), Sunny Bucks (Convenience Store), Wesley Chapel, Sleeth Art Gallery, Atkinson Theatre.

ADMISSIONS

Freshman Academic Profile: Average high school GPA 3.32. 28% in top 10% of high school class, 59% in top 25% of high school class, 81% in top 50% of

high school class. 88% from public high schools. SAT Math middle 50% range 440–568. SAT Critical Reading middle 50% range 420–540. SAT Writing middle 50% range 420–540. ACT middle 50% range 19–25. Minimum paper TOEFL 500. Minimum computer TOEFL 200. **Basis for Candidate Selection:** *Very important factors considered include:* Rigor of secondary school record. *Important factors considered include:* Class rank, academic GPA, standardized test scores, alumni/ae relation, character/personal qualities, extracurricular activities, first generation, interview, level of applicant's interest, talent/ability, volunteer work. *Other factors considered include:* Application essay, recommendation(s), geographical residence, religious affiliation/commitment, state residency, work experience. **Freshman Admission Requirements:** High school diploma is required and GED is accepted. *Academic units recommended:* 4 English, 2 mathematics, 2 science, (2 science labs), 1 foreign language, 2 social studies, 2 history, 1 visual/performing arts, 1 computer science. **Freshman Admission Statistics:** 1,353 applied, 81% admitted, 36% enrolled. **Transfer Admission Requirements:** High school transcript, college transcript(s), statement of good standing from prior institution(s). Minimum college GPA of 2.50 required. Lowest grade transferable C–. **General Admission Information:** Application fee $35. Notification on a rolling basis, beginning on or about 9/15. Nonfall registration accepted. Admission may be deferred for a maximum of 1 yr. Credit offered for CEEB Advanced Placement tests.

COSTS AND FINANCIAL AID

Annual tuition $23,130. Room and board $7,140. Required fees $850. Average book expense $2,500. **Required Forms and Deadlines: Types of Aid:** *Need-based scholarships/grants:* ACG and SMART Grants. *Loans: Student Employment:* Federal Work-Study Program available. Institutional employment available. Highest amount earned per year from on-campus jobs $1,000. Off-campus job opportunities are fair. **Financial Aid Statistics:** 99% freshmen, 98% undergrads receive any aid.

See page 1324.

WESTERN CAROLINA UNIVERSITY

102 Camp Building, Cullowhee, NC 28723
Phone: 828-227-7317 **Financial Aid Phone:** 828-227-7290
E-mail: admiss@email.wcu.edu **CEEB Code:** 5897
Fax: 828-227-7319 **Website:** www.wcu.edu **ACT Code:** 3172

This public school was founded in 1889. It has a 682-acre campus.

RATINGS
Admissions Selectivity Rating: 82   **Fire Safety Rating:** 83   **Green Rating:** 85

STUDENTS AND FACULTY

Enrollment: 7,205. **Student Body:** 53% female, 47% male, 8.8% out-of-state, 3% international (38 countries represented). Asian 1%, African American 6%, Caucasian 83%, Hispanic 2%, Native American 1%.
Retention and Graduation: 26% freshmen graduate within 4 years. **Faculty:** Student/faculty ratio 14.67:1. 473 full-time faculty, 78% hold PhDs, 5% are members of minority groups, 45% are women. 2.1% of classes are taught by teaching assistants.

ACADEMICS

Degrees: Bachelor's, master's, post-bachelor's certificate, post-master's certificate. **Classes:** Most classes have 20–29 students. Most lab/discussion sessions have 10–19 students. **Majors with Highest Enrollment:** Criminal justice/safety studies; elementary education and teaching; nursing/registered nurse (RN, ASN, BSN, MSN). **Special Study Options:** Cooperative education program, distance learning, double major, dual enrollment, English as a Second Language (ESL), exchange student program (domestic), honors program, independent study, internships, student-designed major, study abroad, teacher certification program. **Honors programs:** Western has a residential Honors College designed to enhance the academic and social university experience for high-achieving students. The college consists of honors courses throughout liberal studies with an emphasis on special projects and undergraduate research in the major. Also, special housing, academic, leadership and social programs are available for honors students. Special programs offered to physically disabled students include note-taking services, reader services, tape recorders, tutors. **Career services:** Alumni network, alumni services, career assessment, internships. **Career services highlights include:** Co-op and internship experiences are very common among WCU students. Some departments require them for degree completion. Intern and co-op opportunities are available domestically and internationally.

FACILITIES

Housing: Coed dorms, special housing for disabled students, men's dorms, women's dorms, fraternity/sorority housing, apartments for married students, wellness housing, theme housing. 89% of campus accessible to physically disabled. **Special Academic Facilities/Equipment:** Fine Arts Gallery, Mountain Heritage Center, Reading Center, North Carolina Center for the Advancement of Teaching, Speech/Hearing Center, Center for Applied Technology, CATA Lab (high technology computer lab), Fine and Performing Arts Center, Institute for the Economy and the Future, Public Policy Institute. **Computers:** 90% of classrooms, 10% of dorms, 100% of libraries, 70% of dining areas, 100% of student union, 50% of common outdoor areas have wireless network access. Students can register for classes online. Administrative functions (other than registration) can be performed online. Undergraduates are required to own a computer.

CAMPUS LIFE

Environment: Rural. **Activities:** Choral groups, concert band, dance, drama/theater, jazz band, literary magazine, marching band, music ensembles, musical theater, pep band, radio station, student government, student newspaper, student-run film society, television station, campus ministries, international student organization, Model UN. **Organizations:** 103 registered organizations, 7 honor societies, 12 religious organizations. 11 fraternities, 8 sororities. **Athletics (Intercollegiate):** *Men:* Baseball, basketball, cheerleading, cross-country, football, golf, track/field (outdoor), track/field (indoor). *Women:* Basketball, cheerleading, cross-country, golf, soccer, softball, tennis, track/field (outdoor), track/field (indoor), volleyball. **On-Campus Highlights:** University Center, Campus Recreation Center, Hunter Library, Fine & Performing Arts Center, Ramsey Regional Activity Center, Courtyard Dining Hall is a new facility that opened in summer 2009. It provides students with the following options: All-you-can-eat, foodcourt with 4 restaurants, McAlisters Deli, Starbucks, and a C-store. **Environmental Initiatives:** $5.25 Million Energy Performance Contracting for several buildings on campus. This will include several energy improvements on campus for water, HVAC, lighting, building envelope and renewable energy. Developing and improving WCU Reducing our Carbon Paw Print Campaign. This year we started the Sustainability Council. This new group will help enhance our efforts across campus. Energy Management Practices – Updating Strategic Energy Plan (SEP) which includes: Tracking Measures include:—Total Energy Use Btu per Square Foot—Total Energy Cost per Square Foot—Total Water Use Gallons per Square Foot Components of Performance Plan—Energy Data Management—Energy Supply Management—Energy Use in Facilities—Equipment Efficiency—Organization Integration—Water Management In 2007-08 we achieved a 30% btu/sq ft. reduction based on 2002–03 baseline year.

ADMISSIONS

Freshman Academic Profile: Average high school GPA 3.49. 15.1% in top 10% of high school class, 43.1% in top 25% of high school class, 75% in top 50% of high school class. SAT Math middle 50% range 480–560. SAT Critical Reading middle 50% range 460–560. SAT Writing middle 50% range 440–540. ACT middle 50% range 18–23. Minimum paper TOEFL 550. Minimum computer TOEFL 213. Minimum web-based TOEFL 79. **Basis for Candidate Selection:** *Very important factors considered include:* Academic GPA, rigor of secondary school record, standardized test scores, level of applicant's interest, talent/ability. *Important factors considered include:* Class rank, application essay, recommendation(s), character/personal qualities, extracurricular activities, volunteer work, work experience. *Other factors considered include:* Alumni/ae relation, first generation, geographical residence, interview, state residency. **Freshman Admission Requirements:** High school diploma is required and GED is accepted. *Academic units required:* 4 English, 4 mathematics, 3 science, (3 science labs), 2 foreign language, 2 social studies, 1 history, 4 academic electives. *Academic units recommended:* 4 English, 4 mathematics, 3 science, (3 science labs), 2 foreign language, 2 social studies, 1 history, 8 academic electives. **Freshman Admission Statistics:** 12,325 applied, 44% admitted, 29% enrolled. **Transfer Admission Requirements:** College transcript(s), statement of good standing from prior institution(s). Minimum college GPA of 2.0 required. Lowest grade transferable C. **General Admission Information:** Application fee $45. Regular application deadline 3/1. Notification on a rolling basis, beginning on or about 1/15. Nonfall registration accepted. Credit and/or placement offered for CEEB Advanced Placement tests.

COSTS AND FINANCIAL AID

Required Forms and Deadlines: FAFSA, institution's own financial aid form. Priority financial aid filing date 3/15. **Notification of Awards:** Applicants will be notified of awards on a rolling basis beginning 4/1. **Types of Aid:** *Need-based scholarships/grants:* Federal Pell, SEOG, state scholarships/grants, private scholarships, the school's own gift aid. *Loans:* Direct Subsidized Stafford, Direct Unsubsidized Stafford, Direct PLUS, FFEL Subsidized Stafford, FFEL Unsubsidized Stafford, FFEL PLUS, Federal Perkins. *Student Employment:* Federal Work-Study Program available. Institutional employment available. Off-campus job opportunities are fair. **Financial Aid Statistics:** 58% freshmen, 53% undergrads receive need-based scholarship or grant aid. 6% freshmen, 6% undergrads receive non-need-based scholarship or grant aid. 36% freshmen, 37% undergrads receive need-based self-help aid. 4% freshmen, 4% undergrads

receive athletic scholarships. 51% undergrads borrow to pay for school. Average cumulative indebtedness $11,609. **Criteria for awarding institutional aid:** *Non-need-based:* Academics, art, athletics, leadership, music/drama, state/district residency.

WESTERN CONNECTICUT STATE UNIVERSITY

Undergraduate Admissions Office, 181 White Street, Danbury, CT 06810-6855
Phone: 203-837-9000 **Financial Aid Phone:** 203-837-8588
E-mail: admissions@wcsu.edu **CEEB Code:** 3350
Fax: 000 000-0000 **Website:** www.wcsu.edu **ACT Code:** 558

This public school was founded in 1903. It has a 364-acre campus.

RATINGS

Admissions Selectivity Rating: 75   **Fire Safety Rating:** 83   **Green Rating:** 71

STUDENTS AND FACULTY

Enrollment: 5,092. **Student Body:** 55% female, 45% male, 9% out-of-state, international (7 countries represented). Asian 3%, African American 7%, Caucasian 77%, Hispanic 7%.
Retention and Graduation: 73% freshmen return for sophomore year. 13% freshmen graduate within 4 years. 23% grads go on to further study within 1 year. 10% grads pursue arts and sciences degrees. 2% grads pursue law degrees. 3% grads pursue business degrees. 1% grads pursue medical degrees. **Faculty:** Student/faculty ratio 15:1. 212 full-time faculty, 75% hold PhDs, 13% are members of minority groups, 44% are women.

ACADEMICS

Degrees: Associate, bachelor's, certificate, master's. **Classes:** Most classes have 20–29 students. Most lab/discussion sessions have 20–29 students. **Majors with Highest Enrollment:** Criminal justice/police science; elementary education and teaching; nursing/registered nurse (RN, ASN, BSN, MSN). **Special Study Options:** Cooperative education program, cross-registration, distance learning, double major, dual enrollment, English as a Second Language (ESL), honors program, independent study, internships, student-designed major, study abroad, teacher certification program. **Honors programs:** University Scholars Program Special programs offered to physically disabled students include note-taking services, reader services, tape recorders, tutors. **Career services:** career/job search classes, career assessment, internships. **Career services highlights include:** Career assessment utilizes career software, "SIG13", which assesses career interests; maintains an extensive career library which offers a large collection of literature on career fields, job search, company profiles, and graduate/professional school information; and hosts a major Career Fair each year.

FACILITIES

Housing: Coed dorms, women's dorms, apartments for single students, On campus housing assigned on a first-come, first-served basis. 100% of campus accessible to physically disabled. **Special Academic Facilities/Equipment:** Language lab, observatory, electron microscope, nature preserve, computer-enhanced classrooms, business library, Jane Goodall Institute. **Computers:** 50% of classrooms, 80% of dorms, 100% of libraries, 100% of dining areas, 100% of student union, have wireless network access. Students can register for classes online. Administrative functions (other than registration) can be performed online.

CAMPUS LIFE

Environment: City. **Activities:** Choral groups, concert band, dance, drama/theater, jazz band, literary magazine, music ensembles, musical theater, opera, pep band, radio station, student government, student newspaper, symphony orchestra, yearbook, campus ministries, international student organization. **Organizations:** 40 registered organizations, 8 honor societies, 3 religious organizations. 3 fraternities, 4 sororities. **Athletics (Intercollegiate):** *Men:* Baseball, basketball, football, lacrosse, soccer, tennis. *Women:* Basketball, field hockey, lacrosse, soccer, softball, swimming, tennis, volleyball. **On-Campus Highlights:** Student Centers (Midtown and Westside), O'Neill Center, Science Building, White Hall, Ancell Classroom Building. **Environmental Initiatives:** Think Green: Go Blue recycling efforts (with distribution campus wide of an instruction brochure). Building Automation. Controls monitoring

ADMISSIONS

Freshman Academic Profile: Average high school GPA 2.79. 6% in top 10% of high school class, 20% in top 25% of high school class, 61% in top 50% of high school class. 91% from public high schools. SAT Math middle 50% range 440–530. SAT Critical Reading middle 50% range 430–540. SAT Writing middle 50% range 430–530. Minimum paper TOEFL 550. Minimum computer TOEFL 213. Minimum web-based TOEFL 79. **Basis for Candidate Selection:** *Very important factors considered include:* Rigor of secondary school record, standardized test scores, talent/ability. *Important factors considered include:* Class rank, extracurricular activities. *Other factors considered include:* Application essay, recommendation(s), alumni/ae relation, character/personal qualities, interview, racial/ethnic status, state residency, volunteer work, work experience. **Freshman Admission Requirements:** High school diploma is required and GED is accepted. *Academic units required:* 4 English, 3 mathematics, 2 science, (2 science labs), 2 foreign language, 1 social studies, 1 history. **Freshman Admission Statistics:** 4,345 applied, 58% admitted, 37% enrolled. **Transfer Admission Requirements:** College transcript(s), minimum college GPA of 2.0 required. Lowest grade transferable C–. **General Admission Information:** Application fee $50. Notification on a rolling basis, beginning on or about 12/1. Nonfall registration accepted. Admission may be deferred for a maximum of 1 year. Credit offered for CEEB Advanced Placement tests.

COSTS AND FINANCIAL AID

Required Forms and Deadlines: FAFSA, institution's own financial aid form. Financial aid filing deadline 4/15. **Notification of Awards:** Applicants will be notified of awards on a rolling basis beginning 4/15. **Types of Aid:** *Need-based scholarships/grants:* Federal Pell, SEOG, state scholarships/grants, private scholarships, the school's own gift aid. *Loans:* Direct Subsidized Stafford, Direct Unsubsidized Stafford, Direct PLUS, FFEL Subsidized Stafford, FFEL Unsubsidized Stafford, FFEL PLUS, Federal Perkins. *Student Employment:* Highest amount earned per year from on-campus jobs $1,500. Off-campus job opportunities are excellent. **Financial Aid Statistics:** 41% freshmen, 37% undergrads receive need-based scholarship or grant aid. 7% freshmen, 5% undergrads receive non-need-based scholarship or grant aid. 40% freshmen, 38% undergrads receive need-based self-help aid. 63% freshmen, 61% undergrads receive any aid. **Criteria for awarding institutional aid:** *Non-need-based:* Academics.

WESTERN ILLINOIS UNIVERSITY

1 University Circle, 115 Sherman Hall, Macomb, IL 61455-1390
Phone: 309-298-3157 **Financial Aid Phone:** 309-298-2446
E-mail: wiuadm@wiu.edu **CEEB Code:** 1900
Fax: 309-298-3111 **Website:** www.wiu.edu **ACT Code:** 1158

This public school was founded in 1899. It has a 1050-acre campus.

RATINGS

Admissions Selectivity Rating: 71   **Fire Safety Rating:** 75   **Green Rating:** 78

STUDENTS AND FACULTY

Enrollment: 10,553. **Student Body:** 47% female, 53% male, 7% out-of-state, 1% international (70 countries represented). Asian 1%, African American 9%, Caucasian 77%, Hispanic 5%.

Retention and Graduation: 74% freshmen return for sophomore year. 35% freshmen graduate within 4 years. 21% grads go on to further study within 1 year. 14% grads pursue arts and sciences degrees. 1% grads pursue law degrees. 6% grads pursue business degrees. 1% grads pursue medical degrees. **Faculty:** Student/faculty ratio 16:1. 672 full-time faculty, 71% hold PhDs, 14% are members of minority groups, 43% are women. 5% of classes are taught by teaching assistants.

ACADEMICS

Degrees: Bachelor's, doctoral, master's, post-bachelor's certificate. **Classes:** Most classes have 20–29 students. Most lab/discussion sessions have 10–19 students. **Majors with Highest Enrollment:** Business administration and management; criminal justice/law enforcement administration; elementary education and teaching. **Special Study Options:** Distance learning, double major, dual enrollment, English as a Second Language (ESL), external degree program, honors program, independent study, internships, student-designed major, study abroad, teacher certification program, weekend college. **Honors programs:** Illinois Centennial Honors College Special programs offered to physically disabled students include note-taking services, reader services, tape recorders, tutors.

FACILITIES

Housing: Coed dorms, men's dorms, special housing for international students, women's dorms, fraternity/sorority housing, apartments for married students, wellness housing. 95% of campus accessible to physically disabled. **Special Academic Facilities/Equipment:** Art gallery, electron microscope **Computers:** 100% of classrooms, 100% of dorms, 100% of libraries, 100% of dining areas, 100% of student union, 100% of common outdoor areas have wireless network access. Students can register for classes online. Administrative functions (other than registration) can be performed online.

CAMPUS LIFE

Environment: Village. **Activities:** Choral groups, concert band, dance, drama/theater, jazz band, marching band, music ensembles, musical theater, pep band, radio station, student government, student newspaper, symphony orchestra, television station, yearbook, campus ministries, international student organization. **Organizations:** 200 registered organizations, 25 honor societies, 12 religious organizations. 14 fraternities, 11 sororities. **Athletics (Intercollegiate):** *Men:* Baseball, basketball, cross-country, diving, football, golf, soccer, swimming, tennis, track/field (outdoor), track/field (indoor). *Women:* Basketball, cheerleading, cross-country, diving, golf, soccer, softball, swimming, tennis, track/field (outdoor), track/field (indoor), volleyball. **On-Campus Highlights:** University Union, Student Recreation Center, Leslie Malpass Library. **Environmental Initiatives:** n the last year Western has received two Illinois Clean Energy Community Foundation grants for energy efficient lighting upgrades. The most recent award of $59,262 is for an energy-efficient lighting upgrade in Morgan Hall consisting of retrofitting existing fluorescent lighting fixtures with high efficiency electronic ballasts and lamps that use 35 percent less energy than the original 35-year-old equipment. The University recently completed work from a previous Clean Energy Foundation grant to upgrade the lighting in Stipes Hall. The $83,680 project grant is projected to save nearly $15,000 a year in energy costs due to more efficient lighting Western students have been involved in campus beautification through the Litter Patrol, the Adopt-a-Street Program and the We Care Program to keep the campus and community clean and attractive.

ADMISSIONS

Freshman Academic Profile: Average high school GPA 3.01. 7% in top 10% of high school class, 24% in top 25% of high school class, 58% in top 50% of high school class. ACT middle 50% range 18–23. Minimum paper TOEFL 550. Minimum computer TOEFL 213. **Basis for Candidate Selection:** *Very important factors considered include:* Class rank, academic GPA, rigor of secondary school record, standardized test scores. **Freshman Admission Requirements:** High school diploma is required and GED is accepted. *Academic units recommended:* 4 English, 3 mathematics, 3 science, 3 social studies, 2 **Freshman Admission Statistics:** 8,331 applied, 64% admitted, 31% enrolled. **Transfer Admission Requirements:** College transcript(s), minimum college GPA of 2.0 required. Lowest grade transferable D. **General Admission Information:** Application fee $30. Regular application deadline 5/15. Nonfall registration accepted. Admission may be deferred for a maximum of none. Credit offered for CEEB Advanced Placement tests.

COSTS AND FINANCIAL AID

Average book expense $1,150. **Required Forms and Deadlines:** FAFSA. Priority financial aid filing date 2/15. **Notification of Awards:** Applicants will be notified of awards on a rolling basis beginning 1/15. **Types of Aid:** *Need-based scholarships/grants:* Federal Pell, SEOG, state scholarships/grants, private scholarships, the school's own gift aid. *Loans:* FFEL Subsidized Stafford, FFEL Unsubsidized Stafford, FFEL PLUS, Federal Perkins, college/university loans from institutional funds. *Student Employment:* Federal Work-Study Program available. Institutional employment available. Highest amount earned per year from on-campus jobs $6,500. Off-campus job opportunities are fair. **Financial Aid Statistics:** 47% freshmen, 42% undergrads receive need-based scholarship or grant aid. 62% freshmen, 57% undergrads receive need-based self-help aid. 4% freshmen, 3% undergrads receive athletic scholarships. 85% freshmen, 80% undergrads receive any aid. Average cumulative indebtedness $20,550. **Criteria for awarding institutional aid:** *Non-need-based:* Academics, alumni affiliation, art, athletics, leadership, minority status, music/drama.

WESTERN KENTUCKY UNIVERSITY

Potter Hall 117, 1906 College Heights Blvd, Bowling Green, KY 42101-1020
Phone: 270-745-2551 **Financial Aid Phone:** 270-745-2755
E-mail: admission@wku.edu **CEEB Code:** 1901
Fax: 270-745-6133 **Website:** www.wku.edu **ACT Code:** 1562

This public school was founded in 1906. It has a 235-acre campus.

RATINGS

Admissions Selectivity Rating: 70   **Fire Safety Rating:** 96   **Green Rating:** 92

STUDENTS AND FACULTY

Enrollment: 16,436. **Student Body:** 57% female, 43% male, 15% out-of-state, 2% international (55 countries represented). Asian 1%, African American 11%, Caucasian 83%, Hispanic 1%.

Retention and Graduation: 74% freshmen return for sophomore year. 22% freshmen graduate within 4 years. **Faculty:** Student/faculty ratio 19:1. 735 full-time faculty, 72% hold PhDs, 14% are members of minority groups, 48% are women. 1% of classes are taught by teaching assistants.

ACADEMICS

Degrees: Associate, bachelor's, certificate, master's, post-bachelor's certificate, post-master's certificate. **Classes:** Most classes have 20–29 students. Most lab/discussion sessions have 10–19 students. **Majors with Highest Enrollment:** Biology/biological sciences; business administration and management; elementary education and teaching. **Special Study Options:** Cooperative education program, distance learning, double major, dual enrollment, English as a Second Language (ESL), exchange student program (domestic), honors program, independent study, internships, study abroad, teacher certification program, Gatton Academy of Math and Science, Learning Communities/Block Scheduling, Honors College, American Democracy Project. **Honors programs:** University Honors College Gatton Academy of Mathematics and Science Special programs offered to physically disabled students include note-taking services, reader services, tape recorders, tutors. **Career services:** Alumni network, alumni services, career/job search classes, career assessment, internships.

FACILITIES

Housing: Coed dorms, men's dorms, special housing for international students, women's dorms, fraternity/sorority housing, theme housing, Gatton Academy, Learning Communities, Themed Living options—Fit,Honors, Mosiac Communities. **Special Academic Facilities/Equipment:** Kentucky Museum, University Farm, Hardin Planetarium, Media and Technology Hall. **Computers:** 100% of classrooms, 68% of dorms, 100% of libraries, 100% of dining areas, 100% of student union, have wireless network access. Students can register for classes online. Administrative functions (other than registration) can be performed online.

CAMPUS LIFE

Environment: Town. **Activities:** Choral groups, concert band, dance, drama/theater, jazz band, literary magazine, marching band, music ensembles, musical theater, opera, pep band, radio station, student government, student newspaper, student-run film society, symphony orchestra, television station, yearbook, campus ministries, international student organization. **Organizations:** 360 registered organizations, 28 honor societies, 23 religious organizations. 18 fraternities, 13 sororities. **Athletics (Intercollegiate):** *Men:* Baseball, basketball, cross-country, diving, football, golf, riflery, swimming, tennis, track/field (outdoor), track/field (indoor). *Women:* Basketball, cross-country, diving, golf, riflery, soccer, swimming, tennis, track/field (outdoor), track/field (indoor), volleyball. **On-Campus Highlights:** Downing University Center, Preston Health and Activities Center, E.A. Diddle Arena and L.T. Smith Stadium, Mass Media and Technology Hall, Guthrie Tower, Please visit www.wku.edu/tour.html for further information and an interactive tour of the university. **Environmental Initiatives:** Sustainability-oriented staff positions and Sustainability Committee Creation of comprehensive Energy Policy that will guide purchasing, building operation, building design and construction, transportation, and personal energy use more responsibly. LEED guidelines for all new building and renovation.

ADMISSIONS

Freshman Academic Profile: Average high school GPA 3.15. 17% in top 10% of high school class, 38% in top 25% of high school class, 67.5% in top 50% of high school class. SAT Math middle 50% range 430–550. SAT Critical Reading middle 50% range 430–540. ACT middle 50% range 18–24. Minimum paper TOEFL 525. Minimum computer TOEFL 197. **Basis for Candidate Selection:** *Very important factors considered include:* Academic GPA, standardized test scores. **Freshman Admission Requirements:** High school diploma is required and GED is accepted. *Academic units required:* 4 English, 3 mathematics, 3 science, (1 science labs), 2 foreign language, 3 social studies, 1 1/2 credits each: health and PE, history, performing arts. **Freshman Admission Statistics:** 7,757 applied, 95% admitted, 46% enrolled. **Transfer Admission Requirements:** College transcript(s), statement of good standing from prior institution(s). Minimum college GPA of 2.0 required. Lowest grade transferable D°. **General Admission Information:** Application fee $40. Regular application deadline 8/1. Nonfall registration accepted. Admission may be deferred for a maximum of N/A. Credit and/or placement offered for CEEB Advanced Placement tests.

COSTS AND FINANCIAL AID

Annual in-state tuition $7,200. Annual out-of-state tuition $17,784. Room and board $6,351. Average book expense $1,000. **Required Forms and Deadlines:** FAFSA. Priority financial aid filing date 4/1. **Notification of Awards:** Applicants will be notified of awards on a rolling basis beginning 3/1. **Types of Aid:** *Need-based scholarships/grants:* Federal Pell, SEOG, state scholarships/grants, private scholarships, the school's own gift aid, United Negro College Fund. *Loans:* FFEL Subsidized Stafford, FFEL Unsubsidized Stafford, FFEL PLUS, Federal Perkins, Alternative private loans, Federal Parent Plus Loans. *Student Employment:* Federal Work-Study Program available. Institutional employment available. Off-campus job opportunities are good. **Financial Aid Statistics:** 41% freshmen, 38% undergrads receive need-based scholarship or grant aid. 50% freshmen, 32% undergrads receive non-need-based scholarship or grant aid. 40% freshmen, 44% undergrads receive need-based self-help aid. 3% freshmen, 3% undergrads receive athletic scholarships. 95% freshmen, 87%

---

undergrads receive any aid. 56% undergrads borrow to pay for school. Average cumulative indebtedness $17,436. **Criteria for awarding institutional aid:** *Non-need-based:* Academics, alumni affiliation, art, athletics, job skills, leadership, minority status, music/drama, religious affiliation, state/district residency.

WESTERN MARYLAND COLLEGE

2 College Hill, Westminster, MD 21157
Phone: 410-848-7000 **Financial Aid Phone:** 410-857-2233

RATINGS

Admissions Selectivity Rating: 83   **Fire Safety Rating:** 60*   **Green Rating:** 60*

STUDENTS AND FACULTY

Enrollment: 1,687. **Student Body:** 56% female, 44% male, 30% out-of-state, international. Asian 3%, African American 5%, Caucasian 80%, Hispanic 2%, Native American 1%.
Retention and Graduation: 84% freshmen return for sophomore year.

ACADEMICS

Degrees: Majors with Highest Enrollment: Business/commerce; psychology; sociology; Special programs offered to physically disabled students include note-taking services, reader services, tape recorders, tutors. **Career services:** Alumni network, career/job search classes, career assessment, internships.

FACILITIES

Housing: Coed dorms, special housing for disabled students, men's dorms, women's dorms, fraternity/sorority housing, apartments for married students, apartments for single students, single family homes shared by 3–10 students. 80% of campus accessible to physically disabled. **Special Academic Facilities/Equipment:** Art gallery, computer graphics and physiology labs, electron microscope, math spectrometer. **Computers:** Students can register for classes online. Administrative functions (other than registration) can be performed online.

CAMPUS LIFE

Activities: Choral groups, concert band, dance, drama/theater, jazz band, literary magazine, music ensembles, musical theater, pep band, radio station, student government, student newspaper, symphony orchestra, television station, yearbook. **Organizations:** 136 registered organizations, 22 honor societies, 5 religious organizations. 6 fraternities, 4 sororities. **Athletics (Intercollegiate):** *Men:* Baseball, basketball, cross-country, football, golf, lacrosse, soccer, swimming, tennis, track/field (outdoor), track/field (indoor), volleyball, wrestling. *Women:* Basketball, cross-country, field hockey, golf, lacrosse, soccer, softball, swimming, tennis, track/field (outdoor), track/field (indoor), volleyball. **On-Campus Highlights:** The Hoover Library, Peterson Hall, Golf course, Bair stadium, Academic Hall.

ADMISSIONS

Freshman Academic Profile: Minimum paper TOEFL 550. Minimum computer TOEFL 213. **General Admission Information:** Credit and/or placement offered for CEEB Advanced Placement tests.

COSTS AND FINANCIAL AID

Financial Aid Statistics: 85% undergrads receive any aid.

WESTERN MICHIGAN UNIVERSITY

1903 W. Michigan Avenue, Kalamazoo, MI 49008-5211
Phone: 269-387-2000 **Financial Aid Phone:** 269-387-6000
E-mail: ask-wmu@wmich.edu **CEEB Code:** 1902
Fax: 269-387-2096 **Website:** www.wmich.edu **ACT Code:** 2066

This public school was founded in 1903. It has a 1200-acre campus.

RATINGS

Admissions Selectivity Rating: 71   **Fire Safety Rating:** 76   **Green Rating:** 94

STUDENTS AND FACULTY

Enrollment: 13,802. **Student Body:** 29% female, 71% male, 6% out-of-state, 4% international (90 countries represented). Asian 3%, African American 11%, Caucasian 112%, Hispanic 4%, Native American 1%.
Retention and Graduation: Faculty: Student/faculty ratio 19:1. 908 full-time faculty, 80% hold PhDs, 14% are members of minority groups, 40% are women.

ACADEMICS

Degrees: Bachelor's, master's, post-bachelor's certificate, post-master's certificate. **Classes:** Most classes have 20–29 students. Most lab/discussion sessions have 20–29 students. **Majors with Highest Enrollment:** Elementary education and teaching; management science; nursing/registered nurse (RN, ASN, BSN, MSN). **Special Study Options:** Accelerated program, cross-registration, distance learning, double major, dual enrollment, English as a Second Language (ESL), exchange student program (domestic), honors program, independent study, internships, student-designed major, study abroad, teacher certification program. **Honors programs:** The Lee Honors College The mission of the Carl and Winifred Lee Honors College is to provide a lively, rigorous undergraduate program for bright, highly motivated, and active students. **Combined degree programs:** BA/MA, BA/MEng, Computer; Music. Special programs offered to physically disabled students include note-taking services, reader services, tape recorders, tutors. **Career services:** Alumni network, alumni services, career/job search classes, career assessment, internships, regional alumni.

FACILITIES

Housing: Coed dorms, special housing for disabled students, men's dorms, special housing for international students, women's dorms, fraternity/sorority housing, apartments for married students, apartments for single students, wellness housing, theme housingEach hall has a special thematic concept that is developed through programming and student involvment. Examples are: Community Service, Honors, Arts and Athletics, First Year Initiative, Upper Class Students, Diversity. 85% of campus accessible to physically disabled. **Special Academic Facilities/Equipment:** Pilot plant for manufacturing and printing of paper and for fiber recovery, behavior research and development center, nuclear accelerator, center for electron microscopy, particle accelerator lab, Library Department of Special Collections: Cistercian and Monastic Studies Collections, Medieval Studies Collections Carol Ann Haenicke American Women's Poetry Collection, Nineteenth and Twentieth Century Literature and History Collection, Book Arts Collections: Paper and Fine Printing; Aviation **Computers:** 100% of classrooms, 25% of dorms, 100% of libraries, 100% of dining areas, 100% of student union, 100% of common outdoor areas have wireless network access. Students can register for classes online. Administrative functions (other than registration) can be performed online.

CAMPUS LIFE

Environment: City. **Activities:** Choral groups, concert band, dance, drama/theater, jazz band, literary magazine, marching band, music ensembles, musical theater, opera, pep band, radio station, student government, student newspaper, student-run film society, symphony orchestra, campus ministries, international student organization. **Organizations:** 300 registered organizations, 7 honor societies, 21 religious organizations. 16 fraternities, 11 sororities. **Athletics (Intercollegiate):** *Men:* Baseball, basketball, football, ice hockey, soccer, tennis. *Women:* Basketball, cross-country, golf, gymnastics, soccer, softball, tennis, track/field (outdoor), track/field (indoor), volleyball. **On-Campus Highlights:** Bernhard Center, Waldo Library, University Recreation Center, Miller Auditorium, Gilmore Theatre Complex, Lawson Ice Arena and Gabel Natatorium provide swimming and skating facilities including lessons and family activities. **Environmental Initiatives:** Comprehensive strategic planning; green building plans; energy and water reduction; operational practices; green cleaning; recycling; xeriscaping.

ADMISSIONS

Freshman Academic Profile: Average high school GPA 3.24. 12% in top 10% of high school class, 32% in top 25% of high school class, 71% in top 50% of high school class. ACT middle 50% range 20–25. Minimum paper TOEFL 550. Minimum computer TOEFL 213. Minimum web-based TOEFL 80. **Basis for Candidate Selection:** *Very important factors considered include:* Academic GPA. *Important factors considered include:* Rigor of secondary school record, standardized test scores. *Other factors considered include:* Application essay, recommendation(s). **Freshman Admission Requirements:** High school diploma is required and GED is accepted. *Academic units required:* 4 English, 3 mathematics, 2 science, (1 science labs), 2 social studies, 1 history, 2 academic electives. *Academic units recommended:* 4 English, 3 mathematics, 2 science, (1 science labs), 1 foreign language, 2 social studies, 1 history, 1 visual/performing arts, 1 computer science, 1 academic electives. **Freshman Admission Statistics:** 12,379 applied, 83% admitted, 31% enrolled. **Transfer Admission Requirements:** College transcript(s), minimum college GPA of 2.0 required. Lowest grade transferable C. **General Admission Information:** Application fee $35. Regular application deadline 8/1. Notification on a rolling basis, beginning on or about 7/1. Nonfall registration accepted. Admission may be deferred for a maximum of 1 semester. Credit and/or placement offered for CEEB Advanced Placement tests.

COSTS AND FINANCIAL AID

Required Forms and Deadlines: FAFSA. Priority financial aid filing date 3/15. **Notification of Awards:** Applicants will be notified of awards on a rolling basis beginning 3/15. **Types of Aid:** *Need-based scholarships/grants:* Federal Pell, SEOG, state scholarships/grants, private scholarships, the school's own gift aid. *Loans:* Direct Subsidized Stafford, Direct Unsubsidized Stafford, Direct PLUS, Federal Perkins, Alternative Loans. *Student Employment:* Federal Work-Study Program available. Institutional employment available. Highest

amount earned per year from on-campus jobs $5,000. Off-campus job opportunities are excellent. **Financial Aid Statistics:** 86% freshmen, 81% undergrads receive any aid. **Criteria for awarding institutional aid:** *Non-need-based:* Academics, alumni affiliation, art, athletics, minority status, music/drama, state/district residency.

WESTERN NEW ENGLAND COLLEGE

Admissions Office, 1215 Wilbraham R, Springfield, MA 01119
Phone: 413-782-1321 **Financial Aid Phone:** 413-796-2080
E-mail: ugradmis@wnec.edu **CEEB Code:** 3962
Fax: 413-782-1777 **Website: ACT Code:** 1930

This private school was founded in 1919. It has a 215-acre campus.

RATINGS

Admissions Selectivity Rating: 75   **Fire Safety Rating:** 60*   **Green Rating:** 60*

STUDENTS AND FACULTY

Enrollment: 2,716. **Student Body:** 40% female, 60% male, 53% out-of-state, international (6 countries represented). Asian 2%, African American 4%, Caucasian 85%, Hispanic 4%.
Retention and Graduation: 75% freshmen return for sophomore year. 44% freshmen graduate within 4 years. **Faculty:** Student/faculty ratio 15:1. 188 full-time faculty, 89% hold PhDs, 7% are members of minority groups, 37% are women.

ACADEMICS

Degrees: Bachelor's, certificate, master's, terminal associate. **Classes:** Most classes have 20–29 students. Most lab/discussion sessions have 10–19 students. **Majors with Highest Enrollment:** Business/commerce; criminal justice/safety studies; psychology. **Special Study Options:** Accelerated program, cross-registration, distance learning, double major, dual enrollment, exchange student program (domestic), honors program, independent study, internships, liberal arts/career combination, student-designed major, study abroad, teacher certification program, 3+3 law program with Western New England College School of Law. Washington Semester Program. 5 Yr BSBS/MBA and Engr/MBA. 6 Yr BSBE/Law and 6 Yr BiomedEngr/Law. 5 yr BSEM/MSEM. **Honors programs:** The Honors Program at Western New England College gives academically qualified and motivated students the opportunity to join a community of like students and participate in challenging courses taught by some of the College's best faculty. Honors students generally take one honors course per semester for their first three years and work on a senior honors project during their final year. **Combined degree programs:** BA/JD. Special programs offered to physically disabled students include note-taking services, reader services, tape recorders, tutors. **Career services:** Alumni network, career assessment, internships.

FACILITIES

Housing: Coed dorms, special housing for disabled students, apartments for single students. 90% of campus accessible to physically disabled. **Special Academic Facilities/Equipment:** Art Gallery; Math, Writing Science Centers **Computers:** Students can register for classes online. Administrative functions (other than registration) can be performed online.

CAMPUS LIFE

Environment: City. **Activities:** Choral groups, concert band, dance, drama/theater, jazz band, literary magazine, music ensembles, pep band, radio station, student government, student newspaper, yearbook, campus ministries, international student organization. **Organizations:** 60 registered organizations, 8 honor societies. **Athletics (Intercollegiate):** *Men:* Baseball, basketball, cross-country, football, golf, ice hockey, lacrosse, soccer, tennis, wrestling. *Women:* Basketball, cross-country, field hockey, lacrosse, soccer, softball, swimming, tennis, volleyball. **On-Campus Highlights:** Alumni Healthful Living Center, St Germain Campus Center, D'Amour Library, Computer Labs, Rock Cafe.

ADMISSIONS

Freshman Academic Profile: Average high school GPA 3.16. 14% in top 10% of high school class, 42% in top 25% of high school class, 77% in top 50% of high school class. SAT Math middle 50% range 490–600. SAT Critical Reading middle 50% range 470–560. ACT middle 50% range 21–25. Minimum paper TOEFL 500. Minimum computer TOEFL 173. **Basis for Candidate Selection:** *Very important factors considered include:* Academic GPA, recommendation(s), standardized test scores. *Other factors considered include:* Class rank, application essay, rigor of secondary school record, alumni/ae relation, character/personal qualities, extracurricular activities, interview, level of applicant's interest, racial/ethnic status, talent/ability, volunteer work, work experience. **Freshman Admission Requirements:** High school diploma is required and GED is accepted. *Academic units required:* 4 English, 2 mathematics, 1 science, (1 science labs), 1 social studies, 1 history. *Academic units recommended:* 4 English, 4 mathematics, 2 science, (2 science labs), 2 foreign language, 2 social studies, 2 history. **Freshman Admission Statistics:** 4,769 applied, 81% admitted, 18% enrolled. **Transfer Admission Requirements:** High school transcript, college transcript(s), minimum college GPA of 2.3 required. Lowest grade transferable C–. **General Admission Information:** Application fee $50. Notification on a rolling basis, beginning on or about 12/1. Nonfall registration accepted. Admission may be deferred for a maximum of 1 year. Credit and/or placement offered for CEEB Advanced Placement tests.

COSTS AND FINANCIAL AID

Annual tuition $26,822. Room and board $10,980. Required fees $1,944. Average book expense $1,100. **Required Forms and Deadlines:** FAFSAstudent and parent 1040; W-2s. Priority financial aid filing date 4/15. **Notification of Awards:** Applicants will be notified of awards on a rolling basis beginning 3/15. **Types of Aid:** *Need-based scholarships/grants:* Federal Pell, SEOG, state scholarships/grants, private scholarships, the school's own gift aid, ACG, Smart Grants. *Loans:* Direct Subsidized Stafford, Direct Unsubsidized Stafford, Direct PLUS, FFEL PLUS, Federal Perkins, state loans, Private loan programs. *Student Employment:* Federal Work-Study Program available. Institutional employment available. Off-campus job opportunities are good. **Financial Aid Statistics:** 79% freshmen, 74% undergrads receive need-based scholarship or grant aid. 6% freshmen, 4% undergrads receive non-need-based scholarship or grant aid. 70% freshmen, 68% undergrads receive need-based self-help aid. 93% freshmen, 87% undergrads receive any aid. **Criteria for awarding institutional aid:** *Non-need-based:* Academics.

WESTERN OREGON UNIVERSITY

345 N Monmouth Avenue, Monmouth, OR 97361
Phone: 503-838-8211 **Financial Aid Phone:** 503 838 8475
E-mail: wolfgram@wou.edu **CEEB Code:** 4585
Fax: 503-838-8067 **Website:** www.wou.edu **ACT Code:** 3480

This public school was founded in 1856. It has a 157-acre campus.

RATINGS

Admissions Selectivity Rating: 79   **Fire Safety Rating:** 87   **Green Rating:** 71

STUDENTS AND FACULTY

Enrollment: 911. **Student Body:** 59% female, 41% male, 11% out-of-state, international (19 countries represented). **Retention and Graduation:** 72% freshmen return for sophomore year. 33% freshmen graduate within 4 years. **Faculty:** Student/faculty ratio 20:1. 177 full-time faculty, 10% are members of minority groups, 45% are women.

ACADEMICS

Degrees: Associate, bachelor's, master's, post-bachelor's certificate. **Classes:** Most classes have 10–19 students. Most lab/discussion sessions have 20–29 students. **Majors with Highest Enrollment:** Business/commerce; social sciences; teacher education, multiple levels. **Special Study Options:** Distance learning, double major, dual enrollment, English as a Second Language (ESL), honors program, independent study, internships, study abroad, teacher certification program. **Honors programs:** WOU Honors Program Special programs offered to physically disabled students include note-taking services, reader services, tape recorders, tutors. **Career services:** Career/job search classes, internships.

FACILITIES

Housing: Coed dorms, special housing for disabled students, apartments for married students, apartments for single students. 95% of campus accessible to physically disabled. **Special Academic Facilities/Equipment:** Jensen Arctic Museum **Computers:** 70% of classrooms, 90% of dorms, 100% of libraries, 90% of dining areas, 90% of student union, 20% of common outdoor areas have wireless network access. Students can register for classes online. Administrative functions (other than registration) can be performed online.

CAMPUS LIFE

Environment: Village. **Activities:** Choral groups, concert band, dance, drama/theater, jazz band, literary magazine, music ensembles, musical theater, student government, student newspaper, symphony orchestra, campus ministries, international student organization. **Organizations:** 50 registered organizations, 4 honor societies, 6 religious organizations. **Athletics (Intercollegiate):** *Men:* Baseball, basketball, cheerleading, cross-country, football, track/field (outdoor). *Women:* Basketball, cheerleading, cross-country, soccer, softball, track/field (outdoor), volleyball. **On-Campus Highlights:** Wayne and Lynn Hamersly Library, Neal Werner University Center, Paul Jensen Arctic Museum, Campbell Hall Art Gallery, Arbor Park Apartments. **Environmental Initiatives:** Paper recyling.

ADMISSIONS

Freshman Academic Profile: Average high school GPA 3.26. 12% in top 10% of high school class, 37% in top 25% of high school class, 74% in top 50% of high school class. 95% from public high schools. SAT Math middle 50% range 430–550. SAT Critical Reading middle 50% range 420–540. SAT Writing middle 50% range 470–560. ACT middle 50% range 17–22. Minimum paper TOEFL 500. Minimum computer TOEFL 180. **Basis for Candidate Selection:** *Very important factors considered include:* Academic GPA, rigor of secondary school record, standardized test scores. *Important factors considered include:* Class rank. *Other factors considered include:* Recommendation(s), alumni/ae relation, racial/ethnic status, talent/ability. **Freshman Admission Requirements:** High school diploma is required and GED is accepted. *Academic units required:* 4 English, 3 mathematics, 2 science, 2 foreign language, 2 social studies, 1 history. *Academic units recommended:* (1 science labs). **Freshman Admission Statistics:** 2,098 applied, 45% admitted, 97% enrolled. **Transfer Admission Requirements:** College transcript(s), minimum college GPA of 2.0 required. Lowest grade transferable D–. **General Admission Information:** Application fee $50. Notification on a rolling basis, beginning on or about 1/1. Nonfall registration accepted. Admission may be deferred for a maximum of 0. Credit and/or placement offered for CEEB Advanced Placement tests.

COSTS AND FINANCIAL AID

Annual in-state tuition $4,725. Annual out-of-state tuition $15,750. Room and board $7,675. Required fees $1,143. Average book expense $1,125. **Required Forms and Deadlines:** FAFSA. Priority financial aid filing date 3/1. **Notification of Awards:** Applicants will be notified of awards on a rolling basis beginning 2/28. **Types of Aid:** *Need-based scholarships/grants:* Federal Pell, SEOG, state scholarships/grants, private scholarships, the school's own gift aid. *Loans:* Direct Subsidized Stafford, Direct Unsubsidized Stafford, Direct PLUS, Federal Perkins, college/university loans from institutional funds. *Student Employment:* Federal Work-Study Program available. Highest amount earned per year from on-campus jobs $5,000. Off-campus job opportunities are good. **Financial Aid Statistics:** 60% freshmen, 57% undergrads receive need-based scholarship or grant aid. 5% freshmen, 3% undergrads receive non-need-based scholarship or grant aid. 61% freshmen, 65% undergrads receive need-based self-help aid. 4% freshmen, 3% undergrads receive athletic scholarships. 18% freshmen, 29% undergrads receive any aid. 61% undergrads borrow to pay for school. Average cumulative indebtedness $22,037. **Criteria for awarding institutional aid:** *Non-need-based:* Academics, alumni affiliation, art, athletics, leadership, music/drama.

WESTERN STATE COLLEGE OF COLORADO

600 N. Adams, Gunnison, CO 81231
Phone: 970-943-2119 **Financial Aid Phone:** 970-943-3085
E-mail: admissions@western.edu **CEEB Code:** 4946
Fax: 970-943-2363 **Website:** www.western.edu **ACT Code:** 536

This public school was founded in 1911. It has a 228-acre campus.

RATINGS

Admissions Selectivity Rating: 71   **Fire Safety Rating:** 76   **Green Rating:** 91

STUDENTS AND FACULTY

Enrollment: 1,982. **Student Body:** 39% female, 61% male, 22% out-of-state, (6 countries represented). Asian 1%, African American 2%, Caucasian 80%, Hispanic 5%, Native American 1%. **Retention and Graduation:** 60% freshmen return for sophomore year. 20% freshmen graduate within 4 years. 15% grads go on to further study within 1 year. **Faculty:** Student/faculty ratio 16.5:1. 107 full-time faculty, 83% hold PhDs, 3% are members of minority groups, 42% are women.

ACADEMICS

Degrees: Bachelor's. **Classes:** Most classes have 10–19 students. **Majors with Highest Enrollment:** Parks, recreation and leisure studies. **Special Study Options:** Distance learning, double major, dual enrollment, honors program, independent study, internships, liberal arts/career combination, study abroad, teacher certification program. **Honors programs:** Honors Program—based on the National Collegiate Honors Council-modeled City of Text explores urban environments, while the Partners in the Parks: Black Canyon of the Gunnison course immerses students in the ecosystems of one of America's most amazing national parks. Special programs offered to physically disabled students include note-taking services, reader services, tape recorders, tutors. **Career services:** Alumni network, alumni services, career/job search classes, career assessment, internships, regional alumni.

FACILITIES

Housing: Coed dorms, men's dorms, women's dorms, apartments for married students, apartments for single students, theme housing 80% of campus accessible to physically disabled. **Computers:** 100% of classrooms, 50% of dorms, 100% of libraries, 100% of dining areas, 100% of student union, have wireless network access. Students can register for classes online. Administrative functions (other than registration) can be performed online.

CAMPUS LIFE

Environment: Rural. **Activities:** Choral groups, concert band, dance, drama/theater, jazz band, literary magazine, music ensembles, pep band, radio station, student government, student newspaper, student-run film society, symphony orchestra, television station, campus ministries, international student organization. **Organizations:** 60 registered organizations, 8 honor societies, 5 religious organizations. **Athletics (Intercollegiate):** *Men:* Basketball, cross-country, football, track/field (outdoor), track/field (indoor), wrestling. *Women:* Basketball, cross-country, track/field (outdoor), track/field (indoor), volleyball. **On-Campus Highlights:** College Center—new student center, Hurst Hall — renovated science building, Kelley Hall—renovated social sciences, Gym — Highest Elevation NCAA basketball Court, Borick Business—new business building, College Center, Borick, Business Building and Kelley Hall are either LEED certified or seeking LEED certification. Kelley also features solar panels for energy efficiency. The new College Center features campus dining and a first-run movie theatre. **Environmental Initiatives:** President's Climate Committment—which is a significant challenge for one of the coldest locations in the nation and the isolated nature of Gunnison Bio Mass boiler system and LEED certified buildings. 4th construction project seeking will be underway in spring 2010 with biomass bioler which has received a competitive NEED grant food purchasing, pulping and composting

ADMISSIONS

Freshman Academic Profile: Average high school GPA 2.97. 6% in top 10% of high school class, 22% in top 25% of high school class, 49% in top 50% of high school class. SAT Math middle 50% range 450–550. SAT Critical Reading middle 50% range 450–550. SAT Writing middle 50% range 450–550. ACT middle 50% range 18–23. Minimum paper TOEFL 550. Minimum computer TOEFL 213. **Basis for Candidate Selection:** *Very important factors considered include:* Class rank, rigor of secondary school record, standardized test scores, *Other factors considered include:* Application essay, recommendation(s), alumni/ae relation, character/personal qualities, extracurricular activities, first generation, interview, talent/ability, volunteer work. **Freshman Admission Requirements:** High school diploma is required and GED is accepted. *Academic units required:* 4 English, 4 mathematics, 3 science, (2 science labs), 1 foreign language, 2 social studies, 2 history, 3 academic electives. *Academic units recommended:* 4 English, 4 mathematics, 3 science, 2 foreign language, 3 social studies, 3 history. **Freshman Admission Statistics:** 2,311 applied, 72% admitted, 30% enrolled. **Transfer Admission Requirements:** College transcript(s), minimum college GPA of 2.0 required. Lowest grade transferable C. **General Admission Information:** Application fee $40. Regular application deadline 8/1. Notification on a rolling basis, beginning on or about 11/1. Nonfall registration accepted. Admission may be deferred for a maximum of 1 year. Credit and/or placement offered for CEEB Advanced Placement tests.

COSTS AND FINANCIAL AID

Annual in-state tuition $5,180. Annual out-of-state tuition $12,336. Room and board $7,456. Required fees $924. Average book expense $1,500. **Required Forms and Deadlines:** FAFSA. Priority financial aid filing date 4/1. **Notification of Awards:** Applicants will be notified of awards on a rolling basis beginning 4/1. **Types of Aid:** *Need-based scholarships/grants:* Federal Pell, SEOG, state scholarships/grants, the school's own gift aid. *Loans:* Direct Subsidized Stafford, Direct Unsubsidized Stafford, Direct PLUS, Federal Perkins. *Student Employment:* Federal Work-Study Program available. Institutional employment available. Highest amount earned per year from on-campus jobs $1,500. Off-campus job opportunities are good. **Financial Aid Statistics:** 21% freshmen, 19% undergrads receive need-based scholarship or grant aid. 6% freshmen, 8% undergrads receive non-need-based scholarship or grant aid. 38% freshmen, 34% undergrads receive need-based self-help aid. 10% freshmen, 7% undergrads receive athletic scholarships. 82% freshmen, 80% undergrads receive any aid. 75% undergrads borrow to pay for school. Average cumulative indebtedness $17,750. **Criteria for awarding institutional aid:** *Non-need-based:* Academics, art, athletics, leadership, music/drama.

WESTERN WASHINGTON UNIVERSITY

Mail Stop 9009, Bellingham, WA 98225-9009
Phone: 360-650-3440 **Financial Aid Phone:** 360-650-3470
E-mail: admit@cc.wwu.edu **CEEB Code:** 4947
Fax: 360-650-7369 **Website:** www.wwu.edu **ACT Code:** 4490

This public school was founded in 1893. It has a 300-acre campus.

RATINGS

Admissions Selectivity Rating: 85   **Fire Safety Rating:** 79   **Green Rating:** 96

STUDENTS AND FACULTY

Enrollment: 13,249. **Student Body:** 55% female, 45% male, 8% out-of-state, 1% international (30 countries represented). Asian 9%, African American 3%, Caucasian 76%, Hispanic 5%, Native American 3%.
Retention and Graduation: 84% freshmen return for sophomore year. 35% freshmen graduate within 4 years. 13.3% grads go on to further study within 1 year. **Faculty:** Student/faculty ratio 19:1. 498 full-time faculty, 85% hold PhDs, 15% are members of minority groups, 43% are women. 2% of classes are taught by teaching assistants.

ACADEMICS

Degrees: Bachelor's, certificate, master's, post-bachelor's certificate, post-master's certificate. **Classes:** Most classes have 20–29 students. Most lab/discussion sessions have 10–19 students. **Majors with Highest Enrollment:** Political science and government; pre-medicine/pre-medical studies; psychology. **Special Study Options:** Distance learning, double major, English as a Second Language (ESL), exchange student program (domestic), honors program, independent study, internships, student-designed major, study abroad, teacher certification program. **Honors programs:** Honors Program features small classes and interaction between students and faculty. It is an exciting opportunity for accomplished students who would like a more intimate college experience within the setting of a larger institution. Honors students are welcome to pursue any academic major, and all students complete a self-designed capstone senior project. Special programs offered to physically disabled students include note-taking services, reader services, tape recorders, tutors. **Career services:** Alumni network, career/job search classes, career assessment, internships, regional alumni.

FACILITIES

Housing: Coed dorms, special housing for disabled students, apartments for married students, apartments for single students, theme housing, wellness floors, multicultural floors available. 100% of campus accessible to physically disabled. **Special Academic Facilities/Equipment:** Outdoor art museum, planetarium, electronic music studio, air pollution lab, motor vehicle research lab, marine lab, wind tunnel, electron microscope, neutron generator lab. **Computers:** 100% of classrooms, 100% of dorms, 100% of libraries, 100% of dining areas, 100% of student union, 100% of common outdoor areas have wireless network access. Students can register for classes online. Administrative functions (other than registration) can be performed online.

CAMPUS LIFE

Environment: City. **Activities:** concert band, dance, drama/theater, jazz band, literary magazine, marching band, music ensembles, musical theater, opera, pep band, radio station, student government, student newspaper, symphony orchestra, television station, campus ministries, international student organization. **Organizations:** 200 registered organizations, 4 honor societies, 18 religious organizations. **Athletics (Intercollegiate):** *Men:* Basketball, cheerleading, crew/rowing, cross-country, golf, soccer, track/field (outdoor), track/field (indoor). *Women:* Basketball, cheerleading, crew/rowing, cross-country, golf, soccer, softball, track/field (outdoor), track/field (indoor), volleyball. **On-Campus Highlights:** Viking Union Student Center, Red Square, Performing Arts Center, Sehome Arboretum, Student Recreation Center. **Environmental Initiatives:** 100% Green Energy Fee, All Student Bus Pass, Sustainability in the curriculum—sustainable design minor, joint economics/economics degree

ADMISSIONS

Freshman Academic Profile: Average high school GPA 3.5. 24% in top 10% of high school class, 58% in top 25% of high school class, 92% in top 50% of high school class. 90% from public high schools. SAT Math middle 50% range 510–610. SAT Critical Reading middle 50% range 500–620. SAT Writing middle 50% range 490–590. ACT middle 50% range 21–27. Minimum paper TOEFL 550. Minimum computer TOEFL 213. Minimum web-based TOEFL 80. **Basis for Candidate Selection:** *Very important factors considered include:* Rigor of secondary school record. *Important factors considered include:* Application essay, academic GPA, standardized test scores, level of applicant's interest. *Other factors considered include:* Class rank, recommendation(s), character/personal qualities, extracurricular activities, first generation, geographical residence, state residency, talent/ability, volunteer work, work experience. **Freshman Admission Requirements:** High school diploma is required and GED is accepted. *Academic units required:* 4 English, 3 mathematics, 2 science, (1 science labs), 2 foreign language, 3 social studies. **Freshman Admission Statistics:** 9,620 applied, 73% admitted, 38% enrolled. **Transfer Admission Requirements:** College transcript(s), statement of good standing from prior institution(s). Minimum college GPA of 2.0 required. Lowest grade transferable D-. **General Admission Information:** Application fee $50. Regular application deadline 3/1. Notification on a rolling basis, beginning on or about 11/1. Nonfall registration accepted. Admission may be deferred for a maximum of 1 year. Credit and/or placement offered for CEEB Advanced Placement tests.

COSTS AND FINANCIAL AID
Required Forms and Deadlines: FAFSA. Priority financial aid filing date 2/15. **Notification of Awards:** Applicants will be notified of awards on a rolling basis beginning 3/20. **Types of Aid:** *Need-based scholarships/grants:* Federal Pell, SEOG, state scholarships/grants, private scholarships, the school's own gift aid. *Loans:* Direct Subsidized Stafford, Direct Unsubsidized Stafford, Direct PLUS, Federal Perkins, state loans, Private Loans. *Student Employment:* Institutional employment available. Highest amount earned per year from on-campus jobs $2,690. Off-campus job opportunities are good. **Financial Aid Statistics:** 34% freshmen, 31% undergrads receive need-based scholarship or grant aid. 2% freshmen, 1% undergrads receive non-need-based scholarship or grant aid. 33% freshmen, 34% undergrads receive need-based self-help aid. 1% freshmen, 1% undergrads receive athletic scholarships. 41% freshmen, 41% undergrads receive any aid. 50% undergrads borrow to pay for school. Average cumulative indebtedness $15,929. **Criteria for awarding institutional aid:** *Non-need-based:* Academics, alumni affiliation, art, athletics, job skills, leadership, minority status, music/drama, state/district residency.

WESTFIELD STATE COLLEGE

Westfield State, Westfield, MA 01086
Phone: 413-572-5218
E-mail: admission@wsc.ma.edu **CEEB Code:** 3523
Fax: 413-572-0520 **Website:** www.wsc.ma.edu **ACT Code:** 1912

This public school was founded in 1838. It has a 227-acre campus.

RATINGS
Admissions Selectivity Rating: 74　　**Fire Safety Rating:** 60*　　**Green Rating:** 60*

STUDENTS AND FACULTY
Enrollment: 4,078. **Student Body:** 56% female, 44% male, 7% out-of-state, international (1 countries represented). Asian 1%, African American 3%, Caucasian 83%, Hispanic 3%.
Retention and Graduation: 76% freshmen return for sophomore year. 38% freshmen graduate within 4 years. 12% grads pursue arts and sciences degrees. 1% grads pursue law degrees. 5% grads pursue business degrees. **Faculty:** Student/faculty ratio 18:1. 168 full-time faculty, 87% hold PhDs, 10% are members of minority groups, 42% are women.

ACADEMICS
Degrees: Bachelor's, master's, post-bachelor's certificate, post-master's certificate. **Classes:** Most classes have 20–29 students. Most lab/discussion sessions have 10–19 students. **Special Study Options:** Cooperative education program, cross-registration, distance learning, double major, dual enrollment, exchange student program (domestic), honors program, independent study, internships, student-designed major, study abroad, teacher certification program Special programs offered to physically disabled students include note-taking services, reader services, tape recorders, tutors. **Career services:** Career/job search classes, career assessment.

FACILITIES
Housing: Coed dorms, special housing for disabled students, apartments for single students, Living/Learning Unit (Honors/Academic Intensive) Quiet Living Section, All Women Section, Designated smoking Section(other housing smoke free), Movement Science Student Section. **Special Academic Facilities/Equipment:** Art gallery, language lab, electron microscope. **Computers:**

CAMPUS LIFE
Environment: Village. **Activities:** Choral groups, concert band, drama/theater, jazz band, literary magazine, music ensembles, musical theater, pep band, radio station, student government, student newspaper, television station, yearbook. **Athletics (Intercollegiate):** *Men:* Baseball, basketball, cross-country, football, golf, soccer, track/field (outdoor). *Women:* Basketball, cheerleading, cross-country, field hockey, soccer, softball, swimming, volleyball.

ADMISSIONS
Freshman Academic Profile: Average high school GPA 3. SAT Math middle 50% range 460–560. SAT Critical Reading middle 50% range 460–560. Minimum paper TOEFL 550. **Basis for Candidate Selection:** *Very important factors considered include:* Rigor of secondary school record, standardized test scores. *Important factors considered include:* Extracurricular activities, talent/ability. *Other factors considered include:* Application essay, recommendation(s), character/personal qualities, racial/ethnic status, volunteer work, work experience. **Freshman Admission Requirements:** High school diploma is required and GED is accepted. *Academic units required:* 4 English, 3 mathematics, 3 science, (2 science labs), 2 foreign language, 1 social studies, 1 history, 2 academic electives. **Freshman Admission Statistics:** 3,566 applied, 67% admitted, 36% enrolled. **Transfer Admission Requirements:** College transcript(s), minimum college GPA of 2.0 required. Lowest grade transferable C–. **General Admission Information:** Application fee $25. Regular application deadline 3/1. Nonfall registration accepted. Admission may be deferred for a maximum of 1 semester. Credit and/or placement offered for CEEB Advanced Placement tests.

COSTS AND FINANCIAL AID
Annual in-state tuition $970. Annual out-of-state tuition $7,050. Room and board $5,742. Required fees $3,887. Average book expense $800. **Required Forms and Deadlines:** FAFSA. Priority financial aid filing date 3/1. **Notification of Awards:** Applicants will be notified of awards on or about 4/15. **Types of Aid:** *Need-based scholarships/grants:* Federal Pell, SEOG, state scholarships/grants, private scholarships, the school's own gift aid. *Loans:* FFEL Subsidized Stafford, FFEL Unsubsidized Stafford, FFEL PLUS, Federal Perkins, state loans. *Student Employment:* Federal Work-Study Program available. Highest amount earned per year from on-campus jobs $1,000. Off-campus job opportunities are good. **Financial Aid Statistics:** 40% freshmen, 32% undergrads receive need-based scholarship or grant aid. 1% freshmen, 1% undergrads receive non-need-based scholarship or grant aid. 47% freshmen, 38% undergrads receive need-based self-help aid. 87% undergrads borrow to pay for school. Average cumulative indebtedness $12,731.

WESTMINSTER CHOIR COLLEGE
OF RIDER UNIVERSITY

101 Walnut Lane, Princeton, NJ 08540-3899
Phone: 800-962-4647
CEEB Code: 2758
Fax: 609-921-8829 **Website:** www.rider.edu **ACT Code:** 2590

This private school was founded in 1926. It has a 23-acre campus.

RATINGS
Admissions Selectivity Rating: 79　　**Fire Safety Rating:** 60*　　**Green Rating:** 60*

STUDENTS AND FACULTY
Enrollment: 328. **Student Body:** 64% female, 36% male, 56% out-of-state, 4% international. Asian 2%, African American 7%, Caucasian 75%, Hispanic 4%, Native American 1%.
Retention and Graduation: 79% freshmen return for sophomore year.

ACADEMICS
Degrees: Bachelor's, master's. **Majors with Highest Enrollment:** Accounting; business/commerce; elementary education and teaching.

FACILITIES
Housing: Coed dorms.

CAMPUS LIFE
Environment: Town. **Activities:** Choral groups, concert band, dance, jazz band, music ensembles, opera **Organizations:** 8 registered organizations, 4 honor societies.

ADMISSIONS
Freshman Academic Profile: Average high school GPA 3.41. SAT Math middle 50% range 490–610. SAT Critical Reading middle 50% range 490–620. Minimum paper TOEFL 563. Minimum computer TOEFL 202. **Basis for Candidate Selection:** *Very important factors considered include:* Application essay, academic GPA, recommendation(s), rigor of secondary school record, standardized test scores. *Important factors considered include:* level of applicant's interest. *Other factors considered include:* Class rank, alumni/ae relation, character/personal qualities, extracurricular activities, geographical residence, interview, state residency, talent/ability, volunteer work, work experience. **Freshman Admission Requirements:** High school diploma is required

and GED is accepted. *Academic units required:* 4 English, 3 mathematics. *Academic units recommended:* 4 mathematics, 4 science, (2 science labs), 2 foreign language, 2 social studies, 2 history. **Freshman Admission Statistics:** 206 applied, 76% admitted, 56% enrolled. **General Admission Information:** Application fee $45.

COSTS AND FINANCIAL AID
Annual tuition $22,910. Room and board $9,200. Required fees $560. Average book expense $1,000.

WESTMINSTER COLLEGE (MO)

Champ Auditorium Westminster College, Fulton, MO 65251
Phone: 573-592-5251 **Financial Aid Phone:** 800-475-3361
E-mail: admissions@westminster-mo.edu **CEEB Code:** 6937
Fax: 573-592-5255 **Website:** www.westminster-mo.edu **ACT Code:** 2392

This private school, affiliated with the Presbyterian Church, was founded in 1851. It has a 86-acre campus.

RATINGS
Admissions Selectivity Rating: 77   **Fire Safety Rating:** 73   **Green Rating:** 60*

STUDENTS AND FACULTY
Enrollment: 1,067. **Student Body:** 44% female, 56% male, 24% out-of-state, 12% international (66 countries represented). Asian 1%, African American 4%, Caucasian 52%, Hispanic 1%, Native American 1%.
Retention and Graduation: 83% freshmen return for sophomore year. 40% freshmen graduate within 4 years. 30% grads go on to further study within 1 year. 10% grads pursue arts and sciences degrees. 4% grads pursue law degrees. 6% grads pursue business degrees. 3% grads pursue medical degrees. **Faculty:** Student/faculty ratio 14.8:1. 61 full-time faculty, 77% hold PhDs, 3% are members of minority groups, 41% are women.

ACADEMICS
Degrees: Bachelor's. **Classes:** Most classes have 10–19 students. **Majors with Highest Enrollment:** Biology/biological sciences; business/commerce; political science and government. **Special Study Options:** Cooperative education program, cross-registration, double major, dual enrollment, exchange student program (domestic), honors program, independent study, internships, liberal arts/career combination, student-designed major, study abroad, teacher certification program, Urban Studies Program (Chicago). Other off-campus study opportunities supported through Office of International Programs. Coursework and certification are also available through the Center of Leadership and the Remley Women's Center. **Combined degree programs:** BA/MEng, BA/MEng—University of Missouri-Columbia. Special programs offered to physically disabled students include note-taking services, reader services, tape recorders, tutors. **Career services:** Career/job search classes, career assessment, internships, regional alumni.

FACILITIES
Housing: Coed dorms, special housing for disabled students, men's dorms, women's dorms, fraternity/sorority housing, apartments for single students, theme housing. 70% of campus accessible to physically disabled. **Special Academic Facilities/Equipment:** Winston Churchill Memorial Museum, Coulter Science Center, language lab, NMR spectrometer, laser equipment. **Computers:** 100% of classrooms, 100% of libraries, 100% of dining areas, 100% of student union, 40% of common outdoor areas have wireless network access. Students can register for classes online. Administrative functions (other than registration) can be performed online.

CAMPUS LIFE
Environment: Village. **Activities:** Choral groups, dance, drama/theater, literary magazine, music ensembles, pep band, student government, student newspaper, yearbook, campus ministries, international student organization, Model UN. **Organizations:** 49 registered organizations, 15 honor societies, 2 religious organizations. 6 fraternities, 3 sororities. **Athletics (Intercollegiate):** *Men:* Baseball, basketball, cheerleading, cross-country, football, golf, soccer, tennis, track/field (outdoor). *Women:* Basketball, cheerleading, cross-country, golf, soccer, softball, tennis, track/field (outdoor), volleyball. **On-Campus Highlights:** Coulter Science Center, Johnson College Inn (student center), Hunter Activity Center, Library, Wetterau Athletic Facility.

ADMISSIONS
Freshman Academic Profile: Average high school GPA 3.44. 16% in top 10% of high school class, 45% in top 25% of high school class, 78% in top 50% of high school class. 70% from public high schools. SAT Math middle 50% range 490–625. SAT Critical Reading middle 50% range 440–620. SAT Writing

middle 50% range 450–580. ACT middle 50% range 21–28. Minimum paper TOEFL 550. Minimum computer TOEFL 213. **Basis for Candidate Selection:** *Very important factors considered include:* Rigor of secondary school record, standardized test scores, character/personal qualities. *Important factors considered include:* Class rank, academic GPA, recommendation(s), extracurricular activities, volunteer work. *Other factors considered include:* Application essay, alumni/ae relation, interview, talent/ability, work experience. **Freshman Admission Requirements:** High school diploma is required and GED is accepted. *Academic units required:* 4 English, 3 mathematics, 2 science, (2 science labs). *Academic units recommended:* 2 foreign language, 2 social studies, 2 academic electives. **Freshman Admission Statistics:** 1,356 applied, 78% admitted, 25% enrolled. **Transfer Admission Requirements:** College transcript(s), Lowest grade transferable C. **General Admission Information:** Notification on a rolling basis, beginning on or about 10/1. Nonfall registration accepted. Admission may be deferred for a maximum of 1 year. Credit and/or placement offered for CEEB Advanced Placement tests.

COSTS AND FINANCIAL AID
Annual tuition $17,990. Room and board $7,120. Required fees $710. Average book expense $800. **Required Forms and Deadlines:** FAFSA. Priority financial aid filing date 2/15. **Notification of Awards:** Applicants will be notified of awards on a rolling basis beginning 3/15. **Types of Aid:** *Need-based scholarships/grants:* Federal Pell, SEOG, state scholarships/grants, private scholarships, the school's own gift aid. *Loans:* FFEL Subsidized Stafford, FFEL Unsubsidized Stafford, FFEL PLUS, Federal Perkins. *Student Employment:* Federal Work-Study Program available. Institutional employment available. Highest amount earned per year from on-campus jobs $2,500. Off-campus job opportunities are good. **Financial Aid Statistics:** 60% freshmen, 56% undergrads receive need-based scholarship or grant aid. 47% freshmen, 46% undergrads receive need-based self-help aid. 98% freshmen, 98% undergrads receive any aid. 58% undergrads borrow to pay for school. Average cumulative indebtedness $20,018. **Criteria for awarding institutional aid:** *Non-need-based:* Academics, alumni affiliation, leadership, minority status, music/drama, religious affiliation.

WESTMINSTER COLLEGE (PA)

319 South Market Street, New Wilmington, PA 16172
Phone: 724-946-7100
E-mail: admis@westminster.edu **CEEB Code:** 2975
Fax: 724-946-7171 **Website:** www.westminster.edu **ACT Code:** 2975

This private school, affiliated with the Presbyterian Church, was founded in 1852. It has a 350-acre campus.

RATINGS
Admissions Selectivity Rating: 79   **Fire Safety Rating:** 97   **Green Rating:** 60*

STUDENTS AND FACULTY
Enrollment: 1,387. **Student Body:** 64% female, 36% male, 21% out-of-state, (1 countries represented). African American 3%, Caucasian 80%, Hispanic 1%.
Retention and Graduation: 83% freshmen return for sophomore year. 65% freshmen graduate within 4 years. 21% grads go on to further study within 1 year. 3% grads pursue law degrees. 2% grads pursue business degrees. 3% grads pursue medical degrees. **Faculty:** Student/faculty ratio 12:1. 100 full-time faculty, 83% hold PhDs, 5% are members of minority groups, 44% are women.

ACADEMICS
Degrees: Bachelor's, master's. **Classes:** Most classes have 10–19 students. Most lab/discussion sessions have 10–19 students. **Majors with Highest Enrollment:** Biology/biological sciences; business/commerce; education. **Special Study Options:** Double major, exchange student program (domestic), honors program, independent study, internships, liberal arts/career combination, student-designed major, study abroad, teacher certification program. **Combined degree programs:** BA/JD, BA/MA. Special programs offered to physically disabled students include tutors.

FACILITIES
Housing: Special housing for disabled students, men's dorms, women's dorms, fraternity/sorority housing. We offer townhouses for upperclass men and women. 90% of campus accessible to physically disabled. **Special Academic Facilities/Equipment:** On-campus preschool, Moeller pipe organs, planetarium,

observatory, electron microscopes, X-ray diffractor, spectrometer. **Computers:** Administrative functions (other than registration) can be performed online.

CAMPUS LIFE

Environment: Village. **Activities:** Choral groups, concert band, dance, drama/theater, jazz band, literary magazine, marching band, music ensembles, musical theater, pep band, radio station, student government, student newspaper, television station, yearbook. **Organizations:** 60 registered organizations, 21 honor societies, 3 religious organizations. 5 fraternities, 5 sororities. **Athletics (Intercollegiate):** *Men:* Baseball, basketball, cheerleading, cross-country, football, golf, soccer, swimming, tennis, track/field (outdoor), track/field (indoor). *Women:* Basketball, cheerleading, cross-country, golf, soccer, softball, swimming, tennis, track/field (outdoor), track/field (indoor), volleyball.

ADMISSIONS

Freshman Academic Profile: Average high school GPA 3.4. 20% in top 10% of high school class, 55% in top 25% of high school class, 87% in top 50% of high school class. 90% from public high schools. SAT Math middle 50% range 480–590. SAT Critical Reading middle 50% range 470–570. ACT middle 50% range 20–25. Minimum paper TOEFL 550. Minimum computer TOEFL 213. **Basis for Candidate Selection:** *Very important factors considered include:* Rigor of secondary school record, standardized test scores, interview. *Important factors considered include:* Class rank, application essay, recommendation(s), character/personal qualities. *Other factors considered include:* Alumni/ae relation, extracurricular activities, racial/ethnic status, talent/ability, volunteer work, work experience. **Freshman Admission Requirements:** High school diploma is required and GED is accepted. *Academic units required:* 4 English, 3 mathematics, 2 science, (2 science labs), 2 foreign language, 2 social studies, 1 history, 3 academic electives. **Freshman Admission Statistics:** 1,368 applied, 71% admitted, 32% enrolled. **Transfer Admission Requirements:** High school transcript, college transcript(s), essay or personal statement, interview, standardized test scores, minimum college GPA of 2.5 required. Lowest grade transferable c. **General Admission Information:** Application fee $35. Regular application deadline 4/15. Notification on a rolling basis, beginning on or about 9/1. Nonfall registration not accepted. Admission may be deferred for a maximum of 1 year. Credit and/or placement offered for CEEB Advanced Placement tests.

COSTS AND FINANCIAL AID

Annual tuition $26,940. Room and board $8,440. Required fees $1,100. Average book expense $1,000. **Required Forms and Deadlines:** FAFSA, institution's own financial aid form. Priority financial aid filing date 5/1. **Notification of Awards:** Applicants will be notified of awards on a rolling basis beginning 11/1. **Types of Aid:** *Need-based scholarships/grants:* Federal Pell, SEOG, state scholarships/grants, private scholarships, the school's own gift aid. *Loans:* FFEL Subsidized Stafford, FFEL Unsubsidized Stafford, FFEL PLUS, Federal Perkins, Resource Loans. *Student Employment:* Highest amount earned per year from on-campus jobs $1,300. **Financial Aid Statistics:** 81% freshmen, 79% undergrads receive need-based scholarship or grant aid. 80% freshmen, 71% undergrads receive non-need-based scholarship or grant aid. 68% freshmen, 65% undergrads receive need-based self-help aid. 73% undergrads borrow to pay for school. Average cumulative indebtedness $17,930. **Criteria for awarding institutional aid:** *Non-need-based:* Academics, alumni affiliation, leadership, minority status, music/drama.

WESTMINSTER COLLEGE OF SALT LAKE CITY

1840 South 1300 East, Salt Lake City, UT 84105
Phone: 801-832-2200 **Financial Aid Phone:** 801-832-2501
E-mail: admission@westministercollege.edu **CEEB Code:** 4948
Fax: 801-832-3101 **Website:** www.westminstercollege.edu **ACT Code:** 4284

This private school was founded in 1875. It has a 27-acre campus.

RATINGS

Admissions Selectivity Rating: 81 **Fire Safety Rating:** 97 **Green Rating:** 78

STUDENTS AND FACULTY

Enrollment: 2,141. **Student Body:** 56% female, 44% male, 29% out-of-state, 2% international (41 countries represented). Asian 3%, African American 1%, Caucasian 71%, Hispanic 6%, Native American 1%.
Retention and Graduation: 76% freshmen return for sophomore year. 42% freshmen graduate within 4 years. 31% grads go on to further study within 1

year. **Faculty:** Student/faculty ratio 10:1. 136 full-time faculty, 73% hold PhDs, 2% are members of minority groups, 47% are women.

ACADEMICS

Degrees: Bachelor's, master's, post-bachelor's certificate. **Classes:** Most classes have 10–19 students. Most lab/discussion sessions have 10–19 students. **Majors with Highest Enrollment:** Business/commerce; nursing/registered nurse (RN, ASN, BSN, MSN); social sciences. **Special Study Options:** Accelerated program, cooperative education program, distance learning, double major, dual enrollment, English as a Second Language (ESL), honors program, independent study, internships, liberal arts/career combination, student-designed major, study abroad, teacher certification program, weekend college. **Honors programs:** www.westminstercollege.edu/honors/. Special programs offered to physically disabled students include note-taking services, reader services, tape recorders, tutors. **Career services:** Alumni services, career/job search classes, career assessment, internships. **Career services highlights include:** Internship Program.

FACILITIES

Housing: Coed dorms, men's dorms, women's dorms, apartments for single students. 98% of campus accessible to physically disabled. **Special Academic Facilities/Equipment:** Emma Ecceles Jones Conservatory, Gore school of Business, Giovale Library, Dick Science Building, Climbing Wall, Converse Hall, Dolores Dore Eccles Health, Wellness, and Athletic Center. **Computers:** 100% of classrooms, 100% of dorms, 100% of libraries, 100% of dining areas, 100% of student union, 25% of common outdoor areas have wireless network access. Students can register for classes online. Administrative functions (other than registration) can be performed online.

CAMPUS LIFE

Environment: Metropolis. **Activities:** Choral groups, dance, drama/theater, jazz band, literary magazine, music ensembles, musical theater, student government, student newspaper, student-run film society, symphony orchestra, campus ministries, international student organization. **Organizations:** 55 registered organizations, 4 honor societies, 4 religious organizations. **Athletics (Intercollegiate):** *Men:* Basketball, cross-country, golf, lacrosse, skiing (downhill/alpine), snowboarding, soccer, track/field (outdoor), track/field (indoor). *Women:* Basketball, cross-country, golf, lacrosse, skiing (downhill/alpine), snowboarding, soccer, track/field (outdoor), track/field (indoor), volleyball. **On-Campus Highlights:** Shaw Student Center, Giovale Library, Emma Eccles Jones Conservatory, Dolores Dore Eccles Health, Wellness, and Athletic, Residential Village. **Environmental Initiatives:** Blue Sky Visionary and EPA Green Power Partner, with 11% of campus electricity derived from renwable sources. New LEED Gold Meldrum Science Center to be completed this spring. American College & University Presidents' Climate Commitment charter signatory with a target climate neutrality date of 2030.

ADMISSIONS

Freshman Academic Profile: Average high school GPA 3.495. 29% in top 10% of high school class, 60% in top 25% of high school class, 85% in top 50% of high school class. 84% from public high schools. SAT Math middle 50% range 500–630. SAT Critical Reading middle 50% range 510–620. ACT middle 50% range 22–27. Minimum paper TOEFL 550. Minimum computer TOEFL 213. Minimum web-based TOEFL 100. **Basis for Candidate Selection:** *Very important factors considered include:* Academic GPA, rigor of secondary school record. *Important factors considered include:* Class rank, application essay, standardized test scores, interview. *Other factors considered include:* Recommendation(s), alumni/ae relation, character/personal qualities, extracurricular activities, geographical residence, talent/ability. **Freshman Admission Requirements:** High school diploma is required and GED is accepted. *Academic units required:* 4 English, 2 mathematics, 3 science, 2 foreign language, 2 social studies, 1 history, 2 academic electives. *Academic units recommended:* 4 English, 3 mathematics, 3 science, 3 foreign language, 2 social studies, 1 history, 3 academic electives. **Freshman Admission Statistics:** 1,625 applied, 82% admitted, 35% enrolled. **Transfer Admission Requirements:** High school transcript, college transcript(s), essay or personal statement, minimum college GPA of 2.5 required. Lowest grade transferable C–. **General Admission Information:** Application fee $40. Notification on a rolling basis, beginning on or about 9/1. Nonfall registration accepted. Admission may be deferred for a maximum of 1 year. Credit and/or placement offered for CEEB Advanced Placement tests.

COSTS AND FINANCIAL AID

Annual tuition $24,576. Room and board $7,006. Required fees $420. Average book expense $1,000. **Required Forms and Deadlines:** FAFSA. Priority financial aid filing date 4/15. **Notification of Awards:** Applicants will be notified of awards on a rolling basis beginning 3/1. **Types of Aid:** *Need-based scholarships/grants:* Federal Pell, SEOG, state scholarships/grants, private scholarships, the school's own gift aid. *Loans:* FFEL Subsidized Stafford, FFEL Unsubsidized Stafford, FFEL PLUS, Federal Perkins. *Student Employment:* Federal Work-Study Program available. Institutional employment available.

Highest amount earned per year from on-campus jobs $6,934. Off-campus job opportunities are excellent. **Financial Aid Statistics:** 59% freshmen, 60% undergrads receive need-based scholarship or grant aid. 8% freshmen, 6% undergrads receive non-need-based scholarship or grant aid. 48% freshmen, 52% undergrads receive need-based self-help aid. 2% freshmen, 1% undergrads receive athletic scholarships. 98% freshmen, 93% undergrads receive any aid. 54% undergrads borrow to pay for school. Average cumulative indebtedness $20,251. **Criteria for awarding institutional aid:** *Non-need-based:* Academics, alumni affiliation, art, athletics, leadership, minority status, music/drama, religious affiliation.

See page 1326.

WESTMONT COLLEGE

955 La Paz Road, Santa Barbara, CA 93108
Phone: 805-565-6200 **Financial Aid Phone:** 888-963-4624
E-mail: admissions@westmont.edu **CEEB Code:** 4950
Fax: 805-565-6234 **Website:** www.westmont.edu **ACT Code:** 478

This private school, affiliated with the Christian (Nondenominational) Church, was founded in 1937. It has a 133-acre campus.

RATINGS
Admissions Selectivity Rating: 89 **Fire Safety Rating:** 60* **Green Rating:** 60*

STUDENTS AND FACULTY
Enrollment: 1,333. **Student Body:** 61% female, 39% male, 31% out-of-state, 1% international (8 countries represented). Asian 9%, African American 2%, Caucasian 69%, Hispanic 10%, Native American 2%.
Retention and Graduation: 87% freshmen return for sophomore year. 65% freshmen graduate within 4 years. **Faculty:** Student/faculty ratio 12:1. 93 full-time faculty, 89% hold PhDs, 11% are members of minority groups, 31% are women.

ACADEMICS
Degrees: Bachelor's, post-bachelor's certificate. **Classes:** Most classes have 10–19 students. Most lab/discussion sessions have 10–19 students. **Majors with Highest Enrollment:** Cell/cellular and molecular biology; English/language arts teacher education. **Special Study Options:** Accelerated program, double major, exchange student program (domestic), honors program, independent study, internships, student-designed major, study abroad, teacher certification program. **Honors programs:** Some general education courses are designated as honors courses. **Combined degree programs:** 3/2 Engineering Program. Special programs offered to physically disabled students include note-taking services, reader services, tape recorders, tutors. **Career services:** career/job search classes, career assessment, internships.

FACILITIES
Housing: Coed dorms, apartments for single students, The Coed dorms are segregated by floors and/or suites. Men and women do not share hallways and bathrooms. There are selected visiting hours for members of the opposite sex. 65% of campus accessible to physically disabled. **Special Academic Facilities/Equipment:** Reynolds Art Gallery features the gallery, art studios and classrooms; Carroll Observatory houses a 24-inch reflector telescope; Mericos Whittier Science facility includes state of the art technical equipment such as ultracentrifuge, Fouriertransform NMR spectrometer, etc, as well as the pre-med center; Voskuyl Library holds over 150,000 bound volumes; the physics department is developing advanced experiments for the lab; Ellen Porter Hall of Fine Arts showcases ten to twenty live musical and theatrical performances each year; Physiology Lab and Fithess Center for Kinesiology studies. **Computers:** Administrative functions (other than registration) can be performed online.

CAMPUS LIFE
Environment: City. **Activities:** Choral groups, dance, drama/theater, jazz band, literary magazine, music ensembles, musical theater, radio station, student government, student newspaper, student-run film society, symphony orchestra, yearbook, campus ministries. **Organizations:** 50 registered organizations, 7 honor societies, 40 religious organizations. **Athletics (Intercollegiate):** *Men:* Baseball, basketball, cross-country, soccer, tennis, track/field (outdoor). *Women:* Basketball, cross-country, soccer, tennis, track/field (outdoor), volleyball.

ADMISSIONS
Freshman Academic Profile: Average high school GPA 3.77. 45% in top 10% of high school class, 79% in top 25% of high school class, 96% in top 50% of high school class. 70% from public high schools. SAT Math middle 50% range 540–660. SAT Critical Reading middle 50% range 540–650. SAT Writing middle 50% range 540–650. ACT middle 50% range 24–28. Minimum paper TOEFL 560. Minimum computer TOEFL 220. **Basis for Candidate Selection:** *Very important factors considered include:* Academic GPA, standardized test scores, character/personal qualities, religious affiliation/commitment. *Important factors considered include:* Application essay, recommendation(s), rigor of secondary school record, extracurricular activities, interview, racial/ethnic status, talent/ability. *Other factors considered include:* Class rank, alumni/ae relation, first generation, geographical residence, level of applicant's interest, state residency, volunteer work, work experience. **Freshman Admission Requirements:** High school diploma is required and GED is accepted. *Academic units required:* 4 English, 3 mathematics, 3 science, (2 science labs), 2 foreign language, 2 social studies, 4 academic electives. **Freshman Admission Statistics:** 1,651 applied, 73% admitted, 32% enrolled. **Transfer Admission Requirements:** High school transcript, college transcript(s), essay or personal statement, statement of good standing from prior institution(s). Lowest grade transferable C–. **General Admission Information:** Application fee $50. Notification on a rolling basis, beginning on or about 4/1. Nonfall registration accepted. Credit and/or placement offered for CEEB Advanced Placement tests.

COSTS AND FINANCIAL AID
Annual tuition $30,422. Room and board $9,622. Required fees $790. Average book expense $1,386. **Required Forms and Deadlines:** FAFSA, Cal Grant GPA Verification Form (if student is a California resident). Priority financial aid filing date 3/1. **Notification of Awards:** Applicants will be notified of awards on a rolling basis beginning 4/1. **Types of Aid:** *Need-based scholarships/grants:* Federal Pell, SEOG, state scholarships/grants, private scholarships, the school's own gift aid. *Loans:* FFEL Subsidized Stafford, FFEL Unsubsidized Stafford, FFEL PLUS, Federal Perkins, college/university loans from institutional funds, Work-Study. *Student Employment:* Federal Work-Study Program available. Institutional employment available. **Financial Aid Statistics:** 64% freshmen, 55% undergrads receive need-based scholarship or grant aid. 6% freshmen, 5% undergrads receive non-need-based scholarship or grant aid. 570% freshmen, 46% undergrads receive need-based self-help aid. 4% freshmen, 5% undergrads receive athletic scholarships. 85% undergrads receive any aid. 53% undergrads borrow to pay for school. Average cumulative indebtedness $25,008. **Criteria for awarding institutional aid:** *Non-need-based:* Academics, art, athletics, leadership, minority status, music/drama.

WHEATON COLLEGE (IL)

501 College Avenue, Wheaton, IL 60187
Phone: 630-752-5005 **Financial Aid Phone:** 630-752-5021
E-mail: admissions@wheaton.edu **CEEB Code:** 1905
Fax: 630-752-5285 **Website:** www.wheaton.edu **ACT Code:** 1160

This private school was founded in 1860. It has a 80-acre campus.

RATINGS
Admissions Selectivity Rating: 93 **Fire Safety Rating:** 86 **Green Rating:** 77

STUDENTS AND FACULTY
Enrollment: 2,369. **Student Body:** 50% female, 50% male, 75.5% out-of-state, 1% international (22 countries represented). Asian 8%, African American 4%, Caucasian 83%, Hispanic 4%.
Retention and Graduation: 96% freshmen return for sophomore year. 80% freshmen graduate within 4 years. 32% grads go on to further study within 1 year. 19% grads pursue arts and sciences degrees. 2% grads pursue law degrees. 1% grads pursue business degrees. 9% grads pursue medical degrees. **Faculty:** Student/faculty ratio 11:1. 202 full-time faculty, 95% hold PhDs, 10% are members of minority groups, 29% are women.

ACADEMICS
Degrees: Bachelor's, master's, post-bachelor's certificate. **Classes:** Most classes have 10–19 students. Most lab/discussion sessions have 10–19 students. **Majors with Highest Enrollment:** Business/managerial economics; English language and literature; health services/allied health/health sciences. **Special Study Options:** Cross-registration, double major, exchange student program (domestic), independent study, internships, liberal arts/career combination, student-designed major, study abroad, teacher certification program. **Honors programs:** Some departments offer qualified students to submit an honors project. **Combined degree programs:** Liberal Arts/Engineering; Liberal Arts/N. Special programs offered to physically disabled students include

note-taking services, reader services, tape recorders, tutors. **Career services:** Alumni network, alumni services, career/job search classes, career assessment, internships, regional alumni.

FACILITIES

Housing: Coed dorms, men's dorms, women's dorms, apartments for married students, cooperative housing, apartments for single students, housing for disabled provided as needed. 97% of campus accessible to physically disabled. **Special Academic Facilities/Equipment:** World evangelism museum, language lab, observatory, Collection of works/papers of seven British authors, Billy Graham Center Museum **Computers:** 10% of classrooms, 100% of dorms, 100% of libraries, 100% of dining areas, 100% of student union, 75% of common outdoor areas have wireless network access. Students can register for classes online. Administrative functions (other than registration) can be performed online.

CAMPUS LIFE

Environment: Town. **Activities:** Choral groups, concert band, dance, drama/theater, jazz band, literary magazine, music ensembles, musical theater, opera, pep band, radio station, student government, student newspaper, student-run film society, symphony orchestra, television station, yearbook, campus ministries, international student organization, Model UN. **Organizations:** 85 registered organizations, 13 honor societies, 12 religious organizations. **Athletics (Intercollegiate):** *Men:* Baseball, basketball, cross-country, football, golf, soccer, swimming, tennis, track/field (outdoor), track/field (indoor), wrestling. *Women:* Basketball, cross-country, golf, soccer, softball, swimming, tennis, track/field (outdoor), track/field (indoor), volleyball, water polo. **On-Campus Highlights:** Billy Graham Center—archive, museum, Wade Center—collection of English auth, new Science Building opens fall 2010, Todd M. Beamer Student Center, J. Dennis Hastert Center. **Environmental Initiatives:** Environmental Studies Major LEED Certifications Recycling

ADMISSIONS

Freshman Academic Profile: Average high school GPA 3.7. 59% in top 10% of high school class, 83% in top 25% of high school class, 96% in top 50% of high school class. 53% from public high schools. SAT Math middle 50% range 600–700. SAT Critical Reading middle 50% range 600–610. SAT Writing middle 50% range 590–700. ACT middle 50% range 27–31. Minimum paper TOEFL 550. Minimum computer TOEFL 213. Minimum web-based TOEFL 80. **Basis for Candidate Selection:** *Very important factors considered include:* Application essay, academic GPA, recommendation(s), rigor of secondary school record, standardized test scores, character/personal qualities, interview, religious affiliation/commitment. *Important factors considered include:* Extracurricular activities, talent/ability, volunteer work, work experience. *Other factors considered include:* Class rank, alumni/ae relation, first generation, geographical residence, level of applicant's interest, racial/ethnic status, state residency. **Freshman Admission Requirements:** High school diploma is required and GED is accepted. *Academic units recommended:* 4 English. **Freshman Admission Statistics:** 1,950 applied, 71% admitted, 45% enrolled. **Transfer Admission Requirements:** High school transcript, college transcript(s), essay or personal statement, minimum college GPA of 3.0 required. Lowest grade transferable C–. **General Admission Information:** Application fee $50. Regular application deadline 1/10. Regular notification 4/1. Nonfall registration not accepted. Admission may be deferred for a maximum of 1 year. Credit and/or placement offered for CEEB Advanced Placement tests.

COSTS AND FINANCIAL AID

Annual tuition $26,520. Room and board $7,770. Average book expense $800. **Required Forms and Deadlines:** FAFSA, institution's own financial aid form. Priority financial aid filing date 2/15. **Notification of Awards:** Applicants will be notified of awards on a rolling basis beginning 3/1. **Types of Aid:** *Need-based scholarships/grants:* Federal Pell, SEOG, state scholarships/grants, the school's own gift aid. *Loans:* FFEL Subsidized Stafford, FFEL Unsubsidized Stafford, FFEL PLUS, Federal Perkins. *Student Employment:* Federal Work-Study Program available. Institutional employment available. Off-campus job opportunities are excellent. **Financial Aid Statistics:** 50% freshmen, 50% undergrads receive need-based scholarship or grant aid. 18% freshmen, 19% undergrads receive non-need-based scholarship or grant aid. 52% freshmen, 51% undergrads receive need-based self-help aid. 69.2% freshmen, 68.9% undergrads receive any aid. 51% undergrads borrow to pay for school. Average cumulative indebtedness $20,455. **Criteria for awarding institutional aid:** *Non-need-based:* Academics, alumni affiliation, art, minority status, music/drama.

WHEATON COLLEGE (MA)

Office of Admission, Norton, MA 02766
Phone: 508-286-8251 **Financial Aid Phone:** 508-286-8232
E-mail: admission@wheatoncollege.edu **CEEB Code:** 3963
Fax: 508-286-8271 **Website:** wheatoncollege.edu **ACT Code:** 1932

This private school was founded in 1834. It has a 400-acre campus.

RATINGS

Admissions Selectivity Rating: 93   **Fire Safety Rating:** 78   **Green Rating:** 81

STUDENTS AND FACULTY

Enrollment: 1,632. **Student Body:** 62% female, 38% male, 67% out-of-state, 5% international (38 countries represented). Asian 2%, African American 5%, Caucasian 76%, Hispanic 4%.
Retention and Graduation: 88% freshmen return for sophomore year. 73% freshmen graduate within 4 years. 29% grads go on to further study within 1 year. 15% grads pursue arts and sciences degrees. 5% grads pursue law degrees. 9% grads pursue business degrees. 5% grads pursue medical degrees. **Faculty:** Student/faculty ratio 11:1. 139 full-time faculty, 88% hold PhDs, 19% are members of minority groups, 51% are women.

ACADEMICS

Degrees: Bachelor's. **Classes:** Most classes have 10–19 students. Most lab/discussion sessions have 10–19 students. **Majors with Highest Enrollment:** Economics; English language and literature; psychology. **Special Study Options:** Accelerated program, cross-registration, double major, dual enrollment, exchange student program (domestic), honors program, independent study, internships, liberal arts/career combination, student-designed major, study abroad, teacher certification program **Combined degree programs:** BA/MA, BA/MEng, BA/MBA, BA/BFA, BA/BS, BA/Doctor of Optometry. Special programs offered to physically disabled students include note-taking services, reader services, tape recorders, tutors. **Career services:** Alumni network, alumni services, career/job search classes, career assessment, internships, regional alumni. **Career services highlights include:** Wheaton provides stipends ranging from $3,000 to $6,000 for at least 60% of our students to participate in unpaid internships, research opportunities and other out of classroom learning opportunities.

FACILITIES

Housing: Coed dorms, special housing for disabled students, men's dorms, special housing for international students, women's dorms, wellness housing, theme housing, quiet house. 50% of campus accessible to physically disabled. **Special Academic Facilities/Equipment:** Art gallery, language lab, photography darkrooms, dance studio, on-campus nursery school, media center, observatory. **Computers:** 100% of classrooms, 100% of dorms, 100% of libraries, 100% of dining areas, 100% of student union, have wireless network access. Students can register for classes online. Administrative functions (other than registration) can be performed online.

CAMPUS LIFE

Environment: Village. **Activities:** Choral groups, dance, drama/theater, jazz band, literary magazine, music ensembles, musical theater, pep band, radio station, student government, student newspaper, student-run film society, symphony orchestra, yearbook, international student organization, Model UN. **Organizations:** 60 registered organizations, 8 honor societies, 4 religious organizations. **Athletics (Intercollegiate):** *Men:* Baseball, basketball, cross-country, diving, lacrosse, soccer, swimming, tennis, track/field (outdoor), track/field (indoor). *Women:* Basketball, cross-country, diving, field hockey, lacrosse, soccer, softball, swimming, synchronized swimming, tennis, track/field (outdoor), track/field (indoor), volleyball. **On-Campus Highlights:** Mars Arts and Humanities: $20 million arts facility, Haas Athletic Center, Lyon's Den—coffee house, Mary Lyon Hall—college's oldest building, Balfour-Hood Student Center. **Environmental Initiatives:** Formation of a Sustainability Steering Committee charged with institutionalizing sustainability. Dining Services has demonstrated a commitment to sustainability in the dining halls by introducing reusable containers, eliminating food trays; and incorporating sustainable practices throughout dining operations.

ADMISSIONS

Freshman Academic Profile: Average high school GPA 3.5. 42% in top 10% of high school class, 40% in top 25% of high school class, 98% in top 50% of high school class. 59% from public high schools. SAT Math middle 50% range

560–670. SAT Critical Reading middle 50% range 570–680. ACT middle 50% range 27–30. Minimum paper TOEFL 580. Minimum computer TOEFL 243. Minimum web-based TOEFL 90. **Basis for Candidate Selection:** *Very important factors considered include:* Application essay, academic GPA, rigor of secondary school record, character/personal qualities, extracurricular activities, first generation, talent/ability. *Important factors considered include:* Class rank, recommendation(s), alumni/ae relation, interview, volunteer work, work experience. *Other factors considered include:* geographical residence, level of applicant's interest, racial/ethnic status, state residency. **Freshman Admission Requirements:** High school diploma is required and GED is accepted. *Academic units recommended:* 4 English, 4 mathematics, 3 science, (2 science labs), 4 foreign language, 3 social studies, 2 history. **Freshman Admission Statistics:** 3,304 applied, 59% admitted, 22% enrolled. **Transfer Admission Requirements:** High school transcript, college transcript(s), essay or personal statement, statement of good standing from prior institution(s). Minimum college GPA of 3.0 required. Lowest grade transferable C. **General Admission Information:** Application fee $55. Early decision application deadline 11/15. Regular application deadline 1/15. Regular notification 4/1. Nonfall registration accepted. Admission may be deferred for a maximum of 1 year. Credit and/or placement offered for CEEB Advanced Placement tests.

COSTS AND FINANCIAL AID

Annual tuition $39,565. Room and board $9,590. Required fees $285. Average book expense $940. **Required Forms and Deadlines:** FAFSA, CSS/Financial Aid PROFILE, noncustodial PROFILE, business/farm supplement. Parent and Student Federal Tax Returns and W-2s. Financial aid filing deadline 2/1. **Notification of Awards:** Applicants will be notified of awards on or about 4/1. **Types of Aid:** *Need-based scholarships/grants:* Federal Pell, SEOG, state scholarships/grants, private scholarships, the school's own gift aid. *Loans:* FFEL Subsidized Stafford, FFEL Unsubsidized Stafford, FFEL PLUS, Federal Perkins. *Student Employment:* Federal Work-Study Program available. Institutional employment available. Highest amount earned per year from on-campus jobs $2,528. Off-campus job opportunities are good. **Financial Aid Statistics:** 59% freshmen, 53% undergrads receive need-based scholarship or grant aid. 1% freshmen, 1% undergrads receive non-need-based scholarship or grant aid. 59% freshmen, 55% undergrads receive need-based self-help aid. 76% freshmen, 68% undergrads receive any aid. 53% undergrads borrow to pay for school. Average cumulative indebtedness $25,540. **Criteria for awarding institutional aid:** *Non-need-based:* Academics.

WHEELING JESUIT UNIVERSITY

316 Washington Avenue, Wheeling, WV 26003
Phone: 304-243-2359 **Financial Aid Phone:** 304-243-2304
E-mail: admiss@wju.edu **CEEB Code:** 5906
Fax: 304-243-2397 **Website:** www.wju.edu **ACT Code:** 4546

This private school, affiliated with the Roman Catholic Church, was founded in 1954. It has a 70-acre campus.

RATINGS

Admissions Selectivity Rating: 80   **Fire Safety Rating:** 98   **Green Rating:** 60*

STUDENTS AND FACULTY

Enrollment: 1,001. **Student Body:** 59% female, 41% male, 63% out-of-state, 3% international (19 countries represented). Asian 1%, African American 2%, Caucasian 87%, Hispanic 2%.
Retention and Graduation: 77% freshmen return for sophomore year. 49% freshmen graduate within 4 years. 35% grads go on to further study within 1 year. 25% grads pursue arts and sciences degrees. 4% grads pursue law degrees. 10% grads pursue business degrees. 4% grads pursue medical degrees. **Faculty:** 72 full-time faculty, 65% hold PhDs, 10% are members of minority groups, 43% are women.

ACADEMICS

Degrees: Bachelor's, master's. **Classes:** Most classes have 10–19 students. Most lab/discussion sessions have 10–19 students. **Majors with Highest Enrollment:** Business, management, marketing, and related support services, other; nursing/registered nurse (RN, ASN, BSN, MSN); psychology. **Special Study Options:** Distance learning, double major, English as a Second Language (ESL), honors program, independent study, internships, liberal arts/career combination, student-designed major, study abroad, teacher certification program, Off-campus study: Washington, DC. **Honors programs:** The Laut Honors program which is designed to introduces students to aspects of the arts and sciences that are not available in the regular curriculum in order to inspire and awaken curiosity through a variety of enriching experiences offered. **Combined degree programs:** 3-2 engineering program with Case Western

Reserve. Special programs offered to physically disabled students include note-taking services, reader services, tutors. **Career services:** Alumni network, alumni services, career/job search classes, career assessment, internships, regional alumni.

FACILITIES

Housing: Coed dorms, special housing for disabled students, men's dorms, special housing for international students, women's dorms, apartments for married students. 85% of campus accessible to physically disabled. **Special Academic Facilities/Equipment:** Center for Educational Technologies (NASA). **Computers:** 10% of classrooms, 100% of libraries, 100% of dining areas, 100% of student union, 10% of common outdoor areas have wireless network access. Students can register for classes online. Administrative functions (other than registration) can be performed online.

CAMPUS LIFE

Environment: Town. **Activities:** Choral groups, dance, drama/theater, literary magazine, musical theater, pep band, radio station, student government, student newspaper, television station, yearbook, campus ministries, international student organization. **Organizations:** 30 registered organizations, 9 honor societies, 6 religious organizations. **Athletics (Intercollegiate):** *Men:* Baseball, basketball, cross-country, golf, lacrosse, soccer, swimming, track/field (outdoor), track/field (indoor). *Women:* Basketball, cross-country, golf, soccer, softball, swimming, track/field (outdoor), track/field (indoor), volleyball. **On-Campus Highlights:** Coffee Shop located in Swint Hall, McDonough Fitness Center, Creek Bank surrounding campus, Rathskeller-Pub on campus, McDonough indoor swimming pool and racqu.

ADMISSIONS

Freshman Academic Profile: Average high school GPA 3.5. 22% in top 10% of high school class, 50% in top 25% of high school class, 85% in top 50% of high school class. 62% from public high schools. SAT Math middle 50% range 460–560. SAT Critical Reading middle 50% range 470–560. ACT middle 50% range 20–25. Minimum paper TOEFL 550. Minimum computer TOEFL 213. **Basis for Candidate Selection:** *Very important factors considered include:* Academic GPA, standardized test scores. *Important factors considered include:* Application essay, rigor of secondary school record, interview. *Other factors considered include:* Recommendation(s), character/personal qualities, extracurricular activities, level of applicant's interest, talent/ability, volunteer work, work experience. **Freshman Admission Requirements:** High school diploma is required and GED is accepted. *Academic units required:* 4 English, 2 mathematics, 1 science, (1 science labs), 2 social studies, 2 history, 6 academic electives. *Academic units recommended:* 2 foreign language. **Freshman Admission Statistics:** 1,299 applied, 74% admitted, 27% enrolled. **Transfer Admission Requirements:** College transcript(s), minimum college GPA of 2.3 required. Lowest grade transferable C. **General Admission Information:** Application fee $25. Regular notification 8/15. Notification on a rolling basis, beginning on or about 9/1. Nonfall registration accepted. Admission may be deferred for a maximum of 1 semester. Credit and/or placement offered for CEEB Advanced Placement tests.

COSTS AND FINANCIAL AID

Annual tuition $23,590. Room and board $8,640. Required fees $1,040. Average book expense $1,000. **Required Forms and Deadlines:** FAFSA. Priority financial aid filing date 2/15. **Notification of Awards:** Applicants will be notified of awards on a rolling basis beginning 3/15. **Types of Aid:** *Need-based scholarships/grants:* Federal Pell, SEOG, state scholarships/grants, private scholarships, the school's own gift aid. *Loans:* Direct Subsidized Stafford, Direct Unsubsidized Stafford, Direct PLUS, FFEL Subsidized Stafford, FFEL Unsubsidized Stafford, FFEL PLUS, Federal Perkins, Federal Nursing, Private Alternative Loans. *Student Employment:* Federal Work-Study Program available. Institutional employment available. Highest amount earned per year from on-campus jobs $2,200. Off-campus job opportunities are good. **Financial Aid Statistics:** 59% freshmen, 53% undergrads receive need-based scholarship or grant aid. 84% freshmen, 74% undergrads receive non-need-based scholarship or grant aid. 60% freshmen, 60% undergrads receive need-based self-help aid. 6% freshmen, 5% undergrads receive athletic scholarships. 100% freshmen, 98% undergrads receive any aid. 89% undergrads borrow to pay for school. Average cumulative indebtedness $26,334. **Criteria for awarding institutional aid:** *Non-need-based:* Academics, alumni affiliation, athletics, leadership, music/drama.

WHEELOCK COLLEGE

200 The Riverway, Boston, MA 02215
Phone: 617-879-2206 **Financial Aid Phone:** 617-879-2206
E-mail: undergrad@wheelock.edu **CEEB Code:** 3964
Fax: 617-879-2449 **Website:** www.wheelock.edu **ACT Code:** 1934

This private school was founded in 1888. It has a 6-acre campus.

RATINGS
Admissions Selectivity Rating: 73   **Fire Safety Rating:** 86   **Green Rating:** 60*

STUDENTS AND FACULTY
Enrollment: 746. **Student Body:** 90% female, 10% male, 48% out-of-state, 1% international (6 countries represented). Asian 2%, African American 9%, Caucasian 69%, Hispanic 8%, Native American 1%.
Retention and Graduation: 71% freshmen return for sophomore year. 25% grads go on to further study within 1 year. 12% grads pursue arts and sciences degrees. 1% grads pursue law degrees. **Faculty:** Student/faculty ratio 10:1. 63 full-time faculty, 87% hold PhDs, 24% are members of minority groups, 78% are women.

ACADEMICS
Degrees: Bachelor's, master's, post-bachelor's certificate, post-master's certificate. **Classes:** Most classes have 10–19 students. **Majors with Highest Enrollment:** Elementary education and teaching; human development, family studies, and related services, other; social work. **Special Study Options:** Cross-registration, double major, honors program, independent study, internships, liberal arts/career combination, study abroad, teacher certification program **Combined degree programs:** BA/MA. Special programs offered to physically disabled students include note-taking services, reader services, tape recorders, tutors. **Career services:** Alumni network, career/job search classes, career assessment, internships.

FACILITIES
Housing: Coed dorms, men's dorms, women's dorms, Wellness Floor First Year Floors. 67% of campus accessible to physically disabled. **Special Academic Facilities/Equipment:** Art studio, resource center with fully equipped workshop for creating and developing original curriculum tools.

CAMPUS LIFE
Environment: Metropolis. **Activities:** Choral groups, dance, drama/theater, music ensembles, musical theater, student government, symphony orchestra. **Organizations:** 20 registered organizations, 1 honor societies, 1 religious organizations. **Athletics (Intercollegiate):** *Men:* Basketball, tennis. *Women:* Basketball, diving, field hockey, soccer, softball, swimming **On-Campus Highlights:** The Wheelock Family Theater, The Student Center, The Library, Brookline Campus—Hawes Street, The Resource Center.

ADMISSIONS
Freshman Academic Profile: Average high school GPA 3. 11% in top 10% of high school class, 30% in top 25% of high school class, 73% in top 50% of high school class. 85% from public high schools. SAT Math middle 50% range 420–530. SAT Critical Reading middle 50% range 440–520. SAT Writing middle 50% range 430–540. ACT middle 50% range 18–23. Minimum paper TOEFL 173. Minimum computer TOEFL 173. **Basis for Candidate Selection:** *Very important factors considered include:* Application essay, academic GPA, rigor of secondary school record. *Important factors considered include:* Class rank, recommendation(s), character/personal qualities, extracurricular activities, volunteer work. *Other factors considered include:* Standardized test scores, alumni/ae relation, interview, talent/ability, work experience. **Freshman Admission Requirements:** High school diploma is required and GED is accepted. *Academic units required:* 4 English, 3 mathematics, 2 science, (1 science labs), 2 social studies. **Freshman Admission Statistics:** 1,096 applied, 74% admitted, 29% enrolled. **Transfer Admission Requirements:** High school transcript, college transcript(s), essay or personal statement, minimum college GPA of 2.0 required. Lowest grade transferable C. **General Admission Information:** Application fee $35. Regular application deadline 3/1. Notification on a rolling basis, beginning on or about 1/1. Nonfall registration accepted. Admission may be deferred for a maximum of 1 year. Credit offered for CEEB Advanced Placement tests.

COSTS AND FINANCIAL AID
Annual tuition $26,225. Room and board $10,825. Required fees $980. Average book expense $880. **Required Forms and Deadlines:** FAFSA. Financial aid filing deadline 5/1. Priority financial aid filing date 2/15. **Notification of Awards:** Applicants will be notified of awards on a rolling basis beginning 3/5. **Types of Aid:** *Need-based scholarships/grants:* Federal Pell, SEOG, state scholarships/grants, the school's own gift aid, Merit scholarships are available for all freshmen applicants with a 3.0 GPA(or higher) and SAT scores of 1050

(or higher). Scholarhips range from $3000 to $12,000. *Loans:* FFEL Subsidized Stafford, FFEL Unsubsidized Stafford, FFEL PLUS, Federal Perkins, college/university loans from institutional funds. *Student Employment:* Federal Work-Study Program available. Institutional employment available. Highest amount earned per year from on-campus jobs $2,000. Off-campus job opportunities are good. **Financial Aid Statistics:** 77% freshmen, 78% undergrads receive need-based scholarship or grant aid. 14% freshmen, 8% undergrads receive non-need-based scholarship or grant aid. 68% freshmen, 73% undergrads receive need-based self-help aid. 85% freshmen, 81% undergrads receive any aid. 96% undergrads borrow to pay for school. Average cumulative indebtedness $43,115. **Criteria for awarding institutional aid:** *Non-need-based:* Academics, leadership.

WHITMAN COLLEGE

345 Boyer Ave, Walla Walla, WA 99362
Phone: 509-527-5176 **Financial Aid Phone:** 509-527-5178
E-mail: admission@whitman.edu **CEEB Code:** 4951
Fax: 509-527-4967 **Website:** www.whitman.edu **ACT Code:** 4492

This private school was founded in 1883. It has a 117-acre campus.

RATINGS
Admissions Selectivity Rating: 95   **Fire Safety Rating:** 60*   **Green Rating:** 85

STUDENTS AND FACULTY
Enrollment: 1,491. **Student Body:** 58% female, 42% male, 40% out-of-state, 2% international (29 countries represented). Asian 11%, African American 2%, Caucasian 67%, Hispanic 6%, Native American 1%.
Retention and Graduation: 93% freshmen return for sophomore year. 81% freshmen graduate within 4 years. **Faculty:** Student/faculty ratio 10:1. 130 full-time faculty, 95% hold PhDs, 17% are members of minority groups, 44% are women.

ACADEMICS
Degrees: Bachelor's. **Classes:** Most classes have 10–19 students. Most lab/discussion sessions have 20–29 students. **Majors with Highest Enrollment:** Biology/biological sciences; history; political science and government. **Special Study Options:** Accelerated program, cooperative education program, cross-registration, double major, dual enrollment, exchange student program (domestic), honors program, independent study, liberal arts/career combination, student-designed major, study abroad, undergraduate research conference. **Combined degree programs:** BA/JD, BA/MA, 3-2 Forest./Duke; 3-2 Ocean./ Bio. or Geo. Special programs offered to physically disabled students include note-taking services, reader services, tape recorders, tutors. **Career services:** Alumni network, alumni services, career assessment.

FACILITIES
Housing: Coed dorms, special housing for international students, women's dorms, fraternity/sorority housing, apartments for single students, theme housingInterest houses. 85% of campus accessible to physically disabled. **Special Academic Facilities/Equipment:** Art gallery, Asian art collection, anthropology museum, planetarium, outdoor observatory, two electron microscopes, outdoor sculpture walk, technology/video-conferencing center, indoor and outdoor rock-climbing walls, organic garden. **Computers:** 100% of classrooms, 100% of dorms, 100% of libraries, 100% of dining areas, 100% of student union, 40% of common outdoor areas have wireless network access. Students can register for classes online. Administrative functions (other than registration) can be performed online.

CAMPUS LIFE
Environment: Town. **Activities:** Choral groups, concert band, dance, drama/theater, jazz band, literary magazine, music ensembles, musical theater, radio station, student government, student newspaper, student-run film society, symphony orchestra, campus ministries, international student organization, Model UN. **Organizations:** 80 registered organizations, 3 honor societies, 7 religious organizations. 4 fraternities, 3 sororities. **Athletics (Intercollegiate):** *Men:* Baseball, basketball, cross-country, golf, soccer, swimming, tennis. *Women:* Basketball, cross-country, golf, soccer, swimming, tennis, volleyball. **On-Campus Highlights:** Reid Campus Center, Penrose Library, Baker Fergueson Fitness Center, Sheehan Art Gallery, Olin Hall, Harper Joy Theatre. **Environmental Initiatives:** Installed 21kW Solar Panels on roof of Bratton Tennis Center.

Purchase renewable energy credits worth 30% of the colleges annual electricity use. All printing paper is 100% post-consumer recycled.

ADMISSIONS

Freshman Academic Profile: Average high school GPA 3.78. 67% in top 10% of high school class, 90% in top 25% of high school class, 100% in top 50% of high school class. 75% from public high schools. SAT Math middle 50% range 610–700. SAT Critical Reading middle 50% range 630–730. SAT Writing middle 50% range 610–710. Minimum paper TOEFL 560. Minimum computer TOEFL 220. Minimum web-based TOEFL 85. **Basis for Candidate Selection:** *Very important factors considered include:* Application essay, academic GPA, rigor of secondary school record, character/personal qualities. *Important factors considered include:* Recommendation(s), standardized test scores, extra-curricular activities, racial/ethnic status, talent/ability. *Other factors considered include:* Class rank, alumni/ae relation, first generation, geographical residence, interview, level of applicant's interest, state residency, volunteer work, work experience. **Freshman Admission Requirements:** High school diploma is required and GED is accepted. *Academic units recommended:* 4 English, 4 mathematics, 3 science, (2 science labs), 2 foreign language, 2 social studies, 2 history, 1 arts. **Freshman Admission Statistics:** 3,290 applied, 44% admitted, 27% enrolled. **Transfer Admission Requirements:** High school transcript, college transcript(s), essay or personal statement, statement of good standing from prior institution(s). Lowest grade transferable C–. **General Admission Information:** Application fee $50. Early decision application deadline 11/15. Regular application deadline 1/15. Regular notification 4/1. Nonfall registration accepted. Admission may be deferred for a maximum of 1 year. Credit and/or placement offered for CEEB Advanced Placement tests.

COSTS AND FINANCIAL AID

Annual tuition $36,620. Room and board $9,260. Required fees $320. Average book expense $1,400. **Required Forms and Deadlines:** FAFSA, CSS/Financial Aid PROFILE Financial aid filing deadline 2/1. Priority financial aid filing date 11/15. **Notification of Awards:** Applicants will be notified of awards on a rolling basis beginning 12/20. **Types of Aid:** *Need-based scholarships/grants:* Federal Pell, SEOG, state scholarships/grants, private scholarships, the school's own gift aid. *Loans:* FFEL Subsidized Stafford, FFEL Unsubsidized Stafford, FFEL PLUS, Federal Perkins, state loans, Alternative student loans. *Student Employment:* Federal Work-Study Program available. Institutional employment available. Highest amount earned per year from on-campus jobs $2,463. Off-campus job opportunities are good. **Financial Aid Statistics:** 48% freshmen, 44% undergrads receive need-based scholarship or grant aid. 22% freshmen, 13% undergrads receive non-need-based scholarship or grant aid. 39% freshmen, 37% undergrads receive need-based self-help aid. 81% freshmen, 76% undergrads receive any aid. 49% undergrads borrow to pay for school. Average cumulative indebtedness $17,955. **Criteria for awarding institutional aid:** *Non-need-based:* Academics, art, leadership, minority status, music/drama.

WHITTIER COLLEGE

Best 373

13406 Philadelphia Street, P.O. Box 634, Whittier, CA 90608
Phone: 562-907-4238 **Financial Aid Phone:** 562-907-4285
E-mail: admission@whittier.edu **CEEB Code:** 4952
Fax: 562-907-4870 **Website:** www.whittier.edu **ACT Code:** 480

This private school was founded in 1887. It has a 75-acre campus.

RATINGS

Admissions Selectivity Rating: 84   **Fire Safety Rating:** 83   **Green Rating:** 76

STUDENTS AND FACULTY

Enrollment: 1,361. **Student Body:** 53% female, 47% male; 27% out-of-state, 2% international (24 countries represented). Asian 9%, African American 6%, Caucasian 41%, Hispanic 30%, Native American 1%.
Retention and Graduation: 55% freshmen graduate within 4 years. 18% grads go on to further study within 1 year. 7% grads pursue arts and sciences degrees. 2% grads pursue law degrees. 3% grads pursue business degrees. 1% grads pursue medical degrees. **Faculty:** Student/faculty ratio 12.8:1. 96 full-time faculty, 99% hold PhDs, 27% are members of minority groups, 47% are women.

ACADEMICS

Degrees: Bachelor's, master's. **Classes:** Most classes have 10–19 students. Most lab/discussion sessions have 20–29 students. **Majors with Highest**

Enrollment: Biology/biological sciences; business administration and management; psychology. **Special Study Options:** Double major, independent study, internships, liberal arts/career combination, student-designed major, study abroad, teacher certification program. **Combined degree programs:** BA/JD, 3-2 engineering programs. Special programs offered to physically disabled students include note-taking services, reader services, tape recorders. **Career services:** Alumni network, alumni services, career/job search classes, career assessment, internships, regional alumni. **Career services highlights include:** Backpack to Briefcase: The Office of Career Services and the Office of Alumni Relations have teamed up to present a series of workshops throughout the school year to enable students to learn and develop practical career skills and explore diverse career paths, and at the same time showcase Whittier College alumni professionals, who serve as volunteer mentors and workshop leaders.

FACILITIES

Housing: Coed dorms, special housing for international students, living and learning community; special interest housing. 60% of campus accessible to physically disabled. **Special Academic Facilities/Equipment:** Performing arts center, on-campus pre-school/ elementary school, image processing lab, state-of-the-art nightclub, on-air radio studio and production room, video production room **Computers:** 100% of classrooms, 100% of dorms, 100% of libraries, 100% of dining areas, 100% of student union, have wireless network access. Students can register for classes online. Administrative functions (other than registration) can be performed online.

CAMPUS LIFE

Environment: City. **Activities:** Choral groups, dance, drama/theater, jazz band, literary magazine, music ensembles, musical theater, radio station, student government, student newspaper, student-run film society, yearbook, campus ministries, international student organization, Model UN. **Organizations:** 60 registered organizations, 17 honor societies, 6 religious organizations. 4 fraternities, 5 sororities. **Athletics (Intercollegiate):** *Men:* Baseball, basketball, cross-country, diving, football, golf, lacrosse, soccer, swimming, tennis, track/field (outdoor), water polo. *Women:* Basketball, cross-country, diving, lacrosse, soccer, softball, swimming, tennis, track/field (outdoor), volleyball, water polo. **On-Campus Highlights:** The Campus Center, Bonnie Bell Wardman Library, Donald Graham Athletics Center, Ruth B. Shannon Center for the Performing Arts, the Rock (campus icon), The recently renovated Campus Center houses the student services division, campus dining, The Spot (campus cafe),student organization offices, KPOET radio, student newspaper. Quaker Campus, and an outdoor amphitheatre. **Environmental Initiatives:** Climate Commitment signatory; EnergyStar purchasing policy; waste minimization program.

ADMISSIONS

Freshman Academic Profile: Average high school GPA 3.05. 30% in top 10% of high school class, 42% in top 25% of high school class, 82% in top 50% of high school class. SAT Math middle 50% range 470–590. SAT Critical Reading middle 50% range 470–580. SAT Writing middle 50% range 470–570. ACT middle 50% range 19.25–25. Minimum paper TOEFL 550. Minimum computer TOEFL 230. **Basis for Candidate Selection:** *Very important factors considered include:* Application essay, rigor of secondary school record. *Important factors considered include:* Academic GPA, recommendation(s), standardized test scores, character/personal qualities, extracurricular activities, interview, talent/ability, volunteer work. *Other factors considered include:* Class rank, alumni/ae relation, first generation, geographical residence, racial/ethnic status, state residency, work experience. **Freshman Admission Requirements:** High school diploma is required and GED is accepted. *Academic units required:* 3 English, 2 mathematics, 1 science, (1 science labs), 2 foreign language, 1 social studies. *Academic units recommended:* 4 English, 3 mathematics, 2 science, 3 foreign language, 2 social studies. **Freshman Admission Statistics:** 2,263 applied, 72% admitted, 22% enrolled. **Transfer Admission Requirements:** High school transcript, college transcript(s), essay or personal statement, Lowest grade transferable C–. **General Admission Information:** Application fee $50. Notification on a rolling basis, beginning on or about 12/30. Nonfall registration accepted. Admission may be deferred for a maximum of 1 year. Credit and/or placement offered for CEEB Advanced Placement tests.

COSTS AND FINANCIAL AID

Annual tuition $31,950. Room and board $9,050. Required fees $520. Average book expense $1,566. **Required Forms and Deadlines:** FAFSA, institution's own financial aid form Financial aid filing deadline 6/30. Priority financial aid filing date 3/1. **Notification of Awards:** Applicants will be notified of awards on a rolling basis beginning 2/15. **Types of Aid:** *Need-based scholarships/grants:* Federal Pell, SEOG, state scholarships/grants, private scholarships, the school's own gift aid. *Loans:* Direct PLUS, FFEL Subsidized Stafford, FFEL Unsubsidized Stafford, FFEL PLUS, Federal Perkins, Alternative Financing Loans. *Student Employment:* Federal Work-Study Program available. Highest amount earned per year from on-campus jobs $1,250. Off-campus job opportunities are good. **Financial Aid Statistics:** 62% freshmen, 58% undergrads receive need-based scholarship or grant aid. 60% freshmen, 61% undergrads receive non-need-based scholarship or grant aid. 69% freshmen, 70% undergrads receive need-based self-help aid. 92% freshmen, 89% undergrads receive any aid. 78% undergrads borrow to pay for school. Average cumulative indebtedness $40,220. **Criteria for awarding institutional aid:** *Non-need-based:* Academics, alumni affiliation, art, music/drama.

WHITWORTH COLLEGE

300 West Hawthorne Road, Spokane, WA 99251
Phone: 509-777-4786 **Financial Aid Phone:** 509-777-4306
E-mail: admission@whitworth.edu **CEEB Code:** 4953
Fax: 509-777-3758 **Website: ACT Code:** 4494

This private school, affiliated with the Presbyterian Church, was founded in 1890. It has a 200-acre campus.

RATINGS
Admissions Selectivity Rating: 89   **Fire Safety Rating:** 89   **Green Rating:** 60*

STUDENTS AND FACULTY
Enrollment: 2,233. **Student Body:** 61% female, 39% male, 37% out-of-state, 1% international (15 countries represented). Asian 4%, African American 3%, Caucasian 86%, Hispanic 2%, Native American 1%.
Retention and Graduation: 89% freshmen return for sophomore year. 59% freshmen graduate within 4 years. 50% grads go on to further study within 1 year. **Faculty:** Student/faculty ratio 12:1. 123 full-time faculty, 74% hold PhDs, 10% are members of minority groups, 42% are women.

ACADEMICS
Degrees: Bachelor's, master's. **Classes:** Most classes have 10–19 students. Most lab/discussion sessions have 10–19 students. **Majors with Highest Enrollment:** Business/commerce; elementary education and teaching; English language and literature. **Special Study Options:** Cooperative education program, cross-registration, double major, dual enrollment, English as a Second Language (ESL), exchange student program (domestic), honors program, independent study, internships, liberal arts/career combination, student-designed major, study abroad, teacher certification program Special programs offered to physically disabled students include note-taking services, reader services, tape recorders

FACILITIES
Housing: Coed dorms, men's dorms, women's dorms, Theme houses within walking distance to the campus. 80% of campus accessible to physically disabled. **Special Academic Facilities/Equipment:** Language laboratory, art gallery, computer labs. **Computers:** Students can register for classes online. Administrative functions (other than registration) can be performed online.

CAMPUS LIFE
Environment: City. **Activities:** Choral groups, concert band, dance, drama/theater, jazz band, music ensembles, musical theater, pep band, radio station, student government, student newspaper, symphony orchestra, yearbook. **Organizations:** 50 registered organizations, 5 honor societies, **Athletics (Intercollegiate): Men:** Baseball, basketball, cheerleading, cross-country, football, golf, soccer, swimming, tennis, track/field (outdoor). *Women:* Basketball, cheerleading, cross-country, golf, soccer, softball, swimming, tennis, track/field (outdoor), volleyball. **On-Campus Highlights:** Hixon Union Building (Student Union)—cafe, Weyerhauser Hall (Teaching Theatre), Boppell Hall—new dormitory for upperclassmen, Athletic Complex, Library.

ADMISSIONS
Freshman Academic Profile: Average high school GPA 3.7. 41% in top 10% of high school class, 74% in top 25% of high school class, 92% in top 50% of high school class. 87% from public high schools. SAT Math middle 50% range 540–650. SAT Critical Reading middle 50% range 540–660. SAT Writing middle 50% range 530–640. ACT middle 50% range 23–28. Minimum paper TOEFL 550. Minimum computer TOEFL 250. **Basis for Candidate Selection:** *Very important factors considered include:* Class rank, application essay, recommendation(s), rigor of secondary school record, standardized test scores. *Important factors considered include:* Alumni/ae relation, character/personal qualities, extracurricular activities, geographical residence, interview, talent/ability. *Other factors considered include:* Racial/ethnic status, religious affiliation/commitment, volunteer work. **Freshman Admission Requirements:** High school diploma is required and GED is accepted. *Academic units recommended:* 4 English, 3 mathematics, 3 science, (2 science labs), 2 foreign language, 3 social studies, 3 history. **Freshman Admission Statistics:** 2,686 applied, 63% admitted, 28% enrolled. **Transfer Admission Requirements:** High school transcript, college transcript(s), essay or personal statement, standardized test scores, statement of good standing from prior institution(s). Minimum college GPA of 2.5 required. Lowest grade transferable C–. **General Admission**

Information: Regular application deadline 3/1. Notification on a rolling basis, beginning on or about 12/20. Nonfall registration accepted. Admission may be deferred for a maximum of 12. Credit offered for CEEB Advanced Placement tests.

COSTS AND FINANCIAL AID
Annual tuition $23,850. Room and board $7,030. Required fees $304. Average book expense $792. **Required Forms and Deadlines:** FAFSA. Priority financial aid filing date 3/1. **Notification of Awards:** Applicants will be notified of awards on a rolling basis beginning 4/1. **Types of Aid:** *Need-based scholarships/grants:* Federal Pell, SEOG, state scholarships/grants, private scholarships, the school's own gift aid. *Loans:* Direct Subsidized Stafford, Direct Unsubsidized Stafford, Direct PLUS, Federal Perkins, college/university loans from institutional funds. *Student Employment:* Highest amount earned per year from on-campus jobs $2,500. **Financial Aid Statistics:** 67% freshmen, 67% undergrads receive need-based scholarship or grant aid. 11% freshmen, 8% undergrads receive non-need-based scholarship or grant aid. 52% freshmen, 55% undergrads receive need-based self-help aid. 93% freshmen, 90% undergrads receive any aid. 73% undergrads borrow to pay for school. Average cumulative indebtedness $18,478. **Criteria for awarding institutional aid:** *Non-need-based:* Academics, alumni affiliation, art, music/drama, religious affiliation.

WICHITA STATE UNIVERSITY

1845 Fairmount, Wichita, KS 67260
Phone: 316-978-3085 **Financial Aid Phone:** 800-522-2978
E-mail: admissions@wichita.edu **CEEB Code:** 6884
Fax: 316-978-3174 **Website:** www.wichita.edu **ACT Code:** 1472

This public school was founded in 1895. It has a 330-acre campus.

RATINGS
Admissions Selectivity Rating: 73   **Fire Safety Rating:** 60*   **Green Rating:** 76

STUDENTS AND FACULTY
Enrollment: 10,951. **Student Body:** 54% female, 46% male, 4% out-of-state, 6% international (114 countries represented). Asian 6%, African American 6%, Caucasian 59%, Hispanic 5%, Native American 1%.
Retention and Graduation: 70% freshmen return for sophomore year. 15% freshmen graduate within 4 years. **Faculty:** Student/faculty ratio 20:1. 448 full-time faculty, 79% hold PhDs, 17% are members of minority groups, 42% are women. 10% of classes are taught by teaching assistants.

ACADEMICS
Degrees: Associate, bachelor's, certificate, diploma, doctoral, master's, post-bachelor's certificate, post-master's certificate, terminal associate, transfer associate. **Classes:** Most classes have 10–19 students. Most lab/discussion sessions have 20–29 students. **Majors with Highest Enrollment:** accounting; elementary education and teaching; psychology. **Special Study Options:** Accelerated program, cooperative education program, cross-registration, distance learning, double major, dual enrollment, English as a Second Language (ESL), exchange student program (domestic), honors program, independent study, internships, study abroad, teacher certification program. **Honors programs:** Emory Lindquist Honors Program. The Honors Program offers freshman/sophomore seminars, lower division regular classes, honors colloquia, and honors upper division sections of regular classes. Students can also choose to do independent study projects. The Honors Program also offers a Senior Project, which is an opportunity for students to earn special honors recognition in a student's academic major. Special programs offered to physically disabled students include note-taking services, reader services, tape recorders, tutors. **Career services:** Alumni network, alumni services, career/job search classes, career assessment, internships, regional alumni. **Career services highlights include:** To empower our clients (students, alumni, faculty, staff and community members) with the skills, knowledge and resources necessary for effective career development, and to build partnerships with employers to expand client career opportunities.

FACILITIES
Housing: Coed dorms, fraternity/sorority housing, apartments for married students, apartments for single students, Some dorm floors are reserved for students majoring in Fine Arts, Health Professions, and for students in the Emory Lindquist Honors Program. 98% of campus accessible to physically disabled. **Special Academic Facilities/Equipment:** Art museum, performance hall, media resource center, observatory, national institute of aviation research, supersonic wind tunnels, 24-hour study room in library, outdoor sculpture collection. **Computers:** Students can register for classes online. Administrative functions (other than registration) can be performed online.

CAMPUS LIFE

Environment: Metropolis. **Activities:** Choral groups, concert band, dance, drama/theater, jazz band, literary magazine, music ensembles, musical theater, opera, pep band, radio station, student government, student newspaper, student-run film society, symphony orchestra, television station, campus ministries, international student organization, Model UN. **Organizations:** 140 registered organizations, 11 honor societies, 10 religious organizations. 11 fraternities, 10 sororities. **Athletics (Intercollegiate):** *Men:* Baseball, basketball, bowling, cheerleading, cross-country, golf, rugby, swimming, tennis, track/field (outdoor). *Women:* Basketball, bowling, cheerleading, cross-country, golf, softball, swimming, tennis, track/field (outdoor), volleyball. **On-Campus Highlights:** Rhatigan Student Center, Ulrich Museum of Art, Heskett Center, outdoor sculpture collection, Charles Koch arena, Wichita State University, founded in 1895 as a Congregational institution, is distinguished from other state supported schools in Kansas by its urban setting. Wichita State's location in the largest city in Kansas enhances the traditional classroom experience by providing students greater opportunities in resources, contacts with business and government leaders, employment, and internships. **Environmental Initiatives:** Recycle Program.

ADMISSIONS

Freshman Academic Profile: Average high school GPA 3.31. 18% in top 10% of high school class, 45% in top 25% of high school class, 77% in top 50% of high school class. SAT Math middle 50% range 500–623. SAT Critical Reading middle 50% range 470–600. ACT middle 50% range 21–26. Minimum paper TOEFL 530. Minimum computer TOEFL 197. Minimum web-based TOEFL 72. **Basis for Candidate Selection:** *Very important factors considered include:* Class rank, academic GPA, rigor of secondary school record, standardized test scores. **Freshman Admission Requirements:** High school diploma is required and GED is accepted. *Academic units required:* 4 English, 4 mathematics, 3 science, 3 social studies, 1 computer proficiency **Freshman Admission Statistics:** 2,963 applied, 89% admitted, 53% enrolled. **Transfer Admission Requirements:** College transcript(s), minimum college GPA of 2.0 required. Lowest grade transferable C. **General Admission Information:** Application fee $30. Nonfall registration accepted. Admission may be deferred for a maximum of 2 years. Credit and/or placement offered for CEEB Advanced Placement tests.

COSTS AND FINANCIAL AID

Required Forms and Deadlines: FAFSA. Priority financial aid filing date 3/1. **Notification of Awards:** Applicants will be notified of awards on a rolling basis beginning 3/15. **Types of Aid:** *Need-based scholarships/grants:* Federal Pell, SEOG, state scholarships/grants, private scholarships, the school's own gift aid, Bureau of Indian Affairs. *Loans:* FFEL Subsidized Stafford, FFEL Unsubsidized Stafford, FFEL PLUS, Federal Perkins. *Student Employment:* Federal Work-Study Program available. Institutional employment available. Highest amount earned per year from on-campus jobs $14,224. Off-campus job opportunities are excellent. **Financial Aid Statistics:** 21% freshmen, 20% undergrads receive need-based scholarship or grant aid. 18% freshmen, 12% undergrads receive non-need-based scholarship or grant aid. 20% freshmen, 31% undergrads receive need-based self-help aid. 3% freshmen, 3% undergrads receive athletic scholarships. 73% freshmen, 58% undergrads receive any aid. 57% undergrads borrow to pay for school. Average cumulative indebtedness $15,769. **Criteria for awarding institutional aid:** *Non-need-based:* Academics, alumni affiliation, art, athletics, leadership, music/drama.

WIDENER UNIVERSITY

One University Place, Chester, PA 19013
Phone: 610-499-4126 **Financial Aid Phone:** 610-499-4152
E-mail: admissions.office@widener.edu **CEEB Code:** 2642
Fax: 610-499-4676 **Website:** www.widener.edu **ACT Code:** 3652

This private school was founded in 1821. It has a 110-acre campus.

RATINGS

Admissions Selectivity Rating: 76   **Fire Safety Rating:** 60*   **Green Rating:** 60*

STUDENTS AND FACULTY

Enrollment: 3,247. **Student Body:** 55% female, 45% male, 37% out-of-state, 2% international (38 countries represented). Asian 3%, African American 14%, Caucasian 69%, Hispanic 3%.
Retention and Graduation: 72% freshmen return for sophomore year. 41% freshmen graduate within 4 years. 20% grads go on to further study within 1 year. **Faculty:** Student/faculty ratio 12:1. 310 full-time faculty, 89% hold PhDs, 12% are members of minority groups, 50% are women.

ACADEMICS

Degrees: Associate, bachelor's, certificate, master's. **Classes:** Most classes have 10–19 students. Most lab/discussion sessions have fewer than 10 students. **Majors with Highest Enrollment:** Business/commerce; civil engineering; nursing/registered nurse (RN, ASN, BSN, MSN). **Special Study Options:** Accelerated program, cooperative education program, distance learning, double major, English as a Second Language (ESL), honors program, independent study, internships, liberal arts/career combination, student-designed major, study abroad, teacher certification program, weekend college. **Honors programs:** Honors Program in General Education. **Combined degree programs:** BA/MD, BA/MA, BA/MEng. Special programs offered to physically disabled students include note-taking services, reader services, tape recorders, tutors. **Career services:** Alumni network, alumni services, career/job search classes, career assessment, regional alumni.

FACILITIES

Housing: Coed dorms, men's dorms, women's dorms, fraternity/sorority housing, cooperative housing, apartments for single students, wellness housing, theme housing. **Special Academic Facilities/Equipment:** Art gallery, restaurant lab, child development center education lab, recording studio, commercial graphics lab, physical therapy lab, science labs, engineering labs, nursing labs, multimedia classrooms, Media Center. **Computers:** Students can register for classes online. Administrative functions (other than registration) can be performed online.

CAMPUS LIFE

Environment: Town. **Activities:** Choral groups, concert band, dance, drama/theater, jazz band, literary magazine, music ensembles, pep band, radio station, student government, student newspaper, student-run film society, television station, yearbook, campus ministries, international student organization. **Organizations:** 80 registered organizations, 29 honor societies, 3 religious organizations. 7 fraternities, 3 sororities. **Athletics (Intercollegiate):** *Men:* Baseball, basketball, cross-country, football, golf, lacrosse, soccer, swimming, tennis, track/field (outdoor), track/field (indoor). *Women:* Basketball, cheerleading, cross-country, field hockey, lacrosse, soccer, softball, swimming, tennis, track/field (outdoor), track/field (indoor), volleyball. **On-Campus Highlights:** University Center, Java City and Residential Restaurant, Schwartz Athletic Center, Greek Row, Art Gallery, PMC Museum, Media Center, Observatory.

ADMISSIONS

Freshman Academic Profile: Average high school GPA 3.3. 13% in top 10% of high school class, 39% in top 25% of high school class, 73% in top 50% of high school class. 55% from public high schools. SAT Math middle 50% range 460–560. SAT Critical Reading middle 50% range 440–540. Minimum paper TOEFL 500. Minimum computer TOEFL 173. **Basis for Candidate Selection:** *Very important factors considered include:* Class rank, academic GPA, rigor of secondary school record, standardized test scores, *Other factors considered include:* Application essay, recommendation(s), alumni/ae relation, character/personal qualities, extracurricular activities, interview, level of applicant's interest, talent/ability, volunteer work. **Freshman Admission Requirements:** High school diploma is required and GED is accepted. *Academic units required:* 4 English, 3 mathematics, 3 science, 2 foreign language, 3 social studies, 3 academic electives. *Academic units recommended:* 4 English, 4 mathematics, 4 science, (2 science labs), 2 foreign language, 4 social studies, 3 academic electives. **Freshman Admission Statistics:** 4,636 applied, 70% admitted, 22% enrolled. **Transfer Admission Requirements:** College transcript(s), minimum college GPA of 2.0 required. Lowest grade transferable C. **General Admission Information:** Application fee $35. Notification on a rolling basis, beginning on or about 10/1. Nonfall registration accepted. Admission may be deferred for a maximum of 1 academic year. Credit offered for CEEB Advanced Placement tests.

COSTS AND FINANCIAL AID

Average book expense $1,200. **Required Forms and Deadlines:** FAFSA. Priority financial aid filing date 2/15. **Notification of Awards:** Applicants will be notified of awards on a rolling basis beginning 3/15. **Types of Aid:** *Need-based scholarships/grants:* Federal Pell, SEOG, state scholarships/grants, private scholarships, the school's own gift aid, Federal Nursing Scholarships. *Loans:* FFEL Subsidized Stafford, FFEL Unsubsidized Stafford, FFEL PLUS, Federal Perkins. *Student Employment:* Federal Work-Study Program available. Institutional employment available. Off-campus job opportunities are good. **Financial Aid Statistics:** 73% freshmen, 64% undergrads receive need-based scholarship or grant aid. 72% freshmen, 63% undergrads receive non-need-based scholarship or grant aid. 75% freshmen, 70% undergrads receive need-based self-help aid. 98% freshmen, 90% undergrads receive any aid. 87% undergrads borrow to pay for school. Average cumulative indebtedness $38,372. **Criteria for awarding institutional aid:** *Non-need-based:* Academics, leadership, music/drama.

WILBERFORCE UNIVERSITY

1055 N. Bickett Road, P.O. Box 1001, Wilberforce, OH 45384
Phone: 800-367-8568
E-mail: kchristm@shorter.wilberforce **CEEB Code:** 1906
Fax: 937-376-4751 **Website:** www.wilberforce.edu **ACT Code:** 3360

This private school was founded in 1856. It has a 125-acre campus.

RATINGS
Admissions Selectivity Rating: 60*   **Fire Safety Rating:** 60*   **Green Rating:** 60*

STUDENTS AND FACULTY
Enrollment: 1,180. **Student Body:** 60% female, 40% male, 39% out-of-state (2 countries represented). African American 90%, Caucasian 5%, Hispanic 1%. **Retention and Graduation: Faculty:** Student/faculty ratio 17:1. 49 full-time faculty, 67% are members of minority groups, 45% are women.

ACADEMICS
Degrees: Bachelor's. **Special Study Options:** Accelerated program, cooperative education program, cross-registration, distance learning, double major, external degree program, honors program, independent study, internships, liberal arts/career combination, student-designed major, study abroad. **Career services:** Career/job search classes, career assessment, internships.

FACILITIES
Housing: Coed dorms, men's dorms, women's dorms, apartments for married students. **Special Academic Facilities/Equipment:** African Methodist Church archives.

CAMPUS LIFE
Activities: Choral groups, concert band, dance, jazz band, literary magazine, music ensembles, radio station, student government, student newspaper, yearbook. **Organizations:** 4 religious organizations. 4 fraternities, 4 sororities.

ADMISSIONS
Freshman Academic Profile: Minimum paper TOEFL 500. **Freshman Admission Requirements:** High school diploma is required and GED is accepted. *Academic units required:* 4 English, 2 mathematics, 2 science, 2 social studies, 5 academic electives. **Freshman Admission Statistics:** 2,405 applied, 22% admitted, 36% enrolled. **Transfer Admission Requirements:** College transcript(s), minimum college GPA of 2.0 required. Lowest grade transferable C. **General Admission Information:** Application fee $20. Regular application deadline 6/1. Nonfall registration accepted. Credit and/or placement offered for CEEB Advanced Placement tests.

COSTS AND FINANCIAL AID
Annual tuition $9,720. Room and board $5,320. Required fees $1,060. Average book expense $1,000. **Required Forms and Deadlines:** FAFSA, institution's own financial aid form, state aid form **Types of Aid:** *Need-based scholarships/grants:* United Negro College Fund. *Loans:* FFEL Subsidized Stafford, FFEL PLUS. *Student Employment:* Federal Work-Study Program available. Highest amount earned per year from on-campus jobs $2,000. Off-campus job opportunities are good.

WILKES UNIVERSITY

84 W South St, Wilkes-Barre, PA 18766
Phone: 570-408-4400 **Financial Aid Phone:** 570-408-2000
E-mail: admissions@wilkes.edu **CEEB Code:** 2977
Fax: 570-408-4904 **Website:** www.wilkes.edu **ACT Code:** 3756

This private school was founded in 1933. It has a 27-acre campus.

RATINGS
Admissions Selectivity Rating: 73   **Fire Safety Rating:** 60*   **Green Rating:** 71

STUDENTS AND FACULTY
Enrollment: 2,133. **Student Body:** 48% female, 52% male, 21% out-of-state, 2% international (18 countries represented). Asian 2%, African American 3%, Caucasian 83%, Hispanic 2%.
Retention and Graduation: 80% freshmen return for sophomore year. 50% freshmen graduate within 4 years. **Faculty:** Student/faculty ratio 15:1. 149 full-time faculty, 89% hold PhDs, 8% are members of minority groups, 47% are women.

ACADEMICS
Degrees: Bachelor's, doctoral, master's. **Classes:** Most classes have 10–19 students. Most lab/discussion sessions have 10–19 students. **Majors with Highest Enrollment:** Business administration and management; nursing/registered nurse (RN, ASN, BSN, MSN); pharmacy (pharmd [usa], pharmd or bs/bpharm [canada]). **Special Study Options:** Cooperative education program, cross-registration, distance learning, double major, dual enrollment, English as a Second Language (ESL), external degree program, honors program, independent study, internships, student-designed major, study abroad, teacher certification program, weekend college Special programs offered to physically disabled students include note-taking services, reader services, tape recorders, tutors. **Career services:** Alumni network, alumni services, career/job search classes, career assessment, internships, regional alumni.

FACILITIES
Housing: Coed dorms, men's dorms, women's dorms, apartments for single students. **Special Academic Facilities/Equipment:** Art gallery, performing arts center, electron microscope, television studio. **Computers:** Students can register for classes online. Administrative functions (other than registration) can be performed online.

CAMPUS LIFE
Environment: City. **Activities:** Choral groups, dance, drama/theater, jazz band, literary magazine, music ensembles, musical theater, pep band, radio station, student government, student newspaper, television station, yearbook, campus ministries, international student organization. **Organizations:** 65 registered organizations, 19 honor societies, **Athletics (Intercollegiate):** *Men:* Baseball, basketball, cross-country, football, golf, soccer, tennis, wrestling. *Women:* Basketball, cross-country, field hockey, lacrosse, soccer, softball, tennis, volleyball.

ADMISSIONS
Freshman Academic Profile: 25% in top 10% of high school class, 53% in top 25% of high school class, 86% in top 50% of high school class. SAT Math middle 50% range 480–600. SAT Critical Reading middle 50% range 460–580. SAT Writing middle 50% range 450–570. Minimum paper TOEFL 500. Minimum computer TOEFL 183. Minimum web-based TOEFL 61. **Basis for Candidate Selection:** *Very important factors considered include:* Class rank, rigor of secondary school record. *Important factors considered include:* Academic GPA, standardized test scores, character/personal qualities, extracurricular activities. *Other factors considered include:* Recommendation(s), alumni/ae relation, interview, talent/ability, volunteer work, work experience. **Freshman Admission Requirements:** High school diploma is required and GED is accepted. *Academic units recommended:* 4 English, 3 mathematics, 3 science, (2 science labs), 2 foreign language, 3 social studies, 1 computer science. **Freshman Admission Statistics:** 2,641 applied, 76% admitted, 27% enrolled. **Transfer Admission Requirements:** College transcript(s), statement of good standing from prior institution(s). Minimum college GPA of 2.0 required. Lowest grade transferable C. **General Admission Information:** Application fee $40. Notification on a rolling basis, beginning on or about 9/1. Nonfall registration accepted. Admission may be deferred for a maximum of 1 year. Credit and/or placement offered for CEEB Advanced Placement tests.

COSTS AND FINANCIAL AID
Annual tuition $24,690. Room and board $11,100. Required fees $1,320. Average book expense $1,100. **Required Forms and Deadlines:** FAFSA. Priority financial aid filing date 3/1. **Notification of Awards:** Applicants will be notified of awards on a rolling basis beginning 3/1. **Types of Aid:** *Need-based scholarships/grants:* Federal Pell, SEOG, state scholarships/grants, private scholarships, the school's own gift aid. *Loans:* FFEL Subsidized Stafford, FFEL Unsubsidized Stafford, FFEL PLUS, Federal Perkins, Federal Nursing, state loans, college/university loans from institutional funds. *Student Employment:* Federal Work-Study Program available. Institutional employment available. Off-campus job opportunities are good. **Financial Aid Statistics:** 69% freshmen, 59% undergrads receive need-based scholarship or grant aid. 72% freshmen, 58% undergrads receive non-need-based scholarship or grant aid. 80% freshmen, 73% undergrads receive need-based self-help aid. 97% freshmen, 95% undergrads receive any aid. 88% undergrads borrow to pay for school. Average cumulative indebtedness $31,935. **Criteria for awarding institutional aid:** *Non-need-based:* Academics, leadership, minority status, music/drama.

WILLAMETTE UNIVERSITY

900 State Street, Salem, OR 97301
Phone: 503-370-6303 **Financial Aid Phone:** 503-370-6273
E-mail: libarts@willamette.edu **CEEB Code:** 4954
Fax: 503-375-5363 **Website:** www.willamette.edu **ACT Code:** 3504

This private school, affiliated with the Methodist Church, was founded in 1842. It has a 72-acre campus.

RATINGS

Admissions Selectivity Rating: 93   **Fire Safety Rating:** 77   **Green Rating:** 84

STUDENTS AND FACULTY

Enrollment: 1,853. **Student Body:** 56% female, 44% male, 68% out-of-state, 1% international (16 countries represented). Asian 7%, African American 2%, Caucasian 61%, Hispanic 6%, Native American 1%.
Retention and Graduation: 88% freshmen return for sophomore year. 71% freshmen graduate within 4 years. 24% grads go on to further study within 1 year. 5% grads pursue arts and sciences degrees. 7% grads pursue law degrees. 5% grads pursue business degrees. 4% grads pursue medical degrees. **Faculty:** Student/faculty ratio 10:1. 213 full-time faculty, 96% hold PhDs, 17% are members of minority groups, 45% are women.

ACADEMICS

Degrees: Bachelor's, first professional, first professional certificate, master's. **Classes:** Most classes have 10–19 students. **Majors with Highest Enrollment:** Biology/biological sciences; economics; psychology. **Special Study Options:** Accelerated program, cross-registration, double major, dual enrollment, exchange student program (domestic), independent study, internships, student-designed major, study abroad, teacher certification program. **Honors programs:** Our challenging curriculum includes a variety of opportunities for individualized honors study, for example: Presidential Scholars (senior year), Carson Undergraduate Research Program, Science Collaborative Research Program, various departmental honors programs. **Combined degree programs:** BA/JD, 5 year (BA/MBA);4-2 program in eng(BA/MS). Special programs offered to physically disabled students include note-taking services, reader services, tape recorders, tutors. **Career services:** Alumni network, career/job search classes, career assessment, internships. **Career services highlights include:** Willamette University has a long tradition of academic internships. Three internship programs are in place: to explore career choices (Insight Internship), to gain deeper knowledge of a chosen field (Major Program Internship), or a program which places an emphasis on bridging the gap between liberal arts study and professional responsibilities (Professional Internship). Generally these internships offer one course credit as part of the student's regular academic load though some one-half and two credit internships are available. Internships are an effective means to selecting an interesting, sustaining career; helping students assign meaning and context to their course work; and smoothing the transition from college to work or graduate study. Interns are regularly placed with agencies of the Oregon state government, the Salem city government and the Oregon State Legislature. Other facilities include the Oregon School for the Blind, the Oregon State Hospital and the Salem public schools. Majors in economics, politics, sociology and psychology frequently undertake internships at such sites. Rhetoric and media studies majors may intern with local radio and television stations; English majors intern with the local newspaper or with art organizations; exercise science majors with parks and recreation programs; and others in a variety of settings. Students seeking an internship opportunity will find it at Willamette! Sites in the Salem area which have hosted Willamette interns: • Legislative internships are available with many senators and representatives at the Oregon State Capitol – located across the street from campus. • Historic Deepwood Estate offers a variety of projects geared toward students majoring in the humanities; the gardens and nature trails provide opportunities for biology and environmental science majors as well. • Auburn Elementary School in Salem offers an internship focusing on issues facing children and how they are addressed in the school system. • Marion County Children's Mental Health Services offers internships in counseling. • SAIF Corporation offers internships in industrial psychology. • Silver Falls Soccer Club offers internships in coaching. • The District Attorney's office offers internships in victim's assistance. Internships are available at distant sites as well. These programs often occur during the summer, in which case the academic credit is completed on campus with the assistance of the on-campus supervisor. Some of the organizations which have recently served as internship sites are: • Oregon Public Broadcasting in Portland, Ore.—summer intern-

ship for students studying journalism and telecommunications • Albany Police Department, Albany, Ore.—experience in the criminal justice system • Conari Press in Berkeley, Calif.—editing • Hart Crowser, environmental consulting firm in Lake Oswego, Ore.—site assessment and remedial technologies • Olympic National Forest in Olympia, Wash.—watershed restoration and geology • Corporate Realty Advisors/CRESA in Portland, Ore.—summer research and marketing internship in commercial real estate • The Taylor Family Foundation in Lafayette, Calif.—corporate fundraising • TCI Media Services in Seattle, Wash.—advertising and communication. For further information please refer to www.willamette.edu/cla/intern/index.html.

FACILITIES

Housing: Coed dorms, fraternity/sorority housing, apartments for single students, Substance-free Residence, Environmental Residence (Terra House), Intensive Study (24 hour quiet study) Residence. 95% of campus accessible to physically disabled. **Special Academic Facilities/Equipment:** Student Art purchased annually,and displayed in all public access buildings, Hallie Ford Museum of Art,Collections and papers of Congressional leaders from Oregon,Electron Microscope Lab (scanning and transmission), Herbarium, Japanese and Botanical Gardens, Carnegie Library(fully restored). **Computers:** 100% of classrooms, 100% of dorms, 100% of libraries, 100% of dining areas, 100% of student union, 50% of common outdoor areas have wireless network access. Students can register for classes online. Administrative functions (other than registration) can be performed online.

CAMPUS LIFE

Environment: City. **Activities:** Choral groups, concert band, dance, drama/theater, jazz band, literary magazine, music ensembles, musical theater, opera, student government, student newspaper, student-run film society, symphony orchestra, yearbook, campus ministries, international student organization, Model UN. **Organizations:** 107 registered organizations, 7 honor societies, 5 religious organizations. 4 fraternities, 3 sororities. **Athletics (Intercollegiate):** *Men:* Baseball, basketball, crew/rowing, cross-country, football, golf, soccer, swimming, tennis, track/field (outdoor), track/field (indoor). *Women:* Basketball, crew/rowing, cross-country, golf, soccer, softball, swimming, tennis, track/field (outdoor), track/field (indoor), volleyball. **On-Campus Highlights:** Hallie Ford Museum of Art, Montag Student Center, Sparks Sports and Recreation Center, Willamette Bistro, Mill Stream on campus. **Environmental Initiatives:** Kaneko Commons Residential Hall Ford Hall—Academic Building Purchased Zena Forest—nearby 308-acre sustainable forest for research and teaching. New construction achieved LEED Gold status in 2007. Photo voltaic panels, solar hot water heating, rainwater reclamation for flushing toilets, FSC wood products, Indoor Air Quality measures, low/no VOC materials and products, sustainability educational signage, high recycled content materials, energy efficient boilers, lighting control system, Energy Management System controls, 50% reduction in irrigation, low flow plumbing fixtures, use of plate to plate heat exchangers, sun shades, 95% recycle of construction waste, reflective roof coatings, use of local materials & labor, FSC cert furnishings, Fat Spaniel PV panel monitoring, electrical use monitoring, FLEX CAR program initiated, purchase of Green Power, energy star appliances, and more. Development and approval of a sustainability law certificate program in the University Law School (2007), and planning for a sustainable MBA tract in the MBA program and sustainability concentration in the undergraduate curriculum (2008). Active work groups integrated with curriculum in Law, MBA and undergraduate that research and seek solutions to campus sustainaibility objectives. 2009–2010 projects include Efficacy of purchasing Carbon Offsets (Law), efficacy of Solar Panels on Campus(MBA, Wind Generation (CLA) Solutions for green and post consumer Waste (MBA). President M. Lee Pelton has done much to institutionalize sustainability in both our infrastructure and our educational mission. He created the university wide Sustainability Council in November of 2004, with representation throughout the university, including staff, students, faculty, and administrators. The Sustainability Council is charged with promoting sustainability and environmental literacy, advancing strategic initiatives and best practices on campus (including all new construction and renovations), and enhancing sustainability beyond the campus.Please see www.willamette.edu/about/sustainability/ for more details. In 2007, President Pelton created the Willamette Center for Sustainable Communities (CSC). The CSC is charged with advancing the faculty research and teaching in the area of sustainability, developing meaningful research and learning opportunities for students, and encouraging the adoption of sustainability both on campus and beyond . For more information, see www.willamette.edu/centers/csc/.

ADMISSIONS

Freshman Academic Profile: Average high school GPA 3.72. 49% in top 10% of high school class, 80% in top 25% of high school class, 100% in top 50% of high school class. 80% from public high schools. SAT Math middle 50% range 560–650. SAT Critical Reading middle 50% range 560–670. SAT Writing middle 50% range 550–660. ACT middle 50% range 25–30. Minimum paper TOEFL 550. Minimum computer TOEFL 213. **Basis for Candidate Selection:** *Very important factors considered include:* Class rank, application essay, academic

GPA, rigor of secondary school record, standardized test scores. *Important factors considered include:* Recommendation(s), interview. *Other factors considered include:* Alumni/ae relation, character/personal qualities, extracurricular activities, first generation, geographical residence, racial/ethnic status, talent/ability. **Freshman Admission Requirements:** *Academic units required:* 4 English, 4 mathematics, 3 science, (3 science labs), 1 foreign language, 2 social studies. *Academic units recommended:* 4 English, 4 mathematics, 3 science, (4 science labs), 1 foreign language, 2 social studies, 2 history. **Freshman Admission Statistics:** 5,739 applied, 60% admitted, 16% enrolled. **Transfer Admission Requirements:** High school transcript, college transcript(s), essay or personal statement, statement of good standing from prior institution(s). Lowest grade transferable C. **General Admission Information:** Application fee $50. Notification on a rolling basis, beginning on or about 10/1. Nonfall registration accepted. Admission may be deferred for a maximum of 1 year. Credit and/or placement offered for CEEB Advanced Placement tests.

COSTS AND FINANCIAL AID

Annual tuition $35,400. Room and board $8,350. Required fees $210. Average book expense $920. **Required Forms and Deadlines:** FAFSA. Priority financial aid filing date 2/1. **Notification of Awards:** Applicants will be notified of awards on a rolling basis beginning 4/1. **Types of Aid:** *Need-based scholarships/ grants:* Federal Pell, SEOG, state scholarships/grants, private scholarships, the school's own gift aid. *Loans:* FFEL Subsidized Stafford, FFEL Unsubsidized Stafford, FFEL PLUS, Federal Perkins. *Student Employment:* Federal Work-Study Program available. Institutional employment available. Highest amount earned per year from on-campus jobs $2,000. Off-campus job opportunities are excellent. **Financial Aid Statistics:** 65% freshmen, 62% undergrads receive need-based scholarship or grant aid. 25% freshmen, 14% undergrads receive non-need-based scholarship or grant aid. 59% freshmen, 59% undergrads receive need-based self-help aid. 96% freshmen, 95% undergrads receive any aid. 63% undergrads borrow to pay for school. Average cumulative indebtedness $23,643. **Criteria for awarding institutional aid:** *Non-need-based:* Academics, alumni affiliation, leadership, minority status, music/drama, religious affiliation.

WILLIAM JEWELL COLLEGE

500 College Hill, Liberty, MO 64068
Phone: 816-781-7700
E-mail: admission@william.jewell.edu **CEEB Code:** 6941
Fax: 816-415-5040 **Website:** www.jewell.edu **ACT Code:** 2394

This private school was founded in 1849. It has a 200-acre campus.

RATINGS
Admissions Selectivity Rating: 89   **Fire Safety Rating:** 79   **Green Rating:** 62

STUDENTS AND FACULTY
Enrollment: 1,210. **Student Body:** 60% female, 40% male, 30% out-of-state, international (5 countries represented). Asian 1%, African American 4%, Caucasian 65%, Hispanic 2%, Native American 1%.
Retention and Graduation: 78% freshmen return for sophomore year. 52% freshmen graduate within 4 years. 25% grads go on to further study within 1 year. 5% grads pursue arts and sciences degrees. 3% grads pursue law degrees. 4% grads pursue business degrees. 1% grads pursue medical degrees. **Faculty:** Student/faculty ratio 10:1. 76 full-time faculty, 86% hold PhDs, 5% are members of minority groups, 50% are women.

ACADEMICS
Degrees: Bachelor's, certificate. **Classes:** Most classes have fewer than 10 students. Most lab/discussion sessions have 30–39 students. **Majors with Highest Enrollment:** Business/commerce; nursing/registered nurse (RN, ASN, BSN, MSN); psychology. **Special Study Options:** Accelerated program, double major, dual enrollment, honors program, independent study, internships, liberal arts/career combination, student-designed major, study abroad, teacher certification program, Pryor Leadership Studies. **Honors programs:** The Oxbridge Honors Program combines British tutorial methods of instruction with opportunities for a year of study in Oxford or Cambridge. **Career services:** Alumni network, alumni services, career/job search classes, career assessment, internships, regional alumni. **Career services highlights include:** The Pryor Leadership Program requires 2 internships—one in service; one career-related. Over 50% of Jewell students participate in some form of internship or similar experiential learning opportunity.

FACILITIES
Housing: Coed dorms, men's dorms, women's dorms, fraternity/sorority housing, off-campus housing utilized like residence halls. ADA compliant housing available for disabled students. 80% of campus accessible to physically disabled. **Special Academic Facilities/Equipment:** Radio station, art gallery, observatory, language and computer labs, high-ropes course, teleconferencing center. **Computers:** 80% of classrooms, 20% of dorms, 25% of libraries, 80% of dining areas, 90% of student union, have wireless network access. Students can register for classes online. Administrative functions (other than registration) can be performed online.

CAMPUS LIFE
Environment: Town. **Activities:** Choral groups, concert band, dance, drama/theater, jazz band, literary magazine, music ensembles, pep band, radio station, student government, student newspaper, symphony orchestra, campus ministries. **Organizations:** 70 registered organizations, 13 honor societies, 7 religious organizations. 4 fraternities, 4 sororities. **Athletics (Intercollegiate):** *Men:* Baseball, basketball, cheerleading, cross-country, football, golf, soccer, tennis, track/field (outdoor), track/field (indoor). *Women:* Basketball, cheerleading, cross-country, golf, soccer, softball, tennis, track/field (outdoor), track/field (indoor), volleyball. **On-Campus Highlights:** The Perch—campus coffee shop, Mabee Center—athletic facility, The Quad—central campus quadrangle, Yates College Union—student union buil, Ely Triangle—first-year residence hall, Fitness Center. **Environmental Initiatives:** Campus recycling program. All future construction projects will follow LEED standards. 350 Campaign Carbon Dioxide reduction.

ADMISSIONS
Freshman Academic Profile: Average high school GPA 3.68. 33% in top 10% of high school class, 60% in top 25% of high school class, 90% in top 50% of high school class. 90% from public high schools. SAT Math middle 50% range 500–610. SAT Critical Reading middle 50% range 540–660. ACT middle 50% range 23–29. Minimum paper TOEFL 550. Minimum computer TOEFL 213. Minimum web-based TOEFL 80. **Basis for Candidate Selection:** *Very important factors considered include:* Rigor of secondary school record. *Important factors considered include:* Class rank, academic GPA, recommendation(s), standardized test scores. *Other factors considered include:* Application essay, alumni/ae relation, character/personal qualities, extracurricular activities, first generation, interview, talent/ability, volunteer work, work experience. **Freshman Admission Requirements:** High school diploma is required and GED is accepted. *Academic units required:* 4 English, 3 mathematics, 3 science, (1 science labs), 2 foreign language, 3 social studies. *Academic units recommended:* 4 English, 4 mathematics, 3 science, (1 science labs), 3 foreign language, 3 social studies, 2 academic electives. **Freshman Admission Statistics:** 1,585 applied, 63% admitted, 27% enrolled. **Transfer Admission Requirements:** College transcript(s), statement of good standing from prior institution(s). Minimum college GPA of 2.5 required. Lowest grade transferable C–. **General Admission Information:** Application fee $25. Regular application deadline 8/15. Notification on a rolling basis, beginning on or about 9/15. Nonfall registration accepted. Admission may be deferred for a maximum of 1 year, w/ a. Credit and/or placement offered for CEEB Advanced Placement tests.

COSTS AND FINANCIAL AID
Annual tuition $24,300. Room and board $6,700. Required fees $300. Average book expense $1,100. **Required Forms and Deadlines:** FAFSA, Priority financial aid filing date 3/1. **Notification of Awards:** Applicants will be notified of awards on a rolling basis beginning 2/15. **Types of Aid:** *Need-based scholarships/grants:* Federal Pell, SEOG, state scholarships/grants, the school's own gift aid. *Loans:* FFEL Subsidized Stafford, FFEL Unsubsidized Stafford, FFEL PLUS, Federal Perkins, Federal Nursing, Non-Federal Private Loans. *Student Employment:* Federal Work-Study Program available. Institutional employment available. Highest amount earned per year from on-campus jobs $1,300. Off-campus job opportunities are excellent. **Financial Aid Statistics:** 75% freshmen, 66% undergrads receive need-based scholarship or grant aid. 75% freshmen, 66% undergrads receive non-need-based scholarship or grant aid. 52% freshmen, 50% undergrads receive need-based self-help aid. 7% freshmen, 11% undergrads receive athletic scholarships. 99% freshmen, 96% undergrads receive any aid. 73% undergrads borrow to pay for school. Average cumulative indebtedness $22,123. **Criteria for awarding institutional aid:** *Non-need-based:* Academics, alumni affiliation, art, athletics, music/drama.

See page 1328.

WILLIAM PATERSON UNIVERSITY

Admissions Hall, 300 Pompton Road, Wayne, NJ 07470
Phone: 973-720-2125 **Financial Aid Phone:** 973-720-2202
E-mail: admissions@wpunj.edu **CEEB Code:** 2518
Fax: 973-720–2910 **Website:** ww2.wpunj.edu **ACT Code:** 2584

This public school was founded in 1855. It has a 370-acre campus.

RATINGS
Admissions Selectivity Rating: 70   **Fire Safety Rating:** 95   **Green Rating:** 77

STUDENTS AND FACULTY
Enrollment: 8,608. **Student Body:** 56% female, 44% male, 2% out-of-state, 1% international (31 countries represented). Asian 6%, African American 14%, Caucasian 53%, Hispanic 18%.
Retention and Graduation: 77% freshmen return for sophomore year. 16% freshmen graduate within 4 years. 27% grads go on to further study within 1 year. 18% grads pursue arts and sciences degrees. 15% grads pursue business degrees. **Faculty:** Student/faculty ratio 15:1. 379 full-time faculty, 91% hold PhDs, 32% are members of minority groups, 47% are women.

ACADEMICS
Degrees: Bachelor's, master's, post-bachelor's certificate, post-master's certificate. **Classes:** Most classes have 10–19 students. **Majors with Highest Enrollment:** Business/commerce; communication studies/speech communication and rhetoric; psychology. **Special Study Options:** Accelerated program, cross-registration, distance learning, double major, dual enrollment, English as a Second Language (ESL), exchange student program (domestic), honors program, independent study, internships, study abroad, teacher certification program, Cluster courses (a program that provides opportunities for students and faculty to study and learn together in courses grouped in interdisciplinary clusters of three. Three faculty members teach these courses that meet together once every week to help students see the interdisciplinary connections). University Honors Program (Honors major tracks are available, and "honors" general education courses are offered.) International exchange program. **Honors programs:** University Honors Program offers honors major tracks as well as honors general education courses. For more information please visit our Honors College homepage at: www.wpunj.edu/icip/honors/default.htm. Special programs offered to physically disabled students include note-taking services, reader services, tape recorders, tutors. **Career services:** alumni services, career/job search classes, career assessment **Career services highlights include:** Career Counseling and job search assistance. Unique combination of career services for all students as well as advisement services for undeclared and transfer students.

FACILITIES
Housing: Coed dorms, special housing for disabled students, apartments for single students. °A floor for women is available in one of the residence halls. °°Apartment style housing is available in groups of single students who are 21 or older or are 20 with 58 or more credits. Academic interest housing is available; High Mountain East is freshmen scholars and High Mountain West houses upperclass students who maintain a 2.5 GPA or better. One residence hall is reserved for students who are 21 or older. 88% of campus accessible to physically disabled. **Special Academic Facilities/Equipment:** Art galleries; Collection of NJ State Documents; Collection of William Paterson's private papers; Interactive television classroom; Neurobiology facility; E-Trading Campus Network with ATM technology; Center for Computer Art and Animation; State-of-the-art electron microscopy facility; Teleconference Center with uplink and downlink capabilities; 44,000 square foot, state-of-the-art studio art facility; Center for Electro-Acoustic Music (CEM); E-Trade Financial Learning Center, a real-time simulated trading and financial educational facility; Russ Berrie Institute for Professional Sales including real-time Sales Laboratory. **Computers:** Students can register for classes online. Administrative functions (other than registration) can be performed online.

CAMPUS LIFE
Environment: Metropolis. **Activities:** Choral groups, concert band, dance, drama/theater, jazz band, literary magazine, music ensembles, student government, student newspaper, student-run film society, television station, yearbook, campus ministries, international student organization, Model UN. **Organizations:** 61 registered organizations, 21 honor societies, 4 religious organizations. 11 fraternities, 10 sororities. **Athletics (Intercollegiate):** *Men:* Baseball, basketball, football, soccer, swimming. *Women:* Basketball, cheerleading, field hockey, soccer, softball, swimming, volleyball. **On-Campus Highlights:** Student Center: Coffee Cafe (Starbucks), College of Business E-Trading Center, Power Art Gallery, Atrium Lobby, Library, New Student Center Facility, New Center for Student Services. **Environmental Initiatives:** ACUPCC, NJHEPS challenge, LEED Standard adoption.

ADMISSIONS
Freshman Academic Profile: 6% in top 10% of high school class, 24% in top 25% of high school class, 64% in top 50% of high school class. 86% from public high schools. SAT Math middle 50% range 450–540. SAT Critical Reading middle 50% range 440–520. Minimum paper TOEFL 550. Minimum computer TOEFL 213. Minimum web-based TOEFL 79. **Basis for Candidate Selection:** *Very important factors considered include:* Class rank, rigor of secondary school record, standardized test scores. *Important factors considered include:* Academic GPA, level of applicant's interest. *Other factors considered include:* Application essay, recommendation(s), alumni/ae relation, character/personal qualities, extracurricular activities, geographical residence, interview, talent/ability, volunteer work. **Freshman Admission Requirements:** High school diploma is required and GED is accepted. *Academic units required:* 4 English, 3 mathematics, 2 science, (2 science labs), 2 social studies, 5 additional college preparatory courses (in advanced math, literature, foreign language and social science) are also required. **Freshman Admission Statistics:** 6,843 applied, 63% admitted, 31% enrolled. **Transfer Admission Requirements:** College transcript(s), minimum college GPA of 2.00 required. Lowest grade transferable C. **General Admission Information:** Application fee $50. Regular application deadline 5/1. Notification on a rolling basis, beginning on or about 10/1. Nonfall registration accepted. Admission may be deferred for a maximum of 1 semester. Credit and/or placement offered for CEEB Advanced Placement tests.

COSTS AND FINANCIAL AID
Annual in-state tuition $6,375. Annual out-of-state tuition $12,933. Room and board $6,640. Required fees $4,117. **Required Forms and Deadlines:** FAFSA. Priority financial aid filing date 4/1. **Notification of Awards:** Applicants will be notified of awards on a rolling basis beginning 3/15. **Types of Aid:** *Need-based scholarships/grants:* Federal Pell, SEOG, state scholarships/grants, the school's own gift aid. *Loans:* FFEL Subsidized Stafford, FFEL Unsubsidized Stafford, FFEL PLUS, Federal Perkins, state loans. *Student Employment:* Federal Work-Study Program available. Institutional employment available. Highest amount earned per year from on-campus jobs $3,200. Off-campus job opportunities are good. **Financial Aid Statistics:** 34% freshmen, 30% undergrads receive need-based scholarship or grant aid. 11% freshmen, 8% undergrads receive non-need-based scholarship or grant aid. 54% freshmen, 48% undergrads receive need-based self-help aid. 82% freshmen, 83% undergrads receive any aid. **Criteria for awarding institutional aid:** *Non-need-based:* Academics, music/drama.

See page 1330.

WILLIAM PENN UNIVERSITY

201 Trueblood Avenue, Oskaloosa, IA 52577
Phone: 641-673-1012
E-mail: admissions@wmpenn.edu **CEEB Code:** 6943
Fax: 641-673-2113 **Website:** www.wmpenn.edu **ACT Code:** 1372

This private school, affiliated with the Quaker Church, was founded in 1873. It has a 53-acre campus.

RATINGS
Admissions Selectivity Rating: 65   **Fire Safety Rating:** 60*   **Green Rating:** 60*

STUDENTS AND FACULTY
Enrollment: 1,462. **Student Body:** 48% female, 52% male, 28% out-of-state, 1% international. African American 8%, Caucasian 89%, Hispanic 3%.
Faculty: Student/faculty ratio 14:1. 35 full-time faculty, 49% hold PhDs, 3% are members of minority groups, 29% are women.

ACADEMICS
Degrees: Associate, bachelor's, transfer associate. **Classes:** Most classes have fewer than 10 students. **Majors with Highest Enrollment:** Business/commerce; education; psychology. **Special Study Options:** Cooperative education program, double major, English as a Second Language (ESL), independent study, internships, study abroad, teacher certification program, College for Working Adults. Special programs offered to physically disabled students include tape recorders, tutors. **Career services:** Alumni services, career/job search classes, internships.

FACILITIES
Housing: Coed dorms, women's dorms, apartments for married students, apartments for single students. 75% of campus accessible to physically disabled. **Special Academic Facilities/Equipment:** Foyer Gallery, Mid-East art and artifact collection.

CAMPUS LIFE

Environment: Rural. **Activities:** Choral groups, drama/theater, jazz band, literary magazine, music ensembles, musical theater, radio station, student government, student newspaper, yearbook. **Organizations:** 34 registered organizations, 3 honor societies, 4 religious organizations. 3 fraternities, 3 sororities. **Athletics (Intercollegiate):** *Men:* Baseball, basketball, cheerleading, cross-country, football, golf, soccer, track/field (outdoor), wrestling. *Women:* Basketball, cheerleading, cross-country, soccer, softball, track/field (outdoor), volleyball.

ADMISSIONS

Freshman Academic Profile: Average high school GPA 2.78. 7% in top 10% of high school class, 25% in top 25% of high school class, 60% in top 50% of high school class. 97% from public high schools. Minimum paper TOEFL 500. Minimum computer TOEFL 173. **Basis for Candidate Selection:** *Very important factors considered include:* Rigor of secondary school record. *Important factors considered include:* Class rank, standardized test scores, character/personal qualities. *Other factors considered include:* Application essay, recommendation(s), alumni/ae relation, extracurricular activities, interview, talent/ability, volunteer work, work experience. **Freshman Admission Requirements:** High school diploma is required and GED is accepted. *Academic units recommended:* 3 English, 2 mathematics, 2 science, 2 foreign language, 2 social studies, 2 history, 2 academic electives. **Freshman Admission Statistics:** 781 applied, 62% admitted, 48% enrolled. **Transfer Admission Requirements:** College transcript(s), minimum college GPA of 2.0 required. Lowest grade transferable D. **General Admission Information:** Application fee $20. Notification on a rolling basis, beginning on or about 10/1. Nonfall registration accepted. Credit offered for CEEB Advanced Placement tests.

COSTS AND FINANCIAL AID

Annual tuition $11,924. Room and board $4,140. Required fees $356. Average book expense $675. **Required Forms and Deadlines:** FAFSA. Priority financial aid filing date 7/1. **Notification of Awards:** Applicants will be notified of awards on a rolling basis beginning 1/1. **Types of Aid:** *Need-based scholarships/grants:* Federal Pell, SEOG, state scholarships/grants, private scholarships, the school's own gift aid. *Loans:* FFEL Subsidized Stafford, FFEL Unsubsidized Stafford, FFEL PLUS, Federal Perkins. *Student Employment:* Federal Work-Study Program available. Institutional employment available. Off-campus job opportunities are excellent. **Financial Aid Statistics:** 74% undergrads borrow to pay for school. Average cumulative indebtedness $18,624. **Criteria for awarding institutional aid:** *Non-need-based:* Academics, alumni affiliation, athletics, leadership, music/drama, religious affiliation.

WILLIAM TYNDALE COLLEGE

35700 W. Twelve Mile Road, Farmington Hills, MI 48331-3147
Phone: 800-483-0707
E-mail: admissions@williamtyndale.edu **CEEB Code:** 1167
Fax: 248-553-5963 **Website:** www.williamtyndale.edu **ACT Code:** 2252

This private school was founded in 1945. It has a 28-acre campus.

RATINGS
Admissions Selectivity Rating: 84   **Fire Safety Rating:** 60*   **Green Rating:** 60*

STUDENTS AND FACULTY

Enrollment: 278. **Student Body:** 45% female, 55% male, 7% out-of-state, 3% international (6 countries represented). Asian 1%, African American 31%, Caucasian 63%, Native American 1%.
Retention and Graduation: 66% freshmen return for sophomore year. 21% freshmen graduate within 4 years. **Faculty:** Student/faculty ratio 8:1. 4 full-time faculty, 50% hold PhDs, 50% are women.

ACADEMICS

Degrees: Associate, bachelor's, certificate. **Classes:** Most classes have fewer than 10 students. **Majors with Highest Enrollment:** Business/commerce; counseling psychology; religion/religious studies, other. **Special Study Options:** Accelerated program, distance learning, double major, dual enrollment, independent study, internships Special programs offered to physically disabled students include note-taking services, tutors.

FACILITIES

Housing: Coed dorms. 100% of campus accessible to physically disabled.

CAMPUS LIFE

Environment: Village. **Activities:** Choral groups, drama/theater, music ensembles, student government, student newspaper. **Organizations:** 2 registered organizations, 2 honor societies. **On-Campus Highlights:** Billy T's Cafe.

ADMISSIONS

Freshman Academic Profile: Average high school GPA 3.3. 20% in top 10% of high school class, 60% in top 25% of high school class, 40% in top 50% of high school class. 76% from public high schools. ACT middle 50% range 23–24. Minimum paper TOEFL 500. Minimum computer TOEFL 173. **Basis for Candidate Selection:** *Very important factors considered include:* Rigor of secondary school record, standardized test scores, *Other factors considered include:* Application essay, recommendation(s), character/personal qualities, interview, religious affiliation/commitment. **Freshman Admission Requirements:** High school diploma is required and GED is accepted. *Academic units recommended:* 4 English, 3 mathematics, 3 science, 2 foreign language, 2 social studies, 2 history, 1 FA. **Freshman Admission Statistics:** 40 applied, 50% admitted, 80% enrolled. **Transfer Admission Requirements:** High school transcript, college transcript(s), statement of good standing from prior institution(s). Minimum college GPA of 2.0 required. Lowest grade transferable C. **General Admission Information:** Nonfall registration accepted. Admission may be deferred for a maximum of 1 year. Credit and/or placement offered for CEEB Advanced Placement tests.

COSTS AND FINANCIAL AID

Annual tuition $8,550. Room and board $3,520. Required fees $100. Average book expense $1,328. *Student Employment:* Federal Work-Study Program available. Institutional employment available. Highest amount earned per year from on-campus jobs $1,500. Off-campus job opportunities are good. **Financial Aid Statistics:** 60% freshmen, 60% undergrads receive any aid.

WILLIAM WOODS UNIVERSITY

One University Avenue, Fulton, MO 65251
Phone: 573-592-4221 **Financial Aid Phone:** 573-592-4236
E-mail: admissions@williamwoods.edu
Fax: 573-592-1146 **Website:** www.williamwoods.edu **ACT Code:** 2396

This private school, affiliated with the Disciples of Christ Church, was founded in 1870. It has a 170-acre campus.

RATINGS
Admissions Selectivity Rating: 76   **Fire Safety Rating:** 74   **Green Rating:** 60*

STUDENTS AND FACULTY

Enrollment: 1,118. **Student Body:** 75% female, 25% male, 19% out-of-state, 4% international. African American 3%, Caucasian 87%, Hispanic 2%, Native American 1%.
Retention and Graduation: 76% freshmen return for sophomore year. 39% freshmen graduate within 4 years. **Faculty:** Student/faculty ratio 13:1. 50 full-time faculty, 4% are members of minority groups, 52% are women.

ACADEMICS

Degrees: Associate, bachelor's, master's, post-master's certificate. **Classes:** Most classes have fewer than 10 students. Most lab/discussion sessions have fewer than 10 students. **Majors with Highest Enrollment:** Animal sciences; business/commerce; education. **Special Study Options:** Accelerated program, cross-registration, double major, dual enrollment, honors program, independent study, internships, liberal arts/career combination, student-designed major, study abroad, teacher certification program, Hollywood semester. Special programs offered to physically disabled students include note-taking services, reader services, tape recorders, tutors. **Career services:** Career/job search classes, career assessment.

FACILITIES

Housing: Coed dorms, special housing for disabled students, men's dorms, special housing for international students, women's dorms, fraternity/sorority housing, apartments for single students. 80% of campus accessible to physically disabled. **Special Academic Facilities/Equipment:** Weitzman Court Room Mildred Cox Gallery, Gladys Woods Kemper Center for the Arts, ASL Interpreting Lab, Equestrian Facilities. **Computers:** Administrative functions (other than registration) can be performed online.

CAMPUS LIFE

Environment: Village. **Activities:** Choral groups, dance, drama/theater, literary magazine, musical theater, radio station, student government, student newspaper. **Organizations:** 42 registered organizations, 3 honor societies, 1 religious organizations. 2 fraternities, 4 sororities. **Athletics (Intercollegiate):** *Men:* Baseball, golf, soccer. *Women:* Basketball, golf, soccer, softball, volleyball. **On-Campus Highlights:** Center for Human Performance, McNutt Student Center.

ADMISSIONS

Freshman Academic Profile: Average high school GPA 3.3. 15% in top 10% of high school class, 40% in top 25% of high school class, 77% in top 50% of high school class. SAT Math middle 50% range 420–570. SAT Critical Reading middle 50% range 455–575. ACT middle 50% range 19–25. Minimum paper TOEFL 500. Minimum computer TOEFL 173. Minimum web-based TOEFL 61. **Basis for Candidate Selection:** *Very important factors considered include:* Class rank, academic GPA, rigor of secondary school record. *Important factors considered include:* Recommendation(s), standardized test scores, extracurricular activities. *Other factors considered include:* Character/personal qualities, interview. **Freshman Admission Requirements:** High school diploma is required and GED is accepted. *Academic units required:* 3 English, 3 mathematics. *Academic units recommended:* 4 English, 3 mathematics, 3 science, 1 foreign language, 3 social studies, 2 history, 4 academic electives. **Freshman Admission Statistics:** 792 applied, 68% admitted, 43% enrolled. **Transfer Admission Requirements:** College transcript(s), statement of good standing from prior institution(s). Minimum college GPA of 2.5 required. Lowest grade transferable C. **General Admission Information:** Application fee $25. Notification on a rolling basis, beginning on or about 9/1. Nonfall registration accepted. Admission may be deferred for a maximum of 1. Credit and/or placement offered for CEEB Advanced Placement tests.

COSTS AND FINANCIAL AID

Annual tuition $14,700. Room and board $5,900. Required fees $420. Average book expense $1,000. **Required Forms and Deadlines:** FAFSA, institution's own financial aid form. Priority financial aid filing date 3/1. **Notification of Awards:** Applicants will be notified of awards on a rolling basis beginning 3/15. **Types of Aid:** *Need-based scholarships/grants:* Federal Pell, SEOG, state scholarships/grants, private scholarships, the school's own gift aid. *Loans:* FFEL Subsidized Stafford, FFEL Unsubsidized Stafford, FFEL PLUS, Federal Perkins, college/university loans from institutional funds. *Student Employment:* Federal Work-Study Program available. Institutional employment available. Highest amount earned per year from on-campus jobs $800. Off-campus job opportunities are good. **Financial Aid Statistics:** 56% freshmen, 61% undergrads receive need-based scholarship or grant aid. 13% freshmen, 11% undergrads receive non-need-based scholarship or grant aid. 42% freshmen, 49% undergrads receive need-based self-help aid. 2% freshmen, 3% undergrads receive athletic scholarships. 100% freshmen, 95% undergrads receive any aid. 85% undergrads borrow to pay for school. Average cumulative indebtedness $13,865. **Criteria for awarding institutional aid:** *Non-need-based:* Academics, alumni affiliation, art, athletics, leadership, music/drama, religious affiliation, state/district residency.

WILLIAMS COLLEGE

Best 373

33 Stetson Court, Williamstown, MA 01267
Phone: 413-597-2211 **Financial Aid Phone:** 413-597-4181
E-mail: admission@williams.edu **CEEB Code:** 3965
Fax: 413-597-4052 **Website:** www.williams.edu **ACT Code:** 1936

This private school was founded in 1793. It has a 450-acre campus.

RATINGS

Admissions Selectivity Rating: 99   **Fire Safety Rating:** 60*   **Green Rating:** 92

STUDENTS AND FACULTY

Enrollment: 2,032. **Student Body:** 52% female, 48% male, 86% out-of-state, 7% international (73 countries represented). Asian 12%, African American 10%, Caucasian 61%, Hispanic 10%.
Retention and Graduation: 98% freshmen return for sophomore year. 93% freshmen graduate within 4 years. **Faculty:** Student/faculty ratio 7:1. 271 full-time faculty, 98% hold PhDs, 20% are members of minority groups, 40% are women.

ACADEMICS

Degrees: Bachelor's, master's. **Classes:** Most classes have fewer than 10 students. Most lab/discussion sessions have 10–19 students. **Majors with Highest Enrollment:** Economics; English language and literature/letters, other; visual and performing arts. **Special Study Options:** Cross-registration, double major, independent study, internships, student-designed major, study abroad. **Combined degree programs:** Combined program in liberal arts and eng. Special programs offered to physically disabled students include note-taking services,

reader services, tape recorders, tutors. **Career services:** Alumni network, alumni services, career/job search classes, internships, regional alumni.

FACILITIES

Housing: Coed dorms, cooperative housing. **Special Academic Facilities/Equipment:** Hopkins Observatory; Williams College Museum of Art; Adams Memorial Theatre; Chapin Rare Books Library; Spencer Studio Art Building, '62 Center for Theatre and Dance, Hopkins Experimental Forest. **Computers:** 100% of classrooms, 100% of dorms, 100% of libraries, 100% of dining areas, 100% of student union, 100% of common outdoor areas have wireless network access. Students can register for classes online. Administrative functions (other than registration) can be performed online.

CAMPUS LIFE

Environment: Village. **Activities:** Choral groups, dance, drama/theater, literary magazine, music ensembles, radio station, student government, student newspaper, student-run film society, symphony orchestra, yearbook, international student organization. **Organizations:** 110 registered organizations, 3 honor societies, 8 religious organizations. **Athletics (Intercollegiate):** *Men:* Baseball, basketball, crew/rowing, cross-country, diving, football, golf, ice hockey, lacrosse, skiing (downhill/alpine), skiing (nordic/cross-country), soccer, squash, swimming, tennis, track/field (outdoor), track/field (indoor), wrestling. *Women:* Basketball, crew/rowing, cross-country, diving, field hockey, golf, ice hockey, lacrosse, skiing (downhill/alpine), skiing (nordic/cross-country), soccer, softball, squash, swimming, tennis, track/field (outdoor), track/field (indoor), volleyball. **On-Campus Highlights:** Paresky Student Center, Schow Science Library, Williams College Museum of Art, '62 Center for Theatre and Dance, Chandler Gymnasium. **Environmental Initiatives:** Renewable Energy: 26.7 kW photovoltaic array installed on the library shelving building. Infrastructure Improvements: Undertaking $1.5 million in energy conservation projects—lighting, motors, lab hood improvements, etc. Installed real time electricity meters in almost all campus buildings, and make data available on the sustainability webpage. Buildings: LEED certification of new academic buildings

ADMISSIONS

Freshman Academic Profile: 88% in top 10% of high school class, 99% in top 25% of high school class, 100% in top 50% of high school class. 58% from public high schools. SAT Math middle 50% range 650–760. SAT Critical Reading middle 50% range 660–760. ACT middle 50% range 30–34. **Basis for Candidate Selection:** *Very important factors considered include:* Application essay, academic GPA, recommendation(s), rigor of secondary school record, standardized test scores. *Important factors considered include:* Class rank, extracurricular activities, talent/ability. *Other factors considered include:* Alumni/ae relation, character/personal qualities, first generation, geographical residence, racial/ethnic status, volunteer work, work experience. **Freshman Admission Requirements:** High school diploma or equivalent is not required. *Academic units recommended:* 4 English, 4 mathematics, 3 science, (3 science labs), 4 foreign language, 3 social studies. **Freshman Admission Statistics:** 6,017 applied, 20% admitted, 44% enrolled. **Transfer Admission Requirements:** High school transcript, college transcript(s), essay or personal statement, standardized test scores, statement of good standing from prior institution(s). Minimum college GPA of 3.5 required. Lowest grade transferable C–. **General Admission Information:** Application fee $60. Early decision application deadline 11/10. Regular application deadline 1/1. Regular notification 4/1. Nonfall registration not accepted. Admission may be deferred for a maximum of negotiable. Placement offered for CEEB Advanced Placement tests.

COSTS AND FINANCIAL AID

Annual tuition $39,250. Room and board $10,390. Required fees $240. Average book expense $800. **Required Forms and Deadlines:** FAFSA, CSS/Financial Aid PROFILE, noncustodial PROFILE, business/farm supplement. Parent and student federal taxes and W2s. Financial aid filing deadline 2/1. **Notification of Awards:** Applicants will be notified of awards on or about 4/1. **Types of Aid:** *Need-based scholarships/grants:* Federal Pell, SEOG, state scholarships/grants, private scholarships, the school's own gift aid. *Loans:* Direct Subsidized Stafford, Direct Unsubsidized Stafford, Direct PLUS, Federal Perkins, college/university loans from institutional funds. *Student Employment:* Federal Work-Study Program available. Institutional employment available. **Financial Aid Statistics:** 53% freshmen, 52% undergrads receive need-based scholarship or grant aid. 53% freshmen, 52% undergrads receive need-based self-help aid. 53% freshmen, 50% undergrads receive any aid. 43% undergrads borrow to pay for school. Average cumulative indebtedness $8,103.

WILLISTON STATE COLLEGE

PO Box 1326, Williston, ND 58802-1326
Phone: 701-774-4210
E-mail: Lacey.Madison@wsc.nodak.edu
Fax: 701-774-4211 **Website:** www.wsc.nodak.edu

This public school was founded in 1961. It has a 80-acre campus.

RATINGS
Admissions Selectivity Rating: 71   **Fire Safety Rating:** 60*   **Green Rating:** 60*

STUDENTS AND FACULTY
Enrollment: 937. **Student Body:** 71% female, 29% male, 19% out-of-state, 2% international (2 countries represented). African American 1%, Caucasian 91%, Hispanic 1%, Native American 4%.
Faculty: Student/faculty ratio 12:1. 38 full-time faculty, 39% are women.

ACADEMICS
Degrees: Associate, certificate, diploma, terminal associate, transfer associate. **Classes: Special Study Options:** Cooperative education program, distance learning, dual enrollment, external degree program, independent study, internships, liberal arts/career combination. Special programs offered to physically disabled students include note-taking services, reader services, tape recorders, tutors.

FACILITIES
Housing: Coed dorms, special housing for disabled students, men's dorms, women's dorms, Athletic Housing units, Married/Family Housing units. 90% of campus accessible to physically disabled.

CAMPUS LIFE
Environment: Rural. **Activities:** Choral groups, drama/theater, literary magazine, pep band, student government. **Organizations:** 18 registered organizations, 1 honor societies, 1 religious organizations. **Athletics (Intercollegiate):** *Men:* Baseball, basketball, golf. *Women:* Basketball, golf, volleyball.

ADMISSIONS
Freshman Academic Profile: Average high school GPA 2.83. 12% in top 10% of high school class, 22% in top 25% of high school class, 71% in top 50% of high school class. ACT middle 50% range 16–22. Minimum paper TOEFL 330. Minimum computer TOEFL 195. **Freshman Admission Requirements:** High school diploma is required and GED is accepted. *Academic units recommended:* 4 English, 3 mathematics, 3 science, (3 science labs), 1 foreign language, 3 social studies. **Transfer Admission Requirements:** College transcript(s), statement of good standing from prior institution(s). Lowest grade transferable D. **General Admission Information:** Application fee $35. Notification on a rolling basis, beginning on or about 1/1. Nonfall registration accepted. Credit and/or placement offered for CEEB Advanced Placement tests.

COSTS AND FINANCIAL AID
Required Forms and Deadlines: FAFSA. Priority financial aid filing date 3/15. **Notification of Awards:** Applicants will be notified of awards on a rolling basis beginning 5/15. **Types of Aid:** *Need-based scholarships/grants:* Federal Pell, SEOG, state scholarships/grants, private scholarships, the school's own gift aid. *Loans:* FFEL Subsidized Stafford, FFEL Unsubsidized Stafford, FFEL PLUS, Federal Perkins. *Student Employment:* Federal Work-Study Program available. Institutional employment available. Off-campus job opportunities are good. **Criteria for awarding institutional aid:** *Non-need-based:* Academics, athletics, minority status.

WILMINGTON COLLEGE (DE)

320 Dupont Highway, New Castle, DE 19720
Phone: 302-328-9401
E-mail: mlee@wilmcoll.edu **CEEB Code:** 5925
Fax: 302-328-5902 **Website:** www.wilmcoll.edu **ACT Code:** 635

This private school was founded in 1967. It has a 15-acre campus.

RATINGS
Admissions Selectivity Rating: 60*   **Fire Safety Rating:** 60*   **Green Rating:** 60*

STUDENTS AND FACULTY
Enrollment: 4,399. **Student Body:** 53% female, 47% male, 3% out-of-state,. Asian 1%, African American 14%, Caucasian 64%, Hispanic 2%.

Retention and Graduation: 87% freshmen return for sophomore year. 50% grads go on to further study within 1 year. 9% grads pursue arts and sciences degrees. 10% grads pursue law degrees. 80% grads pursue business degrees. 1% grads pursue medical degrees. **Faculty:** Student/faculty ratio 18:1.

ACADEMICS
Degrees: Associate, bachelor's, certificate, master's, post-master's certificate. **Majors with Highest Enrollment:** Business/commerce; education. **Special Study Options:** Accelerated program, cooperative education program, distance learning, double major, independent study, internships, teacher certification program, weekend college Special programs offered to physically disabled students include tutors. **Career services:** alumni services, career/job search classes, career assessment, internships

FACILITIES
Housing: All housing is off campus.

CAMPUS LIFE
Environment: Village. **Activities:** Student government **Organizations:** 1 honor societies, **Athletics (Intercollegiate):** *Men:* Baseball, basketball, cross-country, soccer. *Women:* Basketball, softball

ADMISSIONS
Freshman Academic Profile: Minimum paper TOEFL 500. **Basis for Candidate Selection:** *Important factors considered include:* Recommendation(s), rigor of secondary school record. **Freshman Admission Requirements:** High school diploma is required and GED is accepted.High school diploma is required and GED is not accepted. **Transfer Admission Requirements:** College transcript(s), minimum college GPA of 2.0 required. Lowest grade transferable C. **General Admission Information:** Application fee $25. Nonfall registration accepted. Admission may be deferred for a maximum of 1 year. Credit offered for CEEB Advanced Placement tests.

COSTS AND FINANCIAL AID
Annual tuition $6,060. Required fees $50. Average book expense $500. **Required Forms and Deadlines:** FAFSA. **Types of Aid:** *Need-based scholarships/grants: Loans: Student Employment:* Federal Work-Study Program available. Highest amount earned per year from on-campus jobs $1,000. Off-campus job opportunities are excellent.

WILMINGTON COLLEGE (OH)

same, Wilmington, OH, 45177,
Phone: ex. 260
E-mail: admissions@wilmington.edu **CEEB Code:** 1909
Fax: 937-383-8542 **Website:** www.wilmington.edu **ACT Code:** 3362

This private school, affiliated with the Quaker Church, was founded in 1870. It has a 65-acre campus.

RATINGS
Admissions Selectivity Rating: 70   **Fire Safety Rating:** 60*   **Green Rating:** 60*

STUDENTS AND FACULTY
Enrollment: 1,395. **Student Body:** 56% female, 44% male, 5% out-of-state, 1% international. African American 9%, Caucasian 71%, Hispanic 1%, Native American 1%.
Retention and Graduation: 68% freshmen return for sophomore year. 50% freshmen graduate within 4 years. **Faculty:** 68 full-time faculty.

ACADEMICS
Degrees: Bachelor's, master's. **Classes:** Most classes have 10–19 students. **Majors with Highest Enrollment:** Bible/biblical studies. **Special Study Options:** Cross-registration, double major, dual enrollment, honors program, independent study, internships, liberal arts/career combination, student-designed major, study abroad, teacher certification program, weekend college Special programs offered to physically disabled students include note-taking services, reader services, tape recorders, tutors. **Career services:** alumni services, internships

FACILITIES
Housing: Coed dorms, women's dorms, fraternity/sorority housing, apartments for single students 100% of campus accessible to physically disabled. **Special Academic Facilities/Equipment:** Hiroshima-Nagasaki memorial collection and peace resource center, education lab, language lab, three farms, observatory, electron microscope.

CAMPUS LIFE

Environment: Rural. **Activities:** Choral groups, drama/theater, literary magazine, music ensembles, musical theater, student government, student newspaper, yearbook, campus ministries, international student organization. **Organizations:** 48 registered organizations, 3 honor societies, 3 religious organizations. 6 fraternities, 5 sororities. **Athletics (Intercollegiate):** *Men:* Baseball, basketball, cheerleading, cross-country, football, golf, soccer, swimming, tennis, track/field (outdoor), wrestling. *Women:* Basketball, cheerleading, cross-country, golf, soccer, softball, swimming, tennis, track/field (outdoor), volleyball. **On-Campus Highlights:** Residence Hall room, Athletic Center, Student Center/Dining Hall, Computer labs, Class room.

ADMISSIONS

Freshman Academic Profile: Average high school GPA 3.2. 13% in top 10% of high school class, 38% in top 25% of high school class, 69% in top 50% of high school class. SAT Math middle 50% range 430–570. SAT Critical Reading middle 50% range 430–540. ACT middle 50% range 17-23. Minimum paper TOEFL 500. Minimum computer TOEFL 173. **Basis for Candidate Selection:** *Very important factors considered include:* Academic GPA. *Important factors considered include:* Class rank, rigor of secondary school record, standardized test scores, alumni/ae relation, character/personal qualities, talent/ability. *Other factors considered include:* Recommendation(s), extracurricular activities, interview, level of applicant's interest, volunteer work. **Freshman Admission Requirements:** High school diploma is required and GED is accepted. *Academic units required:* 4 English, 2 mathematics, 2 science, (2 science labs). *Academic units recommended:* 2 foreign language, 2 social studies. **Freshman Admission Statistics:** 1,700 applied, 93% admitted, 21% enrolled. **Transfer Admission Requirements:** College transcript(s), statement of good standing from prior institution(s). Minimum college GPA of 2.0 required. Lowest grade transferable C–. **General Admission Information:** Application fee $25. Regular application deadline 8/1. Notification on a rolling basis, beginning on or about 12/1. Nonfall registration accepted. Admission may be deferred for a maximum of 1 year. Credit and/or placement offered for CEEB Advanced Placement tests.

COSTS AND FINANCIAL AID

Student Employment: Federal Work-Study Program available. Institutional employment available. Off-campus job opportunities are excellent.

WILSON COLLEGE

1015 Philadelphia Avenue, Chambersburg, PA 17201
Phone: 717-262-2002 **Financial Aid Phone:** 717-262-2016
E-mail: admissions@wilson.edu **CEEB Code:** 2979
Fax: 717-262-2546 **Website:** **ACT Code:** 3758

This private school, affiliated with the Presbyterian Church, was founded in 1869. It has a 300-acre campus.

RATINGS

Admissions Selectivity Rating: 78   **Fire Safety Rating:** 74   **Green Rating:** 80

STUDENTS AND FACULTY

Enrollment: 497. **Student Body:** 95% female, 5% male, 26% out-of-state, 5% international (10 countries represented). Asian 1%, African American 4%, Caucasian 84%, Hispanic 2%, Native American 4%.
Retention and Graduation: 82% freshmen return for sophomore year. 30% grads go on to further study within 1 year. 6% grads pursue arts and sciences degrees. 9% grads pursue law degrees. 8% grads pursue business degrees. 8% grads pursue medical degrees. **Faculty:** Student/faculty ratio 9:1. 42 full-time faculty, 83% hold PhDs, 5% are members of minority groups, 50% are women.

ACADEMICS

Degrees: Associate, bachelor's, master's. **Classes:** Most classes have 10–19 students. Most lab/discussion sessions have 10–19 students. **Majors with Highest Enrollment:** Business/commerce; elementary education and teaching; veterinary/animal health technology/technician and veterinary assistant. **Special Study Options:** Cooperative education program, cross-registration, double major, English as a Second Language (ESL), honors program, independent study, internships, liberal arts/career combination, student-designed major, study abroad, teacher certification program. **Honors programs:** Wilson Scholars Program. Special programs offered to physically disabled students include note-taking services, reader services, tape recorders, tutors. **Career services:** Alumni network, alumni services, career/job search classes, career assessment, internships. **Career services highlights include:** I am proudest of the variety of services we offer and the increased # of services. An alum commented last week on how much more we offer in the Career Development Center.

FACILITIES

Housing: Women's dorms. Students of junior standing or above are guaranteed single residence hall room. We also offer women with children housing, maximum of 2 children. 70% of campus accessible to physically disabled. **Special Academic Facilities/Equipment:** Archives, Bogigian Art gallery, Dance Studio, Helen M. Beach '24 Veterinary Medical Center, Penn Hall Equestrian Center, Natural History Museum, electron microscope, NMR spectrometer. **Computers:** 50% of classrooms, 100% of dining areas, 100% of student union, 15% of common outdoor areas have wireless network access. Students can register for classes online. Administrative functions (other than registration) can be performed online.

CAMPUS LIFE

Environment: Village. **Activities:** Choral groups, dance, drama/theater, literary magazine, music ensembles, radio station, student government, student newspaper, yearbook, campus ministries, international student organization. **Organizations:** 35 registered organizations, 1 honor societies, 4 religious organizations. **Athletics (Intercollegiate):** *Women:* Basketball, field hockey, gymnastics, lacrosse, soccer, softball, tennis. **On-Campus Highlights:** Penn Hall Equestrian Center, Helen M. Beach '24 Veterinary Medical Center, Complex for Science, Math & Technology, Prentis Hall Women with Children Residence, Lenfest Commons with Fitness Center and Coffee House. **Environmental Initiatives:** Organic farm, alternative energy production, environmental sustainability mission statement of college

ADMISSIONS

Freshman Academic Profile: Average high school GPA 3.38. 10% in top 10% of high school class, 37% in top 25% of high school class, 84% in top 50% of high school class. 84% from public high schools. SAT Math middle 50% range 420–540. SAT Critical Reading middle 50% range 460–550. SAT Writing middle 50% range 430–540. ACT middle 50% range 18–22. Minimum paper TOEFL 500. Minimum computer TOEFL 173. Minimum web-based TOEFL 61. **Basis for Candidate Selection:** *Very important factors considered include:* Rigor of secondary school record. *Important factors considered include:* Class rank, academic GPA, recommendation(s). *Other factors considered include:* Application essay, standardized test scores, alumni/ae relation, character/personal qualities, extracurricular activities, interview, talent/ability, volunteer work, work experience. **Freshman Admission Requirements:** High school diploma is required and GED is accepted. *Academic units required:* 4 English, 3 mathematics, 2 science, (2 science labs), 2 foreign language, 4 social studies. **Freshman Admission Statistics:** 477 applied, 55% admitted, 34% enrolled. **Transfer Admission Requirements:** High school transcript, college transcript(s), essay or personal statement, minimum college GPA of 2.0 required. Lowest grade transferable C. **General Admission Information:** Application fee $35. Notification on a rolling basis, beginning on or about 9/15. Nonfall registration accepted. Admission may be deferred for a maximum of 1 year. Credit and/or placement offered for CEEB Advanced Placement tests.

COSTS AND FINANCIAL AID

Required Forms and Deadlines: FAFSA, institution's own financial aid form, state aid form. Priority financial aid filing date 4/30. **Notification of Awards:** Applicants will be notified of awards on a rolling basis beginning 2/15. **Types of Aid:** *Need-based scholarships/grants:* Federal Pell, SEOG, state scholarships/grants, private scholarships, the school's own gift aid. *Loans:* FFEL Subsidized Stafford, FFEL Unsubsidized Stafford, FFEL PLUS, Federal Perkins, college/university loans from institutional funds. *Student Employment:* Federal Work-Study Program available. Institutional employment available. Highest amount earned per year from on-campus jobs $1,500. Off-campus job opportunities are fair. **Financial Aid Statistics:** 87% freshmen, 74% undergrads receive need-based scholarship or grant aid. 8% freshmen, 8% undergrads receive non-need-based scholarship or grant aid. 72% freshmen, 67% undergrads receive need-based self-help aid. 99% freshmen, 97% undergrads receive any aid. 89.83% undergrads borrow to pay for school. Average cumulative indebtedness $34,074. **Criteria for awarding institutional aid:** *Non-need-based:* Academics, alumni affiliation, religious affiliation, state/district residency.

WINGATE UNIVERSITY

Campus Box 3059, Wingate, NC 28174
Phone: 704-233-8200 **Financial Aid Phone:** 704-233-8209
E-mail: admit@wingate.edu **CEEB Code:** 5908
Fax: 704-233-8110 **Website:** www.wingate.edu **ACT Code:** 3176

This private school, affiliated with the Baptist Church, was founded in 1896. It has a 390-acre campus.

RATINGS

Admissions Selectivity Rating: 79   **Fire Safety Rating:** 73   **Green Rating:** 60*

STUDENTS AND FACULTY

Enrollment: 1,462. **Student Body:** 53% female, 47% male, 37% out-of-state, 3% international (10 countries represented). Asian 2%, African American 14%, Caucasian 75%, Hispanic 2%, Native American 1%.
Retention and Graduation: 36% freshmen graduate within 4 years. 20% grads go on to further study within 1 year. 9% grads pursue arts and sciences degrees. 2% grads pursue law degrees. 8% grads pursue business degrees. 1% grads pursue medical degrees. **Faculty:** Student/faculty ratio 14:1. 105 full-time faculty, 94% hold PhDs, 5% are members of minority groups, 47% are women.

ACADEMICS

Degrees: Bachelor's, first professional, master's. **Classes:** Most classes have 20–29 students. Most lab/discussion sessions have 10–19 students. **Majors with Highest Enrollment:** Biology/biological sciences; business/commerce; sport and fitness administration/management. **Special Study Options:** Cross-registration, double major, dual enrollment, honors program, independent study, internships, study abroad, teacher certification program, A Bachelor in Liberal Arts is offered to non-traditional students looking to complete a degree. This programs is offered at the Wingate Metro Center in Matthews, NC. **Honors programs:** Our University Honors program offers students 18 hours of honors courses covering a spectrum of disciplines. Students may travel to New York City as part of the program. Special programs offered to physically disabled students include note-taking services, tape recorders, tutors.

FACILITIES

Housing: men's dorms, women's dorms, apartments for single students. 95% of campus accessible to physically disabled. **Special Academic Facilities/Equipment:** Douglas Helms Art Gallery, outdoor recreation lab, Batte Fine Arts Center. **Computers:** Administrative functions (other than registration) can be performed online.

CAMPUS LIFE

Environment: Village. **Activities:** Choral groups, drama/theater, jazz band, literary magazine, music ensembles, musical theater, student government, student newspaper, television station, yearbook. **Organizations:** 45 registered organizations, 10 honor societies, 8 religious organizations. 4 fraternities, 4 sororities. **Athletics (Intercollegiate):** *Men:* Baseball, basketball, cheerleading, cross-country, football, golf, lacrosse, soccer, swimming, tennis. *Women:* Basketball, cheerleading, cross-country, golf, soccer, softball, swimming, tennis, volleyball. **On-Campus Highlights:** George A. Batte Jr. Fine Arts Center; Kondike Grill; Irwin Belk Football Stadium; Ethel's Cafe (in the Ethel K. Smith Library); Jefferson Clubhouse; Batte Fine Arts Center, a 44,000 sq. foot facility provides a venue foe musicians, singers, actors, and artists. The center features a 554 theatre, among other facilities. Ethel's Cafe provides a quiet environment to study while enjoying coffee, pastries, and other refreshments. Jefferson Clubhouse, houses a convinience store, gym, swinmming pool, Health Services, and the offices of Greek Life.

ADMISSIONS

Freshman Academic Profile: Average high school GPA 3.48. 21.7% in top 10% of high school class, 42.5% in top 25% of high school class, 76.5% in top 50% of high school class. 85% from public high schools. SAT Math middle 50% range 450–570. SAT Critical Reading middle 50% range 440–540. ACT middle 50% range 18–24. Minimum paper TOEFL 550. Minimum computer TOEFL 213. **Basis for Candidate Selection:** *Very important factors considered include:* Class rank, rigor of secondary school record. *Important factors considered include:* Academic GPA, recommendation(s), standardized test scores. *Other factors considered include:* character/personal qualities, extracurricular activities, talent/ability. **Freshman Admission Requirements:** High school diploma is required and GED is accepted. *Academic units recommended:* 4 English, 3 mathematics, 2 science, (1 science labs), 2 foreign language, 2 social studies. **Freshman Admission Statistics:** 3,119 applied, 61% admitted, 22% enrolled. **Transfer Admission Requirements:** High school transcript, college transcript(s), statement of good standing from prior institution(s). Minimum college GPA of 2.0 required. Lowest grade transferable C. **General Admission Information:** Application fee $30. Notification on a rolling basis, beginning on or about 9/15. Nonfall registration accepted. Admission may be deferred for a maximum of 1 year. Credit and/or placement offered for CEEB Advanced Placement tests.

COSTS AND FINANCIAL AID

Annual tuition $16,000. Room and board $6,750. Required fees $1,050. Average book expense $1,000. **Required Forms and Deadlines:** FAFSA. Priority financial aid filing date 5/1. **Notification of Awards:** Applicants will be notified of awards on a rolling basis beginning 3/1. **Types of Aid:** *Need-based scholarships/grants:* Federal Pell, SEOG, state scholarships/grants, private scholarships, the school's own gift aid. *Loans:* Direct Subsidized Stafford, Direct Unsubsidized Stafford, Direct PLUS, FFEL Subsidized Stafford, FFEL Unsubsidized Stafford, FFEL PLUS. *Student Employment:* Federal Work-Study Program available. Institutional employment available. Highest amount earned per year from on-campus jobs $1,200. Off-campus job opportunities are good.

Financial Aid Statistics: 56% freshmen, 51% undergrads receive need-based scholarship or grant aid. 79% freshmen, 72% undergrads receive non-need-based scholarship or grant aid. 40% freshmen, 45% undergrads receive need-based self-help aid. 10% freshmen, 9% undergrads receive athletic scholarships. 97% freshmen, 96% undergrads receive any aid. 70% undergrads borrow to pay for school. Average cumulative indebtedness $18,759. **Criteria for awarding institutional aid:** *Non-need-based:* Academics, alumni affiliation, art, athletics, leadership, music/drama, religious affiliation, state/district residency.

WINONA STATE UNIVERSITY

Office of Admissions/Maxwell Hall, Winona State Uni, Winona, MN 55987
Phone: 507-457-5100 **Financial Aid Phone:** 507-457-5090
E-mail: admissions@winona.edu **CEEB Code:** 6680
Fax: 507-457-5620 **Website:** www.winona.edu **ACT Code:** 2162

This public school was founded in 1858. It has a 40-acre campus.

RATINGS

Admissions Selectivity Rating: 75   **Fire Safety Rating:** 85   **Green Rating:** 93

STUDENTS AND FACULTY

Enrollment: 7,872. **Student Body:** 60% female, 40% male, 34% out-of-state, 3% international (53 countries represented). Asian 2%, African American 1%, Caucasian 91%, Hispanic 1%.
Retention and Graduation: 75% freshmen return for sophomore year. 26% freshmen graduate within 4 years. 15% grads go on to further study within 1 year. 10% grads pursue arts and sciences degrees. 1% grads pursue law degrees. 6% grads pursue business degrees. 1% grads pursue medical degrees. **Faculty:**

ACADEMICS

Degrees: Associate, bachelor's, master's, post-bachelor's certificate, post-master's certificate. **Classes:** Most classes have 20–29 students. Most lab/discussion sessions have 20–29 students. **Majors with Highest Enrollment:** Business administration and management; elementary education and teaching; nursing/registered nurse (RN, ASN, BSN, MSN). **Special Study Options:** Accelerated program, cross-registration, distance learning, double major, dual enrollment, English as a Second Language (ESL), external degree program, independent study, internships, student-designed major, study abroad, teacher certification program Special programs offered to physically disabled students include note-taking services, reader services, tape recorders **Career services:** alumni services, career assessment, internships. **Career services highlights include:** While we do not offer career/job search 'classes,' we do provide nearly 150 workshops and presentations annually reaching an average of 5000 students; we also have podcasts on a variety of topics available online 24/7.

FACILITIES

Housing: Coed dorms, special housing for disabled students, men's dorms, women's dorms, apartments for single students, Residential College-Residence halls with classrooms and faculty offices. 100% of campus accessible to physically disabled. **Special Academic Facilities/Equipment:** Paul Watkins Art Gallery. **Computers:** 100% of classrooms, 50% of dorms, 100% of libraries, 100% of dining areas, 100% of student union, 85% of common outdoor areas have wireless network access. Students can register for classes online. Administrative functions (other than registration) can be performed online. Undergraduates are required to own a computer.

CAMPUS LIFE

Environment: Town. **Activities:** Choral groups, concert band, dance, drama/theater, jazz band, literary magazine, music ensembles, musical theater, pep band, radio station, student government, student newspaper, student-run film society, symphony orchestra, television station, campus ministries, international student organization, Model UN. **Organizations:** 208 registered organizations, 14 honor societies, 10 religious organizations. 2 fraternities, 3 sororities. **Athletics (Intercollegiate):** *Men:* Baseball, basketball, cross-country, football, golf. *Women:* Basketball, cross-country, golf, gymnastics, soccer, softball, tennis, track/field (outdoor), track/field (indoor), volleyball. **On-Campus Highlights:** The Library, Lourdes Hall—Residential College, Central Courtyard and Clock Tower, The Smaug—Kryzsko Commons, Wabasha Hall Fitness Center. **Environmental Initiatives:** Sustainable buildings, local foods, transportation.

ADMISSIONS

Freshman Academic Profile: Average high school GPA 3.26. 10% in top 10% of high school class, 33% in top 25% of high school class, 73% in top 50% of high school class. 68% from public high schools. SAT Math middle 50% range 510–640. SAT Critical Reading middle 50% range 440–600. ACT middle 50% range 21–25. Minimum paper TOEFL 520. Minimum computer TOEFL 190. Minimum web-based TOEFL 68. **Basis for Candidate Selection:** *Very im-*

portant factors considered include: Class rank, rigor of secondary school record, standardized test scores. Important factors considered include: Academic GPA. Other factors considered include: Recommendation(s). **Freshman Admission Requirements:** High school diploma is required and GED is accepted. Academic units required: 4 English, 3 mathematics, 3 science, (3 science labs), 2 foreign language, 2 social studies, 1 history, 1 academic electives. **Freshman Admission Statistics:** 6,500 applied, 71% admitted, 39% enrolled. **Transfer Admission Requirements:** College transcript(s), minimum college GPA of 2.4 required. Lowest grade transferable D. **General Admission Information:** Application fee $20. Regular application deadline 3/1. Notification on a rolling basis, beginning on or about 9/1. Nonfall registration accepted. Admission may be deferred for a maximum of 1 year. Credit and/or placement offered for CEEB Advanced Placement tests.

COSTS AND FINANCIAL AID

Required Forms and Deadlines: FAFSA. **Notification of Awards:** Applicants will be notified of awards on a rolling basis beginning 3/1. **Types of Aid:** Need-based scholarships/grants: Federal Pell, SEOG, state scholarships/grants, private scholarships, the school's own gift aid. Loans: FFEL Subsidized Stafford, FFEL Unsubsidized Stafford, FFEL PLUS, Federal Perkins, state loans, college/university loans from institutional funds. Student Employment: Federal Work-Study Program available. Institutional employment available. Highest amount earned per year from on-campus jobs $2,200. Off-campus job opportunities are fair. **Financial Aid Statistics:** 77% freshmen, 72% undergrads receive any aid. **Criteria for awarding institutional aid:** Non-need-based: Academics, alumni affiliation, art, athletics, minority status, music/drama, state/district residency.

WINSTON-SALEM STATE UNIVERSITY

601 MLK, Jr. Drive, Winston-Salem, NC 27110
Phone: 336-750-2070
E-mail: admissions@wssu1.adp.wssu.edu **CEEB Code:** 5909
Fax: 336-750-2079 **Website:** www.wssu.edu **ACT Code:** 3178

This public school was founded in 1892. It has a 94-acre campus.

RATINGS

Admissions Selectivity Rating: 60*   **Fire Safety Rating:** 60*   **Green Rating:** 60*

STUDENTS AND FACULTY

Enrollment: 5,254. **Student Body:** 70% female, 30% male, 6% out-of-state, international. Asian 1%, African American 84%, Caucasian 12%, Hispanic 1%. **Retention and Graduation:** 72% freshmen return for sophomore year. **Faculty:** Student/faculty ratio 16:1. 275 full-time faculty, 63% hold PhDs, 62% are women.

ACADEMICS

Degrees: Bachelor's, master's, post-bachelor's certificate, post-master's certificate. **Classes:** Most classes have fewer than 10 students. **Special Study Options:** Cooperative education program, double major, dual enrollment, exchange student program (domestic), honors program, independent study, internships, liberal arts/career combination, study abroad, teacher certification program. Special programs offered to physically disabled students include tutors. **Career services:** Alumni services, internships.

FACILITIES

Housing: Coed dorms, men's dorms, women's dorms **Special Academic Facilities/Equipment:** Art gallery.

CAMPUS LIFE

Activities: Choral groups, jazz band, marching band, music ensembles, radio station, student government, student newspaper, yearbook. **Organizations: On-Campus Highlights:** CLEON Thompson Student Center, Fitness Center, O'Kelly Library.

ADMISSIONS

Basis for Candidate Selection: Very important factors considered include: Class rank, rigor of secondary school record, standardized test scores, Other factors considered include: Alumni/ae relation, character/personal qualities, extracurricular activities, interview, talent/ability. Admission Statistics: 1,353 applied, 80% admitted, 46% enrolled. **Transfer Admission Requirements:** College transcript(s), Lowest grade transferable C. **General Admission Information:** Application fee $20. Nonfall registration accepted.

COSTS AND FINANCIAL AID

Annual in-state tuition $1,575. Annual out-of-state tuition $7,868. **Required Forms and Deadlines:** FAFSA. Financial aid filing deadline 4/1. Priority

financial aid filing date 3/15. **Notification of Awards:** Applicants will be notified of awards on or about 5/15. **Types of Aid:** Need-based scholarships/grants: Federal Pell, SEOG, state scholarships/grants, private scholarships, the school's own gift aid, Federal Nursing Scholarships. Loans: FFEL Subsidized Stafford, FFEL Unsubsidized Stafford, FFEL PLUS, Federal Perkins, state loans, college/university loans from institutional funds. Student Employment: Federal Work-Study Program available. Institutional employment available. Highest amount earned per year from on-campus jobs $800. Off-campus job opportunities are good. **Financial Aid Statistics:** 69% freshmen, 82% undergrads receive need-based scholarship or grant aid. 9% freshmen, 6% undergrads receive non-need-based scholarship or grant aid. 65% freshmen, 78% undergrads receive need-based self-help aid. 7% freshmen, 5% undergrads receive athletic scholarships.

WINTHROP UNIVERSITY

701 Oakland Avenue, Rock Hill, SC 29733
Phone: 803-323-2137 **Financial Aid Phone:** 803-323-2189
E-mail: admissions@winthrop.edu **CEEB Code:** 5910
Fax: 803-323-2137 **Website:** www.winthrop.edu **ACT Code:** 3884

This public school was founded in 1886. It has a 418-acre campus.

RATINGS

Admissions Selectivity Rating: 76   **Fire Safety Rating:** 60*   **Green Rating:** 76

STUDENTS AND FACULTY

Enrollment: 4,757. **Student Body:** 69% female, 31% male, 13% out-of-state, 2% international (51 countries represented). Asian 2%, African American 28%, Caucasian 67%, Hispanic 2%. **Retention and Graduation:** 72% freshmen return for sophomore year. 11% grads go on to further study within 1 year. 20% grads pursue arts and sciences degrees. 3% grads pursue law degrees. 25% grads pursue business degrees. 5% grads pursue medical degrees. **Faculty:** Student/faculty ratio 14:1. 282 full-time faculty, 82% hold PhDs, 12% are members of minority groups, 49% are women.

ACADEMICS

Degrees: Bachelor's, master's, post-bachelor's certificate. **Classes:** Most classes have 20–29 students. Most lab/discussion sessions have 20–29 students. **Majors with Highest Enrollment:** Biology/biological sciences; business/commerce; design and visual communications. **Special Study Options:** Cooperative education program, cross-registration, distance learning, double major, exchange student program (domestic), honors program, independent study, internships, study abroad, teacher certification program. Special programs offered to physically disabled students include note-taking services, reader services, tape recorders **Career services:** Alumni network, alumni services, career assessment, internships, regional alumni.

FACILITIES

Housing: Coed dorms, men's dorms, women's dorms, fraternity/sorority housing, apartments for married students, apartments for single students. 85% of campus accessible to physically disabled. **Special Academic Facilities/Equipment:** Art gallery, on-campus nursery and kindergarten. **Computers:** 25% of classrooms, 10% of dorms, 100% of libraries, 100% of dining areas, 100% of student union, 10% of common outdoor areas have wireless network access. Students can register for classes online. Administrative functions (other than registration) can be performed online.

CAMPUS LIFE

Environment: Town. **Activities:** Choral groups, concert band, dance, drama/theater, jazz band, literary magazine, music ensembles, musical theater, opera, pep band, radio station, student government, student newspaper, yearbook, campus ministries, international student organization, Model UN. **Organizations:** 184 registered organizations, 23 honor societies, 10 religious organizations. 8 fraternities, 9 sororities. **Athletics (Intercollegiate):** Men: Baseball, basketball, cross-country, golf, soccer, tennis, track/field (outdoor). Women: Basketball, cross-country, golf, soccer, softball, tennis, track/field (outdoor), volleyball. **On-Campus Highlights:** Java City, Winthrop Coliseum, Frisbee-Golf Course. **Environmental Initiatives:** Very strong recycling program. Commitment to have all new buildings be green certified. Outstanding record of reducing energy use by upgrading historic buildings through things like new windows.

ADMISSIONS

Freshman Academic Profile: Average high school GPA 3.59. 18% in top 10% of high school class, 38% in top 25% of high school class, 86% in top 50% of high school class. SAT Math middle 50% range 480–570. SAT Critical Reading middle 50% range 470–570. ACT middle 50% range 20–24. Minimum paper TOEFL 520. Minimum computer TOEFL 190. **Basis for Candidate Selection:** *Very important factors considered include:* Rigor of secondary school record. *Important factors considered include:* Class rank, academic GPA, standardized test scores. *Other factors considered include:* Application essay, recommendation(s), extracurricular activities, interview, talent/ability, volunteer work. **Freshman Admission Requirements:** High school diploma is required and GED is accepted. *Academic units required:* 4 English, 3 mathematics, 3 science, (3 science labs), 2 foreign language, 2 social studies, 1 history, 4 academic electives, 1 P.E. or ROTC **Freshman Admission Statistics:** 3,996 applied, 70% admitted, 43% enrolled. **Transfer Admission Requirements:** College transcript(s), statement of good standing from prior institution(s). Minimum college GPA of 2.0 required. Lowest grade transferable C. **General Admission Information:** Application fee $40. Regular application deadline 5/1. Notification on a rolling basis, beginning on or about 12/1. Nonfall registration accepted. Admission may be deferred for a maximum of 1 semester. Credit offered for CEEB Advanced Placement tests.

COSTS AND FINANCIAL AID

Average book expense $950. **Required Forms and Deadlines:** FAFSA. Priority financial aid filing date 3/1. **Notification of Awards:** Applicants will be notified of awards on a rolling basis beginning 3/15. **Types of Aid:** *Need-based scholarships/grants:* Federal Pell, SEOG, state scholarships/grants, private scholarships, the school's own gift aid. *Loans:* Direct Subsidized Stafford, Direct Unsubsidized Stafford, FFEL PLUS, Federal Perkins. *Student Employment:* Federal Work-Study Program available. Institutional employment available. Highest amount earned per year from on-campus jobs $1,750. Off-campus job opportunities are fair. **Financial Aid Statistics:** 60% freshmen, 49% undergrads receive need-based scholarship or grant aid. 8% freshmen, 5% undergrads receive non-need-based scholarship or grant aid. 48% freshmen, 48% undergrads receive need-based self-help aid. 4% freshmen, 4% undergrads receive athletic scholarships. 95.97% freshmen, 83% undergrads receive any aid. **Criteria for awarding institutional aid:** *Non-need-based:* Academics, art, athletics, job skills, music/drama.

WISCONSIN LUTHERAN COLLEGE

8800 West Bluemound Road, Milwaukee, WI 53226
Phone: 414-443-8811 **Financial Aid Phone:** 414-443-8856
E-mail: admissions@wlc.edu **CEEB Code:** 1513
Fax: 414-443-8514 **Website:** www.wlc.edu **ACT Code:** 4699

This private school, affiliated with the Lutheran Church, was founded in 1973. It has a 21-acre campus.

RATINGS

Admissions Selectivity Rating: 77   **Fire Safety Rating:** 60*   **Green Rating:** 68

STUDENTS AND FACULTY

Enrollment: 707. **Student Body:** 56% female, 44% male, 23% out-of-state, 2% international (9 countries represented). Asian 2%, African American 4%, Caucasian 89%, Hispanic 2%.
Retention and Graduation: 76% freshmen return for sophomore year. 51% freshmen graduate within 4 years. **Faculty:** Student/faculty ratio 10:1. 60 full-time faculty, 67% hold PhDs, 33% are women.

ACADEMICS

Degrees: Bachelor's. **Classes:** Most classes have 10–19 students. Most lab/discussion sessions have fewer than 10 students. **Majors with Highest Enrollment:** Biology/biological sciences; communication studies/speech communication and rhetoric; psychology. **Special Study Options:** Double major, dual enrollment, English as a Second Language (ESL), independent study, internships, student-designed major, study abroad, teacher certification program Special programs offered to physically disabled students include note-taking services, reader services, tape recorders, tutors. **Career services:** Alumni network, career assessment, internships.

FACILITIES

Housing: Men's dorms, women's dorms, apartments for single students. 90% of campus accessible to physically disabled. **Special Academic Facilities/Equipment:** Center for Arts and Performance, Science Hall. **Computers:** Students can register for classes online.

CAMPUS LIFE

Environment: Metropolis. **Activities:** Choral groups, concert band, dance, jazz band, music ensembles, pep band, student government, student newspaper, campus ministries, international student organization. **Organizations:** 31 registered organizations, **Athletics (Intercollegiate):** *Men:* Baseball, basketball, cross-country, football, golf, soccer, tennis, track/field (outdoor), track/field (in-

door). *Women:* Basketball, cross-country, golf, soccer, softball, tennis, track/field (outdoor), track/field (indoor), volleyball. **On-Campus Highlights:** Residence Halls, Center for Arts and Performance, Chapel, The Warrior Underground, The Recreation Complex, Science Hall, Warrior Fields.

ADMISSIONS

Freshman Academic Profile: Average high school GPA 3.34. 17.7% in top 10% of high school class, 43.1% in top 25% of high school class, 77% in top 50% of high school class. ACT middle 50% range 21–26. Minimum paper TOEFL 550. Minimum computer TOEFL 213. **Basis for Candidate Selection:** *Important factors considered include:* Academic GPA, recommendation(s), rigor of secondary school record, standardized test scores, character/personal qualities, level of applicant's interest, religious affiliation/commitment. *Other factors considered include:* Class rank, application essay, alumni/ae relation, extracurricular activities, first generation, interview, racial/ethnic status, talent/ability, volunteer work, work experience. **Freshman Admission Requirements:** High school diploma is required and GED is accepted. *Academic units required:* 4 English, 3 mathematics, 2 science, (1 science labs), 2 foreign language, 2 history, 3 academic electives. *Academic units recommended:* 4 English, 4 mathematics, 3 science, (2 science labs), 4 foreign language, 2 history, 3 academic electives. **Freshman Admission Statistics:** 646 applied, 76% admitted, 46% enrolled. **Transfer Admission Requirements:** College transcript(s), statement of good standing from prior institution(s). Minimum college GPA of 2.5 required. Lowest grade transferable CD. **General Admission Information:** Application fee $20. Notification on a rolling basis, beginning on or about 9/1. Nonfall registration accepted. Admission may be deferred for a maximum of 1 semester. Credit and/or placement offered for CEEB Advanced Placement tests.

COSTS AND FINANCIAL AID

Annual tuition $21,040. Room and board $7,700. Required fees $140. Average book expense $700. **Required Forms and Deadlines:** FAFSA, institution's own financial aid form, business/farm supplement. Priority financial aid filing date 3/1. **Notification of Awards:** Applicants will be notified of awards on a rolling basis beginning 3/15. **Types of Aid:** *Need-based scholarships/grants:* Federal Pell, SEOG, state scholarships/grants, private scholarships, the school's own gift aid. *Loans:* FFEL Subsidized Stafford, FFEL Unsubsidized Stafford, FFEL PLUS, state loans, Private Educational Loans. *Student Employment:* Federal Work-Study Program available. Institutional employment available. Highest amount earned per year from on-campus jobs $2,800. Off-campus job opportunities are excellent. **Financial Aid Statistics:** 79% freshmen, 75% undergrads receive need-based scholarship or grant aid. 8% freshmen, 7% undergrads receive non-need-based scholarship or grant aid. 72% freshmen, 69% undergrads receive need-based self-help aid. 100% freshmen, 98% undergrads receive any aid. 71% undergrads borrow to pay for school. Average cumulative indebtedness $17,596. **Criteria for awarding institutional aid:** *Non-need-based:* Academics, art, leadership, music/drama.

WITTENBERG UNIVERSITY

Best 373

PO Box 720, Springfield, OH 45501
Phone: 937-327-6314 **Financial Aid Phone:** 937-327-7321
E-mail: admission@wittenberg.edu **CEEB Code:** 1922
Fax: 937-327-6379 **Website:** www.wittenberg.edu **ACT Code:** 3364

This private school, affiliated with the Lutheran Church, was founded in 1845. It has a 71-acre campus.

RATINGS

Admissions Selectivity Rating: 82   **Fire Safety Rating:** 95   **Green Rating:** 79

STUDENTS AND FACULTY

Enrollment: 1,745. **Student Body:** 57% female, 43% male, 27% out-of-state, 2% international (26 countries represented). Asian 1%, African American 5%, Caucasian 76%, Hispanic 1%.
Retention and Graduation: 78% freshmen return for sophomore year. 58% freshmen graduate within 4 years. 38% grads go on to further study within 1 year. 55% grads pursue arts and sciences degrees. 12% grads pursue law degrees. 9% grads pursue business degrees. 14% grads pursue medical degrees. **Faculty:** Student/faculty ratio 12:1. 140 full-time faculty, 93% hold PhDs, 9% are members of minority groups, 41% are women.

ACADEMICS

Degrees: Bachelor's, master's. **Classes:** Most classes have 10–19 students. Most lab/discussion sessions have 10–19 students. **Majors with Highest En-

The Princeton Review's Complete Book of Colleges

rollment: Biology/biological sciences; business/commerce; education. **Special Study Options:** Cross-registration, double major, dual enrollment, honors program, independent study, internships, liberal arts/career combination, student-designed major, study abroad, teacher certification program. **Honors programs:** Honors Program, 3-2 Engineering Program, Pre-Health Programs Special programs offered to physically disabled students include note-taking services, reader services, tape recorders, tutors. **Career services:** Alumni network, alumni services, career/job search classes, career assessment, internships, regional alumni. **Career services highlights include:** Lutheran College Washington Semester.

FACILITIES

Housing: Coed dorms, special housing for international students, women's dorms, fraternity/sorority housing, apartments for married students, apartments for single students, university-owned houses around campus. 81% of campus accessible to physically disabled. **Special Academic Facilities/Equipment:** Language lab, electron microscope, observatory. **Computers:** 50% of classrooms, 100% of libraries, 100% of dining areas, 100% of student union, 100% of common outdoor areas have wireless network access. Students can register for classes online. Administrative functions (other than registration) can be performed online.

CAMPUS LIFE

Environment: Town. **Activities:** Choral groups, concert band, dance, drama/theater, jazz band, literary magazine, music ensembles, musical theater, opera, pep band, radio station, student government, student newspaper, student-run film society, symphony orchestra, yearbook, campus ministries, international student organization. **Organizations:** 126 registered organizations, 24 honor societies, 10 religious organizations. 6 fraternities, 5 sororities. **Athletics (Intercollegiate):** *Men:* Baseball, basketball, cross-country, diving, football, golf, lacrosse, soccer, swimming, tennis, track/field (outdoor), track/field (indoor). *Women:* Basketball, cheerleading, cross-country, diving, field hockey, golf, lacrosse, soccer, softball, swimming, tennis, track/field (outdoor), track/field (indoor), volleyball. **On-Campus Highlights:** HPERC Athletic Center, Benham Prince Student Center, Chakers Theatre, Weaver Observatory, Thomas Library. **Environmental Initiatives:** Campus-wide recycling. Minimization of packaging materials on received goods. Recycling of building materials. ECOHOUSE, an environmentally themed residence for 10 students.

ADMISSIONS

Freshman Academic Profile: Average high school GPA 3.44. 27% in top 10% of high school class, 50% in top 25% of high school class, 81% in top 50% of high school class. 80% from public high schools. SAT Math middle 50% range 500–620. SAT Critical Reading middle 50% range 500–620. ACT middle 50% range 22–28. Minimum paper TOEFL 550. Minimum computer TOEFL 213. **Basis for Candidate Selection:** *Very important factors considered include:* Class rank, academic GPA, rigor of secondary school record. *Important factors considered include:* Application essay, recommendation(s), character/personal qualities, extracurricular activities, talent/ability, volunteer work. *Other factors considered include:* Standardized test scores, alumni/ae relation, first generation, interview, work experience. **Freshman Admission Requirements:** High school diploma is required and GED is accepted. *Academic units required:* 4 English, 3 mathematics, 3 science, (2 science labs), 2 foreign language, 2 history. *Academic units recommended:* 4 English, 4 mathematics, 5 science, (2 science labs), 3 foreign language, 3 history. **Freshman Admission Statistics:** 3,222 applied, 72% admitted, 21% enrolled. **Transfer Admission Requirements:** College transcript(s), minimum college GPA of 2.0 required. Lowest grade transferable C. **General Admission Information:** Application fee $40. Early decision application deadline 11/15. Notification on a rolling basis, beginning on or about 1/1. Nonfall registration accepted. Admission may be deferred for a maximum of 1 year. Credit and/or placement offered for CEEB Advanced Placement tests.

COSTS AND FINANCIAL AID

Required Forms and Deadlines: FAFSA. Priority financial aid filing date 3/1. **Notification of Awards:** Applicants will be notified of awards on a rolling basis beginning 3/1. **Types of Aid:** *Need-based scholarships/grants:* Federal Pell, SEOG, state scholarships/grants, private scholarships, the school's own gift aid. *Loans:* FFEL Subsidized Stafford, FFEL Unsubsidized Stafford, FFEL PLUS, Federal Perkins, college/university loans from institutional funds, private "alternative" loans. *Student Employment:* Federal Work-Study Program available. Institutional employment available. Off-campus job opportunities are excellent. **Financial Aid Statistics:** 76% freshmen, 73% undergrads receive need-based scholarship or grant aid. 76% freshmen, 72% undergrads receive need-based self-help aid. 100% freshmen, 99% undergrads receive any aid. 68% undergrads borrow to pay for school. Average cumulative indebtedness $29,332. **Criteria for awarding institutional aid:** *Non-need-based:* Academics, alumni affiliation, art, leadership, minority status, music/drama, religious affiliation, state/district residency.

See page 1332.

WOFFORD COLLEGE

429 North Church Street, Spartanburg, SC 29303-3663
Phone: 864-597-4130 **Financial Aid Phone:** 864-597-4160
E-mail: admission@wofford.edu **CEEB Code:** 5912
Fax: 864-597-4147 **Website:** www.wofford.edu **ACT Code:** 3886

This private school, affiliated with the Methodist Church, was founded in 1854. It has a 170-acre campus.

RATINGS

Admissions Selectivity Rating: 93   **Fire Safety Rating:** 72   **Green Rating:** 82

STUDENTS AND FACULTY

Enrollment: 1,429. **Student Body:** 50% female, 50% male, 39% out-of-state, 1% international (13 countries represented). Asian 3%, African American 7%, Caucasian 84%, Hispanic 2%.
Retention and Graduation: 87% freshmen return for sophomore year. 77% freshmen graduate within 4 years. 47% grads go on to further study within 1 year. 15% grads pursue arts and sciences degrees. 11% grads pursue law degrees. 3% grads pursue business degrees. 16% grads pursue medical degrees. **Faculty:** Student/faculty ratio 11:1. 117 full-time faculty, 93% hold PhDs, 10% are members of minority groups, 38% are women.

ACADEMICS

Degrees: Bachelor's. **Classes:** Most classes have 10–19 students. Most lab/discussion sessions have 20–29 students. **Majors with Highest Enrollment:** Biology/biological sciences; business/managerial economics; finance. **Special Study Options:** Accelerated program, cross-registration, double major, dual enrollment, independent study, internships, student-designed major, study abroad, teacher certification program, Presidential International Scholar program; "Success Initiative, Bonner Scholars, Community of Scholars, Learning Communities and Creative Writing Concentration. **Combined degree programs:** BA/MEng. Special programs offered to physically disabled students include note-taking services, reader services, tape recorders, tutors. **Career services:** Alumni network, alumni services, career/job search classes, career assessment, internships, regional alumni. **Career services highlights include:** Institute for Professional Development.

FACILITIES

Housing: Coed dorms, apartments for single students, wellness housing. 85% of campus accessible to physically disabled. **Special Academic Facilities/Equipment:** Campus is an Arboretum, Art galleries, Franklin W. Olin Building (teaching technology center), Milliken Science Center. **Computers:** 100% of classrooms, 10% of dorms, 100% of libraries, 100% of dining areas, 100% of student union, 40% of common outdoor areas have wireless network access. Students can register for classes online. Administrative functions (other than registration) can be performed online.

CAMPUS LIFE

Environment: City. **Activities:** Choral groups, concert band, dance, drama/theater, literary magazine, music ensembles, pep band, student government, student newspaper, yearbook, campus ministries. **Organizations:** 105 registered organizations, 10 honor societies, 8 religious organizations. 8 fraternities, 4 sororities. **Athletics (Intercollegiate):** *Men:* Baseball, basketball, cross-country, football, golf, riflery, soccer, tennis, track/field (outdoor), track/field (indoor). *Women:* Basketball, cross-country, golf, riflery, soccer, tennis, track/field (outdoor), track/field (indoor), volleyball. **On-Campus Highlights:** The Roger Milliken Arboretum, Roger Milliken Science Center/Great Oaks, Main Building/Leonard Auditorium, Franklin W. Olin Building, Village Student Housing, Gibbs Stadium Richardson Physical Activities Building Russell C. King Field and Switzer Stadium Joe E. Taylor Athletic Center. **Environmental Initiatives:** Establishment of an innovative and inter-disciplinary Environmental Studies program (a BS/BA major are offered through this program). Wofford has retrofitted an old mill building in Glendale, SC, to serve as a field studies center for the new program and other college programs. The building itself will be the first LEED certified project for the College. This program will offer many opportunities to facilitate sustainable initiatives especially locally. The college has hired a director for the environmental studies program. Santee Cooper Lecture Series on Sustainability & Energy. This endowed two-year series is designed to introduce the campus and Spartanburg community to preeminent experts from the field of sustainability. For more information, go to www.wofford.edu/newsroom/story.aspx?id=60490. Office of Community Sustainability is working to integrate sustainable practices into all aspects of campus life through its Gold, Black & Green campaign. We have launched a pilot program for a

Sustainable Living Initiative which targets residence halls and other areas of student life; we've held community forums on sustainability to foster greater stake holdership in the future of Wofford's sustainability initiative; we have worked with campus offices to facilitate sustainable best practices for events and operations; our Bonner Scholar program and new sustainability fellowship create permanent student roles both for Spartanburg and on-campus activities related to sustainability.

ADMISSIONS

Freshman Academic Profile: Average high school GPA 3.5. 57% in top 10% of high school class, 87% in top 25% of high school class, 98% in top 50% of high school class. 65% from public high schools. SAT Math middle 50% range 580–680. SAT Critical Reading middle 50% range 560–670. SAT Writing middle 50% range 560–660. ACT middle 50% range 22–29. Minimum paper TOEFL 550. Minimum computer TOEFL 213. **Basis for Candidate Selection:** *Very important factors considered include:* Academic GPA, rigor of secondary school record. *Important factors considered include:* Class rank, application essay, standardized test scores, character/personal qualities, extracurricular activities, talent/ability, volunteer work. *Other factors considered include:* Recommendation(s), alumni/ae relation, first generation, geographical residence, interview, racial/ethnic status, work experience. **Freshman Admission Requirements:** High school diploma is required and GED is accepted. *Academic units recommended:* 4 English, 4 mathematics, 3 science, (3 science labs), 3 foreign language, 2 social studies, 1 history, 1 visual/performing arts, 1 computer science, 1 academic electives. **Freshman Admission Statistics:** 2,442 applied, 58% admitted, 28% enrolled. **Transfer Admission Requirements:** High school transcript, college transcript(s), essay or personal statement, standardized test scores, statement of good standing from prior institution(s). Minimum college GPA of 2.5 required. Lowest grade transferable C. **General Admission Information:** Application fee $35. Early decision application deadline 11/15. Regular application deadline 2/1. Regular notification 3/15. Nonfall registration accepted. Admission may be deferred for a maximum of 1 year. Credit and/or placement offered for CEEB Advanced Placement tests.

COSTS AND FINANCIAL AID

Annual tuition $30,280. Room and board $8,480. Average book expense $1,050. **Required Forms and Deadlines:** FAFSA. Priority financial aid filing date 3/15. **Notification of Awards:** Applicants will be notified of awards on or about 3/31. **Types of Aid:** *Need-based scholarships/grants:* Federal Pell, SEOG, state scholarships/grants, the school's own gift aid. *Loans:* FFEL Subsidized Stafford, FFEL Unsubsidized Stafford, FFEL PLUS, Federal Perkins. *Student Employment:* Federal Work-Study Program available. Institutional employment available. Highest amount earned per year from on-campus jobs $1,940. Off-campus job opportunities are good. **Financial Aid Statistics:** 52% freshmen, 52% undergrads receive need-based scholarship or grant aid. 19% freshmen, 20% undergrads receive non-need-based scholarship or grant aid. 28% freshmen, 29% undergrads receive need-based self-help aid. 9% freshmen, 11% undergrads receive athletic scholarships. 51.38% undergrads receive any aid. 45% undergrads borrow to pay for school. Average cumulative indebtedness $22,199. **Criteria for awarding institutional aid:** *Non-need-based:* Academics, athletics, leadership, music/drama, religious affiliation, state/district residency.

as a Second Language (ESL), exchange student program (domestic), independent study, internships, liberal arts/career combination, student-designed major, study abroad, weekend college Special programs offered to physically disabled students include note-taking services, tape recorders, tutors. **Career services:** Alumni services, career assessment, internships.

FACILITIES

Housing: Coed dorms, off-campus overflow apartments. 90% of campus accessible to physically disabled. **Special Academic Facilities/Equipment:** Art Gallery; Architecture Gallery. **Computers:** 100% of classrooms, 100% of libraries, 100% of dining areas, have wireless network access. Students can register for classes online. Administrative functions (other than registration) can be performed online. Undergraduates are required to own a computer.

CAMPUS LIFE

Environment: City. **Activities:** Student government. **Organizations:** 20 registered organizations, 3 honor societies, 2 fraternities, 2 sororities.

ADMISSIONS

Freshman Academic Profile: SAT Math middle 50% range 400–530. SAT Critical Reading middle 50% range 390–520. ACT middle 50% range 16–23. Minimum paper TOEFL 500. Minimum computer TOEFL 173. **Basis for Candidate Selection:** *Very important factors considered include:* Academic GPA, rigor of secondary school record, standardized test scores. *Other factors considered include:* Class rank, application essay, recommendation(s), alumni/ae relation, extracurricular activities, first generation, interview, level of applicant's interest, volunteer work, work experience. **Freshman Admission Requirements:** High school diploma is required and GED is accepted. *Academic units recommended:* 4 English, 3 mathematics, 2 science, (2 science labs), 2 foreign language, 1 social studies, 2 history. **Freshman Admission Statistics:** 514 applied, 41% admitted, 61% enrolled. **Transfer Admission Requirements:** College transcript(s), minimum college GPA of 2.5 required. Lowest grade transferable C. **General Admission Information:** Application fee $50. Notification on a rolling basis, beginning on or about 11/1. Nonfall registration accepted. Admission may be deferred for a maximum of 2 years. Credit offered for CEEB Advanced Placement tests.

COSTS AND FINANCIAL AID

Annual tuition $28,465. Room and board $9,293. Required fees $390. Average book expense $1,700. **Required Forms and Deadlines:** FAFSA, institution's own financial aid form. Priority financial aid filing date 3/2. **Notification of Awards:** Applicants will be notified of awards on a rolling basis beginning 3/15. **Types of Aid:** *Need-based scholarships/grants:* Federal Pell, SEOG, state scholarships/grants, private scholarships, the school's own gift aid. *Loans:* FFEL Subsidized Stafford, FFEL Unsubsidized Stafford, FFEL PLUS, Federal Perkins. *Student Employment:* Federal Work-Study Program available. Institutional employment available. Off-campus job opportunities are good. **Financial Aid Statistics:** 78% freshmen, 83% undergrads receive need-based scholarship or grant aid. 3% freshmen, 2% undergrads receive non-need-based scholarship or grant aid. 72% freshmen, 80% undergrads receive need-based self-help aid. 79% freshmen, 86% undergrads receive any aid. 90.7% undergrads borrow to pay for school. Average cumulative indebtedness $47,059. **Criteria for awarding institutional aid:** *Non-need-based:* Academics.

WOODBURY UNIVERSITY

7500 Glenoaks Boulevard, Burbank, CA 91510-7846
Phone: 818-767-0888 **Financial Aid Phone:** 818-767-0888
E-mail: admissions@woodbury.edu **CEEB Code:** 4955
Fax: 818-767-7520 **Website: ACT Code:** 481

This private school was founded in 1884. It has a 22-acre campus.

RATINGS
Admissions Selectivity Rating: 73   **Fire Safety Rating:** 78   **Green Rating:** 60*

STUDENTS AND FACULTY
Enrollment: 1,269. **Student Body:** 53% female, 47% male, % out-of-state, 10% international (41 countries represented). Asian 10%, African American 5%, Caucasian 41%, Hispanic 33%.
Retention and Graduation: 80% freshmen return for sophomore year. **Faculty:** Student/faculty ratio 11:1. 59 full-time faculty, 83% hold PhDs, 12% are members of minority groups, 56% are women.

ACADEMICS
Degrees: Bachelor's, master's. **Classes:** Most classes have 10–19 students. **Majors with Highest Enrollment:** architecture and related services, other; business administration and management; fashion/apparel design. **Special Study Options:** Accelerated program, double major, dual enrollment, English

---

WORCESTER POLYTECHNIC INSTITUTE

Admissions Office, Bartlett Center, 100 Institute Rd, Worcester, MA 01609
Phone: 508-831-5286 **Financial Aid Phone:** 508-831-5469
E-mail: admissions@wpi.edu **CEEB Code:** 3969
Fax: 508-831-5875 **Website:** www.wpi.edu **ACT Code:** 1942

This private school was founded in 1865. It has a 80-acre campus.

RATINGS
Admissions Selectivity Rating: 93   **Fire Safety Rating:** 81   **Green Rating:** 89

STUDENTS AND FACULTY
Enrollment: 3,391. **Student Body:** 28% female, 72% male, 49% out-of-state, 9% international (83 countries represented). Asian 6%, African American 3%, Caucasian 74%, Hispanic 6%, Native American 1%.
Retention and Graduation: 95% freshmen return for sophomore year. 67% freshmen graduate within 4 years. 26% grads go on to further study within 1 year. 2% grads pursue law degrees. 2% grads pursue business degrees. 2% grads

pursue medical degrees. **Faculty:** Student/faculty ratio 14:1. 251263 full-time faculty.

ACADEMICS

Degrees: Bachelor's, master's, post-bachelor's certificate, post-master's certificate. **Classes:** Most classes have fewer than 10 students. Most lab/discussion sessions have 20–29 students. **Majors with Highest Enrollment:** computer science; electrical, electronics and communications engineering; mechanical engineering. **Special Study Options:** Accelerated program, cooperative education program, cross-registration, distance learning, double major, dual enrollment, English as a Second Language (ESL), honors program, independent study, liberal arts/career combination, student-designed major, study abroad, teacher certification program, Completion of degree-required projects at off-campus locations (international and domestic) supervised by WPI faculty. This program requires the students to reside at the site for 2 months after having prepared for the experience for two months while on campus. **Honors programs:** Chemistry and Biochemistry Scholars Program: Students selected for this highly competitive program will be given the opportunity to participate in faculty research within these departments beginning in the freshman year. In addition to the scholars program, each CBSP Scholar receives an academic merit scholarship. Scholarship amounts will vary, but typically range between $12,500 and $25,000, and are renewable for four years. **Combined degree programs:** BS/MS, BS/MBA, BS/MEng. Special programs offered to physically disabled students include note-taking services, reader services, tape recorders, tutors. **Career services:** Alumni network, alumni services, career/job search classes, career assessment, internships, regional alumni. **Career services highlights include:** Two hands-on, professional-level projects that are the equivalent of three courses each are a requirement in our curriculum. They provide students with the opportunity to apply theory to practice through real-world problems and to find solutions that can be implemented by the project sponsors. As an example, one company implemented eight of nine student recommendations and saved $35,000 a day!

FACILITIES

Housing: Coed dorms, special housing for disabled students, special housing for international students, fraternity/sorority housing, apartments for single students, 4 co-ed residential houses/special interest housing. 90% of campus accessible to physically disabled. **Special Academic Facilities/Equipment:** Several off-campus project centers, TV studio, robotics lab, CAD-CAM lab, laser labs, electron microscopes, wind tunnel, manufacturing engineering applications center, VLSI design lab, nuclear reactor. **Computers:** 100% of classrooms, 100% of dorms, 100% of libraries, 100% of dining areas, 100% of student union, 100% of common outdoor areas have wireless network access. Students can register for classes online. Administrative functions (other than registration) can be performed online.

CAMPUS LIFE

Environment: City. **Activities:** Choral groups, concert band, dance, drama/theater, jazz band, literary magazine, marching band, music ensembles, musical theater, pep band, radio station, student government, student newspaper, student-run film society, symphony orchestra, yearbook, international student organization. **Organizations:** 200 registered organizations, 20 honor societies, 4 religious organizations. 13 fraternities, 3 sororities. **Athletics (Intercollegiate):** *Men:* Baseball, basketball, crew/rowing, cross-country, diving, football, soccer, swimming, track/field (outdoor), track/field (indoor), wrestling. *Women:* Basketball, crew/rowing, cross-country, diving, field hockey, soccer, softball, swimming, track/field (outdoor), track/field (indoor), volleyball. **On-Campus Highlights:** Student-invented fountain, Campus Center, Robotics Lab, Wind Tunnels, Fire Protection Engineering Lab, new biomedical and life sciences research center at Gateway Park, new pub-style restaurant on campus, new apartment-style residence hall, new Sports and Recreation Center opening in 2012. **Environmental Initiatives:** Creation of the President's Task Force on Sustainability, the creation of a Sustainability Coordinator position, and the creation of a Student Sustainability Coordination position. In 2007, WPI's Board of Trustees voted to adopt a policy calling for all future buildings on campus to be enviornmentally friendly and LEED-certified structures. WPI is proud to have two LEED-certified buildings; our new residence hall, East Hall, is certified at the LEED Gold level, and the Bartlett Center, our Admissions Building is recognized at the certified level. And the newly formed Institute for Energy and Sustainability, collaboration between WPI and other institutions and businesses, funded by a grant from the Massachusetts Clean Energy Center is working to develop jobs in the clean energy sector.

ADMISSIONS

Freshman Academic Profile: Average high school GPA 3.8. 55% in top 10% of high school class, 88% in top 25% of high school class, 99% in top 50% of high school class. 66% from public high schools. SAT Math middle 50% range 630–720. SAT Critical Reading middle 50% range 560–660. SAT Writing middle 50% range 560–660. ACT middle 50% range 26–31. Minimum paper TOEFL 550. Minimum computer TOEFL 213. Minimum web-based TOEFL 79. **Basis for Candidate Selection:** *Very important factors considered include:*

Academic GPA, rigor of secondary school record. *Important factors considered include:* Class rank, application essay, recommendation(s), standardized test scores, character/personal qualities, extracurricular activities. *Other factors considered include:* Alumni/ae relation, first generation, geographical residence, interview, level of applicant's interest, talent/ability, volunteer work, work experience. **Freshman Admission Requirements:** High school diploma is required and GED is accepted. *Academic units required:* 4 English, 4 mathematics, 2 science, (2 science labs). *Academic units recommended:* 4 science, 2 foreign language, 2 social studies, 1 history, 1 computer science. **Freshman Admission Statistics:** 6,284 applied, 63% admitted, 23% enrolled. **Transfer Admission Requirements:** College transcript(s), essay or personal statement, statement of good standing from prior institution(s). Minimum college GPA of 3.0 required. Lowest grade transferable C. **General Admission Information:** Application fee $60. Regular application deadline 2/1. Regular notification 4/1. Nonfall registration accepted. Admission may be deferred for a maximum of 1 year. Credit and/or placement offered for CEEB Advanced Placement tests.

COSTS AND FINANCIAL AID

Annual tuition $38,360. Room and board $11,610. Required fees $560. Average book expense $1,000. **Required Forms and Deadlines:** FAFSA, CSS/Financial Aid PROFILE, noncustodial PROFILE. Financial aid filing deadline 2/1. **Notification of Awards:** Applicants will be notified of awards on or about 4/1. **Types of Aid:** *Need-based scholarships/grants:* Federal Pell, SEOG, state scholarships/grants, private scholarships, the school's own gift aid. *Loans:* FFEL Subsidized Stafford, FFEL Unsubsidized Stafford, FFEL PLUS, Federal Perkins, state loans, college/university loans from institutional funds. *Student Employment:* Federal Work-Study Program available. Institutional employment available. Off-campus job opportunities are good. **Financial Aid Statistics:** 70% freshmen, 64% undergrads receive need-based scholarship or grant aid. 27% freshmen, 17% undergrads receive non-need-based scholarship or grant aid. 46% freshmen, 51% undergrads receive need-based self-help aid. 99% freshmen, 95% undergrads receive any aid. 73.82% undergrads borrow to pay for school. Average cumulative indebtedness $44,340. **Criteria for awarding institutional aid:** *Non-need-based:* Academics, leadership, minority status.

See page 1334.

WORCESTER STATE COLLEGE

486 Chandler Street, Department of Ad, Worcester, MA 01602-2597
Phone: 508-929-8040 **Financial Aid Phone:** 508-929-8058
E-mail: admissions@worcester.edu **CEEB Code:** 3524
Fax: 508-929-8183 **Website:** www.worcester.edu **ACT Code:** 1914

This public school was founded in 1874. It has a 58-acre campus.

RATINGS

Admissions Selectivity Rating: 76   **Fire Safety Rating:** 93   **Green Rating:** 83

STUDENTS AND FACULTY

Enrollment: 4,211. **Student Body:** 59% female, 41% male, 3% out-of-state, 1% international (20 countries represented). Asian 3%, African American 6%, Caucasian 80%, Hispanic 6%, Native American 1%.
Retention and Graduation: 77% freshmen return for sophomore year. 24% freshmen graduate within 4 years. **Faculty:** Student/faculty ratio 17:1. 179 full-time faculty, 74% hold PhDs, 20% are members of minority groups, 52% are women.

ACADEMICS

Degrees: Bachelor's, certificate, master's, post-bachelor's certificate, post-master's certificate. **Classes:** Most classes have 20–29 students. Most lab/discussion sessions have 10–19 students. **Majors with Highest Enrollment:** Business administration and management; criminal justice/safety studies; psychology. **Special Study Options:** Cross-registration, distance learning, double major, English as a Second Language (ESL), exchange student program (domestic), honors program, independent study, internships, liberal arts/career combination, study abroad, teacher certification program, Foreign Exchange Student Program. **Honors programs:** Commonwealth Honors Program: The mission of the honors program at Worcester State College is to offer all qualified students an outstanding undergraduate experience through courses that emphasize innovative pedagogy and the values of liberal learning. Honors classes are small (often fewer than 20 students) and are designed to encourage active and lifelong learning. Small classes and extracurricular programs provide honors students with greater interaction between their peers and a select core of dedicated faculty members. In addition to stimulating classes, honors students also enjoy campus speakers, field trips to cultural centers, occasional luncheons with faculty members, and an annual dinner with the college president. Founded in 1996, the program currently enrolls 150 students and recently earned accreditation as a Commonwealth Honors Program from the Massachusetts Board of Higher Education. **Combined degree programs:** BA/MA, occupational therapy. Special programs offered to physically disabled students include note-taking services, reader services, tape recorders, tutors. **Career services:** Alumni network, alumni services, career/job search classes, career assessment, internships, regional alumni. **Career services highlights include:** Sustainability Fair, Green Work.

FACILITIES

Housing: Coed dorms, special housing for disabled students, men's dorms, women's dorms. 100% of campus accessible to physically disabled. **Special Academic Facilities/Equipment:** Art Studio. **Computers:** 100% of classrooms, 100% of dorms, 100% of libraries, 100% of dining areas, 100% of student union, 100% of common outdoor areas have wireless network access. Students can register for classes online. Administrative functions (other than registration) can be performed online. Undergraduates are required to own a computer.

CAMPUS LIFE

Environment: City. **Activities:** Choral groups, concert band, dance, drama/theater, jazz band, music ensembles, radio station, student government, student newspaper, television station, yearbook, campus ministries, international student organization. **Organizations:** 39 registered organizations, 17 honor societies, 1 religious organizations. **Athletics (Intercollegiate):** *Men:* Baseball, basketball, cheerleading, cross-country, football, golf, ice hockey, soccer, track/field (outdoor), track/field (indoor). *Women:* Basketball, cheerleading, cross-country, field hockey, lacrosse, soccer, softball, tennis, track/field (outdoor), track/field (indoor), volleyball. **On-Campus Highlights:** Wasylean Hall, Student Center Living Room, Science and Technology Building, Food Court, Campus Bookstore. **Environmental Initiatives:** 100 kW photovoltaic installation (solar panels); single stream recycling process; Presidents' Climate Commitment.

ADMISSIONS

Freshman Academic Profile: Average high school GPA 3.06. SAT Math middle 50% range 470–560. SAT Critical Reading middle 50% range 460–550. SAT Writing middle 50% range 450–550. ACT middle 50% range 19–24. Minimum paper TOEFL 550. Minimum computer TOEFL 213. Minimum web-based TOEFL 79. **Basis for Candidate Selection:** *Very important factors considered include:* Academic GPA, rigor of secondary school record, standardized test scores. *Important factors considered include:* Class rank, character/personal qualities. *Other factors considered include:* Application essay, recommendation(s), alumni/ae relation, extracurricular activities, first generation, geographical residence, racial/ethnic status, state residency, talent/ability, volunteer work, work experience. **Freshman Admission Requirements:** High school diploma is required and GED is accepted. *Academic units required:* 4 English, 3 mathematics, 3 science, (1 science labs), 2 foreign language, 1 social studies, 1 history, 2 academic electives. **Freshman Admission Statistics:** 3,559 applied, 59% admitted, 33% enrolled. **Transfer Admission Requirements:** High school transcript, college transcript(s), statement of good standing from prior institution(s). Minimum college GPA of 2.5 required. Lowest grade transferable C–. **General Admission Information:** Application fee $40. Regular application deadline 5/1. Notification on a rolling basis, beginning on or about 12/1. Nonfall registration accepted. Admission may be deferred for a maximum of 1 year. Credit and/or placement offered for CEEB Advanced Placement tests.

COSTS AND FINANCIAL AID

Required Forms and Deadlines: FAFSA. Financial aid filing deadline 5/1. Priority financial aid filing date 3/1. **Notification of Awards:** Applicants will be notified of awards on a rolling basis beginning 3/1. **Types of Aid:** *Need-based scholarships/grants:* Federal Pell, SEOG, state scholarships/grants, private scholarships, the school's own gift aid. *Loans:* FFEL Subsidized Stafford, FFEL Unsubsidized Stafford, FFEL PLUS, Federal Perkins, state loans. *Student Employment:* Federal Work-Study Program available. Institutional employment available. Highest amount earned per year from on-campus jobs $17,184. Off-campus job opportunities are good. **Financial Aid Statistics:** 49% freshmen, 36% undergrads receive need-based scholarship or grant aid. 28% freshmen, 16% undergrads receive non-need-based scholarship or grant aid. 55% freshmen, 45% undergrads receive need-based self-help aid. 57% freshmen, 54% undergrads receive any aid. 42% undergrads borrow to pay for school. Average cumulative indebtedness $17,819. **Criteria for awarding institutional aid:** *Non-need-based:* Academics.

WRIGHT STATE UNIVERSITY

3640 Colonel Glenn Highway, Dayton, OH 45435
Phone: 937-775-5700 **Financial Aid Phone:** 937-775-5721
E-mail: admissions@wright.edu **CEEB Code:** 1179
Fax: 937-775-5795 **Website:** www.wright.edu **ACT Code:** 3295

This public school was founded in 1964. It has a 557-acre campus.

RATINGS

Admissions Selectivity Rating: 71   **Fire Safety Rating:** 96   **Green Rating:** 72

STUDENTS AND FACULTY

Enrollment: 13,024. **Student Body:** 55% female, 45% male, 5% out-of-state, 1% international (67 countries represented). Asian 3%, African American 16%, Caucasian 73%, Hispanic 2%.
Retention and Graduation: 70% freshmen return for sophomore year. 18% freshmen graduate within 4 years. **Faculty:** Student/faculty ratio 17:1. 853 full-time faculty, 44% are women. 13% of classes are taught by teaching assistants.

ACADEMICS

Degrees: Associate, bachelor's, certificate, doctoral, master's, post-master's certificate, terminal associate, transfer associate. **Classes:** Most classes have 20–29 students. Most lab/discussion sessions have fewer than 10 students. **Majors with Highest Enrollment:** Elementary education and teaching; nursing/registered nurse (RN, ASN, BSN, MSN); psychology. **Special Study Options:** Cooperative education program, cross-registration, distance learning, double major, dual enrollment, English as a Second Language (ESL), honors program, independent study, internships, student-designed major, study abroad, teacher certification program, weekend college. **Honors programs:** Honors Program. Special programs offered to physically disabled students include note-taking services, reader services, tape recorders, tutors. **Career services:** Alumni network, alumni services, career/job search classes, career assessment, internships. **Career services highlights include:** WSU has a very flexible set of programs that meet the needs of our students.

FACILITIES

Housing: Coed dorms, special housing for disabled students, apartments for married students, apartments for single students, Honors Dorm. 100% of campus accessible to physically disabled. **Special Academic Facilities/Equipment:** Art gallery located in the Creative Arts Center. **Computers:** 100% of classrooms, 100% of dorms, 100% of libraries, 100% of dining areas, 100% of student union, have wireless network access. Students can register for classes online. Administrative functions (other than registration) can be performed online.

CAMPUS LIFE

Environment: City. **Activities:** Choral groups, concert band, dance, drama/theater, jazz band, literary magazine, music ensembles, musical theater, opera, pep band, radio station, student government, student newspaper, symphony orchestra, television station, campus ministries, Model UN. **Organizations:** 145 registered organizations, 22 honor societies, 9 religious organizations. 8 fraternities, 8 sororities. **Athletics (Intercollegiate):** *Men:* Baseball, basketball, cheerleading, cross-country, diving, golf, soccer, swimming, tennis. *Women:* Basketball, cheerleading, cross-country, diving, soccer, softball, swimming, tennis, track/field (outdoor), volleyball. **On-Campus Highlights:** Student Union, Garden of the Senses, Rec Center, Fitness Center, Nutter Center. **Environmental Initiatives:** Diggs Lab LEED Gold rating; recycling efforts; Student Groups (GangGreen).

ADMISSIONS

Freshman Academic Profile: Average high school GPA 3.06. 15% in top 10% of high school class, 35% in top 25% of high school class, 65% in top 50% of high school class. 85% from public high schools. SAT Math middle 50% range 440–580. SAT Critical Reading middle 50% range 440–560. SAT Writing middle 50% range 430–550. ACT middle 50% range 18–24. Minimum web-based TOEFL 61. **Basis for Candidate Selection:** *Very important factors considered include:* Academic GPA, rigor of secondary school record, standardized test scores. *Important factors considered include:* Class rank. *Other factors considered include:* Recommendation(s), state residency. **Freshman Admission Requirements:** High school diploma is required and GED is accepted. *Academic units required:* 4 English, 3 mathematics, 3 science, (3 science labs), 2 foreign language, 3 social studies, 1 visual/performing arts. **Freshman Admission Statistics:** 6,188 applied, 84% admitted, 45% enrolled. **Transfer Admission Requirements:** College transcript(s), minimum college GPA of 2.0 required. Lowest grade transferable D. **General Admission Information:** Application fee $30. Notification on a rolling basis, beginning on or about 10/1. Nonfall registration accepted. Admission may be deferred for a maximum of Four Quarters. Credit offered for CEEB Advanced Placement tests.

COSTS AND FINANCIAL AID

Required Forms and Deadlines: FAFSA. Priority financial aid filing date 2/15. **Notification of Awards:** Applicants will be notified of awards on a rolling basis beginning 3/15. **Types of Aid:** *Need-based scholarships/grants:* Federal Pell, SEOG, state scholarships/grants, private scholarships, the school's own gift aid, United Negro College Fund, Federal Nursing Scholarships. Choose Ohio First Scholarships. *Loans:* FFEL Subsidized Stafford, FFEL Unsubsidized Stafford, FFEL PLUS, Federal Perkins, Federal Nursing, state loans, college/university loans from institutional funds, Private Loans. *Student Employment:* Federal Work-Study Program available. Institutional employment available. Off-campus job opportunities are good. **Financial Aid Statistics:** 58% freshmen, 50% undergrads receive need-based scholarship or grant aid. 5% freshmen, 3% undergrads receive non-need-based scholarship or grant aid. 69% freshmen, 66% undergrads receive need-based self-help aid. 1% freshmen, 1% undergrads receive athletic scholarships. 84% freshmen, 73% undergrads receive any aid. 73% undergrads borrow to pay for school. Average cumulative indebtedness $25,357. **Criteria for awarding institutional aid:** *Non-need-based:* Academics, alumni affiliation, art, athletics, leadership, minority status, music/drama.

XAVIER UNIVERSITY (OH)

3800 Victory Parkway, Cincinnati, OH 45207-5311
Phone: 513-745-3301 **Financial Aid Phone:** 513-745-3142
E-mail: xuadmit@xavier.edu **CEEB Code:** 1965
Fax: 513-745-4319 **Website:** www.xu.edu **ACT Code:** 3366

This private school, affiliated with the Roman CatholiC–Jesuit Church, was founded in 1831. It has a 146-acre campus.

RATINGS

Admissions Selectivity Rating: 87   **Fire Safety Rating:** 71   **Green Rating:** 78

STUDENTS AND FACULTY

Enrollment: 4,083. **Student Body:** 55% female, 45% male, 39% out-of-state, 1% international (45 countries represented). Asian 2%, African American 12%, Caucasian 80%, Hispanic 3%.
Retention and Graduation: 84% freshmen return for sophomore year. 68% freshmen graduate within 4 years. 25% grads go on to further study within 1 year. 4% grads pursue arts and sciences degrees. 2% grads pursue law degrees. 4% grads pursue business degrees. 5% grads pursue medical degrees. **Faculty:** Student/faculty ratio 13:1. 317 full-time faculty, 77% hold PhDs, 15% are members of minority groups, 48% are women.

ACADEMICS

Degrees: Associate, bachelor's, certificate, master's, terminal associate. **Classes:** Most classes have 20–29 students. Most lab/discussion sessions have 20–29 students. **Majors with Highest Enrollment:** Business/commerce; liberal arts and sciences/liberal studies; nursing/registered nurse (RN, ASN, BSN, MSN). **Special Study Options:** Cooperative education program, cross-registration, double major, dual enrollment, English as a Second Language (ESL), honors program, independent study, internships, study abroad, teacher certification program, weekend college, Service Learning Semester. **Honors programs:** University Scholars Progam Philosophy, Politics and the Public Honors AB **Combined degree programs:** BSBA/MBA in Accounting. Special programs offered to physically disabled students include note-taking services, reader services, tape recorders, tutors. **Career services:** Alumni network, alumni services, career/job search classes, career assessment, internships, regional alumni. **Career services highlights include:** Our premier programs include our Executive Mentor Program in which students are matched with a business executive in their sophomore year to guide, advise and serve as a sounding board on career, academic and life issues. Additionally our Business Profession Program, an intentional four-year career development program for business undergraduates has received national attention.

FACILITIES

Housing: Coed dorms, special housing for disabled students, apartments for single students, theme housing. 95% of campus accessible to physically disabled. **Special Academic Facilities/Equipment:** Student-run art gallery, Montessori lab school. **Computers:** 100% of classrooms, 100% of dorms, 100% of libraries, 100% of dining areas, 100% of student union, 100% of common outdoor areas have wireless network access. Students can register for classes online. Administrative functions (other than registration) can be performed online.

CAMPUS LIFE

Environment: Metropolis. **Activities:** Choral groups, concert band, dance, drama/theater, jazz band, literary magazine, music ensembles, musical theater, opera, pep band, radio station, student government, student newspaper, student-run film society, symphony orchestra, television station, campus ministries, international student organization. **Organizations:** 124 registered organizations, 10 honor societies, 11 religious organizations. **Athletics (Intercollegiate):** *Men:* Baseball, basketball, cheerleading, cross-country, golf, soccer, swimming, tennis, track/field (outdoor), track/field (indoor). *Women:* Basketball, cheerleading, cross-country, golf, soccer, swimming, tennis, track/field (outdoor), track/field (indoor), volleyball. **On-Campus Highlights:** Cintas Center basketball arena and conce, McDonald Library, The Gallagher Student Center, O'Conner Sports Center, Bellarmine Chapel. **Environmental Initiatives:** New construction will be required to be LEED Silver. Active participation in RecycleMania and recycling of the waste stream throughout the year. Investment in large central plant equipment to provide heating and sooling for the majority of the buildings on campus which results in lower heating and cooling expenses due to the higher efficiency of this equipment.

ADMISSIONS

Freshman Academic Profile: Average high school GPA 3.54. 24% in top 10% of high school class, 58% in top 25% of high school class, 85% in top 50% of high school class. 49% from public high schools. SAT Math middle 50% range 510–610. SAT Critical Reading middle 50% range 530–620. SAT Writing middle 50% range 500–600. ACT middle 50% range 23–28. Minimum paper TOEFL 530. Minimum computer TOEFL 197. Minimum web-based TOEFL 71. **Basis for Candidate Selection:** *Very important factors considered include:* Rigor of secondary school record. *Important factors considered include:* Class rank, application essay, academic GPA, recommendation(s), standardized test scores, character/personal qualities. *Other factors considered include:* Alumni/ae relation, extracurricular activities, first generation, level of applicant's interest, talent/ability, volunteer work, work experience. **Freshman Admission Requirements:** High school diploma is required and GED is accepted. *Academic units recommended:* 4 English, 3 mathematics, 3 science, 2 foreign language, 3 social studies, 5 academic electives, 1 Health/physical education **Freshman Admission Statistics:** 7,205 applied, 73% admitted, 22% enrolled. **Transfer Admission Requirements:** High school transcript, college transcript(s), statement of good standing from prior institution(s). Minimum college GPA of 2.0 required. Lowest grade transferable C–. **General Admission Information:** Application fee $35. Regular application deadline 2/1. Notification on a rolling basis, beginning on or about 10/15. Nonfall registration accepted. Admission may be deferred for a maximum of 1 year. Credit and/or placement offered for CEEB Advanced Placement tests.

COSTS AND FINANCIAL AID

Required Forms and Deadlines: FAFSA. Priority financial aid filing date 2/15. **Notification of Awards:** Applicants will be notified of awards on a rolling basis beginning 2/15. **Types of Aid:** *Need-based scholarships/grants:* Federal Pell, SEOG, state scholarships/grants, private scholarships, the school's own gift aid. *Loans:* FFEL Subsidized Stafford, FFEL Unsubsidized Stafford, FFEL PLUS, Federal Perkins. *Student Employment:* Federal Work-Study Program available. Institutional employment available. Highest amount earned per year from on-campus jobs $4,900. Off-campus job opportunities are excellent. **Financial Aid Statistics:** 63% freshmen, 56% undergrads receive need-based scholarship or grant aid. 11% freshmen, 7% undergrads receive non-need-based scholarship or grant aid. 53% freshmen, 48% undergrads receive need-based self-help aid. 4% freshmen, 4% undergrads receive athletic scholarships. 100% freshmen, 95% undergrads receive any aid. 69% undergrads borrow to pay for school. Average cumulative indebtedness $22,769. **Criteria for awarding institutional aid:** *Non-need-based:* Academics, alumni affiliation, art, athletics, leadership, music/drama, religious affiliation.

XAVIER UNIVERSITY OF LOUISIANA

Best 373

One Drexel Drive, New Orleans, LA, 70125,
Phone: 504-520-7388 **Financial Aid Phone:** 504-520-7835
E-mail: apply@xula.edu **CEEB Code:** 6975
Fax: 504-520-7941 **Website:** www.xula.edu **ACT Code:** 1618

This private school, affiliated with the Roman Catholic Church, was founded in 1915. It has a 29-acre campus.

RATINGS
Admissions Selectivity Rating: 77   **Fire Safety Rating:** 84   **Green Rating:** 60*

STUDENTS AND FACULTY
Enrollment: 2,644. **Student Body:** 72% female, 28% male, 51% out-of-state, 2% international (8 countries represented). Asian 10%, African American 74%, Caucasian 2%, Hispanic 1%.
Retention and Graduation: 69% freshmen return for sophomore year. 39% grads go on to further study within 1 year. 14% grads pursue arts and sciences degrees. 1% grads pursue law degrees. 1% grads pursue business degrees. 9% grads pursue medical degrees. **Faculty:** Student/faculty ratio 12.9:1. 227 full-time faculty, 87% hold PhDs, 52% are members of minority groups, 49% are women.

ACADEMICS
Degrees: Bachelor's, master's, post-master's certificate. **Classes:** Most classes have 10–19 students. Most lab/discussion sessions have 20–29 students. **Majors with Highest Enrollment:** Pre-medicine/pre-medical studies; pre-pharmacy studies; psychology. **Special Study Options:** Accelerated program, cooperative education program, cross-registration, double major, dual enrollment, exchange student program (domestic), honors program, independent study, internships, study abroad, African American Studies Minor, Women Studies. Special programs offered to physically disabled students include note-taking services, reader services, tape recorders, tutors. **Career services:** Career/job search classes, career assessment, internships.

FACILITIES
Housing: Coed dorms, special housing for disabled students, men's dorms, women's dorms. 99% of campus accessible to physically disabled. **Computers:** 100% of classrooms, 100% of dorms, 100% of libraries, 100% of dining areas, 100% of student union, 100% of common outdoor areas have wireless network access. Students can register for classes online. Administrative functions (other than registration) can be performed online.

CAMPUS LIFE
Environment: Metropolis. **Activities:** Choral groups, concert band, dance, drama/theater, jazz band, literary magazine, music ensembles, opera, student government, student newspaper, symphony orchestra, television station, yearbook, campus ministries, international student organization. **Organizations:** 88 registered organizations, 8 honor societies, 1 religious organizations. 4 fraternities, 4 sororities. **Athletics (Intercollegiate):** *Men:* Basketball, cross-country, tennis, track/field (outdoor), track/field (indoor). *Women:* Basketball, cross-country, tennis, track/field (outdoor), track/field (indoor), volleyball. **On-Campus Highlights:** New University Center, Gymnasium (The Barn), library, university quadrangle, historic administration building.

ADMISSIONS
Freshman Academic Profile: Average high school GPA 3.16. 20% in top 10% of high school class, 34% in top 25% of high school class, 53% in top 50% of high school class. 81% from public high schools. SAT Math middle 50% range 410–530. SAT Critical Reading middle 50% range 420–530. SAT Writing middle 50% range 420–540. ACT middle 50% range 18–24. Minimum paper TOEFL 550. **Basis for Candidate Selection:** *Very important factors considered include:* Academic GPA, recommendation(s), rigor of secondary school record, standardized test scores. *Important factors considered include:* Class rank, application essay. *Other factors considered include:* Alumni/ae relation, character/personal qualities, extracurricular activities, interview, talent/ability, volunteer work, work experience. **Freshman Admission Requirements:** High school diploma is required and GED is accepted. *Academic units required:* 4 English, 2 mathematics, 1 science, 1 social studies, 8 academic electives. *Academic units recommended:* 4 mathematics, 3 science, 1 foreign language, 1 history. **Freshman Admission Statistics:** 3,278 applied, 67% admitted, 35% enrolled. **Transfer Admission Requirements:** College transcript(s), minimum college GPA of 2.00 required. Lowest grade transferable C. **General Admission Informa-**tion: Application fee $25. Regular application deadline 7/1. Regular notification 10/15. Nonfall registration accepted. Credit and/or placement offered for CEEB Advanced Placement tests.

COSTS AND FINANCIAL AID
Annual tuition $15,300. Room and board $7,000. Required fees $1,000. Average book expense $1,200. **Required Forms and Deadlines:** FAFSA. Priority financial aid filing date 1/1. **Notification of Awards:** Applicants will be notified of awards on a rolling basis beginning 4/1. **Types of Aid:** *Need-based scholarships/grants:* Federal Pell, SEOG, state scholarships/grants, private scholarships, the school's own gift aid, United Negro College Fund. *Loans:* Direct Subsidized Stafford, Direct Unsubsidized Stafford, Direct PLUS, FFEL Subsidized Stafford, FFEL Unsubsidized Stafford, FFEL PLUS, Federal Perkins. *Student Employment:* Federal Work-Study Program available. Institutional employment available. Highest amount earned per year from on-campus jobs $1,000. Off-campus job opportunities are good. **Financial Aid Statistics:** 62% freshmen, 53% undergrads receive need-based scholarship or grant aid. 74% freshmen, 56% undergrads receive non-need-based scholarship or grant aid. 83% freshmen, 78% undergrads receive need-based self-help aid. 3% freshmen, 3% undergrads receive athletic scholarships. 86% freshmen, 24% undergrads receive any aid. 83% undergrads borrow to pay for school. Average cumulative indebtedness $23,067. **Criteria for awarding institutional aid:** *Non-need-based:* Music/drama.

YALE UNIVERSITY

Best 373

PO Box 208234, New Haven, CT 06520-8234
Phone: 203-432-9300 **Financial Aid Phone:** 203-432-2700
E-mail: student.questions@yale.edu **CEEB Code:** 3987
Fax: 203-432-9392 **Website:** www.yale.edu **ACT Code:** 618

This private school was founded in 1701. It has a 320-acre campus.

RATINGS
Admissions Selectivity Rating: 99   **Fire Safety Rating:** 60*   **Green Rating:** 99

STUDENTS AND FACULTY
Enrollment: 5,258. **Student Body:** 50% female, 50% male, 94% out-of-state, 9% international (108 countries represented). Asian 14%, African American 9%, Caucasian 42%, Hispanic 9%, Native American 1%.
Retention and Graduation: 99% freshmen return for sophomore year. 90% freshmen graduate within 4 years. 27% grads go on to further study within 1 year. 9% grads pursue arts and sciences degrees. 6% grads pursue law degrees. 8% grads pursue medical degrees. **Faculty:** Student/faculty ratio 6:1. 1158 full-time faculty, 91% hold PhDs, 18% are members of minority groups, 33% are women. 3% of classes are taught by teaching assistants.

ACADEMICS
Degrees: Bachelor's, master's, post-master's certificate. **Classes:** Most classes have 10–19 students. **Majors with Highest Enrollment:** Economics; history; political science and government. **Special Study Options:** Accelerated program, distance learning, double major, English as a Second Language (ESL), honors program, independent study, internships, liberal arts/career combination, student-designed major, study abroad, teacher certification program **Combined degree programs:** BA/MA, BA/MM in Music, BA/MA, BS/MS. Special programs offered to physically disabled students include note-taking services, reader services, tape recorders, tutors. **Career services:** Alumni network, alumni services, career/job search classes, internships, regional alumni. **Career services highlights include:** In coordination with the Yale Undergraduate Career Services department, the university helps place hundreds of students in internships across the country and around the world every year. UCS utilizes a vast array of resources, including alumni, private firms and research fellowships to place students in a wide variety of internships.

FACILITIES
Housing: Coed dorms, special housing for disabled students, Students are randomly assigned to 1 of 12 residential colleges where they live, eat, socialize, and pursue various academic and extracurricular activities. All undergraduate housing is provided through residential college system. **Special Academic Facilities/Equipment:** Art and history museums, observatory, electron microscopes, nuclear accelerators, center for international and areas studies, child study center, marsh botanical gardens, center for parallel supercomput-

ing. **Computers:** 100% of classrooms, 100% of dorms, 100% of libraries, 100% of dining areas, 100% of student union, 100% of common outdoor areas have wireless network access. Students can register for classes online. Administrative functions (other than registration) can be performed online.

CAMPUS LIFE

Environment: City. **Activities:** Choral groups, concert band, dance, drama/theater, jazz band, literary magazine, marching band, music ensembles, musical theater, opera, pep band, radio station, student government, student newspaper, student-run film society, symphony orchestra, television station, yearbook, campus ministries, international student organization, Model UN. **Organizations:** 350 registered organizations, **Athletics (Intercollegiate):** *Men:* Baseball, basketball, crew/rowing, cross-country, diving, fencing, football, golf, ice hockey, lacrosse, sailing, soccer, squash, swimming, tennis, track/field (outdoor), track/field (indoor). *Women:* Basketball, crew/rowing, cross-country, diving, fencing, field hockey, golf, gymnastics, ice hockey, lacrosse, sailing, soccer, softball, squash, swimming, tennis, track/field (outdoor), track/field (indoor), volleyball. **On-Campus Highlights:** Old Campus, Sterling Memorial Library, Yale British Art Center, Beinecke Rare Book and Manuscript Library, Payne-Whitney Gymnasium, www.yale.edu/admit/visit/index.html. **Environmental Initiatives:** Greenhouse gas commitment of 43% below 2005 levels by 2020 40% of food served in the dining halls is local/organic LEED Silver for all new construction

ADMISSIONS

Freshman Academic Profile: 96% in top 10% of high school class, 100% in top 25% of high school class, 100% in top 50% of high school class. 55% from public high schools. SAT Math middle 50% range 700–780. SAT Critical Reading middle 50% range 700–800. SAT Writing middle 50% range 700–790. ACT middle 50% range 30–34. Minimum paper TOEFL 600. Minimum computer TOEFL 250. Minimum web-based TOEFL 100. **Basis for Candidate Selection:** *Very important factors considered include:* Class rank, application essay, academic GPA, recommendation(s), rigor of secondary school record, standardized test scores, character/personal qualities, extracurricular activities, talent/ability, *Other factors considered include:* Alumni/ae relation, first generation, geographical residence, interview, level of applicant's interest, racial/ethnic status, state residency, volunteer work, work experience. **Freshman Admission Requirements:** High school diploma or equivalent is not required. **Freshman Admission Statistics:** 26,003 applied, 8% admitted, 67% enrolled. **Transfer Admission Requirements:** High school transcript, college transcript(s), essay or personal statement, standardized test scores, statement of good standing from prior institution(s). Lowest grade transferable C. **General Admission Information:** Application fee $75. Regular application deadline 12/31. Regular notification 4/1. Nonfall registration not accepted. Admission may be deferred for a maximum of 1 year. Placement offered for CEEB Advanced Placement tests.

COSTS AND FINANCIAL AID

Annual tuition $36,500. Room and board $11,000. Average book expense $950. **Required Forms and Deadlines:** FAFSA, CSS/Financial Aid PROFILE, noncustodial PROFILE, business/farm supplement. Parent Tax returns. Financial aid filing deadline 3/1. Priority financial aid filing date 3/1. **Notification of Awards:** Applicants will be notified of awards on or about 4/1. **Types of Aid:** *Need-based scholarships/grants:* Federal Pell, SEOG, state scholarships/grants, private scholarships, the school's own gift aid, United Negro College Fund. *Loans:* FFEL Subsidized Stafford, FFEL Unsubsidized Stafford, FFEL PLUS, Federal Perkins, state loans, college/university loans from institutional funds. *Student Employment:* Institutional employment available. **Financial Aid Statistics:** 58% freshmen, 51% undergrads receive need-based scholarship or grant aid. 34% freshmen, 39% undergrads receive need-based self-help aid. 58% freshmen, 52% undergrads receive any aid. 33% undergrads borrow to pay for school. Average cumulative indebtedness $12,297.

YESHIVA UNIVERSITY

500 West 185th Street, New York, NY 10033-3299
Phone: 212-960-5277
E-mail: yuadmit@yu.edu **CEEB Code:** 2990
Fax: 212-960-0086 **Website:** www.yu.edu **ACT Code:** 2992

This private school was founded in 1886. It has a 12-acre campus.

RATINGS
Admissions Selectivity Rating: 60*   **Fire Safety Rating:** 60*   **Green Rating:** 60*

STUDENTS AND FACULTY
Enrollment: 2,866. **Student Body:** 46% female, 54% male, 35% out-of-state, 12% international (53 countries represented). Caucasian 83%, Hispanic 2%.

Retention and Graduation: 90% freshmen return for sophomore year. 49% freshmen graduate within 4 years. **Faculty:** Student/faculty ratio 6.6:1.

ACADEMICS

Degrees: Bachelor's, master's. **Classes:** Most classes have 10–19 students. Most lab/discussion sessions have 10–19 students. **Majors with Highest Enrollment:** jewish/judaic studies; political science and government; psychology. **Special Study Options:** Double major, honors program, independent study, internships, student-designed major, study abroad, teacher certification program **Combined degree programs:** BA/MA, 3-2 and 4-2 engineering programs with Columbia U. **Career services:** Career/job search classes, career assessment, internships.

FACILITIES

Housing: Men's dorms, women's dorms, apartments for married students, apartments for single students. **Special Academic Facilities/Equipment:** Archives and rare book collection, museum of Jewish art, architecture, history, and culture.

CAMPUS LIFE

Activities: Choral groups, concert band, drama/theater, jazz band, literary magazine, music ensembles, musical theater, radio station, student government, student newspaper, yearbook. **Athletics (Intercollegiate):** *Men:* Basketball, tennis, volleyball. *Women:* Basketball, tennis.

ADMISSIONS

Freshman Academic Profile: Average high school GPA 3.46. 48% in top 10% of high school class, 77% in top 25% of high school class, 95% in top 50% of high school class. SAT Math middle 50% range 550–680. SAT Critical Reading middle 50% range 550–690. ACT middle 50% range 22–28. Minimum paper TOEFL 500. **Basis for Candidate Selection:** *Important factors considered include:* Application essay, academic GPA, rigor of secondary school record, standardized test scores, extracurricular activities, interview, talent/ability. *Other factors considered include:* volunteer work, work experience. **Freshman Admission Requirements:** High school diploma is required and GED is accepted. *Academic units recommended:* 4 English, 2 mathematics, 2 science, 2 foreign language, 2 social studies. **Freshman Admission Statistics:** 2,027 applied, 63% admitted, 65% enrolled. **Transfer Admission Requirements:** High school transcript, college transcript(s), essay or personal statement, interview, standardized test scores, Lowest grade transferable 75. **General Admission Information:** Application fee $40. Regular application deadline 2/15. Regular notification 4/1. Nonfall registration accepted. Credit and/or placement offered for CEEB Advanced Placement tests.

COSTS AND FINANCIAL AID

Annual tuition $31,594. Room and board $10,380. Required fees $500. Average book expense $1,224. **Required Forms and Deadlines:** FAFSA, institution's own financial aid form, CSS/Financial Aid PROFILE, state aid form, noncustodial PROFILE, business/farm supplement. Priority financial aid filing date 3/15. **Types of Aid:** *Need-based scholarships/grants:* Federal Pell, SEOG, state scholarships/grants, private scholarships, the school's own gift aid. *Loans:* FFEL Subsidized Stafford, FFEL Unsubsidized Stafford, FFEL PLUS, Federal Perkins, college/university loans from institutional funds. *Student Employment:* Federal Work-Study Program available. Institutional employment available. Highest amount earned per year from on-campus jobs $500. Off-campus job opportunities are good. **Financial Aid Statistics:** 41% freshmen, 40% undergrads receive need-based scholarship or grant aid. 6% freshmen, 4% undergrads receive non-need-based scholarship or grant aid. 35% freshmen, 32% undergrads receive need-based self-help aid. **Criteria for awarding institutional aid:** *Non-need-based:* Academics.

YORK COLLEGE

1125 E. 8th Street, York, NE 68467
Phone: 402-363-5627 **Financial Aid Phone:** 402-363-5625
E-mail: enroll@york.edu
Fax: 402-363-5623 **Website:** www.york.edu **ACT Code:** 2484

This private school, affiliated with the Church of Christ Church, was founded in 1890. It has a 200-acre campus.

RATINGS
Admissions Selectivity Rating: 78   **Fire Safety Rating:** 97   **Green Rating:** 60*

STUDENTS AND FACULTY
Enrollment: 385. **Student Body:** 51% female, 49% male, 69% out-of-state, 1% international (6 countries represented). Asian 2%, African American 5%, Caucasian 72%, Hispanic 4%.

Retention and Graduation: 55% freshmen return for sophomore year. **Faculty:** Student/faculty ratio 7:1. 33 full-time faculty, 36% hold PhDs, 3% are members of minority groups, 27% are women.

ACADEMICS

Degrees: Associate, bachelor's, transfer associate. **Classes:** Most classes have fewer than 10 students. **Majors with Highest Enrollment:** Business administration and management; education; psychology. **Special Study Options:** Double major, dual enrollment, internships, student-designed major, teacher certification program. **Career services:** Alumni network, career assessment. **Career services highlights include:** Most degrees require students to serve in some type of internship before graduation.

FACILITIES

Housing: Special housing for disabled students, men's dorms, women's dorms, apartments for married students. 60% of campus accessible to physically disabled. **Computers:** 100% of libraries, 100% of student union, have wireless network access.

CAMPUS LIFE

Environment: Village. **Activities:** Choral groups, drama/theater, literary magazine, music ensembles, musical theater, student government, student newspaper, yearbook, campus ministries. **Organizations:** 12 registered organizations, 2 honor societies, 1 religious organizations. 4 fraternities, 4 sororities. **Athletics (Intercollegiate):** *Men:* Baseball, basketball, soccer, wrestling. *Women:* Basketball, soccer, softball, volleyball. **On-Campus Highlights:** Mackey Center, Prayer Chapel, Spiritual Life Center/Coffee Shop, Gurganus Hall, Freeman Center.

ADMISSIONS

Freshman Academic Profile: Average high school GPA 3.41. 13% in top 10% of high school class, 25% in top 25% of high school class, 60% in top 50% of high school class. SAT Math middle 50% range 440–560. SAT Critical Reading middle 50% range 450–590. ACT middle 50% range 18–26. Minimum paper TOEFL 500. Minimum computer TOEFL 175. **Basis for Candidate Selection:** *Very important factors considered include:* Class rank, academic GPA, rigor of secondary school record, standardized test scores. *Other factors considered include:* Application essay, recommendation(s), alumni/ae relation, character/personal qualities, extracurricular activities, first generation, level of applicant's interest, religious affiliation/commitment, talent/ability, volunteer work. **Freshman Admission Requirements:** High school diploma is required and GED is accepted. *Academic units required:* 3 English, 2 mathematics, 2 science, 1 social studies, 1 history. *Academic units recommended:* 4 English, 4 mathematics, 4 science, 3 foreign language, 4 social studies, 4 history. **Freshman Admission Statistics:** 531 applied, 57% admitted, 30% enrolled. **Transfer Admission Requirements:** High school transcript, college transcript(s), minimum college GPA of 2 required. Lowest grade transferable 1. **General Admission Information:** Application fee $20. Regular application deadline 8/31. Nonfall registration accepted.

COSTS AND FINANCIAL AID

Annual tuition $12,500. Room and board $4,500. Required fees $1,500. Average book expense $1,500. **Required Forms and Deadlines:** FAFSA. Priority financial aid filing date 4/30. **Notification of Awards:** Applicants will be notified of awards on a rolling basis beginning 3/1. **Types of Aid:** *Need-based scholarships/grants:* Federal Pell, SEOG, state scholarships/grants, private scholarships, the school's own gift aid. *Loans:* Direct Subsidized Stafford, Direct Unsubsidized Stafford, Direct PLUS, FFEL Subsidized Stafford, FFEL Unsubsidized Stafford, FFEL PLUS, Federal Perkins, Federal Nursing, college/university loans from institutional funds. *Student Employment:* Federal Work-Study Program available. Off-campus job opportunities are good. **Financial Aid Statistics:** 89% freshmen, 89% undergrads receive any aid. 89% undergrads borrow to pay for school. **Criteria for awarding institutional aid:** *Non-need-based:* Academics, athletics, leadership, music/drama.

YORK COLLEGE OF PENNSYLVANIA

Country Club Road, York, PA 17403-3651
Phone: 717-849-1600 **Financial Aid Phone:** 717-849-1682
E-mail: admissions@ycp.edu **CEEB Code:** 2991
Fax: 717-849-1607 **Website:** www.ycp.edu **ACT Code:** 3762

This private school was founded in 1787. It has a 190-acre campus.

RATINGS

Admissions Selectivity Rating: 81   **Fire Safety Rating:** 91   **Green Rating:** 60*

STUDENTS AND FACULTY

Enrollment: 5,086. **Student Body:** 55% female, 45% male, 36% out-of-state, international (44 countries represented). Asian 1%, African American 3%, Caucasian 87%, Hispanic 1%.
Retention and Graduation: 78% freshmen return for sophomore year. 42% freshmen graduate within 4 years. 25% grads go on to further study within 1 year. 7% grads pursue arts and sciences degrees. 2% grads pursue law degrees. 14% grads pursue business degrees. 2% grads pursue medical degrees. **Faculty:** Student/faculty ratio 18:1. 154 full-time faculty, 86% hold PhDs, 42% are women.

ACADEMICS

Degrees: Associate, bachelor's, master's. **Classes:** Most classes have 20–29 students. Most lab/discussion sessions have 10–19 students. **Majors with Highest Enrollment:** Biology/biological sciences; business administration and management; nursing/registered nurse (RN, ASN, BSN, MSN). **Special Study Options:** Accelerated program, cooperative education program, double major, dual enrollment, honors program, independent study, internships, liberal arts/career combination, student-designed major, study abroad, teacher certification program. **Honors programs:** Honors Program includes coursework, special academic and career advising and extracurricular enrichment activities **Combined degree programs:** BS/MBA. Special programs offered to physically disabled students include tape recorders, tutors. **Career services:** Alumni network, alumni services, career/job search classes, career assessment, internships, regional alumni. **Career services highlights include:** We are very proud of the experiential education opportunities that all of our students enjoy. Credit-based experiential learning is available in all academic programs and provides reflective learning and practical application of skills. Experiential education offerings vary based upon the academic program, and include internships, independent research, service-learning, course based projects, practica, student teaching, clinical rotations, and many other special learning opportunities. Co-ops are exclusive to our three engineering programs, and students are required to participate in 3 before graduating as well as a number of other hands-on experiences and projects.

FACILITIES

Housing: Coed dorms, men's dorms, women's dorms, fraternity/sorority housing, apartments for single students, wellness housing, theme housing 98% of campus accessible to physically disabled. **Special Academic Facilities/Equipment:** Museum, telecommunications center, science and foreign language labs. All of campus is wired to the computer network. **Computers:** 50% of classrooms, 35% of dorms, 100% of libraries, 100% of dining areas, 80% of student union, 65% of common outdoor areas have wireless network access. Students can register for classes online. Administrative functions (other than registration) can be performed online.

CAMPUS LIFE

Environment: City. **Activities:** Choral groups, concert band, drama/theater, jazz band, literary magazine, music ensembles, musical theater, radio station, student government, student newspaper, symphony orchestra, television station, campus ministries, international student organization, Model UN. **Organizations:** 80 registered organizations, 7 honor societies, 4 religious organizations. 9 fraternities, 7 sororities. **Athletics (Intercollegiate):** *Men:* Baseball, basketball, cheerleading, cross-country, golf, lacrosse, soccer, swimming, tennis, track/field (outdoor), wrestling. *Women:* Basketball, cheerleading, cross-country, field hockey, lacrosse, soccer, softball, swimming, tennis, track/field (outdoor), volleyball. **On-Campus Highlights:** Student Union Spart's Den, TV and Radio Studios, Bookstore, York College Art Galleries, Tyler Run Walking Path.

ADMISSIONS

Freshman Academic Profile: Average high school GPA 3.51. 11.2% in top 10% of high school class, 67.1% in top 25% of high school class, 78.3% in top 50% of high school class. 80% from public high schools. SAT Math middle 50% range 500–590. SAT Critical Reading middle 50% range 490–570. SAT Writing middle 50% range 480–570. ACT middle 50% range 21–25. Minimum paper TOEFL 530. Minimum computer TOEFL 200. **Basis for Candidate Selection:** *Very important factors considered include:* Academic GPA, rigor of secondary school record. *Important factors considered include:* Class rank, standardized test scores, character/personal qualities. *Other factors considered include:* Application essay, recommendation(s), alumni/ae relation, extracurricular activities, interview, level of applicant's interest, talent/ability, volunteer work, work experience. **Freshman Admission Requirements:** High school diploma is required and GED is accepted. *Academic units required:* 4 English, 3 mathematics, 3 science, 2 foreign language, 3 social studies. *Academic units recommended:* 4 mathematics. **Freshman Admission Statistics:** 7,395 applied, 60% admitted, 25% enrolled. **Transfer Admission Requirements:** College transcript(s), minimum college GPA of 2.0 required. Lowest grade transferable C. **General Admission Information:** Application fee $30. Notification on a rolling basis, beginning on or about 10/1. Nonfall registration accepted. Admission may be deferred for a maximum of 1 year. Credit and/or placement offered for CEEB Advanced Placement tests.

COSTS AND FINANCIAL AID

Annual tuition $13,000. Room and board $8,080. Required fees $1,460. Average book expense $1,200. **Required Forms and Deadlines: FAFSA Notification of Awards:** Applicants will be notified of awards on a rolling basis beginning 3/1. **Types of Aid:** *Need-based scholarships/grants:* Federal Pell, SEOG, state scholarships/grants, private scholarships, the school's own gift aid. *Loans:* Direct Subsidized Stafford, Direct Unsubsidized Stafford, Direct PLUS, FFEL Subsidized Stafford, FFEL Unsubsidized Stafford, FFEL PLUS, Federal Perkins, Federal Nursing, college/university loans from institutional funds. *Student Employment:* Federal Work-Study Program available. Institutional employment available. Highest amount earned per year from on-campus jobs $12,022. Off-campus job opportunities are good. **Financial Aid Statistics:** 42% freshmen, 38% undergrads receive need-based scholarship or grant aid. 29% freshmen, 17% undergrads receive non-need-based scholarship or grant aid. 52% freshmen, 51% undergrads receive need-based self-help aid. 86% freshmen, 74% undergrads receive any aid. 69% undergrads borrow to pay for school. Average cumulative indebtedness $20,625. **Criteria for awarding institutional aid:** *Non-need-based:* Academics, alumni affiliation, music/drama.

YORK UNIVERSITY

Bennett Centre for Student Services, 3rd Floor, Toronto, ON M3J 1P3 Canada
Phone: 416-736-5000 **Financial Aid Phone:** 416-872-9675
E-mail: intlenq@yorku.ca **CEEB Code:** 0894
Fax: 416-736-5536 **Website:** www.yorku.ca

This public school was founded in 1959. It has a 550-acre campus.

RATINGS

Admissions Selectivity Rating: 60*   **Fire Safety Rating:** 60*   **Green Rating:** 60*

STUDENTS AND FACULTY

Enrollment: 46,079. **Student Body:** 61% female, 39% male, (170 countries represented).
Retention and Graduation: Faculty: Student/faculty ratio 19:1. 1424 full-time faculty, 44% are women.

ACADEMICS

Degrees: Bachelor's, certificate, diploma, doctoral, master's, post-bachelor's certificate. **Majors with Highest Enrollment:** Psychology. **Special Study Options:** Accelerated program, distance learning, double major, English as a Second Language (ESL), exchange student program (domestic), honors program, independent study, internships, student-designed major, study abroad, teacher certification program. **Combined degree programs:** MBA/LLB, BA/BEd, BSc/BEd, BFA/BEd, MES/LLB, MBA/MFA. Special programs offered to physically disabled students include note-taking services, reader services, tape recorders, tutors. **Career services:** Career/job search classes, career assessment, internships. **Career services highlights include:** The York University International Internship Program (YIIP) provides both York undergraduate and graduate students a non-credit opportunity to apply their academic knowledge to an international work environment and enhance their job-related skills in an international and intercultural setting.

FACILITIES

Housing: Coed dorms, special housing for disabled students, men's dorms, special housing for international students, women's dorms, apartments for married students, apartments for single students, theme housing. **Special Academic Facilities/Equipment:** 5 museums with more than 4.4 million items. Observatory with 2 telescopes. Robotics laboratory. 2 professionally staffed art galleries. 6 student-run art exhibition spaces. 3 theatres. 2 cinemas. 1 screening room. Wide-variety professional standard film and video production facilities. **Computers:** Students can register for classes online. Administrative functions (other than registration) can be performed online.

CAMPUS LIFE

Environment: Metropolis. **Activities:** Choral groups, concert band, dance, drama/theater, jazz band, music ensembles, pep band, radio station, student government, student newspaper, symphony orchestra, yearbook, international student organization, Model UN. **Organizations:** 259 registered organizations, 35 religious organizations. **Athletics (Intercollegiate):** *Men:* Badminton, basketball, cross-country, fencing, football, ice hockey, soccer, swimming, tennis, track/field (outdoor), volleyball, water polo. *Women:* Badminton, basketball, cross-country, fencing, field hockey, ice hockey, rugby, soccer, swimming, tennis, track/field (outdoor), volleyball, water polo. **On-Campus Highlights:** York Lanes: on-campus mall, Tait McKenzie Centre: Sports complex, Student Centre: food court/lounge/club, Accolade East: theatre, art gallery, Central Square: Scott library, food court.

ADMISSIONS

Freshman Academic Profile: Minimum paper TOEFL 560. Minimum computer TOEFL 220. Minimum web-based TOEFL 83. **Basis for Candidate Selection:** *Very important factors considered include:* Academic GPA, rigor of secondary school record. *Important factors considered include:* Standardized test scores. *Other factors considered include:* Class rank, interview. **Freshman Admission Requirements:** High school diploma is required and GED is not accepted. **Transfer Admission Requirements:** College transcript(s), minimum college GPA of 2.5 required. Lowest grade transferable C. **General Admission Information:** Application fee $90. Regular application deadline 2/1. Notification on a rolling basis, beginning on or about 1/1. Nonfall registration accepted. Admission may be deferred for a maximum of 1 year. Credit offered for CEEB Advanced Placement tests.

COSTS AND FINANCIAL AID

Annual in-state tuition $5,761. Annual out-of-state tuition $5,761. Room and board $7,250. Average book expense $1,000. **Required Forms and Deadlines:** FAFSAS. **Types of Aid:** *Loans:* FFEL Subsidized Stafford, FFEL Unsubsidized Stafford, FFEL PLUS, Federal Perkins, Institutionally administered bursaries and international work study positions available on a limited basis. Canadian Student Loans and Provincial Student Loans (for Canadian students). *Student Employment:* Institutional employment available. Off-campus job opportunities are good. **Financial Aid Statistics: Criteria for awarding institutional aid:** *Non-need-based:* Academics, art, music/drama.

SCHOOL SAYS . . .

In this section you'll find hundreds of colleges with extended listings describing admissions, curriculum, internships, and much more. This is your chance to get in-depth information on colleges that interest you. The Princeton Review charges each school a small fee to be listed, and the editorial responsibility is solely that of the college.

ALBERTUS MAGNUS COLLEGE

AT A GLANCE

Albertus Magnus College, a four-year, private, liberal arts college located in the heart of vibrant southern Connecticut, has chosen its small size on purpose. Founded in 1925 by the Dominican Sisters of St. Mary's of the Springs, Albertus Magnus College educates men and women to become leaders in all areas of their lives.

Faculty members at Albertus come from leading universities and are one of the College's greatest assets. Ninety percent of the 75 full and part-time faculty members hold a Ph.D. or the equivalent. The student-staff ratio of 13:1 means that they want to get to know students on an individual basis, and they are readily accessible for academic and personal counseling. The College believes that training in the liberal arts is excellent preparation for life and offers the groundwork for a multitude of professions.

The most popular majors at Albertus include business, communications, criminal justice, education, psychology and sociology. However, there are over 30 areas of study including accounting, art (history and studio), art therapy, biology, business administration, chemistry, child development, communications, counseling and mental health, creative writing, criminal justice, dramatic studies, education (grades 4–12), English, finance, general studies, global studies, graphic design, history, humanities, human services, industrial and organizational psychology, international business, computer information systems, marketing, mathematics, peace and justice studies, performance communications, philosophy and religion, photography, physical sciences, political science, pre-law, pre-medicine, promotional communications, psychology, Spanish, sports communications, sport management, social science, social work and social welfare, sociology, urban studies, and visual arts.

The 50-acre campus is located in a residential neighborhood of New Haven's historic north end. Boasting several turn-of-the-century mansions sprawled over rolling green lawns; the Albertus campus is located in an idyllic New England setting. New Haven is a multicultural city with a population of more than 130,000 people. Both New York City and Boston are easily accessible by train, and for the outdoor enthusiast, there are numerous beaches and hiking trails in the immediate vicinity.

Albertus Magnus College has approximately 500 students in the traditional undergraduate program. The highest percentages of students come from the regional New England states. About 60 percent of the students live on campus in housing that has been converted from large former estate homes. The housing program fosters a strong sense of community spirit, and students often plan informal gatherings and other social events in their residence halls. The Campus Center is a hub of student activities such as comedians, live music, contests, and other unique celebrations.

STUDENT ORGANIZATION AND ACTIVITIES

Being an active part of the Albertus Community is an important part of stepping into your future. After all, the numerous extracurricular activities offered at Albertus are essential to an education committed to engaging your mind, body, and spirit.

Commuter resources: Albertus has an active non-residential student population that takes full advantage of all student activities and athletic opportunities. A Commuter representative is elected each year to the Student Government Association to address concerns and issues of specific importance to commuters.

The Student Government Association is the governing body for all student organizations, publications and clubs. It also operates the House of Bollstadt, the College's pub, which features entertainment such as comedians, hypnotists, theme nights, air hockey, foosball, ping pong, music and television. Students plan major events and activities on campus that include semi-formals, drive-in movies, midnight study breaks, and performances.

The Common Ground is our cyber lounge where students can check their email, work on homework, and enjoy a cup of coffee or tea. It is a popular setting for students to relax in between classes or after a long day.

Other current clubs include:

Animation Club

AMC Choir

Art Club

Best Buddies

Breakwater Literary Magazine

Business Club

Campus Ministry / Faith Works

Computer Club

Dance Team

English Club

The Great Perceiver Newspaper

High On Art Group

History Society

Infused Entity

Magazine Club

Multicultural Student Union

Psychology Club

Outspoken - Gay/Straight Alliance

Residence Hall Association

Science Club

Spanish Club

Students United for a Better World

Women's Leadership Group

ADMISSIONS

Albertus Magnus College welcomes applications from students of all ages, all nationalities, and all ethnic, racial, and religious groups.

The College operates on a rolling admission system. Students are encouraged to contact the Office of Admission for an information packet and application. Students may also visit our website to apply online or download a copy of our application.

Freshmen

Students who either plan to graduate from fully accredited high schools, have received a GED, or have been home schooled with a diploma from an accredited high school.

Transfer

Students who have studied at other accredited institutions. Normally, a cumulative average of 2.0 on a grade scale of 4.0 is required of students transferring from fully accredited institutions. We accept transfer credits from classes in which a grade of C or better was earned. How those credits will transfer into a specific degree program will be determined in an individual session with a representative from the Office of the Registrar.

International

Students who are not United States citizens are encouraged to consider continuing their education at Albertus Magnus College. The small classes and personal attention are a good fit for students who are adjusting culturally to this country. Please note that Albertus Magnus College is unable to offer financial aid or scholarships to international students.

The following items are required of every applicant to Albertus:

1. A completed application form

2. An official high school transcript

3. Official ACT or SAT scores

4. At least one letter of recommendation from a guidance counselor, teacher or college advisor who is familiar with the applicant's academic ability and potential

5. A non-refundable application fee of thirty-five dollars ($35)

6. A personal essay

7. An official college or university transcript for transfer students

The information required above will be used by the Office of Admission in deciding on the merits of applicants. Special consideration may be given to selected candidates whose preparation varies from the recommended pattern, but whose record gives evidence of genuine intellectual ability and interest.

CAMPUS LIFE

The 50-acre campus is located in a residential neighborhood of New Haven's historic north end. Boasting several turn-of-the-century mansions sprawled over rolling green lawns; the Albertus campus is located in an idyllic New England setting. New Haven is a multicultural city with a population of more than 130,000 people. Both New York City and Boston are easily accessible by train, and for the outdoor enthusiast, there are numerous beaches and hiking trails in the immediate vicinity.

Practica and Internships

Practica and internships are required for many majors and recommended for all students. The College gives academic credit for work done outside the classroom that is related to the student's primary field of study. For more information please visit www.albertus.edu.

Study Abroad

Students may spend a semester or full academic year studying abroad in approved American college-sponsored programs. Credits received in these programs are transferable to Albertus. All students are encouraged to take advantage of opportunities for foreign study and travel. Language majors in particular find residence in a country where the language they study is spoken rewarding. Study abroad is arranged through the Department Chair and is generally recommended for a student's junior year.

COST AID

Albertus Magnus College seeks to make it possible for every student accepted for admission to attend the College. Financial assistance is available in the form of scholarships, grants, loans, and employment.

Albertus uses the Free Application for Federal Student Aid (FAFSA) to determine the demonstrated need of each applicant for assistance. We encourage students to complete the FAFSA online at www.fafsa.ed.gov. The Albertus Magnus College school code is 001374.

Students who are accepted for admission and complete their FAFSA prior to February 28 are given first priority for awarding funds.

Each year Albertus Magnus College awards a variety of scholarships and grants. All scholarships and grants awarded from the Office of Admission require the application to the College be submitted and complete by March 15. Students are eligible to receive only one scholarship from the College, and must be graduating from a regionally accredited institution.

Please visit www.albertus.edu for more detailed information about scholarships and financial aid.

Tuition for full-time students during the 2009–2010 academic year is $23,126 . Part-time students (individuals taking fewer than 12 credits a semester) are charged $944 per credit. Room and board totals $9,914. Personal expenses, which should be anticipated, include transportation and other miscellaneous items.

ALVERNIA UNIVERSITY

AT A GLANCE

Located on a beautiful campus on the outskirts of Reading, Pennsylvania, Alvernia University is a private Franciscan institution rooted in the Catholic and liberal arts traditions. Our core institutional values—service, humility, peacemaking, contemplation, and collegiality—extend from the faith of our Franciscan founders, and have a universal ethical appeal. We honor our core Catholic traditions while respecting and welcoming students, faculty, and staff of many religious backgrounds. Alvernia fosters moral leadership and service to others in the interest of peace and justice locally and globally. We prepare our graduates to achieve their personal dreams and professional success, and to be engaged citizens and lifelong learners. Alvernia has been honored by the Templeton Foundation as one of the top 100 character-building colleges in the nation and a model of excellence in education. In addition, we are regularly named to the President's Higher Education Community Service Honor Roll for our commitment to and achievement in community service.

Our 2,800 total students (1,400 of which are traditional undergraduates) choose from over 600 courses and 50 majors and minors in an array of academic programs in our College of Arts and Sciences and College of Professional Programs. All programs are geared toward real-world learning and preparing students for a rewarding career. Study abroad, internships, and international service trips make classroom learning come alive and allow our students to develop practical skills that are valued by employers around the world.

LOCATION AND ENVIRONMENT

Alvernia offers a friendly and welcoming setting that is conducive to learning. The school is set in a tree-lined suburban neighborhood three miles from the center of Reading (population 81,000) in the scenic Blue Mountain area of Eastern Pennsylvania. Reading offers a mix of cultural and entertainment destinations such as the GoggleWorks Center for the Arts, the Reading Public Museum, outlet shopping, minor league sports, and concerts and events at the Sovereign Center. Students also find opportunities for community involvement, internships, and fieldwork experience at many local businesses, agencies, and organizations.

The 121-acre campus, overlooking Angelica Park and set on the Schuylkill River along the majestic Appalachian Mountain Trail, gives students access to a wide range of outdoor activities including hiking, boating, camping, and skiing. In addition, Alvernia is just a few hours by train or car to Philadelphia, New York, Washington, DC, and Baltimore. The Pocono Mountains and the New Jersey and Delaware shores are also close by.

OFF-CAMPUS OPPORTUNITIES

The Washington Center experience is a popular way students expand their educational opportunities beyond the classroom. Earning college credit while spending a semester in Washington, DC, students serve as interns in a congressional office, government agency, major corporation, newspaper, or news network, or an agency devoted to legal affairs, international relations, or business and economics. Others intern with nonprofit groups dealing with the environment, women's issues, the arts, education, science, or labor relations.

Study abroad has become increasingly popular. In recent years, Alvernia students have studied in Great Britain, Germany, Italy, Spain, and in the Semester-at-Sea program.

Some majors require that students earn practical experience working hands-on in their field of interest. These practical opportunities help students make career choices and establish important professional contacts.

MAJORS AND DEGREES OFFERED

Alvernia offers over 50 academic programs of study. Bachelor's degrees are awarded in the following majors: accounting, addiction studies, athletic training, biochemistry, biology (including a medical technology emphasis), business management, chemistry (including a medical technology emphasis), communication, computer information systems, criminal justice administration, education (concentrations in early childhood, middle school, secondary, and special), English, forensic science, general science, history, human resource management, liberal studies, marketing, mathematics, nursing, philosophy, political science, psychology, social work, sport management, theatre, and theology. Pre-professional programs are available in dentistry, law, medicine, and veterinary studies. Alvernia also offers minors and certificate programs.

Master's degrees are awarded in occupational therapy, business administration, nursing, community counseling, education, and liberal studies. A Ph.D. program in leadership is also available.

Since 1967, the Middle States Association of Colleges and Schools has granted Alvernia accreditation. The Education program for elementary and secondary teachers is approved by the Pennsylvania Department of Education. The Occupational Therapy program is fully accredited by the American Occupational Therapy Association. The Bachelor of Science in Nursing has approval by the Pennsylvania State Board of Nursing and is accredited by the Commission on Collegiate Nursing Education. The Athletic Training program is accredited by the Commission on Accreditation of Allied Health Education Programs in cooperation with the Joint Review Committee on Educational Programs in Athletic Training. The Social Work program is accredited by the Council on Social Work Education. The Addiction Studies Program is certified by the Pennsylvania Certification Board. The Business Department is accredited by the Association of Collegiate Business Schools and Programs.

ACADEMIC PROGRAMS

Logical and critical thinking, accurate comprehension, and effective communication are at the heart of Alvernia's academic program. Students' personal development is also highly valued, and the university promotes integrity in academic pursuits, social responsibility, and moral values.

The Genesis Program at Alvernia provides academic advisement for students who have not declared a major. It is an incredible opportunity to dedicate the first few semesters of college to pure exploration of potential fields of study. Through careful examination and counseling, students gain exposure to the opportunities available at Alvernia.

Qualified students may participate in the Alvernia's Honors Program. The Honors Program assists students of outstanding intellectual promise and high motivation who are interested in pursuing future graduate or professional studies or who prefer a more challenging program at the undergraduate level. The program recognizes academic excellence and encourages students to achieve, often letting them work at their own pace. It facilitates a stimulating exchange of ideas and information between students' varied interests and different disciplines. The Honors Program includes co-curricular activities, provides service opportunities, intellectual and social support, and injects significant additional depth in the student's academic program. Honors courses are team-taught by faculty from diverse areas and involve student-led discussions. Students and faculty wishing to do research or explore topics not offered in established courses can arrange independent studies under the direction of a faculty member and often present their work at a departmental seminar.

CAMPUS FACILITIES AND EQUIPMENT

Alvernia's newest academic building, the O'Pake Science Center, a $9.3 million state-of-the-art facility, was opened in 2006. The O'Pake Science Center added 31,582 square feet of classroom, laboratory, and faculty office space to Alvernia's campus. Each of two floors is equipped with five laboratory/classrooms, all of which have smart capability, or Internet access, to bring resources, research, and data from other schools and laboratories into Alvernia's classrooms.

The center of campus academic life is the Franco Library and Learning Center, a beautiful facility that provides a quiet place to study. This facility supports Alvernia's curriculum with a growing collection of information resources including books, periodicals, non-print materials, CD-ROM programs, and online resources. Students enjoy access to a number of interlibrary loan services.

The Student Center includes student organization meeting rooms, seminar rooms, dining facilities, informal gathering areas, and the bookstore. Student services offered at Alvernia include a campus ministry and career, counseling, and health services.

On-campus housing includes traditional residence halls, apartments, suites and townhouses. The newest residence halls were completed in the fall of 2009 and feature contemporary housing for our juniors and seniors. The Village Apartments feature gas fireplaces in atriums and business centers for student use. All of our residential facilities are clean and spacious and equipped with laundry, cable TV, and phones with voice mail. Computer hookup is also available.

Alvernia's campus is fully networked. Students have access to the academic information network and the Internet from their residence hall rooms as well as from other campus locations including classrooms, the library, and labs. All students may hook up personal computers through our secure system. Network access and Alvernia email accounts are available to all students.

TUITION, ROOM, BOARD AND FEES

For the 2010–2011 academic year tuition is $24,980, and room and board is $9,300 (an approximate cost based on the highest priced residence hall and an all you can eat meal plan).

FINANCIAL AID

Ninety-nine percent of students attending Alvernia receive some form of financial aid. Alvernia offers financial aid to students whose personal and family resources are unable to meet the full cost of their Alvernia education. Each year we offer more than $3 million in assistance. Aid usually comes in the form of scholarships, grants, loans, and work-study arrangements. Freshmen who have an outstanding GPA and SAT scores may be eligible for one of the following three merit-based scholarships: the Presidential Scholarship ($12,000), the Trustee's Scholarship ($10,000), and the Veronica Founder's Scholarship ($8,000). Students must be enrolled full-time or half-time to be considered for assistance. Applicants interested in financial aid should submit the FAFSA by mid-February. Continuing Studies students must be accepted in a degree program and complete a matriculation form to be eligible for financial aid.

STUDENT ORGANIZATIONS AND ACTIVITIES

Alvernia encourages students to take advantage of learning opportunities outside of the classroom by participating in any of our more than 50 student clubs, organizations, and service programs. Learning in college takes place by being involved in curricular programs as well as extracurricular activities. Campus organizations offer opportunities to suit the interests of all students, to meet new people, to learn various skills, and to develop leadership abilities.

Athletics are an integral part of the educational mission at Alvernia University. Students may participate in intercollegiate, intramural, and club-level athletic programs. Intercollegiate teams compete at the NCAA Division III level. With a proud athletic tradition, Alvernia competes in the Middle Atlantic States Athletic Conference (MAC), a highly competitive conference, and is also a member of the Eastern Collegiate Athletic Conference.

The Office of Student Activities works with the college's many student organizations to provide a calendar of social, cultural, and other co-curricular activities. The Student Government Association provides an opportunity for leadership through the exercise of personal and group responsibility. All students complete approved community service hours as part of Alvernia's commitment to fostering a reverence for the dignity of all life. Our commitment to peace and justice, and a devotion to the service of others, is especially focused on the materially and spiritually disadvantaged of the local and global community.

ADMISSIONS PROCESS

Our warm Alvernia attitude extends to the ease of applying for admission. Many factors are considered for admission, including academic performance, standardized test scores, class rank, extracurricular activities, and community involvement. Application and admission notification is on a rolling basis; however, applicants are encouraged to submit the admission application as early as possible. In addition to their transcripts and SAT or ACT scores, nursing applicants must also submit two letters of reference.

Alvernia accepts and/or offers special programs for accelerated high school students, non-traditional students (older than 24), transfer students, students with a disability, and international students.

The best way to get to know Alvernia is through a campus visit and tour. Applicants and those considering the school are strongly encouraged to come for an individual campus visit. We will personalize the campus visit to match each student's unique interests. Alvernia also hosts information sessions and open houses throughout the year. They allow prospective freshmen or transfers to meet current students, talk to admissions and financial aid counselors, and meet faculty and coaches. Overnight and shadow visits are also available. We invite you to discover Alvernia.

AMERICAN INTERNATIONAL COLLEGE

WELCOME TO AIC

Our history is tied to America's success. Founded in 1885, American International College was first chartered by the Commonwealth of Massachusetts to educate international immigrants. That's where our commitment to diversity began. Ever since, AIC has been a warm home to students from all over the world and has remained committed to creating and understanding environment where dreams are nurtured and fulfilled.

AT A GLANCE

Today American International College is a private, coeducational, four-year comprehensive institution. We are interracial, interfaith, and international. The college is organized into School of Arts and Sciences; Business Administration; Health Sciences (nursing, occupational therapy and physical therapy); and Continuing and Extended Studies. Currently, AIC is the academic home of approximately 1,600 undergraduate and 1,750 graduate students.

LOCATION AND ENVIRONMENT

The American International Campus is located in the geographic center of the City of Springfield, Massachusetts. Springfield is a typical moderate sized American city of nearly 160,000 people, currently transforming itself from a manufacturing to a service center with a global outreach. It is the hub of a metropolitan statistical area of over 500,000 people.

OFF-CAMPUS OPPORTUNITIES

Springfield is positioned on two major highways that provide quick routes to Hartford, Boston, and New York City. In the spring and fall students can visit the Berkshires, New Hampshire, or Vermont for hiking trips, water sports, and other adventures. In colder weather, hop a bus with other students for a whole day of skiing and snowboarding. There are many local museums, places to dine on high cuisine and down home cooking, performance venues for music and theater, and an international airport less than 30 minutes away. Some of the local highlights are the Basketball Hall of Fame, MassMutual Center for sporting and entertainment events, and Six Flags New England. Students can navigate the city by car, or using the local bus transit system operated by the Pioneer Valley Transit Authority.

UNDERGRADUATE MAJORS

Arts, Education and Sciences

American Studies; Biochemistry; Biology; Chemistry; Communication New Media; Criminal Justice; English; History; Human Biology; Interdepartmental Science; International Studies; Liberal Studies; Political Science; Pre-Education Early Childhood; Pre-Education Elementary; Pre-Education Middle School Education; Pre-Education Moderate Disabilities (Special) Education; Pre-Education Secondary Education; Psychology; Sociology

Business Administration

Accounting; Economics/Finance; General Business; Healthcare Management; Healthcare Marketing; Hospitality & Service Management; International Business; Management; Marketing; Sports and Recreation Management

Health Sciences

Nursing; Occupational Science; Physical Therapy

Continuing and Extended Studies

Accounting; Economics/Finance; General Business; Gerontology; Human Services Administration; Human Services for Diploma Nurses; Liberal Studies; Management; Management and Technology; Marketing; Social Sciences

Graduate Programs

Clinical Psychology; Early Childhood Education; Educational Psychology; Elementary Education; Forensic Psychology; Human Resource Development; Middle/Secondary Education; Reading; School Adjustment Counselor; School Administration; School Guidance Counselor; Special Education; Teaching; Online Pre-Doctoral Action Research Program (Certificate)

Master of Arts and Doctorate

Accounting and Taxation (MS); Business Administration (MBA); Nonprofit Leadership (MS); Public Administration (MPA); Organizational Development; Nursing (MSN); Occupational Therapy (MSOT); Physical Therapy (DPT)

ACADEMIC PROGRAMS

Career Services

The Office of Career Services promotes, coordinates, and provides services to assist students with career guidance and job search strategies. The staff provides not only general information and support, but also individual career counseling to assist in exploring and setting career goals. In addition, there are available resources to assist with career selection and employment outlook and trends in occupational fields.

Students looking for internships and jobs, whether full-time, part-time, or summer employment, can find assistance.

Eugene A. Dexter Student Counseling Center

The Dexter Counseling Center provides confidential assistance to students with problems ranging from coping with the transition to college and personal relationships, to academic and vocational help, to issues that require medical assistance. At the center, you can get referrals for other places to get treatment and support.

English as a Second Language Program (ESL)

The ESL program provides non-native English-speaking students an opportunity to improve their English language skills in preparation for successful matriculation in the college program to which they are admitted. The goals of the program are to help students integrate linguistically, academically, and socially into the college community and to assist the student in the successful completion of graduation requirements.

International Student Office

The international student office has been around from the beginning to provide both, necessary immigration information and programs for international students at American International College. It's a valuable resource for international students, and a great place to start getting to know AIC.

Supportive Learning Services Program

The college has been a pioneer in the field of ensuring full participation and equal educational opportunity for students with disabilities. The college is committed to making reasonable academic, social and physical accommodations for students with disabilities at no charge to the student.

For over 25 years, AIC has also served learning-disabled students with Supportive Learning Services—one of the country's premier LD support programs. This fee-based program offers and extended range of tutoring and accommodating services to the students who require a different approach.

Center for Academic Success

The newly reorganized Center for Academic Success is home to a wealth of academic support services to serve students of various needs. It includes the Academic Resource Center, devoted to promoting and teaching good study skills and providing academic assistance; the ACE program, a federally-funded program designed to assist in the personal growth and professional development of qualifying first-generation students through tutoring, individual counseling, and engagement in campus activities; the Writing Center, a resource for all students at all levels of writing proficiency where they can seek help with general writing skills or specific papers; and broader developmental education and tutoring programs.

Our Campus

Our campus offers a cozy refuge in the heart of a city. There's always room to play in the quad, to meet with friends, or take a moment between classes. In the spring and fall you can relax in the grass, and in the winter, skate on a temporary ice rink.

Aside from our main campus, we also have an athletic facility that includes a fully equipped gym, a brand new stadium and field for use by several teams year round, and even into the evening thanks to newly installed lights, and a new track installed for use by the growing track team and other students.

The Princeton Review's Complete Book of Colleges

Computing on Campus

The college offers several computer labs throughout campus, featuring recently upgraded HP workstations and a communications Mac lab. Computers can go anywhere on campus thanks to a high-speed wireless network accessible from any building, even the dining commons, or the middle of the quad.

The James J. Shea, Sr. Memorial Library

AIC's library is an active learning environment that supports undergraduate instruction, graduate research, and independent study. It also houses the Media Center, the Center for Academic Success, Information Technology, the Communication Center, the Oral History Center, and the College Archives.

Computer terminals in the library provide patrons with access to the Internet, as well as 30 databases and the online catalog. Our databases and online catalog are also available on any computer with an Internet connection with a college-issued user ID.

The Schwartz Campus Center

The campus center houses the offices of the Student Government, the radio station, the student newspaper, the yearbook, and Model Congress, along with many others. It's the perfect place to socialize between classes, grab a quick bite, or check in with the student affairs staff.

The Karen Sprague Cultural Arts Center and The Esther B. Griswold Theatre for the Performing Arts

The West Wing is devoted to the visual and literary arts, with studios and galleries, as well as classroom, conference, and seminar facilities. For most of the year, there are rotating art exhibitions open for viewing anytime, at no cost.

The 500-seat Esther B. Griswold Theatre for the Performing Arts has a proscenium stage with flying space and quality acoustics to permit the presentation of professional musical and dramatic productions. This is the place to see a play, a guest speaker, or a student-run fashion show.

Tuition, Room, Board, and Fees

Undergraduate: Tuition $26,700 Room and board $10,930

Graduate: Tuition: $12,510

FINANCIAL AID

All applicants for need-based financial aid (including AIC Grants, Stafford Loans, Perkins Loans, and Federal Work-Study) must file a FAFSA. If they are notified, on the results of the FAFSA, that they have been selected for verification then they are required to file a signed copy of their parents' most recent U.S. Internal Revenue Service Form 1040 or 1040A including all schedules and W-2s, for income verification purposes. Students also must verify their income by filing a signed copy of their own 1040, 1040A, or 1040EZ with all schedules and W-2 forms. Alternate forms or income verification should be obtained from the Financial Aid Office for those who do not file tax returns. For new students there is no application deadline, but early application is advised, since funds are limited. Upperclassmen must have all application materials, including the processor's analysis of the FAFSA, in the Financial Aid Office on or before May 1.

Continuing Education Students

Financial aid programs are available to continuing education students who register for at least six credits. Programs may include Pell Grants, State Grants, and Stafford Loans.

STUDENT ORGANIZATIONS AND ACTIVITIES

AIC currently offers lots of active clubs and organizations on campus, as well as several honor societies. From student government, to theater, to international politics, it's very easy for students to get involved here, and our community encourages the creation and development of new student organizations. The college also conducts a broad recreational program, providing non-varsity students opportunities to engage in basketball, softball, flag football, soccer, volleyball, dodge ball, as well as many other sports. The recreation department also sponsors special events such as ski trips and extramural tournaments against other regional institutions.

ADMISSIONS PROCESS

The undergraduate admissions process at American International College is designed with the prospective student in mind. The application is conveniently found within the Undergraduate View Book, which you may receive upon request from the Office of Admissions. Students may also apply on-line. To access the online application, go to www.aic.edu and click on Admissions.

American International College employs a policy of "rolling admissions," that is, an application is processed upon receipt and a decision about acceptance is made and immediately communicated to the applicant. Rolling admissions provides both the applicant and the college with a degree of flexibility that eliminates the need to set a specific deadline date for application. However, candidates for admission are encouraged to apply early in the academic year (October, November, December) and may expect an admission decision soon after the necessary credentials have been received. Acceptance to the college is contingent upon the successful completion of high school or its equivalent. A final transcript documenting graduation is required.

Students with academic records satisfactory to American International College are admitted from other colleges in September and January. A transfer student must submit official transcripts of all work undertaken at all institutions attended after high school graduation, whether or not advanced credit is desired.

Students transferring from other accredited colleges are not required to take the SAT.

AMERICAN UNIVERSITY

COLLEGE BASICS

Founded in 1893, American University's 84-acre campus is located in the residential "Embassy Row" neighborhood in the northwest quadrant of Washington, DC. Nestled among embassies and ambassadorial residences, AU's campus offers a safe, suburban environment with easy access via the Metrorail subway system to Washington's countless cultural destinations.

A global center of government, Washington, DC, stands unmatched in academic, professional and cultural resources. Building on the strength of our location, AU's faculty includes scholars, journalists, artists, diplomats, authors and scientists. Combining a liberal arts core curriculum with in-depth professional programs, academics at AU provide the necessary balance between theoretical study and hands-on experience. Our nationally recognized Career Center, ranked 19th in the country by the Princeton Review, will work with you to enhance this experience with access to unique internship and career opportunities available only in Washington, DC. Combine this with our diverse national and international student body and our nationally recognized study abroad program, and American University can open up a world of possibilities.

LOCATION AND ENVIRONMENT

On campus, a majority of undergraduates live in one of seven recently renovated residence halls, all with laundry and cooking facilities on each floor. Dining options include AU's Terrace Dining Room, Subway, Einstein Bros. Bagels, McDonalds and many others. AU's completely wireless campus means that you can take your laptop, PDA or smart phone and work from anywhere. With NCAA Division I Patriot League championship teams, club and intramural sports and a state-of-the-art fitness center, staying active is easy. The over 200 clubs and organizations on AU's campus ensure that you can connect with a group that shares your interests and ideals.

OFF-CAMPUS OPPORTUNITIES

Going to school in Washington, DC, opens up a world of possibilities. You have access to internship and career opportunities found nowhere else in the world. You can visit monuments and sights with national and international significance. With scores of libraries, museums and theatres, culture and knowledge is only ever a few minutes away. Add to that the city's world-renowned restaurants and entertainment venues, and it's clear you'll never be at a loss for something to do. The free shuttle service connecting AU's campus to the Tenleytown/AU Metro station ensures that all of Washington, DC, is easily and safely accessible.

ACADEMICS

College of Arts and Sciences

The College of Arts and Sciences offers numerous majors and minors in the arts, education, humanities, sciences and social sciences as well as premedical and prelaw programs. This liberal arts curriculum is designed not only to impart knowledge, but to build the intellectual skills necessary to be successful in any field.

Kogod School of Business

The Kogod School of Business offers a Bachelor of Science in Business Administration (BSBA) with the option to specialize in one of several business disciplines: Accounting, Entrepreneurship and Innovation, Finance, Information Systems and Technology (IST), International Business, International Finance, International Management, International Marketing, Management, Marketing and Real Estate. Kogod also offers a Bachelor of Science in Business Administration and Language and Culture Studies for those students whose passion for language rivals their passion for business. Kogod's Business and Music (BAM) degree prepares students for a career in the for-profit music sector.

School of Communication

The School of Communication offers five majors: Communication Studies (BA), Journalism (BA), Public Communication (BA), Film and Media Arts (BA) and Foreign Language and Communication Media (BA).

School of International Service

The School of International Service (SIS) offers a major in International Studies (BA) and interdisciplinary degrees in Language and Area Studies (BA). SIS majors combine idealism and pragmatism with a strong sense of community. The school's distinguished faculty is noted for its academic diversity and professional experience in the United States and abroad.

School of Public Affairs

The School of Public Affairs (SPA) offers majors in Justice (BA), Law and Society (BA) and Political Science (BA). The school also offers the interdisciplinary CLEG major, consisting of Communication, Legal Institutions, Economics and Government (BA). There is one consistent theme in these programs: academic study combined with practical experience and a focus on internships and opportunities to participate in special programs. You will work and study with others involved in campus organizations, student government, neighborhood outreach projects and political campaigns.

University Honors Program

The University Honors Program invites the top 15 percent of admitted freshmen and selected transfers to participate each year. The program is characterized by small seminars, individual attention from faculty, unique access to the resources of Washington, DC, individualized Honors advising, preparation and support for national scholarship competitions, an opportunity to live on an Honors floor in a residence hall and the special atmosphere of a community of committed faculty and students.

Degrees offered at American University:

Certificate, Associate, Bachelor's, Postbachelor's certificate, Master's, Doctoral, First-Professional and Combined Bachelors/Masters Degrees

You may earn both a bachelor's and a master's degree in a planned program of study that begins during your junior or senior year. Each AU school or college has its own specific requirements for admission to a combined degree program.

Undergraduate Majors:

American Studies (BA); Anthropology (BA); Art History (BA); Audio Production (BS); Audio Technology (BS); Biochemistry (BS); Biology (BS); Business Administration (BSBA); Business Administration and Language and Cultural Studies (BS); Business and Music (BS); Chemistry (BS); Communication Studies (BA); Journalism (BA); Public Communication (BA); Film and Media Arts (BA); Computer Science (BS); Economics (BA, BS); Elementary Education (BA); Environmental Studies (BA); Fine Arts (BFA); Foreign Language and Communication Media (BA); French Studies (BA); German Studies (BA); Graphic Design (BA); Health Promotion (BS); History (BA); Interdisciplinary Studies (BA, BS); Communication, Legal Institutions, Economics and Government (BA); International Studies (BA); Jewish Studies (BA); Justice (BA); Language and Area Studies:; French/Europe (BA); German/Europe (BA); Russian/Area Studies (BA); Spanish/Latin America (BA); Law and Society (BA); Liberal Studies (BA); Literature (BA); Marine Science (BS); Mathematics (BS); Mathematics, Applied (BS); Multimedia (BA); Music (BA); Musical Theatre (BA); Theatre (BA); Philosophy (BA); Physics (BS); Political Science (BA); Psychology (BA); Russian Studies (BA); Secondary Education (secondary major only); Sociology (BA); Spanish Studies (BA); Statistics (BS); Studio Art (BA); Women's and Gender Studies (BA)

ADMISSIONS

Students can apply using either the AU online application or the Common Application.

Signing up on the AU Prospective Student Portal allows students to apply online, check application status, register for events and interviews and change contact information.

All applications require a $60.00 application fee for processing.

U.S. FRESHMAN ADMISSIONS APPLICATION DEADLINES:

- Fall Semester Early Decision: November 15

- Fall Semester Regular Decision: January 15

U.S. Transfer Student Admission Application Deadlines:

- Fall Semester: March 1 to be considered for scholarships/financial aid

- Fall Semester: July 1

- Spring Semester: November 1

- Summer Semester: April 1

International Freshman Admission Application Deadlines:

- Fall Semester Early Decision Freshmen: November 15

- Fall Semester Regular Decision: January 15

- Spring Semester: September 1

International Transfer Admission Application Deadlines:

- Fall Semester: May 1

- Spring Semester: September 1

STUDENT BODY

AU students have more than 200 undergraduate organizations to choose from. Learn more about clubs and organizations ranging from social and political activity groups to religious and media organizations to student government and performing groups.

One of AU's largest student organizations, the award-winning, student-run Kennedy Political Union brings a diverse group of speakers to AU students. Past speakers include former president Bill Clinton, the Dalai Lama, Madeleine Albright, Rev. Jesse Jackson and Norman Mineta. AU's commencement ceremony offers another opportunity to hear prominent speakers each year.

In addition, the Student Union Board brings concerts and comedians to campus on a regular basis and welcomes volunteer help with production tasks. Previous performers include Jon Stewart, Chris Rock, Green Day and Weezer.

The Student Government represents the interests of undergraduate students at American University. Its objectives are met by sponsoring clubs and organizations that meet the diversified needs of the undergraduate student body and by standing as the voice of the undergraduate student body.

The AU Ambassador Program works with the admissions office to recruit prospective freshman and transfer students to American University. Ambassadors share experiences with prospective students during Showcase AU and Freshman Day, conduct daily tours and day visits, participate in online chats and respond to student e-mails. International students can become an AU Ambassador or participate in the similar AU Diplomat program.

FACILITIES AND EQUIPMENT

AU students have access to a 50,000-watt broadcast center, a state-of-the-art language resource center, multimedia design and development labs, science and computer science laboratories and well-equipped buildings for art and performing arts.

The Katzen Arts Center provides academic space for AU students studying the arts: music, dance, theatre, music theatre, studio art, sculpture, art history, multimedia and graphic design. The center also has a 30,000 square-foot museum that features art and performance installations by local, national and internationally known artists. The Greenberg Theatre hosts quality theatre, music and dance performances by the AU arts programs and professional companies for the AU and Washington, DC, communities.

Computing resources are delivered via a fiber optic network as well as a wireless network. Wireless access for laptop computers and other devices is available everywhere on campus. A HelpDesk for assistance is available via telephone, web, and e-mail.

The Bender Library and Learning Resources Center serves campus information needs with over one million volumes and close to 50,000 sound recordings, videos and other media materials. Its electronic collections include nearly 15,000 electronic journals in all subjects. The library is part of the eight-member Washington Research Library Consortium with a shared online catalog.

Students enjoy our state-of-the-arts fitness center, sports center with indoor and outdoor tracks, soccer and intramural fields and pool. Reeves Field, which is used as a soccer and lacrosse competition site, is recognized as one of the finest fields in the nation.

Our Kay Spiritual Life Center is an interdenominational religious center for over 30 faiths. The center also sponsors a monthly Table Talk series, alternative Spring Break service opportunities and an Interfaith Council.

School Says Tuition and Aid

Applicants must file the FAFSA (Free Application for Federal Student Aid) with the federal processor to be eligible for federal government grants and the CSS Financial Aid Profile form with the College Board by the appropriate deadlines to be eligible for American University grants.

TUITION AND FEES

2010–2011 Costs for Full-time Undergraduates:

Tuition: $36,180

Fees: $517

Average Room and Board: $13,468

The per-credit cost for undergraduate courses is $1,205.

Room and board for non-resident undergraduates living with relatives or off-campus will vary.

For those who would like to stretch out yearly payments, AU offers the American Installment Plan. Admitted students are sent information about the plan with their admit packet.

ARCADIA UNIVERSITY

AT A GLANCE

Founded in 1853, Arcadia is a top-ranked private university in metropolitan Philadelphia offering bachelor's, master's, and doctoral degrees to more than 4,000 students. Undergraduate and graduate students choose from among 75 fields of study and enjoy personal attention in the classroom with an average class size of 16 and a 13:1 student to faculty ratio.

The University's diverse student population represents a cross section of cultural and socioeconomic backgrounds and, at present, Arcadia students come from 46 states and 19 countries. With more than 80% of all full-time undergraduate students residing on campus, Arcadia offers a variety of activities including Division III athletics and more than 55 clubs and organizations.

Arcadia's commitment to students includes opportunities to explore global perspectives, integrate theory with real-world experiences, and benefit from the personal attention that is the hallmark of Arcadia's learning community. Known as the Arcadia Promise, this commitment affirms that students will have a distinctively global, integrative and personal learning experience that prepares them to contribute and prosper in a diverse and dynamic world.

In both 2008 and 2009, the Institute of International Education's *Open Doors Report* ranked Arcadia #1 in the nation for undergraduate participation in study abroad.

U.S. News & World Report ranks Arcadia University among the top master's universities in the North, as one of the top study abroad programs in the nation, and as a "top up-and-coming school."

LOCATION AND ENVIRONMENT

Located in metropolitan Philadelphia, Arcadia features a beautiful rolling campus built around the historic landmark Grey Towers Castle. The University is 12 miles from Center City Philadelphia and only 90 minutes from the Jersey shore and Pennsylvania's Pocono Mountains. Students have access to dozens of museums, galleries, performing arts centers, nightspots, and historic, government, and commercial sites.

INTERNATIONAL STUDY AND OFF-CAMPUS EXPERIENCES

Arcadia University, top-ranked in the nation by *U.S. News & World Report*, offers more than 100 study abroad programs around the world. Students can spend a summer, semester, or full year abroad for approximately the same cost as remaining on the Glenside campus. Through Arcadia's highly innovative Undergraduate Curriculum, students have many pathways to study away while remaining on track to complete their degree in four years.

Arcadia offers two distinct opportunities for students to study abroad during their first year of college. The University's London/Scotland/Spain/Ireland Preview program enables first-year students in good academic standing to earn 2 credits while spending their spring break in London, Scotland, Spain or Ireland for just $495, which includes round-trip airfare, accommodations, and programming. The First Year Study Abroad Experience (FYSAE) gives select incoming students the chance to spend their first or second semester studying abroad. Arcadia's FYSAE and Preview programs have been recognized as among the most innovative international programs in the country by the Princeton Review, the American Council on Education, and *U.S. News & World Report*.

Arcadia offers nine different Majors Abroad Programs (MAPs). Students in these majors spend a year (two semesters) abroad, taking general courses as well as major-related courses at an overseas institution.

Off-campus study in the Philadelphia area includes internships, clinical experiences and fieldwork in most majors.

MAJORS AND DEGREES OFFERED

Arcadia offers Bachelor of Arts degrees in accounting, acting, art and design (art history, pre–art therapy, studio art), biology (allied health, biological basis of behavior, biomedical, conservation, forensics, molecular), business administration (economics, international economics, international human resources, international marketing, management, marketing), chemistry (biochemistry, chemical professions, forensics, health professions), communications (cinema studies, corporate, international cinema, print, video), computer science, computing technology (design, technical), criminal justice, digital media/global media, education (elementary and early childhood, elementary, secondary), English (creative writing, professional writing), fashion studies, fine arts (art education, ceramics, graphic design, interior design, metals and jewelry, painting, photography, pre–art therapy, printmaking), french studies, global legal studies, health administration, history, interdisciplinary science, international business and culture, international studies (globalization, development and human rights, modern Mediterranean world, global public health), Italian studies, liberal studies (applied social science for the global citizen, individualized), management information systems, mathematics (actuarial science), media industries, modern languages, philosophy, political science (international politics, pre-law and political theory, U.S. politics and policy), psychology (pre–art therapy, human resources), scientific illustration, sociology, sound and music, Spanish, Spanish cultural studies, sport psychology, and theater arts and English. Bachelor of Science degrees are offered in accounting, business administration, chemistry, chemistry and business, computer science, international finance, management information systems, marketing, and mathematics. Bachelor of Fine Arts degrees are awarded to students majoring in acting or studio arts with concentrations in ceramics, graphic design, interior design, metals and jewelry, painting, photography, and printmaking. Preparation for certification in art education is offered in conjunction with the B.F.A. program, as is preparation for graduate study in art therapy. A five-year program combines the Bachelor of Arts in education with a Master of Education in special education.

Arcadia's physician assistant studies 4+2 program provides a four-year undergraduate degree in a related field, followed by two years of graduate study in the Physician Assistant Program at Arcadia. Arcadia undergraduates who satisfy the prerequisites are assured admission to the program. The University also offers a combined undergraduate and graduate (4+2.5) program leading to the Doctor of Physical Therapy, with assured admission for undergraduates who meet established criteria. The International Peace and Conflict Resolution Program provides a four-year undergraduate degree followed by two years of study in the Master of Arts in international peace and conflict resolution. The forensic science program provides a four-year undergraduate program in a related field followed by two years in the Master of Science in Forensic Science (M.S.F.S.) program. Arcadia also offers an accelerated 3+2 program leading to the MSFS for entering freshman with strong academic backgrounds.

Arcadia offers several five-year combined programs in education. These include master's degrees in special education, environmental education, literacy education/reading, literacy education/ESL, technology education, and library science.

A dual-degree (3+2) program in engineering is offered in conjunction with Columbia University. An accelerated (3+4) program with Salus University leads to Bachelor of Arts and Doctor of Optometry degrees. A 3+2 program in environmental education leads to a B.A. in biology and a Master of Arts in Education in environmental education. Pre-professional preparation is offered for dentistry, law, medicine, nursing, optometry, veterinary medicine, and other areas.

ACADEMIC PHILOSOPHY

The academic programs at Arcadia University take a personalized approach to education that emphasizes critical thinking and collaborative learning and promotes each student's unique intellectual and personal growth. Close interaction with faculty, including the ability to be a part of research both in the United States and abroad, further allows students to apply their classroom learning in real-world settings.

Arcadia operates on a two semester academic calendar.

CAMPUS FACILITIES AND EQUIPMENT

The campus includes historical buildings as well as extensive modern facilities. A prime academic resource on campus is Landman Library, which offers students increased technology and access to resources both on campus and around the globe. The newly opened Easton Hall academic building features smart classrooms with the latest technology, a café, and an outdoor patio and waterfall, which make great places for students, faculty, and staff to interact.

Arcadia's Kuch Recreation and Athletic Center features the Alumni Gymnasium, which seats 1,500 and includes basketball and volleyball courts. The Lenox Pool is a six-lane wave-resistant swimming pool with adjacent jacuzzi. The Kuch Center also includes the Kuch Hospitality Suite, an indoor track that overlooks the gym, an aerobics/dance studio, fitness center, locker rooms, saunas, first aid/training rooms and the University Bookstore. Construction on a new Student Commons Building will begin in the spring of 2010.

Wireless Internet access is available everywhere on campus and extends to each room in the residence halls. Computer labs—including a Mac lab—are available for student use.

TUITION, ROOM, BOARD AND FEES

For 2009–2010, undergraduate tuition is $30,780 and room and board charges are $10,680 per year. Annual student fees are $480.

FINANCIAL AID

Arcadia believes that a qualified student should not have to choose their college based on financial factors alone. With this philosophy in mind, Arcadia University helps qualified students find the financial assistance they need to attend college. On average, 98 percent of students at Arcadia receive financial aid, and over 97 percent receive grants and scholarships.

Aid is awarded on the basis of need, as determined by the Free Application for Federal Student Aid (FAFSA) and the Arcadia University Financial Aid Application, and is available in the form of grants, loans, and part-time campus employment or some combination of the three. Scholarships are presented annually to entering first-year and transfer students who have achieved academic distinction or have been recognized for outstanding extracurricular accomplishments. In 2009, Distinguished Scholarships, ranging up to $72,000 over four years, and Achievement Awards, ranging up to $52,000 over four years, recognize academic excellence, leadership, and extracurricular accomplishments. A limited number of full-tuition scholarships are available to the top entering first-year undergraduates in the applicant pool. To receive full consideration for financial aid, students should complete their applications and submit the FAFSA and the Arcadia University Financial Aid Application by March 1.

A financial aid calculator for students considering full-time undergraduate enrollment is available at www.arcadia.edu/calculator. This calculator allows students to estimate their eligibility for federal, state, and Arcadia University financial aid (including merit scholarships).

STUDENT ORGANIZATIONS AND ACTIVITIES

With more than 55 clubs and organizations at Arcadia, it's easy to get involved in campus life. Clubs and organizations give students the opportunity to meet people with similar interests and to develop leadership, organizational and management skills. Options include participating in student government, religious and cultural organizations, musical, academic and media-related groups, community service organizations; and athletics.

Arcadia is a member of the National Collegiate Athletic Association (NCAA) Division III and Middle Atlantic States Collegiate Athletic Corporation (MAC), the largest Division III Conference holding NCAA membership. Student-athletes compete in 14 intercollegiate sports. Men's sports include baseball, basketball, golf, soccer, swimming and tennis. Women's sports include basketball, field hockey, lacrosse, soccer, softball, swimming, tennis and volleyball. Men's lacrosse, equestrian and cheerleading are offered as club sports, while intramural sports offer other athletic opportunities.

ADMISSIONS PROCESS

Prospective students are evaluated on the basis of their academic preparation, intellectual achievement, and potential for success. The admissions staff evaluates each application individually. The most important factors in an admissions decision are the student's academic transcript, including the quality of his or her secondary school program, GPA, and class rank. Arcadia also looks closely at standardized test scores, recommendations, and the student's involvement in extracurricular or community activities.

Prospective freshmen must submit a secondary school transcript, official scores from the SAT or ACT, a personal essay, and recommendations from a high school teacher and guidance counselor. The Priority Deadline for freshman applicant review for admission and Arcadia's premier scholarship programs is January 15 for the subsequent fall term.

Students are encouraged to follow a strong high school program of at least 19 academic units. Though not required, it is recommended that students visit the campus. Visit opportunities are varied and include large Open Houses, small frequent info sessions each day and on Saturday by appointment, and one-on-one meetings during the application process. Students applying for transfer admission may apply for the fall or spring semester, and must submit college transcripts from each school they have attended. Transfer students with fewer than 30 college credits are also required to submit their high school transcript and standardized test scores.

ARGOSY UNIVERSITY

THE HUMAN SIDE OF SUCCESS

Argosy University is a post-secondary institution offering a variety of degree programs that focus on the human side of success alongside professional competence.

AT A GLANCE

To compete in today's workforce, you need a solid foundation of knowledge—and the power to put it to work. And that's exactly what an Argosy University education offers.

For students looking for a more personal approach to education, Argosy University may just be the answer. All graduate and undergraduate programs (and there are over 48 nationwide, across 19 campuses and 13 states) emphasize interpersonal skills as well as academic learning. And all are taught by practicing professionals who bring top-level, real-world experience—and clear-eyed realism—into the classroom. So students graduate with both a solid foundation of knowledge, and the power to put it to work. To accommodate busy working adults, many programs at Argosy University are structured flexibly: with both campus and online learning, and evening, weekend and daytime classes. There's also a wide range of financial aid options for students who qualify.

Argosy University is committed to creating a supportive learning environment and providing our students with a wealth of opportunities and resources. Our focus on personal development coupled with a curriculum that includes relevant, real-world skills is designed to provide our students with a high quality education.

LOCATION AND ENVIRONMENT

Argosy University, Atlanta

College of Undergraduate Studies; College of Psychology and Behavioral Sciences; College of Business; College of Education

980 Hammond Drive, Suite 100, Atlanta, GA 30328

770-671-1200 or 888-671-4777

Argosy University, Chicago

College of Undergraduate Studies; College of Psychology and Behavioral Sciences; College of Business; College of Education

225 North Michigan Avenue, Suite 1300, Chicago, IL 60601

312-777-7600 or 800-626-4123

Argosy University, Dallas

College of Undergraduate Studies; College of Psychology and Behavioral Sciences; College of Business; College of Education

5001 Lyndon B. Johnson, Freeway, Heritage Square, Farmers Branch, TX 75244

214-890-9900 or 866-954-9900

Argosy University, Denver

College of Undergraduate Studies; College of Psychology and Behavioral Sciences; College of Business; College of Education

7600 E. Eastman Avenue, Denver, CO 80231

303-248-2700 or 866-431-5981

Argosy University, Hawaii

College of Undergraduate Studies; College of Psychology and Behavioral Sciences; College of Business; College of Education

400 ASB Tower, 1001 Bishop Street

Honolulu, HI 96813

808-536-5555 or 888-323-2777

Argosy University, Inland Empire

College of Undergraduate Studies; College of Psychology and Behavioral Sciences; College of Business; College of Education

636 East Brier Drive, Suite 120, San Bernardino, CA 92408

909-915-3800 or 866-217-9075

Argosy University, Los Angeles

College of Undergraduate Studies; College of Psychology and Behavioral Sciences; College of Business; College of Education

5230 Pacific Concourse, Suite 200, Los Angeles, CA 90045

310-866-4000 or 866-505-0332

Argosy University, Nashville

College of Undergraduate Studies; College of Psychology and Behavioral Sciences; College of Business; College of Education

100 Centerview Drive, Suite 225, Franklin, TN 37214

615-525-2800 or 866-833-6598

Argosy University, Orange County

College of Undergraduate Studies; College of Psychology and Behavioral Sciences; College of Business; College of Education

601 South Lewis Street, Orange, CA 92868

714-620-3700 or 800-716-9598

Argosy University, Phoenix

College of Undergraduate Studies; College of Psychology and Behavioral Sciences; College of Business; College of Education

2233 West Dunlap Avenue, Phoenix, AZ 85021

602-216-2600 or 866-216-2777

Argosy University, San Diego

College of Undergraduate Studies; College of Psychology and Behavioral Sciences; College of Business; College of Education

1650 Murray Canyon Road, Suite 100, San Diego, CA 92108

619-321-3000 or 866-505-0333

Argosy University, San Francisco Bay Area

College of Undergraduate Studies; College of Psychology and Behavioral Sciences; College of Business; College of Education

1005 Atlantic Avenue, Alameda, CA 94501

510-217-4700 or 866-215-2777

Argosy University, Salt Lake City

College of Undergraduate Studies; College of Psychology and Behavioral Sciences; College of Business; College of Education

121 Election Road, Suite 300, Draper, UT 84020

801=601-5000 or 888-639-4990

Argosy University, Sarasota

College of Undergraduate Studies; College of Psychology and Behavioral Sciences; College of Business; College of Education

5250 Seventeenth Street, Sarasota, FL 34235

941-379-0404 or 800-331-5995

Argosy University, Schaumburg

College of Undergraduate Studies; College of Psychology and Behavioral Sciences; College of Business; College of Education

999 North Plaza Drive, Suite 111, Schaumburg, IL 60173

847-969-4900 or 866-290-2777

Argosy University, Seattle

College of Undergraduate Studies; College of Psychology and Behavioral Sciences; College of Business; College of Education

2601-A Elliott Avenue, Seattle, WA 98121

206-283-4500 or 888-283-2777

Argosy University, Tampa

College of Undergraduate Studies; College of Psychology and Behavioral Sciences; College of Business; College of Education

1403 North Howard Avenue, Tampa, FL. 33607

813-393-5290 or 800-850-6488

Argosy University, Twin Cities

College of Undergraduate Studies; College of Psychology and Behavioral Sciences; College of Business; College of Education; College of Health Sciences

1515 Central Parkway, Eagan, MN 55121

651-846-2882 or 888-844-2004

Argosy University, Washington, DC

College of Undergraduate Studies; College of Psychology and Behavioral Sciences; College of Business; College of Education

1550 Wilson Boulevard, Suite 600, Arlington, VA 22209

703-526-5800 or 866-703-2777

MAJORS AND DEGREES OFFERED

Argosy University offers Doctoral, Master's, and Bachelor's degrees in four major disciplines through our College of Undergraduate Studies, College of Psychology and Behavioral Sciences, College of Education, College of Business, and College of Health Sciences. Our College of Health Sciences also offers Associate's degree programs. Program offerings vary by campus.

Associate's: Dental Hygiene, Diagnostic Medical Sonography (Ultrasound), Histotechnology, Medical Assisting, Medical Laboratory Technology, Radiation Therapy, Radiologic Technology, and Veterinary Technology

Bachelor's: Business, Criminal Justice, Liberal Arts, Medical Technology, Psychology, Master's: Business, Education, Health Service, Counseling, and Psychology, Doctoral: Business, Education, Counseling, and Psychology

ACADEMIC PROGRAMS

Accreditation: Argosy University is accredited by the Higher Learning Commission and a member of the North Central Association (30 North LaSalle Street, Suite 2400, Chicago, IL 60602, 1-800-621-7440, www.ncahlc.org.)

The Commission on Accreditation of the American Psychological Association (APA) (750 First Street N.E., Washington, DC 20002-4242, 1-202-336-5979) has granted accreditation to the Doctor of Psychology in Clinical Psychology programs at the following Argosy University campuses:

- Argosy University, Atlanta
- Argosy University, Chicago
- Argosy University, Hawai'i
- Argosy University, Orange County
- Argosy University, Phoenix
- Argosy University, San Francisco Bay Area
- Argosy University, Schaumburg
- Argosy University, Tampa
- Argosy University, Twin Cities
- Argosy University, Washington DC

The Council for Accreditation of Counseling and Related Educational Programs (CACREP), a specialized accrediting body recognized by the Council for Higher Education Accreditation (CHEA), has granted accreditation to the Mental Health Counseling (MA degree) program at Argosy University, Sarasota. Council for Accreditation of Counseling and Related Educational Programs, 599 Stevenson Avenue, Alexandria, VA 22304, 703.823.9800, www.cacrep.org.

The Council for Accreditation of Counseling and Related Educational Programs (CACREP), a specialized accrediting body recognized by the Council for Higher

Education Accreditation (CHEA), has granted accreditation to the Community Counseling (M.A. degree) program at Argosy University, Schaumburg and Argosy University, Washington, DC. Council for Accreditation of Counseling and Related Educational Programs, 599 Stevenson Avenue, Alexandria, VA 22304, 703.823.9800, www.cacrep.org.

The following programs at Argosy University, Twin Cities, are accredited as noted:

The Associate of Applied Science in Diagnostic Medical Sonography Degree Program is accredited by the Commission on Accreditation of Allied Health Education Programs (www.caahep.org) upon the recommendation of the Joint Review Committee on Education in Diagnostic Medical Sonography (JRC-DMS). Commission on Accreditation of Allied Health Education Programs, 1361 Park Street, Clearwater, FL 33756, 1-727-210-2350.

The Argosy University, Twin Cities' Echocardiography concentration in the Associate of Applied Science in Diagnostic Medical Sonography program is accredited by the Commission on Accreditation of Allied Health Education Programs upon the recommendation of the Joint Review Committee on Education in Diagnostic Medical Sonography (JRC-DMS). Commission on Accreditation of Allied Health Education Programs, 1361 Park Street, Clearwater, FL 33756, 1-727-210-2350.

The Associate of Applied Science in Histotechnology Degree Program is accredited by the National Accrediting Agency for Clinical Laboratory Sciences (8410 West Bryn Mawr, Suite 670, Chicago, IL 60631, 1.773.714.8880).

The Associate of Applied Science in Medical Assisting Degree Program is accredited by the Commission on Accreditation of Allied Health Education Programs (www.caahep.org) upon the recommendation of the Curriculum Review Board of the American Association of Medical Assistants Endowment (AAMAE) (1361 Park Street, Clearwater, FL 33756, 1-727-210-2350).

The Associate of Applied Science in Radiologic Technology Degree Program is accredited by the Joint Review Committee on Education in Radiologic Technology (20 North Wacker Drive, Suite 2850, Chicago, IL 60606, 1-312-704-5300).

The Associate of Applied Science in Veterinary Technology Degree Program is accredited through the American Veterinary Medical Association (AVMA) Committee on Veterinary Technician Education and Activities (CVTEA) (1931 North Meacham Road, Suite 100, Schaumburg, IL 60173, 1-847-925-8070).

The Associate of Science in Dental Hygiene Degree Program is accredited by the Commission on Dental Accreditation. The Commission is a specialized accrediting body recognized by United States Department of Education. The Commission on Dental Accreditation can be contacted at 1-312-440-4653 or at 211 East Chicago Avenue, Chicago, IL 60611.

The Associate of Science in Medical Laboratory Technology Degree Program is accredited by the National Accrediting Agency for Clinical Laboratory Sciences (8410 West Bryn Mawr, Suite 670, Chicago, IL 60631, 1-773-714-8880).

The Associate of Science in Radiation Therapy Degree Program is accredited by the Joint Review Committee on Education in Radiologic Technology (20 North Wacker Drive, Suite 2850, Chicago, IL 60606-3182, 1-312-704-5300).

FINANCIAL AID

Financial aid is available for those who qualify—from Federal aid programs and merit-based awards to loans and a work-study program. We work individually with students to guide you through the application process. Our financial aid experts can help determine the types of aid you are eligible to receive. In many cases, payments can be deferred until after graduation. For more information, please contact the Director of Admissions at the campus of your choice or visit www.argosy.edu.

ADMISSIONS PROCESS

Each program of study carries specific admission requirements. A personal contact in our Admissions Department can answer questions, arrange a campus tour, and help you through the admission process. To determine the admission requirements for the program you wish to enter, contact the Office of Admissions at the campus of your choice or visit www.argosy.edu/pr.

School Says . . .

ASSUMPTION COLLEGE

THE COLLEGE SAYS

Established in 1904 by the Augustinians of the Assumption, Assumption College is a coeducational institution known for its classic liberal arts curriculum and strong academic programs in business and professional studies. Our 2,113 undergraduates choose among 39 majors and 44 minors, gaining the depth and breadth of knowledge that is the foundation of lifelong success. Their educational experience is grounded in the rich Catholic intellectual tradition, which cultivates both the intellect and personal values students need to meet the demands of a constantly changing world. Undergraduates and graduate students closely interact with faculty members and staff in a thriving community that forms graduates known for critical intelligence, thoughtful citizenship and compassionate service.

The academic atmosphere is marked by individual attention and the quest for personal excellence. With a student/faculty ratio of just 12:1, Assumption's professors serve as mentors who challenge students to ask questions, find their own answers and grow—intellectually, socially, and spiritually. Students are encouraged to gain hands-on experience at internships and to participate in individual research projects. Ninety-seven percent of Assumption graduates are employed or in graduate school within six months of graduation.

Located on 185 acres, the beautiful Assumption campus is situated in a residential neighborhood just minutes from downtown Worcester, Massachusetts, the second-largest city in New England. At Assumption, 90 percent of the undergraduates live on campus and housing is guaranteed for all four years. The campus is lively seven days a week with academic programming, activities sponsored by student clubs and organizations, community service opportunities, campus ministry programs and intercollegiate, intramural and club sports. The College's state-of-the-art recreation center supports the well-being of all students.

LOCATION AND ENVIRONMENT

Worcester is a college town that is home to more than 30,000 students. Great restaurants, cultural venues and programs, retail and entertainment options, and professional sports teams offer students many off-campus activities. Worcester is also a great location for an array of internship and career opportunities. In addition, Boston and Providence are only an hour's drive away, and there is regular commuter rail service to Boston.

OFF-CAMPUS OPPORTUNITIES

As a member of the Colleges of Worcester Consortium, an association of the 13 higher learning institutions in the Worcester region, Assumption students can register for courses at the other colleges and participate in their social and cultural events. Free shuttle buses run regularly among several of the campuses.

Assumption encourages students to expand their horizons. Undergraduates can spend a semester or a year studying abroad—from France and England, to Japan, the Czech Republic and Australia, to name a few locations. Many students also augment their education and hone professional skills through local, regional, national and international internships. Assumption students have worked at diverse organizations around the globe, from the Department of Commerce, Central America Bureau and the Department of State (NAFTA Agreement), to Smith Barney, Fidelity, Morgan Stanley, ABC News, and the Alliance Francaise in Paris.

MAJORS AND DEGREES OFFERED

The College offers 39 different Bachelor of Arts degrees. The most popular programs include English (concentrations in literature or writing and mass communications), history, political science, psychology, the natural sciences—biology, biotechnology and molecular biology, chemistry and environmental science, education, human services and rehabilitation studies, and business disciplines such as accounting, international business, management, marketing and organizational communication. Minors are offered in 44 areas.

Pre-professional preparation is available for dentistry, medicine, and law. Joint seven-year programs also are available for those interested in physical therapy, podiatry, or optometry. In addition, Assumption offers graduate degrees in business, special education, school counseling, counseling psychology and rehabilitation counseling. The College also has agreements with a number of highly regarded institutions so that students can continue their education in medical technology, engineering (a 3/2 program with University of Notre Dame) and law (3/3 programs with Duquesne and Western New England Law Schools).

ACADEMIC PROGRAMS

The College's classic liberal arts curriculum promotes the lively discussion of the books, ideas, people and events that have shaped civilization. Faculty and students explore the rich Catholic intellectual tradition as they seek "truth" and the nature of the world. In all areas of academic study, students learn not only how to ask questions, but also how to find the answers. That is why so many classes at Assumption are discussions, not lectures, and why the faculty assign cooperative projects and frequent writing and hands-on assignments. The curriculum is designed to teach the student how to think, not simply memorize.

Assumption also offers academic programs and courses that help students achieve their full potential. The College's first-year program engages new students with linked courses from two disciplines and coordinated activities that complement classroom experiences. The same 20 students take courses in the fall and spring semesters, enabling them to make important intellectual connections while also getting to know other students. The Honors Program and the Fortin and Gonthier Foundations of Western Civilization Program encourage students to challenge themselves intellectually. Students broaden their worldview and their practical experiences through study abroad and internships. Cross-registration through the Colleges of Worcester Consortium enables Assumption students to take classes at Clark, WPI and Holy Cross, among others. Air Force and Army ROTC are also available.

Assumption College follows a traditional two-semester calendar, from late August to mid-May, as well as an optional January intersession. The Graduate School and the Center for Continuing and Career Education also offer two summer sessions for students.

In order to graduate, students must have 120 semester credits, with 9 to 12 in the upper division of their major. Assumption requires all students complete a course in English composition and a writing emphasis course, two courses in philosophy, two courses in theology, and three courses in two of the following three areas: mathematics, laboratory science, or foreign language. Students must complete additional courses in literature, humanities and history, three courses in social science, and one course in art, music or theater.

CAMPUS FACILITIES AND EQUIPMENT

Assumption offers first-rate facilities for learning and living and virtually all the campus is wireless. Key facilities include:

The Information Technology Center has computer labs, and classrooms used for collaborative projects, multimedia presentations, foreign language work and leading-edge software and computer systems.

The Richard and Janet Testa Science Center houses the Department of Natural Sciences and features multi-use classrooms with state-of-the-art technology; 10 teaching laboratories, seven laboratories dedicated for faculty and student research; a working greenhouse, conference rooms and student lounge areas.

The Emmanuel d'Alzon Library is an ideal location to study, research and relax. The professional library staff, the collection of 200,000 volumes, 1,125 journal subscriptions and extensive access to local, regional and national library networks and databases are vital resources for students and faculty.

Assumption's Multi-Sport Stadium, a lighted, synthetic turf field with seating for 1,200 is the home of Assumption's intercollegiate field hockey, football, men's and women's lacrosse and men's and women's soccer teams and the College's extensive outdoor intramural programs. The Plourde Recreation Center features a swimming pool, exercise and wellness classes, courts, and a fitness facility that is accessible to all students, faculty and staff.

A variety of housing options are available to accommodate the 90 percent of undergraduates who live on campus. Traditional residence halls, suites, the living/learning center and apartments provide housing options for all four years. All resident students have individual hard-wired and wireless high speed Internet access in their rooms, as well as in the computer labs.

TUITION, ROOM, BOARD AND FEES

For 2009–10, tuition was $29,806; room and board was $10,070. The board plan is required for all first-year students. All student fees amounted to $880.

FINANCIAL AID

This past year, Assumption awarded more than $23 million in financial assistance to students. The College offers need-based financial aid, as well as merit-based assistance. All students who apply for admission are considered for merit scholarships ranging from $2,500–$20,000 annually and recipients are chosen based on their academic excellence and demonstrated student leadership. To qualify for need-based financial aid, students must submit the Free Application for Federal Student Aid (FAFSA) by February 1.

STUDENT ORGANIZATIONS AND ACTIVITIES

The 2,113 undergraduates at Assumption come from 25 states and 9 foreign countries. Ninety percent of the students reside on campus and housing is guaranteed for all four years. Numerous social, athletic, recreational and cultural activities are offered on- and off- campus and make Assumption a dynamic place to live.

Assumption College has 60 clubs and organizations that seek to complement the educational process and offer opportunities for students to develop their interests and talents. Students can participate in academic/professional clubs, arts and entertainment groups, student publications, politics and student government, service projects, special interest groups, or spiritual activities. These clubs and organizations also give students opportunities to develop their leadership and team-building skills.

Assumption offers 23 intercollegiate teams, as well as 10 club and 10 intramural sports. The College is a charter member of the Northeast-10 Conference and competes as an NCAA Division II institution. The intercollegiate sports for men include: baseball, basketball, cross-country, football, golf, hockey, lacrosse, soccer, tennis and track & field (indoor and outdoor). Women's sports include: basketball, cross-country, field hockey, lacrosse, rowing, soccer, softball, swimming, tennis, track & field (indoor and outdoor) and volleyball.

Through the Student Government Association (SGA), the Campus Activities Board (CAB), and the many student clubs and organizations, Assumption College offers a wide range of co-curricular events. This includes many large-scale events, such as Family Weekend, Siblings Weekend, Welcome Week, Midnight Madness and the Spring Concert. Other more frequent events include comedians, coffeehouses, films, lectures, off-campus trips and many special events.

ADMISSIONS PROCESS

Assumption College admits students who demonstrate an active intellect and self-motivation and who have compiled a solid academic record and completed all prescribed high school requirements.

The College encourages prospective students to schedule a campus visit prior to applying for admission. During the summer months, high school students are encouraged to attend group information sessions, tours and interviews Monday-Friday. In the fall semester, prospective students may attend group information sessions on Saturdays, or schedule a campus visit during the week.

To apply, students are required to submit an Assumption online or paper application (the Common and Universal Applications are accepted), a $50 application fee, official high school transcripts, and a letter of recommendation. Assumption is test-score optional, so SAT or ACT scores are not required. Applications, including all supporting documents and recommendations, must be received in the Office of Admissions by February 15. Students who want to be considered for Early Action must apply by November 15.

For more information, please contact:

Assumption College

Office of Admissions

500 Salisbury Street

Worcester, MA 01609

Telephone: 866-477-7776 (toll free) or 508-767-7285

Web: www.assumption.edu

E-mail: admiss@assumption.edu

AURORA UNIVERSITY

AT A GLANCE

Founded in 1893, Aurora University describes itself as "an inclusive community dedicated to the transformative power of learning." Undergraduates can earn bachelor's degrees in any of 40 degree programs. Emphasis is placed on both classroom learning and hands-on learning experienced in internships and clinical experiences. Many of the academic programs offered are in pre-professional fields such as athletic training, business, education, nursing, and social work. In addition, traditional liberal arts majors are offered. The university has a growing program in the fine arts, including art, music and theatre. Scholarships are awarded to outstanding music and theatre students based on auditions.

Located in an attractive residential neighborhood on the southwest side of Aurora, Illinois—the state's second largest city with population of over 170,000—the 30-acre campus is located only minutes from the Illinois Research and Development Corridor, home to dozens of nationally-and internationally-based businesses. Along with the campus in Aurora, undergraduate and graduate degree programs are offered at the George Williams College campus near Lake Geneva, Wisconsin.

The university offers the range of programs characteristic of a university as well as the benefits of the personal attention characteristic of a small college. Students who are open about their major will discover the right field of study through the general education program. Highly motivated students with a high school GPA of 3.0 or above and an ACT of 25 or higher are invited to join the AU Honors Program. At the heart of the program is the opportunity to participate in advanced coursework, innovative seminars, and special events.

The campus centers on "the Quad"—a grassy area at the center of the campus. Surrounding the Quad, housing is offered to undergraduates. The newest academic building completed in 2006 is the Institute for Collaboration, which houses the College of Education as well as classrooms for AU students and 200 elementary students from the West Aurora School District. Total university enrollment is over 4,300, including 2,400 undergraduates. Over 95% of students receive financial aid with over $12 million in scholarships awarded in 2009-2010.

LOCATION AND ENVIRONMENT

Located on the southwest side of Aurora, Illinois, the state's second largest city, Aurora University is nestled in a residential area just minutes from the prestigious high-tech corridor that stretches along I-88 across the northern part of the state. The university is housed on a 30-acre campus with a blend of historic and new academic, administrative, and residential buildings. The university's George Williams College campus and conference center sits 70 miles to the north, along the banks of Geneva Lake in Wisconsin.

The campus is welcoming with faculty members who are passionate about their subject matter and have devoted their professional lives to students. There are no packed lecture halls with teaching assistants. Rather classes are small, 23 students on average, and faculty know students by name. The first-year program recognizes the unique needs of first-year students and guides them through the transition from high school to college.

Campus organizations abound with over 50 musical, literary, religious, social and service groups to consider. Students can develop their leadership skills or make lifelong friends through student government or academic societies. Studies show that students who are involved in activities outside of the classroom are more satisfied with their college experience.

Athletics are an important tradition at Aurora University. About one-fourth of traditional AU students participate in intercollegiate athletics. Students have a choice of 19 intercollegiate NCAA Division III sports for men and women. Lacrosse will be added in 2010. In recent years, Spartan teams have compiled an amazing 51 conference titles. Twelve intramural sports allow students to compete in round robin tournaments with fellow students.

OFF-CAMPUS OPPORTUNITIES

Getting involved in activities on campus is a great way to meet new people and learn skills that will be helpful in life after college. With over 50 clubs and organizations and NCAA division III intercollegiate athletics, it is easy to find other students with similar interests. There are academic and professional clubs, fine arts and cultural opportunities, and many ways to develop leadership skills.

MAJORS AND DEGREES OFFERED

Accounting (B.A. or B.S.); Actuarial Science (B.S.); Art (B.A.); Athletic Training (B.S.); Biology (B.A. or B.S.); Business Administration (B.A. or B.S.); Business and Commerce (B.A. or B.S.); Coaching and Youth Sport Development (B.A.); Communication (B.A.); Computer Science (B.A. or B.S.); Criminal Justice (B.A.); Elementary Education (B.A.); English (B.A.); Finance (B.A. or B.S.); Health Science (B.S.); Allied Health Program; Pre-Dentistry; Pre-Medicine; Pre-Veterinary Medicine; History (B.A.); Management Information Technology (B.A. or B.S.); Marketing (B.A. or B.S.); Mathematics (B.S.); Museum Studies (minor only); Music (minor only); Nursing (B.S.N.); Organizational Management (B.A. or B.S.); Parks and Recreation (B.S.) – Wisconsin campus; Physical Education (B.A. or B.S.); Fitness and Health Promotion; K-12 Teaching Certification; Political Science (B.A.); Pre-Law (supplemental major); Psychology (B.A.); Religion (B.A.); Secondary Education (supplemental major); Social Work (B.S.W.); Sociology (B.A.); Spanish (B.A.); Special Education (B.A.); Theatre (B.A.)

ACADEMIC PROGRAMS

Bachelor of Arts

Bachelor of Science

Bachelor of Science in Nursing

Bachelor of Science in Social Work

Master of Science in Social Work

Master of Business Administration

Master of Science in Recreation Administration

Master of Arts in Curriculum and Instruction

Master of Arts in Educational Leadership

Master of Arts in Special Education

Master of Arts in Teaching with Certification

Master of Science in Mathematics

Master of Arts in Reading Instruction

Post-Baccalaureate Secondary Teaching Certification

ESL/Bilingual Endorsement

Doctor of Education

CAMPUS FACILITIES AND EQUIPMENT

Aurora University's 30-acre campus is home to 23 instructional, recreational, administrative, and residential buildings. Some are historic, while others are new. But all surround "the Quad"—a grassy area at the center of the campus. The newest building completed in 2006 is the Institute for Collaboration, which houses the College of Education as well as classrooms for AU students and faculty offices. New performance venues include the 500-seat Crimi Auditorium and 200-seat Perry Theatre in the Aurora Foundation Center for Community Enrichment. The Schingoethe Museum of Native American Culture welcomes student groups, the general public, and scholars. Just 70 miles to the north sits the university's George Williams College campus and conference center on the banks of Geneva Lake in Wisconsin.

TUITION, ROOM, BOARD AND FEES

2010–2011 Tuition:

Full-time	$18,600 per year
Part-time	$550 per semester hour
Room and Board	$8,170 per year (average)
Activity Fee	$50 per year
Lab Fees	$37 per course
Parking Permit	$25 per year

FINANCIAL AID

Scholarships, many of which are endowed by generous donors to the university, and some grants are awarded to full-time undergraduate students based on their high school grade point average (GPA) and composite ACT score. Awards are renewable for up to four years for students who maintain the required renewable GPA for each scholarship level. Merit awards for the 2009–2010 academic year ranged from $2,000 to $10,000 per year.

Need-based financial aid is based on information received from the Free Application for Federal Student Aid (FAFSA). Need-based financial aid includes grants, loans, and student employment. Grants include the Federal Pell Grant, Federal Supplemental Educational Opportunity Grants (SEOG), State of Illinois MAP Grants, and Aurora University Grants. Loans that are available include the Federal Perkins Loans, Federal Direct Stafford Loans (both subsidized and unsubsidized), Federal Direct Undergraduate PLUS Loans, alternative loans and Aurora University Student Loans (AUSL). Federal Work Study (FWS) and on-campus employment are available.

In order to be considered for scholarships or financial aid, students must first apply and be approved for admission. The FAFSA makes it possible to be considered for all need-based federal and state funding. Students are urged to complete the FAFSA on the Web at www.fafsa.gov.

STUDENT ORGANIZATIONS AND ACTIVITIES

Accounting Club; Aurora University Arts United; Aurora University Student Association; Activities Programming Board; Accounting Club; American Criminal Justice Association; AU Communication Club; Black Student Association; Cheerleading and Dance Team; Circle K International; Club Fit; Colleges Against Cancer; Delta Mu Delta (business club); Drama/Theater Club; Fellowship of Christian Athletes; Feminist Society; Fitness and Health Promotion; Future Attorneys of Aurora; Future Educators of Aurora University; Future Leaders of the World; Games Club; GLOBAL; History Club; Inter Varsity Christian Fellowship; Kappa Delta (International Honor Society); Kappa Delta Pi (International Honor Society in Education); Lambda Pi Eta (National Honorary Society for Speech Communication); Latin American Student Organization; Management Information Technology Club; Model United Nations; Native American Club; Omicron Delta Kappa (National Leadership Honor Society); Organized Action Council; Orgs Council; Paladins (Karate Club); Phi Alpha (Social Work Honor Society); Phi Alpha Theta (National History Honors Society); Phi Eta Sigma (Freshman Honor Society); Photography Club; Physical Educators Club; Political Science Club; Pre-Law Club; Psi Chi (National Honor Society in Psychology); Psychology Club; Science Club; Sigma Tau Delta (English Association); Social Worker Association; Spartan Athletic Training Students Organization; Spartan Physical Educators Club; Spartan Pride; Spartan Student Newspaper; Straight Edge; Student Accounting Society; Student Athlete Advisory Committee; Students for Wellness; Student Nurses Association; Student Rec-Majors Club; Students for Wellness; Third City Epic; Ultimate Frisbee Club; University Chorale

ADMISSION PROCESS

Aurora University welcomes applications early in the senior year of high school. To apply for admission, apply online at www.aurora.edu or call 630-844-5533 or 800-742-5281 to request a paper application. Submit the completed AU application along with official transcripts from your high school or college and official ACT or SAT scores. Admission is determined on a rolling basis. The priority application deadline is May 1 for fall admission. Once admitted, a $100 tuition deposit is required to hold a space in the class. Students planning to live on campus must submit a housing contract and a $100 housing deposit. Both deposits are refundable until May 1.

School Says . . .

BABSON COLLEGE

AT A GLANCE

This small New England school, the nation's top ranked small business college, enrolls about 470 students each year into its freshman class, keeping the student population around 1900. Set in beautiful Wellesley, Massachusetts, Babson's 370-acre residential campus is alive with intellectual, cultural, athletic, and social activities. Babson College offers a strong business curriculum with a liberal arts foundation. Students are immersed in an enriching environment that fosters leadership, teamwork, creativity, communication, and diversity. About 22 percent of undergraduates are international students who represent 66 countries; students of color comprise more 27 percent; and 3percent of the Babson undergraduates are women.

Babson is accredited by the New England Association of Schools and Colleges, the International Association for Management Education, AACSB International—the Association to Advance Collegiate Schools of Business, and the European Quality Improvement System (EQUIS).

COLLEGE BASICS

Babson College defines entrepreneurship education for the world. Our approach is unique. It allows our students to hit the ground running upon graduation, finding and making opportunity that will have a lasting impact on the world. We believe, as do our graduates and their employers, in the value of an interdisciplinary approach combined with experiential education.

LOCATION AND ENVIRONMENT

This 370-acre suburban campus is located in Wellesley, Massachusetts (population 26,650). This is the ideal charming New England town, a classic setting for a college environment. A mere 14 miles outside of Boston, students here are sure to experience the best of both worlds: the quaintness of small town life bordering the cultural and social excitement of the big city. Although Boston is accessible by means of public transportation, approximately half of all students have cars.

CAMPUS FACILITIES AND EQUIPMENT

Babson's contemporary facilities provide students with access to dynamic academic and social resources. Students frequent the Donald W. Reynolds Campus Center, the Richard W. Sorenson Family Visual Arts Center, the Richard W. Sorenson Center for the Arts, the Glavin Family Chapel, and the Arthur M. Blank Center for Entrepreneurship. These centers offer students a state-of-the-art campus experience.

Horn Library houses an extensive business collection of print, media, and computerized information resources. Students have campus-wide access to newspapers, journals, investment analyst reports, corporate records, directories, and international information. They also benefit from numerous electronic research and news services that supplement a selection of the best business and liberal arts books, newspapers, journals, CD-ROMs, audiocassettes, videocassettes, and videodiscs. It also holds the Sir Isaac Newton Collection, archives, and a museum. The school is a member of a library consortium, which allows students to borrow books from other libraries.

The Stephen D. Cutler Center for Investments and Finance, a joint venture between the Finance Division and Horn Library, exemplifies Babson College's innovative, real-world approach to business education and applied research. It is the hub for investment education programs, finance-related student organizations and a forum for thought leadership where industry practitioners, faculty and students collaborate, exchange ideas and learn from one another. The Center's programs and resources enhance understanding of the importance of investments and finance in funding the growth engines of the global economy.

Horn Computer Center is equipped with a lab that remains open 24 hours a day. Wireless access is available in the library and computer center, Reynolds Center, Olin Hall, and all residence halls. Every incoming Babson undergraduate student receives a leased laptop computer with integrated Wi-Fi wireless. After their sophomore year, Babson students return their laptops and receive brand new ones, which are then returned at the end of their senior year. When students graduate, they have the option to purchase a new one at Babson's discounted rate. Babson provides microcomputer accounts for student use complete with Internet access and email.

ACADEMICS

Babson College operates on the semester system with thirteen-week spring and fall semesters, one two-week winter session and two six-week summer sessions.

Students are required to take 50 percent liberal arts courses and 50 percent business courses. Babson offers unique programs including First-Year Seminar, field-based learning programs, independent study, and an honors program. All students start and operate their own businesses with money loaned by Babson during their first year as part of Foundations in Management and Entrepreneurship. Students also have the opportunity to work as consultants to organizations as part of the Management Consulting Field Experience.

All students are encouraged to self-design their course of study. Rarely do students' goals exactly parallel a pre-designed major. This unique opportunity allows students to cultivate their own course of study to best prepare them to meet their immediate career goals upon graduation. Although all students will graduate Babson College with a Bachelor of Science Degree, most courses of study incorporate one or more of the following fields: accounting, economics, entrepreneurship, finance, international business, investment banking, management, management information systems, marketing and quantitative methods. In addition, students may choose to plan their course of study around one of twenty-five optional concentrations in both business and liberal arts disciplines.

ADMISSIONS

Babson College bases its acceptance of students on both academic and nonacademic factors. The academic factors include high school record, recommendations, standardized test scores, and essays. The nonacademic factors include extracurricular activities, shown leadership, character/personal qualities, volunteer work, work experience, creativity and enthusiasm and a willingness to contribute to the Babson community in meaningful ways. Graduation from secondary school is required for admission. The most competitive students have taken approximately 5 solid academic courses per year at the highest available level (Honors, Advanced Placement or International Baccalaureate). The SAT or ACT with writing is required for admission. The TOEFL or IELTS is required for students who are nonnative English speakers. The nonrefundable application fee is $65. The application fee may be waived in cases of financial need. Please contact your school guidance office for more details on fee waivers. Babson offers several application programs. Students may apply Early Decision (binding process), Early Action or Regular Decision. The deadline for Early Decision and Early Action is November 1. The Regular Decision Deadline is January 1. Transfer students may apply for September entrance by April 1 and for January entrance by November 1.

CAMPUS LIFE

Babson offers students an extensive variety of student activities. These extracurriculars include 22 NCAA Division III (11 men's and 11 women's) intercollegiate athletic teams. Intramural sports are also popular student activities. More than 90 student-run clubs, organizations, and publishing opportunities are available across every interest spectrum. Some of these activities include: Dance Groups, Theater, Literary Magazine, Jazz Band, Music Ensembles, Radio Station, Student Government, Student Newspaper, the Yearbook and much, much more. The school also has four fraternities and three sororities. Approximately 10 percent of students are involved in Greek life.

MAJORS AND DEGREES

Students are required to take 50 percent liberal arts courses and 50 percent business courses. Babson offers unique programs including First-Year Seminar, field-based learning programs, independent study, and an honors program. All students start and operate their own businesses with money loaned by Babson during their freshman year as part of Foundations in Management and Entrepreneurship. Students also have the opportunity to work as consultants to organizations as part of the Management Consulting Field Experience. All students are encouraged to self-design their course of study. Rarely do students' goals exactly parallel a pre-designed major. This unique opportunity allows students to cultivate their own course of study to best prepare them to meet their immediate career goals upon graduation. Although all students will graduate Babson College with a Bachelor of Science degree in Business Administration, most courses of study incorporate one or more of the following fields: accounting, economics, entrepreneurship, finance, international business, investment banking, management, management information systems, marketing and quantitative methods. In addition, students may choose to plan their course of study around one of twenty-five optional concentrations in both business and liberal arts disciplines.

TUITION AND FEES

The tuition for the 2010–2011 academic year is approximately $39,040 while room and board is approximately $12,876.

FINANCIAL AID

Babson is committed to educating students from diverse backgrounds, and we will do all we can to make it financially possible for you to attend Babson. In 2009–2010, Babson is awarding $24 million from its own funds to undergraduate students. Federal and state grants, loans, and work-study are awarded based on financial need. Students who wish to apply for financial aid should submit the CSS/Financial Aid PROFILE and FAFSA by February 15.

School Says . . .

BARNARD COLLEGE

AT A GLANCE

Founded in 1889, Barnard College was one of the first colleges to offer young women the chance to earn a college degree. Today, Barnard College remains committed to the education of over 2,360 undergraduate women from more than 40 countries and nearly 50 states. Partnered with Columbia University since 1900, under an agreement unique in the world of higher education, Barnard is an independent college for women maintaining its own Board of Trustees, campus, curriculum, faculty, staff, and admissions process. Barnard also operates from its own endowment, while Columbia University confers degrees to Barnard students. The fully residential campus features countless, independent resources and facilities; students at Barnard also have academic and extra-curricular access to the Columbia campus across the street, including cross-registration for courses, and benefit from both an all women and a coeducational experience. Additionally, Barnard women complete alongside Columbia students on 16 NCAA Division I athletic teams as part of the Ivy League conference. The small, personal, and close-knit character of Barnard is augmented by the resources of a large research university.

LOCATION AND ENVIRONMENT

Barnard is located in New York City and offers students endless cultural, academic, and professional opportunities. New York is an extension of our classrooms and students make use of its resources for both study and exploration. Barnard's Office of Career Development lists over 2,500 student internships throughout New York City each year and classes will often incorporate visits to museums, tours of historic neighborhoods, or participation in civic engagement projects. Barnard's location in the neighborhood of Morningside Heights offers a retreat from the fast pace of Mid-town Manhattan and is often referred to as an educational Mecca with students, staff and faculty from a number of institutions of higher education all calling the Heights "home."-Institutions neighboring the Barnard campus, in addition to Columbia University, include the Manhattan School of Music, Teachers College, Bank Street College of Education, Union Theological Seminary, and the Jewish Theological Seminary.

OFF-CAMPUS OPPORTUNITIES

There are numerous opportunities for Barnard students to explore academics beyond the Barnard gates. Barnard students have full access to Columbia resources including 25 libraries, research facilities, and courses, which complement the Barnard curriculum, even at a graduate or professional level. The Jewish Theological Seminary allows Barnard students to enroll in courses for credit and Juilliard and the Manhattan School of Music allow qualified Barnard musicians to enroll in a lesson exchange program.

Barnard students also explore academics beyond both New York and the United States through over 150 study-abroad programs in more than 50 countries including, but certainly not limited to, Argentina, China, Egypt, Greece, Kenya, Russia and Tibet. Programs focus on cultural immersion, advanced or independent study, and field-based or experiential learning and may include a single semester or a full year of study. Many students also enroll in programs in Beijing, Kyoto, Berlin, or Paris via our partnership with Columbia University. Other Barnard students enroll in a variety of programs offered through other universities, consortiums, and international organizations. Atlanta's Spelman College and Washington, DC's Howard University offer domestic exchange programs with Barnard.

MAJORS AND DEGREES OFFERED

Barnard offers the bachelor of arts (BA) degree, and students choose from more than 50 majors, including Africana studies, American studies, ancient studies, anthropology, architecture, art history, Asian and Middle Eastern cultures, biochemistry, biological studies, chemistry, classics (Greek and Latin), comparative literature, computer science, dance, economics, education, English (including creative writing), environmental science and policy, film studies, foreign area studies, French, German, history, human rights studies, Italian, Jewish studies, mathematics, Medieval and Renaissance studies, music, neuroscience and behavior, philosophy, physics and astronomy, political science, psychology, religion, Slavic studies, sociology, Spanish and Latin American cultures, statistics, theatre, urban studies, and women's studies. With this foundation in the liberal arts and sciences, Barnard women succeed in a variety of career fields, including business, communications, health and public service, and are well prepared for global and diverse settings.

Opportunities for double and joint degrees are also available at Barnard in conjunction with other schools within Columbia University. One option is the five-year BA/MIA or BA/MPA program where Barnard students also earn their masters from Columbia's School of International and Public Affairs. Barnard may also nominate juniors with outstanding records for early admission to Columbia Law School under the Accelerated Program in Interdisciplinary Legal Education and may recommend candidates for an accelerated degree with Columbia's School of Oral and Dental Surgery. Students interested in both the liberal arts and engineering may earn the AB/BS degrees in a five-year (3-2) program with Columbia's Fu Foundation School of Engineering and Applied Science. Advanced music students can apply and audition for the Juilliard School's five-year (3-2) program earning their BA from Barnard and the MM degree from Juilliard. Finally, students may earn an BA from Barnard and a BA from the nearby Jewish Theological Seminary's List College, if admitted to the double degree program.

ACADEMIC PROGRAMS

A Barnard education seeks to provide women with the tools and techniques necessary to think critically and act effectively in the world today. Barnard requires students to complete 122 points of course work (including First-Year English, First-Year Seminar, and two semesters of physical education) in addition to a major for the BA degree. Barnard believes that a successful liberal arts education revolves around central ways of knowing the world. This philosophy forms the basis of the general education requirements within the Nine Ways of Knowing curriculum: reason and value, social analysis, cultures in comparison, language, laboratory science, historical studies, literature, visual and performing arts, and quantitative reasoning. To allow for flexibility within this framework, a student chooses among the designated courses that fulfill each of the nine requirement areas. Thus, each student will shape her own academic program by electing a combination of wide-ranging introductory courses and more specialized upper level courses.

The College has a long-standing commitment to prepare students sufficiently in a subject so that they may undertake a semester- or year-long thesis or project, usually during the senior year, on a topic related to their major. Students are encouraged to explore internships in their field, thereby acquiring information and experience that complement what is learned through formal study. A student may major in two fields by satisfying all the major requirements prescribed by each department.

CAMPUS FACILITIES AND EQUIPMENT

Barnard's Campus covers four acres of prime New York real estate stretching from 116th to 120th Street along Broadway with 15 buildings comprising Barnard's cozy campus. Milbank Hall, a nationally registered historic landmark, contains offices, classrooms, a cutting-edge greenhouse, and the Minor Latham Playhouse. 14-story Altschul Hall houses state-of-the-art science research facilities and equipment, along with classrooms, offices, and laboratories. A full gymnasium is located on the first floor of Barnard Hall, facing the college's main entrance. Brooks, Reid, and Sulzberger Halls along with Hewitt, make up the Quad, the residence life complex serving first-year students situated at the southern end of campus. Four years of campus housing is guaranteed to first-years and housing options include opportunities for coeducational living. The heart of student life is the Diana Center, the brand new student center which opened January of 2010, where students have access to many amenities which augment academic life, including an art gallery, black box theatre, event and dining spaces, art and architecture studios, music practice rooms, and more. Finally, Wollman Library offers three floors of study space and along with Columbia's libraries, with more than 6 million books, 3.5 million microforms, over 58,000 serials and periodicals, and a variety of CD-ROMs, provides access to the 8th largest library system in the world.

TUITION, ROOM, BOARD AND FEES

$37,052 is the total for 2009–2010 tuition and fees at Barnard, and room and board are an additional $12,320.

FINANCIAL AID

Financial aid at Barnard is strictly need-based. A student's need is determined using criteria established by both the federal government and Barnard's Financial Aid office. The financial aid awarded by Barnard should supplement a family's own financial resources, while Barnard covers 100 percent of the remaining need. Financial aid awards typically consist of grants, work-study jobs, and student loans. Students who are awarded Barnard College grants should expect grants throughout their four years at Barnard, providing the students' families maintain their level of need and the students maintain their academic standing. Over 52% of first-year students receive some form of financial aid. Need plays no role in the Barnard admissions process; admission for first-year students is need-blind, and admissibility is evaluated solely on merit.

STUDENT ORGANIZATIONS AND ACTIVITIES

The Barnard College community offers numerous activities and opportunities to an active student body. The College Activities Office engages each student and promotes active and involved citizenship through leadership development, multicultural education, and a foundation in social justice. More than 80 student-run organizations including: Asian American Alliance, Barnard Bulletin, Gospel Choir, Community Impact, Late Nite Theatre, Model United Nations, Mujeres, McIntosh Activities Council, Orchesis Dance Troupe, Russian Cultural Association, Students Against Silence, and Women 's International Business Council. Barnard and Columbia students take part in organizations and activities on both campuses, and Barnard women take leadership roles in many of more than 250 Columbia-sponsored clubs. Women's intercollegiate, intramural, and club athletics are also popular. Barnard's varsity athletes compete at the NCAA Division I level alongside their Columbia peers as part of the Ivy League through the Barnard/Columbia Athletic Consortium. The 16 intercollegiate teams include archery, basketball, crew, cross-country, fencing, field hockey, golf, indoor and outdoor track and field, lacrosse, soccer, softball, squash, swimming and diving, tennis, and volleyball. Intramural and club sports include cycling, equestrian, ice hockey, martial arts, rugby, and sailing.

ADMISSIONS PROCESS

High school transcripts, letters of recommendation, standardized test scores, personal attributes and achievements all play a role in Barnard's highly selective and holistic admissions process. The College seeks women with strong academic records who exhibit the capacity and desire to grow intellectually and personally. While there is not a set group of criteria that an applicant must match, the student must have completed a rigorous college preparatory program or its equivalent, with a recommended 4 years of English, 3 or more years of math, 3 or more years of a foreign language, 3 or more years of laboratory science, and 3 or more years of history. Every applicant is evaluated on both the qualities that she personally espouses and her potential for success at Barnard. Applicants must submit the following test scores: either the ACT with writing, or the SAT Reasoning Test and two SAT Subject Tests. Students for whom English is not their primary language of instruction or who have been in the United States for less than 4 years must submit results from the TOEFL of the IELTS exam. Interviews are optional.

BELMONT UNIVERSITY

AT A GLANCE

Belmont is a private, coeducational, comprehensive university. It is the largest Christian university in Tennessee and among the fastest-growing universities in the nation.

We offer undergraduate degrees in over 75 major areas of study through our seven undergraduate colleges and schools: Arts & Sciences, Business Administration, Mike Curb College of Entertainment and Music Business, Gordon E. Inman College of Health Sciences & Nursing, Religion, University College, and Visual & Performing Arts. In addition, master's degrees are available in Accountancy, Business Administration, Education, English, Music, Nursing, Occupational Therapy, and Sport Administration. Doctoral degrees are offered in Occupational Therapy, Physical Therapy, and Pharmacy.

Where is Belmont located?

Belmont sits in the heart of Nashville, in a quiet area convenient to downtown and adjacent to Music Row.

How many students attend Belmont?

Belmont is home to 5400 undergraduate and graduate students. The student body includes representatives from every state and over 25 different countries.

LOCATION AND ENVIRONMENT

Belmont University occupies a 75-acre campus in southeast Nashville. With more than 500,000 residents, Nashville is a cultural, educational, health-care, commercial, and financial center in the mid-South. Practical educational opportunities, offered through diverse curriculums, provide students with the hands-on experience they need in preparation for a meaningful career. The city's location, halfway between the northern and southern boundaries of the United States, with three intersecting interstate highways and an international airport, makes it accessible to students from across the country.

OFF-CAMPUS OPPORTUNITIES

Several programs at Belmont have agreements with area organizations to provide students practical training. Nursing students gain clinical experience at various local medical centers including Vanderbilt Medical Center, Baptist Hospital, Centennial Medical Center, St. Thomas Hospital, and Summit Hospital. Education students gain classroom experience in Metro-Davidson County Schools. Music business students gain real-world experience through internships in the Nashville music industry as well as in the Los Angeles, California and New York, New York markets through the Belmont West and Belmont East programs of study and internships.

Through a wide variety of international study programs, Belmont offers students the opportunity to broaden and deepen their education while earning credit hours toward their degrees. These programs, which range in duration from two weeks to a year, are available in Australia, the Bahamas, China, Costa Rica, England, France, Germany, Ireland, Italy, Mexico, New Zealand, Nicaragua, Russia, Scotland, South Africa, and Spain.

A unique Washington Center Intern Program, that places Belmont students in individualized internships in the Washington, DC, area, is also available.

MAJORS AND DEGREES OFFERED

Belmont University is accredited by the Commission on Colleges of the Southern Association of Colleges and Schools to award baccalaureate, master's, and doctoral degrees. Belmont grants seven undergraduate degrees: the Bachelor of Arts, the Bachelor of Business Administration, the Bachelor of Fine Arts, the Bachelor of Music, the Bachelor of Science, the Bachelor of Science in Nursing, and the Bachelor of Social Work. Majors or concentrations are offered in:

College of Arts and Sciences

School of Education

Early Childhood Education; Exercise Science; Middle School Education; Physical Education and Health; Secondary Education

School of Humanities

Classics; English; French; German; Spanish; Philosophy

School of Sciences

Applied Discrete Mathematics; Biochemistry and Molecular Biology; Biology; Chemistry; Computer Science; Engineering Physics; Environmental Studies; Mathematics; Medical Imaging Technology; Medical Physics; Medical Technology; Neuroscience; Pharmaceutical Studies; Physics; Psychology; Science and Engineering Management; Web Programming and Development

School of Social Sciences

Audio and Video Production; Communication Studies; European Studies; History; International Politics; Journalism; Mass Communication; Organizational and Corporate Communication; Political Science; Politics and Public Law; Public Relations; Sociology; Video Production

College of Business Administration

Accounting; Business Administration; Economics; Entrepreneurship; Finance; Information Systems Management; International Business; International Economics; Management; Marketing

Mike Curb College of Entertainment and Music Business

Audio Engineering Technology; Entertainment Industry Studies; Music Business; Songwriting

Gordon E. Inman College of Health Sciences & Nursing

Nursing; Social Work

College of Visual and Performing Arts

Department of Art

Art Education; Art History; Design Communications; Studio Art

School of Music

Church Music; Commercial Music; Music Composition; Musical Theatre; Music Education; Music with an Outside Minor; Music Theory; Music Performance; Piano Pedagogy

Department of Theatre and Dance

Theatre and Drama

School of Religion

Biblical Languages; Biblical Studies; Christian Ethics; Christian Leadership; Religion and the Arts; Religious Studies

Interdisciplinary Programs

Social Entrepreneurship; Asian Studies

ACADEMIC PROGRAMS

Uniquely positioned to provide the best of liberal arts and professional education, Belmont University offers celebrated professional programs structured to provide an academically well-rounded education. Belmont University operates on a two-semester schedule with classes beginning in late August and ending in early May. Two summer sessions are also offered. The academic program is arranged by school: the College of Arts and Sciences, the College of Business Administration, the Mike Curb College of Entertainment and Music Business, the Gordon E. Inman College of Health Sciences & School of Nursing, the College of Visual and Performing Arts, University College and the School of Religion.

In addition to the degrees offered through the schools, Belmont University offers an honors program, which was created to provide an enrichment opportunity for students who have potential for superior academic performance and who seek added challenge and breadth to their studies. Students enrolled in the honors program are led in designing and working through a flexible, individual curriculum by a private tutor who is an honors faculty member.

The university's advancements in undergraduate research are credited to a faculty committed to helping students practice their disciplines. The annual Belmont Undergraduate Research Symposium puts Belmont at the forefront of this national movement by providing a public forum for in-depth research at the undergraduate level.

CAMPUS FACILITIES AND EQUIPMENT

Belmont's 75-acre campus includes 11 academic buildings, with the library and other multifunction facilities located in proximity to those classrooms. Some highlights include the Leu Center for the Visual Arts, featuring state-of-the-art studios with natural lighting and spacious work areas and the 3,000-square-foot Leu Art Gallery. The Sam A. Wilson School of Music Building houses classrooms, a resource room, seminar rooms, music practice rooms, a piano lab, and a music technology lab. Belmont's elegant theatre complex, which opened in 2007, includes a 350-seat proscenium theater, a scene shop, and a black box theater. The Jack C. Massey Business Center, a state-of-the-art learning center, houses study lounges, seminar rooms, conference rooms, three computer labs, a financial trading room, and a convenience store. In addition, Massey Business Center houses the 9,000-square-foot Center for Music Business which provides classrooms, an academic resource center, two state-of-the-art recording studios and control rooms, four isolation booths, a MIDI pre-postproduction room, and an engineering repair shop.

The newest academic building on campus is the $22.5 million Gordon E. Inman Center. The building is home to Belmont's College of Health Sciences and Nursing, consisting of schools in Nursing, Occupational Therapy, Physical Therapy, Pharmacy and Social Work. The Inman Center includes state-of-the-art labs, classroom facilities, and a community conference center.

Currently under construction, Belmont's new Health Sciences building will house the university's Schools of Pharmacy, Physical Therapy Psychology as well as include expansion space for the Schools of Nursing, Occupational Therapy and Social Work programs. Scheduled to open in fall 2010, the building will continue the innovation for which Belmont University has become known, containing top-notch laboratories for both student and faculty research.

Home to the 2008 Town Hall Presidential Debate, Belmont University's Curb Event Center (CEC) is a 90,000-square-foot major sport and entertainment complex. The building offers state-of-the-art facilities for athletics, concerts, speakers, tradeshows, meetings, conferences, dinners, receptions and consumer shows. The Belmont Bruins NCAA Division 1 basketball and volleyball teams play in the Curb Event Center, which is maintained and operated by fully digital, computerized systems and represents state-of-the-art production capabilities.

Approximately 3,500 square feet of prime retail space has been set aside on the front section of the Curb Event Center for Belmont students to develop retail or service businesses. The three student-run businesses provide an opportunity to learn first-hand about entrepreneurship

Connected to the Curb Event Center, the Beaman Student Life Center is the hub of campus activities. The BSLC includes a fitness center with strength training and cardiovascular equipment, an aerobics and dance area for a wide variety of classes, two racquetball courts, a recreational gym, a rock-climbing wall and student locker rooms. The facility also features numerous student services including a convenience store, offices and meeting rooms for student organizations, and inviting seating areas for students to study and interact.

TUITION, ROOM, BOARD AND FEES

The total cost of attending Belmont is only 80 percent of the national average for a private college. For a full-time student living on campus the total cost for the 2009–2010 academic year is approximately $30,950, which includes tuition, fees, room and board.

FINANCIAL AID

The financial aid program at Belmont combines merit-based assistance with need-based assistance to make the university education affordable. Institutional merit awards range from full-tuition Presidential Scholarships to various levels of partial merit awards. Athletic and performance scholarships are also available. Belmont also administers traditional state and federal programs, including the Federal Pell Grant, Federal Stafford Student Loan, Federal Perkins Loan, Federal PLUS Loan, and Tennessee Student Assistance Grants and Scholarships. Campus employment is available. Parents may arrange monthly tuition payments through an outside vendor. To apply for assistance, the student must complete the Free Application for Federal Student Aid (FAFSA). FAFSA Code: 003479.

STUDENT ORGANIZATIONS AND ACTIVITIES

All told, more than 80 clubs and organizations are active on Belmont's campus, including academic clubs, honor societies, professional fraternities, special interest and Christian organizations, student government, publications, social fraternities and sororities, music and drama groups, and debate and forensics teams.

The Belmont Bruins compete at the NCAA Division I level in the Atlantic Sun Conference in men's and women's basketball, tennis, cross country, track, soccer, and golf; men's baseball; and women's softball and volleyball. Several Bruin teams made NCAA tournament appearances over the last several years including the men's basketball team which won their conference and made the NCAA tournament for three consecutive years from 2006–2008. An extensive intramural sports program is also available.

ADMISSIONS PROCESS

Belmont admissions officers consider applications based on the total picture that a student's credentials present. High school students will be considered competitive for admission if they present a rigorous course of college-preparatory, academic studies. Students should have an above-average academic and cumulative grade point average and rank in the top half of their graduating class. Any college-level work is also expected to be at the above-average level. A strong correlation between high school grades and entrance examination scores is expected. The personal supplemental information, résumé of activities, and recommendations are also strongly considered as indicators of success at Belmont. Additional requirements such as portfolios or auditions are considered in conjunction with the academic credentials for those programs that require them. Each application is considered on an individual basis. No two applicants will present the same credentials or the same "fit" with the university. Our desire is to work with each student to determine the likelihood of that student to enroll in, graduate from, and use the benefits of the Belmont educational experience.

Further information and application materials may be obtained by contacting:

OFFICE OF ADMISSIONS

Belmont University

1900 Belmont Boulevard

Nashville, TN 37212

Telephone: 615-460-6785

800-56ENROLL (toll free)

Fax: 615-460-5434

Email: buadmission@mail.belmont.edu

World Wide Web: www.belmont.edu

CEEB Code: 1058

ACT Code: 3946

BENTLEY UNIVERSITY

AT A GLANCE

Bentley University is a leader in business education. Centered on education and research in business and related professions, Bentley blends the breadth and technological strength of a university with the values and student focus of a small college. A Bentley education combines an unparalleled array of business courses with hands-on technology experience and a strong foundation in the liberal arts. Students gain expertise for a competitive edge in today's economy and broad-based skills essential for success in all areas of life.

LOCATION AND ENVIRONMENT

Bentley is situated on 163 acres in Waltham, Massachusetts. The university's classic New England campus offers an inviting atmosphere for study and socializing. A location just minutes from Boston puts the city's many resources within easy reach. Students can take advantage of options ranging from theater performances to art exhibits, dance clubs to alternative rock concerts, championship sports to championship shopping. A free shuttle makes regular trips from the campus to Harvard Square in Cambridge—a great location itself and just a quick subway ride from the heart of Boston.

The 4,250 undergraduates who attend Bentley live and learn in an environment that reflects and prepares them for a multicultural world. Students come from approximately 40 states and 70 countries. The topic of diversity is not only addressed in courses but a vibrant facet of campus life. Offices such as the Multicultural Center, Spiritual Life Center, Center for International Students and Scholars, and Women's Center support the university's commitment to cultural awareness.

OFF-CAMPUS OPPORTUNITIES

Hands-on experience is emphasized across the Bentley curriculum. Internships, group consulting projects, study abroad programs, service–learning assignments, and other opportunities allow students to apply classroom theory in the workplace and community.

Each year, through the nationally recognized Bentley Service–Learning, hundreds of students build skills in business, communication, and teamwork while assisting nonprofit and community-based organizations both locally and internationally. Study abroad programs offer valuable insight into different countries and cultures. Students can choose from one-week, single-semester, and full academic year opportunities to study in Australia, Italy, France, China, Brazil, Spain, and many other destinations.

Internships at leading organizations in the U.S. and abroad enable students to fine-tune skills, explore interests, and make meaningful connections in the professional world. More than 80 percent of students complete at least one internship during their Bentley career; and over 40 percent lead directly to job offers.

Bentley University was ranked #12 in Career/Job Services by Princeton Review. This is a result of the various resources available on our campus including a recruiting program that draws some 500 national and international companies, an online job-listing service available to students and alumni; an electronic database of student and alumni résumés; career fairs; and workshops on topics such as effective résumé writing, interviewing, and job-search strategies.

MAJORS AND DEGREES OFFERED

Bentley has a strong curriculum focused on business, technology, and the liberal arts. Students have many options for shaping an academic program that fits their skills, interests, and career goals. Bachelor of Science (BS) degree programs provide in-depth knowledge and skills in specific business disciplines. BS degrees are offered in accountancy, computer information systems, corporate finance and accounting, economics–finance, finance, information design and corporate communication, information systems audit and control, management, managerial economics, marketing, and mathematical sciences.

Bachelor of Arts (BA) degree programs at Bentley University offer majors in media and culture (English), history, global studies, liberal arts, and philosophy. Students can also pursue a minor or concentration to develop expertise in an area outside their chosen major. The Master's Candidate Program allows students to earn a bachelor's degree and a master's degree in five years, rather than the usual six. Bentley also has doctoral programs in accountancy and in business.

Another innovative program offers an optional double major in business and liberal studies. Students combine courses that fulfill General Education requirements with related electives to pursue a concentration in a topical area such as earth, environment and global sustainability. Students take the same number of courses, but add another credential to their degree—and stand out to future employers.

ACADEMIC PROGRAMS

At Bentley University, students benefit from a unique integration of business and the liberal arts. As the largest business school in New England, Bentley offers remarkable depth in topics such as management, marketing, and accountancy. A similarly strong commitment to the liberal arts helps students build skills in critical thinking, decision-making, communication, and other areas essential for a meaningful life and rewarding career. Ethics and social responsibility are key themes in Bentley courses as well as supported by the university's internationally recognized Center for Business Ethics and nationally ranked Service-Learning Center.

Over the course of four years, Bentley students develop a solid understanding of the latest technologies and how businesses use them to stay competitive. The focus on information technology begins early, as all freshmen receive a laptop that is fully loaded and network ready. With wireless coverage all over campus—including classrooms, residence hall rooms, dining halls, and the library—students have fast and convenient access to the Internet, the Bentley network, and many other information sources. This commitment to high-tech learning is supported by an array of academic resources, including classrooms equipped with multimedia technology, student computer laboratories, and a Virtual Lab with specialized software accessible from anywhere on campus.

CAMPUS FACILITIES AND EQUIPMENT

Pride in facilities is a constant at Bentley University. The campus continues to develop and has seen a number of construction projects in recent years, including a renovated athletic center, updated library, and expanded athletic fields.

Unique to Bentley are six high-tech labs: the financial Trading Room, Center for Marketing Technology, the Winer Accounting Center for Electronic Learning and Business Measurement, Center for Languages and International Collaboration, Media Arts Lab and Studios, and Design and Usability Center. The Trading Room, which is among the largest in higher education, combines sophisticated technology and real-time data. Students take part in simulated trading sessions, using resources such as Bloomberg and DataStream to build an investment portfolio, analyze financial risk, and gain firsthand exposure to finance concepts.

TUITION, ROOM, BOARD AND FEES

Tuition for resident and nonresident students for the 2009–2010 academic year is $34,360. Room and board (double room, meal plan) costs are $11,740. Additional expenses include books, supplies, laptop computer, travel, and personal items.

FINANCIAL AID

The university administers approximately $100 million in undergraduate financial assistance every year—a commitment designed to ensure that all academically qualified students have access to educational choices regardless of family income and other resources. Over two-thirds of Bentley undergraduates receive some form of financial assistance, which can include scholarships, grants, loans and/or employment.

STUDENT ORGANIZATIONS AND ACTIVITIES

Bentley offers students many avenues for getting involved, making friends, and having fun. Campus activities include athletic events, music and theater programs, and lectures on topical issues, as well as more than 100 clubs and organizations. Students can choose from academically oriented groups, the creative and performing arts, student government, a campus newspaper and radio station, fraternity and sorority life, and much more.

Bentley fields 23 varsity sports for men and women, with all but the Division I men's ice hockey team competing at the NCAA Division II level. The university is a member of the Northeast-10 Conference and the Division I Atlantic Hockey Association. Many teams regularly qualify for post-season competition, and individual student-athletes routinely earn athletic and academic honors. Recreational athletes at Bentley take part in an ever-growing list of intramural sports and activities. Options include fitness training, ultimate Frisbee, and flag football, along with traditional sports such as soccer, softball, volleyball, and basketball.

ADMISSIONS PROCESS

Students applying for admission to Bentley University are encouraged to complete a competitive college-preparatory program. Recommendations include four years of English, four years of mathematics (preferably algebra I and II, geometry, and pre-calculus or its equivalent), and three to four years each of history, laboratory science, and foreign language.

Along with the Common Application and Bentley Supplement, students must submit a secondary school transcript, letters of recommendation from a teacher and a counselor, and official scores of either the SAT or ACT, including the ACT Writing Test. The university has special applications for international students and transfer students. Applicants whose native language is not English must also have official scores of the Test of English as a Foreign Language (TOEFL) or International English Language Testing System (IELTS) to the Office of Undergraduate Admission.

The application deadline for students planning to enter in September is January 15. For students planning to begin study in January, the deadline is November 15. Candidates for the fall semester are notified by April 1; spring semester candidates are notified on a rolling basis.

The Early Decision program is designed for academic achievers for whom Bentley is the first choice. Students who are admitted through this binding program agree to withdraw any applications submitted to other colleges and universities. The Early Decision application deadline is November 1.

The Early Action program is intended for applicants who are seriously considering Bentley, but are not prepared to commit through the Early Decision program. Early Action students receive an earlier admission decision than regular applicants, but can consider other academic options. The application deadline is November 15.

For more information, students should contact:

Office of Undergraduate Admission Bentley University

175 Forest Street

Waltham, MA 02452-4705

United States

Phone: 781-891-2244 or 800-523-2345 (toll-free)

Fax: 781-891-3414

Email: ugadmissions@bentley.edu

Website: www.bentley.edu

BETHANY COLLEGE (WV)

AT A GLANCE

Bethany, a small college of national distinction, was founded March 2, 1840. For 170 years, Bethany College has been a highly contemporary institution based in the tradition of the liberal arts. The College's program of classical liberal arts education prepares students for a lifetime of work and a life of significance. Teaching and learning form the mission of Bethany College. Central to this broad purpose is providing a liberal arts education for students, including the preparation of professionals, in an atmosphere of study, work, and service.

Bethany College is an academic community founded on the close interaction between students and faculty in the educational process. Bethany College values intellectual rigor and freedom, diversity of thought and lifestyle, personal growth within a community context, and responsible engagement with public issues.

Founded by Alexander Campbell, who provided the land and funds for the first building and served as the first president, Bethany has been a four-year private liberal arts college affiliated with the Christian Church (Disciples of Christ), since its inception. This religious body, of which Campbell was one of the principal founders, continues to support and encourage the College, but exercises no sectarian control. Students from virtually every religious community attend Bethany.

LOCATION AND ENVIRONMENT

Bethany's 1,300-acre campus is located in the northern panhandle of West Virginia in the foothills of the Allegheny Mountains. Located just 40 minutes from the Pittsburgh International Airport, Pittsburgh, America's Most Livable City, is just a 50-minute drive from campus. Wheeling, W.Va.; Washington, Pa.; and Steubenville, Ohio are less than a half-hour away.

MAJORS AND DEGREES OFFERED

The College offers a wide array of studies, awarding Bachelor of Science and Bachelor of Arts degrees in more than 25 fields of study, many with options for emphasis. Students also have the option of including one or more optional minors as part of their programs.

ACADEMIC PROGRAMS

Accounting; Biology; Business Administration; Chemistry; Communication; Computer Science; Economics; Education; English; Environmental Science (Interdisciplinary); Equine Studies (Interdisciplinary); History; International Relations (Interdisciplinary); Mathematics; Music; Physical Education and Sports Studies; Political Science; Psychology; Religious Studies; Social Studies (Interdisciplinary); Social Work; Spanish; Theatre; Pre-Professional Studies; Pre-Dentistry; Pre-Engineering; Pre-Law; Pre-Medical; Pre-Ministry; Pre-Physical Therapy; Pre-Veterinary

CAMPUS FACILITIES AND EQUIPMENT

The campus features rolling wooded hills and a lush, green academic mall. Facilities include beautiful historic landmarks, modern well-equipped classrooms, spacious sports/recreational areas, indoor and outdoor theaters, art galleries, an equestrian center, a teaching greenhouse and more. The College operates the Mountainside Conference Center, which includes Gresham Inn, and also the Campbell Mansion and Museum.

The 31,140 square-foot Mary Cutlip Center for Library and Information Services contains computers, collaborative learning spaces, a multi-media area. Its holdings include more than 200,000 bound volumes, 50,000 electronic books, 2,000 periodical subscriptions, and nearly 100,000 microforms along with numerous online information resources. The library also contains two extensive special collections. The College is a partner in the Bowen Central Library of Appalachia, a widely acclaimed research library collaborative of the 36 Appalachian College Association institutions. Bethany is also one of seven colleges in three states participating in the Independent College Enterprise, a state-of-the-art collaborative addressing academic computing.

The Thomas Phillips Johnson Health and Recreation Center includes Hummel Fieldhouse (performance gymnasium), three court multi-use gymnasium (Sandwen Arena), Knight Natatorium (Olympic-size pool), two racquetball courts, a free-weight exercise fitness center with cardiovascular equipment, and an indoor jogging track. The Cummins Community Center is a state-of-the-art 24-hour fitness center.

Outdoor Facilities: A multi-purpose stadium (Bison Stadium) with artificial turf and lights that primarily serves football and track and field, Hoag Soccer Field, John Cunningham Soccer Complex, equestrian center, 6 tennis courts, baseball and softball fields, football practice fields, and additional playing fields for intramural and club sports. The equestrian team trains at the Pegasus Farm Equestrian Center.

More than 90 percent of students live in spacious on-campus apartments, residential halls or fraternity/sorority houses, which include internet, cable TV and voice-mail access. Computer labs with Internet and library access, e-mail, digital media labs, rehearsal halls, research and language labs, The McCann Learning Center for academic support, and other amenities are provided.

TUITION, ROOM, BOARD AND FEES

The 2009–10 costs for resident students enrolled in the fall 2009 semester or later are:

Tuition	$20,565
Fees	$900
Room and Board	$8,700 to $9,100 (depending on option)
Books and Supplies (est)	$1,000
Personal/Transportation (est)	$1,000
Total	$32,165 (approximate)

* Total cost may vary depending on housing option.

FINANCIAL AID

Bethany College is committed to making a financial commitment to our students. If your desire is to receive a Bethany education, our financial aid office will do everything we can to make it affordable for you and your family.

The College awards scholarships based on academic performance, leadership capability and other academic factors.

Additionally, need-based aid is awarded to all eligible students in accordance with FAFSA results. Financial aid packages generally consist of loans, grants, scholarships and student employment.

STUDENT ORGANIZATIONS AND ACTIVITIES

Bethany's 20 varsity athletic teams (10 Women's and 10 Men's) compete in the NCAA Division III Presidents Athletic Conference (PAC) and the Eastern College Athletic Association (ECAC).

Bethany also offers more than 50 student organizations: scholastic and honorary, government, special interest and departmental.

Greek organizations include Phi Kappa Tau, Delta Tau Delta, Phi Mu, Alpha Xi Delta, Alpha Sigma Phi, Zeta Tau Alpha, Kappa Alpha Order, Beta Theta Pi, Sigma Nu, Delta Epsilon Pi.

Student Clubs and Service/Philanthropic Organizations include:

Alpha Phi Omega; American Chemical Society (ASC); Amnesty International; Baseball Club; Bethanians for Life; Big Brothers/Big Sisters; Circle K; Collegiate Middle Level Association (CMLA); Drama Club; Economics and Business Club; Environmental Science Club; Equestrian Club; Film Club; Fire and Rescue Club; French Club; Gay Straight Alliance (GSA); German Club; International Relations Club; International Students Association (ISA); Japanese Club; Judo Club; Math and Computer Science Club (MCSC); Men's Lacrosse; National Broadcasting Society (NBS) (Alpha Epsilon Rho); Outdoors Club; Photography Club; Physical Education Club; Political Awareness Society; Psychology Club; Public Relations Student Society of America (PRSSA); Soccer Club; Social Awareness; Society of Physics Students (SPS); Society of Professional Journalists (SPJ); Softball Club; Spanish Club; Special Education Club; Student Activities Council (SAC); Student Art Guild; Student Athletic Advisory Committee (SAAC); Student Literacy Association; Student National Education Association (SNEA); Tri Beta; Writers Club; Campus Media includes:; Bethany Political Journal; Bethanian Yearbook; Folio Magazine; Harbinger; Tower Online; WTVX TV-3; WVBC 88.1 FM

ADMISSIONS PROCESS

Bethany College specializes in a personalized admission process for each student. As a small school, our admission counselors evaluate each applicant individually —because of this, we are not limited by designated 'cut-offs.'

Enrollment Fast Facts

- Application Deadline: Rolling

- Interview Required: No, but strongly recommended

- SAT average: 1050

- ACT average: 23

- Average GPA: 3.30

- Enrollment Toll Free Number: (800) 922-7611

- Enrollment E-mail: admission@bethanywv.edu

BLOOMFIELD COLLEGE

AT A GLANCE

Founded in 1868, Bloomfield College (BC) is an independent, four-year, liberal arts college enrolling more than 2,300 students from around the world. The College's mission is to prepare students to attain academic, personal, and professional excellence in a multicultural and global society. Bloomfield College offers more than 60 degree programs in the liberal arts and sciences, creative arts and technology, and professional studies, which include accounting, business administration, computer information systems, criminal justice, education, game development, network engineering, nursing, pre-chiropractic, sciences, and more.

Bloomfield is accredited by the Middle States Association of Colleges and Schools, and the nursing program is accredited by the Commission on Collegiate Nursing Education and the New Jersey Board of Nursing. The College is chartered by the state of New Jersey, and its academic programs are approved by the New Jersey Commission on Higher Education. The accounting program is a Registered Accounting Curriculum for Public Accountancy in the state of New Jersey and meets the state's educational requirements for candidates applying to sit for the CPA examination.

Students have many opportunities to engage in co-curricular programs that enrich their educational experience. In addition to Student Government, Nursing Student Association, Association of Latin American Students, International Student Association, Haitian Student Association, and other clubs and organizations, students can actively participate in various service-learning, global awareness, professional and leadership development programs and activities. Campus publications include *In Print,* the College yearbook, and *On the Green,* a magazine for alumni and friends.

The Student Center is the social and recreational focus of the College community and houses meeting rooms, a snack bar, lounges, and the Center for Student Leadership and Engagement, which provides opportunities for student socialization, leadership, and co-curricular learning.

Bloomfield College has a full program of championship NCAA Division II intercollegiate sports, intramural sports, and recreational activities. Men's intercollegiate sports include basketball, baseball, soccer, cross country and tennis. Women's intercollegiate sports are basketball, softball, soccer, cross-country and volleyball. Bloomfield College is also a member of the Central Atlantic Collegiate Conference (CACC), the Eastern College Athletic Conference (ECAC) and the New Jersey Association of Intercollegiate Athletics for Women (NJAIAW).

In addition to general on-campus housing, the College provides special residence halls for first-year students, theme houses, and a new suite-style residence hall. A complete residence-life program provides academic, social, and recreational programs for resident students.

The Center for Academic Development offers individual tutoring and group workshops to all students. Academic advising is ongoing, and students meet with their advisor before registering each semester.

Other support services include the Honors Program, Support for Achievement in Graduate Education, Educational Opportunity Fund Program, career counseling and placement, women's services, and the Wellness Center, which includes health services, the chaplain, and personal counseling. An extensive English for Academic Purposes program for students for whom English is a second language is also offered.

LOCATION AND ENVIRONMENT

Located in Bloomfield, New Jersey, a suburban, residential community 12 miles from New York City, the College attracts resident students from areas across the world as well as commuter students from the New Jersey/New York metropolitan area. Bloomfield is easily accessible by bus, train, and car from northern New Jersey, New York City, and Rockland and Westchester counties in New York.

OFF-CAMPUS OPPORTUNITIES

Bloomfield College is a member of the College Consortium for International Studies (CCIS). Students have the choice of more than seventy-five study-abroad programs in thirty countries around the world, for a semester, a summer, or a full academic year.

MAJORS AND DEGREES OFFERED

Bloomfield College offers more than 60 academic programs in the Bachelor of Arts and Bachelor of Science degrees. Majors and their concentrations include accounting, allied health technologies (diagnostic medical sonography, nuclear medicine technology, respiratory care, and vascular medicine technology), biology (general biology, pre-chiropractic studies, pre-medical studies, and pre-podiatry), business administration (with specializations in economics, finance, human resource management, international business management, management, management information systems, marketing, and supply chain management), chemistry (biochemistry, general chemistry, and pre-medical), clinical laboratory science (cytotechnology and medical laboratory science), computer information systems (database, network/security, and programming), creative arts and technology (animation, digital video, fine arts, game development, graphics for print and digital media, interactive multimedia, and music technology), e-commerce (applications design, applications programming, and support/implementation), education (elementary/early childhood, elementary with subject matter specialization, secondary, and special education), English (communications, literature, and writing), history, mathematics (applied mathematics), network engineering (Internet technology and LAN specialist), nursing (generic nursing and RN to BSN), philosophy, political science (general, human services, public administration, and public policy), psychology (general psychology and human services), religion, and sociology (criminal justice, general sociology, and human services).

Bloomfield College maintains a joint Bachelor of Science/Doctor of Chiropractic degree program with 13 accredited chiropractic colleges. Three versions of the prechiropractic program are offered, each preparing students for admission to colleges offering the Doctor of Chiropractic (D.C.) degree.

Bloomfield offers certificate programs in digital media, diversity training, game design, game programming, gerontology, network engineering, and supply chain management. In addition to the traditional format, there is also an accelerated version of the RN to BSN program allowing quicker degree completion.

The College recently launched its first post-graduate degree - the Master of Science in Accounting (MAcc). The MAcc program provides a strong technical foundation as well as a practical understanding of the context within which business decisions must be evaluated. This ten course program is designed to be completed in two academic years with courses being offered year round. The curriculum allows students to meet the 150-hour rule currently required by most states to sit for the CPA exam.

ACADEMIC PROGRAMS

Degree candidacy requires the successful completion of at least 33 course units; a full course unit is equivalent to 4 semester hours. A minimum of 16 course units must be completed at an advanced level. Four categories of courses are offered at the College: general education courses, distribution courses, specific major and major required courses, and elective courses. Course requirements for the degree vary among majors.

Other special programs available at Bloomfield include an RN to BSN transfer program for registered nurses who already have a two-year degree; the Educational Opportunity Fund Program, a state-funded program of educational and special services for disadvantaged students; English as a second language; an honors program; and various internship programs.

The Bloomfield College academic calendar consists of fifteen-week fall and spring semesters and an optional summer session consisting of two seven-week terms.

CAMPUS FACILITIES AND EQUIPMENT

Renovated Talbott Hall is the technology hub and media center of the College. The lower level houses classrooms featuring laptop and desktop computers, conference rooms, a general computer lab, and a comfortable lounge area. A Web-based radio station, which is part of the College's communications program, occupies the lower mezzanine area level.

The Bloomfield College library houses a collection of more than 68,000 titles, including subscriptions to more than 520 periodicals, an up-to-date reference collection, and thousands of reels of microfilm and microfiche as well as musical recordings and scores, films, and DVDs. The library has an online card catalog, thousands of electronic journals available through 15 databases, and holds a variety of CD-ROMs in the humanities, nursing, and social sciences. Bloomfield College's library holds an unique collection of books about Broadway and theater arts which make up a collection known as the Larry Qualls Collection. Library instruction and research assistance make the library a complete learning center. The library also contains the Media Center, which consists of three electronic classrooms, a distance learning room, and a screening room.

In addition to numerous computer labs, the College has wireless connectivity in most buildings on campus, including the library, the Student Center, and student residences, with plans for many more locations.

Tuition, Room, Board, and Fees

Tuition in 2010–11 for full-time students is $20,800 per year. Room and board for resident students is $10,600 per year. Fees total approximately $1,200.

FINANCIAL AID

Bloomfield College students receive approximately $38 million in scholarships and financial aid, with more than 90 percent of the full-time day student population receiving some form of financial assistance. Academic scholarships are administered by the Office of Admission; athletic scholarships are administered by the athletics department. College, state, and federal programs, such as grants, loans, and work-study, are administered by the Office of Financial Aid. The priority deadline for filing the FAFSA for Bloomfield College financial aid is March 15. Applicants who meet the March 15 deadline are considered for Bloomfield College scholarships and campus-based financial aid, including PACE, an interest-free loan for parents.

FACULTY

A highly qualified and diverse faculty instructs more than 2,100 students of all ages in day, evening, and accelerated sessions, with a student-faculty ratio of 14:1. Approximately 75 percent of the full-time faculty members have earned doctorates or terminal degrees.

STUDENT ORGANIZATIONS AND ACTIVITIES

The Bloomfield College Student Government serves as a vehicle of communication for student concerns, interests, and educational needs. The administrative staff and the College faculty serve as advisors to all student government activities and enterprises.

ADMISSIONS PROCESS

Bloomfield College admits qualified applicants who demonstrate the motivation, desire, and potential to benefit from and contribute to programs of study in the liberal arts and sciences, creative arts and technology, and professional studies. The College evaluates applicants in a comprehensive manner, with emphasis placed on the applicant's academic history, quality of curriculum, performance on standardized tests such as SAT and/or ACT, extracurricular involvement, results of one-on-one interviews, and recommendations from teachers and counselors. Once admitted, students are placed according to their academic preparation and achievement.

All applicants are encouraged to visit the College to discuss their academic and career plans with an admission counselor. Accepted students may participate in the Bloomfield overnight program where they can experience the campus first-hand including talking with students, faculty members, and administrators about academic programs and student activities, as well as the issues of admission and financial assistance. Applications are accepted throughout the year, with a priority application deadline of March 14 for the fall semester and November 15 for the spring semester. Applicants are notified within two weeks of the College's receipt of required materials. Applications received after these dates are considered on a space-available basis. Admission is open to all qualified students without regard to race, color, creed, religion, national or ethnic origin, sex, age, or physical disability. The College welcomes applications from high school seniors, transfer students, and adult students returning to school. Students may apply online at **www.bloomfield.edu/apply**. For further information, students should contact:

BLOOMFIELD COLLEGE OFFICE OF ADMISSIONS

One Park Place

Bloomfield, NJ 07003

Phone: 973-748-9000 Ext. 230 | 800-848-4555 (toll-free)

E-mail: admission@bloomfield.edu

Website: http://www.bloomfield.edu/admissions

BOSTON UNIVERSITY

AT A GLANCE

Boston University offers you a bustling, thriving intellectual atmosphere where you'll find diversity in all aspects of life—from geographic and ethnic diversity to diversity of thought and interests. Just steps away from some of the best museums, shopping, and restaurants in Boston, our campus offers both buzzing city streets and beautiful tree-lined paths along the Charles River. At BU, you'll learn from a world-renowned faculty dedicated to undergraduate education. Even as a freshman or sophomore, you'll find yourself in small classes (our average class size is 27 students) and you can choose your major from more than 250 programs of study, which include biology, broadcast journalism, business, computer engineering, elementary education, international relations, physical therapy, psychology, and theatre, to name a few. You can also choose to enter as an "undecided" major and take up to two years to figure out what you want to study. Your classes will include students from all 50 US states and more than 100 foreign countries, which means that no matter what you're learning about, you'll get a global perspective. You can choose to get involved with one (or more!) of our 500+ campus organizations, including Alianza Latina, Chordially Yours, Engineers Without Borders, the Outing Club, the Debate Society, or the In-Line Skating Team. At Boston University opportunity knocks every day …are you ready to open the door?

LOCATION AND ENVIRONMENT

Boston provides an environment rich in intellectual and cultural stimuli; no other city in the world can compete with Boston's remarkable concentration of higher education facilities. Boston attractions include numerous museums, libraries, major league baseball at Fenway Park, the Boston Symphony Orchestra, and a thriving theater district. The city has an atmosphere of excitement, the result of the many college students who live here. In fact, students make up 20 percent of Boston's population during the academic year. Boston is the quintessential college town. The city provides many opportunities for internship and research positions as well. The Boston University Undergraduate Research Opportunities Program (UROP) helps students locate research positions both within and beyond the university; BU Career Services works to provide students with internships or part-time jobs in any number of fields.

OFF-CAMPUS OPPORTUNITIES

Boston University also has one of the world's most extensive study abroad programs, providing opportunities for students to work and study all over the world. Among the University's study abroad offerings are language and liberal arts programs; programs that combine studies with internships; fieldwork programs for students wishing to pursue academic or scientific research; and summer programs. Study abroad programs are available in Argentina, Australia, China, Denmark, Ecuador, England, France, Germany, Guatemala, Ireland, Israel, Italy, Japan, Mexico, New Zealand, Niger, Peru, Senegal, Spain, Switzerland, Syria, and Turkey. There are also programs available in Washington, D.C. and Los Angeles.

MAJORS AND DEGREES OFFERED

The university awards the BA, BS, BSBA, BSEd, BAS, BLS, BAA, MusB, and BFA undergraduate degrees. Ten of Boston University's 17 colleges and schools have undergraduate study programs. The listing below shows the wide variety of study options available to undergraduates.

College of Arts & Sciences students may pursue degrees in American studies; Ancient Greek; Ancient Greek and Latin; anthropology; anthropology and religion; archaeology; art history; astronomy; astronomy and physics; biochemistry and molecular biology; biology; biology with a specialization in behavioral biology; biology with a specialization in cell biology, molecular biology, and genetics; biology with a specialization in ecology and conservation; biology with a specialization in neurobiology; biology with a specialization in quantitative biology; chemistry; chemistry: biochemistry; chemistry: teaching; Chinese language and literature; classical civilization; classics and philosophy; classics and religion; comparative literature; computer science; earth sciences; East Asian studies; economics; economics and mathematics; English; environmental analysis and policy; environmental science; French language and literature; geography with specialization in human geography; geography with specialization in physical geography; geophysics and planetary sciences; German language and literature; Hispanic language and literatures; history;

international relations; Italian studies; Japanese language and literature; Latin; Latin American studies; linguistics; linguistics and philosophy; marine science; mathematics; mathematics and computer science; mathematics and philosophy; music (nonperformance); neuroscience; philosophy; philosophy and physics; philosophy and political science; philosophy and psychology; philosophy and religion; physics; planetary and space sciences; political science; psychology; religion; Russian/East European studies; Russian language and literature; and sociology. Special curricula are also available, including the Boston University Collaborative Degree program (allowing you to earn dual degrees), seven-year programs in liberal arts and dentistry and liberal arts and medicine, the modular medical integrated curriculum, and a variety of combined BA/MA degree programs. Pre-medical, pre-veterinary, and pre-dental studies are supported through the College of Arts & Sciences with nearly any major.

Through the College of Communication, students can pursue concentrations in advertising, film, television, journalism (including broadcast journalism, magazine journalism, news-editorial journalism, and photojournalism), mass communication, and public relations.

At the College of Engineering, students may choose from programs in biomedical, computer, electrical, mechanical, mechanical with specialization in aerospace, and mechanical with specialization in manufacturing engineering. Students may also pursue the Engineering/Medical Integrated Curriculum to begin medical school courses in their junior year.

The School of Education allows students to pursue bilingual education, deaf studies, early childhood education, elementary education, English education, history and social science education, Latin and classical studies education, mathematics education, modern foreign languages education, science education, and special education.

The School of Hospitality Administration's intense curriculum trains students in the management of hotels, restaurants, food and beverage service, travel and tourism, and entertainment.

The School of Management allows students to pursue concentrations in accounting, entrepreneurship, finance, general management, international management, law, management information systems, marketing, operations and technology management, and organizational behavior.

At the College of Fine Arts, students may pursue studies in the School of Music (composition and theory, music education, musicology, and performance), the School of Theater (acting, theatre arts, design, management, production), and the School of Visual Arts (art education, graphic design, painting, and sculpture).

At the Sargent College of Health & Rehabilitation Sciences, students may pursue concentrations in athletic training; health science; human physiology; nutrition; and speech, language, and hearing sciences. Also available are a five-year combined BS/MS degree program in occupational therapy and six-year combined BS/DPT programs in physical therapy and athletic training/physical therapy (AD/DPT).

The College of General Studies offers a two-year, liberal arts-based program centered on a core curriculum and rigorous team teaching. The program allows students to advance to the university's degree-granting schools and colleges in their junior year.

The Science & Engineering Program is a five-semester program aimed at students interested in studying the natural sciences or engineering.

ACADEMIC PROGRAMS

Boston University is committed to providing well-rounded instruction, merging the fundamentals of a liberal arts program with preparation for the professional job market. University Honors College provides the most exceptional students with a challenging curriculum in the arts, sciences, social sciences, and professions. Additionally, outstanding freshmen and sophomores in the School of Management may be invited to participate in an honors program designed specifically for management students.

CAMPUS FACILITIES AND EQUIPMENT

Boston University's academic and athletic facilities are some of the best in the country. The Life Sciences and Engineering building includes 41 laboratories for faculty-led research, while the $80 million, 235,000 square-foot Photonics Center houses state-of-the-art laboratories devoted to developing new light-based technologies. The School of Management has 4,000 data connections throughout the school, providing Internet access from every classroom seat and from hallway kiosks. The Student Village, Boston University's most ambitious building project in 50 years, is the centerpiece of campus life, providing students with superior recreation, athletics, living, dining, and outdoor spaces. In addition to two high-rise residences and a Track and Tennis Center, the Village includes the ultramodern Fitness and Recreation Center and the state-of-the-art Agganis Arena, offering space for University sporting events as well as concerts and family shows.

TUITION, ROOM, BOARD AND FEES

Tuition for the 2009–2010 academic year was $37,910; standard room and board was $11,848. Additional mandatory fees equaled $530. Allowances for the cost of books, supplies, travel, and other incidental expenses brought the total cost of attendance for a resident student to $53,000. Costs for the 2010–2011 academic year have not yet been announced.

FINANCIAL AID

Boston University Financial Assistance offers comprehensive services to help students and their families finance the cost of a BU education. The university offers a wide variety of financial assistance programs and provides resources to help inform students and their families about payment strategies and financing options. Merit awards, need-based grants, loans, student employment, and a payment plan are all offered.

Because Boston University believes scholars should be encouraged and recognized for their efforts and abilities, the university is committed to offering a variety of scholarships to selected freshmen. University need-based grants are offered based on several factors, including calculated financial eligibility, academic achievement, and the availability of funds for a student's program of study. While every effort is made to assist students with limited resources, the university does not have sufficient funds to offer a grant award to every admitted student who has calculated financial eligibility. Those who present the strongest academic credentials are most likely to be offered grant or scholarship aid.

STUDENT ORGANIZATIONS AND ACTIVITIES

Boston University students excel every day, participating in academic clubs, cultural or religious organizations, cutting-edge research, community service groups, and professional internships. There are 500+ student organizations and more than 50 intramural and club sports that students can participate in throughout the year. A separate student government exists at each school and college to manage student affairs, and the Student Union, the governing body that presides over all of the university's student governments, includes members who represent all branches of the university.

ADMISSIONS PROCESS

The Board of Admissions evaluates each prospective student individually. The board's main focus centers on the merits of a student's high school record, but required standardized test scores (SAT and SAT Subject Tests or ACT), personal qualities and integrity, interests, teacher and counselor references, and other relevant attributes are also considered carefully. All candidates must have graduated from high school or earned an equivalency diploma to be considered. For admission to the College of Fine Arts, students must either audition or submit a portfolio. A few select programs require interviews.

Students should consult the Boston University website at *www.bu.edu/admissions* for additional information. Boston University also considers students with transferable credit from other institutions for admission. Boston University considers applicants for September or January admission, depending on the program of interest.

Boston University offers early decision (which is a binding agreement), early admission, and deferred admission options. All applications for early decision must be submitted by November 1 and applications for regular decision must be submitted by January 1. Accelerated program and select scholarship applications must be submitted by December 1.

Transfer students seeking January admission must submit their application forms by November 1. Those seeking September admission must submit their application forms by April 1.

Transfer students cannot be admitted to the Accelerated Liberal Arts Medical or Dental Programs or the Science & Engineering Program. Transfer students also may not apply for January admission to the College of Fine Arts School of Theater. They also cannot apply as "undeclared" to any school or college.

Boston University accepts qualified applicants regardless of age, color, disability, national origin, race, religion, sexual orientation, or gender to all of its activities and programs.

BRYANT UNIVERSITY

AT A GLANCE

Founded in 1863, Bryant is the one university that is driving a paradigm shift in undergraduate education by shattering the thinking that Liberal Arts and Business are separate paths.

Continuing a 147-year tradition, a Bryant education empowers students to realize their personal best in life and their chosen professions. Bryant is the choice for individuals seeking the best integration of business and liberal arts, utilizing state-of-the-art technology. Our innovative real-world curriculum is made even more profound by an unwavering focus on character and ethics. The result is a transformative, life-defining experience that will help you take full advantage of the opportunities and challenges that lie ahead.

Bryant's 3,347 full-time undergraduate students represent 27 states and 50 countries. They enjoy all the advantages of small classes and close relationships among students, faculty, and administrators. In this environment, students come to understand the interactions among various academic disciplines and their practical applications in the global community.

LOCATION AND ENVIRONMENT

Bryant University is situated on a beautiful 428-acre campus in Smithfield, Rhode Island. The campus is only 15 minutes away from the state capital, Providence; 45 minutes from Boston; and three hours from New York City. In addition to an array of activities on campus, students can enjoy cultural experiences, sports events, and excellent restaurants off campus.

Students are able to take advantage of internship and employment opportunities at many small and large businesses, Fortune 500 companies, and nonprofit organizations within driving distance of Bryant. Transportation includes buses (free for students) that travel to and from campus, a train station in Providence, and airports near Providence and in Boston.

Off-campus Opportunities

The Amica Center for Career Education, recently named one of the top 10 university career and job placement services in the country by the Princeton Review, offers students opportunities to expand their learning beyond the classroom. Through relationships with more than 300 companies, the Amica Career Center helps students get practical internships at organizations such as Walt Disney World, Fidelity Investments, PricewaterhouseCoopers, the New England Patriots, Textron, several local media outlets, and a variety of nonprofit organizations.

Qualifying students may participate in Bryant's Study Abroad Program, where they can choose to study with partners in 46 different countries. The University also offers a Sophomore International Experience, a two-week overseas course where students learn about other cultures and how businesses operate globally.

MAJORS AND DEGREES OFFERED

Bryant's College of Arts and Sciences offers degrees in applied economics, actuarial mathematics, applied mathematics and statistics, applied psychology, communication, environmental science, global studies, history, literary and cultural studies, politics and law, and sociology. The College of Business offers a degree in business administration with concentrations in accounting, computer information systems, entrepreneurship, finance, financial services, management, and marketing. The College of Business also offers a degree in information technology, as well as an international business degree with concentrations in computer information systems, finance, management, and marketing. Students can pursue one of 28 minors in business and liberal arts. To view additional areas of study, go to http://www.bryant.edu/areasofstudy.

Bryant's Graduate School of Business offers a full-time or part-time Master of Business Administration (MBA); a Master of Science in Taxation (MST); and a Master of Professional Accountancy (MPAc).

ACADEMIC PROGRAMS

Bryant's rigorous academic programs are accredited by the New England Association of Schools and Colleges (NEASC). The University's College of Business is accredited by AACSB International – The Association to Advance Collegiate Schools of Business, a distinction earned by only 5 percent of universities worldwide.

Students pursuing a four-year baccalaureate degree must complete a core curriculum that integrates business, liberal arts, and technology. The Honors Program allows motivated students to stretch their intellectual limits each semester.

Bryant faculty are dedicated to helping students develop to their intellectual potential. Ninety-nine percent of tenured and tenure-track faculty hold Ph.D.s or the highest degree in their field of expertise. They continuously engage in research, publishing, consulting, community service, and practical experience. With a 17:1 student-to-faculty ratio, each student can develop relationships with faculty for guidance and support.

CAMPUS FACILITIES AND EQUIPMENT

Bryant's modern campus is anchored by the Unistructure, the center of academic and social activity. The Bryant Center houses the bookstore, student organization offices, and a food court. The Koffler Center and Communications Complex feature several computer labs, a state-of-the-art digital television studio and editing suites, as well as Bryant's student-run radio station.

The George E. Bello Center for Information and Technology has an abundance of wired and wireless data ports and banks of high-speed computers. The C.V. Starr Financial Markets Center receives real-time data transferred by live feeds through Reuters 3000®, the leading information service for finance professionals. The Bello Center also houses The Douglas and Judith Krupp Library. It holds more than 150,000 volumes and thousands of reference databases and online resources, making it one of the most comprehensive business library collections in the region.

Students can balance their academic pursuits with their overall well-being by utilizing the Elizabeth and Malcolm Chace Wellness and Athletic Center. This impressive facility features a fully-equipped fitness center, a six-lane swimming pool, circuit-training equipment and free weights, and a group exercise room. The University has a variety of athletic fields and the 4,000-seat Bulldog Stadium.

Bryant is home to the John H. Chafee Center for International Business, which houses the World Trade Center Rhode Island, the only World Trade Center based at a university in the country. The Chafee Center is also home to the Rhode Island Export Assistance Center, the U.S.-China Institute, and the Confucius Institute at Bryant University. These organizations offer students hands-on experience in a variety of international endeavors.

TUITION, ROOM, BOARD AND FEES

For 2010–2011, tuition is $33,033. As part of their tuition, freshmen receive new laptop computers fully loaded with software and network-ready for Bryant's wireless campus.

Residence hall room and board fees for 2010–2011 is $12,215 with a $312 student activity fee. Approximately 87 percent of students live on campus. There are several housing arrangements, including the first-year complex, suite-style residence halls, the Suite Village for upperclassmen, and townhouse apartments for seniors. In addition, sections of Hall 15 are reserved for select students majoring in international business.

Tuition and fees are subject to change.

FINANCIAL AID

Bryant has a comprehensive program of merit- and need-based financial aid. Eighty-nine percent of Bryant students received some form of aid last year. Merit scholarships, need-based grants, loans, grants, and work-study awards are available. Students interested in applying for need-based grants, work-study, and education loans must file a Free Application for Federal Student Aid (FAFSA). The FAFSA can be found online at http://www.fafsa.ed.gov, in high school guidance offices, or through the Bryant University Financial Aid Office. The FAFSA filing deadline at Bryant University is February 15. The FAFSA can be submitted as early as January 1.

For financial aid information:

Telephone: 401-232-6020 or 800-248-4036 (toll-free)

Fax: 401-232-6319

E-mail: finaid@bryant.edu

Website: http://admission.bryant.edu

STUDENT ORGANIZATIONS AND ACTIVITIES

Bryant's has more than 80 student clubs and organizations that benefit many social causes, provide recreational enjoyment, promote intellectual exploration, and offer opportunities to develop new talents and passions. Organizations include the Student Programming Board, the Multicultural Student Union, the Arts & Culture Club, the Marketing Association, the Student Senate, and Big Brothers Big Sisters. There are many places on campus for students to gather and enjoy music, comedy, and other kinds of entertainment.

Sports and recreation play an integral role in the health and well-being of students. Students participate in and cheer for Bryant's 22 intercollegiate varsity sports teams, which compete at the NCAA Division I level. In addition, students can play club and intramural sports throughout the academic year.

ADMISSION PROCESS

Bryant University seeks students who are motivated learners and have a history of academic achievement. Minimum entrance requirements include: four years each of English and preparatory mathematics, including a year beyond Algebra II (with a preference for pre-calculus or calculus in the senior year); and two years each of history or social science, a laboratory science, and a foreign language. Remaining secondary course work should be in foreign language, mathematics, science, and social studies. Entering students may receive credit through the Advanced Placement (AP) Program or the College-Level Examination Program (CLEP) administered by the College Board. Credit is also awarded for International Baccalaureate (IB) Higher Level exams.

SAT or ACT scores must be submitted. The Admission Committee considers recommendations from the secondary school's guidance office and faculty concerning character and personal qualifications not shown in the academic record. Interviews, though not required, may be scheduled in advance of a campus visit.

Applications must be submitted to the Office of Admission with a nonrefundable fee of $50 by November 15 (early decision I), December 1 (early action), January 14 (early decision II), or February 1 (regular decision). It is the responsibility of the applicant to request that the secondary school guidance office send a copy of his or her school record directly to Bryant and to have SAT or ACT scores sent to the University. International applicants must also submit TOEFL scores and a completed Certification of Finances form.

For more information, contact:

Michelle Beauregard

Director of Admission

Bryant University

1150 Douglas Pike

Smithfield, RI 02917-1285

United States

(401) 232-6100

(800) 622-7001

admission@bryant.edu

http://admission.bryant.edu

BRYN ATHYN COLLEGE

Founded in 1877, Bryn Athyn College is a private, Christian, liberal arts college dedicated to teaching and learning in an environment that acknowledges spiritual purpose in life.

AT A GLANCE

Founded in 1877, Bryn Athyn College is a coeducational, Christian, liberal arts college, affiliated with the New Church. While our perspective is global, reflecting the inclusive, service-oriented Christianity taught in the theological writings of Emanuel Swedenborg, our educational methods are personal, focused on your unique learning style and special talents. We offer academic programs easily tailored to meet the needs of our students. Our educational approach also incorporates experiential learning—through service learning, internships and international experiences. Bryn Athyn College is devoted to helping students prepare for lives of meaningful service.

LOCATION AND ENVIRONMENT

Bryn Athyn College's 130-acre campus is located in beautiful Bryn Athyn, Pennsylvania, just 20 miles northeast of downtown Philadelphia. Bryn Athyn is a warm and thriving suburban community—and also a national historic landmark district. The close-knit community takes pride in its educational and historic institutions and its many beautiful outdoor spaces. The community's ties to the College are tight—Bryn Athyn's neighbors enjoy many events in the College's Mitchell Performing Arts Center, Glencairn Museum, and Bryn Athyn Cathedral. And, everyone enjoys access to the nearby Pennypack Ecological Restoration Trust with eight miles of public trails.

OFF-CAMPUS OPPORTUNITIES

Bryn Athyn's proximity to the country's sixth largest city, Philadelphia, is an asset to our students in many ways. The "City of Brotherly Love" is easily accessible by car, bus, or train. Our students appreciate the amenities of this historic and dynamic city, especially its cultural, educational, social and athletic attractions. The city also provides access to ample agencies for community service projects and corporations and organizations for a variety of internship and employment opportunities. Outdoor types can find plenty of hiking, biking, kayaking and other outdoor adventures in this diverse metropolitan area. Professional sports fans can follow the Eagles, Phillies, Sixers or Flyers. There's something for everyone in Philly.

If you prefer the small town feeling, Bryn Athyn is within easy distance of a number of cozy small Pennsylvania towns—Chestnut Hill, Newtown, Jenkintown, Doylestown, and New Hope all have shops, restaurants, and plenty of small town charm.

MAJORS AND DEGREES OFFERED

As a Bryn Athyn student, you can choose from Bachelors degree majors in Biology, Education, English, History, and Religion, or expand the possibilities with our Interdisciplinary Major (ID). Our ID major offers the option of combining two areas of study into a single cohesive program. These options include Art/Art History, Biology, Business Management, English, History, Mathematics, Philosophy, Psychology, and Religion. The integration of values and spirituality enrich every facet of our academic programs and campus life, helping us create an educational experience that maintains a spiritual focus while embracing variety and individuality.

ACADEMIC PROGRAMS

Our educational philosophy is grounded in the teachings of the New Church and the benefits of a comprehensive liberal arts education. Our approach to academics incorporates a strong liberal arts foundation, spiritual values that permeate the curriculum, and experiential learning opportunities embedded in the core program. The teachings of the New Church inform our curriculum and will help you explore what it means to live an engaged and useful life.

Things to note about academics at Bryn Athyn:

100% of courses are taught by professors so your classroom experiences will be high quality and intellectually engaging.

A student-to-faculty ratio of 7:1 means you'll know your professors and will get a personalized education to meet your needs.

Our generous endowment makes our quality education affordable.

Experiential learning, taking shape through service, international experiences, and an extensive internship program, is an integral part of the Bryn Athyn academic experience. This program is designed to broaden your skills, knowledge, and worldview through exploring what it means to live an engaged and useful life.

CAMPUS FACILITIES AND EQUIPMENT

Bryn Athyn College is a 130-acre campus that includes classroom buildings like Pendleton Hall, the Swedenborg Library, Mitchell Center for Performing Arts, dormitories for residential students, and the Asplundh Field House athletic facilities. The campus also boasts many new additions for the 2009-2010 school year, including the Brickman Center for Student Life and the state-of-the-art Doering Center for Science and Research. In addition to academic and student life buildings, our campus includes the Bryn Athyn Historic District: Glencairn Museum, Cairnwood Estate (special events facility), and the majestic Bryn Athyn Cathedral.

TUITION, ROOM, BOARD, AND FEES

The costs for tuition, comprehensive fees, and room and board for the 2010-2011 academic year is $24,080.

Tuition Fees: The tuition fee per year at Bryn Athyn College is $13,188.

Board and Room Fees: The regular room and board charge for all students living on campus per year is $8,540.

Comprehensive Fees: The comprehensive fee is intended to help meet the cost of classroom supplies and teaching tools, laboratory fees, social activities, athletic supplies, etc. The comprehensive fee per year at Bryn Athyn College is $2,352.

FINANCIAL AID

Bryn Athyn College is committed to giving all students interested in pursuing their studies at Bryn Athyn College access to a quality education. Our generous endowment makes the affordability of our education possible.

Financial assistance is available in many forms, and most students are eligible for one or more types of assistance. In addition to offering federal and state aid, Bryn Athyn College also offers both merit based scholarships and generous need-based institutional aid. 95% of students who applied for financial aid received some assistance (federal, state, institutional, and/or merit).

STUDENT ORGANIZATIONS AND ACTIVITIES

Student clubs and organizations are the fuel that keeps the campus engine going. At Bryn Athyn, you'll embrace opportunities to take on leadership positions and become involved in activities that are important to you. A variety of activities—recreational, service, religious, athletic, social, and cultural—exist both on and off campus. And our students don't hesitate to start a new club when they find others who share an interest or passion that's not currently offered.

Clubs and organizations include:

CARE – Community Service Organization

Student Government – represent students' interests to the wider campus community

Social Committee – plans social activities throughout the year

Outing Club – plans outdoor recreation and adventure

Business Club – promotes interest in and knowledge about business

International Student Organization – supports and celebrates our international students

The Bryn Athyn Beacon – our student newspaper

At Bryn Athyn you can pursue your interest in music, theater, art, and athletics. We recognize the power of dance and sport for developing spiritual strength and moral integrity. We aim to build successful teams where the whole is greater than any of its individual parts.

Arts and Athletics include:

Women: Volleyball, indoor soccer, lacrosse

Men's: Soccer, indoor soccer, lacrosse, ice hockey

Badminton

Volleyball Club

Dance Ensemble

The Never B Flats – women's a cappella group

Bryn Athyn College Orchestra

College Chorale

Bryn Athyn Cathedral Choir

Bryn Athyn Theatre Productions

ADMISSIONS PROCESS

Bryn Athyn College takes a holistic approach to evaluating applications. In addition to secondary school transcripts and standardized test scores, the Bryn Athyn College Admissions Committee uses essays, recommendations and personal interviews to determine if applicants are qualified and would be a good fit for the College. Candidates for admission not only have solid academic backgrounds but will also contribute positively to the moral and religious life of the College.

Bryn Athyn College has a rolling admissions policy. Applications are accepted throughout the year. Priority deadlines for admissions are as follows:

Fall entry – Feb. 1

Winter entry – Oct. 1

Spring entry – Jan. 1

A completed application file consists of the following:

Completed application form, or completed online application

Official secondary school transcript(s)

SAT and/or ACT scores

School Report form

TOFEL or IELTS scores (international students only)

International Student Financial Aid Application (international students only)

Teacher Recommendation form (home-schooled students only)

College Official's Report (transfer students only)

The College gives advanced standing and academic credit to students whose scores on Advanced Placement (AP) tests meet our criteria or who have participated in the International Baccalaureate Diploma (IB) Program.

BUCKNELL UNIVERSITY

With academic programs in the arts, engineering, humanities, management, and social and natural sciences – and broad opportunities outside of class—Bucknell University prepares students for professional and personal success.

AT A GLANCE

Begun in 1846 as a "literary institution" in what its founders described as the "wilds of Pennsylvania," Bucknell University has long embraced academic vigor. Today, Bucknell is a top-ranked university offering a personalized and comprehensive liberal arts education to exceptionally talented students from across the U.S. and around the world. With academic programs in the arts, engineering, humanities, management, and social and natural sciences, and broad opportunities outside of class, Bucknell is now much more than a literary institution: It is a place that prepares students for success in an increasingly complex and interconnected global society.

LOCATION AND ENVIRONMENT

With its green spaces, red brick buildings, and striking vistas, Bucknell's 400-acre campus is a quintessential college environment in the heart of scenic central Pennsylvania. The shops of historic downtown Lewisburg lie within walking distance of campus. The University is located within three to four hours of New York City, Washington, D.C., Philadelphia, and Pittsburgh by car. For more information about Bucknell's location, see www.bucknell.edu/explore.

OFF-CAMPUS OPPORTUNITIES

Bucknell is a residential university, so nearly all of students live on campus. Learning, service, research and recreation happen off campus, too. Students frequently volunteer as close as the local nursing home, community center, and fire-and-rescue company and as far away as New Orleans and Nicaragua. Every year, students also travel off campus to conduct research with faculty mentors. Destinations have included Alaska and the Sudan.

Many students explore their career options and network with alumni through summer internships with corporations, government organizations, and non-profits locally and nationally. An externship program provides job shadowing opportunities for sophomores.

More than 40 percent of students spend a summer, semester, or year abroad through one of University's own "in" programs or 130 other approved programs in Africa, Asia, Australia, the Caribbean, Europe, and South America.

Throughout a student's time at Bucknell and even after graduation, the university offers career services including advising, networking, mock interviews, internship and externship support, and employer fairs to students throughout their four years at Bucknell. The placement rate is consistently high: 93 percent of the Class of 2008 was employed or in graduate school within nine months of graduation.

MAJORS AND DEGREES OFFERED

Bucknell's 3,500 undergraduates can choose from more than 50 majors and 60 minors. Students can build robots, write and perform in their own plays, or debate solutions to global issues. Engineers can make art, artists can analyze DNA, and philosophers can make music. Each student chooses his or her own pathway, but what unites everyone is a shared enthusiasm for learning and a desire to achieve deeper levels of understanding about life and the world.

The College of Arts and Sciences offers bachelor's degrees in science, arts, music, and education. Master's degrees are available in select disciplines.

The School of Management offers bachelor of science degrees in business administration with majors in accounting and management.

The College of Engineering offers a bachelor of science degree in seven majors, a five-year dual degree in engineering and management, a five-year dual degree in engineering and the liberal arts, and a five-year combined bachelor's and master's degree.

For details about any academic program, see www.bucknell.edu/catalog.

ACADEMIC PROGRAMS

Bucknell's academic programs are enlivening and inspiring, largely because of the professors. They encourage free-flowing ideas and stimulating discussions across campus, getting to know students personally and challenging them to do their best. The professors are also dedicated scholars who frequently receive awards and grants for their work. Often, they engage students in research and creative projects outside of class. By doing so, they provide students with mentorship and guidance for the future. The student-faculty ratio is 10:1.

In addition to the faculty, visiting scholars and speakers come to Bucknell regularly. Recent visitors include F.W. deKlerk, Robert F. Kennedy Jr., David McCullough, Barbara Ehrenreich, Leonard Pitts, and Doris Kearns Goodwin.

Distinctive programs that complement the curriculum include, but are not limited to:

- Residential Colleges – http://www.bucknell.edu/rescolleges
- Seven theme-based living and learning environments combine classroom and co-curricular activities
- Themes: Arts, Environmental, Global, Humanities, Languages and Cultures, Social Justice, Society and Technology
- Participating first-year students take a class together and join in programs and social activities that complement their classroom learning
- Bucknell Environmental Center – http://www.bucknell.edu/environmentalcenter
- Faculty, staff, and students collaborate on environmental and nature-related learning, teaching, scholarship, and service
- Initiatives: Campus Greening, Susquehanna River, Nature and Human Communities
- Service-Learning – www.bucknell.edu/servicelearning
- Educational experiences link academic course work with efforts to meet a community need
- Opportunities include Bucknell Brigade to Nicaragua, Katrina Recovery Trips, Alternative Spring Break trips, tutoring in local schools, and international service
- Institute for Leadership in Technology and Management – www.bucknell.edu/iltm
- This two-summer program bridges the disciplines of engineering and management for select students in engineering, management, and the liberal arts
- In the first summer, a group of 18 rising juniors participates in an intensive, six-week, on-campus program focusing on globalization, ethics, communication skills, critical thinking, teamwork, and leadership; students hear lectures and attend workshops by Bucknell faculty and corporate leaders, travel to selected industrial and business sites, and work with companies on significant and real-world management and technological projects
- In the second summer, the students (now rising seniors) participate in off-campus internships involving work at the confluence of technology and management

CAMPUS FACILITIES AND EQUIPMENT

Bucknell's 400-acre campus includes facilities for art, engineering, music, the sciences, theatre and dance, and a 1,200-seat performance hall. Bertrand Library holds nearly 833,000 volumes, provides access to more than 26,000 periodicals, and offers thousands of audiovisual materials and multimedia equipment. Computer labs are available across campus, and most of campus is wireless-accessible. Classrooms are equipped with projectors and computers, some with computers for each student. All student residences are connected to the residential network, which features a high-speed data connection for each student. Science and engineering programs offer sophisticated instrumentation available for student use, including a structural testing lab, an atomic force microscope, and a nuclear magnetic resonance spectrometer.

TUITION, ROOM, BOARD, AND FEES

For the 2010–11 academic year, tuition and fees are set at:

Tuition: $42,112

Standard double room: $5,768

Meals: around $4,170

Student activities fee: $230

FINANCIAL AID

Please do not view the "sticker price" list above as an obstacle to attending Bucknell. The University offers a range of financial aid options to students with demonstrated financial need as calculated by the university. These include scholarships, grants, loans, and student employment. Bucknell considers each family's situation on an individual basis and reevaluates cases annually to accommodate families' changes in financial resources.

• About 50 percent of students receive financial aid from Bucknell, and 62 percent receive financial aid of some form.

• The average financial aid award for first-year students with financial need in the fall of 2009 was about $25,000 including scholarships, loans, and work study.

• The average loan total upon graduation is about $19,000.

• With its unique combination of professional programs and the liberal arts, Bucknell offers an education that provides lifelong personal and career benefits. Consider it an investment worth making.

Important Note: If you are applying for financial aid, you must submit your CSS PROFILE by November 15 for Early Decision I and January 15 for Early Decison II and Regular Decision applications.

STUDENT ORGANIZATIONS AND ACTIVITIES

Outside of class, students participate in more than 150 student-run clubs and organizations. These groups focus on anything from social and environmental causes to cultural awareness, poetry slams, dance, pottery, video games, or politics. Bucknell offers Division I athletics along with intramural and club sports. Students can enrich their religious and spiritual lives through multiple University and student-led faith organizations. About half of sophomore, juniors, and seniors participate in Greek life.

ADMISSIONS PROCESS

Bucknell seeks dynamic, well-rounded students who embrace challenge, ask provocative questions, and are prepared to take advantage of the rich opportunities we offer. Bucknell encourages prospective students and their families to visit campus to determine whether Bucknell is a good fit. View visit options at www.bucknell.edu/visitbucknell.

The University focuses on academic achievement, evidence of significant talent or ability, personal character, and leadership skills. Grades and recommendations are extremely important, but Bucknell also values applicants who cultivate passions outside of the classroom and contribute to their schools and communities in thoughtful and unique ways. Students who are willing to take healthy intellectual risks in both their academic and personal endeavors are also well suited to join Bucknell's community.

To apply for admission, fill out and submit the Common Application as well as the Bucknell Application Supplement. You can do this on the Common Application website: www.commonapp.org. There is a $60 required application fee. Early Decision students should also complete an Early Decision Form.

Deadlines

• For students seeking to begin college in the fall, Regular Decision applications should be filed before January 15 for notification by April 1.

• SAT and/or ACT results must be submitted before March 1.

• Early Decision candidates may apply for Early Decision I consideration by November 15 or Early Decision II consideration by January 15.

• Transfer student information is available on our website. Applications for transfer students should be submitted by March 15 for studies beginning the following fall and by November 1 for the spring semester.

To request application information by mail, please call 570-577-1101.

For detailed information about admissions at Bucknell, go to www.bucknell.edu/admissions.

CABRINI COLLEGE

AT A GLANCE

Cabrini College is a co-educational Catholic college that welcomes students of all faiths and cultures. Founded in 1957 by the Missionary Sisters of the Sacred Heart of Jesus, Cabrini is located on 112 acres in the Main Line suburb of Radnor, Pennsylvania. Cabrini has 1,452 full-time undergraduate students and more than 1,000 reside on-campus.

The top majors at Cabrini are as follows: Education (Early Childhood, Elementary, Special Education, and Secondary Education), English, Communication, Business, Biology/Pre-Med, Graphic Design, and Psychology. The College operates on a Rolling Admissions Basis. There is a two-week turnaround time once a prospective student has submitted the application, application fee, official copy of their high school transcript, and an official copy of their SAT or ACT scores. An essay and one letter of recommendation or teacher evaluation are also required. Merit based scholarships are awarded to students whose SAT/ACT and G.P.A. meet the academic criteria. The average SAT score for an incoming Cabrini student is a combined Math and Verbal score of 955 and the average G.P.A. is a 3.0. The average class size at Cabrini is 17 with a student/teacher ratio of 16:1.

Cabrini's commitment to social justice spans more than two decades: it was among the first in higher education to implement community service into the curriculum, and the first in Pennsylvania to require community service of all undergraduates. In 2005, Cabrini signed a formal agreement with Catholic Relief Services (CRS) to support global service initiatives.

Cabrini offers a foundation for career success. There are more than 30 majors and professional programs, co-op educational experiences and internships, academically focused living and learning communities, and an honors program. Within 10 months of graduation, 97 percent of Cabrini graduates are employed or in graduate school.

The National Survey of Student Engagement consistently shows that Cabrini first-year students and seniors score higher than those at more than 700 colleges and universities in several benchmarks of effective educational practice, such as level of academic challenge, student-faculty interaction, enriching educational experiences, and supportive campus environment.

A Division III school, Cabrini students are able to participate in sports while maintaining excellent grades. Cabrini College has earned more conference championships than any other school in the Colonial States Athletic Conference (CSAC).

LOCATION AND ENVIRONMENT

Cabrini College is located on a beautiful campus setting in Radnor, Pennsylvania, just 30 minutes from downtown Philadelphia, a city brimming with great food, museums, music, and professional sports teams. The King of Prussia Mall is located less than 10 minutes from campus and minutes from downtown Wayne, which boasts a movie theater, restaurants, and shops. Cabrini is located only a few hours from New York, Washington, DC, and Harrisburg.

OFF-CAMPUS OPPORTUNITIES

Internship opportunities are readily available with easy access to companies such as Vanguard, Unisys, Pfizer, Merck, ING, KPMG, CHOP, ABC, NBC, and numerous other places where Cabrini students gain valuable hands-on experience.

MAJORS AND DEGREES OFFERED

Cabrini students can earn a Bachelor of Arts, Bachelor of Science, Bachelor of Science in Education, or a Bachelor of Science in Social Work by majoring in any one of the Programs offered at Cabrini. At the graduate level, the College offers a Master of Education, Teacher Certifications, and Master of Science in Organization Leadership.

ACADEMIC PROGRAMS

The benefit of a liberal arts education is that Cabrini offers various Majors and Minors so students can find the right one for them.

Academic Majors

Business: Accounting, Business Administration, Finance, Human Resources Management, Marketing

Communication

Criminology

Education: Early Childhood Education, Educational Studies, Elementary Education, Secondary Education Certification, Special Education

English

Exercise Science and Health Promotion

Graphic Design

History and Political Science: American Studies, History, Political Science

Individualized Major

Information Science and Technology: Computer Information Science, Information Systems

Mathematics

Philosophy & Liberal Studies

Psychology

Religious Studies

Romance Languages and Literatures: French, Italian, Spanish

Science (Non Degree Granting): Pre-Nursing, Pre-Occupational Therapy, Pre-Pharmacy, Pre-Physical Therapy

Social Work

Sociology

CAMPUS FACILITIES AND EQUIPMENT

Located in suburban Philadelphia, Cabrini's wireless 112-acre campus features state-of-the-art academic and athletic resources. The centerpiece of Cabrini is its turn-of-the-century Mansion, a National Historic Landmark. The Antoinette Iadarola Center for Science, Education, and Technology has state-of-the-art science labs and research tools for students. It also houses the Center for Teaching and Learning, a learning commons that provides individualized support for students in math, writing and specific subjects. The Communications Center is a campus-based professional style media center, home to the campus television studio, award-winning radio station (WYBF), and newsroom. Cabrini's Dixon Field, an artificial turf surface with seating for 700 fans, is located beside the Dixon Center, which houses the pool, squash courts, basketball courts, workout gym, and exercise science lab.

STUDENT ORGANIZATIONS AND ACTIVITIES

With dozens of clubs and organizations at Cabrini, it's easy to get involved in campus life. Students have opportunities to meet others who have similar interests and are encouraged to start their own club or organization.

Cabrini students participate in almost 60 clubs and organizations, ranging from intramural sports like dodge ball and volleyball, to professional organizations like the Accounting Association and the American Institute for Graphic Arts. Students are active in religious, musical and academic clubs as well as community service organizations and athletics.

Cabrini is a member of the National Collegiate Athletic Association (NCAA) Division III and Colonial States Athletic Conference (CSAC). Men's sports include basketball, cross country, golf, lacrosse, soccer, swimming, tennis and track &field. Women's sports include basketball, cross country, field hockey, lacrosse, soccer, softball, swimming, tennis, track &field, and volleyball.

ADMISSIONS PROCESS

The Admissions Process is Rolling Admissions, where students can apply until the class is full. To be considered for admission, students must submit the following: Application, Application Fee, Official High School Transcript, and an Official Copy of the SAT or ACT scores. An essay and one letter of recommendation or teacher evaluation are also required. Students whose files are complete will hear back from an admissions representative within two weeks. Merit scholarships are awarded based on SAT/ACT scores and the high school G.P.A.

CALIFORNIA COLLEGE OF THE ARTS

AT A GLANCE

CCA empowers students to make art that matters. Founded in 1907, the college is noted for the interdisciplinarity and breadth of its programs. It offers studies in 20 undergraduate and seven graduate majors in the areas of fine arts, architecture, design, and writing. The college has world-class facilities at its two campuses, in Oakland and San Francisco. More than 450 highly regarded artists and scholars instruct a population of approximately 1,360 undergraduate and 430 graduate students. The average class size is 18.

The college has several dedicated on-campus spaces for the exhibition of student work, and individual departments and courses frequently present off-campus shows of student work. Many of these exhibitions are organized by the students themselves, which gives them valuable hands-on gallery experience. Student exhibitions on both campuses change weekly. The CCA Wattis Institute for Contemporary Arts, housed on the San Francisco campus, presents several exhibitions every year featuring internationally prominent contemporary artists. Often these artists personally come to campus to lecture and participate in studios and critiques.

The Center for Art and Public Life, based on CCA's Oakland campus, organizes a wide range of programs (exhibitions, student project grants, community art collaborations, and more) that put students into direct contact with the diverse communities of the Bay Area and beyond.

Artist talks, lectures, and other special events take place on both campuses almost every day.

CCA's intimate residential communities are a vibrant part of campus life. Students have a variety of affordable housing options that foster community spirit and can lead to lifelong friendships. Throughout the year, the residential-life staff hosts social and educational programs ranging from movie nights and barbecues to museum trips and professional lectures. Approximately 80 percent of CCA first-year students live on campus. First-year students and international students who meet all admissions and housing deadlines are given priority for housing. College housing is accessible to both the Oakland and San Francisco campuses via the college shuttle and public transportation. The First Year Community, located on the Oakland campus, provides leadership opportunities, themed halls, and many ways for first-year students to meet new people and connect to the college and the art community.

Students are encouraged to join existing clubs and organizations or to form new ones. Clubs and activities range in focus from community building to politics to physical fitness. Students may also choose to get involved in student government. The Student Council sponsors a range of activities throughout the year, including all-college dinners, films, receptions, and shuttles to San Francisco galleries.

Our students are active in many pre-professional groups that are affiliated with corresponding Bay Area professional chapters: American Institute of Architecture Students (AIAS), American Institute of Graphic Arts (AIGA), Industrial Designers Society of America (IDSA), and International Interior Design Association (IIDA).

CCA alumni have been at the forefront of nearly every major art movement of the past century. Noted alumni include the painters Nathan Oliveira and Raymond Saunders; the conceptual artists David Ireland and Dennis Oppenheim; the ceramicists Robert Arneson, Viola Frey, and Peter Voulkos; the filmmaker Wayne Wang; and the designers Lucille Tenazas and Michael Vanderbyl.

And CCA students do not wait for graduation to begin making their mark:

- Our Architecture students, together with students from numerous other programs (from Interior Design to Glass and Ceramics), are currently competing in the extremely high-profile Solar Decathlon, working with a budget exceeding $1 million to create a technologically cutting-edge, beautifully designed, and comfortable solar-powered house.

- Three of our Architecture students just took first place in the Association of Collegiate Schools of Architecture's Green Community International Student Design Competition. Their prize-winning submission, *Urban Reef*, reimagines San Francisco's Pier 70 as a public showplace for green energy and sustainable food production.

- The Council for Interior Design Accreditation just awarded one of its three major national scholarships to one of our Interior Design students, and CCA's two nominees for the Angelo Donghia Scholarship in interior design both claimed top honors: up to $30,000 each to complete their senior years in 2009–10.

- One of our Industrial Design students just signed a contract with Universal Toys to manufacture *Jungle Walkers*, a toy he first conceived as a freshman-year class project. It will be sold at FAO Schwartz this Christmas.

- Two of our MFA students placed in the 2009 SMART Art: Trash Into Treasure competition, in which entrants were challenged to redesign discarded materials into works of art.

- CCA's five 2009 Center Student Grant recipients are actively engaged in community arts projects in Columbia, the Dominican Republic, and here in San Francisco.

- A student in our brand-new Animation Program was one of only 12 selected (out of a whopping 2,500 applicants) for the prestigious Pixar Animation Studios animation internship in summer 2008.

Our students have won the Adobe Design Achievement Award, the James Dyson Award in industrial design, and awards from the Art Directors Club, STEP Inside Design, Type Directors Club, and *ID* magazine. Their work has been featured in the Cannes Film Festival, and the Slamdance Film Festival, the Milan Furniture Fair, the International Contemporary Furniture Fair, and the International Home and Housewares Show.

ACADEMICS

CCA students develop their individual voices and styles as part of a dynamic conversation that engages global currents of thought and practice. While learning to create meaningful art and design, they also learn to make a positive impact on the world. They study in a multidisciplinary context in which crossing boundaries is encouraged and celebrated.

CCA's First Year Program emphasizes skill building, experimentation, and critical thinking. In thoughtfully designed studio and academic courses, students develop their creative practices and are introduced to foundation skills that will apply to all of their subsequent studies. In their second year, they formally join one of CCA's 20 different major programs.

Our faculty members are a diverse group of artists, designers, architects, and writers. They support the students in their explorations while challenging them to take risks, clarify and deepen their processes of inquiry, and refine their techniques. They also advise students, helping them select a major and design an individual path of study.

Students at all levels are exposed to numerous learning opportunities, both curricular and extracurricular, from project-based community learning to summer study-abroad courses, sponsored studios, and internships with recognized commercial firms, nonprofits, and other arts organizations. CCA offers many courses related to issues of sustainability, diversity, and interdisciplinary investigations. It also has established international exchange programs with schools in Australia, Belgium, Denmark, France, Germany, Ireland, Israel, Italy, Japan, the Netherlands, Scotland, Spain, Sweden, and Switzerland. Financial aid is available for study abroad.

CAMPUS FACILITIES AND EQUIPMENT

CCA offers outstanding facilities for making art at its two campuses, in San Francisco and Oakland. Studios and technology resources are usually accessible 16 to 24 hours daily.

CCA's libraries (one on each campus) hold more than 60,000 books, periodicals, and audiovisual titles as well as an extensive visual resource collection. They subscribe to approximately 300 hard-copy periodicals and more than 2,500 full-text online periodicals. On the San Francisco campus there is also a materials library (one of very few such libraries at an educational institution) that contains thousands of material samples.

Students have access to a wide range of digital technologies. Both campuses have media centers, with equipment available for checkout. Wireless access is available throughout both campuses. The San Francisco campus has a brand-new facility for digital film and media with a 2,000-square foot production stage, three video editing suites, an audio recording suite, and a digital postproduction lab. Oakland media facilities include multiple computer labs (including a new 18-station lab and a dedicated 4D lab), an editing and sound suite, an animation homework lab, and a stop-motion lab.

The computer labs are generally available to all students when they are not being used for classes. The two campuses together have 14 dedicated computer labs: eight classroom labs, two open labs, a photography lab, a textiles lab, a core lab, and an animation lab. The labs are equipped with Intel-based Macintosh computers capable of running Windows and Mac OS X. The labs offer a diverse and complete range of software for print and web graphics, audio/video editing, and 3D modeling and animation. Available hardware includes slide and flatbed scanning devices, Cintiq displays, audio/video decks, graphics tablets, CD/DVD burners, and large-format color printers. There is also a rapid prototyping studio for 3D printing that has two laser cutters, a 3D prototyping machine, and a CNC router.

The Oakland campus is home to the First Year Program and the programs in Animation, Ceramics, Community Arts, Glass, Jewelry / Metal Arts, Photography, Printmaking, Sculpture, Textiles, Visual Studies, and Writing and Literature. The ceramics facilities include numerous gas and electric kilns, a large car kiln, and a glaze lab. The jewelry and metalworking facilities include professional jeweler's benches with flexible shafts and a wide range of tools. Sculpture facilities include a bronze foundry, a waxworking area, a plaster and mold-making room, a metal fabrication studio, and a woodworking shop. The glass facility has a two-bench hot shop with a glass furnace and equipment for casting, fusing, and coldworking. Textiles facilities include a computerized weaving lab, a digital Jacquard TC-1 loom, computer-operated dobby looms, 32 floor looms, a print studio with 15 padded print tables, a dye lab, and a fiber sculpture studio. For printmaking there are lithography presses, a 40x60 American French Tool etching press and other etching presses, relief presses, a polymer plate maker, approximately 100 litho stones, a silkscreening and papermaking complex, and a letterpress lab. The two-floor photography center has two large black-and-white darkrooms, 12 individual darkrooms for color printing, a 42-inch RA4 color processor, high-end Macs, a mural darkroom for both black-and-white and color printing, an alternative-processes lab, a dedicated lighting studio, and more.

The San Francisco campus houses the programs in Architecture, Fashion Design, Furniture, Graphic Design, Illustration, Industrial Design, Interior Design, Media Arts, and Painting/Drawing as well as all of the graduate programs. The fashion studio has facilities for cutting, draping, knitting, and sewing. The wood and furniture facilities include a bench room, a machine room, and a spray booth. Students have access to spacious shared studios for painting, drawing, and architecture, and seniors in the Painting/Drawing Program have individual studios, as do all Fine Arts graduate students. There is a graduate center and a graduate writing building.

ADMISSIONS

CCA reviews every application on an individualized basis, taking into account the applicant's academic and personal achievements, creative abilities, activities and interests, personal essay, recommendations, and portfolio. Undergraduate applicants must have a high school diploma or the equivalent. First-year applicants should follow a college preparatory program in high school, including courses in studio art and art history whenever possible.

CCA is strongly committed to making its arts education accessible and affordable. More than 75 percent of our students receive CCA scholarship assistance; the college uses more than $15 million of its own funds each year to provide scholarships for our most promising students. Many other grants and work-study positions are available. In all, 88 percent of CCA students receive some kind of financial assistance, totaling more than $37 million per year.

There are two priority deadlines for fall undergraduate admissions: February 1 and March 1. To be eligible for CCA merit scholarships, you must submit your application by February 1 (there is no separate scholarship application). All other undergraduate applicants must submit their materials by March 1 to receive first consideration for admission, housing, and financial aid (other than CCA merit scholarships). If you are applying to enter in the spring semester, the priority deadline is October 1.

Admissions decisions are made on a rolling basis (that is, applications are reviewed in the order they are received). There is a nonrefundable application fee of $60. It is possible to register for courses as a nondegree student.

Students are encouraged to apply online at www.cca.edu/admissions. To request more information please contact:

Office of Enrollment Services

California College of the Arts

1111 Eighth Street

San Francisco CA 94107-2247

phone: 800.447.1ART

web: www.cca.edu

email: enroll@cca.edu

CALIFORNIA UNIVERSITY OF PENNSYLVANIA

AT A GLANCE

The mission of California University of Pennsylvania is to build character and careers for our students. Although building careers may be expected of universities, building character is less often their focus. But the rationale for building character, as well as careers, is best seen in these words by Theodore Roosevelt: "To educate a person in mind but not in morals is to educate a menace to society."

Since 1852, eager students have seized the opportunity to develop their character and careers at California University of Pennsylvania. In so doing, they have improved their lives and the lives of those around them.

To achieve its mission, the University relies upon committed faculty, motivated students, challenging programs and exceptional facilities. We invite you to meet our faculty and students, to evaluate our academic offerings, and to tour our classrooms, laboratories and residence halls.

Cal U is a student-centered university that is committed above all to academic excellence and intellectual rigor in the context of personal and institutional integrity, civility and responsibility. We provide a welcoming, family atmosphere. Cal U is large enough to offer a variety of programs, yet small enough that most students are known by name.

LOCATION AND ENVIRONMENT

California University of Pennsylvania is nestled in western Pennsylvania's beautiful Monongahela Valley, in a bend on the scenic Monongahela River. The lower campus consists of 32 buildings situated on 92 beautifully maintained acres. The 98-acre George H. Roadman University Park, located one mile away, includes Adamson Stadium and a variety of sports fields and recreation facilities. The upper campus also is home to Vulcan Village, a garden-style apartment complex for students.

OFF-CAMPUS OPPORTUNITIES

In the southwestern corner of Pennsylvania, the University is a short drive from camping, hiking, fishing, hunting, whitewater rafting, canoeing, and skiing. Students have easy access to the Pittsburgh metropolitan area, located only 35 miles north of the campus.

MAJORS AND DEGREES OFFERED

Students may choose from more than 150 four-year degree options and concentrations. The University requires a minimum of 120 semester credits, including satisfactory completion of all required credits, for graduation. Students in all curricula must complete a minimum of 30 credits of their last 60 credits at California University of Pennsylvania.

ACADEMIC PROGRAMS

The College of Education and Human Services carries on the University's long tradition of excellence in teacher education and offers a variety of other professional programs, as well. Other programs in the College include athletic training, gerontology, physical therapist assistant, sport management studies and professional golf management. Also available is a B.S. Ed. in communication disorders, a pre-professional degree that prepares students for future graduate training before employment as a speech-language pathologist, and social work, which provides career opportunities in a variety of human service settings.

The College of Liberal Arts offers a diverse array of major and minor programs of study, including anthropology, art, criminology, English, justice studies, history, political science, psychology, sociology, theater and more. In addition, a broad, general education course of study, based on the liberal arts, encourages students to explore a variety of course offerings and to become aware of the ways many different disciplines understand and view the world.

The Eberly College of Science and Technology offers associate and bachelor's degree programs designed to prepare students to meet current and future requirements of specific professions and/or to undertake advanced studies. Programs include biology, chemistry, Earth sciences and mathematics, as well as a variety of technology-based programs. Environmental studies, computer science, robotics and business administration programs also are housed in this College. Each program in the Eberly College includes both general and professional education components to ensure that students receive a well-rounded education as well as the necessary technical training required for a successful career.

CAMPUS FACILITIES AND EQUIPMENT

Residence Life

California University offers a variety of residence life options for students, designed to fit freshman through graduate students. Six new suite-style residence halls house students on the lower campus, and a garden-style apartment complex is located on the upper campus at Vulcan Village. All housing is air-conditioned and furnished. Most students on the lower campus share a bathroom with only one other person; many apartments at Vulcan Village have private baths for each suitemate.

Students who live on the lower campus must purchase a food service plan, but Vulcan Village apartments have fully equipped kitchens, so a meal plan is optional. All student rooms have free Internet, cable and phone access.

Manderino Library

The Louis L. Manderino Library offers a physical collection of more than 280,000 print titles, 430,000 print volumes, 7,300 audiovisual materials, 19,000 government documents and 4,000 Pennsylvania documents. Through the library's website, users have 24-hour-a-day access to more than 50,000 online books and reference resources, over 36,000 online full-text periodical titles, and numerous electronic databases. PILOT, the library's online public access catalog, is a user-friendly resource that can be used to locate books and other resources in the library's collection. Manderino Library also offers public access computers, wireless Internet connectivity on all floors, and 20 wireless laptop computers that students can borrow for use in the library. The Manderino Library Gallery hosts a series of Smithsonian Institution Traveling Exhibition Service programs year-round.

Other Services

Computer labs are available in many departments, in all residence halls, and in special locations such as the Media Access Center (MAC) Lab in the Natali Student Center and the Instructional Computing Facility in Noss Hall.

Career Services assists students in developing, evaluating and effectively implementing career plans. An Internship Center offers students an opportunity to acquire college-level knowledge and skills outside a traditional classroom setting through affiliations with community organizations, governmental agencies or private businesses.

The Princeton Review's Complete Book of Colleges

TUITION, ROOM, BOARD AND FEES

California University is a member of the Pennsylvania State System of Higher Education, and the Board of Governors of the State System sets its tuition. Tuition usually is set in July for the academic year that begins in August.

The 2009–10 tuition for a resident of Pennsylvania attending full-time (12 to 18 credits) was $2777 per semester. For a full-time nonresident, tuition was $4444 per semester. Room costs for 2009–10 ranged from $2853 to $4162. Board prices ranged from $1284 to $1576. Based on a full-time schedule, fees for 2009-10 included a $103 technology fee, an $85 service fee, a $260 Student Association fee, an $81 student union building fee, an $84 student center operations and maintenance fee, and a $277 academic support fee. The cost of books, materials, and supplies varies with each program.

FINANCIAL AID

There are several types of financial available. Grants and scholarships are considered "gift aid" because they do not have to be repaid. Loans and work-study employment are considered "self help aid" because loans have to be repaid and by working, students earn money for educational expenses. Loans are by far the largest source of financial aid for the majority of students and families. Most grants, some loans (Subsidized Stafford and the Perkins Loan), and Federal Work-Study are need-based financial aid programs. The Unsubsidized Stafford and the Parent Loan for Undergraduate Students (PLUS) are considered non-need-based. Scholarships can be based upon merit, financial need or both.

Approximately 93 percent of all students attending California University receive some type of financial aid. The Free Application for Federal Student Aid (FAFSA), along with the cost of education, will determine whether a student has financial need. To receive financial aid, students must complete the FAFSA or Renewal FAFSA. The forms can be obtained from high school guidance counselors, public libraries, or the financial aid office of a college or university, including the Financial Aid Office at California University.

STUDENT ORGANIZATIONS AND ACTIVITIES

More than 120 clubs and student organizations are offered through academic departments and the Student Association Inc. These groups provide social, educational, community service and leadership opportunities for students. Their range is as varied as the interests of the student members.

ADMISSIONS PROCESS

To be considered for admission as a degree-seeking student at California University, applicants must submit the following:

1. Completed application form

2. Application fee

3. Official high school transcript that includes class rank if applicable (or GED certificate and scores)

4. SAT or ACT scores (may be waived for applicants who have been out of high school for at least two years or who have an associate, R.N. or baccalaureate degree)

Transfer students must submit official transcripts from all colleges and universities attended.

Students can apply and pay their application fee online by visiting www.calu.edu. All applications are individually evaluated. As soon as applications are complete, decisions are reached and applicants are notified. This process usually takes less than two weeks.

Admission standards have been established by the university to select those students who will be most likely to succeed.

1. Academics. An applicant must be a graduate of an approved or accredited secondary school or have an equivalent preparation as determined by any state's Department of Education.

2. Assessment and Ability Standards. An ability to do work in higher education should be evident from an assessment examination such as the SAT. In certain circumstances, other kinds of evidence may be used to determine the ability to do such work.

3. Character and Personality. Applicants must be able to demonstrate that they possess the personality traits, interests, attitudes and personal characteristics necessary for higher education. Recommendation letters are welcomed.

4. Admission to Special Curricula. A student seeking admission to a special curriculum may be required to complete additional requirements or have earned specific credentials.

The Admissions Office considers as many variables as possible in making admission decisions: class rank, cumulative grade-point average, type of curriculum completed in relation to proposed major, guidance counselor or other recommendations, on-campus interview, standardized test scores, activities and maturity. Each of these variables contributes to the overall assessment of individual applicants.

CASTLETON STATE COLLEGE

AT A GLANCE

Founded in 1787, Castleton State College is the 18th oldest higher-learning institute in the United States and the oldest in the state of Vermont. The historic village of Castleton in western Vermont is home to the college's 165-acre campus. Of the 1,800 undergraduates who attend Castleton full-time, nearly 1,100 hail from the state of Vermont. Other students come to Castleton from Vermont's New England neighbors and the Mid-Atlantic States.

Castleton State College is dedicated to providing an education that embraces the principles of liberal arts and the fundamentals of career preparation. Among the innovative aspects of Castleton's curriculum is a program called Soundings, in which first-year students must attend a series of events in order to earn their academic credits. The Soundings events range from theater and dance to debates and speeches by renowned leaders. Freshman also enroll in First-Year Seminar, a normal general education course with an additional component designed to teach them the skills they'll need to thrive in a collegiate environment.

Castleton's ten residence halls house a total of nearly 1000 students. Every room in the residence halls includes two (or more) Internet connections, a cable television outlet, and phone line. On-campus students enjoy meals at the Huden Dining Hall. Students who live off-campus find housing in the village of Castleton, as well as nearby Fair Haven and Rutland. All students may bring automobiles to campus.

Castleton recently completed a $25.7 million series of projects to enlarge and renovate the Campus Center and the gymnasium, to improve athletic fields and build a 1,600-seat stadium. Football and marching band also began in the fall of 2009.

The array of student activities at Castleton is wide. With over 40 student groups to choose from, Castleton's undergrads are involved in club sports, the marching band, the student newspaper, the campus radio station, the outing club, rugby, and dozens of other recreations. Other clubs focus on majors or prospective careers. And yet others strive to service the college or surrounding communities. Men can choose from ten varsity sports: baseball, basketball, cross-country, football, golf, ice hockey, lacrosse, skiing, soccer, and tennis. Women choose from ten: basketball, cross-country, field hockey, ice hockey, lacrosse, skiing, soccer, softball, tennis, and volleyball. A large number of Castleton's undergrads participate in intramural or recreational sports. And skiing, snowboarding, and other snow sports are favorite pastimes all around.

LOCATION AND ENVIRONMENT

Castleton's campus is located in western Vermont. Rutland, one of Vermont's largest cities, is 12 miles east. Albany, Boston, Burlington, Hartford, Montreal, and New York City can all be reached by car or via the public transportation options in Rutland. Outdoor enthusiasts regularly take advantage of the college's proximity to the ski slopes at Pico, Killington, Okemo, and Bromley Mountain. Lake Bomoseen and the Green Mountains also offer excellent outdoor recreation, not to mention pristine environments for living as well as learning.

OFF-CAMPUS OPPORTUNITIES

Castleton offers great opportunities in community service, internships, and service-learning through the Stafford Center for the Support and Study of the Community.

Two annual Career Fairs allow all students to make job contacts and begin networking.

Off-campus employment is available in nearby Rutland and at Killington, the largest ski area in the East.

MAJORS AND DEGREES OFFERED

Bachelor Degrees

Art

Athletic Training

Biology

Business Administration

Accounting

Management

Marketing

Communication

Digital Media

Journalism

Mass Media

Public Relations

Computer Information Systems

Criminal Justice

Environmental Science

Exercise Science

Geology

Health Science

History

Literature

Mathematics (Statistics)

Multidisciplinary Studies

Music

Nursing

Philosophy

Physical Education (Teaching Licensure, Sports Administration)

Psychology (Developmental, Forensic)

Social Sciences

Social Studies

Social Work

Sociology (Criminology)

Spanish Language and Literature

Sports Medicine (Athletic Training, Exercise Science)

Theatre Arts

Associate Degrees

Business

Chemistry

Communication

Computer Programming

Criminal Justice

General Studies

Nursing

Education Licensure Programs

Elementary Education

Secondary Education

Special Education

Graduate Programs

Master of Arts in Education (Curriculum and Instructio,. Education Leadership, Language Arts and Reading. Special Education)

Certificate of Advanced Graduate Study

ACADEMIC PROGRAMS

Castleton's academic programs allow students to build a firm foundation in liberal arts at the same time that they prepare for particular careers. By graduation, all four-year undergraduates must fulfill a core curriculum of 42 liberal arts credits. Many students use their freshman year to explore various academic opportunities and majors. Students who arrive at Castleton with specific career paths in mind may opt to begin work in the chosen major immediately. By the end of sophomore year, each four-year student must declare an academic major.

Typically, each student takes five courses per semester. Fall and spring semester are 15 weeks long; courses are also offered in three four-week blocks during the summer. Castleton employs traditional methods of grading, including pass/fail options. While internships and fieldwork can strengthen many academic degrees, they are required for students in the following programs: communication, criminal justice, education, and social work.

Two-year students already enrolled at Castleton may transfer to four-year tracks if they are pursuing degrees in business, communications, computer information systems, criminal justice, or general studies. Castleton will recognize as many as 64 credits (or the amount needed to earn the associate's degree) from students who arrive at the college with a two-year degree from another accredited institution.

First-year students who earn a GPA of 3.5 or higher will be inducted into Castleton's chapter of the national freshman honor society, Phi Eta Sigma. Similarly, the Castleton Chapter of Alpha Chi acknowledges the academic achievements of outstanding juniors and seniors. Education, psychology, Spanish, and theater arts majors are eligible for discipline-related honors societies as well. The Dean's List consists of students who achieve at least a 3.5 GPA; the President's List of Outstanding Students recognizes undergraduates who achieve a 4.0.

CAMPUS FACILITIES AND EQUIPMENT

Castleton's Calvin Coolidge Library contains more than half a million books, microforms, periodicals, non-print media sources, and online and CD databases. The library's electronic system is both networked and up-to-date, and can be accessed via the world wide web. Established inter-library relationships allow students to choose from expanded offerings. The audiovisual media center, which operates in cooperation with the library, offers a variety of instructional and practical services in areas such as film production and slide transparency.

In the College's Stafford Academic Center, students can enjoy the benefits of a state-of-the-art multimedia lecture room, the Computing Center, and distance-learning facilities. The education, mathematics, and nursing departments are housed in Stafford as well.

In addition to providing well-equipped laboratories and computer facilities, Castleton's science center boasts labs for faculty and student research, an observatory, a greenhouse, and a state-of-the-art auditorium with seating for 120.

The Fine Arts Center is the home of the newly renovated 500-seat Casella Theater, as well television studios and workspaces for students studying art, drama, dance, and music.

Glenbrook Gymnasium provides students with an expansive indoor activity area, a pool, a new state-of-the-art fitness center, an athletic training room, and the Human Performance Center.

In total, computer labs around campus offer more than 225 computers for students to use.

TUITION, ROOM, BOARD AND FEES
2009–2010

Vermont resident tuition - $7,992

Non-resident tuition - $17,232

Room and Board - $7,808

Fees for new students - $200

Fees for continuing students - $828

Non-resident total - $26, 068

Resident total - $16,828

FINANCIAL AID

Eighty-six percent of Castleton's full-time undergrads are recipients of college, state, federal, or other financial aid, including grants, scholarships, work-study programs, and loans. To be eligible for financial aid, students must submit the Free Application for Federal Student Aid (FAFSA) form preferably by April 1 of the academic year prior to enrollment. After February 15, aid is first-come, first-served. Financial aid is offered on a need basis.

The Castleton Honors Program provides the majority of scholarships. The amount of funding can vary from $1,000 to $6,000 a year. To be eligible, incoming students must score at least a total of 1100 on the SAT (Critical Reading and Math only) and have a GPA of 3.3 or higher. Transfer students must have a GPA of at least 3.0/4.0 to be considered for scholarships. Students interested in music or Spanish programs may apply for program-specific scholarships.

STUDENT ORGANIZATIONS AND ACTIVITIES

The Student Association serves as the primary body of student government on campus. Each student who is enrolled in at least eight credit hours is considered a member of the association. The association's elected representatives are granted membership in many College committees as well. Beyond the Student Association, students develop skills in leadership and decision-making through participation in student organizations.

ADMISSIONS PROCESS

Applicants are assessed according to their prior achievement in high-school classrooms and on standardized tests. Additionally, recommendations are strongly considered. Applicants will be admitted to Castleton based on their demonstrated capacity to excel in a post-secondary education atmosphere.

Application forms can be obtained via the College website listed below. Incoming students may enroll in either the fall or spring semester. Applications are considered on a rolling basis. Applicants will receive notification from the admissions office after their folders have been completed.

To learn more about Castleton State College or to set up a visit, please contact:

DIRECTOR OF ADMISSIONS MAURICE OUIMET

Castleton State College

Castleton, VT 05735

Telephone: 802-468-1213

800-639-8521 (toll free)

Fax: 802-468-1476

Email: info@castleton.edu

World Wide Web: www.castleton.edu

School Says . . .

CENTRAL CONNECTICUT STATE UNIVERSITY

AT A GLANCE

Selected as one of the "Great Colleges for the Real World" and honored as a "Leadership Institution" by the Association of American Colleges & Universities, Central Connecticut State University (CCSU) is a comprehensive public university dedicated to learning in the liberal arts and sciences and to education for the professions. Comprising five schools_Arts & Sciences, Business, Education & Professional Studies, Engineering & Technology, and Graduate Studies, CCSU offers full- and part-time undergraduate programs in more than 100 areas of study.

Conveniently located in New Britain, CCSU's innovative undergraduate curriculum inspires student learning in a wide range of fields, while extensive internship and co-op opportunities help students prepare for rewarding careers. The University's Division I athletics teams provide exciting opportunities to play or watch.

LOCATION AND ENVIRONMENT

CCSU is located in suburban New Britain, conveniently located in the center of Connecticut, approximately 2 hours from Boston or New York. The campus has been recently renovated. The University is surrounded by a pleasant neighborhood, with shopping and dining facilities nearby.

OFF-CAMPUS OPPORTUNITIES

CCSU's Center for Advising and Career Exploration coordinates a comprehensive Co-op Education Program as well as internships at local and area corporations, agencies, and government offices. Annual career fairs bring some 200 area and regional businesses to campus. CCSU Co-op students annually earn $4 million, and more than 65% are offered full-time career starting jobs with their Co-op employers.

The School of Education has many connections to area schools, including several Professional Development Schools, which provide CCSU students nearly unique opportunities to perfect their teaching skills in a full range of elementary and secondary classrooms.

The School of Engineering & Technology offers a wide array of internship opportunities in area engineering, manufacturing, and technology businesses.

The George R. Muirhead Center for International Education offers students a rich variety of study-abroad opportunities at more than 40 locations throughout the world and provides academic and cultural programs that promote a better understanding of peoples and cultures.

And the University and the New Britain Museum of American Art (an internationally acclaimed museum) have a partnership allowing students and faculty to visit the museum for free.

MAJORS AND DEGREES OFFERED

CCSU is accredited by the New England Association of Schools and Colleges (NEASC). The University operates on a two-semester calendar and offers four summer sessions plus one winter session. Undergraduate programs include: Accounting; Anthropology; Art (Art History); Athletic Training; Biochemistry; Biology (Ecology; Biodiversity; Evolutionary; Environmental Science; General); Biomolecular Sciences; Chemistry; Civil Engineering; Civil Engineering Technology; Communication (Broadcast Journalism; Media Studies; Organizational Communications; Promotion/Public Relations); Computer Engineering Technology; Computer Science; Construction Management; Criminology; Design (Graphic/Information); Earth Sciences; Economics (General; Operations Research); Education (Elementary; K–12; Secondary; Special Education); Electronics Technology; Engineering & Technology Education; Engineering Technology; English; Entrepreneurship; Exercise Science; Finance; French; Geography (Environmental; General Regional; Planning; Geographic Information Science; Tourism); German; History; Hospitality & Tourism; Industrial Technology (Electro-Mechanical Technology; Environmental & Occupational Safety; Graphics Technology; Manufacturing; Networking Technology; Technology Management); Interdisciplinary Science (Environmental Interpretation; Physical Sciences); International Business; International Studies; Italian; Journalism; Management (Entrepreneurship; Human Resource); Management Information Systems; Manufacturing Engineering Technology; Marketing; Mathematics (Actuarial; Statistics); Mechanical Engineering; Mechanical Engineering Technology; Music; Nursing (BSN & RN to BSN); Philosophy; Physical Education (Exercise Science & Health Promotion); Physics; Political Science (General; Public Administration); Psychology; Social Sciences; Social Work; Sociology; Spanish; Theatre.

Degrees: BA; BFA (Theatre); BS; BSN; Teacher Certification (elementary; secondary; K–12)

ACADEMIC PROGRAMS

CCSU also offers a number of interdisciplinary programs as well as independently designed majors. The Honors Program, a challenging interdisciplinary program of study for academically qualified students, offers half- and full-tuition merit scholarships and a variety of other benefits and resources, including a new Honors Lab.

The academic excellence of CCSU's innovative undergraduate education was nationally recognized when the Association of American Colleges & Universities selected CCSU as a "Leadership Institution," one of only 16 in the nation and the only one in Connecticut. Together with such other prestigious institutions as Colgate University, Duke University, and the University of Michigan, CCSU stands as a national example of quality undergraduate education. Central Connecticut State University is fast realizing its aspiration to become the best public comprehensive university in the region.

CAMPUS FACILITIES AND EQUIPMENT

CCSU offers an attractive campus with new and renovated buildings adding to the classic collegiate style of its historical architecture. The academic buildings feature technologically state-of-the-art "smart classrooms" and seminar rooms, and the entire campus offers wireless access. The Student Center provides lounges, dining services, conference and game rooms, information services, and a range of other support services. Three theatres offer space for plays, concerts, and guest lectures. The S.T. Chen Art Gallery hosts shows by student, faculty, and visiting artists. The Student Technology Center features 250 computers plus printers and scanners for student use. Campus-based TV and radio stations provide exciting entertainment as well as opportunities to learn about the professions. The Elihu Burritt Library provides access to over 2 million books through an online catalog, a wide array of electronic databases and online resources, and special collections ranging from the unparalleled collection of Polish American materials to the Equity Archive. The University also offers many new athletic facilities, including an Olympic-sized swimming pool, modern exercise equipment, a state-of-the-art fitness center, a weight-training room, and an athletic training center. In the Kaiser Annex students can walk, jog, and play tennis or a pickup basketball game. CCSU recently opened new football, soccer, softball, and baseball fields to complement its basketball and volleyball arena. The residence halls and classrooms are fully networked. Approximately 20% of the students live on campus in nine residence halls.

TUITION, ROOM, BOARD AND FEES

Expenses for the 2008–09 academic year include tuition (in-state: $7,414; out-of-state: $17,106), room and board ($9,308 [approx.]); expenses for books, transportation, fees, and other expenses range from $5000 (in residence) to $6000 (off-campus residence).

FINANCIAL AID

Approximately 75% of CCSU full-time students receive some form of financial aid. CCSU's office of Financial Aid works with students to help them meet educational expenses from their first year until graduation. To apply for financial aid students must complete the FAFSA form. For more information, call 860.832.2200, e-mail FinancialAid3@ccsu.edu, or on the Web at www.ccsu.edu/finaid.

STUDENT ORGANIZATIONS AND ACTIVITIES

There are 120 student clubs and organizations, which cover a broad range of interests: academic--such as the Anthropology or the Investment clubs; athletic--such as the crew or flying clubs; cultural—for example, the art club, the jazz band, and other musical organizations; ethnic—such as the Black Student Union, Latin American Students Organization, and the Muslim Student Association; religious—such as Hillel and the Newman Club; and such honors organizations as Delta Mu Delta, Lambda Delta, and Kappa Delta Pi. On-campus entertainment is wide and varied, including, most recently, "Devils Den@ 10," student-run entertainment on Thursday evenings.

ADMISSIONS PROCESS

CCSU is a learning community of students with a broad range of abilities, interests, and backgrounds. We value excellence and achievement in academic scholarship, community involvement, and extracurricular activities. Our admissions process evaluates the readiness of applicants to succeed based on past demonstrations of academic and personal successes. The preferred deadlines for best consideration are May 1 (for fall semester) and December 1 (for spring).

First-year applicants are considered on the basis of performance in college preparatory classes, rank in class, SAT or ACT test scores, recommendations, and community and extracurricular involvement and leadership. A personal essay is required. For some applicants an interview with a representative of the Office of Recruitment & Admissions may be necessary. If the applicant ranks in the top 20% of his/her class, is an A-B student, and has SAT scores of 1100 or higher, the student should consider finding out about CCSU's Honors Program by calling 860-832-2938 for details. CCSU accepts most Advanced Placement (AP) courses for college credit, provided the minimum CCSU required score is achieved. Check with Admissions for the required scores.

Admission criteria include graduation from a regionally accredited secondary school. High school work should include college preparatory courses in: English (four years); Mathematics (covering algebra I, geometry, and algebra II); Science (two years including one-year lab science); Social sciences (two to three years including U.S. history). Coursework in foreign language is recommended (at least three consecutive years of the same foreign language up through the third level will satisfy the foreign language proficiency required of all CCSU-enrolled students). Students whose preparation does not follow this pattern may still qualify for admission if, in the judgment of the Director of Recruitment and Admissions, there is strong evidence that they have the potential to complete a degree program or if they meet other established criteria as authorized by the University President under authority delegated by the Board of Trustees of the Connecticut State University System. Applicants who are not graduates of a secondary school should submit their secondary school transcript up to the time of withdrawal and a copy of their high school equivalency diploma and scores.

Students interested in enrolling part-time on a non-degree basis should contact Continuing Education at (860) 832-2255.

The most important thing for the applicant to remember is to provide as much information as possible - achievements, awards, and examples of leadership - when applying.

HOW TO APPLY: Students are encouraged to apply online at www.ccsu.edu. For paper applications, please provide the Office of Recruitment & Admissions with 1) completed application for undergraduate admission 2) official high school transcript, SAT or ACT test scores, recommendations, and essay and 3) a non-refundable application fee of $50. All correspondence should be sent to the Office of Recruitment and Admissions, CCSU, P.O. Box 4010, 1615 Stanley Street, New Britain, CT 06050-4010.

Tours and information sessions may be arranged by calling 860.832.2289 or via e-mail at: admissions@ccsu.edu.

CHAPMAN UNIVERSITY

AT A GLANCE

Originally organized in 1861, Chapman University has steadily evolved from a small traditional church-related liberal arts school, into a vibrant midsize and nationally recognized university with renowned programs in areas such as film and television production, business and economics, theatre, dance, music, and teacher education.

Set in suburban and historic "Old Towne Orange," California, Chapman's beautiful tree-lined campus features a blending of historic and contemporary structures, tranquil gardens, world-class recreational facilities, and "smart" classrooms. With wireless technology throughout the campus, Chapman was recently named one of the top 50 "Best Wired" campuses by Yahoo!

Chapman's academic preparation and wide breadth of excellence is evidenced by the University's accomplished alumni, who include Loretta Sanchez ('88), member of Congress; David Bonior ('85), member of Congress and former house minority whip; Jose Gomez ('75) member of the Panamanian National Assembly; television and film producers John Copeland ('73), Jon Garcia ('90) and John David Currey ('98); cinematographer Gene Jackson ('70); television sports analyst, Steve Lavin ('88); Tony Award nominee and Broadway star of *Showboat*, Michel Bell ('68); Indy car racing star, Jacques Lazier ('93); former major league baseball stars Tim Flannery ('80), Marty Castillo ('80), Gary Lucas ('76) and Randy Jones ('72); and George L. Argyros ('65), philanthropist and former U.S. Ambassador to Spain.

LOCATION AND ENVIRONMENT

Chapman University is located in Orange County's beautiful south coast, famous for its ideal climate, cultural and recreational opportunities, and varied natural resources. With the San Diego and Los Angeles metropolitan areas in close proximity, students can attend concerts, see professional sports, or go to world famous theme parks like Disneyland and Knott's Berry Farm. There are outdoor activities throughout the year, with Pacific beaches only 10 miles from campus and winter ski resorts only 90-minutes away. Add to these benefits an average year-round temperature of 71° F, and it's no surprise that Places Rated Almanac recently named Orange County, California, "the #1 place to live in North America."

On campus, Chapman students take part in the dynamic student activities program. There are over 70 student run clubs, including community service organizations, eleven national fraternities and sororities, 20 NCAA D-III intercollegiate athletic programs, an active intramural sports program, and music, art, and theatre productions.

Though Chapman students are predominantly from California, the student body is diverse, with students hailing from 46 states and 34 foreign countries. Chapman students have distinguished themselves in a variety of forums. In the preceding five years, Chapman students have been recognized as Truman Scholars, Coro Fellows, USA Today All-USA College Academic Team members, NCAA All-Americans, and NCAA Academic All-Americans.

OFF-CAMPUS OPPORTUNITIES

Chapman's Career Development Center provides a variety of services to students, graduates, and former students. These include: internship opportunities, an on-campus recruiting program, full-time job postings and computer-networked job listings, individual career counseling and career assessment, a career resource library, job search and resume writing skills development, interview coaching, and an Alumni Mentor Program. The center will assist teachers in establishing a self-managed educational placement file.

Chapman students are encouraged to participate in study abroad programs in many academic fields in almost every part of the world. Students studying abroad through Chapman-approved programs are enrolled in a full course of study at the host institution, but receive academic credit from Chapman. The study abroad program directly supports Chapman's emphasis on encouraging students to recognize and develop their roles as global citizens in an increasingly interdependent world.

MAJORS AND DEGREES OFFERED

Chapman University confers degrees in the following field of study:

Accounting

Art

Athletic training

Biochemistry

Biological Sciences

Business administration

Chemistry

Communications

Computer information systems

Computer science

Creative Writing

Dance

Digital Arts

Economics

Engineering (civil)

English

Film Production

Film Studies

French

Health Sciences

History

Liberal studies (teaching)

Mathematics

Music

Peace studies

Philosophy

Pre-law

Pre-medicine

Political science

Psychology

Psychobiology

Public relations and advertising

Religious Studies

Screen Acting

Screenwriting

Sociology

Spanish

Television and Broadcast Journalism

Theatre

ACADEMIC PROGRAMS

Chapman University strives to provide every student with a comprehensive, liberal arts-based course of study which will result in producing an engaging, articulate and communicative world citizen with specific skills to offer. Academic departments are divided into the Wilkinson College of Humanities and Social Sciences; the Argyros School of Business and Economics (AACSB); the College of Educational Studies (CTC); the Dodge College of Film and Media Arts (CILECT); the College of Performing Arts (NASM); the School of Law (ABA); the Schmid College of Science; and University College, the off-campus program for working adults. Chapman is also home to the APTA-accredited graduate program in Physical Therapy. The A. Gary Anderson Center for Economic Research is recognized throughout the world for its excellence in economic forecasting. Chapman was recently named a "Character-Building College" by the Templeton Foundation.

CAMPUS FACILITIES AND EQUIPMENT

Chapman's park-like and ivy-covered, tree-lined campus is set in beautiful and historic Old Towne Orange and features a blending of fully refurbished historic structures with state-of-the-art internet and satellite connected learning environments. The Leatherby Libraries house eight individual libraries, each specific to one of the University's areas of study, as well as a holocaust library and museum. The 90,000 square foot Argyros Forum includes the primary campus dining area, conference and classroom facilities, and associated students offices. Bertea Hall, Oliphant Hall, and Moulton Center are home to the renowned College of Performing Arts (Theatre, Dance, and the NASM-accredited Conservatory of Music which includes a complete music library, classrooms, recital halls (5), concert hall, and practice rooms, 250-seat Waltmar Theatre, and Guggenheim Art Gallery. Memorial Hall (executive offices and Chapman Auditorium), Roosevelt Hall (faculty offices), Wilkinson Hall (Economic Science Institute), Reeves Hall (College of Educational Studies and classrooms), and Smith Hall (Psychology faculty offices and classrooms) are all buildings listed on the National Register of Historic Places. Although designated as historic, each of these structures has been fully refurbished internally and externally to provide both a historic and contemporary learning environment. The Lastinger Athletics Complex includes a 3,000-seat indoor arena, 3,500-seat outdoor stadium, 500-seat swim stadium, four championship tennis courts, and training and fitness facilities for the campus and surrounding community. Beckman Hall for business and technology houses the mathematics and computer sciences programs, as well as the AACSB-accredited Argyros School of Business and Economics. The Hashinger Science Center features laboratories for nuclear science, radiation, crystallography, genetics, food science, and physical therapy. Wilkinson Hall and Chapman's Economic Science Institute is home to 2002 Nobel Economics laureate, Vernon Smith and his team of scholars. Five residence halls and six on-campus apartment buildings are conveniently located on the edge of the campus with a new residence hall and conference center currently under construction. Marion Knott Studios houses the University's renowned Dodge College of Film and Media Arts including the undergraduate school of film and television, the graduate Conservatory of Motion Pictures, and the think tank-style Institute for the Study of Media and the Public Interest. Knott Studios also includes two 18,000-square foot sound stages, pre and post-production facilities, computer and digital editing labs, and 500-seat cinema. Kennedy Hall is home to Chapman's ABA-accredited School of Law, and Liberty Plaza which includes a reflection pond and replica Lincoln chair featuring a memorial to President Ronald Reagan facing a 5-ton section of the Berlin Wall brought to campus in 2000.

TUITION, ROOM, BOARD AND FEES

Undergraduate tuition (annual, 12-18 semester credits) room, board, and fees for the 2010–2011 academic are as follows:

Annual tuition: $37,500

Accident/Sickness plan: 380

Associated students fee: 120

Wellness Center fee: 244

Orientation fee: 145

Total tuition/fees: $38,389

School Says . . .

Room/board cost for academic year 2010–2011:

Room & Board: $13,000

Parking fee: 280

Total room/board $13,280

FINANCIAL AID

Almost 90% of 2009 freshman received some form of need based aid, merit, or talent scholarship. Awards are made through a combination of grants, scholarships, loans, and work-study programs. Awards may be renewed throughout a student's term of study. A student's financial needs are usually met through a combination of internal assets and federal and state funding. Chapman awards merit scholarships, regardless of financial need, to all eligible admitted new students using a standardized test score/ entering grade point average-driven formula. Chapman also offers talent scholarships in areas such as art, music, dance, theatre, writing, film and television, and science awarded regardless of financial need. Audition, submission of portfolio, or supplemental application materials will be required to be considered for talent awards.

STUDENT ORGANIZATIONS AND ACTIVITIES

Programs and services offered include over 70 clubs and organizations, career development, community outreach, multicultural programs, student health and counseling, international student services, PEER and health education, and new student orientation. Six national fraternities, and six national sororities are active and all include special programming directed toward stewardship and community service activities.

A complete and comprehensive offering of intramural sports and activities involve the entire campus community to create an involving, electric, and outdoor-oriented environment.

Intercollegiate athletics are a big part of undergraduate life at Chapman and almost 20 percent of students compete in varsity sports. Chapman is an independent in the NCAA Division III, often qualifying for championships. Last year, 4 students were named NCAA All-American and 14 were honored as Academic All-Americans. Chapman competes in men's baseball, basketball, water polo, crew, cross-country, football, golf, lacrosse, soccer, and tennis; and women's basketball, crew, cross country, soccer, softball, swimming, tennis, track and field, volleyball, and water polo.

ADMISSIONS PROCESS

Chapman University seeks accomplished students who will thrive in a challenging academic environment. Admission to Chapman is selective. In 2009, 51% of the applicant pool was offered admission to the University. Prospective students are evaluated on the strength of their secondary school course work and GPA, and SAT I or ACT scores. Interested students are encouraged to visit the campus, schedule a campus tour, and participate in an information session hosted by an admission officer. Arrangements can be made by contacting the Office of Admission. Chapman offers a non-binding Early Action deadline for freshman applicants. To apply in the Early Action period, students must submit the application before November 15. The regular freshman application deadline is January 15. The deadline for transfer applications is March 1. Chapman is a member of The Common Application group and the application and instructions can be found at www.commonapp.org.

Students may request more information by contacting:

Office of Admission

Chapman University

One University Drive

Orange, CA 92866

Telephone: (714) 997-6711 888-CUAPPLY (toll free)

Fax: 714-997-6713

E-mail: admit@chapman.edu

CLEMSON UNIVERSITY

AT A GLANCE

Ranked No. 22 among the nation's top public institutions, Clemson University is a science- and engineering-oriented research university that maintains a strong commitment to teaching and student success. Clemson is an inclusive, student-centered community characterized by high academic standards, a culture of collaboration, a competitive drive to excel and a determination to make a difference.

Clemson's enrollment is about 19,000, and the campus population is carefully managed to maintain small classes and a student-to-faculty ratio more common to private colleges. Students can select from approximately 80 undergraduate and 110 graduate degree programs offered by five colleges: Agriculture, Forestry and Life Sciences; Architecture, Arts and Humanities; Business and Behavioral Science; Engineering and Science; and Health, Education and Human Development.

Research is important at Clemson, and not just with the faculty and graduate students. By their senior year, nearly 80 percent of undergraduate students are involved in a Creative Inquiry or other research project. Another important aspect of Clemson is its dedication to improving the world through public service. Clemson students typically contribute more than 126,000 service hours in a given year, earning the University national recognition as a "Campus with a Conscience."

Clemson is well-known for its prominent NCAA Division I athletic programs and for the spirit of its fans. But athletics hasn't cornered the market on competitive zeal. Students take just as much satisfaction in winning academic and organization challenges with other universities.

Another defining aspect of the school is that Clemson students are very happy here. Clemson has scored No. 1 and No. 2 in the past two years, according to the Princeton Review, as the university with the happiest students. And 91 percent of seniors and freshmen say they would choose Clemson again if given the opportunity to start their college educations over.

With its college-town, lakefront setting against a backdrop of mountains and forests, Clemson is characterized by a strong sense of community, a commitment to service and a love of winning—in academics, in athletics and in life.

ADMISSIONS:

864-656-2287

www.clemson.edu/prospective-students

Campus Tours:

864-656-4789

www.clemson.edu/visitors/scheduletour

LOCATION AND ENVIRONMENT

Location

Clemson, S.C.

Environment

Clemson is spread out on a 1,400-acre campus along the shores of Hartwell Lake; it's located in the middle of the I-85 corridor between Atlanta, Ga., and Charlotte, N.C. The Blue Ridge Mountains are well within sight, and the climate is as warm as the welcome you'll receive when you make a visit to campus.

OFF-CAMPUS OPPORTUNITIES

Cooperative Education

Undergraduates can obtain professional work experience at hundreds of different companies and organizations through the University's Cooperative Education program. This voluntary program allows students to alternate periods of academic study with periods of related work at organizations ranging from small consulting firms to Fortune 500 companies.

Study Abroad

When you take advantage of Clemson's international study abroad programs, you can study almost anywhere in the world. From France to Malta, Fiji to The Galapagos Islands, chances are there's a program of study there. In many cases, studying abroad costs the same as studying at Clemson. In fact, many scholarships and financial aid plans will cover costs.

Community Service

When you want to make a difference, Clemson's Community Service Office provides plenty of opportunities. You can join a student service organization, find on-going service projects, participate in one-time service events either on campus or in the community, or explore national and international service opportunities. If you want to find people who need your help, learn more about yourself, develop relationships, or if you just want to have fun, this is a great way to do it.

STUDENT ORGANIZATIONS AND ACTIVITIES

Extracurricular activities are a vital part of any student's life. If you're a dancer or a musician, want to build houses for Habitat for Humanity, or join a fraternity or sorority, you can find your niche at Clemson. There are more than 300 student clubs and organizations to try.

MAJORS AND DEGREES OFFERED

Clemson offers more than 80 undergraduate and 110 graduate degree programs through five academic colleges: Agriculture, Forestry and Life Sciences; Architecture, Arts and Humanities; Business and Behavioral Science; Engineering and Science; and Health, Education and Human Development.

To find out what majors are available go to: www.clemson.edu/academics/majors/html

ACADEMIC PROGRAMS

The step from high school to college can be enormous. The standards are different, the work is more demanding, and the personal freedoms are much greater. For students who are making the transition from high school to college, Clemson has developed student success programs to help meet the academic challenges.

The Academic Success Center offers tutoring and supplemental instruction to all students without additional charges. Supplemental instruction allows students enrolled in specific courses to work with student leaders who have already successfully completed the courses and who have been trained to lead study sessions. Student leaders work with the professor of the course, attend class and do homework with their assigned students. They also host study sessions three times a week where they review course content and teach learning and study strategies.

The First Year Experience is a comprehensive program for all first-year students who live on campus. The program assists freshmen in making the transition from the high school and home environment to the Clemson University community.

Living-learning communities offer the chance for students to live and work with others who have similar interests and goals. There are living options for students interested in business, engineering and science, civics and service, honors courses, professional golf management and much more. Recognized as a national model, the communities are designed to help students be more successful by offering on-site advising and academic support, common course assignments, guest speakers, service opportunities and a variety of social activities.

Calhoun Honors College offers honors courses and the opportunity to be actively involved in research. Honors students enjoy priority registration, free tickets for cultural events on campus and honors research grants. Many also live in honors housing.

Communication Across the Curriculum is a program designed to help all students — whether they're studying engineering, biology, history or architecture — become strong communicators. Clemson's mission is not to train students on just the technical aspects of their chosen profession, but rather to prepare them to become leaders in their field. To do that, it's vital that students become good communicators and proficient in the latest communication technology so they can sell their ideas and inspire those they will lead.

Creative Inquiry includes carefully planned research projects that teach by allowing students to apply classroom learning to real-life situations. Led by a special task force of representatives from all academic colleges, these projects include hands-on research opportunities, require several semesters of dedication and give students and teachers a whole new world of learning environments. Some students end up traveling around the state, the country and even abroad to gather and share information. Projects are integrated in each college with the goal of building students' capabilities to find, analyze and evaluate information while applying it in a team-based atmosphere.

Freshman Reading is designed to enrich the intellectual environment of Clemson students, to encourage them to look at things from different perspectives and to be open to new ideas. The summer before their freshman year, students receive a copy of the year's selected book. They read the book and write a paper before arriving on campus in the fall. During Orientation, students come to Littlejohn Coliseum to hear the author speak and break into small groups to discuss what they've read and heard.

CAMPUS FACILITIES AND EQUIPMENT

Clemson University's modern laboratories and classrooms are well-equipped for instruction, research and lectures. Facilities exist beyond the main campus, stretching around the state and even abroad.

Michelin® Career Center

Designed to help launch the promising careers of Clemson graduates, the Michelin Career Center offers resume critiques, campus interviewing, career fairs, experiential education and internship programs, workshops and much more. It has been listed as No. 3 in Best Career Services by the Princeton Review in its 2010 college rankings.

Housing

Located within a 10- to 15-minute walk to class, Clemson's 22 residence halls and five apartment complexes offer a vast selection of living arrangements.

Fike Recreation Center

Fike is a 200,000 square foot recreation center that features a fitness atrium complete with a suspended running track that overlooks the indoor courts. It's also equipped with indoor swimming facilities, fitness studios, racquetball courts, state-of-the-art cardio equipment, weights, locker rooms and even a climbing wall. If you're into staying in shape, Fike is the place to be.

Hendrix Student Center

The Hendrix Center is the hub of campus activity and is located a step away from most housing. Here you can find people taking a yoga class or enjoying a meal at the food court. It's home to the University Bookstore and offers plenty of quiet places to stop and study. It has a movie theater, ice cream parlor and much more.

Health Center

Redfern Health Center provides medical services, counseling and psychological services, and health-related programs like alcohol and drug education. It's one of the nation's few on-campus accredited health centers.

TUITION, ROOM, BOARD AND FEES

2009–2010 Academic Year

S.C Resident Full Time

Tuition and Fees	$11,478
Room and Board (approximate)	$ 6,774
Books and Supplies (approximate)	$ 922
Total	$19,174

Nonresident Full Time

Tuition and Fees	$25,788
Room and Board (approximate)	$6,774
Books and Supplies (approximate)	$ 922
Total	$33,484
Other Expenses	
Estimated Personal Expenses	$1,966
One-time computer cost°	$1,250

°All students are required to own a laptop computer. For details, go to *www.clemson.edu/prospectivestudents/nextsteps.*

FINANCIAL AID

Academic scholarships are available at Clemson, and they're awarded based on academic merit. Financial aid may also be available on the basis of need to supplement the amount students and their families can contribute to college expenses. Clemson offers financial aid in the form of grants, scholarships, loans and part-time employment.

STUDENT ORGANIZATIONS AND ACTIVITIES

At Clemson, school spirit is a color—Solid Orange—and it's hard to miss on fall Saturdays in Death Valley when more than 80,000 fans cheer on the Clemson Tigers. Take a walk through campus on any night, and you'll see the campus alive with students playing intramural sports, going to concerts, attending Greek mixers or gathering to meet with any of Clemson's 300 student organizations.

ADMISSIONS PROCESS

Students can apply by visiting www.clemson.edu/prospectivestudents to quickly submit their applications online. Application fees may be processed online using a credit card or an electronic check. Freshman applicants should arrange to have their high school transcripts sent directly from their high schools and SAT or ACT scores sent directly from the testing service.

Students applying for admission must take the SAT or ACT.°

°Writing portion is mandatory.

THE COLLEGE OF NEW JERSEY

AT A GLANCE

The College of New Jersey (TCNJ) has created a culture of constant questioning. In small classes, students and faculty members collaborate in a rewarding process. They seek to understand fundamental principles, apply key concepts, reveal new problems and pursue lines of inquiry to gain a fluency of thought in their disciplines. This transformative process is at the core of the educational experience at the College.

Many students extend their classroom work by participating in research with faculty members or studying abroad. Often, professors and students co-author papers published in academic journals. The mentor relationship helps students discuss career options and land pertinent fellowships, internships, and summer research positions.

TCNJ admits a diverse class each year full of ambitious students, eager to build on their earlier education and plunge into new topics. The most successful admits are prepared to steer their own academic pursuits toward post-graduation goals of graduate school, professional training, or satisfying careers.

Prestigious graduate schools, including the University of Pennsylvania, Georgetown Law School, Maxwell School at Syracuse University, NYU Law School, and Harvard, Yale, and Northwestern Universities, routinely welcome TCNJ alumni into their ranks. Eighty-five percent of TCNJ students who apply to medical school are accepted.

Many top corporations recruit TCNJ graduates, providing avenues into rewarding jobs directly after graduation. Other barometers of student success include the 100 percent pass rate of education majors taking the state teacher preparation test and the 85 percent three-year pass rate for nursing students going for their license. The variety of learning opportunities at the College prepares students to prosper in any arena after leaving the campus.

LOCATION AND ENVIRONMENT

Neoclassical Georgian Colonial architecture, meticulous landscaping and thoughtful design merge to meet the evolving needs of TCNJ students. Students enjoy a campus with 289 acres of trees, lakes, and open spaces within the suburban setting of Ewing Township, New Jersey. Two out of three undergraduate students live in campus residence halls. The residence halls vary in configuration from the freshman towers to suites and townhouse arrangements for upper class students. An on-campus 600-bed apartment complex is set to open in fall 2009. The college ensures that on-campus housing is available to all students in their first two years.

More that 150 student organizations flourish at the College. Anyone can find an intramural sports team, Greek organization, cultural club, or academic group to suit his or her interests. Many students make friends and enjoy their leisure time participating in one of these groups. In addition, the College Union Board organizes events, including concerts, performances, and comedy nights. The college's highly successful Division III teams also provide an opportunity to socialize and cheer on fellow classmates. Nearby cities, such as Trenton, Philadelphia, and New York, allow for abundant entertainment, employment, and social options. Many courses incorporate field trips to New York City or Washington, DC.

OFF-CAMPUS OPPORTUNITIES

TCNJ administers an extensive international study program, featuring exchange programs in locations as diverse as London and the University of Santiago. Some students choose to attend one of the 131 available institutions in the U.S., while others venture to one of the 33 countries offering full-year or semester-long programs.

Student internships, both on and off campus, expose students to career options as they gain professional skills. With the college's location in the center of corporate activity close to New York and Philadelphia, many internships are available - some with pay and some for credit.

Faculty members lend their advice and help students locate and procure appropriate opportunities including fellowships, research positions and internships. Students may also use resources at the Office of Career Services to find positions in New York, Philadelphia, or any of the corporations, government agencies, or research organizations closer to campus.

MAJORS AND DEGREES OFFERED

The College of New Jersey hosts seven schools: Arts and Communication; Business; Culture and Society; Education; Engineering; Nursing, Health & Exercise Science; Science. The College offers programs leading to the Bachelor of Arts, Bachelor of Fine Arts, Bachelor of Music, Bachelor of Science, and Bachelor of Science in Nursing.

TCNJ grants degrees in the following majors: accountancy, art°, art history, digital arts, fine arts, graphic design, interactive multimedia, biology°, business administration (specializations: finance, general business, information systems management, international business, management, marketing), chemistry°, communication studies, computer science, economics, early childhood education°, education of the deaf and hard of hearing°, elementary education°, health and exercise science°, special education for the developmentally handicapped°, engineering (biomedical engineering, computer engineering, electrical engineering, mechanical engineering, and engineering science-civil engineering), English° (options: liberal arts, journalism, professional writing), history°, international studies, criminology and justice studies, mathematics° (option: statistics), music°, nursing, philosophy, physics° (options: scientific computer programming and earth science), political science, psychology, sociology (option: pre-social work), Spanish°, technology education°, and women's and gender studies.

(° programs in which students may prepare for teacher certification)

Students may also choose to complete a minor, in one of the previously mentioned fields or another subject area, such as African American studies, classical studies, comparative literature, religion, public administration, French, Italian, and Spanish.

Joint degrees are also available at TCNJ. In conjunction with UMDNJ, students can pursue a seven-year combined BS/MD degree. A seven-year combined BS/OD degree program is also available through the State University of New York College of Optometry. There is also a four-and-a half-year combined BS/MA degree in law and justice with Rutgers University. Students can study for five years to receive their dual certification in the education of the deaf and hard of hearing and elementary education/master of arts in teaching.

ACADEMIC PROGRAMS

A Liberal Learning Curriculum ensures that all students are grounded in the beliefs and values of civic responsibility and intellectual and scholarly growth and that they receive a well-rounded education in the liberal arts.

In 2004, the College completed a transformation of its curriculum requiring fewer, more in-depth courses. All courses have been transformed and contain a significant out of class requirement and will provide for even more student and faculty interaction.

The small classes enable dialog between students, and every class at TCNJ is taught by a professor, not a graduate student. The College shapes its curricula and educational experiences around the concept of the accomplished and engaged learner.

The required First-Year Seminar, the cornerstone of the new Liberal Learning program, introduces students to the habits of mind and the methodologies of research; it's seminar format of no more than 15 students reinforces the message that students are not to be passive recipients of knowledge but rather active contributors to their own learning. Requirements are grouped as diversity and community engagement goals, proficiencies and depth requirements that can be self designed or designated interdisciplinary concentrations.

Top students may enroll in TCNJ's honors program, designed to provide a core curriculum with additional challenges and opportunities for individualized work. Most honors classes take an interdisciplinary approach to the history of civilizations, its accomplishments, and its problems. Independent study arrangements fall easily within the parameters of the honors program, as well.

CAMPUS FACILITIES AND EQUIPMENT

Learning, like everything else, is contextual. The surroundings in which students learn and the tools they use influence their experience. Not surprisingly, the college supports its educational aspirations with careful attention to the quality of its facilities. In the first decade of the 21st century, more than $250 million in ongoing and new facilities construction is ensuring that TCNJ students continue to have an environment that not only meets their academic, athletic, social and living needs but extends their reach--resulting in higher scholarship, better health and fitness, closer community, and greater comfort.

TUITION, ROOM, BOARD AND FEES

Because TCNJ is a public institution, costs are lower than most equivalent private institutions. The tuition and fees for undergraduates in the 2008-2009 academic year are as follow:

In-state tuition and fees: $12,308

Out-of-state tuition and fees: $20,415

Room and board (all students): $9,612

FINANCIAL AID

Close to 50 percent of full-time undergraduates benefit from financial aid, which can come in the form of merit-based scholarships, work-study programs, loans, or government or institutional grants. All students seeking financial aid must submit the Free Application for Federal Student Aid (FAFSA) form or renewal FAFSA to apply. The Title IV FAFSA Code for The College is 002642.

Students may compete for the College's merit scholarships, which are funded by the state government as well as private donors. These awards are offered to those applicants with top SAT scores and class rankings. Over the last six years, TCNJ has given scholarships totaling more than $12 million.

STUDENT ORGANIZATIONS AND ACTIVITIES

Classroom learning at TCNJ is complemented by an extensive and acclaimed Leadership Development Program. Life outside the classroom is not something our students do on the side. It's an extension of the learning experience. At every turn from the first year on, students blur the boundary between living and learning, closing the gap between "student" and "life."

For fun or experience, students can participate in any of the more than 150 TCNJ clubs, catering to interests as diverse as theater, professional training, writing, fraternities and sororities, and athletics. TCNJ teams play in the NCAA Division III, as non-scholarship student athletes. The men field teams in 11 sports, while them women compete in 10. The college holds the record for championship and runner-up titles since Division III was started in 1979.

For those looking for something a little less competitive, intramural sports, including flag football, volleyball, softball, floor hockey, and basketball, have thriving coed leagues of their own. Intramural teams play in state, regional, and national tournaments. The college was proud to send its top-ten flag football team to the recent championship in New Orleans.

TCNJ students administer both the Student Finance Board and College Union Board. They organize popular student events, bringing people to the campus such as Matt Nathanson, Ludacris, Third Eye Blind, John Leguizamo, Ann Coulter, George Carlin, Angela Davis and Eddie Palmieri.

ADMISSIONS PROCESS

The admissions committee at TCNJ accepts a class of motivated, ambitious, and highly talented students. Most successful applicants have taken 16 college-preparatory units in high school. They also show impressive class ranks and SAT scores. Most students admitted into the class fall within the top 10 percent of their graduating class. The committee also considers extracurricular involvement, individual pursuits, and community participation. Students applying to the art and music departments are evaluated on additional criteria specific to their intended course of study.

Those applying for September admission must have their applications submitted by February 15. TCNJ offers an early-decision program to those who know the College is their first choice: applications received by November 15 will receive a response by December 30. A small number of students begin classes in January, and they must apply by November 1. For further information, please contact:

OFFICE OF ADMISSIONS

The College of New Jersey

PO Box 7718

Ewing, NJ 08628-0718

Telephone: 609-771-2132

E-mail: admiss@vm.tcnj.edu

THE COLLEGE OF SAINT ROSE

AT A GLANCE

Passion. Knowledge. Purpose. These words define the foundation of The College of Saint Rose. Saint Rose is a distinguished college interwoven within a remarkable city. Saint Rose is a distinct educational advantage for a College dedicated to cultivating intellectual dynamic leaders appreciative of diversity and active citizenship. Saint Rose is about challenging students to achieve new levels of excellence. It is about inspiring intellectual thought, critical writing, and artistic expression. It is about a strong liberal education curriculum with an intensive system of career preparation. It is about conveying the importance of faith, ethics, and integrity to students as they continue through a lifetime of decision-making and relationship-building. It is about dreaming what others have not dreamed and taking risks that others have not taken.

LOCATION AND ENVIRONMENT

The College of Saint Rose is a private, independent, coeducational, liberal arts institution located in Albany, New York. Through its 63 undergraduate and 33 graduate programs, Saint Rose serves more than 5,000 students from 20 states and eighteen countries.

OFF-CAMPUS OPPORTUNITIES

At Saint Rose, students can experience a world-class education by studying in one of more than 30 countries (Australia, Ireland, England, New Zealand, Spain, Italy, France, Greece, Africa, Central and South America, just to name a few).

Through a unique partnership, Saint Rose and the Albany-Colonie Regional Chamber of Commerce offer intensive internships with corporations throughout the Capital Region.

During the past year, students have put their education into practice by working with 72 local businesses and have developed valuable contacts that serve as employment leads after college.

In addition to traditional internships, communications majors may also participate in the Media Education Program, a cooperative effort between Saint Rose, the City of Albany, and Time Warner Cable.

Students majoring in childhood, adolescence, early childhood, and special education program are prepared for the challenges of the classroom through several field experiences including classroom observation and a semester-long student teaching assignment. Communication disorders majors participate in several field experiences in area medical centers and schools, as well as in the Emery Educational and Clinical Services Center, a full-scale on-campus clinic within the College's Thelma P. Lally School of Education.

The College's location in Albany, the epicenter of New York State government, provides exciting internship options for history and political science majors. The Saint Rose campus is slightly more than a mile from the historic state capitol, legislative offices, city hall, and the headquarters of many state agencies.

In the Capital Region's Tech Valley area, Math, Science and Computer majors have put their education into practice by choosing from a number of internships locally and across the nation; field experiences including those held at the Pacific Whale Foundation in Hawaii. Several students have participated in scientific research conducted by professors on campus, funded by National Science Foundation research grants.

MAJORS AND DEGREES OFFERED

The College of Saint Rose offers the following degrees:

BA, BS, BFA, BA/MA, BA/JD, BS/MS, BS/MBA, MA, MS, MBA, and MS in Education. Combined Degree Programs: Qualified students may participate in the 3+3 law option with Albany Law School, or the 3+2 engineering option with Union College, Clarkson University, Rensselaer Polytechnic Institute, or Alfred University, wherein they complete selected bachelor's degree programs at Saint Rose in three years and transfer to the cooperating institution to finish the professional program. Students are also eligible for our 4+2 Occupational Therapy (BS or BA/MS) or 4+3 Clinical Doctorate in Physical Therapy (BS or BA/DPT).

ACADEMIC PROGRAMS

School of Mathematics and Science:

Biochemistry, Biology, Biology 7–12 Education, Biology/Cytotechnology, Bioinformatics, Chemistry, Chemistry 7–12 Education, Computer Information Systems, Computer Science, Criminal Justice, Environmental Affairs, Forensics, Geology, Mathematics, Mathematics 7–12 Education, Pre-dental, Pre-medical, Pre-veterinary, Psychology, Religious Studies, Social Work, Sociology; 3+1 Medical Technology

School of Business:

Accounting, Business Administration

Concentrations:

Finance, Financial Planning, Information Technology Management (ITM), Management, Management in Human Resources, Managerial Accounting, Marketing, Public Sector Accounting and Auditing, Small Business and Entrepreneurship, Sport Management, Taxation, Individualized or Interdisciplinary

School of Arts and Humanities:

American Studies, Art Education (K–12), Studio Arts (B.F.A.), Graphic Design (B.F.A.), Communications, English, English 7–12 Education, History, History/Political Science, Political Science, Social Studies 7–12 Education, Music Education (K–12), Music Industry, Music, Pre-law, Philosophy/Religious Studies, Spanish, Spanish 7–12 Education, and Women's Studies

School of Education:

Technology Education; Communication Sciences & Disorders; Early Childhood Education (Birth–Grade 2); Childhood Education (Grades 1–6); and

Adolescence Education (Grades 7–12):

Students who wish to teach Grades 7–12 major in the subject area in which they plan to teach. Adolescence Education majors include: Biology 7–12; Chemistry 7–12; Earth Science 7–12; English 7–12; Math 7–12; Social Studies 7–12; Spanish 7–12

Special Education Dual Degree Programs:

Early Childhood/Special Education (dual degree program that certifies students to teach in regular and inclusive settings for Birth-Grade 2)

Childhood Education/Special Education (dual degree program that certifies students to teach in regular and inclusive settings for Grades 1–6)

Middle Childhood Extensions:

Childhood Education majors have the option of earning a Grades 7–9 extension to the B.S. degree; Adolescence Education majors have the option of earning a Grades 5–6 extension to the B.S. degree.

CAMPUS FACILITIES AND EQUIPMENT

The Massry Center for the Arts Within the $14 million Massry Center for the Arts 46,000 square feet of wireless and smart classrooms, practice and performance space, the College's music students experience the finest sound quality as they rehearse and perform a wide variety of orchestral and choral works. The facility features a 400-seat performance hall, acoustically perfect instrumental and choral rehearsal suites, applied teaching studios, and piano keyboard laboratories. On December 9, the heart and soul of the College collectively sang with joy as the College announced a $2 million gift by the Massry family that will permanently and symbolically ensure that the visual and performing arts will always be a centerpiece of a Saint Rose education. The largest gift ever by this prominent Capital Region family, it helped fund the construction of the new Massry Center for the Arts on Madison Avenue.

Center for Communications and Interactive Media (spring 2010) the new Center for Communications and Interactive Media is a 20,000 square foot facility. It will house new TV and radio studios, a live recording studio, video and film viewing room, multimedia computer labs and offices for the College's communications and music industry faculty. When completed in late fall 2010, it will join the Massry Center for the Arts and the Campus Theatre to form an arts and communications section of the Saint Rose campus.

The Christian Plumeri Sports Complex (spring 2010)—The College is also investing more than $2.5 million to create an outdoor sports complex with a baseball field, softball field and an artificial turn soccer/lacrosse field as well as a natural grass practice field. These fields will be home for the Saint Rose Golden Knights who have regularly won bids to NE-10 conference and Division II national tournaments as well as for the College's intramural and club sports.

Thelma P. Lally School of Education. This new 56,000 square-foot building features the Joy Emery Educational and Clinical Services Center, the Patricia Standish Curriculum Library, and the Carl E. Touhey Multimedia Forum, as well as classrooms, computer labs, and faculty offices. This building is a national model for the training of skilled teachers, speech pathologists, counselors, and school leaders.

Additionally, a $7.5 million Events and Athletics Center, features a new gymnasium, new team and training rooms, a state-of-the-art fitness center, and two-story lobby. With the creation of this facility, The College of Saint Rose provides an on-campus venue worthy of welcoming best-selling authors, Nobel Prize winners, and world-famous performers. This space will also serve as a unique collegiate basketball venue in the Capital Region, large enough to showcase the premier Saint Rose NCAA intercollegiate athletics program, and to accommodate the Golden Knights loyal fan base.

The College of Saint Rose has spent $7 million recently on new technology. The College's Networked Writing Lab allows students to write in teams and edit each other's work. The journalism, science, business, and education departments also have their own computer labs with software specific to those career fields so that students are trained in the latest technology in their particular industry.

Features of the Saint Rose campus include: a full-scale television studio for communications majors and an internet radio station. The Center for Art and Design houses the Saint Rose Art Gallery as well as extensive photography labs, graphic design computers, and one of the largest screen-printing facilities in the state of New York; the Science Center; the Music Center featuring the Alice and Henry Cooper Finks Music Library, Patricia Brady-Danzig Performance Hall, Saints and Sinners Sound Studio; and The Hubbard Interfaith Sanctuary, which provides a welcoming space for interfaith programs as well as individual prayer and reflection.

TUITION, ROOM, BOARD AND FEES

2006–07 Full-time Undergraduate Costs

Tuition: $18,672

Fee(s): $600

Residence & Board: $7,922-$8,206

FINANCIAL AID

Approximately 90 % of full-time students receive financial aid in the form of scholarships, grants, need and non-need based grants, loans or part-time employment.

STUDENT ORGANIZATIONS AND ACTIVITIES

Saint Rose offers more than thirty-five academic and special interest clubs or groups to choose from. The student government organization, the Student Association (SA), consists of elected students who want to make life at the College enjoyable, interesting, and as meaningful as possible.

Saint Rose is a member of the NCAA Division II and the prestigious Northeast-10 Conference. Men's sports include baseball, basketball, cross-country, golf, soccer, swimming, and tennis. Women's sports include basketball, cross-country, softball, soccer, swimming, tennis, and volleyball.

ADMISSIONS PROCESS

December 1 (Early Action -non Binding)

February 1 (Regular & Scholarship deadline)

School Says . . .

COLUMBIA COLLEGE (MO)

AT A GLANCE

Columbia College opens doors for its students to experience new discoveries, new relationships and new areas of knowledge that can be explored through thought-provoking, honest dialogue—both in and out of the classroom. Academics are strong, grounded in the liberal arts and sciences and offered in a learning environment characterized by civility and respect. Students feel at home on the beautiful campus, located in Columbia, Mo., thanks to the private college's close-knit community where opportunities to get involved are plentiful.

Each year, more than 1,200 students attend the traditional Day Campus and represent more than 22 states and 44 countries. At Columbia College, students choose from 40 outstanding majors and pre-professional programs. Undergraduate and graduate degrees are offered at the home campus in Columbia, Mo., as well as at 34 locations across the nation and online. Our worldwide alumni network of 60,000-strong helps students find internships and jobs after graduation.

Personal service and attention have been hallmarks at the institution since it was founded in 1851—traditions that can be seen and felt with a student-faculty ratio of 14-to-1 and meaningful relationships with professors and classmates. More than 80 percent of our faculty have earned the highest academic degrees possible in their fields.

Whether you're an athlete or a fan, you'll appreciate Cougar Athletics with award-winning NAIA Division I varsity sports in men's and women's basketball, men's soccer and women's volleyball and softball.

Columbia College welcomes students of all religious affiliations, while maintaining a covenant with the Christian Church (Disciples of Christ). The covenant dates back to our founding as Christian Female College, the first women's college west of the Mississippi River to be chartered by a state legislature. In 1970, the college opened its doors to both women and men and changed its name to Columbia College.

LOCATION AND ENVIRONMENT

At Columbia College, you have the best of both worlds when it comes to experiences. You'll live on a campus of 30 beautiful acres, where you'll bump into friends and faculty everywhere you go. You'll also be part of a big, exciting neighborhood as you share the city with more than 30,000 other college students from Stephens College and the University of Missouri, which is why Columbia is often referred to as Collegetown, U.S.A. Plus, the city has consistently been ranked among the best places to live in the nation by national publications and offers a surprisingly affordable cost of living, ideal for the needs and budgets of its large student population. You can walk downtown and experience the fascinating cuisines, eclectic entertainment, excellent shopping, exciting outdoor adventures and a variety of cultural events such as the True/False Film Festival.

OFF-CAMPUS OPPORTUNITIES

Many of our students can list one or more real-world professional experiences on their résumés by the time they graduate. Our students have presented cutting-edge research to a prestigious professional gathering, landed internships with the FBI and at Walt Disney World, volunteered at a local elementary school and traveled to New York, England and China as members of the Jane Froman Singers. Our students also have the opportunity to explore new cultures through study abroad programs to countries like England, Japan, Australia, New Zealand, Italy and France.

MAJORS AND DEGREES OFFERED

Columbia College awards the Associate in Arts, Associate in General Studies, Associate in Science, Bachelor of Science, Bachelor of Arts, Bachelor of Arts in General Studies, Bachelor of Fine Arts, Master of Business Administration, Master of Arts in Teaching and Master of Science in Criminal Justice. Students can major in accounting, American studies, art, biology, business administration, ceramics, chemistry, computer information systems, computer science, criminal justice administration, English, environmental studies, financial services, fire service administration, forensic science, graphic design, history, human resource management, human services, illustration, interdisciplinary studies, international business, management, management information systems, marketing, mathematics, printing and drawing, philosophy and religious studies, photography, political science, pre-communication science and disorders, printmaking, psychology, sociology, speech communication and sports management. The college also offers an outstanding teacher education program.

Students can minor in art history, art studio, criminology, education, environmental science, ethics, philosophy and religious studies, geography, international relations, legal studies, music, ROTC, Spanish and women's studies. Columbia College also offers pre-professional programs in dental, engineering, law, medicine and veterinary.

ACADEMIC PROGRAMS

If you are a first-time freshman confident in the major you have chosen, the college will commit to offering you all the classes you require to graduate in four years through the Four-Year Graduation Plan.

Columbia College also offers a unique program for teachers. Students can earn a Bachelor of Arts plus a Master of Arts in Teaching in a little more than four years through the DAYSTAR teacher education program. Graduates are eligible to be certified to teach at the elementary, middle or secondary school level anywhere in the state of Missouri.

CAMPUS FACILITIES AND EQUIPMENT

We hear time and again about the beauty of our campus from students, parents and visitors. Our campus is a wonderful mix of historic and contemporary buildings situated on 30 park-like acres. Yet all the buildings are within a five-minute walk no matter where you are located on campus. We take great pride in preserving our historic buildings, many of which are 100-150 years old. We are also proud of our new buildings, such as the Atkins-Holman Student Commons and the Southwell Athletic Complex, which are designed to tastefully blend in with the existing historic structures. The college also is pleased to host the Larson Art Gallery, featuring artwork from students and professionals year-round. The college continues to thrive and is in the process of developing plans and raising funds for a new science building.

We have three residence halls; Banks, Hughes and Miller, along with upperclassmen apartments. Each residence hall features extra-spacious rooms; individually controlled heating and air conditioning; voicemail, e-mail and Internet services; cable television; computer labs with printers; study lounges; laundry facilities; and access to a kitchenette with a microwave station. Banks Hall also includes a Wellness Floor exclusively reserved for students committed to a substance-free lifestyle.

TUITION, ROOM, BOARD AND FEES

For the 2009–2010 academic year, tuition is $14,576; and room and board is $5,898.

FINANCIAL AID

The Student Guide to America's 100 Best College Scholarships ranked Columbia College as one of the nation's most affordable top-rated colleges in the country. In addition to maintaining competitive tuition costs, Columbia College also awards more than $4 million in financial aid and scholarships every year. The majority of our students receive financial aid in one form or another.

STUDENT ORGANIZATIONS AND ACTIVITIES

As a Columbia College student, you'll quickly discover that your initiative and involvement are keys to your own success. Maybe that's why nearly 100 percent of our Day Campus students are involved in at least one of the 40 student clubs and organizations offered.

At Columbia College, you'll have the opportunity to become a respected voice on the Student Government Association, an admired actor in the Elysium Players, a responsible resident assistant, or an inspiring leader from the Emerging Leaders Institute, just to name a few of the possibilities. Student interest groups include student government, emerging leaders institute, honorary clubs and organizations, academic clubs and organizations, social clubs and service clubs. It's also easy to start your own club or organization with assistance from Campus Life.

Columbia College also offers competitive athletic programs with five NAIA Division I varsity teams in men's and women's basketball, men's soccer, women's softball and women's volleyball. Every one of our athletic programs has produced All-Americans and All-America Scholar-Athletes in the past 10 years. Our women's volleyball team has brought home the NAIA national championship title three times. And for eight of the past 10 years two or more Columbia College coaches have been recognized as conference or regional coach of the year.

ADMISSIONS PROCESS

While Columbia College is selective about admission, students with a minimum high school cumulative GPA of 2.5 who rank in the top half of their graduating class, or score at the 50th percentile or above on the ACT, SAT or GED generally can expect to be admitted to the college. We also welcome transfer students who have maintained a minimum cumulative grade point average of 2.0. We accept college credits from previous accredited college-level coursework, as well as from programs like CLEP, Advanced Placement, International Baccalaureate, dual credit, proficiency exams and DANTES.

With more than 3,000 colleges and universities in the country, it can be a challenge to find the school that best fits you. There's no better way to make a final decision than to visit the colleges on your short list. Columbia College offers three Preview Days each year, or you can contact the Admissions Office at (800) 231-2391, ext. 7352, to schedule a date that's convenient for you. Columbia College accepts applications throughout the year and the non-refundable application fee is $35. The fee is waived for applications received by Jan. 1 for the fall semester. So plan a visit today and learn about the opportunities that await you.

School Says . . .

COLUMBIA UNIVERSITY

AT A GLANCE

The School of General Studies of Columbia University is the finest liberal arts college in the country dedicated specifically to students with nontraditional backgrounds seeking a traditional education at an Ivy League university. Most students at the School of General Studies (GS) have, for personal or professional reasons, interrupted their education, never attended college, or are only able to attend part-time. GS is unique among colleges of its type because its students are fully integrated into the Columbia undergraduate curriculum: they take the same courses, with the same faculty, and earn the same degree as all other Columbia undergraduates.

General Studies students come from varied backgrounds and all walks of life. They have the option to study either full- or part-time. Many work full-time while pursuing a degree, and many have family responsibilities; others attend classes full-time, experiencing Columbia's more traditional college life. In the classroom the diversity and varied personal experience of the student body promotes discussion and debate, fostering an environment of academic rigor and intellectual development. The School has more than 1,300 undergraduate degree candidates and more than 500 Postbaccalaureate Premedical students. The average age of a GS student is 29. Approximately half of GS students attend classes full-time. Seventy percent of the School's students continue on to graduate and professional study after graduation. In recent years, the acceptance rate for General Studies Postbaccalaureate Premedical Program students applying to U.S. medical schools has been more than 90 percent.

In addition to its bachelor's degree program, the School of General Studies offers combined undergraduate/graduate degree programs with Columbia's Schools of Social Work, International and Public Affairs, Law, Business, Dental Medicine, Teachers College, and the College of Physicians and Surgeons.

LOCATION AND ENVIRONMENT

Columbia University is located in Morningside Heights, on the Upper West Side of Manhattan. The University's neighbors include the Union Theological Seminary, the Jewish Theological Seminary, the Manhattan School of Music, St. Luke's Hospital, Women's Hospital, Riverside Church, and the Cathedral of St. John the Divine. The diversity of intellectual and social activities offered by these institutions is one of Columbia's great assets as a university; another is its location in New York City, which offers students at Columbia a rich and almost boundless variety of social, cultural, and recreational opportunities that are themselves an education.

OFF-CAMPUS OPPORTUNITIES

Columbia students may enhance their academic experiences through various study-abroad programs around the world. For example, students may spend a term at the Reid Hall Program in the Montparnasse district of Paris, the Berlin Consortium for German Studies, Kyoto Consortium for Japanese Studies, or the Language Program in Beijing, China. Additionally, students may apply to participate in one of the Columbia approved study abroad programs located in countries all over the world.

MAJORS AND DEGREES OFFERED

The School of General Studies grants the B.A. and B.S. degrees and offers the following majors: African studies; African American studies; American studies; ancient studies; anthropology; applied mathematics; archaeology; architecture; architecture, history and theory; art history; art history–visual arts; Asian American studies; astronomy; astrophysics; biochemistry; biology; biophysics; chemistry; classical studies; classics; comparative ethnic studies; comparative literature and society; computer science; computer science-mathematics; creative writing; dance; drama and theater arts; earth science; East Asian studies; East Central European studies; economics; economics–mathematics; economics–operations research; economics–philosophy; economics–political science; economics–statistics; English and comparative literature; environmental biology; environmental science; evolutionary biology of the human species; film studies; French; French and Francophone studies; German literature and cultural history; Hispanic studies; history; information science, Italian cultural studies; Italian literature; Latin American and Caribbean studies; Latino studies; mathematics; mathematics–statistics; Middle East and Asian languages and cultures; music; neuroscience and behavior; philosophy; physics; political science; political science-statistics; psychology; regional studies; religion; Russian language and culture; Russian literature and culture; Slavic studies; sociology; statistics; urban studies; visual arts; women's and gender studies; and Yiddish studies. Individually designed majors are also available. In addition, the School offers two undergraduate dual-degree programs: one in conjunction with Columbia's School of Engineering and Applied Science and the other in conjunction with the Jewish Theological Seminary.

ACADEMIC PROGRAMS

The School of General Studies offers a traditional liberal arts education designed to provide students with the broad knowledge and intellectual skills that foster continued education and growth in the years after college, as well as providing a sound foundation for positions of responsibility in the professional world. Requirements for the bachelor's degree comprise three elements: (1) core requirements, intended to develop in students the ability to write and communicate clearly; to understand the modes of thought that characterize the humanities, social sciences, and sciences; to gain familiarity with central cultural ideas through literature, fine arts, and music; and to acquire a working proficiency in a foreign language; (2) major requirements, designed to give students sustained and coherent exposure to a particular discipline in an area of strong intellectual interest; and (3) elective courses, in which students pursue particular interests and skills for their own personal growth or for their relationship to future professional or personal objectives. Students are required to complete a minimum of 124 credits for the bachelor's degree; 60 of these may be in transfer credit, but at least 64 credits (including the last 30 credits) must be completed at Columbia. In addition to the usual graduation honors (cum laude, magna cum laude, and summa cum laude), honors programs for superior students are available in a majority of the University's departments.

Campus facilities and equipment

The Columbia University libraries constitute the nation's sixth-largest academic library system, with a collection of more than 9.5 million volumes, more than 5.8 million microform pieces, and 26 million manuscript items in 850 separate collections. Of the twenty-two libraries in the system, five are designated Distinctive Collections because of their unusual depth and nationally recognized excellence. All library divisions are available to General Studies students. The University's Computer Center is one of the largest and most powerful university installations in the world and has remote units and terminals in several parts of the campus to enhance its accessibility. The Fairchild Life Science Building houses research facilities, laboratories, electron microscopes, and a vast amount of biochemical equipment used for teaching and research. The University's physics building has been the scene of many important developments in the recent history of physics, including the invention of the laser and the first U.S. demonstration of nuclear fission.

TUITION, ROOM, BOARD AND FEES

For the 2009–2010 academic year, tuition was $1,7270 per credit, room and board costs were $$1,600 per month, fees were approximately $1,800, and books and supplies were $2,000.

FINANCIAL AID

The School of General Studies awards financial aid based upon need and academic ability. Approximately 70 percent of General Studies degree candidates receive some form of financial aid, including Federal Pell Grants, New York State TAP Grants, Federal Stafford and unsubsidized Stafford Loans, Federal Perkins Loans, General Studies Scholarships, and Federal Work-Study Program awards. The average award of the General Studies Scholarship is $6,000–$8,000. Priority application deadlines for new students are June 1 for the fall semester and October 15 for the spring semester.

STUDENT ORGANIZATIONS AND ACTIVITIES

One student represents General Studies students in the University Senate, a decision-making body comprised of students, faculty and administrative staff members from each division of the University. In addition, two General Studies students sit as voting members on the Committee on Instruction, which oversees the curriculum of the School. The General Studies Student Council elects officers each year and sponsors activities for students. The Observer, the School's student-run magazine, is published several times each year. The Premedical Association (PMA) sponsors events related to the medical school admissions process.

Additionally, students are eligible to participate in any of the more than 250 student organizations on campus.

ADMISSIONS PROCESS

The admission policy is geared to the maturity and varied backgrounds of its students. Aptitude and motivation are considered along with past academic performance, standardized test scores, and employment history. Admissions decisions are based on a careful review of each application and reflect the Admissions Committee's considered judgment of the applicant's maturity, academic potential and present ability to undertake course work at Columbia.

Admission requirements include a completed application form; a 1,500- to 2,000-word autobiographical statement describing the applicant's past educational history and work experience, present situation, and future plans; two letters of recommendation from academic or professional evaluators; an official high school transcript; official transcripts from all colleges and universities attended; official SAT or ACT scores (applicants may also take the General Studies Admissions Examination); and a nonrefundable application fee of $65.

Students from outside the United States may apply to the School of General Studies to start or to complete a baccalaureate degree. In addition to the materials described above, international applicants must submit official TOEFL scores.

Application deadlines are March 1 for early action (nonbinding) and June 1 for the fall semester, October 1 for early action (nonbinding) and November 1 for the spring semester, and April 1 for the summer semester. Applicants from countries outside the U.S. are urged to apply by August 15 for the spring semester and April 1 for the fall semester. Applications are reviewed as they are completed, and applicants are notified of decisions shortly thereafter.

For more information, please contact:

OFFICE OF ADMISSIONS AND FINANCIAL AID

School of General Studies

408 Lewisohn Hall

2970 Broadway

Columbia University, Mail Code 4101

New York, New York 10027

United States

Phone: 212-854-2772

E-mail: gsdegree@columbia.edu

Website: http://www.gs.columbia.edu

CONNECTICUT COLLEGE

One of the nation's premiere liberal arts colleges, Connecticut College is a small, highly selective, residential, private institution drawing national and international students.

AT A GLANCE

Chartered in 1911, Connecticut College was founded in the spirit of political and social equality, self-determination, and shared governance. The College actively seeks out students who are not only smart and intellectually curious, but who also bring a wide range of life experiences and perspectives that enable this spirit to endure within the College community. The College's near century-old Honor Code defines campus life and is observed by all students, faculty, and staff. Intellectually and academically, the Honor Code inspires students to challenge themselves and their peers to see the world from diverse perspectives, to remain receptive to new ideas and experiences, and, by instilling a sense of mutual respect, to consider how their actions and education may ultimately better the common good. The College offers over 50 majors and minors and participates in the NCAA Division III New England Small College Athletic Conference (NESCAC.) The College is nationally known for career and internship placement and has been called a "college with a conscience," as one of the top schools sending students to Teach for America or the Peace Corps. Enrollment at the College for 2009–2010 is 1,850. In the past three years, thirteen Connecticut College students have been awarded Fulbright Scholarships.

LOCATION AND ENVIRONMENT

Connecticut College is located two hours from Boston and two and a half hours from New York City, in historic New London, Connecticut, a small city (pop. 28,000) founded in 1646. The College's 750-acre campus, which is maintained as an Arboretum, features a centralized series of granite and limestone buildings adjacent to wooded trails. At the heart of the campus, Tempel Green sweeps down to offer commanding views of Long Island Sound. The College's athletic and fitness center is located along the Thames River.

OFF-CAMPUS OPPORTUNITIES

The College is located convenient to shopping and to the New London transportation center, which features train, bus, and ferry service to points along the eastern seaboard. New London is a diverse community home to numerous restaurants and cafes, galleries, and historic sites. The city also serves as the region's legal, medical, and social service center. The College operates a shuttle service for students to area locations and provides two ZipCars for students, although students are permitted to have cars on campus. The College's career and volunteer offices work closely with students to arrange for volunteer or internship opportunities. Many students volunteer in local schools or after school programs and may, in conjunction with coursework, receive teaching certification for elementary or secondary education.

MAJORS AND DEGREES OFFERED

Connecticut College offers over 47 majors and 42 minors, including self-designed study, as part of a liberal-arts curriculum designed for intellectual breadth, critical thinking, and acquisition of the fundamental skills and habits of a mind conducive to lifelong inquiry. Courses lead toward a Bachelor of Arts degree. Students complete General Education Requirements to ensure broad engagement with the range of disciplines that constitute the liberal arts. Connecticut College students launch their inquiry across disciplines and geographic boundaries and consider the campus and course catalogue open to them in this pursuit. The College, for example, offers free music lessons to all students. Through a course of study, students in a variety of majors may become certified for elementary, secondary, or private school education or receive a certificate demonstrating experience in Museum Studies. The most popular majors at the College are economics, government, English, psychology, international relations, and biological sciences. The College's dance program is internationally reputed, as is its theater program, which offers students the opportunity to study at the Eugene O'Neill Theater Center in Waterford, Connecticut and/or the Eugene O'Neill Moscow Art Theater in Russia.

ACADEMIC PROGRAMS

Students benefit from small classes that foster discussion and lead to personalized relationships with professors who serve as teacher-scholars. Professors frequently spark the interest that will inspire a student for their lifetime. The faculty to student ratio is 1 to 9. Average class size is 19. First-year students enroll in a seminar course (in which maximum enrollment is 16.) Ninety percent of full-time faculty member have a PhD or other terminal degree.

More than half of all students study away in a variety of domestic or international programs. Study away is a crucial component of a Connecticut College education, as it complements and informs a liberal arts curriculum (students who choose to study away do so primarily through the College's affiliation with institutions in over 40 countries.) The College also maintains domestic affiliations, including those with the Williams-Mystic Seaport Program, the Maritime Biological Laboratory Ecosystems Center at Woods Hole, and the Twelve College Exchange. In addition, students study away through Connecticut College's Study Away-Teach Away (SATA) program, in which a group of 10 to 15 students and one or two professors travel overseas and affiliate with a foreign university. SATA programs have been conducted in the Czech Republic, Peru, Egypt, Ghana, Greece, India, Italy, Mexico, Morocco, South Africa, Spain, Tanzania, and Vietnam.

To ensure that students consider the practical application of their study, the College provides each student with $3,000 to fund an internship or research project between their junior and senior year. About 80 percent of all students attend a series of seminars and work in conjunction with professors and career services to become eligible for the funding. One in five students conducts their internship overseas. Recent internships have been conducted with such organizations as The Field Museum of Chicago, J.P. Morgan in Hong Kong, Azafady in Madagascar, Vera Wang, New Line Cinema, and, CBS Sports.

To illustrate how several areas of study may be fused to best equip a student to understand and resolve complex issues, the College operates a series of interdisciplinary centers. The Centers are certificate-granting programs within the College that serve as an intellectual commons to bring together professors, students, and outside experts. There are five Centers, each with their own focus: The Toor Cummings Center for International Studies and the Liberal Arts; The Ammerman Center for Arts and Technology; The Holleran Center for Community Action and Public Policy; The Goodwin-Niering Center for Conservation Biology and Environmental Studies; and, the Center for the Comparative Study of Race and Ethnicity. Students combine their coursework with an integrated project and a paid overseas or domestic internship organized through the Center to receive a certificate from their chosen Center.

CAMPUS FACILITIES AND EQUIPMENT

Connecticut College occupies 750 acres (all of which is included in the Connecticut College Arboretum) on a hill overlooking the Thames River and Long Island Sound. The Arboretum's diverse acreage includes the landscaped grounds of the campus as well as the surrounding plant collections and natural areas. The resources of the Arboretum support the College's mission of preparing the next generation of citizen leaders to craft a sustainable relationship with the natural world. The symbiosis of the Environmental Studies major and the Goodwin-Niering Center provides an outstanding model of an ethically and environmentally sound community and places the College in a singular environment that offers a quality of life unique among liberal arts institutions.

Located at the center of the campus, the Charles E. Shain Library consists of more than 616,000 books and bound periodicals, 151,000 media and computing materials, and 5,599 subscriptions to periodicals. The collection is augmented through a consortium with Trinity College and Wesleyan University that provides fast access to more than 2.2 million items.

Other key buildings, include: Hale Laboratory; the Frank Loomis Palmer Auditorium; the F.W. Olin Science Center; Dayton Arena; the College Athletic Center; the Lyn and David Silfen Track and Field; and, Cummings Arts Center, which includes the Greer Music Library.

In the fall of 2009, the College opened a new $8 million fitness center overlooking the Thames River. The center more than triples the amount of exercise and wellness space at the College.

TUITION, ROOM, BOARD, AND FEES

Tuition, fees, room, and board cost $51,115 in 2009-2010. Housing is guaranteed for all students for four years. Ninety-nine percent of students live on campus. There is no Greek system.

FINANCIAL AID

Connecticut College offers need-based financial aid and meets 100 percent of demonstrated need. In 2009–10, the College awarded $20 million in institutional grants. Forty percent of students received some form of institutional aid. The average aid award was $32,000.

In 2006, Connecticut College began replacing or reducing need-based loan eligibility with institutional grants for students whose family income was less than $75,001 and contribution was less than $15,001.

STUDENT ORGANIZATIONS AND ACTIVITIES

As a small, residential liberal arts college, Connecticut College encourages students to pursue many interests outside the classroom, with the Crozier-Williams Student Center serving as the main hub for extracurricular activity as the site of club offices, WCNI-FM radio station, the weekly *College Voice* newspaper, and forums for live music, debate, dance, and poetry. Galleries, student run cafes, and performance spaces are found throughout campus. The Tansill Theater, a blackbox theater, is frequently home to student written productions. Students participate in dozens of clubs and organizations, including the Pegotty Investment Club, the Connecticut College Asian/Asian-American Student Association, Students Taking Action Now: Darfur (STAND,) Hillel, the Multifaith Student Council, and Habitat for Humanity. Students compete in a range of varsity, club, and intramural sports. The campus LGBTQ Center and Womens Center both host events focused on issues of sexuality, equity, and gender, while Unity House is the campus multicultural center and works with the Dean of Multicultural Affairs to host events focused on issues of race.

ADMISSIONS PROCESS

Connecticut College is one of the nation's most highly selective colleges. In 2008-2009, 36 percent of applicants were offered a place in the class of 2013. The College requires the Common Application and Supplement to the Common Application. An interview is recommended but not required. The submission of standardized tests (SAT Reasoning, SAT Subject, or ACT) is optional, although students whose primary language is not English are required to submit TOEFL scores or an equivalent. The College expects applicants will have taken the most appropriately rigorous courses available.

Application deadlines: Early Decision I, Nov. 15 for all ED1 application materials; Early Decision II and Regular Decision, Jan. 1 for all application materials. Financial Aid application dates: ED I, Nov. 15; ED II, Jan. 15; Regular Decision, Feb. 1.

CORCORAN COLLEGE OF ART AND DESIGN

AT A GLANCE

At the Corcoran College of Art + Design, individual attention and career opportunities are emphasized in a vibrant and active creative community. Our students access a diverse range of museums, monuments, and other cultural resources on hand, and form bonds with faculty and staff only a college of our size and caliber can provide.

Both in the studio and the classroom, our students receive individualized attention in a friendly, caring atmosphere. They find themselves not only on a first-name basis with their admissions counselor, but with faculty and staff as well. The collaborative relationships formed with instructors allow students to receive knowledge and feedback from those with a true understanding of their work.

Each year's senior class has the opportunity to showcase their work in a major gallery by participating in the undergraduate Senior Thesis Exhibitions. The series of week-long, rotating exhibitions in the Corcoran's Gallery 31 features photojournalism, photography, graphic design, digital media design, and fine art produced by members of the graduating class. Students are responsible for all aspects of their thesis exhibitions, from exhibition design to installation—an experience vital to their professional and artistic development. The individual shows culminate in May with the All-Senior Exhibition, a dynamic show installed in the Corcoran's museum galleries, representing all disciplines and featuring work by students graduating from the Bachelor's degree programs.

Notable alumni and students include Tara Donovan, American installation artist and 2008 MacArthur Fellow; Bjorn Egeli, American-Norwegian portrait painter; Tim Gunn, American fashion expert and television personality; Leigh Holliday, mixed media artist and fine arts teacher for children with ADD/ADHD and autism; David Lynch, American filmmaker, painter, composer, video artist, and performance artist; Chris Moukarbel, site-specific video and installation artist; Sonya Rapoport, American artist; Ian Svenonius, American musician and author; and Duff Goldman, American Pastry Chef and television personality. Graduates of the Corcoran's degree programs find themselves well connected to practicing artists in their fields, both in Washington, D.C. and beyond.

LOCATION AND ENVIRONMENT

From the National Gallery at the Smithsonian Institution to the political protests on the National Mall, the Corcoran is located at the center of the city's diverse range of museums, monuments, and other cultural resources; most of which are free. You'll join a network of more than 120,000 students pursuing degrees in this lively metropolitan region. Washington, D.C. alone contains more than a dozen colleges and universities, where Corcoran students can take select courses to enhance their curriculum. And with more than 100 local galleries and an expanding arts presence on Fourteenth Street and the U Street corridor, D.C. is home to one of the most dynamic contemporary art scenes in the country.

OFF-CAMPUS OPPORTUNITIES

Student life at the Corcoran is closely linked to Washington, D.C. itself. The city becomes an extended campus and offers limitless opportunities for cultural, social, artistic, academic, and professional growth. With numerous internships and jobs for college students available in the metropolitan area, this community is a magnet for young people from across the country and the world.

Corcoran is a member of the Association of Independent Colleges of Art and Design (AICAD), a consortium of 44 art colleges and universities from across the United States, Canada, Europe, and Asia (www.aicad.org). AICAD's mobility program allows students from member schools to apply to spend a semester at another AICAD college of their choice. Students also have the opportunity to study at AICAD's New York studio via the studio or internship program.

The Corcoran actively pursues partnerships with colleges in other countries where students may study abroad. Current Affiliations include Escuela de Bellas Artes in San Miguel de Allende, Mexico; the Studio Art Centers International (SACI) in Florence, Italy; Ladakh, study and hike at the top of the world, India; and the Lad. Additionally, students are encouraged to find study abroad programs in any country that offer specialization in their majors. Recently students have studied at the Glasgow College of Art, Scotland; Canberra School of Art, Australia; Danish School of Journalism, Denmark; Tallinn University, Estonia; and the Design Academy Eindhoven, Holland.

Additionally, the Corcoran is one of only 15 members of the Consortium of Universities of the Washington Metropolitan Area, a group of D.C. colleges and universities who have joined to provide a broad range of opportunities and resources to its students. Corcoran students may take classes at many of the area schools—including the George Washington University and Georgetown University—to extend their already rich curricular offerings.

MAJORS AND DEGREES OFFERED

The Corcoran is the only four-year college of art and design in Washington, D.C. The College's curriculum is centered on the idea of direct and intense creative education and emphasizes a conservatory approach to instruction, which means classes are small, professors are accessible, and classmates know one another. The College's undergraduate community includes more than 350 students pursuing a wide range of Bachelor of Fine Arts, Bachelor of Arts, and Associate of Fine Arts degrees.

Master of Arts programs at the Corcoran College of Art + Design offer rich, expansive, and uniquely integrated academic curricula grounded in real-world experiences. Our 200 graduate students work with faculty comprised of some of the leading experts in art and design, contribute to exhibition-related projects in the Corcoran Gallery of Art, and take advantage of the extraordinary cultural resources available in Washington, D.C.

The College holds national accreditation by the Middle States Commission on Higher Education since 1985. The Commission on Higher Education is an institutional accrediting agency recognized by the U.S. Secretary of Education and the Commission on Recognition of Postsecondary Accreditation. The College is also an accredited institutional member of the National Association of Schools of Art and Design and the Government of the District of Columbia Educational Licensure Commission licenses the College to grant AFA, BFA, BA, and MA degrees.

Bachelor of Fine Arts°: Fine Art (with concentrations in Ceramics, Digital Media, Drawing, Painting, Printmaking, and Sculpture), Fine Art Photography, Photojournalism, Graphic Design, Digital Media Design, Interior Design

Bachelor of Arts: Art Studies with three concentrations: Contemporary Art and Museum Culture, Theory and Studio Practice, Writing in the Arts

Bachelor of Fine Arts/Master of Arts in Teaching (five-year program) Students in any BFA major can pursue the five-year BFA/MAT degree program, which prepares students to work as an art educator in secondary schools, museums, and community art centers.

Associate of Fine Arts: Digital Media Design, Fine Art, Graphic Design, Photography

Master of Arts: History of Decorative Arts (an academic partnership with the Smithsonian Institution, Interior Design, Exhibition Design, Art Education, Art and the Book, Teaching (MAT)

Coming in fall 2011: Master of Arts in New Media Photojournalism

°Direct entry options available in all majors for first-time freshmen.

ACADEMIC PROGRAMS

In the first year of study, students develop essential visual and technical skills in a wide variety of media as well as in their chosen area of study. A distinctive aspect of the Corcoran's Foundation program is team-teaching in several studio courses, encouraging maximum participation, interchange, and dialogue between students and faculty. Students are exposed to multiple points of view to promote independent thinking, expand perceptual phenomena, and build a creative vocabulary.

Students can select a major upon entry or during their second year, choosing between Fine Art, Graphic Design, Interior Design, Digital Media Design, Fine Art Photography, Photojournalism, Art Studies, or the combined BFA/MAT art education degree. Sophomore studio courses are designed to bridge the ongoing development of technical skills and the increasing personal knowledge of artistic expression. Conceptual abilities are also challenged by academic requirements in art history and humanities.

In the junior and senior year, the focus shifts towards one's personal vision, individual initiative, and professional development. Internships, individual projects, directed studies, and advanced academic and studio electives hone each student's specific career goals. The degree studies culminate in formal exhibitions of senior thesis projects in a formal gallery of the Corcoran Gallery of Art.

CAMPUS FACILITIES AND EQUIPMENT

The Corcoran College of Art + Design's Downtown campus is located a block from the White House in the heart of Washington, D.C. Student services, the Library, studios, tutoring resource center, classrooms, faculty and administrative offices, and the world-renown Corcoran Gallery of Art are housed Downtown. The Georgetown campus is home to our Interior Design, Exhibition Design, Art and the Book, Graphic Design, Digital Media Design, and freshmen year courses. Georgetown houses the design center's state-of-the-art computer laboratories. All students will have the opportunity to take classes at both of our campuses.

The College is within easy walking distance of several desirable Washington neighborhoods. Corcoran housing is conveniently located between the downtown and Georgetown campuses. Through an arrangement with an established apartment facility, the College provides furnished studios and one-bedroom apartments. Fully secured, and with laundry, gym, and parking facilities, the housing provides a good option for students who want to partake in traditional college life.

TUITION, ROOM, BOARD AND FEES

The tuition and fee total for the 2010–2011 academic year is 29,180 for full-time students taking 12–18 credits per semester. The room charge is $9,700. Expenses for books and art supplies are estimated at $2, 600 annually but will vary with personal preference.

The Corcoran participates in many federal and state loans and grant programs. Our merit scholarship program awards a wide range of multi-year awards to students based on academic and artistic achievement.

FINANCIAL AID

The Corcoran strives to make the process of determining how to fund a College education as easy as possible, and offers comprehensive merit scholarships and need-based financial aid programs for new students. Through a combination of institutional merit scholarships and grants, federal and state aid, and tuition payment plans, we help make the personalized Corcoran education affordable. Typically, almost all new undergraduate students receive some form of financial aid, including need- and merit-based scholarships. Corcoran participates in all of the major financial aid programs offered by the U.S. Department of Education and provides institutional funds to supplement federal or state financial aid. We provide a payment plan through Academic Management Services as well as information about other options for our students to meet their educational expenses.

The Corcoran College of Art + Design is committed to helping students meet their educational expenses and encourages potentially eligible students to apply for financial aid as soon after January 1 as possible for the coming fall term. More information is available at www.corcoran.edu.

STUDENT ORGANIZATIONS AND ACTIVITIES

The Office of Student Affairs at the Corcoran College of Art + Design provides a variety of services to undergraduate and graduate students, including academic advising, mental health and counseling services, career services for current students and alumni, study abroad and mobility opportunities, and non-academic student activities. The office assists students in getting involved with the campus community and the local arts community through their orientation programs. In addition, Student Affairs sponsors a wide variety of educational, career, cultural, and social events and activities throughout the year, including bus trips and gallery visits, health and wellness programs, and student-sponsored art shows and sales. As members of the Corcoran Gallery of Art, students are able to take advantage of numerous special opportunities offered by the gallery.

ADMISSIONS PROCESS

The Corcoran College of Art + Design enrolls approximately 600 degree students. Students from more than 20 countries and throughout the United States attend the Corcoran, contributing to the cultural, ethnic, and artistic diversity of the College community. We seek applications from candidates who are committed to the professional study of the visual arts and demonstrate artistic, as well as intellectual talent. As a rolling admission institution, we review applications year-round for programs beginning in the fall or spring semesters.

The Admissions Committee prioritizes their review of applications beginning with the candidate's academic record (high school and college/university); a portfolio of artwork; personal attributes (interview, recommendations, essays, extracurricular activities); and official results of standardized tests such as the SAT, ACT, or the TOEFL. All applicants are encouraged to contact our office to arrange for a campus tour, personal interview, and portfolio review. Portfolios may be submitted on CD, or DVD. Full application requirements are available online at www.corcoran.edu. Candidates may also meet with our representatives for interviews and portfolio reviews during National Portfolio Days, which are held nationally (www.portfolio-day.net), or by appointment as we travel across the country for high school visits and college fairs.

For further information contact:

Office of Admissions

Corcoran College of Art + Design

500 Seventeenth Street, NW

Washington, DC 20006-4804

(202) 639-1814/(888) CORCORAN

E-mail: admissions@corcoran.org

www.corcoran.edu

COTTEY COLLEGE

AT A GLANCE

Cottey College, a two-year, independent, liberal arts college for women, is a place where women learn to become leaders, find their voice, and are encouraged to succeed. Looking for intellectual engagement? Cottey's low 9:1 student to faculty ratio and average class size of 13 means you'll get individual attention from your professors. Our professors, 89 percent of whom have the Ph.D. or terminal degree in their field, teach Cottey's classes, not graduate assistants. Want to become a leader? Cottey has a four-level leadership certification program and a leadership course, offering academic credit, that is open to all students. Want to broaden your global horizons? Cottey offers an educational trip to a European city for every second-year student over spring break.

Cottey's mission to provide the best educational opportunities for women comes from its founder. Cottey was founded in 1884 by Virginia Alice Cottey, who believed that women deserved the same educational opportunities as men. Virginia Alice and her sisters pooled their $3,000 life savings to establish their school. On September 8, 1884, Vernon Seminary, as it was called then, opened with 28 students in a two-story red brick schoolhouse. In 1887, the school was chartered by the State of Missouri as Cottey College and produced its first collegiate graduate, Olive Gatewood.

Today Cottey's campus comprises 14 buildings on 11 city blocks and a 33-acre wooded recreation area with a lodge. The residential student capacity of 350 students typically represents 40 states and as many as 26 countries annually. The campus and the times may have changed, but the principles of a Cottey education have not. Cottey still emphasizes high academic standards with unique opportunities for personal growth through residential, cultural, and intellectual experiences.

LOCATION AND ENVIRONMENT

Cottey is located in Nevada, Missouri, a town of approximately 9,000 residents. The local climate offers pleasant falls, mild winters and colorful springs as campus and community gardens burst into bloom. Of course there are also beautiful city parks, roller skating and bowling facilities, a six-screen movie theater, active community theater and choir group, a newly redesigned water park/swimming pool, and an excellent YMCA facility.

Nevada is a welcoming community. Many students find host families and a home-away-from-home through individual churches' "Adopt-a-Student" programs and Cottey students are vital volunteers in many of Nevada's charitable organizations. Students who are looking to become a part of this community are able to find their place easily and are encouraged to become contributing members of this friendly town.

To learn more about Nevada and Vernon County, we encourage you to visit the official site of the Nevada/Vernon County Chamber of Commerce, http://www.visitnevadamo.com/, and the official City of Nevada site, http://www.nevadamo.org.

Nevada is a great place to call home during your two years at Cottey.

OFF-CAMPUS OPPORTUNITIES

Cottey College: A Leadership Lab

Over 40 clubs and organizations at Cottey represent our students' interests in academics, culture, recreation, social concerns, religion, and volunteerism. With all these groups, there are plenty of leadership positions that need to be filled each year. Cottey is a veritable "leadership lab" where young women like you can gain valuable leadership experiences that will help shape your future, your education, and your career path. You'll also be a part of helping to shape student life at Cottey, while developing leadership skills and self-confidence in new areas.

Many students also become involved in the programs at Cottey's Helen and George Washburn Center for Women's Leadership, which was established to build girl's and women's lives through enrichment, education, and leadership development. The CWL not only brings in special guest lecturers and notable speakers, but Cottey students can get leadership certification through the LEO (Leadership, Experiences, Opportunity) program which provides student leaders with an opportunity to document and receive recognition for their experiences inside and outside the classroom and further develop leadership skills. The LEO program offers four levels of certification. Approximately 60 students participate in the LEO program annually.

- Participation in LEO enables students to discover their own leadership style.

- LEO allows students to connect with women leaders both on campus and in the community.

- In LEO, students focus on the leadership aspects of the activities they are already doing.

- The Center for Women's Leadership hosts special events for LEO students including dinners, guest speakers, and trips to cultural events. Throughout the year students participate in a variety of enrichment events and workshops to reach their LEO goals.

Cottey offers a credit course on leadership team-taught by Cottey's president and other faculty members.

Cottey students may participate in a one-hour credit service learning course which involves a trip to Guatemala.

"Being a leader, being a woman in a man's world does not mean you need to be a man or act like one. You should use your skills and the talents you have as a woman to lead others."

Stephanie Mosbrucker

MAJORS AND DEGREES OFFERED

Associate in Arts

Associate in Science

ACADEMIC PROGRAMS

Academic Departments: Anthropology & Sociology; Art; Biology; Business & Economics; Chemistry; Computer Science; Dance; Education; English; Foreign Languages; History & Political Science; International Relations; Journalism; Mass Communication; Mathematics; Music; Philosophy & Religion; Physical Education; Physics & Astronomy; Psychology; Theater/Speech

Learning Opportunities: Leadership; Learning Communities; Internships

CAMPUS FACILITIES AND EQUIPMENT

The campus occupies 14 buildings on 11 city blocks, and a 33-acre wooded recreational area with lodge.

TUITION, ROOM, BOARD AND FEES

2010–11 Academic Year

For 2010–11, the total cost at Cottey is $21,100. This includes:

Tuition $14,400

Room and board° $6,000

Student activity fee $300

Technology fee $200

Student Health Service fee $200

° For P.E.O. and Reeves residents. Students living in Robertson Hall add $600 to annual cost. Also, there is an additional $800 charge for single rooms in any residence hall

Payment Plan

Families may elect to pay the balance remaining after financial aid in full each semester or make monthly payments with a 1% monthly interest charge.

Fall Semester Payment Due Dates

August 15

September 15

October 15

Spring Semester Payment Due Dates

December 15

January 15

February 15

FINANCIAL AID

The financial aid staff is committed to helping students and their families understand and navigate the financial aid process. We know families are concerned about financing a college education. The good news is that Cottey has been able to remain affordable due to its strong financial foundation, endowment, and the continued financial support of the P.E.O. Sisterhood, a philanthropic educational organization dedicated solely to furthering education for women. A Cottey degree is a smart investment!

We offer a comprehensive program of financial assistance options, including scholarships, grants, student employment, and loans.

More than $5.2 million in financial aid was awarded to our students in 2009-10.

Typically, 98% of Cottey students receive some kind of financial aid.

The average financial aid package for the 2009-10 academic year was $16,900.

FAQs (Frequently Asked Questions)

1. I probably don't qualify for aid. Should I apply anyway?

Yes! All students should apply for financial aid even if they think they probably won't be eligible. Not all types of financial aid are based on need.

2. When should I complete the FAFSA?

Complete the FAFSA as soon as possible after January 1 at www.fafsa.ed.gov.

[Cottey's priority deadline for completing the FAFSA is March 1.]

3. What happens after I file the FAFSA?

You'll get either a paper Student Aid Report (SAR) or an e-mail with a link to your SAR on the Web. If you listed Cottey's federal school code (002458), the financial aid office will receive an Institutional Student Information Record (ISIR) which will be used to determine your eligibility for aid. Once we have determined your eligibility for aid we will send a financial aid award letter to you.

4. What types of financial aid are available?

There are grants, scholarships, student employment, and student loans. A financial aid package may consist of a combination of all of these sources.

5. How do I apply for a P.E.O. scholarship?

When you are accepted for admission we will notify your state P.E.O. scholarship chair. She will contact you and advise you of the procedure to follow to be considered for a scholarship. Be sure to apply for admission before December of your senior year in high school. State P.E.O. scholarships have application deadlines ranging from January 15 - April 1.

6. If my family has special financial circumstances, what should I do?

You may appeal for reevaluation of your financial aid eligibility because of changes in your family's financial situation. Examples of special circumstances might include loss of employment, disability, loss of untaxed income, death of a parent, or unusually high medical expenses. Call the financial aid office and request a Special Condition form.

STUDENT ORGANIZATIONS AND ACTIVITIES
Campus Activities Office

The coordinator of campus activities and calendar works with student organization officers and sponsors, other College faculty and staff and numerous agents and performers to schedule and promote activities and events on campus. The coordinator also organizes student developmental programming, provides support to student organizations and sponsors, conducts leadership training, and coordinates individual and series ticket sales.

Campus Clubs and Organizations:

AIDS Activists Coming Together (AACT)

Alpha Mu Gamma

Amnesty International

Angels for Pets

Anime

Associated Cottey College Artists (ACCA)

BACCHUS (Boosting Alcohol Consciousness Concerning the Health of University Students)

Body Works (dance)

Class Organizations: Senior Class and Freshman Class

Cottey Big Sisters

Cottey College Handbell Choir

Cottey Diversity Corps (CDC)

Delta Psi Omega (national honorary dramatics fraternity)

Explorer's Club (participates in such activities as camping, cookouts, canoeing, rock climbing, etc.)

Feminist Majority Foundation

Food Freaks Anonymous (cooking)

Golden Key (Cottey's honorary service organization)

Image Tree (creative writing magazine)

International Friendship Circle (IFC)

Intersociety

InterVarsity Christian Fellowship

Japanese Club

Mu Sigma Epsilon (campus honorary music society)

Phi Beta Lambda (collegiate level association of student members preparing for a career in business)

Phi Theta Kappa (Epsilon Chapter) (national scholastic honorary society for two-year colleges)

Prayer Shawl Ministry

Pride Alliance (GLBTS)

Psi Beta (national honor society in psychology and sociology)

Residence Hall Organizations: P.E.O. Hall, Reeves Hall, and Robertson Hall

Retrospect (Cottey's annual yearbook)

Rotaract (affiliated with Rotary International)

Sigma Kappa Delta (the national honor society for English)

Societies: Alphan, Delphian, Emerson, and Magnoperian

The Spectrum (Cottey's student newspaper)

Student Activities Committee (SAC)

Students Against a Vanishing Environment (S.A.V.E.)

Student Government Association

CURRY COLLEGE

AT A GLANCE

Curry College is a private, four-year, liberal arts-based institution located on a wooded 137-acre campus in Milton, MA just seven miles from downtown Boston. Curry College today offers 20 undergraduate majors, as well as four graduate programs. The college serves a combined enrollment of approximately 4,000 students, consisting of over 2,000 traditional students from over 40 states and 32 countries; 1,600 continuing education students; and 400 graduate students. More than 1,400 of its students reside on the Curry campus.

Under the leadership of President Kenneth K. Quigley, there's a culture of excellence that exists at Curry College as it continues to rise to a place of prominence and great promise among New England's finest colleges. As we enter our 131st year, we invite you to meet the people of Curry on the Web or at an upcoming campus event to truly experience excellence in action.

LOCATION AND ENVIRONMENT

The wooded, 137-acre Milton campus is one of the most attractive small college campuses in New England. Right on campus, you'll have at your fingertips the resources to help you excel academically, socially, and physically and find endless sources of entertainment, action, and challenge.

Unlike other isolated suburban or rural campuses, Curry is just a stone's throw away from Boston, one of the most exciting cities in the world. As a result, Curry can offer its students an exceptional advantage through access to Boston's cultural and educational institutions. The opportunity for internships and entertainment in this New England capital is a significant part of the Curry experience.

Curry's location has yet another advantage: it is less than two miles from the scenic Blue Hills, a natural reservation which offers skiing, hiking, horseback riding, and a range of resources for environmental education and recreation. The Milton campus is a beautiful retreat in the woods, with the excitement of the City waiting right outside.

Back on campus, students also enjoy the comfort Curry's tight-knit, friendly community and the security services provided by the Department of Public Safety, which administers a highly professional system for the enforcement of rules and regulations designed to promote the general safety and security of persons and properties on the campus.

Curry College is home to a caring and committed community where visitors are always welcome. We invite you to visit our interactive campus map online to learn about our campus facilities and to consider visiting Curry in person. We hope to see you on campus soon!

MAJOR AND DEGREES OFFERED

At Curry, we recognize the potential in all of our students. We take a personalized approach to education that allows you to build on your dreams while you simultaneously explore new ideas and uncover talents, strengths, and abilities you never thought you had. A Curry education will lead you to a level of excellence that will touch all facets of your life. You can select from 20 majors and 65-plus minors and concentrations ranging from biology to theatre. Challenge yourself with the Curry Honors Program as well as support through the Program for Advancement of Learning. You can choose from a wide array of extracurricular activities ranging from 13 NCAA Division III athletic teams to an outstanding theater program. The Curry College experience is as unique as you are and the opportunities are endless. At Curry, you can achieve excellence in the classroom—and beyond.

OFF CAMPUS OPPORTUNITIES

As an alumnus/alumna of Curry College, you are always welcome to use the Office of Career Services. We recognize that you have different challenges than current students, whether it's undertaking a career change, dealing with a job loss, or brushing up on your job search skills. You have free access to individual career counseling, including skills/interests assessments, career exploration, and job search planning; assistance in selecting and applying to graduate school; resume and cover letter reviews; online and print resources; and job postings.

Facilities and Equipment

In the fall of 2009, Curry College opened a new student center. The 84,000 square foot facility is full of state-of-the-art areas for dinning, studying, athletics, student activities, or simply lounging around. The student center has become a place to study between classes, to meet up with friends for dinner, work out or even take on your roommate in a game of billiards or foosball.

The Gertrude M. Webb Learning Center is a unique, Tudor-style building with several thousand square feet of space dedicated to PAL students. The architecture of the learning center is based in the earlier part of this century and features majestic touches including cathedral ceilings and ornate fireplaces. The Kennedy Academic Center, located on South Campus, houses many of Curry's classrooms as well as PC and MAC computer labs. The John S. Hafer Academic Building, erected in 1965, is located on the Academic Quadrangle on North Campus and houses many of Curry's classrooms. The Hafer Building is also a popular location on campus for hosting cultural activities and guest speakers. In 2001, our state-of-the art television studio, the Hirsh Communication Center, complete with full TV production facilities, was added to the facility. In August 2006, the Academic and Performance Center, opened to the College community. The new three-story, 30,000 square-foot building has eight classrooms, including an amphitheatre-style lecture hall and a stock trading classroom, faculty office suites, a student lounge, conference and breakout meeting rooms, and a two-story atrium with a smart-café offering quick and healthy eating options. In addition, the building includes a 229-seat multi-purpose auditorium, the first dedicated performance space for Curry College students.

TUITION, ROOM AND BOARD, AND FEES

Annual Tuition and Fees 2009–2010

Tuition	$28,000
Fees	$1,830
Room	$6,210
Board	$4,900
Total (exclusive of PAL)	
Resident	$40,940°°
Commuter	$29,370
PAL Fee	$6,250
	(if applicable)

°°The total cost for resident students is based on 14 meals per week and a multiple occupancy room. The plan including 17 meals per week would increase the cost by $490. The 10 meals per week plan would decrease the total cost by $1,080. A single occupancy room would increase the total cost by $1,630. Additional fees may apply.

FINANCIAL AID

Recognizing that meeting the total cost of a higher education today can be challenging for students and families, Curry College provides a variety of financing options and participates in federal and state financial aid programs. The Student Financial Services staff is committed to helping you create a financial plan that will allow you to reach your enrollment goals. In order to be considered for need-based financial aid, students must complete a FAFSA annually. You can fill out a FAFSA online at www.fafsa.ed.gov or use the paper application. If you would like us to mail you a paper FAFSA application, please contact our office and we would be happy to mail one to you. FAFSA forms are also available at any high school. Financial aid comes in three forms: grants and scholarships; loans; and student employment. Curry College provides students with millions of dollars in financial aid each year. The college uses its own endowment funds, gifts from friends, foundations and corporations, alumni, parents, and other donors to be able to provide this funding to our students. We believe in the potential of every Curry College student and realize that financing a student's education can be a difficult task for a family. Curry also receives substantial funding from the various state and federal financial aid programs.

STUDENT ORGANIZATIONS AND ACTIVITIES

College is a time for making lifelong connections—with new people, new interests, and passions—a time of endless possibilities. It's a time to go beyond life as you know it now and do the things you've always dreamed of doing. At Curry College, you'll instantly become part of a unique, upbeat community with all the resources to help you excel academically, socially, and physically. Whether you're a resident student or commuter student, we'll help you find your niche. Right on campus you'll find countless sources of entertainment, action, and challenge. You can unwind at the Colonel's Corner snack bar over a game of pool, meet friends at a movie night, take a turn behind the mic, or just listen, at a coffeehouse or comedy night. Work out in the weight room or exercise your voice in the *Currier Times* newspaper or campus chorale. Join one of the many student clubs and organizations or volunteer for community service projects.

Life as a Curry student extends beyond the campus, too. You can hike or ski in the nearby Blue Hills Reservation, and will have easy access to big city excitement and resources just seven miles away in downtown Boston. The staff in the offices of Student Affairs—Student Activities, Residence Life, Public Safety, Health and Counseling, and the Chaplaincy—are all committed to helping you develop your personal goals and establish relationships within the Curry College community. We encourage your involvement and leadership in all aspects of college life.

ADMISSIONS PROCESSES AND REQUIREMENTS

As you explore enrollment at Curry College, the Office of Admission encourages you to visit the campus. To be considered for admission to Curry College, we require you to submit the following:

- A completed application with a nonrefundable fee of $50
- An official high school transcript
- Results of the SAT or ACT
- A letter of recommendation from a guidance counselor or high school teacher
- A college essay

D'YOUVILLE COLLEGE

AT A GLANCE

Focused on professional studies and the liberal arts, D'Youville College is a private institution with a coed student body of 3,000. Founded in 1908, D'Youville has a proud history: The College was the first in western New York to grant undergraduate degrees to female students. Today, D'Youville offers degrees in over thirty-five different undergraduate and graduate programs. The College's holistic approach to education, as well as the 14:1 student-faculty ratio, encourages personal development alongside of academic pursuits.

D'Youville hosts one of the nation's biggest four-year, private nursing programs. The multiple-option Nursing Degree Program allows students to choose between BSN, BSN/MS (five years), and RN to BSN courses of study. Students can also undertake a five-year program resulting in a combined bachelor's/master's (BS/MS) degree in the areas of accounting, education, information technology, occupational therapy, international business, physician assistant and dietetics. Those seeking master's degrees may apply in elementary, secondary, special education, community health nursing, occupational therapy, international business, and health services administration. There is also a 7 year, bachlor's and doctorate of chiropractic and 6 year, bachelor's and doctorate of physical therapy. Upon graduating from D'Youville, 96 percent of students either secure jobs in their chosen field or go on to graduate school.

The College's location by the Niagara River and Lake Erie provides breathtaking vistas, enjoyed by students living in Marguerite Hall. The Koessler Administration Building houses the president's offices as well as the offices of admissions, financial aid, student accounts, and the registrar. The Learning Center and Kavinoky Theatre also share that building. When it's time to relax, students head to the Student Center, outfitted with a gymnasium, swimming pool, weight-training room, dance studio, general recreation center, pub, and dining facilities.

Campus life thrives thanks to student organizations including social groups, academic clubs, and the College newspaper. For athletes of any persuasion, the ski club, intramural teams, and NCAA Division III intercollegiate sports (baseball, basketball, volleyball, golf, cross-country, crew, soccer, and softball) provide athletic activities.

LOCATION AND ENVIRONMENT

Located in Buffalo, the D'Youville campus enjoys a residential setting. The downtown shopping center, the Kleinhans Music Hall, the Albright-Knox Art Gallery, two museums, and several theaters are all nearby. Toronto, a mere 90 miles away, offers additional metropolitan attractions, and Niagara Falls can be reached in just 25 minutes. Skiers can make it to Holiday Valley in about an hour. Buffalo can be reached via the New York State Thruway, Amtrak, Greyhound and Trailways bus lines, and most major airlines.

D'Youville connects itself to the community by forging relationships with local schools, hospitals, and social groups. Buffalo is home to more than 60,000 college students in all.

Specific departments affiliate with the appropriate area organizations. For instance, the nursing program works with 13 local hospitals and public health agencies. Nearby elementary, junior high, and secondary schools, as well as special education centers, are available for student teaching assignments for those in the education program. D'Youville students pursuing degrees in occupational therapy, physical therapy, and the physician assistant program can get hands-on experience at clinics across the country. D'Youville also maintains its own Chiropractic Clinic.

MAJORS AND DEGREES OFFERED

D'Youville students can pursue the degrees of Bachelor of Arts (BA), Bachelor of Science (BS), Bachelor of Science in Nursing (BSN), five-year, two-degree, BS+MS programs. Also combined BS+DC or BS +DPT programs. In 2010 D'Youville is accepting applications for the new 6 year, Pharmacy Program. Students choose from majors including bachelor degrees in Accounting, Biology, Biology, Chemistry, Interdisciplinary Studies (Education), English, Exercise and Sports Studies, Global Studies, Health Services, History, Information Technology, Mathematics, Management, Nursing, Pharmacy, Philosophy, Pre-Professional, science (pre-medical, pre-dental, pre-veterinary, pre-law), Psychology, Sociology. For the BS+MS programs, achieved over five years, these include accounting, dietetics, international business, nursing, occupational therapy, physician assistant, informational technology (BS)+ international business (MS), and education.

Additionally, there is a 6 year, BS+ DPT, physical therapy program and a 7 year, BS + DC, chiropractic program.

We are now offering a doctoral degree, Ed.D. in Health Policy and Health Education Physical Therapy, and Chiropractic.

ACADEMIC PROGRAMS

Students select a major based on their interests and career goals. Any area of study provides a solid background for post-college pursuits. In order to graduate, students must fulfill the requirements of their department, complete the core requirements, pass a total of 120 credit hours, and maintain a minimum grade point average of 2.0. The core requirements cover humanities, 24 hours; social science, 12 hours; science, 7 hours; mathematics/computer science, 6 hours; and electives, 9 hours. Most students take five or six classes, approximately 16 credit hours, each semester. Internships can compliment classroom experiences in any course of study.

Students who are undecided regarding their major can benefit from participation in the Career Discovery Program. Over the course of two years, students explore career options through classes and internships.

The academic year is divided into two fifteen-week semesters. Students complete the final exams for the first semester prior to winter break. Summer programs, lasting eight weeks, are also available for certain classes.

In order to better prepare for D'Youville courses, students can find assistance at the College Learning Center. For help in a specific subject, the Tutor Bank provides trained peer tutors.

CAMPUS FACILITIES AND EQUIPMENT

Living on campus is a great way to make the most of your college years. A D'Youville education extends further than the classroom, and being a campus resident is a major part of that education. Living on campus, students often make friendships that last a lifetime. Close proximity to the labs and library makes it easier to use free moments for study. Living on campus also puts you closer to campus events.

Marguerite Hall, a twelve-story co-ed residence hall, is home to up to 308 students. Each floor in Marguerite houses approximately 28 students. Students can select from several options including single gender floors, coed floors, intensive study floors, and an over-21 floor. Based on availability, students may select a single, double or triple room. Singles are not available for freshmen.

The new Student Apartment Complex has one and four, fully furnished bedroom apartments with cooking facilities. These are available to upperclassmen.

Twenty-four-hour security coverage is provided in the residence halls. All visitors must sign in and be accompanied by their student host. Limited campus parking is available to residence students.

Computer and Network Services (CANS) provides the infrastructure and technical support necessary for many services on campus including email, web access, file and print sharing, and application support for distance learning, the library and administrative offices. We take pride in being a wired campus, providing high-speed network access in our offices, classrooms and dorms. Dialup and VPN access is also provided on a limited basis, and technical support is available free of charge to the college community.

TUITION, ROOM, BOARD AND FEES

In 2010–2011, tuition totaled $20,800 annually, and $9800 for room and board. A mandatory College fee is assessed according to the number of credit hours a student enrolls in. There is a $40 Student Association fee, which defrays the costs of concerts, yearbooks, guest lectures, and other activities. Additionally, there is a $25 orientation fee and $20 liability insurance fee.

FINANCIAL AID

Financial aid is intended to ensure that D'Youville is financially accessible to students of all backgrounds. The allocations of grants, loans, and work-study opportunities are determined by review of the Free Application for Federal Student Aid.

Ninety percent of D'Youville freshmen receive financial aid. This includes nearly $2,000,000 in grants and scholarships. Grants include: Federal Pell Grants and Supplemental Education Opportunity Grants, New York State Tuition Assistance Program, and Aid for Part-Time Study. Federal Work-Study programs, federally insured loans, and flexible payment plans are also available.

All applicants are reviewed for academic scholarships at the time of acceptance. Notifications of awards are made upon acceptance. Awards include: Presidential Honors Scholarships, Academic Initiative Scholarships, Achievement Scholarships and Transfer Achievement Scholarships. These scholarships are based on academic performance and could be worth up to $58,600.

All continuing students may apply for thousands of dollars from endowed and restricted scholarships.

Canadian students receive a 20 percent tuition waiver unless the student receives a RN Nursing waiver. All undergraduate Canadian students are eligible for academic scholarships.

Nursing students in the BSN completion program for RNs receive a 50% tuition-only waiver.

D'Youville is a member of the Council of Independent Colleges Tuition Exchange Program and the Tuition Exchange Program, Inc. Both are tuition remission program.

STUDENT ORGANIZATIONS AND ACTIVITIES

Student representatives elected to the Student Association (SA) work with the administration and faculty to make decisions regarding the College's academic, social, and moral life. The SA comprises the executive council and student senate, and any D'Youville attendees can run for a position or participate in any of the 17 related academic and social organizations.

Extracurricular activities are an important part of college life and at D'Youville we want your academic experience to be safe, successful and fun. Several key services and programs will help you meet your goals and enjoy your time outside of the classroom.

Our intercollegiate program is a Division III member of the National Collegiate Athletic Association, competing in the Allegheny Mountain Collegiate Conference. A variety of recreational activities are available as well as a fitness center, swimming pool and game room.

Students can also join academic, cultural, and recreational clubs, serve on campus wide committees, contribute to student publications, perform in the arts, attend special events, and take advantage of many volunteer opportunities.

As a new student, you will be invited to attend an orientation program for freshmen, families, transfers, certificate or graduate students. Here you'll learn about program requirements, course selection with an academic advisor, registration, and information seminars.

The D'Youville Freshman Experience (DFX) is designed to help make your first year exciting, fun and challenging. At orientation, you'll be assigned a college mentor and registered for the FOCUS Freshmen Seminar. There are also activities and leadership opportunities (D'Youville Leads) as well as a Peer Mentor Program coordinated through the Leadership Development Institute.

ADMISSIONS PROCESS

Admission to D'Youville College is moderately competitive. Our selection process identifies those qualified men and women who will benefit most from the programs the college offers. In making admissions decisions, we consider grades, class rank, standardized test scores, recommendations, and any additional information you can provide.

To apply you'll need to submit a completed application along with a $25 processing fee, official high school transcripts or, if you're a transfer student, official transcripts from colleges previously attended. Freshmen must also submit SAT or ACT scores and letters of recommendation. Review the admission requirements for the major of your choice on our website.

Applications are reviewed on a rolling basis for all programs except the Physicians Assistant program. You can expect to receive an admissions decision within three weeks of the time we receive all the necessary forms, test scores, and transcripts. The sooner you complete your application, the sooner you'll receive a decision.

Admission to D'Youville College is granted without regard to age, race, gender, national origin, religious affiliation, or disability.

DAEMEN COLLEGE

AT A GLANCE

Located in the beautiful suburbs north of Buffalo, New York, Daemen College is a private college offering strong liberal arts majors, exceptional professional degrees, and widely acclaimed Graduate programs. Daemen is distinguished by a low student/faculty ratio and consistently small class sizes, which encourage students to interact with professors and grow as individuals. Daemen students have their education enriched by challenging opportunities that engage them in learning experiences through international education programs, collaborative research with faculty, clinical and field experiences, internships for credit, and service learning positions. Daemen students embrace an academically challenging atmosphere where they are encouraged to develop a strong repertoire of knowledge and skills. Daemen College meets the individual goals and needs of each student, preparing them for leadership and professional life in a global economy.

LOCATION AND ENVIRONMENT

Daemen's beautiful 39-acre campus is located in Amherst, New York, a peaceful suburb of Buffalo. *Money* magazine has reported Amherst, New York as one of America's safest cities. Due to its proximity to Buffalo (New York State's second largest city), Daemen's campus is close to many major rail, plane, and motor routes. While the campus setting is tranquil and residential, Buffalo is a vibrant cultural city, bustling with world-class entertainment, such as the Philharmonic Orchestra, the Albright-Knox Art Gallery, and the Shea's Theater. The greater Buffalo area is rich with sports and recreational activities all year round, whether it be skiing and swimming, or watching our professional sports teams. The surrounding Niagara Frontier boasts numerous historic and scenic locations. For example, Niagara Falls is only 30 minutes away and the attractive, international city of Toronto is just two hours by car. On campus, the numerous trees and open green spaces create a lovely environment to work and study, and compliment the nearby urban environment.

OFF-CAMPUS OPPORTUNITIES

Daemen's office of Global Programs operates and coordinates distinctive global programs (in Europe, Asia, Latin America/Caribbean, and Africa) designed to facilitate students' professional aspirations. In today's global economy, it makes sense to learn all you can about different cultures, political systems, and histories. International study is a staple of the Daemen experience and the College offers semesters abroad, summer programs, and accelerated January term trips.

Daemen's Center of Cooperative Education and Career Development provides students and graduates with a wide variety of services specially geared to the vocational and self-development needs of the College community before and after graduation. The Center helps students find an internship or co-op position so that they can gain real-world experience in their area of interest. Students often express how prepared they feel to have had the chance to experience what careers in their fields are really like. An added bonus, internship employers frequently offer Daemen interns full-time positions after graduation. Employers run the gamut and include business, the sports industry, the arts, industry, government, health-related entities, non-profits, educational institutions, and cultural organizations. The opportunities are local, national, or international – including excellent opportunities with the Washington Internship Institute.

Daemen believes in "learning through service." While at Daemen virtually all undergraduate students engage in various service learning activities. Students from every major and class level participate as individuals or groups in short-term and long-term projects or assignments that benefit the local, national, or global communities. Students work with environmental organizations, refugee groups, build environment agencies, tax credits for the poor programs, residents of nursing homes, hospitals and clinics, tutoring children, mentoring in city schools, and service activities in various cities throughout the city and the world – just to name a few of the hundreds of possibilities.

MAJORS AND DEGREES OFFERED

Daemen College offers BA, BFA, BS, MS, DNP and DPT programs.

Majors offered at Daemen include: Accounting BS/MS, Art; Applied Design/Print-making, Drawing, Graphic Design, Illustration, Painting, Sculpture, Visual Arts Education K–12, Arts Administration BA/MS, Athletic Training BS/MS, Biology; Adolescence Education 7–12, Environmental Studies, Biochemistry; Pre-Professional, Business Administration; Human Resource Management, International Business, Management Information Systems, Marketing, Sport Management, Education; Childhood Education 1–6, Childhood Education/ Special Education1–6, Early Childhood Education/Special Education B–12, English; Adolescence Education 7–12, Communications/Public Relations, French; Adolescence Education 7–12, Health Care Studies; Community Health, Complementary and Alternative Health Care Practices, Health and Fitness Training, History, History and Government; Adolescence Education 7–12, Environmental Studies, Mathematics; Adolescence Education 7–12, Natural Sciences; Environmental Studies, Forensic Science, Health Science, Individualized Studies, Nursing, Physical Therapy BS,NS/DPT, Physician Assistant BS/MS, Political Science, Psychology, Religious Studies, Social Work, Spanish; Adolescence Education 7–12, Interdisciplinary studies; Environmental Studies, Health Care Studies, Individualized Study, and Pre-Professional Programs; Pre-Dentistry, Pre-Law, Pre-Medicine, and Pre-Veterinary.

Graduate MS programs include Accounting; Professional Accountancy BS/MS, Athletic Training BS/MS, Arts Administration BS/MS, Education; Adolescence Education 7–12, Childhood Education 1–6, Special Education 1–6, Executive Leadership and Change, Global Business, Nursing; Adult Nurse Practitioner, Nursing Education, Nursing Executive Leadership, Palliative Care Nursing, and Physician Assistant.

Doctorate programs include Doctor of Nursing Practice and Direct Entry Doctor of Physical Therapy. In addition Physical Therapy offers an Orthopedic Manual Physical Therapy Fellowship Program.

ACADEMIC PROGRAMS

Daemen College is committed to complimenting the depth of study in a major field with a well-rounded academic understanding in the liberal arts. The College's core curriculum ensures that every student graduates with the following seven core competencies: critical thinking and creative problem solving; oral, written and visual communication; information and multi-media technologies; civic responsibility; contextual understanding; affective judgment; and moral and ethical discernment. This innovative core curriculum competes with those of Ivy League Institutions and prepares the student in a holistic manner which not only makes them more marketable upon graduation, but instructs them on alternative ways of approaching education and learning.

Classes at Daemen are taught by professors—not teaching assistants. Daemen provides students with small classes and a caring and committed faculty, allowing for a personalized educational experience. Academics at Daemen will challenge you to test your knowledge, raise your expectations, and think critically and creatively. Daemen's core competencies, honors program, academic exchanges, global programs, and undergraduate research are just a few examples of what makes the College challenging and distinctive.

Daemen students are well prepared for professional success. The vast majority of them obtain a position of choice or admission to graduate study in less than a year after graduation. They are leaders in their communities, with a strong dedication to the improvement of the communities in which they live.

CAMPUS FACILITIES AND EQUIPMENT

Modern apartment-style residence halls provide separate housing for male and female students, in addition to our existing five-story residence hall for freshmen. All residence halls have kitchens, laundry facilities, lounges, and in-room phone/Internet connections.

Full-service meals are served in the main dining hall, with an a la carte selection in the snack bar. The recreation room and Cyber Cafe are popular spots for socializing and relaxing during the day or evening.

New in 2009 the Research and Information Commons has transformed the campus, both aesthetically and academically. This is a technological showcase that has become the hub of academic research, as well as the academic and social heart of the campus.

TUITION, ROOM, BOARD AND FEES

Tuition for the 2009–2010 academic year is $20,720, with additional room and board fees of $9,450. (Cost varies according to meal plan and residence facility.)

FINANCIAL AID

Learning to navigate the financial aid system can be a daunting task. That's why Daemen has trained professionals on hand to assist you every step of the way. Their Admissions Staff and Financial Aid Officers are available to assist you and your family with the financial aid application process, and to ensure that you understand the necessary paperwork and deadlines required in order for you to receive the best financial aid package available.

Daemen College does not want financial issues to keep any admitted student from attending. That's why they strive to create individualized financial aid packages for you and your family that will meet your needs and enable you to get the most out of your college education. With this philosophy in mind, Daemen College offers merit-based and need-based financial assistance, as well as aid based on a combination of financial need and academic achievement. More than 96% of current Daemen students receive some form of financial assistance. In addition to the College's own scholarships, Daemen College participates in all federal and state programs.

STUDENT ORGANIZATIONS AND ACTIVITIES

Student activities provide for the development of the whole person outside of the classroom. The Director of Student Activities on campus helps students participate in recognized organizations, form new ones, and plan events. All students are encouraged to join in extracurricular activities. With over 50 student organizations the possibilities for involvement at Daemen are limitless. Whether your interests are in art or skiing, there is bound to be something that grabs your interest and introduces you to students who share similar passions.

Daemen knows that there's more to being a student than just sitting in a classroom or studying at the library. Daemen believes that *now* is the time to discover exactly *who* you are; cultivating your hidden talents, taking new risks and challenging yourself to grow are all part of the Daemen experience. Daemen encourages all of their students to become actively engaged in the campus community.

Daemen College has enjoyed a tremendous amount of recent success from its athletic programs. They have won nine American Mideast Conference North titles in the past seven years. The Wildcats are a member of the National Association of Intercollegiate Athletics and the highly competitive American Mideast Conference. Our student athletes work hard to achieve success on the field and in the classroom.

Daemen College Intercollegiate Athletics include:

Men's: Basketball, Cross Country, Golf, Soccer

Women's: Basketball, Cross Country, Soccer, Volleyball

More casual athletes take part in club or intramural sports and keep fit in the exercise and weight rooms.

ADMISSIONS PROCESS

Daemen College offers a test optional policy. Applicants are not required to submit standardized test scores (SAT, ACT) as part of the admission application. Our decision to make test scores optional reflects our commitment to enrolling students who reflect intellectual curiosity, persistence in reaching a goal, talent, motivation, and determination to make a difference in their lives and the lives of others. We rely on high school GPA, transcripts (including grade performance and rigor of courses selected), extracurricular activities, class rank, and counselor or teacher recommendations in making our admission decisions. We value strong writing skills, a solid secondary school program, and a student's potential for making an important contribution to our campus community. We will also give careful consideration to applications from students whose preparation is unusual and who can provide strong recommendations as to their ability to succeed in a college program of study. We encourage an on campus interview and any other information a prospective student wishes to provide.

Daemen has a rolling admissions policy. However, due to program and residence-hall capacity limits, we highly encourage you to send your deposit as soon as you have made your decision.

The best way to get to know Daemen is in person. On your visit, we'll take you on a campus tour, arrange for you to meet professors and current students, and plan a one-on-one meeting with an Admissions Counselor.

To schedule your appointment, contact the Office of Admissions at 800-462-7652 or register inline at www.daemen.edu/admissions. You may make an individual visit anytime, attend our fall and spring Open Houses, or join us for many of our other special admissions events. We hope to see you on campus soon!

DESALES UNIVERSITY

DeSales University is a medium-sized, Catholic liberal arts university for men and women administered by the Oblates of St. Francis de Sales.

AT A GLANCE

Founded in 1964, DeSales University is a Catholic liberal arts university that offers courses in a wide range of disciplines. DeSales provides personal attention, small class size, and a feeling of community. The University uses a holistic approach to help students develop a "sense of self," enabling every student to reach their personal and academic potential. This student-centered philosophy is conveyed by an enthusiastic, accessible faculty.

LOCATION AND ENVIRONMENT

DeSales University' suburban campus is located 15 minutes south of Bethlehem and Allentown, Pa., and only 1 hour from Philadelphia, 90 minutes from Scranton and Wilkes-Barre, Pa., less than 2 hours from New York City, and 3 hours from Baltimore. The campus is 480 acres with more than 16 major buildings.

OFF-CAMPUS OPPORTUNITIES

Allentown and Bethlehem are a short 15-minute drive from campus and offer many dining, shopping, and outdoor activities, including the Promenade Shops at Saucon Valley, just minutes from campus. The Lehigh Valley, AKA 'College Valley,' boasts beautiful hiking and biking trails, historic sites, museums, cultural festivals, and Dorney Park and Wildwater Kingdom. Skiing at nearby Blue Mountain and other Pocono resorts is just a short drive away. The Poconos also offer white water rafting trips down the Lehigh and Delaware Rivers.

MAJORS AND DEGREES OFFERED

DeSales University offers 35 bachelor's degrees including 10 pre-professional programs, and six graduate programs through the departments of business, humanities, math and computer science, social science, performing arts, natural science, nursing and health, and theology and philosophy. Our newest majors include digital art, marriage and family studies, and international business.

ACADEMIC PROGRAMS

DeSales University defines "global competence" as using an open, inquisitive mind to understand the norms and expectations of other cultures, and using this acquired knowledge to communicate and to work effectively outside of one's usual environment in the promotion of human solidarity. DeSales University presents opportunities for students to enlarge their worldview, from activities and concerts to short- and long-term study abroad programs.

The University's cultural affairs committee offers a diverse series of weekly performances that bring cultural liveliness to campus. Flamenco dancing, a Cuban percussion group, and a Japanese tea ceremony are recent examples of our Wednesday in the Commons series.

Study abroad programs through DeSales present the opportunity for our students to live and work in this vibrantly interdependent world and range from semester long study to short stay travel of 10 days. Our students have spent semesters in England, Australia, Italy, Latin America, among others. More importantly, DeSales is employing a new model of intensive hands on engagement through short-stay co-curricular trips of students, faculty, and staff. Trips to Ireland, Germany, Peru, and South Africa for short stay intensive travel have been combined with academic courses, the activities of student organizations such as SIFE or PACE, or out of season competition for our athletic teams.

Freshman students are asked to participate in the Character U program, a self-assessment program based on the Golden Counsels of St. Francis de Sales. Each month, University programming addresses one of these Golden Counsels or traits including patience, trust and cooperation, and perseverance.

The University's Academic Resource Center can offer assistance in reading comprehension, study skills, time management and effective writing techniques. Additionally they can help find a tutor if you need it or provide you with the opportunity to become a peer tutor.

CAMPUS FACILITIES AND EQUIPMENT

Trexler Library has a collection of more than 500,000 items and there are electronic databases of newspapers, journal articles, and the Oxford Dictionary of National Biography. There are computer and multimedia labs and a staff who will help with any research topic. Trexler Library has wireless access both with personal laptops or laptops that can be borrowed to use in the building. The Library's resources can be accessed from anywhere on campus. There is online access to databases and full text journal articles. Students can also instant message a librarian with a question.

The DeSales University Center is one of the newest additions to the campus and features many menu choices—especially for healthy eaters—in a food court setting. The University Center also has wireless laptop capability so you can eat and surf, as well as panoramic views of campus.

The Priscilla Payne Hurd Science Center, a 37,500 square foot facility, is equipped with up-to-date computers, labs, and medical equipment. The Hurd Science Center also features a sterile molecular/cell biology suite, complete with a freezer room, bench room, support room, dark room, and instrument room. An ecology/environmental lab with a growing chamber, an analytical/physical chemistry/inorganic laboratory, and a bioinformatics/physics lab also inhabit the two-story building.

Tuition, Room, Board, and Fees

Tuition and Fees (2009–10):	$26,000
Room and Board:	$9,750
Student & Technology Fee:	$1,235
Total:	$36,985

FINANCIAL AID

Nine out of ten DeSales University students receive financial aid in the form of grants, scholarships, work-study, and loans. About 85 percent of the students receive grants directly from DeSales University, and funds are also available from federal and state programs to those who qualify. The amount of aid received and the composition of an aid package will depend on financial need and on academic achievement and potential.

Academic scholarships are also available through DeSales University. All applicants for admission are automatically considered for each of the scholarships offered by the University.

STUDENT ORGANIZATIONS AND ACTIVITIES

DeSales University has more than 31 campus organizations, including the Student Activities crew, which helps plan student events, bus trips, and on-campus performances. Recent renovations to the McShea Student Center include the Dog Pound, a student activities lounge open to students for entertainment and socializing, and Café McShea, an internet café with late night hours. Both new areas are just the beginning of increased special events such as independent movie nights, comedians, music acts, and expanded space for programs sponsored by various student organizations.

DeSales University has 16 intercollegiate varsity sports teams and all are members of the NCAA Division III, Middle Atlantic States Collegiate Athletic Corporation (MAC) Freedom Conference, and the Eastern College Athletic Conference (ECAC).

The University's men's sports are baseball, basketball, cross-country, golf, lacrosse, soccer, tennis, and track and field. Women's sports are basketball, cross-country, field hockey, soccer, softball, tennis, track & field, and volleyball. The University also has six club sports: cheerleading, cycling, disc golf, equestrian, ice hockey, and men's volleyball

There are 30 intramural sports for all seasons, or student can visit the state-of-the-art Billera Hall fitness center, which offers aerobic, Nautilus, and free-weight training.

ADMISSIONS PROCESS

To Apply for Admission you need to:

Complete a DeSales University application and submit it with a nonrefundable $30 fee to our Admissions Office.

Have your high school guidance department send your official high school transcript to our Admissions Office.

Have your standardized test scores (SAT or ACT) sent to our Admissions Office. Our code number for SAT scores is 2021.

Have a guidance counselor and teacher complete the recommendation forms and send to our Admissions Office.

DRAKE UNIVERSITY

AT A GLANCE

Drake University provides a thriving intellectual environment offering more than 70 majors, covering subjects from the liberal arts to professional and pre-professional programs. The University employs professors who demonstrate a dedication to students along with academic prowess. Students benefit from the low 14:1 student-faculty ratio, and they never take classes from graduate students or teaching assistants. Drake enrolls a heterogeneous group of 5,617 students, from 47 states and more than 50 foreign countries. Drake prides itself on alumni success, noting that more than 99.1 percent of Drake graduates embark on careers or start graduate programs during their first six months out of school.

Drake grants master's degrees in: accounting, business administration, communication leadership, education, financial management, and public administration. Students may also pursue their Doctor of Pharmacy, Doctor of Jurisprudence, and Doctor of Education degrees. Joint degrees are also available in MBA/JD, MPA/JD, MBA/PharmD, MPA/PharmD, and PharmD/JD.

LOCATION AND ENVIRONMENT

Students take advantage of Drake's location in Des Moines, Iowa, the state capital and a thriving business center. Internships are available in fields such as government, banking, insurance, publishing, nonprofit organizations, and health care, and nearly 80 percent of students participate in at least one internship during their four years at the University.

OFF-CAMPUS OPPORTUNITIES

Many students take advantage of overseas studies options offered by the Center for International Programs and Services. Through the Center's work with international institutions and consortia, semester- and year-long programs are offered in more than 60 countries.

MAJORS AND DEGREES OFFERED

Those studying in the College of Arts and Sciences receive a classic liberal arts education, preparing them for futures in science, mathematics, politics, or the arts. Students may earn their Bachelor of Arts and Bachelor of Science degrees in the following areas: anthropology and sociology; astronomy; biochemistry, cell and molecular biology; biology; chemistry; computer science; English; environmental policy; environmental science; history; international relations; law, politics, and society; mathematics; mathematics education (secondary); philosophy; physics; politics; psychology; religion; rhetoric and communication studies; sociology; study of culture and society; and writing. Some students design their own majors, while others opt for open enrollment and do not immediately declare a major. The University also administers preprofessional study in dentistry, engineering, law, medicine and veterinary medicine. Concentrations are available in anthropology, geography, Latin American studies, primate studies, women's studies and most fields that offer majors.

Students who attend the School of Fine Arts pursue their Bachelor of Arts, Bachelor of Fine Arts, Bachelor of Music, and Bachelor of Music Education degrees. The available fields include art, music, and theatre arts with a dual focus on teaching excellence and artistic creativity. Holding accreditation from by the National Association of Schools of Art and Design, Drake's Department of Art and Design offers instruction in art history, graphic design, and studio art (drawing, painting, printmaking, and sculpture). Students in the Department of Music select from degrees in applied music (instrumental, piano or vocal music performance) and music education. Other alternatives exist, such as a Bachelor of Arts degree with a music major, a Bachelor of Music degree with elective studies in business, and a Bachelor of Music with a jazz studies concentration. Those who wish to study theatre, acting, directing, theatre design, musical theatre, and theatre education enroll in the Department of Theatre Arts.

Students enrolled in the Drake University College of Business and Public Administration complete their undergraduate degree of Bachelor of Science in Business Administration in four years. Available majors include accounting, actuarial science, economics, entrepreneurial management, finance, general business, information systems, international business, management, and marketing. Concentrations in insurance and law and business are also available. The College allows interdisciplinary majors, combinations of majors, and open business (undeclared) status. The College is accreditation by the AACSB International—The International Association to Advance Collegiate Schools of Business.

First-year students admitted directly to the PharmD program in the College of Pharmacy and Health Sciences complete a two-year prepharmacy program then are guaranteed consideration for admission into a four-year PharmD program. A health sciences major with three tracks—clinical and applied sciences, health services management, and pharmaceutical sciences—is also available. The College is accredited by the Accreditation Council for Pharmacy Education and belongs to the American Association of Colleges of Pharmacy.

Students who wish to pursue Bachelor of Arts majors in advertising (management and creative tracks), electronic media (broadcast news and radio/television), magazines, news/Internet, and public relations study in the School of Journalism and Mass Communication. The School allows an open enrolled (undeclared) option and holds accreditation from the Accrediting Council on Education in Journalism and Mass Communication.

Interdisciplinary concentrations are offered in behavior analysis of developmental disabilities, global public health and comparative studies and human resources management.

In addition, the College of Arts and Sciences, the College of Business and Public Administration, and the School of Journalism offer combined 3+3 programs with the Drake Law School. Students in this program can obtain their undergraduate degrees in three years in one of the aforementioned colleges or schools, then pursue a law degree for the next three years at the Law School.

Programs at the School of Education lead to degrees in elementary or secondary education. Students may earn a Bachelor of Science or Bachelor of Arts degree that is tailored to prepare graduates for employment in elementary or secondary schools. Other options include adding middle school and coaching endorsements to teaching credentials. Drake University has belonged to the American Association of Colleges for Teacher Education since the association's founding.

ACADEMIC PROGRAMS

From their first classes on the Drake campus, students have the chance to learn in an individualized, challenging, and supportive environment. Research opportunities abound; students work closely with their professors and often publish their findings. With more than 160 student-run organizations on campus, there is an outlet for students to investigate career paths and network with professionals in their field.

Students benefit from a combination of liberal arts training and professional preparation. Through the Drake Curriculum, all students take interactive classes that develop their critical thinking and expressive skills. Students also receive personalized academic advising. At the end of their four years, students undertake the Senior Capstone, which is a research project, thesis, or other major work that shows the concepts and skills the student has acquired at Drake. Drake's Honors Program is open to top students who wish to undertake a rigorous, interdisciplinary course of study.

CAMPUS FACILITIES AND EQUIPMENT

Students have access to the Cowles Library and its more than more than 600,000 books and journals, 100,000 federal and state government documents, 777,000 microform records, 118 electronic databases, and approximately 22,000 scholarly online journals. The collections also include DVDs and music CDs, as well as a digital repository of scholarship and historical material unique to Drake. Many classes utilize the resources in specialized collections in the Law School, College of Pharmacy and Health Sciences, Center for Teacher Education, and School of Fine Arts. Between the Dwight D. Opperman Hall and Law Library, there are 330,000 volumes, along with computer labs and study facilities. The Studio Theater, the Monroe Recital Hall, and the Hall of the Performing Arts are housed in the Harmon Fine Arts Center. Another performance hall, Sheslow Auditorium with a capacity of 755 seats, is located in Old Main. The Bell Center offers a gym, pool, aerobic dance room, fitness room, basketball, volleyball, and badminton courts. Additional athletic facilities are available in the Knapp Center, such as racquetball, volleyball and basketball courts, a jogging track, and a weight room. More than 7,000 people can congregate in Knapp for major events. Basketball courts and a track are available at the Fieldhouse, while the Tennis Center provides six indoor and six outdoor tennis courts.

TUITION, ROOM, BOARD AND FEES

Tuition and fees total $35,090 in 2010–2011. Room and board cost $8,130 annually.

FINANCIAL AID

More than 98 percent of full-time students at Drake have their education financed to some degree with the help of financial aid. In the 2008–2009 school year, a typical financial aid package totaled $21,130. More than 5,000 awards, worth $60 million, are given annually, in the form of need- or merit-based grants and scholarships.

STUDENT ORGANIZATIONS AND ACTIVITIES

With more than 160 organizations operating on campus, students can always find activities that suit their interests. Elected student representatives run the Student Senate. Students also hold seats on some committees in the Faculty Senate. The Student Activities Board is charged with putting on special events, including cultural celebrations, social functions, guest speakers, and concerts. Drake also maintains the Residence Hall Association, composed of students who manage the logistics and activities surrounding residential life.

ADMISSIONS PROCESS

While admission is selective, Drake University considers the full record of each candidate for admission. Since the University prefers students with varied talents and interests, there is no single and inflexible set of admission standards applied to all candidates for admission. The admission process involves a comprehensive review of a student s academic background (courses and grades), standardized test scores (ACT or SAT), personal essay, recommendations, and activities both in high school and the community. Drake University does not discriminate on the basis of age, sex, sexual orientation, race, religion, color, national or ethnic origin, or disability.

A completed application for first-year admission contains the following items: a completed application form, the $25 nonrefundable application fee (the fee is waived for those who apply online), the High School Report and Counselor Recommendation Form, an official high school transcript, and ACT or SAT scores and a personal essay. Students applying to transfer to Drake are required to submit official transcripts for all previous college-level coursework.

Application for admission to undergraduate degree programs, except pre-pharmacy, may be made for any fall, spring, or summer term. Beginning October 15, students are notified of the admission decision within four to six weeks of the date that all materials are received. March 1 is the priority deadline for consideration for admission and merit- and need-based financial aid. Freshman applicants to the pre-pharmacy program in the College of Pharmacy and Health Sciences must the December 1 deadline. Transfer students are only admitted to the professional PharmD program.

Candidates should contact:

Drake University

Office of Admission

2507 University Avenue

Des Moines, IA 50311

800-44-DRAKE, x3181

515-271-3181 (locally and outside the U.S)

Fax: 515-271-2831

www.choose.drake.edu

admission@drake.edu

ELMHURST COLLEGE

AT A GLANCE

A private liberal arts college in the heart of metropolitan Chicago, Elmhurst College ranks in the top tier of its category, according to *U.S. News & World Report*. With a student-faculty ratio of only 13:1, Elmhurst offers a personal approach where every student counts. All classes at Elmhurst are taught by professors, not teaching assistants, and about 84 percent of the College's 127 full-time faculty hold the highest degree in their field.

The College is located in Elmhurst, Illinois, a quiet suburb that ranks Number 1 in a *Chicago* magazine survey of the "best places to live." Downtown Chicago is a 30-minute train ride away, offering a wealth of professional, cultural, and recreational opportunities.

Students come to Elmhurst from many states and countries, and from nearly every religious, racial, and ethnic background. The student body comprises nearly 3,000 undergraduates and about 300 graduate students.

LOCATION AND ENVIRONMENT

Elmhurst College is located 16 miles west of downtown Chicago in the quiet suburb of Elmhurst, a community of 43,000 that has been called "the quintessential Chicago suburb." Within walking distance from campus are two art museums, a library, an eight-screen movie house, lots of great restaurants, and more.

The College is just a short train ride from downtown Chicago, where students enjoy unlimited access to world-class cultural and professional opportunities--from internships to sporting events to concerts of all kinds.

Elmhurst's campus looks like a college ought to look, with big trees, broad lawns, and 24 classy red brick buildings. The campus is a 38-acre arboretum with 650 varieties of trees and plants.

OFF-CAMPUS OPPORTUNITIES

Elmhurst offers international education experiences in many countries, including Spain, the Netherlands, Poland, Bulgaria, and England. Students can go abroad for a semester, a year, or a month during the College's distinctive January Term.

Other off-campus opportunities include a wealth of internship and job-shadowing experiences. One student recently shadowed a renowned neurosurgeon in San Francisco, for example; another worked on staff at the Mayo Clinic in Rochester, Minnesota. A third traveled to New York to participate in a high-level discussion of medical ethics.

MAJORS AND DEGREES OFFERED

Elmhurst offers more than 50 majors, ranging from accounting to exercise science to jazz studies. Students may complete a double major, add a minor, or create their own interdisciplinary major. The Honors Program provides extra opportunities for students who are especially talented, curious, and motivated. We also offer a range of pre-professional programs leading to graduate study in health care, law, and more. Nine graduate programs lead to the master's degree.

ACADEMIC PROGRAMS

Elmhurst is a private, four-year college in the liberal arts tradition. The curriculum combines liberal learning and professional preparation to prepare students for lives of meaningful work and personal fulfillment.

Academic programs at Elmhurst are characterized by their real-world connections and demonstrated responsiveness to student needs. Students conduct research and defend their results. They analyze data, think critically, solve problems collaboratively, study and write across the disciplines, and learn to formulate new ideas and to convey them with maximum impact.

All classes at Elmhurst are taught by professors, not teaching assistants, and about 84 percent of the College's 127 full-time faculty hold the highest degree in their field. With a student-faculty ratio of only 13:1, faculty members get to know their students as individuals.

CAMPUS FACILITIES AND EQUIPMENT

Elmhurst's facilities include a newly renovated student center and an excellent library and computer center. At the Speech-Language-Hearing Clinic, student clinicians practice their skills and treat patients. Old Main, built in 1879, is on the National Register of Historic Places. The Tyrrell Fitness Center offers more than 6,000 square feet of weight training and physical fitness equipment. Facilities are open throughout the day and evening and are readily accessible to all students.

TUITION, ROOM, BOARD AND FEES

Full-time tuition for 2009–2010 is $27,270; room (double occupancy) is $4,496; standard meal plan is $3,012. For more details, see our Tuition & Fees pages at www.elmhurst.edu.

FINANCIAL AID

Elmhurst provides financial aid to about 87 percent of full-time students. Financial aid programs include scholarships (based on academic merit), and grants, loans, and student employment (based on financial need). More than 600 students work on campus. The College makes admission decisions independently from any consideration of financial need.

STUDENT ORGANIZATIONS AND ACTIVITIES

Students come to Elmhurst from many states and countries, and from nearly every religious, racial, and ethnic background. The student body comprises nearly 3,000 undergraduates and about 300 graduate students.

Life at Elmhurst is active and creative. Students get involved in more than 100 activities, from theatre to intramurals to the Mock Trial Team. The student newspaper wins awards; the radio station has been on the air since 1947. The campus regularly hosts performances, art exhibits, and an array of excellent guest speakers.

Elmhurst's 18 varsity sports teams compete in the CCIW, one of the top conferences in NCAA Division III athletics. We're big enough to offer a wide choice of sports, but small enough that you can really contribute to your team's success. In the past decade, Bluejay teams have won conference championships in five sports. And they compete in first-rate facilities.

ADMISSION PROCESS

Rolling admission begins on October 1 and continues until all spaces are filled.

Here's how to apply:

• First, complete the application for admission. It's available online at www.elmhurst.edu or by mail from the Elmhurst Admission Office.

• Next, submit your high school transcript, your ACT or SAT scores, and a recommendation from a teacher or counselor. (An essay and a campus interview are recommended but not required.)

• If you're applying as a transfer student, also submit an official transcript from all colleges or universities you've attended.

ELMIRA COLLEGE

AT A GLANCE

Founded in 1855, Elmira College is a private, coeducational, liberal arts college. Elmira, a city of 35,000, is located in the beautiful Finger Lakes Region of Upstate New York.

Campus: 42 historic acres which include 7 classroom buildings, 11 dormitories, 2 administrative office buildings, library, health center, campus center, President's Home and Mark Twain Study. A major athletic facility completes the total campus. Eight college buildings are listed on the National Register of Historic Places.

Academic calendar: Two twelve-week terms followed in April and May by a unique six-week Term III devoted to travel, field experience, research, independent study, and innovative courses.

Enrollment: 1,200 students, thirteen percent of whom are valedictorians or salutatorians of their high schools or prep schools, from 35 states and 31 foreign countries.

Faculty: All have earned the Ph.D. or the highest degree in their field required for undergraduate instruction; 12:1 student faculty ratio. No classes are taught by teaching assistants.

Average Class Size: 16 students per class; 90% of all offerings have 25 or fewer students; 35% have fewer than 12 students. Elmira ranks in the Top Five colleges in the eleven Northern states for small class size.

Athletics: NCAA Division III in men's and women's intercollegiate sports. Member of the Eastern College Athletic Conference, the New York State Women's Collegiate Athletic Association, and the Empire 8 Conference.

LOCATION AND ENVIRONMENT

Elmira, a city of 35,000, is located in the beautiful Finger Lakes Region of Upstate New York. Nestled in the lush, rolling hills of the southern Finger Lakes region, Elmira is a thriving, forward-thinking American community, with fresh air and wide-open spaces in harmony with the modern amenities of a larger city. Nearby, you can attend superb, live entertainment; soar back into American aviation's lofty past; tour historic neighborhoods; investigate Mark Twain's imagination or visit the beautiful lakes that give this region its name.

Within a ten-block radius of the Elmira College campus, there are many restaurants, a performing arts center, a fine arts museum, and shopping. There are about 60 churches, serving most denominations, within walking distance of campus.

Elmira is the place that many scholars say Samuel Clemens (Mark Twain) did his best work, penning the American literary classic The Adventures of Huckleberry Finn and many other works in his study. In 1870, Clemens married Elmira College alumna Olivia Langdon of the Class of 1864. In 1983, the Langdon family gave the study and the historic Quarry Farm to Elmira College. Now Quarry Farm is used as a residence for visiting Twain scholars from all over the world. The Center for Mark Twain Studies at Quarry Farm offers year-round educational programs.

OFF-CAMPUS OPPORTUNITIES

Elmira College offers a wide range of exciting off-campus opportunities. During the Spring Term, for instance, Elmira College students have traveled with faculty to San Salvador in the Bahamas, Spain, France, Russia, England, Italy, Germany, Ecuador, Scotland, the Czech Republic, Peru, Egypt, Belgium, Greece, Mexico, Australia, the American West, Alaska, and Hawaii.

The highly selective and competitive Junior Year Abroad (JYA) program facilitates the study of foreign language and cultures. Generally, financial aid applies to the JYA program; however, tuition exchange programs do not apply. Interested students apply in the Fall Term of their sophomore year.

All Elmira College students participate in a community service activity for a minimum of 60 hours. This service is an academic course required for graduation. New students register for Community Service before beginning their first term at Elmira, with the expectation that they will complete the requirement by the end of their first year. Many find the experience so rewarding that they continue volunteering to help others all four years.

MAJORS AND DEGREES OFFERED

Elmira College offers majors in more than 35 academic areas, but our range of program options is even greater. In ten of these subjects you may pursue either a Bachelor of Science or a Bachelor of Arts degree. While the B.S. degree encourages specialization in a specific area, the B.A. degree offers a broader education in the liberal arts and sciences. Students must earn a stipulated number of credits in the major—with a passing grade—as well as complete the General Degree Requirements.

Academic Majors Include:
Accounting
American Studies
Anthropology and Sociology
Art
Biology
Biology - Chemistry
Business Administration
Chemistry
Classical Studies
Criminal Justice
Economics
Education
Educational Studies
Engineering-Chemical
English Literature
Environmental Studies
Foreign Languages
History
Human Services
Individualized Studies
International Studies
Mathematics
Medical Technology
Music
Nursing
Philosophy & Religion
Political Science
Pre-Medical
Psychology
Public Affairs
Social Studies
Sociology and Anthropology
Speech & Hearing
Speech and Language Disabilities
Theatre

ACADEMIC PROGRAMS

With a faculty-student ratio of 12:1, you will have the chance to express your ideas in class. Debate the nature of the universe with fellow students and professors. And learn from each other: well over half our students are from beyond New York State, representing 35 states, six Canadian provinces and 31 foreign countries. You will end up discussing your future one-on-one with people, who are committed to your success.

The requirements for baccalaureate degrees granted by Elmira College have been established by members of the faculty so that each graduate receives a broad general education, explores different fields of knowledge, examines one or more of those fields intensively, and applies the knowledge acquired in the classroom to realistic and appropriate work experiences.

Special Academic Programs:

Interested in becoming a doctor or lawyer? Elmira College offers a variety of academic programs that will prepare students for a range of career choices. Special Academic Programs include: Chemical Engineering, Army & Air Force ROTC, Pre-Law, Pre-Professional Programs, English as a Second Language, a 4+1 MBA Program, and Athletic Coaching Certificate.

Our Distinctive Academic Programs make the Elmira College experience unique. Required community service and internships allow students to grow and gain practical experience in a workplace dynamic. Encore, the College's performing arts appreciation requirement, and off-campus opportunities, such as, the Junior Year Abroad program and the United Nations Semester, expose students to a diversity of experiences not always found in a traditional classroom. The six-week Term III provides students with an exceptional opportunity to immerse themselves into one or two subjects intensely. Additionally (as you probably know by now), Elmira College is one of the best places in the world to study the work and life of Mark Twain.

TUITION, ROOM, BOARD AND FEES
2008–2009 Full-time Student Charges
Dorm Students°
Tuition: $32,000
Room: $5,700
Board: $4,400
Student Activities Fee: $400
Technology Fee: $400
Health Center Fee: $400

° Elmira College is a residential campus. All Undergraduate students, except those who live with parents locally, are required to live on campus.

Town Students
Tuition: $32,000
Technology Fee: $150
Health Center Fee: $400
Student Activities Fee: $400
Special Events Fee: $250

FINANCIAL AID
Elmira College Financial Aid is based on need and merit. Free Application for Federal Student Aid (FAFSA) is required and Financial Aid PROFILE is accepted. Grants and distinctive Honor Scholarships are awarded to students based on academic achievement, leadership activity, and financial need. Awards start at $6,000 per year and range up to full tuition for Valedictorians. Students may also be eligible for federal and state grants, loans, and work on campus.

- No student has ever paid the full cost of an Elmira College education since its founding in 1855.

- Elmira College awards more than $10 million each year in academic scholarships and awards.

- 100% of students demonstrating need receive financial assistance.

- Elmira College administers more than $36 million each year in scholarships and awards, grants, loans and work-study programs.

STUDENT ORGANIZATIONS AND ACTIVITIES
Students are welcome to join one of more than 100 clubs or organizations any time during the academic year. During Summer Registration, new students can browse our Club and Organization Guide and sign up to receive more information from club officers. Two Activities Fairs, one during Fall Orientation and another in mid-September, offer the opportunity to meet current club members, ask questions, and see photos of past events and projects.

Some of our clubs and organizations include: Classics Society, French Club, Political Science Club, Silent Voices, Spanish Club, Circle K, Compeer, EC Ambassadors, Orientation Leaders, Pupils Assisted in Learning (PAL), Red Cross Club, SCOPE, Work for a Cure, Christian Fellowship, Christian Fellowship, Hillel/Jewish Student Association, and the Ski Club.

National Honor Societies include: Phi Beta Kappa, Psi Chi, Kappa Delta Pi, Phi Eta Sigma, Phi Alpha Theta, Alpha Phi Sigma, Omicron Delta Kappa, Beta Beta Beta, Sigma Beta Delta, Lambda Iota Tau, National Residence Hall Honorary, Pi Sigma Alpha, Sigma Theta Tau, Lambda Alpha, Pi Gamma Mu, and Alpha Sigma Lambda.

Elmira is an NCAA Division III college, as well as a member of the Eastern College Athletic Conference, the New York State Women's Collegiate Athletic Association and the Empire 8 Conference. We field varsity teams in men's and women's basketball, cheerleading, field hockey, men's and women's golf, men's and women's ice hockey, men's and women's lacrosse, men's and women's soccer, softball, men's and women's tennis and women's volleyball. National rankings and post-season tournaments have become annual traditions for the Soaring Eagles.

Elmira College offers its students the chance to compete in collegiate athletics at many levels. The goal of the Junior Varsity and Intramural program is to offer students a chance to participate in athletics without the focus on skill level. Intramural sports range anywhere from flag football to ultimate frisbee. The success of our intramural program can be seen every Term III as our students softball teams compete daily.

ADMISSIONS PROCESS
We offer two admissions plans for freshmen applicants. Early Decision and Regular Admission.

International students may apply only under the Regular Admission program.

Regular Admission

If you are applying to several colleges, here is what you do for Elmira College:

1. Submit a completed application to Elmira College. You can fill out an application online, or print an application that you can send in. We also accept the Common Application and Universal Application.

2. Have your counselor send your official transcript, including senior year courses and grades to date. Have your official SAT I or ACT scores sent to Elmira College.

3. Have at least one letter of recommendation sent to the college.

4. Write a great essay.

5. While not required, we strongly suggest you sit down with an Elmira College admissions counselor for an interview. You can schedule your interview by calling the Office of Admissions at 800-935-6472.

Early Decision

If Elmira College is your first choice college, Early Decision is the program for you. We'll make a decision on your application as soon as it is complete, but you do have to meet the deadlines. There are two Early Decision programs; the first deadline is November 15, and the second is January 15. We promise to notify you of our decision by December 15 for Early Decision I applicants and by January 31 for Early Decision II applicants.

EMMANUEL COLLEGE

Emmanuel College, founded by the Sisters of Notre Dame de Namur in 1919, is a coed, residential, Catholic liberal arts and sciences college located in the city of Boston. Emmanuel's beautiful 17-acre campus is neighbored by a world-class medical center, five other colleges, two major art museums and Fenway Park. Its unique location enables students to explore real-world experiences through internships, research and strategic partnerships within the Longwood Medical and Academic Area and the city of Boston.

AT A GLANCE

Emmanuel College, founded by the Sisters of Notre Dame de Namur in 1919, is a coed, residential, Catholic liberal arts and sciences college located in the city of Boston. The College's student body includes more than 1,700 undergraduate students from 31 countries and 30 states; its neighbors include the world-class surgeons of the Longwood Medical and Academic Area, the Monets and Gauguins of the Museum of Fine Arts and 250,000 college students at institutions across the city. With a history of providing high-quality, values-based academic programs, Emmanuel offers opportunities to learn, teach, explore and research in more than 25 areas of study. Through a supportive learning environment that fosters academic excellence, intellectual integrity and a strong social conscience, Emmanuel students develop the skills and confidence to succeed and make a difference in an ever-changing world.

LOCATION AND ENVIRONMENT

Residing in Boston's Fenway neighborhood, Emmanuel students are encouraged to view Boston as their extended classroom. Its unique location enables students and faculty to explore real-world experiences through internships, research and strategic partnerships in and around the city. Within a few steps from campus students can find: The Emerald Necklace, a vibrant system of parks that connect throughout Boston; the Longwood Medical and Academic Area, one of the most prestigious medical, academic and research districts in the world; the Museum of Fine Arts and Isabella Stewart Gardner Museum, and Fenway Park—the home of the Boston Red Sox.

The College's campus, meanwhile, is a vibrant community alive with energy of teaching and learning, of exploration and research. Emmanuel is the only college in the country to boast a 12-story, 300,000 square-foot private research facility right on campus: Merck Research Laboratories-Boston. The College recently opened the new Maureen Murphy Wilkens Science Center, completed renovations on its Art Department, and restored nearby Roberto Clemente Field, which serves as home field for Emmanuel athletics.

OFF-CAMPUS OPPORTUNITIES

At Emmanuel, internships are considered an integral component of a student's education experience – in fact, many departments require an internship. The College's location in the city of Boston gives students access to some of the most renowned financial, cultural, medical and academic institutions in the world. Eighty percent of Emmanuel students, from across all academic disciplines, participate in internships to apply the knowledge they have gained in the classroom within a professional environment, to enhance their skills and to build a network of professional contacts.

At the core of Emmanuel College's mission is a commitment to social justice and service to the community. Students have ample opportunities to participate in community service, including programs like Alternative Spring Break and service-learning courses. The three main branches of community service outreach available at Emmanuel are The Jean Yawkey Center for Community Leadership, The Carolyn A. Lynch Institute and the Campus Ministry Office. The College also offers service opportunities through partnering agencies in the city of Boston.

Emmanuel is part of the Colleges of the Fenway (COF) consortium, which allows students to cross register for courses at neighboring colleges, utilize shared resources, participate in intramurals and/or play in the COF's orchestra. COF schools include: Emmanuel College, Massachusetts College of Art and Design, Massachusetts College of Pharmacy and Health Sciences, Simmons College, Wentworth Institute of Technology and Wheelock College.

Emmanuel partners with the Colleges of the Fenway GEO Center to provide students with opportunities to study and travel abroad. The GEO Center, located on Emmanuel's campus, offers resources for preparing students to experience the global environment. Students can spend a year, semester, summer or school break in over 70 countries, choosing from more than 550 suggested programs. Emmanuel students have studied everywhere from Italy and Uganda to China and Argentina.

MAJORS AND DEGREES OFFERED

Emmanuel offers opportunities in the pursuit of learning, teaching, exploration and research in more than 25 areas of study. Students are also encouraged to pursue an individualized major by tailoring a course of study from the College's offerings.

Areas of Study

Accounting; American Studies; Art; Art History°; Art Therapy; Digital Photography°; Graphic Design and Technology; Studio Art; Biochemistry; Biology; Neuroscience; Biostatistics; Catholic Studies°; Chemistry; Forensic Science; Economics°; Education; Elementary; Secondary; English; Communication, Media; and Cultural Studies; Literature; Writing and Literature; Gender and Women's Studies°; Global Studies and International Affairs; Health Care°; History; Information Technology°; Latin American Studies°; Management; Accounting°; Organizational Leadership°; Sport Management; Mathematics; Music°; Performing Arts°; Philosophy°

Political Science (International Relations and Comparative Politics); American Politics and Government; Psychology; Counseling and Health; Developmental; General/Experimental; Neuroscience; Religious Studies°; Sociology; Crime and Justice; Human Services; Social Inequality and Social Justice; Spanish; Pre-law; Pre-med

°denotes minor

ACADEMIC PROGRAMS

Emmanuel offers a rigorous liberal arts and sciences curriculum supported by an individualized approach. The academic requirements of Emmanuel College have been established and designed to ensure that every student experiences the range of skills and content that are implied by the liberal arts mission of the College. Through required courses drawn from a cross-section of the liberal arts disciplines, students are exposed to models of analytical reasoning, symbolic thinking, observation, creativity, critical thinking, moral reasoning, self-knowledge; and significant intellectual content from the fields of history, literature, the arts, philosophy, religion, the social sciences, the natural sciences and the study cultures outside the United States. Additionally, such courses require student work that enhances the ability of students to comprehend and to function intellectually in the variety of disciplinary modes that constitute the liberal arts.

Emmanuel College's Office of Academic Advising provides students with the support needed to attain their academic goals and serves as a model of the Emmanuel experience. All first-year students receive an academic advisor, who assists them in navigating the first few semesters of college, helping them to understand the liberal arts and sciences curriculum and its value, and to develop a unique academic plan.

All new students are also required to take a first-year seminar of his or her choice in the fall or spring semester. In small classes, working closely with each other and a member of the faculty, students are introduced to the academic traditions of the liberal arts and sciences, and to the expectations and values of our academic community.

Each year, students who demonstrate superior academic ability and promise are invited to participate in Emmanuel College's Honors Program. This four-year academic and co-curricular program combines a rigorous, discussion-based curriculum with complementary opportunities such as cultural activities, faculty-directed research projects and service in the community. The program begins with the yearlong Honors Colloquium for first-year students and includes: four interdisciplinary, writing intensive seminars; a service-learning component; and an independent research project.

For those students who are uncertain of a major or are exploring majors, Emmanuel College offers the Majors Exploration Program (MEP), which helps students explore careers that will be satisfying and subsequently determine an appropriate major for that career path. Through MEP, students complete the online career tool, FOCUS, which teaches students about themselves and their career ideas through questions about their own interests, values, personality, skills and extracurricular activities.

Additionally, students have access to Emmanuel's Academic Resource Center (ARC), which offers specially designed programs to help students meet their academic goals, and one-on-one guidance from the Internship and Career Development Office.

Facilities And Equipment

The new Maureen Murphy Wilkens Science Center expands opportunities for interactive teaching and learning, enabling the College to better prepare students in the sciences and enhance the academic experience for students and faculty in all fields. The center includes: teaching laboratories for biology, chemistry, biochemistry, physics, psychology/neuroscience; faculty research space and offices; student study areas; and new classrooms for all disciplines.

The College's Jean Yawkey Center includes a gymnasium with 2.5 basketball/volleyball courts and 1,430 seating capacity, a fitness center, training room, locker room facilities, and athletic staff offices and conference rooms. The facility also houses the Jean Yawkey Center for Community Leadership, which is dedicated to developing service opportunities and leadership skills for Emmanuel students and providing programs for young people in Boston area schools and community organizations. Through the Jean Yawkey Center for Community Leadership, Emmanuel students volunteer in schools throughout the city as mentors and tutors.

Emmanuel College recently partnered with the city of Boston on a comprehensive restoration of Roberto Clemente Field, located across the street from campus. The upgraded facility, which serves as home field for the Emmanuel softball, men's and women's soccer and men's and women's lacrosse teams, includes: A 120,000 sq. ft. NCAA-regulation synthetic turf field; a three-lane rubberized track; practice facilities for expanded track and field events; and new MUSCO lighting.

Since Merck Research Laboratories-Boston opened its doors on Emmanuel's campus in October 2004, the College's students have gained access and opportunity to a world few undergraduates ever get to see. This unique partnership gives Emmanuel access to cutting-edge research equipment, supports faculty-student research initiatives, and provides student stipends for summer research projects. Through the Merck Scholars Program, each year Emmanuel students are awarded scholarships based on outstanding academic performance in the sciences.

CAMPUS LIFE

With more than 90 different co-curricular clubs, activities and organizations on campus, Emmanuel is a community alive with a strong sense of mission, a vibrant, confident faith and a joyful spirit. Emmanuel students are challenged to act, to lead, to give generously to others, and to get involved. Students find ample opportunities to take part in academic clubs, honor societies, media clubs, performing arts, cultural organizations, intramurals, leadership roles and special interest groups. They put their beliefs into action through educational programs and volunteer service through Campus Ministry. As an NCAA Division III school, Emmanuel offers an athletic program that includes 17 varsity teams, including the recently added men's and women's lacrosse programs.

TUITION AND FINANCIAL AID

Emmanuel College is committed to making a liberal arts and sciences education affordable for our students and their families. We understand that financing a quality private education can be a challenge. That is why we believe that paying for an education is a partnership between the student, their family and Emmanuel.

At Emmanuel, financial assistance programs include a combination of scholarships, institutional grants, federal and state grants, federal loans and part-time employment. Merit scholarships are based on a combination of students' high school academic achievement and extracurricular activities.

To apply for financial aid, students must complete the Free Application for Federal Student Aid (FAFSA) and an Emmanuel College Application for Financial Aid. Once a FAFSA is completed, students are automatically considered for Emmanuel College grant aid. Some students will also be eligible to receive federal, state and other grant or scholarship funding. These funds may be awarded in addition to merit or other scholarship funds students receive from Emmanuel. Students who complete a FAFSA may also receive low-interest student loans, including the Federal Stafford Loan and Federal Work Study.

For more information, visit www.emmanuel.edu and click on "Tuition and Aid."

TUITION, ROOM, BOARD AND FEES

Emmanuel College is committed to providing students with a quality education at an affordable cost. And we offer billing options and payment plans to ensure that you're able to pay for college in the way most convenient for you.

2009–2010 Tuition and Fees

Tuition: $29,200

Room and Board: $11,950 (double occupancy)

Fees: $165, Estimated Student Health

Insurance: $1,059

Total: $ 41,150 (plus own health insurance), $42,209 (including Emmanuel insurance)

ADMISSIONS

For more information or to apply for admission, please visit www.emmanuel.edu. We require an Emmanuel College application or the Common Application (available online), an essay, a secondary school transcript which includes first semester grades, two letters of recommendation and the SAT or ACT test. Students whose native language is not English should submit the TOEFL.

EMORY AND HENRY COLLEGE

AT A GLANCE

Founded in 1836, Emory & Henry is the oldest college in Southwest Virginia. It is one of the few Southern colleges to have operated more than 170 years under the same name and with the same affiliation: the United Methodist Church. The campus and surrounding village is home to students as well as E&H professors, administrators and retired college employees. It is an academic environment that underscores the broad dedication within the community to each student's enlightenment and success.

COLLEGE BASICS

Noted for its exceptional beauty, Emory & Henry remains firmly grounded in its 173-year commitment to excellence in liberal arts education. Dedicated to creating informed minds and global citizens, Emory & Henry translates an emphasis on civic virtues to active service learning. A hallmark of the College's civic engagement is its leadership in advancing a pragmatic understanding of sustainable communities and practices.

LOCATION AND ENVIRONMENT

Emory & Henry is located in Emory, Virginia, which is approximately 25 miles north of Bristol, a city that offers large shopping areas, movies, and restaurants. The area surrounding Emory is known for its scenic beauty, recreational opportunities, and talented craftsmen. Within an hour's drive are slopes for snow skiing, lakes for waterskiing, the Appalachian Trail for hiking, and locations for horseback riding, canoeing, and many other sports. The historic town of Abingdon, Virginia, which lies just 7 miles south of Emory, is the home of the renowned Barter Theatre, the oldest professional theater in the United States. Abingdon's downtown district includes shopping areas, movie theaters, restaurants, and museums. The city also hosts the annual Virginia Highlands Festival, bringing together musicians, artists, and craftsmen for exhibitions and competition.

ACADEMICS

Emory & Henry College is a transformative academic community. Our education is distinguished by progress—sometimes sudden, sometimes gradual – toward an expanded sense of personal potential and an enlightened sense of civic responsibility. This transformation, this increase in excellence, is the foundation of our campus culture. Its impact is lasting and profound. Emory & Henry offers a liberal arts program with an emphasis on writing, reasoning, value inquiry, and knowledge of global concerns. All students complete a core curriculum that integrates classroom work with study and research beyond the classroom—and the campus, ultimately contributing to a deep understanding of regional and cultural differences and challenges. The core curriculum includes an emphasis on student proficiencies in writing, communication, quantitative literacy, ethical reasoning and critical thinking. Undergraduate programs of study include art, athletic training, biology, business administration, chemistry, computer information management, economics, education, English, geography, history, languages, mass communications, mathematics, music, philosophy, physical education, physics, political science, psychology, religion, sociology and anthropology, and theater. Special and interdisciplinary programs of study offered are environmental studies, international studies, pre-engineering, pre-law, pre-medicine, and public policy and community service. Emory & Henry operates on a semester calendar from late August to mid-December and from mid-January to mid-May. A summer session runs from late May to early July. First-year students typically carry a four-course load of 13 to 14 credit hours per semester. Upperclass students carrying a full load complete five courses (14 to 15 credit hours) each semester. Thirty-eight courses are required for graduation. Classes meet on Monday-Wednesday-Friday or Tuesday-Thursday schedules. One important feature of the Emory & Henry curriculum is its orientation toward helping students make a smooth transition from high school to college. The Powell Resource Center provides academic support, advising, career services, and personal counseling. The Writing Center helps students in every department to use writing for effective communication.

ADMISSIONS

Emory & Henry College offers an Early Action Plan with a deadline of Dec. 1 with acceptance decisions made by Jan. 1. Students who wish to be considered for talent-based and merit-based scholarships in art, music, theatre, pre-health, pre-ministry and the Honors Program must apply through this program. All other applicants are considered on a rolling basis after Jan. 1. In most instances, admissions decisions are made within two weeks of receipt of a completed application. Admission to Emory & Henry is determined on the basis of both academic achievement and personal qualifications. An applicant's secondary school preparation must include the following: 4 years of English, 3 years of mathematics (algebra I, algebra II, and geometry), 2 years of laboratory sciences (biology, chemistry and/or physics), 2 years of a single foreign language, and 2 years of history and social studies. It is strongly recommended that one year of study in the fine arts be included. Strong emphasis also is placed on involvement and leadership in extracurricular and community activities. Merit-based scholarships are offered to students need-blind. Eligibility for need-based grants are determined by submitting the Free Application for Federal Student Aid (FAFSA) as soon as possible after Jan. 1. Indicate that you want results sent to Emory & Henry College, code 003709. Virginia residents need to submit the Virginia Tuition Assistance Grant (VTAG) application by July 31.

CAMPUS FACILITIES AND EQUIPMENT

McGlothlin-Street Hall is a 70,000-square-foot academic center that houses the Departments of Biology, Business, Chemistry, Education, Environmental Studies, Geography, International Studies, and Psychology; a 104-seat auditorium; and a tiered sixty-seat auditorium. Classrooms and laboratories in McGlothlin-Street Hall are equipped with the most current technological equipment, including Internet access and interactive TV. Miller-Fulton Hall contains computerized classrooms used for instruction in such fields as accounting and computer science. Science departments located in Miller-Fulton and McGlothlin-Street Halls feature a variety of equipment, such as a microcomputer-based laboratory for physics students, computerized chromatography for chemistry students, a DNA sequencer in the Biology Department, and biofeedback equipment. In 2006, the construction on two new student residence halls was completed. The residence halls, which are located in Emory a few blocks from the main campus, enhance the E&H academic village where professors, students and administrators live, work and learn together. Built in 1889 the newly renovated Byars Hall houses three stories of classrooms, seminar rooms choir and ensemble rehearsal halls, a digital art lab, a dark room, two large art studios, practice rooms for instrumental music, and a theatre support room. Wiley Hall, which was built in 1929, has undergone a massive restoration. The historic building houses numerous administrative offices as well as some faculty offices and classroom space. The library collection consists of more than 350,000 items, including books, periodicals, government documents, audio and videotapes, compact discs, DVDs, and electronic databases. The library contains a group of computers reserved for library research, an open computer lab, and a computer classroom.

CAMPUS LIFE

Students at Emory & Henry are encouraged to take part in campus decision making. They have voting representatives on nearly every faculty committee and on the Board of Trustees. The central body in campus government is the Student Senate, which brings together representatives of the student body, faculty, and administration. Students have opportunities for involvement in a variety of campus activities: service clubs, Christian fellowship, fraternities, sororities, sports clubs, honor groups, and multicultural groups. Student staffs produce a yearbook, an online magazine, and a literary magazine; others operate a 9,000-watt FM public radio station with a coverage area that extends some 40 miles beyond the campus. Musically talented students have opportunities to participate in a choral program and a pep band. The prestigious Concert Choir has toured throughout the United States and in parts of Europe. The Barter Theatre, a professional theater in nearby Abingdon, works with Emory and Henry College to provide a theater education program that integrates college-level drama study with the benefits of experience on a professional stage.

MAJORS AND DEGREES

Emory & Henry College offers programs of study in art, athletic training, biology, business administration, chemistry, computer information management, economics, education (early childhood through high school, including many subject-area options), English, environmental studies, geography, history, international studies (East Asia, European community, or Middle Eastern and Islamic studies), languages, mass communications, mathematics, music, philosophy, physical education, physics, political science, psychology, public policy and community service; religion, sociology and anthropology, and theater (in association with the Barter Theatre, the state theatre of Virginia). Preprofessional preparation in dentistry, law, medicine, and veterinary medicine may be completed within several of the programs. The Bachelor of Arts degree is awarded in all programs of study and the Bachelor of Science degree in selected areas. Individualized programs of study may be developed in consultation with a faculty adviser.

OFF CAMPUS OPPORTUNITIES

The Appalachian Center for Community Service is available for students committed to community service and integrates service learning into many classes. The King Health and Physical Education Center includes a new fitness center and enhances the College athletics program. Varsity sports for men are baseball, basketball, cross-country, football, golf, soccer, and tennis; women compete in basketball, cross-country, soccer, softball, swimming, tennis, and volleyball. Several sports are played on a club basis. A large percentage of E&H students engage in community projects that often involve policy research and advocacy aimed at benefiting the region. An aggressive internship program provides on-the-job opportunities for students in most of the College's programs, providing academic credit for off-campus work in community agencies and businesses. Many students have completed internships in the surrounding communities, while others have opted for internships outside the region, including several in Washington, D.C., in positions related to the Congress or the federal government. Emory & Henry students participate in a wide variety of study-abroad programs. From Rome to Beijing and from Eastern Europe to East Asia, Emory & Henry students experience cultures and people in a way that enriches their perspective on their studies, their lives, and their futures. Emory & Henry helps students prepare for these experiences through language study and with courses offered through a comprehensive international studies program. The College has exchange agreements with colleges and universities in Asia, Europe, and Central and South America. Students who desire other types of travel/study are assisted by the E&H International Education Program in locating suitable programs.

TUITION AND AID

Our Financial Aid Office works to ensure students receive an Emory & Henry education with a minimal amount of debt. Compared to other private colleges, our annual out-of-pocket expenses are among the lowest in Virginia. The average award to our incoming first-year students including only grants and scholarships is $ 23,469. Approximately 98 percent of all students receive financial aid. Virginia residents may qualify for the Tuition Assistance Grant (TAG), currently a $3,000 value. In recent years, the rate of alumni giving has been among the highest among colleges and universities in the nation. This percentage of giving says volumes about the high degree of satisfaction Emory & Henry graduates have with their education. This level of giving also has translated into tremendous support for scholarships that are offered to Emory & Henry students.

School Says Tuition And Fees

For 2009–10, resident students pay a comprehensive fee of $33,180, which includes tuition, room, and board. This cost is significantly offset for most students by scholarships and financial aid.

EMORY UNIVERSITY

AT A GLANCE

Emory University is internationally recognized for its outstanding liberal arts college, highly ranked professional schools, and comprehensive healthcare system. Emory College, the four-year undergraduate division of Emory University, offers a broad and rigorous liberal arts curriculum with over 70 majors and 55 minors to choose from. Emory provides the opportunities, resources and facilities of a major research university and with 5,500 undergraduate students, the small classes and faculty attention of a smaller liberal arts college. Take a look at all Emory has to offer- you'll see why Emory students feel inspired to do more with what they learn here.

LOCATION AND ENVIRONMENT

One of Emory's most compelling features is its proximity to the vibrant city of Atlanta. Located only fifteen minutes from downtown, Emory's campus is situated on more than 600 acres of property in the historic residential neighborhood of Druid Hills. As home to the third highest concentration of Fortune 1000 companies in the country, Atlanta has become a cultural, technological, and financial hub of both the Southeast and the nation. In fact, with 45 universities, colleges and institutions of higher learning, and endless cultural, intellectual, and social opportunities- Atlanta ranks as one of the best college towns in the United States.

OFF-CAMPUS OPPORTUNITIES

At Emory, students enjoy a balance of rigorous academics, real-world experiences, and an exciting social life, which are all enhanced by the campus's close proximity to Atlanta. Recently voted one of the nation's "most livable cities," you'll find there's more to this Southern city than warm weather. Eclectic restaurants and independent shops surround campus, and a quick subway ride takes you to Atlanta's sports facilities, parks, concerts, and arts venues. Nearly 90% of Emory students supplement their studies with internships or research at places like the Centers for Disease Control, the Carter Center, the Yerkes Primate Center, CNN, Home Depot, the Coca-Cola Company, American Cancer Society and many other companies and organizations with offices in Atlanta. Engaged scholarship and volunteerism are a major component of a student's experience as they are woven into the curriculum; on any given day Emory students can be found engaged in numerous service projects around campus and throughout the city of Atlanta. The opportunities to engage in the community are endless, from working in urban school districts to studying the inhabitants of local streams and rivers.

MAJORS AND DEGREES OFFERED

From small classroom settings to lectures given by prominent scholars and opportunities for study abroad, research and internships, Emory provides a rich environment for learning. Expert faculty members focused on teaching choose Emory for the opportunity to work with intelligent and ambitious students. The curriculum is grounded in the liberal arts, providing a challenging, broad-based education that emphasizes critical thinking and gives students the skills needed to pursue any career or succeed in graduate study. With a 7:1 student to faculty ratio, 87% of classes have fewer than 30 students and 90% of classes are taught by full-time faculty members. Moreover, unique seminar-style classes of 15 students are offered to all first-year students. This is just one of the ways students say that they feel surrounded by nurturing and supportive faculty who are readily available for advice and guidance.

ACADEMIC PROGRAMS

Undergraduate programs in humanities, sciences, business, and nursing allow Emory students to explore their interests and talents in the classroom and in the field. Emory cultivates engaged scholars who make a difference in their communities with critical thinking skills and hands-on experience in ethical leadership, service, and research. Our students come from far and wide to live and learn within a diverse community of talented artists, accomplished researchers, inspired scholars, and skilled educators.

Moreover, at Emory you won't just find students getting an education. Emory students are twice as likely to do research outside of the classroom as their peers. While studying environmental science, why not help build a greener building as part of the LEED initiative? Instead of simply reading about ancient history, why not help preserve ancient relics at the Carlos Museum on campus? How about transferring the class discussion during a political science seminar into an internship at a think tank or at the Georgia State Capitol? Take a look at the resources for learning at Emory and think about what you could do with them. You might discover the desire to choreograph modern dance or to assist in the development of an AIDS vaccine. Regardless of what you choose to tackle first, Emory will give you the tools to transform the world.

In 2009, Emory celebrated worldwide service and partnerships including: the first public exhibition of works from the extraordinary archives of Georgia-born, Pulitzer Prize winner, Alice Walker, opening in the spring at the Woodruff Library. Additionally, the international art exhibit- Tutankhamen: The Golden King and the Great Pharaohs, was hosted by Emory's Michael C. Carlos Museum and organized by National Geographic, in partnership with the Egyptian Supreme Council of Antiquities. The Tut exhibit in Atlanta was a great gesture of friendship and goodwill between the University and the nation of Egypt. An Emory University Presidential Distinguished Professor, the Dalai Lama announced his plans to return to the University in 2010. He also presented a monetary gift to the Emory-Tibet Science Initiative marking a continuation of the strong relationship and collaboration in Western and Tibetan Buddhist intellectual traditions.

CAMPUS FACILITIES AND EQUIPMENT

Emory is a dynamic place that is constantly in a state of growth and improvement. In congruence with the university's commitment to the environment, Emory is a national leader in the construction of "green buildings" which meet certification standards set by Leadership in Energy and Environmental Design (LEED). Over half of the campus is protected "green space". Recent projects include two new buildings to expand facilities for physical science and mathematical research; a new performing arts center; the creation of a pedestrian-friendly campus with more walking paths and common gathering areas; an apartment-style living complex for upper-class students; a multimedia library addition; a new Center for Ethics; a nine building LEED certified Freshman Residence Hall Complex; and a new psychology building.

Thanks to numerous benefactors over the years, Emory is able to consistently improve student resources ranging from facilities and communications to faculty and staff. On the cutting edge of teaching technology, wired classrooms, satellite conferencing, computer labs, ethernet ports, and wireless access points are available throughout campus. Students often use our computer labs for group work, so our Cox Computing Center is a sleek, high-tech space designed specifically for collaborative activity. Students who wish to integrate technology into academic work may do so at the Center for Interactive Teaching, where they can access resources including digital video systems, presentation design, web design, and audio and video editing. From technology to state of the art living environments and an amazing Physical Education center, Emory has created an environment for excellence.

TUITION, ROOM, BOARD AND FEES

Undergraduate Expenses 2009-2010

Tuition $37,500

Fees $536

Room $6,666

Board $4,230

Estimated Books and Supplies $1,100

Estimated Travel and Incidentals $2,100

Total $52,132

FINANCIAL AID

We understand that paying for a college education is a big investment. The undergraduate admission process at Emory is need-blind, and the Office of Financial Aid is committed to meeting 100% of each student's demonstrated need. Emory offers an array of need-based and merit-based financial assistance, and a number of scholarships, grants, loans, and work-study opportunities are available. 60% of undergraduate students receive financial assistance. Additionally, the Emory Advantage program reduces the debt burden for families with annual total incomes of $100,000 or less who demonstrate a need for financial aid. Emory University is also a member of the QuestBridge Scholars Program, an initiative to identify high-achieving, low-income students nationwide. Through the College Match Program high school seniors chosen as finalists have the potential to receive a scholarship package that includes full cost of tuition, books, room and board. We are committed to opening our doors to all qualified students who want a world-class education and to use their talents to impact the world. You can learn even more at: http://www.emory.edu/admission/financial_aid/index.html.

STUDENT ORGANIZATIONS AND ACTIVITIES

Emory students know how to balance hard work with having fun. With all students living on campus for their first two years, this active community is enhanced by a close-knit living environment. The student body is highly involved in extracurricular activities, dedicating 6-10 hours per week to nearly 300 clubs, teams, and organizations. Whether it's Jazz Ensemble, Ultimate Frisbee, Division III Varsity sports, The Emory Wheel (student newspaper), Student Government Association, Concert Choir, or Outdoor Emory, there's an organization for you. Furthermore, more than 80% of our students are involved in Volunteer Emory to share their passion for service and enthusiasm for Emory by volunteering on-campus and throughout the local community. Emory was one of just three schools nationwide that was awarded the Presidential Award for Community Service for commitment to volunteering, service-learning, and civic engagement. In 2009, Emory students completed 150,000 hours of service with more than 200 community partners on projects related to poverty, homelessness, chronic disease, medical services, and environmental conservation. Emory's campus thrives on constant activity, and students are encouraged to get involved, share opinions, and flourish in their new environment.

ADMISSIONS PROCESS

Emory University offers a distinctive undergraduate experience as students have two unique options to begin their education. Entering students can apply to Emory College, which offers a liberal arts education within the heart of a Tier 1 research university. Or, students also can apply to Oxford College where students spend the first two years on Emory's original campus 38 miles east of Atlanta. Oxford offers a small-college setting of 700 students with the same academic strengths, innovative teaching, and unique opportunities for leadership as the Emory College campus in Atlanta. As juniors, students continue from Oxford to the Atlanta campus. A sense of community defines both campuses.

Emory's Admission Committee closely assesses high school coursework and grades. Within the context of the curriculum available at your high school, we look for academically challenging coursework. In addition, we consider your extracurricular involvements as a member of the community, paying close attention to your commitment and leadership in after-school activities. SAT I and ACT (with writing) scores are important but not as important as the rigor of the coursework and grades earned. The middle 50th percent range for successful applicants is 1950–2220 for the SAT and 29–33 for the ACT Composite. 90% of Emory's freshman class came from the top 10% of their graduating high school class with an average unweighted GPA of 3.8.

FELICIAN COLLEGE

AT A GLANCE

Felician College is a liberal arts, coeducational, Catholic, Franciscan college located in northern New Jersey. Founded in 1942 by the Felician Sisters, Felician College currently enrolls 2,350 students in more than 55 undergraduate and graduate programs in the arts and sciences, business and management sciences, health sciences and teacher education. Felician College's NCAA Division II athletic teams compete in basketball, soccer, baseball, softball, cross country, men's golf and women's volleyball. The cheer squad entertains fans and fosters sportsmanship at all home games for both men's and women's basketball.

With a mission to provide a values-oriented education based in the liberal arts, Felician College prepares students for meaningful lives and careers in today's global marketplace. Day, evening and weekend programs are offered to meet the needs of Felician's diverse student body, and students may take course work through semester or accelerated trimester formats. Two summer sessions are also available each year for non-matriculated students.

Felician College is accredited by the Middle States Association of Colleges and Schools and carries program accreditation from the National League for Nursing Accrediting Commission, National Accrediting Agency for Clinical Laboratory Sciences and Teacher Education Accrediting Council. Felician is an active member of the International Assembly for Collegiate Business Education.

On the graduate level, Felician College offers a Master of Business Administration (MBA); Master of Science in Nursing (MSN) in Adult Nurse Practitioner, Family Nurse Practitioner, and Education; a Master of Arts in Religious Education; Master of Arts in Counseling Psychology; Master of Arts in Education and Educational Leadership; and Master of Arts in Education for School Nursing, Health Education, and School Nursing and Health Education. Additionally, Felician offers joint programs in the health sciences terminating on the doctoral or master's level in Audiology, Podiatric Medicine Chiropractic Studies, Physician Assistant Studies, Physical Therapy, Optometry, and Occupational Therapy collaboration with several universities including the University of Medicine and Dentistry of New Jersey (UMDNJ).

LOCATION AND ENVIRONMENT

Felician College is located on two beautifully landscaped campuses in Lodi and Rutherford, New Jersey. Both campuses, set in tree-lined suburban towns, are a 20-minute bus or train ride from New York City and a few miles from the New Jersey Meadowlands sports complex. With classes offered on both campuses, free shuttle buses transport students between the campuses, which are located just a few miles apart.

The College houses an impressive library collection with more than 120,000 books, professional journals, periodicals, microforms, CD-ROMs, and PCs for online learning. A curriculum library serves as a resource center for the teacher education programs.

MAJORS AND DEGREES OFFERED

Felician College offers programs of study in the arts and sciences, business and management sciences, nursing and health management, and teacher education.

Departmental majors for a Bachelor of Arts degree include art with concentrations in fine art, graphic design and new media; biology; communications with concentrations in journalism and digital video production; computer science with concentrations in information assurance/computer security and health information management; criminal justice; English; history; humanities with concentrations in liberal studies and global peace and justice studies; mathematics; music; natural sciences including general science and mathematical science; philosophy (pre-law track); psychology; religious studies; social sciences including international education/foreign language and political science; and sociology.

Bachelor of Arts degree programs are offered in elementary education (K–5); elementary education (K–5) with P-3 endorsement; elementary education with subject specialization (5–8); secondary education (K–12); elementary (K–5) and teacher of students with disabilities (K–12) endorsement.

In the Division of Business, Felician offers five areas of study that award a Bachelor of Science in accounting, business administration, international business, management, and marketing in addition to a five-year BS/ MBA program.

The Nursing and Health Management division offers a generic Bachelor of Science in Nursing degree program for high school graduates and an upper division Bachelor of Science in nursing degree program for registered nurses. Students who complete the four-year generic nursing degree program are eligible to take the examination for licensure as a Registered Nurse (RN) given by the New Jersey Board of Nursing. A bachelor's degree in clinical laboratory science is also available in conjunction with UMDNJ School of Health Related Professions. For this degree, a student may concentrate in cytotechnology, medical technology, or toxicology. Also offered in conjunction with UMDNJ is a Bachelor of Science program in allied-health technology. Students may study medical sonography, nuclear medicine technology, respiratory care, or vascular technology.

With a STUDENTS FIRST philosophy, Felician College provides a number of services designed to meet a variety of needs—the Center for Learning, Nursing Skills Laboratory and a childcare center are housed on campus. To help students plan for their futures, the Career Services Center coordinates field experiences, career seminars, internships and job placements. The Honors Program provides an opportunity for students with strong academic records to conduct scholarly research and develop leadership skills through service learning.

ACADEMIC PROGRAMS

A candidate for the BA in liberal arts is required to complete an organized program of study comprising 120 semester hours distributed among prescribed and elective courses. Four interdisciplinary courses are required in the Core Curriculum focusing on "The College Mission." In addition, students must complete 46 to 48 credits of General Education courses beyond the 12-credit Core. Each baccalaureate degree student in Arts and Sciences is required to prepare a written and oral senior research project. A minimum of 45 credit hours must be earned at the College. A student who pursues an AA degree is required to complete 64 to 68 credits in an approved program of study.

A candidate for the BA in elementary or special education is required to complete a program of 126 to 130 semester hours, including credits in general education, professional education, and a major in the arts and sciences. Field experience begins in the freshman year and students participate in a practicum in the junior year. Students conduct supervised teaching during the senior year in a public elementary school. The education programs are approved by the National Association of State Directors of Teacher Education and Certification (NASDTEC).

Clinical experiences in the medical laboratory techniques begin during the first semester, continue throughout each semester and include a summer internship.

TUITION, ROOM, BOARD AND FEES

The cost of undergraduate tuition for 2010–2011 is $24,950 per year for full-time students. The annual cost of room and board is $10,150 per year.

FINANCIAL AID

Felician College participates in federal, state and institutional aid programs for financial assistance. Financial aid is available to qualified students through grants, loans, and work-study. A number of academic scholarships are awarded annually ranging from $4,000 to full tuition for four years based on merit or need. A tuition payment plan is also available. More than half the students attending Felician College receive financial aid.

STUDENT ORGANIZATIONS AND ACTIVITIES

Felician College offers a competitive athletic program. The College is a member of the National Collegiate Athletic Association (NCAA) Division II. The Golden Falcons athletic teams compete in men's baseball, soccer, basketball, cross-country and golf, as well as women's softball, soccer, basketball, volleyball, cross-country. The athletic department also sponsors cheerleading and dance teams as well as numerous intramural sports activities.

With residence halls on the Rutherford campus, students may elect to reside in one of the spacious suites in Elliott Terrace or Milton Court, which accommodate up to 600 students. The campuses offer comfortable student lounge areas, meeting rooms, dining halls, gymnasium, fitness center and a campus Quad for outdoor recreation.

With student events and activities dotting the calendar throughout the year, campus life bounds with energy. There are more than 23 clubs and organizations on campus to meet the special interests of the students. At orientation, new students are introduced to college life through a broad program that begins with pre-admission interviews followed by an orientation day and ongoing orientation sessions. A special theme, chosen by students, sets the tone for the year's orientation program.

ADMISSIONS PROCESS

Applicants for admission are considered for the fall semester (late August/early September) and the spring semester (January) on a rolling basis. Students are informed of an admission decision within approximately four weeks of the completion of their file. A completed file includes a transcript from an accredited high school (with date of graduation) or high school equivalency certificate, satisfactory SAT or ACT scores, 500-word personal statement and a physician's certificate of health.

Students are eligible to transfer to Felician. Transcripts of previous college work from recognized junior or four-year colleges are required and an evaluation will be made upon receipt of official college transcripts— students are eligible to transfer up to 90 credits. Admission requirements may be adjusted for adults on the basis of maturity and experience. Felician College offers credit for acceptable scores on the College Board Advanced Placement tests and College-Level Examination Program (CLEP) tests.

Open Houses and tours of all facilities are available through the Office of Admission. For more information on admissions, contact:

Felician College

262 South Main Street

Lodi, NJ 07644

223 Montross Avenue

Rutherford, NJ 07070

Telephone: 201.559.6131

World Wide Web: www.felician.edu

FLORIDA ATLANTIC UNIVERSITY

AT A GLANCE

Florida Atlantic University is a public research university with multiple campuses along the southeast Florida coast serving a uniquely diverse community. It promotes academic and personal development, discovery, and lifelong learning. FAU fulfills its mission through excellence and innovation in teaching, outstanding research, public engagement, and distinctive scientific alliances; all within an environment that fosters inclusiveness. Florida Atlantic University was established by the Florida State Legislature in 1961 as the fifth university in the state system. When it originally opened in 1964, FAU was the first university in the country to offer only upper-division and graduate-level work, on the theory that freshmen and sophomores could be served by the community college system. Located in rapidly growing Southeast Florida, the University responded to the need to provide increased access to educational opportunities by opening its doors to freshmen in 1984. Today, with its developed system of distributed campuses, where the same high-quality education is offered at seven different locations, Florida Atlantic University serves as a model for urban, regional universities of the future. It offers a comprehensive array of undergraduate and graduate programs, and enrolls students who reflect the rich cultural diversity of the region. FAU has Eminent Scholar Chairs in multiple disciplines and is the home of nationally recognized research centers. The University's burgeoning Research Park is facilitating exciting new research and learning initiatives by bringing high tech industries into close collaboration with FAU's faculty and students. In recognition of the University's research funding and doctoral programs, the Florida Board of Regents has designated FAU as one of the states public research universities. Florida Atlantic University is a member of the Southern Association of Colleges and Schools, the National Association of State Universities and Land-Grant Colleges, and the Council of Graduate Schools in the United States.

ACADEMICS

Florida Atlantic University's colleges include the College of Architecture, Urban and Public Affairs, the Dorothy F. Schmidt College of Arts and Letters, the College of Business, Charles E. Schmidt College of Biomedical Science, the College of Education, the College of Engineering and Computer Science, the Graduate College, the Christine E. Lynn College of Nursing, and the Charles E. Schmidt College of Science. Together, these colleges offer over one hundred and seventy different academic degree programs. In 1999, FAU opened a new residential Honors College, which provides a unique and challenging four-year curriculum for the brightest students from Florida and beyond. In addition, the University is home to one of the largest lifelong learning and continuing education programs in the Nation.

ADMISSIONS

Admission to the University as an undergraduate is limited to applicants who have graduated from regionally accredited high schools or who hold a General Equivalency Degree (GED). Evaluation is based on the academic course grade point average combined with acceptable results on the Scholastic Aptitude Test (SAT) or the American College Test (ACT). Candidates for admission should have 18 academic high school units, including 4 units of English, 3 units of mathematics, 3 units of natural science, 3 units of social science, 2 units of one foreign language in sequence, and 3 academic electives. Score reports will be accepted directly from the testing agency or from the student's official high school transcript. FAU's SAT school code number is 5229. FAU's ACT school code number is 0729. Applicants who have completed the GED (General Educational Development) should request official high school transcripts (if applicable) and an official GED score report from the Florida Department of Education. The Florida Department of Education GED Division can be reached at 1-877-352-4331. Admission for freshman students requires an application for admission, a non-refundable $30.00 application fee, official transcripts from an accredited high school, and the results of the SAT or ACT administrations. All admitted freshmen must confirm their intention to enroll and secure their place with the freshman class by submitting a required $200.00 admissions tuition deposit. Please contact the Undergraduate Admissions office for details or visit our website: www.fau.edu/admissions. Admission into FAU as a transfer with fewer than 60 transferable credits requires the applicant to be in good academic standing at their previous, regionally accredited colleges or universities, the applicant must present a cumulative GPA of 2.5 or higher, and must meet all freshman admissions requirements. Please submit an application for admission, a non-refundable $30.00 application fee, official transcripts from high school and previously attended colleges, and the results of the SAT or ACT administrations. For students with 60 or more transferable credits, please submit an application for admission, a non-refundable $30.00 application fee, and official transcripts from each previously attended college. Please note that meeting the minimum admission requirements does not guarantee admission into the university. For application deadlines or further information, please contact:

Office of Undergraduate Admissions, Florida Atlantic University, 777 Glades Road Boca Raton, FL 33431. Telephone: 561-297-3040. Fax: 561-297-2758. World Wide Web: www.fau.edu/admissions.

CAMPUS LIFE

By joining one of FAUs 150 student clubs and organizations, students have the opportunity to make new acquaintances outside of the classroom. Getting involved on campus helps students develop leadership, management, and interpersonal skills while contributing to the FAU community. Students are welcome to participate in Academic Organizations, Honor Societies, Spiritual/Religious Organizations, Personal Interest Clubs, Diversity Association Organizations, Service Organizations, Sports Clubs, and Greek Life.

LOCATION AND ENVIRONMENT

The University's campus locations along the Florida Gold and Treasure coasts, which boast a temperate climate and beautiful beaches, innovative industry, and unique cultural opportunities, provide a stimulating environment for its outstanding scholars and researchers. FAU's main campus in Boca Raton is on an 850-acre site located only three miles from the Atlantic Ocean. The campus is conveniently located half way between Palm Beach and Fort Lauderdale and offers a broad range of academic programs, activities, and services. Students attending FAU- Boca Raton have some honored guests: burrowing owls. In fact, the Audubon Society has named the site a burrowing owl sanctuary and FAU varsity athletic teams are known as the Owls in their honor. Our campuses throughout South Florida can be conveniently reached from Interstate 95 or from the Florida Turnpike.

MAJORS AND DEGREES OFFERED

Florida Atlantic University prepares its undergraduate students to be productive and thoughtful citizens by offering a broad liberal education coupled with the development of competency in fields of special interest. FAU encourages students to think creatively and critically and provides intellectual tools needed for lifelong learning. A variety of curricular and extracurricular opportunities enables students to appreciate the rich diversity that characterizes their region and world.

Florida Atlantic University's 10 colleges include the College of Architecture, Urban and Public Affairs, the Dorothy F. Schmidt College of Arts and Letters, the College of Business, Charles E. Schmidt College of Biomedical Science, the College of Education, the College of Engineering and Computer Science, the Graduate College, the Christine E. Lynn College of Nursing, and the Charles E. Schmidt College of Science and the Harriet L. Wilkes Honors College in Jupiter; which is the first public honors institution to be built from the ground up in the United States.

Through its partnerships with other educational institutions, local businesses, industries, and civic and cultural organizations, FAU enhances the economic, human, and cultural development of the surrounding communities and beyond.

Students at Florida Atlantic University may participate in a work-study program that coincides their classroom learning with hands-on experience. Many local businesses and government laboratories participate in the program each year. Students who wish to study overseas can become involved in FAU international programs in various locations from China to Germany.

FAU has developed a new program in medical sciences offered in cooperation with the University of Miami School of Medicine. Students in this program take their first two years of medical school at FAU and complete their clinical studies at the University of Miami.

TUITION, ROOM, BOARD AND FEES

Undergraduate tuition is $139.55 per semester credit for Florida residents and $584.41 per semester credit for non-Florida residents (subject to change). Graduate tuition is $293.94 per semester credit for Florida residents and $920.66 for non-Florida residents. In addition, the estimated nine-month budget for room and board on campus is $9,582; books and supplies cost approximately $900.

FINANCIAL AID

FAU distributes more than $120 million in scholarships, grants, loans and work-study annually, based on the policies of the College Scholarship Service of the College Board. Aid packages may be adjusted over the course of a student's academic career, but assistance can be earned from the first year of attendance all the way through graduate study.

Students seeking need-based aid must submit the Free Application for Federal Student Aid (FAFSA). It is recommended that students planning on fall admission turn in their FAFSA forms by the previous January, though the deadline for priority applications is March 1. Typically, the application procedure takes six to eight weeks. Students are notified about their financial aid packages after they are informed of their acceptance to the University.

Merit-based scholarships are also available for outstanding students. Funding is reserved for top performers in academics, athletics, and the arts. For further information, please refer to the FAU catalog under Financial Assistance.

FORDHAM UNIVERSITY

AT A GLANCE

Founded in 1841, Fordham is a world-renowned Jesuit, Catholic university with two campuses in New York City. In our programs and policies, we draw on the nearly 500-year history of the Jesuits, a distinguished, intellectual and spiritual community within the Catholic Church. We offer numerous academic challenges and expect excellence; we care for the whole person; we ask the members of our community to be men and women for others—to put their education in service to the common good.

LOCATION AND ENVIRONMENT

Fordham's Rose Hill campus is located in the Bronx, one of New York's most diverse, multifaceted boroughs; only a 20-minute ride from Grand Central Terminal. The quintessential college campus is spread across 85 green, leafy acres, with several athletic fields and distinguished Gothic buildings.

Fordham's Lincoln Center campus is located in midtown Manhattan, in one of the nation's premier cultural destinations. Situated on eight landscaped acres, the campus is adjacent to the Lincoln Center for the Performing Arts and a few blocks from Central Park, Columbus Circle and the headquarters of major media corporations.

OFF-CAMPUS OPPORTUNITIES

New York is the nation's biggest college town, with more than 465,000 students enrolled in dozens of college and universities. The Manhattan location of Fordham's Lincoln Center campus is home to the biggest, the best and the most of everything: the Metropolitan Museum of Art and the United Nations, Wall Street and SoHo, Broadway and Chinatown, Harlem and Times Square. Students can take advantage of the city's clean, fast, efficient public transportation system and find ways of volunteering, performing, interning—to join an exceptionally inclusive local community. The Rose Hill campus is in the heart of the Borough of Parks, the home of the Yankees, the origin of a million immigrant success stories: The Bronx. It's home to the country's largest metropolitan zoo—the Bronx Zoo; and one of the country's premier urban gardens and plant research facilities—the New York Botanical Garden.

MAJORS AND DEGREES OFFERED

The undeniable strength of Fordham's academic program is the unbreakable link between its widely regarded core curriculum and 50 outstanding major areas of study offered within Fordham College at Rose Hill, Fordham College at Lincoln Center and the College of Business Administration. Many students choose to major in widely recognized departments, such as biology, communications, English or psychology, while others pursue smaller programs unique to the liberal arts colleges—classical languages, philosophy or theology.

Fordham offers a variety of degrees and programs within its three traditional undergraduate colleges. Among a full slate of programs in the humanities, social sciences and physical and natural sciences, Fordham College at Rose Hill offers several unique programs. Special programs include a new four-year bachelor of science in engineering physics, and an interdisciplinary concentration in American Catholic Studies, sponsored by the University's Francis and Ann Curran Center for American Catholic Studies.

In the College of Business Administration (CBA), students can select among seven degree programs and two dual degree programs. The Global Learning Opportunities and Business Experiences (G.L.O.B.E.) Program within CBA combines coursework in history, literature and language, as well as global business courses, study abroad experiences and/or an international internship.

The theatre program at Fordham College at Lincoln Center offers a comprehensive B.A. grounded in hands-on experience. Theatre majors work with award-winning faculty and stellar guest artists in small classes and ambitious mainstage productions. In addition to the rich mix of majors and courses, Fordham also offers an innovative four-year B.F.A. program in dance, conducted in partnership with The Ailey School of the Alvin Ailey American Dance Theater. The Fordham Law School and our graduate schools in business administration, religion, arts and sciences, education and social services, provide additional opportunities for advanced education.

ACADEMIC PROGRAMS

The University offers numerous programs and services to expand the minds and hearts of students. Academic advising at Fordham puts into practice the Jesuit ideal of cura personalis, the care of the whole person.

The Service Learning Program allows students to integrate serious scholarship with civic action.

The 3-3 Law Program permits qualified students to enroll at Fordham's top-ranked School of Law after three years of undergraduate study.

The Pre-Medical and Pre-Health Professions Advising Program claims a proud history of guiding students into the country's finest medical schools; boasting a 90 percent acceptance rate for a recent graduating class.

Fordham's extensive relationships with firms and organizations provide 2,600 internship opportunities every year.

The University offers access to year-long, semester-long and summer study abroad programs in more than 55 countries, on six continents including the London School of Economics and La Sorbonne in Paris.

The Manresa Program is a living-learning opportunity for freshmen, who live and study together in the newly renovated Tierney Hall, engage with faculty in interactive seminars and participate in activities that nurture the development of the whole person.

The University's Honors Programs are intentionally small, unabashedly intense and deeply supportive of exceptional academic ability.

CAMPUS FACILITIES AND EQUIPMENT

Our athletic facilities include fitness centers and sports fields; the Vince T. Lombardi Memorial Center for intramurals, swimming, water polo and track; and the Walsh Athletic Training Center, a 3,200-square-foot varsity weight training and conditioning facility.

Our award-winning public radio station, WFUV 90.7 FM, pulls in about 300,000 listeners each week. Students are active in all operations of the station, now in its 61st year.

Fordham's libraries house more than 2.2 million volumes and offer access to extensive library archives and special collections. The William D. Walsh Family Library at Rose Hill is also home to the Fordham Museum of Greek, Etruscan and Roman Art.

Fordham's biological field station, the Louis Calder Center, is set on 113-forested acres in Armonk, New York.

Fordham's 12,000-square-foot Visual Arts Complex at the Lincoln Center campus includes drawing studios; a computer imaging lab; film and video editing screening facilities; an architectural workspace; and two galleries.

Fordham is home to the oldest Catholic university press in America, Fordham University Press, with 500 titles in print and one million dollars in sales every year.

Fordham offers essential labs and equipment for students studying in a range of fields including chemistry, biology and the languages. Students in communications and media studies take advantage of the Edward Walsh Digital Media lab, a fully equipped multimedia lab and AVID editing equipment. And our undergraduates benefit from a University-wide network of more than 200 technology-enabled classrooms.

TUITION, ROOM, BOARD, AND FEES

Tuition for the academic year 2009–2010: $35,825; Room and board: $13,716 for double occupancy, including meal plan. For more information, visit www.fordham.edu/tuition.

FINANCIAL AID

As a Jesuit University, Fordham is committed to providing an outstanding education to qualified students. We try our best to support students and families who don't have the resources to pay our full tuition. Fordham also claims a long tradition of welcoming and supporting first-generation college students. More than 80 percent of our students typically receive some form of financial aid, including both need-based and merit-based aid.

Fall freshman applicants should file the FAFSA and CSS Profile forms by February 1. Spring freshman applicants should file by November 1.

STUDENT ORGANIZATIONS AND ACTIVITIES

Fordham students run 135 clubs and organizations—award-winning newspapers and celebrated musical groups, ambitious academic societies and vibrant cultural groups. A few examples: Mimes and Mummers is one of the nation's oldest collegiate theatrical troupes. Our top-ranked Fordham Debate Society is the eighth oldest collegiate debate society in the United States.

Fordham claims a proud history of intercollegiate athletic competition. We support 22 NCAA Division I teams; cheerleading; seven club teams, including our league champion ice hockey team; a spirited intramural program; and many recreational programs.

ADMISSIONS PROCESS

Admission to Fordham is highly selective. We consider our applicants' academic records, standardized test scores, letters of recommendation, co-curricular activities and admission essays—not in isolation, but as parts of a unified whole. This information helps to convey what applicants might do at Fordham, how Fordham might help them and how they might contribute to the community. Applicants can complete and deliver an application online or through the mail. You can apply in one of two ways: Regular Decision or Early Action. Freshman applicants should complete four years of high school English, three to four years of science, three to four years of math, three to four years of social studies and two to three years of a foreign language. Students who want to pursue a math, science, or pre-medical curriculum should have at least four years of math and one each of physics and chemistry. Business students should have four years of college preparatory mathematics. Most successful candidates will have maintained an A/A– average.

FROSTBURG STATE UNIVERSITY

Small classes, dedicated faculty and individualized attention allow Frostburg State University students to explore new possibilities and find direction here in the beautiful mountains of Western Maryland.

AT A GLANCE

Frostburg State University has provided paths to success for students for more than 100 years. Situated in the beautiful mountains of Allegany County, FSU is the premier four-year University System of Maryland institution west of the Baltimore-Washington area. A comprehensive regional university with a diverse student body, FSU serves as an educational and cultural center for the Western Maryland region and plays a vital role in regional economic development initiatives. Strong programs in liberal arts and sciences, business, education and environmental studies, as well as nationally acclaimed community service programs, draw students from around the world at both the undergraduate and graduate levels. Small classes, dedicated faculty and individualized attention allow Frostburg students to explore new possibilities and find direction.

LOCATION AND ENVIRONMENT

Located in the beautiful mountains of Western Maryland, Frostburg is within minutes of tons of outdoor pursuits and just over two hours away from Baltimore, Pittsburgh and Washington, D.C. All the buildings on FSU's medium-sized campus are within easy walking distance of one another, but shuttles are available, too.

The view is fantastic, and yes, we have snow in the winter. You'll love it.

Off-Campus Opportunities

FSU is in the historic town of Frostburg, with a business district within walking distance from campus that features stores, pubs, cafes, pizza shops, convenience stores and restaurants to suit most tastes and budgets. Bus service, free to students, is available to nearby larger communities for more shopping, food and entertainment.

And if you love the outdoors, you should know that within minutes from campus, you can:

- Downhill and cross-country ski, snowboard, whitewater raft, kayak, sail, swim, fish and camp at Deep Creek Lake (41 minutes)
- Camp, swim, fish and boat at Rocky Gap State Park (20 minutes)
- Bike on the C&O Canal Towpath (10 minutes)
- Hike or bike the Great Allegheny Passage (2 minutes)
- See the views from Dan's Rock (go at sunrise and prepare to be amazed…15 minutes)

MAJORS AND DEGREES OFFERED

Frostburg offers 45 undergraduate majors—some traditional, some unique—in performance and visual arts, humanities, natural and social sciences, business, physical and teacher education.

Bachelor's Degrees Programs

Accounting (combined BS/MBA option); Applied Physics (bachelor's/master's collaborative program; dual-degree program); Art and Design (teaching certification option); Athletic Training ; Biology (pre-health professions option; concentrations in biotechnology and environmental science; teaching certification option); Business Administration (concentrations in finance, general management, human resource management, integrated business, marketing and small business/entrepreneurship); Chemistry (track in traditional chemistry; concentrations in professional chemistry and biochemistry; teaching certification option); Communication Studies ; Computer Information Systems; Computer Science ; Earth Science (concentration in environmental science; teaching certification option); Economics (concentrations in business economics, public policy economics and quantitative economics); Early Childhood/Elementary Education ; Elementary Education ; Education: K-12 Programs (teaching certification); Education: Secondary Programs (teaching certification); Education: Secondary/Adult Generic Special Education (teaching certification); Engineering (concentrations in electrical engineering, materials engineering, industrial chemistry and engineering management); Engineering—Dual-degree Program; English (concentrations in literature, creative writing and professional writing; teaching certification option); Environmental Analysis and Planning ; Ethnobotany; Exercise and Sports Science ; Foreign Languages and Literature (concentrations in French and Spanish; teaching certification option); Geography (concentrations in mapping sciences and global systems analysis); Health and Physical Education (major with teaching certification); Health Science Administration (collaborative program); History (concentrations in international history and history of the Americas); Information Technology; Information Technology Management (collaborative program); International Studies (concentrations in international business, international politics, international economics and international development); Interpretive Biology and Natural History ; Law: Bachelor/Juris Doctor Program (dual-degree program); Law and Society (concentrations in criminal justice and legal studies); Liberal Studies ; Mass Communications ; Mathematics (teaching certification option); Mechanical Engineering (collaborative program) ; Music (concentrations in vocal performance and music management; teaching certification option; track in instrumental performance); Nursing (R.N. to B.S.N. completion program); Philosophy ; Physics (tracks in traditional physics and engineering physics; teaching certification option); Political Science ; Psychology (certificate in child and family psychology); Recreation and Parks Management (concentrations in adventure sports, community program delivery, hospitality management and tourism and therapeutic recreation); Social Science (teaching certification option); Social Work ; Sociology (tracks in general sociology and applied social research; option in data analysis); Theatre (tracks in acting, directing, production/design and general theatre) ; Urban and Regional Planning ; Wildlife and Fisheries

Master's Degree Programs

Master of Arts in Teaching (elementary and secondary); Master of Business Administration ; Master of Education (administration and supervision, curriculum and instruction, interdisciplinary, reading, school counseling and special education); Master of Science in Applied Computer Science ; Master of Science in Biological Sciences (applied ecology/conservation biology and wildlife/fisheries biology); Master of Science in Counseling Psychology ; Master of Science in Recreation and Parks Management ; Professional Master of Engineering (collaborative program)

Accreditation

In addition to regional accreditation by the Middle States Commission on Higher Education, several individual FSU programs and colleges have also earned accreditation:

- College of Business (AACSB International)

- College of Education's teacher education programs (NCATE, with recognition by 14 professional content associations for compliance with national standards, and the Maryland State Department of Education)

- Athletic Training Education (CAAHEP)

- Recreation and Parks Management (NRPA/AALR)

- Social Work (Council on Social Work Education)

- Mechanical Engineering collaborative program (ABET)

- M.S. in Counseling Psychology (MPAC).

FSU's Counseling and Psychological Services office is recognized by International Association of Counseling Services, and the Brady Health Center is recognized by the Accreditation Association for Ambulatory Health Care.

ACADEMIC PROGRAMS

Learning communities are offered for freshmen, where you study a handful of special themed courses with the same small group of students who share similar interests. Lifelong friendships often start here.

The FSU Honors Program is set up for promising and motivated students (3.50 high school GPA or minimum 1800 SAT score) to receive research stipends, special courses and housing options.

Our professors value out-of-classroom experiences. Interested in biology? Step outside and delve in the natural plant and wildlife surrounding our campus. Want to study history? The Frostburg area is rich with heritage of pre-Revolution America. Does teaching interest you? Experiences in real-life classrooms are offered as soon as you enroll in the educational professions major. Is business more your speed? Capstone courses have students working with real businesses helping them create marketing, growth or other business plans.

Internships are available in almost every major, and there are study abroad opportunities on almost every continent.

There is also plenty of academic support available, including assistance with papers, peer and group tutoring, placement testing and help with study skills and techniques.

CAMPUS FACILITIES AND EQUIPMENT

Frostburg State University boasts:

- Advanced facilities (including a new science center with a variety of specialized labs and an impressive performing arts center) and the latest technology—which undergraduate students actually get to use.

- Wireless and fiber optics networks (and a 24/7 student computer lab).

- Residence halls with single- and double-room occupancy available, as well as an independent on-campus apartment complex. Residence halls feature high-speed Internet, e-mail, cable TV, laundry—and all of it for free. If you live on campus, bring your car and park it for free, too.

- A library with a wealth of research and reference materials, including more than half a million items including books, periodicals, audio-visual materials, maps, art prints and U.S. and Maryland government information resources. In addition, the library subscribes to 60 electronic databases providing access to 20,000 full-text electronic journals. You also have access to the resources of all the institutions in the University System of Maryland through *catalogUSMAI*.

TUITION, ROOM, BOARD, AND FEES

Frostburg's costs are competitive with other public institutions, so you won't leave college with a mountain of debt.

Full-time tuition for Maryland State residents for the 2009–10 school year is $5,000; tuition for students residing in contiguous counties in Pennsylvania, Virginia and West Virginia is $11,356. All other out-of-state tuition is $15,196.

Mandatory fees (such as technology, athletics, activities, etc.) are $1,684 per year per student. Room fees range from $3,474 to $4,794 per year; board fees range from $2,984 to $3,830 per year. Meal plans can be used at various venues throughout the campus.

Other fees may apply based on academic program or specialized activities.

FINANCIAL AID

In addition to institutional and private scholarships, a number of state and federal programs are available to reduce the cost of attending Frostburg. The FSU Financial Aid Office works closely with each individual student to help him or her meet educational requirements.

STUDENT ORGANIZATIONS AND ACTIVITIES

Frostburg offers plenty of activities—including concerts from local and top-name bands, national speakers, comedians and big events. The Lane University Center (under renovation until January 2011) features a coffee bar, food court and fitness room, as well as get-away trips to New York City, ski resorts, whitewater rafting spots, museums, shopping outlets and more.

Chances are you'll find something that interests you in our 90+ clubs and organizations. If you don't, we encourage you to start your own. We also have 21 NCAA Division III athletic teams. Several national Greek fraternities and sororities have chapters at FSU; these organizations are a good way to experience brotherhood/sisterhood on campus and beyond, as well as enhance your networking, leadership and service skills.

FSU has also been nationally recognized for its community service programs. Student volunteers assist the elderly, tutor/mentor area youth and work to save the environment. FSU students have also traveled over their spring break to in-need locations and join in national movements like Hunger and Homeless Week, Special Olympics, Make a Difference Day, V-Day and Relay for Life.

ADMISSIONS PROCESS

Frostburg State University operates on a rolling admission basis, although we may have to close admissions when no further space for students is available. Applicants from high school should apply in the fall or early winter of the senior year. Beginning on Sept. 15, the admissions office will start accepting applications for the fall semester of the following year.

Admission for the spring semester is granted on a space-available basis. Applications will be considered if received no later than Dec. 1 for the subsequent spring semester. The University does accept applications from first-year students who would like to begin in the spring semester.

Freshmen applicants must complete the FSU Online Application, which includes an essay (gobobcats.frostburg.edu), and submit it with a $30 non-refundable application fee (by mail or provide credit card information). The Request for Academic Record should be given to the guidance counselor or other appropriate official at your high school. SAT scores are required for most freshman applicants.

Transfer applicants must also complete the entire FSU Online Application and submit it with a $30 non-refundable application fee, with official transcripts from each institution of higher education attended. If currently enrolled, an official transcript of the final grades must be submitted. If the applicant has less than 24 transferable credits, the student must also submit an official high school transcript and SAT scores.

GEORGIA COLLEGE & STATE UNIVERSITY

AT A GLANCE

As the state's designated public liberal arts university, Georgia College & State University is committed to combining the educational experiences typical of esteemed private liberal arts colleges with the affordability of public higher education. The faculty is dedicated to challenging students and fostering excellence in the classroom and beyond. GCSU seeks to endow its graduates with a passion for achievement, a lifelong curiosity, and exuberance for learning.

GCSU was chartered in 1889 as Georgia Normal and Industrial College. The institution had several name changes over the years and became coeducational in 1967. In August of 1996, the Board of Regents approved a new name, Georgia College & State University, and a change of mission, which designated the university to serve the entire state of Georgia as the public liberal arts university.

Recent national recognition of Georgia College involves its selection as the only public school in Georgia to be included in "Colleges of Distinction" and being named in the annual report on "America's 100 Best College Buys."

LOCATION AND ENVIRONMENT

Milledgeville is approximately 100 miles southeast of Atlanta, and 30 miles northeast of Macon. The town, which is the former capital of Georgia, has a population of over 20,000 and is a center of history and culture featuring beautiful homes and historic buildings. Located on the fall line in a setting of rolling hills and recreational lakes, Milledgeville's natural beauty is among its most appealing assets.

The university is an integral part Milledgeville's downtown environment and it enhances the town with its architectural blending of majestic buildings of red brick and white Corinthian columns. Georgia's Old Governor's Mansion, one of the finest examples of Greek revival architecture in the United States, is the founding building of the university. "West Campus," comprised of the athletic complex and the Village at West Campus apartment community, is located on a 546-acre site one mile away from the main campus.

Off-Campus Opportunities

Service Learning allows students to apply classroom knowledge to the benefit of others under the auspices of nonprofit agencies with the particular experience tailored to a specific class or major. Participation in Community Service allows students to gain important experience in implementation of various projects and tasks, reveals a sense of commitment and responsibility, and offers wide-ranging leadership opportunities. Participation in *Study Abroad programs* provides experience and understanding of the global context of the society in which we live. Cross-cultural experiences help students appreciate and respect cultural diversity and develop an important sense of the role Americans play around the world. *Internships* offer paid and unpaid practical work experience directly related to a student's major. Not only do internships enhance skills and knowledge first gained in the classroom, but such experiences provide important networking advantages for students preparing to graduate and seeking career opportunities. Participation in *undergraduate research* resulting in presentations or publication, such as in GCSU's own *Corinthian*, indicates a student's commitment to critical thinking, development of analytical skills, self-motivation, and thirst for knowledge.

MAJORS AND DEGREES OFFERED

The College of Liberal Arts and Sciences provides academic programs in the fine and applied arts; the humanities; the behavioral and social sciences; the physical, biological, and mathematical sciences; and various professional fields. Students may choose from over 50 different degree programs at the undergraduate and graduate levels. There are a variety of opportunities for students to participate in internships, field placements, research projects, and study abroad.

The John H. Lounsbury College of Education offers teacher education programs that are accredited by the National Council for the Accreditation of Teacher Education (NCATE) and is the recipient of the 2007 Wisniewski Award for "singularly significant contributions to the theory and practice of teacher education." Most of the undergraduate initial certification programs at GCSU are nationally recognized by Specialty Program Areas. Early Childhood, Middle Grades, and Special Education-Interrelated comprise the undergraduate degrees. Initial certification for Secondary Education is offered at the Masters level. Music Education and Health Education are located in their respective departments in the College of Liberal Arts (Music) and College of Health Sciences (Kinesiology).

The student who enrolls in the J. Whitney Bunting College of Business is first provided with educational opportunities in the broad areas of arts and humanities, natural sciences, and the social sciences. During the junior and senior years, there is an opportunity for in-depth understanding of the entire field of business, as well as for the selection of a major and/or minor field of study that is consistent with the individual's career objectives. The J. Whitney Bunting College of Business is nationally accredited by and is a member of AACSB International, the Association to Advance Collegiate Schools of Business. The following degrees are offered: BS, BBA, MBA, MMIS, and MAcc

The mission of the College of Health Sciences is to provide undergraduate and graduate programs in disciplines that emphasize health education, promotion, maintenance, and restoration. By engaging in the university's liberal arts experience, College of Health Sciences graduates attain intellectual integrity, appreciation of diversity, and commitment to the best for self, family, society, and the world. Students emerge with a worldview that promotes leadership, initiative, accountability, stewardship, ethical respect for self and others, and the ability to effect change in a dynamic society.

ACADEMIC PROGRAMS

The Center for Student Success has a strong commitment to the retention of GCSU students through the First-Year Experience programs, each of which seek to establish a solid base of academic success skills. Focus is directed to academic advisement at GCSU that is a faculty-based system that assures each student contact with a faculty member who can guide a student's course selection and assist in career preparation.

Our Residential Learning Communities bridge the gap between learning inside and outside of the classroom. Incoming students have the ability to apply to one of seven living-learning communities based upon their interests. Activities are designed to provide participants with experiences beneficial to their personal development while at GCSU.

The Georgia Education Mentorship (GEM) program matches outstanding GCSU students with exemplary leaders in fields such as business, education, politics, healthcare, law, and industry. These executives serve as mentors for participating students, promoting their personal and professional growth by providing opportunities for them to identify and understand the principles and practices of leadership and success that benefit both the professional world and the community.

The Georgia College Honors and Scholars Program is an integrated program of learning that presents challenging opportunities for students with proven academic strength. The program promotes student interaction with faculty through small group discussion, supervised projects, internships, interdisciplinary studies, and service learning. Through capstone experiences such as a senior thesis, a creative project, or an internship, the Honors and Scholars Program extends study into the student's academic major.

CAMPUS FACILITIES AND EQUIPMENT

Approximately $150 million of construction has transformed the GCSU campus in the last ten years. New campus venues include the Wellness Depot (a student fitness facility created from an 1853 train station), a new student activities center (adapted from a former Methodist church), renovated bookstore, expanded dining facilities, and a complete replacement of all campus housing -- creating on-campus suites and off-campus apartments.

One of the most impressive additions to campus is the renovation and expansion of the Library and Information Technology Center. Now one of the largest library complexes in Georgia, the GCSU Library and Information Technology Center houses close to 200,000 volumes and holds subscriptions to more than 23,000 serials. The library also possesses several special collections, including the Flannery O'Connor Collection, the GCSU Horology Collection, and Senator Paul Coverdell's Papers. The library is a selective depository of United States Government Documents.

GCSU infuses a strong emphasis on technology into its liberal arts environment. The comprehensive wireless system frees faculty and students to surf the web from virtually anywhere on campus. GCSU has also received national acclaim for its innovative partnership and programs utilizing Apple Computer products and creative uses of Apple's iPod to enhance learning environments.

TUITION, ROOM, BOARD AND FEES

For the 2009–2010 year, freshman tuition and fees for a full-time Georgia resident equal $3,551 per semester. Full-time out-of-state freshman tuition and fees total $12,070 per semester. Current housing and meal plan rates vary and can be reviewed at the GCSU website.

FINANCIAL AID

Through financial aid programs, GCSU makes every effort to assure that no qualified student will be denied the opportunity to attend school because of lack of funds.

Financial aid awards at Georgia College are based on scholastic ability, financial need, contribution to the campus community, or a combination thereof. Students may receive aid in the form of scholarships, grants, loans, or work opportunities. All students are encouraged to apply by using the Free Application for Federal Student Aid (FAFSA). First consideration will be given to any student whose file is complete by March 1. Students must have a complete file by July 1 to guarantee aid will be available at the beginning of the fall term.

STUDENT ORGANIZATIONS AND ACTIVITIES

Georgia College students may participate in a variety of activities that are coordinated or organized through the Office of Student Activities. Such activities include concerts, drama productions, comedians, intramurals, movies, and more. Over 200 registered student organizations include club sports, special interest groups, academic organizations, honor societies, student media, student government, and Greek organizations, to name a few. The Intramural Program provides team as well as individual sports. The university offers a number of indoor and outdoor campus facilities for student use as well.

ADMISSIONS PROCESS

The successful freshman applicant will demonstrate his or her potential for success by completing a rigorous college preparatory curriculum with a competitive grade point average, show strong SAT or ACT score results, and provide a well-developed personal essay. The middle 50 percent of the admitted students for fall 2008 had SAT Critical Reading and Mathematics sub scores ranging from 1060 to 1220, and high school academic grade point averages ranging from 3.24 to 3.75. These numbers are provided only as guidelines.

Admissions decisions are based on the total student portfolio and demonstrated potential for contribution to the university and probability for success in the unique environment of GCSU.

Freshmen applicants must submit to the Office of Admissions, Campus Box 23, Milledgeville, GA 31061, the following documents for admission consideration, no later than April 1 (November 1 for Early Action):

1. Application for admission

2. Application fee

3. Official high school transcript

4. Official SAT and/or ACT score report, including Writing sample(s)—GCSU school codes are 5252 (SAT) and 0828 (ACT)

5. Official transcripts from all colleges attended, if any

6. Personal Essay

7. While not mandatory, a resume of activities and a teacher recommendation letter are encouraged.

GEORGIAN COURT UNIVERSITY

WHO WE ARE

For more than 100 years, Georgian Court University (GCU) has helped students achieve academic excellence, realize their professional and personal goals, and acquire the skills and knowledge needed to make a lasting difference in the lives of others. Founded by the Sisters of Mercy in 1908, GCU is New Jersey's only Mercy University, and one of only two Catholic universities in the state. Students of all faiths, races and economic backgrounds come to Georgian Court where they find success in every aspect of their college experience—an experience that reflects and incorporates the Mercy core values of respect, integrity, justice, compassion and service.

Georgian Court's strong liberal arts foundation prepares students for the many challenges and changes they will encounter in life. Small classes, which average just 14 students, allow them to work closely with dedicated faculty who are respected experts in science, education, art, music, literature, business, history, criminal justice and many other fields. At Georgian Court, students eagerly participate in rigorous courses while exploring broad themes and values-based experiences.

The school's stunning 156-acre campus is a National Historic Landmark nestled in suburban Lakewood, New Jersey. Campus buildings reflect impressive Georgian architecture, prompting the university's name, Georgian Court. Once a lavish, winter home for the wealthy in the early 1900s, Georgian Court today retains the estate's magnificent statuary, lush gardens, and breathtaking landscaping. The campus and its proximity to the beaches of the Jersey Shore make GCU an inviting place to live and learn.

AT A GLANCE

Georgian Court University, which has an enrollment of 3,023 students, offers 30 undergraduate programs—including new majors in nursing; dance; tourism, hospitality, and recreation management; and exercise science, wellness, and sports. Also, a new sports management concentration, a specialty track prepares graduates for the business side of professional athletics and sports-oriented careers. Students interested in pre-professional programs can pursue courses in pre-engineering, pre-law, pre-medicine, and pre-pharmacy.

All courses are delivered through GCU's two highly regarded colleges: the Women's College and University College.

The Women's College at Georgian Court University, open to residential and commuter students, helps women develop the skills and knowledge needed to achieve in all aspects of life. Its comprehensive liberal arts education emphasizes strong leadership, the importance of contributing to society, and bolsters women's confidence to pursue professional and personal excellence.

Research shows that students at women's colleges develop high self-esteem, participate fully in and out of the classroom, and enjoy career success. GCU's Women's College is where students speak up, develop their personal toolkit for success, and demonstrate intellectual and civic engagement.

GCU's University College encompasses coeducational, nonresidential graduate programs and certificates, and more than 16 undergraduate programs geared to nontraditional learners—students who have family obligations, job demands, and limited time to attend class. University College features flexible scheduling, technology-enhanced courses, and classes at convenient locations. University College programs are offered in the evening at the GCU main campus in Lakewood, and during the day and evening at GCU at Woodbridge, GCU at Cumberland County College, and GCU at New Jersey Coastal Communiversity in Wall.

GCU residents and commuters enjoy trips to museums, theater events and concerts. GCU Learning-Living Communities allow those with shared interests in International Cultures, the Arts, and Outdoor Adventures to join discussion groups, attend lectures, and enjoy off-campus outings.

GCU students aren't just educated. They are empowered. At Georgian Court, students demonstrate academic leadership through the University Honors Program, while their professional growth is nurtured through Women in Leadership Development (WILD), a four-year program that cultivates students' skills through hands-on workshops; seminars with career coaches, and discussions with prominent women in business, education and government.

GCU is a member of the Central Atlantic Athletic Conference and participates in eight NCAA Division II sports: basketball, cross-country, lacrosse, soccer, softball, tennis, track and field, and volleyball. In 2008, the soccer team made its first NCAA Division II championship appearance, and the volleyball team won its first NCAA tournament. In 2009, GCU softball players were one win away from appearing in the NCAA Division II World Series, and in 2010, remained a top-ranked conference team.

GCU students enjoy access to the school's eco-friendly, $26 million Wellness Center. The 67,000-square-foot building houses a 1,200-seat arena; an exercise science laboratory; classroom and office space; two professional dance studios; a fitness center; and the university bookstore. Outdoors, the complex includes new fields for softball, soccer and lacrosse, tennis courts and an eight-lane track.

There are three residence halls—Maria Hall, St. Joseph Hall, and St. Catherine Hall—as well as a new chapel, a residence hall for Sisters of Mercy and visiting faculty members, and GCU's historic Gilded Age Mansion, home to GCU's popular interactive history theater productions.

LOCATION AND ENVIRONMENT

Georgian Court University is in Lakewood, a suburban city midway between New York City and Philadelphia, and only minutes from the spectacular Jersey Shore. The campus is near Route 9, the Garden State Parkway, and Interstate 195. New Jersey Transit bus access is within walking distance, giving students quick, inexpensive transportation to places throughout the tri-state.

MAJORS AND DEGREES

The schools of Georgian Court University—the School of Arts and Sciences, the School of Business, and the School of Education—are integrated into the Women's College and University College.

The Bachelor of Arts is awarded in: applied arts and sciences; art; biology; chemistry; communications; criminal justice; dance; elementary education; English; history; humanities; mathematics; music; physics; psychology; sociology; and Spanish. The Bachelor of Science is awarded in: accounting; allied health technologies; biochemistry; biology; business administration; chemistry; clinical laboratory sciences; exercise science, wellness, and sports; natural sciences; nursing; tourism, hospitality, and recreation management; and physics. Social work majors earn a Bachelor of Social Work, and artists earn a Bachelor of Fine Arts.

GCU offers more than 50 minor field sequences, certification programs, and concentrations, including: anthropology; bilingual/bicultural studies; coaching women athletes; communications; criminal justice; economics; gerontology; graphic design/illustration; holistic health; human resource management; marketing; nuclear medicine technology; philosophy; political science; and more. Interdisciplinary minors are offered in international area studies, Latin American studies, and women's studies.

The most popular majors at GCU are psychology, English, business administration, history, and biology. In addition, more than 25 percent of Georgian Court students pursue a second major or certification in education.

Learning at GCU is not limited to the classroom. Internships and practical experiences are offered in most majors, and independent study is available.

ACADEMICS AND BEYOND

A Georgian Court University education develops students in mind, body, and spirit. Its wide-ranging liberal arts education is intellectually rigorous, and GCU's emphasis on service learning develops the spirit. With this dual approach, GCU graduates become successful professionals, compassionate neighbors, concerned citizens, and ethical civic leaders.

The undergraduate curriculum capitalizes on students' college preparation and embraces their aptitudes, talents, and interests. Service learning opportunities, like working with needy families in Guyana or rebuilding homes destroyed by Hurricane Katrina, allow GCU students to put their education into action.

Candidates for a bachelor's degree at Georgian Court must complete 120 credit hours. With departmental approval, students may elect a second major. Elementary education majors are required to choose a second liberal arts major. A minimum cumulative GPA of 2.0 and a minimum cumulative major GPA of 2.5 are required for graduation.

Georgian Court University hosts 16 academic honor societies which recognize outstanding student achievement in biology, business administration, chemistry, education, English, mathematics, physics, psychology, social work, and sociology.

GCU students study abroad in places like Honduras, Ireland and other countries, and Georgian Court University offers joint-degree programs with partner institutions like the University of Medicine and Dentistry of New Jersey.

CAMPUS FACILITIES AND EQUIPMENT

The Arts and Science Center is Georgian Court's largest academic building, providing classrooms, seminar rooms, offices, art studios, and a computer lab. The state-of-the-art Audrey Birish George Science Center, opened in 2005, houses laboratory and instruction space for scientific study.

Other buildings include: the Sister Mary Joseph Cunningham Library; the Raymond Hall Complex, where the School of Education, a computer center and the GCU Dining Hall are located; Farley Center, home to the School of Business and the Department of Psychology, a computer lab, student lounge, and conference center; and GCU's newest addition, the Wellness Center.

TUITION, ROOM, BOARD, AND FEES

Full-time tuition for 2009–10 is $23,246. Room/board for the Women's College is $9,386. Full-time undergraduate fees are $1,244. Textbooks/instructional materials cost extra and vary by course.

FINANCIAL AID

As a private university, Georgian Court works to keep the cost of a college degree affordable, and 95 percent of first-year, full-time students receive financial aid through federal, state, and institutional sources, including scholarships, grants, loans, and work-study. GCU also offers a $2,500 Women's Leadership Award for qualified full-time resident students who demonstrate outstanding leadership and service to school, community, or church. GCU also participates in the New Jersey Educational Opportunity Fund. For financial aid consideration, candidates must complete the Free Application for Federal Student Aid (FAFSA) at http://www.fafsa.ed.gov.

ORGANIZATIONS AND ACTIVITIES

The Student Government Association organizes extracurricular activities, charity fund-raisers, and other events. Through SGA, elected students shape campus life and participate in all major university committees alongside members of the faculty and administration.

ADMISSIONS

GCU welcomes applications from qualified students of all faiths and backgrounds. The University strives to enroll students who can benefit most from its academic program. Entrance is based on individual merit. The high school record of achievement must reflect solid performance, and candidates for admission must have completed 16 academic (Carnegie) units. In 2009, most GCU freshmen ranked in the upper half of their high school class.

Submission of SAT or ACT scores is optional. Consideration is given to the applicant's extracurricular activities and letters of recommendation submitted by teachers, counselors, employers, or similarly qualified people. A campus interview is highly recommended, and guided tours are available.

Qualified applicants whose first choice is Georgian Court University and who apply by November 15 may be considered for early decision. A mature, well-qualified student who wishes to enter the university after three years of high school may apply for early entrance.

Transfer students are accepted into the freshman, sophomore, and junior classes for fall and spring semesters. All transfer applicants must be in good standing at their previous college. Applicants with fewer than 24 credits must fulfill all requirements for admission to the freshman class. International students in need of a student visa must present official documents at least six months before the semester start, and must have a minimum TOEFL score of 550 on the paper-based test or 213 on the computer-based test. International students must complete a GCU financial support form and should be prepared to assume full financial responsibility for their educational and personal expenses.

APPLICATION AND INFORMATION

To apply for admission, first-time freshman applicants should send an application, high school transcript, and nonrefundable $40 application fee payable to the GCU Office of Admissions. Transfer students should submit those materials and transcripts from all colleges they've attended. Freshman applicants are urged to submit applications as early as possible during their senior year of high school. Completed applications are due by August 1 for fall admission and by January 1 for spring admission. Printable and electronic applications are at http://www.georgian.edu. Schedules and registration for campus visits are at http://www.georgian.edu/admissions.

For information, prospective students should contact:

Office of Admissions

Georgian Court University

900 Lakewood Avenue

Lakewood, New Jersey 08701-2697

United States

Phone: 732-987-2760 or 800-458-8422 Ext. 2760

Fax: 732-987-2000

E-mail: admissions@georgian.edu

Website: http://www.georgian.edu/admissions

GONZAGA UNIVERSITY

AT A GLANCE

Gonzaga University, founded in 1887, is an independent, comprehensive university with a distinguished background in the Catholic, Jesuit, and humanistic tradition. Gonzaga emphasizes the moral and ethical implications of learning, living, and working in today's global society. Through the University Core Curriculum, each student develops a strong liberal arts foundation, which many alumni cite as a most valuable asset. In addition, students specialize in any of more than 75 academic programs and majors. Gonzaga enrolls approximately 4,729 undergraduates and 2,908 graduate and law students.

Gonzaga's 131-acre campus combines the old and new: College Hall, the original administration building, and DeSmet Residence Hall with the modern architectural structures of Foley Library, Hughes Life Sciences Building, Jundt Art Center and Museum, and the PACCAR Center for Applied Science. The campus is characterized by sprawling green lawns and majestic evergreen trees. Towering above the campus are the stately spires of St. Aloysius Church, the well-recognized landmark featured in the University logo.

Gonzaga encompasses five undergraduate schools: Arts and Sciences, Business Administration, Education, Engineering and Applied Science, and Professional Studies. The University offers the BA, BBA, BEd, BS, BSCE, BSCpE, BSCS, BSEE, BSEM, BSME, and BSN degrees.

Gonzaga offers several unique options for students. The Honors Program provides a rigorous liberal arts curriculum for intellectually curious students who thrive in a competitive academic environment. Business leaders mentor the Hogan Entrepreneurial Leadership Program students, and internships are an integral part of the program. The award-winning Gonzaga Alumni Mentor Program (GAMP) connects current students and recent graduates with alumni in their professional areas of interest. Students in the Comprehensive Leadership Program take a leadership certificate curriculum that may be combined with any major, and they participate in valuable, interactive leadership experiences. The Army ROTC unit prepares select women and men as leaders in service for their communities and their country. Gonzaga's nationally ranked debate team includes all skill levels. The Mock Trial Team competes nationally and involves students majoring in many different areas of study. Internships, research with faculty, and community service learning enhance class time while providing students first-hand experience.

LOCATION AND ENVIRONMENT

As the hub of the Inland Northwest, Spokane plays a vital role in shaping the University's character. While offering urban advantages such as museum exhibits, shopping, symphony, Broadway and ballet performances, Spokane still maintains an intimate, friendly, and community atmosphere. Used for running and cycling, part of the 37-mile Centennial Trail, runs through campus and to Coeur d' Alene, Idaho. Within a short distance of campus, students snow and water ski, hike, cycle, rock climb, swim, camp, and golf. With an average rainfall of only 16.7 inches per year, outdoor activities are easily accessible.

The 24 residence halls on campus, both single-sex and coed, house 40 to 360 students each. Freshmen and sophomores are required to live on campus. The ZagNet network provides students round-the-clock electronic access to email, Internet, campus intranet, and library holdings, all directly from residence hall rooms. Resident Directors and Assistants, along with a Resident Chaplain, provide a fun, secure, and nurturing environment.

OFF-CAMPUS OPPORTUNITIES

Recognizing the importance of an international perspective for learning, Gonzaga offers study abroad programs in Australia, Benin, China, Costa Rica, Ecuador, El Salvador, England, France, Italy, Japan, Mexico, the Netherlands, Spain, Turks and Caicos, and Zambia. Gonzaga's campus in Florence, Italy is the most popular option.

MAJORS AND DEGREES OFFERED

Gonzaga offers the following areas of study in the five undergraduate schools. The College of Arts and Sciences offers applied communication studies, art, biochemistry, biology (research option), broadcast and electronic media studies, chemistry, classical civilizations, criminal justice, economics, English (writing track option), environmental studies, French, history, integrated studies, international studies (including international relations and Asian, European, and Latin American studies), Italian studies, journalism, mathematics, mathematics/computer science, music (including emphases in composition, general studies, performance and a jazz minor), music education, philosophy, physics, political science, psychology, public relations, religious studies, sociology, Spanish, and theatre arts. Additionally, the School offers concentrations in Catholic studies and women's and gender studies and minors only in advertising, dance, German, and Italian. Students interested in the following areas take tracks of classes respectively in pre-dentistry, pre-law, pre-medicine, pre-physical therapy, and pre-veterinary studies. The School of Business Administration offers majors in accounting or business administration (with concentrations in economics, entrepreneurship (through the Hogan Program), finance, human resource management, individualized study, international business, law and public policy, management information systems, marketing, and operations and supply chain management). As well as granting teacher certification on both the elementary and secondary levels, the School of Education offers degrees in physical education, special education, and sport management. The School of Engineering and Applied Science offers computer science and civil, computer, electrical, and mechanical engineering degrees, as well as an engineering management degree and a 5-year BSEM/MBA option. Also, The School of Professional Studies offers human physiology and nursing degrees. Advanced degrees in accounting, business, education, law, leadership studies, nursing, philosophy, and religious studies, and teaching English as a second language are also offered.

ACADEMIC PROGRAMS

The core curriculum (a basic set of courses in thought and expression, philosophy, religious studies, mathematics, and English literature) is at the foundation of every student's academic experience at Gonzaga. In keeping with the Jesuit ethos of the University, all students share a framework of 31 credits: a trio block of thought and expression courses including English composition, critical thinking, and speech communication; three additional courses in philosophy; three religious studies courses; and one course each in math and English literature. Various schools in the University add courses that complement the core such as modern/classical language requirements, history and science classes, additional math courses, etc. Often, classes at Gonzaga require oral presentations or use of the written and discussion-based communication skills emphasized in the core curriculum.

CAMPUS FACILITIES AND EQUIPMENT

The Foley Library contains more than 800,000 volumes and microform titles, with two special collections of material especially rich in the areas of philosophy and classical civilization, as well as the nation's most extensive collection of works concerning the famous Jesuit poet Gerard Manley Hopkins. The historic College Hall houses the recently-renovated Harry & Colleen Magnuson Theatre, a 24-hour computer lab, a Florentine-style University Chapel, and numerous classrooms and faculty offices.

Students are able to produce sophisticated multimedia presentations and research hundreds of libraries across the country from their own residence hall rooms or from one of the 10 labs on campus. The Communications Building offers an arts lab for the Bulletin (the weekly student-published newspaper), KAGU, the University's radio station, and GUTV, a state-of-the-art TV production station where students learn all aspects of broadcast and electronic media studies. The Herak Center for Engineering offers state-of-the-art CAD/CAM, electronic, digital, microwave, and calibration labs, and the PACCAR Center for Applied Science, which opened in 2008, adds more classroom space, a robotics lab, a computer science lab with a high-speed cluster computer array, and the rapidly growing Electric Utility Transmission & Distribution program.

The Martin Athletic Centre boasts a 13,000 sq. ft. state-of-the-art fitness center, and next door, the 6000-seat McCarthey Athletic Center houses the men's and women's basketball games as well as concerts and events throughout the year. Opened in 2007, Washington Trust Field at Patterson Baseball Complex hosts the Gonzaga baseball program.

TUITION, ROOM, BOARD AND FEES

Tuition for the 2009–2010 academic year is $29,200; room and board is estimated at $7,976. Including tuition, room and board, books, fees, transportation, and living expenses, Gonzaga estimates $41,751 as the total cost of attendance for the 2009–2010 year.

FINANCIAL AID

Over 95 percent of students receive financial aid. The average package for 2007–2008 was $22,643 awarded in the form of grants, scholarships, loans, and campus employment. A number of merit-based, merit/need-based, athletic, music, debate, and other program scholarships are awarded to students each year. Students should file the Free Application for Federal Student Aid (FAFSA) by the priority date of February 1. Gonzaga is committed to working with students and families to finance their investment in a quality education.

STUDENT ORGANIZATIONS AND ACTIVITIES

GU students enjoy a wide variety of activities on and off campus. The Gonzaga Student Body Association (GSBA) oversees over one hundred academic, social, and cultural clubs and provides the structure of student government. Some of the most popular clubs include the Outdoors Club, THIRST (a non-denominational worship group), GUTS (an improvisational comedy team), and the Hawaii Pacific Islanders Club. GSBA organizes service and conservation projects, dances, and countless other activities to channel and challenge the talents and passions of motivated men and women who seek to make a difference.

As the leading provider of service hours in the entire city of Spokane, Gonzaga University encourages students to volunteer their services at any of the area non-profit organizations. University Ministry, the Gonzaga Student Body Association, Unity Multicultural Education Center and the Office of Intercultural Relations, and the Center for Community Action and Service Learning (CCASL) provide organized projects through which students become involved in the greater Spokane community.

Division I, West Coast Conference sports include baseball (men), basketball, crew, cross-country/track, golf, soccer, tennis, and volleyball (women). Approximately 85% of students participate in intramural and club sports such as ultimate frisbee and rugby. The Harry & Colleen Magnuson Theatre hosts main-stage plays (including musicals), dance recitals, GUTS, and numerous one-acts and student directed scenes. Gonzaga's musical groups include a nationally recognized University Choir, a Chorale, the GU Symphony, the Jazz Band, the Gregorian Schola, The Big Bing Theory—an a cappella group, and numerous other ensembles. GU's students also host programs on Gonzaga's TV and radio stations. Additionally, many students participate in University Ministry events, such as retreats, the annual Pilgrimage hike, THIRST, Masses, Christian Life Communities, and interdenominational and/or interfaith services.

ADMISSIONS PROCESS

The University seeks diligent, inquisitive applicants with diverse backgrounds who will benefit from the rigorous Jesuit instruction at Gonzaga as well as enhance the University environment. A Common Application (www.commonapp.org) or the Universal College Application (www.universalcollegeapp.com) and the Gonzaga supplement, SAT (Writing Section not used universally) or ACT scores (Writing Section not required), a teacher recommendation, a counselor report, an activities list or resume, and an essay are required. Transfer students and students with any college credit must submit official transcripts from all colleges. Transfer students must also complete a transfer student clearance report. International students must also submit official transcripts from all colleges attended. Additionally, international students must submit official results of their TOEFL examination. The Non-binding Early Action application deadline for freshmen is November 15th (postmarked). The main advantages of the Early Action Program are early communication of admission and potential scholarship notice (by January 15th). The Regular Decision application date is February 1 (postmarked). Students applying Regular Decision by this date will receive an admission decision by the beginning of April. After February 1, applications will be accepted only if space is available.

GRACELAND UNIVERSITY

There is always something great going on at Graceland University's main campus in Lamoni, Iowa (founded in 1895) and our Independence, Missouri campus (1999). Graceland students and faculty are on the go, on our campuses and around the world.

AT A GLANCE

Graceland University creates and maintains high academic standards of excellence by prioritizing a close student/faculty learning environment, providing nurturing communities that foster intellectual engagement and curiosity, and embracing the philosophy that learning is not confined to the classroom. Graceland integrates a strong tradition in the liberal arts with targeted professional learning.

LOCATION AND ENVIRONMENT

Situated on 170 acres of rolling hills and trees, our main campus in Lamoni, IA is home to about 1,000 students. It is a short, one-hour drive to busy Des Moines, Iowa, or two hours to Kansas City. We offer a beautiful, safe residential campus where diversity of thought and culture are celebrated. You are warmly welcomed at Graceland and in Lamoni from the minute you arrive. You instantly have friends and become a valued member in an all-are-included home away from home.

We integrate learning inside and outside of the classroom and provide limitless opportunities for involvement in educational service, leadership and entertainment activities. The Independence Campus offers online learning opportunities, graduate and undergraduate, in nursing, religion and education.

You will see horses and buggies around town. The Lamoni area is home to a large community of Amish who provide an old-world ambience. Life at Graceland includes forums and guest speakers on the hot issues of the day; community service projects; poetry readings at the local coffee house; world-class entertainment; and quiet time on our pastoral campus.

Off-Campus Opportunities

Lamoni is a small, friendly town with a big heart. There is an old-fashioned pizza place, a modern (wired) coffee house, a university-owned movie theatre called the Coliseum and a dance club called Choices—all just a five-minute walk from campus. Nature surrounds Lamoni. You can hike around a beautiful lake or use new, city bike trails. Popular lakes at Slip Bluff County Park and Nine Eagles State Park offer swimming, boating, fishing and camping and both are only a few miles away. There are close bonds between Graceland and the town of Lamoni, home to about 2,500 residents.

MAJORS AND DEGREES OFFERED

Bachelor's Degrees

Accounting

Art: Studio Art

Art: Visual Communications

Athletic Training

Basic Science

Biology

Business Administration

Chemistry

Communications

Computer Science and Information Technology

Criminal Justice

Economics

Education

English

Film, Theatre, and Performance Studies

Health

Health Care Management

History

Human Services

International Studies

Liberal Studies

Mathematics

Music

Nursing

Physical Education

Psychology

Publication Writing and Design

Recreation

Religion and Philosophy

Sport Management

Wellness Program Management

Pre-Professional Programs

Pre-Chiropractic

Pre-Dentistry

Pre-Forensic Science

Pre-Law

Pre-Medicine

Pre-Optometry

Pre-Pharmacy

Pre-Veterinary Medicine

Masters Programs

Master of Arts in Christian Ministries

Master of Arts in Religion

Master of Education

Master of Science in Nursing

ACADEMIC PROGRAMS

From the beginning, Graceland students learn in an individualized, challenging and supportive environment, with a 15:1 student/faculty ratio. Students immediately meet key professors in 'First Year Experience' classes. GU offers over 50 academic majors and programs. You will work closely with professors who are both teachers and scholars. Most hold a doctorate or the highest degree in their field. Leadership opportunities abound. Our Honors program, highly acclaimed by participants, is designed for motivated students who want to expand their learning beyond the regular curriculum.

Students in Free Enterprise (SIFE) participate in national and international service efforts and our team has won regional championships nine of the last 10 years. Our 80-strong SIFE team placed first in the U.S. and second in the world (at the competition in Paris) in 2006. Winter Term separates the two traditional semesters and allows students to interact with faculty in action-oriented learning experiences on campus and around the world… for example, building a home in Nicaragua or touring European art museums.

Your Graceland Experience will combine a personalized education and an ongoing adventure that will stay with you for the rest of your life. Once a Gracelander, always a Gracelander. Our graduates go on to stellar careers in the sciences, the arts, nursing, education, business, athletics and humanitarian service. Our alumni will tell you that the Graceland Experience helped focus their passions and shape their futures.

In addition to its traditional programs Graceland offers many options for distance learners. Programs offered online by the School of Nursing include the Bachelor in Healthcare Management, RN-B.S.N., RN-M.S.N., and M.S.N. programs. The M.S.N. program has three tracks: family nurse practitioner, nurse educator, and health-care administrator. The Graceland University School of Education offers a Master of Education with an emphasis in collaborative learning and teaching and special education. The Community of Christ Seminary also offers master's programs in religion and Christian ministries at a distance. The Master of Education program is offered in Cedar Rapids, Des Moines, and Lamoni, Iowa; Independence, Missouri; and online. The Community of Christ Seminary at Graceland offers a Master of Arts in Religion and a Master of Arts in Christian Ministries in blended delivery systems. The Community of Christ Seminary also offers master's programs in religion and Christian ministries for distance learners.

CAMPUS FACILITIES AND EQUIPMENT

The brand new Resch Science and Technology Hall was dedicated in 2009 and provides state-of-art-sciences and math facilities. Nearly everything, including lab equipment, is new and industry-standard in Resch Hall. The Helene Center for the Visual Arts (2004) includes 29,000 square feet of classrooms, studios and exhibit space. It is regarded by artists as "the perfect place to get creative." The large north-facing windows, an important feature, provide optimum light. The Shaw Center for the Performing Arts includes an 800-seat auditorium, a 150-seat studio theatre, a 40-foot proscenium stage with orchestra pit, a world-class Casavant pipe organ and a Kurzweil synthesizer.

Campus computer facilities include three microcomputer labs with Macintosh and personal computers, and industry-standard equipment for desktop publishing and graphics design. Graceland's Enter.Net.C@fe provides 24-hour internet access in a cozy atmosphere. Our Closson Athletic Center boasts an indoor track and field facility, a beautiful hardwood basketball and volleyball court and an indoor pool. We have a new FieldTurf, artificial turf football field which is the envy of other universities, a wonderful outdoor track facility and a top soccer complex, home to our perennial conference champion men's and women's teams. Our men's soccer team won the NAIA National Championship in 2006.

The Frederick Madison Smith Library uses the latest technologies to provide information services that students need. Ten fully networked computer workstations offer access to the Internet and many research databases, including seven reference databases and more than 45 periodical databases, many providing access to full-text articles. Access to LIBBIE, the library's online catalog, and to the online reference sources is available to all patrons who use the library on the campus network as well as off-campus users via the Internet. Articles and books may be ordered from a worldwide network of research libraries. Students log on to the library's home page to ask reference questions.

TUITION, ROOM, BOARD, AND FEES

Graceland University has been listed in America's 100 Best College Buys. We are committed to managing our costs, now and in the future, while maintaining the quality of education we provide every student. Costs for traditional students for the 2010–11 academic year are below. Online program costs vary.

	Annual	Semester
Tuition	$20,680	$10,340
Room	2,810	1,405
Board	4,230	2,115
Activity Fee	300	150
Total Direct Costs	$28,020	$14,410

FINANCIAL AID

Student Financial Aid is available for those students who qualify. All aid is based upon financial need, academic achievement, and/or meritorious performance. Financial aid is viewed as a supplement to the effort of the family to finance their student's college education. In order to receive federal or state financial aid, students must file a Free Application for Federal Student Aid (FAFSA) each year using code #001866 and maintain satisfactory academic progress. Institutional Scholarships and Grants may be awarded to full-time students in the areas of academic, athletics, performing arts, Community of Christ Leadership, and congregational matches. When Graceland University receives all documents needed to complete a Financial Aid Package an award notice will be sent to the student for review. Over 94% of Graceland's students receive some form of financial aid.

STUDENT ORGANIZATIONS AND ACTIVITIES

Graceland sponsors over 45 student clubs and organizations, including opportunities for non-traditional and special-interest student groups to participate. We boast 19 varsity and 10 junior varsity sports, and eight performing arts groups. Anyone who wants to play or perform at Graceland has ample opportunity.

The basic residential and social unit of student life is known as a "House." The house system at GU is a unique program based on the principle of inclusion. The importance of each student is recognized. Unlike fraternities and sororities, every student is involved in the house system. Members of each house elect five students, known as the house council, to hold key leadership positions. Under their direction, social, religious, and academic support activities are planned for house members. By cooperative effort, the house organizes its own social, religious, and intramural programs. Each student determines the extent of his/her participation in all house activities. Our students love this "community" approach to residential life.

You can meet students from China, Kosovo, Nepal and more. Our students hail from 47 states and 41 countries. Seventeen percent or our students are international students, the second highest ratio among small universities in Iowa. We are committed to providing an environment that is free of alcohol and tobacco. When you meet the friendly people in our Campus Ministries office, you will learn that whatever your faith tradition, your spiritual life will be nurtured as much as you desire while you are at Graceland.

ADMISSIONS PROCESS

To be considered for acceptance at Graceland, you must meet two of the following three criteria: rank in the upper 50% of your high school class, have a 2.5 grade point average (based on a 4.0 system) and a minimum composite ACT score of 21, or a minimum combined SAT score of 960. International students also need to score at or above 450 on TOEFL and prove ability to cover expenses while enrolled. Transfer students need a minimum 2.0 GPA on previous college coursework.

GRANTHAM UNIVERSITY

Grantham University's 100% online degree programs are designed so you can fit education into your life instead of arranging your life around your education.

AT A GLANCE

Established in 1951, Grantham University, then the Grantham School of Electronics, began by offering F.C.C. License certification courses to veterans returning home from World War II. Today, Grantham specializes in online education for the working adult student. Our mission is to provide accessible, affordable, professionally relevant degree programs in a continuously changing global society.

For nearly 60 years, Grantham University has contributed to the formal education of thousands of working adults, military service members and veterans. Students all across the United States and in many countries around the world have discovered the benefits and convenience of the Grantham distance education model. Grantham University's degree programs are 100% online and are designed to meet the needs of busy working adult students. There are no required login times, so students can complete their coursework at times and places that fit their busy schedule.

Why Grantham:

- 100% Online Degree Programs
- Earn Credit for What You Already Know
- Simple Application Process
- Student Success Teams
- Scholarships & Tuition Grants

Grantham offers a variety of undergraduate degrees including: Accounting, Business Administration, Criminal Justice, Computer Science, Engineering Technology, Health Systems Management and Nursing, as well as graduate degree programs in Business, Health Systems Management, Healthcare Administration, Project Management, Information Management, Information Technology and Nursing.

Grantham's faculty, administration, and advisors are comprised of educators, business executives, industry professionals; entrepreneurs and retired military officers. Among them are Commander Everett Alvarez, Jr. (Ret.), a distinguished Naval officer and government executive; Dr. Herbert I. London, founder, endowed chair, and former Dean of Students at New York University's Gallatin School of Individualized Study; John Ashford, an advisor to Fortune 100 companies as chairman and CEO of The Hawthorn Group; Rear Admiral Karen Harmeyer, former Chief Staff Officer, Navy Surgeon General, OPNAV 093R; and Lieutenant General Thomas Rhame (Ret.), Vice President of Finance and Administration for the Association of the United States Army.

In a highly competitive job market, staying relevant in the workforce requires continuing education and professional development. Whether you need a degree to obtain a promotion, sharpen your skills, or keep pace with new ideas and technological advances, Grantham University has a program for you.

Grantham University is accredited by the Accrediting Commission of the Distance Education and Training Council, 1601 18th Street, N.W., Washington, D.C. 20009 (www.detc.org).

MAJORS AND DEGREES OFFERED

Associate Degree Programs:

Business Administration

Business Management

Computer Science

Criminal Justice

Electronics and Computer Engineering Technology

Engineering Management Technology

General Studies

Medical Coding and Billing

Multidisciplinary Studies

Bachelor Degree Programs:

Accounting

Business Administration

Business Management

Computer Engineering Technology

Computer Science

Criminal Justice

  -Homeland Security

  -Computer Science

Electronics Engineering Technology

Engineering Management Technology

General Studies

Health Systems Management

Multidisciplinary Studies

Nursing: RN-BSN Completion Program

Master's Degree Programs:

Business Administration

  -Project Management

  -Information Management

Healthcare Administration

Health Systems Management

Information Technology

Information Management—Project Management

Information Management Technology

Nursing:

  -RN to MSN Option

  -Case Management

  -Nursing Education

  -Nursing Informatics

  -Nursing Management & Organizational Leadership

ACADEMIC PROGRAMS

Grantham University offers a variety of degree programs through three colleges: The Mark Skousen School of Business, The College of Arts and Sciences and the College of Engineering and Computer Science.

Students must complete a minimum of 62 credit hours for an associate degree, of which 25% of the credit hours must be completed with Grantham. The Bachelor's programs require a minimum of 122 credit hours, of which 25% of the credit hours must be completed with Grantham. The Master's degree programs require 36 credit hours, of which 27 credit hours must be completed with Grantham.

Course content is delivered via the Grantham student learning environment, Angel. All undergraduate degree-seeking students are required to successfully complete GU100 — Student Success (one-credit hour course) in conjunction with their first academic course. GU100 is designed to help you become familiar with Grantham, our policies and procedures; provide an introduction to online learning; and introduce student success strategies, such as study skills, note taking strategies, memory devices, and more.

Students are given 8 weeks to complete each course; however, you may accelerate course completion based on study habits and time devoted to the material.

Grantham University makes every effort to apply college credit for military training and previous coursework whenever possible. CLEP tests, DSST exams, AP and DANTES, along with military and work-related training courses, may be eligible for transfer credit.

CAMPUS FACILITIES AND EQUIPMENT
Distance Learning Programs

Grantham University's degree programs are offered through distance education, or e-learning formats, none of which have a residency requirement. Grantham students are not required to log onto the Internet on specific days or at specific times; however, all courses contain weekly milestones that must be met. This unique method of learning is advantageous for those students with full-time jobs, or who have family or other commitments that do not allow them to participate in a regular classroom environment. Other students who are attracted to the Grantham's distance education model are those who travel extensively or find that the nearest college or university may be hundreds of miles away. Grantham University also attracts thousands of military students who appreciate the benefit of being able to complete classes from almost anywhere in the world. These military students do not have to worry about frequent deployments or transfers interrupting their education because they can take their coursework with them and complete it when and where it is convenient.

TUITION, ROOM, BOARD, AND FEES

Grantham University's tuition rate for full-time enrollments is $265 per credit hour. Required textbooks and software are covered by a Textbook and Software Grant. Shipping is included for APO/FPO and North American delivery addresses.

Tuition for students enrolling in individual courses is $265 per credit hour. Required textbooks and software are covered by a Textbook and Software Grant. Shipping is included for APO/FPO and North American delivery addresses.

At the time of enrollment, a new student will be assessed a one-time $30 Enrollment Processing Fee.

Grantham University offers various scholarships in addition to extended payment plans to assist students with financing their education. In addition, Grantham University offers a military scholarship and discount program for active duty, reserve, guard, veterans and military family members, as well as scholarships for law enforcement professionals. Prospective students who require financing for tuition and fees may contact Grantham's Admissions Department for more information—admissions@grantham.edu.

ADMISSIONS PROCESS

Grantham University does not discriminate on the basis of race, color, or national or ethnic origin in admitting students to its programs or in administering its educational policies, admissions policies, scholarship programs or other University administered programs. Admission policies are based on inclusiveness—Grantham believes that everyone should have the opportunity to pursue a college degree.

Once a student has shown an interest in Grantham, he/she will be required to submit the Admissions Application Transfer Credit Evaluation form, along with other necessary documents requested by the Admissions team. Upon receipt, the University will commence the process of review and assessment.

Grantham accepts applications on a continuous basis throughout the year. A student has the option of enrolling as a degree candidate or on a course-by-course basis (non-degree). Students interested in applying can visit: http://www.grantham.edu/gu-admissions/apply-now to download an application.

Applicants with high school or previous education in a foreign country, who do not reside in an English-speaking country (e.g., the United States, Canada, England, Ireland, Australia, New Zealand), must demonstrate English language proficiency. Official documentation must be submitted with the admission file and admission granted before the applicant may begin the program.

Prospective students with questions should e-mail: admissions@grantham.edu or call 800-955-2527 to speak with an Admissions Representative.

HAWAI'I PACIFIC UNIVERSITY

AT A GLANCE

Hawai'i Pacific University (HPU) is a private, nonprofit university with an international student population of approximately 8,200 students. HPU is one of the most culturally diverse universities in America with students from all 50 U.S. states and more than 100 countries. Founded in 1965, HPU prides itself on maintaining strong academic programs, small class sizes, individual attention to students, and a diverse faculty and student population. HPU offers more than 50 acclaimed undergraduate programs and 12 distinguished graduate programs. HPU is recognized as a "Best in the West" college by the Princeton Review and a "Best Buy" by Barron's business magazine. HPU is accredited by the Western Association of Schools and Colleges, the National League for Nursing Accrediting Commission, and the Council on Social Work Education, to name a few.

The diversity of the student body stimulates learning about other cultures firsthand, both inside and outside of the classroom. There is no majority population at HPU. Students are encouraged to examine the values, customs, traditions, and principles of others to gain a clearer understanding of their own perspectives. HPU students develop friendships with students from throughout the United States and the world and form important connections for success in the global economy of the twenty-first century.

HPU faculty members are renowned for the personal interest they take in each of their students. HPU is proud to offer more than 500 full-time and part-time faculty members with outstanding academic and business credentials from around the world, ensuring that HPU students can easily access a world's worth of knowledge and experiences. A vast majority of HPU faculty members hold the highest degrees in their fields. The student-faculty ratio is 15:1, and the average class size is less than 20.

HPU has NCAA Division II intercollegiate sports. Men's athletic programs include baseball, basketball, cross-country, golf, soccer, and tennis. Women's athletics include basketball, cross-country, soccer, softball, tennis, and volleyball.

The housing office at HPU offers many services and living options for students. Residence halls with cafeteria service are available on the windward Hawai'i Loa campus, while off-campus apartments are available in the Honolulu and Waikiki areas for those seeking more independent living arrangements.

LOCATION AND ENVIRONMENT

Hawaii Pacific University's main campus in downtown Honolulu provides a fast-paced, exciting urban environment in the heart of the business community. The downtown campus comprises six buildings in the center of Honolulu's business district and is home to the College of Business Administration and the College of Humanities & Social Sciences. The campus location makes it easy for students to commute to and also find and maintain internship opportunities at neighboring businesses. One of the downtown buildings is the HPU Frear Center, which houses state-of-the-art classrooms, a communication lab, and a high-tech information systems classroom. HPU's Meader Library provides a multitude of general and specialized resources, including a business reference collection, a National Endowment for the Humanities (NEH) collection, and many online databases and journals. The circulating book collections support communications, computer studies, education, literature, social sciences, and other curriculum areas. Also available are study areas, group study rooms, computer work stations, and wireless Internet. The Tutoring and Testing center provides free tutoring in all core subjects. The expanded downtown computer lab boasts 420 plus computers for student use.

Eight miles away, the 135-acre windward Hawai'i Loa campus, which is set in the lush foothills of the Ko'olau mountains, is the home of the College of Nursing & Health Sciences and the College of Natural & Computational Sciences. The Hawai'i Loa campus has residence halls, dining commons, the Educational Technology Center, a student center, and outdoor recreational facilities including a soccer field, tennis courts, a softball field, and an exercise room.

Academic life on the Hawai'i Loa campus revolves around the Amos N. Starr and Juliette Montague Cooke Academic Center (AC). The AC houses classrooms, organic chemistry, nuclear magnetic resonance, and regular laboratories, faculty and staff offices, a theater, an art gallery, and the Atherton Library which includes circulating and reference book collections in the areas of art, history, marine science, nursing, and Hawai'i and the Pacific. Additionally, the library provides access to electronic books (e-books), databases, study rooms, IBM computers, and wireless Internet. Computers are also available for library research, e-mail, and word processing. HPU is also affiliated with the Oceanic Institute, a major research center specializing in marine biology, marine aquaculture, biotechnology and ocean resource management. It is located on a 56-acre site at Makapu'u Point on the southeastern coast of O'ahu, Hawaii. Learning, internship and research opportunities for graduates and undergraduates abound in this hands-on learning environment. All three sites are conveniently linked by free shuttle.

MAJORS AND DEGREES

Hawai'i Pacific University offers programs that lead to the undergraduate degrees of Bachelor of Arts (B.A.), Bachelor of Science (B.S.), Bachelor of Science in Business Administration (B.S.B.A.), Bachelor of Science in Nursing (B.S.N.), and Bachelor of Social Work (B.S.W.).

Undergraduate majors include the B.A. in: Anthropology • Asian Studies • Communication • East-West Classical Studies • Economics • English • Environmental Studies • History • Human Resource Development • Human Services (General and concentrations in Nonprofit Management, , and Substance Abuse Counseling) • International Relations • International Studies • Journalism (concentrations in Broadcast, Design, Photojournalism, and Print) • Justice Administration • Multimedia (concentrations in Digital Media, Media Studies, Video Production, and web Design) • Political Science • Pre-Law • Psychology • Social Science • Sociology • Teaching English as a Second Language. The B.S. is available in: Advertising/Public Relations (concentrations in Strategic Creative and Strategic Planning/ Account Management) • Biochemistry • Biology (concentrations in General Biology and Human & Health Sciences) • Computer Science • Diplomacy and Military Studies • Environmental Science • Health Science • Marine Biology • Mathematics (concentrations in 3-2 Engineering, Applied Math, Math Education and Pure Math) • Oceanography • Pre-chiropractic • Pre-medical Studies • Pre-physical therapy. The B.S.B.A. is available in: • Accounting • Business Economics • Computer Information Systems • Entrepreneurial Studies • Finance • General Business • Human Resource Management • International Business • Management • Marketing • Public Administration • Travel Industry ManagementThe Bachelor of Education (B.Ed.), the Bachelor of Science in Nursing (B.S.N.) and Bachelor of Social Work (B.S.W.) are also available. Dual degrees, double majors, and minors are also offered.

In addition to the undergraduate programs, HPU offers twelve graduate programs. The Master of Arts (M.A.) is offered in: • Communications • Diplomacy and Military Studies • Global Leadership and Sustainable Development • Human Resource Management • Organizational Change • Teaching English as a Second Language. The Master of Business Administration (M.B.A.) is available in: • Accounting • E-business • Economics • Finance • Human Resource Management • Information Systems • International Business • Management • Marketing • Travel Industry Management. Other graduate programs include: • Master of Education in Secondary Education (M.Ed.) • Master of Science in Information Systems (M.S.I.S.) • Master of Science in Marine Science (M.S.M.S.) • Master of Science in Nursing (M.S.N.) • Master of Social Work (M.S.W.).

OFF-CAMPUS PROGRAMS AND OPPORTUNITIES

As part of its emphasis on international education and global citizenship, Hawai'i Pacific University offers study abroad opportunities that complement and enhance students' academic experience. Study abroad opportunities are available in Australia, Austria, Brazil, France, Germany, Great Britain, Japan, Korea, Mexico, , Spain, Sweden, Taiwan, and Thailand. HPU undergraduates and graduates who have completed at least one semester of studies at HPU and intend to complete a degree at HPU are eligible to apply.

The Career Services Center offers a comprehensive education / internship program to further develop student's studies and, elevate their career related position through experience. HPU intertwines academic and co-curricular programs with the world of work so that students gain academic credit, work experience, and a salary. HPU students have done co-ops and internships at some of the world's best known companies and organizations, including American Express Financial Advisors; Deloitte & Touche, LLP; FBI; Hilton Hotels; Microsoft; Oceanic Institute; Polo Ralph Lauren; and Walt Disney World. The staff at the Career Services Center continues to work with students before and after graduation, assisting with everything from resume writing to job interview preparation.

TUITION, ROOM, BOARD, AND FEES

For the 2009–10 academic year, tuition is $14,860 for most majors, while books, supplies, and health insurance cost approximately $2,610. Tuition for marine science majors is $17,540, and tuition for junior- or senior-year nursing majors is $21,760. The cost to live in on-campus residence halls or off-campus apartments is comparable; room and board are $11,094 for a double occupancy room. There is an additional $500 refundable security deposit required for residence halls and off-campus apartments.

FINANCIAL AID

HPU offers most forms of federal financial aid, including student grant and loan programs, as well as loans for parents of dependent students. Over 60 percent of the University's students benefit from federal financial aid programs, or a wide range of institutional scholarships. Students should complete the Free Application for Federal Student Aid (FAFSA) to be considered for federal aid programs. While aid can be awarded throughout the academic year, students should complete the application prior to the March 1 priority deadline to be considered for all available funding. Visit www.hpu.edu/financialaid for current Financial Aid and Scholarship information.

STUDENT ORGANIZATIONS AND ACTIVITIES

A variety of on-campus activities and events are organized for students by the Student Life Office, including Movie on the Mall, Music on the Mall, intramural sports tournaments, and recreational activities. Annual events include Club Carnival, Welcome Week, Da Freakshow, Halloween Hoopla, and Pacific Bowl. HPU students can join one of the more than 70 student clubs; run for office in the Associated Students of Hawai'i Pacific University (ASHPU), the University's governing body; participate in Army or Air Force ROTC; write for the student newspaper, Kalamalama; edit the school's literary journal, Hawai'i Pacific Review; or join HPU's stage and pep band or International Choral program.

ADMISSIONS REQUIREMENTS

Hawai'i Pacific University seeks students who are motivated and show academic promise. The Admissions Office requires that applicants complete and forward the admission application and their high school transcripts. Transfer students should also submit college transcripts. SAT and/or ACT scores should be submitted if these scores are not posted in their transcripts. First-time freshmen are expected to have a minimum GPA of 2.5 (on a 4.0 scale) in college-preparatory courses. HPU recommends that students complete 4 years of English, 4 years of history or social science, 3 years of math, and 2 years of science. Transfer students with 24 or more postsecondary credits are required to have a GPA of 2.0 or above. For students with less than 24 credits, a combination of college and high school GPA is used.

The Marine Science and Environmental Science Programs require a GPA of 3.0 or above and 3 years of science, including biology, chemistry (physics is recommended), as well as mathematics through trigonometry (calculus is recommended). Transfer students must demonstrate ability in science and math at the college level. Students not meeting the above criteria are encouraged to enroll at HPU without declaring a major to demonstrate the ability to do college-level work in science and math.

APPLICATION INFORMATION

Candidates are notified of admission decisions on a rolling basis, usually within two weeks of receipt of application materials. Early entrance and deferred entrance are available.

For further information and for application materials, students should contact:

Office of Admissions

Hawai'i Pacific University

1164 Bishop Street, Suite 200

Honolulu, Hawai'i 96813

Phone: 808-544-0238 / 866-CALL-HPU (toll-free in U.S. and Canada)

Fax: 808-544-1136

E-mail: admissions@hpu.edu

Website: www.hpu.edu/prev

HILLSDALE COLLEGE

AT A GLANCE

Hillsdale College is a private, coeducational, nonsectarian institution of higher learning founded in 1844 by men and women "grateful to God for the inestimable blessings resulting from the prevalence of civil and religious liberty and intelligent piety in the land, and believing that the diffusion of sound learning is essential to the perpetuity of these blessings." The College maintains independence from direct and indirect state and federal government aid. Far-reaching private support from a national constituency has enabled Hillsdale to continue its trusteeship of the intellectual and spiritual inheritance derived from the Judeo-Christian faiths and Greco-Roman cultures.

The undergraduate enrollment for fall 2009 was 1,350, of whom 48 percent were men. The College draws students from 47 states and 7 foreign countries. Approximately 40 percent of students are from Michigan. The entering freshman class in 2009 had an average high school grade point average of 3.75 and mean test scores well above the national averages, ACT 28 and SAT 1950.

The Hillsdale faculty is in a 10-to-1 ratio to students and is compromised of 117 full-time members. Each student has a faculty adviser for core and major coursework who direct the program of study and provide academic and career counseling. While teaching is their first priority, faculty members also engage in research and scholarly writing supported by summer and sabbatical leaves funded by the College, and are often invited to comment on the national scene.

Special student services provided by the College include a career planning and placement office, academic tutoring, and a health service staffed by a physician and a resident nurse.

LOCATION AND ENVIRONMENT

Located in rural southern Michigan, the nearly 200-acre stately Hillsdale College campus includes both modern and historic buildings. The Indiana and Ohio turnpikes are each 30 minutes away, and the College is within close reach of metropolitan areas as large as Detroit and Chicago. The town of Hillsdale is a county seat with a population of 10,000. Stores, churches, restaurants and movie theaters are all within walking distance of the campus.

OFF-CAMPUS OPPORTUNITIES

For 35 years, the Washington Hillsdale Internship Program (WHIP) has provided students the opportunity to participate in full-time, academically intensive internships in the nation's capital. The program has been significantly bolstered with the 2008 establishment of the Hillsdale College Allan P. Kirby, Jr. Center for Constitutional Studies and Citizenship in Washington, D.C. In addition to study opportunities in D.C., Hillsdale students also take advantage of programs in England with Oxford University and Regents College, as well as the University of St. Andrews in Scotland. Science students benefit from Hillsdale's 685-acre field research laboratory in northern Michigan, as well as from a marine biology program in the Florida Keys, internship opportunities with the Omaha Zoo, and a summer research program in South Africa. Foreign language students frequently study abroad in Argentina, France, Germany and Spain.

MAJORS AND DEGREES OFFERED

Hillsdale awards Bachelor of Arts and Bachelor of Science degrees in accounting, art, biochemistry, biology, chemistry, classical studies, computational mathematics, economics, education, English, financial management, French, German, Greek, history, Latin, marketing/management, mathematics, music, philosophy, physical education, physics, political science, psychology, religion, Spanish, speech and theater. Interdisciplinary majors in American studies, Christian studies, comparative literature, European studies, international studies in business and foreign language, political economy, and sociology and social thought are also available. Pre-professional programs are offered in allied health services (including optometry, physical therapy, nursing, and medical technology), dentistry, engineering, environmental sciences, forestry, law, medicine, osteopathy, theology, and veterinary medicine. Hillsdale also offers 2-2 and 3-2 cooperative programs in engineering.

ACADEMIC PROGRAMS

Hillsdale operates on a two-semester schedule. Two 3-week summer sessions are also offered.

The College believes that a sound classical liberal arts education includes study in the humanities, natural sciences and social sciences, and each student is required to complete a structured core of courses in these areas. All students declare a major by the end of the sophomore year. To graduate, students must complete at minimum 124 hours of course work and fulfill the requirements of at least one major field. Each baccalaureate program is based on the completion of four years of study in the liberal arts. The B.A. program includes a foreign language proficiency requirement. The B.S. program requires additional studies in mathematics and the natural sciences.

The honors program enables exceptionally talented students interested in an interdisciplinary community of learning to develop their intellectual potential through an accelerated college core and honors seminars in the junior and senior years. Discussions, guest lectures and travel opportunities contribute to the social cohesiveness of the group. All Honors students complete a senior thesis on an interdisciplinary topic of their choosing.

The Center for Constructive Alternatives conducts four weeklong symposia during the academic year and is one of the largest college lecture series in America. Each brings to the campus distinguished scholars and public figures of national and international renown in a diverse range of fields. All students are required to enroll in two full seminars for credit prior to graduation.

CAMPUS FACILITIES

The Hillsdale College Mossey Library maintains a collection of more than 300,000 volumes. In addition to the main study and research collections, the Library also contains a number of rare and special holdings. Connected to other Michigan libraries through MelCat, and with college libraries nationwide via interlibrary loan, students have access to most any material necessary for on-campus research.

Lane and Kendall halls at the front of campus serve as the primary academic facilities in the humanities and contain classroom space and faculty offices, as well as a special laboratory for experimental psychology. The Strosacker Science Center houses the departments of biology, chemistry and physics. The Joseph H. Moss Family Laboratory Wing, completed in 2008, is a 17,000-square-foot addition that includes a microbiology/cell biology lab, anatomy/physiology lab with human cadaver access, conservation genetics lab, water lab, greenhouse, and organic/general chemistry labs. The 32,000-square-foot Herbert Henry Dow Science Building provides additional classrooms, research laboratories and a computer lab. The Mary Randall Preschool is a circular laboratory school in which nursery school children are taught by students specializing in early childhood education and psychology. The Hillsdale Academy, a K–12 private model school, provides additional opportunities for classroom observation.

The Roche Sports Complex is a facility available to varsity athletes and the general student body alike. The building houses the 60,000-square-foot Jesse Philips Arena, which features a six-lane, 200-meter running track and basketball/volleyball court. The building also houses the pool/diving John "Jack" McAvoy Natatorium, an exercise physiology and sports medicine facility, three racquetball courts, extensive locker room space, and a weight/fitness room. Adjacent is the 7,000-seat capacity Frank "Muddy" Waters Stadium, which features a Pro Grass Artificial Surface football field and all-weather, Olympic-quality Mondo™ eight-lane running track, along with outdoor tennis courts and fields for soccer, baseball and women's softball.

The Sage Center for the Arts is home to the departments of art, theatre and speech. This 47,000-square-foot facility contains studios, classroom space, an exhibition gallery, a prop and scene-construction shop, a sound studio, graphics lab, Black Box theatre, and Markel Auditorium, a 353-seat performance hall (with orchestra pit). Completed in 2003, the 32,809-square-foot Howard Music Hall houses office, studio, classroom, rehearsal and performance space for the John E.N. and Dede Howard Department of Music. Notable features include the McNamara Rehearsal Hall, Conrad Recital Hall, and studio space for percussion and jazz studies. Lower-level practice rooms are available to students during business hours without reservation.

Dedicated in January 2008, the 53,000-square-foot Grewcock Student Union is the center of student life. The two-story structure houses the cafeteria, bookstore, student mail center, offices for student activities and publications, a 100" flat screen television lounge, formal lounge and conference room, AJ's Café, and game area. The entire building is wireless, and any student with an ID can check out a laptop at the main desk.

TUITION, ROOM, BOARD & FEES

Annual tuition for 2009–10 academic year was $19,380, room was $3,850, board was $3,900, and mandatory fees were $540. Books, supplies, and personal expenses (including travel, recreation, and clothing) are estimated at $2,800 per year.

FINANCIAL AID

Financial aid at Hillsdale is available in many forms. Academic scholarships are awarded on a competitive basis; the application for admission also serves as the application for merit-based aid. The priority deadline for academic scholarship consideration is January 1. Athletic scholarships are also available on a competitive basis in men's baseball and football, men's and women's basketball, track and cross-country, and women's swimming and volleyball. The departments of art and music award a select number of scholarships based on strength of portfolio/audition. To apply for aid on the basis of financial need, students are required to file Hillsdale's Confidential Family Financial Statement (CFFS) in January or February of the year of prospective enrollment at Hillsdale. Grants and loans are available from the College. Students may defer payment of up to $500 per semester while working on campus.

STUDENT ORGANIZATIONS AND ACTIVITIES

Hillsdale's Charger athletes compete in eleven intercollegiate NCAA Division II varsity sports as part of the Great Lakes Intercollegiate Athletic Conference (GLIAC). In the past 20 years, the College has produced 180 athletic and academic All-Americans, 24 conference champions, and 17 teams that have finished tenth or better nationally. An active intramural program is also available. Four national fraternities, three national sororities, and more than seventy other social, academic, spiritual and service organizations provide Hillsdale students with a diverse array of co-curricular opportunities. A resident drama troupe and dance company, a bagpipe and drum corps, a concert choir and chamber chorale, a jazz program with big band and combos, instrumental chamber ensembles from string quartets to percussion ensemble, and a College-community orchestra and band constitute the College's performing arts organizations.

ADMISSIONS PROCESS

Admission is a privilege extended to students who will benefit from and contribute to the academic, social and spiritual environments of the College. Students may apply any time after the completion of the junior year of high school. A formal application includes a completed application form, writing samples in the form of essays, a resume of extra-curricular activities, official score reports from the ACT or SAT examination, official transcripts from high schools and colleges from which students have received academic credit, two letters of recommendation, and a nonrefundable application fee of $35 (free if submitted online). An on-campus interview is highly encouraged. Application plans include Early Decision (November 15), Early Action (January 1), and Regular Decision (February 15). Hillsdale College has been distinguished since its founding by voluntarily adhering to a nondiscriminatory policy regarding race, religion, sex, and national or ethnic origin—long before the government began regulating such matters. Transfer applications are evaluated similarly to non-transfers; students must submit a transfer form from the Dean of Students at the college most recently attended. International applicants follow regular entrance procedures in addition to demonstrating a proficiency in English by satisfactory performance on the Test of English as a Foreign Language (TOEFL) or the Michigan Test of English Proficiency.

All records and forms should be directed to:

Admissions Office

Hillsdale College

Hillsdale, Michigan 49242-1298

United States

Phone: (517) 607-2327

Fax: (517) 607-2223

E-mail: admissions@hillsdale.edu

Online: hillsdale.edu

HOFSTRA UNIVERSITY

AT A GLANCE

Hofstra University is building on its reputation as a center of academic excellence. With an outstanding faculty, advanced technological resources and state-of-the-art facilities, Hofstra is recognized both nationally and internationally as a university on the rise. The global spotlight shone on the University when it hosted the third, and final, 2008 presidential debate and made the Hofstra name immediately recognizable to people all over the world. Every semester we offer a wide range of lectures, conferences, artistic performances and forums to engage students and the community.. The University will open New York's newest medical school in 2011, further proof of its institutionalmomentum.

Yet even as it grows in stature and reputation, Hofstra remains student-focused, providing individual attention and an environment that fosters interaction, critical thinking and analysis. . Undergraduate class size is small, averaging just 22 students, and the student-to-faculty ratio is 14-to-1.

LOCATION AND ENVIRONMENT

Something is always in bloom on the 240-acre Hofstra campus. A nationally recognized arboretum, the campus is home to both ivy-covered classroom buildings and sleek, modern buildings. The New Academic Building, an award-winning architecturally-distinct structure that houses a theater, music rehearsal space, faculty offices and seminar rooms, is one of the newest structures on campus.

With New York City just 25 miles away—a short ride by train or car, students take advantage of theaters, museums, concerts and professional sports as well as the many internship opportunities the city offers. Broadway shows, The Metropolitan Museum of Art, Madison Square Garden, Chinatown and Little Italy, and Wall Street all are within easy reach.

Students can also explore Long Island, which offers world-class beaches and parks; the Hamptons; sport fishing and boating; Nassau Coliseum, home of the New York Islanders; and conveniently located shopping malls.

Off-Campus Opportunities

Hofstra extends learning beyond the classroom through an active internship program and many study abroad opportunities. The internship program takes advantage of the proximity of New York City, allowing students to gain on-the-job experience in areas such as finance, business, media, advertising, and entertainment. Through study abroad programs in Europe, Asia, South America and elsewhere, students can explore the world while earning college credits.

MAJORS AND DEGREES OFFERED

Hofstra offers degrees in more than 140 undergraduate programs of study.

Programs of Study Offered

Accounting; Accounting/Taxation; African Studies; American Studies; Anthropology; Anthropology-Archaeology; Applied Physics; Art History; Asian Studies; Athletic Training; Audio/Radio; Biochemistry; Biology; Business Economics; Business Education; Chemistry; Chinese; Chinese Studies; Classics; Community Health; Comparative Literature; Computer Science; Computer Science & Mathematics; Creative Arts; Dance; Dance Education; Drama; Early Childhood and Childhood Education; Early Childhood Education; Economics; Electrical Engineering; Elementary Education; Engineering; Engineering Science—Biomedical; Engineering Science—Civil; Engineering Science—Production & Manufacturing; English—Creative Writing & Literature; English—English & American Literature; English—Publishing Studies & Literature; English Education; Entrepreneurship; Entrepreneurship/Human Resources; Environmental Resources; Exercise Specialist; Film Studies/Production; Finance; Fine Arts—Ceramics; Fine Arts—Design; Fine Arts—Painting; Fine Arts—Photography; Fine Arts—Sculpture—Jewelry; Fine Arts Education; Foreign Language Education—French; Foreign Language Education—German; Foreign Language Education—Italian; Foreign Language Education—Russian; Foreign Language Education—Spanish; Forensic Science; French; Geography; Geology; German; Global Studies; Health Education; Health Science; Hebrew; History; Humanities; Ibero-American Studies; Industrial Engineering; Information Technology; International Business; Italian; Jewish Studies; Journalism; Labor Studies; Latin; Latin American & Caribbean Studies; Legal Studies in Business; Legal Education Accelerated Program; Liberal Arts; Linguistics; Management; Management/Human Resources; Marketing; Marketing/Marketing Research; Mass Media Studies; Mathematical Business Economics; Mathematical Economics; Mathematical Economics; Mathematics; Mathematics—Actuarial Science; Mathematics—Applied Mathematics; Mathematics—Chemistry; Mathematics—Computer Science; Mathematics—Engineering; Mathematics—Physics; Mathematics Education; Mathematics Education; Mechanical Engineering; Music—History/Literature; Music—Jazz & Commercial Music; Music—Music Merchandising; Music—Performance; Music—Theory & Composition; Music Education; Natural Sciences; Philosophy; Physical Education; Physician Assistant Studies; Physics; Physics Education; Political Science; Pre-Dental; Pre-Law; Pre-Medical/Pre-Health; Pre-Veterinary; Psychology; Public Relations; Religion; Russian; Science Education—Biology; Science Education—Chemistry; Science Education—Earth Science; Science Education—Physics; STEM (Science, Technology, Engineering and Math); Social Studies Education; Sociology; Spanish; Speech Communication & Rhetorical Studies; Speech-Language-Hearing Sciences; Theater Arts—Performance Sequence; Theater Arts—Production Sequence; University Without Walls; Urban Ecology; Video/Television; Video/Television & Business; Video/Television & Film; Women's Studies

ACADEMIC PROGRAMS

Hofstra University is composed of Hofstra College of Liberal Arts and Sciences, the Frank G. Zarb School of Business, School of Communication, School of Education, Health and Human Services, School of Law, Honors College, and School for University Studies. Honors College is a program for high-achieving students;); and School for University Studies was developed for students who have demonstrated their potential in non-traditional ways..

Within these schools are many innovative programs designed to meet the needs of our diverse student body. These include Legal Education Accelerated Program (LEAP), a program that allows students to earn both a B.A. and J.D. in six years; and First-Year Connections, an academic, residential and social program that helps first-year students connect to all the resources and opportunities available at the University.

CAMPUS FACILITIES AND EQUIPMENT

The Hofstra campus contains 115 buildings, including state-of-the-art teaching facilities, 37 residence halls, and libraries containing 1.2 million print volumes and providing 24/7 electronic access to more than 90,000 journals and electronic books. C.V. Starr Hall, home to the Zarb School of Business, features the Martin B. Greenberg Trading Room, one of the most advanced academic trading rooms in the nation. The School of Communication's Dempster Hall contains one of the largest noncommercial broadcast facilities in the Northeast as well as a cutting-edge converged newsroom and multimedia classroom. In addition, there are six theaters, including a new black box theater, and an accredited museum.

Recreational and athletic facilities include an indoor, Olympic-sized swimming pool, a recreational center, an indoor sports and entertainment arena and well-maintained athletic fields.

There are 21 eateries, a post office, a salon and a full-service bank.

TUITION, ROOM, BOARD AND FEES

The annual cost of tuition and fees at Hofstra University for 2009–2010 for a full-time undergraduate student is $29,980. The minimum housing and dining plan is $9,890. Books and supplies cost approximately $1,000; personal expenses and transportation generally amount to $2,640. For the full tuition and fees schedule, visit hofstra.edu/tuition.

FINANCIAL AID

A college degree has always been the surest way to success. To help students achieve their educational goals, Hofstra University offers several financial aid options. For 2009-2010, Hofstra awarded more than $65 million in merit- and need-based financial aid. The average award for first-year students with financial need was $15,176, while the average financial aid package for first-year students who had no financial need was $12,633. Nearly 900 first-year students received merit-based scholarships from Hofstra University, ranging from $4,500 to full-tuition scholarships. About 85 percent of all Hofstra students received some form of financial aid, including more than 90 percent of first-year students. For more detailed information, students should visit http://www.hofstra.edu/FinancialAid.

STUDENT ORGANIZATIONS AND ACTIVITIES

Hofstra has a dynamic campus life, with more than 170 student clubs and organizations, including about 30 fraternities and sororities; 18 varsity sports; and more than 500 cultural events each year. Students can choose from organizations as diverse as the Geology Club, Danceworks, and the Hofstra Organization of Latin Americans.

Hofstra's Division I athletic program includes baseball, field hockey, , softball, volleyball, wrestling and men's and women's basketball, cross-country, golf, lacrosse, soccer and tennis. Students who are not Division I athletes can join the student section "Lion's Den" or participate with more than 25 percent of our students in numerous intramural sports.

Students can also attend debates, lectures, and readings by the many scholars, business leaders, writers, and celebrities who visit campus each year. Some great events include the annual "Great Writers, Great Readings" series, the Center for Civic Engagement's Day of Dialogue, and the Distinguished Faculty Lectures.

ADMISSIONS PROCESS

Hofstra University seeks to enroll talented first-year and transfer students from diverse backgrounds and locations, with varied interests. Applications are accepted for fall and spring admission.

The Admission Committee reviews each application individually to assess academic achievement, curricular rigor, leadership potential, depth of extracurricular activities, standardized test scores and overall interest in attending Hofstra University. The application process provides an opportunity for the applicant to share information that may not be apparent on a transcript or through a test score.

Questions about the application process should be directed to the Admission Office in Bernon Hall:

In writing:

100 Hofstra University

Hempstead, New York 11549-1000

By telephone: 516-463-6700 or 1-800-HOFSTRA

E-mail: admission@hofstra.edu

For more information, visit our website: hofstra.edu/admission

ILLINOIS INSTITUTE OF TECHNOLOGY

A private, independent, Ph.D.-granting, coeducational research university founded in 1890, Illinois Institute of Technology (IIT) offers today's students a superb education in engineering, business, architecture, the sciences, psychology, and the humanities, in an environment geared toward the undergraduate student.

IIT's Mission is to provide distinctive and relevant education in an environment of scientific, technological, and professional knowledge creation and innovation.

Our Vision is that IIT will be internationally recognized in distinctive areas of education and research, using as its platform the global city of Chicago, driven by a professional and technology-oriented focus, and based on a culture of innovation and excellence.

Through committed faculty members, close personal attention, and its signature interprofessional programs (IPRO) which provide between 40-50 project based learning opportunities each semester, Illinois Institute of Technology provides a challenging academic program focused on the integration of education and the professional world.

ACADEMIC OPPORTUNITIES

Illinois Tech offers 27 undergraduate majors including aerospace engineering, applied mathematics, architectural engineering, architecture, biochemistry, biology, biomedical engineering, business administration, business administration and applied science, chemical engineering, chemistry, civil engineering, computer engineering, computer science, electrical engineering, humanities, information technology & management, industrial technology & management, journalism of technology, science and business, materials science and engineering, molecular biochemistry and biophysics, physics. In addition, IIT has over 54 minors including artificial intelligence, energy/environment/economics, organizational psychology, polymer science and engineering. A students education is further enhanced by the the 29 specializations which include cell and tissue engineering, finance, and marketing. Dual Admission Programs offered are B.S./D.O. (osteopathic medicine), B.S./J.D. (law), B.S./M.B.A.(business), B.S./Pharm.D.(pharmacy). Special programs are also available in undergraduate research, math and science education, pre-law, pre-medicine, and pre-optometry.

BEYOND THE CLASSROOM

Historically, IIT graduates in all fields have enjoyed an 85% placement rate in the workplace and in graduate and professional school programs within six months of graduation. A 10:1 student/faculty ratio invites direct mentoring by faculty who are groundbreaking leaders in their respective fields. Combining the resources of a top research university with the small classes and personal attention of a liberal arts college, IIT allows students to deepen their knowledge and gain a better sense of their place in the world. And since that world continually faces unanticipated challenges as new advances and technologies emerge in every field, IIT offers an education that gives students the power to navigate complex ideas, demystify technology for others, and take on important problems as they arise. Much of the learning here happens through collaboration with faculty members who offer insightful and relevant perspectives—whether by incorporating the latest materials in design projects or exploring questions posed by their own research in the lab. IIT has established the Office of Undergraduate Research in order to enhance existing programs at IIT and provide new opportunities for mentored collaborative research experiences for undergraduates.

Reality-based education IIT's Interprofessional Projects (IPRO) program isn't found at any other college or university. Students on an IPRO team take on real challenges facing today's corporations, nonprofits, entrepreneurs, government organizations, and faculty and student researchers. IPRO instructors don't lecture, they coach. Students work as an integral part of a team to research, brainstorm, analyze, experiment, build, demonstrate—whatever it takes to create a solution and advance the project to the next level. Undergraduates develop teamwork, problem-solving, decision-making, project-management, communication, and leadership skills—while enjoying work within a team and building experience and career credentials. IPROs (and their cousins, EnPROs, based on new venture ideas that may even be your own) have proven so worthwhile that every student takes part in at least two of the semester long projects while at IIT.

The addition of the University Technology Park at IIT (UTP), an incubator for technology companies located on the Main Campus, and the university's access to more than 29 research facilities, amplifies student's access to outstanding research and professional opportunities. IIT has a rich history with Chicago's professional world, giving students the ability to create relationships and connections with countless multinational businesses and organizations in the city.

CAMPUS & STUDENT LIFE

Our students come to us from 50 states and over 90 countries. 69% men/31% women, 14% international, 42% in top 10% of high school class. 2,576 undergraduate students, 3,714 graduate and 1,119 law students make up the entire student body of IIT including the Stuart School of Business, Chicago-Kent College of Law and the Institute of Design.

The internationally famous 120-acre main campus is based on a master plan developed by the late Ludwig Mies van der Rohe, one of the most influential architects of the century, who served for twenty years as director of IIT's College of Architecture. IIT is located in the heart of Chicago, Illinois, just 10 minutes from the Loop. Students are able to experience one of the greatest cultural cities in the world. More than 70% of IIT undergraduates live on campus in 13 residence halls, six fraternity houses and two sorority houses. The newest student residence, State Street Village was featured in Time magazine. It has balconies with sweeping views of the Chicago skyline and lounges and multimedia entertainment centers.

Students are encouraged to participate in many social, cultural, and athletic opportunities. Student activities include the campus newspaper, the WIIT radio station, special interest clubs, theater and music groups, intramural and varsity athletics, fraternities and sororities, honor and professional societies, student government, residence hall organizations, and the student-run Union Board. IIT has more than 100 student organizations on campus such as rock climbing club intramural athletics and enjoy events such as Chicago's famous theater and improv performances, Taste of IIT, Homecoming Week and International Festival and Pumpkin launch. Counseling, job placement, and student health services are included in the various campus services. The library has access to more than 22 million volumes. Recreational activities include weekly movies, intramural sports, a swimming pool, a recreation center, and discount tickets to area events.

In the athletic arena, IIT student athletes challenge themselves both physically and mentally. In the classroom, they are committed to the highest standard of academic excellence. They compete on a national stage in cross-country, soccer, swimming and diving, men's baseball and women's volleyball. Our athletes have earned All-American and All-Conference Honors in the National Association Intercollegiate Athletics (NAIA) Division I.

COST & FINANCIAL AID

The Office of Financial Aid works hard to bring the cost of an IIT education within reach of anyone with the talent and desire to be here. Annual tuition for 2010–11 is $31,163. Other expenses are approximately $11,000 for room and board (depending on selections) and $1,000 for fees. 97% of IIT students receive financial aid. Every student is evaluated for significant merit-based scholarships upon admission. Our highest undergraduate academic honor, the Camras Scholars Program, challenges the top 1% of our applicant pool to apply and interview with a faculty member for a place as a Camras Scholar. Chosen Camras Scholars are awarded a full-tuition scholarship in their first-year and a $31,500 scholarship in subsequent three-years (four-years for Architecture majors). Special deadlines apply. ROTC and athletic scholarships are also available to qualified students. Students applying for need-based aid must submit the Free Application for Federal Student Aid (FAFSA).

APPLYING TO IIT

In our application review process, each student is considered on an individual and holistic basis by the Admissions Committee. Our counselors and faculty evaluate not only academic standing, but also extracurricular, social, and community-based activities and leadership. We want to know a student's future goals—whether specific or broad. Overall, we seek to enroll students whose diverse intellectual and professional interests will enable them to make full use of the resources available to them at IIT. We may be just the right school for students who share our goals of innovation and integrity as part of their academic and professional interests. We encourage students to meet one of our Early Decision or Early Action deadlines. Special application deadlines do apply for the College of Architecture, special programs, and some scholarships (see admission.iit.edu for details) We start accepting applications in July of 2010 and will continue to accept them beyond the academic year.

CONTACT US

Office of Undergraduate Admission

10 West 33rd Street, Perlstein hall Room 101

Chicago, Illinois 60616

312.567.3025

800.448.2329 (toll free)

admission.iit.edu

admission@iit.edu

Illinois Institute of Technology is accredited by the Higher Learning Commission of the North Central Association of Colleges and Schools. http://www.ncahigher-learningcommission.org/

It is the intention of Illinois Institute of Technology to act in accordance with all regulations of the federal, state, and local governments with respect to providing equality of opportunity in employment and in education, insofar as those regulations may pertain to IIT. IIT prohibits and will act to eliminate discrimination on the basis of race, color, religion, national origin, gender, sexual orientation, age, disability, or veteran status.

Illinois Institute of Technology provides individuals with disabilities reasonable accommodations to participate in university activities, programs and services. Individuals with disabilities requiring an accommodation to participate in an activity, program or service should call the activity, program or service director. disabilities@iit.edu

IMMACULATA UNIVERSITY

Immaculata University is a Catholic, coeducational, comprehensive liberal arts university dedicated to educating students of all faiths. Approximately 1000 men and women attend the College of Undergraduate Studies. The University is located 20 miles west of Philadelphia.

AT A GLANCE

Immaculata University is a comprehensive Catholic liberal arts institution serving men and women of all ages through the College of Undergraduate Studies, the College of Lifelong Learning, and the College of Graduate Studies. Founded originally as Villa Maria College, the institution was granted a college charter in 1920, making it the first Catholic college for women in the Philadelphia area. In 1929, the name was formally changed to Immaculata College.

Immaculata's origins date from 1906 when the Sisters, Servants of the Immaculate Heart of Mary, purchased the present site in Chester County from seven farmers and the Pennsylvania Railroad. The initial 198 campus acres have grown to approximately 375 today, while the two original residence hall-classroom structures are now part of a complex of 13 principal buildings, representing a multi-million dollar investment. Off-campus sites and online courses extend geographic range and scope of the University.

In June 2002, Immaculata College received confirmation of university status from the Pennsylvania Department of Education and is now known as Immaculata University.

LOCATION AND ENVIRONMENT

Approximately 1,000 traditional-age men and women attend the College of Undergraduate Studies, with 90 percent of them living in University-sponsored housing. The College of Lifelong Learning includes undergraduate programs that are open to adult men and women. Students represent seventeen states and seventeen countries, giving the campus both ethnic and geographic diversity. Resident students live in four residence halls containing double rooms.

The main building, Villa Maria Hall, is of neo-Renaissance architecture in gray stone with a red tile roof. The other thirteen major campus buildings are also of gray stone with red tile roofs, unifying the aesthetic appearance of the campus.

Immaculata's 375-acre campus is located in historic Chester County, 20 miles west of Philadelphia and 10 miles south of Valley Forge.

OFF-CAMPUS OPPORTUNITIES

The area is primarily suburban, with numerous colleges and universities offering a wide range of cultural and social activities. Many places of interest in Philadelphia and Lancaster are easily reached by car, train, or bus. The campus is 15 minutes from the King of Prussia Mall, the second largest mall in the U.S. Southern New Jersey shore resorts and New York City are within 1½ hours by car, with Pocono Mountain ski resorts and Washington, D.C., only 2½ hours away by car or train. The University provides numerous opportunities for internships in the business, educational, and scientific communities throughout the area.

MAJORS AND DEGREES OFFERED

The College of Undergraduate Studies at Immaculata offers the Bachelor of Arts, Bachelor of Music, Bachelor of Science, Associate of Arts, and Associate of Science degrees. Undergraduate major fields of study include accounting, allied health, biology, biology/psychology, business administration, chemistry, communication, criminology/sociology, education, English, exercise science, family and consumer sciences, fashion merchandising, finance, food service management, French, general science, health-care management, history, information technology, international business/foreign language, marketing management, mathematics, mathematics/computer science, music, music education, music therapy, nursing, nutrition/dietetics, political science/international relations, prelaw, pre-medicine, pre–physical therapy, pre–veterinary medicine, psychology, sociology, sociology/social work, Spanish, Spanish/psychology, Spanish/social work, and theology. Allied health concentrations include: clinical laboratory science, diagnostic medical sonography, invasive cardiovascular technology, nuclear medicine technology, and surgical technology. IU also offers partnership programs with Thomas Jefferson University (TJU) in physical therapy, occupational therapy, bioscience technologies, radiologic sciences. These programs allow students to seamlessly matriculate into TJU after three years of study at IU.

ACADEMIC PROGRAMS

Two factors are emphasized in the educational program at Immaculata: a comprehensive liberal arts background and a major field of concentration that prepares students to begin a career or to attend graduate school. The honors program, an option for gifted students, offers an array of courses designed to give those who participate a special involvement in the learning process.

The Mary Bruder Center houses the offices for personal, career, and graduate study counseling and for educational and career testing. Workshops and seminars in resume writing, interviewing, career options, internship opportunities, and graduate fellowships are offered at regular intervals.

Both summer-abroad and junior-year-abroad programs combine travel with academic study to heighten the experience of students who seek these opportunities.

Every undergraduate major department offers numerous internship opportunities for students in agencies, businesses, institutions, or corporations related to their study. Some majors, such as nutrition, fashion merchandising, and music therapy require a multi-week internship for the degree to be granted.

CAMPUS FACILITIES AND EQUIPMENT

The Gabriele Library houses 130,000 volumes and offers 714 periodical subscriptions. In addition to the computer center, students have access to networked computers in the library, an interactive language lab with a video screen, and a multifaceted science lab with computer-simulated experiments; they also have Internet/Intranet access from their residence halls. Well-equipped laboratories, art studios, media centers, and a 1,150-seat theater give students a variety of settings in which to pursue their interests.

State-of-the-art computer labs include the Campus Learning and Language Laboratory, the Sister Maria Socorro Studio Laboratory for Mathematics and Science, a new Biology Laboratory, and the Loyola Executive Technology Center. Classrooms and the library utilize wireless technology in the smart classrooms.

TUITION, ROOM, BOARD, AND FEES

For 2009–10, tuition and fees are $26,540 and room and board are $10,920. An additional $1,000 is estimated to cover books and personal spending. A fixed tuition rate is currently in place. This guarantees the same tuition cost for a maximum of four years for all full-time students entering the College of Undergraduate Studies.

FINANCIAL AID

Financial aid is available in the form of scholarships, grants, loans, and part-time campus employment through the resources of Immaculata, federal and state governments, and private endowments. Scholarships are awarded for academic excellence. Approximately 90 percent of the students receive some form of aid, and all students who demonstrate need are offered financial aid packages. The University requires that students submit the Free Application for Federal Student Aid (FAFSA) to be considered for financial aid. The University sends financial aid packages to accepted students as their files are completed by the middle of March. The FAFSA reporting code is 003276.

STUDENT ORGANIZATIONS AND ACTIVITIES

Both resident and nonresident students participate in more than fifty student clubs and organizations that represent interests in athletics, student government, academic disciplines, community action, music, dance, theater, and student publications.

The Student Association of Immaculata University (SAIU) governs most aspects of student life for both resident and commuter students. The resident assistant program moderates residence life by holding open meetings to discuss safety issues and to set residence hall regulations. Students serve on the various University policymaking committees and handle all student activity funds. The Student Association of Immaculata University provides the unity, enthusiasm, and leadership that are integral parts of the traditional undergraduate experience.

Immaculata University celebrates unique traditions as a part of the overall collegiate experience, such as Freshman Investiture, the academic capping of the newest members of the University community. Carol Night, one of Immaculata's best-loved traditions, involves students, faculty members, alumni, and families singing around the Christmas tree in the rotunda of Villa Maria Hall.

Intercollegiate sports include women's basketball, cross-country, field hockey, golf, lacrosse, soccer, softball, tennis, and volleyball and men's baseball, basketball, cross-country, golf, lacrosse, soccer, tennis and baseball. Immaculata competes in Division III athletics as part of the Colonial Athletic Conference. A new turf field, stadium, gymnasia, fitness room, and pool are available for student use and provide numerous opportunities for physical activities and wellness programs.

ADMISSIONS PROCESS

Applications are accepted from prospective freshman and transfer students on a rolling admissions basis, and decisions are made three to four weeks after an applicant's file is complete.

In order to be considered for admission to the College of Undergraduate Studies, students must submit an official secondary school transcript indicating course selection for the senior year and SAT or ACT scores. The reporting code for the SAT is 2320, and the reporting code for the ACT is 3596. An essay and recommendations are required. The Admission Committee requires 14 or more course units, as follows: 4 units of English, 2 units of social science, 2 units of mathematics, 2 units of science (1 lab), and 2 consecutive years of the same foreign language. Most candidates exceed this curriculum. The mid-range GPA for the past two years was 3.2.

Transfer students are required to submit official college transcripts and high school transcript (if less than 24 transferable credits).

All admission credentials should be sent to the College of Undergraduate Studies. Students can apply online at the University's website. Students also have the option to apply through the Common Application. The application fee is waived for students who apply prior to December 15 or who visit the campus and complete an application during their visit.

IONA COLLEGE

AT A GLANCE

Located on 35 acres in suburban New Rochelle, NY, Iona was founded by the Congregation of Christian Brothers in 1940. Iona has approximately 3,500 undergraduate students and 4,500 total students. There are five residence halls on the main campus; an additional non-residential campus houses the Rockland Graduate Center in Pearl River, NY. As part of the College's mission statement, students are encouraged to integrate the spiritual, intellectual, emotional and physical dimensions of their lives and are immersed in a community where ethical decisions and service to others are primary considerations. Iona is one of the only colleges in the region to hold several prestigious national accreditations in business (AACSB), social work (CSWE), teacher education (NCATE), computer science (ABET), journalism and mass communication (ACEJMC), psychology (NASP) and marriage and family therapy (COAMFTE).

ACADEMICS

Iona College offers BA, BS and BBA degrees for undergraduate students. The Bachelor of Arts and Bachelor of Science degrees require a total of 120 credits for completion for most majors; the Bachelor of Business Administration requires a total of 126 credits. An honors program is available for the most academically gifted students—the course of study is designed to develop intellectual curiosity, analytic abilities, and awareness of ethical and civic responsibilities. The faculty/student ratio is 13:1 and classes are taught by professors, never teaching assistants. Combined five-year bachelor's/master's programs are available in computer science, criminal justice, English, history, psychology and computational/computer science. On the graduate level, the College offers Master of Arts, Science and Business Administration degrees, as well as certificates, and post-master's/advanced certificates. Graduate students in the School of Arts and Science can choose to study computer science, counseling (substance abuse, mental health, marriage and family therapy), criminal justice, education, educational technology, English, finance, history, Italian, psychology, public relations, Spanish, and telecommunications. Through the AACSB-accredited Hagan School of Business, students seeking to earn an MBA can concentrate on financial management, information systems, management, human resource management, marketing, general accounting, public accounting and health care management. A fast-track MBA program is structured to enable students to earn the degree in 13- 15 months. Advanced certificates in business continuity and risk management, sports and entertainment management, infrastructure management, e-commerce and international business are offered. Part-time and adult students returning to college can pursue a bachelor's degree in Professional Studies (BPS), through the Professional Studies Program.

ADMISSIONS

Admission decisions at Iona are based on a wide range of criteria. Most important is an applicant's academic record, including the level of curriculum and grades earned. Also considered are SAT I or ACT scores, grade trends, a writing sample, activities and recommendations. For the class entering in September of 2009, the average grade point average was an 89 percent or 3.4; middle 50 percent on the SAT ranged from 1080 to 1300. Slightly over 7,300 applications were submitted and about 4,300 (59%) of the applications were accepted and offered admission. Campus visits are available on most weekdays classes are in session and on selected Saturdays; appointments are recommended. To schedule a visit, please contact our Campus Visit Center at (914) 633-2622 or email eenglish@iona.edu.

CAMPUS FACILITIES AND EQUIPMENT

In recent-years, Iona College has undertaken an ambitious multi-million renovation and building campaign that has transformed the campus. A newly-expanded and renovated main library (with multimedia seminar room, group study facilities, digital archive room, classrooms with dual-boot Apple computers, Smartboards and other interactive equipment and refurbished auditorium) opened in fall 2009. The Hynes Athletics Center saw new construction and updates (modern workout equipment, an aerobic/dance studio, a pool, rowing tank and more. New residence halls, arts center and student union (with a radio station, extensive room for clubs, comfortable lounges, bookstore, a food court and café) complete the changes. A new residence hall, to accommodate the growing demands of students from outside the region, is proposed for 2012.

CAMPUS LIFE

The Office of Student Development organizes and oversees hundreds of on and off-campus events throughout the year, and students can participate in more than 60 student-run organizations. Iona College encourages students to broaden their educational experience through study abroad; it sponsors summer, semester, and intersession programs in Australia, England, France, Ireland, Italy and Spain. Campus Ministries provides multiple opportunities for students to engage in service and ministry projects, while Iona in Mission offers students the chance to travel to aid the less fortunate in the US and abroad. The College has a vibrant athletics program with more than 400 student-athletes in Iona's 21 NCAA Division I teams in the Metro Atlantic Athletic Conference (MAAC). The men's cross country team placed second in the nation at the NCAA championship for the third consecutive year.

COLLEGE BASICS

Iona College is a diverse community of learners and scholars dedicated to academic excellence in the tradition of the Christian Brothers and American Catholic Higher Education. The College is currently listed in Tier 1 in "America's Best Colleges" 2010 (category- Master's Universities in the North), *U.S. News & World Report;* "A Best Business School"—*BusinessWeek;* "A Best Northeaster College" 2010—The Princeton Review and more.

LOCATION AND ENVIRONMENT

Iona is located just 20 minutes north of Manhattan. Its proximity to New York City provides students with exceptional cultural, educational, internship and career opportunities. Recruiters from top Fortune 500 companies participate in Iona's Internship/Career Expo every year, and students have held internships at some of the best-known corporations in New York City and the surrounding area.

MAJORS AND DEGREES

Iona College offers over 40 majors and minors including accounting, biochemistry, biology (general, pre-professional), business administration, chemistry, computer science, criminal justice, economics, education (childhood, adolescence), English, environmental science, finance, foreign languages (French, Italian, Spanish), history, information systems, interdisciplinary studies, science, international business, international studies, management, marketing, mass communication (advertising, journalism, public relations, TV/video), mathematics and applied mathematics, medical technology, philosophy, physics, political science, psychology, religious studies, social work, sociology, speech communication studies, and speech/language pathology and audiology. Five-year combined bachelor's and master's degree programs are offered in computer science, English, history, and psychology. Additional minors include film studies, fine and performing arts, peace and justice studies, pre-law, sports and entertainment studies, women's studies, and writing. A number of programs offer a business minor.

OFF CAMPUS OPPORTUNITIES

With the creation of the Office of Off-Campus Housing, programs have been created to involve and inform neighbors about student's initiatives and events. The Center for Campus Ministries actively seeks student involvement for its outreach programs such as partnerships with Habitat for Humanity, Project Sunshine, Midnight Runs and more. Students are encouraged to attend events in nearby New York City where internship opportunities also abound.

TUITION AND FEES

Undergraduate tuition for the 2010–11 academic year is $28,850. Room and board is an additional $12,100.

FINANCIAL AID

Iona uses a system of academic scholarships in combination with need-based financial aid to help students enroll. For 2009–10 academic year, 94% of undergraduates received some financial aid, with the average aid award near $21,751. To apply for financial aid, students should file the Free Application for Federal Student Aid (FAFSA) and the Iona College Financial Aid Application forms.

ITHACA COLLEGE

AT A GLANCE

Ithaca's vibrant, residential campus overlooks Cayuga Lake and is home to 6,400 undergraduate students. As a nationally recognized comprehensive institution, Ithaca offers an excellent foundation in the liberal arts as well as strong professional programs at the undergraduate level. Moreover, all of our degree programs are supplemented by options for independent and interdisciplinary studies, dual majors, minors, and elective courses in other academic fields.

Nearly every state and 80 countries are represented in the undergraduate student population; 2,750 men and 3,650 women are currently enrolled. Some 500 additional students are enrolled in graduate programs.

Founded in 1892 as the Ithaca Conservatory of Music, the school eventually grew into a private college, offering academic programs in several professional fields. At mid-century the institutions curricula in liberal arts were unified, and the large and diversified School of Humanities and Sciences now forms the core of the Ithaca educational experience.

In the 1960s the College moved from downtown Ithaca to its current home on South Hill. Here, the College's 650 acres command a majestic vista of the city of Ithaca and Cayuga Lake.

ACADEMICS

Located in the heart of New York State's Finger Lakes region in one of the nation's top college towns, Ithaca College offers a first-rate education on a first-name basis. With nearly 100 academic programs, an intimate student-faculty ratio of 12 to 1 and a focus on active learning and involvement, it's the perfect place to prepare for a lifetime of success.

Whether you know exactly what you want to do after graduation or need to explore your options, Ithaca has a program to suit you. In our Schools of Business, Communications, Health Sciences and Human Performance, Humanities and Sciences, and Music and the Division of Interdisciplinary and International Studies, we combine the breadth of a university with the intimate feel of a college.

First-year students from all areas of the College can choose from among several special seminar-style classes that combine rigorous study with transition-to-college topics.

Our AACSB-accredited School of Business offers a wide range of courses covering the world of business. From our new sustainably designed business school building to the real-time stock ticker in our trading room, you'll have the tools at your fingertips to shape a successful start to your career.

Our renowned Park School of Communications begins training future professionals from day one. Students manage the College's television station, two radio stations, two campus magazines, and a weekly newspaper—all of which consistently win top honors from regional and national professional organizations.

Students in our School of Music are part of one of the nation's most highly regarded music programs. From your first year at Ithaca, you'll be learning from the best and performing on a regular basis in our modern recital halls. Ithaca ensembles regularly perform at regional, national, and international venues, as well.

Other popular options include our five-year B.S./M.S. program in occupational therapy and six-year B.S./D.P.T. program in physical therapy, each leading to professional certification; our one-year MBA program; New York State teacher certification programs in more than a dozen fields; and joint agreements with other schools that provide opportunities to study engineering or optometry.

Are you still undecided? Our Exploratory Program allows you to sample classes from all of the schools before deciding on a major. And if your interests are not encapsulated by a single major, you can turn to our planned studies program, which gives you the opportunity to combine several academic areas into a customized program that suits you.

An Ithaca education emphasizes real-world learning in the classroom and beyond. Our students gain valuable experience in a variety of settings, including on-campus labs and clinics, through original faculty-student research projects, and via a nationwide internship network that accommodates students of all majors. That focus pays off; surveys show that 97 percent of our alumni find employment and/or attend graduate school within a year of graduation.

ADMISSIONS

Admission to Ithaca College is based on high school record, personal recommendations, SAT or ACT scores, and, for some programs, an audition or portfolio is required. Admission is selective and competitive; individual talents and circumstances are always given serious consideration by the admission committee. On average, some 12,900 men and women apply for 1,500 places in the freshman class; applicants are notified of their status as soon as possible after all admission materials are received. We advise you to submit your application early in your senior year of high school and no later than February 1. Early decision applicants must submit materials no later than November 1. Ithaca College accepts the Common Application; contact the Office of Admission or your high school guidance office for more information or visit www.commonapp.org. Applicants will receive a decision no later than December 15 for early decision and April 15 for regular decision. Students offered admission are asked to respond by May 1, the candidate reply date established by the College Board.

Transfer applicants generally follow the same admission procedures as freshmen. Applications for fall admission should be submitted by March 1; applications for spring admission should be submitted by November 1.

CAMPUS LIFE

Ithaca's campus life is sparked by some 150 student organizations, 26 intercollegiate sports teams, and hundreds of lectures, film screenings, and other events. Each year, dozens of distinguished guests and alumni give lectures and performances, teach master classes, and share their perspectives and professional expertise. Our NCAA Division III teams enjoy frequent success: they hold 15 national titles in football (3), women's soccer (2), women's crew (2), wrestling (3), baseball (2), field hockey, softball, and gymnastics. Music and theater performances by students are frequent, and national acts visit campus often; recently the Mountain Goats, Something Corporate, and Mae performed here.

LOCATION AND ENVIRONMENT

Ithaca is located in the center of upstate New York's Finger Lakes region; approximately 100,000 people live in the surrounding county. Major air and bus lines serve the city, which is about 60 miles south of Syracuse, 60 miles north of Binghamton, and an hour's flight from New York City.

MAJORS AND DEGREES

Ithaca College offers more than 2,000 courses and more than 100 degree programs and confers the bachelor of arts, bachelor of science, bachelor of fine arts, bachelor of music, master of business administration, master of science, master of music, master of arts in teaching, and doctor of physical therapy degrees.

OFF CAMPUS OPPORTUNITIES

You'll have access to extensive opportunities for internships in business, communications, music, athletic training, speech-language pathology, health policy studies, community health education, humanities, natural sciences, and more. If you attend the School of Communications, you might apply to spend a semester at our communications program in Los Angeles. Ready access to internships and industry experts make this program a fast-paced working and learning experience. Any student may apply to our internship-focused program in Washington, D.C.

Study abroad is also popular. Programs are available at the College's own London Center or through our study centers and exchange programs in Singapore, Sweden, Spain, the Czech Republic, Japan, and elsewhere. There are also opportunities for study at some 50 affiliated programs throughout the world.

JOHNS HOPKINS UNIVERSITY

COLLEGE BASICS

The Johns Hopkins undergraduate experience is all about exploration and discovery.

AT A GLANCE

Ever since its founding in 1876, Johns Hopkins has made the undergraduate experience all about exploration and discovery. We believe in learning through independent inquiry for anyone in any major. Our students work in every discipline and with every subject imaginable, from Beowulf to bioengineering. And they do it all with the resources of Baltimore and Washington, D.C., at their fingertips, from the comfort of an active and close-knit campus community. You'll have the opportunity to make your own discoveries and the guidance you need to get there: in groups; through faculty mentorships; and through internships, study abroad, and the cultural connections of one of the most exciting cities around.

ACADEMICS

Classes are small here, and the resources are big. That means you get to know your professors and classmates the way you would at a small liberal arts college, but you have all of the opportunities of a major research institution with a global reach, right at your fingertips as an undergraduate. Many students complete independent projects with professors, mentors, and teams. Lots more take advantage of study abroad, internships, semesters in Washington, D.C., and advanced graduate study. Johns Hopkins has schools, centers, and affiliates all over the Baltimore/Washington, D.C., area—often linked by free shuttle bus—and across the country and around the world. Cross registration, independent projects, and internships are all encouraged options. Several generous awards—such as the Provost's Undergraduate Research Awards and the Woodrow Wilson Undergraduate Research Fellowships—are available to give participants the chance to complete projects of their own design under the guidance of a faculty mentor. Instead of a rigid core of compulsory courses, Johns Hopkins leaves you free to concentrate on what you love, or to explore more broadly. Academic and faculty advisers, career advisers, and pre-professional advisers help you chart the waters.

ADMISSIONS

Each year we review more than 16,000 applications, from which we must select a freshman class of around 1,250. Also each year, transfer students from other colleges and universities apply for entrance during their sophomore or junior years. Each application we receive represents an individual, and the Admissions Committee considers each one individually. High school students should inquire by the fall term of senior year and complete and submit applications by January 1 (by November 1 for Early Decision). We accept both the Universal College Application and the Common Application; both require a Johns Hopkins supplement. To apply, complete Part I of the application and submit it as soon as possible, but no later than the deadline, with your $70 nonrefundable application fee. This will open your application file. Supporting materials may be received at any time up until the application deadline. Two essays and teacher recommendations are also required parts of the application. Visit http://apply.jhu.edu/apply/apply.html for detailed information about the application process.

PLEASE NOTE this important policy: Students wishing to enroll in the biomedical engineering (BME) major must indicate BME as their first-choice major on their application. Students are admitted specifically into the BME major, based on evaluation of credentials and space available. Students can be admitted to the university without acceptance to the BME major. No separate application is required. Notification of acceptance into the BME major is given at the time of decision notification. A limited number of transfer majors for matriculated students may be available through the Biomedical Engineering Department at the close of each academic year.

STANDARDIZED TEST REQUIREMENTS

Applicants must submit scores from all SAT tests, including Subject Tests, or ACT tests taken. For freshman, the SAT Reasoning Test or the ACT with Writing Test are required. For those submitting SAT scores, Johns Hopkins recommends submitting SAT Subject Test scores, and if submitted, requests results from three tests. For transfer students, SAT Reasoning Test scores are optional; SAT Subject Tests are not required. For international students, the TOEFL is required of applicants whose native language is not English and who attend a non-English-speaking high school. If you attend an English-language school but do not speak English at home, you should take the TOEFL. If your native language is not English and you attend high school in the U.S., you must take the TOEFL if you have been here for fewer than five years. A minimum score of 600 on the written test is preferred. The preferred sub-scores for the Internet-based TOEFL (iBT) are 26 (Reading), 26 (Listening), 22 (Writing), and 25 (Speaking). A Critical Reading SAT score of 670 or higher may be substituted for the TOEFL.

CAMPUS FACILITIES AND EQUIPMENT

Student life is centered around the 140 acres of Homewood campus. A park-like setting within the city of Baltimore, our campus has had many renovations in recent years. The Mattin Center offers space for student groups and artistic endeavors. The center features a theater, café, art studios, darkrooms, music practice rooms, dance studios, the Digital Media Center, multipurpose rooms, and meeting spaces. The Ralph S. O'Connor Recreation Center, open for use by all students, houses basketball and volleyball courts, a rock-climbing wall, a weight room, and fitness training and aerobics areas, as well as access to the Athletic Center's swimming facilities. Popular fitness classes include yoga, pilates, kickboxing, step aerobics, spinning, West African dance, sports conditioning, and, believe it or not, Ballet for Jocks. Charles Commons, a two-building residential complex, features suites with single rooms, kitchenettes, and in many cases, living rooms. The complex is also home to a number of student amenities and common areas. Our campus is also home to many academic resources, including the Baltimore Museum of Art, the Homewood Museum, a world-class archaeological collection, and the six-story Milton S. Eisenhower Library that contains nearly 3 million books.

CAMPUS LIFE

There are at least 325 student groups and organizations on campus. All Johns Hopkins student groups are governed and managed by students, and there is literally something for everybody, from theater and performing arts groups, to political, special interest, and cultural groups, to publications, student government, and religious groups. Published since 1896, the News-Letter is one of the oldest student papers in the country, and it's where Pulitzer Prize-winning journalist Russell Baker got his start. In 122 years of competition, the men's lacrosse team has won 44 national championships, including the 2005 and 2007 NCAA Division I National Championship, and twice represented the United States in the Olympic Games. For the past 10 years, the women's lacrosse team has also competed in Division I. Outside of lacrosse, one out of six Johns Hopkins students participates in Division III or club athletics, and more than half participate in the popular intramural program.

TUITION AND FEES

Tuition: $39,150

Room and Board: $12,040°

Matriculation Fee: $500 (onetime fee only)

Books and Supplies: $1,200 (estimated)

Personal Expenses: $1,000 (estimated)

°In a typical room with a 14-meal/Dining Dollars plan

JOHNSON & WALES UNIVERSITY

AT A GLANCE

Founded in Providence in 1914, Johnson & Wales University (JWU) is a private, career-oriented institution. The University's 16,000 students attend classes at campuses in Providence, R.I.; North Miami, Fla.; Denver, Colo., and Charlotte, N. C. Most are recent graduates of high school business, college-preparatory, and vocational/technical programs, representing 50 states and 96 countries. The university's 475 full-time and 242 part-time undergraduate faculty members (all campuses) are oriented toward instruction rather than research. Many are chosen for their professional experience in business, culinary arts, hospitality services, or technology. The student-faculty ratio university wide is 28:1. The academic focus of the university is on degree programs in business, culinary arts, hospitality and technology. M.B.A. programs include global business leadership (with a concentration in accounting, financial management, international trade, organizational leadership, or marketing) and hospitality & tourism global business leadership (with concentrations in finance and marketing). M.A. programs in teaching include business, food service, and Special Ed. The university also offers a doctoral program in educational leadership. The university maintains 24 residence halls throughout its four campuses. Student services include academic counseling and testing, a tutorial center, and health services. The university's Experiential Education & Career Services Office provides extensive career planning and placement services. Our 80,000 alumni from 140 countries pursue careers around the world. . Johnson & Wales is accredited by the New England Association of Schools and Colleges. The hospitality programs in Providence are accredited by the Accreditation Commission for Programs in Hospitality Administration.

LOCATION AND ENVIRONMENT

The location of each of the university's campuses enables students to take advantage of a variety of internship and part-time work activities. The urban setting of the Providence Campus provides students proximity to the city's many cultural and recreational facilities. The North Miami Campus is a short trip from the sun and fun of Fort Lauderdale and the culture and diversity of Miami. The Denver Campus offers students great opportunities as Fortune magazine's "second best city in America to work and live." The Charlotte Campus is located in a vibrant urban setting that combines commercial and residential life. More than three hundred Fortune 500 companies have offices in Charlotte, which is known as the second largest financial center in the U.S.

OFF-CAMPUS OPPORTUNITIES

Many of our majors offer internships at university-owned facilities to expand learning beyond the classroom. The hotel and restaurant management programs feature an internship at the Johnson & Wales Inn, Radisson Airport Hotel, or the DoubleTree Hotel; all are full-service hotel complexes owned and/or operated by the university (the Radisson and DoubleTree are corporate franchises). For all majors optional selective career internships are available throughout the U.S. and worldwide, such as Marriott International; Hyatt Regency Hotels; Food Network; Foxwoods Resort and Casino; and Putnam Investments. Most internships are one term in duration and carry 13.5 quarter hours of credit. Study abroad programs are also offered.

MAJORS AND DEGREES OFFERED

The degree programs described below are for the 2010–2011 academic year and are subject to change. Students may pursue concentrations related to their program of study to further tailor their degrees to their specific interests and career goals. They also have the opportunity to take concentrations through the School of Arts & Sciences.

Johnson & Wales University's Providence Campus offers degree programs in accounting, creative advertising, strategic advertising, marketing , baking and pastry arts, business administration, business/information systems analysis, graphic design and digital media, criminal justice, culinary arts, culinary arts and food service management, culinary nutrition, electronics engineering, engineering design and configuration management, entrepreneurship, equine business management, equine business management/riding, fashion merchandising and retail marketing, finance, food service entrepreneurship, hotel and lodging management, international business, international hotel and tourism management, management, marketing, network engineering, baking & pastry arts and food service management, restaurant, food and beverage management, software engineering, sports/entertainment/event management, technology services management and travel, tourism and hospitality management.

In its Continuing Education division, JWU's Providence Campus offers associate and bachelor degrees in business, culinary arts, hospitality and technology.

The North Miami Campus offers degree programs in baking and pastry arts, business administration, criminal justice, culinary arts, culinary arts and food service management, fashion merchandising and retail marketing, hotel and lodging management, management, marketing, pastry arts and food service management, restaurant, food and beverage management, sports/entertainment/event management, and travel, tourism and hospitality management.

The Denver Campus offers degree programs in advertising and marketing communications, baking and pastry arts, business administration, criminal justice, culinary arts, culinary arts and food service management, culinary nutrition, entrepreneurship, fashion merchandising and retail marketing, hotel and lodging management, international business, management, marketing, baking & pastry arts and food service management, restaurant, food and beverage management, and sports/entertainment/event management.

The Charlotte Campus offers degree programs in accounting, baking and pastry arts, business administration, culinary arts, culinary arts and food service management, fashion merchandising and retail marketing, hotel and lodging management, international hotel and tourism management, management, marketing, baking & pastry arts and food service management, restaurant, food and beverage management, and sports/entertainment/event management.

ACADEMIC PROGRAMS

Johnson & Wales University offers its programs within an academic structure of three 11-week terms. The university's "upside-down" curriculum provides immediate focus in the student's chosen major. Many programs include laboratory studies as well as formal internship requirements. Special advanced placement programs are featured for high school seniors with exceptional skills in culinary arts or baking and pastry arts. In addition, the university awards credit for certain courses based on the successful completion of Challenge, CLEP or Portfolio Assessments. All degree candidates must successfully complete the required number of courses and/or quarter credit hours, as prescribed in the various curricula, with a minimum average of 2.0 or higher, depending on the program.

CAMPUS FACILITIES AND EQUIPMENT

The facilities of the Providence Campus are located throughout the intimate state of Rhode Island and in nearby Massachusetts. The Downcity Campus is home to the university's College of Business, The Hospitality College, and the School of Technology. The Harborside Campus, located nearby in Providence, houses the university's College of Culinary Arts. This campus has five student residence halls as well as classrooms and laboratories, production kitchens, bakeshops, dining rooms, a storeroom, and meat-cutting facilities. This campus is also home to the Alan Shawn Feinstein Graduate School and the School of Education. Other facilities at this campus include the University Recreation and Athletic Center and a dining center. In Florida, the campus is located in the heart of North Miami, between Miami and Ft. Lauderdale. Facilities include classrooms, production/demonstration kitchens, a bakeshop, residence halls and a conference center. The Denver Campus, located in the Park Hill neighborhood, combines stately turn-of-the-century buildings and newer student centers in a quiet park landscape. The campus has computers in every classroom and laboratory. The Charlotte Campus is located in the heart of Gateway Village in Uptown Charlotte. The academic center is home to a 200-seat auditorium with a production kitchen; top-of-the-line culinary laboratories, classrooms, seminar rooms and computer labs. A 750-bed student residence center with dining facilities is located within walking distance of the academic building.

TUITION, ROOM, BOARD AND FEES

Tuition at all campuses for 2009–2010 is $22,149. Basic room and board plans range from $8,274 to $10,383. There is also a general fee of $1,065 charged to all students, and an orientation fee of $276 for new students. Books and supplies are estimated at $800–$900 per year, depending upon the program. Room and board fees may vary at each campus.

FINANCIAL AID

Johnson & Wales students are eligible to apply for a variety of financial aid programs, including Federal programs, university-based student scholarship programs and state-supported grants and scholarships. In the past, approximately 90 percent of the university's entering students have received some sort of financial assistance. Students must submit the Free Application for Federal Student Aid (FAFSA) to the Federal Student Aid Processor after January 1 to be considered for financial aid. Early application is strongly suggested for full consideration.

STUDENT ORGANIZATIONS AND ACTIVITIES

Students are involved in a variety of extracurricular activities. Nearly 20 percent of the students at the university are members of national student organizations such Business Professionals of America, DECA, Future Business Leaders of America, Family, Career, Community Leaders of America, National FFA, SkillsUSA and TSA. The Student Activities office and fraternities and sororities are among the many groups that schedule social functions throughout the academic year. Sports and fitness programs include aerobics, baseball, basketball, sailing, soccer, tennis, golf, wrestling, ice hockey, and volleyball.

ADMISSIONS PROCESS

Johnson & Wales University prepares driven students who are seeking a competitive advantage in the global economy.. Academic qualifications are important, but an applicant's motivation and interest in doing well are given special consideration. Graduation from high school or equivalent credentials are required for admission. It is recommended that students applying for admission into the culinary arts and baking & pastry arts programs have some prior education or experience in food service. Although no tests are required for most programs, all applicants are encouraged to submit scores from the SAT or ACT. Students who wish to apply for the Honors Program must have either a score of at least 500 math and 500 critical reading on the SAT or a score of 21 math and 21 verbal on the ACT. High school juniors may apply for early admission under the Early Enrollment Program (EEP). Transfer students are required to submit official high school and college transcripts and to have a minimum GPA of 2.0 for most programs. Credits to be transferred from other institutions are evaluated on the basis of their equivalent at Johnson & Wales. Johnson & Wales does not require an application fee. After submitting the application, the student is responsible for requesting that appropriate transcripts be forwarded to the Admissions Office of the university. While there is no deadline, students are advised to apply as early as possible before the intended date of enrollment to ensure full consideration of their application. Applications are accepted for terms beginning in September, December, and March and for the summer sessions. Inquiries and applications should be addressed to: Kenneth DiSaia, Vice President of Enrollment Management, Johnson & Wales University, 8 Abbott Park Place, Providence, Rhode Island 02903. Telephone: 401-598-1000 1-800-DIAL-JWU (toll-free) Fax: 401-598-4901 E-mail: jwu@admissions.jwu.edu.

KETTERING UNIVERSITY

AT A GLANCE

Kettering University has taken college education and put a spin on it. Billed as "America's premiere co-op university" this college, based in Flint, Michigan, has more than 500 corporate partners, corporations, and agencies that employ Kettering's co-op students throughout hundreds of locations in North America, Europe, and Asia.

The philosophy of this fully accredited school is that students work while they earn their college education, and in essence, Kettering's corporate partners "grow their own" engineers, scientists and managers. The program is four and a half years long, with students' time split evenly between classroom training (in processes, products, corporate culture, and technology, with an emphasis in engineering, the sciences, and business) and paid full-time professional co-op work experience off-site.

Kettering's corporate partners represent major industries that include leaders in business innovation and manufacturing technology. The list of current co-op companies reads like an honor roll of America's top corporations, representing automotive, aerospace, medical, chemical, computer, plastics, and delivery systems industries—just to name a few. Graduates have the skills and experience to succeed in key executive leadership positions, as many have done. Year after year, almost all Kettering graduates have a full-time job offer or are accepted into a top graduate program by the time they receive their diploma.

LOCATION AND ENVIRONMENT

Flint is located in east-central Michigan, just 60 miles west of Lake Huron and the Canadian border, and 60 miles north of Detroit. Flint has approximately 115,000 residents and has a metropolitan area of 450,000. The College Cultural Center Complex is located j just one-and-a-half miles from campus and houses a museum, a performing arts auditorium, a planetarium, and the Flint Public Library. The proximity to outdoor activities, city culture, and Flint's own distinctive resources provides students with access to a wide range of activities and opportunities.

OFF-CAMPUS OPPORTUNITIES

More than half of a Kettering student's time is spent off campus, fulfilling professional co-op work requirements outside the Flint area. On average, students spend 11 academic semesters working for their co-op employer and nine academic semesters in the classroom. The corporations and agencies that employ Kettering students are located throughout North America, Europe and Asia. Approximately 70 percent of students work for a corporation located in their hometown, which allows them to live at home during the work experience portion of their education. On average, students earn between $40,000 and $65,000 over the entire professional co-op program.

MAJORS AND DEGREES OFFERED

The four and a half year professional cooperative education program allows students to earn designated Bachelor of Science degrees in:

APPLIED MATHEMATICS

APPLIED PHYSICS

BIOCHEMISTRY

BUSINESS ADMINISTRATION

CHEMICAL ENGINEERING

CHEMISTRY

COMPUTER ENGINEERING

COMPUTER SCIENCE

ELECTRICAL ENGINEERING

ENGINEERING PHYSICS

INDUSTRIAL ENGINEERING

MECHANICAL ENGINEERING

and a designated Bachelor of Art in

BUSINESS ADMINISTRATION

Kettering also offers more than 45 minors, concentrations, specialties, courses of study and dual degrees, in areas such as Fuel Cell, Applied Optics, Pre-Law, Computer Gaming and Data Security, and Pre-Med. Additionally, the school offers seven Master's Degrees, including an accredited MBA program. Please visit our website for more details on these programs.

ACADEMIC PROGRAMS

The unique structure of Kettering's program allows students to fulfill the academic requirements of 160 credit hours throughout a four and a half year period. This is completed over nine academic semesters and up to 11 co-op work semesters. Students also complete a capstone thesis project on behalf of their co-op employer during their senior year for credit toward the 160 required hours. The academic year consists of two 11-week academic terms on-campus in Flint and two 12-week academic terms working for the corporate employer; students alternate their time between Flint and the employer's site. On average, a freshman student who spends 24 weeks during the academic year working for the professional co-op employer earns $11,000.

CAMPUS FACILITIES AND EQUIPMENT

Kettering University opened its $42 million Mechanical Engineering & Chemistry Center in 2003. This state-of-the-art facility is loaded with hands-on learning laboratories such as automotive labs with several unique test cells and the most advanced chemistry labs around! Engineering and chemistry facilities of this caliber are usually found only in graduate-level programs.

The Academic Building houses more classrooms, laboratories, and department offices. More than 100,000 square feet of this facility is dedicated to labs, which are stocked with equipment to demonstrate and experiment with methods in the engineering industry, from basic machining to emerging technologies. The entire campus, including residence hall rooms, campus apartments, and labs, is networked, providing each student with 24-hour access to computer resources and the Internet.

The library contains more than 118,000 volumes, more than 390 periodicals, and various online services. Special facilities include a microfilm area, database search services, record and tape listening- and videotape viewing-facilities, and a special collection of SAE, SME, and ASME technical papers.

TUITION, ROOM, BOARD AND FEES*

Tuition for the 2009–2010 academic year: $27,584

Room Rate: $4,000

Board, including 19 meals per week: $2,390

Technology Fee: $200

Student Activity Fee: $224

Residence Hall Activity Fee: $24

Orientation Fee (one-time only): $150

*Please remember that tuition and fees are subject to change at any time.

FINANCIAL AID

Kettering University offers all the traditional need and merit-based financial aid, including a generous merit scholarship program. All Kettering students also benefit from the substantial co-op salaries that they earn throughout their years in school. The average range of salaries over the entire period is from $40,000 to $65,000. About 70 percent of students are able to live at home during their work experience terms, and are then able to contribute more of their salaries to their educational expenses. Many students win scholarships from agencies and organizations from their local communities. The primary purpose of Kettering's financial aid program is to supplement students' financial need after co-op earnings and parents' contributions. Aid is given as grants, scholarships, loans, and work-study awards. Students who wish to apply for financial aid should complete the FAFSA.

STUDENT ORGANIZATIONS AND ACTIVITIES

Kettering students enjoy the activities and participate in the organizations that make college exciting and unique.

College is a place to get to know people, and to make contacts students will have throughout their professional lives. Students can make these vital connections at Kettering University by participating in one of the more than 50 clubs and organizations represented on campus. Whatever their social or professional interests, there are opportunities to work together with other students who share those interests, planning and organizing activities, and perfecting essential leadership and teamwork skills.

Outside of class, students will find plenty of ways to enjoy their free time at Kettering. The following list represents just a few of Kettering's many clubs and organizations:

Firebirds (autocross club), Student Government, International Club, Aquaneers (scuba diving club), Campus Crusade for Christ, Christians In Action (CIA), Cycling Club, Bulldog Band ,Outdoors Club, SADD, Tech Sailors, Hockey Club Karate Club Black Unity Congress, Political Awareness Club (PAC), Intramural Sports (including basketball, cross country, golf, soccer, swimming, tennis and volleyball) and Swing Club.

Kettering also has one of the largest student chapters of the Society of Automotive Engineers (SAE), and their Delta Epsilon Chi Chapter (college version of DECA) annually wins top awards in state and national competitions.

Students compete in an intense intramural athletic program and are involved in clubs and professional organizations. Approximately a third of Kettering students join the 14 national fraternities and six sororities that are represented on campus. The school's active student government produces programs to develop peers' leadership skills, self-confidence, interpersonal relations, and organizational operations. Because enrolled students represent approximately 48 states and 18 countries, they have a lot to share with and learn from one another.

ADMISSIONS PROCESS

Admission to Kettering University is competitive and based on scholastic achievement and extracurricular interests, activities, and achievements. Applicants are required to have completed the following courses (one credit represents two semesters or one year of study): two credits algebra, one credit geometry, a half credit trigonometry, two credits laboratory science (one of these credits must be from physics or chemistry, and both are strongly recommended), and three credits English. A minimum of 16 credits is required, but 20 credits are strongly encouraged. Applicants must submit SAT or ACT scores. Most Kettering University students rank at or near the top 10 percent of their high school class.

Although applications are accepted all year long, prospective students are encouraged to file their application early in their senior year. Early application significantly improves students' chances for early co-op employment. Kettering University also accepts transfer students. Admission decisions for transfer applicants are based on college records for those who have completed at least 30 credits. The Application fee is $35. Interested students can apply online at www.admissions.kettering.edu.

KEYSTONE COLLEGE

AT A GLANCE

Keystone College is a small, private college that serves students in the liberal arts tradition. Keystone College has a long history of serving students through progress. What began as Keystone Academy in 1868 has now become one of the most popular and most diverse institutions in northeastern Pennsylvania. Thousands of students have written their college stories at Keystone College, and for good reason! Keystone enhances every student's story through its unique pledge to graduates: "The Keystone Promise". This guarantee of success includes a promise in writing that within six months after graduating from Keystone and fulfilling the requirements of the Career Development Center, graduates will have received at least one job offer, or where appropriate, be accepted into a transfer or graduate program. In the event this does not occur, additional courses and career counseling are provided at no additional charge.

Also included in the Keystone College story is a personalized educational experience. With a 13:1 student-to-faculty ratio the College is able to ensure the individual attention that students deserve. Keystone offers a variety of opportunities for experiential learning. Students have completed internships for such organizations as Dateline NBC, the Philadelphia Eagles, the U.S. Secret Service, Late Night with Conan O'Brien, and the United States Olympic Committee. Students may also choose to take their studies or internships abroad. Recently, Keystone students have studied or worked in London, England; Prague, Czech Republic; Bangkok, India; Melbourne, Australia; Ireland; Spain; and Costa Rica. Hands-on learning is also available without stepping foot off campus. Among top-notch facilities for the visual arts, theatre, the sciences and technology are unique offerings like The Chef's Table, which is a student-run restaurant for culinary arts students; the Oppenheim Family Children's Center, a daycare and preschool where education students can train; and the campus's woodlands, streams, and ponds, which provide a natural classroom for students in environmental programs.

In addition to its commitment to its student body, Keystone College is fully dedicated to the protection of our environment. Through several green initiatives, the College has greatly reduced the size of the carbon footprint left behind by the campus. These initiatives include the purchase of four electric vans which replaced three gas powered vehicles; the purchase of Energy Star rated appliances throughout campus; special parking for carpoolers; Trayless Tuesdays, the utilization of biomass packaging, and serving locally grown and organic food in dining areas.

The strength of The Keystone Family makes the picturesque campus a source of intellectual growth, cultural awareness, environmental stewardship, and service opportunities.

LOCATION AND ENVIRONMENT

Keystone College is located in northeastern Pennsylvania, just twenty minutes outside the city of Scranton. The College truly provides the best of both worlds for students; a safe, quiet campus ideal for learning, yet within easy distance to everything from hiking, mountain biking, and skiing, to movie theaters, shopping, pubs, concerts, museums, and the main cities on the east coast (NYC and Philadelphia). A number of offices on this historic campus are located in Victorian homes. The campus is shaded and beautifully landscaped. The woodland area of campus is fed by a special classification trout stream and is home to several miles of nature trails.

OFF-CAMPUS OPPORTUNITIES

Downhill skiing: Elk Mountain Ski Resort and Sno Mountain (formerly Montage), and other ski areas in the Pocono Mountains of Pennsylvania.

Steamtown Mall

Viewmont Mall

The Shoppes at Montage- a premium retail area

Cinemark Movie Theatre

The Crossings Shopping Outlets

Northeastern Pennsylvania Philharmonic

Everhart Museum

The Scranton Cultural Center

New York Yankees farm team.

Pittsburgh Penguins Ice Hockey development team

Wachovia Arena for concerts

Toyota Pavilion for concerts

Sno Cove Water Park

Lahey Fun Park—miniature golf, batting cages, and go-cart racing

MAJORS AND DEGREES OFFERED

Bachelor of Arts; Bachelor of Science; Associate in Arts; Associate in Fine Arts; Associate in Science; Associate in Applied Science; Accelerated Teaching Certificates; Certificate Programs

ACADEMIC PROGRAMS

MAJORS: Accounting; Biology ; Business; Communications; Criminal Justice; Culinary Arts; Early Childhood Education; Elementary Education; Environmental Biology; Environmental Resource Management; Environmental Studies; Fine Arts; Forensic Biology; Forest/Resource Management; Health Sciences; Information Technology; Landscape Architecture; Organizational Leadership; Pre-Law advising track; Pre-Medical tracks; Psychology; Social Sciences; Sport and Recreation Management; Teaching: Child and Society; Teaching: Art Education; Teaching: Math Education; Teaching: Social Studies Education; Undecided/Pre-Major; Visual Arts; Wildlife Biology

MINORS: Accounting; Art; Biology; Business; Chemistry; Communications; Criminal Justice; Criminal Justice Investigation; Digital Media; Environmental Science; Forensic Biology; Finance; Homeland Security; Human Resource Management; Information Technology; Leadership; Management ; Marketing; Mathematics; Political Science; Psychology; Sociology; Sport and Recreation Management; Theater

CAMPUS FACILITIES AND EQUIPMENT

State-of-the art Smart Classrooms

The Chef's Table restaurant (Student-run)

WKCV-FM radio station

Oppenheim Children's Center

Cupillari Astronomical Observatory

Riparian Hiking Trails

Delayed harvest trout stream

Student Success Center

Wireless Campus

Willary Water Resource Center

U.S. Mid-Atlantic Urban Forestry Center

Countryside Conservancy

GPS/GIS classes

State of the art Forensic Science and DNA laboratory equipment

TUITION, ROOM, BOARD AND FEES

For the 2010–2011 Academic Year:

Tuition & Fees: $19,850/year

Room & Board: $8,950/year

Cost per credit: $400

FINANCIAL AID

Students need only submit the FAFSA form in order to determine eligibility for aid at Keystone College. Merit scholarships are awarded to students based on academic achievement and leadership activities during high school; these scholarships range from $5,000 to full tuition and are renewable each year. Students are notified of these scholarship awards at the point of acceptance.

Keystone also participates in the ACG and Smart Grant program. Students should ensure that their guidance office submits a final transcript to Keystone in order to determine eligibility.

STUDENT ORGANIZATIONS AND ACTIVITIES

ACT 101

Art Society

Campus Activities Board

Campus Prayer and Bible Study Club

Commuter Council

Criminal Justice Club

Forensic Science Club

Honors Program

Intercollegiate Leadership

Inter-Hall Council

Intramural Sports

Junior Professional Chefs of NEPA

Keystone Players

Keystone Service Club

Keystone Steppers Mofyah Club

Marquis Club

Multicultural Affairs Student Organization (MCASA)

Nokomian Student Yearbook

Opposing Prejudice Ending Negativity (OPEN)

Phi Theta Kappa National Honors Fraternity

Prevention Activities Committee

Rotaract

S.I.F.E (Students in Free Enterprise)

Snow Team

Sport Management and Recreation Team (S.M.A.R.T.)

Student Senate

"The Key" Student Newspaper

"The Plume" Student Literary Magazine

T.O.P.S. (Twenty-One Plus) Club

WKCV Radio

ADMISSIONS PROCESS

ADMISSION REQUIREMENTS:

Application for Admission (online or paper, Common Application is accepted)

Official High School Transcript

Official College Transcripts from all schools attended, if applicable

SAT or ACT scores

One Teacher Evaluation

Personal Essay

TOEFL or the equivalent for students whose primary language is not English

Art students: must have a portfolio interview

International Students: must submit a certification of finances

Any other documents that you feel would be helpful to the admissions committee

DEADLINES:

Keystone College practices a rolling admissions process; however students should adhere to the following final deadlines for application submission.

For students entering in the Fall Semester:

Freshmen: July 1

Transfers: August 1

International Students: June 1

For students entering in the Spring Semester:

Freshmen: December 15

Transfers: December 15

International Students: November 1

Students are notified of the admissions decision generally within two weeks of the College receiving the completed application.

KING'S COLLEGE (PA)

AT A GLANCE

King's is a liberal arts Catholic college that offers growth and personal development in a supportive environment. Founded in 1946 by the Congregation of Holy Cross from the University of Notre Dame,

we're located on a small urban campus in Wilkes-Barre, Pennsylvania.

Small classes and labs allow for meaningful interaction with professors. Our average class size is 18 students, average lab size is 13 students, and the student/faculty ratio is 13:1. This personal attention translates into better graduation rates than at institutions with larger classroom environments.

At King's we offer 35 Majors in Business, Humanities, Social Sciences, Education, Sciences and Allied Health programs, 7 Pre-professional programs and 10 Special Concentrations. With our 40 clubs and activities and 19 NCAA Division III athletic programs for men and women there is plenty to do outside the classroom.

King's consistently ranks high in the top college national review issues of several major publications.

For 16 straight years, King's has been ranked in the top tier of *U.S. News & World Report's* list of Best Colleges in the United States.

Barron's Best Buys in College Education selected King's among the nation's top 10% of colleges for its eighth consecutive edition.

The American Association of Colleges and Universities' Greater Expectations Initiative named King's as one of only 16 "Leadership Institutions" nationwide for visionary innovations in undergraduate education.

The John Templeton Foundation Honor Roll for Character-Building Colleges recognizes King's in its select group of 100 colleges nationwide.

In addition to King's ranking in national publications, many of our individual academic programs are accredited by several highly respected organizations.

AACSB International—The Association to Advance Collegiate Schools of Business for the William G. McGowan School of Business, one of only 43 undergraduate schools of business in the country to be accredited.

National Council for the Accreditation of Teacher Education.

The Commission on Accreditation of Healthcare Management Education.

The Accreditation Review Commission on Education for Physician Assistants.

A ten-year re-accreditation from the Middle States Commission on Higher Education.

Our accomplishments and national reputation add value to your degree because employers know that as a King's graduate you challenged yourself. . .and succeeded.

LOCATION AND ENVIRONMENT

King's College is ideally situated in northeastern Pennsylvania within driving distance to New York and Philadelphia, Washington, D.C. and East Coast attractions. Our campus is close to the Pocono Mountains, offering skiing, snowboarding, kayaking and biking trails. The local area features Triple A baseball, the Wilkes-Barre/Scranton Penguins ice hockey team and several venues for concerts.

Our atmosphere is friendly and inviting, with a strong sense of community. Our campus is walkable and accessible, yet you will find impressive facilities, equal to those at much larger institutions. Classes average 18 students allowing for personal interaction with professors, which translates into better graduation rates than at institutions with larger classroom environments.

OFF-CAMPUS OPPORTUNITIES

It's not all limited to campus, we've got malls, theatres and restaurants minutes away as well as specialty shops, cultural events, ethnic celebrations and festivals.. Our bookstore is located in a Barnes & Noble/Starbucks Café. The nearby Pocono Mountains offer great snowboarding, kayaking and biking. Local venues offer concerts, Triple A baseball and minor league hockey.

MAJORS AND DEGREES OFFERED

McGowan School of Business

Accounting; Business Administration; Finance; Human Resource Management; International Business; Marketing; Humanities and; Social Sciences; Computers and Information Systems; Criminal Justice; Economics; English—Literature; English—Professional Writing; Environmental Studies; French; History; Mass Communications; Philosophy; Political Science; Psychology; Sociology; Spanish; Theatre; Theology; Education; Pre-school-Grade 4; Secondary Certification; Special Education; Sciences; Biology; Chemistry; Computer Science; Environmental Science; General Science; Mathematics; Neuroscience; Allied Health; Athletic Training Education; Clinical Laboratory Science/Medical Technology; Physician Assistant (Five-year Master's); 7 Pre-Professional Programs; 10 Special Concentrations

CAMPUS FACILITIES AND EQUIPMENT

We offer a state-of-the-art sports medicine clinic for our athletic training program. New science labs and equipment enable hands-on research. We have a radio station oncampus and offer audio and video editing equipment, along with desktop publishing equipment featuring LCD screens for those interested in communications or media.

The McGowan School of Business is completely wireless, offering students the ability to log in anywhere. The D. Leonard Corgan Library offers an amazing collection of books, periodicals and catalogs to provide students with the informational resources they need to enhance your skills.

Residence halls offer a variety of living arrangements from single rooms to apartments. There are 24-hour computer labs in several residence halls and lest you think we're all work and no fun, each lounge features cable television These facilities are all secure, accessible either by student ID card or by the desk attendant on staff 24-hours a day. King's takes pride in our campus security efforts and can assure you that safety is a top priority here.

ATHLETICS FACILITIES

The 33-acre Robert L. Betzler Fields at McCarthy Stadium is one of the finest facilities in the MAC for football, field hockey, baseball, softball, soccer, and lacrosse.

The 13,000 square-foot John J. Dorish Field House features locker rooms, an equipment room, and an outdoor weight training facility.

The William S. Scandlon Physical Education Center has a state-of-the-art sports medicine clinic, swimming pool, handball and racquetball courts, wrestling room, new locker rooms, and the Robert McGrane Basketball Arena with a seating capacity of 3,200. Outdoor basketball courts are adjacent to the Center.

Our brand new fitness center includes 25,000 pounds of free weights, five full rack stations with platforms for strength lifting, 6,000 pounds of dumbbells, eight Hammer Strength units, and a number of weight training machines. The top floor consists of nearly 30 cardiovascular exercise machines, including treadmills, stationary bikes, elliptical and rowing machines.

The tennis teams play on the newly-surfaced courts at Kirby Park, one of the top facilities in the MAC. (The Kingston Indoor Tennis Center is utilized during the winter.)

The golf team plays at the Wyoming Valley Country Club, a par 72, 6,391-yard course that is only 10 minutes from campus.

TUITION, ROOM, BOARD AND FEES

When determining the cost of a college education, one should also take into consideration the value. *U.S.News & World Report* has ranked King's among America's best colleges for 16 straight years and Barrons consistently considers us one of the best buys in college education.

Approximately 95% of all full-time students attending King's College receive financial assistance, with the average scholarship being $10,555. We encourage every student to apply for financial aid no matter what their family circumstances are. Only after you have applied and been considered for all available assistance will you have a true idea of what your costs will be.

King's offers deferred payment plans, which allows families to make monthly payments on the balance of tuition, fees, room and board less any financial aid received.

FINANCIAL AID

Applicants for financial aid will be considered for all need-based programs, which include private, state and federal grants (gifts), loans and work study programs. King's even has financial aid programs specific to transfer students, so all applicants should take the time to review their options.

Federal campus-based work program allows students to earn money through employment to help pay for educational costs. Average annual amount is $1,200. FAFSA must be filed each year by May 1 to be considered.

The Office of Financial Aid is here to educate you about the various financial aid programs available and to answer your questions. We'll make the application process as simple and painless as possible because our goal is have you join us at King's. Contact us at 1-888-KINGS-PA or finaid@kings.edu.

STUDENT ORGANIZATIONS AND ACTIVITIES

King's recognizes that involvement in student clubs and organizations is an important part of your educational experience. There are a large number of organizations to support your academic, social, and special interests, providing opportunities for leadership, recreation, and the development of special abilities and skills. King's offers the opportunity to participate in a club in the following general areas:

ACADEMIC

Business Related Organizations

Health Related Organizations

Arts & Sciences Organizations

INTERNATIONAL

Foreign Languages Club

Multicultural/International Club

MEDIA & PUBLISHING

Media Club

The Crown (student newspaper)

Regis (yearbook)

WRKC (radio station)

MUSIC / ARTS

Campion Society

King's Players

Monarch Dancers

Music Ensembles at King's

SCOP (fine arts magazine)

SERVICE

Blood Council

Circle K Club

Emergency Response Team (ERT)

Knights of Columbus

Sigma Kappa Sigma (EKE-men)

Sigma Kappa Tau (EKT-women)

SPECIAL INTEREST

Commuter Life Association

Debate Team

Monarch Ambassadors

Residence Hall Council

ROTC

Ski and Snowboard Club

Track and Field

ADMISSIONS PROCESS
APPLYING TO KING'S FOR FRESHMEN

The Office of Admission offers two methods for candidates to apply for admission: The SAT/ACT Traditional Choice and the Standardized Test Option/ Essay Choice. Applicants are required to state their preference prior to the application review and the decision is non-reversible.

SAT/ACT Traditional Choice:

Completed application

Official high school transcripts

SAT I or ACT scores

Guidance counselor recommendation

Essay

$30 Application fee (waived if done online)

Standardized Test Option/Essay Choice:

Completed application

Official high school transcripts

Official graded writing sample from either junior or senior year submitted and notarized by the high school guidance office

Guidance counselor recommendation

Essay

$30 Application fee (waived if done online)

General Guidelines

While each application for admission is reviewed individually, here are some general guidelines:

The most important criteria in the admission decision are a student's four-year academic record, GPA, strength of curriculum and overall rank in class. Recommendations, the personal statement, co-curricular activities, leadership and community service help to complete your profile. March 1 is the preferred application deadline for first-year students. Applications may be submitted after September 1 and are reviewed on a rolling admission basis. Decisions are released in mid-October. Once we have received your application materials, we will notify you with a decision in two to three weeks. Students choosing the standardized test option are required to notify the Office of Admission on the application. A students' decision is non-reversible and must be made prior to application review.

APPLYING FOR TRANSFER STUDENTS

Transferring to King's could not be easier, especially if you're transferring from LCCC. King's offers generous financial assistance packages so don't let cost be a deterrent.

Individual interviews and campus tours may be scheduled Monday through Friday throughout the year. Group information sessions and campus tours are offered on Saturdays during the academic year.

LAKE ERIE COLLEGE

AT A GLANCE

Lake Erie College, founded in 1856, is an independent, coeducational institution located in the city of Painesville in northeastern Ohio. Instruction is provided at the baccalaureate and master's degree levels to academically qualified individuals. Programs of study, founded in the liberal arts, are offered in the following areas: education, equine studies, fine arts, languages and communication, management studies, social sciences, and science and math. Lake Erie College accommodates both residential and commuting students of various ages on a full-time and part-time basis. Local, national, and international students benefit from the College's traditional emphasis on intercultural programs.

Intercollegiate sports play an important role in student life. Athletic teams compete at the NCAA Division II level. Men compete in baseball, basketball, cross-country, football, golf, lacrosse, wrestling, soccer, tennis and track and field. Women compete in basketball, cross-country, lacrosse, soccer, softball, tennis, track and field, swimming and diving and volleyball. The College also sponsors an intercollegiate equestrian team.

Lake Erie College invites students to feel at home in one of four residence halls. Each spacious room is equipped with high-speed Internet access, individual phone lines, cable access, and furniture (desks, beds, and chairs). The College's residence halls have laundry facilities, community lounges, and kitchen areas. Upperclassmen have the opportunity to experience apartment-style living in a College-owned complex adjacent to the campus. Since many students bring their cars to the campus, convenient parking is available near each residence hall.

LOCATION AND ENVIRONMENT

Lake Erie College is located on 57 acres of naturally wooded land in Painesville, Ohio. Painesville is an attractive community in northeast Ohio, 28 miles east of Cleveland and 3 miles south of Lake Erie. The Cleveland Museum of Art; Playhouse Square; Lake Metro Parks; Holden Arboretum; professional baseball, football, and basketball teams; theaters; comedy clubs; and other recreational attractions are located nearby. The area is served by two national highways, U.S. 90 and 20, and state routes 2 and 44.

MAJORS AND DEGREES OFFERED

At the undergraduate level, Lake Erie College offers the Bachelor of Arts, Bachelor of Science, and Bachelor of Fine Arts degrees. Majors are available in accounting, arts management, biology, business administration, chemistry, communications, criminal justice, dance, early childhood education, English, environmental science, equine facilities management, equestrian teacher/trainer studies, fine arts (multidisciplinary), fine arts (with concentrations in art, dance, music, and theater), forensic psychology, human resource management, international business, legal studies, marketing, mathematics, middle childhood education, modern foreign language (French, German, Italian, and Spanish), music, psychology, pre-professional studies (dentistry, law, medicine, pharmacy, and veterinary science), pre-physical therapy, pre-occupational therapy, secondary/young adult education, social sciences (history and sociology), sports management, and therapeutic horsemanship. Students may also pursue an individualized academic major.

ACADEMIC PROGRAMS

The philosophy of Lake Erie College is that the well-being and enrichment of society are dependent upon the abilities of individuals to think both creatively and critically, to make reasoned and informed decisions, and to assume responsibility for their personal actions and continuing education.

Education at Lake Erie College promotes the knowledge and understanding of various cultures and the growth of personal and social responsibilities associated with the acquisition of knowledge and the mastery of skills. The liberal arts and career-oriented disciplines the College offers are not mutually exclusive bodies of knowledge, and the best education is one that promotes the integration of both types of disciplines. The process of education is as vital as the subject matter communicated. It is through intercultural awareness, directed practice in discerning relationships among disciplines, and making informed judgments that a person becomes educated and acquires the flexibility necessary to meet the rapidly changing demands of the marketplace and the world.

One hundred twenty-eight semester hours are required to earn a bachelor's degree.

STUDY ABROAD OPPORTUNITIES

The experience that stands out for most students happens thousands of miles from campus. Because being immersed in a foreign culture truly represents the Lake Erie College liberal arts philosophy, the College encourages every student to take advantage of the 10 to 14- day study tours abroad offered each year. Recent destinations include China, Scotland, Switzerland, England, Spain, France and Costa Rica. The College subsidizes a large part of the trip, making it easily affordable for all students.

Through the College's Academic Program Abroad, students live and study at one of many international colleges or universities while earning Lake Erie College credits. This affords students the opportunity to study within the special educational experience that is part of living in another country, speaking another language, and learning another culture. Academic experiences abroad range in duration from one semester to an entire year, depending upon individual schedules..

CAMPUS FACILITIES AND EQUIPMENT

The scenic Lake Erie College campus provides the ideal setting to pursue an academic career; it reflects the College's commitment to provide a high-quality education in a personalized environment. The focal point of the campus is College Hall, which was completed in 1859. College Hall is a center for classroom and student administrative activities.

The Arthur S. Holden Center houses a telecommunications center, a computer center, computerized classrooms, conference rooms, and faculty offices. In the Holden Center, students also find the bookstore, Storm Café, a cafeteria, student life offices, student government offices, Lake Erie College security, and student mailboxes. Since its dedication in 1997, this facility has been Lake Erie College's premier student center.

The Fine Arts Building houses the 200-seat C. K. Rickel Theatre, the B. K. Smith Gallery, Mac Graphics Lab, art studios, the dance studio, photography laboratories, faculty offices, and classrooms. The Austin Hall of Science includes laboratories, classrooms, and offices and will be completely renovated in 2009 to include added laboratory spaces, smart classrooms, and improved study areas for students.

The new Athletic, Recreation, and Wellness Center, completed in August 2004, includes two full-size gymnasiums, an indoor track, a complete fitness center, multiple locker rooms, an athletic training room, classrooms, a team conference room, and coaches' offices. Adjacent to the center is Jack Slattery Field, with fields for soccer and softball. Lake Erie College student athletes also have access to Ritchie Gym, a state-of-the-art training facility complete with weight training room and swimming pool.

Kilcawley Hall houses the President's Office, the Institutional Advancement Office, Human Resources, and College Relations.

The Lincoln Library/Learning Resource Center maintains a collection of more than 90,000 books and subscribes to more than 750 periodicals. Audiovisual services, educational media and media production centers, two computerized indexes, and two computer laboratories are also located in the library.

Renovated in the summer of 2008, the 85-acre George M. Humphrey Equestrian Center is located just 5 miles from the campus. Served daily by the College van, the equestrian center includes an indoor arena of 100 feet by 225 feet, with seating for 1,000 spectators, and an indoor warm-up area of 75 feet by 130 feet. The Clarence T. Reinberger Equestrian Work Center has an additional indoor ring of 80 feet by 96 feet. Other facilities include the Equine Stud Farm Laboratory and breeding facilities, stabling for 100 horses and learning center. The equestrian center also features outdoor riding rings with all-weather footing and a hunt field with several cross-country obstacles.

TUITION, ROOM, BOARD, AND FEES

Tuition per year for 2010–2011 is $25,675 for full-time students (12–18 credit hours) and $665 per credit hour for part-time students. The room charges per year are $4,054 based on double occupancy. Residential students may choose from three meal plans, with the fourteen-meal-per-week plan equaling $3,864 per year. Yearly fees (student activity, library, and computer) are $1,366 for full-time students and $51 per credit hour for part-time students. At the established sites, the fees for the Academic Program Abroad are comparable to a semester's costs on the Lake Erie campus.

FINANCIAL AID

Lake Erie College offers a number of competitive scholarship programs that are not based on need. Most incoming freshman students receive a renewable scholarship ranging from $3,000 to $12,000 per academic year based on cumulative high school grade point average, standardized test scores, letters of recommendation, and an essay.

Five Presidential Honors Scholarships, which cover 90 percent of tuition, are awarded to incoming students ranking in the top 5 percent of their graduating high school class and achieving a minimum ACT score of 27 or minimum SAT score of 1800 (minimum combination of the three section scores). The award is competitive, with an essay required after the initial GPA and ACT/SAT test score requirements are met. The essay, admissions application, and transcripts are reviewed by a selection committee, and 5 winners are selected. Recipients of the scholarship must live on campus, maintain at least a 3.5 GPA, and take part in the Scholars Program.

Other forms of financial aid, all based on need, include scholarships, grants (federal, state, local, and College), loans (federal and state), and work-study programs; the priority date for need-based aid is March 1. Approximately 98 percent of full-time undergraduate students receive financial aid. Prospective students can complete a Financial Aid Estimator under the financial aid tab at www.lec.edu. To apply for aid, students must submit a Free Application for Federal Student Aid (FAFSA), Form 1040, and other documents required by Lake Erie. The deadline for priority consideration is March 1.

ADMISSIONS PROCESS

A composite evaluation is made of each applicant, with special attention given to high school credentials. A college-preparatory background is highly recommended and should include 4 units of English, 3 units of mathematics, 3 units of science, 3 units of social studies, and 6 additional units from other academic areas; 2 units of foreign language are advised. A personal essay, two letters of recommendation, high school transcripts and ACT and/or SAT scores are required. Lake Erie College welcomes students of all races and backgrounds.

Lake Erie College operates with a rolling admission policy; however, it is recommended that students complete their application and financial aid processes by May 1 in order to maximize their academic and financial aid opportunities. Applicants are notified of the admission decision within two weeks of receipt of all materials.

For further information, students may contact:

Office of Admissions

Lake Erie College

391 West Washington Street

Painesville, Ohio 44077

United States

Phone: 440-375-7050

Toll Free: 800-916-0904

Email: admissions@lec.edu

Website: http://www.lec.edu

LAKE FOREST COLLEGE

AT A GLANCE

Founded in 1857, Lake Forest College has a long tradition of academic excellence and is known for its innovative curriculum. In addition to majors in the humanities, social sciences, and natural sciences, the College features programs of study in pre-law, pre-medicine, communications, business, finance, computer science, and still other practical areas. Lake Forest prepares students to lead successful lives, and many go on to competitive graduate programs and top jobs. Abundant internships, research opportunities, personal guidance from professors, and connections to nearby Chicago also set the Lake Forest apart.

Students learn in a rigorous academic environment in small class settings where professors do all the teaching and also serve as advisors and mentors. Professors are accomplished scholars, published authors, and recipients of prestigious grants. Many have come from some of the top PhD programs in the country.

Students represent 47 states and 71 countries around the world and international and ethnic minorities make up more than 25 percent of the student body. Together they comprise a learning community that prepares them to succeed in a global society.

More than ninety student groups provide a host of extracurricular opportunities that develop leadership skills and enhance students' campus experience and post-college prospects. Lake Forest College offers recreational music, art, and theater programs, as well as 17 varsity sports and intramural and club sports. It competes in NCAA Division III.

LOCATION AND ENVIRONMENT

Just an hour's train ride to Chicago, the College is located in the town of Lake Forest, Illinois, 30 miles north of the city along the shores of Lake Michigan. The 107-acre residential campus is a safe academic home in a beautiful wooded suburban setting within walking distance to the train to downtown Chicago, historic Lake Forest, and the beaches of Lake Michigan.

The College is only 25 miles from O'Hare International Airport and is also served by Midway Airport and Mitchell International Airport in Milwaukee.

The campus is surrounded by lush wooded neighborhoods, ravines, natural prairies, the beautiful beaches along Lake Michigan, and an extensive network of bike and running trails. Nearby Chicago boasts nearly 70 world-class museums, more than 200 theaters, seven major league sports teams, and one of the nation's top opera companies. Chicago is known for its cleanliness, abundant green space, good transportation system, and friendly people.

OFF-CAMPUS OPPORTUNITIES

Lake Forest encourages students to take advantage of study, internship, and research opportunities in Chicago, around the United States, and abroad. Internship opportunities are plentiful in the Chicago area and students have interned at places such as the Art Institute of Chicago, Chicago Blackhawks, Chicago Board of Trade, Chicago Council on Global Affairs, Edelman Public Relations Worldwide, Morgan Stanley, NBC Chicago, Second City, and the John G. Shedd Aquarium, among others.

In addition to a well-established internship program, Lake Forest College provides students with a wide variety of opportunities for off-campus study. Semester-long options in the United States include the Chicago Arts Program, Oak Ridge Science Semester, Chicago Urban Studies Program, Chicago Program in Business and Society, Newberry Library Program in the Humanities, and the Washington Semester Program at American University.

There are many options for international study, such as Lake Forest's own international internship program in Paris, France; the Ancient Civilizations Program in Greece, which uses historical and archaeological sites and museums to study the ancient Aegean world; as well as semester-long programs in Granada, Spain, and China. As a member of the Associated Colleges of the Midwest, Lake Forest also offers programs in Botswana, Costa Rica, England, India, Italy, Japan, Russia, and Tanzania. The off-campus program director works with students to facilitate participation in other approved off-campus study programs.

MAJORS AND DEGREES OFFERED

The academic calendar is based on two 15-week semesters, beginning in August and January. Students normally take four course credits per semester (the equivalent of 16 semester hours).

There are no teaching assistants at the College. Courses are taught in small classroom settings by professors who are experts in their fields and who also serve students as one-on-one advisors. In addition to classroom studies, students are encouraged to complete an internship, conduct original research, and study abroad for a semester.

A Lake Forest graduate will have studied a broad range of ideas; developed real competence in writing, speaking, and quantitative skills; and gained significant experience in humanities, natural sciences and mathematics, and social sciences while completing requirements for a major in an academic department or interdisciplinary program. The College's General Education Curriculum, advising system, and major requirements are designed to support these educational ideals.

Lake Forest awards the Bachelor of Arts (BA) degree in both traditional academic departments and interdisciplinary programs. Areas of study include: African American studies, American studies, anthropology, area studies, studio art, art history, Asian studies, biology, border studies, business, chemistry, cinema studies, classical studies, communication, computer science, economics, education (elementary and secondary), engineering (dual degree), English (literature and writing), environmental studies, finance, history, international relations, Islamic world studies, Latin American studies, legal studies, mathematics, media design and technology, metropolitan studies, modern languages and literatures (Arabic, Chinese, French, German, Italian, Japanese, Russian, and Spanish), media studies, music, neuroscience, philosophy, physics, politics, psychology, religion, rhetoric, social justice, sociology, theater, women's and gender studies. Lake Forest also offers pre-professional programs in law, medicine, dentistry, and veterinary medicine.

ACADEMIC PROGRAMS

The First-Year Studies Program (FIYS)

First-year studies classes are small in size (12–14 students) to encourage interaction and discussion. The FIYS professors also serve as the students' primary academic advisors and help them navigate the College's academic offerings during their first year. With more than twenty topics to choose from, first-year studies courses cover a wide range of academic interests from music, art, and politics to neuroscience, terrorism and religion, many with a focus on Chicago or directly utilizing the resources available there. Chicago plays an integral role in the FIYS program. Students travel to the city with their class during orientation week, providing a first-hand introduction to how the educational, cultural, and social resources of Chicago will influence their coursework and experiences during their four years at Lake Forest.

Honors Fellow Program

As part of the first-year student admission application process, select students are invited to apply to the Honors Fellow Program. Honors fellows produce independent thesis scholarship, research, and symposium presentations, and provide intellectual leadership on campus.

The Richter Apprentice Scholars Program

This program provides students, early in their academic careers, with the opportunity to conduct independent, individual research with Lake Forest faculty. In the summer after their first year, each student in the Richter Program is employed for a ten-week period and does independent research one-on-one with a faculty member. Students are selected through their applications to the program during the admissions process.

The Independent Scholar Program

This program allows students to develop an academic major of their own, working closely with a faculty advisor, culminating in a thesis or a creative project. Recent topics include: sports management, ancient Mediterranean civilizations, graphic design, business theory, medieval studies, lighting design for the theater, metaphysics, and feminist theory.

CAMPUS FACILITIES AND EQUIPMENT

A new recreation, sports, and fitness facility opened in April 2010 and includes three new multipurpose courts, a suspended running track, an aerobic and dance studio, a batting/golf cage, strength, cardio, and fitness spaces, among other amenities.

The Donnelley and Lee Library is a twenty-first century library and information technology center incorporating the latest learning and technological innovations while providing a comfortable environment for collaboration and study. Features include wireless network; 24-hour computing labs; numerous study spaces and workstations; a production and rhetoric room; "smart" classrooms, and a café.

The Mohr Student Center is a student-centered social space that is the hub of social activity on campus. It features pool tables and other games, stage and performance space, large-screen TVs, lounges, deli/snack bar, and an outdoor terrace with seating.

Center for Chicago Programs

Chicago provides a hands-on resource for student learning through research, internships, study, and fun. At the Center for Chicago Programs on campus, students can plan visits to the city and professors can get help incorporating Chicago resources into their classrooms. The Center also brings well-known Chicagoans to the College for lectures and performances.

The Dixon Science Research Center is designed for student-faculty research and contains 13 laboratories with state-of-the-art equipment including a nuclear magnetic resonance spectrometer, a solid-state gamma-ray spectrometer, a multi-imaging phosphorimager, digital-storage oscilloscopes, and fluorescence microscopes.

TUITION, ROOM, BOARD AND FEES

Tuition: $34,206.00

Room: $3,966.00

Board: $4,040.00

Fees: $390.00

FINANCIAL AID

Lake Forest College provides an affordable, high-quality education through maintaining a strong commitment to supporting each student's demonstrated financial need. Financial assistance is available to all who qualify and submit all admission, financial aid, and scholarship applications by the deadlines.

The College offers academic scholarships ranging from $5,000 to $16,000 and talent scholarships ranging from $1,000 to $5,000 for recognized dedication in the fine arts, foreign languages, leadership, music, sciences (including math and computers), theater, or writing.

STUDENT ORGANIZATIONS AND ACTIVITIES

Lake Forest College is a place to study, work, and live. With the diversity of the student body there is an eclectic mix of activities and opportunities outside the classroom.

Student organizations include student government, international interest groups, Greek Life, academic honor societies, community service, publications and media, music and performance, spiritual and religious groups, and many others.

Students have a voice in how the College is run and are actively involved in governance committees such as the College Council and have representation on the Board of Trustees. Student writers and performers can showcase their talents on stage with the Garrick Players, by hosting a show on WMXM, the College's FM radio station, or through the student newspaper, literary magazines, chorus and instrumental ensembles. Academic honor societies enjoy active student participation as do the community service groups and many special-interest clubs. The College provides and maintains a comprehensive intramural and intercollegiate athletic program. There are two national fraternities and five national sororities, all housed within the residence halls. All students have equal opportunity to take advantage of the richness of the College's programs.

Lake Forest College competes in the NCAA Division III fielding nine women's and eight men's intercollegiate varsity teams. Women's teams include basketball, cross-country, handball, ice hockey, soccer, softball, swimming and diving, tennis, and volleyball. Men's teams include basketball, cross-country, football, handball, ice hockey, soccer, swimming and diving, and tennis. The College also offers an extensive roster of intramural and club sports.

The College's Center for Chicago Programs facilitates engagement with the resources of Chicago which often complements programs for student organizations as well as provides students with information on cultural and social activities happening downtown. The train to Chicago is a short walk from campus and students enjoy traveling to the city for fun and entertainment. The College shuttle provides service 7 days a week to popular shopping areas and destinations around campus.

ADMISSIONS PROCESS

The criteria used for selection include assessment of a student's program of study, academic achievement, aptitude, intellectual curiosity, qualities of character and personality, and activities.

Standardized test scores (ACT/SAT) are optional, except for international or home-schooled candidates, and those applying for some academic scholarships. A personal interview is required for students who do not submit scores.

LANDMARK COLLEGE

AT A GLANCE
Our Integrated Approach

While many colleges offer special programs for students with learning difficulties, Landmark College is one of the only accredited colleges in the U.S. designed exclusively for students with dyslexia, attention deficit hyperactivity disorder (AD/HD), or other specific learning disabilities.

Why does Landmark's approach succeed? Because we teach the skills and strategies necessary for success in college and the workforce. At Landmark, you learn how to learn, and this knowledge helps you become more confident and independent.

All of this is achieved through an integrated approach to learning. Landmark College strongly believes that bright students who learn differently can also learn to achieve and thrive.

Students at Landmark get far more personal, directed assistance than at other colleges. Each student receives individualized attention from classroom instructors in courses tailored to meet your individual learning style. We have courses for skills development, college credit, and Associate Degree Programs for individuals who have average to superior intellectual potential. Our experienced advisors meet frequently with you to review and guide your progress. All instructors are trained professional educators, not teaching assistants or peer tutors.

Growth and Discovery

Your time at Landmark College is a time of exploration and learning. A time for you to discover your own personal strengths and abilities. A time for you to grow into your full potential.

It's also a time to make friends, discover talents, and explore interests. The college offers you a wide variety of sports and social activities, both on our beautiful wooded campus and in the surrounding community.

In addition to athletics, activities, and all the off-campus resources of beautiful New England, an important aspect of student life at Landmark College is life in the residence halls. If you choose to live on campus, along with social and educational programs, you'll develop a strong sense of community. There's a true commitment to learning inside and outside of the classroom. Student development professionals also live in each residence hall.

LOCATION AND ENVIRONMENT

Landmark College is located in southeastern Vermont. In summer and spring, you can hike, run, mountain bike, and swim. In winter, students find an atmosphere perfect for snowboarding, cross-country and downhill skiing, and winter camping. For those who prefer something more urban, Boston is two and a half hours away by car and New York City is only four and a half hours away.

OFF-CAMPUS OPPORTUNITIES

Students enjoy exploring the diverse social and cultural offerings in the local Vermont towns of Putney and Brattleboro, and Massachusetts' Northampton. These areas all have bustling downtowns with shops, restaurants, and entertainment. Brattleboro has a vibrant arts community with galleries, music, and theater. Northampton is home to Smith College and a thriving crafts scene.

Larger cities like Boston, Montreal, and New York are close enough for day and weekend trips.

At Landmark College, interactive learning abroad is a reality. Every year, our students have the opportunity to study at locations around the world. January experiences in Costa Rica, as well as summer semesters in England, Ireland, Greece, India, Italy, and Spain enable our students to experience other cultures. While expanding their horizons, they are engaged in rigorous college course work, taught by our own professional faculty members.

MAJORS AND DEGREES OFFERED

AA Business Administration

AA Business Studies

AA Liberal Arts

AA General Studies

ACADEMIC PROGRAMS

Your path through Landmark College can be one of many. Our programs offer you many opportunities to develop the academic skills and strategies that match your abilities.

We offer Associate's Degrees in Business Administration, Business Studies, Liberal Arts and General Studies. Our other programs include Study Abroad, a College Skills Summer Session, a High School Summer Session, and a Summer Transition to College Session for recent High School Graduates.

CAMPUS FACILITIES AND EQUIPMENT

The campus includes several multipurpose classroom buildings, five traditional residence halls, two apartment and condominium-style residential buildings, and a fine arts building housing two theaters.

The campus library houses a growing print, audiovisual, and digital materials collection as well as specialized areas for research, instruction, LD research, and media production. Other campus facilities include the Academic Support Center, a Woman's Resource Center, the Click Sports Center and the Strauch Family Student Center.

TUITION, ROOM, BOARD AND FEES

The comprehensive fees listed below include the cost of taking classes and living at Landmark College. They include all courses, residence hall, and meal plan.

Fees for the 2008–2009 Academic Year (30 weeks):

Tuition: $47,500

Room Fee: $4,250

Board Fee: $4,250

Damage Deposit: $300

Health Insurance: $450 (International Students $644)

Total: $56,750

FINANCIAL AID

By researching, applying to, and choosing Landmark College, you've decided on your educational path. Now you need to get the funding to pursue your goal.

The Financial Aid Office is here to help you navigate the financial obstacles that you may encounter along the way. While you look for outside sources to help make your Landmark College education a reality, we work from the inside. We'll provide information and guidance on applying for federal grants and loans, as well as other sources.

Every family is encouraged to apply for financial assistance through Landmark College. Determining how best to finance a college education can create a lot of questions and concerns. All families are eligible for some form of assistance.

In addition to primary resources of family income and savings, students may be eligible for federal grants, loans, or Landmark College scholarships. Landmark College's tuition and fees can also lead to tax advantages for qualified students and families.

The Financial Aid Office is here to assist with this process and answer all of your questions.

Cathy Mullins

Director of Financial Aid

Office Telephone: 802-387-6736

Fax: 802-387-6868

E-mail: cmullins@landmark.edu

STUDENT ORGANIZATIONS AND ACTIVITIES

When you come to Landmark College, you have the chance to learn about yourself in more ways than you would expect. We believe that there's more to education than just what you find in textbooks and classrooms. We offer you growth in all areas of your life body, mind, and spirit.

The Division of Student Life contributes to your educational experience by providing numerous opportunities, programs, and services so you can get involved. These are designed to enhance your intellectual, social, ethical, physical, and cultural development. You'll discover current favorites and learn to enjoy new activities. We'll help you build the self-esteem you need to push your horizons as far as you can go.

At Landmark College, you'll find people who understand where you're coming from whether they're fellow students or the faculty members and staff. You'll relax in an atmosphere where we all recognize your capabilities. We want you to strive for success at everything you try. Why? Because we know you can do it.

We endeavor to work with you and for you. We'll encourage you to become involved in the campus community, and to take advantage of the leadership role you can play here and in the world. The friendships, experiences, and connections that you will make at Landmark College will create an exciting environment where you will live and learn. Our goal is to provide the widest possible spectrum of activities, and to offer something that will appeal to every student.

Clubs and weekly activities range from jazz band, poetry readings, fencing, Business Management Club, Women's Resources, Multicultural Club, on-campus movies, spiritual life, chorus, to the community garden project. Dances, clubs, and athletic events at the school featuring our Pep Band and mascot "Jerry Jaws" are only a small part of the on-campus events.

Activities at Landmark College take advantage of Vermont's natural beauty, as well as providing opportunities to visit sites further afield. Trips to Fenway Park in Boston to see the Red Sox or to Montreal to experience French-Canadian culture are part of the yearly program.

The student-run Campus Activities Board is a subcommittee of our Student Government Association, and is responsible for scheduling the wide range of activities provided by the college.

ADMISSIONS PROCESS

Our admissions process is as straightforward as we can make it. Here is a brief overview (full details are in the application package or visit our website: www.landmark.edu).

WHAT WE CONSIDER

We are looking for students who meet two essential criteria:

—Average to superior intellectual potential, AND

—Diagnosis of dyslexia, AD/HD, or other specific learning disability

THE STEPS WE FOLLOW

The admissions process has three steps:

1. You complete the application and personal statement (preferably in your own handwriting) and submit these to the Admissions Office with the application fee.

2. You ensure that all required records and recommendations get to us in time for consideration by the Admissions Committee.

3. Our Admissions Committee reviews your completed application package and determines whether to:

Request further documentation

Invite you for an interview

Decline your application

Admit you directly to a degree program

LAWRENCE TECHNOLOGICAL UNIVERSITY

AT A GLANCE

Lawrence Technological University is a premier private university providing superior education through innovative programs, cutting-edge technology, small class sizes, and a commitment to theory and practice. The University's Leadership Program, integrated into all bachelor's degrees, helps students gain critical thinking, teamwork, and communication skills.

The University, including its graduate programs, is accredited by the Higher Learning Commission and is a member of the North Central Association of Colleges and Schools. Lawrence Tech placed in the top tier category of Best University-Masters-Midwest in the *U.S. News and World Report's* 2010 America's Best Colleges rankings. In addition to the overall citation, Lawrence Tech tied for 49th of 100 schools listed in the category of 2010 Best Engineering Programs. Other honors include recognition by the Princeton Review and a designation as a Military Friendly School by *G.I. Jobs*.

Lawrence Tech offers an undergraduate honors program for highly motivated and qualified students. The Quest Program also encourages students to go above and beyond their studies and explore their interests on a deeper level. A scholars program is available, designed to ease the transition from high school to college by providing support services.

Lawrence Tech's student-faculty ratio is 12:1. Most undergraduate classes have 19 or fewer students, and less than 1 percent of the classes have more than 50. More than 500 students live in University Housing. Women make up 26 percent of the student body, and 29 states and 40 nations are represented on campus.

LOCATION AND ENVIRONMENT

The University is located in Southfield, a dynamic suburb of more than 78,000 people. The campus is close to major freeways and about a 30-minute drive north of downtown Detroit and Detroit Metro Airport. Southeastern Michigan offers a rich variety of recreational and cultural activities, with public transportation making most areas accessible to students. Research, manufacturing, scientific, and business enterprises are located nearby, aiding students who work full- or part-time while attending classes as well as those in co-op and internships.

OFF-CAMPUS OPPORTUNITIES

Students can participate in applied research partnerships that offer remarkable hands-on experience. Professional organizations provide additional opportunities to network with industry leaders.

Lawrence Tech's Detroit Studio and Innovation Center allows students to explore community-based architectural, urban design, and community development projects. Architecture students regularly build homes for Habitat for Humanity.

The Global Engineering Program arranges for engineering students to work and study abroad. The Study-Abroad Program is open to all students.

The University also maintains relationships with universities in Asia, Canada, Europe, Mexico, and the Middle East.

MAJORS AND DEGREES OFFERED

Lawrence Tech is a 4,500-student university offering over 100 undergraduate, master's, and doctoral programs in Architecture and Design, Arts and Sciences, Engineering, and Management. Most programs are available during the day or evening; some are offered on weekends and online. Dual majors and customized degree programs combining either associate and bachelor's programs or bachelor's and master's programs also are available. Pre-professional preparation includes pre-dental, pre-law, and pre-medical programs. The University also features 35 accelerated certificate programs in emerging fields, including alternative energy, life sciences, defense, and film, designed to help students quickly retool for a changing economy.

The College of Architecture and Design offers bachelor's degrees in architecture, game art, imaging (concentrations in digital arts and digital design), industrial design, interior architecture, and transportation design. Lawrence Tech enrolls more architectural students than any other school in Michigan, and is one of the top 10 largest architecture schools in the nation.

The College of Arts and Sciences offers bachelor's degrees in chemical biology, chemistry, computer science (concentrations in business software development, game software development, network software development, and scientific software development), English and communication arts, environmental chemistry, humanities, mathematics, mathematics and computer science, media communication, molecular and cell biology, physics, physics and computer science, and psychology (concentrations in clinical psychology, industrial/organizational psychology, and pre-med/biobehavioral psychology).

The College of Management offers undergraduate degrees in business management and information technology.

Bachelor's degrees offered by the College of Engineering are architectural engineering (combining bachelor's and master's studies), audio engineering technology, biomedical engineering, civil engineering, computer engineering, construction management, electrical engineering (concentrations in computer engineering, electronic engineering, and energy engineering), engineering technology, industrial operations engineering, and mechanical engineering (concentrations in alternative energy, automotive engineering, manufacturing engineering, mechanical system design, and thermal system design).

Minors include aeronautical engineering, business management, chemistry, computer science, economics, energy engineering, English, general sciences, history, mathematics, philosophy, physics, psychology, Spanish, technical and professional communication, and television and video production.

Associate degrees are offered in chemical technology, communications engineering technology, construction engineering technology, general studies, manufacturing engineering technology, mechanical engineering technology, and radio and television broadcasting.

Undergraduate certificates can be earned in alternative energy engineering technology, animation and visual effects for film, biochemical engineering, bioelectronics, biomechanics, building information modeling and computer visualization, computer science, electrical power systems, embedded systems, entrepreneurial strategy, film and audio technique, film and production techniques, industrial/organizational psychology, set design, technical and professional communication, television and video production, and video and audio technique.

THEORY AND PRACTICE

Lawrence Tech provides students the tools they need to compete and succeed within their chosen profession. Whether inside or outside of the classroom, the University's theory and practice approach to learning gives opportunities to combine practical knowledge with real-world applications.

Students designed and built a solar-powered home that now serves as an environmental information center in Troy, a nearby suburb. The eco-friendly home demonstrates the University's commitment to sustainability.

In another project, students are educational partners with the regional utility and assess the operation of the first and largest hydrogen technology park of its type in the world.

Lawrence Tech is the recipient of numerous grants and awards for the development and implementation of innovative materials and practices that are expected to double the lifespan of concrete bridges and new armor protection for soldiers.

Student engineering teams design, build, and race hybrid Baja and Formula-style vehicles. Students also compete in bridge building and assembling, designing zero energy homes, and in airplane design, robotics, and concrete canoe competitions.

Lawrence Tech's Lear Entrepreneurial Center teaches engineering students how to create, promote, and bring to market products and services.

CAMPUS FACILITIES AND EQUIPMENT

Lawrence Tech's modern 102-acre campus includes a variety of academic, recreational, and housing facilities—many built within the last several years.

Lawrence Tech is Michigan's first wireless laptop computer campus and is ranked among the nation's top 50 "unwired" universities. All undergraduates are provided high-end laptop or tablet computers that are customized with the software they need to succeed. Additional computers, workstations, terminals, and microcomputers are located in campus labs.

The University has two residence halls, featuring one- and two-bedroom apartment-style suites that accommodate two to four students. Single rooms also are available. All utilities, wireless Internet access, basic cable TV, and individual telephone lines and voicemail are included.

The library offers a wide selection of print and electronic materials, including numerous online databases and full-text periodical titles accessible on and off campus. The library also hosts visual resources and digital images. Librarians provide research guidance and instruction. As a key part of the research community in Michigan, the library participates in the reciprocal borrowing and sharing of resources with many other institutions.

Other facilities include architectural and design studios; senior project lab and studio space; fabrication labs; wind tunnel; wood, metal, and model shops; physics, chemistry, biology, and tissue labs; bioengineering lab; mechatronics lab, anechoic chamber for sound studies; structural testing center; alternative energy, mechanical, and electrical labs; thermal science lab; graphics lab; and the Denso Instructional Technology Lab. Lawrence Tech also owns a nearby Frank Lloyd Wright-designed home that is used as a study center.

The A. Alfred Taubman Student Services Center consolidates all student support services—from admissions through career services—into a convenient one-stop center. This innovative 42,000-square-foot building, which utilizes many energy-efficient and environmentally friendly features and technologies, serves as a "living laboratory" and is part of a region-wide storm water management effort. The Center for Innovative Materials Research is a state-of-the-art laboratory for the research, development, and testing of materials for defense and infrastructure applications. Students participate in related research projects as part of their academic programs.

The Automotive Engineering Institute provides students opportunities to conduct sponsored research on a unique 4 x 4 vehicle chassis dynamometer, which measures many areas of vehicle performance.

TUITION, ROOM, BOARD, AND FEES

Tuition for all undergrads includes a laptop or tablet computer. The 2009–10 tuition for students majoring in arts and sciences and management is $686 per credit hour for freshmen and $734 per credit hour for sophomores. The tuition for juniors and seniors majoring in arts and sciences and management is $767 per credit hour. In architecture and design and engineering, tuition for freshmen and sophomores is $767–$774 per credit hour; for juniors and seniors, it is $792–$799 per credit hour. A normal course load is 12–17 credits per semester. The undergraduate registration fee is $135 each semester. International students on temporary visas must have sufficient funds to pay for an entire year of tuition, room and board, and books at the time of first registration. Additional fees for specific labs and studio courses vary.

Room costs vary, but average $5,573 per year. Average board is $3,780, with a variety of meal plans available.

FINANCIAL AID

Approximately 70 percent of students receive financial assistance, and the University awards nearly $40 million in scholarships, grants, loans, and work-study funds each academic year. The average annual financial aid package is nearly $15,000. Many privately funded scholarships are awarded to qualified students, based on need and/or scholastic performance. Part-time employment is available at the University on a first-come, first-served basis for full-time students. Student loans are also available from a variety of sources—state, federal, and private. Prospective students are urged to contact the Office of Financial Aid for information on deadlines and requirements for eligibility (ltu.edu/financial_aid).

STUDENT ORGANIZATIONS AND ACTIVITIES

More than 50 student clubs and organizations, including fraternities, sororities, honor societies, and student chapters of professional groups are active on campus and sponsor a variety of activities during the year. The Student Government sponsors and supports a variety of campus activities.

Recreational facilities include the Don Ridler Field House, which features a fitness track, gymnasium, racquetball courts, game room, saunas, and weight and conditioning room. Intramural and club sports teams in badminton, basketball, billiards, curling, flag football, golf, hockey, racquetball, soccer, softball, table tennis, tennis, volleyball, and wallyball are active throughout the academic year. The Lawrence Tech Blue Devils ice hockey team competes in the North Region of the American College Hockey Association.

ADMISSIONS PROCESS

A high school diploma or the equivalent is required of all students applying to baccalaureate or associate degree programs. Most baccalaureate applicants must have a minimum 2.5 overall GPA in academic subjects; architecture students must have a minimum 2.75 overall GPA. ACT or SAT results are required of all entering freshmen. An essay and a letter of recommendation from a mentor, high school teacher, or counselor are required. Lawrence Tech's ACT code is 2020 and SAT is 1399. Required high school courses vary with the curriculum, and Lawrence Tech offers a number of basic studies courses designed to augment incoming students' backgrounds if deficiencies exist.

Programs start in August and January. An optional summer semester begins in May. Entry in the fall semester is advised but not required. Students must submit transcripts from all schools attended, along with a nonrefundable $30 application fee. To obtain a digital viewbook and an application form, students should visit ltu. edu or contact:

Lawrence Technological University

Office of Admissions

21000 West Ten Mile Road

Southfield, MI 48075-1058

800.CALL.LTU or 248.204.3160

admissions@ltu.edu

ltu.edu

LAWRENCE UNIVERSITY

AT A GLANCE

Our 1,425 students come from nearly every state and more than 50 countries to enjoy the distinctive benefits of this engaged—and engaging—community. It's a close-knit, residential, 24/7 campus filled with smart and talented people pursuing an astonishing variety of academic and extracurricular interests. Lawrence students are comfortable being themselves—and quite comfortable letting others be themselves, too. Our picturesque, residential campus is nestled on the banks of the Fox River in Appleton, Wisconsin (pop. 70,000; metro pop. 225,000), an area recognized annually by national publications for its safety and high quality of life.

With about 12 percent of our students and 13 percent of our faculty coming from beyond the United States, Lawrence is one of the most internationally diverse liberal arts colleges in the country.

ACADEMICS

Lawrence University—home to a world-class liberal arts college and conservatory of music, both devoted exclusively to undergraduate education—believes that college should not be a one-size-fits-all experience.

Like most private colleges, Lawrence offers a small student-to-faculty ratio (9:1) and average class size (15). Unlike most private colleges, however, Lawrence teaches an extraordinary number of individualized courses—honors projects, tutorials, studio lessons—with one student working directly under the guidance of one professor. Of the 2,000 courses Lawrence teaches each year, nearly two-thirds have total enrollments of one. By the time they graduate, 90% of our students will have had at least one individualized class.

Lawrence offers a number of other meaningful points of distinction: Freshman Studies, a nationally-renowned first-year seminar that integrates material and Lawrence professors from the arts, humanities, sciences, and social sciences to teach students how to think critically, argue civilly, and write confidently; the Honor Code, which ensures academic integrity, promotes mutual trust and respect, and values cooperation and collaboration over competition in all aspects of campus life; Bjorklunden, a 425-acre estate on Lake Michigan in Door County, Wisconsin, serves as Lawrence's northern campus, hosting retreats and seminars for Lawrence students through the academic year; and our Conservatory of Music—with a superb faculty of performers, composers, scholars and teachers—seamlessly integrates professional education in music with the liberal arts.

ADMISSIONS

Whether you apply to our college of liberal arts and sciences or our conservatory of music (or both, as a double-degree candidate), the admission staff will consider the strength of your curriculum, academic performance (grades and rank, if applicable), recommendations, extracurricular activities, and standardized test results (if you choose to submit them; Lawrence does not require ACT or SAT results for admission). We do not require personal interviews—but we strongly encourage and offer them in abundance on campus, on the road or online.

Additionally, music candidates are judged on musicianship, performance potential, recommendations of teachers, and general academic ability. All music applicants must perform an audition—either on campus, at one of our regional sites, or on a high-quality digital recording—as well as submit a music resume and music teacher's recommendation.

Roughly half of Lawrence's students graduated in the top 10 percent of their high school class. Lawrence accepts the Common Application. We offer three application plans: Early Decision (November 15 deadline; December 1 notification); Early Action (December 1 deadline; January 15 notification); Regular Decision (January 15 deadline; April 1 notification). Conservatory applicants and international students typically apply through Regular Decision. Lawrence also encourages applications from transfer students.

CAMPUS FACILITIES AND EQUIPMENT

The brand-new Warch Campus Center, a LEED-Gold building, is home to our dining services (provided by Bon Appetit), retail outlets, 134-seat cinema, and stunning views of the Fox River. Seeley G. Mudd Library, one of the top libraries among liberal arts colleges, has, among its hundreds of thousands of books, government documents, and periodical subscriptions, more than 20,000 recordings and videos along with thousands of musical scores. In addition to the online catalog, the library can access national computerized bibliographic databases. Science facilities include 23 general laboratories for student use; 25 special laboratories for research, including a laser physics lab; a graphics and computational physics lab; four environmentally controlled rooms; animal rooms for psychology and biology; a greenhouse; multiple electron microscopes; a variety of spectroscopic instruments (nuclear magnetic resonance, infrared, UV-visible, atomic absorbance); and an X-ray diffractometer. The Music-Drama Center and the Shattuck Hall of Music house private practice studios, classrooms, a recital hall, large and small ensemble rehearsal halls, a digital recording studio, performance facilities for the theater department, and WLFM, Lawrence's Internet-based radio station. Lawrence has two theaters: Stansbury, with a proscenium stage, seats 500 people; Cloak is an experimental theater, adaptable to arena- or thrust-stage productions. The Memorial Chapel seats 1,250 people and is the primary venue for convocations, performances by Lawrence's large ensembles, and other public events and concerts. The Wriston Art Center offers a first-rate facility for the studio art and art history programs. It includes an outdoor amphitheater, three galleries, two- and three-dimensional art studios, and houses the university's outstanding permanent collection. The Buchanan Kiewit Recreation Center offers an indoor track; swimming pool; weight/exercise room; dance room; racquetball courts; gymnasium; and saunas. Alexander Gymnasium, Whiting Field, and the Banta Bowl (a 5,300-seat football stadium) house 22 varsity (NCAA Division III) and four club sports teams.

CAMPUS LIFE

Lawrence offers the kind of campus life that only a fully residential community can. (Housing is required and guaranteed.) Nearly all of our students live on campus in one of our seven residence halls or theme houses, apartments and small residences. Every day on campus, you will find countless concerts, recitals, theater performances, intercollegiate athletic competitions, poetry slams, artist exhibitions and lectures. More than 80 student clubs and organizations provide a wide variety of activities, ranging from performances by major music ensembles and an international film series to the annual Trivia Weekend (the longest-running and most notorious trivia contest in the country), crew on the Fox River, and winter camping along Lake Michigan.

COLLEGE BASICS

Lawrence University is an internationally recognized college of liberal arts and sciences and a conservatory of music—both dedicated exclusively to undergraduate education.

LOCATION AND ENVIRONMENT

Lawrence is proud to make its home in Appleton, a city of 70,000 people, located on the banks of the historic Fox River in northeast Wisconsin. The metropolitan area (pop. 250,000) is not only one of the safest metro areas in the United States, it is also frequently cited in national publications as one of the country's best places to live and work. Our 84-acre campus, adjacent to Appleton's thriving downtown, overlooks the northward-flowing Fox River. Appleton offers the cultural and commercial advantages (and airport) of a larger urban area with the recreational opportunities and convenience of a Midwestern town.

TUITION AND FEES

Tuition and fees $34,326; room and board: $7,053.

LE MOYNE COLLEGE

Le Moyne College is a four-year, coeducational Jesuit College of approximately 2,500 undergraduate students that uniquely balances a comprehensive liberal arts education with preparation for specific career paths or graduate study.

AT A GLANCE

Founded by the Society of Jesus in 1946, Le Moyne is the second youngest of the twenty-eight Jesuit colleges and universities in the United States. Its emphasis is on the education of the whole person and on the search for meaning and value as integral parts of an intellectual life. Learning, leadership and service are the hallmarks of a Le Moyne College education. Those values are evident in the College's undergraduate majors in 31 areas of study, as well as in its pre-professional studies and graduate programs in business administration, education, nursing and physician assistant studies.

Le Moyne's personal approach to education is reflected in the quality of contact between students and faculty members. With approximately 158 full-time faculty members, Le Moyne has a student-faculty ratio of 13:1 and an average class size of 21.

LOCATION AND ENVIRONMENT

Le Moyne's 160-acre, tree-lined campus is located in a residential setting 10 minutes from downtown Syracuse, the heart of New York State, whose metropolitan population is about 700,000. Just a few miles outside the city are the rolling hills, picturesque lakes, and miles of open country for which central New York is renowned.

OFF CAMPUS OPPORTUNITIES

Syracuse is convenient to most major cities throughout the Northeast, New England, and Canada and offers a wide array of shopping centers and restaurants, many near Le Moyne. Syracuse offers year-round entertainment in the form of rock concerts at the Landmark Theatre, professional baseball and hockey, the Bristol Omni-theatre, the Syracuse Symphony Orchestra, the Syracuse Stage, the Everson Museum of Art, and the Armory Square district downtown, which offers one-of-a-kind eateries, pubs, and coffeehouses in addition to a wide variety of social and cultural events. Central New York is home to an extensive network of state and county parks, recreational areas, and other facilities that offer an abundance of recreational opportunities, including swimming, boating, hiking, downhill and cross-country skiing, snowboarding, and golf.

MAJORS AND DEGREES

Le Moyne College awards the Bachelor of Arts degree in biological sciences, communication (advertising, filmmaking, media studies, print journalism, public relations, television/radio), computer science, criminology (human services, international affairs, law enforcement, research), economics, English (creative writing, literature), French, history, mathematics (actuarial science, pure mathematics, statistics), peace and global studies, philosophy, physics, political science, psychology, religious studies, sociology (anthropology, criminology and criminal justice, human services, research and theory), Spanish, and theatre arts. The Bachelor of Science degree is awarded in biochemistry, biological sciences (health professions, molecular biology, neurobiology), chemistry, economics, environmental studies, general science, natural systems science, physics, psychology and work and employment relations. The Bachelor of Science in business is awarded in accounting, applied management analysis, finance, information systems, management and leadership, and marketing. A Bachelor of Science in Nursing is also offered.

Students may minor in Catholic studies, classical humanities, film, gender and women's studies, Irish literature, Italian, Latin, management information systems, music, urban and regional studies, or visual arts as well as most of the major fields of study offered. Preprofessional programs are offered in dentistry, law, medicine, optometry, physical therapy, physician assistant studies, podiatry, and veterinary science. Students may prepare for teaching careers through certification programs in adolescent education, dual adolescent/special education, dual childhood/special education, middle childhood specialist studies, and TESOL.

Le Moyne College and the L. C. Smith College of Engineering and Computer Science at Syracuse University have a dual-degree program in which students may earn a bachelor's degree from Le Moyne and a master's degree in engineering from Syracuse University in as few as five years. Concentrations include aerospace, chemical, electrical, and mechanical engineering as well as computer science and other fields of engineering.

Formal accelerated 3-4 programs are offered in dentistry, optometry, and podiatry in cooperation with the State University of New York at Buffalo School of Dental Medicine, Pennsylvania College of Optometry, and the New York College of Podiatric Medicine. Predental students may also participate in an early assurance program with the State University of New York at Buffalo School of Dental Medicine. Cooperative 3-2 dual-degree programs in engineering are available with Clarkson University, Manhattan College, and University of Detroit Mercy.

SUNY Upstate Medical University in Syracuse offers students pursuing careers in the health-related professions an accelerated 3-3 doctoral-level transfer program in physical therapy as well as two-year cooperative transfer programs in medical technology and respiratory care. Premedical students at Le Moyne are also offered the opportunity to participate in a medical school early assurance program. An early assurance program for premedical students is also available through the State University of New York at Buffalo School of Medicine.

ACADEMIC PROGRAMS

While each major department has its own sequence requirements for the minimum 120 credit hours needed for the Le Moyne degree, the College is convinced that there is a fundamental intellectual discipline that should characterize the graduate of a superior liberal arts college. Le Moyne's core curriculum provides this foundation by including studies of English language and literature, philosophy, history, religious studies, natural science, and social science.

For exceptional students, Le Moyne offers an integral honors program that includes an interdisciplinary humanities sequence as well as departmental honors courses.

The study-abroad program allows qualified students to spend a semester or year in almost any country throughout the world. Le Moyne College has study-abroad programs or affiliations in China, Czech Republic, Dominican Republic, Germany, Italy, Spain, and the United Kingdom. Students can also use partner programs to study in locations such as Australia, Costa Rica, Egypt, France, Ireland, Japan, and South Africa. Le Moyne is a participant in the sixty-member New York State Visiting Student Program.

As part of the mission of preparing future leaders, Le Moyne College places a strong emphasis on career preparation through internships and other forms of experiential education. Academic departments and the Office of Career Services both provide programs and services for students interested in interning part-time and full-time, both locally and in major cities such as New York and Washington, D.C. The Offices of Service Learning and the Academic Deans are also involved in experiential education to promote learning outside the classroom. In the sciences, students take part in campus research with mentor faculty members. Others receive assistance in pursuing outstanding opportunities off campus in leading research laboratories and health-care settings. The College has maintained a long-standing relationship with the "Washington center" internship programs, where students from all majors complete full-time semester-long internships in Washington, D.C., with government, business, or major nonprofit organizations. Faculty members in the Political Science Department assist students interested in opportunities in Albany, New York State's seat of government, with either the New York State Senate or Assembly. Finally, the education programs at Le Moyne put students into school classrooms starting immediately as freshmen and continuing each year until graduation.

Le Moyne students may enroll in Army and Air Force ROTC programs in conjunction with Syracuse University.

CAMPUS FACILITIES AND EQUIPMENT

Le Moyne students benefit from an ongoing commitment to technological excellence. The College's thirty-four buildings are equipped with accounting, biology, chemistry, computer science, physics, psychology, and statistics laboratories. The W. Carroll Coyne Center for the Performing Arts houses generous production, performance, and classroom space; the latest light and sound technology; scene and costume shops; an aerobics and dance studio; and rehearsal rooms for instrumental and choral music. Academic facilities also include an extensively renovated color television studio; a radio/recording studio; a receiver-antenna satellite dish; transmission and scanning electron microscopes; a nuclear magnetic resonance spectrometer; a gas chromatograph/mass spectrophotometer; a 230,000-volume, open-stack library; and extensive on-site computer facilities. A wireless network allows students easy access to the campus network and Internet. All classrooms have been converted to smart classrooms, with multimedia capabilities that expand and enrich the learning process. Le Moyne students have access to other libraries through the Central New York Library Resources Council, and the campus Academic Support Center is available to students for instructional support. Athletic facilities include a new soccer/lacrosse turf field; softball and baseball fields; tennis, basketball, and racquetball courts; a weight-training and fitness center; practice fields; and two gymnasiums. A recreation center houses an Olympic-size indoor swimming pool, jogging track, indoor tennis and volleyball courts, and additional basketball, racquetball, and fitness areas.

TUITION, ROOM, BOARD AND FEES

For 2009–10, Le Moyne's tuition was $25,110. Room and board charges were $9990. Additional fees amounted to approximately $720, and books and supplies cost approximately $700.

FINANCIAL AID

Financial aid is offered to a large percentage of Le Moyne's students through scholarships, grants, loans, and work-study assignments. Le Moyne offers a generous program of merit-based academic and athletic scholarships as well as financial aid based on a student's need and academic promise. Federal funds are available through the Federal Pell Grant, Federal Work-Study, Federal Supplemental Educational Opportunity Grant, and Federal Perkins Loan programs. A student's eligibility for need-based financial aid is determined from both the Free Application for Federal Student Aid (FAFSA) and the Le Moyne Financial Aid Application Form. It is recommended that these forms be mailed by February 1.

STUDENT ORGANIZATIONS AND ACTIVITES

A wide range of student-directed activities, athletics, clubs, and service organizations complement the academic experience. Intramural sports are very popular with Le Moyne students; nearly 85 percent of the students participate. Le Moyne also has seventeen NCAA intercollegiate teams (eight for men and nine for women). More than 80 percent of students live in residence halls, apartments, and town houses on campus. The Residence Hall Councils and the Le Moyne Student Programming Board organize a variety of campus activities, including concerts, dances, a weekly film series, student talent programs, and special lectures as well as off-campus trips and skiing excursions.

The College encourages student leadership in all activities with positions open to students in all class years. Students are represented by a Student Senate and have formal representation through the senate on most College-wide committees involved in decision making and policy formation.

ADMISSIONS PROCESS

Le Moyne seeks qualified students who are well prepared for serious academic study. Secondary school preparation must have included at least 17 college-preparatory high school units, 4 of which must be in English, 4 in social studies, 3–4 in mathematics, 3–4 in foreign language, and 3–4 in science. It is also recommended that prospective science and mathematics majors complete 4 units of mathematics and science. The SAT or ACT is required and should be taken by December or January of the senior year in high school. Campus visits are strongly recommended, as the admission process is a personal one. As bases for selection, academic achievement and secondary school recommendations are of primary importance; SAT or ACT scores are important as they relate to the record of achievement and to recommendations. Out-of-state students are encouraged to apply.

The Admission Committee reviews applications and mails decisions on a rolling admission cycle beginning January 1. The priority deadline for applications is February 1; all students who wish to be considered for academic merit scholarships should have a completed application on file in the Office of Admission before this date. Students who wish to be considered under the early-decision program must have a completed application submitted by December 1. Early-decision applicants are notified by December 15. Transfer students are encouraged to apply before June 1 for the fall semester and December 1 for the spring semester. Orientation programs for incoming freshmen and transfer students take place in midsummer.

LEWIS & CLARK COLLEGE

AT A GLANCE

On a stunning campus in one of the most exciting and progressive cities anywhere, the next generation of global thinkers gathers to discard conventional thinking, civic complacency, and outmoded preconceptions. Leaders, visionaries, and problem-solvers, we come together to explore new ways of knowing through classic liberal learning and innovative collaboration.

At Lewis & Clark College in Portland, Oregon, we welcome all who are alive to inquiry, open to diversity, and eager to shape the new global century. Through our undergraduate programs in the arts, humanities, and sciences, and through our graduate and professional studies in education, counseling, and law, we undertake original research, interdisciplinary studies, and community service. We push beyond what is known in order to discover something new every day.

Reflecting the College's national and global reach, approximately 84 percent of Lewis & Clark's 1,921 undergraduate students come from outside Oregon, representing nearly every state and 58 countries.

LOCATION AND ENVIRONMENT

Founded in 1867, Lewis & Clark College moved to its present location in Portland's southwest hills in 1942. The 137- acre campus sits on a wooded hilltop just six miles from Portland's exciting downtown, offering stunning views of snow-covered Mount Hood.

Portland is a very livable city with an excellent public transportation system that includes buses, light-rail, and the Portland Street Car. In addition, a free College shuttle runs frequently into the heart of the city and back to campus. The scenic Willamette River bisects Metropolitan Portland, which is home to approximately 2 million people. There are endless things to do in Portland: Park space occupying 10,477 acres of parks, 33 music groups, 35 theater and dance companies, 90 galleries and museums, and more than 1,000 restaurants. The city also offers professional baseball, hockey, soccer, and the NBA's Portland Trailblazers.

Just 50 miles east of campus rises Mount Hood and its 10-month-a-year skiing and snow-boarding. The rugged Oregon coastline is just 90 miles to the west. Throughout the state lie innumerable hiking, climbing, and backpacking opportunities.

OFF-CAMPUS OPPORTUNITIES

Overseas and off-campus study programs have been a big part of Lewis & Clark for over 45 years. Each year, about 300 students participate in two dozen programs abroad and in selected areas of the United States. During the next few years, programs will be offered in the Arizona Borderlands, Australia, Chile, China, Cuba, Dominican Republic, East Africa, Ecuador, England, France, Germany, Ghana, Greece, India, Italy, Japan, Morocco, New York, New Zealand, Russia, Scotland, Senegal, Spain, Vietnam and Washington, D.C.

Whether their off-campus study is domestic or abroad, students earn credit (equivalent to a full semester or year) for their academic work. Depending on the specific program content, it is possible to earn General Education and/or major credit during these programs. Typically, over 50% of students participate in one of these programs prior to graduating from Lewis & Clark. Students can use Lewis & Clark's financial aid and scholarships for assistance in these programs.

MAJORS AND DEGREES OFFERED

The College offers one degree: the Bachelor of Arts. Students have a wide selection of majors from which to choose: art (studio), art history, biochemistry and molecular biology, biology, chemistry, communication, computer science, computer science and mathematics, East Asian studies, economics (international, management, public policy, and theory), English, environmental studies, foreign languages, French, German, Hispanic studies, history, international affairs, mathematics, music, philosophy, physics, political science, psychology, religious studies, sociology/anthropology, and theater. Students may also design their own major, pursue a double major, or select from 25 minors. Pre-professional programs are available in dentistry, education, law, and medicine. Dual degree programs in engineering (3-2 or 4-2) are available in conjunction with Columbia University in New York, Washington University in St. Louis, the University of Southern California in Los Angeles, and the OGI School of Science & Engineering in Beaverton, Oregon. A dual degree, 4-2 B.A/M.B.A. program is available in conjunction with the Simon Graduate School of Business at the University of Rochester. A dual degree, 4-1 B.A/M.A.T program is available in conjunction with Lewis & Clark's Graduate School of Education and Counseling.

ACADEMIC PROGRAMS

A liberal arts education at Lewis & Clark connects classical learning with fresh inquiry and exciting research that pushes the frontiers of knowledge. Lewis & Clark considers the following elements essential to a liberal arts education:

1. Mastery of the fundamental techniques of intellectual inquiry: effective writing and speaking, active reading, and critical and imaginative thinking.

2. Exposure to the major assumptions, knowledge, and approaches in the fine arts, humanities, natural sciences and social sciences.

3. Critical understanding of important contemporary and historical issues.

4. Awareness of international and cross-cultural issues and gender relations.

5. Application of theory and knowledge to the search for informed, thoughtful and responsible solutions to important human problems.

The curriculum combines structure and freedom. Depth and breadth of subject matter are highly valued, but equally important are creativity and critical thinking. There are many opportunities for students to take their learning to a higher level, such as honors projects within academic departments, independent research, and internships.

Two 15-week semesters make up the academic year, and each semester students normally take four 4-semester-hour courses, and one or more activity courses. The average student course load is 16 credits per semester. The requirement for graduation is 128 semester hours—approximately eight classes each year.

CAMPUS FACILITIES AND EQUIPMENT

Located on Palatine Hill on a former estate, Lewis & Clark offers students a campus of unmatched physical beauty, along with academic and residential buildings designed to support a rigorous academic environment and strong sense of community.

The academic buildings include: the Aubrey R. Watzek library, which is open 24 hours on weekdays during the school year and houses over 710,000 items including books, documents, audiovisual materials, microforms, and periodicals. Through the Summit catalog, access to approximately 28 million items from 36 member institutions in the Pacific Northwest. Also houses the most extensive collection of printed materials known to exist on the Lewis and Clark Expedition. Evans Music Center, which includes a 410-seat recital hall equipped with an orchestra pit and stage elevator, 22 practice rooms, 43 pianos, two harpsichords, four pipe organs including an 85-rank Casavant pipe organ, a Baroque organ, Javanese gamelan, and an electronic music studio with CD production capability; Fir Acres Theatre, which houses a 225-seat Main Stage performance/teaching theatre and a black-box experimental theatre (also used as dance studio) along with a scene shop, costume room, green room and design lab; the Olin Center (physics and chemistry), the Biology-Psychology building, and BoDine (mathematical sciences), which all house well-equipped classrooms and extensive laboratory spaces for our natural sciences. Among our notable science facilities are a scanning electron microscope, a molecular modeling lab, a gas chromatograph/mass spectrometer, a high-pressure liquid chromatograph, 300 MHz FTNRM spectrometer, inert spectrophotometers, infrared spectrometers, observatory with Newtonian and solar telescopes, computer-enhanced optical microscope, a solid-state physics lab with variable temperature cryostat and superconducting magnet, a lab for studying the biomechanics of animal locomotion, an astrophysics lab and a lab for studying parallel computing. Nearby Tryon Creek State Park and the Columbia River Gorge are frequently used as laboratories for field courses in biology and geology.

Among other academic buildings are the Fields Center, which includes studio facilities for drawing, painting, sculpture, ceramics, computer graphics, graphic design, and photography; the Miller Center and Howard Hall (opened in 2005), are home to the humanities and social sciences with state-of-the-art classrooms, small auditoriums, and the Keck Interactive Language Lab.

Our computer facilities include several labs in academic buildings available for student use. More than 130 Mac, IBM, and compatible computers are available for students, along with peripherals such as color scanners, color printers, digital cameras and digital-video editing equipment. All residence halls have wireless network access. The institution has a 200 Mbps (Megabits per second) connection to the internet.

TUITION, ROOM, BOARD AND FEES

In 2009–10, tuition and fees were $35,233 and room and board were $9,006. Students have several meal plan options. Books and miscellaneous expenses were approximately $2,040.

FINANCIAL AID

During the 2008–09 academic year approximately 69 percent of Lewis & Clark students received some form of financial assistance. Individual aid packages ranged from $500 to $45,576. Institutional, state, and federal resources including grants, loans and work-study may be part of an aid package. Eligibility for need-based funds is based primarily on an analysis of the income and asset information submitted on the Free Application for Federal Student Aid (FAFSA) and the College Board's CSS/Financial Aid PROFILE. Household size and the number of students in college (excluding parents) are also considered in the analysis. Students must submit the FAFSA and PROFILE by February 15 in order to get priority consideration for financial aid.

STUDENT ORGANIZATIONS AND ACTIVITIES

With over 40 student organizations, there's never a lack of things to do at Lewis & Clark. Cultural events include lectures, symposia, art exhibits, plays, musical events, and dance performances. Athletics play an important role on campus, where 19 varsity teams, nine club teams, and numerous intramural sports keep students physically active. Nature-lovers will enjoy the College Outdoors Program, which offers activities such as hiking, backpacking, rafting, skiing, and kayaking in the wilderness of the Pacific Northwest. There are also plenty of opportunities for volunteering in and around the Portland area.

Lewis & Clark is committed to residential education, to creating a community dedicated to the exploration of ideas, values, beliefs and backgrounds, to the discovery of lifelong friendships; and to collaboration, both formal and informal, with peers, faculty, and staff. There is no Greek system at Lewis & Clark.

About 67 percent of undergraduates live on campus in residence halls; most of our residential space is co-ed. Along with personal living space (usually shared by two to four students) are several community venues within the residence halls, including coffee houses, convenience stores, art centers, outdoor basketball courts, recreation and fitness centers, lounges, and game rooms.

ADMISSIONS PROCESS

Commitment to academic excellence and personal and intellectual growth is imperative for successful Lewis & Clark applicants. Lewis & Clark is very selective, and every part of the application matters: academic records, essays, involvement in activities at school and in the community, leadership, and the strength of recommendations. Students are encouraged to visit our campus. Interviews are available but not required. The best-prepared applicants will have had four years of English, four years of mathematics, three to four years of history or social sciences, three years of laboratory sciences, two to three years of a foreign language, and one year of fine arts. Required credentials include: an essay; an official transcript including senior grades from first semester; a counselor recommendation; and one academic teacher recommendation. Lewis & Clark requires the SAT or ACT, except if the student is applying via the Portfolio Path (see www.lclark.edu for details). Students apply using either the on-line or paper version of the Common Application. The $50 application fee is waived for students applying on-line. Keep in mind these deadlines: First-year applicants—November 1 for non-binding Early Action (notification, January 1) and February 1 for Regular Decision (notification, April 1). Transfer applicants are reviewed on a rolling basis.

LIBERTY UNIVERSITY

Liberty University, the world's largest Christian university, is dedicated to academic excellence and spiritual growth. Liberty offers more than 60 programs of study and an average student-professor ratio of 23:1.

AT A GLANCE

Liberty University is committed to providing its students with a high-quality educational experience in a distinctly Christian environment. Certificate, associate, bachelor's, master's, and doctorate-level degrees are available from Liberty in residential, online and blended formats. Liberty has 20 NCAA Division I athletic teams and many club sports teams, including hockey. Weekly convocation services on campus bring spiritual, political, business and other influential leaders to LU students.

LOCATION AND ENVIRONMENT

Liberty University's 6,500-acre campus is situated in Central Virginia near the foothills of the Blue Ridge Mountains. The campus is just off Virginia highways 460 and 29 in the city of Lynchburg, about 180 miles southwest of Washington, D.C. This historic and picturesque setting provides a natural playground for outdoor enthusiasts, with mountains, lakes, waterfalls and more within a short drive.

OFF-CAMPUS OPPORTUNITIES

The city of Lynchburg offers a unique blend of shopping and outdoor recreation. Several large public parks provide college students and city residents with trail systems for running and biking. Liberty University is located off Lynchburg's main shopping and dining thoroughfare, Wards Road, where River Ridge Mall, and many chain stores and restaurants are located. Lynchburg also has a historic, riverside downtown area full of unique shops, cafes, restaurants and more. Within a 30-minute drive of the university campus are the Peaks of Otter, a particulary scenic portion of the Blue Ridge Mountains. Virginia's Natural Bridge is also located nearby, as are Crabtree Falls and the National D-Day Memorial. Local sports enthusiasts enjoy watching the Lynchburg Hillcats minor league baseball team.

MAJORS AND DEGREES OFFERED

All academic programs at LU consist of hands-on learning experiences. A fashion merchandising student might decorate a room in a professor's house or an aviation student will take his or her first solo flight; learning experiences at LU will expand students' résumé and life experiences. Certificate, associate, bachelor's, master's, and doctorate level degrees are available at Liberty in residential, online and blended formats.

Liberty Baptist Theological Seminary offers all the standard seminary degrees plus a few unique degree options, including Global Apologetics, Children's Ministry and Christian Leadership. More than 4,000 students are enrolled in the seminary's residential, online and blended format programs. E-mail LTS@liberty.edu for more information, or go to www.liberty.edu and click on seminary.

Liberty University School of Law is committed to excellence, with the class of 2008 achieving a 94.4 percent pass rate for the Virginia Bar exam. The School of Law facilities include a 34,000-square-foot law library, two mock trial courtrooms and a Supreme Courtroom that is an exact replica of the U.S. Supreme Courtroom in Washington, D.C., LU's student negotiation teams consistently win competitions and are ranked among the best in the nation. Go to http://law.liberty.edu/ for more information.

Liberty University Online has been ranked among the nation's top 10 online colleges for the past two years in a row by the Online Education Database. Its flexible format allows students to complete their degree at home in many fields, such as nursing, religion, business and more. Military students and their spouses can receive special LU Online benefits and discounts. Go to www.luonline.com for more information or call an Admissions Counselor at (800) 424-9595.

Schools/Colleges at LU

College of Arts and Sciences

Center for Academic Support and Advising Services

Helms School of Government

School of Aeronautics

School of Business

School of Communication

School of Education

School of Engineering and Computational Sciences

School of Law

School of Religion

Most popular majors at LU

Religion

Business

Communication Studies

Nursing

Psychology

Education

Unique Degrees LU Offers

Aviation

Fashion Merchandising & Interiors

Inter Cultural Studies

Pastoral Leadership & Biblical Exposition

Software Engineering

Worship & Music Studies

ACADEMIC PROGRAMS

The Liberty Honors Program offers Ivy League-sized classes to students who are interested in challenging themselves academically. Students are required to have a 3.5 GPA and 1270 SAT or 29 ACT to be admitted into this program. Call the Honors Program Office at (434) 592-3304 for more information.

The Study Abroad program offers students the opportunity to live and study in a culture different from the home campus, broadening and challenging their intellectual prospects in the midst of the global marketplace.

The Office of International Student Services hosts an international student orientation and other events to assist with international student's transition to America. Liberty currently enrolls more than 910 international students from 80 different countries.

The Center for Global Ministries provides students with cross-cultural mission experiences abroad and in the U.S. Short and long-term mission trips are available through this center. The Center for Global Ministries also puts on a missions conference at LU every semester.

The Student Advocate Office offers scholarship symposiums to students in search of additional financial aid.

Air Force and Army ROTC are both available at Liberty.

CAMPUS FACILITIES AND EQUIPMENT

Liberty University's campus includes a diverse range of academic, recreational and other facilities.

Resident students have five styles of residence halls in which they can choose to live. On-campus dining options include a traditional cafeteria style dining hall, Doc's Diner, Jazzman's Café, Sub Connection, Chick-fil-A, Tsunami Sushi, Pete's Arena Pizza, Jump Asian Express, Café a la Cart, Pizza Hut and more.

LU's state-of-the-art athletic facilities include the Tolsma Indoor Track, the LaHaye Ice Center, Matthes-Hopkins Complex and Soccer Field, the Worthington Baseball Stadium, the Vines Center, Williams Stadium and Football Operation Center.

New facilities added to the Liberty campus this year include a new indoor soccer complex, a paintball complex, a Barnes & Noble campus bookstore, archery fields, a motocross track and Liberty Mountain Snowflex Center—a year-round snowless ski slope.

Wireless internet is available campus wide. Go to www.libertyu.com for a virtual tour of the campus.

TUITION, ROOM, BOARD, AND FEES
Resident Undergraduate Student Costs

Full Time Tuition: $16,792 (per year)

Housing: $6,296-$7,592 (depending upon student's housing choice)

Activity/Student Center Fee: $530

Technology Fee: $584

Transportation Fee: $158

FINANCIAL AID

More than 95 percent of all Liberty students receive financial aid.

Liberty University has many scholarship opportunities available to students. The Liberty Champion, Pastor/Alumni Scholarship and New Student Book Dollars (for the campus bookstore) are three scholarships that many Liberty students receive. Scholarships can also be awarded for academic achievement, for students in the Honors Program and for athletes. Scholarship amounts vary throughout the year, so interested students should apply and confirm your enrollment early to obtain the highest amount of scholarships. Scholarships are secured after a student contributes his or her $250 confirmation deposit, which secures their place in LU's incoming class.

Many students also receive outside scholarships and grants, such as the Virginia Tuition Assistance Grant (VTAG). The VTAG is given to most college students from Virginia who are attending a private college or university in the commonwealth. The amount of this grant varies from year to year.

To learn more about financial aid at Liberty, apply for college loans, fill out the FAFSA, and more go to www.liberty.edu/financialaid or http://liberty.financialaidtv.com. Liberty's School Code for the FAFSA is 010392.

STUDENT ORGANIZATIONS AND ACTIVITIES

Liberty currently has 20 NCAA Division I athletic teams: Baseball, Men's Basketball, Women's Basketball, Softball, Men's Cross Country, Women's Cross Country, Football, Men's Golf, Men's Soccer, Women's Soccer, Men's Tennis, Women's Tennis, Men's Indoor and Outdoor Track & Field, Women's Indoor and Outdoor Track & Field, Men's Wrestling, Women's Volleyball, Women's Lacrosse and Women's Swimming.

Campus SERVE is a student-led initiative on Liberty's campus to bring Christianity into the local community, through service. Students who participate in this program often visit nursing homes or sponsor activities for children in government subsidized housing projects.

LU's Student Activities Office (SAO) is the fire-starter for many on-campus social events. The SAO runs motocross events, a trail race series for runners, archery tournaments, flag football, paintball tournaments and more. This office also operates Liberty's intramural sports and LU's seven competitive club teams: Women's Hockey, Men's Hockey, Men's Lacrosse, Men's Volleyball and Women's Equestrian.

Other major campus social events include Christian concerts (past artists include Switchfoot, tobyMac, and the Newsboys), karaoke nights, video game tournaments and more.

ADMISSIONS PROCESS

To apply to Liberty University go to www.libertyu.com or call an Admissions Counselor at (800) 543-5317 (Mon.–Fri. 8 a.m.-9 p.m. and Sat. 10 a.m.–6 p.m. ET). All applicants are required to submit an admissions essay, official SAT or ACT scores, high school and, if applicable, college transcripts. Some accepted students may be required to take College Learning Strategies 101 during their first semester at Liberty. This study skills course is designed to help high school students transition to a college academic workload.

E-mail admissions@liberty.edu for more information.

LIM COLLEGE

AT A GLANCE

LIM College is where business meets fashion. LIM College is located in New York City, the world's undisputed fashion capital. The campus is comprised of four locations in Midtown Manhattan, all within walking distance of each other, and our brand new residence hall on the Upper East Side.

LIM College is accredited by the Commission on Higher Education of the Middle States Association of Colleges and Schools.

The LIM College curriculum stresses both professional and academic preparation, a combination which ensures student success. Students at LIM College receive highly individualized attention as they study the fashion industry. The student body consists of approximately 1350 undergraduates. This small size means that students have near-universal access to instructors, staff, and administrators, up to and including the President.

The curriculum requires students to complete a core set of courses in fashion, business, and the liberal arts, and also emphasizes the importance of hands-on experience. This unique approach opens numerous options to graduates, whom the College prepares for work in management, marketing, and merchandising in both the traditional fashion world and fashion-related businesses.

The Center for Career Development is one of LIM College's chief assets. Every student receives extensive career assistance throughout their time at the College, beginning in the first semester. This counseling helps direct students to positions within their field of study. LIM College is extremely proud of its placement record: historically, more than 90 percent of graduates have been employed in their fields of study within six months of graduation, a remarkable feat within the highly competitive fashion industry.

LIM College's housing is currently located at the brand-new 1760 Third Avenue Residence on Manhattan's Upper East Side. It's just minutes away from fantastic restaurants and shopping, the remarkable sights and sounds of Museum Mile and Central Park, and two blocks from the subway. 24-hour security and a trained live-in staff ensure students' safety and comfort. Double and triple furnished rooms offer private bathrooms and a flat-screen TV with DVD player transmitting 130 digital cable stations, as well as a refrigerator and microwave. Each student receives free local telephone service with their own voicemail, as well as high-speed Internet service. This state-of-the-art building also features a game room, a fully-equipped 3,500 sq. ft. fitness center, and a computer center.

LIM College welcomes all who are interested to attend its Open House program. This program allows students and their families to tour the College with current students, learn about career opportunities in the fashion industry, explore academic programs and financing options, and meet with faculty and administrators.. LIM College also offers many other opportunities to visit including information sessions on Tuesdays, Thursdays, Fridays, and some Saturdays. Transfer Nights and other special events are scheduled periodically as well.

LIM College's student body is diverse, but they have one thing in common: a passion for fashion. As of Fall 2009, approximately 1350 students were enrolled at LIM College. 79% of the student body is from the Tri-State (NY, NJ, and CT) area. 24% of students live in LIM College housing. 94% of students are female. 80% of students receive some form of financial aid.

LOCATION AND ENVIRONMENT

LIM College students benefit from an amazing location in the heart of New York City. World-famous sights, including St. Patrick's Cathedral, Central Park, the Museum of Modern Art, the Garment District, and Rockefeller Center are all a short walk away from the College.

The fashion universe literally waits just beyond LIM College's front door. New York City is the center of many fashion and fashion-related industries, including cosmetics, textiles, visual merchandising, styling, and fashion publishing. The College's location and prestige guarantee that students will interact with many principals in these areas. Additionally, the curriculum frequently incorporates New York City's vast resources. For example, a student taking LIM's Fashion Magazines course could visit showrooms and magazine offices, meet designers, and enjoy other similar experiences. No other city offers the breadth of experiences and fashion-related opportunities that New York does.

ACADEMICS

Students learn in a variety of settings at LIM College. Classroom instruction is supplemented by required internships performed under the supervision of industry professionals. The entire curriculum is aimed at preparing students for entry-level executive positions throughout the fashion industry.

LIM College offers four majors: Fashion Merchandising, Visual Merchandising, Marketing, and Management. Students can earn the Bachelor of Business Administration (BBA) degree in these fields or a Bachelor of Professional Studies (BPS) in Fashion Merchandising. An Associate degree is also offered in Fashion Merchandising. Qualified students who already hold a bachelor's degree in another area may apply for a one-year Associate degree program (ACCESS).

LIM College also offers concentrations within its majors. The current list of concentrations includes: Fashion Merchandising, Visual Merchandising, Styling, Event Planning, Cosmetics, Fashion Publishing, Entrepreneurship, International Marketing, Retailing, and Fashion Communications.

The curriculum includes a required course consisting of field trips to various businesses within the fashion industry, as well as a required guest lecture course featuring fashion leading industry executives.

All students receive extensive work experience as part of their LIM College education. This internship program helps students become truly prepared for successful careers within the industry. During the freshman and sophomore years, student complete five-week internships called Work Projects I & II. Work Project I focuses on retailing, while Work Project II allows students to branch into other fields, such as management, publishing, cosmetics, advertising and public relations, or fashion forecasting. Both Work Projects dovetail with academic courses the students took during the fall semesters. The third and final internship is the semester-long Senior Co-op, which is a required four-day-a-week placement in a field related to the student's chosen area of specialization. Co-ops may take students to fashion magazines, public relations firms, buying offices, or other essential areas of the fashion industry. The Senior Co-op serves as an ideal culmination of the academic experience and a perfect transition into the business world, preparing undergraduates for the challenge and excitement of their future careers.

LIM College operates on a two-semester calendar and students may enter in either semester.

The College also offers summer and Saturday programs for high school students. Courses include Fashion Magazines, Fashion Show Production, Event Planning, Fashion Photography, Marketing Communications, Fashion Buying, and Fashion Styling, and combine traditional coursework with hands-on activities. These classes are a great way for high school students to jump into the world of fashion. The Fashion U program allows visiting transfer students to take up to 9 credits at LIM College over the summer and gain valuable experience in New York City.

CAMPUS FACILITIES AND EQUIPMENT

LIM College is situated in four buildings in Midtown Manhattan, on 45th, 53rd, 54th Streets and on 5th Avenue. All facilities house a blend of classrooms, administrative offices, computer labs, studios, and student lounges.

The Adrian G. Marcuse Library contains approximately 13,000 volumes pertaining to the liberal arts, fashion merchandising and related fields, as well as 130 professional and academic journals. The Library also offers access to an extensive array of online databases worldwide.

Personal computers are available for use throughout the College. The student/computer ratio is 5:1. LIM College also offers wireless internet throughout all four of its locations.

The Math and Writing Centers offer peer tutoring and special programs to supplement and reinforce classroom learning and further develop students' skills in those areas.

TUITION, ROOM, BOARD AND FEES

Tuition for the 2009–2010 academic year is $19,900 and mandatory fees are $525. On average, students spend an additional $1,100 per year on books and supplies. Commuters normally spend $750 to $2,000 for transportation, depending on commuting distance. The LIM College residence hall is comprised of double and triple rooms costing $15,400 and board is approximately $4000 for the academic year. Students should also budget about $2,000 per year for personal expenses.

FINANCIAL AID

LIM College wants every student it admits to be able to attend the College and works hard to make its education affordable to all. Admissions decisions are made independently of financial aid considerations. Approximately 80% of our undergraduates receive financial assistance in some form: grants, scholarships, loans, and work-study are made available to students who qualify.

Students should submit the Free Application for Federal Student Aid (FAFSA) by March 1 to receive priority consideration for financial assistance. Aid in all forms is available on a need basis. Merit scholarships are awarded to those with high academic achievement and other significant talents, regardless of financial need.

LIM College offers merit scholarships to both incoming freshmen and transfer students. The College gives these awards to candidates who demonstrate exceptional academic ability in high school or college.

Please consult our website to learn about other need and non-need based scholarships. You can also contact Student Financial Services for more details.

STUDENT ORGANIZATIONS AND ACTIVITIES

The mission of the Office of Student Life is to provide a supportive social environment and a wealth of cultural opportunities that cultivate personal and academic growth. Club advisors are experienced in their field and can help you connect with key people in the industry. You can meet friends, build a resume, and make the most of your college experience by joining a student club.

Co-curricular organizations include the Student Council, the Fashion Club, the Styling Club, Students in Free Enterprise (SIFE), Fashion Sense magazine and various other clubs formed by students to serve special needs and interests. Students create the annual yearbook (called LIMLIGHT), produce the annual fashion show, which hosted over 1000 guests last year, and organize cultural and social activities. Eligible students may be nominated for Sigma Beta Delta, the national honor society. Other activities/organizations include the Explore New York program, the annual ski trip, and the Multicultural Activities Board.

Each year, LIM College students participate in several different volunteer activities including the Revlon Run/Walk for Women's Cancers and the school Blood Drive.

STUDY ABROAD OPPORTUNITIES

Fashion is a notably international industry, and LIM College recognizes and appreciates that through its off-campus opportunities, all offered for academic credit. For students who are interested in seeing the broad scope of European fashion, there is a short-term study abroad each January. This tour highlights European fashion capitals as well as figures and companies in each of the locations (which are determined on an annual basis).

A second opportunity is a summer experience in Paris, France. This two-week program allows students the opportunity to get their feet wet in one of the industry's oldest and most prestigious world capitals.

LIM College has recently added two new summer programs at American University in Rome and a field trip to China, including stops in Beijing, Hong Kong, and Shanghai.

The highlight of LIM College's study abroad program gives students the chance to study abroad for a full semester during their junior year at University of Westminster in England. The Westminster exchange program includes an internship and is ideal for students who are looking for a longer-term immersion program.

ADMISSIONS

LIM College has a rolling admissions policy. All students are required to submit the LIM College application for admission, an essay, a $40 fee, SAT or ACT scores, two letters of recommendation and official high school transcripts from all high schools attended. After receipt of academic transcripts and test scores some applicants may be asked to complete a personal interview. LIM College strongly suggests all applicants submit an activity sheet or resume.

Transfer students must also submit official transcripts from all colleges attended. The SAT/ACT requirement is waived for transfer students with more than 30 credit hours or who are over 25. International students must also submit TOEFL, IELTS, or PTE scores.

To be considered for Early Action Admission, applicants must complete all the application requirements and the Early Action Applicant form by November 15. An Early Action Applicant Form can be obtained from the LIM College website.

LYNN UNIVERSITY

AT A GLANCE

Located on the southeast Florida coast near Miami and Palm Beach, Lynn University is conveniently situated near three major airports. Our nearly 2,400 students come from more than 80 countries and almost every state. One-quarter of our student body is international.

ACADEMICS

Lynn University faculty members love teaching and challenge you to become active, intentional and purposeful learners. We welcome students who have varying levels of academic abilities and learning styles and a strong desire to excel. Classes average 15 students.

The innovative curriculum is career-focused with a broad-based liberal arts foundation that stresses both critical thinking and real-life applications. Our core curriculum is called "The Dialogues of Learning." It's divided into three areas: Self and Society, Belief and Reason and Justice and Civic Life, and has a number of distinctive features. For example, instead of taking the traditional two years of general education courses before you can begin taking courses in your major, you'll take foundation courses along with major courses throughout your four years of study. Forget traditional college algebra—instead, you'll be taking relevant, real-world math and science classes, and doing writing and public speaking in every class. Your readings will be from Eastern and Western thought, along with ancient and modern-day texts. And you won't be sitting in any lecture halls. Instead, all your classes will be made up of 15 students or less, and half or more of your classes will be taught in seminar format. The Dialogues of Learning ensure that your time, and investment, at Lynn are rewarded—with intensive experiences, fresh insight into and a heightened awareness of yourself, your community and the larger world. Most important, you'll have the knowledge and skills necessary to thrive in a global society and economy.

In addition to colleges of liberal education, business, communication, education and hospitality, Lynn has a school of aeronautics and conservatory of music. Most majors require completion of at least one internship for experience in the major and resume-building.

ADMISSIONS

Lynn has rolling admissions with a priority deadline of March 1. Lynn accepts the Lynn application, the Common Application or the Universal College Application. You can apply online directly at http://www.lynn.edu/admissions/applying-to-lynn/apply-now. Successful applicants generally have a B or better high school GPA. The middle 50 percent of admitted students achieved a combined SAT score (critical reading + math) of 880-1050. Students with an outstanding high school profile will be encouraged to apply for our honors program, which affords additional academic opportunities.

Do you have a clear idea of what you want to get from your college experience? Then Lynn's 3-year degree plan is a powerful strategy to enhance your academic and career path. Beginning in fall 2010, you can apply to become one of a select group of first-year students who can choose to complete their Lynn University degrees in 3 instead of the typical 4 years—a way to achieve your educational aspirations sooner and make a Lynn University degree more affordable. In fact, you'll save an estimated $45,600 (tuition and fees, room and board, books, transportation, and personal expenses) over the cost of a 4-year degree.

You can apply for the 3-year degree plan if you achieve a 3.0 GPA during your first semester and maintain the same GPA during spring semester. If accepted, the dean of the college in which your major is offered will become your academic advisor and will closely guide you in choosing your courses and making sure you are on track.

Like your peers, you'll take a course load of 15 credit hours for the fall and spring semesters plus 2 credits (one course) during the January term. Once selected into the 3-year degree plan, you'll enroll in summer school tuition-free to take 9 credit hours of 200-level Dialogues of Learning (Lynn's core curriculum) courses. The second year and third years, you'll take 18 credits fall and spring semesters and two January term courses (4 credits), for 40 credits each year.

CAMPUS FACILITIES AND EQUIPMENT

Classrooms have SMART boards and the entire campus is wireless. Besides five dormitories, a student center and a library that includes one of the largest African art collections in the southeast, the campus has two pools, state-of-the-art library and communication studios, science labs, athletic and fitness facilities, and a concert hall. The new 750-seat Keith C. and Elaine Johnson Wold Performing Arts Center hosts live theatrical performances by Lynn's drama program, Conservatory of Music concerts and many types of live productions.

COLLEGE BASICS

Lynn's dynamic faculty focuses exclusively on teaching. The individualized attention they provide helps you set your goals and lay out a roadmap to realizing them. The January term, "Dialogues of Innovation," enables you to spend an intensive three-week period exploring subjects in depth. Past J-term courses had students performing live on Broadway in New York City; traveling to Colorado to work behind the scenes at the 2009 ESPN Winter X Games; and seeing firsthand the inauguration of President Barack Obama. Lynn also offers renowned support programs for students with learning differences.

OFF CAMPUS OPPORTUNITIES

The curriculum emphasizes a global view and offers study abroad opportunities for a semester, a year or during the January term. Lynn's career center helps you find internships and jobs with top companies and government organizations around the country and the world. You have the opportunity to build an impressive resume through internships in your major field.

TUITION AND FEES

Tuition for 2010–11 is $29,400. Room and board ranges from $10,900 to $14,100, depending on room type and meal plan.

MARLBORO COLLEGE

AT A GLANCE

Marlboro College is a liberal arts college known for the rigor of its academic program. The philosophy at Marlboro is that of self-governance and students who value learning for its own sake. The curriculum combines wide exploration in many courses within the first two years with more focused research and independent study in the second two years, culminating in a major body of work known as the Plan of Concentration. Marlboro College also offers numerous opportunities to study abroad through the World Studies Program, Asian Studies and other programs.

LOCATION AND ENVIRONMENT

Nestled in the foothills of southern Vermont, Marlboro College offers the benefits of living in the country, with more urban areas nearby. The campus is situated on the side of Potash Hill in the town of Marlboro, Vermont. Most of the 350-acre campus is deliberately preserved as natural forest with trails and streams running through the property. Our location serves to both inspire and inform the unique nature of our undergraduate experience.

Off-Campus Opportunities

With the location of Brattleboro, a town of 12,000, just 10 miles away and Northampton, Massachusetts, 45 minutes away, Marlboro students have access to many resources, activities, and cultural life in central New England and New York. Vans run from the college into Brattleboro multiple times a day and trips to Northeastern cities such as Boston, New York and Montreal occur several weekends each semester.

MAJORS AND DEGREES OFFERED

Marlboro College provides a liberal arts education where students are able to work independently and at the same time closely with their teachers to achieve their academic goals. The college offers more than 30 degree fields in the Arts, the Humanities, the Natural Sciences and the Social Sciences. In developing their own courses of study, students are encouraged, though not required, to draw from more than one area and design an interdisciplinary Plan of Concentration. Degrees offered include Bachelor of Arts, Bachelor of Science and, through the World Studies Program, Bachelor of Arts or Science in International Studies.

American Studies

Anthropology

Art History

Asian Studies

Astronomy

Biochemistry

Biology

Ceramics

Chemistry

Classics

Computer Science

Cultural History

Dance

Economics

Environmental Studies

Film/Video Studies

Foreign Languages

History

Literature

Mathematics

Music

Painting

Philosophy

Photography

Physics

Political Science

Psychology

Religion

Sociology

Theater

Visual Arts

World Studies Progam

Writing

ACADEMIC PROGRAMS

The first two years at Marlboro are designed to give students the opportunity to study broadly in many different courses and areas. With the approval of their faculty advisor, students choose their own course schedules incorporating course work from all four areas of the curriculum: arts, humanities, sciences, and social sciences. The one requirement every student must take within their first three semesters is the Clear Writing Program. When a student moves from the sophomore to the junior year, it is referred to as going "on Plan."

The Plan of Concentration is what sets Marlboro's curriculum apart from other colleges and is Marlboro's alternative to traditional majors. Plans are often interdisciplinary and self-designed with faculty sponsors. In the junior year, Plan students spend time strengthening their knowledge in the particular areas of study on which they are focusing. In the senior year, students complete a great deal of independent study and research. Throughout the whole process of working on their Plan, students benefit from the close academic sponsorship they receive from faculty members. Ultimately, evaluators from outside the college who are considered experts in their field are also included in the final assessment of a student's "Plan of Concentration."

The World Studies Program (WSP) integrates the best traditions of liberal arts learning and international studies with a six-to-eight-month working internship in a foreign culture. Students use their experiences abroad in their Plan of Concentration work. Students in the WSP design and carry out their internships in numerous fields, including photojournalism, business, education, relief work, development, anthropology, and scientific research, to name just a few. Graduates of the program have been accepted to many prestigious graduate schools, and more than two-thirds of the program's graduates now work or study in international fields. The World Studies Program operates in conjunction with the School for International Training in Brattleboro, Vermont, about 15 miles away from Marlboro's campus.

CAMPUS FACILITIES AND EQUIPMENT

Many of the campus buildings were originally farmhouses and barns renovated by the first students who attended Marlboro. These include Dalrymple Hall, which is the main classroom building; the dining hall; the admissions building; Mather, the administrative building. Over many years the College added more buildings, including residence halls, student cabins and cottages, the Whittemore Theater, the Rice-Aron Library, and a post-and-beam campus center, which the students and faculty built through a joint effort. Recently the College has winterized its auditorium and built an art gallery, an art studio, a photography darkroom, an integrated science lab, a DNA lab, and a new residence hall. The Serkin Center for the Performing Arts is an outstanding new facility providing performance and rehearsal space, in support of all performing arts programs. The new Total Health Center opened in 2008.

TUITION, ROOM, BOARD, AND FEES

For the 2009–2010 academic year, the fees are as follows:

Tuition: $33,900

Fees: $1,220

Room: $5,190

Board: $4,230

Total: $44,540

FINANCIAL AID

Students should not refrain from applying to Marlboro College because of perceived inability to meet costs. Marlboro College is committed to helping every student who qualifies for financial aid assemble the resources necessary to attend. More than 80 percent of all Marlboro students receive financial aid. Applicants should contact the Financial Aid Office directly to request a financial aid packet, which includes step-by-step instructions. The deadline for completing the Free Application for Federal Student Aid (FAFSA) is March 1. After that date, the College cannot promise a full financial aid package. The financial aid office can be reached at 802-258-9312 or finaid@marlboro.edu.

STUDENT ORGANIZATIONS AND ACTIVITIES

One particularly unique feature of Marlboro College is the college-wide Town Meeting held every three weeks during each semester. On these Wednesday afternoons, the whole College community, including students, faculty, and staff, gathers after lunch to discuss and debate any variety of college issues. Town Meeting's all-inclusive nature distinguishes it from more traditional student body governments.

Marlboro College is not the type of college that has a football team, unless you count a pick-up game of tag football. Instead, one of the most heavily used student activities is the Outdoor Program, OP for short. The OP offers a variety of activities from week-long orientation trips for new students to weekend mini trips, to winter- and spring-break trips in tropical climates. Some of the popular activities have been rock climbing, hiking, rafting, kayaking, camping, yoga, intramural soccer, broomball and Ultimate Frisbee.

Marlboro College has no fraternities or sororities. Students enjoy a wide range of social, artistic, and cultural activities. A sampling of student activities in one semester would include performances by rock, folk, jazz, and ethnic bands; dances; lectures; poetry readings; recitals; plays; and concerts. Annual events that are considered traditions are Convocation, Cabaret, Broomball Tournament, Community and International Dinners, Gender Bender Ball and Apple Days.

ADMISSIONS PROCESS

Marlboro College seeks students with intellectual promise, a high degree of motivation, self-discipline, creativity, social concern, and the ability and desire to contribute to the College community. The admissions committee—composed of students, admissions counselors and faculty members—assesses student preparedness and academic potential in the unique context of each applicant's personal experience without the confines of G.P.A or standardized test score minimums.

Students may apply to Marlboro under three different application plans.

Early Decision: Deadline-December 1; Notification-December 15

Early Action: Deadline-February 1; Notification-February 15

Regular Admission: Priority Deadline-March 1; Notification-April 1

Please note that if you are applying for financial aid it is important to file the FAFSA no later than March 1.

In order to be considered for admission, please submit the following: a completed Common Application and Marlboro College Supplement with the "Why Marlboro?" personal statement, the $50 nonrefundable application fee, all high school and college transcript(s), an analytic writing sample, and two letters of recommendation (teacher and general). Submission of SAT or ACT scores is optional.

MARQUETTE UNIVERSITY

AT A GLANCE

As Wisconsin's largest private university, Marquette University offers endless opportunities: the chance to live, study and play in the heart of a dynamic city; nationally known programs and powerhouse faculty; a Catholic, Jesuit tradition that emphasizes ethics and lifelong values. For more than 127 years, we have inspired students to Be The Difference in their professional and personal lives.

Our more than 11,000 undergraduate and graduate students come from all 50 states and 70 countries to create a vibrant, diverse, residential learning experience. They learn from professors who believe that there is such a thing as a student-centered university that conducts world-class research.

Our rigorous academic programs are recognized for challenging students to grow intellectually, socially and spiritually. Our demanding core curriculum is grounded in the humanities, social sciences and natural sciences. This liberal arts core, coupled with a student's academic major, provides the balance of knowledge a student will need to succeed as a professional—and a person.

At Marquette, you'll have instant access to top-notch professors who win international awards and grants, publish influential works, and conduct cutting-edge research. And you won't just hear about that research. You'll have the chance to conduct it with faculty mentors, helping to advance your field while getting unrivaled experience.

You will have a diverse experience. As one of approximately 8,000 undergraduates, you will meet students who look, think and act very much like you—and more who don't. More than 90 percent of freshmen live on campus, so you're sure to find your niche in the Marquette family.

We'll ask you tough questions: "What do you believe in?" "What do you stand for?" "Why?" You will be challenged to lead a thoughtful, reflective life.

You will be encouraged to find God in all things. Through retreats, religious services, prayers and conversations within the university community, Marquette fosters an environment that nurtures spiritual growth for students of all faiths.

U.S. News & World Report ranks Marquette 84th among the nation's top 100 universities in the 2010 edition of "America's Best Colleges," and Marquette is one of 44 schools named a "Best Buy School" in the 2010 edition of the *Fiske Guide to Colleges*. Schools are chosen based on the quality of academic offerings in relation to the cost of attendance.

LOCATION AND ENVIRONMENT

With a metro population of almost one million, Milwaukee has all the bonuses you'd expect from a big city—like the arts, major-league sports, fantastic restaurants and shopping—with fewer of the hassles. And right at the heart of the city is Marquette's 90-acre campus, giving you easy access to everything Milwaukee has to offer, including internships, service opportunities and social activities. Your Marquette education will extend from campus classrooms to the larger, more expansive classroom that is the city. It's a place where you can connect what you're learning with what you can do with it.

OFF-CAMPUS OPPORTUNITIES

Your education doesn't need to be limited to Milwaukee. Each year, many Marquette students grab their passports, pack their bags and head off to distant lands to study for a few weeks, a semester or a year. The experience is life-changing. Marquette offers study-abroad and exchange program opportunities on every continent but Antarctica. And if you want to go there, we can probably arrange something for you.

If you prefer to stay in the states, Marquette University's Les Aspin Center for Government is one of the top legislative internship programs in Washington, D.C. For a semester or a summer, you can live, learn and work on Capitol Hill. Take an active role in the legislative process while you work as an intern or aide in the House of Representatives, the Senate or various federal agencies. You'll also take special courses and meet with government officials and dignitaries and become well-connected in a city where connections are everything.

MAJORS AND DEGREES OFFERED

The Carnegie Foundation classifies Marquette as a research university with high research activity, offering a wide variety of degrees. Marquette offers rigorous academic programs in 115 undergraduate majors and excellent advanced education in 34 master's degree programs, 17 doctoral programs, and more than 20 degree and certificate programs. Marquette also is home to the state's only School of Dentistry and a Law School with a reputation as a forum for public policy debate.

ACADEMIC PROGRAMS

At the heart of all Marquette academic programs is the University Core of Common Studies. You'll take courses in nine knowledge areas designed to teach you how to examine, engage and evaluate the world: rhetoric, mathematical reasoning, individual and social behavior, diverse cultures, literature, history of cultures and societies, science and nature, human nature and ethics, and theology. These courses will teach you how to understand and be understood, to act responsibly, and to think for yourself.

Marquette is a direct-entry university, allowing you to begin studying your major right away. Because you can deepen your interest, knowledge and expertise early, you'll practice what you've learned through internships in and beyond Milwaukee. If you are undecided about a major, your academic adviser can help find the right fit for your passions and abilities.

CAMPUS FACILITIES AND EQUIPMENT

More than 90 percent of Marquette's freshmen and sophomores live in nine on-campus residence halls, and most juniors and seniors live off campus in university-owned or independent apartments and houses. The high concentration of residential students gives Marquette a vitality not often found in urban universities. The Raynor Memorial Libraries offer areas for quiet and group study, as well as wireless Internet access and a coffee shop. When students aren't studying, you can find them enjoying our two recreation centers and campus green spots.

TUITION, ROOM, BOARD AND FEES

Full-time tuition for 2010–11 is $30,040. Room and board averages about $9,680, depending on location and meal plan.

FINANCIAL AID

We recognize that Marquette is a great place, but we also know that private school tuition can be rather expensive. That's why the university offers a variety of partial to full-tuition, merit-based scholarships. To apply for need-based financial aid, Marquette requests that you file the Free Application for Federal Student Aid. Financial need that is demonstrated on this form determines our ability to award federal, state, and university-funded grants and loans, as well as some forms of student employment.

STUDENT ORGANIZATIONS AND ACTIVITIES

With about 250 student organizations vying for your time, you won't be bored at Marquette. And because most of our students spend their weekends on campus, there's plenty to do here and around the city. Our students also don't hesitate to get out into the community, and 90 percent of undergraduates participate in service through a wide range of programs, student organizations, service-learning classes and one-day projects.

And when it comes to sports, you're at the right place. Whether you're a big-time intercollegiate athlete or a die-hard spectator, Marquette offers a huge variety of opportunities, including 14 varsity teams that compete in the NCAA Division I Big East Conference. If club and recreational sports are more your speed, we have about 50 coed, men's or women's clubs and intramural teams.

ADMISSIONS PROCESS

For all of its academic programs, Marquette has a priority admission deadline of December 1 (postmark date). Applications postmarked after December 1 will be considered on a space-available basis for admission and scholarship. Admission decisions are based on a thorough review of course selection, academic performance (grade point average), class rank (when applicable), ACT and/or SAT, recommendations, essay, and extracurricular activities. Visit www.marquette.edu/explore for more information about deadlines and requirements.

MARYMOUNT MANHATTAN COLLEGE

At Marymount Manhattan College, you'll find educational advantages of a small college—opportunities to explore your interests, the close-knit atmosphere, guidance from your professors—combined with the once in-a-lifetime opportunities of one of the greatest cities on earth.

AT A GLANCE

Marymount Manhattan College is a four-year, co-educational, non-sectarian, independent liberal arts college located in the highly desirable Upper East Side of Manhattan.

LOCATION AND ENVIRONMENT

MMC's campus extends from our residence hall in Midtown Manhattan to our classroom buildings, and other residence hall, on the Upper East Side of Manhattan. The main campus buildings include the science laboratories, classrooms, studios, galleries, computer labs, club meeting rooms, cafeteria, and performance venues. The College has 2,000 undergraduate students from 48 states and 36 countries.

OFF-CAMPUS OPPORTUNITIES

At MMC, your campus is New York City—that means your whole college experience is a little different. Students hang out in the surrounding restaurants, shop along Third Avenue, and relax in Central Park. MMC has an extensive internship program where student intern in some of the most prestigious companies in the world.

MAJORS AND DEGREES OFFERED

B.A., B.S., B.F.A degrees offered.

17 majors, over 35 minors, special programs and pre-professional tracks.

Divisions include Business Management & Accounting, Fine & Performing Arts, Social Science, Natural Sciences, and Humanities.

ACADEMIC PROGRAMS

Academic Access is a program designed to foster academic success for students with learning disabilities. Through accommodations and multifaceted support, students with learning difficulties will be able to handle the same curriculum as other qualified applicants to Marymount. Academic Access assists learning-disabled students through tutoring services, counseling, advisement, and priority registration. Once accepted into the program, students receive personalized assistance planning their programs based on a careful examination of their psycho-educational evaluations.

MMC students may spend a semester, a summer or January, or a full academic year studying abroad. The College offers a number of opportunities and formats to earn academic credits in programs throughout the world. Studying abroad enhances learning in several ways: students gain an international focus on world events, come to appreciate differing cultural perspectives, and often re-evaluate long-standing ideas and beliefs once taken for granted. An international experience will place you in a global setting that highlights the interrelatedness of nations and the commonality of problems.

The Arthur O. Eve Higher Education Opportunity Program (HEOP) is a New York State funded program that supports five years of undergraduate study. It is specifically designed for students who meet both the educational and economic guidelines established by the New York State Education Department (NYSED). HEOP provides supportive services and **supplementary** financial assistance to students who demonstrate potential for academic success. HEOP has been an integral part of Marymount Manhattan College since 1969.

CAMPUS FACILITIES AND EQUIPMENT

The Commons & Lowerre Family Terrace

The newly opened Commons adjoins the Lowerre Family Terrace, which opened in Fall 2008. These renovations have allowed the College to create nearly 20,000 square feet of contiguous student-centered space at the center of its campus. The Commons, located in the Main Building, offers a new space that fosters interaction among students, faculty and staff. The upper tier (fourth floor) provides a spacious food servery and a staircase that connect to the student lounge. The student lounge (third floor) includes flexible, private areas that can be used for meetings and gatherings, and features a glass canopy and vanishing glass wall system that opens out to the Terrace. The Lowerre Family Terrace links the College's Main and Nugent Buildings providing students with access to the newly renovated Thomas J. Shanahan Library.

The Theresa Lang Center for Producing

Hands-on learning meets state of the art. Here, you'll find studios for experimental video, digital sound design, and graphic design; a non-linear digital video editing suite; and a digital media lab for online publishing and broadcast programming. High-end Macintosh workstations run an array of industry standard software, including Maya, Pro-Tools, and Final Cut Pro.

The Ruth Smadbeck Communication and Learning Center

This on-campus center gives our speech-language pathology and audiology students a level of experience and training they normally wouldn't get until graduate school.

The Theresa Lang Theatre

Interested in theatre? Our professionally equipped facility hosts student performances as well as professional music, dance, opera and theatre companies. On-campus forums about the American theatre have drawn such greats as Stephen Sondheim, John Guare, Wendy Wasserstein, George C. Wolfe and Harold Prince.

The Writing Center

MMC's Writing Center offers the support and resources to help writers at every level improve their ability. The Center hosts a Best Selling Authors Series, monthly writing workshops, courses taught by professional writers and editors, and our annual Writers' Conference.

Art Studios

Whatever your medium, we've got the facilities—drawing, painting, and design studios; a dark room; a printmaking center with lithography and etching presses; a ceramics studio; and a dedicated Mac Lab loaded with the latest computer graphics technology. And if you're serious about photography, you can take classes at the International Center for Photography and apply them toward your MMC degree.

The Great Hall

MMC's four on-campus dance studios include the Great Hall, one of New York City's largest dance studios. The other studios are equally excellent spaces and are equipped with Marley flooring, mirrors, barres and pianos.

The Thomas J. Shanahan Library

With 85,000 books, 4,000 videos and CDs, 735 periodical subscriptions, 4,000 e-books, and over 50 electronic databases (and wireless access), our library reflects our commitment to new technological learning resources. Can't find what you're looking for? You can simultaneously search 15 other local college libraries.

TUITION, ROOM, BOARD, AND FEES

2009–2010 Academic Year Costs

MMC provides exceptional education at a substantially lower tuition than most private colleges in our region. 2009–10 tuition and fees are $22,656 per year and residence and board are $12,874 per year. For 2010–11, please see our website after 4/1/10.

FINANCIAL AID

College can be expensive, but at Marymount Manhattan, more than 85 percent of our students receive some form of financial assistance—which makes MMC an affordable and wise investment. We invite you to investigate your financial aid options and apply for aid. If you have questions, please feel free to contact the Center for Student Services at 212-517-0500.

Scholarships, Grants, Loans, and Work-study are all offered at MMC. Complete FAFSA for consideration for need-based aid.

STUDENT ORGANIZATIONS AND ACTIVITIES

Over 35 clubs and organizations for interests in academics, cultural diversity, religion, community service, social events, arts, and politics. There is an intramural sports program at MMC, but no professional college sports are offered.

ADMISSIONS PROCESS

Undergraduate admission to Marymount Manhattan is competitive, and based on your standardized test scores, high school record, college transcripts (if applicable), counselor/employer recommendations, and an essay.

Freshman Applicants

- Completed application
- Official copy of high school or secondary school transcript or GED score sheet and GED diploma (final transcript, with posted graduation date, required upon registration)
- SAT I and/or ACT scores
- Two recommendations
- Essay (250–500 words)

$60 nonrefundable application fee

Transfer Applicants (completed college credit or high school graduates enrolled in the first semester of college)

- Completed application
- Official transcripts from any and all post-secondary institutions attended
- Official copy of high school or secondary school transcript with graduation date posted
- SAT I and/or ACT scores (may be required)
- One recommendation
- Essay (250–500 words)
- Judicial Record Form
- $60 nonrefundable application fee

International Applicants (non-US)

- Completed application
- Official copy of high school or secondary school transcript (must be issued on school stationary and mailed to our office directly or brought to us by the student in a sealed envelope --- it must list all classes taken each semester with the number of credits/ hours per week or month or semester with final grades earned) or GED score sheet and GED diploma (certified English language translation required, if applicable)
- Official transcripts from any and all accredited post-secondary institutions attended (evaluation may be required by World Education Services, contact Director of International Recruitment for determination (-transfer students only)
- TOEFL examination score (or IELTS score if English is not your native language), or SAT and/or ACT scores if English is your native language. (must be sent to the College by the testing center, You can order the scores for free at the time of exam taking- our code is 2405 or for a fee later).
- I-20 application
- Two recommendations from academic or professional sources. If transferring from another college or university, complete only one recommendation and the Judicial Record Form
- Essay (250–500 words)
- F-1 Student Transfer Certification Form (if currently studying in the U.S.)
- Copy of biographical page of passport
- Personal Interview (recommended)
- $60 nonrefundable application fee

Additional Requirements (if applicable)

- Auditions/interviews required to be considered for the Theatre and Dance programs (Theater applicants must call to schedule auditions early as space is limited, priority deadline of December 15; Dance applicants are not required to call, only to submit the official Dance Application directly to the Dance Office.)
- Portfolio reviews/interviews required to be considered for an Art scholarship. Deadline to submit portfolio is February 1 (fall entry)/December 1 (spring entry).
- Personal interview (may be required)
- Students applying to the Program for Academic Access must submit documentation of a learning disability. Deadline to complete your application is March 1. You must submit all admission requirements AND your LD Testing to complete your application by the deadline.
- To be eligible for HEOP (Higher Education Opportunity Program), students must meet certain academic and financial criteria and be residents of the state of New York. Deadline to complete your application is May 1.
- To apply for need-based federal financial aid, complete the FAFSA after January 1.
- To apply for need-based state financial aid, New York State residents should file the TAP application.

MARYMOUNT UNIVERSITY

AT A GLANCE

Marymount is a comprehensive Catholic university offering undergraduate, graduate, and certificate programs through four schools: Arts and Sciences, Business Administration, Education and Human Services, and Health Professions. The University is located in Arlington, Virginia, just across the Potomac River from the nation's capital.

The University's undergraduate programs combine a strong liberal arts foundation with solid career preparation. Small classes and professors who take a personal interest in student success provide a supportive academic environment. The selective Honors Program draws on all facets of the curriculum to offer highly motivated students extra opportunities for academic enrichment. The University's *Discover Program* offers opportunities for student research, both independent and faculty-mentored, as well as other forms of inquiry learning.

Marymount students enjoy the benefits of the many educational and cultural resources of Washington, DC. Distinguished speakers of national and international stature are frequent visitors to campus; Marymount guests have included Nobel Laureate Desmond Tutu, General Colin L. Powell (USA, Ret.), and fashion designer Michael Kors. Internships provide invaluable hands-on experience in exciting locations in and around Washington, D.C, including Capitol Hill, the National Institutes of Health, the Smithsonian museums, and international businesses. Study Abroad programs offer students the chance to live, study, and complete an internship in virtually every corner of the world.

Marymount's vibrant campus offers something for everyone: athletics, student government, Campus Ministry, volunteer service programs, and more than 30 clubs address diverse interests and provide opportunities for involvement. An NCAA Division III school, Marymount fields men's and women's basketball, cross-country, lacrosse, soccer, and swimming, plus men's golf and women's volleyball.

As a Catholic university, Marymount is a community where people of all faiths and cultures are welcome. The student body represents more than 40 states and nearly 70 countries, adding a wide array of experiences and perspectives that enrich the learning experience.

Visit Marymount and see for yourself all that the University has to offer! Join us for a Campus Visit Day which are held in the fall and spring or arrange for your own visit. A student ambassador will give you a campus tour and answer questions about everything from academics and the social scene to cafeteria food. An admissions counselor will provide details on the admissions process, financial aid and scholarship opportunities, and academic requirements. You can also arrange to talk with faculty or coaches.

To learn more about Marymount University, call (800) 548-7638; e-mail prospective. students@marymount.edu, or visit us online at www.marymount.edu.

LOCATION AND ENVIRONMENT

Marymount's Main Campus and Ballston Center are located in Arlington, Virginia, just minutes from Washington, DC. The public Metrorail system connects the University with the entire metropolitan Washington area. The University also maintains a free shuttle service that connects the Main Campus, Ballston Center, and Ballston MU-Metro station. Students have easy access to national landmarks, cultural sites, restaurants, and shopping.

Marymount's Reston Center is located in western Fairfax County. The Reston Center is an adult education center that offers programs in business, education, and interior design.

OFF-CAMPUS OPPORTUNITIES

University faculty and students takes full advantage of the resources in and around the nation's capital. Popular internship sites include Congressional offices, the Smithsonian museums, the White House, major media outlets, international businesses, and prestigious health care institutions. Students also have access to incredible research facilities such as the Library of Congress. During your Marymount years, you'll have the opportunity to fully experience Washington, DC, and many of the activities are free! Sit in on a Congressional hearing, attend the National Christmas Tree Lighting, or view the latest exhibit at the National Gallery of Art! And if you're a sports fan, DC is home to professional football, basketball, baseball, soccer, and ice hockey teams. Culture, history, world-class museums, restaurants, theatre, sports and music are all just across the Potomac River from Marymount.

MAJORS AND DEGREES OFFERED

The University offers a strong liberal arts education combined with solid career preparation. The following is a listing of Marymount's undergraduate majors and degree programs:

ACADEMIC PROGRAMS

Undergraduates can choose from such diverse fields as business, education, arts and sciences, psychology, technology, and the health professions.

Art (B.A., B.A. with teaching licensure)

  Art Management

  Pre-Art Therapy

Biology (B.S, B.S. with teaching licensure)

General Biology

Molecular and Cellular Biology

Pre-Medicine

  Business Administration (B.B.A., B.B.A./M.B.A)

Accounting

Business Law

Finance

General Business

Hospitality Management

International Business

Management

Marketing

Sport Management

Communication (B.A.)

Computer Science (See Information Technology)

Criminal Justice (B.A.)

Criminal Justice/Forensic Science (B.S.)

Economics in Society (B.A.)

English (B.A., B.A. with teaching licensure)

  Dramatic Arts

  Literature

  Writing

Fashion Design (B.A.)

Fashion Merchandising (B.A.)

Graphic Design (B.A.)

Health Sciences (B.S., B.S./M.S.)

  Health Promotion

  Pre-Physical Therapy

History (B.A.. B.A. with teaching licensure)

Information Technology (B.S., B.S. /M.S.)

  Applied IT

  Computer Science

  Forensic Computing

  Information Systems

Interior Design (B.A.)

Liberal Studies (B.A.)

Mathematics (B.S., B.S. with teaching licensure)

Multidisciplinary Studies (B.A. with teaching licensure for Elementary Education grades PK–6; B.A. with teaching licensure for Special Education, grades K–12)

Nursing (B.S.N.)

Paralegal Studies (B.A.)

Philosophy (B.A.)

Politics (B.A.)

Psychology (B.A)

Sociology (B.A.)

Theology and Religious Studies

Pre-Professional Studies

Pre-Law; Pre-Medicine; Pre-Physical Therapy

Teaching Licensure Programs

Art Education—grades K-12 (B.A. in Art; Elementary Education—grades PK-6 (B.A. in Multidisciplinary Studies); Secondary Education—grades 6-12; Biology (B.S.); English (B.A.); History/Social Science (B.A.); Mathematics (B.S.); Special Education, General Curriculum—grades K–12 (B.A. in Multidisciplinary Studies)

All Marymount undergraduate students complete an internship in their major. Other academic initiatives include the DISCOVER Program, an undergraduate research and inquiry learning endeavor. This multi-dimensional program oversees coordination of a first-year experience class, a summer research program with faculty mentors, the annual student-research conference, and the scheduling of workshops and seminars. The University also offers a selective Honors Program that provides highly-motivated students extra opportunities for academic enrichment. Honors Program benefits include substantial scholarship support, one-one-faculty mentoring, and special seminar and field-trip opportunities. Study Abroad programs are offered around the globe.

The college years are years of transformation. They are a time to explore interests and to grow in knowledge and understanding. The University strives to help students develop critical thinking and principled decision-making skills. A Marymount education puts an emphasis on scholarship, leadership, service, and ethics. These hallmarks serve our graduates well as they pursue personal and professional success beyond Marymount.

CAMPUS FACILITIES AND EQUIPMENT

Marymount University has two locations in Arlington, Virginia—the Main Campus and the Ballston Center. Marymount's Reston Center located in western Fairfax County focuses on meeting the educational needs of adult learners.

A major new facility is currently under construction on the Main Campus. During the fall of 2010, Marymount will open Caruthers Hall, an academic complex, and Rose Benté Lee Ostapenko Hall, a residential dormitory. The two new buildings will be connected by the Malek Family Plaza, a quad area where students will be able to socialize and relax. Caruthers Hall will house teaching and research labs for the sciences and health sciences, as well as classrooms, faculty offices, a computer lab, study lounges, and a café. Rose Benté Lee Ostapenko Hall will provide suite-style housing for more than 230 students.

Currently, the Main Campus consists of the Main House, academic buildings, residence halls, the Emerson G. Reinsch Library, and the Lee University Center. The Main House with its stately white columns is the signature symbol of Marymount University. This beautiful Georgian structure is where Marymount hosts programs honoring outstanding students and faculty, special alumni events, and receptions for distinguished friends and visitors. The Lee University Center is home to the Verizon sports arena, the collegiate swimming facility, and the University bookstore.

Academic facilities on the Main Campus include computer labs and wireless access areas, science labs, and studios for fine and graphic arts, fashion design, and interior design. The Reinsch Library provides print, electronic, and audiovisual material to supplement Marymount's curriculum as well as computers, video viewing stations, and study rooms. Also located in the Library is the Barry Art Gallery which features a variety of exhibitions throughout the year.

Marymount's Ballston Center, located in the Ballston professional district, is home to Marymount's School of Business Administration and the Department of Physical Therapy. It is just minutes from the Main Campus and students travel to and from both locations on free Marymount shuttles. The Ballston Center houses the Verizon Information Security Lab. This state-of-the-art lab provides students with hands-on experience to prepare them for current and future cybersecurity challenges.

The Reston Center, an adult education center, is located in northern Virginia's business and technology corridor.

TUITION, ROOM, BOARD AND FEES

The undergraduate tuition for 2010–11 is $23,160 per academic year; room and board is $10,325 per academic year for double occupancy.

FINANCIAL AID

Marymount has an extensive scholarship and grant program and participates in all federal and state aid programs. To be considered for aid, students must file the Free Application for Federal Student Aid (FAFSA) with the College Scholarship Service. There are three categories of scholarships offered by Marymount University: Academic/Service Scholarships, awarded on the basis of academic and /or service performance; Need-based Scholarships; and Other Scholarships which have variable eligibility criteria. All scholarships are designed for full-time, first-degree, or transfer undergraduates and can be applied to undergraduate tuition only, unless otherwise specified. In fall 2009, 86% of full-time degree-seeking undergraduates received financial assistance.

STUDENT ORGANIZATIONS AND ACTIVITIES

Athletics, student government, volunteer opportunities, and lots of campus activities mean there's always plenty to do at Marymount. More than 30 clubs and organizations are active on campus. An NCAA Division III institution, Marymount fields men's and women's teams in basketball, lacrosse, soccer, swimming, and cross country, as well as women's volleyball and men's golf. Intramural sports are also popular.

The Activities Programming Board, composed of Marymount students and staff, plans and implements ongoing events such as comedy nights, movies, theme parties, dances, music concerts, coffee houses, and trips to off-campus events. Major annual events that Marymount students plan, participate in, and enjoy include SpringFest, a week-long celebration of the arts; HalloweenFest, a trick-or-treat extravaganza for disadvantaged children; and the Special Olympics Basketball Tournament, a community outreach program organized and staffed by Marymount volunteers.

ADMISSIONS PROCESS

The Admissions team reviews the strength of an applicant's academic record, national test scores, breadth of academic preparation, and letters of recommendation. Applicants to the freshman class are considered if a student's high school grade point average in academic courses is 2.5 or better on a 4.0 scale, the combined SAT score is within 100 points of the national average or better, and the student's academic preparation, recommendations, and character indicate that he or she is qualified to undertake Marymount programs. It is recommended that students have at least 4 years of English; 3 years of a foreign language, mathematics, and the social sciences; and 2 years of science. A campus interview is not required but is strongly recommended. It gives students a chance to see if Marymount would be a good fit. The University holds Campus Visit Days in the fall and spring. Visitors are welcome at any time, and appointments with Admissions staff may be made in advance.

Application Information

High school students seeking admission are advised to apply early during their senior year. They should submit an application (which can be completed online), a nonrefundable fee of $40, a high school transcript, SAT or ACT scores, evidence of expected graduation from an accredited high school, and a recommendation from a high school counselor or an appropriate school official. Those who have attended another college or university must also submit transcripts of college-level study and a recommendation from the Dean of Students at the previous institution. The University has a rolling admission policy and notifies applicants soon after the application process is completed and a decision on admission has been made.

MCGILL UNIVERSITY

AT A GLANCE

Founded in 1821 with a bequest by Montreal merchant James McGill, McGill University has earned an international reputation for scholarly achievement and scientific discovery. The only Canadian university selected in the top 25 universities in the world by the Times Higher Education Supplement for six years running, McGill was also ranked the top medical-doctoral school in Canada by Maclean's magazine in 2009.

Innovative research programs and cutting-edge facilities—including our new Life Sciences Complex—attract internationally respected faculty. Our faculty excel at research; in recent years, McGill professors have won the Kyoto Prize, the Gairdner Award, the Templeton Prize, the Balzan Prize and host of other prestigious honours for their life-changing work. McGill's faculty are committed to excellence in teaching, too, bringing their cutting-edge breakthroughs into the classroom.

McGill also attracts the brightest students. The University offers its 35,000 students unparalleled opportunities to enrich their educational experience through hands-on research opportunities, international exchanges, internships, field study, and study-abroad programs. In 2009, two McGill alumni won Nobel prizes.

McGill's 21 faculties and professional schools offer degrees in more than 300 fields of study. McGill offers a full range of bachelor's, master's, and doctoral programs as well as professional degrees in law, dentistry, business and medicine. The world-renowned Faculty of Medicine has four affiliated teaching hospitals and graduates more than 1,000 health care professionals each year.

With almost 20 per cent of its students coming from 160 countries around the globe, McGill has the most internationally diverse student body of any medical-doctoral university in Canada. The ability to balance academic excellence with extracurricular activities is another hallmark of students at McGill. In addition to a rich athletic tradition that includes many Olympians and Rhodes scholars, thousands of McGill students participate in the hundreds of clubs, associations and community groups that enrich Montreal and contribute to a vibrant campus life.

Our website, www.mcgill.ca, provides an excellent introduction to McGill, including descriptions of academic programs and links to major publications, resources and events. An Open House for prospective students is held annually. Our Welcome Centre arranges walking tours and provides the student-for-a-day program, information about accommodation close to campus and much more in the way of support for prospective students and their families.

For information on applying to McGill University, see www.mcgill.ca/prospective.

LOCATION AND ENVIRONMENT

Lively and sophisticated, yet safe and affordable, the bilingual and multicultural city of Montreal boasts four universities and one of the highest number of university students per capita in North America. McGill's main campus, a mosaic of heritage and modern buildings laid out around an oasis of green space, is set in the heart of Montreal's vibrant downtown core. A short drive west of downtown, the Macdonald campus occupies 650 hectares of wooded and waterfront property, providing unique opportunities for fieldwork and research activities.

MAJORS AND DEGREES OFFERED

McGill University offers a number of undergraduate and graduate programs in its schools and faculties:

Faculty of Agricultural and Environmental Sciences

Faculty of Arts

Faculty of Dentistry

Faculty of Education

Faculty of Engineering

Faculty of Law

Desautels Faculty of Management

Faculty of Medicine

Schulich School of Music

Faculty of Religious Studies

Faculty of Science

Centre for Continuing Education

Graduate and Postdoctoral Studies

School of Architecture

School of Communication Sciences and Disorders

School of Computer Science

School of Dietetics and Human Nutrition

School of Information Studies

School of Nursing

School of Physical and Occupational Therapy

McGill School of Environment

School of Social Work

School of Urban Planning

Full details can be found in the course calendars at www.mcgill.ca/courses.

CAMPUS FACILITIES AND EQUIPMENT

McGill has 13 branch libraries and special collections housing over 6 million volumes, about a million e-books, over 40,000 electronic journals and hundreds of databases for different disciplines. The McLennan-Redpath Library Building complex includes provisions of 'high-tech', 'high-touch' computer labs, group study rooms available to students on demand, a variety of individual study spaces, an innovative e-classroom, and informal discussion areas.

Advanced high-speed data networks, both wired and wireless, are available to students, staff and faculty on both campuses.

TUITION, ROOM AND BOARD, AND FEES

All dollar figures quoted are in Canadian funds. Costs are approximate, subject to change and based on a normal course load (30 credits) for the full academic year (fall and winter terms) in 2008–2009.

Students from the province of Quebec (Off-campus/On-campus)

Quebec tuition fees: $1,868/$1,868

Ancillary fees: $1,425-$1,978/$1,425-$1,978

Books and supplies: $1,000/$1,000

Lodging (8 months): $4,600/$8,996-$12,948

Food (8 months): $2,600/-Included above

Other expenses: $2,000/$2,000

Total: Quebec Students: $13,493-$14,046/15,289-$19,794

Students from other parts of Canada (Off-campus/On-campus)

Canadian tuition fees: $5,378/$5,378

Ancillary fees: $1,425-$1,978/$1,425-$1,978

Books and supplies: $1,000/$1,000

Lodging (8 months): $4,600/$8,996-$12,948

Food (8 months): $2,600/-Included above

Other expenses: $2,000/$2,000

Total: Canadian Students: $17,003-$17,556/$18,799-$23,304

U.S. and International students (Off-campus/On-campus)

International tuition fees: $13,965-$15,420/$13,965-$15,420

Ancillary fees: $1,425-$1,978/$1,425-$1,978

Mandatory health insurance (single coverage): $639 /$639

Immigration fees: $250/$250

Books and supplies: $1,000/$1,000

Lodging (8 months): $4,600/$8,996-$12,948

Food (8 months): $2,600/-Included above

Other expenses: $2,000/$2,000

Total: International Students: $26,479-$28,487/$28,275-$34,235

FINANCIAL AID

McGill University has an extensive program of entrance awards to recognize and honor academic excellence. These awards are available to students entering university for the first time to undertake any full-time undergraduate degree program. Entrance scholarships range in value from $3,000 to $10,000 per annum, both renewable and one-year awards. Entrance bursaries range in value up to $10,000 and are based on academic standing and demonstrated financial need. Additional information on scholarships and financial aid can be found online at www.mcgill.ca/studentaid.

STUDENT ORGANIZATIONS AND ACTIVITIES

In addition to a rich athletic tradition that includes many Olympians, thousands of McGill students participate in the hundreds of clubs, associations and community groups that enrich Montreal and contribute to a vibrant campus life. As well, students have the opportunity to participate in University governance, including McGill's Senate and Board of Governors, through the Students' Society of McGill University, the Post-Graduate Students' Society and other organizations.

ADMISSIONS PROCESS

Prospective students are evaluated on the strength of their entire academic dossier. Academic performance over the past three years, the level of programs taken, class rank, and standardized test scores (if applicable) are all given the proper consideration. Applicants should have at least a B+ average or the equivalent, depending on where they have completed their studies. McGill University is very selective. For transfer applicants, the university/college record is reviewed in addition to the above criteria. First-year applicants who wish to enroll in September must meet the following deadlines: January 15 for applicants from U.S. and international high schools, universities and colleges. for first-year entry and university transfer ; February 1 for applicants from Canadian province high schools, other than Quebec, for first-year entry; March 1 for applicants from Quebec CEGEPs for first-year entry; May 1 for student exchange applicants; May 1 for Canadian citizen/permanent resident university transfer applicants from universities in Canada; May 1 for all special and visiting applicants from universities outside Canada; May 1 for NON Canadian citizen/permanent resident special and visiting applicants from universities in Canada; July 1 for Canadian citizen/permanent resident special and visiting applicants from universities in Canada; Confirmation of deadlines is available at www.mcgill.ca/applying. Depending on space availability, January admission is occasionally open to non-Quebec applicants. Refer to McGill's website for program availability and deadlines.

MEREDITH COLLEGE

AT A GLANCE

Meredith was chartered in 1891. Today Meredith is an independent private women's college—one of the largest in the U.S. Meredith offers a comprehensive education with an emphasis on an innovative liberal arts curriculum.

At the undergraduate level, Meredith offers more than 40 programs of study. The Meredith academic experience is enhanced by a commitment to hands-on learning, international education and leadership development, all within the context of a community that is both challenging and supportive. An extensive Undergraduate Research Program encourages student/faculty research in every discipline, while service-learning expands the College's longtime commitment to community service.

Meredith also offers numerous opportunities for graduate and professional study and lifelong learning. Through the John E. Weems Graduate School, Meredith offers coeducational graduate programs in business, nutrition and education. In addition, Meredith offers post-baccalaureate Dietetic Internship and Paralegal Programs. A wide variety of non-credit educational opportunities for men, women and children are available through Community Programs.

The Meredith community is diverse, spirited and culturally engaged. Campus life is shaped by more than 2,200 students from 27 states and 37 countries. Students advance their leadership skills by participating in more than 100 clubs and organizations, playing NCAA Division III sports, producing campus-wide events, taking leadership roles in the community and joining in college traditions.

LOCATION AND ENVIRONMENT

Meredith College is located in Raleigh, North Carolina's capital city. Meredith students are part of the more than 108,000 college students who reside in the Research Triangle Park area, the country's premiere research and development hub.

Off-Campus Opportunities

Study abroad options include summer programs in Switzerland, England, Ireland, Costa Rica and Iceland, plus a variety of semester and year-long travel opportunities throughout the world. A new permanent location in Sansepolcro, Italy, makes study abroad even more accessible for Meredith students. Semester programs at the United Nations in New York City or in Washington, D.C. are also available.

MAJORS AND DEGREES OFFERED

Meredith offers more than 40 majors and concentrations. Each program allows students to pursue intensive study, conduct independent research and work closely with talented, committed professors.

Accounting

American Civilization

Art

-Art Education

-Graphic Design

-Studio Art

Biology

Business Administration

Chemistry .

(Engineering Dual Degree Program Between Meredith and NCSU, College of Engineering)

Child Development

Communication

-Interpersonal Communication

-Mass Communication

Computer Information Systems

Computer Science

Dance

-Performance and Choreography

-Private Studio Teaching

Economics

English

Environmental Studies

Exercise and Sports Science

-Health and Wellness

Family and Consumer Sciences

Fashion Merchandising and Design

-Design

-Merchandising

Food and Nutrition

History

Interior Design

International Studies

Mathematics

(Engineering Dual Degree Program Between Meredith and NCSU, College of Engineering)

Music

-Musical Theatre

-Music Performance

-Piano Pedagogy

Political Science

-Law and Justice

Psychology

Religion

Social Work

Sociology

Spanish

Theatre

-Musical Theatre

-Theatre Performance

ACADEMIC PROGRAMS

Honors and Teaching Fellows programs are offered. Meredith is one of six private colleges participating in the N.C. Teaching Fellows program.

Internships and Cooperative Education are available in all areas of study.

The Cooperating Raleigh Colleges consortium allows students to take courses at other Raleigh colleges and universities. Meredith offers a dual degree program with NC State University's College of Engineering.

The Undergraduate Research Program supports student/faculty partnerships in the pursuit of research and creative activity in all fields. College funds support these projects and underwrite travel costs for students presenting their work at conferences.

CAMPUS FACILITIES AND EQUIPMENT

Meredith's 225-acre campus includes a 1,200-seat amphitheater on a lake, seven residence halls, a music library, art galleries, a research greenhouse, music practice rooms, auditoriums, a theater, concert halls, a student center, computer labs, a child care lab, a learning center, an autism lab, an astronomy observation deck, an indoor swimming pool, a fitness center, a dance studio, lighted tennis courts, a putting green, a new athletic field and track and two miles of greenway connecting our campus to the community. A new apartment building for juniors and seniors opened in Fall 2009.

Carlyle Campbell Library has over 190,000 volumes, 16,000 microforms and journal subscriptions with access to articles from more than 27,000 journals, magazines and newspapers online.

With over 80,000 square feet of space, the science and mathematics building includes unique classroom settings, specialized labs and a telescope observatory deck.

TUITION, ROOM, BOARD AND FEES

Tuition for full-time undergraduate students in 2009–10 is $24,490, with room and board at $7,020, for a total of $31,510. Cost for part-time students is $640 per credit hour, with a graduated fee schedule. Each full-time undergraduate student receives a laptop.

Tuition for graduate students in 2008–09 is $420 per credit hour and $595 per credit hour for MBA students.

FINANCIAL AID

Financial aid programs are available for students with demonstrated need. These grant programs, which do not need to be repaid, include Federal Pell Grants that range from $400 to $4,700; Federal Supplemental Educational Opportunity Grants that range from $100 to $4,000; Meredith College grants; and the North Carolina Legislative Tuition Grant that is available to full-time students who are legal residents of the state, currently about $1,850.

To apply, complete the Free Application for Federal Student Aid (FAFSA). You do not have to wait until you are formally accepted by Meredith to apply.

The Office of Financial Assistance uses the FAFSA form to determine a student's eligibility for grants, loans, scholarships and work-study opportunities. The FAFSA is available online at www.fafsa.ed.gov. Printed copies are available from the Office of Financial Assistance or from a high school guidance counselor. FAFSA forms should be sent directly to the Federal Student Aid Programs by March 1 each year. Meredith College's FAFSA code is 002945. Students must apply for financial aid annually.

STUDENT ORGANIZATIONS AND ACTIVITIES

Meredith sponsors a Presidential Lecture Series, juried student exhibitions, an active concert schedule, visiting artists and exhibitions featuring professional artists.

Students participate in four theatre and dance performance troupes, three choral groups and four musical ensembles.

Meredith students advance their leadership skills in programs such as the Emerging Leader Seminar Series, Sloan Family Student Leadership Program, Sophie Lanneau Women's Leadership Development Program and the LeaderShape® Institute. Meredith was the first women's college in the country to become a campus-based site for LeaderShape®.

Meredith athletes compete in six NCAA Division III sports as a member of the USA South Athletic Conference: basketball, soccer, volleyball, tennis, softball and cross-country. Meredith athletes were conference tournament champions in tennis and soccer for the 2008–09 season.

ADMISSIONS PROCESS

Freshman Applicants

Meredith expects applicants to have taken a challenging academic program, including honors, advanced placement or international baccalaureate level work. Applicants should present a solid grade report with at least a C average in English, foreign language, mathematics, history and natural sciences, and have successfully completed standardized tests including the SAT or ACT. In recent years, the middle 50 percent of enrolling students at Meredith scored between 970 and 1170 on the SAT (Math and Verbal) and 19 and 24 on the ACT. Recommendations from a school official and teacher are also requested.

Freshman Admission Programs

Meredith offers two freshman admission programs: Early Decision and Regular Decision.

- Early Decision is designed for students who are ready to withdraw applications to other schools and enroll at Meredith.

- Regular Decision candidates should apply during fall and early winter of their senior year.

Decisions begin on a rolling basis in early November. Applicants are invited to come for a visit and experience life as a Meredith student. Schedule a visit online, or call 1-800-MEREDITH or email requests to admissions@meredith.edu.

MESSIAH COLLEGE

AT A GLANCE

Messiah College is an independent, nationally ranked, private liberal arts and applied sciences college committed to providing a rigorous education in the context of the Christian tradition. In 2009 it was ranked number five by *U.S. News and World Report* as a Best Baccalaureate College in the North. The College strives to develop each student's intellect, character, and faith, preparing them for successful lives of service, leadership, and reconciliation in church and society.

There are more than 2,800 students at Messiah College, hailing from 43 U.S. states and 30 foreign countries. Collectively, students represent many denominational affiliations; nearly 8 percent of students are ethnic minorities and 2.6 percent are international students. Messiah has a distinctive residential atmosphere and a strong sense of community; 87 percent of students live on campus.

ACADEMICS

Messiah College offers more than 55 academic majors and 6 pre-professional programs. Teacher certification is also available in many disciplines. Students must complete 123 units to graduate except as noted in the requirements for selected majors. In addition to courses required by their major field, all students must complete core general educational requirements that include writing and oral communication, the arts and sciences, language and culture, Christian faith, social responsibility, and physical education. Students fulfill the remaining required units through elective courses.

The College operates on a two semester academic calendar, with a January Term between the fall and spring terms. During January term, students take one intensive, three-week course of study with transcultural travel programs among the innovative courses offered during this term. A three-week May Term immediately follows the Spring Term and is exclusively for cross-cultural studies. Messiah offers study abroad opportunities in more than 40 countries and is ranked eleventh in the U.S. by the Institute of International Education for institutions sending students to study abroad. Qualified students may also participate in the Honors Program or design an individual major or an independent study program. Many students also participate in a variety of local, regional, and international service-learning programs and internships.

The College has been recognized for its focus on service-learning and civic engagement. In 2009, Messiah was named to the National President's Higher Education Community Service Honor Roll, a distinction granted to only seven colleges in Pennsylvania. Messiah also has been identified by *U.S. News and World Report* as a 2010 "Program to Look for" in service-learning and in 2009 the College received the Carnegie Foundation Community Engagement Classification for community outreach and partnerships. Additionally, Messiah's nationally recognized Internship Center has been instrumental in the consistently high post-graduation placement rate of graduates. In 2008, 99 percent of surveyed respondents reported securing employment or acceptance into graduate school within one year of graduation.

Messiah professors are nationally recognized and have been educated at top universities all over the world. They are not only accomplished scholars but also practicing Christians who teach in their areas of expertise and serve as role models for integrating a life of faith with intellectual pursuits. 82 percent hold terminal degrees. Every Messiah professor signs a statement of faith as an indication of his or her commitment to the mission of the College. The student-to-faculty ratio at the College is 13:1. Recent Messiah graduates have distinguished themselves as Rhodes, Fulbright, Carnegie, and Truman scholars.

ADMISSIONS

Messiah seeks students with demonstrated academic promise, who wish to share in the College's multi-denominational, multi-cultural Christian community. Messiah encourages transfer, home school, international, and minority students to apply. The College provides two methods for candidates to apply for admission: the Standard Choice and the Write Choice. Both options require the submission of the application form, high school transcript, application essay, and one Christian Life recommendation form. In addition, the following materials or activities are required to complete an application for admission: Standard Choice—Applicant must submit the New SAT or ACT score results. Write Choice—Applicant must be in the top 20% class ranking, participate in an admissions interview, and submit an additional graded writing sample.

The Admissions Office seeks to admit those candidates who have exhibited scholastic competence and excellence as well as those who are most likely to succeed, benefit from, and contribute to the Messiah College community.

As for decision options, Messiah College operates on a rolling admission basis. On occasion, the Admissions Office may require an interview to clarify academic or personal issues pertaining to a candidate's application for admission. The application for admission must be completed and received prior to the admission interview. Appointments can be made Monday through Friday, 8:00 a.m. to 5:00 p.m. and on some selected Saturdays by contacting the Visit Coordinator at 1-800-233-4220 or by email: admiss@messiah.edu (two weeks' notice is suggested).

CAMPUS FACILITIES AND EQUIPMENT

Messiah's outstanding academic facilities include: Murray Library, a research library with more than 300,000 volumes, the Jordan Science Center that includes the Oakes Museum of Natural History, a state-of-the-art science facility providing technically advanced science laboratories and equipment as well as housing the College's unique treasury of large mammal, insect, seashell, and bird egg collections, Frey Hall, primarily an engineering, mathematics, and business building holding engineering and physics labs but also housing a variety of art studios, Climenhaga Fine Arts Center, complete with a 400-seat performance auditorium, a recital hall, and an art gallery, and Boyer Hall, an academic facility which opened Fall 2003. Messiah's academic facilities are modern and up to date, all completed within the last 25 years.

Students have access to over 350 computers in 18 general computer labs (including 5 in residence halls) as well as computers in department labs. All student rooms on campus are set up for both wired and wireless access to the campus network. Additionally, wireless connections to the campus network are available in all major campus buildings and all academic halls.

Athletic and recreational facilities include: the 90,000 square foot Sollenberger Sports Center with an indoor track, wrestling and gymnastics areas, a natatorium including an 8-lane pool with separate diving well, racquetball and basketball courts, and exercise and fitness equipment; the Starry Athletic Complex with lighted an artificial turf field for field hockey and lacrosse, lighted soccer stadium, eight-lane all weather track, 10 tennis courts, baseball and softball fields, and practice field space.

The College offers both traditional residence halls and apartment-style residences on campus. Staffed by trained, full-time professional Residence Directors, student Assistant Residence Directors, and Student Resident Assistants, these facilities provide an environment which fosters personal growth and responsibility, as students practice living in an intentional Christian community. All residence halls offer carpeting, air conditioning, cable television, Internet, and laundry facilities.

CAMPUS LIFE

As part of an active and dynamic campus community, Messiah students can participate in over 60 student groups and organizations, including theater and music groups, a campus newspaper, and a student-produced radio station. The College's Student Government Organization has a strong history of representing the student body and developing students' leadership skills.

Messiah College maintains one of the most successful NCAA Division III athletics programs in the nation. Messiah athletic teams have garnered 9 national championships. The College's teams also regularly achieve national rankings and conference titles. Messiah athletes have been recognized as all-Americans and have been featured in *Sports Illustrated, USA Today, US News and World Report*, and on national television, while our coaches have received national coaching awards. Overall, Messiah's athletic program is ranked 14th among the 300-plus Division III colleges in the nation. Messiah competes in men's baseball, basketball, cross-country, golf, lacrosse, soccer, swimming, tennis, track and field, and wrestling, as well as women's basketball, cross-country, field hockey, lacrosse, soccer, softball, swimming, tennis, track and field, and volleyball.

Messiah does not have any fraternities or sororities, at either the national or local level.

Students have many opportunities to grow in faith and fellowship at Messiah College, including: Chapel services featuring special music, challenging speakers, shared experiences, and examination of critical spiritual and social issues, Powerhouse, a popular and powerful, student-led praise service, Issachar's Loft, a discipleship program that provides leadership opportunities and weekly fellowship while tackling tough, contemporary social issues, Life groups—small groups that come together through Bible study, prayer, worship, service, and a commitment to each other's well-being.

The College operates a number of campus safety services for students, such as an after-hours transport and escort service, sixteen 24-hour emergency telephone alarm devices, a 24-hour, unarmed, professional security patrol, and student security patrols. In addition, all entrances to the residence halls are electronically operated. A crisis management and response team, emergency text-messaging system, and emergency evacuation plan are also in place on the campus.

LOCATION AND ENVIRONMENT

Messiah College, named a 2008 "Green College" by the National Association of Independent Colleges and Universities, is situated on 471 scenic wooded acres, just 12 miles from Harrisburg, Pennsylvania's capital. The College is approximately two hours from the major urban centers of Philadelphia, Baltimore, and Washington, D.C. There are many recreational and outdoor activities in the immediate vicinity, including the Yellow Breeches Creek, which flows through the campus and the nearby Susquehanna River and Appalachian Trail. The College also operates a satellite campus in Philadelphia, Pennsylvania in conjunction with Temple University.

TUITION AND FEES

In 2009, Messiah College was ranked by *U.S. News and World Report* as third in the region for Great Schools at a Great Price. For the 2009–2010 academic year, tuition is $25,900, room and board (maximum) is $8,170, and average basic fees are $800.

In 2006, the College announced an initiative that seeks to raise an additional $20 million in financial aid over the next five years. Of students who enrolled at Messiah College in 2008, 100% of Messiah students, determined through the College's analysis to have financial need, received financial aid. The average first-year student aid amount for the 2009–2010 school year is $18,402.

MOUNTAIN STATE UNIVERSITY

AT A GLANCE

Mountain State University offers studies at both the undergraduate and master's degree levels, with academic programs focusing on high-demand professional fields as well as the humanities and sciences. Founded in 1933, MSU is a not-for-profit independent institution of higher education. It is West Virginia's largest private university, with the state's third-largest graduate school.

Mountain State University serves students from throughout West Virginia, across the country, and around the world. In addition to its main campus in Beckley, West Virginia, the university offers selected programs at instructional sites across West Virginia and at three branch campuses: Martinsburg, West Virginia; Center Township (greater Pittsburgh area), Pennsylvania; and Orlando, Florida.

Mountain State University is accredited by the Higher Learning Commission and a member of the North Central Association (800-621-7440, www.ncahigherlearningcommission.org). It is authorized by the Pennsylvania Department of Education and licensed by the Florida Commission for Independent Education.

LOCATION AND ENVIRONMENT

Mountain State University's main campus is surrounded by the natural beauty of the southern West Virginia highlands. The area is home to some of the best outdoor recreation opportunities in the nation, including mountain biking, rock climbing, skiing, and whitewater rafting on the famed New and Gauley Rivers. The small city of Beckley combines a welcoming small-town atmosphere with a surprising number of dining, shopping, and entertainment options. For those who are drawn to more urban pursuits, the state capital of Charleston is only about an hour away, and most major eastern U.S. cities are within a day's drive.

OFF-CAMPUS OPPORTUNITIES

Internship and practicum experiences are an integral part of most degree programs. These experiences allow students to gain real-world knowledge and skills while helping them develop a professional network.

MAJORS AND DEGREES OFFERED

Mountain State University offers undergraduate degrees in accounting, applied technology, aviation leadership and management, aviation technology, biology, business administration (concentrations in finance, health care management, hospitality, human resource management, management, and marketing), business studies, computer networking, computer science, criminal justice (concentrations in corrections management, criminal justice, homeland security, and police science), culinary arts, diagnostic medical sonography, elementary and secondary teacher preparation, emergency medical services, environmental studies, fire science, forensics (concentrations in crime scene investigation, fire and arson investigation, forensic pathology, and forensic science)forensic investigation, general engineering, general studies, graphic design, health education and wellness health science, health science education, health studies, human resource management, , information technology (concentrations in computer networking, computer science, information technology, Internet and e-commerce, and website development design), interdisciplinary studies (concentrations in communication studies, ecology, English and literature, environmental studies, HAZMAT/occupational health and safety, health promotion, health sciences, health services management, humanities and fine arts, media studies, natural sciences, pre-law, premedicine, and social and behavioral sciences), legal studies, legal studies/paralegal, liberal studies, medical assisting, mining and environmental engineering, nursing, occupational therapy assistant, office administration, organizational leadership, physical therapist assistant, psychology, psychology of early childhood development, radiologic technology, religious studies, respiratory care, social work, and website development wildlife management.

Master's degree programs are available in criminal justice administration, health science, interdisciplinary studies, nursing (concentrations in administration and education, family nurse practitioner, and nurse anesthesia), physician assistant, and strategic leadership.

Selected programs can be completed online or through other distance-learning options.

ACADEMIC PROGRAMS

To earn a bachelor's degree, students complete a minimum of 120 semester hours, including 36 hours of general studies, and must meet all requirements of their program of study. Students in associate degree programs complete a minimum of 64 hours, including 24 hours of general studies, and must also meet all program requirements. Some associate degrees fulfill the pre-professional studies requirement of the corresponding bachelor's program.

MSU grants credit for nontraditional course work and demonstrated college-level learning. A degree completion program allows adult students who have already earned at least 40 credit hours to earn a bachelor's degree in selected fields on a compressed schedule.

CAMPUS FACILITIES AND EQUIPMENT

Mountain State University works to provide the best possible learning and personal resources to its students. The university library has holdings of more than 95,500 titles and networked access to more than one million titles. The core collection is supported by an online catalog and supplemented by electronic resources that include Proquest, Cumulative Index to Nursing and Allied Health Literature (CINHAL), Social Issues Resources Index (SIRS), Ebscohost, Westlaw, Wilson Web, Newsbank, and Medline.

Specialized learning resources include multimedia classrooms, a video lab, computer-assisted instruction, and lab facilities for students in the sciences, health care professional fields, forensic investigation, and culinary arts. A Testing and Tutoring Center, and a Career and Practicum Services Center, and tutoring services are available at no charge.

A centrally located residence hall accommodates students in comfortably furnished four-person suites (two double rooms and a bath). Each room includes a high-speed Internet connection as well as telephone and cable hookups, and can accommodate a microwave oven and small refrigerator. The hall is air-conditioned and wheelchair accessible. Amenities include laundry facilities and a common area with vending machines and a full kitchen.

TUITION, ROOM, BOARD AND FEES

Mountain State University provides the educational advantages of a private institution at a financially accessible cost. Full-time basic undergraduate tuition and fees for the 2008–2009 academic year were $8,400 (based on two 15-hour semesters) or $280 a credit hour. Tuition varies for some programs, and additional laboratory and clinical fees are sometimes required.

Housing costs for the full academic year ranged from $3,000 for a double room to $4,200 for a private room; meal plans ranged from $2,888 to $3,172. Most first- and second-year students are required to live on campus and purchase a meal plan.

FINANCIAL AID

About 83 percent of MSU's students receive some form of financial aid. Eligible students may receive Federal Pell Grants, Federal Supplemental Educational Opportunity Grants, West Virginia Higher Education Grants, and Federal Stafford Student Loans. Students must submit the Free Application for Federal Student Aid (FAFSA) for determination of eligibility. A number of scholarships based on academic merit and/or financial need are available to students in addition to the Federal Work-Study Program.

STUDENT ORGANIZATIONS AND ACTIVITIES

The Student Government Association (SGA) links students with the university's administration and faculty. Governed by student-elected officers, the SGA works to improve the quality of student life, develop leadership skills in students, and provides representation of student views and opinions on university issues. A Residence Hall Association guides and develops aspects of campus residential life. About 20 additional campus organizations bring students together for fun, service, common interests, and professional growth.

All students receive a complimentary membership in the Beckley-Raleigh County YMCA, located within easy walking distance of campus. The YMCA has a recently renovated fitness center as well as facilities for swimming, workouts, basketball, racquetball, and other sports and activities. An intramural athletics program, open to all students, provides team and individual competition in a variety of sports. The MSU Cougars compete in NAIA Division I men's basketball (where they won the 2004 National Championship) and; women's softball and volleyball.

ADMISSIONS PROCESS

The university's overall admissions policy is open, although some programs have more competitive requirements. Prospective students who have graduated from an accredited high school or received a General Educational Development (GED) certificate are eligible to apply.

Students apply for undergraduate admission by submitting an application, an official high school transcript or GED certificate, a $25 application fee, and a housing application or exemption form. Applications are accepted on a rolling basis and applicants are notified of their acceptance status as soon as the application process is completed. ACT or SAT scores are not required for university admission but are recommended for placement purposes. Competitive programs or courses may have minimum ACT or SAT scores, placement tests, or other requirements.

Transfer credits are evaluated by Student Services (except in the case of international students, whose credit is evaluated through a different process). Credit for courses completed with a grade of C or better is considered for equivalence to Mountain State courses and applicability to university and program requirements.

Mountain State University encourages prospective students and their families to arrange a campus visit. Campus tours and individual meetings are available.

For inquiries of any kind, contact the Information Center toll-free at 866-FOR-MSU1 (866-367-6781) or visit the MSU Website at www.mountainstate.edu.

NAROPA UNIVERSITY

AT A GLANCE

Accredited by The Higher Learning Commission and a member of the North Central Association, Naropa University is a private, nonprofit, nonsectarian liberal arts institution whose mission is contemplative education. This learning approach integrates the best of Eastern and Western educational traditions, enabling students to integrate academic knowledge with self-knowledge through contemplative practice. Founded in 1974 by Chögyam Trungpa Rinpoche, a lineage holder in the Tibetan Buddhist tradition, the university offers BA and BFA degrees through its four-year undergraduate program as well as MA, MDiv and MFA degrees through its graduate school.

The student body currently comprises a mix of 1,069 students, 464 of which are undergraduates. Undergraduates come from 45 states and 8 countries; 61% are female and 39% are male. Naropa's student/faculty ratio is 12:1, and the average class size is 14 students.

LOCATION AND ENVIRONMENT

Naropa University is located in Boulder, Colorado, at the base of the Rocky Mountain foothills and twenty-five miles northwest of Denver. Boulder has earned a reputation for great quality of life with a dynamic arts community. Hiking, skiing and snowboarding enthusiasts have ample opportunity to pursue their sport and recreation activities. Boulder has extensive bike paths, and public transportation provides a frequent and comprehensive bus schedule throughout the day.

Naropa has three Boulder campuses, two of which serve undergraduate programs. The Arapahoe Campus is home to undergraduate advising, administration, a performing arts center, a meditation hall, the Allen Ginsberg Library, a computer lab, student lounges, the bookstore, classrooms for most undergraduate courses and the Naropa Café. The Nalanda Campus, 3.5 miles from the Arapahoe Campus, is home to performing and visual arts programs. The Paramita Campus, 2.3 miles from the Arapahoe Campus, houses the graduate school of psychology.

OFF-CAMPUS OPPORTUNITIES

Naropa University students may study abroad during their junior year or the fall semester of their senior year with the numerous programs offered outside Naropa through other regionally accredited colleges and universities. Studying and living overseas with Naropa fosters intercultural competence and critical thinking and prepares the ground for compassionate engagement with the world. The study abroad advisor assists those seeking study abroad opportunities with other universities.

The Community Studies Center provides opportunities for students and faculty to develop skills for participating in the public life of their communities. Through its emphasis on applied, experiential projects, community-based learning offers innovative tools to forward the knowledge of academic and artistic disciplines, augment student learning and educate a citizenry to perform the public work of a democracy. AmeriCorps scholarship funds are provided for Naropa students involved in community work.

MAJORS AND DEGREES OFFERED

Upon completion of 30 semester credits, a student may declare a major. A total of 120 semester credits is required to earn an undergraduate degree.

Contemplative Psychology integrates Western psychology and Eastern approaches to healing mind and body through concentrations in Somatic Psychology, Psychology of Health and Healing, Transpersonal and Humanistic Psychology, and Psychological Science.

Early Childhood Education nurtures the genuine and compassionate nature of teachers and applies methods drawn from Montessori, Waldorf and Buddhist traditions. The major offers apprentice-style internships with master teachers from these traditions.

Environmental Studies emphasizes experiential learning, natural science, personal growth and an awakened relationship between self and world.

Interdisciplinary Studies invites students to design a major by selecting courses from two or three disciplines at Naropa. Recent examples of senior work include "Documentary Poetics" and "Shambhala Path of Hip-Hop Warriorship."

Music gives students fundamental training in musicianship that includes harmonic analysis, ear training, rhythmic acuity, music theory, improvisation, composition, history and multicultural perspectives.

Peace Studies focuses on the study of peace and explores the causes of violence and war through four related areas of inquiry: history and politics of social change, theory and practice of peacemaking, the arts in peacemaking, and engaged learning.

Religious Studies explores the role of contemplative practice in the world's great religions, especially Buddhism, and places special emphasis on the expression of historical traditions in contemporary life.

Traditional Eastern Arts is the only degree program of its kind in the country combining the practice of sitting meditation and an in-depth study of the philosophy, history and culture of a body-mind awareness discipline. Concentrations are offered in T'ai-chi Ch'uan, Aikido and Yoga Teacher Training.

Visual Arts blends traditional and contemporary visual arts study with contemplative practice and offers courses in several painting media and calligraphic forms, sculpture, pottery and photography. Seniors learn the business of being an exhibiting artist, portfolio production and how to be savvy in career and graduate school markets.

Writing and Literature offers intensive training in the practice and study of writing through small writing workshops, literary studies courses, and exposure to a range of contemporary writing through the Summer Writing Program.

The BFA in Performance offers interdisciplinary training, an emphasis on student-centered creative process and a contemplative approach to performance and performance studies.

ACADEMIC PROGRAMS

Naropa University's learning approach integrates academic study, artistic and contemplative practices, and service to the community in a way that encourages students to develop an understanding of themselves, their individual fields of study and the world around them. A Naropa education allows students to be who they are while exploring who they want to become.

A Naropa education values both the Western liberal arts tradition and the Eastern heritage of Buddhist meditation practice and study. In addition to their academic pursuits, Naropa's students, staff and faculty work together to develop mindfulness and awareness, learning directly from their experience—and from each other—moment by moment.

Through core courses, students are introduced to the values, modes of inquiry and essential skills of contemplative education at Naropa University. Grounded in Naropa's mission, courses strike a living balance between scholarship, contemplative practice, artistic expression and civic engagement. This multidimensional approach to teaching and learning is unique to Naropa, reflecting its singular goal to bridge the gap between knowledge and wisdom.

CAMPUS FACILITIES AND EQUIPMENT

Residential living at Naropa University combines housing, education and community to create an inspired college experience. Required for entering undergraduate students ages twenty and younger who arrive with fewer than 30 credits, Naropa housing incorporates co-curricular programming, peer development, community activities and resident advisors to create a dynamic living/learning environment.

There are two computer labs at Naropa: the main lab in the Administration Building basement on the Arapahoe Campus and a smaller lab on the Paramita Campus. The main lab has fifty-four Windows XP PCs and three Macs, while there are eight Windows XP PCs and three Macs in the Paramita lab. Both labs have laser printers and scanners. All computers are set up for Internet access and word processing. Both labs have lab assistants who can help students with hardware and software. The Nalanda Campus reading room also has five Windows XP PCs and one Mac. Wireless Hot Spots are located at all three campuses for laptop users.

TUITION, ROOM, BOARD AND FEES

Full-time undergraduate tuition for 2009–10 was $23,420 Part-time undergraduates were charged $726 per credit. Both full- and part-time students pay a $250 per semester registration fee. It costs an average of $1,300 per month to live in Boulder. This estimate includes room and board, transportation, books and miscellaneous expenses.

FINANCIAL AID

Naropa University offers institutional grants and scholarships, as well as all types of federal student aid. Some financial aid for international students is also available. Approximately 70 percent of Naropa's degree-seeking students receive financial assistance in the form of loans, student employment, scholarships and grants.

STUDENT ORGANIZATIONS AND ACTIVITIES

Naropa students are encouraged to participate in university governance by taking part in university committees. Town Hall meetings bring together students, faculty and staff to discuss issues of shared concern.

Some student groups active in the last year include: Allies in Action, Amnesty International; A TONO (Latina/o student group); Bombay Gin (literary journal); El Centro de la Gente Committee (multicultural center); Chanoyu Club (tea ceremonies); Community Kitchen, Dharma Clowns, International Student Group; LGBTQIA Group; Naropa Healers, ROOT (Reconnecting on Outer Terrain: outdoor group); Salsa Dance Club; Students of Color Group; Student Union of Naropa; Tendrel Collective (Naropa's diversity journal)

ADMISSIONS PROCESS

A completed application for admission includes a $50 application fee; three essays; two letters of recommendation; official high school transcripts for first-time first-year students and first-year transfer applicants (0 to 30 credits); and official college transcripts for every university attended. Many departments also require supplemental application materials and a phone or in-person interview.

Prospective students are encouraged to visit. The Admissions Office hosts a preview weekend each semester, and guided campus tours are available throughout the year.

The suggested deadline for receiving completed applications for the fall semester is January 15 and for the spring semester is October 15. Applications received after the suggested deadline are reviewed on a space-available basis. For additional information, please contact:

Admissions Office

Naropa University

2130 Arapahoe Avenue

Boulder, Colorado 80302-6697

Telephone: 303-546-3572; 800-772-6951 (toll free)

Fax: 303-546-3583

admissions@naropa.edu

www.naropa.edu

NAZARETH COLLEGE OF ROCHESTER

AT A GLANCE

Founded in 1924, Nazareth College is an independent coeducational college with undergraduate and graduate studies in the liberal arts and sciences and professional programs in health and human services, education, and management. The College is located on 150 scenic acres near Rochester, New York, and currently enrolls 2,000 undergraduate and 1,000 graduate students. Nazareth has a strong commitment to experience-based learning and civic engagement. In the past decade, Nazareth has produced 18 Fulbright recipients and two Pickering Foreign Affairs Fellowships.

More than 40 undergraduate majors and minors are available. Internship opportunities provide students with participatory experience in their field of study. Nazareth competes at the Division III level. Its intercollegiate teams include men's and women's basketball, cross-country, equestrian, golf, lacrosse, soccer, swimming, diving, tennis, volleyball, track and field; and women's field hockey and softball.

LOCATION AND ENVIRONMENT

The Nazareth campus is a short walk from the village of Pittsford, which offers a selection of restaurants and specialty shops, as well as bike trails and boat rides along the Erie Canal. The campus is seven miles from Rochester, the third largest city in the state of New York. Rich in culture and entertainment, the city serves as world headquarters for two major corporations: Eastman Kodak and Bausch and Lomb. A major Xerox facility is also located in Rochester. The city offers a broad array of museums, annual festivals, shopping malls, tourist attractions, professional sporting events, and ski resorts. Two internationally renowned museums—the George Eastman House/International Museum of Film and Photography, and Strong National Museum of Play—make their homes in Rochester.

OFF-CAMPUS OPPORTUNITIES

Nazareth students are able to gain valuable work-related experience off campus no matter what their program of study. Student teaching assignments, clinical work with therapy-related programs, social work placements, and business internships are just a few of the opportunities available.

Nazareth students have access to study abroad programs across five continents. In addition to well-known destinations such as France, Italy, Spain, and Germany, students travel to South America, Asia, Africa, Australia, and the Middle East. Programs include traditional academic semesters abroad, as well as those that address special study in archeology, business, and other topics of interest. The College has institutional relationships with many highly regarded institutions across the globe, allowing students a myriad of choices.

MAJORS AND DEGREES OFFERED

Nazareth offers Bachelor of Arts, Bachelor of Music, and Bachelor of Science in the following areas: accounting, American studies, anthropology, art (studio), art education, art history, biochemistry, biology, business administration, business education, chemistry, communication sciences and disorders (speech pathology), communication and rhetoric, economics, English, environmental science, French, German, history, Inclusive Education, information technology, international business, international studies, Italian, modern foreign languages, management science, mathematics, music, music/business, music education, music history, music performance, music theatre, music theory, music therapy, nursing, peace and justice studies, philosophy, physical therapy (6-year DPT program) political science, psychology, religious studies, social science, social work, sociology, Spanish, and theatre arts.

Nazareth offers pre-professional programs in dentistry, law, medicine, and veterinary science. Students may combine education certification with their declared major to earn certification in elementary, middle and special education (grades 1-9), or secondary education (grades 7-12). Nazareth offers certification in art, music, speech and hearing (birth-grade 12). Most majors are also available as academic minors. Students may pursue interdisciplinary minors in American studies, Asian studies, gerontology, multicultural studies, and women's studies.

Graduate degrees include Master of Arts in Liberal Studies; Master of Science in the following areas: accounting, art education, business & marketing education, computer education/technology specialist, creative arts therapy, human resource management, inclusive education (early childhood, childhood, adolescence), literacy, management, music education, speech-language pathology, social work, TESOL; and a Doctoral program in physical therapy.

CAMPUS FACILITIES AND EQUIPMENT

The College's 150-acre campus features more than 20 buildings of contemporary and Gothic design. The Otto A. Shults Community Center houses a full gymnasium, a 25-meter swimming pool, fitness center, the student union, college radio station, and student personnel offices. Classrooms — including many smart rooms—are located in Smyth Hall, the Arts Center, Carroll Hall, and Golisano Academic Center. Computer labs are found throughout campus, and a campus wi-fi system is installed in all major academic buildings. The Golisano Academic Center houses faculty and administrative offices, a full service dining facility, and multi-faith chapel. Approximately 63 percent of the full-time student body lives on campus.

Nazareth's 11 residence halls include singles, doubles, suites and apartments. A four-story, environmentally friendly residence hall was completed in Fall 08. French majors have the option of rooming at the La Maison Française. The Casa Hispana and Casa Italiana, as well as a German Cultural Center, serve as social, academic, and cultural centers for students wishing to immerse themselves in Spanish, Italian, and German language and customs.

TUITION, ROOM, BOARD AND FEES

Estimated costs for 2010–2011 academic year approx. $36,860 ($25,045 for tuition; $10,715 for room and board; $1,100 for college fees). Books, transportation, and personal expenses are not included in this estimate. Fees may change at any time. For the most current information, contact the Admissions Office.

FINANCIAL AID

Nazareth provides its students with more than $19 million in grant and scholarship assistance; the school is committed to making a Nazareth education affordable for every admitted student. The college also offers an assortment of merit-based awards for those demonstrating excellence in academics, the arts, music and drama. Those seeking aid must submit a completed Free Application for Federal Student Aid (FAFSA); the form must reach federal processors between January 1 and February 15. Those seeking early decision must submit the CSS Profile by November 15.

STUDENT ORGANIZATIONS AND ACTIVITIES

Nazareth offers a wealth of co-curricular choices for students of all interests and backgrounds. Campus clubs and organizations include Amnesty International, Art Club, Asian Club, Association of Student Social Workers, Campus Ministry Council, Cultural Affairs/CALEB, Dance Team, Economics Club, Environmental Club, French Club, German Club, Gleaner (the student newspaper), History Club, iClub, Italian Club, Inter-ethnic Nazareth Coalition, Lambda Association, Math Club, Music Therapy Club, Nazareth Commuter Association, Nazareth Speech, Hearing, and Language Association, Peer Health Educators, Physical Therapy Club, Pre-Med Club, Residence Hall Association, Science Club, Sigilium (yearbook), Spanish Club, Student Activities Council, Theater League, Verity (literary magazine), WNAZ (radio station) and Wilderness Club. The student political voice is heard through the Undergraduate Association.

ADMISSIONS PROCESS

A complete application to Nazareth includes: application form (common app online or paper version mailed), original essay or graded writing sample, letter of recommendation from a teacher or guidance counselor, an official transcript of high school academic achievement, a non-refundable $40 application fee (waived if student visits or submits online application), and Standardized Test scores, if the student decides he/she would like those scores to be used in the admissions process (Nazareth is a Standardized Test Option College).

Early Decision, Early Action and Regular Decision applications are welcome. The deadline for Early Decision applications is November 15; applicants are notified after December 15th; the due date for enrollment deposit is February 1. Those applying for Early Action must submit their application by December 15; notification for Early Action applicants begins January 15; students have until May 1to make a decision about attending Nazareth. Those applying for Regular Decision are encouraged to file before the final deadline of February 15. Regular Decision applicants receive notification of the College's decision after March 1. Admitted applicants must make a final decision on whether they will attend Nazareth by May 1.

The school recommends that the applicants complete a college-preparatory curriculum including English, Mathematics, Social Studies, Science and Foreign Language. Academic achievement is the primary consideration in admissions decisions, but the Admissions Committee also considers special talent in drama, music and art; it also looks at students' co-curricular activities. A campus tour is recommended in order to familiarize you with the college and all that it has to offer. An interview is not a required part of the application, but highly recommended. You can plan a visit or ask for more information by contacting: Office of Admissions, Nazareth College, 4245 East Avenue, Rochester, NY 14618; Telephone: 585-389-2860; Toll Free Line: 800-462-3944; Email: admissions@naz.edu; World Wide Web: www.naz.edu.

THE NEW SCHOOL

AT A GLANCE

The New School is a leading university located in Greenwich Village, in the heart of New York City. Founded nearly a century ago as a bastion of intellectual and artistic freedom, The New School today offers some of the nation's most highly regarded programs in design, liberal arts, management and policy, and the performing arts.

Artists, scholars, and students from across the United States and around the world attend The New School to earn bachelor's, master's, or doctoral degrees, complete certificate programs, or take continuing education classes. The 10,200 matriculated students and 15,000 continuing education students who study on campus or online from anywhere in the world (www.newschool.edu/online) enjoy the benefits of small class sizes, superior resources, and a renowned working faculty who practice what they teach. Find out more about The New School at www.newschool.edu.

For undergraduates, The New School offers four colleges in the arts and the humanities: Parsons The New School for Design, Eugene Lang College The New School for Liberal Arts, Mannes College The New School for Music, and The New School for Jazz and Contemporary Music. (In addition, The New School for General Studies offers a liberal arts bachelor's program designed specifically for working adults and other nontraditional students. Find out more at www.newschool.edu/adultba.)

PARSONS THE NEW SCHOOL FOR DESIGN
www.newschool.edu/parsons

One of the largest and most prestigious degree-granting colleges of art and design in the nation, Parsons The New School for Design has been a leader in the field of art and design since its founding in 1896. Its intensive programs and distinguished faculty embrace innovation, pioneer new uses of technology, and instill in students a global perspective on design. Parsons' more than 15 undergraduate programs are supplemented by interdisciplinary collaboration, international study opportunities, and professional internships with top designers and artists.

EUGENE LANG COLLEGE THE NEW SCHOOL FOR LIBERAL ARTS
www.newschool.edu/lang

Eugene Lang College The New School for Liberal Arts combines the advantages of a small, intimate liberal arts college with the resources of a major university. Lang attracts top students who value individualized attention and the opportunity to be challenged in small seminar-style classes. Committed leaders, scholars, and newsmakers teach these students in an interdisciplinary context. Students may major in a range or disciplines including Environmental Studies, Economics, History, Culture and Media, and the Arts, or map out an individual path of study in the liberal arts.

MANNES COLLEGE THE NEW SCHOOL FOR MUSIC
www.newschool.edu/mannes

Mannes College The New School for Music is a preeminent conservatory of classical music that provides a professional trajectory for serious undergraduate students. The Mannes community is made up of students and a faculty of professional musicians from every corner of the world. Here, aspiring artists learn and play music with scholars, composers, conductors, and performing artists from some of the world's renowned orchestras, ensembles, and opera companies. The school produces more than 400 concerts each year at its two concert halls and venues throughout the New York metropolitan area, most of which feature Mannes students. With only 320 college students, Mannes offers an intimate, supportive atmosphere that allows for close and constructive relationships among students, faculty, and administrators.

THE NEW SCHOOL FOR JAZZ AND CONTEMPORARY MUSIC
www.newschool.edu/jazz

The New School for Jazz and Contemporary Music offers an innovative course of study in which a passionately engaged faculty of professional artists, drawn from New York City's renowned jazz community, guides serious and talented students toward high standards of achievement and the development of an individual creative voice. Since its inception in 1986, the program has been distinguished by a curriculum based on the time-honored tradition of artist as mentor, a focus on small-group performance, and faculty members who have played a major role in the history and evolution of jazz, blues, pop, and new genres. The ultimate proof of the program's success can be heard in the musical voices of a generation of New School Jazz alumni, represented at the highest artistic levels in every musical genre.

For more information about the university, visit **www.newschool.edu**.

LOCATION AND ENVIRONMENT

The New School's New York City location offers access to hundreds of world-class cultural events and venues, including museums, concerts, theaters, restaurants, parks, and the streets themselves. From the main campus in Greenwich Village to Mannes' home on the Upper West Side, New School students live and learn in one of the most vibrant, diverse, and exciting cities in the world.

www.newschool.edu

MAJORS AND DEGREES

PARSONS THE NEW SCHOOL FOR DESIGN
www.newschool.edu/parsons

Parsons offers undergraduate programs in Architectural Design, Art and Design Studies, Communication Design, Design and Management, Design and Technology, Environmental Studies, Fashion Design, Fashion Marketing, Fashion Studies, Fine Arts, Foundation, Graphic Design, Illustration, Integrated Design, Interior Design, Photography, Product Design and Urban Design. Degrees offered are BFA, BBA, BA, BS, AAS, and a joint BA/BFA degree with Eugene Lang College (described below).

EUGENE LANG COLLEGE THE NEW SCHOOL FOR LIBERAL ARTS
www.newschool.edu/lang

Eugene Lang College offers a BA in the following areas of study: The Arts (with tracks in arts in context, theater, dance, music, and visual arts); Culture and Media; Economics; Environmental Studies; Global Studies, History; Interdisciplinary Science; Literary Studies; Philosophy; Psychology; Urban Studies; and Liberal Arts. Within the Liberal Arts major, students may complete interdisciplinary programs of study in Education Studies, Religious Studies, Social Inquiry, and Social Inquiry. Students may also elect a self-designed program of study. Lang College offers dual BA/BFA degrees with Parsons and The New School for Jazz and Contemporary Music (described below).

Lang students can accelerate their progress toward a master's degree by combining undergraduate work with graduate study at one of The New School's graduate schools. Dual bachelor's/master's degree programs offered at Lang include Media

Studies and International Affairs (with The New School); Anthropology, Economics, Liberal Studies, Philosophy, Political Science, Psychology, and Sociology (with The New School for Social Research); and Urban Policy Analysis and Management, Organizational Change Management, and Nonprofit Management (with Milano The New School of Management and Urban Policy).

MANNES COLLEGE THE NEW SCHOOL FOR MUSIC
www.newschool.edu/mannes

Students major in either performance or music in a variety of concentrations (including Orchestral Instruments, Piano, Harpsichord, Voice, Classical Guitar, Orchestral Conducting, Choral Conducting, Composition, and Theory) and can earn a BM, BS, or undergraduate diploma.

THE NEW SCHOOL FOR JAZZ AND CONTEMPORARY MUSIC
www.newschool.edu/jazz

New School Jazz offers concentrations in voice and instrumentals. Students can earn a BFA or joint BA/BFA degree with Eugene Lang College (as described below).

BA/BFA DUAL-DEGREE PROGRAM
www.newschool.edu/babfa

The BA/BFA program at The New School is a five-year dual-degree program through which students can earn a liberal arts bachelor of arts degree from Eugene Lang College The New School for Liberal Arts and a bachelor of fine arts degree from either Parsons The New School for Design or The New School for Jazz and Contemporary Music. The BA/BFA program allows students to explore two areas of interest throughout their studies—with classes and studios located conveniently on one campus.

ACADEMIC PROGRAMS

See the degree section above and visit each school's website for more information on specific programs.

ENVIRONMENTAL STUDIES
www.newschool.edu/environmentalstudies

In fall 2008, The New School launched two new programs of study, focusing on the environment, a Bachelor of Arts and Bachelor of Science in Environmental Studies.

Both degree programs will allow students to focus their work on one of two areas of concentration within the degree programs. For the bachelor of arts degree offered at Eugene Lang College, students can concentrate in urban ecosystems or policy. Students working toward a bachelor of science degree at Parsons can choose to concentrate in Urban Ecosystem Design or Sustainable Design.

Located in the heart of one of the world's largest and most complex urban ecosystems, this innovative program will make the New York City region its focus and laboratory.

OFF-CAMPUS OPPORTUNITIES

The New School believes that students learn both in and outside the classroom. The university offers students access to a wide array of internships with leading New York City organizations, apprenticeships with top designers, and performance opportunities in venues from downtown clubs to Lincoln Center. These opportunities enable students to shape their education and take advantage of all the city has to offer.

PARSONS THE NEW SCHOOL FOR DESIGN
www.newschool.edu/parsons

In 1920, Parsons became the first American school of art and design to found a campus abroad. Today, the school offers its students the opportunity to expand their horizons by studying at art and design schools around the world. During their junior year, bachelor's degree students may enroll for one or two semesters in another school in the United States or abroad. Several departments assist students in securing noncredit internships that provide valuable work experience and professional contacts. Companies and institutions that have offered New School students internships include Marc Jacobs, Polo—Ralph Lauren, HBO, MTV, the *New York Times*, *Rolling Stone* magazine, Marvel Comics, and the Museum of Modern Art.

EUGENE LANG COLLEGE THE NEW SCHOOL FOR LIBERAL ARTS
www.newschool.edu/lang

Many Lang students spend a semester, academic year, or summer abroad taking courses, working as interns, and pursuing volunteer projects. Lang offers foreign study options both through the school (in-house) and through other institutions. Experiential courses at Lang draw on the intellectual and cultural richness of New York City. Many of these courses provide students with tickets to cultural and artistic sites and events around the city. Offerings might include Arts in NYC, Lang at the Guggenheim, Lang at Judson Church, Lang at the Public, and Seeing Performance.

Internships and community activism are an essential part of the undergraduate program in liberal arts at Lang. Student interns receive professional guidance, gain hands-on experience, develop confidence, and establish an expansive network of contacts. Students can pursue internships for academic credit in a variety of fields, including publishing, politics, health care, the arts, radio, television, music, online media, nonprofit administration, and environmental activism.

Recently, Lang students have won coveted spots at MTV, HBO, Beth Israel Hospital, the *Village Voice*, Sony Entertainment, Gay Men's Health Crisis, Miramax Films, and the ACLU.

MANNES COLLEGE THE NEW SCHOOL FOR MUSIC
www.newschool.edu/mannes

A distinct advantage of studying music in New York, a center of the international music scene, is the opportunity to gain professional-level experience at major performance venues. Mannes students have recently performed at Carnegie Hall, Lincoln Center, Symphony Space, the Morgan Library, and other prominent venues throughout the city.

THE NEW SCHOOL FOR JAZZ AND CONTEMPORARY MUSIC
www.newschool.edu/jazz

More than 150 concerts are presented in the jazz program's performance space every year. Jazz students also play at venues outside the school, including the jazz club Sweet Rhythm, where students perform weekly, and appearances at festivals and music conferences worldwide. Students also gain valuable professional experience through performances at special events, including private parties and corporate functions, arranged by the jazz program's Gig Office.

—Continued on next page

THE NEW SCHOOL (continued)

FACILITIES AND EQUIPMENT

New School students have access to excellent resources, including a vast library consortium that houses approximately three million volumes and fully equipped performance spaces, practice rooms, and design studios. Each school's unique facilities are described on its website.

Over the past several years, The New School has invested more than $30 million in a number of fully equipped labs. The Knowledge Union consists of state-of-the-art technology spread over four floors; the 600 networked workstations include all relevant platforms. Servers support work that ranges from traditional print output to online projects using webcasting and secure transaction technology. Specialty work—whether audio or video production, MIDI, recording, or physical computing installation—takes place in private studios across the campus.

Portable production equipment, including video and audio, is readily available. Digital projectors, surround sound, and active whiteboards feed into equipment racks that allow for media presentations of all kinds. The University Computing Center, on the third and fourth floors of Alvin Johnson/J.M. Kaplan Hall, is a hub of technologies. Computers and hands-on classrooms support multimedia, Web design, and desktop publishing as well as word processing and research.

TUITION, ROOM, BOARD AND FEES

The cost of attending The New School varies from program to program and sometimes from student to student. For information on tuition for each program of study and on-campus housing fees, visit www.newschool.edu/tuition.

FINANCIAL AID

Many students enrolled in degree programs at The New School take advantage of financial aid. U.S. citizens or eligible noncitizens must complete the Free Application for Federal Student Aid (FAFSA); degree-seeking undergraduate international students interested in grants or scholarships from The New School should complete the Undergraduate International Student Scholarship Application. Students attending Mannes College The New School for Music and The New School for Jazz and Contemporary Music are not required to fill out this form. For forms and more information, visit www.newschool.edu/financialaid.html.

FULL-TIME AND PART-TIME FACULTY

The New School prides itself on its low student-to-faculty ratio. Thanks to its strong academic programs and dedication to the arts, the school attracts leading professionals in their fields; it is not unusual to find a prominent or award-winning musician, scholar, artist, or designer at the front of the class. See each school's website for more information.

STUDENT ORGANIZATIONS AND ACTIVITIES

Students at The New School play an active role in the life of the university. From informal clubs to student unions, art shows to film festivals, there are hundreds of opportunities for students to get involved outside the classroom. The university recognizes more than 25 student organizations, including Buddhism for Global Peace; Out, Proud Environment at The New School (OPEN); Women of Color; Sketch Comedy Group; The New School Philosophy Club; and Project Africa.

ADMISSION PROCESSES AND REQUIREMENTS

The New School seeks talented and dedicated undergraduates who demand serious study in a nontraditional setting. Additional information about the admissions requirements for each school can be found on its website.

PARSONS THE NEW SCHOOL FOR DESIGN
www.newschool.edu/parsons

Parsons seeks serious, responsible, and highly motivated applicants. Each applicant is reviewed with a focus on experience, achievements, and potential for artistic growth. While Parsons recognizes the benefits of strong artistic preparation, some applicants are admitted on the basis of their academic strengths more than their visual material. For BFA applicants, a large part of the Admissions Committee's decision is based on portfolio evaluations and the Parsons Challenge (a creative exercise that helps Parsons understand how you structure ideas and convey them) as well as academic achievement. For BBA applicants, academic achievement is considered along with the Parsons Challenge. For BS/BA in Environmental Studies applicants, academic achievement is weighted heavily along with a statement of purpose. The AAS program is best suited to students who have some college experience, are clear about their interests within the world of design, and are prepared for rapid immersion in a professional course of study.

All applicants must submit a completed application, a nonrefundable $50 application fee, and original copies of official high school and/or college transcripts. Bachelor's applicants must also submit SAT or ACT scores if they are residents of the United States or TOEFL scores if they are international students (minimum of 580 on the paper-based exam or 237 on the computerized exam). All applicants must submit the multipart Parsons Challenge exercise. A portfolio is required of all BFA applicants except those applying to study design and management. The portfolio must consist of eight to 12 pieces of work, including but not limited to, drawings, paintings, photographs, digital media, or design. A personal interview is recommended for all applicants.

The admission and financial aid deadline for the fall semester is February 1, and the deadline for spring admission is October 15. The Admissions Committee reviews applications and sends students its decision a few weeks after all materials are received.

Admissions Office
Parsons The New School for Design
72 Fifth Avenue, 2nd Floor
New York, NY 10011
212.229.8989
Email: thinkparsons@newschool.edu
www.newschool.edu/parsons

EUGENE LANG COLLEGE THE NEW SCHOOL FOR LIBERAL ARTS
www.newschool.edu/lang

Eugene Lang College encourages students of diverse racial, ethnic, religious, and political backgrounds to apply. The Admissions Committee looks for students who demonstrate an ability to make the best use of college-level resources and contribute to the Lang community. Qualities the college looks for include the ability to question, seriousness of purpose, and the capacity for progressive liberal arts study.

The Admissions Committee takes the whole student into account when making admissions decisions. A student's personal convictions and creative work, as discussed in the personal essay and required interview, are weighed along with scholastic achievement, as represented by transcripts, recommendations, and SAT or ACT scores. Most successful candidates have completed a college-preparatory course load in high school. Applicants are encouraged to take a tour and sit in on a seminar. The early decision application option is strongly recommended for applicants who know that Lang is their first choice.

High school juniors who display a high level of achievement may apply for early entrance, turning in two teacher recommendations with their application materials. Transfer students with a minimum of one year of college work behind them may apply and enroll in upper-level seminars upon acceptance. Those applying internationally follow regular application procedures. Non-native English speakers should submit their TOEFL scores. Students attending other institutions can come to Lang and participate in an internship through the New York Connections program.

Certain programs have special application requirements. Students wishing to enter the five-year dual-degree BA/BFA Jazz Studies program with Jazz and Contemporary Music must audition. Fine arts applicants to the five-year joint BA/BFA program with Parsons The New School for Design must submit a portfolio and a home exercise.

All categories of admitted applicants may begin their studies at Lang in the fall (September) or spring (January) semester. A $50 application fee is required. Waivers may be issued under the College Board's Fee Waiver Service. All required materials must be submitted by the following deadlines: November 15 for spring semester or for fall semester Early Decision; February 1 for freshman general admission and freshman early entrants (April 1 notification). May 15 is the deadline for transfers and visiting students.

Office of Admissions
Eugene Lang College The New School for Liberal Arts
72 Fifth Avenue, 2nd Floor
New York, NY 10011
212.229.5665
Email: lang@newschool.edu
www.newschool.edu/lang

MANNES COLLEGE THE NEW SCHOOL FOR MUSIC
www.newschool.edu/mannes

The Mannes College admissions process is designed to obtain a complete picture of an applicant. In reviewing applications, the Admissions Committee considers performance ability and potential, musical skills, English language aptitude (for applicants whose first language is not English), musical and academic background, and recommendation letters. Applicants must audition in person. In order for an applicant to be considered for an audition and entrance examination appointment within a given audition period, his or her application must be postmarked by the stated deadline. November 15 is the deadline for the main audition period (March 2–9), April 1 is the deadline for the late audition period (May 20–21), and November 1 is the deadline for spring semester entrance.

Most Mannes courses run the entire academic year, so students enroll in September. Undergraduate students transferring from other colleges may enter at the start of the second semester in January, subject to the approval of the Admissions Committee.

Applicants for the piano, violin, cello, flute, and voice concentrations must submit a prescreening recording in order to qualify for an in-person audition. Recordings must be postmarked by the application deadline stated above.

Office of Admissions
Mannes College The New School for Music
150 West 85th Street
New York, NY 10024
800.292.3040 or 212.580.0210 x4862
Email: mannesadmissions@newschool.edu
www.newschool.edu/mannes

THE NEW SCHOOL FOR JAZZ AND CONTEMPORARY MUSIC
www.newschool.edu/jazz

Students applying for the fall semester should submit their applications by January 1. Applicants for the spring (January) semester should apply by September 15. Live auditions are held in February and March. If you would like to schedule a live audition for the citywide audition week in March, you must submit your application by December 15. Applying early allows applicants to take full advantage of financial aid, scholarship, and live audition opportunities at the school. Late applications are due by March 15 for the fall semester and November 1 for the spring semester.

A performance audition is required of all students applying to The New School for Jazz and Contemporary Music. A prescreen tape or CD is required for all applicants on drums, guitar, and voice. The tape or CD must be received within one week of submission of an online application. Vocalists who pass the prescreen must audition live at The New School for Jazz and Contemporary Music; drummers and guitarists may audition live or online or submit an audition tape or CD.

A complete application includes a completed and signed application form (online applicants sign electronically), a nonrefundable application fee of $100 (online credit card payment, check, or money order), a personal statement, a live or recorded audition (prescreen tape or CD for drummers, guitarists, and vocalists); official high school or secondary school transcript or school records; and a letter of recommendation from a teacher, counselor, or professional who is able to comment on your qualifications for study at The New School for Jazz and Contemporary Music. The school will accept one additional recommendation if the applicant chooses to submit one.

Office of Admissions
The New School for Jazz and Contemporary Music
79 Fifth Avenue, 5th floor
New York, NY 10003
212.229.5896 x4589
Email: jazzadm@newschool.edu
www.newschool.edu/jazz

The eight schools that make up the university are The New School for General Studies; The New School for Social Research; Parsons The New School for Design; Eugene Lang College The New School for Liberal Arts; Mannes College The New School for Music; The New School for Drama; and The New School for Jazz and Contemporary Music.

For a list of graduate program offerings at The New School, visit www.newschool.edu/graduateprograms.

NEW YORK SCHOOL OF INTERIOR DESIGN

The New York School of Interior Design's guiding principle is that the interior environment is a fundamental element of human welfare.

AT A GLANCE

Situated in the design capital of the world, the New York School of Interior Design has for nearly one hundred years been preparing aspiring interior designers to join one of the most exciting and important design professions. Today, the value of educational credentials is greater than ever, as the need grows for interior spaces that are functional, safe, beautiful, and sustainable. NYSID continues to prepare leaders to face the newest challenges facing the world of the built environment; designing and building interiors in a socially and environmentally conscientious way.

NYSID is the only institution in the New York City metropolitan area dedicated to the advancement of interior design through education, research, programming, professional development, and outreach. Its nationally ranked graduate and undergraduate programs (*U.S. News & World Report*, 2008, and *DesignIntelligence*, 2009) are taught by a faculty of dedicated scholars and practitioners in a state-of-the-art campus. Most importantly, its graduates excel professionally, receiving the recognition they deserve in leading contract and home magazines.

LOCATION AND ENVIRONMENT

The excitement of being in New York City can be matched nowhere else on the planet, and there is no better place to study the dynamic field of interior design than NYSID with its state-of-the-art facilities in two historic buildings in the heart of it all—the city itself is part of a NYSID education!

Our neighborhood, the Upper East Side, has long been regarded as one of New York City's finest. Besides having Central Park as its backyard, what makes the neighborhood so popular is its location near New York's greatest museums, including the Metropolitan Museum of Art, the Guggenheim and the Frick Collection, as well as one of Manhattan's finest shopping streets — Madison Avenue. Students love the area for its numerous shops, cafes, nightlife, transportation, and housing options. Interior design students appreciate the area's art and antique dealers and the close proximity to the industry's major trade showrooms. New York – It's part of who we are.

OFF-CAMPUS OPPORTUNITIES

NYSID's location is ideal for those looking for job opportunities. Interior designers are being sought by residential and commercial clients who are building, restoring, and renovating, to address the challenging decisions that face designers today. They are employed by interior design and architectural firms, urban planners, and companies that specialize in restaurant, office, or exhibition design as well as the design of interiors for banks, schools, and hospitals. The career placement service at NYSID facilitates finding work in this competitive and dynamic field by maintaining an active list of job openings.

MAJORS AND DEGREES OFFERED

Whether you seek an undergraduate college degree, a graduate degree, or a basic program to begin your interior design education, NYSID has an academic program in Interior Design to suit your needs.

The college offers two undergraduate interior design degree programs: the professional-level, 132-credit Bachelor of Fine Arts (BFA), and the pre-professional-level, 66-credit Associate in Applied Science (AAS). Both degree programs, in conjunction with the requisite work experience, prepare graduates to sit for the NCIDQ exam leading to state certification. The 120-credit Bachelor of Arts (BA) is a liberal arts degree in the history of the interior and the decorative arts.

A 24-credit nondegree certificate program, Basic Interior Design (BID), is offered for those who need to develop a portfolio in order to apply to the BFA or AAS degree program, or for those seeking personal enrichment and entry-level job opportunities in fields related to interior design.

At the graduate level, NYSID offers three distinct opportunities to pursue a graduate degree in interior design. For those without a design background, our 90-credit, professional-level Master of Fine Arts in Interior Design program (MFA-1) prepares students to enter the interior design profession with an advanced degree. A 60-credit, post-professional-level Master of fine Arts in Interior Design program (MFA-2) provides students who already have a design or architecture background the opportunity to further develop and refine their voice as designers and to engage in projects that are more conceptual in nature. The 30-credit, post-professional-level Master of Professional Studies (MPS) program focuses on Sustainable Design and its implementation.

ACADEMIC PROGRAMS

The focus of the CIDA-accredited BFA program is on the development of the professional interior designer's ability to formulate, propose, and carry out creative design solutions in a safe and pleasing fashion. With the required professional experience, the curriculum satisfies educational requirements for membership in national and local interior design associations and allows candidates to sit for the qualifying exams for interior design certification in many states.

The AAS degree program fulfills the minimum of two years of college-level interior design education that is required along with the requisite work experience to be eligible to become a Certified Interior Designer in the State of New York. Required credits earned in AAS courses may be applied to the BFA upon acceptance into the BFA program.

The non-degree Basic Interior Design (BID) certificate program provides an introduction to interior design with emphasis on fundamental skills and knowledge in interiors, architecture, and the visual and decorative arts. On completion, students can continue by applying to a degree program or pursue jobs in fields related to interior design. Introductory courses focus on drawing, design concepts, and design history, building a foundation-level understanding of the technical and aesthetic principles essential to understanding space planning, color, drafting, and materials and finishes.

Applicants who do not have the portfolio of art and design work that is required for acceptance into the BFA and AAS programs can apply to the BID program in which they can complete most of the courses that are in the first year of a degree program while building a portfolio of work for acceptance into a degree program. Credits earned in Basic Interior Design courses may be applied to the AAS and BFA degree programs upon acceptance into these programs.

The BA in the in the History of the Interior & the Decorative Arts program combines the study of design and material culture from a historical perspective with an introduction to basic studio practice. Graduates of the BA program are eligible to apply to the MFA-1 graduate program with one year of advanced standing

CAMPUS FACILITIES AND EQUIPMENT

NYSID is situated in the design capital of the United States, if not the world – New York City. In many important respects, New York City is our campus. Students have access to some of the most coveted and valuable resources critical to any designer's work: world-class museums and galleries, showrooms filled with the work of leading furniture and materials designers, many of the nation's top design firms, and a dizzying array of architectural styles and design approaches found in the City's thousands of residential and commercial buildings. Here, inspiration abounds.

NYSID's Manhattan campus offers everything you would expect from the leader in interior design education: classrooms and labs equipped with CAD and related software, and a one-of-a-kind lighting laboratory; an atelier for independent work that is equipped with computers, a comprehensive materials library, and a high-end digital output center; a library with over 12,000 books, over 100 serial and magazine subscriptions, and access to image and research databases; galleries for the exhibition of student, faculty, and alumni work; and places for students to relax, socialize, study, or grab a quick bite or a cup of coffee.

NYSID offers housing at a state-of-the-art student residential facility at the corner of East 97th Street and Third Avenue. This lively, safe, and easily accessible east-side location makes the NYSID student experience complete. The Residence at 1760 Third Avenue features single, double, and triple accommodations, all with their own bathroom, and provides 24-hour security and concierge service. Each student room is equipped with a refrigerator, microwave oven, and 26-inch DVD-equipped, flat-screen TV. There is free cable, free local and national phone service, and free high-speed internet. Rooms come fully furnished (except for bedding), and the facility has on site a full-service gym, game room, common rooms, laundry room, quiet rooms, and computer kiosks.

TUITION, ROOM, BOARD, AND FEES

Undergraduate (BID, AAS, and BFA) tuition for the 2010–2011 academic year is $765 per credit (a full-time student can expect to pay approximately $12,623 in tuition per semester). BA tuition for 2010–2011 is $11,500 per semester. Graduate tuition for 2010–2011 is $12,750 per semester. Registration/Technology/Student Activity fees equal $280 per semester.

Housing costs vary depending on room types. Rates for nine months are: Standard Double $15,600; Standard Double with Kitchen $16,100; Large Double with Kitchen $16,800; and Single with Kitchen $19,200.

FINANCIAL AID

Most financial aid dollars in the United States, in loans, grants, and work-study, are from federal and state programs. They are awarded to US citizens and permanent residents who qualify according to the financial aid program's criteria. Standards for satisfactory academic progress are measured once per academic year according to federal regulations.

To apply, all applicants must complete the Free Application for Federal Student Aid (online at www.fafsa.ed.gov). If financial need has been established and adequate funding is available, eligible applicants are considered for federal grant, loan, and work-study programs, NYSID institutional aid, and New York State aid, if applicable.

STUDENT ORGANIZATIONS AND ACTIVITIES

Being located in the heart of Manhattan, the opportunities for both professional and recreational activities are endless. NYSID sponsored events have recently included ice skating in Central Park; trips to Broadway shows; bus trips to historic Hudson River Valley houses and Frank Lloyd Wright's Fallingwater; a masquerade ball; movie nights; and a boat cruise in the harbor. NYSID's student chapter of the American Society of Interior Designers (ASID) offers students the opportunity to prepare for rewarding careers by participating in a wide variety of learning experiences and programs that complement their academic training, such as commercial and residential firm office tours, hotel and showroom visits and lectures. The Contract Club organizes monthly tours to prominent commercial interior design and architecture firms, such as Steelcase, Clodagh, and Swanke, Hayden, Connell Architects.

ADMISSIONS PROCESS

It is simple to apply to NYSID; it can be done either by paper or online. Log-in information will be e-mailed to you once you apply so you may track your application through NYSID's online portal. The requirements include the application form and fee; an essay; transcripts of previous academic work; two letters of recommendation; SAT or ACT scores; and a fine arts portfolio of ten to fifteen pieces (AAS and BFA programs only). MFA-2 and MPS graduate applicants should submit a portfolio of their professional-level work. MFA-1 applicants should submit a fine and/or applied arts portfolio, or complete a two-week intensive qualifying workshop offered at NYSID in August.

If you are an undergraduate applicant who does not have a portfolio, you may apply to our Basic Interior Design (BID) certificate program. In the BID program you will develop a portfolio from the work you are doing in your first-semester classes. Using that work you may then apply to our AAS or BFA programs. Since the classes in the BID program are required in the AAS and BFA programs, and the AAS program is equivalent to the first two years of our BFA, it is possible – wherever you begin—to "step-up" to the next higher program without wasting time or money.

The recommended date to submit applications for admission for all programs is March 1. After that date, applications will be accepted on a space-available basis.

NEW YORK UNIVERSITY

AT A GLANCE

New York University is unlike any other institution of higher education in the world. When you enter NYU, you become part of a close-knit community that combines the nurturing atmosphere of a small- to medium-sized college with the myriad cultural offerings and research opportunities of a Global Network University. The energy and resources of New York City and Abu Dhabi serve as extensions of our campuses there, providing unique opportunities for research, internships, and job placement. On campus, NYU's intellectual climate is fostered by a faculty of world-famous scholars, researchers, and artists who teach both undergraduate and graduate courses. Students often work on individual projects with these outstanding professors. NYU students come from all 50 states and over 130 countries. They enroll in one of 11 undergraduate schools, colleges, or programs and choose from over 4,500 courses in over 230 majors.

ACADEMICS

At NYU, students enroll into one of the University's undergraduate schools, colleges, or programs. NYU Abu Dhabi, NYU's new honors college opening fall 2010 in the United Arab Emirates, blends a global academic opportunity with a liberal arts, science, and engineering curriculum. The College of Arts and Science offers an extensive curriculum in liberal arts and science, including preprofessional law, medicine, and dentistry programs. The Global Liberal Studies Program is a rigorous four-year course of study in the liberal arts, language proficiency, and international experience, including a junior-year abroad experience. The Liberal Studies Program is a two-year interdisciplinary liberal arts program for which enrollment is offered to select students; upon successful program completion, the students then enroll as juniors in the undergraduate school, college, or program to which they originally applied. The Leonard N. Stern School of Business ranks among the top 10 nationally, and combines a liberal arts core with an outstanding business curriculum. The Steinhardt School of Culture, Education, and Human Development focuses on the human service professions, including education, health, communications, and the arts. The Tisch School of the Arts combines a liberal arts education with conservatory training. The Gallatin School of Individualized Study allows highly motivated students to design their own curriculum. The Silver School of Social Work combines a liberal arts education with a firm grounding in social work. The Preston Robert Tisch Center for Hospitality, Tourism, and Sports Management offers programs in hotel and tourism management and sports management. The College of Nursing offers liberal arts combined with nursing science.

All students, regardless of major, receive a liberal arts foundation. NYU faculty are among the world's leading intellectuals, including scholars and researchers who have received Nobel, Crafoord, and Pulitzer Prizes; MacArthur, Guggenheim, and Fulbright Fellowships; and Oscar and Emmy Awards. Faculty members teach undergraduate and graduate courses, allowing undergraduate students to become directly involved in research projects with internationally known scholars.

ADMISSIONS

Undergraduate admission to NYU is highly selective. The process involves a comprehensive review of the applicant's academic background, standardized test scores, extracurricular activities, an essay, personal statements, and recommendation letters. Several programs also require the applicant to audition or submit creative materials. Applicants who have successfully completed a broad range of challenging course work throughout high school are the most desirable candidates. Also considered are your unique talents, personal attributes, and future goals.

Applicants must submit official score reports for standardized tests, and may choose from one of the following options: SAT Reasoning Test and two SAT Subject Tests; ACT (with Writing Test); SAT Reasoning Test and two Advanced Placement (AP) Exam scores; three SAT Subject Test scores (one in literature or the humanities, one in math or science, and one nonlanguage of the student's choice); or three AP Exam scores (one in literature or the humanities, one in math or science, and one nonlanguage of the student's choice).

Students who demonstrate evidence of an extraordinary accomplishment outside of normal classroom or scholastic activity, such as a major publication in a national or international journal, a published book, a film or other outstanding visual or performing artistic accomplishment, a scientific or other remarkable discovery, winning a national competition, or the equivalent are required to provide only an SAT score, or two SAT Subject Test scores, or two AP Exam scores.

The admissions staff also visits high schools and hosts receptions nationwide. Check with your college counselor or the Admissions Web site at admissions.nyu.edu for dates and times.

Campus tours or information session appointments can be arranged by calling 212-998-4524 or visiting http://events.embark.com/event/nyu/on_campus/.

CAMPUS FACILITIES AND EQUIPMENT

NYU offers an exceptional range of facilities and student services and an enormously varied program of residence halls, meal plans, and dining locations. Academic facilities include nine libraries and institutes renowned for their research in applied mathematics, physics, neural science, and fine arts. Foreign language and cultural centers offer many lectures, films, and concerts. Students may also access NYU's Wasserman Center for Career Development, advanced computer and multimedia resources, and specialized offices addressing almost every student need, from medical attention to discount theatre tickets. The Kimmel Center for Student Life houses dining facilities, student lounges, computers, club spaces, and the Skirball Center for the Performing Arts, lower Manhattan's largest performance space.

CAMPUS LIFE

With NCAA Division III, intramural, and club athletics, 400 student clubs, and numerous volunteer activities, NYU students participate in ways that match their interests.

Student-run clubs are as varied as the student body. Whether their interests lie in foreign languages, politics, ballroom dancing, writing for the Washington Square News or working at NYU's radio station, students will find something to suit their tastes.

Two gyms—Coles Sports and Recreation Center and the Palladium Athletic Facility—cater to intramurals, recreation classes, and 21 varsity teams. NYU is also partnered with Chelsea Piers, which includes facilities for golf, ice and roller skating, indoor soccer, and sand volleyball.

Hundreds of students annually serve communities across the city, country and world through the Office of Student Activities' C-Team, Alternative Breaks Program, new student OutReach Program, fraternities and sororities, and student organizations. Students deliver meals to the needy and homebound, tutor children, paint public schools, clean up parks, rebuild areas devastated by natural disasters, and more.

COLLEGE BASICS

New York University (NYU) is unlike any other institution of higher education in the world. Whether you're a student in Manhattan's Greenwich Village or at our new portal campus in Abu Dhabi, you'll challenge yourself beyond the classroom and take advantage of NYU's Global Network University.

LOCATION AND ENVIRONMENT

At NYU, New York City is the integral backdrop to the undergraduate experience. NYU's Washington Square campus is located in the heart of Greenwich Village, a historic neighborhood and one of the city's most creative communities that has attracted generations of writers, musicians, artists, and intellectuals. Rather than building walls to separate the campus from the community, NYU embraces the city as an essential element of academic life. New York is a world center of finance, media, and art, offering internships, part-time jobs and research experiences that pair course work with practical experience. The city offers the best in theatre, dance, music, film, museums, and galleries. Undergraduates can be found presenting academic papers at annual conferences; winning prizes at film festivals; working on innovative research projects in laboratories; interning on Wall Street; and completing field work in some of the world's best hospitals and schools.

In addition, NYU's new Abu Dhabi campus puts students in the center of an entrepreneurial capital of ideas and talents. Abu Dhabi, a diverse city in the heart of the Middle East, has developed a progressive agenda in health care, the arts, economic and environmental sustainability, and educational human development. This creates an array of opportunities for students to pursue learning, research, and innovation.

TUITION AND FEES

2009–2010 Costs°

Tuition and fees are $38,765; average room and board (includes up to 19 meals a week) is $13,226.

°Tisch School of the Arts and Stern School of Business rates vary.

MAJORS AND DEGREES

NYU students enroll directly into one of the University's undergraduate schools, colleges, or programs, each of which has earned national recognition: NYU Abu Dhabi, College of Arts and Science; Global Liberal Studies Program; Liberal Studies Program; Leonard N. Stern School of Business; Steinhardt School of Culture, Education, and Human Development; Tisch School of the Arts; Gallatin School of Individualized Study; Silver School of Social Work; Preston Robert Tisch Center for Hospitality, Tourism, and Sports Management; and College of Nursing.

Among the more than 230 undergraduate majors offered by NYU are: Africana Studies, Anthropology, Biochemistry, Economics, Dance, Education, Engineering, Film and Television, Finance, Marketing, Metropolitan Studies, Sociology, Theatre, and Recorded Music.

OFF-CAMPUS OPPORTUNITIES

Students have unparalleled study abroad opportunities within NYU's global network. They may study at one or more of the University's 10 international academic centers—in Accra, Ghana; Berlin, Germany; Buenos Aires, Argentina; Florence, Italy; London, England; Madrid, Spain; Paris, France; Prague, Czech Republic; Shanghai, China; and Tel Aviv, Israel—or in one of many exchange programs NYU has with outstanding research universities around the world. Each international program provides a rich curriculum in which students—who have access to portable financial aid—can complete some of their general degree requirements and, in many fields, take courses in their major. In fact, a number of NYU's schools, colleges, and programs offer specific curricula and majors with an international focus. Students will also take advantage of programs and opportunities made possible by NYU Abu Dhabi, the World's Honors College.

TUITION AND AID

We believe that you should be able to choose a college that offers the best range of educational opportunities. To make this choice possible, we attempt to aid students in need of financial assistance.

There are many financial aid sources at NYU, and all students are invited to apply for financial aid or one of NYU's financing plans. Sixty-seven percent of full-time NYU undergraduates receive some form of financial aid.

Scholarships take into account both financial need and academic merit; however, while merit-based scholarships are available, NYU is committed to using the vast majority of its scholarship funds to assist students whose families are unable to pay the full cost of an NYU education. Low-interest education loans are available for both students and parents. Part-time employment, on and off campus, is another source of funding.

NYU also offers or participates in a variety of payment plans, ranging from interest-free prepayment plans to extensive loan programs that allow families to finance the cost of a college education over many years.

A financial aid package might include any combination of scholarships, loans, or work-study programs. Students wishing to be considered for aid must submit the Free Application for Federal Student Aid (FAFSA). The FAFSA's submission deadline is February 15 for the fall semester and November 1 for the spring semester.

STUDENT ORGANIZATIONS AND ACTIVITIES

NYU is anything but cookie-cutter—that's one of the best things about being a part of a large, global network university. Its culture of openness, opportunity, and tolerance allows NYU's community to thrive. There are so many choices here about what to do that no two students make exactly the same selection. Some come together in groups; others go their own ways.

There are many ways to get involved at NYU—including approximately 400 clubs and organizations, a dynamic student government, a variety of sports teams, myriad community service opportunities, and much more. Students at NYU find their niche by doing what they love. You can determine your future as you contribute to University life, and learn to become a leader in the process!

NIAGARA UNIVERSITY

AT A GLANCE

Founded in 1856 by the Vincentian fathers and brothers, Niagara University (NU) is a private, Catholic, comprehensive, co-educational institution. Located minutes from the scenic Niagara Falls, Niagara University's suburban campus is a blend of historic ivy-covered structures and elegant modern buildings. There are more than 3,000 undergraduates and about 950 graduate students at Niagara. NU is comprised of four academic divisions: the College of Arts and Sciences, College of Education, College of Business Administration, and the College of Hospitality & Tourism Management. While at NU, students have access to a range of support services that help them develop. To assist incoming students who have not decided on a field of study, NU offers the award-winning Academic Exploration Program (AEP). In addition, select students have the opportunity to participate in the honors program, a special academic program designed to stimulate and challenge accomplished students.

The Middle States Association of Colleges and Schools accredits Niagara University. NU also holds the other accreditations and memberships. Its programs in education are accredited by National Council for Accreditation of Teacher Education. Its business programs are accredited the Association to Advance Collegiate Schools of Business (AASCB International). Its social work program is accredited by the Council on Social Work Education and the department of chemistry has the approval of the American Chemical Society. The Commission for Programs in Hospitality Administration accredits NU's Hospitality & Tourism Management curriculum. NU's faculty is dedicated to teaching and takes an active interest in their students' academic and personal growth. With a student-faculty ratio of just 14:1 and an average class size of about 25, students have ample opportunity for personal interaction with their professors.

LOCATION AND ENVIRONMENT

Located in western New York, Niagara University's suburban campus is located outside the quaint village of Lewiston, NY, and within minutes of Niagara Falls, NY. The campus is also about 20 minutes from Buffalo, NY, and 90 minutes from Toronto, Canada. This area boasts a wide variety of resources and attractions, including the world-famous Niagara Falls. In addition, the Canadian border and the vibrant cities of Toronto and Buffalo are easily accessible from NU. The campus community is an ideal size, combining a strong community spirit with a friendly campus setting.

Residence life at NU is creative, social, and educational. Student rooms have comfortable furniture and hookups for telephone, cable television, and computers. Commuting students and resident students discover that the University offers a wide range of programs and activities designed to help new students become a part of the NU community and the surrounding area.

OFF-CAMPUS OPPORTUNITIES

Off-campus and other learning opportunities abound at Niagara University. Students may choose to participate in programs such as: the study abroad program, various internships, cooperative education and/or cross registering at other colleges through the Western New York Consortium.

In keeping with the spirit of St. Vincent de Paul, many Niagara students volunteer off campus through the Niagara University Community Action Program and the Learn & Serve program. Learn & Serve grants students academic credit for volunteer work. These programs are designed to help students utilize their time and talents in service to the less fortunate.

MAJORS AND DEGREES OFFERED

Niagara University (NU) offers over 50 academic programs and majors within the four academic divisions. The University confers Bachelor of Arts, Bachelor of Science, Bachelor of Business Administration, Bachelor of Fine Arts, Associate in Arts, Associate in Science, Associate in Applied Science, Master of Arts, Master of Science, Master of Science in Education, and Master of Business Administration Degrees.

ACADEMIC PROGRAMS

Through the College of Arts and Sciences, students can pursue a Bachelor of Arts in the following areas of study: chemistry, with concentration in chemistry or environmental studies; communications studies; English; French; history; international studies; liberal arts; life sciences; mathematics; philosophy; political science with concentration in political science or environmental studies; psychology; religious studies; social sciences; sociology; and Spanish. NU also offers the Bachelor of Fine Arts degree in theatre studies and the Associate in Arts in general studies. NU offers the Bachelor of Science in biochemistry with a concentration in biochemistry or bioinformatics; biology with concentration in biology, biotechnology, or environmental studies; chemistry with concentration in chemistry, computational chemistry, or environmental studies; computer and information sciences; criminology and criminal justice; mathematics; and social work. The College of Arts and Sciences also offers a five-year B.S./M.S. program in criminal justice. Niagara University also offers several pre-professional partnerships with other universities. In conjunction with the State University of New York at Buffalo, NU offers a 3+4 partnership in dentistry and pharmacy. In conjunction with The Lake Erie College of Osteopathic Medicine, NU also offers a 3+4 partnership in medicine and a 2+3 program in pharmacy. Qualified students are eligible to apply for early assurance at the State University of New York at Buffalo.

For students who do not wish to declare a major, the University offers the award-winning Academic Exploration Program to help them explore fields and hone their individual interests.

Through the College of Business Administration, students can pursue a Bachelor of Business Administration, accounting, or a Bachelor of Science degree iin economics, finance, general business, marketing and management with concentrations in human resources, international business, management, and supply chain management. The College of Business Administration also offers a five-year B.B.A./M.B.A. degree in accounting. Students in this division can also pursue an Associate in Applied Science degree in business.

The College of Education offers Bachelor's degree programs for the New York State initial certification in early childhood and childhood (birth-grade 6), childhood (grades 1-6), childhood and middle childhood (grades 1–9), adolescence (grades 7–12), special education & childhood (grades 1–6) special education and adolescence

(grades 7–12) and TESOL—Teaching English to Speakers of Other Languages (grades K–12). Education majors must choose an academic concentration in English, mathematics, social studies, French, Spanish, biology, chemistry, or business. Education students who choose a concentration in business education can only pursue certification for grades 5–12.

Students in the College of Hospitality & Tourism Management may receive a Bachelor of Science in hotel & restaurant management with concentrations in hotel & restaurant planning and control, foodservice management, restaurant entrepreneurship; sport management with a concentration in sports operations; tourism and recreation management with concentrations in special events & conference management and tourism destination management.

NU also offers pre-professional programs in pre-dental, pre-legal, pre-medical, pre-pharmacy, pre-veterinary; and Army-ROTC.

CAMPUS FACILITIES AND EQUIPMENT

Niagara University is committed to providing students facilities that will enhance their academic, social, cultural, athletic, recreational, and moral development. Below is a sampling of some of these facilities.

The Kiernan Center, NU's fitness and recreation facility, provides a multipurpose gym, a swimming pool and diving pool, an indoor track and racquetball courts, free-weight and Nautilus rooms, and aerobics rooms. In addition, there are several outdoor athletic fields, basketball and tennis courts.

NU also offers student services such as academic and personal counseling, orientation, academic planning and career planning services. The University's library has an extensive collection which exceeds 273,000 hard volumes, 21,000 periodicals, composed of print and electronic subscriptions and 24,140 units of microfilm. The library is affiliated with the On-line Computer Library Center (OCLC) network.

The Academic Complex, which opened in the fall of 2007, is a state-of-the-art facility that houses the College of Business Administration (Bisgrove Hall) and the College of Education. Dunleavy Hall houses the television production centers and a computerized lecture room. The University's other first-rate facilities include the Leary Theatre, the Computer Center, St. Vincent's Hall, the Castellani Art Museum, the student apartments, and the Dwyer Ice Complex, which houses a dual rink ice hockey facility.

TUITION, ROOM, BOARD AND FEES

Fees for the 2009–2010 academic year included: tuition $23,700; room and board $10,250 and student fees $1,000.

FINANCIAL AID

Over 98 percent of the incoming freshmen at NU receive financial assistance. NU offers a merit-based scholarship and grant program, as well as athletic, transfer, service, and talent scholarships. Niagara encourages students of all financial backgrounds to apply to the University.

STUDENT ORGANIZATIONS AND ACTIVITIES

NU has an active, diverse, and social campus culture, with more than 80 student-operated clubs and organizations. Ranging from academic and cultural groups to social and athletic clubs, NU has an activity to suit every taste. Niagara is a member of the NCAA Division I and competes in men's and women's basketball, cross-country, golf, ice hockey, swimming and diving, tennis, and soccer, men's baseball , and women's volleyball and softball. There is also an active intramural and recreational athletic program.

Students seeking off-campus activities need go no further than the Campus Activities Office. This office coordinates many off-campus excursions to local attractions, professional sports competitions, theatre events, and trips to Toronto. Campus Activities also provides local transportation by means of the NU Cruiser. The NU Cruiser transports students to a central area with a bank, grocery store, outlet mall and eateries.

ADMISSIONS PROCESS

Niagara University encourages all men and women whose aptitude and demonstrated academic achievement in high school or college give evidence of their ability to successfully complete the various university programs to apply for admission. Consistent with our Catholic mission, Niagara University welcomes all students, regardless of age, race, creed, color, national origin, sexual orientation, military status, sex, disability, predisposing genetic characteristics, or marital status.

To apply for admission, freshmen students must complete an admissions application; submit a $30.00 application fee, their official high school transcript including official scores from the SAT or ACT, and an personal statement or essay. It is anticipated that all students who apply for admissions will complete and will receive their high school diploma prior to the first day of classes at N.U. Although not required, NU recommends that prospective students schedule an admissions interview and a tour of campus.

Transfer students may apply to enter any of the three semesters—fall, spring, or summer. Transfer students must complete an admissions application, submit a $30.00 application fee, an official high school transcript, official transcript(s) from any college/university previously/presently attending, and, if appropriate, a list of courses being pursued at the time of the application. A personal statement or essay is also required. The dean of each academic division evaluates transfer credit.

Students who complete a strong high school curriculum in three years can apply for early admission. New York State residents who come from an economically and educationally disadvantaged background may apply through the Higher Educational Opportunity Program (HEOP).

International students should refer to our website at www.niagara.edu/admissions/intl.htm for complete application information.

NICHOLS COLLEGE

AT A GLANCE:

Your Success is Our Business

Nichols College strives to develop tomorrow's leaders through a dynamic, career-focused business education.

We transform our students into successful graduates who can respond to challenges, are eager for responsibility, and will assume significant roles in the global economy.

The Nichols experience happens in a welcoming environment where our student is encouraged to learn and grow under the guidance of mentoring faculty and staff committed to student success.

The best way to show you the value of a Nichols degree is to share some statistics from our recent graduating classes.

• An average of 94% were fully employed in professional positions within 6 months

• The average starting salary was nearly $40,000

• 83% of those starting salaries were over $30,000.

1 out of 10 Nichols graduates is a CEO, corporate president or business owner. That's what we mean by success!

LOCATION AND ENVIRONMENT

Nichols is located in Dudley, Massachusetts roughly twenty minutes south of Worcester. We are also within an hour's drive of Boston, Springfield, Hartford, and Providence. Set on over 200 acres of rolling hills we proudly offer a variety of top notch facilities and housing options.

Students can walk to classrooms, the Lombard Dining Hall, Daniels Auditorium, the Library, and the Athletic Center in less than 5 minutes. In addition, you will find that all of our facilities, dorm rooms, classrooms, and Library are equipped with top flight technology to ensure that students are connected everywhere they go.

Please schedule a campus visit with our admissions staff because there is no substitute for seeing it in person.

OFF-CAMPUS OPPORTUNITIES

The greater Worcester area is an active, vibrant and energetic community. Downtown Worcester is in the midst of a dynamic revitalization effort as over $1 billion is being invested in new development projects including CitySquare, the Hanover Theatre for the Performing Arts, and the Blackstone Canal District Initiative.

Whether it's catching the latest concert at the DCU Center, sampling the restaurants on Shrewsbury Street, shopping at Blackstone Valley, or watching the Worcester Tornadoes (Can-Am League baseball), or Worcester Sharks (American Hockey League) in thrilling sports action, Worcester is the place to be for fun and exciting attractions.

MAJORS AND DEGREES OFFERED

There are two undergraduate degrees offered:

• Bachelor of Science in Business Administration (B.S.B.A.)

• Bachelor of Arts (B.A.)

B.S.B.A.

Business students must complete 121 credit hours.

The Business Core curriculum of 37 credits offers a firm grounding in key areas of business including accounting, computer information systems, finance, management and marketing.

In addition, students complete 18–27 credits in their area of specialization.

B.S.B.A. Specializations:

• Accounting

• Arts & Entertainment Management

• Business Communication

• Criminal Justice Management

• Economics

• Finance

• General Business

• Hospitality Management

• Human Resource Management

• International Business

• Legal Studies

• Management

• Management Information Systems

• Marketing

• Sport Management

Qualified applicants who have maintained a 3.0 or better cumulative GPA in high school may be eligible to participate in our 3 year accelerated B.S.B.A program.

B.A.

Liberal Arts students must complete 120 credit hours. The Liberal Arts core of 12 credit hours includes selected studies in the humanities and world culture. In addition, students complete 30 credits in their major.

B.A. Majors:

• Economics

• English

• History

• Mathematics

• Psychology

EDUCATOR PREPARATION

Nichols College Educator Preparation Program prepares you to teach business, history, English or mathematics in middle or secondary schools.

Graduate Options

Traditional MBA

• MBA with an emphasis in Sport Management

• MBA with an emphasis in Security Management

• Master of Organizational Leadership

ACADEMIC PROGRAMS

Professional Development Seminar

Our four-year Professional Development Seminar (PDS) program helps you develop career skills that set you apart.

In the program's 3rd and 4th years, you will increasingly focus on career decision making, refining interview skills, and developing a presentation portfolio of your accomplishments.

Students in particular find the mock interview process helpful. They also enjoy the "Etiquette Dinner" for seniors, and our fashion shows depicting the "Dos and DON'Ts" of professional dress.

Internship Program

An internship lets you test drive a career, develop a work portfolio, and make a network of professional contacts for future employment opportunities. At Nichols, several business specializations require internships, and our students have been placed in top-tier venues from Madison Square Garden to Abbott Labs.

Career Services

Our Career Services Office is renowned throughout New England. The staff maintains a detailed listing of job opportunities and sponsors one of the largest career fairs in the area. Our staff will help you keep your resume current, develop a strong cover letter, and create a complete list of references to help in your job search.

Honors Program

Our undergraduate students have the opportunity to be recognized for outstanding academic achievement.

To be eligible, a student must maintain a GPA of 3.2 or higher and have earned a minimum of 29 credit hours. Participating students complete additional study requirements to earn an extra fourth credit in 300-level or 400-level courses. After achieving a B+ or higher grade in each of the three courses, students are qualified to apply for entrance into a senior-year Honors Scholar Seminar.

Students may select honors courses from across the curriculum. At Commencement, students completing the program with a 3.2 GPA or higher will earn an academic mark of distinction as a Nichols Honors Scholar.

Accelerated Programs

Qualified applicants may be able to take part in one of our unique accelerated programs. Students with above a 3.0 can enter a 3 years B.S.B.A program upon enrollment. In addition to our 3-year degree we also offer a 4+1 M.B.A. option.

CAMPUS FACILITIES AND EQUIPMENT

The state of the art Athletics Center features an indoor climbing wall, squash courts, raquet ball courts, a conference room, administrative offices, a weight room, a fitness room, and four locker rooms.

Once known as the Bison Bowl, Nichols College now plays all of its home football, field hockey and lacrosse games on the new Michael J. Vendetti Multi-Purpose Field. The men's and women's soccer teams also play some of their home contests on the field. The field includes an eight-lane rubberized quarter-mile track surrounding a turf field surface. To facilitate media coverage, there is a new press box with online capabilities and Musco lighting to light the field for night contests.

TUITION, ROOM, BOARD, AND FEES

Tuition: 28,570

Room: 4,900

Board: 4,430

Fees: 300

Total: 38,200

FINANCIAL AID

Nichols awards merit-based and need-based scholarships and grants. You can supplement your Nichols awards with federal and state grants and/or loans. Students with a core G.P.A. of 2.5 or higher are eligible to receive merit grants.

At Nichols College, the average full-time student receives in excess of $26,000 in financial aid from all sources. High-need students may receive up to $35,000 in financial aid. We also have numerous financing plans to fit nearly every budget.

STUDENT ORGANIZATIONS AND ACTIVITIES

Nichols proudly boasts a vibrant residential community. Nearly 90% of our student body lives on campus and a vast majority of our students participate in at least one on-campus group.

Getting connected to other students is a huge part of the college experience. We make sure that's easy and fun to do during your admissions process and through our orientation program.

Campus Organizations: Academic Honor Societies; Delta Mu Delta; Mu Kappa Tau; Omicron Delta Epsilon; Phi Alpha Theta; Zeta Alpha Phi; Athletic Honor Societies; The Student Athlete Advisory Council (SAAC); Elbridge Boyden Society; Student Government and Service Organizations; Campus Activities Board (CAB); Campus Ministry Association; The Student Government Association (SGA); Student Publications and Communications Media; The College Yearbook; The College Literary Magazine; WNRC Radio Station; Club Sports; Paintball Club; Racquetball Club; Men's Ice Hockey Club; Women's Ice Hockey Club; Men's Rugby Club; Women's Volleyball Club; General Interest; Accounting Club; Commuter Club; Criminal Justice Management Club; Economics/Finance Club; History Club; Human Resource Club; Management Club; Marketing Club; MIS Club; Psychology Club; Sport Management Club; Umoja

NCAA Division III Athletics: Nichols competes in The Commonwealth Coast Conference, New England Football Conference, ECAC Northeast Hockey League, and the ECAC Women's East Hockey League.

Men's Teams: Baseball; Basketball; Football; Golf; Ice Hockey; Lacrosse; Soccer; Tennis

Women's Teams: Basketball; Field Hockey; Ice Hockey; Lacrosse; Soccer; Softball; Tennis

ADMISSIONS PROCESS

Nichols College regards each prospective student as an individual, considering each application as it is submitted throughout the academic year. The admissions process is a joint partnership between the applicant and the College. We want to ensure each admitted student is the "right fit," both for the student and for Nichols. Admission candidacy requires that every applicant is either a high school graduate or has earned a high school equivalency diploma (GED). Our typical applicants' credentials vary greatly and many factors go into the admissions decision. We look at the areas of strength and weakness in each candidate and assess the student's ability to succeed at Nichols. Our typical admitted student has a GPA above 2.4, an average SAT score of 1,400 (combined verbal, math and essay scores), and a strong desire to succeed.

Proficiency in certain academic areas is a basic requirement for entrance to the College. Successful candidates for admission will follow a college preparatory course of study prior to applying to Nichols. We encourage students to challenge themselves with a rigorous secondary school curriculum. Though there is no specific schedule of courses required, an ideal four-year program includes the following coursework:

English - 4 units , Social Science - 2 units, Laboratory Science - 2 units, Academic Electives - 5 units, Foreign Language - 2 units and College Preparatory Mathematics - 3 units (recommended courses include: Algebra I, Geometry, Algebra II, and Advanced Mathematics)

NORTHEASTERN UNIVERSITY

AT A GLANCE

Northeastern University is a private research institution offering a comprehensive range of undergraduate and graduate programs leading to degrees from bachelor through doctorate. Over the past century, Northeastern has perfected the integration of study and practice, creating an unparalleled way to learn. Students receive the world's most powerful learning experience through a unique combination of rigorous academics and experiential learning opportunities, anchored by our signature cooperative education program. Experiential learning enables students to link course work with a variety of practical experiences, including global experiences, undergraduate research, and civic engagement opportunities, further enhancing their academics and preparing them for a lifetime of achievement.

LOCATION AND ENVIRONMENT

Northeastern's main campus is located in the heart of Boston's Avenue of the Arts, between the Museum of Fine Arts and Symphony Hall. Also in close proximity is Fenway Park, home of the World Champion Boston Red Sox, and the Fens, part of famous landscape designer Frederick Law Olmstead's Emerald Necklace park system. Northeastern is nestled among four historic and vibrant neighborhoods: the South End, Mission Hill, Roxbury and the Fenway. Through the University's many interactions with the city of Boston, students and faculty alike benefit from the resource-rich and diverse urban environment.

Northeastern's residential campus, situated on 73 acres, consists of 40 academic and administrative building and 37 residence facilities. Freshmen who enter in the fall are guaranteed housing for their first three years. Freshman housing includes ten coed residence halls or an abundance of Living Learning Communities where students are housed with others who share similar interests. Upperclassman can choose from new apartment complexes, many of which offer spectacular views of Boston. Honors students who are admitted into the University Honors Program may choose to live with other Honors students in one of four thematic Living and Learning communities within our newest residence hall, International Village. Residential Life staff enrich the lively community with organized social activities, including move nights, ice cream socials, trips to museums and more. In total, over 7,400 students are housed in university-owned or leased residence facilities. Residence halls have a port-per-pillow internet connections and some newer halls are wireless. Three dining halls and more than 100 Husky vendors give students ample opportunity for culinary variety. Students will find an array of food choices on-campus, including brick-oven pizza, stir-fry, salads and more. One dining hall features a kitchen where guest chefs teach students how to create tasty dishes with relative ease.

OFF-CAMPUS OPPORTUNITIES

Ask students what they enjoy most about being at Northeastern, and one common response is "Boston." It's easy to see why: Boston is the ultimate college town. The city is a hub of cultural, educational and social activity, yet it's small enough to navigate on foot. More than 300,000 college students from around the country and the world call Boston home, and the city is alive with their energy. The Office for Off Campus Student Services is a resource for Northeastern students who choose to live off campus in the surrounding neighborhoods.

MAJORS AND DEGREES OFFERED

Northeastern offers Bachelor of Arts and Bachelor of Science degrees in more than 80 areas of study including:

Bouvé College of Health Sciences: Majors are offered in health science, nursing, pharmacy, physical therapy, and speech-language pathology and audiology.

College of Social Science and Humanities: The Bachelor of Science is offered in African American studies American Sign Language, criminal justice, cultural anthropology, economics, English, history, human services, international affairs linguistics, philosophy, political science, religious studies, sociology, and Spanish.

College of Science: The Bachelor of Science is offered in applied physics, biochemistry, biology, biomedical physics, behavioral neuroscience, chemistry, environmental studies, environmental science, mathematics, physics, and psychology.

College of Art, Media and Design: The Bachelor of Science is offered in art, digital arts, graphic design, journalism, music history, music industry, music technology, theatre, architecture, and studio art.

College of Business Administration: The Bachelor of Science is offered in business administration and in international business. The BS in business administration offers concentrations in accounting, entrepreneurship and small business management, finance, management information systems, marketing, and supply chain management.

College of Computer Science: The Bachelor of Science or Bachelor of Arts is offered in computer science and a Bachelor of Science is offered in information science.

College of Engineering: Majors are offered in chemical engineering, civil and environmental engineering, computer engineering, electrical engineering, industrial engineering, and mechanical engineering.

ACADEMIC PROGRAMS

Northeastern offers a wide variety of curricula through seven undergraduate colleges, eight graduate and professional schools, two part-time undergraduate divisions, and numerous continuing- and special-education programs and institutes. Many dual degrees and minor/concentration options, such as information science and business, computer science and cognitive psychology or political science and international affairs, enable students to balance their studies with programs in the liberal arts and sciences.

CAMPUS FACILITIES AND EQUIPMENT

The campus environment is enriched by all the conveniences students need to complement their busy lifestyles. The state-of-the-art Marino Center offers fitness equipment, basketball courts, a climbing wall, indoor track, free weights and more. Eighteen varsity teams compete in national and international arenas, and almost 40 intramural and club teams offer less demanding competition. In addition to the campus bookstore, students have access to an overnight mail facility, grocery store, ATM machines, and more.

Campus highlights include the full-service Curry Student Center, newly renovated Matthews Arena, Snell Library, the Egan Research Center, the Behrakis Health Sciences Center, and the International Village residence community.

The University provides a broad range of academic and administrative computer resources available to students, faculty, and staff. Accessible 24 hours a day, 7 days a week, the InfoCommons offers an e-bar, Computer Help Desk, training, and more than 200 computers for general use. Internet access is available in Northeastern-owned residence halls through ResNet. The myNEU portal allows students to access many administrative and academic functions online, including e-mail, class schedules, co-op information, student payroll, financial services, and more.

TUITION, ROOM, BOARD AND FEES

For 2009–2010, annual tuition for undergraduates is $34,950. Standard room and board rates are $11,910. Tuition and other costs depend on your pattern of attendance. Whether you choose four of five years for your undergraduate degree, you will only pay tuition for in-class terms and not while on co-op. If you choose to live in campus housing while on co-op, you will be responsible for room and board charges.

FINANCIAL AID

Financial need, academic promise, and the availability of University funds determine how much aid a student receives. Supplemental loans and external scholarships may provide additional financial support. The Office of Student Financial Services prides itself on offering expert advice, friendly service, and personalized support. Regardless of your family income, consider applying for financial aid. Northeastern offers more than $135 million in grant and scholarship assistance, participates in all federal aid programs, and offers an array of alternative financing and payment plans. About 80% of all freshmen received some type of aid. The deadline for all forms of financial aid is February 15.

Northeastern has established several competitive scholarship programs to reward outstanding academic achievement. To be considered for one or more of these prestigious awards, students must apply for undergraduate admission to Northeastern no later than January 15. Only fall freshman applicants may be considered for most of these scholarships. For more information on scholarships, visit http://www.financialaid.neu.edu/.

STUDENT ORGANIZATIONS AND ACTIVITIES

Students have access to over 240 clubs and organizations and an extensive network of advisement and counseling services. Over 5,000 students participate in student organizations. Programs and services sponsored by the African American Institute, the Latino/a Student Cultural Center, the Asian American Center, the International Student & Scholar Institute, and many other organizations enrich Northeastern's social life and cultural fabric. In athletics, Northeastern competes in NCAA Division I and maintains varsity teams in 8 men's and 10 women's sports.

ADMISSIONS PROCESS

Admission to Northeastern is selective and competitive. Building a talented and diverse incoming class is the primary goal of the Admissions Committee. The applicant's academic record is the most important aspect of the admissions application. We give special consideration to applicants who have chosen to challenge themselves in honors, Advanced Placement, International Baccalaureate, and college-level courses. In addition to the applicant's academic record, we also consider the extent to which students have contributed to their school and greater community in a meaningful way. Personal qualities such as leadership, engagement, creative and innovative thinking, and resiliency are important to us.

Last year, more than 34,000 applications were received for 2,800 spots in the class. Students who have carefully explored their college options and have decided that Northeastern is where they want to enroll may choose to apply Early Action. November 1 is the deadline for Early Action. The deadline for the Regular Decision is January 15.

To apply, students should submit the completed application, through the Common Application Web site and the required supplement at the same time. Additional application requirements include the application fee, Official high school record(s), including senior-year first-quarter and mid-term grades; a recommendation from a guidance counselor; a recommendation from a teacher; and the results of the College Board SAT (Northeastern's College Board code is 3667) or the American College Testing Program. Students may enter the university with advanced credit earned on the basis of Advanced Placement (AP) examinations, the College-Level Examination Program (CLEP), the International Baccalaureate (IB) program, and successful completion of accredited college-level courses.

Northeastern does accept transfer students in the fall and spring semesters. Transfer students should include a list of past and anticipated courses and their individual credit values, by term, and submit it with the Northeastern application.

For more information, contact: Office of Undergraduate Admissions Northeastern University 150 Richards Hall 360 Huntington Avenue Boston, MA 02115 Telephone: 617-373-2200 Fax: 617-373-8780 Email: admissions@neu.edu, or visit us online at: www.northeastern.edu/admissions

School Says . . .

NOTRE DAME COLLEGE

AT A GLANCE

Notre Dame College, established in 1922, is an affordable, private, liberal arts college located in South Euclid, a quiet suburban neighborhood just east of Cleveland.

Notre Dame offers quality academic programs in over 30 disciplines including a nationally accredited Education major, a Business major, a Bachelor of Science in Nursing, Intelligence Analysis and Research, and Criminal Justice.

Notre Dame's athletic department has 23 scholarship athletic teams including a new men's football program, which began club competition in the fall of 2009 and will commence intercollegiate play in 2010. The Falcons compete in the American Mideast Conference of the NAIA.

MISSION

A Catholic institution in the tradition of the Sisters of Notre Dame, the College educates a diverse population in the liberal arts for personal, professional and global responsibility. The College believes that truly progressive education selectively blends traditional values with new ideas that represent real growth. Within the scope of a career-oriented liberal arts education, students can grow to meet the challenges of the present and the future.

LOCATION

The College is located in South Euclid, Ohio, 25 minutes from downtown Cleveland and only five minutes from Legacy Village and Beachwood Place, Cleveland's lifestyle retail center. The area combines the excitement and cultural wealth of a major urban and educational center with the relaxed atmosphere of a suburban setting. University Circle in Cleveland, a 500-acre complex containing an unusual blend of cultural, educational, medical, religious and social service institutions, is easily accessible from the College.

Situated on the shores of Lake Erie, Cleveland is the home of the Rock and Roll Hall of Fame and several professional sports teams. The Cleveland Metroparks offer a variety of activities and recreational opportunities. Snowy winters provide abundant opportunities for skiing and tobogganing, and popular ski areas are located a short distance from the city.

The beautiful 53-acre wooded campus provides the perfect setting for the Clara Fritzsche Library; the Administration Building, housing all of the classrooms and offices; Connelly Center, the cafeteria and student center; the Keller Center, the recreational and fitness facility; the Falcon Café, which serves Starbucks products; and five residence halls, including two brand new apartment-style facilities, housing 288 upper class students.

CAMPUS LIFE

A variety of clubs and activities enrich the educational experiences of the College's nearly 1,900 students. The Campus Ministry program promotes the spiritual growth of the Notre Dame College community and facilitates community service, retreats, liturgy and more. The Masquers promote talent in the performing arts and provide entertainment for the College community and general public. Campus publications include the student newspaper *Notre Dame News* and *PIVOT*, the literary magazine. Faculty members and students schedule and coordinate lectures, plays, performances, and concerts.

Most on-campus events are free, and students may purchase tickets at reduced rates for off-campus programs such as performances of the world-famous Cleveland Orchestra, the Cleveland Opera, and road shows of Broadway productions at the Palace Theatre, State Theatre, and Ohio Theatre at Playhouse Square. Performances at the Cleveland Play House are also available.

ATHLETICS

Notre Dame College is a member of the National Association of Intercollegiate Athletics (NAIA) and competes in the American Mideast Conference. It fields 23 scholarship athletic teams, including men's and women's basketball, bowling, cross-country, golf, soccer, swimming and diving, and track and field; men's baseball, football, tennis, and wrestling; and women's lacrosse, softball, and volleyball. Last July, the NCAA announced that Notre Dame had a membership application approved. The Falcons are currently competing as a Candidacy Year-One institution in the NCAA Division-II membership process.

ACADEMICS

The College awards the Bachelor of Arts degree in accounting (business administration); biology; chemistry; communication; education, including early childhood (pre-K–3), middle childhood (4–9), and young adult education and mild-moderate intervention specialist studies; English; graphic design; history/political science; information systems; international business; management; marketing; mathematics; psychology; public administration; sports management; studio art; and theology.

The Bachelor of Science is awarded in biology, chemistry, and mathematics. A student can also design his or her own major that leads to a Bachelor of Arts or Bachelor of Science degree by combining two or three academic areas, such as graphic design, human resource management, and public relations. Notre Dame College also offers a Bachelor of Science in Nursing program. An RN to B.S.N. completion program is also available.

A Master of Education degree is offered with concentrations available in special education, reading, and critical and creative thinking.

Teacher licensure is available in early childhood education, middle childhood education, adolescent/young adult education, and multiage for mild/moderate intervention specialist studies.

The College is accredited by both the North Central Association of Colleges and Schools and NCATE and is registered for the awarding of State Teachers' Licenses by the State of Ohio Department of Education.

The Associate in Arts degree is awarded at the completion of two-year programs in business management and pastoral ministry.

The Center for Pastoral Theology and Ministry grants a two-year catechetical diploma and the College awards a Bachelor of Arts degree.

For the bachelor's degree, students must earn 128 semester hours of credit, with a minimum cumulative grade point average of 2.0. From 36 to 68 semester hours of credit are required in the major field of study.

Through a cooperative education program, students can earn a maximum of six credit hours for paid or volunteer work experience related to their academic field of study. All students are required to complete a coop or internship experience.

Advanced Placement credit is awarded to students who have demonstrated the ability to pursue course work beyond the level of entering freshmen, as indicated by their scores on the Advanced Placement (AP) or College-Level Examination Program (CLEP) tests of the College Board. College credit is given on the basis of a decision made jointly by the academic dean and the department involved.

FACULTY

The faculty has 54 full-time members. It is augmented by highly qualified instructors. Faculty members hold advanced degrees from more than 30 universities in the United States, Canada and Europe.

CAMPUS FACILITIES AND EQUIPMENT

Students with documented learning differences, such as Attention Deficit Disorder (ADD), Attention Deficit Hyperactivity Disorder (ADHD), dyslexia, Asperger's Syndrome and SLD can enroll in our Academic Support Center to receive comprehensive support services. These include tutoring, academic advising and access to a large array of adaptive equipment. In order to be accepted into the Learning Differences Program, students must meet the admission requirements of Notre Dame College. To participate in the Academic Support Center, students must submit documentation of a learning disability.

The Career Services Center provides students with a variety of services to assist with career planning including: résumé writing, interview skills development and locating co-ops and internships.

The Clara Fritzsche Library, housing the modern media center, has a capacity for 100,000 volumes. As a member of OhioLINK, the College also has online access to members throughout the state, with access to more than 31 million library items and more than 90 research databases. The library also houses the smart classroom, a state-of-the-art classroom equipped with laptops for each student and two SMARTBoards.

The Dwyer Learning Center consists of an electronic classroom, a student computer lab, a writing lab, a test proctoring room and a tutoring room. The writing lab is staffed by English faculty members who provide professional writing assistance to students free of charge. The tutoring room is staffed with graduate assistants and upper-class peer tutors for one-on-one study skills and subject specific assistance.

The multi-media lab for graphic design majors offers PC and Macintosh technology for advanced multimedia production capabilities.

The Finn Center for Adult, Graduate and Professional Programs unifies all aspects of adult education at NDC, providing convenient, flexible programs for educational advancement on days, nights, weekends and the Web. Housing the Office of Adult & Graduate Admissions and the Office of Professional Development, the Finn Center offers professional development classes, associate's degrees, bachelor's degrees, post-baccalaureate programs and master's degrees.

TUITION, ROOM, BOARD AND FEES

For the 2009–10 academic year tuition charges were $22,742. Room and board costs were $7,588 for double occupancy. Student fees were $550.

FINANCIAL AID

Notre Dame believes that all qualified students should have the opportunity to attend college, and provides need, merit and athletic-based aid to our students. A comprehensive financial assistance program of more than $25 million assists nearly 93 percent of all full-time students. Students applying for aid must submit the Free Application for Federal Student Aid (FAFSA).

ADMISSIONS PROCESS

Notre Dame College admits students who demonstrate potential for success in rigorous academic work. In fulfilling its mission, the College seeks to attract students of diverse religious, racial and economic backgrounds. Candidates for admission as first-time, full-time freshmen are reviewed on an individual basis, and decisions are based on a broad range of criteria. The most important consideration is the candidate's high school performance, as demonstrated by her/his overall grade average, class rank, grade trends and level of courses completed. Aptitude for verbal and mathematical reasoning, as measured by performance on standardized tests, is also considered. In addition, counselor and teacher recommendations are reviewed.

Notre Dame College recommends that students complete at least 16 units of high school credit in academic subjects as a prerequisite for matriculation in the College. The distribution of these subject areas and the units are as follows: English, 4; mathematics, 3 (to include algebra I, geometry and algebra II); science, 3 (with laboratory experience); social studies, 3; foreign language, 2 (from the same language); and fine arts, 1. Applicants should generally rank in the upper half of their high school graduating class and have a minimum average of C+. Either ACT or SAT scores are accepted.

The College has a fair and generous policy on the transfer of academic credit earned within the preceding five years at a regionally accredited college or university. Students wishing to transfer from other regionally accredited colleges and universities are admitted to advanced standing upon presentation of satisfactory evidence of scholarship and character.

Special consideration may be granted to an applicant whose academic preparation is not consistent with the requirements stated above.

Notre Dame College strongly recommends that prospective students schedule an appointment to visit the campus and talk with an admissions counselor.

A free application is available online at www.NotreDameCollege.edu. The College maintains a rolling admission policy. To apply, students should submit the completed application for undergraduate admission, an official transcript of their high school record and results of the ACT or SAT to:

Office of Admissions

Notre Dame College

4545 College Road

South Euclid, Ohio 44121

United States

Telephone: 877.NDC.OHIO ext. 5355 Fax: 216.373.5278

E-mail: admissions@ndc.edu

Web: www.NotreDameCollege.edu

School Says . . .

OBERLIN COLLEGE

ACADEMICS

In addition to the traditional academic offerings listed below, Oberlin offers a winter term, in which students complete independent and often self-designed projects, either on or off campus. Each January, students explore topics outside of regular course offerings, enabling them to devote their energy to a single project. Projects include, but are not limited to, research projects, internships, reading projects, arts projects, and community service. Oberlin is also home to the Experimental College, a student-run organization that sponsors courses for limited academic credit taught by Oberlin students, townspeople, administrators, and faculty. Each year a heterogeneous list of subjects is offered including crafts, special interests, community service, and academic subjects not found in the regular curriculum.

ADMISSIONS

Admission to both the College of Arts and Sciences and the Conservatory of Music is highly selective. In the Arts and Sciences class entering in 2009, the middle 50 percent of enrolled students scored between 660 and 750 on the Critical Reading portion of the SAT, between 630 and 720 on the Math section and between 650 and 740 on the Writing Section. The middle 50 percent of enrolled students scored between 28 and 32 on the ACT composite. The median unweighted GPA was 3.70 and the middle 50 percent had unweighted GPAs between 3.5 and 3.9 in rigorous high school curriculums. The Conservatory seeks talented music students who have demonstrated records of achievement, potential for further growth and development, the ability to meet Oberlin's demanding standards, and the dedication required to become professional musicians. The most important factor in admission to the Conservatory is the performance audition, or in the case of certain programs, the compositions, tapes, and supporting materials submitted.

CAMPUS FACILITIES AND EQUIPMENT

Oberlin's four libraries contain more than 1.75 million items, including 1.1 million catalogued volumes, which makes Oberlin's library one of the two largest small-college libraries in the nation. The Allen Memorial Art Museum (AMAM) is considered one of the top college and university art museums in the United States. During its renovation period, the AMAM is proud to present 20 of its European and American masterworks in the galleries of the Metropolitan Museum of Art in New York. The works on display, which span the 16th-20th centuries, will be integrated into the Met's galleries, giving visitors the rare opportunity to see the AMAM works with those by the same artists or from similar contexts from the Met's world-renowned collections.

The Conservatory of Music contains more than 150 practice rooms, and houses 207 Steinway grand pianos. There are also two concert halls at the conservatory, music studios, and extensive dance and drama performance space as well. The Litoff Building, which is to be completed in spring 2010, will include a state-of-the-art recording studio and the largest privately held jazz recording collection in the United States. It was designed with the highest environmental building standards in mind; The Litoff Building intends to be the first music facility in the world to attain a gold Leadership in Energy and Environmental Design (LEED) rating, as developed by the U.S. Green Building Council. Recently, the Oberlin Conservatory of Music was awarded the National Medal of Arts by President Barack Obama. The medal is the highest award given by the United States government to artists and arts patrons in recognition of the wealth and depth of their creative expressions.

The Adam Joseph Lewis Center for Environmental Studies has earned national acclaim as a showcase for green building technologies and operating systems. Photovoltaic panels on the center's roof and parking pavilion capture renewable energy from the sun and south-facing windows allow for passive solar heating. Indoors, a specially engineered wetland called the Living Machine purifies non-potable wastewater for reuse in toilets and the landscape. Flows of energy and cycling of materials are monitored and displayed by a sophisticated system (150+ sensors) that gives real-time feedback, teaching about sustainability in the built environment. The Oberlin community has joined the Climate Positive Development Program. A joint initiative of the Clinton Climate Initiative and the U.S. Green Building Council, the program supports the development of large-scale urban projects that demonstrates that cities can grow in ways that aid the environment.

The Science Center is a modern, integrated complex that houses the biology, chemistry, physics and astronomy, and neuroscience departments, as well as the Science Library. Its design promotes maximum collaboration among the science disciplines, as well as between students and faculty mentors. The center is equipped with NMR spectrometers, vacuum deposition chambers, flow cytometers, a confocal microscope, and more. Oberlin is among the first liberal arts colleges in the nation to provide undergraduates with access to a supercomputer that can process gigantic data sets. Purchased in 2005 through a grant from the National Science Foundation, Oberlin's supercomputer has 70 dual, 64-bit nodes - each with 8 gigabytes of RAM, a gigabit ethernet switch, and a 10-terabyte file server. In addition to its applications in chemistry, physics, astrophysics, and computational biology, the computer provided momentum for an interdisciplinary initiative, the Oberlin Center for Computation and Modeling.

Oberlin's Irving E. Houck Computing Center provides a multitude of Macintosh and IBM-compatible computers in several locations on campus. All dorms are wired for connection to the mainframe and the Internet. Many areas of the campus provide wireless access. Oberlin's top-notch athletic facilities include the Jesse Philips Physical Education Center, a modern field house with gold LEED rating, 22 practice and playing fields, indoor and outdoor tracks and tennis courts, a 3,000-seat football stadium, a cross-country course, two pools, a Nautilus center and weight room, basketball and volleyball courts, racquetball and squash courts, a training room, a climbing wall and much more.

CAMPUS LIFE

Students on Oberlin's campus are presented with a rich diversity of extracurricular options. There are over 120 student clubs and organizations funded through the Student Union. Over 500 concerts and recitals are presented annually by students, along with almost 100 theater, musical theater, and opera performances. A large number of visiting artists perform at Oberlin, as do many lecturers and speakers. Oberlin also sponsors an excellent film series, and there are numerous campus parties, dorm and co-op picnics, and special events sponsored by the Student Union.

Oberlin College was honored for the fourth consecutive year with a place on the President's Higher Education Community, Service Honor Roll, a commendation given to colleges and universities for exemplary civic engagement and service to the local community. Oberlin has a longstanding tradition of social responsibility and community service. More than 75 percent of Oberlin undergraduates engage in some form of community service during their time at Oberlin through one of the college's many official programs, student organizations such as Immerse Yourself in Service, and independent projects. Since its establishment in 1994, Oberlin's Bonner Center for Service and Learning (BCSL) has encouraged undergraduates to become engaged citizens through curricular and co-curricular initiatives that enrich both the community and the education of students themselves.

LOCATION AND ENVIRONMENT

Oberlin College is located in the center of Oberlin, Ohio, a town of 8,600 residents, about a 35-minute drive from Cleveland. Oberlin is an idyllic residential town, which is made lively and exciting by the presence of the College. Cultural events dominate the social scene with over 500 concerts and recitals, 50+ theater and dance productions and 200 films annually. Though there are a multitude of bicycles in Oberlin, everything a student needs is within walking distance of campus.

MAJORS AND DEGREES

The College of Arts and Sciences and the Conservatory of Music are both on the same campus. The College offers a Bachelor of Arts; the Conservatory offers a Bachelor of Music and some Master of Music degrees as well. Oberlin also offers a unique five-year "Double Degree" program in which a student attends both the College and the Conservatory and graduates with both the BA and BMus degrees.

CAMPUS OPPORTUNITIES

Oberlin offers an extensive study away program, including several programs sponsored by Oberlin, programs sponsored by the Great Lakes College Association, and a large variety of programs from other sources. Oberlin's Career services office helps students to find a variety of summer internships, and research opportunities can be found through the Career Services office and also through academic departments. Oberlin's Center for Service and Learning helps coordinate a multitude of community service opportunities.

TUITION AND AID

Oberlin meets the full evaluated need of all admitted students. In 2009–2010, approximately 66 percent of students received need-based aid. The average package was about $31,039. Oberlin requires financial aid applicants to complete both the FAFSA and the PROFILE.

TUITION AND FEES

Tuition for the 2009–2010 academic year is $39,686. Room and board fees total $10,480. The student activity fee is $318. Costs for the College of Arts and Sciences and the Conservatory of Music are the same.

OHIO NORTHERN UNIVERSITY

AT A GLANCE

Founded in 1871, Ohio Northern is a competitive, private, coeducational University for 3,666 students (2009–10), offering nationally ranked sciences, arts and professional programs in its five colleges: Arts and Sciences, Business Administration, Engineering, Pharmacy and Law.

From the beginning, students discover the personal attention given to them by faculty and staff. Ohio Northern appeals to highly motivated students who want to get more out of their education than simply a degree. Classroom participation is not only encouraged, but also expected. With a 12 to one student to faculty ratio, students have access to highly qualified professors—80 percent having terminal degrees in their respective fields. They create a can-do environment where students can customize their areas of interest with mentorship and inspiration from faculty who champion their success.

MAJORS AND DEGREES OFFERED:

Students at Ohio Northern University may pursue the following degrees and programs:

Degrees awarded at Northern: B.A., B.F.A., B.M., B.S., B.S.C.L.S., B.S.B.A., B.S.C.E., B.S.C.P.E., B.S.E.E., B.S.M.E., B.S.N., LL.M., Pharm.D., J.D.

College of Arts and Sciences majors: Advertising Design, Applied Mathematics, Art Education, Athletic Training, Biochemistry, Biology, Chemistry, Clinical Laboratory Science, Communication Studies, Construction Management, Creative Writing, Criminal Justice, Education (Early Childhood, Middle Childhood), Environmental and Field Biology, Exercise Physiology (Concentrations is Clinical/Research or Corporate Fitness/Personal Training), Forensic Biology, French, Geography – Area Studies, Geography – Geographic Information Systems, German, General Science (not degree granting), General Studies (not degree granting), Graphic Design, Health Education, History, International Theatre Production, Journalism, Language Arts Education, Literature, Manufacturing Technology, Mathematics, Mathematics/Statistics, Molecular Biology, Music (Concentrations is Music History and Literature or Music Theory and Composition), Music Education, Music Performance, Nursing, Philosophy, Physical Education, Physics (Concentrations in Physics, Applied Physics or Astronomy), Political Science (Concentrations is American Politics or International Relations-Comparative Politics), Professional Writing, Psychology (Concentrations is Behavioral Neuroscience or Clinical and Counseling Psychology), Public Relations, Religion (Concentrations is Eastern or Western Religions), Social Studies, Sociology, Spanish, Sport Management, Studio Arts (Concentrations in 2D or 3D), Technology Education, Theatre, Youth Ministry.

College of Business Administration majors: Accounting, Finance, International Business and Economics, Management, Marketing and Pharmaceutical Business.

College of Engineering majors: Civil Engineering, Computer Engineering, Computer Science, Electrical Engineering, Mechanical Engineering.

College of Pharmacy major: Doctor of Pharmacy (Direct Entry 0–6), Pharmacy/Law

College of Law: Law, Pharmacy/Law

Preprofessional Programs: Predentistry, Prelaw, Premedicine, Preoccupational Therapy, Preoptometry, Prephysical Therapy, Prephysician Assistant, Preseminary, Preveterinary medicine.

Minors: Applied Mathematics, Art, Arts Administration, Asian Studies, Astronomy, Biochemistry, Biology, Biomedical Sciences, Business Administration, Chemistry, Communication Studies, Creative Writing, Criminal Justice, Dance, Design, Electronic Media and Broadcasting, Entrepreneurship, Exercise Physiology, Finance, French, Geography/Area Studies, Geography/GIS, German, History, Journalism, Literature, Management, Marketing, Mathematics, Music, Philosophy, Physics, Political Science, Prelaw, Professional Writing, Psychology, Public Health, Public History/Museum Studies, Public Relations, Religion, Sociology, Spanish, Statistics, Technology Systems, Theatre.

ACADEMICS

The College of Arts and Sciences:

Accomplished scholars, teachers, authors, scientists, researchers, and mentors are at the center of the College of Arts and Sciences, the largest of Ohio Northern's undergraduate colleges. More than 50 areas of study, eight pre-professional programs, and numerous concentrations and options, offer Northern students considerable flexibility and opportunities in their career preparation. Most students complete a minor or second major, or take classes in an additional field of interest. The college's curriculum fuses a lively and challenging classroom environment with many opportunities for undergraduate research, internships, study abroad opportunities and events such as guest lectures.

Chemistry/Biochemistry is a signature program at the University with ACS accreditation, 13 full time professors, research opportunities and state of the art facilities. Graduates go on to their choice of top graduate, medical or professionals schools.

The College of Business Administration:

The James F. Dicke College of Business Administration at Ohio Northern is focused on creating entrepreneurial, ethical and engaged leaders. The college offers a rigorous academic curriculum with a signature major in pharmaceutical business and a forensic accounting option. Internships are required by the college and available year-round as well as a variety of international programs including study abroad, work abroad, and study tours. An office of experiential learning supports students who are looking for these opportunities.

Personal attention and mentoring from faculty, small intimate classes and active student organizations combine with an emphasis on experiential learning, technological proficiency, global awareness, and the entrepreneurial spirit. The college is accredited by the AACSB International - The Association to Advance Collegiate Schools of Business, making it "one of the best business colleges in the world."

The College of Engineering:

Engineering at Ohio Northern University is focused on providing a premier undergraduate experience that inspires creativity and supports innovation. The college features five accredited, disciplinary majors in civil, computer, electrical, and mechanical engineering and computer science.

There is an emphasis on team projects and students participate in many design competitions such as the Concrete Canoe Competition and the Baja SAE off-road vehicle competition.

Many opportunities are available for valuable work experience through the co-op, internship and Engineer-in-Residence programs, with an overall 98 percent job placement rate for graduates.

The College of Pharmacy:

For 125 years the College of Pharmacy has offered a distinctive, comprehensive training for some of the nation's most talented pharmacists.

Pharmacy is a signature program of the University and offers a six-year Doctor of Pharmacy (Pharm.D.) degree accredited by the American Council on Pharmaceutical Education. The program is a direct entry program (0-6) admitting students directly from high school into the college.

The program of study in pharmacy at Ohio Northern is distinctive, because from day one students take pharmacy courses in a rigorous curriculum that utilizes an innovative modular format. The modules organize learning around the human body systems and disease types and implement pharmaceutical science and patient care. Thus, upon graduation, students are well schooled in every aspect of pharmacy and have a 100 percent placement rate.

College of Law:

Founded in 1885, the Ohio Northern University Pettit College of Law is the second oldest of the nine Ohio law schools. The college is accredited by the American Bar Association and is a member of the Association of American Law Schools. Annually, the college enrolls more than 320 students from more than 40 states in its full-time juris doctor degree and LLM programs. Dedicated to the rigorous pursuits of teaching and practicing law, the college's esteemed faculty is focused on providing one-on-one, personal training to students with a passion for legal scholastic excellence. State-of-the-art facilities, a top ranked law library with more than 410,000 volumes and numerous organizations and activities such as Moot Court, Law Review and Student Bar Association provide legal scholars with an excellent education and promising placement.

Ohio Northern University also offers a selective Honors Program open to students of all undergraduate colleges. Each Honors student completes a series of Honors Seminars, contract courses, and a final Honors Project. The Project is a major research, performance, or creative endeavor guided by a full-time faculty member. Acceptance into the ONU Honors Program is highly competitive. Completion of the Honors Program will be recognized on the student's diploma, transcript and at commencement.

ADMISSIONS

Applicants should provide high school transcripts reflecting completion of 16 units of high school credits, 12 of which must be in academic areas. The academic unit requirements vary among the colleges at ONU: College of Arts and Sciences requires 12 units: 4 units in English, 2 in mathematics and 6 in history, socials studies, languages, or natural sciences. College of Business Administration requires 13 academic units: 4 in English, 3 in mathematics (including algebra and geometry), and 6 in history, social studies, languages, or natural sciences. College of Engineering requires 16 academic units: 4 in English, 4 in mathematics (including 2 units of algebra and others in geometry and trigonometry), 2 in science (including physics and preferably chemistry), and 6 in history, social studies, languages, or natural sciences. College of Pharmacy requires 18 academic units: 4 in English, 4 in mathematics (algebra I and II, plane geometry, trigonometry and pre-calculus or calculus), 4 in science (including biology, chemistry, and physics), and 6 in history, social studies, language, and/or natural sciences. The pharmacy college applicant is also highly encouraged to make a visit to campus. All of these materials are due to campus no later than November 1 of the senior year. All applicants must submit standardized test scores (ACT or SAT I). The writing portion is not required but recommended. For top scholarship consideration, all applicants must apply and be accepted by December 1 of the senior year. The Colleges of Arts and Sciences, Business, and Engineering are on rolling admissions.

CAMPUS FACILITIES AND EQUIPMENT

ONU is located in a friendly, rural setting in Northwest Ohio, about an hour from Columbus and other major cities. Situated on nearly 300 beautiful acres, there's plenty of green space around 31 modern, major buildings, including the University's own deluxe Inn. The University is also strongly committed to developing policies and practices that are environmentally friendly. ONU Green website outlines initiatives www.onu.edu/green

The more than 95,000-square-feet Mathile Center for the Natural Sciences at Ohio Northern University is a student-centered academic research and learning facility that strengthens signature programs in pharmacy and chemistry/biochemistry and blends hands-on teaching excellence with advanced technology in a functional modern environment.

CAMPUS LIFE

Excitement, creativity and tradition are the cornerstone of campus life at Ohio Northern. Students of all backgrounds come together to form a common bond in and outside of the classroom. There are nearly 200 clubs and organizations to get involved in and all provide opportunities for developing leadership skills.

At Northern, excellence in academics and athletics go hand in hand. ONU participates in the Ohio Athletic Conference and in NCAA Division III. Teams include 11 men's sports and 10 women's sports. During the 2008–09 season, ONU won both the Men's and Women's OAC All-Sports trophies for the third consecutive year. Northern's NCAA tournament teams were: Men's Cross Country, Soccer, Wrestling, Indoor Track and Field, Swimming and Diving, Outdoor Track and Field. The women's tournament teams were: Volleyball, Softball, Tennis and Outdoor Track and Field. Twelve of 21 teams were nationally ranked during the 2008–09 season. Overall, there were 25 First Team All Conference honorees, 44 OAC individual champions, and 138 individuals (71 men and 67 women) who earned All Conference Honors. Visit www.onusports.com!

The culture of the campus is one of respect, friendship, and community. ONU offers ecumenical and interfaith opportunities for spiritual growth and development. Active religious life programs include groups such as Habitat for Humanity, Northern Christian Fellowship, Fellowship of Christian Athletes, Chapel Band and Choir and the Newman Club.

Greek life is an active part of campus life at ONU where approximately 20 percent of ONU students are members of the six national fraternities and four national sororities. Service and philanthropy are core values of the Greek organizations. In addition, members are also involved in other student organizations on campus, adding a unique mixture of diversity to their chapters.

The arts are the most exciting and rapidly expanding programs at Ohio Northern University. Monthly exhibitions of student artwork, ten theatrical productions and upwards of forty instrumental and voice performances annually by the respective departments allow a myriad of opportunities for any and all majors within the University.

Multicultural students contribute to the diversity and richness of the ONU student body. The Office of Multicultural Development (OMD) encourages students to take an active role in all University activities and seeks to develop an identity for multicultural students. A variety of programs are hosted each year including regular cultural celebrations that feature speakers, performers, music, films, dinners, exhibits and workshops. There are many student organizations students can be a part of including: Asian American Student Union, The Black Student Union, The Indian Student Association, The Latino Student Union, The Muslim Student Union, Men of Distinction, Sister Circle, The Gospel Ensemble, Open Doors, World Student Organization, and Vision Builders.

TUITION AND FEES

2010–11 Fees Per Year	Tuition & Fees	Room & Board	Total
Arts and Sciences	$32,859	$4,347	$41,793°
Business Administration	$32,859	$4,347	$41,793°
Engineering	$35,097	$4,347	$44,031°
Pharmacy	$36,936	$4,347	$45,870°

°Total is based on tuition, double-occupancy room, 19-meal-per-week plan and a technology fee of $240 per year. The average student spends $900 per year on books and fees.

OHIO WESLEYAN UNIVERSITY

AT A GLANCE

An Ohio Wesleyan University education is distinguished by its unique combination of liberal arts study, pre-professional training, and wide array of internships, research opportunities, study-travel, and study abroad opportunities that allow students to test their academic assumptions in real-world settings. OWU is one of only five independent undergraduate schools in the nation whose graduates rank in the top 20 both in the number of PhDs earned and in the number of business leaders. The University, which was founded in 1842 by the United Methodist Church, is dedicated to instilling the service ethic in its undergraduates, linking classroom theory and practical application, and preparing students for success in a global society. Students attend classes in stately historical buildings such as Elliott Hall, the University's first building, and in modern facilities such as the $35 million Conrades-Wetherell Science Center.

Approximately 1,850 men and women undergraduates attend OWU. The student body comes from 47 states and 57 countries; most live on the lovely 200-acre campus. Residences include 6 large halls, a variety of smaller special interest domiciles, and seven fraternity houses (the school's five sorority houses are not residential). In 2010, the University will open three new residences specifically for upperclassmen and women.

Ohio Wesleyan has the highest percentage of international students among undergraduate, bachelor's-degree-granting colleges in the state of Ohio and one of the highest percentages among similar colleges in the United States.

Ohio Wesleyan is widely known for its national and international mission teams and local community service learning. Nearly every student participates in at least one service learning opportunity or philanthropic activity each year, and the University has been recognized by the President's Honor Roll for its service initiatives. Students also publish the nation's oldest independent student newspaper, produce four major theater pieces, and stage a number of concerts featuring OWU's large ensembles and smaller musical groups. Cultural- and ethnic-interest groups are represented by such diverse groups as the Student Union on Black Awareness, Sisters United, VIVA and SANGAM (which promote understanding of Latin American and and South Asian cultures respectively), Hillel, the Muslim Students Association, and many other religious and cultural affiliations.

OWU has 22 varsity athletic teams: 11 men's teams and 11 women's teams. Several teams are nationally ranked each year in Division III of the NCAA. The women's soccer team won its second consecutive national championship in 2002 following an undefeated season with 20 shutouts. Men's soccer earned the national crown in 1998 and has won the conference title 18 of the last 26 years; men's basketball won the NCAA Division III title in 1986. In 2001, the women's basketball team reached the national semifinals, and the men's team reached the round of 16 in the NCAA Division III tournament in 2008. In 2009, OWU captured the North Coast Athletic Conference All-Sports Trophy for the third consecutive year and the ninth time overall. Many head coaches are multiple NCAC Coaches of the Year.

OWU's intramural and club sports programs enjoy wide support throughout the student body. Students find ample facilities for training and fitness in the Branch Rickey Physical Education Center and the Health and Wellness Center. The surrounding area provides opportunities for backpacking, boating, camping, golf, skiing, and swimming.

LOCATION AND ENVIRONMENT

Hometown, Delaware (pop. 34,000) offers OWU students a quiet, small-city setting in one of the fastest-growing counties in the nation, only 30 minutes from Ohio's state capital, Columbus, which is America's sixteenth-largest city. Columbus provides students with numerous opportunities for internships, access to international research projects, cultural events, shopping centers, and restaurants.

VISITING OHIO WESLEYAN

Transportation:

The Port Columbus International Airport in Columbus is a 45-minute drive from campus.

Driving Instructions:

The campus is located near the junction of US Routes 23 and 36. From Route 36 (William St. in Delaware), head south on Sandusky St. Turn left into the parking lot off Sandusky St. and follow signs to Admissions.

If you're staying overnight...:

Numerous hotels and motels are located in Delaware and the northwest Columbus area. Delaware, found in the approximate center of Ohio, is 20 miles north of downtown Columbus and 120 miles southwest of Cleveland.

OFF-CAMPUS OPPORTUNITIES

The Ohio Wesleyan curriculum strengthens students' awareness of international cultures and issues. A large portion of the undergraduate population arrives from outside the United States. OWU offers significant opportunities for study overseas. Study abroad programs are available in more than 20 countries, including Ohio Wesleyan's affiliation programs in Cork, Ireland, and Salamanca, Spain. Programs are also offered in Tanzania and Ghana, China, Colombia, England, India/Nepal, Japan, Russia, and Scotland. Students are encouraged to develop study abroad plans anywhere in the world their curiosity leads.

Many students also participate in the Wesleyan in Washington, New York Arts, and Philadelphia Center programs, which offer meaningful internships in government, the arts, communication, public service, and more.

MAJORS AND DEGREES OFFERED

Ohio Wesleyan confers the Bachelor of Arts degree in accounting, astronomy, botany, microbiology, genetics, and zoology, chemistry, computer science, economics (including accounting, international business, and management), education (elementary and secondary licensing in 17 areas), English literature and writing, environmental science, fine arts, French, geography, geology, German, history, humanities-classics, journalism, mathematics, music (applied or history/literature), neuroscience, philosophy, physical education, physics, planetary science, politics and government, psychology, religion, sociology/anthropology, Spanish, and theatre and dance. Interdisciplinary majors include black world studies; East Asian Studies; environmental studies, international studies, urban studies; ancient, medieval and Renaissance studies; Latin American studies; and women's and gender studies, as well as pre-dentistry, pre-law, pre-medicine, pre-public administration, pre-theology, and pre-veterinary medicine.

The University awards two professional degrees: the Bachelor of Fine Arts and the Bachelor of Music and combined-degree programs in engineering, medical technologies, optometry, and physical therapy.

OWU has 137 full-time faculty members; the student-faculty ratio is approximately 12:1. All full-time tenure-track faculty members have earned the terminal degree in their field of expertise.

ACADEMIC PROGRAMS

Ohio Wesleyan stresses the importance of acquiring a broad general education that fosters insight into our cultural and historical past. The curriculum also emphasizes the value of specialization through its major requirements and is designed to encourage independent thought through the development of logic, problem-solving skills, and communication. OWU ensures that students improve these skills through competency requirements in English composition and foreign language and distribution requirements in the natural and social sciences, the humanities, and the arts. All majors require students to complete eight to 15 courses. .

The University's four-year honors program designates select freshmen as Merit Scholars and allows them to work one-to-one with faculty advisors on original creative work, self-designed reading programs, and research. Independent study is encouraged for juniors and seniors. The school is home to chapters of more than 20 scholastic honorary societies; the University's chapter of Phi Beta Kappa is 103 years old.

The Sagan National Colloquium exemplifies the goals of education at Ohio Wesleyan. It focuses on one issue of major societal importance and addresses the issue through lectures, performances, discussions, specially designed classes, and student-initiated projects. The purpose of the colloquium is to unite the liberal and civic arts; beginning in 2010, the Colloquium added a series of special classes, many of which involve international travel, designed and taught by faculty designated as Sagan Fellows.

In 2009, the University also initiated a series of competitive Theory Into Practice grants, which allow both faculty and students to apply for funds for advanced research projects.

CAMPUS FACILITIES AND EQUIPMENT

Ohio Wesleyan's libraries are teaching libraries that actively support the curriculum, student and faculty research. The Leon A. Beeghly Library and three branch libraries house an extensive collection of more than 505,000 holdings. Special collections include The Archives of the Ohio United Methodism Center, The Ohio Wesleyan University Historical Collection, and the Rare Books, Manuscripts, and Artifacts Collection. Ohio Wesleyan is a member of OhioLINK, which allows students to connect to a consortium of Ohio academic libraries.

The $35 million science center renovation includes an atrium designed to facilitate and showcase student and faculty collaborative research, an expanded science library, improved classrooms, laboratories, state-of-the–art instrumentation, student lounges, and faculty offices.

The new Meek Aquatics and Recreation Center offers a 10-lane pool, a 13-foot diving well, and 1- and 3-meter boards. It is heated and cooled by more than 90 geothermal wells and is Ohio Wesleyan's first "green" building.

TUITION, ROOM, BOARD AND FEES

The cost of attending OWU for the 2010–2011 academic year is $45,674.

Tuition: $35,918

Mandatory fees $480

Room $4,806

Board $4,470

Books and personal expenses (average): $1,100 per year.

Additional, nominal fees are charged for some studio art courses, off-campus study, student teaching programs, and private music lessons for non-music majors.

FINANCIAL AID

OWU awards financial assistance to almost every entering freshman who demonstrates need. Aid packages include a combination of grants, loans, and employment. Federal and state aid are often part of an aid package. Nearly 70 percent of all undergraduates receive need-based financial assistance; another 25 percent are granted merit-based aid. More than three-quarters of aid is awarded in the form of grants and scholarships.

The University awards several merit scholarship programs, ranging from $5,000 to full tuition. The school awarded more than 2,000 scholarships to new and prospective students for 2010–2011.

Private loan programs and flexible payment plans are available to all students, regardless of demonstrated financial need.

STUDENT ORGANIZATIONS AND ACTIVITIES

The student body of OWU is deeply involved in all aspects of campus life. It is a matter of pride among students, alumni, faculty, and administrators that undergraduates play a major role within the entire University community. Major departments incorporate the contributions of student academic boards in planning coursework and requirements. The school provides both the encouragement and the necessary resources for students to start new organizations to meet the needs and interests of any group.

OWU is home to more than 100 student clubs and organizations with each organization managed by its officers, committees, and treasurer. The campus is extremely active in community service; the fraternity and sorority scene is lively, both socially and within the community.

ADMISSIONS PROCESS

Admission to OWU is competitive. Academic record and strength of the student's academic program are the most important factors, followed closely by teacher and counselor recommendations, SAT or ACT scores; many other factors, such as creativity, community service, and leadership are carefully considered. A minimum 16-course preparatory program is required. Four units of English and three each of mathematics, social studies, science, and foreign language are recommended, but variations of this program are considered. SAT Subject Tests may be used for advanced placement but are not required for admission. Candidates for the Bachelor of Music degree must audition (tapes are accepted). OWU offers early action and transfer admission. The University *strongly* recommends, but does not require, campus interviews. OWU admitted 65 percent of the applicants it reviewed in 2009–2010.

The University encourages students to apply as early as possible in the senior year, particularly if they wish to be considered for merit and/or need-based financial aid. Admissions decisions are made on a rolling basis once all application materials (application, transcript, recommendations, and SAT or ACT scores) are received; the first decisions are delivered in January. Students must notify the school of their intent by May 1. Early Action I deadline is November 30; Early Action II deadline in January 15. Applications arriving after March 1 are considered on a space-available, rolling admission basis.

OTTERBEIN UNIVERSITY

AT A GLANCE

Otterbein University combines an award-winning liberal arts core curriculum with experiential learning and pre-professional training in the restored village suburb of Westerville near Columbus, Ohio. Our lovely, wooded 140-acre campus includes state of the art academic classrooms, athletic and recreation centers, radio and television studios, art classrooms and exhibit space, and equine facility. Our innovative faculty ignites student passion for learning. Small class sizes and a student faculty ratio of 12/1 lead to individual attention and supportive relationships, encouraging our 3100 students to reach their full potential. We offer 56 academic majors, 41 minors plus over 150 student organizations.

Otterbein lays claim to many "firsts" or "near firsts." Among these are being the first to admit women without restrictions on what they could study, one of the first to admit students of color, the first to include women faculty and among the first to offer a program balancing classical liberal arts and practical career training.

The mission of Otterbein is to educate students in a context that fosters the development of humane values. Otterbein sponsors traditional and continuing education programs at the Baccalaureate and Master's levels and our commitment is to the liberal arts. Through globalization of its curriculum and encouraging education abroad programs, Otterbein strives to enable its students to become global citizens.

Otterbein doesn't impose specific values on students, it challenges them to define their values and live "the examined life." It views a comprehensive liberal arts education as one that expands the soul and mind and provides a consistent influence over a lifetime.

LOCATION AND ENVIRONMENT

Otterbein is set apart by its superb location in the heart of Westerville, a restored village suburb at the edge of the 15th largest city in the nation, Columbus, Ohio: A charming, comfortable setting for study yet with enormous opportunities for internships, cultural events, shopping and dining and exciting social venues right next door.

Hot spots on campus: The Otterbean Cafe, the campus coffee house and is a popular gathering spot for socializing and group discussions. The Clements Recreation Center is a popular fitness destination. The Campus Center houses the main dining hall. Theme houses where groups of students with a common interest can live and host events are also gathering places.

OFF-CAMPUS OPPORTUNITIES

Hot spots off campus: In Westerville, popular coffee houses include Heavenly Cup and Starbucks. Two popular Westerville restaurants include Classic Pizza and The Old Bag of Nails Pub. Two malls are located within 15 minutes on either side of campus: Easton Towne Center and Polaris Fashion Place are extremely popular with students. Gallery Hops in the Short North Gallery district, and concerts at Nationwide Arena and PromoWest Pavillion are frequented by students. For outdoor recreation, the Columbus area MetroParks system affords miles of tree-lined jogging and bike paths. The Columbus Zoo—made famous by Jack Hanna's appearances on Letterman—is one of the country's best.

MAJORS AND DEGREES OFFERED

Accounting: BA, BS; Accounting, Public: BA, BS; Actuarial Science: BS; Allied Health: BS; Art: BA; Athletic Training:BA, BS; Biochemistry:BA, BS; Broadcasting: BA; Business Administration: BA, BS; Chemistry:BA, BS; Computer Science: BA, BS; Economics:BA, BS; Education/Early Childhood & MIddle Childhood: BSE (Students planning to teach at the secondary level seek BA or BS degrees in their subject area); English:BA; Environmental Science: BA. BS; Equine Business and Facility Management: BA, BS; Equine Health Technology: BA, BS; Equine Science Preveterinary and Pregraduate Studies: BA, BS; French: BA; Health Education: BA; Health Promotion and Fitness: BA; History: BA; Individualized: BA, BS; International Studies: BA; Journalism: BA; Life Science: BA, BS; Mathematics: BA, BS; Molecular Biology: BA, BA; Music: BA; Music Performance: BM ; Music and Business: BA; Music Education:BME; Musical Theatre: BFA; Nursing: BSN; Organizational Communication: BA; Philosophy: BA; Physical Education: BA; Physics: BA, BS; Political Science: BA; Psychology: BA, BS; Public Relations: BA; Religion: BA; Sociology: BA; Spanish: BA; Speech Communication: BA; Sport Management: BA; Theatre: BA, BFA

ACADEMIC PROGRAMS

Special minors:

Art History; Arts Administration; Black Studies; Dance; German; Japanese; Language and Culture of the Deaf Community; Legal Studies; Sound Production (open to BA music majors only); Women's Studies

Special Programs:

Dual degree engineering (3+2) guaranteed progress into engineering at Case Western University, Cleveland or Washington University, St. Louis.

Pre-professional Studies:

Pre-Dentistry; Pre-Law; Pre-Medicine; Pre-Physical Therapy; Pre-Veterinary Medicine

CAMPUS FACILITIES AND EQUIPMENT

Otterbein's 140-acre campus includes 50 buildings. The historic Towers Hall was constructed in 1872. The college completed interior renovation of Towers Hall designed to update the facilities and technology and still recapture the essence of the time period in which Towers was built are evident throughout the building. The Edwin L. and Mary Louise Roush Hall, dedicated June 1993 is the first general purpose academic facility built on the Otterbein campus since Towers and houses the business and graduate programs. Cowan Hall houses theatre and speech facilities, including an extensive scene shop, underwent major renovation in 2004–05 to improve the acoustics, scene shop, lobby and The Fritsche Theatre.

The most recent renovation on campus centers on the $20 million restoration and renovation of the Schear-McFadden Science Building and Weitkamp Planetarium/Observatory. Opening in the fall of 2009, Otterbein's investment in the sciences benefits the Life Science, Chemistry, Physics, Equine Science, and Nursing programs. With an additional 30,000 square feet added on to the facility, including Atrium, students have the opportunity to work in not only a new state-of-the-art facility, but with state of the art equipment as well. Expanding on is already strong investment in the sciences, Otterbein will also open the new $4.92 Center for Equine Studies in the fall of 2009. The new facility calls for 52 total stalls, as well as improved indoor and outdoor riding arenas, pastures, classrooms, and riding trail. Also, completed in the fall of 2006, The Department of Art's facility was constructed with the special needs of artists in mind. The new Miller Gallery is also located in this building, with state-of-the-art lighting for optimal exhibition viewing. Otterbein also runs The Frank Museum of Art, a renovated church near campus that has rotating exhibitions from the college's collection. The other half of the same building opened in the fall of 2007 and is home to the Department of Communication. The newly developed space offers state-of-the-art broadcasting (both radio and television) studios, journalism laboratories, classrooms, as well as student and faculty workspace. Other facilities on campus include the Battelle Fine Arts Center, which is home to programs in music and dance, and the Courtright Memorial Library.

Housing Facilities: Alongside consistent renovations of its traditional housing, Otterbein recently invested in 2 new on campus Suite-Style Residence Halls. The C. Brent DeVore Suites opened in 2006 and for the first time offered sophomore students the option of suite-style living on campus. The $9 million dollar facility is so popular that the college invested in a second suite-style residence hall, which opened in the fall of 2008. With an additional 400 beds on campus, Otterbein is continuing its strong commitment to be both a living and learning community.

Athletic Facilities: The Frank and Vida Clements Recreation and Fitness Center, opened in the fall of 2002, is a $9.5 million center providing facilities for athletic training, sport management, and health and fitness programs with a 75,000 square-foot field house, a high-tech cardiovascular fitness area, fully-equipped training and rehabilitation center, coaching offices, classrooms and a student lounge area. In Fall 2005, the Cardinals football program moved into its new home in Memorial Stadium, a $3.2 million grandstand built on the same site of the original Memorial Stadium, both of which were dedicated to student and alumni veterans.

TUITION, ROOM, BOARD AND FEES

2009–2010 school year

Tuition: $27,321

Room: $3,714

Board: $3,891

FINANCIAL AID

95% of our students receive financial assistance including over $18 million in scholarships and grants.

Students applying for need-based financial aid must complete the FAFSA form with a priority deadline of April 1.

Otterbein offers the following scholarships:

President's Scholar Awards - $12,500

Otterbein Scholar Awards - $8,000

Otterbein Scholar Awards - $6,000

Otterbein Transfer Scholar Awards - $2,500

National Merit Finalist - $2000

International Baccalaureate Scholarships - $1,000 to 7,000

Endowed Scholarships - $800 - 5000

Ammons-Thomas Awards - $500 - 5000

Community Service Awards - $1500

Talent Awards - $500 - 4000

Legacy Awards - $1000

Premier Departmental Scholar Awards - $1000 – 2000

Deans Awards - $1000 -4000

STUDENT ORGANIZATIONS AND ACTIVITIES

Student Clubs and Organizations

ACADEMIC INTEREST GROUPS:

Accounting Club; Actuarial Club of Otterbein College; American chemical society Student Affiliate; Association for Computing Machinery; Ohio Collegiate Music Education Association; Otterbein College Assoc. of Animal Health; Care Professionals; Otterbein College Middle Level Assoc.; Otterbein Club of Athletic Training Students; Otterbein Nursing Students Association; Pre-Law Club; Public Relations Student Society of America; (PRSSA); Sociology Club; Sports Management Club; Student Education Association (OSEA); Teacher Education Committee

GOVERNANCE:

Academic Council; Administrative Council; Affirmative Action Committee; Appeals Council; Constitution Review Committee; Cultural Affairs Committee; Curriculum Committee; Distinction Committee; Faculty Council; Governance, Bylaws and Communication; Committee; Judicial Council; Otterbein College Senate; Personnel Committee; Retention Committee; Student Life Committee; Student Media Board; Student Trustee; Traffic Council; United Greek Governing Board

HONORARIES:

Alpha Epsilon Delta, pre-medicine; Alpha Lambda Delta, freshmen women's academic; Delta Omicron, music; Mortar Board; Order of Omega, Greek leadership; Phi Alpha Theta (History); Phi Eta Sigma, freshmen men's academic; Phi Sigma Iota, foreign language; Pi Kappa Delta, forensics/speech; Psi Chi, psychology; Sigma Zeta, science; Torch and Key, scholarship

MEDIA:

Aegis, humanities journal; Ottervine, Otterbein Campus news publication; Quiz and Quill, student literary magazine; Sibyl Yearbook; Student Media Board; Tan & Cardinal, weekly student newspaper; WOBN-FM and WOCC-TV3

RELIGIOUS LIFE:

Campus Crusade for Christ/Athletes in Action; Otterbein Christian Fellowship; Religious Life Council

GREEK FRATERNITY:

Interfraternity Council (IFC); United Greek Governing Board; Alpha Phi Alpha; Alpha Sigma Phi (Phoenix); Eta Phi Mu; Lambda Gamma Epsilon (Kings); Pi Beta Sigma (Pi Sig); Pi Kappa Phi (Country Club); Sigma Delta Phi (Sphinx); Zeta Phi (Rats); Omega Psi Phi

GREEK SORORITY:

Panhellenic Council; United Greek Governing Board; Alpha Kappa Alpha; Delta Sigma Theta; Epsilon Kappa Tau (EKT); Kappa Phi Omega (Kappa Phi); Sigma Alpha Tau (Owls); Tau Delta (Deltas); Tau Epsilon Mu (TEM); Theta Nu; Zeta Phi Beta

SPECIAL INTEREST GROUPS:

African American student Union (AASU); Asian student Interest Association (ASIA); Campus Green Party; Campus Programming Board (CPB); Commuter Association; Emerging Leaders; Free Thinkers Club; Freezone; International students Association (ISA) Host & Tour; Model United Nations Club; Orientation Leaders; Otterbein College Crew Club; Otterbein College Democrats; Otterbein Equestrian Team; Otterbein Film Club; Otterbein Peace Coalition; Otterbein Young Republicans; Outdoor Adventure Club; Sisters United; Student Athletic Advisory Committee; Volleyball Club; Women's Forum

SPORTS:

Baseball (M); Basketball (M/W); Cross Country (M/W); Equestrian Team (M/W); Football (M); Golf (M/W); Indoor Track (M/W); Lacrosse (M); Outdoor Track (M/W); Soccer (M/W); Softball (M/W); Tennis (M/W); Volleyball (W); Intramurals available in basketball, softball, football, and volleyball; Cheerleading

MUSICAL GROUPS & THEATRE:

Big Band; Camerata; Cap and Dagger; Cardinal Dance Team; Cardinal Marching Band; Chamber Ensembles; Concert Band; Concert Choir; Gospel Choir; Jazz Ensemble; Men's Glee Club; Opera Theatre; Opus One (vocal jazz ensemble); Otterbein Vocal Ensemble; Pep Band; Percussion Ensemble; String Ensemble; Westerville Symphony; Wind Ensemble; Women's Chorale

SERVICE GROUPS:

Community Service T.E.A.M.; Habitat for Humanity; Leadership in Volunteer Experience (LIVE); M.O.S.T. (Mentoring Organizational; Students Today); Rotaract

ADMISSIONS PROCESS

Otterbein College seeks to admit students who are best qualified to benefit from the educational offerings of the College and to contribute to the campus community. Each applicant's credentials are reviewed individually; Admission decisions are based on academic performance, standardized test scores, and the potential for future growth and success. Special talents and participation in extracurricular and community activities will also be considered. Preference is given to applicants who have successfully completed a college preparatory curriculum. Students are admitted without regard to gender, race, sexual orientation, creed, color, nation origin or handicap.

Application process:

Otterbein admits students on a rolling basis beginning in mid-October with a recommended deadline of March 1. After that, students will be admitted on a space-available basis; some programs may be closed by then.

A completed application file includes:

1. Application - either paper with $25 fee or on-line with fee waived (www.otterbein.edu)

2. Official copy of high school transcript

3. Official record of ACT or SAT scores. Test scores will be accepted if reported on an official transcript.

PENNSYLVANIA COLLEGE OF TECHNOLOGY

Penn College is a special mission affiliate of Penn State, committed to applied technology education. Located in Williamsport, it is the second largest campus in the Penn State system, enrolling approximately 6,500 students.

Bachelor- and associate-degree and certificate majors represent more than 100 career fields related to:

- business and computer technologies
- construction and design technologies
- health sciences
- hospitality
- industrial and engineering technologies
- integrated studies
- natural resources management
- transportation technology

STUDENT BODY

In addition to fraternities, sororities, clubs, and organizations—many of which are affiliated with national and professional organizations—Penn College offers 15 intercollegiate athletic teams and various club sports and intramural sport activities.

Matthew Grimminger, Heavy Construction Equipment, explains that getting involved outside of classes is very important. He says, "It's real important to me to be involved with your friends and getting out to play some sports…It lets you relax and relieves stress so you can keep up with the school work and enjoy it both at the same time."

ACADEMICS

Classrooms and laboratories offer extensive "hands-on" experiences that prepare graduates for success in the workplace. Applied technology in each major gives students the opportunity to learn the most current advances in their fields of study. To ensure an ever-present connection to the workforce, business, and industry, advisers provide guidance on matters of curriculum, facilities, and equipment.

Small classes (1:20 faculty-to-student ratio)—and no graduate assistants teaching classes—mean students have access to faculty. "The interactions and the relationships that the students build with the faculty here is just unbelievable," says Jennifer Fritz, Physician Assistant. She goes on to say that the bonds she has with her instructors have "done a world of good for my education."

"The faculty in my major are amazing. They are a huge wealth of knowledge because all of them have worked out in some type of manufacturing field before they started working at the college," says Timothy Senavaitis, Manufacturing Engineering Technology. "This is important because I don't know how it is in the real world and somebody teaching me from experience is extremely valuable."

For those who need alternatives beyond the traditional, on-campus programs of study, Penn College also offers a variety of courses and bachelor-degree completion programs via distance learning. Bachelor's degrees that can be completed through distance learning include: Applied Health Studies, Automotive Technology Management, Dental Hygiene, Health Information Management, Nursing, and Technology Management.

Taking courses online made it possible for Crista Dailey, Technology Management, to earn her degree while working full time and raising a family. She says that "it provided me with the flexibility I needed to complete my education."

Bachelor-degree, associate-degree, and certificate majors combine hands-on experience with theory and management education. Among the majors with the most students enrolled in Fall 2009 were Nursing, Building Construction, Residential Construction Technology & Management, Construction Management, and Information Technology.

For those who are undecided or have specific career goals not addressed in other programs, Penn College offers associate-degree General Studies and Individual Studies majors. For those undecided about a career or college major, counseling and career services are available.

Bachelor of Science:

Accounting

Applied Health Studies

Applied Human Services

Automotive Technology Management

Aviation Maintenance Technology

Building Automation Technology

Building Science & Sustainable Design (Architectural Technology, Building Construction Technology)

Business Administration (Banking & Finance, Human Resource Management, Management, Marketing, Small Business & Entrepreneurship)

Civil Engineering Technology

Computer-Aided Product Design

Construction Management

Culinary Arts and Systems

Dental Hygiene (Health Policy & Administration, Special Population Care)

Electronics and Computer Engineering Technology

Graphic Communications Management

Graphic Design

Health Information Management

HVAC Technology

Information Technology (Information Technology Security Specialist, Network Specialist, Web & Applications Development)

Legal Assistant/Paralegal Studies

Manufacturing Engineering Technology

Nursing

Physician Assistant

Plastics and Polymer Engineering Technology

Residential Construction Technology and Management

Technology Management

Welding and Fabrication Engineering Technology

Associate of Applied Arts:

Advertising Art

Mass Media Communication

Associate of Arts:

General Studies

Studio Arts

Associate of Applied Science:

Accounting

Architectural Technology

Automated Manufacturing Technology

Automotive Service Sales and Marketing

Automotive Technology (Ford ASSET & Honda PACT)

Aviation Technology

Baking and Pastry Arts

Building Construction Technology

Building Construction Technology: Masonry

Business Management

Civil Engineering Technology

Collision Repair Technology

Computer-Aided Drafting Technology

Culinary Arts Technology

Dental Hygiene

Diesel Technology

Early Childhood Education

Electric Power Generation Technology

Electrical Technology

Electromechanical Maintenance Technology

Electronics and Computer Engineering Technology (Communications & Fiber Optics, Electronics & Computer Engineering, Nanofabrication Technology, Robotics & Automation)

Emergency Medical Services

Forest Technology

Graphic Communications Technology

Health Arts

Health Arts: Practical Nursing

Health Information Technology

HVAC Technology

Heavy Construction Equipment Technology (Caterpillar Equipment, Operator, Technician)

Hospitality Management

Human Services

Individual Studies

Information Technology (Network Administration, Network Technology, Technical Support Technology, Web & Applications Technology)

Landscape/Nursery Technology: Turfgrass Management

Legal Assistant/Paralegal

Machine Tool Technology

Nursing

Occupational Therapy Assistant

Ornamental Horticulture (Horticulture Retail Management, Landscape Technology, Plant Production)

Physical Fitness Specialist

Plastics and Polymer Technology

Radiography

Surgical Technology

Surveying Technology

Welding Technology

Certificates:

Automotive Service Technician

Aviation Maintenance Technician

Collision Repair Technician

Construction Carpentry

Diesel Technician

Electrical Occupations

Health Information Coding Specialist

Machinist General

Nurse/Health Care Paralegal Studies

Paramedic Technician

Plumbing

Practical Nursing

Welding

ADMISSIONS

Application deadline for fall is July 1. Submit application and $50 application fee online at www.pct.edu/princeton or contact the Admissions Office for an application.

Applicants for bachelor-degree majors must submit SAT/ACT test scores in addition to high school transcripts to be considered for admission.

Applicants must satisfactorily complete placement testing and satisfy other major-specific admission criteria in order to be offered acceptance into a major program of study.

Information on all Penn College majors, as well as details on admissions and enrollment, is offered at www.pct.edu/princeton.

Pennsylvania College of Technology

One College Avenue

Williamsport, PA 17701

(800) 367-9222 or (570) 327-4761

Fax: 570.321.5551

admissions@pct.edu

www.pct.edu/princeton

CAMPUS LIFE

The main campus is located in Williamsport (North central Pennsylvania)—no more than a four-hour drive from major cities including Philadelphia, New York, Pittsburgh, and Washington, D.C.

Air service is provided at the Williamsport Regional Airport.

In addition to the main campus, the College operates an aviation facility at the regional airport and nearby centers for the earth sciences and advanced automotive technologies.

Students benefit from internships, work-based, and other experiences outside of the classroom. For many, these experiences are the first step toward a full-time job after graduation. "I fit right in at my internship and was able to learn a lot of things about the accounting field," says JoAnna Prusak, Accounting. "Also, after my internship was done they offered me a full-time position which I gladly accepted." JoAnna also was a Volunteer Income Tax Assistant for two years. She states, "In the two years that I have participated in the VITA program, there have been a number of different people that I have helped out, some of which have been difficult. Dealing with these people has been a useful and real world experience of what I will run into in the future."

COST AID

Four out of five Penn College students receive some form of financial aid. Regardless of family income, students are encouraged to apply for financial aid, including grants, loans, scholarships, and work-study options. For the most current information, visit www.pct.edu/finaid.

In 2009–10, Pennsylvania residents attending Penn College paid approximately $21,530 per year and out-of-state residents, approximately $24,680 per year. These estimated costs are based upon tuition and fees for an average 15 credits per semester, plus estimated expenses for housing, meals, books, and supplies. For the most current information, visit www.pct.edu/finaid/cost.htm.

School Says . . .

PITZER COLLEGE

AT A GLANCE

Pitzer is a comprehensive liberal arts college founded in 1963 as the sixth member of The Claremont Colleges and ranks as the fifth most diverse private coed national liberal arts college. Our emphasis on interdisciplinary learning, intercultural understanding, and social responsibility distinguishes us from most other American colleges and universities. Interdisciplinary learning encourages you to explore how different academic fields intersect and draw on each other's wisdom and ideas; intercultural understanding enables you to see issues and events from cultural perspectives different from your own; and social responsibility shows you how to transform knowledge into action as you strive to make the world a better place to live for yourself and future generations.

What's more, Pitzer requires fewer general education courses than most other colleges, so you get to take more of the courses that appeal to your individual interests. You can also choose among a range of courses that connect classroom learning to real-world experience, whether it's working inside a labor union, assisting with a faculty member's research, advising a neighboring city about economic development, or helping underprivileged children prepare for a future that includes college. Such experiences help you grasp the deeper implications of your actions and how your education at Pitzer prepares you to make a difference in society.

Pitzer offers an intimate academic and social community alongside access to the resources of a larger university through membership in The Claremont Colleges, and students are allowed to cross-register at the other Claremont Colleges. This opportunity greatly enhances the range of courses available to students. The total enrollment of all the colleges is about 7,300 students.

In addition, Pitzer has completed phase one of a three-phase residence hall construction project in which we expect to become, upon its completion, the only college in the nation to have all Gold LEED certified buildings by the U.S. Green Building Council.

LOCATION AND ENVIRONMENT

We are located in the city of Claremont (population 35,000) at the base of the San Gabriel Mountains, about 35 miles east of Los Angeles and 78 miles west of Palm Springs. Pitzer is a short distance from rock climbing at Joshua Tree National Park; the Getty, Norton Simon, and other LA County museums; beaches of Southern California; and skiing at Mt. Baldy and Big Bear. Claremont's quaint village, a short walk from campus, has a wide variety of restaurants, galleries, and shops.

OFF-CAMPUS OPPORTUNITIES

More than 72 percent of our students participate in study abroad programs with an emphasis on community involvement at sites throughout the world. Pitzer administers its own language and culture programs and exchanges in Argentina, Australia, Botswana, Bulgaria, Canada, China, Costa Rica, Denmark, Ecuador, England, Finland, France, Germany, Ghana, Ireland, Japan, Korea, Latvia, Mexico, Morocco, Nepal, South Africa, Spain, Thailand, and Turkey and 14 exchanges with U.S. institutions. Students in all majors can arrange a semester of study abroad but those who prefer not to take a full semester away from Pitzer may participate in Pitzer summer programs in Costa Rica and Japan.

MAJORS AND DEGREES OFFERED

Pitzer grants the bachelor of arts degree in 44 fields of study: American studies; anthropology; art; art history, Asian American studies; biology; biology/chemistry; Black studies; chemistry; Chicano studies; classics; dance; economics; English and world literature; environmental science; environmental studies;;; gender and feminist studies; history; human biology; international and intercultural studies (Latin American and Caribbean studies, African studies, Asian studies, European studies and Third World studies); linguistics; management engineering; mathematical economics; mathematics; media studies; molecular biology; music; neuroscience; organismal biology; organizational studies; philosophy; physics; political economy; political studies; psychology; religious studies; science and management; science, technology, and society; sociology; Spanish; and theater. There is also the opportunity to create one's own major.

Minors are also available in anthropology, art, art history, Asian American studies, biology, black studies, classics, dance, economics, English and world literature, environmental studies, gender and feminist studies, history, linguistics, mathematics, media studies, music, philosophy, science, technology and society, sociology, Spanish and theater.

ACADEMIC PROGRAMS

To earn the bachelor of arts degree, students are required to complete 32 courses, about one-third of which are in the field of major. Pitzer co-sponsors a science program with Claremont McKenna and Scripps Colleges. The Keck Science Center has state-of-the-art laboratories for teaching and research and a large biological field station. Pitzer joins Western University of Health Sciences in nearby Pomona to offer a seven-year program culminating in the BA and the Doctor of Osteopathic Medicine degrees.

CAMPUS FACILITIES AND EQUIPMENT

Pitzer provides a variety of special resources and facilities. These facilities include the arboretum (featuring ecologically and sustainable landscapes); computer centers (one laboratory features Macintosh computers, another features PC-compatible computers); the Gold Student Center (housing a fitness room for aerobics and weight training, simulated rock climbing, martial arts and yoga classes, a recreational room, a student-run snack bar, a swimming pool, a video production studio); the W. M. Keck Science Center (housing biology, chemistry, and physics labs); the psychology lab; and the writing lab.

In addition, Pitzer shares a variety of facilities with the other Claremont Colleges: Honnold/Mudd Library, Rancho Santa Ana Botanic Garden, Bernard Biological Field Station, Chicano/Latino Student Affairs Center, Office of Black Student Affairs, Asian American Resource Center, Baxter Student Health Services, Monsour Counseling and Psychological Services, McAlister Center for Religious Activities, campus security, and Huntley Bookstore.

TUITION, ROOM, BOARD AND FEES

Cost for the 2008–2009 academic year are as follows:

Tuition: 35,840

Room: 7,290

Board: 4,200

Fees: 3,490

Books and personal expenses: $2,000 (estimated)

Travel expenses will vary.

Costs are subject to change for the 2010–11 academic year.

FINANCIAL AID

Pitzer's financial aid program supports the goals of the admission program: to enroll a student body of quality and diversity. Financial aid is based on financial need. Approximately 42 percent of the students receive financial aid in the form of grants, loans, and work study. To apply for aid, you must complete and submit the CSS/Financial Aid PROFILE and the Free Application for Federal Student Aid (FAFSA) by February 1. California residents must apply for a CAL Grant by March 2.

STUDENT ORGANIZATIONS AND ACTIVITIES

The spirit of involvement extends well beyond the classroom, and is the essence of a Pitzer education. Opportunities abound within the college to participate in more than 50 student organizations, intramural sports, community service programs, and social activities, as well as the 150 clubs and organizations available consortium-wide. Students participate in all college committees and play a key part in the governance of the college. Pitzer joins Pomona College to field NCAA Division III teams in baseball, basketball, cross-country, football, golf, soccer, softball, swimming and diving, tennis, track and field, volleyball, and water polo. In addition, there are numerous club sports to participate in, including cycling, lacrosse, badminton, fencing, and rugby.

ADMISSIONS PROCESS

Pitzer College strives to attract a diverse student body with demonstrated academic ability, maturity, and independence. Each applicant is evaluated on an individual basis. Your application should show the ways in which you feel you will profit from and contribute to Pitzer College. Pitzer expects that students seeking admission would have selected a rigorous academic program in high school. Your senior year is very important and should include a variety of solid academic courses.

Early Decision: If Pitzer is clearly your first choice, we invite you to use this option. This application deadline is November 15.

Regular Admission: First-year applicants seeking regular admission should have their admission applications submitted by January 1.

Pitzer's admission policy for first-year students provides applicants with greater flexibility in presenting application materials that accurately reflect their diverse academic abilities and potentials.

Pitzer exempts students graduating in the top 10 percent of their class, or those who have an unweighted cumulative GPA of 3.50 or higher in academic subjects from having to submit any standardized tests. Applicants not falling into either one of those categories will be required to submit at least one of the following options:

(a) ACT scores, or (b) SAT scores, or (c) Two or more Advanced Placement test scores of at least 4: one must be in English or English language, and one must be in mathematics or a natural science, or (d) Two International Baccalaureate exam scores: one must be in English 1A and one must be in the Mathematics Methods (Standard Level), or a higher level course in mathematics, or (e) Two exams: one recent junior or senior year graded, analytical writing sample from a humanities or social science course, and one mathematics examination, preferably a final or end-of-semester exam in the most advanced mathmetics course possible (at least at the algebra II level. The samples must include the student's name, the teacher's comments, grades, and the assignment.

Pitzer College adheres to the May 1 National Candidate's Reply Date Agreement.

PRINCETON UNIVERSITY

AT A GLANCE

Princeton combines the strengths of a major research university with the qualities of an outstanding liberal arts college. Princeton prepares its 5,000 undergraduates for lives of leadership and service.

Chartered in 1746, Princeton is the fourth-oldest college in the nation. It is a private, non-sectarian university that seeks to fulfill its informal motto, first expressed by the University's 13th president, Woodrow Wilson: *"Princeton in the nation's service and in the service of all nations."*

LOCATION AND ENVIRONMENT

Princeton is a residential campus set on 500 park-like acres located in the town of Princeton (pop: 30,000) in central New Jersey. Known for its beauty and architectural variety, including the famed "Collegiate Gothic" style of architecture, the campus is home to historic landmarks such as Nassau Hall, which was built in 1756 and played an important role during the American Revolution.

Princeton students enjoy convenient transportation options to New York City and Philadelphia, both only an hour away. Other nearby attractions include numerous parks, cultural venues, and commercial hubs. For arts lovers, the McCarter Theatre is a campus treasure located within easy walking distance.

ACADEMICS

Princeton undergraduates pursue either the bachelor of arts (A.B.) or the bachelor of science in engineering (B.S.E.) degree. Students in the A.B. degree program choose a concentration (major) in one of 34 departments in the arts, humanities, social sciences, and natural sciences, including undergraduate programs in the Woodrow Wilson School of Public and International Affairs and the School of Architecture. The B.S.E. degree is granted by the School of Engineering and Applied Science, which has six engineering departments.

Princeton offers doctoral programs in a range of subjects in the humanities, natural sciences, social sciences, School of Architecture, School of Engineering and Applied Science, and within the Woodrow Wilson School of Public and International Affairs.

In addition to their major course of study, students are encouraged to enroll in one or more of the University's 42 certificate programs, which offer diverse fields of study. For example, a student may wish to concentrate in ecology and evolutionary biology while pursuing a certificate in musical performance.

Undergraduates benefit from small class sizes and one-on-one advising with faculty, particularly while working on independent projects such as the junior paper and senior thesis. The university's 1,172 faculty members are leaders in their disciplines, and it is not uncommon for students to receive instruction from a Nobel laureate, Pulitzer Prize winner, or MacArthur fellow. During their freshman year, students are introduced to many of Princeton's finest faculty through the freshman seminars program, which offers small discussion-focused classes on a variety of topics. One such freshman seminar may study the chemistry of chocolate; another may explore the ideas and arguments of "great books."

From the outset, students are encouraged to bring a multidisciplinary approach to their studies, pulling together what they discover in different classes and through their own research. This approach may be informal, based on a student's particular avenue of study, or it may be more formally structured, such as with the integrated science curriculum that combines the study of physics, mathematics, computer science, and molecular biology.

A global perspective is emphasized across the curriculum, with special opportunities such as the Study Abroad Program and the Princeton Institute for International and Regional Studies. Launched in 2009, the Bridge Year Program provides selected students with opportunities for international service learning before the start of the freshman year.

FACILITIES AND EQUIPMENT

Academic support services include academic advising centered in each of the six residential colleges (for A.B. students) and in the engineering school (for B.S.E. students); the McGraw Center, which offers workshops and individual consultations with students as they evolve as scholars; and the Writing Program, which strengthens students' writing skills through a required seminar. Ongoing tutoring sessions also are available at the program's Writing Center.

Throughout their undergraduate careers, Princeton students are supported by a range of first-rate academic resources, including libraries, laboratories, and one of the leading university art museums in the country. The largest library on campus, Firestone Library, contains more than 70 miles of shelving and a vast range of electronic resources. The Peter B. Lewis Library, designed by renowned architect Frank Gehry, offers impressive print and digital collections in the sciences. In the past several years, new initiatives in African American studies and neuroscience have resulted in expanded activities.

Slated for completion in fall 2010, the new state-of-art and environmentally sustainable science facility will house the chemistry department and provide laboratory space for research and teaching.

Numerous venues for the arts as well as a range of athletic facilities also are available.

TUITION AND FEES

Estimated cost of attendance for 2009–2010:

Tuition: $35,340

Room charge: $6,340

Board rate: $5,340

Estimated miscellaneous expenses (books, supplies, laundry, telephone, recreation, etc.): $3,600

Total: $50,620

FINANCIAL AID

Princeton offers one of the strongest need-based financial aid programs in the country, ensuring that all qualified students, regardless of financial need, can afford to attend. There is no income cutoff on Princeton's aid application; any family who feels they may need help paying for a Princeton education is welcome to apply for aid.

Since 2001, when Princeton initiated its landmark no-loan financial aid program, the university has been a leader in changing the face of financial aid policy. Central to the program is Princeton's groundbreaking "no-loan" policy; the university offers every aid recipient a financial aid package that replaces loans with grant aid that students do not pay back.

If admitted, applicants can be confident that their financial need, as determined by Princeton's aid office, will be met. Today, more than half of each entering class benefits from Princeton's financial aid program. As a result, Princeton has been able to enroll growing numbers of students from low- and middle-income backgrounds. The average aid package for the Class of 2013 was $37,680.

CAMPUS LIFE

Princeton is a residential campus that provides a close-knit living environment for its undergraduates. Through its six residential colleges, students pursue a host of recreational and academic activities. The residential colleges also serve as home base for academic advising for students, who learn about all that the university has to offer from faculty and staff advisers, peer mentors, and fellow students.

With more than 300 student organizations, as well as an extensive calendar of cultural and athletic events, students find it easy to pursue their interests or explore new ones. The Frist Campus Center serves as the hub of campus life, and is home to the Women's Center, the Davis International Center, the LGBT Center, the Pace Center for civic engagement, and the Undergraduate Student Government, as well as many other student clubs and organizations.

For many students, social life at Princeton includes becoming a member of an eating club. The 10 historic eating clubs are open to juniors and seniors and are run independently of the university. Fraternities and sororities are not recognized as official student organizations on campus.

Princeton is an NCAA Division I school.

The university offers 38 varsity sports and 35 club teams. Each year more than 1,000 students participate in intercollegiate varsity and junior varsity sports. In any given year, more than half of Princeton's varsity athletic teams compete in national championships.

ADMISSIONS

Princeton's admission process goes beyond simply looking for academically accomplished students. For each freshman class, Princeton brings together a varied mix of high-achieving, intellectually gifted students from diverse backgrounds to create an exceptional learning community. Princeton cares about what students have accomplished in and out of the classroom. The admission process is highly selective. In recent years, the university has offered admission to only about 10 percent of applicants.

Students applying to Princeton are asked to describe their talents, academic accomplishments, and personal achievements. A transcript and recommendations also are required. To be considered for admission to Princeton, students must submit the results of the SAT Reasoning Test or ACT (with Writing, where offered). In addition, all applicants must submit the results of two different SAT Subject Tests. The university accepts both online and paper applications. Princeton does not offer a transfer admission process.

Under Princeton's admission policy, need for financial aid is not in any way a disadvantage. Princeton welcomes applications from talented students of diverse economic backgrounds.

QUINNIPIAC UNIVERSITY

AT A GLANCE

Quinnipiac, founded in 1929, is a private, co-educational, non-sectarian University - a residential campus in a uniquely attractive New England setting. Quinnipiac's mission is to provide a supportive and stimulating environment for the intellectual and personal growth of undergraduate, graduate, and law students.

The university offers broadly based undergraduate programs together with graduate programs in selected professional fields. At the undergraduate level, through integrated liberal arts and professional curricula, programs in the Schools of Business, Communications, Education, Health Sciences, and the College of Arts and Sciences prepare students for career entry or advanced studies. Graduate programs are designed to provide professional qualifications for success in business, education, health sciences, communications, and law.

An education at Quinnipiac embodies the university's commitment to three important values: excellence in education, a student centered campus, and a spirit of community. The entire university shares a service orientation toward students and their needs. Its collegial atmosphere fosters a strong sense of community, identity, and purpose among faculty, staff, and students.

LOCATION AND ENVIRONMENT:
THREE SETTINGS, ONE UNIVERSITY

Hamden, Connecticut: 8 miles north of New Haven, 20 miles south of Hartford, midway between Boston and New York City. Quinnipiac is a suburban campus with 600 acres on three sites. The *Mount Carmel campus* is adjacent to Sleeping Giant State Park, with 1,700 acres of hills and trails for hiking and walking. A picturesque setting provides an enjoyable academic and residential campus experience for 5600 undergraduate and 1,,800 graduate students. A campus shuttle system provides easy access to theater, shopping, museums, sports, recreation, and a variety of dining and entertainment options in Hamden and New Haven. The nearby *York Hill campus* is home to the TD Bank Sports Center plus new suite-style residence halls with kitchens to accommodate 1,800 students, a 2,000 car parking garage and student/recreation center. The *North Haven campus*, just 4 miles away, provides the upper level and graduate students in the School of Health Sciences with a state of the art setting on 100 acres, soon to be joined by other graduate programs.

Students from over 28 states and 15 countries study at Quinnipiac. Ninety-five percent of the incoming 1600 freshmen choose to live on campus. Housing options include traditional residence halls, suites, and suites with full kitchens. Housing is also available for seniors on a space available basis or seniors may choose to live off campus in a variety of apartments/condos and houses.

Driving time to Quinnipiac from Boston or New York City is about two hours. Metro-North railroad from Grand Central Terminal in New York City and Amtrak Northeast Corridor trains also arrive in New Haven. The campus is a 10-minute taxi ride (students can take the campus shuttle) from the station. Bradley Airport (BDL), just north of Hartford is the nearest international airport, about 40 minutes from campus. Students can also arrive at John F. Kennedy, Newark, or LaGuardia airports in the New York area and travel via Connecticut Limousine to New Haven.

All programs at Quinnipiac offer an excellent combination of classroom learning with internships or clinical affiliations. Students in the health sciences are placed in clinical affiliations as part of their course work. Students in business, communications, and liberal arts have nearby corporations, health care agencies, or media outlets available for internships.

Career Services, offered by each of the academic schools, can provide excellent assistance in resume writing and job placement. The results of a survey of recent alumni show that close to 90 percent were either employed or in graduate school within six months of graduation. Each year about half of students in internships are offered permanent jobs as a result of their work.

Students in all majors can also take advantage of study abroad opportunities either during the summer months or during the academic year. Program sites include: Ireland, Australia; Austria; Czech Republic; England; France; Spain; Italy; Netherlands; Russia; South Africa; Spain and Independent Programs, and through affiliates such as AIFS, API, and Semester at Sea. Study abroad is an experience of a lifetime allowing you to live a different country for a period of time while earning credits at your home institution. Any student in any major can apply to study abroad with at least a 3.0 GPA.

MAJORS AND DEGREES OFFERED

Undergraduate students can choose from more than 50 majors through the College of Arts and Sciences plus the Schools of Business, Education, Communications and Health Sciences. About 30% of all entering freshmen remain at Quinnipiac through their graduate degree program.

Graduate students specialize in law, business, organizational leadership, health management, computer information systems, journalism, interactive communications, public relations, education, and health science programs for physician assistant, pathologist's assistant, medical and laboratory sciences, molecular and cell biology, and nurse practitioner. Several are offered online.

ACADEMIC PROGRAMS

The School of Business, which is AACSB accredited, offers majors in: accounting, advertising, biomedical marketing, information systems management, economics, entrepreneurship, finance, international business, management and marketing. The Lender School of Business Center has case method classrooms, a high-tech Financial Technology Center 'trading room' and small team study rooms for project work.

The School of Health Sciences majors include: athletic training/sports medicine, biomedical science, diagnostic imaging, health/science studies, microbiology/molecular biology, nursing, occupational therapy (a 5 ½-year freshmen entry-level BS/MOT Master's program), physician assistant (6-year freshmen entry-level BS/MHS Master's program), physical therapy (a 6½ year freshmen entry-level BS/DPT doctorate). The North Haven facility has state-of-the-art labs including a diagnostic imaging suite, orthopedics lab, a model adaptive apartment, clinical skills labs, intensive care unit, pediatric/neonatal lab, clinical simulation labs and a biomechanics lab.

The College of Arts and Sciences majors include: biology, biochemistry, chemistry, English, computer science, criminal justice, gerontology, history, interactive digital design, legal studies, mathematics, political science, psychology, social services, sociology, Spanish and theater.

In the School of Communications, majors include: film, video and interactive media, communications, journalism, and public relations. The Ed McMahon Center for Communications provides a state of the art facility with a fully digital high-definition production studio, a news technology center, audio production studio and editing suites.

For those interested in teaching, completion of an undergraduate major in an area in the liberal arts or natural sciences, combined with junior and senior year courses in the School of Education, ending with a fifth year full-time graduate education program, culminates in the Master of Arts in Teaching degree.

A pre-med program is designed to provide the undergraduate student interested in a career as a health professional the appropriate background necessary to meet the entrance requirements of a variety of different medical schools.

TECHNOLOGY, OPPORTUNITIES AND LIBRARY RESOURCES

Quinnipiac is among the top wired—or wireless—campuses in the country, and this is reflected in its facilities, services and programs. All incoming students must purchase a University recommended laptop computer (currently DELL) for use in the classroom and in the residence halls. Service is provided through the 'help desk.' The campus is 100% wireless.

Academic life focuses on the Bernhard Library, open 24 x 7. Automated library systems and over 100 personal computer workstations and 600 data ports are located throughout the library, along with individual study carrels and team study rooms.

Students seeking to improve their grades use the Learning Center for free tutoring help as well as sessions to improve study techniques, writing skills and research abilities. Since 2000, Quinnipiac has adopted a writing-across-the-curriculum approach to teaching writing throughout the University. All undergraduate majors seek to promote good critical thinking and communication skills.

The Honors Program fosters the needs and interests of our most academically talented and committed students. Service Learning courses integrate meaningful community service with instruction and refection to enrich the learning experience, teach civic responsibility and strengthen communities.

TUITION, ROOM, BOARD AND FEES

Tuition and Fees for 2009–10 are $32,400, with $12,380 for room and board.

FINANCIAL AID

The Quinnipiac University Financial Aid Office works with all applicants to assure that they receive the maximum state and federal aid for which they are eligible. The University offers merit-based scholarships to incoming freshmen in the fall semester (admission application deadline February 1st) for which no financial need is required. There is no additional application necessary for scholarship consideration and students are notified by the admissions office. If you have any questions, please feel free to call the Office of Financial Aid at (203) 582-8750 or (800) 462-1944. Or you can e-mail us at: finaid@quinnipiac.edu. Quinnipiac University's FAFSA ID code is 001402.

STUDENT ORGANIZATIONS AND ACTIVITIES

Quinnipiac University has more than 75 clubs and organizations: including student government, newspaper, yearbook, radio station, service organizations, community activities, religious fellowships (Hillel, Christian Fellowship, Branches), diversity awareness (Black Student Union, Latino Cultural Society, Asian and Pacific Islander Association), dance and drama productions, and Greek life, along with numerous recreation activities, providing a balanced college experience. An active Intramural program has team competition in more than 20 sports.

Quinnipiac Bobcats: www.quinnipiacbobcats.com. The Division I athletic program in 19 sports includes: Men: basketball, baseball, cross country, lacrosse, ice hockey, tennis, and soccer. Women: basketball, softball, cross country and track (indoor and outdoor), field hockey, ice hockey, lacrosse, soccer, tennis, competitive cheer and volleyball. Quinnipiac competes in the NEC (Northeast Conference) and the ECAC in Men's and Women's Ice Hockey.

The athletic facilities include a multi-purpose gymnasium, locker rooms, training rooms, steam room, and a 24,000-square-foot, fully-equipped recreation and fitness center, with a suspended indoor track, outdoor lighted tennis, plus the TD Bank Sports Center with twin 3500 seat arenas for ice hockey and basketball.

ADMISSIONS PROCESS (ROLLING ADMISSIONS)

High school students should begin applying for admissions early in their senior year. Visit www.quinnipiac.edu/apply for application information. Quinnipiac is a member of the Common Application. A completed application consists of the application form, official high school transcript, SAT I test scores (QU SAT code - 3712) or ACT scores (QU ACT code - 0582) senior year, first-quarter grades, essay, and one letter of recommendation. Students are asked to supply official SAT and/or ACT test scores. The University will select the highest (critical reading plus math or ACT composite) scores for admission or merit aid.

The admissions office begins reviewing applications as soon as they are complete, and begins notifying students of their decisions in early January. Students applying for the physical therapy, nursing and physician assistant programs should apply by November 1st. We recommend February 1st as the deadline for all other applicants.

All programs subscribe to the nationally recognized candidate reply date of May 1. Any students placed on a waitlist who responds that they are interested in being considered if spaces are available will be notified as soon after May 1 as possible. In general, Quinnipiac admits between 50–55% of their applicants.

Transfer students who have or will receive an associate's degree prior to entrance do not need to provide high school transcripts and SAT results. We must receive transcripts of all courses taken at other colleges. The physician assistant program is not available to transfer students.

To schedule an interview, tour, group information session or register for an open house, go to http://www.quinnipiac.edu/visit. For questions, email admissions@quinnipiac.edu or call us at 800-462-1944, or 203-582-8600. Visit the website at: http://www.quinnipiac.edu.

RADFORD UNIVERSITY

AT A GLANCE

Students come to Radford University for the small class sizes, residential community, dedicated professors, and academic excellence. Since its founding in 1910, the University has grown to encompass the following Colleges: College of Business and Economics, the College of Education and Human Development, the College of Humanities and Behavioral Sciences, the College of Science and Technology, the Waldron College of Health and Human Services, the College of Visual and Performing Arts, and the College of Graduate and Professional Studies. Currently, 87 percent of the approximately 9,200 students attending the University are pursuing an undergraduate degree in one of the over 100 program options. The 38 graduate programs grant the MS, MA, MBA, MFA, MSN, MSW, EdS, and PsyD degrees.

More than one third of students, including all freshmen, live on campus in one of the fifteen residence halls, all configured as two-room suites. A variety of learning/residential communities are available to suit the interests and needs of students. Upperclass students who choose to live off-campus typically rent an apartment within walking distance of the University. The student body is composed of students from many parts of Virginia in addition to 39 other states and 43 foreign countries.

The University offers students ample opportunity to participate in overseas study programs. Radford organizes activities including guest speakers, theatre performances, concerts, film screenings, Greek events, student publications, radio and television stations, and intramural sports competitions. People congregate in the Hurlburt Student Center to utilize the lounges, recreation facilities, study rooms, and meeting areas. Starbucks, Chik-Fil-A, Salsarita's and other dining options are also available in the student center. Dalton Hall houses a food court, which includes Sbarro Pizzeria, Au Bon Pain, Wendy's and Ben & Jerry's. The campus bookstore, post office and a dining hall are also found in Dalton. The Dedmon Center is home to the University's 19 NCAA Division I athletic teams; it also provides comprehensive sports and fitness facilities.

LOCATION AND ENVIRONMENT

The University's hometown of Radford, Virginia, located approximately half an hour outside of Roanoke in the western part of the state, is set amid the scenic Blue Ridge Mountains. The town's population of 16,200 provides a variety of restaurants and shops. Students who enjoy the outdoors take advantage of the campus's proximity to The Blue Ridge Parkway, the Appalachian Trail, New River, and Claytor Lake. Available activities include skiing, hiking, canoeing, biking, and camping. The campus is convenient to I-81 for motorists and close to the Roanoke airport for those traveling by plane.

MAJORS AND DEGREES OFFERED

At Radford, students may work toward their BA, BS, BFA, BM, BBA, BSN or BSW degree. For undergraduates, the following majors are offered: accounting; anthropology; art; biology; chemistry; communication; communication sciences and disorders; computer science and technology; criminal justice; dance; economics; English; exercise sport and health education; fashion; finance; foods and nutrition; foreign languages; geography; geology; history; information science and systems; interdisciplinary studies (education); interior design; management; marketing; mathematics and statistics; media studies; medical technology; music; music therapy; nursing; philosophy and religious studies; physical science; political science; psychology; recreation, parks, and tourism; social science; social work; sociology; and theatre.

ACADEMIC PROGRAMS

To be eligible for an undergraduate degree, students must complete at least 120 semester hours of college-level academic work. Honors courses are available to students enrolled in the Honors Academy and to any qualified student. The Office of New Student Programs coordinates several programs designed to ease the transition from high school to college. The University 100 class and Success Starts Here are programs that help first-year students become active and successful college students. The LARC (Learning Assistance Resource Center) provides tutoring and mentoring programs for student support. Quest, Radford's summer orientation program, allows incoming students to acclimate themselves to campus, receive advising, register for classes, and make friends before coming to school in the fall. An Army ROTC program is also available to interested and qualified students. The academic calendar consists of two semesters, August to December (fall) and January to May (spring), and summer sessions.

CAMPUS FACILITIES AND EQUIPMENT

More than 500,000 books and periodicals are available to students in the McConnell Library. When researching, students utilize these volumes as well as film, microfilm, records, compact audio discs, and tapes. The catalog can be searched on the computer. Also, the University participates in interlibrary loans to supplement the on-campus collection. In addition to the available computer labs, Radford's campus is completely wireless.

The newly renovated Peters Hall is home to the College of Education and Human Development. With smart board technology, a state of the art Teaching Resource Center, dance studios and an indoor climbing wall, this building is not only conducive to learning, but an enjoyable place for students to spend their free time as well.

The newest addition to campus is the recently completed Covington Center for Visual and Performing Arts and is one of the most technologically advanced centers for the arts in Southwest Virginia. The 50,000 square foot building houses performance, exhibition, rehearsal and work space for RU students and faculty.

FACULTY

More than 80 percent of Radford University's faculty members hold terminal degrees in their fields of study. With a student-faculty ratio of 18:1, Radford is committed to interaction between faculty members and students both in and out of the classroom. In addition to their primary responsibilities of teaching and advising students, faculty members are engaged in research, publication, and other professional activities. Fewer than 5 percent of Radford's undergraduate classes are taught by graduate instructors.

TUITION, ROOM, BOARD AND FEES

In the 2008–2009 school year, in-state undergraduates paid $6,536 for tuition and fees. Out-of-state students paid $15,550. An additional $6,622 was charged for room and board. In addition, students spend roughly $800 on books and supplies.

FINANCIAL AID

Students may receive need- or merit-based financial aid awards in the form of loans, work-study programs, private or government grants, or department-based fellowships. Some scholarships are given for outstanding demonstrations of leadership, character, or academic work. Those applying for financial aid must turn in the Free Application for Federal Student Aid (FAFSA) to Federal Student Aid Programs by the March 1 deadline. Transfer students are also required to submit the Financial Aid Transcript form, showing their former colleges or universities, whether or not they received financial aid.

In order to qualify for the Radford University Foundation's scholarship competition, students must ensure that their first-year applications arrive at the Office of Admissions and become complete (including official high school transcript and standardized test scores) by December 15. Those applicants with top high-school records can become finalists through an essay competition. Full scholarships, which include the equivalent of in-state tuition and fees, room and board, and a book stipend, are available. Partial scholarships are also available.

STUDENT ORGANIZATIONS AND ACTIVITIES

All Radford undergraduates are part of the Student Government Association, and elected representatives voice student opinions as part of the following committees: the executive council, cabinet, senate, house of representatives, off-campus student council, graduate student council, class representatives council, black student affairs council, international student affairs council, and diversity promotions council.

RU has over 250 clubs and organizations available for students, including the Radford Redcoats, equestrian team; RU Outdoors; Ultimate Frisbee; social sororities and fraternities; academic, service, sport and religious organizations are all popular options for students to get involved in.

ADMISSIONS PROCESS

The Admissions Committee at RU evaluates each applicant's academic record, looking for signs of scholastic and personal potential. Factors include high school course selection, GPA, academic trend, class rank, SAT I or ACT scores, and extracurricular pursuits. It is recommended that students take the following classes in high school: 4 units of English, 4 units of college-preparatory mathematics (including Algebra 1 & 2 and Geometry), 3-4 units of foreign language, 4 units of lab science, and 4 units of social science. Applicants intending to pursue a degree in nursing should have both biology and chemistry on their transcripts. The University does not discriminate on the basis of race, sex, handicap, age, veteran status, national origin, religious or political affiliation, or sexual preference.

New freshman applicants must submit all of the following materials in their completed application: the application form, the nonrefundable application fee, an official high school transcript, and official SAT I or ACT scores. Transfer applicants are required to send the application form and fee along with official transcripts from all of their previously attended colleges and universities. For fall admission, the early action deadline is December 15 and the regular decision deadline is February 1 for new freshmen. The priority deadline for new transfer applicants is June 1. Applications that arrive later than the deadlines listed will be evaluated as space is available.

Campus visits can be arranged between 8 a.m. and 5 p.m., Monday through Friday. Prospective students may also attend a campus tour at 10 a.m., noon, and 2 p.m. on Monday and Friday, 10 a.m. and 2 p.m. on Tuesday, Wednesday, and Thursday, and at 10 a.m., 11 a.m., and noon on Saturday during the school year.

REED COLLEGE

AT A GLANCE

Intellectual. Quirky. Rigorous. Laid back. Classical. Liberal. College guides grapple to define the Reed College experience, but they all tend to agree on two points: Reed is one of the most distinctive colleges in the nation and it is not for everyone. Reed attracts serious students_and often brings out the best in them. Always engaged, often engrossed, and occasionally engulfed in a demanding, exhilarating educational adventure, "Reedies" thrive on a mix of classical study, critical analysis, and guided inquiry that rewards creativity, independence, and reflection. Classes are small, faculty make themselves accessible, and students adhere to an honor principle both in and out of the classroom.

Reed recruits nationally, with California, the Pacific Northwest, and the Boston to Washington corridor well represented and 8 percent international students. A recent survey of graduating seniors at 52 liberal arts colleges found Reed students one and a half times more likely to be satisfied with their education than the national average and twice as likely to say they would choose Reed again. Reed ranks second among U.S. liberal arts colleges in percentage of graduates going on to earn doctoral degrees and fourth among all institutions of higher education. The breadth, depth, and rigor of the curriculum provide great preparation for nearly any career. Many Reed alumni found or lead companies and organizations, earn medical or law degrees, write books or create works of art, or work to make life on the planet better for all.

LOCATION AND ENVIRONMENT

Talk about the best of both worlds! Located in a quiet residential neighborhood on 116-acre campus of verdant lawns, winding paths, statuesque trees, a wooded natural wetland preserve, and a spring-fed lake frequented by migratory birds and other wildlife, Reed is a short bicycle or bus ride from the energy and excitement of downtown Portland, which is widely cited as the nation's most livable urban center. Portland boasts a wealth of diverse cultural, entertainment, shopping, and dining opportunities in an environment characterized by a combination of youthful exuberance and Pacific Northwest reserve. The Oregon Coast is an hour to the west and Mt. Hood an hour to the east (but reserve early to be sure of securing weekend accommodations at Reed's own ski cabin).

On the campus itself, century-old brick Tudor gothic buildings are interspersed with newer traditionally designed and remodeled facilities. The library, classrooms, and laboratories resonate with the history of decades of inquiry and discovery, supported with modern technology. Extensive facility expansion and renovation financed by $112 million development campaign has increased the overall square footage of Reed's buildings by almost 30 percent and added seven acres of contiguous property to the northwest corner of the campus. Five new eco-friendly residence halls opened in 2008, making it possible for 75% of Reed students to live on campus. For those who want it, housing on campus is all but guaranteed for all four years, because a healthy percentage of Reed students enjoy living in Portland neighborhoods near campus.

OFF-CAMPUS OPPORTUNITIES

Reed undergraduates may participate in a number of domestic exchange and study abroad opportunities. Domestic exchange programs are run in conjunction with Howard University in Washington, D.C.; Sarah Lawrence College in New York; and Sea Semester, based in Woods Hole, Massachusetts. Reed's nearly 40 Study abroad programs are established at universities around the world. Reed encourages students to pursue independent study off campus and must be developed with the assistance of appropriate Reed faculty members, the director for off-campus studies, and the registrar.

MAJORS AND DEGREES OFFERED

Reed confers the bachelor of arts degree in a wide selection of fields, both in traditional academic departments and in interdisciplinary combinations. Undergraduates are encouraged to design interdisciplinary majors; such majors must be planned with the approval of faculty advisers from each department involved.

Reed offers a number of 3-2 (dual degree) programs; these allow undergraduates to earn a three-year bachelor's degree from Reed, then earn a professional degree from a cooperating institution (Cal Tech, Columbia, Duke, RPI, the University of Washington) in two additional years.

ACADEMIC PROGRAMS

The curriculum at Reed is both demanding and wide-ranging. Through required studies, Reed students receive a solid grounding in the liberal arts and sciences.

All freshmen must complete "Hum 110," a survey of Greek, Roman, and other Mediterranean scholars from Homer to Petronius. Distribution requirements set a substantial portion of a student's curriculum for the first two years at Reed. Freshmen and sophomores must complete two courses in each of the four major divisions of the college. No specific courses are required; students are free to pursue their interests within the strictures of the requirements.

Reed juniors must pass a comprehensive exam in their major, to allow faculty members the chance to determine the student's readiness for his or her senior thesis project. The required senior thesis is the capstone experience of a Reed education. Every senior must produce an original independent research project over the course of the final year.

Reed strongly believes that learning should be undertaken for its own sake, not for the sake of letter grades. Accordingly, students do not receive grade reports unless they wish to. A student's transcript does include letter grades for all courses taken, but students can better gauge their progress through professors' written evaluations of their work and one-on-one meetings with faculty. Most prefer this system, which eliminates competition among students and allows them to focus entirely on the content of their academic work.

CAMPUS FACILITIES AND EQUIPMENT

The Reed College campus was established on a tract of land known in 1910 as Crystal Springs Farm. The social center of the college is the Gray Campus Center. It includes a commons building, student union, kitchen, dining room, private meeting rooms, student activities offices, bookstore, and mail services. The Gray Campus Center includes the 6,000-square-foot Kaul Auditorium, which is designed for multimedia presentations, musical performances, lectures, meetings, dinners, and special events. In a park-like setting near the heart of the city, the rolling lawns and open spaces of Reed's 116-acre campus include some of the largest and finest specimen trees in the Portland area. At the center of the campus is the canyon, a beautiful wooded upland surrounding a spring-fed lake and emergent marsh. A walking trail around the lake provides numerous opportunities to observe migratory birds and other woodland wildlife. The college recently built a fish passageway that creates a link from the upper Reed Lake area to the Crystal Springs stream below.

Eight new residence halls have been built since 1997. Naito and Sullivan Hall were completed in the fall of 1997, and Bragdon Hall was completed in January 1998. Naito and Sullivan feature outstanding views of the west hills and downtown Portland. Bragdon Hall takes full advantage of the view overlooking Reed Lake and the canyon interior. The eco-friendly cluster of Aspen, Bidwell Sequoia, and Sitka opened in August 2008. A new Spanish House also opened in 2008, completed a language house cluster that includes Chinese House, French House, German House, and Russian House. In 2003, Reed opened the Educational Technology Center (ETC) for computer-assisted learning as well as a new library wing.

TUITION, ROOM, BOARD AND FEES

Tuition (and fees) for the 2009–2010 academic year is $39,440. A $260 student body fee is added. Room and board is an additional $10,250, bringing the yearly total cost to $49,950.

FINANCIAL AID

Reed provides financial assistance to roughly 50% its undergraduates. The college maintains a need-based assistance program that allows students of all economic backgrounds to attend the college; it further guarantees that full need will be met for all continuing students who maintain good academic standing and who meet all other requirements of the aid process (such as application deadlines). The college makes every effort to make admission decisions on a need-blind basis but cannot guarantee that it will have the funds to do so. Each year, approximately half of all first-year and transfer students receive aid packages equaling their full demonstrated need. The college budgeted approximately $23 million for grant aid in 2009-2010; individual awards ranged from $1,000 to $50,000. For the 2009–2010 academic year, the average financial aid package, including grants, loans, and work opportunities, was approximately $33,000. The college is the primary source of grant money for its students. Reed also administers federal grants and a number of other awards. Students may take Perkins Loans and other federally subsidized loans; campus employment and work-study programs also figure into many aid packages.

STUDENT ORGANIZATIONS AND ACTIVITIES

Reed shuns exclusive organizations and activities, so the college has no Greek organizations and no NCAA or NAIA athletic teams (more about sports below). All campus organizations are student-created and student-run. The student activity fund of approximately $90,000 is administered by the Student Senate. Student organizations must lobby the Student Senate for funding annually, after which the Senate oversees a vote in which the entire student body decides what organizations should be funded. Thus, the number and nature of campus organizations at Reed changes every year to meet current student interests. Reed may not compete at the NCAA or NAIA level, but most students participate in sports on an informal basis. Intramural sports and club sports proliferate in basketball, fencing, rugby, sailing, soccer, squash and ultimate Frisbee. A three-semester physical education requirement demonstrates that the school recognizes the importance of physical fitness and the salutary effects of exercise.

ADMISSIONS PROCESS

Reed seeks students who demonstrate a commitment to learning and to the ideals embodied by a rigorous and stimulating liberal arts education. Freshman and transfer applications are welcome. The admission committee attempts to determine which candidates will benefit most from a Reed education as well as who is most likely to succeed at Reed. The ideal incoming class is diverse in its range of talents, interests, ethnic and socioeconomic backgrounds, and perspectives, yet constituted of students who share a common passion for academic inquiry. The admission committee places most emphasis on an applicant's record of previous academic accomplishment. Successful applicants have usually pursued a rigorous secondary school curriculum that includes honors and advanced courses and typically includes 4 years of English, at least 3 years of a foreign or classical language, 3 to 4 years of mathematics, 3 to 4 years of science, and 3 to 4 years of history or social studies. Because secondary school curricula vary widely in quality and content, Reed sets no fixed requirements in this area. With rare exceptions, incoming students have obtained a secondary school diploma prior to enrollment. The admissions committee sets no "cutoff points" for high school grades, college grades (for transfer students), or standardized test scores. Reed seeks candidates who demonstrate excellence of character, motivation, intellectual curiosity, individual responsibility, and social consciousness. The admission committee recognizes the importance of creating a diverse community in which individual differences contribute to the vitality of the campus. Reed strongly recommends a personal interview, especially for early decision candidates but an interview is not required. Early decision applications should arrive at Reed by November 15 (Option 1) or December 20 (Option 2). Early decision at Reed is binding: students who are accepted under early decision are expected to matriculate. The deadline for regular freshman admission applications is January 15. Transfer candidates should apply no later than March 1.

RIPON COLLEGE

AT A GLANCE

Together with the other members of our tight-knit learning community, at Ripon you'll learn more deeply, live more fully, and achieve more success. You'll be surprised to discover that here you have more opportunities to be involved, to lead, to speak out, to make a difference, to explore new interests than you would at a college 10 times our size. Through collaborative learning, group living, teamwork, and networking, you'll tap into the power of a community where we all work together to ensure your success at Ripon and beyond.

LOCATION AND ENVIRONMENT

All of the best residential liberal arts colleges strive to be true learning communities like Ripon. We succeed better than most because our enrollment of just over 1,000 students is perfect for fostering connections inside and outside the classroom. Our students flourish in this environment of mutual respect, where shared values are elevated and diverse ideas are valued. If you are seeking academic challenge and want to benefit from an environment of personal attention and support then you should take a closer look at Ripon.

In classes that average 20 students, your professors are able to know you, your strengths, and your capabilities extraordinarily well. They'll tailor your course work to make sure you're always challenged to perform at the top of your game. Yet they're always ready to provide extra support when you need it. Faculty collaborate with you on research projects, suggest independent study topics, and connect you with internships and other active learning experiences.

OFF-CAMPUS OPPORTUNITIES

U.S. or abroad? Three weeks, one semester, two semesters? We offer you more than 40 different programs to choose from, each one officially sanctioned by and affiliated with Ripon. Although most programs are connected with a major or minor program, all are open to every Ripon student, regardless of major.

U.S. Programs: Chicago Urban Studies Semester; Fisk University-Ripon Exchange Program; Newberry Seminar in the Humanities; Oak Ridge Science Semester; Washington Semester; Woods Hole Marine Biology.

International Programs: Budapest Semester; Central European Studies Program in the Czech Republic; Cost Rica; Cross-Cultural Study Center in Seville, Spain; Florence Program; France and Spain; Bonn, Germany Program; Global Studies Program in Turkey; India Studies; Japan Study; London and Florence Program in the Arts; Madrid Program; Montpellier, France; Paris, France; Ripon and York St. John Exchange; Russia Program; Sea Semester at Woods Hole; Swansea Program; Tanzania; Toledo, Spain; University of Wales in Bangor; Sea Education Association (marine biology abroad).

MAJORS AND DEGREES OFFERED

Majors include anthropology, art, art history, biology, business administration, chemistry, chemistry/biology, communication, computer science, economics, educational studies, English, environmental sciences, exercise science, foreign languages, French, German, global studies, history, Latin American area studies, mathematics, music, philosophy, physics, politics and government, psychobiology, psychology, religion, sociology/anthropology, Spanish, theater.

Pre-professional programs include dentistry, journalism, law and government, library and information science, medicine, ministry, optometry, physical therapy, veterinary medicine.

Dual-degree programs include engineering, forestry, allied health sciences/medical technology, and social welfare.

Certification programs include education certification, early childhood, elementary, elementary/middle school, secondary, secondary/middle, music K–12, and physical education K–12.

Programs are also available in leadership studies, women's studies, Army ROTC, and sports medicine/athletic training.

ACADEMIC PROGRAMS

Ripon's liberal arts curriculum is designed to introduce you to a wide variety of disciplines. About 40 percent of our students complete double or triple majors, while some create special self-designed majors. Excellent communications skills written and oral as well as critical-thinking and problem-solving skills, are the hallmark of a Ripon education, no matter what your major. In addition, our leadership studies program and our newly established ethical leadership program provide a strong foundation for leadership skills.

A Ripon education will take you anywhere! You could study psychology and play basketball at Ripon, and then become a five-time Grammy winner like jazz singer Al Jarreau (1962). You could guide the space shuttle into orbit like Jeff Bantle (1980), a chief flight director with NASA, or become an international opera star like Gail Dobish (1976). Perhaps you'll set records in medical science like neonatologist Dr. John Muraskas (1978), who is on record for saving the world's smallest premature baby, or cover world events, like Richard Threlkeld (1959), former Moscow correspondent for CBS News. Or perhaps you'll end up in Donald Trump's inner circle like Ashley Cooper (1982), a senior manager of Trump National Golf Club who has served as an advisor to The Donald on "The Apprentice."

CAMPUS FACILITIES AND EQUIPMENT

Located on 250 tree-lined, rolling acres adjacent to downtown Ripon, the campus looks and feels like a college should. Ripon's 25 first-rate buildings are a striking combination of historic (10 campus structures listed on the national register of historic buildings) and modern architecture. Constant improvements, like a new apartment-style residence hall, a multimillion dollar renovation of one of our main classroom buildings, upgrades to the student union, the campus bookstore, our dining facilities, and numerous student activity spaces maintain Ripon's ability to meet the needs of today and tomorrow.

Technology services include high-speed Internet and e-mail, telephone, and video communication. Intranet and Internet services are accessible from systems located throughout the college. Our campus wide network provides access from every room, and several wireless "hot-spots" in key areas let you access the world without tying you down.

Our science labs contain a variety of high-tech instruments, including a 300-Mhz FTNMR Spectrometer, spectrophotometers, an X-ray diffraction instrument, chromatographs, a spectrofluorimeter, modern electroanalytical instrumentation, a HeliumCadmium Laser Lab, transmission and scanning electron microscopes, a super-speed refrigerated centrifuge, a Zeiss universal microscope with digitizing tablet and two Nikon diaphot inverted microscopes. Ripon also houses a small planetarium classroom, but since research is not limited to the lab, Ripon's Ceresco Prairie Conservancy provides the ultimate outdoor classroom—a 130-acre area natural prairie ecosystem where students can not only study science but also become involved in service learning through prairie restoration.

The library staff provides friendly, efficient circulation, reference, instruction, and interlibrary loan services that aid in research. The library also houses the college archives, a computer lab, and more than a dozen online databases. Library holdings include 164,000 volumes, 800 current periodicals, and microfilms.

The C.J. Rodman Center for the Arts is home to a theater with a state-of-the-art computerized lighting system, a recital hall with one of only 50 existing Bedient organs, an art gallery, and a sculpture garden.

The J.M. Storzer Center includes an Olympic-size pool, a first-class gymnasium, tennis and racquetball courts, a dance studio, training facilities, and a weight room. Our outdoor playing fields and courts are the best in their class. In addition, a large, modern exercise facility was recently added in the main student residence area.

TUITION, ROOM, BOARD AND FEES

Ripon is one of just 81 colleges and universities in the country recognized as a Best Value by The Princeton Review in the 2008 edition of *America's Best Value Colleges*. Nearly 100 percent of Ripon students receive some form of merit-based scholarship and/or need-based grants and loans.

Tuition is $23,970, room and board is $6,770, and fees are $275, for a total cost of $31,015.

FINANCIAL AID

We recognize and reward your success in high school with Ripon's institutionally funded scholarships, based not only on academic merit, but also on special achievements in other areas such as the creative arts. Our scholarships range from $1,000 to full tuition. Ripon participates in all federal and state need-based financial aid programs. Our financial aid counselors will work individually with you and your family to investigate every possible financial resource for which you are eligible.

STUDENT ORGANIZATIONS AND ACTIVITIES

The list of student clubs and organizations is ever-changing, reflecting our students' ever-changing interests. A recent addition is FUERZA Alliance, designed to educate students about Latino cultures and to provide services to the Spanish-speaking community of Ripon. Student initiated and sponsored club sports include Rugby and Lacrosse. These competitive teams travel throughout the Midwest.

Every day at Ripon is packed with a host of activities that include: Concerts we have eight vocal and instrumental groups that perform regularly on campus, as well as many individual student and faculty recitals. The Caestecker Fine Arts Series and the Chamber Music at Ripon Series annually bring national performers to campus. The Ethical Leadership Program sponsors an annual ethics conference which included nationally-known personalities Tim Russert, Miles Brand, and Bud Selig. The Theatre Department sponsors two major productions annually, plus a series of student-directed one-acts. Our most recent Ripon Film Festival (an annual showcase for independent films from around the country) included the premiere of a feature-length horror film written, directed by, and starring a Ripon student.

Ripon's NCAA Division III Intercollegiate Teams compete in the Midwest Conference.

Men's varsity sports: baseball, basketball, cross-country, cycling, football, golf, soccer, swimming and diving, tennis, and indoor and outdoor track and field.

Women's varsity sports: basketball, cross-country, cycling, golf, soccer, softball, swimming and diving, tennis, indoor and outdoor track and field.

ADMISSIONS PROCESS

Ripon enrolls students who will contribute to and benefit from the academic and residential programs we provide. Ripon does not discriminate on the basis of gender, sexual orientation, race, color, age, religion, national and ethnic origin, or disability in the administration of its educational policies, admission practices, scholarship and loan programs, athletic, and other college-administered programs.

The faculty committee on academic standards establishes the criteria for admission. The school considers a variety of factors, including secondary school record, standardized test scores (SAT or ACT), recommendations, a written essay, and extracurricular or community service activities. Ripon's admission process reflects the personal attention students can expect to receive during their college careers, and applicants are encouraged to provide any additional information that they consider helpful.

For more information contact:

Admission Office
Ripon College
300 Seward Street
PO Box 248
Ripon, WI 54971
Telephone: 800-947-4766
E-mail: adminfo@ripon.edu

ROBERT MORRIS UNIVERSITY (IL)

AT A GLANCE

Robert Morris University is an independent, not-for-profit, multi-campus institution offering associate, baccalaureate, and graduate degree programs that focus on integrating theory, concepts, and applications. Robert Morris University prepares students to be practitioners in their chosen fields, socially responsible to their communities, and foundations for their families. Robert Morris University is accredited by the Higher Learning Commission and is a member of the North Central Association, 30 North LaSalle Street, Suite 2400, Chicago, Illinois 60602, and (312) 263-0456.

With over a 90-year history of excellence, Robert Morris University offers professional, career-focused education in a collegiate setting to diverse communities. Through the teaching and learning process, students achieve intellectual, personal and cultural growth. Robert Morris University is dedicated to providing opportunities for academically capable students from diverse backgrounds the competencies necessary for entry into and advancement within career fields.

Robert Morris University is a member of the National Association of Intercollegiate Athletics (NAIA) and the Chicagoland Collegiate Athletic Conference (CCAC), Division II. The University offers men's and women's basketball, cross-country, golf, soccer, volleyball and hockey, as well as women's cheerleading, dance, lacrosse, rowing, swimming, tennis, track and softball.

LOCATION AND ENVIRONMENT

Chicago Campus, 401 S. State Street, Chicago, IL 60605

Located across the street from the renowned Harold Washington Public Library in the heart of the city's bustling cultural and financial districts. Minutes away from museums, the lakefront, sports arenas, theaters, and all forms of public transportation.

Housing is available for out-of-state students attending RMU's Chicago Campus. The University Center and Fornelli Hall's housing options is centrally located in Chicago, just steps away from theaters, concert halls, retailers, restaurants, and art galleries as well as Chicago's beautiful Lake Michigan, famous skyline, and expansive parks. Both locations are sure to provide students with an exciting residential environment in a stimulating urban setting.

DuPage Campus, 905 Meridian Lake Drive, Aurora, IL 60504

50,000 square feet in a new modern building in Meridian Lakes Business Park in Aurora. This is in a community that is accessible, convenient, in a great location and close to the Metra. Enjoy what the City of Aurora has to offer: great history, the Fox Valley mall, outstanding golf courses and many restaurants.

Lake County Campus, 1507 Waukegan Road, Waukegan, IL 60085

Located in the northern Chicago suburb of Waukegan. New, modern facilities with a unique, open-space design. Featuring hi-tech computer labs and an expanded library.

Bensenville Campus, 1000 Tower Lane, Bensenville, IL 60106

Surrounding areas has an ever-increasing demand for qualified employees in business and computer technology. Convenient commuter campus with easy access to expressways.

Elgin Campus, 1707 North Randall Road, Suite 170, Elgin, IL 60123

Located in the Fisher Nut Building in Chicago suburb of Elgin. New, modern facilities for students pursuing a Bachelor's of Business Administration Degree.

Orland Park Campus, 82 Orland Square, Orland Park, IL 60462

Recently named one of the most livable cities in the country. Near golf courses, parks, trails, and the Orland Square Mall. Beautiful two-building campus features over 65,000 square feet, including student lounge, outdoor atrium and a newly completed Technology Center.

Peoria Campus, 211 Fulton Street, Peoria, IL 61602

Strengthens RMC's commitment to serving central Illinois. Located in a modern office building in the heart of Peoria's business district. Offering the latest technological facilities in education.

Schaumburg Campus, 1000 East Woodfield Road, Schaumburg, IL 60173

Convenient location in this bustling Chicago suburb offers Master's Degree courses. Located near Woodfield mall, this location offers day and evening courses for students wishing to obtain a Master's Degree.

Springfield Campus, 3101 Montvale Drive, Springfield, IL 62704

Ideally situated in Abraham Lincoln's hometown and the Illinois state capital. Offers plenty of opportunities for historic, cultural and recreational activities as well as access to a thriving business district.

OFF-CAMPUS OPPORTUNITIES

Housing is available for out-of-state students attending RMU's Chicago Campus. Both the Fornelli Hall and University Center housing options are centrally located in Chicago, just steps away from theaters, concert halls, retailers, restaurants, and art galleries as well as Chicago's beautiful Lake Michigan, famous skyline, and expansive parks. 320 North Michigan is sure to provide students with an exciting residential environment in a stimulating urban setting.

MAJORS AND DEGREES OFFERED

Our career-focused degrees are designed to prepare you for the most in-demand jobs in the fastest growing industries. Our caring faculty members—many of whom are active professionals in their fields—will give you all the support you need to succeed. And you can complete your bachelor's degree in as little as three years or a graduate degree in as little as 18 months.

ACADEMIC PROGRAMS

Master's Degrees

- Master of Business Administration

Concentrations in: Accounting; Accounting/Finance; Human Resource Management; Management; Management/Finance

- Master of Information Systems

Dual Degree Program

- Bachelor's and Master's Degree Advantage

Bachelor's Degrees

- Bachelor of Business Administration Degree

Concentrations in: Accounting; Health/Fitness Management; Hospitality Management; Management

- Dual Degree Program
- Bachelor of Applied Science Degree in Computer Studies

Networking

- Bachelor of Applied Science Degree in Graphic Design
- Bachelor of Professional Studies Degree

Concentrations in: Architectural Technology; Law Office Administration; Advanced Culinary Arts; Applied Health Sciences ; Associate Degrees

- Business Administration
- CAD/Drafting (Architectural/Mechanical)
- Computer Network Specialist
- Culinary Arts
- Fitness & Exercise
- Graphic Design
- Interior Space Planning & Design
- Medical Assisting
- Nursing
- Paralegal
- Pharmacy Technology
- Surgical Technology

The Princeton Review's Complete Book of Colleges

TUITION, ROOM, BOARD AND FEES

Can I afford RMU? Definitely. Robert Morris University is an affordable investment in your future. In fact, once you're admitted to the University, you may be eligible to apply for a variety of financial aid programs to help you pay for the cost of your education. In 2008–2009, RMU awarded more than $20 million in scholarships to our students.

2010-2011°

All fees on a per quarter basis

Full-Time: $6,700

Full-time tuition covers all credit course enrollments except an overload. All students taking 12, 16, 20, or 24 quarter hours per quarter will be charged the full-time tuition. Any student given permission by the Director of Education to take more than 24 hours will be charged extra for the additional courses.

Tuition is assessed each term based on enrolled hours on the day representing the official census for verification of enrollment. No tuition adjustment is done for repeated, incomplete, or failed coursework previously charged.

Part-Time (6 - 11 Credit Hours): $4,466

Less-Than-Part-Time Study (Less than 6 Credit Hours): $2,233

Graduate Tuition Rate Per Course: $2200

School of Computer Studies Fee (per quarter)°° $360

Institute of Art and Design Fee(per quarter)°°$250

School of Health Studies - Medical Assisting Fee (per quarter)°° $100

School of Health Studies - Surgical Technician Fee(per quarter)°° $950

School of Health Studies - Nursing Fee (per quarter)°° $950

Institute of Culinary Arts Fee (per quarter)°° $900

Housing Rates

Chicago - Fornelli Hall $2700

Chicago - University Center $4000 (including meal plan)

Study Abroad Fees

10 week programs $4700

6 week programs $2600

Program Deposit Fees (on student account)

Surgical Technology Program Deposit $200

Nursing Program Deposit $200

Security Deposit Fees (held in reserve)

Housing Security Deposit $300

Study Abroad Security Deposit $300

Application Fee $30

(Payable with all applications for admission and non-refundable.)

° 2010–2011 Tuition will be effective as of July 1, 2010.

FINANCIAL AID

There are many ways to finance an education. At Robert Morris University, we look for them all. An admissions representative will help you complete the financial aid forms and explore the many scholarship opportunities available. When your forms have been processed, you will also learn what grants and loans may be available, as well as how a part-time job can help. We know how important getting a degree can be for your future – how spending some money today can lead to a great salary tomorrow. At Robert Morris University, you have many options. Let us show you.

STUDENT ORGANIZATIONS AND ACTIVITIES

College should be more than time spent in a classroom. At Robert Morris University there are plenty of opportunities to experience growth beyond the classroom and have fun. Student life at our seven campuses helps to create a community of students. You can join one of our many clubs or student organizations from the accounting club to the soccer club. Share your interests, network, learn about future careers and bond with other students. Participate in your favorite sport or root for one of our many sports teams. Work out at the fitness center or just relax and enjoy a cup of coffee at the café. Enjoy the college experience and be a part of a dynamic campus community.

ADMISSIONS PROCESS

We'll base our admission decision on a review of your academic record and professional experience. Throughout the process, we'll consider you as an individual. In order to do that, we'll need the information listed below, though these requirements may change if you're an adult, transfer, returning, international student, or have been home-schooled.

General Admission Requirements

High school diploma, college coursework, or GED score

Work or community service experience

Standardized examination results

Demonstrated character necessary for success in college

Nursing and Surgical Technology Students

Nursing students must possess a high school GPA of 2.5 or higher, an ACT score of 21 or higher and successful completion of algebra, biology and chemistry within previous 5 years.

Surgical Technology students must possess a high school GPA of 2.5 or higher and an ACT score of 18 or higher.

International Students

No matter how you say it, we know you will feel welcome at Robert Morris University, where we help your dreams become a reality. The following information will assist you in applying for a student visa to our college. Please note that all documents must be submitted at the same time.

Admissions application ($100 application fee, non-refundable)

TOEFL documentation with a minimum score of 500 paper based, 173 computer based, or 61 internet based (the TOEFL code for Robert Morris University is 1670).

An evaluation of your high school and any college transcripts stating you have the equivalent of a U.S. high school diploma. An official evaluation may be obtained through WES, ECE or AACRAO.

Copy of valid passport

Copy of current I-20, if applicable. This is necessary only if transferring from another U.S. college or high school. A copy of the I-20 from the previous school must be provided along with the official college or high school transcript.

Current bank statement (original copy) indicating a minimum balance of $42,000 (U.S.).

Permanent foreign address of student

Once all required documentation° has been received and is accurate, it will be evaluated for admissions requirements and I-20 eligibility. This process can take up to two weeks after all required documents are received.

Home-Schooled Students

If you were home-schooled, you must submit a transcript of classes, curriculum documentation and state certification. In addition, you must take a nationally standardized examination to demonstrate an achievement level acceptable to the University.

ROCHESTER INSTITUTE OF TECHNOLOGY

AT A GLANCE

RIT is one of the world's leading career-oriented, technological universities. At RIT, some of the world's most talented, ambitious, and creative students find a remarkable array of academic programs; diverse, talented and accessible faculty; an unusual emphasis on experiential learning; and a vibrant, connected community that is home to students from more than 100 countries. RIT's eight colleges offer more than 90 undergraduate programs in areas such as engineering, computing, information technology, engineering technology, business, hospitality, art, design, science, psychology, public policy, game design and development and biomedical sciences. Regardless of background or academic interest, students find that RIT offers a stimulating environment for intellectual and personal growth.

ACADEMICS

Regardless of background or academic interest, students find that RIT offers an innovative and creative environment for intellectual and personal growth. RIT's eight colleges offer more than 90 undergraduate programs in areas such as engineering, computing, information technology, engineering technology, business, hospitality, art, design, science, psychology, public policy, game design and development and biomedical sciences. To complement their specialized field of study, students select from more than 90 minors available at RIT. Students can also complete a master's degree in five years through one of the university's accelerated BS/MS or BS/MBA programs. Other academic enrichments include an Honors program, study abroad, undergraduate research, internships, cooperative education, and double majors.

ADMISSIONS

RIT seeks a diverse and multicultural student body. Entering students come from a variety of geographic, social, cultural, economic, and ethnic backgrounds. Admission to RIT is competitive, but the admission process is a personal one. The university is interested in learning about students' interests, abilities, and goals in order to provide the best information and guidance as they select the college that is right for them. Students applying for freshman admission for the fall quarter (September) may apply through an Early Decision Plan or Regular Decision Plan. The Early Decision Plan is designed for students who consider RIT their first-choice college and wish to make an early commitment regarding admission. Early Decision requires that candidates file their applications and supporting documents by December 1 in order to receive admission notification by January 15. Freshmen who choose not to apply for Early Decision are considered under our Regular Decision Plan. Regular Decision applicants who have provided all required application materials by February 1 will receive admission notification by March 15. Applications received after February 1 will be reviewed on a space-available basis, with notification letters mailed four to six weeks after the application is complete. Students interested in being considered for merit-based (academic and extracurricular) scholarships or the RIT Honors program must apply by February 1. All applications for transfer admission are reviewed as they are received, and notification letters are mailed four to six weeks after the application is complete. Factors considered in our admission decisions include, but are not limited to, past high school and/or college performance (particularly in required academic subjects), admission test scores, competitiveness of high school or previous college, and academic program selected. Recommendations from those familiar with your academic performance and interviews with admissions counselors are often influential. Most students applying to RIT choose a specific academic program as part of the admission process. This is important because there are a variety of academic programs, and admission requirements may differ from one program to another. For example, a student applying for admission to our computer science program would present a strong academic record with particular strength in mathematics, while a student applying for a fine art or design major would need to show artistic talent through a required portfolio. For students who wish to explore their options before declaring a major, RIT offers the following undeclared options: University Studies (for students wishing to explore programs in two or more colleges); Undeclared Art & Design; Undeclared Business; Undeclared Crafts; Engineering Exploration; Liberal Arts Exploration; and General Science Exploration.

CAMPUS FACILITIES AND EQUIPMENT

The campus is filled with the latest equipment, software, laboratories, and conveniences to give students the tools they need to excel. RIT offers academic facilities that are rarely matched on other university campuses, and students use the latest technology to solve problems creatively. RIT plays leadership role in academic computing and gives students maximum access to research and information resources via two OC3 connections to the Internet, 20,000 network connections, and an eight-million-foot fiber-optic backbone. RIT is one of a select group of universities with access to the Internet 2 research network.

CAMPUS LIFE

Clubs and Organizations exist to bring students of similar interest together and provide them with opportunities to become effective leaders. These groups enhance the quality of student life by fostering social interaction, leadership development, school spirit and an affinity to RIT. Clubs and Organizations promote activities, diversity, service and learning outside of the classroom. Currently there are approximately 200 active clubs, 10 Major Student Organizations, and 29 Greek Organizations on campus.

COLLEGE BASICS

As one of the world's leading career-oriented, technological universities, RIT's goal is to prepare students for 21st century career success.

LOCATION AND ENVIRONMENT

RIT's 1,300-acre campus is located in the suburbs, about six miles from downtown Rochester, NY. More than 6,800 diverse, creative, ambitious students live on campus in residence halls or apartments, and the self-contained, suburban location gives the campus a safe, residential atmosphere. RIT also maintains campuses in Croatia, Dubai, and Kosovo.

MAJORS AND DEGREES

Few universities provide RIT's variety of career-oriented programs. Our eight colleges offer more than 90 bachelor's degree programs in art and design, business, engineering, science and mathematics, criminal justice, photography, film, environmental studies, hospitality and service management, computer science, information technology, bioinformatics urban studies, advertising and public relations and many more.

OFF CAMPUS OPPORTUNITIES

Rochester provides a perfect setting—it's large enough to provide the dining, shopping, and night life opportunities found in a bigger city, yet small and friendly enough to be inviting and accessible. In fact, Rochester was ranked 10th best among large cities in the Northeast in a recent Money magazine Best Places to Live in America survey. The greater Rochester area is home to more than 1 million people, making it the third-largest metropolitan area in New York State. Rochester's reputation as an active and inventive community is supported by extensive cultural and intellectual opportunities.

TUITION AND FEES

For 2009–10, tuition and fees cost $28,866; room and board averaged $9,642; and books, transportation, and other expenses averaged $1,925.

FINANCIAL AID

RIT's Office of Financial Aid and Scholarships assists students and their families in identifying sources of financial aid to help meet the cost of a quality education. Currently, more than 12,000 RIT undergraduate and graduate students receive over $243 million dollars in financial assistance from federal, state, and institutional resources, in the form of scholarships, grants, loans, and part-time employment.

ROCKFORD COLLEGE

AT A GLANCE

For more than 160 years, Rockford College has provided a quality four-year education for students from around the region and around the world. Located on Rockford's eastside, the College has a beautiful 130-acre wooded campus. It's not unusual to see students hanging out or studying outside when the weather is nice, or squirrels, turkeys and other wildlife scampering about.

Rockford College is Rockford's only comprehensive four-year college. With more than 70 majors, minors and concentrations to choose from, a return-to-college adult accelerated bachelor's program, as well as master's programs in business and teaching, we're bound to have what you're looking for in a liberal arts college. Sciences, social sciences, English, languages, business, education, performing arts, and more, it's here, being taught by a renowned faculty. And the learning doesn't stop in the classroom. Community-based learning is an important part of the learning experience so many courses offer opportunities to put legs on what you've learned in the classroom. Practical experiences and internships provide students with hands-on learning and networking opportunities.

At Rockford College, we believe it is important to change our own world and the lives of those around us, so there are more than enough opportunities to get involved inside and outside the campus community. Make your voice heard in student government, prepare a dish for the International Food Fair or display your leadership skills in over 25 academic clubs and organizations. You can also join the group of students that spend each spring break building homes for Habitat for Humanity in Starkville, Miss., work with Maya's House or the Rockford Rescue Mission, encourage others to vote, and more. It's your right (and responsibility) to be as active as you possibly can be.

What about athletics? Our students pour their hearts and souls into their competitions. Sure, they like to win (and they do), but they also know that varsity sports allow them to showcase their leadership skills, improve their physical prowess and boost their team-building talents. Rockford College is a fierce competitor in the NCAA Division III.

Opportunities abound at Rockford College, but we can't tell you about all of them. See for yourself: check out an upcoming Visit Day or schedule a personal visit. We can't wait to share our story because it's changed our world.

Think. Act. Change your world.

LOCATION AND ENVIRONMENT

The city of Rockford is one of Illinois' major cities. Within a few miles of campus, there are numerous restaurants, theatres, clubs, coffeehouses, museums, gardens and galleries.

Rockford even has pro and semi-pro sports—AHL hockey, baseball and football—and so many fairways that *Golf Digest* calls Rockford one of the best mid-size cities for golf.

We're just 90 minutes away from Chicago, Madison and Milwaukee. That means triple the job, internship and entertainment opportunities.

OFF-CAMPUS OPPORTUNITIES

A variety of internships are available. Study abroad around the world or visit Regent's College, located in the heart of London, England. If you prefer a trip in the United States, Rockford College participates in the Washington semester.

MAJORS AND DEGREES OFFERED

Rockford College offers undergraduate degrees in Accounting, Anthropology and Sociology (concentrations in Criminal Justice and Social Work), Art (concentrations in studio arts such as Ceramics, Drawing, Painting, Photography, Printmaking and Sculpture, as well as Graphic Design), Art History, Biochemistry, Biology, Business Administration (Management Track and Marketing Track), Chemistry, Classics, Computer Science (Management Information Systems), Economics (Finance Track, International Economics Track, Public Policy Track), Elementary Education, English, French (Literature and Culture Track, International Studies Track), History, Humanities, International Studies, Latin, Mathematics, Music, Musical Theatre Performance, Nursing (Basic BSN Track, BSN Completion Track), Philosophy, Physical Education (Sports Management, Teaching Track), Political Science, Psychology, Romance Languages, Science and Mathematics, Social Sciences, Spanish (Literature Track, Language and Culture Track, International Studies Track), Special Education and Theatre Arts.

In addition, Rockford offers meticulously designed pre-professional programs for those interested in health professions: (Pre-Dentistry, Pre-Medicine, Pre-Pharmacy, Pre-Veterinary Medicine), Pre-Law and Pre-Social Work.

Rockford College students may also minor in any of the following areas: Ancient and Medieval Studies, Classical Civilization, Coaching, Communications, Greek, Human Development, Peace and Conflict Studies, Physics, Religious Studies and Secondary Education (6-12).

ACADEMIC PROGRAMS

More than anything else, a Rockford College education is <u>practical</u>. By the time you graduate, you'll be well prepared to take your place as a citizen and a leader. You can change the world.

The liberal arts curriculum requires both broad-based learning and concentration in a major area. To graduate, students must complete a minimum of 124 credit hours. Rockford College operates on a two-semester calendar and also offers summer courses. The college admits academically strong students to its Honors Program in Liberal Arts, whose extensive core curriculum and thorough distribution requirements place particular emphasis on the humanities. Students must apply separately for admission to the Honors Program. All students may participate in the Forum Series, which focuses on great ideas, significant scholars and influential artists. Rockford College hosts a chapter of Phi Beta Kappa as well as other scholastic honor societies.

CAMPUS FACILITIES AND EQUIPMENT

Once you pass through our gates, the first thing you will see will be our 1,000-seat Sam Greeley Field. Next, you will come to The Jane Addams International Peace Garden.

Rockford College students can enjoy Internet access in every room, nice-sized rooms (singles and doubles), lounges with big screen televisions and plenty of friends from all over.

Thanks to our campus-wide high-speed wireless network, students can surf the Internet from just about any place on campus—indoors or out. The wooded, rolling hills surrounding our campus are home to not just students, but also to wildlife. Our dining room offers food for everyone, including fresh baked breads, homemade soups, a deli and a salad bar, ethnic favorites and, of course, desserts. If you're visiting as a prospective student, lunch is on us!

Our major academic buildings include the Howard Colman Library (170,000 bound volumes, over 800 periodical subscriptions). Starr Science Building is home to the science departments. The facility includes biology and psychology teaching and research laboratories, chemistry laboratories (teaching and research) with a well-equipped instrumentation lab and nursing laboratories.

Clark Arts Center is home to the fine and performing arts programs. The facility includes 570-seat Maddox Theatre equipped with high-tech lighting and sound equipment; an experimental theater; sculpture garden; art studios, including those for ceramics, lithography and printmaking; an art gallery; a darkroom and performance and practice space for music and dance.

Seaver Physical Education Building houses a pool, a basketball court, a fitness center, a training room, a free-weight room, locker rooms and classrooms.

Free tutoring is available at the Rockford College Learning Center in the Starr Science Building. A student lounge, classrooms and faculty offices are located in Scarborough Hall.

TUITION, ROOM, BOARD AND FEES

Academic year 2009–2010 tuition is $24,250. A double occupancy room costs $3,850 per year. Board plans vary. Students should expect to spend about $1,200 per year on books and $3,250 on additional expenses (transportation, discretionary spending, and other expenses).

FINANCIAL AID

Rockford College awards financial aid on the basis of financial need and academic achievement.

Students must enroll in a minimum of 6 credit hours per semester to be eligible for aid. Rockford College uses the Free Application for Federal Student Aid (FAFSA) to determine need and to award need-based aid, which includes college grants and loans and state and federal aid programs. Students are encouraged to submit aid applications by March 1. Students remain eligible for Rockford College aid when they study at Regent's College in London.

Presidential Scholarships are awarded each fall to new first-year and new transfer students who attend full-time. All recipients must live on campus and become active participants in campus life. The Presidential Scholarships are highly competitive and are limited to 10 recipients per year. Award amounts reach up to $20,000.

Criteria are as follows:

First-Year Students

- 3.50 minimum GPA
- 27 minimum ACT/SAT equivalent

Transfer Students

- 3.50 minimum GPA
- 30 completed college credits

Trustee Scholarships are awarded each fall to new first-year and new transfer students who attend full-time. The Trustee Scholarships are competitive and limited to 25 recipients per year. Award amounts reach up to $15,000.

Criteria are as follows:

First-Year Students

- 3.35 minimum GPA
- 25 minimum ACT/SAT equivalent

Transfer Students

- 3.35 minimum GPA
- 12 completed college credits

Qualified students will receive an application for the Presidential or Trustee scholarship from the Office of Admission. The Trustee and Presidential Scholarships are available to Domestic students. GPA is calculated on a 4-point scale.

The deadline to have all Presidential and/or Trustee Scholarship application materials in by is January 31.

Dean's Scholarships are awarded each fall and spring to new first-year and new transfer students who attend full-time. Dean's Scholarships recognize a high level of academic achievement and co-curricular activity involvement. Award amounts reach up to $9,000.

Merit Awards are given each fall and spring to new first-year and new transfer students who attend full-time. Merit Awards recognize strong academic achievement and co-curricular activity involvement. Award amounts reach up to $7,500.

Regent Awards are given each fall and spring to new first-year and new transfer students who attend full-time. Regent Awards are based on academic achievement and co-curricular activity involvement. Award amounts reach up to $5,000.

To apply for the Dean's Scholarship, Merit or Regent Awards, simply apply for admission to Rockford College. These scholarships are available to Domestic and International students.

STUDENT ORGANIZATIONS AND ACTIVITIES

Rockford College offers more than enough opportunities to get involved inside and outside the campus community. Over 25 clubs and organizations await—and if there isn't a club that sparks your interest, start your own!

The Jane Addams Center is a one-stop-shop for information on volunteer and service-related activities. Rake leaves for a good cause, collect diapers for young mothers, encourage community members to vote, or show the world you're a drama queen by helping local kids put on a play. You can do as little or as much as you'd like.

What about athletics? Rockford College is a fierce competitor in the NCAA Division III. If competitive sports aren't for you, join in on intramurals.

ADMISSIONS PROCESS

The Office of Admission considers each application individually with the goal of assessing candidates' potential for academic success at the college. The school looks primarily at an applicant's record of academic and personal achievement, including class rank, GPA, quality of high school curriculum and standardized test scores (ACT or SAT I). Applicants must demonstrate at least a 2.65 (4.0 scale) high school GPA, placement in the top half of their class and minimum standardized test scores of 19 for the ACT or a composite 910 on the SAT. All application files must include official transcripts and standardized test score reports. Students may submit applications any time after the completion of their junior year in high school. Transfer students are assessed based on their college coursework (once they have completed at least 12 hours of college-level study) and must provide transcripts from all colleges and universities they have attended. Transfer students must show a minimum college GPA of 2.3.

An international admissions representative handles all applications from international students. Applicants must submit TOEFL or IELTS-academic scores.

Rockford College admits applicants on a rolling basis; however, there is a fall application deadline of August 1st.

To receive additional information, please contact:

Office of Admission

Blanche Walker Burpee Center

Rockford College

5050 East State Street

Rockford, IL 61108-2393

Telephone: 815-226-4050 or 800-892-2984 (toll free in the U.S. and Canada)

Fax: 815-226-2822

E-mail: RCAdmissions@rockford.edu

Website: www.rockford.edu

ROSEMONT COLLEGE

Starting with you and developing the unique talents of each student is at the heart of a Rosemont education.

AT A GLANCE

Founded in 1921 by the Society of the Holy Child Jesus, Rosemont College is a private, coeducational institution in the Catholic educational tradition that—through close mentoring, excellent academic support, and student life service—focuses on nurturing the strengths of each student.

LOCATION AND ENVIRONMENT

Located on the Main Line, 11 miles west of Philadelphia, on the border of Montgomery and Delaware Counties, Rosemont is situated on 56 acres in a secure historic residential neighborhood.

OFF-CAMPUS OPPORTUNITIES

The greater Philadelphia area is home to 72 other colleges and universities, and more than 250,000 college students, and offers an amazing number of exciting destinations from bike trails to museums to outdoor markets.

MAJORS AND DEGREES OFFERED

Rosemont offers 22 majors allowing students to gain a solid grasp of the subjects that interest them, even if they want to focus on more than one thing. Each program offers an in-depth study of a particular area, as well as privileges at eight nearby colleges and universities.

Majors

- Accounting B.S.
- Biology, B.A.
o Pre-Med track
o Pre-Nursing track
o Pre-dental track
- Business B.S.
- Chemistry, B.A.
o Biochemistry track
- Communication, B.A.
- Economics, B.S
- Education, B.S.
o Elementary Education
o Secondary Education Certification with liberal arts co-major
- English, B.A.
- French, B.A.
- History, B.A.
- History of Art, B.A.
- Humanities B.A.
- International Business B.S.
- Philosophy, B.A.
- Political Science, B.A.
o Pre-Law track
- Psychology, B.A.
- Religious Studies, B.A.
- Social Science, B.A.
- Sociology B.A., B.S.
o Deaf Studies Track
o Forensic Sociology/Criminology
o Applied Sociology/Sociological Practices
- Spanish, B.A.
- Studio Art and Design, B.A., B.F.A
o Studio Art Track
o Graphic Design Track
o Interior Design Track
- Women's Studies, B.A.

Rosemont also offers a number of pre-professional, certification, and special programs.

Special Programs & Dual Degrees

- B.S. in Biology/Health Sciences plus a graduate certificate in Health Care Administration (Three years in the Undergraduate College plus one year in Rosemont's School of Graduate and Professional Studies)

- Nursing program with Villanova University (Transfer to Villanova after sophomore year at Rosemont)

- Dental program with Temple University (Transfer to Temple after junior year at Rosemont)

- B.A. in Psychology plus a Master of Arts in Elementary or Secondary School Counseling with certification (Three years in the Undergraduate College plus two years in Rosemont's Schools of Graduate and Professional Studies)

- B.A. in Psychology plus a Master of Arts in Professional Counseling (Three years in the Undergraduate College plus two and a half years in Rosemont's Schools of Graduate and Professional Studies)

- B.A. in English/Communication plus a Master of Arts in English and Publishing (Three years in the Undergraduate College plus one year in Rosemont's Schools of Graduate and Professional Studies)

- B.A. in English/Communication plus a Master of Arts in English Literature (Three years in the Undergraduate College plus one year in Rosemont's Schools of Graduate and Professional Studies)

- B.A. in English/Communication plus a Master of Fine Arts in Creative Writing (Three years in the Undergraduate College plus one year in Rosemont's Schools of Graduate and Professional Studies)

- B.S. in Business plus an MBA (Three years in the Undergraduate College plus one and a half years in Rosemont's Schools of Graduate and Professional Studies)

- Three-plus-Four Fast Track Medical Program with Drexel University College of Medicine (Enter medical school after three years at Rosemont and prior to receiving your B.A., which will be conferred by Rosemont after your first year of medical school education)

- Early Assurance Medical Program (Four-plus-four) with Drexel University College of Medicine

ACADEMIC PROGRAMS

Rosemont's liberal arts curriculum aims to develop students with open and discerning minds who have the ability to make reasoned, moral decisions. Faculty members deeply involved in and committed to each student's success, bring a wealth of real-world experience to the classroom.

Students can personalize their Rosemont education to make the most of who they are—emphasizing their strengths and remaining connected to what they want to do. At every step, students benefit from close attention and mentorship from professors who know the student as an individual. Students are here to gather knowledge and skills that will prepare them for a successful career and a rich, rewarding life. They will gain a solid understanding of their major by combining things they learn in class with internships, field placement, and study abroad. Or they can get a head start on their graduate studies through a dual-degree program.

CAMPUS FACILITIES AND EQUIPMENT

Rosemont College's 56-acre campus is comprised of 12 academic, administrative, and residence buildings.

Student Academic Support Center: A comprehensive resource for academic assistance including advising, experiential learning, and learning support services. All services are offered to all students at no cost.

Gertrude Kistler Memorial Library: Home to more than 159,000 volumes, approximately 563 current periodicals, and numerous electronic indexes and databases. The Library has an extensive collection of children's literature and is the home of the Multicultural Resource Center and its collection of over 3,000 multicultural books and resources.

Athletic Facilities: Rosemont's current facilities include a multipurpose grass playing field, six tennis courts, a gymnasium used for basketball and volleyball, and a fitness center which provides aerobic and weightlifting equipment.

TUITION, ROOM, BOARD, AND FEES

Many students and families are surprised to discover how affordable a Rosemont education can be. Tuition for 2009–2010 is $13,115 per semester. The total 2009–10 comprehensive fees (tuition, room, board, and mandatory fees) for a student living on campus is $36,810. Additional personal expenses include books and supplies, transportation, and other personal everyday expenditures.

FINANCIAL AID

Rosemont understand that paying for a college education is a substantial commitment—and an important investment—for our students and their families. The College will work with each student to develop an individualized financial aid package—regardless of financial background.

STUDENT ORGANIZATIONS AND ACTIVITIES

Everybody goes to class—it's how you spend the rest of your time that defines your college experience. The things you do outside of class are a vital part of a student's education. While participating in activities students develop fundamental skills that will serve them for the rest of their life.

Rosemont fields nine varsity sports teams and competes in NCAA Division III's Colonial States Athletic Conference (CSAC).

Men's sports:

- Basketball
- Soccer
- Tennis

Coming soon: Cross Country (2010), Golf (2010), and Lacrosse (2011)

Women's sports:

- Basketball
- Field Hockey
- Lacrosse
- Softball
- Tennis
- Volleyball

Coming soon: Cross Country (2010)

Students pursue their interest and share them with others by contributing to—or leading—Rosemont's 23 student-run clubs, organizations, ensembles, and publications.

Academic Clubs:

- Book Club
- Film Critics Guild
- French Club
- Honors Society
- Italian Club
- Jest and Gesture Society
- Pre-Health Club
- Pre-Law Society

Cultural and Religious Organizations:

- Alliance
- Association of Latin American Students
- Campus Women for Christ
- Harmony
- International Club
- Irish Heritage Society
- Muslim Student Association
- Organization of African American Students

Performance Ensemble:

- Ram Squad (step and dance team)

Publications:

- The Cornelian (yearbook)
- The Rambler (newspaper)
- Thorn (literary magazine)

Student Government:

- Rosemont Activities Council (RAC)
- Rosemont Student-Athlete Advisory Committee (RSAAC)
- Student Government Association

Admissions Process

Rosemont begins reviewing applications for the following academic year in September. There is no early decision date and no application deadline. Students may apply on line (no fee) at www.rosemont.edu/uwc/admissions or call 888.2ROSEMONT or 610.526.966 for an application. Rosemont also accepts the Common Application (www.commonapp.org).

SAINT ANSELM COLLEGE

AT A GLANCE

As a four-year Catholic liberal arts college in the Benedictine tradition, Saint Anselm College seeks to provide an educational experience that promotes your intellectual, spiritual, and personal growth. Saint Anselm College encourages you not only to challenge yourself academically, but also to lead a life that is both creative and generous.

Because democracy depends on active participation of citizens, Saint Anselm College is committed to graduating men and women who view themselves as citizens of their communities and of the world.

ACADEMICS

Students at Saint Anselm College are provided with an outstanding liberal arts education. Students normally take 15+ courses directly related to their major; the remainder of the courses needed to graduate consist of liberal arts core curriculum and a variety of electives. Students in the Honors Program will take honors courses in order to earn their Honors Degree.

Saint Anselm College believes that there are certain things one must know to be an educated person in the 21st century. As freshmen and sophomores, all students take part in Saint Anselm's nationally recognized humanities program. This interdisiplinary program known as "Portraits of Human Greatness" focuses on a series of group seminars, readings and lectures that explore various facets of western civilization.

Saint Anselm College is also home to the New Hampshire Insitute of Politics (NHIOP). The NHIOP is a place where students of all majors interact with world leaders, members of Congress, scholars, jounalists, public policy makers, public officials, and innovators of all types. All Saint Anselm College students will have courses held at the NHIOP. Saint Anselm College is a leader in Civic Engagement and encourages all students to explore what it means to be a citizen in a democratic society.

Saint Anselm takes part in the College Board's Advanced Placement program. Students who earn a score of 3 or greater on most AP examinations may gain credit and advanced placement in the related course of study. Students who have taken examinations through the College-Level Examination Program may be awarded credit and advanced placement if they earn satisfactory scores.

ADMISSIONS

In reviewing applicants to the freshman class, the admissions committee considers each prospective student individually and carefully. The committee assesses each applicant's secondary school performance, SAT or ACT scores, recommendation letters, and the written essay included in the application for admission. Of highest priority is the applicant's secondary school transcript, with a specific focus on both the rigor of course study and the marks received. Saint Anselm invites transfer and international students to apply.

Saint Anselm College has the following admission deadlines:

Early Action, November 15

Nursing Majors, January 15

International Students, February 15

Regular Decision, March 1st

It is highly suggested that all students visit the Saint Anselm College campus for a tour, information session and/or interview.

For more information, students should contact:

Office of Admission

Saint Anselm College

100 Saint Anselm Drive

Manchester, NH 03102-1310

Telephone: 603-641-7500 or 888-426-7356 (toll-free)

Fax: 603-641-7550

Email: admission@anselm.edu

World Wide Web: www.anselm.edu

MAJORS AND DEGREES OFFERED

At Saint Anselm College, students may pursue the Bachelor of Arts degree in the following academic programs and majors: in accounting, biochemistry, biology, business, chemistry, classics, communication, computer science, computer science with business, computer science with mathematics, criminal justice, economics, education (secondary and elementary) English, environmental science, financial economics, fine arts, French, history, international business, international relations, liberal studies in the great books, mathematics, mathematics with economics, natural science, philosophy, physics, politics, psychology, sociology, Spanish, and theology. A program that leads to the Bachelor of Science in Nursing (BSN) degree is also offered at the College.

Saint Anselm students may pursue pre-professional programs in dentistry, law, medicine, and theology.

A 3-2 engineering program is offered in partnership with the University of Notre Dame, University of Massachusetts-Lowell, Catholic University of America, and Manhattan College.

ADMISSIONS

In reviewing applicants to the freshman class, the admissions committee considers each prospective student individually and carefully. The committee assesses each applicant's secondary school performance, SAT I or ACT scores, recommendation letters, and the written essay included in the application for admission. Of highest priority is the applicant's secondary school transcript, with a specific focus on both the rigor of course study and the marks received. Saint Anselm invites transfer and international students to apply. Saint Anselm College has the following admission deadlines: Early Action, November 15th and Regular Decision, March 1st. Nursing majors need to apply on or before January 15th and International Students should apply by Feb. 15th. It is highly suggested that all students visit the Saint Anselm College campus for a tour, information session and/or interview. For more information, students should contact: Office of Admission Saint Anselm College 100 Saint Anselm Drive Manchester, NH 03102-1310 Telephone: 603-641-7500 or 888-426-7356 (toll-free) Fax: 603-641-7550 Email: admission@anselm.edu World Wide Web: www.anselm.edu.

CAMPUS FACILITIES AND EQUIPMENT

Saint Anselm College has over 60 different campus facilities. The John Maurus Carr Activities Center is a versatile recreational area that includes a new three story fitness center as well as racquetball courts. The Davison Hall dining area, open all day long, provides a spacious and pleasant atmosphere in which students enjoy spending time. Additional facilities include the Academic Resource Center, the Cushing Student Center (where students will find career and academic counseling services), health services, the Multicultural Center, the Meelia Center for Community Service, Stoutenburgh Gymnasium (where varsity games are played), Sullivan Ice Arena, and The New Hampshire Institute of Politics -home of the 1st in the nation Presidential Primary and the largest television studio north of Boston.

Saint Anselm residential housing accommodates more than 1,800 students in various living arrangements, from traditional residence halls to suites, townhouses, and apartments. More than 88 percent of students choose to live on campus and enjoy a balance of academic study, rest and relaxation, and social life.

Housing is guaranteed for all four years to students who enter as freshmen. Each residence hall has a staff of student resident assistants (RAs) and a residence director (RD) who assist students and are responsible for maintaining the College's residence hall regulations.

CAMPUS LIFE

Student government helps to create an atmosphere of camaraderie and unity on campus. Saint Anselm's student government consists of three branches: Campus Activities Board, the Class Councils, and the Student Senate. The student government's primary goal is to ensure that all students have as many educational opportunities open to them as possible. Student government coordinates academic, cultural, and social, functions, all of which are essential to a broad liberal arts education.

There are over 80 organizations catering to a wide variety of interests. Among these are the Abbey Players (theater group), choral groups, the debate group, an economics club, a jazz band, a local Knights of Columbus chapter, a music society, an outing club, a pre-law society, a pre-med society, and a the Meelia Center for Community Service.

Saint Anselm offers men's intercollegiate sports in baseball, basketball, cross-country, football, golf, ice hockey, lacrosse, skiing, soccer, and tennis and offers women's sports in basketball, cross-country, field hockey, ice hockey, lacrosse, skiing, soccer, softball, tennis, and volleyball. Intramural sports at the College include basketball, ice hockey, indoor and outdoor soccer, racquetball, softball, tennis, and volleyball. There are men's and women's club sports in Alpine, cycling, ice hockey rugby, ski and snowboard, swimming, synchronized skating and track.

COLLEGE BASICS

Saint Anselm College encourages you not only to challenge yourself academically, but also to lead a life that is both creative and generous. Saint Anselm student are active both in and out of the classroom.

LOCATION AND ENVIRONMENT

Nestled in its breathtaking New Hampshire surroundings, the Saint Anselm campus melds traditional and contemporary architecture to create a beautiful academic environment. Students from 12 countries and 31 states attend the College. Roughly 88 percent of Saint Anselm's students enjoy on-campus housing in apartments, dormitories, suites, and townhouses.

Situated on the outer edge of Manchester, New Hampshire's largest city, Saint Anselm College provides the advantages of a chiefly residential neighborhood in a suburban locale. Manchester has a great deal to offer, including a variety of movie theaters, restaurants, and shopping malls. Furthermore, public transportation runs hourly between Manchester and the campus. Southern New Hampshire provides a perfect atmosphere for students desiring a dynamic college lifestyle. The exciting city of Boston, the majestic mountains, and Hampton Beach on the Atlantic Ocean are all within an hour's drive from campus.

OFF-CAMPUS OPPORTUNITIES

The majority of departments throughout Saint Anselm College offer internship positions to students who wish to apply their classroom knowledge to a real-life work experience. Students normally acquire internship positions as juniors or seniors. Internships are offered in Boston, in and around Manchester, New York City, or in Washington, D.C..

Saint Anselm encourages students to consider spending a year, semester, or summer studying in another country (usually during the junior year). Studying abroad presents an invaluable opportunity to gain a more informed perspective on your world, your country, and yourself.

In recent years, students have studied marine biology on Australia's Great Barrier Reef, art history in the museums of Florence, finance in London, language in Spain and France, and political history in Ireland.

Students' experiences studying abroad often remain the most memorable times of their college careers. In addition to the obvious cultural benefits gained from living abroad, students often make intellectual and personal gains as well. Experience studying abroad is a desirable qualification on your resume.

In lieu of participating in study abroad during the academic year, students can sign up for faculty-led programs which include travel to such destinations as France, Greece, Italy, Mexico, Berlize and Spain during the summer. .

TUITION AND FEES

The 2009–2010 school year tuition is $29,720 and room and board costs are $11,240.

FINANCIAL AID

Saint Anselm provides students with financial aid opportunities through both private and federal aid programs. The College provides financial aid to offset the reasonable monetary investment that the student and family are expected to contribute. 88 percent of the College's undergraduates receive some degree of financial aid. Saint Anselm's financial aid opportunities include grants, loans, scholarships, and employment positions. Merit awards (Presidential Scholarships) are awarded to outstanding students. Two forms are required in applying for aid; the student must submit the CSS/Financial Aid PROFILE and the Free Application for Federal Student Aid (FAFSA) by March 15.

SAINT LOUIS UNIVERSITY

AT A GLANCE

Saint Louis University is a Catholic, Jesuit university ranked among the top research institutions in the nation. SLU fosters the intellectual and character development of 12,733 students on campuses in St. Louis and Madrid, Spain. Founded in 1818, it's the oldest university west of the Mississippi River and the second-oldest Jesuit university in the United States. Through teaching, research, health care and community service, Saint Louis University has provided one-of-a-kind education, leadership and service for 191 years.

SLU's urban, residential campus in St. Louis includes the new $82 million Edward A. Doisy Research Center and $81 million Chaifetz Arena, a new on-campus multipurpose arena and a hub for Billiken sports activity.

With nearly 100 undergraduate programs and more than 50 graduate and professional programs, including highly ranked programs in business, law and engineering, students are sure to find the one that's right for them. Students also can take advantage of special opportunities such as direct-entry nursing and health sciences programs, early admission to the University's medical and law schools and study-abroad programs.

SLU education extends far beyond the classroom.

The University offers students something rare in higher education: the opportunity to study at a place where academic achievement and scientific advancement unite with community commitment and Jesuit values. Here, 99 percent of faculty members hold a Ph.D. or the highest degree in their field. SLU students get to do more than just sit in class; they collaborate with premier scholars and researchers and conduct research that will change the face of their disciplines—and the lives of others.

SLU students come from all 50 states and nearly 90 foreign countries. Six months after graduation, 96 percent of our graduates are either working or in graduate or professional school. SLU alumni have written books and movies, become mayors of major cities, presidents of countries and even worked with Mother Theresa. They are also highly successful doctors, lawyers, physical therapists, engineers and social workers.

Learn more about SLU at slu.edu and beabilliken.com.

LOCATION AND ENVIRONMENT

At Saint Louis University, students are in the center of everything. SLU's campus in Midtown St. Louis stretches across more than 230 acres of flowers, fountains and lush greenery. Students and visitors alike appreciate a "green oasis" in the middle of a bustling city. Get a taste of campus and schedule your own visit at visit.slu.edu.

The St. Louis metro region boasts nearly 3 million people, with more than 350,000 residents in the city itself. The city's small-town feel coupled with the amenities of a large city has helped St. Louis achieve its ranking as one of the best cities for young professionals. The city is home to the famous Gateway Arch, a number of Fortune 500 and Fortune 1000 companies and a variety of cultural, historic and sporting attractions.

Students don't have to travel far from SLU to experience St. Louis. Just steps away from SLU's urban campus is one of the city's esteemed arts districts, rich with theatre and music. Students also can hop onto a light rail train or bus and taste the world at delicious restaurants before hitting St. Louis' can't-miss concert scene. With three professional teams and a bevy of independent teams, St. Louis always is high on any sports fan's list of must-see cities.

But that's not all SLU has to offer. The University expanded internationally in 1969 by establishing a campus in Madrid, Spain. The Madrid campus has been recognized by Spain's higher education authority as an official foreign university, the first United States institution ever so recognized. Each semester, more than 200 students arrive at the Madrid campus for a study-abroad experience. Attracted by the quality educational reputation of the St. Louis and Madrid campuses, more than 250 universities in the United States send study-abroad students to SLU's Madrid campus.

OFF-CAMPUS OPPORTUNITIES

Midtown St. Louis offers access to affordable living as well as the excitement of the Grand Center arts district, the cultural heart of St. Louis. The booming performing arts neighborhood features opportunities for art, theatre, dance and music just steps away from SLU's campus. Don't miss the historic Fox Theatre with some of the most memorable concerts and Broadway shows or the famous St. Louis Symphony Orchestra in Powell Symphony Hall.

Just minutes away by car, bus or light rail train, you can play in Forest Park, the 1904 World's Fair site that's larger than even New York City's Central Park and home to the city's world-class art museum, zoo, science center and history museum. Check out the Delmar Loop, one of the "10 Great Streets in America," or head to "The Hill," a nationally noted neighborhood for authentic Italian cuisine, including St. Louis' famous toasted ravioli. Or go downtown for food and fun – St. Louis is noted for being one of the nation's best sports cities. Residents root for the St. Louis Cardinals baseball team, St. Louis Blues hockey team, St. Louis Rams football team, and a number of independent sports teams. In addition, the Saint Louis University Billikens excite the city with 18 NCAA Division I sports—SLU is St. Louis' only Division I school.

The St. Louis metro region boasts nearly 3 million people, with more than 350,000 residents in the city itself. The city's small-town feel coupled with the amenities of a large city helped St. Louis achieve its ranking as one of the best cities for young professionals.

ACADEMIC PROGRAMS

Saint Louis University offers nearly 90 undergraduate programs of study, more than 50 graduate and professional programs and undergraduate degrees in the following areas:

Doisy College of Health Sciences

Athletic Training °; Clinical Laboratory Science; Cytotechnology; Health Informatics and Health Information Management ; Investigative and Medical Sciences; Nuclear Medicine Technology; Nutrition and Dietetics (Culinary Emphasis); Occupational Science and Occupational Therapy °; Physical Therapy °; Radiation Therapy; Still Deciding (Health Sciences); Health Management

School of Nursing

Nursing

College of Arts and Sciences

American Studies; Art History; Biochemistry; Biology; Chemistry; Classical Humanities; Communication; Communication Sciences and Disorders; Computer Science; Criminal Justice; Economics (B.A.); English; Environmental Science; Environmental Studies; French; Geology; Geophysics; German; Greek and Latin Languages and Literature; History; International Studies; Italian Studies; Latin American Studies; Mathematics; Meteorology; Music; Philosophy; Physics (B.A.); Political Science; Psychology; Russian; Sociology; Spanish; Still Deciding; Studio Art; Theater; Theological Studies; Women's Studies

John Cook School of Business

Business Administration; Accounting; Economics (B.S.); Finance; Information Technology Management; International Business; Management and Entrepreneurship; Marketing; Still Deciding (Business)

Parks College of Engineering, Aviation and Technology

Aerospace Engineering; Aviation Management; Biomedical Engineering; Civil Engineering; Computer Engineering; Electrical Engineering; Engineering Physics; Flight Science ^; Interdisciplinary Engineering; Mechanical Engineering; Still Deciding (Engineering)

College of Education and Public Service

Early Childhood Education; Early Childhood Special Education; Elementary Education; Middle School Education; Secondary Education; Special Education for Mild/Moderate Disabilities; Education (without certification); Urban Affairs; Still Deciding

School of Social Work

Social Work ; Still Deciding

College of Philosophy and Letters

Philosophy; Still Deciding^^

KEY

° A five-year, direct-entry master's degree program.

^ Students are strongly encouraged to apply by December 1 for the Flight Science program.

°° Physical Therapy is a direct-entry doctoral program. Students must apply by December 1 for consideration.

^^For students who are "Still Deciding" but have not yet narrowed their interests to a particular college or school at the University.

Students who are "Still Deciding" but have narrowed their interests to either the College of Arts and Sciences, Doisy College of Health Sciences, John Cook School of Business, College of Education and Public Service or Parks College of Engineering, Aviation and Technology should choose the "Still Deciding" program that corresponds with the appropriate college or school.

For the most up-to-date selection of majors offered, visit slu.edu.

CAMPUS FACILITIES AND EQUIPMENT

Under the leadership of University President Lawrence Biondi, S.J., Saint Louis University has fueled the ongoing renaissance of Midtown St. Louis. Saint Louis University improvements and expansions have totaled approximately $840 million since 1987. The University now stretches across more than 230 acres of flowers, fountains and lush greenery. Visitors often say it's the "nicest city campus in the country."

Saint Louis University recently unveiled the two most significant building projects in its history. The new $82 million Edward A. Doisy Research Center offers SLU's world-class researchers a world-class facility. The $81 million Chaifetz Arena is the now home for Billiken men's and women's basketball, volleyball and hosts concerts, family shows, sporting events, trade shows and other events. The arena complex consists of a 10,600-seat arena, athletics practice facility and offices and support facilities for all Division I sports and the athletic department.

Recent campus additions also include a new 40,000-foot expansion to its Simon Recreation Center and a renovated Busch Student Center. The SLU Laclede Park Recreational Complex includes three lakes, walking paths, a picnic area, waterfall, softball field and recreation fields. The campus is also home to the historic Cupples House, a fully restored mansion built in 1890, as well as several unique art galleries and St. Francis Xavier College Church.

TUITION, ROOM, BOARD AND FEES

Annual tuition for full-time undergraduate students is $30,940. Room and board amounts to approximately $8,760 per student (depending on specific residence hall and board plan). Fees average $450 per year.

FINANCIAL AID

Saint Louis University takes its Jesuit mission seriously. SLU is committed to serving others, in part, by providing financial access to a remarkable education.

For fiscal year 2008, 96 percent of SLU's first-time freshmen received some sort of scholarship or financial assistance, as did 84 percent of all SLU students. More than $249 million in total financial aid was awarded to students at Saint Louis University during the last fiscal year.

Scholarships are awarded based on academic merit, talents, service, leadership and financial need. In addition to SLU financial aid programs, the state of Missouri and the federal government also provide assistance.

Contact SLU's office of scholarship and financial aid at (314) 977-2350, (800) SLU-FOR-U or finaid@slu.edu.

STUDENT ORGANIZATIONS AND ACTIVITIES

Students support more than 140 clubs, honor societies and service organizations; 18 NCAA Division I teams; intramural sports; and community service efforts that engage the SLU community in more than 800,000 volunteer hours in a typical year.

Talent and commitment matter at SLU, and high levels of energy and dedication exist in everything our students pursue: academic societies, athletics, performing arts and media groups, student government, cultural and political organizations, and fraternities and sororities. Students come out in force to support Billiken sports, and the Simon Recreation Center is popular with both serious and more casual athletes. Co-curricular life extends throughout the campus with numerous lectures, films, festivals, concerts and plays.

ADMISSIONS PROCESS

For information about the admission process at Saint Louis University or to schedule a campus visit, call the office of undergraduate admission at (800) SLU-FOR-U, e-mail visitslu@slu.edu, or check out visit.slu.edu.

SAINT MARY'S COLLEGE, NOTRE DAME, IN

Saint Mary's is a four-year Catholic residential, women's institution in the liberal arts tradition, educating women who seek to challenge themselves and their world.

AT A GLANCE

Saint Mary's College ranks among the nation's top 100 liberal arts colleges in the U.S. News & World Report 2010 annual survey. Saint Mary's is a spiritually-based, student-centered college with an enrollment of approximately 1,600 women from 45 states and five countries. Our faculty consists of top scholars who are recognized for excellence in their fields of study. All of our classes are taught by faculty, not teaching assistants. Class sizes average 15 students and there is a student to faculty ratio of 10:1. The College offers five bachelor's degrees in 32 major areas of study and six nationally accredited academic programs: social work, art, music, teacher education, chemistry, and nursing.

Founded in 1844, Saint Mary's is a pioneer in the education of women, and is sponsored by the Sisters of the Holy Cross. Supported by faculty who act as both teachers and mentors, students are exceptionally well prepared for their chosen careers and/or their pursuit of advanced degrees.

LOCATION AND ENVIRONMENT

Saint Mary's is located in Notre Dame, Indiana, just north of South Bend and across the street from the University of Notre Dame. Our suburban campus includes 98 acres of rolling hills, manicured lawns, historic buildings, and state-of-the-art classrooms alongside the Saint Joseph River. Approximately 90 miles east of Chicago, Saint Mary's is easily accessible by car, train (both Amtrak and the South Shore Line commuter train), and air (via the South Bend Regional Airport or Chicago's Midway and O'Hare Airports). Coach USA runs a regional bus service from the Chicago airports to the Notre Dame campus.

The University of Notre Dame expands the opportunities for Saint Mary's students through a co-exchange program. Students can take classes and attend sporting events at Notre Dame, as well as participate in a variety of clubs, sports, activities and organizations such as Notre Dame's marching band, or write for the *Observer*, the daily newspaper published jointly by both colleges.

OFF-CAMPUS OPPORTUNITIES

Saint Mary's College is next to the cities of South Bend and Mishawaka, both of which offer a wide array of shops, restaurants, movie theatres, art galleries, golf courses, parks, and walking and bike paths. South Bend also boasts its own symphony, zoo, art museum, and performing arts center. The beaches of Lake Michigan are less than an hour away, and Chicago and Indianapolis are "day-trips." We invite you to visit the cities of South Bend and Mishawaka Web sites at www.southbendin.gov and www.visitmishawaka.com for more information.

MAJORS AND DEGREES OFFERED

Saint Mary's helps students reach their potential through rigorous academics and a supportive environment. Acknowledging the need to prepare women for an array of careers, our top-ranked liberal arts education gives students a broad, deep foundation of knowledge. They will develop strong quantitative skills, the ability to analyze complex issues, competency in modern languages, and excellent writing and communication skills.

Majors:

Accounting; Art; Biology; Business Administration; Chemistry; Communication Studies; Communicative Disorders; Computational Mathematics; Economics; Elementary Education; English Literature; English Writing; English Literature and Writing; French; History; Humanistic Studies; Italian; Management Information Systems; Mathematics; Music; Music Education; Nursing; Philosophy; Political Science; Psychology; Religious Studies; Social Work; Sociology; Spanish; Statistics and Actuarial Mathematics; Student-Designed major; Theatre

ACADEMIC PROGRAMS

Cross Currents Student Advising

This program guides students to think critically about their place in the world as they determine their career and life goals. The Cross Currents program interweaves established campus growth experiences—such as peer mentoring, career assessment, internship opportunities, and a collegiate speaker series—with career advisement for students as they navigate each academic year.

Dual Degree in Engineering Program at Saint Mary's

In addition to completing a Bachelor of Arts or Bachelor of Science degree from Saint Mary's College in four years, students also earn an engineering degree in chemical, computer science, electrical, environmental geosciences, or mechanical engineering from the University of Notre Dame in their fifth year.

Pre-Professional Studies

Saint Mary's College offers advising designed to assist students preparing for law school, medical, or dental school, and other allied health programs. Articulation agreements are offered for physical and occupational therapy master's programs.

Accelerated Nursing Program

For women with a baccalaureate degree in another major from an accredited college or university, Saint Mary's College offers the Accelerated Option Program in Nursing. The program leads to a Bachelor of Science degree with a major in nursing.

Certificate in Intercultural Leadership

A cornerstone for the Center for Women's Intercultural Leadership (CWIL) at Saint Mary's, this two-three year program integrates classes, retreats, mentoring, and study abroad experiences into an electronic portfolio that can be used to demonstrate acquired leadership skills to graduate schools and future employers.

Student Independent Study and Research (SISTAR)

Saint Mary's College offers students and faculty a unique and extraordinary opportunity to conduct research and engage in creative activity with each other through SISTAR grants. These prestigious awards are given to student-faculty partnerships to support research and study for two months during the summer. The student, usually a rising senior, pursues her research as a junior colleague with the faculty partner. The student's research may complement the faculty member's in a similar area, or the team may share a project.

Study Abroad

Saint Mary's has been placing students in study abroad programs for over 30 years. Approximately 42% of our students take advantage of semester-long, semester-break and summer study abroad and service-learning experiences. We offer eleven international adventures during the academic year and many other short immersion trips during semester and summer break. Study abroad is affordable at Saint Mary's because most of a student's financial aid will apply to our yearlong and semester-long programs. Other means of support are available to qualified students for the semester break and summer programs.

Yearlong and semester-long programs:

Córdoba, Argentina

Innsbruck, Austria

Fremantle, Australia

Dijon, France

Mumbai, India

Maynooth, Ireland

Rome, Italy

Pietermaritzburg, South Africa

Seville, Spain

Seoul, South Korea

Women's Studies in Europe

Semester-break programs:

El Salvador Spring Break

Haiti

Honduras Spring Break

Jamaica

Poland to Prague

Summer programs:

Argentina

China

Ecuador

European Summer Study

France Summer Program

Greece

Honduras

Internship in London, England

Internship in Seville, Spain

South Korea

Spain Summer Program

Uganda Summer Practicum with the Sisters of the Holy Cross

CAMPUS FACILITIES AND EQUIPMENT

Students will find both stately historical buildings such as Le Mans Hall with its iconic bell tower and new and updated academic buildings such as Spes Unica, and the remodeled Madeleva Hall, providing students with the latest in technology. The campus is also home to the Cushwa-Leighton Library and its Huisking Instructional Technology Resource Center, Angela Athletic Facility, and the Student Center. Moreau Center for the Arts houses several theaters and exhibit rooms, such as Little Theatre, Hammes, Sister Rosaire, and Little Theatre Galleries, as well as O'Laughlin Auditorium, the largest venue of its type in the area, seating 1,300. Because Saint Mary's is a residential college, 81 percent of the College's students live on campus in one of five residence halls, which include Opus Hall senior apartments.

TUITION, ROOM, BOARD, AND FEES

Tuition and Fees for the 2010–11 academic year for a resident student:

Tuition: $30,360

Room (Double Room average): 5,840

Board: $3,640

These figures do not include other student expenses such as books, travel, spending money, private music lessons, and other miscellaneous fees.

Tuition charges cover a full-time academic program of 12–18 credit hours per semester. Additional tuition charges may apply if the student enrolls in more than 18 credit hours.

The per credit hour cost for part-time students will be $1,200, and the charge for extra credit hours (above 18/semester) will be $596. Room charges vary according to living arrangements. All fees are subject to change.

FINANCIAL AID

The real cost of college can vary dramatically based on financial aid. Our Financial Aid Office will work with you every step of the way to ensure you receive the optimal award to attend Saint Mary's College. More than 92 percent of Saint Mary's students receive some form of financial aid, totaling more than $35 million in the form of institutional grants, scholarships, loans, and work opportunities. Of these funds, over $18 million are awarded by Saint Mary's College in the form of grants and scholarships. Saint Mary's has also partnered with Nelnet Business Solutions to offer a low-cost payment plan options. For additional information, go to our Web site at saintmarys.edu/pay-bill or contact the Financial Aid Office at (866) 502-7788; email finaid@saintmarys.edu.

STUDENT ORGANIZATIONS AND ACTIVITIES

Students can choose from more than 60 student-led organizations. Saint Mary's is a NCAA Division III school in eight varsity sports including: basketball, cross country, golf, soccer, softball, swimming/diving, tennis, and volleyball. The College offers more than 30 intramural sports.

Students gain real world experience through leadership opportunities, which include the Diverse Students' Leadership Conference, the Saint Mary's Board of Trustees, the Alumnae Board, and in student government. Through the Office for Civic and Social Engagement (OCSE), eighty percent of Saint Mary's College students participate in service by the time they graduate (the national average is 55%). Saint Mary's College has been named to the President's Higher Education Community Service Honor Roll for four years. This is the highest federal recognition a college or university can receive for its commitment to volunteering, service learning, and civic engagement.

ADMISSIONS PROCESS

Early Decision and Application Deadlines

Applicants who meet the November 15 Early Decision application deadline will be notified of their admission decision by December 15. These accepted students receive early notification of merit scholarship and financial assistance, and receive first choice in housing. Acceptance deposit must be submitted by January 15.

Applicants who file and complete their applications by December 1 are notified of their admission status by mid-January. Those submitted between December 1 and February 15 are evaluated within four to six weeks following receipt of all materials. Those submitted after February 15 are admitted as space becomes available.

Application Review

The academic review for the first-year student applicants covers the following criteria:

• GPA in core academic courses, rigor of curricular choices;

• The best combination of scores received on either the SAT or ACT with writing;

• Writing proficiency as evidence by a required essay;

• A personal meeting with an admission counselor is recommended and can be arranged by the Admission Office.

College Preparatory Curriculum Requirements:

Complete a minimum of 16 academic units of college preparatory curriculum that includes:

• Four years of high school English;

• Three years of college prep math;

• Two years of science;

• Two years of social science; history

• Two years of the same foreign language;

• Three years of additional course work in any combination of the above subjects.

HOMESCHOOLED STUDENTS

Saint Mary's reviews transcripts of work completed either through homeschooling or traditional high school and gives greater weight to SAT or ACT scores and the student essay when graded work cannot be presented. Personal interviews are highly recommended for homeschooled students.

INTERNATIONAL STUDENTS

International students must fill out the international application and additional materials by February 15. Saint Mary's offers one four-year, full-tuition scholarship including fees, room, board, and books to one well-qualified and deserving international student. In addition, international students are eligible for merit scholarships and a limited amount of need-based assistance. See our Web site for details at saintmarys.edu/scholarships-international.

ADVANCED STANDING

You can receive college credit and/or exemption from college requirements for the following: College Board SAT Subject Tests, Advance Placement Examinations, the College Level Examination Program (CLEP), higher-level International Baccalaureate (IB); and some dual enrollment programs. Results must be submitted before registration and will be evaluated by the Academic Affairs Office.

Contact our Admission Office at (800) 551-7621 or admission@saintmarys.edu

SAINT MARY'S COLLEGE (MD)

AT A GLANCE

St. Mary's College of Maryland is designated the Honors College of the State of Maryland in recognition of the quality of our students, faculty and curriculum. St. Mary's offers an undergraduate, liberal arts education and small-college experience like those found at exceptional private colleges. Home to approximately 2,000 students, the campus is located on the St. Mary's River in the heart of the Chesapeake region, about 70 miles outside of Washington, D.C.

The school shares the hallmarks of private institutions: an outstanding faculty, talented students, high academic standards, a challenging curriculum, small classes, a sense of community, and a spirit of intellectual inquiry. By combining the virtues of public and private education, St. Mary's provides a unique alternative for students and their families. The special identity underpins the College's success and its reputation for excellence.

In 1992, the Maryland legislature designated this public, coeducational institution the state's honors college. Over 98% of the faculty holds the Ph.D. or other terminal degree and 11 of the current faculty have received Fulbright Awards. Although professors are exceptionally active in research and writing, the faculty's primary interest and central concern is teaching. The College is home to the Zeta Chapter of Phi Beta Kappa.

Small classes, dedicated teachers, and an informal atmosphere encourage faculty and students to share in the intellectual life of the College, both in and out of the classroom. Professors serve as academic advisers, work with students in extracurricular programs, involve students in research, and mentor them in individualized projects.

More than 50% of St. Mary's graduates continue on to graduate school. St. Mary's alumni have distinguished themselves in every academic field and creative pursuit. When the State of Maryland surveys graduates of its public colleges and universities, St. Mary's alumni consistently report higher levels of satisfaction with their education than do alumni of other institutions.

ACADEMICS

St. Mary's offers a wide and diverse variety of majors and minors and a Master of Arts in Teaching (M.A.T.) for certification in early childhood, elementary and secondary education.

St. Mary's also provides students the opportunity to explore cross-disciplinary studies in African and African Diaspora Studies, Asian Studies, Environmental Studies, Museum Studies, Neurosciences, and Women, Gender and Sexuality Studies. Cross-disciplinary studies can increase intellectual community across disciplines, encourage cohesion in the choice of electives, and promote combinations of methods and materials that challenge the boundaries of knowledge.

Many St. Mary's students consider careers in professional fields such as medicine, the law, and business. Our pre-professional programs work with interested students throughout their four years by providing academic advice, career exploration, and help applying to professional programs. These include pre-dentistry, pre-engineering (3-2 program with the University of Maryland at College Park), pre-law, pre-medicine, pre-nursing (3-2 program with Johns Hopkins University), pre-optometry, pre-pharmacy, and pre-veterinary science.

The Paul H. Nitze Scholars Program is designed for highly motivated students with exceptional academic potential and a proven record of leadership and service. Students accepted into this program have more flexibility in curricular choices than other students. As a small cohort of peers, Nitze Scholars meet some of the components of the general education curriculum through a series of thematically organized interdisciplinary courses with special components such as a study-tour abroad and collaborative activities on campus.

In compliance with St. Mary's College's position as Maryland's public honors college, the St. Mary's Project (SMP) is the capstone of study at the College. The project is an eight-credit, independent, sustained endeavor of research or creative expression that is supervised by a faculty mentor and presented in a public forum.

St. Mary's College of Maryland offers semester and year-long international exchange programs, study tours, and international internship opportunities. Participation in our signature programs at Oxford in England, Alba in Italy, Shanghai in China, Chiang Mai in Thailand, or The Gambia in West Africa is at about the same cost as attending St. Mary's.

St. Mary's operates on a two-semester academic calendar. Students customarily complete four courses, or 16 credits, each semester and must complete 128 credits for graduation. Students do not need to declare a major until the end of their sophomore year.

ADMISSIONS

St. Mary's College is a selective institution. We admit students with records of high academic achievements, personal abilities, and accomplishments of superior quality. High school or college grades, the quality of course selection, standardized test scores, and letters of recommendation provide evidence of academic accomplishment and potential. These measures are supplemented by the required application essay and resume of co-curricular activities. Individual involvement outside the classroom and in the community also is given attention. Activities that have resulted in honors and awards, or other recognition of special talents, should be listed on the application.

At St. Mary's, we are proud to be a public honors college and are looking for students who are ready to be challenged. We accept applications from first-year and transfer students for the fall and spring semesters. Our Early Decision Deadlines are November 1 and December 1. When students apply under the Early Decision option, they are indicating to us that St. Mary's is their top choice and will attend if admitted. Notification of a decision is approximately one month past the Early Decision deadline. Regular Decision applicants must apply by January 1 and notification will be no later than April 1. Fall transfer applicants must apply February 1 and spring transfer students must apply by November 1. For details, visit www.smcm.edu.

Prospective students are strongly encouraged to come to campus for an interview with an admissions counselor and tour. These visits should be scheduled in advance by calling 800-492-7181.

CAMPUS FACILITIES AND EQUIPMENT

A unique aspect of St. Mary's culture is the influence of the river. Our campus is located on 319 acres and sits on a horseshoe bend of the St. Mary's River just upstream from the confluence of the Potomac River and Chesapeake Bay. You just can't help being affected. It is no wonder we have earned 13 national sailing championships. You don't have to be an expert; the waterfront is open to recreational and novice sailors alike. With our unique location, students also swim, kayak, windsurf, row and are drawn to environmental research. Once you see the campus you'll know you have arrived at a college like no other.

Living at college should be a pleasurable experience. Almost 90% of our students live on campus all four years, contributing a wonderful and safe learning and living environment. Our students enjoy the options of residence halls, suites, apartments and townhouses, and find living on campus an essential part of their college experience.

When our students are not in the classroom, they are busy doing independent research, traveling abroad, interning, and volunteering in the community. They unwind by enjoying the waterfront recreation, watching movies in Cole Cinema, partaking in our 90 clubs and organizations, and competing in intramural and varsity athletics. Our facilities are state-of-the-art and the abundant opportunities provide students a wonderful balance of work and play.

LOCATION AND ENVIRONMENT

St. Mary's College of Maryland is located on a horseshoe bend of the St. Mary's River just upstream from the confluence of the Potomac River and the Chesapeake Bay. In 1634, the first English settlers arrived here by boat and founded the fourth oldest permanent English colony in North America. By the Act of Toleration adopted by the colonists, St. Mary's City became an early site of religious freedom in the New World, and toleration remains an abiding precept of life at the College, where diversity of thought and expression are highly valued.

TUITION AND FEES

Basic educational fees for 2008–2009:

Tuition and Fees:

$10,472 per year (Maryland Resident)

$21,322 per year (Out-of-State Resident)

Room: $5,315

Board: $3,910

MAJORS AND DEGREES

Anthropology
Art and Art History
Asian Studies
Biochemistry
Biology
Chemistry
Computer Science
Economics
Educational Studies
Engineering: Dual-Degree Program with University of Md.
English
History
Human Studies
International Languages and Cultures (Chinese, French, German, Latin American Studies, Spanish, courses in Translation)
Mathematics
Music
Natural Science
Philosophy
Physics
Political Science
Psychology
Public Policy Studies
Religious Studies
Sociology
Student Designed Major
Theater, Film and Media Studies

OFF-CAMPUS OPPORTUNITIES

Located about 20 minutes from the College is Solomons Island, a quiet waterfront fishing village offering museums and attractions, shopping, waterfront dining, sailing and other water sports. Historic Leonardtown, located 20 minutes from St. Mary's, boasts one of the state's few preserved town squares. Maryland's state capital, Annapolis, is located 70 miles from the College. The Nation's Capital, Washington, D.C., is 75 miles from the College and the harbor city of Baltimore is approximately 120 miles from campus.

Tuition and Aid

St. Mary's College believes that qualified students should have an opportunity for a college education. The primary responsibility for paying for the cost of education is the family's. However, as a public institution, St. Mary's College recognizes that students and their families are not always able to fund the full cost of a college education. For this, the school offers a variety of programs designed to assist in meeting college expenses. These programs include scholarships, grants, loans, work opportunities, and a tuition payment plan. In the end, the goal is to ensure that qualified applicants have the opportunity to obtain a liberal arts education at St. Mary's.

To be considered for need-based aid, including federal, state and college grants, loan, and employment programs, students must fill out the Free Application for Federal Student Aid (FAFSA). In order to be considered for merit-based aid from St. Mary's, students need only to apply to the College. Every accepted student is automatically reviewed by the Scholarship Review Committee with consideration in the areas of academic record, standardized test scores, strength of curriculum, essay, recommendations, and co-curricular resume.

School Says . . .

SAINT PETER'S COLLEGE

AT A GLANCE

Saint Peter's College is a Jesuit, Catholic, coeducational, liberal arts college that seeks to develop the whole person in preparation for a lifetime of learning, leadership, and service in a diverse and global society.

Saint Peter's College main campus comprises nearly 25 acres in the heart of Jersey City, the second largest city in New Jersey. The College is 12 minutes by train from New York City and seconds from "The Gold Coast," the rejuvenated Jersey City waterfront district that is home to some of the nation's most respected financial, insurance and real estate companies including Goldman, Sachs and Co., American Express, Morgan Stanley, Merrill Lynch, and Deutsche Bank. The College has a branch campus for adults in Englewood Cliffs; courses are also offered at various corporate sites and at a location right within the Jersey City waterfront.

The total enrollment at Saint Peter's College in fall 2009 was 3,115 undergraduate and graduate students. This figure includes 2,300 full-time, day session undergraduate students at the Jersey City Campus. In 1993, the College opened a new, traditional-style dormitory, Whelan Hall; in 1994, Saint Peter Hall, a former Jesuit residence, was opened as a new residence for students. In 2001, another student residence, Millennium Hall, was opened. Currently, a total of 1100 students, about 50 percent of the full-time day session undergraduates, reside on campus. Saint Peter's College students, born in at least 60 different countries, reflect the increasing diversity of our nation. Excluding international students, approximately 29.1 percent of Jersey City day session full-time undergraduate students identify themselves as Hispanic; 23.4 percent as African American; and 10 percent as Asian. Saint Peter's College students come from at least 25 states. New Jersey is home to 80 percent of Jersey City day session full-time undergraduates; while 16 percent come from other states and 4 percent from foreign countries.

LOCATION AND ENVIRONMENT

The main campus of Saint Peter's College, the Jersey City campus, is divided by Kennedy Boulevard in the heart of Jersey City. Jaroschak Field, for athletic and recreational activities, is located about a mile away. Much of the College's personality comes from its location in Jersey City, where, for nearly 125 years, some of the best teachers in the nation have educated the children of long-established families along with those of recent arrivals. Within the past decade, Jersey City, located directly across the Hudson River from lower Manhattan, has developed its waterfront area into an impressive hub for business and finance.

In 1975, Saint Peter's established a branch campus at Englewood Cliffs in Bergen County. The campus, located on the Palisades about 15 miles up the Hudson River from Jersey City, enrolls primarily working adults from nearby corporate parks and medical centers who are pursuing undergraduate and graduate degrees through evening and weekend study.

OFF-CAMPUS OPPORTUNITIES

Supervised, off-campus cooperative education opportunities and internships are available in all fields. Students in SPC's nationally ranked Cooperative Education Program may earn a maximum of 9 academic credits and up to $10,000. Sixty percent of Saint Peter's undergraduates take advantage of the unique and exciting opportunities afforded by the College's proximity to the nation's business, financial, and media capital, New York City. They work, earning college credit and a salary, with firms such as Atlantic Records, WKTU, Panasonic, Unilever, ABC, Walgreens, Merrill Lynch, the National Basketball Association, MLB Productions, Madison Square Garden, Hackensack University Medical Center, and the NJ Sports and Exposition Authority.

Up to 15 credits are awarded through the Washington Center Program in Washington, D.C., which provides experience working in the nation's capital in a wide range of internship positions. Study abroad is arranged through the International Student Exchange Program, which conducts programs at more than 60 universities in Europe, Asia, Africa, and Latin America.

MAJORS AND DEGREES OFFERED

As befits a school founded in the classic Jesuit liberal arts tradition, Saint Peter's has a rich and varied range of academic offerings. Undergraduate programs include:

Accountancy, Africana Studies°, American Studies, Art History, Asian Studies, Biology (*Environmental Science and Forensic Science concentrations available*), Biological Chemistry, Biotechnology, Business Law°, Business Management, Chemistry (*Forensic Science concentration available*), Classical Civilization, Classical Languages & Literatures, Clinical Laboratory Sciences (Joint programs with UMDNJ) Cytotechnology and Medical Technology, Communications, Computer Science (CIS/MIS, *E-Commerce concentration available*), Criminal Justice, Economics and Finance, Elementary and Secondary Education, English Literature, Finance°, Fine Arts, Graphic Arts, History, International and Intercultural Studies°, International Business and Trade, Journalism°, Latin American Studies, Marketing Management, Mathematical Economics, Mathematics, Modern Languages and Literatures, Music°, Natural Sciences, Nursing, Philosophy, Physics, Physics and Electrical Engineering (5-year joint program w/NJIT), Political Science, Psychology, Social Justice°, Sociology, Spanish, Theater Arts°, Theology, Urban Studies, Visual Arts, and Women's Studies°

°Minor program only

Pre–Professional Joint Programs are also offered. These programs allow undergraduate students to begin pursuing a graduate degree as early as their junior year, thereby reducing the overall length of time required to earn both the undergraduate and graduate degree. Programs include: Accountancy (3-3 at SPC), Dentistry (3-4 w/UMDNJ), Law (3-3 with SHU), Medicine (3-4 w/UMDNJ), Occupational Therapy (3-3 w/ SHU), Pharmacy (3-4 at Rutgers), Physician Assistant (3-3 w/SHU), Physician Assistant (3-3 w/UMDNJ), Physical Therapy (3-3 w/UMDNJ).

ACADEMIC PROGRAMS

Saint Peter's academic programs are designed to offer students a wide breadth of knowledge along with providing the skills necessary to be successful in their chosen field. The College's academic departments offer more than 50 major programs, an Honors Program, individualized majors, and opportunities to earn credit for internships, service learning and other off-campus learning experiences

Undergraduate day courses are offered on a semester calendar, evening and Saturday courses on a trimester basis. Day and evening summer sessions are available on both campuses. A four-year honors program provides academically talented students an opportunity to do extensive scholarly research and participate in small seminars that emphasize class discussion. Selected students are invited to join this program and, upon successful completion, are awarded degrees *in cursu honorum*. The College recognizes the Advanced Placement (AP) program and generally offers credit for scores of 3 or better.

All students complete a core curriculum requirement consisting of at least 60 credits, distributed as follows: 3 credits each of composition and fine arts; 6 credits each of literature, a modern language, history, social sciences, philosophy, and theology; 6 to 8 credits of mathematics; 9 credits of natural science; and a 3 credit values course. The remainder of the academic program is devoted to the major field of specialization. Students must earn 120 credits to graduate.

Students may pursue a double major by completing requirements for two separate majors or may design a composite major in consultation with the appropriate academic dean. Minors are available in 29 areas of concentration.

CAMPUS FACILITIES AND EQUIPMENT

The Edward and Theresa O'Toole Library contains more than 50,000 sq. ft. of space. Students benefit from interlibrary loan arrangements as well as access to the New Jersey state-supported university library system. Students may obtain referral cards to other metropolitan area libraries and have access to the research collections of the New York Public Library and the Science, Industry, and Business Library, both located in midtown Manhattan, minutes from the campus. The library at the branch campus at Englewood Cliffs offers an additional 25,000 volumes.

Saint Peter's was one of the first colleges in the nation to adopt a wireless Ethernet throughout the campus. Students are offered individual e-mail accounts and Internet connectivity through the campus local area network (LAN). All offices, classrooms, and meeting spaces are connected to the Internet and the networked library resources.

The College operates 14 labs in the academic buildings on campus. In addition to general purpose computer labs distributed throughout the academic buildings, each residential hall has a mini-lab open 24 hours a day, 7 days a week. Saint Peter's also has several specialized computer labs to support learning in specific academic areas. The Fine Arts department operates a networked Graphic Arts lab with Apple and PC computer stations. The Modern Language department has its own computerized language lab and the Psychology department has a dedicated computer instruction lab.

Saint Peter's extends its commitment to integrating state of the art technology with high quality instruction beyond the use of computers. Gannon Hall, the science building, recently underwent an $8 million renovation and now offers sophisticated laboratory support to the College's course offerings in the natural sciences. The College has also implemented smart classroom technologies in all of its facilities, combining fully networked computer systems with powerful multimedia capabilities.

With a $2 million federal grant to establish the nation's first and only center for microplasma research, the College is garnering a national and international reputation for research in this emerging science.

The Yanitelli Recreational Life Center is a modern multi-million dollar facility offering five indoor tennis courts, a state-of-the-art fitness center with strength training and cardiovascular equipment, an Olympic-sized swimming pool, free weight room, racquetball, squash, indoor track, and three regulation basketball courts. The Center is home to the College's extensive intramural program as well as its 17 Division I athletic teams.

TUITION, ROOM, BOARD AND FEES

Undergraduate tuition for the 2009–2010 school year is a flat rate of $26,825 for 12-18 credits per semester. Annual tuition and fees are $27,500. Annual room and board is $10,900. Annual tuition for graduate students is $19,848 (24 credits at $827 per credit).

FINANCIAL AID

97% of full-time undergraduates receive financial assistance from Saint Peter's, with an average total package of more than $20,000. Saint Peter's College admits students regardless of financial status. The only form required is the Free Application for Federal Student Aid (FAFSA). It is recommended that students file the FAFSA by March 15 for fullest consideration of all federal, state (including EOF), and institutional sources available. All applications for admission are reviewed for academic scholarships, athletic scholarships, and need-based grants. Students should call the Office of Student Financial Aid (201-761-6073) for more information.

STUDENT ORGANIZATIONS AND ACTIVITIES

Academic life at Saint Peter's College is enriched by many programs and services that complement classroom instruction. The Counseling Center assists students with their social, psychological, and academic adjustment to college. At the Career Development Center, students can receive assistance in career planning and help in the search for meaningful jobs. The Cooperative Education Program gives participants a chance to earn money and college credit for practical work experience. Students can also take advantage of a center for information and assistance in applying for admission to graduate, law, or medical schools. The Campus Ministry Office offers religious services, seminars, and counseling. Students can also make use of the Office of Community Service and Service Learning. The Office of Campus Activities sponsors annual events on campus featuring popular entertainment, guest lecturers, and social events, both on and off campus. New York City, just a short distance away, offers countless cultural opportunities.

Each year over 1,000 men and women participate in an extensive intramural program. On the varsity level, Saint Peter's competes in basketball, baseball, bowling, cross-country, golf, swimming, soccer, softball, track, and volleyball. Saint Peter's is a member of the Metro Atlantic Athletic Conference.

ADMISSIONS PROCESS

Saint Peter's College requires students to have the following academic units:

four years of English

three years of college prep math

two years of history

two years of a foreign language

two years of science, with at least on year of lab science

at least three additional units in any combination of the subject areas listed above.

To satisfy admissions requirements, the complete admissions file must include:

a completed application

an official high school transcript

official ACT or SAT scores

two letters of recommendation

personal statement/essay

Notification of the admission decision is made on a rolling basis once the admission file is complete. Students are awarded an academic scholarship based on the academic index comprised of GPA and SAT scores. Scholarships range from $5,000 to full tuition, room and fees.

SAINT VINCENT COLLEGE

Founded in 1846, Saint Vincent College is a coeducational, Catholic, liberal arts college sponsored by the Order of Saint Benedict. Its mission is to provide quality undergraduate and graduate education for men and women to enable them to integrate their professional aims with the broader purposes of human life. Saint Vincent prepares you for a successful career – and a rewarding life. Caring faculty and administrators push you to believe in yourself and reach for your best. Challenging classes help you build knowledge in many fields. Experiences off campus, whether service in the inner city or an internship abroad, make you adaptable and respectful of different cultures and traditions. Such strengths and abilities make you not only a valuable professional but also someone who can make a difference in the lives of others.

AT A GLANCE

Saint Vincent College is an educational community rooted in the tradition of the Catholic faith, the heritage of Benedictine monasticism, and the love of values inherent in the liberal approach to life and learning.

LOCATION AND ENVIRONMENT

Located in Latrobe, Pennsylvania, 35 miles east of Pittsburgh, on the foothills of the Allegheny Mountains, the College offers panoramic views of the Laurel Highlands, which offer recreational activities such as skiing, hiking and camping. The 200-acre campus is known for its beauty, friendliness and safety. More than $40 million has been invested in campus facilities during the past five years including a new freshman residence hall and the Robert S. Carey Student Center.

OFF-CAMPUS OPPORTUNITIES

Life doesn't happen only in a classroom. That's why Saint Vincent encourages you to get out of the classroom and into real-world situations through internships, research, service learning and learning abroad. Such experiences enrich your learning, expand your view of the world, and give you an advantage when it comes to applying to graduate school or launching a career.

MAJORS AND DEGREES OFFERED

Bachelor of Arts Degrees are offered through the four Schools at Saint Vincent College: School of Humanities and Fine Arts, School of Social Sciences, Communication, and Education, Alex G. McKenna School of Business, Economics, and Government, and the Herbert W. Boyer School of Natural Sciences, Mathematics, and Computing. Programs are offered in Accounting, Anthropology, Art History, Art Education, Arts Administration, Biochemistry, Bioinformatics, Biology, Biotechnology, Business Education, Catholic Theology, Chemistry, Communication, Computing and Information Science, Economics, Early Childhood Education, Elementary Education, Secondary Education, Engineering, English, Entrepreneurship, Environmental Chemistry, Environmental Policy, Environmental Science, Environmental Studies, Finance, Fine Arts, French, General Administration of Justice, German Graphic Arts, Health Science, History, International Studies, Italian, Latin, Liberal Arts, Management, Marketing, Mathematics, Music, Music History, Music Performance, Occupational Therapy, Pharmacy, Philosophy, Physical Therapy, Physician Assistant, Physics, Physics Education, Political Science, Psychology, Psychology Education, Public Administration, Public History, Public Policy Analysis, Religious Education, Sociology, Spanish, Studio Arts and Theology. Master's Degrees are also offered in education, science and business.

ACADEMIC PROGRAMS

Pre-professional programs are offered in chiropractic, dental, law, medicine, optometry and veterinary with specialized laboratories, astronomy observatory, planetarium, radiotelescope and television production studio. Saint Vincent emphasizes service learning and study abroad opportunities that expand horizons and leave students more attuned to their community and world. On recent service trips, students volunteered in Newark, New Orleans, Brazil, and Calcutta. Students can also study abroad for a semester, academic year, or summer in such countries as Argentina, China, Egypt, Great Britain, France, India, Italy, Japan, Poland, Russia, South Africa, Taiwan and Turkey. Saint Vincent's liberal arts curriculum requires students in all majors to take basic courses in philosophy, English, social sciences, natural sciences, mathematics and religious studies. For students looking to intensify the intellectual experience, Saint Vincent also offers an Honors Program with opportunities for independent scholarly work.

CAMPUS FACILITIES AND EQUIPMENT

Specialized laboratories include astronomy, bioinformatics, ecology, genetics, geology, human anatomy, life sciences, microbiology, optics, organic chemistry, and physiology. Students also make use of the astronomy observatory, planetarium, radiotelescope, and television production studio. There are 24 technology-equipped classrooms. Wireless access points are available at a growing number of spots throughout campus. Of special note are the Fred M. Rogers Center and the Winnie Palmer Nature Reserve.

TUITION, ROOM, BOARD AND FEES

2010–2011 tuition, $26,350, room and board $8,754 fees $1,185. Approximately 97% of students received some form of aid.

FINANCIAL AID

Saint Vincent offers merit-based aid, need-based aid and competitive scholarships. To apply for need-based aid, which includes federal, state and institutional grants and loans, students and their parents must complete the Free Application for Federal financial Aid (FAFSA) as soon as possible after January 1. This is the only form needed to apply for aid at Saint Vincent College.

STUDENT ORGANIZATIONS AND ACTIVITIES

On campus are more than 60 student-run social, political, cultural, service, recreational and religious clubs and organizations, an active campus ministry, and a programming board that brings nationally known speakers and bands to campus. Saint Vincent offers career advising for all students, a strong alumni network and internship and job placement opportunities. Saint Vincent competes in the National Collegiate Athletic Association (NCAA) Division III in the Presidents' Athletic Conference. Men's varsity sports include baseball, basketball, cross country, fencing, football, golf, ice hockey, lacrosse, soccer, swimming, tennis and track. Women's varsity sports are basketball, cross country, fencing, field hockey, golf, lacrosse, soccer, softball, swimming, tennis, volleyball and equestrian. Intramurals and club sports are aerobics, basketball, billiards, dodgeball, equestrian, fencing, flag football, ice hockey, soccer, softball, street hockey, ultimate Frisbee, volleyball and weightlifting.

ADMISSION PROCESS

Admission to Saint Vincent is competitive. The foremost consideration is a student's academic potential. SAT scores of accepted students range from 950 to 1155 (25th–75th percentiles). 42% of students were in the top 20% of their high school graduating classes. Saint Vincent has a rolling admission policy.

SAVANNAH COLLEGE OF ART AND DESIGN

ACADEMICS

Undergraduate programs at SCAD embrace a wide range of major areas and are designed to challenge students to perform at a high level, preparing them for professional careers. A well-rounded curriculum provides students with core courses in foundation studies and general education leading to focused major programs emphasizing development of academic knowledge, technical and analytical skills, aesthetic sensibility, and the ability to express ideas visually and verbally. Students are expected to begin assembling a portfolio their first year and to maintain a collection of their best work through graduation. To encourage academic and professional success, portfolios are reviewed and evaluated on a regular basis by faculty members.

SCAD offers the following undergraduate degrees: B.A., B.F.A. In addition more than 50 minor programs are offered to complement any undergraduate program.

Graduate programs at SCAD are designed for dedicated, self-motivated students who are committed to the pursuit of excellence through advanced study. Graduate curricula are structured to include knowledge of the literature of the discipline and to ensure ongoing student engagement in research and/or appropriate professional practice and training experiences. Graduate courses require students to analyze, explore, question, reconsider and synthesize old and new knowledge and skills. The graduate experience culminates in student teaching or in a thesis or final project demonstrating a mature and resolved body of work and/or research.

SCAD offers the following graduate degrees: M.Arch., M.A., M.A.T., M.F.A., M.U.D.

ADMISSIONS

SCAD is committed to the pursuit of excellence and welcomes applicants from the United States and abroad who have the same high standards. SCAD maintains selective admission policies, accounting for a student body that is enthusiastic about the programs of study and capable of advancing rapidly. Applicants who meet or exceed the minimum admission requirements are not guaranteed admission.

New students may enter fall, winter, spring or summer quarter, although most students begin in the fall. Summer course offerings may be limited. Online applications are preferred. Applicants also may download, complete and send the application with fee to the appropriate mailing address.

Early application is encouraged for priority admission and scholarship consideration. For fall admission, first-time freshmen should apply by Feb. 15. Transfer and graduate students should apply for fall admission by April 15. For all entry terms, applications for admission should be completed at least 90 days prior to intended enrollment; however, applications may be submitted at any time and are considered based on student qualifications and space availability. All students may submit supplementary materials to enhance their application for admission and for scholarship consideration.

All admitted students are automatically considered for institutional scholarships. These funds are limited and are awarded to the earliest qualifiers based on materials submitted for review.

AT A GLANCE

The Savannah College of Art and Design is the most comprehensive art and design university in the world, offering more degree programs and specializations than any other art and design university. SCAD is a private, nonprofit, accredited institution that offers bachelor's and master's degrees in distinctive locations and online to prepare talented students for professional careers. The diverse student body of 9,500 comes from all 50 United States and nearly 100 countries worldwide. The education and career preparation of each student is nurtured and cultivated by a faculty of more than 600 professors with extraordinary academic credentials and valuable professional experience. Through individual attention in an inspiring university environment, and with advanced, professional-level technology, equipment and learning resources, SCAD is uniquely qualified to provide an exceptional education and unparalleled career preparation. SCAD has locations in Atlanta and Savannah, Georgia, USA, in Lacoste, France, and in Hong Kong beginning Fall 2010. Online programs are offered through SCAD eLearning.

SCAD is accredited by Southern Association of Colleges and Schools, National Architectural Accrediting Board, Council for Interior Design Accreditation, Georgia Professional Standards Commission, South Carolina Commission on Higher Education. SCAD is a member of American Academy in Rome, Atlanta Regional Council for Higher Education, EDUCAUSE, eLearning Guild, Georgia Foundation for Independent Colleges, National Association of Independent Colleges and Universities, Sloan Consortium, Southeastern College Art Conference, U.S. Distance Learning Association.

The SCAD website (www.scad.edu) has information about degree programs, majors, admission, financial aid and scholarships.

Virtual Adviser is available 24 hours a day, seven days a week at www.scad.edu/admission.

Live chats with SCAD admission representatives can be accessed Monday through Friday at www.scad.edu/livechat.

Facebook connects prospective students at www.facebook.com/scadadmission.

Twitter www.twitter.com/welcometoscad

YouTube www.youtube.com/aboutscad

Flickr www.flickr.com/scaddotedu

CAMPUS FACILITIES AND EQUIPMENT

Specialized educational resources facilitate research and build knowledge. In every department and program, SCAD students work with advanced, professional-level technology, equipment and resources. For example, SCAD is a Digidesign Certified Pro School for sound design and students can become ProTools certified before graduating. Sequential art students create work using Cintiq displays.

Students of the building arts use the latest electronic design software including Bentley MicroStation V8, 3D Studio VIZ, SURFCAM AutoCAD, Autodesk Maya and Revit. Fibers students work with Compu-Dobby looms, an electronic Jacquard loom and a Mimaki textile printer. The advanced technology labs for furniture and industrial design students include computer numerically controlled equipment for rapid prototyping and production as well as a large envelope five-axis CNC router. Computer resources include SolidWorks and Rhino 3D.

Five 3-D printers allow students to print ABS and polycarbonate 3-D models of their computer-generated designs.

Metals and jewelry students explore a wide range of technology in facilities for precision casting, finishing, enameling, lapidary, anodizing, CAD/CAM, forming and stone setting processes. Resources include a laser welder and microscope system, a Dimension prototype printer for ABS plastic, two Solidscape 66 prototypers specifically designed for jewelry printing and two Roland JWX-10 CNC milling machines. Advanced modeling tools include SensAble pens with ClayTools software. Accessory design students use specialized equipment such as men's and women's shoe lasts, a shoe finishing machine and cylinder industrial sewing machines. Industry-standard Lectra RomansCAD software is used for designing bags and shoes. Fashion students use industry-standard dress forms, cutting tables, professional sewing machines and specialty finishing equipment. Computer labs offer an Infinity Plus plotter for patternmaking and a Mimaki textile printer, as well as software including Kaledo, Vision Fashion Studio, Gerber Suite, Lectra U4ia and Virtual Fashion Pro.

Photography students work in both digital and film/chemistry labs equipped with Macintosh computers, Adobe CS software, Imacon scanners and wide-format inkjet printers. Students can expose and process RA-4 photographic materials using a Durst Theta printer in Atlanta and an Epsilon printer in Savannah.

Film and digital media students work with equipment found at major production and postproduction facilities, and use digital technology, nonlinear editing systems, digital audio workstations and comprehensive labs for screenwriting, scheduling and budgeting. Production facilities and equipment include Steadicam EFP and Panavision Panaflex G2 cameras, Super Panther and Fisher dollies, chroma key/green studio and sound stage. The department houses nearly 40 high-end Avid Adrenaline and Symphony Nitris workstations and editing suites. Cameras include Panasonic VariCam high definition; 16 mm, super 16 mm and 35 mm; and Red One digital.

CAMPUS LIFE

Location options in Savannah and Atlanta, Georgia, Lacoste, France, Hong Kong or online offer students a variety of learning environments to suit their individual interests and lifestyles. At every location, student life at SCAD is active and engaging within and beyond the classroom. The SCAD experience includes programs and activities that promote student interaction, leadership and community service, and encourage a healthy lifestyle.

With more than 70 student organizations, SCAD students have many opportunities to meet others who share common interests—from Japanese anime to whitewater rafting.

SCAD sponsors student groups affiliated with professional organizations as well as clubs related to academic programs, international cultures or religions. Leadership development opportunities are promoted through all student organizations including the Student Activities Council and United Student Forum, SCAD's award-winning online student news and Internet radio stations. For students who want to become involved in the community, Service Opportunities for Students provides an array of volunteer programs.

COLLEGE BASICS

Founded

In 1978 by Richard G. Rowan, Paula S. Wallace, May L. Poetter and Paul E. Poetter

Type of institution

Independent, nonprofit, tax-exempt, accredited

President

Paula S. Wallace

Mascot

Art the Bee

Colors

Gold and black

LOCATION AND ENVIRONMENT

In Savannah, SCAD offers a full university experience in a charming historic environment abundant with parks and near the beautiful beaches of the coastal South.

In Atlanta, SCAD is located in the center of a fast-paced, major metropolitan marketplace, with more than 100 art galleries and 1,000 international businesses.

SCAD plans to open a Hong Kong facility in the near future. Within this sophisticated international city, SCAD envisions transforming the former North Kowloon Magistracy building in Hong Kong's Sham Shui Po district into a leading site for the study of digital media in Asia.

SCAD's residential study-abroad location in Lacoste, France, offers immersion in the rich culture of Provence. Course offerings each quarter are varied to apply to all majors and are taught by SCAD professors.

Through SCAD eLearning, a SCAD education is offered to a global online community. Students have the flexibility to decide when and where to attend class.

MAJORS AND DEGREES

Accessory Design (B.F.A., M.A., M.F.A.), Advertising (B.A., B.F.A., M.A., M.F.A.), Animation (B.F.A., M.A., M.F.A.), Architectural History (B.F.A., M.A., M.F.A.), Architecture (B.F.A., Professional M.Arch., Postprofessional M.Arch.), Art History (B.F.A., M.A.), Arts Administration (M.A.), Cinema Studies (M.A.), Commercial Photography (M.A.), Design for Sustainability (M.A.), Design Management (M.A., M.F.A.), Digital Photography (M.A.), Documentary Photography (M.A.), Dramatic Writing (B.F.A., M.F.A.), Equestrian Studies (B.A.), Fashion (B.F.A., M.A., M.F.A.), Fashion Marketing and Management (B.F.A.), Fibers (B.F.A., M.A., M.F.A.), Film and Television (B.F.A., M.A., M.F.A.), Furniture Design (B.F.A., M.A., M.F.A.), Graphic Design (B.A., B.F.A., M.A., M.F.A.), Historic Preservation (B.F.A., M.A., M.F.A.), Illustration (B.A., B.F.A., M.A., M.F.A.), Illustration Design (M.A.), Industrial Design (B.F.A., M.A., M.F.A.), Interactive Design and Game Development (B.A., B.F.A., M.A., M.F.A.), Interior Design (B.F.A., M.A., M.F.A.), International Preservation (M.A.), Luxury and Fashion Management (M.A., M.F.A.), Metals and Jewelry (B.F.A., M.A., M.F.A.), Motion Media Design (B.F.A., M.A., M.F.A.), Painting (B.F.A., M.A., M.F.A.), Performing Arts (B.F.A., M.F.A.), Photography (B.A., B.F.A., M.A., M.F.A.), Printmaking (B.F.A., M.A., M.F.A.), Production Design (B.F.A., M.A., M.F.A.), Sculpture (B.F.A., M.A., M.F.A.), Sequential Art (B.A., B.F.A., M.A., M.F.A.), Service Design (B.F.A., M.F.A.), Sound Design (B.F.A., M.A., M.F.A.), Teaching (M.A.T.), Urban Design (M.U.D.).

Most degree programs have corresponding undergraduate minors. Minors are also offered in arts and entertainment management, British-American studies, business management and entrepreneurship, ceramic arts, concept art for games, creative writing, cultural landscape, dance, decorative arts, drawing, electronic design, exhibition design, interaction design, marine design, menswear, museum studies, new media art, portrait arts, scientific illustration, storyboarding, technical direction and vocal performance.

TUITION AND AID

Undergraduate tuition for the 2010–2011 academic year is $29,070 USD. The housing fee for the academic year ranges from $6,950 and $7460 for dormitory style to $8,390 and 8,450 for apartment style. Basic meal plan rate is $1,430 per quarter. There is a one-time enrollment fee of $500, and a nonrefundable housing reservation fee of $250 for students who sign up for SCAD housing. Approximately 90 percent of SCAD students receive some form of financial assistance. Approximately $23 million (USD) in institutional scholarships is awarded annually to the entering class. SCAD scholarships range from $1,500 (USD) per year to full tuition. Federal and state aid also available.

SCRIPPS COLLEGE

AT A GLANCE

From its founding in 1926 as one of the few institutions in the West dedicated to educating women for professional careers as well as personal growth, Scripps College has championed the qualities of mind and spirit described by its founder, newspaper entrepreneur and philanthropist Ellen Browning Scripps. Scripps remains a women's college because it believes that having women at the core of its concerns provides the best environment for intellectually ambitious women to learn from a distinguished teaching faculty and from each other.

Scripps College emphasizes a challenging Core Curriculum based on interdisciplinary humanistic studies, combined with rigorous training in the disciplines, as the best possible foundation for any goals a woman may pursue. This central feature of a Scripps education consists of a closely integrated sequence of three interdisciplinary courses that focus on our ideas about the world and the methods we use to generate these ideas. Scripps women learn to see the connections not only among academic subjects, but also among the major areas of their own lives, so that alumnae often remark that Scripps "prepared me for life." Above all, Scripps College gives women an intensive, challenging education that will help them to lead, in the words of its founder, lives filled with "confidence, courage, and hope."

LOCATION AND ENVIRONMENT

Scripps College is listed on the National Register of Historic Places. Located in Claremont, California, a college town with a population of 36,500, Scripps is located 35 miles east of Los Angeles. Within driving distance are mountains, beaches, and deserts, all of which can be enjoyed in the beautiful southern California climate. As a member of the Claremont Consortium, Scripps shares facilities and resources with Claremont McKenna, Harvey Mudd, Pitzer, and Pomona Colleges.

OFF-CAMPUS OPPORTUNITIES

Scripps College students can take courses at any of the Claremont Colleges, so they have over 2,500 classes from which to choose. More than half of the student body participates in study abroad programs in any of 37 countries. Career Planning and Resources, among other services, offers students a wide range of internship opportunities. Students may pursue a joint Scripps/Claremont Graduate University combined degree that results in a B.A. and master's degree in five years. The seven master's degree programs offered are in American politics, business administration, economics, international studies, philosophy, public policy and religion. Engineering students have the opportunity to participate in a 3-2 program, through which they spend three years on the Scripps campus and two years at an engineering campus (choices include Boston University, Columbia University, Harvey Mudd College, Rensselaer Polytechnic Institute, USC, and Washington University in St. Louis) and graduate with a combined B.A./B.S. degree.

MAJORS AND DEGREES OFFERED

The following majors are available at Scripps College or through cross-registration at other Claremont Colleges: accounting; American studies; anthropology; art conservation; art history; Asian studies; Asian languages; Asian-American studies; biology; biology-chemistry; Black studies; chemistry; Chicano/Latino studies; Chinese; classics; computer science; dance; economics; engineering; English; environment, economics and politics; environmental science; environmental studies; European studies; French studies; gender and women's studies; geology; German studies; Hispanic studies; history; human biology; humanities: interdisciplinary studies in culture; Italian; Japanese; Jewish studies; Latin American Studies; legal studies; linguistics; management engineering; mathematics; media studies; molecular biology; music; neuroscience; organismal biology and ecology; organizational studies; philosophy; physics; politics and international relations; psychology; religious studies; Russian; science and management; science, technology, and society; sociology; studio art; and theatre.

ACADEMIC PROGRAMS

At least 32 courses are required for the Bachelor of Arts degree at Scripps College. Included in these courses are the Core Curriculum requirements, breadth requirements (in fine arts, foreign language(s), letters, mathematics, natural sciences, social sciences, and writing), coursework for the chosen major, and elective courses or courses for a minor. Students also complete one course each that fulfills a requirement of race and ethnic studies and gender and women's studies. More than one quarter of Scripps College students double major and students may also pursue a self-designed major. Students may elect to pursue an honors program in their chosen major. All students complete a senior thesis and/or—in the case of music, dance, studio art, or theater—possibly a senior performance or project.

There are two semesters to each academic year at Scripps College, and the year runs from early September to mid-May.

CAMPUS FACILITIES AND EQUIPMENT

The center of community life at Scripps is the Malott Commons. Here, students have most of their meals (in a choice of four dining areas), pick up their mail, and meet friends at the student-run Motley Coffeehouse for a cappuccino or for live music. It is also home to Career Planning and Resources, Seal Court, the Student Activities and Residential Life Office and lounge, and the student store. The Malott Commons hosts a myriad of cultural, educational, and social events such as speakers, open mic events, literary readings, and meetings.

With 2,000,000 volumes, the Claremont Colleges' library system is the third largest private academic library in California. Scripps' College science facilities are jointly shared with Claremont McKenna and Pitzer Colleges, offering faculty and facility resources no small college alone could sustain. The European Union Center of California and the Humanities Institute are both special education and research facilities housed on the Scripps campus.

In late 2008, the Sallie Tiernan Field House was completed, offering students a 24,000 square foot, state-of-the-art recreational and athletic facility with an aerobics studio, cardio machine room, weight room, and other spaces for fitness and health education. The Field House is located next to Scripps' 25-meter swimming pool.

TUITION, ROOM, BOARD AND FEES

Costs for the 2009–2010 academic year:

Tuition and fees: $38,700

Room and board: $11,850

Total: $50,550

FINANCIAL AID

Scripps College seeks out the very best students and continues to meet 100% of each eligible student's demonstrated financial need. Financial aid is awarded to over one-half of Scripps students, and this aid can include grants, scholarships, part-time student employment and low-interest loans. Financial need determines the type and amount of awards. High-achieving students are also eligible to compete for merit scholarships through the James E. Scripps and New Generation Scholarship programs. The deadline for merit-based scholarship applications is November 1. Scripps College also awards National Merit Scholarships, enrolling 10 National Merit Scholars in the 2009 entering class.

Mandatory financial aid forms: FAFSA and CSS/ Financial Aid PROFILE

Filing dates vary by the admission plan under which a student applies. Financial aid filing deadlines may be found at: http://www.scrippscollege.edu/financial-aid/index.php.

STUDENT ORGANIZATIONS AND ACTIVITIES

More than 200 clubs and organizations are available at the Claremont Colleges. Students can also choose from a variety of five-college and Scripps campus events, 11 NCAA Division III sports teams, and intramural and club sports teams. Scripps' intercollegiate sports teams are composed of students from Claremont McKenna, Harvey Mudd, and Scripps Colleges (CMS). In addition, the five-time national championship title holder, Claremont Colleges Ballroom Dance Company (CCBDC), is a five-college organization with some 80 student participants who host frequent performances, workshops and dance activities.

ADMISSIONS PROCESS

The desired Scripps College applicant is involved, intellectually curious, and interested in exploring an intensive liberal arts curriculum. High academic achievement is expected, as is personal success. Scripps also highly regards leadership, motivation, honesty, and creativity.

Every part of a student's application is important to the Admission Committee. The quality of a student's academic work is key, and a recommended course of study includes five academic subjects in each year of high school, for a total of 4 years of English, 4 years of mathematics, 3 years of social studies, 3 years of laboratory science (biology, chemistry, or physics), and either 3 years of a foreign language or 2 years each of two different languages. Honors, Advanced Placement, or International Baccalaureate courses are highly regarded by the Committee. Applicants are encouraged to interview either with a member of the professional staff or a trained alumna. Also required are an essay and a graded analytical paper from the junior or senior year of high school. Art or music supplements are welcomed. Scripps College is an exclusive user of the Common Application.

SAT scores for class entering fall of 2009:

Middle 50 percent critical reading: 640–730

Middle 50 percent math: 620–700

Middle 50 percent writing: 650–730

Average Weighted GPA for class entering fall of 2008: 3.9

Early Decision Application Deadlines: November 1 (ED1), January 1 (ED2)

Academic Scholarship Application Deadline: November 1

Regular Decision Application Deadline: January 1

SEATTLE UNIVERSITY

AT A GLANCE

Seattle University, founded in 1891, is one of 28 Jesuit colleges and universities in the United States. The undergraduate student body numbers 4,253 and includes representatives from 55 states and territories and 76 nations. Seattle University provides an ideal environment for motivated students interested in self-reliance, awareness of different cultures, social justice, and the fulfillment that comes from making a difference. Our location in the center of one of the nation's most diverse and progressive cities attracts a student body, faculty, and staff rich in diversity. Our urban setting promotes the development of leadership skills and independence and provides the opportunity for students to apply what they learn through internships, clinical experiences, and volunteer work.

The student life program includes over 80 extracurricular clubs and organizations. Three residence halls and an on-campus apartment complex house 1,700 students, and undergraduate housing is available all four years. Approximately 89% of the freshmen and sophomores live on campus. The Connolly Athletic Center serves as the major facility for varsity and intramural athletics and recreation. It features two swimming pools, two gymnasiums, and saunas. A 6-acre complex provides fields for outdoor sports.

Seattle University is accredited by the Northwest Commission on Colleges and Universities, the Accreditation Board for Engineering and Technology, AACSB International-Association to Advance Collegiate Schools of Business, the American Chemical Society, the Commission on Accreditation of Allied Health Education Programs, the National Association of Schools of Public Affairs and Administration, the National Council for Accreditation of Teacher Education, Association of Theological Schools, the Commission on Collegiate Nursing Education, Council on Social Work Education, and the American Bar Association.

LOCATION AND ENVIRONMENT

Seattle University is located in a port city of unsurpassed natural beauty. As the Pacific Northwest's largest city (and the 14th largest metropolitan area in the United States), Seattle is a scenic and cultural center in a setting that includes breathtaking mountain views of the Cascades to the east and the Olympics to the west. In addition to being situated along Puget Sound, Seattle also contains Lakes Union and Washington.

The campus is located in the center of the city. Seattle's sights and sounds, rich ethnic diversity, celebrated restaurants, first-run entertainment, major-league athletics, theater, opera, and ballet enhance campus life.

OFF-CAMPUS OPPORTUNITIES

Seattle University offers three international study programs—programs for French in France, Latin American Studies in Mexico, Chinese in China, and three reciprocal exchange programs with the University of Graz in Austria, Sophia University in Japan, and Taejon University in Korea. Additional study abroad programs in other nations, in conjunction with other colleges' overseas programs, are also offered.

Seattle University is affiliated with the Council for International Educational Exchange, a consortium of colleges and universities that sponsor a variety of academic programs around the world.

MAJORS AND DEGREES OFFERED

Seattle University offers the following undergraduate degrees: Bachelor of Arts, Bachelor of Science, Bachelor of Science in Nursing, Bachelor of Social Work, Bachelor of Criminal Justice, and the Bachelor of Arts in Business Administration. The University offers 53 majors and 31 minors in five academic units: The Albers School of Business and Economics; The College of Arts and Sciences; The College of Nursing; The College of Science and Engineering; and The Matteo Ricci College.

Undergraduate Programs include accounting; art history; Asian studies, biochemistry; biology; business administration; business economics; chemistry; clinical laboratory science; communication; computer engineering, computer science; criminal justice; cultural anthropology; diagnostic ultrasound; e-commerce, environmental science; environmental studies; economics; electronic commerce; engineering (civil, computer, electrical, environmental, and mechanical); English/creative writing; exercise science; film studies; finance; fine, applied, and performing arts; French; general science; German; history; humanities; humanities for teaching; international business; international studies; journalism; liberal studies; management; marketing; mathematics; military science/ROTC; music; nursing; philosophy; physics; political science; pre-law; pre-medical/pre-dental; psychology; public affairs; sociology; Spanish; string performance; theology/religious studies; and women studies.

ACADEMIC PROGRAMS

Students at Seattle University take a program of liberal studies called the core curriculum. The university core curriculum has several distinguishing characteristics: it provides an integrated freshman year; gives order and sequence to student learning; provides experience in the methods and content of the range of liberal arts, sciences, philosophy, and theology; calls for active learning in all classes, for practice in writing and thinking, and for an awareness of values; fosters a global perspective and a sense of social and personal responsibility. Our academic offerings provide leadership opportunities and enable graduates to serve society through a demanding liberal arts and social sciences foundation. In the Jesuit educational tradition we teach students how to think, not what to think.

Seattle University offers two honors program options for students seeking the greatest possible challenge. The University Honors Program is a small select two year long learning community. It is humanities focused, and its fully integrated curriculum examines the most significant texts and ideas of Western culture. The Core Honors Program involves seminar sections of nine required courses in English, history, philosophy, social science, and theology/religious studies. This option is particularly suited to students in profession-oriented majors where participation in University Honors is less feasible due to specific major requirements and scheduling conflicts. Admission is competitive and requires a separate application.

CAMPUS FACILITIES AND EQUIPMENT

The University is located on 48 acres in the First Hill neighborhood in the center of Seattle. There are 28 buildings recently enhanced by additions, renovations, and new construction. Total assets are valued at $497.2 million and the endowment is $214.8 million.

TUITION, ROOM, BOARD AND FEES

For the 2009–2010 academic year, full-time tuition is $29,340; room and meals are $8,805. The estimate for books, supplies, fees and personal expenses is an additional $5,353. Travel costs vary among students. Costs are subject to change. Seattle University operates on a quarter calendar with fall term beginning in late September.

FINANCIAL AID

Approximately 90 percent of new freshmen receive an average financial aid award of $22,053 per year. These awards usually include scholarships, grants, loans, and Federal Work-Study. Last year, Seattle University awarded more than $72.3 million in aid to undergraduates - nearly $30.6 million of that came from the university's own funds. Students are required to apply for financial aid by February 1, as awards are made early each spring for the following fall quarter. Applications that are received after this deadline will be evaluated in the order received for any remaining aid. Students must submit the Free Application for Federal Student Aid (FAFSA) and be accepted for admission to be considered for financial assistance. There are a number of scholarships for freshmen that are awarded on the basis of academic achievement, extracurricular involvement, and community service. Transfer scholarships are also available.

STUDENT ORGANIZATIONS AND ACTIVITIES

All undergraduates belong to the Associated Students of Seattle University (ASSU), the central student organization on campus, which is organized around an elected president, an executive vice president, and an activities vice president. Additionally, a 12-member representative council oversees every facet of the student body and is responsible for policy-making, a diverse activities program, and the communication of student needs to the administration and faculty.

ADMISSIONS PROCESS

Seattle University is committed to qualitative decision-making based upon evaluations of students as a whole. Decisions are based primarily upon individual course selection, performance, and trends. The expected academic program comprises 16 units of coursework, including 4 years of English, 3 years of social studies or history, 2 years of a foreign language, 3 years of college-preparatory mathematics, and 2 units of lab science (3 are preferred). Laboratory physics and chemistry, as well as 4 units of college-preparatory mathematics are required for engineering; we require laboratory chemistry and biology for admission to the nursing program. Also required for all programs are offical scores from either the ACT or the SAT I. The middle 50 percent of enrolling freshmen have secondary school averages of 3.3–3.8 (on a 4.0 scale).

Essays or personal statements are required for admission and are carefully considered during application review. College credit is awarded to those who have successfully earned minimum scores on Advanced Placement or International Baccalaureate examinations.

Applications and information can be obtained by contacting the Admissions Office. Secondary school students who have completed at least six semesters are encouraged to complete the application process by February 1 of their senior year. Transfer students must submit official transcripts from all post-secondary institutions attended, regardless of whether course work was completed. The recommended financial aid/admission deadline for transfers is March 1. Applications are accepted after these dates but financial aid funds may no longer be available.

Campus visits can be scheduled Monday through Friday and many Saturdays. Guests can attend a class, meet with faculty, participate in a campus tour, and speak individually with representatives from admissions. Students can apply directly or online via our website, www.seattleu.edu. Seattle University is a member of The Common Application and the Universal College Application.

SETON HALL UNIVERSITY

AT A GLANCE

Since its founding by Bishop James Roosevelt Bayley in 1856, Seton Hall University has dedicated itself to providing "a home for the mind, the heart, and the spirit."

FOR THE MIND: We offer more than 60 majors and concentrations taught by 860 full-time faculty members across six undergraduate schools with practical, real-world emphasis. FOR THE HEART: We offer a compassionate, diverse and collaborative environment that focuses on academic and ethical development. FOR THE SPIRIT: Our faith and spiritual commitments inspire faculty to educate students to become servant leaders in their personal and professional lives, and in a diverse society.

"There is pride and excitement in being part of the Seton Hall community. There's a spirit, a passion for the place."

Leonard Jones

Political Science and English

Hillsdale, NJ

Seton Hall's campus spans 58 acres and is home to 5,300 undergraduate students, with 82 percent of its freshmen living on campus. While Seton Hall certainly enjoys a reputation of being a large institution, our campus community is actually close-knit and inclusive. Students receive personal attention with an average class size of 25 to 30 students and a student-to-faculty ratio of 14:1. Students, faculty and staff come from around the world, representing all 50 states and 67 countries, creating a diverse yet unified campus environment.

LOCATION AND ENVIRONMENT

Seton Hall provides students with the best of both worlds. Nestled in the charming suburban Village of South Orange, New Jersey, our campus is only 14 miles from one of the world's most exciting cities. You are close to the action, fun and excitement of New York City, yet you are still able to live your day-to-day life in a more relaxed atmosphere.

Our campus is just a few minutes away from the Village center of South Orange. There you will find clothing stores, grocery stores, ice cream and coffee shops, restaurants, hair stylists and a movie/performing arts theater.

Once in town, it's easy to hop on a train and arrive in the heart of midtown Manhattan in just 30 minutes. Known as the capital of finance, fashion, art and entertainment, the Big Apple offers the best of everything. After arriving in New York City, visit the neighborhood and destination of your choice to enjoy world-renowned restaurants, popular night spots and concert venues, unforgettable sightseeing, Tony Award-winning plays and musicals, and unbeatable shopping.

"If you intend to sit in your room all day, this isn't the school for you. Go to New York City, find internships, have fun. The opportunities are there. Absorb all you can."

Andrew Trzaska

Broadcasting, Visual and Interactive Media, Political Science

North Muskegon, MI

Consider all the international companies and organizations based in the New York/New Jersey Metropolitan area. Seton Hall's prime location puts you at the center of endless opportunities where students can take advantage of internships with museums, nonprofit and government agencies, law and accounting firms, television and print media…the list goes on and on.

MAJORS AND DEGREES OFFERED

Seton Hall University is committed to academic excellence. During their first two years, undergraduate students are exposed to a world of ideas from great scholars that open their minds to new perspectives and achievements of many cultures. This approach helps many of our students choose their majors and minors while giving them plenty of time to focus on these areas in their third and fourth years.

And if you're worried that you will be just one of many students vying for your professors' time, you can relax. At Seton Hall, you are more than just a number. Most classes average 25 students and fewer than 4 percent of courses are taught by teaching assistants. Our low student-to-faculty ratio of 14:1 ensures that you get the personal attention you need.

"Seton Hall faculty pay more attention to the needs of the students than is typical at other universities."

Gerald Ruscingno

Senior Faculty Associate

College of Arts and Science, Biology

We offer core courses in broad range of disciplines within our six undergraduate schools and colleges:

-**College of Arts and Sciences**—Offering an impressive 33 majors and 34 minors in fields ranging from English, art and music to physics, biology and health professions, the College of Arts & Sciences is the largest undergraduate college at Seton Hall University.

-**College of Education and Human Services**—Graduates of this school have a nearly 100 percent job placement rating. The College of Education and Human Services is accredited by the National Council for Accreditation of Teacher Education.

-**College of Nursing**—Accredited by the New Jersey State Board of Nursing and the National League for Nursing, it is the oldest and largest nursing school in New Jersey. Students work toward degrees in the B.S.N., M.S.N., M.A. and Ph.D. programs the school offers. The College of Nursing educates more than one-third of New Jersey's nurses and there is and there is not a hospital in the state of New Jersey that does not employee a Seton Hall University nursing graduate.

-**Immaculate Conception Seminary School of Theology**—offers programs for seminarians studying for Catholic priesthood as well as a B.A. degree in Catholic Theology for lay people. Founded in 1861, it is the major seminary of the Catholic Archdiocese of Newark.

-**Stillman School of Business**—ranked one of top 10 undergraduate business programs at Catholic Colleges, the Stillman School of Business is accredited by the Association to Advance Collegiate School of Business (AACSB). The school offers, programs in accounting, economics, finance, information technology management, management, marketing and sport management.

-**Whitehead School of Diplomacy and International Relations**—as the first professional school of international affairs established after the Cold War, the Whitehead School is the newest school at Seton Hall University. Among its faculty are six current and former ambassadors and U.N. officials. The school also has an exclusive alliance with the United Nations Association of the United States of America.

"Students come to Seton Hall from everywhere. The University gives us a great way to transition into the global community."

Lauren Jackson

Marketing and Sport Management

Queens, NY

Choosing Seton Hall is just the start of your academic journey. Our rigorous programs, dedicated faculty and small classes will support you as you prepare to become a responsible leader in a global society.

CAMPUS FACILITIES AND EQUIPMENT

Seton Hall places a strong emphasis on the use of state-of-the-art technology, facilities and support services to aid in its students' development:

- Our award-winning Mobile Computing Program provides all incoming, full-time freshman a new, fully loaded laptop. Two years later, you'll trade it in for a newer, upgraded model, and when you graduate in four years, it is yours to keep.

- Seton Hall's Recreation Center serves the recreational and fitness needs of the Seton Hall community. Here students can go for a swim in our Olympic sized pool, run on the indoor track or tear up the six indoor basketball courts. Our new fitness center features a free-weight center, new cardiovascular equipment, and plasma screen televisions complete with wireless listening capabilities.

- The Walsh library is a state-of-the-art research facility complete with a computerized catalog, 200 computer terminals for undergraduates, four electronic multimedia facilities and approximately one million holdings. The library also provides students free access to numerous databases of scholarly research.

- The University Center houses most of Seton Hall's cultural, social and recreational activities. The University Center includes the Galleon Dining Room, the Pirate's Cove (lounge and coffee house), Theatre-in-the-Round, a study lounge and the student government office.

- The University offers students such services as aptitude testing, career counseling services, personal counseling and disability support services.

- The University's newest addition is the McNulty Science and Technology Center, which is home to state-of-the-art biology and chemistry labs, an atrium and auditorium, as well as an observatory and greenhouse.

TUITION, ROOM, BOARD AND FEES

Seton Hall offers a flat-tuition rate for students taking between 12–18 credit hours. The 2009–2010 flat-rate tuition is $30,470, including the Mobile Computing Program fee. Room and Board fees range depending on meal plans; however, an average cost is $11,700.

FINANCIAL AID

Paying for college is a major investment. That's why Seton Hall University is committed to providing you with the resources needed to make your dreams a reality. Here at Seton Hall, 90 percent of our students receive some form of financial aid and 72 percent of entering freshmen receive scholarships or grants directly from the University.

At Seton Hall, all you need to begin the process of applying for need-based financial aid is the completion and submission of the Free Application for Federal Student Aid (FAFSA) form. Merit-based aid does not require a FAFSA but completing it is strongly encouraged, as these scholarships rarely pay the entire cost of attendance. Most scholarships do not require a separate application.

STUDENT ORGANIZATIONS AND ACTIVITIES

Your experiences at Seton Hall extend far beyond the classroom. As a student, you're always learning, whether you're joining a Greek organization, broadcasting live at our award-winning radio station, WSOU, touring with our Chamber Choir or serving as in our Student Government Association. From student media to professional societies to religious organizations, our 100-plus clubs and organizations offer something for everyone.

Sports are a big part of life at Seton Hall and there is almost nothing more thrilling than Pirate Athletics. With 17 men's and women's varsity athletic teams competing in the BIG EAST Conference, Seton Hall gives you the opportunity to see college athletics at their most competitive level. In addition to varsity athletics, you can join a club sport or gather a team to play one of 18 different intramural sports, in which about 70 percent of the student population participate.

ADMISSIONS PROCESS

When selecting new students, Seton Hall University looks at secondary school performance records and three-part SAT or ACT scores, plus guidance counselor and teacher evaluations. Applicants must have graduated from an accredited secondary school or have received satisfactory marks on the GED test. The University requires that applicants complete 16 high school credits: four in English, two in foreign language (consecutively), one in laboratory science, three in mathematics, two in social studies, and four in accepted academic electives.

Applicants requesting a transfer to the University must have at least a 2.5 GPA (some academic programs may require a higher GPA) and must have performed satisfactorily at the previous school attended. Credit is generally awarded for grades of C or better in university-level curriculum taken at recognized institutions; students may transfer up to 100 credit hours to apply toward a bachelor's program at Seton Hall. The preferred application deadlines for transfer students are June 1 for the fall semester and December 1 for the spring semester.

Freshman applicants must provide high school transcript, SAT or ACT scores, and complete either a print or online application. Applicants must also submit a teacher evaluation, counselor report and a personal essay. Personal interviews are offered but are not required.

Admission to the University is granted on a rolling basis; however, Seton Hall's early action deadline is November 15. Students applying non-binding early action will receive an admission decision on or before December 30. Seton Hall's preferred deadline for regular admission is March 1.

For more information, contact the Office of Undergraduate Admission:

Website: www.shu.edu

Telephone: 1-800-THE-HALL

E-mail: thehall@shu.edu

SKIDMORE COLLEGE

AT A GLANCE

Skidmore College is an independent, coeducational liberal arts college located in Saratoga Springs, NY. With a student body of 2,400 and a faculty of 297 professors, the college offers a wide array of academic majors in the liberal arts as well as in career-specific fields such as business, social work, education, and the fine and performing arts.

Founded in 1903 as a school for women, Skidmore was chartered as a four-year degree-granting college in 1922. The college made the decision in the 1960s to build an entirely new campus. In the 1970s Skidmore began admitting men and was chartered by Phi Beta Kappa. A program for the master of arts degree in liberal studies was added in 1993.

Skidmore's academic program is designed to promote creative thinking across the disciplines. Skidmore believes that creative thought matters and the curriculum emphasizes strong foundations in the liberal arts and interdisciplinary study, and builds upon the college's founding principle of linking theoretical and applied learning. It is not unusual for students to design cross-disciplinary double majors such as art history and business, or education and Spanish, and the curriculum's flexibility allows for self-determined majors as well.

The college's 100 plus student clubs and organizations include student government, a cappella singing groups, The Skidmore News (student newspaper), WSPN Radio, comedy and cabaret troupes and a number of cultural awareness groups. Skidmore athletes compete at the NCAA Division III level, and the college fields 19 intercollegiate teams. The riding and women's tennis teams have won national championships in recent years. Students are active in the intramural sports program and enjoy abundant opportunities for personal fitness and recreation, both on campus and in the nearby Adirondack Mountains.

ADMISSIONS JOURNAL

At Skidmore creative thought matters. Every life, every career, every endeavor is made more profound with creative ability at its core. We believe that a key purpose of liberal arts education is to encourage, challenge, and explore creative thought. We do this through our curriculum, campus, environment, and teaching approaches, which work together to provide students with an intellectual foundation while encouraging them to explore the areas of study that most align with who they are and where they want to go. If you believe that your life and success will be shaped by your ability to think, create, and communicate then Skidmore is the place for you.

Skidmore encourages you to step out, to try new things, to use diverse perspectives and experiences to guide your thoughts, creativity, and actions. At Skidmore, you'll be encouraged to question all that you have learned and believed, to encounter and evaluate the new. Your fields of interest and your activities will expand in ways you can't imagine. There are many examples: the physics major who excels in studio art; the sophomore who discovered a passion for politics by helping out with grassroots campaigning; the junior who changed majors because of a study experience in India.

LOCATION AND ENVIRONMENT

Set on 850 acres in Saratoga Springs, New York, Skidmore College offers undergraduates the beauty and serenity of a rural setting and convenient access to a historic town of 30,000. New Yorkers have long flocked to Saratoga Springs to take advantage of its resorts, horse-racing and culture of many varieties. Each summer, performing arts ensembles such as the Philadelphia Orchestra, New York City Ballet and Harlem Boys Choir take up residence at the Saratoga Performing Arts Center. Performances also include a wide variety of current popular music. Skidmore is in an ideal location; it is within an hour's drive of state parks, lakes, and major ski areas throughout eastern New York, western Massachusetts, and Vermont. Saratoga Springs is 30 miles north of New York's capital of Albany. Buses link Saratoga Springs to New York City, Boston, Montreal, and other regional major cities. Train service to New York City and Montreal is also available seven days a week. Albany International Airport is served by major airlines. The College is located near Exit 15 of I-87 (the Northway).

OFF-CAMPUS OPPORTUNITIES

Skidmore's membership in the Hudson-Mohawk Association of Colleges and Universities enables students to cross register at any of 14 other colleges and universities in the area. The Washington Semester, conducted through American University in Washington, D.C., offers an intensive workshop experience through course work, seminars, research projects, and internships with government committees. Skidmore's Study Abroad program enables students to study in England, France, Spain and China. Skidmore is also affiliated with other study-abroad programs, facilitating study for a semester or a year in many locations in Asia, Australia, Europe, and Latin America.

Arrangements for student internships are made through academic departments or through the Office of Career Planning and Field Experience Programs. Internships are available in such diverse fields as government, social work, the arts (dance, theater, and museum work), business, scientific research, and medicine.

MAJORS AND DEGREES OFFERED

Skidmore College grants a Bachelor of Arts degree in the following liberal arts subjects: American studies, anthropology, biology, chemistry, classical studies, computer science, economics, English, environmental studies, foreign languages and literatures (French, German, and Spanish), geosciences, government, history, history of art, mathematics, music, neuroscience, philosophy, physics, psychology, religion, and sociology. The Bachelor of Science degree is granted in areas of a more professional nature, including business, dance, education, exercise science, social work, studio art, and theater. There are 33 interdepartmental majors. Self-determined majors, double majors, and minors are also available.

The College offers 3-2 programs with the Thayer School of Engineering at Dartmouth College and with Clarkson University. Also available is a 4-1 MBA program offered with the School of Management at Clarkson, a 3-2 MBA program offered through Rensselaer Polytechnic Institute, a 4-1 MBA program with Union College, and a 4-1 Master of Arts in Teaching program with Union College. Through a cooperative program with the Cardozo Law School, Skidmore students may obtain a bachelor's degree and a law degree in six years. In addition, Skidmore has certification programs in teaching and social work and pre-professional programs in law and medicine.

ACADEMIC PROGRAMS

Skidmore College is renowned for its blending of traditional liberal arts study with opportunities to delve deeply into pre-professional disciplines. Skidmore's liberal studies core curriculum, which requires students to complete two or more interdisciplinary courses, is widely respected. It begins with the selection of a first year seminar. Students choose one from a myriad of topics. Faculty seminar leaders function as their students' first year advisors. Skidmore's core requirements cover a wide range of disciplines, requiring at least one course in each of the following disciplines: the arts; humanities; foreign language; nonwestern culture; science; and social science. Students must select a major by the end of their sophomore year; they may choose from 64 options, including self-designed majors, interdepartmental concentrations, and minors.

The College observes a two-semester academic calendar. Internship opportunities follow directly after the second semester ends in May. Students typically take four or five courses per semester. In addition to two summer terms for Skidmore students, the College offers a summer study through PASS, a six-week program that allows high school students to earn college credit for two courses.

The College implemented a Master of Arts in Liberal Studies program in 1993.

Skidmore College employs 229 full-time instructors and 68 part-time faculty members, including some with special appointments. 94 percent of Skidmore's faculty members in the liberal arts have earned doctoral degrees. The students/full-time faculty ratio is 9:1, the average class size is 16. Skidmore's faculty is actively involved in both research and publication in their areas of expertise; however, instructors here look upon teaching as their principal responsibility. Faculty advisors assist students in choosing courses and in planning their comprehensive academic programs.

CAMPUS FACILITIES AND EQUIPMENT

Scribner Library, housing approximately 400,000 volumes, has been designated a depository for United States government documents. Students have access to 40 libraries in the region through the College's membership in an area council. Skidmore also participates in the Lockheed/Dialog system for information search and retrieval. Dana Science Center has laboratories and sophisticated equipment for the biology, chemistry, physics, and geoscience departments including two electron microscopes and a confocal scanning microscope. The Filene Music Building contains a large recital hall, practice and listening rooms, and a music library. Other special facilities include a language laboratory in Bolton Hall; the Art Building (open 24 hours), with studio space, numerous kilns, and ceramics, weaving, and jewelry-making studios; the Skidmore Theatre; and dance studios. Students have access to a computer center served by a cluster of nine SunSPARC-2 workstations. The spectacular Tang Teaching Museum and Art Gallery enriches the campus scene with experimental programming closely allied with the college's interdisciplinary focus. September 2006 saw two major additions to the campus. The Northwoods Apartments opened with 380 single room units across ten new buildings. All are geothermally heated and cooled. A new dining hall also opened. The new facility offers extensive vegetarian options, fresh made pasta, locally grown organic items and a broad range of daily choices. The new Zankel Music Center with a 700-seat auditorium will be opened in January 2010.

TUITION, ROOM, BOARD, AND FEES

For the 2009–2010 academic year, tuition and fees for all students were an estimated $40,420. Room and board for students living in Skidmore residence halls was an estimated $10,776. Student general and activity fees total $800.

FINANCIAL AID

Skidmore awards financial aid based on demonstrated need. The Free Application for Federal Student Aid (FAFSA), a copy of the federal income tax form, and the CSS PROFILE must be filed each year. The application date is January 15 for entering freshmen. The College hosts an annual Filene Music Scholarship Competition to award four $40,000 ($10,000 per year) scholarships on the basis of musical ability without regard to financial need. Five $10,000 merit scholarships in math and science are also awarded annually. Other grants are available for superior math and science students. Detailed information concerning scholarships, grants, loans, and/or work awards can be obtained through the Office of Financial Aid.

STUDENT ORGANIZATIONS AND ACTIVITIES

Skidmore students participate in all aspects of academic and social life on campus. They play a major role in governing the College through the Student Government Association (SGA) and numerous major College committees. The SGA is authorized by the Board of Trustees; it is committed to the goals of responsible behavior and democratic self-government. The SGA concerns itself with a broad range of issues including educational policy, freshman orientation, SGA elections, social events, student publications, and student organizations and clubs. Elected faculty members and students serve side-by-side on three panels: the Academic Integrity Board, the All-College Council, and the Social Integrity Board.

ADMISSIONS PROCESS

Those seeking admission to Skidmore's freshman class should complete a secondary school curriculum that includes at least 16 credits in college-preparatory courses. The Admissions Committee is also pleased to consider applications from qualified high school juniors who plan to accelerate and enter college early. Applicants typically have completed 4 years of English, 4 years of a foreign language, 4 years of mathematics, 4 years of social studies, and 3–4 years of laboratory science. Applicants must provide a secondary school transcript, standardized test scores (SAT with writing or ACT with writing), letters of recommendation from two teachers of academic subjects, and a report from their guidance counselor. Skidmore recommends that applicants submit scores for three SAT Subject Tests. The school also strongly recommends a campus visit and interview. Through its participation in the Higher Education Opportunity Program (HEOP), Skidmore enrolls capable, energetic, and ambitious New Yorkers who, because of their academic and financial situations, would not otherwise gain admission to the College under traditional requirements.

An applicant for admission registers by completing the Common Application and submitting it with a $65 fee. All information should be postmarked by January 15. Applications from early decision candidates should be submitted by November 15 for the Round I early decision plan or by January 15 for the Round II early decision plan. Transfer candidates are urged to apply by April 1 for the next fall term and by November 15 for the next spring term.

ST. EDWARD'S UNIVERSITY

AT A GLANCE

St. Edward's University offers the best of both worlds—a small, personal learning community in a vibrant city. A private, Catholic, liberal arts university with about 5,300 students, St. Edward's emphasizes service, ethics and the development of an international perspective. Students get to know their professors in small classes with an average size of 20 students.

St. Edward's was founded by the Congregation of Holy Cross in 1885. This Catholic heritage endures today through the Holy Cross ideals of thinking critically, acting ethically, appreciating diversity, striving for social justice and developing the courage to take risks. About half of the students identify as Catholic, with the rest coming from a wide variety of faith backgrounds. Among undergraduates, 32 percent are Hispanic, 4 percent are African American, 3 percent are Asian/Pacific Islander, and 3 percent are international students. The university also has 930 graduate students.

LOCATION AND ENVIRONMENT

Austin, the capital of Texas, is a regional center for politics, education and culture. The city lies in the Texas Hill Country along the Colorado River. With a population of 780,000, Austin offers unlimited opportunities to enjoy the arts, including galleries, museums and theaters. National and local music acts find the spotlight at more than 200 venues, including those along Sixth Street, the most popular stretch of nightspots in town. Dubbed the "Live Music Capital of the World," Austin hosts the world-renowned South by Southwest music, film and interactive media festival each spring. The Austin City Limits festival brings dozens of bands to Zilker Park for three days each fall. With a diverse population made up of more than 50 percent minorities, Austin also offers a variety of city events, such as Mardi Gras, the Pecan Street Festival, the Bob Marley Fest, and more.

Outdoor enthusiasts take advantage of 300 days of sunshine, more than 200 parks, and three major lakes. They also find a wealth of opportunity for kayaking, canoeing, rowing, tubing, swimming, wind surfing, water skiing, cycling, mountain biking, hiking, rock climbing, frisbee golf, camping and more. When it's time to refuel, Austin offers an incredible variety of coffee shops and restaurants, with cuisines including Tex-Mex, barbeque, Ethiopian, sushi, Indian and raw vegan. It's not surprising that Austin has been named the country's coolest, best-read, most computer-literate and most fit city, as well as the third best place to live in the United States.

MAJORS AND DEGREES OFFERED

St. Edward's offers bachelor's degrees through five schools. Students in the School of Behavioral and Social Sciences can earn undergraduate degrees in:

-- Criminal Justice

-- Criminology

-- Environmental Science and Policy

-- Forensic Science

-- Global Studies

-- History

-- Latin American Studies

-- Political Science

-- Psychology

-- Social Work

-- Sociology

School of Management and Business students can earn degrees in:

-- Accounting

-- Accounting Information Technology

-- Business Administration

-- Digital Media Management

-- Economics

-- Entrepreneurship

-- Finance

-- International Business

-- Management

-- Marketing

Degrees through the School of Natural Sciences are available in:

-- Biochemistry

-- Bioinformatics

-- Biology

-- Chemistry

-- Computer Information Science

-- Computer Science

-- Environmental Chemistry

-- Forensic Chemistry

-- Mathematics

The School of Humanities offers degrees in:

-- Art

-- Communication

-- English Literature

-- English Writing and Rhetoric

-- Graphic Design

-- Liberal Studies

-- Philosophy

-- Photocommunications

-- Religious Studies

-- Spanish

-- Theater Arts

The School of Education also prepares students to teach in early childhood, elementary, middle school or secondary settings. Certification subject areas include art, kinesiology, English/language arts, bilingual education, biology, chemistry, history, mathematics, social studies, Spanish and theater. Students may also pursue certification in secondary religious education for Catholic schools.

Students who have not chosen a major participate in the innovative Academic Exploration Program, designed to familiarize students with their own strengths and interests as well as the university's academic programs.

In addition, St. Edward's offers pre-professional programs in Dentistry, Engineering, Law, Medicine and Physical Therapy. Eleven master's programs are also available:

-- Master of Accounting

-- Master of Arts in College Student Development

-- Master of Arts in Counseling

-- Master of Arts in Human Services

-- Master of Arts in Teaching

-- Master of Business Administration

-- Master of Business Administration in Digital Media Management

-- Master of Liberal Arts

-- Master of Science in Computer Information Systems

-- Master of Science in Organizational Leadership and Ethics

-- Master of Science in Project Management

ACADEMIC PROGRAMS

Each student completes an intensive, 57-credit-hour general education program that covers three areas: foundational skills (college math, computational skills, English writing, foreign language and oral communication); cultural foundations (a six-course cluster including American Dilemmas, Literature and Human Experience, and Contemporary World Issues); and foundation for values and decisions (a five-course cluster that includes Ethics and Science in Perspective). A course called Capstone—focusing on oral and written examination, analysis, and problem solving of a controversial topic—is the culmination of the general education program.

Students are encouraged to include internships, research and study abroad in their college experience. The university recently established a satellite campus in Angers, France, where students can take classes for the same tuition they'd pay in Austin. Additional study abroad destinations include Germany, Mexico, Argentina and Scotland.

CAMPUS FACILITIES AND EQUIPMENT

The university's 160-acre campus is located on a hilltop that is the highest point in the city of Austin. Downtown is a 10-minute drive away, and city bus lines stop at the edge of campus.

With a collage of modern and historic buildings, the St. Edward's campus reflects a legacy of progress. The university has opened six residence halls and two major classroom buildings since 2000. Unless living at their parents' home, freshmen must stay in residence halls. Sophomores may also choose on-campus housing including the university apartments. On-campus residence halls include communal kitchens, laundry rooms, and computer facilities.

Classrooms are equipped with the latest technology, and a wireless network spans the heart of campus. The Fine Arts Center includes studios and professional-grade labs for photo processing. The 65,000-square-foot John Brooks Williams Natural Sciences Center-North Building opened in fall 2006 and features state-of-the-art laboratories and a rooftop greenhouse. The Robert and Pearle Ragsdale Center, the hub of campus life, includes the South Congress Market cafeteria, the Jones Auditorium, the Mabee Ballrooms, the Student Life Office, a computer lab, and study rooms. At the Recreation and Convocation Center students can take advantage of a fitness center, an indoor pool, and basketball, volleyball, and racquetball/handball courts.

TUITION, ROOM, BOARD AND FEES

Tuition and fees for the 2010–2011 academic year total $26,484. Room and board costs average $8,816, with variations according to selection of residence hall and meal plan.

FINANCIAL AID

St. Edward's University is dedicated to making education affordable for its students and their families. Financial assistance at St. Edward's is provided through federal, state, and university sources and includes grants, scholar awards, loans, and work-study. As part of the admission process, each student is automatically reviewed for scholar awards based on academic performance. Students awarded academic scholarships are granted between $5,000 and $14,000 annually for all four years. To be considered, students must rank within the top 25 percent of their graduating high-school classes and earn SAT critical reading plus math scores of at least 1100 or ACT scores of at least 24. Other considerations include participation in extracurricular activities and strength of the admissions essay. Interested students should submit their applications for admission by Feb. 1 for scholar award consideration and the best financial assistance package.

All applicants are encouraged to file the Free Application for Federal Student Aid, or FAFSA. March 1 is the priority deadline to complete the FAFSA for students who plan to start in the fall semester. Freshmen who received grants for the 2009–2010 year were awarded an average of $14,447 in assistance, not including loans and campus jobs, and 89 percent of freshmen received some form of aid. Annually, St. Edward's awards more than $38.5 million in financial assistance. Families not applying for financial aid should inquire about payment options through the Office of Student Financial Services.

STUDENT ORGANIZATIONS AND ACTIVITIES

While classes are small and personal, St. Edward's offers a large variety of student organizations—more than 90 in all. Extracurricular activities include academic and professional organizations, cultural groups, spirit groups, service-oriented clubs, honor societies and special interest organizations. The student body is encouraged to be vocal, and the Student Government Association—consisting of elected members of the student body and representatives from constituencies around campus—is the primary vehicle for the student voice.

Aspiring writers contribute to the university's student-run newspaper, creative journal, and academic journal. Students taking part in the University Programming Board and the Residence Hall Association coordinate campus-wide events. St. Edward's hosts popular comedians, independent film screenings, poetry readings, and well-known local bands. The university's volunteer fair provides service-oriented students with an incredible number of possibilities to get involved in the surrounding community.

As an NCAA Division II member, St. Edward's offers plenty of opportunities for its athletes. Men's teams include baseball, basketball, golf, soccer, and tennis. Women have teams in basketball, golf, soccer, softball, tennis and volleyball. In the past three years, men's and women's varsity teams have won 19 Heartland Conference championships. Club and intramural sports offer competitive opportunities for students who don't wish to play at the varsity level.

ADMISSIONS PROCESS

The University accepts applications on a rolling basis, and applicants may use the print or online application from St. Edward's or the Common Application. A student will be notified of the admission decision four to six weeks after the Office of Admission has received the student's completed file. A file is not complete until each of the following has been submitted: the application form, the nonrefundable application fee, results from the SAT or ACT, an official high school transcript, an essay, and a teacher or counselor recommendation letter.

All applicants to St. Edward's are reviewed individually and evaluated according to demonstrations of academic accomplishment, writing skill, extracurricular participation, and results on standardized tests. Candidates for admission should be ranked in the top half of their high-school class and earn a minimum score of 500 on each section of the SAT or a composite score of 21 on the ACT. Students are required to submit the results of the applicable writing test.

For more specific information on the policies and procedures of admission, visit the University web site at www.gotostedwards.com.

For additional information, please contact:

Office of Admission

St. Edward's University

3001 South Congress Avenue

Austin, TX 78704-6489

Telephone: 512-448-8500 or 800-555-0164 (toll free)

Fax: 512-464-8877

E-mail: seu.admit@stedwards.edu

Web: www.gotostedwards.com

ST. LAWRENCE UNIVERSITY

AT A GLANCE

St. Lawrence University is a private, independent, non-denominational, university that seeks to provide a stimulating and rigorous liberal arts education to undergraduate students chosen for their intellectual potential and seriousness of purpose. Chartered in 1856, it is New York State's oldest continuously coeducational college or university. St. Lawrence's 2,200 students arrive from 41 states and 44 countries. The school is situated in Canton, New York (pop. 6,500), midway between the Adirondacks Mountains and Ottawa, Canada's national capital. The University provides unmatched access to social and cultural opportunities, international government, and outdoor recreation.

LOCATION AND ENVIRONMENT

St. Lawrence University provides a distinctive learning environment, offering 37 majors, 37 minors, and 3 graduate programs in education. Its First-Year Program is nationally recognized. St. Lawrence offers international study programs in 15 nations; it also belongs to the International Student Exchange Program. The University offers three off-campus programs within the United States, including a semester program in the Adirondack wilderness. St. Lawrence is currently undergoing an educational renaissance; bold academic initiatives are underway to maximize the learning potential of each and every student. A major facilities upgrade, fueled by more than $200 million, is providing expanded resources to undergraduates.

OFF-CAMPUS OPPORTUNITIES

St. Lawrence University offers international programs in 15 countries: Australia, Austria, Canada, China, Costa Rica, Denmark, England, France, India, Italy, Japan, Kenya, Spain, Thailand and Trinidad and Tobago; students can also direct-enroll in foreign universities in more than 35 additional countries through the International Student Exchange Program (ISEP).

The University also offers three off-campus study programs within the United States. These are located at: American University, Washington, D.C.; Fisk University, Nashville, Tennessee; and the Adirondack Semester, near Tupper Lake, New York.

MAJORS AND DEGREES OFFERED

Students may major in: African studies, anthropology, Asian studies, biochemistry, biology, biology/physics, conservation biology, Canadian studies, chemistry, computer science, conservation biology, economics, economics/mathematics, English, environmental studies, Estudios Hispanicos, fine arts, Francophone studies, geology, geology/physics, German studies, global studies, government, history, international economics/modern languages, mathematics, mathematics/computer science, multifield (self-designed), multi-language, music, neuroscience, performance & communication arts, philosophy, physics, psychology, religious studies, and sociology.

Students may pursue an optional minor in: African studies, African-American studies, anthropology, Asian studies, biology, Canadian studies, Caribbean and Latin American studies, chemistry, computer science, economics, education, English, Estudios Hispanicos, European studies, film & representation studies, fine arts, Francophone studies, gender & sexuality studies, geology, German studies, global studies, government, history, Japanese studies, mathematics, multi-field, music, Native American studies, outdoor studies, peace studies, performance & communication arts, philosophy, physics, psychology, religious studies, sociology, sports studies and exercise science, and statistics.

ACADEMIC PROGRAMS

The University confers the Bachelor of Arts and Bachelor of Science degrees; it also awards graduate degrees in education.

37 majors are available, as is the option to declare a double major (see Majors and Degrees Offered.)

The University offers 37 optional minors (see Majors and Degrees Offered.)

Qualified students may pursue five-year programs in business administration (this program leads to the MBA) and engineering, combining coursework at St. Lawrence with work at other institutions.

Specialized advising is available for postgraduate work in dentistry, law, medicine, and veterinary medicine.

The St. Lawrence distribution requirements involve coursework in six areas.

All students are expected to demonstrate writing competence before graduating.

The University provides extensive opportunities for honors projects and independent work.

CAMPUS FACILITIES AND EQUIPMENT

The University's two libraries, the Owen D. Young Library and Launders Science Library, contain more than half a million volumes, electronic resources, and ample space for reading and research.

Students also enjoy an arts center with recital hall, two theaters, and an art gallery as well as a 7,000-piece art collection. It has undergone recent significant renovations and additional renovation plans are underway.

St. Lawrence's science complex—including the new, Gold LEED-certified Johnson Hall of Science—is connected to the science library and computing center.

A 15,000-square-foot Student Center opened spring 2004, and new student townhouse-style residences for seniors opened fall 2003.

Recreational facilities include cross-country ski and running trails; a 133-station fitness center; a three-story climbing wall; indoor and outdoor tennis courts; and two gymnasium/fieldhouse complexes, one with a 9-lane/400-meter track and five tennis/basketball courts and the other with a 200-meter track, three tennis courts, and ten squash courts. Facilities also include a pool, ice arena, equestrian center, golf course, indoor golf facility, boathouse, astroturf field, baseball, soccer and softball fields.

TUITION, ROOM, BOARD AND FEES

For the 2009–2010 academic year, the comprehensive fee (including tuition, fees, and typical room and board) is $49,925.

Typically, annual personal costs and book expenditures cost an additional $1,650.

FINANCIAL AID

St. Lawrence University offers merit scholarships as well as need-based financial assistance.

The school grants aid in some form to more than 80 percent of its students. Aid packages typically consist of grants, student loans, and campus jobs.

Aid applicants must submit the Free Application for Federal Student Aid (FAFSA) between January 1 and February 1, and request that results be sent to St. Lawrence. Applicants must also submit the CSS PROFILE form.

STUDENT ORGANIZATIONS AND ACTIVITIES

Undergraduates commence their studies with the First-Year Program, which places approximately 30 first-year students in communities that live and learn together.

Once they achieve upper-class status, students may choose to live in traditional residence halls, interest-based theme suites, theme cottages, Greek houses, or senior townhouses.

St. Lawrence provides a full range of services to students, including comprehensive career planning as well as graduate and professional school guidance

Students seeking co-curricular activities can choose from nearly 100 organizations, including everything from student government to interest groups to arts and culture.

St. Lawrence boasts 32 intercollegiate teams including NCAA Division I teams in men's and women's ice hockey. All other teams compete in the NCAA's Division III. Club sports are also available, as is participation in a broad range of popular intramural sports.

The University is home to numerous recreational facilities, including: a 133-station fitness center; a three-story climbing wall; cross-country ski and running trails; and indoor and outdoor tennis courts. Students enjoy access to two gymnasium/field-house complexes; one has a 9-lane/400-meter track as well as five basketball/tennis courts, while the other has a 200-meter track, ten squash courts, and three tennis courts. Other facilities include an Astroturf field; baseball, softball, and soccer fields; an equestrian center; a golf course; an indoor golf facility; an ice arena; a boathouse; and a pool.

ADMISSIONS PROCESS

St. Lawrence seeks undergraduates with the capacity to manage a demanding academic regimen successfully. In addition, the ideal student contributes substantially to the quality of community life. The University strives to enroll students who represent the broadest possible range of economic, ethnic, geographic, and social backgrounds. The admissions committee values academic achievement, but ability in athletics, community service, or the creative arts is also considered a strong indicator of a student's capacity to benefit from his or her time at St. Lawrence. The University is test optional; students may choose whether they would like the results of their SAT Reasoning Test and/or ACT used during the evaluation process. Students are strongly encouraged to plan a campus visit; interviews may be scheduled to occur on campus. In certain areas, off-campus interviews are also an option.

The University makes no requirement of applicants' high school curricula; however, successful applicants generally demonstrate extensive preparation in the humanities, mathematics, the natural sciences, and the social sciences. Advanced Placement, IB and honors work are looked upon favorably, as they demonstrate the applicants intellectual curiosity and maturity. These are qualities that are highly sought by the admission committee.

St. Lawrence uses the Common Application exclusively and students are free to use any version of the Common Application. An application supplement is required and is available on-line. The application processing fee is $60. Applicants pursuing regular decision should submit all materials by February 1; they will be notified by late March. Students whose first choice is St. Lawrence may apply for Early Decision: the deadlines for Early Decision applications are November 15 and January 15. Early decision applicants are notified approximately one month after the deadline. Applicants for transfer to St. Lawrence should submit all application materials by November 1 for the spring semester or March 1 for the fall semester.

To request an application or for more information, students should contact:

OFFICE OF ADMISSIONS AND FINANCIAL AID

St. Lawrence University

Canton, NY 13617

Telephone: 315-229-5261

800-285-1856 (toll free)

admissions@stlawu.edu

www.stlawu.edu

ST. JOSEPH'S COLLEGE

Since 1916, St. Joseph's College has provided an affordable liberal arts education to a diverse group of students. Independent and coeducational, St. Joseph's prepares students for lives of integrity, social responsibility and service - lives that are worthy of the College's motto, *Esse non videri*—"To be and not to seem."

AT A GLANCE

At St. Joseph's College, we believe that qualified students deserve a top quality education for the best value. We've been transforming lives since 1916, consistently earning a place among the top 20 comprehensive colleges in the North as ranked by *U.S.News & World Report*. In the inaugural *Forbes Magazine Best Colleges Guide*, St. Josephs ranks as one of the top four-year private colleges in New York State. We offer stellar academics, innovative programs, accomplished professors and solid community connections – all while ensuring that tuition costs are reasonable and more than 70 percent of students receive financial aid. The end result: At St. Joseph's College, students earn a top-tier education while paying one of the lowest tuition rates of any private college in New York.

LOCATION AND ENVIRONMENT

Founded in 1916, St. Joseph's College is an independent, private institution with two campuses, one in the Clinton Hill section of Brooklyn (urban setting), New York and the other on Long Island in the town of Patchogue (suburban setting). The Brooklyn campus enrollment is over 1200 students, and the Long Island campus has over 5000 students.

OFF-CAMPUS OPPORTUNITIES

Brooklyn Campus

Our campus in Brooklyn is located in the safe Clinton Hill Historic District, home to several prestigious schools and a hub of cultural and intellectual activity. Manhattan career opportunities and cultural attractions lie within easy reach via public transportation. The Brooklyn Campus is surrounded by historic and unique architecture, tree-lined streets and new eateries and shops. The College developed its property on Vanderbilt Avenue into an attractive and attended parking facility.

Long Island Campus

Located in the Village of Patchogue on Great South Bay, our 27-acre Long Island campus is about 50 miles from Manhattan and 60 miles from Montauk Point in Suffolk County. Patchogue offers fine harbors, shops, restaurants, athletic fields and tennis courts right in the village.

MAJORS AND DEGREES OFFERED

Majors

Accounting

Biology

Business Administration

Chemistry (Only at the Brooklyn Campus)

Child Study

Computer Information Systems

Criminal Justice

English

History

Human Relations

Mathematics

Psychology

Recreation

Social Sciences

Economics

Political Science

Sociology

Spanish

Speech Communication

Minors

Accounting

American Studies

Business Administration

Chemistry

Computer Information Systems

Computer Science

Economics

English

History

Latino Studies

Mathematics

Music

Political Science

Religious Studies

Sociology

Spanish

Speech

Theatre

Certificate Programs

No matter what major you choose, you can earn an additional certificate. Certificate programs help you delve deeper into your specific interests, help you focus your career goals and give you a head start when entering the work world. We offer Certificate Programs in:

Criminology/Criminal Justice

Gerontology

Information Technology

Leadership & Supervision

Management

Marketing, Advertising & Public Relations

Religious Studies

Affiliated Programs

Want a fast track to an advanced degree? Try these special affiliated programs at St. Joseph's:

St. Joseph's College Accounting Program

(B.S. plus M.B.A., a five-year program)

Podiatric Medicine: St. Joseph's College/New York College of Podiatric Medicine.

(Leads to a Doctor of Podiatric Medicine, D.P.M.)

Computer Science: St. Joseph's College/Polytechnic University

(B.A. or B.S. plus M.S. in Computer Science, a five-year program)

Graduate Programs

St. Joseph's College provides a top-notch education that generates the knowledge and skills necessary for personal and professional success in today's world. We have recently expanded our programs to offer nine master's degrees, plus an Executive Master's in Business Administration online:

Executive M.B.A.

M.A. in Childhood or Adolescence Special Education with an annotation in Severe and Multiple Disabilities

M.A. in Infant/Toddler Early Childhood Special Education

M.A. in Literacy and Cognition

M.B.A. in Accounting

M.B.A. in Health Care Management

M.S. in Human Services Management and Leadership

M.S. in Management

M.S. in Management: with concentrations in Organizational Management, Health Care Management and Human Resources Management.

M.S. with a major in Nursing

ACADEMIC PROGRAMS

St. Joseph's has an outstanding honors program, which offers eligible students the opportunity to participate in a three-semester honors program as part of their bachelor's degree. The program provides an enriched and rigorous academic experience, meeting the special needs of those students who have demonstrated extraordinary academic accomplishment and ability and who are committed to achieving their full potential. In addition, St. Joseph's offers a freshmen year experience to help students make a seamless transition from high school to college. Study abroad opportunities are also available on each campus.

CAMPUS FACILITIES AND EQUIPMENT

Brooklyn Campus Facilities

SJC's Brooklyn Campus offers easy access to transit lines and brings students from every part of the New York Metropolitan area to the College each day. Students enjoy the freedom of campus life, while profiting from the many cultural and educational advantages of being in New York City. The Brooklyn campus provides architecturally stunning halls in the historical Clinton Hill section of Brooklyn, NY. The Brooklyn campus also offers state-of-the art technology, a gymnasium and fitness center, an outdoor theatre and The Dillon Child Study Center, which offers toddler, preschool and kindergarten programs based on the child development approach to the education of young children.

Long Island Campus Facilities

The 27-acre Long Island Campus, located in Patchogue adjacent to Great Patchogue Lake, is an ideal setting for studying, socializing and partaking in extracurricular activities. Just off of Sunrise Highway, the College is easily accessible from all parts of Long Island.

The Long Island Campus features modern, state-of-the-art facilities, including the recent completion of the Business Technology Center, the John A. Danzi Athletic Center, the Clare Rose Playhouse, the ultra-modern Callahan Library, O'Connor Hall (which includes the D'Ecclesiis Auditorium for fine arts and student theater productions) and Gregg Alfano Field, home to the Golden Eagles baseball, softball and soccer teams.

TUITION, ROOM, BOARD, AND FEES

Tuition for the fall 2009 is $16,200 and $530 per credit for NY State and out-of-area residents.

Housing is available for Brooklyn campus students. Costs vary by year, to learn more, please contact the admissions office at 718.940.5800.

FINANCIAL AID

Students should be sure to consult the St. Joseph's College catalogs for more information concerning financial aid programs, policies and requirements.

Financial aid applications are also available in the Office of Financial Aid on each campus.

Follow these instructions to apply for financial aid

1. Complete the Free Application for Federal Student Aid (FAFSA) online designating St. Joseph's College, Brooklyn NY as a recipient. You will be asked to enter St. Joseph's federal Title IV school code, which is 002825 for the Brooklyn Campus.

2. Complete the New York State Tuition Assistance Program (TAP) application online. Full-time semester students should use code No. 0755. Part-time students should complete the New York State Aid for Part-time Study (APTS) application. The APTS application is available at the Office of Financial Aid. For more information about New York State programs, please visit New York State Higher Education Services Corporation on the Web.

3. Complete any other requirements as requested by the Office of Financial Aid.

STUDENT ORGANIZATIONS AND ACTIVITIES

St. Joseph's College students have a plethora of extracurricular activity opportunities within reach through our Office of Co-Curricular Programs. Joining the Student Government Association, clubs, athletics, organizations and committees emphasizes leadership, community service and effective communication. We also arrange for a student's health insurance. To learn more about our student life opportunities, please visit our website at www.sjcny.edu.

ADMISSIONS PROCESS

What are the admissions requirements?

St. Joseph's College is a selective institution. Applicants are evaluated on an individual basis. The College enrolls students that are academically talented and diverse. Successful admissions candidates typically have:

- a high school diploma or its equivalent

- solid grades in a strong college preparatory curriculum

- standardized test scores that demonstrate the promise of success in college-level courses

Students can obtain a copy of our application or also apply online, by visiting www.sjcny.edu.

When should I apply? When is the application deadline?

St. Joseph's College admits students on a rolling basis, though there are priority dates.

For the fall semester, the scholarship priority date is March 15 for freshmen and August 1 for transfer students. For the spring semester, the priority date is January 1 for both freshmen and transfer students.

What else do I need to submit in addition to my application?

Applicants for Brooklyn and Long Island must also submit high school transcripts and SAT or ACT scores. A personal statement/essay and two letters of recommendation are also requested.

Students wishing to transfer to St. Joseph's should file their applications at least three months in advance of the expected date of matriculation. Transfer students must request that official transcripts from all former colleges, marked catalogs of former colleges and a listing of courses in progress be sent to the St. Joseph's College Office of Admissions.

We provide a block transfer of courses (up to 64 credits) for students who have earned an associate in arts, or an associate in science (with science emphasis) degree in a transfer program at an accredited community or junior college.

STATE UNIVERSITY OF NEW YORK—
COLLEGE OF ENVIRONMENTAL SCIENCE AND FORESTRY

AT A GLANCE

ESF is the premier college in the United States for academic programs focused on the science, design, engineering, and management of our environment and natural resources. Founded in 1911 as the New York State College of Forestry at Syracuse University, ESF is also one of the nation's oldest environmental colleges. As the College begins its centennial year, its mission has expanded to address the wide range of environmental issues facing our global society. The College is a part of NY State's 64 campus system for higher education, and was re-chartered in 1972 as the State University of New York College of Environmental Science and Forestry. ESF currently offers 22 undergraduate and 30 graduate degree programs, including 8 Ph.D. programs, and is nationally-recognized for its outstanding value, small class size, and student engagement in learning.

ESF students share a common concern for the environment. They are hardworking, active learners who want to use their knowledge and experience to confront society's tough questions and make the world a better place to live. They come to the College from throughout the United States to pursue a focused professional education that prepares them for a great variety of career pathways and opportunities for advanced study.

The College's academic programs serve some of the fastest growing and most productive sectors of the nation's "green" economy. Students are broadly educated, prepared for responsibilities as citizens, and trained to be problem-solvers, managers and leaders. The hallmarks of the undergraduate educational experience at ESF include career-oriented programs with an unmatched range of course offerings, along with experiential learning provided through field experiences, internships and student-faculty research projects. Faculty members are responsible for delivering all undergraduate instruction in addition to meeting their research, graduate level teaching and public service responsibilities. More than 90% of the Faculty have completed a Ph.D. or terminal degree, and more than 80% are employed in full-time positions.

ESF graduates experience excellent employment opportunities and are admitted to the nation's best graduate schools. In a typical year, more than 95% are employed or enrolled in advanced study within six months of graduation.

The academic, cultural, and social lives of ESF students are enhanced through the College's long-standing partnership with neighboring Syracuse University. ESF students live in SU residence halls and can access many of the University's academic and student life resources while paying affordable SUNY tuition rates. The College owns more than 25,000 acres of forest property located throughout NY State, and operates several regional campuses and field stations that provide special research and experiential learning opportunities. The ESF Ranger School campus at Wanakena, located in the heart of the 6 million acre Adirondack State Park, offers degree programs in land surveying and forest technology.

LOCATION AND ENVIRONMENT

Syracuse, a metropolitan area of nearly 732,000 people located in the heart of upstate NY, is a leader in healthcare and the manufacture of pharmaceuticals, automotive parts, medical equipment, aerospace and defense systems. It offers many cultural and recreational opportunities, including a symphony orchestra, museums, live theater, and historic places. Area residents closely follow the NCAA Division I intercollegiate athletics program featured at Syracuse University, along with minor league teams in hockey and baseball. The driving time to Syracuse from New York City, Philadelphia, Boston, Toronto, and Montreal is about five hours; from Buffalo and Albany, about three hours. Outdoorsmen have easy access to the Finger Lakes and Adirondack Park. The city is served by a modern international airport and major bus and rail lines. Syracuse has been recognized as one of America's "greenest" cities for its environmental efforts.

MAJORS AND DEGREES OFFERED

The College of Environmental Science and Forestry offers three undergraduate degrees: the Bachelor of Science (BS), the Bachelor of Landscape Architecture (BLA), and the Associate in Applied Science (AAS). BS degree programs include aquatic and fisheries science, bioprocess engineering, biotechnology, chemistry, conservation biology, construction management, environmental biology, environmental science, environmental studies, environmental resources engineering, forest ecosystem science, forest health, forest resources management, natural history and interpretation, natural resources management, paper engineering, paper science, and wildlife science. The BLA degree, which requires five years of study, is awarded in landscape architecture. AAS degrees are awarded in forest technology or land surveying technology at ESF's Ranger School campus.

ACADEMIC PROGRAMS

ESF offers an undergraduate Honors Program and more than 60 service-learning courses. Specialized study options within the biology program include plant physiology, entomology, environmental microbiology, pest management, plant physiology, plant science, zoology, and additional areas. A five-week period of summer field study, usually taken at ESF's Cranberry Lake Biological Station, is a required part of the biology program. Options for specialization within the chemistry program include biochemistry and polymer chemistry. The College offers three engineering programs focused on environmental and chemical engineering specializations. The natural resources management curriculum focuses on environmental, water, and recreation resources and requires a four week period of summer field study. The environmental studies program offers options in environmental communication, environmental policy and law, and biological science applications. The nationally-ranked landscape architecture curriculum requires participation in an off-campus independent study project in the fifth year. Students majoring in biology or chemistry may complete teacher certification through a joint program with Syracuse University. Many undergraduates complete some of their liberal arts requirements through courses offered at SU while paying SUNY tuition. Transfer agreements also exist with SUNY Upstate Medical University in Syracuse to offer several health-related programs, including a 3+3 degree in physical therapy. ESF's new bioprocess engineering program is focused on the production of biofuels, and is the first program of its kind in the Northeast.

CAMPUS FACILITIES AND EQUIPMENT

Specialized facilities and equipment include electron microscopes, plant growth chambers, air conditioned greenhouses, an animal environmental simulation chamber, a bioacoustical laboratory, a radioisotope laboratory, nuclear magnetic resonance spectrometers, gas chromatography apparatus, a mass spectrometer, ultracentrifuges, and X ray and infrared spectrophotometers. The photogrammetric and geodetic facilities of the environmental resources engineering department are among the most extensive available in the United States. The paper science and engineering laboratory has a semi commercial paper mill with accessory equipment. The construction management program has access to a strength of materials laboratory, a pilot scale plywood laboratory, and a machining laboratory. The landscape architecture faculty has a one of a kind environmental simulation laboratory with a visual simulator. Eight greenhouses and a forest insectary are used to produce plant and insect materials for the classroom and laboratory. Extensive collections are available, including wood samples from all over the world, botanical materials, insects, birds, mammals, and fishes. A new six-story chemistry facility with 36 laboratories opened in 1997. Laboratories for environmental resources engineering and sustainable construction management, as well as student computing labs, were totally renovated in 2007.

The F. Franklin Moon Library provides more than 135,000 cataloged items and more than 2,000 print and electronic journals. ESF's library facilities and services are supplemented by the collections available to students through Syracuse University and SUNY Upstate Medical University, both of which are within easy walking distance.

ESF's regional campuses in Tully, Warrensburg, Cranberry Lake, Newcomb, and Wanakena NY offer a great diversity of forest sites used as outdoor teaching laboratories and for intensive research. ESF operates several additional field stations to support its instruction, research, and public service programs, including one in Costa Rica.

FINANCIAL AID

Many financial aid programs are available for ESF students, and more than 85 percent receive support. Types of financial aid include academic (merit) and need-based scholarships, low interest student loans, and student employment. Students are encouraged to apply for aid by completing the Free Application for Federal Student Aid (FAFSA). Special scholarships funded by the College Foundation are often available to students residing outside NY State.

STUDENT ORGANIZATIONS AND ACTIVITIES

The College has a representative Undergraduate Student Association, and representatives also participate in student government at Syracuse University. ESF's student government organizes and presents social activities, and representatives attend College administrative meetings, communicate concerns and ideas to the administration, and serve as a conduit of information back to the student body. ESF students participate in more than 300 clubs and organizations at Syracuse University, in addition to more than 40 offered on the ESF campus. Student community service efforts have led to the College being listed among a select group of institutions on the President's Higher Education Community Service Honor Roll. Students typically provide more than 65,000 of community service throughout Syracuse and Central New York each year.

ESF is a member of the National Association of Intercollegiate Athletics (NAIA), and our "Mighty Oaks" athletics teams compete in men's and women's soccer, cross country and golf with colleges located across NY State and in surrounding states. The athletics program also features a traditional timber sports team (Woodsmen's Team) for men and women.

ADMISSIONS PROCESS

Students interested in the academic programs offered at ESF have four enrollment options: Early Action, Regular Freshman Admission, Guaranteed Transfer Admission, and Regular Transfer Admission.

The Early Action option is for freshman candidates who wish to complete the admission process early in their senior year of high school. Early Action candidates must have their application completed by November 15 and are notified of the decision by January 1.

Students not admitted under the Early Action option are considered for Regular (Rolling) Freshman Admission. The Regular Admission plan has a suggested application deadline of January 15, and students are notified on a rolling basis until the entering class is filled. All freshman candidates should demonstrate strong academic performance in a college preparatory program with emphasis on mathematics and science. Freshman candidates may apply for admission to a specific program of study or enter the College's "undeclared" program option.

Guaranteed Transfer Admission (GTA) candidates apply to ESF as high school seniors but are offered delayed admission to their sophomore or junior year of college. Students who plan to attend another college prior to transferring to ESF select this option to ensure a place at ESF for their chosen entry date. This option may be offered to students who do not meet the College's selective admission criteria at their time of application.

Students applying as transfer students from other institutions are admitted to ESF on the basis of their previous college coursework and overall academic aptitude. Consideration is given to both the quality and the appropriateness of each student's prior academic experience. Students normally spend one or two years at any college of their choice. ESF has worked with a number of four year and two-year colleges in New York, Connecticut, Maryland, Massachusetts, New Jersey, Pennsylvania, and Rhode Island to develop Cooperative Transfer Programs to facilitate transfer credit evaluation. All admission acceptances are conditional upon satisfactory completion of coursework in progress.

Students may apply for fall or spring admission. Admission decisions are made on a rolling basis until the class is filled. Decisions for the fall semester are made beginning on or about December 15, and decisions for the spring semester are made beginning on or about October 15. Students may request an application form directly from the Office of Undergraduate Admissions at ESF or submit their application online at www.suny.edu or at www.esf.edu. ESF also accepts The Common Application form.

Requests for more information should be directed to:

Office of Undergraduate Admissions

SUNY College of Environmental Science and Forestry

1 Forestry Drive

Syracuse, NY 13210-2779

Telephone: 315-470-6600

Fax: 315-470-6933

Email: esfinfo@esf.edu

World Wide Web: www.esf.edu

STATE UNIVERSITY OF NEW YORK—PURCHASE

BASICS

Located on a wooded 500-acre suburban campus in Westchester County only 35 minutes by outside of New York City, Purchase College, a public coeducational college, features a learning environment that's typical of a small, private college. Now enrolling 4200 students, the college founded by Governor Nelson Rockefeller in 1967 as the cultural gem of the SUNY system, enjoys an extraordinary reputation for its arts programs and high rankings for its liberal arts and sciences programs. Purchase College attracts students and faculty from around the world seeking a place where they can develop their talents, expand their minds, and prepare for a life of creative independence.

Uniquely combining the intellectual traditions and spirit of discovery of the liberal arts and sciences with the energy and excitement of professional training in the performing and the visual arts, Purchase College encourages students to "think wide open." Creativity, individual accomplishment, and diversity are strongly emphasized in the curriculum. A Purchase education culminates in a Senior Project that is designed by the student in consultation with a faculty advisor and ultimately serves as an excellent springboard to a career or to graduate or professional school. The professional training BFA programs offer many apprenticeships and other professional opportunities in nearby New York City.

Our Alumni includes actors Edie Falco, Parker Posey and Stanley Tucci; filmmaker Chris Wedge (Ice Age, Robots); a Pulitzer Prize winning playwright; a MacArthur Genius Award winning author and environmentalist; an internationally known cancer researcher; top business executives; the Chief Political Correspondent for The New York Times; Broadway stage designers and lighting technicians; award-winning choreographers and dancers; singer/songwriter Regina Spektor, and hip-hop artist Amanda Diva.

ACADEMIC PROGRAMS

Interdisciplinary learning and thinking are the hallmarks of a Purchase college education. That commitment to enabling students to be educated across multiple disciplines is exemplified in many academic programs including New Media, Gender Studies, Latin American Studies, Media Society and the Arts, and Arts Management. Students may also pursue a self-determined interdisciplinary course of study with the assistance of a dedicated faculty committee. The college has recently developed a new School of Film and Media Studies to more formally enable the flexible integration of media-related studies and allow students to gain knowledge in almost all areas of the wide-ranging field. In addition, our Student Affairs and Academic Affairs areas have been merged to assure maximum integration of a student's intellectual and extracurricular life Community outreach, service-learning programs, career-related internships, and volunteer opportunities about to help students develop leadership skills and engage more deeply with the world beyond campus.

The core curriculum at Purchase College requirements serves to engage all undergraduate students in essential learning offering the serious examination of essential ideas in the context of small classes. The college also encourages students to follow an 8-Semester plan that enable student to participate in high impact academic and extracurricular activities including Study Abroad, internships, and service learning as well as graduate in a timely fashion.

Over 95 percent of the liberal arts and sciences faculty at the college have earned a Ph.D. or equivalent degree, and include widely published authors, scientists and scholars. Bona fide professionals in their respective fields teach Purchase College conservatory and art/design school courses in the master-apprentice tradition.

MAJORS & DEGREES OFFERED

The College offers traditional undergraduate majors, including anthropology, art history, biochemistry, biology, chemistry, math and computer science, economics, English literature, foreign languages and cultures, history, math, philosophy, political science, psychology and sociology, as well as majors in relatively new, interdisciplinary fields such as Afro-American & African studies; arts management, Asian studies; cinema studies, drama studies, Latin American Studies; women's studies; creative and dramatic writing; journalism; environmental studies; new media, and media, society and the arts. Innovative new areas of study that integrate the College's strengths in the arts, liberal arts and the sciences are added regularly. Purchase also provides nationally recognized training in acting; dance; dramatic writing; film; music composition and performance; jazz studies; studio production; theatre design/technology; drawing; painting; sculpture; 3-D media and graphic design; book and/or printmaking; and photography and recently launched a liberal arts degree in visual arts. Purchase College awards the B.A., B.S., B.F.A., Mus.B., Music Performer's Certificate and Music Artists Diploma, as well as the M.A. and M.F.A.

ADMISSIONS

Admission to Purchase College is competitive and involves a thorough evaluation of high school coursework, standardized test scores (SAT or ACT), an essay, and other supporting documents. In general, the Admissions Committee looks for indicators that a student will be academically successful in a college curriculum and graduate within four years. We recommend that freshman applicants complete a minimum of 16 college preparatory courses (which in New York State includes Regents coursework) including a minimum of 4 units of English, 3 units of math, 2 units of lab science, 2 units of social science, 2 units of foreign language, and 3 units of electives. The SAT or the ACT are required. All applicants to the Performing and Visual Arts programs must provide either a resume or repertoire list, writing sample or essay, and take part in a audition, portfolio review or screening interview, depending upon the program. The college also requires freshman entering the Creative Writing program to provide a creative writing portfolio. Transfer students need official transcripts from all the colleges they have attended.

Many adult and non-traditional learners take classes at Purchase College through The School of Liberal Studies and Continuing Education, either for their degrees or as non-matriculated students. The School of LS&CE also offers classes that provide professional development for teachers, graduate test preparation, and certification for arts managers, fundraisers, engineers and early childhood educators. For more details and assistance, please contact: Office of Admissions Purchase College, State University of New York Tele.: (914) 251-6300 E-mail: admissions@purchase.edu

STUDENT BODY

While the majority of Purchase College students are from New York State, the college ranks among the highest in the SUNY system for out-of-state students. At Purchase, you might share a class with someone from NYC, take in a concert with someone else from the Midwest or the West Coast, and hang out with another student from overseas. About 65 percent of students are enrolled in the humanities, natural and social sciences; the other 35 percent study in one of the professional performing and visual arts programs.

CAMPUS LIFE AND FACILITIES

Students make a difference in everything that happens on campus. The Purchase College Student Government is a strong advocate for students' views, and there are more than 40 active clubs and organizations, including the Jazz Club, the Literary Society, the Pre-Med Club, the Organization of African Peoples in America, Hillel, the Gay, Lesbian and Transgendered Union, the Anime Club and the X-Gen/Christian Fellowship. The student radio station and a student-run newspaper are always looking for talent. The Purchase College Panthers field a dozen varsity men's and women's NCAA Division III teams; and there are plenty of intramural sports and activities for every interest and experience level. Even with NYC so near, Purchase students enjoy local bands, poetry slams, art shows, special events, dance concerts, plays and music recitals right on campus. The College boasts its own dance troupe, symphony orchestra, opera company, repertory theatre, jazz orchestra, and contemporary music ensemble. And, the Terra Ve Cafe© on campus was recently named the fifth best "vegetarian-friendly" dining option at a U.S. college or university. You can hear more directly from some of your future classmates at the "Experience Purchase" page of the College's Web site: www.purchase.edu.

In addition to our academic buildings and facilities, the campus is home to the largest Performing Arts Center between Boston and NYC that hosts more than 600 performances a year and to the Neuberger Museum of Art, one of the nation's ten largest university-based art museums. Both will enrich your studies and provide many opportunities for entertainment. The College believes that artists and scholars inspire and stimulate one another and that both forms of knowledge and discovery are essential to success in the 21st century.

School Says . . .

SWARTHMORE COLLEGE

Swarthmore celebrates the life of the mind and gives students of uncommon intellectual ability the knowledge, insight, skills, and experience to become leaders for the common good.

AT A GLANCE

Swarthmore, one of the nation's finest institutions of higher learning, is a college like no other. Private, yet open to all regardless of financial need. American, yet decidedly global in outlook and diversity, drawing students from around the world and all 50 states. Small, yet with the financial strength to offer students and faculty generous resources to push their own and the world's understanding of disciplines from Arabic to plasma physics, from microbiology to dance, from engineering to art history.

Swarthmoreans are CEO patent-holders who bring technology to underserved markets, investment bankers looking for alternative forms of energy, lawyers who become college presidents, doctors who serve in Congress, winners of the Nobel Prize. A Swarthmorean founded the first liberal arts college in Ghana. Another led the team that developed the Hubble Space Telescope. Swarthmoreans invented hypertext and helped women win the right to vote.

So much of what Swarthmore stands for, from its commitment to curricular breadth and rigor to its demonstrated interest in facilitating discovery and fostering ethical intelligence among exceptional young people, lies in the quality and passion of its faculty. Professors at Swarthmore are leading scholars and researchers in their fields, yet remain deeply committed to serving their students as outstanding teachers and mentors. A student/faculty ratio of 8:1 ensures that students have close, meaningful engagement with their professors, preparing them to translate the skills and understanding gained at Swarthmore into the mark they want to make on the world.

LOCATION AND ENVIRONMENT

Located 11 miles southwest of Philadelphia, Swarthmore's idyllic, 399-acre campus is an arboretum, complete with rolling lawns, creek, wooded hills, and hiking trails. From its state-of-the-art LEED certified science center to its new residence halls with environmentally responsible design, Swarthmore's buildings and architecture stand as national models of curricular and co-curricular undergraduate facilities.

OFF-CAMPUS OPPORTUNITIES

Swarthmore College is a member of the Tri-College consortium, linking our campus to Bryn Mawr and Haverford Colleges, academically and socially. Students are also able to take courses at the University of Pennsylvania. The College offers shuttles to the other Tri-Co schools, local community service sites, movie theaters and shopping complexes, as well as to the city of Philadelphia. Public transportation is readily available with a train station located on campus; the ride to Philadelphia takes approximately 20 minutes.

MAJORS AND DEGREES OFFERED

Swarthmore College awards two degrees, the Bachelor of Arts and the Bachelor of Science. The following courses of study are offered at the College:

Art and Art History

Asian Studies

Astronomy

Biology

Black Studies

Chemistry and Biochemistry

Classics

Cognitive Science

Comparative Literature

Computer Science

Dance

Economics

Educational Studies

Engineering

English Literature

Environmental Studies

Film and Media Studies

Gender and Sexuality Studies

History

Interpretation Theory

Islamic Studies

Latin American Studies

Linguistics

Mathematics and Statistics

Medieval Studies

Modern Languages and Literatures (including Arabic, Chinese, French, German, Japanese, Russian, and Spanish)

Music

Peace and Conflict Studies

Philosophy

Physics

Political Science

Psychology

Public Policy

Religion

Sociology and Anthropology

Theater

ACADEMIC PROGRAMS

The College offers more than 600 courses a year; an exceptional honors program; individual special majors; a program in education that leads to Pennsylvania secondary school certification; and undergraduate research opportunities in the sciences, social sciences, humanities, and engineering.

Swarthmore's Honors Program features faculty working with small groups of dedicated and accomplished students; an emphasis on independent learning; students entering into a dialogue with peers, teachers, and examiners; a demanding program of study in major and minor fields; and an examination at the end of two years' study by outside scholars.

CAMPUS FACILITIES AND EQUIPMENT

The 399-acre campus is an arboretum. Arts resources include an art gallery, dance studios, cinema, and theater performance space. Highlights of Swarthmore's library facilities include the Friends Historical Library and the Peace Collection. The athletics facilities include a lighted stadium complex, a 400-meter dual durometer track, a synthetic grass playing field, fitness center, and indoor tennis courts. The Science Center is LEED certified. The College's two newest residence halls feature loft-style rooms and environmentally friendly green roofs.

TUITION, ROOM, BOARD, AND FEES

For 2009–2010, the College charges including tuition, room, board, and student activity fee total $49,600. The activity fee covers not only the usual student services—health, library, laboratory fees, for example—but admission to all social, cultural, and athletic events on campus.

FINANCIAL AID

Swarthmore maintains a need-blind admissions policy for U.S. citizens and permanent residents, wherein admission and financial aid decisions are made independently. Financial aid is also available for some international students. All Swarthmore aid awards are loan-free and are packaged to meet the full demonstrated need for admitted students.

STUDENT ORGANIZATIONS AND ACTIVITIES

With more than 100 student clubs and organizations on campus, dozens of community service groups, 22 varsity athletic teams, free lectures and performances occurring daily on campus, and full academic schedules, Swarthmore students are rarely idle. The student culture encourages involvement and a strong sense of community.

ADMISSIONS PROCESS

In an effort to seek a variety of students leading to a well-rounded class, the admissions staff carefully considers a number of criteria without a rigid emphasis on any one factor in particular. Applicants are evaluated based upon the following:

- High school record (as well as strength of curriculum)
- Rank in class (if high school ranks)
- Standardized tests
- Extracurricular commitments
- Essays (included in application)
- Recommendations (two from academic teachers, one from counselor)
- Interview (highly recommended but not required)

SWEET BRIAR COLLEGE

AT A GLANCE

Since its founding in 1901, Sweet Briar College has been deeply committed to the education of women. It is consistently ranked as one of the top, national liberal arts and sciences colleges in the country. And in 2010, Sweet Briar was recognized by the Princeton Review as a private college "Best Buy." The excellent academic reputation, beautiful campus, and attention to the individual, attract smart, confident women who want to excel.

At Sweet Briar, faculty and staff members are committed to helping each individual young woman reach her full potential both inside and outside the classroom. As a result, the College has put together a series of guarantees (titled "The Sweet Briar Promise") to ensure that every student has a college experience that will land her exactly where she wants to be after college.

The College has a wide geographic, ethnic, and socioeconomic representation. About 650 women from more than forty states and fifteen countries are enrolled at Sweet Briar's Virginia campus; another 125 students are enrolled in Sweet Briar's coed Junior Year in France and Junior Year in Spain programs.

A Sweet Briar education sets in motion the conviction that any goal is achievable, and prepares young women for a lifetime of success. Classes average twelve students, and a student to faculty ratio of 9:1 ensures academic interaction and personal attention.

LOCATION AND ENVIRONMENT

Sweet Briar is located in central Virginia in the foothills of the Blue Ridge Mountains. The spacious campus of 3,250 acres contains hiking trails, nature preserves, and spectacular views. The core buildings, designed by Ralph Adams Cram, form the Sweet Briar College National Historic District.

The College opened a 53,000 square foot Fitness and Athletic Center addition to its gymnasium in November 2009, as well as a new "green" residence hall/townhouse facility in August 2009. The FAC includes multiple volleyball/tennis courts, a suspended indoor running track, racquetball courts, lots of student common space, and a movie theater. The "Green Village" is composed of 5 buildings, each with 3 townhomes, providing an independent living option for 60 seniors and juniors. Other recent additions to campus include a student commons that opened in 2002 and a fine arts facility that opened in 2006. Sweet Briar is the only college in the country with a residential artists' colony on its campus, the Virginia Center for the Creative Arts. The on-campus equestrian center, one of the largest and best-designed college facilities in the country, attracts both competitive and recreational riders.

The community atmosphere of the College is enhanced by the large proportion of faculty and administrators who also live on campus.

The College is 12 miles north of Lynchburg, Virginia; less than an hour south of Charlottesville, VA; and about 3 hours southwest of Washington, D.C.

OFF-CAMPUS OPPORTUNITIES

By the time they graduate, almost half of each Sweet Briar class will have studied abroad.

Sweet Briar owns and operates two study abroad programs (in France and in Spain); maintains formal exchange agreements with universities in Germany, Italy, Japan, and Scotland; and allows students to explore any study abroad program offered through another college or university giving students almost unlimited opportunity for an international study experience. Scholarship assistance is available for students who wish to study abroad.

The Sweet Briar Junior Year in France Program (JYF) is the oldest coeducational intercollegiate American program in Paris. The Sweet Briar Junior Year in Spain Program (JYS) offers students the opportunity to study at the University of Seville, one of Spain's most prestigious universities. In 2006, both the JYF and JYS programs began offering a 5-week session in May/June so that students are able to have an international study experience and not miss an academic semester on campus. In addition, Sweet Briar works with students to select appropriate programs and destinations throughout the world for study during the academic year or for a summer session.

Sweet Briar participates in the Tri-College Consortium along with Randolph College and Lynchburg College. In addition to taking courses at the other colleges, students can also participate in social and cultural activities on those college campuses.

MAJORS AND DEGREES OFFERED

Sweet Briar awards the Bachelor of Arts, Bachelor of Science, or Bachelor of Fine Arts degree in the following majors: Anthropology, Archaeology, Art History, Biochemistry and Molecular Biology, Biology, Business, Chemistry, Classics, Dance, Economics, Engineering Management, Engineering Science, English, English and Creative Writing, Environmental Science, Environmental Studies, French, German, German Studies, Government, History, International Affairs, Italian Studies, Liberal Studies (Education), Mathematical Economics, Mathematics, Mathematics-Physics, Modern Languages and Literatures, Music, Philosophy, Physics, Psychology, Religion, Sociology, Spanish, Studio Art, and Theatre.

Additional area studies, minors, and certificate programs include: Arts Management, Communications, Equine Studies, Film Studies, Gender Studies, Italian, Latin American Studies, Law & Society, Leadership, Musical Theatre, and pre-professional programs in law, medicine, and veterinary medicine.

Students may design interdisciplinary majors focusing on a topic of special interest or may construct a personalized major.

In May 2004, Sweet Briar began offering the Master of Education and the Master of Arts in Teaching degrees. The MAT is a full-time program, which can be completed in 11 months (including teacher licensure requirements); the M.Ed. can be completed full-time or part-time to allow working professionals the opportunity to join the program. Both graduate programs are coed.

ACADEMIC PROGRAMS

Sweet Briar College supports students in realizing their full potential through the "Sweet Briar Promise" - a series of six guarantees that provides each student the opportunity to have a resume-building internship, study abroad, develop and apply her leadership skills, personalize her academic program, conduct primary research with a faculty mentor, and build an advising team of faculty, staff, and alumnae professionals so that she is best prepared for success after college.

The general education program has 4 components: English 104 (composition), Skills Requirements, Experiences Requirements, and Knowledge Area Requirements. Our general education approach is based on the belief that students will benefit more from their college experience and be better prepared for life after college if they understand the value of a liberal arts curriculum and actively cultivate, in and out of the classroom, their intellectual, social, cultural, creative, and recreational potential to prepare for a life of continual growth, responsibility, and fulfillment. The curriculum emphasizes comprehensive understanding, analysis, reflection, creation, and communication across disciplines. Independent studies, available at all levels, and seminars are included in most majors, with a culminating senior course or exercise required in most majors.

Sweet Briar has ten honorary societies including a chapter of Phi Beta Kappa.

The four-year Honors Program is nationally recognized for its innovative partnering of interdisciplinary academic and co-curricular programs. Honors students take special tutorials, known as honors variants and honors seminars. Seniors may choose to complete a yearlong research project culminating in an honors thesis on an original topic in the major department.

Sweet Briar provides free of charge to all students academic support services that include assistance with papers and study strategies, a personalized time management system, stress management advice, tutoring information, and one-on-one peer mentoring. The Academic Resource Center (ARC) also provides support and learning strategies for students with a diagnosed learning difference.

Sweet Briar operates on a traditional, two-semester calendar.

CAMPUS FACILITIES AND EQUIPMENT

Sweet Briar has the largest private undergraduate library collection in the state of Virginia with resources including more than 240,000 volumes, 1,000 journal subscriptions, 430,000 microforms, 6,800 audiovisual materials, and special libraries in art, music, and the sciences.

In 2009, Sweet Briar upgraded its computer network to a state-of-the-art wireless platform that allows high-speed Internet access from all academic and administrative buildings, as well as residence hall rooms. Connection to the campus network is also possible from most outdoor, student-used spaces.

Students enrolled in science courses use modern equipment that enhances faculty-student collaborative research. A sample of equipment used by students on a regular basis includes a scanning electron microscope with digital imaging system, DNA sequencing equipment, two nuclear magnetic resonance spectrometers (NMR; 400 MHz and 60 MHz), an atomic absorption spectrometer (AAS), a modular LASER laboratory, a gas chromatograph/mass spectrograph (GC/MS), a scanning tunneling microscope, a 10-inch diameter reflecting telescope, a 20,000 Pound Capacity Universal Testing Machine, a Rockwell Hardness Tester, and many additional pieces of equipment provided from grant funds provided by the National Science Foundation.

TUITION, ROOM, BOARD AND FEES

For the 2009–2010 academic year, tuition was $28,860 and room and board totaled $10,460. Books, supplies, and student fees average about $1,500. Personal expenses average $1,000.

FINANCIAL AID

Sweet Briar offers merit scholarships to qualified applicants that range up to $15,000 per year. Scholarships are awarded based on the applicant's high school gpa and best standardized test score. There is no separate application required.

Need-based financial aid is offered based on a family's demonstrated need as determined by the Free Application for Federal Student Aid (FAFSA). More than 90% of students receive some type of institutional financial support.

Scholarships for non-U.S. citizens are also available on a competitive basis.

STUDENT ORGANIZATIONS AND ACTIVITIES

Students who benefit the most from the Sweet Briar experience are those who get involved in the co-curricular activities on campus. Sweet Briar students recognize that one of the advantages of a women's college is the opportunity for women to be involved and to hold leadership roles in organizations and activities.

More than fifty campus organizations are available, including honor societies, community service groups, a multicultural club, a student newspaper, drama and dance clubs, a radio station, and singing groups. Students plan and participate in an extensive array of concerts, films, and dance and theatre productions as well as workshops and master classes by visiting scholars and performers. Recent visitors have included writer, Salman Rushdie; environmental attorney, Robert F. Kennedy, Jr.; and columnist, Christine Brennan.

Varsity athletes compete in NCAA Division III field hockey, lacrosse, soccer, softball, swimming, tennis, and volleyball. Sweet Briar's riding program, both competitive and instructional, has consistently garnered national recognition.

Students participate actively in the governance of the College through offices and committee positions of the Student Government Association. The Association and its committees are largely responsible for the self-governance of the student body.

ADMISSIONS PROCESS

Sweet Briar seeks talented women who are adventurous, enthusiastic about learning, and want to take an active part in their education. In addition to academic achievement, the Admissions Committee looks for qualities such as academic promise, independent thinking, upholding of ethical principles, creativity, and an appreciation of diversity. Sweet Briar welcomes students of all economic, ethnic, geographic, religious, and social backgrounds.

Requirements include a minimum of 4 units in English, 3 in mathematics, 3 in social studies, 2 sequential years in a foreign language, and 3 units in science, as well as additional units in these subjects to total 16. Most candidates have 20 such academic units. Special attention is given to the difficulty of the applicant's curriculum, her class rank, and the school attended; scores on the SAT or ACT are required. An interview at the College is recommended but not required.

Sweet Briar has dropped its early decision application program in favor of being responsive to all applicants. An application deadline of February 1 is maintained, but students are invited to apply for admission as early as September of their senior year. Sweet Briar will notify each student of acceptance within one month of the date her application becomes complete. Transfer applications for the fall semester are due by May 1. A completed application includes a transcript of the candidate's academic work, scores on the required tests, recommendations from the guidance counselor and a teacher, and an essay written by the candidate. There is a $40 application fee, but it may be waived if it is deemed to be a financial burden. Sweet Briar also accepts the Common Application. All materials should be sent to the address below; information may be requested from the same office.

Dean of Admissions

Box B

Sweet Briar College

Sweet Briar, Virginia 24595

Telephone: 434.381.6142

800.381.6142 (toll-free)

Fax: 434.381.6152

E-mail: admissions@sbc.edu

World Wide Web: http://www.sbc.edu

TEMPLE UNIVERSITY

AT A GLANCE

Temple University attracts the nation's brightest and most motivated minds from all 50 states and 130 foreign countries. Offering the perfect combination of large-school resources and a small-school feel, Temple has something for every kind of student. At home in Philadelphia, Pennsylvania, Temple is nationally recognized for innovative achievements in teaching and research. Students have the opportunity to choose between suburban and city campuses. Temple University strives to instill a sense of global perspective in our students and offers the ability to study at our campuses in Rome, Italy and Tokyo, Japan. On all of our campuses, the Temple faculty includes instructors who are distinguished and active members in their fields. Professors bring the critical perspective of scholars and the practical knowledge of their discipline to their classrooms. With an average class-size of just 27, students have the access they need to thrive within the classroom. Temple is renowned in areas such as Business, Communications, Education, Art, Music, Science, and the Health Professions, and Temple graduates have the know-how and confidence to achieve success and make lasting contributions. Driven by the knowledge that the greatest students are students that are having fun, Temple goes to great lengths to make sure students are never at a loss for things to do. With a campus that is home to 20,000 students, activities are as diverse as the student body. In addition to cultural, athletic, and social events on campus, students always have the nation's 6th largest city at their fingertips.

LOCATION AND ENVIRONMENT

The city of Philadelphia is the cornerstone of life at Temple. One of the largest cities on the East Coast, Philadelphia is home to a variety of forward-looking businesses, progressive work in technology and science, and thriving artistic output. While the city is the product of a rich history, it is also a center for 21st century innovation and culture. With plays, concerts, museums, major league sporting events, shopping, clubs, and restaurants, Philadelphia provides students with tremendous opportunities for resources and fun. As an alternative to the urban setting, students can attend Temple University Ambler, set on 187 acres 30 minutes outside of the city. Ambler is a great choice for students who want all the resources of a world-renowned research university in a small and quiet setting. Temple also offers three additional campuses/sites in the Philadelphia region. Free shuttles connect all of our campuses giving Temple students ample opportunities to experience the many sides of Temple University.

OFF-CAMPUS OPPORTUNITIES

For Temple, "off-campus" is synonymous with opportunity. Whether it's hopping the subway to an internship with a Fortune 500 Company, hailing a cab to see priceless works of art at Philadelphia's museums, or flying to one of the dozens of study-abroad programs we have to offer, the world off-campus serves us as a classroom without walls.

Temple students are encouraged to incorporate travel and study into their academic experience. In addition to the tremendous opportunities of Philadelphia, the world abroad presents students with an exciting and affordable way to gain invaluable global perspective. Boasting a list of locales from Scotland to France and from Ghana to Beijing and campuses in Rome and Tokyo, a Temple education becomes more than just books and papers - it's about experience.

MAJORS AND DEGREES OFFERED

Temple University offers 134 undergraduate majors through 12 undergraduate schools and colleges. Temple has become nationally recognized in areas such as business, communications, education, engineering, health professions, liberal arts, science and technology, tourism and hospitality, horticulture, music and the arts.

ACADEMIC PROGRAMS

Academics form the foundation of your college life, and at Temple, GenEd is the heart of that experience. GenEd provides connections through dozens of new courses that are fresh, relevant and exciting—courses like The Jazz Century, Sustainable Environments, The Bionic Human and Global Cities. All have a focus on complex 21st century problems, from global climate change to global terrorism. Many of them will take you into the city through PEX, the Philadelphia passport program, free or discounted admission to cultural events across the city: museums, dance performances, historic buildings, local schools and community centers, green roofs and neighborhood gardens.

Temple University offers an extensive breadth of academic programs that provide graduates with an esteemed education. Temple's mission is to provide students with the resources they need to become leaders in their fields. Whether it's cutting-edge technology, a diverse educational experience, or small classes, Temple succeeds in producing graduates that are critical thinkers in addition to working professionals. By integrating the foundations of a student's field in major coursework with a scholarly approach to conceptual ideas through our general education curriculum, Temple prepares students for the rigors of the workplace and the complexity of the world around them. Temple recognizes that education should be personalized to meet the diverse needs of a diverse student body. First-year students can participate in courses and programs that are designed to meet their unique needs. Additionally, the University Honors Program provides tremendous opportunities for students seeking a more rigorous intellectual challenge. Wholly, Temple University's academic programs are founded on a comprehensive and personalized approach to education that enables students to thrive.

CAMPUS FACILITIES AND EQUIPMENT

Temple University's facilities are on the cutting-edge of technology and expose today's students to tomorrow's innovation. Home to the TECH Center, one of the largest student computer labs in the country, Temple students have access to nearly 2,000 computers in over a dozen computer labs across campus. With a campus that is nearly 90% wireless, students have limitless access to information and 24-hour access to their courses through the Temple Blackboard® system. Temple also strives to bring technology into the classroom by outfitting them with "smart" technology as can be seen in Temple's Alter Hall, a new state-of-the-art building for our Fox School of Business. Also new to campus in 2009, the Tyler School of Art building on Main Campus is one of the finest and most advanced facilities of its kind in the nation. On the social scene, Temple's Student Center offers students lounges, a food court, a non-alcoholic nightclub, and a movie theater. Temple's Liacouras Walk is home to restaurants and shops that make campus a city within a city. To stave off that weight from the world-famous Philly cheese steaks, students have access to the Independence Blue Cross Student Recreation Center where they can workout with state-of-the art equipment, take fitness classes, or run the top-floor indoor track. Also, Temple is the proud home of the 11,000 seat Liacouras Center that serves campus as the state-of-the-art home for men's and women's basketball and a variety of top-ticket concerts throughout the year. Temple has been called a "boomtown" as it continues to make improvements and additions to an already vibrant and modern campus.

TUITION, ROOM, BOARD AND FEES

In 2009–2010, full-time undergraduates that are Pennsylvania residents pay $11,724 per year. Students that are residents of other states pay $21,004 per year. Room and board and annual fees cost an additional $9,300 per year on average. Specific schools and colleges within the university, including the Boyer College of Music and Dance, the Tyler School of Art, the College of Health Professions and Social Work, the College of Engineering and the Fox School of Business, may charge slightly different tuitions.

FINANCIAL AID

Two-thirds of Temple attendees are awarded financial aid in the form of a combination of grants, loans, and work-study programs. Those seeking financial aid are asked to submit the Free Application for Federal Student Aid (FAFSA). The deadline for the FAFSA is March 1st. Students transferring to Temple need to submit a financial aid transcript whether they received aid at their previous institution or not. Merit-based scholarships are awarded to top students annually and vary in value. These scholarships may be renewed for each of a student's four years.

STUDENT ORGANIZATIONS AND ACTIVITIES

Temple's campuses are always pulsating with activity. Whether it's a movie night in the residence halls or grabbing a slice of pizza at the campus food court, the Temple experience centers upon living on campus. With 10,000 students that live on or around campus, Temple students never run out of things to do. More than 200 clubs and organizations provide opportunities for socializing, political debate and community service. Temple is also home to 23 NCAA Division I athletics and offers students free tickets to games. For the student who wants to do more than watch, students can get involved with a large variety of intramural sports teams. For students who wish to indulge their cultural side, Temple's prestigious art, music, dance, and theater departments offer over 75 performances and exhibitions annually. Temple University also offers plenty of opportunities for students to take a break from the books with events like "Free Food and Fun Fridays" and an array of low-priced trips to ski resorts, amusements parks, and local attractions. But with downtown Philadelphia less than two miles from campus, Temple students take advantage of the city they call home. With attractions like the Philadelphia Museum of Art, Olde City, South Street, the Italian Market, Main Street Manayunk and the Avenue of the Arts, students find a world of fun to be experienced in their backyard.

ADMISSIONS PROCESS

Temple University takes a holistic approach to the admissions process by taking into consideration every piece of information that a student chooses to provide. Applications are reviewed by the admissions committee in an individualized context. But to standardize the process for all of our applicants, the admissions committee will look at three things specifically. The first and most important piece of information is the student's high school record. Generally, students should have a strong and consistent 3.25 GPA (B+) in academic coursework. Students are required to submit scores from college entrance exams (SAT or ACT). For the SAT, the admissions committee would like to see that a student has a score that is close to Temple's average, which ranges from 500–600 on each section. The Writing section of the SAT is also considered as part of the admissions review process. Temple's average for the ACT is a 23 composite score, and the Writing section of this test is required and considered. Given our holistic approach, Temple also gives consideration to the student's essay, extracurricular activities, recommendation letters and special awards and honors. All applicants are automatically assessed for merit scholarships and the University Honors Program.

The best way to apply to Temple is online at www.temple.edu/undergrad. Temple's application deadline is March 1st. For questions, Temple encourages students to visit our website at www.temple.edu/undergrad or email us at tuadm@temple.edu.

THOMAS MORE COLLEGE

AT A GLANCE

With just the right balance of suburban calm and big-city excitement, modern facilities and old-fashioned attention, Thomas More College is the perfect place to earn your college degree. Our intimate campus and small class sizes ensure you will never get lost in the crowd. Thomas More's wide range of programs and activities helps you pursue any dream or interest. The College's Roman Catholic tradition emphasizes your spiritual and personal growth along with academic achievement. As a result, you will thoroughly enjoy your time here, and you will leave with critical thinking and ethical leadership skills that are so important in life. There's more to learn and more to like at Thomas More College.

LOCATION AND ENVIRONMENT

Thomas More College is ideally located in beautiful Crestview Hills, Kentucky, just 10 minutes from downtown Cincinnati, Ohio, and 10 minutes from the Greater Cincinnati International Airport.

MAJORS AND DEGREES OFFERED

UNDERGRADUATE

Accountancy°

Art°

Art History°

Biology°

Business Administration°

Chemistry°

Communication°

Computer Information Systems°

Criminal Justice°

Economics°

Education

English°

Environmental Science

Exercise Science°°

Forensic Science

French°°

Gerontology°°

History°

Humanities°

International Studies°

Mathematics°

Medical Technology

Music°°

Nursing

Philosophy°

Physics°

Political Science°°

Pre-Engineering

Pre-Legal Studies°°

Pre-Dental

Pre-Medical

Pre-Pharmacy

Pre-Veterinary

Pre-Occupational or Physical Therapy

Psychology°

Sociology°

Spanish°

Sports Entertainment Marketing

Theatre°

Theology°

Web Design °°

° Also offered as a two-year degree program.

°° Only offered as a two-year degree program

GRADUATE

Master of Arts in Teaching

Master of Business Administration

CAMPUS FACILITIES

The Thomas More experience begins in the academic building yet transcends the confines of the four walls of a classroom. For a small, private, liberal arts school, Thomas More is packed with big ideas, featured facilities and powerful programs that are sure to make a big impact on your life stretching your mind, feeding your soul, and lifting your spirit.

The main campus of Thomas More College is situated on over 100 beautiful acres within walking distance of the Crestview Towncenter which includes shopping, dining and numerous retail options. Unique features of the campus include the fully-equipped Observatory, the state-of-the-art Library Center, new athletic complex, newly renovated Seiler Commons dining facility and the Holbrook Student Center. These are just some of the featured cornerstones of excellence and opportunity for Thomas More students.

The Biology Field Station located on the Ohio River provides a unique opportunity for undergraduate research. The field station includes a research center, undergraduate housing for research students, classrooms, conference space and boat docks. Thomas More College works with numerous government agencies in conducting river research and monitoring water quality. These opportunities allow for experiential learning at the undergraduate level and the basis for our students to publish and present at local, regional and national conferences.

CAMPUS LIFE

With more than 35% of our traditional students living on campus in four residence halls, residence life is an important part of the total Thomas More experience. Forming the nucleus of the campus community, resident students experience first hand the important interaction and life skills that will help shape their lives. Our residence halls create a comfortable and safe living-learning environment, which encourages personal growth and development through a variety of activities and social interaction. Each resident is a 'citizen' in this special community, contributing to an atmosphere of harmony and maturity.

For those who choose not to live on campus, it is easy and convenient to become an active member of the campus community. Student activities, intramural sports, campus ministry, clubs and organizations and greek life provide a vibrant atmosphere and active social life. Whether as a fan or player, participating in NCAA athletics as a member of the President's Athletic conference provides a wonderful atmosphere on campus.

Athletics

Thomas More College is a member of the Presidents' Athletic Conference (one of the most competitive NCAA

Division III conferences in the country) and sponsors a total of 16 men's and women's varsity athletic teams. The Saints have a rich athletic tradition that includes a national championship, consistent berths in the NCAA tournaments, conference tournament titles and individual honors. For information about athletics at Thomas More College, visit www.thomasmore.edu/athletics

ADMISSIONS PROCESS

The admissions staff at Thomas More offers a personal experience as you navigate the college search process. Never hesitate to contact our staff for assistance, to plan a personalized visit to campus or with questions about Thomas More or the admissions process in general.

The College makes the admission process simple and easy! There are three ways to Apply:

1. Save $25 by applying online at www.thomasmore.edu.

2. Complete a paper application and submit by mail with your $25 application fee.

3. Download a paper application from www.thomasmore.edu and submit by mail with your $25 application fee.

Do You Qualify?

Freshman must rank in the top half of their high school class, have a high school average of C or better, and a minimum of 20 on the ACT or 980 on the SAT. Transfer students with less than 24 hours of transferable credit must meet the freshman admission criteria, while those with more than 24 hours must have a College GPA of 2.0 or higher. We also look at your extracurricular activities, as well as life or work experience, as important indicators of your ability to succeed at Thomas More.

TUITION, ROOM, BOARD AND FEES

For the school year of 2009–2010 the cost per semester is:

Tuition

Full-Time student 12–18 credit hours: $11,250

Part-Time student 1–11 credit hours: $530 per credit hour

Nursing Differential: $30 per credit hour

Fees

Technology Fee for full-time student: $300

Technology Fee for part-time student: $30/ credit hour, max $300

Student Activity Fee: $60

Reservation Deposit: $100

Room

Housing Security Deposit: $100

Double Occupancy: $1,555

Single Occupancy: $1,875

Two Bedroom Suites: $1,875

Board

19 meal plan with $50 flex dollars: $1,725

14 meal plan with $100 flex dollars: $1,470

10 meal plan with $100 flex dollars: $1,240

FINANCIAL AID

The Office of Financial Aid works to keep tuition affordable for students and their families, while maintaining high standards of quality throughout the College's academic and extracurricular programs. Our track record of helping students experience a high-quality private education at the most affordable price underscores our mission of expanding access to educational opportunities.

Located in the Administrative Building at Thomas More College, the Office of Financial Aid is staffed with professionals eager to assist you and your family with the application process or answer any questions about financial aid. We are here to inform you of the many sources of financial support and help you navigate your way through the process.

Given the high percentage of Thomas More students receiving awards, chances are you may be eligible for a combination of grants, loans, scholarships and part-time work as part of a financial aid package. Students are encouraged to get their applications in by March 15th for full consideration of our scholarships and awards. But don't leave it to chance, contact the Office of Financial Aid to learn more and earn more for your education.

FOR YOUR WHOLE LIFE

Thomas More College offers an experience that you will carry with you *For Your Whole Life*. Visit the website, www.thomasmore.edu to explore more about how this small, liberal arts Catholic College can meet you needs and provide the opportunities of a lifetime.

TRANSYLVANIA UNIVERSITY

AT A GLANCE

Transylvania, a small, private liberal arts college of about 1,100 men and women, is consistently ranked among the best small colleges in the nation. The name, from the Latin that means "across the woods," refers to the heavily forested Transylvania settlement in which the University was founded in 1780. Transylvania was the first college west of the Allegheny Mountains and the sixteenth in the nation. The University established the first schools of medicine and law in what was then the West and educated the doctors, lawyers, ministers, political leaders, and others who helped shape the young nation. Transylvania also founded the first college literary magazine in the West, The Transylvanian, still published by students today.

Transylvania continues as a pioneer in higher education, preparing future leaders in business, government, education, the sciences, and the arts. While professors engage in research and other scholarly activities, they never lose sight of their primary role, being great teachers. With their dedication to students it is not surprising that Transylvania faculty members have dominated Kentucky Professor of the Year awards, winning six times in the last nine years. Students work closely with professors in small classes, many with fewer than 10 students. Due in large part to these close collaborations with faculty, a high percentage of graduates attend selective medical, law, and other graduate and professional programs.

Transylvania students are an active and involved group, and they benefit from tremendous opportunities for learning outside the classroom and off-campus. Transylvania has over sixty active student organizations, covering a range of student interests. Over two-thirds of students study abroad, and many participate in internships, research projects, and volunteer activities.

LOCATION AND ENVIRONMENT

Transylvania is located in Lexington, Kentucky, a city of 270,000 and a growing center of commerce, culture, research, and education. Known as the horse capital of the world, Lexington is surrounded by the rolling green pastures of the famous Bluegrass region of central Kentucky. The area is also home to over 30,000 college students. Transylvania's park-like campus is just a 5-minute walk from downtown, with easy access to restaurants, shops, and entertainment. The proximity to downtown is also an advantage for students who want convenient part-time jobs and internship opportunities in law offices, financial firms, hospitals, non-profits, and other organizations.

OFF-CAMPUS OPPORTUNITIES

Experiencing diverse cultures through international study is a vital part of a Transylvania education, with over two-thirds of students participating in study abroad. It is common for Transylvania students to study abroad for a summer, a term, or a year. In recent years, Transylvania students have studied in 52 foreign countries. Scholarships are available for both semester-long and summer study abroad. Summer study programs, including those in Austria, Brazil, China, Costa Rica, Ecuador, France, Germany, Italy, Japan, Mexico, and Spain, are available through Transylvania's affiliation with the Kentucky Institute for International Studies. Transylvania also cooperates with the English-Speaking Union to offer advanced students scholarships for summer study at Cambridge and Oxford Universities. Students may participate in seminars or internships in Washington, D.C., through the Washington Center and in the Canadian Parliamentary Internship Program in Ottawa. Internships with congressional offices, Kentucky state government, city government, and local firms are easily arranged.

MAJORS AND DEGREES OFFERED

The Bachelor of Arts degree is awarded in the following majors: accounting, anthropology, art history, art studio, biology, business administration (concentrations in finance, hospitality management, management, and marketing), chemistry (concentrations in chemistry and in biochemistry), classics, computer science, drama, economics, education, English, exercise science, French, German, history, mathematics, music, music technology, philosophy, physical education, physics, political science, psychology, religion, sociology, Spanish, and writing, rhetoric, and communication. Individually designed majors also may be arranged. Minors are available in most majors and in; classical studies, communication, environmental studies, hospitality management, international affairs, multicultural studies, and women's studies. Advising and undergraduate preparation are provided for pre-professional programs in dentistry, engineering, law, medicine, ministry, pharmacy, physical therapy, and veterinary medicine. A cooperative program in engineering allows students to earn a B.A. in physics or liberal studies from Transylvania in three years and a B.S. in engineering from the University of Kentucky or Vanderbilt University in two years. A cooperative program in accounting allows students to earn a B.A. in accounting from Transylvania in four years and an M.S. in accounting from the University of Kentucky in one year; graduates qualify to take the CPA exam following the completion of the B.A.

ACADEMIC PROGRAMS

The academic year is based on a 4-4-1 academic calendar, with two 14-week terms (fall and winter) and a one-month May term. During the May term, students may participate in a variety of programs on or off campus. Students normally take four courses in each of the fall and winter terms and one course in the May term. Thirty-six courses are required to graduate. Freshmen participate in a two-term program called Foundations of the Liberal Arts, which features small-group discussions with a faculty leader; lectures, films, concerts, and other presentations; and a tutorial program in basic communication, critical thinking, and study skills. Students must complete requirements designed to ensure broad familiarity with the major areas of learning and human endeavor in the humanities and fine arts, social sciences, natural sciences and mathematics, logic, and languages.

CAMPUS FACILITIES AND EQUIPMENT

Two Georgian-style buildings combine elegance with high-tech facilities to offer the latest advances in teaching and learning. The Cowgill Center for Business, Economics, and Education includes a multimedia classroom where professors from any discipline can use a large display screen to show the entire class information from one of the twenty-five networked student computers. A specialized area for education majors includes a laboratory classroom for teacher training. The Lucille C. Little Theater, used for faculty- and student-directed productions and drama classes, is a technically innovative facility that includes computerized lighting and sound, flexible staging options, and movable seating. The Frances Carrick Thomas/J. Douglas Gay, Jr. Library offers sophisticated computerized databases, which are invaluable for research and can be accessed from any computer connected to Transylvania's server. The Mitchell Fine Arts Center provides music program facilities, including practice rooms, a recital hall, and an auditorium. It also houses the Career Development Center, which helps students research career options, improve job search skills, arrange internships and part-time jobs, and apply to graduate schools and to professional positions. Mitchell is also home to the new state-of-the-art Fine Arts Technology Lab. The Shearer Art Building is dedicated to instructional space, student and faculty studios, and a student gallery. Other modern facilities include the newly renovated L. A. Brown Science Center, the

Haupt Humanities Building, and the Clive M. Beck Athletic and Recreation Center, which includes a state-of-the-art fitness center. About 80 percent of students live on campus in seven residence halls - two for men, one for women, and four for men and women. These include traditional-style accommodations, apartment-style living for upperclass students, and suite-style rooms. Thomson Hall, opened in fall 2008, was only the second residence hall in the southeast to earn the EPA's Energy Star certification. All rooms are air-conditioned and completely furnished, with access to Transylvania's cable television and computer networks. Each residence hall has ample lounge and study space and easy access to computer labs and recreational facilities. Dining options include a cafeteria, two grills, and a coffee shop. The William T. Young Campus Center offers a competition-size indoor pool, a gymnasium, and other meeting and recreation facilities.

TUITION, ROOM, BOARD AND FEES

Transylvania charges an annual tuition that covers fall, winter, and May terms for a normal full-time schedule of courses. Special instruction fees are charged in addition for certain designated courses, such as applied music and May Term travel courses. For 2009–10, tuition and fees were $25,280 and room and board (double occupancy) were $7,700.

FINANCIAL AID

Transylvania is committed to providing financial aid to students and their families. Four types of financial assistance are available: scholarships, which are based on academic performance and leadership. Grants, loans, and work-study are based on financial need. About 90 percent of Transylvania students receive some form of financial assistance, and many receive more than one type of aid. Outstanding entering freshmen may qualify for one of twenty full-tuition William T. Young Scholarships, each worth more than $100,000 over four years. Submission of Transylvania's Application for Admission and Scholarships is all that is necessary to be considered for academic scholarships at Transylvania. Students who are interested in need-based aid must file the Free Application for Federal Student Aid (FAFSA).

STUDENT ORGANIZATIONS AND ACTIVITIES

Transylvania offers more than sixty cocurricular organizations, covering a range of student interests, and most students participate in several of these. The athletics program, in NCAA Division III, includes eight varsity sports for men, ten for women, and more than a dozen intramural sports. Transylvania also has four national sororities and four national fraternities.

ADMISSIONS PROCESS

Each applicant is considered individually on the basis of academic records, SAT scores and/or ACT scores, activities, interests, essays, and recommendations. Admission is also offered to transfer students, international students and nontraditional students.

Transylvania enrolled 297 new students for the 2009–10 academic year. The middle 50 percent composite ACT score for the freshman class was 23 to 29. Nearly fifty percent were in the top 10 percent of their high school class.

Submission of a Transylvania Application for Admission and Scholarships or submission of the Common Application is all that is necessary to be considered for admission and most merit scholarships at Transylvania. The early action deadline is December 1 for applicants who wish to learn of their admission by January 15 and who want to be considered for all Transylvania scholarships. February 1 is the regular admission and scholarships deadline for applicants who wish to be considered for all Transylvania scholarships except the William T. Young Scholarship. Applicants who apply after February 1 are considered on a space-available basis. The deadline for applications for the winter term, which begins in January, is December 1.

Students considering Transylvania are urged to visit the campus, and high school seniors are encouraged to stay overnight in a dorm with a student admissions assistant. Weekday visits may include a customized campus tour, the opportunity to attend classes; talk with professors, coaches, students, and admissions and financial aid counselors; and enjoy meals on campus. Visits should be arranged with the Office of Admissions, preferably one to two weeks in advance. Open houses are held in the fall and winter, and a college planning workshop for high school juniors and sophomores is held in the spring.

To request application materials and additional information, contact:

Office of Admissions

Transylvania University

300 North Broadway

Lexington, KY 40508-1797

Telephone: (859) 233-8242 or (800) 872-6798

E-mail: admissions@transy.edu

Website: www.transy.edu

TRINE UNIVERSITY

AT A GLANCE

Trine University is a private, independent, coeducational institution offering associate, baccalaureate and masters degrees. Our 1,466 students receive a private, career-oriented education and personal attention, within a hands-on learning environment. Our teaching-focused faculty contains experts in the fields of engineering, business, education, criminal justice, communication, sport management, forensic science, golf management, mathematics and sciences. Trine has a full-time faculty of 72 members. Most hold doctoral degrees and/or are registered professional engineers. The student/faculty ratio is 17:1.

LOCATION AND ENVIRONMENT

Trine University's 400-acre main campus is located in Angola, the heart of northeast Indiana's scenic lake resort region. With more than 100 lakes, the area offers fishing, camping, skiing, boating and fine dining. Pokagon State Park is five miles from campus. Trine is situated near the crossroad of two major interstate highways (Interstate 80/90 and Interstate 69), less than a three-hour drive from Cleveland, Detroit, Chicago, Cincinnati and Indianapolis.

ACADEMICS

Trine University's goal is to provide graduates with skills and perspectives to enhance lifelong learning opportunities and to improve communication with other professionals. Our academic programs are designed to ensure breadth of knowledge and to promote intellectual inquiry. All students are required to gain competencies in computer literacy, humanities, mathematics, science, social science, oral and written communication. The Allen School of Engineering & Technology (ABET accredited) concentrates on providing a fundamental, application-oriented engineering education. In addition to specialized fields, students are required to complete courses in communication skills, socio-humanistic studies, and analysis and design. The Ketner School of Business, one of the few nationally accredited (ACBSP) business programs in the region, includes a broad range of hands-on, practical experiences that acquaint students with the practices, procedures, and problems of contemporary business. Teacher preparation first began at Trine University in 1884, and in that tradition, the Franks School of Education is nationally accredited by NCATE and IDE/OELD. The Jannen School of Arts & Sciences is known for its career-oriented, challenging, and competitive programs in communication, criminal justice, forensic science, mathematics, informatics, language and humanities, and sciences. The Trine Virtual Campus makes key programs available anywhere, anytime through the World Wide Web. Nationally known guest lecturers are frequent visitors to campus, and internships and field trips are considered vital to the total educational experience.

MAJORS AND DEGREES

The Allen School of Engineering & Technology awards bachelor's degrees in chemical, civil, computer, electrical and mechanical engineering, computer science and design engineering technology. It also awards a master of engineering (civil, computer and mechanical majors). The Franks School of Education awards bachelor's degrees in elementary, health/physical, mathematics, science and social studies. The Jannen School of Arts & Sciences awards bachelor's degrees in communication, psychology, biology, chemistry, computer science, criminal justice, forensic science, mathematics, informatics, pre-legal and social science general studies, and self-designed general studies. The Ketner School of Business awards bachelor of business administration degrees in accounting, entrepreneurship, finance, hospitality and tourism management, sport management, fitness and recreational programming, management, marketing and golf management.

ADMISSIONS

Trine University admits applicants on the basis of scholastic achievement and academic potential. Selection is made without regard to race, religion, color, gender, sexual orientation, or age. Interested students are encouraged to make individual visits to campus and talk with faculty and students. Trine has a rolling admission process, and applicants are notified of their status within two weeks after completing the application. Applications are considered complete once the Office of Admission has received the following: application (online, no application fee), official high school transcript, and official ACT or SAT score. Standard admission requirements include English (four years), mathematics (three years), science (three years), and social studies (two years). In addition to the standard admission requirements, the Allen School of Engineering & Technology requires a semester of trigonometry, a year of chemistry, and a year of physics.

CAMPUS FACILITIES AND EQUIPMENT

Trine University's upper campus is completely wireless and includes the Aerospace Engineering Building (which contains 4-by-4-by-6-foot subsonic and 4-inch supersonic wind tunnels, aircraft structures, a machine shop, and student project laboratory), Best Hall (which houses the Jannen School of Arts & Sciences), C.W. Sponsel Administration Center (home to the president's office, alumni and development, and academic affairs), Fawick Hall (state-of-the-art technical facility which holds the Allen School of Engineering & Technology), Forman Hall (which contains Centennial Station coffeehouse and Trine Welcome Center), Shambaugh Hall (home to Ketner School of Business), Taylor Hall (Humanities Institute, Wells Theater), Ford Hall (which includes the Franks School of Education), and the student villas (upperclassmen townhouse-style residences with private rooms). Lower campus is home to Hershey Hall (which contains the Ketner Sports Complex, Gettig Fitness Center, two racquetball courts, three basketball courts, and weight room), the University Center and Center for Technology and Online Resources, which contains Whitney Commons dining hall, a bookstore, mailroom, 320-seat Fabiani Theatre, radio station, fitness center, rock climbing wall, and Center for Digital Excellence. Trine University's Zollner Golf Course, an 18-hole championship course, occupies the southwest corner. The University's 13 residence halls offer various living options, including apartment-style, townhouse and traditional options: Alwood, Cameron, Conrad and Platt halls, Moss Street, University Center, Widmann, Moyer, Seculoff, Bukoff, and Wilson apartments, and Trine and Ingledue villas. Every residence is wireless and each room is wired to the university network and the Internet. The ARC (Athletic and Recreation Center), Trine's most recent addition to an ever-expanding sports complex, houses a 200-meter indoor track and facilities for intramurals, tennis, baseball, volleyball and various other sports. The campus safety program includes 24-hour campus security personnel, first aid, CPR and emergency response procedures (five security kiosks are positioned throughout campus and provide immediate response by local law enforcement and fire department personnel). Campus safety has also incorporated an emergency alert text system that apprises students and staff of campus emergencies.

CAMPUS LIFE

Trine University supports and encourages student participation in extracurricular activities. Approximately 40 percent of our students participate in NCAA Division III intercollegiate athletics. Thunder athletics offers 21 varsity sports: baseball (M), basketball (M/W), cross- country (M/W), football (M), golf (M/W), indoor track and field (M/W), lacrosse (M/W), soccer (M/W), softball (W), tennis (M/W), track and field (M/W), volleyball (W), and wrestling (M). Field hockey (W) will be introduced for fall 2010. Of the more than 60 clubs and student organizations, two have had recent success in national competitions: the American Criminal Justice Association and the Bass Anglers Club. Other groups include Blue Crew student athletic support group, Cheer Squad, Christian Campus House, Drama Club, Habitat for Humanity, Marching Band, Pep Band, Ski Club, Student Senate, student newspaper (The Triangle), student yearbook (The Modulus), and student radio station (The Revolution, WEAX 88.3FM). Also active on campus are professional and honorary societies.

TUITION AND FEES

Tuition for the 2009–2010 academic year is $24,100; standard room and board is $8,300.

TRINITY COLLEGE (CT)

AT A GLANCE

Trinity College is an independent, nonsectarian liberal arts college located in the historic capital city of Hartford, Connecticut. Founded in 1823, Trinity is one of the oldest colleges in the country, and is consistently ranked among the best. It brings the great tradition of the liberal arts into the 21st century with a dynamic living and learning community where education doesn't stop at the classroom door.

Our 2,200 students work closely with faculty and extend their education through campus activities and organizations. They engage with the city of Hartford through internships, community learning and service, and explore the wider world through study abroad and international initiatives on campus. With an 11 to 1 student-faculty ratio, each and every student is challenged and encouraged by Trinity's outstanding faculty. Students are offered a rigorous curriculum that is firmly grounded in the traditional liberal arts, but that also incorporates newer fields, an interdisciplinary approach, and urban engagement.

With 38 majors and more than 970 courses to choose from, students are immersed in a community of learning that is facilitated by a stimulating academic environment, small classes, and exceptional facilities, including fully networked classrooms and dorms. Opportunities to explore the arts abound on campus and students can nurture and hone artistic skills. More than 40 percent of our students play varsity and club sports, and many more participate in intramurals and fitness activities.

As a student at Trinity College, you will explore new worlds, thoughts, and ideas, and become prepared for the challenge and change of a successful, fulfilling life.

LOCATION AND ENVIRONMENT

Trinity is situated on a beautiful, 100-acre campus in Connecticut's capital city of Hartford, midway between Boston and New York. Hartford is a city with a rich history that offers many opportunities for urban engagement. Mark Twain lived here, as did Harriet Beecher Stowe. Dentist Horace Wells discovered anesthesia here. It is the home of the oldest continuously published newspaper in America as well as the oldest public art museum, the Wadsworth Atheneum. Trinity effectively uses the city as a classroom with access to assets and resources that is matched by few liberal arts colleges of our size.

Anyone who visits the College sees the beauty of the campus, with its hilltop location, mix of historic and contemporary buildings, and abundant trees and lawns. Trinity is one of the earliest examples of "Collegiate Gothic"; many of the original buildings are modeled after the architecture of Oxford and Cambridge and symbolize Trinity's roots in the classical liberal arts. A major campus and community revitalization initiative has created several new state-of-the-art facilities, including the Raether Library and Information Technology Center on campus and the neighboring innovative Learning Corridor of magnet schools and academic resources. Also, in 2006, the award-winning Koeppel Community Sports Center opened its doors as a multi-use athletic facility on the southern edge of campus.

Off campus, the 256-acre Field Station at Church Farm in Ashford, Connecticut, is dedicated to research in the natural sciences and a wide range of environmental educational endeavors. Plans are being developed for use of Church Farm buildings to support programs in the arts.

As a Trinity student, you have numerous opportunities to engage in volunteer work, internships, research and community learning projects. Many courses—from art history to political science and from economics to neuroscience—incorporate aspects of city life. There are hundreds of internships that allow you to continue your education while exploring career opportunities. And whatever your tastes, there are cultural and entertainment events throughout the city and a shuttle service provided by the College.

OFF-CAMPUS OPPORTUNITIES

Trinity students have a wide variety of opportunities to take advantage of the College's special relationship to the City of Hartford. The Community Learning Initiative comprises nearly 30 courses each year that weave direct contact with local people and institutions directly into the learning process. Such urban engagement builds on Trinity's liberal arts foundation, and for some students, has led to independent studies or collaborative research papers published in scholarly journals.

Trinity offers over 200 internship opportunities that represent excellent preparation for life after college. Students can explore career interests in a wide variety of fields, including law, banking, journalism, communications, health, engineering, computer science, government, and non-profit organizations. Trinity challenges its students to make a difference in the real world - starting with their Hartford community. Students can choose from a wide range of community service activities, from child-mentoring programs to senior citizen buddy programs, from the Boys and Girls Club at Trinity to Habitat for Humanity.

Trinity's study abroad programs provide unforgettable learning experiences that broaden perspectives and deepen understanding. Among the rich menu of study abroad choices are Trinity's own campus in Rome, our Shanghai semester, and our network of global learning sites, as well as intercollegiate exchange and study abroad programs. Equally valuable are many study-away programs in the U.S., including Trinity/La Mama Performing Arts in New York City, research and internships in Washington, D.C., maritime studies at Mystic Seaport, and theater courses at the National Theater Institute. Students can also take advantage of the Twelve College Exchange Program.

Trinity also created the new Center for Urban and Global Studies to integrate the College's well-established tradition of urban engagement with its strong global programs. The center, which is the first of its kind at a liberal arts college in the United States, takes advantage of Trinity's location and will strengthen the long-standing mutually beneficial relationship between the College and Hartford. Playing off Trinity's global reach, it will improve existing and develop new learning and research opportunities in world cities.

MAJORS AND DEGREES OFFERED

Undergraduates completing the necessary requirements receive the Bachelor of Arts or the Bachelor of Science degrees from Trinity College. There is also a five-year Trinity/Rensselaer at Hartford program in engineering and computer science, which leads to both a bachelor's degree and a master's degree.

Trinity offers more than 970 courses in 38 majors. Options include cross-disciplinary majors, such as American studies, and self-designed majors, such as environmental studies, as well as interdisciplinary minors, such as human rights. At Trinity, your education is student-centered, and our array of curricular options will provide you with the tools to help you to meet your goals.

Trinity offers majors in: American Studies, Anthropology, Art History, Biochemistry, Biology, Chemistry, Classical Civilization, Classics, Computer Coordinate, Computer Science, Economics, Educational Studies, Engineering, English, Environmental Science, French, German, History, International Studies, Italian, Jewish Studies, Mathematics, Modern Languages (including Chinese and Japanese), Music, Neuroscience, Philosophy, Physics, Political Science, Psychology, Public Policy, Religion, Russian, Sociology, Spanish, Studio Arts, Theater and Dance, and Women, Gender and Sexuality.

As you can see, Trinity's curriculum is both broad and flexible, encouraging you to challenge yourself as you follow your interests and select a major.

ACADEMIC PROGRAMS

At Trinity, the curriculum features the First-Year Seminar Program, where a small group of students and a faculty member explore a topic through critical reading and discussion, analysis and writing. It's a shared introduction to intellectual life at Trinity and an important way to meet other students and make friends because students in the same seminar live in the same residence hall together with a student mentor.

There are many special curricular options, including the Guided Studies, Interdisciplinary Science, InterArts and Cities Programs, as well as the Trinity/La MaMa Performing Arts Program in New York. Trinity is also home to the first undergraduate Human Rights Program in the United States, as well as the unique Center for Urban and Global Studies.

The key words here are variety and flexibility – if you don't see exactly what you want, that doesn't mean we don't have it. Independent study? Study abroad? Open semester? Engineering? Neuroscience? Law courses? How about an academic leave of absence to work on a political campaign or hike the Appalachian Trail? Many Trinity students pursue these and other existing opportunities. And it is very easy to work with faculty to create your own opportunities. Your motivation and imagination are your only limits.

CAMPUS FACILITIES AND EQUIPMENT

The campus is fully wired, with every student room connected to the campus network and the Internet. The newly expanded Raether Library and Information Technology Center combines the resources of one of the leading small-college library facilities in the nation with an array of electronic resources, including digital media labs and video-conferencing capabilities. The library houses more than 900,000 volumes and more than 12,000 periodicals, as well as the Watkinson Library rare-book collections.

The science labs offer our undergraduates an opportunity to work hands-on with sophisticated equipment, including a research nuclear magnetic resonance spectrometer, a scanning electron microscope, incubators and climatically controlled growth chambers.

Focal points for the visual arts are the Widener Gallery in the Austin Arts Center and the Broad Street Gallery. In addition to a proscenium theater and a more intimate black box performance space, each art medium has its own studio.

The Ferris Athletic Center houses a fully-equipped fitness center, an Olympic-size pool, premier international-size squash courts, crew tanks, an indoor track, a field house, basketball and tennis courts. Outdoor features include an all-weather track, soccer fields, softball and baseball diamonds, tennis courts, an artificial turf field hockey field, and a new field turf playing surface for football and lacrosse. In addition, the new Koeppel Community Sports Center serves as home-ice for Trinity men's and women's ice hockey teams, as well as a place for community academic and athletic mentoring programs..

TUITION, ROOM, BOARD AND FEES

Estimated college fees for 2008–2009 are as follows:

Tuition: $36,864

Room & Board: $9,900

General Fee: $1,860

FINANCIAL AID

Through the generosity of alumni and friends, the College has an endowment sufficient to give our students an education that's worth considerably more than the actual tuition charged. If you decide that Trinity is the right college for you, we are determined not to let money stand in your way. We are committed to making a Trinity education accessible to promising students who are unable to meet the full educational costs. Approximately 40 percent of our students receive need-based financial aid in the form of grants, low-interest loans, and campus employment. If you have any questions about financial aid at Trinity during any point in your college search, you should not hesitate to contact the Office of Student Financial Services at 860-297-2046 or e-mail financial_aid@trincoll.edu.

STUDENT ORGANIZATIONS AND ACTIVITIES

While the number in our student body is relatively small, their interests are incredibly diverse. With over a hundred student organizations on campus, the opportunities for active involvement are wide open—whether continuing something in which you've already been involved or something that is completely new to you. Student organizations include community service organizations, cultural organizations, media groups, such as the College newspaper and radio station, academic clubs, fraternities, and club sports. And if you have an interest that isn't covered by an existing organization, then start one! It will probably be impossible for you not to find at least one activity that appeals to you, whether on campus or in the city. Academics are the most important part of your education, but they aren't the only part. We encourage you to get involved beyond the classroom. The opportunities are right at hand.

ADMISSIONS PROCESS

Selecting candidates for admission to Trinity is a complex but personalized process. The components of your evaluation include your academic credentials. Your grades are very important, but so is the strength of the academic programs in which you participated. We require one form of standardized test; either the SAT, ACT, or any two SAT Subject tests. Non-native speakers of English are encouraged to submit the TOEFL.

In addition, two teachers' recommendations are required. Teachers give us insight into your scholarship, work habits, and classroom contributions. Personal qualities are considered, too. What talents, skills, or qualities can you bring to the life of the campus? What contributions have you made to your school and community? We aren't as concerned with the number of your activities as we are with the quality and depth of them.

If we may be of assistance, please don't hesitate to call upon us in the Office of Admissions at 860-297-2180 or e-mail admissions.office@trincoll.edu.

TRUMAN STATE UNIVERSITY

Truman State University is Missouri's premier liberal arts and sciences university and the only highly selective public institution in the state. As one of the very few publicly funded liberal arts schools in the nation, Truman successfully combines affordability with the type of education and personal attention typically only offered at a private institution.

Truman has established an impeccable reputation in the Midwest and throughout the nation for the high-quality undergraduate programs offered. In fact, for the thirteenth consecutive year, *U.S. News & World Report* has ranked Truman State University as the number one master's level public institution in the Midwest. A commitment to student achievement and learning is the focus of the University.

The Truman campus is beautifully situated on 140 acres in Kirksville, a town of approximately 17,000 located in the northeast corner of Missouri. The historic downtown area is within walking distance of the Truman campus and provides a connection to the Kirksville community with local restaurants, shops, and entertainment.

Undergraduate degrees offered by Truman include the Bachelor of Arts (B.A.), Bachelor of Science (B.S.), Bachelor of Music (B.M.), Bachelor of Fine Arts (B.F.A.), and Bachelor of Science in Nursing (B.S.N.). Truman offers more than forty areas of study in the following disciplines: Accounting, Agricultural Science, Art, Art History, Athletic Training, Biology, Business Administration, Chemistry, Classics, Communication, Communication Disorders, Computer Science, Creative Writing, Economics, English, Exercise Science, French, German, Health Science, History, Interdisciplinary Studies, Justice Systems, Linguistics, Mathematics, Music, Nursing, Philosophy and Religion, Physics, Political Science, Psychology, Romance Languages, Russian, Sociology/Anthropology, Spanish, and Theatre.

Professional paths include but are not limited to dentistry, engineering, law, medicine, optometry, pharmacy, physical therapy, occupational therapy and veterinary medicine.

The teaching degree at Truman is the Master of Arts in Education. Students wishing to pursue a teaching career first complete a bachelor's degree in an academic discipline and then apply for admission into professional study at the master's level. Master's programs in special education, early childhood education, elementary education, middle school education, and secondary education are available.

Truman also offers Master's level degrees in Accountancy (MA), Music (MA), Communication Disorders (MA), English (MA) and Biology (MS).

The Liberal Studies Program is the heart of Truman's curriculum and is intended to serve as a foundation for all major programs of study. The philosophy behind the Liberal Studies Program is based upon a commitment that Truman has made to provide students with essential skills needed for lifelong learning, breadth across the traditional liberal arts and sciences through exposure to various discipline-based modes of inquiry, and interconnecting perspectives that stress interdisciplinary thinking and integration as well as linkage to other cultures and experiences.

Students at Truman complete a "capstone," or culminating experience their senior year. This experience prompts seniors to reflect on the knowledge they have gained throughout their learning experience and to integrate the knowledge, skills, and attitudes of liberal learning with an in-depth understanding of the major.

Truman also offers a challenging General Honors Program. Students have the opportunity to select the most rigorous honors courses to satisfy the liberal arts component of their respective programs. Those who successfully complete this program benefit from an even richer academic experience at Truman and receive special recognition at graduation. Departmental honors are also available in several disciplines.

Students at Truman are active both inside and outside of the classroom. More than 500 Truman students participate in enriching and life-changing study abroad experiences each year. Students can participate in programs ranging from a couple weeks to a year in duration, and can choose from numerous destinations worldwide. In recent years, Truman has continued to rank among the top 15 in the nation among master's level institutions for number of students studying abroad, according to the "Open Doors" survey conducted by the Institute of International Education.

Truman offers a wide variety of experiential internships, a required component of some academic programs. The "Truman in Washington" program provides work-experience opportunities in the nation's capitol in such areas as foreign affairs/diplomacy, government affairs, criminal justice, international relations, health and human services, and communications as well as other areas. Truman also offers internship opportunities with the Missouri State Legislature. In recent years, students have completed internships with United States senators, the United States Supreme Court, the governor of Missouri, business and industry managers, advertising agencies, physical therapists, and artists.

With approximately 250 student organizations to choose from, encompassing service, Greek, honorary, professional, religious, social, political and recreational influences, Truman students have tremendous opportunities to become involved on campus and in the Kirksville community. Truman student organizations sponsor a number of events throughout the year, such as Truman Live, International Idol, guest speakers, poetry slams, musical performances, dance recitals, volunteering events, and ever-popular food nights.

The Kohlenberg Lyceum Series also provides a variety of cultural programs that interest students throughout the year. Past programs have included brilliant performances by the Peking Acrobats, the Missouri Contemporary Ballet, the Vienna Choir Boys, Canadian Brass, and Alvin Ailey II.

Truman's Student Activity Board sponsors a variety of entertainment events. Recent SAB concerts include CAKE, Dashboard Confessional, Regina Spektor, MXPX, and Ben Folds. Comedic acts like Lewis Black, Jim Gaffigan, and Demetri Martin have also come to Truman's campus in recent years.

Students take advantage of numerous academic resources and facilities available to them. Improvements to campus facilities have included the renovation and expansion of Truman's Science facility, Magruder Hall, which was completed for the spring 2006 semester. Renovations to Barnett Hall include a new Convergence Media Center encompassing facilities for the student-produced newspaper, Midwest travel magazine, radio station, and TV studio. Students also enjoy dining, socializing, and relaxing in the newly renovated Student Union Building.

Additional facilities include a biofeedback laboratory, a speech and hearing clinic for Communication Disorders students, an organic chemistry lab, an independent learning center for Nursing students, an observatory, a 400-acre university farm, a multicultural affairs center, student health center, and a career center. Athletic facilities include a 5,000-seat football stadium, a 3,000-seat arena with three basketball courts, an Olympic-size swimming pool, soccer and rugby fields, baseball and softball fields, tennis courts, a dance studio, and a Student Recreation Center.

Residence halls also provide comfortable and enriching living environments for students. Many of the halls have been renovated within the last five years. All residence halls offer lounges, kitchenettes, laundry facilities, high-speed internet (including wireless), cable TV, and many other amenities. Students can dine in dining halls or in the food court style dining in the Student Union Building.

Tuition for Missouri residents for the 2009–10 academic year is $6,458; out-of-state tuition is $11,309. The average room and board rate for both Missouri residents and nonresidents is $6,854. Additional fees include a one-time $305 freshman orientation fee, and annual fees including an $82 activities fee, a $100 athletic fee, a $52 Student Health Center fee, a $50 parking fee for those with a vehicle, and costs of books and personal expenses.

Truman offers automatic scholarships ranging from $500 to $3,000. Competitive scholarship awards vary from $500 up to full tuition, room and board, plus a $4,000 study-abroad stipend. The application for admission also serves as the application for the automatic and competitive scholarship programs, and it is free to apply.

A limited number of scholarships are awarded to students for excellence in fine arts, debate or foreign language. These scholarships are available for instrumental, or vocal music; acting or dramatic production; studio art or art history; speech or debate; and foreign languages offered at Truman. Of special interest to piano students is the Truman Piano Fellowship Competition, a February competition offering scholarships to top pianists.

Truman, a National Collegiate Athletic Association Division II member, offers 21 men's and women's sports. The NCAA and the University authorize a limited number of grants to outstanding athletes. The value of this aid may vary with each individual recipient.

Truman accepts the Free Application for Federal Student Aid (FASFA) and participates in all Federal Title IV financial aid programs. Financial aid estimates are available upon request.

Each applicant is evaluated for admission based upon academic and co-curricular record, ACT or SAT results, and the admission essay. Truman requires the following high school core: 4 units of English, 3 units of mathematics (4 recommended), 3 units of social studies/history, 3 units of natural science, 1 unit of fine arts and 2 units of the same foreign language.

Students interested in being considered for all scholarships are encouraged to apply by December 15 of their senior year. The recommended final deadline to apply for the fall semester is March 1. There is no application fee. Students may apply online at the website listed below. For further information or to schedule a campus visit, students should contact:

Office of Admission

Truman State University

100 East Normal

Kirksville, Missouri 63501

Telephone: 660.785.4114 or 800.892.7792

Fax: 660.785.7456

E-mail: admissions@truman.edu

http://admissions.truman.edu

UNION COLLEGE (NY)

AT A GLANCE

Union College, chartered by the state of New York in 1795, is one of the nation's oldest and most distinguished liberal arts colleges. Union is a leader in educating students to be engaged, innovative, and ethical contributors to an increasingly diverse, global and technologically complex society. The curriculum emphasizes collaboration with students and faculty through small classes and undergraduate research, an international experience in all disciplines, and learning through service to the campus and community. The student population of approximately 2,100 full-time undergraduates, with nearly equal numbers of men and women, comes from 39 U.S. states and 35 foreign countries. The Class of 2013 is the most diverse in Union history, with 21 percent multicultural students and 4 percent international students.

LOCATION AND ENVIRONMENT

Union is located on 100 acres in the city of Schenectady, 15 miles from Albany, the capital of New York state. The first planned campus in America, it was designed by noted French architect Joseph Ramée and features many beautiful gardens and natural woodlands. Union is part of Upstate New York's picturesque Capital Region, whose population of approximately 900,000 includes 55,000 college and university students. A short drive from the Albany International Airport, Union is three hours by car from New York City and Boston, and four hours from Montreal. Nearby natural attractions include the Catskills, Adirondacks, Green Mountains and the Massachusetts Berkshires.

OFF-CAMPUS OPPORTUNITIES

Union offers international study programs in more than two dozen countries. The College focuses on creating innovative opportunities that combine elements of entrepreneurship, research or community service with the chance for students to pursue their academic interests and individual passions. Approximately 60 percent of students study abroad. Most programs are led by Union faculty. Students also may work with a faculty advisor to design their own program of study. Three-week mini-terms, for one credit, are offered during winter break in various U.S. cities and countries, from Argentina to Vietnam. Many students get involved in continuing hurricane relief efforts in New Orleans, and the Civil Rights Public History Mini-Term explores the American Civil Rights Movement in key cities and states. Union's innovative Minerva Fellows program sends graduating seniors to developing countries to work with welfare and anti-poverty initiatives.

MAJORS AND DEGREES OFFERED

Union offers 36 majors, double majors, combined majors and minors, interdepartmental and multidisciplinary concentrations, and area, ethnic and cultural studies programs. The self-designed Organizing Theme Major involves multiple disciplines. Most students take three courses in each of the three 10-week terms that comprise Union's trimester system. The average introductory class has 20 students; the average upper level class, 12. Union offers Bachelor of Arts (B.A.) and Bachelor of Science (B.S.) degrees. Students may declare up to two minors. Union also offers a Leadership in Medicine program with Albany Medical College and Union Graduate College; the Law and Public Policy program with Albany Law School; and five-year bachelor's/M.B.A. or bachelor's/M.A.T. programs with Union Graduate College. Union's 14 academic honor societies include Phi Beta Kappa, the first chapter established in New York (1817).

ACADEMIC PROGRAMS

Union's interdisciplinary approaches bring together concepts from engineering and the liberal arts and sciences so that students graduate with a broad background that goes beyond the traditional major. Students must complete a minimum of 36 courses (up to 40 for engineering degrees) and satisfy all departmental and general education requirements. Gen Ed requirements include a first-year preceptorial and sophomore research seminar, which promote skills in reading, writing, research and analyzing texts. Distribution requirements in the humanities, literature, social sciences, linguistic and cultural competency, quantitative mathematical reasoning and the sciences promote a breadth of knowledge about the social and natural world, and key skills in analysis, literacy and numeracy. Approved interdisciplinary "clusters" on particular intellectual themes are designed to prompt awareness of interdisciplinary connections and understanding of issues from multiple perspectives.

The Union Scholars program is an enriched experience for students with unusual academic capabilities and talents. It includes a more extensive first-year seminar; opportunities to work with faculty on independent study projects during sophomore year; increased opportunities for study abroad; and participation in colloquia and departmental honors programs junior and senior years. Union vigorously encourages student research in all disciplines. At Union's Steinmetz Symposium each spring, more than 400 students present the results of their scholarly and creative activities. Many students co-author publications and present at conferences, such as the National Conference on Undergraduate Research (NCUR). Many participate in internships at businesses, hospitals and social service organizations. The Michael Rapaport '59 Ethics Across the Curriculum promotes courses in all departments that provide training in everyday ethics. Writing Across the Curriculum requires all students to take five designated courses from at least two divisions and one Senior Writing Experience.

CAMPUS FACILITIES AND EQUIPMENT

Union's nearly 100 buildings include the 16-sided Nott Memorial, a National Historic Landmark used for study, symposia, exhibits and special events. The F.W. Olin Center is a high-technology classroom and laboratory building with interactive computerization capabilities. The Science and Engineering Center houses the Center for Bioengineering and Computational Biology and contains specialized research tools available for student use, including a nuclear magnetic resonance spectrometer, a Pelletron accelerator and a scanning electron microscope.

Schaffer Library houses more than 600,000 volumes, 1,600 journals and two on-line databases that provide access to a quarter million printed books, documents and musical scores. Flanking the library are the Humanities and Social Sciences Buildings. The Visual Arts Building includes the Burns Atrium, exhibiting work by students, faculty and alumni. The recently renovated and expanded Taylor Music Building, an all-Steinway facility, includes the Fred L. Emerson Auditorium, featuring state-of-the-art recording technology. The Yulman Theater is the College's major performance space. Union's central computer facility consists of multi-user servers on a campus wide fiber-optic-based network that includes Linux, Windows Server and Apple Macintosh Xserves. Currently under construction is the $18-million Peter Irving Wold Science and Engineering Center, which will provide a home for interdisciplinary studies across departments. It is slated for completion in 2011.

Residential options for students include apartment-style housing, theme houses, residence halls and College Park Hall, which houses upper class students. The Reamer Campus Center, a hub of activity for the entire campus, houses dining facilities, an auditorium, the bookstore, a radio station, the Unity Lounge, a prayer room and multiple student activities spaces. Among the athletic facilities are Alumni Gymnasium, with an eight-lane swimming/diving pool; multi-use rooms for dance, aerobics and yoga; Breazzano Fitness Center; the 3,000-seat Messa Rink at Achilles Center; several fields and tracks; the Viniar Athletic Center for basketball and volleyball; and the Travis J. Clark '00 Strength Training Facility for varsity athletes. The Becker Career Center helps students with career planning, internships, and graduate school and job searches.

STUDENT ORGANIZATIONS AND ACTIVITIES

Union has more than 100 campus clubs and activities, including performance, dance and arts clubs; cultural, religious and ethnic interest groups; the student newspaper, *Concordiensis*, and radio station, WRUC; sports clubs; 17 Greek organizations; more than a dozen theme houses; academic and honor societies; service groups; a cappella singing ensembles; political interest and advocacy groups; and intercollegiate academic competitions, such as the Ethics Bowl and the mini-Baja Club. New groups are formed regularly. Cultural events include concerts, theater, dance, film and art exhibits at the Mandeville Gallery. Student Activities coordinates an active concert schedule. Union's comprehensive athletics program offers 25 varsity intercollegiate sports, organized intramurals, club sports, and recreational and fitness activities. Union is a member of the NCAA, Liberty League and ECAC Hockey. Men's and women's ice hockey compete in NCAA Division I programs; other teams are Division III.

Seven social and academic spaces in the center of campus make up the student-run Minerva House System. Each student belongs to one of the houses, and all faculty members have house affiliations. This unique program encourages students and faculty members to contribute in a variety of ways to Union's social, residential, and intellectual life. Minerva programs range from coffee houses and cooking demonstrations to book clubs and discussions about current events. About 90 percent of all students live in residence halls or college-owned houses, including traditional dorms, Minerva Houses, Greek houses, townhouses and College Park Hall, a renovated hotel. The Kenney Community Center connects students with Big Brothers Big Sisters, Habitat for Humanity, tutoring programs and civic projects.

TUITION, ROOM, BOARD AND FEES

The comprehensive fee for 2009–10 was $50,439. This includes tuition, mandatory fees, and room and board.

FINANCIAL AID

Union is committed to admitting an economically diverse student body and to meeting the full demonstrated need of all admitted students. The College offers more than $32 million annually in aid. The average Union need-based scholarship is $27,000; the average merit scholarship is $10,000. Those families who are unable to pay full tuition and fees are typically covered by a financial aid package consisting of a grant, loan and work opportunity. About half of all applicants apply for financial aid; more than 60 percent of all students receive assistance. Scholarship awards are based on academic performance and financial need. Candidates for aid should complete the Free Application for Federal Student Aid (FAFSA) and the College Scholarship Service's PROFILE form and mail them directly to the appropriate agencies by Feb. 1.

ADMISSION PROCESS

Some 5,000 applicants seek freshman class positions; about half are in the top 10 percent of their secondary school class. In evaluating each application, admissions counselors look at the prospective student's grades, rigor of courses taken, class rank, teacher recommendations and extracurricular involvement. Typically, 16 units of secondary school preparation are required for admission. These should include credits in certain fundamental subjects, such as English; foreign language, mathematics, social studies and science. It is strongly recommended that students visit Union for an admission interview and student-guided tour. Alumni interviews may be requested online. A student can choose not to submit his or her SAT or ACT scores for review, except for accelerated programs, which require applicants to submit the SAT and two SAT Subject Tests.

Early decision (ED) candidates have two options. The application deadline (including all supporting credentials) for Option I is Nov. 15, with notification by Dec. 15. Option II has a Jan. 15 deadline (including all supporting credentials) and Feb. 15 notification. Applications for regular decision (RD) admission must be filed by Jan.15; decisions are mailed by April 1. Applications to the Leadership in Medicine program are due no later than Dec. 15, and for Law and Public Policy, by Jan. 1. Those deferred under ED and all regular applicants are given a final decision by April 1. Accepted students have until May 1 to commit.

UNITED STATES AIR FORCE ACADEMY

AT A GLANCE

The Air Force Academy was established in 1954 to train and motivate Air Force cadets pursuing careers in the military. The Academy emphasizes character building, military discipline, physical fitness and academic excellence. An Academy education builds valuable leadership skills in all areas.

Approximately 4,000 students attend the Academy, with about 1,300 as entering students (fourth-class). The makeup of the student body reflects that of the corps of Air Force officers: approximately 20 percent women and 23 percent minority. Cadets arrive from all 50 states and a number of other countries. All cadets must live on campus and wear uniforms.

The Academy is accredited by the North Central Association of Colleges and Schools. Engineering programs are approved by the Engineering Accreditation Commission of the Accreditation Board for Engineering and Technology. Computer courses are approved by the Computing Sciences Accreditation Board. The Commission on Professional Training of the American Chemical Society establishes the requirements made of biochemistry and chemistry majors.

Cadets are required to engage in club, intramural or intercollegiate athletics each semester. Options for intramural activity include basketball, boxing (men), cross-country, flag football, flickerball, mountain biking, racquetball, rugby (men's and women's), soccer, softball, team handball, tennis, ultimate Frisbee, volleyball and wallyball.

The Academy fields intercollegiate teams in Division I of the NCAA; its teams compete both regionally and nationally. The men compete in baseball, basketball, boxing, cheerleading, cross-country, diving, fencing, football, golf, gymnastics, ice hockey, lacrosse, rifle, soccer, swimming, tennis, track, water polo and wrestling. Women compete in basketball, cheerleading, cross-country, diving, fencing, gymnastics, rifle, soccer, swimming, tennis, track and volleyball. More than 80 extracurricular activities are available to cadets, including competitive and recreational clubs, hobby clubs, mission support clubs, professional organizations and sports groups.

Qualified graduates of the Academy may commence flight training after graduating. About three-quarters of all cadets undertake graduate study within 10 years of graduation. Every year, many graduates of the Academy are granted fellowships and scholarships, including the Guggenheim, Marshall, NCAA, National Science Foundation and Rhodes.

LOCATION AND ENVIRONMENT

Located in the foothills of the Rocky Mountains' Rampart Range, the Academy is truly surrounded by natural beauty. The campus sits upon a 7,000-foot mesa; the campus and its immediate area are among the state's most popular tourist attractions. Contemporary architecture is featured on campus; the space age Cadet Chapel, with its seventeen 150-foot aluminum spires, set the tone for the entire cadet area. This modern setting aptly reflects the campus' mission: to educate, train and inspire men and women to become officers of character, motivated to lead the United States Air Force in service to our nation. The campus is located just north of Colorado Springs, a city of nearly 360,000, which sits at the foot of Pikes Peak (14,100 feet). The state capital, Denver, is just 55 miles to the north. This metropolis of more than 2.5 million offers a plethora of cultural, educational and recreational opportunities. Cadets also enjoy horseback riding, hunting, snowboarding, skiing, whitewater rafting and many other outdoor activities in the nearby mountains and its resorts.

OFF-CAMPUS OPPORTUNITIES

Cadets chosen to participate in a semester-long exchange program may attend the Military Academy, Naval Academy, Coast Guard Academy or foreign air force academies in Canada, Chile, France, Germany and Spain. Other international programs are usually one to three weeks in duration visiting one of 40 countries.

MAJORS AND DEGREES OFFERED

Graduates receive a Bachelor of Science degree and a commission as second lieutenants in the Air Force. Students may pursue their degree in any of 32 majors: aeronautical engineering, astronautical engineering, basic sciences, behavioral sciences, biology, chemistry, civil engineering, computer engineering, computer science, economics, electrical engineering, engineering mechanics, English, environmental engineering, foreign area studies, general engineering, geospatial science, history, humanities, legal studies, management, mathematical sciences, mechanical engineering, meteorology, military strategic studies, operations research, physics, political science, social sciences, space operations, system engineering and system engineering management. Cadets may minor in foreign languages and philosophy.

ACADEMIC PROGRAMS

The school year for entering students begins in late June or early July; incoming cadets commence their tenure at the Academy with a rigorous 38-day summer training program designed to test their physical and mental abilities. This training is conducted by upper-class cadets while commissioned officers serve as advisers. Cadets who successfully complete this program are admitted as fourth-class cadets in the cadet wing. Academic courses begin in early August and run through May. Cadets begin by focusing on core curriculum in engineering, humanities, science and the social sciences. Cadets choose a specialized academic major during their second year.

Core courses are designed to prepare cadets for a wide range of duties as Air Force officers. They include courses in academic subjects; military training and leadership; and athletics and physical education. All cadets must also complete the requirements of an academic major. Other graduation requirements include: demonstration of ability to serve and to lead; demonstration of character befitting a member of a professional military; along with maintenance of a minimum Military Performance Average (MPA), Grade Point Average (GPA) and Physical Education Average of 2.0. Cadets have numerous options in selecting elective courses.

All cadets must enter as freshmen. Cadets who have previously completed comparable core course work at other institutions may earn transfer or validation credit for their work. Those who receive transfer credit may take other courses at the Academy in place of their core courses. Advanced study classes are open to cadets who meet academic prerequisites, including a minimum grade point average. Cadets learn all operational procedures of the Air Force through the Academy's aviation program. Optional courses are available in basic flying, navigation, parachuting and soaring. Students who complete these courses may earn pilot or glider certificates issued by the Federal Aviation Administration. Once they have graduated from the academy, select cadets may enter Air Education and Training Command flight programs to train as pilots or navigators. Cadets may pursue summer studies in aviation and military training. These programs prepare them for the responsibilities of an Air Force officer. A number of optional assignments are available, both at the Air Force Academy and at other military installations.

CAMPUS FACILITIES AND EQUIPMENT

The Air Force Academy has excellent facilities to sustain the academic, athletic and military goals of its programs. Classrooms are designed to accommodate small sessions of 12 to 20 students. A few larger classes meet in lecture halls, as do assemblies. The Academy provides its science students with fully equipped laboratories, as well as an aeronautics laboratory that houses rocket engines, shock tubes and wind tunnels. A LAN links every classroom, dorm room, laboratory, and faculty and staff office on campus. All entering cadets are required to purchase microcomputers, which they may use for both academic and personal purposes. The library houses more than 1.5 million volumes, and its collection includes an entire floor designated to historical materials pertaining to aeronautics.

TUITION, ROOM, BOARD AND FEES

The government of the United States bears the entire cost of an Air Force Academy education. There are no charges for tuition, room, board, medical or dental care. Academy cadets earn a monthly salary, with which they are expected to purchase clothing, supplies and personal items. Cadets who manage their money carefully will meet all obligations and have a small sum left over for personal expenses.

FINANCIAL AID

All cadets attend the Air Force Academy on full scholarship, as described above.

STUDENT ORGANIZATIONS AND ACTIVITIES

Cadets learn important leadership skills through their duties in the cadet wing, an organization through which upper-class cadets take responsibility for enforcing the honor system and honor education, leading under-class cadets in military drills and enforcing the human relations, ethics and character development programs of the Academy. First-class cadets (fourth-year students) supervise the operations of the cadet wing and they hold the rank of cadet officer and command its groups, squadrons, flights and elements.

ADMISSIONS PROCESS

Every year, young U.S. citizens (both men and women) receive appointments to the Academy. They arrive from all of the nation's states and territories. A limited number of foreign nationals are also admitted. Applicants must be between the ages of 17 and 23 as of July 1 of their projected year of admission, must be unmarried and without dependents. They must be principled individuals and must be physically fit. An official nomination is a required part of any application to the Academy. Most nominations come from members of Congress and are submitted for students living in their districts and states. Representatives and senators nominate high school juniors who have demonstrated academic excellence, who possess leadership qualities (as demonstrated by academic and extracurricular records), who are physically fit, who have the respect of their peers and associates, and who desire a career in the military. It is not necessary for applicants to know their congressional representatives personally to receive their nomination. Other categories than congressional exist and interested applicants should consult their guidance counselor or local Admissions Liaison Officer to learn more about other available nomination categories. Students wishing to enter the Academy upon completion of high school should submit applications as soon after January 31 of their junior year as possible. Applicants who receive a nomination must pass a physical aptitude assessment (PAE) and a medical exam. They must also submit standardized test scores (SAT or ACT). Applicants should carefully read the instructions that accompany the application package. These instructions clearly detail the proper procedure for submitting an application. The application package includes, among other materials, sample letters to members of Congress, senators and the President requesting nomination to the Academy. Applicants seeking help with application requirements should contact an Admissions Liaison Officer; there is at least one in every state.

Applications are available to high school juniors. To request an application, write to:

HQ USAFA/RRS

2304 Cadet Drive, Suite 2300

USAF Academy, CO 80840-5025

Telephone: 719-333-2520

Website: www.academyadmissions.com

THE UNIVERSITY OF ALABAMA AT BIRMINGHAM

AT A GLANCE

The University of Alabama at Birmingham (UAB) continues to attract the best and brightest students from around Alabama, the nation, and 109 countries around the globe. The average ACT score of entering students continues to trend upward, currently at 24.3, consistently besting state and national averages.

UAB is a fully accredited research university and academic health center with an annual enrollment of more than 16,000 students. As the University has grown, so have its contributions to the state, the nation, and the world. UAB is committed to education, research, and service programs of excellent quality and far-reaching scope. In terms of federal research and development funding, UAB ranks twenty-sixth nationally and first in the state of Alabama, receiving more funding than all Alabama universities combined. In such an environment, undergraduate students can pursue a wide array of research opportunities and gain valuable experience that pays off later in graduate studies or career development.

LOCATION AND ENVIRONMENT

The UAB campus offers the best of both worlds—the energy and opportunity of a big city nestled in the serene foothills of the Appalachian Mountains. Cosmopolitan Birmingham is home to a thriving arts and culture scene, as well as a "knowledge economy," in which students have access to more than 3,000 internships, co-ops, and clinical activities a year, and more than 150 active student organizations.

Birmingham earned the name "The Magic City" during its first boom days. The expression still rings true as the metropolitan area continues to mirror UAB's phenomenal growth and reflects the many cultural opportunities available within the city. Birmingham is easily reached from major national routes (Interstates 20, 59, and 65) and UAB is only minutes away from the Birmingham International Airport.

MAJORS AND DEGREES OFFERED

College of Arts and Sciences: African-American Studies, Art (concentrations in art education, art history, ceramic sculpture, drawing, graphic design, painting, photography, printmaking, sculpture), Communication Studies [concentrations in Communication Management, Mass Communications (journalism, broadcasting, public relations), English (concentration in creative writing, linguistics, professional writing and public discourse), Foreign Language (concentrations in French, Spanish), Music (concentrations in music education, music technology), Philosophy, Theatre (concentrations in design/technology, performance), Biology (concentrations in marine science, molecular biology), Chemistry (concentrations in biochemistry, forensic chemistry, polymer/materials science, chemistry education), Computer and Information Sciences (concentration in computer networking), Mathematics (concentrations in applied math, scientific computation), Natural Science, Physics (concentrations in biophysics, physics education), Anthropology, Criminal Justice, Economics, History, International Studies, Neuroscience, Political Science, Psychology, Social Work, Sociology (concentration in social psychology),

School of Business: Accounting (concentrations in forensic accounting and information technology/auditing), Economics (concentrations in economic analysis and policy, philosophy and political economy, quantitative methods), Finance (concentrations in investments and institutions, financial management), Industrial Distribution (concentrations in medical equipment and supplies marketing, industrial products), Information Systems, Management, Marketing

School of Education: Early Childhood Education, Elementary Education, Health Education, High School Education, Physical Education, Special Education

School of Engineering: Biomedical Engineering, Civil Engineering, Electrical Engineering, Materials Engineering, Mechanical Engineering

School of Health Professions: Health Information Management, Health Sciences, Medical Technology, Nuclear Medicine Technology), Respiratory Therapy

School of Nursing: Nursing

Exploratory Studies: Undeclared Majors

Pre-Professional Programs: pre-dentistry, pre-medicine, pre-optometry, pre-nurse anesthesia, pre-law, pre-occupational therapy, pre-physical therapy, pre-surgical physician assistant.

Honors Programs

The UAB Honors Academy offers several special programs that present rare and valuable opportunities to explore knowledge from new angles, enriching the overall educational experience for future success. Students can take advantage of smaller class sizes, individual attention from faculty, and a community of like-minded, motivated students.

The University Honors Program concentrates the vast resources of a major research university in a small, liberal arts setting. Students participate in challenging interdisciplinary courses, honors seminars, independent research projects, extracurricular activities and community service.

The Science and Technology Honors Program offers students interested in a science or technology career the opportunity to work closely with world-renowned researchers. Students combine research experience with specialized courses in a scientifically focused learning community and can earn up to 12 hours of graduate credit toward a doctorate as an undergraduate.

The Global and Community Leadership Honors Program is designed to provide unique learning opportunities for students throughout their academic experience. Students will be able to participate in special honors courses relating to global and community issues, and in international and community learning experiences, with the objective of becoming prepared for leadership roles on a global, national, or local level.

The Experiential Learning Scholars Program offers students an undergraduate education that intentionally combines class work and applicable, real-life experiences. Students thoughtfully construct learning plans suited to their unique academic and career aspirations.

Qualified students interested in a career in medicine, optometry, or dentistry may be accepted to professional school at UAB before they even begin college through the Early Admission to Medical Professional Schools Program. Students enjoy specialty seminars, classes, and research opportunities.

CAMPUS FACILITIES

The UAB campus occupies more than 100 major buildings, more than 11 million gross square feet, and almost 90 square blocks near downtown Birmingham. The undergraduate area of campus is concentrated within an eight-square-block area, however, giving students the convenience and togetherness that is so important to the college experience.

The cornerstone of UAB's Campus Green is the 150,000-square-foot Campus Recreation Center, which features an indoor recreational pool with an oval running track, a lap pool, indoor basketball courts, a multi-purpose court, a climbing wall, cardio fitness areas and well-equipped weight-lifting areas. Nearby on the Green is Blazer Hall, a state-of-the-art residence facility for freshman that features suite-style rooms, 14 study lounges, a Residence Life Center and other amenities. Across the way is the Commons on the Green, a full-service dining facility open seven days a week with a variety of international cuisines. The new 95,000-square-foot Heritage Hall is one of the anchor buildings for the Campus Green and houses the College of Arts & Sciences.

The Mervyn H. Sterne Library houses a collection of more than 1.5 million items selected to support teaching and research at UAB. In addition to books and subscriptions to more than 1,600 periodicals, the collection consists of microforms and other print and nonprint materials. In addition to Sterne Library, the Lister Hill Library of the Health Sciences provides a comprehensive collection of materials for medical study and research.

UAB is home to the Alys Robinson Stephens Performing Arts Center, with state-of-the-art concert halls and practice facilities. This beautiful facility draws national and international performers, enhancing the strong cultural opportunities in Birmingham.

TUITION, ROOM, BOARD AND FEES

Enjoy the benefits of a world-class university at a fraction of the cost.

Tuition and fees shown are based on fall 2009 rates and a course load of 12 credit hours each semester (fall and spring). Because tuition and fees are billed per semester hour, the actual costs may vary.

Fall 2009 First-Year Freshman (estimated)

First-Year Freshman	In-State	Out-of-State
Tuition and Fees	$5,144	$11,480
Books and Supplies	$900	$900
Meal Plan	$3,380–$3,650	$3,380–$3,650
Residence Hall	$4,460	$4,460
Grand Total	$14,024–$14,294	$120,360–$19,400

FINANCIAL AID

UAB's financial aid package consists of loans, employment, and grants and scholarships, enabling students from all economic backgrounds to attend UAB. UAB offers a growing number of scholarships to provide support for eligible students who attend UAB. Newly admitted students are considered for all academic scholarships for which they are qualified. Awards are distributed on a first-come, first-served basis; students are encouraged to apply as early as possible. Financial aid applications are available in early January for the following academic year, with a priority packaging deadline of March 1.

STUDENT ORGANIZATIONS AND ACTIVITIES

Part of the UAB experience is student life, consisting of a rich mix of academic organizations, honor clubs, social fraternities and sororities, volunteer groups, and activities ranging from intramural sports and SGA to supporting Blazer sports. With more than 150 campus organizations to keep students involved, UAB offers the chance to make lifelong friendships while assisting in the development of skills essential to leadership and teamwork.

The legacy of Coach Gene Bartow lives on in the arena that bears his name, where the men's basketball team has earned 13 post-season NCAA births (three times to the "Sweet 16" and once to the "Elite Eight") and nine NIT appearances. This winning attitude drives scholar-athletes in six men's and ten women's sports, as cheerleaders, Golden Girls, the painted fans of "Gang Green," and the 150-member Marching Blazers Band cheer them on to victory.

ADMISSIONS PROCESS

UAB is an equal educational opportunity institution. The requirements for regular admission for entering freshmen include minimum high school GPA of 2.25 on a 4.0 scale in core subjects; a minimum ACT score of 20 or SAT score of 950; and completion of no fewer than 17 core courses including four years of English, three years of social studies, three years of math (including algebra 1 and 2, geometry, and either algebra 3, pre-cal, trigonometry, AP calculus, or other senior college-preparatory math), three years of science (including two with lab components),one year of foreign language and three additional courses of the student's choice.

For tentative action, a transcript may be sent during the student's senior year in high school. A final transcript must be sent upon graduation.

An application may be submitted as early as one year prior to admission. A completed application, a nonrefundable $35 application fee ($30 for online U.S. applications), and all supporting documentation must be received by the Office of Undergraduate Admission by the priority deadline for the term for which admission is requested. The application priority deadline for fall term is May 1. For an application and further information, students should contact:

UAB Undergraduate Admission

Hill University Center, Room 260

1530 3rd Avenue, South

Birmingham, Alabama 35294-1150

United States

Phone: 205-934-8221

800-421-8473 (toll-free)

E-mail: undergradadmit@uab.edu

Web site: www.uab.edu/apply

THE UNITED STATES MILITARY ACADEMY

AT A GLANCE

As the nation's oldest service academy, West Point offers young men and women a first-rate and highly respected college education. Through progressive development in four complementary programs – academic, military, physical, and moral-ethical—everything cadets experience during their 47 months at West Point is focused on developing them as educated leaders of character who, upon graduation, will serve at least five years on active duty in a variety of exciting career opportunities while serving as commissioned officers in the U.S. Army.

LOCATION AND ENVIRONMENT

West Point is located approximately 50 miles north of New York City in the picturesque Hudson Valley region. Flanked by the Hudson River and Storm King Mountain, West Point maintains some of the finest educational and military-training facilities in the nation on its 16,000 acres.

MAJORS AND DEGREES OFFERED

Every West Point graduate earns a Bachelor of Science degree and a commission as a second lieutenant in the U.S. Army. The curriculum complements the core program by providing the opportunity for in-depth study through the elective program. There are more than 40 majors available. The majors cover the liberal arts, sciences and engineering disciplines one would expect to find in a high-quality, selective college or university of comparable size. At West Point, cadets may enter most majors without restriction. No special grade-point averages are established for entry, but there may be a limitation as to the number of cadets in a particular major. Cadets choose to major in specialized areas, including philosophy and literature, basic science, chemical engineering, chemistry, civil engineering, computer science, economics, electrical engineering, electronic and information technology systems, engineering management, engineering psychology, environmental engineering, environmental geography, environmental science, environmental studies, foreign area studies (Latin America, Europe, Middle East, Eurasia, East Asia), foreign languages (Arabic, Chinese, French, German, Portuguese, Russian, Spanish), geospatial information science, history, human geography, information systems engineering, law and legal studies, kinesiology, leadership, life science, management, mathematical sciences, mathematical studies, mechanical engineering, mechanical engineering studies, military art and science, nuclear engineering, nuclear engineering science, operations research, physics, political science, psychology, sociology, systems engineering, and systems management.

ACADEMIC PROGRAMS

In addition to offering a top-notch college education, the West Point curriculum develops character, competence, and intellectual abilities—the essential broad base of knowledge necessary for success as a commissioned officer in the U.S. Army. A broad background in the arts and sciences is the focal point of the academic program, which also prepares cadets for future graduate study. The core curriculum ranges in size from 26 to 30 courses, depending on the major.

West Point classes are small, averaging 12 to 18 cadets. Consequently, cadets receive individual attention and may request tutorial sessions, if needed. Cadets with exceptional ability may take advanced and honors courses.

West Point's Centers of Excellence serve to enhance the quality of the academic program. They coordinate professional expertise and concentrate technical resources in order to enrich cadet education, enhance cadet academic performance, improve faculty teaching, promote faculty and cadet research, and provide outreach and support to the Army.

Cadets study military science and participate in class instruction on the principles of small-unit tactics and leadership during a two-week intercession period between the first and second semesters. Field training is concentrated on during the summer as each cadet gains opportunities to learn and practice the military skills and principles that are learned in the classroom.

CAMPUS FACILITIES AND EQUIPMENT

West Point has carefully crafted an electronic environment in which every course has integrated computer use. Cadets and faculty at West Point enjoy the benefits of a first-class information technology environment. Every cadet has a notebook computer and a PDA, and everyone is connected to a large array of powerful academic computing services at West Point and has unlimited access to the internet. Cadets register for classes, get grades and counseling reports, and receive and send homework assignments using the West Point network.

Computer-aided math, design, and simulation; dynamic news sources; world-wide electronic mail; spreadsheets, statistical analyses, and database access; library research; and electronic bulletin boards all contribute to an academic environment rich with information resources and electronic media tools.

Graduates of West Point are well-versed in the use of information technology and services, and are ready for the challenges awaiting them in the high technology Army of the present and future.

TUITION, ROOM, BOARD AND FEES

The full cost of a four-year education at West Point, including tuition, room, board, and medical and dental expenses, is paid by the U.S. Government. As members of the Army, cadets also receive an annual salary of more than $10,000, which pays for uniforms, books, a notebook computer, supplies, and incidental living expenses. An initial deposit of about $3,000 is required to cover uniform costs and initial expenses during the first year.

FINANCIAL AID

All tuition, room, board, and medical and dental expenses are paid by the U.S. Government, so there are no financial aid programs needed at West Point. Scholarship awards may offset the cost of the required initial deposit.

STUDENT ORGANIZATIONS AND ACTIVITIES

Cadets, like college students everywhere, find time for social activities. Cadets hold social functions in the ski lodge, the golf club, a remodeled railroad depot, two lake cabins, and even on West Point's excursion boats.

Throughout the year special weekends are held for each class, which include formal banquets and dances, and other activities. Events surrounding the traditional Army-Navy game culminate the first semester of activities. Broadway touring company plays, nationally and internationally known musicians and comedians, concerts, dances, and other live entertainment play in Eisenhower Hall, the cadet activities center, on many weekends.

There are more than 100 extracurricular clubs to enhance athletic, recreational, hobby, academic, and religious interests of the individual cadet.

In addition to an intercollegiate athletic program that features 25 varsity teams, there are more than 25 competitive club sports teams and an extensive intramural program. There are sailing and crew teams, cycling, marathon and triathlon teams, sport parachuting, orienteering, mountaineering, and skeet and trap teams, as well as a ski team.

There are flying, fishing, and inline hockey clubs, as well as a ballroom dance club, a chess club, close-combat team, mountain bike club and whitewater canoe club. The Cadet Glee Club is one of the most well-known collegiate singing groups in the world. Their nationwide concert schedule often includes appearances throughout the United States and on national television. There are a radio station, pipes and drums, a hop band, and a Gospel choir. There are many academic clubs, a scoutmaster's council, and numerous religious clubs.

ADMISSIONS PROCESS

Each year West Point admits approximately 1,200 young men and woman. These new members of the Corps of Cadets come from all corners of the United States and represent every race, religion, and culture in the country.

To become a cadet you must meet the requirements specified by public law, and you must be qualified academically, physically, and medically. Each candidate must also obtain a nomination from a member of the United States Congress Each candidate can apply to his or her two United States Senators, local representative in Congress, and the vice president of the United States, or from the Department of Army in one of the service-connected categories.

Candidates are evaluated for admission on the basis of academic performance (high school academic record and SAT and/or ACT Plus Writing scores), demonstrated leadership potential, fitness assessment, and medical qualification.

A candidate must be at least 17 but not older than 23 on July 1st of the year of admission, be a U.S. citizen at the time of enrollment, be unmarried, and not be pregnant or have a legal obligation to support a child or children. A candidate must have an above-average high school or college academic record and turn in a strong performance on the timed ACT Plus Writing and/or the SATs.

West Point encourages a strong college-preparatory academic background as a prerequisite for admission. The Admissions Committee looks for four years of English with a strong emphasis on composition, grammar, literature, and speech; four years of math, including algebra, plane geometry, intermediate algebra and trigonometry; two years of a foreign language; two years of a laboratory science, such as chemistry and physics; and one year of U.S. history. Additional courses in geography, government, and economics are helpful. Courses in pre-calculus and calculus, and a basic computer course are extremely helpful.

Candidates for admission should begin the admissions process in the winter of their junior year of high school and should begin the nomination process at the same time.

UNIVERSITY OF ARKANSAS

AT A GLANCE

Located in Fayetteville, the University of Arkansas, founded in 1871, is both the major land-grant university for Arkansas and the state's flagship university. It has a proud legacy of internationally significant scientific and intellectual achievements in many academic fields. It also enjoys a reputation of being a great educational institution, producing over its 139-year history more than 125,000 graduates who have provided leadership in all walks of life.

On July 1, 2005, the University of Arkansas completed the Campaign for the Twenty-First Century, raising more than a billion dollars. The success of this campaign placed the university among only 13 public institutions in America at the time to reach the billion dollar mark during similar campaigns and significantly augmented the institution's endowment funds and ability to serve students.

The university offers more than 200 areas of study in a comprehensive range of fields, and is moderate in size among major research institutions with nearly 20,000 students, of which more than 15,000 are undergraduates. Its diverse student population includes nearly 1,200 international students from 100 countries.

LOCATION AND ENVIRONMENT

Fayetteville, a city of over 64,000 residents, is the predominant city in a metroplex that includes Springdale (home of Tyson Foods), Rogers, and Bentonville (home of Wal-Mart Stores Inc., the world's largest corporation).

The Northwest Arkansas metroplex was ranked seventh by the Milken Report's Best Performing Cities, a report that measures U.S. cities' economic performance. The Fayetteville-Springdale-Rogers area is ranked by the U.S. Census Bureau as being the sixth fastest-growing metro area in the nation.

Situated on the Ozark Mountain Plateau, Fayetteville offers a friendly environment with beautiful scenery, a moderate climate, excellent schools, and an unemployment rate well below national averages. Fayetteville is vibrant with the cultural life that would be expected in any major university town. The area is a haven for writers, artists, poets, and musicians.

OFF-CAMPUS OPPORTUNITIES

The study abroad office works eagerly with students to identify opportunities in virtually any country around the world. Students in all majors are eligible to go abroad and can start as early as the summer following freshman year. It is not necessary to know a foreign language, as students can study in English speaking countries or in programs where classes are taught in English. Often students make multiple trips abroad in the course of their college careers.

There are numerous additional scholarships available for study abroad, including a $4 million endowment specifically for undergraduate international study. Scholarships and federal financial aid (including Pell grants and Stafford loans) can be used for study abroad.

MAJORS AND DEGREES OFFERED

The Fay Jones School of Architecture offers Architecture; Architectural Studies; Landscape Architecture; and Landscape Architectural Studies.

J. William Fulbright College of Arts and Sciences offers African American Studies; American Studies; Anthropology; Art; Biology; Chemistry; Classical Studies; Communication; Criminal Justice; Drama; Earth Science; Economics; English; European Studies; French; Geography; Geology; German; History; International Relations; Journalism; Latin American Studies; Mathematics; Middle East Studies ; Music; Philosophy; Physics; Political Science; Pre-professional Programs; Psychology; Public Administration; Russian Studies; Social Work; Sociology; and Spanish.

Sam M. Walton College of Business offers Accounting; Economics; Finance; Information Systems; International Business; General Business; Management; Marketing; and Transportation/Logistics.

College of Education and Health Professions offers Career/Technical Education; Communication Disorders; Childhood Education; Health Sciences; Kinesiology; Middle Level Education; Nursing (BSN); Recreation; Vocational Education; and Teacher Certification through Master of Arts in Teaching (MAT) Program.

College of Engineering offers Biological Engineering; Chemical Engineering; Civil Engineering; Computer Science & Computer Engineering; Electrical Engineering; Industrial Engineering; and Mechanical Engineering.

Dale Bumpers College of Agricultural, Food and Life Sciences offers Agricultural Business; Ag Education, Communications, & Technology; Animal Science; Apparel Studies; Crop Management; Environmental, Soil & Water Science; Food, Human Nutrition & Hospitality; Food Science; Horticulture Landscape & Turf; Human Development, Family Sciences, & Rural Sociology; Human Environmental Sciences; Interior Design; and Poultry Science,.

The Honors College offers all academic majors to students enrolled concurrently in the home college or school of their academic majors.

ACADEMIC PROGRAMS

The school operates on a traditional two-semester academic year schedule, with two regular summer sessions and some special concurrent summer sessions. The majority of undergraduate degree offerings follow a four-year plan requiring from 124 to 136 course hours for graduation; there are some exceptions to this requirement, such as the five-year, design-oriented architecture program, which requires 163 hours.

The endowed Honors College enables students to pursue honors programs in any college or department and provides undergraduate research and study abroad opportunities. Requirements vary among programs and schools. More information is available by visiting http://honorscollege.uark.edu.

CAMPUS FACILITIES AND EQUIPMENT

The University of Arkansas libraries consist of the David W. Mullins Library (the main facility), the Fine Arts Library, Chemistry Library, Physics Library, and the Robert A. & Vivian Young Law Library. These libraries contain more than 1.77 million volumes, 5.5 million microforms, 340,337 audio-visual items, and 18,576 periodical subscriptions. The university's libraries also offer electronic access to more than 16,700 online journals in a wide variety of subject areas.

The university is a member of Internet2, providing a high speed connection to other national and international research networks. In addition, a wide variety of computing resources are available including e-mail, free internet connections, and Web page development, to all students, faculty and staff.

TUITION, ROOM, BOARD AND FEES

The school is among the most affordable of major research universities. Tuition and fees for 2009-2010 are estimated at $6,400 for Arkansas residents and $15,278 for out-of-state residents. Room and board rates average $7,422 annually. For undergraduate students, the resident tuition rate is $167 per credit hour and nonresident tuition is $440.86 per credit hour.

FINANCIAL AID

Undergraduates receive over $88 million in federal grants-in-aid, loans, scholarships, and work-study funds. Students will need to complete the FAFSA to be considered for federal financial aid and need to submit an application for admission by June 30, and scholarship applications by November 15.

Scholarships are awarded on a competitive basis and include: Sturgis, Bodenhamer, Boyer, and Honors College Fellowships ($12,500 per year), Chancellor's Scholarships (up to $8,000 per year), Silas Hunt Distinguished Scholarships (up to $8,000 per year), Arkansas Alumni Association Endowed Scholarships ($5,000 per year), Honors College Academy Scholarships ($4,000 per year), University Scholarships ($4,000 per year), Nonresident Tuition Award (waiver of out-of-state tuition), Transfer Student Scholarships ($2,000 per year), Arkansas Alumni Association Scholarships (variable), and Alumni Legacy Scholarships (waiver of out-of-state tuition).

STUDENT ORGANIZATIONS AND ACTIVITIES

The university offers a vibrant campus life for its student population. University residence halls accommodate approximately 4,600 students. In addition, Fayetteville offers off-campus housing opportunities, many along university bus routes.

There are more than 340 registered student organizations, including special interest organizations, religious organizations, cultural organizations, honorary and professional service organizations, and student government. Students may also choose to participate in the Greek system, which is made up of 11 sororities and 16 fraternities.

Culturally and intellectually, the academic semesters are filled with musical performances, theatre productions, art exhibits, concerts, poetry readings and visiting speakers - both on campus and at the nearby Walton Arts Center. The University's Distinguished Lecture Series has featured President George H. W. Bush; Anderson Cooper, a CNN news anchor; Benazir Bhutto, former Pakistani Prime Minister; Ehud Barak, former Israeli Prime Minister; Apollo Ohno, U.S. Olympian; and political commentators James Carville and Mary Matalin.

ADMISSIONS PROCESS

Students interested in applying to the University of Arkansas for the fall semester are urged to apply through the early admission process. By applying prior to November 15, students are able to register for housing and orientation early; however, regular fall applications will be accepted until August 15.

Entering freshmen are advised to prepare for admission in high school by taking 4 units of English, 4 of math, 3 of social studies, 3 of natural sciences, and 2 of electives. A minimum 3.0 high school GPA and an ACT composite score of 20 (930 SAT, combined critical reading and math scores) are required for admission, but other students may be admitted after an individual review. The ACT code is 0144, and the SAT code is 6866.

Transfer students need a cumulative GPA of at least 2.0 on all college courses taken and must be in good academic standing when applying for admission. Students completing fewer than 24 transferable hours will need to meet all requirements for freshman admission in addition to those for transfer students.

To apply, complete the application for admission available by visiting http://apply. uark.edu. The application deadline for the fall semester is August 15; the spring deadline is December 20. The student must also request that official transcripts be mailed to the office of admissions. A preliminary admission is provided for those high school seniors who have a transcript of six or seven semesters, but a final transcript is needed to certify high school graduation. Official ACT or SAT scores no more than 5 years old must be submitted by all entering freshmen and transfer students with fewer than 24 transferable hours.

Students wishing to apply for scholarships are encouraged to complete and return a separate scholarship application to the office of academic scholarships with all appropriate materials by the priority deadline, November 15. A scholarship application is available by visiting http://scholarships.uark.edu.

UNIVERSITY OF CALIFORNIA—LOS ANGELES

UCLA is an amazing place—a great research university and one of the nation's elite institutions, with a campus environment that merges residential life into a vibrant academic community.

AT A GLANCE

As one of the world's premier research universities, UCLA offers unimagined diversity, unmatched depth of scholarship, and limitless possibility. UCLA's strength is its size: 4,000 faculty, 5,000 courses, 109 academic departments, 130 undergraduate majors, more than 950 student organizations, and the cultural and social opportunities equal to a large city.

LOCATION AND ENVIRONMENT

UCLA is located on 419 acres in the community of Westwood, a wooded suburban West Los Angeles neighborhood bordered by Beverly Hills, Bel-Air, and Brentwood. The campus has an average year-round temperature of 73 degrees, low humidity, and 330 days of sunshine a year.

OFF-CAMPUS OPPORTUNITIES

The UCLA campus is 15 minutes from the beach, two hours to the mountains, and a short distance to Santa Monica, Hollywood, the ocean, mountain and national park recreation areas, and the vibrant social, cultural, artistic, and sports scenes of greater Los Angeles.

UCLA itself is a major part of the Los Angeles cultural scene, offering more art, music, culture, and sports than most cities. On campus are seven major performance halls and theaters, special exhibitions, two world-class museums, and art galleries. Hosted on a daily basis are performances by world-renowned musicians and theater companies, first-run film sneak previews (often featuring stars and directors in attendance and in conversation), unique art and cultural events, and programs from the world's largest university-based film and television archive.

MAJORS AND DEGREES OFFERED

UCLA offers 190 fields of study, 130 undergraduate majors, and some 3,000 undergraduate courses taught by 4,000 faculty members. Bachelors, Masters, and PhDs are offered in all of the liberal arts and science fields, as well as in 11 graduate and professional schools.

ACADEMIC PROGRAMS

At UCLA students have immediate, first-year access to a vast selection of studies that only a world-class university can offer.

Incoming freshmen can begin their UCLA experience with a *Freshman Cluster* (www.ugeducation.ucla.edu/clusters), an innovative program that involves students in a stimulating, multidisciplinary exploration of challenging, timely topics. Clusters are a year-long learning communities that connect freshman with distinguished UCLA faculty, introduce them to interdisciplinary teaching, and provide opportunities to strengthen skills necessary in a research university.

Students can also choose among 200 small group seminars in the *Fiat Lux* program (www.ugeducation.ucla.edu/fiatlux). *Fiat Lux* offers more than 200 classes each year to bring the talents and expertise of a premier research university into a small classroom setting where students and faculty engage in critical thinking together.

Undergraduate students can perform important, publishable research in close collaboration with senior faculty—often as early as their freshman year (www.ugeducation.ucla.edu/ugresearch). Each year, thousands of UCLA students participate in seminars, research tutorials, and departmental honors programs. Two undergraduate research centers—Humanities and Social Sciences; Life Sciences and Physical Sciences—help undergraduates identify faculty mentors from every discipline.

The *Honors Programs* (www.ugeducation.ucla.edu/honors/) provide an enriched educational experience through interdisciplinary seminars, engaging classroom presentations, individualized mentoring, and special honors courses designed to encourage and reward critical thinking. The *Honors Program* also offers the *Honors Collegium*, which is open to all UCLA students. The Collegium creates a community atmosphere in small, interdisciplinary courses with extensive interaction between students and faculty from throughout the campus, including the graduate professional schools. More than 70 Collegium courses are offered each year.

The faculty is part of the driving force behind the world-renowned reputation. They inspire, challenge, guide, nourish, and ultimately reward their students, course after course. Among the UCLA faculty: five have been awarded Nobel Prizes, three have been awarded Pulitzer Prizes, ten have won the National Medal of Science, and more than 300 have earned Fulbright Scholarship to teach and do international research.

At UCLA, community service is a cornerstone of undergraduate education. The Center for Community Learning (www.ugeducation.ucla.edu/communitylearning) sends students into the diverse communities of Los Angeles in programs that merge a volunteer experience with academic coursework. Programs include tutoring, research and credit-earning internships, AmeriCorps service—even academic minors in Civic Engagement and Disability Studies.

Want to study abroad? UCLA's Education Abroad Program (www.international.ucla.edu/eap) offers opportunities in 140 exchange programs in more than 30 countries. You can go abroad for a year, a summer, or an academic quarter, or work on international internships, independent research, and field studies.

CAMPUS FACILITIES AND EQUIPMENT

UCLA houses many of the most advanced educational facilities for undergraduate study and research, including the top-ranked UCLA library system that includes two major general collections—the Charles E. Young Research Library and the College Library for undergraduates—and special-subject libraries in the arts, medicine, languages, law, management, music, science, and engineering. Laboratories for undergraduate study are often closely linked with faculty research. The recent new additions to the campus residential community include advanced computing labs, academic counseling, classroom, a working TV station and a theater for stage productions—right where most students live.

UCLA is home to the nation's most successful collegiate athletic program, with teams winning over 100 national championships—more than any other university. On campus is Pauley Pavilion, home to the legendary teams in basketball, volleyball, and women's gymnastics.

For recreation, students have access to the expansive workout facilities at the John Wooden Center and can participate in more than 45 intramural sports. Additionally, students can use the UCLA Marina Aquatic Center located 10 miles from campus in scenic Marina del Rey.

At UCLA, diversity is a core value, and the campus is one of the most ethnically and culturally diverse universities in the nation. UCLA is home to the Academic Advancement Program (AAP) (www.ugeducation.ucla.edu/aap/), the nation's largest and most successful university student diversity program. AAP provides tutoring, personal and academic counseling, career guidance, graduate mentoring, scholarships, research, stipends, and opportunities to participate in inventive science programs.

TUITION, ROOM, BOARD, AND FEES

The 2009–10 cost for UCLA's Tuition, Room, Board, and Fees was approximately $25,000 for CA residents and $46,000 for non-residents. Fees are subject to change without notice by The UC Regents. Visit www.registrar.ucla.edu/fees for updates.

FINANCIAL AID

UCLA's Financial Aid Office evaluates eligibility for aid and ensures delivery of funds to undergraduate and graduate students. Need and non-need based aid is available. Assessment of financial need and eligibility for aid (university scholarships, grants, work-study and loans) is based on the evaluation of the Free Application for Federal Student Aid (FAFSA). Financial Aid information is available at www. fao.ucla.edu.

STUDENT ORGANIZATIONS AND ACTIVITIES

At UCLA, the opportunities for involvement are endless: some 950 student organizations—more than any other university—spanning social, political, personal, ethnic, and cultural interests, as well as a daily student newspaper, seven specialized student magazines, a campus radio station, a yearbook, three undergraduate research journals, and a literary magazine. Fraternities and sororities are both available, along with many local community service and religious organizations near campus.

ADMISSIONS PROCESS

UCLA selects students using the carefully designed Holistic Review Process, which takes into account an applicant's achievements, both academic and non-academic, in the context of the opportunities available to the student. Among other factors, the Holistic Review process specifically considers academic grade-point average; performance on standardized tests; the quality, quantity, and level of coursework taken; sustained participation in activities that develop academic and intellectual abilities; leadership and initiative; employment and personal responsibilities; and, overcoming life challenges relating to personal and family situations.

UNIVERSITY OF CENTRAL FLORIDA

AT A GLANCE

The University of Central Florida is a comprehensive research university with approximately 53,000 students. As one of the nation's fastest growing universities and the 3rd largest in the nation, UCF enrolls a diverse student body representing 50 states and over 120 countries. The University offers educational and research programs that complement the economy, with strong components in aerospace engineering, business, education, film, health, nursing, social sciences, and hospitality management. UCF's programs in communication and the fine arts help to meet the cultural and recreational needs of a growing metropolitan area. The University also offers many graduate programs leading to masters and doctoral degrees.

UCF has established extensive partnerships with businesses and industry in the central Florida area that provide students with exceptional research and learning experiences. These partnerships bring practical learning environments to UCF students through co-op and internship programs. Joint curriculum development strategies include BE2020, which is a widely modeled business curriculum incorporating classes taught by local business and industry executives.

The on-campus and campus-affiliated housing facilities include traditional residence halls, apartment-style options, and Greek housing that accommodates approximately 10,000 students. Several thousand students live in apartments located within walking distance of the campus. Approximately 400 students live in on-campus Greek housing.

LOCATION AND ENVIRONMENT

The University of Central Florida: Competitive Advantages

A Focus on Undergraduate Education: We're committed to teaching and providing advising and academic support services for all students. Our undergraduates have access to state-of-the-art wireless buildings, high-tech classrooms and research labs, Web-based classes and an undergraduate Research and Mentoring program.

A Talented Student Body: As one of the fastest growing universities in the southeast, total enrollment has reached 53,000; 45,000 are undergraduates. Our emphasis on excellence in undergraduate education has produced many rewarding results: a Goldwater Scholarship awardee, a Rhodes Scholarship finalist, a Clarion awardee in Radio/Television, a Zonta International Amelia Earhart fellowship awardee, and a nationally ranked Computer Science programming team.

Career Opportunities: Our Career Services professionals help students gain practical experiences at NASA, schools, hospitals, high-tech companies, local municipalities, and the entertainment industry. UCF faculty sit on boards and planning committees, and our graduates make their mark in engineering, business, computer science, education, health care, science, tourism, film and public service.

An International Presence: With an international focus to our curricula and research programs, we currently enroll international students from 122 nations. Our study abroad programs and other study and research opportunities include agreements with 98 institutions and 36 countries, including Australia, France, Germany, Holland, Italy, Russia, South Africa, Spain and Wales.

A Spacious, Modern Campus, plus Orlando: UCF's 1,415-acre campus provides a safe and serene setting for learning, with natural lakes and woodlands. The university provides housing for 10,000 students on campus and through affiliated housing. The bustle of Orlando lies a short distance away: the Orlando Magic, the Orlando Predators, the Kennedy Space Center, major film studios, Walt Disney World, Universal Orlando, Sea World, and sandy beaches are all nearby.

OFF-CAMPUS OPPORTUNITIES

Career Services and Experiential Learning offers programs in which student's alternate semesters of classroom study with equal periods of paid employment in government, industry, or business. The Department of Foreign Languages offers summer study programs in Canada, Eastern Europe, France, Germany, Italy, Japan, Poland, Spain, Sweden, and Russia. Courses are available in the subject areas of language (all levels), art, and civilization. UCF is also a participant in the National Student Exchange Consortium.

MAJORS AND DEGREES OFFERED

The University offers the degrees of Bachelor of Arts, Bachelor of Fine Arts, Bachelor of Science, Bachelor of Science in Business Administration, Bachelor of Science in Education, Bachelor of Science in Engineering, Bachelor of Science in Nursing, and Bachelor of Science in Social Sciences.

These degrees are available in the colleges listed below, with majors or areas of specialization as indicated.

The College of Arts and Humanities offers degrees in art, cinema studies, digital media, English, film, modern language combination, French, history, humanities, music, music education, philosophy, Spanish, and theater.

The College of Business Administration offers degrees in accounting, economics, finance, general business administration, management, and marketing. The College also offers a minor in international business.

The College of Education offers degrees in art education, early childhood education, elementary education, English language arts education, exceptional education, foreign language education, mathematics education, science education, sports and fitness, social science education, and technical education and industry training.

The College of Engineering and Computer Science offers degrees in aerospace engineering, civil engineering, computer engineering, computer science, electrical engineering, environmental engineering, industrial engineering, and mechanical engineering.

The College of Health and Public Affairs offers degrees in athletic training, communicative disorders, criminal justice, health information management, health services administration, health sciences, legal studies, medical laboratory sciences, physical therapy (master's program), public administration, and social work.

The College of Nursing offers degrees in nursing.

The College of Sciences offers degrees in advertising/public relations, anthropology, biology, chemistry, forensic science, interpersonal and organizational communications, journalism, mathematics, physics, political science, psychology, radio/television, sociology, and statistics.

The Rosen College of Hospitality Management offers degrees in Hospitality Management, Event Management, and in Restaurant and Foodservice Management.

The College of Medicine and the Burnett School of Biomedical Sciences offers degrees in Biotechnology, Medical Laboratory Sciences, and molecular biology and microbiology. Pre-professional programs are offered in chiropractic, medicine, optometry, osteopathy, pharmacy, physical therapy, physical assistant, podiatry, dentistry and veterinary medicine.

Degrees in Interdisciplinary Studies are available through the Office of Undergraduate Studies.

CAMPUS FACILITIES AND EQUIPMENT

In addition to the academic programs offered on the Orlando campus, students can work toward a degree at campuses located in Cocoa, Daytona Beach and South Lake. These regional campuses work cooperatively with local community colleges to provide all four years of course work in many academic areas. The library houses nearly 1.4 million volumes and subscribes to more than 10,000 periodicals and journals. In addition, students have access to an online computer catalog that provides information on the collections of the State University System libraries. An extensive online network of more than 500 computer terminals and a network of nearly 1,000 IBM PC's cover the campus. The Institute for Simulation and Training gives students the opportunity to pursue undergraduate research. The School of Optics allows faculty members and students to work directly with industrial personnel in conducting basic and applied research at the regional and national level. The Central Florida Research Park, located next to the UCF campus, houses more than ninety important high-technology firms and agencies. This proximity fosters relationships between industry and the University, which strengthens the academic programs at UCF.

TUITION, ROOM, BOARD AND FEES

Approximate Tuition, Health Fee, Room and Board Annual Rates 2009–2010:

Approximate Total	Florida Resident	Non-Florida Resident
Tuition and Fees	$4,525	$20,004
Room	$4,900	$4,900
Board	$3,200	$3,200
Books (estimate)	$800	$800
Annual Cost	$13,425	$28,904

Based on 15 credit hours per semester, double room and meal plan.

FINANCIAL AID

Financial aid is awarded according to each student's demonstrated need in relation to college costs and may include grants, loans, scholarships and part-time employment. Programs based on need include the Federal Perkins Loan, Federal Pell Grant, Florida Student Assistance Grant, Federal Work-Study, Florida College Career Work-Study Program, and Federal Stafford Student Loan. To qualify for these programs, students must complete the Free Application for Federal Student Aid. The priority application deadline is March 1. Approximately 70 percent of UCF students receive some form of financial aid.

STUDENT ORGANIZATIONS AND ACTIVITIES

Students participate in more than 350 organizations, including special interest clubs, multicultural associations, fraternities and sororities, honor societies, and academic and pre-professional organizations. The Office of Student Involvement schedules a wide array of extracurricular programs, including concerts, movies, and guest speakers.

The University of Central Florida is a member of the NCAA and Conference USA. All teams compete on the NCAA Division 1 Level. UCF's men's teams compete in intercollegiate baseball, basketball, football, golf, soccer, and tennis. Women's teams compete in basketball, cross-country, golf, rowing, soccer, softball, tennis, track, and volleyball. Intercollegiate coed club activities include championship cheerleading, crew, and waterskiing teams. The university intramural sports program offers disc golf, flag football, floor hockey, racquetball, soccer, softball, tennis, and volleyball.

ADMISSIONS PROCESS

A freshman applicant is a student with fewer than 12 hours of college coursework after high school graduation. The most important criteria in the admission decision for these applicants is the high school academic record, quality and level of difficulty of courses, grade point average, grade trends, and SAT I or ACT test scores. UCF operates on a rolling admission basis. Students are generally notified of their admission decision within two to three weeks after receipt of the application and all supporting documents. If the number of qualified applicants exceeds the number that the university is permitted to enroll, a waiting list will be established.

All applicants must have earned a minimum of 18 high school academic units (year-long courses that are not remedial in nature). These include 4 units of English (3 must include substantial writing), 4 units of mathematics at or above algebra I, 3 units of natural science (2 must include a laboratory), 3 units of social science, 2 units of one foreign language, and 2 units of academic electives. Grades in honors courses, International Baccalaureate, Advanced Placement, AICE and dual enrollment courses are given additional weight in the GPA computation. Students must meet the Department of Education minimum eligibility to be considered for admission. Applicants should understand that the satisfaction of minimum requirements does not automatically guarantee admission to UCF.

Transfer applicants with fewer than 60 semester hours of college course work must submit official high school transcripts, SAT I or ACT test scores, and all official college transcripts. Transfer students with more than 60 semester hours or who have earned an Associate in Arts degree or a state-wide articulated Associate in Science degree from a Florida public community college need only to submit all official college transcripts. A transfer credit summary evaluation is provided to students once they are offered admission to UCF.

Students are encouraged to apply several months in advance and can apply online at www.admissions.ucf.edu. It is recommended that freshman students apply early during the fall semester of their senior year. Applications are accepted up to one year prior to the start of the term for which entry is desired. Priority application deadlines are May 1 for the fall term (July 1 for transfers), November 1 for the spring term, and March 1 for the summer term.

UNIVERSITY OF CHICAGO

AT A GLANCE

A private university chartered in 1890, the University of Chicago quickly became a world leader in research. In addition, UChicago's coherent program of general education for undergraduates has been replicated throughout the nation. Drawn to theoretical inquiry and open discussion, UChicago's 5,000 undergraduates enjoy small classes and spirited give-and-take discussions where they are free to break down artificial disciplinary barriers and frequently explore research and coursework outside their selected fields. This atmosphere of free and open inquiry not only attracts exceptional students and faculty from around the globe, including at total of 85 Nobel laureates, but has also led to the development of academic disciplines in fields ranging from literary criticism and urban sociology to ecology and the study of religions, as well as world-renowned programs in anthropology, physics, and economics.

The University of Chicago encourages a close-knit learning environment on campus, and promotes this by guaranteeing each student on-campus housing for four years. Chicago's ten residence halls, including modern dorm complexes and neo-Gothic buildings, are distinct communities made up of undergraduate students as well as Resident Heads, who are advanced graduate students or faculty members. These communities are a focal point for campus life and, along with hundreds of clubs and organizations, uphold the traditions of the College.

LOCATION AND ENVIRONMENT

The University's neighborhood, Hyde Park, is a vibrant yet relaxed residential community, seven miles from downtown Chicago. More than 60% of the faculty and their families call Hyde Park home. The University's 211-acre campus is distinguished by its English Gothic style architecture and its designation as a botanic garden. With its stimulating diversity Hyde Park boasts a thriving cultural scene ranging from the Checkerboard Blues Lounge and the Museum of Science and Industry to The Point, a park on a promontory extending into Lake Michigan and a site for sunbathing and barbeques. Hyde Park is home to a community whose common bond is a shared passion for the type of invigorating discussion bred by such close proximity to UChicago's many educational resources.

ACADEMIC PROGRAMS

Bachelor of Arts or Bachelor of Science degrees are awarded in the following programs:

Anthropology

Archeology°

Art History

Astronomy and

Astrophysics°

Big Problems°

Biological Chemistry

Biological Sciences

Chemistry

Chicago Studies°

Cinema and Media Studies

Classical Studies

Comparative Human Development

Comparative Literature

Comparative Race Studies°

Computer Science

Computational Neuroscience°

Creative Writing°

Early Christian Literature

East Asian Languages and Civilization

Economics

Education°

English Language and Literature

Environmental Studies

Fundamentals: Issues and Texts

Gender Studies

Geographical Studies

Geophysical Sciences

Germanic Studies

History

History, Philosophy, and Social Sciences (HIPS)

Human Rights°

Interdisciplinary Studies in the Humanities

International Studies

Jewish Studies

Latin American Studies

Law, Letters, and Society

Linguistics

Mathematics

Medieval Studies

Music

Near Eastern Languages and Civilizations

Philosophy

Physics

Political Science

Psychology

Public Policy Studies

Religion and the Humanities

Religious Studies

Romance Languages and Literatures

Russian Civilization

Slavic Languages and Literatures

Sociology

South Asian Languages and Civilizations

Statistics

Tutorial Studies

Theatre and Performance Studies

Visual Arts

°Interdisciplinary option

CAMPUS FACILITIES AND EQUIPMENT

Campus facilities offer a broad array of academic, cultural, and other resources, including the Oriental Institute Museum; the David and Alfred Smart Museum of Art; Court Theatre; the University of Chicago Hospitals; the Ryerson Astronomical Observatory; and the Department of Ecology and Evolution's rooftop greenhouse. The Biological Sciences Learning Center is the most up-to-date biology teaching and medical facility of its kind in the nation. Each student has a college advisor, and other support is offered by staff in the residence halls, counselors in the career and planning office, tutors, and the campus ministries.

TUITION, ROOM, BOARD, AND FEES

For freshmen living on campus, the cost of attending the University of Chicago for the 2009–2010 academic year is $54,340. Of that, tuition amounts to $38,550, room and board totals $11,697, fees come to $831, and average personal expenses and books are estimated at $3,262.

STUDENT ORGANIZATIONS AND ACTIVITIES

Chicago students are involved in more than 400 student organizations. Community service, academic interest, and cultural awareness groups provide a wide range of opportunities, perspectives, and support. In addition to three student newspapers, a campus radio station, and music, art, theater, and film organizations, the award-winning Model United Nations Team, Debate Society, and College Bowl Team offer forums for competition. An annual scavenger hunt and the winter festival Kuvia-sungnerk (from an Eskimo word roughly translated as "pursuit of happiness") are among the traditional "UChicago" events on campus. With one of the most extensive intramural and club sports programs in the country, Chicago students take athletics seriously, and more than 70 percent participate in intramurals. Varsity athletics attract 14 percent of the undergraduate student population, where competition at the NCAA Division III level has resulted in numerous Academic All-American awards plus team league championships in women's cross-country, soccer, softball and tennis, and men's basketball, wrestling, and cross country.

ADMISSIONS PROCESS

No formula exists for the successful Chicago applicant; all have displayed the capacity to inquire, to contribute to their schools and communities, and to succeed at the tasks before them. Among 1335 students in the Class of 2013 (High School graduation year 2009), approximately 85 percent graduated in the top 10 percent of their high school classes. The middle 50 percent of admitted students had a combined score of between 1320 and 1530 on the SAT or between 29 and 34 on the ACT.

To apply for admission or to obtain more information about the University of Chicago, please write to the Office of College Admissions, The University of Chicago, 1101 East 58th Street, Suite 105, Chicago, Illinois 60637, or call 773-702-8650.

Information can also be obtained on the web from the University of Chicago College Admissions home page at collegeadmissions.uchicago.edu

School Says . . .

UNIVERSITY OF THE CUMBERLANDS

AT A GLANCE

Founded in 1889, University of the Cumberlands is committed to providing a superior education in an exceptional Christian atmosphere. The University emphasizes the growth of the individual student and strives to instill in students the desire to be agents of change in the world and to use knowledge for the benefit of others, as well as themselves.

University of the Cumberlands is a four-year, coed liberal arts college offering a broad curriculum with more than 46 programs of study from which to choose. The student body consists of 1,843 students representing 40 states and 30 countries. Most students live on campus in the University's eleven residence halls. A director assisted by student staff members supervises each hall.

Students benefit from such special services as the Career Services Center, Center for Leadership Studies, Academic Resource Center, and free tutorial assistance.

University of the Cumberlands is accredited by the Commission of Colleges of the Southern Association of Colleges and Schools (1866 Southern Lane, Decatur, Georgia 30033-4097: Telephone number 404-676-4501) to award the Bachelor of Science, the Bachelor of Arts, the Bachelor of Music, the Bachelor of General Studies, the Master of Arts in Education, and the Master of Arts in Teaching, the Master of Arts in Physician Assistant Studies, the Master of Arts in Professional Counseling, the Master of Business Administration, the Education Specialist, and the Doctor of Education degrees. The University's Teacher Education and Certification programs are also approved by the Kentucky State Department of Education.

LOCATION AND ENVIRONMENT

University of the Cumberlands is located in Williamsburg, Kentucky, which is in the southern part of the mountains of Eastern Kentucky. Williamsburg is about two hundred miles south of Cincinnati, about an equal distance from Louisville, about eighty miles north of Knoxville, and about 100 miles south of Lexington. The business section of the city lies in a small valley of the Cumberland River; the University and chief residence section are situated on the surrounding hills. It is a place of natural beauty and healthful surroundings.

Williamsburg is one of the older cities of the state. It has long been known for its larger number of beautiful residences, for its churches and schools, and for the hospitality of its people.

UC offers a picturesque campus with stately buildings and rolling green lawns nestled in the foothills of the Appalachian mountain range with the main campus situated on three hills which divide it into three distinct parts and afford a magnificent view of the surrounding area. The University's buildings, which are situated on these hills and a viaduct, spanning the south and middle hills, provide an easy and pleasant passageway to each part of the campus.

Within a few miles of campus are Laurel Lake, Cumberland Falls State Park, Cumberland Gap National Park, and the Daniel Boone National Forest.

OFF-CAMPUS OPPORTUNITIES

Study Abroad

Ministry Opportunities

Internships

MAJORS AND DEGREES OFFERED

Major fields of study include accounting, art°, biological science°, biology, business administration, chemistry, church music, communication arts, communication and theatre arts°, criminal justice, early elementary education°, English°, exercise and sport science°, fitness and sport management, health, health education°, history, history and political science, human services, journalism, management information systems, mathematics°, middle school education°, music°, philosophy and religion, physical science°, physician assistant studies, physics, political science, psychology, public health, religion, social studies°, Spanish°, special education°, and theatre arts. Minor fields of study include biblical languages, and French°. Pre-professional and special curricula are offered in medical technology, military science, pre-dentistry, pre-engineering, pre-law, pre-medicine, pre-optometry, pre-pharmacy, pre-physical therapy, pre-veterinary medicine, and religious vocations.

°Denotes teacher certification available

ACADEMIC PROGRAMS

University of the Cumberlands seeks to provide academic specialization within the broad framework of a liberal arts education. To supplement the in-depth knowledge acquired within each major, 37 semester hours of general studies from the areas of Christian faith and values, cultural and aesthetic values, the English language, humanities, leadership and community service, natural and mathematical sciences, physical education, and social sciences are required. Students must earn 128 semester hours to graduate with a bachelor's degree.

The academic year begins in late August, with the first semester ending in mid-December. The second semester runs from early January to early May. Two five-week undergraduate summer sessions and two four-week graduate summer sessions are also offered. Orientation, pre-registration, and academic advising by faculty members begin in the summer preceding entrance.

Students may receive credit for passing the College Board, the College-Level Examination Programs (CLEP), and special departmental tests. Highly qualified students have the opportunity to undertake advanced independent study.

CAMPUS FACILITIES AND EQUIPMENT

UC's campus contains 36 buildings in the architectural style of the early 1900s. Recent additions to campus include the state-of-the-art Hutton School of Business, a 27,000 square foot addition to the science building, featuring well-equipped labs providing graduate-level research opportunities, a new women's residence hall and a baseball complex. The McGaw Music Building contains individual rehearsal and studio areas as well as a recital hall. The Norma Perkins Hagan Memorial Library houses thousands of book titles, current serial subscriptions, and microform titles. Sophisticated computer equipment provides access to an additional 20 million items from many of the nation's outstanding libraries. The instructional media center includes a children's library, a computerized language lab, and a listening library.

Other special academic features include a computer center, an art gallery, a word processing center for English composition, a theatre, the Career Services Center, a 600-seat chapel, four large lecture halls, and the Distance Learning laboratory.

TUITION, ROOM, BOARD AND FEES

For 2010–2011, the basic academic year expenses are $17,000 for tuition and fees and $6,826 for room and board. The average cost for books and supplies is approximately $1,000 per academic year.

FINANCIAL AID

University of the Cumberlands sponsors a large financial aid program that coordinates money from federal, state, private, and University sources. Last year, 95 percent of UC students shared more than $27 million in aid. Academic and athletic scholarships are available.

STUDENT ORGANIZATIONS AND ACTIVITIES

Don't let the small size of our campus fool you. There are enough activities going on every day at UC to fill a dozen college careers. Whether your interest lies in athletics, creative expression, student government, academic enrichment, community service, spiritual development, or in any combination of these areas, you'll find an outlet here for your energy.

Many academic departments sponsor clubs and academic honor societies for students with a particular interest in the discipline, so be sure to visit the departments that interest you or contact a faculty member in that department for more information.

Each year, University of the Cumberlands hosts numerous guest performers and speakers and celebrates the talents of its students and faculty through a variety of lectures, concerts, art exhibitions, and theatrical productions. Many of these events are free of charge, and most are open to the public.

In addition, UC offers ten varsity sports for both men and women. Competing in the Mid-South Conference, UC is a member of the NAIA and is Division I.

The Student Government Association is dedicated to giving students a voice through elected representatives. In addition to promoting student concerns and working as a liaison between students and college administrators, the SGA provides a number of important services, and sponsors a number of student-centered events throughout the year.

ADMISSIONS PROCESS

The purpose of the admission process is to identify applicants who are likely to succeed academically at University of the Cumberlands and at the same time contribute positively to the campus community. The process considers such factors as high school records (including courses taken, grade trends, and rank in class), scores on the American College Test (ACT), or on the Scholastic Aptitude Test (SAT), application essay (not required of all applicants), extracurricular activities and honors, and personal contact.

UNIVERSITY OF DELAWARE

AT A GLANCE

Founded in 1743, the University of Delaware is one of very few institutions who are both public and private (state-assisted with private charter). Students from every state and 100 foreign countries choose Delaware due to its medium size (15,000 undergraduate and 3,000 graduate students) and private offerings, including a $1 billion+ endowment, 125+ majors and 100 minors, smaller classes with 95% taught by full-time faculty, and a vibrant arts community. Located on a classic campus at the center of the East Coast, Delaware is home to a winning Division I athletic program (Go Blue Hens!), the first Study Abroad Program in the U.S. (now on all 7 continents), one of the country's oldest honors programs, and a nationally-recognized Undergraduate Research Program.

LOCATION AND ENVIRONMENT

One of the most beautiful campuses on the East Coast, the University of Delaware in Newark, Delaware, is located at the center of the "megacity" that stretches from New York City to Washington, D.C.. The town of Newark is a charming place, with its very own Main Street full of shops, restaurants, and nightspots catering to the college community. Delaware's location, in a state known as the "Corporate Capital of America," benefits students through access to intellectual resources, professional relationships, and countless opportunities for internships, jobs, and entry into top graduate schools. Delaware's 1,000-acre campus is minutes from I-95 and is easily accessible by car, train, and air, with two airports less than an hour away (Philadelphia & BWI), and both New York City and Washington, D.C., accessible in about two hours by train or car.

Students at the University and visitors to UD believe that Delaware's central campus looks as a college campus should, with a lush central Green, winding brick paths, and historic Georgian architecture. A glimpse beyond the classical setting reveals miles of cables and wires running beneath the ground and into the walls of the library, residence halls, classrooms, labs, and every building on campus. Students are encouraged to bring laptops so that they can plug in for class, for research, and for staying in touch with friends, faculty, and the world.

OFF-CAMPUS OPPORTUNITIES

University of Delaware graduates are in demand due to the opportunities they take advantage of during their undergraduate years. About 20 percent of Delaware grads continue directly on to graduate school. The University's Bank of America Career Services Center reports that over 90 percent of Delaware grads who don't go on to graduate schools find full-time jobs within six months of leaving the University. Fifteen major career fairs are hosted on campus each year with over 600 employers in attendance. In addition, more than 300 corporations and non-profits participate in the Campus Interview Program and contribute to the 20,000 employment possibilities listed at the Career Services Center.

MAJORS AND DEGREES OFFERED

From Accounting to Wildlife Conservation, students at the University of Delaware can choose from over 125 majors and 100 minors. In fact, close to one-third of Delaware students choose to do more, pursuing double majors and multiple minors. Academic programs of study are found in our seven colleges: Arts & Sciences; Agriculture & Natural Resources; Lerner College of Business & Economics; Earth, Ocean, & Environment; Education & Public Policy; Engineering; and Health Sciences. Students can explore the many options with our major finder at http://www.udel.edu/majorfinder/.

125+ Majors (and 100 Minors)

Accounting; Agricultural Education; Agriculture & Natural Resources; Animal & Food Sciences ; Anthropology; Anthropology Education; Apparel Design; Applied Nutrition; Art Interests (includes Fine Arts, BFA or BA, and Visual Communications, BFA); Art History; Athletic Training; Biochemistry; Biological Science Education; Biological Sciences (includes biotechnology, Cellular & Molecular Biology & Genetics, and Ecology & Organismic Biology); Black American Studies (includes Black Arts, Literature & Cultural Studies, Black Gender Study, and Law, Public Policy & Social Justice); Business - Undeclared; Chemical Engineering; Chemistry/Environmental Chemistry (BA or BS) ; Chemistry Education; Civil Engineering; Cognitive Science (BS); Communication (includes Interpersonal and Mass); Comparative Literature; Computer Engineering; Computer Science (BA or BS); Computer Science - Information Systems; Criminal Justice (includes Law & Society); Dietetics; Early Childhood Education ; Earth Science Education; East Asian Studies; Economics (BA or BS) (includes Applied Economics and Economic Theory & Econometrics) ; Economics Education; Electrical Engineering; Elementary Teacher Education (with certification options in: Elementary Education, Middle School English, Middle School Mathematics, Middle School Science, Middle School Social Studies, and Special Education); Energy & Environmental Policy; Engineering - Undeclared; Engineering Technology; English (includes Creative Writing, Drama, Ethnic/Cultural Studies, Film Literary Studies, and Professional Writing); English Education; Entomology; Environmental Engineering; Environmental Science (includes Atmospheric Science, Ecology & Organismal Biology, Environmental Chemistry, Environmental Soil Science, GeoScience, Hydrology, Marine Science, Pollution Control, Sustainable Energy Technology, and Water Resources, Quality, & Technology); European Studies; Environmental Soil Science; Environmental Studies (includes Environmental Economics & Resource Policy, International Environmental Politics & Policy, Environmental Law, Policy & Politics, and Environment, Society & Sustainability); Exercise Science; Fashion Merchandising; Finance; Food & Agribusiness Marketing & Management; Food Science; Foreign Languages & Literatures (includes ancient Greek & Roman Studies, French Educaiton, French Studies, French/Political Science, German Education, German Studies, German/Political Science, Italian Education, Italian Studies, Latin Educaiton & Classics, Russian Studies, Spanish Education, Spanish/Political Science, Spanish Studies, and Three Languages); Geography; Geography Education; Geology (BA or BS) (includes Coastal & Marine GeoScience, Geophysics, and Paleobiology); Health & Physical Education; Health Behavior Science ; Health Studies - Occupational Therapy Option; History (includes American, European, and World); History Education; History - Foreign Languages includes Classics, French, German, Russian, and Spanish); Hotel, Restaurant & Institutional Management; Human Services (includes clinical Services and Administration & Family Policy); Information Systems; International Business Studies; International Relations (includes Development, Diplomacy, Political Economy, and U.S. Foreign Policy); Landscape Horticulture & Design (includes Public Horticulture); Latin American Studies; Management; Management Information Systems; Marketing; Material Culture Preservation; Mathematical Sciences (BA or BS); Mathematics & Economics; Mathematics Education (BA or BS); Mechanical Engineering (includes Aerospace); Medical Technology (Biomedical Sciences); Music (includes Music Management); Music, Applied - Instrumental; Music, Applied - Piano; Music, Applied - Voice; Music Education - General/Choral; Music Education - Instrumental; Music Theory/Composition; Natural Resource Management; Nursing; Nutritional Sciences; Operations Management; Organizational & Community Leadership; Pharmacy Interest; Philosophy; Physics (BA or BS) (includes Astronomy/Astrophysics); Physics Education; Plant Science (includes Plant Protection); Political Science (includes American Politics, Global Studies, Public Law, and Public Policy & Administration); Political Science Education; Pre-Veterinary Medicine & Animal Biosciences; Psychology (BA or BS); Psychology Education; Public Policy; Quantitative Biology (BS); Resource Economics (includes Environmental Economics and Sustainable Development); Sociology (includes Emergency & Environmental Management, Health Services, Law & Society, and Social Welfare); Sociology Education; Sport Management; Statistics; University Studies - Undeclared; Wildlife Conservation; Women's Studies

ACADEMIC PROGRAMS

Delaware students experience learning in a variety of ways, including the First Year Experience, University Honors Program, Service-Learning, Study Abroad, and Undergraduate Research.

First Year Experience

All freshmen at UD have a First Year Experience (FYE) that allows them to meet other students in their major, learn about resources at Delaware, and feel more at home on campus. FYE is designed to help students succeed in any major, including University Studies. FYE is one of the reasons for Delaware's 90% retention rate, a figure that's 20% higher than the national average.

University Honors Program

At the intellectual heart of the University is the University Honors Program (UHP). Entrance into the Program is highly selective, with about 450 new freshmen enrolled each year. Advantages of the Honors Program include smaller classes, private music instruction, academic scholarships, superb teaching, special housing options, personal attention, interdisciplinary colloquia, "great books" tutorials, lectures, and student-run activities and field trips.

Service-Learning

Service-Learning at UD allows students to participate in an organized service experience that heightens their academic experience. As part of their course work, students will provide a service to a community - From Newark to Wilmington to Costa Rica to Vietnam - and then reflect on these real-world experiences in light of the academic theories and information being taught in the course.

Study Abroad

Over 40% of our student body choose to study abroad at least once with 12% (and rising each year) studying abroad more than once. The reasons are compelling: UD credits applicable toward any major; UD faculty; UD's reasonable tuition rate; special study abroad scholarships; & exotic destinations on any of the seven continents including - that's right - Antarctica.

Undergraduate Research

The University of Delaware is recognized as a national leader in fostering undergraduate research by offering research apprenticeships with faculty mentors in a variety of disciplines. About 700 undergraduates (including freshmen) take advantage of the opportunity each year.

CAMPUS FACILITIES AND EQUIPMENT

Although the University traces its roots to 1743, it remains firmly planted in the 21st century with continuing construction and enhancements to campus facilities. Within the past 20 years, Delaware students have benefitted from hundreds of millions of dollars worth of improvements and additions to campus including: the Independence Complex, a breathtaking community of residence halls (named in honor of UD's three alumni who signed the Declaration of Independence); the $48 million Roselle Center for the Arts, featuring multiple performance theatres, private study rooms, and a practice space large enough for Delaware's 350-member Marching Band; the Exelon Trading Center, a 2,200-square-foot space designed to replicate the trading floors on Wall Street; the $17.5 million architectural jewel that is Gore Hall; Rullo Field Hockey Stadium, where students often play until 1 a.m.; Bayard Sharpe Hall -- a technologically enhanced gothic cathedral featuring intimate concerts and lectures; multi-million dollar renovation of laboratory spaces throughout campus; and a new state-of-the-art Student Multimedia Design Center in Morris Library.

Extensive facilities and resources exist to meet the needs of UD students. Over 7,000 students live on campus in one of 65 residence halls and dine in any of more than 16 eateries. Morris Library, a six-acre structure, houses millions of books, journals, and items on microtext, with additional access to over 75 networked databases. Students can plug in their own computers or log on at one of 28 microcomputing sites on campus. Socializing, performing, and engaging in a variety of entertainment options takes place at Perkins Student Center, Trabant University Center, the Roselle Center for the Arts, on the Green, in the residence halls, or at one of the smaller theatres on campus. Athletic facilities abound at the University, including the 23,000-seat Delaware Stadium; 5,000-seat Bob Carpenter Sports/Convocation Center; Rust & Gold Ice Skating Arenas (home of the Ice Skating Development Center and training ground for Olympic skaters); outdoor hockey rink; track, softball, and practice fields; indoor and outdoor swimming pools; Outdoor Recreation Resource Center; and indoor climbing wall, fitness centers, and weight rooms.

TUITION, ROOM, BOARD AND FEES

Delaware Residents

Tuition $ 7,780

Room°° $ 5,128

Board°° $ 3,350

Health Service Fee $466

Comprehensive Student Fee $180

Student Center Fee $220

TOTAL $17,124

Cost Per Credit Hour $325

Non-Residents

Tuition $20,260

Room°° $5,128

Board°° $3,350

Health Service Fee $466

Comprehensive Student Fee $180

Student Center Fee $220

TOTAL $29,604

Cost Per Credit Hour $845

° Optional Winter and Summer Sessions are charged separately.

FINANCIAL AID

The University of Delaware awards more than $100 million annually in aid. Our commitment to making a University of Delaware education affordable is seen in our reasonable tuition for in-state and out-of-state students and in our variety of scholarships, financial aid programs, and financing plans. These include Merit Scholarships, Athletic Scholarships, Music Scholarships, Art Scholarships, Additional Scholarships, Need-based Aid, and Outside Resources.

Additional information can be found online at http://www.udel.edu/finance.

STUDENT ORGANIZATIONS AND ACTIVITIES

The Fightin' Blue Hens are a spirited community with the mix of academics, campus activities, and athletics that fit the profile of a national university. UD supports 23 varsity sports, 11 men's and 12 women's, all NCAA Division I members of the Colonial Athletic Association, except women's rowing, which is independent. You could say that athletics are a big part of the UD culture, since over 80% of the undergraduate body participates in intramurals, varsity, club, band, cheerleading, or other sports.

In addition to athletics, the University is home to close to 300 campus organizations covering a spectrum of interests and communities. Visit the Web at www. udel.edu/RSO/ for a complete list. The UD undergraduate experience begins with DelaWorld 101, the summer and fall orientation program for new students. Annual events on the Green, at the Bob Carpenter Center, in theatres across campus, and in the Trabant University or Perkins Student Centers keep students entertained and active. Delaware students fill their free time with movie nights; Mallstock; and concerts and performances such as Elton John, Jon Stewart, Common, O.A.R., Margaret Cho, and Dane Cook. In addition, there are 38 Greek letter organizations, including 17 NIC fraternities, 11 NPC sororities, and 5 National PanHellenic Council chapters (traditionally African-American membership).

ADMISSIONS PROCESS

The complete admissions process and requirements can be found on the UD website at www.udel.edu/apply.

School Says . . .

THE UNIVERSITY OF FINDLAY

AT A GLANCE

Recognized as one of America's Best Private Colleges, The University of Findlay has much to offer! Affiliated with the Church of God since our beginnings, we are a comprehensive university founded in 1882 with a strong liberal arts tradition. UF offers nearly 60 exciting majors, 23 varsity D-II NCAA sports, more than 60 clubs and organizations, theater, art, music and so much more — there is something for every type of student! Our most popular majors include pre-veterinary medicine, equestrian studies, business, pharmacy, and education.

Our Fall 2009 enrollment of more than 4,100 students includes full-time and part-time students pursuing associate's, bachelor's or master's degrees, as well as doctor's degrees in pharmacy and physical therapy. The diverse student body encompasses more than 1,300 students living on campus. In addition, approximately 500 international students from 25 countries and territories attend Findlay.

Faculty and staff are focused on students, with personal attention, individual academic advising and a caring environment cited by students and alumni as hallmarks of their education at Findlay. Classes are taught by professors, not graduate assistants. Most faculty have worked in their chosen professions, bringing a wealth of experience to the classroom, where their true love is teaching.

Discover who you will be at The University of Findlay!

LOCATION AND ENVIRONMENT

The University of Findlay is located in a small city that is pleasant and progressive. The city of Findlay has been designated as a "dreamtown" by Bizjournals.com, among the most attractive small cities in the U.S. The study gave high marks to the community for its strong economy, light traffic and moderate cost of living, with well-educated adults and easy access to big-city attractions.

The campus has a great location just 45 minutes from Toledo, Ohio, two hours from Cleveland and Columbus, Ohio, and five hours from Chicago.

OFF-CAMPUS OPPORTUNITIES

The University offers career planning and placement services that assist students in determining career goals, developing job search skills, locating internship, cooperative education and degree-related work experience, and in finding paid employment in their fields, and in selecting and applying to graduate programs.

MAJORS AND DEGREES OFFERED

College of Business

The College of Business is home to some of the most popular majors at The University of Findlay. Building on a strong foundation that promotes problem solving, sound decision-making and the integration of the latest technological applications, UF's business programs allow you the opportunity to declare majors in one or two disciplines.

UF also offers a Master of Business Administration degree that is available both in a traditional setting and entirely online.

Our business majors are:

Accounting; Financial Accounting; Managerial Accounting; Business Management; Economics; Entrepreneurship; Finance; Hospitality Management; Human Resource Management; International Business; Marketing; Operations & Logistics

College of Education

UF's teacher education program is constantly evolving to meet the changing requirements of the state and national education systems. Accredited by the National Council for Accreditation of Teacher Education and the Higher Learning Commission, our program emphasizes practical experience, the integration of technology in classrooms and the benefits of service learning.

At UF, you will explore the teaching profession through a combination of general education classes, professional education courses and field experiences. As early as your freshman year, you will be in the schools - observing, participating and learning - to prepare you for an exciting career as an educator.

Findlay also offers a Master of Arts in Education degree for those who wish to continue their training.

Our education programs are:

Adolescent/Young Adult; Integrated English/Language Arts; Integrated Mathematics; Integrated Science; Integrated Social Studies; Life Science; Early Childhood; Intervention Specialist Education/Mild to Moderate Disabilities; Middle Childhood; Language Arts/Math; Language Arts/Science; Language Arts/Social Studies; Math/Science; Math/Social Studies; Science/Social Studies; Multi-Age; Drama/Theatre; Health Education; Japanese; Physical Education; Spanish; Visual Arts

College of Health Professions

Our College of Health Professions is home to some of our most in-demand programs including occupational therapy, physical therapy, and nuclear medicine technology. In the majority of the college's majors, you will gain hands-on experience through clinical training in some of the 500 hospitals, outpatient clinics and rehabilitation centers that are associated with the University.

On the cutting edge in health professions education, UF provides master's degree-level programs in occupational therapy and athletic training. In addition, the College of Health Professions offers doctor of physical therapy program.

Athletic Training (MAT); Health Education; Health Science; Pre-Occupational Therapy; Pre-Physical Therapy; Health Studies; Gerontology; Health Care Management; Personal Training; Psychology; Medical Technology; Nuclear Medicine Technology; Occupational Therapy (MOT); Physical Education; Physician Assistant; Pre-Nursing (Non-degree granting course of study in cooperation with Mt. Carmel College of Nursing or Lourdes College); Social Work; Strength & Conditioning

Closely allied with the College of Health Professions is the College of Pharmacy, which offers a six-year program with direct entry from high school. The program offers small classes with excellent faculty, combined with tutoring services, collaboration with other health professions students on campus and state-of-the-art teaching facilities, including specially designed laboratories. All students admitted to pharmacy will graduate from UF with a Pharm.D. as long as all academic and professional standards are met.

College of Liberal Arts

The College of Liberal Arts offers programs that will equip you with the indispensable tools you will need for that first job and for a lifetime of achievements. Our programs range from sociology and political science to English and history.

We also offer a Master of Arts in Teaching English to Speakers of Other Languages (TESOL) and Bilingual Education.

Our programs are:

Art; Art Management; Children's Book Illustration; Criminal Justice Administration; Digital Media; English (Creative Writing, General Writing, Literature, Teaching); English as an International Language; Forensic Science; DNA/Serology; Toxicology; Graphic Design; Health Communication; History; Japanese; Journalism; Law and the Liberal Arts; Organizational Communication (Interpersonal Track, Professional Track, Public Track); Philosophy/Applied Philosophy; Political Science; Psychology (General Major; Public Relations; Religious Studies ; Biblical Studies (Christian Studies); Comparative Religion Studies; Individualized Studies; Sociology; Spanish; Teaching English to Speakers of Other Languages (TESOL)/Bilingual Education; Theatre; Music Theatre; Performance; Production Design and Technology

College of Sciences

From environmental management to Internet security, UF's College of Sciences can train you for many of the fastest-growing careers in today's marketplace. At UF, you can observe an equine surgery, study gene replication, develop new computer software, analyze exposure risks to hazardous chemicals and more. Our rigorous academic programs, experienced faculty and focus on hands-on training will prepare you for a successful career in the sciences.

We also offer a Master of Science in Environmental, Safety and Health Management.

Our majors are:

Animal Science; Animal Science (Pre-Veterinary Medicine, Science; Biology (recommended for students interested in medical school); Chemistry (recommended for students interested in medical school); Computer Science (Business, Computer Systems, Information Assurance, Mathematics, Web and Database); Environmental, Safety and Occupational Health Management; Equestrian Studies; English Riding/Training; Western Riding/Training; Equine Business Management   ; Mathematics (Applied Emphasis for Actuary Preparation, Applied Emphasis for Computer Science, Applied Emphasis for Engineering Science, Applied Emphasis for Operations Research, Pure Mathematics; Pre-Veterinary Medicine, Animal Science

CAMPUS FACILITIES AND EQUIPMENT

The University of Findlay has more than 70 acres at the main campus on North Main Street, which includes major academic, administrative and athletic buildings; residence halls, townhouses, apartment-style cottages and special interest houses; and a number of facilities housing faculty and staff offices and academic units.

The campus has experienced rapid growth, adding buildings including the Phil Gardner Fitness Center, the Kenneth L. Frost Science Center, the Virginia B. Gardner Fine Arts Pavilion, the Edward and Joyce Brewer Center for Health Sciences, and the Ralph and Gladys Koehler Fitness and Recreation Complex. In addition, the University operates a 32-acre facility on the east side of Findlay, containing the English equestrian studies program and University Equine Veterinary Services Inc. The University's 73-acre farm is located eight miles south of campus and houses the western riding and animal science/pre-veterinary medicine programs. A five-acre site on State Route 12 east of Findlay provides hands-on training simulations for the All Hazards Training Center.

Most recently, the University acquired and renovated the 62,000-square-foot Davis Street Building in 2007 to provide additional academic space and laboratory facilities with the latest technological features to support instruction, and in 2009, opened a 31,000-square-foot animal science building that combines a working barn with first-rate academic facilities for pre-veterinary medicine.

STUDENT ORGANIZATIONS AND ACTIVITIES

Students may participate in any of more than 60 organizations, including special interest clubs, student media, student government, music and theatre groups, service clubs, and academic honorary organizations.

The fine arts flourish on campus with a variety of theatre productions, art exhibits and vocal and instrumental music concerts that offer creative outlets and training for students and serve as a source of cultural enrichment for the community.

Some additional activities include:

Music & theater groups

Greek system

Student Government Association

WLFC-FM radio station

UF-TV student television station

Spiritual life groups

Academic honorary organizations

Student-run newspaper, The Pulse

As a Division II member of the National Collegiate Athletic Association (NCAA), Findlay participates in 21 intercollegiate sports and is a member of the Great Lakes Intercollegiate Athletic Conference (GLIAC). Its equestrian teams compete in the Intercollegiate Horse Show Association (IHSA).

NCAA Sports at The University of Findlay:

Baseball (M); Basketball (M); Basketball (W); Cross country (M); Cross country (W); Football; Golf (M); Golf (W); Soccer (M); Soccer (W); Softball (W); Swimming (M); Swimming (W); Indoor track (M); Indoor track (W); Outdoor track (M); Outdoor track (W); Tennis (M); Tennis (W); Volleyball (W); Wrestling (M); English equestrian (IHSA); Western equestrian (IHSA)

ADMISSIONS PROCESS

Admission as a first-time, full-time undergraduate student to The University of Findlay requires an earned diploma from an accredited high school in a college preparatory course of study or a GED certificate. Candidates for admission should successfully complete the following requirements: four units of English, three units of social science (including one in history), three units of mathematics, two units of science and two units of foreign language.

Students who intend to major in equestrian studies, equine business management or animal science-pre-veterinary medicine option are encouraged to complete the application as early as possible, due to limited space available in these programs.

The profile for the fall 2009 class was: SAT Average of 1599, ACT Average of 23.6, and a GPA average of 3.4.

Application Instructions

Students should complete the Application for Undergraduate Admission after they've finished their junior year course work. Students can apply online at www.findlay.edu or request a paper application from the Office of Undergraduate Admissions. No application fee is required.

Applicants should send an official high school transcript that includes class rank, attendance information, a calculated GPA, and proficiency tests results. Post-secondary option participants should submit transcripts of all college-level work.

Applicants may send the results of the ACT and/or SAT tests directly to The University of Findlay by listing the following codes during test registration: ACT-3272, SAT-1223.

In order to enroll, all candidates must submit their final transcript after graduation.

Tuition, Room, Board and Fees (2009-2010)

Tuition: $12,508/semester

Room: $2,134/semester

Board: $2,143/semester

Student Fees: $624/semester (includes Activity Fee, Insurance and General Service Fee)

FINANCIAL AID

To apply for financial aid, the student must complete the Free Application for Federal Student Aid (FAFSA). Ninety percent of students attending The University of Findlay receive some form of financial assistance. Students received $29 million in financial aid in 2008–09 through scholarships, work study grants, and/or government loans.

Scholarships:

If eligible, scholarships range from $9,000 to $14,000 per year for 2009–10. These scholarships are deducted from your tuition each year subject to the student staying in good academic standing.

UNIVERSITY OF HARTFORD

AT A GLANCE

The University of Hartford, a fully accredited, independent, nonsectarian institution, is composed of the College of Arts and Sciences; the College of Engineering, Technology and Architecture; the College of Education, Nursing, and Health Professions; Hillyer College; the Barney School of Business; the Hartford Art School; and The Hartt School.

Our students come from nearly all 50 states and 61 countries make up the full-time undergraduate enrollment of approximately 4,700 men and women. Students participate in about 100 organized student groups, including clubs devoted to special interests or political, professional, religious, or civic activities. Athletics include intercollegiate (NCAA Division I) and intramural sports. These activities, as well as the recreational and fitness needs of the university, are served by a modern 130,000-square-foot Sports Center. Students are also involved in school publications and AM and FM radio stations, and the Hartt School, the Hartford Art School, and the University Players present a variety of concerts, exhibitions, and theatrical productions each year.

The university's Career Development and Placement Center provides career counseling and information on occupations, employers, testing, and graduate schools; serves as a reference and credential source; and provides graduating students with an on-campus recruiting program. Courses, programs, and educational counseling are provided by the Office of Graduate and Adult Academic Services for part-time adult students.

AT A GLANCE

The University of Hartford offers the personal attention of a smaller university blended with the programs of a large school. We're near the city but have a campus of 300 acres of grass and trees..the best of both worlds for you.

LOCATION AND ENVIRONMENT

The university is located in the peaceful residential suburb of West Hartford. The West Hartford area offers hundreds of shops and restaurants along with many opportunities for students to discover new cultural and intellectual experiences. With museums, theaters, libraries, the XL Center, other colleges, a symphony orchestra, shopping, great restaurants, an international airport, and local and intercity transportation systems, the opportunities are only limited by the individual's imagination.

OFF CAMPUS OPPORTUNITIES

Through the Hartford Consortium for Higher Education, Hartford students have the opportunity to register for select courses at Saint Joseph College, and Trinity College. Opportunities are available to teaching and human services majors in the College of Education, Nursing, and Health Professions for field and/or clinical experiences where applicable. The cooperative education office is available to custom-tailor work experiences within many of the University's programs.

ACADEMICS

The University of Hartford is known nationally for the breadth and depth of its programs. Hartford's seven schools and colleges offer 86 undergraduate majors. The university encourages students to sample a variety of academic areas and enroll in courses in any of the colleges in campus. Students interested in interdisciplinary majors can combine courses from the different schools within the university. Students are assigned academic advisors who help guide them in curriculum choices, career exploration, and the transition to university life. The All-University curriculum was developed in order to help students learn more about how different academic disciplines approach related problems. Courses in different fields of expertise are team taught, and topics are examined from the perspective of several academic disciplines. Students who are undecided on their majors are assisted by a special program at the university. Individual students will also find help in the areas of writing proficiency, reading comprehension, and research and test-taking skills at the reading and writing center, which is available to the entire student body. The Math Tutoring Lab, which is staffed by full-time faculty members and math majors, offers further help for students in math. Selected students are encouraged to participate in the Honors Program. Honors students have the opportunity to graduate with an Honors degree.

MAJORS AND DEGREES OFFERED

The Bachelor of Arts is offered in art history, biology, chemistry, cinema, communication, computer science, criminal justice, drama, economics, English, foreign languages and literatures, history, multimedia and web design & development, international studies, Judaic studies, mathematics, music, philosophy, physics, political economy, politics and government, rhetoric and professional writing, psychology, and sociology.

The Bachelor of Science in secondary education is offered in the fields of English and mathematics.

Students can earn the Bachelor of Fine Arts in ceramics, dance, drawing, illustration, music theater, painting, photography, printmaking, actor training, sculpture, video, and visual communication design.

The Bachelor of Music is offered at the Hartt School with majors in performance (guitar, orchestral instrument, organ, piano, and voice), composition, jazz studies, music education, music history, music management, music production and technology, opera, performing arts management, piano accompanying and ensemble, and theory.

The Bachelor of Science is awarded in biology, clinical lab science-lab tech, chemistry, chemistry-biology, computer science, early childhood education, elementary education, health sciences (upper division only), human services, mathematics, mathematics-management science, nursing (for registered nurses only), physics, radiological technology, respiratory therapy, and special education (offering dual certification and covering emotional disabilities, learning disabilities, and mental retardation).

The Bachelor of Science in Business Administration (BSBA) is offered in accounting, economics and finance, entrepreneurial studies, finance and insurance, management, and marketing.

Additional BS programs are offered in the College of Engineering, Technology and Architecture and include ABET-accredited BSEE, BSME, BSCE, BSCompE, and interdisciplinary BSE options. The most popular BSE options are acoustics/music, biomedical engineering, and environmental engineering

Bachelor of Science degrees are also offered in architectural engineering technology, computer engineering technology, electronic engineering technology, and mechanical engineering technology.

Additional special programs include the Doctor of Physical Therapy (freshman entry); Master's degree in prosthetics and orthotics (freshman entry); the five-year music education program; five-year double-major programs; Bachelor of Music with an emphasis in management, offered by the Hartt School in conjunction with the Barney School of Business; and the Bachelor of Science in Engineering with a music-acoustics major, offered by the College of Engineering.

CAMPUS FACILITIES AND EQUIPMENT

The West Hartford campus houses the buildings and facilities of our seven colleges and schools.

The newest additions to the campus are the Handel Center for Performing Arts for students in theater and dance. The Integrated Science, Engineering and Technology Complex houses 37,000 square feet of new state-of-the-art classrooms and laboratories as well as a complete renovation of the existing science and engineering facilities. The Renee Samuels Center provides state-of-the art digital equipment and studios specifically designed for Media Arts and Photography.

The Harry Jack Gray Center is the home of the Mildred P. Allen Memorial Library; the William H. Mortensen Library; the Museum of American Political Life; the Harry J. Gray Conference Center; the Joseloff Gallery; the University Bookstore; the School of Communication; and studios for art, radio, and television. The library has approximately 572,000 items, including books, musical scores, recordings, periodicals, journals, and microfilm units. The Hartford Consortium for Higher Education, the Hartford Library, and the Interlibrary-Loan systems also offer extensive resources.

The University of Hartford has a Computer Center that houses the central computer systems and operates a high-performance campus wide network that connects student residential housing, all academic buildings on campus, and the university's remote locations. A high-speed T1 line connects the university's network to the Internet. Each student resident has his or her own Ethernet connection to the campus network. The library is connected to the campus network and provides network access in study carrels and study rooms. The library's online systems include the online catalog for book, audio, and video collection; CD-ROM databases; and Internet resources, including 1,000 electronic journals. Easy-to-use Web access for many of the library's online resources and electronic reserves are part of the ongoing improvements to the library's systems. Access is available to all of the university network resources--on campus at university facilities and off campus by using computers with modems. Computing labs, used by all students of the university, are provided at three locations around the campus. The labs are equipped with PCs and Macs, computer workstations, and are connected to the campus network and the Internet. Word processing, spreadsheet, database management, and graphics programs are some of the types of software made available to students. On-duty lab assistants are available to help students with any questions or problems. There are also specialized computer facilities for instruction and learning, including the Gilman Center for Communication Technology for English and journalism instruction; Information Technology Center for business students; the Computer Assisted Learning Center; the Center for Computer and Electronic Music; the Computer Aided Design/Computer Aided Manufacturing Laboratory; and the Dana Computer Lab with workstations for computer science. Additional facilities consist of the Hoffman Computer Lab for health professions, the Graphic Design Lab for art instruction, the Educational Computing Lab, and the GIS Computer Lab for engineering instruction.

TUITION, ROOM, BOARD, AND FEES:

Costs for 2010–11

Tuition $28,582

Double Room (Complexes) $7,114

Freshman Meal Plan $4,458

Fees $1,270

Total $41,424

Over 90 percent of University of Hartford students receive a scholarship or grant from the university. For most students, the cost of a University of Hartford education is significantly reduced by financial assistance.

The average "out of pocket" expense for new students this year was $17,850.

FINANCIAL AID

The university's financial aid program, which administers over $90 million annually including student loans, consists of scholarships, grants, loans, and work-study opportunities provided through the federal government, private agencies, interested individuals, and the University. Factors contributing to disbursal of university funds are the college or school in which the student is enrolled, availability of funds, applicant pool, and competition for funds. About 92 percent of all full-time undergraduate students receive assistance; the average amount is $23,574 per year. Students who have demonstrated outstanding academic achievement are eligible for full and partial-tuition scholarships.

STUDENT BODY

The Student Government Association (SGA) represents all full-time students at the University. Through SGA, students and faculty work together to develop and coordinate the co-curriculars of the university. In addition, students are represented on all major administrative committees, including the Board of Regents.

ADMISSIONS

The admissions decision is based on a combination of the following: quality of the secondary school curriculum, course selection, academic performance in secondary school, recommendations of the secondary school principal or guidance counselor, ACT or SAT scores, evidence of a desire to succeed, and leadership qualities shown by academic and extracurricular activities. Music and art applicants are required to audition, show portfolios, and take other tests depending upon the program to which they are applying.

The University has a rolling admission policy.

For more information, students should contact:

Richard A. Zeiser

Dean of Admission

University of Hartford

West Hartford, CT 06117-0395

Phone: 860-768-4296

Toll free: 800-947-4303

Fax: 860-768-4961

E-mail: admission@hartford.edu

Website: http://admission.hartford.edu

School Says . . .

UNIVERSITY OF MAINE AT FORT KENT

AT A GLANCE

The University of Maine at Fort Kent (UMFK) offers the combination of high-quality education and personalized attention today's students are looking for. The small campus population of 1,100 ensures that professors know their students by name. The favorable student-faculty ratio of 18:1 provides many opportunities for interaction. At the same time, the University is large enough to offer a wide variety of academic and extracurricular opportunities. The University's diverse student body includes individuals from small towns and big cities across the United States and Canada, as well as from Europe, Africa, South America, and Asia.

UMFK was founded in 1878 as the Madawaska Training School to educate teachers for what was known as the Madawaska Territory. Over the next century, the school evolved and refined its program into a comprehensive liberal arts-based institution. In 1970, it became part of the seven-campus University of Maine System.

The University's two residence halls, Crocker Hall, and the Lodge, offer housing; the dining facility, Nowland Hall, provides meal service for the student body. Computer, cable TV, and phone hookups are provided in every room, and the halls also have lounges, game rooms, and free laundry facilities. Resident students and commuters alike participate in a variety of campus activities, including theatrical and musical performances, intercollegiate and intramural athletics, and numerous student organizations.

LOCATION AND ENVIRONMENT

The town of Fort Kent is situated on the banks of the Fish and St. John Rivers in an area originally settled by French-speaking Acadians from Maritime Canada. The St. John Valley community is noted as one of the country's few truly international, bilingual-bicultural regions, and the University of Maine at Fort Kent is known as a great place to learn and grow within that community.

The campus has convenient access to numerous areas of scenic natural beauty, as well as recreational opportunities, including ski areas and resorts, Baxter State Park, the Allagash Wilderness Waterway, and the Gaspé Peninsula in Canada's Quebec Province.

The University of Maine at Fort Kent is in proximity to the Maine Winter Sports Center, which is the home to Olympic biathlon training. The facility typically offers on-snow training from Thanksgiving to Easter and also offers summer training on its paved roller ski–training and advanced-training loops and cross-country running trails. Mountain-biking trails are also available at the site. The center features a three-story lodge with showers, locker rooms, and waxing facilities. Former Olympians provide world-class coaching in cross-country skiing and biathlon.

MAJORS AND DEGREES OFFERED

The University of Maine at Fort Kent is a four-year baccalaureate-granting institution that offers the Bachelor of Arts in English and French; the Bachelor of Science in behavioral science, biology, business management, computer applications, e-commerce, education (K–12), environmental studies, nursing, rural public safety administration, social sciences, teacher certification (both elementary and secondary education), and University studies; the Associate of Arts in business, computer science, criminal justice, general studies, and human services; and the Associate of Science in forest technology.

ACADEMIC PROGRAMS

Dedicated to providing a solid liberal arts education within programs designed to equip students for the twenty-first century, the University of Maine at Fort Kent divides the academic year into two 16-week semesters. Both day and evening classes run from early September through early May. Summer classes and workshops are also offered, beginning in May and usually ending in late July. All students, regardless of degree program and major, are required to complete a general education core curriculum and meet certain requirements for graduation. Each degree program and major also has a number of specific requirements that are described in the University catalog.

Entering freshmen are assigned an adviser who is a member of a special advising team devoted to ensuring the success of every student's first year at UMFK.

After the first year, students choose a faculty academic adviser in their field of study, who guides them toward completion of their program requirements.

CAMPUS FACILITIES AND EQUIPMENT

UMFK is home to the state-of-the-art Northern Maine Center for Rural Health Sciences and Northern Aroostook Technology Center. The facilities serve as a home for the University's nursing program and also house the most modern classrooms and teleconferencing center in northern Maine.

Additional buildings on UMFK's 54-acre campus include the Cyr Hall classroom complex and computer laboratory, Fox Auditorium, the Sportscenter, the Old Model School, the Computer Center, and Nadeau Hall, which houses an e-commerce lab, faculty offices, a nursing lab, a music lab, an on-campus health clinic, and a satellite conference center. In addition to its own collections, Blake Library provides students with a variety of available databases and electronic access to more than 1 million volumes in libraries of the University of Maine System. The Acadian Archives Building, which preserves, celebrates, and disseminates information about the region's history and houses documents and artifacts. This building contains a conference room, reading room, work room, reference desk, a bank of computers, and research materials stacks as well as personnel space, a collections area, and an accessioning room.

The University also owns or has access to a number of off-campus facilities that are available to students, and enhance academic programs by providing opportunity for hands-on study. The Elmer Violette Wilderness Camp, located on the Allagash Wilderness Waterway in the famed North Maine Woods, is frequently used by the Environmental Studies and Forestry Programs to conduct fieldwork. The wilderness camp includes housing and classroom facilities. Other academic programs also use the camp at various times throughout the year.

Other off-campus UMFK facilities include a 1,000-acre wooded lot bordering St. Froid Lake, a biological park near the campus, and access points to the Fish and St. John Rivers.

TUITION, ROOM, BOARD, AND FEES

In 2009–2010, tuition is $6,030 per year for Maine residents and $15,180 per year for out-of-state students. Nonresident students who qualify for the New England Regional Program paid $9,060 per year for tuition. Room and board costs for 2009–2010 are $7,080. Required University fees for new students were $773, which include application, matriculation, orientation, student activity, and technology fees. Tuition and fee figures listed are based on 15 credit hours per semester.

FINANCIAL AID

The University of Maine at Fort Kent Office of Financial Aid administers scholarships, grants, loans, and work assistance to more than 80 percent of enrolled students. The University requires all applicants for financial aid to file the Free Application for Federal Student Aid (FAFSA), which is available from the UMFK Office of Financial Aid, from high school guidance offices, and online at http://www.fafsa.cd.gov. UMFK has a preferred filing date of March 1. Consideration is given at any time during the year; however, early application is recommended because awards depend on the availability of funds.

ADMISSIONS PROCESS

The UMFK Office of Admissions considers each applicant on an individual basis. Consideration is given to academic preparation, maturity, personal motivation, and goals. Particular attention is given to secondary school performance, especially in the junior and senior years. SAT or ACT scores are not required for admission to the University of Maine at Fort Kent.

Application for admission is made by completing a University of Maine System application form or by applying online at the University's Web site. A nonrefundable fee of $40 must be submitted to the UMFK Office of Admissions. The University follows a rolling admissions schedule and accepts applications at any time during the year. Students are usually accepted for entry in either September or January.

Applications and additional information are available from:

Office of Admissions

University of Maine at Fort Kent

23 University Drive

Fort Kent, Maine 04743

United State

Phone: 207-834-7600

888-TRY-UMFK (879-8635; toll-free)

Fax: 207-834-7609

Email: umfkadm@maine.edu

Website: http://umfk.maine.edu

UNIVERSITY OF MAINE

AT A GLANCE

The University of Maine educational experience rises from our resources as a public research institution combined with our commitment to teaching in a small university atmosphere. Excellence is a top priority—reflected in academic standards and programs, research, faculty and the student body. Nationally recognized faculty, state-of-the-art living and learning facilities, exciting cultural programs, and enviable quality of life are instruments in student success. Students come here for the quality of education they acquire and the quality of life we offer.

LOCATION AND ENVIRONMENT

Orono, a classic college town bounded by the Stillwater and Penobscot rivers, is eight miles north of Bangor, a city consistently ranked as one of the most desirable places to live for its natural beauty, safety, quality of life and affordability.

The university is designed to provide a functional and aesthetically pleasing residential campus overlooking the Stillwater River. More than 200 buildings, most of which are constructed of native red brick, grace a 600-acre campus that contains towering pines, birch and poplar, all native to the area. Walking, biking and cross-country skiing trails are a popular feature of the campus.

The University of Maine is 10 minutes from Maine's third-largest city, Bangor, and its international airport. Along with these convenient travel connections the University is an easy driving distance to several ski resorts. Campus is located only an hour from Bar Harbor, which is home to Acadia National Park, and Baxter State Park, the northern terminus for the Appalachian Trail.

OFF-CAMPUS OPPORTUNITIES

An expansive worldview is an essential part of today's education since tomorrow's workforce will function in an increasingly global economy. To help students gain this perspective, the University of Maine offers numerous study abroad programs. Opportunities exist in more than 40 countries in Western and Eastern Europe, South America, Canada, Australia, Africa, New Zealand and Asia. Many programs are offered in English language instruction, while others provide the opportunity for studying or obtaining fluency in another language. Programs are available for one or two semesters, or the summer, and are available in all disciplines.

ACADEMIC PROGRAMS

Founded in 1865 as part of the Land Grant movement, the University of Maine is not just a place to prepare for a good job: it is also a place to prepare for a rich and fulfilling life. A University of Maine education is based on a foundation in the liberal arts to ensure that graduates are broadly educated and can contribute in many ways beyond their technical expertise. A big part of this education takes place outside the classroom by immersion in a university community that celebrates the arts, treasures the truth, defends freedom of thought and expression, and cherishes human racial, ethnic and cultural diversity. Academic majors are distributed throughout five academic colleges: the College of Business Public Policy and Health; the College of Education and Human Development; the College of Engineering; the College of Liberal Arts and Sciences and the College of Natural Sciences Forestry, and Agriculture. In addition, the Honors College, the second-oldest honors program in the country, offers high-achieving and intellectually curious students from all colleges a stimulating, enhanced academic experience.

The University of Maine remains true to its land-grant heritage in yet another important way: it is committed to public service and to improving the quality of human life. Faculty and staff, and undergraduate and graduate students all contribute to improving our society through research, education, and direct community service. By enrolling at the University of Maine students are committing themselves to working for a better, more just, more tolerant society.

CAMPUS FACILITIES AND EQUIPMENT

As Maine's public research institution, the University of Maine strives to assist business, industry and individuals through many of its state-of-the-art research and field laboratory facilities. The university also conducts outreach activities to convey its knowledge and resources to all areas of the state.

The University of Maine is the cultural and artistic center for central Maine. The Collins Center for the Arts, several museums and the Jordan Planetarium all contribute to the artistic and cultural offerings of the area.

FINANCIAL AID

The University is committed to providing financial assistance to qualified students through a combination of scholarships, grants, student employment, and loans. Students applying for financial aid should file the Free Application for Federal Student Financial Aid (FAFSA) before March 1.

The Student Financial Aid Office administers a variety of Federal, State and University aid programs to help University of Maine students finance their education. Financial aid staff award, process, and disburse financial aid funds. They also advise students and their families, the campus community, and the general public on issues related to financial aid.

STUDENT ORGANIZATIONS AND ACTIVITIES

There's never a dull moment at the University of Maine! There are events and activities every day of the week with over 200 student organizations including social groups, community service groups, political groups, Greek organizations, and more. Students can also cheer for the 17 teams of the NCAA Division 1 Black Bears at the Alfond Arena and the Alfond Stadium.

One of the best features of Maine life is its recreation opportunities and outdoor activities. Campus Recreation offers everything from recreation facilities to intramural sports, to sports clubs to fitness classes. MaineBound provides trips and courses in rock climbing, canoeing, and kayaking, camping, and hiking just to name a few. The MaineBound Adventure Center offers a state-of-the art indoor climbing facility and outdoor equipment rental program.

UMaine also provides many cultural activities for the University and the surrounding community. Each year the Department of Art Gallery and UMaine Museum of Art show works by internationally and regionally known artists and UMaine students. The Hudson Museum offers exhibits of cultural art and artifacts. For stargazing, Jordan Planetarium offers many public shows throughout the year. For a wide variety of performances including theatre, dance, and music, the Maine Center for the Arts offers a broad spectrum of nationally and internationally renowned performers.

Perhaps the largest part of campus life is actually living on campus. Currently, there are 19 residence halls. In the halls there is a mixture of students from all classes and all majors, offering a well-rounded experience. In addition, many halls will offer Living/Learning Communities—both fun and educational—for their residents.

Another very important part of student life on campus is food. There are two dining halls, conveniently located near the residence halls, along with many other dining options. The Oakes Room Cafe in Fogler Library provides a great place to get a coffee and a snack. The Marketplace and Wells Central offer comfort foods, ethnic specialties, pizzas, sandwiches and grilled items.

ADMISSIONS PROCESS

Admission to the University of Maine is selective and based on a combination of factors that demonstrates a promise of academic success. Criteria considered for admission include academic credentials, scholastic achievement and personal motivation. Space availability in certain programs may also be considered when selecting candidates for admission.

The University of Maine participates in a nonrestrictive Early Action program. Applications for fall semester and all supporting documents submitted electronically or postmarked by December 15 will be reviewed by the end of January. Early Action candidates will be given first consideration for merit scholarships awarded by the Admissions Office.

Applications for the fall semester completed after December 15, Early Action candidates deferred to the regular admission process, and applications for the spring semester will be reviewed on a rolling admission basis as long as space is available. An admission decision will typically be made within four to six weeks from the receipt of the application and all supporting documents.

UNIVERSITY OF MARYLAND, BALTIMORE COUNTY

AT A GLANCE

University of Maryland, Baltimore County (UMBC) attracts motivated students and rewards them with the resources and attention they need to succeed. A selective, medium-sized public research university, UMBC provides students with opportunities for hands-on research experience working with professors at the top of their fields. This past fall, *U.S. News & World Report* ranked UMBC number one among "Up and Coming" national universities, "schools everyone should be watching." *U.S. News* also ranked UMBC number four for undergraduate teaching at national universities—the highest ranked public university in the category—tied with Stanford just behind Dartmouth, Princeton, and Yale. *The Princeton Review* recently identified UMBC as one of the nation's "Best Value" colleges and universities and ranked us second on its "Most Diverse Student Population" list. UMBC President Freeman A. Hrabowski, III, has been named "one of the 10 best college presidents" by *Time Magazine*. The Carnegie Foundation ranks UMBC in the category of Research Universities with high research activity. UMBC is a two-time winner of the U.S. Presidential Award for Excellence in Science, Mathematics and Engineering Mentoring. The University's academic reputation and industry partnerships help place students in promising careers and leading graduate programs. One-third of UMBC students immediately go on to leading graduate or professional schools such as Harvard, Johns Hopkins, Stanford, and Yale. Three UMBC graduates have received one of the world's most selective academic awards, the Gates Cambridge Fellowship. At UMBC, students find out quickly that learning at an honors university can take place in many ways. Undergraduates have access to the latest technology in areas from geography to art history to chemistry. The Goddard Earth Science and Technology Center brings NASA scientists, UMBC professors, and students together to study the earth. Students in UMBC's Imaging Research Center (IRC) gain professional experience with companies such as the Discovery Channel, CNN, and PBS. UMBC also has a Howard Hughes Medical Institute laboratory, a privately sponsored research facility dedicated to the study of the structural building blocks of the AIDS virus. The UMBC climate is friendly and energetic; 9,700 undergraduates have enough ideas and interests to support more than 250 groups, including Greek organizations, recreational sports clubs, community outreach efforts, and campus events. Students enthusiastically follow UMBC NCAA Division I athletic teams and attend games in the UMBC Stadium and Retriever Activities Center. UMBC students are from nearly all 50 states and over 100 foreign countries. Approximately 72% of freshman students live on campus, with 14% from out of state. The undergraduate student population is 48% female, 23% Asian American, 14% African American, 3% Hispanic American and Native American. UMBC houses nearly 3,900 students, 1,600 live in UMBC's three new residence suites and apartment communities. Residential communities feature nine living-learning programs, including the Center for Women and Information Technology; Intercultural Living Exchange; Shriver Living Learning Center; Visual and Performing Arts.

COLLEGE BASICS

An Honors University with the teaching and student support traditions of a small liberal arts college, UMBC is also among the most rapidly developing and diverse research universities in the nation.

LOCATION AND ENVIRONMENT

Located a few miles south of Baltimore, UMBC is 15 minutes from downtown Baltimore and 45 minutes from Washington, D.C. The Baltimore-Washington area is known for its music, sports, museums, restaurants, and historical traditions. UMBC's 530-acre campus includes more than 40 buildings accessed by a two-mile elliptical drive, with housing and dining facilities on one side and core facilities (classroom/lab buildings, a library, galleries, a student union, a bookstore, a gymnasium, an Olympic-size pool, and tennis courts) surrounding a central walkway. BWTech@UMBC Research and Technology Park, adjacent to the campus, attracts firms in the high-technology fields, including engineering, information technology, and the life sciences. Close to the campus, techcenter@UMBC is a magnet for high-technology start-up and emerging companies and offers students internship opportunities with cutting-edge firms.

OFF-CAMPUS OPPORTUNITIES

Surrounded by business, government, and metropolitan centers, UMBC places students in over 1,200 co-ops and internships in more than 500 organizations each year in the Baltimore-Washington area. UMBC matches students with such employers as the federal Centers for Medicare and Medicaid, Bank of America, Silicon Graphics, MBNA, the Smithsonian Institution, NASA, and the National Aquarium. The university encourages students to participate in study abroad experiences during the semester or travel-study opportunities during winter and summer breaks. The Shriver Center links the resources of the campus to urgent social problems, places students in co-ops and internships at hundreds of businesses and organizations, organizes and manages community service projects that bring the resources of the university to people in need, and connects students to a wide range of social service projects.

ACADEMICS

UMBC's academic calendar consists of fall and spring semesters, a four-week mini session in January, and summer sessions from six to eight weeks. To receive a UMBC degree, students complete 120 to 128 credits plus two physical education courses. In addition to the requirements for the chosen major, the general education program (GEP), provides a solid basis for a lifetime of learning. GEP courses encompass humanities and fine arts, mathematics and natural sciences, social sciences, and languages and culture. The Honors College at UMBC is a special option for students seeking a community of like-minded people for whom the quest for knowledge is its own reward. All Honors College students must take at least one honors course per semester. Students choose from honors versions of core courses, special honors seminars, and plenty of other honors courses.

ADMISSIONS

In fall 2009, the average incoming freshman had a 3.6 cumulative GPA, 52% ranked in the top quarter of his or her senior class, and had a combined SAT I score of 1184. Approximately 68.9% of freshman applicants are admitted each year. Academic performance and curriculum strength play an important part in the decision. An essay is required, and a letter of recommendation is strongly encouraged. Transfer students with at least 30 semester hours of college-level work are admitted based on the strength of college success. A minimum 2.5 GPA is recommended for full consideration. Prospective freshmen are encouraged to submit applications by the early action deadline of November 1. The final deadline is February 1 for full consideration for admission, campus housing, financial aid, and scholarships. The priority deadline for transfer students is March 15 for fall admission and November 1 for spring admission for students seeking admission to special programs or wishing to be considered for campus housing, financial aid, or scholarships. The final deadline for applications is May 31 for fall and December 15 for spring. For further information, students or parents may contact:

Dale Bittinger

Director of Undergraduate Admissions and Orientation

Office of Undergraduate Admissions and Orientation

UMBC

1000 Hilltop Circle

Baltimore, Maryland 21250

Telephone: 410-455-2291 or 800-UMBC-4U2

Fax: 410-455-1094

Web: www.umbc.edu

CAMPUS FACILITIES AND EQUIPMENT

UMBC's landmark building, the Albin O. Kuhn Library and Gallery, contains over 1 million books and bound volumes of journals, an extensive reference collection, 4,200 journal and database subscriptions, more than 200 computers, wireless and wired connections for laptops, and more than 3 million other items, including slides, photographs, maps, musical scores, recordings, and microforms. The Commons, UMBC's state-of-the-art student center, the hub of campus life includes a food court, general lounges, the University bookstore, meeting spaces, a student recreation center, a full-service bank, student organization offices, retail-type spaces, wireless computer connectivity, and Web-accessible kiosks. UMBC students have access to research opportunities and equipment such as conducting AIDS research on one of the world's largest nuclear magnetic resonance spectrometers in the only Howard Hughes Medical Institute lab at a public university in Maryland. New facilities include a Public Policy Building and a state-of-the-art Information Technology/Engineering Building. In the next few years, UMBC will open a new Performing Arts and Humanities Facility, housing seven departments and new performance space that will showcase the University's strong arts and humanities programs and create a regional and national appreciation of UMBC as a cultural attraction.

CAMPUS LIFE

The campus climate is friendly and energetic. UMBC's more than 9,700 undergraduates have enough ideas and interests to support more than 250 student groups, including Greek organizations and recreational sports clubs, such as fencing and sailing; community outreach efforts, such as Habitat for Humanity; and campus events, including lectures, films, concerts, and plays. Students enthusiastically follow UMBC NCAA Division I athletic teams, such as basketball, lacrosse, and soccer and attend games in the UMBC Stadium and Retriever Activities Center, which includes a multipurpose gym, auxiliary gym, weight room, and classrooms. Elections are held each year for officers in UMBC's Student Government Association (SGA). The SGA represents the student body on a number of administrative committees, including the Undergraduate Council, the Library Committee, and the Student Health Advisory Committee.

MAJORS AND DEGREES

Programs leading to Bachelor of Arts, Bachelor of Fine Arts, and Bachelor of Science degrees: acting, Africana studies, American studies, aging services, ancient studies, biochemistry and molecular biology, bioinformatics and computational biology, biological sciences, business technology administration, chemical engineering, chemistry and biochemistry, chemistry education, computer engineering and computer science, cultural anthropology, dance, economics and financial economics, emergency health services, English, environmental science and environmental studies, gender and women's studies, geography, health administration and policy, history, information systems, interdisciplinary studies, mathematics and statistics, mechanical engineering, media and communication studies, modern languages and linguistics, music, philosophy, physics education, physics, political science, psychology, social work, sociology, theater, visual and performing arts, and visual arts. New programs include business technology administration, computer gaming, media and communication studies and physics education. An interdisciplinary studies program allows students to design their own course of study according to their specific educational and career goals. UMBC offers pre-professional studies programs, including two-and four-year advisement programs to prepare students for clinical training in dental hygiene, medical and research technology, medicine, nursing, pharmacy, physical therapy, and veterinary medicine. Minors include Africana studies, American studies, ancient studies, anthropology, applied politics, art history and theory, astronomy, biological sciences, chemistry, computer science, dance, East Asian history, economics, emergency health services, environmental geography, gender and women's studies, geography, history, international affairs, international economics, Judaic studies, legal policy, literature, mathematics, modern languages and linguistics, music, philosophy, physics, political science, political thought, psychology, public administration, religious studies, social welfare, sociology, statistics, theater, writing, and media and communication studies.

FINANCIAL AID

More than 45% of undergraduates receive some financial aid. UMBC uses the Free Application for Federal Student Aid (FAFSA) to help determine a student's financial need. Aid is awarded to qualified applicants on a first-come, first-served basis. Since aid is awarded only to admitted students, early application for admission is also important. Well-qualified freshmen are automatically considered for general merit scholarships once they are admitted to the University. The Scholars Programs at UMBC provide special opportunities for outstanding entering freshmen who want to focus their education through intense study in their major. Scholars participate in a wide range of academic and cultural enrichment activities, extracurricular travel, or summer study. The selection process for specialty scholarships includes application, an interview, and, in some cases, nomination from a high school official.

TUITION AND FEES

Tuition and fees for 2009–2010 were $8,872 for Maryland residents and $18,213 for out-of-state students. Room and board averaged $9,050. Miscellaneous expenses, books, and transportation cost about $1,500 per year.

COLLEGE BASICS

UMass Boston is known as a model urban university and for its dedicated and diverse student population, solid academic reputation, affordability and proximity to the cultural riches of the city of Boston.

AT A GLANCE

Notable for its solid academic reputation, active faculty, modest class size and flexible schedules, UMass Boston is the city's only public university. Its proximity to cultural and social riches and urban sophistication, moderate cost structure, and dedicated, highly diverse student body make the campus a desirable academic destination. The picturesque harborside campus is accessible by both public and private transportation, and help is available to locate appropriate housing options. A rich mix of student organizations provides social options connecting to both the campus and the surrounding metropolitan environs. With more than 100 undergraduate programs, 38 masters and 13 doctoral degree programs, UMass Boston surely has something for you.

CAMPUS LIFE

No matter your interest, UMass Boston has an activity to engage you socially and intellectually. Be it student government, literary endeavors, championship chess, working with inner city youth, academically affiliated clubs, affinity groups, athletics opportunities, or a course-credit-based leadership development program, you can find the right activity to complement your classroom experience. UMass Boston is a community of scholars with pride in academic excellence, diversity, research, and service, tightly woven into the public and community service needs of Greater Boston. Our students come from an extraordinary range of backgrounds, talents and interests and represent all levels of the economic, political, spiritual and ethnic spectra. Many come straight from high school, others transfer from two- and four-year colleges; most are from Massachusetts, but many arrive from other states and countries.

ACADEMICS

Five undergraduate colleges and one graduate college award bachelor's degrees: the College of Liberal Arts and the College of Science and Mathematics (32 majors, and 17 programs of study between them), the College of Management, the College of Nursing and Health Sciences (both a regular BSN, an accelerated BSN and an online RN-to-BSN program, as well as a program in Exercise & Health Sciences), the College of Public and Community Service (five majors and three career concentrations) and the Graduate College of Education (one undergraduate major). Pre-med, pre-law, and a teacher licensure program are also offered, along with programs for honors study, credit by examination, and advanced placement.

These colleges also offer graduate level programs, including master's and doctoral degree programs and graduate certificate programs. Two graduate colleges—the Graduate College of Education and the McCormack Graduate School of Policy Studies—offer graduate degree, graduate certificate and CAGS programs. Altogether, UMass Boston offers 38 master's degree programs, 13 doctoral degrees and more than 20 graduate certificate programs.

The academic calendar runs from early September through the end of May, with a one-month optional winter session in January and summer school sessions in June, July and August.

COLLEGE OF SCIENCE AND MATHEMATICS

Distribution, core curriculum, and writing comprise the 3 required elements of our general education curriculum. Requirements of the major must also be fulfilled. The colleges both offer an individual major option.

COLLEGE OF MANAGEMENT

Fulfilling the general education, management, and elective course requirements earns graduates a BS degree with a strong liberal arts foundation and the theoretical, technical, and functional training needed to succeed in business.

COLLEGE OF NURSING AND HEALTH SCIENCES

A BS program in nursing offers a liberal arts foundation and intensive study in the principles and practices of nursing. The program in Exercise & Health Sciences prepares graduates for the technical aspects of a professional discipline with a foundation in liberal arts.

COLLEGE OF PUBLIC AND COMMUNITY SERVICE

Nationally acclaimed as a model for competency-based education, the college offers an innovative curriculum with a strong emphasis on social justice. Students draw upon a variety of learning options including classroom study, self-directed study, project-based learning, and the demonstration of competence gained through relevant prior experience.

THE GRADUATE COLLEGE OF EDUCATION

Offer a single BA program in Early Education and Care in Inclusive Settings. As a non-licensure program, this major focuses on the professional concerns of inclusive early education and child care.

Honors programs are open to high achievers in all colleges.

ADMISSIONS

Freshman candidates must have at least 16 academic units in high school including four years of English, three of mathematics, three of science including two with laboratory requirements, two years of social science including one of US history, two years of a single foreign language, and two of electives in the arts or computer science (excluding vocational training.) Candidates must present satisfactory scores on either the SAT or ACT. Students must have a strong academic background (as determined by a re-calculated GPA.) Academic program choices, motivation, achievement and annual progress are closely scrutinized. Reading and writing skills are measured using English grades, the application essay and standardized test scores. A separate international application is required of international students. The Test of English as a Foreign Language (TOEFL) is required of all students educated in a non-English educational system. We consider transfer students by reviewing all college academic credentials. In general, a minimum 2.5 GPA is required, though specific programs require higher. A campus visit with a group information session is strongly encouraged. Contact 617-287-6000 or www.umb.edu for more information.

CAMPUS FACILITIES AND EQUIPMENT

The University's Healey Library holds a collection of more than 600,000 volumes, 25,000 electronic and print journals and newspapers, 30,000 electronic books, 85 databases, and over 2,500 videos, DVDs, and films representing all fields of study on the campus. The library's electronic resources are available on and off campus, 24/7. UMass Boston is a member of three library consortia, and participates in the state-wide virtual catalog, providing yet wider accessibility to scholarly and study resources. The Information Technology Division (ITD) provides seven-days-a-week access to general purpose computer labs with some 220 Dell Pentium Four and 60 Apple Macintosh G5/G4s, as well as other specialized, course-related facilities including Adaptive Computer, Graduate and Faculty, and Media and Language Labs, plus a media viewing center. ITD houses equipment from Dell, Sun and Apple, and operating systems include Windows XP, Unix, Linux and Apple OS. With more than 70 Smart Classrooms, network connections throughout the campus, and wireless access in the Library and Campus Center, a wide variety of IT and data communications resources is available to students. The campus uses a WebCT/Blackboard learning management system, a fiber optic infrastructure with Gigabit backbone and 10 MB switched connectivity. The Kennedy Presidential Library is linked to UMass Boston by a number of educational programs, enabling students to utilize the more than 28 million pages of documents, 6.5 million feet of film, and 100,000+ still photographs in that library's archives. Next door, the Archives of the Commonwealth of Massachusetts are also a rich depository covering more than 550 years of Massachusetts history. A state-of-the-art Campus Center provides easy access to student services, dining services and spectacular meeting spaces, along with computer terminals and wireless Internet access.

UNIVERSITY OF MASSACHUSETTS—LOWELL

AT A GLANCE

The academic experience at UML offers students comprehensive, broad-based programs characterized by a continuing effort to break down traditional barriers between disciplines, and between the classroom and the "real world." Most programs include an internship that provides an opportunity for students to put into practice what they've learned in the classroom. Resources including an Honors program, multimedia computer labs, and an active peer tutoring program ensure that all students have access to the opportunities and services that support their success.

UMass Lowell offers 15 doctoral, 31 master's and 38 bachelor's degree programs that incorporate 74 concentrations in science, engineering, health, humanities, social sciences, fine arts, education and management. Signature programs include sound recording technology, plastics engineering and meteorology, as well as new programs in forensics and entrepreneurship. Virtually every major offers a Plus 1 program that allows students to graduate in five years with both a bachelor's and master's degree.

Internationally recognized for excellence in science and engineering, the campus is a leader in nanotechnology, nanomanufacturing, biomanufacturing, bioinformatics and advanced materials research.

LOCATION AND ENVIRONMENT

UMass Lowell is surrounded by a region rich with heritage and culture. The campus is located 25 miles from Boston and within an hour of ocean beaches and New Hampshire mountains.

The City of Lowell, a thriving city of 110,000, offers everything from the Merrimack Repertory Theater to white water rafting, the Kerouac Festival to great baseball with the Red Sox-affiliated minor league Lowell Spinners. Ethnic restaurants, cobblestone streets, a lively arts community - it's a renaissance city.

MAJORS AND DEGREES OFFERED

American Studies
  General
  Thematic Option
Biology
  General
  Bioinformatics
  Biotechnology
  Ecology
Business Administration
  Accounting
  Entrepreneurship
  Finance
  Management Information Systems
  Management
  Marketing
Chemistry
  Forensics Option
Engineering
  Chemical Engineering
    Nuclear option
  Civil and Environmental Engineering
  Computer Engineering
  Electrical Engineering
  Mechanical Engineering
  Plastics Engineering

Clinical Laboratory Sciences
  Clinical Laboratory Sciences
  Medical Technology
  Nutritional Sciences
Computer Science
  General
  Bioinformatics
Criminal Justice
Economics
English
  Literature
  Writing
Environmental Science
  Environmental Studies
  Geoscience
  Atmospheric Science, Meteorology
Exercise Physiology (leading to a Doctor of Physical Therapy degree)
Fine Arts
  Art
  Design
Health Education
  Community Health
  Environmental Health
History
  General
  Art History
Liberal Arts°
  Art History
  Comparative Arts
  Cultural Studies
  Developmental Disabilities
  Gender Studies
  Legal Studies
  Theater Arts
Math
  General
  Applied Math
  Computer Science
  Statistics/Actuarial Science
  Teaching
Modern Languages
  Spanish
  Spanish/French
  Spanish/Italian

Music

   Music Business

   Music Performance

      Instrumental

      Voice

   Music Studies° (leading to a master's degree in Music Education)

   Sound Recording Technology

Nursing°

Physics

   General

   Optics

   Radiological Health

Philosophy

   General

   Communications & Critical Thinking

Political Science

Psychology°

Sociology

°Requires two concentrations

ACADEMIC PROGRAMS

First Year Program

We want you to start off on the right foot. So the First Year program provides learning communities, a freshman leadership program and an ongoing schedule of educational and recreational activities.

Honors Program: www.uml.edu/honors

The Honors Program is for people who want to take their academics to another level. The University-wide program offers students in-depth study in small classes, individualized advising, relationships with faculty mentors, research opportunities, professional development grants for workshops and conferences and scholarships. Honors students may choose to live on honors floors in campus residence halls and may be eligible to earn a degree with the designation "Commonwealth Honors Program Scholar."

Centers for Learning: www.class.uml.edu

Everyone needs a little help sometime and it's available at the Centers for Learning and Academic Support Services. CLASS offers individual and group tutoring (peer tutors cover more than 70 subject areas) and help choosing your courses, editing a paper or boosting your study skills.

Career Services: www.uml.edu/career

In addition to helping you find a job when you graduate, the Career Services office is a resource for internships, co-ops and part-time and summer jobs. The staff will help you identify a career path and how to get there, connect you to alumni so you can get feedback on a career, facilitate on-campus and virtual employer interviews, hold daily drop-in hours and conduct multiple skill-building workshops throughout the year. Career Services maintains a resource library and searchable databases of available positions.

CAMPUS FACILITIES AND EQUIPMENT

The UMass Lowell campus stretches over 100 acres along both sides of the Merrimack River. Academic buildings are clustered on UMass Lowell North and South, while UMass Lowell East is home to residence halls and research labs.

UMass Lowell East also houses a 12,000-square-foot, state-of-the- art Campus Recreation Center that attracts hundreds of students daily to its basketball, racquetball and squash courts, its one-eighth-mile seamless rubber compound running track and its dual-level fitness area that houses dozens of pieces of cardiovascular and strength training equipment.

School Says . . .

The first of two multi-story parking garages was opened in 2007. There are plans on the drawing board for a nanotechnology research center and new residence halls.

We are determined to provide you with the right tools in classrooms, laboratories and residence halls. The multimedia labs on campus are regularly upgraded. Every student has a free email account, and the campus is completely wireless. Our electronic library, which ranks among the best, can be accessed anywhere on-and-off campus, including in residence halls.

TUITION, ROOM, BOARD AND FEES

Annual Undergraduate Costs 2008–2009

Total Tuition and Fees

In-State Residents: $9,181

Out-of-State Residents: $21,201

New England Regional Program: $9,908

Residence Hall Room $4,902

Meals (Full Plan) $2,617

Total Room and Board $7,519

FINANCIAL AID

Maintaining Access

UMass Lowell is committed to making quality higher education accessible to all qualified students. In 2008, the campus met 93 percent of need for its students. In the same year, the campus awarded more than $60 million in need and non-need based aid.

Scholarships for Freshmen

More than 150 UMass Lowell scholarships are available to eligible students each year. Scholarships are awarded by the academic college or department

STUDENT ORGANIZATIONS AND ACTIVITIES

UMass Lowell's 6,000 undergraduate students are ethnically, culturally and economically diverse. Students are active in a wide variety of community service activities and volunteer work throughout the community.

There are more than 100 active clubs and organizations as diverse as publishing a weekly newspaper, producing multicultural festivals and learning to crochet. Academic clubs avoid the all-work-and-no-play principle by going skiing, canoeing and spelunking.

In addition to a nationally-ranked Division I hockey team and 17 other varsity sports, the University sponsors an active recreational sports program.

Whatever you do, you'll be surrounded by one of UMass Lowell's great assets: the people. Among your classmates, professors and administrators, you'll encounter a wide range of ideas, traditions and languages - people who share your aspirations and commitment, people who offer you support and encouragement. You'll be welcomed into the community and form friendships that last a lifetime.

Residence halls offer a choice of living environments. All residence halls are secured 24/7 with electronic access and overnight professional security. Building exteriors and parking lots are lit, scanned by security cameras and regularly patrolled. Between 7 p.m. and 1 a.m., our Student Escort Vans are available to shuttle students around campus.

ADMISSIONS PROCESS

UMass Lowell has a rolling admissions policy, meaning that applications are reviewed and decisions made as soon as a student's application package is complete. However, there is a preferred deadline of February 15 for fall semester applications. We encourage high school seniors to apply as soon as their first quarter grades are in.

Check on the website (www.uml.edu/admissions) to see everything required and to download an Application Checklist.

UNIVERSITY OF NEW ENGLAND

AT A GLANCE

The University of New England (UNE) is an independent, coeducational, comprehensive university committed to academic excellence and the enhancement of the quality of life for the people, organizations, and communities it serves. The university fosters critical inquiry through a student-centered, academic environment rich in research, scholarship, creative activity, and service while providing opportunities for acquiring and applying knowledge in selected clinical, professional, and community settings.

UNE's 4,493 students are enrolled in a wide variety of academic programs at the undergraduate, graduate, and first-professional levels in four colleges: the College of Arts and Sciences, the College of Health Professions, the College of Pharmacy, and the College of Osteopathic Medicine (housing Maine's only medical school). At the undergraduate level, we have approximately 2,441 students enrolled from 35 different states and several foreign countries in over 40 undergraduate degree programs.

UNE traces its history to 1831 with the founding of Westbrook College, one of Maine's oldest institutions of learning. Today's university represents the joining of three unique higher education institutions through the combining of St. Francis College and the New England College of Osteopathic Medicine in 1978, and Westbrook College in 1996.

LOCATION AND ENVIRONMENT

The University of New England has two campuses located in the picturesque southern coastal beach communities of Maine. The 540-acre Biddeford Campus in Biddeford, home to the College of Arts and Sciences and the College of Osteopathic Medicine, is situated on a beautiful coastal site where the Saco River flows into the Atlantic Ocean and includes more than 4,000 feet of water frontage. Located 20 miles to the north is the PortlandCampus, home to the Westbrook College of Health Professions, set on 41 acres in a quiet residential setting in Portland. Students at both campuses can enjoy the vibrant social life offered in nearby metropolitan Boston (located 90 miles to the south of Biddeford) or Portland and the dynamic outdoor recreational activities that have made Maine a prime tourist destination. Southern Maine is conveniently serviced by a number of airlines at the Portland International Jetport and by bus and train service with stations in Biddeford/Saco and Portland, making our campuses very accessible to all areas of the Northeastern United States and beyond.

OFF-CAMPUS OPPORTUNITIES

The university is committed to supplementing the traditional learning process with practical applications. All students are encouraged to participate in cooperative education programs, field placements, and practicums. These experiences provide valuable learning situations and increase a student's exposure to job-related opportunities, and are required for graduation by most majors. Students also have the opportunity to arrange a study abroad experience. UNE's Center for International Educationpromotes the goals of international cooperation and understanding through rigorous academic programs, overseas study opportunities, student-faculty research projects and a host of special programs designed to address current issues in international relations and cultural studies.

MAJORS AND DEGREES OFFERED

UNE offers highly competitive undergraduate and graduate programs in a variety of areas. The university confers the Associates of Science, Bachelor of Arts, Bachelor of Science, Master of Public Health, Master of Science, Master of Science in Education, Master of Social Work, Doctor of Physical Therapy, Doctor of Pharmacy, and Doctor of Osteopathic Medicine degrees along with several post-graduate and graduate certificate programs.

Associate degrees are offered in nursing. Bachelor degrees are offered in: animal behavior, applied exercise science, aquaculture and aquarium science, art education, athletic training, biochemistry, biological sciences, business, chemistry, communications, dental hygiene, elementary education, English, environmental science, environmental studies, health sciences (for occupational therapy five-year entry-level master's degree), history, liberal studies (including pre-law), marine biology, mathematics, medical biology (health and medical sciences tracks for pre-dental, pre-medicine, and pre-veterinary), neuroscience, nursing, political science,, psychology, psychology and social relations, sociology, and sport management.

Individualized majors, various minors, pre-physical therapy designation, accelerated pre-physician assistant programs, pre-pharmacy, and secondary education certification (Teacher Certification Program) is also available at the undergraduate level.

Masters degree programs are offered in applied biosciences, education, medical education leadership, nurse anesthesia, marine sciences, occupational therapy, physician assistant, public health, and social work. Doctor degree programs are offered in osteopathic medicine, pharmacy, and physical therapy. Graduate certificate programs are offered in addictions counseling, gerontology, and public health.

ACADEMIC PROGRAMS

All undergraduate programs at UNE have a core curriculum as a common thread. Designed to provide a foundation in the liberal arts, the core reflects the values of the college and is designed to prepare students for living informed, thoughtful, and active lives in a complex and changing society. It provides an innovative common learning experience for all UNE undergraduates. It invites students to explore four college-wide themes - (1) Environmental Awareness, (2) Social and Global Awareness, (3) Critical Thinking: Human Responses to Problems and Challenges, and (4) Citizenship. Skills of communications, mathematics, and critical thinking are taught throughout the core.

Student Support Services provides a wide-range of services to assist students with psychological and emotional health, academic support, educational and career planning, and equal opportunities during their academic experience. The Office of Career Services provides academic and career exploration assistance, assistance in applying to graduate schools, self-assessment and personal interest exploration, resume help, job listings, and job fairs. Learning Assistance Services, another department within Student Support Services, offers a comprehensive array of academic support including placement testing, courses, workshops, tutoring, and individual consultations.

CAMPUS FACILITIES AND EQUIPMENT

Both the Biddeford and Portland Campuses feature 45 buildings with a variety of uses to support the needs of the university community. The $8 million Marine Science Education and Research Center on the university Campus is the only facility of its kind on any university campus. It features flow-through seawater laboratories and a marine mammal rehabilitation center. The Pickus Center, is a state-of-the-art biomedical research facility on the Biddeford campus. Laboratory space in the new Peter and Cécile Morgane Hall includes two biology labs, two chemistry labs, two physics labs, one biochemistry lab, one genetics lab, and several small research labs with associated prep rooms. The new George and Barbara Bush Center houses The Windward Café, The Bush Legacy Library, The Bush Memorabilia Exhibit space and 'a President's Board Room. The new College of Pharmacy building houses classrooms, a pharmacy practice lab, a sterile products lab, a pharmaceutics lab, a drug information center and six research labs. The Harold Alfond Center for Health Sciences on the Biddeford Campus is a state-of-the-art science education facility and a major medical, health and natural sciences resource for the region. The collections of the Jack S. Ketchum Library (Biddeford Campus) and Josephine S. Abplanalp Library (Portland Campus) provide access to over 150,000 volumes and print journals, more than 22,000 print and electronic full-text journal titles, and 6,000 electronic books.

Computer laboratories are conveniently located throughout each campus and in each library (also providing access via the Internet to many computer databases) along with campus-wide wireless technology service. Other academic facilities include Decary Hall, Gregory Hall, Marcil Hall, and Stella Maris Hall on the Biddeford Campus and Alexander Hall, Alumni Hall, Blewett Science Center, Coleman Dental Hygiene Building, Hersey Hall, Parker Pavillion, and Proctor Hall on the Portland Campus.

Both campuses also provide a variety of facilities in support of community life. The 55,000 square-foot Campus Center on the university Campus houses both a sports complex and student union. The sports complex includes a gymnasium with indoor track, collegiate swimming pool, fully equipped fitness center, racquetball courts and athletic training room. The student union provides multipurpose rooms, snack bar, University bookstore, and offices. The Finley Recreation Center on the Portland Campus provides a variety of fitness, health, wellness, and recreational programs and includes a gymnasium, fitness center, and multi-purpose room. Both campuses provide residence halls and dining halls for residential students. The University Campus has nine residence halls, including the recently completed Featherman Hall. The Portland Campus has three residence halls.

TUITION, ROOM, BOARD AND FEES

For 2010–2011, full-time (12 to 18 credits) undergraduate comprehensive annual costs are $40,740. This includes:

Full-time tuition $28,300

Room and Board $11,410 (traditional double occupancy)

General Services Fee $1,030

FINANCIAL AID

In 2010–2011, 98.5% percent of all full-time freshmen received some form of financial assistance including scholarships, grants, loans and employment. The Financial Aid Office uses the Free Application for Federal Student Aid (FAFSA) as its primary application for institutional, federal, and state aid programs. The University of New England has a generous scholarship program based on academic performance, scholarships range from $2,000 to over $21,000 per year.

STUDENT ORGANIZATIONS AND ACTIVITIES

Both campuses offer a variety of cultural and social events.

The Student Senate plays a vital role in the student life at both campuses and supports various events and programs through funding derived from the General Services Fee.

The university encourages students to become involved in activities, clubs, and sports. Popular interests include scuba diving, skiing, hiking, biking, swimming, photography, and community service. There are over forty student clubs and organizations between the two campuses as well as an extensive student leadership development program.

UNE's Athletic Department operates an NCAA Division III varsity athletics program. Varsity sports for men are basketball, cross-country, golf, ice hockey, lacrosse, soccer, and ; varsity sports for women are basketball, cross-country, field hockey, lacrosse, soccer, softball, swimming and volleyball. Intramural teams in basketball, floor hockey, softball, skiing, and volleyball are popular.

ADMISSIONS PROCESS

The university welcomes applications from students who are seriously pursuing an education of high quality. UNE has a February 15th freshman application deadline, and a December 1st priority application deadline with a December 31st notification date. . Transfer and international students have a Dec 1st application deadline for January admission, and a March 15th application deadline for September admission. Applications received after deadline dates are reviewed on a space available basis.

Students applying for admission are expected to submit a completed application, a $40 nonrefundable application fee, transcripts of all academic work (high school and college), two letters of recommendation, a written essay and scores on either the ACT or SAT (TOEFL is required of students whose primary language is not English). International students must also complete an International Student Supplemental Application. Students applying for admission should have completed a curriculum that includes English, mathematics, science, and social sciences. Those considering majors in the life or health sciences should show strength and preparation in mathematics and science. All prospective students are strongly encouraged to visit the campuses of the University of New England for an information session and tour. Tours are held weekdays and on select Saturdays. Appointments may be requested by letter, online at our website, or telephone.

UNIVERSITY OF NEW HAVEN

AT A GLANCE

Founded in 1920, the University of New Haven is a private, co-educational institution that offers a wide range of majors in a small, intimate college environment. UNH attracts students who are interested in a Liberal Arts education with an emphasis on career preparation through internships, co-operative education, research, community service, and more! With nearly 100 different programs of study for 3,600 students, UNH offers a personalized experience that focuses on "experiential learning" reflecting the belief that students learn best if they are actively engaged in real-world applications of what they learn.

UNH is a leading provider of study abroad education, offering students over 300 options worldwide. Our partnerships with Cultural Experiences Abroad (CEA) and the Center for International Studies (CIS) allow our students to study in a number of different countries, experiencing global cultures in either a traditional college campus setting or at global campus centers in high profile cities like Barcelona, Madrid, Rome, Venice, London and Sydney. UNH also offers unique programs such as: our intensive study abroad program which offers 2-week abroad sessions with a UNH faculty member during intersession for six credits at a number of locations such as London, Dubai, Rome and more. We also offer our Freshman Semester Abroad program (FSA) where students study in Florence, Italy and Seville, Spain during their first semester of Freshman year.

As a member of the Northeast 10 Conference, UNH competes in 17 Division II varsity sports (8 men's and 9 women's) baseball, basketball, cross-country, football, lacrosse, soccer, softball, tennis, track, and volleyball. Opened in December 2007, the new 58,000-square-foot David A. Beckerman Recreation Center adds another dimension to athletic opportunities at UNH. It features a fitness center with aerobic equipment, weights, and televisions; multi-purpose rooms for yoga, aerobics, Pilates, spinning, and other wellness activities; two basketball/volleyball courts; a multi-sport court for rollerblading, floor hockey, indoor soccer, and other activities; an elevated indoor running track; and lounge areas including a juice bar/café.

LOCATION AND ENVIRONMENT

The University of New Haven is located in suburban West Haven, Connecticut. UNH is conveniently situated 75 miles from New York City and 135 miles from Boston. Only minutes away from the beautiful beaches along Long Island Sound, the university offers a shuttle to downtown New Haven and other local areas.

UNH offers a variety of types of residence options for students to choose from ranging from a traditional residence hall to apartment-style housing with suites of two or more bedrooms. In 2005, UNH started a Living Learning Community (LLC) program where students combine their residence hall and academic experience by interacting with faculty members outside of the classroom and living with students in the same academic area of interest as theirs. Participants also enjoy special trips and opportunities geared towards their major of interest. Currently, UNH offers LLC's in Business, Criminal Justice, Education, Engineering, Fire Science, Forensic Science, Interior Design, Marine Biology, Music/Music Industry/Music & Sound Recording, Academic Service-Learning (community service) and Freshman Connections (all other majors).

MAJORS AND DEGREES OFFERED

The University of New Haven mixes traditional degrees along with some unique programs throughout the four academic colleges. The College of Arts and Sciences offers traditional majors like Art, Biology, Biotechnology, Chemistry, Economics, Education (BA/MS), English, History, Liberal Studies, Mathematics, Psychology, and Political Science; as well as unique majors in the areas of Communication, Mass Communication, Dental Hygiene, Environmental Science, Global Studies, Graphic Design, Interior Design, Interior Design – Pre-Architecture, Marine Biology, Music, Music Industry, Music & Sound Recording, Nutrition & Dietetics, and Theatre Arts. The College of Business offers degrees in Management, Accounting, Finance, Hotel & Restaurant Management, Management of Sports Industries, Marketing, and Tourism & Event Management. The Tagliatela College of Engineering offers degrees in Chemistry, General Engineering, Chemical Engineering, Civil Engineering, Computer Engineering, Electrical Engineering, Mechanical Engineering, System Engineering, Computer Science, and Information Technology with concentrations in Web & Database Development, and Network & Security Administration. The Henry C. Lee College of Criminal Justice and Forensic Sciences offers degrees in Criminal Justice, Forensic Science, Fire Science and Legal Studies. UNH offers eight separate Criminal Justice degrees in Investigative Services, Crime Analysis, Law Enforcement Administration, International Justice and Security, Forensic Psychology, Juvenile and Family Justice, Victim Services and Corrections. The Henry C. Lee College of Criminal Justice and Forensic Sciences also contains four distinct degrees in the area of Fire Science: Arson Investigation, Fire Science Administration, Fire Science Technology and Fire Protection Engineering. The University of New Haven also has a fifth college called University College. University College houses areas like Graduate Admissions with nearly 30 graduate degree programs, the Center for Adult and Professional Studies, the Center for K-12 and Community Outreach, the Center for Corporate Education, and the ELS Language Center.

CAMPUS FACILITIES AND EQUIPMENT

Virtually all of the university's classrooms have been converted into "Smart Classrooms," where professors can seamlessly integrate multimedia presentations while sharing data with students in real time. "Smart Classrooms" feature an integrated system that includes an instructor workstation with touch-sensitive projection controls, document camera, DVD/CD and distributed sound.

The Marvin K. Peterson Library offers over 240,000 volumes, 1,400 print journal and newspaper subscriptions, electronic access to over 19,000 full-text journal and newspaper titles, approximately 550,000 pieces of microfiche, 12,000 volumes of microfilm, and 162,000 paper U.S. Government documents. Students have access to numerous Internet stations and ports throughout the library and recently a coffee shop and lounge area opened for students to study and take a break.

UNH offers a variety of facilities in each of our colleges where students can use hands-on methods to learn the latest techniques and trends in their respective fields. In the College of Arts and Sciences our facilities include a new Convergent Media Center, Digital Sound Recording Studio, Analog Sound Recording Studio, Additional Practice Sound Recording rooms, Music Ensemble Room, Multiple Music Practice Facilities, Communication Studio, Radio Station, Dental Center, Nutrition & Food Labs, Graphic and Interior Design Facilities, Field Courses in Marine Biology and Environmental Science in Long Island Sound and local marshlands, Dodds Theater, and Seton Art Gallery.

In our Criminal Justice and Forensic Science programs we have areas such as our National Crime Scene Training & Technology Center, our National Cold Case Center, the Henry C. Lee Institute of Forensic Science, our Cyber Crime Lab, a DNA Lab with state-of-the-art Genetic Analyzers, the Center for Victims' Rights, and Institute for Public Affairs. In our Fire Science program we have areas for students to study in such as our brand new Arson Investigation Lab with portable classrooms that are replicas of a living room, bedroom and kitchen. Students get to investigate an actual fire scene in a highly technological and controlled environment. Other facilities include our Fire Detection and Control Lab, Dynamics Lab, Sprinkler Lab, Crime Scene Training & Technology Center and Fire Equipment Display. Legal Studies students receive practical hands-on training in local law offices and courtrooms. They study alternative methods for resolving disputes through civil or criminal legal systems as well as the application of law to public policy concerns and governmental regulations. The Tagliatela College of Engineering was recently remodeled to incorporate Interdisciplinary Laboratory Classrooms where students work on hands-on projects using robots, fuel cells, and engineering design software, among other tools in the labs. All students have access to the following laboratories their Freshman year, they include: the Multidisciplinary Engineering Lab, the Instrumentation and Mechanics Laboratory, a Thermo/Fluids Laboratory, the Interfacing and Control Laboratory, the Computer Science/Computer Engineering Lab, the Steinhauser Study Center, multiple chemistry and chemical engineering labs and a fully-equipped machine shop. The College of Business uses a Student Enrichment Center featuring an internet café dubbed the Hazel Nut Café. The Hazel Nut Café is run by College of Business students as an experiential learning activity and the technologically advanced Communication laboratory. The College of Business also uses the Samuel S. Bergami Learning Center for Finance and Technology where students can work with cutting-edge software packages and data feeds that rival those found on professional trading floors.

TUITION, ROOM, BOARD AND FEES

Cost for the 2009–2010 Academic year is: Tuition – $28,250, Student Fees – $1,220, and Room & Board – $12,200.

SCHOLARSHIPS AND FINANCIAL AID

Students are automatically considered for merit-based academic scholarships by simply applying for admission to UNH. Students must complete their admission application by May 1 for the fall semester or by January 2 for the spring semester in order to be eligible for merit-based awards.

UNH offers generous financial assistance to qualified undergraduates in the form of state, federal, and proprietary funds. About 80 percent of current full-time students receive federal funds through the Federal Pell Grant, Federal Supplemental Educational Opportunity Grant, Federal Supplemental Opportunity Grant, Federal Work-Study, Federal Perkins Loan, Federal Stafford Student Loan, and Federal PLUS Loan programs. Connecticut residents are also eligible for state sponsored aid. In addition, some students receive financial assistance from other state funds or from private organizations and foundations. The priority deadline for Financial Aid is March 1 for the fall semester and December 1 for the spring semester. Students must fill out the Free Application for Federal Student Aid (FAFSA), which is available online at www.fafsa.ed.gov in order to be qualified for need-based aid at UNH.

STUDENT ORGANIZATIONS AND ACTIVITIES

The Undergraduate Student Government Association (USGA) oversees all aspects of undergraduate life, organizing campus social and cultural activities, supporting the student-run radio station and student-produced publications, and overseeing the budget for all undergraduate organizations.

There are more than 100 campus clubs and organizations, including chapters of several professional societies, religious groups, social clubs, student councils, cultural clubs, and national fraternities and sororities.

ADMISSIONS PROCESS AND VISITING CAMPUS

UNH has an Early Action Admissions Policy; we begin to review applications on September 1st and continue until programs are filled. UNH offers three non-binding admission programs for fall admission. To be considered for certain programs applicants must follow the established timelines and important dates. Early Action I Applications are due by November 15, Early Action II Applications are due by January 15, Regular Decision Applications are due after January 15, and Spring Admission Applications are due by Mid-January. Students who apply under Early Action I are eligible for a number of different benefits if they meet the enrollment deposit deadline which include consideration for additional scholarships, early class registration, living learning communities, housing preferences, honors program and freshman study abroad opportunities.

Students may apply using our online application or paper copy, the Common Application or the Universal Application. To be considered for admission, candidates must complete the application form and submit it along with a nonrefundable $75 paper application fee or $25 online application. An application is considered complete once we receive the application, personal essay, transcript(s), standardized test scores (SAT I or ACT), and one letter of recommendation.

We encourage all prospective students and their families to visit us and see what the University of New Haven has to offer. UNH offers a variety of campus visits for students and their families to choose from seven days a week! Visits to choose from include daily campus information sessions and tours, Open Houses, Summer Preview Days, Enhanced Visits, Accepted Student Days, Charger Days, Explore UNH Days and much more! To view our campus visit calendar and register for an event, visit our website at www.newhaven.edu/visitus.

On-Campus Interviews are an opportunity for a prospective student to learn more specific information about programs and opportunities, and enables our Admissions Staff to ensure that our university fits the needs of the student. For those students who cannot make a trip to campus UNH offers a number of Regional Interviews during the fall where students can be interviewed in or near their hometown.

For further information about the University and admissions, students may contact:

Office of Undergraduate Admissions

Phone: 203-932-7319 or Toll-free 800-DIAL-UNH ext. 7319

Fax: 203-931-6093

E-mail: adminfo@newhaven.edu

Or visit our website: www.newhaven.edu

UNIVERSITY OF OREGON

AT A GLANCE

At the University of Oregon (UO), you'll be part of a community dedicated to making a difference in the world. Whether you want to change a community, a law, or one person's mind, the UO will provide you with the inspiration and resources you'll need to succeed.

You'll discover that many of the UO's academic programs are internationally recognized for academic excellence. The architecture, sustainable design, chemistry, economics, English, psychology, molecular biology, biochemistry, physics, neuroscience, special education, entrepreneurship, and sports business programs all rank among the top ten in the U.S. Programs in comparative literature, finance, historic preservation, and mathematics rank in the top twenty in the U.S.

With a student-teacher ratio of 19:1 and an average class size of 22 students, you'll find it's easy to connect with faculty members and your peers. You'll also have all the resources of a major research university, with 271 comprehensive academic programs (including new programs in cinema studies, African studies, Latin American studies, and queer studies) and more than 250 student organizations.

Set in a 295-acre arboretum, the University of Oregon is aesthetically and environmentally green. Academic programs and student activities will bring you to the forests, mountains, and rivers of Oregon's wilderness areas. The world's first green chemistry teaching methods were developed by UO students and faculty. The Lillis Business Complex was the first certified green business school facility in the United States. Students have access to nationally recognized programs in sustainable business, architecture, and technology. Our Campus Recycling Program is a national award-winner, and the university recently signed an agreement to eliminate the UO's carbon footprint.

You'll learn to see the world differently, attending classes alongside students from all fifty states, three U.S. territories and eighty-five countries. You'll learn from people with religious, cultural, and ethnic heritages different from your own. Your global degree options include 28 languages, as well as international, ethnic, religious, African, Asian, Latin American, Judaic, and Russian and East European studies. The UO offers 165 study programs in 95 countries. You'll experience the history, arts, social institutions, customs, and beliefs of new cultures, all while earning credit toward your UO degree. The IE3 Global Graduates Program offers new UO alumni professional experience in internships worldwide.

LOCATION AND ENVIRONMENT

The UO is located in the center of Eugene (metropolitan area population 343,140), a classic college town that's small enough to bike across but large enough to offer diverse art, music, and social venues. The Hult Center for the Performing Arts and the Grammy-winning Oregon Bach Festival lure a variety of nationally acclaimed musical acts each year. *Rolling Stone* included Eugene in its list of top ten college towns that rock.

Eugene loves the outdoors, offering more than 100 city parks, 250 miles of bicycle trails, rock climbing areas, and beautiful public gardens, all within the city limits. Getting here is easy. Eugene is served by several major airlines and is on the main north-south Amtrak artery connecting Seattle and San Diego.

With 19 NCAA Division 1 teams, as well as 44 club sports, you'll have your choice of sports to play or teams to cheer for. The excitement begins in the fall, when you'll root for the Ducks' football team at Autzen Stadium. In the winter, the men's and women's basketball teams thrill the crowds at the state-of-the-art Matthew Knight Arena. In the spring, UO track stars compete at the world-famous Hayward Field, often the site for NCAA championships and U.S. Olympic Track and Field Trials.

Three campus museums are valuable resources in the sciences and visual arts. The Jordan Schnitzer Museum of Art offers exhibitions of classical and contemporary art. The Museum of Natural and Cultural History features Native American artifacts, archaeological finds, and historically and scientifically significant items. Students appear in music, dance, and theater performances in newly refurbished facilities, including proscenium and "black box" performance spaces. Films, lectures, and cultural events are an everyday part of campus life.

OFF-CAMPUS OPPORTUNITIES

The Career Center offers off-campus internships in fields related to your academic major or extracurricular interests. Both paid and volunteer internships are widely available to all majors. The Global Graduates international program provides academic credit while you gain career experience through overseas internships.

Pine Mountain Observatory, near Bend, Oregon, offers study options in physics and astronomy. You can participate in an annual Archaeology Field School in central Oregon's Northern Great Basin. The Oregon Institute of Marine Biology on the Pacific coast gives you access to deep sea, coastal watershed, and estuary habitat.

Cooperatively run by students, the top-ranked Outdoor Program takes you beyond the campus to Oregon's great outdoors. You can choose from activities like snowboarding, skiing, rock climbing, hiking, surfing, white water rafting, and kayaking.

MAJORS AND DEGREES OFFERED

Undergraduate academic majors, minors, certificates, and preparatory programs offered include:

School of Architecture and Allied Arts

Architecture; art; art history; ceramics; community arts; digital arts; fibers; historic preservation; interior architecture; landscape architecture; material and product studies; metalsmithing and jewelry; multimedia; nonprofit administration; painting; photography; planning, public policy, and management; printmaking; product design; sculpture; and visual design.

College of Arts and Sciences

African studies; anthropology; Asian studies; biochemistry; biology; chemistry; Chinese; cinema studies; classical civilization; classics; clinical laboratory science-medical technology;° comparative literature; computer and information science; computer information technology; dentistry;° East Asian studies; economics; engineering;° English; environmental science; environmental studies; ethnic studies; European studies; folklore; forensic science;° French; general science; geography; geological sciences; German; German studies; Greek; health sciences;° history; humanities; human physiology; independent study; international studies; Italian; Japanese; Judaic studies; Latin; Latin American studies; law;° linguistics; marine biology; mathematics; mathematics and computer science; medicine;° medieval studies; nursing;° occupational therapy;° optometry;° peace studies; pharmacy;° philosophy; physical therapy;° physician assistant;° physics; podiatry;° political science; psychology; queer studies; religious studies; Romance languages; Russian and East European studies; Scandinavian; second-language acquisition and teaching; social work;° sociology; Southeast Asian studies; Spanish; theater arts; veterinary medicine;° women's and gender studies; and writing, speaking, and critical reasoning.

Charles H. Lundquist College of Business

Accounting; business administration with concentrations in entrepreneurship; finance; information systems and operations; management; marketing; sports business; and global management.

College of Education

Communication disorders and sciences; educational foundations; educational studies; family and human services; special education; and teacher education.°

School of Journalism and Communication

Communication studies; journalism; journalism: advertising; journalism: communication studies; journalism: electronic media; journalism: magazine; journalism: news-editorial; and journalism: public relations.

School of Music and Dance

Dance; music; music composition; music education; music education: elementary education; music: jazz studies; and music performance.

An ° denotes preparatory programs.

ACADEMIC PROGRAMS

The UO is on a quarter system, and you'll spend about one third of your education on each of three areas of course work: the general education requirements, requirements for your major, and elective credit. Your general education requirements will include courses in the natural sciences, social sciences, and humanities, as well as multicultural course work.

Freshman Interest Groups (FIGs) bring together a small group of first-year students interested in the same academic area in three related interdisciplinary courses. Freshman Seminars are small-group discussion courses taught by some of the UO's most outstanding faculty members. These academically rigorous FIG programs provide a helpful transition to college-level course work.

The Professional Distinctions Program gives you a competitive edge in the job market by complementing your major course work with a practical area of concentration. You'll build skills through career workshops, internships, and other professional experiences.

The Robert D. Clark Honors College offers the academic rigor of a small liberal arts college with all the resources of a major research university. The Clark Honors College (CHC) is a community of scholars—exceptional students and premier resident faculty members—who are actively engaged in the life of the mind. Your courses in the CHC will include 21 or fewer students, and complement any major. The CHC application process is competitive, with 200 spots available each year and applications averaging more than 1,000.

Upon acceptance to the UO, qualified students will be invited to join the College Scholars program. You'll have access to specialized courses, internship opportunities, and special scholarships. Faculty members provide assistance to develop your plan to achieve department honors or professional distinctions upon graduation.

CAMPUS FACILITIES AND EQUIPMENT

The University of Oregon Libraries, an Association of Research Libraries member, houses the largest research collection in the state, including 3 million volumes and 46,000 journal subscriptions, both print and electronic.

Wireless internet connection is available in all UO buildings, and computer labs are open in the library and residence halls, and in academic facilities across campus.

Science facilities at the UO are among the best in the nation. Research and laboratory courses offer students firsthand experience with electron microscopes and microprobes, advanced optical microscopy, seismic array, atomic absorption and emissions, and one of the only MRi units in the country in an educational setting. The new Lokey Laboratories offer advanced nanotechnology facilities.

TUITION, ROOM, BOARD, AND FEES
Resident

Undergraduate tuition and fees for the 2009–10 academic year: $7,428. On-campus residence halls, including room and board: $8,640 per academic year for double occupancy. Books and supplies: $1,050. Personal expenses: $2,412. Total: $19,530.

Nonresident

Undergraduate tuition and fees for the 2009–10 academic year: $23,718. On-campus residence halls, including room and board: $8,640 per academic year for double occupancy. Books and supplies: $1,050. Personal expenses: $2,412. Total: $35,820.

FINANCIAL AID

The UO makes a concerted effort to enable you to attend, regardless of your family's income. Financial aid in the form of grants, loans, and employment is available to qualifying students. 63% of our students receive scholarships and financial aid that are awarded through the federal government, university, and academic departments.

Eligibility information

To apply for financial aid, you must file the Free Application for Federal Student Aid (FAFSA) in early February. The UO's federal school code is 003223.

Incoming freshmen will be considered automatically for Dean's Scholarships, Staton Scholarships, Laurel Scholarships, and General University Scholarships by completing the UO admission application by January 15. The Presidential Scholarship and Diversity Excellence Scholarship require separate applications due January 15. For more information, visit financialaid.uoregon.edu.

- Dean's Scholarships are awarded each year to academically successful entering freshmen and range from $1,000 to $7,000 per year.
- General University and Laurel Scholarships are awarded each year and range from $1,000 to $2,000 per year.
- Presidential Scholarships are awarded each year to Oregon's brightest incoming freshmen in the amount of $7,800 per year, renewable for up to four years of study.
- Diversity Excellence Scholarships (DES) awards are tuition-remission scholarships with awards ranging from partial to full tuition and fee waivers.
- Staton Scholarships in the amount of $5,500 are awarded each year to incoming Oregon students with extraordinary financial need, and are renewable for up to four years. Students must apply for admission by January 15, 2011 and complete the FAFSA to receive consideration.
- Western Undergraduate Exchange (WUE) offers selected freshmen from certain western states the opportunity to study at the University of Oregon for 150 percent of UO resident tuition.

STUDENT ORGANIZATIONS AND ACTIVITIES

The Associated Students of the University of Oregon offers more than 250 student organizations, including cultural organizations, fraternities and sororities, student government, campus ministries, political groups, performing arts groups, international student clubs, and honor societies. Learn more at asuo.uoregon.edu.

The UO Student Vote Coalition led the nation in registering student voters in each of the past three presidential elections. The UO also ranks 11th in the nation for current Peace Corps volunteers.

ADMISSIONS PROCESS

The early notification deadline for fall 2011 is November 1, 2010. The standard admission deadline for fall 2011 is January 15, 2011. To be eligible for freshman admission, you must have a high school GPA of at least 3.00, be a graduate of a standard or accredited high school, and submit SAT or ACT scores. A cumulative GPA of 3.4 or better on a 4.00 scale and completion of at least sixteen units of academic course work qualifies you for automatic admission.

We require the following college-preparatory courses: Four years of English in preparatory composition and literature; three years of mathematics including first-year algebra and two additional years of college-preparatory mathematics; two years of science in such areas as biology, chemistry or physics; and three years of social science that could include one year of U.S. history, one year of global studies such as world history or geography, and one elective. Two years of the same second language in high school or two college terms of the same second language are also required.

Other factors considered for admission include the strength of high school course work, grade trend, class rank, and senior-year course load. Academic potential and special talents also are considered.

To apply, submit a completed application for admission, transcripts, SAT or ACT scores, and nonrefundable $50 application fee to the Office of Admissions.

For information and an application, contact:

Office of Admissions

1217 University of Oregon

Eugene, OR 97403-1217

USA

Phone: 541-346-3201

Toll-free: 800-BE-A-DUCK

Website: http://admissions.uoregon.edu

Virtual Tour: http://admissions.uoregon.edu/virtualtour

UNIVERSITY OF SAN FRANCISCO

AT A GLANCE

When the Jesuits founded the University of San Francisco in 1855, it was a one-room schoolhouse. Now, it is one of the West Coast's largest Catholic universities. Some things haven't changed: class size is still small, and student/faculty ratio is still low. USF has been dedicated to helping students learn the skills they need to improve their world for over 150 years. USF's Jesuit education is committed to providing all students with individual attention. Both love of learning and the willingness to face the challenge of serving society are fostered in programs in the arts, the sciences, business, education, nursing, and law.

San Francisco itself is a laboratory for students. The city and its university have interconnected histories, and today, this vibrant partnership gives students the wonderful opportunity to bring classroom theory into real, twenty-first-century life. There are 4,929 undergraduates on the 55-acre residential campus, and these students come from all 50 states and 80 countries. All students under the age of 21 and within two years of high school graduation must live on campus unless they have permanent residence within forty miles of the university. Students have access to facilities including libraries, a health and recreation center with an Olympic-size swimming pool, a coffeehouse, and several dining areas. Right outside is the city of San Francisco, and it has "facilities" of its own: the ballet, opera, museum exhibits, concerts, theater, and sports events. In addition, students have the opportunity to live with their peers in a cozy, laid-back environment within the residence halls. There are traditional residence halls and also University apartment-style facilities on campus. Both Hayes-Healy and Gillson Hall are for freshmen students. Sophomores are assigned to live in Phelan Hall, while most of the upperclassmen live in Lone Mountain Hall and Loyola Village. Double rooms are standard, but there are a few single rooms for upperclassmen. There are laundry facilities, study/computer rooms, and television lounges in every residence hall. Most floors in each dormitory also contain a community kitchen.

There are several dining facilities on campus that are convenient to the residence halls and classrooms. The Market has a dining environment similar to a food court with options for vegetarians and those who only consume organic foods. Other selections include a student-run coffeehouse, and a convenience store/cafe.

There are over 80 student-run associations for undergraduates at USF, including culturally focused clubs, leadership and community service organizations, honor and professional societies, and club sports and intramural programs. These associations include the oldest continuously performing theater group west of the Mississippi River: The College Players, an award-winning FM radio station, a weekly newspaper, and a literary magazine. The Career Services Center is one of the most active offices, aiding students in choosing a career path and learning about employment and internship opportunities. The exciting Koret Health and Recreation Center offers facilities for exercise, racquetball, swimming, court games, and socializing.

There are graduate programs in the arts and sciences, business, education, law, and nursing.

LOCATION AND ENVIRONMENT

The beautiful University of San Francisco campus is 55 acres, and is located in a residential neighborhood. Downtown San Francisco and the Pacific Ocean are just minutes away, and the 1,000-acre Golden Gate Park is only a few blocks away. There are many benefits of an urban campus, and San Francisco's diversity and compact geography allow students to discover research facilities, community involvement options, and work opportunities found in few other cities.

OFF-CAMPUS OPPORTUNITIES

USF students have many opportunities for university-sponsored study abroad programs, such as ones to Sophia University (Tokyo), Oxford (England), and Innsbruck (Austria) through USF's St. Ignatius Institute, a program at Universidad Iberoamericana in Mexico City, and a joint program with Hungary's Péter Pázmány Catholic University in Budapest. USF is connected to Gonzaga University's study abroad program in Florence (Italy) and to Loyola University of Chicago's program in Rome. The Institute of European and Asian Studies, of which USF is an associate member, offers programs in Durham and London, England; Paris, Dijon, and Nantes, France; Berlin and Freiburg, Germany; Vienna, Austria; Madrid and Salamanca, Spain; Milan, Italy; Tokyo and Nagoya, Japan; Moscow, Russia; Adelaide and Canberra, Australia; Beijing, China; and Singapore. There are many other study abroad opportunities as well. Students receive assistance from USF in all aspects of the program: choosing a location, completing applications, arranging financial matters, registering for academic credit, obtaining a passport and visa, and organizing travel plans.

MAJORS AND DEGREES OFFERED

BA and BS degrees are available through USF. The College of Arts and Sciences offers majors in Advertising, Architecture and Community Design, Arts History/Arts Management, Asian Studies, Biology, Chemistry, Communication Studies, Comparative Literature and Culture, Computer Science, Design, Economics, Engineering 3/2, English, Environmental Science, Environmental Studies, Exercise and Sports Science, Fine Arts, French, History, Latin American Studies, Mathematics, Media Studies, Performing Arts and Social Justice, Philosophy, Physics, Politics, Pre-Professional Health Studies, Psychology, Sociology, Spanish, Theology and Religious Studies, undeclared arts/science, and Visual Arts. The School of Business and Professional Studies offers degrees in Accounting, Business Administration, Entrepreneurship, Finance, Hospitality Industry Management, International Business, Management, and Marketing. Qualified high school graduates and second-baccalaureate candidates can pursue a four-year baccalaureate program through the School of Nursing. Students can receive teacher certification at the elementary or secondary level by completing a fifth year of study in the Dual Degree in Teacher Preparation program.

The Pre-Professional Health Committee at USF advises and recommends students to medical and dental professional health schools, as well as to schools for pharmacy, optometry, veterinary medicine, and podiatry. The pre-medical or other pre-health science requirements can be taken as part of, or in addition to, the requirements of an academic major. The Pre-Professional Health Committee helps students with the application process, creates a professional file for each student, gathers and sends recommendations to professional schools, gives interviews in preparation for application, and endorses approved candidates through a committee letter of recommendation that is sent to all professional schools the student selects.

ACADEMIC PROGRAMS

It is hoped that students leave USF with a well-rounded education and with a focus and awareness of social justice. A curriculum of 128 credits is required for the degree. General education requirements from six particular categories of knowledge make up 51 credits of the curriculum, including a nine-credit block of basic skills courses and 80 to 83 credits divided between major requirements and electives. Superior students may be selected for an honors program that provides a high academic challenge.

USF urges qualified high school students to study subjects traditionally reserved for colleges as early as possible. To this end, advanced placement courses, as certified by the College Board's Advanced Placement Program tests, are honored. USF also cooperates with the College-Level Examination Program (CLEP). Students interested in obtaining this credit are required to take the CLEP tests before registering for their freshman courses.

A special program is available through the St. Ignatius Institute. The Institute offers a distinguished Great Books curriculum – a historical sequence of courses based on classical works of literature, theology, and philosophy, from ancient Greece to the contemporary world.

Army ROTC is also available at USF, and qualified applicants and continuing students have access to ROTC scholarships.

Two semesters make up the academic year, and there are also summer sessions and a January intersession.

CAMPUS FACILITIES AND EQUIPMENT

USF students enjoy access to the more than 700,000 volumes at Gleeson Library and access to the Computer Center, the Applied Math Laboratory, the Institute of Chemical Biology, and the Physics Research Laboratories, all in the Harney Science Center. The Instructional Media Center is located in Cowell Hall, along with the home base of nursing classes and the Nursing Skills Laboratory. KDNZ and KUSF, the University's AM and FM radio stations, make their home in Phelan Hall. The Headquarters for the School of Business and Professional Studies is Malloy Hall, which also holds an additional computer laboratory and special seminar rooms.

TUITION, ROOM, BOARD AND FEES

Estimated cost of tuition for the 2008–2009 school year is $36,000. Room and board are $11,990 for the academic year. An additional $5,480 per year is generally required for books, fees, travel, and other expenses.

FINANCIAL AID

Many scholarships, grants, loans, and work-study programs are available for USF students, and all students must submit the Free Application for Federal Student Aid (FAFSA). Over two-thirds of all University students receive some form of financial assistance. Students have access to many jobs both on and off campus.

New freshman applicants with a minimum cumulative grade point average of 3.8 and a combined SAT I score of 1320 (Critical Reading + Math sections only) or an ACT composite score of 30 can participate in the University Scholars Program. University Scholars receive a non-need-based scholarship that covers a large portion of tuition costs for four years of undergraduate work. Scholars must maintain a GPA of 3.25 to remain eligible. Students eligible for University Scholars are identified during the admission process, and interested students must apply for admission by the November 15 early action deadline.

STUDENT ORGANIZATIONS AND ACTIVITIES

Every undergraduate student is a member of the Associated Students of the University of San Francisco (ASUSF). There are three purposes to the ASUSF: to represent the official student viewpoint, to recommend policies, and to fund activities and services. There are three branches: the executive branch, the Student Senate, and the Student Court. The main representative body of the undergraduate day students is the Senate, and it monitors the expenditures of the $200,000-plus student budget.

USF offers over 80 different clubs and organizations. They give students opportunities to be involved in leadership and professional organizations, honor societies, culturally focused clubs, fraternities and sororities, club sports and intramurals.

ADMISSIONS PROCESS

Admission is selective, and each application receives an individual review. USF desires a high-quality and diverse student body, and thus encourages applications from men and women of all races, nationalities, and religious beliefs. Prospective students are evaluated on many criteria, including high school grade point average, the application essay, a personal recommendation, and satisfactory test scores. All applicants must take the SAT I or the ACT, and international applicants must take the TOEFL or IELTS. A completed application file is made up of the application form, an essay, all academic transcripts, test scores, and one letter of recommendation. For the fall semester, November 15 is the deadline for early action and January 15 is the deadline for regular action.

For additional information, please contact:

Office of Admission

University of San Francisco

2130 Fulton Street

San Francisco, CA 94117-1046

Telephone: 415-422-6563

800-CALL-USF (toll free outside California)

Fax: 415-422-2217

E-mail: admission@usfca.edu

World Wide Web: www.usfca.edu

UNIVERSITY OF SCRANTON

AT A GLANCE

The University of Scranton is a Catholic and Jesuit university known for outstanding academic quality, a beautiful and technology-rich campus, and a sense of community that helps you feel right at home. At Scranton, you can feed your mind, find all kinds of friends and become part of a community that will enrich your spirit.

Located in Pennsylvania's Pocono Northeast region, our 56-acre hillside campus is in the heart of a city of 75,000, just two hours from New York City, Philadelphia and Hartford.

The University of Scranton is devoted to the Jesuit maxim of *cura personalis*, which for us means that we respect and cherish you for your unique talents and aspirations. We recognize the integral role that campus life plays in the overall education of the student. Because, in so many ways, learning does not stop at the classroom door, Scranton provides a range of activities and support services for leadership development, personal enrichment, and simply for fun and recreation.

Giving back to and partnering with the community are integral parts of The University of Scranton. The University is one of only 119 schools in the country that earned the 2008 Community Engagement Classification designated by the Carnegie Foundation for the Advancement of Teaching. This recognizes Scranton for success in curricular engagement and outreach partnerships. At the University, 160 courses have service-learning components and 11 academic departments have a service learning requirement.

Scranton faculty members have a passion for teaching. It shows in the innovative ways they engage students in the educational experience and is evident in their care for students as individuals. When it comes to scholarly activity, Scranton professors rival the best. Their works are published widely in prestigious scholarly journals. They are featured in national media and are frequent presenters at national and international conferences. Their research projects, many of which are conducted with the assistance of students, are often supported by competitive grants.

In a new ranking in 2010 edition, Scranton was third among the six Master's Universities in the North, and among only 80 in the nation, recognized for a "Strong Commitment to Teaching." According to U.S. News and World Report, this peer assessment ranking identifies "schools where the faculty has an unusually strong commitment to undergraduate teaching - schools that emphasize this aspect of academic life."

Our students are high achievers, too. Since 1972, University of Scranton students have received 124 Fulbright's and other prestigious fellowships. In addition, students earned four Truman Scholarships and seven Goldwater Scholarships in the past seven years alone. Of the 353 senior applicants to medical schools over the last 10 years, an average of 81% were accepted. In the past six years, nearly 300 Scranton graduates have received acceptance into at least 70 law schools throughout the United States, including some of the nation's most prestigious, such as Boston College, Cornell University, Duke University, Georgetown University and the University of Notre Dame.

Because more majors mean more opportunities for you, Scranton offers 59 bachelor's degree programs, 43 minors, 25 master's degree programs and a doctor of physical therapy program through four colleges and schools.

The University of Scranton is nationally recognized for its academic excellence. For the past 16 years U.S. News has ranked Scranton among the 10 finest master's universities in the North and named Scranton as one of only 77 "Up and Coming" schools to watch in the nation.

In addition U.S. News ranked the University 10th among "Great Schools at a Great Price," which relates academic quality to the cost of attendance. This is the fifth consecutive year Scranton has made this listing of just 15 schools in the nation. For the fourth consecutive year the University's Kania School of Management was included among the elite colleges listed in the U.S. News & World Report's "America's Best Graduate Schools."

For two consecutive years, the University has made the list of 600 universities published in Forbes.com's "America's Best Colleges. Also, Princeton Review listed Scranton among "The Best 371 Colleges" in the nation for the eighth consecutive year and the Kania School of Management among the "Best 301 Business Schools" for the fifth consecutive year. Barron's includes Scranton among only 247 colleges in the nation listed in the ninth edition of their "Best Buys in College Education" – only 19 schools in Pennsylvania made the list.

MAJORS AND DEGREES OFFERED

Majors are available in:

Accounting

Biochemistry

Biochemistry, Cell & Molecular Biology

Biology

Biomathematics

Biophysics

Business Administration

Chemistry

Chemistry/Business

Chemistry/Computers

Classical Languages

Communication

Community Health Education

Computer Engineering

Computer Information Systems

Computer Science

Counseling and Human Services

Criminal Justice

Cultural Studies

Early Childhood/Primary (Pre-K–4) Education

Economics (Business)

Economics (Social Science)

Electrical Engineering

Electronic Commerce

Electronics/Business

English

Environmental Science

Exercise Science

Finance

Forensic Chemistry

French

German

Health Administration

History

Human Resources Studies

Individualized Major

International Business

International Language/Business

International Studies

Italian

Management

Marketing

Mathematics

Media and Information Technology

Medical Technology

Middle School (Grades 4–8) Education

Military Science

Modern Languages

Neuroscience

Nursing

Occupational Therapy (Master's)

Operations Management

Philosophy

Physical Therapy (DPT)

Physics

Political Science

Pre-Engineering

Pre-Law

Pre-Medical

Psychology

Secondary Education

Sociology

Spanish

Theatre

Theology/Religious Studies

World Languages/Cultures

Applicants are also allowed to enroll in undecided areas and choose a major in their sophomore year.

CAMPUS FACILITIES AND EQUIPMENT

We've built 25 new buildings and renovated 38 others since 1984. The new Patrick & Margaret DeNaples Center opened in January 2008, providing 118,000 square feet of meeting, dining and office space in a building that is the hub of campus life. Christopher and Margaret Condron Hall, which opened in the fall of 2008, provides 386 beds of suite-style sophomore housing. The John & Jacquelyn Dionne Campus Green, dedicated in August 2008, provides a football field-sized green at the heart of campus. A new, 200,000 sq.ft. unified science center is slated for completion in the fall of 2011. In total, the University is investing more than $180 million in projects to transform its 56-acre campus.

TUITION, ROOM, BOARD AND FEES

Undergraduate tuition for freshmen in the 2009–10 academic year is $32,824, room and board charges are $10,990 and fees are $300.

FINANCIAL AID

Financial aid assists about 88 percent of freshmen, and includes scholarships, grants, loans and work-study. There are full- and partial-tuition academic scholarships available, which are awarded on a merit basis, taking into consideration high academic achievement and standardized test scores.

STUDENT ORGANIZATIONS AND ACTIVITIES

Because learning does not stop at the classroom door, we provide opportunities to participate in an array of social, educational, wellness and retreat activities.

You will be able to participate in more than 75 clubs and organizations. If your interests are journalism or writing you can become involved in *The Aquinas* (student newspaper), *Esprit* (literary journal), *Windhover* (yearbook) or Royal Network News (campus electronic news). You can become active in the arts through the University Players, University Bands and University Singers. You can develop as a leader through student government or explore politics with the Campus Democrats and College Republicans. You can even choose clubs that link to academic majors or that celebrate ethnic and cultural roots. And you can experience the satisfaction of helping others through Students for Social Justice, Habitat for Humanity and the Community Outreach Office.

Scranton fields NCAA Division III varsity teams in nine sports for men and nine sports for women. Our teams compete in NCAA Division III's Landmark Conference, a group of seven like-minded colleges and universities in the Mid-Atlantic states. In addition, more than 3,000 students each year participate in leagues, weekend special events and tournaments through the Intramural and Recreation Program.

ADMISSIONS PROCESS

Scranton welcomes men and women of all races, national origins and religious beliefs. We look for high-achieving students who have shown that they are prepared for a challenging college program through their high school course selection and level, grades, class rank and SAT/ACT scores. Also important are involvement in activities, athletics and service, and work experience. A campus visit with an informational interview or small group presentation is encouraged.

The University of Scranton offers an Early Action program with a November 15 deadline. Students who apply early will receive notification of admission on December 15. For students who choose not to apply for Early Action, we operate on a rolling admissions basis, with an application deadline of March 1 and a confirmation deadline of May 1. Students may apply without submitting SAT/ACT scores if they are in the top 20% of their graduating class. If their high school does not rank, students must have a GPA of at least 3.5 on a 4.0 scale. The SAT/ACT Optional application deadline is November 15.

THE UNIVERSITY OF TAMPA

AT A GLANCE

The University of Tampa is a private, medium-sized, comprehensive university in the heart of Tampa. The university offers exciting learning experiences in over 120 areas of study. All programs offer students a combination of challenging coursework and real world experience. Situated on a beautiful 100-acre campus, the university is adjacent to the Hillsborough River and downtown Tampa. Students enjoy a traditional self-contained campus, only steps away from the excitement and opportunities of the bustling city. At the center of campus lies Plant Hall, once a luxurious hotel for the rich and famous. This historical landmark is complemented by modern surroundings and excellent facilities including a student union, art studios and gallery, theatres, computer resource center, complete athletic facilities, science labs, and new residence halls. Over 6,200 students (5,200 full-time undergraduates) are enrolled at the university. UT students represent 50 states and over 100 countries. Students choose from more than 140 different clubs and organizations including honors societies, social clubs, Greek Life, community service and others. The University of Tampa has one of the top NCAA Division II sports programs in the nation, winning twelve national championships including recent championships in Baseball (2006 & 2007), Women's Volleyball (2006), and Women's Soccer (2007).

LOCATION AND ENVIRONMENT

Located on the west central coast of Florida, Tampa has far more to offer than just beautiful beaches and a pleasant climate. Tampa Bay is one of the fastest growing areas in the United States. The city is a leading center for the arts, international business, law, education, media, and health and scientific research. Forbes magazine and Newsweek magazine consistently pick Tampa Bay as one of the best places to live in the United States.

OFF CAMPUS OPPORTUNITIES

Across the river in downtown Tampa is the Museum of Art, Tampa Bay Center for the Performing Arts, the Florida Aquarium, the St. Petersburg Times Forum, and an outstanding public library. Busch Gardens is only several miles from campus and Walt Disney World and Universal Studios are only 90 minutes away. Tampa International Airport is five miles from campus

MAJOR AND DEGREES OFFERED

The University of Tampa offers Bachelor's degrees in accounting, advertising & public relations, art, athletic training & sports medicine, biochemistry, biology, chemistry, communication, criminology, digital arts, economics, education (elementary and secondary certification), electronic media arts & technology, English, entrepreneurship, environmental science, exercise science & sport studies, film & media arts, finance, financial services operations & systems, forensic science, government and world affairs, graphic design, history, international business, international & cultural studies, liberal studies, management, management information systems, marine science (biology and chemistry), marketing, mathematical programming, mathematics, music, music education, nursing, performing arts, philosophy, physical education, psychology, public health, social sciences, sociology, Spanish, sport management, theatre, and writing. Minors and concentrations are offered in adult fitness, advertising, aerospace studies, American Government, art history, arts administration & management, biology/business, biology/molecular, biology/organismal & evolutionary, business administration, dance/theatre, French, humanities, international studies, law & government, law & justice, military science, recreation, speech/theatre, urban studies, women's studies, and world affairs. Pre-professional programs offered include pre-dentistry, pre-law, pre-medicine, pre-veterinary science, allied health, art therapy, and chemistry. Certificate programs include early childhood education, European studies, French, German, gerontology, international studies, Italian, Latin American studies, Spanish and TESOL. An undergraduate Evening College (School of Continuing Studies) offers fifteen degree programs designed for adults who want to study part-time. Three summer sessions also offer excellent learning and professional advancement opportunities. At the graduate level, the business school offers the Master of Business Administration degree and Master of Science degrees in accounting, finance, innovation management, and marketing. A Master of Science in Nursing, Master of Arts in Teaching, and Master of Education degrees are also offered to students.

ACADEMIC PROGRAMS

The University of Tampa's undergraduate curriculum is designed to give students a broad academic and cultural background as well as a concentrated study in a major. Students complete a comprehensive core curriculum known as the Baccalaureate Experience, which is highlighted by the unique and innovative first year program known as Gateways. Gateways is an extensive orientation program which encourages student development via exploration of global issues, career possibilities, and development of critical thinking and communication skills. International experience has always been a major focus at the University of Tampa. Students are essentially educated and prepared to live and work internationally. Academic opportunities in this area are available to students immediately and in 2010 there are over 20 faculty led study abroad opportunities available to students. For qualifying students, the university has a rigorous and rewarding Honors Program of expanded instruction and student research.

CAMPUS FACILITIES AND EQUIPMENT

$230 million has been invested in new academic facilities, technology, and residence halls since 1998, making this national historic landmark the model of a modern university. 85% of all residence halls are new within the last decade and most of the others have been renovated. The Vaughn Student Center and residence hall complex serves as the hub of student life. Here students find food courts, a two-story cyber cafe, recreational areas, the Reeves Theatre, student office space, Barnes & Noble campus store and a 9th floor conference center with magical views of downtown Tampa. The new Stadium Center residence hall opened in Fall 2007 with state-of-the-art amenities and eight separate dining venues. Other outstanding facilities and resources include The John H. Sykes College of Business, a waterfront Marine Science Field Station and research vessels, the library's online computer catalog system, the Ferman Music Center, Reeves Theatre, 1,000-seat Falk Theatre, the R.K. Bailey Art Studio, and excellent sports facilities. The $20 million Sykes Center for Faith and Values is currently under construction and will open in 2010.

TUITION, ROOM, BOARD, AND FEES

The cost for the 2009–2010 academic year is $22,482 for tuition & fees and $8,296 for room & board. The average financial aid award for students at the University of Tampa in 2009 was $17,500 with 91% of students receiving financial assistance.

FINANCIAL AID

A high-quality, private education at the University of Tampa presents students with exceptional value and is not as difficult to finance as some students may think. Each family's situation is evaluated individually for need-based assistance. Academic achievements, leadership potential, athletic skills, and other special talents are also recognized, regardless of need. Academic scholarships are awarded to all entering first year students with a 3.0 unweighted grade point average or above. Transfer, leadership, departmental, Phi Theta Kappa, International Baccalaureate and ROTC scholarships are also available.

STUDENT ORGANIZATIONS AND ACTIVITIES

Students choose from more than 140 student clubs and organizations including honors societies, social clubs, and community service groups amongst many others. Visit The University of Tampa website at www.ut.edu to learn more about student organizations and activities.

ADMISSIONS PROCESS

The University of Tampa is an academically competitive institution that offers several non-binding early action admission dates. Check The University of Tampa website at www.ut.edu for specific admission details.

School Says . . .

UNIVERSITY OF WYOMING

AT A GLANCE

The University of Wyoming (UW) combines major university benefits and small-school advantages, with more than 180 programs of study, an outstanding faculty, and world-class research facilities all set against the idyllic backdrop of southeastern Wyoming's rugged mountains and high plains. As a major research institution, UW's research goals, which benefit Wyoming and the world, are continually being pushed to the boundaries and beyond by its professors and students. It is this academic ambition that has allowed UW to provide high-quality undergraduate and graduate education, research, and service since 1886. UW continues to remain true to its goal of serving the educational needs of students today while preparing them for the complex world of tomorrow. UW's number of Rhodes, Goldwater, and Truman Scholars in the past decade demonstrates this commitment.

Wyoming, unique among the 50 states, has only one university. UW enjoys tremendous support from within its state as well as from an alumni network that spans the globe. More than 12,538 students from all parts of the U.S. and 77 other countries attend UW classes in Laramie and at outreach sites around the state. The variety of students at UW enriches the educational experience for all by fostering a multicultural environment that encourages sharing and learning about those with different heritages and cultural backgrounds. It is this dialogue that continues to promote respect and appreciation for diversity. Undergraduate education is a high priority at UW with 91 percent of undergraduate courses taught by faculty and not graduate assistants. With an average class size of 29 students, UW students receive more individual attention in the classroom making their educational experience rewarding and valuable.

Opportunities for excitement and involvement are abundant at UW! There are more than 200 recognized campus clubs and organizations, including 16 national fraternities and sororities, honor and professional societies, political and religious organizations and special interest groups. Students also have the opportunity to participate in over 60 different intramural and club sports. UW competes in the Division I NCAA Mountain West Conference athletics in 17 men's and women's sports. UW houses 2,400 students in six residence halls and freshmen are required to live on campus their first year. While primarily coed, the residence halls offer a number of unique living environments, including quiet/study floors, special interest floors, honors floors, single sex floors and other academic living environments.

ACADEMICS

Being a student at UW offers you more than just a first-rate education experience, it offers you an adventure and a challenge. The University of Wyoming is a welcoming community of 12,500 students with the benefits of a larger university; such as awesome research opportunities and NCAA Division 1-A athletics while still having the individual feel of a small school with reasonable class sizes and individual attention.

The UW academic calendar consists of two semesters and a complete summer session. Depending on their degree program, students will be required to complete 120 to 157 credit hours for graduation. Undergraduate programs for most majors can be completed in four years. Student may choose to double major within the same college or they may pursue majors in two separate colleges for a cross college major. Minors are also available in many areas. UW offers a unique breadth of academic programs of study because it is the only four-year public university in Wyoming. Students entering undecided or who want to tailor their education have many options. UW hosts colleges in Agriculture, Arts & Sciences, Business, Education, Engineering and Applied Science, and Health Sciences. At a professional level, UW also has a Law School and Pharmacy School.

UW prepares students to choose rewarding careers and to lead successful lives that make positive contributions in a complex multicultural society. This foundation is centered in the University Studies Program, which provides students a core curriculum that assists in developing oral and written communication, mathematics, science, diversity, global awareness, government and cultures. The University Honors Program provides academically ambitious undergraduates innovative and intellectual learning opportunities. Award-winning faculty, unique and challenging course work and senior research projects are the hallmarks of this program. UW is also committed to providing its students an international experience through actively recruiting international students and providing resources for students to study abroad.

ADMISSIONS

High school graduates with less than 30 transferable college credit hours should have successfully completed thirteen high school courses that include 4 years of English, 3 years of mathematics, 3 years of science (including a physical science), and 3 years of cultural context courses (behavioral or social sciences, visual or performing arts, humanities or foreign languages). A minimum cumulative grade point average (GPA) of 3.0 and an ACT score of 20 or combined math and verbal SAT score of 960 is required for admission. Admissions with conditions is available to students who do not meet these standards but have a minimum 2.25 GPA and an ACT score of 20 or an combined math and verbal SAT score of 960. Transfer students with 30 or more transferable semester credit hours must have a minimum cumulative GPA of 2.0. To be considered for admission, students must submit a completed UW Application for Admission, submit official high school/college transcripts, submit ACT or SAT scores, and pay a $40, non-refundable application fee. Students may apply and pay the application fee online at the address listed below. UW strongly encourages all prospective students and their parents to visit the campus.

For more information or to schedule a campus visit, students should contact:

Admissions Office

Department 3435

1000 East University Avenue

Laramie, Wyoming 82071

Telephone: 307.766.5160

800. DIAL.WYO (342.5996) (toll free)

Email: why-wyo@uwyo.edu

World Wide Web: www.uwyo.edu

CAMPUS FACILITIES AND EQUIPMENT

UW's students, faculty and staff are what make the university truly exceptional. The modern facilities of the campus reinforce UW's commitment as an extensive research university to both students and faculty. In the last five years UW has spent more than $120 million on major renovation and building projects and another $200 million in construction projects are underway. Students have the opportunity to take classes in state of the art classrooms while benefiting from the individual attention UW offers.

CAMPUS LIFE

Students at the University of Wyoming have lots of opportunities to be involved; with UW having over 200 recognized student organizations. There is an organization to fit everyone's interests, from honoraries to Greek life to religious groups to sports activities. Check out all the current groups available by going to www.uwyo.edu/rso.

Whether you like to hit the slopes or dance the night away you'll find plenty to do when you're not hitting the books. The Laramie landscape is an outdoor playground providing opportunities for rock climbing, skiing/snowboarding, hiking, biking, and much more just 15 minutes from campus. If indoor entertainment is more your style, the university brings a wide variety of national art, international culture, concerts and an array of entertainment acts to campus. If that's not enough, Denver and the Colorado Front Range is just a short drive away. At UW, it's the best of both worlds: the comfort of being educated in a "college town" with the adventure opportunities of the great outdoors and the bustling city life.

COLLEGE BASICS

The University of Wyoming ranks among the top research universities in the United States, but still maintains comfortable class sizes and a hands-on approach to learning.

TUITION AND FEES

UW tuition and fees for full-time undergraduates for the 2010–11 academic year are $3,927 for Wyoming residents and $12,237 for nonresidents (figures based on an average class load of 15 credit hours). Room and Board (dual occupancy, unlimited meal plan) in the 2010–11 academic year is $8,360. Other estimated expenses include $1,200 for books and supplies, $889 for travel expenses, and $2200 for personal expenses.

FINANCIAL AID

Nearly 90 percent of all UW students receive financial assistance to attend UW. Over $85 million is available to UW students through the form of scholarships, loans, grants and work-study opportunities. The Free Application for Federal Student Aid (FAFSA) is required for need-based assistance (loans, grants, work-study) and also for scholarships. The priority deadline for financial aid is March 1st. Most scholarships at UW are based on academic merit. UW participates in the Western Undergraduate Exchange (WUE), and offers the Rocky Mountain Scholars Award up to $20,000 ($5,000/year for four years) for non-resident students. For more information on scholarships and how to qualify, go to www.uwyo.edu/scholarships.

School Says . . .

VANDERBILT UNIVERSITY

AT A GLANCE

In 1873, Commodore Cornelius Vanderbilt endowed Vanderbilt University in the hope that it would "strengthen the ties which should exist between all sections of our common country." Today, Vanderbilt is a highly selective, medium-sized university with a total enrollment of just over 12,000. In line with the Commodore's dream, students join the campus from all over the country and around the world.

Vanderbilt has 6,794 undergraduates, and all entering students are required to live on campus for four years. On-campus residence halls are shared by students in all four undergraduate schools. The university has a strong sense of community, and the housing staff works with the Vanderbilt Student Government to organize social, cultural, and educational events on campus. On-campus housing options include traditional single and double rooms, apartments, townhouses, and suites. About 42 percent of undergraduates participate in Greek life, and though fraternities and sororities do not have residential houses, Greek organizations play an active role in undergraduate life.

First-year students live at The Commons, a living-learning residential community comprised of 10 residence houses, The Commons Center, and the Dean of Commons residence. A faculty member lives in each of the residence houses, serving as a mentor to students and working with elected students from the house to design programming throughout the year. The Commons Center includes dining facilities, a health club, post office, mini-market, and a coffee bar open 24 hours a day. Students also frequent the Sarratt Student Center which houses recreational facilities such as a movie theater, a ticket box office, a pub, student organization offices, meeting rooms, an art gallery, and facilities for the student produced radio station and newspapers. Other student facilities include a state-of-the-art recreation center.

ACADEMICS

Students apply to one of the four undergraduate schools: the College of Arts and Science, the School of Engineering, Peabody College of Education and Human Development, and the Blair School of Music. The College of Arts and Science provides all Vanderbilt students the opportunity to experience a wide range of academic disciplines and subjects. Through AXLE (Achieving eXcellence in Liberal Education), students refine their skills in writing, mathematics, foreign languages, the humanities, natural sciences, and the social sciences. The School of Engineering educates engineers for practice in industry, government, consulting, teaching, and research careers. In addition to technical courses, each student's program includes a rich complement of course work in the humanities and social sciences, resulting in a balanced foundation for future achievement and for the assumption of leadership roles in his or her chosen field. The curriculum at Peabody College allows students to pursue a traditional teaching degree or to study human and organizational development, child development, child studies, or cognitive studies. All Peabody students receive a strong liberal arts foundation, combined with a solid program of pre-professional courses and a multitude of internship and practicum opportunities. Peabody undergraduates must complete requirements in communication, the humanities, mathematics, the natural sciences, and the social sciences. The Blair School offers majors in composition and theory, musical arts, musical arts and teacher education, and performance. Instruction is available in all orchestral instruments, as well as piano, organ, euphonium, multiple woodwinds, saxophone, classical guitar, and voice. The curriculum combines intensive musical training with liberal arts studies.

ADMISSIONS

Vanderbilt seeks accomplished students who are prepared to benefit from a demanding undergraduate program. The Admissions Committee evaluates every aspect of a candidate's application and achievements, both academic and extracurricular. The typical applicant will have completed 20 or more units in a challenging high school curriculum, including at least two years of foreign language study. School of Engineering applicants must complete at least 4 units of mathematics; calculus and physics are strongly recommended. Admissions decisions are based on strength of high school transcript, standardized test results (either the SAT Reasoning Test or ACT with Writing), personal essays, official recommendations, and extracurricular activities. SAT Subject Tests are not required. In addition to completing standard application materials, candidates for the Blair School of Music must audition on their primary instrument. Campus visits are recommended for all prospective students although a student's demonstrated interest in Vanderbilt is not a consideration in admissions decisions. Students should visit http://admissions.vanderbilt.edu to learn more about group information sessions, campus tours, half-and full-day visit programs, and opportunities to attend classes and to "shadow" a current Vanderbilt student. Vanderbilt does not conduct on-campus interviews, but optional alumni interviews are available in many locations. Vanderbilt offers Early Decision for students who have selected Vanderbilt as their first choice. Early Decision I applications are due November 1; admissions decisions are mailed by December 15. Early Decision II applications are due January 3, with a response date of February 15. Regular Decision applications are due January 3, and a decision will be mailed by April 1. Vanderbilt exclusively accepts the Common Application for both freshman and transfer admission. Applicants must submit "Part 1: The Vanderbilt Common Application Supplement," the Common Application, and a $50 application fee. Part 1 and the application fee may be submitted before or with the Common Application itself. All parts of the application should be submitted electronically or postmarked by the appropriate deadline.

CAMPUS FACILITIES AND EQUIPMENT

Vanderbilt University sits 1.5 miles southwest of downtown Nashville on a 330-acre, park-like campus that was designated a national arboretum in 1988. The university comprises over 200 buildings, including a world-class medical center, 44 residence halls, and 9 libraries. The most recent additions to campus include The Commons Center, and 10 new or newly renovated residence houses designed specifically for first-year students. Seven of these buildings have received the gold LEED (Leadership in Energy and Environmental Design) certification. Other recently completed buildings include Buttrick Hall, which houses several interdisciplinary centers, the Ingram Studio Arts Center, and an 18,000 square foot Student Life Center. In addition, the Historic Old Gym has been renovated recently as part of the Office of Undergraduate Admissions.

CAMPUS LIFE

Vanderbilt Student Government is responsible for maintaining a lively educational atmosphere on campus. Elected representatives of VSG work in conjunction with the nearly 400 student-run organizations to bring noted speakers and events to campus. Students can join a variety of pre-professional, cultural, religious, political, and social organizations. Vanderbilt's Honor Code has governed the undergraduate academic experience since the first final examination in 1875. Every year, one senior has the honor of serving a four-year term as the Young Alumni Trustee of the university's Board of Trust. Vanderbilt has a thriving college athletics program. Recent accomplishments include the football team's Music City Bowl victory, a trip to the Sweet Sixteen for the men's basketball team, Southeastern Conference regular season and tournament championships for the baseball team, and a national championship for the women's bowling team. A founding member of the SEC, Vanderbilt sponsors 16 Division I (FBS) teams.

LOCATION AND ENVIRONMENT

Vanderbilt is located in the city of Nashville, home to a diverse population of 1.25 million and marked by a special touch of Southern charm. As the capital of Tennessee, Nashville is an important cultural and commercial hub in the mid-South, and is often referred to as Music City. Located equidistant from the northern and southern U.S. borders, Nashville sits at the intersection of three major interstate highways, and the international airport is served by all major airlines . Beyond the city limits, the surrounding area contains 81 parks and recreation areas, and over 30,000 acres of lakes, offering ample opportunity for sports year round.

MAJORS AND DEGREES

Degrees are offered in African American and Diaspora studies; American studies; Ancient Mediterranean studies; anthropology; Asian studies; art; biological sciences; biomedical engineering; chemical engineering; chemistry; child development; child studies; civil engineering; classical languages; classics; cognitive studies; communication of science and technology; communication studies;; computer engineering; computer science; earth and environmental sciences; East Asian studies; ecology, evolution, and organismal biology; economics; economics and history; education (early childhood, elementary, secondary, and special education); electrical engineering; engineering science; English; English and history;film sutdies; French; French and European studies; film studies; German; German and European studies; history; history of art; human and organizational development; Italian and European studies; Jewish studies; Latin American studies; mathematics; mechanical engineering; medicine, health, and society; molecular and cellular biology; musical arts; musical arts and teacher education; music composition and theory; music performance; neuroscience; philosophy; physics; political science; psychology; public policy studies; religious studies; Russian; Russian studies; Russian and European studies; sociology; Spanish, Spanish and European studies; Spanish and Portuguese; Spanish, Portuguese, and European studies; theatre; women's and gender studies; and individually designed majors.

OFF CAMPUS OPPORTUNITIES

During their undergraduate career, students are encouraged to study overseas in Vanderbilt's approximately 80 programs worldwide. Study abroad provides students the opportunity to develop language skills and a deeper cultural awareness. Students receive course credit for overseas study and do not pay extra tuition to participate in programs abroad; financial aid packages also apply to all Vanderbilt study abroad programs. Students may also participate in programs sponsored by other universities.

TUITION AND AID

About 60 percent of the university's undergraduates receive some type of financial aid. Vanderbilt's undergraduate admissions process is need-blind for domestic students, and the university will meet 100% of demonstrated need for all admitted students. Need-based aid is awarded based on the CSS/Financial Aid PROFILE and the FAFSA. Beginning with the entering class in 2009, Vanderbilt no longer includes need-based loans in financial aid packages. Need-based loans have been replaced with a combination of grant, scholarship, and work-study assistance from various sources including Vanderbilt, federal, state, and private entities. Under certain conditions and based upon individual family circumstances, loans from federal and other sources may be made available to students upon their request.

Vanderbilt awards merit-based scholarships to approximately 5% of first-year applicants who demonstrate exceptional accomplishment and intellectual promise. Three signature scholarship programs comprise the majority of these honor scholarships. Recipients are guaranteed full-tuition awards, plus summer stipends for study abroad, research, or service projects. All three programs require a separate application in addition to the application for admission. The signature programs are the Cornelius Vanderbilt Scholarships (for students who combine outstanding academic achievements with strong leadership and contributions outside the classroom), the Ingram Scholarships (for students who have demonstrated an exceptional commitment to community service), and the Chancellor's Scholarship (for students who have worked to build strong high school communities by bridging gaps among economically, socially, and racially diverse groups). Vanderbilt also offers scholarships to National Merit and National Achievement Finalists.

TUITION AND FEES

The costs for 2009–2010 include: tuition, $37,632; room and board, $12,650; books and supplies, $1,292; and the student activities and recreation fee, $946. First-year engineering students are required to have a laptop computer which meets requirements specified by the School of Engineering. All costs are subject to change.

VAUGHN COLLEGE OF AERONAUTICS AND TECHNOLOGY

AT A GLANCE

Located in New York City, Vaughn College of Aeronautics and Technology has offered a quality, small campus experience to students since 1932. We have an enrollment of more than 1,300 students, and offer master's, bachelor's and associate degree programs in engineering, technology, management, and aviation. What sets Vaughn College apart is its small size, unique faculty and student interaction, and ideal location in the heart of the New York metropolitan area. Additionally, Vaughn College is committed to making education affordable for students. Vaughn's reasonable tuition can be an important consideration in your decision-making process. In recent years, the opportunities generated by technology have crossed all segments of American industry. There is a high demand for jobs in electronics, engineering firms, computer software companies, fiber optics communication corporations, local, state and federal government, defense and airport authorities, as well as major transportation companies. Accordingly, our distinguished alumni enjoy positions in many varied fields, from airport management and engineering to manufacturing and electronics. They have built successful careers in organizations such as the Federal Aviation Administration (FAA), IBM and Xerox, Kodak, the Metropolitan Transit Authority (MTA), The Port Authority of New York and New Jersey (PANYNJ), United Technologies, Cessna Citation, and Sikorsky. The analytical, technical, and communications skills developed by more than 5,000 Vaughn alumni make them integral parts of any corporate team, as well as lifelong students of the high-tech world in which we all live.

ACADEMICS

All students in associate and baccalaureate degree programs complete a core curriculum as part of their degree requirements. The core curriculum is derived from the mission of the College and reflects what the institution believes is important and elemental to students' education and development. In general, the core instills in students critical-thinking skills, values appropriate to an educated person, the ability to communicate, and the curriculum provides context for advanced learning. The baccalaureate core consists of three components - academic skills (13 credits, including a year of English composition, a course in oral communication, and pre-calculus), the liberal arts (12 credits, including a year of world and American literature), and math and science (15 credits).

ADMISSIONS

Vaughn College offers equal educational opportunity to all students without regard to age, citizenship status, color, disability, marital status, national origin, race, religion, creed, veteran status, gender or sexual orientation. Applications are accepted throughout the year. Applicants for admission must provide: Vaughn College of Aeronautics and Technology admissions application an official copy of their high school transcript official college transcript(s) - if applicable a copy of their high school diploma or GED with scores immunization records SAT I for all bachelor of science applicants. The admissions counseling staff is available to advise applicants and their parents and to provide up-to-date advisement material to high school guidance offices. Each applicant is evaluated individually and is kept informed about his or her status by admission status notices, which are issued as changes in status occur. For more information, contact the office of admissions at: 1.866.6VAUGHN, ext. 118.

CAMPUS FACILITIES AND EQUIPMENT

Each laboratory provides the work/study environment suited to the requirements of each program. Students experience the technology that they will ultimately use once employed. This practical, hands-on experience helps qualify students for immediate employment upon graduation. From the new photonics laboratory to the CATIA/NASTRAN computer center, the College's faculty members are committed to providing students with the knowledge and tools they are likely to find in today's businesses. The flight simulator center, with its two FRASCAS, two Redbirds and one Canadair two-engine regional jet are major components of the flight students' experience on campus. Vaughn College has invested significant resources in its computing infrastructure. Network access to computing labs, classrooms, faculty offices and student is provided via a high-speed, fiber optic network backbone, with secure wireless access available in many academic and all residential locations.

All campus computer labs are equipped with state-of-the-art HP computers running Microsoft Office 2007 Professional edition, and many other industry standard software programs. These computing labs are used for teaching and learning during the day and are available for general student use during non-class hours. All labs are also equipped with high-speed laser printers.

In addition to providing well-connected academic and residential facilities, Vaughn College has also invested heavily in modern instructional technology. Twelve classrooms have been equipped with large screen computer and video projection equipment. While this audio-visual equipment is used to present course content in a digital format in the classroom, the College also provides digital access to course content outside of the classroom using an online learning management system. Both of these technologies serve to augment the traditional classroom based learning approach.

Plans are underway for the construction of a new library. The new library will incorporate the new technologies that are currently being used in the existing library in addition to providing more complete references to meet more of the needs of a traditional student body and new graduate-level academic programs. More information can be found on the College's Web site, www.vaughn.edu.

CAMPUS LIFE

Vaughn College supports a variety of student organizations. Activities are moderated by members of the faculty and staff. Distinguished professional societies have chartered student chapters. Students interested in joining should contact the office of student affairs.

LOCATION AND ENVIRONMENT

Vaughn College of Aeronautics and Technology is located at 86-01 23rd Avenue, Flushing, NY 11369. Located in the New York City borough of Queens, Vaughn offers many opportunities for a vast array of technology and aviation companies. Vaughn has a six-acre campus and is convenient to major transportation routes. As part of the institution's strategic plan, a 200-bed residential building just opened, a new master's degree in airport management and a bachelor of science in engineering have also been added.

MAJORS AND DEGREES

Vaughn offers master's, bachelor's and associate degree programs in engineering, electronic engineering technology, mechanical engineering technology, mechatronic engineering, flight, general management, airline management, airport management, aviation maintenance management, aviation maintenance, animation and digital technologies, aeronautical engineering technology, and air traffic control (a non-degree program). Most Popular Majors: general management, airline management, airport management, animation and digital technologies, electronic engineering technology, aircraft operations, and aviation maintenance technology. Most Interesting Majors: aircraft operations (flight), airline management, airport management electronic technology, general management, aeronautical, and engineering technology.

OFF CAMPUS OPPORTUNITIES

Vaughn is located in New York City and students can take advantage of every opportunity this amazing city has to offer.

STUDENT ORGANIZATIONS AND ACTIVITIES

Vaughn College supports a variety of student organizations. Activities are moderated by members of the faculty and staff. Distinguished professional societies have chartered student chapters. Students interested in joining should contact the office of student activities and development.

TUITION, ROOM, BOARD AND FEES

In 2009–10, full-time tuition (12 to 18 credits per semester) is $8,150. Students taking fewer than 11 credits pay $550 per credit. The semester fee, which covers the cost of orientation courses, Internet and computer usage, and student-support services, activities, and leadership programs, is $200.

Estimated fees for room and board are approximately $10,380, depending on room size and meal plan selected.

FINANCIAL AID

Vaughn College of Aeronautics and Technology provides financial aid packages, which may include scholarships, grants, loans and work study to students with strong academic records and/or demonstrated need. Counseling and assistance is available at the financial aid office at the College. All financial information is confidential to the extent possible.

Applicants for financial aid must complete the Free Application for Federal Student Aid (FAFSA) and a New York State Tuition Assistance Program (TAP) application if appropriate.

Financial aid is determined by a variety of factors, such as income, assets, family size and other family information. Every applicant has unique circumstances and the financial aid office is committed to helping students and their parents through the process. It is strongly recommended that students file for financial assistance as early in the year prior to enrollment as possible.

Financial aid eligibility requires that the student maintain satisfactory academic progress and program pursuit after enrolling.

WASHINGTON COLLEGE

AT A GLANCE

The first college of the new nation, Washington College was founded in 1782 to educate citizens for the vital task of democracy. With its close ties to the nation's founding, Washington College bears a history that distinguishes it among the nation's selective liberal arts colleges. George Washington was prominent among the colonial leaders who worked to establish this institution of higher learning, and his example continues to shape the Washington College experience.

We believe that a broad, general education in the liberal arts is not only mentally liberating, but also the most effective way to prepare you for a successful career and a productive life. In the first two years of college, we encourage you to explore many interests and to try new areas of study, to encounter different perspectives, and to challenge old ways of thinking. We also encourage our students to pursue creative endeavors, athletic competition, recreational activities and campus leadership roles.

LOCATION AND ENVIRONMENT

Washington College takes full advantage of its unique place in history, its distinctive setting in the environmentally sensitive Chesapeake Bay region, and its proximity to mid-Atlantic urban centers of political power through academic programs, internship opportunities and institutional partnerships. The College's setting on Maryland's Eastern Shore is an extension of the campus, serving as a personal learning laboratory for students' intellectual, social and personal growth. The C.V. Starr Center for the Study of the American Experience and the Center for Environment & Society were developed specifically to take advantage of the region's history, its rural and maritime cultures, and its natural resources. New to the curriculum this year is the Chesapeake Semester, a four-course immersion program devoted to helping students understand the complexity of issues affecting the health of the Chesapeake Bay and the people whose lives depend on it.

The College is set on the scenic Chester River on Maryland's Eastern Shore, between the Atlantic and the Chesapeake, just 75 miles from Washington, D.C.. The College maintains a small fleet of boats—including a new 46-foot research vessel used as a floating classroom—supporting coursework in underwater archaeology, marine and estuarine biology, environmental chemistry, and environmental studies; the College also boasts nationally ranked programs in rowing and sailing.

Small Campus, Big Opportunities

With a student body of 1,300 undergraduates, the College remains defiantly small in a world that more often values size and scale, and it celebrates the interaction between student and professor. The average class size is 17 students; only 1 in 7 classes has more than 25 students. Faculty reach beyond the classroom to create challenges and opportunities that expand students' intellects and creativity through collaborative research, through independent and self-directed study, and through the rigor of creating a senior project that demonstrates the power of a maturing intellect.

Washington College offers an array of internships and field experiences, including fellowships for the study of American history, internships with theatres and museums, model diplomacy programs, and a summer archaeology field school. Each year, the College sends one student to the Center for the Study of the American Presidency.

Writing Across the Curriculum

Washington College is recognized for its rich literary arts environment—the Rose O'Neill Literary House hosts a wonderful series of significant writers and editors supported by the Sophie Kerr Program, and each year, one graduating senior is awarded the Sophie Kerr Prize, the largest undergraduate literary award in the world. Last year's winner took home $68,000. Regardless of discipline, the College is committed to helping all students become better writers. Writing-intensive courses help cultivate students' proficiency in the language arts, as well as the sophisticated use of evolving information technologies.

Academic Enrichment

The Douglass Cater Society of Junior Fellows is the College's flagship academic enrichment program—one that rewards creativity, initiative and intellectual curiosity with competitive grants to support self-directed undergraduate research, internships and scholarship anywhere in the world. Membership is open to rising juniors and seniors, but the College's Presidential Fellows program, open to first-year students by invitation, puts you on the fast track to academic distinction. Presidential Fellows can opt to become Cater Apprentices, partnered with upperclass students who have completed Junior Fellows research projects. Both programs encourage students to get together for intellectual exchange and social outings.

Study Abroad

Washington College offers one of the most extensive study abroad programs of any small liberal arts college. Among more than 40 offerings are summer programs in international business (China) and economic development (Tanzania), yearlong exchanges in Morocco and Ireland, and semesters abroad in England and Japan.

MAJORS AND DEGREES OFFERED

With 46 majors and academic programs, Washington College provides you the opportunity to shape an academic program that fits your intellectual interests and career aspirations. In addition to major and minor fields of study, the College offers regional concentrations in studies of Africa, Asia, Latin America, the Near East and Western Europe.

We operate on a two-semester academic calendar. Students customarily complete four courses, or 16 credits, each semester, and choose a program of study at the end of the sophomore year.

Washington College awards the degrees of bachelor of arts and bachelor of science. In certain fields, we also offer programs leading to the master of arts degree.

ACADEMIC PROGRAMS

American Studies

Anthropology

Archaeology

Art and Art History

Behavioral Neuroscience

Biochemistry

Biology

Black Studies

Business Management

Chemistry

Chesapeake Regional Studies

Clinical Psychology

Computer Science

Creative Writing

Criminal Justice

Dance

Drama

Earth & Planetary Science

Economics

Elementary Education

Engineering 3+2

English

Environmental Studies

Geographic Information Systems

Gender Studies

History

Human Development

Humanities

Information Systems

International Literature & Culture

International Studies

Mathematics

Modern Languages

Music

Nursing 3+2

Pharmacy 3+4

Philosophy & Religion

Physics

Political Science

Pre-Law Studies

Premedical Studies

Pre-Veterinary Studies

Psychology

Secondary Education

Social Welfare

Sociology

CAMPUS FACILITIES

Washington College recently completed a capital campaign that has dramatically transformed the physical campus. The Gibson Performing Arts Center, opened in August 2009, is a glittering showcase offering several venues in which students can learn, rehearse, practice, perform and exhibit their works. The $24 million facility encompasses a main stage, an experimental theatre, music recital hall, and art gallery, as well as all the latest tools and technology that support professional-caliber theatres and exhibition spaces. An exhibition of 19th century landscape masterpieces marked the opening of the Kohl Art Gallery.

Just three months later, Washington College opened the doors of Hodson Hall Commons, a new dining hall and student center complex. The glass and brick structure features a large student lounge, a small theatre/café and several specialty eateries in addition to the main dining hall.

Chester and Sassafras Halls, completed in Summer 2009, were the first buildings on campus to utilize geothermal heating and cooling. *U.S. News & World Report* included Washington College among its Best Colleges offering "green" residence halls.

According to *Lacrosse* Magazine, Roy Kirby, Jr. Stadium is among the top ten venues for collegiate lacrosse in the nation. The stadium, completed in 2008, is the only Division IIII venue to make the cut. In 2009, Athey Park, the College's baseball park, was built to mirror Kirby Stadium.

Scientific Instrumentation and Technology

Our faculty and students use the latest technology to their best personal advantage, whether that's extracting, cloning and sequencing DNA in the lab, accessing primary sources for a Shakespeare project via the library's Early English Books Online database, or simply using an electronic dropbox to send a paper to your professor. The biology department recently acquired a Nuclear Magnetic Spectrometer to support student research. In the psychology department, students use brain mappers and eye trackers in experiments testing cognitive function. Archaeology students use a seabed scanning device and a Remotely Operated Vehicle (ROV) to search the Chester River floor for clues of Native American and colonial settlements, and to explore underwater wreckage.

TUITION, ROOM, BOARD AND FEES

Basic educational fees for 2009–2010

Tuition (full-time)	$34,690
Student Service Fee	$660
Campus Housing	$3,790
Meal Plans per year	
19/week	$3,670
14/week	$3,340

All first-year and transfer students pay a $210 orientation fee for the fall semester and $155 for the spring semester.

FINANCIAL AID

Washington College is committed to providing educational excellence and equity for all students. We strive to provide monetary assistance to students who can benefit from a Washington College education, but who, without such assistance, would be unable to attend. Washington College offers several types of financial aid to help qualified students meet their college expenses. College-sponsored tuition scholarships, tuition grants, work/study, and low-interest loans are available. In addition, eligible students can receive assistance from federal, state and independent aid programs.

National Honor Society members who are accepted to Washington College are automatically considered Washington Scholars, qualifying for $40,000 tuition scholarships ($10,000 for four years). Some students receive even more. Since 1996, approximately 50% of all entering freshmen have been NHS members. To qualify, students must be inducted into NHS before March 1 of their senior year.

STUDENT ORGANIZATIONS AND ACTIVITIES

We cherish our residential tradition for the abundant occasions it affords for around-the-clock academic, social and personal growth. Students may choose to go Greek, join special interest and co-curricular clubs ranging from Amnesty International to Writers Union, participate in program-specific honor society activities, or volunteer in the community. Nearly a third of our students compete in 18 different varsity sports, and another third participate in club sports and intramural activities. The Student Events Board offers a variety of activities that everyone on campus can enjoy. While students reap the benefits of living in one of the best small college towns on the East Coast and the relaxed informality characteristic of the Chesapeake Bay region, they also take advantage of the campus's proximity to three urban centers—Washington, D.C., Baltimore, and Philadelphia. From this corner of the world, students can easily step out into the broader community for internships, volunteer work and recreation.

ADMISSIONS PROCESS

Washington College is a selective institution. In order to assess an applicant's "fit" with the College, the Admission Committee requires the submission of all relevant academic records and test scores, an activity profile, an essay/personal statement, and two letters of recommendation. In some cases, an on-campus interview may also be required.

Prospective applicants are strongly encouraged to come to campus for an information session and tour. These visits should be scheduled in advance by calling 800-422-1782, ext. 7700.

Prospective students may apply online using the Common Application. Preference in admission and financial aid decisions is given to students who apply on or before February 1. Early Decision applicants have an application deadline of November 15; Early Action applicants have a deadline of December 1, and Regular applicants have a deadline of March 1. Admitted applicants must pay a $300.00 enrollment deposit by May 1. For details, visit www.washcoll.edu.

WEBBER INTERNATIONAL UNIVERSITY

AT A GLANCE

Webber International University was established in 1927 by world-renowned economist Roger Babson. This four-year nonaffiliated coeducational institution is situated on a stunning 110-acre campus perched along the Lake Caloosa shoreline. Webber International University's location offers students convenient access to popular attractions such as Disney World and Busch Gardens, among others. Webber receives its accreditation from the Southern Association of Colleges and Schools. The University prides itself on its strong tradition of high moral standards and exemplary academic achievement. Webber has cultivated an atmosphere that promotes success through hard work and scholastic merit. Roughly 160 women and 310 men are enrolled in Webber's undergraduate program. About 80 percent of those students are Florida residents; the remaining 20 percent come from 21 states across the nation and nearly 40 countries around the world. The University's off-campus placement programs provide students with practical, on-the-job business experience. Webber also offers field trips designed to enhance undergraduates' business education pursuits.

The University fields intercollegiate sports teams in baseball, basketball, cross-country, football, golf, soccer, tennis, and track and field for men and in basketball, cheerleading, cross-country, golf, soccer, softball, tennis, track and field, and volleyball for women. Students may also participate in Webber's intramural athletics program. The University's sports complex includes a beach volleyball court, a fitness room, two gymnasiums, racquetball courts, a soccer field, a junior Olympic-size swimming pool, and tennis courts. Undergraduates may also participate in lakeside and water sports such as beach volleyball, canoeing, fishing, and kayaking.

Webber International University offers a large assortment of social clubs and organizations including athletic boosters, Eta Sigma Delta and the Society of Hosteurs, FCA, an international club, a marketing club, Phi Beta Lambda, a sport management club, a student government association, a tourism society, and Webber ambassadors. These organizations, among others, help to fund the numerous social events at Webber.

LOCATION AND ENVIRONMENT

Webber International University is located in the small rural community of Babson Park, which lies at the center of Florida's citrus groves near a variety of freshwater lakes. The area has a welcoming and tranquil atmosphere. Babson Park is convenient to the many popular recreational amenities and tourist attractions of Florida's central region.

OFF-CAMPUS OPPORTUNITIES

Webber International University offers study abroad opportunities to undergraduates pursuing a bachelor's degree. Students may complete either one or two semesters in Paris, Nice, and Lille, France, or Barcelona, Spain.

CAMPUS FACILITIES AND EQUIPMENT

Webber's computer resources centers are data processing hubs and teaching facilities whose equipment offers the most up-to-date technology, encouraging outstanding student performance in business, communication, and creativity.

TUITION, ROOM, BOARD AND FEES

For the 2009–2010 academic year, the annual fee (including room and board, the student activities fee, and tuition) is $25,692. The annual fee for commuting students totaled $17,850. These costs are adjusted periodically. Webber International University projects that $1,400 is sufficient for books and supplies. Laboratory fees are not included in this amount.

FINANCIAL AID

The Student Financial Aid Department is available to guide and assist students in meeting educational costs. Financial aid is distributed on the basis of academic performance, applicant need, and potential. Roughly 90 percent of undergraduates at the University are awarded financial assistance. Students applying for need-based assistance must file the Free Application for Federal Student Aid (FAFSA). Numerous forms of aid, such as Federal Work-Study awards, grants, loans, and scholarships are employed to meet undergraduate needs. A small number of non-need-based scholarships are also offered; these are awarded based on academic achievement, on college and community service, or on athletic performance in basketball, cheerleading, cross-country, football, golf, soccer, softball, tennis, track and field, or volleyball. Students seeking aid must resubmit applications annually. Webber International University participates in the Federal Perkins Loan, Federal Supplemental Educational Opportunity Grant, and Federal Work-Study programs. Prospective applicants must apply for any government-funded grant for which they are qualified, such as the Federal Pell Grant; Florida residents are required to apply for a Florida Student Assistance Grant and the Florida Tuition Voucher Program. Federal Stafford Student Loans are offered as well. Students seeking financial aid should submit their applications prior to April 1 in order to qualify for specific financial aid opportunities.

STUDENT ORGANIZATIONS AND ACTIVITIES

At Webber International University, not all learning takes place in the classroom. Active involvement in social programs, recreational activities and personal-growth experiences create special moments and long-lasting university memories. The Student Government Association, Webber's primary governing organization, is comprised of elected undergraduate representatives and a staff advisor. The SGA addresses nonacademic aspects of campus life. It oversees the activities of student organizations and involves undergraduates in campus procedures and policies. Representatives from many different undergraduate organizations participate in the Student Government Association, as do elected representatives from the University's student body.

ADMISSIONS PROCESS

Prospective students must be high school graduates.

WELLS COLLEGE

AT A GLANCE

Wells College is a coeducational, private, liberal arts college enrolling **568** students from across the United States and throughout the world. Today, true to its heritage, Wells maintains a national reputation for academic excellence. The College prides itself on offering one of the most collaborative learning environments in higher education today. The top five reasons to consider Wells: (1) Wells offers students a personal education: the average class size is **14** and professors know students by name (2) **90%** of Wells faculty members have doctoral degrees and all classes are taught by professors - not teaching assistants (3) Wells students prepare for careers and entrance into top graduate and professional schools through experiential learning: internships, research with faculty members, and community service (4) Wells offers an extensive study abroad program with affiliated programs in 17 different countries (5) All students at Wells benefit from an academic experience similar to honors programs available only to a small number of students at other institutions. Throughout their four years, they work toward a senior thesis that is comparable to graduate-level study. Wells prides itself on offering one of the most collaborative learning environments in higher education.

ACADEMICS

This is not your ordinary education. The Wells experience is deeply personal and intensely focused on superior academic achievement. Wells offers 18 majors and over 40 minors. With one professor for every TEN students, professors really get to know everyone. The average class size has FOURTEEN students and is taught seminar-style, with discussions taking precedence over lectures. Fundamental to the Wells curriculum is an interdisciplinary approach to the liberal arts with the opportunity to experience intimate classes and innovative teaching methods. Through Wells' experiential learning program, students have opportunities to participate in quality internships, off campus study programs, and academic research projects. Experiential learning in the curriculum enables students to test theories learned in the classroom with real-life situations and intertwine it with a rigorous academic program.

ADMISSIONS

Wells students are intellectually curious, open-minded, and creative. They are comfortable expressing themselves, listening to others and sharing ideas. They are caring citizens of the world, eager to travel beyond the campus and outside their comfort zones. Wells students love to learn. If you love learning, you'll love the Wells experience.

Candidates for admission are expected to complete a solid college preparatory program throughout their four years in secondary school. The college recommends a program which provides the best background for study at Wells, including four years of English grammar, composition, and literature; four years of History; three years of mathematics; two years of laboratory science; and coursework in a foreign language. Student's records are enhanced by the addition of courses such as computer science, art, and music, when appropriate curricular choices are offered. To apply for admission to Wells College candidates must submit completed application forms to the Admissions Office by March 1 of the year of entrance.

In addition, the following credentials are required: a transcript of all secondary school work, including the recommendation of the high school principal or school counselor; scores from either the College Entrance Examination Board SAT Reasoning Test or the American College Testing Program (ACT); two letters of recommendation from teachers in academic subject areas. A personal interview is recommended.

Admissions Deadline Options:

Early Decision. December 15: Students whose first choice is Wells College are encouraged to apply under the early decision option. This is a binding admissions option; if admitted; early decision applicants agree to accept Wells offer of admission and agree to withdraw their applications from all other colleges.

Early Action. December 15: Students who would like to receive an early review of their application files are encouraged to apply under the early action option. This is a non-binding admissions option.

Regular Admission. March 1: All other applications to the college should be received by the regular admission deadline. Applications are reviewed after this date and decisions are mailed by April 1.

CAMPUS LIFE

Wells students enjoy all of the advantages of living in a closely-knit community. A well-respected Honor Code shapes the educational and social atmosphere of the campus. Wells supports more than 40 clubs and organizations including a literary magazine and newspaper, music and drama groups, and political organizations, in addition to student-sponsored events, lectures, and performances. Wells is also a Division III member of the NCAA. Wells women compete in seven intercollegiate sports: cross country, field hockey, tennis, lacrosse, soccer, softball and swimming. Wells men compete in five intercollegiate sports: basketball, cross country, lacrosse, soccer and swimming. There are several new teams coming to campus: the co-ed intercollegiate golf team debuts this spring and the women's basketball team will begin at the club level next year and be elevated to intercollegiate status in 2010–11.

LOCATION AND ENVIRONMENT

The beautiful 365-acre lakeside campus is situated in the heart of the Finger Lakes Resort Region of New York State in the historical village of Aurora on Cayuga Lake. The campus is 30 minutes from Ithaca, one hour from Syracuse and Rochester, and approximately five hours from New York City.

MAJORS AND DEGREES

Wells College offers the Bachelor of Arts degree with majors in the following areas (concentrations within the majors appear in parentheses): American Studies (African-American Studies, American Cultures); Biological and Chemical Sciences (Biochemistry, Molecular Biology, Biology, Chemistry); Economics and Management (Economics, Management); English (Creative Writing, Literature); Environmental Studies (Environmental Policies and Values, Environmental Sciences); Foreign Languages, Literatures, and Cultures (French, German, Spanish); History; International Studies; Mathematical and Physical Sciences (Computer Science, Mathematics, Physics, Applied Physics); Performing Arts (Music, Theatre and Dance); Psychology; Public Affairs: Ethics, Politics, and Social Policy (Ethics and Philosophy, Government and Politics); Religion (Historical and Comparative Studies, Religion and Culture); Sociology and Anthropology (Sociology, Anthropology/Cross-cultural Sociology), Visual Arts (Art History, Studio Art); Women's Studies. A NEW MAJOR IN MEDIA AND FILM STUDIES DEBUTS IN THE FALL OF 2010. In consultation with the dean and faculty, students may also design their own concentrations and majors. In addition, Wells offers programs that lead to provisional certification in elementary and secondary education.

TUITION AND FEES

For the 2009–10 year: Tuition: $28,180; Room and board: $9,000; Fees: $1,500

School Says . . .

WEST VIRGINIA WESLEYAN COLLEGE

AT A GLANCE

It's Wesleyan—Expect Great Things. Founded in 1890, Wesleyan is a private four-year co-educational residential college that is affiliated with The United Methodist Church. Small interactive classes and a dedicated and accessible faculty whose priorities are teaching and advising allow students to benefit from a highly personalized educational experience.

Over 80 percent of Wesleyan's faculty hold the highest degree in their respective teaching field and the student faculty ratio is 14:1. The curriculum foundation begins with a general studies liberal arts program where students complete one-third of their course of study. The College offers over 40 majors and over 40 minors of study including the Five-Year Undergraduate/Master of Business Administration Program and several new Master's programs in Education, Nursing, and Athletic Training. The Honors Program is offered to recognize and challenge the College's most academically- talented students. The most popular academic majors include business, education, exercise science and athletic training, biology, political science, and psychology.

West Virginia Wesleyan is accredited by the Commission on Institutions of Higher Education of the North Central Association of Colleges and Schools and approved by the University Senate of The United Methodist Church. It is a member of the National Association of Schools of Music and is approved by the West Virginia Department of Education and the National Council for the Accreditation of Teacher Education. The College participates in the Interstate Certification Project whereby a number of states certify teachers graduating from Wesleyan's Department of Education. The athletic training program is accredited by the Commission on Accreditation of Allied Health Education Programs. Degree programs offered in business and economics, including the Master of Business Administration program, are accredited by the International Assembly for Collegiate Business Education.

All academic programs either require or strongly encourage the completion of an internship experience. Wesleyan's academic calendar is 4-4-1 that includes an optional May Term which over 50 students pursue study abroad courses. The Advising and Career Center assists students with course scheduling, academic advising, internships and study abroad, resume writing, job searches, and graduate and professional school placement. The Learning Center provides tutoring services as well as comprehensive services for students with diagnosed learning disabilities.

Information technology is emphasized throughout the curriculum. As part of a partnership with the Dell University Program, all students are required to have a notebook computer throughout their undergraduate study. Through this partnership a student chooses from three "Wesleyan Configured" models. The models include a base model, a mid-level model, and a high-end model. Each system comes preloaded with a "Wesleyan Software Image" and includes a three-year warranty and a three year accidental damage insurance policy. The College's helpdesk is an authorized Dell repair facility; so that all repairs on the notebook computers are handled locally. The high-technology campus fiber-optic system ensures everyone rapid Internet and email access from all major campus buildings and every residence hall room.

The Annie Merner Pfeiffer Library provides digital, multimedia, and print information sources in support of teaching and learning at the College. Library resources, including the catalog, electronic books and journals, reserve readings, digital collections, and reference tools are available on the campus network around the clock. The Library has over 150,000 print titles, 100,000 electronic books, 15,000 electronic journal titles, and 10,000 media materials in its collections. Of the more than 1,350 undergraduate students, 53 percent are from West Virginia, while the other 47 percent originate from 39 states and 19 countries. 12 percent of Wesleyan's American students are minority students.

Over 85 percent of Wesleyan's students live on-campus and the College guarantees on-campus housing for all undergraduate students. Housing options include double and single rooms, suites, and apartments. Campus dining is provided and prepared by a contracted professional catering service. Meals are served in the French A. See Dining Center and meal options also include dining in the "Cat's Claw Restaurant" and carry-out lunches at "Sunny Bucks."

Wesleyan has a balanced and diverse student life program that includes more than 70 campus organizations. Included among these are a campus radio station, newspaper, student government, departmental clubs, fraternities and sororities, and religious organizations. Over 87 percent of Wesleyan students participate in community service activities that include the complete administration of a youth basketball program to Special Olympics, to tutoring, mentoring, and educational activities to senior citizens programs to more global programs such as hurricane relief and international service trips.

The College also offers a structured leadership program to interested students. The Campus Activities Board organizes entertainment programs each weekend while the Arts Alive Series presents a wide range of cultural events throughout the year. The Wesleyan Outdoor Recreation Life Department (W.O.R.L.D.) takes advantage of the campus' location to private a wide range of weekend activities including snow skiing, hiking, biking, caving, horseback riding, and whitewater rafting. Wesleyan also features 18 NCAA division II sports and has captured the West Virginia Conference Commissioner's Cup, an award that is given to the best overall athletic program, 14 consecutive years.

While Wesleyan is affiliated with The United Methodist Church, students of all faiths are welcome and active. The College holds a weekly optional worship service every Tuesday morning and a Catholic Mass each Saturday evening. Other religious groups include Inter-Varsity Christian Fellowship, United Methodist Youth Movement, Religious Life Council, and Campus Crusade for Christ.

Wesleyan features a beautiful 100-plus acre park-like campus with 23 architecturally coordinated buildings. Tall oaks and flowering shrubs and trees can be found throughout the campus. All students are permitted to bring automobiles and the campus is less than one-half mile from downtown Buckhannon. The local community offers movie theatres, department stories, and a wide selection of local and fast-food restaurants.

LOCATION AND ENVIRONMENT

Situated in the foothills of the Allegheny Mountains, Wesleyan's beautiful 100-acre campus is located in the quaint, residential town of Buckhannon, West Virginia. Buckhannon has been included in Norman Crampton's book, The Top 100 Best Small Towns in America, a Random House Publication. Many students are drawn to this personal and picturesque setting and the numerous outdoor opportunities located in close proximity to campus. The local community offers a movie theatre, department stores, and a wide variety of locally-owned and fast-food restaurants. Wesleyan is a short two-hour drive from Pittsburgh, Pennsylvania, and 90 minutes from Charleston, West Virginia, the state capital.

OFF-CAMPUS OPPORTUNITIES

Wesleyan encourages all students to expand their education beyond the traditional classroom. Many students have studied abroad in such places as England, Ireland, Wales, Germany, Spain, Kenya, Scotland, and Australia. Professional internships are available in the Buckhannon area, Charleston, WV, Washington, D.C.; New York City; Pittsburgh, Pennsylvania; and other states and countries.

MAJORS AND DEGREES OFFERED

West Virginia Wesleyan offers five undergraduate degrees: the Bachelor of Arts in art (painting & drawing, graphic design, and intermedia), arts administration, chemistry, Christian education and church leadership, communication studies, criminal justice, economics, education (elementary and secondary), English (literature, teaching, and writing), environmental studies, history, international studies, music, musical theatre, philosophy, physics, political science, psychology, public relations, religion, sociology, and theatre arts; the Bachelor of Fine Arts in Musical Theatre, Theatre Performance, and Technical Theatre; the Bachelor of Music Education; the Bachelor of Science in accounting, athletic training, biology, business administration, chemistry, computer information science, computer science, environmental science, exercise science, management, marketing, materials chemistry, mathematics, and physical education.

Students may also choose an interdepartmental major or an individualized major. Pre-professional programs are available in dentistry, law, medicine, ministry, optometry, pharmacy, physical therapy, and veterinary medicine.

ACADEMIC PROGRAMS

Wesleyan's liberal arts curriculum begins with a broad base view in a variety of core courses designed to enrich the student's whole view. The classes range from the humanities to contemporary issues and can be intermingled with the courses in the individual's major throughout the four-year program.

Wesleyan's Honors Program is offered for superior students who meet the specific requirements and demonstrate a high quality of academic excellence. Challenging, yet rewarding, classes, along with culturally enriching outings, offer Honors students a diverse and unique educational experience.

The 4-4-1 academic calendar at Wesleyan is a unique feature for students. During the optional May term, many students take advantage of the study abroad courses offered through Wesleyan.

CAMPUS FACILITIES AND EQUIPMENT

Wesleyan's 23 buildings include 10 modern residence hall units (including the renovated and suite-style Fleming Hall, new for 2009). The Annie Merner Pfeiffer Library is a "wireless" environment and spacious facility that contains more than 105,000 volumes, 700 periodicals, and 10,000 media materials. Located in the center of campus is Wesley Chapel, the largest sanctuary in West Virginia, and Martin Religious Center. The chapel serves as a focal point of campus, as many campus events, both religious and cultural, are held there. The hub of the campus, Benedum Campus and Community Center, is an impressive building that houses a convenience store, bookstore, swimming pool, student development offices, study lounges, and a cabaret-style restaurant, The Cat's Claw. The Rockefeller Health and Physical Education Center includes a main gymnasium that seats 3,700 spectators, an intramural gymnasium, weight and nautilus training rooms, and an indoor astro-turf training area. Other vital buildings on campus include Christopher Hall of Science, which has state-of-the-art science equipment; Middleton Hall, which houses Admission and Financial Planning Offices as well as the Nursing Department; and the Lynch-Raine Administration Building. In addition, the multimillion dollar Virginia Thomas Law Center for the Performing Arts, opened in 2009, offers the most advanced performing arts facility of it's kind in the region.

TUITION, ROOM, BOARD AND FEES

The 2009–2010 costs at Wesleyan are $22,030 for tuition, $6800 for room and board, and $800 for student fees, which includes a student activity fee, facilities fee, and a technology fee. These costs do not include books, travel, clothing, the laptop computer, medical insurance, or other personal expenses. Wesleyan offers an interest-free monthly payment plan during the academic year.

FINANCIAL AID

The College offers financial aid on the basis of a variety of criteria: scholastic achievements, special talents and abilities, and financial need. A number of scholarships are available including awards for academics, athletics, performing arts, leadership, community service, and visual arts. Student employment is available in most areas of the College community, financed through a blend of institutional and federal funds. Students may apply for low-cost federal loans. Students should file the Free Application for Federal Student Aid by February 15. The institutional code for Wesleyan is 003830. Wesleyan also offers an early estimator financial aid service to assist with the costs of a Wesleyan education. Currently, more than 95 percent of all students receive grants or scholarships from Wesleyan.

STUDENT ORGANIZATIONS AND ACTIVITIES

The Community Council, one of the first college-based community governing bodies in the country, is structured in favor of student representation. Its student representatives and four student officers are elected by their respective classes or major organizations. This group meets weekly with members of the administration, faculty, and staff, and has long been recognized as an effective force in bringing about change and fostering debate on campus issues.

ADMISSIONS PROCESS

Students are selected by the Office of Admission on the basis of ability, interests, academic preparation, character, and promise, as indicated by their own statements on the application, as well as by high school or college records, recommendations, and standardized test results.

Open without discrimination to all qualified students, the College reserves the right to refuse to admit any applicant who, because of low scholarship or citizenship record, is deemed by the Admission and Academic Standing Council to be unlikely to succeed within the standards the College seeks to maintain.

Persons wishing to be admitted directly from high school should present an application for admission with $35 fee (waived for on-line applications); a transcript of record from an accredited high school showing courses pursued, grades earned, and credits earned in at least grades 9 through 11; and a record of either SAT (Reasoning Test) or ACT (American College Test) scores. Applicants from non-accredited high schools or completing General Educational Development may be considered for admission if satisfactory ability and achievement are demonstrated.

Persons seeking to transfer from another accredited college or university may be admitted to advanced standing upon presentation of an application for admission with $35 fee (waived for on-line applications); an official transcript showing all credits attempted at all post-secondary institutions previously attended; a high school transcript certifying graduation and showing courses pursued and grades earned and, if the cumulative grade point average is less than 2.5, either SAT or ACT scores.

Wesleyan will accept transfer credit courses compatible with its academic program. Grades and hours so earned shall count toward graduation. The College accepts no more than 60 semester hours of credit from a junior or community college.

Students who transfer to Wesleyan with an associate degree from a regionally accredited community or junior college may be admitted with the degree credited as fulfilling Wesleyan's general studies requirements when the total educational background, including high school record, shows compatibility with Wesleyan's general studies requirements. Deficiencies in general studies requirements, as determined by the Admission and Academic Standing Council, must be satisfied after enrollment at Wesleyan.

Former students who were not in good standing may seek to be readmitted after meeting the conditions stated at the time of suspension and upon completion of the appropriate forms. Transcripts of any credits completed at other institutions of higher learning should be filed with the application for readmission.

Wesleyan participates in the Advanced Placement Program of the College Entrance Examination Board. Students who have taken and satisfactorily passed college-level courses in high school and who have passed the Advanced Placement Examination of the Educational Testing Service at the level of three or higher may apply to the College for credit or advanced placement in these subjects. These examinations are administered in the spring. Applicants must have results sent to the Office of Admission for verification prior to the fall semester.

The College recognizes the International Baccalaureate Diploma Program. Students who have successfully completed the IB Program and earn a score of four or above on higher-level examinations may apply to the College for credit or advanced placement in the appropriate subjects. These exams are administered in the spring. Applicants must have the results sent to the Office of Admission for verification prior to the fall semester.

WESTMINSTER COLLEGE

AT A GLANCE

Westminster College offers students a unique learning environment, a vibrant community, and a track record of success. Enrolling approximately 3,000 students, Westminster College is the only private, comprehensive liberal arts college in Utah. Students are encouraged to take advantage of a dynamic urban setting with unparalleled access to an ecological wonderland, and the college uses that larger setting as an extension of its classrooms through internships, field work, undergraduate research, and an impressive outdoor recreation program. The learning environment is led by faculty members who are here because they love to teach. Deeply committed to each student's success, Westminster College is a challenging and supportive community of learners.

ACADEMICS

Westminster encourages students to think for themselves, draw conclusions ... and change their minds. Through engaging college-wide learning goals, students experiment with ideas, raise questions, and critically examine alternatives. That philosophy is just one reason that Westminster offers a unique environment for learning. Others include our commitment to students and their learning; our emphasis on an active and engaged style of learning; a campus that is warm, welcoming, and active; and graduates who have mastered the skills that employers want and society needs. By integrating a liberal arts foundation with professional education, Westminster exhibits features of both a liberal arts college and a comprehensive university.

Courses are designed to involve students in active, experiential, cross-disciplinary, and collaborative learning. Each student must complete at least 124 semester hours to receive a bachelor's degree and while approximately 40 hours consist of liberal arts, students are also exposed to practical, career-oriented experiences. Credit is awarded for successful scores on Advanced Placement and CLEP examinations. The College has a 4-4-1 calendar, consisting of two 15-week semesters followed by a one-month May term, as well as a summer session. May Term is Westminster's intensive semester: a month of offbeat and inspiring classes, laid-back trips around Utah and adventures outside of the U.S. After a year of hitting the books, May Term is a truly unique experience taking you outside of the classroom and leading you to discoveries about yourself and the world. And the best part is students who attend full-time during fall and spring semesters earn free May-term tuition.

Student may also enroll in Reserve Officer Training Corps programs through cooperative agreements with a nearby University.

ADMISSIONS

We seek students who will thrive in our classrooms and bring vibrancy to our campus. We review each application individually and take into consideration individual talents and character; quality of academic preparation, which includes both difficulty of course work and grades; extracurricular activities; recommendations, and ACT or SAT scores. Westminster admits students whose academic records indicate that they possess the skills and maturity necessary for success in college work. Students are admitted without discrimination as to race, color, nationality, creed, sex, physical handicaps, or veteran status. Although the college does not require a specific pattern of school subjects, it does strongly recommend a solid college preparatory high school academic program.

Transfer students must have a minimum 2.5 academic GPA to be considered for admission. In addition to all other admissions criteria, international students must have at least a 3.0 GPA in non U.S. high school or college work and a Test of English as a Foreign Language (TOEFL) score of at least 550 (or equivalent). The College has recently introduced the Westminster English as a Second Language Institute, a comprehensive summer program providing academic and practical ESL instruction for international students who need to strengthen their language skills before enrollment.

Application and Information

To apply for admission, a student must submit an application for admission, personal essay, a recommendation, an application fee, and official transcripts of previous high school and/or college class work. Freshman applicants must submit ACT or SAT scores. Applicants are notified of their admission status within two weeks of receipt of all required materials. Westminster operates rolling admissions, so it's best to send your application in as soon as possible. To preserve the faculty-student ratio, classes are limited. Westminster College reserves the right to close the class earlier than dates specified if enrollment goals are met before those dates. New applicants are accepted for the start of all sessions. For application forms and additional information, students should contact Westminster at the following address:

Office of Admissions

Westminster College

1840 South 1300 East

Salt Lake City, Utah 84105

United States

Phone: 801-832-2200 800-748-4753 (toll-free)

Web site: http://www.westminstercollege.edu

CAMPUS LIFE

Located in the eclectic Sugar House neighborhood of Salt Lake City, Westminster provides a welcome academic haven for learners. Distinguished by old-growth trees, a small creek, and a graceful blend of old and new architecture, the College campus provides plenty of green space to enjoy in the midst of the city. The College's on-campus housing, which accommodates 500 students, includes new apartment-style suites featuring entertainment systems and cooking facilities. Off-campus rental housing is readily available in the neighborhood.

Westminster is an easy-going, laid-back welcoming place with students from many different backgrounds and cultures who have all kinds of different interests, passions, and talents. With more than 50 student clubs and organizations, 13 men's and women's intercollegiate sports teams, and an active intramural program, students have plenty of opportunities to make friends and get involved. Additionally, the campus calendar is jam-packed with lectures, plays, poetry readings, and concerts, as well as student-sponsored events such as "Wild Wednesdays." The biggest challenge may be deciding which activities to attend!

In 2007, *Outside* magazine gave Salt Lake plenty of kudos for its progressive thinking, and describes it as "a near-perfect location for avid outdoor adventures" and in 2008 *Forbes* magazine ranked SLC #1 for job growth.

Downtown Salt Lake is 10 minutes away from campus by bus, car, or bicycle. The city offers internship and employment opportunities, cultural resources, clubs and restaurants, big-time professional sports, and great shopping. A metropolitan area of approximately 1.3 million people, Salt Lake has been rated as one of the ten most fun places to live, was home of the 2002 Winter Olympics, and offers easy access to the Sundance Film Festival.

The Wasatch Mountains, a section of the Rockies that borders the Salt Lake Valley on the east, are famous for the "greatest snow on earth." With approximately 500 inches of annual snowfall, these mountains are ideal for winter sports enthusiasts as well as for those who enjoy summer hiking, biking, and camping. Ten world-class ski and snowboard resorts lie within an hour's drive of campus, and sixteen national parks and recreational areas are within a day's drive or less. Golf, backpacking, mountain biking, kayaking, wakeboarding, mountain climbing, canyoneering, spelunking, and rafting are all within easy reach of campus.

MAJORS AND DEGREES

Westminster College offers more than seventy academic programs. Bachelor of Arts and Bachelor of Science degrees are awarded in the following areas: Accounting, Art, Arts Administration, Aviation: Flight Operations, Aviation: Management, Biology, Chemistry, Communication, Computer Information Systems, Computer Science, Economics, Economics Pre-law, Elementary Education , English, Environmental Studies, Finance, Financial Services, Fine Arts, History, International Business, Justice Studies, Mathematics, Neuroscience, Nursing, Philosophy, Physics, Political Studies, Pre-Professional Programs (Dentistry, Studies, Management, Marketing, Mathematics, Music, Neuroscience, Nursing, Philosophy, Physics, Political Studies, Psychology, Social Sciences, SociologySpanish and Latin American Studies, Special Education, Theatre,. Pre-professional programs include pre-dental, pre-law, and pre-medical. Other academic programs include Chinese, Engineering 3-2, and Honors. In addition to the above-listed majors, the college offers minors in many of those program areas plus minors only subjects ranging from anthropology to paleontology

TUITION AND AID

For 2009–2010, more than 98 percent of freshmen at Westminster received some form of financial aid, averaging approximately $20,571. Aid programs include need-based institutional grants and need-based federal aid programs, such as grants, loans, and employment (Federal Work-Study Program). The Free Application for Federal Student Aid (FAFSA) is the only form required for new students seeking financial aid. Students wishing to apply for federal aid programs should plan to submit applications by early April. Merit-based scholarships are available to incoming freshmen and transfer students as well as to continuing students through a generous endowment and institutional aid programs. Every full-time student is automatically considered for merit-based scholarships awarded by the College. The scholarships are based on their GPA from previous academic course work. Scholarships are also offered for music, theatre, athletics and extra curricular achievements.

TUITION AND FEES

Tuition and fees for 2009–2010 were $24,996 for the academic year for a full-time student (12 to 16 semester credit hours). This figure includes costs for the fall semester, spring semester, and May term. Room and board costs were $7,006 for the same period. Books and supplies were estimated at $1,000 per year.

WILLIAM JEWELL COLLEGE

COLLEGE BASICS

William Jewell College is committed to bringing together talented students and gifted faculty mentors within a vibrant community sparked by a rigorous and intentional liberal arts curriculum. A full range of personal and professional development experiences are presented by the selective national liberal arts college's location within the Kansas City metroplex of more than two million.

AT A GLANCE

Among the oldest colleges west of the Mississippi, William Jewell College is one of a select group of 265 national liberal arts colleges named by the Carnegie Foundation for the Advancement of Teaching. Distinctive programs include the internationally renowned Oxbridge Honors and Pryor Leadership programs. The Harriman-Jewell Series is considered one of the great performing arts series in the country. More than 700 world-class performances and 17 American recital debuts, including that of Luciano Pavarotti in 1973, have come to Kansas City by way of this program. Jewell offers a recognized major in Applied Critical Thought and Inquiry, allowing students to graduate with double majors and some with triple majors in just four years.

LOCATION AND ENVIRONMENT

Just 20 minutes from downtown Kansas City, Missouri, Jewell offers 1,100 students all the amenities of a beautiful liberal arts campus setting. The 200-acre campus is perched above the town of Liberty and its historic town square. With more than 900 students living on campus and 60 clubs and organizations, life at Jewell is vibrant. Students have the opportunity to learn and apply practical life and business skills while making friends and participating in the life of the College.

CAMPUS FACILITIES AND EQUIPMENT

A new $13 million sorority complex opened in fall 2009. The sorority complex complements the three multi-million dollar fraternity houses, which were completed in 2000. The Yates-Gill College Union was dedicated in the fall of 2006, adding 15,000 square feet to what is now a 60,000-square foot College Union. A beautiful atrium, new meeting and dining rooms, wireless internet, Wii access and a new coffee shop now enhance the building's amenities for students, faculty and staff. Also in 2006, the College dedicated a new academic building to support leadership development programs, the Fred and Shirley Pryor Center for Leadership Development. Also housed in the building are offices for the Tucker Leadership Lab, which facilitates team-building exercises on a high and low ropes course, which is also located on campus. The Mabee Center for Physical Education is an exceptional facility for physical fitness. It houses a competition swimming and diving pool, basketball courts, squash and racquetball courts, an indoor track and a weight room. Greene Stadium's Sprinturf playing field accommodates football and soccer matches in a variety of weather conditions, and the Peters Track provides a competitive environment for track and field events.

Students in the sciences have access to state-of-the-art research equipment and are engaged in faculty-directed research as undergraduates. The Pillsbury Observatory is equipped with a 14-inch Celestron telescope on a Byers Class 2 mount in a 5-meter dome and is also available for student research. Jewell's renowned music department is housed in the Pillsbury Music Center, which includes large and small rehearsal space, practice facilities, keyboard/computer lab and the Forbis Recital Hall. The Liberty Symphony Orchestra offers string and wind students the opportunity to gain invaluable orchestral experience at a high level, often playing alongside their teachers and other area professionals. William Jewell is the home of the Quimby Pipe Organ Company's Op. 55, a magnificent instrument that is housed in Gano Chapel and is used for Jewell and area-wide events. Organ students regularly practice and perform on this outstanding instrument.

ACADEMICS

The William Jewell College experience focuses on enhancing the student's ability to apply learning to complex ethical, scientific and cultural problems. The College places a high value on experiential learning and gives students the opportunity to "live what they learn." Students who complete the College's 38-hour liberal arts core plus three applied learning experiences receive a second major in Applied Critical Thought and Inquiry (ACT-In). As a result, all students can graduate with double majors in four years. The ACT-In option is a reflection of the College's philosophy that education must take students beyond thinking and inquiring, and to action. William Jewell prepares students to spend their lives playing an active role in their communities by creating opportunities to apply what they have learned through critical thought and inquiry.

In addition to ACT-In, a number of other distinctive programs are available to Jewell students. The internationally recognized Oxbridge Honors Program, supported by the Hall Family Foundation, combines British tutorial methods of instruction with a year of study in Oxford or Cambridge. It is the only program of its kind in the nation. Jewell's undergraduate Nonprofit Leadership major is one of only 13 nationwide and ranks among the top three in academic rigor. Students will fulfill all of the nonprofit competencies established by American Humanics and meet the guidelines for graduate study in philanthropy, the nonprofit sector and nonprofit leadership established by the Nonprofit Academic Centers Council (NACC). The Pryor Leadership Studies Program includes course work, community service projects and internships that help students enhance their leadership skills in a variety of settings.

William Jewell has created an intentional progression of courses and experiences designed to prepare students for a lifetime of growth and change. Jewell students graduate equipped with deep content knowledge in their major(s), a host of social and real-world experiences, personal maturity and the intellectual habits of mind for success in a world of change and challenge. Each student's educational and personal development journey is shaped by the College's commitment to the following:

• Immersing students in a community of talented peers with high expectations;

• Top faculty who personally engage, challenge, and mentor students;

• A rigorous and intentional curriculum that is both competency and issues based;

• An ideal location that offers exceptional opportunities for students;

• Personal development: ethics, faith, service, and leadership.

William Jewell College believes that graduation in four years should be an expectation for all students. Our Four-Year Graduation Guarantee makes the cost of a great liberal arts education even more affordable and provides students with the momentum they need to transition into graduate school or career choices. Students who follow academic advising guidelines are guaranteed to graduate four years (eight consecutive semesters) from the date of their original matriculation. Students following these basic guidelines who do not meet graduation requirements after four years may take up to an additional 16 credit hours required for graduation within one year of the originally projected graduation date, free of tuition and fees.

ADMISSIONS

Students interested in admission to William Jewell must complete a secondary school curriculum that includes at least 15 credits in college-preparatory courses; four additional academic electives are recommended as well. Required credits include 4 years of English, 3 years of math, 3 years of social science, 3 years of science, and 2 years of foreign language. Applicants must complete either the William Jewell College application or the Common Application and provide an official secondary school transcript, standardized test scores (SAT or ACT, writing sections recommended), a writing sample, and a secondary school report form. Students interested in Oxbridge Honors must also submit two academic letters of recommendation. Home-schooled students must submit one letter of recommendation and complete the homeschool supplement. Applicants to the direct-entry nursing program must submit the nursing supplement form. The $25 application fee is waived for online applications. Priority consideration for merit scholarships is given to applications postmarked by Dec. 1. Additional application materials are required for consideration for the Jewell Scholarship.

TUITION AND FEES

For the 2009–2010 academic year, tuition for all students is $24,300, and typical room and board is $6,700. William Jewell participates in Tuition Exchange, Midwest Student Exchange, the Council of Independent Colleges and Baptist Student Exchange.

WILLIAM PATERSON UNIVERSITY

AT A GLANCE

William Paterson University, a public school founded in 1855, has grown to become a comprehensive, liberal arts institution committed to academic excellence and student success. Accredited by the Middle States Association of Schools and Colleges, it offers 43 undergraduate and 20 graduate degrees and professional development programs through its five colleges: Arts and Communication; Cotsakos College of Business; Education; Humanities and Social Sciences; and Science and Health.

William Paterson is located in suburban Wayne, New Jersey. The approximately 10,819 full- and part-time students, who enjoy the resources of a large university as well as the individual attention available at a smaller school, relax and study on the 370-acre campus amid the University's woods and waterfalls. It offers a wide variety of student activities, modern on-campus housing, and the most up-to-date educational facilities. Financial aid is also available to qualified students.

LOCATION AND ENVIRONMENT

Each course of study at William Paterson is enhanced by world-class academic facilities and resources; curricula that address classic and contemporary issues in higher education; and a distinguished faculty comprised of award-winning teacher-scholars—92 percent of fulltime faculty hold the highest degree in their field.

Many social, cultural, and recreational opportunities complement academic programs. The University's residential capacity is nearly 2,600 students in ten residence halls. A 4,000-seat recreation center is a short walk from the residence halls, and Wightman Gym houses a competition-sized pool. The "Pioneer spirit" is evident in the University's 12 intercollegiate sports with numerous NCAA Division III post-season tournament appearances.

The University also presents many enlightening and entertaining cultural events, among them the Distinguished Lecturer Series, concerts, art exhibitions, and theatrical productions. In addition, it offers a wide variety of continuing education programs designed for both professionals and the general public.

OFF-CAMPUS OPPORTUNITIES

Students participate in internships in many leading area companies and businesses that both help them clarify career goals and forge relationships that can result in post-graduation jobs. Study abroad programs are also available to sophomores and juniors. Students may also elect to study in the University's distance learning programs.

MAJORS AND DEGREES OFFERED

Students can pursue B.A., B.S., B.F.A., B.M., and B.S.N. degrees in any of the University's five colleges. Bachelor of arts degrees are granted in African, African American, and Caribbean studies, anthropology, art, art history, Asian studies, communication, communication disorders, early childhood education, earth science, economics, elementary education, English, French and Francophone studies, geography, history, Latin American and Latino studies, liberal studies, mathematics, music, philosophy, political science, psychology, secondary education, sociology, Spanish, and women's and gender studies.

Bachelor of science program degrees include accounting, applied health, athletic training, biology, biotechnology, business administration, chemistry, computer science, environmental science, exercise science, mathematics, physical education, professional sales, and public health.

The bachelor of fine arts program degree is awarded in fine arts. In the bachelor of music program, students can choose between performance, jazz, and music management. And, nursing students can receive a bachelor of science in nursing.

Students may also pursue certification in early childhood, elementary, secondary, and special education.

ACADEMIC PROGRAMS

In order to graduate, the baccalaureate degree requires 128 credits (120 credits for students entering as of fall 2010). Approximately 53 to 54 of those credits are earned in general education classes. Another 30 to 60 come from work in the student's major, and 20 to 40 can be earned in electives. The general education specifications and major requirements vary for degrees, including the B.F.A. and the B.M. The Career Development and Advisement Center counsels and advises students who are undecided as to their major, as well as their career choices.

Programs in the University Honors College offer students further challenges and include biopsychology, cognitive science, humanities, independent study, life science and environmental ethics, management, marketing, music, performing and literary arts, and social sciences. There are also pre-professional programs in dentistry, engineering, law, medicine (which includes dentistry, optometry, podiatry, and veterinary science), pharmacy, physical therapy, and speech-language pathology. Military experience may also be evaluated for credit.

CAMPUS FACILITIES AND EQUIPMENT

Facilities are easily accessible to students in various academic, cultural, and recreational programs. The David and Lorraine Cheng Library's bound collection area has increased by 33 percent and its seating capacity by 100 percent. Cultural activities are supported by Shea Center for Performing Arts, which contains a 922-seat theater, as well as band, choral, and orchestral practice rooms and classrooms. The Ben Shahn Center for Visual Arts features an extensive art gallery, as well as art studios and classrooms, while the Power Art Center houses faculty offices and studios for three-dimensional design, photography, sculpture, ceramics, printmaking, woodworking, and painting.

Athletic facilities include an indoor pool, outdoor tennis courts, and a lighted athletics field complex. Also, the recreation center includes a 4,000-seat facility with various athletic courts and exercise rooms. Hobart Hall, a state-of-the-art communication facility, houses television studios, a multipurpose computer lab, film studio, a radio station, and an uplink and four downlink satellite dishes. The Atrium, an academic building, contains a writing center, multimedia language lab, tutorial center, and computing support facilities. Among other academic resources are a nursing instructional facility, speech and hearing clinic, a child-care center, and comprehensive science research facilities.

The site of the Allan and Michele Gorab Alumni House contains a pond, wetlands, woods, as well as a living laboratory for courses in biology and the environmental sciences. The 1600 Valley Road facility houses the Cotsakos College of Business and its state-of-the-art Financial Learning Center, the Russ Berrie Institute, the Russ Berrie Professional Sales Lab, the College of Education, the Center for Continuing and Professional Education, and classrooms. The University Commons complex, including the redesigned John Victor Machuga Student Center, is the heart of the campus, where the entire University community gathers and interacts. This state-of-the-art campus center provides students with an exquisite setting for a vast array of social and extracurricular activities, dining venues, and student support services, all under one roof.

TUITION, ROOM, BOARD AND FEES

Full-time students from New Jersey pay $10,838 for tuition and fees in 2009/2010. Tuition for out-of-state students is $17,592. Room and board runs roughly $10,280 annually. For those in-state residents who want to live on-campus, the total is approximately $21,118, and for out-of-state residents, approximately $27,872. These totals may vary subject to decisions by the University's Board of Trustees.

FINANCIAL AID

William Paterson provides a first-rate education at a highly reasonable cost. In accordance with the University's commitment to value in education, federal and state need-based financial aid programs are offered in the forms of grants, loans, scholarships, and work-study programs. In order to apply for financial aid, students should submit Free Application for Federal Student Aid (FAFSA) with the United States Department of Education by April 1.

Recently, scholarship/grant awards totaling approximately $32,890,000were distributed at the University. First-year students and upperclassmen compete for academic scholarships. And both the William Paterson Foundation and the Alumni Association award more than 200 scholarships for academic achievement, exceptional character qualities, leadership excellence, and financial need.

STUDENT ORGANIZATIONS AND ACTIVITIES

There are more than 50 student clubs covering interests from anthropology to the student-run television station. The University also offers various opportunities for students to become involved in leadership roles. They may pursue leadership opportunities in student government or in one of the many academic, social, programmatic, and media groups on campus.

William Paterson's athletic teams participate in the NCAA's Division III, as well as in club and intramural sports. Both men and women have teams in basketball, soccer, and swimming. In addition, the men field baseball and football teams (the baseball team won national championships in 1992 and 1996). Women also participate in field hockey, softball, tennis, and volleyball.

ADMISSIONS PROCESS

APPLICATION DEADLINES

Application, fee, and supporting official transcripts for freshman, transfer, second-degree and re-admit students must be received by the deadline dates shown below:

Fall: June 1

Spring: December 1

All forms, transcripts, and the $50 application fee must be received from first-year applicants or transfer students by those dates. Candidates should bear in mind that the cut-off dates may be earlier if the combination of continuing students and new applications begin to exceed availability.

PROOF OF HIGH SCHOOL GRADUATION

In order to comply with state and federal regulations regarding financial aid, all applicants (freshman, transfer, second baccalaureate, and re-admit students) MUST submit proof of high school graduation or equivalency (copy of high school diploma or high school transcripts with date of graduation posted) prior to enrollment. A high school equivalency diploma recognized by New Jersey may be presented in place of the above requirements.

SAT/ACT REQUIREMENTS

Entering freshman students must have taken the SAT or the American College Test (ACT) and have their scores sent to the Office of Admissions, William Paterson University. To submit your scores, indicate code 2518 for the SAT and code 2584 for the ACT.

TRANSFER APPLICANTS

William Paterson accepts students for the fall and spring semesters (June 1 and December 1) for full- or part-time study. When applying, students must present at least 12 college-level credits with a minimum 2.0 grade point average (GPA); computer science and nursing majors must have a GPA of at least 2.5, and teacher certification program applicants must have a GPA of at least 2.75. There are some limitations on the number of credits accepted, e.g., a maximum of 70 credits from a two-year institution or 90 credits from a four-year college or university. More details on transferring credits may be obtained from our Admissions staff.

William Paterson University welcomes all visitors and requests for information. Campus tours are conducted weekdays by appointment. The Office of Admissions will gladly schedule a tour for you or answer any questions. To make arrangements to visit the University or for more information about our programs, contact:

Office of Admissions

William Paterson University of New Jersey

Wayne, NJ 07470

Telephone: 973-720-2125

Fax: 973-720-2910

E-mail: admissions@wpunj.edu

Web: www.wpunj.edu

WITTENBERG UNIVERSITY

AT A GLANCE

Founded in 1845 in Springfield, Ohio, Wittenberg is a private, coeducational, liberal arts and sciences college affiliated with the Evangelical Lutheran Church in America. In keeping with its mission, Wittenberg provides an education dedicated to intellectual inquiry and wholeness of person within a diverse residential community. Reflecting its Lutheran heritage, Wittenberg also challenges students to become responsible global citizens, to discover their callings, and to lead personal, professional, and civic lives of creativity, service, compassion, and integrity.

Wittenberg enrolls approximately 2,000 full-time students, representing more than 41 states and 19 countries around the world.

Wittenberg's students live on or near campus, making the campus a full-time, 24-hour-a-day, 7-day-a-week campus. All first- and second-year students reside in the residence halls; juniors and seniors have the option to remain in the residence halls, move off campus into a house or apartment, or live in a fraternity or sorority house.

Wittenberg's strong arts and sciences programs and community service make its graduates attractive to prominent medical, law, and graduate programs. More than 20 percent of Wittenberg graduates begin graduate programs immediately after graduation, and 70 percent eventually pursue an advanced degree at some point in their careers. Wittenberg ranks in the 92nd percentile in Ph.D. production of all U.S. four-year colleges over the last 25 years. Graduates have enjoyed successful careers in a variety of fields, including education, business, science, fine and performing arts, politics, medicine, ministry, dentistry, and law.

Wittenberg competes in the nationally renowned Division III North Coast Athletic Conference (NCAC), which consists of 10 academically selective colleges and universities in Ohio, Pennsylvania, and Indiana. The NCAC features championship competition in 23 sports-11 for men and 12 for women. There is also a full list of club sports for men and women, including crew, ice hockey, golf, rugby, and volleyball. Wittenberg is accredited by the Higher Education Commission of the North Central Association of Colleges and Schools, the American Association of University Women, the American Chemical Society, the National Council for the Accreditation of Teacher Education, and the National Association of Schools of Music.

LOCATION AND ENVIRONMENT

Located in Springfield, Ohio, Wittenberg's campus rests on 95 wooded, rolling acres in a residential neighborhood. Springfield is both a "living laboratory" and a "college town." With a population of 68,000, Springfield offers the cultural events and internship opportunities found in larger urban areas, as well as the friendliness and sense of community typical of small towns.

Students have access to a wide range of real learning opportunities that include the advantages, challenges, and realities of small-city life. Students intern with local businesses, social service agencies, hospitals, and schools and volunteer in a variety of community settings.

Springfield's proximity to Dayton (25 miles), Columbus (45 miles), and Cincinnati (75 miles) gives students convenient access to concerts, shopping, parks, museums, airports, and sporting events.

OFF-CAMPUS OPPORTUNITIES

Wittenberg offers a variety of off-campus opportunities in Springfield for community service, internships, and part-time jobs. Classroom education is also put to work through off-campus educational opportunities and study-abroad programs.

One of a select few universities requiring community service of all its students, Wittenberg believes students learn more of themselves when they give of themselves. Through the Office of Community Service, students serve at many local social service agencies for children, the elderly, the environment, literacy, youth mentoring, or the physically disabled.

Off-campus academic opportunities include an extensive student-teaching program, a marine biology/freshwater ecology program in the Bahamas, a local government management internship program, the Africana Studies/community service program in Lesotho, and the Lutheran College Washington, D.C. Semester Program. Students have also held internships across the country, including the U.S. Library of Congress, ABC Primetime Live, The Children's Museum of Indianapolis, and the National Institutes of Health.

The University maintains a full-time Office of International Education to assist students with selecting study-abroad programs and to counsel them on integrating international study with their academic and career goals. Through memberships in several consortia, more than 20 percent of Wittenberg students participate in study-abroad programs at 40 sites in more than 20 countries in Europe, Asia, and Latin America.

MAJORS AND DEGREES OFFERED

Wittenberg offers five undergraduate degrees: Bachelor of Arts (BA), Bachelor of Science (BS), Bachelor of Music (BMus), Bachelor of Music Education (BME), and Bachelor of Fine Arts (BFA). Wittenberg also offers a Masters in Education degree.

We offer 31 majors: American Studies, art, biochemistry & molecular biology, biology, business, chemistry, communication, computer science, East Asian Studies, economics, education, English, earth science, French, geography, geology, German, history, interdepartmental, international studies, mathematics, music, philosophy, physics, political science, psychology, religion, Russian and Central Eurasian Studies, sociology, Spanish, and theatre and dance.

In addition to the above, Wittenberg offers these additional minors: Africana Studies, Chinese, computational science, creative writing, dance, environmental studies, global studies, Japanese, journalism, marine science, pre-modern and ancient world studies, statistics, urban studies, and women's studies.

ACADEMIC PROGRAMS

To experience an education possessing both breadth and depth, students complete courses of study in two broad categories—a comprehensive education in the liberal arts & sciences and a major program of study. The comprehensive program is based on 16 learning goals that involve developing skills and competencies in writing, research, foreign language, speaking, mathematics, and computing. Students also perform community service and take courses in religion and philosophy, fine and performing arts, natural sciences, social sciences, and other cultures. Opportunities exist for independent studies, honors theses or projects, and experiential learning. Popular majors include biology, education, English, management, and psychology. In 2002, Wittenberg's internationally respected East Asian Studies program received a $2 million Freeman Foundation grant, which has ensured that all students, regardless of their course of study, have an encounter with Asia as part of their undergraduate experience.

The Wittenberg Honors Program, which offers special seminars, honors theses or projects, and a variety of academic and cultural activities, is available for outstanding students who want to challenge themselves and enhance their academic program.

Wittenberg has cooperative education programs with other leading research institutions, including Case Western Reserve, Columbia University, Duke University, Johns Hopkins University, and Washington University in St. Louis, to help students complete their majors. These special programs include accounting, engineering, environmental studies, marine/aquatic biology, nursing, and occupational therapy.

Pre-professional programs include accounting, education, law, theology, and the pre-health fields of pre-medicine, pre-dentistry, pre-veterinary, and pre-optometry. With approval, students may plan interdepartmental majors composed of courses selected from several departments that reflect a unified purpose or theme.

CAMPUS FACILITIES AND EQUIPMENT

Wittenberg's campus consists of 26 major buildings, including nine academic buildings; a modern, automated library; an outstanding Health, Physical Education, and Recreation Center; and seven residence halls.

Wittenberg recently dedicated two modern academic facilities, the state-of-the-art Barbara Deer Kuss Science Center and the university's humanities building, Hollenbeck Hall. All are designed to enhance learning and to encourage interaction and collaboration among the faculty and students. The athletics facilities received more than $2 million in improvements in 2005, including the addition of the Bob Rosencrans Fitness Center and upgrades to the track and field. In the fall of 2006 Wittenberg's new residence hall, a cutting-edge facility with 157 rooms in 49,249 square feet of living space, opened. Currently, in a commitment to renovate the historic heart of campus, the University has almost completed the renovation of Blair Hall, which houses the education program.

TUITION, ROOM, BOARD AND FEES

Basic costs for full-time undergraduates for the 2010–2011 academic year are:

Tuition: $34,874

Room: $4,690

Board: $4,342

Activity fee: $300

Technology fee: $250

Books (approximate): $1000

Total: $45,456

FINANCIAL AID

Wittenberg is committed to providing financial assistance to eligible and deserving students and offers both need-based and merit-based assistance. Need-based assistance includes grants, loans, and work-study programs. Approximately 70 percent of Wittenberg students qualify for need-based aid, and the average financial assistance award is $21,098 per year. To be considered, applicants must file the Free Application for Federal Student Aid (FAFSA) by March 15.

All accepted students are automatically considered for academic scholarships and special awards.

The Community Service Scholar Award rewards superior achievements in community service. Wittenberg also offers scholarships recognizing leadership skills and talent in art, dance, music, and theatre. These scholarships require a separate audition/application process. The Student Leader Fellowship Award and Civic and Urban Engagement Award also recognize outstanding student leaders in school and community. In addition, the university offers a computational science scholarship.

STUDENT ORGANIZATIONS AND ACTIVITIES

With more than 125 organizations and clubs, students can easily foster their academic and personal interests and develop management and leadership skills. Student groups are formed on topics ranging from cultural and social awareness to recreational to religious involvement and communication.

Approximately 30 percent of the students are involved in Greek life. Many academic departments have honor societies and clubs for specific majors. Weekend activities include lectures, art exhibits, concerts, dances, movies, coffeehouses, and comedians. New organizations and activities are created regularly to meet the changing interests of students.

ADMISSIONS PROCESS

Admission to Wittenberg is selective and is based on the following information:

high school record, including the strength of the high school and its curriculum,

and trends in the students academic work; SAT or ACT scores; co-curricular activities and community participation; recommendations; and an essay. Wittenberg is a test optional school. International students and transfer students are encouraged to apply. An on-campus interview is not required, but it is highly recommended. Students may apply using the Wittenberg application, the Common Application, or the free online application at http://www4.wittenberg.edu/administration/prospect/apply/.

The deadlines for applying are as follows for incoming freshmen:

Early Decision: November 15

Early Action I: December 1

Early Action II: January 15

Regular Action: March 15

Students must apply by February 15 to be considered for merit-based scholarships. Transfer applications deadlines are December 1 for spring semester and July 1 for fall semester. The international student application deadline is March 15.

WORCESTER POLYTECHNIC INSTITUTE

AT A GLANCE

You want to be on the first Mars mission, find alternative energy sources, or cure cancer. WPI wants to help you make an impact. Our students do much more than study science and technology. They delve into the arts and humanities. They complete projects on campus and around the globe, connecting what they've learned in the classroom with pressing real-life challenges—from health to the environment to global competitiveness. Students grow - personally, professionally, and intellectually - as they discover how to apply their talents and turn ideas into tangible solutions.

WPI's aim is to educate students broadly, so they achieve greatly. Though WPI has been around for more than 140 years, our approach to education, like our students, is innovative and practical. Small classes, a flexible curriculum, and one-on-one interaction with professors at the top of their fields make learning at WPI an experience unlike any other.

WPI has been widely recognized for its quality. It was the only technological university out of 16 national Leadership Institutions selected by the Association of American Colleges and Universities to serve as models of outstanding practices in liberal education. WPI consistently ranks among the top national universities by U.S. News & World Report and in 2009 was ranked number 12 for the highest percentage of classes under 20 students. WPI faculty members have also been recognized as CASE Professors of the Year for the past two years.

LOCATION AND ENVIRONMENT

With its beautiful architecture, grassy quad, and ivy-covered walls, WPI has a traditional New England campus. Students stop and chat with friends and professors on tree-lined paths. They play pool or get a coffee between classes at the Campus Center. They study by the fountain in Reunion Plaza, get a group together for bowling at Gompei's Gutters, stop and smell the roses in the formal English garden behind Higgins House, or see a student play at the Little Theatre.

Home to 12 other colleges and universities and over 35,000 college students, greater Worcester is a great college town. WPI is a member of the Colleges of Worcester Consortium, through which WPI students may register for courses at other colleges and take advantage of a wide range of cultural programming offered by consortium members. A shuttle provides free transportation between campuses.

Late-night diners, clubs, museums, concert venues, and theaters are right down the hill from WPI in Worcester's vibrant downtown. Boston is less than an hour away by commuter rail if you want to catch Red Sox fever. There's great skiing and boarding at nearby Wachusett Mountain. If you want to go a bit farther, Worcester is centrally located with easy access to Providence, New York City, the Berkshire and White Mountains, and Cape Cod.

OFF-CAMPUS OPPORTUNITIES

In Worcester you'll find:

35,000+ college students at 13 colleges and universities

14,800 seats at the DCU Center for arena concerts and sporting events

5,000 objects of arms and armor at the Higgins Armory Museum

53 parks including the largest urban nature sanctuary in New England and the Olmstead-designed Elm Park

36 galleries and 5,000 years of art at the Worcester Art Museum

20 ski trails at nearby Wachusett Mountain

2 minor league sports teams (Tornadoes, baseball; Sharks, hockey)

2 polar bears, one residing at the Ecotarium, and the other on the roof of Polar Beverages

1 Gompei the goat (WPI mascot)

MAJORS AND DEGREES OFFERED

WPI offers over 35 areas of study in engineering, science, management, and the liberal arts leading to the Bachelor of Science (B.S.) or Bachelor of Arts (B.A.) degree. Exciting new interdisciplinary programs, driven by real-world demand, include interactive media and game development, environmental engineering, and the nation's first undergraduate program in robotics engineering.

We offer pre-professional programs (law, medicine, dentistry, and veterinary) and a five-year BS/MS program. You can even create your own major or minor. Not surprisingly, over 40 percent of students change their major at least once. A comprehensive academic advising program and a wide array of academic support services help students make the right choices and reach their goals.

WPI students have received some of the nation's highest academic honors. Over just the last eight years, two students have received the prestigious Marshall Scholarship, 14 have been awarded Goldwater scholarships, five have received the Rotary Ambassadorial Scholarship, three have won National Science Foundation Fellowships, two have been named to the USA Today All-USA College Academic Team, and one has been named an NIH-Oxford/Cambridge Biomedical Research Scholar.

ACADEMIC PROGRAMS

At WPI, learning is about more than just theories and ideas. Students put what they learn into practice through a unique project-enriched curriculum. Each undergraduate complete two projects: one directly related to their major and one in which they work with a team of students to solve a problem at the intersection of society and technology. Students gain valuable professional skills, a talent for teamwork, and the confidence to dive right in—no matter what the challenge.

WPI's academic program is built to be flexible. Students take the equivalent of three courses (as courses or project work) during each of four 7-week terms (two in the fall and two in the spring). It is also designed to encourage collaboration, not competition. Students work closely on projects and in project-oriented classes. Learning to work in teams prepares students to get results and become leaders, no matter what path they take in life.

WPI's award-winning Global Perspective Program, with 25 project centers on five continents, is one of the most comprehensive and highly regarded global studies programs in the nation. Most WPI students complete projects off campus; over half complete project work outside the United States in places like Thailand, Namibia, Costa Rica, and Italy. Global project experiences not only give students the chance to work in teams to solve meaningful real-life problems for people around the world, they immerse students in other cultures and give them a powerful sense of self-confidence.

Top-tier employers seek out WPI graduates for their real-world experience and ability to work collaboratively. With a placement rate of over 90 percent, students are recruited by leading organizations such as Pfizer, General Electric, Fidelity Investments, IBM and Google. Not surprisingly, WPI graduates' starting salaries are higher than those of many other college graduates, according to the National Association of Colleges and Employers. Each year, WPI graduates are accepted at many prestigious graduate schools, including MIT, Yale University, Princeton University, Johns Hopkins University and Tufts University Medical School.

CAMPUS FACILITIES AND EQUIPMENT

With all of the amazing things WPI students and faculty do, our outstanding research facilities should come as no surprise. The new 125,000-square-foot WPI Life Sciences and Bioengineering Center at Gateway Park is a state-of-the-art research center housing faculty from four departments. Our two atomic force microscopes let you see individual atoms on a material's surface. The Fire Science Laboratory enables students and faculty to evaluate fire safety measures in actual fire simulations. Laser holography labs, computer music labs, medical imaging labs, a bioprocess lab - they're all here, and lots more.

Recent additions to WPI's undergraduate teaching facilities include a newly constructed chemistry laboratory center that facilitates team-based work and a new $11 million Undergraduate Life Sciences Laboratory Center, that is the focal point for undergraduate teaching and research in biology and biotechnology, biomedical engineering, chemistry and biochemistry, and chemical engineering.

WPI will be opening a brand new sports and recreation center in 2012 including a four-court gymnasium, indoor jogging track, 14,000 sq. ft. of fitness space, racquetball and squash courts, competition pool, workout studios, and rowing tanks.

TUITION, ROOM, BOARD AND FEES

(2009–2010)

Tuition: $36,890.00

Social Fee: $250.00

Health Fee: $300.00

Total: $37,440.00

Typical Room: $6,530.00

Typical Board Plan: $4,630.00

Books and Supplies: $1,000.00

Personal Expenses: $1,000.00

Total: $50,600.00

FINANCIAL AID

It's no secret. A great education costs a lot of money, but think about the return on your investment. College graduates in general earn over the course of their careers at least $1 million more than those without a degree. For WPI graduates, starting salaries frequently exceed the national averages and graduates are able to move quickly up the ranks to positions of influence as a result of their excellent preparation. In fact, Forbes.com recently ranked WPI No. 9 on a list of the "Top Colleges for Getting Rich."

APPLYING FOR FINANCIAL AID

Students should file the FAFSA and CSS Profile on or near their admissions application deadline. WPI should receive all financial aid materials by February 1. Applications after this date will be reviewed subject to funds available.

Most applicants (including early applicants) will receive a financial aid package within two weeks of their acceptance. We'll inform you of the Financial Aid Committee's decision no later than April 15 for regular decision admissions, and you'll have until the Candidates Common Reply Date (May 1) to either accept or decline the offer.

Academic Scholarships

WPI offers academic scholarships to freshman applicants based upon academic performance, standardized test scores, leadership, extracurricular involvement and community service. All admitted applicants are considered and there is no separate application required.

Scholarships vary in amounts, but typically range between $10,000 and $25,000, and are renewable for four years. Valedictorians and Salutatorians are guaranteed a minimum scholarship of $17,000. National Merit, National Achievement, and National Hispanic Recognition Finalists are guaranteed a minimum of $17,000.

STUDENT ORGANIZATIONS AND ACTIVITIES

WPI has 20 varsity (NCAA Division III) athletics teams and 34 club and intramural athletics. WPI won the "Worcester Cup" for the fourth time in six years, recognizing it as the top collegiate program in Worcester County. WPI has 13 fraternities and three sororities, 20 music and performing arts groups, dozens of academic clubs, international organizations, religious groups and other organizations. Overall, there are more than 200 student clubs and activities.

ADMISSIONS PROCESS

WPI Admissions offers a variety of application options. Students can apply using the WPI application (paper or on-line). We also accept the Common Application and the Universal Application. A $60 application fee is required for all applicants. (WPI endorses the fee waiver policy of the College Board, as well as accepts fee waivers from guidance or college counselors.)

ACADEMIC REQUIREMENTS

four years of math (including pre-calculus)

four years of English

two years of lab science

Other requirements include:

High school transcript

Science or math recommendation

Guidance counselor's recommendation

Personal essay

SAT or ACT scores or alternate materials through WPI's "Flex Path"

TOEFL or IELTS Exam scores for international students whose first language is not English

Interviews

While interviews are optional, this is your chance to meet one-on-one with an Admissions staff member or a trained Admissions intern. We'll have the chance to learn more about you, and can answer specific questions you may have.

Deadlines

Early Action (Round 1) - Nov. 10

Early Action (Round 2) - Jan. 1

Regular Decision - Feb. 1

January Admission - Freshmen and Transfer Students - Nov. 15 (Rolling notification)

Fall Admission - Transfer Students - Apr. 15° (Rolling notification)

INDEXES

INDEXES

ALPHABETICAL INDEX

University of San Francisco 885, 1306
University of Southern California 893
Vanguard University of Southern California 932
Westmont College 977
Whittier College 981
Woodbury University 996

COLORADO

Adams State College 11
Art Institute of Colorado 43
Colorado Christian University 195
Colorado College 196
Colorado School of Mines 196
Colorado State University 197
Colorado State University-Pueblo 198
Colorado Technical University 199
DeVry University (Denver) 237
Fort Lewis College 293
Johnson and Wales University—Denver 381
Jones International University 383
Naropa University 514, 1168
Regis University 614
Rocky Mountain College of Art + Design 629
The American University of Paris (CO) 29
United States Air Force Academy 777, 1268
University of Colorado at Colorado Springs 801
University of Colorado at Denver 802
University of Colorado at Denver and Health
    Sciences Center—Health Sciences Program 803
University of Colorado—Boulder 803
University of Denver 809
University of Northern Colorado 868
Western State College of Colorado 972

CONNECTICUT

Albertus Magnus College 18, 1006
Central Connecticut State University 145, 1050
Charter Oak State College 153
Connecticut College 211, 1064
Eastern Connecticut State University 255
Fairfield University 277
Gibbs College—Norwalk 313
Lyme Academy College of Fine Arts 435
Mitchell College 491
Post University 599
Quinnipiac University 607, 1202
Sacred Heart University 637
Saint Joseph College (CT) 641
Southern Connecticut State University 687
Trinity College (CT) 765, 1262
United States Coast Guard Academy 778
University of Bridgeport 789
University of Connecticut 804
University of Hartford 815, 1288
University of New Haven 858, 1302
Wesleyan University 962
Western Connecticut State University 968
Yale University 1000

DELAWARE

Goldey-Beacom College 315
University of Delaware 808, 1284
Wesley College (DE) 961
Wilmington College (DE) 990

DISTRICT OF COLUMBIA

American University 28, 1012
Catholic University of America, The 140
Corcoran College of Art and Design 214, 1066
Gallaudet University 302
Georgetown University 308
George Washington University, The 306
Howard University 356
Trinity (Washington) University 764
University of the District of Columbia 810

FLORIDA

Baptist College of Florida 56
Barry University 63
Beacon College 67
Bethune-Cookman College 83
Carlos Albizu University—CAU 133
Clearwater Christian College 173
DeVry University (Orlando,FL) 239
Eckerd College 261
Embry Riddle Aeronautical University (FL) 266
Flagler College 284
Florida A&M University 285
Florida Atlantic University 286, 1092
Florida College 286
Florida Gulf Coast University 287
Florida Institute of Technology 287
Florida International University 288
Florida Southern College 289
Florida State University 290
Florida State University 290
Hodges University 348
Jacksonville University 375
Johnson and Wales University
    at North Miami 382
Lynn University 437, 1150
New College of Florida 519
New World School of the Arts 524
Northwood University, Florida Campus 547
Nova Southeastern University 550
Palm Beach Atlantic University 575
Ringling College of Art and Design 621
Rollins College 630
Saint Leo University 644
St. Thomas University 713
Stetson University 736
Trinity College of Florida 766
University of Central Florida 797, 1278
University of Florida 813
University of Miami 841
University of North Florida 866
University of South Florida 892

University of Tampa 897, 1310
University of West Florida 913
Warner Southern College 946
Webber International University 957, 1320

GEORGIA

Agnes Scott College 13
Albany State University 17
Armstrong Atlantic State University 41
Art Institute of Atlanta, The 43
Atlanta Christian College 48
Augusta State University 50
Berry College 78
Brenau University The Women's College 98
Brewton-Parker College 100
Clark Atlanta University 169
Clayton State University 172
Columbus State University 204
Covenant College 218
DeVry University (Alpharetta, GA) 235
DeVry University (Decatur, GA) 236
Emmanuel College (GA) 270
Emory University 271, 1088
Georgia College & State University 308, 1098
Georgia Institute of Technology 309
Georgia Southern University 310
Georgia Southwestern State University 311
Georgia State University 311
Kennesaw State University 391
LaGrange College 401
Mercer University—Macon 467
Morehouse College 500
North Georgia College and State University 534
Oglethorpe University 554
Piedmont College 591
Reinhardt College 615
Savannah College of Art and Design 662, 1230
Savannah State University 663
Shorter College 674
Southern Polytechnic State University 691
Spelman College 697
Toccoa Falls College 760
University of Georgia 814
University of West Georgia 913
Valdosta State University 928
Wesleyan College 961

HAWAII

Brigham Young University—Hawaii 104
Chaminade University of Honolulu 151
Hawai'i Pacific University 340, 1108
University of Hawai'i—West O'ahu 817
University of Hawaii at Hilo 816
University of Hawaii at Manoa 816

INTERNATIONAL

INDEX BY SIZE

4,000–10,000

INDEX BY TUITION

INDEX BY SELECTIVITY

86

85

84

83

82

NOTES

NOTES

NOTES

NOTES

NOTES

NOTES

NOTES

NOTES

NOTES

NOTES

NOTES

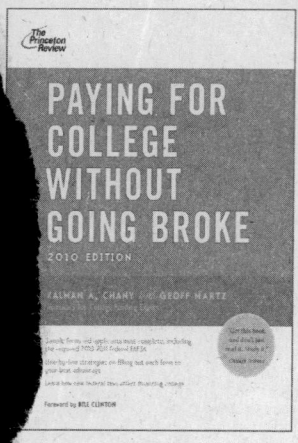

Funding It

Paying for College Without Going Broke, 2010 Edition
978-0-375-42942-2 • $20.00/C$24.95

Ace the APs

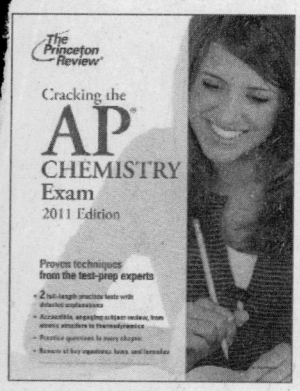

Cracking the AP Biology Exam, 2011 Edition
978-0-375-42996-5 • $18.99/C$20.99

Cracking the AP Calculus AB & BC Exams, 2011 Edition
978-0-375-42988-0 • $19.99/C$22.99

Cracking the AP Chemistry Exam, 2011 Edition
978-0-375-42989-7 • $18.99/C$20.99

Cracking the AP Economics Macro & Micro Exams, 2011 Edition
978-0-375-42997-2 • $18.00/C$20.00

Cracking the AP English Language & Composition Exam, 2011 Edition
978-0-375-42998-9 • $18.00 /C$20.00

Cracking the AP English Literature & Composition Exam, 2011 Edition
978-0-375-42999-6 • $18.00/C$20.00

Cracking the AP Environmental Science Exam, 2011 Edition
978-0-375-42776-3 • $18.00/C$20.00

Cracking the AP European History Exam, 2011 Edition
978-0-375-42990-3 • $18.99/C$20.99

Cracking the AP Human Geography Exam, 2011 Edition
978-0-375-42777-0 • $18.00/C$20.00

Cracking the AP Physics B Exam, 2011 Edition
978-0-375-42778-7 • $18.00/C$20.00

Cracking the AP Physics C Exam, 2011 Edition
978-0-375-42779-4 • $18.00/C$20.00

Cracking the AP Psychology Exam, 2011 Edition
978-0-375-42780-0 • $18.00/C$20.00

Cracking the AP Spanish Exam with Audio CD, 2011 Edition
978-0-375-42781-7 • $24.99/C$27.99

Cracking the AP Statistics Exam, 2011 Edition
978-0-375-42782-4 • $19.99/C$22.99

Cracking the AP U.S. Government & Politics Exam, 2011 Edition
978-0-375-42783-1 • $18.99/C$20.99

Cracking the AP U.S. History Exam, 2011 Edition
978-0-375-42991-0 • $18.99/C$20.99

Cracking the AP World History Exam, 2011 Edition
978-0-375-42995-8 • $18.99/C$20.99

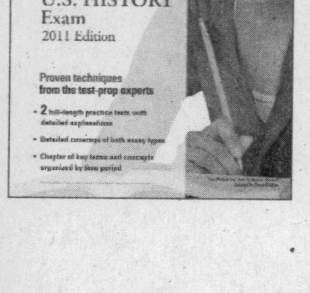

**Available everywhere books are sold and at
PrincetonReviewBooks.com**

NOTES

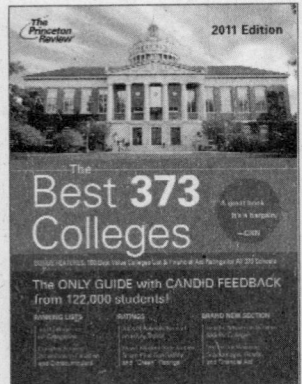